W9-CPO-012

STRAND PRICE $25.00
STRAND BOOK STORE

STRONG'S EXHAUSTIVE CONCORDANCE OF THE BIBLE

---

showing every word of the text of the King James Version of the canonical books of the Bible and every occurrence of each word in regular order together with the

Words of Jesus Identified in Boldface Red Letter

Brief dictionaries of the Hebrew and Greek words of the original with references to the English words

JAMES STRONG, S.T.D., LL.D.

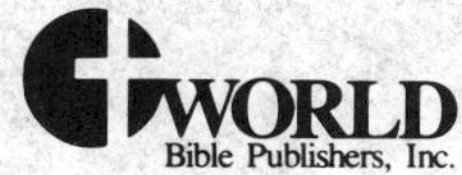

Library of Congress Cataloging in Publication Data

Strong, James, 1822-1894.
Strong's exhaustive concordance of the Bible, with words of Jesus in red letter.

1. Bible—Concordances, English. 2. Hebrew language—Dictionaries—English. 3. Greek language, Biblical—Dictionaries—English. I. Title.
II. Title: Exhaustive concordance of the Bible.
BS425.S8 1980 220.5′2 80-11952

ISBN 0-529-06679-3 (regular)
ISBN 0-529-06680-7 (thumb-indexed)

PRINTED AND BOUND IN THE UNITED STATES OF AMERICA

First Edition Printed April 1894

Forty-sixth Printing 1991

General Preface

THIS work, as the title page indicates, consists of several portions somewhat distinct but mutually related, all having reference to one great object, a thorough verbal index to the Holy Scriptures, as they exist in the three most important forms now known to British and American readers and scholars, namely, the partly Hebrew and partly Greek original text, and the King James Version. The basis of the whole work is the first and much the largest portion, to which this Preface more particularly applies. The design and use of the succeeding portions are explained in the Prefaces to them respectively.

The present work is entitled "The Exhaustive Concordance" to the text of the English Bible ordinarily in use, because it is the only one hitherto constructed that gives all the words of that book and all the passages where they are found. In this respect no Concordance can ever be made more perfect.

In its preparation three great features have been constantly kept in view—*completeness, simplicity,* and *accuracy.* It is intended to be a permanent standard for purposes of reference: so full in its vocabulary and lists that every one consulting it will be sure to find a passage easily and quickly, by seeking it under any word whatever that it contains; so plain in its arrangement that children cannot miss their way in using it; so correct in its citations, both numerical and verbal, that the most scholarly may implicitly depend upon it.* A mere comparison with other works of the kind hitherto produced, however useful they may have been in their place, will reveal the fact that none of them perfectly or adequately combines these advantages; and it will especially be evident that they all fall short in the most essential requisite, namely, completeness.

For this reason no preceding work of the kind has been taken as a basis for the present one; it is entirely independent of them all. The passages were collected directly from the sacred text, and they have been repeatedly compared with it, both in the manuscript and in type, in so careful and thorough a manner as to test satisfactorily their exhaustiveness and exactness. The comparatively few passages—chiefly unimportant particles, which have at last been found to have escaped all previous verification—are given in the APPENDIX at the close of this vocabulary.

By observing the subjoined Directions, in the associated use of the HEBREW and GREEK DICTIONARIES, the reader will have substantially a Concordance-Lexicon of the King James Version and the Hebrew Old Testament and the Greek New Testament.

*The most unsparing industry and scrupulous care have been exercised to weed out all errors, as the work was passing through the press, by means of varied and minute verification with the English and the original texts; but in a task so extended and of such intricacy and peculiar detail, the author cannot hope to have escaped all errata, whether typographical or clerical. He feels confident, however, that in the most essential part of the work, namely, the MAIN CONCORDANCE, which gives the means of readily finding any passage in the King James Version—the purpose for which a Concordance is usually consulted—this will rarely if ever be found defective. He will be thankful to any of his readers who will do him the favor of pointing out any errors that they may discover in it, with a view to their future correction.

Directions and Explanations

Look for the passage sought under any one of its words exactly as it is spelled in the Bible,* choosing for convenience sake the most striking or significant word in the passage that you can recall.†

The leading word in each article is printed in bold face letter in the several citations, and always abbreviated to its initial letter, followed by a period-mark (.). Every word of Jesus has been carefully identified and checked and set in bold face red letter type in the Exhaustive Concordance and in italicized red letter type in the Key Word Comparison.

Phrases, groups or combinations of words (not printed as compounds in ordinary Bibles), will be found under each of their words separately. The chapter-headings and marginal notes of reference-Bibles and similar works are of course not included in the citations; but the *titles* to the Books, to the Psalms severally, and the *subscriptions* to the Epistles are, as they represent parts of the original texts.

The following forty-seven unimportant words of very frequent occurrence are cited (in the Appendix) by reference to chapter and verse only, inasmuch as no person would think of searching out a text by means of them, and the quotation in full of the passages where they are found would be nearly tantamount to reprinting the entire Bible under each of them:

a	*as*	*for*	*him*	*is*	*not*	*out*	*that*	*them*	*to*	*us*	*with*
an	*be*	*from*	*his*	*it*	*O*	*shall*	*the*	*they*	*unto*	*was*	*ye*
and	*but*	*he*	*I*	*me*	*of*	*shalt*	*thee*	*thou*	*up*	*we*	*you*
are	*by*	*her*	*in*	*my*	*our*	*she*	*their*	*thy*	*upon*	*were*	

In the use of the *reference-column* appended to the passages, which is the key to the connection with the subsequent portions of the work, the following particulars will be sufficient to note here.

The appended *number* indicates that the leading word in the passage quoted is there the translation in the King James Version of the Hebrew or Greek word correspondingly numbered in the Dictionaries given in the latter portions of this work; upright numerals (1, 2, 3, etc.) being used for the Old Testament (that is, Hebrew or Chaldee), and sloping or "italic" ones *(1, 2, 3,* etc.) for the New Testament (that is, Greek). The lexical explanations may thus be found and used by any person, whether acquainted with the original languages or not. The absence of a number at the end of the passage shows that the word in question is not there the rendering of any particular term in the original, having either been supplied by the translators for the purpose of greater clearness (in which case in ordinary Bibles it is printed *in italics*), or being the representative merely of some inflectional *form* (auxiliary, preposition, adjunct, etc.), or peculiar *idiom* of a Hebrew or Greek term (which in that case is to be sought under the principal associated word of the same passage).

The following abbreviations of the names of the several books of the Bible are uniformly employed, no two of them being designated by the same formula:

ABBREVIATIONS OF THE NAMES OF THE BOOKS OF THE BIBLE

Ge—Genesis
Ex—Exodus
Le—Leviticus
Nu—Numbers
De—Deuteronomy
Jos—Joshua
Jg—Judges
Ru—Ruth
1Sa—I Samuel
2Sa—II Samuel
1Ki—I Kings
2Ki—II Kings
1Ch—I Chronicles
2Ch—II Chronicles
Ezr—Ezra
Ne—Nehemiah
Es—Esther

Job—Job
Ps—Psalms
Pr—Proverbs
Ec—Ecclesiastes
Ca—Canticles (Song of Solomon, Song of Songs)
Isa—Isaiah
Jer—Jeremiah
La—Lamentations
Eze—Ezekiel
Da—Daniel
Ho—Hosea
Joe—Joel
Am—Amos
Ob—Obadiah
Jon—Jonah
Mic—Micah
Na—Nahum

Hab—Habakkuk
Zep—Zephaniah
Hag—Haggai
Zec—Zechariah
Mal—Malachi
Mt—Matthew
Mk—Mark
Lu—Luke
Joh—John
Ac—Acts
Ro—Romans
1Co—I Corinthians
2Co—II Corinthians
Ga—Galatians
Eph—Ephesians
Php—Philippians
Col—Colossians

1Th—I Thessalonians
2Th—II Thessalonians
1Ti—I Timothy
2Ti—II Timothy
Tit—Titus
Phm—Philemon
Heb—Hebrews
Jas—James
1Pe—I Peter
2Pe—II Peter
1Jo—I John
2Jo—II John
3Jo—III John
Jude—Jude
Re—Revelation (Apocalypse)

*The standard of verification employed is *"The Parallel Bible,"* minion (a large 8 vol. edition of the Oxford Press, England; impression of 1886), to which the spelling, punctuation, and use of (initial) capitals and hyphen have been rigidly conformed.

†From a failure to recollect a passage accurately, persons often search for it in a Concordance under some word which it really does not contain. If readers do not find in this Concordance the passage sought for under the word which has been chosen for that purpose, they may be sure that such a mistake of their own is the reason. In that case they have only to look for it under some other word. If they can remember only one word of the passage, they could scarcely recognize or identify it, should they actually find it.

Main Concordance

A.

AARON (a'-ur-un) See also AARON'S; AARONITES.

Ex	4:14	Is not **A.** the Levite thy brother?	175
Ex	4:27	the Lord said to **A.**, Go into the	175
Ex	4:28	Moses told **A.** all the words of the	175
Ex	4:29	Moses and **A.** went and gathered	175
Ex	4:30	**A.** spake all the words which the	175
Ex	5:1	afterward Moses and **A.** went in,	175
Ex	5:4	Wherefore do ye, Moses and **A.**, let	175
Ex	5:20	they met Moses and **A.**, who stood	175
Ex	6:13	Lord spake unto Moses and unto **A.**,	175
Ex	6:20	and she bare him **A.** and Moses:	175
Ex	6:23	**A.** took him Elisheba, daughter of	175
Ex	6:26	These are that **A.** and Moses, to	175
Ex	6:27	these are that Moses and **A.**	175
Ex	7:1	and **A.** thy brother shall be thy	175
Ex	7:2	and **A.** thy brother shall speak	175
Ex	7:6	Moses and **A.** did as the Lord	175
Ex	7:7	and **A.** fourscore and three years	175
Ex	7:8	Lord spake unto Moses and unto **A.**,	175
Ex	7:9	then thou shalt say unto **A.**, Take	175
Ex	7:10	And Moses and **A.** went in unto	175
Ex	7:10	and **A.** cast down his rod before	175
Ex	7:19	Lord spake unto Moses, Say unto **A.**,	175
Ex	7:20	Moses and **A.** did so, as the Lord	175
Ex	8:5	Say unto **A.**, Stretch forth thine	175
Ex	8:6	**A.** stretched out his hand over the	175
Ex	8:8	Pharaoh called for Moses and **A.**,	175
Ex	8:12	Moses and **A.** went out from	175
Ex	8:16	Say unto **A.**, stretch out thy rod,	175
Ex	8:17	for **A.** stretched out his hand with	175
Ex	8:25	Pharaoh called for Moses and for **A.**	175
Ex	9:8	Lord said unto Moses and unto **A.**,	175
Ex	9:27	sent, and called for Moses and **A.**,	175
Ex	10:3	Moses and **A.** came in unto	175
Ex	10:8	Moses and **A.** were brought again	175
Ex	10:16	Pharaoh called for Moses and **A.** in	175
Ex	11:10	Moses and **A.** did all these wonders	175
Ex	12:1	the Lord spake unto Moses and **A.**	175
Ex	12:28	Lord had commanded Moses and **A.**,	175
Ex	12:31	he called for Moses and **A.** by night,	175
Ex	12:43	the Lord said unto Moses and **A.**,	175
Ex	12:50	the Lord commanded Moses and **A.**,	175
Ex	15:20	the prophetess, the sister of **A.**,	175
Ex	16:2	murmured against Moses and **A.**	175
Ex	16:6	Moses and **A.** said unto all the	175
Ex	16:9	Moses spake unto **A.**, Say unto all	175
Ex	16:10	as **A.** spake unto the whole	175
Ex	16:33	Moses said unto **A.**, Take a pot,	175
Ex	16:34	so **A.** laid it up before the	175
Ex	17:10	and Moses, **A.**, and Hur went up	175
Ex	17:12	and **A.** and Hur stayed up his	175
Ex	18:12	and **A.** came, and all the elders of	175
Ex	19:24	thou shalt come up, thou, and **A.**	175
Ex	24:1	up unto the Lord thou and **A.**,	175
Ex	24:9	Then went up Moses, and **A.**,	175
Ex	24:14	and, behold, **A.** and Hur are with	175
Ex	27:21	**A.** and his sons shall order it from	175
Ex	28:1	take thou unto thee **A.** thy	175
Ex	28:1	n the priest's office, even **A.**,	175
Ex	28:2	shalt make holy garments for **A.**	175
Ex	28:4	shall make holy garments for **A.**	175
Ex	28:12	and **A.** shall bear their names	175
Ex	28:29	**A.** shall bear the names of the	175
Ex	28:30	and **A.** shall bear the judgment of	175
Ex	28:35	And it shall be upon **A.** to minister	175
Ex	28:38	that **A.** may bear the iniquity of	175
Ex	28:41	thou shalt put them upon **A.** thy	175
Ex	28:43	they shall be upon **A.**, and upon	175
Ex	29:4	**A.** and his sons thou shalt bring	175
Ex	29:5	and put upon **A.** the coat, and the	175
Ex	29:9	shalt gird them with girdles, **A.**	175
Ex	29:9	thou shalt consecrate **A.** and his	175
Ex	29:10,	15, 19 **A.** and his sons shall put their	175
Ex	29:20	upon the tip of the right ear of **A.**,	175
Ex	29:21	and sprinkle it upon **A.**, and upon	175
Ex	29:24	shalt put all in the hands of **A.**,	175
Ex	29:27	even of that which is for **A.**, and	175
Ex	29:29	the holy garments of **A.** shall be	175
Ex	29:32	**A.** and his sons shall eat the flesh	175
Ex	29:35	thus shalt thou do unto **A.**, and to	175
Ex	29:44	I will sanctify also both **A.** and	175
Ex	30:7	**A.** shall burn thereon sweet	175
Ex	30:8	when **A.** lighteth the lamps at even,	175
Ex	30:10	**A.** shall make an atonement upon	175
Ex	30:19	For **A.** and his sons shall wash	175
Ex	30:30	thou shalt anoint **A.** and his sons,	175
Ex	31:10	and the holy garments for **A.** the	175
Ex	32:1	themselves together unto **A.**, and	175
Ex	32:2	**A.** said unto them, Break off the	175
Ex	32:3	and brought them unto **A.**,	175
Ex	32:5	when **A.** saw it he built an altar	175
Ex	32:5	**A.** made proclamation, and said,	175
Ex	32:21	Moses said unto **A.**, What did this	175
Ex	32:22	**A.** said, Let not the anger of my	175
Ex	32:25	(for **A.** had made them naked unto	175
Ex	32:35	they made the calf, which **A.** made.	175
Ex	34:30	when **A.** and all the children of	175
Ex	34:31	**A.** and all the rulers of the	175
Ex	35:19	the holy garments for **A.**, the	175
Ex	38:21	by the hand of Ithamar, son to **A.**	175
Ex	39:1	made the holy garments for **A.**;	175
Ex	39:27	fine linen of woven work for **A.**,	175
Ex	39:41	and the holy garments for **A.** the	175
Ex	40:12	thou shalt bring **A.** and his sons	175
Ex	40:13	thou shalt put upon **A.** the holy	175
Ex	40:31	Moses and **A.** and his sons washed	175
Le	1:7	the sons of **A.** the priest shall put	175
Le	3:13	the sons of **A.** shall sprinkle the	175
Le	6:9	Command **A.** and his sons, saying,	175
Le	6:14	the sons of **A.** shall offer it before	175
Le	6:16	the remainder thereof shall **A.**	175
Le	6:18	males among the children of **A.**	175
Le	6:20	This is the offering of **A.** and of	175
Le	6:25	Speak unto **A.** and to his sons,	175
Le	7:10	and dry, shall all the sons of **A.**	175
Le	7:33	He among the sons of **A.**, that	175
Le	7:34	and have given them unto **A.** the	175
Le	7:35	the portion of the anointing of **A.**,	175
Le	8:2	Take **A.** and his sons with him,	175
Le	8:6	Moses brought **A.** and his sons,	175
Le	8:14,	18 **A.** and his sons laid their hands	175
Le	8:22	the ram of consecration: and **A.**	175
Le	8:30	and sprinkled it upon **A.**, and	175
Le	8:30	sanctified **A.**, and his garments,	175
Le	8:31	Moses said unto **A.**, and to his	175
Le	8:31	as I commanded, saying, **A.** and	175
Le	8:36	So **A.** and his sons did all things	175
Le	9:1	the eighth day, that Moses called **A.**	175
Le	9:2	he said unto **A.**, Take thee a young	175
Le	9:7	Moses said unto **A.**, Go into the	175
Le	9:8	**A.** therefore went unto the altar,	175
Le	9:9	the sons of **A.** brought the blood	175
Le	9:21	And the right shoulder **A.** waved	175
Le	9:22	**A.** lifted up his right hand toward	175
Le	9:23	Moses and **A.** went into the	175
Le	10:1	Nadab and Abihu, the sons of **A.**,	175
Le	10:3	Moses said unto **A.**, This is it that	175
Le	10:3	And **A.** held his peace.	175
Le	10:4	the sons of Uzziel the uncle of **A.**,	175
Le	10:6	Moses said unto **A.** and unto	175
Le	10:8	the Lord spake unto **A.**, saying,	175
Le	10:12	Moses spake unto **A.** and unto	175
Le	10:16	the sons of **A.** which were left	175
Le	10:19	**A.** said unto Moses, Behold, this	175
Le	11:1	Lord spake unto Moses and to **A.**,	175
Le	13:1	the Lord spake unto Moses and **A.**,	175
Le	13:2	then he shall be brought unto **A.**	175
Le	14:33	Lord spake unto Moses and unto **A.**,	175
Le	15:1	Lord spake unto Moses and to **A.**,	175
Le	16:1	the death of the two sons of **A.**,	175
Le	16:2	Speak unto **A.** thy brother, that	175
Le	16:3	Thus shall **A.** come into the holy	175
Le	16:6	**A.** shall offer his bullock of the sin	175
Le	16:8	**A.** shall cast lots upon the two goats	175
Le	16:9	**A.** shall bring the goat upon which	175
Le	16:11	**A.** shall bring the bullock of the sin	175
Le	16:21	**A.** shall lay both his hands upon the	175
Le	16:23	**A.** shall come into the tabernacle	175
Le	17:2	Speak unto **A.**, and unto his sons,	175
Le	21:1	unto the priests the sons of **A.**, and	175
Le	21:17	Speak unto **A.**, saying, Whosoever	175
Le	21:21	hath a blemish of the seed of **A.** the	175
Le	21:24	Moses told it unto **A.**, and to his	175
Le	22:2	Speak unto **A.** and to his sons, that	175
Le	22:4	What man soever of the seed of **A.**	175
Le	22:18	Speak unto **A.**, and to his sons, and	175
Le	24:3	Shall **A.** order it from the evening	175
Nu	1:3	thou and **A.** shall number them by	175
Nu	1:17	Moses and **A.** took these men which	175
Nu	1:44	which Moses and **A.** numbered, and	175
Nu	2:1	Lord spake unto Moses and unto **A.**,	175
Nu	3:1	also are the generations of **A.** and	175
Nu	3:2, 3	are the names of the sons of **A.**	175
Nu	3:4	the priest's office in the sight of **A.**	175
Nu	3:6	and present them before **A.** the	175
Nu	3:9	thou shalt give the Levites unto **A.**	175
Nu	3:10	thou shalt appoint **A.** and his sons	175
Nu	3:32	Eleazar the son of **A.** the priest	175
Nu	3:38	shall be Moses, and **A.** and his sons	175
Nu	3:39	which Moses and **A.** numbered at	175
Nu	3:48	is to be redeemed, unto **A.** and to	175
Nu	3:51	that were redeemed unto **A.** and to	175
Nu	4:1	Lord spake unto Moses and unto **A.**,	175
Nu	4:5	when the camp setteth forward, **A.**	175
Nu	4:15	when **A.** and his sons have made an	175
Nu	4:16	the office of Eleazar the son of **A.**	175
Nu	4:17	Lord spake unto Moses and unto **A.**,	175
Nu	4:19	**A.** and his sons shall go in, and	175
Nu	4:27	At the appointment of **A.** and his	175
Nu	4:28,	33 hand of Ithamar the son of **A.**	175
Nu	4:34	Moses and **A.** and the chief of the	175
Nu	4:37	which Moses and **A.** did number	175
Nu	4:41	whom Moses and **A.** did number	175
Nu	4:45	whom Moses and **A.** numbered	175
Nu	4:46	whom Moses and **A.** and the chief	175
Nu	6:23	Speak unto **A.** and unto his sons,	175
Nu	7:8	the hand of Ithamar the son of **A.**	175
Nu	8:2	Speak unto **A.**, and say unto him,	175
Nu	8:3	**A.** did so; he lighted the lamps	175
Nu	8:11	**A.** shall offer the Levites before the	175
Nu	8:13	shalt set the Levites before **A.**, and	175
Nu	8:19	given the Levites as a gift to **A.** and	175
Nu	8:20	And Moses, and **A.**, and all the	175
Nu	8:21	and **A.** offered them as an offering	175
Nu	8:21	**A.** made an atonement for them	175
Nu	8:22	of the congregation before **A.**, and	175
Nu	9:6	came before Moses and before **A.**	175
Nu	10:8	the sons of **A.**, the priests, shall	175
Nu	12:1	and Miriam and **A.** spake against	175

Nu 12:4 suddenly unto Moses, and unto **A.**, 175
Nu 12:5 and called **A.** and Miriam: 175
Nu 12:10 and **A.** looked upon Miriam, and 175
Nu 12:11 **A.** said unto Moses, Alas, my lord, 175
Nu 13:26 and came to Moses, and to **A.**, and 175
Nu 14:2 against Moses and against **A.**: and 175
Nu 14:5 Moses and **A.** fell on their faces 175
Nu 14:26 Lord spake unto Moses and unto **A.**, 175
Nu 15:33 brought him unto Moses and **A.**, 175
Nu 16:3 against Moses and against **A.**, and 175
Nu 16:11 and what is **A.**, that ye murmur 175
Nu 16:16 thou, and they, and **A.**, to morrow: 175
NU 16:17 and **A.**, each of you his censer. 175
Nu 16:18 congregation with Moses and **A.** 175
Nu 16:20 Lord spake unto Moses and unto **A.**, 175
Nu 16:37 Speak unto Eleazar the son of **A.** 175
Nu 16:40 which is not of the seed of **A.**, come 175
Nu 16:41, 42 against Moses and against **A.**, 175
Nu 16:43 And Moses and **A.** came before the 175
Nu 16:46 Moses said unto **A.**, Take a censer 175
Nu 16:47 **A.** took as Moses commanded, and 175
Nu 16:50 **A.** returned unto Moses unto the 175
Nu 17:6 the rod of **A.** was among their rods 175
Nu 17:8 the rod of **A.** for the house of Levi 175
Nu 18:1 the Lord said unto **A.**, Thou and 175
Nu 18:8 the Lord spake unto **A.**, Behold, I 175
Nu 18:20 the Lord spake unto **A.**, Thou 175
Nu 18:28 the Lord's heave offering to **A.** the 175
Nu 19:1 Lord spake unto Moses and unto **A.**, 175
Nu 20:2 against Moses and against **A.** 175
Nu 20:6 And Moses and **A.** went from the 175
Nu 20:8 thou and **A.** thy brother, and speak 175
Nu 20:10 And Moses and **A.** gathered the 175
Nu 20:12, 23 Lord spake unto Moses and **A.**, 175
Nu 20:24 **A.** shall be gathered unto his people 175
Nu 20:25 Take **A.** and Eleazar his son, and 175
Nu 20:26 strip **A.** of his garments, and put 175
Nu 20:26 and **A.** shall be gathered unto his 175
Nu 20:28 Moses stripped **A.** of his garments 175
Nu 20:28 and **A.** died there in the top of the 175
Nu 20:29 congregation saw that **A.** was dead, 175
Nu 20:29 they mourned for **A.** thirty days 175
Nu 25:7 the son of Eleazar, the son of **A.** the 175
Nu 25:11 the son of **A.** the priest, hath turned 175
Nu 26:1 and unto Eleazar the son of **A.** the 175
Nu 26:9 and against **A.** in the company of 175
Nu 26:59 and she bare unto Amram **A.** and 175
Nu 26:60 And unto **A.** was born Nadab and 175
Nu 26:64 a man of them whom Moses and **A.** 175
Nu 27:13 as **A.** thy brother was gathered. 175
Nu 33:1 under the hand of Moses and **A.** 175
Nu 33:38 **A.** the priest went up into mount 175
Nu 33:39 **A.** was a hundred and twenty and 175
De 9:20 Lord was very angry with **A.** to 175
De 9:20 and I prayed for **A.** also the 175
De 10:6 there **A.** died, and there he was 175
De 32:50 as **A.** thy brother died in mount 175
Jos 21:4 and the children of **A.** the priest, 175
Jos 21:10 Which the children of **A.**, being of 175
Jos 21:13 Thus they gave to the children of **A.** 175
Jos 21:19 All the cities of the children of **A.**, 175
Jos 24:5 I sent Moses also and **A.**, and I 175
Jos 24:33 And Eleazar the son of **A.** died; 175
Jg 20:28 the son of **A.**, stood before it in 175
1Sa 12:6 Lord that advanced Moses and **A.**, 175
1Sa 12:8 then the Lord sent Moses and **A.**, 175
1Ch 6:3 the children of Amram; **A.**, and 175
1Ch 6:3 The sons also of **A.**; Nadab and 175
1Ch 6:49 But **A.** and his sons offered upon 175
1Ch 6:50 these are the sons of **A.**; Eleazar 175
1Ch 6:54 of the sons of **A.**, of the families of 175
1Ch 6:57 And to the sons of **A.** they gave the 175
1Ch 15:4 David assembled the children of **A.**, 175
1Ch 23:13 of Amram; **A.** and Moses: and **A.** 175
1Ch 23:28 office was to wait on the sons of **A.** 175
1Ch 23:32 and the charge of the sons of **A.** 175
1Ch 24:1 are the divisions of the sons of **A.** 175
1Ch 24:1 The sons of **A.**; Nadab and 175
1Ch 24:19 to their manner, under **A.** their 175
1Ch 24:31 their brethren the sons of **A.** in the 175
2Ch 13:9 the sons of **A.**, and the Levites, and 175
2Ch 13:10 unto the Lord, are the sons of **A.**, 175
2Ch 26:18 but to the priests the sons of **A.**, 175
2Ch 29:21 the priests the sons of **A.** to offer 175
2Ch 31:19 Also of the sons of **A.** the priests, 175
2Ch 35:14 because the priests the sons of **A.** 175
2Ch 35:14 and for the priests the sons of **A.** 175
Ezr 7:5 Eleazar, the son of **A.** the chief 175
Ne 10:38 the priest the son of **A.** shall be 175
Ne 12:47 them unto the children of **A.** 175
Ps 77:20 flock by the hand of Moses and **A.** 175
Ps 99:6 Moses and **A.** among his priests, 175
Ps 105:26 He sent Moses his servant; and **A.** 175
Ps 106:16 Moses also in the camp, and **A.** 175
Ps 115:10 O house of **A.**, trust in the Lord: 175
Ps 115:12 he will bless the house of **A.** 175
Ps 118:3 Let the house of **A.** now say, that 175
Ps 135:19 bless the Lord, O house of **A.**: 175
Mic 6:4 I sent before thee Moses, **A.**, and 175
Lu 1:5 wife was of the daughters of **A.**, *2*
Ac 7:40 Saying unto **A.**, Make us gods to *2*
Heb 5:4 that is called of God, as was **A.** *2*
Heb 7:11 not be called after the order of **A.**? *2*

AARONITES (a'-ur-un-ites)
1Ch 12:27 Jehoida was the leader of the **A.**, 175
1Ch 27:17 the son of Kemuel: of the **A.**, 175

AARON'S (a'-ur-uns)
Ex 6:25 Eleazar **A.** son took him one of the 175
Ex 7:12 but **A.** rod swallowed up their rods. 175
Ex 28:1 Eleazar and Ithamar, **A.** sons. 175
Ex 28:3 that they may make **A.** garments 175
Ex 28:36 and they shall be upon **A.** heart, 175
Ex 28:38 And it shall be upon **A.** forehead 175
Ex 28:40 for **A.** sons thou shalt make coats, 175
Ex 29:26 of the ram of **A.** consecration, 175
Ex 29:28 it shall be **A.** and his sons' by a 175
Le 1:5 the priests, **A.** sons, shall bring 175
Le 1:8 the priests, **A.** sons, shall lay the 175
Le 1:11 the priests, **A.** sons, shall sprinkle 175
Le 2:2 he shall bring it to **A.** sons the 175
Le 2:3, 10 of the meat offering shall be **A.** 175
Le 3:2 **A.** sons the priests shall sprinkle 175
Le 3:5 **A.** sons shall burn it on the altar 175
Le 3:8 **A.** sons shall sprinkle the blood 175
Le 7:31 but the breast shall be **A.** and his 175
Le 8:12 the anointing oil upon **A.** head, 175
Le 8:13 Moses brought **A.** sons, and put 175
Le 8:23 put it upon the tip of **A.** right ear, 175
Le 8:24 he brought **A.** sons, and Moses 175
Le 8:27 he put all upon **A.** hands, and 175
Le 9:12, 18 and **A.** sons presented unto him 175
Le 24:9 it shall be **A.** and his sons': and 175
Nu 17:3 thou shalt write **A.** name upon 175
Nu 17:10 Bring **A.** rod again before the 175
Ps 133:2 upon the beard, even **A.** beard: 175
Heb 9:4 pot that had manna and **A.** rod *2*

ABADDON (ab-ad'-dun)
Re 9:11 name in the Hebrew tongue is **A.**, *3*

ABAGTHA (ab-ag'-thah)
Es 1:10 Bigtha, and **A.**, Zethar, and Carcas, 5

ABANA (ab-ay'-nah)
2Ki 5:12 Are not **A.** and Pharpar, rivers of 71

ABARIM (ab'-ar-im) See also IJE-ABARIM.
Nu 27:12 Get thee up into this mount **A.**, 5682
Nu 33:47 pitched in the mountains of **A.**, 5682
Nu 33:48 departed from the mountains of **A.**, 5682
De 32:49 get thee up into this mountain **A.**, 5682

ABASE See also ABASED; ABASING.
Job 40:11 every one that is proud, and **a.** 8213
Isa 31:4 nor **a.** himself for the noise of 6031
Eze 21:26 is low, and **a.** him that is high, 8213
Da 4:37 that walk in pride he is able to **a.** 8214

ABASED
Mt 23:12 **shall exalt himself shall be a.**, *5013*
Lu 14:11 **that exalteth himself shall be a.**; *5013*
Lu 18:14 **that exalteth himself shall be a.**; *5013*
Php 4:12 I know both how to be **a.**, and I *5013*

ABASING
2Co 11:7 **a.** myself that ye might be exalted, *5013*

ABATED
Ge 8:3 and fifty days the waters were **a.** 2637
Ge 8:8 him to see if the waters were **a.** 7043
Ge 8:11 nor knew that the waters were **a.** 7043
Le 27:18 shall be **a.** from thy estimation. 1639
De 34:7 not dim, nor his natural force **a.** 5127
Jg 8:3 their anger was **a.** towards him. 7503

ABBA (ab'-bah)
Mk 14:36 And he said, **A., Father, all things** *5*
Ro 8:15 of adoption, whereby we cry, **A.** *5*
Ga 4:6 into your hearts, crying, **A.**, Father. *5*

ABBAS See BARABBAS.

ABDA (ab'-dah)
1Ki 4:6 and Adoniram the son of **A.** 5653
Ne 11:17 and **A.** the son of Shammua, 5653

ABDEEL (ab'de-el)
Jer 36:26 and Shelemiah the son of **A.**, to 5655

ABDI (ab'-di)
1Ch 6:44 the son of Kishi, the son of **A.**, 5660
2Ch 29:12 Kish the son of **A.**, and Azariah 5660
Ezr 10:26 and Jehiel, and **A.**, and Jeremoth, 5660

ABDIEL (ab'-de-el)
1Ch 5:15 Ahi the son of **A.**, the son of Guni, 5661

ABDON (ab'-dun)
Jos 21:30 Mishal with her suburbs, **A.** with 5658
Jg 12:13 And after him **A.** the son of 5658
Jg 12:15 And **A.** the son of Hillel the 5658
1Ch 6:74 Moshal with her suburbs, and **A.** 5658
1Ch 8:23 Eliel and **A.**, and Zichri and 5658
1Ch 8:30 his firstborn son **A.**, and Zur, and 5658
1Ch 9:36 **A.**, then Zur, and Kish, and Baal, 5658
2Ch 34:20 and **A.** the son of Micah, and 5658

ABED-NEGO (ab-ed'-ne-go)
Da 1:7 Meshach; and to Azariah, of **A.** 5664
Da 2:49 Shadrach, Meshach, and **A.**, over 5665
Da 3:12, 13, 14, 16, 19, 20, 22, 23, 26, 26, 28, 29, 30
Shadrach, Meshach, and **A.** 5665

ABEL (a'-bel) See also ABEL-BETH-MAACHAH; ABEL-MAIM; ABEL-MEHOLAH; ABEL-MIZRAIM; ABEL-SHITTIM.
Ge 4:2 bare his brother **A.**. And **A.** was 1893
Ge 4:4 And **A.**, he also brought of the 1893
Ge 4:4 the Lord had respect unto **A.** and 1893
Ge 4:8 Cain talked with **A.** his brother: 1893
Ge 4:8 that Cain rose up against **A.** his 1893
Ge 4:9 Lord said unto Cain, Where is **A.** 1893
Ge 4:25 me another seed instead of **A.**, 1893
1Sa 6:18 even unto the great stone of **A.**, 59
2Sa 20:14 all the tribes of Israel unto **A.**, 62
2Sa 20:15 they came and besieged him in **A.** 62
2Sa 20:18 They shall surely ask counsel at **A.**: 59
Mt 23:35 **from the blood of righteous A. unto** *6*
Lu 11:51 **From the blood of A. unto the** *6*
Heb 11:4 By faith **A.** offered unto God a more *6*
Heb 12:24 better things than that of **A.** *6*

ABEL-BETH-MASCHAH (a''-bel-beth-ma'-a-kah)
1Ki 15:20 and smote Ijon, and Dan, and **A.**, 62
2Ki 15:29 and took Ijon, and **A.**, and 62

ABEL-MAIM (a''-bel-ma'-im)
2Ch 16:4 they smote Ijon, and Dan, and **A.**, 66

ABEL-MEHOLAH (a''-bel-me-ho'-lah) See also MEHOLATHITE.
Jg 7:22 and to the border of **A.**, unto 65
1Ki 4:12 from Beth-shean to **A.**, even unto 65
1Ki 19:16 Elisha the son of Shaphat of **A.** 65

ABEL-MIZRAIM (a''-bel-miz'-ra-im)
Ge 50:11 the name of it was called **A.**, which 67

ABEL-SHITTIM (a''-bel-shit'-tim)
Nu 33:49 from Beth-jesimoth even unto **A.** 63

ABEZ (a'-bez)
Jos 19:20 And Rabbith, and Kishion, and **A.**, 77

ABHOR See also ABHORRED; ABHORREST; ABHORRETH; ABHORRING.
Le 26:11 and my soul shall not **a.** you. 1602
Le 26:15 if your soul **a.** my judgments, so 1602
Le 26:30 your idols, and my soul shall **a.** you. 1602
Le 26:44 neither will I **a.** them, to destroy 1602
De 7:26 thou shalt utterly **a.** it; for it is a 8581
De 23:7 Thou shalt not **a.** an Edomite; 8581
De 23:7 thou shalt not **a.** an Egyptian: 8581
1Sa 27:12 his people Israel utterly to **a.** him 887
Job 9:31 and mine own clothes shall **a.** me. 8581
Job 30:10 They **a.** me, they flee far from me, 8581
Job 42:6 Wherefore I **a.** myself, and repent 3988
Ps 5:6 the Lord will **a.** the bloody and 8581
Ps 119:163 I hate and **a.** lying: but thy 8581
Pr 24:24 the people curse, nations shall **a.** 2194

Jer 14:21 Do not **a.** us, for thy name's sake, 5006
Am 5:10 and they **a.** him that speaketh 8581
Am 6:8 I **a.** the excellency of Jacob, and 8374
Mic 3:9 Israel, that **a.** judgment, and 8581
Ro 12:9 **A.** that which is evil; cleave to *655*

ABHORRED
Ex 5:21 ye have made our savour to be **a.** 887
Le 20:23 things, and therefore I **a.** them. 6973
Le 26:43 because their soul **a.** my statutes. 1602
De 32:19 when the Lord saw it, he **a.** them, 5006
1Sa 2:17 men **a.** the offering of the Lord. 5006
2Sa 16:21 shall hear that thou art **a.** of thy 887
1Ki 11:25 and he **a.** Israel, and reigned 6973
Job 19:19 All my inward friends **a.** me: 8581
Ps 22:24 he hath not despised nor **a.** the 8262
Ps 78:59 was wroth, and greatly **a.** Israel: 3988
Ps 89:38 thou hast cast off and **a.**, thou 3988
Ps 106:40 that he **a.** his own inheritance, 8581
Pro 22:14 he that is **a.** of the Lord shall fall 2194
La 2:7 he hath **a.** his sanctuary, he hath 5010
Eze 16:25 hast made thy beauty to be **a.**, 8581
Zec 11:8 and their soul also **a.** me. 973

ABHORREST
Isa 7:16 the land that thou **a.** shall be 6973
Ro 2:22 that **a.** idols, dost thou commit *948*

ABHORRETH
Job 33:20 So that his life **a.** bread, and 2092
Ps 10:3 the covetous, whom the Lord **a.**, 5006
Ps 36:4 that is not good; he **a.** not evil. 3988
Ps 107:18 Their soul **a.** all manner of meat; 8581
Isa 49:7 to him whom the nation **a.**, to a 8581

ABHORRING
Isa 66:24 they shall be an **a.** unto all flesh. 1860

ABI (a'-bi) See also ABI-ALBON; ABI-EZER.
2Ki 18:2 His mother's name also was **A.**, 21

ABIA (ab-i'-ah) See also ABIAH; ABIJAH; ABIJAM.
1Ch 3:10 **A.** his son, Asa his son, 29
Mt 1:7 Roboam begat **A.**; and **A.** begat *7*
Lu 1:5 Zacharias, of the course of **A.** : *7*

ABIAH (ab-i'-ah) See also ABIA.
1Sa 8:2 and the name of his second, **A.** : 29
1Ch 2:24 **A.** Hezron's wife bare him Ashur 29
1Ch 6:28 the firstborn Vashni, and **A.** 29
1Ch 7:8 Jerimoth, and **A.**, and Anathoth, 29

ABI-ALBON (ab'-i'-al'bun)
2Sa 23:31 **A.** the Arbathite, Azmaveth the 45

ABIASAPH (ab-i'-as-af) See also EBI-ASAPH.
Ex 6:24 Assir, and Elkanah, and **A.** : 23

ABIATHAR (ab-i'-uth-ur) See also ABIATHAR'S.
1Sa 22:20 son of Ahitub, named **A.**, escaped, 54
1Sa 22:21 And **A.** shewed David that Saul had 54
1Sa 22:22 David said unto **A.**, I knew it that 54
1Sa 23:6 when **A.** the son of Ahimelech fled 54
1Sa 23:9 and he said to **A.** the priest, Bring 54
1Sa 30:7 And David said to **A.** the priest, 54
1Sa 30:7 And **A.** brought thither the ephod 54
2Sa 8:17 and Ahimelech the son of **A.**, were 54
2Sa 15:24 **A.** went up, until all the people 54
2Sa 15:27 and Jonathan the son of **A.**, 54
2Sa 15:29 Zadok therefor and **A.** carried the 54
2Sa 15:35 not there with thee Zadok and **A.** 54
2Sa 15:35 thou shalt tell it to Zadok and **A.** 54
2Sa 17:15 said Hushai unto Zadok and to **A.** 54
2Sa 19:11 king David sent to Zadok and to **A.** 54
2Sa 20:25 and Zodak and **A.** were the priests: 54
1Ki 1:7 the son of Zeruiah, and with **A.** 54
1Ki 1:19 sons of the king, and **A.** the priest, 54
1Ki 1:25 the captains of the host, and **A.** the 54
1Ki 1:42 Jonathan the son of **A.** the priest 54
1Ki 2:22 for him, and for **A.** the priest, 54
1Ki 2:26 unto **A.** the priest said the king, 54
1Ki 2:27 Solomon thrust out **A.** from being 54
1Ki 2:35 did the king put in the room of **A.** 54
1Ki 4:4 and Zadok and **A.** were the priests: 54
1Ch 15:11 And David called for Zadok and **A.** 54
1Ch 18:16 and Abimelech the son of **A.**, were 54
1Ch 24:6 priest, and Ahimelech the son of **A.**, 54
1Ch 27:34 the son of Benaiah, and **A.** : 54
Mr 2:26 **in the days of A. the high priest,** *8*

ABIATHAR'S (ab-i'-uth-urs)
2Sa 15:36 Zadok's son, and Jonathan **A.** 54

ABIB (a'-bib) See also TEL-ABIB.
Ex 13:4 day came ye out in the month **A.** 24
Ex 23:15 time appointed of the month **A.**; 24
Ex 34:18 in the time of the month **A.**: for in 24
Ex 34:18 the month **A.** thou camest out from 24
De 16:1 Observe the month of **A.**, and keep 24
De 16:1 in the month of **A.** the Lord thy God 24

ABIDA (ab'-id-ah) See also ABIDAH.
1Ch 1:33 and Epher, and Henoch, and **A.**. 28

ABIDAH (ab'-id-ah) See also ABIDA
Gen 25:4 and Hanoch, and **A.**, and Eldaah, 28

ABIDAN (ab'-id-an)
Nu 1:11 Of Benjamin; **A.** the son of Gideoni. 27
Nu 2:22 of the sons of Benjamin shall be **A.** 27
Nu 7:60 On the ninth day **A.** the son of 27
Nu 7:65 offering of **A.** the son of Gideoni. 27
Nu 10:24 of the children Benjamin was **A.** 27

ABIDE See also ABIDETH; ABIDING; ABODE.
Ge 19:2 we will **a.** in the street all night. 3885
Ge 22:5 **A.** ye here with the ass; 3427
Ge 24:55 Let the damsel **a.** with us a few 3427
Ge 29:19 **a.** with me. 3427
Ge 44:33 let thy servant **a.** instead of the lad 3427
Ex 16:29 **a.** ye every man in his place, 3427
Le 8:35 Therefore shall ye **a.** at the door of 3427
Le 19:13 shall not **a.** with thee all night 3885
Nu 22:5 they **a.** over against me: 3427
Nu 31:19 **a.** without the camp seven days: 2583
Nu 31:23 Every thing that may **a.** the fire, 935
Nu 35:25 he shall **a.** in it unto the death of 3427
De 3:19 **a.** in your cities which I have 3427
Jos 18:5 Judah shall **a.** in their coast on 5975
Jos 18:5 Joseph shall **a.** in their coasts on 5975
Ru 2:8 **a.** here fast by my maidens: 1692
1Sa 1:22 and there **a.** for ever. 3427
1Sa 5:7 God of Israel shall not **a.** with us: 3427
1Sa 19:2 and **a.** in a secret place, and hide 3427
1Sa 22:5 **A.** not in the hold; 3427
1Sa 22:23 **A.** thou with me, fear not: 3427
1Sa 30:21 whom they had made also to **a.** at 3427
2Sa 11:11 the ark, and Israel, and Judah, **a.** 3427
2Sa 15:19 return to thy place, and **a.** with 3427
2Sa 16:18 with him will I **a.**. 3427
1Ki 8:13 a settled place for thee to **a.** in 3427
2Ch 25:19 **a.** now at home; 3427
2Ch 32:10 ye **a.** in the siege in Jerusalem? 3427
Job 24:13 nor **a.** in the paths thereof. 3427
Job 38:40 and **a.** in the covert to lie in wait? 3427
Job 39: 9 to serve thee, or **a.** by thy crib? 3885
Ps 15:1 who shall **a.** in thy tabernacle? 1481
Ps 61:4 I will **a.** in thy tabernacle 1481
Ps 61:7 He shall **a.** before God for ever: 3427
Ps 91:1 shall **a.** under the shadow 3885
Pr 7:11 her feet **a.** not in her house: 7937
Pr 19:23 he that hath it shall **a.** satisfied; 3885
Ec 8:15 shall **a.** with him of his labour 3867
Jer 10:10 the nations shall not be able to **a.** 3557
Jer 42:10 If ye will still **a.** in this land, 3427
Jer 49:18 no man shall **a.** there, 3427
Jer 49:33 there shall no man **a.** there, 3427
Jer 50:40 so shall no man **a.** there, 3427
Ho 3:3 Thou shalt **a.** for me many days; 3427
Ho 3:4 children of Israel shall **a.** many 3427
Ho 11:6 the sword shall **a.** on his cities, 2342
Joe 2:11 and who can **a.** it? 3557
Mic 5:4 and they shall **a.**. 3427
Na 1:6 who can **a.** in the fierceness of his 6965
Mal 3:2 may **a.** the day of his coming? 3557
Mt 10:11 **and there a. till ye go thence.** *3306*
Mk 6:10 **a. till ye depart from that place.** *3306*
Lu 9:4 **there a., and thence depart.** *3306*
Lu 19:5 **for to-day I must a. at thy house.** *3306*
Lu 24:29 constrained him, saying, **A.** with *3306*
Joh 12:46 **believeth on me should not a. in** 3306
Joh 14:16 **that, he may a. with you for ever:** *3306*
Joh 15:4 **A. in me, and I in you** *3306*
Joh 15:4 **except it a. in the vine;** *3306*
Joh 15:4 **no more can ye, except ye a. in me** *3306*
Joh 15:6 **If a man a. not in me, he is cast** *3306*
Joh 15:7 **If ye a. in me, and my words a. in** *3306*
Joh 15:10 **ye shall a. in my love.** *3306*
Joh 15:10 **and a. in his love.** *3306*

Ac 15:34 it pleased Silas to **a.** there still. *1961*
Ac 16:15 come into my house, and **a.** there. *3306*
Ac 20:23 and afflictions **a.** me. *3306*
Ac 27:31 Except these **a.** in the ship, *3306*
Ro 11:23 if they **a.** not still in unbelief, *1961*
1Co 3:14 any man's work **a.** which he hath *3306*
1Co 7:8 if they **a.** even as I. *3306*
1Co 7:20 every man **a.** in the same calling *3306*
1Co 7:24 every man,....therein **a.** with God. *3306*
1Co 7:40 she is happier if she so **a.**, *3306*
1Co 16:6 And it may be that I will **a.**, yea, *3887*
Php 1:24 to **a.** in the flesh is more needful *1961*
Php 1:25 know that I shall **a.** and continue *3306*
1Ti 1:3 to **a.** still at Ephesus, *4357*
1Jo 2:24 Let that therefore **a.** in you, *3306*
1Jo 2:27 ye shall **a.** in him. *3306*
1Jo 2:28 little children, **a.** in him; *3306*

ABIDETH
Nu 31:23 all that **a.** not the fire ye shall 935
2Sa 16:3 he **a.** at Jerusalem: 3427
Job 39:28 She dwelleth and **a.** on the rock, 3885
Ps 49:12 man being in honour **a.** not: 3885
Ps 55:19 even he that **a.** of old. 3427
Ps 119:90 established the earth, and it **a.**. 5975
Ps 125:1 cannot be removed, but **a.** for ever. 3427
Pr 15:31 reproof of life **a.** among the wise. 3885
Ec 1:4 the earth **a.** for ever. 5975
Jer 21:9 He that **a.** in this city shall die 3427
Joh 3:36 the wrath of God **a.** on him. *3306*
Joh 8:35 **the servant a. not in the house for** *3306*
Joh 8:35 **but the Son a. ever.** *3306*
Joh 12:24 **ground and die, it a. alone:** *3306*
Joh 12:34 of the law that Christ **a.** for ever: *3306*
Joh 15:5 **He that a. in me, and I in him,** *3306*
1Co 13:13 now **a.** faith, hope, charity, *3306*
2Ti 2:13 he **a.** faithful: he cannot deny *3306*
Heb 7:3 **a.** a priest continually. *3306*
1Pe 1:23 which liveth and **a.** for ever. *3306*
1Jo 2:6 He that saith he **a.** in him. *3306*
1Jo 2:10 **a.** in the light, *3306*
1Jo 2:14 the word of God **a.** in you, *3306*
1Jo 2:17 doeth the will of God **a.** for ever. *3306*
1Jo 2:27 received of him **a.** in you, *3306*
1Jo 3:6 Whosoever **a.** in him sinneth not: *3306*
1Jo 3:14 He that loveth not his brother **a.** in *3306*
1Jo 3:24 hereby we know that he **a.** in us, *3306*
2Jo 1:9 **a.** not in the doctrine of Christ, *3306*
2Jo 1:9 He that **a.** in the doctrine *3306*

ABIDING
Nu 24:2 he saw Israel **a.** in his tents 7931
Jg 16.9 **a.** with her in the chamber 3427
Jg 16:12 **a.** in the chamber. 3427
1Sa 26:19 driven me out this day from **a.** 5596
1Ch 29:15 there is none **a.** 4728
Lu 2:8 shepherds **a.** in the field, *63*
Joh 5:38 **ye have not his word a. in you:** *3306*
Ac 16:12 were in that city **a.** certain days. *1304*
1Jo 3:15 no murderer hath eternal life **a.** *3306*

ABIEL (a'-be-el)
1Sa 9:1 name was Kish, the son of **A.**, 22
1Sa 14:51 father of Abner was the son of **A.** 22
1Ch 11:32 Hurai of the brooks of Gaash, **A.** 22

ABIEZER or **ABI-EZER** (ab-i-e'-zur) See also ABIEZRITE; JEEZER.
Jos 17:2 for the children of **A.** and for the 44
Jg 6:34 and **A.** was gathered after him. 44
Jg 8:2 better than the vintage of **A**? 44
2Sa 23:27 **A** the Anethothite, Mebunnai the 44
1Ch 7:18 Hammoleketh bare Ishod, and **A** 44
1Ch 11:28 Ikkesh the Tekoite, **A** the Antothite 44
1Ch 27:12 captain for the ninth month was **A** 44

ABI-EZRITE (ab-i-ez'-rite) See also ABI-EZRITES.
Jg 6:11 that pertained unto Joash the **A.**: 33

ABI-EZRITES
Jg 6:24 it is yet in Ophrah of the **A.** 33
Jg 8:32 his father, in Ophrah of the **A.** 33

ABIGAIL (ab'-e'gul)
1Sa 25:3 Nabal: and the name of his wife **A.**: 26
1Sa 25:14 But one of the young men told **A.**, 26
1Sa 25:18 Then **A.** made haste, and took two 26
1Sa 25:23 when **A.** saw David, she hasted, 26
1Sa 25:32 David said to **A.**, Blessed be the Lord 26
1Sa 25:36 And **A.** came to Nabel; and, behold, 26

1Sa 25:39 David sent and communed with **A.**,........ 26
1Sa 25:40 servants of David were come to **A.** 26
1Sa 25:42 And **A.** hasted, and arose, and rode....... 26
1Sa 27:3 **A.** the Carmelitess, Nabal's wife. 26
1Sa 30:5 **A.** the wife of Nabal the Carmelite. 26
2Sa 2:2 and **A.** Nabal's wife the Carmelite......... 26
2Sa 3:3 **A.** the wife of Nabal the Carmelite; 26
2Sa 17:25 in to **A.** the daughter of Nahash, ... 26
1Ch 2:16 Whose sisters were Zeruiah, and **A.**. 26
1Ch 2:17 and **A.** bare Amasa: and the father 26
1Ch 3:1 the second Daniel, of **A.** the................ 26

ABIHAIL (ab-e-ha'-il)
Nu 3:35 of Merari was Zuriel the son of **A.**: 32
1Ch 2:29 name of the wife of Abishur was **A.**, ... 32
1Ch 5:14 These are the children of **A.** the son...... 32
2Ch 11:18 and **A.** the daughter of Eliab the 32
Es 2:15 the daughter of **A.** the uncle of............ 32
Es 9:29 Esther the queen, the daughter of **A.**,.... 32

ABIHU (a-bi'-hew)
Ex 6:23 and she bare him Nadab and **A.**, ... 30
Ex 24:1 thou, and Aaron, Nadab, and **A.**, ... 30
Ex 24:9 Moses, and Aaron, Nadab, and **A.**, ... 30
Ex 28:1 office, even Aaron, Nadab and **A.**, ... 30
Le 10:1 Nadab and **A.**, the sons of Aaron, ... 30
Nu 3:2 Nadab the firstborn, and **A.**,................ 30
Nu 3:4 Nadab and **A.** died before the Lord,....... 30
Nu 26:60 unto Aaron was born Nadab, and **A.**, ... 30
Nu 26:61 And Nadab and **A.** died, when they........ 30
1Ch 6:3 sons also of Aaron; Nadab, and **A.**,....... 30
1Ch 24:1 The sons of Aaron; Nadab, and **A.**, ... 30
1CH 24:2 But Nadab and **A.** died before their 30

ABIHUD (a-bi'-hud)
1Ch 8:3 Addar, and Gera, and **A.**, ... 31

ABIJAH (a-bi'-jah) See also ABIA; ABIJAM.
1Ki 14:1 At that time **A.** the son of Jeroboam 29
1Ch 24:10 seventh to Hakkoz, the eighth to **A.**, ... 29
2Ch 11:20 which bare him **A.**, and Attai, and 29
2Ch 11:22 Rehoboam made **A.** the son of............. 29
2Ch 12:16 and **A.** his son reigned in his stead. 29
2Ch 13:1 year of king Jeroboam began **A.** to 29
2Ch 13:2 was war between **A.** and Jeroboam. 29
2Ch 13:3 And **A.** set the battle in array with 29
2Ch 13:4 **A.** stood up upon mount Zemaraim, ... 29
2Ch 13:15 Jeroboam and all Israel before **A.** 29
2Ch 13:17 And **A.** and his people slew them 29
2Ch 13:19 And **A.** pursued after Jeroboam,............ 29
2Ch 13:20 strength again in the days of **A.** 29
2Ch 13:21 But **A.** waxed mighty, and married 29
2CH 13:22 rest of the acts of **A.**, and his ways, ... 29
2Ch 14:1 So **A.** slept with his fathers,................ 29
2Ch 29:1 And his mother's name was **A.**, ... 29
Ne 10:7 Meshullam, **A.**, Mijamin,...................... 29
Ne 12:4 Iddo, Ginnetho, **A.**, ... 29
Ne 12:17 Of **A.**, Zichri; of Miniamin, of 29

ABIJAM (a-bi'-jum) See also ABIJAH.
1Ki 14:31 And **A.** his son reigned in his stead. 38
1Ki 15:1 reigned **A.** over Judah. 38
1Ki 15:7 the rest of the acts of **A.**, and all 38
1Ki 15:7 was war between **A.** and Jeroboam. 38
1Ki 15:8 And **A.** slept with his fathers; and 38

ABILENE (ab-i-le'-ne)
Lu 3:1 **Lysanias the tetrarch of A.**,............... *9*

ABILITY
Le 27:8 according to his **a.** that vowed........... 5381
Ezr 2:69 They gave after their **a.** 3581
Ne 5:8 We after our **a.** have redeemed 1767
Da 1:4 such as had **a.** in them..................... 3581
Mt 25:15 **according to his several a.**; *1411*
Ac 11:29 every man according to his **a.**,........... *2141*
1Pe 4:11 as of the **a.** which God giveth;........... *2479*

ABIMAEL (a-bim'-ah-el)
Ge 10:28 And Obal, and **A.**. and Sheba,............... 39
1Ch 1:22 And Ebal, and **A.**. and Sheba............... 39

ABIMELECH (a-bim'-e-lek) See also ABIMELECH'S; AHIMELECH.
Ge 20:2 and **A.** king of Gerar sent, and took....... 40
Ge 20:3 But God came to **A.** in a dream 40
Ge 20:4 But **A.** had not come near her: 40
Ge 20:8 **A.** rose early in the morning, ... 40
Ge 20:9 Then **A.** called Abraham, and said 40
Ge 20:10 **A.** said unto Abraham, What sawest...... 40
Ge 20:14 And **A.** took sheep, and oxen, and......... 40
Ge 20:15 **A.** said, Behold, my land is before......... 40
Ge 20:17 and God healed **A.**, and his wife,........... 40
Ge 20:18 all the wombs of the house of **A.**, ... 40
Ge 21:22 that **A.** and Phichol the chief captain 40
Ge 21:25 And Abraham reproved **A.** because 40
Ge 21:26 **A.** said I wot not who hath done........... 40
Ge 21:27 and oxen, and gave them unto **A.**;.......... 40
Ge 21:29 **A.** said unto Abraham, What mean......... 40
Ge 21:32 then **A.** rose up, and Phichol the.......... 40
Ge 26:1 And Isaac went unto **A.** king of the 40
Ge 26:8 **A.** king of the Philistines looked............ 40
Ge 26:9 And **A.** called Isaac, and said,............... 40
Ge 26:10 **A.** said, What is this thou hast done 40
Ge 26:11 **A.** charged all his people, saying, ... 40
Ge 26:16 And **A.** said unto Isaac, Go from us; 40
Ge 26:26 Then **A.** went to him from Gerar, ... 40
Jg 8:31 a son, whose name he called **A.**. 40
Jg 9:1 And **A.** the son of Jerubbaal went.......... 40
Jg 9:3 their hearts inclined to follow **A.**; 40
Jg 9:4 **A.** hired vain and light persons, ... 40
Jg 9:6 and went, and made **A.** king,................ 40
Jg 9:16 in that ye have made **A.** king,............... 40
Jg 9:18 made **A.**, the son of his maidservant. 40
Jg 9:19 then rejoice ye in **A.**, and let him.......... 40
Jg 9:20 But if not, let fire come out from **A.**, ... 40
Jg 9:20 the house of Millo, and devour **A.**. 40
Jg 9:21 and dwelt there, for fear of **A.** his.......... 40
Jg 9:22 When **A.** had reigned three years.......... 40
Jg 9:23 God sent an evil spirit between **A.** 40
Jg 9:23 dealt treacherously with **A.**: 40
Jg 9:24 **A.** their brother, which slew them: 40
Jg 9:25 way by them: and it was told **A.**. 40
Jg 9:27 did eat and drink, and cursed **A.**. 40
Jg 9:28 Who is **A.**, and who is Shechem,............. 40
Jg 9:29 my hand then would I remove **A.**. 40
Jg 9:29 he said to **A.**, Increase thine army,......... 40
Jg 9:31 he sent messengers unto **A.** privily,........ 40
Jg 9:34 And **A.** rose up, and all the people 40
Jg 9:35 And **A.** rose up, and the people that...... 40
Jg 9:38 Who is **A.**, that we should serve him?.... 40
Jg 9:39 of Shechem, and fought with **A.**. 40
Jg 9:40 **A.** chased him, and he fled before 40
Jg 9:41 And **A.** dwelt at Arumah; and Zebul........ 40
Jg 9:42 out into the field; and they told **A.**......... 40
Jg 9:44 **A.**, and the company that was with........ 40
Jg 9:45 And **A.** fought against the city all 40
Jg 9:47 And it was told **A.**, that all the men........ 40
Jg 9:48 **A.** gat him up to mount Zalmon,............ 40
Jg 9:48 and **A.** took an axe in his hand,............ 40
Jg 9:49 and followed **A.**, and put them to the..... 40
Jg 9:50 went **A.** to Thebez, and encamped 40
Jg 9:52 And **A.** came unto the tower, ... 40
Jg 9:55 men of Israel saw that **A.** was dead, ... 40
Jg 9:56 God rendered the wickedness of **A.**, ... 40
Jg 10:1 after **A.** there arose to defend Israel...... 40
2Sa 11:21 smote **A.** the son of Jerubbesheth? 40
1Ch 18:16 and **A.** the son of Abiathar,................... 40
Ps 34:*title* changed his behaviour before **A.**;........... 40

ABIMELECH'S (a-bim'-e-leks)
Ge 21:25 **A.** servants had violently taken............ 40
Jg 9:53 a piece of a millstone upon **A.** head. 40

ABINADAB (a-bin'-ah-dab)
1Sa 7:1 and brought it into the house of **A.**......... 41
1Sa 16:8 Jesse called **A.**, and made him pass 41
1Sa 17:13 and next unto him **A.**, and the third....... 41
1Sa 31:2 Philistines slew Jonathan, and **A.**, ... 41
2Sa 6:3 brought it out of the house of **A.**........... 41
2Sa 6:3 the sons of **A.**, drave the new cart. 41
2Sa 6:4 brought it out of the house of **A.**........... 41
1Ki 4:11 son of **A.**, in all the region of Dor; 41
1Ch 2:13 begat his firstborn Eliah, and **A.** the....... 41
1Ch 8:33, 9:39 and Malchishua, and **A.**,................. 41
1Ch 10:2 Philistines slew Jonathan, and **A.**, ... 41
1Ch 13:7 in a new cart out of the house of **A.**: 41

ABINOAM (a-bin'-o-am)
Jg 4:6 sent and called Barak the son of **A.** 42
Jg 4:12 that Barak the son of **A.** was gone 42
Jg 5:1 Deborah and Barak the son of **A.** 42
Jg 5:12 thy captivity captive, thou son of **A.** 42

ABIRAM (a-bi'-rum)
Nu 16:1 Dathan and **A.**, the sons of Eliab,.......... 48
Nu 16:12 Moses sent to call Dathan, and **A.**,......... 48
Nu 16:24 tabernacle of Korah, Dathan, and **A.**. 48
Nu 16:25 up and went unto Dathan and **A.**; 48
Nu 16:27 tabernacle of Korah, Dathan, and **A.**, ... 48
Nu 16:27 Dathan and **A.** came out, and stood 48
Nu 26:9 Eliab; Nemuel, and Dathan, and **A.**......... 48
NU 26:9 Dathan and **A.**, which were famous........ 48
De 11:6 what he did unto Dathan and **A.**,........... 48
1Ki 16:34 he laid the foundations thereof in **A.**........ 48
Ps 106:17 and covered the company of **A.**............. 48

ABISHAG (ab'-e-shag)
1Ki 1:3 and found **A.** a Shunammite.................. 49
1K1 1:15 and **A.** the Shunammite ministered.......... 49
1Ki 2:17 give me **A.** the Shunammite to wife. 49
1Ki 2:21 she said, Let **A.** the Shunammite be 49
1Ki 23:22 dost thou ask **A.** the Shunammite.......... 49

ABISHAI (ab'-e-shahee)
1Sa 26:6 and to **A.** the son of Zeruiah. 52
1Sa 26:6 **A.** said, I will go down with thee. 52
1Sa 26:7 So David and **A.** came to the people 52
1Sa 26:8 said **A.** to David, God hath delivered...... 52
1Sa 26:9 David said to **A.**, Destroy him not:......... 52
2Sa 2:18 sons of Zeruiah there, Joab, and **A.**, ... 52
2Sa 2:24 also and **A.** pursued after Abner:............ 52
2Sa 3:30 Joab and **A.** his brother slew Abner, ... 52
2Sa 10:10 he delivered into the hand of **A.**............ 52
2Sa 10:14 then fled they also before **A.**,................ 52
2Sa 16:9 Then said **A.** the son of Zeruiah unto..... 52
2Sa 16:11 David said to **A.**, and to all his.............. 52
2Sa 18:2 a third part under the hand of **A.**........... 52
2Sa 18:5 the king commanded Joab and **A.**............ 52
2Sa 18:12 hearing the king charged thee and **A.** 52
2Sa 19:21 But **A.** the son of Zeruiah answered........ 52
2Sa 20:6 David said to **A.**, Now shall Sheba.......... 52
2Sa 20:10 So Joab and **A.** his brother pursued 52
2Sa 21:17 **A.** the son of Zeruiah succoured him, ... 52
2Sa 23:18 And **A.**, the brother of Joab, the son...... 52
1Ch 2:16 the sons of Zeruiah; **A.**, and Joab, ... 52
1Ch 11:20 **A.** the brother of Joab, he was chief 52
1Ch 18:12 **A.** the son of Zeruiah slew of the.......... 52
1Ch 19:11 he delivered unto the hand of **A.**............ 52
1Ch 19:15 likewise fled before **A.** his brother,........ 52

ABISHALOM (a-bish'-ah-lum) See also ABSALOM.
1Ki 15:2, 10 Maachah, the daughter of **A.**............ 53

ABISHUA (a-bish'-u-ah)
1Ch 6:4 begat Phinehas, Phinehas begat **A.**, ... 50
1Ch 6:5 **A.** begat Bukki, and Bukki begat........... 50
1Ch 6:50 Phinehas his son, **A.** his son,................ 50
1Ch 8:4 And **A.**, and Naaman, and Ahoah,........... 50
Ezr 7:5 The son of **A.**, the son of Phinehas, ... 50

ABISHUR (ab'-e-shur)
1Ch 2:28 the sons of Shammai; Nadab and **A.**........ 51
1Ch 2:29 name of the wife of **A.** was Abihail, ... 51

ABITAL (ab'-e-tal)
2Sa 3:4 the fifth, Shephatiah the son of **A.**; 37
1Ch 3:3 The fifth, Shephatiah of **A.**: 37

ABITUB (ab'-e'tub)
1Ch 8:11 of Hushim he begat **A.**, and Elpaal,......... 36

ABIUD (a-bi'-ud)
Mt 1:13 Zorobabel begat **A.**; and **A.** begat.......... *10*

ABJECTS
Ps 35:15 **a.** gathered themselves together 5222

ABLE See also BLAMEABLE; CHANGEABLE; CHARGEABLE; COMFORTABLE; COMPARABLE; CONFORMABLE; CORRUPTIBLE; DAMNABLE; DECEIVABLENESS; DELECTABLE; DESIRABLE; DETESTABLE; DURABLE; ENABLED; FAVOURABLE; FORCIBLE; HONOURABLE; INCORRUPTIBLE; INCREDIBLE; INCURABLE; INEXCUSABLE; INFALLIBLE; LAMENTABLE; MISERABLE; MOVEABLE; PEACEABLE; POSSIBLE; PROFITABLE; QUENCHABLE; REBUKABLE; REPROVABLE; REASONABLE; SATIABLE; SEARCHABLE; VARIABLENESS.
Ge 13:6 the land was not **a.** to bear them, ... 5375
Ge 15:5 if thou be **a.** to number them 3201
Ge 33:14 and the children be **a.** to endure, ... 7272
Ex 10:5 one cannot be **a.** to see the earth: 3201
Ex 18:18 thou art not **a.** to perform it............. 3201
Ex 18:21 provide out of all the people **a.**.......... 2428
Ex 18:23 then thou shalt be **a.** to endure,......... 3201
Ex 18:25 Moses chose **a.** men out of all........... 2428
Ex 40:35 Moses was not **a.** to enter into the 3201
Le 5:7 be not **a.** to bring a lamb, ... 5060, 1767
Le 5:11 he be not **a.** 5381
Le 12:8 be not **a.** to bring a lamb, ... 4672, 1767
Le 14:22 such as he is **a.** to get; 5381
Le 14:31 such as he is **a.** to get, the one for 5381
Le 14:32 whose hand is not **a.** to get that 5381
Le 25:26 himself be **a.** to redeem it; 5381
Le 25:28 if he be not **a.** to restore it 4672, 1767
Le 25:49 he be **a.**, he may redeem himself. 5381

Nu 1:3 all that are **a.** to go forth to war... 3318
Nu 1:20, 22, 24, 26, 28, 30, 32, 34, 36, 38, 40,42,
45 all that were **a.** to go forth to war... 3318
Nu 11:14 I am not **a.** to bear all this people... 3201
Nu 13:30 we are well **a.** to overcome it... 3201
Nu 13:31 not **a.** to go up against the people;... 3201
Nu 14:16 the Lord was not **a.** to bring this... 3201
Nu 22:11 I shall be **a.** to overcome them,... 3201
Nu 22:37 am I not **a.** indeed to promote thee... 3201
Nu 26:2 all that are **a.** to go to war... 3318
De 1:9 am not **a.** to bear you myself alone:... 3201
De 7:24 no man be **a.** to stand before thee,... 3320
De 9:28 Lord was not **a.** to bring them... 3201
De 11:25 no man be **a.** to stand before you:... 3320
De 14:24 thou art not **a.** to carry it;... 3201
De 16:17 man shall give as he is **a.**,... 4979, 3027
Jos 1:5 There shall not any man be **a.** to... 3320
Jos 14:12 I shall be **a.** to drive them out,...
Jos 23:9 hath been **a.** to stand before you... 5975
Jg 8:3 what was **I a.** to do... 3201
1Sa 6:20 Who is **a.** to stand before this holy... 3201
1Sa 17:9 If he be **a.** to fight with me,... 3201
1Sa 17:33 Thou art not **a.** to go against this... 3201
1Ki 3:9 **a.** to judge this thy so great people?... 3201
1Ki 9:21 children of Israel also were not **a.**... 3201
2Ki 3:21 all that were **a.** to put on armour,... 2296
2Ki 18:23 thou be **a.** on thy part to set riders... 3201
2Ki 18:29 he shall not be **a.** to deliver you... 3201
1Ch 5:18 men **a.** to bear buckler and sword,... 5375
1Ch 9:13 **a.** men for the work of the service... 2428
1Ch 26:8 **a.** men for strength for the service,... 2428
1Ch 29:14 that we should be **a.** to offer... 6113, 3581
2Ch 2:6 is **a.** to build him an house,... 3581
2Ch 7:7 **a.** to receive the burnt offerings,... 3201
2Ch 20:6 that none is **a.** to withstand thee?...
2Ch 20:37 they were not **a.** to go to Tarshish... 6113
2Ch 25:5 choice men, **a.** to go forth to war,...
2Ch 25:9 Lord is **a.** to give thee much more...
2Ch 32:13 any ways **a.** to deliver their lands... 3201
2Ch 32:14 your God should be **a.** to deliver... 3201
2Ch 32:15 was **a.** to deliver his poeple... 3201
Ezr 10:13 we are not **a.** to stand without,... 3581
Ne 4:10 we are not **a.** to build the wall... 3201
Job 41:10 who then is **a.** to stand before me?...
Ps 18:38 that they were not **a.** to rise:... 3201
Ps 21:11 they are not **a.** to perform... 3201
Ps 36:12 shall not be **a.** to rise... 3201
Ps 40:12 I am not **a.** to look up;... 3201
Pr 27:4 who is **a.** to stand before envy?...
Ec 8:17 yet shall he not be **a.** to find it... 3201
Isa 36:8 thou be **a.** on thy part to set riders... 3201
Isa 36:14 he shall not be **a.** to deliver you... 3201
Isa 47:11 thou shalt not be **a.** to put it off:... 3201
Isa 47:12 if so be thou shalt be **a.** to profit,... 3201
Jer 10:10 the nations shall not be **a.** to abide... 3201
Jer 11:11 they shall not be **a.** to escape;... 3201
Jer 49:10 he shall not be **a.** to hide himself:... 3201
La 1:14 I am not **a.** to rise up... 3201
Eze 7:19 their gold shall not be **a.** to deliver... 3201
Eze 33:12 shall the righteous be **a.** to live... 3201
Eze 46:5 as he shall be **a.** to give,... 4991, 3027
Eze 46:11 the lambs as he is **a.** to give,... 4991, 3027
Da 2:26 Art thou **a.** to make known unto... 3546
Da 3:17 God whom we serve is **a.** to deliver... 3202
Da 4:18 not **a.** to make known unto me the... 3202
Da 4:18 but thou art **a.**; for the spirit of... 3546
Da 4:37 walk in pride he is **a.** to abase... 3202
Da 6:20 **a.** to deliver thee from the lions?... 3202
Am 7:10 land is not **a.** to bear all his words... 3201
Zep 1:18 nor their gold shall be **a.** to deliver... 3201
Mt 3:9 God is **a.** of these stone to raise... *1410*
Mt 9:28 **Believe ye that I am a. to do this?**... *1410*
Mt 10:28 **but are not a. to kill the soul;**... *1410*
Mt 10:28 **fear him which is a. to destroy**... *1410*
Mt 19:12 **He that is a. to receive it, let him**... *1410*
Mt 20:22 **Are ye a. to drink of the cup that I** *1410*
Mt 20:22 They say unto him, We are **a.**... *1410*
Mt 22:46 no man was **a.** to answer him... *1410*
Mt 26:61 am **a.** to destroy the temple of God,... *1410*
Mt 4:33 as they were **a.** to hear... *1410*
Mt 22:46 no man was **a.** to answer him... *1410*
Mt 26:61 am **a.** to destroy the temple of God,... *1410*
Mk 4:33 as they were **a.** to hear... *1410*
Lu 1:20 shalt be dumb, and not **a.** to speak,... *1410*
Lu 3:8 God is **a.** of these stones to raise... *1410*
Lu 12:26 **ye then be not a. to do that thing**... *1410*
Lu 13:24 **to enter in, and shall not be a.**... *2480*
Lu 14:29 **is not a. to finish it, all that**... *2480*
Lu 14:30 **began to build, and was not a. to**... *2480*
Lu 14:31 **whether he be a. with ten**... *1415*
Lu 21:15 **not be a. to gainsay nor resist**... *1410*
Joh 10:29 **no man is a. to pluck them out of**... *1410*
Joh 21:6 now they were not **a.** to draw it... *2480*
Ac 6:10 were not **a.** to resist the wisdom... *2480*
Ac 15:10 neither our fathers nor we were **a.**... *2480*
Ac 20:32 the word of his grace, which is **a.**... *1410*
Ac 25:5 which among you are **a.**, to go down... *1415*
Ro 4:21 what he had promised, he was **a.**... *1415*
Ro 8:39 shall be **a.** to separate us from the... *1410*
Ro 11:23 God is **a.** to graff them in again... *1415*
Ro 14:4 for God is **a.** to make him stand... *1415*
Ro 15:14 **a.** also to admonish one another... *1410*
1Co 3:2 hitherto ye were not **a.** to bear it,... *1410*
1Co 3:2 neither yet now are ye **a.**... *1410*
1Co 6:5 not one that shall be **a.** to judge... *1410*
1Co 10:13 to be tempted above that ye are **a.**;... *1410*
1Co 10:13 that ye may be **a.** to bear it... *1410*
2Co 1:4 may be **a.** to comfort them which... *1410*
2Co 3:6 hath made us **a.** ministers of the... *2427*
2Co 9:8 God is **a.** to make all grace abound... *1415*
Eph 3:18 **a.** to comeprehend with all saints... *1840*
Eph 3:20 Now unto him that is **a.** to do... *1410*
Eph 6:11 that ye may be **a.** to stand against... *1410*
Eph 6:13 thay ye may be **a.** to withstand in... *1410*
Eph 6:16 ye shall be **a.** to quench all the... *1410*
Php 3:21 he is **a.** even to subdue all things... *1410*
2Ti 1:12 persuaded that he is **a.** to keep... *1415*
2Ti 2:2 shall be **a.** to teach others also... *2425*
2Ti 3:7 never **a.** to come to the knowledge... *1410*
2Ti 3:15 scriptures, which are **a.** to make... *1410*
Tit 1:9 he may be **a.** by sound doctrine... *1415*
Heb 2:18 he is **a.** to succour them that are... *1410*
Heb 5:7 was **a.** to save him from death,... *1410*
Heb 7:25 Wherefore he is **a.** also to save... *1410*
Heb 11:19 that God was **a.** to raise him up,... *1415*
Jas 1:21 which is **a.** to save your souls... *1410*
Jas 3:2 **a.** also to bridle the whole body... *1415*
Jas 4:12 lawgiver, who is **a.** to save and to... *1410*
2Pe 1:15 ye may be **a.** after my decease to... *2192*
Jude 24 Now unto him that is **a.** to keep... *1410*
Re 5:3 was **a.** to open the book, neither... *1410*
Re 6:17 who shall be **a.** to stand?... *1410*
Re 13:4 who is **a.** to make war with him?... *1410*
Re 15:8 was **a.** to enter into the temple,... *1410*

ABLY See ABOMINABLY; BLAMEABLY.

ABNER (ab'-nur) See also ABNER'S.
1Sa 14:50 of the captain of his host was **A.**,... 74
1Sa 14:51 Ner the father of **A.** was the son of... 74
1Sa 17:55 said unto **A.**, the captain of the host,... 74
1Sa 17:55 **A.**, whose son is this youth?... 74
1Sa 17:55 **A.** said, As thy soul liveth, O king,... 74
1Sa 17:57 **A.** took him, and brought him... 74
1Sa 20:25 and Jonathan arose, and **A.** sat by... 74
1Sa 26:5 and **A.** the son of Ner, the captain... 74
1Sa 26:7 **A.** and the people lay round about... 74
1Sa 26:14 David cried to the people, and to **A.**... 74
1Sa 26:14 saying, Answerest thou not, **A.**?... 74
1Sa 26:14 **A.** answered and said, Who art thou... 74
1Sa 26:15 David said to **A.**, Art not thou a... 74
2Sa 2:8 **A.** the son of Ner, captain of Saul's... 74
2Sa 2:12 **A.** the son of Ner, and the servants... 74
2Sa 2:14 **A.** said to Joab, Let the young men... 74
2Sa 2:17 **A.** was beaten, and the men of Israel,... 74
2Sa 2:19 And Asahel pursued after **A.**; and... 74
2Sa 2:19 nor to the left from following **A.**... 74
2Sa 2:20 **A.** looked behind him, and said,... 74
2Sa 2:21 And **A.** said to him, Turn thee aside... 74
2Sa 2:22 **A.** said again to Asahel, Turn thee... 74
2Sa 2:23 **A.** with the hinder end of the spear... 74
2Sa 2:24 also and Abishai pursued after **A.**:... 74
2Sa 2:25 themselves together after **A.**,... 74
2Sa 2:26 Then **A.** called to Joab, and said,... 74
2Sa 2:29 **A.** and his men walked all that... 74
2Sa 2:30 Joab returned from following **A.**:... 74
2Sa 3:6 that **A.** made himself strong for the... 74
2Sa 3:7 Ishbosheth said to **A.**, Wherefore... 74
2Sa 3:8 Then was **A.** very wroth for the... 74
2Sa 3:9 So do God to **A.**, and more also,... 74
2Sa 3:11 And he could not answer **A.** a word... 74
2Sa 3:12 And **A.** sent messengers to David... 74
2Sa 3:16 Then said **A.** unto him, Go, return... 74
2Sa 3:17 And **A.** had communication with... 74
2Sa 3:19 And **A.** also spake in the ears of... 74
2Sa 3:19 **A.** went also to speak in the ears of... 74
2Sa 3:20 So **A.** came to David and Hebron,... 74
2Sa 3:20 David made **A.** and the men that... 74
2Sa 3:21 **A.** said unto David, I will arise and... 74
2Sa 3:21 David sent **A.** away; and he went in... 74
2Sa 3:22 **A.** was not with David in Hebron;... 74
2Sa 3:23 **A.** the son of Ner came to the king,... 74
2Sa 3:24 behold, **A.** came unto thee; why is... 74
2Sa 3:25 Thou knowest **A.** the son of Ner,... 74
2Sa 3:26 he sent messengers after **A.**, which... 74
2Sa 3:27 when **A.** was returned to Hebron,... 74
2Sa 3:28 for ever from the blood of **A.** the... 74
2Sa 3:30 and Abishai his brother slew **A.**,... 74
2Sa 3:31 sackcloth, and mourn before **A.**... 74
2Sa 3:32 And they buried **A.** in Hebron; and... 74
2Sa 3:32 voice, and wept at the grave of **A.**;... 74
2Sa 3:33 the king lamented over **A.**, and said,... 74
2Sa 3:33 Died **A.** as a fool dieth?... 74
2Sa 3:37 that it was not of the king to slay **A.**... 74
2Sa 4:1 Saul's son heard that **A.** was dead... 74
2Sa 4:12 and buried it in the sepulchre of **A.**... 74
1Ki 2:5 unto **A.** the son of Ner, and unto... 74
1Ki 2:32 to wit, **A.** the son of Ner, captain of... 74
1Ch 26:28 Saul the son of Kish, and **A.** the son... 74
1Ch 27:21 of Benjamin, Jaasiel the son of **A.**:... 74

ABNER'S (ab'-nurs)
2Sa 2:31 of Benjamin, and of **A.** men, so that... 74

ABOARD
Ac 21:2 we went **a.**, and set forth... *1910*

ABODE See also ABODEST.
Ge 29:14 **a.** with him the space of a month,... 3427
Ge 49:24 But his bow **a.** in strength, and... 3427
Ex 24:16 glory of the Lord **a.** upon mount... 7931
Ex 40:35 because the cloud **a.** thereon,... 7931
Nu 9:17 the place where the cloud **a.**, there... 7931
Nu 9:18 as long as the cloud **a.** upon the... 7931
Nu 9:20 **a.** in their tents, and according... 2583
Nu 9:21 when the cloud **a.** from even... 1961
Nu 9:22 the children of Israel **a.** in their... 2583
Nu 11:35 unto Hazeroth; and **a.** at... 1961
Nu 20:1 and the people **a.** in Kadesh;... 3427
Nu 22:8 princes of Moab **a.** with Balaam,... 3427
Nu 25:1 And Israel **a.** in Shittim, and the... 3427
De 1:46 So ye **a.** in Kadesh many days,... 3427
De 1:46 according unto the days that ye **a.**... 3427
De 3:29 So we **a.** in the valley over against... 3427
De 9:9 then I **a.** in the mount forty days... 3427
Jos 2:22 and **a.** there three days, until the... 3427
Jos 5:8 they **a.** in their places in the camp,... 3427
Jos 8:9 and **a.** between Beth-el and Ai,... 3427
Jg 5:17 Gilead **a.** beyond Jordan:... 7931
Jg 5:17 and **a.** in his breaches... 7931
Jg 11:17 and Israel **a.** in Kadesh... 3427
Jg 19:4 and he **a.** with him three days:... 3427
Jg 20:47 **a.** in the rock Rimmon four months... 3427
Jg 21:2 and **a.** there till even before God... 3427
1Sa 1:23 the woman **a.**, and gave her son... 3427
1Sa 7:2 while the ark **a.** in Kirjath-jearim,... 3427
1Sa 13:16 **a.** in Gibeah of Benjamin:... 3427
1Sa 22:6 Saul **a.** in Gibeah under a tree... 3427
1Sa 23:14 David **a.** in the wilderness... 3427
1Sa 23:18 and David **a.** in the wood,... 3427
1Sa 23:25 and **a.** in the wilderness of Maon... 3427
1Sa 25:13 two hundred **a.** by the stuff... 3427
1Sa 26:3 David **a.** in the wilderness, and he... 3427
1Sa 30:10 for two hundred **a.** behind which... 5975
2Sa 1:1 David had **a.** two days in Ziklag;... 3427
2Sa 11:12 Uriah **a.** in Jerusalem that day... 3427
2Sa 15:8 while I **a.** in Geshur in Syria... 3427
1Ki 17:19 him up into a loft, where he **a.**,... 3427
2Ki 19:27 I know thy **a.**, and thy going out,... 3427
Ezr 8:15 there **a.** we in tents three days:... 2583
Ezr 8:32 came to Jerusalem, and **a.** there... 3427
Isa 37:28 I know thy **a.**, and thy going out,... 3427
Jer 38:28 So Jeremiah **a.** in the court of the... 3427
Mt 17:22 while they **a.** in Galilee, Jesus... *390*
Lu 1:56 **a.** with her about three months,... *3306*
Lu 8:27 **a.** in any house, but in the tombs,... *3306*
Lu 21:37 he went out, and **a.** in the mount... *835*
Joh 1:32 like a dove, and it **a.** upon him... *3306*
Joh 1:39 saw where he dwelt, and **a.** with... *3306*
Joh 4:40 he **a.** there two days... *3306*
Joh 7:9 he **a.** still in Galilee... *3306*
Joh 8:44 **a. not in the truth, because there**... *2476*
Joh 10:40 and there he **a.**... *3306*

Joh 11:6 **a.** two days still in the same place 3306
Joh 14:23 **and make our a. with him.** 3438
Ac 1:13 where **a.** both Peter, and James, *2650*
Ac 12:19 Judaea to Caesarea, and there **a.**. *1304*
Ac 14:3 Long time therefore **a.** they *1304*
Ac 14:28 **a.** long time with the disciples, *1304*
Ac 17:14 Silas and Timotheus **a.** there still. *5278*
Ac 18:3 he **a.** with them, and wrought: *3306*
Ac 20:3 And there **a.** three months *4160*
Ac 20:6 where we **a.** seven days. *1304*
Ac 21:7 saluted the brethren, and **a.** with *3306*
Ac 21:8 one of the seven, and **a.** with him. *3306*
Ga 1:18 see Peter, and **a.** with him fifteen *1961*
2Ti 4:20 Erastus **a.** at Corinth: *3306*

ABODEST

Jg 5:16 **a.** thou among the sheepfolds, to 3427

ABOLISH See also ABOLISHED.

Isa 2:18 the idols he shall utterly **a.**. 2498

ABOLISHED

Isa 51:6 my righteousness shall not be **a.**. 2865
Eze 6:6 and your works may be **a.**. 4229
2Co 3:13 to the end of that which is **a.**: *2673*
Eph 2:15 Having **a.** in his flesh the enmity. *2673*
2Ti 1:10 Christ, who hath **a.** death, *2673*

ABOMINABLE

Le 7:21 or any **a.** unclean thing, 8263
Le 11:43 ye shall not make yourselves **a.** 8262
Le 18:30 not any one of these **a.** customs, 8441
Le 19:7 it is **a.**; it shall not be accepted. 6292
Le 20:25 ye shall not make your souls **a.** 8262
De 14:3 Thou shalt not eat any **a.** thing. 8441
1Ch 21:6 the king's word was **a.** to Joab. 8581
2Ch 15:8 put away the **a.** idols out of all 8251
Job 15:16 How much more **a.** and filthy is 8581
Ps 14:1 they have done **a.** works, 8581
Ps 53:1 and have done **a.** iniquity: 8581
Isa 14:19 thy grave like an **a.** branch, 8581
Isa 65:4 of **a.** things is in their vessels; 6292
Jer 16:18 detestable and **a.** things 8441
Jer 44:4 do not this **a.** thing that I hate 8441
Eze 4:14 neither came there **a.** flesh into 6292
Eze 8:10 and **a.** beasts, and all the idols 8263
Eze 16:52 thou hast committed more **a.** than 8581
Mic 6:10 the scant measure that is **a.**? 2194
Na 3:6 I will cast **a.** filth upon thee, 8251
Tit 1:16 him, being **a.**, and disobedient, *947*
1Pe 4:3 banquetings, and **a.** idolatries; *111*
Re 21:8 unbelieving, and the **a.**, and *948*

ABOMINABLY

1Ki 21:26 he did very **a.** in the following idols, 8581

ABOMINATION See also ABOMINATIONS.

Ge 43:32 is an **a.** unto the Egyptians, 8441
Ge 46:34 every shepherd is an **a.** unto the 8441
Ex 8:26, 26 the **a.** of the Egyptians 8441
Le 7:18 it shall be an **a.**, 6292
Le 11:10 they shall be an **a.** unto you: 8263
Le 11:11 be even an **a.** unto you; 8263
Le 11:11 ye shall have their carcases in **a.** 8262
Le 11:12 that shall be an **a.** 8263
Le 11:13 shall have in **a.** among the fowls; 8262
Le 11:13 they are an **a.**: 8263
Le 11:20 an **a.** unto you. 8263
Le 11:23 four feet, shall be an **a.** unto you. 8263
Le 11:41 the earth shall be an **a.**; 8263
Le 11:42 shall not eat; for they are an **a.**. 8263
Le 18:22 with womankind; it is **a.**, 8441
Le 20:13 of them have committed an **a.**: 8441
De 7:25 for it is an **a.** to the Lord thy God. 8441
De 7:26 shalt thou bring an **a.** into thine 8441
De 12:31 for every **a.** to the Lord, which he 8441
De 13:14 such **a.** is wrought among you; 8441
De 17:1 an **a.** unto the Lord 8441
De 17:4 such **a.** is wrought in Israel: 8441
De 18:12 these things are an **a.** unto the 8441
De 22:5 all that do so are **a.** unto the 8441
De 23:18 both these are **a.** unto the Lord 8441
De 24:4 that is **a.** before the Lord; 8441
De 25:16 unrighteously, are an **a.** unto 8441
De 27:15 molten image, an **a.** unto 8441
1Sa 13:4 Israel also was had in **a.** 887
1Ki 11:5 the **a.** of the Ammonites 8251
1Ki 11:7 the **a.** of Moab. 8251
1Ki 11:7 the **a.** of the children of Ammon. 8251
2Ki 23:13 the **a.** of the Zidonians, and for 8251
2Ki 23:13 Chemosh the **a.** of the Moabites, 8251
2Ki 23:13 Milcom the **a.** of the children 8441
Ps 88:8 thou hast made me an **a.** unto 8441
Pr 3:32 the froward is **a.** to the Lord: 8441
Pr 6:16 seven are an **a.** unto him: 8441
Pr 8:7 and wickedness is an **a.** to my lips. 8441
Pr 11:1 false balance is **a.** to the Lord: 8441
Pr 11:20 are of a froward heart are **a.** to 8441
Pr 12:22 Lying lips are **a.** to the Lord: 8441
Pr 13:19 it is **a.** to fools to depart from evil. 8441
Pr 15:8 wicked is an **a.** to the Lord: 8441
Pr 15:9 way of the wicked is an **a.** unto the 8441
Pr 15:26 thoughts of the wicked are an **a.** to 8441
Pr 16:5 proud in heart is an **a.** to. 8441
Pr 16:12 **a.** to kings to commit wickedness: 8441
Pr 17:15 both are **a.** to the Lord. 8441
Pr 20:10 both of them are alike **a.** to the 8441
Pr 20:23 Divers weights are an **a.** unto 8441
Pr 21:27 sacrifice of the wicked is **a.**: 8441
Pr 24:9 and the scorner is an **a.** to men 8441
Pr 28:9 even his prayer shall be **a.**. 8441
Pr 29:27 an unjust man is an **a.** to the just: 8441
Pr 29:27 is upright in the way is **a.** to the 8441
Isa 1:13 incense is an **a.** unto me; 8441
Isa 41:24 an **a.** is he that chooseth you. 8441
Isa 44:19 make the residue thereof an **a.**? 8441
Isa 66:17 eating swine's flesh, and the **a.**, 8263
Jer 2:7 made mine heritage an **a.**. 8441
Jer 6:15 when they had committed **a.**? 8441
Jer 8:12 when they had committed **a.**? 8441
Jer 32:35 do this **a.**, to cause Judah to sin. 8441
Eze 16:50 were haughty, and committed **a.** 8441
Eze 18:12 the idols, hath committed **a.**, 8441
Eze 22:11 **a.** with his neighbour's wife; 8441
Eze 33:26 ye work **a.**, and ye defile every 8441
Da 11:31 place the **a.** that maketh desolate. 8251
Da 12:11 the **a.** that maketh desolate set up, 8251
Mal 2:11 and an **a.** is committed in Israel 8441
Mt 24:15 **see the a. of desolation,** *946*
Mk 13:14 **shall see the a. of desolation,** *946*
Lu 16:15 **is a. in the sight of God.** *946*
Re 21:27 worketh **a.**, or maketh a lie: *946*

ABOMINATIONS

Le 18:26 not commit any of these **a.**; 8441
Le 18:27 all these **a.** have the men of the 8441
Le 18:29 shall commit any of these **a.**, 8441
De 18:9 after the **a.** of these nations. 8441
De 18:12 and because of these **a.** the Lord 8441
De 20:18 you not to do after all their **a.**, 8441
De 29:17 have seen their **a.**, and their idols, 8251
De 32:16 **a.** provoked they him to anger. 8441
1Ki 14:24 all the **a.** of the nations 8441
2Ki 16:3 according to the **a.** of the heathen, 8441
2Ki 21:2 after the **a.** of the heathen, 8441
2Ki 21:11 Judah hath done these **a.**, 8441
2Ki 23:24 the **a.** that were spied in the land. 8251
2Ch 28:3 after the **a.** of the heathen 8441
2Ch 33:2 like unto the **a.** of the heathen, 8441
2Ch 34:33 Josiah took away all the **a.** out of 8441
2Ch 36:8 and his **a.** which he did, 8441
2Ch 36:14 after all the **a.** of the heathen; 8441
Ezr 9:1 according to their **a.**, 8441
Ezr 9:11 with their **a.**, which have filled 8441
Ezr 9:14 the people of these **a.**? 8441
Pr 26:25 for there are seven **a.** in his heart. 8441
Isa 66:3 their soul delighteth in their **a.** 8251
Jer 4:1 put away thine **a.** out of my sight, 8251
Jer 7:10 delivered to do all these **a.**? 8441
Jer 7:30 have set their **a.** in the house 8251
Jer 13:27 whoredom, and thine **a.** on the 8251
Jer 32:34 they set their **a.** in the house, 8251
Jer 44:22 **a.** which ye have committed; 8441
Eze 5 :9 the like, because of all thine **a.**. 8441
Eze 5:11 and with all thine **a.** therefore, 8441
Eze 6:9 have committed in all their **a.** 8441
Eze 6:11 Alas for all the evil **a.** of the house. 8441
Eze 7:3 recompense upon thee all thine **a.**, 8441
Eze 7:4 **a.** shall be in the midst of thee: 8441
Eze 7:8 recompense thee for all thine **a.** 8441
Eze 7:9 according to thy ways and thine **a.** 8441
Eze 7:20 made the images of their **a.** 8441
Eze 8:6 **a.** that the house of Israel 8441
Eze 8:6, 13, 15 thou shalt see greater **a.** 8441
Eze 8:9 wicked **a.** that they do here. 8441
Eze 8:17 Judah that they commit the **a.** 8441
Eze 9:4 that cry for all the **a.** that be done 8441
Eze 11:18 all the **a.** thereof from thence. 8441
Eze 11:21 detestable things and their **a.**, 8441
Eze 12:16 may declare all their **a.** among the 8441
Eze 14:6 faces from all your **a.** 8441
Eze 16:2 cause Jerusalem to know her **a.**, 8441
Eze 16:22 in all thine **a.** and thy whoredoms 8441
Eze 16:36 with all the idols of thy **a.**, 8441
Eze 16:43 lewdness above all thine **a.**. 8441
Eze 16:47 nor done after their **a.**: 8441
Eze 16:51 thou hast multiplied thine **a.** more 8441
Eze 16:51 in all thine **a.** which thou hast done. 8441
Eze 16:58 borne thy lewdness and thine **a.**, 8441
Eze 18:13 hath done all these **a.**; 8441
Eze 18:24 doeth according to all the **a.** 8441
Eze 20:4 cause them to know the **a.** of their. 8441
Eze 20:7 Cast ye away every man the **a.** of 8251
Eze 20:8 cast away the **a.** of their eyes, 8251
Eze 20:30 commit ye whoredom after their **a.**? 8251
Eze 22:2 thou shalt shew her all her **a.** 8441
Eze 23:36 declare unto them their **a.**; 8441
Eze 33:29 desolate because of all their **a.** 8441
Eze 36:31 iniquities and for your **a.** 8441
Eze 43:8 defiled my holy name by their **a.** 8441
Eze 44:6 suffice you of all your **a.**, 8441
Eze 44:7 because of all your **a.**. 8441
Eze 44:13 bear their shame, and their **a.** 8441
Da 9:27 the overspreading of **a.** he shall 8251
Ho 9:10 **a.** were according as they loved. 8251
Zec 9:7 and his **a.** from between his teeth: 8251
Re 17:4 full of **a.** and filthiness of *946*
Re 17:5 mother of harlots and **a.** of the *946*

ABOUND See also ABOUNDED; ABOUNDETH; ABOUNDING.

Pr 28:20 A faithful man shall **a.** with. 7227
Mt 24:12 **because iniquity shall a.,** *4129*
Ro 5:20 the offence might **a.**. But where *4121*
Ro 5:20 grace did much more **a.**: *5248*
Ro 6:1 that grace may **a.**? *4121*
Ro 15:13 that ye may **a.** in hope, through *4052*
2Co 1:5 sufferings of Christ **a.** in us, so our *4052*
2Co 8:7 as ye **a.** in every thing, in faith, *4052*
2Co 8:7 that ye **a.** in this grace also. *4052*
2Co 9:8 to make all grace **a.** toward you: *4052*
2Co 9:8 may **a.** to every good work: *4052*
Php 1:9 that your love may **a.** yet more *4052*
Php 4:12 and I know how to **a.** *4052*
Php 4:12 both to **a.** and to suffer need. *4052*
Php 4:17 that may **a.** to your account. *4121*
Php 4:18 I have all and **a.** *4052*
1Th 3:12 make you to increase and **a.** in *4052*
1Th 4:1 so ye would **a.** more and more. *4052*
2Pe 1:8 if these things be in you, and **a.**, *4121*

ABOUNDED

Ro 3:7 hath more **a.** through my lie unto *4052*
Ro 5:15 hath **a.** unto many. *4052*
Ro 5:20 But where sin **a.**, grace did much *4121*
2Co 8:2 **a.** unto the riches of their liberality. *4052*
Eph 1:8 Wherein he hath **a.** toward us in *4052*

ABOUNDETH

Pr 29:22 a furious man **a.** in transgression. 7227
2Co 1:5 consolation also **a.** by Christ. *4052*
2Th 1:3 all toward each other **a.**; *4121*

ABOUNDING

Pr 8:24 no fountains **a.** with water. 3513
1Co 15:58 always **a.** in the work of the Lord, *4052*
Col 2:7 **a.** therein with thanksgiving. *4052*

ABOUT See also THEREABOUT; WHEREABOUT.

Ge 23:17 were in all the borders round **a.**,
Ge 35:5 the cities that were round **a.** them,
Ge 37:7 round **a.**, and made obeisance
Ge 38:24 came to pass **a.** three months after
Ge 39:11 it came to pass **a.** this time
Ge 41:25 shewed Pharaoh what he is **a.** to
Ge 41:28 What God is **a.** to do he sheweth
Ge 41:42 and put a gold chain **a.** his neck; 5921
Ge 41:48 which was round **a.** every city,
Ge 42:24 he turned himself **a.** from them,
Ge 46:34 servants' trade hath been **a.**
Ex 7:24 the Egyptians digged round **a.**
Ex 9:18 to-morrow **a.** this time I will cause
Ex 11:4 **A.** midnight will I go out into . . . Egypt:
Ex 12:37 **a.** six hundred thousand on foot that
Ex 13:18 God led the people **a.**, through 5437
Ex 16:13 the morning the dew lay round **a.**
Ex 19:12 bounds unto the people round **a.**,
Ex 19:23 Set bounds **a.** the mount, and 854

Ex 25:11 a crown of gold round **a**..
Ex 25:24 thereto a crown of gold round **a**..
Ex 25:25 border of an hand breadth round **a**.,
Ex 25:25 to the border thereof round **a**..
Ex 27:17 All the pillars round **a**. the court
Ex 28:32 a binding of woven work round **a**.
Ex 28:33 round **a**. the hem thereof; and bells
Ex 28:33 of gold between them round **a**.:
Ex 28:34 upon the hem of the robe round **a**..
Ex 29:16 sprinkle it round **a**. upon the altar.
Ex 29:20 the blood upon the altar round **a**..
Ex 30:3 the sides thereof round **a**.,
Ex 30:3 unto it a crown of gold round **a**.
Ex 32:28 fell of the people that day **a**. three
Ex 37:2 a crown of gold to it round **a**..
Ex 37:11 thereunto a crown of gold round **a**..
Ex 37:12 border of an handbreadth round **a**.;
Ex 37:12 for the border thereof round **a**..
Ex 37:26 the sides thereof round **a**.,
Ex 37:26 unto it a crown of gold round **a**.
Ex 38:16 the hangings of the court round **a**.
Ex 38:20 and of the court round **a**.,
Ex 38:31 the sockets of the court round **a**.,
Ex 38:31 all the pins of the court round **a**..
Ex 39:23 with a band round **a**. the hole,
Ex 39:25 **a**. between the pomegranates;
Ex 39:26 round **a**. the hem of the robe
Ex 40:8 shalt set up the court round **a**.,
Ex 40:33 he reared up the court round **a**. the
Le 1:5 sprinkle the blood round **a**. upon
Le 1:11 sprinkle his blood round **a**. upon
Le 3:2 the blood upon the altar round **a**..
Le 3:8 sprinkle the blood thereof round **a**.
Le 3:13 thereof upon the altar round **a**..
Le 6:5 Or all that **a**. which he hath sworn 5921
Le 7:2 sprinkle round **a**. upon the altar.
Le 8:15 horns of the altar round **a**. with
Le 8:19, 24 blood upon the altar round **a**..
Le 9:12 sprinkled round **a**. upon the altar.
Le 9:18 sprinkled upon the altar round **a**.,
Le 14:41 to be scraped within round **a**.,
Le 16:18 the horns of the altar round **a**.
Le 25:31 which have no wall round **a**. them
Le 25:44 the heathen that are round **a**. you;
Nu 1:50 encamp round **a**. the tabernacle
Nu 1:53 the Levites shall pitch round **a**.
Nu 2:2 far off **a**. the tabernacle of the 5439
Nu 3:26 by the altar round **a**.,
Nu 3:37 the pillars of the court round **a**.,
Nu 4:4 tabernacle of the congregation, **a**.
Nu 4:14 wherewith they minister **a**. 5921
Nu 4:26 altar round **a**., and their cords,
Nu 4:32 the pillars of the court round **a**.,
Nu 11:8 people went **a**., and gathered it, 7751
Nu 11:24 set them round **a**. the tabernacle
Nu 11:31 the other side, round **a**. the camp.
Nu 11:32 for themselves round **a**. the camp.
Nu 16:24 up from **a**. the tabernacle of Korah, 5439
Nu 16:34 Israel that were round **a**. them fled
Nu 16:49 that died **a**. the matter of Korah. 5921
Nu 22:4 lick up all that are round **a**. us,
Nu 32:33 the cities of the country round **a**..
Nu 34:12 with the coasts thereof round **a**.
Nu 35:2 suburbs for the cities round **a**.
Nu 35:4 a thousand cubits round **a**..
De 6:14 the people which are round **a**. you;
De 12:10 rest from all your enemies round **a**..
De 13:7 the people which are round **a**. you,
De 17:14 as all the nations that are **a**. me; 5439
De 21:2 round **a**. him that is slain:
De 25:19 rest from all thine enemies round **a**.,
De 31:21 imagination which they go **a**., 6213
De 32:10 he led him **a**., he instructed him, 5437
Jos 2:5 to pass **a**. the time of shutting of
Jos 3:4 you and it, **a**. two thousand
Jos 4:13 **A**. forty thousand prepared for
Jos 6:3 ye men of war, and go round **a**.
Jos 6:11 compassed the city, going **a**. it 5362
Jos 6:15 they rose early **a**. the dawning of
Jos 7:3 let **a**. two or three thousand men
Jos 7:4 up thither of the people **a**. three
Jos 7:5 men of Ai smote of them **a**. thirty
Jos 8:12 he took **a**. five thousand men, and
Jos 10:13 not to go down **a**. a whole day.
Jos 11:6 to-morrow **a**. this time will I
Jos 15:12 of the children of Judah round **a**.
Jos 16:6 the border went **a**. eastward unto 5437
Jos 18:20 by the coasts thereof round **a**.,
Jos 19:8 **a**. these cities to Baalath-beer,
Jos 21:11 the suburbs thereof round **a**. it.
Jos 21:42 with their suburbs round **a**. them:
Jos 21:44 the Lord gave them rest round **a**.,
Jos 23:1 from all their enemies round **a**.,
Jg 2:12 the people that were round **a**. them,
Jg 2:14 hands of their enemies round **a**.,
Jg 3:29 they slew of Moab at that time **a**.
Jg 7:21 every man in his place round **a**.
Jg 8:10 with them, **a**. fifteen thousand men,
Jg 8:26 chains that were **a**. their camels'
Jg 9:49 of Shechem died also, **a**. a thousand
Jg 16:27 upon the roof **a**. three thousand
Jg 17:2 silver that were taken from thee, **a**.
Jg 19:22 Belial, beset the house round **a**.,
Jg 20:5 beset the house round **a**. upon me.
Jg 20:29 set liers in wait round **a**. Gibeah.
Jg 20:31 in the field, **a**. thirty men of Israel.
Jg 20:39 the men of Israel **a**. thirty persons:
Jg 20:43 Benjamites round **a**., and chased 3803
Ru 1:4 and they dwelled there **a**. ten years.
Ru 1:19 all the city was moved **a**. them, 5921
Ru 2:17 and it was **a**. an ephah of barley.
1Sa 1:20 the time was come **a**. after Hannah
1Sa 4:2 in the field **a**. four thousand men.
1Sa 4:20 And **a**. the time of her death
1Sa 5:8 of the God of Israel be carried **a**., 5437
1Sa 5:8 ark of the God of Israel **a**. thither. 5437
1Sa 5:9 after they had carried it **a**., 5437
1Sa 5:10 brought **a**. the ark of the God of 5437
1Sa 9:13 **a**. this time ye shall find him.
1Sa 9:16 To morrow **a**. this time I will send
1Sa 9:22 which were **a**. thirty persons.
1Sa 9:26 to pass **a**. the spring of the day,
1Sa 13:15 present with him, **a**. six hundred
1Sa 14:2 with him were **a**. six hundred
1Sa 14:14 was **a**. twenty men, within as it
1Sa 14:21 from the country round **a**.,
1Sa 15:12 set him up a place, and is gone **a**., 5437
1Sa 15:27 as Samuel turned **a**. to go away, 5437
1Sa 17:42 when the Philistine looked **a**., 5027
1Sa 20:12 **a**. to morrow any time, or the
1Sa 21:5 kept from us **a**. these three days,
1Sa 22:2 with him **a**. four hundred men.
1Sa 22:6 servants were standing **a**. him;) 5921
1Sa 22:7 his servants that stood **a**. him, 5921
1Sa 22:17 the footmen that stood **a**. him, 5921
1Sa 23:13 David and his men, which were **a**.
1Sa 23:26 his men round **a**. to take them.
1Sa 25:13 there went up after David **a**. four
1Sa 25:38 **a**. ten days after, that the Lord
1Sa 26:5 the people pitched round **a**. him.
1Sa 26:7 Abner and the people lay round **a**.,
1Sa 31:9 land of the Philistines round **a**.,
2Sa 3:12 to bring **a**. all Israel unto thee. 5437
2Sa 4:5 and came **a**. the heat of the day to
2Sa 5:9 David built round **a**. from Millo
2Sa 7:1 Lord had given him rest round **a**.
2Sa 14:20 To fetch **a**. this form of speech 5437
2Sa 18:15 compassed **a**. and smote Absalom, 5437
2Sa 20:26 Jairite was a chief ruler **a**. David.
2Sa 22:6 sorrows of hell compassed me **a**.; 5437
2Sa 22:12 made darkness pavilions round **a**.
2Sa 24:6 to Dan-jaan, and **a**. to Zidon, 5439
1Ki 2:5 his girdle that was **a**. his loins,
1Ki 2:15 howbeit the kingdom is turned **a**., 5437
1Ki 3:1 the wall of Jerusalem round **a**..
1Ki 4:24 had peace on all sides round **a**.
1Ki 4:31 fame was in all nations round **a**..
1Ki 5:3 for the wars which were **a**. him 5437
1Ki 6:5 built chambers round **a**., against
1Ki 6:5 the walls of the house round **a**.
1Ki 6:5 he made chambers round **a**.:
1Ki 6:6 he made narrowed rests round **a**.,
1Ki 6:29 the walls of the house round **a**. 4524
1Ki 7:12 the great court round **a**. was with
1Ki 7:15 did compass either of them **a**. 5437
1Ki 7:18 two rows round **a**. upon the one
1Ki 7:20 two hundred in rows round **a**.
1Ki 7:23 it was round all **a**.,
1Ki 7:23 cubits did compass it round **a**.
1Ki 7:24 under the brim of it round **a**.
1Ki 7:24 compassing the sea round **a**.:
1Ki 7:36 and additions round **a**..
1Ki 8:14 And the king turned his face **a**.,
1Ki 18:32 he made a trench **a**. the altar, 5439
1Ki 18:35 the water ran round **a**. the altar
1Ki 19:2 of them by to morrow **a**. this time.
1Ki 20:6 unto thee to morrow **a**. this time,
1Ki 22:6 prophets together, **a**. four hundred
1Ki 22:36 throughout the host **a**. the going
2Ki 1:8 with a girdle of leather **a**. his loins.
2Ki 3:25 the slingers went **a**. it, and smote 5437
2Ki 4:16 **A**. this season, according to the
2Ki 6:14 and compassed the city **a**. 5362
2Ki 6:17 chariots of fire round **a**. Elisha.
2Ki 7:1 To morrow **a**. this time shall a
2Ki 7:18 shall be to morrow **a**. this time in
2Ki 8:21 which compassed him **a**., 413
2Ki 11:7 the house of the Lord **a**. the king. 413
2Ki 11:8 shall compass the king round **a**.,
2Ki 11:11 in his hand, round **a**. the king, 5921
2Ki 17:15 heathen that were round **a**. them,
2Ki 23:5 in the places round **a**. Jerusalem;
2Ki 25:1 built forts against it round **a**.
2Ki 25:4 were against the city round **a**.:)
2Ki 25:10 the walls of Jerusalem round **a**..
2Ki 25:17 upon the chapiter round **a**.,
1Ch 4:33 villages that were round **a**. the
1Ch 6:55 the suburbs thereof round **a**. it.
1Ch 9:27 lodged round **a**. the house of God,
1Ch 10:9 land of the Philistines round **a**.,
1Ch 11:8 he built the city round **a**.,
1Ch 11:8 even from Millo round **a**.:
1Ch 15:22 he instructed **a**. the song, because
1Ch 18:17 the sons of David were chief **a**. the
1Ch 22:9 from all his enemies round **a**.:
1Ch 28:12 of all the chambers round **a**.,
2Ch 2:9 house which I am **a**. to build shall
2Ch 4:2 cubits did compass it round **a**.
2Ch 4:3 which did compass it round **a**.:
2Ch 4:3 compassing the sea round **a**..
2Ch 13:13 caused an ambushment to come **a**. 5437
2Ch 14:7 make **a**. them walls, and towers, 5437
2Ch 14:14 smote all the cities round **a**. Gerar;
2Ch 15:15 the Lord gave them rest round **a**..
2Ch 17:9 went **a**. throughout all the cities 5437
2Ch 17:10 lands that were round **a**. Judah,
2Ch 18:31 they compassed **a**. him to fight:
2Ch 18:34 **a**. the time of the sun going down
2Ch 20:30 God gave him rest round **a**..
2Ch 23:2 And they went **a**. in Judah, 5437
2Ch 23:7 shall compass the king round **a**.,
2Ch 23:10 the temple, by the king round **a**..
2Ch 26:6 built cities **a**. Ashdod, and
2Ch 33:14 compassed **a**. Ophel, and raised it
2Ch 34:6 with their mattocks round **a**..
Ezr 1:6 that were **a**. them strengthened 5439
Ezr 10:15 Tikvah were employed **a**. this 5921
Ne 5:17 among the heathen that are **a**. us.
Ne 6:16 all the heathen that were **a**. us
Ne 12:28 plain country round **a**. Jerusalem,
Ne 12:29 had builded them villages round **a**.
Ne 13:21 them, Why lodge ye **a**. the wall? 5048
Job 1:5 of their feasting were gone **a**., 5362
Job 1:10 **a**. him, and **a**. his house, and **a**. 1157
Job 8:17 roots are wrapped **a**. the heap, 5440
Job 10:8 fashioned me together round **a**.;
Job 11:18 yea, thou shalt dig **a**. thee, and 5439
Job 16:13 archers compass me round **a**.,
Job 19:12 encamp round **a**. my tabernacle.
Job 20:23 When he is **a**. to fill his belly, God
Job 22:10 Therefore snares are round **a**.
Job 29:5 when my children were **a**. me; 5439
Job 30:18 bindeth me **a**. as the collar of my 247
Job 37:12 turned round **a**. by his counsels:
Job 40:22 of the brook compass him **a**..
Job 41:14 his teeth are terrible round **a**.
Ps 3:6 themselves against me round **a**.
Ps 7:7 of the people compass thee **a**.:
Ps 17:9 enemies, who compass me **a**.
Ps 18:5 sorrows of hell compassed me **a**.:
Ps 18:11 his pavilion round **a**. him were
Ps 27:6 above mine enemies round **a**. me:
Ps 32:7 shalt compass me **a**. with songs
Ps 32:10 mercy shall compass him **a**.
Ps 34:7 encampeth round **a**. them that
Ps 40:12 compassed me **a**.: mine iniquities
Ps 44:13 derision to them that are round **a**.
Ps 48:12 Walk **a**. Zion, and go round 5439
Ps 48:12 Zion, and round **a**. her:
Ps 49:5 of my heels shall compass me **a**.?
Ps 50:3 very tempestuous round **a**. him.

Ps 55:10 Day and night they go **a.** it upon 5437
Ps 59:6, 14 like a dog, and go round **a.** the city
Ps 73:6 pride compasseth them **a.** as a
Ps 76:11 let all that be round **a.** him bring
Ps 78:28 round **a.** their habitations
Ps 79:3 like water round **a.** Jerusalem;
Ps 79:4 to them that are round **a.** us
Ps 88:17 They came round **a.** me daily like
Ps 88:17 they compassed me **a.** together
Ps 89:7 reverence of all them that are **a.** 5439
Ps 89:8 to thy faithfulness round **a.** thee?
Ps 97:2 and darkness are round **a.** him:
Ps 97:3 burneth up his enemies round **a.**
Ps 109:3 They compassed me **a.** also with
Ps 118:10 All nations compassed me **a.**:
Ps 118:11 me **a.**; yea, they compassed me **a.**:
Ps 118:12 They compassed me **a.** like bees;
Ps 125:2 As the mountains are round **a.**
Ps 125:2 so the Lord is round **a.** his people
Ps 128:3 olive plants round **a.** thy table
Ps 139:11 the night shall be light **a.** me 1157
Ps 140:9 of those that compass me **a.**,
Ps 142:7 righteous shall compass me **a.**;
Pr 1:9 thy head, and chains **a.** thy neck
Pr 3:3 bind them **a.** thy neck; write 5921
Pr 6:21 thine heart, and tie them **a.** thy 5921
Pr 20:19 He that goeth **a.** as a talebearer 1980
Ec 1:6 and turneth **a.** unto the north;
Ec 1:6 it whirleth **a.** continually,
Ec 2:20 I went **a.** to cause my heart 5437
Ec 12:5 the mourners go **a.** the streets: 5437
Ca 3:2 I will rise now, and go **a.** the city 5437
Ca 3:3 The watchmen that go **a.** the city 5437
Ca 3:7 threescore valiant men are **a.** it, 5439
Ca 5:7 watchmen that went **a.** the city 5437
Ca 7:2 heap of wheat set **a.** with lilies 5473
Isa 3:18 tinkling ornaments **a.** their feet,
Isa 15:8 cry is gone round **a.** the borders of
Isa 23:16 Take an harp, go **a.** the city, 5437
Isa 26:20 and shut thy doors **a.** thee: hide 1157
Isa 28:27 neither is a cart wheel turned **a.**
Isa 29:3 will camp against thee round **a.**,
Isa 42:25 it hath set him on fire round **a.**,
Isa 49:18 Lift up thine eyes round **a.**,
Isa 50:11 compass yourselves **a.** with sparks:
Isa 60:4 Lift up thine eyes round **a.**, and
Jer 1:15 all the walls thereof round **a.**,
Jer 2:36 Why gaddest thou **a.** so much 235
Jer 4:17 are they against her round **a.**;
Jer 6:3 their tents against her round **a.**:
Jer 12:9 birds round **a.** are against her:
Jer 14:18 the prophet and the priest go **a.** 5503
Jer 17:26 from the places **a.** Jerusalem, 5439
Jer 21:14 shall devour all things round **a.** it
Jer 25:9 all these nations round **a.**,
Jer 31:22 How long wilt thou go **a.**, 2559
Jer 31:39 and shall compass **a.** to Goath
Jer 32:44, 33:13 in the places **a.** Jerusalem, 5439
Jer 41:14 cast **a.** and returned, and went 5437
Jer 46:5 fear was round **a.**, saith the Lord
Jer 46:14 sword shall devour round **a.** thee,
Jer 48:17 ye that are **a.** him, bemoan him; 5439
Jer 48:39 a dismaying to all them **a.** him 5439
Jer 49:5 from all those that be **a.** thee; 5439
Jer 50:14 in array against Babylon round **a.**:
Jer 50:15 Shout against her round **a.**:
Jer 50:29 camp against it round **a.**;
Jer 50:32 it shall devour all round **a.** him
Jer 51:2 they shall be against her round **a.**
Jer 52:4 built forts against it round **a.**
Jer 52:7 were by the city round **a.**:)
Jer 52:14 the walls of Jerusalem round **a.**
Jer 52:22 upon the chapiters round **a.**,
Jer 52:23 were an hundred round **a.**
La 1:17 his adversaries should be round **a.**
La 2:3 fire, which devoureth round **a.**
La 2:22 solemn day my terrors round **a.**,
La 3:7 hath hedged me **a.**, that I cannot 1157
Eze 1:4 a brightness was **a.** it, 5439
Eze 1:18 rings were full of eyes round **a.**
Eze 1:27 as the appearance of fire round **a.**
Eze 1:27 it had brightness round **a.**
Eze 1:28 of the brightness round **a.**
Eze 4:2 battering rams against it round **a.**
Eze 5:2 and smite **a.** it with a knife: 5439
Eze 5:5, 6 countries that are round **a.** her
Eze 5:7 nations that are round **a.** you;
Eze 5:12 fall by the sword round **a.** thee;
Eze 5:14, 15 nations that are round **a.** thee,
Eze 6:5 scatter your bones round **a.** your
Eze 6:13 among their idols round **a.** their
Eze 8:10 pourtrayed upon the wall round **a.**
Eze 8:16 were **a.** five and twenty men, with
Eze 10:12 full of eyes round **a.**, even the
Eze 11:12 the heathen that are round **a.** you
Eze 12:14 all that are **a.** him to help him, 5439
Eze 16:10 I girded thee **a.** with fine linen,
Eze 16:37 I will even gather them round **a.**
Eze 16:57 and all that are round **a.** her,
Eze 16:57 which despise thee round **a.**
Eze 23:24 and shield and helmet round **a.**:
Eze 27:11 were upon thy walls round **a.**,
Eze 27:11 shields upon thy walls round **a.**;
Eze 28:24 all that are round **a.** them,
Eze 28:26 despise them round **a.** them;
Eze 31:4 rivers running round **a.** his plants,
Eze 32:22 his graves are **a.** him: 5439
Eze 32:23 her company is round **a.** her grave;
Eze 32:24 her multitude round **a.** her grave,
Eze 32:25, 26 her graves are round **a.** him:
Eze 34:26 places round **a.** my hill a blessing;
Eze 36:4 of the heathen that are round **a.**;
Eze 36:7 Surely the heathen that are **a.** you, 5439
Eze 36:36 heathen that are left round **a.** you
Eze 37:2 me to pass by them round **a.**:
Eze 40:5 the outside of the house round **a.**,
Eze 40:14 unto the post of the court round **a.**
Eze 40:16 posts within the gate round **a.**,
Eze 40:16 windows were round **a.** inward:
Eze 40:17 made for the court round **a**:
Eze 40:25 in the arches thereof round **a.**,
Eze 40:29 round **a.**: it was fifty cubits long,
Eze 40:30 the arches round **a.** were five and
Eze 40:33 in the arches thereof round **a.**: it
Eze 40:36 the windows to it round **a.**:
Eze 40:43 hand broad, fastened round **a.**:
Eze 41:5 round **a.** the house on every side
Eze 41:6 for the side chambers round **a.**,
Eze 41:7 a winding **a.** still upward to the
Eze 41:7 the winding **a.** of the house went
Eze 41:7 still upward round **a.** the house:
Eze 41:8 the height of the house round **a.**:
Eze 41:10 twenty cubits round **a.** the house
Eze 41:11 five cubits round **a.**
Eze 41:12 five cubits thick round **a.**,
Eze 41:16 galleries round **a.** on their three
Eze 41:16 cieled with wood round **a.**,
Eze 41:17 by all the wall round **a.**
Eze 41:19 through all the house round **a.**
Eze 42:15 and measureed it round **a.**
Eze 42:16, 17 the measuring reed round **a.**
Eze 42:19 He turned **a.** to the west side, and
Eze 42:20 had a wall round **a.**, five hundred
Eze 43:12 limit thereof round **a.** shall be
Eze 43:13 the edge thereof round **a.** shall be
Eze 43:17 border **a.** it shall be half a cubit: 5439
Eze 43:17 bottom thereof shall be a cubit **a.**; 5439
Eze 43:20 and upon the border round **a.**:
Eze 45:1 in all the borders thereof round **a.**
Eze 45:2 in breadth, square round **a.**;
Eze 45:2 and fifty cubits round **a.**
Eze 46:23 a row of building round **a.** in them,
Eze 46:23 round **a.** them four,
Eze 46:23 under the rows round **a.**
Eze 47:2 led me **a.** the way without unto 5437
Eze 48:35 was round **a.** eighteen thousand
Da 5:7 have a chain of gold **a.** his neck, 5922
Da 5:16 a chain of gold **a.** thy neck, 5922
Da 5:29 put a chain of gold **a.** his neck, 5922
Da 5:31 kingdom, being **a.** threescore and
Da 9:16 a reproach to all that are **a.** us 5439
Da 9:21 me **a.** the time of the evening
Ho 7:2 own doings have beset them **a.**; 5437
Ho 11:12 Ephraim compassed me **a.** with
Joe 3:11 yourselves together round **a.**:
Joe 3:12 to judge all the heathen round **a.**
Am 3:11 even round **a.** the land;
Jon 2:3 the floods compassed me **a.**: all
Jon 2:5 The waters compassed me **a.**, even
Jon 2:5 the depth closed me round **a.**, the
Jon 2:5 weeds were wrapped **a.** my head
Jon 2:6 with her bars was **a.** me for 1157
Na 3:8 that had the waters round **a.** it,
Hab 1:4 the wicked doth compass **a.** the
Zec 2:5 unto her a wall of fire round **a.**,
Zec 7:7 cities thereof round **a.** her,
Zec 9:8 And I will encamp **a.** mine house
Zec 12:2 unto all the people round **a.**,
Zec 12:6 devour all the people round **a.**, 1157
Zec 14:14 wealth of all the heathen round **a.** 1157
Mt 1:11 **a.** the time they were carried *1909*
Mt 3:4 girdle **a.** his loins; *4012*
Mt 3:5 all the region round **a.** Jordan, *4066*
Mt 4:23 And Jesus went **a.** all Galilee, *4013*
Mt 8:18 Jesus saw great multitudes **a.** *4012*
Mt 9:22 Jesus turned him **a.**, and when *1994*
Mt 9:35 Jesus went **a.** all the cities and *4013*
Mt 14:21 were **a.** five thousand men, *5616*
Mt 14:35 all that country round **a.**, and *4066*
Mt 18:6 **millstone were hanged a. his neck,** *1909*
Mt 20:3 **he went out a. the third hour,** *4012*
Mt 20:5 **Again he went out a. the sixth and** *4012*
Mt 20:6 **And a. the eleventh hour he went** *4012*
Mt 20:9 **were hired a. the eleventh hour,** *4012*
Mt 21:33 **hedged it round a., and digged** *4060*
Mt 27:46 And **a.** the ninth hour Jesus cried *4012*
Mk 1:6 girdle of a skin **a.** his loins; *4012*
Mk 1:28 all the region round **a.** Galilee *4066*
Mk 2:2 not so much as **a.** the door; *4814*
Mk 3:5 when he had looked round **a.** on *4017*
Mk 3:8 and they **a.** Tyre and Sidon, *4012*
Mk 3:32 And the multitude sat **a.** him, *4012*
Mk 3:34 And he looked round **a.** on them *2945*
Mk 3:34 on them which sat **a.** him, *4012*
Mk 4:10 they that were **a.** him 4012
Mk 5:13 they were **a.** two thousand;) and *5613*
Mk 5:30 turned him **a.** in the press, and *1994*
Mk 5:32 he looked round **a.** to see her *4017*
Mk 6:6 he went round **a.** the villages, *2945*
Mk 6:36 into the country round **a.**, and into *2945*
Mk 6:44 were **a.** five thousand men *5616*
Mk 6:48 **a.** the fourth watch of the night *4012*
Mk 6:55 that whole region round **a.**, *4066*
Mk 6:55 carry **a.** in beds those that were *4064*
Mk 8:9 had eaten were **a.** four thousand: *5613*
Mk 8:33 But when he had turned **a.** and *1994*
Mk 9:8 when they had looked round **a.**, *4017*
Mk 9:14 he saw a great multitude **a.** them, *4012*
Mk 9:42 **millstone were hanged a. his neck,** *4012*
Mk 10:23 Jesus looked round **a.**, and saith *4017*
Mk 11:11 and when he had looked round **a.** *4017*
Mk 12:1 **and set an hedge a. it,** *5418*
Mk 14:51 cloth cast **a.** his naked body; *1909*
Mk 15:17 thorns, and put it **a.** his head *4060*
Lu 1:56 And Mary abode with her **a.** three *5616*
Lu 1:65 on all that dwelt round **a.** them: *4037*
Lu 2:9 glory of the Lord shone round **a.** *4034*
Lu 2:37 she was a widow of **a.** fourscore *5613*
Lu 2:49 **be a. my Father's business?** *1722*
Lu 3:3 into all the country **a.** Jordan, *4066*
Lu 3:23 began to be **a.** thirty years of age, *5616*
Lu 4:14 through all the region round **a.** *4066*
Lu 4:37 place of the country round **a.** *4066*
Lu 6:10 looking round **a.** upon them all, *4017*
Lu 7:9 at him, and turned him **a.**, *4762*
Lu 7:17 all the region round **a.** *4066*
Lu 8:37 country of the Gardarenes round **a.** *4066*
Lu 8:42 **a.** twelve years of age, and she lay *5613*
Lu 9:12 and country round **a.**, and lodge, *2945*
Lu 9:14 were **a.** five thousand men *5616*
Lu 9:28 **a.** an eight days after these, *5616*
Lu 10:40 Martha was cumbered **a.** much *4012*
Lu 10:41 **and troubled a. many things:** *4012*
Lu 12:35 **Let your loins be girded a., and** *4024*
Lu 13:8 **till I shall dig a. it, and dung it:** *4012*
Lu 17:2 **hanged a. his neck, and he cast** *4012*
Lu 19:43 **shall cast a trench a. thee, and** *4016*
Lu 22:41 withdrawn from them **a.** a stone's *5616*
Lu 22:49 When they which were **a.** him *4012*
Lu 22:59 **a.** the space of one hour after *5616*
Lu 23:44 And it was **a.** the sixth hour, and *5616*
Lu 24:13 Jerusalem **a.** threescore furlongs.
Joh 1:39 for it was **a.** the tenth hour *5613*
Joh 3:25 and the Jews **a.** purifying *4012*
Joh 4:6 well: and it was **a.** the sixth hour *5616*
Joh 6:10 in number **a.** five thousand *5616*
Joh 6:19 rowed **a.** five and twenty or thirty *5613*
Joh 7:14 **a.** the midst of the feast Jesus
Joh 7:19 **Why go ye a. to kill me?** *2212*
Joh 7:20 who goeth **a.** to kill thee? *2212*
Joh 10:24 came the Jews round **a.** him, *2944*

Joh 11:18 **a.** fifteen furlongs off: *5618*
Joh 11:44 face was bound **a.** with a napkin. *4019*
Joh 19:14 and **a.** the sixth hour: *5616*
Joh 19:39 **a.** an hundred pound weight. *5616*
Joh 20:7 the napkin, that was **a.** his head, *1909*
Joh 21:20 Then Peter, turning **a.**, seeth the *1994*
Ac 1:15 together were **a.** an hundred and *5613*
Ac 2:10 of Libya **a.** Cyrene, *2596*
Ac 2:41 them **a.** three thousand souls. *5616*
Ac 3:3 seeing Peter and John **a.** to go *3195*
Ac 4:4 of the men was **a.** five thousand. *5616*
Ac 5:7 **a.** the space of three hours after, *5613*
Ac 5:16 cities round **a.** unto Jerusalem, *4038*
Ac 5:36 men, **a.** four hundred, joined *5616*
Ac 9:3 there shined round **a.** him a light *4015*
Ac 9:29 they went **a.** to slay him. *2021*
Ac 10:3 **a.** the ninth hour of the day, *5616*
Ac 10:9 to pray **a.** the sixth hour: *4012*
Ac 10:38 went **a.** doing good, and healing *1330*
Ac 11:19 persecution that arose **a.** Stephen *1909*
Ac 12:1 Now **a.** that time Herod the king *2596*
Ac 12:8 Cast thy garment **a.** thee, and *4016*
Ac 13:11 went **a.** seeking some to lead him *4013*
Ac 13:18 **a.** the time of forty years suffered *5613*
Ac 13:20 **a.** the space of four hundred and *5613*
Ac 14:6 the region that lieth round **a.** *4066*
Ac 14:20 the disciples stood round **a.** him, *2944*
Ac 15:2 the apostles and elders **a.** this *4012*
Ac 18:14 when Paul was now **a.** to open his *3195*
Ac 19:7 all the men were **a.** twelve. *5616*
Ac 19:23 no small stir **a.** that way *4012*
Ac 19:34 **a.** the space of two hours cried *5613*
Ac 20:3 as he was **a.** to sail into Syria, *3195*
Ac 21:31 And as they went **a.** to kill him, *2212*
Ac 22:6 **a.** noon, suddenly there shone *4012*
Ac 22:6 light round **a.** me. *4012*
Ac 24:6 Who also hath gone **a.** to profane *3985*
Ac 25:7 from Jerusalem stood round **a.**, *3936*
Ac 25:15 **A.** whom, when I was at *4012*
Ac 25:24 **a.** whom all the multitude of the *4012*
Ac 26:13 shining round **a.** me and them *4034*
Ac 26:21 and went **a.** to kill me. *3985*
Ac 27:27 Adria, **a.** midnight the shipmen *2596*
Ac 27:30 the shipmen were **a.** to flee out *2212*
Ro 4:19 when he was **a.** an hundred years *4225*
Ro 10:3 and going **a.** to establish their *2212*
Ro 15:19 from Jerusalem, and round **a.** *2945*
1Co 9:5 power to lead **a.** a sister, a wife, *4013*
1Co 9:13 which minister **a.** holy things live
2Co 4:10 Always bearing **a.** in the body *4064*
Eph 4:14 and carried **a.** with every wind of *4064*
Eph 6:14 having your loins girt **a.** with *4024*
1Ti 5:13 wandering **a.** from house to *4022*
1Ti 6:4 doting **a.** questions and strifes of *4012*
2Ti 2:14 that they strive not **a.** words to no
Tit 3:9 strivings **a.** the law; for they are *3163*
Heb 8:5 he was **a.** to make the tabernacle: *3195*
Heb 9:4 overlaid round **a.** with gold, *3840*
Heb 11:30 after they were compassed **a.** *2944*
Heb 11:37 they wandered **a.** in sheepskins *4022*
Heb 12:1 we also are compassed **a.** with so *4029*
Heb 13:9 Be not carried **a.** with divers and *4064*
Jas 3:3 and we turn **a.** their whole body. *3329*
Jas 3:4 yet are they turned **a.** with a very *3329*
1Pe 5:8 walketh **a.**, seeking whom he may *4043*
Jude 7 Gomorrha, and the cities **a.** them *4012*
Jude 7 disputed **a.** the body of Moses, *4012*
Jude 12 carried **a.** of winds; trees whose *4064*
Re 1:13 girt **a.** the paps with a golden *4024*
Re 4:3 a rainbow round **a.** the throne, *2943*
Re 4:4 And round **a.** the throne were four *2943*
Re 4:6 and round **a.** the throne, were four *2943*
Re 4:8 six wings **a.** him *2943*
Re 5:11 angels round **a.** the throne and *2943*
Re 7:11 all the angels stood round **a.** the *2943*
Re 7:11 and **a.** the elders and the four beasts
Re 8:1 **a.** the space of half an hour *5613*
Re 10:4 their voices, I was **a.** to write: *3195*
Re 16:21 every stone **a.** the weight of a *5613*
Re 20:9 the camp of the saints **a.**, *2944*

ABOVE

Ge 1:7 which were **a.** the firmament: 5921
Ge 1:20 **a.** the earth in the open 5921
Ge 3:14 cursed **a.** all cattle, and **a.** every
Ge 6:16 in a cubit shalt thou finish it **a.**; 4605
Ge 7:17 and it was lift up **a.** the earth. 5921
Ge 27:39 and of the dew of heaven from **a.**; 5921
Ge 28:13 Lord stood **a.** it, and said, I am 5921
Ge 48:22 one portion **a.** thy brethren, which 5921
Ge 49:25 with blessings of heaven **a.**, 5921
Ge 49:26 prevailed **a.** the blessings of my 5921
Ex 18:11 dealt proudly he was **a.** them. 5921
Ex 19:5 treasure unto me **a.** all people:
Ex 20:4 of any thing that is in heaven **a.**, 4605
Ex 25:21 the mercy seat **a.** upon the ark; 4605
Ex 25:22 with thee from **a.** the mercy seat, 5921
Ex 26:14 a covering **a.** of badgers' skins. 4605
Ex 26:24 be coupled together **a.** the head 5921
Ex 28:27, 28 **a.** the curious girdle of the 4605
Ex 29:13 and the caul that is **a.** the liver. 5921
Ex 29:22 and the caul **a.** the liver, and the
Ex 30:14 from twenty years old and **a.**, 4605
Ex 36:19 covering of badgers' skins **a.** that. 4605
Ex 39:20 **a.** the curious girdle of the ephod. 4605
Ex 39:21 it might be **a.** the curious girdle 5921
Ex 40:19 covering of the tent **a.** upon it; 4605
Ex 40:20 the mercy seat **a.** upon the ark: 4605
Le 3:4 and the caul **a.** the liver, with 5921
Le 3:10 flanks, and the caul **a.** the liver, 5921
Le 3:15 and the caul **a.** the liver, with 5921
Le 4:9 flanks, and the caul **a.** the liver, 5921
Le 7:4 and the caul that is **a.** the liver, 5921
Le 8:16 inwards, and the caul **a.** the liver,
Le 8:25 and the caul **a.** the liver, and the
Le 9:10 **a.** the liver of the sin offering, 4480
Le 9:19 kidneys, and the caul **a.** the liver: 5921
Le 11:21 which have legs **a.** their feet, 4605
Le 27:7 from sixty years old and **a.**; 4605
Nu 3:49 of them that were over and **a.** 5921
Nu 4:25 is **a.** upon it, and the hanging for 4605
Nu 12:3 Moses was very meek, **a.** all the
Nu 16:3 lift ye up yourselves **a.** the 5921
De 4:39 he is God in heaven **a.**, 4605
De 5:8 that is in heaven **a.**, or that is in 4605
De 7:6 **a.** all people that are upon the face
De 7:14 Thou shalt be blessed **a.** all people:
De 10:15 even you **a.** all people, as it is this
De 14:2 **a.** all the nations that are upon
De 17:20 his heart be not lifted up **a.** his
De 25:3 and beat him **a.** these with many 5921
De 26:19 high **a.** all nations which he hath 5921
De 28:1 set thee on high **a.** all nations of 5921
De 28:13 thou shalt be **a.** only, 4605
De 28:43 is within thee shall get up **a.** thee 5921
De 30:5 and multiply thee **a.** thy fathers
Jos 2:11 he is God in heaven **a.**, 4605
Jos 3:13 waters that come down from **a.**; 4605
Jos 3:16 waters which came down from **a.** 4605
Jg 5:24 Blessed **a.** women shall Jael the
Jg 5:24 blessed shall she be **a.** women in
1Sa 2:29 and honourest thy sons **a.** me, to
2Sa 22:17 He sent from **a.**, he took me; 4791
2Sa 22:49 hast lifted me up on high **a.** them
1Ki 7:3 covered with cedar **a.** upon the 4605
1Ki 7:11 And **a.** were costly stones, 4605
1Ki 7:20 had pomegranates also **a.**, 4605
1Ki 7:25 the sea was set **a.** upon them, 4605
1Ki 7:29 there was a base **a.**: 4605
1Ki 7:31 within the chapiter and **a.** was a 4605
1Ki 8:7 and the staves thereof **a.** 4605
1Ki 8:23 no God like thee, in heaven **a.**, 4605
1Ki 14:9 But hast done evil **a.** all that were
1Ki 14:22 they had committed, **a.** all that
1Ki 16:30 in the sight of the Lord **a.** all that
2Ki 21:11 hath done wickedly **a.** all that the
2Ki 25:28 set his throne **a.** the throne of 5921
1Ch 5:2 Judah prevailed **a.** his brethren,
1Ch 16:25 he also is to be feared **a.** all gods. 5921
1Ch 23:27 from twenty years old and **a.**: 4605
1Ch 27:6 **a.** the thirty: and in his course 5921
1Ch 29:3 house of my God, over and **a.** all 4605
1Ch 29:11 and thou art exalted as head **a.** all.
2Ch 2:5 for great is our God **a.** all gods.
2Ch 4:4 the sea was set **a.** upon them, 4605
2Ch 5:8 the staves thereof **a.** 4605
2Ch 11:21 daughter of Absalom **a.** all his
2Ch 24:20 priest, which stood **a.** the people, 5921
2Ch 25:5 from twenty years old and **a.**, 4605
2Ch 34:4 images, that were on high **a.** 5921
Ne 3:28 From **a.** the horse gate repaired
Ne 7:2 man, and feared God **a.** many.
Ne 8:5 (for he was **a.** all the people;) and 5921
Ne 9:5 which is exalted **a.** all blessing 5921
Ne 12:37 of the wall, **a.** the house of David, 5921
Ne 12:39 And from **a.** the gate of Ephraim, 5921
Ne 12:39 **a.** the old gate, and **a.** the fish 5921
Es 2:17 king loved Esther **a.** all the women,
Es 3:1 and set his seat **a.** all the princes 5921
Es 5:11 he had advanced him **a.** the princes 5921
Job 3:4 let not God regard it from **a.**, 4605
Job 18:16 and **a.** shall his branch be cut off. 4605
Job 28:18 the price of wisdom is **a.** rubies.
Job 31:2 portion of God is there from **a.**? 4605
Job 31:28 denied the God that is **a.** 4605
Ps 8:1 hast set thy glory **a.** the heavens. 5921
Ps 10:5 judgments are far **a.** out of his 4791
Ps 18:16 He sent from **a.**, he took me, he 4791
Ps 18:48 yea, thou liftest me up **a.** those
Ps 27:6 lifted up **a.** mine enemies round 5921
Ps 45:7 the oil of gladness **a.** thy fellows.
Ps 50:4 call to the heavens from **a.**, 5921
Ps 57:5 exalted, O God, **a.** the heavens; 5921
Ps 57:5, 11 let thy glory be **a.** all the earth. 5921
Ps 57:11 exalted, O God, **a.** the heavens: 5921
Ps 78:23 commanded the clouds from **a.**, 4605
Ps 95:3 God, and a great king **a.** all gods. 5921
Ps 96:4 praised: he is to be feared **a.** all 5921
Ps 97:9 Lord, art high **a.** all the earth: 5921
Ps 97:9 thou art exalted far **a.** all gods. 5921
Ps 99:2 and he is high **a.** all the people. 5921
Ps 103:11 as the heaven is high **a.** the earth, 5921
Ps 104:6 the water stood **a.** the mountains. 5921
Ps 108:4 thy mercy is great **a.** the heavens: 5921
Ps 108:5 exalted, O God, **a.** the heavens: 5921
Ps 108:5 and thy glory **a.** all the earth; 5921
Ps 113:4 the Lord is high **a.** all nations, 5921
Ps 113:4 and his glory **a.** the heavens. 5921
Ps 119:127 commandments **a.** gold; yea, **a.**
Ps 135:5 and that our Lord is **a.** all gods.
Ps 136:6 stretched out the earth **a.** the 5921
Ps 137:6 prefer not Jerusalem **a.** my chief 5921
Ps 138:2 magnified thy word **a.** all thy 5921
Ps 144:7 Send thine hand from **a.**; rid me, 4791
Ps 148:4 ye waters that be **a.** the heavens 4791
Ps 148:13 glory is **a.** the earth and heaven. 4791
Pr 8:28 established the clouds **a.** 4605
Pr 15:24 The way of life is **a.** to the wise, 4605
Pr 31:10 for her price is far **a.** rubies
Ec 2:7 and small cattle **a.** all that were
Ec 3:19 a man hath no preeminence **a.** a 4480
Isa 2:2 and shall be exalted **a.** the hills;
Isa 6:2 **A.** it stood the seraphims: 4605
Isa 7:11 or in the height **a.** 4605
Isa 14:13 **a.** the stars of God: 4605
Isa 14:14 I will ascend **a.** the heights of the 5921
Isa 45:8 Drop down, ye heavens, from **a.**, 4605
Jer 4:28 the heavens **a.** be black: 4605
Jer 15:8 increased to me **a.** the sand of the
Jer 17:9 The heart is deceitful **a.** all things,
Jer 31:37 If heaven **a.** can be measured, 4605
Jer 35:4 was **a.** the chamber of Maaseiah 4605
Jer 52:32 set his throne **a.** the throne of the 4605
La 1:13 From **a.** hath he sent fire into my 4791
Eze 1:22 stretched forth over their heads **a.** 4605
Eze 1:26 And **a.** the firmament that was 4605
Eze 1:26 appearance of a man **a.** upon it. 4605
Eze 10:1 firmament that was **a.** the head 5921
Eze 10:19 God of Israel was over them **a.** 4605
Eze 11:22 God of Israel was over them **a.** 4605
Eze 16:43 **a.** all thine abominations. 5921
Eze 29:15 itself any more **a.** the nations: for 5921
Eze 31:5 his height was exalted **a.** all the
Eze 37:8 the skin covered them **a.** 4605
Eze 41:17 To that **a.** the door, even unto the 5921
Eze 41:20 From the ground unto **a.** the door 5921
Da 6:3 Daniel was preferred **a.** the 5922
Da 11:5 and he shall be strong **a.** him, and 5921
Da 11:36 and magnify himself **a.** every god, 5921
Da 11:37 for he shall magnify himself **a.** all. 5921
Am 2:9 I destroyed his fruit from **a.**, 4605
Mic 4:1 and it shall be exalted **a.** the hills;
Na 3:16 merchants **a.** the stars of heaven:
Mt 10:24 **The disciple is not a. his master,** *5228*
Mt 10:24 **nor the servant a. his lord.** *5228*
Lu 3:20 Added yet this **a.** all, that he *1909*
Lu 6:40 **The disciple is not a. his master:** *5228*
Lu 13:2 **sinners a. all the Galilaeans,** *3844*
Lu 13:4 **they were sinners a. all men that** *3844*
Joh 3:31 cometh from **a.** is **a.** all: *509*
Joh 3:31 cometh from heaven is **a.** all. *1883*
Joh 6:13 which remained over and **a.**

Joh 8:23 **are from beneath; I am from a.** *507*
Joh 19:11 **except it were given thee from a.** *509*
Ac 2:19 I will shew wonders in heaven **a.**, ... *507*
Ac 4:22 the man was **a.** forty years old, ... *4117*
Ac 26:13 **a.** the brightness of the sun, ... *5228*
Ro 10:6 is, to bring Christ down from **a.**:) ....
Ro 14:5 one day **a.** another: *3844*
1Co 4:6 not to think of men **a.** that which *5228*
1Co 10:13 to be tempted **a.** that ye are able; *5228*
1Co 15:6 seen of **a.** five hundred brethren *1883*
2Co 1:8 out of measure, **a.** strength, ... *5228*
2Co 11:23 abundant, in stripes **a.** measure *5234*
2Co 12:2 **a.** fourteen years ago (whether in *4253*
2Co 12:6 **a.** that which he seeth me to be, ... *5228*
2Co 12:7 I should be exalted **a.** measure ....
2Co 12:7 should be exalted **a.** measure, ...
Ga 1:14 Jews' religion **a.** many my equals *5228*
Ga 4:26 Jerusalem which is **a.** is free, ... *507*
Eph 1:21 Far **a.** all principality, and power, ... *5231*
Eph 3:20 exceeding abundantly **a.** all that *5228*
Eph 4:6 who is **a.** all, and through all, ... *1909*
Eph 4:10 ascended up far **a.** all heavens, ... *5231*
Eph 6:16 **A.** all, taking the shield of faith, ... *1909*
Php 2:9 a name which is **a.** every name: *5228*
Col 3:1 seek those things which are **a.**, ... *507*
Col 3:2 Set your affections on things **a.**, ... *507*
Col 3:14 **a.** all these things put on charity, ... *1909*
2Th 2:4 **a.** all that is called God, ... *1909*
Phm 16 Not now as a servant, but **a.** a *5228*
Heb 1:9 the oil of gladness **a.** thy fellows. *3844*
Heb 10:8 **A.** when he said, Sacrifice and *511*
Jas 1:17 every perfect gift is from **a.**, ... *509*
Jas 3:15 descendeth not from **a.**, but is *509*
Jas 3:17 the wiscom that is from **a.** is first *509*
Jas 5:12 But **a.** all things, my brethren, ... *4253*
1Pe 4:8 **a.** all things have fervent charity *4253*
3Jo 2 I wish **a.** all things that thou *4012*

ABRAHAM (a'-bra-ham) See also ABRAHAM'S; ABRAM.

Ge 17:5 but thy name shall be **A.**; 85
Ge 17:9 God said unto **A.**, Thou shalt keep 85
Ge 17:15 God said unto **A.**, As for Sarai thy 85
Ge 17:17 **A.** fell upon his face, and laughed, ... 85
Ge 17:18 **A.** said unto God, Oh that Ishmael 85
Ge 17:22 and God went up from **A.** 85
Ge 17:23 And **A.** took Ishmael his son, and 85
Ge 17:24 **A.** was ninety years old and nine, ... 85
Ge 17:26 selfsame day was **A.** circumcised, ... 85
Ge 18:6 **A.** hastened into the tent unto 85
Ge 18:7 **A.** ran unto the herd, and fetcht 85
Ge 18:11 **A.** and Sarah were old and well 85
Ge 18:13 the Lord said unto **A.**, Wherefore 85
Ge 18:16 **A.** went with them to bring them 85
Ge 18:17 Shall I hide from **A.** that thing 85
Ge 18:18 Seeing that **A.** shall surely become 85
Ge 18:19 that the Lord may bring upon **A.** 85
Ge 18:22 but **A.** stood yet before the Lord. 85
Ge 18:23 **A.** drew near, and said, Wilt thou 85
Ge 18:27 **A.** answered and said, Behold now, ... 85
Ge 18:33 as he had left communing with **A.** 85
Ge 18:33 and **A.** returned unto his place. 85
Ge 19:27 **A.** gat up early in the morning to 85
Ge 19:29 God remembered **A.**, and sent Lot 85
Ge 20:1 **A.** journeyed from thence toward 85
Ge 20:2 **A.** said of Sarah his wife, She is my 85
Ge 20:9 Abimelech called **A.**, and said unto 85
Ge 20:10 Abimelech said unto **A.**, What 85
Ge 20:11 **A.** said, Because I thought, surely 85
Ge 20:14 gave them unto **A.**, and restored 85
Ge 20:17 So **A.** prayed unto God: and God 85
Ge 21:2 and bare **A.** a son in his old age, ... 85
Ge 21:3 **A.** called the name of his son that 85
Ge 21:4 **A.** circumcised his son Isaac 85
Ge 21:5 **A.** was an hundred years old, when 85
Ge 21:7 Who would have said unto **A.**, that 85
Ge 21:8 **A.** made a great feast the same day 85
Ge 21:9 which she had born unto **A.**, ... 85
Ge 21:10 she said unto **A.**, Cast out this 85
Ge 21:12 God said unto **A.**, Let it not be 85
Ge 21:14 **A.** rose up early in the morning, ... 85
Ge 21:22 captain of his host spake unto **A.**, ... 85
Ge 21:24 And **A.** said, I will swear. 85
Ge 21:25 **A.** reproved Abimelech because of a 85
Ge 21:27 **A.** took sheep and oxen, and gave 85
Ge 21:28 **A.** set seven ewe lambs of the flock 85
Ge 21:29 Abimelech said unto **A.**, What mean 85
Ge 21:33 **A.** planted a grove in Beer-sheba, ... 85
Ge 21:34 **A.** sojourned in the Philistines' land 85
Ge 22:1 that God did tempt **A.**, and said 85
Ge 22:1 unto him, **A.**: and he said, Behold, ... 85
Ge 22:3 **A.** rose up early in the morning, ... 85
Ge 22:4 day **A.** lifted up his eyes, and saw 85
Ge 22:5 **A.** said unto his young men, Abide 85
Ge 22:6 **A.** took the wood of the burnt 85
Ge 22:7 Issac spake unto **A.** his father, and 85
Ge 22:8 **A.** said, My son, God will provide 85
Ge 22:9 **A.** built an altar there, and laid the 85
Ge 22:10 **A.** stretched forth his hand, and 85
Ge 22:11 him out of heaven, and said, **A.**, **A.** 85
Ge 22:13 **A.** lifted up his eyes, and looked, ... 85
Ge 22:13 **A.** went and took the ram, and 85
Ge 22:14 **A.** called the name of that place 85
Ge 22:15 the angel of the Lord called unto **A.** 85
Ge 22:19 So **A.** returned unto his young men, ... 85
Ge 22:19 and **A.** dwelt at Beer-sheba 85
Ge 22:20 it was told **A.**, saying, Behold, ... 85
Ge 23:2 and **A.** came to mourn for Sarah, ... 85
Ge 23:3 **A.** stood up from before his dead, ... 85
Ge 23:5 the children of Heth answered **A.**, ... 85
Ge 23:7 **A.** stood up, and bowed himself to 85
Ge 23:10 Ephron the Hittite answered **A.** 85
Ge 23:12 **A.** bowed down himself before the 85
Ge 23:14 Ephron answered **A.**, saying unto 85
Ge 23:16 And **A.** hearkened unto Ephron; 85
Ge 23:16 **A.** weighed to Ephron the silver, ... 85
Ge 23:18 Unto **A.** for a possession in the 85
Ge 23:19 after this, **A.** buried Sarah his wife 85
Ge 23:20 made sure into **A.** for a possession 85
Ge 24:1 **A.** was old, and well stricken in age: 85
Ge 24:1 Lord had blessed **A.** in all things. 85
Ge 24:2 **A.** said unto his eldest servant of 85
Ge 24:6 **A.** said unto him, Beware thou that 85
Ge 24:9 put his hand under the thigh of **A.** 85
Ge 24:12 O Lord God of my master **A.**, I pray 85
Ge 24:12 shew kindness unto my master **A.** 85
Ge 24:27 be the Lord God of my master **A.**, ... 85
Ge 24:42 said, O Lord God of my master **A.**, ... 85
Ge 24:48 the Lord God of my master **A.**, ... 85
Ge 25:1 Then again **A.** took a wife, and her 85
Ge 25:5 **A.** gave all that he had unto Issac 85
Ge 25:6 concubines, which **A.** had, **A.** gave 85
Ge 25:8 Then **A.** gave up the ghost, and died 85
Ge 25:10 The field which **A.** purchased of the 85
Ge 25:10 there was **A.** buried, and Sarah his 85
Ge 25:11 the death of **A.**, that God blessed 85
Ge 25:12 Sarah's handmaid, bare unto **A.**: 85
Ge 25:19 **A.** begat Isaac: 85
Ge 26:1 famine that was in the days of **A.** 85
Ge 26:3 the oath which I sware unto **A.** 85
Ge 26:5 Because that **A.** obeyed my voice, ... 85
Ge 26:15 had digged in the days of **A.** 85
Ge 26:18 they had digged in the days of **A.** 85
Ge 26:18 stopped them after the dath of **A.**: 85
Ge 26:24 and said, I am the God of **A.** thy 85
Ge 28:4 And give thee the blessing of **A.**, ... 85
Ge 28:4 a stranger, which God gave unto **A.** 85
Ge 28:13 I am the Lord God of **A.** thy father, ... 85
Ge 31:42 the God of my father, the God of **A.**, ... 85
Ge 31:53 The God of **A.**, and the God of Nahor, ... 85
Ge 32:9 Jacob said, O God of my father **A.**, ... 85
Ge 35:12 the land which I gave **A.** and Isaac, ... 85
Ge 35:27 which is Hebron, where **A.** and 85
Ge 48:15 before whom my fathers **A.** and 85
Ge 48:16 and the name of my fathers **A.** and 85
Ge 49:30 which **A.** bought with the field of 85
Ge 49:31 There they buried **A.** and Sarah his 85
Ge 50:13 which **A.** bought with the field for a 85
Ge 50:24 unto the land which he sware to **A.**, ... 85
Ex 2:24 remembered his covenant with **A.**, ... 85
Ex 3:6 the God of thy father, the God of **A.**, ... 85
Ex 3:15 God of your fathers, the God of **A.**, ... 85
Ex 3:16 God of **A.**, Issac, and of Jacob, ... 85
Ex 4:5 God of their fathers, the God of **A.**, ... 85
Ex 6:3 I appeared unto **A.**, unto Isaac, and 85
Ex 6:8 which I did sware to give it to **A.**, ... 85
Ex 32:13 Remember **A.**, Isaac, and Israel, ... 85
Ex 33:1 the land which I sware unto **A.**, ... 85
Le 26:42 also my convenant with **A.** will I 85
Nu 32:11 see the land which I sware unto **A.**, ... 85
De 1:8 Lord sware unto your fathers, **A.**, ... 85
De 6:10 he sware unto thy fathers, to **A.**, ... 85
De 9:5 Lord sware unto thy fathers, **A.**, ... 85
De 9:27 Remember thy servants, **A.**, Isaac, ... 85
De 29:13 hath sworn unto thy fathers, to **A.**, ... 85
De 30:20 Lord sware unto thy fathers, to **A.**, ... 85
De 34:4 is the land which I sware unto **A.**, ... 85
Jos 24:2 even Terah, the father of **A.**, ... 85
Jos 24:3 I took your father **A.** from the 85
1Ki 18:36 came near, and said, Lord God of **A.**, ... 85
2Ki 13:23 because of his covenant with **A.**, ... 85
1Ch 1:27 Abram; the same is **A.** 85
1Ch 1:28 The sons of **A.**; Isaac, and Ishmael 85
1Ch 1:34 And **A.** begat Isaac. The sons of 85
1Ch 16:16 covenant which he made with **A.**, ... 85
1Ch 29:18 O Lord God of **A.**, Isaac, and of 85
2Ch 20:7 and gavest it to the seed of **A.** 85
2Ch 30:6 again unto the Lord God of **A.**, ... 85
Ne 9:7 and gavest him the name of **A.**; 85
Ps 47:9 even the people of the God of **A.**: 85
Ps 105:6 O ye seed of **A.** his servant, ... 85
Ps 105:9 Which covenant he made with **A.**, ... 85
Ps 105:42 his holy promise, and **A.** 85
Isa 29:22 saith the Lord, who redeemed **A.**, ... 85
Isa 41:8 the seed of **A.** my friend. 85
Isa 51:2 Look unto **A.** your father, and unto 85
Isa 63:16 though **A.** be ignorant of us, ... 85
Jer 33:26 to be rulers over the seed of **A.**, ... 85
Eze 33:24 **A.** was one, and he inherited the 85
Mic 7:20 truth to Jacob, and the mercy to **A.**, ... 85
Mt 1:1 the son of David, the son of **A.** *11*
Mt 1:2 **A.** begat Isaac; and Isaac begat *11*
Mt 1:17 the generations from **A.** to David *11*
Mt 3:9 We have **A.** to our father: *11*
Mt 3:9 to raise up children unto **A.** *11*
Mt 8:11 **shall sit down with A.,** *11*
Mt 22:32 **I am the God of A., and the God of.** . *11*
Mr 12:26 **I am the God of A.** *11*
Lu 1:55 As he spake to our fathers, to **A.**, ... *11*
Lu 1:73 he sware to our father **A.**, ... *11*
Lu 3:8 We have **A.** to our father: *11*
Lu 3:8 to raise up children unto **A.** *11*
Lu 3:34 which was the son of **A.**, ... *11*
Lu 13:16 **this woman, being a daughter of A.,** . *11*
Lu 13:28 **when ye shall see A., and Isaac,** *11*
Lu 16:23 **and seeth A. afar off,** *11*
Lu 16:24 **Father A., have mercy on me,** *11*
Lu 16:25 **But A. said, Son, remember that** *11*
Lu 16:29 **A. saith unto him, They have Moses** .. *11*
Lu 16:30 **Nay, father A.: but if one went** *11*
Lu 19:9 **forsomuch as he also is a son of A.** .. *11*
Lu 20:37 **he calleth the Lord the God of A,** *11*
Joh 8:39 answered and said unto him, **A.** is *11*
Joh 8:39 **ye would do the works of A.** *11*
Joh 8:40 **this did not A.** *11*
Joh 8:52 **A.** is dead, and the prophets; *11*
Joh 8:53 Art thou greater than our father **A.**, ... *11*
Joh 8:56 **A. rejoiced to see my day:** *11*
Joh 8:57 and hast thou seen **A.**? *11*
Joh 8:58 **Before A. was, I am.** *11*
Ac 3:13 The God of **A.**, and of Isaac, ... *11*
Ac 3:25 saying unto **A.**, And in thy seed *11*
Ac 7:2 appeared unto our father **A.** *11*
Ac 7:8 circumcision: and so **A.** begat ....
Ac 7:16 the sepulchre that **A.** bought *11*
Ac 7:17 which God had sworn to **A.**, ... *11*
Ac 7:32 God of thy fathers, the God of **A.**, ... *11*
Ac 13:26 children of the stock of **A.**, ... *11*
Ro 4:1 **A.** our father, as pertaining *11*
Ro 4:2 if **A.** were justified by works, ... *11*
Ro 4:3 **A.** believed God, and it was counted *11*
Ro 4:9 faith was reckoned to **A.** for *11*
Ro 4:12 that faith of our father **A.**, ... *11*
Ro 4:13 not to **A.**, or to his seed, through *11*
Ro 4:16 which is of the faith of **A.**; *11*
Ro 9:7 because they are the seed of **A.**, ... *11*
Ro 11:1 of the seed of **A.**, of the tribe of *11*
2Co 11:22 Are they the seed of **A.**? so am I. *11*
Ga 3:6 Even as **A.** believed God, ... *11*
Ga 3:7 are the children of **A.** *11*
Ga 3:8 preached before the gospel unto **A.**, ... *11*
Ga 3:9 blessed with faithful **A.** *11*
Ga 3:14 the blessing of **A.** might come *11*
Ga 3:16 to **A.** and his seed were the *11*
Ga 3:18 God gave it to **A.** by promise. *11*
Ga 4:22 **A.** had two sons, the one by *11*
Heb 2:16 but he took on him the seed of **A.** *11*
Heb 6:13 when God made promise to **A.**, ... *11*
Heb 7:1 **A.** returning from the slaughter *11*
Heb 7:2 To whom also **A.** gave a tenth *11*
Heb 7:4 **A.** gave the tenth of the spoils *11*
Heb 7:5 they come out of the loins of **A.**: *11*
Heb 7:6 received tithes of **A.**, ... *11*

Heb 7:9 payed tithes in **A.**. *11*
Heb 11:8 By faith **A.**, when he was called to *11*
Heb 11:17 By faith **A.**, when he was tried, *11*
Jas 2:21 Was not **A.** our father justified by *11*
Jas 2:23 **A.** believed God, and it was imputed *11*
1Pe 3:6 Sara obeyed **A.**, calling him lord: *11*

ABRAHAM'S (a'-bra-hams)
Ge 17:23 every male among the men of **A.** 85
Ge 20:18 because of Sarah **A.** wife. 85
Ge 21:11 thing was very grievous in **A.** sight 85
Ge 22:23 eight Milcah did bear to Nahor, **A.** 85
Ge 24:15 son of Milcah, the wife of Nahor, **A.** 85
Ge 24:34 And he said, I am **A.** servant. 85
Ge 24:52 when **A.** servant heard their words, 85
Ge 24:59 and her nurse, and **A.** servant, and 85
Ge 25:7 these are the days of the years of **A.** 85
Ge 25:12 are the generations of Ishmael, **A.** 85
Ge 25:19 are the generations of Isaac, **A.** 85
Ge 26:24 multiply thy seed for my servant **A.** 85
Ge 28:9 the daughter of Ishmael **A.** 85
1Ch 1:32 the sons of Keturah, **A.** concubine: 85
Lu 16:22 **carried by the angels into A. bosom:** *11*
Joh 8:33 We be **A.** seed, and were never in *11*
Joh 8:37 **I know that ye are A. seed;** *11*
Joh 8:39 **If ye were A. children, ye would do** *11*
Ga 3:29 then are ye **A.** seed, and heirs *11*

ABRAM (a'-brum) See also ABRAHAM; ABRAM'S.
Ge 11:26 lived seventy years, and begat **A.**, 87
Ge 11:27 Terah begat **A.**, Nahor, and Haran; 87
Ge 11:29 And **A.** and Nahor took them wives: 87
Ge 11:31 And Terah took **A.** his son, and Lot 87
Ge 12:1 the Lord had said unto **A.**, Get thee 87
Ge 12:4 So **A.** departed, as the Lord had 87
Ge 12:4 **A.** was seventy and five years old 87
Ge 12:5 **A.** took Sarai his wife, and Lot 87
Ge 12:6 **A.** passed through the land unto 87
Ge 12:7 Lord appeared unto **A.**, and said, 87
Ge 12:9 **A.** journeyed, going on still toward 87
Ge 12:10 and **A.** went down into Egypt to 87
Ge 12:14 when **A.** was come into Egypt, the 87
Ge 12:16 And he entreated **A.** well for her 87
Ge 12:18 Pharaoh called **A.**, and said, What 87
Ge 13:1 **A.** went up out of Egypt, he, and 87
Ge 13:2 And **A.** was very rich in cattle, 87
Ge 13:4 and there **A.** called on the name of 87
Ge 13:5 Lot also, which went with **A.**, had 87
Ge 13:8 **A.** said unto Lot, Let there be no 87
Ge 13:12 **A.** dwelled in the land of Canaan, 87
Ge 13:14 the Lord said unto **A.**, after that 87
Ge 13:18 Then **A.** removed his tent, and 87
Ge 14:13 one that had escaped, and told **A.** 87
Ge 14:13 and these were confederate with **A.** 87
Ge 14:14 when **A.** heard that his brother was 87
Ge 14:19 Blessed be **A.** of the most high God, 87
Ge 14:21 the king of Sodom said unto **A.**, 87
Ge 14:22 **A.** said to the king of Sodom, 87
Ge 14:23 thou shouldest say, I have made **A.** 87
Ge 15:1 the word of the Lord came unto **A.** 87
Ge 15:1 in a vision, saying, Fear not, **A.**: 87
Ge 15:2 **A.** said, Lord God, what wilt thou 87
Ge 15:3 **A.** said, Behold, to me thou hast 87
Ge 15:11 came down upon the carcasses, **A.** 87
Ge 15:12 a deep sleep fell upon **A.**; 87
Ge 15:13 he said unto **A.**, Know of a surety 87
Ge 15:18 the Lord made a covenant with **A.**, 87
Ge 16:2 Sarai said unto **A.**, Behold now, the 87
Ge 16:2 And **A.** hearkened to the voice of 87
Ge 16:3 after **A.** had dwelt ten years in the 87
Ge 16:3 and gave her to her husband **A.** 87
Ge 16:5 Sarai said unto **A.**, My wrong be 87
Ge 16:6 **A.** said unto Sarai, Behold, thy 87
Ge 16:15 Hagar bare **A.** a son; and **A.** called 87
Ge 16:16 **A.** was fourscore and six years old, 87
Ge 16:16 when Hagar bare Ishmael to **A.**. 87
Ge 17:1 when **A.** was ninety years old and 87
Ge 17:1 the Lord appeared to **A.**, 87
Ge 17:5 **A.** fell on his face: and God talked 87
Ge 17:5 thy name any more be called **A.**, 87
1Ch 1:27 **A.**; the same is Abraham. 87
Ne 9:7 Lord the God, who didst choose **A.**, 87

ABRAM'S (a'-brums)
Ge 11:29 the name of **A.** wife was Sarai; 87
Ge 11:31 his daughter in law, his son **A.** wife; 87
Ge 12:17 because of Sarai, **A.** wife. 87
Ge 13:7 a strife between the herdmen of **A.** 87
Ge 14:12 they took Lot, **A.** brother's son. 87
Ge 16:1 Now Sarai, **A.** wife, bare him no 87
Ge 16:3 And Sarai, **A.** wife, took Hagar her 87

ABROAD
Ge 10:18 of the Canaanites spread **a.** 5310
Ge 11:4 lest we be scattered **a.** upon the 6527
Ge 11:8 the Lord scattered them **a.** from 6527
Ge 11:9 did the Lord scatter them **a.** 6527
Ge 15:5 he brought him forth **a.**, and 2351
Ge 19:17 had brought them forth **a.**, 2351
Ge 28:14 and thou shalt spread **a.** to the 6555
Ex 5:12 So the people were scattered **a.** 6527
Ex 9:29 I will spread **a.** my hands unto 6566
Ex 9:33 from Pharaoh, and spread **a.** his 6566
Ex 12:46 carry forth aught of the flesh **a.** 2351
Ex 21:19 walk **a.** upon his staff, 2351
Ex 40:19 And he spread **a.** the tent over 6566
Le 13:7 But if the scab spread much **a.** in 6581
Le 13:12 And if a leprosy break out **a.** in 6524
Le 13:22 And if it spread much **a.** in the 6581
Le 13:27 if it be spread much **a.** in the 6581
Le 14:8 tarry **a.** out of his tent seven days. 2351
Le 18:9 at home, or born **a.**, 2351
Nu 11:32 they spread them all **a.** for 7849
De 23:10 then shall he go **a.** out of the 2351
De 23:12 whither thou shalt go forth **a.**: 2351
De 23:13 when thou wilt ease thyself **a.**, 2351
De 24:11 Thou shalt stand **a.**, and the 2351
De 24:11 shall bring out the pledge **a.** 2351
De 32:11 spreadeth **a.** her wings, taketh 6566
Jg 12:9 daughters, whom he sent **a.**, 2351
Jg 12:9 took in thirty daughters from **a.** 2351
1Sa 9:26 he and Samuel, **a.**. 2351
1Sa 30:16 they were spread **a.** upon all the 5203
2Sa 22:43 did spread them **a.** 7554
1Ki 2:42 and walkest **a.** any whither,
2Ki 4:3 vessels **a.** of all thy neighbours, 2351
1Ch 13:2 **a.** unto our brethren everywhere, 6555
1Ch 14:13 themselves **a.** in the valley 6584
2Ch 26:8 Uzziah: and his name spread **a.**
2Ch 26:15 his name spread far **a.**; 7350
2Ch 29:16 it out **a.** into the brook Kidron 2351
2Ch 31:5 as the commandment came **a.**, 6555
Ne 1:8 I will scatter you **a.** among the 6327
Es 1:17 deed of the queen shall come **a.** 3318
Es 3:8 is a certain people scattered **a.** 6340
Job 4:11 lion's whelps are scattered **a.**. 6504
Job 15:23 wandereth **a.** for bread, saying, 5074
Job 40:11 Cast **a.** the rage of thy wrath 6327
Ps 41:6 when he goeth **a.**, he telleth it. 2351
Ps 77:17 thine arrows also went **a.**. 1980
Pr 5:16 thy fountains be dispersed **a.**, 2351
Isa 24:1 **a.** the inhabitants thereof. 6327
Isa 28:25 doth he not cast **a.** the fitches, 6327
Isa 44:24 spreadeth **a.** the earth by myself; 7554
Jer 6:11 pour it out upon the children **a.**, 2351
La 1:20 **a.** the sword bereaveth, at home 2351
Eze 34:21 till ye have scattered them **a.**; 2351
Zec 1:17 prosperity shall yet be spread **a.**; 6327
Zec 2:6 spread you **a.** as the four winds 6566
Mt 9:26 went **a.** into all that land. *1831*
Mt 9:31 **a.** his fame in all that country. *1310*
Mt 9:36 scattered **a.**, as sheep having no *4496*
Mt 12:30 **not with me scattereth a.** *4650*
Mt 26:31 **the flock shall be scattered a.** *1287*
Mk 1:28 fame spread **a.** throughout all *1831*
Mk 1:45 blaze **a.** the matter, insomuch that *1310*
Mk 4:22 **but that it should come a.** *1519,5318*
Mk 6:14 (for his name was spread **a.**:) *1519,1096*
Lu 1:65 these sayings were noised **a.** *1255*
Lu 2:17 made known **a.** the saying *1232*
Lu 5:15 more went there a fame **a.** of him: *1330*
Lu 8:17 **be known and come a.** *1519,5318*
Joh 11:52 of God that were scattered **a.**. *1287*
Joh 21:23 went this saying **a.** among the *1831*
Ac 2:6 when this was noised **a.**, *1096,5456*
Ac 8:1 all scattered **a.** throughout the *1289*
Ac 8:4 they that were scattered **a.** went *1289*
Ac 11:19 scattered **a.** upon the persecution *1289*
Ro 5:5 love of God is shed **a.** in our hearts *1632*
Ro 16:19 your obedience is come **a.** unto all *864*
2Co 9:9 He hath dispersed **a.**; he hath *4650*
1Th 1:8 faith to God-ward is spread **a.**; *1831*
Jas 1:1 tribes which are scattered **a.**, *1290*

ABSALOM (ab'-sal-um) See also ABISHALOM; ABSALOM'S.
2Sa 3:3 the third, **A.** the son of Maacah 53
2Sa 13:1 that **A.** the son of David had a fair 53
2Sa 13:20 And **A.** her brother said unto her, 53
2Sa 13:22 And **A.** spake unto his brother 53
2Sa 13:22 Amnon neither good nor bad: for **A.** 53
2Sa 13:23 **A.** had sheepshearers in Baal-hazor, 53
2Sa 13:23 and **A.** invited all the king's 53
2Sa 13:24 And **A.** came to the king, and said, 53
2Sa 13:25 the king said to **A.**, Nay, my son, 53
2Sa 13:26 Then said **A.**, If not, I pray thee, 53
2Sa 13:27 **A.** pressed him, that he let Amnon 53
2Sa 13:28 Now **A.** had commanded his 53
2Sa 13:29 And the servants of **A.** did unto 53
2Sa 13:29 Amnon as **A.** had commanded. 53
2Sa 13:30 **A.** hath slain all the king's sons. 53
2Sa 13:32 by the appointment of **A.** this hath 53
2Sa 13:34 But **A.** fled. And the young man 53
2Sa 13:37 But **A.** fled, and went to Talmai, 53
2Sa 13:38 So **A.** fled, and went to Geshur, 53
2Sa 13:39 David longed to go forth unto **A.**: 53
2Sa 14:1 that the king's heart was toward **A.**. 53
2Sa 14:21 bring the young man **A.** again. 53
2Sa 14:23 went to Geshur, and brought **A.** to 53
2Sa 14:24 So **A.** returned to his own house, 53
2Sa 14:25 much praised as **A.** for his beauty: 53
2Sa 14:27 unto **A.** there were born three sons, 53
2Sa 14:28 **A.** dwelt two full years in Jerusalem, 53
2Sa 14:29 **A.** sent for Joab, to have sent him 53
2Sa 14:31 Then Joab arose, and came to **A.** 53
2Sa 14:32 **A.** answered Joab, Behold, I sent 53
2Sa 14:33 when he had called for **A.**, he came 53
2Sa 14:33 the king: and the king kissed **A.** 53
2Sa 15:1 that **A.** prepared him chariots and 53
2Sa 15:2 And **A.** rose up early, and stood 53
2Sa 15:2 then **A.** called unto him, and said, 53
2Sa 15:3 **A.** said unto him, See, thy matters 53
2Sa 15:4 **A.** said moreover, Oh that I were 53
2Sa 15:6 on this manner did **A.** to Israel 53
2Sa 15:6 so **A.** stole the hearts of the men of 53
2Sa 15:7 **A.** said unto the king, I pray thee, 53
2Sa 15:10 But **A.** sent spies throughout all the 53
2Sa 15:10 ye shall say, **A.** reigneth in Hebron 53
2Sa 15:11 And with **A.** went two hundred men 53
2Sa 15:12 **A.** sent for Ahithophel the Gilonite, 53
2Sa 15:12 people increased continually with **A.** 53
2Sa 15:13 of the men of Israel are after **A.**. 53
2Sa 15:14 for we shall not else escape from **A.** 53
2Sa 15:31 is among the conspirators with **A.**. 53
2Sa 15:34 say unto **A.**, I will be thy servant, 53
2Sa 15:37 came into the city, and **A.** came into 53
2Sa 16:8 the kingdom into the hand of **A.** 53
2Sa 16:15 And **A.**, and all the people the men 53
2Sa 16:16 David's friend, was come unto **A.**, 53
2Sa 16:16 Hushai said unto **A.**, God save the 53
2Sa 16:17 **A.** said to Hushai, Is this thy 53
2Sa 16:18 Hushai said unto **A.**, Nay; but whom 53
2Sa 16:20 said **A.** to Ahithophel, Give counsel 53
2Sa 16:21 Ahithophel said unto **A.**, Go in unto 53
2Sa 16:22 So they spread **A.** a tent upon the 53
2Sa 16:22 and **A.** went in unto his father's 53
2Sa 16:23 both with David and with **A.** 53
2Sa 17:1 Ahithophel said unto **A.**, Let me 53
2Sa 17:4 And the saying pleased **A.** well, 53
2Sa 17:5 Then said **A.**, Call now Hushai 53
2Sa 17:6 When Hushai was come to **A.**, **A.** 53
2Sa 17:7 Hushai said unto **A.**, The counsel 53
2Sa 17:9 among the people that follow **A.** 53
2Sa 17:14 **A.** and all the men of Israel said, 53
2Sa 17:14 the Lord might bring evil upon **A.**. 53
2Sa 17:15 and thus did Ahithophel counsel **A.** 53
2Sa 17:18 a lad saw them, and told **A.**: 53
2Sa 17:24 And **A.** passed over Jordan, he and 53
2Sa 17:25 **A.** made Amasa captain of the host 53
2Sa 17:26 Israel and **A.** pitched in the land of 53
2Sa 18:5 with the young man, even with **A.** 53
2Sa 18:5 the captains charge concerning **A.** 53
2Sa 18:9 and **A.** met the servants of David. 53
2Sa 18:9 And **A.** rode upon a mule, 53
2Sa 18:10 Behold, I saw **A.** hanged in an oak. 53
2Sa 18:12 that none touch the young man **A.** 53
2Sa 18:14 them through the heart of **A.**, 53
2Sa 18:15 about and smote **A.**, and slew him. 53
2Sa 18:17 they took **A.**, and cast him into a 53
2Sa 18:18 Now, **A.** in his life time had taken 53
2Sa 18:29 said, Is the young man **A.** safe? 53
2Sa 18:32 Cushi, Is the young man **A.** safe? 53
2Sa 18:33 O my son **A.**, my son, my son, **A.**! 53
2Sa 18:33 died for thee, O **A.**, my son, my son! 53
2Sa 19:1 king weepeth and mourneth for **A.** 53

2Sa 19:4 with a loud voice, O my son **A.**, 53
2Sa 19:4 O **A.**, my son, my son! 53
2Sa 19:6 I perceive, that if **A.** had lived, 53
2Sa 19:9 now he is fled out of the land for **A.**. 53
2Sa 19:10 And **A.**, whom we anointed over us, 53
2Sa 20:6 do us more harm than did **A.** 53
1Ki 1:6 and his mother bare him after **A.**. 53
1Ki 2:7 I fled because of **A.** thy brother. 53
1Ki 2:28 though he turned not after **A.**. 53
1Ch 3:2 The third, **A.** the son of Maachah 53
2Ch 11:20 took Maachah the daughter of **A.**; 53
2Ch 11:21 loved Maachah the daughter of **A.** 53
Ps 3:*title* Psalm of David, when he fled from **A.** 53

ABSALOM'S (ab'-sal-ums)
2Sa 13:4 I love Tamar, my brother **A.** sister, 53
2Sa 13:20 desolate in her brother **A.** house. 53
2Sa 14:30 And **A.** servants set the field on fire. 53
2Sa 17:20 **A.** servants came to the woman 53
2Sa 18:18 it is called unto this day, **A.** place 53

ABSENCE
Lu 22:6 in the **a.** of the multitude. *817*
Php 2:12 now much more in my **a.**, *666*

ABSENT
Ge 31:49 when we are **a.** one from another. 5641
1Co 5:3 For I verily, as **a.** in body, but *548*
2Co 5:6 we are **a.** from the Lord: *1553*
2Co 5:8 rather to be **a.** from the body, *1553*
2Co 5:9 that, whether present or **a.**, *1553*
2Co 10:1 being **a.** am bold toward you: *548*
2Co 10:11 by letters when we are **a.**, such *548*
2Co 13:2 **a.** now I write to them *548*
2Co 13:10 write these things being **a.**, *548*
Php 1:27 come and see you, or else be **a.**, *548*
Col 2:5 though I be **a.** in the flesh, *548*

ABSTAIN
Ac 15:20 they **a.** from pollutions of idols, *567*
Ac 15:29 ye **a.** from meats offered to idols, *567*
1Th 4:3 that ye should **a.** from fornication: *567*
1Th 5:22 **A.** from all appearance of evil. *567*
1Ti 4:3 commanding to **a.** from meats, *567*
1Pe 2:11 **a.** from fleshly lusts, which war *567*

ABSTINENCE
Ac 27:21 after long **a.** Paul stood forth in *776*

ABUNDANCE
De 28:47 for the **a.** of all things; 7230
De 33:19 they shall suck of the **a.** of the 8228
1Sa 1:16 out of the **a.** of my complaint 7230
2Sa 12:30 the spoil of the city in great **a.**. 7235
1Ki 1:19 and fat cattle and sheep in **a.**, 7230
1Ki 1:25 fat cattle and sheep in **a.**, 7230
1Ki 10:10 came no more such **a.** of spices 7230
1Ki 10:27 as the sycomore trees....for **a.**. 7230
1Ki 18:41 there is a sound of **a.** of rain. 1995
1Ch 22:3 David prepared iron in **a.** for the 7230
1Ch 22:3 brass in **a.** without weight; 7230
1Ch 22:4 Also cedar trees in **a.** 369,4557
1Ch 22:14 iron without weight; for it is in **a.** 7230
1Ch 22:15 workmen with thee in **a.**, 7230
1Ch 29:2 mable stones in **a.** 7230
1Ch 29:21 sacrifices in **a.** for all Israel: 7230
2Ch 1:15 as the sycomore trees....for **a.**. 7230
2Ch 2:9 to prepare me timber in **a.** 7230
2Ch 4:18 vessels in great **a.** 7230
2Ch 9:1 spices, and gold in **a.**, 7230
2Ch 9:9 of spices great **a.**, and precious 7230
2Ch 9:27 as the sycomore trees....in **a.**. 7230
2Ch 11:23 gave them victual in **a.**. 7230
2Ch 14:15 sheep and camels in **a.**, 7230
2Ch 15:9 fell to him out of Israel in **a.**, 7230
2Ch 17:5 he had riches and honour in **a.** 7230
2Ch 18:1 had riches and honour in **a.**, 7230
2Ch 18:2 killed sheep and oxen for him in **a.**, 7230
2Ch 20:25 found among them in **a.** both riches 7230
2Ch 24:11 gathered money in **a.**. 7230
2Ch 29:35 the burnt offerings were in **a.**, 7230
2Ch 31:5 children of Israel brought in **a.** 7235
2Ch 32:5 made darts and shields in **a.** 7230
2Ch 32:29 flocks and herds in **a.** 7230
Ne 9:25 fruit trees in **a.**: 7230
Es 1:7 royal wine in **a.**, according to the 7227
Job 22:11 and **a.** of waters cover thee. 8229
Job 36:31 he giveth meat in **a.** 4342
Job 38:34 that **a.** of waters may cover 8229
Ps 37:11 delight themselves in the **a.** of 7230
Ps 52:7 trusted in the **a.** of his riches, 7230
Ps 72:7 **a.** of peace so long as the moon 7230
Ps 105:30 land brought forth frogs in **a.**, 8317
Ec 5:10 he that loveth **a.** with increase: 1995
Ec 5:12 but the **a.** of the rich will not 7647
Isa 7:22 for the **a.** of milk that they shall 7230
Isa 15:7 the **a.** they have gotten, 3502
Isa 47:9 great **a.** of thine enchantments 6109
Isa 60:5 **a.** of the sea shall be converted 1995
Isa 66:11 with the **a.** of her glory. 2123
Jer 33:6 reveal unto them the **a.** of peace 6283
Eze 16:49 and **a.** of idleness was in her 7962
Eze 26:10 By reason of the **a.** of his horses 8229
Zec 14:14 silver, and apparel, in great **a.**. 7230
Mt 12:34 **out of the a. of the heart the** *4051*
Mt 13:12 **and he shall have more a.** *4052*
Mt 25:29 **and he shall have a.** *4052*
Mk 12:44 **did cast in of their a.;** *4052*
Lu 6:45 **of the a. of the heart his mouth** *4051*
Lu 12:15 **consisteth not in the a. of the** *4052*
Lu 21:4 **these have of their a. cast in unto** *4052*
Ro 5:17 they which receive **a.** of grace *4050*
2Co 8:2 the **a.** of their joy and their deep *4050*
2Co 8:14 your **a.** may be a supply for their *4051*
2Co 8:14 that their **a.** also may be a supply *4051*
2Co 8:20 blame us in this **a.** which is *100*
2Co 12:7 through the **a.** of the revelations, *5236*
Re 18:3 the **a.** of her delicacies. *1411*

ABUNDANT
Ex 34:6 and **a.** in goodness and truth, 7227
Isa 56:12 much more **a.**. 1419
Jer 51:13 many waters, **a.** in treasures, 7227
1Co 12:23 we bestow more **a.** honour; *4055*
1Co 12:23 have more **a.** comeliness. *4055*
1Co 12:24 given more **a.** honour *4055*
2Co 4:15 that the **a.** grace might through *4121*
2Co 7:15 his inward affection is more **a.** *4056*
2Co 9:12 is **a.** also by many thanksgivings *4052*
2Co 11:23 in labours more **a.**, in stripes *4056*
Php 1:26 may be more **a.** in Jesus Christ *4052*
1Ti 1:14 of our Lord was exceeding **a.** *5250*
1Pe 1:3 according to his **a.** mercy hath *4183*

ABUNDANTLY
Ge 1:20 Let the waters bring forth **a.** 8317
Ge 1:21 the waters brought forth **a.**, 8317
Ge 8:17 they may breed **a.** in the earth, 8317
Ge 9:7 bring forth **a.** in the earth, and 8317
Ex 1:7 fruitful, and increased **a.**, and 8317
Ex 8:3 river shall bring forth frogs **a.**, 8317
Nu 20:11 the water came out **a.**, 7227
1Ch 12:40 oxen, and sheep **a.**: for there 7230
1Ch 22:5 David prepared **a.** before his 7230
1Ch 22:8 Thou has shed blood **a.**, 7230
2Ch 31:5 all things brought they in **a.**. 7230
Job 12:6 whose hand God bringeth **a.**
Job 36:28 distil upon man **a.**. 7227
Ps 36:8 They shall be **a.** satisfied with 7301
Ps 65:10 waterest the ridges thereof **a.** 7301
Ps 132:15 I will **a.** bless her provision: 1288
Ps 145:7 They shall **a.** utter the memory 5042
Ca 5:1 drink, yea, drink **a.**. O beloved. 7937
Isa 15:3 every one shall howl, weeping **a.**. 3381
Isa 35:2 it shall blossom **a.**, and rejoice 6524
Isa 55:7 for he will **a.** pardon. 7235
Jo 10:10 **might have it more a.** *4053*
1Co 15:10 I laboured more **a.** than they all; *4054*
2Co 1:12 and more **a.** to you-ward. *4056*
2Co 2:4 I have more **a.** unto you. *4056*
2Co 10:15 according to our rule **a.**, *1519,4050*
2Co 12:15 the more **a.** I love you, the less I *4056*
Eph 3:20 able to do exceeding **a.** above *1537,4053*
1Th 2:17 endeavoured the more **a.** to see *4056*
Tit 3:6 Which he shed on us **a.** through *4146*
Heb 6:17 willing more **a.** to shew unto the *4054*
2Pe 1:11 shall be ministered unto you **a.** *4146*

ABUSE See also ABUSED; ABUSING.
1Sa 31:4 thrust me through, and **a.** me. 5953
1Ch 10:4 these uncircumcised come and **a.** 5953
1Co 9:18 I **a.** not my power in the gospel. *2710*

ABUSED
Jg 19:25 they knew her, and **a.** her 5953

ABUSERS
1Co 6:9 **a.** of themselves with mankind, *733*

ABUSING
1Co 7:31 that use this world, as not **a.** it: *2710*

ACCAD (ak'-kad)
Ge 10:10 Babel, and Erech, and **A.**, and 390

ACCEPT See also ACCEPTED; ACCEPTEST; ACCEPTETH; ACCEPTING.
Ge 32:20 peradventure he will **a.** of me. 5375
Ex 22:11 the owner of it shall **a.** thereof, 3947
Le 26:41 they then **a.** of the punishment 7521
Le 26:43 they shall **a.** of the punishment 7521
De 33:11 **a.** the work of his hands: 7521
1Sa 26:19 me, let him **a.** an offering: 7306
2Sa 24:23 The Lord thy God **a.** thee. 7521
Job 13:8 Will ye **a.** his person? will ye 5375
Job 13:10 if ye do secretly **a.** persons. 5375
Job 32:21 Let me not, I pray you, **a.** any 5375
Job 42:8 for him will I **a.**: 5375
Ps 20:3 **a.** thy burnt sacrifice; 1878
Ps 82:2 **a.** the persons of the wicked? 5375
Ps 119:108 **A.**, I beseech thee, the freewill 7521
Pr 18:5 to **a.** the person of the wicked, 5375
Jer 14:10 the Lord doth not **a.** them; 7521
Jer 14:12 I will not **a.** them: 7521
Eze 20:40 there will I **a.** them, and there will 7521
Eze 20:41 will **a.** you with your sweet savour, 7521
Eze 43:27 I will **a.** you, saith the Lord God. 7521
Am 5:22 meat offerings, I will not **a.** them; 7521
Mal 1:8 pleased with thee, or **a.** thy 5375
Mal 1:10 neither will I **a.** an offering at 7521
Mal 1:13 should I **a.** this of your hand? 7521
Ac 24:3 We **a.** it always, and in all places, *588*

ACCEPTABLE
Le 22:20 it shall not be **a.** for you. 7522
De 33:24 let him be **a.** to his brethren, 7522
Ps 19:14 be **a.** in thy sight, O Lord, 7522
Ps 69:13 is unto thee, O Lord, in an **a.** time: 7522
Pr 10:32 of the righteous know what is **a.** 7522
Pr 21:3 justice and judgment is more **a.** 977
Ec 12:10 preacher sought to find out **a.** 2656
Isa 49:8 In an **a.** time have I heard thee, 7522
Isa 58:5 a fast, and an **a.** day to the Lord? 7522
Isa 61:2 proclaim the **a.** year of the Lord, 7522
Jer 6:20 your burnt offerings are not **a.**, 7522
Da 4:27 O king, let my counsel be **a.** unto 8232
Lu 4:19 **To preach the a. year of the Lord.** *1184*
Ro 12:1 living sacrifice, holy, **a.** unto God, *2101*
Ro 12:2 and **a.**, and perfect, will of God. *2101*
Ro 14:18 **a.** to God, and approved of men. *2101*
Ro 15:16 up of the Gentiles might be **a.**, *2144*
Eph 5:10 Proving what is **a.** unto the Lord. *2101*
Php 4:18 a sweet smell, a sacrifice **a.**, *1184*
1Ti 2:3 this is good and **a.** in the sight of *587*
1Ti 5:4 good and **a.** before God. *587*
1Pe 2:5 **a.** to God by Jesus Christ. *2144*
1Pe 2:20 this is **a.** with God. *5485*

ACCEPTABLY
Heb 12:28 serve God **a.** with reverence and *2102*

ACCEPTANCE
Isa 60:7 come up with **a.** on mine altar, 7522

ACCEPTATION
1Ti 1:15 worthy of all **a.**, that *594*
1Ti 4:9 saying and worthy of all **a.**. *594*

ACCEPTED
Ge 4:7 doest well, shalt thou not be **a.**? 7613
Ge 19:21 I have **a.** thee concerning this 5375
Ex 28:38 they may be **a.** before the Lord. 7522
Le 1:4 and it shall be **a.** for him to make 7521
Le 7:18 the third day, it shall not be **a.**, 7521
Le 10:19 been **a.** in the sight of the Lord? 3190
Le 19:7 is abominable; it shall not be **a.** 7521
Le 22:21 shall be perfect to be **a.**; 7522
Le 22:23 for a vow it shall not be **a.**. 7521
Le 22:25 they shall not be **a.** for you. 7521
Le 22:27 it shall be **a.** for an offering made 7521
Le 23:11 before the Lord, to be **a.** for you: 7522
1Sa 18:5 and he was **a.** in the sight of all 3190
1Sa 25:35 and have **a.** thy person. 5375
Es 10:3 and **a.** of the multitude of his 7521
Job 42:9 the Lord also **a.** Job. 5375
Isa 56:7 their sacrifices shall be **a.** upon 7522
Jer 37:20 let my supplication....be **a.** 5307
Jer 42:2 Let....our supplication be **a.** 5307
Lu 4:24 **No prophet is a. in his own** *1184*

Ac 10:35 worketh righteousness, is **a.** *1184*
Ro 15:31 may be **a.** of the saints; *2144*
2Co 5:9 we may be **a.** of him. *2101*
2Co 6:2 I have heard thee in a time **a.,** *1184*
2Co 6:2 behold, now is the **a.** time; *2144*
2Co 8:12 it is **a.** according to that a man *2144*
2Co 8:17 For indeed he **a.** the exhortation; *1209*
2Co 11:4 gospel, which ye have not **a.,** *1209*
Eph 1:6 wherein he hath made us **a.** in *5487*

ACCEPTEST
Lu 20:21 neither **a.** thou the person of any, *2983*

ACCEPTETH
Job 34:19 him that **a.** not the persons of *5375*
Ec 9:7 God now **a.** thy works. *7521*
Ho 8:13 the Lord **a.** them not; 7521
Ga 2:6 God **a.** no man's person:) *2983*

ACCEPTING
Heb 11:35 were tortured, not **a.** deliverance; *4327*

ACCESS
Ro 5:2 we have **a.** by faith into this grace *4318*
Eph 2:18 we both have **a.** by one Spirit *4318*
Eph 3:12 **a.** with confidence by the faith of *4318*

ACCHO (ak'-ko)
Jg 1:31 drive out the inhabitants of **A.,** 5910

ACCOMPANIED
Ac 10:23 brethren from Joppa **a.** him. *4905*
Ac 11:12 these six brethren **a.** me, *2064, 4862*
Ac 20:4 **a.** him into Asia Sopater of Berea; *4902*
Ac 20:38 And they **a.** him unto the ship. *4311*

ACCOMPANY See also ACCOMPANIED; ACCOMPANYING.
Heb 6:9 things that **a.** salvation, *2192*

ACCOMPANYING
2Sa 6:4 **a.** the ark of God: 5973

ACCOMPLISH See also ACCOMPLISHED, ACCOMPLISHING.
Le 22:21 to **a.** his vow, 6381
1Ki 5:9 and thou shalt **a.** my desire, 6213
Job 14:6 till he shall **a.,** as an hireling, 7521
Ps 64:6 they **a.** a diligent search: 8552
Isa 55:11 it shall **a.** that which I please, 6213
Jer 44:25 ye will surely **a.** your vows, 6965
Eze 6:12 thus will I **a.** my fury upon them. 3615
Eze 7:8 and **a.** mine anger upon thee: 3615
Eze 13:15 Thus will I **a.** my wrath upon the 3615
Eze 20:8, 21 to **a.** my anger against them 3615
Da 9:2 that he would **a.** seventy years in 4390
Lu 9:31 which he should **a.** at Jerusalem. *4137*

ACCOMPLISHED
2Ch 36:22 word of the Lord . . . might be **a.,** 3615
Es 2:12 days of their purifications **a.,** 4390
Job 15:32 It shall be **a.** before his time, 4390
Pr 13:19 The desire **a.** is sweet to the soul: 1961
Isa 40:2 her warfare is **a.,** that her 4390
Jer 25:12 when seventy years are **a.,** that I 4390
Jer 25:34 and of your dispersions are **a.;** 4390
Jer 29:10 after seventy years be **a.** at 4390
Jer 39:16 and they shall be **a.** in that
La 4:11 The Lord hath **a.** his fury; 3615
La 4:22 punishment of thine iniquity is **a.,** 8552
Eze 4:6 And when thou hast **a.** them, 3615
Eze 5:13 Thus shall mine anger be **a.,** 3615
Eze 5:13 when I have **a.** my fury in them. 3615
Da 11:36 till the indignation be **a.:** 3615
Da 12:7 and when he shall have **a.** to 3615
Lu 1:23 days of his ministration were **a.,** *4130*
Lu 2:6 the days were **a.** that she should *4130*
Lu 2:21 eight days were **a.** *4130*
Lu 2:22 when the days . . . were **a.,** *4130*
Lu 12:50 **straitened till it be a.!** *5055*
Lu 18:31 **the Son of man shall be a.** *5055*
Lu 22:37 **must yet be a. in me,** *5055*
Joh 19:28 all things were now **a.,** *5055*
Ac 21:5 when we had **a.** those days. *1822*
1Pe 5:9 are **a.** in your brethren *2005*

ACCOMPLISHING
Heb 9:6 **a.** the service of God. *2005*

ACCOMPLISHMENT
Ac 21:26 the **a.** of the days of purification, *1604*

ACCORD See also ACCORDING.
Le 25:5 which groweth of its own **a.** 5599
Jos 9:2 and with Israel, with one **a.** 6310
Ac 1:14 continued with one **a.** in prayer *3661*
Ac 2:1 were all with one **a.** in one place *3661*
Ac 2:46 daily with one **a.** in the temple, *3661*
Ac 4:24 up their voice to God with one **a.,** *3661*
Ac 5:12 they were all with one **a.** in *3661*
Ac 7:57 and ran upon him with one **a.,** *3661*
Ac 8:6 the people with one **a.** gave heed *3661*
Ac 12:10 opened to them of his own **a.:** *844*
Ac 12:20 but they came with one **a.** to him, *3661*
Ac 15:25 being assembled with one **a.,** to *3661*
Ac 18:12 made insurrection with one **a.** *3661*
Ac 19:29 rushed with one **a.** into the *3661*
2Co 8:17 of his own **a.** he went unto you. *830*
Php 2:2 love, being of one **a.,** of one mind. *4861*

ACCORDING
Ge 6:22 **a.** to all that God commanded him,
Ge 7:5 **a.** unto all that the Lord commanded
Ge 18:10 return unto thee **a.** to the time
Ge 18:14 **a.** to the time of life, and Sarah shall
Ge 18:21 done altogether **a.** to the cry of it,
Ge 21:23 **a.** to the kindness that I have done
Ge 25:13 by their names, **a.** to their
Ge 25:16 twelve princes **a.** to their nations.
Ge 27:8 **a.** to that which I command thee.
Ge 27:19 I have done **a.** as thou badest me: arise,
Ge 30:34 I would it might be **a.** to thy word
Ge 33:14 **a.** as the cattle that goeth before 7272
Ge 34:12 and I will give **a.** as ye shall say
Ge 36:40 the dukes that came of Esau, **a.**
Ge 36:43 **a.** to their habitations in the land
Ge 39:17 she spake unto him **a.** to these
Ge 40:5 each man **a.** to the interpretation
Ge 41:11 we dreamed each man **a.** to the
Ge 41:12 to each man **a.** to his dream he
Ge 41:40 **a.** unto thy word shall all my 5921
Ge 41:54 dearth began to come, **a.** as
Ge 43:7 we told him **a.** to the tenor of 5921
Ge 43:33 before him, the firstborn **a.** to his
Ge 43:33 and the youngest **a.** to his youth:
Ge 44:2 he did **a.** to the word that Joseph
Ge 44:7 thy servants should do **a.** to this
Ge 44:10 let it be **a.** unto your words:
Ge 45:21 **a.** to the commandment of 5921
Ge 47:12 with bread, **a.** to their families. 6310
Ge 49:28 every one **a.** to his blessing he 834
Ge 50:6 and bury thy father, **a.** as he
Ge 50:12 sons did unto him **a.** as he 3651
Ex 6:16 the sons of Levi **a.** to their
Ex 6:17 Libni, and Shimi, **a.** to their
Ex 6:19 are the families of Levi **a.** to
Ex 6:25 of the fathers of the Levites **a.**
Ex 6:26 land of Egypt **a.** to their armies 5921
Ex 8:10 Be it **a.** to thy word: that thou
Ex 8:13 the Lord did **a.** to the word of
Ex 8:31 **a.** to the word of Moses; and he
Ex 12:3 every man a lamb, **a.** to the
Ex 12:4 take it **a.** to the number of
Ex 12:4 every man **a.** to his eating shall 6310
Ex 12:21 a lamb **a.** to your families, and
Ex 12:25 the Lord will give you, **a.** as he
Ex 12:35 Israel did **a.** to the word of
Ex 16:16 every man **a.** to his eating, 6310
Ex 16:16 every man, **a.** to the number of
Ex 16:18, 21 every man **a.** to his eating. 6310
Ex 17:1 **a.** to the commandment of the 5921
Ex 21:22 **a.** as the woman's husband will
Ex 21:31 **a.** to this judgment shall it be
Ex 22:17 he shall pay money **a.** to the
Ex 24:4 twelve pillars, **a.** to the twelve tribes
Ex 25:9 **A.** to all that I shew thee, after
Ex 25:35 **a.** to the six branches that
Ex 26:30 **a.** to the fashion thereof which
Ex 28:8 the same, **a.** to the work
Ex 28:10 the rest on the other stone, **a.** to
Ex 28:21 **a.** to their names, like the 5921
Ex 28:21 with his name shall they be **a.** to
Ex 29:35 **a.** to all things which I have
Ex 29:41 do thereto **a.** to the meat offering
Ex 29:41 and **a.** to the drink offering
Ex 30:37 not make to yourselves **a.** to the
Ex 31:11 **a.** to all that I have commanded
Ex 32:28 the children of Levi did **a.** to
Ex 36:1 **a.** to all that the Lord had
Ex 37:21 **a.** to the six branches going out
Ex 37:29 **a.** to the work of the apothecary.
Ex 38:21 as it was counted, **a.** to the 5921
Ex 39:5 the same, **a.** to the work therof;
Ex 39:14 the stones were **a.** to the names 5921
Ex 39:14 twelve, **a.** to their names, like the 5921
Ex 39:14 every one with his name, **a.** to the 5921
Ex 39:32 did **a.** to all that the Lord
Ex 39:42 **A.** to all that the Lord
Ex 40:16 Thus did Moses: **a.** to all that
Le 4:3 do sin **a.** to the sin of the people;
Le 4:35 **a.** to the offerings made by fire 5921
Le 5:10 burnt offering, **a.** to the manner:
Le 5:12 **a.** to the offerings made by fire 5921
Le 9:16 offered it **a.** to the manner
Le 10:7 did **a.** to the word of Moses.
Le 12:2 **a.** to the days of the separation
Le 25:15 **A.** to the number of years after
Le 25:15 **a.** unto the number of years of
Le 25:16 **A.** to the multitude of years 6310
Le 25:16 **a.** to the fewness of years thou 6310
Le 25:16 **a.** to the number of the years of
Le 25:50 price of his sale shall be **a.** unto
Le 25:50 **a.** to the time of an hired servant
Le 25:51 **a.** unto them he shall give again 6310
Le 25:52 **a.** unto his years shall he give 6310
Le 26:21 more plagues upon you **a.** to
Le 27:8 **a.** to his ability that vowed 6310
Le 27:16 thy estimation shall be **a.** to the 6310
Le 27:17 year of jubile, **a.** to thy
Le 27:18 **a.** to the years that remain, 5921,6310
Le 27:25 estimations shall be **a.** to the
Le 27:27 then he shall redeem it **a.** to
Le 27:27 then it shall be sold **a.** to thy
Nu 1:18 20, 22, 24, 26, 28, 30, 32, 34, 36, 38, 40,
42 **a.** to the number of the names,
Nu 1:54 **a.** to all that the Lord commanded
Nu 2:10 the camp of Reuben **a.** to their
Nu 2:18 the camp of Ephraim **a.** to their
Nu 2:34 **a.** to all that the Lord commanded
Nu 1:34 after their families, **a.** to the 5921
Nu 3:16 Moses numbered them **a.** to the 5921
Nu 3:20 families of the Levites **a.** to the
Nu 3:22, 34 **a.** to the number of all the
Nu 3:51 Aaron and to his sons, **a.** to the 5921
Nu 4:31 **a.** to all their service in the
Nu 4:33 families of the sons of Merari, **a.**
Nu 4:37 **a.** to the commandment of the 5921
Nu 4:41 number **a.** to the commandment. 5921
Nu 4:45 Moses and Aaron numbered **a.** to 5921
Nu 4:49 **A.** to the commandment of the 5921
Nu 4:49 Moses, every one **a.** to his service, 5921
Nu 4:49 and **a.** to his burden: thus were 5921
Nu 6:21 **a.** to the vow which he vowed, 6310
Nu 7:5 every man **a.** to his service 6310
Nu 7:7 **a.** to their service: 6310
Nu 7:8 **a.** unto their service, 6310
Nu 8:4 **a.** unto the pattern which the
Nu 8:20 **a.** unto all that the Lord
Nu 9:3 **a.** to all the rites of it, and **a.** to
Nu 9:5 **a.** to all that the Lord commanded
Nu 9:12 **a.** to all the ordinances of the
Nu 9:14 unto the Lord; **a.** to the
Nu 9:14 and **a.** to the manner thereof,
Nu 9:20 **a.** to the commandment of the 5921
Nu 9:20 and **a.** to the commandment of 5921
Nu 10:13 their journey **a.** to the 5921
Nu 10:14 camp of the children of Judah **a.**
Nu 10:18 camp of Reuben set forward **a.**
Nu 10:22 of Ephraim set forward **a.** to
Nu 10:28 of the children of Israel **a.** to
Nu 14:17 be great, **a.** as thou hast spoken,
Nu 14:19 this people **a.** unto the greatness
Nu 14:20 I have pardoned **a.** to thy word:
Nu 14:29 all that were numbered of you, **a.**
Nu 15:12 **A.** to the number that ye shall
Nu 15:12 to every one **a.** to their number.
Nu 15:24 **a.** to the manner, and one kid of
Nu 17:2 a rod **a.** to the house of their
Nu 17:2 of all their princes **a.** to the house
Nu 17:6 for each prince one, **a.** to their
Nu 18:16 redeem, **a.** to thine estimation,
Nu 23:23 **a.** to this time it shall be said
Nu 24:2 saw Israel abiding in his tents **a.**
Nu 26:18 children of Gad **a.** to those that
Nu 26:22 families of Judah **a.** to those
Nu 26:25 families of Issachar **a.** to those.
Nu 26:27 of the Zebulunites **a.** to those
Nu 26:37 of the sons of Ephraim **a.** to
Nu 26:43 of the Shuhamites, **a.** to those

Book	Ref.	Context	No.
Nu	26:47	of the sons of Asher **a.** to those	
Nu	26:50	the families of Naphtali **a.** to	
Nu	26:53	**a.** to the number of names	
Nu	26:54	be given **a.** to those that were	6310
Nu	26:55	**a.** to the names of the tribes of their	
Nu	26:56	**A.** to the lot shall...possession	5921,6310
Nu	29:6	**a.** unto their manner, for a sweet	
Nu	29:18	shall be **a.** to their number, after	
Nu	29:21,	24 **a.** to their number, after the	
Nu	29:27	shall be **a.** to their number, after	
Nu	29:30	**a.** to their number, after the	
Nu	29:33	shall be **a.** to their number, after	
Nu	29:37	**a.** to their number, after the	
Nu	29:40	**a.** to all that the Lord commanded	
Nu	30:2	do **a.** to all that proceedeth out of	
Nu	33:2	Moses wrote their goings out **a.** to	
Nu	33:2	these are their journeys **a.** to	
Nu	33:54	**a.** to the tribes of your fathers ye	
Nu	34:14	children of Reuben **a.** to the house	
Nu	34:14	children of Gad **a.** to the house	
Nu	35:8	the Levites **a.** to his inheritance	6310
Nu	35:24	the revenger of blood **a.** to these	5921
Nu	36:5	children of Israel **a.** to the word	5921
De	1:3	**a.** unto all that the Lord had	
De	1:30	**a.** to all that he did for you in	
De	1:41	**a.** to all that the Lord our God	
De	1:46	**a.** unto the days that ye abode	
De	3:24	**a.** to thy works, and **a.** to thy	
De	4:34	**a.** to all that the Lord your God	
De	9:10	**a.** to all the words, which the Lord	
De	10:4	**a.** to the first writing, the ten	
De	10:9	his inheritance, **a.** as the Lord thy	
De	10:10	**a.** to the first time, forty days	
De	12:15	**a.** to the blessing of the Lord thy	
De	16:10	**a.** as the Lord thy God hath	
De	16:17	**a.** to the blessing of the Lord thy	
De	17:10	shalt do **a.** to the sentence,	5921,6310
De	17:10	observe to do **a.** to all that they	
De	17:11	**A.** to the sentence of the law	5921
De	17:11	and **a.** to the judgment which	5921
De	18:16	**A.** to all that thou desiredst of the	
De	23:23	**a.** as thou hast vowed unto the	
De	24:8	**a.** to all that the priests the	
De	25:2	**a.** to his fault, by a certain	1767
De	26:13	**a.** to all thy commandments	
De	26:14	and have done **a.** to all that thou	
De	29:21	**a.** to all the curses of the	
De	30:2	**a.** to all that I command thee this	
De	31:5	**a.** unto all the commandments	
De	32:8	**a.** to the number of the children	
De	34:5	Moab, **a.** to the word of the Lord.	5921
Jos	1:7	observe to do **a.** to all the law	
Jos	1:8	thou mayest observe to do **a.** to	
Jos	1:17	**A.** as we hearkened unto Moses	
Jos	2:21	**A.** unto your words, so be it.	
Jos	4:5	**a.** unto the number of the tribes	
Jos	4:8	**a.** to the number of the tribes of	
Jos	4:10	**a.** to all that Moses commanded	
Jos	7:14	be brought **a.** to your tribes:	
Jos	7:14	shall come **a.** to the families	
Jos	8:8	**a.** to the commandment of the	
Jos	8:27	**a.** unto the word of the Lord	
Jos	8:34	**a.** to all that is written in the	
Jos	10:32,	35,37 **a.** to all that he had done	
Jos	11:23	**a.** to all that the Lord said unto	
Jos	11:23	inheritance unto Israel **a.** to their	
Jos	12:7	Israel for a possession **a.** to their	
Jos	13:15	children of Reuben inheritance **a.**	
Jos	13:24	even unto the children of Gad **a.**	
Jos	15:12	children of Judah round about **a.**	
Jos	15:13	**a.** to the commandment of the	413
Jos	15:20	tribe of the children of Judah **a.**	
Jos	16:5	children of Ephraim **a.** to their	
Jos	17:4	**a.** to the commandment of the	413
Jos	18:4	**a.** to the inheritance of them;	6310
Jos	18:10	the children of Israel **a.** to their	
Jos	18:11	came up **a.** to their families:	
Jos	18:20	round about, **a.** to their families.	
Jos	18:21,	28 children of Benjamin **a.** to	
Jos	19:1,	8 children of Simeon **a.** to their	
Jos	19:10,	16 children of Zebulun **a.** to their	
Jos	19:17,	23 the children of Issachar **a.** to	
Jos	19:24,	31 children of Asher **a.** to their	
Jos	19:32,	39 the children of Naphtali **a.** to	
Jos	19:40,	48 the children of Dan **a.** to their	
Jos	19:50	**A.** to the word of the Lord they	5921
Jos	21:33	All the cities of the Gershonites **a.**	
Jos	21:44	**a.** to all that he sware unto their	
Jos	22:9	**a.** to the word of the Lord by the	5921
Jos	24:5	**a.** to that which I did among	
Jg	8:35	**a.** to all the goodness which he	
Jg	9:16	done unto him **a.** to the deserving	
Jg	11:10	if we do not so **a.** to thy words.	
Jg	11:36	to me **a.** to that which hath	
Jg	11:39	who did with her **a.** to his vow	
Jg	20:10	**a.** to all the folly that they have	
Jg	21:23	wives, **a.** to their number, of them	
Ru	3:6	did **a.** to all that her mother in law	
1Sa	2:35	that shall do **a.** to that which is in	
1Sa	6:4	**a.** to the number of the lords of	
1Sa	6:18	**a.** to the number of all the cities	
1Sa	8:8	**A.** to all the works which they	
1Sa	13:8	**a.** to the set time that Samuel had	
1Sa	14:7	behold, I am with thee **a.** to thy	
1Sa	17:23	spake **a.** to the same words:	
1Sa	23:20	come down **a.** to all the desire of	
1Sa	25:9	they spake to Nabal **a.** to all those	
1Sa	25:30	**a.** to all the good that he hath	
2Sa	3:39	reward the doer of evil **a.** to his	
2Sa	7:17	**A.** to all these words, and **a.** to all	
2Sa	7:21	sake, and **a.** to thine own heart,	
2Sa	7:22	**a.** to all that we have heard with	
2Sa	9:11	**A.** to all that my lord the king	
2Sa	14:20	**a.** to the wisdom of an angel of	
2Sa	22:21	the Lord rewarded me **a.** to my	
2Sa	22:21	**a.** to the cleanness of my hands	
2Sa	22:25	Lord hath recompensed me **a.** to	
2Sa	22:25	**a.** to my cleanness in his eye sight.	
2Sa	24:19	David, **a.** to the saying of Gad,	
1Ki	2:6	Do therefore **a.** to thy wisdom,	
1Ki	3:6	**a.** as he walked before thee in	
1Ki	3:12	Behold, I have done **a.** to thy	
1Ki	4:28	every man **a.** to his charge.	
1Ki	5:6	give hire for thy servants **a.** to all	
1Ki	5:10	cedar trees and fir trees **a.** to all	
1Ki	6:3	**a.** to the breadth of the house;...	5921,6440
1Ki	6:38	and **a.** to all the fashion of it.	
1Ki	7:9	**a.** to the measures of hewed	
1Ki	7:36	**a.** to the proportion of every one,	
1Ki	8:32	give him **a.** to his righteousness	
1Ki	8:39	give to every man **a.** to his ways,	3605
1Ki	8:43	and do **a.** to all that the stranger	
1Ki	8:56	rest unto his people Israel, **a.** to	
1Ki	9:4	**a.** to all that I have commanded	
1Ki	9:11	with gold, **a.** to his desire,)	
1Ki	11:37	and thou shalt reign **a.** to all that	
1Ki	12:24	returned to depart, **a.** to the word	
1Ki	13:5	out from the altar, **a.** to the sign	
1Ki	13:26	slain him, **a.** to the word of the	
1Ki	14:18	**a.** to the word of the Lord, which	
1Ki	14:24	they did **a.** to all the abominations	
1Ki	15:29	destroyed him, **a.** unto the	
1Ki	16:12	Baasha, **a.** to the word of the Lord,	
1Ki	16:34	Segub, **a.** to the word of the Lord,	
1Ki	17:1	**a.** to my word	6310
1Ki	17:5	did **a.** unto the word of the Lord:	
1Ki	17:15	**a.** to the saying Elijah:	
1Ki	17:16	oil fail, **a.** to the word of the Lord,	
1Ki	18:31	**a.** to the number of the tribes of	
1Ki	20:4	O king, **a.** to thy saying, I am thine,	
1Ki	21:26	following idols, **a.** to all things as	
1Ki	22:38	**a.** unto the word of the Lord	
1Ki	22:53	**a.** to all that his father had done.	
2Ki	1:17	he died **a.** to the word of the Lord	
2Ki	2:22	**a.** to the saying of Elisha	
2Ki	4:16	About this season, **a.** to the time	
2Ki	4:17	unto her, **a.** to the time of life.	
2Ki	4:44	left thereof, **a.** to the word of the	
2Ki	5:14	**a.** to the saying of the man of God:	
2Ki	6:18	with blindness **a.** to the word of	
2Ki	7:16	barley for a shekel, **a.** to the word	
2Ki	9:26	ground, **a.** to the word of the Lord.	
2Ki	10:17	destroyed him, **a.** to the saying of	
2Ki	10:30	**a.** to all that was in mine heart,	
2Ki	11:9	did **a.** to all things that Jehoiada	
2Ki	14:3	he did **a.** to all things as Joash	
2Ki	14:6	**a.** unto that which is written in the	
2Ki	14:25	**a.** to the word of the Lord God of	
2Ki	15:3	**a.** to all that his father Amaziah	
2Ki	15:34	**a.** to all that his father Uzziah	
2Ki	16:3	fire, **a.** to the abominations of the	
2Ki	16:10	**a.** to all the workmanship thereof.	
2Ki	16:11	altar **a.** to all that king Ahaz had	
2Ki	16:16	the priest, **a.** to all that king Ahaz	
2Ki	17:13	**a.** to all the law which I	
2Ki	18:3	**a.** to all that David his father did	
2Ki	21:8	they will observe to do **a.** to all	
2Ki	21:8	**a.** to all the law that my servant	
2Ki	22:13	to do **a.** unto all that which is	
2Ki	23:16	polluted it, **a.** to the word of the	
2Ki	23:19	**a.** to all the acts that he had done	
2Ki	23:25	might, **a.** to all the law of Moses;	
2Ki	23:32	**a.** to all that his fathers had done.	
2Ki	23:35	to give the money **a.** to the	5921
2Ki	23:35	of every one **a.** to his taxation, to	
2Ki	23:37	**a.** to all that his fathers had done.	
2Ki	24:2	destroy it, **a.** to the word of the	
2Ki	24:3	Manasseh, **a.** to all that he did;	
2Ki	24:9	sight of the Lord, **a.** to all that	
2Ki	24:19	**a.** to all that Jehoiakim had done.	
1Ch	6:19	the families of the Levites **a.** to	
1Ch	6:32	waited on their office **a.** to their	
1Ch	6:49	**a.** to all that Moses the servant of	
1Ch	9:9	brethren, **a.** to their generations,	
1Ch	11:3	**a.** to the word of the Lord by	
1Ch	11:10	**a.** to the word of the Lord	
1Ch	12:23	of Saul to him, **a.** to the word of	
1Ch	15:15	**a.** to the word of the Lord.	
1Ch	16:40	**a.** to all that is written in the law	
1Ch	17:15	**A.** to all these words, and **a.** to all	
1Ch	17:17	regarded me **a.** to the estate of a	
1Ch	17:19	**a.** to thine own heart, hast thou	
1Ch	17:20	**a.** to all that we have heard with	
1Ch	23:11	reckoning, **a.** to their father's	
1Ch	23:31	**a.** to the order commanded unto	
1Ch	24:3	**a.** to their offices in their service.	
1Ch	24:4	sons of Ithamar **a.** to the house	
1Ch	24:19	**a.** to their manner, under Aaron,	
1Ch	25:1	the number of the workmen **a.** to	
1Ch	25:2	prophesied **a.** to the order of the	5921
1Ch	25:6	**a.** to the king's order to Asaph,	5921
1Ch	26:13	**a.** to the house of their fathers,	
1Ch	26:31	**a.** to the generations of his fathers.	
1Ch	28:15	**a.** to the use of every candlestick	
2Ch	3:4	length of it was **a.** to the breadth	5921
2Ch	3:8	the length whereof was **a.** to the	5921
2Ch	4:7	gold **a.** to their form,	
2Ch	6:23	giving him **a.** to his righteousness	
2Ch	6:30	render unto every man **a.** unto all	
2Ch	6:33	**a.** to all that the stranger calleth to	
2Ch	7:17	and do **a.** to all that I have	
2Ch	7:18	**a.** as I have covenanted with	
2Ch	8:13	offering **a.** to the commandment	
2Ch	8:14	**a.** to the order of David his	
2Ch	17:14	numbers of them **a.** to the house	
2Ch	23:8	**a.** to all things that Jehoiada the	
2Ch	24:6	**a.** to the commandment of Moses	
2Ch	25:5	**a.** to the houses of their fathers,	
2Ch	26:4	sight of the Lord, **a.** to all that	
2Ch	26:11	**a.** to the number of their account	
2Ch	27:2	**a.** to all that his father Uzziah	
2Ch	29:2	**a.** to all that David his father	
2Ch	29:15	came, **a.** to the commandment of	
2Ch	29:25	**a.** to the commandment of David,	
2Ch	30:6	and Judah, and **a.** to the	
2Ch	30:16	**a.** to the law of Moses the man of	
2Ch	30:19	he be not cleansed **a.** to the	
2Ch	31:2	every man **a.** to his service,	6310
2Ch	31:16	their service in their charges **a.**	
2Ch	32:25	rendered not again **a.** to the	
2Ch	33:8	**a.** to the whole law and the	
2Ch	34:32	did **a.** to the covenant of God,	
2Ch	35:4	**a.** to the writing of David king of	
2Ch	35:4	and **a.** to the writing of Solomon	
2Ch	35:5	the holy place **a.** to the divisions	
2Ch	35:6	may do **a.** to the word of the Lord	
2Ch	35:10	**a.** to the king's commandment.	
2Ch	35:12	that they might give **a.** to the divisions	
2Ch	35:13	with fire **a.** to the ordinance:	
2Ch	35:15	**a.** to the commandment of David,	
2Ch	35:16	**a.** to the commandment of king	
2Ch	35:26	**a.** to that which was written in the	
Ezr	3:4	**a.** to the custom, as the duty of	
Ezr	3:7	**a.** to the grant that they had of	
Ezr	6:9	**a.** to the appointment of the	
Ezr	6:13	**a.** to that which Darius the king	6903
Ezr	6:14	**a.** to the commandment of the	4481
Ezr	6:14	and **a.** to the commandment of	
Ezr	6:17	twelve he goats, **a.** to the number	
Ezr	7:6	**a.** to the hand of the Lord his God	
Ezr	7:9	to Jerusalem, **a.** to the good hand	

Ezr 7:14 **a.** to the law of thy God which is in
Ezr 9:1 doing **a.** to their abominations,
Ezr 10:3 **a.** to the counsel of my Lord, and
Ezr 10:3 and let it be done **a.** to the law
Ezr 10:5 do **a.** to this word. And they sware,
Ezr 10:8 come within three days, **a.** to the
Ne 2:8 **a.** to the good hand of my God
Ne 5:12 should do **a.** to this promise.
Ne 5:13 people did **a.** to this promise.
Ne 5:19 **a.** to all that I have done for this
Ne 6:6 be their king, **a.** to these words.
Ne 6:7 reported to the king **a.** to these
Ne 6:14 **a.** to these their works, and on
Ne 8:18 a solemn assembly, **a.** unto the
Ne 9:27 **a.** to thy manifold mercies thou
Ne 9:28 didst thou deliver them **a.** to thy
Ne 12:24, 45 **a.** to the commandment of
Ne 13:22 and spare me **a.** to the greatness
Ne 13:24 but **a.** to the language of each
Es 1:7 royal wine in abundance, **a.** to the
Es 1:8 the drinking was **a.** to the law;
Es 1:8 that they should do **a.** to every
Es 1:15 we do unto the queen Vashti **a.**
Es 1:21 did **a.** to the word of Memucan:
Es 1:22 into every province **a.** to the writing
Es 1:22 should be published **a.** to the
Es 2:12 she had been twelve months, **a.** to
Es 2:18 and gave gifts, **a.** to the state of
Es 3:12 and there was written **a.** to all
Es 3:12 every people of every province **a.**
Es 4:16 king, which is not **a.** to the law:
Es 4:17 and did **a.** to all that Esther had
Es 8:9 written **a.** to all that Mordecai
Es 8:9 unto every province **a.** to the
Es 8:9 Jews **a.** to their writing, and **a.** to
Es 9:13 to do to morrow also **a.** unto this
Es 9:27 **a.** to their writing, and **a.** to their
Es 9:31 **a.** as Mordecai the Jew and
Job 1:5 offered burnt offerings **a.** to the
Job 20:18 **a.** to his substance shall the
Job 33:6 I am **a.** to thy wish in God's
Job 34:11 every man to find **a.** to his ways.
Job 34:33 Should it be **a.** to thy mind? he
Job 36:27 they pour down rain **a.** to the
Job 42:9 and did **a.** as the Lord commanded
Ps 7:8 **a.** to my righteousness, and **a.** to
Ps 7:17 I will praise the Lord **a.** to his
Ps 18:20 The Lord rewarded me **a.** to my
Ps 18:20 **a.** to the cleanness of my hands
Ps 18:24 hath the Lord recompensed me **a.**
Ps 18:24 **a.** to the cleanness of my hands
Ps 20:4 Grant thee **a.** to thine own heart,
Ps 25:7 **a.** to thy mercy remember thou
Ps 28:4 them **a.** to their deeds, and **a.** to
Ps 33:22 upon us, **a.** as we hope in thee.
Ps 35:24 Judge me, O Lord my God, **a.** to thy
Ps 48:10 **A.** to thy name, O God, so is thy
Ps 51:1 Have mercy upon me, O God, **a.** to
Ps 51:1 **a.** unto the multitude of thy
Ps 62:12 renderest to every man **a.** to his
Ps 69:16 turn unto me **a.** to the multitude
Ps 74:5 A man was famous **a.** as he had
Ps 78:72 So he fed them **a.** to the integrity
Ps 79:11 **a.** to the greatness of thy power
Ps 90:11 even **a.** to thy fear, so is thy
Ps 90:15 **a.** to the days wherein thou hast
Ps 103:10 rewarded us **a.** to our iniquities
Ps 106:45 and repented **a.** to the multitude
Ps 109:26 O Lord my God: O save me **a.** to
Ps 119:9 taking heed thereto **a.** to thy word.
Ps 119:25 quicken thou me **a.** to thy word.
Ps 119:28 strengthen thou me **a.** unto thy
Ps 119:41 even thy salvation, **a.** to thy word.
Ps 119:58 merciful unto me **a.** to thy word
Ps 119:65 O Lord, **a.** unto thy word.
Ps 119:76 be for my comfort, **a.** to thy word
Ps 119:91 this day **a.** to thine ordinances:
Ps 119:107 quicken me, O Lord, **a.** unto thy
Ps 119:116 Uphold me **a.** unto thy word, that
Ps 119:124 Deal with thy servant **a.** unto
Ps 119:149 hear my voice **a.** unto thy
Ps 119:149 quicken me **a.** to thy judgment
Ps 119:154 and deliver me: quicken me **a.** to
Ps 119:156 quicken me **a.** to thy judgments.
Ps 119:159 quicken me, O Lord, **a.** to thy
Ps 119:169 me understanding **a.** to thy word
Ps 119:170 before thee: deliver me **a.** to thy word
Ps 150:2 praise him **a.** to his excellent
Pr 12:8 shall be commended **a.** to his 6310
Pr 24:12 render to every man **a.** to his
Pr 24:29 I will render to the man **a.** to
Pr 26:4 Answer not a fool **a.** to his folly,
Pr 26:5 Answer a fool **a.** to his folly, lest
Ec 1:6 and the wind returneth again **a.** 5921
Ec 8:14 **a.** to the work of the wicked;
Ec 8:14 **a.** to the work of the righteous:
Isa 8:20 if they speak not **a.** to this word,
Isa 9:3 they joy before thee **a.** to the joy
Isa 10:26 **a.** to the slaughter of Midian at
Isa 21:16 Within a year, **a.** to the years of
Isa 23:15 forgotten seventy years, **a.** to the
Isa 27:7 or is he slain **a.** to the slaughter of
Isa 44:13 the figure of a man, **a.** to the
Isa 59:18 **A.** to their deeds, accordingly he 5921
Isa 63:7 **a.** to all that the Lord hath 5921
Isa 63:7 he hath bestowed on them **a.** to
Isa 63:7 and **a.** to the multitude of his
Jer 2:28 for **a.** to the number of thy cities
Jer 3:15 And I will give you pastors **a.** to
Jer 11:4 and do them, **a.** to all which I
Jer 11:13 For **a.** to the number of thy cities
Jer 11:13 and **a.** to the number of the
Jer 13:2 girdle **a.** to the word of the Lord,
Jer 17:10 **a.** to his ways, and **a.** to the fruit
Jer 21:2 the Lord will deal with us **a.** to
Jer 21:14 But I will punish you **a.** to the
Jer 25:14 recompense them **a.** to their
Jer 25:14 **a.** to the works of their own hands.
Jer 26:20 against this land **a.** to all the
Jer 27:12 to Zedekiah king of Judah **a.** to
Jer 31:32 Not **a.** to the covenant that I made
Jer 32:8 **a.** to the word of the Lord, and
Jer 32:11 both that which was sealed **a.** to
Jer 32:19 to give every one **a.** to his ways,
Jer 32:19 and **a.** to the fruit of his doings:
Jer 35:10 and done **a.** to all that Jonadab
Jer 35:18 and done **a.** unto all that he hath
Jer 36:8 did **a.** to all that Jeremiah the
Jer 38:27 **a.** to all these words that the king
Jer 40:3 Lord hath brought it, and done **a.**
Jer 42:4 **a.** to your words;
Jer 42:5 if we do not even **a.** to all things
Jer 42:20 and **a.** unto all that the Lord our
Jer 50:21 do **a.** to all that I have commanded
Jer 50:29 recompense her **a.** to her work;
Jer 50:29 **a.** to all that she hath done, do
Jer 52:2 **a.** to all that Jehoiakim had done.
La 3:32 compassion **a.** to the multitude
La 3:64 **a.** to the work of their hands
Eze 4:4 **a.** to the number of the days
Eze 4:5 their iniquity, **a.** to the number of
Eze 4:9 make thee bread thereof, **a.** to the
Eze 5:7 have done **a.** to the judgments
Eze 7:3 and will judge thee **a.** to thy ways,
Eze 7:8 I will judge thee **a.** to thy ways,
Eze 7:9 I will recompense thee **a.** to thy
Eze 7:27 and **a.** to their deserts will I judge
Eze 8:4 **a.** to the vision that I saw in the
Eze 14:4 that cometh **a.** to the multitude
Eze 18:24 committeth iniquity, and doeth **a.**
Eze 18:30 every one **a.** to his ways, saith the
Eze 20:44 not **a.** to your wicked ways,
Eze 20:44 nor **a.** to your corrupt doings,
Eze 23:24 judge thee **a.** to their judgments
Eze 24:14 **a.** to thy ways, and
Eze 24:14 **a.** to thy doings,
Eze 24:24 **a.** to all that he hath done shall
Eze 25:14 in Edom **a.** to mine anger and
Eze 25:14 **a.** to my fury;
Eze 35:11 do **a.** to thine anger, and
Eze 35:11 **a.** to thine envy
Eze 36:19 **a.** to their way and
Eze 36:19 **a.** to their doings I judged them.
Eze 39:24 **A.** to their uncleanness and
Eze 39:24 **a.** to their transgressions
Eze 40:24 and the arches thereof **a.** to these
Eze 40:28 measured the south gate **a.** to
Eze 40:29 and the arches thereof, **a.** to these
Eze 40:32 and he measured the gate **a.** to
Eze 40:33 the arches thereof, were **a.** to
Eze 40:35 the north gate, and measured it **a.**
Eze 42:11 both **a.** to their fashions, and
Eze 42:11 **a.** to their doors.
Eze 42:12 **a.** to the doors of the chambers
Eze 43:3 **a.** to the appearance of the vision
Eze 43:3 even **a.** to the vision that I saw
Eze 44:24 judge it **a.** to my judgments:
Eze 45:8 give to the house of Israel **a.** to
Eze 45:25 **a.** to the sin offering,
Eze 45:25 **a.** to the burnt offering,
Eze 45:25 and **a.** to the meat offering,
Eze 45:25 and **a.** to the oil.
Eze 46:7 for the lambs **a.** as his hand shall
Eze 47:10 their fish shall be **a.** to their kinds,
Eze 47:12 bring forth new fruit **a.** to his
Eze 47:13 ye shall inherit the land **a.** to the
Eze 47:21 divide this land unto you **a.** to the
Da 4:8 whose name was Belteshazzar, **a.**
Da 4:35 and he doeth **a.** to his will in the
Da 6:8 **a.** to the law of the Medes and
Da 6:12 is true, **a.** to the law of the Medes
Da 8:4 but he did **a.** to his will, and
Da 9:16 O Lord, **a.** to all thy righteousness,
Da 11:3 with great dominion, and do **a.**
Da 11:4 to his posterity, nor **a.** to his
Da 11:16 shall do **a.** to his own will, and
Da 11:36 And the king shall do **a.** to his
Ho 3:1 **a.** to the love of the Lord
Ho 9:10 their abominations were **a.** as
Ho 10:1 **a.** to the multitude of his fruit he
Ho 10:1 **a.** to the goodness of his land
Ho 12:2 **a.** to his ways; **a.** to his doings
Ho 13:2 and idols **a.** to their own
Ho 13:6 **A.** to their pasture, so were they
Jon 3:3 **a.** to the word of the Lord.
Mic 7:15 **A.** to the days of thy coming out
Hab 3:9 made quite naked, **a.** to the
Hag 2:5 **A.** to the word that I covenanted
Zec 1:6 **a.** to our ways, and **a.** to our
Zec 5:3 cut off as on this side **a.** to it; 3644
Zec 5:3 cut off as on that side **a.** to it. 3644
Mal 2:9 **a.** as ye have not kept my ways, 6310
Mt *general* *title* Gospel **A.** to S. [St.] Matthew *2596*
Mt 2:16 **a.** to the time which he had *2596*
Mt 9:29 **A. to your faith be it unto you** *2596*
Mt 16:27 **he shall reward every man a. to** *2596*
Mt 25:15 **to every man a. to his several** *2596*
Mk *general* *title* The Gospel **A.** to S. [St.] Mark *2596*
Mk 7:5 Why walk not thy disciples **a.** to *2596*
Lu *general* *title* The Gospel **A.** to S [St.] Luke *2596*
Lu 1:9 **A.** to the custom of the priest's *2596*
Lu 1:38 be it unto me **a.** to thy word *2596*
Lu 2:22 **a.** to the law of Moses were *2596*
Lu 2:24 **a.** to that which is said in the law *2596*
Lu 2:29 in peace, **a.** to thy word: *2596*
Lu 2:39 **a.** to the law of the Lord, *2596*
Lu 5:14 **and offer for thy cleansing, a. as**
Lu 12:47 **neither did a. to his will,** *4314*
Lu 23:56 **a.** to the commandment *2596*
Joh *general* *title* The Gospel **A.** to S. [St.] John *2596*
Joh 7:24 **Judge not a. to the appearance,** *2596*
Joh 18:31 judge him **a.** to your law. *2596*
Ac 2:30 **a.** to the flesh, he would raise up *2596*
Ac 4:35 unto every man **a.** as he had need *2530*
Ac 7:44 should make it **a.** to the fashion *2596*
Ac 11:29 every man **a.** to his ability, *2531*
Ac 13:23 **a.** to his promise raised unto *2596*
Ac 22:3 taught **a.** to the perfect manner *2596*
Ac 22:12 a devout man **a.** to the law, *2596*
Ac 24:6 would have judged **a.** to our law. *2596*
Ro 1:3 of the seed of David **a.** to the flesh; *2596*
Ro 1:4 **a.** to the spirit of holiness, *2596*
Ro 2:2 the judgment of God is **a.** to truth *2596*
Ro 2:6 to every man **a.** to his deeds: *2596*
Ro 2:16 **a.** to my gospel. *2596*
Ro 4:18 **a.** to that which was spoken, So *2596*
Ro 8:27 **a.** to the will of God. *2596*
Ro 8:28 **a.** to his purpose. *2596*
Ro 9:3 my kinsmen **a.** to the flesh: *2596*
Ro 9:11 **a.** to election might stand, not of *2596*
Ro 10:2 have a zeal of God, but not **a.** to *2596*
Ro 11:5 **a.** to the election of grace. *2596*
Ro 11:8 (**A.** as it is written, God hath given *2531*
Ro 12:3 **a.** as God hath dealt to every
Ro 12:6 differing **a.** to the grace *2596*
Ro 12:6 **a.** to the proportion of faith; *2596*
Ro 15:5 **a.** to Christ Jesus: *2596*
Ro 16:25 **a.** to my gospel, *2596*
Ro 16:25 **a.** to the revelation of the mystery, *2596*
Ro 16:26 **a.** to the commandment of the *2596*
1Co 1:31 **a.** as it is written, He that glorieth, *2531*

1Co 3:8 a. to his own labour. ... 2596
1Co 3:10 A. to the grace of God which is ... 2596
1Co 15:3 died for our sins a. to the ... 2596
1Co 15:4 a. to the scriptures: ... 2596
2Co 1:17 do I purpose a. to the flesh, ... 2596
2Co 4:13 a. as it is written, I believed, ... 2596
2Co 5:10 a. to that he hath done, ... 4314
2Co 8:12 a. to that a man hath and not a. ... 2526
2Co 9:7 a. as he purposeth in his heart, ... 2531
2Co 10:2 as if we walked a. to the flesh. ... 2596
2Co 10:13 but a. to the measure of the rule ... 2596
2Co 10:15 a. to our rule abundantly, ... 2596
2Co 11:15 and shall be a. to their works. ... 2596
2Co 13:10 a. to the power which the Lord ... 2596
Ga 1:4 a. to the will of God and our Father: .. 2596
Ga 2:14 a. to the truth of the gospel, ... 4314
Ga 3:29 heirs a. to the promise. ... 2596
Ga 6:16 And as many as walk a. to this ...
Eph 1:4 A. as he hath chosen us in him ... 2531
Eph 1:5 a. to the good pleasure of his will, ... 2596
Eph 1:7 a. to the riches of his grace; ... 2596
Eph 1:9 a. to his good pleasure ... 2596
Eph 1:11 a. to the purpose of him who ... 2596
Eph 1:19 a. to the working of his mighty ... 2596
Eph 2:2 a. to the course of this world, ... 2596
Eph 2:2 a. to the prince of the power ... 2596
Eph 3:7 a. to the gift of the grace of God ... 2596
Eph 3:11 A. to the eternal purpose which he ... 2596
Eph 3:16 a. to the riches of his glory, ... 2596
Eph 3:20 a. to the power that worketh in us, ... 2596
Eph 4:7 grace a. to the measure of the ... 2596
Eph 4:16 a. to the effectual working ... 2596
Eph 4:22 a. to the deceitful lusts; ... 2596
Eph 6:5 a. to the flesh, with fear and ... 2596
Php 1:20 A. to my earnest expectation and ... 2596
Php 3:21 a. to the working whereby he is ... 2596
Php 4:19 a. to his riches in glory by Christ ... 2596
Col 1:11 a. to his glorious power, ... 2596
Col 1:25 a. to the dispensation of God ... 2596
Col 1:29 striving a. to his working, ... 2596
Col 3:22 obey in all thing your masters a. ... 2596
2Th 1:12 a. to the grace of our God ... 2596
1Ti 1:11 A. to the glorious gospel of the ... 2596
1Ti 1:18 a. to the prophecies which went ... 2596
1Ti 6:3 which is a. to godliness; ... 2596
2Ti 1:1 a. to the promise of life ... 2596
2Ti 1:8 a. to the power of God; ... 2596
2Ti 1:9 not a. to our works, but a. to his ... 2596
2Ti 2:8 a. to my gospel: ... 2596
2Ti 4:14 Lord reward him a. to his works: ... 2596
Tit 1:1 a. to the faith of God's elect, ... 2596
Tit 1:3 a. to the commandment of God ... 2596
Tit 3:5 but a. to his mercy he saved us, ... 2596
Tit 3:7 a. to the hope of eternal life ... 2596
Heb 2:4 a. to his own will? ... 2596
Heb 7:5 tithes of the people a. to the law, ... 2596
Heb 8:4 offer gifts a. to the law: ... 2596
Heb 8:5 a. to the pattern shewed to thee ... 2596
Heb 8:9 Not a. to the covenant that I made ... 2596
Heb 9:19 a. to the law, he took the blood ... 2596
Jas 2:8 fulfill the royal law a. to the ... 2596
1Pe 1:2 Elect a. to the foreknowledge of ... 2596
1Pe 1:3 a. to his abundant mercy hath ... 2596
1Pe 1:14 not fashioning yourselves a. to ... 2596
1Pe 1:17 judgeth a. to every man's work, ... 2596
1Pe 3:7 a. to knowledge, giving honour ... 2596
1Pe 4:6 judged a. to men in the flesh, ... 2596
1Pe 4:6 but live a. to God in the spirit. ... 2596
1Pe 4:19 that suffer a. to the will of God ... 2596
2Pe 1:3 A. as his divine power hath given ... 5613
2Pe 2:22 a. to the true proverb, The dog is ...
2Pe 3:13 a. to his promise, look for new ... 2596
2Pe 3:15 a. to the wisdom given unto him ... 2596
1Jo 5:14 if we ask any thing a. to his will, ... 2596
Re 2:23 **a. to your works.** ... 2596
Re 18:6 double a. to her works: ... 2596
Re 20:12, 13 a. to their works. ... 2596
Re 21:17 a. to the measure of a man, that ...
Re 22:12 **to give every man a. as his work** ... 5613

ACCORDINGLY
Isa 59:18 a. he will repay, fury to his ... 5922

ACCOUNT See also ACCOUNTED; ACCOUNTING; ACCOUNTS.
2Ki 12:4 of every one that passeth the a., ...
1Ch 27:24 was the number put in the a. of ... 4557
2Ch 26:11 number of their a. by the hand ... 6486
Job 33:13 he giveth not a. of any of his ... 6030
Ps 144:3 son of man, that thou makest a. ... 2803
Ec 7:27 one by one, to find out the a.; ... 2808
Mt 12:36 **they shall give a. thereof in the** ... 3056
Mt 18:23 **would take a. of his servants.** ... 3056
Lu 16:2 **give an a. of thy stewardship;** ... 3056
Ac 19:40 whereby we may give an a. of this ... 3056
Ro 14:12 every one of us shall give a. of ... 3056
1Co 4:1 Let a man so a. of us, as of the ... 3049
Php 4:17 fruit that may abound to your a. ... 3056
Phm 4:18 put that on mine a.; ... 1677
Heb 13:17 as they that must give a., ... 3056
1Pe 4:5 shall give a. to him that is ready ... 3056
2Pe 3:15 And a. that the longsuffering ... 2233

ACCOUNTED
De 2:11 Which also were a. giants, as the ... 2803
De 2:20 (That also was a. a land of giants: ... 2803
1Ki 10:21 it was nothing a. of in the days ... 2803
2Ch 9:20 of silver; it was not any thing a. ... 2803
Ps 22:30 it shall be a. to the Lord for a ... 5608
Isa 2:22 wherein is he to be a. of? ... 2803
Mk 10:42 **they which are a. to rule over** ... 1380
Lu 20:35 **which shall be a. worthy to** ... 2661
Lu 21:36 **that ye may be a. worthy to** ... 2661
Lu 22:24 which of them should be a. the ... 1380
Ro 8:36 we are a. as sheep for the ... 3049
Ga 3:6 it was a. to him for righteousness. ... 3049

ACCOUNTING
Heb 11:19 A. that God was able to raise ... 3049

ACCOUNTS
Da 6:2 that the princes might give a. ... 2941

ACCURSED
De 21:23 he that is hanged is a. of God;) ... 7045
Jos 6:17 the city shall be a., ... 2764
Jos 6:18 keep yourselves from the a. ... 2764
Jos 6:18 lest ye make yourselves a., ... 2763
Jos 6:18 when ye take of the a. thing, and ... 2764
Jos 7:1 a trespass in the a. thing: ... 2764
Jos 7:1 took of the a. thing: ... 2764
Jos 7:11 have even taken of the a. thing, ... 2764
Jos 7:12 because they were a.: ... 2764
Jos 7:12 except ye destroy the a. from ... 2764
Jos 7:13 an a. thing in the midst of thee, ... 2764
Jos 7:13 until ye take away the a. thing ... 2764
Jos 7:15 taken with the a. thing shall be ... 2764
Jos 22:20 commit a trespass in the a. thing, ... 2764
1Ch 2:7 who transgressed in the thing a. ... 2764
Isa 65:20 an hundred years old shall be a. ... 7043
Ro 9:3 that myself were a. from Christ ... 331
1Co 12:3 calleth Jesus a.: and that no man ... 331
Ga 1:8 preached unto you, let him be a. ... 331
Ga 1:9 have received, let him be a. ... 331

ACCUSATION
Ezr 4:6 wrote they unto him an a. against ... 7855
Mt 27:37 over his head his a. written, ... 156
Mk 15:26 his a. was written over, ... 156
Lu 6:7 might find an a. against him. ... 2724
Lu 19:8 thing from any man by false a., ... 4811
Joh 18:29 What a. bring ye against this ... 2724
Ac 25:18 they brought none a. of such ... 156
1Ti 5:19 receive not an a., but before two ... 2724
2Pe 2:11 bring not railing a. against them ... 2920
Jude 9 a railing a., but said, The Lord ... 2920

ACCUSE See also ACCUSED; ACCUSETH; ACCUSING.
Pr 30:10 A. not a servant unto his master, ... 3960
Mt 12:10 that they might a. him. ... 2723
Mk 3:2 sabbath day; that they might a. ... 2723
Lu 3:14 neither a. any falsely; and be ... 4811
Lu 11:54 his mouth, that they might a. ... 2723
Lu 23:2 they began to a. him, ... 2723
Lu 23:14 whereof ye a. him: ... 2723
Joh 5:45 **Do not think that I will a. you to** .. 2723
Joh 8:6 that they might have to a. him. ... 2723
Ac 24:2 Tertullus began to a. him, ... 2723
Ac 24:8 these things, whereof we a. him. ... 2723
Ac 14:13 whereof they now a. me. ... 2723
Ac 25:5 go down with me, and a. this man, ... 2723
Ac 25:11 whereof these a. me, no man may ... 2723
Ac 28:19 ought to a. my nation of. ... 2723
1Pe 3:16 ashamed that falsely a. your ... 1908

ACCUSED
Da 3:8 Chaldeans came near, and a. ... 399,7170
Da 6:24 those men which had a. ... 399,7170
Mt 27:12 he was a. of the chief priests ... 2723
Mk 15:3 the chief priests a. him of many ... 2723
Lu 16:1 **the same was a. unto him that he** .. 1225
Lu 23:10 scribes stood and vehemently a. ... 2723
Ac 22:30 wherefore he was a. of the Jews, ... 2723
Ac 23:28 the cause wherefore they a. him, ... 1458
Ac 23:29 be a. of questions of their law, ... 1458
Ac 25:16 before that he which is a. have ... 2723
Ac 26:2 things whereof I am a. of the ... 1458
Ac 26:7 king Agrippa, I am a. of the Jews. ... 1458
Tit 1:6 children not a. of riot, or ... 1722,2724
Re 12:10 which a. them before our God ... 2723

ACCUSER See also ACCUSERS.
Re 12:10 for the a. of our brethren is cast ... 2725

ACCUSERS
Joh 8:10 **where are those thine a.?** ... 2725
Ac 23:30 gave commandment to his a. ... 2725
Ac 23:35 when thine a. are also come. ... 2725
Ac 24:8 Commanding his a. to come unto ... 2725
Ac 25:16 have the a. face to face, ... 2725
Ac 25:18 when the a. stood up, ... 2725
2Ti 3:3 trucebreakers, false a., ... 1228
Tit 2:3 not false a., not given to much ... 1228

ACCUSETH
Joh 5:45 **there is one that a. you, even** ... 2723

ACCUSING
Ro 2:15 their thoughts the mean while a. ... 2723

ACCUSTOMED See also UNACCUSTOMED.
Jer 13:23 that are a. to do evil. ... 3928

ACELDAMA (as-el'-dam-ah)
Ac 1:19 A., that is to say, The field of ... 184

ACHAIA (ak-ah'-yah)
Ac 18:12 Gallio was the deputy of A., ... 882
Ac 18:27 to pass into A., the brethren wrote, ... 882
Ac 19:21 passed through Macedonia and A., ... 882
Ro 15:26 them of Macedonia and A. to make ... 882
Ro 16:5 who is the firstfruits of A. unto ... 882
1Co 16:15 firstfruits of A., and that they have ... 882
2Co 1:1 saints which are in all A.: ... 882
2Co 9:2 A. was ready a year ago; ... 882
2Co 11:10 of boasting in the regions of A. ... 882
1Th 1:7 that believe in Macedonia and A. ... 882
1Th 1:8 not only in Macedonia and A., but ... 882

ACHAICUS (ak-ah'-yah-cus)
1Co 16:17 Fortunatus and A.: ... 883
subscr. Stephanas, and Fortunatus, and A., ...

ACHAN (a'-kan) See also ACHAR.
Jos 7:1 for A., the son of Carmi, the son ... 5912
Jos 7:18 his household man by man; and A., ... 5912
Jos 7:19 and Joshua said unto A., My son, ... 5912
Jos 7:20 And A. answered Joshua, and said, ... 5912
Jos 7:24 and all Israel with him, took A. ... 5912
Jos 22:20 Did not A. the son of Zerah ... 5912

ACHAR (a'-kar) See also ACHAN.
1Ch 2:7 And the sons of Carmi; A., the ... 5917

ACHAZ (a'-kaz) See also AHAZ.
Mt 1:9 Joatham begat A.; ... 881
Mt 1:9 and A. begat Ezekias; ... 881

ACHBOR (ak'-bor)
Ge 36:38 and Baal-hanan the son of A. ... 5907
Ge 36:39 Baal-hanan the son of A. died, ... 5907
2Ki 22:12 And A. the son of Michaiah, and ... 5907
2Ki 22:14 and A., and Shaphan, and Asahiah, ... 5907
1Ch 1:49 Baal-hanan the son of A. reigned ... 5907
Jer 26:22 namely, Elnathan the son of A., ... 5907
Jer 36:12 Elnathan the son of A., and ... 5907

ACHIM (a'-kim)
Mt 1:14 and Sadoc begat A.; ... 885
Mt 1:14 and A. begat Eliud; ... 885

ACHISH (a'-kish)
1Sa 21:10 and went to A. the king of Gath. ... 397
1Sa 21:11 the servants of A. said unto him, ... 397
1Sa 21:12 was sore afraid of A. the king ... 397
1Sa 21:14 Then said A. unto his servants, ... 397
1Sa 27:2 unto A., the son of Maoch, king ... 397
1Sa 27:3 David dwelt with A. at Gath, ... 397
1Sa 27:5 David said unto A., If I have ... 397
1Sa 27:6 A. gave him Ziklag that day: ... 397
1Sa 27:9 and returned, and came to A. ... 397
1Sa 27:10 A. said, Whither have ye made ... 397

1Sa 27:12 **A.** believed David, saying, He hath 397
1Sa 28:1 **A.** said unto David, Know thou 397
1Sa 28:2 David said to **A.**, Surely thou shalt 397
1Sa 28:2 **A.** said to David, Therefore will I 397
1Sa 29:2 passed on in the rereward with **A.**. 397
1Sa 29:3 **A.** said unto the princes of the 397
1Sa 29:6 **A.** called David, and said unto him, 397
1Sa 29:8 David said unto **A.**, But what have I 397
1Sa 29:9 **A.** answered and said to David, 397
1Ki 2:39 servants of Shimei ran away unto **A.** 397
1Ki 2:40 and went to Gath to **A.** to seek his 397

ACHMETHA (ak'-meth-ah)
Ezr 6:2 And there was found at **A.**, in the 307

ACHOR (a'-kor)
Jos 7:24 them unto the valley of **A.**. 5911
Jos 7:26 was called, The valley of **A.**, unto 5911
Jos 15:7 toward Debir from the valley of **A.**, 5911
Isa 65:10 and the valley of **A.** a place for the 5911
Ho 2:15 and the valley of **A.** for a door of 5911

ACHSA (ak'-sah) See also ACHSAH.
1Ch 2:49 the daughter of Caleb was **A.**. 5915

ACHSAH (ak'-sah) See also ACHSA.
Jos 15;16 him will I give **A.** my daughter 5915
Jos 15:17 and he gave him **A.** his daughter 5915
Jg 1:12 and taketh it, to him will I give **A.** 5919
Jg 1:13 took it: and he gave him **A.** his 5919

ACHSHAPH (ak'-shaf)
Jos 11:1 of Shimron, and to the king of **A.**, 407
Jos 12:20 the king of **A.**, one; 407
Jos 19:25 and Hali, and Beten, and **A.**, 407

ACHZIB (ak'-zib) See also CHEZIB.
Jos 15:44 Keilah, and **A.**, and Mereshah; 392
Jos 19:29 at the sea from the coast to **A.**: 392
Jg 1:31 nor of **A.**, nor of Helbah, 392
Mic 1:14 the houses of **A.** shall be a lie 392

ACKNOWLEDGE See also ACKNOWLEDGED; ACKNOWLEDGETH; ACKNOWLEDGING.
De 21:17 he shall **a.** the son of the hated 5234
De 33:9 neither did he **a.** his brethren, 5234
Ps 51:3 I **a.** my transgressions: 3045
Pr 3:6 In all thy ways **a.** him, 3045
Isa 33:13 ye that are near, **a.** my might. 3045
Isa 61:9 all that see them shall **a.** them, 5234
Isa 63:16 Israel **a.** us not: 5234
Jer 3:13 Only **a.** thine iniquity, 3045
Jer 14:20 We **a.**, O Lord, our wickedness, 3045
Jer 24:5 so will I **a.** them that are carried 5234
Da 11:39 a strange god, whom he shall **a.** 5234
Ho 5:15 till they **a.** their offence,
1Co 14:37 let him **a.** that the things that I *1921*
1Co 16:18 therefore **a.** ye them that are such. *1921*
2Co 1:13 than what ye read or **a.**; *1921*
2Co 1:13 ye shall **a.** even to the end; *1921*

ACKNOWLEDGED
Ge 38:26 And Judah **a.** them, 5234
Ps 32:5 I **a.** my sin unto thee, and mine 3045
2Co 1:14 ye have **a.** us in part. *1922*

ACKNOWLEDGETH
1Joh 2:23 he that **a.** the Son hath the Father

ACKNOWLEDGING
2Ti 2:25 repentance to the **a.** of the truth; *1922*
Tit 1:1 and the **a.** of the truth which is *1922*
Phm 6 by the **a.** of every good thing *1922*

ACKNOWLEDGMENT
Col 2:2 to the **a.** of the mystery of God, *1922*

ACQUAINT See also ACQUAINTED; ACQUAINTING.
Job 22:21 **A.** now thyself with him, 5532

ACQUAINTANCE
2Ki 12:5 it to them, every man of his **a.**: 4378
2Ki 12:7 receive no more money of your **a.**, 4378
Job 19:13 and mine **a.** are verily estranged 3045
Job 42:11 all they that had been of his **a.** 3045
Ps 31:11 a fear to mine **a.**: 3045
Ps 55:13 my guide, and mine **a.**. 3045
Ps 88:8 Thou hast put away mine **a.** 3045
Ps 88:18 mine **a.** into darkness. 3045
Lu 2:44 among their kinsfolk and **a.**. *1110*
Lu 23:49 all his **a.**, and the women that *1110*
Ac 24:23 he should forbid none of his **a.** *2398*

ACQUAINTED
Ps 139:3 and art **a.** with all my ways. 5532
Isa 53:3 man of sorrows, and **a.** with grief: 3045

ACQUAINTING
Ec 2:3 **a.** mine heart with wisdom; 5090

ACQUIT
Job 10:14 thou wilt not **a.** me from mine 5352
Na 1:3 will not at all **a.** the wicked: 5352

ACRABBIM See MAALEH-ACRABBIM.

ACRE See also ACRES.
1Sa 14:14 as it were an half **a.** of land, 4618

ACRES
Isa 5:10 ten **a.** of vineyard shall yield 6776

ACT See also ACTS; EXACT.
Isa 28:21 to pass his **a.**, his strange **a.** 5656
Isa 59:6 **a.** of violence is in their hands. 6467
Joh 8:4 taken in adultery, in the very **a.** *1888*

ACTIONS See also EXACTIONS.
1Sa 2:3 by him **a.** are weighed. 5949

ACTIVITY
Ge 47:6 if thous knowest any men of **a.** 2428

ACTS
De 11:3 his **a.**, which he did in the midst 4639
De 11:7 seen all the great **a.** of the Lord 4639
Jg 5:11 the righteous **a.** of the Lord,
Jg 5:11 even the righteous **a.**
1Sa 12:7 all the righteous **a.** of the Lord,
2Sa 23:20 who had done many **a.**, he slew 6467
1Ki 10:6 heard in mine own land of thy **a.** 1697
1Ki 11:41 the rest of the **a.** of Solomon, 1697
1Ki 11:41 in the book of the **a.** of Solomon? 1697
1Ki 14:19 the rest of the **a.** of Jeroboam, how 1697
1Ki 14:29 the rest of the **a.** of Rehoboam, and 1697
1Ki 15:7 the rest of the **a.** of Abijam, and 1697
1Ki 15:23 rest of all the **a.** of Asa, and all his 1697
1Ki 15:31 the rest of the **a.** of Nadab, and all 1697
1Ki 16:5 the rest of the **a.** of Baasha, and 1697
1Ki 16:14 the rest of the **a.** of Elah, and all 1697
1Ki 16:20 the rest of the **a.** of Zimri, and his 1697
1Ki 16:27 the rest of the **a.** of Omri which he 1697
1Ki 22:39 the rest of the **a.** of Ahab, and all 1697
1Ki 22:45 the rest of the **a.** of Jehoshaphat, 1697
2Ki 1:18 the rest of the **a.** of Ahaziah which 1697
2Ki 8:23 the rest of the **a.** of Joram, 1697
2Ki 10:34 the rest of the **a.** of Jehu, and all 1697
2Ki 12:19 the rest of the **a.** of Joash, and all 1697
2Ki 13:8 the rest of the **a.** of Jehoahaz, 1697
2Ki 13:12 the rest of the **a.** of Joash, 1697
2Ki 14:15 the rest of the **a.** of Jehoash which 1697
2Ki 14:18 the rest of the **a.** of Amaziah, 1697
2Ki 14:28 the rest of the **a.** of Jeroboam, and 1697
2Ki 15:6 the rest of the **a.** of Azariah, 1697
2Ki 15:11 the rest of the **a.** of Zachariah, 1697
2Ki 15:15 the rest of the **a.** of Shallum, and 1697
2Ki 15:21 the rest of the **a.** of Menahem, 1697
2Ki 15:26 the rest of the **a.** of Pekahiah, 1697
2Ki 15:31 the rest of the **a.** of Pekah, 1697
2Ki 15:36 the rest of the **a.** of Jotham, 1697
2Ki 16:19 the rest of the **a.** of Ahaz 1697
2Ki 20:20 the rest of the **a.** of Hezekiah, and 1697
2Ki 21:17 the rest of the **a.** of Manasseh, and 1697
2Ki 21:25 the rest of the **a.** of Amon which 1697
2Ki 23:19 **a.** that he had done in Beth-el. 4640
2Ki 23:28 the rest of the **a.** of Josiah, and all 1697
2Ki 24:5 the rest of the **a.** of Jehoiakim, 1697
1Ch 11:22 who had done many **a.**; 6467
1Ch 29:29 Now the **a.** of David the king, first 1697
2Ch 9:5 in mine own land of thine **a.**, and 1697
2Ch 9:29 the rest of the **a.** of Solomon, 1697
2Ch 12:15 Now the **a.** of Rehoboam, first and 1697
2Ch 13:22 the rest of the **a.** of Abijah, and 1697
2Ch 16:11 behold, the **a.** of Asa, first and last, 1697
2Ch 20:34 the rest of the **a.** of Jehoshaphat, 1697
2Ch 25:26 the rest of the **a.** of Amaziah, first 1697
2Ch 26:22 the rest of the **a.** of Uzziah, 1697
2Ch 27:7 the rest of the **a.** of Jotham, and 1697
2Ch 28:26 Now the rest of his **a.** and of all his 1697
2Ch 32:32 the rest of the **a.** of Hezekiah, and 1697
2Ch 33:18 the rest of the **a.** of Manasseh, and 1697
2Ch 35:26 the rest of the **a.** of Josiah, and his 1697
2Ch 36:8 the rest of the **a.** of Jehoiakim, 1697
Es 10:2 all the **a.** of his power and of his 4640
Ps 103:7 his **a.** unto the children of Israel. 5949
Ps 106:2 Who can utter the mighty **a.** of
Ps 145:4 and shall declare thy mighty **a.**
Ps 145:6 the might of thy terrible **a.**:
Ps 145:12 to the sons of men his mighty **a.**,
Ps 150:2 Praise him for his mighty **a.**:
Ac *general* *title* The **A.** of the Apostles *4234*

ADADAH (ad'-ad-ah)
Jos 15:22 Kinah, and Dimonah, and **A.**, 5735

ADAH (a'-dah)
Ge 4:19 the name of the one was **A.**, 5711
Ge 4:20 and **A.** bare Jabal: he was the 5711
Ge 4:23 **A.** and Zillah, Hear my voice; 5711
Ge 36:2 **A.** the daughter of Elon the 5711
Ge 36:4 And **A.** bare to Esau Eliphaz; 5711
Ge 36:10 Eliphaz the son of **A.** the wife of 5711
Ge 36:12 these were the sons of **A.** Esau's 5711
Ge 36:16 Edom: these were the sons of **A.** 5711

ADAIAH (ad-a-i'-yah)
2Ki 22:1 was Jedidah, the daughter of **A.** 5718
1Ch 6:41 the son of Zerah, the son of **A.**, 5718
1Ch 8:21 **A.**, and Beraiah, and Shimrath, 5718
1Ch 9:12 and **A.** the son of Jeroham, the 5718
2Ch 23:1 and Maaseiah the son of **A.**, and 5718
Ezr 10:29 Malluch, and **A.**, Jashub, and 5718
Ezr 10:39 and Nathan, and **A.**, 5718
Ne 11:5 the son of Hazaiah, the son of **A.**, 5718
Ne 11:12 and **A.** the son of Jeroham, the son 5718

ADALIA (ad-al-i'-yah)
Es 9:8 Poratha, and **A.**, and Aridatha, 118

ADAM (ad'-um) See also ADAM'S.
Ge 2:19 brought them unto **A.** to see what 120
Ge 2:19 whatsoever **A.** called every living 120
Ge 2:20 **A.** gave names to all cattle, 120
Ge 2:20 but for **A.** there was not found an 120
Ge 2:21 a deep sleep to fall upon **A.**, 121
Ge 2:23 **A.** said, This is now bone of my 120
Ge 3:8 **A.** and his wife hid themselves 120
Ge 3:9 And the Lord God called unto **A.**, 120
Ge 3:17 And unto **A.** he said, Because 121
Ge 3:20 **A.** called his wife's name Eve; 120
Ge 3:21 Unto **A.** also and to his wife did the 120
Ge 4:1 And **A.** knew Eve his wife; 120
Ge 4:25 **A.** knew his wife again; 120
Ge 5:1 the book of the generations of **A.**. 121
Ge 5:2 called their name **A.**, in the day 120
Ge 5:3 **A.** lived an hundred and thirty years 121
Ge 5:4 And the days of **A.** after he had 121
Ge 5:5 the days that **A.** lived 121
De 32:8 when he separated the sons **A.**, 120
Jos 3:16 very far from the city **A.**, 121
1Ch 1:1 **A.**, Sheth, Enosh, 121
Job 31:33 I covered my transgressions as **A.**, 121
Lu 3:38 which was the son of **A.**, *76*
Ro 5:14 death reigned from **A.** to Moses, *76*
1Co 15:22 as in **A.** all die, even so in Christ *76*
1Co 15:45 The first man **A.** was made a *76*
1Co 15:45 the last **A.** was made *76*
1Ti 2:13 For **A.** was first formed, *76*
1Ti 2:14 And **A.** was not deceived, *76*
Jude 14 Enoch also, the seventh from **A.**, *76*

ADAMAH (ad'-am-ah)
Jos 19:36 And **A.**, and Ramah, and Hazor, 128

ADAMANT
Eze 3:9 As an **a.** harder than flint 8068
Zec 7:12 made their hearts as an **a.** stone, 8068

ADAMANT-STONE See ADAMANT and STONE.

ADAMI (ad'-am-i)
Jos 19:33 from Allon to Zaanannim, and **A.**, 129

ADAM'S (ad'-ums)
Ro 5:14 similitude of **A.** transgression, *76*

ADAN See NEBUZAR-ADAN.

ADAR (a'-dar) See also ADDAR; ATAROTH-ADAR.
Jos 15:3 and went up to **A.**, and fetched a 146
Ezr 6:15 on the third day of the month **A.**, 144
Es 3:7 twelfth month, that is, the month **A.** 143
Es 3:13 which is the month **A.**, 143
Es 8:12 month, which is the month **A.** 143
Es 9:1 that is the month **A.**, 143
Es 9:15 fourteenth day also of the month **A.**, 143
Es 9:17 thirteenth day of the month **A.**; 143
Es 9:19 the fourteenth day of the month **A.**
Es 9:21 fourteenth day of the month **A.**. 143

ADBEEL (ad'-be-el)
Ge 25:13 and Kedar, and **A.**, and Mibsam, ... 110
1Ch 1:29 then Kedar, and **A.**, and Mibsam, ... 110

ADD See also ADDED; ADDETH.
Ge 30:24 Lord shall **a.** to me another son. 3254
Le 5:16 shall **a.** the fifth part thereto, and......... 3254
Le 6:5 shall **a.** the fifth part more thereto,...... 3254
Le 27:13 then he shall **a.** a fifth part................ 3254
Le 27:15, 19 then he shall **a.** the fifth part......... 3254
Le 27:27 and shall **a.** a fifth part...................... 3254
Le 27:31 he shall **a.** thereto the fifth part 3254
Nu 5:7 **a.** unto it the fifth part thereof,.......... 3254
Nu 35:6 to them ye shall **a.** forty and two 5414
De 4:2 Ye shall not **a.** unto the word 3254
De 12:32 thou shalt not **a.** thereto, nor 3254
De 19:9 then shalt thou **a.** three cities............. 3254
De 29:19 to **a.** drunkenness to thirst:.................. 5595
2Sa 24:3 Now the Lord thy God **a.** unto the...... 3254
1Ki 12:11 I will **a.** to your yoke:.......................... 3254
1Ki 12:14 heavy, and I will **a.** to your yoke: 3254
2Ki 20:6 And I will **a.** unto thy days fifteen 3254
1Ch 22:14 thou mayest **a.** thereto.......................... 3254
2Ch 10:14 I will **a.** thereto: my father 3254
2Ch 28:13 ye intend to **a.** more to our sins 3254
Ps 69:27 **A.** iniquity unto their iniquity: 5414
Pr 3:2 peace, shall they **a.** to thee.................. 3254
Pr 30:6 **A.** thou not unto his words, lest he 3254
Isa 29:1 **a.** ye year to year;.............................. 5595
Isa 30:1 that they may **a.** sin to sin:.................. 5595
Isa 38:5 I will **a.** unto thy days fifteen............. 3254
Mt 6:27 **can a. one cubit unto his stature?** *4369*
Lu 12:25 **can a. to his stature one cubit?**..... *4369*
Php 1:16 to **a.** affliction to my bonds: *2018*
2Pe 1:5 **a.** to your faith virtue; *2023*
Re 22:18 If any man shall **a.** unto these, ... *2007*
Re 22:18 God shall **a.** unto him the *2007*

ADDAN (ad'-dan)
Ezr 2:59 Tel-harsa, Cherub, **A.**, and Immer: 135

ADDAR (ad'-dar) See also ADAR; ATAROTH-ADDAR; HAZAR-ADDAR.
1Ch 8:3 And the sons of Bela were, **A.**, and 146

ADDED
De 5:22 great voice: and he **a.** no more.......... 3254
1Sa 12:19 we have **a.** unto all our sins this 3254
Jer 36:32 there were **a.** besides unto them.......... 3254
Jer 45:3 Lord hath **a.** grief to my sorrow; 3254
Da 4:36 excellent majesty was **a.** unto me....... 3255
Mt 6:33 **these things shall be a. unto you**··· *4369*
Lu 3:20 **A.** yet this above all, that he shut *4369*
Lu 12:31 **these things shall be a. unto you**··· *4369*
Lu 19:11 he **a.** and spake a parable, ... *4369*
Ac 2:41 there were **a.** unto them about *4369*
Ac 2:47 And the Lord **a.** to the church.............. *4369*
Ac 5:14 believers were the more **a.** to the....... *4369*
Ac 11:24 much people was **a.** unto the Lord. *4369*
Ga 2:6 in conference **a.** nothing to me: *4323*
Ga 3:19 was **a.** because of transgressions,........ *4369*

ADDER See also ADDERS'.
Ge 49:17 serpent by the way, an **a.** in the......... 8207
Ps 58:4 the deaf **a.** that stoppeth her ear;........ 6620
Ps 91:13 shalt tread upon the lion and **a.**.......... 6620
Pr 23:32 a serpent, and stingeth like an **a.**. 6848

ADDERS'
Ps 140:3 **a.** poison is under their lips................. 5919

ADDETH
Job 34:37 he **a.** rebellion unto his sin,................ 3254
Pr 10:22 he **a.** no sorrow with it........................ 3254
Pr 16:23 **a.** learning to his lips. 3254
Ga 3:15 no man disannulleth, or **a.**.................. *1928*

ADDI (ad'-di)
Lu 3:28 which was the son of **A.**, which *78*

ADDICTED
1Co 16:15 they have **a.** themselves to the........... *5021*

ADDITION See also ADDITIONS.
1Ki 7:30 at the side of every **a.**. 3914

ADDITIONS
1Ki 7:29 certain **a.** made of thin work. 3914
1Ki 7:36 and **a.** round about............................ 3914

ADDON (ad'-don)
Ne 7:61 Tel-haresha, Cherub, **A.**, and............. 114

ADER (a'-dur)
1Ch 8:15 And Zebadiah, and Arad, and **A.**,......... 5738

ADIEL (a'-de-el)
1Ch 4:36 and Asaiah, and **A.**, and Jesimiel, ... 5717
1Ch 9:12 and Maasiai the son of **A.**, ... 5717
1Ch 27:25 was Azmaveth the son of **A.**: 5717

ADIN (a'-din)
Ezr 2:15 The children of **A.**, four hundred........ 5720
Ezr 8:6 Of the sons also of **A.**; Ebed the........ 5720
Ne 7:20 The children of **A.**, six hundred 5720
Ne 10:16 Adonijah, Bigvai, **A.**,......................... 5720

ADINA (ad'-in-ah)
1Ch 11:42 **A.** the son of Shiza the Reubenite, ... 5721

ADINO (ad'-in-o)
2Sa 23:8 the same was **A.** the Eznite: he........... 5722

ADITHAIM (ad-ith-a'-im)
Jos 15:36 Sharaim, and **A.**, and Gederah, ... 5723

ADJURE See also ADJURED.
1Ki 22:16 How many times shall I **a.** thee 7650
2Ch 18:15 How many times shall I **a.** thee 7650
Mt 26:63 I **a.** thee by the living God,................ *1844*
Mk 5:7 I **a.** thee by God, that thou................ *3726*
Ac 19:13 We **a.** you by Jesus whom Paul *3726*

ADJURED
Jos 6:26 Joshua **a.** them at that time,............... 7650
1Sa 14:24 for Saul had **a.** the people, ... 422

ADLAI (ad'-la-i)
1Ch 27:29 was Shaphat the son of **A.**: 5724

ADMAH (ad'-mah)
Ge 10:19 Sodom, and Gomorrah, and **A.**, ... 126
Ge 14:2 of Gomorrah, Shinab king of **A.**, ... 126
Ge 14:8 of Gomorrah, and the king of **A.**,......... 126
De 29:23 **A.**, and Zeboim, which the Lord 126
Ho 11:8 how shall I make thee as **A.**?............... 126

ADMATHA (ad'-math-ah)
Es 1:14 Shethar, **A.**, Tarshish, Meres, ... 133

ADMINISTERED
2Co 8:19 which is **a.** by us to the glory of........ *1247*
2Co 8:20 abundance which is **a.** by us:............. *1247*

ADMINISTRATION See also ADMINISTRATIONS.
2Co 9:12 For the **a.** of this service.................. *1248*

ADMINISTRATIONS
1Co 12:5 are differences of **a.**, but the............. *1248*

ADMIRATION
Jude 16 having men's persons in **a.**................. *2296*
Re 17:6 her, I wondered with great **a.**. *2295*

ADMIRED
2Th 1:10 to be **a.** in all them that believe *2296*

ADMONISH See also ADMONISHED; ADMONISHING.
Ro 15:14 able also to **a.** one another................ *3560*
1Th 5:12 over you in the Lord, and **a.** you; *3560*
2Th 3:15 but **a.** him as a brother. *3560*

ADMONISHED
Ec 4:13 who will no more be **a.**. 2094
Ec 12:12 by these, my son, be **a.**: 2094
Jer 42:19 know certainly that I have **a.**............. 5749
Ac 27:9 already past, Paul **a.** them, ... *3867*
Heb 8:5 as Moses was **a.** of God when........... *5537*

ADMONISHING
Col 3:16 **a.** one another in psalms and............ *3560*

ADMONITION
1Co 10:11 they are written for our **a.**,.............. *3559*
Eph 6:4 the nurture and **a.** of the Lord........... *3559*
Tit 3:10 after the first and second **a.** reject;..... *3559*

ADNA (ad'-nah) See also ADNAH.
Ezr 10:30 **A.**, and Chelal, Benaiah, Maaseiah,..... 5733
Ne 12:15 Of Harim, **A.**; of Meraioth, ... 5733

ADNAH (ad'-nah) See also ADNA.
1Ch 12:20 fell to him of Manasseh, **A.**,............... 5734
2Ch 17:14 **A.** the chief, and with him mighty....... 5734

ADO
Mk 5:39 **Why make ye this a., and weep?** ... *2350*

ADONI See ADONI-BEZEK; ADONI-ZEDEK.

ADONI-BEZEK (ad''-on-i-be'-zek)
Jg 1:5 And they found **A.** in Bezek:.............. 137
Jg 1:6 **A.** fled; and they pursued after him, ... 137
Jg 1:7 **A.** said, Threescore and ten kings,........ 137

ADONIJAH (ad-on-i'-jah) See also TOB-ADONIJAH.
2Sa 3:4 the fourth, **A.** the son of Haggith;........ 138
1Ki 1:5 **A.** the son of Haggith exalted............. 138
1Ki 1:7 and they following **A.** helped him. 138
1Ki 1:8 belonged to David, were not with **A.**..... 138
1Ki 1:9 And **A.** slew sheep and oxen and......... 138
1Ki 1:11 Hast thou not heard that **A.** the son..... 138
1Ki 1:13 why then doth **A.** reign? 138
1Ki 1:18 And now, behold, **A.** reigneth; 138
1Ki 1:24 hast thou said, **A.** shall reign after 138
1Ki 1:25 and say, God save king **A.**. ....
1Ki 1:41 And **A.** and all the guests that were..... 138
1Ki 1:42 and **A.** said unto him, Come in; 138
1Ki 1:43 Jonathan answered and said to **A.**, ... 138
1Ki 1:49 guests that were with **A.** were afraid,... 138
1Ki 1:50 **A.** feared because of Solomon, ... 138
1Ki 1:51 Behold, **A.** feareth king Solomon:......... 138
1Ki 2:13 And **A.** the son of Haggith came to 138
1Ki 2:19 to speak unto him for **A.**..................... 138
1Ki 2:21 the Shunammite be given to **A.** 138
1Ki 2:22 ask Abishag the Shunammite for **A.**?..... 138
1Ki 2:23 if **A.** have not spoken this word............ 138
1Ki 2:24 **A.** shall be put to death this day.......... 138
1Ki 2:28 for Joab had turned after **A.**,.............. 138
1Ch 3:2 the fourth, **A.** the son of Haggith:......... 138
2Ch 17:8 Jehonathan, and **A.**, and Tobijah, ... 138
Ne 10:16 **A.**, Bigvai, Adin, ... 138

ADONIKAM (ad-on-i'-kam)
Ezr 2:13 The children of **A.**, six hundred........... 140
Ezr 8:13 And of the last sons of **A.**, whose........ 140
Ne 7:18 The children of **A.**, six hundred........... 140

ADONIRAM (ad-on-i'-ram). See also ADORAM.
1Ki 4:6 **A.** the son of Abda was over the.......... 141
1Ki 5:14 and **A.** was over the levy..................... 141

ADONI-ZEDEK (ad''-on-i-ze'-dek)
Jos 10:1 when **A.** king of Jerusalem had............ 139
Jos 10:3 **A.** king of Jerusalem sent unto 139

ADOPTION
Ro 8:15 ye have received the Spirit of **a.**, ... *5206*
Ro 8:23 waiting for the **a.**, to wit, the............ *5206*
Ro 9:4 to whom pertaineth the **a.**, and........... *5206*
Ga 4:5 we might receive the **a.** of sons........... *5206*
Eph 1:5 unto the **a.** of children by Jesus *5206*

ADORAIM (ad-o-ra'-im)
2Ch 11:9 And **A.**, and Lachish, and Azekah, ... 115

ADORAM (ad-o'-ram). See also ADONIRAM.
2Sa 20:24 And **A.** was over the tribute: 151
1Ki 12:18 Then king Rehoboam sent **A.**,.............. 151

ADORN See also ADORNED; ADORNETH; ADORNING.
1Ti 2:9 that women **a.** themselves in............. *2885*
Tit 2:10 they may **a.** the doctrine of God *2885*

ADORNED
Jer 31:4 thou shalt again be **a.** with thy........... 5710
Lu 21:5 how it was **a.** with goodly stones *2885*
1Pe 3:5 **a.** themselves, being in subjection *2885*
Re 21:2 as a bride **a.** for her husband............. *2885*

ADORNETH
Isa 61:10 a bride **a.** herself with her jewels. 5710

ADORNING
1Pe 3:3 **a.** let it not be that outward **a.**........... *2889*

ADRAMMELECH (a-dram'-mel-ek)
2Ki 17:31 burnt their children in fire to **A.** 152
2Ki 19:37 **A.** and Sharezer his sons smote 152
Isa 37:38 **A.** and Sharezer his sons smote 152

ADRAMYTTIUM (a-dram-mit'-te-um)
Ac 27:2 entering into a ship of **A.**,.................... *98*

ADRIA (a'-dre-ah)
Ac 27:27 driven up and down in **A.**, ... *99*

ADRIEL (a'-dre-el)
1Sa 18:19 that she was given unto **A.** the......... 5741
2Sa 21:8 whom she brought up for **A.** the 5741

ADULLAM (a-dul'-lam) See also ADULLAMITE.
Jos 12:15 of Libnah, one; the king of **A.**, ... 5725
Jos 15:35 Jarmuth, and **A.**, Socoh, and 5725
1Sa 22:1 and escaped to the cave **A.**: and 5725
2Sa 23:13 harvest time unto the cave of **A.**;....... 5725
1Ch 11:15 rock to David, into the cave of **A.**; 5725

2Ch 11:7 And Beth-zur, and Shoco, and **A.**,...... 5725
Ne 11:30 Zanoah, **A.**, and in their villages,........ 5725
Mic 1:15 he shall come unto **A.** the glory......... 5725

ADULLAMITE (a-dul'-lam-ite)
Ge 38:1 turned in to a certain **A.**, whose........ 5726
Ge 38:12 he and his friend Hirah the **A.**.......... 5726
Ge 38:20 by the hand of his friend the **A.**........ 5726

ADULTERER See also ADULTERERS.
Le 20:10 the **a.** and the adulteress shall.......... 5003
Job 24:15 the eye also of the **a.** waiteth for....... 5003
Isa 57:3 the seed of the **a.**.......................... 5003

ADULTERERS
Ps 50:18 hast been partaker with **a.**.............. 5003
Jer 9:2 they be all **a.**,............................. 5003
Jer 23:10 the land is full of **a.**;....................... 5003
Ho 7:4 They are all **a.**,............................. 5003
Mal 3:5 the sorcerers, and against the **a.**,...... 5003
Lu 18:11 **extortioners, unjust, a.**,.................. *3432*
1Co 6:9 nor idolaters, nor **a.**,...................... *3432*
Heb 13:4 whoremongers and **a.** God will.............. *3432*
Jas 4:4 Ye **a.** and adulteresses,..................... *3432*

ADULTERESS See also ADULTERESSES.
Le 20:10 adulterer and the **a.** shall surely......... 5003
Pr 6:26 and the **a.** will hunt for the.......... 802,376
Ho 3:1 beloved of her friend, yet an **a.**,........ 5003
Ro 7:3 she shall be called an **a.**:.................. *3428*
Ro 7:3 so that she is no **a.**,......................... *3428*

ADULTERESSES
Eze 23:45 after the manner of **a.**,..................... 5003
Eze 23:45 because they are **a.**,......................... 5003
Jas 4:4 Ye adulterers and **a.**,........................ *3428*

ADULTERIES
Jer 13:27 I have seen thine **a.**,........................ 5004
Eze 23:43 her that was old in **a.**,....................... 5004
Ho 2:2 out of her sight, and her **a.**.............. 5005
Mt 15:19 **murders, a., fornications,**................ *3430*
Mk 7:21 **evil thoughts, a., fornications,**......... *3430*

ADULTEROUS
Pr 30:20 such is the way of an **a.** woman;......... 5003
Mt 12:39 **An evil and a. generation seeketh**.. *3428*
Mt 16:4 **A wicked and a. generation**............. *3428*
Mk 8:38 **in this a. and sinful generation;**.... *3428*

ADULTERY See also ADULTERIES.
Ex 20:14 Thou shalt not commit **a.**.................. 5003
Le 20:10 the man that committeth **a.**............... 5003
Le 20:10 he that committeth **a.**........................ 5003
De 5:18 Neither shalt thou commit **a.**............ 5003
Pr 6:32 committeth **a.** with a woman............. 5003
Jer 3:8 backsliding Israel committed **a.**.......... 5003
Jer 3:9 and committed **a.** with stones............ 5003
Jer 5:7 they then committed **a.**, and............ 5003
Jer 7:9 ye steal, murder, and commit **a.**,....... 5003
Jer 23:14 they commit **a.**, and walk in lies:........ 5003
Jer 29:23 in Israel, and have committed **a.**........ 5003
Eze 16:32 a wife that committeth **a.**,................ 5003
Eze 23:37 they have committed **a.**, and blood..... 5003
Eze 23:37 their idols have they committed **a.**,..... 5003
Ho 4:2 stealing, and committing **a.**,.............. 5003
Ho 4:13 your spouses shall commit **a.**.............. 5003
Ho 4:14 when they commit **a.**:......................... 5003
Mt 5:27 **Thou shalt not commit a.**:................. *3431*
Mt 5:28 **hath committed a. with her**.............. *3431*
Mt 5:32 **causeth her to commit a.**:................ *3429*
Mt 5:32 **that is divorced committeth a.**......... *3429*
Mt 19:9 **marry another, committeth a.**.......... *3429*
Mt 19:9 **is put away doth commit a.**............. *3429*
Mt 19:18 **Thou shall not commit a.**,............... *3431*
Mk 10:11 **committeth a. against her**............... *3429*
Mk 10:12 **to another, she committeth a.**......... *3429*
Mk 10:19 **Do not commit a.**,.......................... *3431*
Lu 16:18 **marrieth another, committeth a.**:.. *3431*
Lu 16:18 **from her husband committeth a.**... *3431*
Lu 18:20 **Do not commit a., Do not kill,**...... *3431*
Joh 8:3 unto him a woman taken in **a.**;.......... *3430*
Joh 8:4 was taken in **a.**, in the very act......... *3431*
Ro 2:22 should not commit **a.**,........................ *3431*
Ro 2:22 dost thou commit **a.**?........................ *3431*
Ro 13:9 Thou shalt not commit **a.**, Thou......... *3431*
Ga 5:19 **A.**, fornication, uncleanness,............. *3430*
Jas 2:11 Do not commit **a.**, said also............... *3431*
Jas 2:11 Now if thou commit no **a.**,................. *3431*
2Pe 2:14 Having eyes full of **a.**,...................... *3428*
Re 2:22 **and them that commit a. with her.** *3431*

ADUMMIM (a-dum'-mim)
Jos 15:7 that is before the going up to **A.**,........ 131
Jos 18:17 over against the going up of **A.**,.......... 131

ADVANCED
1Sa 12:6 Lord that **a.** Moses and Aaron,.......... 6213
Es 3:1 and **a.** him, and set his seat above..... 5375
Es 5:11 he had **a.** him above the princes........ 5375
Es 10:2 whereunto the king **a.** him,............... 1431

ADVANTAGE See also ADVANTAGED; ADVANTAGETH.
Job 35:3 thou saidst, What **a.** will it be............ 5532
Ro 3:1 What **a.** then hath the Jew?.............. *4053*
2Co 2:11 Lest Satan should get an **a.** of us:...... *4122*
Jude 16 in admiration because of **a.**............... *5622*

ADVANTAGED
Lu 9:25 **For what is a man a.**,..................... *5623*

ADVANTAGETH
1Co 15:32 what **a.** it me, if the dead rise........... *3786*

ADVENTURE See also ADVENTURED; PERADVENTURE.
De 28:56 would not **a.** to set the sole of her..... 5254
Ac 19:31 not **a.** himself into the theatre........... *1325*

ADVENTURED
Jg 9:17 fought for you, and **a.** his life far,...... 7993

ADVERSARIES
Ex 23:22 and an adversary unto thine **a.**.......... 6696
De 32:27 **a.** should behave themselves............ 6862
De 32:43 render vengeance to his **a.**,............... 6862
Jos 5:13 Art thou for us, or for our **a.**?........... 6862
1Sa 2:10 **a.** of the Lord shall be broken to....... 7378
2Sa 19:22 should this day be **a.** unto me?.......... 7854
Ezr 4:1 the **a.** of Judah and Benjamin............ 6862
Ne 4:11 And our **a.** said, They shall not.......... 6862
Ps 38:20 render evil for good are mine **a.**;....... 7853
Ps 69:19 mine **a.** are all before thee............... 6887
Ps 71:13 **a.** to my soul;.................................. 7853
Ps 81:14 turned my hand against their **a.**........ 6862
Ps 89:42 hast set the right hand of his **a.**;....... 6862
Ps 109:4 For my love they are my **a.**:.............. 7853
Ps 109:20 the reward of mine **a.**..................... 7853
Ps 109:29 Let mine **a.** be clothed with............... 7853
Isa 1:24 I will ease me of mine **a.**,................. 6862
Isa 9:11 shall set up the **a.** of Rezin against..... 6862
Isa 11:13 and the **a.** of Judah shall be cut.......... 6887
Isa 59:18 he will repay, fury to his **a.**,.............. 6862
Isa 63:18 our **a.** have trodden down thy.......... 6862
Isa 64:2 make thy name known to thine **a.**,..... 6862
Jer 30:16 devoured; and all thine **a.**,................ 6862
Jer 46:10 avenge him of his **a.**:........................ 6862
Jer 50:7 and their **a.** said, We offend not,........ 6862
La 1:5 Her **a.** are the chief,.......................... 6862
La 1:7 the **a.** saw her, and did mock............. 6862
La 1:17 his **a.** should be round about him:....... 6862
La 2:17 set up the horn of thine **a.**................. 6862
Mic 5:9 lifted up upon thine **a.**,...................... 6862
Na 1:2 Lord will take vengeance on his **a.**,.... 6862
Lu 13:17 all his **a.** were ashamed;..................... *480*
Lu 21:15 **which all your a. shall not be able**.. *480*
1Co 16:9 unto me, and there are many **a.**......... *480*
Php 1:28 in nothing terrified by your **a.**:........... *480*
Heb 10:27 which shall devour the **a.**.................. *5227*

ADVERSARY See also ADVERSARIES.
Ex 23:22 and an **a.** unto thine adversaries......... 6887
Nu 22:22 stood in the way for an **a.** against...... 7854
1Sa 1:6 her **a.** also provoked her sore............. 6869
1Sa 29:4 lest in the battle he be an **a.**............. 7854
1Ki 5:4 is neither **a.** nor evil occurrent........... 7854
1Ki 11:14 the Lord stirred up an **a.** unto.......... 7854
1Ki 11:23 God stirred him up another **a.**,.......... 7854
1Ki 11:25 he was an **a.** to Israel all the days...... 7854
Es 7:6 The **a.** and enemy is this wicked......... 6862
Job 31:35 mine **a.** had written a book.......... 376,7379
Ps 74:10 how long shall the **a.** reproach?......... 6862
Isa 50:8 who is mine **a.**?...................... 1166,4941
La 1:10 The **a.** hath spread out his hand......... 6862
La 2:4 with his right hand as an **a.**,............... 6862
La 4:12 have believed that the **a.** and the....... 6862
Am 3:11 An **a.** there shall be even round......... 6862
Mt 5:25 **Agree with thine a. quickly,**............. *476*
Mt 5:25 **at any time the a. deliver**................. *476*
Lu 12:58 **with thine a. to the magistrate,**....... *476*
Lu 18:3 **saying, Avenge me of mine a.**.......... *476*
1Ti 5:14 give none occasion to the **a.**............... *480*
1Pe 5:8 because your **a.** the devil,................... *476*

ADVERSITIES
1Sa 10:19 saved you out of all your **a.**.............. 7451
Ps 31:7 hast known my soul in **a.**;................... 6869

ADVERSITY See also ADVERSITIES.
2Sa 4:9 redeemed my soul out of all **a.**,......... 6869
2Ch 15:6 God did vex them with all **a.**.............. 6869
Ps 10:6 I shall never be in **a.**.......................... 7451
Ps 35:51 But in mine **a.** they rejoiced,.............. 6761
Ps 94:13 give him rest from the days of **a.**,...... 7451
Pr 17:17 a brother is born for **a.**..................... 6869
Pr 24:10 If thou faint in the day of **a.**,............. 6869
Ec 7:14 in the day of **a.** consider:.................... 7451
Isa 30:20 the Lord give you the bread of **a.**,...... 6862
Heb 13:3 and them which suffer **a.**,.................. *2558*

ADVERTISE
Nu 24:14 I will **a.** thee what this people.......... 3289
Ru 4:4 And I thought to **a.** thee,........... 1540,241

ADVICE
Jg 19:30 consider of it, take a., and speak......... 5779
Jg 20:7 give here your **a.** and counsel............ 1697
1Sa 25:33 blessed be thy **a.**, and blessed be....... 2940
2Sa 19:43 that our **a.** should not be first had...... 1697
2Ch 10:9 What **a.** give ye that we may............. 3289
2Ch 10:14 answered them after the **a.** of........... 6098
2Ch 25:17 Amaziah king of Judah took **a.**,.......... 3289
Pr 20:18 and with good **a.** make war............... 8458
2Co 8:10 herein I give my **a.**: for this is............ *1106*

ADVISE See also ADVISED.
2Sa 24:13 **a.**, and see what answer I shall.......... 3045
1Ki 12:6 How do ye **a.** that I may answer......... 3289
1Ch 21:12 **a.** thyself what word I shall............... 7200

ADVISED
Pr 13:10 with the well **a.** is wisdom................. 3289
Ac 27:12 the more part **a.** to depart......... *1012,5087*

ADVISEMENT
1Ch 12:19 the Philistines upon **a.** sent him.......... 6098

ADVOCATE
1Jo 2:1 **a.** with the Father, Jesus Christ......... *3875*

A-DYING See DYING.

AENEAS (e'-ne-as)
Ac 9:33 found a certain man named **AE.**.......... *132*
Ac 9:34 And Peter said unto him, **AE.**............. *132*

AENON (e'-non)
Joh 3:23 baptizing in **AE.** near to Salim,............ *137*

AFAR
Ge 22:4 Abraham . . . . saw the place **a.** off...... 7350
Ge 37:18 when they saw him **a.** off,................ 7350
Ex 2:4 his sister stood **a.** off,........................ 7350
Ex 20:18 they removed, and stood **a.** off.......... 7350
Ex 20:21 the people stood **a.** off, and Moses...... 7350
Ex 24:1 worship ye **a.** off............................. 7350
Ex 33:7 pitched it without the camp, **a.** off...... 7368
Nu 9:10 in a journey **a.** off,............................. 7350
1Sa 26:13 Stood on the top of a hill **a.** off;......... 7350
2Ki 2:7 went, and stood to view **a.** off:.......... 7350
2Ki 4:25 when the man of God saw her **a.** off,.. 5048
Ezr 3:13 the noise was heard **a.** off,................ 7350
Ne 12:43 Jerusalem was heard even **a.** off........ 7350
Job 2:12 they lifted up their eyes **a.** off........... 7350
Job 36:3 I will fetch my knowledge from **a.**,...... 7350
Job 36:25 man may behold it **a.** off.................. 7350
Job 39:25 and he smelleth the battle **a.** off,........ 7350
Job 39:29 her eyes behold **a.** off...................... 7350
Ps 10:1 Why standest thou **a.** off, O Lord?...... 7350
Ps 38:11 my kinsmen stand **a.** off.................... 7350
Ps 65:5 them that are **a.** off upon the sea:...... 7350
Ps 138:6 the proud he knoweth **a.** off............. 4801
Ps 139:2 understandest my thought **a.** off......... 7350
Pr 31:14 she bringeth her food from **a.**............ 4801
Isa 23:7 her own feet shall carry her **a.** off...... 7350
Isa 59:14 justice standeth **a.** off:........................ 7350
Isa 66:19 isles **a.** off, that have not heard......... 7350
Jer 23:23 saith the Lord, and not a God **a.**......... 7350
Jer 30:10 I will save thee from **a.**,..................... 7350
Jer 31:10 declare it in the isles **a.** off,............... 4801
Jer 46:27 I will save thee from **a.** off,................ 7350
Jer 51:50 remember the Lord **a.** off,.................... 7350
Mic 4:3 rebuke strong nations **a.** off;............... 7350
Mt 26:58 Peter followed him **a.** off................... *3113*
Mt 27:55 women were there beholding **a.**.......... *3113*
Mk 5:6 when he saw Jesus **a.** off,.................... *3113*

Mk 11:13 seeing a fig tree **a.** off *3113*
Mk 14:54 Peter followed him **a.** off, *3113*
Mk 15:40 women looking on **a.** off: *3113*
Lu 16:23 **and seeth Abraham a. off,** *3113*
Lu 17:12 lepers, which stood **a.** off: *4207*
Lu 18:13 **the publican, standing a. off,** *3113*
Lu 22:54 Peter followed **a.** off. *3113*
Lu 23:49 stood **a.** off, beholding these *3113*
Ac 2:39 and to all that are **a.** off, *3112*
Eph 2:17 peace to you which were **a.** off, *3112*
Heb 11:13 but having seen them **a.** off, *4207*
2Pe 1:9 is blind, and cannot see **a.** off, *3467*
Re 18:10 Standing **a.** off for the fear of her *3113*
Re 18:15 shall stand **a.** off for the fear of *3113*
Re 18:17 as many as trade by sea, stood **a.** *3113*

AFFAIRS
1Ch 26:32 pertaining to God, and **a.** of the 1697
Ps 112:5 he will guide his **a.** 1697
Da 2:49 the **a.** of the province of Babylon: 5673
Da 3:12 whom thou hast set over the **a.** of 5673
Eph 6:21 also may know my **a.**, *2596*
Eph 6:22 ye might know our **a.**, *4012*
Php 1:27 I may hear of your **a.**, that ye *4012*
2Ti 2:4 entangleth himself with the **a.** of *4230*

AFFECT See also AFFECTED; AFFECTETH.
Ga 4:17 They zealously **a.** you, but not *2206*
Ga 4:17 that ye might **a.** them. *2206*

AFFECTED
Ac 14:2 and made their minds evil **a.** *2559*
Ga 4:18 be zealously **a.** always in a good *2206*

AFFECTETH
La 3:51 Mine eye **a.** mine heart 5953

AFFECTION See also AFFECTIONED; AFFECTIONS.
1Ch 29:3 because I have set my **a.** to the 7521
Ro 1:31 without natural **a.**, implacable, *794*
2Co 7:15 his inward **a.** is more abundant *4698*
Col 3:2 Set your **a.** on things above, *5426*
Col 3:5 uncleanness, inordinate **a.**, *3806*
2Ti 3:3 Without natural **a.**, trucebreakers, *794*

AFFECTIONATELY
1Th 2:8 So being **a.** desirous of you, we *2442*

AFFECTIONED
Ro 12:10 Be kindly **a.** one to another *5387*

AFFECTIONS
Ro 1:26 God gave them up unto vile **a.**: *3806*
Ga 5:24 crucified the flesh with the **a.** *3804*

AFFINITY
1Ki 3:1 Solomon made **a.** with Pharaoh 2859
2Ch 18:1 and joined **a.** with Ahab 2859
Ezr 9:14 and join in **a.** with the people 2859

AFFIRM See also AFFIRMED.
Ro 3:8 and as some **a.** that we say,) *5346*
1Ti 1:7 they say, nor whereof they **a.** *1226*
Tit 3:8 I will that thou **a.** constantly, *1226*

AFFIRMED
Lu 22:59 another confidently **a.**, saying, *1340*
Ac 12:15 she constantly **a.** that it was even *1340*
Ac 25:19 whom Paul **a.** to be alive. *5335*

AFFLICT See also AFFLICTED; AFFLICTEST.
Ge 15:13 they shall **a.** them four hundred 6031
Ge 31:50 If thou shalt **a.** my daughters, 6031
Ex 1:11 over them taskmasters to **a.** them. 6031
Ex 22:22 Ye shall not **a.** any widow, 6031
Ex 22:23 If thou **a.** them in any wise, 6031
Le 16:29 ye shall **a.** your souls, 6031
Le 16:31 you, and ye shall **a.** your souls, 6031
Le 23:27 ye shall **a.** your souls, and offer an 6031
Le 23:32 ye shall **a.** your souls: in the ninth 6031
Nu 24:24 shall **a.** Asshur, and shall **a.** Eber, 6031
Nu 29:7 and ye shall **a.** your souls: 6031
Nu 30:13 every binding oath to **a.** the soul, 6031
Jg 16:5 that we may bind him to **a.** him: 6031
Jg 16:6 thou mightest be bound to **a.** thee. 6031
Jg 16:19 and she began to **a.** him, 6031
2Sa 7:10 shall the children of wickedness **a.** 6031
1Ki 11:39 I will for this **a.** the seed of David, 6031
2Ch 6:26 when thou dost **a.** them; 6031
Ezr 8:21 **a.** ourselves before our God, 6031
Job 37:23 plenty of justice: he will not **a.** 6031
Ps 44:2 how thou didst **a.** the people, 7489
Ps 55:19 God shall hear, and **a.** them, 6031
Ps 89:22 nor the son of wickedness **a.** him. 6031
Ps 94:5 and **a.** thine heritage. 6031
Ps 143:12 destroy all them that **a.** my soul: 6887
Isa 9:1 afterward did more grievously **a.** 3513
Isa 51:23 into the hand of them that **a.** 3013
Isa 58:5 a day for a man to **a.** his soul? 6031
Isa 64:12 hold thy peace, and **a.** us very sore? 6031
Jer 31:28 down, and to destroy, and to **a.**; 7489
La 3:33 For he doth not **a.** willingly 6031
Am 5:12 they **a.** the just, they take a bribe, 6887
Am 6:14 and they shall **a.** you 3905
Na 1:12 I will **a.** thee no more. 6031
Zep 3:19 I will undo all that **a.** thee: 6031

AFFLICTED
Ex 1:12 But the more they **a.** them, the 6031
Le 23:29 shall not be **a.** in that same day, 6031
Nu 11:11 Wherefore hast thou **a.** thy 7489
De 26:6 evil entreated us, and **a.** us, 6031
Ru 1:21 the Almighty hath **a.** me? 7489
2Sa 22:28 the **a.** people thou wilt save: 6041
1Ki 2:26 thou hast been **a.** in all 6031
1Ki 2:26 wherein my father was **a.** 6031
2Ki 17:20 all the seed of Israel, and **a.** them, 6031
Job 6:14 To him that is **a.** pity should be 4523
Job 30:11 he hath loosed my cord, and **a.** 6031
Job 34:28 and he heareth the cry of the **a.** 6041
Ps 18:27 thou wilt save the **a.** people; 6041
Ps 22:24 abhorred the affliction of the **a.**; 6041
Ps 25:16 me; for I am desolate and **a.** 6041
Ps 82:3 do justice to the **a.** and needy. 6041
Ps 88:7 hast **a.** me with all thy waves. 6031
Ps 88:15 I am **a.** and ready to die from my 6041
Ps 90:15 thou hast **a.** us, 6031
Ps 102: *title* A prayer of the **a.**, when he 6041
Ps 107:17 because of their iniquities, are **a.** 6031
Ps 116:10 I was greatly **a.**: 6031
Ps 119:67 Before I was **a.** I went astray: 6031
Ps 119:71 good for me that I have been **a.**; 6031
Ps 119:75 thou in faithfulness hast **a.** me. 6031
Ps 119:107 I am **a.** very much: 6031
Ps 129:1,2 Many a time have they **a.** me 6887
Ps 140:12 maintain the cause of the **a.**, and 6041
Pr 15:15 All the days of the **a.** are evil: 6041
Pr 22:22 neither oppress the **a.** in the gate: 6041
Pr 26:28 hateth those that are **a.** by it; 1790
Pr 31:5 the judgment of any of the **a.** 6040
Isa 9:1 lightly **a.** the land of Zebulun, 7043
Isa 49:13 and will have mercy upon his **a.** 6041
Isa 51:21 Therefore hear now this, thou **a.**, 6041
Isa 53:4 smitten of God, and **a.** 6031
Isa 53:7 He was oppressed, and he was **a.**, 6031
Isa 54:11 O thou **a.**, tossed with tempest, and 6041
Isa 58:3 wherefore have we **a.** our soul, 6031
Isa 58:10 satisfy the **a.** soul; 6031
Isa 60:14 The sons also of them that **a.** thee 6031
Isa 63:9 In all their affliction he was **a.**, 6862
La 1:4 priests sigh, her virgins are **a.**, 3013
La 1:5 for the Lord hath **a.** her for the 3013
La 1:12 wherewith the Lord hath **a.** me 3013
Mic 4:6 her that I have **a.**; 7489
Na 1:12 Though I have **a.** thee, 6031
Zep 3:12 of thee an **a.** and poor people, 6041
Mt 24:9 **they deliver you up to be a.,** *2347*
2Co 1:6 And whether we be **a.**, *2346*
1Ti 5:10 if she have relieved the **a.**, *2346*
Heb 11:37 being destitute, **a.**, tormented; *2346*
Jas 4:9 Be **a.**, and mourn, and weep: *5003*
Jas 5:13 Is any among you **a.**? *2553*

AFFLICTEST
1Ki 8:35 their sin, when thou **a.** them: 6031

AFFLICTION See also AFFLICTIONS.
Ge 16:11 the Lord hath heard thy **a.** 6040
Ge 29:32 the Lord hath looked upon my **a.**; 6040
Ge 31:42 God hath seen mine **a.** 6040
Ge 41:52 in the land of my **a.** 6040
Ex 3:7 surely seen the **a.** of my people 6040
Ex 3:17 bring you up out of the **a.** of Egypt 6040
Ex 4:31 he had looked upon their **a.**, 6040
De 16:3 the bread of **a.**; 6040
De 26:7 and looked on our **a.**, 6040
1Sa 1:11 look on the **a.** of thine handmaid, 6040
2Sa 16:12 the Lord will look on mine **a.**, 5869
1Ki 22:27 feed him with bread of **a.** 3905
1Ki 22:27 and with water of **a.**, 3905
2Ki 14:26 the Lord saw the **a.** of Israel, 6040
2Ch 18:26 feed him with bread of **a.** 3905
2Ch 18:26 and with water of **a.**, 3905
2Ch 20:9 and cry unto thee in our **a.**, 6869
2Ch 33:12 when he was in **a.**, he besought 6887
Ne 1:3 in great **a.** and reproach: 7451
Ne 9:9 didst see the **a.** of our fathers 6040
Job 5:6 **a.** cometh not forth of the dust, 205
Job 10:15 see thou mine **a.**; 6040
Job 30:16 days of **a.** have taken hold upon 6040
Job 30:27 the days of **a.** prevented me. 6040
Job 36:8 in cords of **a.**; 6040
Job 36:15 He delivereth the poor in his **a.**, 6040
Job 36:21 hast thou chosen rather than **a.** 6040
Ps 22:24 the **a.** of the afflicted; 6039
Ps 25:18 Look upon mine **a.** and my pain; 6040
Ps 44:24 our **a.** and our oppression? 6040
Ps 66:11 thou laidst **a.** upon our loins. 4157
Ps 88:9 eye mourneth by reason of **a.**: 6040
Ps 106:44 he regarded their **a.**, 6862
Ps 107:10 bound in **a.** and iron; 6040
Ps 107:39 through oppression, **a.**, and 7451
Ps 107:41 he the poor on high from **a.**, 6040
Ps 119:50 my comfort in my **a.**: 6040
Ps 119:92 then have perished in mine **a.** 6040
Ps 119:153 Consider mine **a.**, 6040
Isa 30:20 water of **a.**, yet shall not 3905
Isa 48:10 in the furnace of **a.** 6040
Isa 63:9 In all their **a.** he was afflicted, 6869
Jer 4:15 **a.** from mount Ephraim 205
Jer 15:11 of evil and in the time of **a.** 6869
Jer 16:19 my refuge in the day of **a.**, 6869
Jer 30:15 Why criest thou for thine **a.**? 7667
Jer 48:16 and his **a.** hasteth fast 7451
La 1:3 gone into captivity because of **a.**, 6040
La 1:7 remembered in the days of her **a.** 6040
La 1:9 O Lord, behold my **a.**: 6040
La 3:1 I am the man that hath seen **a.** 6040
La 3:19 Remembering mine **a.** and my 6040
Ho 5:15 in their **a.** they will seek me early. 6862
Am 6:6 not grieved for the **a.** of Joseph. 7667
Ob 13 not have looked on their **a.** 7451
Jon 2:2 reason of mine **a.** unto the Lord, 6869
Na 1:9 **a.** shall not rise up the second time. 6869
Hab 3:7 I saw the tents of Cushan in **a.**: 205
Zec 1:15 they helped forward the **a.** 7451
Zec 8:10 out or came in because of the **a.**: 6862
Zec 10:11 pass through the sea with **a.**, 6869
Mk 4:17 **when a. or persecution ariseth** *2347*
Mk 13:19 **in those days shall be a.,** *2347*
Ac 7:11 Egypt and Chanaan, and great **a.**; *2347*
Ac 7:34 I have seen the **a.** of my people *2561*
2Co 2:4 out of much **a.** and anguish of *2347*
2Co 4:17 light **a.**, which is but for a moment, *2347*
2Co 8:2 How that in a great trial of **a.** *2347*
Php 1:16 to add **a.** to my bonds: *2347*
Php 4:14 ye did communicate with my **a.** *2347*
1Th 1:6 the word in much **a.**, *2347*
1Th 3:7 our **a.** and distress by your faith: *2347*
Heb 11:25 Choosing rather to suffer **a.** with *4797*
Jas 1:27 and widows in their **a.**, *2347*
Jas 5:10 an example of suffering **a.**, and *2552*

AFFLICTIONS
Ps 34:19 Many are the **a.** of the righteous: 7451
Ps 132:1 remember David, and all his **a.**: 6031
Ac 7:10 delivered him out of all his **a.**, *2347*
Ac 20:23 bonds and **a.** abide me. *2347*
2Co 6:4 in **a.**, in necessities, in distresses, *2347*
Col 1:24 which is behind of the **a.** of Christ *2347*
1Th 3:3 man should be moved by these **a.**: *2347*
2Ti 1:8 partaker of the **a.** of the gospel *4777*
2Ti 3:11 Persecutions, **a.**, which came *3804*
2Ti 4:5 **a.**, do the work of an evangelist, *2553*
Heb 10:32 endured a great fight of **a.**; *3804*
Heb 10:33 both by reproaches and **a.**; *2347*
1Pe 5:9 the same **a.** are accomplished *3804*

AFFORDING
Ps 144:13 That our garners may be full, **a.** 6329

AFFRIGHT See also AFFRIGHTED.
2Ch 32:18 to **a.** them, and to trouble them; 3372

AFFRIGHTED
De 7:21 Thou shalt not be **a.** at them: 6206
Job 18:20 that went before were **a.**. 270,8178
Job 39:22 He mocketh at fear, and is not **a.**; 2865
Isa 21:4 fearfulness **a.** me: 1204
Jer 51:32 and the men of war are **a.** 926
Mk 16:5 white garment; and they were **a.**. *1568*
Mk 16:6 And he saith unto them, Be not **a.**: *1568*
Lu 24:37 But they were terrified and **a.**, *1719*
Re 11:13 remnant were **a.**, and gave glory *1719*

A-FISHING See FISHING.

AFOOT
Mk 6:33 ran **a.** thither out of all cities, *3979*
Ac 20:13 minding himself to go **a.**. *3978*

AFORE See also AFOREHAND; AFORETIME; BEFORE.
2Ki 20:4 came to pass, **a.** Isaiah was gone 3808
Ps 129:6 which withereth **a.** it groweth up: 6924
Isa 18:5 **a.** the harvest, when the bud is 6440
Eze 33:22 **a.** he that was escaped came: 6440
Ro 1:2 had promised **a.** by his prophets *4279*
Ro 9:23 he had **a.** prepared unto glory. *4282*
Eph 3:3 (as I wrote **a.** in few words, *4270*

AFOREHAND
Mk 14:8 **she is come a. to anoint my body** *4301*

AFORETIME
Ne 13:5 **a.** they laid the meat offerings, 6440
Job 17:6 **a.** I was as a tabret. 6440
Isa 52:4 My people went down **a.** into 7223
Jer 30:20 Their children also shall be as **a.**, 6924
Da 6:10 his God, as he did **a.**. 4481,6928,1836
Joh 9:13 him that **a.** was blind. *4218*
Ro 15:4 things were written **a.** were *4270*

AFRAID
Ge 3:10 I was **a.**, because I was naked; 3372
Ge 18:15 I laughed not; for she was **a.** 3372
Ge 20:8 and the men were sore **a.**. 3372
Ge 28:17 And he was **a.**, and said, 3372
Ge 31:31 Because I was **a.**: for I said, 3372
Ge 32:7 Then Jacob was greatly **a.** and 3372
Ge 42:28 failed them, and they were **a.**, 2729
Ge 42:35 bundles of money, they were **a.**. 3372
Ge 43:18 And the men were **a.**, because 3372
Ex 3:6 he was **a.** to look upon God. 3372
Ex 14:10 and they were sore **a.**: and the 3372
Ex 15:14 people shall hear, and be **a.**: 7264
Ex 34:30 they were **a.** to come nigh him. 3372
Le 26:6 none shall make you **a.**: 2729
Nu 12:8 then were ye not **a.** to speak 3372
Nu 22:3 Moab was sore **a.** of the people, 1481
De 1:17 ye shall not be **a.** of the face of man; 1481
De 1:29 Dread not, neither be **a.** of them. 3372
De 2:4 and they shall be **a.** of you: 3372
De 5:5 ye were **a.** by reason of the fire, 3372
De 7:18 Thou shalt not be **a.** of them: but 3372
De 7:19 all the people of whom thou art **a.**. 3373
De 9:19 For I was **a.** of the anger and hot 3025
De 18:22 thou shalt not be **a.** of him 1481
De 20:1 be not **a.** of them: for the Lord 3372
De 28:10 and they shall be **a.** of thee. 3372
De 28:60 of Egypt, which thou wast **a.** of; 3025
De 31:6 fear not, nor be **a.** of them: 6206
Jos 1:9 not **a.**, neither be thou dismayed 6206
Jos 9:24 we were sore **a.** of our lives 3372
Jos 11:6 Be not **a.** because of them: 3372
Jg 7:3 Whosoever is fearful and **a.**, 2730
Ru 3:8 that the man was **a.**, and turned 2729
1Sa 4:7 And the Philistines were **a.**, for 3372
1Sa 7:7 they were **a.** of the Philistines. 3372
1Sa 17:11 were dismayed, and greatly **a.**. 3372
1Sa 17:24 fled from him, and were sore **a.**. 3372
1Sa 18:12 And Saul was **a.** of David, 3372
1Sa 18:15 very wisely, he was **a.** of him. 1481
1Sa 18:29 Saul was yet the more **a.** of David; 3372
1Sa 21:1 Ahimelech was **a.** at the meeting 2729
1Sa 21:12 was sore **a.** of Achish the king of 3372
1Sa 23:3 we be **a.** here in Judah: 3373
1Sa 28:5 he was **a.**, and his heart 3372
1Sa 28:13 the king said unto her, Be not **a.**: 3372
1Sa 28:20 was sore **a.**, because of the words 3372
1Sa 31:4 would not: for he was sore **a.**. 3372
2Sa 1:14 How wast thou not **a.** to stretch 3372
2Sa 6:9 David was **a.** of the Lord that day, 3372
2Sa 14:15 the people have made me **a.**: 3372
2Sa 17:2 and will make him **a.**: 2729
2Sa 22:5 of ungodly men made me **a.**; 1204
2Sa 22:46 they shall be **a.** out of their close 2296
1Ki 1:49 that were with Adonijah were **a.**, 2729
2Ki 1:15 down with him: be not **a.** of him. 3372
2Ki 10:4 But they were exceedingly **a.**, 3372
2Ki 19:6 Be not **a.** of the words which thou 3372
2Ki 25:26 they were **a.** of the Chaldees. 3372
1Ch 10:4 would not; for he was sore **a.**. 3372
1Ch 13:12 David was **a.** of God that day, 3372
1Ch 21:30 he was **a.** because of the sword 1204
2Ch 20:15 Be not **a.** nor dismayed by reason 3372
2Ch 32:7 be not **a.** nor dismayed for the 3372
Ne 2:2 Then I was very sore **a.**, 3372
Ne 4:14 Be not ye **a.** of them: 3372
Ne 6:9 they all made us **a.**, saying, 3372
Ne 6:13 was he hired, that I should be **a.**, 3372
Es 7:6 Haman was **a.** before the king 1204
Job 3:25 which I was **a.** of is come unto me. 3025
Job 5:21 shalt thou be **a.** of destruction 3372
Job 5:22 neither shalt thou be **a.** of the 3372
Job 6:21 see my casting down, and are **a.**. 3372
Job 9:28 I am **a.** of all my sorrows, I 3025
Job 11:19 none shall make thee **a.**; 2729
Job 13:11 not his excellency make you **a.**? 1204
Job 13:21 let not thy dread make me **a.**. 1204
Job 15:24 anguish shall make him **a.**; 1204
Job 18:11 Terrors shall make him **a.** on every 1204
Job 19:29 Be ye **a.** of the sword: 1481
Job 21:6 when I remember I am **a.**, 926
Job 23:15 when I consider, I am **a.** of him. 6342
Job 32:6 wherefore I was **a.**, and durst 2119
Job 33:7 my terror shall not make thee **a.**, 1204
Job 39:20 Canst thou make him **a.** as a 7493
Job 41:25 the mighty are **a.**: 1481
Ps 3:6 I will not be **a.** of ten thousands 3372
Ps 18:4 floods of ungodly men made me **a.**. 1204
Ps 18:45 shall fade away, and be **a.** 2727
Ps 27:1 of whom shall I be **a.**? 6342
Ps 49:16 Be not thou **a.** when one is made 3372
Ps 56:3 time I am **a.**, I will trust in thee. 3372
Ps 56:11 not be **a.** what man can do unto me. 3372
Ps 65:8 in the uttermost parts are **a.** at 3372
Ps 77:16 they were **a.**: the depths also 2342
Ps 83:15 make them **a.** with thy storm. 926
Ps 91:5 Thou shalt not be **a.** for the 3372
Ps 112:7 He shall not be **a.** of evil tidings: 3372
Ps 112:8 is established, he shall not be **a.**, 3372
Ps 119:120 I am **a.** of thy judgments. 3372
Pr 3:24 thou shalt not be **a.**: 6342
Pr 3:25 Be not **a.** of sudden fear, 3372
Pr 31:21 She is not **a.** of the snow for her 3372
Ec 12:5 they shall be **a.** of that which is 3372
Isa 8:12 fear ye their fear, nor be **a.**. 6206
Isa 10:24 be not **a.** of the Assyrian: 3372
Isa 10:29 Ramah is **a.**; Gibeah of Saul is 2729
Isa 12:2 I will trust, and not be **a.**: 6342
Isa 13:8 And they shall be **a.**: pangs and 926
Isa 17:2 none shall make them **a.**. 2729
Isa 19:16 and it shall be **a.** and fear because 2729
Isa 19:17 mention thereof shall be **a.** in 6342
Isa 20:5 they shall be **a.** and ashamed 2865
Isa 31:4 he will not be **a.** of their voice, 2865
Isa 31:9 princes shall be **a.** of the ensign, 2865
Isa 33:14 The sinners in Zion are **a.**; 6342
Isa 37:6 Be not **a.** of the words 3372
Isa 40:9 lift it up, be not **a.**; 3372
Isa 41:5 the ends of the earth were **a.**, 2729
Isa 44:8 Fear ye not, neither be **a.**: 7297
Isa 51:7 neither be ye **a.** of their revilings. 2865
Isa 51:12 that thou shouldest be **a.** of a man 3372
Isa 57:11 of whom hast thou been **a.** or 1672
Jer 1:8 Be not **a.** of their faces: 3372
Jer 2:12 be horribly **a.**, be ye very desolate, 8175
Jer 10:5 Be not **a.** of them; for they cannot 3372
Jer 26:21 he was **a.**, and fled, and went into 3372
Jer 30:10 none shall make him **a.**. 2729
Jer 36:16 heard all the words, they were **a.** 6342
Jer 36:24 Yet they were not **a.**, 6342
Jer 38:19 I am **a.** of the Jews 1672
Jer 39:17 of the men of whom thou art **a.**. 3025
Jer 41:18 **a.** of them, because of Ishmael 3372
Jer 42:11 Be not **a.** of the king of Babylon. 3372
Jer 42:11 of whom ye are **a.**; 3373
Jer 42:11 be not **a.** of him, saith the Lord 3372
Jer 42:16 the famine, whereof ye were **a.**, 1672
Jer 46:27 and none shall make him **a.**. 2729
Eze 2:6 son of man, be not **a.** of them, 3372
Eze 2:6 neither be **a.** of their words, 3372
Eze 2:6 be not **a.** of their words, 3372
Eze 27:35 their kings shall be sore **a.**, 8175
Eze 30:9 make the careless Ethiopians **a.**, 2729
Eze 32:10 their kings shall be horribly **a.** 8175
Eze 34:28 none shall make them **a.**. 2729
Eze 39:26 none made them **a.**. 2729
Da 4:5 I saw a dream which made me **a.**, 1763
Da 8:17 when he came, I was **a.**, 1204
Joe 2:22 Be not **a.**, ye beasts of the field: 3372
Am 3:6 the people not be **a.**? 2729
Jon 1:5 Then the mariners were **a.**, 3372
Jon 1:10 Then were the men exceedingly **a.**, 3372
Mic 4:4 none shall make them **a.**: 2729
Mic 7:17 they shall be **a.** of the Lord 6342
Na 2:11 none made them **a.**? 2729
Hab 2:17 beasts, which made them **a.**, 2865
Hab 3:2 heard thy speech, and was **a.**: 3372
Zep 3:13 none shall make them **a.**. 2729
Mal 2:5 was **a.** before my name. 2865
Mt 2:22 he was **a.** to go thither: *5399*
Mt 14:27 **it is I; be not a.** *5399*
Mt 14:30 the wind boisterous, he was **a.**; *5399*
Mt 17:6 fell on their face, and were sore **a.**. *5399*
Mt 17:7 **Arise, and be not a.** *5399*
Mt 25:25 **And I was a., and went and hid** *5399*
Mt 28:10 **Be not a.: go tell my brethren** *5399*
Mk 5:15 his right mind: and they were **a.**. *5399*
Mk 5:36 **Be not a., only believe.** *5399*
Mk 6:50 **it is I; be not a.** *5399*
Mk 9:6 to say; for they were sore **a.**. *1630*
Mk 9:32 and were **a.** to ask him. *5399*
Mk 10:32 and as they followed, they were **a.**. *5399*
Mk 16:8 any man; for they were **a.**. 5399
Lu 2:9 and they were sore **a.**. *5399*
Lu 8:25 And they being **a.** wondered, *5399*
Lu 8:35 and they were **a.**. *5399*
Lu 12:4 **Be not a. of them that kill** *5399*
Lu 24:5 as they were **a.**, and bowed down *1719*
Joh 6:19 unto the ship: and they were **a.**. *5399*
Joh 6:20 **It is I; be not a.,** *5399*
Joh 14:27 **be troubled, neither let it be a.** *1168*
Joh 19:8 he was the more **a.**; *5399*
Ac 9:26 but they were all **a.** of him, *5399*
Ac 10:4 looked on him, he was **a.**, *1719*
Ac 18:9 **Be not a., but speak, and hold** *5399*
Ac 22:9 saw indeed the light, and were **a.**; *1719*
Ac 22:29 and the chief captain also was **a.**, *5399*
Ro 13:3 Wilt thou then not be **a.** of the *5399*
Ro 13:4 if thou do that which is evil, be **a.**; *5399*
Ga 4:11 I am **a.** of you, lest I have bestowed *5399*
Heb 11:23 and they were not **a.** of the king's *5399*
1Pe 3:6 are not **a.** with any amazement. *5399*
1Pe 3:14 and be not **a.** of their terror, *5399*
2Pe 2:10 they are not **a.** to speak evil of *5141*

AFRESH
Heb 6:6 to themselves the Son of God **a.**, *388*

AFTER See also AFTERNOON; AFTERWARD; HEREAFTER.
Ge 1:11 fruit tree yielding fruit **a.** his
Ge 1:12 herb yielding seed **a.** his kind,
Ge 1:12 seed was in itself, **a.** his kind;
Ge 1:21 **a.** their kind,
Ge 1:21 and every winged fowl **a.** his
Ge 1:24 the living creature **a.** his kind,
Ge 1:24 the beast of the earth **a.** his kind:
Ge 1:25 **a.** his kind, and cattle **a.** their
Ge 1:25 creepeth upon the earth **a.** his
Ge 1:26 man in our image, **a.** our likeness:
Ge 4:17 **a.** the name of his son, Enoch.
Ge 5:3 his own likeness, **a.** his image;
Ge 5:4 **a.** he had begotten Seth 310
Ge 5:7 **a.** he begat Enos 310
Ge 5:10 **a.** he begat Cainan 310
Ge 5:13 **a.** he begat Mahalaleel 310
Ge 5:16 **a.** he begat Jared 310
Ge 5:19 **a.** he begat Enoch eight hundred 310
Ge 5:22 **a.** he begat Methuselah 310
Ge 5:26 **a.** he begat Lamech 310
Ge 5:30 **a.** he begat Noah 310
Ge 6:4 also **a.** that, when the sons of God 310
Ge 6:20 fowls **a.** their kind, and of cattle **a.**
Ge 6:20 creeping thing of the earth **a.** his
Ge 7:10 it came to pass **a.** seven days,
Ge 7:14 beast **a.** his kind

Book	Ref.	Context	Strong's
Ge	7:14	and all the cattle **a.**	
Ge	7:14	**a.** his kind, and every fowl **a.** his	
Ge	8:3	**a.** the end of the hundred and	
Ge	8:19	creepeth upon the earth, **a.** their	
Ge	9:9	with your seed **a.** you;	310
Ge	9:28	Noah lived **a.** the flood three	310
Ge	10:1	unto them were sons born **a.** the	310
Ge	10:5	one **a.** his tongue, **a.** their families,	
Ge	10:20,	31 **a.** their families, **a.** their	
Ge	10:31	in their lands, **a.** their nations.	
Ge	10:32	sons of Noah, **a.** their	
Ge	10:32	divided in the earth **a.** the flood.	310
Ge	11:10	begat Arphaxad two years **a.** the	310
Ge	11:11	Shem lived **a.** he begat Arphaxad	310
Ge	11:13	Arphaxad lived **a.** he begat Salah	310
Ge	11:15	Salah lived **a.** he begat Eber	310
Ge	11:17	Eber lived **a.** he begat Peleg	310
Ge	11:19	Peleg lived **a.** he begat Reu	310
Ge	11:21	Reu lived **a.** he begat Serug	310
Ge	11:23	Serug lived **a.** he begat Nahor	310
Ge	11:25	Nahor lived **a.** he begat Terah	310
Ge	13:14	**a.** that Lot was separated from	310
Ge	14:17	**a.** his return from the slaughter	310
Ge	15:1	**A.** these things the word of the	310
Ge	16:3	**a.** Abraham had dwelt ten years	7093
Ge	16:13	here looked **a.** him that seeth me?	310
Ge	17:7	me and thee and thy seed **a.** thee	310
Ge	17:7	God unto thee, and to the seed **a.**	310
Ge	17:8	to thy seed **a.** thee.	310
Ge	17:9	thy seed **a.** thee in their generations.	310
Ge	17:10	between me and you and thy seed **a.**	310
Ge	17:19	with his seed **a.** him.	310
Ge	18:5	**a.** that ye shall pass on:	310
Ge	18:11	be with Sarah **a.** the manner of women	
Ge	18:12	**A.** I am waxed old shall I have	310
Ge	18:19	children and his household **a.** him,	310
Ge	18:25	to do **a.** this manner,	3651
Ge	19:6	shut the door **a.** him,	310
Ge	19:31	came in unto us **a.** the manner of all	
Ge	22:1,	20 it came to pass **a.** these things,	310
Ge	23:19	And **a.** this, Abraham buried Sarah	310
Ge	24:55	the least ten; **a.** that she shall go.	310
Ge	24:67	Isaac was comforted **a.** his mother's	310
Ge	25:11	it came to pass **a.** the death of	310
Ge	25:26	And **a.** that came his brother out,	310
Ge	26:18	the Philistines had stopped them **a.**	310
Ge	26:18	he called their names **a.** the names	
Ge	31:23	pursued **a.** him seven days'	310
Ge	31:30	thou sore longedst **a.** thy father's	
Ge	31:36	thou hast so hotly pursued **a.** me?	310
Ge	32:29	that thou dost ask **a.** my name?	
Ge	33:2	Leah and her children **a.**,	314
Ge	33:7	**a.** came Joseph near and Rachel.	310
Ge	35:5	did not pursue **a.** the sons of Jacob.	310
Ge	35:12	thy seed **a.** thee will I give the land.	310
Ge	36:40	to their families, **a.** their places,	
Ge	37:17	Joseph went **a.** his brethren,	310
Ge	38:24	about three months **a.**, that it	
Ge	39:7	it came to pass **a.** these things,	310
Ge	39:19	**A.** this manner did thy servant	
Ge	40:1	it came to pass **a.** these things,	310
Ge	40:13	cup into his hand, **a.** the former	
Ge	41:3	seven other kine came up **a.** them	310
Ge	41:6	the east wind sprung up **a.** them.	310
Ge	41:19	seven other kine came up **a.** them,	310
Ge	41:23	the east wind, sprung up **a.** them:	310
Ge	41:27	came up **a.** them are seven years;	310
Ge	41:30	shall arise **a.** them seven years of	310
Ge	44:4	Up, follow **a.** the men;	310
Ge	45:15	**a.** that his brethren talked with him,	310
Ge	45:23	And to his father he sent **a.** this	
Ge	48:1	it came to pass **a.** these things,	310
Ge	48:4	give this land to thy seed **a.** thee	310
Ge	48:6	which thou begettest **a.** them.	310
Ge	48:6	shall be called **a.** the name of	5921
Ge	50:14	**a.** he had buried his father.	310
Ex	3:20	and **a.** that he will let you go.	310
Ex	5:19	in evil case, **a.** it was said,	
Ex	7:25	seven days were fulfilled, **a.** that	310
Ex	10:14	neither **a.** them shall be such.	310
Ex	11:8	and **a.** that I will go out.	310
Ex	14:4	that he shall follow **a.** them;	310
Ex	14:8	he pursued **a.** the children of Israel:	310
Ex	14:9	the Egyptians pursued **a.** them,	310
Ex	14:10	the Egyptians marched **a.** them;	310
Ex	14:23	went in **a.** them to the midst of the	310
Ex	14:28	that came into the sea **a.** them;	310
Ex	15:20	all the women went out **a.** her with	310
Ex	16:1	**a.** their departing out of the land	
Ex	17:1	from the wilderness of Sin, **a.**	
Ex	18:2	**a.** he had sent her back,	310
Ex	21:9	shall deal with her **a.** the manner	
Ex	23:2	to decline **a.** many to wrest	310
Ex	23:24	nor serve them, nor do **a.** their	
Ex	25:9	**a.** the pattern of the tabernacle,	
Ex	25:40	**a.** their pattern, which was	
Ex	28:15	**a.** the work of the ephod thou	
Ex	28:43	his seed **a.** him.	310
Ex	29:29	Aaron shall be his sons' **a.** him,	310
Ex	30:12	sum of the children of Israel **a.**	
Ex	30:13	half a shekel **a.** the shekel of the	
Ex	30:24	five hundred shekels, **a.** the shekel	
Ex	30:25	compound **a.** the art of the	
Ex	30:32	ye make any other like it, **a.**	
Ex	30:35	a confection **a.** the art of the	
Ex	32:4	with a graving tool, **a.** he had	
Ex	33:8	looked **a.** Moses, until he was gone	310
Ex	34:15	they go a whoring **a.** their gods,	310
Ex	34:16	go a whoring **a.** their gods, and	310
Ex	34:16	make thy sons go a whoring **a.**	310
Ex	34:27	for **a.** the tenor of these words I	5921
Ex	37:19	Three bowls made **a.** the fashion	
Ex	38:24	shekels, **a.** the shekel of the	
Ex	38:25	threescore and fifteen shekels, **a.**	
Ex	38:26	**a.** the shekel of the sanctuary,	
Le	5:15	**a.** the shekel of the sanctuary,	
Le	11:14	vulture, and the kite **a.** his kind;	
Le	11:15	Every raven **a.** his kind;	
Le	11:16	cuckow, and the hawk **a.** his kind,	
Le	11:19	the stork, the heron **a.** her kind,	
Le	11:22	**a.** his kind, and the bald locust **a.**	
Le	11:22	**a.** his kind, and the grasshopper **a.**	
Le	11:29	the mouse, and the tortoise **a.** his	
Le	13:7	**a.** that he hath been seen of the	310
Le	13:35	in the skin **a.** his cleansing;	310
Le	13:55	**a.** that it is washed:	310
Le	13:56	somewhat dark **a.** the washing of	310
Le	14:8	**a.** that he shall come into the camp,	310
Le	14:43	**a.** that he hath taken away the	310
Le	14:43	and **a.** he hath scraped the house,	310
Le	14:43	and **a.** it is plaistered;	310
Le	14:48	**a.** the house was plaistered:	310
Le	15:28	and **a.** that she shall be clean.	310
Le	16:1	**a.** the death of the two sons of	310
Le	17:7	**a.** whom they have gone a whoring.	310
Le	18:3	**A.** the doings of the land of Egypt,	
Le	18:3	**a.** the doings of the land of Canaan,	
Le	19:31	neither seek **a.** wizards, to be	413
Le	20:5	all that go a whoring **a.** him, to	310
Le	20:6	the soul that turneth **a.** such as	413
Le	23:11	**a.** the sabbath the priest shall wave it	
Le	20:6	**a.** wizards, to go a whoring **a.**	310
Le	23:15	from the morrow **a.** the sabbath,	
Le	23:16	unto the morrow **a.** the seventh	
Le	25:15	number of years **a.** the jubile	310
Le	25:29	within a whole year **a.** it is sold;	
Le	25:46	inheritance for your children **a.**	310
Le	25:48	**A.** that he is sold he may be	310
Le	26:33	will draw out a sword **a.** you:	310
Le	27:3	**a.** the shekel of the sanctuary.	310
Le	27:18	if he sanctify his field **a.** the jubile,	310
Nu	1:1	**a.** they were come out of the	
Nu	1:2	**a.** their families, by the house of	
Nu	1:18	declared their pedigrees **a.** their	
Nu	1:20	by their generations, **a.** their	
Nu	1:22	**a.** their families, by the house of	
Nu	1:24	of Gad, by their generations, **a.**	
Nu	1:26	of Judah, by their generations, **a.**	
Nu	1:28	Issachar, by their generations, **a.**	
Nu	1:30	Zebulun, by their generations, **a.**	
Nu	1:32	**a.** their families, by the house of	
Nu	1:34	Manasseh, by their generations, **a.**	
Nu	1:36	Benjamin, by their generations, **a.**	
Nu	1:38	of Dan, by their generations, **a.**	
Nu	1:40	of Asher, by their generations, **a.**	
Nu	1:42	throughout their generations, **a.**	
Nu	1:47	the Levites **a.** the tribe of their	
Nu	2:34	every one **a.** their families,	
Nu	3:15	the children of Levi **a.** the house	
Nu	3:47	**a.** the shekel of the sanctuary	
Nu	3:50	threescore and five shekels, **a.**	
Nu	4:2	**a.** their families, by the house of	
Nu	4:15	**a.** that, the sons of Kohath shall	310
Nu	4:29	number them **a.** their families,	
Nu	4:34	**a.** their families, and **a.** the house	
Nu	4:44	**a.** their families, were three	
Nu	4:46	**a.** their families, and **a.** the house	
Nu	6:19	**a.** the hair of his separation is	310
Nu	6:20	and **a.** that the Nazarite may drink	310
Nu	6:21	so he must do **a.** the law of his	5921
Nu	7:13	bowl of seventy shekels, **a.** the	
Nu	7:19	**a.** the shekel of the sanctuary;	
Nu	7:25,	31,37,43,49,55,61,67,73,79 of seventy shekels, **a.** the shekel of	
Nu	7:85	and four hundred shekels, **a.** the	
Nu	7:86	ten shekels apiece, **a.** the shekel	
Nu	7:88	**a.** that it was anointed.	310
Nu	8:15	And **a.** that shall the Levites go	310
Nu	8:22	And **a.** that went the Levites in	310
Nu	9:1	**a.** they were come out of the land	
Nu	9:17	**a.** that the children of Israel	310
Nu	12:14	and **a.** that let her be received in	310
Nu	13:25	searching of the land **a.** forty	7093
Nu	14:34	**A.** the number of the days in	
Nu	15:13	do these things **a.** this manner,	3602
Nu	15:39	seek not **a.** your own heart and	310
Nu	15:39	and your own eyes, **a.** which	310
Nu	16:29	visited **a.** the visitation of all men;	
Nu	18:16	**a.** the shekel of the sanctuary,	
Nu	25:8	he went **a.** the man of Israel	310
Nu	25:13	shall have it, and his seed **a.** him,	310
Nu	26:1	it came to pass **a.** the plague,	310
Nu	26:12	sons of Simeon **a.** their families:	
Nu	26:15	The children of Gad **a.** their	
Nu	26:20	sons of Judah **a.** their families	
Nu	26:23	Of the sons of Issachar **a.** their	
Nu	26:26	sons of Zebulun **a.** their families:	
Nu	26:28	sons of Joseph **a.** their families	
Nu	26:35	are the sons of Ephraim **a.** their	
Nu	26:37	These are the sons of Joseph **a.**	
Nu	26:38	The sons of Benjamin **a.** their	
Nu	26:41	are the sons of Benjamin **a.** their	
Nu	26:42	These are the sons of Dan **a.** their	
Nu	26:42	These are the families of Dan **a.**	
Nu	26:44	Of the children of Asher **a.** their	
Nu	26:48	sons of Naphtali **a.** their families:	
Nu	26:57	numbered of the Levites **a.** their	
Nu	27:21	for him **a.** the judgment of Urim	
Nu	28:24	**A.** this manner ye shall offer	
Nu	28:26	offering unto the Lord, **a.** your	
Nu	29:18,	21,24,27,30,33,37 number, **a.** the	
Nu	30:15	make them void **a.** that he hath	310
Nu	32:15	if ye turn away from **a.** him,	310
Nu	32:42	thereof, and called it Nobah, **a.** his	
Nu	33:3	on the morrow **a.** the passover	
Nu	33:38	**a.** the children of Israel were	
Nu	35:28	**a.** the death of the high priest	310
De	1:4	**A.** he had slain Sihon the king of	310
De	1:8	to their seed **a.** them.	310
De	3:11	the breadth of it, **a.** the cubit of	
De	3:14	and called them **a.** his own name,	5921
De	4:37	therefore he chose their seed **a.**	310
De	4:40	with thy children **a.** thee,	310
De	4:45	**a.** they came forth out	
De	4:46	**a.** they were come forth out	
De	6:14	Ye shall not go **a.** other gods,	310
De	8:19	and walk **a.** other gods, and serve	310
De	9:4	**a.** that the Lord thy God hath	
De	10:15	he chose their seed **a.** them,	310
De	11:4	as they pursued **a.** you,	310
De	1:28	to go **a.** other gods, which ye	310
De	12:8	Ye shall not do **a.** all the things	
De	12:15,	20,21 thy soul lusteth **a.**,	
De	12:25	with thy children **a.** thee, when	310
De	12:28	with thee, and with thy children **a.**	310
De	12:30	following them, **a.** that they be	310
De	12:30	thou enquire not **a.** their gods,	
De	13:2	Let us go **a.** other gods,	310
De	13:4	Ye shall walk **a.** the Lord your God,	310
De	14:13	kite, and the vulture **a.** his kind,	
De	14:14	And every raven **a.** his kind,	
De	14:15	cuckow, and the hawk **a.** his kind,	
De	14:18	stork, and the heron **a.** her kind,	
De	14:26	whatsoever thy soul lusteth **a.**,	
De	16:13	**a.** that thou hast gathered in thy	
De	18:9	learn to do **a.** the abominations	
De	20:18	That they teach you not to do **a.**	
De	21:13	**a.** that thou shalt go in unto her,	310
De	22:2	thee until thy brother seek **a.** it,	
De	24:4	**a.** that she is defiled;	310

Book	Ref	Context	No.
De	24:9	**a.** that ye were come forth out	
De	28:14	to go **a.** other gods to serve them.	310
De	29:22	that shall rise up **a.** you,	310
De	31:16	go a whoring **a.** the gods of the	310
De	31:27	how much more **a.** my death?	310
De	31:29	I know that **a.** my death ye will	310
Jos	1:1	Now **a.** the death of Moses	310
Jos	2:5	pursue **a.** them quickly;	310
Jos	2:7	the men pursued **a.** them the way	310
Jos	2:7	as soon as they which pursued **a.**	310
Jos	3:2	came to pass **a.** three days,	7097
Jos	3:3	remove from your place, and go **a.**	310
Jos	5:4	**a.** they came out of Egypt.	
Jos	5:11	on the morrow **a.** the passover	
Jos	5:12	**a.** they had eaten of the old corn	
Jos	6:9	and the reward came **a.** the ark,	310
Jos	6:13	but the reward came **a.** the ark of	310
Jos	6:15	compassed the city **a.** the same	
Jos	7:25	burned them with fire, **a.** they	
Jos	8:6	(For they will come out **a.** us)	310
Jos	8:16	called together to pursue **a.** them:	310
Jos	8:16	and they pursued **a.** Joshua,	310
Jos	8:17	that went not out **a.** Israel: and	310
Jos	8:17	left the city open, and pursued **a.**	
Jos	9:16	**a.** they had made a league with	310
Jos	10:14	no day like that before it or **a.** it,	310
Jos	10:19	stay ye not, but pursue **a.** your	310
Jos	13:23	of the children of Reuben **a.** their	
Jos	13:28	of the children of Gad **a.** their	
Jos	19:47	called Leshem, Dan, **a.** the name	
Jos	20:5	the avenger of blood pursue **a.** him,	310
Jos	22:27	and you, and our generations **a.** us,	310
Jos	23:1	it came to pass a long time **a.**	310
Jos	24:6	Egyptians pursued **a.** your fathers	310
Jos	24:20	consume you, **a.** that he hath done	310
Jos	24:29	it came to pass **a.** these things,	310
Jg	1:1	Now **a.** the death of Joshua	310
Jg	1:6	fled; and they pursued **a.** him,	310
Jg	2:10	arose another generation **a.** them,	310
Jg	2:17	went a whoring **a.** other gods,	310
Jg	3:22	the haft also went in **a.** the blade;	310
Jg	3:28	he said unto them, Follow **a.** me:	310
Jg	3:28	they went down **a.** him,	310
Jg	3:31	And **a.** him was Shamgar the son	310
Jg	4:14	ten thousand men **a.** him	310
Jg	4:16	Barak pursued **a.** the chariots,	310
Jg	4:16	and **a.** the host,	310
Jg	5:14	**a.** thee, Benjamin, among thy	310
Jg	6:34	Abi-ezer was gathered **a.** him.	310
Jg	6:35	who also was gathered **a.** him:	310
Jg	7:23	pursued **a.** the Midianites.	310
Jg	8:5	I am pursuing **a.** Zebah and	310
Jg	8:12	pursued **a.** them, and took the two	310
Jg	8:27	went thither a whoring **a.** it:	310
Jg	8:33	went a whoring **a.** Baalim,	310
Jg	10:1	**a.** Abimelech there arose to defend	310
Jg	10:3	**a.** him arose Jair, a Gileadite,	310
Jg	12:8	**a.** him Ibzan of Beth-lehem judged	310
Jg	12:11	**a.** him Elon, a Zebulonite,	310
Jg	12:13	**a.** him Abdon the son of Hillel,	310
Jg	13:11	Manoah arose, and went **a.** his wife,	310
Jg	13:18	Why askest thou thus **a.** my	
Jg	14:8	**a.** a time he returned to take her,	
Jg	15:1	it came to pass within a while **a.**	
Jg	15:7	and **a.** that I will cease.	310
Jg	16:22	to grow again **a.** he was shaven.	834
Jg	18:7	**a.** the manner of the Zidonians,	
Jg	18:29	the name of the city Dan, **a.** the	
Jg	19:3	her husband arose, and went **a.** her,	310
Jg	20:45	pursued hard **a.** them unto Gidom,	310
Ru	1:15	return thou **a.** thy sister in law.	310
Ru	1:16	or to return from following **a.** thee:	310
Ru	2:2	glean ears of corn **a.** him in whose	310
Ru	2:3	gleaned in the field **a.** the reapers:	310
Ru	2:7	let me glean and gather **a.** the	310
Ru	2:9	they do reap, and go thou **a.** them:	310
Ru	2:18	to her that she had reserved **a.** she	
Ru	4:4	I am **a.** thee. And he said, I will	310
1Sa	1:9	**a.** they had eaten in Shiloh,	310
1Sa	1:9	and **a.** they had drunk.	310
1Sa	1:20	**a.** Hannah had conceived, that	
1Sa	5:9	**a.** they had carried it about,	310
1Sa	6:12	the lords of the Philistines went **a.**	310
1Sa	7:2	house of Israel lamented **a.** the	310
1Sa	8:3	but turned aside **a.** lucre,	310
1Sa	10:5	**A.** that thou shalt come to the hill	310
1Sa	11:5	Saul came **a.** the herd out of the	310
1Sa	11:7	Whosoever cometh not forth **a.** Saul	310
1Sa	11:7	and **a.** Samuel,	310
1Sa	12:21	for then should ye go **a.** vain things,	310
1Sa	13:4	called together **a.** Saul to Gilgal.	310
1Sa	13:14	the Lord hath sought him a man **a.**	
1Sa	14:12	armourbearer, Come up **a.** me:	310
1Sa	14:13	his armourbearer **a.** him:	310
1Sa	14:13	his armourbearer slew **a.** him.	310
1Sa	14:22	they also followed hard **a.** them	310
1Sa	14:36	Let us go down **a.** the Philistines	310
1Sa	14:37	Shall I go down **a.** the Philistines?	310
1Sa	15:31	So Samuel turned again **a.** Saul;	310
1Sa	17:27	answered him **a.** this manner,	
1Sa	17:30	and spake **a.** the same manner:	
1Sa	17:30	him again **a.** the former manner.	
1Sa	17:35	I went out **a.** him, and smote him,	310
1Sa	17:53	returned from chasing **a.** the	310
1Sa	18:30	**a.** they went forth,	167
1Sa	20:37,	38 Jonathan cried **a.** the lad,	311
1Sa	22:20	Abiathar, escaped, and fled **a.**	310
1Sa	23:25	he pursued **a.** David in the	310
1Sa	23:28	Saul returned from pursuing **a.**	310
1Sa	24:8	out of the cave, and cried **a.** Saul,	310
1Sa	24:14	**A.** whom is the king of Israel come	310
1Sa	24:14	**a.** whom dost thou pursue?	310
1Sa	24:14	**a.** a dead dog, **a.** a flea.	310
1Sa	24:21	not cut off my seed **a.** me,	310
1Sa	25:13	there went up **a.** David	310
1Sa	25:19	behold, I come **a.** you.	310
1Sa	25:38	about ten days **a.**, that the Lord	
1Sa	25:42	damsels of hers that went **a.** her;	7272
1Sa	25:42	she went **a.** the messengers of	310
1Sa	26:3	Saul came **a.** him into the	310
1Sa	26:18	my lord thus pursue **a.** his servant?	310
1Sa	30:8	Shall I pursue **a.** this troop?	310
2Sa	1:1	Now it came to pass **a.** the death	310
2Sa	1:6	horsemen followed hard **a.** him.	
2Sa	1:10	he could not live **a.** that he was	310
2Sa	2:1	it came to pass **a.** this,	310
2Sa	2:19	Asahel pursued **a.** Abner;	310
2Sa	2:24	Joab also and Abishai pursued **a.**	310
2Sa	2:25	gathered themselves together **a.**	310
2Sa	2:28	pursued **a.** Israel no more,	310
2Sa	3:26	he sent messengers **a.** Abner,	310
2Sa	5:13	**a.** he was come from Hebron:	310
2Sa	7:12	I will set up thy seed **a.** thee,	310
2Sa	8:1	**a.** this it came to pass,	310
2Sa	10:1	it came to pass **a.** this,	310
2Sa	11:1	**a.** the year was expired, at the	
2Sa	11:3	And David sent and enquired **a.**	
2Sa	12:28	city, and it be called **a.** my name.	5921
2Sa	13:1	it came to pass **a.** this,	310
2Sa	13:17	bolt the door **a.** her.	310
2Sa	13:18	bolted the door **a.** her.	310
2Sa	13:23	**a.** two full years, that Absalom	
2Sa	14:26	head at two hundred shekels **a.**	
2Sa	15:1	it came to pass **a.** this,	310
2Sa	15:7	it came to pass **a.** forty years,	7093
2Sa	15:13	the men of Israel are **a.** Absalom,	310
2Sa	15:16	and all his household **a.** him.	7272
2Sa	15:17	went forth, and all the people **a.**	7272
2Sa	15:18	six hundred men which came **a.**	7272
2Sa	17:1	I will arise and pursue **a.** David	310
2Sa	17:6	saying, Ahithophel hath spoken **a.**	
2Sa	17:6	shall we do **a.** his saying? if not;	
2Sa	17:21	it came to pass, **a.** they were	310
2Sa	18:16	returned from pursuing **a.** Israel:	310
2Sa	18:18	and he called the pillar **a.** his own	5921
2Sa	18:22	let me, I pray thee, also run **a.**	310
2Sa	20:2	of Israel went up from **a.** David,	310
2Sa	20:6	pursue **a.** him, lest he get him	310
2Sa	20:7	there went out **a.** him Joab's men,	310
2Sa	20:7	of Jerusalem, to pursue **a.** Sheba	310
2Sa	20:10	Abishai his brother pursued **a.**	310
2Sa	20:11	he that is for David, let him go **a.**	310
2Sa	20:13	went on **a.** Joab, to pursue **a.** Sheba	310
2Sa	20:14	together, and went also **a.** him.	310
2Sa	21:1	three years, year **a.** year;	310
2Sa	21:14	**a.** that God was intreated for the	310
2Sa	21:18	it came to pass **a.** this,	310
2Sa	23:4	of the earth by clear shining **a.** rain.	
2Sa	23:9	And **a.** him was Eleazar the son	310
2Sa	23:10	the people returned **a.** him only to	310
2Sa	23:11	And **a.** him was Shammah	310
2Sa	24:10	David's heart smote him **a.** that	310
1Ki	1:6	his mother bare him **a.** Absalom.	310
1Ki	1:13	Solomon thy son shall reign **a.** me,	310
1Ki	1:14	I also will come in **a.** thee,	310
1Ki	1:17	Solomon thy son shall reign **a.** me,	310
1Ki	1:20	throne of my lord the king **a.** him.	310
1Ki	1:24	Adonijah shall reign **a.** me,	310
1Ki	1:27	the throne of my lord the king **a.**	310
1Ki	1:30	shall reign **a.** me, and he shall sit	310
1Ki	1:35	Then ye shall come up **a.** him,	310
1Ki	1:40	all the people came up **a.** him,	310
1Ki	2:28	for Joab had turned **a.** Adonijah,	310
1Ki	2:28	though he turned not **a.** Absalom.	310
1Ki	3:12	neither **a.** thee shall any arise like	310
1Ki	3:18	And it came to pass the third day **a.**	
1Ki	6:1	**a.** the children of Israel were	
1Ki	7:11	costly stones, **a.** the measures of	
1Ki	7:31	the mouth thereof was round **a.**	
1Ki	7:37	**A.** this manner he made the ten	
1Ki	9:21	Their children that were left **a.**	310
1Ki	11:2	turn away your heart **a.** their gods:	310
1Ki	11:4	his wives turned away his heart **a.**	310
1Ki	11:5	Solomon went **a.** Ashtoreth	310
1Ki	11:5	**a.** Milcom the abomination of the	310
1Ki	11:6	went not fully **a.** the Lord,	310
1Ki	11:10	he should not go **a.** other gods:	310
1Ki	11:15	**a.** he had smitten every male in	
1Ki	12:14	spake to them **a.** the counsel of	
1Ki	13:14	went **a.** the man of God,	310
1Ki	13:23	**a.** he had eaten bread, and **a.** he	310
1Ki	13:31	it came to pass, **a.** he had buried	310
1Ki	13:33	**A.** this thing Jeroboam returned not	310
1Ki	15:4	to set up his son **a.** him, and to	310
1Ki	16:24	**a.** the name of Shemer, owner of	5921
1Ki	17:7	**a.** a while, that the brook dried	7093
1Ki	17:13	**a.** make for thee and for thy son.	314
1Ki	17:17	it came to pass **a.** these things,	310
1Ki	18:1	**a.** many days, that the word of the	
1Ki	18:28	and cut themselves **a.** their manner	
1Ki	19:11	and **a.** the wind an earthquake;	310
1Ki	19:12	And **a.** the earthquake a fire;	310
1Ki	19:12	and **a.** the fire a still small voice.	310
1Ki	19:20	he left the oxen, and ran **a.** Elijah,	310
1Ki	19:21	Then he arose, and went **a.** Elijah,	310
1Ki	20:15	**a.** them he numbered all the people,	310
1Ki	21:1	it came to pass **a.** these things,	310
2Ki	1:1	against Israel **a.** the death of Ahab.	310
2Ki	5:20	as the Lord liveth, I will run **a.** him,	310
2Ki	5:21	So Gehazi followed **a.** Naaman.	310
2Ki	5:21	Naaman saw him running **a.** him,	310
2Ki	6:24	it came to pass **a.** this,	310
2Ki	7:14	king sent **a.** the host of the Syrians,	310
2Ki	7:15	they went **a.** them unto Jordan:	310
2Ki	8:2	**a.** the saying of the man of God:	
2Ki	9:25	I and thou rode together **a.** Ahab	310
2Ki	9:27	Jehu followed **a.** him,	310
2Ki	10:29	Jehu departed not from **a.** them,	310
2Ki	14:17	Joash king of Judah lived **a.** the	310
2Ki	14:19	they sent **a.** him to Lachish,	310
2Ki	14:22	**a.** that the king slept with his	310
2Ki	17:15	and went **a.** the heathen	310
2Ki	17:33	**a.** the manner of the nations	
2Ki	17:34	they do **a.** the former manners:	
2Ki	17:34	do they **a.** their statutes, or **a.** their	
2Ki	17:34	or **a.** the law and commandment	
2Ki	17:40	they did **a.** their former manner.	
2Ki	18:5	so that **a.** him was none like him	310
2Ki	21:2	**a.** the abominations of the heathen,	
2Ki	23:3	to walk **a.** the Lord,	310
2Ki	23:25	neither **a.** him arose there any like	310
2Ki	25:5	the Chaldees pursued **a.** the king,	310
1Ch	2:24	And **a.** that Hezron was dead	310
1Ch	5:1	not to be reckoned **a.** the birthright.	
1Ch	5:25	went a whoring **a.** the gods	310
1Ch	6:31	in the house of the Lord, **a.** that	
1Ch	7:4	generations, **a.** the house of their	
1Ch	7:9	number of them, **a.** their genealogy	
1Ch	8:8	**a.** he had sent them away;	4480
1Ch	9:25	in their villages, were to come **a.**	
1Ch	10:2	hard **a.** Saul, and **a.** his sons;	310
1Ch	11:12	And **a.** him was Eleazar the son	310
1Ch	14:14	said unto him, Go not up **a.** them;	310
1Ch	15:13	sought him not **a.** the due order	
1Ch	17:11	I will raise up thy seed **a.** thee,	310
1Ch	18:1	Now **a.** this it came to pass,	310
1Ch	19:1	Now it came to pass **a.** this,	310
1Ch	20:1	**a.** the year was expired,	6256
1Ch	20:4	it came to pass **a.** this, that there	310
1Ch	23:24	sons of Levi **a.** the house of their	
1Ch	24:30	Levites **a.** the house of their fathers.	

1Ch 27:1 of Israel **a.** their number, to wit,
1Ch 27:7 Zebadiah his son **a.** him: 310
1Ch 27:34 And **a.** Ahithophel was Jehoiada 310
1Ch 28:8 inheritance for your children **a.** you 310
1Ch 29:14 able to offer so willingly **a.** this sort?
1Ch 29:21 Lord, on the morrow **a.** that day,
2Ch 1:12 there any **a.** thee have the like. 310
2Ch 2:17 **a.** the numbering wherewith 310
2Ch 3:3 length by cubits **a.** the first measure
2Ch 4:20 burn **a.** the manner before the
2Ch 8:8 who were left **a.** them in the land, 310
2Ch 8:13 Even **a.** a certain rate every day,
2Ch 10:5 again unto me **a.** three days.
2Ch 10:14 answered them **a.** the advice of
2Ch 11:16 And **a.** them out of all the tribes 310
2Ch 11:20 And **a.** her he took Maachah 310
2Ch 13:9 priests **a.** the manner of the nations
2Ch 13:19 Abijah pursued **a.** Jeroboam, 310
2Ch 17:4 and not **a.** the doings of Israel
2Ch 18:2 **a.** certain years he went down to 7093
2Ch 18:19 one spake saying **a.** this manner, 3602
2Ch 18:19 another saying **a.** that manner. 3602
2Ch 20:1 It came to pass **a.** this also, 310
2Ch 20:35 And **a.** this did Jehoshaphat 310
2Ch 21:18 And **a.** all this the Lord smote him, 310
2Ch 21:19 **a.** the end of two years, his
2Ch 22:4 his counsellors **a.** the death of his 310
2Ch 22:5 He walked also **a.** their counsel,
2Ch 23:21 **a.** that they had slain Athaliah
2Ch 24:4 it came to pass **a.** this, 310
2Ch 24:17 Now **a.** the death of Jehoiada 310
2Ch 25:14 it came to pass, **a.** that Amaziah 310
2Ch 25:15 sought **a.** the gods of the people,
2Ch 25:20 they sought **a.** the gods of Edom.
2Ch 25:25 lived **a.** the death of Joash son of 310
2Ch 25:27 **a.** the time that Amaziah did
2Ch 25:27 sent to Lachish **a.** him, and slew 310
2Ch 26:2 **a.** that the king slept with his 310
2Ch 26:17 Azariah the priest went in **a.** him, 310
2Ch 28:3 **a.** the abominations of the
2Ch 30:16 **a.** their manner, according to the
2Ch 31:2 **a.** their courses, every man 5921
2Ch 32:1 **A.** these things, and the 310
2Ch 32:9 **A.** this did Sennacherib king of 310
2Ch 33:14 Now **a.** this he built a wall 310
2Ch 34:3 he began to seek **a.** the God of
2Ch 34:21 to do **a.** all that is written in this
2Ch 34:31 to walk **a.** the Lord, 310
2Ch 35:4 **a.** your courses, according to the
2Ch 35:5 **a.** the division of the families of
2Ch 35:20 **A.** all this, when Josiah had 310
2Ch 36:14 transgressed very much **a.** all the
Ezr 2:61 Gileadite, and was called **a.** their 5921
Ezr 2:69 They gave **a.** their ability unto
Ezr 3:10 praise the Lord, **a.** the ordinance 5921
Ezr 5:4 **a.** this manner, What are the
Ezr 5:12 **a.** that our fathers had provoked 4481
Ezr 7:1 Now **a.** these things, 310
Ezr 7:18 that do **a.** the will of your God.
Ezr 7:25 And thou, Ezra, **a.** the wisdom of
Ezr 9:10 what shall we say **a.** this? 310
Ezr 9:13 And **a.** all that is come upon us 310
Ezr 10:16 chief of the fathers, **a.** the house of
Ne 3:16 **A.** him repaired Nehemiah 310
Ne 3:17 **A.** him repaired the Levites, 310
Ne 3:18 **A.** him repaired their brethren, 310
Ne 3:20 **A.** him Baruch the son of Zabbai 310
Ne 3:21 **A.** him repaired Meremoth 310
Ne 3:22 And **a.** him repaired the priests, 310
Ne 3:23 **A.** him repaired Benjamin 310
Ne 3:23 **A.** him repaired Azariah 310
Ne 3:24 **A.** him repaired Binnui 310
Ne 3:25 **A.** him Pedaiah the son of Parosh. 310
Ne 3:27 **A.** them the Tekoites repaired 310
Ne 3:29 **A.** them repaired Zadok 310
Ne 3:29 **A.** him repaired also Shemaiah 310
Ne 3:30 **A.** him repaired Hananiah 310
Ne 3:30 **A.** him repaired Meshullam 310
Ne 3:31 **A.** him repaired Malchiah 310
Ne 4:13 I even set the people **a.** their
Ne 5:8 We **a.** our ability, have redeemed 1767
Ne 6:4 sent unto me four times **a.** this
Ne 6:4 and I answered them **a.** the same
Ne 7:63 and was called **a.** their name. 5921
Ne 9:28 But **a.** they had rest, they did
Ne 10:34 **a.** the houses of our fathers,
Ne 11:8 And **a.** him Gabbai, Sallai, 310
Ne 12:32 **a.** them went Hoshaiah, 310
Ne 12:38 went over against them, and I **a.** 310
Ne 13:6 and **a.** certain days obtained I 7093
Ne 13:19 not be opened till **a.** the sabbath: 310
Es 1:22 to every people **a.** their language,
Es 2:1 **A.** these things, when the wrath 310
Es 2:12 **a.** that she had been twelve 7093
Es 3:1 **A.** these things did king Ahasuerus 310
Es 3:12 to every people **a.** their language;
Es 8:9 thereof, and unto every people **a.**
Es 9:26 they called these days Purim **a.** 5921
Job 3:1 **A.** this opened Job his mouth, 310
Job 10:6 thou enquirest **a.** mine iniquity,
Job 10:6 and searchest **a.** my sin?
Job 18:20 come **a.** him shall be astonied 314
Job 19:26 though **a.** my skin worms destroy 310
Job 21:3 and **a.** that I have spoken, mock on. 310
Job 21:21 in his house **a.** him, 310
Job 21:33 and every man shall draw **a.** him, 310
Job 29:22 **A.** my words they spake not again; 310
Job 30:5 (they cried **a.** them 5921
Job 30:5 as **a.** a thief;)
Job 31:7 mine heart walked **a.** mine eyes, 310
Job 37:4 **A.** it a voice roareth: 310
Job 39:8 he searcheth **a.** every green thing 310
Job 39:10 will he harrow the valleys **a.** thee? 310
Job 41:32 He maketh a path to shine **a.** him; 310
Job 42:7 **a.** the Lord had spoken these words 310
Job 42:8 lest I deal with you **a.** your folly,
Job 42:16 **A.** this lived Job an hundred and 310
Ps 4:2 love vanity, and seek **a.** leasing?
Ps 10:4 will not seek **a.** God: God is not
Ps 16:4 shall be multiplied that hasten **a.**
Ps 27:4 that will I seek **a.**; that I may
Ps 28:4 give them **a.** the work of their
Ps 35:4 put to shame that seek **a.** my
Ps 38:12 They also that seek **a.** my life
Ps 40:14 that seek **a.** my soul to destroy it;
Ps 42:1 As the hart panteth **a.** the water 5921
Ps 42:1 so panteth my soul **a.** thee, O God. 413
Ps 49:11 they call their lands **a.** their own
Ps 49:17 his glory shall not descend **a.** him. 310
Ps 51:*title* **a.** he had gone in to Bath-sheba. 834
Ps 54:3 and oppressors seek **a.** my soul:
Ps 63:8 My soul followeth hard **a.** thee: 310
Ps 68:25 players on instruments followed **a.**; 310
Ps 70:2 confounded that seek **a.** my soul:
Ps 78:34 returned and enquired early **a.**
Ps 86:14 violent men have sought **a.** my
Ps 103:10 not dealt with us **a.** our sins; nor
Ps 104:21 The young lions roar **a.** their prey,
Ps 110:4 Thou art a priest for ever **a.** the 5921
Ps 119:40 I have longed **a.** thy precepts:
Ps 119:85 The proud . . . which are not **a.** thy law
Ps 119:88 Quicken me **a.** thy lovingkindness;
Ps 119:150 nigh that follow **a.** mischief:
Ps 143:6 my soul thirsteth **a.** thee, as a
Ps 144:12 as corner stones, polished **a.** the
Pr 2:3 if thou criest **a.** knowledge, and
Pr 6:25 **a.** her beauty in thine heart;
Pr 7:22 He goeth **a.** her straightway, 310
Pr 15:9 he loveth him that followeth **a.**
Pr 20:7 his children are blessed **a.** him. 310
Pr 20:25 and **a.** vows to make enquiry. 310
Pr 21:21 that followeth **a.** righteousness
Pr 28:19 he that followeth **a.** vain persons
Ec 1:11 come with those that shall come **a.** 314
Ec 2:12 man do that cometh **a.** the king? 310
Ec 2:18 unto the man that shall be **a.** me. 310
Ec 3:22 bring him to see what shall be **a.** 310
Ec 4:16 also that come **a.** shall not rejoice 314
Ec 6:12 who can tell a man what shall be **a.** 310
Ec 7:14 that man should find nothing **a.** 310
Ec 9:3 and **a.** that they go to the dead. 310
Ec 10:14 what shall be **a.** him, 310
Ec 11:1 thou shalt find it **a.** many days.
Ec 12:2 nor the clouds return **a.** the rain: 310
Ca 1:4 Draw me, we will run **a.** thee: 310
Isa 1:23 and followeth **a.** rewards:
Isa 5:17 lambs feed **a.** their manner, and
Isa 10:24 against thee, **a.** the manner of
Isa 10:26 so shall he lift it up **a.** the manner
Isa 11:3 not judge **a.** the sight of his eyes,
Isa 11:3 neither reprove **a.** the hearing of
Isa 23:15, 17 **a.** the end of seventy years
Isa 24:22 and **a.** many days shall they be
Isa 43:10 formed, neither shall there be **a.** 310
Isa 44:13 maketh it **a.** the figure of a man,
Isa 45:14 they shall come **a.** thee; 310
Isa 49:20 **a.** thou hast lost the other, shall
Isa 51:1 ye that follow **a.** righteousness,
Isa 65:2 **a.** their own thoughts; 310
Jer 2:2 when thou wentest **a.** me in the 310
Jer 2:5 have walked **a.** vanity, 310
Jer 2:8 walked **a.** things that do not profit. 310
Jer 2:23 I have not gone **a.** Baalim? 310
Jer 2:25 and **a.** them will I go. 310
Jer 3:7 **a.** she had done all these things, 310
Jer 3:17 **a.** the imagination of their evil 310
Jer 5:8 morning: every one neighed **a.** 413
Jer 7:6 neither walk **a.** other gods to 310
Jer 7:9 **a.** other gods whom ye know not; 310
Jer 8:2 **a.** whom they have walked, 310
Jer 9:14 have walked **a.** the imagination 310
Jer 9:14 of their own heart, and **a.** Baalim, 310
Jer 9:16 I will send a sword **a.** them, 310
Jer 9:22 as the handful **a.** the harvestman, 310
Jer 11:10 they went **a.** other gods to serve 310
Jer 12:6 have called a multitude **a.** thee: 310
Jer 12:15 **a.** that I have plucked them out 310
Jer 13:6 **a.** many days, that the Lord said 7093
Jer 13:9 **A.** this manner will I mar the 3602
Jer 13:10 walk **a.** other gods, to serve them, 310
Jer 16:11 have walked **a.** other gods, 310
Jer 16:12 **a.** the imagination of his evil heart, 310
Jer 16:16 **a.** will I send for many hunters, 310
Jer 18:12 we will walk **a.** our own devices, 310
Jer 23:17 every one that walketh **a.** the
Jer 24:1 **a.** that Nebuchadrezzar king of 310
Jer 25:6 go not **a.** other gods to serve them, 310
Jer 25:26 of Sheshach shall drink **a.** them. 310
Jer 28:12 **a.** that Hananiah the prophet had 310
Jer 29:2 (**A.** that Jeconiah the king, 310
Jer 29:10 **a.** seventy years be accomplished 6310
Jer 30:17 Zion, whom no man seeketh **a.**.
Jer 30:18 palace shall remain **a.** the manner 5921
Jer 31:19 **a.** that I was turned, I repented; 310
Jer 31:19 and **a.** that I was instructed, 310
Jer 31:33 **A.** those days, saith the Lord. 310
Jer 32:18 into the bosom of their children **a.** 310
Jer 32:39 of their children **a.** them: 310
Jer 34:8 **a.** that the king Zedekiah had 310
Jer 35:15 go not **a.** other gods to serve them, 310
Jer 36:27 **a.** that the king had burned the 310
Jer 39:5 the Chaldeans' army pursued **a.** 310
Jer 40:1 **a.** that Nebuzar-adan the captain 310
Jer 41:4 day **a.** he had slain Gedaliah, and
Jer 41:16 **a.** that he had slain Gedaliah 310
Jer 42:7 **a.** ten days, that the word of the 7093
Jer 42:16 shall follow close **a.** you 310
Jer 49:37 I will send the sword **a.** them, 310
Jer 50:21 waste and utterly destroy **a.** them, 310
Jer 51:46 and **a.** that in another year shall 310
Jer 52:8 the Chaldeans pursued **a.** the king, 310
Eze 5:2, 12 I will draw out a sword **a.** them. 310
Eze 6:9 which go a whoring **a.** their idols: 310
Eze 7:27 I will do unto them **a.** their way,
Eze 9:5 Go ye **a.** him through the city, 310
Eze 11:12 **a.** the manners of the heathen
Eze 11:21 whose heart walketh **a.** the heart
Eze 12:14 I will draw out the sword **a.** them. 310
Eze 16:23 came to pass **a.** all thy wickedness, 310
Eze 16:47 walked **a.** their ways, nor done **a.**
Eze 20:16 for their heart went **a.** their idols. 310
Eze 20:24 eyes were **a.** their fathers' idols. 310
Eze 20:30 **a.** the manner of your fathers?
Eze 20:30 whoredom **a.** their abominations? 310
Eze 23:15 **a.** the manner of the Babylonians
Eze 23:30 thou hast gone a whoring **a.** the 310
Eze 23:45 shall judge them **a.** the manner of
Eze 23:45 and **a.** the manner of women that
Eze 23:48 may be taught not to do **a.** your
Eze 29:16 when they shall look **a.** them: 310
Eze 33:20 I will judge you every one **a.** his
Eze 33:31 heart goeth **a.** their covetousness. 310
Eze 34:6 none did search or seek **a.** them.
Eze 36:11 I will settle you **a.** your old estates.
Eze 38:8 **A.** many days thou shalt be
Eze 39:14 **a.** the end of seven months shall
Eze 39:26 **A.** that they have borne their
Eze 40:1 fourteenth year **a.** that the city was 310
Eze 40:21 the arches thereof were **a.** the
Eze 40:22 **a.** the measure of the gate that
Eze 40:24 **A.** that he brought me toward

Eze 41:5 A. he measured the wall of the
Eze 43:13 a. the cubits: The cubit is a cubit
Eze 44:10 astray away from me a. their 310
Eze 44:26 And a. he is cleansed, 310
Eze 45:11 the measure thereof shall be a.
Eze 46:12 a. his going forth one shall shut 310
Eze 46:17 a. it shall return to the prince:
Eze 46:19 A. he brought me through the
Eze 48:31 be a. the names of the tribes of 5921
Da 2:39 And a. thee shall arise another 870
Da 3:29 no other God that can deliver a. 1836
Da 4:26 a. that thou shalt have known 1767
Da 7:6 A. this I beheld, and lo another, 870
Da 7:7 A. this I saw in the night visions, 870
Da 7:24 and another shall rise a. them; 311
Da 8:1 a. that which appeared unto me at 310
Da 9:26 And a. threescore and two weeks 310
Da 11:13 come a. certain years 7093
Da 11:18 A. this shall he turn his face unto
Da 11:23 And a. the league made with him
Ho 2:5 I will go a. my lovers, 310
Ho 2:7 And she shall follow a. her lovers,
Ho 2:13 she went a. her lovers, 310
Ho 5:8 a. thee, O Benjamin 310
Ho 5:11 walked a. the commandment 310
Ho 6:2 A. two days will he revive us: in
Ho 7:4 who ceaseth from raising a. he
Ho 11:10 They shall walk a. the Lord: 310
Ho 12:1 and followeth a. the east wind:
Joe 2:2 neither shall be any more a. it, 310
Am 2:4 a. the which their fathers have 310
Am 2:7 pant a. the dust of the earth on 5921
Am 4:4 and your tithes a. three years:
Am 4:10 pestilence a. the manner of Egypt:
Am 7:1 growth a. the king's mowings 310
Zec 2:8 A. the glory hath he sent me unto 310
Zec 6:6 the white go forth a. them; 310
Zec 7:14 the land was desolate a. them, 310
Mt 1:12 a. they were brought to Babylon, 3326
Mt 3:11 but he that cometh a. me 3694
Mt 5:6 **they which do hunger and thirst a.**
Mt 5:28 **looketh on a woman to lust a. her**
Mt 6:9 **A. this manner therefore pray ye:** 3779
Mt 6:32 **a. all these things do the Gentiles** 1934
Mt 10:38 **and followeth a. me, is not worthy** 3694
Mt 12:39 **generation seeketh a. a sign;** 1934
Mt 15:12 were offended, a. they heard this
Mt 15:23 for she crieth a. us. 3693
Mt 16:4 **generation seeketh a. a sign;** 1934
Mt 16:24 **If any man will come a. me,** 3694
Mt 17:1 a. six days Jesus taketh Peter, 3326
Mt 18:32 **lord, a. that he had called him,**
Mt 23:3 **but do not ye a. their works:** 2596
Mt 24:29 **Immediately a. the tribulation** 3326
Mt 25:19 **A. a long time the lord of those** 3326
Mt 26:2 **Ye know that a. two days is the** 3326
Mt 26:32 **But a. I am risen again, I will go** 3326
Mt 26:73 And a. a while came unto him 3326
Mt 27:31 a. that they had mocked him, 3753
Mt 27:53 of the graves a. his resurrection, 3326
Mt 27:63 A. three days I will rise again 3326
Mk 1:7 cometh one mightier than I a. me, 3694
Mk 1:14 a. that John was put in prison, 3326
Mk 1:17 **Come ye a. me,** 3694
Mk 1:20 and went a. him. 3694
Mk 1:36 that were with him followed a. 2614
Mk 2:1 into Capernaum a. some days; 1223
Mk 4:28 **a. that the full corn in the ear** 1534
Mk 8:12 **Why doth this generation seek a.** 1934
Mk 8:25 A. that he put his hands again 1534
Mk 8:31 and a. three days rise again. 3326
Mk 8:34 **Whosoever will come a. me,** 3694
Mk 9:2 a. six days Jesus taketh with him 3326
Mk 9:31 **a. that he is killed, he shall rise**
Mk 12:34 no man a. that durst ask him 3765
Mk 13:24 **a. that tribulation, the sun shall** 3326
Mk 14:1 A. two days was the feast of the 3326
Mk 14:28 **But a. that I am risen,** 3326
Mk 14:70 And a little a., they that stood by 3326
Mk 16:12 A. that he appeared in another 3326
Mk 16:14 not them which had seen him a.
Mk 16:19 a. the Lord had spoken unto them, 3326
Lu 1:24 And a. those days his wife 3326
Lu 1:59 a. the name of his father. 1909
Lu 2:27 a. the custom of the law, 2596
Lu 2:42 a. the custom of the feast 2596
Lu 2:46 a. three days they found him in 3326
Lu 5:27 a. these things he went forth, 3326
Lu 6:1 second sabbath a. the first, that 1207
Lu 7:11 it came to pass the day a., 1836
Lu 9:23 **If any man will come a. me,** 3694
Lu 9:28 an eight days a. these sayings, 3326
Lu 10:1 A. these things the Lord 3326
Lu 12:4 **a. that have no more that they** 3326
Lu 12:5 **which a. he hath killed hath power** 3326
Lu 12:30 **the nations of the world seek a.:** 1934
Lu 13:9 **a. that thou shalt cut it** 1519,3195
Lu 14:27 **and come a. me, cannot be my** 3694
Lu 14:29 **a. he hath laid the foundation,**
Lu 15:4 **and go a. that which is lost, until** 1909
Lu 15:13 **not many days a. the younger** 3326
Lu 17:23 **or, see there: go not a. them,**
Lu 19:14 **and sent a message a. him,** 3694
Lu 20:40 And a. that they durst not ask 2089
Lu 21:8 **go ye not therefore a. them.** 3694
Lu 21:26 **and for looking a. those things** 4329
Lu 22:20 also the cup a. supper, 3326
Lu 22:58 a. a little while another saw him, 3326
Lu 22:59 about the space of one hour a.
Lu 23:26 that he might bear it a. Jesus. 3693
Lu 23:55 followed a., and beheld the 2628
Joh 1:15 He that cometh a. me is preferred 3694
Joh 1:27 He it is, who coming a. me is 3694
Joh 1:30 A. me cometh a man which is 3694
Joh 1:35 the next day a., John stood, 1887
Joh 2:6 a. the manner of the purifying 2596
Joh 2:12 A. this he went down to 3326
Joh 3:22 A. these things came Jesus and 3326
Joh 4:43 Now a. two days he departed 3326
Joh 5:1 A. this there was a feast of the 3326
Joh 5:4 first a. the troubling of the water 3326
Joh 6:1 A. these things Jesus went over 3326
Joh 6:23 a. that the Lord had given thanks:)
Joh 7:1 A. these things Jesus walked in 3326
Joh 8:15 **Ye judge a. the flesh; I judge no** 2596
Joh 11:7 a. that saith he to his disciples, 3326
Joh 11:11 and a. that he saith unto them, 3326
Joh 12:19 the world is gone a. him. 3694
Joh 13:5 A. that he poureth water into a 1534
Joh 13:12 So a. he had washed their feet, 3753
Joh 13:27 a. the sop Satan entered into him 3326
Joh 19:28 a. this, Jesus knowing that all 3326
Joh 19:38 a. this Joseph of Arimathaea, 3326
Joh 20:26 a. eight days again his disciples 3326
Joh 21:1 A. these things Jesus shewed 3326
Joh 21:14 a. that he was risen from the dead.
Ac 1:2 a. that he through the Holy Ghost
Ac 1:3 a. his passion by many infallible 3326
Ac 1:8 **receive power, a. that the Holy**
Ac 3:24 those that follow a., as many 2517
Ac 5:4 and a. it was sold, was it not in
Ac 5:7 three hours a., when his wife, not
Ac 5:37 A. this man rose up Judas of 3326
Ac 5:37 drew away much people a. him: 3694
Ac 7:5 and to his seed a. him, 3326
Ac 7:7 **and a. that shall they come forth,** 3326
Ac 7:36 a. that he had shewed wonders
Ac 7:45 our fathers that came a. brought 3326
Ac 9:23 a. that many days were fulfilled, 5613
Ac 10:24 And the morrow a. they entered 3326
Ac 10:37 a. the baptism which John 3326
Ac 10:41 a. he rose from the dead 3326
Ac 12:4 intending a. Easter to bring him 3326
Ac 13:15 And a. the reading of the law 3326
Ac 13:20 And a. that he gave unto them 3326
Ac 13:22 a man a. mine own heart 2596
Ac 13:25 there cometh one a. me, 3326
Ac 13:36 For David, a. he had served his
Ac 14:24 a. they had passed throughout
Ac 15:1 a. the manner of Moses, ye cannot
Ac 15:13 And a. they had held their peace, 3326
Ac 15:16 A. this I will return, and will 3326
Ac 15:17 men might seek after the Lord, 1567
Ac 15:23 they wrote letters by them a. this
Ac 15:33 a. they had tarried there a space,
Ac 15:36 And some days a. Paul said unto 3326
Ac 16:7 A. they were come to Mysia,
Ac 16:10 And a. he had seen the vision, 5613
Ac 17:27 if haply they might feel a. him,
Ac 18:1 A. these things Paul departed 3326
Ac 18:18 And Paul a. this tarried there yet
Ac 18:23 a. he had spent some time there,
Ac 19:4 which should come a. him, 3326
Ac 19:21 A. these things were ended, 5613
Ac 19:21 A. I have been there, I must also 3326
Ac 20:1 And a. the uproar was ceased, 3326
Ac 20:6 a. the days of unleavened bread 3326
Ac 20:18 a. what manner I have been with 4459
Ac 20:29 a. my departing shall grievous 3326
Ac 20:30 to draw away disciples a. them 3694
Ac 21:1 it came to pass, that a. we were 5613
Ac 21:15 And a. those days we took up our 3326
Ac 21:21 neither to walk a. the customs
Ac 21:36 multitude of the people followed a.,
Ac 22:29 a. he knew that he was a Roman,
Ac 23:3 to judge me a. the law, and 2596
Ac 23:25 a letter a. this manner: 4023
Ac 24:1 a. five days Ananias the high 3326
Ac 24:10 Then Paul, a. that the governor
Ac 24:14 a. the way which they call heresy, 2596
Ac 24:17 a. many years I came to bring 1223
Ac 24:24 And a. certain days, when Felix 3326
Ac 24:27 a. two years Porcius Festus came 4137
Ac 25:1 a. three days he ascended from 3326
Ac 25:13 a. certain days king Agrippa and 1230
Ac 25:26 thee, O king Agrippa, that, a.
Ac 26:5 that a. the most straitest sect of 2596
Ac 27:14 not long a. there arose against it
Ac 27:21 a. long abstinence Paul stood 5225
Ac 28:6 a. they had looked a great while,
Ac 28:11 a. three months we departed 3326
Ac 28:13 a. one day the south wind blew, 3326
Ac 28:17 a. three days Paul called the chief 3326
Ac 28:25 a. that Paul had spoken one word,
Ro 2:5 a. thy hardness and impenitent 2596
Ro 3:11 none that seeketh a. God 1567
Ro 5:14 had not sinned a. the similitude 1909
Ro 6:19 I speak a. the manner of men
Ro 7:22 I delight in the law of God a. the 2596
Ro 8:1 walk not a. the flesh, but a. 2596
Ro 8:4 walk not a. the flesh, but a. 2596
Ro 8:5 that are a. the flesh do mind the 2596
Ro 8:5 that are a. the Spirit the things of 2596
Ro 8:12 not to the flesh, to live a. the flesh. 2596
Ro 8:13 if ye live a. the flesh, ye shall die: 2596
Ro 9:30 followed not a. righteousness,
Ro 9:31 which followed a. the law of
Ro 10:20 unto them that asked not a. me 1905
Ro 14:19 therefore follow a. the things 1377
1Co 1:21 for a. that in the wisdom of God 1894
1Co 1:22 and the Greeks seek a. wisdom:
1Co 1:26 wise men a. the flesh, 2596
1Co 7:7 one a. this manner, and another 3779
1Co 7:40 so abide, a. my judgment: 2596
1Co 10:6 we should not lust a. evil things, 1938
1Co 10:18 Behold Israel a. the flesh: 2596
1Co 11:25 A. the same manner also he 5615
1Co 12:28 a. that miracles, then gifts 1899
1Co 14:1 Follow a. charity, and desire
1Co 15:6 A. that, he was seen of above five 1899
1Co 15:7 A. that, he was seen of James; 1899
1Co 15:32 If a. the manner of men I have 2596
2Co 5:16 know we no man a. the flesh: yea, 2596
2Co 5:16 we have known Christ a. the flesh, 2596
2Co 7:9 made sorry a. a godly manner, 2596
2Co 7:11 ye sorrowed a. godly sort, 2596
2Co 9:14 long a. you for the exceeding 1971
2Co 10:3 we do not war a. the flesh: 2596
2Co 10:7 a. the outward appearance? 2596
2Co 11:17 I speak it not a. the Lord, 2596
2Co 11:18 that many glory a. the flesh, 2596
Ga 1:11 which was preached of me is not a. 2596
Ga 1:18 Then a. three years I went up to 2596
Ga 2:1 fourteen years a. I went up 1223
Ga 2:14 a. the manner of the Gentiles,
Ga 3:15 I speak a. the manner of men; 2596
Ga 3:17 thirty years a., cannot disannul, 3326
Ga 3:25 But a. that faith is come, we are
Ga 4:9 now, a. that ye have known God,
Ga 4:23 was born a. the flesh; 2596
Ga 4:29 he that was born a. the flesh 2596
Ga 4:29 persecuted him that was born a. 2596
Eph 1:11 all things a. the counsel of his own 2596
Eph 1:13 also trusted, a. that ye heard the
Eph 1:13 whom also a. that ye believed, ye
Eph 1:15 a. I heard of your faith in the
Eph 4:24 a. God is created in righteousness 2596
Php 1:8 how greatly I long a. you all 1971
Php 2:26 For he longed a. you all, 1971
Php 3:12 I follow a., if that I may

Col 2:8 **a.** the tradition of men, *2596*
Col 2:8 **a.** the rudiments of the world, *2596*
Col 2:8 and not **a.** Christ. *2596*
Col 2:22 **a.** the commandments and *2596*
Col 3:10 **a.** the image of him that created *2596*
1Th 2:2 **a.** that we had suffered before,
2Th 2:9 whose coming is **a.** the working *2596*
2Th 3:6 and not **a.** the tradition *2596*
1Ti 5:15 already turned aside **a.** Satan. *3694*
1Ti 5:24 some men they follow **a.**. *1872*
1Ti 6:10 while some coveted **a.**, they have
1Ti 6:11 follow **a.** righteousness, godliness,
2Ti 4:3 but **a.** their own lusts *2596*
Tit 1:1 the truth which is **a.** godliness; *2596*
Tit 1:4 own son **a.** the common faith: *2596*
Tit 3:4 **a.** that the kindness and love of *3753*
Tit 3:10 **a.** the first and second admonition *3326*
Heb 3:5 which were to be spoken **a.**;
Heb 4:7 **a.** so long a time; *3326*
Heb 4:11 **a.** the same example of unbelief. *1722*
Heb 5:6 **a.** the order of Melchisedec. *2596*
Heb 5:10 an high priest **a.** the order of *2596*
Heb 6:15 **a.** he had patiently endured, he
Heb 6:20 **a.** the order of Melchisedec. *2596*
Heb 7:2 **a.** that also king of Salem, *1899*
Heb 7:11 rise **a.** the order of Melchisedec, *2596*
Heb 7:11 be called **a.** the order of Aaron? *2596*
Heb 7:15 **a.** the similitude of Melchisedec *2596*
Heb 7:16 not **a.** the law of a carnal *2596*
Heb 7:16 but **a.** the power of an *2596*
Heb 7:17 **a.** the order of Melchisedec. *2596*
Heb 7:21 **a.** the order of Melchisedec:) *2596*
Heb 8:10 **a.** those days, saith the Lord; *3326*
Heb 9:3 And **a.** this the judgment: *3326*
Heb 9:17 a testament is of force **a.** men
Heb 9:27 but **a.** this the judgment: *3326*
Heb 10:12 **a.** he had offered one sacrifice
Heb 10:15 for **a.** that he had said before, *3326*
Heb 10:16 **a.** those days, saith the Lord, *3326*
Heb 10:26 **a.** that we have received the *3326*
Heb 10:32 **a.** ye were illuminated, ye endured
Heb 10:36 **a.** ye have done the will of God,
Heb 11:8 which he should **a.** receive *3195*
Heb 11:30 Jericho fell down, **a.** they were
Heb 12:10 chastened us **a.** their own *2596*
Jas 3:9 **a.** the similitude of God. *2596*
1Pe 3:5 **a.** this manner in the old time *3779*
1Pe 5:10 by Christ Jesus, **a.** that ye have
2Pe 1:15 ye may be able **a.** my decease *3326*
2Pe 2:6 that **a.** should live ungodly; *3195*
2Pe 2:10 that walk **a.** the flesh in *3694*
2Pe 2:20 For if **a.** they have escaped
2Pe 2:21 **a.** they have known it, to turn
2Pe 3:3 walking **a.** their own lusts, *2596*
2Jo 6 we walk **a.** his commandments. *2596*
3Jo 6 forward on their journey **a.** a *516*
Jude 7 and going **a.** strange flesh, *3694*
Jude 11 and ran greedily **a.** the error of
Jude 16 complainers, walking **a.** their *2596*
Jude 18 who should walk **a.** their own *2596*
Re 4:1 **A.** this I looked, and, behold, *3326*
Re 7:1 **a.** these things I saw four angels *3326*
Re 7:9 **A.** this I beheld, and, lo, *3326*
Re 11:11 And **a.** three days and an half *3326*
Re 12:15 as a flood **a.** the woman, *3694*
Re 13:3 the world wondered **a.** the beast *3694*
Re 15:5 And **a.** that I looked, *3326*
Re 18:1 **a.** these things I saw another angel *3326*
Re 18:14 the fruits that thy soul lusted **a.**
Re 19:1 **a.** these things I heard a great *3326*
Re 20:3 **a.** that he must be loosed *3326*

AFTERNOON
Jg 19:8 they tarried until **a.**, and 5186,3117

AFTERWARD See also AFTERWARDS.
Ge 10:18 and **a.** were the families of the 310
Ge 15:14 **a.** shall they come out with 310,3651
Ge 32:20 and **a.** I will see his face; 310,3651
Ge 38:30 And **a.** came out his brother, 310
Ex 5:1 **a.** Moses and Aaron went in, and 310
Ex 34:32 **a.** all the children of Israel 310,3651
Le 14:19 **a.** he shall kill the burnt offering: 310
Le 14:36 **a.** the priest shall go in to see 310,3651
Le 16:26 **a.** come into the camp. 310,3651
Le 16:28 **a.** he shall come into the camp. 310,3651
Le 22:7 and shall **a.** eat of the holy things; 310
Nu 5:26 **a.** shall cause the woman to drink 310
Nu 12:16 **a.** the people removed from 310
Nu 19:7 **a.** he shall come into the camp, 310
Nu 31:2 **a.** shalt thou be gathered unto thy 310
Nu 31:24 **a.** ye shall come into the camp. 310
Nu 32:22 **a.** ye shall return, and be guiltless 310
De 17:7 **a.** the hands of all the people. 314
De 24:21 thou shalt not glean it **a.**: 310
Jos 2:16 and **a.** may ye go your way. 310
Jos 8:34 **a.** he read all the words of the 310,3651
Jos 10:26 **a.** Joshua smote them, and 310,3651
Jos 24:5 and **a.** I brought you out. 310
Jg 1:9 **a.** the children of Judah went down 310
Jg 7:11 **a.** shall thine hands be strengthened 310
Jg 16:4 came to pass **a.**, that he loved 310,3651
Jg 19:5 and **a.** go your way. 310
1Sa 24:5 **a.**, that David's heart smote 310,3651
1Sa 24:8 David also arose **a.**, and went 310,3651
2Sa 3:28 **a.** when David heard it, he said, 310,3651
1Ch 2:21 **a.** Hezron went in to the daughter 310
2Ch 35:14 **a.** they made ready for themselves, 310
Ezr 3:5 **a.** offered the continual burnt 310,3651
Ne 6:10 **A.** I came unto the house of
Ps 73:24 and **a.** receive me to glory, 310
Isa 1:26 **a.** thou shalt be called, 310,3651
Isa 9:1 **a.** did more grievously afflict 314
Jer 21:7 **a.**, saith the Lord, I will 310,3651
Jer 34:11 **a.** they turned, and caused 310,3651
Jer 46:26 **a.** it shall be inhabited, 310,3651
Jer 49:6 **a.** I will bring again the 310,3651
Eze 41:1 **A.** he brought me to the temple,
Eze 43:1 **A.** he brought me to the gate,
Eze 47:1 **A.** he brought me again unto the
Eze 47:5 **A.** he measured a thousand;
Da 8:27 **a.** I rose up, and did the king's
Ho 3:5 **A.** shall the children of Israel 310
Joe 2:28 come to pass **a.**, that I will 310,3651
Mt 4:2 he was **a.** an hungred. *5305*
Mt 21:29 **but a. he repented, and went** *5305*
Mt 21:32 **ye had seen it, repented not a.,** *5305*
Mt 25:11 **A. came also the other virgins,** *5305*
Mk 4:17 **a., when affliction or persecution** *1534*
Mk 16:14 **A.** he appeared unto the eleven *5305*
Lu 4:2 they were ended, he **a.** hungered. *5305*
Lu 8:1 it came to pass **a.**, that he went *2517*
Lu 17:8 **a. thou shalt eat and drink?** *3326,5023*
Lu 18:4 **but a. he said within himself,** *3326,5023*
Joh 5:14 **A.** Jesus findeth him in the *3326,5023*
Ac 13:21 And **a.** they desired a king: *2547*
1Co 15:23 **a.** they that are Christ's at his *1899*
1Co 15:46 **a.** that which is spiritual. *1899*
Heb 4:8 would he not **a.** have spoken *3326,5023*
Heb 12:11 **a.** it yieldeth the peaceable fruit *5305*
Heb 12:17 ye know how that **a.**, when he *3347*
Jude 5 **a.** destroyed them that believed *1208*

AFTERWARDS See also AFTERWARD.
Ge 30:21 And **a.** she bare a daughter, 310
Ex 11:1 **a.** he will let you go hence: 310,3651
De 13:9 and **a.** the hand of all the people. 314
1Sa 9:13 **a.** they eat that be bidden. 310,3651
Job 18:2 and **a.** we will speak. 310
Pr 20:17 **a.** his mouth shall be filled with 310
Pr 24:27 **a.** build thine house. 310
Pr 28:23 rebuketh a man **a.** shall find 310
Pr 29:11 a wise man keepeth it in till **a.** 268
Eze 11:24 **A.** the spirit took me up, and
Joh 13:36 **but thou shalt follow me a.** *5305*
Ga 1:21 **A.** I came into the regions of *1899*
Ga 3:23 which should **a.** be revealed.

AGABUS (ag'-ab-us)
Ac 11:28 one of them named **A.**, *13*
Ac 21:10 a certain prophet, named **A.** *13*

AGAG (a'-gag) See also AGAGITE.
Nu 24:7 his king shall be higher than **A.**, 90
1Sa 15:8 took **A.** the king of the Amalekites 90
1Sa 15:9 But Saul and the people spared **A.**, 90
1Sa 15:20 have brought **A.** the king of Amalek, 90
1Sa 15:32 Bring ye hither to me **A.** the king 90
1Sa 15:32 And **A.** came unto him delicately. 90
1Sa 15:32 **A.** said, Surely the bitterness of 90
1Sa 15:33 And Samuel hewed **A.** in pieces 90

AGAGITE (ag'-ag-ite)
Es 3:1, 10 the son of Hammedatha the **A.**, 91
Es 8:3 away the mischief of Haman the **A.**, 91
Es 8:5 the son of Hammedatha the **A.**, 91
Es 9:24 the son of Hammedatha the **A.**, 91

AGAIN
Ge 4:2 And she **a.** bare his brother Abel. 3254
Ge 4:25 And Adam knew his wife **a.**: 5750
Ge 8:10 **a.** he sent forth the dove out of 3254
Ge 8:12 returned not **a.** unto him 3254
Ge 8:21 I will not **a.** curse the ground 3254
Ge 8:21 neither will I **a.** smite any more 3254
Ge 14:16 brought **a.** his brother Lot, and 7725
Ge 15:16 they shall come hither **a.**: 7725
Ge 18:29 And he spake unto him yet **a.**, 3254
Ge 19:9 And they said **a.**, This one fellow
Ge 22:5 and worship, and come **a.** to you. 7725
Ge 24:5 bring thy son **a.** unto the land 7725
Ge 24:6,8 bring not my son thither **a.**. 7725
Ge 24:20 ran **a.** unto the well to draw water, 5750
Ge 25:1 Then **a.** Abraham took a wife, 3254
Ge 26:18 Isaac digged **a.** the wells of water, 7725
Ge 28:15 will bring thee **a.** into this land; 7725
Ge 28:21 I come **a.** to my father's house in 7725
Ge 29:3 put the stone **a.** upon the well's 7725
Ge 29:33, 34,35 conceived **a.**, and bare a 5750
Ge 30:7 conceived **a.**, and bare Jacob a 5750
Ge 30:19 conceived **a.**, and bare Jacob the 5750
Ge 30:31 I will **a.** feed and keep thy flock. 7725
Ge 35:9 And God appeared unto Jacob **a.**, 5750
Ge 37:14 and bring me word **a.**. 7725
Ge 37:22 to deliver him to his father **a.**. 7725
Ge 38:4 conceived **a.**, and bare a son; and 5750
Ge 38:5 **a.** conceived, and bare a son; and 5750
Ge 38:26 he knew her **a.** no more. 3254
Ge 40:21 butler unto his butlership **a.**; 7725
Ge 42:24 and returned to them **a.**, and 7725
Ge 42:37 I will bring him to thee **a.**. 7725
Ge 43:2 Go **a.**, buy us a little food. 7725
Ge 43:12 the money that was brought **a.** 7725
Ge 43:12 carry it **a.** in your hand; 7725
Ge 43:13 and arise, go **a.** unto the man: 7725
Ge 43:21 we have brought it **a.** in our hand. 7725
Ge 44:8 money,...we brought **a.** unto thee 7725
Ge 44:25 Go **a.**, and buy us a little food. 7725
Ge 46:4 I will also surely bring thee up **a.**:
Ge 48:21 and bring you **a.** unto the land of 7725
Ge 50:5 bury my father, and I will come **a.**. 7725
Ex 4:7 Put thine hand into thy bosom **a.**. 7725
Ex 4:7 he put his hand into his bosom **a.**; 7725
Ex 4:7 it was turned **a.** as his other flesh. 7725
Ex 10:8 Moses and Aaron were brought **a.** 7725
Ex 10:29 I will see thy face **a.** no more. 3254
Ex 14:13 ye shall see them **a.** no more 3254
Ex 14:26 may come **a.** upon the Egyptians, 7725
Ex 15:19 the Lord brought **a.** the waters 7725
Ex 21:19 If he rise **a.**, and walk abroad
Ex 23:4 thou shalt surely bring it back **a.**. 7725
Ex 24:14 until we come **a.** unto you: 7725
Ex 33:11 And he turned **a.** into the camp: 7725
Ex 34:35 Moses put the vail upon his face **a.**, 7725
Le 13:6 look on him **a.** the seventh day: 8145
Le 13:7 he shall be seen of the priest **a.**: 8145
Le 13:16 if the raw flesh turn **a.**, 7725
Le 14:39 shall come **a.** the seventh day, 7725
Le 14:43 if the plague come **a.**, and break 7725
Le 20:2 **A.**, thou shalt say to the children
Le 24:20 so shall it be done to him **a.**
Le 25:48 may be redeemed **a.**; one of his
Le 25:51 he shall give **a.** the price of his 7725
Le 25:52 his years shall he give him **a.** 7725
Le 26:26 shall deliver you your bread **a.** 7725
Nu 11:4 the children of Israel also wept **a.**, 7725
Nu 12:14 after that let her be received in **a.**
Nu 12:15 not till Miriam was brought in **a.**
Nu 17:10 Bring Aaron's rod **a.** before the 7725
Nu 22:8 and I will bring you word **a.**, as 7725
Nu 22:15 And Balak sent yet **a.** princes, 3254
Nu 22:25 and he smote her **a.**. 3254
Nu 22:34 thee, I will get me back **a.**. 7725
Nu 23:16 Go **a.** unto Balak, and say thus. 7725
Nu 32:15 he will yet **a.** leave them in the 3254
Nu 33:7 and turned **a.** unto Pi-hahiroth, 7725
Nu 35:32 come **a.** to dwell in the land, 7725
De 1:22 bring us word **a.** by what way 7725
De 1:25 and brought us word **a.**, and said, 7725
De 5:30 Get you into your tents **a.**. 7725
De 13:16 for ever; it shall not be built **a.** 5750
De 15:3 thou mayest exact it **a.**: but that
De 18:16 Let me not hear **a.** the voice of 3254
De 22:1 shalt in any case bring them **a.** 7725

Book	Ref	Context	No.
De	22:2	thou shalt restore it to him **a.**	7725
De	22:4	surely help to lift them up **a.**	
De	23:11	he shall come into the camp **a.**	
De	24:4	not take her **a.** to be his wife,	7725
De	24:13	shalt deliver him the pledge **a.**	7725
De	24:19	thou shalt not go **a.** to fetch it: it	7725
De	24:20	shalt not go over the boughs **a.**:	310
De	28:68	shall bring thee into Egypt **a.**	7725
De	28:68	Thou shalt see it no more **a.**: and	3254
De	30:9	will **a.** rejoice over thee for good,	7725
De	33:11	hate him, that they rise not **a.**	
Jos	5:2	and circumcise **a.** the children of	7725
Jos	8:21	then they turned **a.**, and slew the	7725
Jos	14:7	I brought him word **a.** as it was	7725
Jos	18:4	and they shall come **a.** to me	
Jos	18:8	describe it, and come **a.** to me,	7725
Jos	18:9	came **a.** to Joshua to the host of	
Jos	22:28	that we may say **a.**, Behold the	
Jos	22:32	and brought them word **a.**	7725
Jg	3:12	the children of Israel did evil **a.**	3254
Jg	3:19	turned **a.** from the quarries	7725
Jg	4:1	the children of Israel **a.** did evil	3254
Jg	4:20	**A.** he said unto her, Stand in the	
Jg	6:18	I will tarry until thou come **a.**	7725
Jg	8:9	When I come **a.** in peace, I will	7725
Jg	8:33	the children of Israel turned **a.**	7725
Jg	9:37	And Gaal spake **a.** and said,	3254,5750
Jg	10:6	the children of Israel did evil **a.**	3254
Jg	11:8	we turn **a.** to thee now, that thou	7725
Jg	11:9	If ye bring me home **a.** to fight	7725
Jg	11:13	restore those lands **a.** peaceably	7725
Jg	11:14	Jephthah sent messengers **a.**	3254,5750
Jg	13:1	the children of Israel did evil **a.**	3254
Jg	13:8	thou didst send come **a.** unto us,	5750
Jg	13:9	the angel of God came **a.** unto the	5750
Jg	15:19	he had drunk, his spirit came **a.**,	7725
Jg	16:22	hair of his head began to grow **a.**	
Jg	19:3	unto her, and to bring her **a.**,	7725
Jg	19:7	therefore he lodged there **a.**	7725
Jg	20:22	and set their battle **a.** in array in	3254
Jg	20:23	Shall I go up **a.** to battle	3254
Jg	20:25	ground of the children of Israel **a.**	5750
Jg	20:28	Shall I yet **a.** go out to battle	3254
Jg	20:41	the men of Israel turned **a.**, the	
Jg	20:48	the men of Israel turned **a.**	7725
Jg	21:14	Benjamin came **a.** at that time;	7725
Ru	1:11	Naomi said, Turn **a.**, my	7725
Ru	1:12	Turn **a.**, my daughters, go your	7725
Ru	1:14	lifted up their voice, and wept **a.**:	5750
Ru	1:21	Lord hath brought me home **a.**	7725
Ru	4:3	Naomi, that is come **a.** out of the	7725
1Sa	3:5	I called not; lie down **a.**	7725
1Sa	3:6	the Lord called yet **a.**, Samuel	3254
1Sa	3:6	I called not, my son; lie down **a.**	7725
1Sa	3:8	And the Lord called Samuel **a.** the	3254
1Sa	3:21	the Lord appeared **a.** in Shiloh:	3254
1Sa	4:5	so that the earth rang **a.**	
1Sa	5:3	and set him in his place **a.**	7725
1Sa	5:11	and let it go **a.** to his own place,	7725
1Sa	6:21	Philistines have brought **a.** the ark	7725
1Sa	9:8	the servant answered Saul **a.**,	3254
1Sa	15:25,	30 and turn **a.** with me, that	7725
1Sa	15:31	So Samuel turned **a.** after Saul;	7725
1Sa	16:10	**A.**, Jesse made seven of his sons	
1Sa	17:30	the people answered him **a.** after	7725
1Sa	19:8	And there was war **a.**: and David	3254
1Sa	19:15	Saul sent the messengers **a.** to	
1Sa	19:21	And Saul sent messengers **a.**	3254
1Sa	20:17	Jonathan caused David to swear **a.**,	3254
1Sa	23:4	David enquired of the Lord yet **a.**	3254
1Sa	23:23	and come ye **a.** to me with the	7725
1Sa	25:12	turned their way, and went **a.**,	7725
1Sa	27:4	he sought no more **a.** for him	3254
1Sa	29:4	that he may go **a.** to his place	7725
1Sa	30:12	when...his spirit came **a.** to him:	7725
2Sa	1:9	He said unto me **a.**, Stand, I pray	
2Sa	2:22	And Abner said **a.** to Asahel,	3254,5750
2Sa	3:11	not answer Abner a word **a.**,	5750
2Sa	3:26	Abner, which brought him **a.**	5750
2Sa	3:34	all the people wept **a.** over him	3254
2Sa	5:22	the Philistines came up yet **a.**	3254
2Sa	6:1	**A.**, David gathered together all	5750
2Sa	12:23	can I bring him back **a.**?	5750
2Sa	14:13	the king doth not fetch home **a.**	7725
2Sa	14:14	which cannot be gathered up **a.**;	
2Sa	14:21	bring the young man Absalom **a.**	7725
2Sa	14:29	when he sent **a.** the second time,	5750
2Sa	15:8	Lord shall bring me **a.** indeed to	7725
2Sa	15:25	he will bring me **a.**, and shew me	7725
2Sa	15:29	Abiathar carried the ark of God **a.**	7725
2Sa	16:19	And **a.**, whom should I serve?	8145
2Sa	18:22	Then said Ahimaaz....yet **a.** to	3254
2Sa	19:24	until the day he came **a.** in peace	
2Sa	19:30	my lord the king is come **a.** in	7725
2Sa	19:37	servant, I pray thee, turn back **a.**,	7725
2Sa	20:10	struck him not **a.**, and he died	8138
2Sa	21:15	Philistines had yet war **a.** with	5750
2Sa	21:18	was **a.** a battle with the Philistines	5750
2Sa	21:19	there was **a.** a battle in Gob with	5750
2Sa	22:38	not **a.** until I had consumed	7725
2Sa	24:1	And **a.** the anger of the Lord was	3254
1Ki	1:45	so that the city rang **a.**. This is	
1Ki	2:30	Benaiah brought the king word **a.**,	7725
1Ki	2:41	Jerusalem to Gath, and was come **a.**	7725
1Ki	8:33	shall turn **a.** to thee, and confess	7725
1Ki	8:34	and bring them **a.** unto the land	7725
1Ki	12:5	for three days, then come **a.** to me	7725
1Ki	12:12	Come to me **a.** the third day	7725
1Ki	12:20	that Jeroboam was come **a.**,	7725
1Ki	12:21	to bring the kingdom **a.** to	7725
1Ki	12:27	this people turn **a.** unto their lord	7725
1Ki	12:27	go **a.** to Rehoboam king of Judah	7725
1Ki	13:4	he could not pull it in **a.** to him	7725
1Ki	13:6	my hand may be restored me **a.**	7725
1Ki	13:6	king's hand was restored him **a.**,	7725
1Ki	13:9	nor turn **a.** by the same way that	7725
1Ki	13:17	nor turn **a.** to go by the way that	7725
1Ki	13:33	but made **a.**...priests of the high	7725
1Ki	17:21	this child's soul come into him **a.**	7725
1Ki	17:22	soul of the child came into him **a.**,	7725
1Ki	18:37	hast turned their heart back **a.**	322
1Ki	18:43	And he said, Go **a.** seven times	7725
1Ki	19:6	and drink, and laid him down **a.**	7725
1Ki	19:7	the angel of the Lord came **a.** the	7725
1Ki	19:20	Go back **a.**: for what have I done	7725
1Ki	20:5	the messengers came **a.**, and said,	7725
1Ki	20:9	departed, and brought him word **a.**	7725
2Ki	1:6	turn **a.** unto the king that sent you,	7725
2Ki	1:11	**A.** also he sent unto him another	7725
2Ki	1:13	sent **a.** a captain of the third fifty	7725
2Ki	2:18	when they came **a.** to him, (for he	7725
2Ki	4:22	to the man of God, and come **a.**	7725
2Ki	4:29	salute thee, answer him not **a.**:	
2Ki	4:31	Wherefore he went **a.** to meet	7725
2Ki	4:38	Elisha came **a.** to Gilgal;	7725
2Ki	4:43	He said **a.**, Give the people,	
2Ki	5:10	thy flesh shall come **a.** to thee,	7725
2Ki	5:14	his flesh came **a.** like unto the flesh	7725
2Ki	5:26	when the man turned **a.** from his	
2Ki	7:8	came **a.**, and entered into another	7725
2Ki	9:18	he cometh not **a.**	7725
2Ki	9:20	even unto them, and cometh not **a.**:	7725
2Ki	9:36	Wherefore they came **a.**, and told	7725
2Ki	13:25	the son of Jehoahaz took **a.**	7725
2Ki	19:9	sent messengers **a.** unto Hezekiah,	7725
2Ki	19:30	shall yet **a.** take root downward,	3254
2Ki	20:5	Turn again, and tell Hezekiah the	7725
2Ki	21:3	For he built up **a.** the high places	7725
2Ki	22:9	and brought the king word **a.**,	7725
2Ki	22:20	they brought the king word **a.**	7725
2Ki	24:7	the king of Egypt came not **a.** any	3254
1Ch	13:3	bring **a.** the ark of our God to us:	5437
1Ch	14:13	Philistines yet **a.** spread	3254
1Ch	14:14	Therefore David enquired **a.** of	5750
1Ch	20:5	was war **a.** with the Philistines;	5750
1Ch	20:6	yet **a.** there was war at Gath,	5750
1Ch	21:12	what word I shall bring **a.** to him	7725
1Ch	21:27	put his sword **a.** into the sheath	7725
2Ch	6:25	bring them **a.** unto the land which	7725
2Ch	10:5	Come **a.** unto me after three days	7725
2Ch	10:12	Come **a.** to me on the third day	7725
2Ch	11:1	bring the kingdom **a.** to Rehoboam	7725
2Ch	12:11	brought them **a.** into the guard	7725
2Ch	13:20	did Jeroboam recover strength **a.**	5750
2Ch	18:18	**A.** he said, Therefore hear the	
2Ch	18:32	turned back **a.** from pursuing	7725
2Ch	19:4	he went out **a.** through the people	7725
2Ch	20:27	to go **a.** to Jerusalem with joy;	7725
2Ch	24:11	carried it to his place **a.**	7725
2Ch	24:19	to bring them **a.** unto the Lord;	7725
2Ch	25:10	out of Ephraim, to go home **a.**:	
2Ch	28:11	and deliver the captives **a.**,	
2Ch	28:17	For **a.** the Edomites had come	5750
2Ch	30:6	**a.** unto the Lord God of Abraham,	7725
2Ch	30:9	if ye turn **a.** unto the Lord,	7725
2Ch	30:9	they shall come **a.** into this land:	7725
2Ch	32:25	Hezekiah rendered not **a.**	7725
2Ch	33:3	For he built **a.** the high places	7725
2Ch	33:13	**a.** to Jerusalem into his kingdom	7725
2Ch	34:16	brought the king word back **a.**,	5750
2Ch	34:28	So they brought the king word **a.**	7725
Ezr	2:1	**a.** unto Jerusalem and Judah,	7725
Ezr	4:13	the walls set up **a.**, then will they	
Ezr	4:16	if this city be builded **a.**, and the	
Ezr	6:5	and brought **a.** unto the temple	1946
Ezr	6:21	Israel, which were come **a.** out of	7725
Ezr	9:14	we **a.** break thy commandments,	7725
Ne	7:6	**a.** to Jerusalem and to Judah,	7725
Ne	8:17	**a.** out of the captivity made booths,	7725
Ne	9:28	they did evil **a.** before thee:	7725
Ne	9:29	that thou mightest bring them **a.**	7725
Ne	13:9	brought I **a.** the vessels of the	7725
Ne	13:21	if ye do so **a.**, I will lay hands on	8138
Es	4:10	**A.** Esther spake unto Hatach,	
Es	6:12	Mordecai came **a.** to the king's	7725
Es	7:2	the king said **a.** unto Esther on	1571
Es	8:3	Esther spake yet **a.** before the	3254
Job	2:1	**A.** there was a day when the sons	
Job	6:29	not be iniquity; yea, return **a.**,	5750
Job	10:9	wilt thou bring me into dust **a.**?	7725
Job	10:16	and **a.** thou shewest thyself	7725
Job	12:14	down, and it cannot be built **a.**:	
Job	12:23	nations, and straiteneth them **a.**	
Job	14:7	cut down, that it will sprout **a.**,	5750
Job	14:14	If a man die, shall he live **a.**? all	
Job	20:15	and he shall vomit them up **a.**:	
Job	29:22	After my words they spake not **a.**;	8138
Job	34:15	man shall turn **a.** unto dust	7725
Ps	18:37	neither did I turn **a.** till they were	7725
Ps	37:21	payeth not **a.**: but the righteous	7999
Ps	60:1	O turn thyself to us **a.**	7725
Ps	68:22	I will bring **a.** from Bashan,	7725
Ps	68:22	I will bring my people **a.**	7725
Ps	71:20	shalt quicken me **a.**, and shalt	7725
Ps	71:20	bring me up **a.** from the depths	7725
Ps	78:39	passeth away, and cometh not **a.**	7725
Ps	80:3	Turn us **a.**, O God, and cause thy	7725
Ps	80:7	Turn us **a.**, O God of hosts,	7725
Ps	80:19	Turn us **a.**, O Lord God of hosts,	7725
Ps	85:6	Wilt thou not revive us **a.**:	7725
Ps	85:8	let them not turn **a.** to folly	7725
Ps	104:9	turn not **a.** to cover the earth	7725
Ps	107:26	they go down **a.** to the depths:	
Ps	107:39	**A.**, they are minished and brought	
Ps	126:1	the Lord turned **a.** the captivity	
Ps	126:4	Turn **a.** our captivity, O Lord,	7725
Ps	126:6	shall doubtless come **a.** with	
Ps	140:10	pits, that they rise not up **a.**	
Pr	2:19	that go unto her return **a.**,	7725
Pr	3:28	thy neighbour, Go, and come **a.**,	7725
Pr	19:17	he hath given will he pay him **a.**	7999
Pr	19:19	yet thou must do it **a.**	3254
Pr	19:24	much as bring it to his mouth **a.**	7725
Pr	23:35	I awake? I will seek it yet **a.**	5750
Pr	24:16	seven times, and riseth up **a.**:	
Pr	26:15	grieveth him to bring it **a.** to his	7725
Ec	1:6	the wind returneth **a.** according	7725
Ec	1:7	thither they return **a.**	7725
Ec	3:20	the dust, and all turn to dust **a.**	7725
Ec	4:4	**A.**, I considered all travail, and	
Ec	4:11	**A.**, if two lie together, then they	1571
Ec	8:14	**a.**, there be wicked men, to whom	
Isa	7:10	the Lord spake **a.** unto Ahaz,	3254
Isa	8:5	The Lord spake also unto me **a.**,	3254
Isa	10:20	shall no more **a.** stay upon him	3254
Isa	11:11	the Lord shall set his hand **a.**	3254
Isa	24:20	it shall fall, and not rise **a.**	3254
Isa	37:31	**a.** take root downward, and	3254
Isa	38:8	I will bring **a.** the shadow of the	7725
Isa	46:8	it **a.** to mind, O ye transgressors	7725
Isa	49:5	to bring Jacob **a.** to him,	7725
Isa	49:20	shall say **a.** in thine ears, The	5750
Isa	51:22	thou shalt no more drink it **a.**:	5750
Isa	52:8	the Lord shall bring **a.** Zion	7725
Jer	3:1	man's, shall he return unto her **a.**	5750
Jer	3:1	yet return **a.** to me, saith the Lord	
Jer	12:15	will bring them **a.**, every man to	7725
Jer	15:19	return, then will I bring thee **a.**,	7725
Jer	16:15	I will bring them **a.** into their land	7725
Jer	18:4	so he made it **a.** another vessel,	7725
Jer	19:11	that cannot be made whole **a.**:	5750

Jer 23:3 will bring them **a.** to their folds; 7725
Jer 24:4 **A.** the word of the Lord came
Jer 24:6 I will bring them **a.** to this land: 7725
Jer 25:5 Turn ye **a.** now every one from 7725
Jer 27:16 be brought **a.** from Babylon: 7725
Jer 28:3 **a.** into this place all the vessels 7725
Jer 28:4 will bring **a.** to this place Jeconiah 7725
Jer 28:6 bring **a.** the vessels of the Lord's 7725
Jer 29:14 I will bring you **a.** into the place 7725
Jer 30:3 bring **a.** the captivity of my people 7725
Jer 30:18 I will bring **a.** the captivity of 7725
Jer 31:4 **A.** I will build thee, and thou shalt 5750
Jer 31:4 thou shalt **a.** be adorned with thy 5750
Jer 31:16 they shall come **a.** from the land 7725
Jer 31:17 that thy children shall come **a.** to 7725
Jer 31:21 turn **a.**, O virgin of Israel, turn **a.** 7725
Jer 31:23 I shall bring **a.** their captivity; 7725
Jer 32:15 vineyards shall be possessed **a.** 5750
Jer 32:37 will bring them **a.** unto this place, 7725
Jer 33:10 **A.** there shall be heard in this 5750
Jer 33:12 **A.** in this place, which is desolate 5750
Jer 33:13 of Judah, shall the flocks pass **a.** 5750
Jer 36:28 Take thee **a.** another roll, 7725
Jer 37:8 the Chaldeans shall come **a.**, and 7725
Jer 41:16 whom he had brought **a.** from 7725
Jer 46:16 let us go **a.** to our own people, 7725
Jer 48:47 bring **a.** the captivity of Moab 7725
Jer 49:6 I will bring **a.** the captivity of the 7725
Jer 49:39 will bring **a.** the captivity of Elam, 7725
Jer 50:19 And I will bring Israel **a.** to his 7725
La 3:40 our ways, and turn **a.** to the Lord. 7725
Eze 3:20 **A.**, When a righteous man doth 7725
Eze 4:6 lie **a.** on thy right side, and thou 8145
Eze 5:4 take of them **a.**, and cast them 5750
Eze 7:7 sounding **a.** of the mountains. 1906
Eze 8:6 turn thee yet **a.**, and thou shalt 5750
Eze 8:13 Turn thee yet **a.**, and thou shalt 5750
Eze 8:15 O son of man? turn thee yet **a.**, 5750
Eze 11:14 **A.** the word of the Lord came unto me,
Eze 12:26 **A.** the word of the Lord came to
Eze 14:12 word of the Lord came **a.** to me,
Eze 16:1 **A.** the word of the Lord came
Eze 16:53 I shall bring **a.** their captivity, 7725
Eze 16:53 then will I bring **a.** the captivity
Eze 18:1 word of the Lord came unto me **a.**,
Eze 18:27 **A.**, when the wicked man turneth
Eze 21:8 **A.** the word of the Lord came
Eze 21:18 word of the Lord came unto me **a.**,
Eze 23:1 word of the Lord came **a.** unto me,
Eze 24:1 **A.** in the ninth year, in the tenth
Eze 25:1 The word of the Lord came **a.**
Eze 26:21 shalt thou never be found **a.**, 5750
Eze 27:1 The word of the Lord came **a.**
Eze 28:1 The word of the Lord came **a.**
Eze 28:20 **A.** the word of the Lord came
Eze 29:14 bring **a.** the captivity of Egypt, 7725
Eze 30:1 the word of the Lord came **a.** unto
Eze 33:1 **A.** the word of the Lord came
Eze 33:14 **A.**, when I say unto the wicked,
Eze 33:15 restore the pledge, give **a.** that he 7999
Eze 34:4 neither have ye brought **a.** 7725
Eze 34:16 bring **a.** that which was driven 7725
Eze 37:4 **A.** he said unto me, Prophesy
Eze 37:15 The word of the Lord came **a.**
Eze 39:25 bring **a.** the captivity of Jacob, 7725
Eze 39:27 When I have brought them **a.** 7725
Eze 47:1 Afterward he brought me **a.** unto 7725
Eze 47:4, 4 **A.** he measured a thousand,
Da 2:7 They answered **a.** and said, 8579
Da 9:25 the street shall be built **a.**, and 7725
Da 10:18 there came **a.** and touched me 3254
Ho 1:6 And she conceived **a.**, and bare a 5750
Joe 3:1 bring **a.** the captivity of Judah, 7725
Am 7:8 not **a.** pass by them any more: 3254
Am 7:13 prophesy not **a.** any more at 3254
Am 8:2 not **a.** pass by them any more. 3254
Am 8:14 shall fall, and never rise up **a.** 5750
Am 9:14 And I will bring **a.** the captivity 7725
Jon 2:4 look **a.** toward thy holy temple. 3254
Mic 7:19 He will turn **a.**, he will have 7725
Zep 3:20 At that time will I bring you **a.**,
Hag 2:20 **a.** the word of the Lord came 8145
Zec 2:1 I lifted up mine eyes **a.**, and
Zec 2:12 and shall choose Jerusalem **a.** 5750
Zec 4:1 that talked with me came **a.**, 7725
Zec 4:12 answered **a.**, and said unto him, 8145
Zec 8:1 **A.** the word of the Lord of hosts
Zec 8:15 **a.** have I thought in these days 7725
Zec 10:6 will bring them **a.** to place them; 7725
Zec 10:9 with their children, and turn **a.** 7725
Zec 10:10 bring them **a.** also out of the land 7725
Zec 12:6 be inhabited **a.** in her own place, 5750
Mal 2:13 And this have ye done **a.**, 8145
Mt 2:8 bring me word **a.**, that I may *518*
Mt 4:7 **It is written a., Thou shalt not** *3825*
Mt 4:8 **A.**, the devil taketh him up *3825*
Mt 5:33 **A., ye have heard that it hath been** *3825*
Mt 7:2 **it shall be measured to you a.** *488*
Mt 7:6 **and turn a. and rend you** *4762*
Mt 11:4 **and shew John a. those things** *518*
Mt 13:44 **A., the kingdom of heaven** *3825*
Mt 13:45, 47 **A., the kingdom of heaven** *3825*
Mt 16:21 and be raised **a.** the third day *1453*
Mt 17:9 **until the son of man be risen a** *450*
Mt 17:23 **third day he shall be raised a** *1453*
Mt 18:19 **A. I say unto you, That if two of** *3825*
Mt 19:24 **And a. I say unto you, It is easier** *3825*
Mt 20:5 **A. he went out about the sixth** *3825*
Mt 20:19 **the third day he shall rise a.** *450*
Mt 21:36 **A., he sent other servants more** *3825*
Mt 22:1 spake unto them **a.** by parables, *3825*
Mt 22:4 **A.**, he sent forth other servants, *3825*
Mt 26:32 **after I am risen a. I will go** *1453*
Mt 26:42 He went away **a.** the second time, *3825*
Mt 26:43 came and found them asleep **a.**: *3825*
Mt 26:44 went away **a.**, and prayed the *3825*
Mt 26:52 **Put up a. thy sword into his place,** *654*
Mt 26:72 And **a.** he denied with an oath, *3825*
Mt 27:3 brought **a.** the thirty pieces of *654*
Mt 27:50 Jesus, when he had cried **a.** with *3825*
Mt 27:63 After three days I will rise **a.** *1453*
Mk 2:1 **a.** he entered into Capernaum *3825*
Mk 2:13 he went forth **a.** by the seaside; *3825*
Mk 3:1 he entered **a.** into the synagogue; *3825*
Mk 3:20 the multitude cometh together **a.**, *3825*
Mk 4:1 began **a.** to teach by the sea side: *3825*
Mk 5:21 when Jesus was passed over **a.** by *3825*
Mk 7:31 **a.**, departing from the coasts of *3825*
Mk 8:13 entering into the ship **a.** departed *3825*
Mk 8:25 he put his hands **a.** upon his eyes, *3825*
Mk 8:31 after three days rise **a.** *450*
Mk 10:1 resort unto him **a.**; and, as he *3825*
Mk 10:1 was wont, he taught them **a.** *3825*
Mk 10:10 his disciples asked him **a.** of the *3825*
Mk 10:24 But Jesus answereth **a.**, and saith *3825*
Mk 10:32 he took **a.** the twelve, and began *3825*
Mk 10:34 **the third day he shall rise a.** *450*
Mk 11:27 And they come **a.** to Jerusalem: *3825*
Mk 12:4 **and a. he sent unto them another** *3825*
Mk 12:5 **And a. he sent another; and him** *3825*
Mk 13:16 **is in the field not turn back a** *1994*
Mk 14:39 **a.** he went away, and prayed, *3825*
Mk 14:40 he found them asleep **a.**, *3825*
Mk 14:61 **A.** the high priest asked him, *3825*
Mk 14:69 a maid saw him **a.**, and began to *3825*
Mk 14:70 he denied it **a.**. And a little after, *3825*
Mk 14:70 they that stood by said **a.** to Peter, *3825*
Mk 15:4 And Pilate asked him **a.**, saying, *3825*
Mk 15:12 Pilate answered and said **a.** unto *3825*
Mk 15:13 And they cried out **a.**, Crucify him. *3825*
Lu 2:34 and rising **a.** of many in Israel; *386*
Lu 2:45 turned back **a.** to Jerusalem, *5290*
Lu 4:20 he gave it **a.** to the minister, and *591*
Lu 6:30 **thy goods ask them not a.** *523*
Lu 6:34 **to sinners, to receive as much a.** *618*
Lu 6:35 **lend, hoping for nothing a.; and** *560*
Lu 6:38 **measured to you a.** *488*
Lu 8:37 the ship, and returned back **a.** *5290*
Lu 8:55 her spirit came **a.**, and she arose *1994*
Lu 9:8 of the old prophets was risen **a.** *450*
Lu 9:19 one of the old prophets is risen **a.** *450*
Lu 9:39 him that he foameth **a.**, *3326*
Lu 9:42 delivered him **a.** to his father. *591*
Lu 10:6 **if not, it shall turn to you a.** *344*
Lu 10:17 the seventy returned **a.** with joy, *5290*
Lu 10:35 **when I come a., I will repay thee** *1880*
Lu 13:20 And **a.** he said, **Whereunto shall** *3825*
Lu 14:6 could not answer him **a.** to these *470*
Lu 14:12 **lest they also bid thee a., and a** *479*
Lu 15:24 **my son was dead, and is alive a.;** *326*
Lu 15:32 **brother was dead, and is alive a.;** *326*
Lu 17:4 **turn a. to thee, saying, I repent:** *1994*
Lu 18:33 **the third day he shall rise a.** *450*
Lu 20:11 **a. he sent another servant:** *4388*
Lu 20:12 **And a. he sent a third: and** *4388*
Lu 23:11 robe, and sent him **a.** to Pilate. *375*
Lu 23:20 willing to release Jesus, spake **a.** *3825*
Lu 24:7 crucified, and the third day rise **a.** *450*
Joh 1:35 **A.** the next day after John stood, *3825*
Joh 3:3 **Except a man be born a., he** *509*
Joh 3:7 **Ye must be born a.** *509*
Joh 4:3 and departed **a.** into Galilee. *3825*
Joh 4:13 **of this water shall thirst a.:** *3825*
Joh 4:46 Jesus came **a.** into Cana of Galilee, *3825*
Joh 4:54 This is **a.** the second miracle that *3825*
Joh 6:15 he departed **a.** into a mountain *3825*
Joh 6:39 **should raise it up a. at the last** *450*
Joh 8:2 he came **a.** into the temple, *3825*
Joh 8:8 **a.** he stooped down, and wrote *3825*
Joh 8:12 Then spake Jesus **a.** unto them, *3825*
Joh 8:21 Then said Jesus **a.** unto them, **I go** *3825*
Joh 9:15 Then **a.** the Pharisees also asked *3825*
Joh 9:17 They say unto the blind man **a.**, *3825*
Joh 9:24 Then **a.** called they the man *1537,1208*
Joh 9:26 said they to him **a.**, What did he *3825*
Joh 9:27 wherefore would you hear it **a.**? *3825*
Joh 10:7 Then said Jesus unto them **a.**, *3825*
Joh 10:17 **my life, that I might take it a** *3825*
Joh 10:18 **and I have power to take it a.** *3825*
Joh 10:19 a division therefore **a.** among the *3825*
Joh 10:31 the Jews took up stones **a.** to stone *3825*
Joh 10:39 Therefore they sought **a.** to take *3825*
Joh 10:40 And went away **a.** beyond Jordan *3825*
Joh 11:7 **Let us go into Judaea a.** *3825*
Joh 11:8 and goest thou thither **a.**? *3825*
Joh 11:23 unto her, **Thy brother shall rise a.** *450*
Joh 11:24 I know that he shall rise **a.** in the *450*
Joh 11:38 **a.** groaning in himself *3825*
Joh 12:22 **a.** Andrew and Philip tell Jesus. *3825*
Joh 12:28 and will glorify it **a.** *3825*
Joh 12:39 because that Esaias said **a.**, *3825*
Joh 13:12 and was set down **a.**, he said *3825*
Joh 14:3 **I will come a., and receive you** *3825*
Joh 14:28 **I go away, and come a. unto you.**
Joh 16:16 **and a., a little while, and ye shall.** *3825*
Joh 16:17 and **a.**, a little while 3825
Joh 16:19 **and a., a little while, and** *3825*
Joh 16:22 **but I will see you a.,** *3825*
Joh 16:28 **a., I leave the world, and go to the** *3825*
Joh 18:7 Then asked he them **a., Whom** *3825*
Joh 18:27 Peter then denied **a.**: *3825*
Joh 18:33 into the judgment hall **a.**, *3825*
Joh 18:38 he went out **a.** unto the Jews, *3825*
Joh 18:40 Then cried they all **a.**, saying, *3825*
Joh 19:4 Pilate therefore went forth **a.**, *3825*
Joh 19:9 went **a.** into the judgment hall, *3825*
Joh 19:37 And **a.** another scripture saith, *3825*
Joh 20:9 he must rise **a.** from the dead. *450*
Joh 20:10 the disciples went away **a.** unto *3825*
Joh 20:21 said Jesus to them **a.**, *3825*
Joh 20:26 And after eight days **a.** his disciples *3825*
Joh 21:1 Jesus shewed himself **a.** to the *3825*
Joh 21:16 He saith to him **a.** the second time, *3825*
Ac 1:6 this time restore **a.** the kingdom. *600*
Ac 7:26 would have set them at one **a.**, *1515*
Ac 7:39 their hearts turned back **a.** into *4762*
Ac 10:15 the voice spake unto him **a.** the *3825*
Ac 10:16 the vessel was received up **a.** into *3825*
Ac 11:9 voice answered me **a.** from *1537,1208*
Ac 11:10 all were drawn up **a.** into heaven. *3825*
Ac 13:33 he hath raised up Jesus **a.**; *450*
Ac 13:37 he, whom God raised **a.**, saw no *1453*
Ac 14:21 they returned **a.** to Lystra, *5290*
Ac 15:16 will build **a.** the tabernacle *456*
Ac 15:16 I will build **a.** the ruins thereof. *456*
Ac 15:36 us go **a.** and visit our brethren *1994*
Ac 17:3 suffered, and risen **a.** from the *450*
Ac 17:32 will hear thee **a.** of this matter, *3825*
Ac 18:21 I will return **a.** unto you, *3825*
Ac 20:11 was come up **a.**, and broken
Ac 21:6 and they returned home **a.** *5290*
Ac 22:17 I was come **a.** to Jerusalem, *5290*
Ac 27:28 sounded **a.**, and found it fifteen *3825*
Ro 4:25 raised **a.** for our justification. *1453*
Ro 8:15 the spirit of bondage **a.** to fear; *3825*
Ro 8:34 yea rather, that is risen **a.**, *1453*
Ro 10:7 bring up Christ **a.** from the dead.) *321*
Ro 11:23 is able to graff them in **a.** *3825*
Ro 11:35 shall be recompensed unto him **a.**? *467*
Ro 15:10 **a.** he saith, Rejoice, ye Gentiles, *3825*
Ro 15:11 **a.**, Praise the Lord, all ye Gentiles; *3825*

Ro 15:12 And **a.**, Esaias saith, *3825*
1Co 3:20 And **a.**, The Lord knoweth the *3825*
1Co 7:5 and come together **a.**, that Satan *3825*
1Co 12:21 nor **a.** the head to the feet, I have *3825*
1Co 15:4 rose **a.** the third day according *1453*
2Co 1:16 and to come **a.** out of Macedonia *3825*
2Co 2:1 not come **a.** to you in heaviness *3825*
2Co 3:1 begin **a.** to commend ourselves? *3825*
2Co 5:12 we commend not ourselves **a.** unto *3825*
2Co 5:15 which died for them, and rose **a.** *1453*
2Co 10:7 let him of himself think this **a.**, *3825*
2Co 11:16 say **a.**, Let no man think me a fool; *3825*
2Co 12:19 **A.**, think ye that we excuse *3825*
2Co 12:21 And lest, when I come **a.**, *3825*
2Co 13:2 come **a.**, I will not spare: ... *1519,3588,3825*
Ga 1:9 so say I now **a.**, if any man preach *3825*
Ga 1:17 returned **a.** unto Damascus. *3825*
Ga 2:1 went up **a.** to Jerusalem *3825*
Ga 2:18 For if I build **a.** the things which I *3825*
Ga 4:9 how turn ye **a.** to the walk *3825*
Ga 4:9 ye desire **a.** to be in bondage? *3825,509*
Ga 4:19 of whom I travail in birth **a.** *3825*
Ga 5:1 not entangled **a.** with the yoke of *3825*
Ga 5:3 For I testify **a.** to every man *3825*
Php 1:26 by my coming to you **a.**. *3825*
Php 2:28 when ye see him **a.**, ye may rejoice, .. *3825*
Php 4:4 and **a.** I say, Rejoice. *3825*
Php 4:10 care of me hath flourished **a.**; *330*
Php 4:16 ye sent once and **a.** unto my *1364*
1Th 2:18 even I Paul, once and **a.**; *1364*
1Th 3:9 can we render to God **a.** for you, *467*
1Th 4:14 Jesus died and rose **a.**, even so *450*
Tit 2:9 in all things; not answering **a.**; *483*
Phm 12 Whom I have sent **a.**: thou *375*
Heb 1:5 And **a.**, I will be to him a Father, *3825*
Heb 1:6 And **a.**, when he bringeth in the *3825*
Heb 2:13 And **a.**, I will put my trust in him *3825*
Heb 2:13 And **a.**, Behold I and the children *3825*
Heb 4:5 in this place **a.**, If they shall enter *3825*
Heb 4:7 **A.**, he limiteth a certain day, *3825*
Heb 5:12 ye have need that one teach you **a.** *3825*
Heb 6:1 not laying **a.** the foundation of *3825*
Heb 6:6 to renew them **a.** unto repentance; *3825*
Heb 10:3 there is a remembrance **a.** made *364*
Heb 10:30 And **a.**, The Lord shall judge his *3825*
Heb 11:35 their dead raised to life **a.**: *386*
Heb 13:20 that brought **a.** from the dead *321*
Jas 5:18 he prayed **a.**, and the heaven gave *3825*
1Pe 1:3 which hath begotten us **a.** unto *313*
1Pe 1:23 Being born **a.**, not of corruptible *313*
1Pe 2:23 he was reviled, reviled not **a.**; *486*
2Pe 2:20 they are **a.** entangled therein, and *3825*
2Pe 2:22 dog is turned to his own vomit **a.**; *1994*
1Jo 2:8 **A.**, a new commandment I write *3825*
Re 10:8 from heaven spake unto me **a.**, *3825*
Re 10:11 prophesy **a.** before many peoples, *3825*
Re 19:3 **a.** they said, Alleluia *1208*
Re 20:5 the rest of the dead lived not **a.** *326*

AGAINST

Ge 4:8 Cain rose up **a.** Abel his brother, 413
Ge 14:15 And he divided himself **a.** them, 5921
Ge 15:10 laid each piece one **a.** another: 7125
Ge 16:12 **a.** every man,
Ge 16:12 and every man's hand **a.**
Ge 20:6 withheld thee from sinning **a.** me:
Ge 21:16 sat her down over **a.** him a good 5048
Ge 21:16 she sat over **a.** him, and lifted up 5048
Ge 30:2 anger was kindled **a.** Rachel: and
Ge 32:25 that he prevailed not **a.** him,
Ge 34:30 gather themselves together **a.** me, 5921
Ge 37:18 near unto them, they conspired **a.** 834
Ge 39:9 this great wickedness, and sin **a.**
Ge 40:2 Pharaoh was wroth **a.** two of his 5921
Ge 40:2 **a.** the chief of the butlers, and **a.** 5921
Ge 41:36 **a.** the seven years of famine, which
Ge 42:22 unto you, saying, Do not sin **a.** the
Ge 42:36 away: all these things are **a.** 5921
Ge 43:18 he may seek occasion **a.** us, and 5921
Ge 43:25 ready the present **a.** Joseph came 5704
Ge 44:18 and let not thine anger burn **a.**
Ge 50:20 ye thought evil **a.** me; but God 5921
Ex 1:10 unto our enemies, and fight **a.**
Ex 4:14 of the Lord was kindled **a.** Moses,
Ex 7:15 stand by the river's brink **a.** he 7125
Ex 8:12 he had brought **a.** Pharaoh.
Ex 9:17 yet exaltest thou thyself **a.** my people,
Ex 10:16 **a.** the Lord your God, and **a.** you.
Ex 11:7 But **a.** any of the children of Israel
Ex 11:7 move his tongue, **a.** man or beast:
Ex 12:12 and **a.** all the gods of Egypt
Ex 14:2 the sea, over **a.** Baal-zephon: 6440
Ex 14:5 of his servants was turned **a.** 413
Ex 14:25 the Lord fighteth for them **a.**
Ex 14:27 the Egyptians fled **a.** it; 7125
Ex 15:7 overthrown them that rose up **a.** 6965
Ex 15:24 the people murmured **a.** Moses, 5921
Ex 16:2 Israel murmured **a.** Moses and 5921
Ex 16:7 heareth your murmurings **a.** the 5921
Ex 16:7 are we, that you murmur **a.** us? 5921
Ex 16:8 murmurings which ye murmur **a.** 5921
Ex 16:8 are not **a.** us, but **a.** the Lord. 5921
Ex 17:3 the people murmured **a.** Moses, 5921
Ex 19:11 be ready **a.** the third day: for the
Ex 19:15 the people, Be ready **a.** the third
Ex 20:16 not bear false witness **a.** thy
Ex 23:29 beast of the field multiply **a.** thee. 5921
Ex 23:33 land, lest they make thee sin **a.**
Ex 25:27 Over **a.** the border shall the rings 5980
Ex 25:37 they may give light over **a.** 5676,6440
Ex 26:17 set in order one **a.** another: thus 413
Ex 26:35 the candlestick over **a.** the table 5227
Ex 28:27 **a.** the other coupling thereof 5980
Ex 32:10 my wrath may wax hot **a.** them,
Ex 32:11 thy wrath wax hot **a.** thy people,
Ex 32:12 and repent of this evil **a.** thy
Ex 32:33 Whosoever hath sinned **a.** me,
Ex 37:14 Over **a.** the border were the rings, 5980
Ex 39:20 **a.** the other coupling thereof, 5980
Ex 40:24 congregation, over **a.** the table, 5227
Le 4:2 sin through ignorance **a.** any of
Le 4:2 not to be done, and shall do **a.**
Le 4:13 have done somewhat **a.** any of
Le 4:14 which they have sinned **a.** it is 5921
Le 4:22 somewhat through ignorance **a.**
Le 4:27 **a.** any of the commandments
Le 5:19 certainly trespassed **a.** the Lord.
Le 6:2 commit a trespass **a.** the Lord,
Le 17:10 blood; I will even set my face **a.**
Le 19:16 **a.** the blood of thy neighbour: 5921
Le 19:18 nor bear any grudge **a.** the
Le 20:3 I will set my face **a.** that man,
Le 20:5 **a.** that man, and **a.** his family,
Le 20:6 even set my face **a.** that soul,
Le 26:17 set my face **a.** you, and ye shall
Le 26:40 trespass which they trespassed **a.**
Nu 5:6 to do a trespass **a.** the Lord, and
Nu 5:7 give it unto him **a.** whom he
Nu 5:12 and commit a trespass **a.** him,
Nu 5:13 and there be no witness **a.** her,
Nu 5:27 done trespass **a.** her husband.
Nu 8:2 lamps shall give light over **a.** 4136,6440
Nu 8:3 therefore over **a.**...candlestick, ... 4136,6440
Nu 10:9 to war in your land **a.** the enemy 5921
Nu 10:21 did set up the tabernacle **a.** they 5704
Nu 11:18 Sanctify yourselves **a.** to morrow,
Nu 11:33 Lord was kindled **a.** the people,
Nu 12:1 Miriam and Aaron spake **a.** Moses
Nu 12:8 not afraid to speak **a.** my servant
Nu 12:9 anger of the Lord was kindled **a.** them;
Nu 13:31 be not able to go up **a.** the people; 413
Nu 14:2 Israel murmured **a.** Moses and **a.** 5921
Nu 14:9 Only rebel not ye **a.** the Lord,
Nu 14:27 congregation, which murmur **a.** 5921
Nu 14:27 Israel, which they murmur **a.** me. 5921
Nu 14:29 upward, which have murmured **a.** 5921
Nu 14:35 gathered together **a.** me: in this 5921
Nu 14:36 congregation to murmur **a.** him, 5921
Nu 16:3 gathered themselves together **a.** 5921
Nu 16:3 Moses and **a.** Aaron, and said 5921
Nu 16:11 company are gathered together **a.** 5921
Nu 16:11 what is Aaron, that ye murmur **a.** 5921
Nu 16:19 the congregation **a.** them unto 5921
Nu 16:38 these sinners **a.** their own souls,
Nu 16:41 children of Israel murmured **a.** 5921
Nu 16:41 Moses, and **a.** Aaron, saying, 5921
Nu 16:42 gathered **a.** Moses and **a.** Aaron, 5921
Nu 17:5 whereby they murmur **a.** you. 5921
Nu 17:10 be kept for a token **a.** the rebels;
Nu 20:2 together **a.** Moses and **a.** Aaron. 5921
Nu 20:18 lest I come out **a.** thee with the 7125
Nu 20:20 Edom came out **a.** him 7125
Nu 20:24 rebelled **a.** my word at the water 4775
Nu 21:1 then he fought **a.** Israel, and took
Nu 21:5 spake **a.** God, and **a.** Moses,
Nu 21:7 spoken **a.** the Lord, and **a.** thee;
Nu 21:23 out **a.** Israel into the wilderness:
Nu 21:23 to Jahaz, and fought **a.** Israel.
Nu 21:26 who had fought **a.** the former king
Nu 21:33 the king of Bashan went out **a.** 7125
Nu 22:5 they abide over **a.** me: 4136
Nu 22:22 in the way for an adversary **a.** him.
Nu 22:25 crushed Balaam's foot **a.** the wall: 413
Nu 22:34 thou stoodest in the way **a.** me: 7125
Nu 23:23 there is no enchantment **a.** Jacob,
Nu 23:23 is there any divination **a.** Israel:
Nu 24:10 And Balak's anger was kindled **a.** 413
Nu 25:3 of the Lord was kindled **a.** Israel.
Nu 25:4 before the Lord **a.** the sun, 5048
Nu 26:9 who strove **a.** Moses and **a.** Aaron 5921
Nu 26:9 when they strove **a.** the Lord: 5921
Nu 27:3 **a.** the Lord in the company 5921
Nu 27:14 ye rebelled **a.** my commandment
Nu 30:9 bound their souls, shall stand **a.** 5921
Nu 31:3 and let them go **a.** the Midianites, 5921
Nu 31:7 they warred **a.** the Midianites, as 5921
Nu 31:16 to commit trespass **a.** the Lord in
Nu 32:13 Lord's anger was kindled **a.** Israel,
Nu 32:23 ye have sinned **a.** the Lord: and
Nu 35:30 one witness shall not testify **a.**
De 1:1 in the plain over **a.** the Red sea, 4136
De 1:26 rebelled **a.** the commandment of
De 1:41 We have sinned **a.** the Lord, we
De 1:43 **a.** the commandment of the Lord,
De 1:44 came out **a.** you, and chased you, 7125
De 2:15 the hand of the Lord was **a.** them,
De 2:19 over **a.** the children of Ammon, 4136
De 2:32 Sihon came out **a.** us, he and all 7125
De 3:1 king of Bashan came out **a.** us, 7125
De 3:29 in the valley over **a.** Beth-peor. 4136
De 4:26 earth to witness **a.** you this day,
De 4:46 in the valley over **a.** Beth-peor, 4136
De 5:20 shalt thou bear false witness **a.**
De 6:15 Lord thy God be kindled **a.** thee,
De 7:4 anger of the Lord be kindled **a.**
De 8:19 I testify **a.** you this day that ye
De 9:7 have been rebellious **a.** the Lord. 5973
De 9:16 behold, ye had sinned **a.** the Lord
De 9:19 wherewith the Lord was wroth **a.** 5921
De 9:23 rebelled **a.** the commandment of
De 9:24 ye have been rebellious **a.** the Lord. 5973
De 11:17 Lord's wrath be kindled **a.** you,
De 11:30 in the champaign over **a.** Gilgal, 4136
De 15:9 eye be evil **a.** thy poor brother,
De 15:9 and he cry unto the Lord **a.** thee, 5921
De 19:11 rise up **a.** him, and smite him 5921
De 19:15 One witness shall not rise up **a.**
De 19:16 a false witness rise up **a.** any man
De 19:16 testify **a.** him that which is wrong;
De 19:18 testified falsely **a.** his brother;
De 20:1 to battle **a.** thine enemies, and 5921
De 20:3 approach this day unto battle **a.** 5921
De 20:4 to fight for you **a.** your enemies, 5973
De 20:10 a city to fight **a.** it, then proclaim 5921
De 20:12 but will make war **a.** thee, then 5973
De 20:18 ye sin **a.** the Lord your God.
De 20:19 a long time, in making war **a.** it 5921
De 20:19 thereof by forcing an ax **a.** them: 5921
De 20:20 shalt build bulwarks **a.** the city 5921
De 21:10 forth to war **a.** thine enemies, 5921
De 22:14 give occasions of speech **a.** her,
De 22:17 given occasions of speech **a.** her,
De 22:26 a man riseth **a.** his neighbour, 5921
De 23:4 they hired **a.** thee Balaam 5921
De 23:9 host goeth forth **a.** thine enemies, 5921
De 24:15 lest he cry **a.** thee unto the Lord, 5921
De 28:7 enemies that rise up **a.** thee to 5921
De 28:7 shall come out **a.** thee one way, 413
De 28:25 shalt go out one way **a.** them, 413
De 28:48 the Lord shall send **a.** thee, in
De 28:49 Lord shall bring a nation **a.** thee 5921
De 29:7 the king of Bashan, came out **a.** 7125
De 29:20 jealousy shall smoke **a.** that man,
De 29:27 anger of the Lord was kindled **a.**
De 30:19 and earth to record this day **a.**
De 31:17 my anger shall be kindled **a.** them
De 31:19 a witness for me **a.** the children
De 31:21 this song shall testify **a.** them as 6440
De 31:26 may be there for a witness **a.** thee.
De 31:27 have been rebellious **a.** the Lord; 5973
De 31:28 and earth to record **a.** them.
De 32:49 of Moab that is over **a.** Jericho; 6440

De 32:51 Because ye trespassed **a.** me
De 33:11 the loins of them that rise **a.** him,
De 34:1 Pisgah that is over **a.** Jericho 6440
De 34:6 of Moab, over **a.** Beth-peor: 4136
Jos 1:18 doth rebel **a.** thy commandment,
Jos 3:16 passed over right **a.** Jericho 5048
Jos 5:13 stood a man over **a.** him with his 5048
Jos 7:1 anger of the Lord was kindled **a.**
Jos 7:13 Sanctify yourselves **a.** to morrow:
Jos 7:20 I have sinned **a.** the Lord God
Jos 8:3 the people of war, to go up **a.** Ai:
Jos 8:4 ye shall lie in wait **a.** the city, even
Jos 8:5 when they come out **a.** us 7125
Jos 8:14 men of the city went out **a.** Israel 7125
Jos 8:14 that there were liers in ambush **a.**
Jos 8:22 issued out of the city **a.** them; 7125
Jos 8:33 over **a.**...Gerizim,...over **a.**...Ebal; 4136
Jos 9:1 over **a.** Lebanon, 4136
Jos 9:18 the congregation murmured **a.** 5921
Jos 10:5 before Gibeon, and made war **a.** it 5921
Jos 10:6 are gathered together **a.** us 413
Jos 10:21 none moved his tongue **a.** any of
Jos 10:25 to all your enemies **a.** whom ye
Jos 10:29 him, unto Libnah, and fought **a.** 5973
Jos 10:31, 34 encamped **a.** it, and fought 5921
Jos 10:31, 34 encamped...and fought **a.** it;
Jos 10:36 unto Hebron; and they fought **a.** 5921
Jos 10:38 him, to Debir; and fought **a.** it: 5921
Jos 11:5 of Merom, to fight **a.** Israel 5973
Jos 11:7 people of war with him, **a.** them 5921
Jos 11:20 should come **a.** Israel in battle, 7125
Jos 18:17 **a.** the going up of Adummim, 5227
Jos 18:18 over **a.** Arabah northward, 4136
Jos 19:47 Dan went up to fight **a.** Leshem, 5973
Jos 22:11 over **a.** the land of Canaan, 4136
Jos 22:12 at Shiloh, to go up to war **a.** them 5921
Jos 22:16 committed **a.** the God of Israel,
Jos 22:16 might rebel this day **a.** the Lord?
Jos 22:18 seeing ye rebel to day **a.** the Lord,
Jos 22:19 not **a.** the Lord, nor rebel **a.** us,
Jos 22:22 or if in transgression **a.** the Lord,
Jos 22:29 God forbid that we should rebel **a.**
Jos 22:31 this trespass **a.** the Lord:
Jos 22:33 intend to go up **a.** them in battle, 5921
Jos 23:16 anger of the Lord be kindled **a.**
Jos 24:9 Moab, arose and warred **a.** Israel,
Jos 24:11 the men of Jericho fought **a.** you,
Jos 24:22 Ye are witnesses **a.** yourselves
Jg 1:1 **a.** the Canaanites first, to fight **a.**
Jg 1:3 we may fight **a.** the Canaanites;
Jg 1:5 in Bezek: and they fought **a.** him
Jg 1:8 Judah had fought **a.** Jerusalem,
Jg 1:9 down to fight **a.** the Canaanites,
Jg 1:10 And Judah went **a.** the Canaanites 413
Jg 1:11 thence he went **a.** the inhabitants 413
Jg 1:22 they also went up **a.** Beth-el:
Jg 2:14 anger of the Lord was hot **a.** Israel,
Jg 2:15 the hand of the Lord was **a.** them
Jg 2:20 anger of the Lord was hot **a.** Israel,
Jg 3:8 anger of the Lord was hot **a.** Israel,
Jg 3:10 prevailed **a.** Chushan-rishathaim 5921
Jg 3:12 Eglon the king of Moab **a.** Israel, 5921
Jg 4:24 and prevailed **a.** Jabin the king 5921
Jg 5:14 there a root of them **a.** Amalek;
Jg 5:20 in their courses fought **a.** Sisera 5973
Jg 5:23 to the help of the Lord **a.** the
Jg 6:2 the hand of Midian prevailed **a.** 5921
Jg 6:3 east, even they came up **a.** them; 5921
Jg 6:4 And they encamped **a.** them, and 5921
Jg 6:31 Joash said unto all that stood **a.** 5921
Jg 6:32 Let Baal plead **a.** him, because he
Jg 6:39 Let not thine anger be hot **a.** me,
Jg 7:2 Israel vaunt themselves **a.** me, 5921
Jg 7:22 the Lord set every man's sword **a.**
Jg 7:24 Come down **a.** the Midianites, 7125
Jg 9:18 risen up **a.** my father's house 5921
Jg 9:31 behold, they fortify the city **a.** 5921
Jg 9:33 people that is with him come out **a.** 413
Jg 9:34 they laid wait **a.** Shechem in four 5921
Jg 9:43 he rose up **a.** them, and smote 5921
Jg 9:45 Abimelech fought **a.** the city all
Jg 9:50 encamped **a.** Thebez, and took it 413
Jg 9:52 unto the tower, and fought **a.** it,
Jg 10:7 anger of the Lord was hot **a.** Israel,
Jg 10:9 passed over Jordan to fight also **a.**
Jg 10:9 and **a.** Benjamin, and **a.** the house
Jg 10:10 Lord, saying, We have sinned **a.**
Jg 10:18 will begin to fight **a.** the children
Jg 11:4 children of Ammon made war **a.** 5973
Jg 11:5 of Ammon made war **a.** Israel, 5973
Jg 11:8 fight **a.** the children of Ammon,
Jg 11:9 again to fight **a.** the children
Jg 11:12 come **a.** me to fight in my land? 413
Jg 11:20 pitched in Jahaz, and fought **a.** 5973
Jg 11:25 **a.** Israel, or did he ever fight **a.** 5973
Jg 11:27 I have not sinned **a.** thee,
Jg 11:27 thou doest me wrong to war **a.** me:
Jg 11:32 children of Ammon to fight **a.** them;
Jg 12:1 over to fight **a.** the children of Ammon,
Jg 12:3 over **a.** the children of Ammon, 413
Jg 12:3 unto me this day, to fight **a.** me?
Jg 14:4 that he sought an occasion **a.** the
Jg 14:5 a young lion roared **a.** him 7125
Jg 15:10 Why are ye come up **a.** us? And 5921
Jg 15:14 the Philistines shouted **a.** him: 7125
Jg 16:5 what means we may prevail **a.**
Jg 18:9 Arise, that we may go up **a.** them: 5921
Jg 19:2 **a.** him, and went away from him 5921
Jg 19:10 **a.** Jebus, which is Jerusalem: 5227
Jg 20:5 the men of Gibeah rose **a.** me, 5921
Jg 20:9 Gibeah; we will go up by lot **a.** it; 5921
Jg 20:11 Israel were gathered **a.** the city, 413
Jg 20:14 to battle **a.** the children of Israel 5973
Jg 20:18 shall go up first to the battle **a.** 5973
Jg 20:19 in the morning, and encamped **a.** 5921
Jg 20:20 went out to battle **a.** Benjamin; 5973
Jg 20:20 array to fight **a.** them at Gibeah
Jg 20:23 battle **a.** the children of Benjamin 5973
Jg 20:23 And the Lord said, Go up **a.** him.) 413
Jg 20:24 Israel came near **a.** the children 413
Jg 20:25 Benjamin went forth **a.** them 7125
Jg 20:28 I yet again go out to battle **a.** 5973
Jg 20:30 Israel went up **a.** the children of 413
Jg 20:30 put themselves in array **a.** Gibeah, 413
Jg 20:31 Benjamin went out **a.** the people 7125
Jg 20:34 came **a.** Gibeah ten thousand 5048
Jg 20:43 **a.** Gibeah toward the sunrising 5227
Ru 1:13 hand of the Lord is gone out **a.** me
Ru 1:21 the Lord hath testified **a.** me,
1Sa 2:25 If one man sin **a.** another, the
1Sa 2:25 but if a man sin **a.** the Lord, who
1Sa 3:12 In that day I will perform **a.** Eli 413
1Sa 4:1 Israel went out **a.** the Philistines 7125
1Sa 4:2 put themselves in array **a.** Israel: 7125
1Sa 5:9 the hand of the Lord was **a.** the city
1Sa 7:6 We have sinned **a.** the Lord
1Sa 7:7 the Philistines went up **a.** Israel 413
1Sa 7:10 Philistines drew near to battle **a.**
1Sa 7:13 the hand of the Lord was **a.** the
1Sa 9:14 Samuel came out **a.** them, 7125
1Sa 11:1 came up, and encamped **a.** 5921
1Sa 12:3 witness **a.** me before the Lord,
1Sa 12:5 The Lord is witness **a.** you, and
1Sa 12:9 and they fought **a.** them
1Sa 12:12 of the children of Ammon came **a.** 5921
1Sa 12:14 not rebel **a.** the commandment
1Sa 12:15 but rebel **a.** the commandment
1Sa 12:15 the hand of the Lord be **a.** you,
1Sa 12:15 as it was **a.** your fathers
1Sa 12:23 that I should sin **a.** the Lord in
1Sa 14:5 northward over **a.** Michmash, 4136
1Sa 14:5 southward over **a.** Gibeah 4136
1Sa 14:20 every man's sword was **a.** his
1Sa 14:33 Behold, the people sin **a.** the Lord,
1Sa 14:34 sin not **a.** the Lord in eating with
1Sa 14:47 and fought **a.** all his enemies on
1Sa 14:47 **a.** Moab, and **a.** the children of
1Sa 14:47 **a.** Edom, and **a.** the kings of Zobah,
1Sa 14:47 and **a.** the Philistines:
1Sa 14:52 war **a.** the Philistines all the days 5921
1Sa 15:7 Shur, that is over **a.** Egypt 6440
1Sa 15:18 the Amalekites, and fight **a.** them
1Sa 17:2 battle in array **a.** the Philistines 7125
1Sa 17:9 if I prevail **a.** him, and kill him,
1Sa 17:21 army **a.** army 7125
1Sa 17:28 Eliab's anger was kindled **a.** David,
1Sa 17:33 not able to go **a.** this Philistine 413
1Sa 17:35 when he arose **a.** me, I caught him 5921
1Sa 17:55 Saul saw David go forth **a.** the 7125
1Sa 18:21 of the Philistines may be **a.** him
1Sa 19:4 the king sin **a.** his servant, **a.** David;
1Sa 19:4 because he hath not sinned **a.** thee,
1Sa 19:5 wilt thou sin **a.** innocent blood,
1Sa 20:30 Then Saul's anger was kindled **a.**
1Sa 22:8 all of you have conspired **a.** me, 5921
1Sa 22:8 son hath stirred up my servant **a.** 5921
1Sa 22:13 Why have ye conspired **a.** me, 5921
1Sa 22:13 that he should rise up **a.** me, to 413
1Sa 23:1 the Philistines fight **a.** Keilah,
1Sa 23:3 come to Keilah **a.** the armies of 413
1Sa 23:9 secretly practised mischief **a.** 5921
1Sa 23:28 pursuing after David, and went **a.** 7125
1Sa 24:6 to stretch forth mine hand **a.** him,
1Sa 24:7 suffered them not to rise **a.** Saul 413
1Sa 24:10 not put forth mine hand **a.** my
1Sa 24:11 I have not sinned **a.** thee; yet thou
1Sa 25:17 evil is determined **a.** our master, 413
1Sa 25:17 and **a.** all his household: for he is 5921
1Sa 25:20 his men came down **a.** her; 7125
1Sa 25:22, 34 light any that pisseth **a.**
1Sa 26:9 stretch forth his hand **a.** the Lord's
1Sa 26:11 I should stretch forth mine hand **a.**
1Sa 26:19 Lord have stirred thee up **a.** me,
1Sa 26:23 not stretch forth mine hand **a.** the
1Sa 27:10 David said, **A.** the south of Judah, 5921
1Sa 27:10 **a.** the south of the Jerahmeelites, 5921
1Sa 27:10 and **a.** the south of the Kenites 413
1Sa 28:15 the Philistines make war **a.** me,
1Sa 29:8 I may not go fight **a.** the enemies
1Sa 30:23 delivered...company that came **a.** 5921
1Sa 31:1 the Philistines fought **a.** Israel:
1Sa 31:3 And the battle went sore **a.** Saul, 413
2Sa 1:16 thy mouth hath testified **a.** thee,
2Sa 3:8 Am I a dog's head, which **a.** Judah
2Sa 5:23 come upon them over **a.** the 4136
2Sa 6:7 the Lord was kindled **a.** Uzzah;
2Sa 8:10 he had fought **a.** Hadadezer,
2Sa 10:9 the front of the battle was **a.** him 413
2Sa 10:9 put them in array **a.** the Syrians: 7125
2Sa 10:10 in array **a.** the children of Ammon 7125
2Sa 10:13 unto the battle **a.** the Syrians:
2Sa 10:17 set themselves in array **a.** David, 7125
2Sa 11:23 Surely the men prevailed **a.** us, 5921
2Sa 11:25 make thy battle more strong **a.** 413
2Sa 12:5 anger was greatly kindled **a.**
2Sa 12:11 I will raise up evil **a.** thee out of 5921
2Sa 12:13 I have sinned **a.** the Lord. And
2Sa 12:26 Joab fought **a.** Rabbah of the
2Sa 12:27 I have fought **a.** Rabbah, and have
2Sa 12:28 encamp **a.** the city, and take it: 5921
2Sa 12:29 and fought **a.** it, and took it
2Sa 14:7 family is risen **a.** thine handmaid, 5921
2Sa 14:13 thought such a thing **a.** the people 5921
2Sa 16:13 on the hill's side over **a.** him, 5980
2Sa 17:21 Ahithophel counselled **a.** you 5921
2Sa 18:6 people went out into the field **a.** 7125
2Sa 18:12 I not put forth mine hand **a.** the 413
2Sa 18:13 should have wrought falsehood **a.**
2Sa 18:13 wouldest have set thyself **a.** 5048
2Sa 18:28 lifted up their hand **a.** my lord
2Sa 18:31 this day of all them that rose up **a.** 5921
2Sa 18:32 all that rise **a.** thee to do thee hurt, 5921
2Sa 20:15 they cast up a bank **a.** the city, 413
2Sa 20:21 hath lifted up his hand **a.** the king,
2Sa 21:5 and that devised **a.** us that we
2Sa 21:15 and fought **a.** the Philistines: and
2Sa 22:40 rose up **a.** me hast thou subdued
2Sa 22:49 also...above them that rose up **a.**
2Sa 23:8 lift up his spear **a.** eight hundred, 5921
2Sa 23:18 up his spear **a.** three hundred, 5921
2Sa 24:1 anger of the Lord was kindled **a.**
2Sa 24:1 he moved David **a.** them to say,
2Sa 24:4 the king's word prevailed **a.** Joab, 413
2Sa 24:4 and **a.** the captains of the host 5921
2Sa 24:17 thine hand, I pray thee, be **a.** me,
2Sa 24:17 and **a.** my father's house
1Ki 2:23 have not spoken this word **a.** his
1Ki 6:5 **a.** the wall of the house he built 5921
1Ki 6:5 **a.** the walls of the house round
1Ki 6:10 And then he built chambers **a.** all 5921
1Ki 7:4 light was **a.** light in three ranks 413
1Ki 7:5 light was **a.** light in three 4136,413
1Ki 7:20 over **a.** the belly which was by 5980
1Ki 7:39 eastward over **a.** the south 4136
1Ki 8:31 any man trespass **a.** his neighbour,
1Ki 8:33 because they have sinned **a.** thee,
1Ki 8:35 rain, because they have sinned **a.**
1Ki 8:44 go out to battle **a.** their enemy, 5921
1Ki 8:46 If they sin **a.** thee, (for there is no
1Ki 8:50 people that have sinned **a.** thee,
1Ki 8:50 they have transgressed **a.** thee,

1Ki 11:26, 27 he lifted up his hand **a.** the king
1Ki 12:19 So Israel rebelled **a.** the house of
1Ki 12:21 to fight **a.** the house of Israel, to 5973
1Ki 12:24 nor fight **a.** your brethren the 5973
1Ki 13:2 And he cried **a.** the altar in the 5921
1Ki 13:4 of God, which had cried **a.** the 5921
1Ki 13:4 hand, which he put forth **a.** him, 5921
1Ki 13:32 cried by the word of the Lord **a.** 5921
1Ki 13:32 and **a.** all the houses of the high 5921
1Ki 14:10 Jeroboam him that pisseth **a.**
1Ki 14:25 of Egypt came up **a.** Jerusalem: 5921
1Ki 15:17 king of Israel went up **a.** Judah, 5921
1Ki 15:20 of the hosts which he had **a.** 5921
1Ki 15:27 of Issachar, conspired **a.** him; 5921
1Ki 16:1 Jehu the son of Hanani **a.** Baasha, 5921
1Ki 16:7 the word of the Lord **a.** Baasha, 413
1Ki 16:7 and **a.** his house, even for all 413
1Ki 16:9 his chariots, conspired **a.** him, 5921
1Ki 16:11 **a.** a wall, neither of his kinsfolks,
1Ki 16:12 which he spake **a.** Baasha by Jehu 413
1Ki 16:15 were encamped **a.** Gibbethon, 5921
1Ki 16:22 prevailed **a.** the people that
1Ki 20:1 besieged Samaria, and warred **a.**
1Ki 20:12 themselves in array **a.** the city. 5921
1Ki 20:22 king of Syria will come up **a.** thee. 5921
1Ki 20:23 let us fight **a.** them in the plain,
1Ki 20:25 we will fight **a.** them in the plain,
1Ki 20:26 up to Aphek, to fight **a.** Israel. 5973
1Ki 20:27 all present, and went **a.** them: 7125
1Ki 20:29 they pitched one over **a.** the other 5227
1Ki 21:10 before him, to bear witness **a.** him,
1Ki 21:13 men of Belial witnessed **a.** him,
1Ki 21:13 even **a.** Naboth, in the presence
1Ki 21:21 off from Ahab him that pisseth **a.**
1Ki 22:6 I go **a.** Ramoth-gilead to battle, 5921
1Ki 22:15 shall we go **a.** Ramoth-gilead 413
1Ki 22:32 they turned aside to fight **a.** him: 5921
1Ki 22:35 stayed up in his chariot **a.** the 5227
2Ki 1:1 Then Moab rebelled **a.** Israel
2Ki 3:5 king of Moab rebelled **a.** the king
2Ki 3:7 king of Moab hath rebelled **a.** me:
2Ki 3:7 wilt thou go with me **a.** Moab 413
2Ki 3:21 the kings were come up to fight **a.**
2Ki 3:27 was great indignation **a.** Israel: 5921
2Ki 5:7 how he seeketh a quarrel **a.** me
2Ki 6:8 king of Syria warred **a.** Israel,
2Ki 7:6 king of Israel hath hired **a.** us 5921
2Ki 8:28 the war **a.** Hazael king of Syria 5973
2Ki 8:29 Ramah, when he fought **a.** Hazael
2Ki 9:8 from Ahab him that pisseth **a.**
2Ki 9:14 son of Nimshi conspired **a.** Joram 413
2Ki 9:21 they went out **a.** Jehu, and met 7125
2Ki 10:9 I conspired **a.** my master, and 5921
2Ki 12:17 went up, and fought **a.** Gath, and 5921
2Ki 13:3 anger of the Lord was kindled **a.**
2Ki 13:12 his might wherewith he fought **a.** 5973
2Ki 14:19 they made a conspiracy **a.** him 5921
2Ki 15:10 thy son of Jabesh conspired **a.** 5921
2Ki 15:19 Pul the king of Assyria came **a.** 5921
2Ki 15:25 conspired **a.** him, and smote him 5921
2Ki 15:30 son of Elah made a conspiracy **a.** 5921
2Ki 15:37 the Lord began to send **a.** Judah
2Ki 16:7 king of Israel, which rise up **a.** 5921
2Ki 16:9 of Assyria went up **a.** Damascus 413
2Ki 16:11 made it **a.** king Ahaz came from 5704
2Ki 17:3 **A.** him came up Shalmaneser 5921
2Ki 17:7 children of Israel had sinned **a.**
2Ki 17:9 things that were not right **a.** 5921
2Ki 17:13 testified **a.** Israel, and **a.** Judah,
2Ki 17:15 which he testified **a.** them; and
2Ki 18:7 rebelled **a.** the king of Assyria,
2Ki 18:9 of Assyria came up **a.** Samaria, 5921
2Ki 18:13 come up **a.** all the fenced cities 5921
2Ki 18:17 with a great host **a.** Jerusalem.
2Ki 18:20 trust, that thou rebellest **a.** me?
2Ki 18:25 come up without the Lord **a.** this 5921
2Ki 18:25 Go up **a.** this land, and destroy it 5921
2Ki 19:8 of Assyria warring **a.** Libnah: 5921
2Ki 19:9 he is come out to fight **a.** thee:
2Ki 19:20 **a.** Sennacherib king of Assyria I 413
2Ki 19:22 and **a.** whom hast thou exalted 5921
2Ki 19:22 even **a.** the Holy One of Israel. 5921
2Ki 19:27 coming in, and thy rage **a.** me 413
2Ki 19:28 thy rage **a.** me and thy tumult 413
2Ki 19:32 with shield, nor cast a bank **a.** 5921
2Ki 21:23 servants of Amon conspired **a.** 5921
2Ki 21:24 that had conspired **a.** king Amon; 5921
2Ki 22:13 wrath of the Lord that is kindled **a.**
2Ki 22:17 my wrath shall be kindled **a.** this
2Ki 22:19 what I spake **a.** this place, 5921
2Ki 22:19 and **a.** the inhabitants thereof, 5921
2Ki 23:17 hast done **a.** the altar of Beth-el. 5921
2Ki 23:26 his anger was kindled **a.** Judah,
2Ki 23:29 went up **a.** the king of Assyria 5921
2Ki 23:29 the king Josiah went **a.** him; 7125
2Ki 24:1 he turned and rebelled **a.** him.
2Ki 24:2 sent **a.** him bands of the Chaldees,
2Ki 24:2 sent them **a.** Judah to destroy it,
2Ki 24:10 king of Babylon came **a.**
2Ki 24:11 came **a.** the city, and his servants 5921
2Ki 24:20 Zedekiah rebelled **a.** the king of
2Ki 25:1 and all his host, **a.** Jerusalem, 5921
2Ki 25:1 **a.** it; and they built forts **a.** it 5921
2Ki 25:4 the Chaldees were **a.** the city 5921
1Ch 5:11 children of Gad dwelt over **a.** 5048
1Ch 5:20 And they were helped **a.** them, 5921
1Ch 5:25 transgressed **a.** the God of their
1Ch 8:32 in Jerusalem, over **a.** them 5048
1Ch 9:38 brethren at Jerusalem, over **a.** 5048
1Ch 10:1 the Philistines fought **a.** Israel; 5921
1Ch 10:3 And the battle went sore **a.** Saul, 5921
1Ch 10:13 which he committed **a.** the Lord,
1Ch 10:13 even **a.** the word of the Lord, 5921
1Ch 11:11 up his spear **a.** three hundred 5921
1Ch 11:20 up his spear **a.** three hundred, 5921
1Ch 12:19 came with the Philistines **a.** Saul 5921
1Ch 12:21 they helped David **a.** the band 5921
1Ch 13:10 anger of the Lord was kindled **a.**
1Ch 14:8 heard of it, and went out **a.** them 6640
1Ch 14:10 Shall I go up **a.** the Philistines? 5921
1Ch 14:14 them over **a.** the mulberry trees. 4136
1Ch 18:10 he had fought **a.** Hadarezer,
1Ch 19:10 the battle was set **a.** him before 413
1Ch 19:10 put them in array **a.** the Syrians. 7125
1Ch 19:11 set themselves in array **a.** the 7125
1Ch 19:17 set the battle in array **a.** them. 413
1Ch 19:17 the battle in array **a.** the Syrians, 7125
1Ch 21:1 And Satan stood up **a.** Israel, 5921
1Ch 21:4 the king's word prevailed **a.** Joab 5921
1Ch 24:31 cast lots over **a.** their brethren 5980
1Ch 24:31 over **a.** their younger brethren. 5980
1Ch 25:8 they cast lots, ward **a.** ward, 5980
1Ch 26:12 having wards one **a.** another, 5980
1Ch 26:16 ward **a.** ward. 5980
1Ch 27:24 there fell wrath for it **a.** Israel; 5921
2Ch 4:10 east end, over **a.** the south 4136
2Ch 6:22 if a man sin **a.** his neighbour, and
2Ch 6:24 because they have sinned **a.** thee;
2Ch 6:26 rain, because they have sinned **a.**
2Ch 6:34 go out to war **a.** their enemies 5921
2Ch 6:36 If they sin **a.** thee, (for there is no
2Ch 6:39 people which have sinned **a.** thee.
2Ch 8:3 Hamath-zobah, and prevailed **a.** 5921
2Ch 9:29 of Iddo the seer **a.** Jeroboam 5921
2Ch 10:19 Israel rebelled **a.** the house of
2Ch 11:1 were warriors, to fight **a.** Israel, 5973
2Ch 11:4 shall not go up, nor fight **a.** your 5973
2Ch 11:4 returned from going **a.** Jeroboam. 413
2Ch 12:2 Shishak king of Egypt came up **a.** 5921
2Ch 12:2 they had transgressed **a.** the Lord,
2Ch 12:9 Shishak king of Egypt came up **a.** 5921
2Ch 13:3 also set the battle in array **a.** him 5973
2Ch 13:6 up, and hath rebelled **a.** his lord 5921
2Ch 13:7 have strengthened themselves **a.** 5921
2Ch 13:12 sounding trumpets to cry alarm **a.** 5921
2Ch 13:12 fight ye not **a.** the Lord God 5973
2Ch 14:9 there came out **a.** them Zerah 413
2Ch 14:10 Then Asa went out **a.** him, 6440
2Ch 14:11 thy name we go **a.** this multitude. 5921
2Ch 14:11 God; let not man prevail **a.** thee. 5973
2Ch 16:1 king of Israel came up **a.** Judah, 5921
2Ch 16:4 captains of his armies **a.** the cities 413
2Ch 17:1 strengthened himself **a.** Israel 5921
2Ch 17:10 made no war **a.** Jehoshaphat 5973
2Ch 18:22 Lord hath spoken evil **a.** thee 5921
2Ch 18:34 up in his chariot **a.** the Syrians 5227
2Ch 19:10 they trespass not **a.** the Lord,
2Ch 20:1 came **a.** Jehoshaphat to battle 5921
2Ch 20:2 cometh a great multitude **a.** thee 5921
2Ch 20:12 we have no might **a.** this great 6440
2Ch 20:12 company that cometh **a.** us; 5921
2Ch 20:16 To morrow go ye down **a.** them: 5921
2Ch 20:17 to morrow go out **a.** them: 6440
2Ch 20:22 ambushments **a.** the children of 5921
2Ch 20:22 Seir, which were come **a.** Judah;
2Ch 20:23 **a.** the inhabitants of mount Seir, 5921
2Ch 20:29 the Lord fought **a.** the enemies 5973
2Ch 20:37 prophesied **a.** Jehoshaphat, 5921
2Ch 21:16 the Lord stirred up **a.** Jehoram 5921
2Ch 22:5 king of Israel to war **a.** Hazael 5921
2Ch 22:7 went out with Jehoram **a.** Jehu 413
2Ch 24:19 the Lord; and they testified **a.**
2Ch 24:21 conspired **a.** him, and stoned him 5921
2Ch 24:23 the host of Syria came up **a.** him: 5921
2Ch 24:24 executed judgment **a.** Joash.
2Ch 24:25 own servants conspired **a.** him 5921
2Ch 24:26 are they that conspired **a.** him; 5921
2Ch 25:10 anger was greatly kindled **a.**
2Ch 25:15 anger of the Lord was kindled **a.**
2Ch 25:27 they made a conspiracy **a.** him 5921
2Ch 26:6 and warred **a.** the Philistines,
2Ch 26:7 God helped him **a.** the Philistines, 5921
2Ch 26:7 and **a.** the Arabians that dwelt 5921
2Ch 26:13 to help the king **a.** the enemy. 5921
2Ch 26:16 transgressed **a.** the Lord his God,
2Ch 27:5 the Ammonites, and prevailed **a.** 5921
2Ch 28:10 you, sins **a.** the Lord your God?
2Ch 28:12 stood up **a.** them that came from 5921
2Ch 28:13 we have offended **a.** the Lord
2Ch 28:13 great, and there is fierce wrath **a.** 5921
2Ch 28:19 and transgressed sore **a.** the Lord.
2Ch 28:22 trespass yet more **a.** the Lord.
2Ch 30:7 trespassed **a.** the Lord God of
2Ch 32:1 into Judah, and encamped **a.** the 5921
2Ch 32:2 purposed to fight **a.** Jerusalem, 5921
2Ch 32:9 he himself laid siege **a.** Lachish, 5921
2Ch 32:16 his servants spake yet more **a.** the 5921
2Ch 32:16 God, and **a.** his servant Hezekiah. 5921
2Ch 32:17 Lord God of Israel, and to speak **a.** 5921
2Ch 32:19 **a.** the God of Jerusalem, 413
2Ch 32:19 as **a.** the gods of the people 5921
2Ch 33:24 And his servants conspired **a.** him, 5921
2Ch 33:25 that had conspired **a.** king Amon; 5921
2Ch 34:27 when thou heardest his words **a.** 5921
2Ch 34:27 and **a.** the inhabitants thereof, 5921
2Ch 35:20 king of Egypt came up to fight **a.**
2Ch 35:20 and Josiah went out **a.** him 7125
2Ch 35:21 I come not **a.** thee this day, but 5921
2Ch 35:21 **a.** the house wherewith I have 413
2Ch 36:6 **A.** him came up Nebuchadnezzar 5921
2Ch 36:13 rebelled **a.** king Nebuchadnezzar,
2Ch 36:16 the wrath of the Lord arose **a.** his
Ezr 4:5 And hired counsellors **a.** them, 5921
Ezr 4:6 **a.** the inhabitants of Judah 5921
Ezr 4:8 wrote a letter **a.** Jerusalem unto 5922
Ezr 4:19 made insurrection **a.** kings, 5922
Ezr 7:23 should there be wrath **a.** the realm 5922
Ezr 8:22 help us **a.** the enemy in the way:
Ezr 8:22 wrath is **a.** all them that forsake 5921
Ezr 10:2 We have trespassed **a.** our God,
Ne 1:6 which we have sinned **a.** thee
Ne 1:7 have dealt very corruptly **a.** thee,
Ne 2:19 will ye rebel **a.** the king? 5921
Ne 3:10 even over **a.** his house 5048
Ne 3:16 over **a.** the sepulchres of David, 5048
Ne 3:19 **a.** the going up to the armoury 5048
Ne 3:23 Benjamin and Hashub over **a.** 5048
Ne 3:25 over **a.** the turning of the wall, 5048
Ne 3:26 **a.** the water gate toward the east, 5048
Ne 3:27 over **a.** the great tower that lieth 5048
Ne 3:28 every one over **a.** his house 5048
Ne 3:29 Zadok the son of Immer over **a.** 5048
Ne 3:30 Meshullam . . . over **a.** his chamber 5048
Ne 3:31 over **a.** the gate Miphkad, 5048
Ne 4:8 fight **a.** Jerusalem, and to hinder it.
Ne 4:9 a watch **a.** them day and night, 5921
Ne 5:1 wives **a.** their brethren the Jews. 413
Ne 5:7 I set a great assembly **a.** them. 5921
Ne 6:12 pronounced this prophecy **a.** me: 5921
Ne 7:3 every one to be over **a.** his house 5048
Ne 9:10 that they dealt proudly **a.** 5921
Ne 9:26 disobedient, and rebelled **a.** thee,
Ne 9:26 prophets which testified **a.** them
Ne 9:29 And testifiedst **a.** them, that thou
Ne 9:29 commandments, but sinned **a.** thy
Ne 9:30 testifiedst **a.** them by thy spirit in
Ne 9:34 wherewith thou didst testify **a.**
Ne 12:9 were over **a.** them in the watches. 5048
Ne 12:24 brethren over **a.** them, to praise 5048
Ne 12:24 ward over **a.** ward. 5980
Ne 12:37 fountain gate, which was over **a.** 5048

Book	Ref	Context	No.
Ne	12:38	that gave thanks went over **a.**	4136
Ne	13:2	but hired Balaam **a.** them, that	5921
Ne	13:15	sabbath day: and I testified **a.**	
Ne	13:21	Then I testified **a.** them, and said	
Ne	13:27	transgress **a.** our God in marrying	
Es	2:1	and what was decreed **a.** her	5921
Es	3:14	they should be ready **a.** that day	
Es	5:1	over **a.** the king's house:	5227
Es	5:1	over **a.** the gate of the house	5227
Es	5:9	full of indignation **a.** Mordecai	5921
Es	6:13	thou shalt not prevail **a.** him, but	
Es	7:7	determined **a.** him by the king	413
Es	8:3	that he had devised **a.** the Jews	5921
Es	8:13	Jews should be ready **a.** that day	
Es	9:24	devised **a.** the Jews to destroy	5921
Es	9:25	which he devised **a.** the Jews,	5921
Job	2:3	although thou movedst me **a.** him,	
Job	6:4	do set themselves in array **a.** me	
Job	7:20	why hast thou set me as a mark **a.**	
Job	8:4	If thy children have sinned **a.** him,	
Job	9:4	hath hardened himself **a.** him,	413
Job	10:17	renewest thy witnesses **a.** me,	5048
Job	10:17	changes and war are **a.** mine	5973
Job	11:5	speak, and open his lips **a.** thee;	5973
Job	13:26	thou writest bitter things **a.** me,	5921
Job	14:20	Thou prevailest for ever **a.** him,	
Job	15:6	yea, thine own lips testify **a.** thee	
Job	15:13	that thou turnest thy spirit **a.** God,	413
Job	15:24	they shall prevail **a.** him, as a king	
Job	15:25	he stretcheth out his hand **a.** God,	413
Job	15:25	strengtheneth himself **a.** the	413
Job	16:4	I could heap up words **a.** you, and	5921
Job	16:8	wrinkles, which is a witness **a.** me:	
Job	16:10	gathered themselves together **a.**	5921
Job	17:8	innocent shall stir up himself **a.**	5921
Job	18:9	the robber shall prevail **a.** him	5921
Job	19:5	ye will magnify yourselves **a.**	5921
Job	19:5	and plead **a.** me my reproach:	5921
Job	19:11	hath also kindled his wrath **a.** me,	5921
Job	19:12	and raise up their way **a.** me, and	5921
Job	19:18	I arose, and they spake **a.** me	
Job	19:19	they whom I loved are turned **a.** me	
Job	20:27	and the earth shall rise up **a.** him	
Job	21:27	ye wrongfully imagine **a.** me	5921
Job	23:6	**a.** me with his great power?	5978
Job	24:13	They are of those that rebel **a.** the	
Job	27:7	riseth up **a.** me as the unrighteous	
Job	30:12	they raise up **a.** me the ways of	5921
Job	30:21	thou opposest thyself **a.** me	
Job	31:21	up my hand **a.** the fatherless,	5921
Job	31:38	If my land cry **a.** me, or that the	5921
Job	32:2	**a.** Job was his wrath kindled,	
Job	32:3	Also **a.** his three friends was his	
Job	32:14	hath not directed his words **a.** me:	413
Job	33:10	he findeth occasions **a.** me,	5921
Job	33:13	Why dost thou strive **a.** him?	413
Job	34:6	Should I lie **a.** my right? my	5921
Job	34:29	done **a.** a nation, or **a.** a man only:	5921
Job	34:37	and multiplieth his words **a.** God	
Job	35:6	sinnest, what doest thou **a.** him?	
Job	38:23	reserved **a.** the time of trouble,	
Job	38:23	**a.** the day of battle and war?	
Job	39:16	She is hardened **a.** her young	
Job	39:23	The quiver rattleth **a.** him, the	5921
Job	42:7	My wrath is kindled **a.** thee, and **a.**	
Ps	2:2	counsel together, **a.** the Lord,	5921
Ps	2:2	and **a.** his anointed, saying,	5921
Ps	3:1	many are they that rise up **a.** me	5921
Ps	3:6	have set themselves **a.** me round	5921
Ps	5:10	for they have rebelled **a.** thee	
Ps	7:13	he ordaineth his arrows **a.** the	
Ps	10:8	his eyes are privily set **a.** the poor	
Ps	13:4	say, I have prevailed **a.** him;	
Ps	15:3	up a reproach **a.** his neighbour	5921
Ps	15:5	taketh reward **a.** the innocent	5921
Ps	17:7	from those that rise up **a.** them	
Ps	18:39	under me those that rose up **a.** me	
Ps	18:48	rise up **a.** me: thou hast delivered	
Ps	21:11	For they intended evil **a.** thee:	5921
Ps	21:12	thine arrows upon thy strings **a.**	5921
Ps	27:3	host should encamp **a.** me, my	5921
Ps	27:3	though war should rise **a.** me, in	5921
Ps	27:12	false witnesses are risen up **a.** me,	
Ps	31:13	they took counsel together **a.** me,	5921
Ps	31:18	proudly and contemptuously **a.**	5921
Ps	34:16	the Lord is **a.** them that do evil,	
Ps	35:1	fight **a.** them that fight **a.** me	
Ps	35:3	way **a.** them that persecute me:	7125
Ps	35:15	gathered themselves together **a.**	5921
Ps	35:20	devise deceitful matters **a.** them	5921
Ps	35:21	mouth wide **a.** me, and said, Aha,	5921
Ps	35:26	that magnify themselves **a.** me	5921
Ps	36:11	Let not the foot of pride come **a.**	
Ps	37:1	envious **a.** the workers of iniquity	
Ps	37:12	The wicked plotteth **a.** the just,	
Ps	38:16	they magnify themselves **a.**	5921
Ps	41:4	my soul; for I have sinned **a.** thee	
Ps	41:7	hate me whisper together **a.** me:	5921
Ps	41:7	**a.** me do they devise my hurt	5921
Ps	41:9	bread, hath lifted up his heel **a.** me	5921
Ps	43:1	plead my cause **a.** an ungodly	
Ps	44:5	tread them under that rise up **a.**	
Ps	50:7	O Israel, and I will testify **a.** thee:	
Ps	50:20	Thou sittest and speakest **a.** thy	
Ps	51:4	**A.** thee, thee only, have I sinned,	
Ps	53:5	the bones of him that encampeth **a.**	
Ps	54:3	strangers are risen up **a.** me,	5921
Ps	55:12	that did magnify himself **a.** me;	5921
Ps	55:18	peace from the battle that was **a.**	
Ps	55:20	his hands **a.** such as be at peace	
Ps	56:2	for they be many that fight **a.** me,	
Ps	56:5	their thoughts are **a.** me for evil	5921
Ps	59:1	me from them that rise up **a.** me	
Ps	59:3	the mighty are gathered **a.** me;	5921
Ps	62:3	ye imagine mischief **a.** a man?	5921
Ps	65:3	Iniquities prevail **a.** me: as for	
Ps	69:12	that sit in the gate speak **a.** me;	
Ps	71:10	mine enemies speak **a.** me;	
Ps	73:9	set their mouth **a.** the heavens,	
Ps	73:15	I should offend **a.** the generation	
Ps	74:1	smoke **a.** the sheep of thy pasture?	
Ps	74:23	tumult of those that rise up **a.**	
Ps	78:17	**a.** him by provoking the most High	
Ps	78:19	Yea, they spake **a.** God; and said,	
Ps	78:21	so a fire was kindled **a.** Jacob,	
Ps	78:21	and anger also came up **a.** Israel;	
Ps	79:8	O remember not **a.** us former	
Ps	80:4	be angry **a.** the prayer of thy	
Ps	81:14	my hand **a.** their adversaries	5921
Ps	83:3	have taken crafty counsel **a.** thy	5921
Ps	83:3	consulted **a.** thy hidden ones	5921
Ps	83:5	they are confederate **a.** me,	5921
Ps	86:14	O God, the proud are risen **a.** thee:	5921
Ps	91:12	lest thou dash thy foot **a.** a stone	
Ps	92:11	the wicked that rise up **a.** me	5921
Ps	94:16	rise up for me **a.** the evildoers?	5973
Ps	94:16	or who will stand up for me **a.** the	5973
Ps	94:21	**a.** the soul of the righteous,	5921
Ps	102:8	are mad **a.** me are sworn **a.** me	
Ps	105:28	and they rebelled not **a.** his word	
Ps	106:26	he lifted up his hand **a.** them,	
Ps	106:40	the Lord kindled **a.** his people,	
Ps	107:11	they rebelled **a.** the words of God,	
Ps	109:2	the deceitful are opened **a.** me:	5921
Ps	109:2	**a.** me with a lying tongue	
Ps	109:3	and fought **a.** me without a cause	
Ps	109:20	them that speak evil **a.** my soul	5921
Ps	119:11	heart, that I might not sin **a.** thee	
Ps	119:23	also did sit and speak **a.** me:	
Ps	119:69	proud have forged a lie **a.** me:	5921
Ps	124:2	our side, when men rose up **a.** us:	5921
Ps	124:3	when their wrath was kindled **a.** us:	
Ps	129:2	yet they have not prevailed **a.** me	
Ps	137:9	thy little ones **a.** the stones	413
Ps	138:7	stretch forth thine hand **a.** the	5921
Ps	139:20	they speak **a.** thee wickedly,	
Ps	139:21	I grieved with those that rise up **a.**	
Pr	3:29	Devise not evil **a.** thy neighbour,	5921
Pr	8:36	sinneth **a.** me wrongeth his own	
Pr	14:35	his wrath is **a.** him that causeth	
Pr	17:11	messenger shall be sent **a.** him	
Pr	19:3	his heart fretteth **a.** the Lord	5921
Pr	20:2	to anger sinneth **a.** his own soul	
Pr	21:30	nor understanding nor counsel **a.**	5048
Pr	21:31	the horse is prepared **a.** the day	
Pr	24:1	Be not thou envious **a.** evil men,	
Pr	24:15	**a.** the dwelling of the righteous;	
Pr	24:28	Be not a witness **a.** thy neighbour	
Pr	25:18	false witness **a.** his neighbour	
Pr	30:31	**a.** whom there is no rising up	5973
Ec	4:12	And if one prevail **a.** him, two	
Ec	7:14	God also hath set the one over **a.**	5980
Ec	8:11	sentence **a.** an evil work is not	
Ec	9:14	great king **a.** it, and besieged it,	413
Ec	9:14	and built great bulwarks **a.** it:	5921
Ec	10:4	spirit of the ruler rise up **a.** thee,	5921
Isa	1:2	and they have rebelled **a.** me	
Isa	2:4	nation shall not lift up sword **a.**	413
Isa	3:5	shall behave himself proudly **a.**	
Isa	3:5	and the base **a.** the honourable	
Isa	3:8	and their doings are **a.** the Lord,	413
Isa	3:9	countenance doth witness **a.** them;	
Isa	5:25	the Lord kindled **a.** his people,	
Isa	5:25	stretched forth his hand **a.** them,	5921
Isa	5:30	roar **a.** them like the roaring of	5921
Isa	7:1	toward Jerusalem to war **a.** it,	5921
Isa	7:1	but could not prevail **a.** it	5921
Isa	7:5	have taken evil counsel **a.**	5921
Isa	7:6	Let us go up **a.** Judah, and vex it,	
Isa	9:11	the adversaries of Rezin **a.** him,	5921
Isa	9:21	they together shall be **a.** Judah	5921
Isa	10:6	send him **a.** an hypocritical nation,	
Isa	10:6	and **a.** the people of my wrath	5921
Isa	10:15	Shall the ax boast itself **a.** him	5921
Isa	10:15	shall the saw magnify itself **a.**	5921
Isa	10:15	if the rod should shake itself **a.**	
Isa	10:24	and shall lift up his staff **a.** thee,	5921
Isa	10:32	shake his hand **a.** the mount of	
Isa	13:17	I will stir up the Medes **a.** them,	5921
Isa	14:4	proverb **a.** the king of Babylon,	5921
Isa	14:8	no feller is come up **a.** us	5921
Isa	14:22	For I will rise up **a.** them,	5921
Isa	19:2	I will set the Egyptians **a.** the	
Isa	19:2	fight every one **a.** his brother,	
Isa	19:2	every one **a.** his neighbour; city **a.**	
Isa	19:2	city, and kingdom **a.** kingdom	
Isa	19:17	which he hath determined **a.** it	5921
Isa	20:1	fought **a.** Ashdod, and took it;	
Isa	23:8	hath taken his counsel **a.** Tyre,	5921
Isa	23:11	**a.** the merchant city, to destroy	413
Isa	25:4	terrible ones is as a storm **a.** the	
Isa	27:4	set the briers and thorns **a.** me in	
Isa	29:3	I will camp **a.** thee round about,	5921
Isa	29:3	lay siege **a.** thee with a mount,	5921
Isa	29:3	and I will raise forts **a.** thee	5921
Isa	29:7	of all the nations that fight **a.**	5921
Isa	29:7	fight **a.** her and her munition,	
Isa	29:8	be, that fight **a.** mount Zion	5921
Isa	31:2	arise **a.** the house of the evildoers,	5921
Isa	31:2	and **a.** the help of them that work	5921
Isa	31:4	shepherds is called forth **a.** him,	5921
Isa	32:6	and to utter error **a.** the Lord, to	413
Isa	36:1	**a.** all the defenced cities of Judah,	5921
Isa	36:5	trust, that thou rebellest **a.** me?	
Isa	36:10	Lord **a.** this land to destroy it?	5921
Isa	36:10	Go up **a.** this land, and destroy it	413
Isa	37:8	king of Assyria warring **a.** Libnah:	5921
Isa	37:21	**a.** Sennacherib king of Assyria:	413
Isa	37:23	**a.** whom hast thou exalted thy	5921
Isa	37:23	even **a.** the Holy One of Israel	413
Isa	37:28	thy coming in, and thy rage **a.** me	413
Isa	37:29	Because thy rage **a.** me, and thy	413
Isa	37:33	with shields, nor cast a bank **a.** it	5921
Isa	41:11	incensed **a.** thee shall be ashamed	
Isa	41:12	war **a.** thee shall be as nothing,	
Isa	42:13	he shall prevail **a.** his enemies	5921
Isa	42:24	Lord, he **a.** whom we have sinned?	
Isa	43:27	teachers have transgressed **a.** me	
Isa	45:24	incensed **a.** him shall be ashamed	
Isa	54:15	**a.** thee shall fall for thy sake	5921
Isa	54:17	is formed **a.** thee shall prosper;	5921
Isa	54:17	every tongue that shall rise **a.** thee	
Isa	57:4	**A.** whom do ye sport yourselves?	5921
Isa	57:4	**a.** whom make ye a wide mouth,	5921
Isa	59:12	and our sins testify **a.** us: for	
Isa	59:13	and lying **a.** the Lord,	
Isa	59:19	shall lift up a standard **a.** him	
Isa	63:10	enemy, and he fought **a.** them	
Isa	66:24	transgressed **a.** me: for their	
Jer	1:15	and **a.** all the walls thereof round	5921
Jer	1:15	and **a.** all the cities of Judah	5921
Jer	1:16	my judgments **a.** them touching	5921
Jer	1:18	brasen walls **a.** the whole land,	5921
Jer	1:18	**a.** the kings of Judah,	
Jer	1:18	**a.** the princes	
Jer	1:18	**a.** the priests thereof, and **a.** the	
Jer	1:19	And they shall fight **a.** thee; but	413
Jer	1:19	not prevail **a.** thee; for I am with	
Jer	2:8	pastors also trangressed **a.** me,	
Jer	2:29	ye all have transgressed **a.** me,	
Jer	3:13	thou hast transgressed **a.** the Lord	

Jer 3:25 have sinned **a.** the Lord our God,
Jer 4:12 also will I give sentence **a.** them.
Jer 4:16 **a.** Jerusalem, that watchers come 5921
Jer 4:16 their voice **a.** the cities of Judah 5921
Jer 4:17 field, are they **a.** her round about; 5921
Jer 4:17 she hath been rebellious **a.** me,
Jer 5:11 dealt very treacherously **a.** me,
Jer 6:3 pitch their tents **a.** her 5921
Jer 6:4 Prepare ye war **a.** her; arise, 5921
Jer 6:6 and cast a mount **a.** Jerusalem: 5921
Jer 6:23 set in array as men for war **a.** thee, 5921
Jer 8:14 drink, because we have sinned **a.**
Jer 8:18 I would comfort myself **a.** sorrow,
Jer 11:17 hath pronounced evil **a.** thee, 5921
Jer 11:17 they have done **a.** themselves
Jer 11:19 they have devised devices **a.** me, 5921
Jer 12:8 it crieth out **a.** me: therefore 5921
Jer 12:9 the birds round about are **a.** her; 5921
Jer 12:14 Lord **a.** all mine evil neighbours, 5921
Jer 13:14 I will dash them one **a.** another, 413
Jer 14:7 though our iniquities testify **a.** us,
Jer 14:7 are many; we have sinned **a.** thee.
Jer 14:20 for we have sinned **a.** thee.
Jer 15:6 will I stretch out my hand **a.** thee, 5921
Jer 15:8 brought upon them **a.** the mother 5921
Jer 15:20 and they shall fight **a.** thee, 413
Jer 15:20 they shall not prevail **a.** thee:
Jer 16:10 pronounced all this great evil **a.** 5921
Jer 16:10 committed **a.** the Lord our God?
Jer 18:8 If that nation, **a.** whom I have 5921
Jer 18:11 **a.** you, and devise a device **a.** you: 5921
Jer 18:18 let us devise devices **a.** Jeremiah; 5921
Jer 18:23 all their counsel **a.** me to slay me: 5921
Jer 19:15 evil that I have pronounced **a.** it, 5921
Jer 20:10 and we shall prevail **a.** him,
Jer 21:2 king of Babylon maketh war **a.** 5921
Jer 21:4 fight **a.** the king of Babylon, and **a.**
Jer 21:5 myself will fight **a.** you with an
Jer 21:10 I have set my face **a.** this city for
Jer 21:13 I am **a.** thee, O inhabitant of the 413
Jer 21:13 Who shall come down **a.** us? or 5921
Jer 22:7 I will prepare destroyers **a.** thee, 5921
Jer 23:2 saith the Lord God of Israel **a.** the 5921
Jer 23:30 **a.** the prophets, saith the Lord. 5921
Jer 23:31 Behold, I am **a.** the prophets, saith 5921
Jer 23:32 **a.** them that prophesy false 5921
Jer 25:9 my servant, and will bring them **a.** 5921
Jer 25:9 and **a.** the inhabitants thereof, 5921
Jer 25:9 **a.** all these nations round about, 5921
Jer 25:13 which I have pronounced **a.** it, 5921
Jer 25:13 Jeremiah hath prophesied **a.** all 5921
Jer 25:30 prophesy thou **a.** them all these 413
Jer 25:30 **a.** all the inhabitants of the earth. 413
Jer 26:9 were gathered **a.** Jeremiah 413
Jer 26:11 to die: for he hath prophesied **a.** 413
Jer 26:12 sent me to prophesy **a.** this house 413
Jer 26:12 and **a.** this city all the words that 413
Jer 26:13 that he hath pronounced **a.** you 5921
Jer 26:19 he had pronounced **a.** them? 5921
Jer 26:19 we procure great evil **a.** our souls. 5921
Jer 26:20 **a.** this city and **a.** this land 5921
Jer 27:13 Lord hath spoken **a.** the nation 413
Jer 28:8 **a.** many countries, 413
Jer 28:8 and **a.** great kingdoms, 5921
Jer 28:16 hast taught rebellion **a.** the Lord 413
Jer 29:32 taught rebellion **a.** the Lord. 5921
Jer 31:20 since I spake **a.** him, I do
Jer 31:39 over **a.** it upon the hill Gareb, 5048
Jer 32:24 of the Chaldeans, that fight **a.** it, 5921
Jer 32:29 Chaldeans, that fight **a.** this city, 5921
Jer 33:8 whereby they have sinned **a.** me;
Jer 33:8 they have transgressed **a.** me.
Jer 34:1,7 fought **a.** Jerusalem, and **a.** all 5921
Jer 34:7 **a.** Lachish, and **a.** Azekah: for 413
Jer 34:22 they shall fight **a.** it, and take it, 5921
Jer 35:17 that I have pronounced **a.** them: 5921
Jer 36:2 have spoken unto thee **a.** Israel, 5921
Jer 36:2 **a.** Judah, and **a.** all the nations, 5921
Jer 36:7 the Lord hath pronounced **a.** this 413
Jer 36:31 that I have pronounced **a.** them; 413
Jer 37:8 come again, and fight **a.** this 5921
Jer 37:10 of the Chaldeans that fight **a.** you,
Jer 37:18 have I offended **a.** thee, or **a.** thy
Jer 37:18 or **a.** this people, that ye have put
Jer 37:19 Babylon shall not come **a.** you, 5921
Jer 37:19 nor **a.** this land? 5921
Jer 38:5 he that can do any thing **a.** you
Jer 38:22 on, and have prevailed **a.** thee:
Jer 39:1 and all his army **a.** Jerusalem, 413
Jer 40:3 because ye have sinned **a.** the Lord,
Jer 43:3 son of Neriah setteth thee on **a.** us,
Jer 44:7 this great evil **a.** your souls, 413
Jer 44:11 I will set my face **a.** you for evil,
Jer 44:23 because ye have sinned **a.** the Lord,
Jer 44:29 my words shall surely stand **a.** you 5921
Jer 46:1 the prophet **a.** the Gentiles; 5921
Jer 46:2 **A.** Egypt,
Jer 46:2 **a.** the army of 5921
Jer 46:12 hath stumbled **a.** the mighty,
Jer 46:22 army, and come **a.** her with axes,
Jer 47:1 the prophet **a.** the Philistines, 413
Jer 47:7 charge **a.** Ashkelon, and **a.** the 413
Jer 48:1 **A.** Moab thus saith the Lord of
Jer 48:2 they have devised evil **a.** it; 5921
Jer 48:26, 42 magnified himself **a.** the Lord 5921
Jer 49:14 ye together, and come **a.** her, 5921
Jer 49:19 **a.** the habitation of the strong: 413
Jer 49:20 Lord, that he hath taken **a.** Edom; 413
Jer 49:20 hath purposed **a.** the inhabitants 413
Jer 49:30 hath taken counsel **a.** you, 5921
Jer 49:30 hath conceived a purpose **a.** you. 5921
Jer 49:34 Jeremiah the prophet **a.** Elam 413
Jer 50:1 that the Lord spake **a.** Babylon 413
Jer 50:1 and **a.** the land of the Chaldeans 413
Jer 50:3 there cometh up a nation **a.** her, 5921
Jer 50:7 they have sinned **a.** the Lord,
Jer 50:9 come up **a.** Babylon an assembly 5921
Jer 50:9 set themselves in array **a.** her;
Jer 50:14 in array **a.** Babylon round about: 5921
Jer 50:14 for she hath sinned **a.** the Lord.
Jer 50:15 Shout **a.** her round about: she 5921
Jer 50:21 Go up **a.** the land of Merathaim, 5921
Jer 50:21 even **a.** it, 5921
Jer 50:21 and **a.** the inhabitants 413
Jer 50:24 thou hast striven **a.** the Lord.
Jer 50:26 **a.** her from the utmost border,
Jer 50:29 together the archers **a.** Babylon: 413
Jer 50:29 bend the bow, camp **a.** it round 5921
Jer 50:29 proud **a.** the Lord, **a.** the Holy One 413
Jer 50:31 I am **a.** thee, O thou most proud, 413
Jer 50:42 **a.** thee, O daughter of Babylon. 5921
Jer 50:45 that he hath taken **a.** Babylon; 413
Jer 50:45 **a.** the land of the Chaldeans: 413
Jer 51:1 raise up **a.** Babylon, 5921
Jer 51:1 and **a.** them 413
Jer 51:1 midst of them that rise up **a.** me,
Jer 51:2 they shall be **a.** her round about. 5921
Jer 51:3 **A.** him that bendeth let the 413
Jer 51:3 **a.** him that lifteth himself up 413
Jer 51:5 sin **a.** the Holy One of Israel.
Jer 51:11 for his device is **a.** Babylon, to 5921
Jer 51:12 **a.** the inhabitants of Babylon. 413
Jer 51:14 they shall lift up a shout **a.** thee. 5921
Jer 51:25 **a.** thee, O destroying mountain, 413
Jer 51:27 prepare the nations **a.** her, 5921
Jer 51:27 call together **a.** her the kingdoms 5921
Jer 51:27 appoint a captain **a.** her; cause 5921
Jer 51:28 Prepare **a.** her the nations with 5921
Jer 51:29 of the Lord shall be performed **a.** 5921
Jer 51:46 violence in the land, ruler **a.** ruler. 5921
Jer 51:60 that are written **a.** Babylon. 413
Jer 51:62 thou hast spoken **a.** this place. 413
Jer 52:3 that Zedekiah rebelled **a.** the king
Jer 52:4 **a.** Jerusalem, and pitched **a.** it, 5921
Jer 52:4 and built forts **a.** it round about. 5921
La 1:13 and it prevaileth **a.** them:
La 1:15 an assembly **a.** me to crush my 5921
La 1:18 rebelled **a.** his commandment:
La 2:3 burned **a.** Jacob like a flaming
La 2:16 opened their mouth **a.** thee: 5921
La 3:3 Surely **a.** me is he turned; he
La 3:3 turneth his hand **a.** me all the
La 3:5 He hath builded **a.** me, and 5921
La 3:46 have opened their mouths **a.** us. 5921
La 3:60 all their imaginations **a.** me.
La 3:61 all their imaginations **a.** me; 5921
La 3:62 lips of those that rose up **a.** me,
La 3:62 their device **a.** me all the day. 5921
La 5:22 us; thou art very wroth **a.** us. 5921
Eze 1:20 were lifted up over **a.** them: 5980
Eze 1:21 were lifted up over **a.** them: 5980
Eze 2:3 nation that hath rebelled **a.** me:
Eze 2:3 fathers have transgressed **a.** me,
Eze 3:8 thy face strong **a.** their faces, 5980
Eze 3:8 forehead strong **a.** their foreheads. 5980
Eze 3:13 noise of the wheels over **a.** them, 5980
Eze 4:2 lay siege **a.** it, and build a fort 5921
Eze 4:2 **a.** it, and cast a mount **a.** it; 5921
Eze 4:2 set the camp also **a.** it, and set 5921
Eze 4:2 battering rams **a.** it round 5921
Eze 4:3 and set thy face **a.** it, and it shall 413
Eze 4:3 and thou shalt lay siege **a.** it. 5921
Eze 4:7 and thou shalt prophesy **a.** it. 5921
Eze 5:8 Behold, I, even I, am **a.** thee, and 5921
Eze 6:2 of Israel, and prophesy **a.** them, 413
Eze 11:4 prophesy **a.** them, prophesy, O 5921
Eze 13:2 prophesy **a.** the prophest of Israel 413
Eze 13:8 I am **a.** you, saith the Lord God. 413
Eze 13:17 **a.** the daughters of thy people, 413
Eze 13:17 and prophesy thou **a.** them, 5921
Eze 13:20 Behold, I am **a.** your pillows, 413
Eze 14:8 And I will set my face **a.** that man, and
Eze 14:13 land sinneth **a.** me by trespassing
Eze 15:7 And I will set my face **a.** them;
Eze 15:7 Lord, when I set my face **a.** them.
Eze 16:37 gather them round about **a.** thee, 5921
Eze 16:40 also bring up a company **a.** thee, 5921
Eze 16:44 shall use this proverb **a.** thee, 5921
Eze 17:15 But he rebelled **a.** him in sending
Eze 17:20 that he hath trespassed **a.** me.
Eze 19:8 Then the nations set **a.** him on 5921
Eze 20:8 they rebelled **a.** me, and would
Eze 20:8 accomplish my anger **a.** them in
Eze 20:13 the house of Israel rebelled **a.** me
Eze 20:21 the children rebelled **a.** me:
Eze 20:21 to accomplish my anger **a.** them
Eze 20:27 have committed a trespass **a.** me.
Eze 20:38 and them that transgress **a.**
Eze 20:46 and prophesy **a.** the forest of the 413
Eze 21:2 places, and prophesy **a.** the land 413
Eze 21:3 Lord; Behold, I am **a.** thee, and 413
Eze 21:4 **a.** all flesh from the south to 413
Eze 21:15 of the sword **a.** all their gates, 5921
Eze 21:22 battering rams **a.** the gates, 5921
Eze 21:31 I will blow **a.** thee in the fire of 5921
Eze 22:3 idols **a.** herself to defile herself, 5921
Eze 23:22 I will raise up thy lovers **a.** thee, 5921
Eze 23:22 bring them **a.** thee on every side; 5921
Eze 23:24 shall come **a.** thee with chariots, 5921
Eze 23:24 of people, which shall set **a.** thee 5921
Eze 23:25 And I will set my jealousy **a.** thee,
Eze 24:2 set himself **a.** Jerusalem this 413
Eze 25:2 set my face **a.** the Ammonites, 413
Eze 25:2 and prophesy **a.** them; 5921
Eze 25:3 thou saidst, Aha, **a.** my sanctuary, 413
Eze 25:3 **a.** the land of Israel, when it was 413
Eze 25:3 **a.** the house of Judah, when they 413
Eze 25:6 all thy despite **a.** the land of Israel; 413
Eze 25:12 Edom hath dealt **a.** the house of
Eze 26:2 Tyrus hath said **a.** Jerusalem, 5921
Eze 26:3 Behold, I am **a.** thee, O Tyrus, 5921
Eze 26:3 many nations to come up **a.** thee, 5921
Eze 26:8 and he shall make a fort **a.** thee, 5921
Eze 26:8 a mount **a.** thee, and lift up the 5921
Eze 26:8 buckler **a.** thee. 5921
Eze 26:9 set engines of war **a.** thy walls,
Eze 27:30 their voice to be heard **a.** thee, 5921
Eze 28:7 draw their swords **a.** the beauty of 5921
Eze 28:21 set thy face **a.** Zidon, 413
Eze 28:21 and prophesy **a.** it, 5921
Eze 28:22 Behold, I am **a.** thee, O Zidon; 5921
Eze 29:2 set thy face **a.** Pharaoh king of 5921
Eze 29:2 prophesy **a.** him, and **a.** all Egypt: 5921
Eze 29:3 I am **a.** thee, Pharaoh king of 5921
Eze 29:10 therefore I am **a.** thee, 413
Eze 29:10 and **a.** thy rivers, 413
Eze 29:18 to serve a great service **a.** Tyrus: 413
Eze 29:18 service that he had served **a.** it: 5921
Eze 29:20 labour wherewith he served **a.** it,
Eze 30:11 shall draw their swords **a.** Egypt, 5921
Eze 30:22 I am **a.** Pharaoh king of Egypt, 413
Eze 33:30 of thy people still are talking **a.**
Eze 34:2 prophesy **a.** the shepherds of 5921
Eze 34:10 I am **a.** the shepherds; and I will 413
Eze 35:2 set thy face **a.** mount Seir, 5921
Eze 35:2 and prophesy **a.** it, 5921
Eze 35:3 O mount Seir, I am **a.** thee, 413
Eze 35:3 stretch out mine hand **a.** thee, 5921
Eze 35:11 used out of thy hatred **a.** them;
Eze 35:12 spoken **a.** the mountains of Israel, 5921
Eze 35:13 mouth ye have boasted **a.** me, 5921

Book	Ref.	Context	No.
Eze	35:13	have multiplied your words a. me:	5921
Eze	36:2	the enemy hath said a. you,	5921
Eze	36:5	a. the residue of the heathen,	5921
Eze	36:5	and a. all Idumea,	5921
Eze	38:2	set thy face a. God, the land of	413
Eze	38:2	and Tubal, and prophesy a.	5921
Eze	38:3	I am a. thee, O God, the chief	413
Eze	38:8	many people, a. the mountains	5921
Eze	38:16	come up a. my people of Israel,	5921
Eze	38:16	I will bring thee a. my land,	5921
Eze	38:17	that I would bring thee a. them?	5921
Eze	38:18	shall come a. the land of Israel,	5921
Eze	38:21	sword a. him throughout all my	5921
Eze	38:21	man's sword shall be a. his brother.	
Eze	38:22	will plead a. him with pestilence	
Eze	39:1	thou son of man, prophesy a. God,	5921
Eze	39:1	the Lord God; Behold, I am a. thee,	413
Eze	39:23	because they trespassed a. me,	
Eze	39:26	they have trespassed a. me,	
Eze	40:13	and twenty cubits, door a. door.	5048
Eze	40:18	of the gates over a. the length	5980
Eze	40:23	over a. the gate toward the north,	5048
Eze	41:15	over a. the separate place which	6440
Eze	41:16	over a. the door, ceiled with wood	5048
Eze	42:1	was over a. the separate place,	5048
Eze	42:3	Over a. the twenty cubits which	5048
Eze	42:3	court, and over a. the pavement	5048
Eze	42:3	was gallery a. gallery in three	413,6440
Eze	42:7	without over a. the chambers,	5980
Eze	42:10	over a. the separate place,	6440
Eze	42:10	and over a. the building	6440
Eze	44:12	I lifted up mine hand a. them,	5921
Eze	45:6	over a. the oblation of the holy	5980
Eze	45:7	over a. one of the portions,	5980
Eze	46:9	but shall go forth over a. it.	5227
Eze	47:20	a man come over a. Hamath.	5704,5227
Eze	48:13	over a. the border of the priests	5980
Eze	48:15	a. five and twenty thousand,	5921,6440
Eze	48:18	in length over a. the oblation	5980
Eze	48:18	it shall be over a. the oblation	5980
Eze	48:21	a. the five and twenty	413,6440
Eze	48:21	a. the five and twenty	5921,6440
Eze	48:21	over a. the portions for the prince:	5980
Da	3:19	visage was changed a. Shadrach,	5922
Da	3:29	a. the God of Shadrach, Meshach,	5922
Da	5:5	over a. the candlestick upon the	6903
Da	5:6	his knees smote one a. another.	
Da	5:23	up thyself a. the Lord of heaven;	5922
Da	6:4	occasion a. Daniel concerning	
Da	6:5	find any occasion a. this Daniel,	5922
Da	6:5	find it a. him concerning the law	
Da	7:21	with the saints, and prevailed a.	
Da	7:25	great words a. the most High,	6655
Da	8:7	he was moved with choler a. him,	413
Da	8:12	given him a. the daily sacrifice	5921
Da	8:25	stand up a. the Prince of princes:	5921
Da	9:7	that they have trespassed a. thee.	
Da	9:8	because we have sinned a.	
Da	9:9	though we have rebelled a. him;	
Da	9:11	because we have sinned a. him.	
Da	9:12	which he spake a. us,	5921
Da	9:12	and a. our judges	5921
Da	11:2	stir up all a. the realm of Grecia.	
Da	11:7	and shall deal a. them, and shall	
Da	11:14	stand up a. the king of the south:	5921
Da	11:16	cometh a. him shall do according	413
Da	11:24	forecast his devices a. the strong	5921
Da	11:25	his courage a. the king of the south	5921
Da	11:25	they shall forecast devices a. him.	5921
Da	11:28	shall be a. the holy covenant;	5921
Da	11:30	of Chittim shall come a. him:	
Da	11:30	indignation a. the holy covenant:	5921
Da	11:32	do wickedly a. the covenant shall	
Da	11:36	marvellous things a. the God	5921
Da	11:40	come a. him like a whirlwind,	5921
Ho	4:7	increased, so they sinned a. me:	
Ho	5:7	dealt treacherously a. the Lord:	
Ho	6:7	they dealt treacherously a. me.	
Ho	7:13	they have transgressed a. me:	
Ho	7:13	yet they have spoken lies a. me.	5921
Ho	7:14	and wine, and they rebel a. me.	
Ho	7:15	do they imagine mischief a. me.	413
Ho	8:1	an eagle a. the house of the Lord,	5921
Ho	8:1	covenant, and trespassed a. my law.	5921
Ho	8:5	mine anger is kindled a. them:	
Ho	10:9	Gibeah a. the children of iniquity	5921
Ho	10:10	people shall be gathered a. them,	5921
Ho	13:16	for she hath rebelled a. her God:	
Joe	3:19	violence a. the children of Judah,	
Am	1:8	I will turn mine hand a. Ekron:	5921
Am	3:1	that the Lord hath spoken a. you,	5921
Am	3:1	a. the whole family which I	5921
Am	5:1	up a. you, even a lamentation,	5921
Am	5:9	strengtheneth the spoiled a. the	5921
Am	5:9	shall come a. the fortress.	5921
Am	6:14	a. you a nation, O house of Israel,	5921
Am	7:9	will rise a. the house of Jeroboam	5921
Am	7:10	Amos hath conspired a. thee in	5921
Am	7:16	sayest, Prophesy not a. Israel,	5921
Am	7:16	drop not thy word a. the house of	5921
Ob	1	and let us rise up a. her in battle.	5921
Ob	7	thee, and prevailed a. thee;	
Ob	10	For thy violence a. thy brother	
Jon	1:2	that great city, and cry a. it;	5921
Jon	1:13	and was tempestuous a. them.	5921
Mic	1:2	Lord God be witness a. you,	
Mic	2:3	a. this family do I devise an evil,	5921
Mic	2:4	shall one take up a parable a. you,	5921
Mic	3:5	they even prepare war a. him.	5921
Mic	4:3	shall not lift up a sword a. nation,	413
Mic	4:11	nations are gathered a. thee,	5921
Mic	5:1	troops: he hath laid siege a. us:	5921
Mic	5:5	raise a. him seven shepherds,	5921
Mic	6:3	have I wearied thee? testify a. me.	
Mic	7:6	daughter riseth up a. her mother,	
Mic	7:6	in law a. her mother in law:	
Mic	7:8	Rejoice not a. me, O mine enemy:	
Mic	7:9	the Lord, because I have sinned a.	
Na	1:9	do ye imagine a. the Lord?	413
Na	1:11	that imagineth evil a. the Lord,	5921
Na	2:4	one a. another in the broad ways:	
Na	2:13	I am a. thee, saith the Lord of	413
Na	3:5	Behold, I am a. thee, saith the	413
Hab	2:6	parable a. him,	5921
Hab	2:6	and a taunting proverb a.	
Hab	2:10	and hast sinned a. thy soul.	
Hab	3:8	the Lord displeased a. the rivers?	
Hab	3:8	was thine anger a. the rivers?	
Hab	3:8	was thy wrath a. the sea,	
Zep	1:16	a. the fenced cities,	5921
Zep	1:16	and a. the high towers.	5921
Zep	1:17	they have sinned a. the Lord:	
Zep	2:5	the word of the Lord is a. you;	5921
Zep	2:8	themselves a. their border.	5921
Zep	2:10	themselves a. the people	5921
Zep	2:13	stretch out his hand a. the north,	5921
Zep	3:11	thou hast transgressed a. me:	
Zec	1:12	a. which thou hast had indignation	
Zec	7:10	evil a. his brother in your heart.	
Zec	8:10	men every one a. his neighbour.	
Zec	8:17	in your hearts a. his neighbour;	
Zec	9:13	O Zion, a. thy sons, O Greece,	5921
Zec	10:3	was kindled a. the shepherds,	5921
Zec	12:2	both a. Judah	5921
Zec	12:2	and a. Jerusalem.	5921
Zec	12:3	earth be gathered together a. it.	5921
Zec	12:7	magnify themselves a. Judah.	5921
Zec	12:9	nations that come a. Jerusalem.	5921
Zec	13:7	Awake, O sword, a. my shepherd,	5921
Zec	13:7	and a. the man that is my fellow,	5921
Zec	14:2	nations a. Jerusalem to battle;	413
Zec	14:3	forth, and fight a. those nations,	
Zec	14:12	that have fought a. Jerusalem;	5921
Zec	14:13	up a. the hand of his neighbour.	5921
Zec	14:16	of all the nations which came a.	5921
Mal	1:4	The people a. whom the Lord	
Mal	2:10	every man a. his brother,	
Mal	2:14	a. whom thou hast dealt	
Mal	2:15	a. the wife of his youth.	
Mal	3:5	a swift witness a. the sorcerers,	
Mal	3:5	and a. the adulterers,	
Mal	3:5	and a. false swearers.	
Mal	3:5	and a. those that oppress	
Mal	3:13	words have been stout a. me,	5921
Mal	3:13	have we spoken so much a. thee?	5921
Mt	4:6	thou dash thy foot a. a stone.	4314
Mt	5:11	all manner of evil a. you falsely,	2596
Mt	5:23	thy brother hath aught a. thee;	2596
Mt	10:1	them power a. unclean spirits,	
Mt	10:18	a. them and the Gentiles.	
Mt	10:21	shall rise up a. their parents,	1909
Mt	10:35	a man at variance a. his father.	2596
Mt	10:35	and the daughters a. her mother,	2596
Mt	10:35	daughter in law a. her mother in	2596
Mt	12:14	held a council a. him,	2596
Mt	12:25	kingdom divided a. itself,	2596
Mt	12:25	city or house divided a. itself,	2596
Mt	12:26	he is divided a. himself;	1909
Mt	12:30	He that is not with me is a. me;	2596
Mt	12:31	the blasphemy a. the Holy Ghost	
Mt	12:32	a word a. the Son of man,	2596
Mt	12:32	speaketh a. the Holy Ghost,	2596
Mt	16:18	gates of hell shall not prevail a. it.	2729
Mt	18:15	thy brother shall trespass a. thee,	1519
Mt	18:21	how oft shall my brother sin a. me,	1519
Mt	20:11	murmured a. the goodman of the	2596
Mt	20:24	indignation a. the two brethren.	4012
Mt	21:2	Go into the village over a. you,	561
Mt	23:13	the kingdom of heaven a. men:	1715
Mt	24:7	nation shall rise a. nation,	1909
Mt	24:7	and kingdom a. kingdom:	1909
Mt	26:55	Are ye come out as a. a thief	1909
Mt	26:59	sought false witness a. Jesus,	2596
Mt	26:62	is it which these witness a. thee?	2649
Mt	27:1	took counsel a. Jesus to put him	2596
Mt	27:13	many things they witness a. thee?	
Mt	27:61	sitting over a. the sepulchre.	561
Mk	3:6	counsel with the Herodians a. him,	2596
Mk	3:24	kingdom be divided a. itself,	1909
Mk	3:25	a house be divided a. itself,	1909
Mk	3:26	if Satan rise up a. himself,	1909
Mk	3:29	shall blaspheme a. the Holy Ghost	1519
Mk	6:11	feet for a testimony a. them.	
Mk	6:19	Herodias had a quarrel a. him,	
Mk	9:40	he that is not a. us is on our part	2596
Mk	10:11	committeth adultery a. her.	1909
Mk	11:2	way into the village over a. you:	2713
Mk	11:25	if ye have aught a. any:	2596
Mk	12:12	had spoken the parable a. them:	4314
Mk	12:41	Jesus sat over a. the treasury,	2713
Mk	13:3	mount of Olives over a. the temple,	2713
Mk	13:8	nation shall rise a. nation,	1909
Mk	13:8	and kingdom a. kingdom:	1909
Mk	13:9	sake, for a testimony a. them.	
Mk	13:12	children shall rise up a. their	1909
Mk	14:5	they murmured a. her.	1690
Mk	14:48	Are ye come out, as a. a thief,	1909
Mk	14:55	sought for witness a. Jesus to put	2596
Mk	14:56	bare false witness a. him,	2596
Mk	14:57	and bare false witness a. him,	2596
Mk	14:60	is it which these witness a. thee?	
Mk	15:4	many things they witness a. thee.	
Mk	15:39	which stood over a. him,	1537, 1727
Lu	2:34	which shall be spoken a.;	483
Lu	4:11	thou dash thy foot a. a stone.	4314
Lu	5:30	murmured a. his disciples,	4314
Lu	6:7	might find an accusation a. him.	
Lu	6:49	a. which the stream did beat	4366
Lu	7:30	counsel of God a. themselves,	1519
Lu	8:26	Gadarenes, which is over a. Galilee	495
Lu	9:5	your feet for a testimony a. them.	1909
Lu	9:50	he that is not a. us is for us.	2596
Lu	10:11	on us, we do wipe off a. you:	
Lu	11:17	Every kingdom divided a. itself	1909
Lu	11:17	a house divided a. a house,	1909
Lu	11:18	Satan also be divided a. himself,	1909
Lu	11:23	he that is not with me is a. me:	2596
Lu	12:10	speak a word a. the Son of man,	1519
Lu	12:10	blasphemeth a. the Holy Ghost.	1519
Lu	12:52	three a. two, and two a. three	1909
Lu	12:53	a. the son,	1909
Lu	12:53	and the son a. the father;	1909
Lu	12:53	the mother a. the daughter,	1909
Lu	12:53	and the daughter a. the mother;	1909
Lu	12:53	mother in law a. her daughter in	1909
Lu	12:53	daughter in law a. her mother in	1909
Lu	14:31	to make war a. another king,	
Lu	14:31	to meet him that cometh a. him	1909
Lu	15:18,	21 I have sinned a. heaven,	1519
Lu	17:3	If thy brother trespass a. thee,	1519
Lu	17:4	if he trespass a. thee seven times	1519
Lu	19:30	Go ye into the village over a. you;	2713
Lu	20:19	had spoken his parable a. them.	4314
Lu	21:10	Nation shall rise a. nation,	1909
Lu	21:10	and kingdom a. kingdom:	1909
Lu	22:52	Be ye come out, as a. a thief,	1909
Lu	22:53	ye stretched forth no hands a. me:	1909
Lu	22:65	blasphemously spake they a. him.	1519
Joh	12:7	a. the day of my buring has she	1519
Joh	13:18	lifted up his heel a. me.	1519
Joh	13:29	we have need of a. the feast;	

Joh 18:29 accusation bring ye a. this man? *2596*
Joh 19:11 no power at all a. me, *2596*
Joh 19:12 himself a king speaketh a. Caesar. *483*
Ac 4:14 they could say nothing a. it. *471*
Ac 4:26 gathered together a. the Lord, *2596*
Ac 4:26 and a. his Christ. *2596*
Ac 4:27 a truth a. thy holy child Jesus, *1909*
Ac 5:39 ye be found even to fight a. God.
Ac 6:1 of the Grecians a. the Hebrews, *4314*
Ac 6:11 blasphemous words a. Moses, *1519*
Ac 6:11 and a. God.
Ac 6:13 a. this holy place, *2596*
Ac 8:1 persecution a. the church *1909*
Ac 9:1 a. the disciples of the Lord, *1519*
Ac 9:5 for thee to kick a. the pricks. *4314*
Ac 9:29 and disputed a. the Grecians: *4314*
Ac 13:45 spake a. those things which *483*
Ac 13:50 raised persecution a. Paul *1909*
Ac 13:51 dust of their feet a. them, *1909*
Ac 14:2 evil affected a. the brethren. *2596*
Ac 16:22 rose up together a. them: *2596*
Ac 18:12 insurrection with one accord a.
Ac 19:16 and prevailed a. them, *2596*
Ac 19:36 these things cannot be spoken a., *368*
Ac 19:38 have a matter a. any man, *4314*
Ac 20:15 came the next day over a. Chios; *481*
Ac 21:28 every where a. the people, *2596*
Ac 22:24 wherefore they cried so a. him. *2019*
Ac 23:9 to him, let us not fight a. God.
Ac 23:30 what they had a. him. *4314*
Ac 24:1 informed the governor a. Paul. *2596*
Ac 24:19 if they had aught a. me. *4314*
Ac 25:2 informed him a. Paul, *2596*
Ac 25:3 desired favour a. him, *2596*
Ac 25:7 grievous complaints a. Paul, *2596*
Ac 25:8 neither a. the law of the Jews, *1519*
Ac 25:8 neither a. the temple, *1519*
Ac 25:8 nor yet a. Caesar, *1519*
Ac 25:15 to have judgment a. him. *2596*
Ac 25:16 concerning the crime laid a. him.
Ac 25:18 A. whom, when the accusers *4012*
Ac 25:19 certain questions a. him of their *4314*
Ac 25:27 the crimes laid a. him. *2596*
Ac 26:10 to death, I gave my voice a. them. *2702*
Ac 26:11 being exceedingly mad a. them, *1693*
Ac 26:14 hard for thee to kick a. the pricks. *4314*
Ac 27:7 scarce were come over a. Cnidus, *2596*
Ac 27:7 under Crete, over a. Salmone; *2596*
Ac 27:14 arose a. it a tempestuous wind, *2596*
Ac 28:17 committed nothing a. the people, *1727*
Ac 28:19 when the Jews spake a. it, *483*
Ac 28:22 every where it is spoken a. *483*
Ro 1:18 from heaven a. all ungodliness *1909*
Ro 1:26 into that which is a. nature: *3844*
Ro 2:2 a. them which commit such. *1909*
Ro 2:5 wrath a. the day of wrath *1722*
Ro 4:18 Who a. hope believed in hope, *3844*
Ro 7:23 warring a. the law of my mind, *497*
Ro 8:7 carnal mind is enmity a. God: *1519*
Ro 8:31 God be for us, who can be a. us? *2596*
Ro 9:20 who art thou that repliest a. God? *470*
Ro 11:2 to God a. Israel, saying, *2596*
Ro 11:18 Boast not a. the branches. *2620*
1Co 4:6 puffed up for one a. another. *2596*
1Co 6:1 having a matter a. another, *4314*
1Co 6:18 sinneth a. his own body. *1519*
1Co 8:12 ye sin so a. the brethren, *1519*
1Co 8:12 ye sin a. Christ. *1519*
1Co 9:17 if a. my will, a dispensation *210*
2Co 10:2 I think to be bold a. some, *1909*
2Co 10:5 itself a. the knowledge of God, *2596*
2Co 13:8 we can do nothing a. the truth, *2596*
Ga 3:21 law then a. the promises of God? *2596*
Ga 5:17 the flesh lusteth a. the Spirit, *2596*
Ga 5:17 and the Spirit a. the flesh: *2596*
Ga 5:23 a. such there is no law. *2596*
Eph 6:11 able to stand a. the wiles of the *4314*
Eph 6:12 we wrestle not a. flesh and blood, *4314*
Eph 6:12 but a. principalities, a. powers, *4314*
Eph 6:12 a. the rulers of the darkness of *4314*
Eph 6:12 a. spiritual wickedness in high *4314*
Col 2:14 ordinances that was a. us, *2596*
Col 3:13 if any man have a quarrel a. any: *4314*
Col 3:19 be not bitter a. them. *4314*
1Ti 5:11 a. Christ, they will marry; *2691*
1Ti 5:19 A. an elder receive not an *2596*
1Ti 6:19 a good foundation a. the time to *1519*
2Ti 1:12 committed unto him a. that day. *1519*
Heb 12:3 contradiction of sinners a. himself, *1519*
Heb 12:4 unto blood, striving a. sin. *4314*
Jas 2:13 and mercy rejoiceth a. judgment *2620*
Jas 3:14 and lie not a. the truth. *2596*
Jas 5:3 rust of them shall be a witness a. you,
Jas 5:9 Grudge not one a. another, *2596*
1Pe 2:11 which war a. the soul; *2596*
1Pe 2:12 they speak a. you as evildoers, *1909*
1Pe 3:12 the Lord is a. them that do evil. *1909*
2Pe 2:11 accusation a. them before the *2596*
2Pe 3:7 reserved unto fire a. the day of *1519*
3Jo 10 a. us with malicious words: *5396*
Jude 9 bring a. him a railing accusation, *2018*
Jude 15 ungodly sinners have spoken a. *2596*
Re 2:4 I have somewhat a. thee, *2596*
Re 2:14 I have a few things a. thee, *2596*
Re 2:16 will fight a. them with the sword. *3326*
Re 2:20 I have a few things a. thee, *2596*
Re 11:7 shall make war a. them, *3326*
Re 12:7 his angels fought a. the dragon; *2596*
Re 13:6 his mouth is blasphemy a. God, *4314*
Re 19:19 war a. him that sat on the horse, *3326*
Re 19:19 and a. his army. *3326*

AGAR (a'-gar) See also HAGAR.
Ga 4:24 gendereth to bondage, which is A. *28*
Ga 4:25 For this A. is mount Sinai *28*

AGATE See also AGATES.
Ex 28:19 the third row a ligure, a a., and 7618
Ex 39:12 And the third row a ligure, and a., 7618
Eze 27:16 fine linen, and coral, and a. 3539

AGATES
Isa 54:12 I will make thy windows of a., 3539

AGE See also AGED; AGES.
Ge 15:15 shalt be buried in a good old a. 7872
Ge 18:11 well stricken in a.; and it ceased 3117
Ge 21:2 bare Abraham a son in his old a.,
Ge 21:7 have born him a son in his old a.
Ge 24:1 was old, and well stricken in a.: 3117
Ge 25:8 Abraham . . . died in a good old a., 7872
Ge 37:3 he was the son of his old a.:
Ge 44:20 child of his old a., a little one;
Ge 47:28 whole a. of Jacob was an hundred 3117
Ge 48:10 the eyes of Israel were dim for a., 2207
Nu 8:25 And from the a. of fifty years 1121
Jos 23:1 waxed old and stricken in a. 3117
Jos 23:2 I am old and stricken in a.: 3117
Jg 8:32 Gideon . . . died in a good old a., 7872
Ru 4:15 and a nourisher of thine old a.: 7872
1Sa 2:33 shall die in the flower of their a. 582
1Ki 14:4 eyes were set by reason of his a. 7869
1Ki 15:23 in the time of his old a. he was
1Ch 23:3 from the a. of thirty years and 1121
1Ch 23:24 from the a. of twenty years and 1121
1Ch 29:28 died in a good old a., full of days, 7872
2Ch 36:17 or him that stooped for a.: 3486
Job 5:26 come to thy grave in a full a., 3624
Job 8:8 I pray thee, of the former a., 1755
Job 11:17 And thine a. shall be clearer 2465
Job 30:2 in whom old a. was perished? 3624
Ps 39:5 mine a. is as nothing before thee: 2465
Ps 71:9 me not off in the time of old a.;
Ps 92:14 still bring forth fruit in old a.; 7872
Isa 38:12 Mine a. is departed, and is 1755
Isa 46:4 even to your old a. I am he; 2209
Zec 8:4 his staff in his hand for very a. 3117
Mk 5:42 she was of the a. of twelve years.
Lu 1:36 also conceived a son in her old a.:
Lu 2:36 was of a great a., and had lived *2250*
Lu 3:23 about thirty years of a., being (as
Lu 8:42 about twelve years of a., and she lay
Joh 9:21 we know not: he is of a.; *2244*
Joh 9:23 said his parents, He is of a.; *2244*
1Co 7:36 she pass the flower of her a., *5230*
Heb 5:14 to them that are of full a., *5046*
Heb 11:11 when she was past a., because she *2244*

AGED
2Sa 19:32 Barzillai was a very a. man, 2204
Job 12:20 away the understanding of the a. 2205
Job 15:10 the grayheaded and very a. men, 3453
Job 29:8 and the a. arose, and stood up. 2205
Job 32:9 neither do the a. understand 2205
Jer 6:11 a. with him that is full of days. 2205
Tit 2:2 That the a. men be sober, grave, *4246*
Tit 2:3 The a. women likewise, that they *4247*
Phm 9 being such an one as Paul the a., *4246*

AGEE (ag'-ee)
2Sa 23:11 him was Shammah the son of A. 89

AGES
Eph 2:7 That in the a. to come he might *165*
Eph 3:5 Which in other a. was not made *1074*
Eph 3:21 throughout all a., world without *1074*
Col 1:26 hid from a. and from generations, *165*

AGO See also AGONE.
1Sa 9:20 asses that were lost three days a., 3117
2Ki 19:25 Hast thou not heard long a. how 7350
Ezr 5:11 was builded these many years a., 6928
Isa 22:11 unto him that fashioned it long a. 7350
Isa 37:26 Hast thou not heard long a., 7350
Mt 11:21 repented long a. in sackcloth *3819*
Mk 9:21 How long is it a. since this came
Lu 10:13 they had a great while a. *3819*
Ac 10:30 And Cornelius said, Four days a. *575*
Ac 15:7 how that a good while a. God made *575*
2Co 8:10 also to be forward a year a. *575*
2Co 9:2 that Achaia was ready a year a.; *575*
2Co 12:2 in Christ above fourteen years a., *4253*

AGONE See also AGO.
1Sa 30:13 because three days a. I fell sick.

AGONY
Lu 22:44 being in an a. he prayed more *74*

AGREE See also AGREED; AGREETH.
Mt 5:25 A. with thine adversary quickly, *2132*
Mt 18:19 That if two of you shall a. on *4856*
Mt 20:13 didst not thou a. with me for a *4856*
Mk 14:59 neither so did their witness a. *2470*
Ac 15:15 a. the words of the prophets; *4856*
1Jo 5:8 blood: and these three a. in one. *1526*
Re 17:17 fulfill his will, and to a., *4160,3391,1106*

AGREED
Am 3:3 walk together, except they be a.? 3259
Mt 20:2 And when he had a. with the *4856*
Mk 14:56 their witness a. not together. *2470*
Joh 9:22 for the Jews had a. already, *4934*
Ac 5:9 How is it that ye have a. together *4856*
Ac 5:40 And to him they a.: *3982*
Ac 23:20 The Jews have a. to desire thee *4934*
Ac 28:25 they a. not among themselves, *800*

AGREEMENT
2Ki 18:31 and a. with me by a present,
Isa 28:15 with hell are we at a.; 2374
Isa 28:18 and your a. with hell shall not 2380
Isa 36:16 Assyria, Make an a. with me by
Da 11:6 king of the north to make an a.: 4339
2Co 6:16 what a. hath the temple of God *4783*

AGREETH
Mk 14:70 and thy speech a. thereto. *3662*
Lu 5:36 a. not with the old. *4856*

AGRIPPA (ag-rip'-pah)
Ac 25:13 king A. and Bernice came *67*
Ac 25:22 Then A. said unto Festus, *67*
Ac 25:23 when A. was come, *67*
Ac 25:24 And Festus said, King A., *67*
Ac 25:26 specially before thee, O king A., that *67*
Ac 26:1 Then A. said unto Paul, *67*
Ac 26:2 I think myself happy, king A. *67*
Ac 26:7 For which hope's sake, king A., *67*
Ac 26:19 Whereupon, O king A., *67*
Ac 26:27 King A., believest thou the prophets? *67*
Ac 26:28 Then A. said unto Paul, *67*
Ac 26:32 Then said A. unto Festus, *67*

AGROUND
Ac 27:41 they ran the ship a.; *2027*

AGUE
Le 26:16 consumption, and the burning a., 6920

AGUR (a'-gur)
Pr 30:1 The words of A. the son of Jakeh, 94

AH See also AHA.
Ps 35:25 A., so would we have it: let them 253
Isa 1:4 A. sinful nation, a people laden 1945
Isa 1:24 A., I will ease me of mine 1945
Jer 1:6 Then said I, A., Lord God! behold, 162
Jer 4:10 A., Lord God! surely thou hast 162
Jer 14:13 A., Lord God! behold, the prophets, 162
Jer 22:18 A. my brother! or, A. sister! 1945
Jer 22:18 saying, A. Lord! or A. his glory! 1945
Jer 32:17 A. Lord God! behold, thou hast 162

Jer 34:5 will lament thee, saying **A.** lord! 1945
Eze 4:14 Then said I, **A.** Lord God! 162
Eze 9:8 cried, and said, **A.** Lord God! 162
Eze 11:13 and said, **A.** Lord God! 162
Eze 20:49 Then said I, **A.** Lord God! 162
Eze 21:15 **a.**! it is made bright, 253
Mk 15:29 **A.**, thou that destroyest the *3758*

AHA See also AH.
Ps 35:21 said, **A.**, **a.**, our eye hath seen it. 253
Ps 40:15 that say unto me, **A.**, **a.**. 253
Ps 70:3 of their shame that say, **A.**, **a.**. 253
Isa 44:16 saith, **A.**, I am warm, 253
Eze 25:3 Because thou saidst, **A.**, against 253
Eze 26:2 **A.**, she is broken that was the gates 253
Eze 36:2 enemy hath said against you, **A.**, 253

AHAB (a'-hab) See also AHAB'S.
1Ki 16:28 and **A.** his son reigned in his stead 256
1Ki 16:29 began **A.** the son of Omri to reign 256
1Ki 16:29 and **A.** the son of Omri reigned 256
1Ki 16:30 **A.** the son of Omri did evil 256
1Ki 16:33 **A.** made a grove; and **A.** did more 256
1Ki 17:1 said into **A.**, As the Lord God of 256
1Ki 18:1 Go, shew thyself unto **A.**; and I will 256
1Ki 18:2 Elijah went to shew himself unto **A.**. 256
1Ki 18:3 **A.** called Obadiah, which was the 256
1Ki 18:5 **A.** said unto Obadiah, Go into the 256
1Ki 18:6 **A.** went one way by himself, and 256
1Ki 18:9 thy servant into the hand of **A.**,
1Ki 18:12 and so when I come and tell **A.**, 256
1Ki 18:16 So Obadiah went to meet **A.**, and 256
1Ki 18:16 and **A.** went to meet Elijah. 256
1Ki 18:17 it came to pass, when **A.** saw Elijah, 256
1Ki 18:17 that **A.** said unto him, Art thou he 256
1Ki 18:20 So **A.** sent unto all the children of 256
1Ki 18:41 Elijah said unto **A.**, Get thee up, eat 256
1Ki 18:42 So **A.** went up to eat and to drink. 256
1Ki 18:44 And he said, Go up, say unto **A.**, 256
1Ki 18:45 And **A.** rode, and went to Jezreel 256
1Ki 18:46 and ran before **A.** to the entrance 256
1Ki 19:1 **A.** told Jezebel all that Elijah had 256
1Ki 20:2 sent messengers to **A.** king of Israel 256
1Ki 20:13 there came a prophet unto **A.**. 256
1Ki 20:14 **A.** said, By whom? And he said, 256
1Ki 20:34 Then said **A.**, I will send thee away
1Ki 21:1 the palace of **A.** king of Samaria. 256
1Ki 21:2 **A.** spake unto Naboth, saying, 256
1Ki 21:3 Naboth said to **A.**, The Lord forbid 256
1Ki 21:4 **A.** came into his house heavy and 256
1Ki 21:15 Jezebel said to **A.**, Arise, take 256
1Ki 21:16 **A.** heard that Naboth was dead, 256
1Ki 21:16 that **A.** rose up 256
1Ki 21:18 go down to meet **A.** king of Israel, 256
1Ki 21:20 **A.** said to Elijah, Hast thou found 256
1Ki 21:21 and will cut off from **A.** him 256
1Ki 21:24 Him that dieth of **A.** in the city 256
1Ki 21:25 But there was none like unto **A.**, 256
1Ki 21:27 to pass, when **A.** heard those words, 256
1Ki 21:29 Seest thou how **A.** humbleth himself 256
1Ki 22:20 Lord said, Who shall persuade **A.**, 256
1Ki 22:39 Now the rest of the acts of **A.**, 256
1Ki 22:40 So **A.** slept with his fathers; 256
1Ki 22:41 the fourth year of **A.** king of Israel. 256
1Ki 22:49 said Ahaziah the son of **A.** unto 256
1Ki 22:51 Ahaziah the son of **A.** began to reign 256
2Ki 1:1 against Israel after the death of **A.**. 256
2Ki 3:1 Jehoram the son of **A.** began to reign 256
2Ki 3:5 it came to pass, when **A.** was dead, 256
2Ki 8:16 the fifth year of Joram the son of **A.** 256
2Ki 8:18 as did the house of **A.**; 256
2Ki 8:18 for the daughter of **A.** was his wife: 256
2Ki 8:25 twelfth year of Joram the son of **A.** 256
2Ki 8:27 walked in the way of the house of **A.**, 256
2Ki 8:27 as did the house of **A.**: for he was 256
2Ki 8:27 the son in law of the house of **A.** 256
2Ki 8:28 he went with Joram the son of **A.** 256
2Ki 8:29 see Joram the son of **A.** in Jezreel, 256
2Ki 9:7 thou shalt smite the house of **A.** 256
2Ki 9:8 the whole house of **A.** shall perish: 256
2Ki 9:8 and I will cut off from **A.** him 256
2Ki 9:9 I will make the house of **A.** like the 256
2Ki 9:25 I and thou rode together after **A.** 256
2Ki 9:29 year of Joram the son of **A.** 256
2Ki 10:1 **A.** had seventy sons in Samaria. 256
2Ki 10:10 spake concerning the house of **A.**: 256
2Ki 10:11 all that remained of the house of **A.** 256
2Ki 10:17 he slew all that remained unto **A.** 256
2Ki 10:18 unto them, **A.** served Baal a little; 256
2Ki 10:30 and hast done unto the house of **A.** 256
2Ki 21:3 and made a grove, as did **A.** 256
2Ki 21:13 and the plummet of the house of **A.**: 256
2Ch 18:1 and joined affinity with **A.** 256
2Ch 18:2 certain years he went down to **A.** 256
2Ch 18:2 **A.** killed sheep and oxen for him 256
2Ch 18:3 **A.** king of Israel said unto 256
2Ch 18:19 Who shall entice **A.** king of Israel,
2Ch 21:6 like as did the house of **A.**: 256
2Ch 21:6 he had the daughter of **A.** to wife: 256
2Ch 21:13 to the whoredoms of the house of **A.**, 256
2Ch 22:3 in the ways of the house of **A.**: 256
2Ch 22:4 of the Lord like the house of **A.**: 256
2Ch 22:5 went with Jehoram the son of **A.** 256
2Ch 22:6 down to see Jehoram the son of **A.** 256
2Ch 22:7 anointed to cut off the house of **A.** 256
2Ch 22:8 judgment upon the house of **A.**, 256
Jer 29:21 of **A.** the son of Kolaiah, and of 256
Jer 29:22 make thee like Zedekiah and like **A.**, 256
Mic 6:16 all the works of the house of **A.**, 256

AHAB'S (a'habs)
1Ki 21:8 So she wrote letters in **A.** name, 256
2Ki 10:1 them that brought up **A.** children, 256

AHARAH (a-har'-ah) See also AHER; AHIRAM; EHI.
1Ch 8:1 the second, and **A.** the third, 315

AHARHEL (a-har'-hel)
1Ch 4:8 families of **A.** the son of Harum, 316

AHASAI (a-ha'-sa-i)
Ne 11:13 the son Azareel, the son of **A.**, 273

AHASBAI (a-has'-ba-i)
2Sa 23:34 Eliphalet the son of **A.**, the son of 308

AHASUERUS (a-has-u-e'-rus) See also AHASUERUS'.
Ezr 4:6 in the reign of **A.**, in the beginning 325
Es 1:1 in the days of **A.**, 325
Es 1:1 (this is **A.** which reigned from India 325
Es 1:2 when the king **A.** sat on the throne 325
Es 1:9 house which belonged to king **A.**. 325
Es 1:10 in the presence of **A.** the king, 325
Es 1:15 the commandment of the king **A.** 325
Es 1:16 in all the provinces of the king **A.**. 325
Es 1:17 The king **A.** commanded Vashti 325
Es 1:19 Vashti come no more before king **A.**; 325
Es 2:1 the wrath of king **A.** was appeased, 325
Es 2:12 turn was come to go in to king **A.**, 325
Es 2:16 So Esther was taken unto king **A.** 325
Es 2:21 sought to lay hand on the king **A.**. 325
Es 3:1 After these things did king **A.** 325
Es 3:6 throughout the whole kingdom of **A.**, 325
Es 3:7 in the twelfth year of king **A.**, they 325
Es 3:8 Haman said unto king **A.**, There 325
Es 3:12 in the name of king **A.** was it 325
Es 6:2 sought to lay hand on the king **A.** 325
Es 7:5 Then the king **A.** answered and 325
Es 8:1 On that day did the king **A.** give 325
Es 8:7 Then the king **A.** said unto Esther 325
Es 8:12 day in all the provinces of king **A.**, 325
Es 9:2 all the provinces of the king **A.**, 325
Es 9:20 the provinces of the king **A.**, both 325
Es 9:30 of the kingdom of **A.**, with words 325
Es 10:1 the king **A.** laid a tribute upon the 325
Es 10:3 the Jew was next unto king **A.**, 325
Da 9:1 first year of Darius the son of **A.**, 325

AHASUERUS' (a-has-u-e'-rus)
Es 8:10 he wrote in the king **A.** name, 325

AHAVA (a-ha'-vah) See also IVA.
Ezr 8:15 the river that runneth to **A.**; 163
Ezr 8:21 a fast there, at the river of **A.**, 163
Ezr 8:31 we departed from the river of **A.** 163

AHAZ (a'-haz) See also ACHAZ.
2Ki 15:38 **A.** his son reigned in his stead. 271
2Ki 16:1 **A.** the son of Jotham king of Judah 271
2Ki 16:2 Twenty years old was **A.** when he 271
2Ki 16:5 they besieged **A.**, but could not 271
2Ki 16:7 So **A.** sent messengers to 271
2Ki 16:8 **A.** took the silver and gold that was 271
2Ki 16:10 king **A.** went to Damascus to meet 271
2Ki 16:10 king **A.** sent to Urijah the priest 271
2Ki 16:11 king **A.** had sent from Damascus: 271
2Ki 16:11 priest made it against king **A.** came 271
2Ki 16:15 king **A.** commanded Urijah the 271
2Ki 16:16 to all that king **A.** commanded. 271
2Ki 16:17 **A.** cut off the borders of the bases, 271
2Ki 16:19 rest of the acts of **A.** which he did, 271
2Ki 16:20 **A.** slept with his fathers, and was 271
2Ki 17:1 In the twelfth year of **A.** king of 271
2Ki 18:1 of **A.** king of Judah began to reign 271
2Ki 20:11 it had gone down in the dial of **A.** 271
2Ki 23:12 the top of the upper chamber of **A.**, 271
1Ch 3:13 **A.** his son, Hezekiah his son, 271
1Ch 8:35 and Melech, and Tarea, and **A.** 271
1Ch 8:36 And **A.** begat Jehoiadah; and 271
1Ch 9:41 and Melech, and Tahrea, and **A.**.
1Ch 9:42 And **A.** begat Jarah; and Jarah 271
2Ch 27:9 **A.** his son reigned in his stead. 271
2Ch 28:1 **A.** was twenty years old when he 271
2Ch 28:16 At that time did king **A.** send unto 271
2Ch 28:19 brought Judah low because of **A.** 271
2Ch 28:21 **A.** took away a portion out of the 271
2Ch 28:22 against the Lord: this is that king **A.**. 271
2Ch 28:24 **A.** gathered together the vessels of 271
2Ch 28:27 And **A.** slept with his fathers, and 271
2Ch 29:19 all the vessels, which king **A.** in his 271
Isa 1:1 in the days of Uzziah, Jotham, **A.**, 271
Isa 7:1 the days of **A.** the son of Jotham, 271
Isa 7:3 Go forth now to meet **A.**, thou, 271
Isa 7:10 the Lord spake again unto **A.**, 271
Isa 7:12 But **A.** said, I will not ask, 271
Isa 14:28 that king **A.** died was this burden. 271
Isa 38:8 is gone down in the sun dial of **A.**, 271
Ho 1:1 **A.** and Hezekiah, kings of Judah, 271
Mic 1:1 in the days of Jotham, **A.**, and 271

AHAZIAH (a-haz-i'-ah) See also AZARIAH; JEHOAHAZ.
1Ki 22:40 **A.** his son reigned in his stead. 274
1Ki 22:49 Then said **A.** the son of Ahab unto 274
1Ki 22:51 **A.** the son of Ahab began to reign 274
2Ki 1:2 And **A.** fell down through a lattice 274
2Ki 1:18 rest of the acts of **A.** which he did, 274
2Ki 8:24 and **A.** his son reigned in his stead 274
2Ki 8:25 did **A.** the son of Jehoram king of 274
2Ki 8:26 Two and twenty years old was **A.** 274
2Ki 8:29 **A.** the son of Jehoram king of Judah 274
2Ki 9:16 **A.** king of Judah was come down 274
2Ki 9:21 and **A.** king of Judah went out, 274
2Ki 9:23 his hands, and fled, and said to **A.**, 274
2Ki 9:23 There is treachery, O **A.**. 274
2Ki 9:27 when **A.** king of Judah saw this, 274
2Ki 9:29 began **A.** to reign over Judah. 274
2Ki 10:13 Jehu met with the brethren of **A.** 274
2Ki 10:13 answered, We are the brethren of **A.**; 274
2Ki 11:1 the mother of **A.** saw that her son 274
2Ki 11:2 daughter of king Joram, sister of **A.**, 274
2Ki 11:2 took Joash the son of **A.**, 274
2Ki 12:18 and **A.**, his fathers, kings of Judah, 274
2Ki 13:1 twentieth year of Joash the son of **A.** 274
2Ki 14:13 the son of Jehoash the son of **A.**, 274
1Ch 3:11 Joram his son, **A.** his son, Joash 274
2Ch 20:35 join himself with **A.** king of Israel, 274
2Ch 20:37 thou hast joined thyself with **A.**, 274
2Ch 22:1 made **A.** his youngest son king in 274
2Ch 22:1 So **A.** the son of Jehoram king of 274
2Ch 22:2 Forty and two years old was **A.** 274
2Ch 22:7 the destruction of **A.** was of God 274
2Ch 22:8 and the sons of the brethren of **A.**, 274
2Ch 22:8 that ministered to **A.**, 274
2Ch 22:9 he sought **A.**: and they caught him, 274
2Ch 22:9 So the house of **A.** had no power 274
2Ch 22:10 Athaliah the mother of **A.** saw that 274
2Ch 22:11 the king, took Joash the son of **A.**, 274
2Ch 22:11 (for she was the sister of **A.**,) hid 274

AHBAN (ah'-ban)
1Ch 2:29 and she bare him **A.**, and Molid 257

AHER (a'-hur) See also AHARAH.
1Ch 7:12 Ir, and Hushim, the sons of **A.** 313

AHI (a'-hi)
1Ch 5:15 **A.** the son of Abdiel, the son of 277
1Ch 7:34 **A.**, and Rohgah, Jehubbah, and 277

AHIAH (a-hi'-ah) See also AHIJAH.
1Sa 14:3 and **A.**, the son of Ahitub, 281
1Sa 14:18 Saul said unto **A.**, Bring hither the 281
1Ki 4:3 Elihoreph and **A.**, the sons of 281
1Ch 8:7 And Naaman, and **A.**, and Gera, 281

AHIAM (a-hi'-am)
2Sa 23:33 Shammah the Hararite, **A.** the 279
1Ch 11:35 **A.** the son of Sacar the Hararite 279

AHIAN (a-hi'-an)
1Ch 7:19 the sons of Shemidah were, **A.**, 291

AHIEZER (a-hi-e'-zer)
Nu 1:12 **A.** the son of Ammishaddai. 295
Nu 2:25 of the children of Dan shall be **A.** 295
Nu 7:66 On the tenth day **A.** the son of 295
Nu 7:71 this was the offering of **A.** the son 295
Nu 10:25 over his host was **A.** the son of 295
1Ch 12:3 The chief was **A.**, then Joash, the 295

AHIHUD (ahi'-hud)
Nu 34:27 of Ashar, **A.** the son of Shelomi 282
1Ch 8:7 them, and begat Uzza, and **A.** 284

AHIJAH (a-hi'-jah) See also AHIAH; AHIMELECH.
2Ki 11:29 **A.** the Shilonite found him in 281
2Ki 8:30 **A.** caught the new garment that 281
2Ki 12:15 which the Lord spake by **A.** the 281
2Ki 14:2 there is **A.** the prophet, which told 281
2Ki 14:4 and came to the house of **A.** 281
2Ki 14:4 But **A.** could not see; for his eyes 281
2Ki 14:5 the Lord said unto **A.**, Behold, the 281
2Ki 14:6 when **A.** heard the sound of her feet, 281
2Ki 14:18 spake by the hand of his servant **A.** 281
2Ki 15:27 Baasha the son of **A.**, of the house 281
2Ki 15:29 which he spake by his servant **A.** 281
2Ki 15:33 began Baasha the son of **A.** to reign 281
2Ki 21:22 the house of Baasha the son of **A.**, 281
2Ki 9:9 the house of Baasha the son of **A.**: 281
1Ch 2:25 Bunah, and Oren, and Ozem, and **A.** 281
1Ch 11:36 Hepher the Mecherathite, **A.** the 281
1Ch 26:20 **A.** was over the treasures of the 281
2Ch 9:29 and in the prophecy of **A.** the 281
2Ch 10:15 by the hand of **A.** the Shilonite to 281
Ne 10:26 And **A.**, Hanan, Anan, 281

AHIKAM (a-hi'-kam)
2Ki 22:12 Hilkiah the priest, and **A.** the son 296
2Ki 22:14 So Hilkiah the priest, and **A.**, and 296
2Ki 25:22 he made Gedaliah the son of **A.**, 296
2Ch 34:20 king commanded Hilkiah, and **A.** 296
Jer 26:24 the hand of **A.** the son of Shaphan 296
Jer 39:14 him unto Gedaliah the son of **A.** 296
Jer 40:5 back also to Gedaliah the son of **A.** 296
Jer 40:6 Jeremiah unto Gedaliah the son of **A.** 296
Jer 40:7 Gedaliah the son of **A.** governor 296
Jer 40:9 the son of **A.** the son of Shaphan 296
Jer 40:11 over them Gedaliah the son of **A.** 296
Jer 40:14 the son of **A.** believed them not. 296
Jer 40:16 the son of **A.** said unto Johanan the 296
Jer 41:1 came unto Gedaliah the son of **A.** 296
Jer 41:2 and smote Gedaliah the son of **A.** 296
Jer 41:6 Come to Gedaliah the son of **A.** 296
Jer 41:10 committed to Gedaliah the son of **A.**: 296
Jer 41:16, 18 had slain Gedaliah the son of **A.**, 296
Jer 43:6 left with Gedaliah the son of **A.** 296

AHILUD (a-hi'-lud)
2Sa 8:16 Jehoshaphat the son of **A.** was 286
2Sa 20:24 Jehoshaphat the son of **A.** was 286
1Ki 4:3 Jehoshaphat the son of **A.**, the 286
1Ki 4:12 Baana the son of **A.**; to him 286
1Ch 18:15 Jehoshaphat the son of **A.**, recorder. 286

AHIMAAZ (a-him'-a-az)
1Sa 14:50 was Ahinoam, the daughter of **A.**: 290
2Sa 15:27 **A.** thy son, and Jonathan the son 290
2Sa 15:36 **A.** Zadok's son, and Jonathan 290
2Sa 17:17 Jonathan and **A.** stayed by 290
2Sa 17:20 Where is **A.** and Jonathan? 290
2Sa 18:19 Then said **A.** the son of Zadok, Let 290
2Sa 18:22 Then said **A.** the son of Zadok yet 290
2Sa 18:23 **A.** ran by the way of the plain, 290
2Sa 18:27 foremost is like the running of **A.** 290
2Sa 18:28 **A.** called, and said unto the king, 290
2Sa 18:29 **A.** answered, When Joab sent the 290
1Ki 4:15 **A.** was in Naphtali; he also took 290
1Ch 6:8 begat Zadok, and Zadok begat **A.**, 290
1Ch 6:9 **A.** begat Azariah, and Azariah 290
1Ch 6:53 Zadok his son, **A.** his son. 290

AHIMAN (a-hi'-man)
Nu 13:22 where **A.**, Sheshai, and Talmai. 289
Jos 15:14 **A.**, and Talmai, the children of 289
Jg 1:10 they slew Sheshai, and **A.**, and 289
1Ch 9:17 Talmon, and **A.**, and their brethren: 289

AHIMELECH (a-him'-el-ek) See also AHIMELECH'S; ABIMELECH; AHIAH.
1Sa 21:1 came David to Nob to **A.** the priest: 288
1Sa 21:1 **A.** was afraid at the meeting of 288
1Sa 21:2 David said unto **A.** the priest, The 288
1Sa 21:8 David said unto **A.**, And is there 288
1Sa 22:9 coming to Nob, to **A.** the son of 288
1Sa 22:11 Then the king sent to call **A.** the 288
1Sa 22:14 Then **A.** answered the king, and 288
1Sa 22:16 king said, Thou shalt surely die, **A.**, 288
1Sa 22:20 one of the sons of **A.** the son of 288
1Sa 23:6 when Abiathar the son of **A.** fled 288
1Sa 26:6 answered David and said to **A.** 288
2Sa 8:17 Ahitub, and **A.**, the son of Abiathar, 288
1Ch 24:3 and **A.** of the sons of Ithamar, 288
1Ch 24:6 **A.** the son of Abiathar, and before 288
1Ch 24:31 David the king, and Zadok, and **A.**, 288
Ps 52:*title* David is come to the house of **A.** 288

AHIMELECH'S (a-him'-el-eks)
1Sa 30:7 to Abiathar the priest, **A. son,** 288

AHIMOTH (a-hi'-moth)
1Ch 6:25 sons of Elkanah; Amasai, and **A.** 287

AHINADAB (a-hin'-ad-ab)
1Ki 4:14 **A.** the son of Iddo had Mahanaim: 292

AHINOAM (a-hin'-o-am)
1Sa 14:50 the name of Saul's wife was **A.**, 293
1Sa 25:43 David also took **A.** of Jezreel; 293
1Sa 27:3 **A.** the Jezreelitess, and Abigail 293
1Sa 30:5 two wives were taken captives, **A.** 293
2Sa 2:2 **A.** the Jezreelitess, and Abigail 293
2Sa 3:2 his firstborn was Amnon, of **A.** 293
1Ch 3:1 the firstborn Amnon, of **A.** the 293

AHIO (a-hi'-o)
2Sa 6:3 and Uzzah and **A.**, the sons of 283
2Sa 6:4 and **A.** went before the ark. 283
1Ch 8:14 And **A.**, Shashak, and Jeremoth, 283
1Ch 8:31 And Gedor, and **A.**, and Zacher. 283
1Ch 9:37 And Gedor, and **A.**, and Zechariah, 283
1Ch 13:7 and Uzzah and **A.** drave the cart. 283

AHIRA (a-hi'-rah)
Nu 1:15 Of Naphtali; **A.** the son of Enan. 299
Nu 2:29 Naphtali shall be **A.** the son of Enan. 299
Nu 7:78 the twelfth day **A.** the son of Enan, 299
Nu 7:83 this was the offering of **A.** the son 299
Nu 10:27 of the children of Naphtali was **A.** 299

AHIRAM (a-hi'-rum) See also AHARAH; AHIRAMITES.
Nu 26:38 **A.**, the family of the Ahiramites: 297

AHIRAMITES (a-hi'-ram-ites)
Nu 26:38 of Ahiram, the family of the **A.**: 298

AHISAMACH (a-his'-am-ak)
Ex 31:6 with him Aholiab, the son of **A.**, 294
Ex 35:34 both he, and Aholiab, the son of **A.**, 294
Ex 38:23 with him was Aholiab, son of **A.**, 294

AHISHAHAR (a-hish'-a-har)
1Ch 7:10 Zethan, and Tharshish, and **A.** 300

AHISHAR (a-hi'-shar)
1Ki 4:6 And **A.** was over the household: 301

AHITHOPHEL (a-hith'-o-fel)
2Sa 15:12 Absalom sent for **A.** the Gilonite, 302
2Sa 15:31 **A.** is among the conspirators with 302
2Sa 15:31 the counsel of **A.** into foolishness. 302
2Sa 15:34 for me defeat the counsel of **A.** 302
2Sa 16:15 to Jerusalem, and **A.** with him. 302
2Sa 16:20 said Absalom to **A.**, Give counsel 302
2Sa 16:21 **A.** said unto Absalom, Go in unto 302
2Sa 16:23 counsel of **A.**, which he counselled 302
2Sa 16:23 so was all the counsel of **A.** 302
2Sa 17:1 **A.** said unto Absalom, Let me now 302
2Sa 17:6 **A.** hath spoken after this manner: 302
2Sa 17:7 the counsel that **A.** hath given is 302
2Sa 17:14 is better than the counsel of **A.** 302
2Sa 17:14 to defeat the good counsel of **A.**, 302
2Sa 17:15 Thus and thus did **A.** counsel 302
2Sa 17:21 hath **A.** counselled against you. 302
2Sa 17:23 when **A.** saw that his counsel was 302
2Sa 23:34 Eliam thw son of **A.** the Gilonite, 302
1Ch 27:33 **A.** was the king's counsellor: 302
1Ch 27:34 after **A.** was Jehoida the son of 302

AHITUB (a-hi'-tub)
1Sa 14:3 Ahiah, the son of **A.**, I-chabod's 285
1Sa 22:9 to Ahimelech the son of **A.** 285
1Sa 22:11 the son of **A.**, and all his father's 285
1Sa 22:12 Saul said, Hear now, thou son of **A.** 285
1Sa 22:20 the sons of Ahimelech the son of **A.**, 285
2Sa 8:17 Zadok the son of **A.**, and Ahimelech 285
1Ch 6:7 Amariah, and Amariah begat **A.**, 285
1Ch 6:8 And **A.** begat Zadok, and Zadok 285
1Ch 6:11 Amariah, and Amariah begat **A.**, 285
1Ch 6:12 **A.** begat Zadok, and Zadok begat 285
1Ch 6:52 Amariah his son, **A.** his son, 285
1Ch 9:11 **A.**, the ruler of the house of God: 285
1Ch 18:16 And Zadok the son of **A.**, and 285
Ezr 7:2 the son of Zadok, the son of **A.**, 285
Ne 11:11 the son of **A.**, was the ruler of the 285

AHLAB (ah'-lab)
Jg 1:31 of Zidon, nor of **A.**, nor of Achzib, 303

AHLAI (ah'-lahee)
1Ch 2:31 And the children of Sheshan; **A.** 304
1Ch 11:41 the Hittite, Zabad the son of **A.**, 304

AHOAH (a-ho'-ah) See also AHOHITE.
1Ch 8:4 Abishua, and Naaman, and **A.**, 265

AHOHITE (a-ho'-hite)
2Sa 23:9 Eleazar the son of Dodo the **A.** 1121,266
2Sa 23:28 Zalmon the **A.**, Maharai the 266
1Ch 11:12 Eleazar the son of Dodo, the **A.**, 266
1Ch 11:29 the Hushathite, Ilai the **A.**, 266
1Ch 27:4 the second month was Dodai an **A.**, 266

AHOLAH (a-ho'-lah)
Eze 23:4 names of them were **A.** the elder, 170
Eze 23:4 were their names; Samaria is **A.**, 170
Eze 23:5 **A.** played the harlot when she was 170
Eze 23:36 Son of man, wilt thou judge **A.** 170
Eze 23:44 so went they in unto **A.** and unto 170

AHOLIAB (a-ho'-lee-ab)
Ex 31:6 behold, I have given with him **A.**, 171
Ex 35:34 he may teach, both he, and **A.**, 171
Ex 36:1 Then wrought Bezaleel and **A.**, 171
Ex 36:2 And Moses called Bezaleel and **A.**, 171
Ex 38:23 And with him was **A.**, son of 171

AHOLIBAH (a-hol'-ib-ah)
Eze 23:4 the elder, and **A.** her sister: 172
Eze 23:4 is Aholah, and Jerusalem **A.** 172
Eze 23:11 when her sister **A.** saw this, she 172
Eze 23:22 Therefore, O **A.**, thus saith the Lord. 172
Eze 23:36 wilt thou judge Aholah and **A.**? 172
Eze 23:44 and unto **A.**, the lewd women. 172

AHOLIBAMAH (a-hol'-ib-a'-mah)
Ge 36:2 and **A.** the daughter of Anah 173
Ge 36:5 And **A.** bare Jeush, and Jaalam, 173
Ge 36:14 these were the sons of **A.**, the 173
Ge 36:18 are the sons of **A.** Esau's wife; 173
Ge 36:18 were the dukes that came of **A.** 173
Ge 36:25 and **A.** the daughter of Anah. 173
Ge 36:41 Duke **A.**, duke Elah, duke Pinon, 173
1Ch 1:52 Duke **A.**, duke Elah, duke Pinon, 173

AHUMAI (a-hoo'-mahee)
1Ch 4:2 and Jahath begat **A.**, and Lahad. 267

AHUZAM (a-hoo'-zam)
1Ch 4:6 And Naarah bare him **A.**, and 275

AHUZZATH (a-huz'-zath)
Ge 26:26 **A.** one of his friends, and Phichol 276

AI (a'-i) See also AIATH; AIJA; HAI.
Jos 7:2 sent men from Jericho to **A.**, 5857
Jos 7:2 the men went up and viewed **A.** 5857
Jos 7:3 thousand men go up and smite **A.**; 5857
Jos 7:4 and they fled before the men of **A.** 5857
Jos 7:5 men of **A.** smote of them about 5857
Jos 8:1 and arise, go up to **A.**: 5857
Jos 8:1 given into thy hand the king of **A.**, 5857
Jos 8:2 thou shalt do to **A.** and her king 5857
Jos 8:3 people of war, to go up against **A.**; 5857
Jos 8:9 and abode between Beth-el and **A.**, 5857
Jos 8:9 on the west side of **A.**: but Joshua 5857
Jos 8:10 of Israel, before the people to **A.** 5857
Jos 8:11 pitched on the north side of **A.**: 5857
Jos 8:11 was a valley between them and **A.** 5857
Jos 8:12 between Beth-el and **A.**, on the 5857
Jos 8:14 when the king of **A.** saw it, that 5857
Jos 8:16 the people that were in **A.** were 5892
Jos 8:17 there was not a man left in **A.** or 5857
Jos 8:18 that is in thy hand toward **A.**; 5857
Jos 8:20 the men of **A.** looked behind them, 5857
Jos 8:21 again, and slew the men of **A.** 5857
Jos 8:23 And the king of **A.** they took alive, 5857
Jos 8:24 slaying all the inhabitants of **A.** in 5857
Jos 8:24 all the Israelites returned unto **A.**, 5857
Jos 8:25 thousand, even all the men of **A.** 5857
Jos 8:26 destroyed all the inhabitants of **A.** 5857
Jos 8:28 And Joshua burnt **A.**, and made it 5857
Jos 8:29 the king of **A.** he hanged on a tree 5857

Jos 9:3 had done unto Jericho and to **A.**, 5857
Jos 10:1 heard how Joshua had taken **A.**, 5857
Jos 10:1 her king, so he had done to **A.** and 5857
Jos 10:2 because it was greater than **A.**, 5857
Jos 12:9 king of **A.**, which is beside Beth-el, 5857
Ezr 2:28 The men of Beth-el and **A.**, 5857
Ne 7:32 The men of Beth-el and **A.**, 5857
Jer 49:3 Howl, O Heshbon, for **A.** is spoiled: 5857

AIAH (a-i'-ah) See also AJAH.
2Sa 3:7 was Rizpah, the daughter of **A.**: 345
2Sa 21:8 sons of Rizpah the daughter of **A.**, 345
2Sa 21:10 Rizpah the daughter of **A.** took 345
2Sa 21:11 daughter of **A.**, the concubine of 345
1Ch 1:40 the sons of Zibeon; **A.**, and Anah 345

AIATH (a-i'-ath) See also AI.
Isa 10:28 He is come to **A.**, he is passed to 5857

AIDED
Jg 9:24 which **a.** him in the killing 2388,3027

AIJA (a-i'-jah) See also AI.
Ne 11:31 Geba dwelt at Michmash, and **A.**, 5857

AIJALON (a-ij-el-on) See also AJALON.
Jos 21:24 **A.** with her suburbs, Gath-rimmon 357
Jg 1:35 would dwell in mount Heres in **A.**, 357
Jg 12:12 was buried in **A.** in the country of 357
1Sa 14:31 that day from Michmash to **A.**: 357
1Ch 6:69 And **A.** with her suburbs, and 357
1Ch 8:13 the fathers of the inhabitants of **A.**, 357
2Ch 11:10 And Zorah, and **A.**, and Hebron, 357

AIJELETH (a-ii'-el-eth)
Ps 22:*title* chief Musician upon **A.** Shahar, 365

AILED
Ps 114:5 What **a.** thee, O thou sea, that

AILETH
Ge 21:17 said unto her, What **a.** thee, Hagar?
Jg 18:23 said unto Micah, What **a.** thee,
Jg 18:24 ye say unto me, What **a.** thee?
1Sa 11:5 What **a.** the people that they weep?
2Sa 14:5 king said unto her, What **a.** thee?
2Ki 6:28 king said unto her, What **a.** thee
Isa 22:1 What **a.** thee now, that thou art

AIN (a'-in) See also EN.
Nu 34:11 to Riblah, on the east side of **A.**; 5871
Jos 15:32 **A.**, and Rimmon: all the cities are 5871
Jos 19:7 **A.**, Remmon, and Ether, and 5871
Jos 21:16 **A.** with her suburbs, and Juttah 5871
1Ch 4:32 their villages were, Etam, and **A.** 5871
Ps 119:12 *title* [ע] **A.**

AIR
Ge 1:26, 28 the fowl of the **a.**, and over 8064
Ge 1:30 every fowl of the **a.**, and to every 8064
Ge 2:19 the field, and every fowl of the **a.**; 8064
Ge 2:20 gave names . . . to the fowl of the **a.**, 8064
Ge 6:7 fowls of the **a.**; for it repenteth me 8064
Ge 7:3 Of fowls also of the **a.** by sevens, 8064
Ge 9:2 upon every fowl of the **a.**, 8064
De 4:17 winged fowl that flieth in the **a.**, 8064
De 28:26 all fowls of the **a.**, and unto the 8064
1Sa 17:44 thy flesh unto the fowls of the **a.**, 8064
1Sa 17:46 carcases . . . unto the fowls of the **a.**, 8064
2Sa 21:10 the birds of the **a.** to rest on them 8064
1Ki 14:11 shall the fowls of the **a.** eat: 8064
1Ki 16:4 shall the fowls of the **a.** eat. 8064
1Ki 21:24 field shall the fowls of the **a.** eat. 8064
Job 12:7 fowls of the **a.**, and they shall tell 8064
Job 28:21 kept close from the fowls of the **a.** 8064
Job 41:16 no **a.** can come between them. 7307
Ps 8:8 The fowls of the **a.**, and the fish of 8064
Pr 30:19 The way of an eagle in the **a.**; 8064
Ec 10:20 bird of the **a.** shall carry the voice, 8064
Mt 6:26 Behold the fowls of the **a.**: *3772*
Mt 8:20 the birds of the **a.** have nests; *3772*
Mt 13:32 birds of the a. come and lodge in *3772*
Mk 4:4 the fowls of the a. came and *3772*
Mk 4:32 fowls of the a. may lodge under *3772*
Lu 8:5 the fowls of the a. devoured it. *3772*
Lu 9:58 and birds of the a. have nests; *3772*
Lu 13:19 the fowls of the a. lodged in the *3772*
Ac 10:12 things, and fowls of the **a.** *3772*
Ac 11:6 and fowls of the **a.** *3772*
Ac 22:23 clothes, and threw dust into the **a.**, *109*
1Co 9:26 not as one that beateth the **a.**: *109*
1Co 14:9 for ye shall speak into the **a.** *109*
Eph 2:2 prince of the power of the **a.**, *109*
1Th 4:17 to meet the Lord in the **a.**: and *109*
Re 9:2 the sun and the **a.** were darkened *109*
Re 16:17 poured out his vial into the **a.**; *109*

AJAH (a'-jah) See also AIAH.
Ge 36:24 children of Zibeon; both **A.**, and 345

AJALON (aj'-a-lon) See also AIJALON.
Jos 10:12 thou, Moon, in the valley of **A.** 357
Jos 19:42 Shaalabbin, and **A.**, and Jethlah, 357
2Ch 28:18 had taken Beth-shemesh, and **A.**, 357

AKAN (a'-kan) See also JAAKAN; JAKAN.
Ge 36:27 Bilhan, and Zaavan, and **A.** 6130

AKKUB (ak'-kub)
1Ch 3:24 Pelaiah, and **A.**, and Johanan, 6126
1Ch 9:17 Shallum, and **A.**, and Talmon, 6126
Ezr 2:42 of Talmon, the children of **A.**, the 6126
Ezr 2:45 of Hagabah, the children of **A.**, 6126
Ne 7:45 the children of **A.**, the children of 6126
Ne 8:7 Sherebiah, Jamin, **A.**, Shabbethai, 6126
Ne 11:19 Moreover the porters, **A.**, Talmon, 6126
Ne 12:25 Talmon, **A.**, were porters keeping 6126

AKRABBIM (ac-rab'-bim) See also MAALEHACRABBIM.
Nu 34:4 from the south to the ascent of **A.**, 6137
Jg 1:36 from the going up to **A.**, from the 6137

AL See AL-TASCHITH.

ALABASTER
Mt 26:7 having an **a.** box of very precious *211*
Mk 14:3 having an **a.** box of ointment *211*
Lu 7:37 brought an **a.** box of ointment, *211*

ALABASTER-BOX See ALABASTER and BOX.

ALAMETH (al'-am-eth)
1Ch 7:8 and Abiah, and Anathoth, and **A.**, 5964

ALAMMELECH (a-lam'-mel-ek)
Jos 19:26 **A.**, and Amad, and Mishael; 487

ALAMOTH (al'-am-oth)
1Ch 15:20 with psalteries on **A.**; 5961
Ps 46:*title* A Song upon **A.** 5961

ALARM
Nu 10:5 When ye blow an **a.**, then the 8643
Nu 10:6 When ye blow an **a.** the second 8643
Nu 10:6 they shall blow an **a.** for their 8643
Nu 10:7 blow, ye shall not sound an **a.** 7321
Nu 10:9 blow an **a.** with the trumpets; 7321
2Ch 13:12 with sounding trumpets to cry **a.** 7321
Jer 4:19 sound of the trumpet, the **a.** of war 8643
Jer 49:2 I will cause an **a.** of war to be heard 8643
Joe 2:1 sound of **a.** in my holy mountain: 7321
Zep 1:16 A day of the trumpet and **a.** 8643

ALAS
Nu 12:11 Aaron said unto Moses, **A.**, my, 994
Nu 24:23 **A.**, who shall live when God doeth 188
Jos 7:7 Joshua said, **A.**, O Lord 162
Jg 6:22 Gideon said, **A.**, O Lord God! 162
Jg 11:35 **A.**, my daughter! thou hast 162
1Ki 13:30 mourned over him, saying, **A.**, my 1945
2Ki 3:10 the king of Israel said, **A.**! 162
2Ki 6:5 **A.**, master! for it was borrowed. 162
2Ki 6:15 **A.**, my master! how shall we do? 162
Jer 30:7 **A.**! for that day is great, 1945
Eze 6:11 **A.** for all the evil abominations 253
Joe 1:15 **A.** for the day! for the day of the 162
Am 5:16 say in all the highways, **A.**! **a.**! 1930
Re 18:10 **A. a.**, that great city Babylon, *3759*
Re 18:16 **A.**, **a.** that great city, that was *3759*
Re 18:19 **A.**, **a.** that great city, wherein *3759*

ALBEIT
Eze 13:7 Lord saith it; **a.** I have not spoken?
Phm 19 **a.** I do not say to thee how thou *2443*

ALBON See ABI-ALBON.

ALEMETH (al-e'-meth)
1Ch 6:60 and **A.** with her suburbs, and 5904
1Ch 8:36 Jehoadah begat **A.**, and Azmaveth, 5904
1Ch 9:42 Jarah begat **A.**, and Azmaveth. 5904

ALEPH
Ps 110:1 *title* [א] **A.**

ALEXANDER (al-ex-an'-dur)
Mk 15:21 the father of **A.** and Rufus, *223*
Ac 4:6 John, and **A.**, and as many as were *223*
Ac 19:33 they drew **A.** out of the multitude, *223*
Ac 19:33 **A.** beckoned with the hand, *223*
1Ti 1:20 Of whom is Hymenaeus and **A.**; *223*
2Ti 4:14 **A.** the coppersmith did me much *223*

ALEXANDRIA (al-ex-an'-dree-ah) See also ALEXANDRIANS.
Ac 18:24 Apollos, born at **A.**, an eloquent *221*
Ac 27:6 a ship of **A.** sailing into Italy; *221*
Ac 28:11 we departed in a ship of **A.**, *221*

ALEXANDRIANS (al-ex-an'-dree-uns)
Ac 6:9 **A.**, and of them of Cilicia and of *221*

ALGUM (al'-gum) See also ALMUG.
2Ch 2:8 and **a.** trees, out of Lebanon: 418
2Ch 9:10 **a.** trees and precious stones. 418
2Ch 9:11 king made of the **a.** trees terraces 418

ALGUM-TREES See ALGUM and TREES.

ALIAH (a-li'-ah) See also ALVAH.
1Ch 1:51 were; duke Timnah, duke **A.**, 5933

ALIAN (a-li'-un) See also ALVAN.
1Ch 1:40 of Shobal; **A.**, and Manahath, 5935

ALIEN See also ALIENS.
Ex 18:3 I have been an **a.** in a strange 1616
De 14:21 thou mayest sell it unto an **a.**: 5237
Job 19:15 I am an **a.** in their sight. 5237
Ps 69:8 an **a.** unto my mother's children. 5237
Isa 61:5 the **a.** shall be your ploughmen 5236

ALIENATE See also ALIENATED.
Eze 48:14 nor **a.** the first fruits of the land; 5674

ALIENATED
Eze 23:17 and her mind was **a.** from them. 3363
Eze 23:18 then my mind was **a.** from her, 3363
Eze 23:18 like as my mind was **a.** from her 5361
Eze 23:22 whom thy mind is **a.**, and I will 5361
Eze 23:28 them from whom thy mind is **a.**: 5361
Eph 4:18 being **a.** from the life of God *526*
Col 1:21 that were sometime **a.** and enemies *526*

ALIENS
La 5:2 our houses to **a.** 5237
Eph 2:12 being **a.** from the commonwealth *526*
Heb 11:34 to flight the armies of the **a.** *245*

ALIKE
De 12:22 the clean shall eat of them **a.** 3162
De 15:22 the clean person shall eat it **a.**, 3162
1Sa 30:24 they shall part **a.** 3162
Job 21:26 They shall lie down **a.** in the dust, 3162
Ps 33:15 He fashioneth their hearts **a.**; 3162
Ps 139:12 darkness and the light are both **a.**
Pr 20:10 both of them are **a.** abomination 1571
Pr 27:15 and a contentious woman are **a.** 7737
Ec 9:2 All things come **a.** to all: 834
Ec 11:6 whether they both shall be **a.** good. 259
Ro 14:5 another esteemeth every day **a.**

ALIVE See also QUICK.
Ge 6:19 to keep them **a.** with thee; 2421
Ge 6:20 come unto thee, to keep them **a.** 2421
Ge 7:3 to keep seed **a.** upon the face of 2421
Ge 7:23 and Noah only remained **a.**, and
Ge 12:12 but they will save thee **a.** 2421
Ge 43:7 Is your father yet **a.**? 2416
Ge 43:27 of whom you spake? Is he yet **a.**? 2416
Ge 43:28 he is yet **a.** 2416
Ge 45:26 told him, saying, Joseph is yet **a.**, 2416
Ge 45:28 Joseph my son is yet **a.**: 2416
Ge 46:30 because thou art yet **a.** 2416
Ge 50:20 to save much people **a.** 2421
Ex 1:17 but saved the men children **a.** 2421
Ex 1:18 have saved the men children **a.**? 2421
Ex 1:22 every daughter ye shall save **a.** 2421
Ex 4:18 see whether they be yet **a.** 2416
Ex 22:4 be certainly found in his hand **a.**,
Le 10:16 sons of Aaron which were left **a.**,
Le 14:4 cleansed two birds **a.** and clean, 2416
Le 16:10 be presented **a.** before the Lord, 2416
Le 26:36 And upon them that are left **a.**
Nu 16:33 went down **a.** into the pit, and the 2416
Nu 21:35 until there was none left him **a.**: 8300
Nu 22:33 I had slain thee, and saved her **a.** 2421
Nu 31:15 Have ye saved all the women **a.**? 2421
Nu 31:18 keep **a.** for yourselves. 2421
De 4:4 **a.** every one of you this day. 2416
De 5:3 who are all of us here **a.** this day. 2416
De 6:24 that he might preserve us **a.**, 2421
De 20:16 save **a.** nothing that breatheth: 2421
De 31:27 while I am yet **a.** with you this 2416
De 32:39 I kill, and I make **a.**; I wound, 2421
Jos 2:13 And that ye will save **a.** my father, 2421
Jos 6:25 Joshua saved Rahab the harlot **a.**, 2421
Jos 8:23 the king of Ai they took **a.**, 2416
Jos 14:10 the Lord hath kept me **a.** 2421
Jg 8:19 if ye had saved them **a.**, I would 2421

Jg 21:14 which they had saved **a.** of the 2421
1Sa 2:6 The Lord killeth, and maketh **a.**: 2421
1Sa 15:8 Agag the king of the Amalekites **a.**, 2416
1Sa 27:9 left neither man nor woman **a.**, 2421
1Sa 27:11 saved neither man nor woman **a.**, 2421
2Sa 8:2 with one full line to keep **a.**. 2421
2Sa 12:18 while the child was yet **a.**, 2416
2Sa 12:21 weep for the child, while it was **a.**; 2416
2Sa 12:22 While the child was yet **a.**, I fasted 2416
2Sa 18:14 while he was yet **a.** in the midst of 2416
1Ki 18:5 to save the horses and mules **a.**, 2421
1Ki 20:18 come out for peace, take them **a.**; 2416
1Ki 20:18 be come out for war, take them **a.** 2416
1Ki 20:32 said, Is he yet **a.**? he is my brother 2416
1Ki 21:15 for Naboth is not **a.**, but dead. 2416
2Ki 5:7 Am I God, to kill and to make **a.**, 2421
2Ki 7:4 if they save us **a.**, we shall live; 2421
2Ki 7:12 catch them **a.**, and get into the 2416
2Ki 10:14 he said, Take them **a.** 2416
2Ki 10:14 And they took them **a.**, 2416
2Ch 25:12 other ten thousand left **a.** 2416
Ps 22:29 none can keep **a.** his own soul. 2421
Ps 30:3 thou hast kept me **a.**, 2421
Ps 33:19 and to keep them **a.** in famine. 2421
Ps 41:2 will preserve him, and keep him **a.**; 2421
Pr 1:12 swallow them up **a.** as the grave; 2416
Ec 4:2 than the living which are yet **a.** 2416
Jer 49:11 I will preserve them **a.**; 2421
Eze 7:13 although they were yet **a.**: 2416
Eze 13:18 save the souls **a.** that come unto 2421
Eze 13:19 save the souls **a.** that should not 2421
Eze 18:27 he shall save his soul **a.**. 2421
Da 5:19 whom he would be kept **a.**; 2418
Mt 27:63 said, while he was yet **a.**, After *2198*
Mk 16:11 when they had heard that he was **a.**, *2198*
Lu 15:24 **my son was dead, and is a. again;** *326*
Lu 15:32 **brother was dead, and is a. again;** *326*
Lu 24:23 angels, which said that he was **a.** *2198*
Ac 1:3 he shewed himself **a.** after his *2198*
Ac 9:41 and widows, presented her **a.** *2198*
Ac 20:12 they brought the young man **a.** *2198*
Ac 25:19 whom Paul affirmed to be **a.**. *2198*
Ro 6:11 dead indeed unto sin, but **a.** unto *2198*
Ro 6:13 as those that are **a.** from the dead, *2198*
Ro 7:9 I was **a.** without the law once: *2198*
1Co 15:22 so in Christ shall all be made **a.** *2227*
1Th 4:15 we which are **a.** and remain *2198*
1Th 4:17 are **a.** and remain shall be caught *2198*
Re 1:18 **behold, I am a. for evermore,** *2198*
Re 2:8 **which was dead, and is a.;** *2198*
Re 19:20 both were cast **a.** into a lake of fire *2198*

ALL See also ALBEIT; ALMIGHTY; ALMOST; ALREADY; ALTOGETHER; ALTHOUGH; ALWAY.

Ge 1:26 the cattle, and over **a.** the earth, 3605
Ge 1:29 is upon the face of **a.** the earth, 3605
Ge 2:1 finished, and **a.** the host of them. 3605
Ge 2:2 the seventh day from **a.** his work 3605
Ge 2:3 rested from **a.** his work which God 3605
Ge 2:20 **a.** cattle, and to the fowl of the air, 3605
Ge 3:14 thou art cursed above **a.** cattle, 3605
Ge 3:14 thou eat **a.** the days of thy life: 3605
Ge 3:17 eat of it **a.** the days of thy life; 3605
Ge 3:20 she was the mother of **a.** living. 3605
Ge 4:21 **a.** such as handle the harp and 3605
Ge 5:5 **a.** the days that Adam lived were 3605
Ge 5:8 **a.** the days of Seth were 3605
Ge 5:11 **a.** the days of Enos were 3605
Ge 5:14 **a.** the days of Cainan were 3605
Ge 5:17 **a.** the days of Mahalaleel were 3605
Ge 5:20 **a.** the days of Jared were 3605
Ge 5:23 **a.** the days of Enoch were 3605
Ge 5:27 **a.** the days of Methuselah were 3605
Ge 5:31 **a.** the days of Lamech were 3605
Ge 6:2 wives of **a.** which they chose. 3605
Ge 6:12 for **a.** flesh had corrupted his way 3605
Ge 6:13 of **a.** flesh is come before me; 3605
Ge 6:17 upon the earth, to destroy **a.** flesh, 3605
Ge 6:19 of **a.** flesh, two of every sort shalt 3605
Ge 6:21 unto thee of **a.** food that is eaten, 3605
Ge 6:22 according to **a.** that God 3605
Ge 7:1 Come thou and **a.** thy house into 3605
Ge 7:3 keep seed alive upon the face of **a.** 3605
Ge 7:5 Noah did according unto **a.** that 3605
Ge 7:11 the same day were **a.** the fountains 3605
Ge 7:14 and **a.** the cattle after their kind, 3605
Ge 7:15 the ark, two and two of **a.** flesh, 3605
Ge 7:16 in male and female of **a.** flesh, 3605
Ge 7:19 **a.** the high hills, that were under 3605
Ge 7:21 And **a.** flesh died that moved upon 3605
Ge 7:22 **A.** in whose nostrils was the 3605
Ge 7:22 of **a.** that was in the dry land, died. 3605
Ge 8:1 and **a.** the cattle that was with him 3605
Ge 8:17 of **a.** flesh, both of fowl, and of 3605
Ge 9:2 fowl of the air, upon **a.** that moveth 3605
Ge 9:2 and upon **a.** the fishes of the sea; 3605
Ge 9:3 herb have I given you **a.** things. 3605
Ge 9:10 from **a.** that go out of the ark, to 3605
Ge 9:11 neither shall **a.** flesh be cut off any 3605
Ge 9:15 you and every living creature of **a.** 3605
Ge 9:15 become a flood to destroy **a.** flesh. 3605
Ge 9:16 and every living creature of **a.** flesh 3605
Ge 9:17 between me and **a.** flesh that is 3605
Ge 9:29 **a.** the days of Noah were 3605
Ge 10:21 Unto Shem also, the father of **a.** 3605
Ge 10:29 **a.** these were the sons of Joktan. 3605
Ge 11:6 and they have **a.** one language; 3605
Ge 11:8 upon the face of **a.** the earth: 3605
Ge 11:9 the language of **a.** the earth: 3605
Ge 11:9 upon the face of **a.** the earth. 3605
Ge 12:3 in thee shall **a.** families of the 3605
Ge 12:5 **a.** their substance that they had, 3605
Ge 12:20 and his wife, and **a.** that he had. 3605
Ge 13:1 and his wife, and **a.** that he had, 3605
Ge 13:10 beheld **a.** the plain of Jordan, that 3605
Ge 13:11 chose him **a.** the plain of Jordan; 3605
Ge 13:15 **a.** the land which thou seest, to 3605
Ge 14:3 **A.** these were joined together in 3605
Ge 14:7 and smote **a.** the country of the 3605
Ge 14:11 they took **a.** the goods of Sodom 3605
Ge 14:11 and **a.** their victuals, and went 3605
Ge 14:16 he brought back **a.** the goods, 3605
Ge 14:20 And he gave him tithes of **a.**. 3605
Ge 15:10 And he took unto him **a.** these, 3605
Ge 16:12 in the presence of **a.** his
Ge 17:8 **a.** the land of Canaan, for an
Ge 17:23 and **a.** that were born in his house, 3605
Ge 17:23 **a.** that were bought with his money, 3605
Ge 17:27 And **a.** the men of his house, born 3605
Ge 18:18 and **a.** the nations of the earth 3605
Ge 18:25 Shall not the Judge of **a.** the earth 3605
Ge 18:26 then I will spare **a.** the place for 3605
Ge 18:28 wilt thou destroy **a.** the city for 3605
Ge 19:2 tarry **a.** night, and wash your feet, 3885
Ge 19:2 we will abide in the street **a.** night. 3885
Ge 19:4 **a.** the people from every quarter: 3605
Ge 19:17 neither stay thou in **a.** the plain; 3605
Ge 19:25 **a.** the plain, and **a.** the inhabitants 3605
Ge 19:28 Gomorrah, and toward **a.** the land 3605
Ge 19:31 after the manner of **a.** the earth: 3605
Ge 20:7 die, thou, and **a.** that are thine. 3605
Ge 20:8 called **a.** his servants, and told **a.** 3605
Ge 20:16 **a.** that are with thee, and with **a.** 3605
Ge 20:18 closed up **a.** the wombs of the 3605
Ge 21:6 so that **a.** that hear will laugh 3605
Ge 21:12 **a.** that Sarah hath said unto thee, 3605
Ge 21:22 with thee in **a.** that thou doest 3605
Ge 22:18 **a.** the nations of the earth be blessed 3605
Ge 23:10 of **a.** that went in at the gate 3605
Ge 23:17 **a.** the trees that were in the field
Ge 23:17 that were in **a.** the borders round about
Ge 23:18 before **a.** that went in at the gate 3605
Ge 24:1 had blessed Abraham in **a.** things 3605
Ge 24:2 that ruled over **a.** that he had 3605
Ge 24:10 **a.** the goods of his master were his 3605
Ge 24:20 and drew for **a.** his camels 3605
Ge 24:36 hath he given **a.** that he hath. 3605
Ge 24:54 with him, and tarried **a.** night: 3885
Ge 24:66 Isaac **a.** things that he had done. 3605
Ge 25:4 **A.** these were the children of 3605
Ge 25:5 gave **a.** that he had unto Isaac. 3605
Ge 25:18 died in the presence of **a.** his 3605
Ge 25:25 **a.** over like an hairy garment; 3605
Ge 26:3 seed, I will give **a.** these countries, 3605
Ge 26:4 unto thy seed **a.** these countries; 3605
Ge 26:4 **a.** the nations of the earth be 3605
Ge 26:11 Abimelech charged **a.** his people, 3605
Ge 26:15 For **a.** the wells which his father's 3605
Ge 27:33 I have eaten of **a.** before thou 3605
Ge 27:37 and **a.** his brethren have I given 3605
Ge 28:11 tarried there **a.** night, because 3885
Ge 28:14 in thy seed shall **a.** the families 3605
Ge 28:15 and will keep thee in **a.** places 3605
Ge 28:22 **a.** that thou shalt give me I will 3605
Ge 29:3 thither were **a.** the flocks gathered: 3605
Ge 29:8 until **a.** the flocks be gathered 3605
Ge 29:13 he told Laban **a.** these things. 3605
Ge 29:22 Laban gathered together **a.** the 3605
Ge 30:32 I will pass through **a.** thy flock 3605
Ge 30:32 from thence **a.** the speckled and 3605
Ge 30:32 and **a.** the brown cattle among 3605
Ge 30:35 and **a.** the she goats that were 3605
Ge 30:35 some white in it, and **a.** the brown 3605
Ge 30:40 **a.** the brown in the flock of Laban; 3605
Ge 31:1 away **a.** that was our father's; 3605
Ge 31:1 father's hath he gotten **a.** this glory. 3605
Ge 31:6 know that with **a.** my power I have 3605
Ge 31:8 then **a.** the cattle bare speckled: 3605
Ge 31:8 bare **a.** the cattle ringstraked. 3605
Ge 31:12 eyes, and see, **a.** the rams which 3605
Ge 31:12 I have seen **a.** that Laban doeth 3605
Ge 31:16 For **a.** the riches which God hath 3605
Ge 31:18 carried away **a.** his cattle, and **a.** 3605
Ge 31:21 So he fled with **a.** that he had; and 3605
Ge 31:34 And Laban searched **a.** the tent, 3605
Ge 31:37 Whereas thou hast searched **a.** my 3605
Ge 31:37 what hast thou found of **a.** thy 3605
Ge 31:43 and **a.** that thou seest is mine. 3605
Ge 31:54 tarried **a.** night in the mount. 3885
Ge 32:10 of the least of **a.** the mercies, 3605
Ge 32:10 of **a.** the truth, which thou hast 3605
Ge 32:19 third, and **a.** that followed 3605
Ge 33:8 What meanest thou by **a.** this 3605
Ge 33:13 them one day, **a.** the flock will die. 3605
Ge 34:19 was more honorable than **a.** the 3605
Ge 34:24 hearkened **a.** that went out of 3605
Ge 34:24 **a.** that went out of the gate
Ge 34:25 city boldly, and slew **a.** the males. 3605
Ge 34:29 **a.** their wealth, and **a.** their little 3605
Ge 34:29 and spoiled even **a.** that was in the 3605
Ge 35:2 and to **a.** that were with him, 3605
Ge 35:4 unto Jacob **a.** the strange gods 3605
Ge 35:4 and **a.** their earrings which were
Ge 35:6 Beth-el, he and **a.** the people that 3605
Ge 36:6 and **a.** the persons of his house, 3605
Ge 36:6 **a.** his beasts, and **a.** his substance, 3605
Ge 37:3 loved Joseph more than **a.** his 3605
Ge 37:4 him more than **a.** his brethren, 3605
Ge 37:35 **a.** his sons and **a.** his daughters 3605
Ge 39:3 made **a.** that he did to prosper 3605
Ge 39:4 and **a.** that he had he put into his 3605
Ge 39:5 and over **a.** that he had, that the 3605
Ge 39:5 blessing of the Lord was upon **a.** 3605
Ge 39:6 he left **a.** that he had in Joseph's 3605
Ge 39:8 and he hath committed **a.** that he 3605
Ge 39:22 to Joseph's hand **a.** the prisoners 3605
Ge 40:17 uppermost basket there was of **a.** 3605
Ge 40:20 that he made a feast unto **a.** his 3605
Ge 41:8 he sent and called for **a.** the 3605
Ge 41:8 and **a.** the wise men thereof: and 3605
Ge 41:19 I never saw in **a.** the land of Egypt 3605
Ge 41:29 throughout **a.** the land of Egypt: 3605
Ge 41:30 **a.** the plenty shall be forgotten 3605
Ge 41:35 let them gather **a.** the food of 3605
Ge 41:37 and in the eyes of **a.** his servants 3605
Ge 41:39 as God hath shewed thee **a.** this, 3605
Ge 41:40 word shall **a.** my people be ruled: 3605
Ge 41:41 I have set thee over **a.** the land 3605
Ge 41:43 ruler over **a.** the land of Egypt. 3605
Ge 41:44 his hand or foot in **a.** the land 3605
Ge 41:45 out over **a.** the land of Egypt.
Ge 41:46 throughout **a.** the land of Egypt. 3605
Ge 41:48 And he gathered up **a.** the food of 3605
Ge 41:51 hath made me forget **a.** my toil, 3605
Ge 41:51 and **a.** my father's house. 3605
Ge 41:54 dearth was in **a.** lands; but in **a.** 3605
Ge 41:55 **a.** the land of Egypt was famished, 3605
Ge 41:55 said unto **a.** the Egyptians, Go 3605
Ge 41:56 was over **a.** the face of the earth: 3605
Ge 41:56 Joseph opened **a.** the storehouses, 3605
Ge 41:57 **a.** countries came into Egypt to 3605
Ge 41:57 famine was so sore in **a.** lands. 3605
Ge 42:6 he it was that sold to **a.** the people 3605
Ge 42:11 We are **a.** one man's sons; we are 3605
Ge 42:17 And he put them **a.** together into 622
Ge 42:29 told him **a.** that befell unto them; 3605
Ge 42:36 **a.** these things are against me. 3605
Ge 45:1 not refrain himself before **a.** them 3605
Ge 45:8 Pharaoh, and lord of **a.** his house, 3605
Ge 45:8 throughout **a.** the land of Egypt 3605
Ge 45:9 hath made me lord of **a.** Egypt: 3605

Ge	45:10	thy herds, and **a.** that thou hast:	3605
Ge	45:11	**a.** that thou hast, come to poverty.	3605
Ge	45:13	tell my father of **a.** my glory in	3605
Ge	45:13	Egypt, and of **a.** that ye have seen;	3605
Ge	45:15	kissed **a.** his brethren, and wept	3605
Ge	45:22	To **a.** of them he gave each man	3605
Ge	45:26	the good of **a.** the land of Egypt	3605
Ge	45:26	governor over **a.** the land of Egypt.	3605
Ge	45:27	told him **a.** the words of Joseph,	3605
Ge	46:1	And Israel took his journey with **a.**	3605
Ge	46:6	Jacob, and **a.** his seed with him:	3605
Ge	46:7	**a.** his seed brought he with him	3605
Ge	46:15	**a.** the souls of his sons and his	3605
Ge	46:22	Jacob: **a.** the souls were fourteen.	3605
Ge	46:25	Jacob: **a.** the souls were seven.	3605
Ge	46:26	**A.** the souls that came with Jacob	3605
Ge	46:26	**a.** the souls were threescore and	3605
Ge	46:27	**a.** the souls of the house of Jacob,	3605
Ge	46:32	their herds, and **a.** that they have.	3605
Ge	47:1	**a.** that they have, are come out of	3605
Ge	47:12	and **a.** his father's household, with	3605
Ge	47:13	there was no bread in **a.** the land;	3605
Ge	47:13	**a.** the land of Canaan fainted	
Ge	47:14	Joseph gathered up **a.** the money	3605
Ge	47:15	**a.** the Egyptians came unto Joseph,	3605
Ge	47:17	for **a.** their cattle for that year	3605
Ge	47:20	Joseph bought **a.** the land of Egypt	3605
Ge	48:15	God which fed me **a.** my life long	
Ge	48:16	which redeemed me from **a.** evil,	3605
Ge	49:28	**A.** these are the twelve tribes of	3605
Ge	50:7	with him went up **a.** the servants	3605
Ge	50:7	**a.** the elders of the land of Egypt,	3605
Ge	50:8	**a.** the house of Joseph, and his	3605
Ge	50:14	**a.** that went up with him to bury	3605
Ge	50:15	**a.** the evil which we did unto him	3605
Ex	1:5	and **a.** the souls that came out of	3605
Ex	1:6	and **a.** his brethren, and **a.** that	3605
Ex	1:14	**a.** manner of service in the field: **a.**	3605
Ex	1:22	And Pharaoh charged **a.** his people,	3605
Ex	3:20	and smite Egypt with **a.** my wonders	3605
Ex	3:15	my memorial unto **a.** generations	
Ex	4:19	**a.** the men are dead which sought	3605
Ex	4:21	**a.** those wonders before Pharaoh,	3605
Ex	4:28	Moses told Aaron **a.** the words of	3605
Ex	4:28	him, and **a.** the signs which he had	3605
Ex	4:29	gathered together **a.** the elders	3605
Ex	4:30	Aaron spake **a.** the words which	3605
Ex	5:12	throughout **a.** the land of Egypt	3605
Ex	5:23	hast thou delivered thy people at **a.**	3605
Ex	6:29	of Egypt **a.** that I say unto thee	3605
Ex	7:2	speak **a.** that I command thee:	3605
Ex	7:19	ponds, and upon **a.** their pools of	3605
Ex	7:19	throughout **a.** the land of Egypt,	3605
Ex	7:20	**a.** the waters that were in the	3605
Ex	7:21	throughout **a.** the land of Egypt.	3605
Ex	7:24	And **a.** the Egyptians digged round	3605
Ex	8:2	smite **a.** thy borders with frogs:	3605
Ex	8:4	people, and upon **a.** thy servants	3605
Ex	8:16	throughout **a.** the land of Egypt	3605
Ex	8:17	**a.** the dust of the land became lice	
Ex	8:17	throughout **a.** the land of Egypt	3605
Ex	8:24	and into **a.** the land of Egypt:	3605
Ex	9:4	nothing die of **a.** that is the	3605
Ex	9:6	morrow, and **a.** the cattle of Egypt	3605
Ex	9:9	small dust in **a.** the land of Egypt,	3605
Ex	9:9	throughout **a.** the land of Egypt.	3605
Ex	9:11	and upon **a.** the Egyptians,	3605
Ex	9:14	**a.** my plagues upon thine heart,	3605
Ex	9:14	is none like me in **a.** the earth	3605
Ex	9:16	declared throughout **a.** the earth.	3605
Ex	9:19	and **a.** that thou hast in the field;	3605
Ex	9:22	may be hail in **a.** the land of Egypt	
Ex	9:24	none like it in **a** the land of Egypt	3605
Ex	9:25	throughout **a.** the land of Egypt	3605
Ex	9:25	**a.** that was in the field, both man	3605
Ex	10:6	and the houses of **a.** thy servants,	3605
Ex	10:6	houses of **a.** the Egyptians;	3605
Ex	10:12	even **a.** that the hail hath left.	3605
Ex	10:13	land **a.** that day,	3605
Ex	10:13	and **a.** that night;	3605
Ex	10:14	went up over **a.** the land of Egypt,	3605
Ex	10:14	rested in **a.** the coasts of Egypt:	3605
Ex	10:15	of the land, and **a.** the fruit of the	3605
Ex	10:15	through **a.** the land of Egypt.	3605
Ex	10:19	locust in **a.** the coasts of Egypt.	3605
Ex	10:22	darkness in **a.** the land of Egypt	3605
Ex	10:23	**a.** the children of Israel had light	3605
Ex	11:5	And **a.** the firstborn in the land	3605
Ex	11:5	and **a.** the firstborn of beasts.	3605
Ex	11:6	throughout **a.** the land of Egypt,	3605
Ex	11:8	**a.** these thy servants shall come	3605
Ex	11:8	and **a.** the people that follow thee:	3605
Ex	11:10	**a.** these wonders before Pharaoh:	3605
Ex	12:3	Speak ye unto **a.** the congregation	3605
Ex	12:9	nor sodden at **a.** with water, but	
Ex	12:12	smite **a.** the firstborn in the land	3605
Ex	12:12	against **a.** the gods of Egypt I will	3605
Ex	12:20	in **a.** your habitations shall ye eat	3605
Ex	12:21	Then Moses called for **a.** the elders	3605
Ex	12:29	the Lord smote **a.** the firstborn	3605
Ex	12:29	and **a.** the firstborn of cattle	3605
Ex	12:30	**a.** his servants,	3605
Ex	12:30	and **a.** the Egyptians;	3605
Ex	12:33	they said, We be **a.** dead men	3605
Ex	12:41	**a.** the hosts of the Lord went out	3605
Ex	12:42	observed of **a.** the children of	3605
Ex	12:47	**A.** the congregation of Israel shall	3605
Ex	12:48	to the Lord, let **a.** his males be	3605
Ex	12:50	Thus did **a.** the children of Israel;	3605
Ex	13:2	Sanctify unto me **a.** the firstborn,	3605
Ex	13:7	seen with thee in **a.** thy quarters	3605
Ex	13:12	Lord **a.** that openeth the matrix,	3605
Ex	13:13	and **a.** the firstborn of man among	3605
Ex	13:15	that the Lord slew **a.** the firstborn	3605
Ex	13:15	sacrifice to the Lord **a.** that	3605
Ex	13:15	but **a.** the firstborn of my children	3605
Ex	14:4	upon Pharaoh, and upon **a.** his host	
Ex	14:7	chosen chariots, and **a.** the chariots	3605
Ex	14:9	**a.** the horses and chariots of	3605
Ex	14:17	honour upon Pharaoh, and upon **a.**	3605
Ex	14:20	not near the other **a.** the night.	3605
Ex	14:21	to go back by a strong east wind **a.**	3605
Ex	14:23	the sea, even **a.** Pharaoh's horses,	3605
Ex	14:28	and **a.** the host of Pharaoh that	3605
Ex	15:15	**a.** the inhabitants of Canaan shall	3605
Ex	15:20	hand; and **a.** the women went out	3605
Ex	15:26	keep **a.** his statutes, I will put none	3605
Ex	16:1	**a.** the congregation of the children	3605
Ex	16:6	said unto **a.** the children of Israel,	3605
Ex	16:9	**a.** the congregation of the children	3605
Ex	16:22	**a.** the rulers of the congregation	3605
Ex	17:1	**a.** the congregation of the children	3605
Ex	18:1	heard of **a.** that God had done	3605
Ex	18:8	**a.** that the Lord had done unto	3605
Ex	18:8	for Israel's sake, and **a.** the travail	3605
Ex	18:9	**a.** the goodness which the Lord	3605
Ex	18:11	the Lord is greater than **a.** gods:	3605
Ex	18:12	**a.** the elders of Israel, to eat	3605
Ex	18:14	saw **a.** that he did to the people,	3605
Ex	18:14	alone, and **a.** the people stand	3605
Ex	18:21	provide out of **a.** the people able	3605
Ex	18:22	let them judge the people at **a.**	3605
Ex	18:23	and **a.** this people shall also go	3605
Ex	18:24	and did **a.** that he had said	3605
Ex	18:25	chose able men out of **a.** Israel,	3605
Ex	18:26	judged the people at **a.** seasons:	3605
Ex	19:5	treasure unto me above **a.** people:	3605
Ex	19:5	for **a.** the earth is mine:	3605
Ex	19:7	before their faces **a.** these words	3605
Ex	19:8	**a.** the people answered together,	3605
Ex	19:8	**A.** that the Lord hath spoken we	3605
Ex	19:11	in the sight of **a.** the people upon	3605
Ex	19:16	so that **a.** the people that was in	3605
Ex	20:1	And God spake **a.** these words,	3605
Ex	20:9	shalt thou labour, and do **a.** thy	3605
Ex	20:11	and earth, the sea, and **a.** that in	3605
Ex	20:18	**a.** the people saw the thunderings,	3605
Ex	20:24	in **a.** places where I record my	3605
Ex	22:9	For **a.** manner of trespass,	3605
Ex	22:23	and they cry at **a.** unto me, I will	
Ex	22:26	If thou at **a.** take thy neighbour's	
Ex	23:13	in **a.** things that I have said unto	3605
Ex	23:17	**a.** thy males shall appear before	3605
Ex	23:22	his voice, and do **a.** that I speak;	3605
Ex	23:27	will destroy **a.** the people to whom	3605
Ex	23:27	and I will make **a.** thine enemies	3605
Ex	24:3	**a.** the words of the Lord,	3605
Ex	24:3	and **a.** the judgments:	3605
Ex	24:3	**a.** the people answered with one	3605
Ex	24:3	**A.** the words which the Lord hath	3605
Ex	24:4	Moses wrote **a.** the words of the	3605
Ex	24:7	**A.** that the Lord hath said will we	3605
Ex	24:8	you concerning **a.** these words.	3605
Ex	25:9	**a.** that I shew thee, after the	3605
Ex	25:9	the pattern of **a.** the instruments	3605
Ex	25:22	of **a.** things which I will give thee	3605
Ex	25:36	**a.** it shall be one beaten work of	3605
Ex	25:39	he make it, with **a.** these vessels.	3605
Ex	26:8	shall be **a.** of one measure,	
Ex	26:17	**a.** the boards of the tabernacle.	3605
Ex	27:3	**a.** the vessels thereof thou shalt	3605
Ex	27:17	**A.** the pillars round about the	3605
Ex	27:19	**A.** the vessels of the tabernacle	3605
Ex	27:19	in **a.** the service thereof,	3605
Ex	27:19	and **a.** the pins thereof,	3605
Ex	27:19	and **a.** the pins of the court,	3605
Ex	28:3	unto **a.** that are wise hearted,	3605
Ex	28:31	the robe of the ephod **a.** of blue.	3632
Ex	28:38	shall hallow in **a.** their holy gifts;	
Ex	29:12	pour **a.** the blood beside the	3605
Ex	29:13	take **a.** the fat that covereth the	3605
Ex	29:24	put **a.** in the hands of Aaron,	3605
Ex	29:35	**a.** things which I have commanded	3605
Ex	30:27	**a.** his vessels, and the candlestick	3605
Ex	30:28	burnt offering with **a.** his vessels,	3605
Ex	31:3	and in **a.** manner of workmanship,	3605
Ex	31:5	**a.** manner of workmanship.	3605
Ex	31:6	hearts of **a.** that are wise hearted	3605
Ex	31:6	**a.** that I have commanded thee;	3605
Ex	31:7	**a.** the furniture of the tabernacle,	3605
Ex	31:8	candlestick with **a.** his furniture,	3605
Ex	31:9	offering with **a.** his furniture,	3605
Ex	31:11	**a.** that I have commanded thee	3605
Ex	32:3	And **a.** the people brake off the	3605
Ex	32:13	**a.** this land that I have spoken of	3605
Ex	32:26	**a.** the sons of Levi gathered	3605
Ex	33:8	that **a.** the people rose up, and	3605
Ex	33:10	**a.** the people saw the cloudy	3605
Ex	33:10	and **a.** the people rose up and	3605
Ex	33:16	and thy people, from **a.** the people	3605
Ex	33:19	**a.** my goodness pass before thee,	3605
Ex	34:3	be seen throughout **a.** the mount;	3605
Ex	34:10	**a.** thy people I will do marvels,	3605
Ex	34:10	have not been done in **a.** the earth,	3605
Ex	34:10	**a.** the people among which thou	3605
Ex	34:19	**A.** that openeth the matrix is mine;	3605
Ex	34:20	**A.** the firstborn of thy sons thou	3605
Ex	34:23	**a.** your men-children appear	3605
Ex	34:30	**a.** the children of Israel saw Moses,	3605
Ex	34:31	Aaron and **a.** the rulers of the	3605
Ex	34:32	**a.** the children of Israel came nigh:	3605
Ex	34:32	commandment **a.** that the Lord	3605
Ex	35:1	**a.** the congregation of the children	3605
Ex	35:4	spake unto **a.** the congregation	3605
Ex	35:10	**a.** that the Lord hath commanded;	3605
Ex	35:13	**a.** his vessels, and the shewbread,	3605
Ex	35:16	**a.** his vessels, the layer and his foot,	3605
Ex	35:20	**a.** the congregation of the children	3605
Ex	35:21	for **a.** his service, and for the holy	3605
Ex	35:22	and tablets, **a.** jewels of gold:	3605
Ex	35:25	And **a.** the women that were wise	3605
Ex	35:26	**a.** the women whose heart stirred	3605
Ex	35:29	them willing to bring for **a.** manner	3605
Ex	35:31	in **a.** manner of workmanship;	3605
Ex	35:35	to work **a.** manner of work, of the	3605
Ex	36:1	**a.** manner of work for the service	3605
Ex	36:1	according to **a.** that the Lord had	3605
Ex	36:3	**a.** the offering, which the children	3605
Ex	36:4	**a.** the wise men,	3605
Ex	36:4	**a.** the work of the sanctuary,	3605
Ex	36:7	sufficient for **a.** the work to make	3605
Ex	36:9	the curtains were **a.** of one size	3605
Ex	36:22	**a.** the boards of the tabernacle.	3605
Ex	37:22	**a.** of it was one beaten work of	3605
Ex	37:24	it, and **a.** the vessels thereof	3605
Ex	38:3	made **a.** the vessels of the altar,	3605
Ex	38:3	**a.** the vessels thereof made he of	3605
Ex	38:16	**A.** the hangings of the court round	3605
Ex	38:17	**a.** the pillars of the court were	3605
Ex	38:20	**a.** the pins of the tabernacle,	3605
Ex	38:22	**a.** that the Lord commanded	3605
Ex	38:24	**A.** the gold that was occupied	3605
Ex	38:24	for the work in **a.**	3605
Ex	38:30	and **a.** the vessels of the altar,	3605
Ex	38:31	and **a.** the pins of the tabernacle,	3605
Ex	38:31	and **a.** the pins of the court	3605
Ex	39:22	ephod of woven work, **a.** of blue	3632
Ex	39:32	was **a.** the work of the tabernacle	3605
Ex	39:32	according to **a.** that the Lord	3605
Ex	39:33	**a.** his furniture, his taches, his	3605
Ex	39:36	and **a.** the vessels thereof, and the	3605

Book	Ref	Text	No.
Ex	39:37	**a.** the vessels thereof, and the oil	3605
Ex	39:39	his staves, and **a.** his vessels,	3605
Ex	39:40	**a.** the vessels of the service of the	3605
Ex	39:42	to **a.** that the Lord commanded	3605
Ex	39:42	of Israel made **a.** the work	3605
Ex	39:43	Moses did look up **a.** the work.	3605
Ex	40:9	and **a.** that is therein, and shalt	3605
Ex	40:9	it, and **a.** the vessels thereof;	3605
Ex	40:10	burnt offering, and **a.** his vessels,	3605
Ex	40:16	**a.** that the Lord commanded him,	3605
Ex	40:36	Israel went onward in **a.** their	3605
Ex	40:38	the sight of **a.** the house of Israel,	3605
Ex	40:38	throughout **a.** their journeys.	3605
Le	1:9	priest shall burn **a.** on the altar,	3605
Le	1:13	priest shall bring it **a.**, and burn	3605
Le	2:2	with **a.** the frankincense thereof;	3605
Le	2:13	with **a.** thine offerings thou shalt	3605
Le	2:16	with **a.** the frankincense thereof:	3605
Le	3:3	and **a.** the fat that is upon the	3605
Le	3:9	the inwards, and **a.** the fat that is	3605
Le	3:14	**a.** the fat that is upon the inwards,	3605
Le	3:16	savour: **a.** the fat is the Lord's.	3605
Le	3:17	**a.** your dwellings, that ye eat	3605
Le	4:7	pour **a.** the blood of the bullock	3605
Le	4:8	take off from it **a.** the fat of the	3605
Le	4:8	**a.** the fat that is upon the inwards,	3605
Le	4:11	and **a.** his flesh, with his head,	3605
Le	4:18	pour out **a.** the blood at the bottom	3605
Le	4:19	take **a.** his fat from him, and burn	3605
Le	4:26	he shall burn **a.** his fat upon the	3605
Le	4:30	pour out **a.** the blood thereof at	3605
Le	4:31	shall take away **a.** the fat thereof,	3605
Le	4:34	shall pour out **a.** the blood thereof	3605
Le	4:35	**a.** the fat thereof, as the fat of the	3605
Le	6:3	in any of **a.** these that a man doeth,	3605
Le	6:5	Or **a.** that about which he hath	3605
Le	6:7	anything of **a.** that he hath done	3605
Le	6:9	upon the altar **a.** night unto the	3605
Le	6:15	**a.** the frankincense which is upon	3605
Le	6:18	**A.** the males among the children	3605
Le	6:29	**A.** the males among the priests	3605
Le	7:3	shall offer of it **a.** the fat thereof;	3605
Le	7:9	And **a.** the meat offering that is	3605
Le	7:9	and **a.** that is dressed in the	3605
Le	7:10	oil, and dry, shall **a.** the sons of	3605
Le	7:18	eaten at **a.** on the third day, it	
Le	7:19	**a.** that be clean shall eat thereof.	3605
Le	8:3	gather thou **a.** the congregation	3605
Le	8:10	**a.** that was therein, and sanctified	3605
Le	8:11	anointed the altar and **A.** his vessels,	3605
Le	8:16	he took **a.** the fat that was upon	3605
Le	8:25	**a.** the fat that was upon the	3605
Le	8:27	put **a.** upon Aaron's hands, and	3605
Le	8:36	sons did **a.** things which the Lord	3605
Le	9:5	**a.** the congregation drew near	3605
Le	9:23	Lord appeared unto **a.** the people	3605
Le	9:24	when **a.** the people saw, they	3605
Le	10:3	and before **a.** the people I will be	3605
Le	10:6	wrath come upon **a.** the people:	3605
Le	10:11	children of Israel **a.** the statutes	3605
Le	11:2	eat among **a.** the beasts that are	3605
Le	11:9	ye eat of **a.** that are in the waters:	3605
Le	11:10	**a.** that have not fins and scales in	3605
Le	11:10	of **a.** that move in the waters,	3605
Le	11:20	**A.** fowls that creep,	3605
Le	11:20	going upon **a.** four,	
Le	11:21	thing, that goeth upon **a.** four,	
Le	11:23	**a.** other flying creeping things,	3605
Le	11:27	among **a.** manner of beasts	3605
Le	11:27	that go on **a.** four,	
Le	11:31	unclean to you among **a.** that	3605
Le	11:34	Of **a.** meat which may be eaten,	3605
Le	11:34	and **a.** drink that may be drunk	3605
Le	11:42	whatsoever goeth upon **a.** four,	
Le	11:42	feet among **a.** creeping things	3605
Le	13:12	leprosy cover **a.** the skin of him	3605
Le	13:13	leprosy have covered **a.** his flesh.	3605
Le	13:13	it is **a.** turned white: he is clean	3605
Le	13:46	**A.** the days wherein the plague	3605
Le	14:8	clothes, and shave off **a.** his hair,	3605
Le	14:9	**a.** his hair off his head and his	3605
Le	14:9	even **a.** his hair he shall shave off:	3605
Le	14:36	**a.** that is in that house be not	3605
Le	14:45	and **a.** the morter of the house;	3605
Le	14:46	**a.** the while that it is shut up shall	3605
Le	14:54	law for **a.** manner of plague of	3605
Le	15:16	wash **a.** his flesh in water, and be	3605
Le	15:24	And if any man lie with her at **a.**,	
Le	15:24	**a.** the bed whereon he lieth shall	3605
Le	15:25	of her separation; **a.** the days of	3605
Le	15:26	whereon she lieth **a.** the days of	3605
Le	16:2	not at **a.** times into the holy place	3605
Le	16:16	trangressions in **a.** their sins:	3605
Le	16:17	for **a.** the congregation of Israel.	3605
Le	16:21	**a.** the iniquities of the children	3605
Le	16:21	**a.** their transgressions in **a.** their	3605
Le	16:22	bear upon him **a.** their iniquities	3605
Le	16:29	no work at **a.**, whether it be one	3605
Le	16:30	be clean from **a.** your sins before	3605
Le	16:33	**a.** the people of the congregation.	3605
Le	16:34	for **a.** their sins once a year.	3605
Le	17:2	and unto **a.** the children of Israel,	3605
Le	17:14	For it is the life of **a.** flesh; the	3605
Le	17:14	life of **a.** flesh is the blood thereof:	3605
Le	18:24	in **a.** these the nations are defiled	3605
Le	18:27	(For **a.** these abominations have	3605
Le	19:2	Speak unto **a.** the congregation of	3605
Le	19:7	it be eaten at **a.** on the third day,	
Le	19:13	thee **a.** night until the morning.	
Le	19:20	not at **a.** redeemed, nor freedom	
Le	19:23	have planted **a.** manner of trees	3605
Le	19:24	**a.** the fruit thereof shall be holy	3605
Le	19:37	observe **a.** my statutes,	3605
Le	19:37	and **a.** my judgments,	3605
Le	20:5	family, and will cut him off, and **a.**	3605
Le	20:22	keep **a.** my statutes,	3605
Le	20:22	and **a.** my judgments,	3605
Le	20:23	for they committed **a.** these things,	3605
Le	21:24	and unto **a.** the children of Israel.	3605
Le	22:3	**a.** your seed among your	3605
Le	22:18	and unto **a.** the children of Israel,	3605
Le	22:18	for **a.** his vows,	3605
Le	22:18	and for **a.** his freewill offerings,	3605
Le	23:3	of the Lord in **a.** your dwellings.	3605
Le	23:14	generations in **a.** your dwellings.	3605
Le	23:21	in **a.** your dwellings throughout	3605
Le	23:31	generations in **a.** your dwellings.	3605
Le	23:38	beside **a.** your vows,	3605
Le	23:38	beside **a.** your freewill offerings,	3605
Le	23:42	**a.** that are Israelites born shall	3605
Le	24:14	**a.** that heard him lay their hands	3605
Le	24:14	let **a.** the congregation stone him.	3605
Le	24:16	**a.** the congregation shall certainly	3605
Le	25:7	**a.** the increase thereof be meat.	3605
Le	25:9	sound throughout **a.** your land.	3605
Le	25:10	liberty throughout **a.** the land	
Le	25:10	unto **a.** the inhabitants thereof:	3605
Le	25:24	in **a.** the land of your possession	3605
Le	26:14	not do **a.** these commandments;	3605
Le	26:15	will not do **a.** my commandments,	3605
Le	26:18	yet for **a.** this hearken unto me,	
Le	26:27	not for **a.** this hearken unto me,	
Le	26:44	yet for **a.** that, when they be in	1571
Le	27:9	**a.** that any man giveth of such	3605
Le	27:10	shall at **a.** change beast for beast,	
Le	27:13	But if he will at **a.** redeem it,	
Le	27:25	**a.** thy estimations shall be	3605
Le	27:28	unto the Lord of **a.** that he hath,	3605
Le	27:30	**a.** the tithe of the land, whether of	3605
Le	27:31	at **a.** redeem ought of his tithes,	
Le	27:33	and if he change it at **a.**, then	
Nu	1:2	ye the sum of **a.** the congregation	3605
Nu	1:3	**a.** that are able to go forth to war	3605
Nu	1:18	assembled **a.** the congregation	3605
Nu	1:20,	22,24,26,28,30,34,36,38,40,42 **a.** that were able to go forth to war;	3605
Nu	1:45	were **a.** those that were numbered	3605
Nu	1:45	**a.** that were able to go forth to war	3605
Nu	1:46	Even **a.** they that were numbered	3605
Nu	1:50	over **a.** the vessels thereof,	3605
Nu	1:50	and over **a.** things	3605
Nu	1:50	tabernacle, and **a.** the vessels	3605
Nu	1:54	did according to **a.** that the Lord	3605
Nu	2:9,16	**A.** that were numbered in the	3605
Nu	2:24	**A.** that were numbered of the	3605
Nu	2:31	**A.** they that were numbered in the	3605
Nu	2:32	**a.** those that were numbered of the	3605
Nu	2:34	to **a.** that the Lord commanded	3605
Nu	3:8	they shall keep **a.** the instruments	3605
Nu	3:12	of **a.** the firstborn that openeth the	3605
Nu	3:13	Because **a.** the firstborn are mine;	3605
Nu	3:13	I smote **a.** the firstborn in the land	3605
Nu	3:13	unto me **a.** the firstborn in Israel,	3605
Nu	3:22	to the number of **a.** the males,	3605
Nu	3:26	the cords of it for **a.** the service	3605
Nu	3:28	number of **a.** the males, from a	3605
Nu	3:31	hanging, and **a.** the service thereof.	3605
Nu	3:34	to the number of **a.** the males,	3605
Nu	3:36	**a.** the vessels thereof,	3605
Nu	3:36	and **a.** that serveth thereto,	3605
Nu	3:39	**A.** that were numbered of the	3605
Nu	3:39	**a.** the males from a month old and	3605
Nu	3:40	Number **a.** the firstborn of the	3605
Nu	3:41	**a.** the firstborn among the children	3605
Nu	3:41	**a.** the firstlings among the cattle	3605
Nu	3:42	**a.** the firstborn among the children	3605
Nu	3:43	And **a.** the firstborn males by the	3605
Nu	3:45	Levites instead of **a.** the firstborn	3605
Nu	4:3	**a.** that enter into the host, to do	3605
Nu	4:9	snuffdishes, and **a.** the oil vessels	3605
Nu	4:10	put it and **a.** the vessels thereof	3605
Nu	4:12	**a.** the instruments of ministry,	3605
Nu	4:14	**a.** the vessels thereof, wherewith	3605
Nu	4:14	basons, **a.** the vessels of the altar;	3605
Nu	4:15	**a.** the vessels of the sanctuary,	3605
Nu	4:16	the oversight of **a.** the tabernacle,	3605
Nu	4:16	and of **a.** that therein is,	3605
Nu	4:23	**a.** that enter in to perform the	3605
Nu	4:26	**a.** the instruments of their	3605
Nu	4:26	and **a.** that is made for them:	3605
Nu	4:27	**a.** the service of the sons of the	3605
Nu	4:27	in **a.** their burdens,	3605
Nu	4:27	and in **a.** their service: and ye	3605
Nu	4:27	them in charge **a.** their burdens.	3605
Nu	4:31	according to **a.** their service in the	3605
Nu	4:32	with **a.** their instruments,	3605
Nu	4:32	and with **a.** their service:	3605
Nu	4:33	according to **a.** their service,	3605
Nu	4:37,	41 **a.** that might do service in the	3605
Nu	4:46	**A.** those that were numbered of	3605
Nu	5:9	offering of **a.** the holy things of the	3605
Nu	5:30	shall execute upon her **a.** this law.	3605
Nu	6:4	**A.** the days of his separation	3605
Nu	6:5	**A.** the days of the vow of his	3605
Nu	6:6	**A.** the days that he separateth	3605
Nu	6:8	**A.** the days of his separation he is	3605
Nu	7:1	**a.** the instruments thereof,	3605
Nu	7:1	both the altar and **a.** the vessels	3605
Nu	7:85	**a.** the silver vessels weighed	3605
Nu	7:86	**a.** the gold of the spoons was	3605
Nu	7:87	**A.** the oxen for the burnt offering	3605
Nu	7:88	And **a.** the oxen for the sacrifice of	3605
Nu	8:7	and let them shave **a.** their flesh	3605
Nu	8:16	of the firstborn of **a.** the children	3605
Nu	8:17	For **a.** the firstborn of the children	3605
Nu	8:18	Levites for **a.** the firstborn of the	3605
Nu	8:20	Aaron, and **a.** the congregation	3605
Nu	8:20	unto **a.** that the Lord commanded	3605
Nu	9:3	appointed season: according to **a.**	3605
Nu	9:3	according to **a.** the ceremonies	3605
Nu	9:5	to **a.** that the Lord commanded	3605
Nu	9:12	according to **a.** the ordinances of	3605
Nu	10:3	**a.** the assembly shall assemble	3605
Nu	10:25	was the rereward of **a.** the camps	3605
Nu	11:6	nothing at **a.**, beside this manna,	3605
Nu	11:11	burden of **a.** this people upon me?	3605
Nu	11:12	Have I conceived **a.** this people?	3605
Nu	11:13	flesh to give unto **a.** this people?	3605
Nu	11:14	able to bear **a.** this people alone,	3605
Nu	11:22	**a.** the fish of the sea be gathered	3605
Nu	11:29	would God that **a.** the Lord's	3605
Nu	11:32	the people stood up **a.** that day,	3605
Nu	11:32	and **a.** that night,	3605
Nu	11:32	and **a.** the next day,	3605
Nu	11:32	they spread them **a.** abroad	3605
Nu	12:3	above **a.** the men which were upon	3605
Nu	12:7	who is faithful in **a.** mine house	
Nu	13:3	**a.** those men were heads of the	3605
Nu	13:26	Aaron, and to **a.** the congregation	3605
Nu	13:26	and unto **a.** the congregation,	3605
Nu	13:32	**a.** the people that we saw in it are	3605
Nu	14:1	**a.** the congregation lifted up their	3605
Nu	14:2	**a.** the children of Israel murmured	3605
Nu	14:5	their faces before **a.** the assembly	3605
Nu	14:7	spake unto **a.** the company of the	3605
Nu	14:10	**a.** the congregation bade stone	3605
Nu	14:10	before **a.** the children of Israel.	3605
Nu	14:11	me, for **a.** the signs which I have	3605
Nu	14:15	kill **a.** this people as one man,	
Nu	14:21	**a.** the earth shall be filled with	3605
Nu	14:22	Because **a.** those men which have	3605

Book	Ref	Context	No.
Nu	14:29	and **a.** that were numbered of you,	3605
Nu	14:35	do it unto **a.** this evil congregation.	3605
Nu	14:36	**a.** the congregation to murmur	3605
Nu	14:39	these sayings unto **a.** the children	3605
Nu	15:13	**A.** that are born of the country	3605
Nu	15:22	and not observed **a.** these commandments	
Nu	15:23	**a.** that the Lord hath commanded	3605
Nu	15:24	**a.** the congregation shall offer one	3605
Nu	15:25	atonement for **a.** the congregation	3605
Nu	15:26	be forgiven **a.** the congregation	3605
Nu	15:26	**a.** the people were in ignorance.	3605
Nu	15:33	and unto **a.** the congregation.	3605
Nu	15:35	**a.** the congregation shall stone him	3605
Nu	15:36	**a.** the congregation brought him	3605
Nu	15:39	remember **a.** the commandments	3605
Nu	15:40	do **a.** my commandments, and be	3605
Nu	16:3	**a.** the congregation are holy,	3605
Nu	16:5	Korah and unto **a.** his company,	3605
Nu	16:6	censers, Korah, and **a.** his company;	3605
Nu	16:10	**a.** thy brethren the sons of Levi	3605
Nu	16:11	and **a.** thy company are gathered	3605
Nu	16:16	Be thou and **a.** thy company before	3605
Nu	16:19	gathered **a.** the congregation	3605
Nu	16:19	appeared unto **a.** the congregation.	3605
Nu	16:22	the God of the spirits of **a.** flesh,	3605
Nu	16:22	wroth with **a.** the congregation?	3605
Nu	16:26	ye be consumed in **a.** their sins.	3605
Nu	16:28	Lord hath sent me to do **a.** these	3605
Nu	16:29	die the common death of **a.** men,	3605
Nu	16:29	after the visitation of **a.** men;	3605
Nu	16:30	**a.** that appertained unto them,	3605
Nu	16:31	an end of speaking **a.** these words,	3605
Nu	16:32	them up, and their houses, and **a.**	3605
Nu	16:32	unto Korah, and **a.** their goods.	3605
Nu	16:33	**a.** that appertained to them, went	3605
Nu	16:34	**a.** Israel that were round about	3605
Nu	16:41	**a.** the congregation of the children	3605
Nu	17:2	their fathers, of **a.** their princes	3605
Nu	17:9	**a.** the rods from before the Lord	3605
Nu	17:12	we die, we perish, we **a.** perish	3605
Nu	17:9	unto **a.** the children of Israel:	3605
Nu	18:3	the charge of **a.** the tabernacle:	3605
Nu	18:4	for **a.** the service of the tabernacle:	3605
Nu	18:8	offerings of **a.** the hallowed	3605
Nu	18:11	with **a.** the wave offerings of the	3605
Nu	18:12	**A.** the best of the oil,	3605
Nu	18:12	and **a.** the best of the wine,	3605
Nu	18:15	openeth the matrix in **a.** flesh,	3605
Nu	18:19	**A.** the heave offerings of the holy	3605
Nu	18:21	**a.** the tenth in Israel for an	3605
Nu	18:28	offering unto the Lord of **a.** your	3605
Nu	18:29	Out of **a.** your gifts ye shall offer	3605
Nu	18:29	offering of the Lord, of **a.** the best	3605
Nu	19:14	**a.** that come into the tent,	3605
Nu	19:14	and **a.** that is in the tent,	3605
Nu	19:18	the tent, and upon **a.** the vessels,	3605
Nu	20:14	Thou knowest **a.** the travel that	3605
Nu	20:27	in the sight of **a.** the congregation.	3605
Nu	20:29	when **a.** the congregation saw that	3605
Nu	20:29	for Aaron thirty days, even **a.** the	3605
Nu	21:23	Sihon gathered **a.** his people	3605
Nu	21:25	And Israel took **a.** these cities:	3605
Nu	21:25	in **a.** the cities of the Amorites,	3605
Nu	21:25	in Heshbon, and in **a.**	3605
Nu	21:26	taken **a.** his land out of his hand,	3605
Nu	21:33	he, and **a.** his people, to the battle	3605
Nu	21:34	into thy hand, and **a.** his people,	3605
Nu	21:35	and his sons, and **a.** his people,	3605
Nu	22:2	the son of Zippor saw **a.** that Israel	3605
Nu	22:4	this company lick up **a.** that are	3605
Nu	22:38	any power at **a.** to say any thing?	
Nu	23:6	sacrifice, he, and **a.** the princes	3605
Nu	23:13	of them, and shalt not see them **a.**:	3605
Nu	23:25	Neither curse them at **a.**,	
Nu	23:25	nor bless them at **a.**.	
Nu	23:26	**A.** that the Lord speaketh, that I	3605
Nu	24:17	destroy **a.** the children of Sheth.	3605
Nu	25:4	Take **a.** the heads of the people,	3605
Nu	25:6	Moses, and in the sight of **a.** the	3605
Nu	26:2	sum of **a.** the congregation of the	3605
Nu	26:2	**a.** that are able to go to war in	3605
Nu	26:43	**A.** the families of the Shuahmites,	3605
Nu	26:62	**a.** males from a month old and	3605
Nu	27:2	princes and **a.** the congregation,	3605
Nu	27:16	the God of the spirits of **a.** flesh,	3605
Nu	27:19	and before **a.** the congregation;	3605
Nu	27:20	upon him, that **a.** the congregation	3605
Nu	27:21	and **a.** the children of Israel with	3605
Nu	27:21	even **a.** the congregation.	3605
Nu	27:22	and before **a.** the congregation:	3605
Nu	29:40	to **a.** that the Lord commanded	3605
Nu	30:2	according to **a.** that proceedeth out	3605
Nu	30:4	her: then **a.** her vows shall stand,	3605
Nu	30:6	if she had at **a.** an husband,	
Nu	30:11	then **a.** her vows shall stand,	3605
Nu	30:14	establisheth **a.** her vows,	3605
Nu	30:14	or **a.** her bonds,	3605
Nu	31:4	throughout **a.** the tribes of Israel,	3605
Nu	31:7	and they slew **a.** the males.	3605
Nu	31:9	**a.** the women of Midian captives,	
Nu	31:9	**a.** their cattle,	
Nu	31:9	and **a.** their flocks,	3605
Nu	31:9	and **a.** their goods.	3605
Nu	31:10	And they burnt **a.** their cities	3605
Nu	31:10	**a.** their goodly castles, with fire.	3605
Nu	31:11	took **a.** the spoil,	3605
Nu	31:11	and **a.** the prey, both of men and	3605
Nu	31:13	**a.** the princes of the congregation,	3605
Nu	31:15	Have ye saved **a.** the women alive?	3605
Nu	31:18	**a.** the women children, that have	3605
Nu	31:20	And purify **a.** your raiment,	3605
Nu	31:20	and **a.** that is made of skins,	3605
Nu	31:20	and **a.** work of goats' hair,	3605
Nu	31:20	and **a.** things made of wood.	3605
Nu	31:23	**a.** that abideth not the fire ye shall	3605
Nu	31:27	and between **a.** the congregation:	3605
Nu	31:30	flocks, of **a.** manner of beasts,	3605
Nu	31:35	and two thousand persons in **a.**,	3605
Nu	31:51	of them, even **a.** wrought jewels.	3605
Nu	31:52	**a.** the gold of the offering that they	3605
Nu	32:13	forty years, until **a.** the generation,	3605
Nu	32:15	and ye shall destroy **a.** this people.	3605
Nu	32:21	go **a.** for you armed over Jordan	3605
Nu	32:26	**a.** our cattle, shall be there in the	3605
Nu	33:3	in the sight of **a.** the Egyptians.	3605
Nu	33:4	Egyptians buried **a.** their firstborn,	3605
Nu	33:52	shall drive out **a.** the inhabitants	3605
Nu	33:52	and destroy **a.** their pictures, and	3605
Nu	33:52	destroy **a.** their molten images,	3605
Nu	33:52	pluck down **a.** their high places:	3605
Nu	35:3	their goods, and for **a.** their beasts.	3605
Nu	35:7	**a.** the cities which ye shall give to	3605
Nu	35:29	generations in **a.** your dwellings.	3605
De	1:1	**a.** Israel on this side Jordan	3605
De	1:3	unto **a.** that the Lord had given	3605
De	1:7	unto **a.** the places nigh thereunto,	3605
De	1:18	**a.** the things which ye should do.	3605
De	1:19	**a.** that great and terrible	3605
De	1:30	to **a.** that he did for you in Egypt	3605
De	1:31	son, in **a.** the way that ye went,	3605
De	1:41	to **a.** that the Lord our God	3605
De	2:7	thee in **a.** the works of thy hand:	3605
De	2:14	until **a.** the generation of the men	3605
De	2:16	when **a.** the men of war were	3605
De	2:32	**a.** his people, to fight at Jahaz.	3605
De	2:33	and his sons, and **a.** his people.	3605
De	2:34	we took **a.** his cities at that time,	3605
De	2:36	Lord our God delivered **a.** unto us:	3605
De	3:1	he and **a.** his people, to battle at	3605
De	3:2	and **a.** his people, and his land,	3605
De	3:3	king of Bashan, and **a.** his people:	3605
De	3:4	we took **a.** his cities at that time,	3605
De	3:4	**a.** the region of Argob, the kingdom	3605
De	3:5	**A.** these cities were fenced with	3605
De	3:7	But **a.** the cattle, and the spoil of	3605
De	3:10	**A.** the cities of the plain,	3605
De	3:10	and **a.** Gilead, and **a.** Bashan,	3605
De	3:13	the rest of Gilead, and **a.** Bashan,	3605
De	3:13	**a.** the region of Argob,	3605
De	3:13	with **a.** Bashan,	3605
De	3:14	Manasseh took **a.** the country of	3605
De	3:18	**a.** that are meet for the war.	3605
De	3:21	**a.** that the Lord your God hath	3605
De	3:21	the Lord do unto **a.** the kingdoms	3605
De	4:3	**a.** the men that followed Baal-peor,	3605
De	4:6	which shall hear **a.** these statutes,	3605
De	4:7	in **a.** things that we call upon him	3605
De	4:8	so righteous as **a.** this law,	3605
De	4:9	thy heart **a.** the days of thy life:	3605
De	4:10	may learn to fear me **a.** the days	3605
De	4:19	even **a.** the host of heaven,	3605
De	4:19	God hath divided unto **a.** nations	3605
De	4:29	with **a.** thy heart	3605
De	4:29	and with **a.** thy soul.	3605
De	4:30	and **a.** these things are come upon	3605
De	4:34	according to **a.** that the Lord	3605
De	4:49	**a.** the plain on this side Jordan	3605
De	5:1	Moses called **a.** Israel, and said	3605
De	5:3	are **a.** of us here alive this day.	3605
De	5:13	shalt labour, and do **a.** thy work:	3605
De	5:22	**a.** your assembly in the mount	3605
De	5:23	even **a.** the heads of your tribes,	3605
De	5:26	For who is there of **a.** flesh, that	3605
De	5:27	hear **a.** that the Lord our God	3605
De	5:27	unto us **a.** that the Lord our God	3605
De	5:28	said **a.** that they have spoken.	3605
De	5:29	**a.** my commandments always,	3605
De	5:31	unto thee **a.** the commandments,	3605
De	5:33	walk in **a.** the ways which the	3605
De	6:2	thy God, to keep **a.** his statutes	3605
De	6:2	sons's son, **a.** the days of thy life;	3605
De	6:5	Lord thy God with **a.** thine heart,	3605
De	6:5	and with **a.** thy soul,	3605
De	6:5	and with **a.** thy might.	3605
De	6:11	And houses full of **a.** good things,	3605
De	6:19	To cast out **a.** thine enemies from	3605
De	6:22	and upon **a.** his household,	3605
De	6:24	commanded us to do **a.** these	3605
De	6:25	to do **a.** these commandments	3605
De	7:6	above **a.** people that are upon the	3605
De	7:7	for ye were the fewest of **a.** people:	3605
De	7:14	shalt be blessed above **a.** people:	3605
De	7:15	take away from thee **a.** sickness,	3605
De	7:15	upon **a.** them that hate thee.	3605
De	7:16	consume **a.** the people which the	3605
De	7:18	unto Pharaoh, and unto **a.** Egypt;	3605
De	7:19	God do unto **a.** the people of whom	3605
De	8:1	**A.** the commandments which I	3605
De	8:2	remember all the way which the	3605
De	8:13	multiplied, and **a.** that thou hast	3605
De	8:19	do at **a.** forget the Lord thy God,	
De	9:10	according to **a.** the words,	3605
De	9:18	of **a.** your sins which ye sinned,	3605
De	10:12	thy God, to walk in **a.** his ways,	3605
De	10:12	Lord thy God with **a.** thy heart	3605
De	10:12	and with **a.** thy soul,	3605
De	10:14	earth also, with **a.** that therein is.	3605
De	10:15	even you above **a.** people, as it is	3605
De	11:3	of Egypt, and unto **a.** his land;	3605
De	11:6	and **a.** the substance that was in	3605
De	11:6	in the midst of **a.** Israel:	3605
De	11:7	seen **a.** the great acts of the Lord	3605
De	11:8	ye keep **a.** the commandments	3605
De	11:13	to serve him with **a.** your heart	3605
De	11:13	and with **a.** your soul,	3605
De	11:22	keep **a.** these commandments	3605
De	11:22	your God, to walk in **a.** his ways,	3605
De	11:23	Lord drive out **a.** these nations	3605
De	11:25	you upon **a.** the land that ye shall	3605
De	11:32	to do **a.** the statutes and judgments	3605
De	12:1	**a.** the days that ye live upon the	3605
De	12:2	shall utterly destroy **a.** the places,	3605
De	12:5	shall choose out of **a.** your tribes	3605
De	12:7	in **a.** that ye put your hand unto,	3605
De	12:8	**a.** the things that we do here this	3605
De	12:10	you rest from **a.** your enemies	3605
De	12:11	ye bring **a.** that I command you;	3605
De	12:11	**a.** your choice vows which ye vow	3605
De	12:14	shalt do **a.** that I command thee.	3605
De	12:15	kill and eat flesh in **a.** thy gates,	3605
De	12:18	before the Lord thy God in **a.**	3605
De	12:28	Observe and hear **a.** these words	3605
De	13:3	God with **a.** your heart	3605
De	13:3	and with **a.** your soul.	3605
De	13:9	the hand of **a.** the people.	3605
De	13:11	**a.** Israel shall hear, and fear,	3605
De	13:15	it utterly, and **a.** that is therein,	3605
De	13:16	gather **a.** the spoil of it into the	3605
De	13:16	the city, and **a.** the spoil thereof	3605
De	13:18	to keep **a.** his commandments	3605
De	14:2	above **a.** the nations that are	3605
De	14:9	eat of **a.** that are in the waters:	3605
De	14:9	**a.** that have fins and scales shall	3605
De	14:11	Of **a.** clean birds ye shall eat.	3605
De	14:20	But of **a.** clean fowls ye may eat.	3605
De	14:22	tithe **a.** the increase of thy seed,	3605
De	14:28	bring forth **a.** the tithe of thine	3605
De	14:29	bless thee in **a.** the work of thine	3605
De	15:5	to do **a.** these commandments	3605
De	15:10	God shall bless thee in **a.** thy works	3605
De	15:10	in **a.** that thou puttest thine hand	3605

De 15:18 bless thee in **a.** that thou doest. 3605
De 15:19 **A.** the firstling males that come 3605
De 16:3 of Egypt **a.** the days of thy life. 3605
De 16:4 seen with thee in **a.** thy coast 3605
De 16:4 remain **a.** night until the morning. 3885
De 16:15 bless thee in **a.** thine increase, 3605
De 16:15 and in **a.** the works of thine hands, 3605
De 16:16 shall **a.** thy males appear before 3605
De 16:18 thou make thee in **a.** thy gates, 3605
De 17:7 the hands of **a.** the people. 3605
De 17:10 according to **a.** that they inform 3605
De 17:13 And **a.** the people shall hear, and 3605
De 17:14 **a.** the nations that are about me; 3605
De 17:19 read therein **a.** the days of his life: 3605
De 17:19 to keep **a.** the words of this law 3605
De 18:1 Levites, and **a.** the tribe of Levi, 3605
De 18:5 chosen him out of **a.** thy tribes, 3605
De 18:6 any of thy gates out of **a.** Israel, 3605
De 18:6 come with **a.** the desire of his mind 3605
De 18:7 as **a.** his brethren the Levites do, 3605
De 18:12 For **a.** that do these things are 3605
De 18:16 **a.** that thou desiredst of the Lord 3605
De 18:18 them **a.** that I shall command him. 3605
De 19:8 **a.** the land which he promised 3605
De 19:9 keep **a.** these commandments to 3605
De 20:11 **a.** the people that is found therein 3605
De 20:14 **a.** that is in the city, 3605
De 20:14 even **a.** the spoil thereof, 3605
De 20:15 shalt thou do unto **a.** the cities 3605
De 20:18 to do after **a.** their abominations, 3605
De 21:6 And **a.** the elders of that city, 3605
De 21:14 shalt not sell her at **a.** for money, 3605
De 21:17 double portion of **a.** that he hath. 3605
De 21:21 And **a.** the men of his city shall 3605
De 21:21 **a.** Israel shall hear, and fear. 3605
De 21:23 remain **a.** night upon the tree, 3885
De 22:3 **a.** lost thing of thy brother's, 3605
De 22:5 for **a.** that do so are abomination. 3605
De 22:19, 29 not put her away **a.** his days. 3605
De 23:6 prosperity **a.** thy days forever. 3605
De 23:20 God may bless thee in **a.** that 3605
De 24:8 to **a.** that the priests the Levites 3605
De 24:19 God may bless thee in **a.** the work 3605
De 25:16 **a.** that do such things, 3605
De 25:16 and **a.** that do unrighteously, 3605
De 25:18 of thee, even **a.** that were feeble 3605
De 25:19 from **a.** thine enemies round about, 3605
De 26:2 the first of **a.** the fruit of the earth, 3605
De 26:12 **a.** the tithes of thine increase 3605
De 26:13 to **a.** thy commandments which 3605
De 26:14 **a.** that thou hast commanded me 3605
De 26:16 and do them with **a.** thine heart, 3605
De 26:16 and with **a.** thy soul. 3605
De 26:18 keep **a.** his commandments; 3605
De 26:19 **a.** nations which he hath made, 3605
De 27:1 Keep **a.** the commandments which 3605
De 27:3 upon them **a.** the words of this law, 3605
De 27:8 the stones **a.** the words of this law. 3605
De 27:9 the Levites spake unto **a.** Israel, 3605
De 27:14 and say unto **a.** the men of Israel 3605
De 27:15 And **a.** the people shall answer 3605
De 27:16, 17,18,19,20,21,22,23,24,25 And **a.** the people shall say, Amen. 3605
De 27:26 confirmeth not **a.** the words of
De 27:26 **a.** the people shall say, Amen. 3605
De 28:1 and to do **a.** his commandments 3605
De 28:1 high above **a.** nations of the earth: 3605
De 28:2 **a.** these blessings shall come on 3605
De 28:8 in **a.** that thou settest thine hand 3605
De 28:10 **a.** people of the earth shall see 3605
De 28:12 bless **a.** the work of thine hand: 3605
De 28:15 to do **a.** his commandments 3605
De 28:15 **a.** these curses shall come upon 3605
De 28:20 vexation, and rebuke, in **a.** that 3605
De 28:25 into **a.** the kingdoms of the earth. 3605
De 28:26 shall be meat unto **a.** fowls of the 3605
De 28:32 longing for them **a.** the day long: 3605
De 28:33 **a.** thy labours, shall a nation which 3605
De 28:37 among **a.** nations whither the Lord 3605
De 28:40 olive trees throughout **a.** thy coasts, 3605
De 28:42 **A.** thy trees and fruit of thy land. 3605
De 28:45 **a.** these curses shall come upon 3605
De 28:47 for the abundance of **a.** things; 3605
De 28:48 nakedness, and in want of **a.** things: 3605
De 28:52 shall besiege thee in **a.** thy gates, 3605
De 28:52 trustedst, throughout **a.** thy land: 3605
De 28:52 shall besiege thee in **a.** thy gates, 3605
De 28:52 throughout **a.** thy land, which the 3605
De 28:55 shall distress thee in **a.** thy gates. 3605
De 28:57 for want of **a.** things secretly in 3605
De 28:58 to do **a.** the words of this law 3605
De 28:60 upon thee **a.** the diseases of Egypt, 3605
De 28:64 shall scatter thee among **a.** people, 3605
De 29:2 And Moses called unto **a.** Israel, 3605
De 29:2 Ye have seen **a.** that the Lord did 3605
De 29:2 and unto **a.** his servants, 3605
De 29:2 and unto **a.** his land; 3605
De 29:9 ye may prosper in **a.** that ye do. 3605
De 29:10 **a.** of you before the Lord your 3605
De 29:10 officers, with **a.** the men of Israel, 3605
De 29:20 **a.** the curses that are written in 3605
De 29:21 evil out of **a.** the tribes of Israel, 3605
De 29:21 **a.** the curses of the covenant that 3605
De 29:24 Even **a.** nations shall say, 3605
De 29:27 to bring upon it **a.** the curses that 3605
De 29:29 may do **a.** the words of this law. 3605
De 30:1 when **a.** these things are come 3605
De 30:1 to mind among **a.** the nations, 3605
De 30:2 according to **a.** that I command 3605
De 30:2 with **a.** thine heart, 3605
De 30:2 and with **a.** thy soul; 3605
De 30:3 gather thee from **a.** the nations, 3605
De 30:6 Lord thy God with **a.** thine heart, 3605
De 30:6 and with **a.** thy soul, that thou 3605
De 30:7 God will put **a.** these curses upon 3605
De 30:8 and do **a.** his commandments. 3605
De 30:10 turn unto the Lord thy God with **a.** 3605
De 30:10 thine heart, and with **a.** thy soul. 3605
De 31:1 spake these words unto **a.** Israel. 3605
De 31:5 unto **a.** the commandments which 3605
De 31:7 sight of **a.** Israel, Be strong and 3605
De 31:9 and unto **a.** the elders of Israel. 3605
De 31:11 When **a.** Israel is come to appear 3605
De 31:11 thou shalt read this law before **a.** 3605
De 31:12 to do **a.** the words of this law: 3605
De 31:18 **a.** the evils which they shall have 3605
De 31:28 unto me **a.** the elders of your tribes, 3605
De 31:30 in the ears of **a.** the congregation 3605
De 32:4 for **a.** his ways are judgment: 3605
De 32:27 and the Lord hath not done **a.** this. 3605
De 32:44 spake **a.** the words of this song, 3605
De 32:45 **a.** these words to **a.** Israel: 3605
De 32:46 hearts unto **a.** the words which I 3605
De 32:46 to do, **a.** the words of this law. 3605
De 33:3 **a.** his saints are in thy hand: 3605
De 33:12 shall cover him **a.** the day long, 3605
De 34:1 shewed him **a.** the land of Gilead, 3605
De 34:2 And **a.** Naphtali, and the land of 3605
De 34:2 Manasseh, and **a.** the land of Judah, 3605
De 34:11 In **a.** the signs and the wonders, 3605
De 34:11 to **a.** his servants, 3605
De 34:11 and to **a.** his land, 3605
De 34:12 And in **a.** that mighty hand, 3605
De 34:12 and in **a.** the great terror 3605
De 34:12 shewed in the sight of **a.** Israel. 3605
Jos 1:2 Jordan, thou, and **a.** this people, 3605
Jos 1:4 **a.** the land of the Hittites, and 3605
Jos 1:5 before thee **a.** the days of thy life: 3605
Jos 1:7 do according to **a.** the law, which 3605
Jos 1:8 according to **a.** that is written 3605
Jos 1:14 **a.** the mighty men of valour, and 3605
Jos 1:16 **A.** that thou commandest us we 3605
Jos 1:17 hearkened unto Moses in **a.** things, 3605
Jos 1:18 words in **a.** that thou commandest 3605
Jos 2:3 come to search out **a.** the country. 3605
Jos 2:9 that **a.** the inhabitants of the land 3605
Jos 2:13 my sisters, and **a.** that they have, 3605
Jos 2:18 and **a.** thy father's household, 3605
Jos 9:19 But **a.** the princes said unto **a.** the 3605
Jos 12:22 throughout **a.** the way, but found 3605
Jos 12:23 told him **a.** things that befell them: 3605
Jos 12:24 into our hands **a.** the land; 3605
Jos 12:24 **a.** the inhabitants of the country 3605
Jos 3:1 he and **a.** the children of Israel, 3605
Jos 3:7 thee in the sight of **a.** Israel, 3605
Jos 3:11 covenant of the Lord of **a.** the earth 3605
Jos 3:13 the Lord, the Lord of **a.** the earth, 3605
Jos 3:15 **a.** his banks **a.** the time 3605
Jos 3:17 and **a.** the Israelites passed over 3605
Jos 3:17 **a.** the people were passed clean 3605
Jos 4:1 when **a.** the people were clean 3605
Jos 4:10 according to **a.** that Moses 3605
Jos 4:11 when **a.** the people were clean 3605
Jos 4:14 Joshua in the sight of **a.** Israel; 3605
Jos 4:14 Moses, **a.** the days of his life. 3605
Jos 4:18 and flowed over **a.** his banks, as 3605
Jos 4:24 That **a.** the people of the earth 3605
Jos 5:1 when **a.** the kings of the Amorites, 3605
Jos 5:1 **a.** the kings of the Canaanites, 3605
Jos 5:4 **A.** the people that came out of 3605
Jos 5:4 males, even **a.** the men of war, 3605
Jos 5:5 Now **a.** the people that came out 3605
Jos 5:5 but **a.** the people that were born 3605
Jos 5:6 years in the wilderness, till **a.** the 3605
Jos 5:8 done circumcising **a.** the people, 3605
Jos 6:3 compass the city, **a.** ye men of war, 3605
Jos 6:5 trumpet, **a.** the people shall shout 3605
Jos 6:17 even it, and **a.** that are therein, 3605
Jos 6:17 **a.** that are with her in the house, 3605
Jos 6:19 But **a.** the silver, and gold, and 3605
Jos 6:21 destroyed **a.** that was in the city, 3605
Jos 6:22 the woman, and **a.** that she hath, 3605
Jos 6:23 her brethren, and **a.** that she had; 3605
Jos 6:23 brought out **a.** her kindred, and 3605
Jos 6:24 with fire, and **a.** that was therein: 3605
Jos 6:25 and **a.** that she had; and she 3605
Jos 6:27 noised throughout **a.** the country. 3605
Jos 7:3 Let not **a.** the people go up; but 3605
Jos 7:3 make not **a.** the people to labour 3605
Jos 7:7 thou at **a.** brought this people over
Jos 7:9 **a.** the inhabitants of the land 3605
Jos 7:15 with fire, he and **a.** that he hath: 3605
Jos 7:23 and unto **a.** the children of Israel, 3605
Jos 7:24 Joshua, and **a.** Israel with him, 3605
Jos 7:24 and his tent, and **a.** that he had: 3605
Jos 7:25 **a.** Israel stoned him with stones, 3605
Jos 8:1 take **a.** the people of war with thee, 3605
Jos 8:3 arose, and **a.** the people of war, 3605
Jos 8:4 from the city, but be ye **a.** ready: 3605
Jos 8:5 and **a.** the people that are with me, 3605
Jos 8:11 And **a.** the people, even the people 3605
Jos 8:13 even **a.** the host that was on the 3605
Jos 8:14 to battle, he and **a.** his people, 3605
Jos 8:15 And Joshua and **a.** Israel made as 3605
Jos 8:16 And **a.** the people that were in Ai 3605
Jos 8:21 when Joshua and **a.** Israel saw 3605
Jos 8:24 slaying **a.** the inhabitants of Ai 3605
Jos 8:24 **a.** fallen on the edge of the sword, 3605
Jos 8:24 **a.** the Israelites returned unto Ai, 3605
Jos 8:25 that **a.** that fell that day, both of 3605
Jos 8:25 even **a.** the men of Ai. 3605
Jos 8:26 destroyed **a.** the inhabitants of Ai. 3605
Jos 8:33 And **a.** Israel, and their elders, 3605
Jos 8:34 he read **a.** the words of the law, 3605
Jos 8:34 **a.** that is written in the book of the 3605
Jos 8:35 word of **a.** that Moses commanded, 3605
Jos 8:35 **a.** the congregation of Israel, 3605
Jos 9:1 when **a.** the kings which were on 3605
Jos 9:1 **a.** the coasts of the great sea over 3605
Jos 9:5 **a.** the bread of their provision 3605
Jos 9:9 of him, and **a.** that he did in Egypt, 3605
Jos 9:10 **a.** that he did to the two kings of 3605
Jos 9:11 our elders and **a.** the inhabitants 3605
Jos 9:17 But **a.** the princes said unto **a.** the 3605
Jos 9:18 And **a.** the congregation murmured 3605
Jos 9:19 But **a.** the princes said unto **a.** the 3605
Jos 9:21 of water unto **a.** the congregation; 3605
Jos 9:24 Moses to give you **a.** the land, 3605
Jos 9:24 **a.** the inhabitants of the land from 3605
Jos 10:2 **a.** the men thereof were mighty. 3605
Jos 10:5 they and **a.** their hosts, and 3605
Jos 10:6 for **a.** the kings of the Amorites
Jos 10:7 **a.** the people of war with him, 3605
Jos 10:7 and **a.** the mighty men 3605
Jos 10:9 and went up from Gilgal **a.** night. 3605
Jos 10:15 returned, and **a.** Israel with him, 3605
Jos 10:21 **a.** the people returned to the camp 3605
Jos 10:24 called for **a.** the men of Israel, 3605
Jos 10:25 the Lord do to **a.** your enemies 3605
Jos 10:28 them, and **a.** the souls that 3605
Jos 10:29 from Makkedah, and **a.** Israel 3605
Jos 10:30 and **a.** the souls that were therein; 3605
Jos 10:31 Libnah, and **a.** Israel with him, 3605
Jos 10:32 and **a.** the souls that were therein, 3605
Jos 10:32 according to **a.** that he had done 3605
Jos 10:34 unto Eglon, and **a.** Israel with him; 3605
Jos 10:35 and **a.** the souls that were therein, 3605
Jos 10:35 according to **a.** that he had done 3605
Jos 10:36 from Eglon, and **a.** Israel with him; 3605
Jos 10:37 thereof, and **a.** the cities thereof, 3605
Jos 10:37 and **a.** the souls that were therein; 3605

Jos 10:37 according to **a.** that he had done... 3605
Jos 10:37 it utterly, and **a.** the souls... 3605
Jos 10:38 and **a.** Israel with him, to Debir;... 3605
Jos 10:39 thereof, and **a.** the cities thereof;... 3605
Jos 10:39 **a.** the souls that were therein;... 3605
Jos 10:40 So Joshua smote **a.** the country of... 3605
Jos 10:40 of the springs, and **a.** their kings:... 3605
Jos 10:40 utterly destroyed **a.** that breathed,... 3605
Jos 10:41 and **a.** the country of Goshen,... 3605
Jos 10:42 And **a.** these kings and their land... 3605
Jos 10:43 returned, and **a.** Israel with him,... 3605
Jos 11:4 they and **a.** their hosts with them,... 3605
Jos 11:5 **a.** these kings were met together,... 3605
Jos 11:6 time will I deliver them up **a.** slain... 3605
Jos 11:7 and **a.** the people of war with him,... 3605
Jos 11:10 the head of **a.** those kingdoms... 3605
Jos 11:11 **a.** the souls that were therein with... 3605
Jos 11:12 And **a.** the cities of those kings,... 3605
Jos 11:12 and **a.** the kings... 3605
Jos 11:14 And **a.** the spoil of these cities,... 3605
Jos 11:15 of **a.** that the Lord commanded... 3605
Jos 11:16 So Joshua took **a.** that land,... 3605
Jos 11:16 and **a.** the south country,... 3605
Jos 11:16 and **a.** the land of Goshen,... 3605
Jos 11:17 under Mount Hermon: and **a.**... 3605
Jos 11:18 a long time with **a.** those kings... 3605
Jos 11:19 Gibeon: **a.** other they took in battle... 3605
Jos 11:21 from **a.** the mountains of Judah,... 3605
Jos 11:21 **a.** the mountains of Israel:... 3605
Jos 11:21 **a.** that the Lord said unto Moses;... 3605
Jos 12:1 Hermon, and **a.** the plain on the... 3605
Jos 12:5 and in **a.** Bashan, unto the border... 3605
Jos 12:24 one: **a.** the kings thirty and one... 3605
Jos 13:2 **a.** the borders of the Philistines,... 3605
Jos 13:2 and **a.** Geshuri,... 3605
Jos 13:4 **a.** the land of the Canaanites,... 3605
Jos 13:5 and **a.** Lebanon, toward the... 3605
Jos 13:6 **A.** the inhabitants of the hill... 3605
Jos 13:6 and **a.** the Sidonians, then will I... 3605
Jos 13:9 **a.** the plain of Medeba unto Dibon;... 3605
Jos 13:10 And **a.** the cities of Sihon king of... 3605
Jos 13:11 **a.** mount Hermon... 3605
Jos 13:11 and **a.** Bashan unto Salcah;... 3605
Jos 13:12 **A.** the kingdom of Og in Bashan,... 3605
Jos 13:16 river, and **a.** the plain by Medeba;... 3605
Jos 13:17 **a.** her cities that are in the plain;... 3605
Jos 13:21 And **a.** the cities of the plain,... 3605
Jos 13:21 and **a.** the kingdom of Sihon... 3605
Jos 13:25 Jazer, and **a.** the cities of Gilead,... 3605
Jos 13:30 from Mahanaim, **a.** Bashan,... 3605
Jos 13:30 **a.** the kingdom of Og king of... 3605
Jos 13:30 **a.** the towns of Jair, which are in... 3605
Jos 15:32 and Rimmon: **a.** the cities are... 3605
Jos 15:46 **a.** that lay near Ashdod, with their... 3605
Jos 16:9 **a.** the cities with their villages... 3605
Jos 17:16 for us: and **a.** the Canaanites... 3605
Jos 19:8 **a.** the villages that were round... 3605
Jos 20:9 appointed for **a.** the children of... 3605
Jos 21:19 **A.** the cities of the children of... 3605
Jos 21:26 **A.** the cities were ten with their... 3605
Jos 21:33 **A.** the cities of the Gershonites... 3605
Jos 21:39 her suburbs; four cities in **a.**... 3605
Jos 21:40 So **a.** the cities for the children of... 3605
Jos 21:41 **A.** the cities of the Levites within... 3605
Jos 21:42 them: thus were **a.** these cities... 3605
Jos 21:43 Lord gave unto Israel **a.** the land... 3605
Jos 21:44 according to **a.** that he sware unto... 3605
Jos 21:44 not a man of **a.** their enemies... 3605
Jos 21:44 Lord delivered **a.** their enemies... 3605
Jos 21:45 house of Israel; **a.** came to pass... 3605
Jos 22:2 **a.** that Moses the servant of the... 3605
Jos 22:2 in **a.** that I commanded you:... 3605
Jos 22:5 Lord your God, and to walk in **a.**... 3605
Jos 22:5 **a.** your heart and with **a.** your soul... 3605
Jos 22:14 **a.** the tribes of Israel;... 3605
Jos 22:20 wrath fell on **a.** the congregation... 3605
Jos 23:1 unto Israel from **a.** their enemies... 3605
Jos 23:2 And Joshua called for **a.** Israel,... 3605
Jos 23:3 seen **a.** that the Lord your God... 3605
Jos 23:3 done unto **a.** these nations because... 3605
Jos 23:4 **a.** the nations that I have cut off,... 3605
Jos 23:6 do **a.** that is written in the book of... 3605
Jos 23:14 I am going the way of **a.** the earth:... 3605
Jos 23:14 know in **a.** your hearts... 3605
Jos 23:14 and in **a.** your souls, that... 3605
Jos 23:14 hath failed of **a.** the good things... 3605
Jos 23:14 concerning you; **a.** are come to... 3605
Jos 23:15 **a.** good things are come upon you,... 3605
Jos 23:15 Lord bring upon you **a.** evil things,... 3605
Jos 24:1 Joshua gathered **a.** the tribes of... 3605
Jos 24:2 Joshua said unto **a.** the people,... 3605
Jos 24:3 throughout **a.** the land of Canaan,... 3605
Jos 24:17 and preserved us in **a.** the way... 3605
Jos 24:17 among **a.** the people through whom... 3605
Jos 24:18 out from before us **a.** the people,... 3605
Jos 24:27 Joshua said unto **a.** the people,... 3605
Jos 24:27 unto us; for it hath heard **a.** the... 3605
Jos 24:31 Israel served the Lord **a.** the days... 3605
Jos 24:31 and **a.** the days of the elders that... 3605
Jos 24:31 known **a.** the works of the Lord,... 3605
Jg 1:25 let go the man and **a.** his family... 3605
Jg 2:4 unto **a.** the children of Israel,... 3605
Jg 2:7 people served the Lord **a.** the days... 3605
Jg 2:7 and **a.** the days of the elders that... 3605
Jg 2:7 seen **a.** the great works of the Lord,... 3605
Jg 2:10 **a.** that generation were gathered... 3605
Jg 2:18 hand of their enemies **a.** the days... 3605
Jg 3:1 not known **a.** the wars of Canaan;... 3605
Jg 3:3 and **a.** the Canaanites, and the... 3605
Jg 3:19 And **a.** that stood by him went out... 3605
Jg 3:29 ten thousand men, **a.** lusty,... 3605
Jg 3:29 **a.** men of valour; and there... 3605
Jg 4:13 gathered together **a.** his chariots,... 3605
Jg 4:13 **a.** the people that were with him,... 3605
Jg 4:15 and **a.** his chariots,... 3605
Jg 4:15 and **a.** his host, with the... 3605
Jg 4:16 **a.** the host of Sisera fell upon the... 3605
Jg 5:31 let **a.** thine enemies perish, O Lord:... 3605
Jg 6:9 out of the hand of **a.** that oppressed... 3605
Jg 6:13 why then is **a.** this befallen us?... 3605
Jg 6:13 and where be **a.** his... 3605
Jg 6:31 unto **a.** that stood against him, Will... 3605
Jg 6:33 Then **a.** the Midianites and the... 3605
Jg 6:35 throughout **a.** Manasseh;... 3605
Jg 6:37 and it be dry upon **a.** the earth... 3605
Jg 6:39 upon **a.** the ground let there be dew... 3605
Jg 6:40 there was dew on **a.** the ground... 3605
Jg 7:1 who is Gideon, and **a.** the people... 3605
Jg 7:6 but **a.** the rest of the people bowed... 3605
Jg 7:7 let **a.** the other people go every... 3605
Jg 7:8 he sent **a.** the rest of Israel every... 3605
Jg 7:12 and the Amalekites and **a.** the... 3605
Jg 7:14 hath God delivered Midian, and **a.**... 3605
Jg 7:18 a trumpet, I and **a.** that are with... 3605
Jg 7:18 also on every side of **a.** the camp,... 3605
Jg 7:21 and **a.** the host ran, and cried, and... 3605
Jg 7:22 fellow, even throughout **a.** the host:... 3605
Jg 7:23 of Asher, and out of **a.** Manasseh,... 3605
Jg 7:24 messengers throughout **a.** mount... 3605
Jg 7:24 **a.** the men of Ephraim gathered... 3605
Jg 8:10 **a.** that were left of **a.** the hosts of... 3605
Jg 8:12 and discomfited **a.** the host... 3605
Jg 8:27 Ophrah: and **a.** Israel went thither... 3605
Jg 8:34 out of the hands of **a.** their enemies... 3605
Jg 8:35 according to **a.** the goodness which... 3605
Jg 9:1 with them, and with **a.** the family... 3605
Jg 9:2 pray you, in the ears of **a.** the men... 3605
Jg 9:2 that **a.** the sons of Jerubbaal,... 3605
Jg 9:3 the ears of **a.** the men of Shechem... 3605
Jg 9:3 **a.** these words: and their hearts... 3605
Jg 9:6 **a.** the men of Shechem gathered... 3605
Jg 9:6 and **a.** the house of Millo, and went,... 3605
Jg 9:14 said **a.** the trees unto the bramble,... 3605
Jg 9:25 they robbed **a.** that came along... 3605
Jg 9:34 rose up, and **a.** the people that... 3605
Jg 9:44 companies ran upon **a.** the people... 3605
Jg 9:45 fought against the city **a.** that day;... 3605
Jg 9:46 when **a.** the men of the tower of... 3605
Jg 9:47 **a.** the men of the tower of Shechem... 3605
Jg 9:48 he and **a.** the people that were... 3605
Jg 9:49 **a.** the people likewise cut down... 3605
Jg 9:49 **a.** the men of the tower of Shechem... 3605
Jg 9:51 thither fled **a.** the men and women,... 3605
Jg 9:51 and **a.** they of the city,... 3605
Jg 9:53 Abimelech's head, and **a.** to brake...
Jg 9:57 **a.** the evil of the men of Shechem... 3605
Jg 10:8 **a.** the children of Israel... 3605
Jg 10:18 over **a.** the inhabitants of Gilead... 3605
Jg 11:8 be our head over **a.** the inhabitants... 3605
Jg 11:11 Jephthah uttered **a.** his words,... 3605
Jg 11:20 but Sihon gathered **a.** his people... 3605
Jg 11:21 delivered Sihon and **a.** his people... 3605
Jg 11:21 so Israel possessed **a.** the land of... 3605
Jg 11:22 possessed **a.** the coasts of the... 3605
Jg 11:26 in **a.** the cities that be along by the... 3605
Jg 12:4 Jephthah gathered together **a.** the... 3605
Jg 13:13 Of **a.** that I said unto the woman... 3605
Jg 13:14 **a.** that I commanded her let her... 3605
Jg 13:23 have shewed us **a.** these things,... 3605
Jg 14:3 brethren, or among **a.** my people,... 3605
Jg 16:2 wait for him **a.** night in the gate of... 3605
Jg 16:2 were quiet **a.** the night, saying,... 3605
Jg 16:3 went away with them, bar and **a.**,... 5973
Jg 16:17 that he told her **a.** his heart, and... 3605
Jg 16:18 that he had told her **a.** his heart,... 3605
Jg 16:18 he hath shewed me **a.** his heart... 3605
Jg 16:27 **a.** the lords of the Philistines were... 3605
Jg 16:30 bowed himself with **a.** his might;...
Jg 16:30 fell upon the lords, and upon **a.**... 3605
Jg 16:31 his brethren and **a.** the house of... 3605
Jg 18:1 that day **a.** their inheritance had...
Jg 18:31 **a.** the time that the house of God... 3605
Jg 19:6 tarry **a.** night, and let thine heart... 3885
Jg 19:9 I pray you tarry **a.** night:... 3885
Jg 19:13 to lodge **a.** night, in Gibeah, or in... 3885
Jg 19:20 howsoever let **a.** thy wants lie... 3605
Jg 19:25 **a.** the night until the morning:... 3605
Jg 19:29 sent her into **a.** the coasts of Israel... 3605
Jg 19:30 that **a.** that saw it said, There was... 3605
Jg 20:1 **a.** the children of Israel went out,... 3605
Jg 20:2 And the chief of **a.** the people,... 3605
Jg 20:2 even of **a.** the tribes of Israel,... 3605
Jg 20:6 sent her throughout **a.** the country... 3605
Jg 20:7 ye are **a.** children of Israel; give... 3605
Jg 20:8 **a.** the people arose as one man,... 3605
Jg 20:10 men of an hundred throughout **a.**... 3605
Jg 20:10 according to **a.** the folly that they... 3605
Jg 20:11 **a.** the men of Israel were gathered... 3605
Jg 20:12 through **a.** the tribe of Benjamin,... 3605
Jg 20:16 Among **a.** this people there were... 3605
Jg 20:17 sword: **a.** these were men of war... 3605
Jg 20:25 men; **a.** these drew the sword... 3605
Jg 20:26 Then **a.** the children of Israel,... 3605
Jg 20:26 and **a.** the people, went up,... 3605
Jg 20:33 And **a.** the men of Israel rose up... 3605
Jg 20:34 chosen men out of **a.** Israel, and... 3605
Jg 20:35 **a.** these drew the sword... 3605
Jg 20:37 smote **a.** the city with the edge of... 3605
Jg 20:44 men; **a.** these were men of valour... 3605
Jg 20:46 **a.** which fell that day of Benjamin... 3605
Jg 20:46 drew the sword; **a.** these were men... 3605
Jg 20:48 and **a.** that came to hand: also... 3605
Jg 20:48 they set on fire **a.** the cities that... 3605
Jg 21:5 among **a.** the tribes of Israel,... 3605
Ru 1:19 that **a.** the city was moved about... 3605
Ru 2:11 fully been shewed me, **a.** that thou... 3605
Ru 2:21 they have ended **a.** my harvest... 3605
Ru 3:5 **A.** that thou sayest unto me I will... 3605
Ru 3:6 **a.** that her mother in law bade her... 3605
Ru 3:11 do to thee **a.** that thou requirest:... 3605
Ru 3:11 for **a.** the city of my people doth... 3605
Ru 3:16 my daughter? And she told her **a.**... 3605
Ru 4:7 confirm **a.** things; a man plucked... 3605
Ru 4:9 the elders, and unto **a.** the people,... 3605
Ru 4:9 this day, that I have bought **a.**... 3605
Ru 4:9 and **a.** that was Chilion's... 3605
Ru 4:11 **a.** the people that were in the gate,... 3605
1Sa 1:4 Peninnah his wife, and to **a.** her... 3605
1Sa 1:11 give him unto the Lord **a.** the days... 3605
1Sa 1:21 man Elkanah, and **a.** his house,... 3605
1Sa 2:14 **a.** that the fleshhook brought up... 3605
1Sa 2:14 So they did in Shiloh unto **a.**... 3605
1Sa 2:22 heard **a.** that his sons did... 3605
1Sa 2:22 unto **a.** Israel;... 3605
1Sa 2:23 evil dealings by **a.** this people... 3605
1Sa 2:28 choose him out of **a.** the tribes of... 3605
1Sa 2:28 give unto the house of thy father **a.**... 3605
1Sa 2:29 fat with the chiefest of **a.** the... 3605
1Sa 2:32 **a.** the wealth which God shall give... 3605
1Sa 2:33 grieve thine heart: and **a.** the... 3605
1Sa 3:12 will perform against Eli **a.** things... 3605
1Sa 3:17 hide anything from me of **a.** the... 3605
1Sa 3:20 And **a.** Israel from Dan even to... 3605
1Sa 4:1 word of Samuel came to **a.** Israel... 3605
1Sa 4:5 into the camp, **a.** Israel shouted... 3605
1Sa 4:8 that smote the Egyptians with **a.**... 3605
1Sa 4:13 into the city, and told it, **a.** the city... 3605
1Sa 5:8 **a.** the lords of the Philistines unto... 3605
1Sa 5:11 gathered together **a.** the lords of... 3605
1Sa 5:11 destruction throughout **a.** the city;... 3605
1Sa 6:4 for one plague was on you **a.**, and... 3605

1Sa 6:18 according to the number of **a.** the 3605
1Sa 7:2 **a.** the house of Israel lamented.......... 3605
1Sa 7:3 Samuel spake unto **a.** the house of..... 3605
1Sa 7:3 unto the Lord with **a.** your hearts,..... 3605
1Sa 7:5 Gather **a.** Israel to Mizpeh, and I....... 3605
1Sa 7:13 against the Philistines **a.** the days....... 3605
1Sa 7:15 Samuel judged Israel **a.** the days........ 3605
1Sa 7:16 judged Israel in **a.** those places.......... 3605
1Sa 8:4 **a.** the elders of Israel gathered.......... 3605
1Sa 8:5 to judge us like **a.** the nations. 3605
1Sa 8:7 of the people in **a.** that they say 3605
1Sa 8:8 According to **a.** the works which........ 3605
1Sa 8:10 Samuel told **a.** the words of the Lord.. 3605
1Sa 8:20 we also may be like **a.** the nations;..... 3605
1Sa 8:21 And Samuel heard **a.** the words of...... 3605
1Sa 9:6 **a.** that he saith cometh surely to......... 3605
1Sa 9:19 tell thee **a.** that is in thine heart. 3605
1Sa 9:20 on whom is **a.** the desire of Israel?..... 3605
1Sa 9:20 and on **a.** thy father's house? 3605
1Sa 9:21 least of **a.** the families of the tribe..... 3605
1Sa 10:9 **a.** those signs came to pass that......... 3605
1Sa 10:11 when **a.** that knew him beforetime...... 3605
1Sa 10:18 Egyptians, and out of the hand of **a.**.... 3605
1Sa 10:19 saved you out of **a.** your adversities ... 3605
1Sa 10:20 had caused **a.** the tribes of Israel....... 3605
1Sa 10:24 And Samuel said to **a.** the people,....... 3605
1Sa 10:24 none like him among **a.** the people?.... 3605
1Sa 10:24 **a.** the people shouted, and said,......... 3605
1Sa 10:25 Samuel sent **a.** the people away,......... 3605
1Sa 11:1 **a.** the men of Jabesh said unto.......... 3605
1Sa 11:2 may thrust out **a.** your right eyes,....... 3605
1Sa 11:2 lay it for a reproach upon **a.** Israel. 3605
1Sa 11:3 send messengers unto **a.** the coasts.... 3605
1Sa 11:4 **a.** the people lifted up their voices,..... 3605
1Sa 11:7 throughout **a.** the coasts of Israel....... 3605
1Sa 11:10 **a.** that seemeth good unto you. 3605
1Sa 11:15 And **a.** the people went to Gilgal;....... 3605
1Sa 11:15 and **a.** the men of Israel rejoiced........ 3605
1Sa 12:1 Samuel said unto **a.** Israel, Behold,...... 3605
1Sa 12:1 voice in **a.** that ye said unto me,........ 3605
1Sa 12:7 **a.** the righteous acts of the Lord,....... 3605
1Sa 12:18 **a.** the people greatly feared the......... 3605
1Sa 12:19 **a.** the people said unto Samuel, ... 3605
1Sa 12:19 added unto **a.** our sins this evil,........ 3605
1Sa 12:20 done **a.** this wickedness: yet turn....... 3605
1Sa 12:20 serve the Lord with **a.** your heart;..... 3605
1Sa 12:24 him in truth with **a.** your heart. 3605
1Sa 13:3 the trumpet throughout **a.** the land..... 3605
1Sa 13:4 And **a.** Israel heard say that Saul....... 3605
1Sa 13:7 and **a.** the people followed him 3605
1Sa 13:19 throughout **a.** the land of Israel:......... 3605
1Sa 13:20 **a.** the Israelites went down to the...... 3605
1Sa 14:7 Do **a.** that is in thine heart: turn........ 3605
1Sa 14:15 the host, in the field; and among **a.**.... 3605
1Sa 14:20 Saul and **a.** the people that were........ 3605
1Sa 14:22 Likewise **a.** the men of Israel........... 3605
1Sa 14:25 And **a.** they of the land came to a...... 3605
1Sa 14:34 And **a.** the people brought every man . 3605
1Sa 14:38 hither, **a.** the chief of the people:....... 3605
1Sa 14:39 **a.** the people that answered him. 3605
1Sa 14:40 unto **a.** Israel, Be ye on one side,...... 3605
1Sa 14:47 fought against **a.** his enemies on 3605
1Sa 14:52 against the Philistines **a.** the days....... 3605
1Sa 15:3 and utterly destroy **a.** that they 3605
1Sa 15:6 to **a.** the children of Israel, ... 3605
1Sa 15:8 destroyed **a.** the people with the........ 3605
1Sa 15:9 the lambs, and **a.** that was good, ... 3605
1Sa 15:11 he cried unto the Lord **a.** night.......... 3605
1Sa 16:11 Jesse, Are here **a.** thy children?.......... 8552
1Sa 17:11 and **a.** Israel heard those words of..... 3605
1Sa 17:19 and **a.** the men of Israel, were........... 3605
1Sa 17:24 And **a.** the men of Israel, when.......... 3605
1Sa 17:46 **a.** the earth may know that there....... 3605
1Sa 17:47 And **a.** this assembly shall know......... 3605
1Sa 18:5 in the sight of **a.** the people,............ 3605
1Sa 18:6 came out of **a.** cities of Israel,........... 3605
1Sa 18:14 behaved himself wisely in **a.** his......... 3605
1Sa 18:16 **a.** Israel and Judah loved David,......... 3605
1Sa 18:22 hath delight in thee and **a.** his........... 3605
1Sa 18:30 himself more wisely than **a.**.............. 3605
1Sa 19:1 to Jonathan his son, and to **a.**........... 3605
1Sa 19:5 a great salvation for **a.** Israel:........... 3605
1Sa 19:7 and Jonathan shewed him **a.** those...... 3605
1Sa 19:18 told him **a.** that Saul had done to 3605
1Sa 19:24 lay down naked **a.** that day............... 3605
1Sa 19:24 and **a.** that night.......................... 3605
1Sa 20:6 If thy father at **a.** miss me, then.............
1Sa 20:6 sacrifice there for **a.** the family. 3605
1Sa 22:1 and **a.** his father's house heard it,....... 3605
1Sa 22:4 with him **a.** the while that David........ 3605
1Sa 22:6 in his hand, and **a.** his servants.......... 3605
1Sa 22:7 make you **a.** captains of thousands...... 3605
1Sa 22:8 That **a.** of you have conspired........... 3605
1Sa 22:11 Ahitub, and **a.** his father's house,....... 3605
1Sa 22:11 they came **a.** of them to the king....... 3605
1Sa 22:14 so faithful among **a.** thy servants........ 3605
1Sa 22:15 nor to **a.** the house of my father:........ 3605
1Sa 22:15 servant knew nothing of **a.** this,......... 3605
1Sa 22:16 thou, and **a.** thy father's house. 3605
1Sa 22:22 the death of **a.** the persons of........... 3605
1Sa 23:8 called **a.** the people together to war,... 3605
1Sa 23:20 according to **a.** the desire of thy........ 3605
1Sa 23:23 knowledge of **a.** the lurking places...... 3605
1Sa 23:23 **a.** the thousands of Judah. 3605
1Sa 24:2 three thousand chosen men out of **a.**.. 3605
1Sa 25:1 **a.** the Israelites were gathered.......... 3605
1Sa 25:6 peace be unto **a.** that thou hast. 3605
1Sa 25:7 them, **a.** the while they were in.......... 3605
1Sa 25:9 Nabal according to **a.** those words...... 3605
1Sa 25:12 again, and came and told him **a.**......... 3605
1Sa 25:16 by night and day, **a.** the while 3605
1Sa 25:17 against our master, and against **a.**...... 3605
1Sa 25:21 have I kept **a.** that this fellow............ 3605
1Sa 25:21 was missed of **a.** that pertained 3605
1Sa 25:22 if I leave of **a.** that pertain to him 3605
1Sa 25:28 not been found in thee **a.** thy days, ...
1Sa 25:30 according to **a.** the good that he 3605
1Sa 26:12 for they were **a.** asleep; because........ 3605
1Sa 26:24 deliver me out of **a.** tribulation........... 3605
1Sa 27:11 manner **a.** the while he dwelleth 3605
1Sa 28:3 dead, and **a.** Israel had lamented........ 3605
1Sa 28:4 and Saul gathered **a.** Israel................ 3605
1Sa 28:20 **a.** along on the earth, ... 4393
1Sa 28:20 eaten no bread **a.** the day,................ 3605
1Sa 28:20 nor **a.** the night............................ 3605
1Sa 29:1 gathered together **a.** their armies........ 3605
1Sa 30:6 soul of **a.** the people was grieved,....... 3605
1Sa 30:8 them, and without fail recover **a.**..............
1Sa 30:16 spread abroad upon **a.** the earth,......... 3605
1Sa 30:16 dancing, because of **a.** the great......... 3605
1Sa 30:18 recovered **a.** that the Amalekites.......... 3605
1Sa 30:19 taken to them: David recovered **a.**...... 3605
1Sa 30:20 And David took **a.** the flocks and 3605
1Sa 30:22 answered **a.** the wicked men and 3605
1Sa 30:31 in Hebron, and to **a.** the places.......... 3605
1Sa 31:6 armourbearer, and **a.** his men,........... 3605
1Sa 31:12 **A.** the valiant men arose, ... 3605
1Sa 31:12 and went **a.** night, and..................... 3605
2Sa 1:11 them; and likewise **a.** the men that..... 3605
2Sa 2:9 Benjamin, and over **a.** Israel. 3605
2Sa 2:28 and **a.** the people stood still, and......... 3605
2Sa 2:29 and his men walked **a.** that night........ 3605
2Sa 2:29 and went through **a.** Bithron, ... 3605
2Sa 2:30 gathered **a.** the people together, ... 3605
2Sa 2:32 Joab and his men went **a.** night,.......... 3605
2Sa 3:12 be with thee, to bring about **a.**.......... 3605
2Sa 3:18 out of the hand of **a.** their enemies..... 3605
2Sa 3:19 of David in Hebron **a.** that seemed...... 3605
2Sa 3:21 will gather **a.** Israel unto my lord 3605
2Sa 3:21 over **a.** that thine heart desireth. 3605
2Sa 3:23 Joab and **a.** the host that was with 3605
2Sa 3:25 and to know **a.** that thou doest........... 3605
2Sa 3:29 and on **a.** his father's house; 3605
2Sa 3:31 and to **a.** the people that were 3605
2Sa 3:32 of Abner; and **a.** the people wept......... 3605
2Sa 3:34 **a.** the people wept again over him...... 3605
2Sa 3:35 when **a.** the people came to cause...... 3605
2Sa 3:36 **a.** the people took notice of it, ... 3605
2Sa 3:36 whatsoever the king did pleased **a.**...... 3605
2Sa 3:37 For **a.** the people and **a.** Israel.......... 3605
2Sa 4:1 and **a.** the Israelites were troubled. 3605
2Sa 4:7 away through the plain **a.** night.......... 3605
2Sa 4:9 my soul out of **a.** adversity, ... 3605
2Sa 5:1 came **a.** the tribes of Israel to........... 3605
2Sa 5:3 So **a.** the elders of Israel came to 3605
2Sa 5:5 years over **a.** Israel and Judah. 3605
2Sa 5:17 **a.** the Philistines came up to seek...... 3605
2Sa 6:1 **a.** the chosen men of Israel,.............. 3605
2Sa 6:2 arose, and went with **a.** the people..... 3605
2Sa 6:5 and **a.** the house of Israel played........ 3605
2Sa 6:5 on **a.** manner of instruments made...... 3605
2Sa 6:11 Obed-edom, and **a.** his household. 3605
2Sa 6:12 Obed-edom, and **a.** that pertaineth..... 3605
2Sa 6:14 before the Lord with **a.** his might;...... 3605
2Sa 6:15 **a.** the house of Israel brought up....... 3605
2Sa 6:19 And he dealt among **a.** the people,..... 3605
2Sa 6:19 So **a.** the people departed every........ 3605
2Sa 6:21 and before **a.** his house, to appoint..... 3605
2Sa 7:1 round about from **a.** his enemies;....... 3605
2Sa 7:3 Go, do **a.** that is in thine heart;......... 3605
2Sa 7:7 **a.** the places wherein I have walked ... 3605
2Sa 7:7 with **a.** the children of Israel............ 3605
2Sa 7:9 **a.** thine enemies out of thy sight,....... 3605
2Sa 7:11 to rest from **a.** thine enemies............ 3605
2Sa 7:17 According to **a.** these words, and....... 3605
2Sa 7:17 And according to **a.** this vision, so...... 3605
2Sa 7:21 thou done **a.** these great things, ... 3605
2Sa 7:22 God beside thee, according to **a.**........ 3605
2Sa 8:4 houghed **a.** the chariot horses,........... 3605
2Sa 8:9 smitten **a.** the host of Hadadezer, ... 3605
2Sa 8:11 of **a.** nations which he subdued;......... 3605
2Sa 8:14 throughout **a.** Edom put he............... 3605
2Sa 8:14 garrisons, and **a.** they of Edom.......... 3605
2Sa 8:15 And David reigned over **a.** Israel;....... 3605
2Sa 8:15 and justice unto **a.** his people. 3605
2Sa 9:7 **a.** the land of Saul thy father;............ 3605
2Sa 9:9 **a.** that pertained to Saul................... 3605
2Sa 9:9 and to **a.** his house. 3605
2Sa 9:11 According to **a.** that my lord the........ 3605
2Sa 9:12 And **a.** that dwelt in the house of....... 3605
2Sa 10:7 and **a.** the host of the mighty men...... 3605
2Sa 10:9 of **a.** the choice men of Israel,........... 3605
2Sa 10:17 he gathered **a.** Israel together, ... 3605
2Sa 10:19 **a.** the kings that were servants to...... 3605
2Sa 11:1 and his servants with him, and **a.**........ 3605
2Sa 11:9 with **a.** the servants of his lord, ... 3605
2Sa 11:18 **a.** the things concerning the war; 3605
2Sa 11:22 shewed David **a.** that Joab had........... 3605
2Sa 12:12 I will do this thing before **a.** Israel,..... 3605
2Sa 12:16 and lay **a.** night upon the earth. 3885
2Sa 12:29 And David gathered **a.** the people 3605
2Sa 12:31 unto **a.** the cities of the children of..... 3605
2Sa 12:31 David and **a.** the people returned 3605
2Sa 13:9 said, Have out **a.** men from me. 3605
2Sa 13:21 king David heard of **a.** these things,.... 3605
2Sa 13:23 Absalom invited **a.** the king's sons....... 3605
2Sa 13:25 Nay, my son, let us not **a.** now go,.... 3605
2Sa 13:27 and **a.** the king's sons go with him. 3605
2Sa 13:29 Then **a.** the king's sons arose,........... 3605
2Sa 13:30 hath slain **a.** the king's sons, ... 3605
2Sa 13:31 **a.** his servants stood by with their 3605
2Sa 13:32 they have slain **a.** the young men........ 3605
2Sa 13:33 that **a.** the king's sons are dead: 3605
2Sa 13:36 and **a.** his servants wept very sore..... 3605
2Sa 14:19 hand of Joab with thee in **a.** this?......... 3605
2Sa 14:19 put **a.** these words in the mouth......... 3605
2Sa 14:20 to know **a.** things that are in the........ 3605
2Sa 14:25 But in **a.** Israel there was none to...... 3605
2Sa 15:6 manner did Absalom to **a.** Israel......... 3605
2Sa 15:10 sent spies throughout **a.** the tribes..... 3605
2Sa 15:14 David said unto **a.** his servants.......... 3605
2Sa 15:16 went forth, and **a.** his household......... 3605
2Sa 15:17 forth, and **a.** the people after him....... 3605
2Sa 15:18 **a.** his servants passed on beside......... 3605
2Sa 15:18 and **a.** the Cherethites, ... 3605
2Sa 15:18 and **a.** the Pelethites, ... 3605
2Sa 15:18 and **a.** the Gittites, six hundred 3605
2Sa 15:22 passed over, and **a.** his men, ... 3605
2Sa 15:22 and **a.** the little ones 3605
2Sa 15:23 **a.** the country wept with a loud......... 3605
2Sa 15:23 **a.** the people passed over: the king.... 3605
2Sa 15:23 **a.** the people passed over, toward..... 3605
2Sa 15:24 Zadok also, and **a.** the Levites.......... 3605
2Sa 15:24 **a.** the people had done passing out..... 3605
2Sa 15:30 went barefoot: and **a.** the people......... 3605
2Sa 16:4 thine are **a.** that pertained unto.......... 3605
2Sa 16:6 and at **a.** the servants...................... 3605
2Sa 16:6 of king David: and **a.** the people 3605
2Sa 16:6 and **a.** the mighty men...................... 3605
2Sa 16:8 **a.** the blood of the house of Saul,........ 3605
2Sa 16:11 to Abishai, and to **a.** his servants, ... 3605
2Sa 16:14 the king, and **a.** the people that......... 3605
2Sa 16:15 and **a.** the people the men................ 3605
2Sa 16:18 and **a.** the men of Israel, choose,....... 3605
2Sa 16:21 **a.** Israel shall hear that thou art......... 3605
2Sa 16:21 then shall the hands of **a.** that........... 3605
2Sa 16:22 concubines in the sight of **a.** Israel. 3605
2Sa 16:23 so was **a.** the counsel of Ahithophel.... 3605
2Sa 17:2 **a.** the people that are with him.......... 3605
2Sa 17:3 bring back **a.** the people unto thee: 3605
2Sa 17:3 thou seekest is as if **a.** returned: 3605

2Sa 17:3 so **a.** the people shall be in peace....... 3605
2Sa 17:4 pleased Absalom well, and **a.** the 3605
2Sa 17:10 **a.** Israel knoweth that thy father....... 3605
2Sa 17:11 **a.** Israel be generally gathered.......... 3605
2Sa 17:12 of **a.** the men that are with him......... 3605
2Sa 17:13 **a.** Israel bring ropes to that city, ... 3605
2Sa 17:14 and **a.** the men of Israel said,........... 3605
2Sa 17:16 swallowed up, and **a.** the people 3605
2Sa 17:22 arose, and **a.** the people that were..... 3605
2Sa 17:24 Jordan, he and **a.** the men of Israel 3605
2Sa 18:4 by the gate side, and **a.** the people..... 3605
2Sa 18:5 And **a.** the people heard when........... 3605
2Sa 18:5 king gave **a.** the captains charge 3605
2Sa 18:8 scattered over the face of **a.** the......... 3605
2Sa 18:17 **a.** Israel fled every one to his tent. 3605
2Sa 18:28 and said unto the king, **A.** is well. ....
2Sa 18:31 avenged thee this day of **a.** them 3605
2Sa 18:32 **a.** that rise against thee to do........... 3605
2Sa 19:2 into mourning unto **a.** the people:........ 3605
2Sa 19:5 day the faces of **a.** thy servants, ... 3605
2Sa 19:6 had lived, and **a.** we had died............ 3605
2Sa 19:7 worse unto thee than **a.** the evil........ 3605
2Sa 19:8 unto **a.** the people, saying, Behold,...... 3605
2Sa 19:8 **a.** the people came before the king:..... 3605
2Sa 19:9 **a.** the people were at strife.............. 3605
2Sa 19:9 throughout **a.** the tribes of Israel,....... 3605
2Sa 19:11 the speech of **a.** Israel is come.......... 3605
2Sa 19:14 the heart of **a.** the men of Judah, ... 3605
2Sa 19:14 Return thou, and **a.** thy servants......... 3605
2Sa 19:20 the first this day of **a.** the house........ 3605
2Sa 19:28 For **a.** of my father's house were....... 3605
2Sa 19:30 Yea, let him take **a.**, forasmuch.......... 3605
2Sa 19:39 **a.** the people went over Jordan........... 3605
2Sa 19:40 and **a.** the people of Judah 3605
2Sa 19:41 behold, **a.** the men of Israel came to... 3605
2Sa 19:41 and **a.** David's men with him, ... 3605
2Sa 19:42 **a.** the men of Judah answered 3605
2Sa 19:42 we eaten at **a.** of the king's cost?............
2Sa 20:7 and **a.** the mighty men:................... 3605
2Sa 20:12 saw that **a.** the people stood still,....... 3605
2Sa 20:13 **a.** the people went on after Joab, ... 3605
2Sa 20:14 through **a.** the tribes of Israel........... 3605
2Sa 20:14 and to Beth-maachah, and **a.** the........ 3605
2Sa 20:15 **a.** the people that were with Joab........ 3605
2Sa 20:22 woman went unto **a.** the people in...... 3605
2Sa 20:23 was over **a.** the host of Israel: 3605
2Sa 21:9 and they fell **a.** seven together, ...
2Sa 21:14 his father: and they performed **a.**......... 3605
2Sa 22:1 out of the hand of **a.** his enemies, ... 3605
2Sa 22:23 **a.** his judgments were before me: 3605
2Sa 22:31 Lord is tried: he is a buckler to **a.** 3605
2Sa 23:5 ordered in **a.** things, and sure: 3605
2Sa 23:5 **a.** my salvation, and **a.** my desire, ... 3605
2Sa 23:6 **a.** of them as thorns thrust away, ... 3605
2Sa 23:39 Hittite: thirty and seven in **a.**. 3605
2Sa 24:2 now through **a.** the tribes of Israel, ... 3605
2Sa 24:7 and to **a.** the cities of the Hivites,...... 3605
2Sa 24:8 they had gone through **a.** the land, ... 3605
2Sa 24:23 **A.** these things did Araunah, as a....... 3605
1Ki 1:3 damsel throughout **a.** the coasts......... 3605
1Ki 1:9 **a.** his brethren the king's sons,........... 3605
1Ki 1:9 **a.** the men of Judah the king's........... 3605
1Ki 1:19 hath called **a.** the sons of the king,..... 3605
1Ki 1:20 the eyes of **a.** Israel are upon thee,..... 3605
1Ki 1:25 called **a.** the king's sons, and the 3605
1Ki 1:29 redeemed my soul out of **a.** distress, .. 3605
1Ki 1:39 and **a.** the people said, God save 3605
1Ki 1:40 **a.** the people came up after him,........ 3605
1Ki 1:41, 49 **a.** the guests that were with......... 3605
1Ki 2:2 I go the way of **a.** the earth: be......... 3605
1Ki 2:3 prosper in **a.** that thou doest,............ 3605
1Ki 2:4 in truth with **a.** their heart.............. 3605
1Ki 2:4 and with **a.** their soul,...................... 3605
1Ki 2:15 that **a.** Israel set their faces on me,.... 3605
1Ki 2:26 thou hast been afflicted in **a.** 3605
1Ki 2:44 **a.** the wickedness which thine 3605
1Ki 3:13 kings like unto thee **a.** thy days. 3605
1Ki 3:15 made a feast to **a.** his servants.......... 3605
1Ki 3:28 **a.** Israel heard of the judgment.......... 3605
1Ki 4:1 Solomon was king over **a.** Israel. 3605
1Ki 4:7 had twelve officers over **a.** Israel, ... 3605
1Ki 4:10 Sochoh, and **a.** the land of Hepher:..... 3605
1Ki 4:11 Abinadab, in **a.** the region of Dor; 3605
1Ki 4:12 Taanach and Megiddo, and **a.**.............. 3605
1Ki 4:21 Solomon reigned over **a.** kingdoms 3605
1Ki 4:21 Solomon **a.** the days of his life........... 3605
1Ki 4:24 **a.** the region on this side the river, ... 3605
1Ki 4:24 **a.** the kings on this side the river: 3605
1Ki 4:24 peace on **a.** sides round about him...... 3605
1Ki 4:25 Beer-sheba, **a.** the days of Solomon.... 3605
1Ki 4:27 for king Solomon, and for **a.**.............. 3605
1Ki 4:30 excelled the wisdom of **a.** the............ 3605
1Ki 4:30 and **a.** the wisdom of Egypt. 3605
1Ki 4:31 For he was wiser than **a.** men;.......... 3605
1Ki 4:31 was in **a.** nations round about............ 3605
1Ki 4:34 of **a.** people to hear the wisdom......... 3605
1Ki 4:34 Solomon, from **a.** kings of the earth,... 3605
1Ki 5:6 servants according to **a.** that thou 3605
1Ki 5:8 I will do **a.** thy desire concerning 3605
1Ki 5:10 trees according to **a.** his desire.......... 3605
1Ki 5:13 raised a levy out of **a.** Israel; 3605
1Ki 6:10 chambers against **a.** the house,.......... 3605
1Ki 6:12 and keep **a.** my commandments 3605
1Ki 6:18 **a.** was cedar; there was no stone....... 3605
1Ki 6:22 with gold, until he had finished **a.**....... 3605
1Ki 6:29 carved **a.** the walls of the house 3605
1Ki 6:38 house finished throughout **a.** the 3605
1Ki 6:38 according to **a.** the fashion of it.......... 3605
1Ki 7:1 thirteen years, and he finished **a.** 3605
1Ki 7:5 **a.** the doors and posts were square,... 3605
1Ki 7:9 **A.** these were of costly stones, ... 3605
1Ki 7:14 cunning to work **a.** works in brass...... 3605
1Ki 7:14 Solomon, and wrought **a.** his work...... 3605
1Ki 7:23 round **a.** about, and his height ....
1Ki 7:25 **a.** their hinder parts were................. 3605
1Ki 7:33 and their spokes, were **a.** molten. 3605
1Ki 7:37 **a.** of them had one casting, one......... 3605
1Ki 7:40 made an end of doing **a.** the work...... 3605
1Ki 7:45 and **a.** these vessels, which Hiram...... 3605
1Ki 7:47 left **a.** the vessels unweighed, ... 3605
1Ki 7:48 made **a.** the vessels that pertained..... 3605
1Ki 7:51 **a.** the work that king Solomon........... 3605
1Ki 8:1 of Israel, and **a.** the heads of the 3605
1Ki 8:2 **a.** the men of Israel assembled.......... 3605
1Ki 8:3 And **a.** the elders of Israel came, ... 3605
1Ki 8:4 **a.** the holy vessels that were in the.... 3605
1Ki 8:5 And king Solomon, and **a.**.................. 3605
1Ki 8:14 and blessed **a.** the congregation 3605
1Ki 8:14 (and **a.** the congregation of Israel....... 3605
1Ki 8:16 I chose no city out of **a.** the tribes 3605
1Ki 8:22 of **a.** the congregation of Israel, ... 3605
1Ki 8:23 before thee with **a.** their heart:.......... 3605
1Ki 8:38 any man, or by **a.** thy people Israel, ... 3605
1Ki 8:39 hearts of **a.** the children of men;)....... 3605
1Ki 8:40 thee **a.** the days that they live........... 3605
1Ki 8:43 according to **a.** that the stranger........ 3605
1Ki 8:43 that **a.** people of the earth may.......... 3605
1Ki 8:48 unto thee with **a.** their heart, ... 3605
1Ki 8:48 and with **a.** their soul, in the land...... 3605
1Ki 8:50 sinned against thee, and **a.** their 3605
1Ki 8:52 unto them in **a.** that they call 3605
1Ki 8:53 them from among **a.** the people of...... 3605
1Ki 8:54 had made an end of praying **a.**............ 3605
1Ki 8:55 **a.** the congregation of Israel............. 3605
1Ki 8:56 people Israel, according to **a.** that 3605
1Ki 8:56 hath not failed one word of **a.**............ 3605
1Ki 8:58 unto him, to walk in **a.** his ways, ... 3605
1Ki 8:59 of his people Israel at **a.** times,................
1Ki 8:60 That **a.** the people of the earth.......... 3605
1Ki 8:62 the king, and **a.** Israel with him, ... 3605
1Ki 8:63 king and **a.** the children of Israel......... 3605
1Ki 8:65 held a feast, and **a.** Israel with him,.... 3605
1Ki 8:66 **a.** the goodness that the Lord had...... 3605
1Ki 9:1 and **a.** Solomon's desire which he........ 3605
1Ki 9:4 to do according to **a.** that I have........ 3605
1Ki 9:6 at **a.** turn from following me,..................
1Ki 9:7 and a byword among **a.** people: 3605
1Ki 9:9 brought upon them **a.** this evil. 3605
1Ki 9:11 gold, according to **a.** his desire.)........ 3605
1Ki 9:19 **a.** the cities of store that Solomon...... 3605
1Ki 9:19 and in **a.** the land of his dominion....... 3605
1Ki 9:20 And **a.** the people that were left 3605
1Ki 10:2 him of **a.** that was in her heart. 3605
1Ki 10:3 Solomon told her **a.** her questions: 3605
1Ki 10:4 had seen **a.** Solomon's wisdom,.......... 3605
1Ki 10:13 the queen of Sheba **a.** her desire, ... 3605
1Ki 10:15 and of **a.** the kings of Arabia, ... 3605
1Ki 10:21 **a.** king Solomon's drinking vessels...... 3605
1Ki 10:21 **a.** the vessels of the house............... 3605
1Ki 10:23 exceeded **a.** the kings of the earth 3605
1Ki 10:24 **a.** the earth sought to Solomon,......... 3605
1Ki 10:29 so for **a.** the kings of the Hittites, ... 3605
1Ki 11:8 did he for **a.** his strange wives, ... 3605
1Ki 11:13 will not rend away **a.** the kingdom;..... 3605
1Ki 11:16 did Joab remain there with **a.** 3605
1Ki 11:25 to Israel **a.** the days of Solomon, ... 3605
1Ki 11:28 **a.** the charge of the house of 3605
1Ki 11:32 out of **a.** the tribes of Israel:)........... 3605
1Ki 11:34 prince **a.** the days of his life 3605
1Ki 11:37 to **a.** thay thy soul desireth,.............. 3605
1Ki 11:38 hearken unto **a.** that I command......... 3605
1Ki 11:41 acts of Solomon, and **a.** that he did,.... 3605
1Ki 11:42 reigned in Jerusalem over **a.** Israel..... 3605
1Ki 12:1 for **a.** Israel were come to Shechem... 3605
1Ki 12:3 and **a.** the congregation of Israel 3605
1Ki 12:12 Jeroboam and **a.** the people came....... 3605
1Ki 12:16 when **a.** Israel saw that the king........ 3605
1Ki 12:18 **a.** Israel stoned him with stones, ... 3605
1Ki 12:20 **a.** Israel heard that Jeroboam was...... 3605
1Ki 12:20 and made him king over **a.** Israel: 3605
1Ki 12:21 assembled **a.** the house of Judah, ... 3605
1Ki 12:23 and unto **a.** the house of Judah 3605
1Ki 13:11 came and told him **a.** the works......... 3605
1Ki 13:32 altar in Beth-el, and against **a.** the...... 3605
1Ki 14:8 who followed me with **a.** his heart,...... 3605
1Ki 14:9 evil above **a.** that were before thee: ... 3605
1Ki 14:10 away dung, till it be **a.** gone.............. 8552
1Ki 14:13 **a.** Israel shall mourn for him, ... 3605
1Ki 14:18 buried him; and **a.** Israel mourned...... 3605
1Ki 14:21 out of **a.** the tribes of Israel,............. 3605
1Ki 14:22 **a.** that their fathers had done. 3605
1Ki 14:24 according to **a.** the abominations 3605
1Ki 14:26 house; he even took away **a.**:.............. 3605
1Ki 14:26 he took away **a.** the shields of gold..... 3605
1Ki 14:29 Rehoboam, and **a.** that he did,........... 3605
1Ki 14:30 Rehoboam and Jeroboam **a.**................ 3605
1Ki 15:3 walked in **a.** the sins of his father,....... 3605
1Ki 15:5 commanded him **a.** the days of his...... 3605
1Ki 15:6 Jeroboam **a.** the days of his life.......... 3605
1Ki 15:7 acts of Abijam, and **a.** that he did,...... 3605
1Ki 15:12 **a.** the idols that his fathers 3605
1Ki 15:14 perfect with the Lord **a.** his days. 3605
1Ki 15:16 Asa and Baasha king of Israel **a.** 3605
1Ki 15:18 Asa took **a.** the silver and the gold..... 3605
1Ki 15:20 and **a.** Cinneroth,.............................. 3605
1Ki 15:20 with **a.** the land of Naphtali. 3605
1Ki 15:22 made a proclamation throughout **a.** 3605
1Ki 15:23 The rest of **a.** the acts of Asa, ... 3605
1Ki 15:23 and **a.** his might,................................ 3605
1Ki 15:23 and **a.** that he did, and the cities........ 3605
1Ki 15:27 **a.** Israel laid siege to Gibbethon......... 3605
1Ki 15:29 smote **a.** the house of Jeroboam;........ 3605
1Ki 15:31 act of Nadab, and **a.** that he did,........ 3605
1Ki 15:32 Asa and Baasha king of Israel **a.** 3605
1Ki 15:33 son of Ahijah to reign over **a.** Israel.... 3605
1Ki 16:7 for **a.** the evil that he did in the......... 3605
1Ki 16:11 he slew **a.** the house of Baasha: 3605
1Ki 16:12 destroy **a.** the house of Baasha,.......... 3605
1Ki 16:13 For **a.** the sins of Baasha, and the...... 3605
1Ki 16:14 the acts of Elah, and **a.** that he did,.... 3605
1Ki 16:16 wherefore **a.** Israel made Omri, ... 3605
1Ki 16:17 and **a.** Israel with him, and they......... 3605
1Ki 16:25 did worse than **a.** that were before..... 3605
1Ki 16:26 walked in **a.** the way of Jeroboam....... 3605
1Ki 16:30 of the Lord above **a.** that were.......... 3605
1Ki 16:33 Lord God of Israel to anger than **a.**..... 3605
1Ki 18:5 land, unto **a.** fountains of water,......... 3605
1Ki 18:5 and unto **a.** brooks: peradventure............
1Ki 18:5 mules alive, that we lose not **a.** 3605
1Ki 18:19 gather to me **a.** Israel unto mount...... 3605
1Ki 18:20 Ahab sent unto **a.** the children of....... 3605
1Ki 18:21 Elijah came unto **a.** the people,......... 3605
1Ki 18:24 by fire, let him be God. And **a.** 3605
1Ki 18:30 And Elijah said unto **a.** the people, ... 3605
1Ki 18:30 **a.** the people came near unto him. 3605
1Ki 18:36 done **a.** these things at thy word........ 3605
1Ki 18:39 And when **a.** the people saw it, ... 3605
1Ki 19:1 Ahab told Jezebel **a.** that Elijah.......... 3605
1Ki 19:1 how he had slain **a.** the prophets........ 3605
1Ki 19:18 **a.** the knees which have not bowed.... 3605
1Ki 20:1 king of Syria gathered **a.** his host....... 3605
1Ki 20:4 thy saying, I am thine, and **a.** that....... 3605
1Ki 20:7 king of Israel called **a.** the elders 3605
1Ki 20:8 And **a.** the elders............................... 3605
1Ki 20:8 and **a.** the people said,...................... 3605
1Ki 20:9 **A.** that thou didst send for thy 3605
1Ki 20:10 for handfuls for **a.** the people that 3605
1Ki 20:13 thou seen **a.** this great multitude? 3605
1Ki 20:15 he numbered **a.** the people,................ 3605
1Ki 20:15 even **a.** the children of Israel, being.... 3605
1Ki 20:27 numbered, and were **a.** present, ...

1Ki 20:28 I deliver **a.** this great multitude.......... 3605
1Ki 21:26 in following idols, according to **a.**......... 3605
1Ki 22:10, 12 **a.** the prophets prophesied........... 3605
1Ki 22:17 **a.** Israel scattered upon the hills,......... 3605
1Ki 22:19 sitting on his throne, and **a.** the......... 3605
1Ki 22:22 in the mouth of **a.** his prophets........... 3605
1Ki 22:23 **a.** these thy prophets, and the Lord.... 3605
1Ki 22:28 said, If thou return at **a.** in peace,............
1Ki 22:39 acts of Ahab, and **a.** that he did,......... 3605
1Ki 22:39 and **a.** the cities that he built,........... 3605
1Ki 22:43 in **a.** the ways of Asa his father;......... 3605
1Ki 22:53 Lord God of Israel, according to **a.**....... 3605
2Ki 3:6 time, and numbered **a.** Israel............ 3605
2Ki 3:19 every good tree, and stop **a.** wells...... 3605
2Ki 3:21 And when **a.** the Moabites heard......... 3605
2Ki 3:21 **a.** that were able to put on armour,...... 3605
2Ki 3:25 they stopped **a.** the wells of water,..... 3605
2Ki 3:25 and felled **a.** the good trees:............. 3605
2Ki 4:3 abroad of **a.** thy neighbours,.............. 3605
2Ki 4:4 shalt pour into **a.** those vessels,.......... 3605
2Ki 4:13 careful for us with **a.** this care;........... 3605
2Ki 5:12 better than **a.** the waters of............... 3605
2Ki 5:15 to the man of God, he and **a.** his........ 3605
2Ki 5:15 there is no God in **a.** the earth,.......... 3605
2Ki 5:21 to meet him, and said, Is **a.** well?............
2Ki 5:22 **A.** is well. My master hath sent...............
2Ki 6:24 king of Syria gathered **a.** his host,........ 3605
2Ki 7:13 are as **a.** the multitude of Israel.......... 3605
2Ki 7:13 behold, I say, they are even as **a.**........ 3605
2Ki 7:15 lo, **a.** the way was full of garments...... 3605
2Ki 8:4 **a.** the great things that Elisha........... 3605
2Ki 8:6 Restore **a.** that was hers,................... 3605
2Ki 8:6 and **a.** the fruits of the field.............. 3605
2Ki 8:21 Zair, and **a.** the chariots with him:........ 3605
2Ki 8:23 acts of Joram, and **a.** that he did,......... 3605
2Ki 9:5 Jehu said, Unto which of **a.** of us?......... 3605
2Ki 9:7 of **a.** the servants of the Lord,............ 3605
2Ki 9:11 one said unto him, Is **a.** well?...............
2Ki 9:14 Ramoth-gilead, he and **a.** Israel,.......... 3605
2Ki 10:5 will do **a.** that thou shalt bid us;.......... 3605
2Ki 10:9 to **a.** the people, Ye be righteous:........ 3605
2Ki 10:9 but who slew **a.** these?...................... 3605
2Ki 10:11 Jehu slew **a.** that remained of the......... 3605
2Ki 10:11 in Jezreel, and **a.** his great men,.......... 3605
2Ki 10:17 slew **a.** that remained unto Ahab........ 3605
2Ki 10:18 gathered **a.** the people together,.......... 3605
2Ki 10:19 unto me **a.** the prophets of Baal,........ 3605
2Ki 10:19 **a.** his servants, and **a.** his priests:...... 3605
2Ki 10:21 And Jehu sent through **a.** Israel:......... 3605
2Ki 10:21 and **a.** the worshippers of Baal.......... 3605
2Ki 10:22 vestments for **a.** the worshippers......... 3605
2Ki 10:30 to **a.** that was in mine heart, thy.......... 3605
2Ki 10:31 with **a.** his heart: for he departed......... 3605
2Ki 10:32 them in **a.** the coasts of Israel;........... 3605
2Ki 10:33 eastward, **a.** the land of Gilead,.......... 3605
2Ki 10:34 acts of Jehu and **a.** that he did,........... 3605
2Ki 10:34 and **a.** his might,............................ 3605
2Ki 11:1 arose and destroyed **a.** the seed......... 3605
2Ki 11:7 **a.** you that go forth on the sabbath,...... 3605
2Ki 11:9 **a.** things that Jehoiada the priest......... 3605
2Ki 11:14, 18,19,20 **a.** the people of the land....... 3605
2Ki 12:2 the sight of the Lord **a.** his days.......... 3605
2Ki 12:4 **A.** the money of the dedicated............ 3605
2Ki 12:4 **a.** the money that cometh into any...... 3605
2Ki 12:9 put therein **a.** the money.................. 3605
2Ki 12:12 of the house of the Lord, and for **a.**..... 3605
2Ki 12:18 Jehoash king of Judah took **a.** the........ 3605
2Ki 12:18 **a.** the gold that was found in the......... 3605
2Ki 12:19 acts of Joash, and **a.** that he did,......... 3605
2Ki 13:3 the son of Hazael, **a.** their days.......... 3605
2Ki 13:8 of the acts of Jehoahaz, and **a.**............ 3605
2Ki 13:11 he departed not from **a.** the sins of..... 3605
2Ki 13:12 acts of Joash, and **a.** that he did,......... 3605
2Ki 13:22 Israel **a.** the days of Jehoahaz............. 3605
2Ki 14:3 according to **a.** things as Joash........... 3605
2Ki 14:14 he took **a.** the gold and silver,............ 3605
2Ki 14:14 and **a.** the vessels that were found...... 3605
2Ki 14:21 And **a.** the people of Judah took.......... 3605
2Ki 14:24 he departed not from **a.** the sins.......... 3605
2Ki 14:28 acts of Jeroboam, and **a.** that he......... 3605
2Ki 15:3 **a.** that his father Amaziah had............ 3605
2Ki 15:6 acts of Azariah, and **a.** that he did,....... 3605
2Ki 15:16 smote Tiphsah, and **a.** that were......... 3605
2Ki 15:16 him, therefore he smote it; and **a.**........ 3605
2Ki 15:18 he departed not **a.** his days from........ 3605
2Ki 15:20 of **a.** the mighty men of wealth,.......... 3605
2Ki 15:21 acts of Menahem, and **a.** that he......... 3605
2Ki 15:26 of Pekahiah, and **a.** that he did,.......... 3605
2Ki 15:29 Gilead, and Galilee, **a.** the land of....... 3605
2Ki 15:31 of the acts of Pekah, and **a.** that......... 3605
2Ki 15:34 according to **a.** that his father............. 3605
2Ki 15:36 acts of Jotham, and **a.** that he did,....... 3605
2Ki 16:10 according to **a.** the workmanship......... 3605
2Ki 16:11 according to **a.** that king Ahaz........... 3605
2Ki 16:15 of **a.** the people of the land,............... 3605
2Ki 16:15 **a.** the blood of the burnt offering,....... 3605
2Ki 16:15 **a.** the blood of the sacrifice: and......... 3605
2Ki 16:16 to **a.** that king Ahaz commanded......... 3605
2Ki 17:5 came up throughout **a.** the land,......... 3605
2Ki 17:9 them high places in **a.** their cities,....... 3605
2Ki 17:11 incense in **a.** the high places,............. 3605
2Ki 17:13 by **a.** the prophets,............................ 3605
2Ki 17:13 and by **a.** the seers, saying,............... 3605
2Ki 17:13 to **a.** the law which I commanded......... 3605
2Ki 17:16 **a.** the commandments of the Lord....... 3605
2Ki 17:16 worshipped **a.** the host of heaven,....... 3605
2Ki 17:20 Lord rejected **a.** the seed of Israel,..... 3605
2Ki 17:22 of Israel walked in **a.** the sins........... 3605
2Ki 17:23 by **a.** his servants the prophets.......... 3605
2Ki 17:39 deliver you out of the hand of **a.**.......... 3605
2Ki 18:3 to **a.** that David his father did............ 3605
2Ki 18:5 was none like him among **a.** the.......... 3605
2Ki 18:12 his covenant, and **a.** that Moses......... 3605
2Ki 18:13 up against **a.** the fenced cities........... 3605
2Ki 18:15 gave him **a.** the silver that was........... 3605
2Ki 18:21 king of Egypt unto **a.** that trust on...... 3605
2Ki 18:33 delivered at **a.** his land out of....................
2Ki 18:35 **a.** the gods of the countries,............... 3605
2Ki 19:4 thy God will hear **a.** the words........... 3605
2Ki 19:11 of Assyria have done to **a.** lands,......... 3605
2Ki 19:15 thou alone, of **a.** the kingdoms........... 3605
2Ki 19:19 of his hand, that **a.** the kingdoms........ 3605
2Ki 19:24 sole of my feet have I dried up **a.**......... 3605
2Ki 19:35 behold, they were **a.** dead corpses...... 3605
2Ki 20:13 **a.** the house of his precious things,..... 3605
2Ki 20:13 **a.** the house of his armour,............... 3605
2Ki 20:13 **a.** that was found in his treasures:...... 3605
2Ki 20:13 nor in **a.** his dominion, that................ 3605
2Ki 20:15 **A.** the things that are in mine........... 3605
2Ki 20:17 days come, that **a.** that is in thine........ 3605
2Ki 20:20 acts of Hezekiah, and **a.** his might,...... 3605
2Ki 21:3 of Israel; and worshipped **a.** the.......... 3605
2Ki 21:5 altars for **a.** the host of heaven........... 3605
2Ki 21:7 which I have chosen out of **a.**............. 3605
2Ki 21:8 observe to do according to **a.** that....... 3605
2Ki 21:8 **a.** the law that my servant Moses....... 3605
2Ki 21:11 above **a.** that the Amorites................ 3605
2Ki 21:14 and a spoil to **a.** their enemies;.......... 3605
2Ki 21:17 the acts of Manasseh, and **a.** that...... 3605
2Ki 21:21 **a.** the way that his father walked........ 3605
2Ki 21:24 of the land slew **a.** them that had........ 3605
2Ki 22:2 in **a.** the way of David his father,......... 3605
2Ki 22:13 me, and for the people, and for **a.**....... 3605
2Ki 22:13 **a.** that which is written concerning...... 3605
2Ki 22:16 thereof, even **a.** the words............... 3605
2Ki 22:17 me to anger with **a.** the works of........ 3605
2Ki 22:20 shall not see **a.** the evil which I.......... 3605
2Ki 23:1 unto him **a.** the elders of Judah........... 3605
2Ki 23:2 and **a.** the men of Judah.................. 3605
2Ki 23:2 **a.** the inhabitants of Jerusalem........... 3605
2Ki 23:2 the prophets, and **a.** the people,......... 3605
2Ki 23:2 their ears **a.** the words of the book..... 3605
2Ki 23:3 and his statutes with **a.** their heart...... 3605
2Ki 23:3 and **a.** their soul,............................ 3605
2Ki 23:3 **a.** the people stood to the covenant..... 3605
2Ki 23:4 **a.** the vessels that were made for....... 3605
2Ki 23:4 and for **a.** the host of heaven:............ 3605
2Ki 23:5 and to **a.** the host of heaven............. 3605
2Ki 23:8 **a.** the priests out of the cities........... 3605
2Ki 23:19 And **a.** the houses also of the high..... 3605
2Ki 23:19 according to **a.** the acts that he had..... 3605
2Ki 23:20 he slew **a.** the priests of the high........ 3605
2Ki 23:21 king commanded **a.** the people,........... 3605
2Ki 23:22 **a.** the days of the kings of Israel,......... 3605
2Ki 23:24 and **a.** the abominations that were........ 3605
2Ki 23:25 to the Lord with **a.** his heart,............. 3605
2Ki 23:25 and with **a.** his soul,......................... 3605
2Ki 23:25 and with **a.** his might,........................ 3605
2Ki 23:25 according to **a.** the law of Moses;........ 3605
2Ki 23:26 **a.** the provocations that Manasseh....... 3605
2Ki 23:28 the acts of Josiah, and **a.** that he......... 3605
2Ki 23:32 to **a.** that his fathers had done............ 3605
2Ki 23:37 sight of the Lord, according to **a.**......... 3605
2Ki 24:3 sins of Manasseh, according to **a.**......... 3605
2Ki 24:5 of Jehoiakim, and **a.** that he did,......... 3605
2Ki 24:7 **a.** that pertained to the king of........... 3605
2Ki 24:9 sight of the Lord, according to **a.**......... 3605
2Ki 24:13 carried out thence **a.** the treasures...... 3605
2Ki 24:13 cut in pieces **a.** the vessels of gold...... 3605
2Ki 24:14 he carried away **a.** Jerusalem,............ 3605
2Ki 24:14 **a.** the princes, and **a.** the mighty........ 3605
2Ki 24:14 **a.** the craftsmen and smiths:.............. 3605
2Ki 24:16 And **a.** the men of might, even........... 3605
2Ki 24:16 **a.** that were strong and apt for war,..... 3605
2Ki 24:19 according to **a.** that Jehoiakim............. 3605
2Ki 25:1 and **a.** his host, against Jerusalem,...... 3605
2Ki 25:4 and **a.** the men of war fled by night..... 3605
2Ki 25:5 and **a.** his army were scattered........... 3605
2Ki 25:9 and **a.** the houses of Jerusalem,........... 3605
2Ki 25:10 And **a.** the army of the Chaldees,........ 3605
2Ki 25:14 **a.** the vessels of brass wherewith....... 3605
2Ki 25:16 **a.** these vessels was without weight.... 3605
2Ki 25:17 upon the chapiter round about, **a.**........ 3605
2Ki 25:23 when **a.** the captains of the armies,..... 3605
2Ki 25:26 **a.** the people, both small and great,...... 3605
2Ki 25:29 continually before him, **a.** the days...... 3605
2Ki 25:30 every day, **a.** the days of his life......... 3605
1Ch 1:23 **A.** these were the sons of Joktan......... 3605
1Ch 1:33 **A.** these are the sons of Keturah......... 3605
1Ch 2:4 **A.** the sons of Judah were five........... 3605
1Ch 2:6 and Dara: five of them in **a.**............... 3605
1Ch 2:23 **A.** these belonged to the sons of........ 3605
1Ch 3:9 These were **a.** the sons of David,....... 3605
1Ch 4:27 did **a.** their family multiply, like........... 3605
1Ch 4:33 **a.** their villages that were round......... 3605
1Ch 5:10 **a.** the east land of Gilead.................. 3605
1Ch 5:16 and in **a.** the suburbs of Sharon,.......... 3605
1Ch 5:17 **A.** these were reckoned by.................. 3605
1Ch 5:20 and **a.** that were with them: for.......... 3605
1Ch 6:48 appointed unto **a.** manner of............... 3605
1Ch 6:49 **a.** the work of the place most holy,...... 3605
1Ch 6:49 to **a.** that Moses the servant of God.... 3605
1Ch 6:60 **A.** their cities throughout their.......... 3605
1Ch 7:3 five: **a.** of them chief men................. 3605
1Ch 7:5 brethren among **a.** the families........... 3605
1Ch 7:5 of might, reckoned in **a.** by their......... 3605
1Ch 7:8 **A.** these are the sons of Becher.......... 3605
1Ch 7:11 **A.** these the sons of Jediael, by.......... 3605
1Ch 7:40 **A.** these were the children of Asher,... 3605
1Ch 8:38 **A.** these were the sons of Azel.......... 3605
1Ch 8:40 **A.** these are the sons of Benjamin....... 3605
1Ch 9:1 So **a.** Israel were reckoned by............. 3605
1Ch 9:9 **A.** these men were chief of the.......... 3605
1Ch 9:22 **A.** these which were chosen to be...... 3605
1Ch 9:29 **a.** the instruments of the sanctuary,..... 3605
1Ch 10:6 and **a.** his house died together............ 3605
1Ch 10:7 **a.** the men of Israel that were in......... 3605
1Ch 10:11 And when **a.** Jabesh-gilead................ 3605
1Ch 10:11 heard **a.** that the Philistines had.......... 3605
1Ch 10:12 They arose, **a.** the valiant men,.......... 3605
1Ch 11:1 Then **a.** Israel gathered themselves..... 3605
1Ch 11:3 **a.** the elders of Israel to the king........ 3605
1Ch 11:4 and **a.** Israel went to Jerusalem,......... 3605
1Ch 11:10 him in his kingdom, and with **a.**.......... 3605
1Ch 12:15 when it had overflown **a.** his.............. 3605
1Ch 12:15 put to flight **a.** them of the valleys,...... 3605
1Ch 12:21 they were **a.** mighty men of valour,...... 3605
1Ch 12:32 and **a.** their brethren were at their...... 3605
1Ch 12:33 war, with **a.** instruments of war,......... 3605
1Ch 12:37 tribe of Manasseh, with **a.** manner...... 3605
1Ch 12:38 **A.** these men of war, that could......... 3605
1Ch 12:38 make David king over **a.** Israel:.......... 3605
1Ch 12:38 **a.** the rest also of Israel were of......... 3605
1Ch 13:2 unto **a.** the congregation of Israel,........ 3605
1Ch 13:2 that are left in **a.** the land of Israel,...... 3605
1Ch 13:4 And **a.** the congregation said that......... 3605
1Ch 13:4 right in the eyes of **a.** the people......... 3605
1Ch 13:5 David gathered **a.** Israel together,........ 3605
1Ch 13:6 And David went up, and **a.** Israel,........ 3605
1Ch 13:8 and **a.** Israel played before God.......... 3605
1Ch 13:8 with **a.** their might, and with............. 3605
1Ch 13:14 house of Obed-edom, and **a.** that he.... 3605
1Ch 14:8 David was anointed king over **a.**.......... 3605
1Ch 14:8 **a.** the Philistines went up to seek....... 3605
1Ch 14:17 of David went out into **a.** lands;.......... 3605
1Ch 14:17 the fear of him upon **a.** nations.......... 3605
1Ch 15:3 David gathered **a.** Israel together........ 3605
1Ch 15:27 and **a.** the Levites that bare the ark,... 3605
1Ch 15:28 Thus **a.** Israel brought up the ark....... 3605
1Ch 16:9 talk ye of **a.** his wondrous works........ 3605

1Ch 16:14 his judgments are in **a.** the earth........ 3605
1Ch 16:23 Sing unto the Lord, **a.** the earth;........ 3605
1Ch 16:24 works among **a.** nations.................... 3605
1Ch 16:25 also is to be feared above **a.** gods....... 3605
1Ch 16:26 **a.** the gods of the people are idols:..... 3605
1Ch 16:30 Fear before him, **a.** the earth:........... 3605
1Ch 16:32 fields rejoice, and **a.** that is therein...... 3605
1Ch 16:36 And **a.** the people said, Amen, and...... 3605
1Ch 16:40 according to **a.** that is written in.......... 3605
1Ch 16:43 And **a.** the people departed every........ 3605
1Ch 17:2 David, Do **a.** that is in thine heart;....... 3605
1Ch 17:6 I have walked with **a.** Israel, spake..... 3605
1Ch 17:8 **a.** thine enemies from before thee,...... 3605
1Ch 17:10 I will subdue **a.** thine enemies............ 3605
1Ch 17:15 According to **a.** these words, and......... 3605
1Ch 17:15 according to **a.** this vision, so did........ 3605
1Ch 17:19 thine own heart, hast thou done **a.**...... 3605
1Ch 17:19 known **a.** these great things............... 3605
1Ch 17:20 God beside thee, according to **a.**......... 3605
1Ch 18:4 houghed **a.** the chariot horses,........... 3605
1Ch 18:9 David had smitten **a.** the host of......... 3605
1Ch 18:10 him **a.** manner of vessels of gold......... 3605
1Ch 18:11 he brought from **a.** these nations;....... 3605
1Ch 18:13 **a.** the Edomites became David's......... 3605
1Ch 18:14 So David reigned over **a.** Israel,......... 3605
1Ch 18:14 and justice among **a.** his people.......... 3605
1Ch 19:8 and **a.** the host of the mighty men....... 3605
1Ch 19:10 chose out of **a.** the choice of Israel,..... 3605
1Ch 19:17 told David; and he gathered **a.**........... 3605
1Ch 20:3 so dealt David with **a.** the cities of...... 3605
1Ch 20:3 And David and **a.** the people.............. 3605
1Ch 21:3 they not **a.** my lord's servants?.......... 3605
1Ch 21:4 and went throughout **a.** Israel, and...... 3605
1Ch 21:5 people unto David. And **a.** they of....... 3605
1Ch 21:12 throughout **a.** the coasts of Israel........ 3605
1Ch 21:23 for the meat offering; I give it **a.**......... 3605
1Ch 22:5 of glory throughout **a.** countries:......... 3605
1Ch 22:9 rest from **a.** his enemies round........... 3605
1Ch 22:15 and **a.** manner of cunning men for....... 3605
1Ch 22:17 also commanded **a.** the princes........... 3605
1Ch 23:2 together **a.** the princes of Israel,......... 3605
1Ch 23:28 in the purifying of **a.** holy things......... 3605
1Ch 23:29 for **a.** manner of measure and size;..... 3605
1Ch 23:31 And to offer **a.** burnt sacrifices........... 3605
1Ch 25:5 **A.** these were the sons of Heman....... 3605
1Ch 25:6 **A.** these were under the hands of....... 3605
1Ch 25:7 in the songs of the Lord, even **a.**......... 3605
1Ch 26:8 **A.** these of the sons of Obed-edom:..... 3605
1Ch 26:11 **a.** the sons and brethren of Hosah...... 3605
1Ch 26:26 and his brethren were over **a.** the....... 3605
1Ch 26:28 And **a.** that Samuel the seer, and........ 3605
1Ch 26:30 in **a.** the business of the Lord, and...... 3605
1Ch 27:1 **a.** the months of the year, of............. 3605
1Ch 27:3 the chief of **a.** the captains of the........ 3605
1Ch 27:31 **A.** these were the rulers of the.......... 3605
1Ch 28:1 assembled **a.** the princes of Israel,...... 3605
1Ch 28:1 the stewards over **a.** the substance..... 3605
1Ch 28:1 and with **a.** the valiant men, unto........ 3605
1Ch 28:4 of Israel chose me before **a.** the......... 3605
1Ch 28:4 to make me king over **a.** Israel:.......... 3605
1Ch 28:5 And of **a.** my sons, (for the Lord........ 3605
1Ch 28:8 sight of **a.** Israel the congregation....... 3605
1Ch 28:8 seek for **a.** the commandments of....... 3605
1Ch 28:9 mind: for the Lord searcheth **a.**.......... 3605
1Ch 28:9 understandeth **a.** the imaginations........ 3605
1Ch 28:12 of **a.** that he had by the spirit,............ 3605
1Ch 28:12 of **a.** the chambers round about,.......... 3605
1Ch 28:13 for **a.** the work of the service of the.... 3605
1Ch 28:13 for **a.** the vessels of service in the...... 3605
1Ch 28:14 of gold, for **a.** instruments................. 3605
1Ch 28:14 of **a.** manner of service;..................... 3605
1Ch 28:14 **a.** instruments of silver by weight,....... 3605
1Ch 28:14 **a.** instruments of every kind of............ 3605
1Ch 28:19 **A.** this, said David, the Lord made...... 3605
1Ch 28:19 upon me, even **a.** the works of this..... 3605
1Ch 28:20 thou hast finished **a.** the work............ 3605
1Ch 28:21 they shall be with thee for **a.** the........ 3605
1Ch 28:21 for **a.** manner of workmanship............ 3605
1Ch 28:21 and **a.** the people will be wholly.......... 3605
1Ch 29:1 king said unto **a.** the congregation,...... 3605
1Ch 29:2 I have prepared with **a.** my might....... 3605
1Ch 29:2 and **a.** manner of precious stones,........ 3605
1Ch 29:3 of my God, over and above **a.** that...... 3605
1Ch 29:5 for **a.** manner of work to be made....... 3605
1Ch 29:10 Lord before **a.** the congregation:......... 3605
1Ch 29:11 **a.** that is in the heaven and in the....... 3605
1Ch 29:11 thou art exalted as head above **a.**......... 3605
1Ch 29:12 of thee, and thou reignest over **a.**;...... 3605
1Ch 29:12 great, and to give strength unto **a.**...... 3605
1Ch 29:14 for **a.** things come of thee, and of........ 3605
1Ch 29:15 sojourners, as were **a.** our fathers:...... 3605
1Ch 29:16 **a.** this store that we have prepared..... 3605
1Ch 29:16 of thine hand, and is **a.** thine own....... 3605
1Ch 29:17 willingly offered **a.** these things:.......... 3605
1Ch 29:19 statutes, and to do **a.** these things,..... 3605
1Ch 29:20 David said to **a.** the congregation,....... 3605
1Ch 29:20 **a.** the congregation blessed the.......... 3605
1Ch 29:21 in abundance for **a.** Israel:................. 3605
1Ch 29:23 and **a.** Israel obeyed him................... 3605
1Ch 29:24 **a.** the princes, and the mighty men,.... 3605
1Ch 29:24 **a.** the sons likewise of king David,...... 3605
1Ch 29:25 exceedingly in the sight of **a.** Israel,.... 3605
1Ch 29:26 son of Jesse reigned over **a.** Israel...... 3605
1Ch 29:30 With **a.** his reign and his might,.......... 3605
1Ch 29:30 **a.** the kingdoms of the countries......... 3605
2Ch 1:2 spake unto **a.** Israel, to the captains.... 3605
2Ch 1:2 and to every governor in **a.** Israel,...... 3605
2Ch 1:3 and **a.** the congregation with him........ 3605
2Ch 1:17 out horses for **a.** the kings of the........ 3605
2Ch 2:5 for great is our God above **a.** gods...... 3605
2Ch 2:17 Solomon numbered **a.** the strangers..... 3605
2Ch 4:4 and **a.** their hinder parts were........... 3605
2Ch 4:16 **a.** their instruments, did Huram.......... 3605
2Ch 4:18 Solomon made **a.** these vessels in....... 3605
2Ch 4:19 Solomon made **a.** the vessels that....... 3605
2Ch 5:1 **a.** the work that Solomon made.......... 3605
2Ch 5:1 **a.** the things that David his father............
2Ch 5:1 and **a.** the instruments, put he........... 3605
2Ch 5:2 elders of Israel, and **a.** the heads........ 3605
2Ch 5:3 **a.** the men of Israel assembled........... 3605
2Ch 5:4 And **a.** the elders of Israel came;........ 3605
2Ch 5:5 **a.** the holy vessels that were in.......... 3605
2Ch 5:6 Solomon, and **a.** the congregation........ 3605
2Ch 5:11 (for **a.** the priests that were present.... 3605
2Ch 5:12 **a.** of them of Asaph, of Heman, of...... 3605
2Ch 6:3 **a.** the congregation of Israel stood...... 3605
2Ch 6:5 among **a.** the tribes of Israel to.......... 3605
2Ch 6:12 of the Lord in the presence of **a.**......... 3605
2Ch 6:13 before **a.** the congregation of Israel,.... 3605
2Ch 6:14 that walk before thee with **a.**.............. 3605
2Ch 6:29 or of **a.** thy people Israel, when.......... 3605
2Ch 6:30 man according unto **a.** his ways,......... 3605
2Ch 6:33 to **a.** that the stranger calleth to......... 3605
2Ch 6:33 that **a.** people of the earth may.......... 3605
2Ch 6:38 return to thee with **a.** their heart........ 3605
2Ch 6:38 **a.** their soul in the land of their......... 3605
2Ch 7:3 when **a.** the children of Israel saw....... 3605
2Ch 7:4 the king and **a.** the people offered....... 3605
2Ch 7:5 the king and **a.** the people dedicated.... 3605
2Ch 7:6 before them, and **a.** Israel stood......... 3605
2Ch 7:8 seven days, and **a.** Israel with him,...... 3605
2Ch 7:11 **a.** that came into Solomon's heart....... 3605
2Ch 7:17 **a.** that I have commanded thee,.......... 3605
2Ch 7:20 and a byword among **a.** nations........... 3605
2Ch 7:22 he brought **a.** this evil upon them........ 3605
2Ch 8:4 **a.** the store cities, which he built......... 3605
2Ch 8:6 **a.** the store cities that Solomon.......... 3605
2Ch 8:6 **a.** the chariot cities, and the cities....... 3605
2Ch 8:6 **a.** that Solomon desired to build.......... 3605
2Ch 8:6 **a.** the land of his dominion................ 3605
2Ch 8:7 As for **a.** the people that were left...... 3605
2Ch 8:16 Now **a.** the work of Solomon was....... 3605
2Ch 9:1 him of **a.** that was in her heart........... 3605
2Ch 9:2 Solomon told her **a.** her questions:...... 3605
2Ch 9:12 the queen of Sheba **a.** her desire,....... 3605
2Ch 9:14 And **a.** the kings of Arabia and.......... 3605
2Ch 9:20 **a.** the drinking vessels of king........... 3605
2Ch 9:20 **a.** the vessels of the house of the....... 3605
2Ch 9:22 Solomon passed **a.** the kings of........... 3605
2Ch 9:23 **a.** the kings of the earth sought.......... 3605
2Ch 9:26 he reigned over **a.** the kings from........ 3605
2Ch 9:28 out of Egypt, and out of **a.** lands......... 3605
2Ch 9:30 Jerusalem over **a.** Israel forty years..... 3605
2Ch 10:1 **a.** Israel come to make him king.......... 3605
2Ch 10:3 and **a.** Israel came and spake to.......... 3605
2Ch 10:12 **a.** the people came to Rehoboam.......... 3605
2Ch 10:16 when **a.** Israel saw that the king......... 3605
2Ch 10:16 So **a.** Israel went to their tents.......... 3605
2Ch 11:3 and to **a.** Israel in Judah and.............. 3605
2Ch 11:13 the Levites that were in **a.** Israel........ 3605
2Ch 11:13 to him out of **a.** their coasts............. 3605
2Ch 11:16 them out of **a.** the tribes of Israel....... 3605
2Ch 11:21 of Absalom above **a.** his wives............ 3605
2Ch 11:23 and dispersed of **a.** his children........... 3605
2Ch 11:23 throughout **a.** the countries of............ 3605
2Ch 12:1 and **a.** Israel with him....................... 3605
2Ch 12:9 he took **a.**: he carried away also......... 3605
2Ch 12:13 chosen out of **a.** the tribes of Israel,.... 3605
2Ch 13:4 me, thou Jeroboam, and **a.** Israel;........ 3605
2Ch 13:15 smote Jeroboam and **a.** Israel............ 3605
2Ch 14:5 away out of **a.** the cities of Judah........ 3605
2Ch 14:8 **a.** these were mighty men of............. 3605
2Ch 14:14 **a.** the cities round about Gerar;.......... 3605
2Ch 14:14 and they spoiled **a.** the cities;............. 3605
2Ch 15:2 Asa, and **a.** Judah and Benjamin;......... 3605
2Ch 15:5 were upon **a.** the inhabitants.............. 3605
2Ch 15:6 did vex them with **a.** adversity........... 3605
2Ch 15:8 **a.** the land of Judah and Benjamin,...... 3605
2Ch 15:9 gathered **a.** Judah and Benjamin,......... 3605
2Ch 15:12 their fathers with **a.** their heart.......... 3605
2Ch 15:12 and with **a.** their soul;...................... 3605
2Ch 15:15 And **a.** Judah rejoiced at the oath:....... 3605
2Ch 15:15 sworn with **a.** their heart, and............ 3605
2Ch 15:17 of Asa was perfect **a.** his days........... 3605
2Ch 16:4 and **a.** the store cities of Naphtali........ 3605
2Ch 16:6 Then Asa the king took **a.** Judah;......... 3605
2Ch 17:2 in **a.** the fenced cities of Judah,.......... 3605
2Ch 17:5 **a.** Judah brought to Jehoshaphat.......... 3605
2Ch 17:9 throughout **a.** the cities of Judah,........ 3605
2Ch 17:10 Lord fell upon **a.** the kingdoms........... 3605
2Ch 17:19 fenced cities throughout **a.** Judah......... 3605
2Ch 18:9 **a.** the prophets prophesied before....... 3605
2Ch 18:11 **a.** the prophets prophesied so,........... 3605
2Ch 18:16 I did see **a.** Israel scattered upon........ 3605
2Ch 18:18 sitting upon his throne, and **a.** the........ 3605
2Ch 18:21 in the mouth of **a.** his prophets........... 3605
2Ch 18:27 And he said, Hearken, **a.** ye people..... 3605
2Ch 19:5 judges in the land throughout **a.**.......... 3605
2Ch 19:11 you in **a.** the matters of the Lord;....... 3605
2Ch 19:11 house of Judah, for **a.** the king's......... 3605
2Ch 20:3 a fast throughout **a.** Judah................ 3605
2Ch 20:4 Lord: even out of **a.** the cities of........ 3605
2Ch 20:6 over **a.** the kingdoms of the heathen?.. 3605
2Ch 20:13 **a.** Judah stood before the Lord,.......... 3605
2Ch 20:15 he said, Hearken ye, **a.** Judah,............ 3605
2Ch 20:18 his face to the ground: and **a.**............ 3605
2Ch 20:29 of God was on **a.** the kingdoms,.......... 3605
2Ch 21:2 **a.** these were the sons of................. 3605
2Ch 21:4 slew **a.** his brethren with the sword,... 3605
2Ch 21:9 and **a.** his chariots with him:.............. 3605
2Ch 21:14 and thy wives, and **a.** thy goods:......... 3605
2Ch 21:17 away **a.** the substance that was.......... 3605
2Ch 21:18 after **a.** this the Lord smote him.......... 3605
2Ch 22:1 to the camp had slain **a.** the eldest....... 3605
2Ch 22:9 sought the Lord with **a.** his heart....... 3605
2Ch 22:10 destroyed **a.** the seed royal of the....... 3605
2Ch 23:2 Levites out of **a.** the cities of Judah,.... 3605
2Ch 23:3 And **a.** the congregation made a.......... 3605
2Ch 23:5 **a.** the people shall be in the courts...... 3605
2Ch 23:6 **a.** the people shall keep the watch...... 3605
2Ch 23:8 and **a.** Judah did according to............ 3605
2Ch 23:8 **a.** things that Jehoiada the priest......... 3605
2Ch 23:10 he set **a.** the people, every man......... 3605
2Ch 23:13 **a.** the people of the land rejoiced,....... 3605
2Ch 23:16 between **a.** the people, and between.... 3605
2Ch 23:17 **a.** the people went to the house of...... 3605
2Ch 23:20 people, and **a.** the people of the......... 3605
2Ch 23:21 **a.** the people of the land rejoiced:....... 3605
2Ch 24:2 the Lord **a.** the days of Jehoiada......... 3605
2Ch 24:5 gather of **a.** Israel money to repair...... 3605
2Ch 24:7 the house of God; and also **a.** the....... 3605
2Ch 24:10 And **a.** the princes.......................... 3605
2Ch 24:10 and **a.** the people rejoiced,............... 3605
2Ch 24:14 continually **a.** the days of Jehoiada....... 3605
2Ch 24:23 destroyed **a.** the princes of the........... 3605
2Ch 24:23 sent **a.** the spoil of them unto the....... 3605
2Ch 25:5 of their fathers, throughout **a.**............ 3605
2Ch 25:7 not with Israel, to wit, with **a.** the...... 3605
2Ch 25:12 the rock, that they **a.** were broken........ 3605
2Ch 25:24 he took **a.** the gold and the silver,....... 3605
2Ch 25:24 and **a.** the vessels that were found...... 3605
2Ch 26:1 **a.** the people of Judah took Uzziah,...... 3605
2Ch 26:4 according to **a.** that his father............ 3605
2Ch 26:14 prepared for them throughout **a.**.......... 3605
2Ch 26:20 **a.** the priests, looked upon him,......... 3605
2Ch 27:2 sight of the Lord, according to **a.**......... 3605
2Ch 27:7 acts of Jotham, and **a.** his wars,.......... 3605
2Ch 28:6 which were **a.** valiant men;................ 3605
2Ch 28:14 princes and **a.** the congregation.......... 3605
2Ch 28:15 clothed **a.** that were naked among....... 3605
2Ch 28:15 carried **a.** the feeble of them upon....... 3605

Book	Ref	Context	No.
2Ch	28:23	the ruin of him, and of **a.** Israel	3605
2Ch	28:26	rest of his acts and of **a.** his ways,	3605
2Ch	29:2	according to **a.** that David his	3605
2Ch	29:16	brought out **a.** the uncleanness	3605
2Ch	29:18	cleansed **a.** the house of the Lord,	3605
2Ch	29:18	offering, with **a.** the vessels thereof	3605
2Ch	29:18	table, with **a.** the vessels thereof	3605
2Ch	29:19	Moreover **a.** the vessels, which	3605
2Ch	29:24	make an atonement for **a.** Israel	3605
2Ch	29:24	should be made for **a.** Israel	3605
2Ch	29:28	**a.** the congregation worshipped,	3605
2Ch	29:28	**a.** this continued until the burnt	3605
2Ch	29:29	and **a.** that were present with him	3605
2Ch	29:32	**a.** these were for a burnt offering	3605
2Ch	29:34	not flay **a.** the burnt offerings:	3605
2Ch	29:36	rejoiced, and **a.** the people,	3605
2Ch	30:1	sent to **a.** Israel and Judah, and	3605
2Ch	30:2	counsel, and his princes, and **a.**	3605
2Ch	30:4	the king and **a.** the congregation	3605
2Ch	30:5	proclamation throughout **a.** Israel,	3605
2Ch	30:6	his princes throughout **a.** Israel	3605
2Ch	30:14	**a.** the altars for incense took they	3605
2Ch	30:22	spake comfortably unto **a.** the	3605
2Ch	30:25	And **a.** the congregation of Judah,	3605
2Ch	30:25	Levites, and **a.** the congregation	3605
2Ch	31:1	Now when **a.** this was finished,	3605
2Ch	31:1	**a.** Israel that were present went	3605
2Ch	31:1	out of **a.** Judah and Benjamin,	3605
2Ch	31:1	they had utterly destroyed them **a.**	
2Ch	31:1	**a.** the children of Israel returned,	3605
2Ch	31:5	and of **a.** the increase of the field;	3605
2Ch	31:5	tithe of **a.** things brought they in	3605
2Ch	31:18	genealogy of **a.** their little ones,	3605
2Ch	31:18	through **a.** the congregation:	3605
2Ch	31:19	to **a.** the males among the priests,	3605
2Ch	31:19	and to **a.** that were reckoned by	3605
2Ch	31:20	did Hezekiah throughout **a.** Judah,	3605
2Ch	31:21	he did it with **a.** his heart, and	3605
2Ch	32:4	people together, who stopped **a.**	3605
2Ch	32:5	built up **a.** the wall that was broken,	3605
2Ch	32:7	for **a.** the multitude that is with	3605
2Ch	32:9	Lachish, and **a.** his power with	3605
2Ch	32:9	king of Judah, and unto **a.** Judah	3605
2Ch	32:13	and my fathers have done unto **a.**	3605
2Ch	32:14	among **a.** the gods of those nations	3605
2Ch	32:21	off **a.** the mighty men of valour,	3605
2Ch	32:22	and from the hand of **a.** other,	3605
2Ch	32:23	magnified in the sight of **a.** nations	3605
2Ch	32:27	for **a.** manner of pleasant jewels;	3605
2Ch	32:28	and stalls for **a.** manner of beasts	3605
2Ch	32:30	Hezekiah prospered in **a.** his works	3605
2Ch	32:31	know **a.** that was in his heart	3605
2Ch	32:33	**a.** Judah and the inhabitants of	3605
2Ch	33:3	worshipped **a.** the host of heaven,	3605
2Ch	33:5	altars for **a.** the host of heaven in	3605
2Ch	33:7	before **a.** the tribes of Israel	3605
2Ch	33:8	**a.** that I have commanded them,	3605
2Ch	33:14	captains of war in **a.** the fenced	3605
2Ch	33:15	and **a.** the altars that he had built	3605
2Ch	33:19	intreated of him, and **a.** his sins,	3605
2Ch	33:22	unto **a.** the carved images,	3605
2Ch	33:25	the people of the land slew **a.** them	3605
2Ch	34:7	and cut down **a.** the idols	3605
2Ch	34:7	throughout **a.** the land of Israel,	3605
2Ch	34:9	and of **a.** the remnant of Israel,	3605
2Ch	34:9	and of **a.** Judah and Benjamin;	3605
2Ch	34:12	**a.** that could skill of instruments	3605
2Ch	34:13	of **a.** that wrought the work	3605
2Ch	34:16	**A.** that was committed to thy	3605
2Ch	34:21	**a.** that is written in this book	3605
2Ch	34:24	even **a.** the curses that are written	3605
2Ch	34:25	with **a.** the works of their hands;	3605
2Ch	34:28	eyes see **a.** the evil that I will	3605
2Ch	34:29	gathered together **a.** the elders	3605
2Ch	34:30	and **a.** the men of Judah, and the	3605
2Ch	34:30	and the Levites, and **a.** the people,	3605
2Ch	34:30	he read in their ears **a.** the words	3605
2Ch	34:31	his statutes, with **a.** his heart,	3605
2Ch	34:31	and with **a.** his soul, to perform	3605
2Ch	34:32	**a.** that were present in Jerusalem	3605
2Ch	34:33	took away **a.** the abominations	3605
2Ch	34:33	out of **a.** the countries	3605
2Ch	34:33	**a.** that were present in Israel	3605
2Ch	34:33	And **a.** his days they departed not	3605
2Ch	35:3	the Levites that taught **a.** Israel,	3605
2Ch	35:7	**a.** for the passover offerings,	3605
2Ch	35:7	for **a.** that were present,	3605
2Ch	35:13	them speedily among **a.** the people	3605
2Ch	35:16	So **a.** the service of the Lord was	3605
2Ch	35:18	neither did **a.** the kings of Israel	3605
2Ch	35:18	the priests, and the Levites, and **a.**	3605
2Ch	35:20	After **a.** this, when Josiah had	3605
2Ch	35:24	**a.** Judah and Jerusalem mourned	3605
2Ch	35:25	lamented for Josiah: and **a.** the	3605
2Ch	36:14	Moreover **a.** the chief of the priests,	3605
2Ch	36:14	much after **a.** the abominations of	3605
2Ch	36:17	for age: he gave them **a.** into	3605
2Ch	36:18	**a.** the vessels of the house of God,	3605
2Ch	36:18	**a.** these he brought to Babylon	3605
2Ch	36:19	**a.** the palaces thereof with fire,	3605
2Ch	36:19	destroyed **a.** the goodly vessels	3605
2Ch	36:22	throughout **a.** his kingdom,	3605
2Ch	36:23	**A.** the kingdoms of the earth hath	3605
2Ch	36:23	there among you of **a.** his people?	3605
Ezr	1:1	throughout **a.** his kingdom, and	3605
Ezr	1:2	hath given me **a.** the kingdoms	3605
Ezr	1:3	among you of **a.** his people? his	3605
Ezr	1:5	with **a.** them whose spirit God had	3605
Ezr	1:6	**a.** they that were about them	3605
Ezr	1:6	things, beside **a.** that was willingly	3605
Ezr	1:11	**A.** the vessels of gold and of silver	3605
Ezr	1:11	**A.** these did Sheshbazzar bring up	3605
Ezr	2:42	in **a.** an hundred thirty and nine	3605
Ezr	2:58	**A.** the Nethinims, and the children	3605
Ezr	2:70	cities, and **a.** Israel in their cities	3605
Ezr	3:5	new moons, and of **a.** the set feasts	3605
Ezr	3:8	and **a.** they that were come out	3605
Ezr	3:11	**a.** the people shouted with a great	3605
Ezr	4:5	their purpose, **a.** the days of Cyrus	3605
Ezr	4:20	which have ruled over **a.** countries	3606
Ezr	5:7	Unto Darius the king, **a.** peace	3606
Ezr	6:12	destroy **a.** kings and people,	3606
Ezr	6:17	for a sin offering for **a.** Israel,	3606
Ezr	6:20	Levites were purified together, **a.**	3605
Ezr	6:20	and killed the passover for **a.**	3605
Ezr	6:21	again out of captivity, and **a.** such	3605
Ezr	7:6	king granted him **a.** his request,	3605
Ezr	7:13	that **a.** they of the people of Israel	3606
Ezr	7:16	**a.** the silver and gold that thou	3606
Ezr	7:16	find in **a.** the province of Babylon,	3606
Ezr	7:21	decree to **a.** the treasurers which	3606
Ezr	7:25	which may judge **a.** the people	3606
Ezr	7:25	river, **a.** such as know the laws	3606
Ezr	7:28	before **a.** the king's mighty princes	3605
Ezr	8:20	**a.** of them were expressed by	3605
Ezr	8:21	for our little ones, and for **a.** our	3605
Ezr	8:22	hand of our God is upon **a.** them	3605
Ezr	8:22	power and his wrath is against **a.**	3605
Ezr	8:25	lords, and **a.** Israel there present,	3605
Ezr	8:34	**a.** the weight was written at that	3605
Ezr	8:35	twelve bullocks for **a.** Israel,	3605
Ezr	8:35	**a.** this was a burnt offering unto	3605
Ezr	9:13	And after **a.** that is come upon us	3605
Ezr	10:3	our God to put away **a.** the wives,	3605
Ezr	10:5	and **a.** Israel, to swear that they	3605
Ezr	10:7	**a.** the children of the captivity,	3605
Ezr	10:8	**a.** his substance should be	3605
Ezr	10:9	**a.** the men of Judah and Benjamin	3605
Ezr	10:9	**a.** the people sat in the street of	3605
Ezr	10:12	**a.** the congregation answered and	3605
Ezr	10:14	rulers of **a.** the congregation stand,	3605
Ezr	10:14	and let **a.** them which have	3605
Ezr	10:16	and **a.** of them by their names,	3605
Ezr	10:17	made an end with **a.** the men that	3605
Ezr	10:44	**A.** these had taken strange wives:	3605
Ne	4:6	**a.** the wall was joined together	3605
Ne	4:8	And conspired **a.** of them together	3605
Ne	4:12	From **a.** places whence ye shall	3605
Ne	4:15	we returned **a.** of us to the wall,	3605
Ne	4:16	were behind **a.** the house of Judah	3605
Ne	5:13	**a.** the congregation said, Amen,	3605
Ne	5:16	and **a.** my servants were gathered	3605
Ne	5:18	ten days store of **a.** sorts of wine:	3605
Ne	5:18	for **a.** this required not I the bread	5973
Ne	5:19	my God, for good, according to **a.**	3605
Ne	6:9	For they **a.** made us afraid, saying,	3605
Ne	6:16	when **a.** our enemies heard thereof,	3605
Ne	6:16	**a.** the heathen that were about us	3605
Ne	7:60	**A.** the Nethinims, and the children	3605
Ne	7:73	and **a.** Israel, dwelt in their cities;	3605
Ne	8:1	**a.** the people gathered themselves	3605
Ne	8:2	and **a.** that could hear with	3605
Ne	8:3	ears of **a.** the people were attentive	3605
Ne	8:5	book in the sight of **a.** the people;	3605
Ne	8:5	(for he was above **a.** the people;)	3605
Ne	8:5	it, **a.** the people stood up:	3605
Ne	8:6	And **a.** the people answered, Amen,	3605
Ne	8:9	taught the people, said unto **a.** the	3605
Ne	8:9	For **a.** the people wept, when they	3605
Ne	8:11	the Levites stilled **a.** the people,	3605
Ne	8:12	And **a.** the people went their way	3605
Ne	8:13	the chief of the fathers of **a.**	3605
Ne	8:15	and proclaim in **a.** their cities, and	3605
Ne	8:17	And **a.** the congregation of them	3605
Ne	9:2	separated themselves from **a.**	3605
Ne	9:5	name, which is exalted above **a.**	3605
Ne	9:6	the heaven of heavens, with **a.**	3605
Ne	9:6	and **a.** things that are therein,	3605
Ne	9:6	the seas, and **a.** that is therein,	3605
Ne	9:6	preservest them **a.**; and the host	3605
Ne	9:10	wonders upon Pharaoh, and on **a.**	3605
Ne	9:10	and on **a.** the people of his land:	3605
Ne	9:25	possessed houses full of **a.** goods,	3605
Ne	9:32	covenant and mercy, let not **a.**	3605
Ne	9:32	our fathers, and on **a.** thy people,	3605
Ne	9:33	Howbeit thou art just in **a.** that is	3605
Ne	9:38	of **a.** this we make a sure covenant,	3605
Ne	10:28	and **a.** they that had separated	3605
Ne	10:29	**a.** the commandments of the Lord	3605
Ne	10:33	and for **a.** the work of the house	3605
Ne	10:35	and the firstfruits of **a.** fruit	3605
Ne	10:35	of **a.** trees, year by year,	3605
Ne	10:37	and the fruit of **a.** manner of trees,	3605
Ne	10:37	tithes in **a.** the cities of our tillage	3605
Ne	11:2	the people blessed **a.** the men,	3605
Ne	11:6	**A.** the sons of Perez that dwelt at	3605
Ne	11:18	**A.** the Levites in the holy city	3605
Ne	11:20	were in **a.** the cities of Judah,	3605
Ne	11:24	at the king's hand in **a.** matters	3605
Ne	12:27	the Levites out of **a.** their places,	3605
Ne	12:47	**a.** Israel in the days of Zerubbabel,	3605
Ne	13:3	Israel **a.** the mixed multitude	3605
Ne	13:6	**a.** this time was not I at Jerusalem:	3605
Ne	13:8	I cast forth **a.** the household stuff	3605
Ne	13:12	brought **a.** Judah the tithe of the	3605
Ne	13:15	grapes, and figs, and **a.** manner of	3605
Ne	13:16	and **a.** manner of ware, and sold	3605
Ne	13:18	**a.** this evil upon us, and upon this	3605
Ne	13:20	sellers of **a.** kind of ware lodged	3605
Ne	13:26	God made him king over **a.** Israel:	3605
Ne	13:27	unto you to do **a.** this great evil,	3605
Ne	13:30	cleansed I them from **a.** strangers,	3605
Es	1:3	made a feast unto **a.** his princes	3605
Es	1:5	feast unto **a.** the people that were	3605
Es	1:8	had appointed to **a.** the officers	3605
Es	1:13	the king's manner toward **a.** that	3605
Es	1:16	but also to **a.** the princes,	3605
Es	1:16	and to **a.** the people that are	3605
Es	1:16	in **a.** the provinces of the king	3605
Es	1:17	queen shall come abroad unto **a.**	3605
Es	1:18	and Media say this day unto **a.**	3605
Es	1:20	throughout **a.** his empire,	3605
Es	1:20	**a.** the wives shall give to their	3605
Es	1:22	into **a.** the king's provinces,	3605
Es	2:3	appoint officers in **a.** the provinces	3605
Es	2:3	together **a.** the fair young virgins	3605
Es	2:15	in the sight of **a.** them that looked	3605
Es	2:17	loved Esther above **a.** the women,	3605
Es	2:17	in his sight more than **a.** the	3605
Es	2:18	a great feast unto **a.** his princes	3605
Es	3:1	set his seat above **a.** the princes	3605
Es	3:2	**a.** the king's servants, that were in	3605
Es	3:6	sought to destroy **a.** the Jews that	3605
Es	3:8	the people in **a.** the provinces of	3605
Es	3:8	laws are diverse from **a.** people;	3605
Es	3:12	**a.** that Haman had commanded	3605
Es	3:13	posts into **a.** the king's provinces,	3605
Es	3:13	and to cause to perish, **a.** Jews,	3605
Es	3:14	was published unto **a.** people, that	3605
Es	4:1	Mordecai perceived **a.** that was	3605
Es	4:7	told him of **a.** that had happened	3605
Es	4:11	**A.** the king's servants, and the	3605
Es	4:13	house, more than **a.** the Jews	3605
Es	4:16	**a.** the Jews that are present in	3605
Es	4:17	**a.** that Esther had commanded	3605
Es	5:11	**a.** the things wherein the king had	3605
Es	5:13	Yet **a.** this availeth me nothing,	3605
Es	5:14	wife and **a.** his friends unto him,	3605
Es	6:10	fail of **a.** that thou hast spoken	3605

Es 6:13 told Zeresh his wife and **a.** his 3605
Es 8:5 are in **a.** the king's provinces: 3605
Es 8:9 to **a.** that Mordecai commanded 3605
Es 8:11 perish, **a.** the power of the people 3605
Es 8:12 Upon one day in **a.** the provinces 3605
Es 8:13 was published unto **a.** people, 3605
Es 9:2 throughout **a.** the provinces of the 3605
Es 9:2 the fear of them fell upon **a.** people. 3605
Es 9:3 And **a.** the rulers of the provinces, 3605
Es 9:4 throughout **a.** the provinces: 3605
Es 9:5 the Jews smote **a.** their enemies 3605
Es 9:20 things, and sent letters unto **a.** 3605
Es 9:20 Jews that were in **a.** the provinces 3605
Es 9:24 enemy of **a.** the Jews, had devised 3605
Es 9:26 for **a.** the words of this letter, 3605
Es 9:27 upon **a.** such as joined themselves 3605
Es 9:29 the Jew, wrote with **a.** authority, 3605
Es 9:30 sent the letters unto **a.** the Jews, 3605
Es 10:2 And **a.** the acts of his power and of 3605
Es 10:3 and speaking peace to **a.** his seed. 3605
Job 1:3 greatest of **a.** the men of the east. 3605
Job 1:5 according to the number of them **a.**: 3605
Job 1:10 **a.** that he hath on every side? 3605
Job 1:11 and touch **a.** that he hath, and he 3605
Job 1:12 **a.** that he hath is in thy power; 3605
Job 1:22 In **a.** this Job sinned not, 3605
Job 2:4 yea, **a.** that a man hath will he give 3605
Job 2:10 In **a.** this did not Job sin with his 3605
Job 2:11 three friends heard of **a.** this evil 3605
Job 4:14 which made **a.** my bones to shake. 7230
Job 8:13 the paths of **a.** that forget God; 3605
Job 9:28 I am afraid of **a.** my sorrows, 3605
Job 12:9 Who knoweth not in **a.** these that 3605
Job 12:10 and the breath of **a.** mankind, 3605
Job 13:1 Lo, mine eye hath seen **a.** this, 3605
Job 13:4 ye are **a.** physicians of no value. 3605
Job 13:27 narrowly unto **a.** my paths; 3605
Job 14:14 **a.** the days of my appointed time 3605
Job 15:20 travaileth with pain **a.** his days, 3605
Job 16:2 miserable comforters are ye **a.**. 3605
Job 16:7 made desolate **a.** my company. 3605
Job 17:7 dim by reason of sorrow, and **a.** my 3605
Job 17:10 But as for you **a.**, do ye return, 3605
Job 19:19 **A.** my inward friends abhorred me: 3605
Job 20:26 **A.** darkness shall be hid in his 3605
Job 24:24 taken out of the way as **a.** other, 3605
Job 27:3 **A.** the while my breath is in me, 3605
Job 27:12 **a.** ye yourselves have seen it; 3605
Job 28:3 and searcheth out **a.** perfection: 3605
Job 28:21 it is hid from the eyes of **a.** living: 3605
Job 29:19 dew lay **a.** night upon my branch. 3885
Job 30:23 the house appointed for **a.** living. 3605
Job 31:4 my ways, and count **a.** my steps? 3605
Job 31:12 would root out **a.** mine increase. 3605
Job 33:1 and hearken to **a.** my words. 3605
Job 33:11 in the stocks, he marketh **a.** my 3605
Job 33:29 Lo, **a.** these things worketh God. 3605
Job 34:15 **A.** flesh shall perish together, 3605
Job 34:19 they **a.** are the work of his hands. 3605
Job 34:21 of man, and he seeth **a.** his goings. 3605
Job 36:19 gold, nor **a.** the forces of strength. 3605
Job 37:7 every man; that **a.** men may know 3605
Job 38:7 **a.** the sons of God shouted for joy? 3605
Job 38:18 earth? declare if thou knowest it **a.** 3605
Job 40:20 **a.** the beasts of the field play. 3605
Job 41:34 He beholdeth **a.** high things: 3605
Job 41:34 over **a.** the children of pride. 3605
Job 42:11 there unto him **a.** his brethren, 3605
Job 42:11 and **a.** his sisters, 3605
Job 42:11 and **a.** they that had been of 3605
Job 42:11 and comforted him over **a.** the evil 3605
Job 42:15 in **a.** the land were no women 3605
Ps 2:12 Blessed are **a.** they that put their 3605
Ps 3:7 thou hast smitten **a.** mine enemies 3605
Ps 5:5 thou hatest **a.** workers of iniquity. 3605
Ps 5:11 let **a.** those that put their trust in 3605
Ps 6:6 **a.** the night make I my bed to 3605
Ps 6:7 old because of **a.** mine enemies. 3605
Ps 6:8 from me, **a.** ye workers of iniquity; 3605
Ps 6:10 Let **a.** mine enemies be ashamed 3605
Ps 7:1 from **a.** them that persecute me, 3605
Ps 8:1 is thy name in **a.** the earth! 3605
Ps 8:6 hast put **a.** things under his feet: 3605
Ps 8:7 **A.** sheep and oxen, yea, and the 3605
Ps 8:9 is thy name in **a.** the earth! 3605
Ps 9:1 forth **a.** thy marvellous works. 3605
Ps 9:14 that I may shew forth **a.** thy praise 3605
Ps 9:17 and **a.** the nations that forget God. 3605
Ps 10:4 God is not in **a.** his thoughts. 3605
Ps 10:5 as for **a.** his enemies, he puffeth 3605
Ps 12:3 Lord shall cut off **a.** flattering lips, 3605
Ps 14:3 They are **a.** gone aside, 3605
Ps 14:3 they are **a.** together become
Ps 14:4 Have **a.** the workers of iniquity 3605
Ps 16:3 in whom is **a.** my delight. 3605
Ps 18:*title* from the hand of **a.** his enemies, 3605
Ps 18:22 **a.** his judgments were before me, 3605
Ps 18:30 he is a buckler to **a.** those that 3605
Ps 19:4 is gone out through **a.** the earth, 3605
Ps 20:3 Remember **a.** thy offerings, and 3605
Ps 20:4 heart, and fulfil **a.** thy counsel. 3605
Ps 20:5 the Lord fulfil **a.** thy petitions. 3605
Ps 21:8 shall find out **a.** thine enemies: 3605
Ps 22:7 **A.** they that see me laugh me to 3605
Ps 22:14 out like water, and **a.** my bones, 3605
Ps 22:17 I may tell **a.** my bones: they look 3605
Ps 22:23 praise him; **a.** ye the seed of Jacob, 3605
Ps 22:23 fear him, **a.** ye the seed of Israel. 3605
Ps 22:27 **A.** the ends of the world shall 3605
Ps 22:27 and **a.** the kindreds of the nations 3605
Ps 22:29 **A.** they that be fat upon earth 3605
Ps 22:29 **a.** they that go down to the dust 3605
Ps 23:6 mercy shall follow me **a.** the days 3605
Ps 25:5 on thee do I wait **a.** the day. 3605
Ps 25:10 **A.** the paths of the Lord are mercy 3605
Ps 25:18 and my pain; and forgive **a.** my 3605
Ps 25:22 O God, out of **a.** his troubles. 3605
Ps 26:7 and tell of **a.** thy wondrous works. 3605
Ps 27:4 in the house of the Lord **a.** the days 3605
Ps 31:11 reproach among **a.** mine enemies, 3605
Ps 31:23 O love the Lord, **a.** ye his saints: 3605
Ps 31:24 heart, **a.** ye that hope in the Lord. 3605
Ps 32:3 through my roaring **a.** the day long. 3605
Ps 32:11 **a.** ye that are upright in heart. 3605
Ps 33:4 Lord is right; and **a.** his works 3605
Ps 33:6 **a.** the host of them by the breath 3605
Ps 33:8 Let **a.** the earth fear the Lord: 3605
Ps 33:8 let **a.** the inhabitants of the world 3605
Ps 33:11 of his heart to **a.** generations.
Ps 33:13 from heaven; he beholdeth **a.** the 3605
Ps 33:14 **a.** the inhabitants of the earth. 3605
Ps 33:15 hearts alike; he considereth **a.** 3605
Ps 34:1 I will bless the Lord at **a.** times: 3605
Ps 34:4 delivered me from **a.** my fears. 3605
Ps 34:6 saved him out of **a.** his troubles. 3605
Ps 34:17 them out of **a.** their troubles. 3605
Ps 34:19 Lord delivereth him out of them **a.** 3605
Ps 34:20 He keepeth **a.** his bones: not one 3605
Ps 35:10 **A.** my bones shall say, Lord, who 3605
Ps 35:28 and of thy praise **a.** the day long. 3605
Ps 38:6 I go mourning **a.** the day long. 3605
Ps 38:9 Lord, **a.** my desire is before thee; 3605
Ps 38:12 imagine deceits **a.** the day long. 3605
Ps 39:8 me from **a.** my transgressions: 3605
Ps 39:12 a sojourner, as **a.** my fathers 3605
Ps 40:16 Let **a.** those that seek thee rejoice 3605
Ps 41:3 make **a.** his bed in his sickness. 3605
Ps 41:7 **A.** that hate me whisper together 3605
Ps 42:7 **a.** thy waves and thy billows are 3605
Ps 44:8 In God we boast **a.** the day long, 3605
Ps 44:17 **A.** this is come upon us; yet have 3605
Ps 44:22 sake are we killed **a.** the day long; 3605
Ps 45:8 **A.** thy garments smell of myrrh, 3605
Ps 45:13 The king's daughter is **a.** glorious 3605
Ps 45:16 make princes in **a.** the earth. 3605
Ps 45:17 thy name to be remembered in **a.** 3605
Ps 47:1 O clap your hands, **a.** ye people; 3605
Ps 47:2 is a great King over **a.** the earth. 3605
Ps 47:7 God is the King of **a.** the earth: 3605
Ps 49:1 Hear this, **a.** ye people; 3605
Ps 49:1 give ear, **a.** ye inhabitants 3605
Ps 49:11 dwelling places to **a.** generations;
Ps 50:11 **a.** the fowls of the mountains: 3605
Ps 51:9 from my sins, and blot out **a.** mine 3605
Ps 52:4 Thou lovest **a.** devouring words, 3605
Ps 54:7 delivered me out of **a.** trouble: 3605
Ps 56:5 **a.** their thoughts are against me. 3605
Ps 57:2 that performeth **a.** things for me. 3605
Ps 57:5, 11 glory be above **a.** the earth. 3605
Ps 59:5 awake to visit **a.** the heathen: 3605
Ps 59:8 have **a.** the heathen in derision. 3605
Ps 62:3 ye shall be slain **a.** of you: as a 3605
Ps 62:8 Trust in him at **a.** times; 3605
Ps 64:8 **a.** that see them shall flee away. 3605
Ps 64:9 And **a.** men shall fear, and shall 3605
Ps 64:10 **a.** the upright in heart shall glory. 3605
Ps 65:2 unto thee shall **a.** flesh come. 3605
Ps 65:5 of **a.** the ends of the earth, and 3605
Ps 66:1 noise unto God, **a.** ye lands: 3605
Ps 66:4 **A.** the earth shall worship thee, 3605
Ps 66:16 Come and hear, **a.** ye that fear God, 3605
Ps 67:2 saving health among **a.** nations. 3605
Ps 67:3, 5 let **a.** the people praise thee. 3605
Ps 67:7 and **a.** the ends of the earth shall 3605
Ps 69:19 adversaries are **a.** before thee. 3605
Ps 70:4 Let **a.** those that seek thee rejoice 3605
Ps 71:8 praise and with thy honour **a.** the 3605
Ps 71:15 salvation **a.** the day; for I know 3605
Ps 71:24 righteousness **a.** the day long: 3605
Ps 72:5 throughout **a.** generations.
Ps 72:11 **a.** kings shall fall down before 3605
Ps 72:11 **a.** nations shall serve him. 3605
Ps 72:17 in him: **a.** nations shall call 3605
Ps 73:14 For **a.** the day long have I been 3605
Ps 73:27 thou hast destroyed **a.** them that 3605
Ps 73:28 that I may declare **a.** thy works. 3605
Ps 74:3 even **a.** that the enemy hath done 3605
Ps 74:8 burned up **a.** the synagogues of God 3605
Ps 74:17 set **a.** the borders of the earth: 3605
Ps 75:3 **a.** the inhabitants thereof are 3605
Ps 75:8 **a.** the wicked of the earth shall 3605
Ps 75:10 **A.** the horns of the wicked also 3605
Ps 76:9 to save **a.** the meek of the earth. 3605
Ps 76:11 your God: let **a.** that be round 3605
Ps 77:12 I will meditate also of **a.** thy work, 3605
Ps 78:14 **a.** the night with a light of fire. 3605
Ps 78:32 For **a.** this they sinned still, and 3605
Ps 78:38 and did not stir up **a.** his wrath. 3605
Ps 78:51 smote **a.** the firstborn in Egypt; 3605
Ps 79:13 forth thy praise to **a.** generations.
Ps 80:12 so that **a.** they which pass by the 3605
Ps 82:5 **a.** the foundations of the earth are 3605
Ps 82:6 **a.** of you are children of the most 3605
Ps 82:8 for thou shalt inherit **a.** nations. 3605
Ps 83:11 **a.** their princes as Zebah, and as 3605
Ps 83:18 art the most high over **a.** the 3605
Ps 85:2 thou hast covered **a.** their sin. 3605
Ps 85:3 hast taken away **a.** thy wrath: 3605
Ps 85:5 out thine anger to **a.** generations? 3605
Ps 86:5 unto **a.** them that call upon thee. 3605
Ps 86:9 **A.** nations whom thou hast made 3605
Ps 86:12 Lord my God, with **a.** my heart: 3605
Ps 87:2 than **a.** the dwellings of Jacob. 3605
Ps 87:7 be there: **a.** my springs are in thee. 3605
Ps 88:7 afflicted me with **a.** thy waves. 3605
Ps 89:1 thy faithfulness to **a.** generations.
Ps 89:4 up thy throne to **a.** generations.
Ps 89:7 of **a.** them that are about him. 3605
Ps 89:16 name shall they rejoice **a.** the day: 3605
Ps 89:40 hast broken down **a.** his hedges; 3605
Ps 89:41 **A.** that pass by the way spoil him: 3605
Ps 89:42 made **a.** his enemies to rejoice. 3605
Ps 89:47 hast thou made **a.** men in vain? 3605
Ps 89:50 reproach of **a.** the mighty people; 3605
Ps 90:1 dwelling place in **a.** generations.
Ps 90:9 **a.** our days are passed away in 3605
Ps 90:14 rejoice and be glad **a.** our days. 3605
Ps 91:11 thee, to keep thee in **a.** thy ways 3605
Ps 92:7 when **a.** the workers of iniquity do 3605
Ps 92:9 **a.** the workers of iniquity shall be 3605
Ps 94:4 and **a.** the workers of iniquity boast 3605
Ps 94:15 **a.** the upright in heart shall follow 3605
Ps 95:3 and a great King above **a.** gods. 3605
Ps 96:1 sing unto the Lord, **a.** the earth. 3605
Ps 96:3 his wonders among **a.** people 3605
Ps 96:4 he is to be feared above **a.** gods. 3605
Ps 96:5 **a.** the gods of the nations are idols: 3605
Ps 96:9 fear before him, **a.** the earth. 3605
Ps 96:12 be joyful, and **a.** that is therein: 3605
Ps 96:12 **a.** the trees of the wood rejoice 3605
Ps 97:6 and **a.** the people see his glory. 3605
Ps 97:7 **a.** they that serve graven images, 3605
Ps 97:7 of idols: worship him, **a.** ye gods. 3605
Ps 97:9 art high above **a.** the earth: 3605
Ps 97:9 thou art exalted far above **a.** gods. 3605
Ps 98:3 **a.** the ends of the earth have seen 3605
Ps 98:4 noise unto the Lord, **a.** the earth: 3605
Ps 99:2 and he is high above **a.** the people. 3605
Ps 100:1 noise unto the Lord, **a.** ye lands. 3605
Ps 100:5 truth endureth to **a.** generations.
Ps 101:8 destroy **a.** the wicked of the land; 3605

Ps 101:8 that I may cut off **a.** wicked doers 3605
Ps 102:8 enemies reproach me **a.** the day; 3605
Ps 102:12 remembrance unto **a.** generations.
Ps 102:15 **a.** the kings of the earth thy 3605
Ps 102:24 are throughout **a.** generations.
Ps 102:26 but thou shalt endure: yea, **a.** of 3605
Ps 103:1 **a.** that is within me, bless his holy 3605
Ps 103:2 and forget not **a.** his benefits: 3605
Ps 103:3 Who forgiveth **a.** thine iniquities; 3605
Ps 103:3 who healeth **a.** thy diseases; 3605
Ps 103:6 judgment for **a.** that are oppressed. 3605
Ps 103:19 and his kingdom ruleth over **a.**. 3605
Ps 103:21 Bless ye the Lord, **a.** ye his hosts; 3605
Ps 103:22 Bless the Lord, **a.** his works 3605
Ps 103:22 in **a.** places of his dominion: 3605
Ps 104:20 wherein **a.** the beasts of the forest 3605
Ps 104:24 in wisdom hast thou made them **a.**: 3605
Ps 104:27 These wait **a.** upon thee; that 3605
Ps 105:2 talk ye of **a.** his wondrous works. 3605
Ps 105:7 his judgments are in **a.** the earth. 3605
Ps 105:21 of his house, and ruler of **a.** his 3605
Ps 105:31 flies, and lice in **a.** their coasts. 3605
Ps 105:35 eat up **a.** the herbs in their land, 3605
Ps 105:36 also **a.** the firstborn in their land, 3605
Ps 105:36 the chief of **a.** their strength. 3605
Ps 106:2 who can shew forth **a.** his praise? 3605
Ps 106:3 doeth righteousness at **a.** times. 3605
Ps 106:31 unto **a.** generations for evermore.
Ps 106:46 **a.** those that carried them
Ps 106:48 and let **a.** the people say, Amen
Ps 107:18 abhorreth **a.** manner of meat;
Ps 107:42 **a.** iniquity shall stop her mouth.
Ps 108:5 and thy glory above **a.** the earth;
Ps 109:11 extortioner catch **a.** that he hath; 3605
Ps 111:2 Lord are great, sought out of **a.** 3605
Ps 111:7 **a.** his commandments are sure. 3605
Ps 111:10 a good understanding have **a.** 3605
Ps 113:4 The Lord is high above **a.** nations, 3605
Ps 116:11 said in my haste, **A.** men are liars. 3605
Ps 116:12 unto the Lord for **a.** his benefits 3605
Ps 116:14 in the presence of **a.** his people. 3605
Ps 116:18 the Lord now in the presence of **a.** 3605
Ps 117:1 O praise the Lord, **a.** ye nations: 3605
Ps 117:1 praise him, **a.** ye people. 3605
Ps 118:10 **A.** nations compassed me about: 3605
Ps 119:6 unto **a.** thy commandments. 3605
Ps 119:13 With my lips have I declared **a.** 3605
Ps 119:14 as much as in **a.** riches. 3605
Ps 119:20 unto thy judgments at **a.** times. 3605
Ps 119:63 of **a.** them that fear thee, and of 3605
Ps 119:86 **A.** thy commandments are faithful: 3605
Ps 119:90 faithfulness is unto **a.** generations:
Ps 119:91 for **a.** are thy servants. 3605
Ps 119:96 I have seen an end of **a.** perfection. 3605
Ps 119:97 it is my meditation **a.** the day. 3605
Ps 119:99 than **a.** my teachers: for thy 3605
Ps 119:118 trodden down **a.** them that err 3605
Ps 119:119 **a.** the wicked of the earth like 3605
Ps 119:128 I esteem **a.** thy precepts 3605
Ps 119:128 concerning **a.** things to be right; 3605
Ps 119:151 **a.** thy commandments are truth. 3605
Ps 119:168 for **a.** my ways are before thee. 3605
Ps 119:172 for **a.** thy commandments are 3605
Ps 121:7 shall preserve thee from **a.** evil: 3605
Ps 128:5 Jerusalem **a.** the days of thy life 3605
Ps 129:5 Let them **a.** be confounded and 3605
Ps 130:8 Israel from **a.** his iniquities 3605
Ps 132:1 David, and **a.** his afflictions: 3605
Ps 134:1 Lord, **a.** ye servants of the Lord, 3605
Ps 135:5 that our Lord is above **a.** gods. 3605
Ps 135:6 in the seas, and **a.** deep places. 3605
Ps 135:9 Pharaoh, and upon **a.** his servants, 3605
Ps 135:11 and **a.** the kingdoms of Canaan: 3605
Ps 135:13 O Lord, throughout **a.** generations.
Ps 136:25 Who giveth food to **a.** flesh: for 3605
Ps 138:2 thy word above **a,** thy name 3605
Ps 138:4 **A.** the kings of the earth shall 3605
Ps 139:3 art acquainted with **a.** my ways. 3605
Ps 139:16 book **a.** my members were written, 3605
Ps 143:5 the days of old; I meditate on **a.** 3605
Ps 143:12 destroy **a.** them that afflict my soul: 3605
Ps 144:13 garners may be full, affording **a.**
Ps 145:9 The Lord is good to **a.**: and his 3605
Ps 145:9 mercies are over **a.** his works. 3605
Ps 145:10 **A.** thy works shall praise thee, O 3605
Ps 145:13 throughout **a.** generations.
Ps 145:14 The Lord upholdeth **a.** that fall, 3605
Ps 145:14 raiseth up **a.** those that be bowed 3605
Ps 145:15 The eyes of **a.** wait upon thee; and 3605
Ps 145:17 Lord is righteous in **a.** his ways, 3605
Ps 145:17 and holy in **a.** his works. 3605
Ps 145:18 The Lord is nigh unto **a.** them that 3605
Ps 145:18 to **a.** that call upon him in truth. 3605
Ps 145:20 preserveth **a.** them that love him: 3605
Ps 145:20 but **a.** the wicked will he destroy 3605
Ps 145:21 and let **a.** flesh bless his holy name 3605
Ps 146:6 earth, the sea, and **a.** that therein 3605
Ps 146:10 God, O Zion, unto **a.** generations.
Ps 147:4 of the stars; he calleth them **a.** 3605
Ps 148:2 Praise ye him, **a.** his angels: 3605
Ps 148:2 praise ye him, **a.** his hosts. 3605
Ps 148:3 praise him, **a.** ye stars of light. 3605
Ps 148:7 the earth, ye dragons, and **a.** deeps. 3605
Ps 148:9 Mountains, and **a.** hills; 3605
Ps 148:9 fruitful trees, and **a.** cedars: 3605
Ps 148:10 Beasts, and **a.** cattle; creeping 3605
Ps 148:11 Kings of the earth, and **a.** people; 3605
Ps 148:11 princes, and **a.** judges of the earth: 3605
Ps 148:14 the praise of **a.** his saints; even of 3605
Ps 149:9 written: this honour have **a.** 3605
Pr 1:13 shall find **a.** precious substance, 3605
Pr 1:14 us; let us **a.** have one purse: 3605
Pr 1:25 have set at nought **a.** my counsel, 3605
Pr 1:30 of my counsel: they despised **a.** 3605
Pr 3:5 in the Lord with **a.** thine heart; 3605
Pr 3:6 In **a.** thy ways acknowledge him, 3605
Pr 3:9 and with the firstfruits of **a.** 3605
Pr 3:15 precious than rubies: and **a.** the 3605
Pr 3:17 ways of pleasantness, and **a.** her 3605
Pr 4:7 **a.** thy getting get understanding. 3605
Pr 4:22 find them, and health to **a.** their 3605
Pr 4:23 Keep thy heart with **a.** diligence; 3605
Pr 4:26 of thy feet, and let **a.** thy ways be 3605
Pr 5:14 I was almost in **a.** evil in the midst 3605
Pr 5:19 her breasts satisfy thee at **a.** times. 3605
Pr 5:21 and he pondereth **a.** his goings. 3605
Pr 6:31 shall give **a.** the substance of his 3605
Pr 8:8 **A.** the words of my mouth are in 3605
Pr 8:9 **a.** plain to him that understandeth, 3605
Pr 8:11 than rubies; and **a.** the things 3605
Pr 8:16 and nobles, even **a.** the judges of 3605
Pr 8:36 **a.** they that hate me love death. 3605
Pr 10:12 strifes: but love covereth **a.** sins. 3605
Pr 14:23 In **a.** labour there is profit: but 3605
Pr 15:15 **A.** the days of the afflicted are 3605
Pr 16:2 **A.** the ways of a man are clean in 3605
Pr 16:4 hath made **a.** things for himself: 3605
Pr 16:11 **a.** the weights of the bag are his 3605
Pr 17:17 A friend loveth at **a.** times, and a 3605
Pr 18:1 intermeddleth with **a.** wisdom. 3605
Pr 19:7 **A.** the brethren of the poor do hate 3605
Pr 20:8 away **a.** evil with his eyes. 3605
Pr 20:27 candle of the Lord, searching **a.** 3605
Pr 21:26 He coveteth greedily **a.** the day 3605
Pr 22:2 the Lord is the maker of them **a.** 3605
Pr 23:17 fear of the Lord **a.** the day long. 3605
Pr 24:4 **a.** precious and pleasant riches. 3605
Pr 24:31 it was **a.** grown over with thorns, 3605
Pr 26:10 great God that formed **a.** things 3605
Pr 28:5 the Lord understand **a.** things. 3605
Pr 29:11 A fool uttereth **a.** his mind: but a 3605
Pr 29:12 to lies, **a.** his servants are wicked. 3605
Pr 30:4 established **a.** the ends of the earth? 3605
Pr 30:27 king, yet go they forth **a.** of them 3605
Pr 31:8 for the dumb in the cause of **a.** 3605
Pr 31:12 and not evil **a.** the days of her life. 3605
Pr 31:21 **a.** her household are clothed with 3605
Pr 31:29 but thou excellest them **a.**. 3605
Ec 1:2 vanity of vanities; **a.** is vanity. 3605
Ec 1:3 What profit hath a man of **a.** his 3605
Ec 1:7 **A.** the rivers run into the sea; 3605
Ec 1:8 **A.** things are full of labour; man 3605
Ec 1:13 by wisdom concerning **a.** things 3605
Ec 1:14 I have seen **a.** the works that are 3605
Ec 1:14 **a.** is vanity and vexation of spirit. 3605
Ec 1:16 **a.** they that have been before me 3605
Ec 2:3 heaven **a.** the days of their life. 4557
Ec 2:5 trees in them of **a.** kind of fruits: 3605
Ec 2:7 **a.** that were in Jerusalem before 3605
Ec 2:8 instruments, and that of **a.** sorts.
Ec 2:9 increased more than **a.** that were 3605
Ec 2:10 my heart rejoiced in **a.** my labour: 3605
Ec 2:10 was my portion of **a.** my labour. 3605
Ec 2:11 Then I looked on **a.** the works that 3605
Ec 2:11 **a.** was vanity and vexation of 3605
Ec 2:14 one event happeneth to them **a.** 3605
Ec 2:16 days to come shall **a.** be forgotten. 3605
Ec 2:17 me: for **a.** is vanity and vexation 3605
Ec 2:18 I hated **a.** my labour which I had 3605
Ec 2:19 he have rule over **a.** my labour 3605
Ec 2:20 to despair of **a.** the labour which 3605
Ec 2:22 what hath man of **a.** his labour, 3605
Ec 2:23 For **a.** his days are sorrows, and 3605
Ec 3:13 enjoy the good of **a.** his labour, 3605
Ec 3:19 yea, they have **a.** one breath; so 3605
Ec 3:19 above a beast: for **a.** is vanity. 3605
Ec 3:20 **A.** go unto one place; 3605
Ec 3:20 **a.** are of the dust, 3605
Ec 3:20 and **a.** turn to dust again. 3605
Ec 4:1 and considered **a.** the oppressions 3605
Ec 4:4 Again, I considered **a.** travail, and 3605
Ec 4:8 is there no end of **a.** his labour; 3605
Ec 4:15 **a.** the living which walk under the 3605
Ec 4:16 There is no end of **a.** the people, 3605
Ec 4:16 of **a.** that have been before them: 3605
Ec 5:9 the profit of the earth is for **a.**: 3605
Ec 5:16 that in **a.** points as he came, so 3605
Ec 5:17 **A.** his days also he eateth in 3605
Ec 5:18 to enjoy the good of **a.** his labour 3605
Ec 5:18 the sun **a.** the days of his life, 4557
Ec 6:2 for his soul of **a.** that he desireth, 3605
Ec 6:6 no good: do not **a.** go to one place? 3605
Ec 6:7 **A.** the labour of man is for his 3605
Ec 6:12 **a.** the days of his vain life which 4557
Ec 7:2 for that is the end of **a.** men; 3605
Ec 7:15 **A.** things have I seen in the days 3605
Ec 7:18 God shall come forth of them **a.** 3605
Ec 7:21 heed unto **a.** words that are spoken; 3605
Ec 7:23 **A.** this have I proved by wisdom: 3605
Ec 7:28 among **a.** those have I not found. 3605
Ec 8:9 **A.** this have I seen, and applied 3605
Ec 8:17 Then I beheld **a.** the work of God, 3605
Ec 9:1 **a.** this I considered in my heart 3605
Ec 9:1 even to declare **a.** this, 3605
Ec 9:1 or hatred by **a.** that is before them. 3605
Ec 9:2 **A.** things come alike to **a.**: there 3605
Ec 9:3 This is an evil among **a.** things 3605
Ec 9:3 that there is one event unto **a.**: 3605
Ec 9:4 joined to **a.** the living there is hope: 3605
Ec 9:9 wife whom thou lovest **a.** the days 3605
Ec 9:9 **a.** the days of thy vanity: for that 3605
Ec 9:11 and chance happeneth to them **a.** 3605
Ec 10:19 but money answereth **a.** things. 3605
Ec 11:5 the works of God who maketh **a.** 3605
Ec 11:8 many years, and rejoice in them **a.**; 3605
Ec 11:8 many. **A.** that cometh is vanity. 3605
Ec 11:9 that for **a.** these things God will 3605
Ec 12:4 and **a.** the daughters of musick shall 3605
Ec 12:8 saith the preacher; **a.** is vanity. 3605
Ca 1:13 unto me; he shall lie **a.** night 3885
Ca 3:6 with **a.** powders of the merchant? 3605
Ca 3:8 They **a.** hold swords, being expert 3605
Ca 4:4 bucklers, **a.** shields of mighty men. 3605
Ca 4:7 Thou art **a.** fair, my love, there is 3605
Ca 4:10 thine ointments than **a.** spices! 3605
Ca 4:14 with **a.** trees of frankincense; 3605
Ca 4:14 aloes, with **a.** the chief spices: 3605
Ca 7:13 are **a.** manner of pleasant fruits, 3605
Ca 8:7 **a.** the substance of his house for 3605
Isa 1:25 away thy dross, and take away **a.** 3605
Isa 2:2 the hills; and **a.** nations shall flow 3605
Isa 2:13 upon **a.** the cedars of Lebanon, 3605
Isa 2:13 and upon **a.** the oaks of Bashan, 3605
Isa 2:14 And upon **a.** the high mountains, 3605
Isa 2:14 upon **a.** the hills that are lifted up 3605
Isa 2:16 And upon **a.** the ships of Tarshish, 3605
Isa 2:16 and upon **a.** pleasant pictures. 3605
Isa 4:5 upon **a.** the glory shall be a defence 3605
Isa 5:25 For **a.** this his anger is not turned 3605
Isa 5:28 are sharp, and **a.** their bows bent, 3605
Isa 7:19 come, and shall rest **a.** of them in 3605
Isa 7:19 of the rocks, and upon **a.** thorns, 3605
Isa 7:19 and upon **a.** bushes. 3605
Isa 7:24 **a.** the land shall become briers 3605
Isa 7:25 And on **a.** hills that shall be digged 3605
Isa 8:7 king of Assyria, and **a.** his glory: 3605
Isa 8:7 come up over **a.** his channels, 3605
Isa 8:7 and go over **a.** his banks: 3605
Isa 8:9 give ear, **a.** ye of far countries: 3605
Isa 8:12 confederacy, to **a.** them to whom 3605
Isa 9:9 And **a.** the people shall know, 3605

Book	Ref	Context	No.
Isa	9:12	with open mouth. For **a.** this	3605
Isa	9:17	speaketh folly. For **a.** this his	3605
Isa	9:21	judah. For **a.** this his anger is	3605
Isa	10:4	For **a.** this his anger is not turned	3605
Isa	10:14	that are left, have I gathered **a.**	3605
Isa	10:23	in the midst of **a.** the land	3605
Isa	11:9	destroy in **a.** my holy mountain:	3605
Isa	12:5	this is known in **a.** the earth	3605
Isa	13:7	Therefore shall **a.** hands be faint,	3605
Isa	14:9	even **a.** the chief ones of the earth;	3605
Isa	14:9	thrones **a.** the kings of the nations	3605
Isa	14:10	**A.** they shall speak and say unto	3605
Isa	14:18	**A.** the kings of the nations,	3605
Isa	14:18	even **a.** of them, lie in glory,	3605
Isa	14:26	stretched out upon **a.** the nations	3605
Isa	15:2	on **a.** their heads shall be baldness,	3605
Isa	16:14	be contemned, with **a.** that great	3605
Isa	18:3	**A.** ye inhabitants of the world,	3605
Isa	18:6	**a.** the beasts of the earth shall	3605
Isa	19:8	shall mourn, and **a.** they that cast	3605
Isa	19:10	**a.** that make sluices and ponds for	3605
Isa	21:2	**a.** the sighing thereof have I made	3605
Isa	21:9	is fallen; and **a.** the graven images	3605
Isa	21:16	and **a.** the glory of Kedar shall fail:	3605
Isa	22:3	**A.** thy rulers are fled together,	3605
Isa	22:3	**a.** that are found in thee are	3605
Isa	22:24	him **a.** the glory of his father's	3605
Isa	22:24	and the issue, **a.** vessels of small	3605
Isa	22:24	the vessels of cups, even to **a.** the	3605
Isa	23:9	to stain the pride of **a.** glory,	3605
Isa	23:9	**a.** the honourable of the earth	3605
Isa	23:17	with **a.** the kingdoms of the world	3605
Isa	24:7	**a.** the merryhearted do sigh	3605
Isa	24:11	**a.** joy is darkened, the mirth of	3605
Isa	25:6	hosts make unto **a.** people a feast	3605
Isa	25:7	covering cast over **a.** people,	3605
Isa	25:7	vail that is spread over **a.** nations	3605
Isa	25:8	wipe away tears from off **a.** faces;	3605
Isa	25:8	shall he take away from off **a.**	3605
Isa	26:12	hast wrought **a.** our works in us	3605
Isa	26:14	made **a.** their memory to perish	3605
Isa	26:15	far unto **a.** the ends of the earth	3605
Isa	27:9	**a.** the fruit to take away his sin;	3605
Isa	27:9	maketh **a.** the stones of the altar	3605
Isa	28:8	For **a.** tables are full of vomit and	3605
Isa	28:24	the plowman plow **a.** day to sow?	3605
Isa	29:7	of **a.** the nations that fight against	3605
Isa	29:7	even **a.** that fight against her and	3605
Isa	29:8	so shall the multitude of **a.** the	3605
Isa	29:11	**a.** is become unto you as the words	3605
Isa	29:20	**a.** that watch for iniquity are cut	3605
Isa	30:5	They were **a.** ashamed of a people	3605
Isa	30:18	blessed are **a.** they that wait for	3605
Isa	31:3	fall down, and they **a.** shall fail	3605
Isa	32:13	upon **a.** the houses of joy in the	3605
Isa	32:20	are ye that sow beside **a.** waters,	3605
Isa	34:1	let the earth hear, and **a.** that is	4393
Isa	34:1	and **a.** things that come forth of it	3605
Isa	34:2	of the Lord is upon **a.** nations,	3605
Isa	34:2	and his fury upon **a.** their armies:	3605
Isa	34:4	And **a.** the host of heaven shall be	3605
Isa	34:4	and **a.** their host shall fall down,	3605
Isa	34:12	**a.** her princes shall be nothing	3605
Isa	36:1	Assyria came up against **a.** the	3605
Isa	36:6	of Egypt to **a.** that trust in him	3605
Isa	36:20	among **a.** the gods of these lands,	3605
Isa	37:11	**A.** lands by destroying them	3605
Isa	37:16	of **a.** the kingdoms of the earth:	3605
Isa	37:17	hear **a.** the words of Sennacherib,	3605
Isa	37:18	have laid waste **a.** the nations,	3605
Isa	37:20	that **a.** the kingdoms of the earth	3605
Isa	37:25	**a.** the rivers of the besieged places	3605
Isa	37:36	behold, they were **a.** dead corpses	3605
Isa	38:13	so will he break **a.** my bones:	3605
Isa	38:15	**a.** my years in the bitterness of my	3605
Isa	38:16	men live, and in **a.** these things	3605
Isa	38:17	cast **a.** my sins behind thy back	3605
Isa	38:20	**a.** the days of our life in the house	3605
Isa	39:2	and **a.** the house of his armour,	3605
Isa	39:2	**a.** that was found in his treasures:	3605
Isa	39:2	nor in **a.** his dominion, that	3605
Isa	39:4	**A.** that is in mine house have they	3605
Isa	39:6	that **a.** that is in thine house,	3605
Isa	40:2	Lord's hand double for **a.** her sins	3605
Isa	40:5	the Lord shall be revealed, and **a.**	3605
Isa	40:6	**A.** flesh is grass,	3605
Isa	40:6	and **a.** the goodliness thereof	3605
Isa	40:17	**A.** nations before him are as	3605
Isa	40:26	he calleth them **a.** by names by	3605
Isa	41:11	**a.** they that were incensed against	3605
Isa	41:29	they are **a.** vanity; their works	3605
Isa	42:10	to the sea, and **a.** that is therein;	4393
Isa	42:15	and hills, and dry up **a.**	3605
Isa	42:22	they are **a.** of them snared in holes,	3605
Isa	43:9	Let **a.** the nations he gathered	3605
Isa	43:14	have brought down **a.** their nobles,	3605
Isa	44:9	graven image are **a.** of them vanity;	3605
Isa	44:11	**a.** his fellows shall be ashamed:	3605
Isa	44:11	of men: let them **a.** be gathered	3605
Isa	44:24	the Lord that maketh **a.** things;	3605
Isa	44:28	my shepherd, and shall perform **a.**	3605
Isa	45:7	I the Lord do **a.** these things	
Isa	45:12	**a.** their host have I commanded	3605
Isa	45:13	and I will direct **a.** his ways:	3605
Isa	45:16	**a.** of them: they shall go to	3605
Isa	45:22	ye saved, **a.** the ends of the earth:	
Isa	45:24	**a.** that are incensed against him	3605
Isa	45:25	shall **a.** seed of Israel be justified,	3605
Isa	46:3	**a.** the remnant of the house of	3605
Isa	46:10	and I will do **a.** my pleasure:	3605
Isa	48:6	Thou hast heard, see **a.** this;	3605
Isa	48:14	**A.** ye, assemble yourselves, and	3605
Isa	49:9	pastures shall be in **a.** high places	3605
Isa	49:11	I will make **a.** my mountains a	3605
Isa	49:18	**a.** these gather themselves	3605
Isa	49:18	surely clothe thee with them **a.**	3605
Isa	49:26	**a.** flesh shall know that I the Lord	3605
Isa	50:2	Is my hand shortened at **a.**, that	
Isa	50:9	**a.** shall wax old as a garment;	3605
Isa	50:11	Behold, **a.** ye that kindle a fire,	3605
Isa	51:3	Zion: he will comfort **a.** her	3605
Isa	51:18	to guide her among **a.** the sons	3605
Isa	51:18	by the hand of **a.** the sons that she	3605
Isa	51:20	fainted, they lie at the head of **a.** the	3605
Isa	52:10	bare his holy arm in the eyes of **a.**	3605
Isa	52:10	**a.** the ends of the earth shall see	3605
Isa	53:6	**A.** we like sheep have gone astray;	3605
Isa	53:6	laid on him the iniquity of us **a.**	3605
Isa	54:12	**a.** thy borders of pleasant stones	3605
Isa	54:13	**a.** thy children shall be taught of	3605
Isa	55:12	**a.** the trees of the field shall clap	3605
Isa	56:7	an house of prayer for **a.** people	3605
Isa	56:9	**A.** ye beasts of the field, come to	3605
Isa	56:9	yea, **a.** ye beasts in the forest	3605
Isa	56:10	they are **a.** ignorant,	3605
Isa	56:10	they are **a.** dumb dogs,	3605
Isa	56:11	they **a.** look to their own way,	3605
Isa	57:13	wind shall carry them **a.** away;	3605
Isa	58:3	pleasure, and exact **a.** your labours	3605
Isa	59:11	We roar **a.** like bears, and mourn	3605
Isa	60:4	eyes round about, and see: **a.** they	3605
Isa	60:6	**a.** they from Sheba shall come:	3605
Isa	60:7	**A.** the flocks of Kedar shall be	3605
Isa	60:14	and **a.** they that despised thee	3605
Isa	60:21	people also shall be **a.** righteous:	3605
Isa	61:2	our God; to comfort **a.** that mourn;	3605
Isa	61:9	**a.** that see them shall acknowledge	3605
Isa	61:11	spring forth before **a.** the nations	3605
Isa	62:2	and **a.** kings thy glory:	3605
Isa	63:3	and I will stain **a.** my raiment	3605
Isa	63:7	according to **a.** that the Lord	3605
Isa	63:9	In **a.** their affliction he was afflicted,	3605
Isa	63:9	carried them **a.** the days of old	3605
Isa	64:6	we are **a.** as an unclean thing,	3605
Isa	64:6	and **a.** our righteousnesses	3605
Isa	64:6	are as filthy rags; and we **a.** do	3605
Isa	64:8	we **a.** are the work of thy hand	3605
Isa	64:9	beseech thee, we are **a.** thy people	3605
Isa	64:11	and **a.** our pleasant things are laid	3605
Isa	65:2	spread out my hands **a.** the day	3605
Isa	65:5	a fire that burneth **a.** the day	3605
Isa	65:8	that I may not destroy them **a.**	3605
Isa	65:12	shall **a.** bow down to the slaughter	3605
Isa	65:25	destroy in **a.** my holy mountain,	3605
Isa	66:2	For **a.** those things hath mine	3605
Isa	66:2	**a.** those things have been, saith	3605
Isa	66:10	glad with her, **a.** ye that love her:	3605
Isa	66:10	with her, **a.** ye that mourn for her:	3605
Isa	66:16	will the Lord plead with **a.** flesh:	3605
Isa	66:18	gather **a.** nations and tongues;	3605
Isa	66:20	**a.** your brethren for an offering	3605
Isa	66:20	out of **a.** nations upon horses,	3605
Isa	66:23	to another, shall **a.** flesh come	3605
Isa	66:24	shall be an abhorring unto **a.** flesh	3605
Jer	1:7	go to **a.** that I shall send thee,	3605
Jer	1:14	upon **a.** the inhabitants of the land	3605
Jer	1:15	I will call **a.** the families of the	3605
Jer	1:15	against **a.** the walls thereof round	3605
Jer	1:15	and against **a.** the cities of Judah	3605
Jer	1:16	touching **a.** their wickedness,	3605
Jer	1:17	unto them **a.** that I command thee:	3605
Jer	2:3	**a.** that devour him shall offend;	3605
Jer	2:4	the Lord, O house of Jacob, and **a.**	3605
Jer	2:24	**a.** they that seek her will not	3605
Jer	2:29	ye **a.** have transgressed against	3605
Jer	2:34	secret search, but upon **a.** these	3605
Jer	3:7	after she had done **a.** these things,	3605
Jer	3:8	when for **a.** the causes whereby	3605
Jer	3:10	**a.** this her treacherous sister Judah	3605
Jer	3:17	**a.** the nations shall be gathered	3605
Jer	4:24	and **a.** the hills moved lightly	3605
Jer	4:25	**a.** the birds of the heavens were	3605
Jer	4:26	and **a.** the cities thereof	3605
Jer	5:16	sepulchre, they are **a.** mighty men	3605
Jer	5:19	our God **a.** these things unto us?	3605
Jer	6:15	nay, they were not at **a.** ashamed,	
Jer	6:28	They are **a.** grievous revolters,	3605
Jer	6:28	and iron; they are **a.** corrupters	3605
Jer	7:2	word of the Lord, **a.** ye of Judah,	3605
Jer	7:10	to do **a.** these abominations?	3605
Jer	7:13	ye have done **a.** these works,	3605
Jer	7:15	I have cast out **a.** your brethren,	3605
Jer	7:23	walk ye in **a.** the ways that I have	3605
Jer	7:25	even sent unto you **a.** my servants	3605
Jer	7:27	speak **a.** these words unto them;	3605
Jer	8:2	and **a.** the host of heaven, whom	3605
Jer	8:3	rather than life by **a.** the residue	3605
Jer	8:3	which remain in **a.** the places	3605
Jer	8:12	they were not at **a.** ashamed,	
Jer	8:16	the land, and **a.** that is in it; the	4393
Jer	9:2	for they be **a.** adulterers, an	3605
Jer	9:25	I will punish **a.** them which are	3605
Jer	9:26	**a.** that are in the utmost corners,	3605
Jer	9:26	for **a.** these nations are	3605
Jer	9:26	and **a.** the house of Israel are	3605
Jer	10:7	**a.** the wise men of the nations,	3605
Jer	10:7	and in **a.** their kingdoms, there is	3605
Jer	10:9	are **a.** the work of cunning men	3605
Jer	10:16	for he is the former of **a.** things;	3605
Jer	10:20	and **a.** my cords are broken:	3605
Jer	10:21	**a.** their flocks shall be scattered	3605
Jer	11:4	do them, according to **a.** which I	3605
Jer	11:6	Proclaim **a.** these words in the	3605
Jer	11:8	them **a.** the words of this covenant,	3605
Jer	11:12	at **a.** in the time of their trouble	
Jer	12:1	wherefore are **a.** they happy that	3605
Jer	12:9	assemble **a.** the beasts of the field,	3605
Jer	12:12	are come upon **a.** high places	3605
Jer	12:14	against **a.** mine evil neighbours,	3605
Jer	13:13	**a.** the inhabitants of this land,	3605
Jer	13:13	**a.** the inhabitants of Jerusalem,	3605
Jer	13:19	be carried away captive **a.** of it,	3605
Jer	14:22	for thou hast made **a.** these things	3605
Jer	15:4	to be removed into **a.** kingdoms of	3605
Jer	15:13	and that for **a.** thy sins,	3605
Jer	15:13	even in **a.** thy borders	3605
Jer	16:10	shew this people **a.** these words,	3605
Jer	16:10	**a.** this great evil against us?	3605
Jer	16:15	from **a.** the lands whither he had	3605
Jer	16:17	mine eyes are upon **a.** their ways:	3605
Jer	17:3	and **a.** thy treasures to the spoil,	3605
Jer	17:3	for sin, throughout **a.** thy borders	3605
Jer	17:9	heart is deceitful above **a.** things,	3605
Jer	17:13	**a.** that forsake thee shall be	3605
Jer	17:19	and in **a.** the gates of Jerusalem;	3605
Jer	17:20	kings of Judah, and **a.** Judah,	3605
Jer	17:20	**a.** the inhabitants of Jerusalem,	3605
Jer	18:23	thou knowest **a.** their counsel	3605
Jer	19:8	because of **a.** the plagues thereof	3605
Jer	19:13	place of Tophet, because of **a.** the	3605
Jer	19:13	incense unto **a.** the host of heaven,	3605
Jer	19:14	house; and said to **a.** the people,	3605
Jer	19:15	and upon **a.** her towns	3605
Jer	19:15	**a.** the evil that I have pronounced	3605
Jer	20:4	to thyself, and to **a.** thy friends:	3605
Jer	20:4	give **a.** Judah into the hand of the	3605
Jer	20:5	deliver **a.** the strength of this city,	3605
Jer	20:5	and **a.** the labours thereof,	3605
Jer	20:5	and **a.** the precious things thereof,	3605
Jer	20:5	**a.** the treasures of the kings of	3605

Book	Ref	Context	No.
Jer	20:6	**a.** that dwell in thine house shall	3605
Jer	20:6	and **a.** thy friends, to whom thou	3605
Jer	20:10	**A.** my familiars watched for my	3605
Jer	21:2	us according to **a.** his wondrous	3605
Jer	21:14	devour **a.** things round about it	3605
Jer	22:20	for **a.** thy lovers are destroyed	3605
Jer	22:22	wind shall eat up **a.** thy pastors,	3605
Jer	22:22	confounded for **a.** thy wickedness	3605
Jer	23:3	the remnant of my flock out of **a.**	3605
Jer	23:8	and from **a.** countries whither I	3605
Jer	23:9	**a.** my bones shake; I am like a	3605
Jer	23:14	are **a.** of them unto me as Sodom,	3605
Jer	23:15	gone forth into **a.** the land	3605
Jer	23:32	shall not profit this people at **a.**,	
Jer	24:9	removed into **a.** the kingdoms of	3605
Jer	24:9	**a.** places whither I shall	3605
Jer	25:1	Jeremiah concerning **a.** the people	3605
Jer	25:2	spake unto **a.** the people of Judah,	3605
Jer	25:2	**a.** the inhabitants of Jerusalem,	3605
Jer	25:4	you **a.** his servants the prophets,	3605
Jer	25:9	take **a.** the families of the north,	3605
Jer	25:9	**a.** these nations round about,	3605
Jer	25:13	that land **a.** my words which I	3605
Jer	25:13	even **a.** that is written in this book,	3605
Jer	25:13	prophesied against **a.** the nations	3605
Jer	25:15	this fury at my hand, and cause **a.**	3605
Jer	25:17	and made **a.** the nations to drink,	3605
Jer	25:19	and his princes, and **a.** his people;	3605
Jer	25:20	And **a.** the mingled people,	3605
Jer	25:20	and **a.** the kings of the land of Uz,	3605
Jer	25:20	and **a.** the kings of the land of the	3605
Jer	25:22	And **a.** the kings of Tyrus,	3605
Jer	25:22	and **a.** the kings of Zidon,	3605
Jer	25:23	Buz, and **a.** that are in the utmost	3605
Jer	25:24	And **a.** the kings of Arabia,	3605
Jer	25:24	and **a.** the kings of the	3605
Jer	25:25	And **a.** the kings of Zimri,	3605
Jer	25:25	and **a.** the kings of Elam,	3605
Jer	25:25	and **a.** the kings of the Medes,	3605
Jer	25:26	And **a.** the kings of the north, far	3605
Jer	25:26	and **a.** the kingdoms of the world,	3605
Jer	25:29	upon **a.** the inhabitants of the	3605
Jer	25:30	thou against them **a.** these words,	3605
Jer	25:30	**a.** the inhabitants of the earth	3605
Jer	25:31	he will plead with **a.** flesh; he will	3605
Jer	26:2	speak unto **a.** the cities of Judah,	3605
Jer	26:2	**a.** the words that I command thee	3605
Jer	26:6	to **a.** the nations of the earth	3605
Jer	26:7	and **a.** the people heard Jeremiah	3605
Jer	26:8	**a.** that the Lord had commanded	3605
Jer	26:8	him to speak unto **a.** the people,	3605
Jer	26:8	prophets and **a.** the people took	3605
Jer	26:9	And **a.** the people were gathered	3605
Jer	26:11	and to **a.** the people, saying, This	3605
Jer	26:12	spake Jeremiah unto **a.** the princes	3605
Jer	26:12	and to **a.** the people,	3605
Jer	26:12	**a.** the words that ye have heard	3605
Jer	26:15	speak **a.** these words in your ears	3605
Jer	26:16	the princes and **a.** the people unto	3605
Jer	26:17	elders of the land, and spake to **a.**	3605
Jer	26:18	to **a.** the people of Judah, saying,	3605
Jer	26:19	king of Judah and **a.** Judah	3605
Jer	26:19	put him at **a.** to death?	
Jer	26:20	to **a.** the words of Jeremiah:	3605
Jer	26:21	the king, with **a.** his mighty men,	3605
Jer	26:21	and **a.** the princes, heard his	3605
Jer	27:6	given **a.** these lands into the hand	3605
Jer	27:7	And **a.** nations shall serve him, and	3605
Jer	27:12	king of Judah according to **a.**	3605
Jer	27:16	the priests and to **a.** this people,	3605
Jer	27:20	and **a.** the nobles of Judah and	3605
Jer	28:1	the priests and of **a.** the people,	3605
Jer	28:3	**a.** the vessels of the Lord's house,	3605
Jer	28:4	with **a.** the captives of Judah, that	3605
Jer	28:5	in the presence of **a.** the people	3605
Jer	28:6	vessels of the Lord's house, and **a.**	3605
Jer	28:7	and in the ears of **a.** the people;	3605
Jer	28:11	in the presence of **a.** the people,	3605
Jer	28:11	from the neck of **a.** nations within	3605
Jer	28:14	upon the neck of **a.** these nations,	3605
Jer	29:1	and to **a.** the people whom	3605
Jer	29:4	**a.** that are carried away captives,	3605
Jer	29:13	search for me with **a.** your heart	3605
Jer	29:14	will gather you from **a.** the nations,	3605
Jer	29:14	from **a.** the places whither I have	3605
Jer	29:16	**a.** the people that dwelleth in this,	3605
Jer	29:18	to **a.** the kingdoms of the earth,	3605
Jer	29:18	among **a.** the nations whither I	3605
Jer	29:20	**a.** ye of the captivity, whom I have	3605
Jer	29:22	curse by **a.** the captivity, of Judah	3605
Jer	29:25	in thy name unto **a.** the people	3605
Jer	29:25	the priest, and to **a.** the priests,	3605
Jer	29:31	to **a.** them of the captivity, saying,	3605
Jer	30:2	Write thee **a.** the words that I have	3605
Jer	30:6	**a.** faces are turned into paleness?	3605
Jer	30:11	I make a full end of **a.** nations	3605
Jer	30:14	**A.** thy lovers have forgotten thee;	3605
Jer	30:16	Therefore **a.** they that devour thee	3605
Jer	30:16	**a.** thine adversaries, every one	3605
Jer	30:16	and **a.** that prey upon thee will I	3605
Jer	30:20	will punish **a.** that oppress them	3605
Jer	31:1	God of **a.** the families of Israel,	3605
Jer	31:12	shall not sorrow any more at **a.**	
Jer	31:24	in **a.** the cities thereof together,	3605
Jer	31:34	for they shall **a.** know me, from	3605
Jer	31:37	I will also cast off **a.** the seed of	3605
Jer	31:37	Israel for **a.** that they have done,	3605
Jer	31:40	**a.** the fields unto the brook of	3605
Jer	32:12	before **a.** the Jews that sat in the	3605
Jer	32:19	**a.** the ways of the sons of men:	3605
Jer	32:23	of **a.** that thou commandest	3605
Jer	32:23	caused **a.** this evil to come upon	3605
Jer	32:27	I am the Lord, the God of **a.** flesh:	3605
Jer	32:32	**a.** the evil of the children of Israel	3605
Jer	32:37	gather them out of **a.** countries	3605
Jer	32:42	brought **a.** this great evil upon this	3605
Jer	32:42	upon them **a.** the good that I	3605
Jer	33:5	and for **a.** whose wickedness I	3605
Jer	33:8	cleanse them from **a.** their iniquity,	3605
Jer	33:8	I will pardon **a.** their iniquities,	3605
Jer	33:9	before **a.** the nations of the earth,	3605
Jer	33:9	which shall hear **a.** the good that	3605
Jer	33:9	tremble for **a.** the goodness	3605
Jer	33:9	**a.** the prosperity that I procure	3605
Jer	33:12	and in **a.** the cities thereof, shall	3605
Jer	34:1	king of Babylon, and **a.** his army,	3605
Jer	34:1	and **a.** the kingdoms of the earth	3605
Jer	34:1	and **a.** the people, fought against	3605
Jer	34:1	and against **a.** the cities thereof,	3605
Jer	34:6	the prophet spake **a.** these words	3605
Jer	34:7	against **a.** the cities of Judah that	3605
Jer	34:8	a covenant with **a.** the people	3605
Jer	34:10	Now when **a.** the princes,	3605
Jer	34:10	**a.** the people, which had entered	3605
Jer	34:17	be removed into **a.** the kingdoms	3605
Jer	34:19	and **a.** the people of the land,	3605
Jer	35:3	**a.** his sons, and the whole house	3605
Jer	35:7	**a.** your days ye shall dwell in tents;	3605
Jer	35:8	in **a.** that he hath charged us,	3605
Jer	35:8	no wine **a.** our days, we, our wives	3605
Jer	35:10	according to **a.** that Jonadab our	3605
Jer	35:15	**a.** my servants the prophets,	3605
Jer	35:17	bring upon Judah and upon **a.** the	3605
Jer	35:17	Jerusalem **a.** the evil that I have	3605
Jer	35:18	and kept **a.** his precepts,	3605
Jer	35:18	and done according unto **a.**	3605
Jer	36:2	and write therein **a.** the words	3605
Jer	36:2	and against **a.** the nations,	3605
Jer	36:3	of Judah will hear **a.** the evil	3605
Jer	36:4	from the mouth of Jeremiah **a.** the	3605
Jer	36:6	read them in the ears of **a.** Judah	3605
Jer	36:8	son of Neriah did according to **a.**	3605
Jer	36:9	to **a.** the people in Jerusalem,	3605
Jer	36:9	**a.** the people that came from the	3605
Jer	36:10	house, in the ears of **a.** the people	3605
Jer	36:11	the book **a.** the words of the Lord,	3605
Jer	36:12	and, lo, **a.** the princes sat there,	3605
Jer	36:12	of Hananiah, and **a.** the princes	3605
Jer	36:13	declared unto them **a.** the words	3605
Jer	36:14	Therefore **a.** the princes sent Jehudi	3605
Jer	36:16	when they had heard **a.** the words,	3605
Jer	36:16	surely tell the king of **a.** these words	3605
Jer	36:17	didst thou write **a.** these words	3605
Jer	36:18	He pronounced **a.** these words	3605
Jer	36:20	**a.** the words in the ears of the king	3605
Jer	36:21	and in the ears of **a.** the princes	3605
Jer	36:23	until **a.** the roll was consumed in	3605
Jer	36:24	servants that heard **a.** these words	3605
Jer	36:28	and write in it **a.** the former words	3605
Jer	36:31	the men of Judah, **a.** the evil that	3605
Jer	36:32	mouth of Jeremiah **a.** the words	3605
Jer	37:21	**a.** the bread in the city was spent	3605
Jer	38:1	had spoken unto **a.** the people,	3605
Jer	38:4	and the hands of **a.** the people,	3605
Jer	38:9	**a.** that they have done to Jeremiah	3605
Jer	38:22	**a.** the women that are left in the	3605
Jer	38:23	they shall bring out **a.** thy wives	3605
Jer	38:27	came **a.** the princes unto Jeremiah,	3605
Jer	38:27	according to **a.** these words that	3605
Jer	39:1	king of Babylon and **a.** his army	3605
Jer	39:3	And **a.** the princes of the king	3605
Jer	39:3	with **a.** the residue of the princes	3605
Jer	39:4	saw them, and **a.** the men of war,	3605
Jer	39:6	king of Babylon slew **a.** the nobles	3605
Jer	39:13	**a.** the king of Babylon's princes;	3605
Jer	40:1	among **a.** that were carried away	3605
Jer	40:4	behold, **a.** the land is before thee:	3605
Jer	40:7	when **a.** the captains of the forces	3605
Jer	40:11	**a.** the Jews that were in Moab,	3605
Jer	40:11	and that were in **a.** the countries,	3605
Jer	40:12	Even **a.** the Jews returned	3605
Jer	40:12	out of **a.** places whither they	3605
Jer	40:13	son of Kareah, and **a.** the captains	3605
Jer	40:15	**a.** the Jews which are gathered	3605
Jer	41:3	Ishmael also slew **a.** the Jews that	3605
Jer	41:6	to meet them, weeping **a.** along	
Jer	41:9	had cast **a.** the dead bodies	3605
Jer	41:10	**a.** the residue of the people	3605
Jer	41:10	and **a.** the people that remained	3605
Jer	41:11	and **a.** the captains of the forces	3605
Jer	41:11	heard of **a.** the evil that Ishmael	3605
Jer	41:12	Then they took **a.** the men,	3605
Jer	41:13	**a.** the people which were with	3605
Jer	41:13	son of Kareah, and **a.** the captains	3605
Jer	41:14	So **a.** the people that Ishmael had	3605
Jer	41:16	son of Kareah, and **a.** the captains	3605
Jer	41:16	him, **a.** the remnant of the people	3605
Jer	42:1	Then **a.** the captains of the forces,	3605
Jer	42:1	and **a.** the people from the least	3605
Jer	42:2	thy God, even for **a.** this remnant;	3605
Jer	42:5	if we do not even according to **a.**	3605
Jer	42:8	and **a.** the captains of the forces	3605
Jer	42:8	and **a.** the people from the least	3605
Jer	42:17	So shall it be with **a.** the men	3605
Jer	42:20	according unto **a.** that the Lord	3605
Jer	43:1	end of speaking unto **a.** the people	3605
Jer	43:1	**a.** the words of the Lord their God,	3605
Jer	43:1	him to them, even **a.** these words,	3605
Jer	43:2	and **a.** the proud men, saying unto	3605
Jer	43:4	**a.** the captains of the forces,	3605
Jer	43:4	and **a.** the people, obeyed not	3605
Jer	43:5	son of Kareah, and **a.** the captains	3605
Jer	43:5	took **a.** the remnant of Judah,	3605
Jer	43:5	were returned from **a.** nations,	3605
Jer	44:1	concerning **a.** the Jews which dwell	3605
Jer	44:2	**a.** the evil that I have brought	3605
Jer	44:2	and upon **a.** the cities of Judah;	3605
Jer	44:4	you **a.** my servants the prophets,	3605
Jer	44:8	a curse and a reproach among **a.**	3605
Jer	44:11	for evil, and to cut off **a.** Judah	3605
Jer	44:12	and they shall **a.** be consumed,	3605
Jer	44:15	**a.** the men which knew that their	3605
Jer	44:15	other gods, and **a.** the women	3605
Jer	44:15	great multitude, even **a.** the people	3605
Jer	44:18	we have wanted **a.** things,	3605
Jer	44:20	Jeremiah said unto **a.** the people,	3605
Jer	44:20	to the women, and to **a.** the people	3605
Jer	44:24	Jeremiah said unto **a.** the people,	3605
Jer	44:24	**a.** the women, Hear the word	3605
Jer	44:24	of the Lord, **a.** Judah that are in	3605
Jer	44:26	**a.** Judah that dwell in the land of	3605
Jer	44:26	in **a.** the land of Egypt, saying,	3605
Jer	44:27	and **a.** the men of Judah that are	3605
Jer	44:28	and **a.** the remnant of Judah,	3605
Jer	45:5	I will bring evil upon **a.** flesh,	3605
Jer	45:5	unto thee for a prey in **a.** places	3605
Jer	46:25	and **a.** them that trust in him:	
Jer	46:28	make a full end of **a.** the nations	3605
Jer	47:2	the land, and **a.** that is therein;	4393
Jer	47:2	and **a.** the inhabitants of the land	3605
Jer	47:4	cometh to spoil **a.** the Philistines,	3605
Jer	48:17	**A.** ye that are about him,	3605
Jer	48:17	bemoan him; and **a.** ye that know	3605
Jer	48:24	**a.** the cities of the land of Moab,	3605
Jer	48:31	and I will cry out for **a.** Moab;	3605
Jer	48:37	**a.** the hands shall be cuttings,	3605
Jer	48:38	upon **a.** the housetops of Moab,	3605
Jer	48:39	and a dismaying to **a.** them about	3605
Jer	49:5	from **a.** those that be about thee;	3605
Jer	49:13	and **a.** the cities thereof shall be	3605
Jer	49:17	shall hiss at **a.** the plagues thereof	3605

Book	Ref	Context	No.
Jer	49:26	**a.** the men of war shall be cut off	3605
Jer	49:29	**a.** their vessels, and their camels;	3605
Jer	49:32	I will scatter into **a.** winds them	3605
Jer	49:32	their calamity from **a.** sides	3605
Jer	49:36	them toward **a.** those winds;	3605
Jer	50:7	**A.** that found them have devoured	3605
Jer	50:10	**a.** that spoil her shall be satisfied,	3605
Jer	50:13	be astonished, and hiss at **a.** her	3605
Jer	50:14	**a.** ye that bend the bow, shoot at	3605
Jer	50:21	**a.** that I have commanded thee	3605
Jer	50:27	Slay **a.** her bullocks; let them go	3605
Jer	50:29	the archers against Babylon: **a.** ye	3605
Jer	50:29	according to **a.** that she hath done,	3605
Jer	50:30	**a.** her men of war shall be cut off	3605
Jer	50:32	shall devour **a.** round about him.	3605
Jer	50:33	and **a.** that took them captives	3605
Jer	50:37	and upon **a.** the mingled people	3605
Jer	51:3	young men; destroy ye utterly **a.**	3605
Jer	51:7	that made **a.** the earth drunken:	3605
Jer	51:19	for he is the former of **a.** things:	3605
Jer	51:24	to **a.** the inhabitants of Chaldea	3605
Jer	51:24	**a.** their evil that they have done	3605
Jer	51:25	which destroyest **a.** the earth:	3605
Jer	51:28	and **a.** the rulers thereof,	3605
Jer	51:28	and **a.** the land of his dominion.	3605
Jer	51:47	**a.** her slain shall fall in the midst	3605
Jer	51:48	and **a.** that is therein, shall sing	3605
Jer	51:49	shall fall the slain of **a.** the earth.	3605
Jer	51:52	through **a.** her land the wounded	3605
Jer	51:60	a book **a.** the evil that should come	3605
Jer	51:60	**a.** these words that are written	3605
Jer	51:61	and shalt read **a.** these words;	3605
Jer	52:2	of the Lord, according to **a.** that	3605
Jer	52:4	**a.** his army, against Jerusalem,	3605
Jer	52:7	up, and **a.** the men of war fled,	3605
Jer	52:8	**a.** his army was scattered from	3605
Jer	52:10	slew also **a.** the princes of Judah	3605
Jer	52:13	and **a.** the houses of Jerusalem,	3605
Jer	52:13	**a.** the houses of the great men,	3605
Jer	52:14	And **a.** the army of the Chaldeans,	3605
Jer	52:14	down **a.** the walls of Jerusalem	3605
Jer	52:17	carried **a.** the brass...to Babylon.	3605
Jer	52:18	the bowls, and the spoons, and **a.**	3605
Jer	52:20	the brass of **a.** these vessels was	3605
Jer	52:22	chapiters round about, **a.** of brass.	3605
Jer	52:23	**a.** the pomegranates upon the	3605
Jer	52:30	**a.** the persons were four thousand	3605
Jer	52:33	before him **a.** the days of his life	3605
Jer	52:34	until the day of his death, **a.** the	3605
La	1:2	among **a.** her lovers she hath none	3605
La	1:2	**a.** her friends have dealt	3605
La	1:3	**a.** her presecutors overtook her	3605
La	1:4	**a.** her gates are desolate; her	3605
La	1:6	daughter of Zion **a.** her beauty is	3605
La	1:7	**a.** her pleasant things that she had	3605
La	1:8	**a.** that honoured her despise her,	3605
La	1:10	hath spread out his hand upon **a.**	3605
La	1:11	**A.** her people sigh, they seek bread;	3605
La	1:12	to you, **a.** ye that pass by? behold,	3605
La	1:13	me desolate and faint **a.** the day.	3605
La	1:15	trodden under foot **a.** my mighty	3605
La	1:18	hear, I pray you, **a.** people,	3605
La	1:21	**a.** mine enemies have heard of my	3605
La	1:22	**a.** their wickedness come before	3605
La	1:22	thou hast done unto me for **a.** my	3605
La	2:2	The Lord hath swallowed up **a.**	3605
La	2:3	fierce anger **a.** the horn of Israel:	3605
La	2:4	and slew **a.** that were pleasant to	3605
La	2:5	hath swallowed up **a.** her palaces:	3605
La	2:15	**A.** that pass by clap their hands at	3605
La	2:16	**A.** thine enemies have opened their	3605
La	3:3	he turneth his hand against me **a.**	3605
La	3:14	I was a derision to **a.** my people;	3605
La	3:14	and their song **a.** the day	3605
La	3:34	feet **a.** the prisoners of the earth,	3605
La	3:46	**A.** our enemies have opened their	3605
La	3:51	heart because of **a.** the daughters	3605
La	3:60	Thou hast seen **a.** their vengeance	3605
La	3:60,	61 **a.** their imaginations against	3605
La	3:62	device against me **a.** the day	3605
La	4:12	and **a.** the inhabitants of the world,	3605
Eze	3:7	**a.** the house of Israel are impudent	3605
Eze	3:10	**a.** my words that I shall speak	3605
Eze	5:4	forth into **a.** the house of Israel.	3605
Eze	5:9	because of **a.** thine abominations.	3605
Eze	5:10	will I scatter into **a.** the winds.	3605
Eze	5:11	with **a.** thy detestable things,	3605
Eze	5:11	and with **a.** thine abominations,	3605
Eze	5:12	third part into **a.** the winds,	3605
Eze	5:14	in the sight of **a.** that pass by	3605
Eze	6:6	In **a.** your dwellingplaces the	3605
Eze	6:9	in **a.** their abominations.	3605
Eze	6:11	Alas for **a.** the evil abominations	3605
Eze	6:13	in **a.** the tops of the mountains,	3605
Eze	6:13	sweet savour to **a.** their idols.	3605
Eze	6:14	in **a.** their habitations: and they	3605
Eze	7:3	upon thee **a.** thine abominations.	3605
Eze	7:8	and will recompense thee for **a.**	3605
Eze	7:12	wrath is upon **a.** the multitude	3605
Eze	7:14	trumpet, even to make **a.** ready;	3605
Eze	7:14	battle: for my wrath is upon **a.**	3605
Eze	7:16	**a.** of them mourning, every one	3605
Eze	7:17	**A.** hands shall be feeble,	3605
Eze	7:17	and **a.** knees shall be weak	3605
Eze	7:18	shame shall be upon **a.** faces,	3605
Eze	7:18	and baldness upon **a.** their heads	3605
Eze	8:10	**a.** the idols of the house of Israel,	3605
Eze	9:4	cry for **a.** the abominations that	3605
Eze	9:8	destroy **a.** the residue of Israel	3605
Eze	11:15	and **a.** the house of Israel wholly,	3605
Eze	11:18	shall take away **a.** the detestable	3605
Eze	11:18	and **a.** the abominations thereof	3605
Eze	11:25	**a.** the things that the Lord had	3605
Eze	12:10	and **a.** the house of Israel that	3605
Eze	12:14	toward every wind **a.** that are	3605
Eze	12:14	to help him, and **a.** his bands;	3605
Eze	12:16	may declare **a.** their abominations	3605
Eze	12:19	be desolate from **a.** that is therein,	4393
Eze	12:19	of **a.** them that dwell therein.	3605
Eze	13:18	that sew pillows to **a.** armholes,	3605
Eze	14:3	face: should I be enquired of at **a.**	
Eze	14:5	they are **a.** estranged from me	3605
Eze	14:6	faces from **a.** your abominations.	3605
Eze	14:11	polluted any more with **a.** their	3605
Eze	14:22	concerning **a.** that I have brought	3605
Eze	14:23	cause **a.** that I have done in it,	3605
Eze	16:4	thou wast not salted at **a.**,	
Eze	16:4	nor swaddled at **a.**.	
Eze	16:22	And in **a.** thine abominations and	3605
Eze	16:23	to pass after **a.** thy wickedness,	3605
Eze	16:30	seeing thou doest **a.** these things,	3605
Eze	16:33	They give gifts to **a.** whores: but	3605
Eze	16:33	givest thy gifts to **a.** thy lovers,	3605
Eze	16:36	**a.** the idols of thy abominations,	3605
Eze	16:37	I will gather **a.** thy lovers, with	3605
Eze	16:37	and **a.** them that thou hast loved,	3605
Eze	16:37	with **a.** them that thou hast hated;	3605
Eze	16:37	they may see **a.** thy nakedness	3605
Eze	16:43	hast fretted me in **a.** these things;	3605
Eze	16:43	above **a.** thine abominations.	3605
Eze	16:47	more than they in **a.** thy ways	3605
Eze	16:51	in **a.** thine abominations which	3605
Eze	16:54	**a.** that thou hast done, in that thou	3605
Eze	16:57	and **a.** that are round about her,	3605
Eze	16:63	toward thee for **a.** that thou	3605
Eze	17:9	in **a.** the leaves of her spring,	3605
Eze	17:18	and hath done **a.** these things, he	3605
Eze	17:21	And **a.** his fugitives	3605
Eze	17:21	with **a.** his bands shall fall by the	3605
Eze	17:21	be scattered toward **a.** winds:	3605
Eze	17:23	shall dwell **a.** fowl of every wing;	3605
Eze	17:24	And **a.** the trees of the field shall	3605
Eze	18:4	Behold, **a.** souls are mine; as the	3605
Eze	18:13	not live: he hath done **a.** these	3605
Eze	18:14	that seeth **a.** his father's sins which	3605
Eze	18:19	kept **a.** my statutes, and hath	3605
Eze	18:21	will turn from **a.** his sins that he	3605
Eze	18:21	and keep **a.** my statutes, and do	3605
Eze	18:22	**A.** his transgressions that he	3605
Eze	18:23	at **a.** that the wicked should die	
Eze	18:24	according to **a.** the abominations	3605
Eze	18:24	**A.** his righteousness that he hath	3605
Eze	18:28	and turneth away from **a.**	3605
Eze	18:30	from **a.** your transgressions;	3605
Eze	18:31	from you **a.** your transgressions,	3605
Eze	20:6,	15 which is the glory of **a.** lands:	3605
Eze	20:26	to pass through the fire **a.** that	3605
Eze	20:28	high hill, and **a.** the thick trees,	3605
Eze	20:31	pollute yourselves with **a.** your	3605
Eze	20:32	into your mind shall not be at **a.**.	
Eze	20:40	there shall **a.** the house of Israel,	3605
Eze	20:40	**a.** of them in the land, serve me:	3605
Eze	20:40	oblations, with **a.** your holy things.	3605
Eze	20:43	your ways, and **a.** your doings,	3605
Eze	20:43	for **a.** your evils that ye have	3605
Eze	20:47	and **a.** faces from the south to the	3605
Eze	20:48	**a.** flesh shall see that I the Lord	3605
Eze	21:4	**a.** flesh from the south to the north:	3605
Eze	21:5	That **a.** flesh may know that I	3605
Eze	21:7	melt, and **a.** hands shall be feeble,	3605
Eze	21:7	faint, and **a.** knees shall be weak	3605
Eze	21:12	be upon **a.** the princes of Israel:	3605
Eze	21:15	the sword against **a.** their gates,	3605
Eze	21:24	so that in **a.** your doings your sins	3605
Eze	22:2	shalt shew her **a.** her abominations.	3605
Eze	22:4	and a mocking to **a.** countries	3605
Eze	22:18	Israel is to me become dross: **a.**	3605
Eze	22:19	Because ye are **a.** become dross,	3605
Eze	23:6	**a.** of them desirable young men,	3605
Eze	23:7	**a.** them that were the chosen men	
Eze	23:7	with **a.** on whom she doted:	3605
Eze	23:7	with **a.** their idols she defiled	3605
Eze	23:12	**a.** of them desirable young men.	3605
Eze	23:15	**a.** of them princes to look to, after	3605
Eze	23:23	and **a.** the Chaldeans, Pekod, and	3605
Eze	23:23	and **a.** the Assyrians with them:	3605
Eze	23:23	**a.** of them desirable young men,	3605
Eze	23:23	**a.** of them riding upon horses	3605
Eze	23:29	shall take away **a.** thy labour,	3605
Eze	23:48	that **a.** women may be taught	3605
Eze	24:24	**a.** that he hath done shall ye do:	3605
Eze	25:6	**a.** thy despite against the land of	3605
Eze	25:8	Judah is like unto **a.** the heathen;	3605
Eze	26:11	shall he tread down **a.** thy streets:	3605
Eze	26:16	Then **a.** the princes of the sea shall	3605
Eze	26:17	terror to be on **a.** that haunt it!	3605
Eze	27:5	made **a.** thy ship boards of fir trees	3605
Eze	27:9	**a.** the ships of the sea with their	3605
Eze	27:12	of the multitude of **a.** kind of riches;	3605
Eze	27:18	for the multitude of **a.** riches; in	3605
Eze	27:21	Arabia, and **a.** the princes of Ked ar,	3605
Eze	27:22	of **a.** spices, and with **a.** precious	3605
Eze	27:24	merchants in **a.** sorts of things,	3605
Eze	27:27	and **a.** thy men of war,	3605
Eze	27:27	and in **a.** thy company	3605
Eze	27:29	And **a.** that handle the oar,	3605
Eze	27:29	the mariners, and **a.** the pilots	3605
Eze	27:34	and **a.** thy company in the midst	3605
Eze	27:35	**A.** the inhabitants of the isles	3605
Eze	28:18	earth in the sight of **a.** them that	3605
Eze	28:19	**A.** they that know thee among the	3605
Eze	28:24	of **a.** that are round about them,	3605
Eze	28:26	judgments upon **a.** those that	3605
Eze	29:2	against him, and against **a.** Egypt:	3605
Eze	29:4	and **a.** the fish of thy rivers shall	3605
Eze	29:5	wilderness, thee and **a.** the fish	3605
Eze	29:6	And **a.** the inhabitants of Egypt	3605
Eze	29:7	break, and rend **a.** their shoulder:	3605
Eze	29:7	and madest all their loins to be at **a.**	3605
Eze	30:5	Lydia, and **a.** the mingled people,	3605
Eze	30:8	**a.** her helpers shall be destroyed.	3605
Eze	30:12	land waste, and **a.** that is therein,	4393
Eze	31:4	unto **a.** the trees of the field.	3605
Eze	31:5	his height was exalted above **a.** the	3605
Eze	31:6	**A.** the fowls of heaven made their	3605
Eze	31:6	**a.** the beasts of the field bring	3605
Eze	31:6	his shadow dwelt **a.** great nations	3605
Eze	31:9	so that **a.** the trees of Eden,	3605
Eze	31:12	in **a.** the valleys his branches are	3605
Eze	31:12	broken by **a.** the rivers of the land;	3605
Eze	31:12	**a.** the people of the earth are gone	3605
Eze	31:13	**a.** the fowls of the heaven remain,	3605
Eze	31:13	and **a.** the beasts of the field shall	3605
Eze	31:14	To the end that none of **a.** the trees	3605
Eze	31:14	**a.** that drink water: for	3605
Eze	31:14	they are **a.** delivered unto death,	3605
Eze	31:15	**a.** the trees of the field fainted for	3605
Eze	31:16	and **a.** the trees of Eden,	3605
Eze	31:16	**a.** that drink water, shall be	3605
Eze	31:18	is Pharaoh and **a.** his multitude,	3605
Eze	32:4	cause **a.** the fowls of the heaven	3605
Eze	32:8	**A.** the bright lights of heaven	3605
Eze	32:12	terrible of the nations, **a.** of them:	3605
Eze	32:12	and **a.** the multitude thereof	3605
Eze	32:13	destroy also **a.** the beasts thereof	3605
Eze	32:15	smite **a.** them that dwell therein,	3605
Eze	32:16	Egypt, and for **a.** her multitude,	3605
Eze	32:20	draw her and **a.** her multitudes	3605
Eze	32:22	is there and **a.** her company:	3605
Eze	32:22	**a.** of them slain, fallen by the	3605
Eze	32:23	round about her grave: **a.** of them	3605

Book	Ref	Context	No.
Eze	32:24	Elam and **a.** her multitude round	3605
Eze	32:24	her grave, **a.** of them slain, fallen	3605
Eze	32:25	the slain with **a.** her multitude:	3605
Eze	32:25	are round about him: **a.** of them	3605
Eze	32:26	Tubal, and **a.** her multitude:	3605
Eze	32:26	**a.** of them uncircumcised, slain	3605
Eze	32:29	her kings, and **a.** her princes,	3605
Eze	32:30	princes of the north, **a.** of them,	3605
Eze	32:30	and **a.** the Zidonians, which are	3605
Eze	32:31	comforted over **a.** his multitude,	3605
Eze	32:31	Pharaoh and **a.** his army slain by	3605
Eze	32:32	Pharaoh and **a.** his multitude,	3605
Eze	33:13	iniquity, **a.** his righteousnesses	3605
Eze	33:29	land most desolate because of **a.**	3605
Eze	34:5	meat to **a.** the beasts of the field,	3605
Eze	34:6	through **a.** the mountains,	3605
Eze	34:6	was scattered upon **a.** the face	3605
Eze	34:12	and will deliver them out of **a.**	3605
Eze	34:13	and in **a.** the inhabited places of	3605
Eze	34:21	and pushed **a.** the diseased with	3605
Eze	35:8	and in **a.** thy rivers, shall they fall	3605
Eze	35:12	I have heard **a.** thy blasphemies	3605
Eze	35:15	Seir, and **a.** Idumea, even **a.** of it:	3605
Eze	36:5	and against **a.** Idumea, which have	3605
Eze	36:5	with the joy of **a.** their heart,	3605
Eze	36:10	multiply men upon you, **a.** the	3605
Eze	36:10	Israel, even **a.** of it: and the cities	3605
Eze	36:24	gather you out of **a.** countries,	3605
Eze	36:25	from **a.** your filthiness,	3605
Eze	36:25	and from **a.** your idols,	3605
Eze	36:29	you from **a.** your uncleannesses:	3605
Eze	36:33	you from **a.** your iniquities	3605
Eze	36:34	in the sight of **a.** that passed by	3605
Eze	37:16	of Ephraim, and for **a.** the house	3605
Eze	37:22	one king shall be king to them **a.**:	3605
Eze	37:22	two kingdoms any more at **a.**:	
Eze	37:23	out of **a.** their dwelling places,	3650
Eze	37:24	they **a.** shall have one shepherd:	3650
Eze	38:4	thee forth, and **a.** thine army,	3650
Eze	38:4	**a.** of them clothed	3650
Eze	38:4	with **a.** sorts of armour,	3650
Eze	38:4	**a.** of them handling swords:	3650
Eze	38:5	**a.** of them with shield and helmet:	3650
Eze	38:6	Gomer, and **a.** his bands;	3650
Eze	38:6	north quarters, and **a.** his bands:	3650
Eze	38:7	prepare for thyself, thou, and **a.**	3650
Eze	38:8	they shall dwell safely **a.** of them.	3650
Eze	38:9	thou, and **a.** thy bands, and many	3650
Eze	38:11	**a.** of them dwelling without walls,	3650
Eze	38:13	Tarshish, with **a.** the young lions	3650
Eze	38:15	**a.** of them riding upon horses,	3650
Eze	38:20	and **a.** creeping things that creep	3650
Eze	38:20	**a.** the men that are upon the face	3650
Eze	38:21	him throughout **a.** my mountains,	3650
Eze	39:4	mountains of Israel, thou, and **a.**	3650
Eze	39:11	bury Gog and **a.** his multitude:	3650
Eze	39:13	Yea, **a.** the people of the land shall	3650
Eze	39:18	**a.** of them fatlings of Bashan.	3650
Eze	39:20	men, and with **a.** men of war,	3650
Eze	39:21	and **a.** the heathen shall see my	3650
Eze	39:23	so fell they **a.** by the sword.	3650
Eze	39:26	and **a.** their trespasses whereby	3650
Eze	40:4	upon **a.** that I shall shew thee;	3650
Eze	40:4	declare **a.** that thou seest to the	3650
Eze	41:17	and by **a.** the wall round about	3650
Eze	41:19	it was made through **a.** the house	3650
Eze	42:11	and **a.** their goings out were both	3650
Eze	43:11	ashamed of **a.** that they have done,	3650
Eze	43:11	and **a.** the forms thereof,	3650
Eze	43:11	and **a.** the ordinances thereof,	3650
Eze	43:11	and **a.** the forms thereof	3650
Eze	43:11	and **a.** the laws thereof:	3650
Eze	43:11	and **a.** the ordinances thereof,	3650
Eze	44:5	hear with thine ears **a.** that I say	3650
Eze	44:5	concerning **a.** the ordinances of	3650
Eze	44:5	**a.** the laws thereof; and mark well	3650
Eze	44:6	suffice you of **a.** your abominations,	3650
Eze	44:7	because of **a.** your abominations	3650
Eze	44:14	for **a.** the service thereof, and	3650
Eze	44:14	for **a.** that shall be done therein.	3650
Eze	44:24	my statutes in **a.** mine assemblies;	3650
Eze	44:30	And the first of **a.** the firstfruits	3650
Eze	44:30	of **a.** things, and	3650
Eze	44:30	every oblation of **a.**, of every sort	3650
Eze	45:1	**a.** the borders thereof round about.	3650
Eze	45:16	**A.** the people of the land shall give	3650
Eze	45:17	**a.** solemnities of the house of Israel:	3650
Eze	45:22	and for **a.** the people of the land	3650
Eze	47:12	shall grow **a.** trees for meat,	3650
Eze	48:13	**a.** the length shall be five and	3650
Eze	48:19	it out of **a.** the tribes of Israel.	3650
Eze	48:20	**A.** the oblation shall be five and	3650
Da	1:4	skilful in **a.** wisdom, and cunning	3650
Da	1:15	fatter in flesh than **a.** the children	3650
Da	1:17	knowledge and skill in **a.** learning	3650
Da	1:17	understanding in **a.** visions and	3650
Da	1:19	among them **a.** was found none like	3650
Da	1:20	and in **a.** matters of wisdom and	3650
Da	1:20	them ten times better than **a.**	3650
Da	1:20	astrologers that were in **a.** his	3650
Da	2:12	**a.** the wise men of Babylon.	3606
Da	2:38	made thee ruler over them **a.**	3606
Da	2:39	shall bear rule over **a.** the earth.	3606
Da	2:40	in pieces and subdueth **a.** things:	3606
Da	2:40	and as iron that breaketh **a.** these,	3606
Da	2:44	and consume **a.** these kingdoms,	3606
Da	2:48	over **a.** the wise men of Babylon.	3606
Da	3:2,3	**a.** the rulers of the provinces,	3606
Da	3:5	dulcimer, and **a.** kinds of musick,	3606
Da	3:7	**a.** the people heard the sound of	3606
Da	3:7	and **a.** kinds of musick, **a.** the	3606
Da	3:10	and **a.** kinds of musick, shall fall	3606
Da	3:15	psaltery, and dulcimer, and **a.**	3606
Da	4:1	**a.** people, nations, and languages,	3606
Da	4:1	that dwell in **a.** the earth;	3606
Da	4:6	in **a.** the wise men of Babylon	3606
Da	4:11	thereof to the end of **a.** the earth:	3606
Da	4:12	and in it was meat for **a.**:	3606
Da	4:12	**a.** flesh was fed of it.	3606
Da	4:18	forasmuch as **a.** the wise men	3606
Da	4:20	the sight thereof to **a.** the earth;	3606
Da	4:21	much, and in it was meat for **a.**;	3606
Da	4:28	**A.** this came upon the king	3606
Da	4:35	And **a.** the inhabitants of the earth	3606
Da	4:37	**a.** whose works are truth,	3606
Da	5:8	came in **a.** the king's wise men:	3606
Da	5:19	**a.** people, nations, and languages,	3606
Da	5:22	though thou knewest **a.** this;	3606
Da	5:23	and whose are **a.** thy ways,	3606
Da	6:7	**A.** the presidents of the kingdom,	3606
Da	6:24	and brake **a.** their bones in pieces	3606
Da	6:25	**a.** people, nations, and languages,	3606
Da	6:25	that dwell in **a.** the earth;	3606
Da	7:7	it was diverse from **a.** the beasts	3606
Da	7:14	**a.** people, nations, and languages,	3606
Da	7:16	and asked him the truth of **a.** this.	3606
Da	7:19	was diverse from **a.** the others,	3606
Da	7:23	shall be diverse from **a.** kingdoms,	3606
Da	7:27	**a.** dominions shall serve and obey	3606
Da	9:6	and to **a.** the people of the land.	3605
Da	9:7	and unto **a.** Israel, that are near,	3605
Da	9:7	**a.** the countries whither thou hast	3605
Da	9:11	**a.** Israel have transgressed thy law,	3605
Da	9:13	Moses, **a.** this evil is come upon us:	3605
Da	9:14	God is righteous in **a.** his works	3605
Da	9:16	according to **a.** thy righteousness,	3605
Da	9:16	a reproach to **a.** that are about us.	3605
Da	10:3	did I anoint myself at **a.**,	
Da	11:2	shall be far richer than they **a.**:	3605
Da	11:2	up **a.** against the realm of Grecia.	3605
Da	11:37	he shall magnify himself above **a.**	3605
Da	11:43	**a.** the precious things of Egypt:	3605
Da	12:7	**a.** these things shall be finished.	3605
Ho	2:11	also cause **a.** her mirth to cease,	3605
Ho	2:11	sabbaths, and **a.** her solemn feasts.	3605
Ho	5:2	I have been a rebuker of them **a.**	3605
Ho	7:2	I remember **a.** their wickedness:	3605
Ho	7:4	They are **a.** adulterers, as an oven	3605
Ho	7:6	their baker sleepeth **a.** the night;	3605
Ho	7:7	They are **a.** hot as an oven,	3605
Ho	7:7	**a.** their kings are fallen: there is	3605
Ho	7:10	Lord their God, nor seek him for **a.**	3605
Ho	9:4	**a.** that eat thereof shall be polluted:	3605
Ho	9:8	is a snare of a fowler in **a.** his	3605
Ho	9:15	**A.** their wickedness is in Gilgal:	3605
Ho	9:15	**a.** their princes are revolters.	3605
Ho	10:14	**a.** thy fortresses shall be spoiled,	3605
Ho	11:7	most High, none at **a.** would exalt	3162
Ho	12:8	in **a.** my labours they shall find	3605
Ho	13:2	**a.** of it the work of the craftsmen:	3605
Ho	13:10	that may save thee in **a.** thy cities?	3605
Ho	13:15	the treasure of **a.** pleasant vessels.	3605
Ho	14:2	take away **a.** iniquity, and receive	3605
Joe	1:2	ear, **a.** ye inhabitants of the land.	3605
Joe	1:5	and howl, **a.** ye drinkers of wine,	3605
Joe	1:12	even **a.** the trees of the field,	3605
Joe	1:13	come, lie **a.** night in sackcloth,	3885
Joe	1:14	and **a.** the inhabitants of the land	3605
Joe	1:19	the flame hath burned **a.** the trees	3605
Joe	2:1	let **a.** the inhabitants of the land	3605
Joe	2:6	**a.** faces shall gather blackness.	3605
Joe	2:12	ye even to me with **a.** your heart,	3605
Joe	2:28	pour out my spirit upon **a.** flesh;	3605
Joe	3:2	I will also gather **a.** nations,	3605
Joe	3:4	and **a.** the coasts of Palestine?	3605
Joe	3:9	let **a.** the men of war draw near;	3605
Joe	3:11	and come, **a.** ye heathen, and	3605
Joe	3:12	judge **a.** the heathen round about.	3605
Joe	3:18	**a.** the rivers of Judah shall flow	3605
Am	1:11	the sword, and did cast off **a.** pity,	
Am	2:3	and will slay **a.** the princes thereof	3605
Am	3:2	of **a.** the families of the earth:	3605
Am	3:2	punish you for **a.** your iniquities.	3605
Am	3:5	and have taken nothing at **a.**?	
Am	4:6	you cleanness of teeth in **a.** your	3605
Am	4:6	want of bread in **a.** your places:	3605
Am	5:16	Wailing shall be in **a.** streets;	3605
Am	5:16	they shall say in **a.** the highways,	3605
Am	5:17	in **a.** vineyards shall be wailing:	3605
Am	6:8	up the city with **a.** that is therein.	4393
Am	7:10	land is not able to bear **a.** his	3605
Am	8:10	**a.** your sons into lamentation;	3605
Am	8:10	bring up sackcloth upon **a.** loins,	3605
Am	9:1	cut them in the head, **a.** of them;	3605
Am	9:5	**a.** that dwell therein shall mourn:	3605
Am	9:9	house of Israel among **a.** nations,	3605
Am	9:10	**A.** the sinners of my people shall	3605
Am	9:12	and of **a.** the heathen, which are	3605
Am	9:13	wine, and **a.** the hills shall melt	3605
Ob	7	**A.** the men of thy confederacy have	3605
Ob	15	Lord is near upon **a.** the heathen:	3605
Ob	16	**a.** the heathen drink continually,	3605
Jon	2:3	**a.** thy billows and thy waves	3605
Mic	1:2	Hear, **a.** ye people; hearken,	3605
Mic	1:2	O earth, and **a.** that therein is:	4393
Mic	1:5	transgression of Jacob is **a.** this,	3605
Mic	1:7	And **a.** the graven images thereof	3605
Mic	1:7	and **a.** the hires thereof shall be	3605
Mic	1:7	and **a.** the idols thereof will I lay	3605
Mic	1:10	it not at Gath, weep ye not at **a.**:	
Mic	2:12	assemble, O Jacob, **a.** of thee;	3605
Mic	3:7	yea, they shall **a.** cover their lips;	3605
Mic	3:9	judgment, and pervert **a.** equity.	3605
Mic	4:5	**a.** people will walk every one in the	3605
Mic	5:9	and **a.** thine enemies shall be cut	
Mic	5:11	throw down **a.** thy strong holds:	3605
Mic	6:16	are kept, and **a.** the works of the	3605
Mic	7:2	among men: they **a.** lie in wait	3605
Mic	7:16	be confounded at **a.** their might:	3605
Mic	7:19	cast **a.** their sins into the depths	3605
Na	1:3	will not at **a.** acquit the wicked:	
Na	1:4	maketh it dry, and drieth up **a.**	3605
Na	1:5	world, and **a.** that dwell therein.	3605
Na	2:9	out of **a.** the pleasant furniture.	3605
Na	2:10	pain is in **a.** loins,	3605
Na	2:10	faces of them **a.** gather blackness.	3605
Na	3:1	city! it is **a.** full of lies and	3605
Na	3:7	that **a.** they that look upon thee	3605
Na	3:10	pieces at the top of **a.** the streets:	3605
Na	3:10	and **a.** her great men were bound	3605
Na	3:12	**A.** thy strongholds shall be like fig	3605
Na	3:19	**a.** that hear the bruit of thee shall	3605
Hab	1:9	They shall come **a.** for violence:	3605
Hab	1:15	take up **a.** of them with the angle,	3605
Hab	2:5	gathereth unto him **a.** nations,	3605
Hab	2:5	and heapeth unto him **a.** people:	3605
Hab	2:6	Shall not **a.** these take up a parable	3605
Hab	2:8	**a.** the remnant of the people shall	3605
Hab	2:8,	17 city, and of **a.** that dwell therein.	3605
Hab	2:19	no breath at **a.** in the midst of it.	3605
Hab	2:20	let **a.** the earth keep silence	3605
Zep	1:2	**a.** things from off the land,	3605
Zep	1:4	hand upon Judah, and upon **a.**	3605
Zep	1:8	and **a.** such as are clothed with	3605
Zep	1:9	will I punish **a.** those that leap on	3605
Zep	1:11	**a.** the merchant people are cut	3605
Zep	1:11	down; **a.** they that bear	3605
Zep	1:18	a speedy riddance of **a.** them that	3605
Zep	2:3	the Lord, **a.** ye meek of the earth,	3605
Zep	2:11	famish **a.** the gods of the earth;	3605
Zep	2:11	one from his place, even **a.** the	3605

Zep 2:14 in the midst of her, a. the beasts 3605
Zep 3:7 and corrupted a. their doings 3605
Zep 3:8 even a. my fierce anger 3605
Zep 3:8 for a. the earth shall be devoured 3605
Zep 3:9 that they may a. call upon the name 3605
Zep 3:11 not be ashamed for a. thy doings, 3605
Zep 3:14 glad and rejoice with a. the heart, 3605
Zep 3:19 time I will undo a. that afflict thee: 3605
Zep 3:20 name and a praise among a. people 3605
Hag 1:11 upon a. the labour of the hands. 3605
Hag 1:12 with a. the remnant of the people, 3605
Hag 1:14 the spirit of a. the remnant of the 3605
Hag 2:4 strong, a. ye people of the land, 3605
Hag 2:7 And I will shake a. nations, 3605
Hag 2:7 and the desire of a. nations 3605
Hag 2:17 hail in a. the labours of your hands; 3605
Zec 1:11 and, behold, a. the earth sitteth still 3605
Zec 2:13 Be silent, O a. flesh, before the 3605
Zec 4:2 and behold a candlestick a. of gold, 3605
Zec 5:6 resemblance through a. the earth. 3605
Zec 6:5 before the Lord of a. the earth. 3605
Zec 7:5 unto a. the people of the land, 3605
Zec 7:5 years, did ye at a. fast unto me,
Zec 7:14 a. the nations whom they knew 3605
Zec 8:10 for I set a. men every one against 3605
Zec 8:12 of this people to possess a. 3605
Zec 8:17 for a. these are things that I hate, 3605
Zec 8:23 take hold out of a. languages of 3605
Zec 9:1 of man, as of a. the tribes of Israel, 3605
Zec 10:11 a. the deeps of the river shall dry 3605
Zec 11:10 I had made with a. the people. 3605
Zec 12:2 of trembling unto a. the people 3605
Zec 12:3 a burdensome stone for a. people: 3605
Zec 12:3 a. that burden themselves with it 3605
Zec 12:3 though a. the people of the earth 3605
Zec 12:6 devour a. the people round about, 3605
Zec 12:9 destroy a. the nations that come 3605
Zec 12:14 A. the families that remain, every 3605
Zec 13:8 that in a. the land, saith the Lord, 3605
Zec 14:2 a. nations against Jerusalem to 3605
Zec 14:5 come, and a. the saints with thee. 3605
Zec 14:9 shall be king over a. the earth: 3605
Zec 14:10 A. the land shall be turned as a 3605
Zec 14:12 the Lord will smite a. the people 3605
Zec 14:14 and the wealth of a. the heathen 3605
Zec 14:15 a. the beasts that shall be in these 3605
Zec 14:16 that is left of a. the nations which 3605
Zec 14:17 will not come up of a. the families
Zec 14:19 and the punishment of a. nations 3605
Zec 14:21 the Lord of hosts: and a. they that 3605
Mal 2:9 and base before a. the people, 3605
Mal 2:10 Have we not a. one father? hath 3605
Mal 3:10 a. the tithes into the storehouse, 3605
Mal 3:12 a. nations shall call you blessed: 3605
Mal 4:1 and a. the proud, yea, 3605
Mal 4:1 and a. that do wickedly, 3605
Mal 4:4 unto him in Horeb for a. Israel, 3605
Mt 1:17 a. the generations from Abraham 3956
Mt 1:22 Now a. this was done, that it 3650
Mt 2:3 and a. Jerusalem with him 3956
Mt 2:4 had gathered a. the chief priests 3956
Mt 2:16 and slew a. the children that were 3956
Mt 2:16 and in a. the coasts thereof, 3956
Mt 3:5 to him Jerusalem, and a. Judaea, 3956
Mt 3:5 a. the region round about Jordan, 3956
Mt 3:15 us to fulfil a. righteousness. 3956
Mt 4:8 and sheweth him a. the kingdoms 3956
Mt 4:9 A. these things will I give thee, 3956
Mt 4:23 Jesus went about a. Galilee, 3650
Mt 4:23 healing a. manner of sickness 3956
Mt 4:23 and a. manner of disease 3956
Mt 4:24 fame went throughout a. Syria: 3650
Mt 4:24 brought unto him a. sick people 3956
Mt 5:11 say a. manner of evil against you 3956
Mt 5:15 giveth light unto a. that are in 3956
Mt 5:18 till a. be fulfilled 3956
Mt 5:34 Swear not at a.; neither by 3654
Mt 6:29 Solomon in a. his glory was not 3956
Mt 6:32 (For after a. these things do the 537
Mt 6:32 ye have need of a. these things. 3956
Mt 6:33 a. these things shall be added 3956
Mt 7:12 Therefore a. things whatsoever 3956
Mt 8:16 and healed a. that were sick: 3956
Mt 9:26 went abroad into a. that land. 3650
Mt 9:31 his fame in a. that country. 3650
Mt 9:35 Jesus went about a. the cities 3956
Mt 10:1 and to heal a. manner of sickness, 3956

Mt 10:1 and a. manner of disease. 3956
Mt 10:22 ye shall be hated of a. men for my 3956
Mt 10:30 of your head are a. numbered. 3956
Mt 11:13 For a. the prophets and the law 3956
Mt 11:27 A. things are delivered unto me 3956
Mt 11:28 Come unto me, a. ye that labour 3956
Mt 12:15 and he healed them a.; 3956
Mt 12:23 And a. the people were amazed, 3956
Mt 12:31 A. manner of sin and blasphemy 3956
Mt 13:32 indeed is the least of a. seeds: 3956
Mt 13:34 A. these things spake Jesus 3956
Mt 13:41 out of his kingdom a. things that 3956
Mt 13:44 and selleth a. that he hath 3956
Mt 13:46 went and sold a. that he had 3956
Mt 13:51 ye understood a. these things? 3956
Mt 13:56 sisters, are they not a. with us? 3956
Mt 13:56 hath this man a. these things? 3956
Mt 14:20 And they did a. eat, and were filled: 3956
Mt 14:35 they sent out into a. that country 3650
Mt 14:35 and brought unto him a. that 3956
Mt 15:37 And they did a. eat, and were 3956
Mt 17:11 first come, and restore a. things 3956
Mt 18:25 and a. that he had, and payment 3956
Mt 18:26 with me, and I will pay thee a.
Mt 18:29 with me, and I will pay thee a.
Mt 18:31 unto their lord a. that was done 3956
Mt 13:32 I forgave thee a. that debt, 3956
Mt 18:34 till he should pay a. that was due 3956
Mt 19:11 A. men cannot receive this saying, 3956
Mt 19:20 A. these things have I kept from 3956
Mt 19:26 with God a. things are possible. 3956
Mt 19:27 we have forsaken a., and followed 3956
Mt 20:6 Why stand ye here a. the day idle? 3650
Mt 21:4 A. this was done, that it might 3650
Mt 21:10 a. the city was moved, saying, 3956
Mt 21:12 and cast out a. them that sold 3956
Mt 21:22 a. things, whatsoever ye shall ask 3956
Mt 21:26 for a. hold John as a prophet. 3956
Mt 21:37 of a. he sent unto them his son,
Mt 22:4 and a. things are ready: 3956
Mt 22:10 and gathered together a. as many 3956
Mt 22:27 And last of a. the woman died 3956
Mt 22:28 for they a. had her. 3956
Mt 22:37 the Lord thy God a. thy heart, 3650
Mt 22:37 and with a. thy soul, 3650
Mt 22:37 and with a. thy mind. 3650
Mt 22:40 a. the law and the prophets. 3650
Mt 23:3 A. therefore whatsoever they bid 3956
Mt 23:5 But a. their works they do for to 3956
Mt 23:8 and a. ye are brethren. 3956
Mt 23:20 and by a. things thereon 3956
Mt 23:27 and of a. uncleanness. 3956
Mt 23:35 may come a. the righteous blood 3956
Mt 23:36 A. these things shall come upon 3956
Mt 24:2 See ye not a. these things? 3956
Mt 24:6 for a. these things must come to 3956
Mt 24:8 A. these are the beginning of 3956
Mt 24:9 ye shall be hated of a. nations for 3956
Mt 24:14 in a. the world for a witness 3650
Mt 24:14 unto a. nations; and then 3956
Mt 24:30 then shall a. the tribes of the 3956
Mt 24:33 when ye shall see a. these things, 3956
Mt 24:34 till a. these things be fulfilled. 3956
Mt 24:39 flood came, and took them a. away; 537
Mt 24:47 make him ruler over a. his goods. 3956
Mt 25:5 they a. slumbered and slept. 3956
Mt 25:7 Then a. those virgins arose, 3956
Mt 25:31 and a. the holy angels with him, 3956
Mt 25:32 him shall be gathered a. nations: 3956
Mt 26:1 Jesus had finished a. these 3956
Mt 26:27 saying, Drink ye a. of it; 3956
Mt 26:31 A. ye shall be offended because of 3956
Mt 26:33 Though a. men shall be offended 3956
Mt 26:35 Likewise also said a. the disciples. 3956
Mt 26:52 for a. they that take the sword 3956
Mt 26:56 But a. this was done, 3650
Mt 26:56 Then a. the disciples forsook him, 3956
Mt 26:59 and a. the council, sought false 3650
Mt 26:70 But he denied before them a., 3956
Mt 27:1 morning was come, a. the chief, 3956
Mt 27:22 They a. say unto him, Let him be 3956
Mt 27:25 Then answered a. the people, 3956
Mt 27:45 there was darkness over a. the land 3956
Mt 28:9 Jesus met them, saying, A. hail.
Mt 28:11 unto the chief priests a. the things 537
Mt 28:18 A. power is given unto me in 3956
Mt 28:19 and teach a. nations, baptising 3956
Mt 28:20 to observe a. things whatsoever 3956

Mk 1:5 out unto him a. the land of Judaea, 3956
Mk 1:5 and were a. baptized of him 3956
Mk 1:27 And they were a. amazed, 3956
Mk 1:28 throughout a. the region round 3650
Mk 1:32 brought unto him a. that were 3956
Mk 1:33 a. the city was gathered together 3650
Mk 1:37 A. men seek for thee. 3956
Mk 1:39 synagogues throughout a. Galilee, 3650
Mk 2:12 went forth before them a.; 3956
Mk 2:12 that they were a. amazed, 3956
Mk 2:13 and a. the multitude resorted 3956
Mk 3:28 A. sins shall be forgiven unto 3956
Mk 4:11 a. these things are done in 3956
Mk 4:13 then will ye know a. parables? 3956
Mk 4:31 is less than a. the seeds that be in 3956
Mk 4:32 becometh greater than a. herbs, 3956
Mk 4:34 expounded a. things to his disciples. 3956
Mk 5:12 And a. the devils besought him, 3956
Mk 5:20 and a. men did marvel. 3956
Mk 5:26 and had spent a. that she had, 3956
Mk 5:33 and told him a. the truth. 3956
Mk 5:40 when he had put them a. out, 537
Mk 6:30 and told him a. things, both 3956
Mk 6:33 ran afoot thither out of a. cities, 3956
Mk 6:39 to make a. sit down by companies 3956
Mk 6:41 fishes divided he among them a. 3956
Mk 6:42 And they did a. eat, 3956
Mk 6:50 For they a. saw him, and were 3956
Mk 7:3 and a. the Jews, except they wash 3956
Mk 7:14 when he had called a. the people 3956
Mk 7:19 purging a. meats? 3956
Mk 7:23 A. these evil things come from 3956
Mk 7:37 He hath done a. things well: 3956
Mk 9:12 and restoreth a. things; 3956
Mk 9:15 And straightway a. the people, 3956
Mk 9:23 a. things are possible to him that 3956
Mk 9:35 the same shall be last of a., 3956
Mk 9:35 and servant of a. 3956
Mk 10:20 a. these have I observed from my 3956
Mk 10:27 with God a. things are possible. 3956
Mk 10:28 Lo, we have left a., and have 3956
Mk 10:44 chiefest, shall be servant of a. 3956
Mk 11:11 looked round about upon a. things, 3956
Mk 11:17 of a. nations the house of prayer? 3956
Mk 11:18 a. the people were astonished at 3956
Mk 11:32 for a. men counted John, that he 537
Mk 12:22 last of a. the women died also. 3956
Mk 12:28 is the first commandment of a.? 3956
Mk 12:29 The first of a. the commandments 3956
Mk 12:30 Lord thy God with a. thy heart, 3650
Mk 12:30 and with a. thy soul, 3650
Mk 12:30 and with a. thy mind, 3650
Mk 12:30 and with a. thy strength: 3650
Mk 12:33 to love him with a. the heart, 3650
Mk 12:33 and with a. the understanding, 3650
Mk 12:33 and with a. the soul, 3650
Mk 12:33 and with a. the strength, 3650
Mk 12:33 more than a. whole burnt offerings 3956
Mk 12:43 hath cast more in, than a. they 3956
Mk 12:44 For a. they did cast in of their 3956
Mk 12:44 did cast in a. that she had, 3956
Mk 12:44 even a. her living. 3650
Mk 13:4 a. these things shall be fulfilled? 3956
Mk 13:10 be published among a. nations. 3956
Mk 13:13 hated of a. men for my name's 3956
Mk 13:23 I have foretold you a. things. 3956
Mk 13:30 till a. these things be done. 3956
Mk 13:37 I say unto a., Watch. 3956
Mk 14:23 and they a. drank of it. 3956
Mk 14:27 A. ye shall be offended because of 3956
Mk 14:29 Although a. shall be offended, 3956
Mk 14:31 Likewise also said they a. 3956
Mk 14:36 a. things are possible unto thee; 3956
Mk 14:50 And they a. forsook him, and fled. 3956
Mk 14:53 were assembled a. the chief priests 3956
Mk 14:55 a. the council sought for witness 3650
Mk 14:64 a. condemned him to be guilty of 3956
Mk 16:15 Go ye into a. the world, 537
Lu 1:3 perfect understanding of a. things 3956
Lu 1:6 walking in a. the commandments 3956
Lu 1:48 from henceforth a. generations 3956
Lu 1:63 And they marvelled a. 3956
Lu 1:65 a. that dwelt round about them: 3956
Lu 1:65 and a. these sayings were noised 3956
Lu 1:65 a. the hill country of Judaea. 3650
Lu 1:66 And a. they that heard them 3956
Lu 1:71 from the hand of a. that hate us; 3956

Lu 1:75 before him, a. the days of our life. 3956
Lu 2:1 that a. the world should be taxed. 3956
Lu 2:3 And a. went to be taxed, 3956
Lu 2:10 which shall be to a. people. 3956
Lu 2:18 a. they that heard it wondered 3956
Lu 2:19 But Mary kept a. these things, 3956
Lu 2:20 praising God for a. the things 3956
Lu 2:31 before the face of a. people; 3956
Lu 2:38 a. them that looked for redemption 3956
Lu 2:39 they had performed a. things 537
Lu 2:47 a. that heard him were astonished 3956
Lu 2:51 kept a. these sayings in her heart. 3956
Lu 3:3 into a. the country about Jordan, 3956
Lu 3:6 And a. flesh shall see the salvation 3956
Lu 3:15 and a. men mused in their hearts 3956
Lu 3:16 answered, saying unto them a., 537
Lu 3:19 a. the evils which Herod had done, 3956
Lu 3:20 Added yet this above a., 3956
Lu 3:21 when a. the people were baptized, 537
Lu 4:5 him a. the kingdoms of the world 3956
Lu 4:6 A. this power will I give thee, 537
Lu 4:7 worship me, a. shall be thine. 3956
Lu 4:13 had ended a. the temptation, 3956
Lu 4:14 fame of him through a. the region 3650
Lu 4:15 being glorified of a. 3956
Lu 4:20 a. them that were in the synagogue 3956
Lu 4:22 And a. bare him witness, 3956
Lu 4:25 famine was throughout a. the land; 3956
Lu 4:28 And a. they in the synagogue, 3956
Lu 4:36 And they were a. amazed, 3956
Lu 4:40 a. they that had any sick 3956
Lu 5:5 we have toiled a. the night, 3650
Lu 5:9 and a. that were with him, 3956
Lu 5:11 they forsook a., and followed him. 537
Lu 5:26 a. amazed, and they glorified God, 537
Lu 5:28 left a., rose up, and followed him. 537
Lu 6:10 looking round about upon them a., 3956
Lu 6:12 continued a. night in prayer to 1273
Lu 6:17 people out of a. Judaea 3956
Lu 6:19 and healed them a. 3956
Lu 6:27 a. men shall speak well of you! 3956
Lu 7:1 when he had ended a. his sayings 3956
Lu 7:16 there came a fear on a.: 537
Lu 7:17 went forth throughout a. Judaea. 3650
Lu 7:17 a. the region round about. 3956
Lu 7:18 shewed him of a. these things. 3956
Lu 7:29 and a. the people that heard him, 3956
Lu 7:35 wisdom is justified of a. her 3956
Lu 8:40 for they were a. waiting for him. 3956
Lu 8:43 a. her living upon physicians 3956
Lu 8:45 When a. denied, Peter and they 3956
Lu 8:47 declared unto him before a. the 3956
Lu 8:52 And a. wept and bewailed her: 3956
Lu 8:54 And he put them a. out, and took 3956
Lu 9:1 and authority over a. devils, 3956
Lu 9:7 heard of a. that was done by him: 3956
Lu 9:10 told him a. that they had done. 3745
Lu 9:13 buy meat for a. this people. 3956
Lu 9:15 did so, and made them a. sit down. 537
Lu 9:17 and were a. filled: 3956
Lu 9:23 he said to them a., If any man will 3956
Lu 9:43 a. amazed at the mighty power of 3956
Lu 9:43 wondered every one at a. things, 3956
Lu 9:48 for he that is least among you a., 3956
Lu 10:19 over a. the power of the enemy: 3956
Lu 10:22 A. things are delivered to me of 3956
Lu 10:27 Lord thy God with a. thy heart, 3650
Lu 10:27 and with a. thy soul, 3650
Lu 10:27 and with a. thy strength, 3650
Lu 10:27 and with a. thy mind; 3650
Lu 11:22 taketh from him a. his armour 3833
Lu 11:41 a. things are clean unto you. 3956
Lu 11:42 rue and a. manner of herbs, 3956
Lu 11:50 That the blood of a. the prophets, 3956
Lu 12:1 to say unto his disciples first of a.,
Lu 12:7 hairs of your head are a. 3956
Lu 12:18 there will I bestow a. my fruits 3956
Lu 12:27 Solomon in a. his glory was not 3956
Lu 12:30 For a. these things do the nations. 3956
Lu 12:31 and a. these things shall be added 3956
Lu 12:41 this parable unto us, or even to a.? 3956
Lu 12:44 make him ruler over a. that he 3956
Lu 13:2 sinners above a. the Galilaeans, 3956
Lu 13:3 ye shall a. likewise perish. 3956
Lu 13:4 sinners above a. men 3956
Lu 13:5 ye shall a. likewise perish. 3956
Lu 13:17 a. his adversaries were ashamed: 3956
Lu 13:17 and a. the people rejoiced 3956
Lu 13:17 for a. the glorious things 3956
Lu 13:27 from me, a. ye workers of iniquity. 3956
Lu 13:28 a. the prophets, in the kingdom 3956
Lu 14:17 for a. things are now ready. 3956
Lu 14:18 And they a. with one consent 3956
Lu 14:29 a. that behold it begin to mock 3956
Lu 14:33 that forsaketh not a. that he hath, 3956
Lu 15:1 a. the publicans and sinners 3956
Lu 15:13 younger son gathered a. together, 537
Lu 15:14 And when he had spent a., 3956
Lu 15:31 and a. that I have is thine. 3956
Lu 16:14 covetous, heard a. these things: 3956
Lu 16:26 And beside a. this, between us 3956
Lu 17:10 ye shall have done a. those things 3956
Lu 17:27 flood came, and destroyed them a. 537
Lu 17:29 heaven, and destroyed them a. 537
Lu 18:12 I give tithes of a. that I possess. 3956
Lu 18:21 A. these have I kept from my 3956
Lu 18:22 sell a. that thou hast, 3956
Lu 18:28 we have left a., and followed thee 3956
Lu 18:31 and a. things that are written 3956
Lu 18:43 a. the people, when they saw it, 3956
Lu 19:7 they saw it, they a. murmured, 537
Lu 19:37 loud voice for a. the mighty works 3956
Lu 19:48 a. the people were very attentive 537
Lu 20:6 a. the people will stone us: 3956
Lu 20:32 Last of a. the woman died also. 3956
Lu 20:38 for a. live unto him. 3956
Lu 20:40 not ask him any question at a.
Lu 20:45 in the audience of a. the people 3956
Lu 21:3 cast in more than they a. 3956
Lu 21:4 a. these have of their abundance 537
Lu 21:4 cast in a. the living that she had. 537
Lu 21:12 before a. these, they shall lay their 537
Lu 21:15 which a. your adversaries shall 3956
Lu 21:17 hated of a. men for my name's 3956
Lu 21:22 that a. things which are written 3956
Lu 21:24 led away captive into a. nations: 3956
Lu 21:29 Behold the fig tree, and a. the 3956
Lu 21:32 not pass away, till a. be fulfilled. 3956
Lu 21:35 on a. them that dwell on the face 3956
Lu 21:36 to escape a. these things 3956
Lu 21:38 And a. the people came early 3956
Lu 22:70 Then said they a., Art thou then 3956
Lu 23:5 teaching throughout a. Jewry, 3650
Lu 23:18 they cried out a. at once, saying, 3829
Lu 23:44 darkness over a. the earth until 3650
Lu 23:48 a. the people that came together 3956
Lu 23:49 And a. his acquaintance, 3956
Lu 24:9 told a. these things unto the eleven, 3956
Lu 24:9 and to a. the rest. 3956
Lu 24:14 talked together of a. these things 3956
Lu 24:19 before God and a. the people: 3956
Lu 24:21 beside a. this, to day is the third 3956
Lu 24:25 a. that the prophets have spoken: 3956
Lu 24:27 at Moses and a. the prophets, 3956
Lu 24:27 unto them in a. the scriptures 3956
Lu 24:44 that a. things must be fulfilled, 3956
Lu 24:47 a. nations, beginning at 3956
Joh 1:3 A. things were made by him; 3956
Joh 1:7 a. men through him might believe. 3956
Joh 1:16 of his fulness have a. we received, 3956
Joh 2:15 drove them a. out of the temple, 3956
Joh 2:24 because he knew a. men, 3956
Joh 3:26 and a. men come to him. 3956
Joh 3:31 cometh from above is above a. 3956
Joh 3:31 cometh from heaven is above a. 3956
Joh 3:35 given a. things into his hand. 3956
Joh 4:25 is come, he will tell us a. things. 3956
Joh 4:29 told me a. things that ever I did. 3956
Joh 4:39 He told me a. that ever I did: 3956
Joh 4:45 seen a. the things that he did 3956
Joh 5:20 and sheweth him a. things 3956
Joh 5:22 committed a. judgment unto the 3956
Joh 5:23 a. men should honour the Son, 3956
Joh 5:28 a. that are in the graves shall 3956
Joh 6:37 A. that the Father giveth me shall 3956
Joh 6:39 of a. which he hath given me 3956
Joh 6:45 they shall be a. taught of God. 3956
Joh 7:21 done one work, and ye a. marvel. 3956
Joh 8:2 and a. the people came unto him; 3956
Joh 10:8 A. that ever came before me 3956
Joh 10:29 gave them me, is greater than a.; 3956
Joh 10:41 but a. things that John spake 3956
Joh 10:48 alone, a. men will believe on him: 3956
Joh 10:49 unto them, Ye know nothing at a., 3762
Joh 12:32 will draw a. men unto me. 3956
Joh 13:3 the Father had given a. things 3956
Joh 13:10 ye are clean, but not a. 3956
Joh 13:11 Ye are not a. clean. 3956
Joh 13:18 I speak not of you a.: 3956
Joh 13:35 By this shall a. men know 3956
Joh 14:26 shall teach you a. things, and 3956
Joh 14:26 a. things to your remembrance, 3956
Joh 15:15 for a. things that I have heard 3956
Joh 15:21 a. these things will they do unto 3956
Joh 16:13 he will guide you into a. truth: 3956
Joh 16:15 A. things that the Father hath are 3956
Joh 16:30 that thou knowest a. things, 3956
Joh 17:2 given him power over a. flesh, 3956
Joh 17:7 known that a. things whatsoever 3956
Joh 17:10 And a. mine are thine, 3956
Joh 17:21 That they a. may be one; 3956
Joh 18:4 a. things that should come upon 3956
Joh 18:38 I find in him no fault at a.
Joh 18:40 Then cried they a. again, saying, 3956
Joh 19:11 have no power at a. against me, 3762
Joh 19:28 a. things were now accomplished. 3956
Joh 21:11 and for a. there were so many,
Joh 21:17 Lord, thou knowest a. things; 3956
Ac 1:1 of a. that Jesus began both to do 3956
Ac 1:8 and in a. Judaea, and in Samaria, 3956
Ac 1:14 These a. continued with one accord 3956
Ac 1:18 and a. his bowels gushed out. 3956
Ac 1:19 it was known unto a. the dwellers 3956
Ac 1:21 companied with us a. the time 3956
Ac 1:24 knowest the hearts of a. men, 3956
Ac 2:1 a. with one accord in one place. 537
Ac 2:2 filled a. the house where they were. 3650
Ac 2:4 were a. filled with the Holy Ghost, 537
Ac 2:7 And they were a. amazed 3956
Ac 2:7 a. these which speak Galilaeans? 3956
Ac 2:12 And they were a. amazed, 3956
Ac 2:14 a. ye that dwell at Jerusalem, 537
Ac 2:17 out of my Spirit upon a. flesh: 3956
Ac 2:32 whereof we a. are witnesses. 3956
Ac 2:36 Therefore let a. the house of Israel 3956
Ac 2:39 and to a. that are afar off, 3956
Ac 2:44 a. that believed were together, 3956
Ac 2:44 and had a. things common; 537
Ac 2:45 and parted them to a. men, 3956
Ac 2:47 having favour with a. the people. 3650
Ac 3:9 a. the people saw him walking 3956
Ac 3:11 a. the people ran together 3956
Ac 3:16 in the presence of you a. 3956
Ac 3:18 by the mouth of a. his prophets, 3956
Ac 3:21 times of restitution of a. things, 3956
Ac 3:21 the mouth of a. his holy prophets 3956
Ac 3:22 a. things whatsoever he shall say 3956
Ac 3:24 and a. the prophets from Samuel 3956
Ac 3:25 shall a. the kindreds of the earth 3956
Ac 4:10 Be it known unto you a., 3956
Ac 4:10 and to a. the people of Israel, 3956
Ac 4:16 to a. them that dwell in Jerusalem; 3956
Ac 4:18 not to speak at a. nor teach in the 2527
Ac 4:21 for a. men glorified God for that 3956
Ac 4:23 reported a. that the chief priests 3745
Ac 4:24 the sea, and a. that in them is: 3956
Ac 4:29 with a. boldness they may speak 3956
Ac 4:31 were a. filled with the Holy Ghost, 537
Ac 4:32 they had a. things common. 537
Ac 4:33 great grace was upon them a. 3956
Ac 5:5 and great fear came on a. 3956
Ac 5:11 And great fear came upon a. 3650
Ac 5:12 a. with one accord in Solomon's 537
Ac 5:17 and a. they that were with him, 3956
Ac 5:20 a. the words of this life. 3956
Ac 5:21 a. the senate of the children of 3956
Ac 5:23 found we shut with a. safety, 3956
Ac 5:34 in reputation among a. the people, 3956
Ac 5:36 and a., as many as obeyed him, 3956
Ac 5:37 a., even as many as obeyed him, 3956
Ac 6:15 a. that sat in the council, looking 537
Ac 7:10 delivered him out of a. his 3956
Ac 7:10 governor over Egypt and a. 3650
Ac 7:11 a dearth over a. the land of Egypt 3650
Ac 7:14 and a. his kindred, threescore 3956
Ac 7:22 in a. the wisdom of the Egyptians, 3956
Ac 7:50 my hands made a. these things? 3956
Ac 8:1 and they were a. scattered abroad 3956
Ac 8:10 To whom they a. gave heed, 3956
Ac 8:27 had the charge of a. her treasure, 3956
Ac 8:37 thou believest with a. thine heart, 3650

Ac 8:40 he preached in **a.** the cities, 3956
Ac 9:14 to bind **a.** that call on thy name 3956
Ac 9:21 **a.** that heard him were amazed, 3956
Ac 9:26 but they were **a.** afraid of him, 3956
Ac 9:31 churches rest throughout **a.** Judaea 3650
Ac 9:32 passed throughout **a.** quarters, 3956
Ac 9:35 And **a.** that dwelt at Lydda 3956
Ac 9:39 and **a.** the widows stood by him 3956
Ac 9:40 But Peter put them **a.** forth, 3956
Ac 9:42 was known throughout **a.** Joppa; 3650
Ac 10:2 feared God with **a.** his house, 3956
Ac 10:8 declared **a.** these things unto them, 537
Ac 10:12 **a.** manner of fourfooted beasts of 3956
Ac 10:22 among **a.** the nation of the Jews, 3650
Ac 10:33 Now therefore are we **a.** here 3956
Ac 10:33 **a.** things that are commanded thee 3956
Ac 10:36 (he is Lord of **a.**:) 3956
Ac 10:37 published throughout **a.** Judaea, 3650
Ac 10:38 **a.** that were oppressed of the devil; 3956
Ac 10:39 witnesses of **a.** things which he did 3956
Ac 10:41 Not to **a.** the people, but unto 3956
Ac 10:43 him give **a.** the prophets witness, 3956
Ac 10:44 the Holy Ghost fell on **a.** them 3956
Ac 11:10 **a.** were drawn up again into 537
Ac 11:14 thou and **a.** thy house shall be 3956
Ac 11:23 and exhorted them **a.**, that with 3956
Ac 11:28 dearth throughout **a.** the world: 3650
Ac 12:11 **a.** the expectation of the people 3956
Ac 13:10 full of **a.** subtilty and **a.** mischief, 3956
Ac 13:10 thou enemy of **a.** righteousness, 3956
Ac 13:22 which shall fulfil **a.** my will 3956
Ac 13:24 repentance to **a.** the people of 3956
Ac 13:29 fulfilled **a.** that was written of him, 537
Ac 13:39 And by him **a.** that believe 3956
Ac 13:39 are justified from **a.** things, 3956
Ac 13:49 throughout **a.** the region 3650
Ac 4:15 and **a.** things that are therein: 3956
Ac 4:16 in times past suffered **a.** nations 3956
Ac 4:27 **a.** that God had done with them, 3745
Ac 15:3 great joy unto **a.** the brethren 3956
Ac 15:4 declared **a.** things that God had 3745
Ac 15:12 Then **a.** the multitude kept silence, 3956
Ac 15:17 **a.** the Gentiles, upon whom my name 3956
Ac 15:17 who doeth **a.** these things 3956
Ac 15:18 Known unto God are **a.** his works 3956
Ac 16:3 **a.** that his father was a Greek 537
Ac 16:26 **a.** the doors were opened, and 3956
Ac 16:28 Do thyself no harm: for we are **a.** 537
Ac 16:32 to **a.** that were in his house 3956
Ac 16:33 baptized, he and **a.** his, straightway 3956
Ac 16:34 believing in God with **a.** his house 3832
Ac 17:5 and set **a.** the city on an uproar,
Ac 17:7 **a.** do contrary to the decrees of 3956
Ac 17:11 the word with **a.** readiness 3956
Ac 17:15 to come to him with **a.** speed, 5613,5033
Ac 17:21 **a.** the Athenians and strangers 3956
Ac 17:22 **a.** things ye are too superstitious 3956
Ac 17:24 the world and **a.** things therein, 3956
Ac 17:25 to **a.** life, and breath, and **a.** things; 3956
Ac 17:26 of one blood **a.** nations of men 3956
Ac 17:26 dwell on **a.** the face of the earth, 3956
Ac 17:30 commandeth **a.** men every where 3956
Ac 17:31 hath given assurance unto **a.** men, 3956
Ac 18:2 Claudius had commanded **a.** Jews 3956
Ac 18:8 believed on the Lord with **a.** his 3650
Ac 18:17 **a.** the Greeks took Sosthenes, 3956
Ac 18:21 must by **a.** means keep this feast 3843
Ac 18:23 over **a.** the country of Galatia
Ac 18:23 strengthening **a.** the disciples 3956
Ac 19:7 And **a.** the men were about twelve 3956
Ac 19:10 that **a.** they which dwelt in Asia 3956
Ac 19:17 this was known to **a.** the Jews 3956
Ac 19:17 and fear fell on them **a.**, 3956
Ac 19:19 and burned them before **a.** men: 3956
Ac 19:26 almost throughout **a.** Asia, 3956
Ac 19:27 whom **a.** Asia and the world 3650
Ac 19:34 **a.** with one voice about the space 3956
Ac 20:18 I have been with you at **a.** seasons, 3956
Ac 20:19 with **a.** humility of mind, 3956
Ac 20:25 I know that ye **a.**, among whom 3956
Ac 20:26 pure from the blood of **a.** men 3956
Ac 20:27 **a.** the counsel of God 3956
Ac 20:28 and to **a.** the flock, over the which 3956
Ac 20:32 **a.** them which are sanctified 3956
Ac 20:35 I have shewed you **a.** things, 3956
Ac 20:36 and prayed with them **a.** 3956
Ac 20:37 And they **a.** wept sore, 3956

Ac 20:38 Sorrowing most of **a.** for the words 3122
Ac 21:5 they **a.** brought us on our way, 3956
Ac 21:18 and **a.** the elders were present 3956
Ac 21:20 and they are **a.** zealous of the law: 3956
Ac 21:21 that thou teachest **a.** the Jews 3956
Ac 21:24 **a.** may know that those things, 3956
Ac 21:27 stirred up **a.** the people, and laid 3956
Ac 21:28 that teacheth **a.** men every where 3956
Ac 21:30 And **a.** the city was moved, 3650
Ac 21:31 **a.** Jerusalem was in an uproar 3650
Ac 22:3 as ye **a.** are this day 3956
Ac 22:5 and **a.** the estate of the elders: 3956
Ac 22:10 **it shall be told thee of a. things** 3956
Ac 22:12 having a good report of **a.** the Jews 3956
Ac 22:15 shalt be his witness unto **a.** men 3956
Ac 22:30 and **a.** their council to appear, 3650
Ac 23:1 I have lived in **a.** good conscience 3956
Ac 24:3 always, and in **a.** places, 3837
Ac 24:3 most noble Felix, with **a.** 3956
Ac 24:5 of sedition among **a.** the Jews 3956
Ac 24:8 take knowledge of **a.** these things, 3956
Ac 24:14 believing **a.** things which are 3956
Ac 25:8 have I offended any thing at **a.**
Ac 25:24 King Agrippa, and **a.** men which 3956
Ac 25:24 whom **a.** the multitude of the Jews 3956
Ac 26:2 touching **a.** the things whereof 3956
Ac 26:3 to be expert in **a.** customs 3956
Ac 26:4 know **a.** the Jews; 3956
Ac 26:14 we were **a.** fallen to the earth, 3956
Ac 26:20 throughout **a.** the coasts of Judaea, 3956
Ac 26:29 but also **a.** that hear me this day, 3956
Ac 27:20 **a.** hope that we should be saved 3956
Ac 27:24 God hath given thee **a.** them 3956
Ac 27:33 besought them **a.** to take meat, 537
Ac 27:35 in presence of them **a.** 3956
Ac 27:36 Then were they **a.** of good cheer, 3956
Ac 27:37 we were in **a.** in the ship 3956
Ac 27:44 they escaped **a.** safe to land 3956
Ac 28:30 and received **a.** that came in unto, 3956
Ac 28:31 with **a.** confidence, no man 3956
Ro 1:5 to the faith among **a.** nations, for 3956
Ro 1:7 To **a.** that be in Rome, 3956
Ro 1:8 through Jesus Christ for you **a.**, 3956
Ro 1:18 against **a.** ungodliness and 3956
Ro 1:29 filled with **a.** unrighteousness, 3956
Ro 3:9 that they are **a.** under sin; 3956
Ro 3:12 They are **a.** gone out of the way, 3956
Ro 3:19 **a.** the world may become guilty 3956
Ro 3:22 by faith of Jesus Christ unto **a.** 3956
Ro 3:22 and upon **a.** them that believe 3956
Ro 3:23 For **a.** have sinned, and come short 3956
Ro 4:11 might be the father of **a.** them that 3956
Ro 4:16 might be sure to **a.** the seed; 3956
Ro 4:16 who is the father of us **a.**, 3956
Ro 5:12 and so death passed upon **a.** men, 3956
Ro 5:12 for that **a.** have sinned: 3956
Ro 5:18 upon **a.** men to condemnation; 3956
Ro 5:18 upon **a.** men unto justification of 3956
Ro 7:8 in me **a.** manner of concupiscence 3956
Ro 8:28 **a.** things work together for good 3956
Ro 8:32 delivered him up for us **a.**, 3956
Ro 8:32 also freely give us **a.** things? 3956
Ro 8:36 we are killed **a.** the day long; 3650
Ro 8:37 Nay, in **a.** these things we are 3956
Ro 9:5 who is over **a.**, God blessed for ever 3956
Ro 9:6 For they are not **a.** Israel, 3956
Ro 9:7 of Abraham, are they **a.** children: 3956
Ro 9:17 declared throughout **a.** the earth 3956
Ro 10:12 same Lord over **a.** is rich 3956
Ro 10:12 unto **a.** that call upon him 3956
Ro 10:16 they have not **a.** obeyed the gospel 3956
Ro 10:18 their sound went into **a.** the earth, 3956
Ro 10:21 **A.** day long I have stretched forth 3650
Ro 11:26 And so **a.** Israel shall be saved: 3956
Ro 11:32 concluded them **a.** in unbelief, 3956
Ro 11:32 that he might have mercy upon **a.** 3956
Ro 11:36 and to him, are **a.** things: 3956
Ro 12:4 and **a.** members have not the 3956
Ro 12:17 honest in the sight of **a.** men 3956
Ro 12:18 live peaceably with **a.** men 3956
Ro 13:7 Render therefore to **a.** their dues: 3956
Ro 14:2 that he may eat **a.** things: 3956
Ro 14:10 for we shall **a.** stand before the 3956
Ro 14:20 **A.** things indeed are pure; 3956
Ro 15:11 Praise the Lord, **a.** ye Gentiles; 3956
Ro 15:11 and laud him, **a.** ye people 3956
Ro 15:13 fill you with **a.** joy and peace in 3956

Ro 15:14 filled with **a.** knowledge, 3956
Ro 15:33 the God of peace be with you **a.** 3956
Ro 16:4 but also **a.** the churches of the 3956
Ro 16:15 and **a.** the saints which are with 3956
Ro 16:19 is come abroad unto **a.** men 3956
Ro 16:24 be with you **a.**. Amen 3956
Ro 16:26 made known to **a.** nations 3956
1Co 1:2 with **a.** that in every place call 3956
1Co 1:5 in **a.** utterance, 3956
1Co 1:5 and in **a.** knowledge; 3956
1Co 1:10 thay ye **a.** speak the same thing, 3956
1Co 2:10 the Spirit searcheth **a.** things, 3956
1Co 2:15 is spiritual judgeth **a.** things, 3956
1Co 3:21 For **a.** things are yours; 3956
1Co 3:22 or things to come; **a.** are yours; 3956
1Co 4:13 the offscouring of **a.** things unto 3956
1Co 6:12 **A.** things are lawful unto me, 3956
1Co 6:12 but **a.** things are not expedient: 3956
1Co 6:12 **a.** things are lawful for me, 3956
1Co 7:7 For I would that **a.** men were 3956
1Co 7:17 And so ordain I in **a.** churches 3956
1Co 8:1 know that we **a.** have knowledge, 3956
1Co 8:6 of whom are **a.** things, and we in 3956
1Co 8:6 by whom are **a.** things, and we by 3956
1Co 9:12 but suffer **a.** things, lest we should 3956
1Co 9:19 though I be free from **a.** men, yet 3956
1Co 9:19 have I made myself servant unto **a.**, 3956
1Co 9:22 I am made **a.** things to **a.** men, 3956
1Co 9:22 that I might by **a.** means save 3956
1Co 9:24 run in a race run **a.**, but one 3956
1Co 9:25 is temperate in **a.** things 3956
1Co 10:1 how that **a.** our fathers were 3956
1Co 10:1 and **a.** passed through the sea; 3956
1Co 10:2 And were **a.** baptized unto Moses 3956
1Co 10:3 And did **a.** eat the same 3956
1Co 10:4 And did **a.** drink the same 3956
1Co 10:11 Now **a.** these things happened 3956
1Co 10:17 for we are **a.** partakers of that one 3956
1Co 10:23 **A.** things are lawful for me, 3956
1Co 10:23 but **a.** things are not expedient: 3956
1Co 10:23 **a.** things are lawful for me, 3956
1Co 10:23 but **a.** things edify not 3956
1Co 10:31 do **a.** to the glory of God 3956
1Co 10:33 I please **a.** men in **a.** things, 3956
1Co 11:2 that ye remember me in **a.** things, 3956
1Co 11:5 even **a.** one as if she were shaven
1Co 11:12 but **a.** things of God 3956
1Co 11:18 For first of **a.** when ye come
1Co 12:6 same God which worketh **a.** in **a.** 3956
1Co 12:11 But **a.** these worketh that one 3956
1Co 12:12 and **a.** the members of that one 3956
1Co 12:13 are we **a.** baptized into one 3956
1Co 12:13 and have been **a.** made to drink 3956
1Co 12:19 And if they were **a.** one member, 3956
1Co 12:26 **a.** the members suffer with it; 3956
1Co 12:26 **a.** the members rejoice with it 3956
1Co 12:29 Are **a.** apostles? are **a.** prophets? 3956
1Co 12:29 are **a.** teachers? are **a.** workers 3956
1Co 12:30 Have **a.** the gifts of healing? 3956
1Co 12:30 do **a.** speak with tongues? 3956
1Co 12:30 do **a.** interpret? 3956
1Co 13:2 and understand **a.** mysteries, 3956
1Co 13:2 and **a.** knowledge; 3956
1Co 13:2 and though I have **a.** faith, 3956
1Co 13:3 though I bestow **a.** my goods to 3956
1Co 13:7 Beareth **a.** things, believeth **a.** 3956
1Co 13:7 hopeth **a.** things, endureth **a.** 3956
1Co 14:5 I would that ye **a.** spake with 3956
1Co 14:18 with tongues more than ye **a.** 3956
1Co 14:21 yet for **a.** that will they not hear 3779
1Co 14:23 and **a.** speak with tongues, 3956
1Co 14:24 But if **a.** prophesy, and there come 3956
1Co 14:24 convinced of **a.**, he is judged of **a.** 3956
1Co 14:26 Let **a.** things be done unto 3956
1Co 14:31 For ye may **a.** prophesy one by one, 3956
1Co 14:31 that **a.** may learn, 3956
1Co 14:31 and **a.** may be comforted 3956
1Co 14:33 as in **a.** churches of the saints 3956
1Co 14:40 Let **a.** things be done decently and 3956
1Co 15:3 delivered unto you first of **a.**
1Co 15:7 then of **a.** the apostles 3956
1Co 15:8 And last of **a.** he was seen of me 3956
1Co 15:10 more abundantly than they **a.** 3956
1Co 15:19 we are of **a.** men most miserable 3956
1Co 15:22 For as in Adam **a.** die, 3956
1Co 15:22 in Christ shall **a.** be made alive 3956
1Co 15:24 he shall have put down **a.** rule 3956

1Co 15:24 and **a.** authority and power. 3956
1Co 15:25 till he hath put **a.** enemies under 3956
1Co 15:27 hath put **a.** things under his feet. 3956
1Co 15:27 But when he saith **a.** things 3956
1Co 15:27 which did put **a.** things under him. 3956
1Co 15:28 And when **a.** things shall be 3956
1Co 15:28 him that put **a.** things under him, 3956
1Co 15:28 that God may be **a.** in **a.** 3956
1Co 15:29 dead, if the dead rise not at **a.**? 3654
1Co 15:39 **A.** flesh is not the same flesh: 4561
1Co 15:51 We shall not **a.** sleep, 3956
1Co 15:51 but we shall **a.** be changed, 3956
1Co 16:12 was not at **a.** to come at this time; 3843
1Co 16:14 Let **a.** your things be done with 3956
1Co 16:20 **A.** the brethren greet you. 3956
1Co 16:24 My love be with you **a.** in Christ 3956
2Co 1:1 with **a.** the saints which are 3956
2Co 1:1 which are in **a.** Achaia: 3650
2Co 1:3 the God of **a.** comfort; 3650
2Co 1:4 in **a.** our tribulation, 3650
2Co 1:20 For **a.** the promises of God in 3745
2Co 2:3 having confidence in you **a.**, 3956
2Co 2:3 that my joy is the joy of you **a.** 3956
2Co 2:5 I may not overcharge you **a.**. 3956
2Co 2:9 ye be obedient in **a.** things. 3956
2Co 3:2 known and read of **a.** men: 3956
2Co 3:18 But we **a.**, with open face 3956
2Co 4:15 For **a.** things are for your sakes. 3956
2Co 5:10 For we must **a.** appear before 3956
2Co 5:14 if one died for **a.**, 3956
2Co 5:14 then were **a.** dead: 3956
2Co 5:15 And that he died for **a.**, 3956
2Co 5:17 behold, **a.** things are become new. 3956
2Co 5:18 And **a.** things are of God, 3956
2Co 6:4 But in **a.** things approving 3956
2Co 6:10 and yet possessing **a.** things. 3956
2Co 7:1 from **a.** filthiness of the flesh 3956
2Co 7:4 joyful in **a.** our tribulation. 3956
2Co 7:11 In **a.** things ye have approved 3956
2Co 7:13 was refreshed by you **a.** 3956
2Co 7:14 but as we spake **a.** things to you 3956
2Co 7:15 the obedience of you **a.**, 3956
2Co 7:16 confidence in you in **a.** things. 3956
2Co 8:7 and in **a.** diligence, 3956
2Co 8:18 throughout **a.** the churches; 3956
2Co 9:8 God is able to make **a.** grace 3956
2Co 9:8 always having **a.** sufficiency in 3956
2Co 9:8 **a.** things, may abound to every 3956
2Co 9:11 in everything to **a.** bountifulness, 3956
2Co 9:13 unto them, and unto **a.** men; 3956
2Co 10:6 to revenge **a.** disobedience, 3956
2Co 11:6 manifest among you in **a.** things. 3956
2Co 11:9 and in **a.** things I have kept 3956
2Co 11:28 the care of **a.** the churches. 3956
2Co 12:12 among you in **a.** patience, 3956
2Co 12:19 but we do **a.** things, dearly 3956
2Co 13:2 and to **a.** other, that, if I come 3956
2Co 13:13 **A.** the saints salute you. 3956
2Co 13:14 Ghost, be with you **a.**. Amen. 3956
Ga 1:2 And **a.** the brethren which are with 3956
Ga 2:14 said unto Peter before them **a.**, 3956
Ga 3:8 In thee shall **a.** nations be blessed. 3956
Ga 3:10 in **a.** things which are written 3956
Ga 3:22 hath concluded **a.** under sin, 3956
Ga 3:26 For ye are **a.** the children of God. 3956
Ga 3:28 for ye are **a.** one in Christ Jesus. 3956
Ga 4:1 though he be lord of **a.**; 3956
Ga 4:12 ye have not injured me at **a.**. 3762
Ga 4:26 which is the mother of us **a.**. 3956
Ga 5:14 For **a.** the law is fulfilled in one 3956
Ga 6:6 that teacheth in **a.** good things. 3956
Ga 6:10 let us do good unto **a.** men, 3956
Eph 1:3 hath blessed us with **a.** spiritual 3956
Eph 1:8 abounded toward us in **a.** wisdom 3956
Eph 1:10 gather together in one **a.** things 3956
Eph 1:11 who worketh **a.** things 3956
Eph 1:15 and love unto **a.** the saints, 3956
Eph 1:21 Far above **a.** principality, 3956
Eph 1:22 put **a.** things under his feet, 3956
Eph 1:22 to be the head over **a.** things 3956
Eph 1:23 of him that filleth **a.** in **a.**. 3956
Eph 2:3 Among whom also we **a.** had our 3956
Eph 2:21 In whom **a.** the building 3956
Eph 3:8 less than the least of **a.** saints, 3956
Eph 3:9 and to make **a.** men see 3956
Eph 3:9 created **a.** things by Jesus Christ: 3956
Eph 3:18 to comprehend with **a.** saints. 3956
Eph 3:19 with **a.** the fulness of God. 3956
Eph 3:20 above **a.** that we ask or think, 3956
Eph 3:21 throughout **a.** ages, world without 3956
Eph 4:2 With **a.** lowliness and meekness, 3956
Eph 4:6 and Father of **a.**, who is above **a.**, 3956
Eph 4:6 and through **a.**, and in you **a.**. 3956
Eph 4:10 up far above **a.** heavens, 3956
Eph 4:10 that he might fill **a.** things. 3956
Eph 4:13 Till we **a.** come in the unity of 3956
Eph 4:15 grow up into him in **a.** things, 3956
Eph 4:19 to work **a.** uncleanliness with 3956
Eph 4:31 Let **a.** bitterness, and wrath, 3956
Eph 4:31 put away from you, with **a.** malice: 3956
Eph 5:3 and **a.** uncleanness, 3956
Eph 5:9 of the spirit is in **a.** goodness 3956
Eph 5:13 **a.** things that are reproved 3956
Eph 5:20 always for **a.** things unto God 3956
Eph 6:13 having done **a.**, to stand. 537
Eph 6:16 Above **a.**, taking the shield of 3956
Eph 6:16 to quench **a.** the fiery darts. 3956
Eph 6:18 Praying always with **a.** prayer 3956
Eph 6:18 with **a.** perseverance and 3956
Eph 6:18 supplication for **a.** saints; 3956
Eph 6:21 make known to you **a.** things: 3956
Eph 6:24 Grace be with **a.** them that love 3956
Php 1:1 to **a.** the saints in Christ Jesus, 3956
Php 1:4 you **a.** making request with joy, 3956
Php 1:7 to think this of you **a.**, 3956
Php 1:7 ye **a.** are partakers of my grace. 3956
Php 1:8 I long after you **a.** in the bowels 3956
Php 1:9 and in **a.** judgment; 3956
Php 1:13 in **a.** the palace, 3650
Php 1:13 and in **a.** other places, 3956
Php 1:20 with **a.** boldness, as always, 3956
Php 1:25 with you **a.** for your futherance 3956
Php 2:14 Do **a.** things without murmurings 3956
Php 2:17 and rejoice with you **a.**. 3956
Php 2:21 For **a.** seek their own, 3956
Php 2:26 he longed after you **a.**, 3956
Php 2:29 with **a.** gladness; and hold such in 3956
Php 3:8 I count **a.** things but loss. 3956
Php 3:8 suffered the loss of **a.** things, 3956
Php 3:21 to subdue **a.** things unto himself. 3956
Php 4:5 be known unto **a.** men. 3956
Php 4:7 passeth **a.** understanding, 3956
Php 4:12 everywhere and in **a.** things I am 3956
Php 4:13 I can do **a.** things through Christ 3956
Php 4:18 But I have **a.**, and abound: 3956
Php 4:19 shall supply **a.** your need 3956
Php 4:22 **A.** the saints salute you, 3956
Php 4:23 Christ be with you **a.**. Amen. 3956
Col 1:4 which ye have to **a.** the saints, 3956
Col 1:6 as it is in **a.** the world; 3956
Col 1:9 knowledge of his will in **a.** wisdom 3956
Col 1:10 unto **a.** pleasing, being fruitful in 3956
Col 1:11 Strengthened with **a.** might, 3956
Col 1:11 unto **a.** patience and 3956
Col 1:16 by him were **a.** things created, 3956
Col 1:16 **a.** things were created by him, 3956
Col 1:17 he is before **a.** things, 3956
Col 1:17 and by him **a.** things consist. 3956
Col 1:18 that in **a.** things he might have 3956
Col 1:19 in him should **a.** fulness dwell; 3956
Col 1:20 to reconcile **a.** things unto himself; 3956
Col 1:28 teaching every man in **a.** wisdom; 3956
Col 2:2 and unto **a.** riches of the full 3956
Col 2:3 are hid **a.** the treasures of wisdom 3956
Col 2:9 dwelleth **a.** the fulness of the 3956
Col 2:10 the head of **a.** principality 3956
Col 2:13 forgiven you **a.** trespasses; 3956
Col 2:19 from which **a.** the body 3956
Col 2:22 Which **a.** are to perish with the 3956
Col 3:8 put off **a.** these; anger, wrath, 3956
Col 3:11 but Christ is **a.**, and in **a.**. 3956
Col 3:14 And above **a.** these things 3956
Col 3:16 dwell in you richly in **a.** wisdom; 3956
Col 3:17 do **a.** in the name of the Lord 3956
Col 3:20 obey your parents in **a.** things: 3956
Col 3:22 obey in **a.** things your masters 3956
Col 4:7 **A.** my state shall Tychicus declare 3956
Col 4:9 make known unto you **a.** things 3956
Col 4:12 complete in **a.** the will of God. 3956
1Th 1:2 to God always for you **a.**, 3956
1Th 1:7 ensamples to **a.** that believe 3956
1Th 2:15 and are contrary to **a.** men: 3956
1Th 3:7 in **a.** our affliction 3956
1Th 3:9 for **a.** the joy wherewith we joy 3956
1Th 3:12 and toward **a.** men, 3956
1Th 3:13 Jesus Christ with **a.** his saints. 3956
1Th 4:6 is the avenger of **a.** such, 3956
1Th 4:10 ye do it toward **a.** the brethren 3956
1Th 4:10 which are in **a.** Macedonia: 3650
1Th 5:5 Ye are **a.** the children of light, 3956
1Th 5:14 be patient toward **a.** men. 3956
1Th 5:15 among yourselves, and to **a.** men. 3956
1Th 5:21 Prove **a.** things; hold fast that 3956
1Th 5:22 Abstain from **a.** appearance of 3956
1Th 5:26 Greet **a.** the brethren with an holy 3956
1Th 5:27 be read unto **a.** the holy brethren. 3956
2Th 1:3 charity of every one of you **a.** 3956
2Th 1:4 faith in **a.** your persecutions 3956
2Th 1:10 admired in **a.** them that believe 3956
2Th 1:11 and fulfil **a.** the good pleasure 3956
2Th 2:4 above **a.** that is called God, 3956
2Th 2:9 with **a.** power and signs 3956
2Th 2:10 And with **a.** deceivableness 3956
2Th 2:12 That they **a.** might be damned 3956
2Th 3:2 for **a.** men have not faith. 3956
2Th 3:11 disorderly, working not at **a.**, but 3367
2Th 3:16 you peace always by **a.** means. 3956
2Th 3:16 The Lord be with you **a.**. 3956
2Th 3:18 Christ be with you **a.**. Amen. 3956
1Ti 1:15 worthy of **a.** acceptation, 3956
1Ti 1:16 shew forth **a.** longsuffering, 3956
1Ti 2:1 that, first of **a.**, supplications, 3956
1Ti 2:1 be made for **a.** men; 3956
1Ti 2:2 for **a.** that are in authority; 3956
1Ti 2:2 peaceable life in **a.** godliness 3956
1Ti 2:4 Who will have **a.** men to be saved, 3956
1Ti 2:6 gave himself a ransom for **a.**, 3956
1Ti 2:11 in silence with **a.** subjection. 3956
1Ti 3:4 in subjection with **a.** gravity; 3956
1Ti 3:11 faithful in **a.** things. 3956
1Ti 4:8 is profitable unto **a.** things, 3956
1Ti 4:9 worthy of **a.** acceptation. 3956
1Ti 4:10 who is the Saviour of **a.** men, 3956
1Ti 4:15 thy profiting may appear to **a.**. 3956
1Ti 5:2 younger as sisters, with **a.** purity. 3956
1Ti 5:20 rebuke before **a.**, that others also 3956
1Ti 6:1 masters worthy of **a.** honour, 3956
1Ti 6:10 money is the root of **a.** evil: 3956
1Ti 6:13 who quickeneth **a.** things, 3956
1Ti 6:17 richly **a.** things to enjoy; 3956
2Ti 1:15 **a.** they which are in Asia be 3956
2Ti 2:7 thee understanding in **a.** things. 3956
2Ti 2:10 I endure **a.** things for the elect's 3956
2Ti 2:24 but be gentle unto **a.** men, 3956
2Ti 3:9 shall be manifest unto **a.** men, 3956
2Ti 3:11 out of them **a.** the Lord delivered 3956
2Ti 3:12 Yea, and **a.** that will live godly 3956
2Ti 3:16 **A.** scripture is given by 3956
2Ti 3:17 furnished unto **a.** good works. 3956
2Ti 4:2 exhort with **a.** longsuffering 3956
2Ti 4:5 watch thou in **a.** things, 3956
2Ti 4:8 but unto **a.** them also that love 3956
2Ti 4:16 but **a.** men forsook me: 3956
2Ti 4:17 and that **a.** the Gentiles might 3956
2Ti 4:21 and **a.** the brethren. 3956
Tit 1:15 Unto the pure **a.** things are pure: 3956
Tit 2:7 In **a.** things shewing thyself 3956
Tit 2:9 to please them well in **a.** things; 3956
Tit 2:10 shewing **a.** good fidelity; 3956
Tit 2:10 of God our Saviour in **a.** things. 3956
Tit 2:11 hath appeared to **a.** men, 3956
Tit 2:14 might redeem us from **a.** iniquity, 3956
Tit 2:15 rebuke with **a.** authority, 3956
Tit 3:2 shewing **a.** meekness unto **a.** men. 3956
Tit 3:15 **A.** that are with me salute thee. 3956
Tit 3:15 Grace be with you **a.**. 3956
Phm 5 and toward **a.** saints; 3956
Heb 1:2 appointed heir of **a.** things, 3956
Heb 1:3 upholding **a.** things by the word 3956
Heb 1:6 And let **a.** the angels of God 3956
Heb 1:11 and they **a.** shall wax old 3956
Heb 1:14 Are they not **a.** ministering spirits, 3956
Heb 2:8 hast put **a.** things in subjection 3956
Heb 2:8 he put **a.** in subjection under him, 3956
Heb 2:8 not yet **a.** things put under him. 3956
Heb 2:10 for whom are **a.** things, 3956
Heb 2:10 and by whom are **a.** things, 3956
Heb 2:11 sanctified are **a.** of one: 3956
Heb 2:15 **a.** their lifetime subject to bondage. 3956
Heb 2:17 in **a.** things it behoved him. 3956
Heb 3:2 Moses was faithful in **a.** his house. 3650

Heb 3:4 but he that built a. things is God 3956
Heb 3:5 verily was faithful in a. his house, 3650
Heb 3:16 not a. that came out of Egypt 3956
Heb 4:4 the seventh day from a. his works 3956
Heb 4:13 but a. things are naked 3956
Heb 4:15 was in a. points tempted 3956
Heb 5:9 unto a. them that obey him; 3956
Heb 6:16 is to them an end of a. strife 3956
Heb 7:2 gave a tenth part of a.; 3956
Heb 7:7 And without a. contradiction 3956
Heb 8:5 a. things according to the pattern 3956
Heb 8:11 for a. shall know me, 3956
Heb 9:3 which is called the Holiest of a.;
Heb 9:8 that the way into the holiest of a.
Heb 9:17 it is of no strength at a. while the 4219
Heb 9:19 every precept to a. the people 3956
Heb 9:19 both the book, and a. the people, 3956
Heb 9:21 and a. the vessels of the ministry 3956
Heb 9:22 almost a. things are by the law 3956
Heb 10:10 body of Jesus Christ once for a. 2178
Heb 11:13 these a. died in faith, not having 3956
Heb 11:39 these a., having obtained a good 3956
Heb 12:8 whereof a. are partakers, 3956
Heb 12:14 Follow peace with a. men, 3956
Heb 12:23 to God the Judge of a., 3956
Heb 13:4 marriage is honourable in a., 3956
Heb 13:18 a. things willing to live honestly 3956
Heb 13:24 Salute a. them that have the rule 3956
Heb 13:24 and a. the saints 3956
Heb 13:25 Grace be with you a.. Amen 3956
Jas 1:2 count it a. joy when ye fall 3956
Jas 1:5 that giveth to a. men liberally, 3956
Jas 1:8 unstable in a. his ways 3956
Jas 1:21 lay apart a. filthiness 3956
Jas 2:10 he is guilty of a. 3956
Jas 3:2 in many things we offend a. 537
Jas 4:16 a. such rejoicing is evil 3956
Jas 5:12 above a. things, my brethren, 3956
1Pe 1:15 holy in a. manner of conversation; 3956
1Pe 1:24 For a. flesh is as grass, 3956
1Pe 1:24 and a. the glory of man 3956
1Pe 2:1 laying aside a. malice, and a. guile, 3956
1Pe 2:1 and a. evil speakings, 3956
1Pe 2:17 Honour a. men. Love the 3956
1Pe 2:18 masters with a. fear; 3956
1Pe 3:8 be ye a. of one mind, 3956
1Pe 4:7 the end of a. things is at hand: 3956
1Pe 4:8 a. things have fervent charity 3956
1Pe 4:11 God in a. things may be glorified 3956
1Pe 5:5 a. of you be subject one to another, 3956
1Pe 5:7 Casting a. your care upon him; 3956
1Pe 5:10 But the God of a. grace, 3956
1Pe 5:14 Peace be with you a. that are in 3956
2Pe 1:3 a. things that pertain unto life 3956
2Pe 1:5 giving a. diligence, add to your 3956
2Pe 3:4 a. things continue as they were 3956
2Pe 3:9 that a. should come to repentance 3956
2Pe 3:11 a. these things shall be dissolved, 3956
2Pe 3:11 ye to be in a. holy conversation
2Pe 3:16 As also in a. his epistles 3956
1Jo 1:5 and in him is no darkness at a. 3762
1Jo 1:7 cleanseth us from a. sin 3956
1Jo 1:9 us from a. unrighteousness, 3956
1Jo 2:16 For a. that is in the world, 3956
1Jo 2:19 that they were not a. of us 3956
1Jo 2:20 and ye know a. things 3956
1Jo 2:27 teacheth you of a. things, 3956
1Jo 3:20 and knoweth a. things 3956
1Jo 5:17 A. unrighteousness is sin: 3956
2Jo 1 a. they that have known the truth; 3956
3Jo 2 I wish above a. things that thou 3956
3Jo 12 hath good report of a. men, 3956
Jude 3 when I gave a. diligence 3956
Jude 15 judgment upon a., 3956
Jude 15 and to convince a. 3956
Jude 15 of a. their ungodly deeds 3956
Jude 15 and of a. their hard speeches 3956
Re 1:2 and of a. things that he saw 3745
Re 1:7 a. kindreds of the earth shall wail 3956
Re 2:23 **and a. the churches shall know** 3956
Re 3:10 **shall come upon a. the world,** 3650
Re 4:11 for thou hast created a. things, 3956
Re 5:6 sent forth into a. the earth 3956
Re 5:13 sea, and a. that are in them, 3956
Re 7:4 of a. the tribes of the children of 3956
Re 7:9 of a. nations, and kindreds, 3956
Re 7:11 a. the angels stood round about 3956
Re 7:17 away a. tears from their eyes 3956
Re 8:3 with the prayers of a. saints 3956
Re 8:7 and a. green grass was burnt up 3956
Re 11:6 smite the earth with a. plagues, 3956
Re 12:5 rule a. nations with a rod of iron: 3956
Re 13:3 a. the world wondered after the 3650
Re 13:7 over a. kindreds, and tongues, 3956
Re 13:8 And a. that dwell upon the earth 3956
Re 13:12 a. the power of the first beast 3956
Re 13:16 causeth a., both small and great, 3956
Re 14:8 because she made a. nations drink 3956
Re 15:4 for a. nations shall come and 3956
Re 18:3 a. nations have drunk of the wine 3956
Re 18:12 and a. thyine wood, 3956
Re 18:12 a. manner vessels of ivory, 3956
Re 18:12 and a. manner vessels of most 3956
Re 18:14 and a. things which were dainty 3956
Re 18:14 shalt find them no more at a. 3364
Re 18:17 shipmaster, and a. the company 3956
Re 18:19 rich a. that had ships in the sea 3956
Re 18:21 and shall be found no more at a. 3364
Re 18:22 shall be heard no more at a. 3364
Re 18:22 shall be heard no more at a. 3364
Re 18:23 shall shine no more at a. in thee; 3364
Re 18:23 shall be heard no more at a. in 3364
Re 18:23 sorceries were a. nations deceived 3956
Re 18:24 a. that were slain upon the earth 3956
Re 19:5 Praise our God, a. ye his servants, 3956
Re 19:17 saying to a. the fowls that fly in 3956
Re 19:18 flesh of a. men, both free and bond, 3956
Re 19:21 a. the fowls were filled with their 3956
Re 21:4 God shall wipe away a. tears 3956
Re 21:5 Behold, I make a. things new 3956
Re 21:7 shall inherit a. things; 3956
Re 21:8 and a. liars, shall have their part 3956
Re 21:19 with a. manner of precious stones 3956
Re 21:25 shall not be shut at a. by day: 3364
Re 22:21 Lord Jesus Christ be with you a. 3956

ALLEGE See ALLEGING.

ALLEGING
Ac 17:3 Opening and a., that Christ 3908

ALLEGORY
Ga 4:24 Which things are an a.: for these 238

ALLELUIA (al-le-loo'-yah)
Re 19:1 people in heaven, saying, A.; 239
Re 19:3 they said, A.. And her 239
Re 19:4 the throne, saying, Amen; A. 239
Re 19:6 mighty thunderings, saying, A. 239

ALLIED
Ne 13:4 the priest,...was a. unto Tobiah: 7138

ALLON (al'-lon) See also ALLON-BACHUTH; ELON.
Jos 19:33 Heleph, from A. to Zaanannim, 438
1Ch 4:37 the son of Shiphi, the son of A., 438

ALLON-BACHUTH (al'-lon-bak'-ooth)
Ge 35:8 and the name of it was called A. 439

ALLOW See also ALLOWED; ALLOWETH; ALLOWING; DISALLOW.
Lu 11:48 **ye a. the deeds of your fathers:** 4909
Ac 24:15 which they themselves also a., 4327
Ro 7:15 that which I do I a. not: 1097

ALLOWANCE
2Ki 25:30 And his a. was a continual a. 737

ALLOWED See also DISALLOWED.
1Th 2:4 But as we were a. of God to be 1381

ALLOWETH
Ro 14:22 in that thing which he a. 1381

ALL-TO (Jg 9:53) See ALL.

ALLURE
Ho 2:14 I will a. her, and bring her into 6601
2Pe 2:18 a. through the lusts of the flesh, 1185

ALMIGHTY
Ge 17:1 said unto him, I am the A. God; 7706
Ge 28:3 And God A. bless thee, 7706
Ge 35:11 God said unto him, I am God A. 7706
Ge 43:14 God A. give you mercy 7706
Ge 48:3 God A. appeared unto me at Luz 7706
Ge 49:25 and by the A., who shall bless thee 7706
Ex 6:3 by the name of God A., 7706
Nu 24:4, 16 which saw the vision of the A., 7706
Ru 1:20 A. hath dealt very bitterly with me 7706
Ru 1:21 and the A. hath afflicted me? 7706
Job 5:17 not thou the chastening of the A.: 7706
Job 6:4 arrows of the A. are within me, 7706
Job 6:14 he forsaketh the fear of the A. 7706
Job 8:3 doth the A. pervert justice? 7706
Job 8:5 make thy supplication to the A.; 7706
Job 11:7 find out the A. unto perfection? 7706
Job 13:3 Surely I would speak to the A., 7706
Job 15:25 himself against the A. 7706
Job 21:15 What is the A., that we should 7706
Job 21:20 shall drink of the wrath of the A. 7706
Job 22:3 Is it any pleasure to the A., 7706
Job 22:17 what can the A. do for them? 7706
Job 22:23 If thou return to the A., 7706
Job 22:25 the A. shall be thy defence, 7706
Job 22:26 have thy delight in the A., 7706
Job 23:16 and the A. troubleth me: 7706
Job 24:1 times are not hidden from the A., 7706
Job 27:2 the A., who hath vexed my soul: 7706
Job 27:10 Will he delight himself in the A.? 7706
Job 27:11 with the A. will I not conceal 7706
Job 27:13 they shall receive of the A. 7706
Job 29:5 When the A. was yet with me, 7706
Job 31:2 inheritance of the A. from on high? 7706
Job 31:35 that the A. would answer me, 7706
Job 32:8 inspiration of the A. giveth them 7706
Job 33:4 breath of the A. hath given me life 7706
Job 34:10 and from the A., that he should 7706
Job 34:12 will the A. pervert judgment 7706
Job 35:13 neither will the A. regard it 7706
Job 37:23 the A., we cannot find him out: 7706
Job 40:2 he that contendeth with the A. 7706
Ps 68:14 When the A. scattered kings 7706
Ps 91:1 under the shadow of the A. 7706
Isa 13:6 as a destruction for the A. 7706
Eze 1:24 as the voice of the A., 7706
Eze 10:5 the A. God when he speaketh 7706
Joe 1:15 as a destruction from the A. 7706
2Co 6:18 saith the Lord A. 3841
Re 1:8 and which is to come, the A. 3841
Re 4:8 Holy, holy, holy, Lord God A., 3841
Re 11:17 O Lord God A., which art, and wast, 3841
Re 15:3 thy works, Lord God A.; 3841
Re 16:7 Lord God A., true and righteous 3841
Re 16:14 that great day of God A. 3841
Re 19:15 and wrath of A. God 3841
Re 21:22 the Lord God A. and the Lamb are 3841

ALMODAD (al-mo'-dad)
Ge 10:26 Joktan begat A., and Sheleph, 486
1Ch 1:20 Joktan begat A., and Sheleph, 486

ALMON (al'-mon) See also ALMON-DIBLATHAIM.
Jos 21:18 A. with her suburbs; four cities 5960

ALMOND See also ALMONDS.
Ec 12:5 the a. tree shall flourish, 8247
Jer 1:11 I see a rod of an a. tree 8247

ALMON-DIBLATHAIM (al''-mon-dib-lath-a'-im)
Nu 33:46 Dibon-gad, and encamped in A. 5963
Nu 33:47 And they removed from A., and 5963

ALMONDS
Ge 43:11 myrrh, nuts, and a. 8247
Ex 25:33 Three bowls made like unto a., 8246
Ex 25:33 bowls made like a. 8246
Ex 25:34 four bowls made like unto a., 8246
Ex 37:19 made after the fashion of a. 8246
Ex 37:19 three bowls made like a. 8246
Ex 37:20 four bowls made like a., 8246
Nu 17:8 blossoms, and yielded a. 8247

ALMOND-TREE See ALMOND and TREE.

ALMOST
Ex 17:4 they be a. ready to stone me 4592
Ps 73:2 as for me my feet were a. gone; 4592
Ps 94:17 my soul had a. dwelt in silence 4592
Ps 119:87 had a. consumed me upon earth; 4592
Pr 5:14 I was a. in all evil 4592
Ac 13:44 came a. the whole city together 4975
Ac 19:26 but a. throughout all Asia, 4975
Ac 21:27 the seven days were a. ended, 3195
Ac 26:28 A. thou persuadest me to be 1722,3641
Ac 26:29 a., and altogether such as I 1722,3641
Heb 9:22 And a. all things are by the law 4975

ALMS See also ALMSDEEDS.
Mt 6:1 **do not your a. before men,** 1654

Mt 6:2 **when thou doest thine a.,** *1654*
Mt 6:3 **when thou doest a., let not** *1654*
Mt 6:4 **That thine a. may be in secret:** *1654*
Lu 11:41 **give a. of such things as ye have;** *1654*
Lu 12:33 **Sell that ye have, and give a.;** *1654*
Ac 3:2 to ask **a.** of them that entered *1654*
Ac 3:3 into the temple asked an **a.** *1654*
Ac 3:10 it was he which sat for **a.** *1654*
Ac 10:2 gave much **a.** to the people, *1654*
Ac 10:4 prayers and thine **a.** are come up *1654*
Ac 10:31 thine **a.** are had in remembrance *1654*
Ac 24:17 I came to bring **a.** to my nation, *1654*

ALMSDEEDS
Ac 9:36 full of good works and **a.** which *1654*

ALMUG (al'-mug) See also ALGUM.
1Ki 10:11 great plenty of **a.** trees, 484
1Ki 10:12 king made of the **a.** trees pillars 484
1Ki 10:12 there came no such **a.** trees, 484

ALMUG-TREES See ALMUG and TREES.

ALOES
Nu 24:6 as the trees of lign **a.** which the 174
Ps 45:8 garments smell of myrrh, and **a.**, 174
Pr 7:17 perfumed my bed with myrrh, **a.**, 174
Ca 4:14 and **a.**, with all the chief spices: 174
Joh 19:39 brought a mixture of myrrh and **a.**, *250*

ALONE
Ge 2:18 good that the man should be **a.**; 905
Ge 32:24 And Jacob was left **a.**; and there 905
Ge 42:38 brother is dead, and he is left **a.**: 905
Ge 44:20 brother is dead, and he **a.** is left. 905
Ex 14:12 thee in Egypt, saying, Let us **a.**, 2308
Ex 18:14 why sittest thou thyself **a.**, 905
Ex 18:18 art not able to perform it thyself **a.** 905
Ex 24:2 And Moses **a.** shall come near the 905
Ex 32:10 Now therefore let me **a.**,
Le 13:46 shall dwell **a.**; without the camp 909
Nu 11:14 able to bear all this people **a.**, 905
Nu 11:17 that thou bear it not thyself **a.**, 905
Nu 23:9 the people shall dwell **a.**, 909
De 1:9 not able to bear you myself **a.** 905
De 1:12 How can I myself **a.** bear your 905
De 9:14 me **a.**, that I may destroy them, 7503
De 32:12 the Lord **a.** did lead him, 909
De 33:28 Israel then shall dwell in safety **a.** 909
Jos 22:20 man perished not **a.** in his iniquity 259
Jg 3:20 which he had for himself **a.** 905
Jg 11:37 let me **a.** two months, 7503
1Sa 21:1 Why art thou **a.**, and no man with 905
2Sa 16:11 let him **a.**, and let him curse;
2Sa 18:24 and behold a man running **a.** 905
2Sa 18:25 And the king said, If he be **a.**, 905
2Sa 18:26 Behold another man running **a.** 905
1Ki 11:29 and they two were **a.** in the field: 905
2Ki 4:27 Let her **a.**; for her soul is vexed 7503
2Ki 19:15 thou art the God, even thou **a.**, of 905
2Ki 23:18 And he said, Let him **a.**;
2Ki 23:18 So they let his bones **a.**, 4422
1Ch 29:1 my son, whom **a.** God hath chosen, 259
Ezr 6:7 the work of this house of God **a.**; 7662
Ne 9:6 Thou, even thou, art Lord **a.**; 905
Es 3:6 scorn to lay hands on Mordecai **a.**; 905
Job 1:15, 16,17,19 am escaped **a.** to tell thee 905
Job 7:16 let me **a.**; for my days are vanity 2308
Job 7:19 let me **a.** till I swallow down my 7503
Job 9:8 **a.** spreadeth out the heavens, 905
Job 10:20 let me **a.**, that I may take comfort 7896
Job 13:13 Hold your peace, let me **a.**, that I
Job 15:19 whom **a.** the earth was given, 905
Job 31:17 have eaten my morsel myself **a.**, 905
Ps 83:18 thou, whose name **a.** is Jehovah, 905
Ps 86:10 wondrous things: thou art God **a.** 905
Ps 102:7 as a sparrow **a.** upon the housetop 909
Ps 136:4 him who **a.** doeth great wonders: 905
Ps 148:13 Lord: for his name **a.** is excellent; 905
Pr 9:12 scornest, thou **a.** shalt bear it. 905
Ec 4:8 There is one **a.**, and there is not a
Ec 4:10 him that is **a.** when he falleth; 259
Ec 4:11 but how can one be warm **a.**?
Isa 2:11, 17 Lord **a.** shall be exalted in that 905
Isa 5:8 placed **a.** in the midst of the earth! 905
Isa 14:31 none shall be **a.** in his appointed 909
Isa 37:16 thou art the God, even thou **a.**, 905
Isa 44:24 stretcheth forth the heavens **a.**; 905
Isa 49:21 Behold, I was left **a.**; these, where 905
Isa 51:2 I called him **a.**, and blessed him, 259
Isa 63:3 I have trodden the winepress **a.**; 905
Jer 15:17 I sat **a.** because of thy hand: 909
Jer 49:31 which dwell **a.** 909
La 3:28 He sitteth **a.** and keepeth silence, 905
Da 10:7 And I Daniel **a.** saw the vision: 905
Da 10:8 Therefore I was left **a.**, and saw 905
Ho 4:17 is joined to idols: let him **a.**
Ho 8:9 a wild ass **a.** by himself: 909
Mt 4:4 **shall not live by bread a.,** *3441*
Mt 14:23 he was there **a.** *3441*
Mt 15:14 **Let them a.: they be blind leaders** *863*
Mt 18:15 **between thee and him a.** *3441*
Mk 1:24 Saying, Let us **a.**: what have we *1439*
Mk 4:10 And when he was **a.**, *2651*
Mk 4:34 and when they were **a.**, *2596,2398*
Mk 6:47 and he **a.** on the land. *3441*
Mk 14:6 **Let her a.; why trouble ye her?** *863*
Mk 15:36 saying, Let **a.**; let us see whether *863*
Lu 4:4 **not live by bread a., but by every** *3441*
Lu 4:34 Saying, Let us **a.**; what have we *1439*
Lu 5:21 Who can forgive sins, but God **a.**? *3441*
Lu 6:4 **but for the priests a.?** *3441*
Lu 9:18 as he was **a.** praying, *2651*
Lu 9:36 Jesus was found **a.** *3441*
Lu 10:40 hath left me to serve **a.**? *3441*
Lu 13:8 **Lord, let it a. this year also,** *863*
Joh 6:15 into a mountain himself **a.** *3441*
Joh 6:22 his disciples were gone away **a.**; *3441*
Joh 8:9 and Jesus was left **a.**, *3441*
Joh 8:16 **for I am not a., but I and the** *3441*
Joh 8:29 **the Father hath not left me a.;** *3441*
Joh 11:48 If we let him thus **a.**, all men will *863*
Joh 12:7 Then said Jesus, **Let her a.** *863*
Joh 12:24 **and die, it abideth a.** *3441*
Joh 16:32 **and shall leave me a.** *3441*
Joh 16:32 **and yet I am not a., because the** *3441*
Joh 17:20 **pray I for these a., but for** *3440*
Ac 5:38 from these men, and let them **a.** *1439*
Ac 19:26 not **a.** at Ephesus, but almost *3440*
Ro 4:23 for his sake **a.**, that it was *3440*
Ro 11:3 and I am left **a.**, and they seek *3441*
Gal 6:4 have rejoicing in himself **a.**, *3441*
1Th 3:1 to be left at Athens **a.**; *3441*
Heb 9:7 went the high priest **a.** once every *3441*
Jas 2:17 not works, is dead, being **a.** *2596,1438*

ALONG
Ex 2:5 walked **a.** by the river's side;
Ex 9:23 the fire ran **a.** upon the ground;
Nu 21:22 will go **a.** by the king's high way,
Nu 34:3 wilderness of Zin **a.** by the coast
De 2:27 I will go **a.** by the highway,
Jos 10:10 and chased them **a.** the way
Jos 15:3 and passed **a.** to Zin,
Jos 15:3 and passed **a.** to Hezron,
Jos 15:6 **a.** by the north of Beth-arabah
Jos 15:10 **a.** unto the side of mount Jearim,
Jos 15:11 and passed **a.** to mount Baalah,
Jos 16:2 and passeth **a.** unto the borders
Jos 17:7 border went **a.** on the right hand
Jos 18:18 And passed **a.** toward the side to
Jos 18:19 And the border passed **a.** to the
Jos 19:13 And from thence passeth on **a.** the
Jg 7:12 of the east lay **a.** in the valley
Jg 7:13 it, that the tent lay **a.**
Jg 9:25 robbed all that came **a.** that way
Jg 9:37 **a.** by the plain of Meonenim
Jg 11:18 went **a.** through the wilderness,
Jg 11:26 cities that be **a.** by the coasts of
Jg 20:37 liers in wait drew themselves **a.**,
1Sa 6:12 went **a.** the highway, lowing as 1980
1Sa 28:20 Saul fell straightway all **a.** 4393,6967
2Sa 3:16 went with her **a.** weeping 1980
2Sa 16:13 Shimei went **a.** on the hill's side
2Ki 11:11 **a.** by the altar and the temple.
2Ch 23:10 **a.** by the altar and the temple,
Jer 41:6 weeping all **a.** as he went: 1980

ALOOF
Ps 38:11 friends stand **a.** from my sore; 5048

ALOTH (a'-loth) See also BEALOTH.
1Ki 4:16 Hushai was in Asher and in **A.** 1175

ALOUD
Gen 45:2 And he wept **a.** 5414,854,6963
1Ki 18:27 Cry **a.**: for he is a god; 6963,1419
1Ki 18:28 they cried **a.**, and cut 1419,3605
Ezr 3:12 many shouted **a.** for joy: 7311,1419
Job 19:7 I cry **a.**, but there is no 7768
Ps 51:14 my tongue shall sing **a.** of thy 7442
Ps 55:17 will I pray, and cry **a.**: and he 1993
Ps 59:16 yea, I will sing **a.** of thy mercy 7442
Ps 81:1 Sing **a.** unto God our strength: 7442
Ps 132:16 her saints shall shout **a.** for joy 7442
Ps 149:5 let them sing **a.** upon their beds. 7442
Isa 24:14 they shall cry **a.** from the sea 6670
Isa 54:1 break forth into singing and cry **a.**, 6670
Isa 58:1 Cry **a.**, spare not, lift up thy voice 1627
Da 3:4 Then an herald cried **a.**, To you 2429
Da 4:14 He cried **a.**, and said thus, Hew 2429
Da 5:7 The king cried **a.** to bring in the 2429
Ho 5:8 cry **a.** at Beth-aven, 7321
Mic 4:9 thou cry out **a.**? is there no king 7452
Mk 15:8 the multitude crying **a.** began to *310*

ALPHA (al'-fah)
Re 1:8 **I am A. and Omega, the** *1*
Re 1:11 **I am A. and Omega, the first and** *1*
Re 21:6 **I am A. and Omega, the beginning** *1*
Re 22:13 **I am A. and Omega, the beginning** *1*

ALPHAEUS (al-fe'-us) See also CLEOPAS.
Mt 10:3 James the son of **A.**, *256*
Mk 2:14 Levi the son of **A.** sitting *256*
Mk 3:18 James the son of **A.**, *256*
Lu 6:15 James the son of **A.**, *256*
Ac 1:13 James the son of **A.**, *256*

ALPHEUS See ALPHAEUS.

ALREADY
Ex 1:5 souls: for Joseph was in Egypt **a.**
2Ch 28:13 offended against the Lord **a.**,
Ne 5:5 are brought unto bondage **a.**,
Ec 1:10 it hath been **a.** of old time, 3528
Ec 2:12 even that which hath been **a.** done. 3528
Ec 3:15 which is to be hath **a.** been; 3528
Ec 4:2 the dead which are **a.** dead, 3528
Ec 6:10 which hath been is named **a.**, 3528
Mal 2:2 I have cursed them **a.**, because
Mt 5:28 **committed adultery with her a.** *2235*
Mt 17:12 **Elias is come a., and they knew** *2235*
Mk 15:44 marvelled if he were **a.** dead: *2235*
Lu 12:49 **what will I, if it be a. kindled?** *2235*
Joh 3:18 **believeth not is condemned a.,** *2235*
Joh 4:35 **they are white a. to harvest.** *2235*
Joh 9:22 for the Jews have agreed **a.**, *2235*
Joh 9:27 I have told you **a.**, and ye did not *2235*
Joh 11:17 had lain in the grave four days **a.**, *2235*
Joh 19:33 saw that he was dead **a.**, *2235*
Ac 11:11 were three men **a.** come unto the
Ac 27:9 because the fast was now **a.** past, *2235*
1Co 5:3 have judged **a.**, as though I were *2235*
2Co 12:21 many which have sinned **a.**, *4258*
Php 3:12 Not as though I had **a.** attained, *2235*
Php 3:12 either were **a.** perfect: *2235*
Php 3:16 whereto we have **a.** attained, let *5348*
2Th 2:7 mystery of iniquity doth **a.** work: *2235*
1Ti 5:15 For some are **a.** turned aside *2235*
2Ti 2:18 that the resurrection is past **a.** *2235*
1Jo 4:3 even now **a.** is it in the world *2235*
Re 2:25 **that which ye have a. hold fast**

ALSO
Ge 1:16 rule the night: he made the stars **a.**
Ge 2:9 life **a.** in the midst of the garden,
Ge 3:6 **a.** unto her husband with her; 1571
Ge 3:18 Thorns **a.** and thistles shall it
Ge 3:21 Unto Adam **a.** and to his wife did
Ge 3:22 and take **a.** of the tree of life, and 1571
Ge 4:4 he **a.** brought of the firstlings of 1571
Ge 4:22 Zillah, she **a.** bare Tubal-cain, an 1571
Ge 4:26 to him also there was born a son; 1571
Ge 6:3 for that he **a.** is flesh: 7683
Ge 6:4 the earth in those days; and **a.** 1571
Ge 6:11 The earth **a.** was corrupt before
Ge 7:3 Of fowls **a.** of the air by sevens, 1571
Ge 8:2 The fountains **a.** of the deep and
Ge 8:8 **A.** he sent forth a dove from him,
Ge 10:21 Unto Shem **a.**, the father of all 1571
Ge 12:15 The princes **a.** of Pharaoh saw
Ge 13:5 And Lot **a.**, which went with 1571
Ge 13:16 shall thy seed **a.** be numbered. 1571
Ge 14:7 and **a.** the Amorites, that dwelt in 1571
Ge 14:16 **a.** brought again his brother Lot, 1571
Ge 14:16 and the women **a.**, and the people. 1571

Ge 15:14 **a.** that nation, whom they shall.......... 1571
Ge 16:13 Have I **a.** here looked after him.......... 1571
Ge 17:16 and give thee a son **a.** of her:.......... 1571
Ge 18:12 pleasure, my lord being old **a.**?..........
Ge 18:23 thou **a.** destroy the righteous.......... 637
Ge 18:24 wilt thou **a.** destroy and not spare.......... 637
Ge 19:21 thee concerning this thing **a.**,.......... 1571
Ge 19:34 make him drink wine this night **a.**;.......... 1571
Ge 19:35 father drink wine that night **a.**.......... 1571
Ge 19:38 she **a.** bare a son, and called his name..........
Ge 20:4 thou slay **a.** a righteous nation?.......... 1571
Ge 20:6 I **a.** withheld thee from sinning.......... 1571
Ge 21:13 **a.** of the son of the bondwoman.......... 1571
Ge 22:20 **a.** born children unto thy brother Nahor;....
Ge 24:14 I will give thy camels drink **a.**.......... 1571
Ge 24:19 I will draw water for thy camels **a.**.......... 1571
Ge 24:44 and I will **a.** draw for thy camels:.......... 1571
Ge 24:46 and I will give thy camels drink **a.**.......... 1571
Ge 24:46 and she made the camels drink **a.**.......... 1571
Ge 24:53 he gave **a.** to her brother and to..........
Ge 26:21 well, and strove for that **a.**.......... 1571
Ge 27:31 he **a.** had made savoury meat,.......... 1571
Ge 27:34 Bless me, even me **a.**, O my father.......... 1571
Ge 27:38 **a.**, O my father. And Esau lifted.......... 1571
Ge 27:45 deprived **a.** of you both in one?.......... 1571
Ge 29:27 and we will give thee this **a.** for.......... 1571
Ge 29:28 Rachel his daughter to wife **a.**..........
Ge 29:30 And he went in **a.** unto Rachel,.......... 1571
Ge 29:30 **a.** Rachel more than Leah, and.......... 1571
Ge 29:33 therefore given me this son **a.**.......... 1571
Ge 30:3 that I may **a.** have children by.......... 1571
Ge 30:6 God hath judged me, and hath **a.**.......... 1571
Ge 30:15 away my son's mandrakes **a.**?.......... 1571
Ge 30:30 I provide for mine own house **a.**?.......... 1571
Ge 31:15 sold us, and hath quite devoured **a.**.......... 1571
Ge 32:6 Esau, and **a.** he cometh to meet.......... 1571
Ge 32:18 lord Esau: and, behold, **a.** he is.......... 1571
Ge 33:7 Leah **a.** with her children came.......... 1571
Ge 35:17 thou shalt have this son **a.**.......... 1571
Ge 37:7 my sheaf arose, and **a.** stood upright;..........
Ge 38:10 Lord: wherefore he slew him **a.**.......... 1571
Ge 38:11 Lest peradventure he die **a.**, as his.......... 1571
Ge 38:22 find her; and **a.** the men of the.......... 1571
Ge 38:24 hath played the harlot; and **a.**,.......... 1571
Ge 40:15 land of the Hebrews: and here **a.**.......... 1571
Ge 40:16 unto Joseph, I **a.** was in my dream,.......... 637
Ge 42:22 behold, **a.** his blood is required.......... 1571
Ge 43:8 both we, and thou, and **a.** our.......... 1571
Ge 43:13 Take **a.** your brother, and arise,..........
Ge 44:9 die, and we **a.** will be my lord's.......... 1571
Ge 44:10 Now **a.** let it be according unto.......... 1571
Ge 44:16 he **a.** with whom the cup is found.......... 1571
Ge 44:29 And if ye take this **a.** from me,.......... 1571
Ge 45:20 **A.** regard not your stuff; for the..........
Ge 46:4 will **a.** surely bring thee up again:.......... 1571
Ge 46:34 until now, both we, and **a.** our.......... 1571
Ge 47:3 both we, and **a.** our fathers.......... 1571
Ge 47:18 lord **a.** hath our herds of cattle;..........
Ge 48:11 God hath shewed me **a.** thy seed.......... 1571
Ge 48:19 he **a.** shall become a people,.......... 1571
Ge 48:19 and he **a.** shall be great:.......... 1571
Ge 50:18 his brethren **a.** went and fell down.......... 1571
Ge 50:23 the children **a.** of Machir the son.......... 1571
Ex 1:10 they join **a.** unto our enemies,.......... 1571
Ex 2:19 and **a.** drew water enough for us,.......... 1571
Ex 3:9 I have **a.** seen the oppression.......... 1571
Ex 4:9 not believe **a.** these two signs,.......... 1571
Ex 4:14 And **a.**, behold, he cometh forth.......... 1571
Ex 6:4 I have **a.** established my covenant.......... 1571
Ex 6:5 I have **a.** heard the groaning of.......... 1571
Ex 7:11 Pharaoh **a.** called the wise men.......... 1571
Ex 7:11 Egypt, they **a.** did in like manner.......... 1571
Ex 7:23 did he set his heart to this **a.**.......... 1571
Ex 8:21 and **a.** the ground whereon they are.... 1571
Ex 8:32 hardened his heart at this time **a.**,.......... 1571
Ex 10:24 let your little ones **a.** go with you.......... 1571
Ex 10:25 Thou must give us **a.** sacrifices.......... 1571
Ex 10:26 Our cattle **a.** shall go with us:.......... 1571
Ex 12:32 **A.** take your flocks and your.......... 1571
Ex 12:32 and be gone; and bless me **a.**.......... 1571
Ex 12:38 multitude went up **a.** with them;.......... 1571
Ex 15:4 **a.** are drowned in the Red sea.......... 1571
Ex 18:23 this people shall **a.** go to their place.......... 1571
Ex 19:22 And let the priests **a.** which come.......... 1571
Ex 21:6 shall **a.** bring him to the door,..........
Ex 21:29 owner **a.** shall be put to death.......... 1571
Ex 21:35 the dead ox **a.** shall divide.......... 1571
Ex 23:9 **A.** thou shalt not oppress a..........
Ex 24:11 **a.** they saw God, and eat and..........
Ex 25:23 Thou shalt **a.** make a table of..........
Ex 29:15 Thou shall **a.** take one ram; and..........
Ex 29:22 **A.** thou shalt take of the ram the..........
Ex 29:44 sanctify **a.** both Aaron and his..........
Ex 30:18 shalt **a.** make a laver of brass,..........
Ex 30:18 foot **a.** of brass, to wash withal:..........
Ex 30:23 thou **a.** unto thee principal spices,..........
Ex 31:13 Speak thou **a.** unto the children..........
Ex 33:12 thou hast **a.** found grace in my.......... 1571
Ex 33:17 I will do this thing **a.** that thou.......... 1571
Ex 35:14 The candlestick **a.** for the light,..........
Ex 37:12 **A.** he made thereunto a border..........
Ex 37:26 **a.** he made unto it a crown of..........
Le 5:2 he **a.** shall be unclean, and..........
Le 7:16 **a.** the remainder of it shall be..........
Le 8:8 **a.** he put in the breastplate the..........
Le 8:9 **a.** upon the mitre, even upon his..........
Le 9:4 **A.** a bullock and a ram for peace..........
Le 9:18 He slew **a.** the bullock and the ram..........
Le 11:29 These **a.** shall be unclean unto..........
Le 11:40 he **a.** that beareth the carcase of..........
Le 13:18 The flesh **a.**, in which, even in..........
Le 13:38 If a man **a.** or a woman have in..........
Le 13:47 The garment **a.** that the plague..........
Le 14:9 **a.** he shall wash his flesh in water,..........
Le 15:18 The woman **a.** with whom man..........
Le 15:20 every thing **a.** that she sitteth upon..........
Le 18:19 **A.** thou shalt not approach unto..........
Le 18:28 That the land spue not you out **a.**..........
Le 20:13 If a man **a.** lie with mankind, as..........
Le 20:27 A man **a.** or woman that hath a..........
Le 22:12 priest's daughter **a.** be married..........
Le 23:27 **A.** on the tenth day of this seventh.......... 389
Le 23:39 **A.** in the fifteenth day of the.......... 389
Le 26:16 I **a.** will do this unto you; I will.......... 637
Le 26:22 I will **a.** send wild beasts among..........
Le 26:24 Then will I **a.** walk contrary.......... 637
Le 26:28 contrary unto you **a.** in fury;..........
Le 26:39 **a.** in the iniquities of their fathers.......... 637
Le 26:40 that **a.** they have walked contrary.......... 637
Le 26:41 that I **a.** have walked contrary.......... 637
Le 26:42 my covenant with Jacob, and **a.**.......... 637
Le 26:42 my covenant with Isaac, and **a.**.......... 637
Le 26:43 The land **a.** shall be left of them,.......... 637
Nu 3:1 These **a.** are generations of..........
Nu 4:22 Take **a.** the sum of the sons of.......... 1571
Nu 6:17 shall offer **a.** his meat offering,..........
Nu 9:2 Let the children of Israel **a.** keep..........
Nu 10:10 **A.** in the day of your gladness,..........
Nu 11:4 children of Israel **a.** wept again,.......... 1571
Nu 11:10 Moses **a.** was displeased..........
Nu 12:2 hath he not spoken **a.** by us?.......... 1571
Nu 15:15 **a.** for the stranger that sojourneth..........
Nu 16:10 and seek ye the priesthood **a.**?.......... 1571
Nu 16:17 thou **a.**, and Aaron, each of you..........
Nu 16:34 Lest the earth swallow us up **a.**..........
Nu 18:2 brethren **a.** of the tribe of Levi,.......... 1571
Nu 18:3 neither they, nor ye **a.**, die.......... 1571
Nu 18:8 I **a.** have given thee the charge..........
Nu 18:28 ye **a.** shall offer an heave offering.......... 1571
Nu 20:11 drank, and their beasts **a.**..........
Nu 22:19 tarry ye **a.** here this night,.......... 1571
Nu 22:33 surely now **a.** I had slain thee,.......... 1571
Nu 24:12 Spake I not **a.** to thy messengers.......... 1571
Nu 24:18 Seir **a.** shall be a possession for..........
Nu 24:24 and he **a.** shall perish for ever.......... 1571
Nu 24:25 and Balak **a.** went his way.......... 1571
Nu 27:13 thou **a.** shalt be gathered unto.......... 1571
Nu 28:26 **A.** in the day of the firstfruits,..........
Nu 30:3 If a woman **a.** vow a vow unto..........
Nu 31:8 Balaam **a.** the son of Beor they..........
Nu 3:4 **a.** the Lord executed judgments..........
Nu 35:2 give **a.** unto the Levites suburbs..........
De 1:37 **A.** the Lord was angry with me.......... 1571
De 1:37 Thou **a.** shalt not go in thither..........
De 2:6 ye shall **a.** buy water of them.......... 1571
De 2:11 Which **a.** were accounted giants,.......... 637
De 2:12 Horims **a.** dwelt in Seir beforetime;..........
De 2:20 (That **a.** was accounted a land of.......... 637
De 3:3 delivered into our hands Og **a.**,.......... 1571
De 3:17 The plain **a.**, and Jordan, and..........
De 3:20 until they **a.** possess the land.......... 1571
De 7:13 multiply thee: he will **a.** bless..........
De 8:5 shalt **a.** consider in thine heart,..........
De 9:8 **A.** in Horeb ye provoked the..........
De 9:19 hearkened unto me at that time **a.**.......... 1571
De 9:20 I prayed for Aaron **a.** the same.......... 1571
De 10:10 hearkened unto me at that time **a.**,.......... 1571
De 10:14 God, the earth **a.**, with all that..........
De 15:17 And **a.** unto thy maidservant.......... 637
De 18:4 The firstfruit **a.** of thy corn,..........
De 20:6 let him **a.** go and return unto..........
De 23:12 Thou shalt have a place **a.**..........
De 26:13 **a.** have given them unto the.......... 1571
De 28:51 which **a.** shall not leave thee..........
De 28:61 **A.** every sickness, and every.......... 1571
De 29:15 **a.** with him that is not here with..........
De 31:2 and come in: **a.** the Lord hath..........
De 32:24 I will **a.** send the teeth of beasts..........
De 32:25 the suckling **a.** with the man of..........
De 33:28 **a.** his heavens shall drop down.......... 637
Jos 1:15 they **a.** have possessed the land.......... 1571
Jos 2:12 ye will **a.** shew kindness unto my.......... 1571
Jos 7:11 they have **a.** transgressed my.......... 1571
Jos 7:11 have **a.** stolen, and dissembled **a.**,.......... 1571
Jos 10:30 And the Lord delivered it **a.**,.......... 1571
Jos 10:39 as he had done **a.** to Libnah,..........
Jos 13:3 the Ekronites; **a.** the Avites:..........
Jos 13:22 Balaam **a.** the son of Beor,..........
Jos 15:19 south land; give me **a.** springs of..........
Jos 17:1 There was **a.** a lot for the tribe..........
Jos 17:2 There was **a.** a lot for the rest..........
Jos 17:9 the coast of Manasseh **a.** was on..........
Jos 19:30 Ummah **a.**, and Aphek, and Rehob:..........
Jos 20:1 The Lord **a.** spake unto Joshua,..........
Jos 22:7 them away **a.** unto the tents,.......... 1571
Jos 24:5 I sent Moses **a.** and Aaron,..........
Jos 24:18 will we **a.** serve the Lord;.......... 1571
Jg 1:15 give me **a.** springs of water..........
Jg 1:18 **A.** Judah took Gaza with the..........
Jg 1:22 they **a.** went up against Beth-el:.......... 1571
Jg 2:3 I **a.** said, I will not drive them.......... 1571
Jg 2:10 And **a.** all that generation were.......... 1571
Jg 2:21 I **a.** will not henceforth drive out.......... 1571
Jg 3:22 the haft **a.** went in after the blade;.......... 1571
Jg 3:31 and he **a.** delivered Israel.......... 1571
Jg 5:4 the clouds **a.** dropped water.......... 1571
Jg 5:15 even Issachar, and **a.** Barak:.......... 3651
Jg 6:35 who **a.** was gathered after him:.......... 1571
Jg 7:18 the trumpets **a.** on every side of.......... 1571
Jg 8:9 he spake **a.** unto the men of Penuel,.......... 1571
Jg 8:22 and thy son, and thy son's son **a.**.......... 1571
Jg 8:31 she **a.** bare him a son, whose name.......... 1571
Jg 9:2 remember **a.** that I am your bone..........
Jg 9:19 and let him **a.** rejoice in you:.......... 1571
Jg 9:49 of the tower of Shechem died **a.**,.......... 1571
Jg 10:9 passed over Jordan to fight **a.**.......... 1571
Jg 10:10 our God, and **a.** served Baalim..........
Jg 10:12 The Zidonians **a.**, and the..........
Jg 15:5 and **a.** the standing corn, with.......... 5704
Jg 17:2 and spakest of **a.** in mine ears,.......... 1571
Jg 19:10 his concubine **a.** was with him..........
Jg 19:16 which was **a.** of mount Ephraim;..........
Jg 19:19 is bread and wine **a.** for me,.......... 1571
Jg 20:48 **a.** they set on fire all the cities..........
Ru 1:5 Mahlon and Chilion died **a.** both.......... 1571
Ru 1:12 to night, and should **a.** bear sons.......... 1571
Ru 1:12 an husband **a.** to night,.......... 1571
Ru 1:17 and more **a.**, if ought but death.......... 3541
Ru 2:16 let fall **a.** some of the handfuls.......... 1571
Ru 2:21 He said unto me **a.**, Thou shalt..........
Ru 3:15 **A.** he said, Bring the vail that..........
Ru 4:5 thou must buy it **a.** of Ruth the..........
1Sa 1:6 adversary **a.** provoked her sore,.......... 1571
1Sa 1:28 **a.** I have lent him to the Lord;.......... 1571
1Sa 2:15 **A.** before they burnt the fat,.......... 1571
1Sa 2:26 with the Lord, and **a.** with men.......... 1571
1Sa 3:12 I begin, I will **a.** make an end..........
1Sa 3:17 and more **a.**, if thou hide.......... 3541
1Sa 4:17 been **a.** a great slaughter among.......... 1571
1Sa 4:17 two sons **a.**, Hophni and Phinehas,.......... 1571
1Sa 8:8 other goods, so do they **a.** unto thee... 1571
1Sa 8:20 we **a.** may be like all the nations;.......... 1571
1Sa 10:11, 12 Is Saul **a.** among the prophets?.......... 1571
1Sa 10:26 And Saul **a.** went to Gibeah;.......... 1571
1Sa 12:14 **a.** the king that reigneth over you.......... 1571
1Sa 13:4 Israel **a.** was had in abomination.......... 1571
1Sa 14:15 they **a.** trembled, and the earth.......... 1571
1Sa 14:21 **a.** turned to be with the Israelites.......... 1571
1Sa 14:22 they **a.** followed hard after them.......... 1571
1Sa 14:44 answered, God do so and more **a.**.......... 3541
1Sa 15:1 Samuel **a.** said unto Saul,..........
1Sa 15:23 **a.** rejected thee from being king..........

1Sa 15:29 **a.** the Strength of Israel will not 1571
1Sa 17:38 **a.** he armed him with a coat of
1Sa 18:5 and **a.** in the sight of Saul's 1571
1Sa 19:11 Saul **a.** sent messengers unto
1Sa 19:20 of Saul, and they **a.** prophesied 1571
1Sa 19:21 third time, and they prophesied **a.** 1571
1Sa 19:22 Then went he **a.** to Ramah, 1571
1Sa 19:23 the Spirit of God was upon him **a.**, 1571
1Sa 19:24 And he stripped off his clothes **a.**, 1571
1Sa 19:24 say, Is Saul **a.** among the prophets? 1571
1Sa 20:15 But **a.** thou shalt not cut off thy
1Sa 22:17 their hand **a.** is with David, 1571
1Sa 23:17 that **a.** Saul my father knoweth 1571
1Sa 23:25 Saul **a.** and his men went to seek
1Sa 24:8 David **a.** arose afterward, and went
1Sa 25:13 David **a.** girded on his sword: 1571
1Sa 25:22 more **a.** do God unto the enemies 3541
1Sa 25:43 they were **a.** both of them his wives
1Sa 25:43 David **a.** took Ahinoam of Jezreel;
1Sa 26:25 things, and **a.** shalt still prevail 1571
1Sa 28:19 the Lord will **a.** deliver Israel 1571
1Sa 28:19 thy sons be with me: the Lord **a.** 1571
1Sa 28:22 hearken thou **a.** unto the voice 1571
1Sa 30:21 **a.** to abide at the brook Besor:
2Sa 1:4 many of the people **a.** are fallen 1571
2Sa 1:4 and Jonathan his son are dead **a.** 1571
2Sa 1:18 (**A.** he bade them teach the
2Sa 2:2 up thither, and his two wives **a.**, 1571
2Sa 2:6 I **a.** will requite you this kindness, 1571
2Sa 2:7 and **a.** the house of Judah have 1571
2Sa 2:24 Joab **a.** and Abishai pursued
2Sa 3:9 So do God to Abner, and more **a.**, 3541
2Sa 3:12 **a.**, Make thy league with me, and,
2Sa 3:19 Abner **a.** spake in the ears of 1571
2Sa 3:19 **a.** to speak in the ears of David 1571
2Sa 3:35 So do God to me, and more **a.**, if I 3541
2Sa 4:2 (for Beeroth **a.** was reckoned to 1571
2Sa 5:2 **A.** in time past, when Saul was 1571
2Sa 5:15 Ibhar **a.**, and Elishua, and
2Sa 5:18 The Philistines **a.** came and
2Sa 7:11 **A.** the Lord telleth thee that he
2Sa 7:19 spoken **a.** of thy servant's house 1571
2Sa 8:3 David smote also Hadadezer,
2Sa 8:11 Which **a.** king David did dedicate
2Sa 10:14 then fled they **a.** before Abishai,
2Sa 11:12 to Uriah, Tarry here to day **a.**, 1571
2Sa 11:17 and Uriah the Hittite died **a.** 1571
2Sa 11:21, 24 Uriah the Hittite is dead **a.** 1571
2Sa 12:13 The Lord **a.** hath put away thy sin; 1571
2Sa 12:14 the child **a.** that is born unto thee 1571
2Sa 13:36 king **a.** and all his servants wept 1571
2Sa 14:7 and we will destroy the heir **a.** 1571
2Sa 15:19 Wherefore goest thou **a.** with us? 1571
2Sa 15:19 art a stranger, and **a.** an exile 1571
2Sa 15:21 even there **a.** will thy servant be
2Sa 15:23 the king **a.** himself passed over
2Sa 15:24 lo Zadok **a.**, and all the Levites 1571
2Sa 15:27 king said **a.** unto Zadok the priest,
2Sa 15:34 hitherto, so will I now **a.** be
2Sa 17:5 Call now Hushai the Archite **a.**, 1571
2Sa 17:10 he **a.** that is valiant, whose heart 1571
2Sa 18:2 surely go forth with you myself **a.** 1571
2Sa 18:22 I pray thee, **a.** run after Cushi 1571
2Sa 18:26 said, He **a.** bringeth tidings 1571
2Sa 19:13 God do so to me, and more **a.**, 3541
2Sa 19:40 and **a.** half the people of Israel 1571
2Sa 19:43 we have **a.** more right in David 1571
2Sa 20:14 together, and went **a.** after him 637
2Sa 20:26 Ira **a.** the Jairite was a chief ruler 1571
2Sa 21:20 and he also was born to the giant 1571
2Sa 22:10 He bowed the heavens **a.**, and came
2Sa 22:20 brought me forth **a.** into a large
2Sa 22:24 I was **a.** upright before him, and
2Sa 22:36 Thou hast **a.** given me the shield
2Sa 22:41 Thou hast **a.** given me the necks
2Sa 22:44 **a.** hast delivered me from the
2Sa 22:49 thou **a.** hast lifted me up on high
2Sa 23:20 he went down **a.** and slew a lion
1Ki 1:6 and he **a.** was a very goodly man; 1571
1Ki 1:14 I **a.** will come in after thee, and
1Ki 1:22 Nathan the prophet **a.** came in
1Ki 1:33 The king **a.** said unto them, Take
1Ki 1:46 **a.** Solomon sitteth on the throne 1571
1Ki 1:48 And **a.** thus said the king, Blessed 1571
1Ki 2:5 Moreover thou knowest **a.** what 1571
1Ki 2:22 ask for him the kingdom **a.**;
1Ki 2:23 God do so to me, and more **a.**, 3541

1Ki 3:13 I have **a.** given thee that which 1571
1Ki 3:18 that this woman was delivered **a.** 1571
1Ki 4:13 to him **a.** pertained the region of
1Ki 4:15 he **a.** took Basmath the daughter 1571
1Ki 4:28 Barley **a.** and straw for the horses
1Ki 4:33 he spake **a.** of beasts, and of fowl,
1Ki 6:22 **a.** the whole altar that was by the
1Ki 6:32 two doors **a.** were of olive tree;
1Ki 6:33 So **a.** made he for the door of the
1Ki 7:2 built **a.** the house of the forest
1Ki 7:8 Solomon made **a.** an house for
1Ki 7:20 two pillars had pomegranates **a.** 1571
1Ki 7:31 and **a.** upon the mouth of it were 1571
1Ki 8:24 thou spakest **a.** with thy mouth, 1571
1Ki 9:21 the children of Israel **a.** were not
1Ki 10:11 And the navy **a.** of Hiram, that 1571
1Ki 10:12 house, harps **a.** and psalteries
1Ki 12:14 **a.** chastised you with whips,
1Ki 13:5 altar **a.** was rent, and the ashes
1Ki 13:11 them they told **a.** to their father
1Ki 13:18 I am a prophet **a.** as thou art; 1571
1Ki 13:24 the lion **a.** stood by the carcase
1Ki 14:23 they **a.** built them high places, 1571
1Ki 14:24 were **a.** sodomites in the land: 1571
1Ki 15:13 And **a.** Maachah his mother, 1571
1Ki 16:7 **a.** by the hand of the prophet 1571
1Ki 16:16 and hath **a.** slain the king: 1571
1Ki 17:20 Lord my God, hast thou **a.** brought
1Ki 18:35 he filled the trench **a.** with water 1571
1Ki 19:2 the gods do to me, and more **a.**, 3541
1Ki 20:3 thy wives **a.** and thy children,
1Ki 20:10 more **a.**, if the dust of Samaria 3541
1Ki 21:19 killed, and **a.** taken possession? 1571
1Ki 21:23 And of Jezebel **a.** spake the Lord, 1571
1Ki 22:22 persuade him, and prevail **a.**: 1571
2Ki 1:11 Again **a.** he sent unto him
2Ki 2:13 He took up **a.** the mantle of Elijah
2Ki 2:14 and when he **a.** had smitten the
2Ki 3:18 the Moabites **a.** into your hand
2Ki 5:1 was **a.** a mighty man in valour,
2Ki 6:31 God do so and more **a.** to me, if 3541
2Ki 7:4 if we sit still here, we die **a.**
2Ki 7:8 and carried thence **a.**, and went
2Ki 8:1 and it shall **a.** come upon the land 1571
2Ki 9:27 Smite him **a.** in the chariot 1571
2Ki 10:2 a fenced city **a.**, and armour;
2Ki 10:5 was over the city, the elders **a.**,
2Ki 11:17 between the king **a.** and the
2Ki 13:6 and there remained the grove **a.** 1571
2Ki 16:14 he brought **a.** the brasen altar,
2Ki 17:19 **A.** Judah kept not the 1571
2Ki 18:2 His mother's name **a.** was Abi,
2Ki 21:11 made Judah **a.** to sin with idols: 1571
2Ki 22:19 **a.** have heard thee, saith the Lord 1571
2Ki 23:5 them **a.** that burned incense unto
2Ki 23:19 the houses **a.** of the high places 1571
2Ki 23:27 remove Judah **a.** out of my sight, 1571
2Ki 24:4 And **a.** for the innocent blood 1571
1Ch 1:14 The Jebusite **a.**, and the Amorite,
1Ch 1:21 Hadoram **a.**, and Uzal, and
1Ch 1:51 Hadad died **a.**. And the dukes of
1Ch 2:9 The sons **a.** of Hezron, that were
1Ch 2:26 Jerahmeel had **a.** another wife,
1Ch 2:49 She bare **a.** Shaaph the father of
1Ch 3:6 Ibhar **a.**, and Elishama, and
1Ch 3:18 Malchiram **a.**, and Pedaiah, and
1Ch 6:3 The sons **a.** of Aaron; Nadab,
1Ch 6:48 Their brethren **a.** the Levites
1Ch 6:67 gave **a.** Gezer with her suburbs,
1Ch 6:79 Kedemoth **a.** with her suburbs
1Ch 7:10 The sons **a.** of Jediael; Bilhan:
1Ch 7:12 Shuppim **a.**, and Huppim,
1Ch 7:25 Rephah was his son, **a.** Resheph,
1Ch 7:28 Shechem **a.** and the towns thereof,
1Ch 8:13 Beriah **a.**, and Shemia, who were
1Ch 8:18 Ishmerai **a.**, and Jezliah, and
1Ch 8:32 these **a.** dwelt with their brethren 637
1Ch 9:29 Some of them **a.** were appointed
1Ch 9:38 they **a.** dwelt with their brethren 637
1Ch 10:13 and **a.** for asking counsel of one 1571
1Ch 11:10 These **a.** are the chief of the
1Ch 11:22 **a.** he went down and slew a lion
1Ch 11:26 **A.** the valiant men of the armies
1Ch 12:38 and all the rest **a.** of Israel were 1571
1Ch 13:2 and with them **a.** to the priests
1Ch 15:27 David **a.** had upon him an ephod
1Ch 16:6 Benaiah **a.** and Jahaziel the

1Ch 16:25 he **a.** is to be feared above all gods
1Ch 16:30 the world **a.** shall be stable, that 637
1Ch 16:38 Obed-edom **a.** the son of Jeduthun
1Ch 17:9 **A.** I will ordain a place for my
1Ch 17:17 **a.** spoken of thy servant's house
1Ch 18:4 David **a.** houghed all the chariot
1Ch 18:11 Them **a.** king David dedicated 1571
1Ch 20:2 brought **a.** exceeding much spoil
1Ch 20:6 he **a.** was the son of the giant 1571
1Ch 21:23 lo, I give thee the oxen **a.** for
1Ch 22:4 **A.** cedar trees in abundance:
1Ch 22:14 **a.** and stone have I prepared;
1Ch 22:17 David **a.** commanded all the
1Ch 23:26 And **a.** unto the Levites; they 1571
1Ch 24:30 The sons **a.** of Mushi; Mahli,
1Ch 26:6 **A.** unto Shemaiah his son were
1Ch 26:10 **A.** Hosah, of the children of
1Ch 27:4 course was Mikloth **a.** the ruler:
1Ch 27:30 Over the camels **a.** was Obil
1Ch 27:32 **A.** Jonathan David's uncle was a
1Ch 28:13 **A.** for the courses of the priests
1Ch 28:14 silver **a.** for all instruments of
1Ch 28:15 and **a.** for the lamps thereof,
1Ch 28:17 **A.** pure gold for the fleshhooks,
1Ch 28:21 **a.** the princes and all the people
1Ch 29:9 David the king **a.** rejoiced with 1571
1Ch 29:17 I know **a.**, my God, that thou
2Ch 2:8 Send me **a.** cedar trees, fir trees,
2Ch 2:14 **a.** to grave any manner of graving,
2Ch 3:7 He overlaid **a.** the house,
2Ch 3:12 the other wing was five cubits **a.**,
2Ch 3:15 **A.** he made before the house
2Ch 4:2 **A.** he made a molten seal of ten
2Ch 4:6 He made **a.** ten lavers, and put
2Ch 4:8 He made **a.** ten tables, and placed
2Ch 4:14 He made **a.** bases, and lavers
2Ch 4:16 The pots **a.**, and the shovels,
2Ch 4:19 the golden altar **a.**, and the tables
2Ch 5:6 **A.** king Solomon, and **a.** the
2Ch 5:12 **A.** the Levites which were the
2Ch 7:6 the Levites **a.** with instruments
2Ch 7:8 **A.** at the same time Solomon
2Ch 8:5 **A.** he built Beth-horon the upper,
2Ch 8:14 the porters **a.** by their courses at
2Ch 9:4 cupbearers **a.**, and their apparel;
2Ch 9:10 And the servants **a.** of Huram, 1571
2Ch 12:5 **a.** left you in the hand of Shishak
2Ch 12:9 he carried away **a.** the shields of
2Ch 12:12 and **a.** in Judah things went well 1571
2Ch 13:2 mother's name **a.** was Michaiah
2Ch 13:3 Jeroboam **a.** set the battle in
2Ch 13:11 the shewbread **a.** set they in order
2Ch 14:5 **A.** he took away out of all the
2Ch 14:15 They smote **a.** the tents of cattle, 1571
2Ch 15:16 And **a.** concerning Maachah the 1571
2Ch 17:7 **A.** in the third year of his reign
2Ch 17:11 **A.** some of the Philistines
2Ch 18:21 him, and thou shalt **a.** prevail: 1571
2Ch 19:11 **a.** the Levites shall be officers
2Ch 20:1 It came to pass after this **a.**,
2Ch 21:4 divers **a.** of the princes of Israel 1571
2Ch 21:10 The same time **a.** did Libnah
2Ch 21:13 and **a.** hast slain thy brethren of 1571
2Ch 21:17 king's house, and his sons **a.**, 1571
2Ch 22:2 mother's name **a.** was Athaliah
2Ch 22:3 He **a.** walked in the ways of the 1571
2Ch 22:5 He walked **a.** after their counsel, 1571
2Ch 23:13 and sounded with trumpets, **a.** 1571
2Ch 23:18 **A.** Jehoiada appointed the offices
2Ch 24:1 his mother's name **a.** was Zibiah
2Ch 24:7 and **a.** all the dedicated things 1571
2Ch 24:12 **a.** such as wrought iron and brass 1571
2Ch 24:20 the Lord, he hath **a.** forsaken you
2Ch 25:6 **a.** an hundred thousand mighty
2Ch 25:24 the hostages **a.**, and returned to
2Ch 26:3 mother's name **a.** was Jecoliah
2Ch 26:10 **A.** he built towers in the desert,
2Ch 26:10 husbandmen **a.**, and vine
2Ch 26:20 yea, himself hasted **a.** to go out, 1571
2Ch 27:1 mother's name **a.** was Jerushah
2Ch 27:5 He fought **a.** with the king of the
2Ch 28:2 **a.** molten images for Baalim 1571
2Ch 28:4 sacrificed **a.** and burnt incense
2Ch 28:5 he was **a.** delivered into the hand
2Ch 28:8 and took **a.** away much spoil 1571
2Ch 28:18 Philistines **a.** had invaded the cities
2Ch 28:18 Gimzo **a.** and the villages thereof:

2Ch 29:7 **A.** they have shut up the doors of...... 1571
2Ch 29:22 they killed **a.** the lambs, and they............
2Ch 29:27 Lord began **a.** with the trumpets,............
2Ch 29:35 **a.** the burnt offerings were in............ 1571
2Ch 30:1 **a.** to Ephraim and Manasseh,............ 1571
2Ch 30:12 **A.** in Judah the hand of God was........ 1571
2Ch 31:1 in Ephraim **a.** and Manasseh,..................
2Ch 31:3 He appointed **a.** the king's portion............
2Ch 31:6 **a.** brought in the tithe of oxen and..... 1571
2Ch 31:19 **A.** of the sons of Aaron the priests,..........
2Ch 32:5 **A.** he strengthened himself, and.............
2Ch 32:17 He wrote **a.** letters to rail on the............
2Ch 32:28 **a.** for the increase of corn, and.............
2Ch 32:30 This same Hezekiah **a.** stopped...............
2Ch 33:4 **A.** he built altars in the house of...............
2Ch 33:6 **a.** he observed times, and used...............
2Ch 33:19 His prayer **a.**, and how God was.............
2Ch 34:13 **A.** they were over the bearers of.............
2Ch 34:27 I have even heard thee **a.**, saith........ 1571
2Ch 35:9 Conaniah **a.**, and Shemaiah and..............
2Ch 36:7 Nebuchadnezzar **a.** carried off the............
2Ch 36:13 And he **a.** rebelled against king.......... 1571
2Ch 36:22 all his kingdom, and put it **a.** in.......... 1571
Ezr 1:1 and put it **a.** in writing, saying,.......... 1571
Ezr 1:7 **A.** Cyrus the king brought forth...............
Ezr 3:4 They kept **a.** the feast of the..................
Ezr 3:7 gave money **a.** unto the masons,.............
Ezr 4:20 mighty kings **a.** over Jerusalem,..............
Ezr 5:10 We asked their names **a.**, to.............. 638
Ezr 5:14 the vessels **a.** of gold and silver.......... 638
Ezr 6:5 And **a.** let the golden and silver........... 638
Ezr 6:11 **A.** I have made a decree, that...............
Ezr 7:19 The vessels **a.** that are given thee...........
Ezr 7:24 **A.** we certify you, that touching.............
Ezr 8:6 Of the sons **a.** of Adin; Ebed the............
Ezr 8:14 Of the sons **a.** of Bigvai; Uthai,..............
Ezr 8:16 **a.** for Joiarib, and for Elnathan,...............
Ezr 8:20 **A.** of the Nethinims, whom....................
Ezr 8:27 **A.** twenty basons of gold, of a.................
Ezr 8:28 Lord; the vessels are holy **a.**;...................
Ezr 8:35 **A.** the children of those that had.............
Ezr 10:4 we **a.** will be with thee: be of....................
Ezr 10:23 **A.** of the Levites; Jozabad, and...............
Ezr 10:24 Of the singers **a.**; Eliashib: and..............
Ezr 10:28 Of the sons **a.** of Bebai;.........................
Ne 1:3 wall of Jerusalem **a.** is broken down,.........
Ne 2:6 me, (the queen **a.** sitting by him,)............
Ne 2:18 as **a.** the king's words that he had....... 637
Ne 3:3 sons of Hassenaah build, who **a.**...............
Ne 3:8 unto him **a.** repaired Hananiah.................
Ne 3:29 After him repaired **a.** Shemaiah...............
Ne 5:3 Some **a.** there were that said. We............
Ne 5:4 There were **a.** that said, We have............
Ne 5:9 **A.** I said, It is not good that ye do:..........
Ne 5:11 **a.** the hundredth part of the money,.........
Ne 5:13 **A.** I shook my lap, and said, So......... 1571
Ne 5:16 Yea, **a.** I continued in the work......... 1571
Ne 5:18 **a.** fowls were prepared for me,................
Ne 6:7 And thou hast **a.** appointed.............. 1571
Ne 6:19 **A.** they reported his good deeds........ 1571
Ne 7:61 And ...went up **a.** from Tel-melah,..........
Ne 8:7 **A.** Jeshua, and Bani, and Sherebiah,.........
Ne 8:18 **A.** day by day, from the first day...........
Ne 9:13 down **a.** upon mount Sinai,......................
Ne 9:20 Thou gavest **a.** thy good spirit to............
Ne 9:23 Their children **a.** multipliedst..................
Ne 9:37 **a.** they have dominion over our...............
Ne 10:32 **A.** we made ordinances for us,................
Ne 10:36 **A.** the firstborn of our sons, and of..........
Ne 11:1 the rest of the people **a.** cast lots,............
Ne 11:15 **A.** of the Levites: Shemaiah the..............
Ne 11:22 The overseer **a.** of the Levites at............
Ne 11:31 The children **a.** of Benjamin from............
Ne 12:9 **A.** Bakbukiah and Unni, their...................
Ne 12:10 Joiakim **a.** beat Eliashib, and...................
Ne 12:22 **a.** the priests, to the reign of..................
Ne 12:29 **A.** from the house of Gilgal, and.............
Ne 12:43 **A.** that day they offered great..................
Ne 12:43 **a.** and the children rejoiced:....................
Ne 13:15 as **a.** wine, grapes, and figs, and......... 637
Ne 13:16 There dwelt men of Tyre **a.** therein,........
Ne 13:22 O my God, concerning this **a.**,........... 1571
Ne 13:23 **a.** saw I Jews that had married.......... 1571
Es 1:9 **A.** Vashti the queen made a feast....... 1571
Es 1:16 wrong to the king only, but **a.**.................
Es 2:8 brought **a.** unto the king's house,............
Es 3:11 given to thee, the people **a.**, to do..........
Es 4:8 **A.** he gave him a copy of the.................
Es 4:16 I **a.** and my maidens will fast............ 1571
Es 5:12 am I invited unto her **a.** with............ 1571
Es 7:8 Will he force the queen **a.** before....... 1571
Es 7:9 Behold **a.**, the gallows fifty cubits....... 1571
Es 8:8 Write ye **a.** for the Jews, as it................
Es 9:13 to do to morrow **a.** according unto..... 1571
Es 9:15 together on the fourteenth day **a.**........ 1571
Job 1:3 **a.** was seven thousand sheep,................
Job 1:6 and Satan came **a.** among them.......... 1571
Job 1:16 speaking, there came **a.** another,............
Job 1:17 came **a.** another, and said, The...............
Job 1:18 came **a.** another and said, Thy.................
Job 2:1 Satan came **a.** among them to........... 1571
Job 5:25 Thou shalt know **a.** that thy seed............
Job 7:1 **a.** like the days of an hireling?..................
Job 9:11 he passeth on **a.**, but I perceive...............
Job 9:20 am perfect, it shall **a.** prove me...............
Job 11:11 vain men: he seeth wickedness **a.**;...........
Job 11:19 **A.** thou shalt lie down, and none.............
Job 12:15 **a.** he sendeth them out, and they............
Job 13:2 know, the same do I know **a.**:............ 1571
Job 13:16 He **a.** shall be my salvation: for an..... 1571
Job 13:27 puttest my feet **a.** in the stocks,.............
Job 14:2 he fleeth **a.** as a shadow, and.................
Job 16:4 I **a.** could speak as ye do: if your....... 1571
Job 16:12 he hath **a.** taken me by my neck,............
Job 16:17 in mine hands: **a.** my prayer....................
Job 16:19 **A.** now, behold, my witness is in....... 1571
Job 17:6 He hath made me **a.** a byword of............
Job 17:7 Mine eye **a.** is dim by reason of..............
Job 17:9 The righteous **a.** shall hold on his............
Job 19:11 He hath **a.** kindled his wrath..................
Job 20:9 The eye **a.** which saw him shall...............
Job 22:28 Thou shalt **a.** decree a thing, and............
Job 24:15 The eye **a.** of the adulterer waiteth..........
Job 24:22 He draweth **a.** the mighty with his............
Job 30:11 they have **a.** let loose the bridle.............
Job 30:31 My harp **a.** is turned to mourning,............
Job 31:28 This **a.** were an iniquity to be............ 1571
Job 32:3 **A.** against his three friends was...............
Job 32:10 me; I **a.** will shew mine opinion.......... 637
Job 32:17 said, I will answer **a.** my part,........... 637
Job 32:17 I **a.** will shew mine opinion................ 637
Job 33:6 I **a.** am formed out of the clay........... 1571
Job 33:19 He is chastened **a.** with pain upon............
Job 36:1 Elihu **a.** proceeded, and said,................
Job 36:10 openeth **a.** their ear to discipline,............
Job 36:29 **A.** can any understand the................ 637
Job 36:33 the cattle **a.** concerning the vapour...... 637
Job 37:1 At this **a.** my heart trembleth,............ 637
Job 37:11 **A.** by watering he wearieth the.......... 637
Job 39:30 young ones **a.** suck up blood:..................
Job 40:8 Wilt thou **a.** disannul my..................... 637
Job 40:14 Then will I **a.** confess unto thee......... 1571
Job 42:9 them: the Lord **a.** accepted Job...............
Job 42:10 **a.** the Lord gave Job twice as..................
Job 42:11 every man **a.** gave him a piece of.............
Job 42:13 He had **a.** seven sons and three..............
Ps 1:3 his leaf **a.** shall not wither; and................
Ps 5:11 let them **a.** that love thy name.................
Ps 6:3 My soul is **a.** sore vexed: but thou,..........
Ps 7:13 He hath **a.** prepared for him the..............
Ps 9:9 The Lord **a.** will be a refuge for the.........
Ps 16:7 **a.** instruct me in the night................. 637
Ps 16:9 my flesh **a.** shall rest in hope............. 637
Ps 18:7 the foundations **a.** of the hills..................
Ps 18:9 He bowed the heavens **a.**, and came............
Ps 18:13 Lord **a.** thundered in the heavens,............
Ps 18:19 me forth **a.** into a large place;..................
Ps 18:23 I was **a.** upright before him, and I............
Ps 18:35 Thou hast **a.** given me the shield.............
Ps 18:40 Thou hast **a.** given me the necks of.........
Ps 19:10 sweeter **a.** than honey and the................
Ps 19:13 **a.** from presumptuous sins;............... 1571
Ps 26:1 I have trusted **a.** in the Lord;..................
Ps 27:7 have mercy **a.** upon me, and.....................
Ps 28:9 feed them **a.**, and lift them up for............
Ps 29:6 maketh them **a.** to skip like a calf;............
Ps 35:3 Draw out **a.** the spear, and stop.............
Ps 37:4 Delight thyself **a.** in the Lord; and............
Ps 37:5 unto the Lord; trust **a.** in him;..................
Ps 38:10 mine eyes, it **a.** is gone from me........ 1571
Ps 38:12 They **a.** that seek after my life...............
Ps 38:20 They **a.** that render evil for good.............
Ps 40:2 me up **a.** out of an horrible pit, out............
Ps 45:10 forget **a.** thine own people, and..............
Ps 52:6 The righteous **a.** shall see, and...............
Ps 55:10 mischief **a.** and sorrow are in the............
Ps 60:7 Ephraim **a.** is the strength of mine..........
Ps 62:12 **A.** unto thee, O, Lord, belongeth.............
Ps 65:8 They **a.** that dwell in the.......................
Ps 65:13 the valleys **a.** are covered over...............
Ps 65:13 they shout for joy, they **a.** sing.......... 637
Ps 68:1 let them **a.** that hate him flee.................
Ps 68:8 the heavens **a.** dropped at the............. 637
Ps 68:18 yea, for the rebellious **a.**, that the....... 637
Ps 69:11 made sackcloth **a.** my garment;..................
Ps 69:21 They gave me **a.** gall for my meat;...........
Ps 69:31 This **a.** shall please the Lord..................
Ps 69:36 The seed **a.** of his servants shall..............
Ps 71:18 **a.** when I am old and greyheaded,...... 1571
Ps 71:19 Thy righteousness **a.**, O God, is.............
Ps 71:22 I will **a.** praise thee with the............ 1571
Ps 71:24 My tongue **a.** shall talk of thy............ 1571
Ps 72:8 have dominion **a.** from sea to sea,...........
Ps 72:12 the poor **a.**, and him that hath no............
Ps 72:15 prayer **a.** shall be made for him...............
Ps 74:16 day is thine, the night **a.** is thine:........ 637
Ps 75:10 horns of the wicked **a.** will I cut..............
Ps 76:2 In Salem **a.** is his tabernacle,...................
Ps 77:12 I will meditate **a.** of all thy work,............
Ps 77:16 the depths **a.** were troubled............... 637
Ps 77:17 thine arrows **a.** went abroad............... 637
Ps 78:14 In the daytime **a.** he led them.................
Ps 78:16 brought streams **a.** out of the rock,..........
Ps 78:20 bread **a.**? can he provide flesh for...... 1571
Ps 78:21 anger **a.** came up against Israel;......... 1571
Ps 78:27 rained flesh **a.** upon them as dust,............
Ps 78:46 He ave **a.** their increase unto the............
Ps 78:48 gave up their cattle **a.** to the hail,...........
Ps 78:55 cast out the heathen **a.** before them,........
Ps 78:62 his people over **a.** unto the sword;...........
Ps 78:70 He chose David **a.** his servant,................
Ps 81:16 He should have fed them **a.** with the........
Ps 83:8 Assur **a.** is joined with them:........... 1571
Ps 84:6 the rain **a.** filleth the pools............... 1571
Ps 89:5 faithfulness **a.** in the congregation........ 637
Ps 89:11 heavens are thine, the earth **a.** is........ 637
Ps 89:21 mine arm **a.** shall strengthen him........ 637
Ps 89:25 I will set his hand **a.** in the sea,.............
Ps 89:27 **A.** I will make him my firstborn,.......... 637
Ps 89:29 His seed **a.** will I make to endure............
Ps 89:43 Thou hast **a.** turned the edge of.......... 637
Ps 92:11 Mine eye **a.** shall see my desire..............
Ps 93:1 the world is **a.** stablished that it.......... 389
Ps 95:4 the strength of the hills is his **a.**.............
Ps 96:10 the world **a.** shall be established.......... 637
Ps 99:4 king's strength **a.** loveth judgment;..........
Ps 105:23 Israel **a.** came into Egypt;.......................
Ps 105:33 smote their vines **a.** and their..................
Ps 105:36 He smote **a.** all the firstborn in...............
Ps 105:37 forth **a.** with silver and gold:..................
Ps 106:9 He rebuked the Red sea **a.**, and it............
Ps 106:16 They envied Moses **a.** in the camp,............
Ps 106:27 their seed **a.** among the nations,..............
Ps 106:28 joined themselves **a.** unto Baal-peor,.........
Ps 106:32 him **a.** at the waters of strife,..................
Ps 106:42 Their enemies **a.** oppressed them,............
Ps 106:46 He made them **a.** to be pitied of...............
Ps 107:32 exalt him **a.** in the congregation...............
Ps 107:38 He blesseth them **a.**, so that they............
Ps 108:8 Ephraim **a.** is the strength of mine...........
Ps 109:3 compassed me about **a.** with words..........
Ps 109:10 seek their bread **a.** out of their................
Ps 109:25 I became **a.** a reproach unto them:...........
Ps 119:3 They **a.** do no iniquity: They.............. 637
Ps 119:23 Princes **a.** did sit and speak.............. 1571
Ps 119:24 Thy testimonies **a.** are my delight............
Ps 119:41 Let thy mercies come **a.** unto me,.............
Ps 119:46 thy testimonies **a.** before kings,...............
Ps 119:48 My hands **a.** will I lift up unto.................
Ps 132:12 **a.** sit upon thy throne for evermore.... 1571
Ps 132:16 I will **a.** clothe her priests with...............
Ps 139:17 How precious **a.** are thy thoughts.............
Ps 141:5 **a.** shall be in their calamities....................
Ps 145:19 he **a.** will hear their cry, and will..............
Ps 148:6 He hath **a.** stablished them for................
Ps 148:14 He **a.** exalteth the horn of his.................
Pr 1:26 I **a.** will laugh at your calamity;.......... 1571
Pr 4:4 He taught me **a.**, and said unto................
Pr 9:2 she hath **a.** furnished her................... 637
Pr 11:25 shall be watered **a.** himself................ 1571
Pr 17:26 **A.** to punish the just is not good,....... 1571

Pr 18:3 cometh, then cometh **a.** contempt, 1571
Pr 18:9 He **a.** that is slothful in his work 1571
Pr 19:2 **A.**, that the soul be without 1571
Pr 21:13 his ears at the cry of the poor, he **a.** 1571
Pr 23:23 and sell it not; **a.** wisdom,
Pr 23:28 She **a.** lieth in wait as for a prey, 637
Pr 24:23 These things **a.** belong to the wise. 1571
Pr 25:1 These are **a.** proverbs of Solomon, 1571
Pr 26:4 according to his folly, lest thou **a.** 1571
Pr 28:16 wanteth understanding is **a.** a
Pr 30:31 A greyhound: an he goat **a.**; 176
Pr 31:15 She riseth **a.** while it is yet night,
Pr 31:28 her husband **a.**, and he praiseth
Ec 1:5 The sun **a.** ariseth, and the sun
Ec 1:17 that this **a.** is vexation of spirit. 1571
Ec 2:1 and, behold, this **a.** is vanity. 1571
Ec 2:7 **a.** I had great possessions of great 1571
Ec 2:8 gathered me **a.** silver and gold, 1571
Ec 2:9 **a.** my wisdom remained with me. 637
Ec 2:14 perceived **a.** that one event 1571
Ec 2:15 in my heart, that this **a.** is vanity. 1571
Ec 2:19 under the sun. This is **a.** vanity. 1571
Ec 2:21 This **a.** is vanity and a great evil. 1571
Ec 2:23 rest in the night. This is **a.** vanity. 1571
Ec 2:24 This **a.** I saw, that it was from the 1571
Ec 2:26 This **a.** is vanity and vexation of 1571
Ec 3:11 **a.** he hath set the world in their 1571
Ec 3:13 **a.** that every man should eat and 1571
Ec 4:4 This is **a.** vanity and vexation of 1571
Ec 4:8 **a.** vanity, yea, it is a sore travail 1571
Ec 4:14 **a.** he that is born in his kingdom 1571
Ec 4:16 they **a.** that come after shall not 1571
Ec 4:16 Surely this **a.** is vanity and vexation 1571
Ec 5:7 there are **a.** divers vanities:
Ec 5:10 with increase: this is **a.** vanity. 1571
Ec 5:16 And this **a.** is a sore evil, that in 1571
Ec 5:17 his days **a.** he eateth in darkness, 1571
Ec 5:19 **a.** to whom God hath given riches 1571
Ec 6:3 and **a.** that he have no burial; 1571
Ec 6:9 this is **a.** vanity and vexation 1571
Ec 7:6 of the fool: this **a.** is vanity. 1571
Ec 7:14 God **a.** hath set the one over 1571
Ec 7:18 **a.** from this withdraw not thine 1571
Ec 7:21 **A.** take no heed unto all words 1571
Ec 7:22 **a.** thine own heart knoweth that 1571
Ec 8:10 had so done: this is **a.** vanity 1571
Ec 8:14 I said that this **a.** is vanity. 1571
Ec 8:16 (for **a.** there is that neither day 1571
Ec 9:3 **a.** the heart of the sons of men is 1571
Ec 9:6 **A.** their love, and their hatred, 1571
Ec 9:12 For man **a.** knoweth not his time: 1571
Ec 9:13 wisdom have I seen **a.** under the 1571
Ec 10:3 Yea **a.**, when he that is a fool 1571
Ec 10:14 A fool **a.** is full of words: a man
Ec 11:2 portion to seven, and **a.** to eight; 1571
Ec 12:5 **A.** when they shall be afraid of 1571
Ca 1:16 my beloved, yea, pleasant: **a.** 637
Ca 7:8 of the boughs thereof: now **a.**
Isa 2:7 Their land **a.** is full of silver and
Isa 2:7 their land is **a.** full of horses,
Isa 2:8 Their land **a.** is full of idols;
Isa 5:2 of it, and **a.** made a winepress 1571
Isa 5:6 I will **a.** command the clouds
Isa 6:1 I saw **a.** the Lord sitting upon
Isa 6:8 **A.** I heard the voice of the Lord,
Isa 7:13 but will ye weary my God **a.**? 1571
Isa 7:20 and it shall **a.** consume the beard. 1571
Isa 8:5 Lord spake **a.** unto me again,
Isa 11:6 The wolf **a.** shall dwell with the
Isa 11:13 The envy **a.** of Ephraim shall
Isa 12:2 he **a.** is become my salvation
Isa 13:3 I have **a.** called my mighty ones 1571
Isa 13:16 Their children **a.** shall be dashed
Isa 13:18 bows **a.** shall dash the young
Isa 14:10 Art thou **a.** become weak as we? 1571
Isa 14:13 I will sit **a.** upon the mount of
Isa 14:23 I will **a.** make it a possession for
Isa 17:3 The fortress **a.** shall cease from
Isa 19:8 The fishers **a.** shall mourn, and
Isa 19:13 Noph are deceived; they have **a.**
Isa 21:12 morning cometh, and **a.** the night: 1571
Isa 22:9 Ye have seen **a.** the breaches of
Isa 22:11 **a.** a ditch between the two walls
Isa 23:12 there **a.** shalt thou have no rest 1571
Isa 24:5 The earth **a.** is defiled under the
Isa 26:12 for thou **a.** hast wrought all our 1571
Isa 26:21 earth **a.** shall disclose her blood,

Isa 28:7 they **a.** have erred through wine, 1571
Isa 28:17 Judgment **a.** will I lay to the line,
Isa 28:29 **a.** cometh forth from the Lord 1571
Isa 29:19 The meek **a.** shall increase their
Isa 29:24 They **a.** that erred in spirit shall
Isa 30:5 but a shame, and **a.** a reproach 1571
Isa 30:22 defile **a.** the covering of thy graven
Isa 31:2 Yet he **a.** is wise, and will bring 1571
Isa 31:5 defending **a.** he will deliver it;
Isa 32:4 The heart **a.** of the rash shall
Isa 32:7 instruments **a.** of the churl are evil:
Isa 33:2 salvation **a.** in the time of trouble. 637
Isa 34:3 Their slain **a.** shall be cast out,
Isa 34:11 the owl **a.** and the raven shall
Isa 34:14 beasts of the desert shall **a.** meet
Isa 34:14 the screech owl **a.** shall rest there, 389
Isa 34:15 shall the vultures **a.** be gathered, 389
Isa 38:22 Hezekiah **a.** had said, what is the
Isa 40:24 and he shall **a.** blow upon them, 1571
Isa 44:19 **a.** I have baked bread upon the 637
Isa 45:16 be ashamed, and **a.** confounded, 1571
Isa 46:11 I will **a.** bring it to pass; 637
Isa 46:11 have purposed it, I will **a.** do it. 637
Isa 48:12 I am the first, I **a.** am the last. 637
Isa 48:13 Mine hand **a.** hath laid the 637
Isa 48:19 Thy seed **a.** had been as the sand,
Isa 48:21 clave the rock **a.**, and the waters
Isa 49:6 I will **a.** give thee for a light to
Isa 49:7 arise, princes **a.** shall worship,
Isa 56:6 **A.** the sons of the stranger, that
Isa 57:8 Behind the doors **a.** and the posts
Isa 57:15 with him **a.** that is of a contrite
Isa 57:18 I will lead him **a.**, and restore
Isa 60:14 sons **a.** of them that afflicted thee
Isa 60:16 Thou shalt **a.** suck the milk of
Isa 60:17 I will **a.** make thy officers peace,
Isa 60:21 people **a.** shall be all righteous:
Isa 62:3 Thou shalt **a.** be a crown of glory
Isa 66:4 I **a.** will choose their delusions, 1571
Isa 66:21 I will **a.** take of them for priests 1571
Jer 1:3 came **a.** in the days of Jehoiakim
Jer 2:8 pastors **a.** transgressed against me,
Jer 2:16 **A.** the children of Noph and 1571
Jer 2:33 **a.** taught the wicked ones thy 1571
Jer 2:34 **A.** in thy skirts is found the blood 1571
Jer 2:36 **a.** shalt be ashamed of Egypt, 1571
Jer 3:6 Lord said **a.** unto me in the days
Jer 3:8 but went and played the harlot **a.** 1571
Jer 4:12 now **a.** will I give sentence against 1571
Jer 6:14 healed **a.** the hurt of the daughter
Jer 6:17 **A.** I set watchmen over you,
Jer 7:27 thou shalt **a.** call unto them;
Jer 9:16 scatter them **a.** among the heathen,
Jer 10:5 **a.** is it in them to do good. 1571
Jer 13:23 then may ye **a.** do good, that are 1571
Jer 14:5 the hind **a.** calved in the field, 1571
Jer 16:1 word of the Lord came **a.** unto me,
Jer 16:8 shalt not **a.** go into the house of
Jer 19:5 They have built **a.** the high places
Jer 20:1 who was **a.** chief governor in the
Jer 23:14 I have seen **a.** in the prophets of
Jer 23:14 strengthen **a.** the hands of evildoers,
Jer 25:14 serve themselves of them **a.** 1571
Jer 26:20 was **a.** a man that prophesied 1571
Jer 27:6 the field have I given him **a.** to 1571
Jer 27:12 **a.** to Zedekiah king of Judah
Jer 27:16 **A.** I spake to the priests and to
Jer 28:14 him the beasts of the field **a.** 1571
Jer 29:24 Thus shalt thou **a.** speak to
Jer 30:19 I will **a.** glorify them, and they
Jer 30:20 children **a.** shall be as aforetime,
Jer 31:36 the seed of Israel **a.** shall cease 1571
Jer 31:37 **a.** cast off all the seed of Israel 1571
Jer 33:21 may **a.** my covenant be broken 1571
Jer 35:15 I have sent **a.** unto you all my servants
Jer 36:6 and **a.** thou shalt read them in the 1571
Jer 38:25 death **a.** what the king said unto thee
Jer 39:6 **a.** the king of Babylon slew all
Jer 40:5 Go back **a.** to Gedaliah the son
Jer 41:3 Ishmael **a.** slew all the Jews that
Jer 43:13 He shall break **a.** the images of
Jer 46:21 **A.** her hired men are in the midst 1571
Jer 46:21 for they **a.** are turned back, 1571
Jer 48:2 **A.** thou shalt be cut down, O 1571
Jer 48:7 treasures, thou shalt **a.** be taken: 1571
Jer 48:8 the valley **a.** shall perish, and the
Jer 48:26 Moab **a.** shall wallow in his vomit,

Jer 48:26 and he **a.** shall be in derision. 1571
Jer 48:34 for the waters **a.** of Nimrim shall 1571
Jer 49:17 **A.** Edom shall be a desolation:
Jer 50:24 for thee, and thou art **a.** taken, 1571
Jer 50:24 thou art found, and **a.** caught, 1571
Jer 51:22 With thee **a.** will I break in
Jer 51:23 I will **a.** break in pieces with
Jer 52:10 slew **a.** all the princes of Judah 1571
Jer 52:17 **A.** the pillars of brass that were
Jer 52:18 the caldrons **a.**, and the shovels,
Jer 52:22 The second pillar **a.** and the
Jer 52:25 took **a.** out of the city an eunuch,
La 2:9 her prophets **a.** find no vision 1571
La 3:8 **A.** when I cry and shout, he 1571
La 3:16 He hath **a.** broken my teeth with
La 4:21 cup **a.** shall pass through unto 1571
Eze 1:5 **A.** out of the midst thereof came
Eze 1:10 four **a.** had the face of an eagle
Eze 3:13 I heard **a.** the noise of the wings
Eze 3:21 **a.** thou hast delivered thy soul
Eze 4:1 Thou **a.**, son of man, take thee a
Eze 4:2 set the camp **a.** against it,
Eze 4:4 Lie thou **a.** upon thy left side,
Eze 4:9 Take thou **a.** unto thee wheat,
Eze 4:11 shalt drink **a.** water by measure,
Eze 5:3 Thou shalt **a.** take thereof a few
Eze 5:11 therefore will I **a.** diminish 1571
Eze 7:2 **A.**, thou son of man, thus saith
Eze 7:18 They shall **a.** gird themselves
Eze 7:22 My face will I turn **a.** from them,
Eze 7:24 will **a.** make the pomp of the strong
Eze 8:13 He said **a.** unto me, Turn thee yet
Eze 8:18 Therefore will I **a.** deal in fury: 1571
Eze 9:1 He cried **a.** in mine ears with a
Eze 9:10 And as for me **a.**, mine eye shall 1571
Eze 10:16 the same wheel **a.** turned not from 1571
Eze 10:17 these lifted up themselves **a.**:
Eze 10:19 the wheels **a.** were beside them,
Eze 12:1 word of the Lord **a.** came unto me,
Eze 12:13 My net **a.** will I spread upon him,
Eze 13:21 Your kerchiefs **a.** will I tear,
Eze 16:10 I clothed thee **a.** with broidered
Eze 16:11 I decked thee **a.** with ornaments,
Eze 16:17 Thou hast **a.** taken thy fair jewels
Eze 16:19 My meat **a.** which I gave thee,
Eze 16:24 That thou hast **a.** built unto thee
Eze 16:26 hast **a.** committed fornication
Eze 16:28 Thou hast played the whore **a.**
Eze 16:39 will **a.** give thee into their hand,
Eze 16:39 shall strip thee **a.** of thy clothes,
Eze 16:40 They shall **a.** bring up a company
Eze 16:41 and thou **a.** shalt give no hire 1571
Eze 16:43 therefore I **a.** will recompense 1571
Eze 16:52 Thou **a.**, which hast judged thy 1571
Eze 16:52 yea, be thou confounded **a.**, 1571
Eze 17:5 He took **a.** of the seed of the land,
Eze 17:7 There was **a.** another great eagle
Eze 17:13 **a.** taken the mighty of the land:
Eze 17:22 I will **a.** take of the highest branch
Eze 18:4 so **a.** the soul of the son is mine:
Eze 19:4 The nations **a.** heard of him;
Eze 20:12 **a.** I gave them my sabbaths to be 1571
Eze 20:15 Yet **a.** I lifted up my hand unto 1571
Eze 20:23 unto them **a.** in the wilderness, 1571
Eze 20:25 I gave them **a.** statutes that were 1571
Eze 20:28 **a.** they made their sweet savour,
Eze 20:39 hereafter **a.**, if ye will not hearken
Eze 21:9 is sharpened, and **a.** furbished: 1571
Eze 21:17 will **a.** smite mine hands together, 1571
Eze 21:19 **A.**, thou son of man, appoint thee
Eze 23:26 **a.** strip thee out of thy clothes,
Eze 23:35 bear thou **a.** thy lewdness and 1571
Eze 23:37 and have **a.** caused their sons, 1571
Eze 24:3 set it on, and **a.** pour water 1571
Eze 24:5 of the flock, and burn **a.** the 1571
Eze 24:15 **A.** the word of the Lord came
Eze 24:25 **A.**, thou son of man, shall it not
Eze 25:13 I will **a.** stretch out mine hand
Eze 26:4 I will **a.** scrape her dust from her,
Eze 27:19 Dan **a.** and Javan going to and fro
Eze 30:6 They **a.** that uphold Egypt shall
Eze 30:10 **a.** make the multitude of Egypt
Eze 30:13 I will **a.** destroy the idols, and I
Eze 30:18 At Tehaphnehes **a.** the day shall
Eze 31:17 They **a.** went down into hell 1571
Eze 32:6 **a.** water with thy blood the land
Eze 32:9 I will **a.** vex the hearts of many

Eze	32:13	I will destroy **a.** all the beasts	
Eze	32:17	came to pass **a.** in the twelfth year,	
Eze	33:30	**A.**, thou son of man, the children	
Eze	36:1	**A.**, thou son of man, prophesy	
Eze	36:26	A new heart **a.** will I give you,	
Eze	36:29	I will **a.** save you from all your	
Eze	36:33	**a.** cause you to dwell in the cities,	
Eze	37:24	shall **a.** walk in my judgments,	
Eze	37:27	tabernacle **a.** shall be with them:	
Eze	38:10	It shall **a.** come to pass, that at	
Eze	39:16	And **a.** the name of the city shall	1571
Eze	40:8	measured **a.** the porch of the gate	1571
Eze	40:12	The space **a.** before the little	
Eze	40:14	He made **a.** posts of threescore	
Eze	40:42	**a.** they laid the instruments	
Eze	41:8	I saw **a.** the height of the house	
Eze	41:14	**A.** the breadth of the face of the	
Eze	43:21	take the bullock **a.** of the sin	
Eze	43:25	shall **a.** prepare a young bullock,	
Eze	44:30	shall **a.** give unto the priest the	
Eze	45:5	shall **a.** the Levites, the ministers	
Eze	47:20	side **a.** shall be the great sea	
Da	6:22	and **a.** before thee, O king, have I	638
Da	7:6	the beast had **a.** four heads;	
Da	8:25	And through his policy **a.** he shall	
Da	8:25	shall **a.** stand up against the Prince	
Da	10:6	His body **a.** was like the beryl,	
Da	11:1	**A.** I in the first year of Darius	
Da	11:8	**a.** carry captives into Egypt	1571
Da	11:14	**a.** the robbers of thy people shall	
Da	11:17	He shall **a.** set his face to enter	
Da	11:22	be broken, yea, **a.** the prince of	1571
Da	11:41	enter **a.** into the glorious land,	
Da	11:42	stretch forth his hand **a.** upon	
Ho	2:11	will **a.** cause all her mirth to cease,	
Ho	3:3	man: so will I **a.** be for thee.	1571
Ho	4:3	sea **a.** shall be taken away.	1571
Ho	4:5	and the prophet **a.** shall fall with	1571
Ho	4:6	hast rejected knowledge, I will **a.**	
Ho	4:6	law of thy God, I will **a.** forget thy	1571
Ho	5:5	Judah **a.** shall fall with them.	1571
Ho	6:11	**A.**, O Judah, he hath set an harvest	1571
Ho	7:11	Ephraim **a.** is like a silly dove	
Ho	8:6	For from Israel was it **a.**: the	
Ho	9:12	yea, woe **a.** to them when I	1571
Ho	10:6	shall be **a.** carried unto Assyria	1571
Ho	10:8	The high places **a.** of Aven, the sin	
Ho	11:3	I taught Ephraim **a.** to go,	
Ho	12:2	hath **a.** a controversy with Judah,	
Ho	12:10	have **a.** spoken by the prophets,	
Joe	1:12	tree, the palm tree **a.**, and	1571
Joe	1:20	The beasts of the field cry **a.**	1571
Joe	2:12	Therefore **a.** now, saith the Lord,	1571
Joe	2:29	And **a.** upon the servants and	1571
Joe	3:2	I will **a.** gather all nations, and will	
Joe	3:6	The children **a.** of Judah and the	
Joe	3:16	Lord **a.** shall roar out of Zion,	
Am	1:5	break **a.** the bar of Damascus,	
Am	2:10	**A.** I brought you up from the land	
Am	3:14	I will **a.** visit the altars of Beth-el:	
Am	4:6	And I **a.** have given you cleanness	1571
Am	4:7	And **a.** I have withholden the rain	1571
Am	7:6	This **a.** shall not be, saith the Lord	
Am	7:12	**A.** Amaziah said unto Amos,	
Am	9:14	they shall **a.** make gardens, and	
Jon	4:11	and their left hand; and **a.** much	
Mic	3:3	Who **a.** eat the flesh of my people,	
Mic	4:11	**a.** many nations are gathered	
Mic	5:13	graven images **a.** will I cut off,	
Mic	6:13	Therefore **a.** will I make thee sick	1571
Mic	7:12	In that day **a.** he shall come even	
Na	3:10	children **a.** were dashed in pieces	1571
Na	3:11	Thou **a.** shalt be drunken: thou	1571
Na	3:11	thou **a.** shalt seek strength	1571
Hab	1:8	Their horses **a.** are swifter than	
Hab	2:5	Yea **a.**, because he transgresseth	637
Hab	2:15	him, and makest him drunken **a.**,	637
Hab	2:16	shame for glory: drink thou **a.**,	1571
Zep	1:4	I will **a.** stretch out mine hand	
Zep	1:9	In the same day **a.** will I punish	
Zep	1:13	they shall **a.** build houses, but	
Zep	2:12	Ye Ethiopians **a.**, ye shall be	1571
Zep	3:12	I will **a.** leave in the midst of	
Zec	3:7	thou shalt **a.** judge my house,	1571
Zec	3:7	and shalt **a.** keep my courts,	1571
Zec	4:9	his hands shall **a.** finish it; and	
Zec	8:6	should it **a.** be marvellous in mine	1571
Zec	8:21	the Lord of hosts: I will go **a.**	1571
Zec	9:2	Hamath **a.** shall border thereby;	1571
Zec	9:5	Gaza **a.** shall see it, and be very	
Zec	9:11	As for thee **a.**, by the blood of thy	1571
Zec	10:10	bring them again **a.** out of the	
Zec	11:8	Three shepherds **a.** I cut off in	
Zec	11:8	lothed them, and their soul **a.**	1571
Zec	12:7	The Lord **a.** shall save the tents of	
Zec	13:2	and **a.** I will cause the prophets	1571
Zec	14:14	Judah **a.** shall fight at Jerusalem;	1571
Mal	1:13	Ye said **a.**, Behold, what a	
Mal	2:9	Therefore have I **a.** made you	1571
Mt	2:8	I may come and worship him **a.**	*2504*
Mt	3:10	And now **a.** the ax is laid unto	*2532*
Mt	5:39	**cheek, turn to him the other a.**	*2532*
Mt	5:40	**thy coat, let him have thy cloke a.**	*2532*
Mt	6:14	**heavenly Father will a. forgive**	*2532*
Mt	6:21	**is, there will your heart be a.**	*2532*
Mt	10:4	Iscariot, who **a.** betrayed him.	*2532*
Mt	10:32	**will I confess a. before my Father.**	*2504*
Mt	10:33	**him will I a. deny before my**	*2504*
Mt	12:45	**be a. unto this wicked generation.**	*2532*
Mt	13:22	**He a. that received seed among**	*1161*
Mt	13:23	**which a. beareth fruit, and**	*1211*
Mt	13:26	**fruit, then appeared the tares a.**	*2532*
Mt	13:29	**ye root up a. the wheat with them**	*260*
Mt	15:3	**Why do ye a. transgress the**	*2532*
Mt	15:16	**ye a. yet without understanding?**	*2532*
Mt	16:1	**a.** with the Sadducees came,	*2532*
Mt	16:18	**And I say a. unto thee, That thou**	*1161*
Mt	17:12	**Likewise shall a. the Son of man**	*2532*
Mt	18:33	**not thou a. have had compassion**	*2532*
Mt	18:35	**shall my heavenly Father do a.**	*2532*
Mt	19:3	The Pharisees **a.** came unto him,	*2532*
Mt	19:28	**ye a. shall sit upon twelve thrones,**	*2532*
Mt	20:4	**Go ye a. into the vineyard, and**	*2532*
Mt	20:7	**them, Go ye a. into the vineyard;**	*2532*
Mt	21:21	**but a. if ye shall say unto this**	*2579*
Mt	21:24	**I a. will ask you one thing,**	*2504*
Mt	22:26	Likewise the second **a.**, and the	*2532*
Mt	22:27	And last of all the woman died **a.**	*2532*
Mt	23:26	**outside of them may be clean a.**	*2532*
Mt	23:28	**Even so ye a. outwardly appear**	*2532*
Mt	24:27	**a. the coming of the Son of man**	*2532*
Mt	24:37	**days of Noe were, so shall a. the**	*2532*
Mt	24:39	**all away; so shall a. the coming**	*2532*
Mt	24:44	**Therefore be ye a. ready: for in**	*2532*
Mt	25:11	**Afterward came a. the other**	*2532*
Mt	25:17	**two, he a. gained other two.**	*2532*
Mt	25:22	**He a. that had received two**	*2532*
Mt	25:41	**Then shall he say a. unto them**	*2532*
Mt	25:44	**Then shall they a. answer him,**	*2532*
Mt	26:13	**there shall a. this, that this**	*2532*
Mt	26:35	Likewise **a.** said all the disciples	*2532*
Mt	26:69	Thou **a.** wast with Jesus of Galilee.	*2532*
Mt	26:71	This fellow was **a.** with Jesus of	*2532*
Mt	26:73	Surely thou **a.** art one of them;	*2532*
Mt	27:41	**a.** the chief priests mocking him	*1161*
Mt	27:44	The thieves **a.**, which were	*2532*
Mt	27:57	**a.** himself was Jesus' disciple:	*2532*
Mk	1:19	who **a.** were in the ship mending	*2532*
Mk	1:38	**towns, that I may preach there a.:**	*2546*
Mk	2:15	publicans and sinners sat **a.**	*2532*
Mk	2:21	**No man a. seweth a piece of new**	*2532*
Mk	2:26	**and gave a. to them which were**	*2532*
Mk	2:28	**of man is Lord a. of the sabbath.**	*2532*
Mk	3:19	Iscariot, which **a.** betrayed him:	*2532*
Mk	4:36	And there were **a.** with him other	
Mk	5:16	and **a.** concerning the swine.	
Mk	7:18	**ye so without understanding a.?**	*2532*
Mk	8:7	to set them **a.** before them.	*2532*
Mk	8:34	unto him with his disciples **a.**,	
Mk	8:38	**of him a. shall the Son of man be**	*2532*
Mk	11:25	**that your Father a. which is in**	*2532*
Mk	11:29	**I will a. ask of you one question,**	*2504*
Mk	12:6	**he sent him a. last unto them,**	*2532*
Mk	12:22	last of all the woman died **a.**	*2532*
Mk	14:9	**this a. that she hath done shall**	*2532*
Mk	14:31	anywise. Likewise **a.** said they all	*2532*
Mk	14:67	**a.** wast with Jesus of Nazareth.	*2532*
Mk	15:31	Likewise **a.** the chief priests	*2532*
Mk	15:40	There were **a.** women looking on	*2532*
Mk	15:41	(Who **a.**, when he was in Galilee,	*2532*
Mk	15:43	which **a.** waited for the kingdom of	*2532*
Lu	1:3	It seemed good to me **a.**, having	*2504*
Lu	1:35	therefore **a.** that holy thing which	*2532*
Lu	1:36	thy cousin Elizabeth, she hath **a.**	*2532*
Lu	2:4	And Joseph **a.** went up from	*2532*
Lu	2:35	pierce through thy own soul **a.**,)	*2532*
Lu	3:9	And now **a.** the axe is laid unto	*2532*
Lu	3:12	Then came **a.** publicans to be	*2532*
Lu	3:21	Jesus **a.** being baptized	*2532*
Lu	4:23	**do a. here in thy country.**	*2532*
Lu	4:41	And devils **a.** came out of many,	*2532*
Lu	4:43	**kingdom of God to other cities a.:**	*2532*
Lu	5:10	And so was **a.** James, and John,	*2532*
Lu	5:36	he spake **a.** a parable unto them;	*2532*
Lu	5:39	**No man a. having drunk old wine**	*2532*
Lu	6:4	**gave a. to them that were with**	*2532*
Lu	6:5	**the Son of man is Lord a. of the**	*2532*
Lu	6:6	**a.** on another sabbath, that he	*2532*
Lu	6:13	whom **a.** he named apostles;	*2532*
Lu	6:14	Simon, (whom he **a.** named Peter,)	*2532*
Lu	6:16	Iscariot, which **a.** was the traitor	*2532*
Lu	6:29	**on the one cheek offer a. the**	*2532*
Lu	6:29	**cloke forbid not to take thy coat a.**	*2532*
Lu	6:31	**to you, do ye a. to them likewise.**	*2532*
Lu	6:32	**sinners a. love those that love**	*2532*
Lu	6:33	**for sinners a. do even the same.**	*2532*
Lu	6:34	**for sinners a. lend to sinners,**	*2532*
Lu	6:36	**as your Father a. is merciful.**	*2532*
Lu	7:8	I **a.** am a man set under authority,	*2532*
Lu	7:49	Who is this that forgiveth sins **a.**?	*2532*
Lu	8:36	They **a.** which saw it told them	*2532*
Lu	9:61	another **a.** said, Lord, I will follow	*2532*
Lu	10:1	Lord appointed other seventy **a.**,	*2532*
Lu	10:39	Mary, which **a.** sat at Jesus' feet,	*2532*
Lu	11:1	as John **a.** taught his disciples.	*2532*
Lu	11:4	**for we a. forgive every one that is.**	*2532*
Lu	11:18	**If Satan a. be divided against**	*2532*
Lu	11:30	**so shall a. the Son of man be to**	*2532*
Lu	11:34	**thy whole body a. is full of light;**	*2532*
Lu	11:34	**thy body a. is full of darkness**	*2532*
Lu	11:40	**make that which is within a.**	*2532*
Lu	11:45	saying thou reproachest us **a.**?	*2532*
Lu	11:46	**Woe unto you a., ye lawyers!**	*2532*
Lu	11:49	**a. said the wisdom of God, I will**	*2532*
Lu	12:8	**A. I say unto you, Whosoever**	*1161*
Lu	12:8	**Son of man a. confess before the**	*2532*
Lu	12:34	**is, there will your heart be a.**	*2532*
Lu	12:40	**Be ye therefore ready a.: for the**	*2532*
Lu	12:54	And he said **a.** to the people,	*2532*
Lu	13:6	He spake **a.** this parable;	*1161*
Lu	13:8	**Lord, let it alone this year a.,**	*2532*
Lu	14:12	said he **a.** to him that bade him,	*2532*
Lu	14:12	**lest they a. bid thee again,**	*2532*
Lu	14:26	**and his own life a., he cannot be**	*2532*
Lu	16:1	he said **a.** unto his disciples,	*2532*
Lu	16:10	**is least is faithful a. in much:**	*2532*
Lu	16:10	**in the least is unjust a. in much.**	*2532*
Lu	16:14	And the Pharisees **a.**, who were	*2532*
Lu	16:22	**the rich man a. died, and was**	*2532*
Lu	16:28	**lest they a. come into this place.**	*2532*
Lu	17:24	**a. the Son of man be in his day.**	*2532*
Lu	17:26	**a. in the days of the Son of man.**	*2532*
Lu	17:28	**a. as it was in the days of Lot;**	*2532*
Lu	18:15	**a.** infants, that he would touch	*2532*
Lu	19:9	as he **a.** is a son of Abraham.	*2532*
Lu	19:19	**to him, Be thou a. over five cities.**	*2532*
Lu	20:3	**I will a. ask you one thing;**	*2504*
Lu	20:11	**they beat him a., and entreated**	*2528*
Lu	20:12	**a third: and they wounded him a.,**	*2532*
Lu	20:31	and in like manner the seven **a.**:	*2532*
Lu	20:32	Last of all the woman died **a.**	*2532*
Lu	21:2	**a.** a certain poor widow casting	*2532*
Lu	22:20	Likewise **a.** the cup after supper,	*2532*
Lu	22:24	there was **a.** a strife among them,	*2532*
Lu	22:39	and his disciples **a.** followed	*2532*
Lu	22:56	said, This man was **a.** with him.	*2532*
Lu	22:58	Thou art **a.** of them. And Peter	*2532*
Lu	22:59	truth this fellow **a.** was with him:	*2532*
Lu	22:68	**And if I a. ask you, ye will not**	*2532*
Lu	23:7	who himself **a.** was at Jerusalem	*2532*
Lu	23:27	of women, which **a.** bewailed and	*2532*
Lu	23:32	And there were **a.** two other,	*2532*
Lu	23:35	the rulers **a.** with them derided	*2532*
Lu	23:36	And the soldiers **a.** mocked him,	*2532*
Lu	23:38	a superscription **a.** was written	*2532*
Lu	23:51	**a.** himself waited for the	*2532*
Lu	23:55	And the women **a.**, which came	*2532*
Lu	24:22	certain women **a.** of our company	*2532*
Lu	24:23	had **a.** seen a vision of angels,	*2532*
Joh	3:23	John **a.** was baptizing in AEnon	*2532*

Joh	4:45	for they a. went unto the feast	2532
Joh	5:18	said a. that God was his Father,	2532
Joh	5:19	soever he doeth, these a. doeth	2532
Joh	5:27	authority to execute judgment a.,	2532
Joh	6:24	disciples, they a. took shipping,	2532
Joh	6:36	That ye a. have seen me, and	2532
Joh	6:67	the twelve, Will ye a. go away?	2532
Joh	7:3	disciples a. may see the works	2532
Joh	7:10	then went he a. up unto the feast,	2532
Joh	7:47	the Pharisees, Are ye a. deceived?	2532
Joh	7:52	Art thou a. of Galilee?	2532
Joh	8:17	It is a. written in your law, that	2532
Joh	8:19	should have known my Father a.	2532
Joh	9:15	again the Pharisees a. asked him	2532
Joh	9:27	will ye a. be his disciples?	2532
Joh	9:40	said unto him, Are we blind a.?	2532
Joh	10:16	this fold: them a. I must bring,	2548
Joh	11:16	Let us a. go, that we may die	2532
Joh	11:33	a. weeping which came with her,	2532
Joh	11:52	that a. he should gather together	2532
Joh	12:9	that they might see Lazarus a.,	2532
Joh	12:10	that they might put Lazarus a.	2532
Joh	12:18	this cause the people a. met him,	2532
Joh	12:26	I am, there shall a. my servant be:	2532
Joh	12:42	the chief rulers a. many believed	2532
Joh	13:9	but a. my hands and my head	2532
Joh	13:14	ye a. ought to wash one another's	2532
Joh	13:32	God shall a. glorify him in himself,	2532
Joh	13:34	that ye a. love one another.	2532
Joh	14:1	ye believe in God, believe a. in me.	2532
Joh	14:3	where I am, there ye may be a.	2532
Joh	14:7	should have known my Father a.:	2532
Joh	14:12	the works that I do shall he do a.;	2548
Joh	14:19	because I live, ye shall live a.	2532
Joh	15:20	me, they will a. perecute you;	2532
Joh	15:20	saying, they will keep yours a.	2532
Joh	15:23	hateth me hateth my Father a.	2532
Joh	15:27	And ye a. shall bear witness.	2532
Joh	17:1	that thy Son a. may glorify thee:	2532
Joh	17:18	have I a. sent them into the world.	2504
Joh	17:19	that they a. might be sanctified	2532
Joh	17:20	for these alone, but for them a.	2532
Joh	17:21	that they a. may be one in us:	2532
Joh	17:24	Father, I will that they a., whom	2548
Joh	18:2	and Judas a., which betrayed him	2532
Joh	18:5	And Judas a., which betrayed him,	2532
Joh	18:17	Art not thou a. one of this man's	2532
Joh	18:25	not thou a. one of his disciples?	2532
Joh	19:23	soldier a part; and a. his coat:	2532
Joh	19:39	And there came a. Nicodemus,	2532
Joh	20:8	Then went in a. that other disciple,	2532
Joh	21:3	say unto him, We a. go with thee.	2532
Joh	21:20	a. leaned on his breast at supper,	2532
Joh	21:25	a. many other things which Jesus	2532
Ac	1:3	To whom a. he shewed himself	2532
Ac	1:11	Which a. said, Ye men of Galilee,	2532
Ac	2:22	midst of you, as ye yourselves a.	2532
Ac	2:26	moreover a. my flesh shall rest	2532
Ac	3:17	ye did it, as did a. your rulers.	2532
Ac	5:2	part of the price, his wife a. being	2532
Ac	5:16	There came a. a multitude out of	2532
Ac	5:32	and so is a. the Holy Ghost,	2532
Ac	5:37	he a. perished; and all, even as	2548
Ac	7:45	Which a. our fathers that came	2532
Ac	8:13	Then Simon himself believed a.:	2532
Ac	8:19	Give me a. this power,	2504
Ac	9:32	he came down a. to the saints	2532
Ac	10:26	I myself a. am a man	2504
Ac	10:45	a. was poured out the gift of the	2532
Ac	11:1	had a. received the word of God	2532
Ac	11:18	God a. to the Gentiles granted	2532
Ac	11:30	Which a. they did, and sent it to	2532
Ac	12:3	proceeded further to take Peter a.	2532
Ac	13:5	had a. John to their minister.	2532
Ac	13:9	Then Saul, (who a. is called Paul,)	2532
Ac	13:22	to whom a. he gave testimony,	2532
Ac	13:33	again; as it is a. written in the	2532
Ac	13:35	he saith a. in another psalm,	2532
Ac	14:1	Jews and a. of the Greeks believed	2532
Ac	14:5	a. of the Jews with their rulers,	
Ac	14:15	We a. are men of like passions	2532
Ac	15:27	shall a. tell you the same things	2532
Ac	15:32	Judas and Silas, being prophets a.	2532
Ac	15:35	Paul a. and Barnabas continued	1161
Ac	15:35	of the Lord, with many others a.	2532
Ac	17:6	upside down are come hither a.;	2532
Ac	17:12	a. of honourable women which	2532
Ac	17:13	at Berea, they came thither a.,	2546
Ac	17:28	as certain a. of your own poets	2532
Ac	17:28	For we are a. his offspring.	2532
Ac	19:17	to all the Jews and Greeks a.	2532
Ac	19:19	them a. which used curious arts	1161
Ac	19:21	been there, I must a. see Rome.	2532
Ac	19:27	a. that the temple of the great	2532
Ac	20:21	to the Jews, and a. to the Greeks	2532
Ac	20:30	A. of your own selves shall men	2532
Ac	21:13	a. to die at Jerusalem for the	2532
Ac	21:16	with us a. certain of the disciples	2532
Ac	21:24	thou thyself a. walkest orderly,	2532
Ac	21:28	brought Greeks a. into the temple,	2532
Ac	22:5	As a. the high priest doth bear	2532
Ac	22:5	from whom a. I received letters	2532
Ac	22:20	was shed, I a. was standing	2532
Ac	22:29	the chief captain a. was afraid,	2532
Ac	23:11	must thou bear witness a. at	2532
Ac	23:30	his accusers a. to say before thee	2532
Ac	23:33	presented Paul a. before him	2532
Ac	23:35	when thine accusers are a. come.	2532
Ac	24:6	a. hath gone about to profane	2532
Ac	24:9	And the Jews a. assented, saying	2532
Ac	24:15	which they themselves a. allow,	2532
Ac	24:26	hoped a. that money	260,1161,2532
Ac	25:22	I would a. hear the man myself.	2532
Ac	25:24	both at Jerusalem, and a. here,	
Ac	26:10	Which thing I a. did in Jerusalem:	2532
Ac	26:26	before whom a. I speak freely:	2532
Ac	26:29	but a. all that hear me this day,	2532
Ac	27:10	lading and ship, but a. of our lives	2532
Ac	27:12	part advised to depart thence a.,	2547
Ac	27:36	and they a. took some meat	2532
Ac	28:9	So when this was done, others a.,	2532
Ac	28:10	a. honoured us with many honours;	2532
Ro	1:6	are ye a. the called of Jesus Christ	2532
Ro	1:13	have some fruit among you a.,	2532
Ro	1:15	preach . . . to you that are at Rome a.	2532
Ro	1:16	Jew first, and a. to the Greek.	2532
Ro	1:24	a. gave them up to uncleanness	2532
Ro	1:27	And likewise a. the men, leaving	2532
Ro	2:9	Jew first, and a. of the Gentile;	2532
Ro	2:10	good, to the Jew first, and a.	2532
Ro	2:12	law shall a. perish without law:	2532
Ro	2:15	conscience a. bearing witness,	4828
Ro	3:7	yet am I a. judged as a sinner?	2504
Ro	3:29	of the Jews only? is he not a. of	2532
Ro	3:29	Yes, of the Gentiles a.:	2532
Ro	4:6	David a. describeth the blessedness	2532
Ro	4:9	or upon the uncircumcision a.?	2532
Ro	4:11	might be imputed unto them a.:	2532
Ro	4:12	who a. walk in the steps of that	2532
Ro	4:16	to that a. which is of the faith of	2532
Ro	4:21	he was able a. to perform	2532
Ro	4:24	But for us a., to whom it shall be	2532
Ro	5:2	By whom a. we have access by faith	2532
Ro	5:3	but we glory in tribulations a.:	2532
Ro	5:11	we a. joy in God through our Lord	2532
Ro	5:15	the offence, so a. is the free gift	2532
Ro	6:4	a. should walk in newness of life	2532
Ro	6:5	we shall be a. in the likeness of	2532
Ro	6:8	believe that we shall a. live with	2532
Ro	6:11	reckon ye a. yourselves to be dead	2532
Ro	7:4	ye a. are become dead to the law	2532
Ro	8:11	shall a. quicken your mortal bodies	2532
Ro	8:17	that we may be a. glorified	2532
Ro	8:21	creature itself a. shall be delivered	2532
Ro	8:23	not only they, but ourselves a.,	2532
Ro	8:26	Spirit a. helpeth our infirmities:	2532
Ro	8:29	foreknow, he a. did predestinate	2532
Ro	8:30	he did predestinate, them he a.	2532
Ro	8:30	he called, them he a. justified:	2532
Ro	8:30	he justified, them he a. glorified.	2532
Ro	8:32	shall he not with him a. freely give	2532
Ro	8:34	who a. maketh intercession for us.	2532
Ro	9:1	a. bearing me witness in the Holy	4828
Ro	9:10	but when Rebecca a. had	2532
Ro	9:24	Jews only, but a. of the Gentiles?	2532
Ro	9:25	As he saith a. in Osee, I will call	2532
Ro	9:27	Esaias a. crieth concerning Israel,	1161
Ro	11:1	For I a. am an Israelite, of the	2532
Ro	11:5	present time a. there is a remnant	2532
Ro	11:16	be holy, the lump is a. holy:	2532
Ro	11:21	heed lest he a. spare not thee	3761
Ro	11:22	otherwise thou a. shalt be cut off.	2532
Ro	11:23	And they a. if they abide not still	1161
Ro	11:31	mercy they a. may obtain mercy	2532
Ro	11:31	so have these a. now not believed,	2532
Ro	13:5	wrath, but a. for conscience sake.	2532
Ro	13:6	for this cause pay ye tribute a.:	2532
Ro	15:7	receive ye one another, as Christ a.	2532
Ro	15:14	I myself a. am persuaded of you,	2532
Ro	15:14	that ye a. are full of goodness,	2532
Ro	15:14	able a. to admonish one another	2532
Ro	15:22	a. I have been much hindered	2532
Ro	15:27	their duty is a. to minister unto	2532
Ro	16:2	of many, and of myself a.	2532
Ro	16:4	a. all the churches of the Gentiles.	2532
Ro	16:7	who a. were in Christ before me	2532
1Co	1:8	Who shall a. confirm you unto	2532
1Co	1:16	And I baptized a. the household	2532
1Co	2:13	Which things a. we speak, not in	2532
1Co	4:8	that we a. might reign with you.	2532
1Co	5:12	what have I to do to judge them a.	2532
1Co	6:14	and will a. raise up us by his own	2532
1Co	7:3	a. the wife unto the husband.	2532
1Co	7:4	a. the husband hath not power of	2532
1Co	7:22	likewise a. he that is called,	2532
1Co	7:34	difference a. between a wife and a	2532
1Co	7:40	I think a. that I have the Spirit	2504
1Co	9:8	saith not the law the same a.?	2532
1Co	10:6	evil things, as they a. lusted.	2548
1Co	10:9	as some of them a. tempted,	2532
1Co	10:10	as some of them a. murmured,	2532
1Co	10:13	the temptation a. make a way to	2532
1Co	11:1	even as I a. am of Christ.	2504
1Co	11:6	not covered, let her a. be shorn:	2532
1Co	11:12	so is the man a. by the woman;	2532
1Co	11:19	must be a. heresies among you,	2532
1Co	11:23	the Lord that which a. I delivered	2532
1Co	11:25	same manner a. he took the cup,	2532
1Co	12:12	are one body: so a. is Christ	2532
1Co	13:12	I know even as a. I am known.	2532
1Co	14:15	pray with the understanding a.:	2532
1Co	14:15	sing with the understanding a.	2532
1Co	14:19	my voice I might teach others a.,	2532
1Co	14:34	under obedience, as a. saith the	2532
1Co	15:1	which a. ye have received,	2532
1Co	15:2	By which a. ye are saved, if ye	2532
1Co	15:3	of all that which I a. received,	2532
1Co	15:8	he was seen of me a.,	2504
1Co	15:14	vain, and your faith is a. vain.	2532
1Co	15:18	they a. which are fallen asleep	2532
1Co	15:21	a. the resurrection of the dead.	2532
1Co	15:28	shall the Son a. himself be subject	2532
1Co	15:40	There are a. celestial bodies,	2532
1Co	15:42	a. is the resurrection of the dead.	2532
1Co	15:48	such are they a. that are earthy:	2532
1Co	15:48	such are they a. that are heavenly.	2532
1Co	15:49	a. bear the image of the heavenly.	2532
1Co	16:4	And if it be meet that I go a.,	2504
1Co	16:10	the work of the Lord, as I a. do.	2532
2Co	1:5	consolation a. aboundeth by Christ	2532
2Co	1:6	sufferings which we a. suffer:	2532
2Co	1:7	shall ye be a. of the consolation.	2532
2Co	1:11	Ye a. helping together by prayer	2532
2Co	1:14	As a. ye have acknowledged us in	2532
2Co	1:14	even as ye a. are ours in the day	2532
2Co	1:22	Who hath a. sealed us, and given	2532
2Co	2:9	For to this end a. did I write,	2532
2Co	2:10	ye forgive any thing, I forgive a.:	2532
2Co	3:6	Who a. hath made us able	2532
2Co	4:10	that the life a. of Jesus might be	2532
2Co	4:11	for Jesus' sake, that the life a.	2532
2Co	4:13	we a. believe, and therefore speak;	2532
2Co	4:14	raise up us a. by Jesus, and shall	2532
2Co	5:5	who a. hath given unto us the	2532
2Co	5:11	and I trust a. are made manifest	2532
2Co	6:1	beseech ye a. that ye receive not	2532
2Co	6:13	my children,) be ye a. enlarged.	2532
2Co	8:6	so he would a. finish in you	2532
2Co	8:6	the same grace a.	2532
2Co	8:7	see that ye abound in this grace a.	2532
2Co	8:10	but a. to be forward a year ago.	2532
2Co	8:11	so there may be a performance a.	2532
2Co	8:14	abundance a. may be a supply for	2532
2Co	8:19	a. chosen of the churches to travel	2532
2Co	8:21	Lord, but a. in the sight of men.	2532
2Co	9:6	sparingly shall reap a. sparingly;	2532
2Co	9:6	shall reap a. bountifully.	2532
2Co	9:12	abundant a. by many thanksgivings	2532
2Co	10:11	such will we be a. in deed when	2532
2Co	10:14	as far as to you a. in preaching	2532
2Co	11:15	his ministers a. be transformed as	2532

2Co 11:18 after the flesh, I will glory **a.** *2504*
2Co 11:21 speak foolishly,) I am bold **a.** *2504*
2Co 13:4 For we **a.** are weak in him, but we *2532*
2Co 13:9 and this **a.** we wish, even your *2532*
Ga 2:1 and took Titus with me **a.** *2532*
Ga 2:10 which I **a.** was forward to do *2532*
Ga 2:13 Barnabas **a.** was carried away *2532*
Ga 2:17 we ourselves **a.** are found sinners. *2532*
Ga 5:21 as I have **a.** told you in time past, *2532*
Ga 5:25 Spirit, let us **a.** walk in the Spirit. *2532*
Ga 6:1 thyself, lest thou **a.** be tempted. *2532*
Ga 6:7 man soweth, that shall he **a.** reap *2532*
Eph 1:11 In whom **a.** we have obtained an *2532*
Eph 1:13 In whom ye **a.** trusted, after that *2532*
Eph 1:13 in whom **a.** after that ye believed, *2532*
Eph 1:15 I **a.**, after I heard of your faith *2504*
Eph 1:21 but **a.** in that which is to come: *2532*
Eph 2:3 **a.** we all had our conversation *2532*
Eph 2:22 In whom ye **a.** are builded together *2532*
Eph 4:9 but that he **a.** descended first into *2532*
Eph 4:10 is the same **a.** that ascended *2532*
Eph 5:2 in love, as Christ **a.** hath loved us, *2532*
Eph 5:25 love your wives, even as Christ **a.** *2532*
Eph 6:9 that your Master **a.** in in heaven; *2532*
Eph 6:21 that ye **a.** may know my affairs, *2532*
Php 1:15 strife; and some **a.** of good will: *2532*
Php 1:20 now **a.** Christ shall be magnified *2532*
Php 1:29 but **a.** to suffer for his sake; *2532*
Php 2:4 man **a.** on the things of others *2532*
Php 2:5 you, which was **a.** in Christ Jesus: *2532*
Php 2:9 God **a.** hath highly exalted him, *2532*
Php 2:18 For the same cause **a.** do ye joy, *2532*
Php 2:19 that I **a.** may be of good comfort, *2504*
Php 2:24 that I **a.** myself shall come shortly *2532*
Php 2:27 not on him only, but on me **a.**, *2532*
Php 3:4 though I might **a.** have confidence *2532*
Php 3:12 for which **a.** I am apprehended *2532*
Php 3:20 whence **a.** we look for the Saviour, *2532*
Php 4:3 I intreat thee **a.**, true yokefellow, *2532*
Php 4:3 with Clement **a.**, and with other *2532*
Php 4:10 wherein ye were **a.** careful, but *2532*
Php 4:15 Now ye Phillippians know **a.**, *2532*
Col 1:6 forth fruit, as it doth **a.** in you, *2532*
Col 1:7 As ye **a.** learned of Epaphras our *2532*
Col 1:8 Who **a.** declared unto us your love *2532*
Col 1:9 For this cause we **a.**, since the day *2532*
Col 1:29 Whereunto I **a.** labour, striving *2532*
Col 2:11 In whom **a.** ye are circumcised *2532*
Col 2:12 with him in baptism, wherein **a.** *2532*
Col 3:4 ye **a.** appear with him in glory. *2532*
Col 3:7 the which ye **a.** walked some time, *2532*
Col 3:8 But now ye **a.** put off all these; *2532*
Col 3:13 Christ forgave you, so **a.** do ye. *2532*
Col 3:15 which **a.** ye are called in one body; *2532*
Col 4:1 knowing that ye **a.** have a Master *2532*
Col 4:3 Withal praying **a.** for us, that God *2532*
Col 4:3 of Christ, for which I am **a.** *2532*
Col 4:16 that it be read **a.** in the church *2532*
1Th 1:5 **a.** in power, and in the Holy Ghost, *2532*
1Th 1:8 but **a.** in every place your faith to *2532*
1Th 2:8 of God only, but **a.** our own souls, *2532*
1Th 2:10 Ye are witnesses, and God **a.**, *2532*
1Th 2:13 For this cause **a.** thank we God *2532*
1Th 2:13 which effectually worketh **a.** in *2532*
1Th 2:14 for ye **a.** have suffered like things *2532*
1Th 3:6 to see us, as we **a.** to see you: *2532*
1Th 4:6 as we **a.** have forewarned you and *2532*
1Th 4:8 **a.** given unto us his holy Spirit. *2532*
1Th 4:14 so them **a.** which sleep in Jesus *2532*
1Th 5:11 edify one another, even as **a.** ye do *2532*
1Th 5:24 that calleth you, who **a.** will do it. *2532*
2Th 1:5 of God, for which ye **a.** suffer: *2532*
2Th 1:11 Wherefore **a.** we pray always for *2532*
1Ti 2:9 In like manner **a.**, that women *2532*
1Ti 3:10 And let these **a.** first be proved; *2532*
1Ti 5:13 but tattlers **a.** and busybodies, *2532*
1Ti 5:20 before all, that others **a.** may fear. *2532*
1Ti 5:25 Likewise **a.** the good works of *2532*
1Ti 6:12 life, whereunto thou art **a.** called, *2532*
2Ti 1:5 I am persuaded that in thee **a.** *2532*
2Ti 1:12 cause I **a.** suffer these things: *2532*
2Ti 2:2 shall be able to teach others **a.** *2532*
2Ti 2:5 if a man **a.** strive for masteries, *2532*
2Ti 2:10 they may **a.** obtain the salvation *2532*
2Ti 2:11 with him, we shall **a.** live with him: *2532*
2Ti 2:12 suffer, we shall **a.** reign with him: *2532*
2Ti 2:12 we deny him, he **a.** will deny us: *2548*
2Ti 2:20 but **a.** of wood and of earth; *2532*
2Ti 2:22 Flee **a.** youthful lusts: but follow *1161*
2Ti 3:1 This know **a.**, that in the last days *1161*
2Ti 3:8 so do these **a.** resist the truth: *2532*
2Ti 3:9 manifest unto all men, as theirs **a.** *2532*
2Ti 4:8 them **a.** that love his appearing. *2532*
2Ti 4:15 Of whom be thou ware **a.**; for he *2532*
Tit 3:3 we . . . **a.** were sometimes foolish *2532*
Tit 3:14 let ours **a.** learn to maintain good *2532*
Phm 9 now **a.** a prisoner of Jesus Christ *2532*
Phm 21 thou wilt **a.** do more than I say. *2532*
Phm 22 withal prepare me **a.** a lodging: *2532*
Heb 1:2 by whom **a.** he made the worlds; *2532*
Heb 2:4 God **a.** bearing them witness, *4901*
Heb 2:14 he **a.** himself likewise took part *2532*
Heb 3:2 as **a.** Moses was faithful in all his *2532*
Heb 4:10 he **a.** hath ceased from his own *2532*
Heb 5:2 he himself **a.** is compassed with *2532*
Heb 5:3 for the people, so **a.** for himself, *2532*
Heb 5:5 So **a.** Christ glorified not himself *2532*
Heb 5:6 As he saith **a.** in another place, *2532*
Heb 7:2 **a.** Abraham gave a tenth part of *2532*
Heb 7:2 and after that **a.** King of Salem, *2532*
Heb 7:9 Levi **a.**, who receiveth tithes, *2532*
Heb 7:12 necessity a change **a.** of the law. *2532*
Heb 7:25 Wherefore he is able **a.** to save *2532*
Heb 8:3 this man have somewhat **a.** to offer. *2532*
Heb 8:6 by how much **a.** he is the mediator *2532*
Heb 9:1 first covenant had **a.** ordinances *2532*
Heb 9:16 there must **a.** of necessity be the
Heb 10:15 the Holy Ghost **a.** is a witness *2532*
Heb 11:11 Through faith **a.** Sara herself *2532*
Heb 11:19 from whence **a.** he received him *2532*
Heb 11:32 of David **a.**, and Samuel, and of *5037*
Heb 12:1 seeing we **a.** are compassed about *2532*
Heb 12:26 not the earth only, but **a.** heaven. *2532*
Heb 13:3 being yourselves **a.** in the body. *2532*
Heb 13:12 Wherefore Jesus **a.**, that he might *2532*
Jas 1:11 so **a.** shall the rich man fade away *2532*
Jas 2:2 in **a.** a poor man in vile raiment; *2532*
Jas 2:11 commit adultery, said **a.**. Do not kill *2532*
Jas 2:19 the devils **a.** believe, and tremble. *2532*
Jas 2:25 Likewise **a.** was not Rahab the *2532*
Jas 2:26 faith without works is dead **a.** *2532*
Jas 3:2 able **a.** to bridle the whole body. *2532*
Jas 3:4 Behold **a.** the ships, which though *2532*
Jas 5:8 Be ye **a.** patient; stablish your *2532*
1Pe 2:5 Ye **a.**, as lively stones, are built up *2532*
1Pe 2:6 Wherefore **a.** it is contained in *2532*
1Pe 2:8 whereunto **a.** they were appointed *2532*
1Pe 2:18 and gentle, but **a.** to the froward. *2532*
1Pe 2:21 because Christ **a.** suffered for us, *2532*
1Pe 3:1 they **a.** may without the word *2532*
1Pe 3:5 in the old time the holy women **a.**, *2532*
1Pe 3:18 For Christ **a.** hath once suffered *2532*
1Pe 3:19 By which **a.** he went and preached *2532*
1Pe 3:21 even baptism doth **a.** now save us *2532*
1Pe 4:6 preached **a.** to them that are dead, *2532*
1Pe 4:13 may be glad **a.** with exceeding joy. *2532*
1Pe 5:1 I exhort, who am **a.** an elder, and *2532*
1Pe 5:1 and **a.** a partaker of the glory *2532*
2Pe 1:19 We have **a.** a more sure word of *2532*
2Pe 2:1 But there were false prophets **a.** *2532*
2Pe 3:10 the earth **a.** and the works that *2532*
2Pe 3:15 brother Paul **a.** according to the *2532*
2Pe 3:16 As **a.** in all his epistles, speaking *2532*
2Pe 3:16 as they do **a.** the other scriptures, *2532*
2Pe 3:17 things before, beware lest ye **a.** *4879*
1Jo 1:3 they ye **a.** may have fellowship *2532*
1Jo 2:2 **a.** for the sins of the whole world. *2532*
1Jo 2:6 ought himself **a.** so to walk, *2532*
1Jo 2:23 the Son hath the Father **a.** *2532*
1Jo 2:24 ye **a.** shall continue in the Son, *2532*
1Jo 3:4 sin transgresseth **a.** the law: *2532*
1Jo 4:11 we ought **a.** to love one another *2532*
1Jo 4:21 loveth God love his brother **a.** *2532*
1Jo 5:1 him **a.** that is begotten of him. *2532*
2Jo 1 but **a.** all they that have known the *2532*
3Jo 12 and we **a.** bear record; and ye *2532*
Jude 8 Likewise **a.** these filthy dreamers *2532*
Jude 14 And Enoch **a.**, the seventh from *2532*
Re 1:7 him, and they **a.** which pierced
Re 1:9 I John, who **a.** am your brother, *2532*
Re 2:6 **the Nicolaitanes, which I a. hate** *2504*
Re 2:15 **So hast thou a. them that hold** *2532*
Re 3:10 **I a. will keep thee from the hour** *2504*
Re 3:21 **even as I a. overcame, and am set** *2504*
Re 6:11 fellowservants **a.** and their *2532*
Re 11:8 where **a.** our Lord was crucified. *2532*
Re 14:17 he **a.** having a sharp sickle *2532*

ALTAR See also ALTARS.

Ge 8:20 Noah builded an **a.** unto the Lord 4196
Ge 8:20 offered burnt offerings on the **a.**. 4196
Ge 12:7 there builded he an **a.** 4196
Ge 12:8 there he builded an **a.** 4196
Ge 13:4 Unto the place of the **a.**, 4196
Ge 13:18 built there an **a.** unto the Lord. 4196
Ge 22:9 Abraham built an **a.** there, 4196
Ge 22:9 laid him on the **a.** 4196
Ge 26:25 he builded an **a.** there, 4196
Ge 33:20 And he erected there an **a.**, 4196
Ge 35:1 make there an **a.** unto God, 4196
Ge 35:3 I will make there an **a.** 4196
Ge 35:7 he built there an **a.**, 4196
Ex 17:15 And Moses built an **a.**, 4196
Ex 20:24 An **a.** of earth thou shalt make 4196
Ex 20:25 if thou wilt make me an **a.** of stone, 4196
Ex 20:26 go up by steps unto mine **a.**, 4196
Ex 21:14 thou shalt take him from mine **a.**, 4196
Ex 24:4 builded an **a.** under the hill, 4196
Ex 24:6 the blood he sprinkled on the **a.** 4196
Ex 27:1 thou shalt make an **a.** 4196
Ex 27:1 the **a.** shall be foursquare: 4196
Ex 27:5 compass of the **a.** beneath, that 4196
Ex 27:5 may be even to the midst of the **a.**. 4196
Ex 27:6 thou shalt make staves for the **a.**, 4196
Ex 27:7 be upon the two sides of the **a.**, 4196
Ex 28:43 when they come near unto the **a.** 4196
Ex 29:12 put it upon the horns of the **a.** 4196
Ex 29:12 beside the bottom of the **a.** 4196
Ex 29:13 burn them upon the **a.**. 4196
Ex 29:16 sprinkle it round about upon the **a.**. 4196
Ex 29:18 burn the whole ram upon the **a.**: 4196
Ex 29:20 sprinkle the blood upon the **a.** 4196
Ex 29:21 the blood that is upon the **a.**, 4196
Ex 29:25 burn them upon the **a.** 4196
Ex 29:36 thou shalt cleanse the **a.**, 4196
Ex 29:37 an atonement for the **a.**, and 4196
Ex 29:37 and it shall be an **a.** most holy: 4196
Ex 29:37 toucheth the **a.** shall be holy. 4196
Ex 29:38 thou shalt offer upon the **a.**; 4196
Ex 29:44 the congregation, and the **a.**: 4196
Ex 30:1 thou shalt make an **a.** to burn. 4196
Ex 30:18 the congregation and the **a.**, 4196
Ex 30:20 when they come near to the **a.** 4196
Ex 30:27 and the **a.** of incense, 4196
Ex 30:28 the **a.** of burnt offering 4196
Ex 31:8 the **a.** of incense, 4196
Ex 31:9 the **a.** of burnt offering 4196
Ex 32:5 he built an **a.** before it; 4196
Ex 35:15 the incense **a.**, and his staves, 4196
Ex 35:16 The **a.** of burnt offering, 4196
Ex 37:25 he made the incense **a.** 4196
Ex 38:1 he made the **a.** of burnt offering 4196
Ex 38:3 he made all the vessels of the **a.**, 4196
Ex 38:4 he made for the **a.** a brasen grate 4196
Ex 38:7 the rings on the sides of the **a.**, 4196
Ex 38:7 made the **a.** hollow with boards
Ex 38:30 and the brasen **a.**, 4196
Ex 38:30 all the vessels of the **a.**, 4196
Ex 39:38 the golden **a.**, and the anointing 4196
Ex 39:39 The brasen **a.**, and his grate 4196
Ex 40:5 thou shalt set the **a.** of gold 4196
Ex 40:6 the **a.** of the burnt offering 4196
Ex 40:7 of the congregation and the **a.**, 4196
Ex 40:10 shalt anoint the **a.** of the burnt 4196
Ex 40:10 all his vessels, and sanctify the **a.**: 4196
Ex 40:10 and it shall be an **a.** most holy. 4196
Ex 40:26 he put the golden **a.** in the tent 4196
Ex 40:29 he put the **a.** of burnt offering 4196
Ex 40:30 tent of the congregation and the **a.**, 4196
Ex 40:32 they came near unto the **a.**, 4196
Ex 40:33 about the tabernacle and the **a.**, 4196
Le 1:5 blood round about upon the **a.** 4196
Le 1:7 shall put fire upon the **a.**, 4196
Le 1:8 the fire which is upon the **a.**: 4196
Le 1:9 the priest shall burn all on the **a.**, 4196
Le 1:11 kill it on the side of the **a.** 4196
Le 1:11 blood round about upon the **a.**. 4196
Le 1:12 the fire which is upon the **a.**: 4196
Le 1:13 burn it upon the **a.**: 4196
Le 1:15 the priest shall bring it unto the **a.**, 4196
Le 1:15 burn it on the **a.**; and the blood 4196

Le	1:15	wrung out at the side of the **a.**:	4196
Le	1:16	cast it beside the **a.**	4196
Le	1:17	the priest shall burn it upon the **a.**,	4196
Le	2:2	burn the memorial of it upon the **a.**,	4196
Le	2:8	he shall bring it unto the **a.**.	4196
Le	2:9	shall burn it upon the **a.**:	4196
Le	2:12	shall not be burnt on the **a.**.	4196
Le	3:2	shall sprinkle the blood upon the **a.**	4196
Le	3:5	shall burn it on the **a.**	4196
Le	3:8	round about upon the **a.**.	4196
Le	3:11	the priest shall burn it upon the **a.**:	4196
Le	3:13	upon the **a.** round about.	4196
Le	3:16	priest shall burn them upon the **a.**:	4196
Le	4:7	blood upon the horns of the **a.**	4196
Le	4:7	the bullock at the bottom of the **a.**	4196
Le	4:10	shall burn them upon the **a.**	4196
Le	4:18	blood upon the horns of the **a.**	4196
Le	4:18	the blood at the bottom of the **a.**	4196
Le	4:19	burn it upon the **a.**.	4196
Le	4:25	it upon the horns of the **a.**	4196
Le	4:25	blood at the bottom of the **a.**	4196
Le	4:26	burn all his fat upon the **a.**,	4196
Le	4:30	it upon the horns of the **a.**	4196
Le	4:30	thereof at the bottom of the **a.**.	4196
Le	4:31	shall burn it upon the **a.**	4196
Le	4:34	it upon the horns of the **a.**	4196
Le	4:34	thereof at the bottom of the **a.**:	4196
Le	4:35	shall burn them upon the **a.**,	4196
Le	5:9	upon the side of the **a.**;	4196
Le	5:9	out at the bottom of the **a.**:	4196
Le	5:12	burn it on the **a.**,	4196
Le	6:9	the burning upon the **a.**	4196
Le	6:9	the fire of the **a.** shall be burning	4196
Le	6:10	with the burnt offering on the **a.**,	4196
Le	6:10	and he shall put them beside the **a.**.	4196
Le	6:12	the fire upon the **a.** shall be	4196
Le	6:13	shall ever be burning upon the **a.**;	4196
Le	6:14	before the Lord, before the **a.**	4196
Le	6:15	shall burn it upon the **a.**	4196
Le	7:2	sprinkle round about upon the **a.**.	4196
Le	7:5	priest shall burn them upon the **a.**	4196
Le	7:31	shall burn the fat upon the **a.**:	4196
Le	8:11	he sprinkled thereof upon the **a.**	4196
Le	8:11	and anointed the **a.** and all	4196
Le	8:15	put it upon the horns of the **a.**	4196
Le	8:15	and purified the **a.**, and poured	4196
Le	8:15	blood at the bottom of the **a.**,	4196
Le	8:16	Moses burnt it upon the **a.**.	4196
Le	8:19	sprinkled the blood upon the **a.**	4196
Le	8:21	burnt the whole ram upon the **a.**:	4196
Le	8:24	sprinkled the blood upon the **a.**	4196
Le	8:28	burnt them on the **a.**	4196
Le	8:30	the blood which was upon the **a.**,	4196
Le	9:7	Go unto the **a.**,	4196
Le	9:8	Aaron therefore went unto the **a.**,	4196
Le	9:9	put it upon the horns of the **a.**,	4196
Le	9:9	the blood at the bottom of the **a.**:	4196
Le	9:10	he burnt upon the **a.**;	4196
Le	9:12	sprinkled round about upon the **a.**.	4196
Le	9:13	and he burnt them upon the **a.**.	4196
Le	9:14	the burnt offering on the **a.**.	4196
Le	9:17	burnt it upon the **a.**,	4196
Le	9:18	which he sprinkled upon the **a.**	4196
Le	9:20	he burnt the fat upon the **a.**:	4196
Le	9:24	upon the **a.** the burnt offering	4196
Le	10:12	eat it without leaven beside the **a.**:	4196
Le	14:20	the meat offering upon the **a.**:	4196
Le	16:12	burning coals of fire from off the **a.**	4196
Le	16:18	he shall go out unto the **a.**	4196
Le	16:18	put it upon the horns of the **a.**	4196
Le	16:20	the **a.**, he shall bring the live goat:	4196
Le	16:25	shall he burn upon the **a.**,	4196
Le	16:33	of the congregation, and for the **a.**,	4196
Le	17:6	sprinkle the blood upon the **a.**	4196
Le	17:11	to you upon the **a.**	4196
Le	21:23	nor come nigh unto the **a.**,	4196
Le	22:22	offering by fire of them upon the **a.**	4196
Nu	3:26	by the **a.** round about,	4196
Nu	4:11	golden **a.** they shall spread a cloth	4196
Nu	4:13	take away the ashes from the **a.**,	4196
Nu	4:14	all the vessels of the **a.**;	4196
Nu	4:26	by the **a.** round about,	4196
Nu	5:25	offer it upon the **a.**:	4196
Nu	5:26	and burn it upon the **a.**,	4196
Nu	7:1	both the **a.** and all the vessels	4196
Nu	7:10	offered for dedicating of the **a.**	4196
Nu	7:10	offered their offering before the **a.**	4196

Nu	7:11	for the dedicating of the **a.**	4196
Nu	7:84	This was the dedication of the **a.**,	4196
Nu	7:88	the dedication of the **a.**, after that	4196
Nu	16:38,	39 plates for a covering of the **a.**	4196
Nu	16:46	put fire therein from off the **a.**,	4196
Nu	18:3	vessels of the sanctuary and the **a.**,	4196
Nu	18:5	the charge of the **a.**:	4196
Nu	18:7	for everything of the **a.**,	4196
Nu	18:17	sprinkle their blood upon the **a.**,	4196
Nu	23:2	on every **a.** a bullock and a ram.	4196
Nu	23:4	upon every **a.** a bullock and a ram.	4196
Nu	23:14	bullock and a ram on every **a.**.	4196
Nu	23:30	a bullock and a ram on every **a.**.	4196
De	12:27	upon the **a.** of the Lord thy God:	4196
De	12:27	shall be poured out upon the **a.**	4196
De	16:21	trees near unto the **a.** of the Lord	4196
De	26:4	set it down before the **a.**	4196
De	27:5	shalt thou build an **a.**	4196
De	27:5	an **a.** of stones:	4196
De	27:6	build the **a.** of the Lord thy God	4196
De	33:10	burnt sacrifice upon thine **a.**.	4196
Jos.	8:30	Then Joshua built an **a.**	4196
Jos.	8:31	an **a.** of whole stones,	4196
Jos.	9:27	and for the **a.** of the Lord,	4196
Jos.	22:10	there an **a.** by Jordan, a great **a.**	4196
Jos.	22:11	have built an **a.** over against	4196
Jos.	22:16	in that ye have builded you an **a.**,	4196
Jos.	22:19	in building you an **a.**	4196
Jos.	22:19	beside the **a.** of the Lord.	4196
Jos.	22:23	That we have built us an **a.**	4196
Jos.	22:26	prepare to build us an **a.**,	4196
Jos.	22:28	Behold the pattern of the **a.** of	4196
Jos.	22:29	to build an **a.** for burnt offerings,	4196
Jos.	22:29	beside the **a.** of the Lord.	4196
Jos.	22:34	called the **a.** Ed:	4196
Jg	6:24	Then Gideon built an **a.** there	4196
Jg	6:25	throw down the **a.** of Baal	4196
Jg	6:26	and build an **a.** unto the Lord	4196
Jg	6:28	the **a.** of Baal was cast down,	4196
Jg	6:28	offered upon the **a.** that was built	4196
Jg	6:30	he hath cast down the **a.** of Baal,	4196
Jg	6:31	because one hath cast down his **a.**	4196
Jg	6:32	because he hath thrown down his **a.**.	4196
Jg	13:20	toward heaven from off the **a.**,	4196
Jg	13:20	in the flame of the **a.**.	4196
Jg	21:4	built there an **a.**,	4196
1Sa	2:28	to offer upon mine **a.**,	4196
1Sa	2:33	I shall not cut off from mine **a.**,	4196
1Sa	7:17	and there he built an **a.**	4196
1Sa	14:35	And Saul built an **a.**	4196
1Sa	14:35	the same was the first **a.**	4196
2Sa	24:18	rear an **a.** unto the Lord	4196
2Sa	24:21	to build an **a.** unto the Lord,	4196
2Sa	24:25	David built there an **a.**	4196
1Ki	1:50	caught hold on the horns of the **a.**.	4196
1Ki	1:51	on the horns of the **a.**, saying, Let	4196
1Ki	1:53	they brought him down from the **a.**.	4196
1Ki	2:28	caught hold on the horns of the **a.**	4196
1Ki	2:29	behold, he is by the **a.**	4196
1Ki	3:4	did Solomon offer upon that **a.**.	4196
1Ki	6:20	and so covered the **a.**	4196
1Ki	6:22	also the whole **a.**	4196
1Ki	7:48	the **a.** of gold, and the table of gold,	4196
1Ki	8:22	Solomon stood before the **a.** of the	4196
1Ki	8:31	the oath come before thine **a.**	4196
1Ki	8:54	he arose from before the **a.**	4196
1Ki	8:64	the brasen **a.** that was before the	4196
1Ki	9:25	upon the **a.** which he built	4196
1Ki	9:25	he burnt incense upon the **a.** that	4196
1Ki	12:32	he offered upon the **a.**.	4196
1Ki	12:33	So he offered upon the **a.** which he	4196
1Ki	12:33	he offered upon the **a.**, and burnt	4196
1Ki	13:1	Jeroboam stood by the **a.**	4196
1Ki	13:2	he cried against the **a.** in the word	4196
1Ki	13:2	and said, O **a.**, **a.**,	4196
1Ki	13:3	the **a.** shall be rent,	4196
1Ki	13:4	which had cried against the **a.** in	4196
1Ki	13:4	he put forth his hand from the **a.**.	4196
1Ki	13:5	the **a.** also was rent, and	4196
1Ki	13:5	the ashes poured out from the **a.**,	4196
1Ki	13:32	against the **a.** in Beth-el,	4196
1Ki	16:32	he reared up an **a.** for Baal	4196
1Ki	18:26	they leaped upon the **a.**	4196
1Ki	18:30	he repaired the **a.** of the Lord	4196
1Ki	18:32	And with the stones he built an **a.**	4196
1Ki	18:32	he made a trench about the **a.**,	4196
1Ki	18:35	the water ran round about the **a.**;	4196

2Ki	11:11	by the **a.** and the temple.	4196
2Ki	12:9	set it beside the **a.**,	4196
2Ki	16:10	saw an **a.** that was at Damascus:	4196
2Ki	16:10	the fashion of the **a.**,	4196
2Ki	16:11	And Urijah the priest built an **a.**	4196
2Ki	16:12	the king saw the **a.**: and	4196
2Ki	16:12	the king approached to the **a.**,	4196
2Ki	16:13	his peace offerings, upon the **a.**.	4196
2Ki	16:14	he brought also the brasen **a.**,	4196
2Ki	16:14	from between the **a.**	4196
2Ki	16:14	put it on the north side of the **a.**	4196
2Ki	16:15	Upon the great **a.** burn	4196
2Ki	16:15	and the brasen **a.** shall be for me	4196
2Ki	18:22	Ye shall worship before this **a.**	4196
2Ki	23:9	came not up to the **a.** of the Lord	4196
2Ki	23:15	the **a.** that was at Beth-el,	4196
2Ki	23:15	both that **a.** and the high place	4196
2Ki	23:16	burned them upon the **a.**,	4196
2Ki	23:17	hast done against the **a.** of Beth-el.	4196
1Ch	6:49	and his sons offered upon the **a.**	4196
1Ch	6:49	and on the **a.** of incense,	4196
1Ch	16:40	upon the **a.** of the burnt offering	4196
1Ch	21:18	set up an **a.** unto the Lord	4196
1Ch	21:22	that I may build an **a.**	4196
1Ch	21:26	built there an **a.** unto the Lord	4196
1Ch	21:26	fire upon the **a.** of burnt offering.	4196
1Ch	21:29	and the **a.** of the burnt offering,	4196
1Ch	22:1	this is the **a.** of the burnt offering	4196
1Ch	28:18	And for the **a.** of incense	4196
2Ch	1:5	the brasen **a.**, that Bezaleel	4196
2Ch	1:6	went up thither to the brasen **a.**	4196
2Ch	4:1	Moreover he made an **a.** of brass,	4196
2Ch	4:19	the golden **a.** also,	4196
2Ch	5:12	stood at the east end of the **a.**,	4196
2Ch	6:12	he stood before the **a.** of the Lord	4196
2Ch	6:22	and the oath come before thine **a.**	4196
2Ch	7:7	brasen **a.** which Solomon had made	4196
2Ch	7:9	kept the dedication of the **a.** seven	4196
2Ch	8:12	on the **a.** of the Lord,	4196
2Ch	15:8	renewed the **a.** of the Lord,	4196
2Ch	23:10	along by the **a.** and the temple,	4196
2Ch	26:16	incense upon the **a.** of incense.	4196
2Ch	26:19	from beside the incense **a.**	4196
2Ch	29:18	the **a.** of burnt offering,	4196
2Ch	29:19	they are before the **a.** of the Lord.	4196
2Ch	29:21	to offer them on the **a.** of the Lord.	4196
2Ch	29:22	sprinkled it on the **a.**:	4196
2Ch	29:22	upon the **a.**: they killed also the	4196
2Ch	29:22	sprinkled the blood upon the **a.**	4196
2Ch	29:24	their blood upon the **a.**,	4196
2Ch	29:27	the burnt offering upon the **a.**	4196
2Ch	32:12	Ye shall worship before one **a.**,	4196
2Ch	33:16	he repaired the **a.** of the Lord,	4196
2Ch	35:16	to offer burnt offerings upon the **a.**	4196
Ezr	3:2	builded the **a.** of the God of Israel,	4196
Ezr	3:3	they set the **a.** upon his bases;	4196
Ezr	7:17	and offer them upon the **a.**	4056
Ne	10:34	to burn upon the **a.** of the Lord	4196
Ps	26:6	so will I compass thine **a.**,	4196
Ps	43:4	Then will I go unto the **a.** of God,	4196
Ps	51:19	they offer bullocks upon thine **a.**.	4196
Ps	118:27	unto the horns of the **a.**.	4196
Isa	6:6	with the tongs from off the **a.**:	4196
Isa	19:19	in that day shall there be an **a.**	4196
Isa	27:9	maketh all the stones of the **a.**	4196
Isa	36:7	Ye shall worship before this **a.**?	4196
Isa	56:7	accepted upon mine **a.**;	4196
Isa	60:7	with acceptance on mine **a.**,	4196
La	2:7	The Lord hath cast off his **a.**,	4196
Eze	8:5	at the gate of the **a.** this image	4196
Eze	8:16	between the porch and the **a.**,	4196
Eze	9:2	stood beside the brasen **a.**	4196
Eze	40:46	the keepers of the charge of the **a.**:	4196
Eze	40:47	the **a.** that was before the house	4196
Eze	41:22	The **a.** of wood was three cubits	4196
Eze	43:13	measures of the **a.** after the cubits:	4196
Eze	43:13	the higher place of the **a.**.	4196
Eze	43:15	So the **a.** shall be four cubits:	741
Eze	43:15	and from the **a.** and upward	741
Eze	43:16	And the **a.** shall be twelve cubits	741
Eze	43:18	are the ordinances of the **a.**	4196
Eze	43:22	they shall cleanse the **a.**,	4196
Eze	43:26	Seven days shall they purge the **a.**	4196
Eze	43:27	your burnt offerings upon the **a.**,	4196
Eze	45:19	four corners of the settle of the **a.**,	4196
Eze	47:1	at the south side of the **a.**.	4196
Joe	1:13	howl, ye ministers of the **a.**	4196

Joe 2:17 weep between the porch and the **a.**, 4196
Am 2:8 laid to pledge by every **a.**, 4196
Am 3:14 the horns of the **a.** shall be cut off, 4196
Am 9:1 the Lord standing upon the **a.**: 4196
Zec 9:15 as the corners of the **a.**. 4196
Zec 14:20 be like the bowls before the **a.**. 4196
Mal 1:7 offer polluted bread upon mine **a.**; 4196
Mal 1:10 do ye kindle fire on mine **a.** for 4196
Mal 2:13 covering the **a.** of the Lord with 4196
Mt 5:23 **bring thy gift to the a.,** *2379*
Mt 5:24 **thy gift before the a.,** *2379*
Mt 23:18 **shall swear by the a.,** *2379*
Mt 23:19 **the gift, or the a.** *2379*
Mt 23:20 **shall swear by the a.,** *2379*
Mt 23:35 **the temple and the a..** *2379*
Lu 1:11 of the **a.** of incense. *2379*
Lu 11:51 **between the a. and the temple:** *2379*
Ac 17:23 I found an **a.** with this inscription, *1041*
1Co 9:13 and they which wait at the **a.** *2379*
1Co 9:13 partakers with the **a.**? *2379*
1Co 10:18 partakers of the **a.**? *2379*
Heb 7:13 no man gave attendance at the **a.** *2379*
Heb 13:10 We have an **a.**, whereof *2379*
Jas 2:21 offered Isaac his son upon the **a.**? *2379*
Re 6:9 under the **a.** the souls *2379*
Re 8:3 stood at the **a.**, having a golden *2379*
Re 8:3 of all saints upon the golden **a.** *2379*
Re 8:5 filled it with fire of the **a.**, *2379*
Re 9:13 horns of the golden **a.** *2379*
Re 11:1 the temple of God, and the **a.**, *2379*
Re 14:18 another angel came out from the **a.**, *2379*
Re 16:7 I heard another out of the **a.** say, *2379*

ALTARS
Ex 34:13 But ye shall destroy their **a.**, 4196
Nu 3:31 the candlestick, and the **a.**, 4196
Nu 23:1 Build me here seven **a.**, 4196
Nu 23:4 I have prepared seven **a.**, 4196
Nu 23:14 and built seven **a.**, 4196
Nu 23:29 Build me here seven **a.**, and prepare 4196
De 7:5 ye shall destroy their **a.**, 4196
De 12:3 ye shall overthrow their **a.**, 4196
Jg 2:2 ye shall throw down their **a.**: 4196
1Ki 19:10, 14 thrown down thine **a.**, 4196
2Ki 11:18 his **a.** and his images 4196
2Ki 11:18 the priest of Baal before the **a.** 4196
2Ki 18:22 whose **a.** Hezekiah hath taken 4196
2Ki 21:3 he reared up **a.** for Baal, 4196
2Ki 21:4 he built **a.** in the house of the Lord, 4196
2Ki 21:5 built **a.** for all the host of heaven 4196
2Ki 23:12 the **a.** that were on the top 4196
2Ki 23:12 the **a.** which Manasseh had made 4196
2Ki 23:20 that were there upon the **a.**, 4196
2Ch 14:3 he took away the **a.** of the strange 4196
2Ch 23:17 brake his **a.** and his images 4196
2Ch 23:17 the priest of Baal before the **a.** 4196
2Ch 28:24 **a.** in every corner of Jerusalem 4196
2Ch 30:14 they arose and took away the **a.** 4196
2Ch 30:14 the **a.** for incense took they away,
2Ch 31:1 the **a.** out of all Judah 4196
2Ch 32:12 away his high places and his **a.**, 4196
2Ch 33:3 he reared up **a.** for Baalim, 4196
2Ch 33:4 Also he built **a.** in the house 4196
2Ch 33:5 built **a.** for all the host of heaven 4196
2Ch 33:15 all the **a.** that he had built 4196
2Ch 34:4 they brake down the **a.** of Baalim 4196
2Ch 34:5 bones of the priests upon their **a.**, 4196
2Ch 34:7 when he had broken down the **a.** 4196
Ps 84:3 even thine **a.**, O Lord of hosts, 4196
Isa 17:8 he shall not look to the **a.**, 4196
Isa 36:7 whose **a.** Hezekiah hath taken 4196
Isa 65:3 burneth incense upon **a.** of brick;
Jer 11:13 set up **a.** to that shameful thing, 4196
Jer 11:13 even **a.** to burn incense unto Baal. 4196
Jer 17:1 upon the horns of your **a.**; 4196
Jer 17:2 their children remember their **a.** 4196
Eze 6:4 your **a.** shall be desolate, 4196
Eze 6:5 your bones round about your **a.** 4196
Eze 6:6 that your **a.** may be laid waste 4196
Eze 6:13 round about their **a.**, 4196
Ho 8:11 Ephraim hath made many **a.** to sin, 4196
Ho 8:11 **a.** shall be unto him to sin. 4196
Ho 10:1 he hath increased the **a.**; 4196
Ho 10:2 he shall break down their **a.** 4196
Ho 10:8 shall come up on their **a.**; 4196
Ho 12:11 their **a.** are as heaps 4196
Am 3:14 I will also visit the **a.** of Beth-el: 4196
Ro 11:3 and digged down thine **a.**; *2379*

AL-TASCHITH (al-tas'-kith)
Ps 57:*title* To the chief Musician, **A.**, 516
Ps 58:*title* chief Musician, **A.**, Michtam of 516
Ps 59:*title* **A.**, Michtam of David; when Saul 516
Ps 75:*title* Musician, **A.**, A Psalm or Song 516

ALTER See also ALTERED; ALTERETH.
Le 27:10 He shall not **a.** it, nor change it, 2498
Ezr 6:11 that whosoever shall **a.** this word, 8133
Ezr 6:12 that shall put to their hand to **a.** 8133
Ps 89:34 covenant will I not break, nor **a.** 8138

ALTERED
Es 1:19 it be not **a.**, That Vashti come 5674
Lu 9:29 of his countenance was **a.**, *1096,2087*

ALTERETH
Da 6:8,12 and Persians, which **a.** not. 5709

ALTHOUGH
Ex 13:17 **a.** that was near; for God said, 3588
Jos 22:17 **a.** there was a plague in the
2Sa 23:5 **A.** my house be not so with God; 3588
2Sa 23:5 **a.** he make it not to grow. 3588
1Ki 20:5 **A.** I have sent unto thee, saying, 3588
Es 7:4 held my tongue, **a.** the enemy 3588
Job 2:3 integrity, **a.** thou movedst me
Job 5:6 **A.** affliction cometh not forth 3588
Job 35:14 **A.** thou sayest thou shalt 637,3588
Jer 31:32 **a.** I was an husband unto them,
Eze 7:13 is sold, **a.** they were yet alive:
Eze 11:16 **A.** I have cast them far off 3588
Eze 11:16 and **a.** I have scattered them 272
Hab 3:17 **A.** the fig tree shall not blossom, 272
Mk 14:29 **A.** all shall be offended, *2532,1487*
Heb 4:3 **a.** the works were finished *2543*

ALL-TO (Jg 9:53) See ALL; ALTOGETHER.

ALTOGETHER
Ge 18:21 whether they have done **a.** 3617
Ex 11:1 thrust you out hence **a.** 3617
Ex 19:18 And mount Sinai was **a.** on a 3605
Nu 16:13 make thyself **a.** a prince over us? 1571
Nu 23:11 behold, thou hast blest them **a.**
Nu 24:10 behold, thou hast **a.** blessed them
Nu 30:14 her husband **a.** hold his peace
De 16:20 which is **a.** just shalt thou follow,
2Ch 12:12 he would not destroy him **a.**: 3617
Es 4:14 For if thou **a.** holdest thy peace
Job 13:5 O that ye would **a.** hold your
Job 27:12 why then are ye thus **a.** vain?
Ps 19:9 are true and righteous **a.** 3162
Ps 39:5 every man at his best state is **a.** 3605
Ps 50:21 thoughtest that I was **a.** such an
Ps 53:3 they are **a.** become filthy; 3162
Ps 62:9 they are **a.** lighter than vanity. 3162
Ps 139:4 lo, O Lord, thou knowest it **a.** 3605
Ca 5:16 is most sweet: yea, he is **a.** lovely. 3605
Isa 10:8 Are not my princes **a.** kings? 3162
Jer 5:5 these have **a.** broken the yoke, 3162
Jer 10:8 they are **a.** brutish and foolish: 259
Jer 15:18 wilt thou be **a.** unto me as a
Jer 30:11 not leave thee **a.** unpunished.
Jer 49:12 that shall **a.** go unpunished?
Joh 9:34 Thou wast **a.** born in sins, *3650*
Ac 26:29 both almost, and **a.** such as *1722,4183*
1Co 5:10 Yet not **a.** with the fornicators *3843*
1Co 9:10 Or saith he it **a.** for our sakes? *3843*

ALUSH (a'-lush)
Nu 33:13 Dophkah, and encamped in **A.** 442
Nu 33:14 removed from **A.**, and encamped 442

ALVAH (al'-vah) See also ALIAH.
Ge 36:40 names; duke Timnah, duke **A.**, 5933

ALVAN (al'-van) See also ALIAN.
Ge 36:23 children of Shobal were these; **A.**, 5935

ALWAY See also ALWAYS.
Ex 25:30 the table shewbread before me **a.** 8548
Nu 9:16 So it was **a.**: the cloud covered it 8548
De 11:1 his commandments, **a.** 3605,3117
De 28:33 oppressed and crushed **a.**: 3605,3117
2Sa 9:10 shall eat bread **a.** at my table. 8548
1Ki 11:36 have a light **a.** before me 3605,3117
2Ki 8:19 to give him **a.** a light, 3605,3117
Job 7:16 I would not live **a.** 5769
Ps 9:18 needy shall not **a.** be fogotten: 5331
Ps 119:112 heart to perform thy statutes **a.**, 5769
Pr 28:14 Happy is the man that feareth **a.**: 8548
Mt 28:20 **I am with you a., even unto** *3956,2250*
Joh 7:6 **but your time is a. ready.** *3842*
Ac 10:2 the people, and prayed to God **a.** *1275*
Ro 11:10 bow down their back **a.** *1275*
2Co 4:11 we which live are **a.** delivered *104*
2Co 6:10 As sorrowful, yet **a.** rejoicing; *104*
Php 4:4 Rejoice in the Lord **a.**: *104*
Col 4:6 Let your speech be **a.** with grace, *104*
1Th 2:16 to fill up their sins **a.**: *104*
2Th 2:13 bound to give thanks **a.** to God *104*
Tit 1:12 the Cretians are **a.** liars, *104*
Heb 3:10 They do **a.** err in their heart: *104*

ALWAYS See also ALWAY.
Ge 6:3 My spirit shall not **a.** strive with 5769
Ex 27:20 to cause the lamp to burn **a.** 8548
Ex 28:38 it shall be **a.** upon his forehead, 8548
De 5:29 all my commandments **a.**, 3605,3117
De 6:24 for our good **a.**, 3605,3117
De 11:12 the Lord thy God are **a.** upon it, 8548
De 14:23 to fear the Lord thy God **a.**, 3605,3117
1Ch 16:15 Be ye mindful **a.** of his covenant; 5769
2Ch 18:7 good unto me, but **a.** evil: 3605,3117
Job 27:10 will he **a.** call upon God? 6256
Job 32:9 Great men are not **a.** wise:
Ps 10:5 His ways are **a.** grievous; 3605,6256
Ps 16:8 I have set the Lord **a.** before me: 8548
Ps 103:9 He will not **a.** chide: 5331
Pr 5:19 be thou ravished **a.** with her love. 8548
Pr 8:30 rejoicing **a.** before him; 3605,6256
Ec 9:8 Let thy garments be **a.** white; 3605,6256
Isa 57:16 neither will I be **a.** wroth: 5331
Jer 20:17 her womb to be **a.** great with me. 5769
Eze 38:8 which have been **a.** waste: 8548
Mt 18:10 **their angels do a. behold the** *1223,3956*
Mt 26:11 **ye have the poor a. with you;** *3842*
Mt 26:11 **but me ye have not a.** *3842*
Mk 5:5 **a.**, night and day, he was in the *1275*
Mk 14:7 **ye have the poor with you a.,** *3842*
Mk 14:7 **but me ye have not a.** *3842*
Lu 18:1 that men ought **a.** to pray, *3842*
Lu 21:36 **pray a., that ye may be** *1722,3956,2540*
Joh 8:29 **I do a. those things that please** *3842*
Joh 11:42 **I knew that thou hearest me a.:** *3842*
Joh 12:8 **the poor a. ye have with you;** *3842*
Joh 12:8 **but me ye have not a.** *3842*
Joh 18:20 **whither the Jews a. resort;** *3842*
Ac 2:25 I foresaw the Lord **a.** before *1223,3956*
Ac 7:51 ye do **a.** resist the Holy Ghost: *104*
Ac 24:3 We accept it **a.**, and in all places, *3839*
Ac 24:16 **a.** a conscience void of offence *1275*
Ro 1:9 mention of you **a.** in my prayers; *3842*
1Co 1:4 thank my God **a.** on your behalf, *3842*
1Co 15:58 **a.** abounding in the work of the *3842*
2Co 2:14 **a.** causeth us to triumph in Christ, *3842*
2Co 4:10 **A.** bearing about in the body *3842*
2Co 5:6 Therefore we are **a.** confident, *3842*
2Co 9:8 that ye, **a.** having all sufficiency *3842*
Ga 4:18 affected **a.** in a good thing, *3842*
Eph 5:20 Giving thanks **a.** for all things *3842*
Eph 6:18 Praying **a.** with all *1722,3956,2540*
Php 1:4 **A.** in every prayer of mine for you *3842*
Php 1:20 with all boldness, as **a.**, so now *3842*
Php 2:12 my beloved, as ye have **a.** obeyed, *3842*
Col 1:3 praying **a.** for you, *3842*
Col 4:12 **a.** labouring fervently for you *3842*
1Th 1:2 We give thanks to God **a.** for you *3842*
1Th 3:6 have good remembrance of us **a.**, *3842*
2Th 1:3 bound to thank God **a.** for you, *3842*
2Th 1:11 Wherefore also we pray **a.** for you, *3842*
2Th 3:16 you peace **a.** by all means. *1223,3956*
Phm 4 mention of thee **a.** in my prayers, *3842*
Heb 9:6 went **a.** into the first tabernacle, *1275*
1Pe 3:15 be ready **a.** to give an answer *104*
2Pe 1:12 **a.** in remembrance of these things, *104*
2Pe 1:15 these things **a.** in remembrance. *1539*

AM
Ge 4:9 **A.** I my brother's keeper?
Ge 15:1 Fear not, Abram: I **a.** thy shield,
Ge 15:7 I **a.** the Lord that brought thee
Ge 17:1 unto him, I **a.** the Almighty God;
Ge 18:12 herself, saying, After I **a.** waxed
Ge 18:13 surety bear a child, which **a.** old?
Ge 18:27 speak unto the Lord, which **a.** but
Ge 22:1 and he said, Behold, here I **a.**
Ge 22:7 and he said, Here **a.** I, my son.
Ge 22:11 Abraham: and he said, Here **a.** I.
Ge 23:4 I **a.** a stranger and a sojourner
Ge 24:24 I **a.** the daughter of Bethuel the

Ge	24:34	he said, I **a.** Abraham's servant	
Ge	25:22	said, If it be so, why **a.** I thus?	
Ge	25:30	for I **a.** faint: therefore was his	
Ge	25:32	Behold, I **a.** at the point to die:	
Ge	26:24	I **a.** the God of Abraham thy father:	
Ge	26:24	I **a.** with thee, and will bless thee,	
Ge	27:1	said unto him, Behold, here **a.** I.	
Ge	27:2	Behold now, I **a.** old, I know not	
Ge	27:11	hairy man, and I **a.** a smooth man:	
Ge	27:18	Here **a.** I; who art thou, my son?	
Ge	27:19	his father, I **a.** Esau thy firstborn;	
Ge	27:24	son Esau? And he said, I **a.**.	
Ge	27:32	I **a.** thy son, thy firstborn Esau.	
Ge	27:46	said to Isaac, I **a.** weary of my life,	
Ge	28:13	said, I **a.** the Lord God of Abraham	
Ge	28:15	And, behold, I **a.** with thee,	
Ge	30:2	and he said, **A.** I in God's stead,	
Ge	30:13	And Leah said, Happy **a.** I,	
Ge	31:11	Jacob: and I said, Here **a.** I.	
Ge	31:13	I **a.** the God of Bethel, where thou	
Ge	32:10	I **a.** not worthy of the least of all	
Ge	32:10	and now I **a.** become two bands.	
Ge	35:11	unto him, I **a.** God Almighty:	
Ge	37:13	And he said to him, Here **a.** I.	
Ge	38:25	whose these are, **a.** I with child:	
Ge	41:44	I **a.** Pharaoh, and without thee	
Ge	43:14	bereaved of my children, I **a.**	
Ge	45:3	said unto his brethren, I **a.** Joseph;	
Ge	45:4	he said, I **a.** Joseph your brother,	
Ge	46:2	Jacob: and he said, Here **a.** I.	
Ge	46:3	I **a.** God, the God of thy father:	
Ge	49:29	**a.** to be gathered unto my people:	
Ge	50:19	for **a.** I in the place of God?	
Ex	3:4	Moses. And he said, Here **a.** I.	
Ex	3:6	he said, I **a.** the God of thy father,	
Ex	3:8	I **a.** come down to deliver them	
Ex	3:11	Who **a.** I, that I should go unto	
Ex	3:14	said unto Moses, I **A.** that I **A.**:	1961
Ex	3:14	Israel, I **A.** hath sent me unto you.	1961
Ex	3:19	I **a.** sure that the king of Egypt	
Ex	4:10	O Lord, I **a.** not eloquent,	
Ex	4:10	but I **a.** slow of speech, and of a	
Ex	6:2	and said unto him, I **a.** the Lord:	
Ex	6:6	children of Israel, I **a.** the Lord,	
Ex	6:7	know that I **a.** the Lord your God,	
Ex	6:8	you for a heritage: I **a.** the Lord.	
Ex	6:12	me, who **a.** of uncircumcised lips?	
Ex	6:29	unto Moses, saying, I **a.** the Lord:	
Ex	6:30	Behold, I **a.** of uncircumcised lips,	
Ex	7:5	shall know that I **a.** the Lord,	
Ex	7:17	shalt know that I **a.** the Lord:	
Ex	8:22	I **a.** the Lord in the midst of the	
Ex	9:29	As soon as I **a.** gone out of the city,	
Ex	10:2	know how that I **a.** the Lord.	
Ex	12:12	execute judgment: I **a.** the Lord.	
Ex	14:4	may know that I **a.** the Lord.	
Ex	14:18	that I **a.** the Lord, when I have	
Ex	15:26	for I **a.** the Lord that healeth thee.	
Ex	16:12	know that I **a.** the Lord your God.	
Ex	18:6	I thy father in law Jethro **a.** come	
Ex	20:2	I **a.** the Lord thy God, which have	
Ex	20:5	for I the Lord thy God **a.** a jealous	
Ex	22:27	that I will hear; for I **a.** gracious.	
Ex	29:46	they shall know that I **a.** the Lord	
Ex	29:46	dwell among them: I **a.** the Lord.	
Ex	31:13	**a.** the Lord that doth sanctify you.	
Le	8:35	die not: for so I **a.** commanded.	
Le	10:13	by fire: for so I **a.** commanded.	
Le	11:44	For I **a.** the Lord your God:	
Le	11:44	and ye shall be holy; for I **a.** holy:	
Le	11:45	For I **a.** the Lord that bringeth you	
Le	11:45	therefore be holy, for I **a.** holy.	
Le	18:2	unto them, I **a.** the Lord your God.	
Le	18:4	therein: I **a.** the Lord your God.	
Le	18:5	shall live in them: I **a.** the Lord.	
Le	18:6	their nakedness: I **a.** the Lord.	
Le	18:21	the name of thy God: I **a.** the Lord.	
Le	18:30	therein: I **a.** the Lord your God.	
Le	19:2	for I the Lord your God **a.** holy.	
Le	19:3	sabbaths: I **a.** the Lord your God.	
Le	19:4	gods: I **a.** the Lord your God.	
Le	19:10	stranger: I **a.** the Lord your God.	
Le	19:12	the name of thy God: I **a.** the Lord.	
Le	19:14	shalt fear thy God; I **a.** the Lord.	
Le	19:16	of thy neighbour: I **a.** the Lord.	
Le	19:18	neighbour as thyself: I **a.** the Lord.	3605
Le	19:25	thereof: I **a.** the Lord your God.	
Le	19:28	any marks upon you: I **a.** the Lord.	3605
Le	19:30	my sanctuary: I **a.** the Lord.	
Le	19:31	by them: I **a.** the Lord your God.	
Le	19:32	and fear thy God: I **a.** the Lord.	
Le	19:34	of Egypt: I **a.** the Lord your God.	
Le	19:36	I **a.** the Lord your God, which	
Le	19:37	and do them: I **a.** the Lord.	
Le	20:7	be ye holy: for I **a.** the Lord	
Le	20:8	I **a.** the Lord which sanctify you.	
Le	20:24	I **a.** the Lord your God, which have	
Le	20:26	for I the Lord **a.** holy, and have	
Le	21:8	Lord, which sanctify you, **a.** holy.	
Le	21:12	God is upon him: I **a.** the Lord.	
Le	22:2	they hallow unto me: I **a.** the Lord.	
Le	22:3	off from my presence: I **a.** the Lord.	
Le	22:8	himself therewith: I **a.** the Lord.	
Le	22:30	until the morrow: I **a.** the Lord.	
Le	22:31	and do them: I **a.** the Lord.	
Le	22:32	of Israel: I **a.** the Lord which	
Le	22:33	to be your God: I **a.** the Lord.	
Le	23:22	stranger: I **a.** the Lord your God.	
Le	23:43	Egypt: I **a.** the Lord your God.	
Le	24:22	country: for I **a.** the Lord your God.	
Le	25:17	thy God: for I **a.** the Lord your God.	
Le	25:38	I **a.** the Lord your God, which	
Le	25:55	Egypt: I am the Lord your God.	
Le	26:1	unto it: for I **a.** the Lord your God.	
Le	26:2	my sanctuary: I **a.** the Lord.	
Le	26:13	I **a.** the Lord your God, which	
Le	26:44	them: for I **a.** the Lord their God.	
Le	26:45	might be their God: I **a.** the Lord.	
Nu	3:13	mine shall they be: I **a.** the Lord.	
Nu	3:41	Levites for me (I **a.** the Lord)	
Nu	3:45	Levites shall be mine: I **a.** the Lord.	
Nu	10:10	God: I **a.** the Lord your God.	
Nu	11:14	I **a.** not able to bear all this people	
Nu	11:21	The people among whom I **a.**,	
Nu	15:41	I **a.** the Lord your God, which	
Nu	15:41	God: I **a.** the Lord your God.	
Nu	18:20	I **a.** thy part and thine inheritance.	
Nu	22:30	**A.** not I thine ass, upon which thou	
Nu	22:37	**a.** I not able indeed to promote	
Nu	22:38	Lo, I **a.** come unto thee: have I now	
De	1:9	I **a.** not able to bear you myself	
De	1:42	fight; for I **a.** not among you;	
De	5:6	I **a.** the Lord thy God, which	
De	5:9	the Lord thy God **a.** a jealous God,	
De	26:3	that I **a.** come unto the country	
De	29:6	know that I **a.** the Lord your God.	
De	31:2	I **a.** an hundred and twenty years	
De	31:27	while I **a.** yet alive with you this	
De	32:39	even I, **a.** he, and there is no god	
Jos	5:14	the host of the Lord **a.** I now come.	
Jos	14:10	I **a.** this day fourscore and five	
Jos	14:11	As yet I **a.** as strong this day as I	
Jos	17:14	inherit, seeing I **a.** a great people,	
Jos	23:2	I **a.** old and stricken in age:	
Jos	23:14	this day I **a.** going the way of all	
Jg	4:19	little water to drink; for I **a.** thirsty.	
Jg	6:10	unto you, I **a.** the Lord your God;	
Jg	6:15	and I **a.** the least in my father's	
Jg	8:5	and I **a.** pursuing after Zebah	
Jg	9:2	I **a.** your bone and your flesh.	
Jg	13:11	the woman? And he said, I **a.**	
Jg	17:9	I **a.** a Levite of Beth-lehem-judah,	
Jg	18:4	hired me, and I **a.** his priest.	
Jg	19:18	Ephraim; from thence **a.** I:	
Jg	19:18	but I **a.** now going to the house	
Ru	1:12	for I **a.** too old to have an husband.	
Ru	2:10	of me, seeing I **a.** stranger?	
Ru	3:9	answered, I **a.** Ruth thine handmaid:	
Ru	3:12	true that I **a.** thy near kinsman:	
Ru	4:4	beside thee; and I **a.** after thee.	
1Sa	1:8	**a.** not I better to thee than ten sons?	
1Sa	1:15	I **a.** a woman of a sorrowful spirit:	
1Sa	1:26	I **a.** the woman that stood by thee.	
1Sa	3:4	and he answered, Here **a.** I.	
1Sa	3:5	and said, Here **a.** I; for thou	
1Sa	3:6,8	went to Eli, and said, Here **a.** I;	
1Sa	3:16	son. And he answered, Here **a.** I.	
1Sa	4:16	Eli, I **a.** he that came out of the	
1Sa	9:19	Saul, and said, I **a.** the seer:	
1Sa	9:21	answered and said, **A.** not I	
1Sa	12:2	and I **a.** old and grayheaded;	
1Sa	12:3	Behold, here I **a.**: witness against	
1Sa	14:7	I **a.** with thee according to thy	
1Sa	16:2	I **a.** come to sacrifice to the Lord.	
1Sa	16:5	Peaceably: I **a.** come to sacrifice	
1Sa	17:8	**a.** not I a Philistine, and ye	
1Sa	17:43	said unto David, **A.** I a dog,	
1Sa	17:58	I **a.** the son of thy servant Jesse	
1Sa	8:18	David said unto Saul, Who **a.** I?	
1Sa	8:23	that I **a.** a poor man, and	
1Sa	22:12	he answered, Here I **a.**, my lord.	
1Sa	28:15	answered, I **a.** sore distressed;	
1Sa	30:13	said, I **a.** a young man of Egypt,	
2Sa	1:3	the camp of Israel **a.** I escaped.	
2Sa	1:7	me. And I answered, Here **a.** I.	
2Sa	1:8	him, I **a.** an Amalekite.	
2Sa	1:13	I **a.** the son of a stranger, an	
2Sa	1:26	I **a.** distressed for thee, my brother	
2Sa	2:20	Asahel? And he answered, I **a.**.	
2Sa	3:8	**A.** I a dog's head, which against	
2Sa	3:39	And I **a.** this day weak, though	
2Sa	7:18	he said, Who **a.** I, O Lord God?	
2Sa	9:8	upon such a dead dog as I **a.**?	
2Sa	11:5	David, and said, I **a.** with child.	
2Sa	14:5	she answered, I **a.** indeed a widow	
2Sa	14:15	that I **a.** come to speak of this	
2Sa	14:32	Wherefore **a.** I come from Geshur?	
2Sa	15:26	behold, here **a.** I, let him do to me	
2Sa	19:20	I **a.** come the first this day of all	
2Sa	19:22	do not I know that I **a.** this day	
2Sa	19:35	I **a.** this day fourscore years old:	
2Sa	20:17	And he answered, I **a.** he. Then	
2Sa	20:19	I **a.** one of them that are peaceable	
2Sa	24:14	I **a.** in a great strait: let us fall	
1Ki	3:7	and I **a.** but a little child: I know	
1Ki	8:20	and I **a.** risen up in the room of	
1Ki	13:14	from Judah? And he said, I **a.**	
1Ki	13:18	I **a.** a prophet also as thou art;	
1Ki	13:31	when I **a.** dead, then bury me in	
1Ki	14:6	for I **a.** sent to thee with heavy	
1Ki	17:12	I **a.** gathering two sticks, that I	
1Ki	18:8	And he answered him, I **a.**:	
1Ki	18:12	as soon as I **a.** gone from thee,	
1Ki	18:36	and that I **a.** thy servant, and that	
1Ki	19:4	for I **a.** not better than my fathers.	
1Ki	19:10	and I, even I only, **a.** left; and	
1Ki	19:14	I only, **a.** left; and they seek my	
1Ki	20:4	saying, I **a.** thine, and all that I	
1Ki	20:13	thou shalt know that I **a.** the Lord.	
1Ki	20:28	ye shall know that I **a.** the Lord.	
1Ki	22:4	I **a.** as thou art, my people as thy	
1Ki	22:34	of the host; for I **a.** wounded.	
2Ki	2:10	see me when I **a.** taken from thee,	
2Ki	3:7	I **a.** as thou art, my people as thy	
2Ki	5:7	**A.** I God, to kill and to make alive,	
2Ki	16:7	I **a.** thy servant and thy son: come	
2Ki	18:25	**A.** I now come up without the Lord	
2Ki	19:23	I **a.** come up to the height of the	
2Ki	21:12	I **a.** bringing such evil upon	
1Ch	17:16	Who **a.** I, O Lord God, and what is	
1Ch	21:13	I **a.** in a great strait: let me fall	
1Ch	29:14	But who **a.** I, and what is my people,	
2Ch	2:6	who **a.** I then, that I should build	
2Ch	2:9	the house which I **a.** about to build	
2Ch	6:10	for I **a.** risen up in the room of	
2Ch	6:10	**a.** set on the throne of Israel,	
2Ch	18:3	I **a.** as thou art, and my people as	
2Ch	18:33	of the host; for I **a.** wounded.	
2Ch	35:23	me away; for I **a.** sore wounded.	
Ezr	9:6	God, I **a.** ashamed and blush to lift	
Ne	6:3	I **a.** doing a great work, so that I	
Ne	6:11	there, that, being as I **a.**, would	
Es	5:12	to morrow **a.** I invited unto her	
Job	1:15	and I only **a.** escaped alone to tell	
Job	1:16	consumed them; and I only **a.**	
Job	1:17	the sword; and I ony **a.** escaped	
Job	1:19	are dead; and I only **a.** escaped	
Job	7:3	So **a.** I made to possess months of	
Job	7:4	and I **a.** full of tossings to and fro.	
Job	7:8	eyes are upon me, and I **a.** not.	
Job	7:12	**A.** I a sea, or a whale, that thou	
Job	7:20	so that I **a.** a burden to myself?	
Job	9:20	if I say, I **a.** perfect, it shall	
Job	9:28	I **a.** afraid of all my sorrows, I know	
Job	9:32	For he is not a man, as I **a.**, that I	
Job	10:7	Thou knowest that I **a.** not wicked;	
Job	10:15	I **a.** full of confusion: therefore	
Job	11:4	doctrine is pure, and I **a.** clean in	
Job	12:3	I **a.** not inferior to you: yea, who	1961
Job	12:4	I **a.** as one mocked of his neighbour,	
Job	13:2	also: I **a.** not inferior unto you.	

Job 16:6 though I forbear, what **a.** I eased?
Job 19:7 cry out of wrong, but I **a.** not heard:
Job 19:10 and I **a.** gone: and mine hope hath
Job 19:15 I **a.** an alien in their sight
Job 19:20 and I **a.** escaped with the skin of
Job 21:6 I remember I **a.** afraid, and
Job 23:15 Therefore **a.** I troubled at his
Job 23:15 I consider, I **a.** afraid of him
Job 30:9 And now **a.** I their song,
Job 30:9 yea, I **a.** their byword
Job 30:19 and I **a.** become like dust and ashes.
Job 30:29 I **a.** a brother to dragons, and a
Job 32:6 said, I **a.** young, and ye are very
Job 32:18 For I **a.** full of matter, the spirit
Job 33:6 Behold, I **a.** according to thy wish
Job 33:6 I also **a.** formed out of the clay
Job 33:9 I **a.** clean without transgression,
Job 33:9 I **a.** innocent; neither is there
Job 34:5 For Job hath said, I **a.** righteous:
Job 40:4 Behold, I **a.** vile; what shall I
Ps 6:2 for I **a.** weak: O Lord, heal me;
Ps 6:6 I **a.** weary with my groaning;
Ps 13:4 trouble me rejoice when I **a.** moved.
Ps 17:3 I **a.** purposed that my mouth shall
Ps 22:2 the night season, and **a.** not silent.
Ps 22:6 But I **a.** a worm, and no man;
Ps 22:14 I **a.** poured out like water, and all
Ps 25:16 for I am desolate and afflicted.
Ps 28:7 trusted in him, and I **a.** helped:
Ps 31:9 O Lord, for I am in trouble:
Ps 31:12 I **a.** forgotten as a dead man out
Ps 31:12 I **a.** like a broken vessel.
Ps 31:22 I **a.** cut off from before thine eyes:
Ps 35:3 say unto my soul, I **a.** thy salvation,
Ps 37:25 I have been young, and now **a.** old;
Ps 38:6 I **a.** troubled;
Ps 38:6 I **a.** bowed down greatly;
Ps 38:8 I **a.** feeble and sore broken:
Ps 38:17 For I **a.** ready to halt, and my
Ps 39:4 that I may know how frail I **a.**.
Ps 39:10 I **a.** consumed by the blow of thine
Ps 39:12 for I **a.** a stranger with thee,
Ps 40:12 so that I **a.** not able to look up;
Ps 40:17 But I **a.** poor and needy:
Ps 46:10 Be still, and know that I **a.** God:
Ps 50:7 I **a.** God, even thy God.
Ps 52:8 But I **a.** like a green olive tree
Ps 56:3 What time I **a.** afraid, I will trust
Ps 69:2 I **a.** come into deep waters, where
Ps 69:3 I **a.** weary of my crying:
Ps 69:8 I **a.** become a stranger unto my
Ps 69:17 I **a.** in trouble: hear me speedily.
Ps 69:20 and I **a.** full of heaviness:
Ps 69:29 But I **a.** poor and sorrowful:
Ps 70:5 But I **a.** poor and needy;
Ps 71:7 I **a.** as a wonder unto many;
Ps 71:18 when I **a.** old and grayheaded,
Ps 73:23 Nevertheless I **a.** continually with
Ps 77:4 I **a.** so troubled that I cannot
Ps 81:10 I **a.** the Lord thy God which
Ps 86:1 hear me: for I **a.** poor and needy.
Ps 86:2 Preserve my soul; for I am holy:
Ps 88:4 I **a.** counted with them that go
Ps 88:4 I **a.** as a man that hath no strength: ... 1961
Ps 88:8 I **a.** shut up, and I cannot come
Ps 88:15 I **a.** afflicted and ready to die from
Ps 88:15 I suffer thy terrors I **a.** distracted.
Ps 102:2 in the day when I **a.** in trouble;
Ps 102:6 I **a.** like a pelican of the wilderness:.... 1961
Ps 102:6 **a.** like an owl of the desert. 1961
Ps 102:7 I watch, and **a.** as a sparrow alone
Ps 102:11 and I **a.** withered like grass.
Ps 109:22 For I **a.** poor and needy,
Ps 109:23 I **a.** gone like the shadow when
Ps 109:23 I **a.** tossed up and down as the
Ps 116:16 truly I **a.** thy servant;
Ps 116:16 I **a.** thy servant;
Ps 119:19 I **a.** a stranger in the earth:
Ps 119:63 I **a.** a companion of all them
Ps 119:83 I **a.** become like a bottle in the
Ps 119:94 I **a.** thine, save me; for I have
Ps 119:107 I **a.** afflicted very much: quicken
Ps 119:120 fear of thee; and I **a.** afraid of
Ps 119:125 I **a.** thy servant; give me
Ps 119:141 I **a.** small and despised: yet do
Ps 120:7 I **a.** for peace: but when I speak,
Ps 139:14 I **a.** fearfully and wonderfully
Ps 139:18 I awake, I **a.** still with thee.
Ps 139:21 **a.** not I grieved with those that rise ... 3605
Ps 142:6 for I **a.** brought very low:
Ps 143:12 for I **a.** thy servant.
Pr 8:14 I **a.** understanding;
Pr 20:9 I **a.** pure from my sin?
Pr 26:19 and saith, **A.** not I in sport?
Pr 30:2 I **a.** more brutish than any man,
Ec 1:16 Lo, I **a.** come to great estate,
Ca 1:5 I **a.** black, but comely, O ye
Ca 1:6 not upon me, because I **a.** black,
Ca 2:1 I **a.** the rose of Sharon, and the
Ca 2:5 for I **a.** sick of love.
Ca 2:16 My beloved is mine, and I **a.** his:
Ca 5:1 I **a.** come into my garden, my
Ca 5:8 ye tell him, that I **a.** sick of love.
Ca 6:3 I **a.** my beloved's, and my beloved
Ca 7:10 I **a.** my beloved's, and his desire
Ca 8:10 I **a.** a wall, and my breasts like
Isa 1:11 I **a.** full of the burnt offerings of
Isa 1:14 I **a.** weary to bear them.
Isa 6:5 Woe is me! for I **a.** undone;
Isa 6:5 because I **a.** a man of unclean
Isa 6:8 Then said I, Here **a.** I; send me.
Isa 10:13 by my wisdom; for I **a.** prudent:
Isa 19:11 I **a.** the son of the wise, the son
Isa 21:8 and I **a.** set in my ward whole
Isa 29:12 and he saith, I **a.** not learned.
Isa 33:24 inhabitant shall not say, I **a.** sick:
Isa 36:10 **a.** I now come up without the
Isa 37:24 of my chariots **a.** I come up
Isa 38:10 I **a.** deprived of the residue of my
Isa 38:14 O Lord, I **a.** oppressed; undertake
Isa 41:4 the first, and with the last; I **a.** he.
Isa 41:10 Fear thou not; for I **a.** with thee:
Isa 41:10 be not dismayed; for I **a.** thy God:
Isa 42:8 I **a.** the Lord; that is my name:
Isa 43:3 For I **a.** the Lord thy God, the
Isa 43:5 Fear not; for I **a.** with thee:
Isa 43:10 and understand that I **a.** he:
Isa 43:11 I, even I, **a.** the Lord;
Isa 43:12 saith the Lord, that I **a.** God.
Isa 43:13 Yea, before the day was I **a.** he;
Isa 43:15 I **a.** the Lord, your Holy One,
Isa 43:25 I, even I, **a.** he that blotteth out
Isa 44:5 One shall say, I **a.** the Lord's;
Isa 44:6 I **a.** the first,
Isa 44:6 and I **a.** the last;
Isa 44:16 and saith, Aha, I **a.** warm,
Isa 44:24 I **a.** the Lord that maketh all
Isa 45:3 **a.** the God of Israel.
Isa 45:5,6 I **a.** the Lord, and there is
Isa 45:18 I **a.** the Lord; and there is none.
Isa 45:22 I **a.** God, and there is none else.
Isa 46:4 and even to your old age I **a.** he;
Isa 46:9 I **a.** God, and there is none else;
Isa 46:9 I **a.** God, and there is none like me,
Isa 47:8 that sayest in thine heart, I **a.**.
Isa 47:10 I **a.**, and none else beside me,
Isa 48:12 I **a.** he; I **a.** the first,
Isa 48:12 I also **a.** the last.
Isa 48:16 the time that it was, there **a.** I:
Isa 48:17 I **a.** the Lord thy God which
Isa 49:21 lost my children, and **a.** desolate,
Isa 49:23 thou shalt know that I **a.** the Lord:
Isa 49:26 that I the Lord **a.** thy Saviour
Isa 51:12 even I, **a.** he that comforteth you:
Isa 51:15 But I **a.** the Lord thy God,
Isa 52:6 in that day that I **a.** he that doth
Isa 56:3 Behold, I **a.** a dry tree.
Isa 58:9 and he shall say, Here I **a.**.
Isa 60:16 that I the Lord **a.** thy Saviour
Isa 65:1 I **a.** sought of them that asked
Isa 65:1 I **a.** found of them that sought
Isa 65:5 for I **a.** holier than thou.
Jer 1:6 I cannot speak: for I **a.** a child.
Jer 1:7 Say not, I **a.** a child:
Jer 1:8 I **a.** with thee to deliver thee,
Jer 1:19 I **a.** with thee, saith the Lord,
Jer 2:23 canst thou say, I **a.** not polluted,
Jer 2:35 sayest, Because I **a.** innocent,
Jer 3:12 for I **a.** merciful, saith the Lord,
Jer 3:14 for I **a.** married unto you:
Jer 4:19 I **a.** pained at my very heart;
Jer 6:11 I **a.** full of the fury of the Lord;
Jer 6:11 I **a.** weary with holding in:
Jer 8:21 daughter of my people **a.** I hurt;
Jer 8:21 I **a.** black; astonishment hath
Jer 9:24 that I **a.** the Lord which exercise
Jer 15:6 I **a.** weary with repenting.
Jer 15:16 for I **a.** called by thy name,
Jer 15:20 I **a.** with thee to save thee and to
Jer 20:7 I **a.** in derision daily, every one
Jer 21:13 I **a.** against thee, O inhabitant of
Jer 23:9 I **a.** like a drunken man, and like
Jer 23:23 **A.** I a God at hand, saith the Lord,
Jer 23:30, 31 I **a.** against the prophets, saith
Jer 23:32 I **a.** against them that prophesy
Jer 24:7 to know me, that I **a.** the Lord;
Jer 26:14 behold, I **a.** in your hand:
Jer 29:23 and **a.** a witness, saith the Lord.
Jer 30:11 For I **a.** with thee, saith the Lord,
Jer 31:9 for I **a.** a father to Israel,
Jer 32:27 I **a.** the Lord, the God of all flesh:
Jer 36:5 Baruch, saying, I **a.** shut up;
Jer 38:19 I **a.** afraid of the Jews that are
Jer 42:11 for I **a.** with you to save you,
Jer 46:28 for I **a.** with thee; for I will make
Jer 50:31 Behold, I **a.** against thee, 3605
Jer 51:25 Behold, I **a.** against thee, O
La 1:11 for I **a.** become vile.
La 1:14 I **a.** not able to rise up.
La 1:20 I **a.** in distress: my bowels are
La 3:1 I **a.** the man that hath seen
La 3:54 mine head; then I said, I **a.** cut off.
La 3:63 sitting down and rising up; I **a.**
Eze 5:8 Behold, I, even I, **a.** against thee,
Eze 6:7, 14 shall know that I **a.** the Lord.
Eze 6:9 I **a.** broken with their whorish heart,
Eze 6:10, 13 shall know that I **a.** the Lord,
Eze 7:4 ye shall know that I **a.** the Lord.
Eze 7:9 ye shall know that I **a.** the Lord.
Eze 7:27 they shall know that I **a.** the Lord.
Eze 11:10, 12 shall know that I **a.** the Lord.
Eze 12:11 I **a.** your sign: like as I have done,
Eze 12:15, 16,20 shall know that I **a.** the Lord.
Eze 12:25 for I **a.** the Lord: I will speak,
Eze 13:8 I **a.** against you, saith the Lord.
Eze 13:9, 14 shall know that I **a.** the Lord.
Eze 13:20 Behold, I **a.** against your pillows,
Eze 13:21, 23 shall know that I **a.** the Lord.
Eze 14:8 ye shall know that I **a.** the Lord.
Eze 15:7 ye shall know that I **a.** the Lord,
Eze 16:62 thou shalt know that I **a.** the Lord:
Eze 16:63 when I **a.** pacified toward thee.
Eze 20:5,7 I **a.** the Lord your God.
Eze 20:12 I **a.** the Lord that sanctify them.
Eze 20:19 I **a.** the Lord your God; walk in
Eze 20:20 know that I **a.** the Lord your God.
Eze 20:26, 38,42,44 know that I **a.** the Lord,
Eze 21:3 I **a.** against thee, and will draw
Eze 22:16 thou shalt know that I **a.** the Lord.
Eze 22:26 and I **a.** profaned among them.
Eze 23:49 shall know that I **a.** the Lord God.
Eze 24:24 shall know that I **a.** the Lord God.
Eze 24:27 they shall know that I **a.** the Lord.
Eze 25:5 ye shall know that I **a.** the Lord.
Eze 25:7 thou shalt know that I **a.** the Lord.
Eze 25:11 they shall know that I **a.** the Lord.
Eze 25:17 shall know that I **a.** the Lord, when
Eze 26:3 Behold, I **a.** against thee, O Tyrus,
Eze 26:6 they shall know that I **a.** the Lord.
Eze 27:3 hast said, I **a.** of perfect beauty.
Eze 28:2 thou hast said, I **a.** a God,
Eze 28:9 I **a.** God? but thou shalt be a man,
Eze 28:22 Behold, I **a.** against thee, O Zidon;
Eze 28:22 that I **a.** the Lord, when I shall have
Eze 28:23 shall know that I **a.** the Lord.
Eze 28:24 shall know that I **a.** the Lord God.
Eze 28:26 know that I **a.** the Lord their God.
Eze 29:3 Behold, I **a.** against thee, Pharaoh
Eze 29:6 shall know that I **a.** the Lord,
Eze 29:9 they shall know that I **a.** the Lord:
Eze 29:10 Behold, therefore I **a.** against thee,
Eze 29:16 shall know that I **a.** the Lord God.
Eze 29:21 they shall know that I **a.** the Lord.
Eze 30:8, 19 shall know that I **a.** the Lord.
Eze 30:22 Behold, I **a.** against Pharaoh.
Eze 30:25, 26 shall I know that I **a.** the Lord.
Eze 32:15 shall they know that I **a.** the Lord.
Eze 33:29 shall they know that I **a.** the Lord,
Eze 34:10 I **a.** against the shepherds; and I
Eze 34:27 they shall know that I **a.** the Lord,
Eze 34:30 I the Lord their God **a.** with them,

Eze 34:31 I a. your God, saith the Lord God...
Eze 35:3 I a. against thee, and I will stretch...
Eze 35:4 thou shalt know that I a. the Lord...
Eze 35:9 ye shall know that I a. the Lord...
Eze 35:12 shalt know that I a. the Lord, ...
Eze 35:15 they shall know that I a. the Lord. ...
Eze 36:9 For, behold, I a. for you, and I will...
Eze 36:11 ye shall know that I a. the Lord...
Eze 36:23 shall know that I a. the Lord,...
Eze 36:38 they shall know that I a. the Lord. ...
Eze 37:6 ye shall know that I a. the Lord...
Eze 37:13 know that I a. the Lord, when...
Eze 38:3 I a. against thee, O Gog, the chief...
Eze 38:23 they shall know that I a. the Lord...
Eze 39:1 I a. against thee, O Gog, the chief...
Eze 39:6 they shall know that I a. the Lord. ...
Eze 39:7 shall know that I a. the Lord,...
Eze 39:22 Israel shall know that I a. the...
Eze 39:27 and a. sanctified in them in the...
Eze 39:28 shall they know that I a. the Lord, ...
Eze 44:28 I a. their inheritance: and ye shall...
Eze 44:28 no possession in Israel: I a. their...
Da 9:22 O Daniel, I a. now come forth to...
Da 9:23 and I a. come to shew thee; for...
Da 10:11 stand upright: for unto thee a. I...
Da 10:12 thy words were heard, and I a. come ...
Da 10:14 Now I a. come to make thee...
Da 10:20 of Persia; and when I a. gone...
Ho 2:2 neither a. I her husband: let her...
Ho 11:9 for I a. God, and not man; the...
Ho 12:8 Yet I a. become rich, I have found...
Ho 12:9 And I that a. the Lord thy God...
Ho 13:4 Yet I a. the Lord thy God from the...
Ho 14:8 I a. like a green fir tree. From me...
Joe 2:27 know that I a. in the midst of Israel,...
Joe 2:27 and that I a. the Lord your God,...
Joe 3:10 let the weak say, I a. strong...
Joe 3:17 ye know that I a. the Lord your...
Am 2:13 Behold, I a. pressed under you,...
Jon 1:9 I a. an Hebrew; and I fear the...
Jon 2:4 I a. cast out of thy sight; yet I will...
Mic 3:8 But truly I a. full of power by the...
Mic 7:1 for I a. as when they have gathered...
Na 2:13 Behold, I a. against thee, saith the...
Na 3:5 Behold, I a. against thee, saith the...
Hab 2:1 what I shall answer when I a....
Zep 2:15 I a., and there is none beside me:...
Hag 1:13 saying, I a. with you, saith the...
Hag 2:4 for I a. with you, saith the Lord of...
Zec 1:14 I a. jealous for Jerusalem and for...
Zec 1:15 And I a. very sore displeased with...
Zec 1:16 I a. returned to Jerusalem with...
Zec 8:3 I a. returned unto Zion, and will...
Zec 10:6 for I a. the Lord their God, and...
Zec 11:5 for I a. rich: and their own...
Zec 13:5 I a. no prophet,...
Zec 13:5 I a. an husbandman;...
Mal 1:14 for I a. a great king, saith...
Mal 3:6 For I a. the Lord, I change not; ...
Mt 3:11 whose shoes I a. not worthy to... 1510
Mt 3:17 my beloved Son, in whom I a. well...
Mt 5:17 **Think not that I a. come to**...
Mt 5:17 **I a. not come to destroy, but to**...
Mt 8:8 I a. not worthy... 1510
Mt 8:9 For I a. a man under authority, ... 1510
Mt 9:13 **a. not come to call the righteous,**...
Mt 9:28 **Believe ye that I a. able to do this?**...
Mt 10:34 **Think not that I a. come to send**...
Mt 10:35 **For I a. come to set a man at**...
Mt 11:29 **for I a. meek and lowly in heart:** .. 1510
Mt 15:24 **a. not sent but unto the lost sheep**...
Mt 16:13 **that I the Son of man a.?**... 1511
Mt 16:15 **But whom say ye that I a.**... 1511
Mt 17:5 my beloved Son, in whom I a. well...
Mt 18:20 **there a. I in the midst of them**... 1510
Mt 20:15 **Is thine eye evil, because I a.**... 1510
Mt 20:22, 23 **with the baptism that I a.**...
Mt 22:32 **I a. the God of Abraham, and the** .. 1510
Mt 24:5 **saying, I a. Christ; and shall**... 1510
Mt 26:32 **But after I a. risen again, I will go**...
Mt 26:61 I a. able to destroy the temple of...
Mt 27:24 I a. innocent of the blood of this... 1510
Mt 27:43 for he said, I am the Son of God... 1510
Mt 28:20 **and, lo, I a. with you alway, even** . 1510
Mk 1:7 whose shoes I a. not worthy to... 1510
Mk 1:11 Son, in whom I a. well pleased...
Mk 8:27 **Whom do men say that I a.?**... 1511
Mk 8:29 **But whom say ye that I a.? And**... 1511
Mk 10:38 **baptism that I a. baptized with?**...
Mk 10:39 **baptism that I a. baptized withal**...
Mk 12:26 **I a. the God of Abraham, and the**...
Mk 13:6 **in my name, saying, I a. Christ;** ... 1510
Mk 14:28 **But after that I a. risen, I will go**...
Mk 14:62 And Jesus said, **I a.: and ye shall** ... 1510
Lu 1:18 for I a. an old man, and my wife...
Lu 1:19 I a. Gabriel, that stand in the... 1510
Lu 1:19 and a. sent to speak unto thee, ...1510
Lu 3:16 whose shoes I a. not worthy to... 1510
Lu 3:22 Son, in thee I a. well pleased...
Lu 4:43 **other cities also: for therefore a.**...
Lu 5:8 for I a. a sinful man, O Lord... 1510
Lu 7:6 for I a. not worthy that thou... 1510
Lu 7:8 For I also a. a man set under... 1510
Lu 9:18 **Whom say the people that I a.?**... 1511
Lu 9:20 **But whom say ye that I a.? Peter**.. 1511
Lu 12:49 **I a. come to send fire on the earth;**...
Lu 12:50 **and how a. I straitened till it**...
Lu 12:51 **Suppose ye that I a. come to give**...
Lu 15:19 **a. no more worthy to be called**... 1510
Lu 15:21 **in thy sight, and a. no more**... 1510
Lu 16:3 **I cannot dig; to beg I a. ashamed**...
Lu 16:4 **I a. resolved what to do,**...
Lu 16:4 **that, when I a. put**...
Lu 16:24 **cool my tongue; for I a. tormented**...
Lu 18:11 **that I a. not as other men are**... 1510
Lu 21:8 **saying, I a. Christ; and the time** ... 1510
Lu 22:27 **I a. among you as he that serveth**.. 1510
Lu 22:33 Lord, I a. ready to go with thee, ... 1510
Lu 22:58 And Peter said, Man, I a. not... 1510
Lu 22:70 he said unto them, **Ye say that I a.**.. 1510
Joh 1:20 but confessed, I a. not the Christ... 1510
Joh 1:21 And he saith, I a. not. Art thou that... 1510
Joh 1:23 I a. the voice of one crying in the...
Joh 1:27 whose shoe's latchet I a. not... 1510
Joh 1:31 therefore a. I come baptizing...
Joh 3:28 I a. not the Christ,... 1510
Joh 3:28 but that I a. sent... 1510
Joh 4:9 me, which a. a woman of Samaria?... 5607
Joh 4:26 **I that speak to thee a. he**... 1510
Joh 5:7 but while I a. coming, another...
Joh 5:43 **I a. come in my father's name, and**...
Joh 6:35 said unto them, **I a. the bread of** ... 1510
Joh 6:41 I a. the bread which came down... 1510
Joh 6:48 **I a. that bread of life**... 1510
Joh 6:51 **I a. the living bread which came** ... 1510
Joh 7:28 **and ye know whence I a.:**... 1510
Joh 7:28 **and I a. not come**...
Joh 7:29 **But I know him: for I a. from him**, 1510
Joh 7:33 **Yet a little while a. I with you,** ... 1510
Joh 7:34, 36 **where I a., thither ye cannot** ... 1510
Joh 8:12 **I a. the light of the world: he that** . 1510
Joh 8:16 **for I a. not alone, but I and the** ... 1510
Joh 8:18 **I a. one that bear witness of**... 1510
Joh 8:23 **I a. from above: ye are of this**... 1510
Joh 8:23 **I a. not of this world**... 1510
Joh 8:24 **believe not that I a. he, ye shall**... 1510
Joh 8:28 **ye know that I a. he, and that I do** 1510
Joh 8:58 **Before Abraham was, I a.**... 1510
Joh 9:5 **As long as I a. in the world,**... 1510
Joh 9:5 **I a. the light of the world**... 1510
Joh 9:9 He is like him: but he said, I a. he... 1510
Joh 9:39 **For judgment I a. come into this**...
Joh 10:7 **I a. the door of the sheep**... 1510
Joh 10:9 **I a. the door: by me if any man**... 1510
Joh 10:10 **a. come that they might have life,**...
Joh 10:11 **I a. the good shepherd: the good** ... 1510
Joh 10:14 **I a. the good shepherd, and know**.. 1510
Joh 10:14 **and a. known of mine**...
Joh 10:36 **because I said, I a. the Son of God?** ...
Joh 11:15 And I a. glad for your sakes that I...
Joh 11:25 **I a. the resurrection, and the life:** .. 1510
Joh 12:26 **and where I a., there shall also my** 1510
Joh 12:46 **I a. come a light into the world,**...
Joh 13:13 **and ye say well; for so I a.**... 1510
Joh 13:19 **ye may believe that I a. he**... 1510
Joh 13:33 **yet a little while I a. with you**... 1510
Joh 14:3 **that where I a., there ye may be** ... 1510
Joh 14:6 **I a. the way, the truth, the life:**... 1510
Joh 14:10 **that I a. in the Father, and the**...
Joh 14:11 **Believe me that I a. in the Father,**...
Joh 14:20 **that I a. in my Father, and ye in**...
Joh 15:1 **I a. the true vine, and my Father**.. 1510
Joh 15:5 **I a. the vine, ye are the branches:**. 1510
Joh 16:28 **the Father, and a. come into the**...
Joh 16:32 **and yet I a. not alone, because**... 1510
Joh 17:10 **mine; and I a. glorified in them**...
Joh 17:11 **now I a. no more in the world**... 1510
Joh 17:14 16 **even as I a. not of the world**... 1510
Joh 17:24 **be with me where I a.; that they**... 1510
Joh 18:5 Jesus saith unto them, **I a. he**... 1510
Joh 18:6 he said unto them, I a. he, they... 1510
Joh 18:8 **I have told you that I a. he: if**... 1510
Joh 18:17 man's disciples? He saith, I a. not... 1510
Joh 18:25 He denied it, and said, I a. not... 1510
Joh 18:35 **A.** I a Jew? Thine own nation... 1510
Joh 18:37 **Thou sayest that I a. a king.**... 1510
Joh 19:21 but that he said, I a. King of the... 1510
Joh 20:17 **for I a. not yet ascended to my**...
Ac 7:32 I a. the God of thy fathers, the...
Ac 7:34 and a. come down to deliver them...
Ac 9:5 **I a. Jesus whom thou persecutest:**.. 1510
Ac 9:10 he said, Behold, I a. here, Lord...
Ac 10:21 Behold, I a. he whom ye seek:... 1510
Ac 10:26 Stand up; I myself also a. a man... 1510
Ac 13:25 Whom think ye that I a.?... 1511
Ac 13:25 I a. not he. But, behold, there... 1510
Ac 13:25 his feet I a. not worthy to loose... 1510
Ac 18:6 I a. clean: from henceforth I will...
Ac 18:10 **For I a. with thee and no man**... 1510
Ac 20:26 that I a. pure from the blood of...
Ac 21:13 for I a. ready not to be bound only,...
Ac 21:39 But Paul said, I a. a man which... 1510
Ac 21:39 which a. a Jew of Tarsus,...
Ac 22:3 I a. verily a man which a. a Jew... 1510
Ac 22:3 which a. a Jew, born in Tarsus,...
Ac 22:8 **I a. Jesus of Nazareth, whom thou**. 1510
Ac 23:6 Men and brethren, I a. a Pharisee,... 1510
Ac 23:6 of the dead I a. called in question...
Ac 24:21 I a. called in question by you this...
Ac 26:2 whereof I a. accused of the Jews. ...
Ac 26:6 And now I stand and a. judged...
Ac 26:7 sake, king Agrippa, I a. accused...
Ac 26:15 **I a. Jesus whom thou persecutest**.. 1510
Ac 26:25 I a. not mad, most noble Festus; ...
Ac 26:26 for I a. persuaded that none of...
Ac 26:29 altogether such as I a., except... 1510
Ac 27:23 the angel of God, whose I a.,... 1510
Ac 28:20 for the hope of Israel I a. bound...
Ro 1:14 I a. debtor both to the Greeks, ... 1510
Ro 1:15 I a. ready to preach the gospel...
Ro 1:16 For I a. not ashamed of the...
Ro 3:7 yet a. I also judged as a sinner?...
Ro 7:14 but I a. carnal, sold under sin... 1510
Ro 7:24 O wretched man that I a.! who...
Ro 8:38 For I a. persuaded, that neither...
Ro 11:1 For I also a. an Israelite, of the... 1510
Ro 11:3 and I a. left alone, and they seek my...
Ro 11:13 inasmuch as I a. the apostle of... 1510
Ro 14:14 and a. persuaded by the Lord...
Ro 15:14 I myself also a. persuaded of you,...
Ro 15:29 And I a. sure that, when I come...
Ro 16:19 a. glad therefore on your behalf: ...
1Co 1:12 one of you saith, I a. of Paul;... 1510
1Co 3:4 For while one saith, I a. of Paul; ... 1510
1Co 3:4 and another, I a. of Apollos;...
1Co 4:4 yet a. I not hereby justified: but...
1Co 9:1 **A.** I not an apostle?... 1510
1Co 9:1 a. I not free? have I not seen... 1510
1Co 9:2 yet doubtless I a. to you: for the... 1510
1Co 9:22 I a. made all things to all men, ...
1Co 10:30 by grace be a partaker, why a. I...
1Co 11:1 of me, even as I also a. of Christ...
1Co 12:15 Because I a. not the hand,... 1510
1Co 12:15 I a. not of the body;... 1510
1Co 12:16 Because I a. not the eye,... 1510
1Co 12:16 I a. not of the body;... 1510
1Co 13:1 I a. become as sounding brass,...
1Co 13:2 have not charity, I a. nothing. ... 1510
1Co 13:12 I know even as also I a. known. ...
1Co 15:9 For I a. the least of the apostles,... 1510
1Co 15:9 that a. not meet... 1510
1Co 15:10 the grace of God I a. what I a.: ... 1510
1Co 16:17 I a. glad of the coming of...
2Co 7:4 I a. filled with comfort, ...
2Co 7:4 I a. exceeding joyful...
2Co 7:14 to him of you, I a. not ashamed;...
2Co 10:1 who in presence a. base among...
2Co 10:1 being absent a. bold toward you:...
2Co 10:2 may not be bold when I a. present...
2Co 11:2 For I a. jealous over you with...
2Co 11:21 (I speak foolishly,) I a. bold also...

2Co 11:22 Are they Hebrews? so **a.** I.
2Co 11:22 Are they Israelites? so **a.** I.
2Co 11:22 they the seed of Abraham? so **a.** I.
2Co 11:23 (I speak as a fool) I **a.** more;
2Co 11:29 I **a.** not weak? who is offended,
2Co 12:10 for when I **a.** weak, *1510*
2Co 12:10 then **a.** I strong. *1510*
2Co 12:11 I **a.** become a fool in glorying;
2Co 12:11 for in nothing **a.** I behind the very
2Co 12:14 the third time I **a.** ready to come
2Co 13:1 is the third time I **a.** coming to you
Ga 2:19 For I through the law **a.** dead.
Ga 2:20 I **a.** crucified with Christ:
Ga 4:11 I **a.** afraid of you, lest I have
Ga 4:12 be as I **a.**; for I **a.** as ye are;
Ga 4:16 **A.** I therefore become your enemy,
Ga 4:18 and not only when I **a.** present
Eph 3:8 who **a.** less than the least of all
Eph 6:20 For which I **a.** an ambassador
Php 1:17 that I **a.** set for the defence
Php 1:23 For I **a.** in a strait betwixt two,
Php 3:12 **a.** apprehended of Christ Jesus.
Php 4:11 in whatsoever state I **a.**, *1510*
Php 4:12 and in all things I **a.** instructed
Php 4:18 I **a.** full, having received of
Col 1:23 I Paul **a.** made a minister;
Col 1:25 I **a.** made a minister, according
Col 2:5 flesh, yet **a.** I with you in the *1510*
Col 4:3 for which I **a.** also in bonds:
1Ti 1:15 to save sinners; of whom I **a.** *1510*
1Ti 2:7 Whereunto I **a.** ordained a
2Ti 1:5 and I **a.** persuaded that in thee
2Ti 1:11 Whereunto I **a.** appointed a
2Ti 1:12 nevertheless I **a.** not ashamed:
2Ti 1:12 and **a.** persuaded that he is able
2Ti 4:6 For I **a.** now ready to be offered,
Jas 1:13 he is tempted, I **a.** tempted of God:
1Pe 1:16 Be ye holy; for I **a.** holy. *1510*
1Pe 5:1 I exhort, who **a.** also an elder,
2Pe 1:13 so long as I **a.** in this tabernacle, *1510*
2Pe 1:17 son in whom I **a.** well pleased.
Re 1:8 **I a. Alpha and Omega, the** *1510*
Re 1:9 I John, who also **a.** your brother,
Re 1:11 **I a. Alpha and Omega, the first** *1510*
Re 1:17 **not; I a. the first and the last:** *1510*
Re 1:18 **I a. he that liveth, and was dead;** *1510*
Re 1:18 **I a. alive for evermore, Amen;** *1510*
Re 2:23 **know that I a. he which searcheth** *1510*
Re 3:17 **Because thou sayest, I a. rich,** *1510*
Re 3:21 **and a. set down with my Father.**
Re 18:7 and **a.** no widow, and shall see *1510*
Re 19:10 I **a.** thy fellow servant, and of thy *1510*
Re 21:6 I **a.** Alpha and Omega, the *1510*
Re 22:9 for I **a.** thy fellowservant, and of *1510*
Re 22:13 **I a. Alpha and Omega, the** *1510*
Re 22:16 **I a. the root and the offspring** *1510*

AMAD (a'-mad)
Jos 19:26 and **A.**, and Misheal; 6008

AMAL (a'-mal)
1Ch 7:35 and Imna, and Shelesh, and **A.** 6000

AMALEK (am'-al-ek) See also AMALEKITE.
Ge 36:12 and she bare to Eliphaz **A.**: 6002
Ge 36:16 Korah, duke Gatam, and duke **A.**: 6002
Ex 17:8 Then came **A.**, and fought with 6002
Ex 17:9 men, and go out, fight with **A.**: 6002
Ex 17:10 said to him, and fought with **A.**: 6002
Ex 17:11 let down his hand, **A.** prevailed. 6002
Ex 17:13 And Joshua discomfited **A.** and 6002
Ex 17:14 put out the remembrance of **A.** 6002
Ex 17:16 the Lord will have war with **A.** 6002
Nu 24:20 And when he looked on **A.**, he 6002
Nu 24:20 **A.** was the first of the nations; 6002
De 25:17 Remember what **A.** did unto thee 6002
De 25:19 blot out the remembrance of **A.** 6002
Jg 3:13 the children of Ammon and **A.**, 6002
Jg 5:14 there a root of them against **A.**; 6002
1Sa 15:2 that which **A.** did to Israel, how 6002
1Sa 15:3 Now go, and smite **A.**, and utterly 6002
1Sa 15:5 And Saul came to a city of **A.**, and 6002
1Sa 15:20 have brought Agag the king of **A.**, 6002
1Sa 28:18 his fierce wrath upon **A.**, 6002
2Sa 8:12 and of **A.**, and of the spoil of 6002
1Ch 1:36 Gatam, Kenaz, and Timna, and **A.** 6002
1Ch 18:11 the Philistines, and from **A.** 6002
Ps 83:7 Gebal, and Ammon, and **A.**; 6002

AMALEKITE (am'-al-ek-ite) See also AMALEKITES.
1Sa 30:13 man of Egypt, servant to an **A.**; 6003
2Sa 1:8 And I answered him, I am an **A.** 6003
2Sa 1:13 am the son of a stranger, an **A.** 6003

AMALEKITES (am'-al-ek-ites)
Ge 14:7 smote all the country of the **A.**, 6003
Nu 13:29 **A.** dwell in the land of the south: 6003
Nu 14:25 (Now the **A.** and the Canaanites 6003
Nu 14:43 For the **A.** and the Canaanites 6003
Nu 14:45 Then the **A.** came down, and the 6003
Jg 6:3 **A.**, and the children of the east 6003
Jg 6:33 all the Midianites and the **A.** and 6003
Jg 7:12 **A.**, and all the children of the east 6003
Jg 10:12 The Zidonians also, and the **A.**, 6003
Jg 12:15 Ephraim, in the mount of the **A.** 6003
1Sa 14:48 an host, and smote the **A.**, and 6003
1Sa 15:6 get you down from among the **A.**, 6003
1Sa 15:6 departed from among the **A.** 6003
1Sa 15:7 Saul smote the **A.** from Havilah 6003
1Sa 15:8 he took Agag the king of the **A.** 6003
1Sa 15:15 have brought them from the **A.**: 6003
1Sa 15:18 utterly destroy the sinners the **A.**, 6003
1Sa 15:20 have utterly destroyed the **A.** 6003
1Sa 15:32 to me Agag the King of the **A.** 6003
1Sa 27:8 and the Gezerites, and the **A.**: 6003
1Sa 30:1 that the **A.** had invaded the south, 6003
1Sa 30:18 all that the **A.** had carried away; 6003
2Sa 1:1 from the slaughter of the **A.**, and 6003
1Ch 4:43 And they smote the rest of the **A.** 6003

AMAM (a'-mam)
Jos 15:26 **A.**, and Shema, and Moladah, 538

AMANA (am-a'-nah)
Ca 4:8 look from the top of **A.**, 549

AMARIAH (am-a-ri'ah)
1Ch 6:7 Meraioth beat **A.** 568
1Ch 6:7 and **A.** begat Ahitub, 568
1Ch 6:11 Azariah begat **A.**, 568
1Ch 6:11 and **A.** begat Ahitub 568
1Ch 6:52 Meraioth his son, **A.** his son, 568
1Ch 23:19 Jeriah the first, **A.** the second, 568
1Ch 24:23 **A.** the second, Jahaziel the third, 568
2Ch 19:11 **A.** the chief priest is over you. 568
2Ch 31:15 Shemaiah, **A.**, and Shecaniah, 568
Ezr 7:3 The son of **A.**, the son of Azariah, 568
Ezr 10:42 Shallum, **A.**, and Joseph. 568
Ne 10:3 Pashur, **A.**, Malchijah, 568
Ne 11:4 son of **A.**, the son of Shephatiah, 568
Ne 12:2 **A.**, Malluch, Hattush, 568
Ne 12:13 of **A.**, Jehohanan; 568
Zep 1:1 the son of **A.**, the son of Hizkiah, 568

AMASA (am'-a-sah)
2Sa 17:25 Absalom made **A.** captain of the 6021
2Sa 17:25 which **A.** was a man's son, 6021
2Sa 19:13 And say ye to **A.**, Art thou not 6021
2Sa 20:4 Then said the king to **A.**, 6021
2Sa 20:5 So **A.** went to assemble the men 6021
2Sa 20:8 which is in Gibeon, **A.** went before 6021
2Sa 20:9 And Joab said to **A.**, Art thou 6021
2Sa 20:9 And Joab took **A.** by the beard 6021
2Sa 20:10 But **A.** took no heed to the sword 6021
2Sa 20:12 And **A.** wallowed in blood in the 6021
2Sa 20:12 he removed **A.** out of the highway 6021
1Ki 2:5 and unto **A.** the son of Jether, 6021
1Ki 2:32 and **A.** the son of Jether, captain 6021
1Ch 2:17 And Abigail bare **A.**: 6021
1Ch 2:17 and the father of **A.** was Jether 6021
2Ch 28:12 and **A.** the son of Hadlai, stood up 6021

AMASAI (am'-as-ahee)
1Ch 6:25 of Elkanah; **A.**, and Ahimoth. 6022
2Ch 28:35 the son of Mahath, the son of **A.**, 6022
2Ch 12:18 Then the spirit came upon **A.**, 6022
2Ch 15:24 Nathaneel, and **A.**, and Zechariah, 6022
2Ch 29:12 Levites arose, Mahath the son of **A.**, 6022

AMASHAI (am'-ash-ahee)
Ne 11:13 and **A.** the son of Azareel, 6023

AMASIAH (am-a-si'-ah)
2Ch 17:16 next him was **A.** the son of Zichri, 6007

AMAZED
Ex 15:15 the dukes of Edom shall be **a.**; 926
Jg 20:41 the men of Benjamin were **a.** 926
Job 32:15 They were **a.**, they answered no 2865
Isa 13:8 they shall be **a.** one at another, 8539
Eze 32:10 will make many people **a.** at thee, 8074
Mt 12:23 all the people were **a.**, *1839*
Mt 19:25 they were exceedingly **a.**, *1605*
Mk 1:27 And they were all **a.**, *2284*
Mk 2:12 insomuch that they were all **a.**, *1839*
Mk 6:51 they were sore **a.** in themselves, *1839*
Mk 9:15 they beheld him, were greatly **a.**, *1568*
Mk 10:32 and they were **a.**; *2284*
Mk 14:33 began to be sore **a.**, *1568*
Mk 16:8 for they trembled and were **a.**: *1611*
Lu 2:48 they saw him, they were **a.**: *1605*
Lu 4:36 And they were all **a.**, *1096,2285*
Lu 5:26 And they were all **a.**, *1611,2983*
Lu 9:43 **a.** at the mighty power of God. *1605*
Ac 2:7 they were all **a.** and marvelled, *1839*
Ac 2:12 were all **a.**, and were in doubt, *1839*
Ac 9:21 all that heard him were **a.** *1839*

AMAZEMENT
Ac 3:10 filled with wonder and **a.** *1611*
1Pe 3:6 and are not afraid with any **a.** *4423*

AMAZIAH (am-a-zi'-ah)
2Ki 12:21 **A.** his son reigned in his stead. 558
2Ki 13:12 where with he fought against **A.** 558
2Ki 14:1 reigned **A.** the son of Joash 558
2Ki 14:8 **A.** sent messengers to Jehoash, 558
2Ki 14:9 the king of Israel sent to **A.** 558
2Ki 14:11 **A.** would not hear. Therefore 558
2Ki 14:11 he and **A.** king of Judah looked 558
2Ki 14:13 Jehoash king of Israel took **A.** 558
2Ki 14:15 and how he fought with **A.** king of 558
2Ki 14:17 **A.** the son of Joash king of Judah 558
2Ki 14:18 the rest of the acts of **A.**, 558
2Ki 14:21 him king instead of his father **A.** 558
2Ki 14:23 In the fifteenth year of **A.** the son 558
2Ki 15:1 Azariah son of **A.** king of Judah 558
2Ki 15:3 to all that his father **A.** had done; 558
1Ch 3:12 **A.** his son, Azariah his son, 558
1Ch 4:34 Jamlech, and Joshah the son of **A.**, 558
1Ch 6:45 son of Hashabiah, the son of **A.**, 558
2Ch 24:27 **A.** his son reigned in his stead. 558
2Ch 25:1 **A.** was twenty and five years old 558
2Ch 25:5 **A.** gathered Judah together, 558
2Ch 25:9 **A.** said to the man of God, 558
2Ch 25:10 Then **A.** separated them, to wit, 558
2Ch 25:11 **A.** strengthened himself, and led 558
2Ch 25:13 of the army which **A.** sent back, 558
2Ch 25:14 **A.** was come from the slaughter 558
2Ch 25:15 of the Lord was kindled against **A.**, 558
2Ch 25:17 **A.** king of Judah took advice, 558
2Ch 25:18 Joash king of Judah sent to **A.** 558
2Ch 25:20 But **A.** would not hear; for it came 558
2Ch 25:21 both he and **A.** king of Judah, 558
2Ch 25:23 Joash the king of Israel took **A.** 558
2Ch 25:25 **A.** the son of Joash king of Judah 558
2Ch 25:26 the rest of the acts of **A.**, 558
2Ch 25:27 the time that **A.** did turn away 558
2Ch 26:1 king in the room of his father **A.** 558
2Ch 26:4 to all that his father **A.** did. 558
Am 7:10 **A.** the priest of Beth-el sent to 558
Am 7:12 **A.** said unto Amos, O thou seer, 558
Am 7:14 answered Amos, and said to **A.**, 558

AMBASSADOR See also AMBASSADORS.
Pr 13:17 but a faithful **a.** is health. 6735
Jer 49:14 an **a.** is sent unto the heathen, 6735
Ob 1 an **a.** is sent among the heathen, 6735
Eph 6:20 For which I am an **a.** in bonds: *4243*

AMBASSADORS
Jos 9:4 and made as if they had been **a.**, 6735
2Ch 32:31 in the business of the **a.** of the 3887
2Ch 35:21 he sent **a.** to him, 4397
Isa 18:2 That sendeth **a.** by the sea, 6735
Isa 30:4 and his **a.** came to Hanes. 4397
Isa 33:7 the **a.** of peace shall weep bitterly. 4397
Eze 17:15 in sending his **a.** into Egypt, 4397
2Co 5:20 we are **a.** for Christ, *4243*

AMBASSAGE
Lu 14:32 **he sendeth an a.,** *4242*

AMBER
Eze 1:4 as the colour of **a.**, 2830
Eze 1:27 I saw as the colour of **a.**, 2830
Eze 8:2 as the colour of **a.** 2830

AMBUSH See also AMBUSHES; AMBUSHMENT.
Jos 8:2 lay thee an **a.** for the city 693
Jos 8:7 ye shall rise up from the **a.**, 693
Jos 8:9 they went to lie in **a.**, 693
Jos 8:12 set them to lie in **a.** between 693
Jos 8:14 liers in **a.** against him 693
Jos 8:19 And the **a.** arose quickly 693

Jos 8:21 saw that the **a.** had taken the city, 693

AMBUSHES
Jer 51:12 up the watchmen, prepare the **a.**: 693

AMBUSHMENT See also AMBUSHMENTS.
2Ch 13:13 Jeroboam caused an **a.** 3993
2Ch 13:13 and the **a.** was behind them. 3993

AMBUSHMENTS
2Ch 20:22 the Lord set **a.** 693

AMEN
Nu 5:22 And the woman shall say, **A.**, **a.** 543
De 27:15, 16 people shall answer and say, **A.** 543
De 27:17, 18,19,20,21,22,23,24,25,26 And all the people shall say, **A.** 543
1Ki 1:36 answered the king, and said, **A.**: 543
1Ch 16:36 And all the people said, **A.**, 543
Ne 5:13 all the congregation said, **A.**, 543
Ne 8:6 the people answered, **A.**, **A.**, 543
Ps 41:13 to everlasting. **A.**, and **A.** 543
Ps 72:19 filled with his glory; **A.**, and **A.** 543
Ps 89:52 for evermore. **A.**, and **A.** 543
Ps 106:48 **A.**, Praise ye the Lord. 543
Jer 28:6 the prophet Jeremiah said, **A.**: 543
Mt 6:13 **and the glory, for ever. A.** *281*
Mt 28:20 **unto the end of the world. A.** *281*
Mk 16:20 the word with signs following. **A.** *281*
Lu 24:53 praising and blessing God. **A.** *281*
Joh 21:25 books that should be written. **A.** *281*
Ro 1:25 Creator, who is blessed for ever. **A.** *281*
Ro 9:5 over all, God blessed for ever. **A.** *281*
Ro 11:36 to whom be glory for ever. **A.** *281*
Ro 15:33 God of peace be with you all. **A.** *281*
Ro 16:20 Jesus Christ be with you. **A.** *281*
Ro 16:24 Jesus Christ be with you all. **A.** *281*
Ro 16:27 through Jesus Christ for ever. **A.** *281*
1Co 14:16 unlearned say **A.** at thy giving of *281*
1Co 16:24 with you all in Christ Jesus. **A.** *281*
2Co 1:20 yea, and in him **A.**, unto the glory *281*
2Co 13:14 Holy Ghost, be with you all. **A.** *281*
Ga 1:5 be glory for ever and ever. **A.** *281*
Ga 6:18 Christ be with your spirit. **A.** *281*
Eph 3:21 all ages, world without end. **A.** *281*
Eph 6:24 Jesus Christ in sincerity. **A.** *281*
Php 4:20 be glory for ever and ever. **A.** *281*
Php 4:23 Jesus Christ be with you all. **A.** *281*
Col 4:18 my bonds. Grace be with you. **A.** *281*
1Th 5:28 of…Christ be with you. **A.** *281*
2Th 3:18 of…Christ be with you all. **A.** *281*
1Ti 1:17 and glory for ever and ever. **A.** *281*
1Ti 6:16 honour and power everlasting. **A.** *281*
1Ti 6:21 Grace be with thee. **A.** *281*
2Ti 4:18 be glory for ever and ever. **A.** *281*
2Ti 4:22 Grace be with you. **A.** *281*
Tit 3:15 Grace be with you all. **A.** *281*
Phm 25 Christ be with your spirit. **A.** *281*
Heb 13:21 be glory for ever and ever. **A.** *281*
Heb 13:25 Grace be with you all. **A.** *281*
1Pe 4:11 dominion for ever and ever. **A.** *281*
1Pe 5:11 dominion for ever and ever. **A.** *281*
1Pe 5:14 all that are in Christ Jesus. **A.** *281*
2Pe 3:18 glory both now and for ever. **A.** *281*
1Jo 5:21 keep yourselves from idols. **A.** *281*
2Jo 13 of thy elect sister greet thee. **A.** *281*
Jude 25 and power, both now and ever. **A.** *281*
Re 1:6 dominion for ever and ever. **A.** *281*
Re 1:7 wail because of him. Even so, **A.** *281*
Re 1:18 **I am alive for evermore, A.**; *281*
Re 3:14 **These things saith the A.**, *281*
Re 5:14 And the four beasts said, **A.** *281*
Re 7:12 Saying, **A.**: Blessing, and glory, *281*
Re 7:12 unto our God for ever and ever. **A.** *281*
Re 19:4 Sat on the throne, saying, **A.**; *281*
Re 22:20 **A.** Even so, come, Lord Jesus. *281*
Re 22:21 Jesus Christ be with you all. **A.** *281*

AMEND See also AMENDS.
2Ch 34:10 to repair and **a.** the house: 2388
Jer 7:3 **A.** your ways and your doings, 3190
Jer 7:5 if ye throughly **a.** your ways. 3190
Jer 26:13 **a.** your ways and your doings, 3190
Jer 35:15 and **a.** your doings, 3190
Joh 4:52 hour when he began to **a.** *2192,2866*

AMENDS
Le 5:16 he shall make **a.** for the harm *7999*

AMERCE
De 22:19 shall **a.** him in an hundred shekels, 6064

AMETHYST
Ex 28:19 a ligure, an agate, and an **a.** 306
Ex 39:12 a ligure, an agate, and an **a.** 306
Re 21:20 a jacinth; the twelfth, an **a.** *271*

AMI (a'-mi)
Ezr 2:57 of Zebaim, the children of **A.** 532

AMIABLE
Ps 84:1 How **a.** are thy tabernacles, 3039

AMINADAB (a-min'-a-dab) See also AMMINADAB.
Mt 1:4 Aram begat **A.**; *284*
Mt 1:4 and **A.** begat Naasson; *284*
Lu 3:33 Which was the son of **A.**, *284*

AMISS
2Ch 6:37 We have sinned, we have done **a.**, 5753
Da 3:29 speak anything **a.** against the God 7955
Lu 23:41 this man hath done nothing **a.** *824*
Jas 4:3 receive not, because ye ask **a.**, *2560*

AMITTAI (a-mit'-tahee)
2Ki 14:25 Jonah, the son of **A.**, the prophet, 573
Jon 1:1 came unto Jonah the son of **A.**, 573

AMMAH (am'-mah) See also METHEG-AMMAH.
2Sa 2:24 they were come to the hill of **A.** 522

AMMI (am'-mi) See also AMMI-NADIB; BENAMMI; LO-AMMI.
Ho 2:1 Say ye unto your brethren, **A.**: 5971

AMMIEL (am'-me-el) See also ELIAM.
Nu 13:12 of Dan, **A.** the son of Gemalli. 5988
2Sa 9:4,5 house of Machir, the son of **A.**, 5988
2Sa 17:27 Machir the son of **A.** of Lo-debar, 5988
1Ch 3:5 Bath-shua the daughter of **A.**: 5988
1Ch 26:5 **A.** the sixth, Issachar the seventh, 5988

AMMIHUD (am-mi'-hud)
Nu 1:10 Elishama the son of **A.**: 5989
Nu 2:18 shall be Elishama the son of **A.** 5989
Nu 7:48 seventh day Elishama the son of **A.**, 5989
Nu 7:53 offering of Elishama the son of **A.** 5989
Nu 10:22 host was Elishama the son of **A.** 5989
Nu 34:20 Simeon, Shemuel the son of **A.** 5989
Nu 34:28 Pedahel the son of **A.** 5989
2Sa 13:37 went to Talmai, the son of **A.**, 5989
1Ch 7:26 Laadan his son, **A.** his son, 5989
1Ch 9:4 Uthai the son of **A.**, the son of 5989

AMMINADAB (am-min'-a-dab) See also AMINADAB; AMMI-NADIB.
Ex 6:23 Elisheba, daughter of **A.**, sister 5992
Nu 1:7 Nahshon the son of **A.** 5992
Nu 2:3 Nahshon the son of **A.** shall be 5992
Nu 7:12 the son of **A.**, of the tribe of Judah 5992
Nu 7:17 offering of Nahshon the son of **A.** 5992
Nu 10:14 his host was Nahshon the son of **A.** 5992
Ru 4:19 begat Ram, and Ram begat **A.**, 5992
Ru 4:20 **A.** begat Nahshon, and Nahshon 5992
1Ch 2:10 Ram begat **A.**; 5992
1Ch 2:10 and **A.** begat Nahshon, 5992
1Ch 6:22 **A.** his son, Korah his son, 5992
1Ch 15:10 **A.** the chief, and his brethren 5992
1Ch 15:11 Shemaiah, and Eliel, and **A.**, 5992

AMMI-NADIB (am-min'-a-dib) See also AMMINADAB.
Ca 6:12 made me like the chariots of **A.** 5993

AMMISHADDAI (am-mi-shad'-dahee)
Nu 1:12 Of Dan; Ahiezer the son of **A.** 5996
Ca 2:25 shall be Ahiezer the son of **A.** 5993
Ca 7:66 tenth day Ahiezer the son of **A.**, 5993
Ca 7:71 offering of Ahiezer the son of **A.** 5993
Ca 10:25 host was Ahiezer the son of **A.** 5993

AMMIZABAD (am-miz'-a-bad)
1Ch 27:6 in his course was **A.** his son. 5990

AMMON (am'-mon) See also AMMONITE.
Ge 19:38 the children of **A.** unto this day. 5983
Nu 21:24 even unto the children of **A.**: 5983
Nu 21:24 of the children of **A.** was strong. 5983
De 2:19 over against the children of **A.**, 5983
De 2:19 the children of **A.** any possession; 5983
De 2:37 of the children of **A.** thou camest 5983
De 3:11 in Rabbath of the children of **A.**? 5983
De 3:16 is the border of the children of **A.**; 5983
Jos 12:2 the border of the chldren of **A.**; 5983
Jos 13:10 the border of the children of **A.**; 5983
Jos 13:25 half the land of the children of **A.**, 5983
Jg 3:13 unto him the children of **A.** 5983
Jg 10:6 and the gods of the children of **A.**, 5983
Jg 10:7 into the hands of the children of **A.** 5983
Jg 10:9 children of **A.** passed over Jordan 5983
Jg 10:11 Amorites, from the children of **A.**, 5983
Jg 10:17 the children of **A.** were gathered 5983
Jg 10:18 to fight against the children of **A.**? 5983
Jg 11:4 children of **A.** made against Israel. 5983
Jg 11:5 when the children of **A.** made war 5983
Jg 11:6 we may fight with the children of **A.** 5983
Jg 11:8, 9 against the children of **A.**, 5983
Jg 11:12 king of the children of **A.**, saying, 5983
Jg 11:13 king of the children of **A.** answered 5983
Jg 11:14 unto the king of the children of **A.**: 5983
Jg 11:15 nor the land of the children of **A.**: 5983
Jg 11:27 of Israel and the children of **A.** 5983
Jg 11:28 the king of the children of **A.** 5983
Jg 11:29 passed over unto the children of **A.** 5983
Jg 11:30 children of **A.** into mine hands, 5983
Jg 11:31 in peace from the children of **A.**, 5983
Jg 11:32 passed over unto the children of **A.** 5983
Jg 11:33 the children of **A.** were subdued 5983
Jg 11:36 enemies, even of the children of **A.** 5983
Jg 12:1 against the children of **A.**, 5983
Jg 12:2 great strife with the children of **A.**; 5983
Jg 12:3 over against the children of **A.**, 5983
1Sa 12:12 the king of the children of **A.** 5983
1Sa 14:47 against the children of **A.**, 5983
2Sa 8:12 of Moab, and of the children of **A.**, 5983
2Sa 10:1 the king of the children of **A.** died, 5983
2Sa 10:2 into the land of the children of **A.** 5983
2Sa 10:3 the princes of the children of **A.** 5983
2Sa 10:6 when the children of **A.** saw that 5983
2Sa 10:6 the children of **A.** sent and hired 5983
2Sa 10:8 And the children of **A.** came out, 5983
2Sa 10:10 array against the children of **A.** 5983
2Sa 10:11 if the children of **A.** be too strong 5983
2Sa 10:14 when the children of **A.** saw that 5983
2Sa 10:14 returned from the children of **A.**, 5983
2Sa 10:19 feared to help the children of **A.** 5983
2Sa 11:1 they destroy the children of **A.**, 5983
2Sa 12:9 with the sword of the children of **A.** 5983
2Sa 12:26 of **A.**, and took the royal city. 5983
2Sa 12:31 all the cities of the children of **A.** 5983
2Sa 17:27 of Rabbah of the children of **A.**, 5983
1Ki 11:7 abomination of the children of **A.** 5983
1Ki 11:33 the god of the children of **A.**, 5983
2Ki 23:13 abomination of the children of **A.**, 5983
2Ki 24:2 and bands of the children of **A.** 5983
1Ch 18:11 and from the children of **A.**, 5983
1Ch 19:1 the king of the children of **A.** died, 5983
1Ch 19:2 into the land of the children of **A.** 5983
1Ch 19:3 princes of the children of **A.** said 5983
1Ch 19:6 of **A.** saw that they had made 5983
1Ch 19:6 of **A.** sent a thousand talents of 5983
1Ch 19:7 of **A.** gathered themselves together 5983
1Ch 19:9 of **A.** came out, and put the battle 5983
1Ch 19:11 array against the children of **A.** 5983
1Ch 19:12 of **A.** be too strong for thee, then 5983
1Ch 19:15 of **A.** saw that the Syrians were 5983
1Ch 19:19 the Syrians help the children of **A.** 5983
1Ch 20:1 of **A.**, and came and besieged 5983
1Ch 20:3 all the cities of the children of **A.** 5983
2Ch 20:1 of **A.**, and with them other beside 5983
2Ch 20:10 the children of **A.** and Moab, 5983
2Ch 20:22 against the children of **A.**, 5983
2Ch 20:23 children of **A.** and Moab stood up 5983
2Ch 27:5 of **A.** gave him the same year an 5983
2Ch 27:5 So much did the children of **A.** pay 5983
Ne 13:23 married wives of Ashdod, of **A.**, 5983
Ps 83:7 Gebal, and **A.**, and Amalek; 5983
Isa 11:14 the children of **A.** shall obey them. 5983
Jer 9:26 of **A.**, and Moab, and all that are 5983
Jer 25:21 and Moab, and the children of **A.** 5983
Jer 49:6 the captivity of the children of **A.**, 5983
Da 11:41 and the chief of the children of **A.** 5983
Am 1:13 transgressions of the children of **A.**, 5983
Zep 2:8 the revilings of the children of **A.** 5983
Zep 2:9 of **A.** as Gomorrah, even the 5983

AMMONITE (am'-mon-ite) See also AMMONITES; AMMONITESS.
De 23:3 An **A.** or Moabite shall not enter 5984
1Sa 11:1 the **A.** came up, and encamped 5984
1Sa 11:2 Nahash the **A.** answered them, 5984
2Sa 23:37 Zelek the **A.**, Naharai the 5984
1Ch 11:39 Zelek the **A.**, Naharai the 5984
Ne 2:10 and Tobiah the servant, the **A.**, 5984
Ne 2:19 the **A.**, and Geshem the Arabian, 5984
Ne 4:3 Now Tobiah the **A.** was by him, 5984
Ne 13:1 the **A.** and the Moabite should not 5984

AMMONITES (am'-mon-ites)
De 2:20 the **A.** call them Zamzummims; 5984

1Sa 11:11 slew the **A.** until the heat of the 5984
1Ki 11:1 women of the Moabites, **A.**, 5984
1Ki 11:5 Milcom the abomination of the **A.** 5984
2Ch 20:1 and with them other beside the **A.** 5984
2Ch 26:8 the **A.** gave gifts to Uzziah: 5984
2Ch 27:5 fought also with the king of the **A.**, 5984
Ezr 9:1 the Perizzites, the Jebusites, the **A.**, 5984
Ne 4:7 and the Arabians, and the **A.**, 5984
Jer 27:3 to the king of the **A.**, and to the 5984
Jer 40:11 among the **A.**, and in Edom. 5984
Jer 40:14 Baalis the king of the **A.** hath 5984
Jer 41:10 departed to go over to the **A.** 5984
Jer 41:15 eight men, and went to the **A.** 5984
Jer 49:1 Concerning the **A.**, thus saith 5984
Jer 49:2 to be heard in Rabbah of the **A.**; 5984
Eze 21:20 come to Rabbath of the **A.**, 1121,5984
Eze 21:28 concerning the **A.**, and 1121,5984
Eze 25:2 set thy face against the **A.** 1121,5984
Eze 25:3 unto the **A.**, Hear the word 1121,5984
Eze 25:5 **A.** a couching place for flocks; 1121,5984
Eze 25:10 men of the east with the **A.**, 1121,5984
Eze 25:10 **A.** may not be remembered 1121,5984

AMMONITESS (am'-mon-i-tess)
1Ki 14:21 mother's name was Naamah an **A.** 5984
1Ki 14:31 was Naamah an **A.** And Abijam 5984
2Ch 12:13 mother's name was Naamah an **A.** 5984
2Ch 24:26 Zabad the son of Shimeath, an **A.**, 5984

AMNON (am'-non) See also AMNON'S.
2Sa 3:2 his firstborn was **A.**, of Ahinoam 550
2Sa 13:1 and **A.** the son of David loved her. 550
2Sa 13:2 **A.** was so vexed, that he fell sick 550
2Sa 13:2 **A.** thought it hard for him to do 550
2Sa 13:3 But **A.** had a friend whose name 550
2Sa 13:4 **A.** said unto him, I love Tamar, 550
2Sa 13:6 So **A.** lay down, and made himself 550
2Sa 13:6 **A.** said unto the king, I pray thee, 550
2Sa 13:9 **A.** said, Have out all men from me. 550
2Sa 13:10 **A.** said unto Tamar, Bring the 550
2Sa 13:10 them into the chamber to **A.** 550
2Sa 13:15 Then **A.** hated her exceedingly; 550
2Sa 13:15 **A.** said unto her, Arise, be gone. 550
2Sa 13:20 Hath **A.** thy brother been with thee? 550
2Sa 13:22 Absalom spake unto his brother **A.** 550
2Sa 13:22 for Absalom hated **A.**, because he 550
2Sa 13:26 I pray thee, Let my brother **A.** go 550
2Sa 13:27 he let **A.** and all the king's sons go 550
2Sa 13:28 and when I say unto you, Smite **A.**; 550
2Sa 13:29 did unto **A.** as Absalom had 550
2Sa 13:32 for **A.** only is dead: for by the 550
2Sa 13:33 **A.** only is dead. But Absalom fled. 550
2Sa 13:39 he was comforted concerning **A.**, 550
1Ch 3:1 the firstborn **A.**, of Ahinoam 550
1Ch 4:20 the sons of Shimon were, **A.**, and 550

AMNON'S (am'-nons)
2Sa 13:7 Go now to thy brother **A.** house 550
2Sa 13:8 So Tamar went to her brother **A.** 550
2Sa 13:28 when **A.** heart is merry with 550

AMOK (a'-mok)
Ne 12:7 Sallu, **A.**, Hilkiah, Jedaiah 5987
Ne 12:20 Of Sallai, Kallai: of **A.**, Eber; 5987

AMON (a'-mon)
1Ki 22:26 and carry him back unto **A.** the 526
2Ki 21:18 and **A.** his son reigned in his stead 526
2Ki 21:19 **A.** was twenty and two years old 526
2Ki 21:23 the servants of **A.** conspired against 526
2Ki 21:24 that had conspired against king **A.**; 526
2Ki 21:25 the rest of the acts of **A.** which he 526
1Ch 3:14 **A.** his son, Josiah his son 526
2Ch 18:25 carry him back to **A.** the governor 526
2Ch 33:20 and **A.** his son reigned in his stead 526
2Ch 33:21 **A.** was two and twenty years old 526
2Ch 33:22 **A.** sacrificed unto all the carved 526
2Ch 33:23 but **A.** trespassed more and more 526
2Ch 33:25 that had conspired against king **A.**; 526
Ne 7:59 of Zebaim, the children of **A.** 526
Jer 1:2 in the days of Josiah the son of **A.** 526
Jer 25:3 year of Josiah the son of **A.** 526
Zep 1:1 the son of **A.**, king of Judah 526
Mt 1:10 Manasses begat **A.**; *300*
Mt 1:10 and **A.** begat Josias; *300*

AMONG See also AMONGST.
Ge 17:10 child **a.** you shall be circumcised
Ge 17:12 shall be circumcised **a.** you, every
Ge 17:23 every male child **a.** the men of
Ge 23:6 thou art a mighty prince **a.** us: 8432
Ge 23:10 Ephron dwelt **a.** the children of 8432
Ge 24:3 daughters of the Canaanites, **a.** 7130
Ge 30:32 all the brown cattle **a.** the sheep,
Ge 30:32 spotted and speckled **a.** the goats:
Ge 30:33 that is not speckled and spotted **a.**
Ge 30:33 and brown **a.** the sheep, that shall
Ge 30:35 and all the brown **a.** the sheep,
Ge 30:41 that they might conceive **a.** the rods.
Ge 34:22 if every male **a.** us be circumcised,
Ge 34:30 me to stink **a.** the inhabitants of
Ge 34:30 **a.** the Canaanites and the
Ge 35:2 strange gods that are **a.** you, 8432
Ge 36:30 Hori, **a.** their dukes in the land
Ge 40:20 chief baker **a.** his servants. 8432
Ge 42:5 of Israel came to buy corn **a.** those 8432
Ge 47:6 knowest any men of activity **a.** them,
Ex 2:5 when she saw the ark **a.** the flags, 8432
Ex 7:5 the children of Israel from **a.** them. 8432
Ex 9:20 the word of the Lord **a.** the servants
Ex 10:2 my signs which I have done **a.** them:
Ex 12:31 get you forth from **a.** my people, 8432
Ex 12:49 stranger that sojourneth **a.** you. 8432
Ex 13:2 whatsoever openeth the womb **a.**
Ex 13:13 and all the firstborn of man **a.** thy
Ex 15:11 Who is like unto thee, O Lord, **a.**
Ex 17:7 Is the Lord **a.** us, 7130
Ex 25:8 that I may dwell **a.** them. 8432
Ex 28:1 him, from **a.** the children of Israel, 8432
Ex 29:45 I will dwell **a.** the children of Israel, 8432
Ex 29:46 that I may dwell **a.** them: 8432
Ex 30:12 that there be no plague **a.** them,
Ex 30:13 **a.** them that are numbered, 5921
Ex 30:14 Every one that passeth **a.** them 5921
Ex 31:14 shall be cut off from **a.** his people. 7130
Ex 32:25 them naked unto their shame **a.**
Ex 34:9 let my Lord, I pray thee, go **a.** us; 7130
Ex 34:10 the people **a.** which thou art 7130
Ex 34:19 and every firstling **a.** thy cattle,
Ex 35:5 Take ye from **a.** you an offering
Ex 35:10 And every wise hearted **a.** you shall
Ex 36:8 **a.** them that wrought the work
Le 6:18 the males **a.** the children of Aaron
Le 6:29 the males **a.** the priests shall eat
Le 7:6 Every male **a.** the priests shall eat
Le 7:33 He **a.** the sons of Aaron, that
Le 7:34 by a statute for ever from **a.** the
Le 11:2 which ye shall eat **a.** all the beasts
Le 11:3 and cheweth the cud, **a.** the beasts,
Le 11:13 have in abomination **a.** the fowls; 4480
Le 11:27 goeth upon his paws, **a.** all manner
Le 11:29 shall be unclean unto you **a.** the
Le 11:31 unclean to you **a.** all that creep:
Le 11:42 or whatsoever hath more feet **a.**
Le 15:31 defile my tabernacle that is **a.** 8432
Le 16:16 that remaineth **a.** them in the 854
Le 16:29 a stranger that sojourneth **a.** you: 8432
Le 17:4 that man shall be cut off from **a.** 7130
Le 17:8 strangers which sojourn **a.** you, 8432
Le 17:9 that man shall be cut off from **a.**
Le 17:10 strangers that sojourn **a.** you, 8432
Le 17:10 cut him off from **a.** his people 7130
Le 17:12 stranger that sojourneth **a.** you 8432
Le 17:13 the strangers that sojourn **a.** you, 8432
Le 18:26 stranger that sojourneth **a.** you: 8432
Le 18:29 cut off from **a.** their people. 7130
Le 19:8 that soul shall be cut off from **a.**
Le 19:16 go up and down as a talebearer **a.**
Le 19:34 be unto you as one born **a.** you, 854
Le 20:3 will cut him off from **a.** his people; 7130
Le 20:5 cut him off,...from **a.** their people. 7130
Le 20:6 cut him off from **a.** his people 7130
Le 20:14 there be no wickedness **a.** you. 8432
Le 20:18 be cut off from **a.** their people 7130
Le 21:1 defiled for the dead **a.** his people:
Le 21:4 being a chief man **a.** his people, to
Le 21:10 the high priest **a.** his brethren,
Le 21:15 he profane his seed **a.** his people:
Le 22:3 all your seed **a.** your generations,
Le 22:32 hallowed **a.** the children of Israel: 8432
Le 23:29 shall be cut off from **a.** his people
Le 23:30 will I destroy from **a.** his people. 7130
Le 24:10 went out **a.** the children of Israel: 8432
Le 25:33 possession **a.** the children of 8432
Le 25:45 strangers that do sojourn **a.** you,
Le 26:11 set my tabernacle **a.** you: 8432
Le 26:12 I will walk **a.** you, 8432
Le 26:22 send wild beasts **a.** you, which
Le 26:25 I will send the pestilence **a.** you; 8432
Le 26:33 I will scatter you **a.** the heathen,
Le 26:38 And ye shall perish **a.** the heathen,
Nu 1:47 were not numbered **a.** them. 8432
Nu 1:49 them **a.** the children of Israel: 8432
Nu 2:33 numbered **a.** the children of Israel; 8432
Nu 3:12 from **a.** the children of Israel 8432
Nu 3:12 that openeth the matrix **a.**
Nu 3:41 firstborn **a.** the children of Israel;
Nu 3:41 the firstlings **a.** the cattle of the
Nu 3:42 the firstborn **a.** the children of Israel
Nu 3:45 **a.** the children of Israel, and the
Nu 4:2 from **a.** the sons of Levi, 8432
Nu 4:18 Kohathites from **a.** the Levites: 8432
Nu 5:21 a curse and an oath **a.** thy people, 8432
Nu 5:27 a curse **a.** her people 7130
Nu 8:6, 14,16,19 **a.** the children of Israel, 8432
Nu 8:19 no plague **a.** the children of Israel,
Nu 9:7 appointed season **a.** the children 8432
Nu 9:13 soul shall be cut off from **a.** his
Nu 9:14 if a stranger shall sojourn **a.** you, 854
Nu 11:1 the fire of the Lord burnt **a.** them,
Nu 11:3 because the fire of the Lord burnt **a.**
Nu 11:4 mixt multitude that was **a.** them 7130
Nu 11:20 the Lord which is **a.** you, 7130
Nu 11:21 The people, **a.** whom I am, 7130
Nu 12:6 If there be a prophet **a.** you, I the
Nu 13:2 send a man, every one a ruler **a.**
Nu 14:11 which I have shewed **a.** them? 7130
Nu 14:13 this people in thy might from **a.** 7130
Nu 14:14 thou Lord art **a.** this people, 7130
Nu 14:42 the Lord is not **a.** you; 7130
Nu 15:14 whosoever be **a.** you in your 8432
Nu 15:23 Moses, and henceforward **a.** your
Nu 15:26 stranger that sojourneth **a.** them; 8432
Nu 15:29 is born **a.** the children of Israel,
Nu 15:29 stranger that sojourneth **a.** them. 8432
Nu 15:30 cut off from **a.** his people. 7130
Nu 16:3 and the Lord is **a.** them: 8432
Nu 16:21 Separate yourselves from **a.** this 8432
Nu 16:33 perished from **a.** the congregation. 8432
Nu 16:45 you up from **a.** this congregation, 8432
Nu 16:47 plague was begun **a.** the people:
Nu 17:6 rod of Aaron was **a.** their rods. 8432
Nu 18:6 from **a.** the children of Israel: 8432
Nu 18:20 neither shalt thou have any part **a.** 8432
Nu 18:20 inheritance **a.** the children of Israel. 8432
Nu 18:23 that **a.** the children of Israel 8432
Nu 18:24 **A.** the children of Israel they 8432
Nu 19:10 stranger that sojourneth **a.** them, 8432
Nu 19:20 shall be cut off from **a.** the 8432
Nu 21:6 sent fiery serpents **a.** the people,
Nu 23:9 not be reckoned **a.** the nations
Nu 23:21 and the shout of a king is **a.** them.
Nu 25:7 rose up from **a.** the congregation, 8432
Nu 25:11 was zealous for my sake **a.** them, 8432
Nu 25:14 a chief house **a.** the Simeonites
Nu 26:62 numbered **a.** the children of Israel, 8432
Nu 26:62 them **a.** the children of Israel. 8432
Nu 26:64 But **a.** these there was not a man
Nu 27:4 done away from **a.** his family, 8432
Nu 27:4 **a.** the brethren of our father. 8432
Nu 27:7 an inheritance **a.** their father's 8432
Nu 31:16 was a plague **a.** the congregation
Nu 31:17 kill every male **a.** the little ones,
Nu 32:30 they shall have possessions **a.** you 8432
Nu 33:4 the Lord had smitten **a.** them:
Nu 33:54 by lot for an inheritance **a.** your
Nu 35:6 And **a.** the cities which ye shall 854
Nu 35:15 and for the sojourner **a.** them: 8432
Nu 35:34 dwell **a.** the children of Israel. 8432
De 1:13 understanding, and known **a.**
De 1:15 tens, and officers **a.** your tribes.
De 1:42 I am not **a.** you; 7130
De 2:14 wasted out from **a.** the host, 7130
De 2:15 to destroy them from **a.** the host, 7130
De 2:16 and dead from **a.** the people, 7130
De 4:3 destroyed them from **a.** you. 7130
De 4:27 shall scatter you **a.** the nations,
De 4:27 left few in number **a.** the heathen,
De 6:15 a jealous God **a.** you) 7130
De 7:14 male or female barren **a.** you,
De 7:14 or **a.** your cattle.
De 7:20 God will send the hornet **a.** them,
De 7:21 the Lord thy God is **a.** you, 7130
De 13:1 If there arise **a.** you a prophet, 7130
De 13:11 such wickedness as this is **a.** you. 7130

De 13:13 Belial, are gone out from **a.** you, 7130
De 13:14 abomination is wrought **a.** you; 7130
De 14:6 cheweth the cud **a.** the beasts,
De 15:4 there shall be no poor **a.** you;
De 15:7 If there be **a.** you a poor man of
De 16:11 and the widow, that are **a.** you, 7130
De 17:2 If there be found **a.** you, 7130
De 17:7 put the evil away from **a.** you. 7130
De 17:15 one from **a.** thy brethren 7130
De 18:2 no inheritance **a.** their brethren: 7130
De 18:10 not be found **a.** you any one
De 18:18 a Prophet from **a.** their brethren, 7130
De 19:19 put the evil away from **a.** you. 7130
De 19:20 no more any such evil **a.** you. 7130
De 21:9 of innocent blood from **a.** you, 7130
De 21:11 seest **a.** the captives a beautiful
De 21:21 thou put evil away from **a.** you; 7130
De 22:21 thou put evil away from **a.** you. 7130
De 22:24 put away evil from **a.** you. 7130
De 23:10 If there be **a.** you any man, that
De 23:16 dwell with thee, even **a.** you, 7130
De 24:7 put evil away from **a.** you. 7130
De 26:11 the stranger that is **a.** you. 7130
De 28:37 **a.** all nations whither the Lord
De 28:54 the man that is tender **a.** you,
De 28:56 tender and delicate woman **a.** you,
De 28:64 the Lord shall scatter thee **a.** all
De 28:65 **a.** these nations shalt thou find no
De 29:17 and gold, which were **a.** them:)
De 29:18 Lest there should be **a.** you man,
De 29:18 **a.** you a root that beareth gall
De 30:1 them to mind **a.** all the nations,
De 31:16 whither they go to be **a.** them, 7130
De 31:17 because our God is not **a.** us? 7130
De 32:26 of them to cease from **a.** men:
De 32:34 and sealed up **a.** my treasures?
De 32:46 the words which I testify **a.** you
De 32:51 **a.** the children of Israel 8432
Jos 3:5 the Lord will do wonders **a.** you. 7130
Jos 3:10 the living God is **a.** you, 7130
Jos 4:6 That this may be a sign **a.** you, 7130
Jos 7:11 put it even **a.** their own stuff
Jos 7:12 destroy the accursed from **a.** you. 7130
Jos 7:13 the accursed thing from **a.** you. 7130
Jos 7:21 When I saw **a.** the spoils a goodly
Jos 8:9 lodged that night **a.** the people. 8432
Jos 8:33 as he that was born **a.** them;
Jos 8:35 that were conversant **a.** them. 7130
Jos 9:7 Peradventure ye dwell **a.** us; 7130
Jos 9:16 and that they dwelt **a.** them. 7130
Jos 9:22 when ye dwell **a.** us? 7130
Jos 10:1 inhabitants of Gibeon....were **a.** 7130
Jos 13:13 the Maachathites dwell **a.** the 7130
Jos 13:22 slay with the sword **a.** them that 413
Jos 14:3 he gave none inheritance **a.** them. 8432
Jos 14:15 Arba was a great man **a.** the
Jos 15:13 a part **a.** the children of Judah, 8432
Jos 16:9 the children of Ephraim were **a.** 8432
Jos 16:10 the Canaanites dwell **a.** the 7130
Jos 17:4 an inheritance **a.** our brethren. 8432
Jos 17:4 an inheritance **a.** the brethren 8432
Jos 17:6 had an heritance **a.** his sons: 8432
Jos 17:9 cities of Ephraim are **a.** the cities 8432
Jos 18:2 remained **a.** the children of Israel
Jos 18:4 **a.** you three men of each tribe:
Jos 18:7 the Levites have no part **a.** you; 7130
Jos 19:49 Joshua the son of Nun **a.** them: 8432
Jos 20:4 a place, that he may dwell **a.** them. 5973
Jos 20:9 stranger that sojourneth **a.** them, 8432
Jos 22:7 gave Joshua **a.** their brethren 5973
Jos 22:14 their fathers **a.** the thousands of
Jos 22:19 take possession **a.** us: 8432
Jos 22:31 perceive that the Lord is **a.** us, 8432
Jos 23:7 ye come not **a.** these nations,
Jos 23:7 remain **a.** you; neither make
Jos 23:12 even these that remain **a.** you, 854
Jos 24:5 that which I did **a.** them: 7130
Jos 24:17 and **a.** all the people through
Jos 24:23 strange gods which are **a.** you, 7130
Jg 1:16 went and dwelt **a.** the people. 854
Jg 1:29 Canaanites dwelt in Gezer **a.** them. 7130
Jg 1:30 the Canaanites dwelt **a.** them, 7130
Jg 1:32 Asherites dwelt **a.** the Canaanites, 7130
Jg 1:33 Naphtali...dwelt **a.** the Canaanites, 7130
Jg 3:5 children of Israel dwelt **a.** the 7130
Jg 5:8 seen **a.** forty thousand in Israel
Jg 5:9 offered themselves willingly **a.**

Jg 5:13 over the nobles **a.** the people:
Jg 5:14 after thee, Benjamin, **a.** thy people;
Jg 5:16 abodest thou **a.** the sheepfolds, 996
Jg 10:16 away the strange gods from **a.** 7130
Jg 12:4 Ephraim **a.** the Ephraimites, 8432
Jg 12:4 and **a.** the Manassites. 8432
Jg 14:3 **a.** the daughters of thy brethren,
Jg 14:3 or **a.** all my people, that thou
Jg 18:1 unto them **a.** the tribes of Israel. 8432
Jg 18:25 Let not thy voice be heard **a.** us,
Jg 20:12 is this that is done **a.** you?
Jg 20:16 **A.** all this people there were
Jg 21:5 there **a.** all the tribes of Israel
Jg 21:12 **a.** the inhabitants of Jabesh-gilead
Ru 2:7 gather after the reapers **a.** the 996
Ru 2:15 Let her glean even **a.** the sheaves,
Ru 4:10 not cut off from **a.** his brethren, 5973
1Sa 2:8 to set them **a.** princes, and to 5973
1Sa 4:3 when it cometh **a.** us. it may 7130
1Sa 4:17 a great slaughter **a.** the people,
1Sa 6:6 had wrought wonderfully **a.** them,
1Sa 7:3 Ashtaroth from **a.** you, 8432
1Sa 9:2 was not **a.** the children of Israel
1Sa 9:22 place **a.** them that were bidden,
1Sa 10:10 and he prophesied **a.** them. 8432
1Sa 10:11 he prophesied **a.** the prophets, 5973
1Sa 10:11, 12 Is Saul also **a.** the prophets?
1Sa 10:22 he hath hid himself **a.** the stuff 413
1Sa 10:23 when he stood **a.** the people, 8432
1Sa 10:24 there is none like him **a.** the people?
1Sa 14:15 **a.** all the people: the garrison,
1Sa 14:30 much greater slaughter **a.** the
1Sa 14:34 Saul said, Disperse yourselves **a.**
1Sa 14:39 **a.** all the people that answered
1Sa 15:6 down from **a.** the Amalekites, 8432
1Sa 15:6 departed from **a.** the Amalekites. 8432
1Sa 15:33 thy mother be childless **a.** women.
1Sa 16:1 have provided me a king **a.** his sons.
1Sa 17:12 man went **a.** men for an old man
1Sa 19:24 Is Saul also **a.** the prophets?
1Sa 22:14 **a.** all thy servants as David
1Sa 31:9 the house of their idols, and **a.** 854
2Sa 6:19 And he dealt **a.** all the people,
2Sa 6:19 even **a.** the whole multitude
2Sa 15:31 Ahithophel is **a.** the conspirators
2Sa 16:20 Give counsel **a.** you what we
2Sa 17:9 There is a slaughter **a.** the people
2Sa 19:28 didst thou set thy servant **a.** them
2Sa 22:50 unto thee, O Lord, **a.** the heathen,
2Sa 23:8 chief **a.** the captains; the same
2Sa 23:18 of Zeruiah, was chief **a.** three.
2Sa 23:18 and had the name **a.** three.
2Sa 23:22 had the name **a.** three mighty men.
1Ki 3:13 **a.** the kings like unto thee all thy
1Ki 5:6 there is not **a.** us any that can
1Ki 6:13 I will dwell **a.** the children of 8432
1Ki 7:51 put **a.** the treasures of the house
1Ki 8:53 them from **a.** all the people of
1Ki 9:7 and a byword **a.** all people:
1Ki 11:20 **a.** the sons of Pharaoh. 8432
1Ki 14:7 I exalted thee from **a.** the people, 8432
1Ki 21:9 a fast, and set Naboth on high **a.**
1Ki 21:12 Naboth on high **a.** the people
2Ki 4:13 I dwell **a.** mine own people. 8432
2Ki 9:2 arise up from **a.** his brethren, 8432
2Ki 11:2 stole him from **a.** the king's sons 8432
2Ki 17:25 26 the Lord sent lions **a.** them,
2Ki 18:5 after him was none like him **a.** all
2Ki 18:35 **a.** all the gods of the countries,
2Ki 20:15 there is nothing **a.** my treasures
2Ki 23:9 bread **a.** their brethren. 8432
1Ch 4:23 and those that dwelt **a.** plants
1Ch 7:5 their brethren **a.** all the families
1Ch 11:20 and had a name **a.** the three.
1Ch 11:24 the name **a.** the three mighties.
1Ch 11:25 he was honourable **a.** the thirty, 4480
1Ch 12:1 and they were **a.** the mighty men,
1Ch 12:4 the Gibeonite, a mighty man **a.**
1Ch 16:8 known his deeds **a.** the people.
1Ch 16:24 Declare his glory **a.** the heathen;
1Ch 16:24 marvellous works **a.** all nations.
1Ch 16:31 men say **a.** the nations, The Lord
1Ch 18:14 judgment and justice **a.** all his
1Ch 21:6 Benjamin counted he not **a.** them: 8432
1Ch 23:6 into courses **a.** the sons of Levi,
1Ch 24:4 **A.** the sons of Eleazar there were
1Ch 24:4 eight **a.** the sons of Ithamar

1Ch 26:12 **A.** these were the divisions of
1Ch 26:12 even **a.** the chief men, having
1Ch 26:19 divisions of the porters **a.** the
1Ch 26:19 of Kore, and **a.** the sons of Merari.
1Ch 26:30 were officers **a.** them of Israel on 5921
1Ch 26:31 **A.** the Hebronites was Jerijah
1Ch 26:31 even **a.** the Hebronites, according
1Ch 26:31 were found **a.** them mighty men
1Ch 27:6 who was mighty **a.** the thirty,
1Ch 28:4 **a.** the sons of my father he liked
2Ch 5:1 put he **a.** the treasures of the
2Ch 6:5 I chose no city **a.** all the tribes
2Ch 7:13 I send pestilence **a.** my people;
2Ch 7:20 and a byword **a.** all nations.
2Ch 11:22 to be ruler **a.** his brethren:
2Ch 20:25 they found **a.** them in abundance
2Ch 22:11 stole him from **a.** the king's sons 8432
2Ch 24:16 buried him in the city of David **a.** 5973
2Ch 24:23 all the princes of the people from **a.**
2Ch 26:6 Ashdod, and **a.** the Philistines.
2Ch 28:15 clothed all that were naked **a.**
2Ch 31:19 to all the males **a.** the priests,
2Ch 31:19 reckoned by genealogies **a.** the
2Ch 32:14 Who was there **a.** all the gods of
2Ch 33:11 took Manasseh **a.** the thorns,
2Ch 33:19 they are written **a.** the sayings 5921
2Ch 35:13 divided them speedily **a.** all the
2Ch 36:23 is there **a.** you of all his people?
Ezr 1:3 is there **a.** you of all his people?
Ezr 2:62 **a.** those that were reckoned
Ezr 2:65 **a.** them two hundred singing
Ezr 10:18 And **a.** the sons of the priests
Ne 1:8 scatter you abroad **a.** the nations:
Ne 4:11 we come in the midst **a.** them, 8432
Ne 5:17 unto us from **a.** the heathen that 4480
Ne 6:6 It is reported **a.** the heathen,
Ne 7:64 **a.** those that were reckoned by
Ne 9:17 thy wonders thou didst **a.** them; 5973
Ne 10:34 we cast the lots **a.** the priests,
Ne 11:17 the second **a.** his brethren,
Ne 13:26 yet **a.** many nations was there no
Es 1:19 and let it be written **a.** the laws of
Es 3:8 scattered abroad and dispersed **a.** 996
Es 4:3 was great mourning **a.** the Jews,
Es 9:21 To stablish this **a.** them, 5921
Es 9:28 should not fail from **a.** the Jews, 8432
Es 10:3 great **a.** the Jews, and accepted
Job 1:6 Satan came also **a.** them. 8432
Job 2:1 came also **a.** them to present 8432
Job 2:8 he sat down **a.** the ashes. 8432
Job 15:19 no stranger passed **a.** them. 8432
Job 17:10 cannot find one wise man **a.** you.
Job 18:19 neither have son nor nephew **a.**
Job 28:10 He cutteth out rivers **a.** the rocks;
Job 30:5 driven forth from **a.** men, 1460
Job 30:7 **A.** the bushes they brayed; 996
Job 33:23 one **a.** a thousand, to shew unto 4480
Job 34:4 know **a.** ourselves what is good 996
Job 34:37 he clappeth his hands **a.** us, 996
Job 36:14 and their life is **a.** the unclean.
Job 39:25 He saith **a.** the trumpets, Ha, Ha; 1767
Job 41:6 part him **a.** the merchants? 996
Job 42:15 inheritance **a.** their brethren. 8432
Ps 9:11 declare **a.** the people his doings.
Ps 12:1 fail from **a.** the children of men.
Ps 18:49 unto thee, O Lord, **a.** the heathen,
Ps 21:10 seed from **a.** the children of men.
Ps 22:18 They part my garments **a.** them,
Ps 22:28 he is the governor **a.** the nations.
Ps 31:11 a reproach **a.** all mine enemies,
Ps 31:11 especially **a.** my neighbours,
Ps 35:18 I will praise thee **a.** much people.
Ps 44:11 hast scattered us **a.** the heathen.
Ps 44:14 makest us a byword **a.** the heathen,
Ps 44:14 shaking of the head **a.** the people.
Ps 45:9 were **a.** thy honourable women:
Ps 45:12 even the rich **a.** the people shall
Ps 46:10 I will be exalted **a.** the heathen,
Ps 55:15 in their dwellings, and **a.** them. 7130
Ps 57:4 My soul is **a.** lions: and I lie 8432
Ps 57:4 even **a.** them that are set on fire,
Ps 57:9 praise thee, O Lord, **a.** the people:
Ps 57:9 will sing unto thee **a.** the nations.
Ps 67:2 thy saving health **a.** all nations.
Ps 68:13 though ye have lien **a.** the pots, 996
Ps 68:17 the Lord is **a.** them, as in Sinai,
Ps 68:18 the Lord God might dwell **a.** them.

Ps 68:25 **a.** them were the damsels ... 8432
Ps 74:9 neither is their **a.** us any that ... 854
Ps 77:14 declared thy strength **a.** the people ...
Ps 78:45 sent divers sorts of flies **a.** them, ...
Ps 78:49 by sending evil angels **a.** them. ...
Ps 78:60 the tent which he placed **a.** men; ...
Ps 79:10 let him be known **a.** the heathen ...
Ps 80:6 our enemies laugh **a.** themselves. ...
Ps 81:2 mighty; he judgeth **a.** the gods. ... 8432
Ps 86:8 **A.** the gods there is none like ...
Ps 88:5 Free **a.** the dead, like the slain ...
Ps 89:6 who **a.** the sons of the mighty can ...
Ps 94:8 ye brutish **a.** the people: and ye ...
Ps 96:3 Declare his glory **a.** the heathen, ...
Ps 96:3 his wonders **a.** all the people. ...
Ps 96:10 Say **a.** the heathen that the Lord ...
Ps 99:6 Moses and Aaron **a.** his priests, ...
Ps 99:6 and Samuel **a.** them that call ...
Ps 104:10 valleys, which run **a.** the hills. ... 996
Ps 104:12 which sing **a.** the branches. ... 996
Ps 105:1 known his deeds **a.** the people. ...
Ps 105:27 they shewed his signs **a.** them, ...
Ps 105:37 one feeble person **a.** their tribes. ...
Ps 106:27 their seed also **a.** the nations, ...
Ps 106:35 were mingled **a.** the heathen, ...
Ps 106:47 and gather us from **a.** the heathen, ...
Ps 108:3 praise thee, O Lord, **a.** the people: ...
Ps 108:3 praises unto thee **a.** the nations. ...
Ps 109:30 yea, I will praise him **a.** the ... 8432
Ps 110:6 He shall judge **a.** the heathen, ...
Ps 126:2 then said they **a.** the heathen, ...
Ps 136:11 brought out Israel from **a.** them: ... 8432
Pr 1:14 Cast in thy lot **a.** us; let us all ... 8432
Pr 6:19 that soweth discord **a.** brethren. ... 996
Pr 7:7 And beheld **a.** the simple ones, ...
Pr 7:7 I discerned **a.** the youths, a young ...
Pr 14:9 **a.** the righteous there is favour. ... 996
Pr 15:31 reproof of life abideth **a.** the wise. ... 7130
Pr 17:2 of the inheritance **a.** the brethren. ... 8432
Pr 23:20 Be not **a.** winebibbers; **a.** riotous ...
Pr 23:28 the transgressors **a.** men. ...
Pr 27:22 a mortar **a.** wheat with a pestle, ... 8432
Pr 30:14 earth, and the needy from **a.** men. ...
Pr 30:30 lion which is strongest **a.** beasts, ...
Pr 31:23 sitteth **a.** the elders of the land. ... 5973
Ec 6:1 sun, and it is common **a.** men: ... 5921
Ec 7:28 one man **a.** a thousand have I ...
Ec 7:28 but a woman **a.** all those have I ...
Ec 9:3 This is an evil **a.** all things that ...
Ec 9:17 cry of him that ruleth **a.** fools. ...
Ca 1:8 O thou fairest **a.** women, go thy ...
Ca 2:2 As the lily **a.** thorns, ... 996
Ca 2:2 so is my love **a.** the daughters. ... 996
Ca 2:3 As the apple tree **a.** the trees of ...
Ca 2:3 so is my beloved **a.** the sons, I sat ... 996
Ca 2:16 am his: he feedeth **a.** the lilies. ...
Ca 4:2 twins, and none is barren **a.** them. ...
Ca 4:5 are twins, which feed **a.** the lilies. ...
Ca 5:9 O thou fairest **a.** women: what is ...
Ca 5:10 the chiefest **a.** ten thousand. ...
Ca 6:1 O thou fairest **a.** women? ...
Ca 6:3 is mine: he feedeth **a.** the lilies. ...
Ca 6:6 and there is not one barren **a.** them. ...
Isa 2:4 he shall judge **a.** the nations, ... 996
Isa 4:3 written **a.** the living in Jerusalem: ...
Isa 5:27 be weary nor stumble **a.** them; ...
Isa 8:15 many **a.** them shall stumble, ...
Isa 8:16 the testimony, seal the law **a.** ...
Isa 10:16 send **a.** his fat ones leanness; ...
Isa 12:4 declare his doings **a.** the people, ...
Isa 24:13 midst of the land **a.** the people, ... 8432
Isa 29:14 to do a marvellous work **a.** this ...
Isa 29:19 and the poor **a.** men shall rejoice ...
Isa 33:14 Who **a.** us shall dwell with the ...
Isa 33:14 **a.** us shall dwell with everlasting ...
Isa 36:20 Who are they **a.** all the gods of these ...
Isa 39:4 there is nothing **a.** my treasures ...
Isa 41:28 even **a.** them, and there was no ...
Isa 42:23 Who **a.** you will give ear to this? ...
Isa 43:9 who **a.** them can declare this, ...
Isa 43:12 there was no strange god **a.** you: ...
Isa 44:4 shall spring up as **a.** the grass, ... 996
Isa 44:14 himself **a.** the trees of the forest: ...
Isa 48:14 which **a.** them hath declared these ...
Isa 50:10 Who is **a.** you that feareth the ...
Isa 51:18 none to guide her **a.** all the sons ...
Isa 57:6 **A.** the smooth stones of the stream ...
Isa 61:9 shall be known **a.** the Gentiles, ...
Isa 61:9 and their offspring **a.** the people: ... 8432
Isa 65:4 Which remain **a.** the graves, ...
Isa 66:19 And I will set a sign **a.** them, ...
Isa 66:19 declare my glory **a.** the Gentiles. ...
Jer 3:19 shall I put thee **a.** the children, ...
Jer 4:3 ground, and sow not **a.** thorns. ... 413
Jer 5:26 For **a.** my people are found ...
Jer 6:15 they shall fall **a.** them that fall: ...
Jer 6:18 O congregation, what is **a.** them. ...
Jer 6:27 for a tower and a fortress **a.** my ...
Jer 8:12 **a.** them that fall: in the time of ...
Jer 8:17 send serpents, cockatrices, **a.** you, ...
Jer 9:16 scatter them also **a.** the heathen, ...
Jer 10:7 **a.** all the wise men of the nations, ...
Jer 11:9 conspiracy is found **a.** the men ...
Jer 11:9 **a.** the inhabitants of Jerusalem. ...
Jer 12:14 the house of Judah from **a.** them. ... 8432
Jer 14:22 **a.** the vanities of the Gentiles ...
Jer 18:13 Ask ye now **a.** the heathen, ...
Jer 24:10 and the pestilence, **a.** them, till ...
Jer 25:16 sword that I will send **a.** them. ... 996
Jer 25:27 sword which I will send **a.** you. ... 996
Jer 29:18 **a.** all the nations whither I have ...
Jer 29:32 a man to dwell **a.** this people; ... 8432
Jer 31:7 shout **a.** the chief of the nations: ...
Jer 32:20 this day, and in Israel, and **a.** ...
Jer 37:4 Jeremiah came in and went out **a.** ... 8432
Jer 37:10 remained but wounded men **a.** ...
Jer 39:14 so he dwelt **a.** the people. ... 8432
Jer 40:1 bound in chains **a.** all that were ... 8432
Jer 40:5 dwell with him **a.** the people: ... 8432
Jer 40:6 dwelt with him **a.** the people that ... 8432
Jer 40:11 **a.** the Ammonites, and in Edom, ...
Jer 41:8 But ten men were found **a.** them ...
Jer 41:8 slew them not **a.** their brethren. ... 8432
Jer 44:8 a reproach **a.** all the nations of ...
Jer 46:18 as Tabor is **a.** the mountains, ...
Jer 48:27 was he found **a.** thieves? ...
Jer 49:15 small **a.** the heathen, ...
Jer 49:15 and despised **a.** men. ...
Jer 50:2 Declare ye **a.** the nations, ...
Jer 50:23 a desolation **a.** the nations! ...
Jer 50:46 is moved, and the cry is heard **a.** ...
Jer 51:27 blow the trumpet **a.** the nations, ...
Jer 51:41 Babylon become an astonishment **a.** ...
La 1:1 she that was great **a.** the nations, ...
La 1:1 and princess **a.** the provinces, ...
La 1:2 **a.** all her lovers she hath none to ...
La 1:3 she dwelleth **a.** the heathen, ...
La 1:17 as a menstruous woman **a.** them. ... 996
La 2:9 her princes are **a.** the Gentiles: ...
La 4:15 wandered, they said **a.** the heathen, ...
La 4:20 we shall live **a.** the heathen. ...
Eze 1:1 as I was **a.** the captives by the ... 8432
Eze 1:13 and down **a.** the living creatures; ... 996
Eze 2:5 hath been a prophet **a.** them. ... 8432
Eze 2:6 and thou dost dwell **a.** scorpions: ... 413
Eze 3:15 astonished **a.** them seven days. ... 8432
Eze 3:25 thou shalt not go out **a.** them: ... 8432
Eze 4:13 eat their defiled bread **a.** the ...
Eze 5:14 and a reproach **a.** the nations ...
Eze 6:8 escape the sword **a.** the nations, ...
Eze 6:9 shall remember me **a.** the nations ...
Eze 6:13 slain men shall be **a.** their idols ... 8432
Eze 9:2 one man **a.** them was clothed ... 8432
Eze 11:1 **a.** whom I saw Jaazaniah the ... 8432
Eze 11:9 will execute judgments **a.** you. ...
Eze 11:16 cast them far off **a.** the heathen, ...
Eze 11:16 scattered them **a.** the countries, ...
Eze 12:10 house of Israel that are **a.** them. ... 8432
Eze 12:12 the prince that is **a.** them ... 8432
Eze 12:15 I shall scatter them **a.** the nations, ...
Eze 12:16 their abominations **a.** the heathen ...
Eze 13:19 will ye pollute me **a.** my people ... 413
Eze 15:2 which is **a.** the trees of the forest? ...
Eze 15:6 As the vine tree **a.** the trees of the ...
Eze 16:14 renown went forth **a.** the heathen ...
Eze 18:18 which is not good **a.** his people, ... 8432
Eze 19:2 lioness: she lay down **a.** lions, ... 996
Eze 19:2 her whelps **a.** young lions. ... 8432
Eze 19:6 he went up and down **a.** the lions, ... 8432
Eze 19:11 exalted **a.** the thick branches, ... 5921, 996
Eze 20:9 heathen, **a.** whom they were, ... 8432
Eze 20:23 would scatter them **a.** the heathen, ...
Eze 20:38 purge out from **a.** you the rebels, ...
Eze 22:15 scatter thee **a.** the heathen, ...
Eze 22:26 sabbaths, I am profaned **a.** them. ... 8432
Eze 22:30 And I sought for a man **a.** them, ...
Eze 23:10 she became famous **a.** women; ...
Eze 25:10 may not be remembered **a.** ...
Eze 27:24 of cedar, **a.** thy merchandise. ...
Eze 27:36 The merchants **a.** the people ...
Eze 28:19 they that know thee **a.** the people ...
Eze 28:25 house of Israel from the people **a.** ...
Eze 29:12 her cities **a.** the cities that are ... 8432
Eze 29:12 the Egyptians **a.** the nations, ...
Eze 30:23, 26 the Egyptians **a.** the nations ...
Eze 30:26 disperse them **a.** the countries; ...
Eze 31:3, 10 his top was **a.** the thick boughs, ... 996
Eze 31:14 their top **a.** the thick boughs, ... 413
Eze 31:18 glory and in greatness **a.** the trees ...
Eze 32:9 bring thy destruction **a.** the nations, ...
Eze 32:21 The strong **a.** the mighty shall ...
Eze 33:6 take any person from **a.** them, ...
Eze 33:33 that a prophet hath been **a.** them. ... 8432
Eze 34:12 the day that he is **a.** his sheep. ... 8432
Eze 34:24 servant David a prince **a.** them ... 8432
Eze 35:11 will make myself known **a.** them, ...
Eze 36:19 I scattered them **a.** the heathen, ...
Eze 36:21 Israel had profaned **a.** the heathen, ...
Eze 36:22 ye have profaned **a.** the heathen, ...
Eze 36:23 great name, which was profaned **a.** ...
Eze 36:24 take you from **a.** the heathen, ...
Eze 36:30 reproach of famine **a.** the heathen. ...
Eze 37:21 the children of Israel from **a.** the ... 996
Eze 39:6 a fire on Magog, and **a.** them ...
Eze 39:21 I will set my glory **a.** the heathen, ...
Eze 39:28 them to be led into captivity **a.** ... 413
Eze 40:46 **a.** the sons of Levi, which come ...
Eze 44:9 stranger that is **a.** the children. ... 8432
Eze 47:22 strangers that sojourn **a.** you, ... 8432
Eze 47:22 which shall beget children **a.** you: ... 8432
Eze 47:22 country **a.** the children of Israel; ...
Eze 47:22 with you **a.** the tribes of Israel, ... 8432
Da 1:6 Now **a.** these were of the children ...
Da 1:19 and **a.** them all was found none ...
Da 4:35 in the army of heaven, and **a.** ...
Da 7:8 there came up **a.** them another ... 997
Da 11:24 shall scatter **a.** them the prey, ...
Da 11:33 that understand **a.** the people ...
Ho 5:9 **a.** the tribes of Israel have I made ...
Ho 7:7 there is none **a.** them that ...
Ho 7:8 hath mixed himself **a.** the people; ...
Ho 8:8 up: now shall they be **a.** ...
Ho 8:10 they have hired **a.** the nations, ...
Ho 9:17 shall be wanderers **a.** the nations. ...
Ho 10:14 shall a tumult arise **a.** thy people, ...
Ho 13:15 he be fruitful **a.** his brethren, ... 996
Joe 2:17 should they say **a.** the people, ...
Joe 2:19 you a reproach **a.** the heathen; ...
Joe 2:25 great army which I sent **a.** ...
Joe 3:2 scattered **a.** the nations, and parted ...
Joe 3:9 Proclaim ye this **a.** the Gentiles; ...
Am 1:1 Amos, who was **a.** the herdmen ...
Am 2:16 that is courageous **a.** the mighty ...
Am 4:10 I have sent **a.** you the pestilence ...
Am 9:9 the house of Israel **a.** all nations, ...
Ob 1 is sent **a.** the heathen, ...
Ob 2 made thee small **a.** the heathen: ...
Ob 4 thou set thy nest **a.** the stars, ... 996
Mic 3:11 Is not the Lord **a.** us? none ... 7130
Mic 4:3 he shall judge **a.** many people, ... 996
Mic 5:2 Ephratah, though thou be little **a.** ...
Mic 5:8 Jacob shall be **a.** the Gentiles ...
Mic 5:8 people as a lion **a.** the beasts ...
Mic 5:8 young lion **a.** the flocks of sheep: ...
Mic 7:2 and there is none upright **a.** men: ...
Na 3:8 that was situate **a.** the rivers, ...
Hab 1:5 Behold ye **a.** the heathen, and ...
Zep 3:20 praise **a.** all people of the earth, ...
Hag 2:3 Who is left **a.** you that saw this ...
Hag 2:5 so my spirit remaineth **a.** you: ... 8432
Zec 1:8 and he stood **a.** the myrtle trees ... 996
Zec 1:10 man that stood **a.** the myrtle trees. ... 996
Zec 1:11 Lord that stood **a.** the myrtle trees, ... 996
Zec 3:7 give the places **a.** these that ... 996
Zec 7:14 a whirlwind **a.** all the nations ... 5921
Zec 8:13 ye were a curse **a.** the heathen, ...
Zec 10:9 And I will sow them **a.** the people: ...
Zec 12:6 like an hearth of fire **a.** the wood, ...
Zec 12:8 and he that is feeble **a.** them at that ...
Zec 14:13 from the Lord shall be **a.** them; ...
Mal 1:10 Who is there even **a.** you that ...

Mal 1:11 shall be great a. the Gentiles;...
Mal 1:11 name shall be great a. the heathen, ...
Mal 1:14 name is dreadful a. the heathen. ...
Mt 2:6 not the least a. the princes of... 1722
Mt 4:23 manner of disease a. the people... 1722
Mt 9:35 and every disease a. the people... 1722
Mt 11:11 A. them that are born of women... 1722
Mt 12:11 What man shall there be a. you,... 1537
Mt 13:7 and some fell a. thorns; and the... 1909
Mt 13:22 that received seed a. the thorns... 1519
Mt 13:25 sowed tares a. the wheat,... 303,3319
Mt 13:32 it is the greatest a. herbs,...
Mt 13:49 the wicked from a. the just... 3319
Mt 16:7 they reasoned a. themselves,... 1722
Mt 16:8 why reason ye a. yourselves,... 1722
Mt 20:26 But it shall not be so a. you:... 1722
Mt 20:26 whosoever will be great a. you,... 1722
Mt 20:27 whosoever will be chief a. you,... 1722
Mt 21:38 they said a. themselves, This is... 1722
Mt 23:11 But he that is greatest a. you shall...
Mt 26:5 there be an uproar a. the people... 1722
Mt 27:35 parted my garments a. them, ...
Mt 27:56 A. which was Mary Magdalene, ... 1722
Mt 28:15 reported a. the Jews until this day... 1722
Mk 1:27 they questioned a. themselves,... 4314
Mk 4:7 some fell a. thorns, and the thorns.1519
Mk 4:18 they which are sown a. thorns;... 1519
Mk 5:3 had his dwelling a. the tombs;... 1722
Mk 6:4 own country, and a. his own kin,.. 1722
Mk 6:41 two fishes divided he a. them all. ...
Mk 8:16 they reasoned a. themselves,... 4314
Mk 8:19 the five loaves a. five thousand,... 1519
Mk 8:20 when the seven a. four thousand,.. 1519
Mk 9:33 that ye disputed a. yourselves... 4314
Mk 9:34 they had disputed a. themselves, ... 4314
Mk 10:26 saying a. themselves, Who then... 4314
Mk 10:43 so shall it not be a. you:... 1722
Mk 10:43 whosoever will be great a. you,... 1722
Mk 12:7 husbandmen said a. themselves,... 4314
Mk 13:10 first be published a. all nations... 1519
Mk 15:31 said a. themselves with the... 4314
Mk 15:40 a. whom was Mary Magdelene, ... 1722
Mk 16:3 they said a. themselves, Who... 4314
Lu 1:1 are most surely believed a. us,... 1722
Lu 1:25 take away my reproach a. men... 1722
Lu 1:28 thee: blessed art thou a. women... 1722
Lu 1:42 Blessed art thou a. women, ... 1722
Lu 2:44 a. their kinsfolk and acquaintance. ... 1722
Lu 4:36 amazed and spake a. themselves,... 4314
Lu 7:16 a great prophet is risen up a. us;... 1722
Lu 7:28 A. those that are born of women...
Lu 8:7 some fell a. thorns: and... 1722,3319
Lu 8:14 that which fell a. thorns are they,. 1519
Lu 9:46 there arose a reasoning a. them,... 1722
Lu 9:48 that is least a. you all, the same... 1722
Lu 10:3 forth as lambs a. wolves... 1722,3319
Lu 10:30 and fell a. thieves, which stripped. 4045
Lu 10:36 unto him that fell a. the thieves?.. 1519
Lu 16:15 which is highly esteemed a. men... 1722
Lu 19:2 was the chief a. the publicans,...
Lu 19:39 the Pharisees from a. the multitude...
Lu 20:14 him they reasoned a. themselves... 4314
Lu 22:17 this, and divide it a. yourselves:...
Lu 22:23 began to enquire a. themselves,... 4314
Lu 22:24 was also a strife a. them, ... 1722
Lu 22:26 he that is greatest a. you,... 1722
Lu 22:27 a. you as he that serveth... 1722,3319
Lu 22:37 reckoned a. the transgressors:... 3326
Lu 22:55 together, Peter sat down a. them. ... 3319
Lu 24:5 seek ye the living a. the dead?... 3326
Lu 24:47 in his name a. all nations,... 1519
Joh 1:14 was made flesh, and dwelt a. ... 1722
Joh 1:26 there standeth one a. you,... 1722,5216
Joh 6:9 what are they a. so many?... 1519
Joh 6:43 them, Murmur not a. yourelves... 3326
Joh 6:52 therefore strove a. themselves, ... 4314
Joh 7:12 much murmuring a. the people ... 1722
Joh 7:35 said the the Jews a. themselves,... 4314
Joh 7:35 unto the dispersed a. the Gentiles, ...
Joh 7:43 was a division a. the people ... 1722
Joh 8:7 He that is without sin a. you, ...
Joh 9:16 And there was a division a. them. ... 1722
Joh 10:19 a. the Jews for these sayings... 1722
Joh 11:54 no more openly a. the Jews; ... 1722
Joh 11:56 they for Jesus, and spake a.... 3326
Joh 12:19 therefore said a. themselves, ... 4314
Joh 12:20 Greeks a. them that came up to... 1537

Joh 12:42 a. the chief rulers also many ... 1537
Joh 15:24 I had not done a. them the works.. 1722
Joh 16:17 of his disciples a. themselves, ... 4314
Joh 16:19 Do ye enquire a. yourselves of... 3326
Joh 19:24 said therefore a. themselves, ... 4314
Joh 19:24 parted my raiment a. them, and...
Joh 21:23 saying abroad a. the brethren, ... 1519
Ac 1:21 Lord Jesus went in and out a. us, ... 1909
Ac 2:22 of God a. you by miracles... 1519
Ac 3:23 destroyed from a. the people...
Ac 4:12 given a. men, whereby we must... 1722
Ac 4:15 they conferred a. themselves, ... 4315
Ac 4:17 it spread no further a. the people,... 1519
Ac 4:34 there any a. them that lacked:... 1722
Ac 5:12 wonders wrought a. the people;... 1722
Ac 5:34 in reputation a. all the people, ...
Ac 6:3 a. you seven men of honest report, ... 1537
Ac 6:8 wonders and miracles a. the... 1722
Ac 10:22 of good report a. all the nation... 5259
Ac 12:18 was no small stir a. the soldiers,... 1722
Ac 13:26 whosoever a. you feareth God,... 1722
Ac 14:14 ran in a. the people, crying out,... 1519
Ac 15:7 while ago God made choice a. us, ... 1722
Ac 15:12 had wrought a. the Gentiles by... 1722
Ac 15:19 a. the Gentiles are turned to God... 575
Ac 15:22 Silas, chief men a. the brethren:... 1722
Ac 17:33 Paul departed from a. them. ... 3319
Ac 17:34 a. the which was Dionysius the... 1722
Ac 18:11 teaching the word of God a. them. ... 1722
Ac 20:25 a. whom I have gone preaching ... 1722
Ac 20:29 grievous wolves enter in a. you, ... 1519
Ac 20:32 an inheritance a. all them which... 1722
Ac 21:19 wrought a. the Gentiles by his... 1722
Ac 21:21 teachest all the Jews which are a. ... 2596
Ac 21:34 some another, a. the multitude:... 1722
Ac 23:10 take him by force from a.... 3319
Ac 24:5 a mover of sedition a. all the Jews...
Ac 24:21 I cried standing a. them, ... 1722
Ac 25:5 which a. you are able, go down... 1722
Ac 25:6 And when he had tarried a. them... 1722
Ac 26:3 customs which are a. the Jews: ... 2596
Ac 26:4 a. mine own nation at Jerusalem, ... 1722
Ac 26:18 inheritance a. them which are... 1722
Ac 27:22 no loss of any man's life a. you,... 1537
Ac 28:4 said a. themselves, No doubt... 4314
Ac 28:25 when they agreed not a. themselves,.. 4314
Ac 28:29 and had great reasoning a.... 1722
Ro 1:5 obedience to the faith a. all nations,... 1722
Ro 1:6 A. whom are ye also the called... 1722
Ro 1:13 have some fruit a. you also,... 1722
Ro 1:13 even as a. other Gentiles. ... 1722
Ro 1:24 the name of God is blasphemed a.... 1722
Ro 8:29 the firstborn a. many brethren... 1722
Ro 11:17 wert graffed in a. them, and with... 1722
Ro 12:3 to every man that is a. you,... 1722
Ro 15:9 confess to thee a. the Gentiles, ... 1722
Ro 16:7 are of note a. the apostles, who ... 1722
1Co 1:10 that there be no divisions a. you;... 1722
1Co 1:11 there are contentions a. you. ... 1722
1Co 2:2 not to know any thing a. you,... 1722
1Co 2:6 speak wisdom a. them that are... 1722
1Co 3:3 there is a. you envying, and strife,... 1722
1Co 3:18 If any man a. you seemeth to be ... 1722
1Co 5:1 there is fornication a. you,... 1722
1Co 5:1 as named a. the Gentiles,... 1722
1Co 5:2 might be taken away from a. you. ... 3319
1Co 5:13 put away from a. yourselves ...
1Co 6:5 there is not a wise man a. you?... 1722
1Co 6:7 utterly a fault a. you, because ... 1722
1Co 11:18 there be divisions a. you; ... 1722
1Co 11:19 there must be also heresies a. you,... 1722
1Co 11:19 approved may be made manifest a.... 1722
1Co 11:30 many are weak and sickly a. you,... 1722
1Co 15:12 how say some a. you that there... 1722
2Co 1:19 Jesus Christ who was preached a.... 1722
2Co 6:17 come out from a. them, ... 3319
2Co 10:1 who in presence am base a. you, ... 1722
2Co 10:12 comparing themselves a. ...
2Co 11:6 manifest a. you in all things... 1519
2Co 11:26 in perils a. false brethren;... 1722
2Co 12:12 a. you in all patience, in signs, ... 1722
2Co 12:21 my God will humble me a. you, ... 4314
Ga 1:16 I might preach him a. the heathen;... 1722
Ga 2:2 which I preach a. the Gentiles, ... 1722
Ga 3:1 set forth, crucified a. you?... 1722
Ga 3:5 worketh miracles a. you, doeth he... 1722
Eph 2:3 A. whom also we all had our... 1722

Eph 3:8 I should preach a. the Gentiles... 1722
Eph 5:3 not be once named a. you, ... 1722
Php 2:15 a. whom ye shine as lights in the... 1722
Col 1:27 mystery a. the Gentiles; which is... 1722
Col 4:16 when this epistle is read a. you, ... 3844
1Th 1:5 men we are a. you for your sake... 1722
1Th 2:7 But we were gentle a. you,... 1722,3319
1Th 2:10 we behaved ourselves a. you that ...
1Th 5:12 a. you, and are over you in the ... 1722
1Th 5:13 And be at peace a. yourselves... 1722
1Th 5:15 follow that which is good, both a.... 1519
2Th 1:10 testimony a. you was believed)... 1909
2Th 3:7 not ourselves disorderly a. you;... 1722
2Th 3:11 which walk a. you disorderly, ... 1722
2Ti 2:2 heard of me a. many witnesses,... 1223
Heb 5:1 priest taken from a. men is... 3319
Jas 1:26 If any man a. you seem to be... 1722
Jas 3:6 so is the tongue a. our members, ... 1722
Jas 3:13 endued with knowledge a. you? ... 1722
Jas 4:1 come wars and fightings a. you? ... 1722
Jas 5:13 Is any a. you afflicted? let him pray. ... 1722
Jas 5:14 Is any sick a. you?... 1722
1Pe 2:12 your conversation honest a. the... 1722
1Pe 4:8 have fervent charity a. yourselves: ... 1519
1Pe 5:1 elders which are a. you I exhort, ... 1722
1Pe 5:2 flock of God which is a. you,... 1722
2Pe 2:1 false prophets also a. the people, ... 1722
2Pe 2:1 shall be false teachers a. you, ... 1722
2Pe 2:8 righteous man dwelling a. them,... 1722
3Jo 9 loveth to have the preeminence a.... 1722
Jude 15 convince all that are ungodly a....
Re 2:13 who was slain a. you, where... 3844
Re 7:15 shall dwell a. them... 1909
Re 14:4 were redeemed from a. men, ...

AMONGST
Ge 3:8 a. the trees of the garden... 8432
Ge 23:9 possessions of a buryingplace a.... 8432

AMORITE (am'-o-rite) See also AMORITES.
Ge 10:16 And the Jebusite, and the A.,... 567
Ge 14:13 dwelt in the plain of Mamre the A., ... 567
Ge 48:22 I took out of the hand of the A. ... 567
Ex 33:2 will drive out the Canaanite, the A.,... 567
Ex 34:11 I drive out before thee the A.,... 567
Nu 32:39 dispossessed the A. which was in it... 567
De 2:24 given into thine hand Sihon the A., ... 567
Jos 9:1 Hittite, and the A., the Canaanite, ... 567
Jos 11:3 east and on the west, and to the A.,... 567
1Ch 1:14 The Jebusite also, and the A.,... 567
Eze 16:3 thy father was an A., and thy ... 567
Eze 16:45 was a Hittite, and your father an A.... 567
Am 2:9 destroyed I the A. before them,... 567
Am 2:10 to possess the land of the A.... 567

AMORITES (am'-o-rites)
Ge 14:17 and also the A., that dwelt in... 567
Ge 15:16 iniquity of the A. is not yet full... 567
Ge 15:21 And the A. and the Canaanites,... 567
Ex 3:8 and the Hittites, and the A.,... 567
Ex 3:17 and the A., and the Perizzites,... 567
Ex 13:5 and the A., and the Hivites, ... 567
Ex 23:23 and bring thee in unto the A.,... 567
Nu 13:29 the A., dwell in the mountains: ... 567
Nu 21:13 cometh out of the coasts of the A.:... 567
Nu 21:13 between Moab and the A.... 567
Nu 21:21 unto Sihon king of the A.,... 567
Nu 21:25 dwelt in all the cities of the A.,... 567
Nu 21:26 city of Sihon the king of the A.,... 567
Nu 21:29 captivity unto Sihon king of the A.... 567
Nu 21:31 Israel dwelt in the land of the A.... 567
Nu 21:32 drove out the A. that were there... 567
Nu 21:34 didst unto Sihon king of the A.,... 567
Nu 22:2 all that Israel had done to the A.... 567
Nu 32:33 the kingdom of Sihon king of the A., ... 567
De 1:4 had slain Sihon the king of the A., ... 567
De 1:7 and go to the mount of the A.,... 567
De 1:19 the way of the mountain of the A., ... 567
De 1:20 come unto the mountain of the A.,... 567
De 1:27 deliver us into the hand of the A.,... 567
De 1:44 A., which dwell in that mountain,... 567
De 3:2 of the A., which dwelt at Heshbon... 567
De 3:8 the hand of the two kings of the A.... 567
De 3:9 and the A. call it Shenir;)... 567
De 4:46 in the land of Sihon king of the A., ... 567
De 4:47 two kings of the A., which were on... 567
De 7:1 and the Girgashites, and the A.,... 567
De 20:17 namely, the Hittites, and the A.,... 567
De 31:4 to Sihon and to Og, kings of the A.,... 567

Jos 2:10 ye did unto the two kings of the **A.**,..... 567
Jos 3:10 and the **A.**, and the Jebusites,............ 567
Jos 5:1 when all the kings of the **A.**,.............. 567
Jos 7:7 deliver us into the hand of the **A.**, ... 567
Jos 9:10 the two kings of the **A.**, that were....... 567
Jos 10:5 Therefore the five kings of the **A.**,....... 567
Jos 10:6 all the kings of the **A.** that dwell......... 567
Jos 10:12 when the Lord delivered up the **A.** 567
Jos 12:2 Sihon king of the **A.**, who dwelt in......... 567
Jos 12:8 the **A.**, and the Canaanites, ... 567
Jos 13:4 unto Aphek, to the borders of the **A.**: .. 567
Jos 13:10 Sihon king of the **A.**, which reigned...... 567
Jos 13:21 kingdom of Sihon king of the **A.**, ... 567
Jos 24:8 brought you into the land of the **A.**, ... 567
Jos 24:11 fought against you, the **A.**, ... 567
Jos 24:12 even the two kings of the **A.**; 567
Jos 24:15 or the gods of the **A.**, in whose land 567
Jos 24:18 even the **A.** which dwelt in the land: 567
Jg 1:34 the **A.** forced the children of Dan......... 567
Jg 1:35 **A.** would dwell in mount Heres 567
Jg 1:36 the coast of the **A.** was from the.......... 567
Jg 3:5 the Canaanites, Hittites, and **A.**, ... 567
Jg 6:10 fear not the gods of the **A.**,................ 567
Jg 10:8 Jordan in the land of the **A.**, ... 567
Jg 10:11 the Egyptians, and from the **A.**, ... 567
Jg 11:19 Sihon king of the **A.**, the king of.......... 567
Jg 11:21 **A.**, the inhabitants of that country........ 567
Jg 11:22 possessed all the coasts of the **A.**,....... 567
Jg 11:23 of Israel hath dispossessed the **A.**......... 567
1Sa 7:14 peace between Israel and the **A.**........... 567
2Sa 21:2 but of the remnant of the **A.**;.............. 567
1Ki 4:19 the country of Sihon king of the **A.**, ... 567
1Ki 9:20 the people that were left of the **A.**,...... 567
1Ki 21:26 according to all things as did the **A.**,.... 567
2Ki 21:11 wickedly above all that the **A.** did, ... 567
2Ch 8:7 of the Hittites, and the **A.**, ... 567
Ezr 9:1 Moabites, the Egyptians, and the **A.**..... 567
Ne 9:8 the **A.**, and the Perizzites, ... 567
Ps 135:11 Sihon king of the **A.**, and Og 567
Ps 136:19 Sihon king of the **A.**: for his mercy 567

AMOS (A'-mos)
Am *general title* **A.**..
Am 1:1 The words of **A.**, who was among...... 5986
Am 7:8 And the Lord said unto me, **A.**, ... 5986
Am 7:10 saying, **A.** hath conspired against........ 5986
Am 7:11 thus **A.** saith, Jeroboam shall die 5986
Am 7:12 Amaziah said unto **A.**, O thou seer, ... 5986
Am 7:14 answered **A.**, and said to Amaziah, ... 5986
Am 8:2 And he said, **A.**, what seest thou?...... 5986
Lu 3:25 which was the son of **A.**, ... *301*

AMOUNTING
2Ch 3:8 gold, **a.** to six hundred talents. ....

AMOZ (A'-moz)
2Ki 19:2 to Isaiah the prophet the son of **A.**. 531
2Ki 19:20 the son of **A.** sent to Hezekiah,........... 531
2Ki 20:1 the son of **A.** came to him, and said...... 531
2Ch 26:22 did Isaiah the prophet, the son of **A.**, ... 531
2Ch 32:20 the son of **A.**, prayed and cried to 531
2Ch 32:32 Isaiah the prophet, the son of **A.**, ... 531
Isa 1:1 The vision of Isaiah the son of **A.**, ... 531
Isa 2:1 The word that Isaiah the son of **A.** 531
Isa 13:1 which Isaiah the son of **A.** did see. 531
Isa 20:2 the Lord by Isaiah the son of **A.**,.......... 531
Isa 37:2 Isaiah the prophet the son of **A.**......... 531
Isa 37:21 the son of **A.** sent unto Hezekiah,......... 531
Isa 38:1 son of **A.** came unto him, and said....... 531

AMPHIPOLIS (am-fip'-o-lis)
Ac 17:1 when they had passed through **A.**........ *295*

AMPLIAS (am'-ple-as)
Ro 16:8 Greet **A.** my beloved in the Lord......... *291*

AMRAM (am'-ram) See also AMRAMITES; AMRAM'S; HEMDAN.
Ex 6:18 the sons of Kohath; **A.**, and Izhar, ... 6019
Ex 6:20 And **A.** took him Jochebed, his 6019
Ex 6:20 and the years of the life of **A.** were.... 6019
Nu 3:19 of Kohath by their families; **A.**,.......... 6019
Nu 26:58 Korathites. And Kohath begat **A.** 6019
Nu 26:59 and she bare unto **A.** Aaron, and........ 6019
1Ch 1:41 **A.**, and Eshban, and Ithran, and......... 2566
1Ch 6:2 **A.**, Izhar, and Hebron, and Uzziel. 6019
1Ch 6:3 children of **A.**; Aaron and Moses,........ 6019
1Ch 6:18 sons of Kohath were, **A.**, and Izhar, ... 6019
1Ch 23:12 sons of Kohath; **A.**, Izhar, Hebron,....... 6019
1Ch 23:13 sons of **A.**; Aaron and Moses: 6019
1Ch 24:20 sons of **A.**; Shubael: of the sons 6019
Ezr 10:34 sons of Bani; Maadai, **A.**, and Uel, ... 6019

AMRAMITES (am'-ram-ites)
Nu 3:27 Kohath was the family of the **A.**......... 6020
1Ch 26:23 Of the **A.**, and the Izharites, the........ 6020

AMRAM'S (am'-rams)
Nu 26:59 name of **A.** wife was Jochebed, ... 6019

AMRAPHEL (am'-raf-el)
Ge 14:1 it came to pass in the days of **A.** 569
Ge 14:9 and **A.** king of Shinar, and Arioch 569

AMZI (am'-zi)
1Ch 6:46 The son of **A.**,the son of Bani,............ 557
Ne 11:12 the son of **A.**, the son of Zechariah, ... 557

AN See In the APPENDIX; also ANOTHER.

ANAB (a'-nab)
Jos 11:21 from **A.**, and from all the................. 6024
Jos 15:50 And **A.**, and Eshtemoh, and Anim, ... 6024

ANAH (a'-nah)
Ge 36:2 Aholibamah, the daughter of **A.**.......... 6034
Ge 36:14, 18 Aholibamah, the daughter of **A.**,..... 6034
Ge 36:20 and Shobal, and Zibeon, and **A.**,......... 6034
Ge 36:24 of Zibeon; both Ajah and **A.**: 6034
Ge 36:24 was that **A.** that found the mules 6034
Ge 36:25 And the children of **A.** were these;..... 6034
Ge 36:25 Aholibamah the daughter of **A.**........... 6034
Ge 36:29 duke Shobal, duke Zibeon, duke **A.**,.... 6034
1Ch 1:38 and Zibeon, and **A.**, and Dishon, ... 6034
1Ch 1:40 the sons of Zibeon; Aiah, and **A.**.......... 6034
1Ch 1:41 The sons of **A.**; Dishon. And the 6034

ANAHARATH (an-a-ha'-rath)
Jos 19:19 Haphraim, and Shihon, and **A.**,............ 588

ANAIAH (an-a-i'-ah)
Ne 8:4 and Shema, and **A.**, and Urijah, ... 6043
Ne 10:22 Pelatiah, Hanan, **A.**, ... 6043

ANAK (a'-nak) See also ANAKIMS.
Nu 13:22 and Talmai, the children of **A.**, ... 6061
Nu 13:28 we saw the children of **A.** there.......... 6061
Nu 13:33 we saw the giants, the sons of **A.**, ... 6061
De 9:2 stand before the children of **A.**! 6061
Jos 15:13 the city of Arba the father of **A.**, ... 6061
Jos 15:14 drove thence the three sons of **A.**,..... 6061
Jos 15:14 and Talmai, the children of **A.**. 6061
Jos 21:11 the city of Arba the father of **A.**, ... 6061
Jg 1:20 expelled thence the three sons of **A.**... 6061

ANAKIMS (an'-ak-ims)
De 1:28 seen the sons of the **A.** there........... 6062
De 2:10 and many, and tall, as the **A.**;........... 6062
De 2:11 were accounted giants, as the **A.**; 6062
De 2:21 as the **A.**; but the Lord destroyed...... 6062
De 9:2 and tall, the children of the **A.**, ... 6062
Jos 11:21 cut off the **A.** from the mountains,...... 6062
Jos 11:22 There was none of the **A.** left 6062
Jos 14:12 heardest in that day how the **A.**......... 6062
Jos 14:15 was a great man among the **A.**. 6062

ANAMIM (an'-am-im)
Ge 10:13 **A.**, and Lehabim, and Naphtuhim,....... 6047
1Ch 1:11 Mizraim begat Ludim, and **A.**, ... 6047

ANAMMELECH (a-nam'-mel-ek)
2Ki 17:31 and **A.**, the gods of Sepharvaim. 6048

ANAN (a'-nan)
Ne 10:26 And Ahijah, Hanan, **A.**,.................... 6052

ANANI (an-a'-ni)
1Ch 3:24 Johanan, and Dalaiah, and **A.**, ... 6054

ANANIAH (an-an-i'-ah) See also ANANIAS.
Ne 3:23 son of Maaseiah, the son of **A.**, ... 6055
Ne 11:32 And at Anathoth, Nob, **A.**,................ 6055

ANANIAS (an-an-i'-as) See also ANANIAH.
Ac 5:1 a certain man named **A.**,.................... *367*
Ac 5:3 But Peter said, **A.**, why hath Satan...... *367*
Ac 5:5 **A.** hearing these words fell down,........ *367*
Ac 9:10 disciple at Damascus, named **A.**;........... *367*
Ac 9:10 said the Lord in a vision, **A.**. *367*
Ac 9:12 **a vision a man named A. coming**.... *367*
Ac 9:13 Then **A.** answered, Lord..................... *367*
Ac 9:17 **A.** went his way, and entered into *367*
Ac 22:12 **A.**, a devout man according to the *367*
Ac 23:2 the high priest **A.** commanded............ *367*
Ac 24:1 after five days **A.** the high priest *367*

ANATH (a'-nath) See also BETH-ANATH.
Jg 3:31 was Shamgar the son of **A.**, which...... 6067
Jg 5:6 the days of Shamgar the son of **A.**, ... 6067

ANATHEMA (a-nath'-em-ah)
1Co 16:22 let him be **A.** Maran-atha. *331*

ANATHOTH (an'-a-thoth) See also ANETOTHITE.
Jos 21:18 **A.** with her suburbs, and Almon......... 6068
1Ki 2:26 Get thee to **A.**, unto thine own fields;. 6068
1Ch 6:60 and **A.** with her suburbs. All their 6068
1Ch 7:8 and Abiah, and **A.**, and Alameth......... 6068
Ezr 2:23 **A.**, an hundred twenty and eight. 6068
Ne 7:27 **A.**, an hundred twenty and eight. 6068
Ne 10:19 Hariph, **A.**, Nebai, ... 6068
Ne 11:32 And at **A.**, Nob, Ananiah, ... 6068
Isa 10:30 be heard unto Laish, O poor **A.** 6068
Jer 1:1 in **A.**, in the land of Benjamin: 6068
Jer 11:21 saith the Lord of the men of **A.**, ... 6068
Jer 11:23 will bring evil upon the men of **A.**, ... 6068
Jer 29:27 thou not reproved Jeremiah of **A.**, ... 6068
Jer 32:7 Buy thee my field that is in **A.**: 6068
Jer 32:8 field, I pray thee, that is in **A.**,.......... 6068
Jer 32:9 my uncle's son, that was in **A.**,.......... 6068

ANCESTORS
Le 26:45 remember the covenant of their **a.**, ... 7223

ANCHOR See also ANCHORS.
Heb 6:19 hope we have as an **a.** of the soul, ... *45*

ANCHORS
Ac 27:29 they cast four **a.** out of the stern, ... *45*
Ac 27:30 have cast **a.** out of the foreship...............
Ac 27:40 they had taken up the **a.**, ... *45*

ANCIENT See also ANCIENTS.
De 33:15 chief things of the **a.** mountains, ... 6924
Jg 5:21 that **a.** river, the river Kishon. 6917
2Ki 19:25 Hast thou not heard... of **a.** times...... 6924
1Ch 4:22 And these are **a.** things.................... 6267
Ezr 3:12 of the fathers, who were **a.** men,........ 2204
Job 12:12 With the **a.** is wisdom;...................... 3453
Ps 77:5 the years of **a.** times. 5769
Pr 22:28 Remove not the **a.** landmark, ... 5769
Isa 3:2 and the prudent, and the **a.**,.............. 2204
Isa 3:5 himself proudly against the **a.**, ... 2204
Isa 9:15 **a.** honourable, he is the head; 2204
Isa 19:11 son of the wise, the son of **a.** kings? .. 6924
Isa 23:7 whose antiquity is of **a.** days?............ 6924
Isa 37:26 Hast thou not heard...of **a.** times, ... 6924
Isa 44:7 since I appointed the **a.** people?......... 5769
Isa 45:21 hath declared this from **a.** time?......... 6924
Isa 46:10 **a.** times the things that are not 6924
Isa 47:6 upon the **a.** hast thou very................ 2204
Isa 51:9 **a.** days, in the generations of old. 6924
Jer 5:15 mighty nation, it is an **a.** nation.,........ 5769
Jer 18:15 in their ways from the **a.** paths,.......... 5769
Eze 9:6 Then they began at the **a.** men.......... 2204
Eze 36:2 the **a.** high places are ours in 5769
Da 7:9 **A.** of days did sit, whose garment...... 6268
Da 7:13 and came to the **A.** of days, ... 6268
Da 7:22 **A.** of days came, and judgment.......... 6268

ANCIENTS
1Sa 24:13 As saith the proverb of the **a.**, ... 6931
Ps 119:100 I understand more than the **a.**, ... 2204
Isa 3:14 enter into judgment with the **a.**.......... 2204
Isa 24:23 and before his **a.** gloriously. 2204
Jer 19:1 and take of the **a.** of the people, ... 2204
Jer 19:1 and of the **a.** of the priests; 2204
Eze 7:26 priest, and counsel from the **a.**. 2204
Eze 8:11 seventy men of the **a.** of the............ 2204
Eze 8:12 the **a.** of the house of Israel do 2204
Eze 27:9 **a.** of Gebal and the wise men............ 2204

ANCLE See also ANCLES.
Ac 3:7 feet and **a.** bones received strength.... *4974*

ANCLE-BONES See ANCLE and BONES.

ANCLES
Eze 47:3 the waters were to the **a.**. 657

AND See in the APPENDIX.

ANDREW (an'-drew)
Mt 4:18 Simon called Peter, and **A.** his *406*
Mt 10:2 called Peter, and **A.** his brother;.......... *406*
Mk 1:16 Simon and **A.** his brother casting *406*
Mk 1:29 into the house of Simon and **A.**, ... *406*
Mk 3:18 **A.**, and Philip, and Bartholomew,......... *406*
Mk 13:3 John and **A.** asked him privately, ... *406*
Lu 6:14 named Peter,) and **A.** his brother, ... *406*
Joh 1:40 **A.**, Simon Peter's brother. *406*
Joh 1:44 Bethsaida, the city of **A.** and Peter. *406*
Joh 6:8 One of his disciples, **A.**, Simon............ *406*
Joh 12:22 Philip cometh and telleth **A.**:.............. *406*

Joh 12:22 and again **A.** and Philip tell Jesus. ... *406*
Ac 1:13 **A.**, Philip, and Thomas, ... *406*

ANDRONICUS (an-dro-ni'-cus)
Ro 16:7 Salute **A.** and Junia, my kinsmen, ... *408*

ANEM (a'-nem) See also EN-GANNIM.
1Ch 6:73 suburbs, and **A.** with her suburbs: ... 6046

ANER (a'-nur)
Ge 14:13 of Eshcol, and brother of **A.**: ... 6063
Ge 14:24 the men which went with me, **A.**, ... 6063
1Ch 6:70 **A.** with her suburbs, and Bileam ... 6063

ANETHOTHITE (an'-e-thoth-ite) See also ANETOTHITE.
2Sa 23:27 Abiezer the **A.**, Mebunnai the ... 6069

ANETOTHITE (an'-e-toth-ite) See ANETHOTHITE; ANTOTHITE.
1Ch 27:12 Abiezer the **A.**, of the Benjamites: ... 6069

ANGEL See also ANGEL'S; ANGELS; ARCHANGEL.
Ge 16:7 the **a.** of the Lord found her by a ... 4397
Ge 16:9 the **a.** of the Lord said unto her, ... 4397
Ge 16:10 **a.** of the Lord said unto her, I will ... 4397
Ge 16:11 the **a.** of the Lord said unto her, ... 4397
Ge 21:17 the **a.** of God called to Hagar out ... 4397
Ge 22:11 the **a.** of the Lord called unto him ... 4397
Ge 22:15 **a.** of the Lord called unto Abraham ... 4397
Ge 24:7 he shall send his **a.** before thee ... 4397
Ge 24:40 will send his **a.** with thee, ... 4397
Ge 31:11 the **a.** of God spake unto me in a ... 4397
Ge 48:16 The **A.** which redeemed me from ... 4397
Ex 3:2 **a.** of the Lord appeared unto him, ... 4397
Ex 14:19 the **a.** of God, which went before ... 4397
Ex 23:20 Behold, I send an **A.** before thee, ... 4397
Ex 23:23 mine **A.** shall go before thee, ... 4397
Ex 32:34 mine **A.** shall go before thee: ... 4397
Ex 33:2 I will send an **a.** before thee; ... 4397
Nu 20:16 he heard our voice, and sent an **a.**, ... 4397
Nu 22:22 the **a.** of the Lord stood in the way ... 4397
Nu 22:23 the ass saw the **a.** of the Lord ... 4397
Nu 22:24 the **a.** of the Lord stood in a path ... 4397
Nu 22:25 And when the ass saw the **a.** of the ... 4397
Nu 22:26 the **a.** of the Lord went further. ... 4397
Nu 22:27 the **a.** of the Lord, she fell down ... 4397
Nu 22:31 he saw the **a.** of the Lord standing ... 4397
Nu 22:32 the **a.** of the Lord said unto him, ... 4397
Nu 22:34 Balaam said unto the **a.** of the ... 4397
Nu 22:35 **a.** of the Lord said unto Balaam, ... 4397
Jg 2:1 an **a.** of the Lord came up from ... 4397
Jg 2:4 when the **a.** of the Lord spake ... 4397
Jg 5:23 Meroz, said the **a.** of the Lord, ... 4397
Jg 6:11 there came an **a.** of the Lord, ... 4397
Jg 6:12 **a.** of the Lord appeared unto him, ... 4397
Jg 6:20 the **a.** of God said unto him, Take ... 4397
Jg 6:21 **a.** of the Lord put forth the end ... 4397
Jg 6:21 Then the **a.** of the Lord departed ... 4397
Jg 6:22 perceived that he was an **a.** ... 4397
Jg 6:22 I have seen an **a.** of the Lord ... 4397
Jg 13:3 the **a.** of the Lord appeared unto ... 4397
Jg 13:6 like the countenance of an **a.** ... 4397
Jg 13:9 the **a.** of God came again unto the ... 4397
Jg 13:13, 16 the **a.** of the Lord said unto ... 4397
Jg 13:15, 17 Manoah said unto the **a.** of the ... 4397
Jg 13:16 Manoah knew not that he was an **a.** ... 4397
Jg 13:18 And the **a.** of the Lord said ... 4397
Jg 13:19 and the **a.** did wondrously; ...
Jg 13:20 the **a.** of the Lord ascended in the ... 4397
Jg 13:21 **a.** of the Lord did no more appear ... 4397
Jg 13:21 Manoah knew that he was an **a.** ... 4397
1Sa 29:9 good in my sight, as an **a.** of God: ...
2Sa 14:17 **a.** of God, so is my lord the king ... 4397
2Sa 14:20 to the wisdom of an **a.** of God, ... 4397
2Sa 19:27 the king is as an **a.** of God: ... 4397
2Sa 24:16 when the **a.** stretched out his hand ... 4397
2Sa 24:16 to the **a.** that destroyed the people, ... 4397
2Sa 24:16 **a.** of the Lord was by the threshing ... 4397
2Sa 24:17 the **a.** that smote the people, ... 4397
1Ki 13:18 and an **a.** spake unto me by the ... 4397
1Ki 19:5 an **a.** touched him, and said unto ... 4397
1Ki 19:7 the **a.** of the Lord came again ... 4397
2Ki 1:3 the **a.** of the Lord said to Elijah ... 4397
2Ki 1:15 the **a.** of the Lord said unto Elijah, ... 4397
2Ki 19:35 the **a.** of the Lord went out. ... 4397
1Ch 21:12 and the **a.** of the Lord destroying ... 4397
1Ch 21:15 God sent an **a.** unto Jerusalem ... 4397
1Ch 21:15 **a.** that destroyed, It is enough, ... 4397
1Ch 21:15 And the **a.** of the Lord stood by ... 4397
1Ch 21:16 saw the **a.** of the Lord stand ... 4397
1Ch 21:18 the **a.** of the Lord commanded ... 4397
1Ch 21:20 Ornan turned back, and saw the **a.**; ... 4397
1Ch 21:27 And the Lord commanded the **a.**; ... 4397
1Ch 21:30 the sword of the **a.** of the Lord. ... 4397
2Ch 32:21 the Lord sent an **a.**, which cut off ... 4397
Ps 34:7 The **a.** of the Lord encampeth ... 4397
Ps 35:5 let the **a.** of the Lord chase them ... 4397
Ps 35:6 let the **a.** of the Lord persecute ... 4397
Ec 5:6 neither say thou before the **a.**, ... 4397
Isa 37:36 the **a.** of the Lord went forth, ... 4397
Isa 63:9 the **a.** of his presence saved them: ... 4397
Da 3:28 who hath sent his **a.**, and delivered ... 4398
Da 6:22 My God hath sent his **a.**, and hath ... 4398
Ho 12:4 he had power over the **a.**, ... 4397
Zec 1:9 the **a.** that talked with me ... 4397
Zec 1:11 they answered the **a.** of the Lord ... 4397
Zec 1:12 **a.** of the Lord answered and said, ... 4397
Zec 1:13 the Lord answered the **a.** that ... 4397
Zec 1:14 the **a.** that communed with me ... 4397
Zec 1:19 I said unto the **a.** that talked ... 4397
Zec 2:3 **a.** that talked with me went forth, ... 4397
Zec 2:3 and another **a.** went out ... 4397
Zec 3:1 the **a.** of the Lord, and Satan ... 4397
Zec 3:3 stood before the **a.** ... 4397
Zec 3:5 And the **a.** of the Lord stood by. ... 4397
Zec 3:6 the **a.** of the Lord protested unto ... 4397
Zec 4:1 **a.** that talked with me came again, ... 4397
Zec 4:4 spake to the **a.** that talked with ... 4397
Zec 4:5 **a.** that talked with me answered ... 4397
Zec 5:5 **a.** that talked with me went forth, ... 4397
Zec 5:10 said I to the **a.** that talked with me, ... 4397
Zec 6:4 I answered and said unto the **a.** ... 4397
Zec 6:5 the **a.** answered and said unto me, ... 4397
Zec 12:8 as the **a.** of the Lord before them. ... 4397
Mt 1:20 **a.** of the Lord appeared unto him ... *32*
Mt 1:24 did as the **a.** of the Lord had bidden ... *32*
Mt 2:13 **a.** of the Lord appeareth to ... *32*
Mt 2:19 behold, an **a.** of the Lord appeareth ... *32*
Mt 28:2 for the **a.** of the Lord descended ... *32*
Mt 28:5 the **a.** answered and said unto the ... *32*
Lu 1:11 appeared unto him an **a.** of the Lord ... *32*
Lu 1:13 the **a.** said unto him, Fear not, ... *32*
Lu 1:18 Zacharias said unto the **a.**, ... *32*
Lu 1:19 the **a.** answering said unto him, ... *32*
Lu 1:26 the **a.** Gabriel was sent from God ... *32*
Lu 1:28 And the **a.** came in unto her, ... *32*
Lu 1:30 **a.** said unto her, Fear not, Mary: ... *32*
Lu 1:34 Then said Mary unto the **a.**, ... *32*
Lu 1:35 the **a.** answered and said unto her, ... *32*
Lu 1:38 And the **a.** departed from her. ... *32*
Lu 2:9 the **a.** of the Lord came upon them, ... *32*
Lu 2:10 the **a.** said unto them, Fear not: ... *32*
Lu 2:13 **a.** a multitude of the heavenly ... *32*
Lu 2:21 which was so named of the **a.** ... *32*
Lu 22:43 there appeared an **a.** unto him ... *32*
Joh 5:4 **a.** went down at a certain season ... *32*
Joh 12:29 others said, An **a.** spake to him. ... *32*
Ac 5:19 the **a.** of the Lord by night opened ... *32*
Ac 6:15 as it had been the face of an **a.** ... *32*
Ac 7:30 an **a.** of the Lord in a flame ... *32*
Ac 7:35 the hand of the **a.** which appeared ... *32*
Ac 7:38 with the **a.** which spake to him ... *32*
Ac 8:26 **a.** of the Lord spake unto Philip, ... *32*
Ac 10:3 an **a.** of God coming in to him, ... *32*
Ac 10:7 the **a.** which spake unto Cornelius ... *32*
Ac 10:22 warned from God by an holy **a.** ... *32*
Ac 11:13 how he had seen an **a.** in his house, ... *32*
Ac 12:7 the **a.** of the Lord came upon him, ... *32*
Ac 12:8 the **a.** said unto him, Gird thyself, ... *32*
Ac 12:9 which was done by the **a.**; ... *32*
Ac 12:10 forthwith the **a.** departed ... *32*
Ac 12:11 the Lord hath sent his **a.**, ... *32*
Ac 12:15 said they, It is his **a.** ...
Ac 12:23 the **a.** of the Lord smote him, ... *32*
Ac 23:8 resurrection, neither **a.**, nor spirit: ... *32*
Ac 23:9 if a spirit or an **a.** hath spoken ... *32*
Ac 27:23 by me this night the **a.** of God, ... *32*
2Co 11:14 transformed into an **a.** of light ... *32*
Ga 1:8 we, or an **a.** from heaven, preach ... *32*
Ga 4:14 received me as an **a.** of God, ... *32*
Re 1:1 he sent and signified it by his **a.** ... *32*
Re 2:1 **the a. of the church of Ephesus** ... *32*
Re 2:8 **the a. of the church in Smyrna** ... *32*
Re 2:12 **to the a. of the church in Pergamos** ... *32*
Re 2:18 **the a. of the church in Thyatira** ... *32*
Re 3:1 **unto the a. of the church in Sardis** ... *32*
Re 3:7 **the a. of the church in Philadelphia.** *32*
Re 3:14 **unto the a. of the church of the** ... *32*
Re 5:2 I saw a strong **a.** proclaiming ... *32*
Re 7:2 another **a.** ascending from the east, ... *32*
Re 8:3 **a.** came and stood at the altar, ... *32*
Re 8:5 the **a.** took the censer, and filled it ... *32*
Re 8:7 The first **a.** sounded, and there ... *32*
Re 8:8 the second **a.** sounded, and as it ... *32*
Re 8:10 the third **a.** sounded, and there fell ... *32*
Re 8:12 the fourth **a.** sounded, and the ... *32*
Re 8:13 an **a.** flying through the midst ... *32*
Re 9:1 the fifth **a.** sounded, and I saw ... *32*
Re 9:11 which is the **a.** of the bottomless pit, ... *32*
Re 9:13 and the sixth **a.** sounded. ... *32*
Re 9:14 saying to the sixth **a.** which had the ... *32*
Re 10:1 And I saw another mighty **a.** come ... *32*
Re 10:5 **a.** which I saw stand upon the sea ... *32*
Re 10:7 of the voice of the seventh **a.**, ... *32*
Re 10:8 open in the hand of the **a.** ... *32*
Re 10:9 I went unto the **a.**, and said unto ... *32*
Re 11:1 and the **a.** stood, saying, Rise, ... *32*
Re 11:15 and the seventh **a.** sounded; ... *32*
Re 14:6 I saw another **a.** fly in the midst ... *32*
Re 14:8 and there followed another **a.**, ... *32*
Re 14:9 the third **a.** followed them ... *32*
Re 14:15, 17 **a.** came out of the temple ... *32*
Re 14:18 another **a.** came out from the altar, ... *32*
Re 14:19 **a.** thrust in his sickle into the earth, ... *32*
Re 16:3 the second **a.** poured out his vial ... *32*
Re 16:4 the third **a.** poured out his vial ... *32*
Re 16:5 I heard the **a.** of the waters say, ... *32*
Re 16:8 the fourth **a.** poured out his vial ... *32*
Re 16:10 the fifth **a.** poured out his vial ... *32*
Re 16:12 the sixth **a.** poured out his vial ... *32*
Re 16:17 the seventh **a.** poured out his vial ... *32*
Re 17:7 and the **a.** said unto me, ... *32*
Re 18:1 I saw another **a.** come down from ... *32*
Re 18:21 a mighty **a.** took up a stone ... *32*
Re 19:17 I saw an **a.** standing in the sun; ... *32*
Re 20:1 and I saw an **a.** come down ... *32*
Re 21:17 measure of a man, that is, of the **a.** ... *32*
Re 22:6 his **a.** to shew unto his servants ... *32*
Re 22:8 before the feet of the **a.** ... *32*
Re 22:16 **have sent mine a. to testify unto** ... *32*

ANGEL'S
Re 8:4 before God out of the **a.** hand. ... *32*
Re 10:10 the little book out of the **a.** hand, ... *32*

ANGELS See also ANGELS'.
Ge 19:1 there came two **a.** to Sodom ... 4397
Ge 19:15 then the **a.** hastened Lot, ... 4397
Ge 28:12 the **a.** of God ascending ... 4397
Ge 32:1 way, and the **a.** of God met him. ... 4397
Job 4:18 and his **a.** he charged with folly: ... 4397
Ps 8:5 him a little lower than the **a.**, ... 430
Ps 68:17 thousand, even thousands of **a.**: ... 8136
Ps 78:49 by sending evil **a.** among them. ... 4397
Ps 91:11 shall give his **a.** charge over thee, ... 4397
Ps 103:20 Bless the Lord, ye his **a.**, ... 4397
Ps 104:4 Who maketh his **a.** spirits; ... 4397
Ps 148:2 Praise ye him, all his **a.**: ... 4397
Mt 4:6 He shall give his **a.** charge ... *32*
Mt 4:11 **a.** came and ministered unto him. ... *32*
Mt 13:39 **and the reapers are the a.** ... *32*
Mt 13:41 **Son of man shall send forth his a.,** ... *32*
Mt 13:49 **the a. shall come forth, and sever** ... *32*
Mt 16:27 **the glory of his Father with his a.;** ... *32*
Mt 18:10 **That in heaven their a. do always** ... *32*
Mt 22:30 **are as the a. of God in heaven.** ... *32*
Mt 24:31 **And he shall send his a. with a great.** *32*
Mt 24:36 **no, not the a. of heaven,** ... *32*
Mt 25:31 **all the holy a. with him,** ... *32*
Mt 25:41 **prepared for the devil and his a.** ... *32*
Mt 26:53 **more than twelve legions of a.?** ... *32*
Mk 1:13 and the **a.** ministered unto him. ... *32*
Mk 8:38 **glory of his Father with the holy a.** ... *32*
Mk 12:25 **are as the a. which are in heaven.** ... *32*
Mk 13:27 **then shall he send his a.,** ... *32*
Mk 13:32 **not the a. which are in heaven,** ... *32*
Lu 2:15 as the **a.** were gone away from ... *32*
Lu 4:10 He shall give his **a.** charge over thee, ... *32*
Lu 9:26 **in his Father's, and of the holy a.** ... *32*
Lu 12:8 **confess before the a. of God:** ... *32*
Lu 12:9 **denied before the a. of God.** ... *32*
Lu 15:10 **in the presence of the a. of God** ... *32*
Lu 16:22 **carried by the a. into Abraham's** ... *32*
Lu 20:36 **for they are equal unto the a.;** ... *2465*
Lu 24:23 had also seen a vision of **a.**, ... *32*

Joh 1:51 **the a. of God ascending and** *32*
Joh 20:12 seeth two **a.** in white sitting, the *32*
Ac 7:53 the law by the disposition of **a.**, *32*
Ro 8:38 nor life, nor **a.**, nor principalities, *32*
1Co 4:9 world, and to **a.**, and to men *32*
1Co 6:3 Know ye not that we shall judge **a.**? *32*
1Co 11:10 on her head because of the **a.**. *32*
1Co 13:1 the tongues of men and of **a.**, *32*
Ga 3:19 and it was ordained by **a.** in the *32*
Col 2:18 humility and worshipping of **a.**, *32*
2Th 1:7 from heaven with his mighty **a.**, *32*
1Ti 3:16 in the Spirit, seen of **a.**, preached *32*
1Ti 5:21 Jesus Christ, and the elect **a.**, *32*
Heb 1:4 made so much better than the **a.**, *32*
Heb 1:5 unto which of the **a.** said he at *32*
Heb 1:6 let all the **a.** of God worship him *32*
Heb 1:7 of the **a.** he saith, *32*
Heb 1:7 Who maketh his **a.** spirits, *32*
Heb 1:13 to which of the **a.** said he at any *32*
Heb 2:2 if the word spoken by **a.** was *32*
Heb 2:5 unto the **a.** hath he not put in *32*
Heb 2:7 a little lower than the **a.**; *32*
Heb 2:9 made a little lower than the **a.** *32*
Heb 2:16 not on him the nature of **a.**; *32*
Heb 12:22 an innumerable company o **a.**, *32*
Heb 13:2 some have entertained **a.** unawares. *32*
1Pe 1:12 things the **a.** desire to look into. *32*
1Pe 3:22 **a.** and authorities and powers being *32*
2Pe 2:4 spared not the **a.** that sinned, *32*
2Pe 2:11 Whereas **a.**, which are greater *32*
Jude 6 **a.** which kept not their first estate, *32*
Re 1:20 **the a. of the seven churches** *32*
Re 3:5 **my Father, and before his a.** *32*
Re 5:11 I heard the voice of many **a.** round *32*
Re 7:1 I saw four **a.** standing on the four *32*
Re 7:2 with a loud voice to the four **a.**, *32*
Re 7:11 all the **a.** stood round about the *32*
Re 8:2 I saw the seven **a.** which stood *32*
Re 8:6 **a.** which had the seven trumpets *32*
Re 8:13 the trumpet of the three **a.**, which *32*
Re 9:14 Loose the four **a.** which are bound *32*
Re 9:15 and the four **a.** were loosed, *32*
Re 12:7 Michael and his **a.** fought against *32*
Re 12:7 and the dragon fought and his **a.**, *32*
Re 12:9 his **a.** were cast out with him *32*
Re 14:10 in the presence of the holy **a.**, *32*
Re 15:1 seven **a.** having the seven last *32*
Re 15:6 seven **a.** came out of the temple, *32*
Re 15:7 gave unto the seven **a.** seven golden *32*
Re 15:8 of the seven **a.** were fulfilled *32*
Re 16:1 saying to the seven **a.**, Go your *32*
Re 17:1 one of the seven **a.** which had the *32*
Re 21:9 unto me one of the seven **a.** which *32*
Re 21:12 at the gates twelve **a.**, *32*

ANGELS'
Ps 78:25 Man did eat **a.** food: 47

ANGER See also ANGERED.
Ge 27:45 Until thy brother's **a.** turn away 639
Ge 30:2 Jacob's **a.** was kindled against 639
Ge 44:18 thine **a.** burn against thy servant: 639
Ge 49:6 in their **a.** they slew a man, 639
Ge 49:7 Cursed be their **a.**, for it was fierce; 639
Ex 4:14 the **a.** of the Lord was kindled 639
Ex 11:8 out from Pharaoh in a great **a.** 639
Ex 32:19 Moses' **a.** waxed hot, and he cast 639
Ex 32:22 Let not the **a.** of my lord wax hot; 639
Nu 11:1 heard it; and his **a.** was kindled; 639
Nu 11:10 the **a.** of the Lord was kindled 639
Nu 12:9 **a.** of the Lord was kindled against 639
Nu 22:22 God's **a.** was kindled because he 639
Nu 22:27 Balaam's **a.** was kindled, and he 639
Nu 24:10 Balak's **a.** was kindled against 639
Nu 25:3 the **a.** of the Lord was kindled 639
Nu 25:4 that the fierce **a.** of the Lord may 639
Nu 32:10, 13 the Lord's **a.** was kindled 639
Nu 32:14 to augment yet the fierce **a.** of the 639
De 4:25 Lord thy God, to provoke him to **a.** 3707
De 6:15 lest the **a.** of the Lord thy God be 639
De 7:4 will the **a.** of the Lord be kindled 639
De 9:18 the Lord, to provoke him to **a.** 3707
De 9:19 I was afraid of the **a.** and hot 639
De 13:17 turn from the fierceness of his **a.**, 639
De 29:20 **a.** of the Lord and his jealousy 639
De 29:23 which the Lord overthrew in his **a.**, 639
De 29:24 meaneth the heat of this great **a.**? 639
De 29:27 the **a.** of the Lord was kindled 639
De 29:28 rooted them out of their land in **a.**, 639
De 31:17 Then my **a.** shall be kindled 639
De 31:29 to provoke him to **a.** through the 3707
De 32:16 provoked they him to **a.** 3707
De 32:21 they have provoked me to **a.** with 3707
De 32:21 I will provoke them to **a.** with a
De 32:22 For a fire is kindled in mine **a.**, 639
Jos 7:1 the **a.** of the Lord was kindled 639
Jos 7:26 turned from the fierceness of his **a.** 639
Jos 23:16 then shall the **a.** of the Lord be 639
Jg 2:12 and provoked the Lord to **a.** 3707
Jg 2:14 the **a.** of the Lord was hot against 639
Jg 2:20 And the **a.** of the Lord was hot 639
Jg 3:8 **a.** of the Lord was hot against Israel, 639
Jg 6:39 Let not thine **a.** be hot against me, 639
Jg 8:3 their **a.** was abated toward him, 7307
Jg 9:30 son of Ebed, his **a.** was kindled 639
Jg 10:7 the **a.** of the Lord was hot against 639
Jg 14:19 his **a.** was kindled, and he went up 639
1Sa 11:6 his **a.** was kindled greatly 639
1Sa 17:28 Eliab's **a.** was kindled against 639
1Sa 20:30 Saul's **a.** was kindled against 639
1Sa 20:34 arose from the table in fierce **a.**, 639
2Sa 6:7 the **a.** of the Lord was kindled 639
2Sa 12:5 David's **a.** was greatly kindled 639
2Sa 24:1 again the **a.** of the Lord was 639
1Ki 14:9 images, to provoke me to **a.**, 3707
1Ki 14:15 groves, provoking the Lord to **a.** 3707
1Ki 15:30 the Lord God of Israel to **a.** 3707
1Ki 16:2 provoke me to **a.** with their sins; 3707
1Ki 16:7 provoking him to **a.** with the work 3707
1Ki 16:13 the Lord God of Israel to **a.** 3707
1Ki 16:26 provoke the Lord God of Israel to **a.** 3707
1Ki 16:33 Israel to **a.** than all the kings of 3707
1Ki 21:22 thou hast provoked me to **a.**, 3707
1Ki 22:53 and provoked to **a.** the Lord God 3707
2Ki 13:3 the **a.** of the Lord was kindled 639
2Ki 17:11 things to provoke the Lord to **a.**: 3707
2Ki 17:17 the Lord, to provoke him to **a.** 3707
2Ki 21:6 to provoke him to **a.** 3707
2Ki 21:15 provoked me to **a.**, since the day 3707
2Ki 22:17 that they might provoke me to **a.** 3707
2Ki 23:19 made to provoke the Lord to **a.**, 3707
2Ki 23:26 wherewith his **a.** was kindled 639
2Ki 24:20 through the **a.** of the Lord it came 639
1Ch 13:10 the **a.** of the Lord was kindled 639
2Ch 25:10 wherefore their **a.** was greatly 639
2Ch 25:10 they returned home in great **a.** 639
2Ch 25:15 the **a.** of the Lord was kindled 639
2Ch 28:25 and provoked to **a.** the Lord God 3707
2Ch 33:6 to provoke him to **a.** 3707
2Ch 34:25 that they might provoke me to **a.** 3707
Ne 4:5 they have provoked thee to **a.** 3707
Ne 9:17 merciful, slow to **a.**, and of great 639
Es 1:12 and his **a.** burned in him 2534
Job 9:5 which overturneth them in his **a.** 639
Job 9:13 God will not withdraw his **a.**, 639
Job 18:4 He teareth himself in his **a.**: 639
Job 21:17 God distributeth sorrows in his **a.** 639
Job 35:15 is not so, he hath visited in his **a.**; 639
Ps 6:1 O Lord, rebuke me not in thine **a.**, 639
Ps 7:6 Arise, O Lord, in thine **a.**, lift up 639
Ps 21:9 fiery oven in the time of thine **a.**: 6440
Ps 27:9 put not thy servant away in **a.**: 639
Ps 30:5 his **a.** endureth but a moment; 639
Ps 37:8 Cease from **a.**, and forsake wrath: 639
Ps 38:3 in my flesh because of thine **a.**; 2195
Ps 56:7 in thine **a.** cast down the people, 639
Ps 69:24 let thy wrathful **a.** take hold of 639
Ps 74:1 doth thine **a.** smoke against the 639
Ps 77:9 in **a.** shut up his tender mercies? 639
Ps 78:21 **a.** also came up against Israel; 639
Ps 78:38 many a time turned he his **a.** away, 639
Ps 78:49 upon them the fierceness of his **a.**, 639
Ps 78:50 He made a way to his **a.**; 639
Ps 78:58 For they provoked him to **a.** with 3707
Ps 85:3 from the fierceness of thine **a.** 639
Ps 85:4 cause thine **a.** toward us to cease. 3708
Ps 85:5 out thine **a.** to all generations? 639
Ps 90:7 we are consumed by thine **a.**, 639
Ps 90:11 Who knoweth the power of thine **a.**? 639
Ps 103:8 gracious, slow to **a.**, and plenteous 639
Ps 103:9 neither will he keep his **a.** for ever
Ps 106:29 Thus they provoked him to **a.** 3707
Ps 145:8 slow to **a.**, and of great mercy 639
Pr 15:1 grievous words stir up **a.** 639
Pr 15:18 that is slow to **a.** appeaseth strife. 639
Pr 16:32 slow to **a.** is better than the mighty, 639
Pr 19:11 discretion of a man deferreth his **a.**; 639
Pr 20:2 whoso provoketh him to **a.** sinneth 5674
Pr 21:14 A gift in secret pacifieth **a.** 639
Pr 22:8 the rod of his **a.** shall fail 5678
Pr 27:4 is cruel, and **a.** is outrageous; 639
Ec 7:9 **a.** resteth in the bosom of fools. 3708
Isa 1:4 the Holy One of Israel unto **a.**, 5006
Isa 5:25 the **a.** of the Lord kindled against 639
Isa 5:25 all this his **a.** is not turned away, 639
Isa 7:4 the fierce **a.** of Rezin with Syria, 639
Isa 9:12 all this his **a.** is not turned away, 639
Isa 9:17 his **a.** is not turned away, but his 639
Isa 9:21 against Judah. For all this his **a.** 639
Isa 10:4 under the slain. For all this his **a.** 639
Isa 10:5 O Assyrian, the rod of mine **a.**, 639
Isa 10:25 and mine **a.** in their destruction 639
Isa 12:1 thine **a.** is turned away, and thou 639
Isa 13:3 called my mighty ones for mine **a.**, 639
Isa 13:9 both with wrath and fierce **a.**, 639
Isa 13:13 in the day of his fierce **a.** 639
Isa 14:6 he that ruled the nations in **a.**, 639
Isa 30:27 from far burning with his **a.**, 639
Isa 30:30 with the indignation of his **a.**, 639
Isa 42:25 poured upon him the fury of his **a.**, 639
Isa 48:9 name's sake will I defer mine **a.**, 639
Isa 63:3 for I will tread them in mine **a.**, 639
Isa 63:6 tread down the people in mine **a.**, 639
Isa 65:3 A people that provoketh me to **a.** 3707
Isa 66:15 to render his **a.** with fury, and his 639
Jer 2:35 surely his **a.** shall turn from me 639
Jer 3:5 Will he reserve his **a.** forever?
Jer 3:12 not cause mine **a.** to fall upon you: 6440
Jer 3:12 and I will not keep **a.** forever.
Jer 4:8 for the fierce **a.** of the Lord is not 639
Jer 4:26 presence of the Lord by his fierce **a.** 639
Jer 7:18 that they may provoke me to **a.** 3707
Jer 7:19 Do they provoke me to **a.**? 3707
Jer 7:20 mine **a.** and my fury shall be poured 639
Jer 8:19 Why have they provoked me to **a.** 3707
Jer 10:24 not in thine **a.**, lest thou bring me 639
Jer 11:17 to provoke me to **a.** in offering 3707
Jer 12:13 because of the fierce **a.** of the Lord. 639
Jer 15:14 for a fire is kindled in mine **a.**, 639
Jer 17:4 have kindled a fire in mine **a.**, 639
Jer 18:23 with them in the time of thine **a.** 639
Jer 21:5 **a.**, and in fury, and in great wrath. 639
Jer 23:20 The **a.** of the Lord shall not return, 639
Jer 25:6 provoke me not to **a.** with the 3707
Jer 25:7 that ye might provoke me to **a.** 3707
Jer 25:37 because of the fierce **a.** of the Lord. 639
Jer 25:38 because of his fierce **a.** 639
Jer 30:24 **a.** of the Lord shall not return, 639
Jer 32:29 other gods, to provoke me to **a.** 3707
Jer 32:30 provoked me to **a.** with the work 3707
Jer 32:31 to me as a provocation of mine **a.** 639
Jer 32:32 provoke me to **a.**, they, their kings, 3707
Jer 32:37 I have driven them in mine **a.**, 639
Jer 33:5 whom I have slain in mine **a.** 639
Jer 36:7 for great is the **a.** and the fury 639
Jer 42:18 As mine **a.** and my fury hath been 639
Jer 44:3 provoke me to **a.**, in that they 3707
Jer 44:6 and mine **a.** was poured forth, 639
Jer 49:37 evil upon them, even my fierce **a.**, 639
Jer 51:45 from the fierce **a.** of the Lord. 639
Jer 52:3 through the **a.** of the Lord it came 639
La 1:12 me in the day of his fierce **a.** 639
La 2:1 with a cloud in his **a.**, 639
La 2:1 his footstool in the day of his **a.**! 639
La 2:3 He hath cut off in his fierce **a.** 639
La 2:6 of his **a.** the king and the priest. 639
La 2:21 slain them in the day of thine **a.**; 639
La 2:22 day of the Lord's **a.** none escaped 639
La 3:43 covered with **a.**, and persecuted us: 639
La 3:66 Persecute and destroy them in **a.** 639
La 4:11 he hath poured out his fierce **a.**, 639
La 4:16 **a.** of the Lord hath divided them; 6440
Eze 5:13 shall mine **a.** be accomplished, 639
Eze 5:15 in **a.** and in fury and in furious 639
Eze 7:3 I will send mine **a.** upon thee, 639
Eze 7:8 accomplish mine **a.** upon thee: 639
Eze 8:17 returned to provoke me to **a.**: 3707
Eze 13:13 overflowing shower in mine **a.**, 639
Eze 16:26 whoredoms, to provoke me to **a.** 3707
Eze 20:8 to accomplish my **a.** against them 639
Eze 20:21 to accomplish my **a.** against them 639
Eze 22:20 so will I gather you in mine **a.** 639

Eze 25:14 in Edom according to mine a. 639
Eze 35:11 I will even do according to thine a., 639
Eze 43:8 I have consumed them in mine a. 639
Da 9:16 let thine a. and thy fury be turned 639
Da 11:20 neither in a., nor in battle. 639
Ho 8:5 mine a. is kindled against them: 639
Ho 11:9 execute the fierceness of mine a., 639
Ho 12:14 provoked him to a. most bitterly: 3707
Ho 13:11 I gave thee a king in mine a., 639
Ho 14:4 for mine a. is turned away from him. 639
Joe 2:13 slow to a., and of great kindness, 639
Am 1:11 his a. did tear perpetually, 639
Jon 3:9 turn away from his fierce a., 639
Jon 4:2 slow to a., and of great kindness, 639
Mic 5:15 I will execute vengeance in a. 639
Mic 7:18 he retaineth not his a. for ever, 639
Na 1:3 The Lord is slow to a., and great 639
Na 1:6 abide in the fierceness of his a.? 639
Hab 3:8 thine a. against the rivers? 639
Hab 3:12 thou didst thresh the heathen in a. 639
Zep 2:2 before the fierce a. of the Lord 639
Zep 2:2 before the day of the Lord's a. come 639
Zep 2:3 hid in the day of the Lord's a. 639
Zep 3:8 even all my fierce a. 639
Zec 10:3 Mine a. was kindled against the 639
Mk 3:5 on them with a., being grieved 3709
Ro 10:19 by a foolish nation I will a. you. 3949
Eph 4:31 and wrath, and a., and clamour, 3709
Col 3:8 put off all these; a., wrath, malice, 3709
Col 3:21 provoke not your children to a.

ANGERED
Ps 106:32 a. him also at the waters of strife, 7107

ANGLE
Isa 19:8 they that cast a. into the brooks 2443
Hab 1:15 take up all of them with the a., 2443

ANGRY
Ge 18:30, 32 Oh let not the Lord be a., and 2734
Ge 45:5 grieved, nor a. with yourselves 2734
Le 10:16 was a. with Eleazar and Ithamar, 7107
De 1:37 was a. with me for your sakes, 599
De 4:21 was a. with me for your sakes, 599
De 9:8 so that the Lord was a. with you 599
De 9:20 the Lord was very a. with Aaron 599
Jg 18:25 lest a. fellows run upon thee, 4751,5315
2Sa 19:42 then be ye a. for this matter? 2734
1Ki 8:46 and thou be a. with them, and 599
1Ki 11:9 And the Lord was a. with Solomon, 599
2Ki 17:18 the Lord was very a. with Israel, 599
2Ch 6:36 be a. with them, and deliver them 599
Ezr 9:14 wouldest not thou be a. with us 599
Ne 5:6 very a. when I heard their cry 2734
Ps 2:12 Kiss the Son, lest he be a., and 599
Ps 7:11 God is a. with the wicked every 2194
Ps 76:7 in thy sight when once thou art a.? 639
Ps 79:5 wilt thou be a. for ever? shall thy 599
Ps 80:4 how long wilt thou be a. against 6225
Ps 85:5 Wilt thou be a. with us for ever? 599
Pr 14:17 that is soon a. dealeth foolishly: 639
Pr 21:19 a contentious and an a. woman. 3708
Pr 22:24 no friendship with an a. man; 639
Pr 25:23 so doth an a. countenance a 2194
Pr 29:22 An a. man stirreth up strife, 639
Ec 5:6 should God be a. at thy voice, 7107
Ec 7:9 Be not hasty in thy spirit to be a.: 3707
Ca 1:6 my mother's children were a. 2734
Isa 12:1 though thou wast a. with me, 599
Eze 16:42 be quiet and will be no more a. 3707
Da 2:12 the king was a. and very furious, 1149
Jon 4:1 and he was very a. 2734
Jon 4:4 Lord, Doest thou well to be a.? 2734
Jon 4:9 thou well to be a. for the gourd? 2734
Jon 4:9 I do well to be a., even unto death. 2734
Mt 5:22 **whosoever is a. with his brother** 3710
Lu 14:21 **the master of the house being a.** 3710
Lu 15:28 **he was a., and would not go in:** 3710
Joh 7:23 **are ye a. at me, because I have** 5520
Eph 4:26 Be ye a., and sin not: let not the 3710
Tit 1:7 not soon a., not given to wine, 3711
Re 11:18 nations were a., and thy wrath 3710

ANGUISH
Ge 42:21 we saw the a. of his soul, when 6869
Ex 6:9 hearkened not…for a. of spirit, 7115
De 2:25 and be in a. because of thee. 2342
2Sa 1:9 a. is come upon me, because my 7661
Job 7:11 I will speak in the a. of my spirit; 6862
Job 15:24 and a. shall make him afraid; 4691
Ps 119:143 Trouble and a. have taken hold 4689
Pr 1:27 distress and a. cometh upon you. 6695
Isa 8:22 and darkness, dimness of a.; 6695
Isa 30:6 the land of trouble and a., 6695
Jer 4:31 the a. as of her that bringeth 6869
Jer 6:24 a. hath taken hold of us. 6869
Jer 49:24 a. and sorrows have taken her, 6869
Jer 50:43 a. took hold of him, and pangs as 6869
Joh 16:21 **she remembereth no more the a.,** 2347
Ro 2:9 and a., upon every soul of man 4730
2Co 2:4 of much affliction and a. of heart 4928

AN-HUNGERED See HUNGERED.

ANIAM (a'-ne-am)
1Ch 7:19 Shechem, and Likhi, and A. 593

ANIM (a'-nim)
Jos 15:50 And Anab, and Eshtemoh, and A., 6044

ANISE
Mt 23:23 **tithe of mint, and a. and cummin,** 432

ANKLE See ANCLE.

ANNA (an'-nah)
Lu 2:36 there was one A., a prophetess, 451

ANNAS (an'-nas)
Lu 3:2 A. and Caiaphas being the high 452
Joh 18:13 led him away to A. first; 452
Joh 18:24 A. had sent him bound unto 452
Ac 4:6 A. the high priest, and Caiaphas, 452

ANNUL See DISANNUL.

ANOINT See also ANOINTED; ANOINTEST; ANOINTING.
Ex 28:41 a. them, and consecrate them, 4886
Ex 29:7 pour it upon his head, and a. him. 4886
Ex 29:36 and thou shalt a. it, to sanctify it. 4886
Ex 30:26 And thou shalt a. the tabernacle 4886
Ex 30:30 thou shalt a. Aaron and his sons, 4886
Ex 40:9 a. the tabernacle, and all that is 4886
Ex 40:10 a. the altar of the burnt offering, 4886
Ex 40:11 thou shalt a. the laver and his foot, 4886
Ex 40:13 the holy garments, and a. him, 4886
Ex 40:15 And thou shalt a. them, 4886
Ex 40:15 as thou didst a. their father, 4886
Le 16:32 And the priest, whom he shall a., 4886
De 28:40 shalt not a. thyself with the oil; 5480
Jg 9:8 trees went forth on a time to a. 4886
Jg 9:15 If in truth ye a. me king over you, 4886
Ru 3:3 Wash thyself therefore, and a. 5480
1Sa 9:16 a. him to be captain over my 4886
1Sa 15:1 The Lord sent me to a. thee 4886
1Sa 16:3 shalt a. unto me him whom I name. 4886
1Sa 16:12 the Lord said, Arise, a. him: 4886
2Sa 14:2 a. not thyself with oil, 5480
1Ki 1:34 and Nathan the prophet a. him 4886
1Ki 19:15 a. Hazael to be king over Syria: 4886
1Ki 19:16 the son of Nimshi shalt thou a. 4886
1Ki 19:16 Elisha…shalt thou a. to be prophet. 4886
Isa 21:5 arise, ye princes, and a. the shield. 4886
Da 9:24 and to a. the most Holy. 4886
Da 10:3 neither did I a. myself at all, 5480
Am 6:6 a. themselves with the chief 4886
Mic 6:15 thou shalt not a. thee with oil; 5480
Mt 6:17 **a. thine head, and wash thy face;** 218
Mk 14:8 **to a. my body to the burying** 3462
Mk 16:1 they might come and a. him. 218
Lu 7:46 **My head with oil thou didst not a.** 218
Re 3:18 **a. thine eyes with eyesalve, that** 1472

ANOINTED See also ANOINTEDST.
Ex 29:2 wafers unleavened a. with oil: 4886
Ex 29:29 a. therein, and to be consecrated 4888
Le 2:4 unleavened wafers a. with oil. 4886
Le 4:3 If the priest that is a. do sin 4899
Le 4:5 And the priest that is a. shall 4899
Le 4:16 is a. shall bring of the bullock's 4899
Le 6:20 the Lord in the day when he is a.; 4886
Le 6:22 the priest of his sons that is a. in 4899
Le 7:12 a. with oil, and cakes mingled 4886
Le 7:36 in the day that he a. them, 4886
Le 8:10 a. the tabernacle and all that was 4886
Le 8:11 a. the altar and all his vessels, 4886
Le 8:12 and a. him, to sanctify him. 4886
Nu 3:3 of Aaron, the priests which were a., 4886
Nu 6:15 wafers of unleavened bread a. 4886
Nu 7:1 set up the tabernacle, and had a. it, 4886
Nu 7:1 vessels thereof, and had a. them, 4886
Nu 7:10 the altar in the day that it was a., 4886
Nu 7:84 it was a., by the princes of Israel; 4886
Nu 7:88 of the altar after that it was a. 4886
Nu 35:25 which was a. with the holy oil. 4886
1Sa 2:10 and exalt the horn of his a., 4899
1Sa 2:35 shall walk before mine a. for ever. 4899
1Sa 10:1 Lord hath a. thee to be captain 4886
1Sa 12:3 before the Lord, and before his a.: 4899
1Sa 12:5 his a. is witness this day, 4899
1Sa 15:17 the Lord a. thee king over Israel? 4886
1Sa 16:6 Surely the Lord's a. is before him. 4899
1Sa 16:13 a. him in the midst of his brethren. 4886
1Sa 24:6 unto my master, the Lord's a., 4899
1Sa 24:6 he is the a. of the Lord. 4899
1Sa 24:10 he is the Lord's a. 4899
1Sa 26:9 his hand against the Lord's a., 4899
1Sa 26:11 mine hand against the Lord's a.: 4899
1Sa 26:16 kept your master, the Lord's a. 4899
1Sa 26:23 against the Lord's a. 4899
2Sa 1:14 to destroy the Lord's a.? 4899
2Sa 1:16 I have slain the Lord's a. 4899
2Sa 1:21 as though he had not been a. with 4899
2Sa 2:4 and there they a. David king 4886
2Sa 2:7 house of Judah have a. me king 4886
2Sa 3:39 this day weak, though a. king; 4886
2Sa 5:3 they a. David king over Israel. 4886
2Sa 5:17 heard that they had a. David king 4886
2Sa 12:7 I a. thee king over Israel, 4886
2Sa 12:20 earth and washed, and a. himself, 5480
2Sa 19:10 Absalom, whom we a. over us, 4886
2Sa 19:21 because he cursed the Lord's a.? 4899
2Sa 22:51 sheweth mercy to his a., 4899
2Sa 23:1 the a. of the God of Jacob, 4899
1Ki 1:39 the tabernacle, and a. Solomon. 4886
1Ki 1:45 and Nathan…have a. him king 4886
1Ki 5:1 a. him king in the room of his 4886
2Ki 9:3 I have a. thee king over Israel. 4886
2Ki 9:6 have a. thee king over the people 4886
2Ki 9:12 Thus saith the Lord, I have a. thee 4886
2Ki 11:12 they made him king, and a. him; 4886
2Ki 23:30 and a. him, and made him king 4886
1Ch 11:3 they a. David king over Israel, 4886
1Ch 14:8 David was a. King over all Israel, 4886
1Ch 16:22 Touch not mine a., and do my 4899
1Ch 29:22 and a. him unto the Lord 4886
2Ch 6:42 turn not away the face of thine a.: 4899
2Ch 22:7 a. to cut off the house of Ahab. 4886
2Ch 23:11 Jehoiada and his sons a. him, 4886
2Ch 28:15 to eat and to drink, and a. them, 4886
Ps 2:2 the Lord, and against his a., 4899
Ps 18:50 sheweth mercy to his a., 4899
Ps 20:6 the Lord saveth his a.; 4899
Ps 28:8 he is the saving strength of his a. 4899
Ps 45:7 thy God, hath a. thee with the oil 4886
Ps 84:9 look upon the face of thine a. 4899
Ps 89:20 with my holy oil have I a. him: 4886
Ps 89:38 hast been wroth with thine a. 4899
Ps 89:51 reproached the footsteps of thine a. 4899
Ps 92:10 I shall be a. with fresh oil. 1101
Ps 105:15 Touch not mine a., 4899
Ps 132:10 turn not away the face of thine a. 4899
Ps 132:17 I have ordained a lamp for mine a. 4899
Isa 45:1 Thus saith the Lord to his a., 4899
Isa 61:1 the Lord hath a. me to preach 4886
La 4:20 a. of the Lord, was taken in their 4899
Eze 16:9 and I a. thee with oil. 5480
Eze 28:14 art the a. cherub that covereth; 4473
Hab 3:13 for salvation with thine a.; 4899
Zec 4:14 the two a. ones, that stand 1121,3323
Mk 6:13 a. with oil many that were sick, 218
Lu 4:18 **hath a. me to preach the gospel** 5548
Lu 7:38 a. them with the ointment. 218
Lu 7:46 **hath a. my feet with ointment** 218
Joh 9:6 a. the eyes of the blind man 2025,1909
Joh 9:11 made clay and a. mine eyes, 2025
Joh 11:2 was that Mary which a. the Lord 218
Joh 12:3 a. the feet of Jesus, and wiped 218
Ac 4:27 child Jesus, whom thou hast a., 5548
Ac 10:38 How God a. Jesus of Nazareth 5548
2Co 1:21 and hath a. us in God. 5548
Heb 1:9 a. thee with the oil of gladness 5548

ANOINTEDST
Ge 31:13 Bethel, where thou a. the pillar, 4886

ANOINTEST
Ps 23:5 thou a. my head with oil; my 1878

ANOINTING
Ex 25:6 spices for **a.** oil, and for sweet.......... 4888
Ex 29:7 Then shalt thou take the **a.** oil,.......... 4888
Ex 29:21 and of the **a.** oil, and sprinkle it.......... 4888
Ex 30:25 it shall be an holy **a.** oil.................... 4888
Ex 30:31 This shall be an holy **a.** oil unto.......... 4888
Ex 31:11 And the **a.** oil, and sweet incense....... 4888
Ex 35:8 the light, and spices for the **a.** oil,....... 4888
Ex 35:15 and his staves, and the **a.** oil,........... 4888
Ex 35:28 and for the **a.** oil,........................... 4888
Ex 37:29 he made the holy **a.** oil,..................... 4888
Ex 39:38 the golden altar and the **a.** oil,........... 4888
Ex 40:9 thou shalt take the **a.** oil,.................. 4888
Ex 40:15 **a.** shall surely be an everlasting.......... 4888
Le 7:35 is the portion of the **a.** of Aaron,........ 4888
Le 7:35 and of the **a.** of his sons,.................. 4888
Le 8:2 and the **a.** oil, and a bullock for.......... 4888
Le 8:10 Moses took the **a.** oil, and anointed..... 4888
Le 8:12 he poured of the **a.** oil upon.............. 4888
Le 8:30 Moses took the **a.** oil,......................... 4888
Le 10:7 the **a.** oil of the Lord is upon you........ 4888
Le 21:10 whose head the **a.** oil was poured,...... 4888
Le 21:12 the crown of the **a.** oil is of his........... 4888
Nu 4:16 daily meat offering, and the **a.** oil,....... 4888
Nu 18:8 given them by reason of the **a.**,........... 4888
Isa 10:27 be destroyed because of the **a.**............ 8081
Jas 5:14 **a.** him with oil in the name of the......... *218*
1Jo 2:27 But the **a.** which ye have received...... *5545*
1Jo 2:27 same **a.** teacheth you of all things,...... *5545*

ANON
Mt 13:20 **and a. with joy receiveth it;**........... *2117*
Mk 1:30 **a.** they tell him of her........................ *2112*

ANOTH See BETH-ANOTH.

ANOTHER See also ANOTHER'S.
Ge 4:25 appointed me **a.** seed instead of.......... 312
Ge 11:3 said one to **a.**, Go to, let us make....... 7453
Ge 15:10 laid each piece one against **a.**........... 7453
Ge 26:21 And they digged **a.** well, and.............. 312
Ge 26:22 from thence, and digged **a.** well;.......... 312
Ge 26:31 and sware to one **a.**........................... 251
Ge 29:19 I should give her to **a.** man:................ 312
Ge 30:24 Lord shall add to me **a.** son................. 312
Ge 31:49 when we are absent one from **a.**.......... 7453
Ge 37:9 he dreamed yet **a.** dream.................... 312
Ge 37:19 they said one to **a.**, Behold, this.......... 250
Ge 42:1 Why do ye look one upon **a.**?...............
Ge 42:21 they said one to **a.**, We are verily........ 250
Ge 42:28 they were afraid, saying one to **a.**,........ 250
Ge 43:7 yet alive? have ye **a.** brother? and............
Ge 43:33 the men marvelled one at **a.**.................. 7453
Ex 10:23 They saw not one **a.**, neither rose.......... 250
Ex 16:15 they said one to **a.**, it is manna:........... 250
Ex 18:16 I judge between one and **a.**,............... 7453
Ex 21:10 If he take him **a.** wife, her food,............ 312
Ex 21:18 strive together, and one smite **a.**......... 7453
Ex 22:5 shall feed in **a.** man's field:.................. 312
Ex 22:9 which **a.** challengeth to be his..................
Ex 25:20 their faces shall look one to **a.**;............ 250
Ex 26:3 coupled together one to **a.**;.................. 269
Ex 26:3 curtains shall be coupled one to **a.**;....... 269
Ex 26:4 uttermost edge of **a.** curtain;....................
Ex 26:5 loops may take hold one of **a.**............... 269
Ex 26:17 set in order one against **a.**:................. 269
Ex 26:19, 21,25 and two sockets under **a.**.................. 259
Ex 36:10 curtains one unto **a.**: and the.............. 259
Ex 36:10 curtains he coupled one unto **a.**............ 259
Ex 36:11 the uttermost side of **a.** curtain,...............
Ex 36:12 the loops held one curtain to **a.**............ 259
Ex 36:13 one unto **a.** with the taches:................ 259
Ex 36:22 equally distant one from **a.**:.................. 259
Ex 36:24, 26 and two sockets under **a.** board....... 259
Ex 37:8 and **a.** cherub on the other end........... 259
Ex 37:9 with their faces one to **a.**;................... 250
Ex 37:19 made like almonds in **a.** branch,........... 259
Le 7:10 Aaron have, one as much as **a.**............ 250
Le 19:11 deal falsely, neither lie one to **a.**......... 5997
Le 20:10 adultery with **a.** man's wife,....................
Le 25:14 ye shall not oppress one **a.**:................. 250
Le 25:17 not therefore oppress one **a.**;.............. 5997
Le 25:46 ye shall not rule one over **a.** with.......... 250
Le 26:37 they shall fall one upon **a.**,................... 250
Le 27:20 if he have sold the field to **a.** man,........ 312
Nu 5:19 with **a.** instead of thy husband,.................
Nu 5:20 to **a.** instead of thy husband,....................
Nu 5:29 when a wife goeth aside to **a.**...................
Nu 8:8 **a.** young bullock shalt thou take.......... 8145
Nu 14:4 they said one to **a.**, Let us make.......... 250
Nu 14:24 because he had **a.** spirit with him,........ 312
Nu 23:13 with me unto **a.** place,......................... 312
Nu 23:27 I will bring thee unto **a.** place;............. 312
Nu 36:9 remove from one tribe to **a.** tribe;......... 312
De 4:34 midst of **a.** nation, by temptations,............
De 20:5 the battle, and **a.** man dedicate it......... 312
De 20:6 in the battle, and **a.** man eat of it......... 312
De 20:7 in the battle, and **a.** man take her......... 312
De 21:15 one beloved, and **a.** hated,.................. 259
De 24:2 she may go and be **a.** man's wife.......... 312
De 25:11 men strive together one with **a.**,.......... 250
De 28:30 **a.** man shall lie with her:.................... 312
De 28:32 shall be given unto **a.** people,.............. 312
De 29:28 cast them into **a.** land, as it is this........ 312
Jg 2:10 thee arose **a.** generation after.............. 312
Jg 6:29 said one to **a.**, Who hath done this...... 7453
Jg 9:37 **a.** company come along by the............. 259
Jg 10:18 princes of Gilead said one to **a.**,.......... 7453
Jg 16:7, 11 I be weak, and be as **a.** man............. 259
Ru 2:8 Go not to glean in **a.** field,.................. 312
Ru 3:14 rose up before one could know **a.**........ 7453
1Sa 2:25 If one man sin against **a.**,..................... 376
1Sa 10:3 **a.** carrying three loaves of bread,......... 259
1Sa 10:3 and **a.** carrying a bottle of wine:........... 259
1Sa 10:6 shalt be turned into **a.** man................ 312
1Sa 10:9 God gave him **a.** heart:........................ 312
1Sa 10:11 the people said one to **a.**,................... 7453
1Sa 13:18 And **a.** company turned the way............ 259
1Sa 13:18 and **a.** company turned to the way........ 259
1Sa 14:16 went on beating down one **a.**..................
1Sa 17:30 he turned from him toward **a.**,.............. 312
1Sa 18:7 And the women answered one **a.**...............
1Sa 20:41 and they kissed one **a.**,...................... 7453
1Sa 20:41 and wept one with **a.**,......................... 7453
1Sa 21:11 did they not sing one to **a.** of him..............
1Sa 29:5 sang one to **a.** in dances, saying,...............
2Sa 11:25 devoureth one as well as **a.**:................ 2090
2Sa 18:20 thou shalt bear tidings **a.** day............... 312
2Sa 18:26 the watchman saw **a.** man running........ 312
2Sa 18:26 Behold **a.** man running alone...................
1Ki 6:27 and their wings touched one **a.**............ 3671
1Ki 7:8 had **a.** court within the porch,............... 312
1Ki 11:23 God stirred him up **a.** adversary,..............
1Ki 13:10 So he went **a.** way, and returned........ 312
1Ki 14:5 shall feign herself to be **a.** woman....... 5234
1Ki 14:6 why feignest thou thyself to be **a.**?....... 5234
1Ki 18:6 Obadiah went **a.** was by himself........... 259
1Ki 20:37 Then he found **a.** man, and said,........... 312
1Ki 21:6 I will give thee **a.** vineyard for it...............
1Ki 22:20 one said on this manner, and **a.**........... 2088
2Ki 1:11 he sent unto him **a.** captain of fifty....... 312
2Ki 3:23 they have smitten one **a.**:................... 7453
2Ki 7:3 said one to **a.**, why sit we here.......... 7453
2Ki 7:6 they said one to **a.**, Lo, the king.......... 250
2Ki 7:8 entered into **a.** tent, and carried........... 312
2Ki 7:9 Then they said one to **a.**, We do......... 7453
2Ki 10:21 Baal was full from one end to **a.**...............
2Ki 14:8 let us look one **a.** in the face....................
2Ki 14:11 looked one **a.** in the face at......................
2Ki 21:16 filled Jerusalem from one end to **a.**;............
1Ch 2:26 Jerahmeel had also **a.** wife,................. 312
1Ch 16:20 from one kingdom to **a.** people;............ 312
1Ch 17:5 and from one tabernacle to **a.**..................
1Ch 24:5 divided by lot, one sort with **a.**;................
1Ch 26:12 having wards one against **a.**,................ 251
2Ch 18:19 and **a.** saying after that manner.......... 2088
2Ch 20:23 every one helped to destroy **a.**........... 7453
2Ch 25:17 Come, let us see one **a.** in the face..........
2Ch 25:21 and they saw one **a.** in the face,...............
2Ch 32:5 **a.** wall without, and repaired.............. 312
Ezr 4:21 **a.** commandment shall be given.................
Ezr 9:11 end to **a.** with their uncleanness...............
Ne 3:19 **a.** piece over against the going........... 8145
Ne 3:21 the son of Koz **a.** piece,.................... 8145
Ne 3:24 the son of Henadad **a.** piece,............. 8145
Ne 3:27 the Tekoites repaired **a.** piece,............ 8145
Ne 3:30 the sixth son of Zalaph, **a.** piece......... 8145
Ne 4:19 upon the wall, one far from **a.**............ 250
Ne 9:3 and **a.** fourth part they confessed..............
Es 1:7 vessels being diverse one from **a.**,.............
Es 1:19 give her royal estate unto **a.**.............. 7468
Es 4:14 arise to the Jews from **a.** place;........... 312
Es 9:19 and of sending portions one to **a.**......... 7453
Es 9:22 one to **a.**, and gifts to the poor........... 7453
Job 1:16 came also **a.**, and said, The fire.......... 2088
Job 1:17 also **a.**, and said, the Chaldeans.......... 2088
Job 1:18 yet speaking, there came also **a.**,......... 2088
Job 13:9 as one man mocketh **a.**, do ye................
Job 19:27 eyes shall behold, and not **a.**;............. 2114
Job 21:25 And **a.** dieth in the bitterness of......... 2088
Job 31:8 let me sow, and let **a.** eat;..................... 312
Job 31:10 let my wife grind unto **a.**,..................... 312
Job 41:16 One is so near to **a.**, that no air........... 259
Job 41:17 They are joined one to **a.**, they........... 250
Ps 16:4 that hasten after **a.** god:....................... 312
Ps 75:7 down one, and setteth up **a.**............... 2088
Ps 105:13 they went from one nation to **a.**,..............
Ps 105:13 from one kingdom to **a.** people;............ 312
Ps 109:8 let **a.** take his office............................. 312
Ps 145:4 shall praise thy works to **a.**, and..............
Pr 25:9 discover not a secret to **a.**:.................. 312
Pr 27:2 Let **a.** man praise thee, and not.......... 2114
Ec 1:4 away, and **a.** generation cometh:..............
Ec 4:10 for he hath not **a.** to help him up........ 8145
Ec 8:9 wherein one man ruleth over **a.**................
Ca 5:9 beloved more than **a.** beloved, O.............
Ca 5:9 **a.** beloved, that thou dost so....................
Isa 3:5 every one by **a.**, and every one by...........
Isa 6:3 And one cried unto **a.**, and said,.......... 2088
Isa 13:8 they shall be amazed one at **a.**;.......... 7453
Isa 28:11 with stammering lips and **a.** tongue....... 312
Isa 42:8 my glory will I not give to **a.**,.............. 312
Isa 44:5 and **a.** shall call himself by................ 2088
Isa 44:5 and **a.** shall subscribe with his............ 2088
Isa 48:11 I will not give my glory unto **a.**............ 312
Isa 57:8 thou hast discovered thyself to **a.**..............
Isa 65:15 call his servants by **a.** name:............... 312
Isa 65:22 not build, and **a.** inhabit;..................... 312
Isa 65:22 they shall not plant, and **a.** eat:............ 312
Isa 66:23 that from one new moon to **a.**,.................
Isa 66:23 and from one sabbath to **a.**, shall.............
Jer 3:1 become **a.** man's, shall he return.......... 312
Jer 13:14 I will dash them one against **a.**............ 250
Jer 18:4 so he made it again **a.** vessel,............... 312
Jer 18:14 come from **a.** place be forsaken?......... 2114
Jer 22:26 into **a.** country, where ye were not....... 312
Jer 25:26 far and near, one with **a.**,.................... 250
Jer 36:28 Take thee again **a.** roll, and write......... 312
Jer 36:32 Then took Jeremiah **a.** roll,.................. 312
Jer 46:16 many to fall, yea, one fell upon **a.**........ 7453
Jer 51:31 One post shall run to meet **a.**,................
Jer 51:31 and one messenger to meet **a.**,.................
Jer 51:46 one year, and after that in **a.** year...........
Eze 1:9 Their wings were joined one to **a.**;.......... 269
Eze 1:11 of every one were joined one to **a.**,....... 376
Eze 3:13 creatures that touched one **a.**,................ 269
Eze 4:8 not turn thee from one side to **a.**,.............
Eze 4:17 astonied one with **a.**, and consume........ 250
Eze 10:9 by one cherub, and **a.** wheel by........... 259
Eze 10:9 **a.** cherub: and the appearance............. 259
Eze 12:3 remove from thy place to **a.** place......... 312
Eze 15:7 and **a.** fire shall devour them;...................
Eze 17:7 There was also **a.** great eagle................ 259
Eze 19:5 she took **a.** of her whelps..................... 259
Eze 22:11 **a.** hath lewdly defiled his daughter........ 376
Eze 22:11 **a.** in thee hath humbled his sister,........ 376
Eze 24:23 mourn one toward **a.**.......................... 250
Eze 33:30 and speak one to **a.**, every one to.......... 259
Eze 37:16 then take **a.** stick, and write upon........ 259
Eze 37:17 join them one to **a.** into one stick;......... 259
Eze 40:13 little chamber to the roof of **a.**...................
Eze 40:26, 49 one on this side, and **a.** on that........ 259
Eze 41:6 one over **a.**, and thirty in order;.................
Eze 41:11 the north, and **a.** door toward the.......... 259
Eze 47:14 shall inherit it, one as well as **a.**:........... 250
Da 2:39 arise **a.** kingdom inferior to thee,........... 317
Da 2:39 and **a.** third kingdom of brass,............... 317
Da 2:43 they shall not cleave one to **a.**,........... 1836
Da 5:6 his knees smote one against **a.**........... 1668
Da 5:17 to thyself, give thy rewards to **a.**;......... 321
Da 7:3 diverse one from **a.**........................... 1668
Da 7:5 And behold **a.** beast, a second, like....... 317
Da 7:6 I beheld, and lo **a.**, like a leopard,......... 317
Da 7:8 came up among them **a.** little horn,........ 317
Da 7:24 and **a.** shall rise after them;................ 321
Da 8:13 **a.** saint said unto that certain............... 259
Ho 3:3 thou shalt not be for **a.** man:....................
Ho 4:4 let no man strive, nor reprove **a.**:......... 376
Joe 1:3 their children **a.** generation.................. 312
Joe 2:8 Neither shall one thrust **a.**;.................. 250
Am 4:7 caused it not to rain upon **a.** city:.......... 259

Na 2:4 against a. in the broad ways: 8264
Zec 2:3 a. angel went out to meet him, 312
Zec 8:21 inhabitants of one city shall go to a., 259
Zec 11:9 rest eat every one the flesh of a.. 7468
Mal 3:16 they....spake ofter one to a.: 7453
Mt 2:12 into their own country a. way. 243
Mt 8:9 and to a., Come, and he cometh; 243
Mt 8:21 And a. of his disciples said unto 2087
Mt 10:23 you in this city, flee ye into a. 243
Mt 11:3 should come, or do we look for a.? 2087
Mt 13:24, 31 A. parable put he forth unto 243
Mt 13:33 A. parable spake he unto them; 243
Mt 19:9 for fornication, and shall marry a., 243
Mt 21:33 Hear a. parable: There was a 243
Mt 21:35 and killed a., and stoned a. 3739
Mt 22:5 his farm, a. to his merchandise.
Mt 24:2 left here one stone upon a., that
Mt 24:10 shall betray one a., 240
Mt 24:10 and shall hate one a.. 240
Mt 25:15 to a. two, and to a. one; to every 3739
Mt 25:32 he shall separate them one from a., 240
Mt 26:71 into the porch, a. maid saw him, 243
Mt 27:38 right hand, and a. on the left. 1520
Mk 4:41 exceedingly, and said one to a., 240
Mk 9:10 questioning one with a. what the 1438
Mk 9:50 and have peace one with a.. 240
Mk 10:11 put away his wife, and marry a., 243
Mk 10:12 her husband, and be married to a., 243
Mk 12:4 he sent unto them a. servant; 243
Mk 12:5 he sent a.; and him they killed, 243
Mk 13:2 not be left one stone upon a.,
Mk 14:19 one, Is it I? and a. said, Is it I? 243
Mk 14:58 will build a. made without hands. 243
Mk 16:12 appeared in a. form unto two of 2087
Lu 2:15 the shepherds said one to a., 240
Lu 6:6 came to pass also on a. sabbath, 2087
Lu 6:11 with a. what they might do to Jesus. 240
Lu 7:8 and to a., Come, and he cometh; 243
Lu 7:19, 20 should come? or look we for a.? 243
Lu 7:32 marketplace, and calling one to a., 240
Lu 8:25 wondered, saying one to a., What 240
Lu 9:56 And they went to a. village. 2087
Lu 9:59 And he said unto a., Follow me. 2087
Lu 9:61 a. also said, Lord, I will follow 2087
Lu 12:1 that they trode one upon a., 240
Lu 14:19 a. said, I have bought five yoke of 2087
Lu 14:20 a. said, I have married a wife, 2087
Lu 14:31 to make war against a. king, 2087
Lu 16:7 said he to a., And how much owest 2087
Lu 16:12 faithful in that which is a. man's, 245
Lu 16:18 marrieth a., committeth adultery: 2087
Lu 19:20 a. came, saying, Lord, behold, 2087
Lu 19:44 in thee one stone upon a.;
Lu 20:11 he sent a. servant: and they beat 2087
Lu 21:6 not be left one stone upon a.,
Lu 22:58 a. saw him, and said, Thou art also 2087
Lu 22:59 a. confidently affirmed, saying, 243
Lu 24:17 these that ye have one to a., as ye 240
Lu 24:32 they said one to a., Did not our 240
Joh 4:33 said the disciples one to a., 240
Joh 4:37 true, One soweth, and a. reapeth. 243
Joh 5:7 while I am coming, a. steppeth 243
Joh 5:32 There is a. that beareth witness 243
Joh 5:43 a. shall come in his own name, 243
Joh 5:44 which receive honor one of a., 240
Joh 13:22 disciples looked one on a., doubting 240
Joh 13:34 give unto you, That ye love one a.; 240
Joh 13:34 loved you, that ye also love one a. 240
Joh 13:35 if ye have love one to a.. 240
Joh 14:16 he shall give you a. Comforter, 243
Joh 15:12 love one a., as I have loved you. 240
Joh 15:17 command you, that love one a. 240
Joh 18:15 Peter followed Jesus, and so did a. 243
Joh 19:37 a. scripture saith, They shall 2087
Joh 21:18 and a. shall gird thee, and carry 243
Ac 1:20 His bishoprick let a. take. 2087
Ac 2:7 marvelled, saying one to a., 240
Ac 2:12 were in doubt, saying one to a. 243
Ac 7:18 a. king arose, which knew not 2087
Ac 7:26 why do ye wrong one to a.? 240
Ac 10:28 or come unto one of a. nation; 246
Ac 12:17 departed and went into a. place. 2087
Ac 13:35 Wherefore he saith also in a. psalm, 2087
Ac 17:7 that there is a. king, one Jesus. 2087
Ac 19:32 cried one thing, and some a.: 243
Ac 19:38 deputies: let them implead one a. 240
Ac 21:6 we had taken our leave one of a., 240

Ac 21:34 some cried one thing, some a., 243
Ro 1:27 burned in their lust one toward a.; 240
Ro 2:1 wherein thou judgest a., thou 2087
Ro 2:15 accusing or else excusing one a.;) 240
Ro 2:21 Thou therefore which teachest a., 2087
Ro 7:3 she be married to a. man, 2087
Ro 7:3 though she be married to a. man. 2087
Ro 7:4 that ye should be married to a., 2087
Ro 7:23 But I see a. law in my members, 2087
Ro 9:21 one vessel unto honour, and a. 3739
Ro 12:5 every one members one of a.. 240
Ro 12:10 one to a. with brotherly love; 240
Ro 12:10 in honour preferring one a.; 240
Ro 12:16 Be of the same mind one toward a.. 240
Ro 13:8 but to love one a.: for he that 240
Ro 13:8 loveth a. hath fulfilled the law. 2087
Ro 14:2 a., who is weak, eateth herbs. 3739
Ro 14:4 that judgest a. man's servant? 245
Ro 14:5 esteemeth one day above a.
Ro 14:5 a. esteemeth every day alike. 3739
Ro 14:13 therefore judge one a. any more : 240
Ro 14:19 things wherewith one may edify a.. 240
Ro 15:5 to be likeminded one toward a. 240
Ro 15:7 Wherefore receive ye one a., 240
Ro 15:14 able also to admonish one a.. 240
Ro 15:20 build upon a. man's foundation: 245
Ro 16:16 Salute one a. with an holy kiss. 240
1Co 3:4 and a., I am of Apollos; are ye not 2087
1Co 3:10 the foundation, and a. buildeth 243
1Co 4:6 be puffed up for one against a.. 2087
1Co 4:7 maketh thee to differ from a.?
1Co 6:1 you, having a matter against a., 2087
1Co 6:7 because ye go to law one with a.. 1438
1Co 7:7 one after this manner, and a. 3588
1Co 10:29 judged of a. man's conscience? 243
1Co 11:21 one is hungry, and a. is drunken. 3739
1Co 11:33 together to eat, tarry one for a.. 240
1Co 12:8 to a. the word of knowledge by 243
1Co 12:9 To a. faith by the same Spirit; 2087
1Co 12:9 to a. the gifts of healing by the 243
1Co 12:10 to a. the working of miracles; 243
1Co 12:10 to a. prophecy; 243
1Co 12:10 to a. discerning of spirits; 243
1Co 12:10 to a. divers kinds of tongues; 2087
1Co 12:10 to a. the interpretation of tongues: 243
1Co 12:25 have the same care one for a. 240
1Co 14:30 If any thing be revealed to a. that 243
1Co 15:39 a. flesh of beasts, 243
1Co 15:39 a. of fishes, and a. birds. 243
1Co 15:40 glory of the terrestrial is a. 2087
1Co 15:41 sun, and a. glory of the moon, 243
1Co 15:41 moon, and a. glory of the stars: 243
1Co 15:41 star differeth from a. star in glory.
1Co 16:20 Greet ye one a. with an holy kiss. 240
2Co 10:16 not to boast in a. man's line of 245
2Co 11:4 a. Jesus, whom we have not 243
2Co 11:4 or if ye receive a. spirit, 2087
2Co 11:4 or a. gospel, which ye have not 2087
2Co 13:12 Greet one a. with a holy kiss. 240
Ga 1:6 grace of Christ unto a. gospel: 2087
Ga 1:7 Which is not a.; but there be 243
Ga 5:13 the flesh, but by love serve one a.. 240
Ga 5:15 if ye bite and devour one a., take 240
Ga 5:15 that ye be not consumed one of a.. 240
Ga 5:26 provoking one a., envying one a. 240
Ga 6:4 in himself alone, and not in a. 2087
Eph 4:2 forbearing one a. in love; 240
Eph 4:25 for we are members one of a. 240
Eph 4:32 be kind one to a., tenderhearted, 240
Eph 4:32 tenderhearted, forgiving one a., 1438
Eph 5:21 Submitting yourselves one to a. in 240
Col 3:9 Lie not one to a., seeing that ye 240
Col 3:13 Forbearing one a., 240
Col 3:13 and forgiving one a., 1438
Col 3:16 admonishing one a. in psalms 1438
1Th 3:12 abound in love one toward a., 240
1Th 4:9 are taught of God to love one a.. 240
1Th 4:18 comfort one a. with these words. 240
1Th 5:11 edify one a., even as also ye do. 1520
1Ti 5:21 without preferring one before a., 4299
Tit 3:3 envy, hateful, and hating one a. 240
Heb 3:13 exhort one a. daily, while it is 1438
Heb 4:8 afterward have spoken of a. day. 243
Heb 5:6 As he saith also in a. place, 2087
Heb 7:11 that a. priest should rise 2087
Heb 7:13 pertaineth to a. tribe, 2087
Heb 7:15 there ariseth a. priest, 2087

Heb 10:24 let us consider one a. to provoke 240
Heb 10:25 but exhorting one a.; and so
Jas 2:25 and had sent them out a. way? 2087
Jas 4:11 Speak not evil one of a., brethren. 240
Jas 4:12 who art thou that judgest a.? 2087
Jas 5:9 Grudge not one against a., 240
Jas 5:16 Confess your faults one to a., 240
Jas 5:16 and pray one for a., that ye may be 240
1Pe 1:22 love one a. with a pure heart 240
1Pe 3:8 having compassion one of a., 4835
1Pe 4:9 Use hospitality one to a. without 240
1Pe 4:10 minister the same one to a., 1438
1Pe 5:5 Yea, all of you be subject one to a., 240
1Pe 5:14 Greet ye one a. with a kiss of 240
1Jo 1:7 we have fellowship one with a., 240
1Jo 3:11 that we should love one a.. 240
1Jo 3:23 love one a., as he gave us 240
1Jo 4:7 Beloved, let us love one a.: 240
1Jo 4:11 us, we ought also to love one a.. 240
1Jo 4:12 If we love one a., God dwelleth in 240
2Jo 5 beginning, that we love one a.. 240
Re 6:4 there went out a. horse that was 243
Re 6:4 they should kill one a.. 240
Re 7:2 And I saw a. angel ascending 243
Re 8:3 And a. angel came and stood 243
Re 10:1 I saw a. mighty angel come 243
Re 11:10 and shall send gifts one to a.; 240
Re 12:3 And there appeared a. wonder in 243
Re 13:11 And I beheld a. beast coming 243
Re 14:6 And I saw a. angel fly in the 243
Re 14:8 And there followed a. angel, 243
Re 14:15, 17 a. angel came out of the temple 243
Re 14:18 a. angel came out from the altar, 243
Re 15:1 And I saw a. sign in heaven, great 243
Re 16:7 And I heard a. out of the altar 243
Re 18:1 a. angel come down from heaven. 243
Re 18:4 And I heard a. voice from heaven, 243
Re 20:12 and a. book was opened, which 243

ANOTHER'S

Ge 11:7 not understand one a. speech. 7453
Ex 21:35 if one man's ox hurt a., that he die; 7453
Joh 13:14 ye also ought to wash one a. feet. 240
1Co 10:24 but every man a. wealth. 2087
Ga 6:2 Bear ye one a. burdens, and so 240

ANSWER See also ANSWERED; ANSWEREST; ANSWERETH; ANSWERING; ANSWERS.

Ge 30:33 shall my righteousness a. for me 6030
Ge 41:16 God shall give Pharaoh an a. of 6030
Ge 45:3 his brethren could not a. him; 6030
De 20:11 if it make thee a. of peace, 6030
De 21:7 And they shall a. and say, 6030
De 25:9 shall a. and say, So shall it be done 6030
De 27:15 the people shall a. and say, Amen. 6030
Jos 4:7 Then ye shall a. them, That the 559
Jg 5:29 yea, she returned a. to herself, 559
1Sa 2:16 then he would a. him, Nay; 559
1Sa 20:10 if thy father a. thee roughly? 6030
2Sa 3:11 he could not a. Abner a word 7725
2Sa 24:13 see what a. I shall return to him 1697
1Ki 9:9 And they shall a., Because they 559
1Ki 12:6 do ye advise, that I may a. 7725,1697
1Ki 12:7 and wilt serve them, and a. them, 6030
1Ki 12:9 that we may a. this people, 7725,1697
1Ki 18:29 neither voice, nor any to a., 6030
2Ki 4:29 if any salute thee, a. him not 6030
2Ki 18:36 commandment was, saying, A. 6030
2Ch 10:6 to return a. to this people? 1697
2Ch 10:9 we may return a. to this people, 1697
2Ch 10:10 Thus shalt thou a. the people 559
Ezr 4:17 sent the king an a. unto Rehum 6600
Ezr 5:5 then they returned a. by letter 8421
Ezr 5:11 And thus they returned us a., 6600
Ne 5:8 peace, and found nothing to a. 1696
Es 4:13 commanded to a. Esther, 7725
Es 4:15 bade them return Mordecai this a.,
Job 5:1 if there be any that will a. thee; 6030
Job 9:3 cannot a. him one of a thousand 6030
Job 9:14 How much less shall I a. him, 6030
Job 9:15 would I not a., but I would make 6030
Job 9:32 I should a. him, and we should 6030
Job 13:22 Then call thou, and I will a. 6030
Job 13:22 let me speak, and a. thou me. 7725
Job 14:15 Thou shalt call, and I will a. thee: 6030
Job 19:16 servant, and he gave me no a.; 6030
Job 20:2 do my thoughts cause me to a., 7725
Job 20:3 understanding causeth me to a. 6030

Job 23:5 the words which he would **a.** me, 6030
Job 31:14 when he visiteth, what shall I **a.** 7725
Job 31:35 that the Almighty would **a.** me, 6030
Job 32:1 these three men ceased to **a.** Job, 6030
Job 32:3 they had found no **a.**, and yet had 4617
Job 32:5 saw that there was no **a.** 4617
Job 32:14 will I **a.** him with your speeches. 7725
Job 32:17 I said, I will **a.** also my part, 6030
Job 32:20 I will open my lips and **a.**. 6030
Job 33:5 If thou canst **a.** me, set thy 7725
Job 33:12 I will **a.** thee, that God is greater 6030
Job 33:32 If thou hast any thing to say, **a.** 7725
Job 35:4 I will **a.** thee and thy 7725,4405
Job 35:12 there they cry, but none giveth **a.**, 6030
Job 38:3 demand of thee, and **a.** thou me. 3045
Job 40:2 he that reproveth God, let him **a.** 6030
Job 40:4 vile; what shall I **a.** thee? 7725
Job 40:5 have I spoken; but I will not **a.**: 6030
Ps 27:7 mercy also upon me, and **a.** me. 6030
Ps 65:5 wilt thou **a.** us, O God 6030
Ps 86:7 call upon thee: for thou wilt **a.** me 6030
Ps 91:15 call upon me, and I will **a.** him: 6030
Ps 102:2 the day when I call **a.** me speedily. 6030
Ps 108:6 with thy right hand, and **a.** me. 6030
Ps 119:42 to **a.** him that reproacheth me: 6030
Ps 143:1 in thy faithfulness **a.** me, and in 6030
Pr 1:28 call upon me, but I will not **a.**; 6030
Pr 15:1 A soft **a.** turneth away wrath: 4617
Pr 15:23 hath joy by the **a.** of his mouth: 4617
Pr 15:28 of the righteous studieth to **a.**: 6030
Pr 16:1 **a.** of the tongue, is from the Lord 4617
Pr 22:21 mightest **a.** the words of truth 7725
Pr 24:26 his lips that giveth a right **a.**. 7725,1697
Pr 26:4 **A.** not a fool according to his 6030
Pr 26:5 **A.** a fool according to his folly, 6030
Pr 27:11 **a.** him that reproacheth me 7725,1697
Pr 29:19 he understand he will not **a.** 4617
Ca 5:6 called him, but he gave me no **a.** 6030
Isa 14:32 shall one then **a.** the messengers 6030
Isa 30:19 he shall hear it, he will **a.** thee. 6030
Isa 36:21 was, saying, **A.** him not. 6030
Isa 41:28 I asked of them, could **a.** 7725
Isa 46:7 yet can he not **a.**, nor save him 6030
Isa 50:2 I called, was there none to **a.**? 6030
Isa 58:9 thou call, and the Lord shall **a.**; 6030
Isa 65:12 when I called, ye did not answer; 6030
Isa 65:24 before they call, I will **a.**; 6030
Isa 66:4 when I called, none did **a.**; 6030
Jer 5:19 then shalt thou **a.** them, Like as 559
Jer 7:27 they will not **a.** thee. 6030
Jer 22:9 Then they shall **a.**, Because they 559
Jer 33:3 Call unto me, and I will **a.** thee, 6030
Jer 42:4 the Lord shall **a.** you, 6030
Jer 44:20 which had given him that **a.**, 6030
Eze 14:4 I the Lord will **a.** him that cometh 6030
Eze 14:7 I the Lord will **a.** him by myself: 6030
Eze 21:7 thou shalt **a.**, For the tidings; 559
Da 3:16 careful to **a.** thee in this matter, 8421
Joe 2:19 Yea, the Lord will **a.** and say 6030
Mic 3:7 for there is no **a.** of God. 4617
Hab 2:1 what I shall **a.** when I am 7725
Hab 2:11 beam out of the timber shall **a.** 6030
Zec 13:6 Then he shall **a.**, Those with 559
Mt 22:46 no man was able to **a.** him a word, *611*
Mt 25:37 **Then shall the righteous a. him,** *611*
Mt 25:40 **King shall a. and say unto them,** *611*
Mt 25:44 **Then shall they also a. him,** *611*
Mt 25:45 **Then shall he a. them,** *611*
Mk 11:29 **ask of you one question, and a. me,** *611*
Mk 11:30 **from heaven, or of men? a. me** *611*
Mk 14:40 wist they what to **a.** him. *611*
Lu 11:7 **shall a. and say, Trouble me not:** *611*
Lu 12:11 **how or what thing ye shall a.,** *626*
Lu 13:25 **he shall a. and say unto you,** *611*
Lu 14:6 could not **a.** him again to these *470*
Lu 20:3 **ask you one thing; and a. me:** *2036*
Lu 20:26 they marvelled at his **a.**, and held *612*
Lu 21:14 **meditate before what ye shall a.** *626*
Lu 22:68 **ye will not a. me, nor let me go.** *611*
Joh 1:22 give an **a.** to them that sent us. *612*
Joh 19:9 Jesus gave him no **a.** *612*
Ac 24:10 more cheerfully **a.** for myself: *626*
Ac 25:16 have licence to **a.** for himself *627*
Ac 26:2 **a.** for myself this day before thee *626*
Ro 11:4 what saith the **a.** of God unto him? *5538*
1Co 9:3 **a.** to them that do examine me *627*
2Co 5:12 somewhat to **a.** them which glory
Col 4:6 how ye ought to **a.** every man. *611*
2Ti 4:16 first **a.** no man stood with me, *627*
1Pe 3:15 **a.** to every man that asketh you *627*
1Pe 3:21 **a.** of a good conscience toward *1906*

ANSWERABLE

Ex 38:18 **a.** to the hangings of the court. 5980

ANSWERED See also ANSWEREDST.

Ge 18:27 And Abraham **a.** and said, 6030
Ge 23:5 the children of Heth **a.** Abraham, 6030
Ge 23:10 and Ephron the Hittite **a.** Abraham 6030
Ge 23:14 and Ephron **a.** Abraham, saying 6030
Ge 24:50 Laban and Bethuel **a.** and said, 6030
Ge 27:37 And Isaac **a.** and said unto Esau, 6030
Ge 27:39 And Isaac his father **a.** and said 6030
Ge 31:14 And Rachel and Leah **a.** and said 6030
Ge 31:31, 36 Jacob **a.** and said to Laban, 6030
Ge 31:43 And Laban **a.** and said unto Jacob, 6030
Ge 34:13 And the sons of Jacob **a.** Shechem 6030
Ge 35:3 unto God, who **a.** me in the day of 6030
Ge 40:18 And Joseph **a.** and said, This is 6030
Ge 41:16 And Joseph **a.** Pharaoh, saying, 6030
Ge 42:22 And Reuben **a.** them, saying, 6030
Ge 43:28 they **a.**, Thy servant our father is 559
Ex 4:1 Moses **a.** and said, But, behold, 6030
Ex 15:21 And Miriam **a.** them, 6030
Ex 19:8 And all the people **a.** together, 6030
Ex 19:19 and God **a.** him by a voice. 6030
Ex 24:3 and all the people **a.** with one voice, 6030
Nu 11:28 And Joshua the son of Nun...**a.** 6030
Nu 22:18 And Balaam **a.** and said unto the 6030
Nu 23:12 and he **a.** and said, 6030
Nu 23:26 But Balaam **a.** and said unto Balak, 6030
Nu 32:31 And the children of Gad...**a.**, 6030
De 1:14 And ye **a.** me, and said, 6030
De 1:41 Then ye **a.** and said unto me, 6030
Jos 1:16 And they **a.** Joshua, saying, 6030
Jos 2:14 men **a.** her, Our life for yours, 559
Jos 7:20 And Achan **a.** Joshua, 6030
Jos 9:24 And they **a.** Joshua, 6030
Jos 15:19 Who **a.**, Give me a blessing; 559
Jos 17:15 Joshua **a.** them, If thou be a great 559
Jos 22:21 the half tribe of Manasseh **a.**, 6030
Jos 24:16 the people **a.** and said, God forbid 6030
Jg 5:29 Her wise ladies **a.** her, 6030
Jg 7:14 And his fellow **a.** and said, 6030
Jg 8:8 and the men of Penuel **a.** him 6030
Jg 8:8 as the men of Succoth had **a.** him. 6030
Jg 8:18 they **a.**, As thou art, so were they; 559
Jg 8:25 they **a.**, We will willingly give them 559
Jg 11:13 of Ammon **a.** unto the messengers 559
Jg 15:6 they **a.**, Samson, the son in law 559
Jg 15:10 And they **a.**, To bind Samson 559
Jg 18:14 **a.** the five men that went to spy 6030
Jg 19:28 and let us be going. But none **a.**. 6030
Jg 20:4 And the Levite...**a.** and said, 6030
Ru 2:4 they **a.** him, The Lord bless thee. 559
Ru 2:6 And the servant...**a.** and said, 6030
Ru 2:11 And Boaz **a.** and said unto her, 6030
Ru 3:9 she **a.**, I am Ruth thine handmaid; 559
1Sa 1:15 Hannah **a.** and said, No, my lord, 6030
1Sa 1:17 Then Eli **a.** and said, Go in peace: 6030
1Sa 3:4 and he **a.**, Here am I. 559
1Sa 3:6 And he **a.**, I called not, my son; 559
1Sa 3:10 Then Samuel **a.**, Speak; for thy 559
1Sa 3:16 And he **a.**, Here am I. 559
1Sa 4:17 And the messenger **a.** and said, 6030
1Sa 4:20 she **a.** not, neither did she regard it. 6030
1Sa 5:8 And they **a.**, Let the ark of the God 559
1Sa 6:4 They **a.**, Five golden emerods, 559
1Sa 9:8 the servant **a.** Saul again, 6030
1Sa 9:12 and they **a.** them, and said, 6030
1Sa 9:19 And Samuel **a.** Saul, and said, 6030
1Sa 9:21 And Saul **a.**, and said, 6030
1Sa 10:12 And one of the same place **a.** 6030
1Sa 10:22 the Lord **a.**, Behold, he hath hid 559
1Sa 11:2 Nahash the Ammonite **a.** them, 559
1Sa 12:5 And they **a.**, He is witness. 559
1Sa 14:12 men of the garrison **a.** Jonathan 6030
1Sa 14:28 Then **a.** one of the people, 6030
1Sa 14:37 he **a.** him not that day. 6030
1Sa 14:39 among all the people that **a.** him. 6030
1Sa 14:44 Saul **a.**, God do so and more: 559
1Sa 16:18 Then **a.** one of the servants, 6030
1Sa 17:27 people **a.** him after this manner, 559
1Sa 17:30 the people **a.** him again after 7725,1697
1Sa 17:58 David **a.**, I am the son of thy servant 559
1Sa 18:7 the women **a.** one another as 6030
1Sa 19:17 Michal **a.** Saul, He said unto me, 559
1Sa 20:28 And Jonathan **a.** Saul, David 6030
1Sa 20:32 And Jonathan **a.** Saul his father, 6030
1Sa 21:4 And the priest **a.** David, 6030
1Sa 21:5 And David **a.** the priest, 6030
1Sa 22:9 Then **a.** Doeg the Edomite, 6030
1Sa 22:12 And he **a.**, Here I am, my lord. 559
1Sa 22:14 Then Ahimelech **a.** the king, 6030
1Sa 23:4 the Lord **a.** him and said, Arise, 6030
1Sa 25:10 And Nabal **a.** David's servants, 6030
1Sa 26:6 **a.** David and said to Ahimelech 6030
1Sa 26:14 Abner **a.** and said, Who art thou 6030
1Sa 26:22 David **a.** and said, Behold the king's 6030
1Sa 28:6 the Lord **a.** him not, neither by 6030
1Sa 28:15 Saul **a.**, I am sore distressed; 6030
1Sa 29:9 And Achish **a.** and said to David, 6030
1Sa 30:8 And he **a.** him, Pursue: 559
1Sa 30:22 Then **a.** all the wicked men 6030
2Sa 1:4 And he **a.**, That the people are fled 559
2Sa 1:7 And I **a.**, Here am I. 559
2Sa 1:8 I **a.** him, I am an Amalekite. 559
2Sa 1:13 he **a.**, I am the son of a stranger, 559
2Sa 2:20 Art thou Ashel? And he **a.**, I am. 559
2Sa 4:9 David **a.** Rechab and Baanah his 603
2Sa 9:6 And he **a.**, Behold thy servant! 559
2Sa 13:12 she **a.** him, Nay, my brother, 559
2Sa 13:32 And Jonadab,...David's brother, **a.** 6030
2Sa 14:5 she **a.**, I am indeed a widow woman, 559
2Sa 14:18 king **a.** and said unto the woman, 6030
2Sa 14:19 And the woman **a.** and said, 6030
2Sa 14:32 Absalom **a.** Joab, Behold, I sent 559
2Sa 15:21 And Ittai **a.** the king, and said, 6030
2Sa 18:3 people **a.**, Thou shalt not go 559
2Sa 18:29 And Ahimaaz **a.**, When Joab sent 559
2Sa 18:32 Cushi **a.**, The enemies of my lord 559
2Sa 19:21 But Abishai the son of Zeruiah **a.** 6030
2Sa 19:26 he **a.**, My lord, O king, my servant 559
2Sa 19:38 the king **a.**, Chimham shall go over 559
2Sa 19:42 men of Judah **a.** the men of Israel, 6030
2Sa 19:43 men of Israel **a.** the men of Judah, 6030
2Sa 20:17 he **a.**, I am he. Then she said 559
2Sa 20:17 And he **a.**, I do hear. 559
2Sa 20:20 And Joab **a.** and said, Far be it, 6030
2Sa 21:1 And the Lord **a.**. It is for Saul, 559
2Sa 21:5 And they **a.** the king, The man 559
2Sa 22:42 the Lord, but he **a.** them not. 6030
1Ki 1:28 Then king David **a.** and said, 6030
1Ki 1:36 And Benaiah...**a.** the king, 6030
1Ki 1:43 Jonathan **a.** and said to Adonijah, 6030
1Ki 2:22 And king Solomon **a.** and said 6030
1Ki 2:30 Thus said Joab, and thus he **a.** me. 6030
1Ki 3:27 Then the king **a.** and said, 6030
1Ki 11:22 he **a.**, Nothing: howbeit let me go 559
1Ki 12:13 the king **a.** the people roughly, 6030
1Ki 12:16 people **a.** the king, saying, 7725,1697
1Ki 13:6 king **a.** and said unto the man of 6030
1Ki 18:8 And he **a.** him, I am: 559
1Ki 18:18 he **a.**, I have not troubled Israel; 559
1Ki 18:21 the people **a.** him not a word. 6030
1Ki 18:24 people **a.** and said, It is well spoken. 6030
1Ki 18:26 was no voice, nor any that **a.**. 6030
1Ki 20:4 And the king of Israel **a.** and 6030
1Ki 20:11 **a.** and said, Tell him, Let not him 6030
1Ki 20:14 And he **a.**, Thou. 559
1Ki 21:6 **a.**, I will not give thee my vineyard 559
1Ki 21:20 And he **a.**, I have found thee: 559
1Ki 22:15 he **a.** him, Go, and prosper: 559
2Ki 1:8 they **a.** him, He was a hairy man, 559
2Ki 1:10 Elijah **a.** and said to the captain 6030
2Ki 1:11 And he **a.** and said unto him, 6030
2Ki 1:12 And Elijah **a.** and said unto them, 6030
2Ki 2:5 And he **a.**, Yea, I know it; hold 559
2Ki 3:8 **a.**, The way through the wilderness 559
2Ki 3:11 of the king of Israel's servants **a.** 6030
2Ki 4:13 she **a.**, I dwell among mine own 559
2Ki 4:14 Gehazi **a.**, Verily she hath no child, 559
2Ki 4:26 the child? And she **a.**, It is well. 559
2Ki 6:2 And he **a.**, Go ye. 559
2Ki 6:3 thy servants. And he **a.**, I will go. 559
2Ki 6:16 And he **a.**, Fear not: for they that 559
2Ki 6:22 he **a.**, Thou shalt not smite them: 559
2Ki 6:28 she **a.**, This woman said unto me, 559
2Ki 7:2 king leaned **a.** the man of God, 6030
2Ki 7:13 one of his servants **a.** and said, 6030
2Ki 7:19 And that lord **a.** the man of God, 6030
2Ki 8:12 he **a.**, Because I know the evil 559

2Ki	8:13	Elisha **a.**, The Lord hath shewed	559
2Ki	8:14	And he **a.**, He told me that thou	559
2Ki	9:19	And Jehu **a.**, What hast thou to do	559
2Ki	9:22	And he **a.**, What peace, so long as	559
2Ki	10:13	And they **a.**, We are the brethren	559
2Ki	10:15	And Jehonadab **a.**, It is. If it be,	559
2Ki	18:36	and **a.** him not a word:	6030
2Ki	20:10	Hezekiah **a.**, It is a light thing	559
2Ki	20:15	And Hezekiah **a.**, All the things	559
1Ch	12:17	David went out...and **a.** and	6030
1Ch	21:3	And Joab **a.**, The Lord make his	559
1Ch	21:26	he **a.** him from heaven by fire	6030
1Ch	21:28	the Lord had answered him in	6030
2Ch	2:11	the king of Tyre **a.** in writing,	559
2Ch	7:22	And it shall be **a.**, Because they	559
2Ch	10:13	And the king **a.** them roughly;	6030
2Ch	10:14	And **a.** them after the adivce of	1697
2Ch	10:16	when...the people **a.** the king,	7725
2Ch	18:3	And he **a.** him, I am as thou art,	559
2Ch	25:9	the man of God **a.**, The Lord is able	559
2Ch	29:31	Then Hezekiah **a.** and said,	6030
2Ch	31:10	priest of the house of Zadok **a.**	559
2Ch	34:15	Hilkiah **a.** and said to Shaphan	6030
2Ch	34:23	she **a.** them, Thus saith the Lord	559
Ezr	10:2	sons of Elam, **a.** and said unto	6030
Ezr	10:12	all the congregation **a.** and said	6030
Ne	2:20	Then **a.** I them, and said unto	7725,1697
Ne	6:4	I **a.** them after the same manner	7725
Ne	8:6	all the people **a.**, Amen, Amen.	6030
Es	1:16	And Memucan **a.** before the king	559
Es	5:4	Esther **a.**, If it seem good unto	559
Es	5:7	The **a.** Esther, and said, My	6039
Es	6:7	And Haman **a.** the king, For the	559
Es	7:3	Esther the queen **a.** and said,	6030
Es	7:5	the king Ahasuerus **a.** and said	559
Job	1:7,9	Satan **a.** the Lord and said,	6030
Job	2:2,4	Satan **a.** the Lord, and said,	6030
Job	4:1	Eliphaz the Temanite **a.** and said,	6030
Job	6:1	But Job **a.** and said,	6030
Job	8:1	Then **a.** Bildad the Shuhite,	6030
Job	9:1	Then Job **a.** and said,	6030
Job	9:16	If I had called, and he had **a.** me;	6030
Job	11:1	**a.** Zophar the Naamathite,	6030
Job	11:2	not the multitude of words be **a.**?	6030
Job	12:1	And Job **a.** and said,	6030
Job	15:1	Then **a.** Eliphaz the Temanite,	6030
Job	16:1	Then Job **a.** and said.	6030
Job	18:1	Then **a.** Bildad the Shuhite,	6030
Job	19:1	Then Job **a.** and said,	6030
Job	20:1	Then **a.** Zophar the Naamathite,	6030
Job	21:1	But Job **a.** and said,	6030
Job	22:1	Then Eliphaz the Temanite **a.**	6030
Job	23:1	Then Job **a.** and said,	6030
Job	25:1	Then **a.** Bildad the Shuhite	6030
Job	26:1	But Job **a.** and said,	6030
Job	32:6	the son of Barachel the Buzite **a.**	6030
Job	32:12	convinced Job, or that **a.** his words:	6030
Job	32:15	were amazed they **a.** no more:	6030
Job	32:16	stood still, and **a.** no more,	6030
Job	34:1	Furthermore Elihu **a.** and said,	6030
Job	38:1	Lord **a.** Job out of the whirlwind,	6030
Job	40:1	Moreover the Lord **a.** Job,	6030
Job	40:3	Then Job **a.** the Lord, and said,	6030
Job	40:6	Then **a.** the Lord unto Job	6030
Job	42:1	Then Job **a.** the Lord,	6030
Ps	18:41	the Lord, but he **a.** them not.	6030
Ps	81:7	I **a.** thee in the secret place of	6030
Ps	99:6	upon the Lord, and he **a.** them.	6030
Ps	118:5	Lord **a.** me, and set me in a large	6030
Isa	6:11	And he **a.**, Until the cities	559
Isa	21:9	he **a.** and said, Babylon is fallen,	6030
Isa	36:21	peace, and **a.** him not a word:	6030
Isa	39:4	Hezekiah **a.**, All that is in mine	559
Jer	7:13	I called you, but ye **a.** not;	6030
Jer	11:5	Then **a.** I, and said, so be it, O Lord.	6030
Jer	23:35	What hath the Lord **a.**?	6030
Jer	23:37	What hath the Lord **a.** thee?	6030
Jer	35:17	unto them, but they have not **a.**	6030
Jer	36:18	Then Baruch **a.** them.	559
Jer	44:15	all the men....**a.** Jeremiah,	6030
Eze	24:20	I **a.** them, The word of the Lord	559
Eze	37:3	I **a.**, O Lord God, thou knowest.	559
Da	2:5	king **a.** and said to the Chaldeans.	6032
Da	2:7	**a.** again and said, Let the king tell	6032
Da	2:8	**a.** and said, I know of certainty	6032
Da	2:10	Chaldeans **a.** before the king, and	6032
Da	2:14	**a.** with counsel and wisdom to	8421
Da	2:15	He **a.** and said to Arioch	6032
Da	2:20	Daniel **a.** and said, Blessed be the	6032
Da	2:26	The king **a.** and said to Daniel,	6032
Da	2:27	**a.** in the presence of the king,	6032
Da	2:47	The king **a.** unto Daniel,	6032
Da	3:16	**a.** and said to the king,	6032
Da	3:24	They **a.** and said unto the king,	6032
Da	3:25	He **a.** and said, Lo, I see four men	6032
Da	4:19	Belteshazzar **a.** and said, My lord,	6032
Da	5:17	Daniel **a.** and said before the king,	6032
Da	6:12	king **a.** and said, The thing is true,	6032
Da	6:13	**a.** they and said before the king,	6032
Am	7:14	**a.** Amos, and said to Amaziah,	6030
Mic	6:5	Balaam the son of Beor **a.** him,	6030
Hab	2:2	And the Lord **a.** me, and said,	6030
Hag	2:12	And the priests **a.** and said, No.	6030
Hag	2:13	the priests **a.** and said, It shall be	6030
Hag	2:14	Then **a.** Haggai, and said,	6030
Zec	1:10	the man that stood....**a.** and said,	6030
Zec	1:11	And they **a.** the angel of the Lord	6030
Zec	1:12	Then the angel of the Lord **a.**	6030
Zec	1:13	And the Lord **a.** the angel	6030
Zec	1:19	And he **a.** me, These are the horns	559
Zec	3:4	And he **a.** and spake	6030
Zec	4:4	So I **a.** and spake to the angel	6030
Zec	4:5	the angel that talked with me **a.**	6030
Zec	4:6	Then he **a.** and spake unto me,	6030
Zec	4:11	Then **a.** I, and said unto him,	6030
Zec	4:12	And I **a.** again, and said unto him,	6030
Zec	4:13	And he **a.** me and said,	559
Zec	5:2	And I **a.**, I see a flying roll;	559
Zec	6:4	Then I **a.** and said unto the angel	6030
Zec	6:5	the angel **a.** and said unto me,	6030
Mt	4:4	he **a.** and said, It is written.	611
Mt	8:8	The centurion **a.** and said, Lord,	611
Mt	11:4	Jesus **a.** and said unto them,	611
Mt	11:25	At that time Jesus **a.** and said,	611
Mt	12:38	scribes and of the Pharisees **a.**,	611
Mt	12:39	he **a.** and said unto them,	611
Mt	12:48	he **a.** and said unto him that told	611
Mt	13:11,	37 He **a.** and said unto them,	611
Mt	14:28	Peter **a.** him and said, Lord,	611
Mt	15:3	he **a.** and said unto them,	611
Mt	15:13	he **a.** and said, Every plant,	611
Mt	15:15	Then **a.** Peter and said unto him,	611
Mt	15:23	he **a.** her not a word.	611
Mt	15:24	he **a.** and said, I am not sent	611
Mt	15:26	he **a.** and said, It is not meet	611
Mt	15:28	Then Jesus **a.** and said unto her,	611
Mt	16:2	He **a.** and said unto them,	611
Mt	16:16	Simon Peter **a.** and said,	611
Mt	16:17	Jesus **a.** and said unto him,	611
Mt	17:4	Then **a.** Peter, and said unto	611
Mt	17:11	Jesus **a.** and said unto them,	611
Mt	17:17	Then Jesus **a.** and said, O faithless	611
Mt	19:4	he **a.** and said unto them,	611
Mt	19:27	Then **a.** Peter and said unto him,	611
Mt	20:13	he **a.** one of them, and said,	611
Mt	20:22	Jesus **a.** and said, Ye know	611
Mt	21:21,	24 Jesus **a.** and said unto them	611
Mt	21:27	they **a.** Jesus, and said, We cannot	611
Mt	21:29	He a. and said, I will not:	611
Mt	21:30	he a. and said, I go, sir;	611
Mt	22:1	Jesus **a.** and spake unto them again	611
Mt	22:29	Jesus **a.** and said unto them,	611
Mt	24:4	Jesus **a.** and said unto them,	611
Mt	25:9	the wise a., saying, Not so;	611
Mt	25:12	he a. and said, Verily I say unto	611
Mt	25:26	His lord a. and said unto him	611
Mt	26:23	he **a.** and said, He that dippeth his	611
Mt	26:25	which betrayed him, **a.** and said,	611
Mt	26:33	Peter **a.** and said unto him,	611
Mt	26:63	the high priest **a.** and said unto	611
Mt	26:66	**a.** and said. He is guilty of death.	611
Mt	27:12	priests and elders, he **a.** nothing.	611
Mt	27:14	he **a.** him to never a word;	611
Mt	27:21	The governor **a.** and said unto them,	611
Mt	27:25	Then **a.** all the people, and said,	611
Mt	28:5	the angel **a.** and said unto the	611
Mk	3:33	he **a.** them, saying, Who is my	611
Mk	5:9	he **a.**, saying, My name is Legion:	611
Mk	6:37	He **a.** and said unto them,	611
Mk	7:6	He **a.** and said unto them,	611
Mk	7:28	she **a.** and said unto him,	611
Mk	8:4	his disciples **a.** him,	611
Mk	8:28	they **a.**, John the Baptist:	611
Mk	9:5	Peter **a.** and said to Jesus,	611
Mk	9:12	he **a.** and told them, Elias verily	611
Mk	9:17	one of the multitude **a.** and said,	611
Mk	9:38	John **a.** him, saying, Master,	611
Mk	10:3	he **a.** and said unto them,	611
Mk	10:5	Jesus **a.** and said unto them,	611
Mk	10:20	he **a.** and said unto him, Master,	611
Mk	10:29	Jesus **a.** and said, Verily I say	611
Mk	10:51	Jesus **a.** and said unto him,	611
Mk	11:14	Jesus **a.** and said unto it,	611
Mk	11:29	Jesus **a.** and said unto them,	611
Mk	11:33	they **a.** and said unto Jesus, We	611
Mk	12:28	perceiving that he had **a.** them well,	611
Mk	12:29	Jesus **a.** him, The first of all the	611
Mk	12:34	saw that he **a.** discreetly,	611
Mk	12:35	Jesus **a.** and said, while he taught	611
Mk	14:20	he **a.** and said unto them,	611
Mk	14:48	Jesus **a.** and said unto them,	611
Mk	14:61	held his peace and **a.** nothing.	611
Mk	15:3	many things: but he **a.** nothing.	611
Mk	15:5	Jesus yet **a.** nothing; so that Pilate	611
Mk	15:9	Pilate **a.** them, saying,	611
Mk	15:12	Pilate **a.** and said again unto them	611
Lu	1:35	the angel **a.** and said unto her,	611
Lu	1:60	his mother **a.** and said,	611
Lu	3:16	John **a.**, saying unto them all,	611
Lu	4:4	Jesus **a.** him, saying,	611
Lu	4:8	Jesus **a.** and said unto him,	611
Lu	7:43	Simon **a.** and said, I suppose that	611
Lu	8:21	he **a.** and said unto them,	611
Lu	8:50	he **a.** him, saying, Fear not:	611
Lu	9:49	John **a.** and said, Master, we saw	611
Lu	10:28	unto him, Thou hast a. right:	611
Lu	10:41	Jesus **a.** and said unto her,	611
Lu	11:45	Then **a.** one of the lawyers, and	611
Lu	13:14	the ruler of the synagogue **a.**	611
Lu	13:15	The Lord then **a.** him, and said,	611
Lu	14:5	**a.** them, saying, Which of you	611
Lu	17:20	he **a.** them and said,	611
Lu	17:37	they **a.** and said unto him,	611
Lu	19:40	he **a.** and said unto them,	611
Lu	20:3	he **a.** and said unto them,	611
Lu	20:7	they **a.**, that they could not tell	611
Lu	20:24	They **a.** and said, Caesar's.	611
Lu	22:51	Jesus **a.** and said, Suffer ye thus	611
Lu	23:3	he **a.** him and said, Thou sayest it.	611
Lu	23:9	he **a.** him nothing.	611
Joh	1:21	thou that prophet? And he **a.**, No.	611
Joh	1:26	John **a.** them, saying, I baptize	611
Joh	1:48	Jesus **a.** and said unto him,	611
Joh	1:49	Nathanael **a.** and saith	611
Joh	1:50	Jesus **a.** and said unto him,	611
Joh	2:18	Then **a.** the Jews and said	611
Joh	2:19	Jesus **a.** and said unto them,	611
Joh	3:3	Jesus **a.** and said unto him,	611
Joh	3:5	Jesus **a.**, Verily, verily,	611
Joh	3:9	Nicodemus **a.** and said	611
Joh	3:10	Jesus **a.** and said unto him, Art	611
Joh	3:27	John **a.** and said, A man can	611
Joh	4:10,	13 Jesus **a.** and said unto her,	611
Joh	4:17	**a.** and said, I have no husband.	611
Joh	5:7	The impotent man **a.**	611
Joh	5:11	he **a.** them, He that made me	611
Joh	5:17	Jesus **a.** them, My Father worketh	611
Joh	5:19	Then **a.** Jesus and said unto them,	611
Joh	6:7	Philip **a.** him, Two hundred	611
Joh	6:26	Jesus **a.** them and said,	611
Joh	6:29	Jesus **a.** and said unto them,	611
Joh	6:43	Jesus therefore **a.** and said	611
Joh	6:68	Then Simon Peter **a.** him,	611
Joh	6:70	Jesus **a.** them, Have not I chosen	611
Joh	7:16	Jesus **a.** them, and said,	611
Joh	7:20	The people **a.** and said,	611
Joh	7:21	Jesus **a.** and said unto them,	611
Joh	7:46	The officers **a.**, Never man	611
Joh	7:47	Then **a.** them the Pharisees,	611
Joh	7:52	They **a.** and said unto him,	611
Joh	8:14	Jesus **a.** and said unto them,	611
Joh	8:19	Jesus **a.**, Ye neither know me,	611
Joh	8:33	**a.** him, We be Abraham's seed,	611
Joh	8:34	Jesus **a.** them, Verily,	611
Joh	8:39	They **a.** and said unto him,	611
Joh	8:48	Then **a.** the Jews, and said	611
Joh	8:49	Jesus **a.**, I have not a devil;	611
Joh	8:54	Jesus **a.**, If I honour myself, my	611
Joh	9:3	Jesus **a.**, Neither hath this man	611
Joh	9:11	He **a.** and said, A man that is	611

Joh 9:20 His parents a. them 611
Joh 9:25 He a. and said, Whether he be a 611
Joh 9:27 He a. them, I have told 611
Joh 9:30 The man a. and said unto them, 611
Joh 9:34 They a. and said unto him, 611
Joh 9:36 He a. and said, Who is he, 611
Joh 10:25 Jesus a. them, I told you, and ye 611
Joh 10:32 Jesus a. them, Many good works 611
Joh 10:33 The Jews a. him, saying, 611
Joh 10:34 Jesus a. them, Is it not 611
Joh 11:9 Jesus a., Are there not twelve 611
Joh 12:23 Jesus a. them, saying, 611
Joh 12:30 Jesus a. and said, This voice 611
Joh 12:34 the people a. him, We have heard 611
Joh 13:7 Jesus a. and said unto him, 611
Joh 13:8 Jesus a. him, If I wash thee not, 611
Joh 13:26 Jesus a., He it is, to whom 611
Joh 13:36 Jesus a. him, Whither I go, 611
Joh 13:38 Jesus a. him, Wilt thou lay 611
Joh 14:23 Jesus a. and said unto him, 611
Joh 16:31 Jesus a. them, Do ye now believe? 611
Joh 18:5 They a. him, Jesus of Nazareth. 611
Joh 18:8 Jesus a., I have told you that I am 611
Joh 18:20 Jesus a. him, I spake openly to 611
Joh 18:23 Jesus a. him, If I have spoken evil, 611
Joh 18:30 They a. and said unto him, 611
Joh 18:34 Jesus a. him, Sayest thou this 611
Joh 18:35 Pilate a., Am I a Jew? 611
Joh 18:36 Jesus a., My kingdom is not of 611
Joh 18:37 Jesus a., Thou sayest that I am 611
Joh 19:7 The Jews a. him, We have a law. 611
Joh 19:11 Jesus a., Thou couldest have no 611
Joh 19:15 chief priests a., We have no king 611
Joh 19:22 Pilate a., What I have written, 611
Joh 20:28 Thomas a., and said unto 611
Joh 21:5 They a. him, No. 611
Ac 3:12 he a. unto the people, ye men of 611
Ac 4:19 Peter and John a. and said unto 611
Ac 5:8 Peter a. unto her, Tell me 611
Ac 5:29 and the other apostles a. and said, 611
Ac 8:24 Then a. Simon, and said, Pray ye, 611
Ac 8:34 the eunuch a. Philip, and said, 611
Ac 8:37 he a. and said, I believe 611
Ac 9:13 Ananias a., Lord, I have heard 611
Ac 10:46 magnify God. Then a. Peter. 611
Ac 11:9 the voice a. me again from heaven, 611
Ac 15:13 James a., saying, Men, 611
Ac 19:15 the evil spirit a. and said, 611
Ac 21:13 Then Paul a., What mean ye to 611
Ac 22:8 I a., Who art thou, Lord? 611
Ac 22:28 chief captain a., With a great sum 611
Ac 24:10 answered, Forasmuch as I know 611
Ac 24:25 trembled, and a., Go thy way 611
Ac 25:4 Festus a., that Paul should be 611
Ac 25:8 While he a. for himself, 626
Ac 25:9 a. Paul, and said, Wilt thou go up 611
Ac 25:12 a., Hast thou appealed unto 611
Ac 25:16 whom I a., It is not the manner 611
Ac 26:1 the hand, and a. for himself: 626
Re 7:13 one of the elders a., saying unto 611

ANSWEREDST
Ps 99:8 Thou a. them, O Lord our God: 6030
Ps 138:3 the day when I cried thou a. me, 6030

ANSWEREST
1Sa 26:14 A. thou not, Abner? 6030
Job 16:3 emboldeneth thee that thou a.? 6030
Mt 26:62 unto him, A. thou nothing? 611
Mk 14:60 saying, A. thou nothing? 611
Mk 15:4 him, saying, a. thou nothing? 611
Joh 18:22 A. thou the high priest so? 611

ANSWERETH
1Sa 28:15 and a. me no more, neither by 6030
1Ki 18:24 the God that a. by fire, let him 6030
Job 12:4 upon God, and he a. him: 6030
Pr 18:13 He that a. a matter before 7725
Pr 18:23 intreaties; but the rich a. roughly. 6030
Pr 27:19 As in water face a. to face, so
Ec 5:20 God a. him in the joy of his 6030
Ec 10:19 but money a. all things. 6030
Mk 8:29 And Peter a. and saith unto 611
Mk 9:19 He a. him, and saith, O faithless 611
Mk 10:24 But Jesus a. again, and saith unto 611
Lu 3:11 He a. and saith unto them, 611
Ga 4:25 and a. to Jerusalem which now is, 4960

ANSWERING
Mt 3:15 Jesus a. said unto him, 611
Mk 11:22 And Jesus a. saith unto them, 611
Mk 11:33 Jesus a. saith unto them, 611
Mk 12:17 Jesus a. said unto them, 611
Mk 12:24 Jesus a. said unto them, 611
Mk 13:2 Jesus a. said unto him, 611
Mk 13:5 Jesus a. them, began to say, 611
Mk 15:2 he a. said unto him, Thou sayest it 611
Lu 1:19 the angel a. said unto him, 611
Lu 4:12 Jesus a. said unto him, 611
Lu 5:5 Simon a. said unto him, Master, 611
Lu 5:22 a. said unto them, What reason 611
Lu 5:31 Jesus a. said unto them, 611
Lu 6:3 Jesus a. them said, Have ye not 611
Lu 7:22 Then Jesus a. said unto 611
Lu 7:40 Jesus a. said unto him, 611
Lu 9:19 They a. said, John the Baptist; 611
Lu 9:20 Peter a. said, The Christ of God. 611
Lu 9:41 Jesus a. said. O faithless 611
Lu 10:27 he a. said, Thou shalt love the 611
Lu 10:30 And Jesus a. said, A certain man 5274
Lu 13:2 Jesus a. said unto them, 611
Lu 13:8 he a. said unto him, Lord, 611
Lu 14:3 Jesus a. spake unto the lawyers 611
Lu 15:29 he a. said to his father, 611
Lu 17:17 Jesus a. said, Were there not ten 611
Lu 20:34 Jesus a. said unto them, 611
Lu 20:39 certain of the scribes a. said, 611
Lu 23:40 the other a. rebuked him, 611
Lu 24:18 Cleopas, a. said unto him, 611
Tit 2:9 well in all things; not a. again: 488

ANSWERS
Job 21:34 a. there remaineth falsehood? 8666
Job 34:36 of his a. for wicked men. 8666
Lu 2:47 at his understanding and a. 612

ANT See also ANTS.
Pro 6:6 Go to the a., thou sluggard; 5244

ANTICHRIST See also ANTICHRISTS.
1Jo 2:18 ye have heard that a. shall come, 500
1Jo 2:22 He is a., that denieth the Father 500
1Jo 4:3 this is that spirit of a., whereof 500
2Jo 7 This is a deceiver and an a. 500

ANTICHRISTS
1Jo 2:18 come, even now are there many a. 500

ANTIOCH (an'-te-ok)
Ac 6:5 and Nicolas a proselyte of A. 491
Ac 11:19 far as Phenice, and Cyprus, and A., 490
Ac 11:20 when they were come to A., 490
Ac 11:22 that he should go as far as A. 490
Ac 11:26 brought him unto A. 490
Ac 11:26 were called Chrtistians first in A. 490
Ac 11:27 from Jerusalem unto A. 490
Ac 13:1 in the church that was at A. 490
Ac 13:14 they came to A. in Pisidia, 490
Ac 14:19 certain Jews from A. and Iconium, 490
Ac 14:21 Iconium, and A., 490
Ac 14:26 and thence sailed to A., 490
Ac 15:22 men of their own company to A. 490
Ac 15:23 Gentiles in A. and Syria 490
Ac 15:30 were dismissed, they came to A. 490
Ac 15:35 Barnabas continued in A., teaching 490
Ac 18:22 the church, he went down to A. 490
Ga 2:11 when Peter was come to A., 490
2Ti 3:11 which came unto me at A., 490

ANTIPAS (an'-tip-as)
Re 2:13 A. was my faithful martyr, 493

ANTIPATRIS (an-tip'-at-ris)
Ac 23:31 and brought him by night to A. 494

ANTIQUITY
Isa 23:7 whose a. is of ancient days? 6927

ANTOTHIJAH (an-to-thi'-jah)
1Ch 8:24 And Hananiah, and Elam, and A., 6070

ANTOTHITE (an'-to-thite) See also ANETOTHITE.
1CH 11:28 The Tekoite, Abi-ezer the A., 6069
1CH 12:3 and Berachah, and Jehu the A., 6069

ANTS
Pr 30:25 The a. are a people not strong, 5244

ANUB (a'-nub)
1Ch 4:8 And Coz begat a., and Zobebah, 6036

ANVIL
Isa 41:7 hammer him that smote the a., 6471

ANY
Ge 3:1 was more subtil than a. beast 3605
Ge 4:15 a mark upon Cain, lest a. finding 3605
Ge 8:12 not again unto him a. more. 5750
Ge 8:21 not again curse the ground a. more 5750
Ge 8:21 again smite a. more every thing 5750
Ge 9:11 shall all flesh be cut off a. more 5750
Ge 9:11 there a. more be a flood to destroy 5750
Ge 14:23 not take a. thing that is thine, 3605
Ge 17:5 name a. more be called Abram, 5750
Ge 17:12 bought with money of a. stranger, 3605
Ge 18:14 Is a. thing too hard for the Lord?
Ge 19:12 Hast thou here a. besides? 4310
Ge 19:22 I cannot do a. thing till thou be
Ge 22:12 neither do thou a. thing unto 3972
Ge 24:16 neither had a. man known her:
Ge 30:31 Thou shalt not give me a. thing: 3972
Ge 31:14 there yet a. protion or inheritance
Ge 35:10 shall not be called a. more Jacob, 5750
Ge 36:31 reigned a. king over the children of
Ge 39:9 neither hath he kept back a. thing 3972
Ge 39:23 a. thing that was under his hand; 3972
Ge 42:16 be proved, whether there be a.
Ge 43:34 five times as much as a. of theirs. 3605
Ge 47:6 if thou knowest a. men of activity
Ex 1:10 when there falleth out a. war, they join
Ex 8:29 Pharaoh deal deceitfully a. more. 3254
Ex 9:29 shall there be a. more hail; 5750
Ex 10:15 there remained not a. green thing 3605
Ex 10:23 neither rose a. from his place 376
Ex 11:6 nor shall be like it a. more. 3254
Ex 11:7 against a. of the children of Israel 3605
Ex 12:39 prepared for themselves a. victual
Ex 16:24 neither was there a. worm
Ex 20:4 unto thee a. graven image,
Ex 20:4 or a. likeness of 3605
Ex 20:4 a. thing that is in heaven above
Ex 20:10 in it thou shalt not do a. work, 3605
Ex 20:17 a. thing that is thy neighbour's. 3605
Ex 21:23 And if a. mischief follow, then
Ex 22:9 or for a. manner of lost thing, 3605
Ex 22:10 or a. beast, to keep; and it die, 3605
Ex 22:20 He that sacrificeth unto a. god,
Ex 22:22 Ye shall not afflict any widow, 3605
Ex 22:23 If thou afflict them in a. wise,
Ex 22:25 If thou lend money to a. of my people
Ex 22:31 neither shall ye eat a. flesh that
Ex 24:14 if a. man have a. matters to do,
Ex 30:32 neither shall ye make a. other
Ex 30:33 Whosoever compoundeth a. like it,
Ex 30:33 whosoever putteth a. of it upon
Ex 31:14 whosoever doeth a. work therein, 3605
Ex 31:15 doeth a. work in the sabbath day, 3605
Ex 32:24 Whosoever hath a. gold,
Ex 34:3 neither let a. man be seen
Ex 34:10 done in all the earth, nor in a. 3605
Ex 34:24 neither shall a. man desire thy
Ex 35:24 found shittim wood for a. work of 3605
Ex 35:33 to make a. manner of cunning 3605
Ex 35:35 even of them that do a. work, 3605
Ex 36:6 man nor woman make a. more 5750
Le 1:2 If a. man of you bring an offering
Le 2:1 when a. will offer a meat offering 5315
Le 2:11 burn no leaven, nor a. honey, in 3605
Le 2:11 a. offering of the Lord made by
Le 4:2 sin through ignorance against a. 3605
Le 4:2 be done, and shall do against a. 259
Le 4:13 have done somewhat against a. of 259
Le 4:22 through ignorance against a. of 259
Le 4:27 if a. one of the common people sin 5315
Le 4:27 he doeth somewhat against a. of 259
Le 5:2 if a soul touch a. unclean thing, 3605
Le 5:11 he put a. frankincense thereon:
Le 5:17 sin, and commit a. of these things 259
Le 6:3 a. of all these that a man doeth, 259
Le 6:7 shall be forgiven him for a. thing 259
Le 6:27 of the blood thereof upon a.
Le 6:30 offering, whereof a. of the blood
Le 7:8 a. man's burnt offering, even the
Le 7:15 not leave a. of it until the morning
Le 7:18 if a. of the flesh of the sacrifice of
Le 7:19 that toucheth a. unclean thing 3605
Le 7:21 that shall touch a. unclean thing, 3605
Le 7:21 or a. unclean beast,

Le	7:21	or **a.** abominable unclean	3605
Le	7:24	may be used in **a.** other use	3605
Le	7:26	of beast, in **a.** of your dwellings	3605
Le	7:27	he that eateth **a.** manner of blood,	3605
Le	11:10	of **a.** living thing which is in the	3605
Le	11:32	And upon whatsoever **a.** of them,	
Le	11:32	whether it be **a.** vessel of wood,	3605
Le	11:32	vessel it be, wherein **a.** work is done	
Le	11:33	vessel, whereinto **a.** of them	
Le	11:35	whereupon **a.** part of their carcase	
Le	11:37	And if **a.** part of their carcase	
Le	11:37	fall upon **a.** sowing seed	3605
Le	11:38	if **a.** water be put upon the seed,	
Le	11:38	**a.** part of their carcase fall	
Le	11:39	if **a.** beast, of which he may eat,	
Le	11:43	abominable with **a.** creeping	3605
Le	11:44	defile yourselves with **a.** manner	3605
Le	13:24	Or if there be **a.** flesh, in the skin	
Le	13:48	or in **a.** thing made of skin;	3605
Le	13:49	the work, or in **a.** thing of skin;	3605
Le	13:51	in **a.** work that is made of skin;	3605
Le	13:52	or in linen, or **a.** thing of skin,	3605
Le	13:53	in the woof, or in **a.** thing of skin;	3605
Le	13:57	or in **a.** thing of skin; it is a	3605
Le	13:59	or **a.** thing of skins, to pronounce	3605
Le	15:2	When **a.** man hath a running issue	376
Le	15:6	he that sitteth on **a.** thing	
Le	15:10	whosoever toucheth **a.** thing that	3605
Le	15:10	he that beareth **a.** of those things	
Le	15:16	if **a.** man's seed of copulation go	
Le	15:22	whosoever toucheth **a.** thing that	3605
Le	15:23	or on **a.** thing whereon she sitteth,	
Le	15:24	And if **a.** man lie with her at all,	
Le	17:10	that eateth **a.** manner of blood;	3605
Le	17:12	shall eat blood, neither shall **a.**	
Le	17:13	catcheth **a.** beast or fowl that may	
Le	18:6	shall approach to **a.** that is near	376
Le	18:21	not let **a.** of thy seed pass through	
Le	18:23	lie with **a.** beast to defile thyself	3605
Le	18:23	neither shall **a.** woman stand before	
Le	18:24	yourselves in **a.** of these things:	3605
Le	18:26	commit **a.** of these abominations;	3605
Le	18:26	**a.** of your own nations, nor **a.**	
Le	18:29	commit **a.** of these abominations;	3605
Le	18:30	not **a.** one of these abominable	
Le	19:17	in **a.** wise rebuke thy neighbour,	
Le	19:18	nor bear **a.** grudge against the	
Le	19:26	not eat **a.** thing with the blood;	
Le	19:28	not make **a.** cuttings in your flesh	
Le	19:28	nor print **a.** marks upon you:	
Le	20:2	giveth **a.** of his seed unto Molech;	
Le	20:4	people of the land do **a.** ways hide	
Le	20:16	a woman approach unto **a.** beast,	3605
Le	20:25	by **a.** manner of living thing that	3605
Le	21:5	nor make **a.** cuttings in their flesh	
Le	21:9	the daughter of **a.** priest, if she	376
Le	21:11	shall he go into **a.** dead body,	3605
Le	21:17	that hath **a.** blemish, let him not	
Le	21:18	a flat nose, or **a.** thing superfluous,	
Le	22:4	toucheth **a.** thing that is unclean	3605
Le	22:5	toucheth **a.** creeping thing,	3605
Le	22:6	soul which hath touched **a.** such	
Le	22:11	priest buy **a.** soul with his money,	
Le	22:23	that hath **a.** thing superfluous or	
Le	22:24	neither shall ye make **a.** offering	
Le	22:25	bread of your God of **a.** of these;	3605
Le	23:22	gather **a.** gleaning of thy harvest:	
Le	23:30	soul it be that doeth **a.** work	3605
Le	24:17	he that killeth **a.** man shall surely	3605
Le	25:25	if **a.** of his kin come to redeem it,	
Le	25:32	the Levites redeem at **a.** time	5769
Le	25:49	**a.** that is nigh of kin unto him of	
Le	26:1	neither shall ye set up **a.** image of	
Le	27:9	all that **a.** man giveth of such	
Le	27:11	And if it be **a.** unclean beast,	3605
Le	27:19	sanctified the field will in **a.** wise	
Le	27:20	it shall not be redeemed **a.** more	
Nu	4:15	they shall not touch **a.** holy thing	
Nu	5:6	man or woman shall commit **a.** sin	3605
Nu	5:10	whatsoever **a.** man giveth the priest,	
Nu	5:12	If **a.** man's wife go aside, and	376
Nu	6:3	shall he drink **a.** liquor of grapes,	3605
Nu	6:9	if **a.** man die very suddenly by him,	
Nu	9:10	If **a.** man of you or of your posterity	376
Nu	9:12	morning, nor break **a.** bone of	
Nu	14:23	shall **a.** of them that provoked me	3605
Nu	15:27	if **a.** soul sin through ignorance,	259
Nu	17:13	Whosoever cometh **a.** thing near	
Nu	18:5	wrath **a.** more upon the children	
Nu	18:20	thou have **a.** part among them:	
Nu	19:11,	13 toucheth the dead body of **a.**	3605
Nu	20:5	neither is there **a.** water to drink	
Nu	20:19	without doing **a.** thing else, go	
Nu	21:5	bread, neither is there **a.** water;	
Nu	21:9	serpent had bitten **a.** man,	
Nu	22:38	I now **a.** power…to say a thing?	
Nu	23:23	there **a.** divination against Israel:	
Nu	29:7	souls: ye shall not do **a.** work	3605
Nu	30:5	not **a.** of her vows, or of her	3605
Nu	30:15	shall **a.** ways make them void	
Nu	31:19	whosoever hath killed **a.** person,	
Nu	31:19	whosoever hath touched **a.** slain,	
Nu	35:11	killeth **a.** person at unawares	
Nu	35:15	Every one that killeth **a.** person	
Nu	35:22	or have cast upon him **a.** thing	3605
Nu	35:23	Or with **a.** stone, wherewith a man	3605
Nu	35:26	if the slayer shall at **a.** time come	
Nu	35:30	killeth **a.** person, the murderer	
Nu	35:30	shall not testify against **a.** person	
Nu	36:3	be married to **a.** of the sons of the	259
Nu	36:8	possesseth an inheritance in **a.**	
De	2:19	children of Ammon **a.** possession;	
De	2:37	unto **a.** place of the river Jabbok,	3605
De	4:16	graven image, the similitude of **a.**	3605
De	4:17	The likeness of **a.** beast that is	3605
De	4:17	the likeness of **a.** winged fowl	3605
De	4:18	likeness of **a.** thing that creepeth	3605
De	4:18	likeness of **a.** fish that is in the	3605
De	4:23	likeness of **a.** thing, which the Lord	3605
De	4:25	graven image, or the likeness of **a.**	3605
De	4:32	there hath been **a.** such thing as	
De	5:8	**a.** graven image, or **a.** likeness	3605
De	5:8	of **a.** thing that is in heaven above,	
De	5:14	that shalt not do **a.** work, thou,	3605
De	5:14	nor **a.** of thy cattle, nor thy	3605
De	5:21	or **a.** thing that is thy neighbour's	3605
De	5:25	voice of the Lord our God **a.** more	
De	7:7	more in number than **a.** people;	3605
De	8:9	thou shalt not lack **a.** thing in it;	3605
De	12:17	nor **a.** of thy vows which thou	3605
De	13:11	do no more **a.** such wickedness	1697
De	14:1	nor make **a.** baldness between	
De	14:3	shalt not eat **a.** abominable thing	3605
De	14:21	shall not eat of **a.** thing that dieth	3605
De	15:7	brethren within **a.** of thy gates	259
De	15:21	if there be **a.** blemish therein, as	
De	15:21	or have **a.** ill blemish, thou shalt	3605
De	16:4	shall there **a.** thing of the flesh,	
De	16:5	passover within **a.** of thy gates,	259
De	16:21	thee a grove of **a.** trees near	3605
De	16:22	shalt thou set thee up **a.** image;	
De	17:1	the Lord thy God **a.** bullock,	
De	17:1	or **a.** evilfavouredness: for that	3605
De	17:2	among you, within **a.** of thy gates	259
De	17:3	moon, or **a.** of the host of heaven,	3605
De	17:15	in **a.** wise set him king over thee,	
De	18:6	a Levite come from **a.** of thy gates	259
De	18:10	not be found among you **a.** one	
De	18:16	let me see this great fire **a.** more,	
De	19:11	if **a.** man hate his neighbour, and	
De	19:15	against a man for **a.** iniquity, or	3605
De	19:15	for **a.** sin, in **a.** sin that he sinneth:	3605
De	19:16	witness rise up against **a.** man to	
De	19:20	commit no more **a.** such evil	1697
De	21:23	in **a.** wise bury him that day	
De	22:1	shalt in **a.** case bring them again	
De	22:6	before thee in the way in **a.** tree,	3605
De	22:7	shalt in **a.** wise let the dam go,	
De	22:8	house, if **a.** man fall from thence	
De	22:13	If **a.** man take a wife, and go in	
De	23:10	among you **a.** man, that is not clean	
De	23:18	of the Lord thy God for **a.** vow:	3605
De	23:19	usury of **a.** thing that is lent	3605
De	23:24	shalt not put **a.** in thy vessel	
De	24:5	he be charged with **a.** business:	3605
De	24:7	found stealing **a.** of his brethren	5315
De	24:10	dost lend thy brother **a.** thing,	3972
De	24:13	In **a.** case thou shalt deliver him	
De	26:14	taken away ought thereof for **a.**	
De	27:5	not lift up **a.** iron tool upon them	
De	27:15	Cursed be the man that maketh **a.**	
De	27:21	with **a.** manner of beast. And all	3605
De	28:14	go aside from any of the words	3605
De	28:55	not give to **a.** of them of the flesh	259
De	29:23	nor **a.** grass groweth therein, like	3605
De	30:4	If **a.** of thine be driven out unto	
De	31:13	have not known **a.** thing, may	
De	32:28	there **a.** understanding in them	
De	32:39	neither is there **a.** that can deliver	
Jos	1:5	There shall not **a.** man be able	
Jos	2:11	remain **a.** more courage in **a.** man,	
Jos	2:19	our head, if **a.** hand be upon him	
Jos	5:1	spirit in them **a.** more, because	
Jos	5:12	children of Israel manna **a.** more;	
Jos	6:10	shout, nor make **a.** noise with	
Jos	6:10	neither shall **a.** word proceed out	
Jos	6:18	And ye, in **a.** wise keep yourselves	
Jos	7:12	neither will I be with you **a.** more,	
Jos	8:31	no man hath lift up **a.** iron: and	
Jos	10:21	against **a.** of the children of Israel	
Jos	11:11	there was not **a.** left to breathe:	3605
Jos	11:14	them neither left they **a.**	3605
Jos	13:33	Moses gave not **a.** inheritance:	3605
Jos	20:3	that killeth **a.** person unawares	
Jos	20:9	killeth **a.** person at unawares	
Jos	21:45	failed not ought of **a.** good thing	3605
Jos	23:12	Else if ye do in **a.** wise go back,	
Jos	23:13	God will no more drive out **a.** of	
Jg	2:14	could not **a.** longer stand before	
Jg	2:21	drive out **a.** from before them	
Jg	4:20	when **a.** man doth come…and say,	
Jg	4:20	Is there **a.** man here? that thou	
Jg	11:25	art thou **a.** thing better than Balak	
Jg	13:4	and eat not **a.** unclean thing:	3605
Jg	13:7	neither eat **a.** unclean thing: for	3605
Jg	13:14	She may not eat of **a.** thing that	3605
Jg	13:14	nor eat **a.** unclean thing: all	3605
Jg	16:17	weak, and be like **a.** other man	3605
Jg	18:7	put them to shame in **a.** thing;	
Jg	18:7	and had no business with **a.** man	
Jg	18:10	there is no want of **a.** thing that	3605
Jg	18:28	had no business with **a.** man; and	
Jg	19:19	there is no want of **a.** thing:	3605
Jg	20:8	not **a.** of us go to his tent, neither	376
Jg	20:8	we **a.** of his turn into his house	376
Jg	21:1	shall not **a.** of us give his daughter	376
Jg	21:12	**a.** male: and they brought them	
Ru	1:11	with me? are there yet **a.** more	
Ru	2:22	meet thee not in **a.** other field	
1Sa	2:2	is there **a.** rock like our God	
1Sa	2:13	when **a.** man offered sacrifice,	3605
1Sa	2:16	if **a.** man said unto him, Let them	
1Sa	3:17	if thou hide **a.** thing from me of	
1Sa	5:5	**a.** that come into Dagon's house,	3605
1Sa	6:3	in **a.** wise return him a trespass	
1Sa	9:2	was higher than **a.** of the people	3605
1Sa	10:23	higher than **a.** of the people from	3605
1Sa	12:3	of whose hand I received **a.** bribe	
1Sa	12:4	thou taken ought of **a.** man's hand	
1Sa	13:22	nor spear found in the hand of **a.**	3605
1Sa	14:24	the man that eateth **a.** food until	
1Sa	14:24	none of the people tasted **a.** food	3605
1Sa	14:28	Cursed be the man that eateth **a.**	
1Sa	14:52	Saul saw **a.** strong man, or **a.**	3605
1Sa	18:25	The king desireth not **a.** dowry,	
1Sa	20:12	my father about to morrow **a.**	
1Sa	20:26	Saul spake not **a.** thing that day:	3972
1Sa	20:39	the lad knew not **a.** thing:	3972
1Sa	21:2	Let no man know **a.** thing of the	3972
1Sa	22:15	let not the king impute **a.** thing	3605
1Sa	25:15	neither missed we **a.** thing,	3972
1Sa	25:22	to him by the morning light **a.**	
1Sa	25:34	Nabal by the morning light **a.**	
1Sa	27:1	to seek me **a.** more	
1Sa	27:1	in **a.** coast of Israel:	3605
1Sa	30:2	slew not **a.**, either great or small,	376
1Sa	30:12	bread, nor drunk **a.** water,	
1Sa	30:19	nor **a.** thing that they had taken	3605
2Sa	2:1	up into **a.** of the cities of Judah?	259
2Sa	2:28	more, neither fought they **a.** more	
2Sa	7:6	I have not dwelt in **a.** house	
2Sa	7:7	with **a.** of the tribes of Israel,	259
2Sa	7:10	of wickedness afflict them **a.** more,	
2Sa	7:22	neither is there **a.** God beside thee,	
2Sa	9:1	Is there yet **a.** that is left of the	
2Sa	9:3	not yet **a.** of the house of Saul,	376
2Sa	10:19	help the children of Ammon **a.** more	
2Sa	13:2	hard for him to do **a.** thing to her	3972
2Sa	14:10	he shall not touch thee **a.** more	
2Sa	14:11	revengers of blood to destroy **a.**,	
2Sa	14:14	doth God respect **a.** person:	

2Sa	14:32	and if there be **a.** iniquity in me,	
2Sa	15:2	**a.** man that had a controversy	3605
2Sa	15:4	every man which hath **a.** suit or	
2Sa	15:5	when **a.** man came nigh to him	
2Sa	15:11	and they knew not **a.** thing.	3605
2Sa	19:22	there **a.** man be put to death	
2Sa	19:28	therefore have I yet to cry **a.** more	
2Sa	19:29	Why speakest thou **a.** more of thy	
2Sa	19:35	can I hear **a.** more the voice of	
2Sa	19:42	or hath he given us **a.** gift?	
2Sa	21:4	shalt thou kill **a.** man in Israel	
2Sa	21:5	in **a.** of the coasts of Israel,	3605
1Ki	1:6	had not displeased him at **a.** time	
1Ki	2:36	go not forth thence **a.** whither.	
1Ki	2:42	and walkest abroad **a.** whither,	
1Ki	3:12	neither after thee shall **a.** arise.	
1Ki	3:13	shall not be **a.** among the kings	376
1Ki	5:6	there is not among us **a.** that can	376
1Ki	6:7	nor ax nor **a.** tool of iron heard	3605
1Ki	8:31	If **a.** man trespass against his	
1Ki	8:38	supplication soever be made by **a.**	3605
1Ki	10:3	all her questions: there was not **a.**	
1Ki	10:20	not the like made in **a.** kingdom.	3605
1Ki	11:22	howbeit let me go in **a.** wise.	
1Ki	15:5	turned not aside from **a.** thing	3605
1Ki	15:17	he might not suffer **a.** to go out	
1Ki	15:29	not to Jeroboam **a.** that breathed,	3605
1Ki	18:26	was no voice, nor **a.** that answered.	
1Ki	18:29	neither voice, nor **a.** to answer,	
1Ki	18:29	nor **a.** that regarded.	
1Ki	20:33	diligently observe whether **a.**	
1Ki	20:39	if by **a.** means he be missing,	
2Ki	2:21	there shall not be from thence **a.** more	
2Ki	4:2	handmaid hath not **a.** thing	3605
2Ki	4:29	if thou meet **a.** man, salute him	
2Ki	4:29	if **a.** salute thee, answer him not	376
2Ki	6:33	I wait for the Lord **a.** longer?	
2Ki	10:5	we will not make **a.** king:	376
2Ki	10:14	forty men; neither left he **a.** of	376
2Ki	10:24	**a.** of the men whom I have brought	
2Ki	12:4	that cometh into **a.** man's heart	
2Ki	12:5	**a.** breach shall be found	376
2Ki	12:13	**a.** vessels of gold,	376
2Ki	14:26	for there was not **a.** shut up,	
2Ki	14:26	nor **a.** left,	
2Ki	14:26	nor **a.** helper for Israel.	
2Ki	18:5	nor **a.** that were before him.	
2Ki	18:33	Hath **a.** of the gods of the nations	376
2Ki	21:8	the feet of Israel move **a.** more	
2Ki	23:25	after him arose there **a.** like him.	
2Ki	24:7	of Egypt came not again **a.** more	
1Ch	1:43	before **a.** king reigned over the	
1Ch	17:6	word to **a.** of the judges of Israel,	259
1Ch	17:9	of wickedness waste them **a.** more,	
1Ch	17:20	neither is there **a.** God beside thee,	
1Ch	19:19	help the children of Ammon **a.** more.	
1Ch	23:26	nor **a.** vessels of it for the service	3605
1Ch	26:28	whosoever had dedicated **a.** thing,	
1Ch	27:1	that served the king in **a.** matter	3605
1Ch	28:21	skilful man, nor **a.** manner of	3605
1Ch	29:25	as had not been on **a.** king	3605
2Ch	1:12	there **a.** after thee have the like	
2Ch	2:14	to grave **a.** manner of graving,	3605
2Ch	6:5	neither chose I **a.** man to be a ruler	
2Ch	6:29	soever shall be made of **a.** man,	3605
2Ch	8:15	concerning **a.** matter, or	3605
2Ch	9:9	neither was there **a.** such spice	
2Ch	9:19	not the like made in **a.** kingdom.	3605
2Ch	9:20	it was not **a.** thing accounted of	3972
2Ch	23:19	which was unclean in **a.** thing	3605
2Ch	32:13	**a.** ways able to deliver their lands	
2Ch	32:15	no god of **a.** nation or kingdom,	3605
2Ch	33:8	I **a.** more remove the foot of Israel	
2Ch	34:13	work in **a.** manner of service:	3605
Ezr	1:4	whosoever remaineth in **a.** place	3605
Ezr	7:24	**a.** of the priests and Levites,	3606
Ne	2:12	neither told I **a.** man what my God	
Ne	2:12	at Jerusalem: neither was there **a.**	
Ne	5:16	wall, neither bought we **a.** land:	
Ne	10:31	the land bring ware or **a.** victuals	
Job	4:20	for ever without **a.** regarding it.	
Job	5:1	there be **a.** that will answer thee;	
Job	5:4	neither is thee **a.** to deliver them.	
Job	6:6	**a.** taste in the white of an egg?	
Job	7:10	shall his place know him **a.** more	
Job	8:12	it withered before **a.** other herb.	3605
Job	9:33	is there **a.** daysman betwixt us,	
Job	10:22	shadow of death, without **a.** order,	
Job	15:11	there **a.** secret thing with thee?	
Job	16:17	for **a.** injustice in mine hands:	
Job	18:19	people, nor **a.** remaining in his	
Job	20:9	his place **a.** more behold him.	
Job	21:22	Shall **a.** teach God knowledge?	
Job	22:3	Is it **a.** pleasure to the Almighty,	
Job	25:3	Is there **a.** number of his armies?	
Job	31:7	**a.** blot hath cleaved to mine hands;	
Job	31:19	**a.** perish for want of clothing,	
Job	31:19	or **a.** poor without covering;	
Job	32:21	pray you, accept **a.** man's person,	
Job	33:13	not account of **a.** of his matters.	3605
Job	33:27	upon men, and if **a.** say, I	
Job	33:32	*(In most editions)* hast **a.** thing to say,	3605
Job	34:27	would not consider **a.** of his ways:	3605
Job	34:31	I will not offend **a.** more:	
Job	36:5	is mighty, and despiseth not **a.**	
Job	36:29	can **a.** understand the spreadings	
Job	37:24	respecteth not **a.** that are wise of	
Ps	4:6	say, Who will shew us **a.** good?	
Ps	14:2	there were **a.** that did understand,	
Ps	33:17	deliver **a.** by his great strength.	
Ps	34:10	shall not want **a.** good thing.	3605
Ps	37:8	fret not thyself in **a.** wise to do	
Ps	38:3	neither is there **a.** rest in my bones	
Ps	49:7	by **a.** means redeem his brother,	
Ps	53:2	there were **a.** that did understand,	
Ps	59:5	to **a.** wicked transgressors.	3605
Ps	74:9	signs: there is no more **a.** prophet:	
Ps	74:9	is there **a.** among us that knoweth	
Ps	81:9	thou worship **a.** strange God.	
Ps	86:8	neither are there **a.** works like	
Ps	91:10	neither shall **a.** plague come nigh	
Ps	109:12	be **a.** to favour his fatherless	
Ps	115:17	**a.** that go down into silence.	3605
Ps	119:133	let not **a.** iniquity have dominion	3605
Ps	135:17	neither is their **a.** breath in their	
Ps	139:24	if there be **a.** wicked way in me,	
Ps	141:4	Incline not my heart to **a.** evil	
Ps	146:2	my God while I have **a.** being	
Ps	147:20	hath not dealt so with **a.** nation:	3605
Pr	1:17	is spread in the sight of **a.** bird	3605
Pr	6:35	He will not regard **a.** ransom;	3605
Pr	14:34	but sin is a reproach to **a.** people.	
Pr	28:17	violence to the blood of **a.** person.	
Pr	30:2	I am more brutish than **a.** man,	
Pr	30:30	and turneth not away from **a.**	3605
Pr	31:5	the judgment of **a.** of the afflicted	3605
Ec	1:10	Is there **a.** thing whereof it may	
Ec	1:11	shall there be **a.** remembrance	
Ec	2:10	withheld not my heart from **a.**	3605
Ec	3:14	nothing can be put to it, nor **a.**	
Ec	5:2	heart be hasty to utter **a.** thing	
Ec	6:5	not seen the sun, nor known **a.**	
Ec	9:5	but the dead know not **a.** thing,	3972
Ec	9:5	they **a.** more a reward; for the	
Ec	9:6	have they **a.** more a portion ever	
Ec	9:6	**a.** thing that is done under the	3605
Isa	1:5	should ye be stricken **a.** more?	
Isa	2:4	shall they learn war **a.** more.	
Isa	2:7	there **a.** end of their treasures;	
Isa	2:7	is their **a.** end of their chariots:	
Isa	19:15	shall their be **a.** work for Egypt,	
Isa	26:18	have not wrought **a.** deliverance	
Isa	27:3	lest **a.** hurt it, I will keep it night	
Isa	30:20	removed into a corner **a.** more,	
Isa	33:20	**a.** of the cords thereof be broken.	3605
Isa	35:9	nor **a.** ravenous beast shall	
Isa	36:18	Hath **a.** of the gods of the	376
Isa	44:8	yea, there is no God; I know not **a.**	
Isa	51:18	neither is there **a.** that taketh her	
Isa	52:14	was so marred more than **a.** man,	
Isa	53:9	neither was **a.** deceit in his mouth.	
Isa	54:4	of thy widowhood **a.** more.	
Isa	56:2	his hand from doing **a.** evil.	3605
Isa	59:4	nor **a.** pleadeth for truth:	
Isa	62:4	land **a.** more be termed Desolate:	
Jer	3:16	neither shall that be done **a.** more.	
Jer	3:17	neither shall they walk **a.** more	
Jer	5:1	there be **a.** that executeth judgment,	
Jer	9:4	and trust ye not in **a.** brother:	3605
Jer	10:20	to stretch forth my tent **a.** more,	
Jer	14:22	Are there **a.** among the vanities	
Jer	17:22	neither do ye **a.** work, but	3605
Jer	18:18	not give heed to **a.** of his words.	3605
Jer	20:9	nor speak **a.** more in his name.	
Jer	22:11	shall not return thither **a.** more:	
Jer	22:30	and ruling **a.** more in Judah.	
Jer	23:24	Can **a.** hide himself in secret	376
Jer	31:12	they shall not sorrow **a.** more at all.	
Jer	31:40	nor thrown down **a.** more for ever.	
Jer	32:27	is there **a.** thing too hard for me?	3605
Jer	33:26	I will not take **a.** of his seed	
Jer	34:10	serve themselves of them **a.** more	
Jer	35:7	nor plant vineyard, nor have **a.**	
Jer	36:24	nor **a.** of his servents that heard	3605
Jer	37:17	Is there **a.** word from the Lord?	
Jer	38:5	he that can do **a.** thing against you.	
Jer	42:21	voice of the Lord your God, nor **a.**	3605
Jer	44:26	more be named in the mouth of **a.**	3605
Jer	48:9	without **a.** to dwell therein.	
Jer	49:33	nor **a.** son of man dwell in it.	
Jer	50:40	shall **a.** son of man dwell therein.	
Jer	51:43	neither doth **a.** son of man pass	
Jer	51:44	shall not flow together **a.** more	
La	1:12	and see if there be **a.** sorrow like	
La	3:49	down, and ceaseth not, without **a.**	
Eze	5:9	whereunto I will not do **a.** more	
Eze	5:11	spare, neither will I have **a.** pity.	
Eze	7:11	multitude, nor of **a.** of theirs:	1991
Eze	7:13	neither shall **a.** strengthen himself	376
Eze	9:6	**a.** man upon whom is the mark;	3605
Eze	12:24	shall be no more **a.** vain vision	
Eze	12:28	my words be prolonged **a.** more,	3605
Eze	14:11	polluted **a.** more with all their	3605
Eze	15:2	is the vine tree more than **a.** tree	3605
Eze	15:3	be taken thereof to do **a.** work?	
Eze	15:3	of it to hang **a.** vessel thereon?	3605
Eze	15:4	burned. Is it meet for **a.** work?	
Eze	15:5	shall it be meet yet for **a.** work,	
Eze	16:5	thee, to do **a.** of these unto thee,	259
Eze	16:41	also shalt give no hire **a.** more	
Eze	16:63	never open thy mouth **a.** more.	
Eze	18:3	ye shall not have occasion **a.** more	
Eze	18:7	And hath not oppressed **a.**, but	376
Eze	18:8	neither hath taken **a.** increase,	
Eze	18:10	the like to **a.** one of these things,	
Eze	18:11	that doeth not **a.** of those duties,	3605
Eze	18:16	Neither hath oppressed **a.**, hath	376
Eze	18:23	Have I **a.** pleasure at all that the	
Eze	21:5	it shall not return **a.** more.	
Eze	23:27	nor remember Egypt **a.** more.	
Eze	24:13	purges from thy filthiness **a.** more,	
Eze	27:36	terror, and never shalt be **a.** more.	
Eze	28:19	and never shalt thou be **a.** more.	
Eze	28:24	nor **a.** grieving thorn of all that	
Eze	29:15	itself **a.** more above the nations:	
Eze	31:8	nor **a.** tree in the garden of God	3605
Eze	32:13	foot of man trouble them **a.** more,	
Eze	33:6	come, and take **a.** person from	
Eze	34:10	shepherds feed themselves **a.** more;	
Eze	34:29	the shame of the heathen **a.** more.	
Eze	36:14	neither bereave thy nations **a.** more,	
Eze	36:15	in thee the shame of the heathen **a.**	
Eze	36:15	reproach of the people **a.** more,	
Eze	36:15	cause thy nations to fall **a.** more	
Eze	37:22	into two kingdoms **a.** more	
Eze	37:23	they defile themselves **a.** more	
Eze	37:23	with **a.** of their transgressions:	3605
Eze	39:7	pollute my holy name **a.** more:	
Eze	39:10	cut down **a.** out of the forests;	
Eze	39:15	when **a.** seeth a man's bone, then	
Eze	39:28	have left none of them **a.** more	
Eze	39:29	hide my face **a.** more from them:	
Eze	44:9	sanctuary, of **a.** stranger that	3605
Eze	44:13	come near to **a.** of my holy things,	3605
Eze	44:18	with **a.** thing that causeth sweat.	
Eze	44:21	Neither shall **a.** priest drink wine,	3605
Eze	44:31	of **a.** thing that is dead of itself,	3605
Eze	46:16	give a gift unto **a.** of his sons,	376
Da	2:10	asked such things at **a.** magician,	3606
Da	2:30	for **a.** wisdom that I have more	
Da	2:30	than **a.** living, but for their sakes	3606
Da	3:28	not serve nor worship **a.** god,	3606
Da	3:29	which speak **a.** thing amiss	
Da	6:4	was there **a.** error or fault found	3606
Da	6:5	We shall not find **a.** occasion	3606
Da	6:7	ask a petition of **a.** God or man	3606
Da	6:12	that shall ask a petition of **a.** God	3606
Da	8:4	before him, neither was there **a.**	
Da	11:15	neither shall there be **a.** strength	
Da	11:37	nor regard **a.** god: for he shall	3605
Ho	13:10	where is **a.** other that may save	
Ho	14:3	neither will we say **a.** more to the	

Ho 14:8 have I to do **a.** more with idols?
Joe 2:2 neither shall be **a.** more after it,
Joe 3:17 pass through her **a.** more.
Am 6:10 Is there yet **a.** with thee? and he
Am 7:8 I will not pass by them **a.** more:
Am 7:13 not again **a.** more at Beth-el:
Am 8:2 not again pass by them **a.** more.
Am 8:7 never forget **a.** of their works. 3605
Ob 18 **a.** remaining of the house of Esau;
Jon 3:7 herd nor flock, taste **a.** thing: 3792
Mic 4:3 shall they learn war **a.** more.
Zep 3:15 thou shalt not see evil **a.** more.
Hag 2:12 or wine, or oil, or **a.** meat, shall 3605
Hag 2:13 by a dead body touch **a.** of these, 3605
Zec 8:10 nor **a.** hire for beast;
Zec 8:10 neither was there **a.** peace
Zec 9:8 shall pass through them **a.** more:
Zec 13:3 when **a.** shall yet prophesy, then 376
Mal 2:13 regardeth not the offering **a.** more,
Mt 4:6 lest at **a.** time thou dash thy foot *3379*
Mt 5:25 **at a. time the adversary deliver** *3379*
Mt 5:40 **if a. man will sue thee at the law,**
Mt 10:5 **and into a city of the Samaritans**
Mt 11:27 **knoweth a. man the Father,** *5100*
Mt 12:19 shall **a.** man hear his voice in *5100*
Mt 13:15 **lest at a. time they should see** *3379*
Mt 13:19 **When a. one heareth the word** *3956*
Mt 16:24 **If a. man will come after me, let** *1536*
Mt 18:19 **agree on earth as touching a.** *3956*
Mt 21:3 **if a. man say ought unto you,** *5100*
Mt 22:16 neither carest thou for **a.** man: *3762*
Mt 22:46 **a.** man from that day forth *5100*
Mt 22:46 forth ask him **a.** more questions. *3765*
Mt 24:17 **take a. thing out of his house:** *5100*
Mt 24:23 **if a. man shall say unto you,** *5100*
Mk 1:44 **See thou say nothing to a. man:** *3367*
Mk 4:12 **a. time they should be converted,** *3379*
Mk 4:22 **neither was a. thing kept secret,** *5100*
Mk 4:23 **If a. man have ears to hear, let** *1536*
Mk 5:4 neither could **a.** man tame him. *3762*
Mk 5:35 thou the Master **a.** further? *2089*
Mk 7:16 **If a. man have ears to hear, let** *1536*
Mk 8:26 **nor tell it to a. in the town** *5100*
Mk 9:8 they saw no man **a.** more, save *3765*
Mk 9:22 if thou canst do **a.** thing, have *1536*
Mk 9:30 that **a.** man should know it *5100*
Mk 9:35 **If a. man desire to be first, the** *1536*
Mk 11:3 **And if a. man say unto you, Why** *1536*
Mk 11:13 he might find **a.** thing thereon: *1536*
Mk 11:16 suffer that **a.** man should carry *1536*
Mk 11:16 carry **a.** vessel through the *1536*
Mk 11:25 **if ye have ought against a.;** *1536*
Mk 12:21 and died, neither left he **a.** seed:
Mk 12:34 that durst ask him **a.** question.
Mk 13:5 **heed lest a. man deceive you:** *5100*
Mk 13:15 **take a. thing out of his house:** *5100*
Mk 13:21 **if a. man shall say to you, Lo,** *5100*
Mk 14:31 I will not deny thee in **a.** wise. *3364*
Mk 14:63 need we **a.** further witnesses? *2089*
Mk 15:44 whether he had been **a.** while dead.
Mk 16:8 said they **a.** thing to *3762*
Mk 16:8 to **a.** man; for they were afraid. *3762*
Mk 16:18 **and if they drink a. deadly thing** *5100*
Lu 3:14 man, neither accuse **a.** falsely;
Lu 4:11 lest at **a.** time thou dash thy foot *3379*
Lu 4:40 that had **a.** sick with divers diseases
Lu 8:17 **neither a. thing hid, that shall not**
Lu 8:27 neither abode in **a.** house, but in
Lu 8:43 neither could be healed of **a.**, *3762*
Lu 9:23 **If a. man will come after me, let** *5100*
Lu 9:36 in those days **a.** of those things *3762*
Lu 10:19 **shall by a. means hurt you.** *3364*
Lu 11:11 **son shall ask bread of a. of you** *5100*
Lu 14:8 **art bidden of a. man to a wedding,** *5100*
Lu 14:26 **a. man come to me, and hate not** *1536*
Lu 15:29 neither transgressed I at **a.** time *3763*
Lu 19:8 taken **a.** thing from *5100*
Lu 19:8 **a.** man by false accusation, I *1536*
Lu 19:31 **if a. man ask you, Why do ye** *5100*
Lu 20:21 acceptest thou the person of **a.**,
Lu 20:27 deny that there is **a.** resurrection; *3361*
Lu 20:28 If **a.** man's brother die, have a *5100*
Lu 20:36 **Neither can they die a. more;** *2089*
Lu 20:40 not ask him **a.** question at all. *3762*
Lu 21:34 **lest at a. time your hearts** *3379*
Lu 22:16 **I will not a. more eat thereof,** *3765*
Lu 22:35 **lacked ye a. thing?** And they *5100*
Lu 22:71 What need we **a.** further witness? *2089*
Lu 24:41 them, **Have ye here a. meat?** *5100*
Joh 1:3 not **a.** thing made that was made. *1520*
Joh 1:18 No man hath seen God at **a.** time; *4455*
Joh 1:46 there **a.** good thing come out of *5100*
Joh 2:25 that **a.** should testify of man: *5100*
Joh 4:33 Hath **a.** man brought him ought *3387*
Joh 5:37 **neither heard his voice at a. time,** *4455*
Joh 6:46 **Not that a. man hath seen the** *5100*
Joh 6:51 **if a. man eat of this bread, he** *5100*
Joh 7:4 no man that doeth **a.** thing in secret, *5100*
Joh 7:17 **If a. man will do his will, he shall** *5100*
Joh 7:37 **If a. man thirst, let him come unto** *5100*
Joh 7:48 Have **a.** of the rulers or of the *3387*
Joh 7:51 Doth our law judge **a.** man, *3588*
Joh 8:33 were never in bondage to **a.** man: *3762*
Joh 9:22 if **a.** man did confess that he was *5100*
Joh 9:31 if **a.** man be a worshipper of God, *5100*
Joh 9:32 that **a.** man opened the eyes of *5100*
Joh 10:9 **if a. man enter in, he shall be** *5100*
Joh 10:28 **neither shall a. man pluck them** *5100*
Joh 11:9 **If a. man walk in the day, he** *5100*
Joh 11:57 if **a.** man knew where he were. *5100*
Joh 12:26 **If a. man serve me, let him follow** *5100*
Joh 12:26 **if a. man serve me, him will my** *5100*
Joh 12:47 **And if a. man hear my words,** *5100*
Joh 14:14 **If ye shall ask a. thing in my** *5100*
Joh 16:30 that **a.** man should ask thee: *5100*
Joh 18:31 for us to put **a.** man to death: *3762*
Joh 21:5 **Children, have ye a. meat?** *3387*
Ac 4:12 is there salvation in **a.** other: *3762*
Ac 4:32 neither said **a.** of them that *1520*
Ac 4:34 there **a.** among them that lacked: *5100*
Ac 9:2 that if he found **a.** of this way, *5100*
Ac 10:14 I have never eaten **a.** thing that *3956*
Ac 10:28 I should not call **a.** man common *3367*
Ac 10:47 Can **a.** man forbid water, that *5100*
Ac 11:8 common or unclean hath at **a.** time *3763*
Ac 13:15 brethren, if ye have **a.** word of *5150*
Ac 17:25 as though he needed **a.** thing, *5100*
Ac 19:2 whether there be **a.** Holy Ghost.
Ac 19:38 have a matter against **a.** man, *5100*
Ac 19:39 if ye enquire **a.** thing concerning *5100*
Ac 24:12 the temple disputing with **a.** man. *5100*
Ac 24:20 have found **a.** evil doing in me, *1536*
Ac 25:5 if there be **a.** wickedness in him. *1536*
Ac 25:8 have I offended **a.** thing at all. *5100*
Ac 25:11 committed **a.** thing worthy of death, *5100*
Ac 25:16 to deliver **a.** man to die, before *5100*
Ac 25:17 without **a.** delay on the morrow *3362*
Ac 25:24 he ought not to live **a.** longer. *3370*
Ac 27:12 if by **a.** means they might attain *4458*
Ac 27:22 shall be no loss of **a.** man's life *3762*
Ac 27:34 hair fall from the head of **a.** of you, *3762*
Ac 27:42 lest **a.** of them should swim out. *5100*
Ac 28:21 neither **a.** of the brethren that *5100*
Ac 28:21 or spake **a.** harm of thee. *5100*
Ro 1:10 if by **a.** means now at length I *4458*
Ro 6:2 to sin, live **a.** longer therein? *2089*
Ro 8:9 if **a.** man have not the Spirit of *5100*
Ro 8:33 lay **a.** thing to the charge of God's
Ro 8:39 nor depth, nor **a.** other creature, *5100*
Ro 9:11 having done **a.** good or evil. *5100*
Ro 11:14 If by **a.** means I may provoke *4458*
Ro 13:8 Owe no man **a.** thing, but to love *3367*
Ro 13:9 there be **a.** other commandment, *1536*
Ro 14:13 judge one another **a.** more: *3370*
Ro 14:14 esteemeth **a.** thing to be unclean, *5100*
Ro 14:21 nor **a.** thing whereby thy brother *3362*
Ro 15:18 dare to speak of **a.** of those things *5100*
1Co 1:15 Lest **a.** should say that I had *3387*
1Co 1:16 not whether I baptized **a.** other. *1536*
1Co 2:2 not to know **a.** thing among you, *5100*
1Co 3:7 neither is he that planteth **a.** thing, *5100*
1Co 3:12 **a.** man build upon his foundation *5100*
1Co 3:14 If **a.** man's work abide which he *1536*
1Co 3:15 If **a.** man's work shall be burned, *1536*
1Co 3:17 If **a.** man defile the temple of God. *1536*
1Co 3:18 If **a.** man among you seemeth to *1536*
1Co 5:11 if **a.** man that is called brother *5100*
1Co 6:1 Dare **a.** of you, having a matter *5100*
1Co 6:12 brought under the power of **a.** *5100*
1Co 7:12 If **a.** brother hath a wife that *1536*
1Co 7:18 **a.** man called being circumcised? *5100*
1Co 7:18 Is **a.** called in uncircumcision? *5100*
1Co 7:36 But if **a.** man think that he *5100*
1Co 8:2 if **a.** man think that he knoweth **a.** *5100*
1Co 8:3 But if **a.** man love God, the same *5100*
1Co 8:9 lest by **a.** means this liberty of *3381*
1Co 8:10 For if **a.** man see thee which hast *5100*
1Co 9:7 a warfare **a.** time at his own *4218*
1Co 9:15 **a.** man should make my glorying *5100*
1Co 9:27 lest that by **a.** means, when I *3381*
1Co 10:19 that the idol is **a.** thing, or that *5100*
1Co 10:19 in sacrifice to idols is **a.** thing? *5100*
1Co 10:27 If **a.** of them that believe not bid *5100*
1Co 10:28 But if **a.** man say unto you. *5100*
1Co 11:16 if **a.** man seem to be contentious, *5100*
1Co 11:34 if **a.** man hunger, let him eat at *5100*
1Co 14:27 If **a.** man speak in an unknown *5100*
1Co 14:30 If **a.** thing be revealed to another
1Co 14:35 And if they will learn **a.** thing, *5100*
1Co 14:37 If **a.** man think himself to be a *1536*
1Co 14:38 But if **a.** man be ignorant, let him *1536*
1Co 16:22 If **a.** man love not the Lord Jesus *1536*
2Co 1:4 them which are in **a.** trouble, *3956*
2Co 2:5 But if **a.** have caused grief, he *5100*
2Co 2:10 To whom ye forgive **a.** thing, *5100*
2Co 2:10 if I forgave **a.** thing, to whom I *1536*
2Co 3:5 to think **a.** thing as of ourselves; *5100*
2Co 5:17 Therefore if **a.** man be in Christ, *1536*
2Co 6:3 Giving no offence in **a.** thing, *3367*
2Co 7:14 if I have boasted **a.** thing to him *1536*
2Co 8:23 Whether **a.** do enquire of Titus.
2Co 10:7 If **a.** man trust to himself that he *5100*
2Co 11:3 But I fear, lest by **a.** means, as *3381*
2Co 11:21 Howbeit whereinsoever **a.** is bold, *5100*
2Co 12:6 lest **a.** man should think of me *5100*
2Co 12:17 **a.** of them whom I sent unto you? *5100*
Ga 1:8 heaven, preach **a.** other gospel
Ga 1:9 If **a.** man preach **a.** other gospel *1536*
Ga 2:2 lest by **a.** means I should run, *3381*
Ga 5:6 neither circumcision availeth **a.** *5100*
Ga 6:15 neither circumcision availeth **a.** *5100*
Eph 2:9 lest **a.** man should boast. *5100*
Eph 5:5 an idolater, hath **a.** inheritance
Eph 5:27 or wrinkle or **a.** such thing; *5100*
Eph 6:8 whatsoever good thing **a.** man *1538*
Php 2:1 therefore **a.** consolation in Christ, *1536*
Php 2:1 if **a.** comfort of love, *1536*
Php 2:1 if **a.** fellowship of the Spirit, *1536*
Php 2:1 if **a.** bowels and mercies, *1536*
Php 3:4 If **a.** other man thinketh that he *1536*
Php 3:11 If by **a.** means I might attain unto *4458*
Php 3:15 if in **a.** thing ye be otherwise *1536*
Php 4:8 **a.** virtue, and if there be **a.** praise, *1536*
Col 2:4 lest **a.** man should beguile you *3387*
Col 2:8 Beware lest **a.** man spoil you *3387*
Col 2:23 not in **a.** honor to the satisfying *5100*
Col 3:13 if **a.** man have a quarrel against **a.** *5100*
1Th 1:8 we need not to speak **a.** thing. *5100*
1Th 2:5 at **a.** time used we flattering words, *4218*
1Th 2:9 not be chargeable unto **a.** of you, *5100*
1Th 4:6 defraud his brother in **a.** matter:
1Th 5:15 render evil for evil unto **a.** man; *5100*
2Th 2:3 man deceive you by **a.** means: *3367*
2Th 3:8 we eat **a.** man's bread for nought; *5100*
2Th 3:8 not be chargeable to **a.** of you: *5100*
2Th 3:10 that if **a.** would not work, neither *1536*
2Th 3:14 And if **a.** man obey not our word *5100*
1Ti 1:10 if there be **a.** other thing that is *1536*
1Ti 5:4 But if **a.** widow have children *5100*
1Ti 5:8 But if **a.** provide not for his own, *5100*
1Ti 5:16 If **a.** man or woman that believeth *1536*
1Ti 6:3 If **a.** man teach otherwise, and *1536*
Tit 1:6 If **a.** be blameless, the husband *1536*
Heb 1:5 of the angels said he at **a.** time, *4218*
Heb 1:13 said he at **a.** time, Sit on my right *4218*
Heb 2:1 lest at **a.** time we should let them *3379*
Heb 3:12 there be in **a.** of you an evil heart *5100*
Heb 3:13 lest **a.** of you be hardened through *5100*
Heb 4:1 **a.** of you should seem to come *5100*
Heb 4:11 **a.** man fall after the same *5100*
Heb 4:12 sharper than **a.** twoedged sword, *3956*
Heb 4:13 Neither is there **a.** creature that
Heb 10:38 shall live by faith: but if **a.** man
Heb 12:15 lest **a.** man fail of the grace of God; *5100*
Heb 12:15 lest **a.** root of bitterness springing *5100*
Heb 12:16 Lest there be **a.** fornicator, or *5100*
Heb 12:19 not be spoken to them **a.** more: *2089*
Jas 1:5 If **a.** of you lack wisdom, let him *5100*
Jas 1:7 shall receive **a.** thing of the Lord. *5100*
Jas 1:13 neither tempteth he **a.** man: *3762*
Jas 1:23 if **a.** man be a hearer of the word, *1536*

Jas 1:26 If **a.** man among you seem to be *1536*
Jas 3:2 If **a.** man offend not in word, *1536*
Jas 5:12 neither by **a.** other oath: but let *5100*
Jas 5:13 Is **a.** among you afflicted? let him *5100*
Jas 5:13 Is **a.** merry? let him sing psalms. *5100*
Jas 5:14 Is **a.** sick among you? let him call *5100*
Jas 5:19 If **a.** of you do err from the truth, *1536*
1Pe 3:1 if **a.** obey not the word, they also *5100*
1Pe 3:6 not afraid with **a.** amazement. *1536*
1Pe 4:11 If **a.** man speak, let him speak *1536*
1Pe 4:11 if **a.** man minister, let him do it *1536*
1Pe 4:16 if **a.** man suffer as a Christian,
2Pe 1:20 of the scripture is **a.** private
2Pe 3:9 not willing that **a.** should perish. *5100*
1Jo 2:1 if **a.** man sin, we have an advocate *5100*
1Jo 2:15 If **a.** man love the world, the love *5100*
1Jo 2:27 ye need not that **a.** man teach you: *5100*
1Jo 4:12 No man hath seen God at **a.** time. *4455*
1Jo 5:14 if we ask **a.** thing according to his *5100*
1Jo 5:16 If **a.** man see his brother sin a sin *1530*
2Jo 10 If there come **a.** unto you, and *1530*
Re 3:20 **if a. man hear my voice, and open** *1530*
Re 7:1 nor on the sea, nor on **a.** tree. *3956*
Re 7:16 hunger no more, neither thirst **a.** *2089*
Re 7:16 sun light on them, nor **a.** heat, *3956*
Re 9:4 neither **a.** green thing, *3956*
Re 9:4 neither **a.** tree; *3956*
Re 11:5 And if **a.** man will hurt them, fire *1536*
Re 11:5 if **a.** man will hurt them, he must *1536*
Re 12:8 place found **a.** more in heaven. *2089*
Re 13:9 If **a.** man have an ear, let him hear, *1536*
Re 14:9 If **a.** man worship the beast and *1536*
Re 18:11 buyeth their merchandise **a.** more: *3765*
Re 18:22 shall be found **a.** more in thee; *2089*
Re 21:4 shall there be **a.** more pain: *2089*
Re 21:27 into it **a.** thing that defileth, *3956*
Re 22:18 If **a.** man shall add unto these *5100*
Re 22:19 if **a.** man shall take away from the *5100*

ANY-MAN See ANY and MAN.

ANY-ONE See ANY and ONE.

ANYTHING See also ANY and THING.
Job 33:32 (*In some editions*) If thou has **a.** to say

ANY-WISE See ANY and WISE.

APACE
2Sa 18:25 And he came **a.**, and drew near.
Ps 68:12 Kings of armies did flee **a.**;
Jer 46:5 their mighty ones...are fled **a.**,

APART
Ex 13:12 thou shalt set **a.** unto the Lord 5674
Le 15:19 she shall be put **a.** seven days; 5079
Le 18:19 as long as she is put **a.** for her 5079
Ps 4:3 the Lord hath set **a.** him that is 6395
Eze 22:10 they humbled her that was set **a.** 5079
Zec 12:12 land shall mourn, every family **a.**; 905
Zec 12:12 the family of the house of David **a.**, 905
Zec 12:12 and their wives **a.**; 905
Zec 12:12 family of the house of Nathan **a.**; 905
Zec 12:12 and their wives **a.**; 905
Zec 12:13 The family of...Levi **a.**, 905
Zec 12:13 and their wives **a.**; 905
Zec 12:13 the family of Shimei **a.**, 905
Zec 12:13 and their wives **a.**; 905
Zec 12:14 every family **a.**, 905
Zec 12:14 and their wives **a.** 905
Mt 14:13 into a desert place **a.** *2596, 2398*
Mt 14:23 into a mountain **a.** to pray: *2596, 2398*
Mt 17:1 into an high mountain **a.**, *2596, 2398*
Mt 17:19 the disciples to Jesus **a.**, *2596, 2398*
Mt 20:17 took the twelve disciples **a.** in *2596, 2398*
Mk 6:31 **ye yourselves a. into a desert** *2596, 2398*
Mk 9:2 mountain **a.** by themselves: *2596, 2398*
Jas 1:21 Wherefore lay **a.** all filthiness *659*

APE See APES.

APELLES (a-pel'-leze)
Ro 16:10 Salute **A.** approved in Christ. *559*

APES
1Ki 10:22 ivory, and **a.**, and peacocks. 6971
2Ch 9:21 ivory, and **a.**, and peacocks. 6971

APHARSACHITES (a-far'-sak-ites) See also APHARSATHCHITES.
Ezr 5:6 and his companions the **A.**, which 671
Ezr 6:6 and your companions the **A.**, which 671

APHARSATHCHITES (a-far'-sath-kites) See also APHARSACHITES; APHARSITES.
Ezr 4:9 Dinaites, the **A.**, the Tarpelites, 671

APHARSITES (a-far'-sites) See also APHARSATHCHITES.
Ezr 4:9 Tarpelites, the **A.**, the Archevites, 670

APHEK (a'fek) See also APHIK.
Jos 12:18 The king of **A.**, one; the king of 663
Jos 13:4 unto **A.**, to the borders of the 663
Jos 19:30 Ummah also, and **A.**, and Rehob: 663
1Sa 4:1 and the Philistines pitched in **A.** 663
1Sa 29:1 together all their armies to **A.** 663
1Ki 20:26 up to **A.**, to fight against Israel. 663
1Ki 20:30 the rest fled to **A.**, into the city; 663
2Ki 13:17 thou shalt smite the Syrians in **A.** 663

APHEKAH (af-e'-kah)
Jos 15:35 Janum, and Beth-tappuah, and **A.**, 664

APHIAH (af-i'-ah)
1Sa 9:1 son of **A.**, a Benjamite, a mighty 647

APHIK (a'-fik) See also APHEK.
Jg 1:31 nor of **A.**, nor of Rehob: 663

APHRAH (af'-rah) See also BETH-LEAPHRAH; OPHRAH.
Mic 1:10 house of **A.** roll thyself in the dust 1036

APHSES (af'-seze)
1Ch 24:15 Hezir, the eithteenth to **A.**, 6483

APIECE
Nu 3:47 take five shekels **a.** by the poll
Nu 7:86 ten shekels **a.**, after the shekel
Nu 17:6 their princes gave him a rod **a.**,
1Ki 7:15 eighteen cubits high **a.** 5982, 259
Eze 10:21 Every one had four faces **a.** 259
Eze 41:24 and the doors had two leaves **a.**,
Lu 9:3 **money, neither have two coats a.** *303*
Joh 2:6 containing two or three firkins **a.** *303*

APOLLONIA (ap-ol-lo'-ne-ah)
Ac 17:1 through Amphipolis and **A.**, *624*

APOLLOS (ap-ol'-los)
Ac 18:24 a certain Jew named **A.**, *625*
Ac 19:1 while **A.** was at Corinth, *625*
1Co 1:12 and I of **A.**; and I of Cephas; *625*
1Co 3:4 another, I am of **A.**; are ye not *625*
1Co 3:5 Who then is Paul, and who is **A.**, *625*
1Co 3:6 **A.** watered: but God gave the *625*
1Co 3:22 Whether Paul, or **A.**, or Cephas, *625*
1Co 4:6 and to **A.** for your sakes; *625*
1Co 16:12 touching our brother **A.**, *625*
Tit 3:13 Bring Zenas the lawyer and **A.** *625*

APOLLYON (ap-ol'-le-on)
Re 9:11 Greek tongue hath this name **A.**, *623*

APOSTLE See also APOSTLES.
Ro *general* *title* The Epistle Of Paul The **A.** *652*
Ro 1:1 called to be an **a.**, separated unto *652*
Ro 11:13 as I am the **a.** of the Gentiles, 652
1Co *general* *title* First Epistle Of Paul The **A.** *652*
1Co 1:1 called to be an **a.** of Jesus Christ *652*
1Co 9:1 Am I not an **a.**? am I not free? *652*
1Co 9:2 If I be not an **a.** unto others, *652*
1Co 15:9 not meet to be called an **a.**, *652*
2Co *general* *title* Second Epistle Of Paul The **A.** *652*
2Co 1:1 Paul, an **a.** of Jesus Christ by the *652*
2Co 12:12 the signs of an **a.** were wrought *652*
Ga *general* *title* The Epistle Of Paul [The **A.**] *652*
Ga 1:1 Paul, an **a.**, (not of men, neither by *652*
Eph *general* *title* The Epistle Of Paul The **A.** *652*
Eph 1:1 Paul, an **a.** of Jesus Christ *652*
Php *general* *title* The Epistle Of Paul The **A.** *652*
Col *general* *title* The Epistle Of Paul The **A.** *652*
Col 1:1 Paul, an **a.** of Jesus Christ by the *652*
1Th *general* *title* First Epistle Of Paul The **A.** *652*
2Th *general* *title* Second Epistle of Paul The **A.** *652*
1Ti *general* *title* First Epistle of Paul The **A.** *652*
1Ti 1:1 Paul, an **a.** of Jesus Christ by the *652*
1Ti 2:7 am ordained a preacher, and an **a.**, *652*
2Ti *general* *title* Second Epistle Of Paul The **A.** *652*
2Ti 1:1 Paul, an **a.** of Jesus Christ *652*
2Ti 1:11 appointed a preacher, and an **a.**, *652*
Tit 1:1 an **a.** of Jesus Christ, according to *652*
Heb *general* *title* The Epistle Of Paul The **A.** *652*
Heb 3:1 consider the **A.** and High Priest *652*
1Pe 1:1 Peter, an **a.** of Jesus Christ, to the *652*
2Pe 1:1 a servant and an **a.** of Jesus *652*

APOSTLES See also APOSTLES'.
Mt 10:2 names of the twelve **a.** are these; *652*
Mk 6:30 the **a.** gathered themselves together *652*
Lu 6:13 whom also he named **a.**; *652*
Lu 9:10 the **a.**, when they were returned, *652*
Lu 11:49 **I will send them prophets and a.,** *652*
Lu 17:5 the **a.** said unto the Lord, *652*
Lu 22:14 the twelve **a.** with him. *652*
Lu 24:10 told these things unto the **a.** *652*
Ac *general* *title* The Acts Of The **A.** [40,]*652*
Ac 1:2 commandments unto the **a.** whom *652*
Ac 1:26 numbered with the eleven **a.** *652*
Ac 2:37 Peter, and to the rest of the **a.**, *652*
Ac 2:43 and signs were done by the **a.** *652*
Ac 4:33 the **a.** witness of the resurrection *652*
Ac 4:36 by the **a.** was surnamed Barnabas *652*
Ac 5:12 hands of the **a.** were many signs *652*
Ac 5:18 laid their hands on the **a.**, *652*
Ac 5:29 Peter and the other **a.** answered *652*
Ac 5:34 to put the **a.** forth a little space; *652*
Ac 5:40 called the **a.**, and beaten them, *652*
Ac 6:6 Whom they set before the **a.** *652*
Ac 8:1 Judea and Samaria, except the **a.** *652*
Ac 8:14 the **a.** which were at Jerusalem *652*
Ac 9:27 him and brought him to the **a.**, *652*
Ac 11:1 **a.** and brethren that were in Judea, *652*
Ac 14:4 with the Jews, and part with the **a.**, *652*
Ac 14:14 when the **a.**, Barnabas and Paul, *652*
Ac 15:2 unto the **a.** and elders about this *652*
Ac 15:4 of the **a.** and elders, and they *652*
Ac 15:6 the **a.** and elders came together *652*
Ac 15:22 Then pleased it the **a.** and elders, *652*
Ac 15:23 The **a.** and elders and brethren *652*
Ac 15:33 the brethren unto the **a.**
Ac 16:4 were ordained of the **a.** and elders *652*
Ro 16:7 who are of note among the **a.**, *652*
1Co 4:9 God hath set forth us the **a.** last, *652*
1Co 9:5 as well as other **a.**, and as the *652*
1Co 12:28 first **a.**, secondarily prophets, *652*
1Co 12:29 Are all **a.**? are all prophets? *652*
1Co 15:7 of James; then of all the **a.** *652*
1Co 15:9 I am the least of the **a.**, that am *652*
2Co 11:5 a whit behind the very chiefest **a.** *652*
2Co 11:13 are false **a.**, deceitful workers. *5570*
2Co 11:13 themselves into the **a.** of Christ. *652*
2Co 12:11 the very chiefest **a.**, though I be *652*
Ga 1:17 to them which were **a.** before me; *652*
Ga 1:19 other of the **A.** saw I none, *652*
Eph 2:20 foundation of the **a.** and prophets, *652*
Eph 3:5 revealed unto his holy **a.** *652*
Eph 4:11 gave some, **a.**; and some, prophets; *652*
1Th 2:6 burdensome, as the **a.** of Christ. *652*
2Pe 3:2 the **a.** of the Lord and Saviour: *652*
Jude 17 before of the **a.** of our Lord Jesus *652*
Re 2:2 **them which say they are a.,** *652*
Re 18:20 ye holy **a.** and prophets; *652*
Re 21:14 names of the twelve **a.** of the Lamb. *652*

APOSTLES'
Ac 2:42 in the **a.** doctrine and fellowship. *652*
Ac 4:35 laid them down at the **a.** feet: *652*
Ac 4:37 the money, and laid it at the **a.** feet. *652*
Ac 5:2 part, and laid it at the **a.** feet. *652*
Ac 8:18 through laying on of the **a.** hands *652*

APOSTLESHIP
Ac 1:25 take part of this ministry and **a.**, *651*
Ro 1:5 received grace and **a.**, for obedience *651*
1Co 9:2 seal of mine **a.** are ye in the Lord. *651*
Ga 2:8 to the **a.** of the circumcision, *651*

APOTHECARIES See also APOTHECARIES'.
Ne 3:8 Hananiah the son of one of the **a.**, 7543

APOTHECARIES'
2Ch 16:14 spices prepared by the **a.** art: 4842

APOTHECARY See also APOTHECARIES.
Ex 30:25 compound after the art of the **a.** 7543
Ex 30:35 confection after the art of the **a.**, 7543
Ex 37:29 according to the work of the **a.** 7543
Ec 10:1 the ointment of the **a.** 7543

APPAIM (ap'-pa-im)
1Ch 2:30 the sons of Nadab: Seled, and **A.**: 649
1Ch 2:31 the sons of **A.**; Ishi. And the sons 649

APPAREL See also APPARELLED.
Jg 17:10 and a suit of **a.**, and thy victuals, 899
1Sa 27:9 the camels, and the **a.**, 899

2Sa 1:24 ornaments of gold upon your **a.**. 3830
2Sa 12:20 himself, and changed his **a.**, 8071
2Sa 14:2 put on now mourning **a.**, 899
1Ki 10:5 his ministers, and their **a.**, 4403
2Ch 9:4 his ministers, and their **a.**; his 4403
2Ch 9:4 cupbearers also, and their **a.**; 4403
Ezr 3:10 they set the priests in their **a.**; 3847
Es 5:1 that Esther put on her royal **a.**, 3847
Es 6:8 Let the royal **a.** be brought 3830
Es 6:9 let this **a.** and horse be delivered 3830
Es 6:10 take the **a.** and the horse, 3830
Es 6:11 Then took Haman the **a.** 3830
Es 8:15 in royal **a.** of blue and white, 3830
Isa 3:22 The changeable suits of **a.**, 4254
Isa 4:1 own bread, and wear our own **a.** 8071
Isa 63:1 this that is glorious in his **a.**, 3830
Isa 63:2 Wherefore art thou red in thine **a.**, 3830
Eze 27:24 in chests of rich **a.**, bound with 1264
Zep 1:8 as are clothed with strange **a.**, 4403
Zec 14:14 gold, and silver, and **a.**, 899
Ac 1:10 men stood by them in white **a.**; *2066*
Ac 12:21 Herod, arrayed in royal **a.**, *2066*
Ac 20:33 no man's silver, or gold, or **a.** *2441*
1Ti 2:9 adorn themselves in modest **a.**, *2689*
Jas 2:2 gold ring, in goodly **a.**, *2066*
1Pe 3:3 of gold or of putting on of **a.**; *2440*

APPARELLED
2Sa 13:18 daughters that were virgins **a.** 3847
Lu 7:25 **they which are gorgeously a.**, *2441*

APPARENTLY
Nu 12:8 speak mouth to mouth, even **a.**, 4758

APPEAL See also APPEALED.
Ac 25:11 I **a.** unto Caesar. *1941*
Ac 28:19 constrained to **a.** unto Caesar; *1941*

APPEALED
Ac 25:12 Hast thou **a.** unto Caesar? *1941*
Ac 25:21 when Paul had **a.** to be reserved *1941*
Ac 25:25 himself hath **a.** to Augustus, *1941*
Ac 26:32 if he had not **a.** unto Caesar. *1941*

APPEAR See also APPEARED; APPEARETH; APPEARING.
Ge 1:9 let the dry land **a.**: and it was so. 7200
Ge 30:37 made the white **a.** which was in 4286
Ex 23:15 none shall **a.** before me empty:) 7200
Ex 23:17 all thy males shall **a.** before 7200
Ex 34:20 none shall **a.** before me empty 7200
Ex 34:23 menchildren **a.** before the Lord 7200
Ex 34:24 to **a.** before the Lord thy God 7200
Le 9:4 to day the Lord will **a.** unto you 7200
Le 9:6 glory of the Lord shall **a.** unto you. 7200
Le 13:57 if it **a.** still in the garment, 7200
Le 16:2 I will **a.** in the cloud upon the 7200
De 16:16 males **a.** before the Lord thy God 7200
De 16:16 they shall not **a.**...empty: 7200
De 31:11 Israel is come to **a.** before the Lord 7200
Jg 13:21 angel of the Lord did no more **a.** 7200
1Sa 1:22 that he may **a.** before the Lord, 7200
1Sa 2:27 Did I plainly **a.** unto the house of 1540
2Ch 1:7 night did God **a.** unto Solomon, 7200
Ps 42:2 shall I come and **a.** before God? 7200
Ps 90:16 thy work **a.** unto thy servants, 7200
Ps 102:16 he shall **a.** in his glory. 7200
Ca 2:12 The flowers **a.** on the earth; 7200
Ca 4:1 goats, that **a.** from mount Gilead. 1570
Ca 6:5 of goats that **a.** from Gilead. 1570
Ca 7:12 whether the tender grape **a.**, 6524
Isa 1:12 When ye come to **a.** before me, 7200
Isa 66:5 but he shall **a.** to your joy, and 7200
Jer 13:26 that thy shame may **a.**, 7200
Eze 21:24 so that...you sins do **a.**; 7200
Mt 6:16 **they may a. unto men to fast,** *5316*
Mt 6:18 **thou a. not unto men to fast** *5316*
Mt 23:27 **which indeed a. beautiful outward,** *5316*
Mt 23:28 **ye also outwardly a. righteous** *5316*
Mt 24:30 **shall a. the sign of the Son of man** *5316*
Lu 11:44 **are as graves which a. not,** *82*
Lu 19:11 of God should imediately **a.**, *398*
Ac 22:30 and all their council to **a.**, *2064*
Ac 26:16 **in the which I will a. unto thee;** *3700*
Ro 7:13 But sin, that it might **a.** sin, *5316*
2Co 5:10 all **a.** before the judgment seat *5319*
2Co 7:12 sight of God might **a.** unto you. *5319*
2Co 13:7 not that we should **a.** approved, *5316*
Col 3:4 Christ, who is our life, shall **a.**, *5319*
Col 3:4 then shall ye also **a.** with him in *5319*
1Ti 4:15 that thy profiting may **a.** *5318, 5600*
Heb 9:24 **a.** in the presence of God for us. *1718*
Heb 9:28 them that look for him shall he **a.** *3700*
Heb 11:3 not made of things which do **a.** *5316*
1Pe 4:18 the ungodly and the sinner **a.**? *5316*
1Pe 5:4 when the chief Shepherd shall **a.**, *5319*
1Jo 2:28 when he shall **a.**, we may have *5319*
1Jo 3:2 doth not yet **a.** what we shall be: *5319*
1Jo 3:2 when he shall **a.**, we shall be like *5319*
Re 3:18 **of thy nakedness do not a.;** *5319*

APPEARANCE See also APPEARANCES.
Nu 9:15 as it were the **a.** of fire, 4758
Nu 9:16 and the **a.** of fire by night. 4758
1Sa 16:7 man looketh on the outward **a.**, 5869
Eze 1:5 this was their **a.**; they had the 4758
Eze 1:13 their **a.** was like burning coals 4758
Eze 1:13 and like the **a.** of lamps: 4758
Eze 1:14 as the **a.** of a flash of lightning 4758
Eze 1:16 The **a.** of the wheels 4758
Eze 1:16 and their **a.** and their work 4758
Eze 1:26 as the **a.** of a sapphire 4758
Eze 1:26 as the **a.** of a man above it. 4758
Eze 1:27 as the **a.** of fire round about 4758
Eze 1:27 the **a.** of his loins even upward, 4756
Eze 1:27 the **a.** of his loins even downward, 4756
Eze 1:27 as it were the **a.** of fire, 4756
Eze 1:28 **a.** of the bow that is in the cloud 4756
Eze 1:28 **a.** of the brightness round about. 4756
Eze 1:28 This was the **a.** of the likeness 4758
Eze 8:2 a likeness as the **a.** of fire: 4758
Eze 8:2 from the **a.** of his loins 4758
Eze 8:2 as the **a.** of brightness, as the 4758
Eze 10:1 the **a.** of the likeness of a throne. 4758
Eze 10:9 and the **a.** of the wheels 4758
Eze 40:3 whose **a.** was like the **a.** of brass, 4758
Eze 41:21 **a.** of the one as the **a.** of the other. 4758
Eze 42:11 like the **a.** of the chambers 4758
Eze 43:3 according to the **a.** of the vision, 4758
Da 8:15 as the **a.** of a man 4758
Da 10:6 his face as the **a.** of lightning, 4758
Da 10:18 like the **a.** of a man, and he 4758
Joe 2:4 **a.** of them is as the **a.** of horses; 4758
Joh 7:24 **Judge not according to the a.,** *3799*
2Co 5:12 glory in **a.**, and not in heart. *4383*
2Co 10:7 on things after the outward **a.**? *4383*
1Th 5:22 Abstain from all **a.** of evil. *1491*

APPEARANCES
Eze 10:10 And as for their **a.**, they four had 4758
Eze 10:22 Chebar, their **a.** and themselves: 4758

APPEARED
Ge 12:7 And the Lord **a.** unto Abram, 7200
Ge 12:7 unto the Lord, who **a.** unto him. 7200
Ge 17:1 And when...the Lord **a.** to Abram, 7200
Ge 18:1 And the Lord **a.** unto him in the 7200
Ge 26:2 And the Lord **a.** unto him, 7200
Ge 26:24 **a.** unto him the same night. 7200
Ge 35:1 God, that **a.** unto thee when thou 7200
Ge 35:7 because there God **a.** unto him, 1540
Ge 35:9 And God **a.** unto Jacob again, 7200
Ge 48:3 God Almighty **a.** unto me at Luz 7200
Ex 3:2 And the angel of the Lord **a.** 7200
Ex 3:16 The Lord God of your fathers,...**a.** 7200
Ex 4:1 The Lord hath not **a.** unto thee. 7200
Ex 4:5 God of Jacob, hath **a.** unto thee. 7200
Ex 6:3 And I **a.** unto Abraham, 7200
Ex 14:27 strength when the morning **a.**; 6437
Ex 16:10 glory of the Lord **a.** in the cloud. 7200
Le 9:23 and the glory of the Lord **a.** unto 7200
Nu 14:10 the glory of the Lord **a.** in the 7200
Nu 16:19 Lord **a.** unto all the congregation. 7200
Nu 16:42 and the glory of the Lord **a.** 7200
Nu 20:6 the glory of the Lord **a.** unto them. 7200
De 31:15 And the Lord **a.** in the tabernacle 7200
Jg 6:12 the angel of the Lord **a.** unto him, 7200
Jg 13:3 **a.** unto the woman, and said unto 7200
Jg 13:10 the man hath **a.** unto me, 7200
1Sa 3:21 the Lord **a.** again in Shiloh: 7200
2Sa 22:16 And the channels of the sea **a.**, 7200
1Ki 3:5 In Gibeon the Lord **a.** to Solomon 7200
1Ki 9:2 the Lord **a.** to Solomon the second 7200
1Ki 9:2 as he had **a.** unto him at Gibeon. 7200
1Ki 11:9 Lord God of Israel, which had **a.** 7200
2Ki 2:11 behold, there **a.** a chariot of fire
2Ch 3:1 where the Lord **a.** unto David 7200
2Ch 7:12 the Lord **a.** to Solomon by night, 7200
Ne 4:21 of the morning till the stars **a.**. 3318
Jer 31:3 The Lord hath **a.** of old 7200
Eze 10:1 there **a.** over them as it were a 7200
Eze 10:8 And there **a.** in the cherubims 7200
Eze 19:11 and she **a.** in her height 7200
Da 1:15 countenances **a.** fairer and fatter 7200
Da 8:1 **a.** unto me,...after that which **a.** 7200
Mt 1:20 behold, the angel of the Lord **a.** *5316*
Mt 2:7 what time the star **a.** *5316*
Mt 13:26 **then a. the tares also** *5316*
Mt 17:3 **a.** unto them Moses and Elias *3700*
Mt 27:53 into the holy city, and **a.** unto *1718*
Mk 9:4 **a.** unto them Elias with Moses: *3700*
Mk 16:9 he **a.** first to Mary Magdalene. *5316*
Mk 16:12 **a.** in another form unto two of *5319*
Mk 16:14 Afterward he **a.** unto the eleven *5319*
Lu 1:11 there **a.** unto him an angel *3700*
Lu 9:8 of some, that Elias had **a.**; *5316*
Lu 9:31 Who **a.** in glory, and spake of his *3700*
Lu 22:43 And there **a.** an angel unto him *3700*
Lu 24:34 and hath **a.** to Simon. *3700*
Ac 2:3 there **a.** unto them cloven tongues *3700*
Ac 7:2 God of glory **a.** unto our father *3700*
Ac 7:30 there **a.** to him in the wilderness. *3700*
Ac 7:35 angel which **a.** to him in the bush. *3700*
Ac 9:17 Jesus, that **a.** unto thee in the way *3700*
Ac 16:9 a vision **a.** to Paul in the night; *3700*
Ac 26:16 **I a. unto thee for this purpose,** *3700*
Ac 27:20 nor stars in many days **a.**, *2014*
Tit 2:11 salvation hath **a.** to all men. *2014*
Tit 3:4 of God our Saviour toward man **a.**, *2014*
Heb 9:26 hath he **a.** to put away sin by *5319*
Re 12:1 **a.** a great wonder in heaven, *3700*
Re 12:3 **a.** another wonder in heaven; *3700*

APPEARETH
Le 13:14 when raw flesh **a.** in him, 7200
Le 13:43 **a.** in the skin of the flesh; 4758
De 2:30 into thy hands, as **a.** this day.
Ps 84:7 every one of them in Zion **a.** 7200
Pr 27:25 The hay **a.**, and the tender grass 1540
Jer 6:1 evil **a.** out of the north, 8259
Mal 3:2 who shall stand when he **a.**? 7200
Mt 2:13 angel of the Lord **a.** to Joseph in *5316*
Mt 2:19 **a.** in a dream to Joseph in Egypt, *5316*
Jas 4:14 a vapour, that **a.** for a little time, *5316*

APPEARING
1Ti 6:14 the **a.** of our Lord Jesus Christ: *2015*
2Ti 1:10 the **a.** of our Saviour Jesus Christ, *2015*
2Ti 4:1 at his **a.** and his kingdom; *2015*
2Ti 4:8 them also that love his **a.**. *2015*
Tit 2:13 the glorious **a.** of the great God *2015*
1Pe 1:7 glory at the **a.** of Jesus Christ: *602*

APPEASE See also APPEASED; APPEASETH.
Ge 32:20 will **a.** him with the present 3722, 6440

APPEASED
Es 2:1 wrath of king Ahasuerus was **a.**, 7918
Ac 19:35 the townclerk had **a.** the people, *2687*

APPEASETH
Pr 15:18 he that is slow to anger **a.** strife. 8252

APPERTAIN See also APPERTAINED; APPERTAINETH; PURTENANCE.
Nu 16:30 with all that **a.** unto them,
Jer 10:7 for to thee doth it **a.** 2969

APPERTAINED
Nu 16:32 all the men that **a.** unto Korah,
Nu 16:33 they, and all that **a.** to them,
Ne 2:8 palace which **a.** to the house,

APPERTAINETH
Le 6:5 it unto him to whom it **a.**,
2Ch 26:18 It **a.** not unto thee, Uzziah

APPETITE
Job 38:39 or fill the **a.** of the young lions, 2416
Pr 23:2 if thou be a man given to **a.** 5315
Ec 6:7 the **a.** is not filled. 5315
Isa 29:8 he is faint, and his soul hath **a.** 8264

APPHIA (af'-fee-ah)
Phm 2 to our beloved **A.**, and Archippus *682*

APPII (ap'-pe-i)
Ac 28:15 to meet us as far as **A.** forum, *675*

APPII-FORUM See APPII and FORUM.

APPLE See also APPLES.
De 32:10 he kept him as the a. of his eye......... 380
Ps 17:8 Keep me as the a. of the eye,..... 380,1323
Pr 7:2 my law as the a. of thine eye. 380
Ca 2:3 as the a. tree among the trees......... 8598
Ca 8:5 I raised thee up under the a. tree: 8598
La 2:18 not the a. of thine eye cease............ 1323
Joe 1:12 palm tree also, and the a. tree, ... 8598
Zec 2:8 toucheth the a. of his eye. 892

APPLES
Pr 25:11 A word fitly spoken is like a. of......... 8598
Ca 2:5 flagons, comfort me with a................ 8598
Ca 7:8 the smell of thy nose like a.;............ 8598

APPLE-TREE See APPLE and TREE.

APPLIED
Ec 7:25 I a. mine heart to know, and............ 5437
Ec 8:9 and a. my heart unto every work....... 5414
Ec 8:16 I a. mine heart to know wisdom, ... 5414

APPLY See also APPLIED.
Ps 90:12 may a. our hearts unto wisdom. 935
Pr 2:2 a. thine heart to understanding; 5186
Pr 22:17 a. thine heart unto my.................... 7896
Pr 23:12 A. thine heart unto instruction,........... 935

APPOINT See also APPOINTED; APPOINTETH; APPOINTING; DISAPPOINT.
Ge 30:28 A. me thy wages, and I will give........ 5344
Ge 41:34 him a. officers over the land, ... 6485
Ex 21:13 then I will a. thee a place,............... 7760
Ex 30:16 and shalt a. it for the service of......... 5414
Le 26:16 I will even a. over you terror............ 6485
Nu 1:50 thou shalt a. the Levites over 6485
Nu 3:10 And thou shalt a. Aaron 6485
Nu 4:19 and a. them every one to his 7760
Nu 4:27 ye shall a. unto them in charge.......... 6485
Nu 35:6 ye shall a. for the manslayer............ 5414
Nu 35:11 Then ye shall a. you cities to be........ 7136
Jos 20:2 A. out for you cities of refuge, ... 5414
1Sa 8:11 and a. them for himself, for his.......... 7760
1Sa 8:12 And he will a. him captains 7760
2Sa 6:21 to a. me ruler over the people 6680
2Sa 7:10 I will a. a place for my people 7760
2Sa 15:15 my lord the king shall a.................... 977
1Ki 5:6 all that thou shalt a........................... 559
1Ki 5:9 the place that thou shalt a. me, ... 7971
1Ch 15:16 the Levites to a. their brethren 5975
Ne 7:3 a. watches of the inhabitants 5975
Es 2:3 And let the king a. officers 6485
Job 14:13 thou wouldst a. me a set time,........... 7896
Isa 26:1 salvation will God a. for walls........... 7896
Isa 61:3 To a. unto them that mourn in 7760
Jer 15:3 I will a. over them four kinds, ... 6485
Jer 49:19 that I may a. over her?.................... 6485
Jer 49:19 who will a. me the time?.................. 3259
Jer 50:44 man, that I may a. over her? 6485
Jer 50:44 and who will a. me the time? 3259
Jer 51:27 a. a captain against her; 6485
Eze 21:19 son of man, a. thee two ways, ... 7760
Eze 21:20 A. a way, that the sword may 7760
Eze 21:22 to a. captains, and to open the 7760
Eze 21:22 to a. battering rams against the 7760
Eze 45:6 ye shall a. the possession of the 5414
Ho 1:11 and a. themselves one head, ... 7760
Mt 24:51 **and a. him his portion with** *5087*
Lu 12:46 **and will a. him his portion with**.... *5087*
Lu 22:29 **I a. unto you a kingdom, as my**.... *1303*
Ac 6:3 we may a. over this business. *2525*

APPOINTED See also DISAPPOINTED.
Ge 4:25 said she, hath a. me another seed...... 7896
Ge 18:14 At the time a. I will return 4150
Ge 24:14 hast a. for thy servant Isaac: 3198
Ge 24:44 woman whom the Lord hath a............ 3198
Ex 9:5 And the Lord a. a set time, ... 7760
Ex 23:15 the time a. of the month Abib; 4150
Nu 9:2 keep the passover at his a. season. 4150
Nu 9:3 ye shall keep it in his a. season: 4150
Nu 9:7 in his a. season among the children 4150
Nu 9:13 of the Lord in his a. season. 4150
Jos 8:14 at a time a., before the plain;........... 4150
Jos 20:7 And they a. Kedesh in Galilee 6942
Jos 20:9 These were the cities a. for all.......... 4152
Jg 18:11 men a. with weapons of war. 2296
Jg 18:16 the six hundred men a...................... 2296
Jg 18:17 men that were a. with weapons......... 2296
Jg 20:38 there was an a. sign between........... 4150
1Sa 13:8 set time that Samuel had a. ....
1Sa 13:11 camest not within the days a.,........... 4150
1Sa 19:20 Samuel standing as a. over 5324
1Sa 20:35 field at the time a. with David, ... 4150
1Sa 21:2 I have a. my servants to such........... 3045
1Sa 25:30 and shall have a. thee ruler over........ 6680
1Sa 29:4 his place which thou hast a. him, ... 6485
2Sa 17:14 Lord had a. to defeat the good 6680
2Sa 20:5 the set time which he had a. him, ... 3259
2Sa 24:15 the morning even to the time a. 4150
1Ki 1:35 I have a. him to be ruler.................. 6680
1Ki 11:18 a. him victuals, and gave him............. 559
1Ki 12:12 as the king had a., saying,................ 1696
1Ki 20:42 whom I a. to utter destruction........... 2764
2Ki 7:17 king a. the lord on whose hand.......... 6485
2Ki 8:6 king a. unto her a certain officer, ... 5414
2Ki 10:24 Jehu a. fourscore men without, ... 7760
2Ki 11:18 And the priest a. officers over the....... 7760
2Ki 18:14 the king of Assyria a. unto............... 7760
1Ch 6:48 Levites were a. unto all manner......... 5414
1Ch 6:49 and were a. for all the work.............. 5414
1Ch 9:29 were a. to oversee the vessels,.......... 4487
1Ch 15:17 So the Levites a. Heman.................. 5975
1Ch 15:19 And Ethan, were a. to sound ....
1Ch 16:4 And he a. certain of the Levites 5414
2Ch 8:14 And he a., according to the order 5975
2Ch 20:21 he a. singers unto the Lord, ... 5975
2Ch 23:18 Jehoiada a. the officers of the........... 7760
2Ch 31:2 And Hezekiah a. the courses............. 5975
2Ch 31:3 He a. also the king's portion ....
2Ch 33:8 which I have a. for your fathers;........ 5975
2Ch 34:22 king had a., went to Huldah ....
Ezr 3:8 and a. the Levites, from twenty.......... 5975
Ezr 8:20 David and the princes had a............. 5414
Ezr 10:14 come at a. times, and with them......... 2163
Ne 5:14 I was a. to be their governor 6680
Ne 6:7 thou hast also a. prophets to............ 5975
Ne 7:1 singers and the Levites were a.,......... 6485
Ne 9:17 in their rebellion a. a capatin 5414
Ne 10:34 at times a. year by year................... 2163
Ne 12:31 and a. two great companies............... 5975
Ne 12:44 were some a. over the chambers 6485
Ne 13:30 and a. the wards of the priests 5975
Ne 13:31 for the wood offering, at times a.,....... 2163
Es 1:8 king had a. to all the officers............ 3245
Es 2:15 the keeper of the women, a., ... 559
Es 4:5 whom he had a. to attend.................. 5975
Es 9:27 and according to their a. time ....
Es 9:31 days of Purim in their times a., ...
Job 7:1 a. time to man upon the earth?........... 6635
Job 7:3 wearisome nights are a. to me. 4487
Job 14:5 thou hast a. his bounds that he.......... 6213
Job 14:14 days of my a. time will I wait, ... 6635
Job 20:29 the heritage a. unto him by God.......... 561
Job 23:14 the thing that is a. for me: 2706
Job 30:23 the house a. for all living................. 4150
Ps 44:11 given us like sheep a. for meat;...............
Ps 78:5 a. a law in Israel, which he.............. 7760
Ps 79:11 preserve thou those that are a. 1121
Ps 81:3 in the new moon, in the time a.,......... 3677
Ps 102:20 loose those that are a. to death; 1121
Ps 104:19 He a. the moon for seasons: 6213
Pr 7:20 will come home at the day a.. 3677
Pr 8:29 when he a. the foundations of............ 2710
Pr 31:8 all such as are a. to destruction. 1121
Isa 1:14 new moons and your a. feasts 4150
Isa 14:31 shall be alone in his a. times. 4151
Isa 28:25 wheat and the a. barley................... 5567
Isa 44:7 since I a. the ancient people? 7760
Jer 5:24 reserveth unto us the a. weeks 2708
Jer 8:7 the stork...knoweth her a. times;........ 4150
Jer 33:25 if I have not a. the ordinances........... 7760
Jer 46:17 he hath passed the time a................. 4150
Jer 47:7 there hath he a. it.......................... 3259
Eze 4:6 have a. thee each day for a year......... 5414
Eze 36:5 have a. my land into their................ 5414
Eze 43:21 he shall burn it in the a. place 4662
Da 1:5 And the king a. them a daily 4487
Da 1:10 who hath a. your meat, and 4487
Da 8:19 at the time a. the end shall be........... 4150
Da 10:1 but the time a. was long: 6635
Da 11:27 the end shall be at the time a........... 4150
Da 11:29 At the time a. he shall return,........... 4150
Da 11:35 it is yet for a time a....................... 4150
Mic 6:9 the rod, and who hath a. it. 3259
Hab 2:3 the vision is yet for an a. time, ... 4150
Mt 26:19 disciples did as Jesus had a. them *4929*
Mt 27:10 as the Lord a. me............................ *4929*
Mt 28:16 where Jesus had a. them. *5021*
Lu 3:13 than that which is a. you. *1299*
Lu 10:1 the Lord a. other seventy also............. *322*
Lu 22:29 **as my Father hath a. unto me;** *1303*
Ac 1:23 a. two, Joseph called Barsabas,.......... *2476*
Ac 7:44 as he had a., speaking unto Moses,..... *1299*
Ac 17:26 determined the times before a.,......... *4384*
Ac 17:31 Because he hath a. a day, ... *2476*
Ac 20:13 for so he had a., minding himself *1299*
Ac 22:10 **which are a. for thee to do** *5021*
Ac 28:23 And when they had a. him a day,......... *5021*
1Co 4:9 as it were a. to death;...................... *1935*
Ga 4:2 until the time a. of the father. *4287*
1Th 3:3 know that we are a. thereunto. *2749*
1Th 5:9 God hath not a. us to wrath,.............. *5087*
2Ti 1:11 Whereunto I am a. a preacher, ... *5087*
Tit 1:5 as I had a. thee:............................. *1299*
Heb 1:2 he hath a. heir of all things, ... *5087*
Heb 3:2 faithful to him that a. him, ... *4160*
Heb 9:27 as it is a. unto men once to die,.......... *606*
1Pe 2:8 whereunto also they were a.. .... *5087*

APPOINTETH See also DISAPPOINTETH.
Da 5:21 he a. over it whomsoever he will. 6966

APPOINTMENT
Nu 4:27 At the a. of Aaron and his sons 6310
2Sa 13:32 by the a. of Absalom this hath........... 6310
Ezr 6:9 according to the a. of the priests 3983
Job 2:11 for they had made an a. together........ 3259

APPREHEND See also APPREHENDED.
2Co 11:32 desirous to a. me:........................... *4084*
Php 3:12 if that I may a. that for which............ *2638*

APPREHENDED
Ac 12:4 when he had a. him,........................ *4084*
Php 3:12 for which also I am a. for Christ *2638*
Php 3:13 I count not myself to have a.: *2638*

APPROACH See also APPROACHED; APPROACHETH; APPROACHING.
Le 18:6 None of you shall a. to any that......... 7126
Le 18:14 thou shalt not a. to his wife:............. 7126
Le 18:19 thou shalt not a. unto a woman.......... 7126
Le 20:16 if a woman a. unto any beast,............ 7126
Le 21:17 let him not a. to offer the bread 7126
Le 21:18 hath a blemish, he shall not a.:.......... 7126
Nu 4:19 they a. unto the most holy things:...... 5066
De 20:2 that the priest shall a. and speak....... 5066
De 20:3 Israel, ye a. this day unto battle 7126
De 31:14 thy days a. that thou must die: 7126
Jos 8:5 people that are with me will a. 7126
Job 40:19 make his sword to a. unto him. 5066
Ps 65:4 thou choosest and causest to a............ 7126
Jer 30:21 and he shall a. unto me:.................. 5066
Jer 30:21 engaged his heart to a. unto me? 5066
Eze 42:13 the priests that a. unto the Lord........ 7138
Eze 42:14 shall a. to those things which are 7126
Eze 43:19 the Levites...which a. unto me, ... 7138
1Ti 6:16 in the light which no man can a.......... *676*

APPROACHED
2Sa 11:20 Wherefore a. ye so nigh unto the....... 5066
2Ki 16:12 and the king a. to the altar, ... 7126

APPROACHETH
Lu 12:33 **where no theif a., neither moth** *1448*

APPROACHING
Isa 58:2 they take delight in a. to God............ 7132
Heb 10:25 the more, as ye see the day a............ *1448*

APPROVE See also APPROVED; APPROVEST; APPROVETH; APPROVING.
Ps 49:13 their posterity a. their sayings........... 7520
1Co 16:3 whosoever ye shall a. by... letters *1381*
Php 1:10 may a. things that are excellent; *1381*

APPROVED
Ac 2:22 a man a. of God among you by *584*
Ro 14:18 acceptable to God, and a. of men....... *1384*
Ro 16:10 Salute Apelles a. in Christ. *1384*
1Co 11:19 which...a. may be made manifest *1384*
2Co 7:11 ye have a. yourselves to be clear....... *4921*
2Co 10:18 he that commendeth himself is a., ... *1384*
2Co 13:7 not that we should appear a., ... *1384*
2Ti 2:15 Study to shew thyself a. unto God, ... *1384*

APPROVEST
Ro 2:18 **a.** the things that are more *1381*

APPROVETH
La 3:36 in his cause, the Lord **a.** not. 7200

APPROVING
2Co 6:4 **a.** ourselves as the ministers of *4921*

APPURTENANCE See PURTENANCE.

APRONS
Ge 3:7 together, and made themselves **a.**. 2290
Ac 19:12 handkerchiefs or **a.**, and the *4612*

APT
2Ki 24:16 all that were strong and **a.** for war, ... 6213
1Ch 7:40 that were **a.** to the war and to ....
1Ti 3:2 given to hospitality, **a.** to teach; *1317*
2Ti 2:24 unto all men, **a.** to teach, patient, ... *1317*

AQUILA (ac'quil-ah)
Ac 18:2 a certain Jew named **A.**, born in *207*
Ac 18:18 with him Priscilla and **A.**; *207*
Ac 18:26 when **A.** and Priscilla had heard, ... *207*
Ro 16:3 Greet Priscilla and **A.** my helpers *207*
Co 16:19 **A.** and Priscilla salute you much *207*
2Ti 4:19 Salute Prisca and **A.**, ... *207*

AR (ar)
Nu 21:15 goeth down to the Dwelling of **A.**, ... 6144
Nu 21:28 it hath consumed **A.** of Moab, ... 6144
De 2:9 I have given **A.** unto the children 6144
De 2:18 Thou art to pass over through **A.**, ... 6144
De 2:29 the Moabites which dwell in **A.**, ... 6144
Isa 15:1 in the night **A.** of Moab is laid 6144

ARA (a'-rah)
1Ch 7:38 Jephunneh, and Pispah, and **A.**. 690

ARAB (a'-rab) See also ARBITE.
Jos 15:52 **A.**, and Dumah, and Eshean, ... 694

ARABAH (ar'-ab-ah) See also BETH-ARABAH.
Jos 18:18 over against **A.** northward, ... 6160
Jos 18:18 and went down unto **A.**: 6160

ARABIA (a-ra'-be-ah) See also ARABIAN.
1Ki 10:15 of all the kings of **A.**, and of the 6152
2Ch 9:14 all the kings of **A.** and governors 6152
Isa 21:13 The burden upon **A.**, In the forest 6152
Isa 21:13 In the forest in **A.** shall ye lodge, ... 6152
Jer 25:24 And all the kings of **A.**, and all 6152
Eze 27:21 **A.**, and all the princes of Kedar, ... 6152
Ga 1:17 I went into **A.**, and returned *688*
Ga 4:25 this Agar is mount Sinai in **A.**, ... *688*

ARABIAN (a-ra'-be-un) See also ARABIANS.
Ne 2:19 and Greshem the **A.**, heard it, they 6163
Ne 6:1 Geshem the **A.**, and the rest of 6163
Isa 13:20 neither shall the **A.** pitch tent 6163
Jer 3:2 thou sat for them, as the **A.** in the 6163

ARABIANS (a-ra'-be-uns)
2Ch 17:11 and the **A.** brought him flocks, ... 6163
2Ch 21:16 of the Philistines, and of the **A.**, ... 6163
2Ch 22:1 band of men that came with the **A.**, ... 6163
2Ch 26:7 the **A.** that dwelt in Gur-baal, ... 6163
Ne 4:7 and the **A.**, and the Ammonites, ... 6163
Ac 2:11 Cretes and **A.**, we do hear them *690*

ARAD (a'-rad)
Nu 21:1 And when king **A.** the Canaanite, ... 6166
Nu 33:40 **A.** the Canaanite, which dwelt in 6166
Jos 12:14 Hormah, one; the king of A, one; 6166
Jg 1:16 which lieth in the south of **A.**; 6166
1Ch 8:15 And Zebadiah, and **A.**, and Ader, ... 6166

ARAH (a'-rah)
1Ch 7:39 the sons of Ulla; **A.**, and Haniel, ... 733
Ezr 2:5 **A.**, seven hundred seventy and five 733
Ne 6:18 in law of Shechaniah the son of **A.**; 733
Ne 7:10 the children of **A.**, six hundred 733

ARAM (a'-ram) See also ARAMITESS; ARAM-NAHARAIM; ARAM-ZOBAH; BETH-ARAM; PADAN-ARAM; SYRIA.
Ge 10:22 and Arphaxad, and Lud, and **A.**. 758
Ge 10:23 the children of **A.**: Uz, and Hul, ... 758
Ge 22:21 and Kemuel the father of **A.**, ... 758
Nu 23:7 of Moab that brought me from **A.**, ... 758
1Ch 1:17 Arphaxad, and Lud, and **A.**, and Uz, ... 758
1Ch 2:23 he took Geshur, and **A.**, with the 758
1Ch 7:34 Rohgah, Jehubbah, and **A.**. 758
Mt 1:3 Esrom begat **A.**; *689*
Mt 1:4 **A.** begat Aminadab; *689*
Lu 3:33 which was the son of **A.**, ... *689*

ARAMITESS (a'-ram-i-tes) See also SYRIAN.
1Ch 7:14 his concubine the **A.** bare Machir 761

ARAM-NAHARAIM (a''-ram-na-ha-ra'-im) See also MESOPOTAMIA.
Ps 60:*title* when he strove with **A.** 763

ARAM-ZOBAH (a''-ram-zo'-bah)
Ps 60:*title* and with **A.**, ... 760

ARAN (a'-ran) See also BETH-ARAN.
Ge 36:28 of Dishan are these; Uz and **A.**. 765
1Ch 1:42 The sons of Dishan; Uz and **A.**. 765

ARARAT (ar'-ar-at) See also ARMENIA.
Ge 8:4 upon the mountains of **A.**. 780
Jer 51:27 against her the kingdoms of **A.**, ... 780

ARAUNAH (a-raw'-nah) See also ORNAN.
2Sa 24:16 threshingplace of **A.** the Jehusite 728
2Sa 24:18 threshingfloor of **A.** the Jehusite. 728
2Sa 24:20 **A.** looked, and saw the king and 728
2Sa 24:20 **A.** went out, and bowed himself 728
2Sa 24:21 **A.** said, Wherefore is my lord 728
2Sa 24:22 **A.** said unto David, Let my lord 728
2Sa 24:23 All these things did **A.**, as a king, ... 728
2Sa 24:23 **A.** said unto the king, The Lord 728
2Sa 24:24 the king said unto **A.**. Nay, but I 728

ARBA (ar'-bah) See also ARBAH; ARBATHITE; ARBITE; KIRJATH-ARBA.
Jos 14:15 which **A.** was a great man among ....
Jos 15:13 even the city of **A.** the father of 704
Jos 21:11 they gave them the city of **A.** 704

ARBAH (ar'-bah) See also ARBA.
Ge 34:27 the city of **A.**, which is Hebron, ... 704

ARBATHITE (ar'-bath-ite)
2Sa 23:31 Abi-albon the **A.**, Azmaveth the 6164
1Ch 11:32 brooks of Gaash, Abiel and **A.**, ... 6164

ARBEL See BETH-ARBEL.

ARBITE (ar'-bite)
2Sa 23:35 the Carmelite, Paarai the **A.**, ... 701

ARCH See ARCHANGEL; ARCHES.

ARCHANGEL
1Th 4:16 with the voice of the **a.**, ... *743*
Jude 9 Michael the **a.**, when contending *743*

ARCHELAUS (ar-ke-la'-us)
Mt 2:22 heard that **A.** did reign in Judaea *745*

ARCHER See also ARCHERS.
Ge 21:20 he grew...and became an **a.**. 7198
Jer 51:3 let the **a.** bend his bow, ... 1869

ARCHERS
Ge 49:23 **a.** have sorely grieved him, ... 1167,2671
Jg 5:11 are delivered from the noise of **a.** 2686
1Sa 31:3 the **a.** hit him, and he 3384,376,7198
1Sa 31:3 sore wounded of the **a.**. 3384
1Ch 8:40 mighty men of valour, **a.**, ... 1869,7198
1Ch 10:3 the **a.** hit him, ... 3384,7198
1Ch 10:3 he was wounded of the **a.** 3384
2Ch 35:23 the **a.** shot at king Josiah; 3384
Job 16:13 His **a.** compass me round about, ... 7228
Isa 21:17 the residue of the number of **a.**, ... 7198
Isa 22:3 they are bound by the **a.** 7198
Jer 50:29 Call together the **a.** against 7228

ARCHES
Eze 40:16 about, and likewise to the **a.** 361
Eze 40:21 posts thereof and the **a.** thereof 361
Eze 40:22 the **a.**thereof were before them. ....
Eze 40:22 their windows, and their **a.**, ... 361
Eze 40:24 and the **a.** thereof according to 361
Eze 40:25 windows in it and in the **a.** thereof 361
Eze 40:26 the **a.** thereof were before them: 361
Eze 40:29 and the posts thereof, and the **a.** 361
Eze 40:29 the **a.** thereof round about: it was 361
Eze 40:30 **a.** round about were five and twenty 361
Eze 40:31 **a.** thereof were toward the outer 361
Eze 40:33 **a.** thereof, were according to these 361
Eze 40:33 windows therein and in the **a.** 361
Eze 40:34 the **a.** thereof were toward the 361
Eze 40:36 and the **a.** thereof, and the windows 361

ARCHEVITES (ar'-ke-vites)
Ezr 4:9 the Apharsites, the **A.**, the 756

ARCHI (ar'-kee) See also ARCHITE.
Jos 16:2 along unto the borders of **A.** 757

ARCHIPPUS (ar-kip'-pus)
Col 4:17 say to **A.**, Take heed to the *751*
Phm 2 **A.** our fellowsoldier, ... *751*

ARCHITE (ar'-kite) See also ARCHI.
2Sa 15:32 Hushai the **A.** came to meet him 757
2Sa 16:16 Hushai the **A.**, David's friend, ... 757
2Sa 17:5 Call now Hushai the **A.** also, ... 757
2Sa 17:14 counsel of Hushai the **A.** is better 757
1Ch 27:33 Hushai the **A.** was the king's 757

ARCTURUS (ark-tu'-rus)
Job 9:9 maketh **A.**, Orion, and Pleiades, ... 5906
Job 38:32 thou guide **A.** with his sons? 5906

ARD (ard) See also ARDITES.
Ge 46:21 Muppim, and Huppim, and **A.**. 714
Nu 26:40 sons of Bela were **A.** and Naaman: 714
Nu 26:40 of **A.**, the family of the Ardites: 714

ARDITES (ar'-dites)
Nu 26:40 of Ard, the family of the **A.** 716

ARDON (ar'-don)
1Ch 2:18 Jesher, and Shobab, and **A.** 715

ARE See in the APPENDIX.

ARELI (a-re'-li) See also ARELITES.
Ge 46:16 Ezbon, Eri, and Arodi, and **A.** 692
Nu 26:17 of **A.**, the family of the Arelites. 692

ARELITES (a-re'-lites) See also ARELI.
Nu 26:17 of Areli, the family of the **A.** 692

AREOPAGITE (a-re-op'-a-jite)
Ac 17:34 which was Dionysius, the **A.**, ... *698*

AREOPAGUS (a-re-op'-a-gus) See also AREOPAGITE; MARS'-HILL.
Ac 17:19 took him, and brought him unto **A.**, ... *697*

ARETAS (ar'-e-tas)
2Co 11:32 under **A.** the king kept the city *702*

ARGOB (ar'-gob)
De 3:4 all the region of **A.**, the kingdom 709
De 3:13 the region of **A.**, with all Bashan, ... 709
De 3:14 Manasseh took all the country of **A.** 709
1Ki 4:13 him also pertained the region of **A.**, ... 709
2Ki 15:25 with **A.** and Arieh, and with him 709

ARGUING
Job 6:25 what doth your **a.** reprove? 3198

ARGUMENTS
Job 23:4 fill my mouth with **a.**. 8433

ARIDAI (a-rid'-a-i)
Es 9:9 Parmashta, and Arisai, and **A.**, ... 742

ARIDATHA (a-rid'-a-thah)
Es 9:8 Poratha, and Adalia, and **A.**, ... 743

ARIEH (a-ri'-eh)
2Ki 15:25 with Argob and **A.**, and with him 745

ARIEL (a'-re-el) See also JERUSALEM.
Ezr 8:16 Then sent I for Eliezer, for **A.**, for 740
Isa 29:1 Woe to **A.**, to **A.**, the city where 740
Isa 29:2 Yet I will distress **A.**, and there 740
Isa 29:2 it shall be unto me as **A.** 740
Isa 29:7 the nations that fight against **A.** 740

ARIGHT
Ps 50:23 that ordereth his conversation **a.** ....
Ps 78:8 that set not their heart **a.**, ... 3559
Pr 15:2 of the wise useth knowledge **a.** 3190
Pr 23:31 the cup, when it moveth itself **a.** 4339
Jer 8:6 heard, but they spake not **a.** 3651

ARIM See KIRJATH-ARIM.

ARIMATHAEA (ar-im-ath-e'-ah)
Mt 27:57 there came a rich man of **A.**, ... *707*
Mk 15:43 Joseph of **A.**, an honourable *707*
Lu 23:51 **A.**, a city of the Jews: *707*
Joh 19:38 Joseph of **A.**, being a disciple of *707*

ARIOCH (a'-re-ok)
Ge 14:1 **A.** king of Ellasar, Chedorlaomer 746
Ge 14:9 and **A.** king of Ellasar; four kings 746
Da 2:14 **A.** the captain of the king's guard, ... 746
Da 2:15 He answered and said to **A.** 746
Da 2:15 **A.** made the thing known to Daniel. 746
Da 2:24 Therefore Daniel went in unto **A.**, ... 746
Da 2:25 Then **A.** brought in Daniel before 746

ARISAI (a-ris'-a-i)
Es 9:9 Parmashta, and **A.**, and Aridai, 747

ARISE See also ARISETH; ARISING; AROSE.
Ge 13:17 **A.**, walk through the land 6965
Ge 19:15 **A.**, take thy wife, and thy two 6965
Ge 21:18 **A.**, lift up the lad, and hold him in 6965
Ge 27:19 **a.**, I pray thee, sit and eat of my 6965
Ge 27:31 Let my father **a.**, and eat of his 6965
Ge 27:43 **a.**, flee thou to Laban my brother 6965
Ge 28:2 **A.**, go to Padan-aram, to the home 6965
Ge 31:13 **a.**, get thee out from this land, 6965
Ge 35:1 **A.**, go up to Beth-el, and dwell 6965
Ge 35:3 And let us **a.**, and go up to Bethel; 6965
Ge 41:30 And there shall **a.** after them 6965
Ge 43:8 with me, and we will **a.** and go; 6965
Ge 43:13 Take also your brother, and **a.**, 6965
De 9:12 **A.**, get thee down quickly from 6965
De 10:11 **A.**, take thy journey before the 6965
De 13:1 If there **a.** among you a prophet, 6965
De 17:8 there **a.** a matter too hard for thee
De 17:8 then shalt thou **a.**, and get thee 6965
Jos 1:2 therefore **a.**, go over this Jordan, 6965
Jos 8:1 and **a.**, go up to Ai: see, I have 6965
Jg 5:12 **a.**, Barak, and lead thy captivity 6965
Jg 7:9 **A.**, get thee down unto the host; 6965
Jg 7:15 **A.**; for the Lord hath delivered 6965
Jg 18:9 **A.**, that we may go up against 6965
Jg 20:40 when the flame began to **a.** up 5927
1Sa 9:3 and **a.**, go seek the asses 6965
1Sa 16:12 **A.**, anoint him: for this is he 6965
1Sa 23:4 **A.**, go down to Keilah; 6965
2Sa 2:14 Let the young men now **a.**, and 6965
2Sa 2:14 And Joab said, Let them **a.** 6965
2Sa 3:21 Abner said unto David, I will **a.** 6965
2Sa 11:20 if so be that the king's wrath **a.**, 5927
2Sa 13:15 Ammon said unto her, **A.**, be 6965
2Sa 15:14 **A.**, and let us flee; 6965
2Sa 17:1 I will **a.** and pursue after David 6965
2Sa 17:21 **A.**, and pass quickly over the 6965
2Sa 19:7 Now therefore **a.**, go forth, 6965
2Sa 22:39 them, that they could not **a.** 6965
1Ki 3:12 after thee shall any **a.** like thee 6965
1Ki 14:2 **A.**, I pray thee, and disguise 6965
1Ki 14:12 **A.** thou therefore, get thee to thine 6965
1Ki 17:9 **A.**, get thee to Zarephath, 6965
1Ki 19:5 said unto him, **A.** and eat 6965
1Ki 19:7 **A.** and eat; because the journey is 6965
1Ki 21:7 **a.**, and eat bread, and let thine 6965
1Ki 21:15 **A.**, take possession of the 6965
1Ki 21:18 **A.**, go down to meet Ahab king of 6965
2Ki 1:3 **A.**, go up to meet the messengers 6965
2Ki 8:1 **A.**, and go thou and thine 6965
2Ki 9:2 **a.** up from among his brethren 6965
1Ch 22:16 **A.** therefore, and be doing, 6965
1Ch 22:19 **a.** therefore, and build ye the 6965
2Ch 6:41 Now therefore **a.**, O Lord God, 6965
Ezr 10:4 **A.**; for this matter belongeth unto 6965
Ne 2:20 we his servants will **a.** and build: 6965
Es 1:18 **a.** too much contempt and wrath
Es 4:14 and deliverance **a.** to the Jews 5975
Job 7:4 When shall I **a.**, and the night 6965
Job 25:3 upon whom doth not his light **a.**? 6965
Ps 3:7 **A.**, O Lord; save me, O my God: 6965
Ps 7:6 **A.**, O Lord, in thine anger, 6965
Ps 9:19 **A.**, O Lord; let not man prevail: 6965
Ps 10:12 **A.**, O Lord; O God, lift up thine 6965
Ps 12:5 now will I **a.**, saith the Lord; 6965
Ps 17:13 **A.**, O Lord, disappoint him, 6965
Ps 44:23 why sleepest thou, O Lord? **a.**, 6974
Ps 44:26 **a.** for our help, and redeem us 6965
Ps 68:1 Let God **a.**, let his enemies be 6965
Ps 74:22 **A.**, O God, plead thine own cause: 6965
Ps 78:6 who should **a.** and declare them to 6965
Ps 82:8 **A.**, O God, judge the earth: 6965
Ps 88:10 shall the dead **a.** and praise thee? 6965
Ps 89:9 when the waves thereof **a.**, thou 7721
Ps 102:13 Thou shalt **a.**, and have mercy 6965
Ps 109:28 they **a.**, let them be ashamed; 6965
Ps 132:8 **A.**, O Lord, into thy rest; 6965
Pr 6:9 when wilt thou **a.** out of thy sleep? 6965
Pr 31:28 children **a.** up, and call her 6965
Ca 2:13 **A.**, my love, my fair one, and 6965
Isa 21:5 **a.**, ye princes, and anoint the 6965
Isa 23:12 **a.**, pass over to Chittim; 6965
Isa 26:19 with my dead body shall they **a.** 6965
Isa 31:2 but will **a.** against the house of 6965
Isa 49:7 Kings shall see and **a.**, 6965
Isa 52:2 **a.**, and sit down, O Jerusalem: 6965
Isa 60:1 **A.**, shine; for thy light is come, 6965
Isa 60:2 but the Lord shall **a.** upon thee, 2224
Jer 1:17 gird up thy loins, and **a.**, 6965
Jer 2:27 they will say, **A.**, and save us 6965
Jer 2:28 let them **a.**, if they can save thee 6965
Jer 6:4 **a.**, and let us go up at noon 6965
Jer 6:5 **A.**, and let us go by night, 6965
Jer 8:4 Shall they fall, and not **a.**? 6965
Jer 13:4 and **a.**, go to Euphrates, and hide 6965
Jer 13:6 **A.**, go to Euphrates, and take the 6965
Jer 18:2 **A.**, and go down to the potter's 6965
Jer 31:6 **A.** ye, and let us go up to Zion
Jer 46:16 **A.**, and let us go again to our own 6965
Jer 49:28 **A.** ye, go up to Kedar, 6965
Jer 49:31 **A.**, get you up unto the wealthy 6965
La 2:19 **A.**, cry out in the night: 6965
Eze 3:22 **A.**, go forth into the plain, 6965
Da 2:39 And after thee shall **a.** another 6966
Da 7:5 **A.**, devour much flesh 6966
Da 7:17 which shall **a.** out of the earth 6966
Da 7:24 ten kings that shall arise: 6966
Ho 10:14 a tumult **a.** among thy people 6965
Am 7:2,5 by whom shall Jacob **a.**? for 6965
Ob 1 **A.** ye, and let us rise up against 6965
Jon 1:2 **A.**, go to Nineveh, that great city, 6965
Jon 1:6 **a.**, call upon thy God, 6965
Jon 3:2 **A.**, go unto Nineveh, 6965
Jon 4:8 when the sun did **a.**, 2224
Mic 2:10 **A.** ye, and depart, for this is not 6965
Mic 4:13 **A.** and thresh, O daughter of 6965
Mic 6:1 **A.** contend thou before the 6965
Mic 7:8 enemy: when I fall, I shall **a.**; 6965
Hab 2:19 **A.**, it shall teach! Behold, it is 5782
Mal 4:2 shall the Sun of righteousness **a.** 2224
Mt 2:13 **A.**, and take the young child *1453*
Mt 2:20 **A.**, and take the young child *1453*
Mt 9:5 **or to say, A., and walk?** *1453*
Mt 9:6 **A., take up thy bed, and go unto** *1453*
Mt 17:7 said, **A., and be not afraid** *1453*
Mt 24:24 **For there shall a. false Christs,** *1453*
Mk 2:9 **or to say, A., and take up thy bed,** *1453*
Mk 2:11 **unto thee, A., and take up thy bed,** *1453*
Mk 5:41 Damsel, I say unto thee, **a.**, *1453*
Lu 5:24 **I say unto thee, A., and take up** *1453*
Lu 7:14 **Young man, I say unto thee, A.** *1453*
Lu 8:54 called, saying, Maid, **a.**, *1453*
Lu 15:18 **I will a. and go to my father,** *450*
Lu 17:19 he said unto him, **A., go thy way:** *450*
Lu 24:38 **why do thoughts a. in your hearts?** *305*
Joh 14:31 **even so I do. A., let us go hence,** *1453*
Ac 8:26 **A.**, and go toward the south *450*
Ac 9:6 **A., and go into the city, and it** *450*
Ac 9:11 **A., and go into the street which** *450*
Ac 9:34 **a.**, and make thy bed. And he *450*
Ac 9:40 him to the body said, Tabitha, **a.** *450*
Ac 10:20 **A.** therefore, and get thee down, *450*
Ac 11:7 **A.**, Peter; slay and eat *450*
Ac 12:7 raised him up, saying, **A.** up *450*
Ac 20:30 of your own selves, shall men **a.**, *450*
Ac 22:10 me, **A., and go unto Damascus;** *450*
Ac 22:16 **a.**, and be baptized, and wash away *450*
Eph 5:14 **a.** from the dead, and Christ shall *450*
2Pe 1:19 the day star **a.** in your hearts: *393*

ARISETH
1Ki 18:44 **a.** a little cloud out of the sea, 5927
Ps 104:22 sun **a.**, they gather themselves 2224
Ps 112:4 Unto the upright there **a.** light 2224
Ec 1:5 The sun also **a.**, and the sun 2224
Isa 2:19, 21 when he **a.** to shake terribly 6965
Nah 3:17 when the sun **a.** they flee away 2224
Mt 13:21 **tribulation or persecution a.** *1096*
Mk 4:17 **affliction or persecution a. for** *1096*
Joh 7:52 for out of Galilee **a.** no prophet *1453*
Heb 7:15 there **a.** another priest, *450*

ARISING
Es 7:7 the king **a.** from the banquet of 6965

ARISTARCHUS (ar-is-tar'-cus)
Ac 19:29 having caught Gaius and **A.**, *708*
Ac 20:4 Thessalonians, **A.** and Secundus; *708*
Ac 27:2 **A.**, a Macedonian of Thessalonica, *708*
Col 4:10 **A.** my fellowprisoner saluteth you, *708*
Phm 24 Marcus, **A.**, Demas, *708*

ARISTOBULUS' (a-ris-to-bu'-lus)
Ro 16:10 them which are of **A.** household, *711*

ARK
Ge 6:14 Make thee an **a.** of gopher wood; 8392
Ge 6:14 rooms shalt thou make in the **a.**, 8392
Ge 6:15 the length of the **a.** shall be three 8392
Ge 6:16 window shalt thou make to the **a.**, 8392
Ge 6:16 the door of the **a.** shalt thou set 8392
Ge 6:18 thou shalt come into the **a.**, 8392
Ge 6:19 shalt thou bring into the **a.**, 8392
Ge 7:1 thou and all thy house into the **a.**; 8392
Ge 7:7 sons' wives with him, into the **a.**, 8392
Ge 7:9 and two unto Noah into the **a.**, 8392
Ge 7:13 of his sons with them, into the **a.**; 8392
Ge 7:15 went in unto Noah into the **a.**, 8392
Ge 7:17 increased, and bare up the **a.**, 8392
Ge 7:18 the **a.** went upon the face of the 8392
Ge 7:23 that were with him in the **a.** 8392
Ge 8:1 cattle that was with him in the **a.** 8392
Ge 8:4 the **a.** rested in the seventh month, 8392
Ge 8:6 Noah opened the window of the **a.** 8392
Ge 8:9 she returned unto him into the **a.**, 8392
Ge 8:9 pulled her in unto him into the **a.** 8392
Ge 8:10 sent forth the dove out of the **a.**; 8392
Ge 8:13 removed the covering of the **a.**, 8392
Ge 8:16 Go forth of the **a.**, 8392
Ge 8:19 went forth out of the **a.** 8392
Ge 9:10 from all that go out of the **a.**, 8392
Ge 9:18 that went forth of the **a.**, 8392
Ex 2:3 she took for him an **a.** for bulrushes, 8392
Ex 2:5 she saw the **a.** among the flags, 8392
Ex 25:10 shall make an **a.** of shittim wood: 727
Ex 25:14 into the rings by the sides of the **a.**, 727
Ex 25:14 the **a.**, may be borne with them 727
Ex 25:15 shall be in the rings of the **a.** 727
Ex 25:16 shalt put into the **a.** the testimony 727
Ex 25:21 the mercy seat above upon the **a.** 727
Ex 25:21 and in the **a.** thou shalt put 727
Ex 25:22 are upon the **a.** of the testimony 727
Ex 26:33 within the vail the **a.** of the 727
Ex 26:34 upon the **a.** of the testimony in the 727
Ex 30:6 that is by the **a.** of the testimony, 727
Ex 30:26 therewith, and the **a.** of the 727
Ex 31:7 the **a.** of the testimony, and the 727
Ex 35:12 The **a.**, and the staves thereof, 727
Ex 37:1 Bezaleel made the **a.** of shittim 727
Ex 37:5 the sides of the **a.**, to bear the **a.** 727
Ex 39:35 The **a.** of the testimony, and the 727
Ex 40:3 therein the **a.** of the testimony, 727
Ex 40:3 and cover the **a.** with the vail 727
Ex 40:5 before the **a.** of the testimony, 727
Ex 40:20 put the testimony into the **a.**, 727
Ex 40:20 and set the staves on the **a.**, 727
Ex 40:20 the mercy seat above upon the **a.** 727
Ex 40:21 brought the **a.** into the tabernacle, 727
Ex 40:21 covered the **a.** of the testimony; 727
Le 16:2 which is upon the **a.** 727
Nu 3:31 the charge shall be the **a.**, and the 727
Nu 4:5 cover the **a.** of testimony with it: 727
Nu 7:89 mercy seat that was upon the **a.** 727
Nu 10:33 and the **a.** of the covenant of the 727
Nu 10:35 when the **a.** set forward, 727
Nu 14:44 nevertheless the **a.** of the covenant 727
De 10:1 make thee an **a.** of wood 727
De 10:2 thou shalt put them in the **a.** 727
De 10:3 made an **a.** of shittim wood, 727
De 10:5 put the tables into the **a.** which 727
De 10:8 to bear the **a.** of the covenant 727
De 31:9 the sons of Levi which bear the **a.** 727
De 31:25 which bare the **a.** of the covenant 727
De 31:26 the side of the **a.** of the covenant 727
Jos 3:3 When ye see the **a.** of the covenant 727
Jos 3:6 Take up the **a.** of the covenant, 727
Jos 3:6 they took up the **a.** of the covenant, 727
Jos 3:8 that bear the **a.** of the covenant, 727
Jos 3:11 Behold, the **a.** of the covenant 727
Jos 3:13 that bear the **a.** of the Lord, 727
Jos 3:14 the priests bearing the **a.** 727
Jos 3:15 as they that bare the **a.** were come 727
Jos 3:15 the priests that bare the **a.** were 727
Jos 3:17 the priests that bare the **a.** of the 727
Jos 4:5 Pass over before the **a.** of the Lord 727
Jos 4:7 before the **a.** of the covenant 727
Jos 4:9 which bare the **a.** of the covenant 727
Jos 4:10 the priests which bare the **a.** stood 727
Jos 4:11 that the **a.** of the Lord passed over, 727

Jos 4:16 command the priests that bear the **a.** 727
Jos 4:18 when the priests that bare the **a.** 727
Jos 6:4 priests shall bear before the **a.** 727
Jos 6:6 Take up the **a.** of the covenant, 727
Jos 6:6 before the **a.** of the Lord 727
Jos 6:7 pass on before the **a.** of the Lord
Jos 6:8 and the **a.** of the covenant 727
Jos 6:9 the rereward came after the **a.**, 727
Jos 6:11 the **a.** of the Lord compassed the 727
Jos 6:12 the priests took up the **a.** of the 727
Jos 6:13 **a.** of the Lord went on continually, 727
Jos 6:13 but the rereward came after the **a.** 727
Jos 7:6 before the **a.** of the Lord 727
Jos 8:33 judges, stood on this side the **a.** 727
Jos 8:33 which bare the **a.** of the covenant 727
Ju 20:27 the **a.** of the covenant of God was 727
1Sa 3:3 where the **a.** of God was, 727
1Sa 4:3 Let us fetch the **a.** of the 727
1Sa 4:4 bring from thence the **a.** of 727
1Sa 4:4 there with the **a.** of the covenant 727
1Sa 4:5 when the **a.** of the covenant 727
1Sa 4:6 that the **a.** of the Lord was come 727
1Sa 4:11 And the **a.** of God was taken; 727
1Sa 4:13 his heart trembled for the **a.** of God 727
1Sa 4:17 and the **a.** of God is taken 727
1Sa 4:18 he made mention of the **a.** of God, 727
1Sa 4:19 that the **a.** of God was taken, 727
1Sa 4:21 because the **a.** of God was taken, 727
1Sa 4:22 for the **a.** of God is taken 727
1Sa 5:1 the Philistines took the **a.** of God, 727
1Sa 5:2 When the Philistines took the **a.** 727
1Sa 5:3 before the **a.** of the Lord 727
1Sa 5:4 the ground before the **a.** of the Lord;
1Sa 5:7 The **a.** of the God of Israel 727
1Sa 5:8 What shall we do with the **a.** of 727
1Sa 5:8 Let the **a.** of the God of Israel be 727
1Sa 5:8 And they carried the **a.** of the God 727
1Sa 5:10 Therefore they sent the **a.** of God 727
1Sa 5:10 as the **a.** of God came to Ekron 727
1Sa 5:10 They have brought about the **a.** of 727
1Sa 5:11 Send away the **a.** of the God of 727
1Sa 6:1 **a.** of the Lord was in the country 727
1Sa 6:2 What shall we do to the **a.** of 727
1Sa 6:3 If ye send away the **a.** of 727
1Sa 6:8 take the **a.** of the Lord, 727
1Sa 6:11 they laid the **a.** of the Lord upon 727
1Sa 6:13 saw the **a.**, and rejoiced to see it 727
1Sa 6:15 the Levites took down the **a.** of 727
1Sa 6:18 whereon they set down the **a.** of 727
1Sa 6:19 because they had looked into the **a.** 727
1Sa 6:21 Philistines have brought again the **a.** 727
1Sa 7:1 fetched up the **a.** of the Lord, 727
1Sa 7:1 Eleazar his son to keep the **a.** of 727
1Sa 7:2 the **a.** abode in Kirjath-jearim, 727
1Sa 14:18 Bring hither the **a.** of God 727
1Sa 14:18 For the **a.** of God was at that time 727
2Sa 6:2 bring up from thence the **a.** of God, 727
2Sa 6:3 they set the **a.** of God upon a new 727
2Sa 6:4 accompanying the **a.** of God: 727
2Sa 6:4 and Ahio went before the **a.** 727
2Sa 6:6 put forth his hand to the **a.** of God, 727
2Sa 6:7 there he died by the **a.** of God 727
2Sa 6:9 How shall the **a.** of the Lord 727
2Sa 6:10 David would not remove the **a.** of 727
2Sa 6:11 the **a.** of the Lord continued 727
2Sa 6:12 because of the **a.** of God 727
2Sa 6:12 went and brought up the **a.** of 727
2Sa 6:13 when they that bare the **a.** of 727
2Sa 6:15 brought up the **a.** of the Lord 727
2Sa 6:16 as the **a.** of the Lord came into the 727
2Sa 6:17 they brought in the **a.** of the Lord, 727
2Sa 7:2 but the **a.** of God dwelleth within 727
2Sa 11:11 The **a.**, and Israel, and Judah, 727
2Sa 15:24 the **a.** of the covenant of God: 727
2Sa 15:24 and they set down the **a.** of God; 727
2Sa 15:25 Carry back the **a.** of God into the 727
2Sa 15:29 carried the **a.** of God again to 727
1Ki 2:26 because thou barest the **a.** of 727
1Ki 3:15 stood before the **a.** of the covenant 727
1Ki 6:19 set there the **a.** of the covenant 727
1Ki 8:1 bring up the **a.** of the covenant 727
1Ki 8:3 the priests took up the **a.** 727
1Ki 8:4 they brought up the **a.** of the Lord, 727
1Ki 8:5 with him before the **a.**, 727
1Ki 8:6 the priests brought in the **a.** of the 727
1Ki 8:7 two wings over the place of the **a.**, 727
1Ki 8:7 and the cherubims covered the **a.** 727
1Ki 8:9 nothing in the **a.** save the two 727
1Ki 8:21 I have set there a place for the **a.**, 727
1Ch 6:31 after that the **a.** had rest 727
1Ch 13:3 let us bring again the **a.** of our God 727
1Ch 13:5 bring the **a.** of God from 727
1Ch 13:6 to bring up thence the **a.** of God 727
1Ch 13:7 they carried the **a.** of God in a new 727
1Ch 13:9 put forth his hand to hold the **a.**; 727
1Ch 13:10 because he put his hand to the **a.** 727
1Ch 13:12 How shall I bring the **a.** of 727
1Ch 13:13 David brought not the **a.** 727
1Ch 13:14 the **a.** of God remained 727
1Ch 15:1 prepared a place for the **a.** of God, 727
1Ch 15:2 None ought to carry the **a.** of God 727
1Ch 15:2 the Lord chosen to carry the **a.** of 727
1Ch 15:3, 14 to bring up the **a.** of the Lord 727
1Ch 15:12 may bring up the **a.** of the Lord 727
1Ch 15:15 the Levites bare the **a.** of God 727
1Ch 15:23, 24 doorkeepers for the **a.** 727
1Ch 15:24 with the trumpets before the **a.** of 727
1Ch 15:25 bring up the **a.** of the covenant 727
1Ch 15:26 helped the Levites that bare the **a.** 727
1Ch 15:27 the Levites that bare the **a.**, 727
1Ch 15:28 Thus all Israel brought up the **a.** 727
1Ch 15:29 the **a.** of the covenant of the Lord 727
1Ch 16:1 they brought the **a.** of God, 727
1Ch 16:4 Levites to minister before the **a.** 727
1Ch 16:6 before the **a.** of the covenant 727
1Ch 16:37 he left there before the **a.** of the 727
1Ch 16:37 minister before the **a.** continually, 727
1Ch 17:1 the **a.** of the covenant of the Lord 727
1Ch 22:19 to bring the **a.** of the covenant 727
1Ch 28:2 an house of rest for the **a.** of 727
1Ch 28:18 covered the **a.** of the covenant 727
2Ch 1:4 But the **a.** of God had David 727
2Ch 5:2 to bring up the **a.** of the covenant 727
2Ch 5:4 the Levites took up the **a.** 727
2Ch 5:5 they brought up the **a.**, 727
2Ch 5:6 assembled unto him before the **a.**, 727
2Ch 5:7 the priests brought in the **a.** 727
2Ch 5:8 their wings over the place of the **a.**, 727
2Ch 5:8 and the cherubims covered the **a.** 727
2Ch 5:9 drew out the staves of the **a.**,
2Ch 5:9 were seen from the **a.** before the 727
2Ch 5:10 nothing in the **a.** save the two 727
2Ch 6:11 in it have I put the **a.**, 727
2Ch 6:41 and the **a.** of thy strength: 727
2Ch 8:11 the **a.** of the Lord hath come 727
2Ch 35:3 Put the holy **a.** in the house 727
Ps 132:8 thou, and the **a.** of thy strength 727
Jer 3:16 The **a.** of the covenant of the Lord: 727
Mt 24:38 **day that Noe entered into the a.,** *2787*
Lu 17:27 **Noe entered into the a., and the** *2787*
Heb 9:4 censer, and the **a.** of the covenant *2787*
Heb 11:7 prepared an **a.** to the saving of *2787*
1Pe 3:20 while the **a.** was a preparing *2787*
Re 11:19 was seen in his temple the **a.** of *2787*

ARKITE (ar'-kite)
Ge 10:17 Hivite, and the **A.**, and the Sinite, 6208
1Ch 1:15 and the **A.**, and the Sinite, 6208

ARM See also ARMED; ARMHOLES, ARMS.
Ex 6:6 you with a stretched out **a.**, 2220
Ex 15:16 by the greatness of thine **a.** 2220
Nu 31:3 **A.** some of yourselves unto the 2502
De 4:34 and by a stretched out **a.**, and by 2220
De 5:15 hand and by a stretched out **a.** 2220
De 7:19 and the stretched out **a.**, 2220
De 9:29 and by thy stretched out **a.** 2220
De 11:2 hand, and his stretched out **a.**, 2220
De 26:8 and with an outstretched **a.**, 2220
De 33:20 teareth the **a.** with the crown of 2220
1Sa 2:31 that I will cut off thine **a.**, and 2220
1Sa 2:31 the **a.** of thy father's house, 2220
2Sa 1:10 the bracelet that was on his **a.**, 2220
1Ki 8:42 and of thy stretched out **a.**;) 2220
2Ki 17:36 great power and a stretched out **a.**, 2220
2Ch 6:32 and thy stretched out **a.**; 2220
2Ch 32:8 With him is an **a.** of flesh; 2220
Job 26:2 the **a.** that hath no strength? 2220
Job 31:22 **a.** fall from my shoulder blade, 3802
Job 31:22 mine **a.** be broken from the bone 248
Job 35:9 by reason of the **a.** of the mighty 2220
Job 38:15 and the high **a.** shall be broken 2220
Job 40:9 Hast thou an **a.** like God? 2220
Ps 10:15 Break thou the **a.** of the wicked 2220
Ps 44:3 neither did their own **a.** save them: 2220
Ps 44:3 but thy right hand, and thine **a.**, 2220
Ps 77:15 with thine **a.** redeemed thy people, 2220
Ps 89:10 thine enemies with thy strong **a.** 2220
Ps 89:13 Thou hast a mighty **a.**: 2220
Ps 89:21 mine **a.** also shall strengthen him 2220
Ps 98:1 **a.**, hath gotten him the victory 2220
Ps 136:12 and with a stretched out **a.**:) 2220
Ca 8:6 as a seal upon thine **a.** 2220
Isa 9:20 every man the flesh of his own **a.** 2220
Isa 17:5 and reapeth the ears with his **a.**; 2220
Isa 30:30 shew the lighting down of his **a.**, 2220
Isa 33:2 be thou their **a.** every morning, 2220
Isa 40:10 and his **a.** shall rule for him: 2220
Isa 40:11 shall gather the lambs with his **a.**, 2220
Isa 48:14 his **a.** shall be on the Chaldeans 2220
Isa 51:5 on mine **a.** shall they trust 2220
Isa 51:9 put on strength, O **a.** of the Lord; 2220
Isa 52:10 Lord hath made bare his holy **a.** 2220
Isa 53:1 to whom is the **a.** of the Lord 2220
Isa 59:16 his **a.** brought salvation unto him; 2220
Isa 62:8 and by the **a.** of his strength, 2220
Isa 63:5 own **a.** brought salvation unto me; 2220
Isa 63:12 Moses with his glorious **a.**, dividing 2220
Jer 17:5 and maketh flesh his **a.**, 2220
Jer 21:5 and with a strong **a.**, 2220
Jer 27:5 and by my outstretched **a.**, 2220
Jer 32:17 great power and stretched out **a.**, 2220
Jer 32:21 and with a stretched out **a.**, 248
Jer 48:25 his **a.** is broken, saith the Lord 2220
Eze 4:7 and thine **a.** shall be uncovered, 2220
Eze 20:33 with a stretched out **a.**, and with 2220
Eze 20:34 hand, and with a stretched out **a.**, 2220
Eze 30:21 I have broken the **a.** of Pharaoh 2220
Eze 31:17 and they that were his **a.**, 2220
Da 11:6 not retain the power of the **a.**; 2220
Da 11:6 neither shall he stand, nor his **a.** 2220
Zec 11:17 the sword shall be upon his **a.**, 2220
Zec 11:17 his **a.** shall be clean dried up, 2220
Lu 1:51 hath shewed strength with his **a.**; *1023*
Joh 12:38 to whom hath the **a.** of the Lord *1023*
Ac 13:17 with an high **a.** brought he them *1023*
1Pe 4:1 **a.** yourselves likewise with the *3695*

ARMAGEDDON (ar-mag-ed'-don)
Re 16:16 in the Hebrew tongue **A.** *717*

ARMED
Ge 14:14 when...he **a.** his trained servants, 7324
Nu 31:5 twelve thousand **a.** for war 2502
Nu 32:17 we ourselves will go ready **a.** 2502
Nu 32:20 if ye will go **a.** before the Lord 2502
Nu 32:21 go all of you **a.** over Jordan 2502
Nu 32:27 every man **a.** for war, 2502
Nu 32:29 every man **a.** to battle, 2502
Nu 32:30 they will not pass over with you **a.**, 2502
Nu 32:32 will pass over **a.** before the Lord 2502
De 3:18 pass over **a.** before your brethren 2502
Jos 1:14 pass before your brethren **a.**, 2571
Jos 4:12 Manasseh, passed over **a.** before 2571
Jos 6:7 that is **a.** pass on before the ark 2502
Jos 6:9 the **a.** men went before the priests 2502
Jos 6:13 the **a.** men went before them: but 2502
Jg 7:11 the **a.** men that were in the host, 2571
1Sa 17:5 he was **a.** with a coat of mail; 3847
1Sa 17:38 Saul **a.** David with his armour, 3847
1Sa 17:38 also he **a.** him with a coat of mail 3847
1Ch 12:2 They were **a.** with bows, 5401
1Ch 12:23 that were ready **a.** to the war, 2502
1Ch 12:24 ready **a.** to the war 2502
2Ch 17:17 **a.** men with bow and shield 5401
2Ch 28:14 the **a.** men left the captives and 2502
Job 39:21 he goeth on to meet the **a.** men 5402
Ps 78:9 The children of Ephraim, being **a.**, 5401
Pr 6:11 and thy want as an **a.** man 4043
Pr 24:34 and thy want as an **a.** man 4043
Isa 15:4 **a.** soldiers of Moab shall cry out 2502
Lu 11:21 **strong man a. keepeth his palace** *2528*

ARMENIA (ar-me'-ne-ah) See also ARARAT.
2Ki 19:37 they escaped into the land of **A.** 780
Isa 37:38 they escaped into the land of **A.** 780

ARMHOLES
Jer 38:12 rotten rags under thine **a.** 679,3027
Eze 13:18 sew pillows to all **a.** 679,3027

ARMIES
Ex 6:26 from...Egypt according to their **a.** 6635
Ex 7:4 forth mine **a.**, and my people 6635

Ex 12:17 your **a.** out of the land of Egypt: 6635
Ex 12:51 of the land of Egypt by their **a.**. 6635
Nu 1:3 number them by their **a.**. 6635
Nu 2:3 pitch throughout their **a.**: and 6635
Nu 2:9 throughout their **a.**. These shall 6635
Nu 2:10 of Reuben according to their **a.** 6635
Nu 2:16 throughout their **a.**. And they 6635
Nu 2:18 of Ephraim according to their **a.** 6635
Nu 2:24 throughout their **a.**. And they 6635
Nu 2:25 on the north side by their **a.** 6635
Nu 10:14, 18 according to their **a.**: and 6635
Nu 10:22 according to his **a.**; and over his 6635
Nu 10:28 of Israel according to their **a.**, 6635
Nu 33:1 their **a.** under the hand of Moses 6635
De 20:9 make captains of the **a.** to lead 6635
1Sa 17:1 together their **a.** to battle, 4264
1Sa 17:8 and cried unto the **a.** of Israel, 4634
1Sa 17:10 I defy the **a.** of Israel this day; 4634
1Sa 17:23 out of the **a.** of the Philistines, 4630
1Sa 17:26 defy the **a.** of the living God? 4634
1Sa 17:36 defied the **a.** of the living God. 4634
1Sa 17:45 the God of the **a.** of Israel, 4634
1Sa 23:3 against the **a.** of the Philistines? 4634
1Sa 28:1 the Philistines gathered their **a.** 4264
1Sa 29:1 together all their **a.** to Aphek: 4264
2Ki 25:23 the captains of the **a.**, they and 2428
2Ki 25:26 captains of the **a.**, arose, and 2428
1Ch 11:26 the valiant men of the **a.** were, 2428
2Ch 16:4 of his **a.** against the cities 2428
Job 25:3 Is there any number of his **a.**? 1416
Ps 44:9 goest not forth with our **a.** 6635
Ps 60:10 didst not go out with our **a.**? 6635
Ps 68:12 Kings of **a.** did flee apace: and 6635
Ca 6:13 As it were the company of two **a.**. 4264
Isa 34:2 his fury upon all their **a.**: he 6635
Mt 22:7 **he sent forth his a., and destroyed** *4753*
Lu 21:20 **Jerusalem compassed with a.,** *4760*
Heb 11:34 turned to flight the **a.** of the aliens *3925*
Re 19:14 And the **a.** which were in heaven *4753*
Re 19:19 and their **a.**, gathered together *4753*

ARMONI (ar-mo'-ni)
2Sa 21:8 unto Saul, **A.** and Mephibosheth; 764

ARMOUR See also ARMOURBEARER.
1Sa 14:1 the young man that bare his **a.**, 3627
1Sa 14:6 that bare his **a.**, Come, and let us 3627
1Sa 17:38 Saul armed David with his **a.**, 4055
1Sa 17:39 girded his sword upon his **a.**, 4055
1Sa 17:54 he put his **a.** in his tent. 3627
1Sa 31:9 his head, and stripped off his **a.**, 3627
1Sa 31:10 his **a.** in the house of Ashtaroth: 3627
2Sa 2:21 take thee his **a.**. But Ashahel would 2488
2Sa 18:15 young men that bare Joab's **a.** 3627
1Ki 10:25 garments, and **a.**, and spices, 5402
1Ki 22:38 they washed his **a.**; according 2185
2Ki 3:21 all that were able to put on **a.**, 2290
2Ki 10:2 horses, a fenced city also, and **a.**; 5402
2Ki 20:13 of his **a.**, and all that was found 3627
1Ch 10:9 they took his head, and his **a.**, 3627
1Ch 10:10 his **a.** in the house of their gods, 3627
Isa 22:8 the **a.** of the house of the forest. 5402
Isa 39:2 the house of his **a.**, and all that 3627
Eze 38:4 clothed with all sorts of **a.**, even
Lu 11:22 **him all his a. wherein he trusted,** *3833*
Ro 13:12 let us put on the **a.** of light. *3696*
2Co 6:7 by the **a.** of righteousness on the *3696*
Eph 6:11 Put on the whole **a.** of God, that *3833*
Eph 6:13 take unto you the whole **a.** of God, *3833*

ARMOURBEARER
Jg 9:54 the young man his **a.**, 5375,3627
1Sa 14:7 his **a.** said unto him, 5375,3627
1Sa 14:12 Jonathan and his **a.**, and said, 5375,3627
1Sa 14:12 Jonathan said unto his **a.**, 5375,3627
1Sa 14:13 and his **a.** after him: 5375,3627
1Sa 14:13 and his **a.** slew after him. 5375,3627
1Sa 14:14 Jonathan and his **a.** made, 5375,3627
1Sa 14:17 Jonathan and his **a.** were not 5375,3627
1Sa 16:21 he became his **a.**. 5375,3627
1Sa 31:4 Then said Saul unto his **a.**, 5375,3627
1Sa 31:4 his **a.** would not; for he was 5375,3627
1Sa 31:5 **a.** saw that Saul was dead, 5375,3627
1Sa 31:6 Saul died,...and his **a.**, and 5375,3627
2Sa 23:27 **a.** to Joab the son of Zeruiah, 5375,3627
1Ch 10:4 Then said Saul to his **a.**, 5375,3627
1Ch 10:4 his **a.** would not; 5375,3627
1Ch 10:5 his **a.** saw that Saul was dead, 5375,3627
1Ch 11:39 **a.** of Joab the son of Zeruiah, 5375,3627

ARMOURY
Ne 3:19 going up to the **a.** at the turning 5402
Ca 4:4 builded for an **a.**, whereon there 8530
Jer 50:25 The Lord hath opened his **a.** 214

ARMS
Ge 49:24 the **a.** of his hands were made 2220
De 33:27 underneath are the everlasting **a.** 2220
Jg 15:14 the cords that were upon his **a.** 2220
Jg 16:12 he brake them from off his **a.** like 2220
2Sa 22:35 bow of steel is broken by mine **a.**. 2220
2Ki 9:24 smote Jehoram between his **a.**, 2220
Job 22:9 the **a.** of the fatherless have been 2220
Ps 18:34 bow of steel is broken by mine **a.**. 2220
Ps 37:17 For the **a.** of the wicked shall be 2220
Pr 31:17 strength, and strengtheneth her **a.**. 2220
Isa 44:12 it with the strength of his **a.** 2220
Isa 49:22 bring thy sons in their **a.**, and thy 2684
Isa 51:5 mine **a.** shall judge the people: 2220
Eze 13:20 I will tear them from your **a.**, 2220
Eze 30:22 of Egypt, and will break his **a.**, 2220
Eze 30:24 I will strengthen the **a.** of the king 2220
Eze 30:24 but I will break Pharaoh's **a.**, 2220
Eze 30:25 I will strengthen the **a.** of the king 2220
Eze 30:25 the **a.** of Pharaoh shall fall down: 2220
Da 2:32 his breast and his **a.** of silver, 1872
Da 10:6 his **a.** and his feet like in colour 2220
Da 11:15 and the **a.** of the south shall not 2220
Da 11:22 with the **a.** of a flood shall they be 2220
Da 11:31 And **a.** shall stand on his part, 2220
Ho 7:15 bound and strengthened their **a.**, 2220
Ho 11:3 taking them by their **a.**; but they 2220
Mk 9:36 when he had taken him in his **a.**, *1723*
Mk 10:16 he took them up in his **a.**, put his *1723*
Lu 2:28 took he him up in his **a.**, *43*

ARMY See also ARMIES.
Ge 26:26 the chief captain of his **a.** 6635
Ex 14:9 and his horsemen, and his **a.**, 2428
De 11:4 what he did unto the **a.** of Egypt, 2428
Jg 4:7 Sisera, the captain of Jabin's **a.**, 6635
Jg 8:6 should give bread unto thine **a.**? 6635
Jg 9:29 Increase thine **a.**, and come out. 6635
1Sa 4:2 they slew of the **a.** in the field 4634
1Sa 4:12 a man of Benjamin out of the **a.**, 4634
1Sa 4:16 I am he that came out of the **a.**, 4634
1Sa 4:16 I fled to day out of the **a.**. 4634
1Sa 17:21 battle in array, **a.** against **a.** 4634
1Sa 17:22 and ran into the **a.**, and came and 4634
1Sa 17:48 David hasted, and ran toward the **a.** 4634
1Ki 20:19 and the **a.** which followed them. 2428
1Ki 20:25 number thee an **a.**, 2428
1Ki 20:25 like the **a.** that thou hast lost, 2428
2Ki 25:5 the **a.** of the Chaldees pursued 2428
2Ki 25:5 all his **a.** were scatted from him. 2428
2Ki 25:10 And all the **a.** of the Chaldees, 2428
1Ch 20:1 Joab led forth the power of the **a.**, 6635
1Ch 27:34 the general of the king's **a.** 6635
2Ch 13:3 in array with an **a.** of valiant 2428
2Ch 14:8 Asa had an **a.** of men that bare 2428
2Ch 20:21 they went out before the **a.**, 2502
2Ch 24:24 **a.** of the Syrians came with a 2428
2Ch 25:7 let not the **a.** of Israel go with 6635
2Ch 25:9 I have given to the **a.** of Israel? 1416
2Ch 25:10 the **a.** that was come to him out of 1416
2Ch 25:13 But the soldiers of the **a.** which 1416
2Ch 26:13 under their hand was an **a.**, 2426, 6635
Ne 2:9 had sent captains of the **a.** 2428
Ne 4:2 the **a.** of Samaria, and said, What 2428
Job 29:25 dwelt as a king in the **a.**, 1416
Ca 6:4, 10 terrible as an **a.** with banners.
Isa 36:2 king Hezekiah with a great **a.** 2426
Isa 43:17 horse, the **a.** and the power; 2428
Jer 32:2 Babylon's **a.** besieged Jerusalem: 2428
Jer 34:1 king of Babylon, and all his **a.**, 2428
Jer 34:7 the king of Babylon's **a.** fought 2428
Jer 34:21 hand of the king of Babylon's **a.**, 2428
Jer 35:11 for fear of the **a.** of the Chaldeans, 2428
Jer 35:11 for fear of the **a.** of the Syrians: 2428
Jer 37:5 Pharaoh's **a.** was come forth out 2428
Jer 37:7 Pharaoh's **a.**, which is come 2428
Jer 37:10 ye had smitten the whole **a.** of 2428
Jer 37:11 when the **a.** of the Chaldeans was 2428
Jer 37:11 for fear of Pharaoh's **a.**, 2428
Jer 38:3 the king of Bablylon's **a.**, 2428
Jer 39:1 all his **a.** against Jerusalem, 2428
Jer 39:5 Chaldeans' **a.** pursued after them, 2428
Jer 46:2 against the **a.** of Pharaoh-necho 2428
Jer 46:22 they shall march with an **a.**, 2428
Jer 52:4 he and all his **a.**, against Jerusalem, 2428
Jer 52:8 **a.** of the Chaldeans pursued after 2428
Jer 52:8 all his **a.** was scattered from him. 2428
Jer 52:14 all the **a.** of the Chaldeans, 2428
Eze 17:17 Pharaoh with his mighty **a.** 2428
Eze 27:10 Lud and Phut were in thine **a.**, 2428
Eze 27:11 The men of Arvad with thine **a.** 2428
Eze 29:18 caused his **a.** to serve a great service. 2428
Eze 29:18 yet had he no wages, nor his **a.**, 2428
Eze 29:19 and it shall be the wages for his **a.**, 2428
Eze 32:31 Pharaoh and all his **a.** slain by 2428
Eze 37:10 an exceeding great **a.** 2428
Eze 38:4 all thine **a.**, horses and horsemen, 2428
Eze 38:15 a great company, and a mighty **a.** 2428
Da 3:20 mighty men that were in his **a.** 2429
Da 4:35 according to his will in the **a.** of 2429
Da 11:7 which shall come with an **a.**, 2428
Da 11:13 after certain years with a great **a.** 2428
Da 11:25 of the south with a great **a.**; 2428
Da 11:25 with a very great and mighty **a.**; 2428
Da 11:26 and his **a.** shall overflow: 2428
Joe 2:11 shall utter his voice before his **a.** 2428
Joe 2:20 far off from you the northern **a.**,
Joe 2:25 my great **a.** which I sent among 2428
Zec 9:8 mine house because of the **a.**, 4675
Ac 23:27 then came I with an **a.**, and *4753*
Re 9:16 number of the **a.** of the horsemen *4753*
Re 19:19 sat on the horse, and against his **a.**. *4753*

ARNAN (ar'-nan)
1Ch 3:21 the sons of **A.**, the sons of Obadiah 770

ARNON (ar'-non)
Nu 21:13 and pitched on the other side of **A.**, 769
Nu 21:13 for **A.** is the border of Moab, 769
Nu 21:14 Red sea, and in the brooks of **A.**, 769
Nu 21:24 possessed his land from **A.** unto 769
Nu 21:26 land out of his hand, even unto **A.**. 769
Nu 21:28 the lords of the high places of **A.** 769
Nu 22:36 Moab, which is in the border of **A.**, 769
De 2:24 and pass over the river **A.** 769
De 2:36 is by the brink of the river of **A.**, 769
De 3:8 river of **A.** unto mount Hermon; 769
De 3:12 Aroer, which is by the river **A.**, 769
De 3:16 from Gilead even unto the river **A.** 769
De 4:48 is by the bank of the river **A.**, 769
Jos 12:1 rising of the sun, from the river **A.** 769
Jos 12:2 is upon the bank of the river **A.**, 769
Jos 13:9 is upon the bank of the river **A.**, 769
Jos 13:16 the river **A.**, and the city that is 769
Jg 11:13 from **A.** even unto Jabbok, and 769
Jg 11:18 and pitched on the other side of **A.**, 769
Jg 11:18 for **A.** was the border of Moab. 769
Jg 11:22 from **A.** even unto Jabbok, and 769
Jg 11:26 that be along by the coasts of **A.**, 769
2Ki 10:33 by the river **A.**, even Gilead and 769
Isa 16:2 of Moab shall be at the fords of **A.** 769
Jer 48:20 tell ye it in **A.**, that Moab is spoiled, 769

AROD (a'-rod) See also ARODITES.
Nu 26:17 **A.**, the family of the Arodites. 720

ARODI (ar'-o-di) See also ARODITES.
Ge 46:16 Ezbon, Eri, and **A.**, and Areli. 722

ARODITES (a'-ro-dites) See also ARODI.
Nu 26:17 Of Arod, the family of the **A.** 722

AROER (ar'-o-ur) See also AROERITE.
Nu 32:34 built Dibon, and Ataroth, and **A.**, 6177
De 2:36 From **A.**, which is by the brink of 6177
De 3:12 we possessed at that time, from **A.**, 6177
De 4:48 From **A.**, which is by the bank of 6177
Jos 12:2 in Heshbon, and ruled from **A.**, 6177
Jos 13:9 From **A.**, that is upon the bank 6177
Jos 13:16 And their coast was from **A.**, that 6177
Jos 13:25 unto **A.** that is before Rabbah; 6177
Jg 11:26 towns, and in **A.** and her towns, 6177
Jg 11:33 And he smote them from **A.**, even 6177
1Sa 30:28 And to them which were in **A.**, 6177
2Sa 24:5 over Jordan, and pitched in **A.**, 6177
2Ki 10:33 from **A.**, which is by the river 6177
1Ch 5:8 the son of Joel, who dwelt in **A.**, 6177
Isa 17:2 The cities of **A.** are forsaken; 6177
Jer 48:19 O inhabitant of **A.**, stand by the 6177

AROERITE (ar'-o-ur-ite)
1Ch 11:44 Jehiel the sons of Hothan the **A.**, 6200

AROSE
Ge 19:15 when the morning **a.**, then the... 5927
Ge 19:33 she lay down, nor when she **a.**... 6965
Ge 19:35 and the younger **a.**, and lay with... 6965
Ge 19:35 she lay down, nor when she **a.**... 6965
Ge 24:10 he **a.**, and went to Mesopotamia,... 6965
Ge 24:61 And Rebekah **a.**, and her damsels,... 6965
Ge 37:7 my sheaf **a.**, and also stood upright;... 6965
Ge 38:19 And she **a.**, and went away... 6965
Ex 1:8 there **a.** up a new king over Egypt,... 6965
De 34:10 there **a.** not a prophet since in... 6965
Jos 8:3 So Joshua **a.**, and all the people... 6965
Jos 8:19 the ambush **a.** quickly out of their... 6965
Jos 18:8 And the men **a.**, and went away:... 6965
Jos 24:9 **a.** and warred against Israel,... 6965
Jg 2:10 **a.** another generation after them,... 6965
Jg 3:20 And he **a.** out of his seat... 6965
Jg 4:9 Deborah **a.**, and went with Barak... 6965
Jg 5:7 until that I Deborah **a.**,... 6965
Jg 5:7 that I **a.** a mother in Israel... 6965
Jg 6:28 when the men of the city **a.** early... 7925
Jg 8:21 And Gideon **a.**, and slew Zebah... 6965
Jg 10:1 after Abimelech there **a.** to defend... 6965
Jg 10:3 And after him **a.** Jair, a Gileadite,... 6965
Jg 13:11 And Manoah **a.**, and went after... 6965
Jg 16:3 Samson lay till midnight, and **a.** at... 6965
Jg 19:3 her husband **a.**, and went after her,... 6965
Jg 19:5 they **a.** early in the morning,... 7925
Jg 19:8 And he **a.** early in the morning on... 7925
Jg 20:8 And all the people **a.** as one man,... 6965
Jg 20:18 And the children of Israel **a.**,... 6965
Ru 1:6 she **a.** with her daughters in law,... 6965
1Sa 3:6 And Samuel **a.** and went to Eli,... 6965
1Sa 3:8 And he **a.** and went to Eli,... 6965
1Sa 5:3 And when they of Ashdod **a.** early... 7925
1Sa 5:4 when they **a.** early on the morrow... 7925
1Sa 9:26 And they **a.** early: and it came... 7925
1Sa 9:26 Saul **a.**, and they went out both... 6965
1Sa 13:15 Samuel **a.**, and gat him up from... 6965
1Sa 17:35 he **a.** against me, I caught him... 6965
1Sa 17:48 came to pass, when the Philistine **a.**,... 6965
1Sa 17:52 the men of Israel and of Judah **a.**,... 6965
1Sa 18:27 Wherefore David **a.** and went,... 6965
1Sa 20:25 Jonathan **a.**, and Abner sat by... 6965
1Sa 20:34 **a.** from the table in fierce anger,... 6965
1Sa 20:41 soon as the lad was gone, David **a.**... 6965
1Sa 20:42 And he **a.** and departed:... 6965
1Sa 21:10 And David **a.**, and fled that day... 6965
1Sa 23:13 David...**a.** and departed out of... 6965
1Sa 23:16 And Jonathan Saul's son **a.**,... 6965
1Sa 23:24 **a.**, and went to Ziph before Saul:... 6965
1Sa 24:4 Then David **a.**, and cut off the skirt... 6965
1Sa 24:8 David also **a.** afterward, and went... 6965
1Sa 25:1 And David **a.**, and went down to... 6965
1Sa 25:41 And she **a.**, and bowed herself... 6965
1Sa 25:42 Abigail hasted, and **a.**,... 6965
1Sa 26:2 Then Saul **a.**, and went down... 6965
1Sa 26:5 David **a.**, and came to the place... 6965
1Sa 27:2 David **a.**, and he passed over with... 6965
1Sa 28:23 hearkened unto their voice. So he **a.**... 6965
1Sa 31:12 All the valiant men **a.**,... 6965
2Sa 2:15 Then there **a.** and went over by... 6965
2Sa 6:2 And David **a.**, and went with all... 6965
2Sa 11:2 that David **a.** from off his bed,... 6965
2Sa 12:17 And the elders of his house **a.**,... 6965
2Sa 12:20 Then David **a.** from the earth,... 6965
2Sa 13:29 Then all the king's sons **a.**,... 6965
2Sa 13:31 the king **a.**, and tare his garments,... 6965
2Sa 14:23 So Joab **a.**, and went to Geshur,... 6965
2Sa 14:31 Then Joab **a.**, and came to Absalom... 6965
2Sa 15:9 So he **a.**, and went to Hebron... 6965
2Sa 17:22 Then David **a.**, and all the people... 6965
2Sa 17:23 he saddled his ass, and **a.**,... 6965
2Sa 19:8 the king **a.**, and sat in the gate,... 6965
2Sa 23:10 He **a.**, and smote the Philistines... 6965
1Ki 1:50 and **a.**, and went, and caught hold... 6965
1Ki 2:40 Shimei **a.**, and saddled his ass,... 6965
1Ki 3:20 And she **a.** at midnight,... 6965
1Ki 8:54 he **a.** from before the altar of the... 6965
1Ki 11:18 And they **a.** out of Midian,... 6965
1Ki 11:40 Jeroboam **a.**, and fled into Egypt,... 6965
1Ki 14:4 Jeroboam's wife did so, and **a.**,... 6965
1Ki 14:17 Jeroboam's wife **a.**, and departed,... 6965
1Ki 17:10 So he **a.** and went to Zarephath... 6965
1Ki 19:3 And when he saw that, he **a.**,... 6965
1Ki 19:8 And he **a.**, and did eat and drink,... 6965
1Ki 19:21 Then he **a.**, and went after Elijah,... 6965
2Ki 1:15 he **a.**, and went down with him... 6965
2Ki 4:30 And he **a.**, and followed her... 6965
2Ki 7:7 they **a.** and fled in the twilight,... 6965
2Ki 7:12 And the king **a.** in the night,... 6965
2Ki 8:2 woman **a.**, and did after the saying... 6965
2Ki 9:6 he **a.**, and went into the house;... 6965
2Ki 10:12 And he **a.** and departed,... 6965
2Ki 11:1 she **a.** and destroyed all the seed... 6965
2Ki 12:20 servants **a.**, and made a conspiracy,... 6965
2Ki 19:35 they **a.** early in the morning,... 7925
2Ki 23:25 after him **a.** there any like him... 6965
2Ki 25:26 the captains of the armies, **a.**,... 6965
1Ch 10:12 They **a.**, all the valiant men,... 6965
1Ch 20:4 **a.** war at Gezer with the... 5975
2Ch 22:10 she **a.** and destroyed all the seed... 6965
2Ch 29:12 Then the Levites **a.**, Mahath the... 6965
2Ch 30:14 they **a.** and took away the altars... 6965
2Ch 30:27 Then the priests the Levites **a.**... 6965
2Ch 36:16 the wrath of the Lord **a.** against... 5927
Ezr 9:5 I **a.** up from my heaviness;... 6965
Ezr 10:5 **a.** Ezra, and made the chief priest,... 6965
Ne 2:12 And I **a.** in the night,... 6965
Es 8:4 Esther **a.**, and stood before the... 6965
Job 1:20 Then Job **a.**, and rent his mantle,... 6965
Job 19:18 I **a.**, and they spake against me... 6965
Job 29:8 the aged **a.**, and stood up... 6965
Ps 76:9 When God **a.** to judgment,... 6965
Ec 1:5 hasteth to his place where he **a.**... 2224
Isa 37:36 when they **a.** early in the morning,... 7925
Jer 41:2 **a.** Ishmael the son of Nethaniah,... 6965
Eze 3:23 Then I **a.**, and went forth into the... 6965
Da 6:19 king **a.** very early in the morning,... 6966
Jon 3:3 Jonah **a.**, and went unto Nineveh,... 6965
Jon 3:6 and he **a.** from his throne,... 6965
Mt 2:14 he **a.** he took the young child and... *1453*
Mt 2:21 he **a.**, and took the young child... *1453*
Mt 8:15 she **a.**, and ministered unto them... *1453*
Mt 8:24 there **a.** a great tempest in the sea,... *1096*
Mt 8:26 he **a.**, and rebuked the winds... *1453*
Mt 9:7 he **a.**, and departed to his house... *1453*
Mt 9:9 And he **a.**, and followed him... *450*
Mt 9:19 Jesus **a.**, and followed him,... *1453*
Mt 9:25 her by the hand, and the maid **a.**... *1453*
Mt 25:7 **all those virgins a., and trimmed**... *1453*
Mt 26:62 the high priest **a.**, and said... *450*
Mt 27:52 of the saints which slept **a.**,... *1453*
Mk 2:12 immediately he **a.**, took up the bed,... *1453*
Mk 2:14 And he **a.** and followed him... *450*
Mk 4:37 there **a.** great storm of wind,... *1096*
Mk 4:39 he **a.**, and rebuked the wind,... *1326*
Mk 5:42 the damsel **a.**, and walked;... *450*
Mk 7:24 he **a.**, and went into the borders... *450*
Mk 9:27 lifted him up; and he **a.**... *450*
Mk 10:1 he **a.** from thence, and cometh... *450*
Mk 14:57 **a.** certain, and bare false witness,... *450*
Lu 1:39 And Mary **a.** in those days, and... *450*
Lu 4:38 he **a.** out of the synagogue,... *450*
Lu 4:39 she **a.** and ministered unto them... *450*
Lu 6:8 he **a.** and stood forth... *450*
Lu 6:48 **a., the stream beat vehemently**... *1096*
Lu 8:24 he **a.**, and rebuked the wind... *1453*
Lu 8:55 again, and she **a.** straightway:... *450*
Lu 9:46 there **a.** a reasoning among them,... *1525*
Lu 15:14 **a. a mighty famine in that land;**... *1096*
Lu 15:20 **he a., and came to his father**... *450*
Lu 23:1 the whole multitude of them **a.**,... *450*
Lu 24:12 **a.** Peter, and ran unto the sepulchre;... *450*
Joh 3:25 there **a.** a question between some... *1096*
Joh 6:18 sea **a.** by reason of a great wind... *1326*
Joh 11:29 she **a.** quickly, and came unto him... *1453*
Ac 5:6 the young men **a.**, wound him... *450*
Ac 6:1 **a.** a murmuring of the Grecians... *1096*
Ac 6:9 there **a.** certain of the synagogue,... *450*
Ac 7:18 king **a.**, which knew not Joseph... *450*
Ac 8:27 he **a.** and went: and, behold, a... *450*
Ac 9:8 Saul **a.** from the earth; and when... *1453*
Ac 9:18 **a.**, and was baptized... *450*
Ac 9:34 thy bed. And he **a.** immediately... *450*
Ac 9:39 Then Peter **a.** and went with them... *450*
Ac 11:19 persecution that **a.** about Stephen... *1096*
Ac 19:23 same time there **a.** no small stir,... *1096*
Ac 23:7 there **a.** a dissension between the... *1096*
Ac 23:9 **a.** a great cry: and the scribes... *1096*
Ac 23:9 of the Pharisees' part **a.**, and... *450*
Ac 23:10 when there **a.** a great dissension... *1096*
Ac 27:14 **a.** against it a tempestuous wind... *906*
Re 9:2 there **a.** a smoke out of the pit,... *305*

ARPAD (ar'-pad) See also ARPHAD.
2Ki 18:34 the gods of Hamath, and of **A.**?... 774
2Ki 19:13 of Hamath, and the king of **A.**,... 774
Isa 10:9 not Hamath as **A.**? is not Samaria... 774
Jer 49:23 Hamath is confounded, and **A.**... 774

ARPHAD (ar'-fad) See also ARPAD.
Isa 36:19 are the gods of Hamath and **A.**?... 774
Isa 37:13 of Hamath, and the king of **A.**,... 774

ARPHAXAD (ar-fax'-ad)
Ge 10:22 Elam, and Asshur, and **A.**, and... 775
Ge 10:24 **A.** begat Salah; and Salah begat... 775
Ge 11:10 begat **A.** two years after the flood:... 775
Ge 11:11 Shem lived after he begat **A.** five... 775
Ge 11:12 **A.** lived five and thirty years,... 775
Ge 11:13 **A.** lived after he begat Salah four... 775
1Ch 1:17 **A.**, and Lud, and Aram,... 775
1Ch 1:18 **A.** begat Shelah, and Shelah... 775
1Ch 1:24 Shem, **A.**, Shelah,... 775
Lu 3:36 which was the son of **A.**,... *742*

ARRAY See also ARRAYED.
Jg 20:20 men of Israel put themselves in **a.**... 6186
Jg 20:22 battle again in **a.** in the place... 6186
Jg 20:22 where they put themselves in **a.**... 6186
Jg 20:30 themselves in **a.** against Gibeah,... 6186
Jg 20:33 themselves in **a.** at Baal-tamar:... 6186
1Sa 4:2 Philistines put themselves in **a.**... 6186
1Sa 17:2 and set the battle in **a.**... 6186
1Sa 17:8 come out to set your battle in **a.**?... 6186
1Sa 17:21 Philistines had put the battle in **a.**,... 6186
2Sa 10:8 put the battle in **a.** at the entering... 6186
2Sa 10:9 and put them in **a.** against the... 6186
2Sa 10:10 that he might put them in **a.**... 6186
2Sa 10:17 the Syrians set themselves in **a.**... 6186
1Ki 20:12 his servants, Set yourselves in **a.**...
1Ki 20:12 themselves in **a.** against the city...
1Ch 19:9 and put the battle in array... 6186
1Ch 19:10 and put them in **a.** against the... 6186
1Ch 19:11 they set themselves in **a.** against... 6186
1Ch 19:17 set the battle in **a.** against them... 6186
1Ch 19:17 when David had put the battle in **a.**... 6186
2Ch 13:3 And Abijah set the battle in **a.**... 631
2Ch 13:3 Jeroboam also set the battle in **a.**... 6186
2Ch 14:10 set the battle in **a.** in the valley... 6186
Es 6:9 **a.** the man withal whom the king... 3847
Job 6:4 set themselves in **a.** against me... 6186
Job 40:10 **a.** thyself with glory and beauty... 3847
Isa 22:7 set themselves in **a.** at the gate... 7896
Jer 6:23 they ride upon horses, set in **a.**... 6186
Jer 43:12 and he shall **a.** himself with the... 5844
Jer 50:9 and they shall set themselves in **a.**... 6186
Jer 50:14 yourselves in **a.** against Babylon... 6186
Jer 50:42 put in **a.**, like a man to the battle,... 6186
Joe 2:5 a strong people set in battle **a.**... 6186
1Ti 2:9 or gold, or pearls, or costly **a.**;... *2441*

ARRAYED
Ge 41:42 **a.** him in vestures of fine linen,... 3847
2Ch 5:12 **a.** in white linen, having cymbals... 3847
2Ch 28:15 and **a.** them, and shod them)... 3847
Es 6:11 **a.** Mordecai, and brought him on... 3847
Mt 6:29 **was not a. like one of these**... *4016*
Lu 12:27 **was not a. like one of these**... *4016*
Lu 23:11 **a.** him in a gorgeous robe, and... *4016*
Ac 12:21 Herod, **a.** in royal apparel,... *1746*
Re 7:13 these which are **a.** in white robes?... *4016*
Re 17:4 And the woman was **a.** in purple... *4016*
Re 19:8 she should be **a.** in fine linen,... *4016*

ARRIVED
Lu 8:26 **a.** at the country of the Gadarenes,... *2668*
Ac 20:15 and the next day we **a.** at Samos,... *3846*

ARROGANCY
1Sa 2:3 not **a.** come out of your mouth:... 6277
Pr 8:13 pride, and **a.**, and the evil way,... 1347
Isa 13:11 the **a.** of the proud to cease,... 1347
Jer 48:29 his **a.**, and his pride,... 1347

ARROW See also ARROWS.
1Sa 20:36 he shot an **a.** beyond him... 2678
1Sa 20:37 was come to the place of the **a.**... 2678
1Sa 20:37 is not the **a.** beyond thee?... 2678
2Ki 9:24 the **a.** went out at his heart,... 2678
2Ki 13:17 The **a.** of the Lord's deliverance,... 2671
2Ki 13:17 and the **a.** of deliverance... 2671
2Ki 19:32 nor shoot an **a.** there... 2671
Job 41:28 **a.** cannot make him flee:... 1121, 7198
Ps 11:2 they make ready their **a.**... 2671

Ps 64:7 God shall shoot at them with an **a.**; 2671
Ps 91:5 for the **a.** that flieth by day; 2671
Pr 25:18 a sword, and a sharp **a.**: 2671
Isa 37:33 nor shoot an arrow there, 2671
Jer 9:8 Their tongue is as an **a.** 2671
La 3:12 set me as a mark for the **a.**. 2671
Zec 9:14 his **a.** shall go forth 2671

ARROWS
Nu 24:8 pierce them through with his **a.**. 2671
De 32:23 I will spend mine **a.** upon them. 2671
De 32:42 make mine **a.** drunk with blood, 2671
1Sa 20:20 I will shoot three **a.** on the side 2671
1Sa 20:21 Go, find out the **a.**. 2671
1Sa 20:21 the **a.** are on this side of thee, 2671
1Sa 20:22 the **a.** are beyond thee; 2671
1Sa 20:36 find out now the **a.** which I shoot. 2671
1Sa 20:38 Jonathan's lad gathered up the **a.**, 2678
2Sa 22:15 he sent out **a.**, and scattered them; 2671
2Ki 13:15 Take bow and **a.** 2671
2Ki 13:15 And he took unto him bow and **a.**. 2671
2Ki 13:18 he said, Take the **a.**. 2671
1Ch 12:12 in hurling stones and shooting **a.** 2671
2Ch 26:15 to shoot **a.** and great stones. 2671
Job 6:4 For the **a.** of the Almighty are 2671
Ps 7:13 he ordaineth his **a.** against the 2671
Ps 18:14 Yea, he sent out his arrows, 2671
Ps 21:12 ready thine **a.** upon thy strings
Ps 38:2 For thine **a.** stick fast in me, 2671
Ps 45:5 Thine **a.** are sharp in the heart 2671
Ps 57:4 whose teeth are spears and **a.**, 2671
Ps 58:7 bendeth his bow to shoot his **a.**, 2671
Ps 64:3 bend their bows to shoot their **a.**, 2671
Ps 76:3 brake he the **a.** of the bow, 7565
Ps 77:17 thine **a.** also went abroad. 2687
Ps 120:4 Sharp **a.** of the mighty, 2671
Ps 127:4 As **a.** are in the hand of a mighty 2671
Ps 144:6 shoot out thine **a.**, and destroy 2671
Pr 26:18 casteth firebrands, **a.**, and death, 2671
Isa 5:28 Whose **a.** are sharp, 2671
Isa 7:24 With **a.** and with bows shall men 2671
Jer 50:9 their **a.** shall be as of a mighty 2671
Jer 50:14 shoot at her, spare no **a.** 2671
Jer 51:11 Make bright the **a.** 2671
La 3:13 hath caused the **a.** of his quiver 1121
Eze 5:16 send upon them the evil **a.** of 2671
Eze 21:21 he made his **a.** bright, he 2671
Eze 39:3 and will cause thine **a.** to fall 2671
Eze 39:9 the bows and the **a.**, and the 2671
Hab 3:11 at the light of thine **a.** they went, 2671

ART See also ARTS.
Ge 3:9 and said unto him, Where **a.** thou?
Ge 3:14 thou **a.** cursed above all cattle,
Ge 3:19 for dust thou **a.**, and unto dust
Ge 4:6 unto Cain, Why **a.** thou wroth?
Ge 4:11 now **a.** thou cursed from the earth,
Ge 12:11 **a.** a fair woman to look upon:
Ge 12:13 I pray thee, thou **a.** my sister:
Ge 13:14 look from the place where thou **a.**
Ge 16:11 Behold, thou **a.** with child, and
Ge 17:8 land wherein thou **a.** a stranger,
Ge 20:3 Behold, thou **a.** but a dead man,
Ge 23:6 Thou **a.** a mighty prince among us:
Ge 24:23 And said, Whose daughter **a.** thou?
Ge 24:47 and said, Whose daughter **a.** thou?
Ge 24:60 Thou **a.** our sister; be thou the
Ge 26:16 thou **a.** much mightier than we.
Ge 26:29 **a.** now the blessed of the Lord.
Ge 27:18 Here am I; who **a.** thou, my son?
Ge 27:24 **A.** thou my very son Esau? And he
Ge 27:32 said unto him, Who **a.** thou?
Ge 28:4 land wherein thou **a.** a stranger,
Ge 29:14 thou **a.** my bone and my flesh.
Ge 29:15 Because thou **a.** my brother,
Ge 32:17 thee, saying, Whose **a.** thou?
Ge 39:9 thee, because thou **a.** his wife:
Ge 41:39 so discreet and wise as thou **a.**
Ge 44:18 for thou **a.** even as Pharaoh.
Ge 45:19 Now thou **a.** commanded, this do
Ge 46:30 face, because thou **a.** yet alive.
Ge 47:8 unto Jacob, How old **a.** thou?
Ge 49:3 Reuben, thou **a.** my firstborn, my
Ge 49:8 thou **a.** he whom thy brethren
Ge 49:9 thou **a.** gone up: he stooped.
Ex 4:25 a bloody husband **a.** thou to me!
Ex 4:26 said, A bloody husband thou **a.**,
Ex 18:18 thou **a.** not able to perform it
Ex 30:25, 35 the **a.** of the apothecary: 4640
Ex 33:3 for thou **a.** a stiffnecked people:
Ex 34:10 the people among which thou **a.**
Le 27:12 valuest it, who **a.** the priest
Nu 14:14 thou Lord **a.** among this people.
Nu 14:14 that thou Lord **a.** seen face to face,
Nu 21:29 thou **a.** undone, O people of
De 2:18 Thou **a.** to pass over through Ar,
De 4:30 When thou **a.** in tribulation,
De 4:38 and mightier than thou **a.**,
De 7:6 For thou **a.** an holy people unto
De 7:19 people of whom thou **a.** afraid.
De 8:10 thou hast eaten and **a.** full,
De 8:12 and **a.** full, and hast built goodly
De 9:1 **a.** to pass over Jordan this day,
De 9:6 for thou **a.** a stiffnecked people.
De 14:2 For thou **a.** an holy people unto the
De 14:21 **a.** an holy people unto the Lord
De 14:24 that thou **a.** not able to carry it;
De 17:14 When thou **a.** come unto the land
De 18:9 **a.** come into the land which the
De 26:1 when thou **a.** come in unto the
De 27:3 law, when thou **a.** passed over,
De 27:9 **a.** become the people of the Lord.
De 28:10 the earth shall see that thou **a.**
De 32:15 thou **a.** waxen fat,
De 32:15 thou **a.** grown thick,
De 32:15 thou **a.** covered with fatness;
De 32:18 that begat thee thou **a.** unmindful,
De 33:29 Happy **a.** thou, O Israel: who is
Jos 5:13 **A.** thou for us, or for our
Jos 13:1 Thou **a.** old and stricken in years,
Jos 17:17 saying, Thou **a.** a great people,
Jg 8:18 As thou **a.**, so were they;
Jg 11:2 **a.** the son of a strange woman.
Jg 11:12 thou **a.** come against me to fight
Jg 11:25 **a.** thou any thing better than Balak
Jg 11:35 **a.** one of them that trouble me:
Jg 12:5 unto him, **A.** thou an Ephraimite?
Jg 13:3 Behold now, thou **a.** barren, and
Jg 13:11 **A.** thou the man that spakest
Ru 2:9 when thou **a.** athirst, go unto the
Ru 2:11 and **a.** come unto a people which
Ru 2:12 wings thou **a.** come to trust.
Ru 3:9 And he said, Who **a.** thou?
Ru 3:9 for thou **a.** a near kinsman
Ru 3:11 that thou **a.** a virtuous woman.
Ru 3:16 said, Who **a.** thou, my daughter?
1Sa 8:5 unto him, Behold, thou **a.** old,
1Sa 10:2 thou **a.** departed from me today,
1Sa 10:5 thou **a.** come thither to the city,
1Sa 17:28 for thou **a.** come down that thou
1Sa 17:33 Thou **a.** not able to go against
1Sa 17:33 for thou **a.** but a youth, and he
1Sa 17:58 Whose son **a.** thou, thou young
1Sa 19:3 father in the field where thou **a.**,
1Sa 21:1 Why **a.** thou alone, and no man
1Sa 24:17 Thou **a.** more righteous than I:
1Sa 26:14 Who **a.** thou that criest to the king?
1Sa 26:15 Abner, **A.** not thou a valiant man?
1Sa 28:12 deceived me? for thou **a.** Saul.
1Sa 29:9 that thou **a.** good in my sight,
1Sa 30:13 thou? and whence **a.** thou?
2Sa 1:8 he said unto me, Who **a.** thou?
2Sa 1:13 that told him. Whence **a.** thou?
2Sa 2:20 and said **A.** thou Asahel?
2Sa 7:22 Wherefore thou **a.** great, O Lord
2Sa 7:24 thou, Lord, **a.** become their God.
2Sa 7:28 O Lord God, thou **a.** that God,
2Sa 9:2 king said unto him, **A.** thou Ziba?
2Sa 12:7 Nathan said to David, Thou **a.**
2Sa 13:4 he said unto him, Why **a.** thou,
2Sa 15:2 Of what city **a.** thou? and he said,
2Sa 15:19 for thou art a stranger, and also
2Sa 15:27 **A.** not thou a seer? return into
2Sa 16:8 thou **a.** taken in thy mischief,
2Sa 16:8 because thou **a.** a bloody man.
2Sa 16:21 shall hear that thou **a.** abhorred
2Sa 18:3 thou **a.** worth ten thousand of us:
2Sa 19:13 **A.** thou not of my bone, and of my
2Sa 20:9 **A.** thou in health, my brother?
2Sa 20:17 the woman said, **A.** thou Joab?
2Sa 22:29 For thou **a.** my lamp, O Lord:
1Ki 1:42 for thou **a.** a valiant man, and
1Ki 2:9 for thou **a.** a wise man, and
1Ki 2:26 for thou **a.** worthy of death:
1Ki 6:12 concerning this house which thou **a.**
1Ki 13:14 **A.** thou the man of God that
1Ki 13:18 I am a prophet also as thou **a.**
1Ki 17:18 **a.** thou come unto me to call my
1Ki 17:24 I know that thou **a.** a man of God,
1Ki 18:7 **A.** thou that my lord Elijah?
1Ki 18:17 **A.** thou he that troubleth Israel?
1Ki 18:36 this day that thou **a.** God in Israel,
1Ki 18:37 know that thou **a.** the Lord God,
1Ki 20:36 as soon as thou **a.** departed from
1Ki 22:4 I am as thou **a.**, my people as thy
2Ki 1:4 bed on which thou **a.** gone up,
2Ki 1:6 on which thou **a.** gone up, but
2Ki 1:16 off that bed on which thou **a.** gone
2Ki 3:7 I am as thou **a.**, my people as thy
2Ki 4:4 And when thou **a.** come in, thou
2Ki 19:15 thou **a.** the God, even thou alone,
2Ki 19:19 know that thou **a.** the Lord God,
1Ch 17:26 And now, Lord, thou **a.** God, and
1Ch 29:11 and thou **a.** exalted as head above
2Ch 14:11 O Lord, thou **a.** our God; let not
2Ch 16:14 prepared by the apothecaries' **a.** 4640
2Ch 18:3 I am as thou **a.**, and my people as
2Ch 20:6 of our fathers, **a.** not thou God in
2Ch 20:7 **A.** not thou our God, who didst
2Ch 25:16 **A.** thou made of the king's
Ezr 7:14 as thou **a.** sent to the king, and of
Ezr 9:15 of Israel; thou **a.** righteous:
Ne 2:2 sad, seeing thou **a.** not sick?
Ne 9:6 Thou, even thou, **a.** Lord alone;
Ne 9:7 Thou **a.** the Lord the God, who
Ne 9:8 thy words; for thou **a.** righteous:
Ne 9:17 but thou **a.** a God ready to pardon,
Ne 9:31 **a.** a gracious and merciful God.
Ne 9:33 thou **a.** just in all that is brought
Es 4:14 knoweth whether thou **a.** come
Job 4:5 thee, and thou **a.** troubled.
Job 15:7 **A.** thou the first man that was
Job 17:14 Thou **a.** my father;
Job 17:14 to the worm, Thou **a.** my
Job 22:3 Almighty, that thou **a.** righteous?
Job 30:21 Thou **a.** become cruel to me: with
Job 31:24 fine gold, thou **a.** my confidence;
Job 33:12 Behold, in this thou **a.** not just;
Job 34:18 say to a king, Thou **a.** wicked?
Job 35:8 may hurt a man as thou **a.**; and
Ps 2:7 Thou **a.** my son; this day have I
Ps 3:3 But thou, O Lord, art a shield
Ps 5:4 For thou **a.** not a God that hath
Ps 8:4 man, that thou **a.** mindful of him?
Ps 10:14 **a.** the helper of the fatherless.
Ps 16:2 Thou **a.** my Lord: my goodness
Ps 22:1 why **a.** thou so far from helping
Ps 22:3 But thou **a.** holy, O thou that
Ps 22:9 But thou **a.** he that took me out
Ps 22:10 thou **a.** my God from my mother's
Ps 23:4 fear no evil; for thou **a.** with me;
Ps 25:5 thou **a.** the God of my salvation;
Ps 31:3 thou **a.** my rock and my fortress;
Ps 31:4 for me: for thou **a.** my strength.
Ps 31:14 O Lord: I said, Thou **a.** my God.
Ps 32:7 Thou **a.** my hiding place; thou
Ps 40:17 thou **a.** my help and my deliverer;
Ps 42:5 Why **a.** thou cast down, O my
Ps 42:5 why **a.** thou disquieted in me?
Ps 42:11 Why **a.** thou cast down, O my
Ps 42:11 why **a.** thou disquieted within me?
Ps 43:2 For thou **a.** the God of my strength,
Ps 43:5 Why **a.** thou cast down, O my soul?
Ps 43:5 why **a.** thou disquieted within me?
Ps 44:4 Thou **a.** my King, O God:
Ps 45:2 Thou **a.** fairer than the children
Ps 63:1 O God, thou **a.** my God; early will
Ps 65:5 who **a.** the confidence of all the
Ps 66:3 How terrible **a.** thou in thy works:
Ps 68:35 thou **a.** terrible out of thy holy
Ps 70:5 thou **a.** my help and my deliverer;
Ps 71:3 thou **a.** my rock and my fortress.
Ps 71:5 thou **a.** my hope, O Lord God;
Ps 71:5 thou **a.** my trust from my youth.
Ps 71:6 thou **a.** he that took me out of
Ps 71:7 but thou **a.** my strong refuge.
Ps 76:4 Thou **a.** more glorious and excellent
Ps 76:7 Thou, even thou, **a.** to be feared:
Ps 76:7 sight when once thou **a.** angry?
Ps 77:14 Thou **a.** the God that doest
Ps 83:18 Jehovah, **a.** the most high over
Ps 86:5 For thou, Lord, **a.** good, and

Book	Ref	Context	No.
Ps	86:10	For thou **a.** great, and doest	
Ps	86:10	thou **a.** God alone.	
Ps	86:15	Lord, **a.** a God full of compassion,	
Ps	89:17	thou **a.** the glory of their strength:	
Ps	89:26	Thou **a.** my father, my God, and	
Ps	90:2	to everlasting thou **a.** God.	
Ps	92:8	But thou, Lord, **a.** most high	
Ps	93:2	of old: thou **a.** from everlasting.	
Ps	97:9	Lord, **a.** high above all the earth:	
Ps	97:9	thou **a.** exalted far above all gods.	
Ps	102:27	But thou **a.** the same, and thy	
Ps	104:1	God, thou **a.** very great; thou **a.**	
Ps	110:4	Thou **a.** a priest for ever after the	
Ps	118:21	and **a.** become my salvation.	
Ps	118:28	Thou **a.** my God, I will praise thee;	
Ps	118:28	thou **a.** my God, I will exalt thee.	
Ps	119:12	Blessed **a.** thou, O Lord: teach	
Ps	119:57	Thou **a.** my portion, O Lord:	
Ps	119:68	Thou **a.** good, and doest good:	
Ps	119:114	Thou **a.** my hiding place and my	
Ps	119:137	Righteous **a.** thou, O Lord, and	
Ps	119:151	Thou **a.** near, O Lord: and all thy	
Ps	137:8	Babylon who **a.** to be destroyed;	
Ps	139:3	**a.** acquainted with all my ways.	
Ps	139:8	up into heaven, thou **a.** there:	
Ps	139:8	bed in hell, behold, thou **a.** there:	
Ps	140:6	unto the Lord, Thou **a.** my God:	
Ps	142:5	Thou **a.** my refuge and my portion	
Ps	143:10	for thou **a.** my God: thy spirit is	
Pr	6:2	Thou **a.** snared with the words of	
Pr	6:2	thou **a.** taken with the words of	
Pr	6:3	when thou **a.** come into the hand	
Pr	7:4	Thou **a.** my sister,	
Pr	24:24	the wicked, Thou **a.** righteous;	
Ec	10:17	Blessed **a.** thou, O land, when	
Ca	1:15	Behold, thou **a.** fair, my love;	
Ca	1:15	behold, thou **a.** fair;	
Ca	1:16	Behold, thou **a.** fair, my beloved,	
Ca	2:14	that **a.** in the clefts of the rock,	
Ca	4:1	Behold, thou **a.** fair, my love;	
Ca	4:1	behold, thou **a.** fair;	
Ca	4:7	Thou **a.** all fair, my love;	
Ca	6:4	Thou **a.** beautiful, O my love,	
Ca	7:6	How fair and how pleasant **a.** thou,	
Isa	14:8	saying, Since thou **a.** laid	
Isa	14:10	**A.** thou also become weak as we?	
Isa	14:10	**a.** thou become like unto us?	
Isa	14:12	How **a.** thou fallen from heaven,	
Isa	14:12	how **a.** thou cut down to the ground,	
Isa	14:19	thou **a.** cast out of thy grave like	
Isa	14:31	whole Palestina, **a.** dissolved:	
Isa	22:1	thou **a.** wholly gone up to the	
Isa	22:2	Thou that **a.** full of stirs,	
Isa	25:1	O Lord, thou **a.** my God;	
Isa	26:15	hast increased the nation: thou **a.**	
Isa	37:16	thou **a.** the God, even thou alone,	
Isa	37:20	may know that thou **a.** the Lord,	
Isa	41:8	But thou, Israel, **a.** my servant,	
Isa	41:9	unto thee, Thou **a.** my servant;	
Isa	43:1	thee by thy name; thou **a.** mine.	
Isa	44:17	Deliver me; for thou **a.** my God.	
Isa	44:21	for thou **a.** my servant;	
Isa	44:21	formed thee; thou **a.** my servant:	
Isa	45:15	thou **a.** a God that hidest thyself,	
Isa	47:8	thou that **a.** given to pleasures,	
Isa	47:13	Thou **a.** wearied in the multitude	
Isa	48:4	I knew that thou **a.** obstinate,	
Isa	49:3	Thou **a.** my servant, O Israel,	
Isa	51:9	**A.** thou not it that hath cut Rahab.	
Isa	51:10	**A.** thou not it which hath dried	
Isa	51:12	who **a.** thou that thou shouldest	
Isa	51:16	and say unto Zion, Thou **a.** my	
Isa	57:8	thyself to another than me, and **a.**	
Isa	57:10	Thou **a.** wearied in the greatness	
Isa	63:2	Wherefore **a.** thou red in thine	
Isa	63:16	Doubtless thou **a.** our father,	
Isa	63:16	thou, O Lord, **a.** our father	
Isa	64:5	behold, thou **a.** wroth; for we	
Isa	64:8	But now, O Lord, thou **a.** our	
Jer	2:21	wholly a right seed: how then **a.**	
Jer	2:23	thou **a.** a swift dromedary	
Jer	2:27	Thou **a.** my father;	
Jer	3:4	My father, thou **a.** the guide of	
Jer	3:22	for thou **a.** the Lord our God.	
Jer	4:30	And when thou **a.** spoiled, what	
Jer	10:6	thou **a.** great, and thy name is	
Jer	12:1	Righteous **a.** thou, O Lord, when I	
Jer	12:2	thou **a.** near in their mouth, and	
Jer	14:9	O Lord, **a.** in the midst of us, and	
Jer	14:22	**A.** not thou he, O Lord our God?	
Jer	15:6	saith the Lord, thou **a.** gone	
Jer	17:14	and I shall be saved: for thou **a.**	
Jer	17:17	Be not a terror unto me: thou **a.**	
Jer	20:7	thou **a.** stronger than I, and hast	
Jer	22:6	Thou **a.** Gilead unto me, and the	
Jer	31:18	for thou **a.** the Lord my God.	
Jer	39:17	the hand of men of whom thou **a.**	
Jer	49:12	and **a.** thou he that shall	
Jer	50:24	and thou **a.** also taken, O	
Jer	50:24	was not aware: thou **a.** found,	
Jer	51:20	Thou **a.** my battle ax and	
La	5:22	hast utterly rejected us; thou **a.**	
Eze	3:5	For thou **a.** not sent to a people	
Eze	16:7	and thou **a.** come to excellent	
Eze	16:34	therefore thou **a.** contrary.	
Eze	16:45	Thou **a.** thy mother's daughter	
Eze	16:45	children; and thou **a.** the sister	
Eze	16:54	in that thou **a.** a comfort unto	
Eze	22:4	Thou **a.** become guilty in thy	
Eze	22:4	and **a.** come even unto thy years:	
Eze	22:5	which **a.** infamous and much	
Eze	22:24	Thou **a.** the land that is not	
Eze	23:30	and because thou **a.** polluted	
Eze	26:17	How **a.** thou destroyed, that wast	
Eze	27:3	Tyrus, O thou that **a.** situate	
Eze	27:3	which **a.** a merchant of the	
Eze	28:2	yet thou **a.** a man, and not God.	
Eze	28:3	Behold, thou **a.** wiser than	
Eze	28:14	Thou **a.** the anointed cherub	
Eze	31:2	his multitude; whom **a.** thou	
Eze	31:18	To whom **a.** thou thus like in	
Eze	32:2	Thou **a.** like a young lion of the	
Eze	32:2	and thou **a.** as a whale in the	
Eze	33:32	And lo, thou **a.** unto them as a	
Eze	38:13	**A.** thou come to take a spoil?	
Eze	38:17	**A.** thou he of whom I have	
Eze	40:4	unto thee **a.** thou brought hither:	
Da	2:26	**A.** thou able to make known	383
Da	2:37	Thou, O king, **a.** a king of kings:	
Da	2:38	Thou **a.** this head of gold.	
Da	4:18	but thou **a.** able; for the spirit	
Da	4:22	It is thou, O king, that **a.** grown	
Da	5:13	**A.** thou that Daniel,	
Da	5:13	which **a.** of the children of the	
Da	5:27	Tekel; Thou **a.** weighed in the	
Da	5:27	and **a.** found wanting.	
Da	9:23	for thou **a.** greatly beloved:	
Ho	2:23	Thou **a.** my people; and they	
Ho	2:23	Thou **a.** my God.	
Ob	2	the heathen: thou **a.** greatly	
Ob	5	by night, (how **a.** thou cut off!)	
Jon	1:8	and of what people **a.** thou?	
Jon	4:2	that thou **a.** a gracious God, and	
Mic	2:7	O thou that **a.** named the house	
Na	1:14	make thy grave: for thou **a.** vile.	
Na	3:8	**A.** thou better than populous No,	
Hab	1:12	**A.** thou not from everlasting,	
Hab	1:13	Thou **a.** of purer eyes than to	
Hab	2:16	thou **a.** filled with shame for glory:	
Zec	4:7	Who **a.** thou, O great mountain?	
Mt	2:6	in the land of Juda, **a.** not	*1488*
Mt	5:25	**whiles thou a. in the way with**	*1488*
Mt	6:9	**Our Father which a. in heaven,**	
Mt	8:29	**a.** thou come hither to torment	
Mt	11:3	**A.** thou he that should come, or	*1488*
Mt	11:23	**thou, Capernaum, which a.**	
Mt	14:33	Of a truth thou **a.** the Son of God.	*1488*
Mt	16:14	Some say that thou **a.** John the	
Mt	16:16	Thou **a.** the Christ, the Son of	*1488*
Mt	16:17	**Blessed a. thou, Simon Bar-jona;**	*1488*
Mt	16:18	**That thou a. Peter,**	*1488*
Mt	16:23	**thou a. an offence unto me:**	*1488*
Mt	22:16	we know that thou **a.** true and	*1488*
Mt	25:24	**that thou a. an hard man,**	*1488*
Mt	26:50	him, **Friend, wherefore a. thou**	
Mt	26:73	Surely thou also **a.** one of them;	*1488*
Mt	27:11	**A.** thou the king of the Jews?	*1488*
Mk	1:11	Thou **a.** my beloved Son, in	*1488*
Mk	1:24	**A.** thou come to destroy us?	
Mk	1:24	who thou **a.**, the Holy One of God.	*1488*
Mk	3:11	saying, Thou **a.** the Son of God.	*1488*
Mk	8:29	saith unto him, Thou **a.** the	*1488*
Mk	12:14	we know that thou **a.** true, and	*1488*
Mk	12:34	**Thou a. not far from the**	*1488*
Mk	14:61	**A.** thou the Christ, the Son of the	*1488*
Mk	14:70	Surely thou **a.** one of them:	*1488*
Mk	14:70	one of them: for thou **a.** a Galilaean,	
Mk	15:2	Pilate asked him, **A.** thou the	*1488*
Lu	1:28	Hail, thou that **a.** highly favoured,	
Lu	1:28	blessed **a.** thou among women.	
Lu	1:42	Blessed **a.** thou among women,	
Lu	3:22	Thou **a.** my beloved Son;	*1488*
Lu	4:34	**a.** thou come to destroy us?	
Lu	4:34	I know thee who thou **a.**	*1488*
Lu	4:41	Thou **a.** Christ the Son of God.	*1488*
Lu	7:19, 20	**A.** thou he that should come?	*1488*
Lu	10:15	**Capernaum, which a. exalted to**	
Lu	10:41	**Martha, Martha, thou a. careful**	
Lu	11:2	**Our Father which a. in heaven,**	
Lu	12:58	**thou a. in the way, give diligence**	
Lu	13:12	**thou a. loosed from thine infirmity.**	
Lu	14:8	**a. bidden of any man to a wedding,**	
Lu	14:10	**when thou a. bidden, go and sit**	
Lu	15:31	**Son, thou a. ever with me,**	*1488*
Lu	16:25	**comforted, and thou a. tormented.**	
Lu	19:21	**because thou a. an austere man;**	
Lu	22:32	**and when thou a. converted,**	
Lu	22:58	Thou **a.** also of them. And Peter	*1488*
Lu	22:67	**A.** thou the Christ? tell us.	*1488*
Lu	22:70	**A.** thou then the Son of God?	*1488*
Lu	23:3	**A.** thou the king of the Jews?	*1488*
Lu	23:40	**a.** in the same condemnation?	*1488*
Lu	24:18	**A.** thou only a stranger in	
Joh	1:19	to ask him, Who **a.** thou?	*1488*
Joh	1:21	**A.** thou Elias? And he saith, I	*1488*
Joh	1:21	**A.** thou that prophet? And he	*1488*
Joh	1:22	Who **a.** thou? that we may give	*1488*
Joh	1:42	**Thou a. Simon the son of Jona:**	*1488*
Joh	1:49	thou **a.** the Son of God;	*1488*
Joh	1:49	thou **a.** the king of Israel	*1488*
Joh	3:2	we know that thou **a.** a teacher	
Joh	3:10	**A. thou a master of Israel,**	*1488*
Joh	4:12	**A.** thou greater than our father	*1488*
Joh	4:19	I perceive that thou **a.** a prophet	*1488*
Joh	5:14	**Behold, thou a. made whole:**	
Joh	6:69	that thou **a.** that Christ, the Son	*1488*
Joh	7:52	**A.** thou also of Galilee?	*1488*
Joh	8:25	Who **a.** thou? And Jesus saith	*1488*
Joh	8:48	that thou **a.** a Samaritan, and hast	*1488*
Joh	8:53	**A.** thou greater than our father	*1488*
Joh	8:57	Thou **a.** not yet fifty years old,	*2192*
Joh	9:28	Thou **a.** his disciple; but we are	*1488*
Joh	11:27	I believe that thou **a.** the Christ,	*1488*
Joh	17:21	**as thou, Father, a. in me, and I in**	
Joh	18:17	**A.** not thou also one of this man's	*1488*
Joh	18:25	**A.** not thou also one of his	*1488*
Joh	18:33	**A.** thou the king of the Jews?	*1488*
Joh	18:37	**A.** thou a king then? Jesus	*1488*
Joh	19:9	Whence **a.** thou? But Jesus gave	*1488*
Joh	19:12	thou **a.** not Caesar's friend:	*1488*
Joh	21:12	Who **a.** thou? knowing that it was	*1488*
Ac	4:24	Lord, thou **a.** God, which hast	
Ac	8:23	thou **a.** in the gall of bitterness,	
Ac	9:5	Who **a.** thou, Lord? And the Lord	*1488*
Ac	10:33	hast well done that thou **a.** come	
Ac	12:15	Thou **a.** mad. But she constantly	
Ac	13:33	Thou **a.** my Son, this day have I	*1488*
Ac	17:29	graven by **a.** and man's device	*5078*
Ac	21:22	they will hear that thou **a.** come	
Ac	21:38	**A.** not thou that Egyptian, which	*1488*
Ac	22:8	Who **a.** thou, Lord? And he said	*1488*
Ac	22:27	Tell me, **a.** thou a Roman?	*1488*
Ac	26:1	said unto Paul, Thou **a.** permitted	
Ac	26:15	Who **a.** thou, Lord? And he said,	*1488*
Ac	26:24	Paul, thou **a.** beside thyself;	
Ro	2:1	Therefore thou **a.** inexcusable,	*1488*
Ro	2:1	whosoever thou **a.** that judgest:	*1488*
Ro	2:17	Behold, thou **a.** called a Jew,	
Ro	2:19	And **a.** confident	
Ro	2:19	that thou thyself **a.** a guide	
Ro	3:4	overcome when thou **a.** judged.	
Ro	9:20	who **a.** thou that repliest against	*1488*
Ro	14:4	Who **a.** thou that judgest another	*1488*
1Co	7:21	**A.** thou called being a servant?	
1Co	7:27	**A.** thou bound unto a wife?	
1Co	7:27	**A.** thou loosed from a wife?	
Ga	4:7	thou **a.** no more a servant,	*1488*
1Ti	6:12	whereunto thou **a.** also called,	
Heb	1:5	Thou **a.** my Son, this day have I	*1488*
Heb	1:12	but thou **a.** the same, and thy	*1488*
Heb	2:6	man that thou **a.** mindful of him?	

Heb 5:5 Thou **a.** my Son, to day have I.......... *1488*
Heb 5:6 Thou **a.** a priest for ever after the............
Heb 7:17, 21 Thou **a.** a priest for ever after.........
Heb 12:5 nor faint when thou **a.** rebuked of him:......
Jas 2:11 **a.** become a transgressor of the..............
Jas 4:11 **a.** not a doer of the law, but a........... *1488*
Jas 4:12 Who **a.** thou that judgest another?...... *1488*
Re 2:5 **from whence thou a. fallen**........... *1488*
Re 2:9 **and poverty, (but thou a. rich)**...... *1488*
Re 3:1 **name that thou livest and a. dead.** . *1488*
Re 3:15 **that thou a. neither cold nor hot:**.. *1488*
Re 3:16 **So then because thou a. lukewarm,** *1488*
Re 3:17 **knowest not that thou a. wretched,** *1488*
Re 4:11 Thou **a.** worthy, O Lord, to receive *1488*
Re 5:9 Thou **a.** worthy to take the book, ... *1488*
Re 11:17 O Lord God Almighty which **a.**, ... *5607*
Re 11:17 and wast, and **a.** to come; ....
Re 15:4 thou only **a.** holy: for all nations..............
Re 16:5 Thou **a.** righteous, O Lord,............... *1488*
Re 16:5 which **a.**, and wast, and *5607*

ARTAXERXES (ar-tax-erx'-ees) See also ARTAXERXES'.
Ezr 4:7 in the days of **A.**, wrote Bishlam, ... 783
Ezr 4:7 unto **A.** king of Persia; and the............ 783
Ezr 4:8 to **A.** the king in this sort: 783
Ezr 4:11 they sent unto him, even unto **A.** 783
Ezr 6:14 and Darius, and **A.** king of Persia. 783
Ezr 7:1 in the reign of **A.** king of Persia, ... 783
Ezr 7:7 in the seventh year of **A.** the king. 783
Ezr 7:11 that the king **A.** gave unto Ezra 783
Ezr 7:12 **A.**, king of kings, unto Ezra the 783
Ezr 7:21 And I, even I **A.** the king,.................. 783
Ezr 8:1 in the reign of **A.**, the king,................ 783
Ne 2:1 in the twentieth year of **A.** the king, ... 783
Ne 5:14 the two and thirtieth year of **A.**........... 783
Ne 13:6 in the two and thirtieth year of **A.** 783

ARTAXERXES' (ar-tax-erx'-eez)
Ezr 4:23 the copy of king **A.** letter was read...... 783

ARTEMAS (ar'-te-mas)
Tit 3:12 When I shall send **A.** unto thee. *734*

ARTIFICER See also ARTIFICERS.
Ge 4:22 an instructer of every **a.**.................... 2794
Isa 3:3 and the cunning **a.**, and the............... 2796

ARTIFICERS
1Ch 29:5 by the hands of **a.** 2796
2Ch 34:11 Even to the **a.** and builders................ 2796

ARTILLERY
1Sa 20:40 Jonathan gave his **a.** unto his lad, ... 3627

ARTS
Ac 19:19 them also which used curious **a.**.......... *4021*

ARUBOTH (ar'-u-both)
1Ki 4:10 The son of Hesed, in **A.**; to him........... 700

ARUMAH (a-ru'-mah)
Jg 9:41 And Abimelech dwelt at **A.**................. 725

ARVAD (ar'-vad) See also ARVADITE.
Eze 27:8 The inhabitants of Zidon and **A.**.......... 719
Eze 27:11 The men of **A.** with thine army 719

ARVADITE (ar'-vad-ite)
Ge 10:18 And the **A.**, and the Zemarite. 721
1Ch 1:16 And the **A.**, and the Zemarite, ... 721

ARZA (ar'-zah)
1Ki 16:9 himself drunk in the house of **A.**........... 777

AS See in the APPENDIX; also FORASMUCH; INASMUCH.

ASA (a'-sah) See also ASA'S.
1Ki 15:8 and **A.** his son reigned in his stead....... 609
1Ki 15:9 of Isr el reigned **A.** over Judah. 609
1Ki 15:11 And **A.** did that which was right 609
1Ki 15:13 **A.** destroyed her idol, and burnt it........ 609
1Ki 15:16 was war between **A.** and Baasha 609
1Ki 15:17 any to go out or come in to **A.**............. 609
1Ki 15:18 **A.** took all the silver and the gold......... 609
1Ki 15:18 king **A.** sent them to Ben-hadad, ... 609
1Ki 15:20 Ben-hadad hearkened unto king **A.**, ... 609
1Ki 15:22 Then king **A.** made a proclamation 609
1Ki 15:22 and king **A.** built with them Geba.......... 609
1Ki 15:23 The rest of all the acts of **A.**, ... 609
1Ki 15:24 And **A.** slept with his fathers, ... 609
1Ki 15:25 over Israel in the second year of **A.** 609
1Ki 15:28 Even in the third year of **A.** king of 609
1Ki 15:32 was war between **A.** and Baasha 609
1Ki 15:33 In the third year of **A.** king of.............. 609
1Ki 16:8 In the twenty and sixth year of **A.** 609
1Ki 16:10, 15 twenty and seventh year of **A.**......... 609
1Ki 16:23 In the thirty and first year of **A.**.......... 609
1Ki 16:29 in the thirty and eighth year of **A.**......... 609
1Ki 22:41 the son of **A.** began to reign.............. 609
1Ki 22:43 he walked in all the ways of **A.** his....... 609
1Ki 22:46 in the days of his father **A.**,................. 609
1Ch 3:10 Abia his son, **A.** his son,...................... 609
1Ch 9:16 and Berechiah, the son of **A.**, ... 609
2Ch 14:1 and **A.** his son reigned in his stead....... 609
2Ch 14:2 **A.** did that which was good and........... 609
2Ch 14:8 **A.** had an army of men that bare......... 609
2Ch 14:10 Then **A.** went out against him, ... 609
2Ch 14:11 **A.** cried unto the Lord his God, ... 609
2Ch 14:12 smote the Ethiopians before **A.**, ... 609
2Ch 14:13 And **A.** and the people that were........... 609
2Ch 15:2 And he went out to meet **A.**, and 609
2Ch 15:2 Hear ye me, **A.**, and all Judah............. 609
2Ch 15:8 when **A.** heard these words, and 609
2Ch 15:10 fifteenth year of the reign of **A.**............ 609
2Ch 15:16 Maachah the mother of **A.** the king,....... 609
2Ch 15:16 **A.** cut down her idol, and stamped......... 609
2Ch 15:17 of **A.** was perfect all his days.............. 609
2Ch 15:19 year of the reign of **A.**. 609
2Ch 16:1 year of the reign of **A.**, Baasha 609
2Ch 16:1 or come in to **A.** king of Judah. 609
2Ch 16:2 Then **A.** brought out silver and gold...... 609
2Ch 16:4 Ben-hadad hearkened unto king **A.**, ... 609
2Ch 16:6 Then **A.** the king took all Judah; 609
2Ch 16:7 time Hanani the seer came to **A.** 609
2Ch 16:10 Then **A.** was wroth with the seer, ... 609
2Ch 16:10 **A.** oppressed some of the people........... 609
2Ch 16:11 the acts of **A.**, first and last, lo, ... 609
2Ch 16:12 **A.** in the thirty and ninth year............. 609
2Ch 16:13 **A.** slept with his fathers, and died........ 609
2Ch 17:2 which **A.** his father had taken............... 609
2Ch 20:32 walked in the way of **A.** his father, ... 609
2Ch 21:12 the ways of **A.** king of Judah,............... 609
Jer 41:9 which **A.** the king had made for........... 609
Mt 1:7 and Abia begat **A.**;............................. *760*
Mt 1:8 and **A.** begat Josaphat;......................... *760*

ASAHEL (as'-a-hel)
2Sa 2:18 there, Joab, Abishai, and **A.**.............. 6214
2Sa 2:18 **A.** was as light of foot as a wild.......... 6214
2Sa 2:19 And **A.** pursued after Abner; and 6214
2Sa 2:20 him, and said, Art thou **A.**?............... 6214
2Sa 2:21 But **A.** would not turn aside from....... 6214
2Sa 2:22 And Abner said again to **A.**, Turn....... 6214
2Sa 2:23 where **A.** fell down and died............. 6214
2Sa 2:30 servants nineteen men and **A.**. 6214
2Sa 2:32 And they took up **A.**, and buried......... 6214
2Sa 3:27 for the blood of **A.** his brother........... 6214
2Sa 3:30 slain their brother **A.** at Gibeon 6214
2Sa 23:24 **A.** the brother of Joab was one........... 6214
1Ch 2:16 Abishai, and Joab, and **A.**, three.......... 6214
1Ch 11:26 were, **A.** the brother of Joab,............... 6214
1Ch 27:7 for the fourth month, was **A.** the 6214
2Ch 17:8 and Zebadiah, and **A.**, and.................. 6214
2Ch 31:13 and Nahath, and **A.**, and Jerimoth,...... 6214
Ezr 10:15 Only Jonathan the son of **A.**, and......... 6214

ASAHIAH (as-a-hi'-ah) See also ASAIAH.
2Ki 22:12 and **A.** a servant of the king's,........... 6222
2Ki 22:14 and **A.**, went unto Huldah the............ 6222

ASAIAH (as-a'-yah) See also ASAHIAH.
1Ch 4:36 and **A.**, and Adiel, and Jesimiel, ... 6222
1Ch 6:30 Haggiah his son, **A.** his son............... 6222
1Ch 9:5 **A.** the first born, and his sons. 6222
1Ch 15:6 sons of Merari; **A.** the chief, ... 6222
1Ch 15:11 Uriel, **A.**, and Joel, Shemaiah, ... 6222
2Ch 34:20 the scribe, and **A.** a servant of 6222

ASAPH (a'-saf) See also ASAPH'S.
2Ki 18:18 Joah the son of **A.** the recorder........... 623
2Ki 18:37 the son of **A.** the recorder, to............. 623
1Ch 6:39 And his brother **A.**, who stood on.......... 623
1Ch 6:39 right hand, even **A.** the son of 623
1Ch 9:15 the son of Zichri, the son of **A.**; 623
1Ch 15:17 **A.** the son of Berechiah;.................... 623
1Ch 15:19 singers, Heman, **A.**, and Ethan, ... 623
1Ch 16:5 **A.** the chief, and next to him............... 623
1Ch 16:5 **A.** made a sound with cymbals;............ 623
1Ch 16:7 the hand of **A.** and his brethren............ 623
1Ch 16:37 **A.** and his brethren, to minister 623
1Ch 25:1 to the service of the sons of **A.**,............ 623
1Ch 25:2 Of the sons of **A.**; Zaccur, and............. 623
1Ch 25:2 the sons of **A.** under the...................... 623
1Ch 25:2 under the hands of **A.**, ... 623
1Ch 25:6 according to the king's order to **A.**,...... 623
1Ch 25:9 the first lot came forth for **A.**............... 623
1Ch 26:1 son of Kore, of the sons of **A.**. 623
2Ch 5:12 all of them of **A.**, of Heman,................ 623
2Ch 20:14 a Levite of the sons of **A.**, came 623
2Ch 29:13 of the sons of **A.**; Zechariah, and......... 623
2Ch 29:30 words of David, and of **A.** the seer. 623
2Ch 35:15 the sons of **A.** were in their place,........ 623
2Ch 35:15 commandment of David, and **A.**, ... 623
Ezr 2:41 the children of **A.**, an hundred............ 623
Ezr 3:10 the sons of **A.** with cymbals,................ 623
Ne 2:8 **A.** the keeper of the king's forest, ... 623
Ne 7:44 The singers: the children of **A.**............. 623
Ne 11:17 the son of **A.**, was the principal............ 623
Ne 11:22 Of the sons of **A.**, the singers were...... 623
Ne 12:35 the son of Zaccur, the son of **A.**........... 623
Ne 12:46 the days of David and **A.** of old............ 623
Ps 50:*title* A Psalm of **A.** The mighty God, ... 623
Ps 73:*title* A Psalm of **A.** Truly God is good.......... 623
Ps 74:*title* Maschil of **A.** O God, why hast 623
Ps 75:*title* A Psalm or Song of **A.** Unto thee, ... 623
Ps 76:*title* A Psalm or Song of **A.** In Judah........... 623
Ps 77:*title* A Psalm of **A.** I cried unto God........... 623
Ps 78:*title* Maschil of **A.** Give ear, O my.............. 623
Ps 79:*title* A Psalm of **A.** O God, the.................... 623
Ps 80:*title* A Psalm of **A.** Give ear, O................... 623
Ps 81:*title* A Psalm of **A.** Sing aloud 623
Ps 82:*title* A Psalm of **A.** God standeth in............. 623
Ps 83:*title* A Song or Psalm of **A.**. Keep not 623
Isa 36:22 Joah, the son of **A.**, the recorder,........... 623

ASAPH'S (a'-safs)
Isa 36:3 the scribe, and Joah, **A.** son, ... 623

ASAREEL (a-sar'e-el)
1Ch 4:16 Ziph, and Ziphah, Tiria, and **A.**............ 840

ASARELAH (as-a-re'-lah) See also JESHARELAH.
1Ch 25:2 Joseph, and Nethaniah. and **A.**. 841

ASA'S (a'-sahz)
1Ki 15:14 nevertheless **A.** heart was perfect........ 609

ASCEND See also ASCENDED; ASCENDETH; ASCENDING.
Jos 6:5 and the people shall **a.** up.................. 5927
Ps 24:3 Who shall **a.** into the hill of the.......... 5927
Ps 135:7 He causeth the vapours to **a.** 5927
Ps 139:8 If I **a.** up into heaven,...................... 5927
Isa 14:13 I will **a.** into heaven, ... 5927
Isa 14:14 I will **a.** above the heights of the........ 5927
Jer 10:13 and he causeth the vapours to **a.** 5927
Jer 51:16 and he causeth the vapours to **a.** 5927
Eze 38:9 Thou shalt **a.** and come like a............ 5927
Joh 6:62 **ye shall see the Son of man a. up**... *305*
Joh 20:17 **I a. unto my Father, and your**........ *305*
Ro 10:6 Who shall **a.** into heaven?.................. *305*
Re 17:8 shall **a.** out of the bottomless pit, ... *305*

ASCENDED
Ex 19:18 and the smoke thereof **a.**.................... 5927
Nu 13:22 And they **a.** by the south,................. 5927
Jos 8:20 the smoke of the city **a.** up.............. 5927
Jos 8:21 the smoke of the city **a.**,.................... 5927
Jos 10:7 So Joshua **a.** from Gilgal, ... 5927
Jos 15:3 and **a.** up on the south side............... 5927
Jg 13:20 that the angel of the Lord **a.** in.......... 5927
Jg 20:40 flame of the city **a.** up to heaven,....... 5927
Ps 68:18 Thou hast **a.** on high, ... 5927
Pr 30:4 Who hath **a.** up into heaven, ... 5927
Joh 3:13 **no man hath a. up to heaven**,........... *305*
Joh 20:17 **for I am not yet a. to my Father:**... *305*
Ac 2:34 David is not **a.** into the heavens: *305*
Ac 25:1 **a.** from Caesarea to Jerusalem *305*
Eph 4:8 When he **a.** up on high, ... *305*
Eph 4:9 (Now that he **a.**, what is it *305*
Eph 4:10 is the same also that **a.** up *305*
Re 8:4 **a.** up before God out of the angel's...... *305*
Re 11:12 they **a.** up to heaven in a cloud; *305*

ASCENDETH
Re 11:7 that **a.** out of the bottomless pit........... *305*
Re 14:11 their torment **a.** up for ever *305*

ASCENDING
Ge 28:12 angels of God **a.** and descending 5927
1Sa 28:13 I saw gods **a.** out of the earth. 5927
Lu 19:28 went before, **a.** up to Jerusalem. *305*
Joh 1:51 **the angels of God a. and**................ *305*
Re 7:2 another angel **a.** from the east, ... *305*

ASCENT
Nu 34:4 to the **a.** of Akbrabim, ... 4608

2S 15:30 up by the **a.** of mount Olivet, 4608
1Ki 10:5 and his **a.** by which he went up 5930
2Ch 9:4 and his **a.** by which he went up 5944

ASCRIBE See also ASCRIBED.
De 32:3 **a.** ye greatness unto our God. 3051
Job 36:3 **a.** righteousness to my Maker. 5414
Ps 68:34 **A.** ye strength unto God: 5414

ASCRIBED
1Sa 18:8 they have **a.** unto David 5414
1Sa 18:8 to me they have **a.** but thousands: 5414

ASENATH (as'-e-nath)
Ge 41:45 and he gave him to wife **A.** the 621
Ge 41:50 **A.** the daughter of Poti-pherah 621
Ge 46:20 Manasseh and Ephraim, which **A.** 621

ASER (a'-sur) See also ASHER.
Lu 2:36 of the tribe of **A.** *768*
Re 7:6 Of the tribe of **A.** were sealed *768*

ASH
Isa 44:14 he planteth an **a.**, and the rain 766

ASHAMED
Ge 2:25 and were not **a.**. 954
Nu 12:14 should she not be **a.** seven days? 3637
Jg 3:25 they tarried till they were **a.** 954
2Sa 10:5 because the men were greatly **a.** 3637
2Sa 19:3 as people being **a.** steal away 3637
2Ki 2:17 they urged him till he was **a.**, 954
2Ki 8:11 until he was **a.**: and the man of 954
1Ch 19:5 the men were greatly **a.** 3637
2Ch 30:15 and the Levites were **a.**, 3637
Ezr 8:22 I was **a.** to require of the king 954
Ezr 9:6 I am **a.** and blush to lift up my face 954
Job 6:20 they came thither, and were **a.**. 2659
Job 11:3 shall no man make thee **a.**? 3637
Job 19:3 ye are not **a.** that ye make 954
Ps 6:10 Let all mine enemies be **a.** 954
Ps 6:10 them return and be **a.** suddenly. 954
Ps 25:2 I trust in thee: let me not be **a.**, 954
Ps 25:3 let none that wait on thee be **a.** 954
Ps 25:3 let them be **a.** which trangress 954
Ps 25:20 let me not be **a.**; for I put 954
Ps 31:1 let me never be **a.** 954
Ps 31:17 Let me not be **a.**, O Lord; 954
Ps 31:17 let the wicked be **a.**, 954
Ps 34:5 their faces were not **a.** 2659
Ps 35:26 be **a.** and brought to confusion 954
Ps 37:19 shall not be **a.** in the evil time: 954
Ps 40:14 Let them be **a.** and confounded 954
Ps 69:6 them that wait on thee,...be **a.** 954
Ps 70:2 Let them be **a.** and confounded 954
Ps 74:21 let not the oppressed return **a.** 3637
Ps 86:17 may see it, and be **a.** 954
Ps 109:28 them be **a.**; but let thy servant 954
Ps 119:6 Then shall I not be **a.**, 954
Ps 119:46 and will not be **a.** 954
Ps 119:78 Let the proud be **a.**; 954
Ps 119:80 that I be not **a.**. 954
Ps 119:116 let me not be **a.** of my hope. 954
Ps 127:5 they shall not be **a.**, 954
Pr 12:4 she that maketh **a.** is as rottenness 954
Isa 1:29 For they shall be **a.** of the oaks 954
Isa 20:5 shall be afraid and **a.** of Ethiopia 954
Isa 23:4 Be thou **a.**, O Zidon: 954
Isa 24:23 and the sun **a.**, 954
Isa 26:11 be **a.** for their envy at the people; 954
Isa 29:22 Jacob shall not now be **a.**, 954
Isa 30:5 They were all **a.** of a people 954
Isa 33:9 Lebanon is **a.** and hewn down: 2659
Isa 41:11 shall be **a.** and confounded: 954
Isa 42:17 they shall be greatly **a.**, 954
Isa 44:9 that they may be **a.** 954
Isa 44:11 all his fellows shall be **a.** 954
Isa 44:11 they shall be **a.** together. 954
Isa 45:16 shall be **a.**, and also confounded, 954
Isa 45:17 shall not be **a.** nor confounded 954
Isa 45:24 incensed against him shall be **a.** 954
Isa 49:23 shall not be **a.** that wait for me. 954
Isa 50:7 that I shall not be **a.**. 954
Isa 54:4 for thou shalt not be **a.** 954
Isa 65:13 but ye shall be **a.** 954
Isa 66:5 they shall be **a.**. 954
Jer 2:26 the thief is **a.** when he is found. 1322
Jer 2:26 so is the house of Israel **a.**; 954
Jer 2:36 thou also shalt be **a.** of Egypt. 954
Jer 2:36 as thou wast **a.** of Assyria. 954
Jer 3:3 thou refusedst to be **a.**. 3637
Jer 6:15 Were they **a.** when they had 954
Jer 6:15 they were not at all **a.**, 954
Jer 8:9 The wise men are **a.**, 954
Jer 8:12 Were they **a.** when they 954
Jer 8:12 at all **a.**, neither could they blush: 954
Jer 12:13 they shall be **a.** of your enemies 954
Jer 14:3 they were **a.** and confounded, 954
Jer 14:4 the plowmen were **a.**, 954
Jer 15:9 hath been **a.** and confounded, 954
Jer 17:13 all that forsake thee shall be **a.**, 954
Jer 20:11 they shall be greatly **a.**; 954
Jer 22:22 surely then shalt thou be **a.** 954
Jer 31:19 I was **a.**, yea, even confounded 954
Jer 48:13 And Moab shall be **a.** of Chemosh, 954
Jer 48:13 house of Israel was **a.** of Beth-el 954
Jer 50:12 she that bare you shall be **a.** 2659
Eze 16:27 of the Philistines, which are **a.** 3637
Eze 16:61 remember thy ways, and be **a.**, 3637
Eze 32:30 they are **a.** of their might; 954
Eze 36:32 be **a.** and confounded for your own 954
Eze 43:10 they may be **a.** of their iniquities: 3637
Eze 43:11 they be **a.** of all that 3637
Ho 4:19 and they shall be **a.** 954
Ho 10:6 Israel shall be **a.** of his own counsel. 954
Joe 1:11 Be ye **a.**, O ye husbandmen; 954
Joe 2:26, 27 My people shall never be **a.**. 954
Mic 3:7 the seers be **a.**, and the diviners 954
Zep 3:11 In that day shalt thou not be **a.** 954
Zec 9:5 her expectation shall be **a.**; 954
Zec 13:4 the prophets shall be **a.** every one 954
Mk 8:38 **therefore shall be a. of me** *1870*
Mk 8:38 **shall the Son of man be a.,** *1870*
Lu 9:26 **whosoever shall be a. of me** *1870*
Lu 9:26 **of him shall the Son of man be a.,** *1870*
Lu 13:17 all his adversaries were **a.** *2617*
Lu 16:3 **I cannot dig; to beg I am a.** *153*
Ro 1:16 am not **a.** of the gospel of Christ: *1870*
Ro 5:5 hope maketh not **a.**; because *2617*
Ro 6:21 whereof ye are now **a.**? *1870*
Ro 9:33 believeth on him shall not be **a.**. *2617*
Ro 10:11 on him shall not be **a.** *2617*
2Co 7:14 I am not **a.**; *2617*
2Co 9:4 we...should be **a.** in this same *2617*
2Co 10:8 destruction, I should not be **a.** *153*
Php 1:20 in nothing I shall be **a.**, *153*
2Th 3:14 with him, that he may be **a.** *1788*
2Ti 1:8 thou therefore **a.** of the testimony *1870*
2Ti 1:12 nevertheless I am not **a.** *1870*
2Ti 1:16 and was not **a.** of my chain: *1870*
2Ti 2:15 workman that needeth not to be **a.**, *422*
Tit 2:8 the contrary part may be **a.**, *1788*
Heb 2:11 is not **a.** to call them brethren, *1870*
Heb 11:16 is not **a.** to be called their God; *1870*
1Pe 3:16 as of evildoers, they may be **a.** *2617*
1Pe 4:16 a Christian, let him not be **a.**; *153*
1Jo 2:28 not be **a.** before him. *153*

ASHAN (a'-shan) See also COR-ASHAN.
Jos 15:42 Libnah, and Ether, and **A.**, 6228
Jos 19:7 Ain, Remmon, and Ether, and **A.**; 6228
1Ch 4:32 Rimmon, and Tochen, and **A.**, five 6228
1Ch 6:59 And **A.** with her suburbs, and 6228

ASHBEA (ash'-be-ah)
1Ch 4:21 of the house of **A.**, 791

ASHBEL (ash'-bel) See also ASHBELITES.
Ge 46:21 Becher, and **A.**, Gera, and Naaman, 788
Nu 26:38 of **A.**, the family of the Ashbelites: 788
1Ch 8:1 Bela his firstborn, **A.** the second, 788

ASHBELITES (ash'-bel-ites)
Nu 26:38 of Ashbel, the family of the **A.**; 789

ASHCHENAZ (ash'-ke-naz) See also ASHKENAZ.
1Ch 1:6 sons of Gomer; **A.**, and Riphath, 813
Jer 51:27 kingdoms of Ararat, Minni, and **A.**; 813

ASHDOD (ash'-dod) See also ASHDODITES; AZOTUS.
Jos 11:22 only in Gaza, in Gath, and in **A.**, 795
Jos 15:46 lay near **A.**, with their villages: 795
Jos 15:47 **A.** with her towns and her villages; 795
1Sa 5:1 brought it from Eben-ezer unto **A.**. 795
1Sa 5:3 of **A.** rose early on the morrow. 795
1Sa 5:5 the threshold of Dagon in **A.** 795
1Sa 5:6 was heavy upon them of **A.**, and 795
1Sa 5:6 even **A.** and the coasts thereof. 795
1Sa 5:7 when the men of **A.** saw that it 795
1Sa 6:17 for **A.** one, for Gaza one, for 795
2Ch 26:6 of **A.**, and built cities about **A.**, 795
Ne 13:23 Jews that had married wives of **A.**, 795
Ne 13:24 spake half in the speech of **A.**. 795
Isa 20:1 year that Tartan came unto **A.**, 795
Isa 20:1 and fought against **A.**, and took it; 795
Jer 25:20 and Ekron, and the remnant of **A.**, 795
Am 1:8 cut off the inhabitant from **A.**, 795
Am 3:9 Publish in the palaces at **A.**, 795
Zep 2:4 shall drive out **A.** at the noonday, 795
Zec 9:6 And a bastard shall dwell in **A.** 795

ASHDODITES (ash'-dod-ites) See also ASHDOTHITES.
Ne 4:7 And the **A.**, heard that the walls 796

ASHDOTH See ASHDOTH-PISGAH.

ASHDOTHITES (ash'-doth-ites) See also ASHDODITES.
Jos 13:3 **A.**, the Eshkalonites, the Gittites, 796

ASHDOTH-PISGAH (ash''-doth-piz'-gah)
De 3:17 salt sea, under **A.** eastward. 798,6449
Jos 12:3 from the south, under **A.** 798,6449
Jos 13:20 And Beth-peor, and **A.**, and 798,6449

ASHER (ash'-ur) See also ASER; ASHERITES.
Ge 30:13 and she called his name **A.** 836
Ge 35:26 Leah's handmaid; Gad, and **A.** 836
Ge 46:17 sons of **A.**; Jimnah, and Ishuah, 836
Ge 49:20 Out of **A.** his bread shall be fat, 836
Ex 1:4 Dan and Naphtali, Gad, and **A.** 836
Nu 1:13 Of **A.**; Pagiel the son of Ocran. 836
Nu 1:40 children of **A.**, by their generations, 836
Nu 1:41 of the tribe of **A.**, were forty and 836
Nu 2:27 by him shall be the tribe of **A.** 836
Nu 2:27 captain of the children of **A.** shall 836
Nu 7:72 prince of the children of **A.**, offered: 836
Nu 10:26 tribe of the children of **A.** was 836
Nu 13:13 of **A.**, Sethur the son of Michael. 836
Nu 26:44 children of **A.** after their families: 836
Nu 26:46 of the daughter of **A.** was Sarah. 836
Nu 26:47 are the families of the sons of **A.** 836
Nu 34:27 of **A.**, Ahihud the son of Shelomi, 836
De 27:13 Reuben, Gad, and **A.**, and Zebulun, 836
De 33:24 of **A.** he said, Let **A.** be blessed 836
Jos 17:7 coast of Manasseh was from **A.** to 836
Jos 17:10 met together in **A.** on the north, 836
Jos 17:11 Manasseh had in Issachar and in **A.** 836
Jos 19:24 tribe of the children of **A.** according 836
Jos 19:31 of the tribe of the children of **A.** 836
Jos 19:34 reacheth to **A.** on the west side, 836
Jos 21:6 out of the tribe of **A.**, and out of 836
Jos 21:30 of **A.**, Mishal with her suburbs, 836
Jg 1:31 did **A.** drive out the inhabitants of 836
Jg 5:17 **A.** continued on the sea shore, 836
Jg 6:35 and he sent messengers unto **A.**, 836
Jg 7:23 of **A.**, and out of all Manasseh, 836
1Ki 4:16 son of Hushai was in **A.** and in 836
1Ch 2:2 Benjamin, Naphtali, Gad, and **A.** 836
1Ch 6:62 out of the tribe of A., and out of 836
1Ch 6:74 of **A.**; Mashal with her suburbs, 836
1Ch 7:30 sons of **A.**; Imnah, and Isuah, 836
1Ch 7:40 All these were the children of **A.**, 836
1Ch 12:36 of **A.**, such as went forth to battle, 836
2Ch 30:11 divers of **A.**, and Manasseh 836
Eze 48:2 the west side, a portion for **A.**, 836
Eze 48:3 border of **A.**, from the east side, 836
Eze 48:34 gate of **A.**, one gate of Naphtali. 836

ASHERITES (ash'-ur-ites)
Jg 1:32 **A.** dwelt among the Canaanites, 843

ASHES
Ge 18:27 which am but dust and **a.** 665
Ex 9:8 you handfuls of **a.** of the furnace, 6368
Ex 9:10 And they took **a.** of the furnace, 6368
Ex 27:3 pans to receive his **a.**, 1878
Le 1:16 by the place of the **a.** 1880
Le 4:12 where the **a.** are poured out, and 1880
Le 4:12 where the **a.** are poured out shall 1880
Le 6:10 take up the **a.** 1880
Le 6:11 carry forth the **a.** 1880
Nu 4:13 And they shall take away the **a.** 1878
Nu 19:9 the **a.** of the heifer, 665
Nu 19:10 he that gathereth the **a.** of 665
Nu 19:17 they shall take of the **a.** of the 6083
2Sa 13:19 Tamar put **a.** on her head, 665
1Ki 13:3 the **a.** that are upon it 1880
1Ki 13:5 the **a.** poured out from the altar, 1880

1Ki 20:38 disguised himself with **a.** upon 665
1Ki 20:41 took the **a.** away from his face; 665
2Ki 23:4 the **a.** of them unto Beth-el 6083
Es 4:1 put on sackcloth with **a.**, 665
Es 4:3 many lay in sackcloth and **a.**. 665
Job 2:8 he sat down among the **a.** 665
Job 13:12 remembrances are like unto **a.**. 665
Job 30:19 I am become like dust and **a.**, 665
Job 42:6 repent in dust and **a.** 665
Ps 102:9 For I have eaten **a.** like bread, 665
Ps 147:16 he scattereth the hoarfrost like **a.**, 665
Isa 44:20 He feedeth on **a.** 665
Isa 58:5 spread sackcloth and **a.** under him? 665
Isa 61:3 to give unto them beauty for **a.**, 665
Jer 6:26 wallow thyself in **a.** 665
Jer 25:34 and wallow yourselves in the **a.**, ye
Jer 31:40 and of the **a.**, and all the fields 1880
La 3:16 he hath covered me with **a.** 665
Eze 27:30 wallow themselves in the **a.** 665
Eze 28:18 I will bring thee to **a.**, 665
Da 9:3 with fasting, and sackcloth, and **a.** 665
Jon 3:6 and sat in **a.**. 665
Mal 4:3 for they shall be **a.** 665
Mt 11:21 **long ago in sackcloth and a..** 4700
Lu 10:13 **sitting in sackcloth and a..** 4700
Heb 9:13 the **a.** of an heifer sprinkling the 4700
2Pe 2:6 Sodom and Gomorrha into **a.** 5077

ASHIMA (ash'-im-ah)
2Ki 17:30 and the men of Hamath made **A.** 807

ASHKELON (ash'-ke-lon) See also ASKELON; ESHKALONITES.
Jg 14:19 and he went down to **A.**, and slew 831
Jer 25:20 **A.** and Azzah, and Ekron. 831
Jer 47:5 **A.** is cut off with the remnant 831
Jer 47:7 **A.**, and against the sea shore? 831
Am 1:8 that holdeth the sceptre from **A.**, 831
Zep 2:4 Gaza shall be forsaken, and **A.** 831
Zep 2:7 houses of **A.** shall they lie down 831
Zec 9:5 **A.** shall see it, and fear; 831
Zec 9:5 and **A.** shall not be inhabited. 831

ASHKENAZ (ash'-ke-naz) See also ASCHENAZ.
Ge 10:3 sons of Gomer; **A.**, and Riphath, 813

ASHNAH (ash'-nah)
Jos 15:33 Eshtaol, and Zoreah, and **A.**, 823
Jos 15:43 Jiphtah, and **A.**, and Nezib, 823

ASHPENAZ (ash'-pe-naz)
Da 1:3 the king spake unto **A.** the master 828

ASHRIEL (ash'-re-el) See also ASRIEL.
1Ch 7:14 of Manasseh; **A.**, whom she bare: 845

ASHTAROTH (ash'-ta-roth) See also ASHTERATHITE; ASHTEROTH; ASTORETH; ASTAROTH; BEESHTERAH.
Jos 9:10 king of Bashan, which was at **A.**, 6252
Jos 12:4 that dwelt at **A.** and at Edrei, 6252
Jos 13:12 Og in Bashan, which reigned in **A.** 6252
Jos 13:31 half Gilead, and **A.**, and Edrei, 6252
Jg 2:13 the Lord, and served Baal and **A.** 6252
Jg 10:6 served Baalim, and **A.**, and the 6252
1Sa 7:3 put away the strange gods and **A.** 6252
1Sa 7:4 Israel did put away Baalim and **A.**, 6252
1Sa 12:10 and have served Baalim and **A.**: 6252
1Sa 31:10 put his armour in the house of **A.**; 6252
1Ch 6:71 and **A.** with her suburbs: 6252

ASHTERATHITE (ash'-ter-a-thite)
1Ch 11:44 Uzzia the **A.**, Shama and Jehiel 6254

ASHTEROTH (ash'-te-roth) See also ASHTAROTH.
Ge 14:5 and smote the Rephaims in **A.** 6255

ASHTEROTH-KARNAIM See ASHTEROTH and KARNAIM.

ASHTORETH (ash'-to-reth) See also ASHTAROTH.
1Ki 11:5 Solomon went after **A.** the 6252
1Ki 11:33 **A.** the goddess of the Sidonians, 6252
2Ki 23:13 for **A.** the abomination of the 6252

ASHUR (ash'-ur) See also ASHURITES; ASHUR; ASSUR; ASSYRIA.
1Ch 2:24 Hezron's wife bare him **A.** the 804
1Ch 4:5 **A.** the father of Tekoa had two 804

ASHURITES (ash'-ur-ites) See also ASSHURIM.
2Sa 2:9 over the **A.**, and over Jezreel. 843
Eze 27:6 the **A.** have made thy benches 843

ASHVATH (ash'-vath)
1Ch 7:33 and **A.**. These are the children 6220

ASIA (a'-she-ah)
Ac 2:9 Pontus, and **A.**, *773*
Ac 6:9 them of Cilicia, and of **A.**, *773*
Ac 16:6 to preach the word in **A.**, *773*
Ac 19:10 all they which dwelt in **A.** *773*
Ac 19:22 stayed in **A.** for a season. *773*
Ac 19:26 but almost throughout all **A.**, *773*
Ac 19:27 all **A.** and the world worshippeth. *773*
Ac 19:31 certain of the chief of **A.**, *775*
Ac 20:4 accompanied him into **A.** *773*
Ac 20:4 of **A.**, Tychicus and Trophimus. *773*
Ac 20:16 would not spend the time in **A.** *773*
Ac 20:18 that I came into **A.**. *773*
Ac 21:27 the Jews which were of **A.**, *773*
Ac 24:18 certain Jews from **A.** *773*
Ac 27:2 by the coasts of **A.**; *773*
1Co 16:19 The churches of **A.** salute you. *773*
2Co 1:8 which came to us in **A.**, *773*
2Ti 1:15 all they which are in **A.** *773*
1Pe 1:1 **A.** and Bithynia, *773*
Re 1:4 seven churches which are in **A.** *773*
Re 1:11 **seven churches which are in A.;** *773*

ASIDE
Ex 3:3 I will now turn **a.**, and see this
Ex 3:4 the Lord saw that he turned **a.**
Ex 32:8 They have turned **a.** quickly out
Nu 5:12 If any man's wife go **a.**, 7847
Nu 5:19 if thou hast not gone **a.** 7847
Nu 5:20 if thou hast gone **a.** 7847
Nu 5:29 when a wife goeth **a.** 7847
Nu 22:23 and the ass turned **a.** 5186
De 5:32 ye shall not turn **a.** to the right
De 9:12 they are quickly turned **a.** out of
De 9:16 ye had turned **a.** quickly out of
De 11:16 ye turn **a.**, and serve other gods,
De 11:28 but turn **a.** out of the way
De 17:20 that he turn not **a.** from the
De 28:14 thou shalt not go **a.** from any 5493
De 31:29 corrupt yourselves, and turn **a.**
Jos 23:6 that ye turn not **a.** therefrom
Jg 14:8 he turned **a.** to see the carcase
Jg 19:12 We will not turn **a.** hither into
Jg 19:15 And they turned **a.** thither, to go
Ru 4:1 Ho, such a one! turn **a.**, sit down
Ru 4:1 And he turned **a.**, and sat down,
1Sa 6:12 turned not **a.** to the right hand
1Sa 8:3 but turned **a.** after lucre, 5186
1Sa 12:20 turn not **a.** from following the
1Sa 12:21 turn ye not **a.**: for then
2Sa 2:21 Turn thee **a.** to thy right hand, or 5186
2Sa 2:21 But Asahel would not turn **a.**
2Sa 2:22 Turn thee **a.** from following me:
2Sa 2:23 Howbeit he refused to turn **a.**:
2Sa 3:27 And when...Joab took him **a.** in 5186
2Sa 6:10 but David carried it **a.** 5186
2Sa 18:30 Turn **a.**, and stand here. 5437
2Sa 18:39 And he turned **a.**, and stood still. 5437
1Ki 15:5 turned not **a.** from anything
1Ki 20:39 behold, a man turned **a.**,
1Ki 22:32 And they turned **a.** to fight
1Ki 22:43 he turned not **a.** from it,
2Ki 4:4 thou shalt set **a.** that which is 5265
2Ki 22:2 turned not **a.** to the right hand 5493
1Ch 13:13 but carried it **a.** into the house of 5186
Job 6:18 paths of their way are turned **a.**; 3943
Ps 14:3 They are all gone **a.**, 5493
Ps 40:4 nor such as turn **a.** to lies. 7847
Ps 78:57 were turned **a.** like a deceitful 2015
Ps 101:3 the work of them that turn **a.** 7750
Ps 125:5 As for such as turn **a.** unto their 5186
Ca 1:7 should I be as one that turneth **a.** 5844
Ca 6:1 whither is thy beloved turned **a.**? 6437
Isa 10:2 To turn **a.** the needy from 5186
Isa 29:21 and turn **a.** the just for a thing of 5186
Isa 30:11 turn **a.** out of the path, 5186
Isa 44:20 heart hath turned him **a.**, 5186
Jer 14:8 a wayfaring man that turneth **a.** 5186
Jer 15:5 who shall go **a.** to ask how thou 5493
La 3:11 He hath turned **a.** my ways,
La 3:35 To turn **a.** the right of a man 5186
Am 2:7 and turn **a.** the way of the meek: 5186
Am 5:12 they turn **a.** the poor 5186
Mal 3:5 and that turn **a.** the stranger 5186
Mt 2:22 he turned **a.** into the parts of *402*
Mk 7:8 **laying a. the commandment of** *863*
Mk 7:33 **a.** from the multitude, *2596, 2398*
Lu 9:10 and went **a.** privately *5298*
Joh 13:4 and laid **a.** his garments; *5087*
Ac 4:15 commanded them to go **a.** out of *565*
Ac 23:19 went with him **a.** privately, and *402*
Ac 26:31 when they were gone **a.**, they *402*
1Ti 1:6 turned **a.** into vain jangling; *1824*
1Ti 5:15 some are already turned **a.** after *1824*
Heb 12:1 let us lay **a.** every weight, and *659*
1Pe 2:1 Wherefore laying **a.** all malice, *659*

ASIEL (a'-se'-el).
1Ch 4:35 of Seraiah, the son of **A.**, 6221

ASK See also ASKED; ASKEST; ASKETH; ASKING.
Ge 32:29 thou dost **a.** after my name? 7592
Ge 34:12 **A.** me never so much dowry and
Nu 27:21 who shall **a.** counsel for him 7592
De 4:32 **a.** now of the days that are past, 7592
De 4:32 **a.** from the one side of heaven
De 13:14 enquire, and make search, and **a.** 7592
De 32:7 **a.** thy father, and he will shew 7592
Jos 4:6 your children **a.** their fathers 7592
Jos 4:21 When your children shall **a.** 7592
Jos 15:18 she moved him to **a.** of her 7592
Jg 1:14 she moved him to **a.** of her 7592
Jg 18:5 **A.** counsel, we pray thee, of God, 7592
1Sa 12:19 our sins this evil, to **a.** us a king 7592
1Sa 25:8 **A.** thy young men, and they will 7592
1Sa 28:16 Wherefore then dost thou **a.** of me, 7592
2Sa 14:18 thee, the thing that I shall **a.** thee. 7592
2Sa 20:18 shall surely **a.** counsel at Abel; 7592
1Ki 2:16 **a.** one petition of thee. 7592
1Ki 2:20 the king said unto her, **A.** on, my 7592
1Ki 2:22 why dost thou **a.** Abishag 7592
1Ki 2:22 **a.** for him the kingdom also; 7592
1Ki 3:5 **A.** what I shall give thee. 7592
1Ki 14:5 cometh to **a.** a thing of thee for 1875
2Ki 2:9 **A.** what I shall do for thee. 7592
2Ch 1:7 **A.** what I shall give thee. 7592
2Ch 20:4 to **a.** help of the Lord: 1245
Job 12:7 **a.** now the beasts, and they shall 7592
Ps 2:8 **A.** of me, and I shall give thee 7592
Isa 7:11 **A.** thee a sign of the Lord 7592
Isa 7:11 **a.** it either in the depth, or in the 7592
Isa 7:12 Ahaz said, I will not **a.**, 7592
Isa 45:11 **A.** me of things to come. 7592
Isa 58:2 **a.** of me the ordinances of justice; 7592
Jer 6:16 and **a.** for the old paths, 7592
Jer 15:5 who shall go aside to **a.** how thou 7592
Jer 18:13 **A.** ye now among the heathen, 7592
Jer 23:33 prophet, or a priest, shall **a.** thee, 7592
Jer 30:6 **A.** ye now, and see 7592
Jer 38:14 I will **a.** thee a thing; 7592
Jer 48:19 **a.** him that fleeth, 7592
Jer 50:5 They shall **a.** the way to Zion 7592
La 4:4 the young children **a.** bread, 7592
Da 6:7 whosoever shall **a.** a petition of 1156
Da 6:12 every man that shall **a.** a petition 1156
Ho 4:12 My people **a.** counsel at their 7592
Hag 2:11 **A.** now the priests concerning 7592
Zec 10:1 **A.** ye of the Lord rain 7592
Mt 6:8 **have need of, before ye a. him,** *154*
Mt 7:7 **A., and it shall be given you;** *154*
Mt 7:9 **if his son a. bread, will he give** *154*
Mt 7:10 **Or if he a. a fish, will be give him.** *154*
Mt 7:11 **good things to them that a. him?** *154*
Mt 14:7 give her whatsoever she would **a.** *154*
Mt 18:19 **anything that they shall a.,** *154*
Mt 20:22 said, **Ye know not what ye a.** *154*
Mt 21:22 **whatsoever ye shall a. in prayer** *154*
Mt 21:24 **I also will a. you one thing,** *2065*
Mt 22:46 **a.** him any more questions. *1905*
Mt 27:20 that they should **a.** Barabbas. *154*
Mk 6:22 **A.** of me whatsoever thou wilt; *154*
Mk 6:23 Whatsoever thou shalt **a.** of me, *154*
Mk 6:24 unto her mother, What shall I **a.**? *154*
Mk 9:32 saying, and were afraid to **a.** him. *1905*
Mk 10:38 **Ye know not what ye a.** *154*
Mk 11:29 **I will also a. of you one question,.** *1905*
Mk 12:34 And no man after that durst **a.** *1905*
Lu 6:9 **I will a. you one thing,; Is it** *1905*
Lu 6:30 **away thy goods a. them not** *523*
Lu 9:45 they feared to **a.** him of that *2065*
Lu 11:9 **A., and it shall be given you;** *154*
Lu 11:11 **If a son shall a. bread of any** *154*
Lu 11:11 **if he a. a fish will he for a fish**
Lu 11:12 **Or if he shall a. an egg, will** *154*
Lu 11:13 **Holy Spirit to them that a. him?** *154*

Lu 12:48 of him they will a. the more 154
Lu 19:31 if any man a. you, 2065
Lu 20:3 I will also a. you one thing; 2065
Lu 20:40 they durst not a. him any 1905
Lu 22:68 And if I also a. you 2065
Joh 1:19 from Jerusalem to a. him, Who 2065
Joh 9:21 he is of age; a. him: he shall 2065
Joh 9:23 his parents, He is of age: a. him. 2065
Joh 11:22 whatsoever thou wilt a. of God, 154
Joh 13:24 that he should a. who it should 4441
Joh 14:13 whatsoever ye shall a. in my 154
Joh 14:14 If ye shall a. any thing in my 154
Joh 15:7 abide in you, ye shall a. what 154
Joh 15:16 whatsoever ye shall a. of the 154
Joh 16:19 they were desirous to a. him, 2065
Joh 16:23 ye shall a. me nothing 2065
Joh 16:23 Whatsoever ye shall a. the 154
Joh 16:24 a., and ye shall receive, that your 154
Joh 16:26 At that day ye shall a. in my name: 154
Joh 16:30 that any man should a. thee: 2065
Joh 18:21 Why askest thou me? a. them 1905
Joh 21:12 none of the disciples durst a. 1833
Ac 3:2 to a. alms of them that entered 154
Ac 10:29 I a. therefore for what intent 4441
1Co 14:35 let them a. their husbands at 1905
Eph 3:20 above all that we a. or think, 154
Jas 1:5 you lack wisdom, let him a. of 154
Jas 1:6 But let him a. in faith, nothing 154
Jas 4:2 ye have not, because ye a. not. 154
Jas 4:3 Ye a., and receive not, because 154
Jas 4:3 ye a. amiss, that ye may 154
1Jo 3:22 whatsoever we a., we receive 154
1Jo 5:14 if we a. any thing according to his 154
1Jo 5:15 we a., we know that we have the 154
1Jo 5:16 not unto death, he shall a., and 154

ASKED
Ge 24:47 And I a. her, and said, 7592
Ge 26:7 the men of the place a. him of 7592
Ge 32:29 And Jacob a. him. 7592
Ge 37:15 and the man a. him, 7592
Ge 38:21 Then he a. the men of that place, 7592
Ge 40:7 And he a. Pharaoh's officers 7592
Ge 43:7 The man a. us straitly 7592
Ge 43:27 And he a. them of their welfare, 7592
Ge 44:19 My lord a. his servants, 7592
Ex 18:7 they a. each other of their welfare; 7592
Jos 9:14 a. not counsel at the mouth of the 7592
Jos 19:50 gave him the city which he a. 7592
Jg 1:1 that the children of Israel a. 7592
Jg 5:25 a. water, and she gave him milk; 7592
Jg 6:29 And when they enquired and a., 1245
Jg 13:6 I a. him not whence he was, 7592
Jg 20:18 and a. counsel of God, 7592
Jg 20:23 and a. counsel of the Lord, 7592
1Sa 1:17 thy petition that thou hast a. 7592
1Sa 1:20 I have a. him of the Lord. 7592
1Sa 1:27 my petition which I a. of him: 7592
1Sa 8:10 the people that a. of him a king. 7592
1Sa 14:37 And Saul a. counsel of God, 7592
1Sa 19:22 and he a. and said, 7592
1Sa 20:6 David earnestly a. leave 7592
1Sa 20:28 a. leave of me to go to Beth-lehem: 7592
1Ki 3:10 Solomon had a. this thing. 7592
1Ki 3:11 Because thou hast a. this thing. 7592
1Ki 3:11 hast not a. for thyself long life; 7592
1Ki 3:11 neither hast a. riches for thyself, 7592
1Ki 3:11 hast a. the life of thine enemies; 7592
1Ki 3:11 hast a. for thyself understanding 7592
1Ki 3:13 thee that which thou hast not a., 7592
1Ki 10:13 whatsoever she a., 7592
2Ki 2:10 Thou hast a. a hard thing: 7592
2Ki 8:6 when the king a. the woman, 7592
2Ch 1:11 thou hast not a. riches, 7592
2Ch 1:11 neither yet hast a. long life; 7592
2Ch 1:11 hast a. wisdom and knowledge 7592
2Ch 9:12 all her desire, whatsoever she a., 7592
Ezr 5:9 Then a. we those elders, 7593
Ezr 5:10 We a. their names also, 7593
Ne 1:2 and I a. them concerning the Jews 7592
Job 21:29 Have ye not a. them that go by 7592
Ps 21:4 He a. life of thee, 7592
Ps 105:40 The people a., and he brought 7592
Isa 30:2 have not a. at my mouth; 7592
Isa 41:28 when I a. of them, could answer 7592
Isa 65:1 I am sought of them that a. not 7592
Jer 36:17 they a. Baruch, 7592
Jer 37:17 the king a. him secretly in his 7592
Jer 38:27 the princes unto Jeremiah, and a. 7592
Da 2:10 a. such things at any magician, 7593
Da 7:16 and a. him the truth of all this. 1156
Mt 12:10 they a. him, saying, 1905
Mt 16:13 he a. his disciples, saying, Whom 2065
Mt 17:10 his disciples a. him, saying. 1905
Mt 22:23 is no resurrection, and a. him, 1905
Mt 22:35 them, which was a lawyer, a. him 1905
Mt 22:41 gathered together, Jesus a. them. 1905
Mt 27:11 and the governor a. him, saying, 1905
Mk 4:10 about him with the twelve a. of 2065
Mk 5:9 And he a. him, What is thy name? 1905
Mk 6:25 unto the king, and a., saying, 154
Mk 7:5 Pharisees and scribes a. him, 1905
Mk 7:17 his disciples a. him concerning the 1905
Mk 8:5 he a. them, How many loaves 1905
Mk 8:23 he a. him if he saw ought. 1905
Mk 8:27 by the way he a. his disciples, 1905
Mk 9:11 And they a. him saying, Why say 1905
Mk 9:16 And he a. the scribes, What 1905
Mk 9:21 And he a. his father, How long is it 1905
Mk 9:28 his disciples a. him privately, Why 1905
Mk 9:33 being in the house he a. them, 1905
Mk 10:2 Pharisees came to him, and a. him, 1905
Mk 10:10 disciples a. him again of the same 1905
Mk 10:17 and a. him, Good master, what 1905
Mk 12:18 no resurrection; and they a. him, 1905
Mk 12:28 a. him, Which is the first 1905
Mk 13:3 John and Andrew a. him privately, 1905
Mk 14:60 the midst, and a. Jesus, saying, 1905
Mk 14:61 Again the high priest a. him, and 1905
Mk 15:2 And Pilate a. him, Art thou the 1905
Mk 15:4 And Pilate a. him again, saying, 1905
Mk 15:44 he a. him whether he had been 1905
Lu 1:63 he a. for a writing table, and wrote, 154
Lu 3:10 And the people a. him, saying, 1905
Lu 8:9 And his disciples a. him, saying, 1905
Lu 8:30 And Jesus a. him, saying, What is 1905
Lu 9:18 and he a. them, saying, Whom say 1905
Lu 15:26 and a. what these things meant 4441
Lu 18:18 a certain ruler a. him, saying, 1905
Lu 18:36 pass by, he a. what it meant. 4441
Lu 18:40 he was come near, he a. him, 1905
Lu 20:21 they a. him, saying, Master, we 1905
Lu 20:27 any resurrection; and they a. him, 1905
Lu 21:7 And they a. him saying, Master, 1905
Lu 22:64 and a. him, saying, Prophesy, who 1905
Lu 23:3 And Pilate a. him, saying, Art 1905
Lu 23:6 he a. whether the man were a 1905
Joh 1:21 And they a. him, What then? 2065
Joh 1:25 they a. him, and said 2065
Joh 4:10 thou wouldest have a. of him, 154
Joh 5:12 Then a. they him, What man is 2065
Joh 9:2 his disciples a. him, 2065
Joh 9:15 the Pharisees also a. him 2065
Joh 9:19 a. them, saying, Is this your son, 2065
Joh 16:24 have ye a. nothing in my name: 154
Joh 18:7 Then a. he them again, Whom 1905
Joh 18:19 The high priest then a. Jesus of 2065
Ac 1:6 they a. of him, saying, Lord, wilt 1905
Ac 3:3 to go into the temple a. an alms. 2065
Ac 4:7 they a., By what power, or by 4441
Ac 5:27 and the high priest a. them, 1905
Ac 10:18 and a. whether Simon, 4441
Ac 23:19 aside privately, and a. him, 2065
Ac 23:34 he a. of what province he was. 1905
Ac 25:20 I a. him whether he would go 3004
Ro 10:20 unto them that a. not after me. 1905

ASKELON (as'-ke-lon) See also ASHKELON.
Jg 1:18 and A. with the coast thereof, 831
1Sa 6:17 for Gaza one, for A. one, for Gath 831
2Sa 1:20 publish it not in the streets of A.; 831

ASKEST
Jg 13:18 Why a. thou thus after my name, 7592
Joh 4:9 being a Jew, a. drink of me. 154
Joh 18:21 Why a. thou me? ask them which 1905

ASKETH
Ge 32:17 my brother meeteth thee, and a. 7592
Ex 13:14 when thy son a. thee 7592
De 6:20 thy son a. thee in time to come, 7592
Mic 7:3 hands earnestly, the prince a., 7592
Mic 7:3 and the judge a. for a reward; 7592
Mt 5:42 Give to him that a. thee, and 154
Mt 7:8 every one that a. receiveth; 154
Lu 6:30 Give to every man that a. of thee; 154
Lu 11:10 every one that a. receiveth; 154
Joh 16:5 none of you a. me, 2065
1Pe 3:15 every man that a. you a reason 154

ASKING
1Sa 12:17 in a. you a king. 7592
1Ch 10:13 for a. counsel of one that had a 7592
Ps 78:18 tempted God in their heart by a. 7592
Lu 2:46 them, and a. them questions. 1905
Joh 8:7 So when they continued a. him, 2065
1Co 10:25 a. no question for conscience sake: 350
1Co 10:27 eat, a. no question for conscience 350

ASLEEP
Jg 4:21 he was fast a. and weary 7290
1Sa 26:12 for they were all a.; 3463
Ca 7:9 those that are a. to speak 3463
Jon 1:5 and he lay, and was fast a. 7290
Mt 8:24 but he was a. 2518
Mt 26:40 and findeth them a., 2518
Mt 26:43 came and found them a. again; 2518
Mk 4:38 a. on a pillow: and they awake 2518
Mk 14:40 he found them a. again, 2518
Lu 8:23 as they sailed he fell a. 879
Ac 7:60 when he had said this, he fell a., 2837
1Co 15:6 but some are fallen a. 2837
1Co 15:18 also which are fallen a. in Christ 2837
1Th 4:13 concerning them which are a., 2837
1Th 4:15 not prevent them which are a. 2837
2Pe 3:4 since the fathers fell a., all things 2837

ASNAH (as'-nah)
Ezr 2:50 The children of A., the children 619

ASNAPPER (as-nap'-pur)
Ezr 4:10 great and noble A. brought over, 620

ASP See also ASPS.
Isa 11:8 shall play on the hole of the a., 6620

ASPATHA (as'-pa-tha)
Es 9:7 and Dalphon, and A., 630

ASPS
De 32:33 and the cruel venom of a., 6620
Job 20:14 the gall of a. within him. 6620
Job 20:16 He shall suck the poison of a. 6620
Ro 3:13 poison of a. is under their lips: 785

ASRIEL (as'-re-el) See also ASHRIEL; ASRIELITES.
Nu 26:31 of A., the family of the Asrielites: 844
Jos 17:2 and for the children of A., 844

ASRIELITES (as'-re-el-ites)
Nu 26:31 of Asriel, the family of the A. 845

ASS See also ASS'S; ASSES.
Ge 22:3 saddled his a., and took two of 2543
Ge 22:5 abide ye here with the a.; 2543
Ge 42:27 give his a. provender in the inn, 2543
Ge 44:13 laded every man his a., 2543
Ge 49:14 Issachar is a strong a. couching 2543
Ex 4:20 set them upon an a., 2543
Ex 13:13 every firstling, of an a. thou shalt 2543
Ex 20:17 nor his ox, nor his a., nor anything 2543
Ex 21:33 an ox or an a. fall therein; 2543
Ex 22:4 whether it be ox, or a., or sheep; 2543
Ex 22:9 for ox, for a., for sheep, 2543
Ex 22:10 deliver unto his neighbour an a., 2543
Ex 23:4 thine enemy's ox or his a. going 2543
Ex 23:5 If thou see the a. of him that 2543
Ex 23:12 thine ox and thine a. may rest, 2543
Ex 34:20 firstling of an a. thou shalt redeem 2543
Nu 16:15 I have not taken one a. from them. 2543
Nu 22:21 and saddled his a., and went with 860
Nu 22:22 Now he was riding upon his a. 860
Nu 22:23 the a. saw the angel of the Lord 860
Nu 22:23 the a. turned aside out of the way 860
Nu 22:23 Balaam smote the a., to turn her 860
Nu 22:25, 27 the a. saw the angel of the Lord, 860
Nu 22:27 he smote the a. with a staff 860
Nu 22:28 Lord opened the mouth of the a., 860
Nu 22:29 Baalam said unto the a., 860
Nu 22:30 the a. said unto Baalam, 860
Nu 22:30 Am not I thine a., 860
Nu 22:32 hast thou smitten thine a. 860
Nu 22:33 And the a. saw me, and turned 860
De 5:14 nor thine ox, nor thine a., 2543
De 5:21 his ox, or his a., or any thing 2543
De 22:3 shalt thou do with his a.; 2543
De 22:4 see thy brother's a. or his ox fall 2543

De 22:10 plow with an ox and an **a.** together ... 2543
De 28:31 thine **a.** shall be violently taken ... 2543
Jos 6:21 ox, and sheep, and **a.**, with the ... 2543
Jos 15:18 she lighted off her **a.**; ... 2543
Jg 1:14 she lighted from off her **a.**; ... 2543
Jg 6:4 neither sheep, nor ox, nor **a.**. ... 2543
Jg 10:4 sons that rode on thirty **a.** colts, ... 5895
Jg 12:14 threescore and ten **a.** colts: ... 5895
Jg 15:15 found a new jawbone of an **a.**, ... 2543
Jg 15:16 With the jawbone of an **a.**, ... 2543
Jg 15:16 upon heaps, with the jaw of an **a.** ... 2543
Jg 19:28 the man took her up upon an **a.**, ... 2543
1Sa 12:3 or whose **a.** have I taken? ... 2543
1Sa 15:3 ox and sheep, camel and **a.** ... 2543
1Sa 16:20 Jesse took an **a.** laden with bread, ... 2543
1Sa 25:20 she rode on the **a.**, ... 2543
1Sa 25:23 hasted, and lighted off the **a.**, ... 2543
1Sa 25:42 arose, and rode upon an **a.**, ... 2543
2Sa 17:23 he saddled his **a.**, and arose, ... 2543
2Sa 19:26 I will saddle me an **a.**, ... 2543
1Ki 2:40 Shimei arose, and saddled his **a.**, ... 2543
1Ki 13:13 Saddle me the **a.**, ... 2543
1Ki 13:13 So they saddled him the **a.** ... 2543
1Ki 13:23 that he saddled for him the **a.**, ... 2543
1Ki 13:24 cast in the way, and the **a.** stood by ... 2543
1Ki 13:27 Saddle me the **a.**. ... 2543
1Ki 13:28 and the **a.** and the lion standing ... 2543
1Ki 13:28 the carcase, nor torn the **a.**. ... 2543
1Ki 13:29 laid it upon the **a.**, ... 2543
2Ki 4:24 Then she saddled an **a.**, ... 860
Job 6:5 Doth the wild **a.** bray ... 6501
Job 24:3 away the **a.** of the fatherless, ... 2543
Job 39:5 hath sent out the wild **a.** free? ... 6501
Job 39:5 loosed the bands of the wild **a.**? ... 6171
Pr 26:3 a bridle for the **a.**, ... 2543
Isa 1:3 and the **a.** his master's crib: ... 2543
Isa 32:20 the feet of the ox and the **a.**. ... 2543
Jer 2:24 A wild **a.** used to the wilderness, ... 6501
Jer 22:19 buried with the burial of an **a.**, ... 2543
Hos 8:9 a wild **a.** alone by himself: ... 6501
Zec 9:9 lowly, and riding upon an **a.**, ... 2543
Zec 9:9 and upon a colt and foal of an **a.** ... 860
Zec 14:15 mule, of the camel, and of the **a.**, ... 2543
Mt 21:2 **ye shall find an a. tied,** ... *3688*
Mt 21:5 meek, and sitting upon an **a.**, ... *3688*
Mt 21:5 and a colt and foal of an **a.**, ... *5268*
Mt 21:7 And brought the **a.**, and the colt, ... *3688*
Lu 13:15 **loose his ox or his a. from the** ... *3688*
Lu 14:5 **Which of you shall have an a. or** .. *3688*
Joh 12:14 when he had found a young **a.**, ... *3678*
2Pe 2:16 **a.** speaking with man's voice ... *5268*

ASSAULT See also ASSAULTED.
Es 8:11 the people...that would **a.**, them, ... 6696
Ac 14:5 when there was an **a.** made ... *3730*

ASSAULTED
Ac 17:5 **a.** the house of Jason, and sought ... *2186*

ASSAY See also ASSAYED; ASSAYING.
Job 4:2 If we **a.** to commune with thee, ... 5254

ASSAYED
De 4:34 hath God **a.** to go and take him ... 5254
1Sa 17:39 and he **a.** to go; for he had not ... 2974
Ac 9:26 **a.** to join himself to the disciples: ... *3087*
Ac 16:7 they **a.** to go into Bithynia; ... *3985*

ASSAYING
Heb 11:29 Egyptians **a.** to do were ... *3984, 2983*

ASS-COLTS See ASS and COLTS.

ASSEMBLE See also ASSEMBLED; ASSEMBLING.
Nu 10:3 shall **a.** themselves to thee ... 3259
2Sa 20:4 **A.** me the men of Judah ... 2199
2Sa 20:5 went to **a.** the men of Judah: ... 2199
Isa 11:12 shall **a.** the outcasts of Israel, ... 622
Isa 45:20 **A.** yourselves and come: ... 6908
Isa 48:14 All ye, **a.** yourselves, and hear; ... 6908
Jer 4:5 and say, **A.** yourselves, and let us ... 622
Jer 8:14 do we sit still? **a.** yourselves, ... 622
Jer 12:9 **a.** all the beasts of the field, ... 622
Jer 21:4 and I will **a.** them into the midst ... 622
Eze 11:17 and **a.** you out of the countries ... 622
Eze 39:17 **A.** yourselves, and come; ... 6908
Da 11:10 **a.** a multitude of great forces: ... 622
Ho 7:14 they **a.** themselves for corn ... 1481
Joe 2:16 Gather the people,...**a.** the elders, ... 6908
Joe 3:11 **A.** yourselves, and come, all ye ... 5789
Am 3:9 **A.** yourselves upon the mountains ... 622
Mic 2:12 surely **a.**, O Jacob, all of thee; ... 622
Mic 4:6 will I **a.** her that halteth, ... 622
Zep 3:8 that may **a.** the kingdoms, ... 6908

ASSEMBLED
Ex 38:8 **a.** at the door of the tabernacle ... 6633
Nu 1:18 they **a.** all the congregation ... 6950
Jos 18:1 congregation...**a.** together at ... 6950
Jg 10:17 of Israel **a.** themselves together, ... 622
1Sa 2:22 **a.** at the door of the tabernacle ... 6633
1Sa 14:20 all the people...**a.** themselves, ... 2199
1Ki 8:1 Solomon **a.** the elders of Israel, ... 6950
1Ki 8:2 **a.** themselves unto king Solomon ... 6950
1Ki 8:5 that were **a.** unto him, ... 3259
1Ki 12:21 he **a.** all the house of Judah, ... 6950
1Ch 15:4 David **a.** the children of Aaron. ... 622
1Ch 28:1 David **a.** all the princes of Israel, ... 6950
2Ch 5:2 Solomon **a.** the elders of Israel, ... 6950
2Ch 5:3 the men of Israel **a.** themselves ... 6950
2Ch 5:6 were **a.** unto him before the ark, ... 3259
2Ch 20:26 they **a.** themselves in the valley ... 6950
2Ch 30:13 **a.** at Jerusalem much people, ... 622
Ezr 9:4 Then were **a.** unto me every one ... 622
Ezr 10:1 there **a.** unto him...a very great ... 6908
Ne 9:1 the children of Israel were **a.** ... 622
Es 9:18 that were at Shushan **a.** together ... 6950
Ps 48:4 kings were **a.**, they passed by ... 3259
Isa 43:9 and let the people be **a.**: ... 622
Jer 5:7 and **a.** themselves by troops ... 1413
Eze 38:7 company that are **a.** unto thee, ... 6950
Da 6:6 presidents and princes **a.** together ... 7284
Da 6:11 these men **a.**, and found Daniel ... 7284
Da 6:15 Then these men **a.** unto the king, ... 7284
Mt 26:3 **a.** together the chief priests, ... *4863*
Mt 26:57 scribes and the elders were **a.** ... *4863*
Mt 28:12 they were **a.** with the elders, ... *4863*
Mk 14:53 were **a.** all the chief priests, ... *4905*
Joh 20:19 were the disciples were **a.** ... *4863*
Ac 1:4 And being **a.** together with them, ... *4871*
Ac 4:31 when they were **a.** together; ... *4863*
Ac 11:26 **a.** themselves with the church, ... *4863*
Ac 15:25 being **a.** with one accord, ... *1096*

ASSEMBLIES
Ps 86:14 and the **a.** of violent men ... 5712
Ec 12:11 fastened by the masters of **a.**, ... 627
Isa 1:13 calling of **a.**, I cannot away with; ... 4744
Isa 4:5 her **a.** a cloud of smoke by day, ... 4744
Eze 44:24 my statutes in all mine **a.**; ... 4150
Am 5:21 not smell in your solemn **a.** ... 6116

ASSEMBLING
Ex 38:8 glasses of the women **a.**, ... 6633
Heb 10:25 the **a.** of ourselves together, ... *1997*

ASSEMBLY See also ASSEMBLIES.
Ge 49:6 into their secret; unto their **a.**, ... 6951
Ex 12:6 **a.** of the congregation of Israel ... 6951
Ex 16:3 kill this whole **a.** with hunger. ... 6951
Le 4:13 be hid from the eyes of the **a.**, ... 6951
Le 8:4 the **a.** was gathered together ... 5712
Le 23:36 it is a solemn **a.**; ... 6116
Nu 8:9 thou shalt gather the whole **a.** ... 5712
Nu 10:2 the calling of the **a.**, and for the ... 5712
Nu 10:3 **a.** shall assemble themselves to ... 5712
Nu 14:5 on their faces before all the **a.** ... 6951
Nu 16:2 princes of the **a.**, famous ... 5712
Nu 20:6 went from the presence of the **a.** ... 6951
Nu 20:8 gather thou the **a.** together, ... 5712
Nu 29:35 ye shall have a solemn **a.** ... 6116
De 5:22 the Lord spake unto all your **a.** ... 6951
De 9:10 fire in the day of the **a.** ... 6951
De 10:4 of the fire, in the day of the **a.** ... 6951
De 16:8 a solemn **a.** to the Lord thy God ... 6116
De 18:16 Horeb in the day of the **a.**, ... 6951
Jg 20:2 themselves in the **a.** of the people, ... 6951
Jg 21:8 from Jabesh-gilead to the **a.**. ... 6951
1Sa 17:47 this **a.** shall know that the Lord ... 6951
2Ki 10:20 Proclaim a solemn **a.** for Baal ... 6116
2Ch 7:9 they made a solemn **a.**: ... 6116
2Ch 39:23 the whole **a.** took counsel ... 6951
Ne 5:7 And I set a great **a.** against them. ... 6952
Ne 8:18 the eighth day was solemn **a.**, ... 6116
Ps 22:16 **a.** of the wicked have inclosed me: ... 5712
Ps 89:7 to be feared in the **a.** of the saints, ... 5475
Ps 107:32 and praise him in the **a.** of the ... 4186
Ps 111:1 in the **a.** of the upright, ... 5475
Pr 5:14 midst of the congregation and **a.**. ... 5712
Jer 6:11 the **a.** of young men together: ... 5475
Jer 9:2 an **a.** of treacherous men. ... 6116
Jer 15:17 I sat not in the **a.** of the mockers, ... 5475
Jer 26:17 spake to all the **a.** of the people, ... 6951
Jer 50:9 Babylon an **a.** of great nations, ... 6951
La 1:15 he hath called an **a.** against me, ... 4150
La 2:6 destroyed his places of the **a.** ... 4150
Eze 13:9 not be in the **a.** of my people, ... 5475
Eze 23:24 and with an **a.** of people, ... 6951
Joe 1:14 call a solemn **a.**, gather the elders ... 6116
Joe 2:15 sanctify a fast, call a solemn **a.** ... 6116
Zep 3:18 are sorrowful for the solemn **a.**, ... 4150
Ac 19:32 for the **a.** was confused; ... *1577*
Ac 19:39 determined in a lawful **a.**. ... *1577*
Ac 19:41 thus spoken, he dismissed the **a.**. ... *1577*
Heb 12:23 **a.** and church of the firstborn, ... *3831*
Jas 2:2 there come unto your **a.** a man ... *4864*

ASSENT See also ASSENTED.
2Ch 18:12 good to the king with one **a.**; ... 6310

ASSENTED
Ac 24:9 And the Jews also **a.**, saying ... *4934*

ASS'S
Ge 49:11 his **a.** colt unto the choice vine; ... 860
2Ki 6:25 an **a.** head was sold for fourscore ... 2543
Job 11:12 man be born like a wild **a.** colt. ... 6501
Joh 12:15 King cometh, sitting on an **a.** colt ... *3688*

ASSES
Ge 12:16 he **a.**, and menservants, ... 2543
Ge 12:16 and maidservants, and she **a.**, ... 860
Ge 24:35 maidservants, and camels, and **a.** ... 2543
Ge 30:43 menservants, and camels, and **a.** ... 2543
Ge 32:5 I have oxen, and **a.**, flocks, ... 2543
Ge 32:15 twenty she **a.**, and ten foals. ... 860
Ge 34:28 their oxen, and their **a.**, ... 2543
Ge 36:24 as he fed the **a.** of Zibeon ... 2543
Ge 42:26 they laded their **a.** with the corn, ... 2543
Ge 43:18 take us for bondmen, and our **a.** ... 2543
Ge 43:24 he gave their **a.** provender. ... 2543
Ge 44:3 sent away, they and their **a.**. ... 2543
Ge 45:23 ten **a.** laden with the good things ... 2543
Ge 45:23 she **a.** laden with corn and bread ... 860
Ge 47:17 herds, and for the **a.** ... 2543
Ex 9:3 upon the horses, upon the **a.**, ... 2543
Nu 31:28 of the beeves, and of the **a.**, ... 2543
Nu 31:30 of the **a.**, and of the flocks, ... 2543
Nu 31:34 threescore and one thousand **a.**, ... 2543
Nu 31:39 And the **a.** were thirty thousand ... 2543
Nu 31:45 thousand **a.** and five hundred, ... 2543
Jos 7:24 his oxen, and his **a.**, ... 2543
Jos 9:4 took old sacks upon their **a.**, ... 2543
Jg 5:10 speak, ye that ride on white **a.**, ... 860
Jg 19:3 with him, and a couple of **a.** ... 2543
Jg 19:10 with him two **a.** saddled, ... 2543
Jg 19:19 straw and provender for our **a.**; ... 2543
Jg 19:21 gave provender unto the **a.** ... 2543
1Sa 8:16 goodliest young men, and your **a.**, ... 2543
1Sa 9:3 **a.** of Kish, Saul's father were lost ... 860
1Sa 9:3 arise, go seek the **a.** ... 860
1Sa 9:5 leave caring for the **a.**, ... 860
1Sa 9:20 And as for thine **a.** that were lost ... 860
1Sa 10:2 The **a.** which thou wentest to seek ... 860
1Sa 10:2 hath left the care of the **a.**, ... 860
1Sa 10:14 And he said, To seek the **a.** ... 860
1Sa 10:16 plainly that the **a.** were found. ... 860
1Sa 22:19 oxen, and **a.**, and sheep. ... 2543
1Sa 25:18 laid them on **a.**. ... 2543
1Sa 27:9 oxen, and the **a.**, and the camels, ... 2543
2Sa 16:1 with a couple of **a.** saddled, ... 2543
2Sa 16:2 The **a.** be for the king's household ... 2543
2Ki 4:22 the young men, and one of the **a.**, ... 860
2Ki 7:7 their horses, and their **a.**, ... 2543
2Ki 7:10 horses tied, and **a.** tied. ... 2543
1Ch 5:21 and of **a.** two thousand, ... 2543
1Ch 12:40 brought bread on **a.**, ... 2543
1Ch 27:30 and over the **a.** was Jehdeiah ... 860
2Ch 28:15 all the feeble of them upon **a.**, ... 2543
Ezr 2:67 **a.**, six thousand seven hundred ... 2543
Ne 7:69 seven hundred and twenty **a.** ... 2543
Ne 13:15 bringing in sheaves, and lading **a.**; ... 2543
Job 1:3 five hundred she **a.**, ... 860
Job 1:14 and the **a.** feeding beside them ... 860
Job 24:5 as wild **a.** in the desert, ... 6501

Job 42:12 a thousand she **a.**. 860
Ps 104:11 the wild **a.** quench their thirst. 6501
Isa 21:7 a chariot of **a.**, and a chariot of 2543
Isa 30:6 upon the shoulders of young **a.**, 5895
Isa 30:24 the young **a.** that ear the ground 5895
Isa 32:14 joy of wild **a.**, a pasture of flocks; 6501
Jer 14:6 **a.** did stand in the high places, 6501
Eze 23:20 whose flesh is as the flesh of **a.**, 2543
Da 5:21 his dwelling was with the wild **a.** 6167

ASSHUR (ash'-ur) See also ASHUR; ASSUR; ASSYRIA.
Ge 10:11 Out of that land went forth **A.**, 804
Ge 10:22 Elam, and **A.**, and Arphaxad, and 804
Nu 24:22 **A.** shall carry thee away captive. 804
Nu 24:24 afflict **A.**, and shall afflict Eber, 804
1Ch 1:17 The sons of Shem; Elam, and **A.**, 804
Eze 27:23 the merchants of Sheba, **A.**, and 804
Eze 32:22 **A.** is there an all her company: 804
Hos 14:3 **A.** shall not save us; we will not 804

ASSHURIM (ash'-u-rim) See also ASHURITES.
Ge 25:3 the sons of Dedan were **A.**, and 805

ASSIGNED
Ge 47:22 priests had a portion **a.** them.
Jos 20:8 they **a.** Bezer in the wilderness 5414
2Sa 11:16 that he **a.** Uriah unto a place 5414

ASSIR (as'-sur)
Ex 6:24 **A.**, and Elkanah, and Abiasaph: 617
1Ch 3:17 Jeconiah; **A.**, Salathiel his son, 617
1Ch 6:22 Korah his son, **A.** his son, 617
1Ch 6:23 Ebiasaph his son, and **A.** his son, 617
1Ch 6:37 The son of Tahath, the son of **A.**, 617

ASSIST
Ro 16:2 and that ye **a.** her in whatsoever *3936*

ASSOCIATE
Isa 8:98 **A.** yourselves, O ye people, 7489

ASSOS (as'-sos)
Ac 20:13 sailed unto **A.**, there intending to *789*
Ac 20:14 he met with us at **A.**, *789*

ASSUAGE See ASSWAGE.

ASSUR (as'-sur) See also ASSHUR.
Ezr 4:2 days of Esar-haddon king of **A.**, 804
Ps 83:8 **A.** also is joined with them: they 804

ASSURANCE
De 28:66 shalt have none **a.** of thy life: 539
Isa 32:17 quietness and **a.** for ever. 983
Ac 17:31 he hath given **a.** unto all men, *4102*
Col 2:2 of the full **a.** of understanding, *4136*
1Th 1:5 and in much **a.**; as ye know *4136*
He 6:11 the full **a.** of hope unto the end: *4136*
He 10:22 in full **a.** of faith, having our *4136*

ASSURE See also ASSURED.
1Jo 3:19 and shall **a.** our hearts before him, *3982*

ASSURED
Le 27:19 and it shall be **a.** to him. 6966
Jer 14:13 **a.** peace in this place. 571
2Ti 3:14 and hast been **a.** of, *4104*

ASSUREDLY
1Sa 28:1 know thou **a.**, that thou shalt go 3045
1Ki 1:13 **A.** Solomon thy son shall reign 3588
1Ki 1:17, 30 saying, **A.** Solomon thy son 3588
Jer 32:41 **a.** with my whole heart 571
Jer 38:17 wilt **a.** go forth unto the king 3318
Jer 49:12 of the cup have **a.** drunken; 8354
Ac 2:36 house of Israel know **a.**, *806*
Ac 16:10 **a.** gathering that the Lord had *4822*

ASSWAGE See ASSWAGED.
Job 16:5 my lips should **a.** your grief 2820

ASSWAGED
Ge 8:1 and the waters **a.**; 7918
Job 16:6 my grief is not **a.** 2820

ASSYRIA (as-sir'-e-ah) See also ASSHUR; ASSYRIAN.
Ge 2:14 which goeth toward the east of **A.**. 804
Ge 25:18 Egypt, as thous goest toward **A.** 804
2Ki 15:19 Pul the king of **A.** came against 804
2Ki 15:20 of silver, to give to the king of **A.**. 804
2Ki 15:20 So the king of **A.** turned back, 804
2Ki 15:29 came Tiglath-pileser king of **A.**, 804
2Ki 15:29 and carried them captive to **A.**. 804
2Ki 16:7 to Tiglath-pilser king of **A.** 804
2Ki 16:8 for a present to the king of **A.**. 804
2Ki 16:9 the king of **A.** hearkened unto him: 804
2Ki 16:9 of **A.** went up against Damascus, 804
2Ki 16:10 to meet Tiglath-pilser king of **A.**, 804
2Ki 16:18 of the Lord for the king of **A.**. 804
2Ki 17:3 came up Shalmaneser king of **A.**; 804
2Ki 17:4 the king of **A.** found conspiracy 804
2Ki 17:4 brought no present to the king of **A.**, 804
2Ki 17:4 therefore the king of **A.** shut him up, 804
2Ki 17:5 Then the king of **A.** came up 804
2Ki 17:6 the king of **A.** took Samaria, 804
2Ki 17:6 and carried Israel away into **A.**, 804
2Ki 17:23 away out of their own land to **A.** 804
2Ki 17:24 the king of **A.** brought men from 804
2Ki 17:26 they spake to the king of **A.**, 804
2Ki 17:27 Then the king of **A.** commanded, 804
2Ki 18:7 he rebelled against the king of **A.**, 804
2Ki 18:9 Shalmaneser king of **A.** came up 804
2Ki 18:11 And the king of **A.** did carry away 804
2Ki 18:11 did carry away Israel unto **A.**, 804
2Ki 18:13 did Sennacherib king of **A.** come 804
2Ki 18:14 sent to the king of **A.** to Lachish, 804
2Ki 18:14 king of **A.** appointed unto Hezekiah 804
2Ki 18:16 and gave it to the king of **A.**. 804
2Ki 18:17 the king of **A.** sent Tartan and 804
2Ki 18:19 the great king, the king of **A.**, 804
2Ki 18:23 pledges to my lord the king of **A.**, 804
2Ki 18:28 of the great king, the king of **A.** 804
2Ki 18:30 into the hand of the king of **A.**. 804
2Ki 18:31 for thus saith the king of **A.**, 804
2Ki 18:33 out of the hand of the king of **A.**? 804
2Ki 19:4 whom the king of **A.** his master 804
2Ki 19:6 the servants of the king of **A.** have 804
2Ki 19:8 and found the king of **A.** warring 804
2Ki 19:10 into the hand of the king of **A.**. 804
2Ki 19:11 what the kings of **A.** have done 804
2Ki 19:17 the kings of **A.** have destroyed the 804
2Ki 19:20 against Sennacherib king of **A.** I 804
2Ki 19:32 Lord concerning the king of **A.**, 804
2Ki 19:36 Sennacherib king of **A.** departed, 804
2Ki 20:6 out of the hand of the king of **A.**; 804
2Ki 23:20 went up against the king of **A.** 804
1Ch 5:6 whom Tilgath-pilneser king of **A.** 804
1Ch 5:26 up the spirit of Pul king of **A.**, 804
1Ch 5:26 spirit of Tilgath-pilneser king of **A.**, 804
2Ch 28:16 Ahaz send unto the kings of **A.** to 804
2Ch 28:20 Tilgath-pilneser king of **A.** came 804
2Ch 28:21 and gave it unto the king of **A.**: 804
2Ch 30:6 out of the hand of the kings of **A.**. 804
2Ch 32:1 Sennacherib king of **A.** came, 804
2Ch 32:4 Why should the kings of **A.** come, 804
2Ch 32:7 nor dismayed for the king of **A.**, 804
2Ch 32:9 did Sennacherib king of **A.** send 804
2Ch 32:10 Thus saith Sennacherib king of **A.**, 804
2Ch 32:11 out of the hand of the king of **A.**? 804
2Ch 32:21 in the camp of the king of **A.**. 804
2Ch 32:22 hand of Sennacherib the king of **A.**, 804
2Ch 33:11 of the host of the king of **A.**, 804
Ezr 6:22 turned the heart of the king of **A.** 804
Ne 9:32 since the time of the kings of **A.** 804
Isa 7:17 from Judah; even the king of **A.**. 804
Isa 7:18 the bee that is in the land of **A.**. 804
Isa 7:20 beyond the river, by the king of **A.**. 804
Isa 8:4 taken away before the king of **A.**. 804
Isa 8:7 the king of **A.**, and all his glory: 804
Isa 10:12 of the stout heart of the king of **A.**, 804
Isa 11:11 which shall be left, from **A.**, and 804
Isa 11:16 which shall be left, from **A.**: like as 804
Isa 19:23 a highway out of Egypt to **A.**, 804
Isa 19:23 and the Egyptian into **A.**, and the 804
Isa 19:24 the third with Egypt and with **A.**, 804
Isa 19:25 and **A.** the work of my hands, 804
Isa 20:1 Sargon the king of **A.** sent him,) 804
Isa 20:4 So shall the king of **A.** lead away 804
Isa 20:6 be delivered from the king of **A.**: 804
Isa 27:13 ready to perish in the land of **A.**, 804
Isa 36:1 that Sennacherib king of **A.** came 804
Isa 36:2 the king of **A.** sent Rabshakeh 804
Isa 36:4 the king of **A.**, What confidence 804
Isa 36:8 thee, to my master the king of **A.**, 804
Isa 36:13 of the great king, the king of **A.** 804
Isa 36:15 into the head of the king of **A.**. 804
Isa 36:16 for thus saith the king of **A.**, 804
Isa 36:18 out of the hand of the king of **A.**? 804
Isa 37:4 whom the king of **A.** his master hath 804
Isa 37:6 the servants of the king of **A.** have 804
Isa 37:8 and found the king of **A.** warring 804
Isa 37:10 into the hand of the king of **A.**. 804
Isa 37:11 what the kings of **A.** have done 804
Isa 37:18 the kings of **A.** have laid waste all 804
Isa 37:21 me against Sennacherib king of **A.**: 804
Isa 37:33 Lord concerning the king of **A.**, 804
Isa 37:37 Sennacherib king of **A.** departed, 804
Isa 38:6 out of the hand of the king of **A.**: 804
Jer 2:18 hast thou to do in the way of **A.**, 804
Jer 2:36 Egypt, as thou wast ashamed of **A.**. 804
Jer 50:17 the king of **A.** hath devoured him; 804
Jer 50:18 as I have punnished the king of **A.**. 804
Eze 23:7 that were the chosen men of **A.**, 804
Ho 7:11 they called to Egypt, they go of **A.**. 804
Ho 8:9 For they are gone up to **A.**, a wild 804
Ho 9:3 they shall eat unclean things in **A.**. 804
Ho 10:6 It shall be also carried unto the **A.** 804
Ho 11:11 as a dove out of the land of **A.** 804
Mic 5:6 they shall waste the land of **A.** 804
Mic 7:12 shall come even to thee from **A.**, 804
Na 3:18 shepherds slumber, O king of **A.** 804
Zep 2:13 against the north, and destroy **A.**; 804
Zec 10:10 Egypt, and gather them out of **A.**; 804
Zec 10:11 pride of **A.** shall be brought down, 804

ASSYRIAN (as-sir'-e'-un) See also ASSYRIANS.
Isa 10:5 O **A.**, the rod of mine anger, 804
Isa 10:24 in Zion, be not afraid of the **A.** 804
Isa 14:25 I will break the **A.** in my land, 804
Isa 19:23 and the **A.** shall come into Egypt, 804
Isa 23:13 till the **A.** founded it for them that 804
Isa 30:31 shall the **A.** be beaten down, 804
Isa 31:8 shall the **A.** fall with the sword, 804
Isa 52:4 **A.** oppressed them without cause. 804
Eze 31:3 the **A.** was a cedar in Lebanon with 804
Ho 5:13 then went Ephraim to the **A.**, 804
Ho 11:5 but the **A.** shall be his king, 804
Mic 5:5 the **A.** shall come into our land: 804
Mic 5:6 thus shall he deliver us from the **A.**, 804

ASSYRIANS (as-sir'-e-uns)
2Ki 19:35 and smote in the camp of the **A.** 804
Isa 19:23 shall serve with the **A.**. 804
Isa 37:36 and smote in the camp of the **A.** 804
La 5:6 and to the **A.**, to be satisfied with 804
Eze 16:28 the whore also with the **A.**, 1121,804
Eze 23:5 her lovers, on the **A.** her neighbors, 804
Eze 23:9 into the hand of the **A.** upon 1121,804
Eze 23:12 upon the **A.** her neighbours, 1121,804
Eze 23:23 and Koa, and all the **A.** with them: 804
Ho 12:1 do make a covenant with the **A.**, 804

ASTAROTH (as'-ta-roth) See also ASHTAROTH.
De 1:4 king of Bashanm, which dwelt at **A.**. 6252

ASTONIED See also ASTONISHED.
Ezr 9:3 of my beard, and sat down **a.**. 8074
Ezr 9:4 sat **a.** until the evening sacrifice. 8074
Job 17:8 upright men shall be **a.** at this, 8074
Job 18:20 that come after him shall be **a.** 8074
Isa 52:14 As man were **a.** at thee; 8074
Jer 14:9 shouldest thou be as a man **a.**, 1724
Eze 4:17 **a.** one with another, and 8074
Da 3:24 Nebuchadnezzar the king was **a.**, 8429
Da 4:19 Daniel,....was **a.** for one hour 8075
Da 5:9 in him, and his lords were **a.** 7672

ASTONISHED See also ASTONIED.
Le 26:32 and your enemies...shall be **a.** 8074
1Ki 9:8 passeth by it shall be **a.**, 8074
Job 21:5 Mark me, and be **a.**, and lay your 8074
Job 26:11 and are **a.** at his reproof. 8539
Jer 2:12 Be **a.**, O ye heavens, at this, 8074
Jer 4:9 and the priests shall be **a.**, 8074
Jer 18:16 that passeth thereby shall be **a.** 8074
Jer 19:8 that passeth thereby shall be **a.** 8074
Jer 49:17 that goeth by it shall be **a.**, 8074
Jer 50:13 that goeth by Babylon shall be **a.**, 8074
Eze 3:15 remained there **a.** among them 8074
Eze 26:16 every moment, and be **a.** at thee. 8074
Eze 27:35 inhabitants of the isles shall be **a.** 8074
Eze 28:19 the people shall be **a.** at thee: 8074
Da 8:27 and I was **a.** at the vision, 8074
Mt 7:28 the people were **a.** at his doctrine: *1605*
Mt 13:54 insomuch that they were **a.**, *1605*
Mt 22:33 they were **a.** at his doctrine *1605*
Mk 1:22 they were **a.** at his doctrine: *1605*
Mk 5:42 **a.** with a great astonishment. *1839*
Mk 6:2 many hearing him were **a.**, *1605*
Mk 7:37 were beyond measure **a.**, *1605*
Mk 10:24 disciples were **a.** at his words. *2284*

Mk 10:26 they were **a.** out of measure, *1605*
Mk 11:18 the people was **a.** at his doctrine *1605*
Lu 2:47 were **a.** at his understanding *1839*
Lu 4:32 they were **a.** at his doctrine: *1605*
Lu 5:9 For he was **a.**, and all that *4023,2285*
Lu 8:56 her parents were **a.**: *1839*
Lu 24:22 made us **a.**, which were early *1839*
Ac 9:6 And he trembling and **a.** said, *2284*
Ac 10:45 were **a.**, as many as came with *1839*
Ac 12:16 saw him, they were **a.** *1839*
Ac 13:12 **a.** at the doctrine of the Lord *1605*

ASTONISHMENT
De 28:28 and **a.** of heart: 8541
De 28:37 thou shalt become an **a.**, 8047
2Ch 7:21 shall be an **a.** to every one 8074
2Ch 29:8 to trouble, to **a.**, and to hissing, 8047
Ps 60:3 made us to drink the wine of **a.** 8653
Jer 8:21 **a.** hath taken hold on me 8047
Jer 25:9 make them an **a.**, and an hissing, 8047
Jer 25:11 desolation, and an **a.**; 8047
Jer 25:18 a desolation, an **a.**, an hissing, 8047
Jer 29:18 a curse, and an **a.**, 8047
Jer 42:18 execration, and an **a.**, 8047
Jer 44:12 an **a.**, and a curse, 8047
Jer 44:22 desolation, and an **a.**, 8047
Jer 51:37 an **a.**, and an hissing, 8047
Jer 51:41 Babylon become an **a.** 8047
Eze 4:16 water by measure, and with **a.** 8078
Eze 5:15 instruction and an **a.**: 8047
Eze 12:19 and drink their water with **a.**, 8078
Eze 23:33 with the cup of **a.** and desolation, 8047
Zec 12:4 smite every horse with **a.**, 8541
Mk 5:42 astonished with a great **a.** *1611*

ASTRAY
Ex 23:4 enemy's ox or his ass going **a.**, 8582
De 22:1 not see thy brother's ox…go **a.**, 5080
Ps 58:3 they go **a.** as soon as they be born, 8582
Ps 119:67 Before I was afflicted I went **a.**: 7683
Ps 119:176 I have gone **a.** like a lost sheep; 8582
Pr 5:23 of his folly he shall go **a.** 7686
Pr 7:25 go not **a.** in her paths 8582
Pr 28:10 causeth the righteous to go **a.** 7686
Isa 53:6 All we like sheep have gone **a.**; 8582
Jer 50:6 have caused them to go **a.**, 8582
Eze 14:11 Israel may go no more **a.** from me, 8582
Eze 44:10 when Israel went **a.**, 8582
Eze 44:10 which went **a.** away from me 8582
Eze 44:15 the children of Israel went **a.**, 8582
Eze 48:11 which went not **a.** 8582
Eze 48:11 when the children of Israel went **a.**, 8582
Eze 48:11 as the Levites went **a.** 8582
Mt 18:12 **and one of them be gone a.** *4105*
Mt 18:12 **and seeketh that which is gone a.?** *4105*
Mt 18:13 **ninety and nine which went not a.** *4105*
1Pe 2:25 ye were as sheep going **a.**; *4105*
2Pe 2:15 and are gone **a.**, following the way *4105*

ASTROLOGER See also ASTROLOGERS.
Da 2:10 things at any magician, or **a.**, 826

ASTROLOGERS
Isa 47:13 now the **a.**, the stargazers, 1895,8064
Da 1:20 **a.** that were in all his realm, 825
Da 2:2 the magicians, and the **a.**, 825
Da 2:27 cannot the wise men, the **a.** 826
Da 4:7 came in the magicians, the **a.**, 826
Da 5:7 cried aloud to bring in the **a.**, 826
Da 5:11 master of the magicians, **a.**, 826
Da 5:15 the **a.**, have been brought in 826

ASUNDER
Le 1:17 shall not divide it **a.**: 826
Le 5:8 his neck, but shall not divide it **a.**:
Nu 16:31 the ground clave **a.** that was
2Ki 2:11 and parted them both **a.**; 996
Job 16:12 but he hath broken me **a.**: he hath
Job 16:13 about, he cleaveth my reins **a.**,
Ps 2:3 Let us break their bands **a.**, and
Ps 129:4 he hath cut **a.** the cords of the
Jer 50:23 hammer of the whole earth cut **a.**
Eze 30:16 No shall be rent **a.**,
Hab 3:6 and drove **a.** the nations;
Zec 11:10 and cut it **a.**, that I might break
Zec 11:14 Then I cut **a.** mine other staff,
Mt 19:6 **together, let not man put a.** *5563*
Mt 24:51 **shall cut him a., and appoint him** *1371*
Mk 5:4 had been plucked **a.** by him, *1288*
Mk 10:9 **let not man put a.** *5562*
Ac 1:18 he burst **a.** in the midst, *2977*
Ac 15:39 they departed **a.** one from the *673*
Heb 4:12 even to the dividing **a.** of soul and
Heb 11:37 they were sawn **a.**, were tempted, *4249*

ASUPPIM
1Ch 26:15 to his sons, the house of **A.** 624
1Ch 26:17 and toward **A.** two and two 624

ASYNCRITUS (a-sin'-cri-tus)
Ro 16:14 Salute **A.**, Phlegon, Hermas, *790*

AT See also THEREAT.
Ge 3:24 and he placed **a.** the east of the 790
Ge 4:7 doest not well, sin lieth **a.** the
Ge 6:6 and it grieved him **a.** his heart 413
Ge 8:6 And it came to pass **a.** the end of
Ge 9:5 **a.** the hand of every beast will I
Ge 9:5 require it, and **a.** the hand of man;
Ge 9:5 **a.** the hand of every man's brother
Ge 13:3 where his tent had been **a.** the
Ge 13:4 he had made there **a.** the first:
Ge 14:17 **a.** the valley of Shaveh, which is 413
Ge 17:21 unto thee **a.** this set time in the
Ge 18:14 **A.** the time appointed I will
Ge 19:1 angels to Sodom **a.** even; and Lot
Ge 19:6 And lot went out **a.** the door unto
Ge 19:11 that were **a.** the door of the house
Ge 20:13 **a.** every place whither we shall 413
Ge 21:2 **a.** the set time of which God had
Ge 21:22 And it came to pass **a.** that time,
Ge 21:32 Thus they made a covenant **a.**
Ge 22:19 and Abraham dwelt **a.** Beer-sheba
Ge 23:10 that went in **a.** the gate of his city,
Ge 23:18 that went in **a.** the gate of his city,
Ge 24:11 by a well of water **a.** the time of
Ge 24:21 And the man wondering **a.** her
Ge 24:30 stood by the camels **a.** the well 5921
Ge 24:55 with us a few days, **a.** the least ten; 176
Ge 24:57 damsel, and inquire **a.** her mouth
Ge 24:63 in the field **a.** the eventide:
Ge 25:32 Behold, I am **a.** the point to die:
Ge 26:8 looked out **a.** window, and 1157
Ge 27:41 for my father are **a.** hand; 7128
Ge 28:19 city was called Luz **a.** the first
Ge 31:10 And it came to pass **a.** the time
Ge 33:10 receive my present **a.** my hand:
Ge 33:19 tent, **a.** the hand of the children
Ge 38:1 it came to pass **a.** that time, that
Ge 38:5 and he was at Chezib, when she
Ge 38:11 Remain a widow **a.** thy father's
Ge 41:1 it came to pass **a.** the end of two
Ge 41:21 ill favored, as **a.** the beginning
Ge 43:16 shall dine with me **a.** noon
Ge 43:18 in our sacks **a.** the first time
Ge 43:19 communed with him **a.** the door
Ge 43:20 came indeed down **a.** the first time
Ge 43:25 against Joseph came **a.** noon:
Ge 43:33 men marvelled one **a.** another 413
Ge 44:12 began **a.** the eldest, and left **a.** the
Ge 45:3 they were troubled **a.** his presence
Ge 48:3 appeared unto me **a.** Luz in the
Ge 49:13 Zebulun shall dwell **a.** the heaven
Ge 49:19 but he shall overcome **a.** the last
Ge 49:23 and shot **a.** him, and hated him:
Ge 49:27 the prey, and **a.** night he shall
Ex 2:5 wash herself **a.** the river; and her 5921
Ex 4:25 of her son, and cast it **a.** his feet,
Ex 5:23 thou delivered the people **a.** all
Ex 8:32 hardened his heart **a.** this time
Ex 9:14 For I will **a.** this time send all my
Ex 12:9 raw, nor sodden **a.** all with water,
Ex 12:18 fourteenth day of the month **a.** even,
Ex 12:18 twentieth day of the month **a.** even
Ex 12:22 shall go out **a.** the door of his
Ex 12:29 **a.** midnight the Lord smote all
Ex 12:41 it came to pass **a.** the end of the
Ex 16:6 **A.** even, then ye shall know that
Ex 16:12 **A.** even ye shall eat flesh, and in 996
Ex 16:13 it came to pass, that **a.** ever the
Ex 18:5 he encamped **a.** the mount of God:
Ex 18:22 judge the people **a.** all seasons:
Ex 18:26 judged the people **a.** all seasons:
Ex 19:15 third day: come not **a.** your wives 413
Ex 19:17 and they stood **a.** the nether part
Ex 22:23 in any wise, and they cry **a.** all
Ex 22:26 If thou **a.** all take thy neighbour's
Ex 28:7 joined **a.** the two edges thereof; 413
Ex 28:14 chains of pure gold **a.** the ends;
Ex 28:22 chains **a.** the ends of wreathen
Ex 29:39 lamb thou shalt offer **a.** even: 996
Ex 29:41 thou shalt offer **a.** even, and shalt
Ex 29:42 **a.** the door of the tabernacle of
Ex 30:8 Aaron lighteth the lamps **a.** even, 996
Ex 32:4 received them **a.** their hand, and
Ex 33:8 stood every man **a.** his tent door,
Ex 33:9 stood **a.** the door of the tabernacle,
Ex 33:10 stand **a.** the tabernacle door:
Ex 34:22 of ingathering **a.** the year's end,
Ex 35:15 for the door **a.** the entering in of
Ex 36:29 together **a.** the head thereof, 413
Ex 38:8 assembled **a.** the door of the
Ex 39:15 breastplate chains **a.** the ends,
Ex 40:8 up the hanging **a.** the court gate
Ex 40:28 set up the hanging **a.** the door of
Le 1:3 voluntary will **a.** the door of the 413
Le 1:15 shall be wrung out **a.** the side of 5921
Le 3:2 of the offering, and kill it **a.** the
Le 4:7 of the bullock **a.** the bottom of the 413
Le 4:7 which is **a.** the door of the
Le 4:18 pour out all the blood **a.** the 413
Le 4:18 **a.** the door of the tabernacle of the
Le 4:25 **a.** the bottom of the altar of burnt 413
Le 4:30 thereof **a.** the bottom of the altar 413
Le 4:34 the blood thereof **a.** the bottom 413
Le 5:9 wrung out **a.** the bottom of the 413
Le 6:20 and half thereof **a.** night
Le 7:18 be eaten **a.** all on the third
Le 8:15 blood **a.** the bottom of the altar, 413
Le 8:31 Boil the flesh **a.** the door of the
Le 8:33 your consecration be **a.** an end: 3117
Le 8:35 shall ye abide **a.** the door
Le 9:9 the blood **a.** the bottom of the 413
Le 13:5 plague in his sight be **a.** a stay, 413
Le 13:37 if the scall be in his sight **a.** a stay,
Le 14:11 before the Lord, **a.** the door of the
Le 15:24 man lie with her **a.** all, and her
Le 16:2 come not **a.** all times into the holy
Le 16:7 before the Lord **a.** the door of the
Le 16:29 do no work **a.** all, whether it be
Le 17:6 of the Lord **a.** the door of the
Le 18:9 be born **a.** home, or born aboard,
Le 19:5 ye shall offer it **a.** your will
Le 19:7 if it be eaten **a.** all on the third day,
Le 19:20 not **a.** all redeemed, nor freedom
Le 22:19 Ye shall offer **a.** your own will **a.**
Le 22:29 Lord, offer it **a.** your own will
Le 23:5 the first month **a.** even is the 996
Le 23:32 ninth day of the month **a.** even,
Le 25:32 the Levites redeem **a.** any time
Le 26:32 therein shall be astonished **a.** it 5921
Le 27:10 if he shall **a.** all change beast for
Le 27:13 But if he will **a.** all redeem it,
Le 27:16 shall be valued **a.** fifty shekels
Le 27:31 And if a man will **a.** all redeem
Le 27:33 if he change it **a.** all, then both it
Nu 3:39 numbered **a.** the commandment 5921
Nu 4:27 **A.** the appointment of Aaron
Nu 6:6 he shall come **a.** no dead body
Nu 6:18 **a.** the door of the tabernacle of
Nu 9:2 the passover **a.** his appointed
Nu 9:3 day of this month, **a.** even, 996
Nu 9:5 first month **a.** even in the 996
Nu 9:11 **a.** even they shall keep it, and eat 996
Nu 9:15 and **a.** even there was upon the
Nu 9:18 **A.** the commandment of the Lord 5921
Nu 9:18 **a.** the commandment of the Lord 5921
Nu 9:23 **A.** the commandment of the Lord 5921
Nu 9:23 **a.** the commandment of the Lord 5921
Nu 9:23 of the Lord, **a.** the commandment 5921
Nu 10:3 themselves to the **a.** the door of 413
Nu 11:6 there is nothing **a.** all besides this
Nu 11:20 until it come out **a.** your nostrils
Nu 11:35 and abode **a.** Hazeroth
Nu 13:30 Let us go up **a.** once, and possess
Nu 16:34 round about them, fled **a.** the cry
Nu 19:19 and shall be clean **a.** even
Nu 20:24 against my word **a.** the water
Nu 21:11 both, and pitched **a.** Ije-abarim,
Nu 21:15 And **a.** the stream of the brooks
Nu 21:30 We have shot **a.** them; Heshbon is
Nu 21:33 his people, to the battle **a.** Edrei
Nu 21:34 Amorites, which dwelt **a.** Heshbon
Nu 22:4 king of the Moabites **a.** that time
Nu 22:20 came unto Balaam **a.** night, and
Nu 22:38 I now any power **a.** all to say any

Nu 23:25 them **a.** all, nor bless them **a.** all
Nu 24:1 he went not. as **a.** other times, to
Nu 27:14 to sanctify me **a.** the water before
Nu 27:21 **a.** his word shall they go out, 5921
Nu 27:21 go out, and **a.** his word they shall 5921
Nu 28:4 lamb shalt thou offer **a.** even; 996
Nu 28:8 lamb shalt thou offer **a.** even; 996
Nu 30:4 father shall hold his peace **a.** her;
Nu 30:6 And if she had **a.** all a husband,
Nu 30:7 it, and held his peace **a.** her,
Nu 30:11 and held his peace **a.** her,
Nu 30:14 altogether hold his peace **a.** her
Nu 30:14 because he held his peace **a.** her,
Nu 31:12 the camp **a.** the plains of Moab, 413
Nu 33:14 and encamped **a.** Rephidim,
Nu 33:16 pitched **a.** Kibroth-hattaavah
Nu 33:17 and encamped **a.** Hazeroth
Nu 33:19 and pitched **a.** Rimmon-parez
Nu 33:21 Libnah, and pitched **a.** Rissah.
Nu 33:26 and encamped **a.** Tahath.
Nu 33:27 Tahathm, and pitched **a.** Tarah.
Nu 33:30 and encamped **a.** Moseroth.
Nu 33:32 and encamped **a.** Hor-hagidgod,
Nu 33:34 and encamped **a.** Ebronah.
Nu 33:35 and encamped **a.** Ezion-gaber.
Nu 33:38 **a.** the commandment of the Lord, 5921
Nu 34:5 goings out of it shall be **a.** the sea
Nu 34:9 out of it shall be **a.** Hazar-enan:
Nu 34:12 out of it shall be **a.** the salt sea:
Nu 35:11 killeth any person **a.** unawares
Nu 35:20 or hurl **a.** him laying of wait,
Nu 35:26 the slayer shall **a.** any time come
De 1:4 dwelt **a.** Astaroth in Edrei:
De 1:9 And I spake unto you **a.**: that time,
De 1:16 I charged your judges **a.** that time,
De 1:18 I commanded you **a.** that time
De 2:32 all his people, to fight **a.** Jahaz.
De 2:34 we took all his cities **a.** that time
De 3:1 to battle **a.** Edrei
De 3:2 Amorites, which dwelt **a.** Heshbon.
De 3:4 we took all his cities **a.** that time,
De 3:8 took **a.** that time out of the hand
De 3:12 which we possessed **a.** that time,
De 3:18 **a.** that time, saying, The Lord
De 3:21 I commanded Joshua **a.** that time,
De 3:23 I besought the Lord **a.** that time,
De 4:14 Lord commanded me **a.** that time
De 4:46 Amorites, who dwelt **a.** Heshbon,
De 5:5 the Lord and you **a.** that time,
De 6:24 us alive, as it is **a.** this day.
De 7:21 shalt not be affrighted **a.** them: 6440
De 7:22 not consume them **a.** once, 4118
De 8:16 do thee good **a.** thy latter end;
De 8:19 if thou do **a.** all forget the Lord
De 9:11 it came to pass **a.** the end of
De 9:18 before the Lord, as **a.** the first,
De 9:19 hearkened unto me **a.** that time
De 9:22 And **a.** Taberah, and **a.** Massah,
De 9:22 and **a.** Kibroth-hattaavah,
De 9:25 as I fell down **a.** the first;
De 10:1 **A.** that time the Lord said unto
De 10:8 **A.** that time the Lord separated
De 10:10 hearkened unto me **a.** that time
De 14:28 **A.** the end of three years thou
De 15:1 **A.** the end of every seven years
De 15:9 the year of release is **a.** hand; 7126
De 16:4 sacrificedst the first day **a.** even,
De 16:6 But **a.** the place which the Lord 413
De 16:6 **a.** even, **a.** the going down of the
De 16:6 **a.** the season that thou camest
De 17:6 **A.** the mouth of two witnesses, 5921
De 17:6 but **a.** the mouth of one witness 5921
De 19:15 **a.** the mouth of two witnesses, 5921
De 19:15 **a.** the mouth of three witnesses, 5921
De 21:14 shalt not sell her **a.** all for money,
De 23:24 thy fill **a.** thine own pleasure;
De 24:5 shall be free **a.** home one year,
De 24:15 **A.** his day thou shalt give him
De 28:29 thou shalt grope **a.** noonday,
De 28:67 and **a.** even thou shalt say,
De 31:10 **A.** the end of every seven years,
De 32:35 day of their calamity is **a.** hand, 7138
De 32:51 **a.** the waters of Meribah-kadesh,
De 33:3 and they sat down **a.** thy feet;
De 33:8 whom thou didst prove **a.** Massah, 5921
De 33:8 and with whom thou didst strive **a.**
Jos 5:2 **A.** that time the Lord said unto
Jos 5:3 the children of Israel **a.** the hill 413
Jos 5:10 **a.** even in the plains of Jericho
Jos 6:16 came to pass **a.** the seventh time,
Jos 6:26 Joshua adjured them **a.** that time,
Jos 7:7 hast thou **a.** all brought this people
Jos 8:5 out against us, as **a.** the first,
Jos 8:6 flee before us, as **a.** the first:
Jos 8:14 his people, **a.** a time appointed,
Jos 8:29 cast it **a.** the entering in of the 413
Jos 9:6 Joshua unto the camp **a.** Gilgal,
Jos 9:10 Bashan, which was **a.** Ashtaroth,
Jos 9:14 counel **a.** the mouth of the Lord
Jos 9:16 to pass **a.** the end of three days
Jos 10:10 with a great slaughter **a.** Gibeon,
Jos 10:16 themelves in a cave **a.** Makkedah.
Jos 10:17 found hid in a cave **a.** Makkedah.
Jos 10:21 the camp to Joshua **a.** Makkedah.
Jos 10:27 it came to pass **a.** the time of the
Jos 10:42 land did Joshua take **a.** one time,
Jos 11:5 pitched together **a.** the waters of 413
Jos 11:10 Joshua **a.** that time turned back,
Jos 11:21 And **a.** that time came Joshua,
Jos 12:4 that dwelt **a.** Ashtroth and **a.**
Jos 15:4 out of that coast were **a.** the sea:
Jos 15:5 of the sea **a.** the uttermost part 5704
Jos 15:7 out thereof were **a.** En-rogel: 413
Jos 15:8 westward, which is **a.** the end of
Jos 15:11 out of the border were **a.** the sea.
Jos 15:63 children of Judah **a.** Jerusalem
Jos 16:3 goings out thereof are **a.** the sea
Jos 16:7 to Jericho, and went out **a.** Jordan.
Jos 16:8 out thereof were **a.** the sea.
Jos 17:9 the outgoings of it were **a.** the sea:
Jos 18:1 Israel assembled together **a.** Shiloh,
Jos 18:9 to Joshua to the host **a.** Shiloh.
Jos 18:12 out thereof were **a.** the wilderness
Jos 18:14 out thereof were **a.** Kirjath-baal, 413
Jos 18:19 **a.** the north bay of the salt sea
Jos 18:19 **a.** the south end of Jordan:
Jos 19:22 of their border were **a.** Jordan:
Jos 19:29 are **a.** the sea from the coast to
Jos 19:33 outgoings thereof were **a.** Jordan:
Jos 19:51 **a.** the door of the tabernacle
Jos 20:4 stand **a.** the entering of the gate
Jos 20:9 killeth any person **a.** unawares
Jos 21:2 they spake unto them **a.** Shiloh
Jos 21:3 **a.** the commandment of the 413
Jos 22:11 **a.** the passage of the children of 413
Jos 22:12 themselves together **a.** Shiloh.
Jg 3:2 **a.** the least such as before knew 7535
Jg 3:29 slew of Moab **a.** that time about
Jg 4:4 she judged Israel **a.** that time.
Jg 4:10 ten thousand men **a.** his feet:
Jg 5:27 **A.** her feet he bowed, he fell, he 996
Jg 5:27 **a.** her feet he bowed, he fell: where 996
Jg 5:28 Sisera looked out **a.** a window, 1157
Jg 7:25 slew **a.** the winepress of Zeeb,
Jg 8:18 were they whom ye slew **a.** Tabor?
Jg 9:5 unto his father's house **a.** Ophrah,
Jg 9:41 Abimelech dwelt **a.** Arumah:
Jg 11:39 it came to pass **a.** the end of two
Jg 12:2 my people were **a.** great strife
Jg 12:6 him **a.** the passages of Jordan: 413
Jg 12:6 there fell **a.** that time of the
Jg 12:10 and was buried **a.** Beth-lehem
Jg 13:23 a meat offering **a.** our hands,
Jg 13:23 as **a.** this time have told us such
Jg 13:25 began to move him **a.** times
Jg 14:4 for **a.** that time the Philistines had
Jg 16:3 midnight, and arose **a.** midnight,
Jg 16:20 I will go out as **a.** other times
Jg 16:28 I may be **a.** once avenged of the
Jg 16:30 dead which he slew **a.** his death
Jg 18:27 a people that were **a.** quiet and
Jg 18:29 of the city was Laish **a.** the first
Jg 19:16 his work out of the field **a.** even,
Jg 19:22 beat **a.** the door, and spake to 5921
Jg 19:26 fell down **a.** the door of the man's
Jg 19:27 was fallen down **a.** the door
Jg 20:15 were numbered **a.** that time
Jg 20:16 one could sling a stone **a.** an hair 413
Jg 20:20 fight against them **a.** Gibeah
Jg 20:30 against Gibeah, as **a.** other times
Jg 20:31 and kill, as **a.** other times, in the
Jg 20:32 down before us, as **a.** the first
Jg 20:33 put themselves in array **a.** Baaltamar
Jg 21:14 Benjamin came again **a.** that time;
Jg 21:22 not give unto them **a.** this time,
Jg 21:24 of Israel departed thence **a.** that
Ru 2:14 **A.** mealtime come thou hither,
Ru 3:7 he went to lie down **a.** the end of
Ru 3:8 And it came to pass **a.** midnight,
Ru 3:8 behold, a woman lay **a.** his feet
Ru 3:10 latter end than **a.** the beginning,
Ru 3:14 And she lay **a.** his feet until the
1Sa 2:22 women that assembled **a.** the door
1Sa 2:29 ye **a.** my sacrifice and **a.** mine
1Sa 3:2 pass **a.** that time, when Eli was
1Sa 3:10 and called as **a.** other times,
1Sa 3:11 in Israel, **a.** which both the ears
1Sa 6:10 and shut up their calves **a.** home:
1Sa 9:8 I have here **a.** hand the fourth
1Sa 10:2 the border of Benjamin **a.** Zezah;
1Sa 13:11 themselves together **a.** Michmash;
1Sa 14:18 the ark of God was **a.** that time
1Sa 16:4 of the own trembled **a.** his
1Sa 17:1 were gathered together **a.** Shocoh,
1Sa 17:15 his father's sheep **a.** Beth-lehem.
1Sa 18:10 with his hand, as **a.** other times:
1Sa 18:19 it came to pass **a.** the time when
1Sa 19:19 David is **a.** Naioth in Ramah.
1Sa 19:22 they be **a.** Naioth in Ramah
1Sa 20:5 fail to sit with he king **a.** meat:
1Sa 20:5 field unto the third day **a.** even.
1Sa 20:6 If thy father **a.** all miss me,
1Sa 20:16 **a.** the hand of David's enemies.
1Sa 20:20 thereof, as though I shot **a.** a mark.
1Sa 20:25 upon his seat, as **a.** other times,
1Sa 20:33 Saul cast a javelin **a.** him to smite 5921
1Sa 20:35 went out into the field **a.** the time
1Sa 21:1 was afraid **a.** the meeting of
1Sa 21:4 themselves **a.** least from women. 389
1Sa 22:8, 13 to lie in wait, as **a.** this day?
1Sa 22:14 in law, and goeth **a.** thy bidding, 413
1Sa 23:29 dwelt in strong holds **a.** En-gedi. 413
1Sa 25:1 buried him in his house **a.** Ramah.
1Sa 25:24 And fell **a.** his feet and said, 5921
1Sa 26:7 stuck in the ground **a.** his bolster:
1Sa 26:8 spear even to the earth **a.** once,
1Sa 26:11 the spear that is **a.** his bolster,
1Sa 26:16 of water that was **a.** his bolster.
1Sa 27:3 David dwelt with Achish **a.** Gath,
1Sa 28:7 hath a familiar spirit **a.** En-dor.
1Sa 30:8 David enquired **a.** the Lord,
1Sa 30:21 also to abide **a.** the brook Besor:
1Sa 31:13 them under a tree **a.** Jabesh,
2Sa 2:32 they came to Hebron **a.** break of
2Sa 3:30 slain their brother Asahel **a.**
2Sa 3:32 and wept **a.** the grave of Abner;
2Sa 4:5 who lay on a bed **a.** noon.
2Sa 6:4 which was **a.** Gilbeah,
2Sa 8:3 to recover his border **a.** the river
2Sa 9:7 shalt eat bread **a.** my table 5921
2Sa 9:10 eat bread alway **a.** my table. 5921
2Sa 9:11 he shall eat **a.** my table, as one 5921
2Sa 9:13 did eat continually **a.** the king's 5921
2Sa 10:5 the king said, Tarry **a.** Jericho
2Sa 10:8 battle in array **a.** the entering in
2Sa 11:1 the year was expired, **a.** the time
2Sa 11:1 But David tarried still **a.**
2Sa 11:9 But Uriah slept **a.** the door of the
2Sa 11:13 and **a.** even he went out to lie
2Sa 13:5 see it, and eat it **a.** her hand.
2Sa 13:6 sight, that I may eat **a.** her hand.
2Sa 14:26 for it was **a.** every year's end
2Sa 14:26 the hair of his head **a.** two
2Sa 15:8 while I abode **a.** Geshur in Syria,
2Sa 15:14 that were **a.** Jerusalem, Arise,
2Sa 16:3 he abideth **a.** Jerusalem: for he
2Sa 16:6 And he cast stones **a.** David,
2Sa 16:6 and **a.** all the servants of the
2Sa 16:13 threw stones **a.** him, and cast 5980
2Sa 16:23 as if a man had inquired **a.** the
2Sa 17:7 given is not good **a.** this time.
2Sa 17:9 of them be overthrown **a.** the
2Sa 19:9 And all the people were **a.** strife
2Sa 19:28 them that did eat **a.** thine own
2Sa 19:32 of sustenance while he lay **a.**
2Sa 19:42 have we eaten **a.** all of the king's
2Sa 20:3 David came to his house **a.**
2Sa 20:8 When they were **a.** the great 5973
2Sa 20:18 surely ask counsel **a.** Abel: and
2Sa 21:18 with the Philistines **a.** Gob:
2Sa 22:16 **a.** the rebuking of the Lord,
2Sa 22:16 **a.** the blast of the
2Sa 23:8 whom he slew **a.** one time.
2Sa 24:8 they came to Jerusalem **a.** the

2Sa 24:24 I will surely buy it of thee **a.** a
1Ki 1:6 had not displeased him **a.** any time
1Ki 2:7 of those that eat **a.** thy table: for
1Ki 2:8 came down to meet me **a.** Jordan,
1Ki 2:26 but I will not **a.** this time put thee
1Ki 2:39 And it came to pass **a.** the end of
1Ki 3:20 And she arose **a.** midnight, and
1Ki 5:14 Lebanon, and two months **a.** home;
1Ki 7:30 undersetters molten, **a.** the side of
1Ki 8:2 unto king Solomon **a.** the feast
1Ki 8:9 which Moses put there **a.** Horeb,
1Ki 8:59 cause of his people Israel **a.** all
1Ki 8:61 keep his commandments as **a.** this
1Ki 8:65 And **a.** that time Solomon held a
1Ki 9:2 had appeared unto him **a.** Gibeon
1Ki 9:6 But if ye shall **a.** all turn from
1Ki 9:8 And **a.** this house, which is high,
1Ki 9:10 And it came to pass **a.** the end of
1Ki 10:22 For the king had **a.** sea a navy of
1Ki 10:26 and with the king at Jerusalem
1Ki 10:28 received the linen yarn **a.** a price
1Ki 11:29 And it came to pass **a.** that time
1Ki 12:27 house of the Lord **a.** Jerusalem,
1Ki 13:20 it came to pass as they sat **a.** the 413
1Ki 14:1 **A.** that time Abijah the son of
1Ki 14:6 as she came in **a.** the door, that he
1Ki 15:18 king of Syria, that dwelt **a.**
1Ki 15:27 Baasha smote him **a.** Gibbethon,
1Ki 18:19 which eat **a.** Jezebel's table
1Ki 18:27 And it came to pass **a.** noon, that
1Ki 18:36 it came to pass **a.** the time of the
1Ki 18:36 I have done all these things **a.** thy
1Ki 18:44 And it came to pass **a.** the seventh
1Ki 19:6 and a cruse of water **a.** his head
1Ki 20:9 to thy servants **a.** the first I will do:
1Ki 20:16 And they went out **a.** noon. But
1Ki 20:22 **a.** the return of the year the king
1Ki 20:26 And it came to pass **a.** the return
1Ki 22:5 I pray thee, **a.** the word of the Lord
1Ki 22:20 go up and fall **a.** Ramoth-gilead?
1Ki 22:28 if thou return **a.** all in peace, the
1Ki 22:34 drew a bow **a.** a venture, and smote
1Ki 22:35 died **a.** even: and the blood ran
1Ki 22:48 ships were broken **a.** Ezion-geber
2Ki 2:3 prophets that were **a.** Beth-el came
2Ki 2:5 prophets that were **a.** Jericho came
2Ki 2:15 were to view **a.** Jericho, saw him,
2Ki 2:18 he tarried **a.** Jericho,) he said unto,
2Ki 4:17 and bare a son **a.** that season that
2Ki 4:37 fell **a.** his feet, and bowed herself 5921
2Ki 5:9 stood **a.** the door of the house of
2Ki 5:20 not receiving **a.** his hands that
2Ki 6:32 and hold him fast **a.** the door: is
2Ki 7:3 four leprous men **a.** the entering
2Ki 8:3 came to pass **a.** the seven years'
2Ki 8:22 Then Libna revolted **a.** the same
2Ki 8:29 the Syrians had given him **a.** Ramah,
2Ki 9:7 servants of the Lord, **a.** the hand
2Ki 9:24 the arrow went out **a.** his heart,
2Ki 9:27 they did so **a.** the going up to Gur,
2Ki 9:30 and looked out **a.** a window 1157
2Ki 9:31 And as Jehu entered in **a.** the gate,
2Ki 10:8 Lay ye them in two heaps **a.** the
2Ki 10:12 as he was **a.** the shearing house
2Ki 10:14 slew them **a.** the pit of the shearing
2Ki 11:6 shall be **a.** the gate of Sur; and a
2Ki 11:6 **a.** the gate behind the guard:
2Ki 12:4 money that every man is set **a.**,
2Ki 13:20 invaded the land **a.** the coming in
2Ki 14:10 glory of this, and tarry **a.** home:
2Ki 14:11 looked one another in the face **a.**
2Ki 14:13 son of Ahaziah, **a.** Beth-shemesh
2Ki 14:20 and he was buried **a.** Jerusalem
2Ki 16:6 **A.** that time Rezin king of Syria
2Ki 16:10 an altar that was **a.** Damascus:
2Ki 17:25 And so it was **a.** the beginning of
2Ki 18:10 And **a.** he end of three years they
2Ki 18:16 **A.** that time did Hezekiah cut off
2Ki 18:33 gods of the nations delivered **a.**
2Ki 19:21 hath shaken her head **a.** thee
2Ki 19:36 returned, and dwelt **a.** Nineveh
2Ki 20:12 **A.** that time Berodach-baladan,
2Ki 23:6 burned it **a.** the brook Kidron,
2Ki 23:8 left hand **a.** the gate of the city
2Ki 23:11 given to the sun, **a.** the entering in
2Ki 23:15 altar that was **a.** Beth-el, and the
2Ki 23:29 he slew him **a.** Megiddo, when he
2Ki 23:33 put him in bands **a.** Riblah in the
2Ki 24:3 Surely **a.** the commandment of 5921
2Ki 24:10 **A.** that time the servants of
2Ki 25:21 slew them **a.** Riblah in the land
2Ki 25:25 the Chaldees that were with him **a.**
1Ch 2:55 the scribes which dwell **a.** Jabez;
1Ch 4:28 And they dwelt **a.** Beer-sheba,
1Ch 4:29 **a.** Bilhah, and **a.** Ezem, and **a.** Tolad,
1Ch 4:30 And **a.** Bethuel, and **a.** Hormah,
1Ch 4:30 Hormah, and **a.** Ziklag,
1Ch 4:31 And **a.** Beth-marcaboth, and
1Ch 4:31 **a.** Beth-birei, and **a.** Shaaraim
1Ch 8:29 **a.** Gibeon dwelt the father of
1Ch 9:34 their generations: these dwell **a.**
1Ch 9:38 with their brethren **a.** Jerusalem,
1Ch 11:11 three hundred slain by him **a.** one
1Ch 11:13 He was with David **a.** Pas-dammim,
1Ch 11:16 Philistines' garrison was then **a.**
1Ch 11:17 Bethlehem, that is **a.** the gate!
1Ch 12:22 For **a.** that time day by day there
1Ch 12:32 their breathren were **a.** their 5921
1Ch 13:3 inquired not **a.** it in the days of 5921
1Ch 14:3 David took more wives **a.**
1Ch 15:13 because ye did it not **a.** the first,
1Ch 15:29 daughter of Saul looking out **a.** a. 1157
1Ch 16:33 wood sing out **a.** the presence of
1Ch 16:39 that was **a.** Gibeon
1Ch 17:9 them any more, as **a.** the beginning
1Ch 19:5 Tarry **a.** Jericho until your beards
1Ch 20:1 year was expired, **a.** the time that
1Ch 20:1 But David tarried **a.** Jerusalem
1Ch 20:4 that there arose war **a.** Gezer
1Ch 20:4 **a.** which time Sibbechai the
1Ch 20:6 was war **a.** Gath, where was a man
1Ch 21:19 David went up **a.** the saying of Gad,
1Ch 21:28 **A.** that time when David saw that
1Ch 21:29 **a.** that season in the high place **a.**
1Ch 23:30 praise the Lord, and likewise **a.**
1Ch 26:18 **A.** Parbar westward,
1Ch 26:18 four **a.** the causeway
1Ch 26:18 and two **a.** Parbar
1Ch 26:31 mighty men of valour **a.** Jazer of
1Ch 28:7 my judgments, as **a.** this day
1Ch 28:21 the people will be wholly **a.** thy
2Ch 1:3 high place that was **a.** Gibeon;
2Ch 1:4 pitched a tent for it **a.** Jerusalem
2Ch 1:6 which was **a.** the tabernacle of
2Ch 1:13 the high place that was **a.** Gibeon
2Ch 1:14 and with the king **a.** Jerusalem
2Ch 1:15 silver and gold **a.** Jerusalem
2Ch 1:16 received the linen yarn **a.** a price
2Ch 3:1 to build the house of the Lord **a.**
2Ch 5:10 which Moses put therein **a.** Horeb,
2Ch 5:12 stood **a.** the east end of the altar,
2Ch 7:8 Also **a.** the same time Solomon
2Ch 8:1 to pass **a.** the end of twenty years,
2Ch 8:14 also by their courses **a.** every gate:
2Ch 8:17 to Eloth, **a.** the sea side in the 5921
2Ch 9:1 Solomon with hard questions **a.**
2Ch 9:25 and with the king **a.** Jerusalem
2Ch 13:18 of Israel were brought under **a.**
2Ch 14:10 in the valley of Zephathah **a.**
2Ch 15:10 gathered themselves together **a.**
2Ch 15:15 all Judah rejoiced **a.** the oath: 5921
2Ch 15:16 and burned it **a.** the brook Kidron
2Ch 16:2 king of Syria, that dwelt **a.**
2Ch 16:7 And **a.** that time Hanani the seer
2Ch 18:4 Enquire, I pray thee, **a.** the word
2Ch 18:9 sat in a void place **a.** the entering
2Ch 18:19 go up and fall **a.** Ramoth-gilead?
2Ch 18:33 a certain man drew a bow **a.** a
2Ch 19:4 Jehoshahat dwelt **a.** Jerusalem:
2Ch 20:16 ye shall find them **a.** the end of
2Ch 22:5 against Hazael king of Syria **a.**
2Ch 22:6 that were given him **a.** Ramah,
2Ch 22:6 Ahab **a.** Jezreel, because he was
2Ch 23:5 part shall be **a.** the king's house;
2Ch 23:5 part **a.** the gate of the foundation:
2Ch 23:13 the king stood **a.** his pillar 5921
2Ch 23:13 **a.** the entering in, and the princes
2Ch 23:19 porters **a.** the gates of the house 5921
2Ch 24:8 And **a.** the king's commandment
2Ch 24:8 and set it without **a.** the gate of
2Ch 24:11 came to pass, that **a.** what time
2Ch 24:21 and stoned him with stones **a.** the
2Ch 24:23 came to pass **a.** the end of he year,
2Ch 25:19 abide now **a.** home; why shouldest
2Ch 25:21 king of Judah, **a.** Beth-hemesh,
2Ch 25:23 son of Jehoahaz, **a.** Beth-shemesh,
2Ch 26:9 built towers in Jerusalem **a.** the 5921
2Ch 26:9 and **a.** the valley gate, and **a.**
2Ch 28:16 **A.** that time did king Ahaz send
2Ch 30:1 house of the Lord **a.** Jerusalem,
2Ch 30:3 could not keep it **a.** that time,
2Ch 30:5 Lord God of Israel **a.** Jerusalem:
2Ch 30:13 there assembled **a.** Jerusalem
2Ch 30:21 that were present **a.** Jerusalem
2Ch 31:13 brother, **a.** the commandment
2Ch 32:9 all Judah that were **a.** Jerusalem,
2Ch 32:33 did honour him **a.** his death
2Ch 33:14 to the entering in **a.** the fish gate,
2Ch 35:15 the porters waited **a.** every gate;
2Ch 35:17 kept the passover **a.** that time,
2Ch 35:23 the archers shot **a.** king Josiah;
2Ch 36:3 put him down **a.** Jerusalem,
2Ch 36:7 put them in his temple **a.** Babylon
Ezr 1:2 him a house **a.** Jerusalem,
Ezr 2:68 the Lord which is **a.** Jerusalem,
Ezr 3:8 unto the house of God **a.** Jerusalem,
Ezr 4:10, 11 the river, and **a.** such a time
Ezr 4:17 Peace, and **a.** such a time
Ezr 4:24 of God which is **a.** Jerusalem
Ezr 5:2 of God which is **a.** Jerusalem:
Ezr 5:3 **A.** the same time came to them
Ezr 5:17 which is there **a.** Babylon,
Ezr 5:17 this house of God **a.** Jerusalem,
Ezr 6:2 there was found **a.** Achmetha,
Ezr 6:3 the house of God **a.** Jerusalem,
Ezr 6:5 the temple which is **a.** Jerusalem
Ezr 6:5 which is **a.** Jerusalem, every
Ezr 6:9 priests which are **a.** Jerusalem,
Ezr 6:12 of God which is **a.** Jerusalem
Ezr 6:17 **a.** the dedication of this house of
Ezr 6:18 of God, which is **a.** Jerusalem;
Ezr 7:12 perfect peace, and **a.** such a time
Ezr 8:17 the chief **a.** the place Casiphia,
Ezr 8:17 Nehinims, **a.** the place Casiphia,
Ezr 8:21 a fast there, **a.** the river 5921
Ezr 8:29 **a.** Jerusalem, in the chambers
Ezr 8:34 weight was written **a.** that time
Ezr 9:4 trembled **a.** the words of the God
Ezr 9:5 **a.** he evening sacrifice I arose up
Ezr 10:3 that tremble **a.** the commandment
Ezr 10:14 in our cities come **a.** appointed
Ne 2:12 in my heart to do **a.** Jerusalem:
Ne 3:19 armoury **a.** the turning of the wall
Ne 4:22 Likewise **a.** the same time said I
Ne 5:17 there were **a.** my table an 5921
Ne 6:1 **a.** that time I had not set up the 5704
Ne 6:7 to preach of thee **a.** Jerusalem,
Ne 7:5 of them which came up **a.** the first,
Ne 9:37 over our cattle, **a.** their pleasure,
Ne 10:34 **a.** times appointed year by year,
Ne 11:1 the people dwelt **a.** Jerusalem:
Ne 11:2 to dwell **a.** Jerusalem
Ne 11:4 And **a.** Jerusalem dwelt certain
Ne 11:6 of Perez that dwelt **a.** Jerusalem
Ne 11:22 overseer of the Levites **a.** Jerusalem
Ne 11:24 of Judah, was **a.** the king's hand
Ne 11:25 dwelt **a.** Kirjath-arba, and in the
Ne 11:25 and **a.** Dibon, and in the villages
Ne 11:25 **a.** Jekabzeel, and in the villages
Ne 11:26 And **a.** Jeshua, and **a.** Moladah,
Ne 11:26 and **a.** Beth-phelet,
Ne 11:27 **a.** Hazar-shual, and **a.**
Ne 11:28 And **a.** Ziklag, and **a.** Mekonah,
Ne 11:29 **a.** En-rimmon, and **a.** Zareah,
Ne 11:29 and **a.** Jarmuth,
Ne 11:30 **a.** Lachish, and the fields
Ne 11:30 **a.** Azekah, and in the villages
Ne 11:31 dwelt **a.** Michmash, and Aija,
Ne 11:32 And **a.** Anathoth, Nob, Ananiah,
Ne 12:25 **a.** the threeholds of the gates
Ne 12:27 And **a.** the dedication of the wall
Ne 12:37 **a.** the fountain gate, which was 5921
Ne 12:37 David, **a.** the going up of the wall,
Ne 12:44 **a.** that time were some appointed
Ne 13:6 this time was not I **a.** Jerusalem:
Ne 13:19 my servants set I **a.** the gates, 5921
Ne 13:31 wood offering, **a.** times appointed,
Es 1:12 come **a.** the king's commandment,
Es 4:8 **a.** Shushan to destroy them,
Es 4:14 thou holdest thy peace **a.** this time,
Es 5:6 said unto Esther **a.** the banquet
Es 5:13 the Jew sitting **a.** the king's gate

Es 6:10 Jew, that sitteth **a.** the king's gate:
Es 7:2 second day **a.** the banquet of wine,
Es 7:3 my life be given me **a.** my petition,
Es 7:3 and my people **a.** my request:
Es 8:3 fell down **a.** his feet, and besought 6440
Es 8:9 king's scribes called **a.** that time
Es 8:14 the decree was given **a.** Shushan
Es 9:14 decree was given **a.** Shushan;
Es 9:15 three hundred men **a.** Shushan;
Es 9:18 the Jews that were **a.** Shushan
Job 2:10 receive good **a.** the hand of God,
Job 3:13 have slept: then had I been **a.** rest,
Job 3:17 and there the weary be **a.** rest
Job 5:22 **A.** destruction and famine thou
Job 5:23 beasts of the field shall be **a.** peace
Job 9:23 laugh **a.** the trial of the innocent
Job 12:5 thought of him that is **a.** ease
Job 15:12 and what do thy eyes wink **a.**,
Job 15:23 of darkness is ready **a.** his hand
Job 16:4 and shake mine head **a.** you
Job 16:12 I was **a.** ease, but he hath broken
Job 17:8 men shall be astonished **a.** this, 5921
Job 18:12 destruction shall be ready **a.** his 5921
Job 18:20 shall be astonished **a.** his day, 5921
Job 19:25 he shall stand **a.** the latter day
Job 21:12 rejoice **a.** the sound of the organ
Job 21:23 being wholly **a.** ease and quiet
Job 22:21 thyself with him, and be **a.** peace
Job 23:15 am I troubled **a.** his presence:
Job 26:11 and are astonished **a.** his reproof
Job 27:23 Men shall clap their hands **a.** him, 5921
Job 29:21 and kept silence **a.** my counsel 3926
Job 31:9 lain wait **a.** my neighbour's door; 5921
Job 31:29 rejoiced **a.** the destruction of him
Job 34:20 shall be troubled **a.** midnight,
Job 37:1 **A.** this also my heart trembleth
Job 39:22 He mocketh **a.** fear, and is not
Job 39:27 eagle mount up **a.** thy command, 5291
Job 41:9 down even **a.** the sight of him?
Job 41:26 sword of him that layeth **a.** him
Job 41:29 laugheth **a.** the shaking of a spear
Ps 7:4 him that was **a.** peace with me;
Ps 9:3 fall and perish **a.** thy presence
Ps 10:5 his enemies, he puffeth **a.** them
Ps 11:2 may privily shoot **a.** the upright
Ps 12:5 from him that puffeth **a.** him
Ps 16:8 because he is **a.** my right hand, I
Ps 16:11 **a.** thy right hand there are
Ps 18:12 **A.** the brightness that was before
Ps 18:15 **a.** thy rebuke, O Lord,
Ps 18:15 **a.** the blast of the breath
Ps 25:13 His soul shall dwell **a.** ease;
Ps 25:30 *title* Psalm and Song **a.** the dedication
Ps 25:4 give thanks **a.** the remembrance
Ps 34:1 I will bless the Lord **a.** all times:
Ps 35:8 come upon him **a.** unawares;
Ps 35:26 together that rejoice **a.** mine hurt:
Ps 37:13 The Lord shall laugh **a.** him:
Ps 39:5 verily every man **a.** his best state
Ps 39:12 hold not thy peace **a.** my tears: 413
Ps 42:7 Deep calleth unto deep **a.** the noise
Ps 52:6 fear, and shall laugh **a.** him: 5921
Ps 55:6 would I fly away, and be **a.** rest,
Ps 55:17 and morning, and **a.** noon, will I
Ps 55:20 such as be **a.** peace with him
Ps 59:6 They return **a.** evening: they make
Ps 59:8 thou, O Lord, shalt laugh **a.** them;
Ps 59:14 And **a.** evening let them return:
Ps 62:8 Trust in him **a.** all times;
Ps 64:4 shoot in secret **a.** the perfect;
Ps 64:4 suddenly do they shoot **a.** him
Ps 64:7 God shall shoot **a.** them with an
Ps 65:8 parts are afraid **a.** thy tokens;
Ps 68:2 perish **a.** the presence of God
Ps 68:8 dropped **a.** the presence of God;
Ps 68:8 even Sinai itself was moved **a.** the
Ps 68:12 she that tarried **a.** home divided
Ps 68:29 of thy temple **a.** Jerusalem 5921
Ps 73:3 For I was envious **a.** the foolish,
Ps 74:6 the carved work thereof **a.** once 3162
Ps 76:6 **A.** thy rebuke, O God of Jacob,
Ps 80:16 **a.** the rebuke of thy countenance
Ps 81:7 I proved thee **a.** the waters of 5291
Ps 83:9 Jabin, **a.** the brook of Kison:
Ps 83:10 which perished **a.** En-dor: they
Ps 91:6 destruction that wasteth **a.** noonday
Ps 91:7 A thousand shall fall **a.** thy side,

Ps 91:7 and ten thousand **a.** thy right hand;
Ps 97:5 The hills melted like wax **a.** the
Ps 97:5 **a.** the presence of the Lord of the
Ps 97:12 give thanks **a.** the remembrance
Ps 99:5 and worship **a.** his footstool;
Ps 99:9 and worship **a.** his holy hill;
Ps 104:7 **A.** thy rebuke they fled; 4480
Ps 104:7 **a.** the voice of thy 4480
Ps 105:22 to bind his princes **a.** his pleasure;
Ps 106:3 doeth righteousness **a.** all times
Ps 106:7 but provoked him **a.** the sea, 5921
Ps 106:7 even **a.** the Red sea 5921
Ps 106:32 angered him also **a.** the waters of 5921
Ps 107:27 man, and are **a.** their wit's end
Ps 109:6 let Satan stand **a.** his right hand 5921
Ps 109:31 he shall stand **a.** the right hand
Ps 110:1 Sit thou **a.** my right hand, until I
Ps 110:5 Lord **a.** thy right hand shall 5921
Ps 114:7 earth, **a.** the presence of the Lord,
Ps 114:7 **a.** the presence of the God of Jacob;
Ps 118:13 Thou hast thrust sore **a.** me that
Ps 119:20 unto thy judgments **a.** all times
Ps 119:45 And I will walk **a.** liberty: for I
Ps 119:62 **A.** midnight I will rise to give
Ps 119:162 I rejoice **a.** thy word, as one that 5921
Ps 123:4 scorning of those that are **a.** ease,
Ps 132:6 Lo, we heard of it **a.** Ephratah:
Ps 132:7 we will worship **a.** his footstool
Ps 135:21 Zion, which dwelleth **a.** Jerusalem
Ps 141:7 are scattered **a.** the grave's mouth,
Pr 1:23 turn you **a.** my reproof:
Pr 1:25 set **a.** nought all my counsel, 6544
Pr 1:26 also will laugh **a.** your calamity;
Pr 4:19 know not **a.** what they stumble
Pr 5:11 and thou mourn **a.** the last,
Pr 5:19 her breasts satisfy thee **a.** all times;
Pr 7:6 for **a.** the window of my house I
Pr 7:12 and lieth in wait **a.** every corner 681
Pr 7:19 For the goodman is not **a.** home,
Pr 7:20 come home **a.** the day appointed
Pr 8:3 She crieth **a.** the gates, 3027
Pr 8:3 **a.** the entry of the city, 3027
Pr 8:3 **a.** the coming in **a.** the doors:
Pr 8:34 watching daily **a.** my gates, 5921
Pr 8:34 waiting **a.** the posts of my doors
Pr 9:14 sitteth **a.** the door of her house,
Pr 14:9 Fools make a mock **a.** sin:
Pr 14:19 **a.** he gates of the righteous 5921
Pr 16:7 enemies to be **a.** peace with him
Pr 17:5 and he that is glad **a.** calamities
Pr 17:17 A friend loveth **a.** all times,
Pr 20:21 be gotten hastily **a.** the beginning;
Pr 21:13 his ears **a.** the cry of the poor,
Pr 23:30 They that tarry long **a.** the wine; 5921
Pr 23:32 **A.** the last it biteth like a serpent,
Pr 24:19 be thou envious **a.** the wicked;
Pr 28:18 in his ways shall fall **a.** once
Pr 29:21 become his son **a.** the length
Pr 30:17 eye that mocketh **a.** his father,
Ec 5:6 should God be angry **a.** thy voice, 5921
Ec 5:8 marvel not **a.** the matter: 5921
Ec 10:2 man's heart is **a.** his right hand;
Ec 10:2 but a fool's heart **a.** his left
Ec 12:4 rise up **a.** the voice of the bird,
Ec 12:6 be broken **a.** the fountain, 5921
Ec 12:6 wheel broken **a.** the cistern 413
Ca 1:7 makest thy flock to rest **a.** noon:
Ca 1:12 While the king sitteth **a.** his table,
Ca 2:9 he looketh forth **a.** the windows, 4480
Ca 7:13 and **a.** our gates are all manner 5921
Ca 8:11 had a vineyard **a.** Baal-hamon;
Isa 1:12 hath required this **a.** your hand,
Isa 1:26 restore thy judges as **a.** the first,
Isa 1:26 counsellors as **a.** the beginning:
Isa 6:4 door moved **a.** the voice of him
Isa 7:3 **a.** the end of the conduit of the 413
Isa 7:23 vines **a.** a thousand silverlings,
Isa 9:1 **a.** the first he lightly afflicted
Isa 10:26 of Midian **a.** the rock of Oreb:
Isa 10:28 **a.** Michmash he hath laid up his
Isa 10:29 taken up their lodging **a.** Geba;
Isa 10:32 shall remain **a.** Nob that day:
Isa 13:6 for the day of the Lord is **a.** hand: 7138
Isa 13:8 shall be amazed one **a.** another; 413
Isa 14:7 the whole earth is **a.** rest,
Isa 14:8 Yea, the fir trees rejoice **a.** thee,
Isa 14:9 thee to meet thee **a.** thy coming:

Isa 16:2 of Moab shall be **a.** the fords
Isa 16:4 for the extortioner is **a.** an end,
Isa 17:7 **A.** that day shall a man look to
Isa 17:14 behold **a.** eveningtide trouble;
Isa 19:1 idols of Egypt shall be removed **a.**
Isa 19:19 **a.** the border thereof to the Lord 681
Isa 20:2 **A.** the same time spake the Lord
Isa 21:3 down **a.** the hearing of it;
Isa 21:3 I was dismayed **a.** the seeing of
Isa 22:7 shall set themselves in array **a.**
Isa 23:5 **a.** the report concerning Egypt,
Isa 23:5 pained **a.** the report of Tyre
Isa 26:11 for their envy **a.** the people;
Isa 27:13 in the holy mount **a.** Jerusalem
Isa 28:15 with hell are we **a.** agreement;
Isa 29:5 it shall be **a.** an instant suddenly
Isa 30:2 and have not asked **a.** my mouth;
Isa 30:4 For his princes were **a.** Zoan,
Isa 30:13 cometh suddenly **a.** an instant
Isa 30:17 shall flee **a.** the rebuke of one; 6440
Isa 30:17 **a.** the rebuke of five shall ye flee: 6440
Isa 30:19 dwell in Zion **a.** Jerusalem:
Isa 30:19 gracious unto thee **a.** the voice
Isa 32:9 Rise up, ye women that are **a.** ease;
Isa 32:11 Tremble, ye women that are **a.** ease;
Isa 33:3 **A.** the noise of the tumult the
Isa 33:3 **a.** the lifting up of thyself the
Isa 37:22 hath shaken her head **a.** thee
Isa 37:37 and dwelt **a.** Nineveh
Isa 39:1 **A.** that time Merodach-baladan,
Isa 42:14 destroy and devour **a.** once 3162
Isa 47:14 shall not be a coal to warm **a.**,
Isa 50:2 Is my hand shortened **a.** all,
Isa 50:2 **a.** my rebuke I dry up the sea,
Isa 51:17 drank **a.** the hand of the Lord
Isa 51:20 lie **a.** the head of all the streets,
Isa 52:14 As many were astonished **a.** thee;
Isa 52:15 shall shut their mouths **a.** him:
Isa 59:10 we stumble **a.** noon day as in the
Isa 60:4 shall be nursed **a.** thy side 5921
Isa 60:14 down **a.** the soles of thy feet; 5921
Isa 64:1 might flow down **a.** thy
Isa 64:2 may tremble **a.** thy presence!
Isa 64:3 flowed down **a.** thy presence
Isa 66:2 and trembleth **a.** my word 5921
Isa 66:5 ye that tremble **a.** his word; 413
Isa 66:8 shall a nation be born **a.** once?
Jer 1:15 every one his throne **a.** the entering
Jer 1:17 be not dismayed **a.** their faces,
Jer 2:12 O ye heavens, **a.** this, 5921
Jer 2:24 up the wind **a.** her pleasure;
Jer 3:17 **A.** that time they shall call
Jer 4:9 shall come to pass **a.** that day,
Jer 4:11 **A.** that time shall it be said to this
Jer 4:19 I am pained **a.** my very heart;
Jer 4:26 down **a.** the presence of the Lord,
Jer 5:22 ye not tremble **a.** my presence,
Jer 6:4 arise, and let us go up **a.** noon
Jer 6:15 they were not **a.** all ashamed,
Jer 6:15 **a.** the time that I visit them they
Jer 7:2 that enter in **a.** these gates to
Jer 7:12 where I set my name **a.** the first,
Jer 8:1 **A.** that time, saith the Lord,
Jer 8:12 they were not **a.** all ashamed,
Jer 8:16 whole land trembled **a.** the sound
Jer 10:2 dismayed **a.** the signs of heaven;
Jer 10:2 heathen are dismayed **a.** them
Jer 10:10 **a.** his wrath the earth shall
Jer 10:18 of the land **a.** this once,
Jer 11:12 they shall not save them **a.** all
Jer 15:8 young men a spoiler **a.** noonday;
Jer 17:11 and **a.** his end shall be a fool
Jer 17:27 in **a.** the gates of Jerusalem
Jer 18:7 **A.** what instant I shall speak
Jer 18:9 And **a.** what instant I shall speak
Jer 20:16 and the shouting **a.** noontide:
Jer 23:23 Am I a God **a.** hand, saith the
Jer 23:32 profit this people **a.** all, saith the
Jer 25:15 winecup of this fury **a.** my hand,
Jer 25:17 I took the cup **a.** the Lord's hand,
Jer 25:28 to take the cup **a.** thine hand
Jer 25:33 the Lord shall be **a.** that day from
Jer 26:19 Judah put him **a.** all to death?
Jer 27:18 **a.** Jerusalem, go not to Babylon
Jer 29:10 years be accomplished **a.** Babylon
Jer 29:25 the people that are **a.** Jerusalem,
Jer 31:1 **A.** the same time, saith the Lord,

Book	Ref	Context	No.
Jer	31:12	shall not sorrow any more **a.** all.	
Jer	32:20	thee a name, as **a.** this day;	5704
Jer	33:7	build them, as **a.** the first.	
Jer	33:11	of the land, as **a.** the first, saith	
Jer	33:15	In those days, and **a.** that time,	
Jer	34:8	people which were **a.** Jerusalem,	
Jer	34:14	**A.** the end of seven years let ye go	
Jer	34:16	whom he had set **a.** liberty	
Jer	34:16	**a.** their pleasure to return	
Jer	35:11	so we dwell **a.** Jerusalem,	
Jer	36:10	court, **a.** the entry of the new	
Jer	36:17	write all these things **a.** his mouth?	
Jer	36:27	wrote **a.** the mouth of Jeremiah	
Jer	39:10	and fields **a.** the same time.	
Jer	40:10	I will dwell **a.** Mizpah, to serve	
Jer	41:3	even with Gedaliah, **a.** Mizpah,	
Jer	43:9	**a.** the entry of Pharaoh's house in	
Jer	44:1	which dwell **a.** Migdol,	
Jer	44:1	and **a.** Tahpanhes, and **a.** Noph,	
Jer	44:6	and desolate, as **a.** this day.	
Jer	44:22	an inhabitant as **a.** this day.	
Jer	44:23	happened unto you, as **a.** this	
Jer	45:1	words in a book **a.** the mouth of	
Jer	46:27	and be in rest and **a.** ease, and	
Jer	47:3	**A.** the noise of the stamping of	
Jer	47:3	**a.** the rushing of his chariots,	
Jer	47:3	and **a.** the rumbling of his wheels,	
Jer	48:11	Moab hath been **a.** ease from his	
Jer	48:41	hearts in Moab **a.** that day shall	
Jer	49:17	hiss **a.** all the plagues thereof.	5921
Jer	49:21	The earth is moved **a.** the noise	
Jer	49:21	**a.** the cry the noise thereof was	
Jer	49:22	**a.** that day shall the heart of the	
Jer	50:11	ye are grown fat as the heifer **a.**	
Jer	50:13	and hiss **a.** all her plagues.	5921
Jer	50:14	shoot **a.** her, spare no arrows:	413
Jer	50:46	**A.** the noise of the taking of	
Jer	51:31	that his city is taken **a.** one end,	
Jer	51:49	so **a.** Babylon shall fall the slain	
La	1:7	and did mock **a.** her sabbaths.	5921
La	1:20	sword bereaveth, **a.** home there	
La	2:15	pass by clap their hands **a.** thee;	5921
La	2:15	wag their head **a.** the daughter	5921
La	3:56	ear **a.** my breathing, **a.** my cry.	
Eze	2:6	nor be dismayed **a.** their looks,	
Eze	3:9	neither be dismayed **a.** their looks,	
Eze	3:15	of the captivity **a.** Tel-abib, that	
Eze	3:16	came to pass **a.** the end of seven	
Eze	3:17	hear the word **a.** my mouth,	
Eze	3:18, 20	blood will I require **a.** thine hand.	
Eze	8:5	northward **a.** the gate of the	
Eze	8:16	**a.** the door of the temple of the	
Eze	9:6	and begin **a.** my sanctuary.	
Eze	9:6	Then they began **a.** the ancient	
Eze	10:19	and every one stood **a.** the door	
Eze	11:1	behold **a.** the door of the gate	
Eze	12:4	go forth **a.** even in their sight	
Eze	12:23	The days are **a.** hand, and the	7126
Eze	14:3	be enquired of **a.** all by them?	
Eze	16:4	thou wast not salted **a.** all,	
Eze	16:4	nor swaddled **a.** all.	
Eze	16:25	place **a.** every head of the way,	413
Eze	16:46	that dwelt **a.** thy left hand;	5921
Eze	16:46	that dwelleth **a.** thy right hand,	
Eze	16:57	as **a.** the time of thy reproach of	
Eze	18:23	**a.** all that the wicked should die?	
Eze	20:32	into your mind shall not be **a.** all,	
Eze	21:19	choose it **a.** the head of the way	
Eze	21:21	of Babylon stood **a.** the parting	413
Eze	21:21	**a.** the head of the two ways, to	
Eze	21:22	**A.** his right hand was the	
Eze	22:13	mine hand **a.** thy dishonest gain	413
Eze	22:13	made, and **a.** thy blood which	5921
Eze	23:42	voice of a multitude being **a.** ease	
Eze	24:18	and **a.** even my wife died; and I	
Eze	26:10	shake **a.** the noise of the horsemen,	
Eze	26:15	not the isle shake **a.** the sound of	
Eze	26:16	shall tremble **a.** every moment,	
Eze	26:16	and be astonished **a.** thee.	
Eze	26:18	shall be troubled **a.** thy departure	
Eze	27:3	situate **a.** the entry of the sea	5921
Eze	27:28	shake **a.** the sound of the cry of thy	
Eze	27:35	isles shall be astonished **a.** thee,	5921
Eze	27:36	the people shall hiss **a.** thee;	5921
Eze	28:19	people shall be astonished **a.** thee:	5921
Eze	29:7	all their lions to be **a.** a stand.	
Eze	29:13	God; **A.** the end of forty years	
Eze	30:18	**A.** Tehaphnehes also the day	
Eze	31:16	to shake **a.** the sound of his fall,	
Eze	32:10	make many people amazed **a.** thee,	5921
Eze	32:10	shall tremble **a.** every moment,	
Eze	33:6	require **a.** the watchman's hand	
Eze	33:7	shalt hear the word **a.** my mouth,	
Eze	33:8	blood will I require **a.** thine hand.	
Eze	34:10	require my flock **a.** their hand,	
Eze	35:15	didst rejoice **a.** the inheritance	
Eze	36:8	for they are **a.** hand to come.	7126
Eze	36:11	you than **a.** your beginnings:	
Eze	37:22	into two kingdoms any more **a.** all:	
Eze	38:10	**a.** the same time shall things	
Eze	38:11	I will go to them that are **a.** rest,	
Eze	38:18	it come to pass **a.** the same time	
Eze	38:20	shall shake **a.** my presence, and	
Eze	39:20	shall be filled **a.** my table with	5921
Eze	40:40	And **a.** the side without, as one	413
Eze	40:40	which was **a.** the porch of the	
Eze	40:44	which was **a.** the side of the north	413
Eze	40:44	one **a.** the side of the east gate	413
Eze	41:12	the separate place **a.** the end	
Eze	44:11	having charge **a.** the gates of	413
Eze	44:17	they enter in **a.** the gates of the	413
Eze	44:25	they shall come **a.** no dead person	413
Eze	46:2	he shall worship **a.** the threshold	5921
Eze	46:3	shall worship **a.** the door of	
Eze	46:19	which was **a.** the side of the gate,	5921
Eze	47:1	**a.** the south side of the altar	
Eze	47:7	**a.** the bank of the river were	413
Eze	48:28	**a.** the south side southward,	413
Eze	48:32	**a.** the east side four thousand	413
Eze	48:33	**a.** the south side four thousand	
Eze	48:34	**A.** the west side four thousand	
Da	1:5	that **a.** the end thereof they might	
Da	1:15	And **a.** the end of ten days their	
Da	1:18	Now **a.** the end of the days that	
Da	2:10	such things **a.** any magician,	
Da	3:5	That **a.** what time ye hear the sound	
Da	3:7	Therefore **a.** that time, when all	
Da	3:8	Wherefore **a.** that time certain	
Da	3:15	that **a.** what time ye hear the	
Da	4:4	was **a.** rest in mine house, and	
Da	4:8	But **a.** the last Daniel came in	5705
Da	4:29	**A.** the end of twelve months he	
Da	4:34	And **a.** the end of the days I	
Da	4:36	**A.** the same time my reason	
Da	5:3	of God which was **a.** Jerusalem;	
Da	6:24	they came **a.** the bottom of the	
Da	8:1	appeared unto me **a.** the first.	
Da	8:2	I was **a.** Shushan in the palace,	
Da	8:17	for **a.** the time of the end shall be	
Da	8:19	for **a.** the time appointed the end	
Da	8:27	I was astonished **a.** the vision,	5921
Da	9:7	**a.** this day; to the men of Judah,	
Da	9:15	as **a.** this day; we have sinned,	
Da	9:21	in the vision **a.** the beginning,	
Da	9:23	**A.** the beginning of thy supplications	
Da	10:3	did I anoint myself **a.** all, till	
Da	11:27	lies **a.** one table; but it shall not	5921
Da	11:27	yet the end shall be **a.** the time	
Da	11:29	**A.** the time appointed he shall	
Da	11:40	And **a.** the time of the end shall	
Da	11:40	king of the south push **a.** him:	
Da	11:43	Ethiopians shall be **a.** his steps.	
Da	12:1	And **a.** that time Michael stand	
Da	12:1	and **a.** that time thy people shall	
Da	12:13	stand in thy lot **a.** the end of	
Ho	1:5	come to pass **a.** that day, that	
Ho	2:16	And it shall be **a.** that day, saith	
Ho	4:12	My people ask counsel **a.** their	
Ho	5:8	cry aloud **a.** Beth-aven, after thee,	
Ho	9:10	in the fig tree **a.** her first time;	
Ho	11:7	none **a.** all would exalt him	3162
Joe	1:15	the Lord is **a.** hand, and as a	7138
Joe	2:1	cometh, for it is nigh **a.** hand;	
Joe	2:9	shall enter in **a.** the window like	1157
Am	3:5	and have taken nothing **a.** all?	
Am	3:9	Publish in the palaces **a.** Ashdod,	
Am	4:3	ye shall go out **a.** the breaches,	
Am	4:3	every cow **a.** that which is before	
Am	4:4	transgress; **a.** Gilgal multiply	
Am	6:1	to them that are **a.** ease in Zion,	
Am	7:13	not again any more **a.** Beth-el:	
Am	8:9	the sun to go down **a.** noon, and	
Ob	7	the men that were **a.** peace with	
Mic	1:10	Declare ye it not **a.** Gath,	
Mic	1:10	weep ye not **a.** all: in the house	
Mic	3:4	his face from them **a.** that time,	
Mic	7:16	and be confounded **a.** all their	
Na	1:3	will not **a.** all acquit the wicked:	
Na	1:5	The mountains quake **a.** him, and	
Na	1:5	and the earth is burned **a.** his	
Na	3:10	dashed in pieces **a.** the top of	
Hab	1:10	And they shall scoff **a.** the kings,	
Hab	2:3	but **a.** the end it shall speak,	
Hab	2:5	neither keepeth **a.** home, who	
Hab	2:19	there is no breath **a.** all in the	
Hab	3:5	coals went forth **a.** his feet.	
Hab	3:11	**a.** the light of thine arrows they	
Hab	3:11	**a.** the shining of thy glittering	
Hab	3:16	my lips quivered **a.** the voice:	
Zep	1:7	Hold thy peace **a.** the presence	
Zep	1:7	the day of the Lord is **a.** hand;	
Zep	1:12	shall come to pass **a.** that time,	
Zep	2:4	out of Ashdod **a.** the noon day,	
Zep	3:19	**a.** that time I will undo all	
Zep	3:20	**A.** that time will I bring you	
Zec	1:11	earth sitteth still, and is **a.** rest	
Zec	1:15	the heathen that are **a.** ease:	
Zec	3:1	Satan standing **a.** his right hand	5921
Zec	3:8	for they are men wondered **a.**:	
Zec	7:5	did ye **a.** all fast unto me, even	
Zec	11:13	I was prised **a.** of them. And I	
Zec	12:8	feeble among them **a.** that day	
Zec	14:7	**a.** evening time it shall be light.	
Zec	14:14	shall also fight **a.** Jerusalem;	
Mal	1:10	accept an offering **a.** your hand.	
Mal	1:13	ye have snuffed **a.** it, saith the	
Mal	2:7	should seek the law **a.** his mouth:	
Mal	2:8	many to stumble **a.** the law;	
Mal	2:13	it with good will **a.** your hand.	
Mt	3:2	kingdom of heaven is **a.** hand.	*1448*
Mt	4:6	lest **a.** any time thou dash thy	*3379*
Mt	4:17	**kingdom of heaven is a. hand.**	*1448*
Mt	5:25	**lest a. any time the adversary**	*3379*
Mt	5:34	**Swear not a. all;**	*2527*
Mt	5:40	**any man will sue thee a. the law**	*2919*
Mt	7:13	**Enter ye in a. the strait gate**	*1223*
Mt	7:28	were astonished **a.** his doctrine:	*1909*
Mt	8:6	my servant lieth **a.** home	*1722*
Mt	9:9	sitting **a.** the receipt of custom;	*1909*
Mt	9:10	as Jesus sat **a.** meat in the house,	*345*
Mt	10:7	**kingdom of heaven is a. hand.**	*1448*
Mt	10:35	**am come to set a man a. variance**	*1369*
Mt	11:22	**Tyre and Sidon a. the day of**	*1722*
Mt	11:25	**A.** that time Jesus answered and	*1722*
Mt	12:1	**A.** that time Jesus went on the	*1722*
Mt	12:41	**repented a. the preaching of**	*1519*
Mt	13:15	**lest a. any time they should see**	*3379*
Mt	13:49	**So shall it be a. the end of the**	*1722*
Mt	14:1	**A.** that time Herod the tetrarch	*1722*
Mt	14:9	them which sat **a.** meat with him	*4873*
Mt	15:17	**whatsoever entereth in a. the**	*1519*
Mt	15:30	and cast them **a.** Jesus' feet;	*3844*
Mt	18:1	**A.** the same time came the	*1722*
Mt	18:29	**fell down a. his feet**	*1519*
Mt	19:4	**a. the beginning made them male**	*575*
Mt	22:33	were astonished **a.** his doctrine.	*1909*
Mt	23:6	**the uppermost rooms a. feasts,**	*1722*
Mt	23:24	**which strain a. a gnat, and**	*1368*
Mt	24:33	**it is near, even a. the doors**	*1909*
Mt	24:41	**shall be grinding a. the mill;**	*1722*
Mt	25:6	**a. midnight there was a cry made,**	
Mt	25:27	**and then a. my coming I should**	
Mt	26:7	it on his head, as he sat **a.** meat.	*345*
Mt	26:18	**My time is a. hand; I will keep**	*1451*
Mt	26:18	**a. thy house with my disciples**	*4314*
Mt	26:45	**the hour is a. hand, and the Son**	*1448*
Mt	26:46	**he is a. hand that doth betray me**	*1448*
Mt	26:60	**A.** the last came two false	
Mt	27:15	Now **a.** that feast the governor	*2596*
Mk	1:15	**the kingdom of God is a. hand:**	*1448*
Mk	1:22	were astonished **a.** his doctrine:	*1909*
Mk	1:32	And **a.** even, when the sun did set,	
Mk	1:33	gathered together **a.** the door	*4314*
Mk	2:14	Alphaeus sitting **a.** the	*1909*
Mk	2:15	Jesus sat **a.** meat in his house,	*2621*
Mk	4:12	**lest a. any time they should be**	*3379*
Mk	5:22	he saw him, he fall **a.** his feet.	*4314*
Mk	5:23	lieth **a.** the point of death:	
Mk	6:3	And they were offended **a.** him.	*1722*
Mk	7:25	and came and fell **a.** his feet	*4314*
Mk	9:12	**many things, and be set a. nought**	*1847*

Book	Ref	Context	No.
Mk	10:22	And he was sad a. that saying,	1909
Mk	10:24	disciples were astonished a. his	1909
Mk	11:1	Bethany, a. the mount of Olives,	4314
Mk	11:18	the people was astonished a. his	1909
Mk	12:2	And a. the season he sent to the	
Mk	12:4	and a. him they cast stones, and	
Mk	12:17	And they marvelled a. him	1909
Mk	12:39	the uppermost rooms a. feasts	1722
Mk	13:29	is nigh, even a. the doors	1909
Mk	13:35	of the house cometh, a. even,	
Mk	13:35	a. midnight, or a. the cockcrowing,	
Mk	14:3	as he sat a. meat, there came a	2621
Mk	14:42	that betrayeth me is a. hand	1448
Mk	14:54	and warmed himself a. the fire	4314
Mk	15:6	Now a. that feast he released	2596
Mk	15:34	a. the ninth hour Jesus cried	
Mk	16:2	sepulchre a. the rising of the sun	
Mk	16:14	the eleven as they sat a. meat,	345
Lu	1:10	praying without a. the time of	
Lu	1:14	many shall rejoice a. his birth	1909
Lu	1:29	she was troubled a. this saying,	1909
Lu	2:18	wondered a. those things which	4012
Lu	2:33	marvelled a. those things which	1909
Lu	2:41	Jerusalem every year a. the feast	
Lu	2:47	astonished a. his understanding	1909
Lu	4:11	up, lest a. any time thou dash	3379
Lu	4:18	to set a. liberty them that are	1722
Lu	4:22	wondered a. the gracious words	1909
Lu	4:32	were astonished a. his doctrine;	1909
Lu	5:5	nevertheless a. thy word I will let	1909
Lu	5:8	he fell down a. Jesus' knees,	4363
Lu	5:9	were with him, a. the draught	1909
Lu	5:27	Levi, sitting a. the receipt of	1909
Lu	7:9	he marvelled a. him, and turned	
Lu	7:37	knew that Jesus sat a. meat in	345
Lu	7:38	stood a. his feet behind him	3844
Lu	7:49	they that sat a. meat with him	345
Lu	8:19	could not come a. him for the	1519
Lu	8:26	they arrived a. the country of	1519
Lu	8:35	sitting a. the feet of Jesus,	3844
Lu	8:41	and fell down a. Jesus' feet, and	3844
Lu	9:31	should accomplish a. Jerusalem	1722
Lu	9:43	amazed a. the mighty power of	1909
Lu	9:43	wondered every one a. all things	1909
Lu	9:61	farewell, which are a. home	
Lu	9:61	home a. my house	1519
Lu	10:14	Tyre and Sidon a. the judgment,	1722
Lu	10:32	when he was a. the place, came	2596
Lu	10:39	which also sat a. Jesus' feet, and	3844
Lu	11:5	shall go unto him a. midnight,	3317
Lu	11:32	they repented a. the preaching of	1519
Lu	12:40	Son of man cometh a. an hour	
Lu	12:46	not for him, and a. an hour when	1722
Lu	13:1	There were present a. that season	1722
Lu	13:24	to enter in a. the strait gate:	1223
Lu	13:25	and to knock a. the door, saying,	
Lu	14:10	of them that sit a. meat with thee	4873
Lu	14:14	recompensed a. the resurrection	1722
Lu	14:15	them that sat a. meat with him	4873
Lu	14:17	sent his servant a. supper time	
Lu	15:29	neither transgressed I a. any	3763
Lu	16:20	which was laid a. his gate, full of	4314
Lu	17:16	fell down on his face a. his feet,	3844
Lu	19:5	to day I must abide a. thy house	1722
Lu	19:23	bank, that a. my coming I might	
Lu	19:29	Bethany, a. the mount called	4314
Lu	19:30	in the which a. your entering ye	1531
Lu	19:37	even now a. the descent of the	4314
Lu	19:42	even thou, a. least in this thy day,	1065
Lu	20:10	a. the season he sent a servant to	1722
Lu	20:26	and they marvelled a. his answer,	1909
Lu	20:37	Moses shewed a. the bush, when	1909
Lu	20:40	not ask him any question a. all,	
Lu	20:46	and the chief rooms a. feasts;	1722
Lu	21:30	that summer is now nigh a. hand	1451
Lu	21:31	kingdom of God is nigh a. hand	1451
Lu	21:34	to yourselves, lest a. any time	3379
Lu	21:37	a. night he went out, and abode	3571
Lu	22:27	he that sitteth a. meat, or he that	345
Lu	22:27	is not he that sitteth a. meat?	345
Lu	22:30	eat and drink a. my table in my	1909
Lu	22:40	And when he was a. the place, he	1909
Lu	23:7	to Herod, who himself also was a.	1722
Lu	23:7	Jerusalem a. that time	1722
Lu	23:11	men of war set him a. nought, and	1848
Lu	23:12	they were a. enmity between	1722
Lu	23:17	release one unto them a. the	2596
Lu	23:18	cried all a. once, saying, Away	3826
Lu	24:12	wondering in himself a. that	
Lu	24:22	which were early a. the sepulchre;	1909
Lu	24:27	And beginning a. Moses and all	575
Lu	24:30	as he sat a. meat with them, he	2625
Lu	24:47	nations, beginning a. Jerusalem	575
Joh	1:18	No man hath seen God a. any	4455
Joh	2:10	Every man a. the beginning doth	4412
Joh	2:13	the Jews' passover was a. hand,	1451
Joh	2:23	was in Jerusalem a. the passover,	1722
Joh	4:21	nor yet a. Jerusalem, worship the	1722
Joh	4:45	seen all the things that he did a.	1722
Joh	4:45	Jerusalem a. the feast: for they	1722
Joh	4:46	whose son was sick a. Capernaum	1722
Joh	4:47	for he was a. the point of death	3195
Joh	4:52	Yesterday a. the seventh hour the	
Joh	4:53	knew that it was a. the same hour,	1722
Joh	5:2	Now there is a. Jerusalem by the	1722
Joh	5:4	an angel went down a. a certain	2596
Joh	5:28	Marvel not a. this: for the hour is	
Joh	5:37	his voice a. any time, nor seen his	4455
Joh	6:21	ship was a. the land whither they	1909
Joh	6:39	raise it up again a. the last day	1722
Joh	6:40	I will raise him up a. the last day	
Joh	6:41	Jews then murmured a. him,	4012
Joh	6:44	raise him up a. the last day	
Joh	6:54	I will raise him up a. the last day	
Joh	6:61	his disciples murmured a. it, he	4012
Joh	7:2	Jews' feast of tabernacle was a.	1451
Joh	7:11	Jews sought him a. the feast, and	1722
Joh	7:23	are ye angry a. me, because I have	
Joh	8:7	let him first cast a stone a. her	1909
Joh	8:9	beginning a. the eldest, even unto	575
Joh	8:59	took they up stones to cast a. him:	1909
Joh	10:22	And it was a. Jerusalem the feast	1722
Joh	10:40	place where John a. first baptized;	
Joh	11:24	in the resurrection at the last day	1722
Joh	11:32	she fell down a. his feet, saying	1519
Joh	11:49	Ye know nothing a. all,	3762
Joh	11:55	Jews' passover was nigh a. hand:	1451
Joh	12:2	one of them that sat a. the table	4873
Joh	12:16	understood not his disciples a. the	4412
Joh	12:20	came up to worship a. the feast:	1722
Joh	13:28	Now no man a. the table knew for	345
Joh	14:20	A. that day ye shall know that I	1722
Joh	16:4	not unto you a. the beginning,	1537
Joh	16:26	A. that day ye shall ask in my	1722
Joh	18:16	Peter stood a. the door without	4314
Joh	18:38	I find no fault in him a. all	
Joh	18:39	release unto you one a. the	1722
Joh	19:11	couldest have no power a. all	
Joh	19:39	Nicodemus, which a. the first	
Joh	19:42	the sepulchre was nigh a. hand	1451
Joh	20:11	Mary stood without a. the	4314
Joh	20:12	one a. the head, and the other a.	4314
Joh	20:19	Then the same day a. evening,	
Joh	21:1	disciples a. the sea of Tiberias;	1909
Joh	21:20	leaned on his breast a. supper,	1722
Ac	1:6	wilt thou a. this time restore	1722
Ac	1:19	all the dwellers a. Jerusalem;	
Ac	2:5	were dwelling a. Jerusalem Jews,	1722
Ac	2:14	all ye that dwelt a. Jerusalem, be	
Ac	3:1	into the temple a. the hour of	1909
Ac	3:2	whom they laid daily a. the gate	4314
Ac	3:10	for alms a. the Beautiful gate of	1909
Ac	3:10	amazement a. that which had	1909
Ac	3:12	why marvel ye a. this? or why	1909
Ac	4:6	gathered together a. Jerusalem	1519
Ac	4:11	which was set a. nought of you	1848
Ac	4:18	not to speak a. all nor teach in	2527
Ac	4:35	laid them down a. the apostles'	3844
Ac	4:37	and laid it a. the apostles' feet	3844
Ac	5:2	and laid it a. the apostles' feet	3844
Ac	5:9	thy husband are a. the door, and	1909
Ac	5:10	down straightway a. his feet, and	3844
Ac	5:15	a. the least the shadow of Peter	2579
Ac	7:13	a. the second time Joseph was	1722
Ac	7:26	would have set them a. one again,	1519
Ac	7:29	Then fled Moses a. this saying,	1722
Ac	7:31	Moses saw it, he wondered a. the	
Ac	7:58	laid down their clothes a. a young	3844
Ac	8:1	And a. that time there was a	1722
Ac	8:1	church which was a. Jerusalem;	1722
Ac	8:14	apostles which were a. Jerusalem	1722
Ac	8:35	and began a. the same scripture,	575
Ac	8:40	But Philip was found a. Azotus:	1519
Ac	9:10	a certain disciple a. Damascus,	1722
Ac	9:13	done to thy saints a. Jerusalem:	1722
Ac	9:19	disciples which were a. Damascus	1722
Ac	9:22	Jews which dwelt a. Damascus,	1722
Ac	9:27	preached boldly a. Damascus in	1722
Ac	9:28	in and going out a. Jerusalem,	1722
Ac	9:32	the saints which dwelt a. Lydda	
Ac	9:35	all that dwelt a. Lydda and Saron,	
Ac	9:36	Now there was a. Joppa a certain	1722
Ac	10:11	sheet knit a. the four corners,	
Ac	10:25	down a. his feet, and worshipped	1909
Ac	10:30	a. the ninth hour I prayed in my	
Ac	11:8	unclean hath a. any time entered	3763
Ac	11:15	them, as on us a. the beginning	1722
Ac	12:13	Peter knocked a. the door of the	
Ac	13:1	church that was a. Antioch	1722
Ac	13:5	when they were a. Salamis, they	1722
Ac	13:12	being astonished a. the doctrine	1909
Ac	13:27	they that dwelt a. Jerusalem, and	1722
Ac	14:8	sat a certain man a. Lystra,	1722
Ac	15:14	declared how God a. the first did	
Ac	16:2	brethren that were a. Lystra and	1722
Ac	16:4	elders which were a. Jerusalem	1722
Ac	16:25	And a. midnight Paul and Silas	2596
Ac	17:13	God was preached of Paul a.	1722
Ac	17:16	Paul waited for them a. Athens,	1722
Ac	17:30	this ignorance God winked a.;	
Ac	18:22	when he had landed a. Caesarea,	1519
Ac	18:24	Apollos, born a. Alexandria, an	
Ac	19:1	Apollos was a. Corinth, Paul	1722
Ac	19:17	Greeks also dwelling a. Ephesus;	
Ac	19:26	not alone a. Ephesus, but almost	
Ac	19:27	our crafts in danger to be set a.	1519
Ac	20:5	before tarried for us a. Troas	1722
Ac	20:14	when he met with us a. Assos,	1519
Ac	20:15	we arrived a. Samos, and	1519
Ac	20:15	tarried a. Trogyllium; and the	1722
Ac	20:16	a. Jerusalem the day of Pentecost	1519
Ac	20:18	have been with you a. all seasons,	
Ac	21:3	into Syria, and landed a. Tyre:	1519
Ac	21:11	So shall the Jews a. Jerusalem	1722
Ac	21:13	but also to die a. Jerusalem for	1519
Ac	21:24	and be a. charges with them, that	1159
Ac	22:3	brought up in this city a. the feet	3844
Ac	23:11	thou bear witness also a. Rome	1519
Ac	23:23	two hundred, a. the third hour of	575
Ac	25:4	should be kept a. Caesarea, and	1722
Ac	25:8	have I offended any thing a. all	
Ac	25:10	I stand a. Caesar's judgment seat,	1909
Ac	25:15	About whom, when I was a.	1519
Ac	25:23	men of the city, a. Festus'	
Ac	25:24	both a. Jerusalem, and also here,	1722
Ac	26:4	which was a. the first among	575
Ac	26:4	nation a. Jerusalem, know all the	1722
Ac	26:13	A. midday, O king, I saw in the	
Ac	26:20	and a. Jerusalem, and throughout	
Ac	26:32	might have been set a. liberty, if	630
Ac	27:3	the next day we touched a. Sidon,	1519
Ac	28:12	And landing a. Syracuse, we	1519
Ro	1:10	if by any means now a. length I	4218
Ro	1:15	gospel to you that are a. Rome	1722
Ro	3:26	To declare, I say, a. this time his	1722
Ro	4:20	he staggered not a. the promise	1519
Ro	8:34	who is even a. the right hand of	1722
Ro	9:9	A. this time will I come, and	2596
Ro	9:32	stumbled a. that stumblingstone;	
Ro	11:5	Even so then a. this present time	1722
Ro	13:12	spent, the day is a. hand: let us	1448
Ro	14:10	set a. nought thy brother? for	1848
Ro	15:26	saints which are a. Jerusalem	1722
Ro	16:1	servant of the church a. Cenchrea:	1722
1Co	1:2	which is a. Corinth, to them that	1722
1Co	7:39	she is a. liberty to be married to	1657
1Co	8:10	sit a. meat in the idol's temple,	2621
1Co	9:7	time a. his own charges? who	4218
1Co	9:13	and they which wait a. the altar	
1Co	11:34	let him eat a. home; that ye come	1722
1Co	14:16	say Amen a. thy giving of thanks,	1909
1Co	14:27	or a. the most by three, and that	
1Co	14:35	their husbands a. home: for it is	1722
1Co	15:6	five hundred brethren a. once:	2178
1Co	15:23	that are Christ's a. his coming	1722
1Co	15:29	if the dead rise not a. all? why	3654
1Co	15:32	fought with beasts a. Ephesus,	1722
1Co	15:52	twinkling of an eye a. the last	1722
1Co	16:8	But I will tarry a. Ephesus until	1722
1Co	16:12	but his will was not a. all	3843
1Co	16:12	to come a. this time;	3568

2Co 1:1 which is **a.** Corinth, with all the ... *1722*
2Co 4:18 While we look not **a.** the things ... *4648*
2Co 4:18 but **a.** the things which are not ... *4648*
2Co 5:6 whilst we are **a.** home in the ... *1722*
2Co 8:14 that now **a.** this time your ... *1722*
Ga 4:12 ye have not injured me **a.** all ... *3762*
Ga 4:13 the gospel unto you **a.** the first ...
Eph 1:1 saints which are **a.** Ephesus, ... *1722*
Eph 1:20 and set him **a.** his own right ... *1722*
Eph 2:12 That **a.** that time ye were ... *1722*
Eph 3:13 faint not **a.** my tribulations ... *1722*
Php 1:1 Christ Jesus which are **a.** Philippi, ... *1722*
Php 2:10 That **a.** the name of Jesus every ... *1722*
Php 4:5 to all men. The Lord is **a.** hand ... *1451*
Php 4:10 that now **a.** the last your care of ... *4218*
Col 1:2 brethren in Christ which are **a.** ... *1722*
Col 2:1 for them **a.** Laodicea, and for ... *1722*
1Th 2:2 know, **a.** Philippi we were bold ... *1722*
1Th 2:5 For neither **a.** any time used we ... *4218*
1Th 2:19 our Lord Jesus **a.** his coming? ... *1722*
1Th 3:1 good to be left **a.** Athens alone; ... *1722*
1Th 3:13 even our Father, **a.** the coming of ... *1722*
1Th 5:13 And be **a.** peace among yourselves ... *1722*
2Th 2:2 the day of Christ is **a.** hand ... *1764*
2Th 3:11 disorderly, working not **a.** all, ... *3367*
1Ti 1:3 to abide still **a.** Ephesus, when ... *1722*
1Ti 5:4 to show piety **a.** home, and to ...
2Ti 1:18 ministered unto me **a.** Ephesus, ... *1722*
2Ti 2:26 captive by him **a.** his will ... *1519*
2Ti 3:11 **a.** Antioch, **a.** Iconium, **a.** Lystra; ... *1722*
2Ti 4:1 and the dead **a.** his appearing ... *2596*
2Ti 4:6 of my departure is **a.** hand ... *2186*
2Ti 4:8 shall give me **a.** that day: ... *1722*
2Ti 4:13 left **a.** Troas with Carpus, when ... *1722*
2Ti 4:16 **A.** my first answer no man stood ... *1722*
2Ti 4:20 Erastus abode **a.** Corinth: ... *1722*
2Ti 4:20 have I left **a.** Miletum sick ... *1722*
Tit 2:5 keepers **a.** home, good, obedient ... *3626*
Heb 1:1 God, who **a.** sundry times and in ...
Heb 1:5, 13 the angels said he **a.** any time, ... *4218*
Heb 2:1 lest **a.** any time we should let ... *3379*
Heb 2:3 which **a.** the first began to be ...
Heb 7:13 man gave attendance **a.** the altar ...
Heb 9:17 no strength **a.** all while the ... *3379*
Heb 12:2 and is set down **a.** the right hand ... *1722*
Heb 13:23 brother Timothy is set **a.** liberty; ... *630*
Jas 3:11 send forth **a.** the same place ... *1537*
1Pe 1:7 and glory **a.** the appearing ... *1722*
1Pe 1:13 unto you **a.** the revelation of ... *1722*
1Pe 2:8 which stumble **a.** the word, being ...
1Pe 4:7 is **a.** hand: be ye therefore ... *1448*
1Pe 4:17 begin **a.** the house of God; and if ... *575*
1Pe 4:17 it first begin **a.** us, what shall the ... *575*
1Pe 5:13 that is **a.** Babylon, elected ... *1722*
1Jo 1:5 and in him is no darkness **a.** all ... *3762*
1Jo 2:28 before him **a.** his coming ... *1722*
1Jo 4:12 man hath seen God **a.** any time ... *4455*
Re 1:3 therein: for the time is **a.** hand ... *1451*
Re 1:17 saw him, I fell **a.** his feet as dead ... *4314*
Re 3:20 **Behold I stand a. the door, and** ... *1909*
Re 8:3 and stood **a.** the altar, having ... *1909*
Re 18:14 shalt find them no more **a.** all ...
Re 18:21 shall be found no more **a.** all ...
Re 18:22 shall be heard no more **a.** all in ...
Re 18:22 shall be found no more **a.** all in ...
Re 18:23 shall shine no more **a.** all in thee: ...
Re 18:23 shall be heard no more **a.** all in thee: ...
Re 19:2 blood of his servants **a.** her hand ... *1537*
Re 19:10 And I fell **a.** his feet to worship ... *1715*
Re 21:12 twelve gates, and **a.** the gates ... *1909*
Re 21:25 not be shut **a.** all by day; for ...
Re 22:10 this book; for the time is **a.** hand ... *1451*

ATAD (a'-tad) See also ABEL-MIZRAIM.
Ge 50:10 came to the threshingfloor of **A.**, ... 329
Ge 50:11 saw the mourning in the floor of **A.**, ... 329

ATARAH (at'-a-rah)
1Ch 2:26 another wife, whose name was **A.**; ... 5851

ATAROTH (at'-a-roth) See also ATAROTH-ADAR; ATROTH.
Nu 32:3 **A.**, and Dibon, and Jazer, ... 5852
Nu 32:34 of Gad built Dibon, and **A.**, ... 5852
Jos 16:2 unto the borders of Archi to **A.**, ... 5852
Jos 16:7 went down from Janohah to **A.**, ... 5852
1Ch 2:54 **A.**, the house of Joab, and half ... 5852

ATAROTH-ADAR (at''-a-roth-a'-dar) See also ATAROTH-ADDAR.
Jos 18:13 the border descended to **A.**, ... 5853

ATAROTH-ADDAR (at''-a-roth-ad'-dar) See also ATAROTH-ADAR.
Jos 16:5 on the east side was **A.**, unto ... 5853

ATE
Ps 106:28 and **a.** the sacrifices of the dead ... 398
Da 10:3 I **a.** no pleasant bread, neither ... 398
Re 10:10 of the angel's hand, and **a.** it up; ... *2719*

ATER (a'-tur)
Ezr 2:16 The children of **A.** of Hezekiah, ... 333
Ezr 2:42 the children of **A.**, the children of ... 333
Ne 7:21 The children of **A.** of Hezekiah, ... 333
Ne 7:45 of Shallum, the children of **A.**, ... 333
Ne 10:17 **A.**, Hizkijah, Azzur, ... 333

ATHA See MARAN-ATHA.

ATHACH (a'-thak)
1Sa 30:30 and to them which were in **A.**, ... 6269

ATHAIAH (ath-a-i'-ah)
Ne 11:4 of Judah; **A.** the son of Uzziah, ... 6265

ATHALIAH (ath-a-li'-ah)
2Ki 8:26 and his mother's name was **A.**, ... 6271
2Ki 11:1 And when **A.**, the mother of ... 6271
2Ki 11:2 from **A.**, so that he was not slain ... 6271
2Ki 11:3 And **A.** did reign over the land ... 6271
2Ki 11:13 when **A.** heard the noise of the ... 6271
2Ki 11:14 and **A.** rent her clothes, and cried ... 6271
2Ki 11:20 and they slew **A.** with the sword ... 6271
1Ch 8:26 and Shehariah, and **A.**, ... 6271
2Ch 22:2 was **A.** the daughter of Omri ... 6271
2Ch 22:10 when **A.** the mother of Ahaziah ... 6271
2Ch 22:11 hid him from **A.**, so that she slew ... 6271
2Ch 22:12 house of God in six years: and **A.** ... 6271
2Ch 23:12 Now when **A.** heard the noise ... 6271
2Ch 23:13 **A.** rent her clothes, and said, ... 6271
2Ch 23:21 they had slain **A.** with the sword ... 6271
2Ch 24:7 sons of **A.**, that wicked woman, ... 6271
Ezr 8:7 of Elam; Jeshaiah the son of **A.**, ... 6271

ATHENIANS (a-the'-ne-uns)
Ac 17:21 (For all the **A.** and strangers ... *117*

ATHENS (ath'-ens) See also ATHENIANS.
Ac 17:15 brought him unto **A.** ... *116*
Ac 17:16 while Paul waited for them at **A.**, ... *116*
Ac 17:22 Ye men of **A.**, I perceive ... *117*
Ac 18:1 Paul departed from **A.**, ... *116*
1Th 3:1 it good to be left at **A.** alone; ... *116*
1Th *subscr.* Thessalonians was written from **A.** ... *116*
2Th *subscr.* Thessalonians was written from **A.** ... *116*

ATHIRST
Jg 15:18 he was sore **a.**, and called on the ... 6770
Ru 2:9 thou art **a.**, go unto the vessels, ... 6770
Mt 25:44 **saw we thee an hungered, or a.** ... *1372*
Re 21:6 I will give to him that is **a.** ... *1372*
Re 22:17 let him that is **a.** come ... *1372*

ATHLAI (ath'-lahee)
Ezr 10:28 Hananiah, Zabbai, and **A.** ... 6270

ATONEMENT See also ATONEMENTS.
Ex 29:33 wherewith the **a.** was made, ... 3722
Ex 29:36 a bullock for a sin offering for **a.** ... 3725
Ex 29:36 when thou hast made an **a.** for it, ... 3722
Ex 29:37 shalt make an **a.** for the altar, ... 3722
Ex 30:10 shall make an **a.** upon the horns ... 3722
Ex 30:10 once in the year shall he make **a.** ... 3722
Ex 30:15 to make **a.** for your souls ... 3722
Ex 30:16 take the **a.** money of the children ... 3725
Ex 30:16 to make an **a.** for your souls ... 3722
Ex 32:30 I shall make an **a.** for your sin ... 3722
Le 1:4 to make **a.** for him ... 3722
Le 4:20 priest shall make an **a.** for them, ... 3722
Le 4:26 and the priest shall make an **a.** ... 3722
Le 4:31 priest shall make an **a.** for him, ... 3722
Le 4:35 shall make an **a.** for his sin ... 3722
Le 5:6, 10, 13 shall make an **a.** for him ... 3722
Le 5:16 the priest shall make an **a.** ... 3722
Le 5:18 an **a.** for him concerning his ... 3722
Le 6:7 an **a.** for him before the Lord: ... 3722
Le 7:7 the priest that maketh **a.** ... 3722
Le 8:34 to make an **a.** for you ... 3722
Le 9:7 and make an **a.** for thyself, ... 3722
Le 9:7 and make an **a.** for them; ... 3722
Le 10:17 make **a.** for them before the Lord? ... 3722
Le 12:7 and make an **a.** for her; ... 3722
Le 12:8 priest shall make an **a.** for her, ... 3722
Le 14:18 and the priest shall make an **a.** ... 3722
Le 14:19 and make an **a.** for him ... 3722
Le 14:20 and the priest shall make an **a.** ... 3722
Le 14:21, 29 to make an **a.** for him, ... 3722
Le 14:31 and the priest shall make an **a.** ... 3722
Le 14:53 and make an **a.** for the house: ... 3722
Le 15:15, 30 the priest shall make an **a.** for ... 3722
Le 16:6 and make an **a.** for himself, ... 3722
Le 16:10 to make an **a.** with him, ... 3722
Le 16:11 and shall make an **a.** for himself, ... 3722
Le 16:16 shall make an **a.** for the holy place, ... 3722
Le 16:17 to make an **a.** in the holy place, ... 3722
Le 16:17 and have made an **a.** for himself, ... 3722
Le 16:18 and make an **a.** for it; ... 3722
Le 16:24 and make an **a.** for himself, ... 3722
Le 16:27 blood was brought in to make **a.** ... 3722
Le 16:30 the priest make an **a.** for you, ... 3722
Le 16:32 And the priest,...shall make the **a.**, ... 3722
Le 16:33 make an **a.** for the holy sanctuary, ... 3722
Le 16:33 shall make an **a.** for the tabernacle ... 3722
Le 16:33 and he shall make an **a.** for the ... 3722
Le 16:34 an **a.** for the children of Israel ... 3722
Le 17:11 to make an **a.** for your souls: ... 3722
Le 17:11 the blood that maketh an **a.** for ... 3722
Le 19:22 the priest shall make an **a.** for ... 3722
Le 23:27 there shall be a day of **a.**: ... 3725
Le 23:28 it is a day of **a.**, ... 3725
Le 23:28 to make an **a.** for you ... 3722
Le 25:9 the day of **a.** shall ye make the ... 3725
Nu 5:8 the ram of the **a.**, ... 3725
Nu 5:8 an **a.** shall be made for him ... 3722
Nu 6:11 and make an **a.** for him, ... 3722
Nu 8:12 to make an **a.** for the Levites ... 3722
Nu 8:19 and to make an **a.** for the children ... 3722
Nu 8:21 and Aaron made an **a.** ... 3722
Nu 15:25 And the priests shall make an **a.** ... 3722
Nu 15:28 shall make an **a.** for the soul ... 3722
Nu 15:28 to make an **a.** for him; ... 3722
Nu 16:46 and make an **a.** for them: ... 3722
Nu 16:47 and made an **a.** for the people ... 3722
Nu 25:13 an **a.** for the children of Israel ... 3722
Nu 28:22 sin offering, to make an **a.** for you ... 3722
Nu 28:30 the goats; to make an **a.** for you ... 3722
Nu 29:5 offering to make an **a.** for you: ... 3722
Nu 29:11 the sin offering of **a.**, ... 3725
Nu 31:50 to make an **a.** for our souls ... 3722
2Sa 21:3 wherewith shall I make the **a.** ... 3722
1Ch 6:49 and to make an **a.** for Israel, ... 3722
2Ch 29:24 to make an **a.** for all Israel: ... 3722
Ne 10:33 to make an **a.** for Israel, ... 3722
Ro 5:11 we have now received the **a.** ... *2643*

ATONEMENTS
Ex 30:10 the sin offering of **a.**; ... 3725

ATROTH (a'-troth) See also ATAROTH.
Nu 32:35 And **A.**, Shophan, and Jaazer, ... 5855

ATTAI (at'-tahee)
1Ch 2:35 to wife, and she bare him **A.** ... 6262
1Ch 2:36 And **A.** begat Nathan, and Nathan ... 6262
1Ch 12:11 **A.** the sixth, Eliel the seventh, ... 6262
2Ch 11:20 which bare him Abijah, and **A.**, ... 6262

ATTAIN See also ATTAINED.
Ps 139:6 it is high, I cannot **a.** unto it ...
Pr 1:5 a man of understanding shall **a.** ... 7069
Eze 46:7 as his hand shall **a.** unto, ... 5381
Ho 8:5 will it be ere they **a.** to innocency? ... 3201
Ac 27:12 means they might **a.** to Phenice, ... *2658*
Php 3:11 I might **a.** unto the resurrection ... *2658*

ATTAINED
Ge 47:9 not **a.** unto the days of the years ... 5381
2Sa 23:19 he **a.** not unto the first three: ... 935
2Sa 23:23 he **a.** not to the first ... 935
1Ch 11:21 howbeit he **a.** not to the first three ... 935
1Ch 11:25 but **a.** not to the first three ... 935
Ro 9:30 have **a.** to righteousness ... *2638*
Ro 9:31 not **a.** to the law of righteousness ... *5348*
Php 3:12 Not as though I had already **a.**, ... *2983*
Php 3:16 whereto we have already **a.**, ... *5348*
1Ti 4:6 whereunto thou hast **a.** ... *3877*

ATTALIA (at-ta-li'-ah)
Ac 14:25 they went down into **A.** ... *825*

ATTEND
Es 4:5 he had appointed to **a.** upon her, 6440
Ps 17:1 **a.** unto my cry, give ear unto my 7181
Ps 55:2 **A.** unto me, and hear me: 7181
Ps 61:1 **a.** unto my prayer. 7181
Ps 86:6 **a.** to the voice of my supplications 7181
Ps 142:6 **A.** unto my cry; for I am brought 7181
Pr 4:1 and **a.** to know understanding. 7181
Pr 4:20 My son, **a.** to my words; 7181
Pr 5:1 My son, **a.** unto my wisdom, 7181
Pr 7:24 and **a.** to the words of my mouth. 7181
1Co 7:35 that ye may **a.** upon the Lord *2145*

ATTENDANCE
1Ki 10:5 and the **a.** of his ministers, 4612
2Ch 9:4 and the **a.** of his ministers, 4612
1Ti 4:13 Till I come, give **a.** to reading, *4337*
Heb 7:13 no man gave **a.** at the altar. *4337*

ATTENDED
Job 32:12 Yea, I **a.** unto you, and, behold, 995
Ps 66:19 hath **a.** to the voice of my prayer. 7181
Ac 16:14 she **a.** unto the things which were *4337*

ATTENDING
Ro 13:6 **a.** continually upon this very thing. *4342*

ATTENT
2Ch 6:40 thine ears be **a.** unto the prayer 7183
2Ch 7:15 mine ears **a.** unto the prayer 7183

ATTENTIVE
Ne 1:6 let now thine ear be **a.**, 7183
Ne 1:11 now thine ear be **a.** to the prayer 7183
Ne 8:3 were **a.** unto the book of the law.
Ps 130:2 let thine ears be **a.** to the voice 7183
Lu 19:48 were very attentive to hear him. *1582*

ATTENTIVELY
Job 37:2 Hear **a.** the noise of his voice, 8085

ATTIRE
Pr 7:10 the **a.** of an harlot, 7897
Jer 2:32 her ornaments, or a bride her **a.**? 7196
Eze 23:15 in dyed **a.** upon their heads, 2871

ATTIRED
Le 16:4 the linen mitre shall he be **a.**: 6801

AUDIENCE
Ge 23:10 in the **a.** of the children of Heth, 241
Ge 23:13 in the **a.** of the people of the land, 241
Ge 23:16 named in the **a.** of the sons of Heth, 241
Ex 24:7 read in the **a.** of the people: 241
1Sa 25:24 in thine **a.** and hear the words 241
1Ch 28:8 and in the **a.** of our God, 241
Ne 13:1 in the **a.** of the people; 241
Lu 7:1 sayings in the **a.** of the people, *189*
Lu 20:45 in the **a.** of all the people he said *191*
Ac 13:16 ye that fear God, give **a.** *191*
Ac 15:12 and gave **a.** to Barnabas and *191*
Ac 22:22 they gave him **a.** unto this word, *191*

AUGHT See NAUGHT; OUGHT.

AUGMENT
Nu 32:14 to **a.** yet the fierce anger of the 5595

AUGUSTUS (aw-gus'-tus) See also AUGUSTUS'; CAESAR.
Lu 2:1 a decree from Caesar **A.**, *828*
Ac 25:21 reserved unto the hearing of **A.**, *828*
Ac 25:25 himself hath appealed to **A.**, *828*

AUGUSTUS' (aw-gus'-tus)
Ac 27:1 a centurion of **A.** band. *828*

AUL
Ex 21:6 bore his ear through with an **a.**; 4836
De 15:17 Then thou shalt take an **a.**, 4836

AUNT
Le 18:14 she is thine **a.** 1733

AUSTERE
Lu 19:21 **because thou art an a. man:** *840*
Lu 19:22 **that I was an a. man,** *840*

AUTHOR
1Co 14:33 God is not the **a.** of confusion, but
Heb 5:9 became the **a.** of eternal salvation *159*
Heb 12:2 the **a.** and finisher of our faith; *747*

AUTHORITIES
1Pe 3:22 **a.** and powers being made subject *1849*

AUTHORITY See also AUTHORITIES.
Es 9:29 Mordecai the Jew,...with all **a.**, 8633
Pr 29:2 When the righteous are in **a.**, the 7235
Mt 7:29 taught them as one having **a.**, *1849*
Mt 8:9 For I am a man under **a.**, *1849*
Mt 20:25 **that are great exercise a. upon** *2715*
Mt 21:23 what **a.** doest thou these things? *1849*
Mt 21:23 and who gave thee this **a.** *1849*
Mt 21:24, 27 **by what a. I do these things.** *1849*
Mk 1:22 as one that had **a.**, *1849*
Mk 1:27 for with **a.** commandeth he even *1849*
Mk 10:42 **their great ones exercise a. upon** *2715*
Mk 11:28 what **a.** doest thou these things? *1849*
Mk 11:28 and who gave thee this **a.** *1849*
Mk 11:29, 33 **by what a. I do these things.** *1849*
Mk 13:34 **gave a. to his servants,** *1849*
Lu 4:36 with **a.** and power he commandeth *1849*
Lu 7:8 am a man set under **a.**, *1849*
Lu 9:1 gave them power and **a.** over all *1849*
Lu 19:17 **have thou a. over ten cities** *1849*
Lu 20:2 what **a.** doest thou these things? *1849*
Lu 20:2 who is he that gave thee this **a.**? *1849*
Lu 20:8 **by what a. I do these things.** *1849*
Lu 20:20 power and **a.** of the governor. *1849*
Lu 22:25 **that exercise a. upon them are** *1850*
Joh 5:27 **hath given him a. to execute** *1849*
Ac 8:27 eunuch of great **a.** under Candace *1413*
Ac 9:14 he hath **a.** from the chief priests *1849*
Ac 26:10 having received **a.** from the chief *1849*
Ac 26:12 went to Damascus with **a.** and *1849*
1Co 15:24 all rule and all **a.** and power. *1849*
2Co 10:8 somewhat more of our **a.**, *1849*
1Ti 2:2 and for all that are in **a.**; *5247*
1Ti 2:12 nor to usurp **a.** over the man, but *831*
Tit 2:15 exhort, and rebuke with all **a.** *2003*
Re 13:2 power, and his seat, and great **a.** *1849*

AVA (a'-vah) See also IVAH.
2Ki 17:24 and from Cuthah, and from **A.**, 5755

AVAILETH
Es 5:13 all this **a.** me nothing, 7737
Ga 5:6 neither circumcision **a.** any thing, *2480*
Ga 6:15 neither circumcision **a.** any thing, *2480*
Jas 5:16 prayer of a righteous man **a.** much. *2480*

AVEN See also BETH-AVEN.
Eze 30:17 young men of **A.** and of Pi-beseth 206
Ho 10:8 high places also of **A.**, the sin of 206
Am 1:5 inhabitant from the plain of **A.**, 206

AVENGE See also AVENGED; AVENGETH; AVENGING.
Le 19:18 Thou shalt not **a.**, nor bear any 5358
Le 26:25 a sword...that shall **a.** the quarrel 5358
Nu 31:2 **A.** the children of Israel of 5358,5360
Nu 31:3 and **a.** the Lord of Midian. 5414,5360
De 32:43 will **a.** the blood of his servants, 5358
1Sa 24:12 and the Lord **a.** me of thee: 5358
2Ki 9:7 I may **a.** the blood of my servants 5358
Es 8:13 to **a.** themselves on their enemies. 5358
Isa 1:24 and **a.** me of mine enemies: 5358
Jer 46:10 he may **a.** him of his adversaries: 5358
Ho 1:4 and I will **a.** the blood of Jezreel 6485
Lu 18:3 **saying, A. me of mine adversary.** *1556*
Lu 18:5 **I will a. her, lest by her continual** *1556*
Lu 18:7 **not God a. his own elect,** *4160,3588,1557*
Lu 18:8 **he will a. them speedily** *4160,3588,1557*
Ro 12:19 Dearly beloved, **a.** not yourselves, *1556*
Re 6:10 dost thou not judge and **a.** our *1556*

AVENGED
Ge 4:24 If Cain shall be **a.** sevenfold, 5358
Jos 10:13 the people had **a.** themselves 5358
Jd 15:7 yet will I be **a.** of you, 5358
Jd 16:28 that I may be at once **a.** of the 5358
1Sa 14:24 that I may be **a.** on mine enemies. 5358
1Sa 18:25 to be **a.** of the king's enemies. 5358
1Sa 25:31 or that my Lord hath **a.** himself: 3467
2Sa 4:8 the Lord hath **a.** my lord 5414,5360
2Sa 18:19 hath **a.** him of his enemies. 8199
2Sa 18:31 Lord hath **a.** thee this day of all 8199
Jer 5:9, 29 shall not my soul be **a.** on such 5358
Jer 9:9 shall not my soul be **a.** on such 5358
Ac 7:24 **a.** him that was oppressed, *4160,1557*
Re 18:20 God hath **a.** you on her *2919,3588,2917*
Re 19:2 hath **a.** the blood of his servants *1556*

AVENGER
Nu 35:12 for refuge from the **a.**; that the 1350
De 19:6 Lest the **a.** of the blood pursue the 1350
De 19:12 into the hand of the **a.** of blood, 1350
Jos 20:3 your refuge from the **a.** of blood. 1350
Jos 20:5 if the **a.** of blood pursue after him, 1350
Jos 20:9 by the hand of the **a.** of blood, 1350
Ps 8:2 still the enemy and the **a.** 5358
Ps 44:16 by reason of the enemy and **a.** 5358
1Th 4:6 the Lord is the **a.** of all such, *1558*

AVENGETH
2Sa 22:48 It is God that **a.** me, 5414,5360
Ps 18:47 It is God that **a.** me, 5414,5360

AVENGING
Jg 5:2 Praise ye the Lord for the **a.** 6544,6546
1Sa 25:26 from **a.** thyself with thine own 3467
1Sa 25:33 from **a.** myself with mine own 3467

AVERSE
Mic 2:8 by securely as men **a.** from war. 7725

AVIM (a'-vim) See also AVIMS; AVITES.
Jos 18:23 And **A.**, and Parah, and Ophrah, 5761

AVIMS (a'-vims) See also AVIM.
De 2:23 And the **A.** which dwelt in 5757

AVITES (a'-vites) See also AVIM.
Jos 13:3 and the Ekronites; also the **A.** 5757
2Ki 17:31 the **A.** made Nibhaz and Tartak, 5757

AVITH (a'-vith)
Ge 36:35 and the name of his city was **A.** 5762
1Ch 1:46 and the name of his city was **A.** 5762

AVOID See also AVOIDED; AVOIDING.
Pr 4:15 **A.** it, pass not by it, turn from it, 6544
Ro 16:17 which ye have learned; and **a.** *1578*
1Co 7:2 Nevertheless, to **a.** fornication, *1223*
2Ti 2:23 and unlearned question **a.**, *3868*
Tit 3:9 But **a.** foolish questions, and *4026*

AVOIDED See also AVOID.
1Sa 18:11 And David **a.** out of his presence 5437

AVOIDING
2Co 8:20 **A.** this, that no man should *4724*
1Ti 6:20 **a.** profane and vain babblings, *1624*

AVOUCHED
De 26:17 thou hast **a.** the Lord this day to 559
De 26:18 the Lord hath **a.** thee this day 559

AWAIT
Ac 9:24 laying **a.** was known of Saul. *1917*

AWAKE See also AWAKED; AWAKEST; AWAKETH; AWAKING; AWOKE.
Jg 5:12 **A.**, Deborah; **a.**, **a.**, utter a 5782
Job 8:6 surely now he would **a.** for thee, 5782
Job 14:12 they shall not **a.**, nor be raised 6974
Ps 7:6 and **a.** for me to the judgment 5782
Ps 17:15 I shall be satisfied, when I **a.**, with 6974
Ps 35:23 Stir up thyself, and **a.** to my 6974
Ps 44:23 **A.**, why sleepest thou, O Lord? 5782
Ps 57:8 **A.** up, my glory, 5782
Ps 57:8 **a.**, psaltery and harp: 5782
Ps 57:8 I myself will **a.** early. 5782
Ps 59:4 **a.** to help me, and behold. 5782
Ps 59:5 **a.** to visit all the heathen: 6974
Ps 108:2 **A.**, psaltery and harp: 5782
Ps 108:2 I myself will **a.** early. 5782
Ps 139:18 when I **a.**, I am still with thee. 6974
Pr 23:35 when shall I **a.**? I will seek it yet 6974
Ca 2:7 nor **a.** my love, till he please. 5782
Ca 3:5 not up, nor **a.** my love, till he 5782
Ca 4:16 **A.**, O north wind; and come, 5782
Ca 8:4 ye stir not up, nor **a.** my love, 5782
Isa 26:19 **A.** and sing, ye that dwell in dust: 6974
Isa 51:9 **A.**, **a.**, put on strength, O arm of 5782
Isa 51:9 the Lord; **a.**, as in the ancient 5782
Isa 51:17 **A.**, **a.**; stand up, O Jerusalem, 5782
Isa 52:1 **A.**, **a.**; put on thy strength, 5782
Da 12:2 in the dust of the earth shall **a.**, 6974
Joe 1:5 **A.**, ye drunkards, and weep; 6974
Hab 2:7 and **a.** that shall vex thee, 6974
Hab 2:19 him that saith to the wood, **A.**; 6974
Zec 13:7 **A.**, O sword, against my shepherd, 5782
Mk 4:38 they **a.** him, and say unto him *1326*
Lu 9:32 when they were **a.**, they saw his *1235*
Joh 11:11 **that I may a. him out of sleep.** *1852*
Ro 13:11 is high time to **a.** out of sleep: *1453*
1Co 15:34 **A.** to righteousness, and sin not; *1594*
Eph 5:14 **A.** thou that sleepest, and arise *1453*

AWAKED See also AWOKE.
Ge 28:16 And Jacob **a.** out of his sleep, 3364
Jg 16:14 And he **a.** out of his sleep, 3364
1Sa 26:12 saw it, nor knew it, neither **a.** 6974
1Ki 18:27 he sleepeth, and must be **a.**. 3364
2Ki 4:31 The child is not **a.** 6974
Ps 3:5 I **a.**; for the Lord sustained me. 6974
Ps 78:65 the Lord **a.** a one out of sleep, 3364
Jer 31:26 Upon this I **a.**, and beheld; 6974

AWAKEST
Ps 73:20 when thou **a.**, thou shalt despise 5782
Pr 6:22 when thou **a.**, it shall talk with 6974

AWAKETH
Ps 73:20 As a dream when one **a.**; 6974
Isa 29:8 but he **a.**, and his soul is empty: 6974
Isa 29:8 but he **a.**, and, behold, he is faint, 6974

AWAKING
Ac 16:27 **a.** out of his sleep, and *1096,1853*

AWARE See also WARE.
Ca 6:12 Or ever I was **a.**, my soul made 3045
Jer 50:24 thou wast not **a.**; thou art found, 3045
Mt 24:50 **in an hour that he is not a. of,** *1097*
Lu 11:44 **over them are not a. of them.** *1492*
Lu 12:46 **and at an hour when he is not a.,** .1097

AWAY See also CASTAWAY.
Ge 12:20 and they sent him **a.**, and his wife,
Ge 15:11 carcasses, Abram drove them **a.**.
Ge 18:3 favour in thy sight, pass not **a.**,
Ge 21:14 and the child, and sent her **a.**:
Ge 21:25 servants had violently taken **a.**.
Ge 24:54 said, Send me **a.** unto my master.
Ge 24:56 send me **a.** that I may go to my
Ge 24:59 they sent **a.** Rebekah, their sister,
Ge 25:6 gifts, and sent them **a.** from Isaac
Ge 26:27 me, and have sent me **a.** from you?
Ge 26:29 and have sent thee **a.** in peace:
Ge 26:31 Isaac sent them **a.**, and they
Ge 27:35 and hath taken **a.** thy blessing.
Ge 27:36 times: he took **a.** my birthright;
Ge 27:36 now he hath taken **a.** my blessing.
Ge 27:44 until thy brother's fury turn **a.**;
Ge 27:45 Until thy brother's anger turn **a.**
Ge 28:5 And Isaac sent **a.** Jacob: and he
Ge 28:6 and sent him **a.** to Padan-aram,
Ge 30:15 take **a.** my son's mandrakes also?
Ge 30:23 Lord hath taken **a.** my reproach:
Ge 30:25 said unto Laban, Send me **a.**,
Ge 31:1 taken **a.** all that was our father's;
Ge 31:9 taken **a.** the cattle of your father,
Ge 31:18 And he carried **a.** all his cattle,
Ge 31:20 And Jacob stole **a.** unawares
Ge 31:26 stolen **a.** unawares to me,
Ge 31:26 and carried **a.** my daughters,
Ge 31:27 didst thou flee **a.** secretly,
Ge 31:27 and steal **a.** from me; and
Ge 31:27 that I might have sent thee **a.**
Ge 31:42 hadst sent me **a.** now empty.
Ge 35:2 Put **a.** the strange gods that are
Ge 38:19 and she arose, and went **a.**, and
Ge 40:15 I was stolen **a.** out of the land
Ge 42:36 and ye will take Benjamin **a.**:
Ge 43:14 may send **a.** your other brother
Ge 44:3 the men were sent **a.**, they and
Ge 45:24 So he sent his brethren **a.**, and
Ex 2:9 Take this child **a.**, and nurse it
Ex 2:17 came and drove them **a.**:
Ex 8:8 may take **a.** the frogs from me,
Ex 8:28 not go very far **a.**: intreat for me.
Ex 10:17 take **a.** from me this death only.
Ex 10:19 which took **a.** the locusts, and
Ex 12:15 first day ye shall put **a.** leaven
Ex 12:28 the children of Israel went **a.**,
Ex 13:19 up my bones **a.** hence with you.
Ex 13:22 He took not **a.** the pillar of the
Ex 14:11 hast thou taken us **a.** to die in the
Ex 15:15 of Canaan shalt melt **a.**
Ex 18:18 thou wilt surely wear **a.**, both
Ex 19:24 the Lord said unto him, **A.**, get 3212
Ex 22:10 die, or be hurt, or driven **a.**,
Ex 23:25 I will take sickness **a.** from the
Ex 33:23 And I will take **a.** mine hand,
Le 1:16 he shall pluck **a.** his crop with his
Le 3:4, 10,15 kidneys, it shall he take **a.**,
Le 4:9 the kidneys, it shall he take **a.**.
Le 4:31 **a.** all the fat thereof,
Le 4:31 as the fat is taken **a.**
Le 4:35 shall take **a.** all the fat thereof,
Le 4:35 the fat of the lamb is taken **a.**
Le 6:2 or in a thing taken **a.** by violence,
Le 6:4 that which he took violently **a.**,
Le 7:4 the kidneys, it shall he take **a.**:
Le 14:40 that they take **a.** the stones
Le 14:43 that he hath taken **a.** the stones,
Le 16:21 shall send him **a.** by the hand of a fit
Le 21:7 a woman put **a.** from her husband
Le 25:25 sold **a.** some of his possession,
Le 26:39 that are left of you shall pine **a.**
Le 26:39 of their fathers shall they pine **a.**
Le 26:44 I will not cast them **a.**, neither
Nu 4:13 take **a.** the ashes from the altar,
Nu 11:6 But now our soul is dried **a.**:
Nu 14:43 ye are turned **a.** from the Lord, 310
Nu 17:10 quite take **a.** their murmurings
Nu 20:21 wherefore Israel turned **a.** from
Nu 21:7 he take **a.** the serpents from us.
Nu 24:22 Asshur shall carry thee **a.** captive.
Nu 25:4 anger of the Lord may be turned **a.**
Nu 25:11 hath turned my wrath **a.** from
Nu 27:4 name of our fathers be done **a.** 1639
Nu 32:15 For if ye turn **a.** from after him,
Nu 36:4 their inheritance be taken **a.** from
De 7:4 turn **a.** thy son from following me,
De 7:15 take **a.** from thee all sickness,
De 13:5 to turn you **a.** from the Lord
De 13:5 So shalt thou put the evil **a.** 1197
De 13:10 he hath sought to thrust thee **a.**
De 15:13 shalt not let him go **a.** empty:
De 15:16 thee, I will not go **a.** from thee; 3318
De 15:18 sendest him **a.** free from thee;
De 17:7 put the evil **a.** from among you. 1197
De 17:12 shalt put **a.** the evil from Israel. 1197
De 17:17 that his heart turn not **a.**:
De 19:13 put **a.** the guilt of innocent blood 1197
De 19:19 put the evil **a.** from among you. 1197
De 21:9 put **a.** the guilt of innocent blood 1197
De 21:21 thou put evil **a.** from among you; 1197
De 22:19 may not put her **a.** all his days.
De 22:21 thou put evil **a.** from among you. 1197
De 22:22 shalt thou put **a.** evil from Israel. 1197
De 22:24 thou put **a.** evil from among you. 1197
De 22:29 may not put her **a.** all his days.
De 23:14 in thee, and turn **a.** from thee.
De 24:4 husband, which sent her **a.**,
De 24:7 shalt put evil **a.** from among you. 1197
De 26:13 brought **a.** the hallowed things 1197
De 26:14 have I taken **a.** aught thereof 1197
De 28:26 and no man shall fray them **a.**
De 28:31 ass shall be violently taken **a.**
De 29:18 heart turneth **a.** this day from
De 30:17 But if thine heart turn **a.**, so that
De 30:17 not hear, but shalt be drawn **a.**,
Jos 2:21 And she sent them **a.**, and they
Jos 5:9 day have I rolled **a.** the reproach
Jos 7:13 ye take **a.** the accursed thing
Jos 8:3 and sent them **a.** by night.
Jos 8:16 Joshua, and were drawn **a.** from
Jos 18:8 the men arose, and went **a.**
Jos 22:6 blessed them, and sent them **a.**
Jos 22:7 when Joshua sent them **a.** also
Jos 22:16 to turn **a.** this day from following
Jos 22:18 ye must turn **a.** this day from
Jos 24:14 **a.** the gods which your fathers 5493
Jos 24:23 therefore put **a.**, said he, the 5493
Jg 3:18 sent **a.** the people that bare the
Jg 4:15 chariot, and fled **a.** on his feet.
Jg 4:17 Howbeit Sisera fled **a.** on his feet
Jg 5:21 river of Kishbon swept them **a.**,
Jg 8:21 and took **a.** the ornaments
Jg 9:21 and Jotham ran **a.**, and fled,
Jg 10:16 And they put **a.** the strange gods 5493
Jg 11:13 Because Israel took **a.** my land,
Jg 11:15 took not **a.** the land of Moab,
Jg 11:38 he sent her **a.** for two months:
Jg 15:17 cast **a.** the jawbone out of his hand,
Jg 16:3 posts, and went **a.** with them, 5265
Jg 16:14 went **a.** with the pin of the beam, 5265
Jg 18:24 taken **a.** my gods which I made,
Jg 18:24 ye are gone **a.**: and what have I
Jg 19:2 went **a.** from him unto her
Jg 20:13 and put **a.** evil from Israel. 1197
Jg 20:31 and were drawn **a.** from the city;
1Sa 1:14 put **a.** thy wine from thee. 5493
1Sa 5:11 Send **a.** the ark of the God of Israel,
1Sa 6:3 send **a.** the ark of the God of Israel,
1Sa 6:8 by the side thereof; and send it **a.**,
1Sa 7:3 then put **a.** the strange gods 5493
1Sa 7:4 the children of Israel did put **a.** 5493
1Sa 9:26 Up, that I may send thee **a.**
1Sa 10:25 And Samuel sent all the people **a.**
1Sa 14:16 behold, the multitude melted **a.**,
1Sa 15:27 as Samuel turned about to go **a.**
1Sa 17:26 taketh **a.** the reproach from Israel
1Sa 19:10 slipped **a.** out of Saul's presence.
1Sa 19:17 me so, and sent **a.** mine enemy.
1Sa 20:13 shew it thee, and send thee **a.**,
1Sa 20:22 for the Lord hath sent thee **a.**
1Sa 20:29 let me get **a.**, I pray thee, and see 4422
1Sa 21:6 in the day when it was taken **a.**
1Sa 23:5 and brought **a.** their cattle,
1Sa 23:26 haste to get **a.** for fear of Saul; 3212
1Sa 24:19 will he let him go well **a.**? 1870
1Sa 25:10 break **a.** every man from his
1Sa 26:12 and gat them **a.**, and no man 3212
1Sa 27:9 alive, and took **a.** the sheep,
1Sa 28:3 had put **a.** those that had familiar 5493
1Sa 28:25 rose up, and went **a.** that night.
1Sa 30:2 but carried them **a.**, and went on
1Sa 30:18 the Amalekites had carried **a.**
1Sa 30:22 that they may lead them **a.**,
2Sa 1:21 of the mighty is vilely cast **a.**,
2Sa 3:21 And David sent Abner **a.**; and he
2Sa 3:22 for he had sent him **a.**, and he is gone
2Sa 3:23 and he hath sent him **a.**, and he is
2Sa 3:24 thou hast sent him **a.**, and he is
2Sa 4:7 gat them **a.** through the plain 3212
2Sa 4:11 and take you **a.** from the earth?
2Sa 5:6 Except thou take **a.** the blind and 5493
2Sa 7:15 But my mercy shall not depart **a.**
2Sa 7:15 Saul, whom I put **a.** before thee, 5493
2Sa 10:4 their buttocks, and sent them **a.**,
2Sa 12:13 Lord also hath put **a.** their sin; 5674
2Sa 13:16 this evil in sending me **a.** is
2Sa 17:18 went both of them **a.** quickly,
2Sa 18:3 for if we flee **a.**, they will not care
2Sa 18:9 that was under him went **a.**
2Sa 19:3 as people being ashamed steal **a.**
2Sa 19:41 the men of Judah stolen thee **a.**,
2Sa 22:46 Strangers shall fade **a.**, and they
2Sa 23:6 as thorns thrust **a.**, because they 5074
2Sa 23:9 the men of Israel were gone **a.**:
2Sa 24:10 take **a.** the iniquity of thy 5674
1Ki 2:31 thou mayest take **a.** the innocent 5493
1Ki 2:39 the servants of Shimei ran **a.**
1Ki 8:46 that they carry them **a.** captives 7617
1Ki 8:48 which led them **a.** captive, 7617
1Ki 8:66 eighth day he sent the people **a.**
1Ki 11:2 surely they will turn **a.** your heart
1Ki 11:3 and his wives turned **a.** his heart
1Ki 11:4 that his wives turned **a.** his heart
1Ki 11:13 I will not rend **a.** all the kingdom;
1Ki 14:8 the kingdom **a.** from the house
1Ki 14:10 take **a.** the remnant of the house
1Ki 14:10 as a man taketh **a.** dung, till it
1Ki 14:26 he took **a.** the treasures of the
1Ki 14:26 he even took **a.** all:
1Ki 14:26 and he took **a.** all the shields
1Ki 15:12 he took **a.** the sodomites out of
1Ki 15:22 took **a.** the stones of Ramah,
1Ki 16:3 I will take **a.** the posterity of
1Ki 19:4 now, O Lord, take **a.** my life;
1Ki 19:10, 14 they seek my life, to take it **a.**
1Ki 20:6 it in their hand, and take it **a.**
1Ki 20:24 Take the kings **a.**, every man out
1Ki 20:34 I will send thee **a.** with this
1Ki 20:34 with him, and sent him **a.**
1Ki 20:41 took the ashes **a.** from his face; 5493
1Ki 21:4 and turned **a.** his face, and would
1Ki 21:21 and will take **a.** thy posterity,
1Ki 22:43 the high places were not taken **a.**; 5493
2Ki 2:3, 5 Lord will take **a.** thy master
2Ki 2:9 before I be taken **a.** from thee.
2Ki 3:2 he put **a.** the image of Baal that 5493
2Ki 4:27 came near to thrust her **a.**
2Ki 5:2 had brought **a.** captive out of
2Ki 5:11 and went **a.**, and said, Behold,
2Ki 5:12 he turned and went **a.** in a rage.
2Ki 6:23 he sent them **a.**, and they went
2Ki 6:32 hath sent to take **a.** mine head?

2Ki 7:15 the Syrians had cast **a.** in their
2Ki 12:3 high places were not taken **a.**: 5493
2Ki 12:18 and he went **a.** from Jerusalem.
2Ki 14:4 the high places were not taken **a.**: 5493
2Ki 17:6 and carried Israel **a.** into Assyria, 1540
2Ki 17:11 Lord carried **a.** before them; 1540
2Ki 17:23 So was Israel carried **a.** out of 1540
2Ki 17:28 had carried **a.** from Samaria 1540
2Ki 17:33 the nations whom they carried **a.** 1540
2Ki 18:11 king of Assyria did carry **a.** Israel 1540
2Ki 18:22 altars Hezekiah hath taken **a.**, 5493
2Ki 18:24 How then wilt thou turn **a.** the
2Ki 18:32 take you **a.** to a land like your own
2Ki 20:18 thou shalt beget, shall they take **a.**;
2Ki 23:11 he took **a.** the horses that the 7673
2Ki 23:19 Josiah took **a.**, and did to them 5493
2Ki 23:24 did Josiah put **a.**, that he might 1197
2Ki 23:34 and took Jehoahaz **a.**: and he
2Ki 24:14 And he carried **a.** all Jerusalem, 1540
2Ki 24:15 and he carried **a.** Jehoiachin to 1540
2Ki 25:11 the fugitives that fell **a.** to the
2Ki 25:11 the captain of the guard carry **a.** 1540
2Ki 25:14 they ministered, took they **a.**.
2Ki 25:15 the captain of the guard took **a.**.
2Ki 25:21 So Judah was carried **a.** out of 1540
1Ch 5:6 king of Assyria carried **a.** captive: 1540
1Ch 5:21 And they took **a.** their cattle; 7617
1Ch 5:26 and he carried them **a.**, even the 1540
1Ch 6:15 carried **a.** Judah and Jerusalem 1540
1Ch 7:21 came down to take **a.** their cattle
1Ch 8:8 after he had sent them **a.**;
1Ch 8:13 who drove **a.** the inhabitants of 1272
1Ch 9:1 were carried **a.** to Babylon for 1540
1Ch 10:12 and took **a.** the body of Saul,
1Ch 12:19 upon advisement sent him **a.**,
1Ch 14:14 turn **a.** from them, and come upon
1Ch 17:13 not take my mercy **a.** from him, 5493
1Ch 19:4 their buttocks, and sent them **a.**.
1Ch 21:8 thee, do **a.** the iniquity of thy 5674
2Ch 6:36 they carry them **a.** captives unto 7617
2Ch 6:42 O Lord God, turn not **a.** the face
2Ch 7:10 sent the people **a.** into their tents,
2Ch 7:19 But if ye turn **a.**, and forsake my
2Ch 9:12 and went **a.** to her own land,
2Ch 12:9 took **a.** the treasures of the house
2Ch 12:9 he carried **a.** also the shields of
2Ch 14:3 took **a.** the altars of the strange 5493
2Ch 14:5 took **a.** out of all the cities of 5493
2Ch 14:13 they carried **a.** very much spoil
2Ch 14:15 and carried **a.** sheep and camels 7617
2Ch 15:8 and put **a.** the abominable idols 5674
2Ch 15:17 the high places were not taken **a.** 5493
2Ch 16:6 and they carried **a.** the stones of
2Ch 17:6 he took **a.** the high places and 5493
2Ch 19:3 thou hast taken **a.** the groves out 1197
2Ch 20:25 came to take **a.** the spoil of them,
2Ch 20:25 more than they could carry **a.**:
2Ch 20:33 high places were not taken **a.**: 5493
2Ch 21:17 carried **a.** all the substance 7617
2Ch 25:12 children of Judah carry **a.** captive,
2Ch 25:27 Amaziah did turn **a.** from following
2Ch 28:5 and carried **a.** a great multitude 7617
2Ch 28:8 children of Israel carried **a.** captive
2Ch 28:8 and took also **a.** much spoil
2Ch 28:17 and smitten Judah, and carried **a.**
2Ch 28:21 Ahaz took **a.** a portion out of the
2Ch 29:6 have turned **a.** their faces from the
2Ch 29:10 his fierce wrath may turn **a.** from
2Ch 29:19 king Ahaz in his reign did cast **a.**
2Ch 30:8 his wrath may turn **a.** from you.
2Ch 30:9 not turn **a.** his face from you,
2Ch 30:14 they arose and took **a.** the altars 5493
2Ch 30:14 the altars for incense took they **a.** 5493
2Ch 32:12 Hezekiah taken **a.** his high places 5493
2Ch 33:15 And he took **a.** the strange gods, 5493
2Ch 34:33 took **a.** all the abominations 5493
2Ch 35:23 Have me **a.**; for I am sore 5674
2Ch 36:20 sword carried he **a.** to Babylon; 1540
Ezr 2:1 those which had been carried **a.**, 1473
Ezr 2:1 the king of Babylon had carried **a.** 1540
Ezr 5:12 carried the people **a.** into Babylon. 1541
Ezr 8:35 of those that had been carried **a.**, 1473
Ezr 9:4 of those that had been carried **a.**; 1473
Ezr 10:3 our God to put **a.** all the wives, 3318
Ezr 10:6 of them that had been carried **a.** 1473
Ezr 10:8 of those that had been carried **a.** 1473
Ezr 10:19 that they would put **a.** their wives; 3318

Ne 7:6 had been carried **a.**, whom 1473
Ne 7:6 the king of Babylon had carried **a.**, 1546
Es 2:6 been carried **a.** from Jerusalem 1546
Es 2:6 captivity which had been carried **a.** 1546
Es 2:6 the king of Babylon had carried **a.**, 1546
Es 4:4 take **a.** his sackcloth from him: 5493
Es 8:3 with tears to put **a.** the mischief 5674
Job 1:15 fell upon them, and took them **a.**;
Job 1:17 and have carried them **a.**,
Job 1:21 and the Lord hath taken **a.**;
Job 4:21 excellency which is in them go **a.**? 5265
Job 6:15 streams of brooks they pass **a.**;
Job 7:9 is consumed and vanisheth **a.**:
Job 7:21 and take **a.** mine iniquity? 5674
Job 8:4 he have cast them **a.** for their
Job 8:20 God will not cast **a.** a perfect man,
Job 9:12 Behold, he taketh **a.**, who can 2862
Job 9:25 they flee **a.**, they see no good.
Job 9:26 are pased **a.** as the swift ships:
Job 9:34 Let him take his rod **a.** from me, 5493
Job 11:14 put it far **a.**, and let not wickedness
Job 11:16 it as waters that pass **a.**:
Job 12:17 he leadeth counsellors **a.** spoiled,
Job 12:19 He leadeth princes **a.** spoiled,
Job 12:20 He removeth **a.** the speech of the
Job 12:20 taketh **a.** the understanding of
Job 12:24 he taketh **a.** the heart of the chief 5493
Job 14:10 But man dieth, and wasteth **a.**:
Job 14:19 thou washest **a.** the things which
Job 14:20 countenance, and sendest him **a.**,
Job 15:12 doth thine heart carry thee **a.**?
Job 15:30 breath of his mouth shall he go **a.**.
Job 20:8 He shall fly **a.** as a dream and
Job 20:8 he shall be chased **a.** as a vision
Job 20:19 taken **a.** an house which he 1497
Job 20:28 his goods shall flow **a.** in the day
Job 21:18 as chaff that the storm carrieth **a.** 1589
Job 22:9 Thou hast sent widows **a.** empty,
Job 22:23 thou shalt put **a.** iniquity far from 7368
Job 24:2 they violently take **a.** flocks, and
Job 24:3 drive **a.** the ass of the fatherless,
Job 24:10 take **a.** the sheaf from the hungry;
Job 27:2 who hath taken **a.** my judgment; 5493
Job 27:8 when God taketh **a.** his soul? 7953
Job 27:20 stealeth him **a.** in the night.
Job 27:21 the east wind carrieth him **a.**,
Job 28:4 up, they are gone **a.** from men.
Job 30:12 they push **a.** my feet, and they
Job 30:15 my welfare passeth **a.** as a cloud
Job 32:22 Maker would soon take me **a.**,
Job 33:21 His flesh is consumed **a.**, that
Job 34:5 God hath taken **a.** my judgment. 5493
Job 34:20 be troubled at midnight, and pass **a.**:
Job 34:20 and the mighty shall be taken **a.** 5493
Job 36:18 lest he take thee **a.** with his 5496
Ps 1:4 the chaff which the wind driveth **a.**.
Ps 2:3 and cast **a.** their cords from us.
Ps 18:22 I did not put **a.** his statutes from 5493
Ps 18:45 The strangers shall fade **a.**,
Ps 27:9 put not thy servant **a.** in anger: 5186
Ps 28:3 Draw me not **a.** with the wicked,
Ps 31:13 they devised to take **a.** my life.
Ps 34:*title* Abimelech; who drove him **a.**,
Ps 37:20 into smoke shall they consume **a.**.
Ps 37:36 Yet he passed **a.**, and lo, he was
Ps 39:10 Remove thy stroke **a.** from me:
Ps 39:11 makest his beauty to consume **a.**
Ps 48:5 were troubled, and hasted **a.**,
Ps 49:17 he dieth he shall carry nothing **a.**:
Ps 51:11 Cast me not **a.** from thy presence;
Ps 52:5 he shall take thee **a.**, and pluck 2846
Ps 55:6 for then would I fly **a.** and be at
Ps 58:7 Let them melt **a.** as waters which
Ps 58:8 let every one of them pass **a.**:
Ps 58:9 he shall take them **a.** as with a
Ps 64:8 all that see them shall flee **a.**
Ps 65:3 thou shalt purge them **a.**.
Ps 66:20 hath not turned **a.** my prayer,
Ps 68:2 As smoke is driven **a.**,
Ps 68:2 so drive them **a.**:
Ps 69:4 restored that which I took not **a.** 1497
Ps 78:38 turned his anger **a.**, and did not
Ps 78:39 a wind that passeth **a.**, and cometh
Ps 79:9 and purge **a.** our sins, for thy
Ps 85:3 Thou hast taken **a.** all thy wrath:
Ps 88:8 hast put **a.** mine acquaintance 7368
Ps 90:5 carriest them **a.** as with a flood;

Ps 90:9 For all our days are passed **a.** in
Ps 90:10 it is soon cut off, and we fly **a.**.
Ps 102:24 O my God, take me not **a.** in the
Ps 104:7 voice of thy thunder they hasted **a.**.
Ps 104:29 takest **a.** their breath, they die,
Ps 106:23 to turn **a.** his wrath, lest he should
Ps 112:10 gnash with his teeth, and melt **a.**:
Ps 119:37 Turn **a.** mine eyes from beholding
Ps 119:39 Turn **a.** my reproach which I fear:
Ps 119:119 Thou puttest **a.** all the wicked of
Ps 132:10 David's sake turn not **a.** the face
Ps 137:3 carried us **a.** captive required
Ps 144:4 are as a shadow that passeth **a.**.
Pr 1:19 taketh **a.** the life of the owners
Pr 1:32 the turning **a.** of the simple shall
Pr 4:15 turn from it, and pass **a.**
Pr 4:16 and their sleep is taken **a.**, unless 1497
Pr 4:24 Put **a.** from thee a froward mouth, 5493
Pr 6:33 reproach shall not be wiped **a.**
Pr 10:3 casteth **a.** the substance of the 1920
Pr 14:32 is driven **a.** in his wickedness:
Pr 15:1 A soft answer turneth **a.** wrath:
Pr 19:26 and chaseth **a.** his mother,
Pr 20:8 throne of judgment scattereth **a.**
Pr 20:30 blueness of a wound cleanseth **a.**
Pr 22:27 why should he take **a.** the bed
Pr 23:5 they fly **a.** as an eagle toward
Pr 24:18 he turn **a.** his wrath from him
Pr 25:4 Take **a.** the dross from the silver, 1898
Pr 25:5 Take **a.** the wicked from before 1898
Pr 25:10 and thine infamy turn not **a.**.
Pr 25:20 taketh **a.** a garment in cold 5710
Pr 25:23 The north wind driveth **a.** rain:
Pr 28:9 turneth **a.** his ear from hearing the
Pr 29:8 but wise men turn **a.** wrath
Pr 30:30 and turneth not **a.** for any;
Ec 1:4 One generation passeth **a.**,
Ec 3:5 A time to cast **a.** stones, and a
Ec 3:6 to keep, and a time to cast **a.**;
Ec 5:15 he may carry **a.** in his hand
Ec 11:10 and put **a.** evil from thy flesh: 5493
Ca 2:10, 13 love, my fair one, and come **a.**.
Ca 2:17 day break, and the shadows flee **a.**,
Ca 4:6 day break, and the shadows flee **a.**,
Ca 5:7 keepers of the walls **a.** my veil
Ca 6:5 Turn **a.** thine eyes from me,
Isa 1:4 they are gone **a.** backward.
Isa 1:13 of assemblies, I cannot **a.** with;
Isa 1:16 put **a.** the evil of your doings 5493
Isa 1:25 and purely purge **a.** thy dross,
Isa 1:25 and take **a.** all thy tin: 5493
Isa 3:1 the Lord of hosts doth take **a.** from 5493
Isa 3:18 the Lord will take **a.** the bravery 5493
Isa 4:1 to take **a.** our reproach.
Isa 4:4 Lord shall have washed **a.** the filth
Isa 5:5 I will take **a.** the hedge thereof, 5493
Isa 5:23 take **a.** the righteousness of the 5493
Isa 5:24 because they have cast **a.** the law
Isa 5:25 all this his anger is not turned **a.**,
Isa 5:29 shall carry it **a.** safe, and none shall
Isa 6:7 and thine iniquity is taken **a.**, 5493
Isa 6:12 the Lord have removed men far **a.**,
Isa 8:4 spoil of Samaria shall be taken **a.**
Isa 9:12, 17,21 his anger is not turned **a.**,
Isa 10:2 to take **a.** the right from the poor 1497
Isa 10:4 all this his anger is not turned **a.**,
Isa 10:27 his burden shall be taken **a.** from 5493
Isa 12:1 thine anger is turned **a.**, and thou
Isa 15:6 for the hay is withered **a.**,
Isa 15:7 carry **a.** to the brook of the willows
Isa 16:10 And gladness is taken **a.**, and joy
Isa 17:1 Damascus is taken **a.** from being 5493
Isa 18:5 **a.** and cut down the branches 5493
Isa 19:6 they shall turn the rivers far **a.**;
Isa 19:7 be driven **a.** and be no more.
Isa 20:4 shall the king of Assyria lead **a.**
Isa 22:4 Therefore said I, Look **a.** from me;
Isa 22:17 Behold, the Lord will carry thee **a.**
Isa 24:4 The earth mourneth and fadeth **a.**,
Isa 24:4 world languisheth and fadeth **a.**.
Isa 25:8 Lord God will wipe **a.** tears from
Isa 25:8 of his people shall he take **a.** 5493
Isa 27:9 is all the fruit to take **a.** his sin; 5493
Isa 28:17 shall sweep **a.** the refuge of lies,
Isa 29:5 shall be as chaff that passeth **a.**:
Isa 30:22 them **a.** as a menstruous cloth; 2219
Isa 31:7 shall cast **a.** his idols of silver, 3988

Book	Ref	Context	No.
Isa	35:10	sorrow and sighing shall flee **a.**.	
Isa	36:7	altars Hezekiah hath taken **a.**,	5493
Isa	36:9	How then wilt thou turn **a.** the face	
Isa	36:17	I come and take you **a.** to a land	
Isa	39:7	thou shalt beget, shall they take **a.**;	
Isa	40:24	shall take them **a.** as stubble.	
Isa	41:9	chosen thee, and not cast thee **a.**.	
Isa	41:16	and the wind shall carry them **a.**,	
Isa	49:19	swallowed thee up shall be far **a.**.	
Isa	49:25	of the mighty shall be taken **a.**.	
Isa	50:1	whom I have put **a.**?	
Isa	50:1	transgressions is your mother put **a.**.	
Isa	50:5	neither turned **a.** back.	
Isa	51:6	heavens shall vanish **a.** like smoke,	
Isa	51:11	sorrow and mourning shall flee **a.**.	
Isa	52:5	my people is taken **a.** for nought?	
Isa	57:1	and merciful men are taken **a.**,	
Isa	57:1	that the righteousness is taken **a.**.	
Isa	57:13	the wind shall carry them all **a.**;	
Isa	58:9	If thou take **a.** from the midst of	5493
Isa	58:13	If thou turn **a.** thy foot from the	
Isa	59:13	and departing **a.** from our God,	
Isa	59:14	judgment is turned **a.** backward,	
Isa	64:6	like the wind, have taken us **a.**.	
Jer	1:3	carrying **a.** of Jerusalem captive	
Jer	2:24	her occasion who can turn her **a.**?	
Jer	3:1	They say, If a man put **a.** his wife,	
Jer	3:8	committed adultery I had put her **a.**,	
Jer	3:19	and shalt not turn **a.** from me	
Jer	4:1	put **a.** thine abominations	5493
Jer	4:4	take **a.** the foreskins of your heart,	5493
Jer	5:10	take **a.** her battlements;	5493
Jer	5:25	your iniquities have turned **a.** these	
Jer	6:4	unto us! for the day goeth **a.**,	
Jer	6:29	for the wicked are not plucked **a.**.	
Jer	7:29	and cast it **a.**, and take up a	
Jer	7:33	and none shall fray them **a.**.	
Jer	8:4	shall he turn **a.**, and not return?	
Jer	8:13	I have given them shall pass **a.**.	
Jer	13:17	Lord's flock is carried **a.** captive.	
Jer	13:19	Judah shall be carried **a.** captive	
Jer	13:19	shall be wholly carried **a.** captive.	
Jer	13:24	that passeth **a.** by the wind of the	
Jer	15:15	me not **a.** in thy longsuffering:	
Jer	16:5	for I have taken **a.** my peace from	
Jer	18:20	to turn **a.** thy wrath from them.	
Jer	22:10	weep sore for him that goeth **a.**:	
Jer	23:2	and driven them **a.**, and have not	
Jer	24:1	Babylon had carried **a.** captive	
Jer	24:5	are carried **a.** captive of Judah,	
Jer	27:20	he carried **a.** captive Jeconiah	
Jer	28:3	king of Babylon took **a.** from this	
Jer	28:6	and all that is carried **a.** captive,	
Jer	29:1	which were carried **a.** captives,	
Jer	29:1	carried **a.** captive from Jerusalem	
Jer	29:4	all that are carried **a.** captives,	
Jer	29:4	to be carried **a.** from Jerusalem	
Jer	29:7	you to be carried **a.** captives,	
Jer	29:14	and I will turn **a.** your captivity,	
Jer	29:14	I caused you to be carried **a.**.	
Jer	32:40	I will turn **a.** from them, to do	
Jer	33:26	will I cast **a.** the seed of Jacob,	
Jer	37:13	Thou fallest **a.** to the Chaldeans.	
Jer	37:14	I fall not **a.** to the Chaldeans.	
Jer	38:22	mire, and they are turned **a.** back.	
Jer	39:9	carried **a.** captive into Babylon	
Jer	39:9	the city, and those that fell **a.**,	
Jer	40:1	carried **a.** captive of Jerusalem	
Jer	40:1	carried **a.** captive unto Babylon.	
Jer	40:7	not carried **a.** captive to Babylon;	
Jer	41:10	carried **a.** captive all the residue	
Jer	41:10	carried them **a.** captive, and	
Jer	41:14	people that Ishmael had carried **a.**	
Jer	43:3	carry us **a.** captives into Babylon	
Jer	43:12	carry them **a.** captives: and he	
Jer	46:5	turned **a.** back? and their mighty	
Jer	46:6	Let not the swift flee **a.**, nor the	
Jer	46:15	Why are thy valiant men swept **a.**?	
Jer	46:21	and are fled **a.** together: they did	
Jer	48:9	may flee and get **a.**: for the cities	3318
Jer	49:19	suddenly make him run **a.** from	
Jer	49:29	their flocks shall they take **a.**:	
Jer	50:6	they have turned them **a.** on the	
Jer	50:17	the loins have driven him **a.**:	
Jer	50:44	suddenly run **a.** from her; and	
Jer	51:50	go **a.**, stand not still: remember	
Jer	52:15	guard carried **a.** captive certain	
Jer	52:15	and those that fell **a.**, that	
Jer	52:18	they ministered, took they **a.**.	
Jer	52:19	took the captain of the guard **a.**.	
Jer	52:27	Judah was carried **a.** captive	
Jer	52:28	whom Nebuchadrezzar carried **a.**	
Jer	52:29	carried **a.** captive from Jerusalem	
Jer	52:30	the captain of the guard carried **a.**	
La	2:6	violently taken **a.** his tabernacle,	
La	2:14	to turn **a.** thy captivity; but have	
La	4:9	for these pine **a.**, stricken through	
La	4:15	when they fled **a.** and wandered,	
La	4:22	more carry thee **a.** into captivity:	
Eze	3:14	spirit lifted me up, and took me **a.**,	
Eze	4:17	and consume **a.** for their iniquity.	
Eze	11:18	take **a.** all the detestable things	5493
Eze	14:6	and turn **a.** your faces from all	
Eze	16:9	I thoroughly washed **a.** thy blood	
Eze	16:50	I took them **a.** as I saw good.	5493
Eze	18:24	But when the righteous turneth **a.**	
Eze	18:26	a righteous man turneth **a.** from	
Eze	18:27	when the wicked man turneth **a.**	
Eze	18:28	he considereth, and turneth **a.**	
Eze	18:31	Cast **a.** from you all your	
Eze	20:7	ye **a.** every man the abominations	
Eze	20:8	they did not every man cast **a.** the	
Eze	23:25	take **a.** thy nose and thine ears;	5493
Eze	23:26	clothes, and take **a.** thy fair jewels.	
Eze	23:29	and shall take **a.** all thy labour,	
Eze	24:16	Son of man, behold, I take **a.** from	
Eze	24:23	shall pine **a.** for your iniquities,	
Eze	26:16	and lay **a.** their robes, and put off	5493
Eze	30:4	they shall take **a.** her multitude,	
Eze	33:4	and take him **a.**, his blood shall	
Eze	33:6	he is taken **a.** in his iniquity; but	
Eze	33:10	we pine **a.** in them, how should	
Eze	34:4	again that which was driven **a.**,	
Eze	34:16	that which was driven **a.**, and will	
Eze	36:26	I will take **a.** the stony heart out	5493
Eze	38:13	to carry **a.** silver and gold,	
Eze	38:13	to take **a.** cattle and goods,	
Eze	43:9	let them put **a.** their whoredom,	7368
Eze	44:10	are gone **a.** far from me, when	
Eze	44:10	**a.** from me after their idols;	
Eze	44:22	nor her that is put **a.**: but they	
Eze	45:9	take **a.** your exactions from my	7311
Da	1:16	Thus Melzar took **a.** the portion	
Da	2:35	carried them **a.**, that no place was	
Da	4:14	the beasts get **a.** from under it,	5111
Da	7:12	had their dominion taken **a.**:	5709
Da	7:14	which shall not pass **a.**, and his	5709
Da	7:26	they shall take **a.** his dominion,	5709
Da	8:11	the daily sacrifice was taken **a.**,	7311
Da	9:16	fury be turned **a.** from thy city	
Da	11:12	hath taken **a.** the multitude, his	
Da	11:31	shall take **a.** the daily sacrifice,	5493
Da	11:44	and utterly to make **a.** many.	2763
Da	12:11	be taken **a.**, and the abomination	5493
Ho	1:6	I will utterly take them **a.**.	
Ho	2:2	therefore put a. her whoredoms	5493
Ho	2:9	and take **a.** my corn in the time	
Ho	2:17	I will take **a.** the names of Baalim	5493
Ho	4:3	the sea also shall be taken **a.**.	
Ho	4:11	and new wine take **a.** the heart	
Ho	5:14	I, even I, will tear and go **a.**;	
Ho	5:14	I will take **a.**, and none shall	
Ho	6:4	as the early dew it goeth **a.**.	
Ho	9:11	their glory shall fly **a.** like a bird,	
Ho	9:17	God will cast them **a.**, because	
Ho	13:3	the early dew that passeth **a.**, as	
Ho	13:11	and took him **a.** in my wrath.	
Ho	14:2	Take **a.** all iniquity, and receive us	
Ho	14:4	mine anger is turned **a.** from him.	
Joe	1:7	and cast it **a.**; the branches thereof	
Joe	1:12	joy is withered **a.** from the sons of	
Am	1:3	I will not turn **a.** the punishment	
Am	1:6	not turn **a.** the punishment thereof;	
Am	1:6	because they carried **a.** captive	
Am	1:9,	11,13 I will not turn **a.** the	
Am	2:1,	4,6 I will not turn **a.** the	
Am	2:16	the mighty shall flee **a.** naked in	
Am	4:2	he will take you **a.** with hooks,	
Am	4:10	and have taken **a.** your horses;	7628
Am	5:23	Take thou **a.** from me the noise	5493
Am	6:3	Ye that put far **a.** the evil day,	5077
Am	7:11	surely be led **a.** captive out of	
Am	7:12	flee thee **a.** into the land of Judah,	
Am	9:1	shall not flee **a.**, and he that	
Ob	11	strangers carried **a.** captive his	
Jon	3:9	and turn **a.** from his fierce anger,	
Mic	1:11	pass ye **a.**, thou inhabitant of	
Mic	2:2	and take them **a.**; so they oppress	7726
Mic	2:4	turning **a.** he hath divided our	
Mic	2:9	have ye taken **a.** my glory for ever.	
Na	2:2	hath turned **a.** the excellency	
Na	2:7	Huzzab shall be led **a.** captive, she	1540
Na	2:8	yet they shall flee **a.**. Stand, stand,	
Na	3:10	yet was she carried **a.**, she went	1473
Na	3:16	cankerworm spoileth, and fleeth **a.**.	
Na	3:17	the sun ariseth they flee **a.**, and	
Zep	2:7	visit them, and turn **a.** their	
Zep	3:11	then I will take **a.** out of the	5493
Zep	3:15	The Lord hath taken **a.** thy	5493
Zec	3:4	Take **a.** the filthy garments from	5493
Zec	7:11	and pulled **a.** the shoulder, and	
Zec	9:7	And I will take **a.** his blood out	5493
Zec	10:11	sceptre of Egypt shall depart **a.**.	
Zec	14:12	Their flesh shall consume **a.** while	
Zec	14:12	their eyes shall consume **a.** in	
Zec	14:12	and their tongue shall consume **a.**	
Mal	2:3	one shall take you **a.** with it.	
Mal	2:6	and did turn many **a.** from iniquity.	
Mal	2:16	saith that he hateth putting **a.**:	
Mal	3:7	are gone **a.** from mine ordinances,	5493
Mt	1:11	they were carried **a.** to Babylon:	*3350*
Mt	1:17	carrying **a.** into Babylon are	*3350*
Mt	1:17	from the carrying **a.** into Babylon	*3350*
Mt	1:19	was minded to put her **a.** privily.	*630*
Mt	5:31	**Whosoever shall put a. his wife,**	*630*
Mt	5:32	**whosoever shall put a. his wife,**	*630*
Mt	5:40	**and take a. thy coat,**	
Mt	5:42	**turn not thou a.**	*654*
Mt	8:31	suffer us to go **a.** into the herd of	*565*
Mt	13:6	**they had no root, they withered a.**	
Mt	13:12	**him shall be taken a. even that**	*142*
Mt	13:19	**and catcheth a. that which was**	*726*
Mt	13:36	Then Jesus sent the multitude **a.**,	*863*
Mt	13:48	**but cast the bad a.**	*1854*
Mt	14:15	send the multitude **a.**,	*630*
Mt	14:22	while he sent the multitudes **a.**.	*630*
Mt	14:23	he had sent the multitudes **a.**,	*630*
Mt	15:23	saying, Send her **a.**; for she crieth	*630*
Mt	15:32	**I will not send them a. fasting,**	*630*
Mt	15:39	And he sent **a.** the multitude,	*630*
Mt	19:3	for a man to put **a.** his wife	*630*
Mt	19:7	and to put her **a.**?	*630*
Mt	19:8	**suffered you to put a. your wives:**	*630*
Mt	19:9	**Whosoever shall put a. his wife,**	*630*
Mt	19:9	**whoso marrieth her which is put a.**	*630*
Mt	19:22	he went **a.** sorrowful; for he had	*565*
Mt	21:19	presently the fig tree withered **a.**.	
Mt	21:20	soon is the fig tree withered **a.**!	
Mt	22:13	**and take him a., and cast him into**	*142*
Mt	24:35	**Heaven and earth shall pass a.,**	*3928*
Mt	24:35	**but my word shall not pass a.**	*3928*
Mt	24:39	**flood came, and took them all a.;**	*142*
Mt	25:29	**shall be taken a. even that which**	*142*
Mt	25:46	**these shall go a. into everlasting**	*565*
Mt	26:42	He went **a.** again the second time,	*565*
Mt	26:42	**cup may not pass a. from me,**	*3928*
Mt	26:44	and went **a.** again, and prayed	*565*
Mt	26:57	led him **a.** to Caiaphas the	*520*
Mt	27:2	they led him **a.**, and delivered him	*520*
Mt	27:31	and led him **a.** to crucify him.	*520*
Mt	27:64	and steal him **a.**, and say unto the	
Mt	28:13	and stole him **a.** while we slept.	
Mt	28:16	the eleven disciples went **a.** into	
Mk	1:43	and forthwith sent him **a.**;	*1544*
Mk	2:20	**bridegroom shall be taken a. from**	*522*
Mk	2:21	**taketh a. from the old, and the**	*142*
Mk	4:6	**it had no root, it withered a.**	
Mk	4:15	**and taketh a. the word that was**	*142*
Mk	4:36	when they had sent **a.** the	*863*
Mk	5:10	not send them **a.** out of the	*649*
Mk	6:36	Send them **a.**, that they may go	*630*
Mk	6:45	while he sent **a.** the people.	*630*
Mk	6:46	he had sent them **a.**, he departed	*657*
Mk	8:3	**if I send them a. fasting to their**	*630*
Mk	8:9	thousand: and he sent them **a.**.	*630*
Mk	8:26	And he sent him **a.** to his house,	*649*
Mk	9:18	with his teeth, and pineth **a.**: and I	
Mk	10:2	for a man to put **a.** his wife?	*630*
Mk	10:4	divorcement, and to put her **a.**.	*630*
Mk	10:11	**Whosoever shall put a. his wife,**	*630*
Mk	10:12	**woman shall put a. her husband,**	*630*

Mk 10:22 and went a. grieved: for he had 565
Mk 10:50 And he, casting a. his garment, 577
Mk 11:21 which thou cursedst is withered a.
Mk 12:3 and sent him a. empty. 649
Mk 12:4 and sent him a. shamefully 649
Mk 13:31 Heaven and earth shall pass a.: 3928
Mk 13:31 but my words shall not pass a. 3928
Mk 14:36 take a. this cup from me: 3911
Mk 14:39 And again he went a., and prayed, 565
Mk 14:44 take him, and lead him a. safely. 520
Mk 14:53 And they led Jesus a. to the high 520
Mk 15:1 and carried him a., and delivered 667
Mk 15:16 soldiers led him a. into the hall, 520
Mk 16:3 Who shall roll a. the stone from 617
Mk 16:4 that the stone was rolled a.: for it 617
Lu 1:25 to take a. my reproach among 851
Lu 1:53 the rich he hath sent empty a. 1821
Lu 2:15 the angels were gone a. from them 565
Lu 5:35 shall be taken a. from them, and 851
Lu 6:29 that taketh a. thy cloke forbid not 142
Lu 6:30 that taketh a. thy goods ask 142
Lu 8:6 it withered a., because it lacked
Lu 8:12 and taketh a. the word out of 142
Lu 8:13 and in time of temptation fall a. 868
Lu 8:38 but Jesus sent him a., saying, 630
Lu 9:12 when the day began to wear a.,
Lu 9:12 Send the multitude a., that they 630
Lu 9:25 lose himself, or be cast a.? 2210
Lu 10:42 which shall not be taken a. from 851
Lu 11:52 taken a. the key of knowledge:
Lu 13:15 and lead him a. to watering? 520
Lu 16:3 for my lord taketh a. from me the 851
Lu 16:18 Whosoever putteth a. his wife, and 630
Lu 16:18 a. from her husband committeth 630
Lu 17:31 not come down to take it a.: and
Lu 19:26 he hath shall be taken a. from him.
Lu 20:10 beat him, and sent him a. empty 1821
Lu 20:11 shamefully, and sent him a. empty. 1821
Lu 21:24 and shall be led a. captive into
Lu 21:32 generation shall not pass a., till
Lu 21:33 earth shall pass a.: but
Lu 21:33 my words shall not pass a.
Lu 23:18 saying, A. with this man, and
Lu 23:26 And as they led him a., they laid 520
Lu 24:2 stone rolled a. from the sepulchre 617
Joh 1:29 taketh a. the sin of the world.
Joh 4:8 his disciples were gone a. unto the 565
Joh 5:13 Jesus had conveyed himself a., a 1593
Joh 6:22 his disciples were gone a. alone; 565
Joh 6:67 unto the twelve, Will ye also go a.? 5217
Joh 10:40 And went a. again beyond Jordan 565
Joh 11:39 Take ye a. the stone. Martha, the
Joh 11:41 Then they took a. the stone from
Joh 11:48 come and take a. both our place
Joh 12:11 the Jews went a., and believed on 5217
Joh 14:28 I go a. and come again unto you 5217
Joh 15:2 he taketh a.: and every branch
Joh 16:7 is expedient for you that I go a.: 565
Joh 16:7 if I go not a., the Comforter will 565
Joh 18:13 And led him a. to Annas first; 520
Joh 19:15 A. with him, a. with him, crucify 142
Joh 19:16 took Jesus, and led him a. 520
Joh 19:31 and that they might be taken a.
Joh 19:38 that he might take a. the body of
Joh 20:1 stone taken a. from the sepulchre.
Joh 20:2 They have taken a. the Lord out of
Joh 20:10 disciples went a. again unto their 565
Joh 20:13 they have taken a. my Lord, and I
Joh 20:15 and I will take him a.
Ac 3:26 in turning a. every one of you from 654
Ac 5:37 drew a. much people after him: 868
Ac 7:27 him a., saying, Who made thee 683
Ac 7:43 will carry you a. beyond Babylon 3351
Ac 8:33 his judgment was taken a.: and
Ac 8:39 the Lord caught a. Philip, that the 726
Ac 10:23 morrow Peter went a. with them, 1831
Ac 13:3 hands on them, they sent them a. 630
Ac 13:8 seeking to turn a. the deputy 1294
Ac 17:10 immediately sent a. Paul and Silas 1599
Ac 17:14 the brethren sent a. Paul to go as 1821
Ac 19:26 turned a. much people, saying, 3179
Ac 20:6 And we sailed a. from Philippi 1602
Ac 20:30 to draw a. disciples after them. 645
Ac 21:36 followed after, crying, A. with him. 142
Ac 22:16 wash a. thy sins, calling on the 628
Ac 22:22 A. with such a fellow from the 142
Ac 24:7 great violence took him a. out of 520
Ac 27:20 should be saved was then taken a. 4014
Ro 11:1 Hath God cast a. his people? 683
Ro 11:2 God hath not cast a. his people 683
Ro 11:15 For if the casting a. of them be 580
Ro 11:26 and shall turn a. ungodliness from 654
Ro 11:27 when I shall take a. their sins. 851
1Co 5:2 might be taken a. from among you.
1Co 5:13 Therefore put a. from among 1808
1Co 7:11 not the husband put a. his wife. 863
1Co 7:12 let him not put her a. 863
1Co 7:31 fashion of this world passeth a.
1Co 12:2 carried a. unto these dumb idols, 520
1Co 13:8 be knowledge, it shall vanish a. 2673
1Co 13:10 which is in part shall be done a. 2673
1Co 13:11 when I became a man, I put a. 2673
2Co 3:7 which glory was to be done a. 2673
2Co 3:11 For of that which is done a. was 2673
2Co 3:14 vail untaken a. in the reading 343
2Co 3:14 which vail is done a. in Christ. 2673
2Co 3:16 the vail shall be taken a. 4014
2Co 5:17 old things are passed a.; behold,
Ga 2:13 Barnabas also was carried a. with 4879
Eph 4:25 Wherefore putting a. lying, speak 659
Eph 4:31 evil speaking, be put a. from you,
Col 1:23 be not moved a. from the hope of 3334
2Th 2:3 except there come a falling a. first, 646
1Ti 1:19 some having put a. concerning 683
2Ti 1:15 are in Asia be turned a. from me; 654
2Ti 3:5 power thereof: from such turn a. 665
2Ti 3:6 women laden with sins, led a.
2Ti 4:4 And they shall turn a. their ears 654
Heb 6:6 they shall fall a., to renew them 3895
Heb 8:13 waxeth old, is ready to vanish a.
Heb 9:26 a. sin by the sacrifice of himself. 115
Heb 10:4 should take a. sins. 851
Heb 10:9 He taketh a. the first, that he may 337
Heb 10:11 which can never take a. sins: 4014
Heb 10:35 Cast not a. therefore your 577
Heb 12:25 we turn a. from him that speaketh 654
Jas 1:10 of the grass he shall pass a.
Jas 1:11 the rich man fade a. in his ways.
Jas 1:14 he is drawn a. of his own lust,
Jas 4:14 little time, and then vanisheth a.,
1Pe 1:4 undefiled, and that fadeth not a.,
1Pe 1:24 the flower thereof falleth a.: 1601
1Pe 3:21 (not the putting a. of the filth of the 595
1Pe 5:4 crown of glory that fadeth not a.
2Pe 3:10 heavens shall pass a. with a great
2Pe 3:17 a. with the error of the wicked, 4879
1Jo 2:17 the world passeth a., and the lust
1Jo 3:5 manifested to take a. our sins;
Re 7:17 God shall wipe a. all tears from 1813
Re 12:15 her to be carried a. of the flood.
Re 16:20 And every island fled a., and the
Re 17:3 So he carried me a. in the spirit 667
Re 20:11 the earth and the heaven fled a.;
Re 21:1 first earth were passed a.; and
Re 21:4 God shall wipe a. all tears from 1813
Re 21:4 the former things are passed a. 565
Re 21:10 he carried me a. in the spirit to a 667
Re 22:19 if any man shall take a. from the 851
Re 22:19 God shall take a. his part out of the 851

AWE
Ps 4:4 Stand in a., and sin not: 7264
Ps 33:8 of the world stand in a. 1481
Ps 119:161 heart standeth in a. of thy word. 6342

AWHILE See WHILE.

AWL See AUL.

AWOKE See also AWAKED.
Ge 9:24 And Noah a. from his wine, 3364
Ge 41:4 and fat kine. So Pharaoh a. 3364
Ge 41:7 and Pharaoh a., and, behold, it 3364
Ge 41:21 as at the beginning. So I a. 3364
Jg 16:20 And he a. out of his sleep, 3364
1Ki 3:15 And Solomon a.; and, behold, it 3364
Mt 8:25 a. him, saying, Lord, save us: 1453
Lu 8:24 they came to him, and a. him, 1326

AX See also AXE.
De 19:5 with the a. to cut down the tree, 1631
De 20:19 by forcing an a. against them: 1631
Jg 9:48 Abimelech took an a. in his hand, 7134
1Sa 13:20 to sharpen every man...his a., 7134
1Ki 6:7 neither hammer nor a. nor any 1631
2Ki 6:5 the a. head fell into the water: 1270
Isa 10:15 Shall the a. boast itself 1631
Jer 10:3 of the workman, with the a. 4621
Jer 51:20 Thou art my battle a. and 4661
Mt 3:10 now also the a. is laid unto the 513

AXE See also AXES. (*Most editions have* AX.)
Lu 3:9 now also the a. is laid unto the 513

AXES
1Sa 13:21 for the forks, and for the a., 7134
2Sa 12:31 and under a. of iron, 4037
1Ch 20:3 with harrows of iron, and with a. 4050
Ps 74:5 he had lifted up a. upon the thick 7134
Ps 74:6 with a. and hammers. 3781
Jer 46:22 and come against her with a., 7134
Eze 26:9 with his a. he shall break down 2719

AX-HEAD See AXE and HEAD.

AXLETREES
1Ki 7:32 and the a. of the wheels 3027
1Ki 7:33 their a., and their naves, 3027

AY See NAY.

AZAL (a'-zal)
Zec 14:5 mountains shall reach unto A. 682

AZALIAH (az-a-li'-ah)
2Ki 22:3 king sent Shaphan the son of A., 683
2Ch 34:8 the son of A., and Maaseiah 683

AZANIAH (az-a-ni'-ah)
Ne 10:9 both Jeshua the son of A., 245

AZARAEL (a-zar'-a-el) See also AZAREEL.
Ne 12:36 his brethren, Shemaiah, and A., 5832

AZAREEL (a-zar'-e-el) See also AZARAEL.
1Ch 12:6 and A., and Joezer, and 5832
1Ch 25:18 The eleventh to A., he, his sons, 5832
1Ch 27:22 Of Dan, A. the son of Jeroham. 5832
Ezr 10:41 A., and Shelemiah, Shemariah, 5832
Ne 11:13 And Amashai the son of A., the son 5832

AZARIAH (az-a-ri'-ah) See also AHAZIAH.
1Ki 4:2 A. the son of Zadok the priest, 5838
1Ki 4:5 And A. the son of Nathan was 5838
2Ki 14:21 all the people of Judah took A., 5838
2Ki 15:1 began A. son of Amaziah king of 5838
2Ki 15:6 And the rest of the acts of A., and 5838
2Ki 15:7 So A. slept with his fathers; and 5838
2Ki 15:8 In the thirty and eighth year of A. 5838
2Ki 15:17 In the nine and thirtieth year of A. 5838
2Ki 15:23 In the fiftieth year of A. king of 5838
2Ki 15:27 In the two and fiftieth year of A. 5838
1Ch 2:8 And the sons of Ethan; A. 5838
1Ch 2:38 begat Jehu, and Jehu begat A., 5838
1Ch 2:39 And A. begat Helez, and Helez 5838
1Ch 3:12 Amaziah his son, A. his son, 5838
1Ch 6:9 And Ahimaaz begat A., 5838
1Ch 6:9 And A. begat Johanan, 5838
1Ch 6:10 And Johanan begat A., (he it is 5838
1Ch 6:11 And A. begat Amariah, and 5838
1Ch 6:13 and Hilkiah begat A., 5838
1Ch 6:14 and A. begat Seriah, and 5838
1Ch 6:36 the son of Joel, the son of A., 5838
1Ch 9:11 And A. the son of Hilkiah, the son 5838
2Ch 15:1 the Spirit of God came upon A. 5838
2Ch 21:2 the sons of Jehoshaphat, A., and 5838
2Ch 21:2 Zechariah, and A., and Michael, 5838
2Ch 22:6 And A. the son of Jehoram king 5838
2Ch 23:1 A. the son of Jeroham, and 5838
2Ch 23:1 A. the son of Obed, and Maaseiah 5838
2Ch 26:17 A. the priest went in after him, 5838
2Ch 26:20 And A. the chief priest, and all 5838
2Ch 28:12 A. the son of Johanan, Berechiah 5838
2Ch 29:12 Amasai, and Joel the son of A., 5838
2Ch 29:12 and A. the son of Jehalelel: 5838
2Ch 31:10 And A. the chief priest of the 5838
2Ch 31:13 and A. the ruler of the house of 5838
Ezr 7:1 the son of Seraiah, the son of A., 5838
Ezr 7:3 The son of Amariah, the son of A., 5838
Ne 3:23 After him repaired A. the son of 5838
Ne 3:24 from the house of A. unto the 5838
Ne 7:7 Nehemiah, A., Raamiah, 5838
Ne 8:7 Kelita, A., Jozabad, Hanan, 5838
Ne 10:2 Seraiah, A., Jeremiah, 5838
Ne 12:33 And A., Ezra, and Meshullam, 5838
Jer 43:2 spake A. the son of Hoshaiah, 5838
Da 1:6 Daniel, Hananiah, Mishael, and A. 5838
Da 1:7 and to A., of Abed-nego. 5838

Da 1:11 Daniel, Hananiah, Mishael, and **A.**, 5838
Da 1:19 and **A.**: therefore stood they 5838
Da 2:17 Mishael, and **A.**, his companions: 5839

AZAZ (a'-zaz)
1Ch 5:8 And Bela the son of **A.**, the son of 5811

AZAZIAH (az-a-zi'-ah)
1Ch 15:21 **A.**, with harps on the Sheminith 5812
1Ch 27:20 Ephraim, Hoshea the son of **A.**: 5812
2Ch 31:13 And Jehiel, and **A.**, and Nahath, 5812

AZBUK (az'-buk)
Ne 3:16 Nehemiah the son of **A.**, the ruler 5802

AZEKAH (a-ze'-kah)
Jos 10:10 and smote them to **A.**, and unto 5825
Jos 10:11 from heaven upon them unto **A.**, 5825
Jos 15:35 and Adullam, Socoh, and **A.**, 5825
1Sa 17:1 pitched between Shochoh and **A.**, 5825
2Ch 11:9 Adoraim, and Lachish, and **A.**, 5825
Ne 11:30 and the fields thereof, at **A.**. 5825
Jer 34:7 against Lachish, and against **A.**: 5825

AZEL (a'-zel) See also JAAZIEL.
1Ch 8:37 Eleasah his son, **A.** his son: 682
1Ch 8:38 **A.** had six sons, whose names are 682
1Ch 8:38 All these were the sons of **A.**. 682
1Ch 9:43 Eleasah his son, **A.** his son 682
1Ch 9:44 **A.** had six sons, whose names are 682
1Ch 9:44 these were the sons of **A.**. 682

AZEM (a'-zem) See also EZEM.
Jos 15:29 Baalah, and Iim, and **A.**, 6107
Jos 19:3 Hazar-shual, and Balah, and **A.**, 6107

AZGAD (az'-gad)
Ezr 2:12 The children of **A.**, a thousand 5803
Ezr 8:12 And of the sons of **A.**; Johanan 5803
Ne 7:17 The children of **A.**, two thousand 5803
Ne 10:15 Bunni, **A.**, Bebai, 5803

AZIEL (a'-ze-el)
1Ch 15:20 And Zechariah, and **A.**, and 5815

AZIZA (a-zi'-zah)
Ezr 10:27 and Jeremoth, and Zabad, and **A.** 5819

AZMAVETH (az-ma'-veth) See also BETH-AZMAVETH.
2Sa 23:31 Abi-albon the Arbathite, **A.** the 5820
1Ch 8:36 Jehoadah begat Alemeth, and **A.**, 5820
1Ch 9:42 and Jarah begat Alemeth, and **A.**, 5820
1Ch 11:33 **A.** the Baharumite, Eliahba 5820
1Ch 12:3 Jeziel, and Pelet, the sons of **A.**; 5820
1Ch 27:25 over the king's treasures was **A.** 5820
Ezr 2:24 The children of **A.**, forty and two. 5820
Ne 12:29 out of the fields of Geba and **A.**: 5820

AZMON (az'-mon) See also HESHMON.
Nu 34:4 Hazar-addar, and pass on to **A.**: 6111
Nu 34:5 shall fetch a compass from **A.** 6111
Jos 15:4 From thence it passed toward **A.**, 6111

AZNOTH-TABOR (az''-noth-ta'-bor)
Jos 19:34 the coast turneth westward to **A.**, 243

AZOR (a'-zor)
Mt 1:13 and Eliakim begat **A.**; *107*
Mt 1:14 And **A.** begat Sadoc; *107*

AZOTUS (a-zo'-tus) See also ASHDOD.
Ac 8:40 But Philip was found at **A.**: *108*

AZRIEL (az'-re-el)
1Ch 5:24 and Ishi, and Eliel, and **A.**, 5837
1Ch 27:19 Naphtali, Jerimoth the son of **A.**: 5837
Jer 36:26 and Seraiah the son of **A.**, and 5837

AZRIKAM (az'-ri-kam)
1Ch 3:23 Elioenai, and Hezekiah, and **A.**, 5840
1Ch 8:38 whose names are these, **A.**, 5840
1Ch 9:14 son of **A.**, the son of Hashabiah, 5840
1Ch 9:44 sons, whose names are these, **A.**, 5840
2Ch 28:7 **A.**, the governor of the house, 5840
Ne 11:15 the son of Hashub, the son of **A.**, 5840

AZUBAH (a-zu'-bah)
1Ki 22:42 And his mother's name was **A.**, 5806
1Ch 2:18 son of Hezron begat children of **A.** 5806
1Ch 2:19 And when **A.** was dead, Caleb 5806
2Ch 20:31 And his mother's name was **A.** 5806

AZUR (a'-zur) See also AZZUR.
Jer 28:1 that Hananiah the son of **A.** the 5809
Eze 11:1 I saw Jaazaniah the son of **A.**, 5809

AZZAH (az'-zah) See also GAZA.
De 2:23 dwelt in Hazarim, even unto **A.**, 5804
1Ki 4:24 from Tiphsah even to **A.**, over all 5804
Jer 25:20 and Ashkelon, and **A.**, and 5804

AZZAN (az'-zan)
Nu 34:26 Paltiel the son of **A.**. 5821

AZZUR (az'-zur) See also AZUR.
Ne 10:17 Ater, Hizkijah, **A.**, 5809

B.

BAAL (ba'-al) See also BAAL-BERITH; BAALE; BAAL-GAD; BAAL-HAMON; BAAL-HANAN; BAAL-HAZOR; BAAL-HERMON; BAALIM; BAAL-MEON; BAAL-PEOR; BAAL-PERAZIM; BAAL'S; BAAL-SHALISHA; BAAL-TAMAR; BAAL-ZEBUB; BAAL-ZEPHON; BAMOTH-BAAL; GUR-BAAL; BEL; KIR-JATH-BAAL; MERIB-BAAL.
Nu 22:41 up into the high places of **B.**, 1168
Jg 2:13 Lord, and served **B.** and Ashtaroth. 1168
Jg 6:25 and throw down the altar of **B.** 1168
Jg 6:28 the altar of **B.** was cast down, 1168
Jg 6:30 hath cast down the altar of **B.**, 1168
Jg 6:31 Will ye plead for **B.**? will ye save 1168
Jg 6:32 Let **B.** plead against him, because 1168
1Ki 16:31 and served **B.**, and worshipped 1168
1Ki 16:32 he reared up an altar for **B.** 1168
1Ki 16:32 in the house of **B.**, 1168
1Ki 18:19 the prophets of **B.** four hundred 1168
1Ki 18:21 but if **B.**, then follow him. 1168
1Ki 18:25 Elijah said unto the prophets of **B.**, 1168
1Ki 18:26 and called on the name of **B.** 1168
1Ki 18:26 saying, O **B.**, hear us. 1168
1Ki 18:40 them, Take the prophets of **B.**; 1168
1Ki 19:18 which have not bowed unto **B.**, 1168
1Ki 22:53 For he served **B.**, and worshipped 1168
2Ki 3:2 for he put away the image of **B.** 1168
2Ki 10:18 unto them, Ahab served **B.** a little; 1168
2Ki 10:19 unto me all the prophets of **B.**, 1168
2Ki 10:19 have a great sacrifice to do to **B.**; 1168
2Ki 10:19 destroy the worshippers of **B.**. 1168
2Ki 10:20 Proclaim a solemn assembly for **B.**. 1168
2Ki 10:21 all the worshippers of **B.** came, 1168
2Ki 10:21 they came into the house of **B.**; 1168
2Ki 10:21 and the house of **B.** was full 1168
2Ki 10:22 for all the worshippers of **B.**. 1168
2Ki 10:23 into the house of **B.**, 1168
2Ki 10:23 said unto the worshippers of **B.**, 1168
2Ki 10:23 but the worshippers of **B.** only. 1168
2Ki 10:25 went to the city of the house of **B.**. 1168
2Ki 10:26 the images out of the house of **B.**, 1168
2Ki 10:27 they brake down the image of **B.**, 1168
2Ki 10:27 and brake down the house of **B.**, 1168
2Ki 10:28 Jehu destroyed **B.** out of Israel. 1168
2Ki 11:18 the land went into the house of **B.**, 1168
2Ki 11:18 and slew Mattan the priest of **B.** 1168
2Ki 17:16 the host of heaven, and served **B.** 1168
2Ki 21:3 and he reared up altars for **B.**, 1168
2Ki 23:4 the vessels that were made for **B.**, 1168
2Ki 23:5 also that burned incense unto **B.**, 1168
1Ch 4:33 about the same cities, unto **B.** 1168
1Ch 5:5 Reaia his son, **B.** his son, 1168
1Ch 8:30 and Kish, and **B.**, and Nadab, 1168
1Ch 9:36 Kish, and **B.**, and Ner, and Nadab, 1168
2Ch 23:17 the people went to the house of **B.**, 1168
2Ch 23:17 and slew Mattan the priest of **B.** 1168
Jer 2:8 the prophets prophesied by **B.**, 1168
Jer 7:9 falsely, and burn incense unto **B.**, 1168
Jer 11:13 altars to burn incense unto **B.**. 1168
Jer 11:17 anger in offering incense unto **B.** 1168
Jer 12:16 taught my people to swear by **B.**; 1168
Jer 19:5 built also the high places of **B.**, 1168
Jer 19:5 fire for burnt offerings unto **B.**, 1168
Jer 23:13 they prophesied in **B.**, and caused 1168
Jer 23:27 have forgotten my name for **B.** 1168
Jer 32:29 they have offered incense unto **B.**, 1168
Jer 32:35 they build the high places of **B.**, 1168
Ho 2:8 gold, which they prepared for **B.** 1168
Ho 13:1 when he offended in **B.**, he died. 1168
Zep 1:4 I will cut off the remnant of **B.** 1168
Ro 11:4 bowed the knee to the image of **B.** *896*

BAALAH (ba'-al-ah) See also BAALE; BALEH; BILHAH; KIRJATH-BAAL.
Jos 15:9 and the border was drawn to **B.**, 1173
Jos 15:10 the border compassed from **B.** 1173
Jos 15:11 and passed along to mount **B.**, 1173
Jos 15:29 **B.**, and Iim, and Azem, 1173
1Ch 13:6 went up, and all Israel, to **B.**, 1173

BAALATH (ba'-al-ath) See also BAALATH-BEER.
Jos 19:44 Eltekeh, and Gibbethon, and **B.**, 1191
1Ki 9:18 **B.**, and Tadmor in the wilderness, 1191
2Ch 8:6 **B.**, and all the store cities 1191

BAALATH-BEER (ba''-al-ath-be'-ur)
Jos 19:8 round about these cities to **B.**, 1192

BAAL-BERITH (ba''al-be'-rith)
Jg 8:33 and made **B.** their god, 1170
Jg 9:4 of silver out of the house of **B.**, 1170

BAALE (ba'-al-eh)
2Sa 6:2 people that were with him from **B.** 1184

BAAL-GAD (ba''-al-gad')
Jos 11:17 even unto **B.** in the valley of 1171
Jos 12:7 the west, from **B.** in the valley 1171
Jos 13:5 from **B.** under mount Hermon 1171

BAAL-HAMON (ba''-al-ha'-mon)
Ca 8:11 Solomon had a vineyard at **B.**; 1174

BAAL-HANAN (ba''-al-ha'-nan)
Ge 36:38 **B.** the son of Achbor reigned 1177
Ge 36:39 And **B.** the son of Achbor died, 1177
1Ch 1:49 when Shaul was dead, **B.** the son 1177
1Ch 1:50 when **B.** was dead, Hadad reigned 1177
1Ch 27:28 the low plains was **B.** the Gederite: 1177

BAAL-HAZOR (ba''-al-ha'-zor) See also HAZOR.
2Sa 13:23 Absalom had sheepshearers in **B.**, 1178

BAAL-HERMON (ba''-al-her'-mon)
Jg 3:3 from mount **B.** unto the entering 1179
1Ch 5:23 from Bashan unto **B.** and Senir, 1179

BAALI (ba'-al-i)
Hos 2:16 and shalt call me no more **B.** 1180

BAALIM (ba'-al-im) See also BAAL.
Jg 2:11 sight of the Lord, and served **B.** 1168
Jg 3:7 and served **B.** and the groves. 1168
Jg 8:33 went a whoring after **B.**, and made 1168
Jg 10:6 and served **B.**, and Ashtaroth, 1168
Jg 10:10 our God, and also served **B.**. 1168
1Sa 7:4 children of Israel did put away **B.** 1168
1Sa 12:10 have served **B.** and Ashtaroth: 1168
1Ki 18:18 and thou hast followed **B.**. 1168
2Ch 17:3 David, and sought not unto **B.**; 1168
2Ch 24:7 Lord did they bestow upon **B.**. 1168
2Ch 28:2 made also molten images for **B.**. 1168
2Ch 33:3 and he reared up altars for **B.**, 1168
2Ch 34:4 they brake down the altars of **B.** 1168
Jer 2:23 polluted, I have not gone after **B.**? 1168
Jer 9:14 after **B.**, which their fathers 1168
Ho 2:13 I will visit upon her the days of **B.**, 1168
Ho 2:17 I will take away the names of **B.** 1168
Ho 11:2 sacrificed unto **B.**, and burned 1168

BAALIS (ba'-al-is)
Jer 40:14 **B.** the king of the Ammonites 1185

BAAL-MEON (ba''-al-me'-on) See also BETH-BAAL-MEON.
Nu 32:38 Nebo, and **B.**, (their names being 1186
1Ch 5:8 even unto Nebo and **B.**: 1186
Eze 25:9 Beth-jeshimoth, **B.**, and 1186

BAAL-PEOR (ba''-al-pe'-or) See also PEOR.
Nu 25:3 Israel joined himself unto **B.** 1187
Nu 25:5 his men that were joined unto **B.**. 1187
De 4:3 what the Lord did because of **B.** 1187
De 4:3 for all the men that followed **B.**, 1187
Ps 106:28 joined themselves also unto **B.**, 1187
Ho 9:10 they went to **B.**, and separated 1187

BAAL-PERAZIM (ba''-al-per'-a-zim)
2Sa 5:20 David came to **B.**, and David 1188
2Sa 5:20 called the name of that place **B.** 1188
1Ch 14:11 So they came up to **B.**; and David...... 1188
1Ch 14:11 called the name of that place **B.** 1188

BAAL'S (ba'-als)
1Ki 18:22 but **B.** prophets are four hundred....... 1168

BAAL-SHALISHA (ba''-al-shal'-i-shah)
2Ki 4:42 there came a man from **B.**,............... 1190

BAAL-TAMAR (ba''-al-ta'-mar)
Jg 20:33 put themselves in array at **B.** 1193

BAAL-ZEBUB (ba''-al-ze'-bub) See also BEELZEBUB.
2Ki 1:2 Go, enquire of **B.** the god of Ekron.... 1176
2Ki 1:3 that ye go to enquire of **B.** the god.... 1176
2Ki 1:6 that thou sendest to enquire of **B.**....... 1176
2Ki 1:16 sent messengers to enquire of **B.**....... 1176

BAAL-ZEPHON (ba''-al-ze'-fon)
Ex 14:2 and the sea, over against **B.** 1189
Ex 14:9 beside Pe-hahiroth, before **B.** 1189
Nu 33:7 Pa-hahiroth, which is before **B.**.......... 1189

BAANA (ba'-an-ah) See also BAANAH.
1Ki 4:12 **B.** the son of Ahilud; to him............. 1195
Ne 3:4 repaired Zadok the son of **B.** 1195

BAANAH (ba'-an-ah) See also BAANA.
2Sa 4:2 the name of the one was **B.**,............. 1195
2Sa 4:5 Rechab and **B.**, went, and came......... 1195
2Sa 4:6 Rechab and **B.** his brother................ 1195
2Sa 4:9 David answered Rechab and **B.** 1195
2Sa 23:29 Heleb the son of **B.**, a Netophathite, .. 1195
1Ki 4:16 **B.** the son of Hushai was in Asher..... 1195
1Ch 11:30 Netophathite, Heled the son of **B.**....... 1195
Ezr 2:2 Mizpar, Bigvai, Rehum, **B.**. 1195
Ne 7:7 Mispereth, Bigvai, Nehum, **B.**. 1195
Ne 10:27 Malluch, Harim, **B.**. 1195

BAARA (ba'-ar-ah)
1Ch 8:8 Hushim and **B.** were his wives, ... 1199

BAASEIAH (ba-as-i'-ah)
1Ch 6:40 the son of **B.**, the son of Malchiah, ... 1202

BAASHA (ba'-ash-ah)
1Ki 15:16 was war between Asa and **B.**........... 1201
1Ki 15:17 **B.** king of Israel went up against....... 1201
1Ki 15:19 and break thy league with **B.** 1201
1Ki 15:21 to pass, when **B.** heard thereof, ... 1201
1Ki 15:22 wherewith **B.** had builded; 1201
1Ki 15:27 **B.** the son of Ahijah, of the house...... 1201
1Ki 15:27 and **B.** smote him at Gibbethon, ... 1201
1Ki 15:28 did **B.** slay him, and reigned............ 1201
1Ki 15:32 was war between Asa and **B.**........... 1201
1Ki 15:33 began **B.** the son of Ahijah to reign.... 1201
1Ki 16:1 the son of Hanani against **B.**, ... 1201
1Ki 16:3 will take away the posterity of **B.**,...... 1201
1Ki 16:4 Him that dieth of **B.** in the city.......... 1201
1Ki 16:5 Now the rest of the acts of **B.**, ... 1201
1Ki 16:6 **B.** slept with his fathers, and was 1201
1Ki 16:7 the word of the Lord against **B.**,........ 1201
1Ki 16:8 Elah the son of **B.** to reign............... 1201
1Ki 16:11 that he slew all the house of **B.**......... 1201
1Ki 16:12 Zimri destroy all the house of **B.**,...... 1201
1Ki 16:12 which he spake against **B.** by Jehu 1201
1Ki 16:13 all the sins of **B.**, and the sins of....... 1201
1Ki 21:22 like the house of **B.**, the son of.......... 1201
2Ki 9:9 like the house of **B.** the son of........... 1201
2Ch 16:1 **B.** king of Israel came up against 1201
2Ch 16:3 go, break thy league with **B.** king 1201
2Ch 16:5 it came to pass, when **B.** heard it, ... 1201
2Ch 16:6 wherewith **B.** was building; 1201
Jer 41:9 king had made for fear of **B.** 1201

BABBLER
Ec 10:11 and a **b.** is no better................ 1167,3956
Ac 17:18 said, What will this **b.** say? *4691*

BABBLING See also BABBLINGS.
Pr 23:29 who hath **b.**? who hath wounds.......... 7879

BABBLINGS
1Ti 6:20 avoiding profane and vain **b.**, ... *2757*
2Ti 2:16 shun profane and vain **b.**: for............. *2757*

BABE See also BABES.
Ex 2:6 behold, the **b.** wept............................ 5288
Lu 1:41 the **b.** leaped in her womb; *1025*
Lu 1:44 the **b.** leaped in my womb for joy....... *1025*
Lu 2:12 the **b.** wrapt in swaddling clothes, ... *1025*
Lu 2:16 Mary, and Joseph, and the **b.** lying..... *1025*
Heb 5:13 of righteousness: for he is a **b.**. *3516*

BABEL (ba'-bel) See also BABYLON.
Ge 10:10 beginning of his kingdom was **B.**,......... 894
Ge 11:9 is the name of it called **B.**; 894

BABES
Ps 8:2 of the mouth of **b.** and sucklings 5768
Ps 17:14 rest of their substance to their **b.**....... 5768
Isa 3:4 and **b.** shall rule over them. 8586
Mt 11:25 **hast revealed them unto b.**........... *3516*
Mt 21:16 **Out of the mouth of b.** *3516*
Lu 10:21 **hast revealed them unto b.**:.......... *3516*
Ro 2:20 teacher of **b.**, which hast the form...... *3516*
1Co 3:1 as unto **b.** in Christ. *3516*
1Pe 2:2 As newborn **b.**, desire the sincere...... *1025*

BABYLON (bab'-il-un) See also BABEL; BABYLONIANS; BABYLONISH; BABYLON'S; CHALDEA; SHESHACH.
2Ki 17:24 of Assyria brought men from **B.**, ... 894
2Ki 17:30 men of **B.** made Succoth-benoth, ... 894
2Ki 20:12 son of Baladan, king of **B.**, sent 894
2Ki 20:14 from a far country, even from **B.**......... 894
2Ki 20:17 this day, shall be carried unto **B.**......... 894
2Ki 20:18 in the palace of the king of **B.**............ 894
2Ki 24:1 king of **B.** came up, and Jehoiakim...... 894
2Ki 24:7 the king of **B.** had taken from............ 894
2Ki 24:10 of **B.** came up against Jerusalem, ... 894
2Ki 24:11 king of **B.** came against the city, ... 894
2Ki 24:12 Judah went out to the king of **B.**, ... 894
2Ki 24:12 king of **B.** took him in the eighth......... 894
2Ki 24:15 he carried away Jehoiachin to **B.**,........ 894
2Ki 24:15 into captivity from Jerusalem to **B.**....... 894
2Ki 24:16 king of **B.** brought captive to **B.**......... 894
2Ki 24:17 the king of **B.** made Mattaniah his 894
2Ki 24:20 rebelled against the king of **B.**. 894
2Ki 25:1 of **B.** came, he, and all his host,........... 894
2Ki 25:6 him up to the king of **B.** to Riblah; 894
2Ki 25:7 of brass, and carried him to **B.**, ... 894
2Ki 25:8 of king Nebuchadnezzar king of **B.**, ... 894
2Ki 25:8 a servant of the king of **B.**, unto 894
2Ki 25:11 that fell away to the king of **B.**,........... 894
2Ki 25:13 carried the brass of them to **B.**. 894
2Ki 25:20 them to the king of **B.** to Riblah:......... 894
2Ki 25:21 king of **B.** smote them, and slew.......... 894
2Ki 25:22 Nebuchadnezzar king of **B.** had 894
2Ki 25:23 of **B.** had made Gedaliah governor, ... 894
2Ki 25:24 the land, and serve the king of **B.**; 894
2Ki 25:27 Evil-merodach king of **B.** in the........... 894
2Ki 25:28 kings that were with him in **B.**;........... 894
1Ch 9:1 away to **B.** for their transgression........ 894
2Ch 32:31 ambassadors of the princes of **B.**,........ 894
2Ch 33:11 with fetters, and carried him to **B.**........ 894
2Ch 36:6 up Nebuchadnezzar king of **B.**,........... 894
2Ch 36:6 him in fetters, to carry him to **B.**. 894
2Ch 36:7 of the house of the Lord to **B.**,............ 894
2Ch 36:7 put them in his temple at **B.**............... 894
2Ch 36:10 brought him to **B.**, with the goodly 894
2Ch 36:18 all these he brought to **B.**.................. 894
2Ch 36:20 the sword carried he away to **B.**; 894
Ezr 1:11 up from **B.** unto Jerusalem. 894
Ezr 2:1 of **B.** had carried away unto **B.**, ... 894
Ezr 5:12 the king of **B.**, the Chaldean, who 895
Ezr 5:12 carried the people away into **B.**........... 895
Ezr 5:13 first year of Cyrus the king of **B.** 895
Ezr 5:14 brought them into the temple of **B.**,..... 895
Ezr 5:14 king take out of the temple of **B.**,........ 895
Ezr 5:17 treasure house, which is there at **B.**, ... 895
Ezr 6:1 the treasures were laid up in **B.**. 895
Ezr 6:5 and brought unto **B.**, be restored, ... 895
Ezr 7:6 This Ezra went up from **B.**; and 894
Ezr 7:9 began he to go up from **B.**, and on...... 894
Ezr 7:16 canst find in all the province of **B.**, ... 895
Ezr 8:1 that went up with me from **B.**............. 894
Ne 7:6 the king of **B.** had carried away............ 894
Ne 13:6 of Artaxerxes king of **B.** came I............ 894
Es 2:6 the king of **B.** had carried away............ 894
Ps 87:4 make mention of Rahab and **B.**............ 894
Ps 137:1 the rivers of **B.**, there we sat down,.... 894
Ps 137:8 O daughter of **B.**, who art to be.......... 894
Isa 13:1 The burden of **B.**, which Isaiah 894
Isa 13:19 And **B.**, the glory of kingdoms, ... 894
Isa 14:4 this proverb against the king of **B.**,...... 894
Isa 14:22 and cut off from **B.** the name,.............. 894
Isa 21:9 and said, **B.** is fallen, is fallen; 894
Isa 39:1 king of **B.**, sent letters and a............. 894
Isa 39:3 far country unto me, even from **B.**. 894
Isa 39:6 this day, shall be carried to **B.**............ 894
Isa 39:7 in the palace of the king of **B.**............. 894
Isa 43:14 For your sake I have sent to **B.**,.......... 894
Isa 47:1 O virgin daughter of **B.**, sit on the....... 894
Isa 48:14 he will do his pleasure on **B.**, ... 894
Isa 48:20 Go ye forth of **B.**, flee ye from the...... 894
Jer 20:4 into the hand of the king of **B.**, ... 894
Jer 20:4 he shall carry them captive into **B.**,...... 894
Jer 20:5 take them, and carry them to **B.**. 894
Jer 20:6 and thou shalt come to **B.**, and 894
Jer 21:2 Nebuchadrezzar king of **B.** 894
Jer 21:4 ye fight against the king of **B.**,............ 894
Jer 21:7 of Nebuchadrezzar king of **B.**,............. 894
Jer 21:10 into the hand of the king of **B.**, ... 894
Jer 22:25 king of **B.**, and into the hand of the 894
Jer 24:1 king of **B.** had carried away................ 894
Jer 24:1 and had brought them to **B.**................ 894
Jer 25:1 of Nebuchadrezzar king of **B.**.............. 894
Jer 25:9 the king of **B.**, my servant, and 894
Jer 25:11 serve the king of **B.** seventy years. 894
Jer 25:12 I will punish the king of **B.**,................ 894
Jer 27:6 the king of **B.**, my servant; and 894
Jer 27:8 the king of **B.**, and that will not........... 894
Jer 27:8 under the yoke of the king of **B.**, ... 894
Jer 27:9 Ye shall not serve the king of **B.**.......... 894
Jer 27:11, 12 under the yoke of the king of **B.**, ... 894
Jer 27:13 that will not serve the king of **B.**? 894
Jer 27:14 Ye shall not serve the king of **B.** 894
Jer 27:16 shortly be brought again from **B.** 894
Jer 27:17 serve the king of **B.**, and live: 894
Jer 27:18 and at Jerusalem, go not to **B.**............ 894
Jer 27:20 Nebuchadnezzar king of **B.** took 894
Jer 27:20 from Jerusalem to **B.**, and all the......... 894
Jer 27:22 They shall be carried to **B.**,................ 894
Jer 28:2 broken the yoke of the king of **B.**........ 894
Jer 28:3 Nebuchadnezzar king of **B.** took 894
Jer 28:3 and carried them to **B.**: 894
Jer 28:4 of Judah, that went into **B.**,................ 894
Jer 28:4 break the yoke of the king of **B.**. 894
Jer 28:6 captive, from **B.** into this place. 894
Jer 28:11 king of **B.** from the neck of all........... 894
Jer 28:14 serve Nebuchadnezzar king of **B.**;........ 894
Jer 29:1 away captive from Jerusalem to **B.**;...... 894
Jer 29:3 king of Judah sent unto **B.**.................. 894
Jer 29:3 to Nebuchadnezzar king of **B.**) 894
Jer 29:4 away from Jerusalem unto **B.**; 894
Jer 29:10 years be accomplished at **B.** 894
Jer 29:15 hath raised us up prophets in **B.**;......... 894
Jer 29:20 I have sent from Jerusalem to **B.**......... 894
Jer 29:21 king of **B.**; and he shall slay them........ 894
Jer 29:22 of Judah which are in **B.**, saying, ... 894
Jer 29:22 the king of **B.** roasted in the fire; 894
Jer 29:28 therefore he sent unto us in **B.**, ... 894
Jer 32:3 the king of **B.**, and he shall take it;...... 894
Jer 32:4 of the king of **B.**, and shall speak 894
Jer 32:5 he shall lead Zedekiah to **B.**,............... 894
Jer 32:28 Nebuchadrezzar king of **B.**,................ 894
Jer 32:36 of the king of **B.** by the sword,........... 894
Jer 34:1 king of **B.**, and all his army,................ 894
Jer 34:2 the king of **B.**, and he shall burn it 894
Jer 34:3 behold the eyes of the king of **B.**, ... 894
Jer 34:3 to mouth, and thou shalt go to **B.**........ 894
Jer 35:11 Nebuchadrezzar king of **B.** came up 894
Jer 36:29 king of **B.** shall certainly come. 894
Jer 37:1 Nebuchadrezzar king of **B.** made 894
Jer 37:17 into the hand of the king of **B.**. 894
Jer 37:19 The king of **B.** shall not come.............. 894
Jer 38:23 by the hand of the king of **B.**.............. 894
Jer 39:1 came Nebuchadrezzar king of **B.**......... 894
Jer 39:3 princes of the king of **B.** came in,........ 894
Jer 39:3 of the princes of the king of **B.**. 894
Jer 39:5 up to Nebuchadnezzar king of **B.** 894
Jer 39:6 Then the king of **B.** slew the sons....... 894
Jer 39:6 the king of **B.** slew all the nobles 894
Jer 39:7 with chains, to carry him to **B.**. 894
Jer 39:9 guard carried away captive into **B.** 894
Jer 39:11 king of **B.** gave charge concerning 894
Jer 40:1 were carried away captive unto **B.**...... 894
Jer 40:4 unto thee to come with me into **B.**, ... 894
Jer 40:4 unto thee to come with me into **B.**, ... 894
Jer 40:5 whom the king of **B.** hath made 894
Jer 40:7 the king of **B.** had made Gedaliah 894
Jer 40:7 not carried away captive to **B.**; 894

Jer 40:9 and serve the king of **B.**, and it... 894
Jer 40:11 the king of **B.** had left a remnant... 894
Jer 41:2 and slew him, whom the king of **B.**... 894
Jer 41:18 Ahikam, whom the king of **B.** made ... 894
Jer 42:11 Be not afraid of the king of **B.**, ... 894
Jer 43:3 and carry us away captives into **B.**... 894
Jer 43:10 Nebuchadrezzar the king of **B.**, ... 894
Jer 44:30 king of **B.**, his enemy, and that... 894
Jer 46:2 king of **B.** smote in the fourth year... 894
Jer 46:13 Nebuchadrezzar king of **B.** should... 894
Jer 46:26 hand of Nebuchadrezzar king of **B.**,... 894
Jer 49:28 which Nebuchadrezzar king of **B.**... 894
Jer 49:30 king of **B.** hath taken counsel... 894
Jer 50:1 that the Lord spake against **B.**... 894
Jer 50:2 **B.** is taken, Bel is confounded, ... 894
Jer 50:8 Remove out of the midst of **B.**,... 894
Jer 50:9 and cause to come up against **B.** ... 894
Jer 50:13 goeth by **B.** shall be astonished,... 894
Jer 50:14 Put yourselves in array against **B.** ... 894
Jer 50:16 Cut off the sower from **B.**,... 894
Jer 50:17 king of **B.** hath broken his bones. ... 894
Jer 50:18 I will punish the king of **B.** and ... 894
Jer 50:23 how is **B.** become a desolation... 894
Jer 50:24 and thou art also taken, O **B.**, ... 894
Jer 50:28 and escape out of the land of **B.**,... 894
Jer 50:29 together the archers against **B.**... 894
Jer 50:34 and disquiet the inhabitants of **B.**... 894
Jer 50:35 and upon the inhabitants of **B.**,... 894
Jer 50:42 against thee, O daughter of **B.**... 894
Jer 50:43 king of **B.** hath heard the report... 894
Jer 50:45 that he hath taken against **B.**:... 894
Jer 50:46 At the noise of the taking of **B.**... 894
Jer 51:1 Behold, I will raise up against **B.**,... 894
Jer 51:2 and will send unto **B.** fanners,... 894
Jer 51:6 Flee out of the midst of **B.**,... 894
Jer 51:7 **B.** hath been a golden cup... 894
Jer 51:8 **B.** is suddenly fallen and destroyed: ... 894
Jer 51:9 We would have healed **B.**, but she... 894
Jer 51:11 for his device is against **B.**,... 894
Jer 51:12 the standard upon the walls of **B.**... 894
Jer 51:12 spake against the inhabitants of **B.**... 894
Jer 51:24 I will render unto **B.** and to all... 894
Jer 51:29 shall be performed against **B.**,... 894
Jer 51:29 make the land of **B.** a desolation... 894
Jer 51:30 mighty men of **B.** have forborn ... 894
Jer 51:31 shew the king of **B.** that his city ... 894
Jer 51:33 of **B.** is like a threshing floor, ... 894
Jer 51:34 the king of **B.** hath devoured me, ... 894
Jer 51:35 and to my flesh be upon **B.**, ... 894
Jer 51:37 **B.** shall become heaps, a dwelling... 894
Jer 51:41 how is **B.** become an astonishment ... 894
Jer 51:42 The sea is come up upon **B.**:... 894
Jer 51:44 I will punish Bel in **B.**, ... 894
Jer 51:44 yea, the wall of **B.** shall fall. ... 894
Jer 51:47 upon the graven images of **B.**... 894
Jer 51:48 that is therein, shall sing for **B.**... 894
Jer 51:49 As **B.** hath caused the slain of... 894
Jer 51:49 so at **B.** shall fall the slain of all... 894
Jer 51:53 **B.** should mount up to heaven, ... 894
Jer 51:54 A sound of a cry cometh from **B.**, ... 894
Jer 51:55 Because the Lord hath spoiled **B.**, ... 894
Jer 51:56 is come upon her, even upon **B.**,... 894
Jer 51:58 walls of **B.** shall be utterly broken, ... 894
Jer 51:59 **B.** in the fourth year of his reign... 894
Jer 51:60 evil that should come upon **B.**,... 894
Jer 51:60 words that are written against **B.** ... 894
Jer 51:61 When thou comest to **B.**, and shalt ... 894
Jer 51:64 Thus shall **B.** sink, and shall not... 894
Jer 52:3 rebelled against the king of **B.**... 894
Jer 52:4 king of **B.** came, he and all his... 894
Jer 52:9 carried him up unto the king of **B.**... 894
Jer 52:10 king of **B.** slew the sons of Zedekiah... 894
Jer 52:11 the king of **B.** bound him in chains,... 894
Jer 52:11 and carried him to **B.**,... 894
Jer 52:12 year of Nebuchadrezzar king of **B.**, ... 894
Jer 52:12 which served the king of **B.**, into... 894
Jer 52:15 that fell to the king of **B.**,... 894
Jer 52:17 carried all the brass of them to **B.** ... 894
Jer 52:26 them to the king of **B.** to Riblah... 894
Jer 52:27 the king of **B.** smote them, and... 894
Jer 52:31 Evil-merodach king of **B.**, in the... 894
Jer 52:32 of the kings that were with him in **B.**, .. 894
Jer 52:34 diet given him of the king of **B.**,... 894
Eze 12:13 I will bring him to **B.** to the land... 894
Eze 17:12 tell them, Behold, the king of **B.** ... 894
Eze 17:12 and led them with him to **B.**;... 894
Eze 17:16 in the midst of **B.** he shall die... 894
Eze 17:20 I will bring him to **B.**, and will ... 894
Eze 19:9 and brought him to the king of **B.**... 894
Eze 21:19 the sword of the king of **B.** may... 894
Eze 21:21 the king of **B.** stood at the parting... 894
Eze 24:2 the king of **B.** set himself against... 894
Eze 26:7 Nebuchadrezzar king of **B.**, a king ... 894
Eze 29:18 of man, Nebuchadrezzar king of **B.** ... 894
Eze 29:19 unto Nebuchadrezzar king of **B.**;... 894
Eze 30:10 of Nebuchadrezzar king of **B.**... 894
Eze 30:24 the arms of the king of **B.**,... 894
Eze 30:25 the king of **B.**, and the arms of... 894
Eze 30:25 the king of **B.**, and he shall... 894
Eze 32:11 The sword of the king of **B.**... 894
Da 1:1 Nebuchadnezzar king of **B.**... 894
Da 2:12 to destroy all the wise men of **B.**, ... 895
Da 2:14 to slay the wise men of **B.**... 895
Da 2:18 with the rest of the wise men of **B.** ... 895
Da 2:24 to destroy the wise man of **B.** ... 895
Da 2:24 Destroy not the wise men of **B.**... 895
Da 2:48 ruler over the whole province of **B.**, ... 895
Da 2:48 over all the wise men of **B.**... 895
Da 2:49 the affairs of the province of **B.**... 895
Da 3:1 of Dura, in the province of **B.**... 895
Da 3:12 the affairs of the province of **B.**,... 895
Da 3:30 Abed-nego, in the province of **B.**... 895
Da 4:6 to bring in all the wise men of **B.** ... 895
Da 4:29 in the palace of the kingdom of **B.** ... 895
Da 4:30 Is not this great **B.**, that I have ... 895
Da 5:7 and said to the wise men of **B.**, ... 895
Da 7:1 first year of Belshazzar king of **B.**... 895
Mic 4:10 and thou shall go even to **B.**;... 894
Zec 2:7 with the daughter of **B.**... 894
Zec 6:10 which are come from **B.**, ... 894
Mt 1:11 they were carried away to **B.** ... *897*
Mt 1:12 after they were brought to **B.**, ... *897*
Mt 1:17 the carrying away into **B.**... *897*
Mt 1:17 carrying away into **B.** unto Christ... *897*
Ac 7:43 carry you away beyond **B.**,... *897*
1Pe 5:13 The church that is at **B.**, ... *897*
Re 14:8 **B.** is fallen, is fallen,... *897*
Re 16:19 great **B.** came in remembrance ... *897*
Re 17:5 **B.** the great, the mother of... *897*
Re 18:2 **B.** the great is fallen, ... *897*
Re 18:10 that great city **B.**, that mighty city!... *897*
Re 18:21 great city **B.** be thrown down, ... *897*

BABYLONIANS (bab-il-o'-ne-ans) See also CHALDEANS.
Ezr 4:9 the **B.**, the Susanchites, the... 896
Eze 23:15 manner of the **B.** of Chaldea,... 1121,894
Eze 23:17 the **B.** came to her into the... 1121,894
Eze 23:23 The **B.**, and all the Chaldeans,... 1121,894

BABYLONISH (bab-il-o'-nish) See also BABYLONIANS.
Jos 7:21 spoils a goodly **B.** garment,... 8152

BABYLON'S (bab'-il-ons)
Jer 32:2 the king of **B.** army besieged... 894
Jer 34:7 When the king of **B.** army fought... 894
Jer 34:21 the hand of the king of **B.** army, ... 894
Jer 38:3 of **B.** army, which shall take it. ... 894
Jer 38:17 go forth unto the king of **B.** princes, ... 894
Jer 38:18 to the king of **B.** princes, then shall ... 894
Jer 38:22 forth to the king of **B.** princes,... 894
Jer 39:13 and all the king of **B.** princes;... 894

BACA (ba'-cah)
Ps 84:6 passing through the valley of **B.**... 1056

BACHRITES (bak'-rites)
Nu 26:35 of Becher, the family of the **B.**:... 1076

BACHUTH See ALLON-BACHUTH.

BACK See also BACKBITERS; BACKBITETH; BACKBITING; BACKBONE; BACKS; BACKSIDE; BACKSLIDER; BACKSLIDING; BACKWARD; HORSEBACK.
Ge 14:16 And he brought **b.** all the goods,... 7725
Ge 19:9 they said, Stand **b.**... 1973
Ge 19:26 his wife looked **b.** from behind...
Ge 38:29 as he drew **b.** his hand,... 7725
Ge 39:9 neither hath he kept **b.** anything... 2820
Ex 14:21 Lord caused the sea to go **b.** by a ...
Ex 18:2 after he had sent her **b.**,...
Ex 23:4 surely bring it **b.** to him again... 7725
Ex 33:23 thou shalt see my **b.** parts:... 268
Nu 9:7 wherefore are we kept **b.**,... 1639
Nu 13:26 and brought **b.** word unto them,... 7725
Nu 22:34 thee, I will get me **b.** again... 7725
Nu 24:11 hath kept thee **b.** from honour... 4513
De 23:13 and shalt turn **b.** and cover that... 7725
Jos 8:20 wilderness turned **b.** upon the ... 2015
Jos 8:26 Joshua drew not his hand **b.**,... 7725
Jos 11:10 and Joshua at that time turned **b.**, ... 7725
Jos 23:12 if ye do in any wise go **b.**,... 7725
Jg 11:35 the Lord, and I cannot go **b.**... 7725
Jg 18:26 he turned and went **b.** unto his... 7725
Ru 1:15 is gone **b.** unto her people,... 7725
Ru 2:6 Moabitish damsel that came **b.**... 7725
1Sa 10:9 he had turned his **b.** to go from... 7926
1Sa 15:11 he is turned **b.** from following me,... 7725
1Sa 25:34 hath kept me **b.** from hurting ... 4513
2Sa 1:22 the bow of Jonathan turned not **b.**,... 268
2Sa 12:23 can I bring him **b.** again? I... 7725
2Sa 15:20 and take **b.** thy brethren: mercy ... 7725
2Sa 15:25 Carry **b.** the ark of God into the ... 7725
2Sa 17:3 I will bring **b.** all the people unto... 7725
2Sa 18:16 Joab held **b.** the people... 2820
2Sa 19:10 a word of bringing the king **b.**? ... 7725
2Sa 19:11 to bring the king **b.** to his house?... 7725
2Sa 19:12 ye the last to bring **b.** the king?... 7725
2Sa 19:37 I pray thee, turn **b.** again,... 7725
2Sa 19:43 first had in bringing **b.** our king? ... 7725
1Ki 13:18 Bring him **b.** with thee into thine... 7725
1Ki 13:19 So he went **b.** with him, and did eat... 7725
1Ki 13:20 the prophet that brought him **b.**: ... 7725
1Ki 13:22 But camest **b.**, and hast eaten... 7725
1Ki 13:23 prophet whom he had brought **b.**... 7725
1Ki 13:26 prophet that brought him **b.** from... 7725
1Ki 13:29 upon the ass, and brought it **b.**... 7725
1Ki 14:9 hast cast me behind thy **b.**:... 1458
1Ki 14:28 and brought them **b.** into the... 7725
1Ki 18:37 hast turned their heart **b.** again. ... 322
1Ki 19:20 Go **b.** again: for what have I done... 7725
1Ki 19:21 And he returned **b.** from him... 7725
1Ki 22:26 and carry him **b.** unto Amon the ... 7725
1Ki 22:33 they turned **b.** from pursuing him... 7725
2Ki 1:5 the messengers turned **b.** unto ... 7725
2Ki 1:5 Why are ye now turned **b.**?... 7725
2Ki 2:13 and went **b.**, and stood by the bank... 7725
2Ki 2:24 And he turned **b.**, and looked on ... 310
2Ki 8:29 king Joram went **b.** to be healed ... 7725
2Ki 15:20 So the king of Assyria turned **b.**, ... 7725
2Ki 19:28 and I will turn thee **b.** by the way... 7725
2Ki 20:9 ten degrees, or go **b.** ten degrees?... 7725
1Ch 21:20 And Ornan turned **b.**, and saw the... 7725
2Ch 13:14 when Judah looked **b.**, behold, ... 6437
2Ch 18:25 and carry him **b.** to Amon the... 7725
2Ch 18:32 turned **b.** again from pursuing... 7725
2Ch 19:4 and brought them **b.** unto the Lord... 7725
2Ch 25:13 the army which Amaziah sent **b.**, ... 7725
2Ch 34:16 brought the king word **b.** again, ... 7725
Ne 2:15 viewed the wall, and turned **b.**, and... 7725
Job 23:12 I gone **b.** from the commandment... 4185
Job 26:9 He holdeth **b.** the face of his...
Job 33:18 He keepeth **b.** his soul from the... 2820
Job 33:30 To bring **b.** his soul from the pit, ... 7725
Job 34:27 they turned **b.** from him, and ... 5493
Job 39:22 neither turneth he **b.** from the... 7725
Ps 9:3 enemies are turned **b.**, they shall... 268
Ps 14:7 the Lord bringeth **b.** the captivity... 7725
Ps 19:13 Keep **b.** thy servant also from... 2820
Ps 21:12 make them turn their **b.**, when... 7926
Ps 35:4 let them be turned **b.** and brought ... 268
Ps 44:10 makest us to turn **b.** from the... 268
Ps 44:18 Our heart is not turned **b.**, neither... 268
Ps 53:3 Every one of them is gone **b.**... 5472
Ps 53:6 God bringeth **b.** the captivity of ... 7725
Ps 56:9 then shall mine enemies turn **b.**... 268
Ps 70:3 Let them be turned **b.** for a... 7725
Ps 78:9 turned **b.** in the day of battle... 2015
Ps 78:41 Yea, they turned **b.** and tempted... 7725
Ps 78:57 But turned **b.**, and dealt... 5472
Ps 80:18 will not we go **b.** from thee:... 5472
Ps 85:1 hast brought **b.** the captivity of... 7725
Ps 114:3 and fled: Jordan was driven **b.**... 268
Ps 114:5 Jordan, that thou wast driven **b.**?... 268
Ps 129:3 plowed upon my **b.**: they made... 1354
Ps 129:5 all be confounded and turned **b.**... 268
Pr 10:13 a rod is for the **b.** of him that is... 1458
Pr 19:29 and stripes for the **b.** of fools. ... 1458
Pr 26:3 a rod for the fool's **b.**... 1458
Isa 14:27 out, and who shall turn it **b.**?... 7725
Isa 31:2 will not call **b.** his words: but ... 5493
Isa 37:29 and I will turn thee **b.** by the way... 7725
Isa 38:17 cast all my sins behind thy **b.**... 1458
Isa 42:17 They shall be turned **b.**, they shall... 268
Isa 43:6 and to the south. Keep not **b.**... 3607

Isa 50:5 neither turned away b.. 268
Isa 50:6 I gave my b. to the smiters, and 1458
Jer 2:27 have turned their b. unto me, 6203
Jer 4:8 of the Lord is not turned b. 7725
Jer 4:28 neither will I turn b. from it. 7725
Jer 6:9 turn b. thine hand as a grape 7725
Jer 8:5 of Jerusalem slidden b. by a 7725
Jer 11:10 They are turned b. to the 7725
Jer 18:17 shew them the b., and not the 6203
Jer 21:4 I will turn b. the weapons of war 5437
Jer 32:33 they have turned unto me the b., 6203
Jer 38:22 and they are turned away b.. 268
Jer 40:5 he was not yet gone b., he said, 7725
Jer 40:5 Go b. also to Gedaliah the son of 7725
Jer 42:4 I will keep nothing b. from you. 4513
Jer 46:5 dismayed and turned away b.? 268
Jer 46:5 are fled apace, and look not b. 3437
Jer 46:21 also are turned b., and are fled 3437
Jer 47:3 fathers shall not look b. to their 3437
Jer 48:10 he that keepeth b. his sword from 4513
Jer 48:39 hath Moab turned the b. with 6203
Jer 49:8 Flee ye, turn b., dwell deep, 6437
La 1:13 he hath turned me b.: he hath 268
La 2:3 he hath drawn b. his right hand 268
Eze 23:35 me behind thy b., therefore bear 1458
Eze 24:14 I will not go b., neither will I 6544
Eze 38:4 And I will turn thee b., 7725
Eze 38:8 the land that is brought b. from 7725
Eze 39:2 I will turn thee b.,and leave but 7725
Eze 44:1 Then he brought me b. the way of 7725
Da 7:6 which had upon the b. of it four 1355
Ho 4:16 Israel slideth b. as a backsliding 5637
Na 2:8 they cry; but none shall look b.. 6437
Zep 1:6 them that are turned b. from the 5253
Zep 3:20 when I turn b. your captivity 7725
Mt 24:18 **return b. to take his clothes** *3694*
Mt 28:2 came and rolled b. the stone *617*
Mk 13:16 **that is in the field not turn b.** *617*
Lu 2:45 turned b. again to Jerusalem, *5290*
Lu 8:37 the ship, and returned b. again. *5290*
Lu 9:62 **looking b., is fit for the kingdom** *3694*
Lu 17:15 turned b., and with a loud voice *5290*
Lu 17:31 **let him likewise not return b.** *3694*
Joh 6:66 many of his disciples went b., *3694*
Joh 20:14 turned herself b., and saw Jesus *3694*
Ac 5:2 And kept b. part of the price, *3557*
Ac 5:3 to keep b. part of the price of the *3557*
Ac 7:39 hearts turned b. again into Egypt. *4762*
Ac 20:20 how I kept b. nothing that was *5288*
Ro 11:10 and bow down their b. alway *3577*
Heb 10:38 but if any man draw b., my soul *5288*
Heb 10:39 we are not of them who draw b. *5289*
Jas 5:4 is of you kept b. by fraud, *650*

BACKBITERS
Ro 1:30 B., haters of God, despiteful, *2637*

BACKBITETH
Ps 15:3 He that b. not with his tongue, 7270

BACKBITING See also BACKBITINGS.
Pr 25:23 angry countenance a b. tongue 5643

BACKBITINGS
2Co 12:20 strifes, b.,whisperings, *2636*

BACKBONE
Le 3:9 it shall he take off hard by the b.; 6096

BACKED See BACKT.

BACKS
Ex 23:27 all thine enemies turn their b. 6203
Jos 7:8 when Israel turneth their b. 6203
Jos 7:12 their b. before their enemies. 6203
Jg 20:42 Therefore they turned their b.
2Ch 29:6 of the Lord, and turned their b. 6203
Ne 9:26 cast thy law behind their b., 1458
Eze 8:16 with their b. toward the temple 268
Eze 10:12 and their b., and their hands, 1354

BACKSIDE
Ex 3:1 flock to the b. of the desert, and 310
Ex 26:12 over the b. of the tabernacle 268
Re 5:1 book written within and on the b. *3693*

BACKSLIDER
Pr 14:14 The b. in heart shall be filled 5472

BACKSLIDING See also BACKSLIDINGS.
Jer 3:6 that which b. Israel hath done? 4878
Jer 3:8 b. Israel committed adultery 4878
Jer 3:11 The b. Israel hath justified herself 4878
Jer 3:12 Return, thou b. Israel, saith the 4878
Jer 3:14 Turn, O b. children, saith the 7726
Jer 3:22 Return, ye b. children, and I will 7726
Jer 8:5 slidden back by a perpetual b.? 4878
Jer 31:22 O thou b. daughter? 7728
Jer 49:4 thy flowing valley, O b. daughter? 7728
Ho 4:16 Israel slideth back as a b. heifer: 5637
Ho 11:7 my people are bent to b. from me: 4878
Ho 14:4 I will heal their b., 4878

BACKSLIDINGS
Jer 2:19 and thy b. shall reprove thee: 4878
Jer 3:22 and I will heal your b.. 4878
Jer 5:6 their b. are increased. 4878
Jer 14:7 our b. are many; 4878

BACKWARD
Ge 9:23 both their shoulders, and went b., 322
Ge 9:23 and their faces were b., and they 322
Ge 49:17 so that his rider shall fall b.. 268
1Sa 4:18 he fell from off the seat b. 322
2Ki 20:10 shadow return b. ten degrees. 322
2Ki 20:11 brought the shadow ten degrees b. 322
Job 23:8 and b., but I cannot perceive 268
Ps 40:14 them be driven b. and put to shame 268
Ps 70:2 be turned b., and put to confusion, 268
Isa 1:4 unto anger, they are gone away b. 268
Isa 28:13 that they might go, and fall b., 268
Isa 38:8 sun dial of Ahaz, ten degrees b.. 322
Isa 44:25 that turneth wise men b., 268
Isa 59:14 judgment is turned away b., 268
Jer 7:24 went b., and not forward. 268
Jer 15:6 saith the Lord, thou are gone b. 268
La 1:8 she sigheth, and turneth b.. 268
Joh 18:6 they went b.,and fell to *1519,3588,3694*

BAD See also WORSE; WORST.
Ge 24:50 cannot speak unto thee b. or good 7451
Ge 31:24, 29 not to Jacob either good or b.. 7451
Le 27:10 nor change it, a good for a b., 7451
Le 27:10 or a b. for a good: and if he 7451
Le 27:12 value it, whether it be good or b. 7451
Le 27:14 estimate it, whether it be good or b., 7451
Le 27:33 not search whether it be good or b., 7451
Nu 13:19 whether it be good or b.; and what 7451
Nu 24:13 good or b. of mine own mind; 7451
2Sa 13:22 brother Amnon neither good nor b. 7451
2Sa 14:17 the king to discern good and b. 7451
1Ki 3:9 discern between good and b. 7451
Ezr 4:12 the rebellious and the b. city, 873
Jer 24:2 not be eaten, they were so b.. 7451
Mt 13:48 **into vessels, but cast the b. away.** *4550*
Mt 22:10 **as they found, both b. and good:** *4190*
2Co 5:10 done, whether it be good or b.. *2556*

BADE See also BADEST; FORBAD.
Ge 43:17 did as Joseph b.; and the man 559
Ex 16:24 up till the morning, as Moses b. 6680
Nu 14:10 congregation b. stone them with 559
Jos 11:9 unto them as the Lord b. him: 559
Ru 3:6 all that her mother in law b. her. 6680
1Sa 24:10 and some b. me kill thee: but 559
2Sa 1:18 b. them teach the children of Judah 559
2Sa 14:19 thy servant Joab, he b. me, and 6680
2Ch 10:12 the king b. saying, Come again 1696
Es 4:15 Then Esther b. them return 559
Mt 16:12 they how that he b. them not *2036*
Lu 14:9 **And he that b. thee and him come** *2564*
Lu 14:10 **when he that b. thee cometh, he** *2564*
Lu 14:12 said he also to him that b. him, *2564*
Lu 14:16 **made a great supper, and b. many:** *2564*
Ac 11:12 the spirit b. me go with them, *2036*
Ac 18:21 b. them farewell, saying, I must *657*
Ac 22:24 b. that he should be examined *2036*

BADEST
Ge 27:19 done according as thou b. me: 1696

BADGERS'
Ex 25:5 b. skins, and shittim wood, 8476
Ex 26:14 a covering above of b. skins. 8476
Ex 35:7 dyed red, and b. skins, and 8476
Ex 35:23 red skins of rams, and b. skins, 8476
Ex 36:19 a covering of b. skins above that 8476
Ex 39:34 the covering of b. skins, 8476
Nu 4:6 the covering of b. skins, 8476
Nu 4:8 with a covering of b. skins, 8476
Nu 4:10 within a covering of b. skins, 8476
Nu 4:11 with a covering of b. skins, 8476
Nu 4:12 a covering of b. skins, and shall 8476
Nu 4:14 upon it a covering of b. skins, 8476
Nu 4:25 the covering of the b. skins. 8476
Eze 16:10 shod thee with b. skin, 8476

BADGER-SKIN See BADGERS' and SKIN.

BADNESS
Ge 41:19 in all the land of Egypt for b. 7455

BAG See also BAGS.
De 25:13 not have in thy b. divers weights, 3599
1Sa 17:40 in a shepherd's b. which he had, 3627
1Sa 17:49 David put his hand in his b., 3627
Job 14:17 transgression is sealed up in a b., 6872
Pr 7:20 taken a b. of money with him, 6872
Pr 16:11 weights of the b. are his work. 3599
Isa 46:6 They lavish gold out of the b. 3599
Mic 6:11 with the b. of deceitful weights? 3599
Hag 1:6 to put it into a b. with holes . 6872
Joh 12:6 he was a thief, and had the b.. *1101*
Joh 13:29 thought, because Judas had the b., *1101*

BAGS
2Ki 5:23 two talents of silver in two b. 2754
2Ki 12:10 they put up in b., and told the 6696
Lu 12:33 **provide yourselves b. which wax** *905*

BAH See HEPHZI-BAH.

BAHARUMITE (ba-ha'-rum-ite) See also BARHUMITE.
1Ch 11:33 Azmaveth the B., Eliahba the 978

BAHURIM (ba-hu'-rim) See also BAHARUMITE.
2Sa 3:16 along weeping behind her to B.. 980
2Sa 16:5 And when king David came to B. 980
2Sa 17:18 and came to a man's house in B. 980
2Sa 19:16 a Benjamite, which was of B., 980
1Ki 2:8 a Benjamite of B., which cursed 980

BAJITH (ba'-jith)
Isa 15:2 is gone up to B., and to Dibon. 1006

BAKBAKKAR (bak-bak'-kar)
1Ch 9:15 B., Heresh, and Galal, and 1230

BAKBUK (bak'-buk)
Ezr 2:51 The children of B., the children 1227
Ne 7:53 The children of B., the children 1227

BAKBUKIAH (bak-buk-i'-ah)
Ne 11:17 B. the second among his 1229
Ne 12:9 B. and Unni, their brethren, 1229
Ne 12:25 Mattaniah, and B., Obadiah, 1229

BAKE See also BAKED; BAKEMEATS; BAKEN; BAKETH.
Ge 19:3 did b. unleavened bread, and they 644
Ex 16:23 b. that which ye will b. 644
Le 24:5 and b. twelve cakes thereof: 644
Le 26:26 ten women shall b. your bread in 644
1Sa 28:24 did b. unleavened bread thereof: 644
2Sa 13:8 in his sight, and did b. the cakes. 1310
Eze 4:12 thou shalt b. it with dung that 5746
Eze 46:20 they shall b. the meat offering; 644

BAKED See also BAKEN.
Ex 12:39 And they b. unleavened cakes 644
Nu 11:8 b. it in pans, and made cakes 1310
1Ch 23:29 and for that which is b. in the pan,
Isa 44:19 I have b. bread upon the coals 644

BAKEMEATS
Ge 40:17 of b. for Pharaoh; 3978,4639,644

BAKEN See also BAKED.
Le 2:4 a meat offering b. in the oven, 644
Le 2:5 be a meat offering b. in a pan,
Le 2:7 offering b. in the frying pan,
Le 6:17 it shall not be b. with leaven. 644
Le 6:21 when it is b., thou shalt 7246
Le 6:21 the b. pieces of the meat offering 8601
Le 7:9 all the meat offering that is b. 644
Le 23:17 they shall be b. with leaven; 644
1Ki 19:6 there was a cake b. on the coals,

BAKETH
Isa 44:15 he kindleth it, and b. bread; 644

BAKER See also BAKERS.
Ge 40:1 and his b. had offended their lord 644
Ge 40:5 and the b. of the king of Egypt, 644
Ge 40:16 When the chief b. saw that the 644
Ge 40:20 of the chief b. among his servants 644

Ge 40:22 But he hanged the chief **b.**: 644
Ge 41:10 both me and the chief **b.**: 644
Ho 7:4 as an oven heated by the **b.**, 644
Ho 7:6 their **b.** sleepeth all the night; 644

BAKERS See also BAKERS'.
Ge 40:2 against the chief of the **b.** 644
1Sa 8:13 and to be cooks, and to be **b.**. 644

BAKERS'
Jer 37:21 piece of bread out of the **b.** street. 644

BALAAM (ba'-la-am) See also BALAAM'S.
Nu 22:5 therefore unto **B.** the son of Beor 1109
Nu 22:7 and they came unto **B.**, and spake 1109
Nu 22:8 princes of Moab abode with **B.**. 1109
Nu 22:9 And God came unto **B.**, and said, 1109
Nu 22:10 And **B.** said unto god, Balak the 1109
Nu 22:12 God said unto **B.**, Thou shalt not 1109
Nu 22:13 **B.** rose up in the morning, and said 1109
Nu 22:14 said, **B.** refuseth to come with us. 1109
Nu 22:16 they came to **B.**, and said to him, 1109
Nu 22:18 **B.** answered and said unto the 1109
Nu 22:20 And God came unto **B.** at night, 1109
Nu 22:21 And **B.** rose up in the morning, 1109
Nu 22:23 and **B.** smote the ass, to turn her 1109
Nu 22:27 fell down under **B.**: and Balaam's 1109
Nu 22:28 she said unto **B.**, What have I done 1109
Nu 22:29 And **B.** said unto the ass, Because 1109
Nu 22:30 ass said unto **B.**, Am not I thine 1109
Nu 22:31 the Lord opened the eyes of **B.**, 1109
Nu 22:34 **B.** said unto the angel of the Lord, 1109
Nu 22:35 angel of the Lord said unto **B.**, Go 1109
Nu 22:35 **B.** went with the princes of Balak. 1109
Nu 22:36 Balak heard that **B.** was come, 1109
Nu 22:37 And Balak said unto **B.**, Did I not 1109
Nu 22:38 **B.** said unto Balak, Lo, I am come 1109
Nu 22:39 **B.** went with Balak, and they came 1109
Nu 22:40 sent to **B.**, and to the princes 1109
Nu 22:41 Balak took **B.**, and brought him 1109
Nu 23:1 And **B.** said unto Balak, Build me 1109
Nu 23:2 Balak did as **B.** had spoken; 1109
Nu 23:2 Balak and **B.** offered on every altar 1109
Nu 23:3 **B.** said unto Balak, Stand by thy 1109
Nu 23:4 And God met **B.**: and he said unto 1109
Nu 23:11 Balak said unto **B.**, What hast thou 1109
Nu 23:16 the Lord met **B.**, and put a word 1109
Nu 23:25 Balak said unto **B.**, Neither curse 1109
Nu 23:26 **B.** answered and said unto Balak 1109
Nu 23:27 Balak said unto **B.**, Come, I pray 1109
Nu 23:28 brought **B.** unto the top of Peor, 1109
Nu 23:29 **B.** said unto Balak, Build me here 1109
Nu 23:30 And Balak did as **B.** had said. 1109
Nu 24:1 **B.** saw that it pleased the Lord 1109
Nu 24:2 And **B.** lifted up his eyes, and he 1109
Nu 24:3 and said, **B.** the son of Beor 1109
Nu 24:10 anger was kindled against **B.**, 1109
Nu 24:10 Balak said unto **B.**, I called thee 1109
Nu 24:12 **B.** said unto Balak, Spake I not 1109
Nu 24:15 said, **B.** the son of Beor hath said, 1109
Nu 24:25 **B.** rose up, and went and returned 1109
Nu 31:8 **B.** also the son of Beor they slew 1109
Nu 31:16 through the counsel of **B.**. 1109
De 23:4 they hired against thee **B.** the son 1109
De 23:5 God would not hearken unto **B.**; 1109
Jos 13:22 **B.** also the son of Beor, the 1109
Jos 24:9 sent and called **B.** the son of Beor 1109
Jos 24:10 But I would not hearken unto **B.**; 1109
Ne 13:2 water, but hired **B.** against them, 1109
Mic 6:5 what **B.** the son of Beor answered 1109
2Pe 2:15 following the way of **B.** the son of *903*
Jude 11 the error of **B.** for reward) *903*
Re 2:14 **doctrine of B., who taught Balac** *903*

BALAAM'S (ba'-la-ams)
Nu 22:25 and crushed **B.** foot against 1109
Nu 22:27 and **B.** anger was kindled. 1109
Nu 23:5 the Lord put a word in **B.** mouth, 1109

BALAC (ba'-lak) See also BALAK.
Re 2:14 **taught B. to cast a stumblingblock** *904*

BALADAN (bal'-adan) See also BERODACH-BALADAN; MERODACH-BALADAN.
2Ki 20:12 the son of **B.**, the king of Babylon, 1081
Isa 39:1 Merodach-baladan, the son of **B.**, 1081

BALAH (ba'-lah) See also BAALAH.
Jos 19:3 Hazar-shual, and **B.**, and Azem, 1088

BALAK (ba'-lak) See also BALAC; BALAK'S.
Nu 22:2 **B.** the son of Zippor saw all that 1111
Nu 22:4 **B.** the son of Zippor was king of 1111
Nu 22:7 spake unto him the words of **B.**. 1111
Nu 22:10 **B.** the son of Zippor, king of 1111
Nu 22:13 and said unto the princes of **B.**, 1111
Nu 22:14 went unto **B.**, and said, Balaam 1111
Nu 22:15 And **B.** sent yet again princes, 1111
Nu 22:16 Thus saith **B.** the son of Zippor, 1111
Nu 22:18 unto the servants of **B.**, 1111
Nu 22:18 If **B.** would give me 1111
Nu 22:35 went with the princes of **B.**. 1111
Nu 22:36 **B.** heard that Baalam was come, 1111
Nu 22:37 **B.** said unto Balaam, Did I not 1111
Nu 22:38 Balaam said unto **B.**, Lo, I am 1111
Nu 22:39 Balaam went with **B.**, and they 1111
Nu 22:40 And **B.** offered oxen and sheep, 1111
Nu 22:41 **B.** took Balaam, and brought him 1111
Nu 23:1 Balaam said unto **B.**, Build me 1111
Nu 23:2 **B.** did as Balaam had spoken; 1111
Nu 23:2 **B.** and Balaam offered on every 1111
Nu 23:3 Balaam said unto **B.**, Stand by thy 1111
Nu 23:5 Return unto **B.**, and thus thou 1111
Nu 23:7 and said, **B.** the king of Moab 1111
Nu 23:11 **B.** said unto Balaam, what hast 1111
Nu 23:13 **B.** said unto him, Come, I pray 1111
Nu 23:15 said unto **B.**, Stand here by thy 1111
Nu 23:16 Go again unto **B.**, and say thus. 1111
Nu 23:17 **B.** said unto him, What hath the 1111
Nu 23:18 and said, Rise up, **B.**, and hear; 1111
Nu 23:25 And **B.** said unto Balaam, 1111
Nu 23:26 and said unto **B.**, Told not I thee, 1111
Nu 23:27 **B.** said unto Balaam, Come, I pray 1111
Nu 23:28 **B.** brought Balaam unto the top 1111
Nu 23:29 Balaam said unto **B.**, Build me 1111
Nu 23:30 **B.** did as Baalam had said, 1111
Nu 24:10 **B.** said unto Balaam, I called thee 1111
Nu 24:12 Balaam said unto **B.**, Spake I not 1111
Nu 24:13 If **B.** would give me his house 1111
Nu 24:25 to his place: and **B.** also went 1111
Jos 24:9 Then **B.** the son of Zippor, king of 1111
Jg 11:25 art thou anything better than **B.** 1111
Mic 6:5 what **B.** king of Moab consulted, 1111

BALAK'S (ba'-laks)
Nu 24:10 And **B.** anger was kindled against 1111

BALANCE See also BALANCES; BALANCINGS.
Job 31:6 Let me be weighed in an even **b.**, 3976
Ps 62:9 to be laid in the **b.**, they are 3976
Pr 11:1 false **b.** is abomination to the 3976
Pr 16:11 just weight and **b.** are the Lord's: 3976
Pr 20:23 and a false **b.** is not good. 3976
Isa 40:12 and the hills in a **b.**? 3976
Isa 40:15 count as the small dust of the **b.** 3976
Isa 46:6 weigh silver in the **b.** and hire a 7070

BALANCES
Le 19:36 Just **b.**, just weights, a just 3976
Job 6:2 my calamity laid in the **b.** together! 3976
Jer 32:10 weighed him the money in the **b.**. 3976
Eze 5:1 then take thee **b.** to weigh, and 3976
Eze 45:10 Ye shall have just **b.**, 3976
Da 5:27 Thou art weighed in the **b.**, 3977
Ho 12:7 the **b.** of deceit are in his hand: 3976
Am 8:5 falsifying the **b.** by deceit? 3976
Mic 6:11 pure with the wicked **b.**, 3976
Re 6:5 had a pair of **b.** in his hand

BALANCINGS
Job 37:16 thou know the **b.** of the clouds, 4657

BALD
Le 11:22 the **b.** locust after his kind, and 5556
Le 13:40 he is **b.**; yet is he clean. 7142
Le 13:41 he is forehead **b.**: yet is he clean. 1371
Le 13:42 if there be in the **b.** head, 7146
Le 13:42 or **b.** forehead, a white 1372
Le 13:42 leprosy sprung up in his **b.** head, 7146
Le 13:42 head or his **b.** forehead. 1372
Le 13:43 be white reddish in his **b.** head, 7146
Le 13:43 or in her bald forehead, 1372
2Ki 2:23 **b.** head; go up, thou **b.** head. 7142
Jer 16:6 make themselves **b.** for them: 7139
Jer 48:37 every head shall be **b.**, and every 7144
Eze 27:31 themselves utterly **b.** for thee, 7139
Eze 29:18 every head was made **b.**, and every 7139
Mic 1:16 Make thee **b.**, and poll thee for thy 7139

BALD-HEAD See BALD and HEAD.

BALD-LOCUST See BALD and LOCUST.

BALDNESS
Le 21:5 They shall not make **b.** upon their 7144
De 14:1 nor make any **b.** between your 7144
Isa 3:24 instead of well set hair **b.**; 7144
Isa 15:2 on all their heads shall be **b.**, 7144
Isa 22:12 to mourning, and to **b.**, 7144
Jer 47:5 **B.** is come upon Gaza; 7144
Eze 7:18 **b.** upon all their heads. 7144
Am 8:10 **b.** upon every head; and I will 7144
Mic 1:16 enlarge thy **b.** as the eagle; 7144

BALL
Isa 22:18 and toss thee like a **b.** into a 1754

BALM See also EMBALM.
Ge 37:25 spicery and **b.** and myrrh, going 6875
Ge 43:11 a little **b.**, and a little honey, 6875
Jer 8:22 Is there no **b.** in Gilead; 6875
Jer 46:11 Go up into Gilead, and take **b.**, 6875
Jer 51:8 take **b.** for her pain, if so be she 6875
Eze 27:17 and honey, and oil, and **b.** 6875

BAMAH (ba'-mah) See also BAMOTH.
Eze 20:29 thereof is called **B.** unto this day 1117

BAMOTH (ba'-moth) See also BAMOTH-BAAL.
Nu 21:19 from Nahaliel to **B.** 1120
Nu 21:20 And from **B.** in the valley, that is 1120

BAMOTH-BAAL (ba''-moth-ba'-al)
Jos 13:17 Dibon, and **B.**, and 1120

BAND See also BANDED; BANDS; SWADDLING BAND.
Ex 39:23 a **b.** round about the hole, that it 8193
1Sa 10:26 him a **b.** of men, whose hearts 2428
1Ki 11:24 captain over a **b.**, when David 1416
2Ki 13:21 they spied a **b.** of men; and they 1416
1Ch 12:18 made them captains of the **b.**. 1416
1Ch 12:21 David against the **b.** of the 1416
2Ch 22:1 the **b.** of men that came with the 1416
Ezr 8:22 the king a **b.** of soldiers and 2428
Job 39:10 unicorn with his **b.** in the furrow? 5688
Da 4:15 even with a **b.** of iron and brass, 613
Da 4:23 in the earth, even with a **b.** of iron 613
Mt 27:27 gathered unto him the whole **b.** *4686*
Mk 15:16 they call together the whole **b.**. *4686*
Joh 18:3 having received a **b.** of men and *4686*
Joh 18:12 Then the **b.** and the captain and *4686*
Ac 10:1 of the **b.** called the Italian **b.**, *4686*
Ac 21:31 chief captain of the **b.**, that all *4686*
Ac 27:1 Julius, a centurion of Augustus' **b.**. *4686*

BANDED
Ac 23:12 of the Jews **b.** together, *4160,4963*

BANDS See also HEADBANDS.
Ge 32:7 herds, and the camels, into two **b.**; 4264
Ge 32:10 and now I am become two **b.**. 4264
Le 26:13 have broken the **b.** of your yoke, 4133
Jg 15:14 his **b.** loosed from off his hands. 612
2Sa 4:2 two men that were captains of **b.**: 1416
2Ki 6:23 So the **b.** of Syria came no more 1416
2Ki 13:20 And the **b.** of the Moabites invaded 1416
2Ki 23:33 Pharaoh-nechoh put him in **b.** at 631
2Ki 24:2 against him **b.** of the Chaldees, 1416
2Ki 24:2 and **b.** of the Syrians, 1416
2Ki 24:2 and **b.** of the Moabites, 1416
2Ki 24:2 and **b.** of the children of Ammon. 1416
1Ch 7:4 were **b.** of soldiers for war, 1416
1Ch 12:23 of the **b.**, that were ready armed 7218
2Ch 26:11 went out to war by **b.**, according 1416
Job 1:17 Chaldeans made out three **b.**, and 7218
Job 38:31 Pleiades, or loose the **b.** of Orion? 4189
Job 39:5 hath loosed the **b.** of the wild ass? 4147
Ps 2:3 break their **b.** asunder, and cast 4147
Ps 73:4 there are no **b.** in their death: 2784
Ps 107:14 and break their **b.** in sunder. 4147
Ps 119:61 The **b.** of the wicked have robbed 2256
Pr 30:27 go they forth all of them by **b.**; 2683
Ec 7:26 and nets, and her hands as **b.**: 612
Isa 28:22 lest your **b.** be made strong: 4147
Isa 52:2 loose thyself from the **b.** of thy 4147
Isa 58:6 loose the bands of wickedness, to 2784
Jer 2:20 thy yoke, and burst thy **b.**; 4147
Eze 3:25 they shall put **b.** upon thee, and 5688
Eze 4:8 I will lay **b.** upon thee, and thou 5688
Eze 12:14 to help him, and all his **b.**; 102
Eze 17:21 with all his **b.** shall fall by the 102

Eze 34:27 have broken the **b.** of their yoke, 4133
Eze 38:6 Gomer, and all his **b.**; 102
Eze 38:6 the north quarters, and all his **b.**: 102
Eze 38:9 the land, thou, and all thy **b.**, 102
Eze 38:22 upon him, upon his **b.**, 102
Eze 39:4 of Israel, thou, and all thy **b.**, 102
Ho 11:4 of a man, with **b.** of love: 5688
Zec 11:7 Beauty, the other I called **B.**; 2256
Zec 11:14 asunder mine other staff, even **B.**, 2256
Lu 8:29 he brake the **b.**, and was driven *1199*
Ac 16:26 and every one's **b.** were loosed. *1199*
Ac 22:30 he loosed him from his **b.**, and *1199*
Ac 27:40 loosed the rudder **b.**, and hoised *2202*
Col 2:19 the body by joints and **b.** having *4886*

BANI (ba'-ni)
2Sa 23:26 Nathan of Zobah, **B.** the Gadite, 1137
1Ch 6:46 The son of **B.**, the son of Shamer, 1137
1Ch 9:4 the son of **B.**, of the children of 1137
Ezr 2:10 The children of **B.**, six hundred 1137
Ezr 10:29 sons of **B.**; Meshullam, and 1137
Ezr 10:34 Of the sons of **B.**; Maadai, Amram, 1137
Ezr 10:38 And **B.**, and Binnui, and Shimei, 1137
Ne 3:17 Rehum the son of **B.**. Next 1137
Ne 8:7 Jeshua, and **B.**, and Sherebiah, 1137
Ne 9:4 Levites, Jeshua, and **B.**, Kadmiel, 1137
Ne 9:4 **B.**, and Chenani, and cried 1137
Ne 9:5 and Kadmiel, **B.**, Hashabniah, 1137
Ne 10:13 Hodijah, **B.**, Beninu. 1137
Ne 10:14 Pahath-moab, Elam, Zatthu, **B.**, 1137
Ne 11:22 Uzzi the son of **B.**, the son of 1137

BANISHED
2Sa 14:13 doth not fetch home again his **b.**. 5080
2Sa 14:14 that his **b.** be not expelled 5080

BANISHMENT
Ezr 7:26 it be unto death, or to **b.**, 8331
La 2:14 false burdens and causes of **b.**. 4065

BANK See also BANKS.
Ge 41:17 I stood upon the **b.** of the river: 8193
De 4:48 is by the **b.** of the river Arnon, 8193
Jos 12:2 upon the **b.** of the river Arnon, 8193
Jos 13:9 is upon the **b.** of the river Arnon, 8193
Jos 13:16 is on the **b.** of the river Arnon, 8193
2Sa 20:15 cast up a **b.** against the city, 5550
2Ki 2:13 and stood by the **b.** of Jordan; 8193
2Ki 19:32 shield, nor cast a **b.** against it 5550
Isa 37:33 shields, nor cast a **b.** against it. 5550
Eze 47:7 at the **b.** of the river were very 8193
Eze 47:12 by the river upon the **b.** thereof, 8193
Da 12:5 this side of the **b.** of the river, 8193
Da 12:5 other on that side of the **b.** of 8193
Lu 19:23 **money into the b., that at my** *5132*

BANKS
Jos 3:15 overfloweth all his **b.** all the time 1415
Jos 4:18 flowed over all his **b.**, as they did 1415
1Ch 12:15 it had overflown all his **b.**; 1428
Isa 8:7 channels, and go over all his **b.** 1415
Da 8:16 man's voice between the b. of Ulai,

BANNER See also BANNERS.
Ps 60:4 given a **b.** to them that fear 5251
Ca 2:4 and his **b.** over me was love. 1714
Isa 13:2 Lift ye up a **b.** upon the high 5251

BANNERS
Ps 20:5 set up our **b.**: the Lord fulfil all 1713
Ca 6:4 terrible as an army with **b.** 1713
Ca 6:10 and terrible as an army with **b.**? 1713

BANQUET See also BANQUETING.
Es 5:4 Haman come this day unto the **b.** 4960
Es 5:5 the king and Haman came to the **b.** 4960
Es 5:6 said unto Esther at the **b.** wine, 4960
Es 5:8 the king and Haman come to the **b.** 4960
Es 5:12 come in with the king unto the **b.** 4960
Es 5:14 merrily with the king unto the **b.** 4960
Es 6:14 hasted to bring Haman unto the **b.** 4960
Es 7:1 the king and Haman came to **b.** 8354
Es 7:2 Esther on the second day at the **b.** 4960
Es 7:7 the king arising from the **b.** of 4960
Es 7:8 into the place of the **b.** of wine; 4960
Job 41:6 Shall the companions make a **b.** 3738
Da 5:10 his lord, came into the **b.** house: 4961
Am 6:7 the **b.** of them that stretched 4797

BANQUETING See also BANQUETINGS.
Ca 2:4 He brought me to the **b.** house, 3196

BANQUETINGS
1Pe 4:3 **b.**, and abominable idolatries: *4224*

BAPTISM See also BAPTISMS.
Mt 3:7 and Sadducees come to his **b.**, *908*
Mt 20:22 **the b. that I am baptized with?** *908*
Mt 20:23 **be baptized with the b. that I am** *908*
Mt 21:25 **The b. of John, whence was it?** *908*
Mk 1:4 preach the **b.** of repentance for *908*
Mk 10:38 **the b. that I am baptized with?** *908*
Mk 10:39 **with the b. that I am baptized** *908*
Mk 11:30 **The b. of John, was it from heaven,** *908*
Lu 3:3 preaching the **b.** of repentance *908*
Lu 7:29 being baptized with the **b.** of John. *908*
Lu 12:50 **I have a b. to be baptized with,** *908*
Lu 20:4 **The b. of John, was it from heaven,** *908*
Ac 1:22 Beginning from the **b.** of John, *908*
Ac 10:37 after the **b.** which John preached: *908*
Ac 13:24 the **b.** of repentance to all the people *908*
Ac 18:25 Lord, knowing only the **b.** of John. *908*
Ac 19:3 And they said, Unto John's **b.**. *908*
Ac 19:4 with the **b.** of repentance, saying *908*
Ro 6:4 buried with him by **b.** into death: *908*
Eph 4:5 One Lord, one faith, one **b.**, *908*
Col 2:12 Buried with him in **b.**, wherein *908*
1Pe 3:21 even **b.** doth also now save us *908*

BAPTISMS
Heb 6:2 Of the doctrine of **b.**, and of laying *909*

BAPTIST (bap'-tist) See also BAPTIST'S.
Mt 3:1 In those days came John the **B.**, *910*
Mt 11:11 **risen a greater than John the B** *910*
Mt 11:12 **from the days of John the B. until** *910*
Mt 14:2 This is John the **B.**; he is risen *910*
Mt 16:14 Some say that thou art John the **B.** *910*
Mt 17:13 he spake unto them of John the **B.**. *910*
Mk 6:14 That John the **B.** was risen from *907*
Mk 6:24 she said, The head of John the **B.**. *910*
Mk 6:25 a charger the head of John the **B.** *910*
Mk 8:28 they answered, John the **B.** *910*
Lu 7:20 John **B.** hath sent us unto thee, *910*
Lu 7:28 **greater prophet than John the B** *910*
Lu 7:33 **John the B. came neither eating** *910*
Lu 9:19 answering said, John the **B.**; *910*

BAPTIST'S (bap'-tists)
Mt 14:8 Give me here John **B.** head in *910*

BAPTIZE See also BAPTIZED; BAPTIZEST; BAPTIZETH; BAPTIZING.
Mt 3:11 I indeed **b.** you with water *907*
Mt 3:11 he shall **b.** you with the Holy Ghost, *907*
Mk 1:4 John did **b.** in the wilderness, *907*
Mk 1:8 he shall **b.** you with the Holy Ghost *907*
Lu 3:16 I indeed **b.** you with water; *907*
Lu 3:16 he shall **b.** you with the Holy Ghost *907*
Joh 1:26 saying, I **b.** with water: but *907*
Joh 1:33 he that sent me to **b.** with water, *907*
1Co 1:17 Christ sent me not to **b.**, but to *907*

BAPTIZED
Mt 3:6 And were **b.** of him in Jordan, *907*
Mt 3:13 Jordan unto John, to be **b.** of him. *907*
Mt 3:14 I have need to be **b.** of thee, and *907*
Mt 3:16 Jesus, when he was **b.**, went up *907*
Mt 20:22 **I shall drink of, and to be b.,** *907*
Mt 20:22 **the baptism that I am b. with?** *907*
Mt 20:23 **and be b. with the baptism** *907*
Mt 20:23 **that I am b. with:** *907*
Mk 1:5 all **b.** of him in the river of Jordan, *907*
Mk 1:8 I indeed have **b.** you with water: *907*
Mk 1:9 and was **b.** of John in Jordan. *907*
Mk 10:38 **and be b. with the baptism** *907*
Mk 10:38 **that I am b. with?** *907*
Mk 10:39 **and with the baptism that I am b.** *907*
Mk 10:39 **withal shall ye be b.** *907*
Mk 16:16 **believeth and is b. shall be saved;** *907*
Lu 3:7 came forth to be **b.** of him, *907*
Lu 3:12 Then came also publicans to be **b.**, *907*
Lu 3:21 when all the people were **b.**, it came *907*
Lu 3:21 that Jesus also being **b.**, *907*
Lu 7:29 being **b.** with the baptism of John. *907*
Lu 7:30 themselves, being not **b.** of him. *907*
Lu 12:50 **I have a baptism to be b. with:** *907*
Joh 3:22 there he tarried with them, and **b.**. *907*
Joh 3:23 and they came, and were **b.** *907*
Joh 4:1 Jesus made and **b.** more disciples *907*
Joh 4:2 (Though Jesus himself **b.** not, *907*
Joh 10:40 place where John at first **b.**; *907*
Ac 1:5 **John truly b. with water;** *907*
Ac 1:5 **ye shall be b. with the Holy Ghost** *907*
Ac 2:38 Repent, and be **b.** every one of you *907*
Ac 2:41 gladly received his word were **b.**: *907*
Ac 8:12 were **b.**, both men and women. *907*
Ac 8:13 he was **b.**, he continued with Philip, *907*
Ac 8:16 only they were **b.** in the name *907*
Ac 8:36 what doth hinder me to be **b.**? *907*
Ac 8:38 and the eunuch; and he **b.** him. *907*
Ac 9:18 forthwith, and arose, and was **b.** *907*
Ac 10:47 water, that these should not be **b.**, *907*
Ac 10:48 commanded them to be **b.** in the *907*
Ac 11:16 **John indeed b. with water;** *907*
Ac 11:16 **ye shall be b. with the Holy Ghost** *907*
Ac 16:15 when she was **b.**, and her household, *907*
Ac 16:33 was **b.**, he and all his, straightway. *907*
Ac 18:8 hearing believed, and were **b.**. *907*
Ac 19:3 Unto what then were ye **b.**? *907*
Ac 19:4 John verily **b.** with the baptism of *907*
Ac 19:5 heard this, they were **b.** in the name *907*
Ac 22:16 and be **b.**, and wash away thy sins, *907*
Ro 6:3 of us as were **b.** into Jesus Christ *907*
Ro 6:3 were **b.** into his death? *907*
1Co 1:13 or were ye **b.** in the name of Paul? *907*
1Co 1:14 I thank God that I **b.** none of you, *907*
1Co 1:15 say that I had **b.** in mine own name. *907*
1Co 1:16 I **b.** also the household of Stephanas: *907*
1Co 1:16 I know not whether I **b.** any other. *907*
1Co 10:2 were all **b.** unto Moses in the cloud *907*
1Co 12:13 For by one Spirit are we all **b.** into *907*
1Co 15:29 they do which are **b.** for the dead, *907*
1Co 15:29 why are they then **b.** for the dead? *907*
Ga 3:27 as have been **b.** into Christ have put *907*

BAPTIZEST
Joh 1:25 said unto him, Why **b.** thou then, *907*

BAPTIZETH
Joh 1:33 is he which **b.** with the Holy Ghost. *907*
Joh 3:26 behold, the same **b.**, and all men *907*

BAPTIZING
Mt 28:19 **b. them in the name of the Father** *907*
Joh 1:28 Jordan, where John was **b.** *907*
Joh 1:31 therefore am I come **b.** with water. *907*
Joh 3:23 John also was **b.** in AEnon *907*

BAR See also BARS.
Ex 26:28 And the middle **b.** in the midst of 1280
Ex 36:33 he made the middle **b.** to shoot 1280
Nu 4:10 skins, and shall put it upon a **b.** 4132
Nu 4:12 skins, and shall put them on a **b.** 4132
Jg 16:3 away with them, **b.** and all, and 1280
Ne 7:3 them shut the doors, and **b.** them: 270
Am 1:5 break also the **b.** of Damascus, 1280

BAR See BARABBAS; BAR-JESUS; BAR-JONAH; BARNABAS; BARSABAS; BARTHOLOMEW; BARTIMAEUS.

BARABBAS (ba-rab'-bas)
Mt 27:16 a notable prisoner, called **B.** *912*
Mt 27:17 **B.**, or Jesus which is called Christ? *912*
Mt 27:20 should ask **B.**, and destroy Jesus. *912*
Mt 27:21 release unto you? They said, **B.**. *912*
Mt 27:26 Then released he **B.** unto them: *912*
Mk 15:7 And there was one named **B.**, *912*
Mk 15:11 that he should rather release **B.** *912*
Mk 15:15 released **B.** unto them, and delivered *912*
Lu 23:18 this man, and release unto us **B.** *912*
Joh 18:40 Not this man, but **B.** *912*
Joh 18:40 Now **B.** was a robber, *912*

BARACHEL (bar'-ak-el)
Job 32:2 the wrath of Elihu the son of **B.** 1292
Job 32:6 Elihu the son of **B.** the Buzite 1292

BARACHIAS (bar'-ak-i'-as)
Mt 23:35 **Zacharias son of B., whom ye slew** *914*

BARAH See BETH-BARAH.

BARAK (ba'-rak)
Jg 4:6 and called **B.** the son of Abinoam 1301
Jg 4:8 **B.** said unto her, If thou wilt go 1301
Jg 4:9 and went with **B.** to Kedesh, 1301
Jg 4:10 **B.** called Zebulun and Naphtali to 1301
Jg 4:12 they shewed Sisera that **B.** the son 1301
Jg 4:14 Deborah said unto **B.**, Up; for this 1301
Jg 4:14 **B.** went down from mount Tabor, 1301
Jg 4:15 the edge of the sword before **B.**; 1301
Jg 4:16 But **B.** pursued after the chariots, 1301
Jg 4:22 behold, as **B.** pursued Sisera, 1301
Jg 5:1 Then sang Deborah and **B.** the son 1301

Jg 5:12 arise, **B.**, and lead thy captivity ... 1301
Jg 5:15 even Issachar, and also **B.**: he was ... 1301
Heb 11:32 to tell of Gedeon, and of **B.**, ... *913*

BARBARIAN See also BARBARIANS; BARBAROUS.
1Co 14:11 unto him that speaketh a **b.**, ... *915*
1Co 14:11 that speaketh shall be a **b.** unto me ... *915*
Col 3:11 **B.**, Scythian, bond nor free: ... *915*

BARBARIANS
Ac 28:4 when the **b.** saw the venomous ... *915*
Ro 1:14 to the Greeks, and to the **B.**; ... *915*

BARBAROUS
Ac 28:2 the **b.** people shewed us no little ... *915*

BARBED
Job 41:7 thou fill his skin with **b.** irons? ... 7905

BARBER'S
Eze 5:1 sharp knife, take thee a **b.** razor, ... 1532

BARE See also BAREFOOT; BAREST; FORBARE.
Ge 4:1 she conceived, and **b.** Cain, and ... 3205
Ge 4:2 she again **b.** his brother Abel ... 3205
Ge 4:17 she conceived, and **b.** Enoch: ... 3205
Ge 4:20 Adah **b.** Jabal: he was the father ... 3205
Ge 4:22 And Zillah, she also **b.** Tubal-cain, ... 3205
Ge 4:25 **b.** a son, and called his name Seth; ... 3205
Ge 6:4 and they **b.** children to them, ... 3205
Ge 7:17 increased, and **b.** up the ark, ... 5375
Ge 16:1 Abram's wife, **b.** him no children: ... 3205
Ge 16:15 And Hagar **b.** Abram a son: and ... 3205
Ge 16:15 his son's name, which Hagar **b.**, ... 3205
Ge 16:16 when Hagar **b.** Ishmael to Abram ... 3205
Ge 19:37 the firstborn **b.** a son, and called ... 3205
Ge 19:38 And the younger, she also **b.** a son, ... 3205
Ge 20:17 maidservants; and they **b.** children ... 3205
Ge 21:2 Sarah conceived, and **b.** Abraham a ... 3205
Ge 21:3 whom Sarah **b.** to him, Isaac ... 3205
Ge 22:24 she **b.** also Tebah, and Gaham, ... 3205
Ge 24:24 Milcah, which she **b.** unto Nahor ... 3205
Ge 24:36 wife **b.** a son to my master ... 3205
Ge 24:47 son, whom Milcah **b.** unto him: ... 3205
Ge 25:2 she **b.** him Zimran, and Jokshan, ... 3205
Ge 25:12 handmaid, **b.** unto Abraham: ... 3205
Ge 25:26 threescore years old when she **b.** ... 3205
Ge 29:32 And Leah conceived, and **b.** a son, ... 3205
Ge 29:33, 34,35 conceived again, and **b.** a ... 3205
Ge 30:1 saw that she **b.** Jacob no children, ... 3205
Ge 30:5 conceived, and **b.** Jacob a son ... 3205
Ge 30:7 maid conceived again, and **b.** Jacob ... 3205
Ge 30:10 Zilpah Leah's maid **b.** Jacob a son ... 3205
Ge 30:12 Leah's maid **b.** Jacob a second ... 3205
Ge 30:17 she conceived, and **b.** Jacob a fifth ... 3205
Ge 30:19 again, and **b.** Jacob the sixth son ... 3205
Ge 30:21 And afterwards she **b.** a daughter, ... 3205
Ge 30:23 And she conceived, and **b.** a son; ... 3205
Ge 31:8 then all the cattle **b.** speckled: ... 3205
Ge 31:8 then **b.** all the cattle ringstraked ... 3205
Ge 31:39 I **b.** the loss of it; of my hand ... 2398
Ge 34:1 which she **b.** unto Jacob, went ... 3205
Ge 36:4 Adah **b.** to Esau Eliphaz; ... 3205
Ge 36:4 and Bashemath **b.** Reuel; ... 3205
Ge 36:5 Aholibamah **b.** Jeush, and Jaalam, ... 3205
Ge 36:12 and she **b.** to Eliphaz Amalek: ... 3205
Ge 36:14 she **b.** to Esau Jeush, and Jaalam, ... 3205
Ge 38:3 And she conceived, and **b.** a son; ... 3205
Ge 38:4 she conceived again, and **b.** a son; ... 3205
Ge 38:5 yet again conceived, and **b.** a son; ... 3205
Ge 38:5 was at Chezib, when she **b.** him ... 3205
Ge 41:50 Poti-pherah priest of On **b.** unto ... 3205
Ge 44:27 Ye know that my wife **b.** me two ... 3205
Ge 46:15 she **b.** unto Jacob in Padan-aram, ... 3205
Ge 46:18 and these she **b.** unto Jacob, ... 3205
Ge 46:20 priest of On **b.** unto him ... 3205
Ge 46:25 and she **b.** these unto Jacob: ... 3205
Ex 2:2 the woman conceived, and **b.** a son: ... 3205
Ex 2:22 And she **b.** him a son, and he called ... 3205
Ex 6:20 and she **b.** him Aaron and Moses: ... 3205
Ex 6:23 and she **b.** him Nadab, and Abihu, ... 3205
Ex 6:25 and she **b.** him Phinehas: these are ... 3205
Ex 19:4 and how I **b.** you on eagles' wings, ... 5375
Le 13:45 and his head **b.**, and he shall put ... 6544
Le 13:55 whether it be **b.** within or ... 7146
Nu 13:23 and they **b.** it between two ... 5375
Nu 26:59 her mother **b.** to Levi in Egypt: ... 3205
Nu 26:59 and she **b.** unto Amram Aaron ... 3205
De 1:31 how that the Lord thy God **b.** thee, ... 5375
De 31:9 the sons of Levi, which **b.** the ark ... 5375
De 31:25 the Levites, which **b.** the ark ... 5375
Jos 3:15 they that **b.** the ark were come ... 5375
Jos 3:15 and the feet of the priests that **b.** ... 5375
Jos 3:17 the priests that **b.** the ark ... 5375
Jos 4:9 which **b.** the ark of the covenant ... 5375
Jos 4:10 the priest which **b.** the ark stood ... 5375
Jos 4:18 when the priests that **b.** the ark ... 5375
Jos 8:33 the Levites, which **b.** the ark ... 5375
Jg 3:18 the people that **b.** the present ... 5375
Jg 8:31 she also **b.** him a son, whose ... 3205
Jg 11:2 And Gilead's wife **b.** him sons; ... 3205
Jg 13:2 his wife was barren, and **b.** not ... 3205
Jg 13:24 And the woman **b.** a son, ... 3205
Ru 4:12 Pharez whom Tamar **b.** unto ... 3205
Ru 4:13 her conception and she **b.** a son ... 3205
1Sa 1:20 Hannah had conceived that she **b.** ... 3205
1Sa 2:21 she conceived, and **b.** three sons ... 3205
1Sa 14:1 unto the young man that **b.** his ... 5375
1Sa 14:6 the young man that **b.** his armour, ... 5375
1Sa 17:41 man that **b.** the shield went before ... 5375
2Sa 6:13 they that **b.** the ark of the Lord ... 5375
2Sa 11:27 became his wife, and **b.** him a ... 3205
2Sa 12:15 the child that Uriah's wife **b.** ... 3205
2Sa 12:24 and she **b.** a son, and he called ... 3205
2Sa 18:15 ten young men that **b.** Joab's ... 5375
2Sa 21:8 Aiah, whom she **b.** unto Saul, ... 3205
1Ki 1:6 his mother **b.** him after Absalom. ...
1Ki 5:15 and ten thousand that **b.** burdens, ... 5375
1Ki 9:23 five hundred and fifty which **b.** ... 7287
1Ki 10:2 camels that **b.** spices, and very ... 5375
1Ki 11:20 the sister of Tahpenes **b.** him ... 3205
1Ki 14:28 the guard **b.** them, and brought ... 5375
2Ki 4:17 the woman conceived, and **b.** a son ... 3205
2Ki 5:23 and they **b.** them before him ... 5375
1Ch 1:32 she **b.** Zimran, and Jokshan, ... 3205
1Ch 2:4 Tamar, his daughter in law, **b.** him ... 3205
1Ch 2:17 Abigail **b.** Amasa; and the father ... 3205
1Ch 2:19 Ephrath, which **b.** him Hur, ... 3205
1Ch 2:21 and she **b.** him Segub ... 3205
1Ch 2:24 then Abiah Hezron's wife **b.** him ... 3205
1Ch 2:29 and she **b.** him Ahban, and Molid ... 3205
1Ch 2:35 servant to wife; and she **b.** him ... 3205
1Ch 2:46 Ephah, Caleb's concubine, **b.** ... 3205
1Ch 2:48 Maachah, Caleb's concubine, **b.** ... 3205
1Ch 2:49 she **b.** also Shaaph the father ... 3205
1Ch 4:6 And Naarah **b.** him Ahuzam, and ... 3205
1Ch 4:9 saying, Because I **b.** him with ... 3205
1Ch 4:17 and she **b.** Miriam, and Shammai, ... 2029
1Ch 4:18 And his wife Jehudijah **b.** Jered ... 3205
1Ch 7:14 Ashriel, whom she **b.**; but his ... 3205
1Ch 7:14 concubine the Aramitess **b.** Machir ... 3205
1Ch 7:16 Maachah the wife of Machir **b.** a ... 3205
1Ch 7:18 his sister Hammoleketh **b.** Ishod, ... 3205
1Ch 7:23 she conceived, and **b.** a son, and he ... 3205
1Ch 12:24 children of Judah that **b.** shield ... 5375
1Ch 15:15 children of the Levites **b.** the ark ... 5375
1Ch 15:26 the Levites that **b.** the ark of the ... 5375
1Ch 15:27 and all the Levites that **b.** the ark, ... 5375
2Ch 8:10 two hundred and fifty, that **b.** rule ... 7287
2Ch 9:1 camels that **b.** spices and gold in ... 5375
2Ch 11:19 Which **b.** him children; Jeush, ... 3205
2Ch 11:20 which **b.** him Abijah, and Attai, ... 3205
2Ch 14:8 an army of men that **b.** targets ... 5375
2Ch 14:8 out of Benjamin, that **b.** shields ... 5375
Ne 4:17 and they that **b.** burdens, with the ... 5375
Ne 5:15 even their servants **b.** rule ... 7980
Pr 17:25 and bitterness to her that **b.** him ... 3205
Pr 23:25 she that **b.** thee shall rejoice ... 3205
Ca 6:9 is the choice one of her that **b.** her ... 3205
Ca 8:5 brought thee forth that **b.** thee ... 3205
Isa 8:3 she conceived, and **b.** a son ... 3205
Isa 22:6 Elam **b.** the quiver with chariots ... 5375
Isa 32:11 strip you, and make you **b.**, and ... 6209
Isa 47:2 make **b.** the leg, uncover the ... 2834
Isa 51:2 father, unto Sarah that **b.** you: ... 2342
Isa 52:10 Lord hath made **b.** his holy arm ... 2834
Isa 53:12 and he **b.** the sin of many, and ... 5375
Isa 63:9 and he **b.** them, and carried them ... 5190
Jer 13:22 discovered, and thy heels made **b.** ... 2554
Jer 16:3 concerning their mothers that **b.** ... 3205
Jer 20:14 day wherein my mother **b.** me be ... 3205
Jer 22:26 out, and thy mother that **b.** thee, ... 3205
Jer 49:10 I have made Esau **b.**, I have ... 2834
Jer 50:12 she that **b.** you shall be ashamed: ... 3205
Eze 12:7 I **b.** it upon my shoulder in their ... 5375
Eze 16:7 whereas thou wast naked and **b.** ... 6181
Eze 16:22 when thou wast naked and **b.**, ... 6181
Eze 16:39 jewels, and leave thee naked and **b.** ... 6181
Eze 19:11 the sceptres of them that **b.** rule, ... 4910
Eze 23:4 and they **b.** sons and daughters ... 3205
Eze 23:29 shall leave thee naked and **b.** ... 6181
Eze 23:37 their sons, whom they **b.** unto me, ... 3205
Ho 1:3 which conceived, and **b.** him a son ... 3205
Ho 1:6 she conceived again, and **b.** him a ... 3205
Ho 1:8 she conceived, and **b.** a son ... 3205
Joe 1:7 he hath made clean **b.**, and cast it ... 2834
Mt 8:17 our infirmities, and **b.** our ... *941*
Mk 14:56 For many **b.** false witness against ... *5576*
Mk 14:57 and **b.** false witness against him, ... *5576*
Lu 4:22 all **b.** him witness, and wondered ... *3140*
Lu 7:14 they that **b.** him stood still ... *941*
Lu 8:8 **and sprang up, and b. fruit an** ... *4160*
Lu 11:27 Blessed is the womb that **b.** thee, ... *941*
Lu 23:29 **and the wombs that never b.**, ... *1080*
Joh 1:15 John **b.** witness of him, and cried, ... *3140*
Joh 1:32 And John **b.** record, saying, I saw ... *3140*
Joh 1:34 I saw, and **b.** record that this ... *3140*
Joh 2:8 **of the feast. And they b. it** ... *5342*
Joh 5:33 **and he b. witness unto the truth** ... *3140*
Joh 12:6 had the bag, and **b.** what was put ... *941*
Joh 12:17 from the dead, **b.** record ... *3140*
Joh 19:35 he that saw it **b.** record, and his ... *3140*
Ac 15:8 **b.** them witness, giving them the ... *3140*
1Co 15:37 body that shall be, but **b.** grain, ... *1131*
1Pe 2:24 who his own self **b.** our sins in his ... *399*
Ro 1:2 Who **b.** record of the word of God, ... *3140*
Ro 22:2 which **b.** twelve manner of fruits, ... *4160*

BAREFOOT
2Sa 15:30 head covered, and he went **b.** ... 3182
Isa 20:2 he did so, walking naked and **b.** ... 3182
Isa 20:3 Isaiah hath walked naked and **b.** ... 3182
Isa 20:4 young and old, naked and **b.**, ... 3182

BAREST
1Ki 2:26 because thou **b.** the ark of the ... 5375
Isa 63:19 thou never **b.** rule over them ... 4910
Joh 3:26 to whom thou **b.** witness, behold, ... *3140*

BARHUMITE (bar'-hu-mite) See also BAHARUMITE.
2Sa 23:31 Azmaveth the **B.**, ... 1273

BARIAH (ba-ri'-ah)
1Ch 3:22 Hattush, and Igeal, and **B.**, and ... 1282

BAR-JESUS (bar'-je'-sus) See also ELYMAS.
Ac 13:6 a Jew, whose name was **B.** ... *919*

BAR-JONA (bar-jo'-nah) See also SIMON.
Mt 16:17 **Blessed art thou, Simon B.** ... *920*

BARK See also BARKED.
Isa 56:10 all dumb dogs, they cannot **b.**; ... 5024

BARKED
Joe 1:7 and **b.** my fig tree: he hath ... 7111

BARKOS (bar'-cos)
Ezr 2:53 The children of **B.**, the children ... 1302
Ne 7:55 The children of **B.**, ... 1302

BARLEY
Ex 9:31 the flax and the **b.** was smitten: ... 8184
Ex 9:31 for the **b.** was in the ear, ... 8184
Le 27:16 an homer of **b.** seed shall be valued ... 8184
Nu 5:15 tenth part of an ephah of **b.** meal; ... 8184
De 8:8 A land of wheat, and **b.**, and vines, ... 8184
Jg 7:13 and, lo, a cake of **b.** bread tumbled ... 8184
Ru 1:22 in the beginning of **b.** harvest ... 8184
Ru 2:17 and it was about an ephah of **b.** ... 8184
Ru 2:23 to glean unto the end of **b.** harvest ... 8184
Ru 3:2 he winnoweth **b.** to-night in the ... 8184
Ru 3:15 he measured six measures of **b.**, ... 8184
Ru 3:17 six measures of **b.** gave he me; ... 8184
2Sa 14:30 he hath **b.** there; go and set it on ... 8184
2Sa 17:28 wheat, and **b.**, and flour ... 8184
2Sa 21:9 beginning of **b.** harvest ... 8184
1Ki 4:28 **B.** also and straw for the horses ... 8184
2Ki 4:42 twenty loaves of **b.**, and full ears ... 8184
2Ki 7:1 two measures of **b.** for a shekel, ... 8184
2Ki 7:16 two measures of **b.** for a shekel, ... 8184
2Ki 7:18 saying, Two measures of **b.** for a ... 8184
1Ch 11:13 parcel of ground full of **b.**; ... 8184
2Ch 2:10 twenty thousand measures of **b.**, ... 8184
2Ch 2:15 and the **b.**, the oil, and the wine, ... 8184
2Ch 27:5 of wheat, and ten thousand of **b.**, ... 8184
Job 31:40 cockle instead of **b.**. The words ... 8184
Isa 28:25 and the appointed **b.** and the rie ... 8184

Jer 41:8 of wheat, and of **b.**, and of oil,........... 8184
Eze 4:9 unto thee wheat, and **b.**, and beans, ... 8184
Eze 4:12 thou shalt eat it as **b.** cakes, ... 8184
Eze 13:19 for handfuls of **b.**, and for pieces........ 8184
Eze 45:13 part of an ephah of an homer of **b.**: 8184
Ho 3:2 and for an homer of **b.**, ... 8184
Ho 3:2 and an half homer of **b.**: 8184
Joe 1:11 for the wheat and for the **b.**; 8184
Joh 6:9 which hath five **b.** loaves and two....... *2916*
Joh 6:13 the fragments of the five **b.** loaves, ... *2916*
Re 6:6 three measures of **b.** for a penny; *2915*

BARN See also BARNFLOOR; BARNS.
Job 39:12 seed, and gather it into thy **b.**?.......... 1637
Hag 2:19 Is the seed yet in the **b.**? 4035
Mt 13:30 **but gather the wheat into my b.**..... *596*
Lu 12:24 **neither have storehouse nor b.;**....... *596*

BARNABAS (bar'-na-bas) See also JOSES.
Ac 4:36 by the apostles was surnamed **B.**, ... *921*
Ac 9:27 But **B.** took him and brought him *921*
Ac 11:22 and they sent forth **B.**, that he............ *921*
Ac 11:25 Then departed **B.** to Tarsus, ... *921*
Ac 11:30 it to the elders by the hands of **B.**........ *921*
Ac 12:25 And **B.** and Saul returned from *921*
Ac 13:1 as **B.**, and Simeon that was called......... *921*
Ac 13:2 Separate me **B.** and Saul for the.......... *921*
Ac 13:7 called for **B.** and Saul, and desired....... *921*
Ac 13:43 proselytes followed Paul and **B.**; *921*
Ac 13:46 then Paul and **B.** waxed bold, ... *921*
Ac 13:50 persecution against Paul and **B.**, ... *921*
Ac 14:12 And they called **B.**, Jupiter; *921*
Ac 14:14 when the apostles, **B.** and Paul, ... *921*
Ac 14:20 he departed with **B.** to Derbe. *921*
Ac 15:2 When therefore Paul and **B.** had........... *921*
Ac 15:2 they determined that Paul and **B.**, ... *921*
Ac 15:12 and gave audience to **B.** and Paul, ... *921*
Ac 15:22 to Antioch with Paul and **B.**; *921*
Ac 15:25 with our beloved **B.** and Paul, ... *921*
Ac 15:35 also and **B.** continued in Antioch, ... *921*
Ac 15:36 some days after, Paul said unto **B.**,....... *921*
Ac 15:37 **B.** determined to take with them.......... *921*
Ac 15:39 and so **B.** took Mark, and sailed........... *921*
1Co 9:6 Or I only and **B.**, have not we *921*
Ga 2:1 up again to Jerusalem with **B.**, ... *921*
Ga 2:9 gave to me and **B.** the right hands....... *921*
Ga 2:13 that **B.** also was carried away *921*
Co 4:10 and Marcus, sister's son to **B.**, ... *921*

BARNEA (bar'-ne-ah) See KADESH-BARNEA.

BARNFLOOR
2Ki 6:27 the **b.**, or out of the winepress?......... 1637

BARNS
Pr 3:10 shall thy **b.** be filled with plenty, ... 618
Joe 1:17 the **b.** are broken down; 4460
Mt 6:26 **do they reap, nor gather into b.;**..... *596*
Lu 12:18 **I will pull down my b., and build**.... *596*

BARREL See also BARRELS.
1Ki 17:12 a handful of meal in a **b.**, and a.......... 3537
1Ki 17:14 The **b.** of meal shall not waste, ... 3537
1Ki 17:16 the barrel of meal wasted not, ... 3537

BARRELS
1Ki 18:33 Fill four **b.** with water, and pour 3537

BARREN
Ge 11:30 Sarai was **b.**; she had no child. 6135
Ge 25:21 for his wife, because she was **b.** 6135
Ge 29:31 but Rachel was **b.** 6135
Ex 23:26 nothing cast their young, nor be **b.**, ... 6135
De 7:14 shall not be male or female **b.**............ 6135
Jg 13:2 his wife was **b.**, and bare not. 6135
Jg 13:3 Behold now, thou art **b.**, ... 6135
1Sa 2:5 so that the **b.** hath born seven; 6135
2Ki 2:19 is naught, and the ground **b.** 7921
2Ki 2:21 any more death or **b.** land.................. 7921
Job 24:21 He evil entreateth the **b.** that........... 6135
Job 39:6 and the **b.** land his dwellings. 4420
Ps 113:9 maketh the **b.** woman to keep 6135
Pr 30:16 The grave; and the **b.** womb; 6115
Ca 4:2 and none is **b.** among them. 7909
Ca 6:6 there is not one **b.** among them. 7909
Isa 54:1 Sing, O **b.**, thou that didst not............ 6135
Joe 2:20 him into a land **b.** and desolate, ... 6723
Lu 1:7 because that Elisabeth was **b.**,........... *4723*
Lu 1:36 month with her, who was called **b.** *4723*
Lu 23:29 **Blessed are the b., and the wombs** .*4723*
Ga 4:27 Rejoice, thou **b.** that bearest not; *4723*
2Pe 1:8 neither be **b.** nor unfruitful in the......... *692*

BARRENNESS
Ps 107:34 A fruitful land into **b.** for the 4420

BARS
Ex 26:26 shalt make **b.** of shittim wood; 1280
Ex 26:27 **b.** for the boards of the other side...... 1280
Ex 26:27 **b.** for the boards of the side of 1280
Ex 26:29 rings of gold for places for the **b.** 1280
Ex 26:29 thou shalt overlay the **b.** with gold....... 1280
Ex 35:11 his **b.**, his pillars, and his sockets; 1280
Ex 36:31 And he made **b.** of shittim wood; 1280
Ex 36:32 five **b.** for the boards of the other 1280
Ex 36:32 **b.** for the boards of the tabernacle...... 1280
Ex 36:34 rings of gold to be places for the **b.**, ... 1280
Ex 36:34 and overlaid the **b.** with gold. 1280
Ex 39:33 his **b.**, and his pillars, and his 1280
Ex 40:18 put in the **b.** thereof, and reared up.... 1280
Nu 3:36 and the **b.** thereof, and the pillars....... 1280
Nu 4:31 boards of the tabernacle, and the **b.**.... 1280
De 3:5 with high walls, gates, and **b.**; 1280
1Sa 23:7 a town that hath gates and **b.**............. 1280
1Ki 4:13 cities with walls and brasen **b.** 1280
2Ch 8:5 cities, with walls, gates, and **b.**; 1280
2Ch 14:7 walls, and towers, gates, and **b.**.......... 1280
Ne 3:3 locks thereof, and the **b.** thereof. 1280
Ne 3:6 and the **b.** thereof. 1280
Ne 3:13 and the **b.** thereof, and a thousand 1280
Ne 3:14 and the **b.** thereof. 1280
Ne 3:15 and the **b.** thereof, and the wall of...... 1280
Job 17:16 shall go down to the **b.** of the pit, ... 905
Job 38:10 place, and set **b.** and doors, ... 1280
Job 40:18 his bones are like **b.** of iron. 4300
Ps 107:16 and cut the **b.** of iron in sunder. 1280
Ps 147:13 strengthened the **b.** of thy gates; 1280
Pr 18:19 are like the **b.** of a castle.................. 1280
Isa 45:2 and cut in sunder the **b.** of iron: 1280
Jer 49:31 which have neither gates nor **b.**, ... 1280
Jer 51:30 dwellingplaces; her **b.** are broken. 1280
La 2:9 hath destroyed and broken her **b.** 1280
Eze 38:11 having neither **b.** nor gates, ... 1280
Jon 2:6 the earth with her **b.** was about me.... 1280
Na 3:13 the fire shall devour thy **b.**................ 1280

BARSABAS (bar'-sab-as) See also JOSEPH; JUDAS; JUSTUS.
Ac 1:23 **B.**, who was surnamed Justus, ... *923*
Ac 15:22 namely, Judas surnamed **B.**, ... *923*

BARTHOLOMEW (bar-thol'-o-mew) See also NATHANAEL.
Mt 10:3 Philip, and **B.**; Thomas.......................*918*
Mk 3:18 Philip, and **B.**, and Matthew, ... *918*
Lu 6:14 Philip and **B.**, ...*918*
Ac 1:13 Philip, and Thomas, **B.**, ...*918*

BARTIMAEUS (bar-ti-me'-us)
Mk 10:46 blind **B.**, the son of Timaeus, sat......... *924*

BARUCH (ba'-rook)
Ne 3:20 After him **B.** the son of Zabbai 1263
Ne 10:6 Daniel, Ginnethon, **B.**, ... 1263
Ne 11:5 Maaseiah the son **B.**, the son of 1263
Jer 32:12 evidence of the purchase unto **B.** 1263
Jer 32:13 And I charged **B.** before them, ... 1263
Jer 32:16 evidence of the purchase unto **B.**......... 1263
Jer 36:4 Then Jeremiah called **B.** the son of..... 1263
Jer 36:4 and **B.** wrote from the mouth of 1263
Jer 36:5 Jeremiah commanded **B.**, saying,........ 1263
Jer 36:8 **B.** the son of Neriah did according 1263
Jer 36:10 Then read **B.** in the book the words... 1263
Jer 36:13 when **B.** read the book in the ears 1263
Jer 36:14 unto **B.**, saying Take in thine 1263
Jer 36:14 **B.** the son Neriah took the roll.......... 1263
Jer 36:15 So **B.** read it in their ears. 1263
Jer 36:16 and said unto **B.**, We will surely 1263
Jer 36:17 they asked **B.**, saying, Tell us now...... 1263
Jer 36:18 **B.** answered them, He pronounced..... 1263
Jer 36:19 Then said the princes unto **B.**, Go, ... 1263
Jer 36:26 to take **B.** the scribe and Jeremiah 1263
Jer 36:27 and the words which **B.** wrote at 1263
Jer 36:32 gave it to **B.** the scribe, the son........ 1263
Jer 43:3 **B.** the son of Neriah setteth thee....... 1263
Jer 43:6 Jeremiah the prophet, and **B.** the 1263
Jer 45:1 the prophet spake unto **B.**................ 1263
Jer 45:2 the God of Israel, unto thee, O **B.**; 1263

BARZILLAI (Bar-zil'-la-i)
2Sa 17:27 and **B.** the Gileadite of Rogelim, ... 1271
2Sa 19:31 **B.** the Gileadite came down from 1271
2Sa 19:32 Now **B.** was a very aged man, ... 1271
2Sa 19:33 the king said unto **B.**, Come thou....... 1271
2Sa 19:34 **B.** said unto the king, How long 1271
2Sa 19:39 king kissed **B.**, and blessed him; 1271
2Sa 21:8 brought up for Adriel the son of **B.** 1271
1Ki 2:7 shew kindness unto the sons of **B.** 1271
Ezr 2:61 children of Koz, the children of **B.**; 1271
Ezr 2:61 took a wife of the daughters of **B.**....... 1271
Ne 7:63 the children of **B.**, which took 1271
Ne 7:63 one of the daughters of **B.**................. 1271

BASE See also ABASE; BASER; BASES; BASEST; DEBASE.
2Sa 6:22 will be **b.** in mine own sight: 8217
1Ki 7:27 cubits was the length of one **b.**, ... 4350
1Ki 7:29 upon the ledges there was a **b.** 3653
1Ki 7:30 every **b.** had four brasen wheels, ... 4350
1Ki 7:31 work of the **b.**, a cubit and a............ 3653
1Ki 7:32 axletrees...were joined to the **b.** 4350
1Ki 7:34 the four corners of one **b.**:................ 4350
1Ki 7:34 undersetters were of the very **b.** 4350
1Ki 7:35 in the top of the **b.** was there a......... 4350
1Ki 7:35 and on the top of the **b.** the ledges..... 4350
Job 30:8 yea, children of **b.** men: 1097,8034
Isa 3:5 the **b.** against the honourable............. 7034
Eze 17:14 That the kingdom might be **b.**, ... 8217
Eze 29:14 they shall be there a **b.** kingdom. 8217
Zec 5:11 and set there upon her own **b.** 4369
Mal 2:9 and **b.** before all the people, ... 8217
1Co 1:28 And **b.** things of the world, ... *36*
2Co 10:1 who in presence am **b.** among *5011*

BASER
Ac 17:5 lewd fellows of the **b.** sort, ... *60*

BASES
1Ki 7:27 And he made ten **b.** of brass; 4350
1Ki 7:28 the work of the **b.** was on this........... 4350
1Ki 7:37 this manner he made the ten **b.** 4350
1Ki 7:38 upon every one of the ten **b.** one....... 4350
1Ki 7:39 he put five **b.** on the right side of....... 4350
1Ki 7:43 And the ten **b.**, ... 4350
1Ki 7:43 and ten lavers on the **b.**: 4350
2Ki 16:17 Ahaz cut off the border so the **b.** 4350
2Ki 25:13 and the **b.**, and the brasen sea 4350
2Ki 25:16 the **b.** which Solomon had made......... 4350
2Ch 4:14 He made also **b.**, ... 4350
2Ch 4:14 and lavers made he upon the **b.**; 4350
Ezr 3:3 they set the altar upon his **b.**; 4350
Jer 27:19 concerning the **b.**, and concerning....... 4369
Jer 52:17 and the **b.**, and the brasen sea 4350
Jer 52:20 bulls that were under the **b.**, ... 4350

BASEST
Eze 29:15 shall be the **b.** of the kingdoms; 8217
Da 4:17 setteth up over it the **b.** of men......... 8215

BASHAN (ba'-shan) See also BASHAN-HAVOTH-JAIR.
Nu 21:33 and went up by the way of **B.**............ 1316
Nu 21:33 and Og the king **B.** went out............. 1316
Nu 32:33 the kingdom of Og king of **B.**, ... 1316
De 1:4 and Og the king **B.**, which dwelt......... 1316
De 3:1 up the way to **B.**............................. 1316
De 3:1 and Og the king of **B.** came out.......... 1316
De 3:3 our hands Og also, the king of **B.**, ... 1316
De 3:4 Argob, the kingdom of Og in **B.**.......... 1316
De 3:10 all Gilead, and all **B.**, unto Salchah...... 1316
De 3:10 cities of the kingdom of Og in **B.** 1316
De 3:11 For only Og king of **B.** remained........ 1316
De 3:13 And the rest of Gilead, and all **B.**,....... 1316
De 3:13 all the region of Argob, with all **B.**, ... 1316
De 4:43 Golan in **B.**, of the Manassites. 1316
De 4:47 and the land of Og king of **B.**, ... 1316
De 29:7 Heshbon, and Og the king of **B.**, ... 1316
De 32:14 and rams of the breed of **B.**, ... 1316
De 33:22 lion's whelp: he shall leap from **B.**...... 1316
Jos 9:10 and the Og king of **B.**, which was at... 1316
Jos 12:4 And the coast of Og king **B.**, ... 1316
Jos 12:5 and in Salcah, and in all **B.**,............... 1316
Jos 13:11 and all mount Hermon, and all **B.**........ 1316
Jos 13:12 All the kingdom of Og in **B.**, ... 1316
Jos 13:30 Coast was from Mahanaim, all **B.**, ... 1316
Jos 13:30 all the kingdom of Og king of **B.**, ... 1316
Jos 13:30 the towns of Jair, which are in **B.**, ... 1316
Jos 13:31 cities of the kingdom of Og in **B.**, ... 1316
Jos 17:1 therefore he had Gilead and **B.**.......... 1316
Jos 17:5 besides the land of Gilead and **B.**, ... 1316
Jos 20:8 tribe of Gad, and Goan in **B.** out.......... 1316
Jos 21:6 half tribe of Manasseh in **B.**, ... 1316
Jos 21:27 of Manasseh they gave Golan in **B.** 1316

Jos 22:7 Moses had given possession in **B.** 1316
1Ki 4:13 the region of Argob, which is in **B.**, 1316
1Ki 4:19 Amorites, and of Og king of **B.**; 1316
2Ki 10:33 river Arnon, even Gilead and **B.**. 1316
1Ch 5:11 them, in the land of **B.** unto Salcah: 1316
1Ch 5:12 Jaanai, and Shaphat in **B.**. 1316
1Ch 5:16 dwelt in Gilead in **B.**, and in her 1316
1Ch 5:23 they increased from **B.** unto 1316
1Ch 6:62 the tribe of Manasseh in **B.**, 1316
1Ch 6:71 Golan in **B.** with her suburbs, 1316
Ne 9:22 and the land of Og king of **B.**. 1316
Ps 22:12 bulls of **B.** have beset me round. 1316
Ps 68:15 The hill of God is as the hill of **B.** 1316
Ps 68:15 a high hill as the hill of **B.**. 1316
Ps 68:22 I will bring again from **B.**, I will 1316
Ps 135:11 Amorites, and Og king of **B.**, 1316
Ps 136:20 Og the king of **B.**: for his mercy 1316
Isa 2:13 up, and upon all the oaks of **B.**, 1316
Isa 33:9 Sharon is like a wilderness; and **B.** 1316
Jer 22:20 cry; and lift up thy voice in **B.**, 1316
Jer 50:19 feed on Carmel and **B.**, and his 1316
Eze 27:6 of **B.** have they made thine oars; 1316
Eze 39:18 bullocks, all of them fatlings of **B.** 1316
Am 4:1 Hear this word, ye kine of **B.**, that 1316
Mic 7:14 let them feed in **B.** and Gilead, 1316
Na 1:4 **B.** languisheth, and Carmel, 1316
Zec 11:2 howl, O ye oaks of **B.**; for the 1316

BASHAN-HAVOTH-JAIR (ba'''-shan-ha''-voth-ha'-ur)
De 3:14 own name, **B.**, unto this day. 1316,2334

BASHEMATH (bash'-e-math) See also BASMATH.
Ge 26:34 and **B.** the daughter of Elon 1315
Ge 36:3 **B.** Ishmael's daughter, sister of 1315
Ge 36:4 Esau Eliphaz; and **B.** bare Reuel; 1315
Ge 36:10 the son of **B.** the wife of Esau. 1315
Ge 36:13 were the sons of **B.** Esau's wife. 1315
Ge 36:17 are the sons of **B.** Esau's wife 1315

BASIN See BASON.

BASKET See also BASKETS.
Ge 40:17 And in the uppermost **b.** there 5536
Ge 40:17 birds did eat them out of the **b.** 5536
Ex 29:3 thou shalt put them into one **b.**, 5536
Ex 29:3 and bring them in the **b.**, 5536
Ex 29:23 wafer out of the **b.** of unleavened 5536
Ex 29:32 and the bread that is in the **b.**, 5536
Le 8:2 and a **b.** of unleavened bread: 5536
Le 8:26 out of the **b.** of unleavened bead, 5536
Le 8:31 that is in the **b.** of consecrations, 5536
Nu 6:15 And a **b.** of unleavened bread, 5536
Nu 6:17 with the **b.** of unleavened bread: 5536
Nu 6:19 one unleavened cake out of the **b.**, 5536
De 26:2 shalt put it in a **b.**, and shalt go 2935
De 26:4 the priest shall take the **b.** out of 2935
De 28:5 Blessed shall be thy **b.** and thy 2935
De 28:17 Cursed shall be thy **b.** and thy 2935
Jg 6:19 the flesh he put in a **b.**, and he 5536
Jer 24:2 One **b.** had very good figs, 1731
Jer 24:2 other **b.** had very naughty figs, 1731
Am 8:1 behold a **b.** of summer fruit 3619
Am 8:2 And I said, A **b.** of summer fruit. 3619
Ac 9:25 let him down by the wall in a **b.** *4711*
2Co 11:33 in a **b.** was I let down by the wall, *4553*

BASKETS
Ge 40:16 I had three white **b.** on my head: 5536
Ge 40:18 The three **b.** are three days: 5536
2Ki 10:7 put their heads in **b.**, and sent 1731
Jer 6:9 as a grapegatherer into the **b.**. 5552
Jer 24:1 two figs were set before the 1736
Mt 14:20 that remained twelve **b.** full. *2894*
Mt 15:37 meat that was left seven **b.** full. *4711*
Mt 16:9 **and how many b. ye took up?** *2894*
Mt 16:10 **and how many b. ye took up?** *4711*
Mk 6:43 twelve **b.** full of the fragments, *2894*
Mk 8:8 meat that was left seven **b.**. *4711*
Mk 8:19 **how many b. full of fragments** *2894*
Mk 8:20 **how many b. full of fragments** *4711*
Lu 9:17 remained to them twelve **b.**. *2894*
Joh 6:13 and filled twelve **b.** with the *2894*

BASMATH (bas'-math) See also BASHEMATH.
1Ki 4:15 took **B.** the daughter of Solomon. 1315

BASON See also BASONS.
Ex 12:22 in the blood that is in the **b.**, 5592
Ex 12:22 with the blood that is in the **b.**; 5592
1Ch 28:17 gave gold by weight for every **b.**; 3713
1Ch 28:17 silver by weight for every **b.** of 3713
Joh 13:5 that he poureth water into a **b.**, *3537*

BASONS
Ex 24:6 half of the blood, and put it in **b.**; 101
Ex 27:3 ashes, and his shovels, and his **b.**, 4219
Ex 38:3 the shovels, and the **b.**, and the 4219
Nu 4:14 the shovels, and the **b.**, all the 4219
2Sa 17:28 beds, and **b.**, and earthen vessels, 5592
1Ki 7:40 the shovels, and the **b.**. So Hiram 4219
1Ki 7:45 and the **b.**: and all these vessels, 4219
1Ki 7:50 the snuffers, and the **b.**, and the 4219
2Ki 12:13 bowls of silver, snuffers, **b.**, 4219
1Ch 28:17 for the golden **b.** he gave gold by 3713
2Ch 4:8 he made an hundred **b.** of gold. 4219
2Ch 4:11 pots, and the shovels, and the **b.**. 4219
2Ch 4:22 the snuffers, and the **b.**, and the 4219
Ezr 1:10 Thirty **b.** of gold, 3713
Ezr 1:10 silver **b.** of second sort 3713
Ezr 8:27 Also twenty **b.** of gold, of a 3713
Ne 7:70 thousand drams of gold, fifty **b.**, 4219
Jer 52:19 the **b.**, and the firepans, and the 5592

BASTARD See also BASTARDS.
De 23:2 A **b.** shall not enter into the 4464
Zec 9:6 and a **b.** shall dwell in Ashdod, 4464

BASTARDS
Heb 12:8 then are ye **b.**, not sons. *3541*

BAT See also BATS.
Le 11:19 kind, and the lapwing, and the **b.**. 5847
De 14:18 the lapwing, and the **b.**. 5847

BATH See also BATHS.
Isa 5:10 of vineyard shall yield one **b.**, 1324
Eze 45:10 a just ephah, and a just **b.**. 1324
Eze 45:11 the **b.** shall be of one measure, 1324
Eze 45:11 that the **b.** may contain 1324
Eze 45:14 the **b.** of oil, ye shall 1324
Eze 45:14 offer the tenth part of a **b.** 1324

BATH See BATH-RABBIM; BATH-SHEBA; BATH-SHUA.

BATHE See also BATHED.
Le 15:5 and **b.** himself in water, and be 7364
Le 15:6 wash his clothes, and **b.** himself 7364
Le 15:7 **b.** himself in water, and be unclean 7364
Le 15:8 wash his clothes, and **b.** himself 7364
Le 15:10 **b.** himself in water, and be unclean 7364
Le 15:11 wash his clothes, and **b.** himself 7364
Le 15:13 and **b.** his flesh in running water. 7364
Le 15:18 shall both **b.** themselves in water 7364
Le 15:21 wash his clothes, and **b.** himself 7364
Le 15:22 **b.** himself in water, and be unclean 7364
Le 15:27 wash his clothes, and **b.** himself 7364
Le 16:26 his flesh in water, and afterward 7364
Le 16:28 clothes, and **b.** his flesh in water, 7364
Le 17:15 **b.** himself in water, and be unclean 7364
Le 17:16 nor **b.** his flesh; 7364
Nu 19:7 he shall **b.** his flesh in water, 7364
Nu 19:8 **b.** his flesh in water, and shall be 7364
Nu 19:19 clothes, and **b.** himself in water, 7364

BATHED
Isa 34:5 my sword shall be **b.** in heaven: 7301

BATH-RABBIM (bath-rab'-bim)
Ca 7:4 Heshbon, by the gate of **B.**: thy 1337

BATHS
1Ki 7:26 it contained two thousand **b.**. 1324
1Ki 7:38 one laver contained forty **b.**: 1324
2Ch 2:10 twenty thousand **b.** of wine, 1324
2Ch 2:10 and twenty thousand **b.** of oil. 1324
2Ch 4:5 received and held three thousand **b.** 1324
Ezr 7:22 and to an hundred **b.** of wine, 1325
Ezr 7:22 and to an hundred **b.** of oil, 1324
Eze 45:14 an homer of ten **b.**; 1324
Eze 45:14 for ten **b.** are an homer. 1324

BATH-SHEBA (bath'-she-bah) See also BATH-SHUA.
2Sa 11:3 one said, Is not this **B.**, the 1339
2Sa 12:24 David comforted **B.** his wife, 1339
1Ki 1:11 Nathan spake unto **B.** the 1339
1Ki 1:15 And **B.** went in unto the king 1339
1Ki 1:16 And **B.** bowed, and did obeisance 1339
1Ki 1:28 answered and said, Call me **B.**. 1339
1Ki 1:31 Then **B.** bowed with her face to 1339
1Ki 2:13 came to **B.** the mother of Solomon. 1339
1Ki 2:18 And **B.** said, Well; I will speak 1339
1Ki 2:19 **B.** therefore went unto king 1339
Ps 51:*title* him, after he had gone in to **B.**. 1339

BATH-SHUA (bath'-shu-ah) See also BATH-SHEBA.
1Ch 3:5 Solomon, four, of **B.** the daughter 1340

BATS
Isa 2:20 to the moles and to the **b.**; 5847

BATTERED
2Sa 20:15 **b.** the wall, to throw it down. 7843

BATTERING
Eze 4:2 set **b.** rams against it
Eze 21:22 appoint **b.** rams against the gates.

BATTERING-RAM See BATTERING and RAM.

BATTLE See also BATTLES.
Ge 14:8 they joined **b.** with them in the 4421
Nu 21:33 all his people, to the **b.** at Edrei. 4421
Nu 31:14 which came from the **b.**. 6635,4421
Nu 31:21 men of war which went to the **b.**, 4421
Nu 31:27 upon them who went out to **b.**, 6635
Nu 31:28 men of war which went out to **b.** 6635
Nu 32:27 before the Lord to **b.**, as my lord 4421
Nu 32:29 man armed to **b.**, before the Lord, 4421
De 2:9 neither contend with them in **b.** 4421
De 2:24 and contend with him in **b.**. 4421
De 3:1 and all his people, to **b.** at Edrei. 4421
De 20:1 When thou goest out to **b.** against 4421
De 20:2 ye are come nigh unto the **b.**, 4421
De 20:3 ye approach this day unto **b.** 4421
De 20:5,6 his house, lest he die in the **b.**, 4421
De 20:7 lest he die in the **b.**, and another 4421
De 29:7 came out against us unto **b.**, 4421
Jos 4:13 unto **b.**, to the plains of Jericho 4421
Jos 8:14 went out against Israel to **b.**, 4421
Jos 11:19 of Gibeon: all other they took in **b.** 4421
Jos 11:20 should come against Israel in **b.**, 4421
Jos 22:33 to go up against them in **b.**, to 6635
Jg 8:13 the son of Joash returned from **b.** 4421
Jg 20:14 unto Gibeah, to go out to **b.** 4421
Jg 20:18 of us shall go up first to the **b.** 4421
Jg 20:20 the men of Israel went out to **b.** 4421
Jg 20:22 and set their **b.** again in array 4421
Jg 20:23 Shall I go up again to **b.** 4421
Jg 20:28 Shall I yet again go out to **b.** 4421
Jg 20:34 of all Israel, and the **b.** was sore: 4421
Jg 20:39 the men of Israel retired in the **b.**, 4421
Jg 20:39 as in the first **b.**. 4421
Jg 20:42 but the **b.** overtook them; and 4421
1Sa 4:1 out against the Philistines to **b.**, 4421
1Sa 4:2 they joined **b.**, Israel was smitten 4421
1Sa 7:10 the Philistines drew near to **b.** 4421
1Sa 13:22 So it came to pass in the day of **b.**, 4421
1Sa 14:20 themselves, and they came to the **b.** 4421
1Sa 14:22 followed hard after them in the **b.**, 4421
1Sa 14:23 the **b.** passed over unto Beth-aven. 4421
1Sa 17:1 together their armies to **b.**, 4421
1Sa 17:2 and set the **b.** in array against 4421
1Sa 17:8 come out to set your **b.** in array? 4421
1Sa 17:13 went and followed Saul to the **b.** 4421
1Sa 17:13 three sons that went to the **b.** 4421
1Sa 17:20 the fight, and shouted for the **b.**. 4421
1Sa 17:21 had put the **b.** in array,
1Sa 17:28 that thou mightest see the **b.**. 4421
1Sa 17:47 for the **b.** is the Lord's and he 4421
1Sa 26:10 he shall descend into **b.**, and perish. 4421
1Sa 28:1 thou shalt go out with me to **b.**, 4264
1Sa 29:4 not go down with us to **b.**, 4421
1Sa 29:4 lest in the **b.** he be an adversary 4421
1Sa 29:9 He shall not go up with us to the **b.**. 4421
1Sa 30:24 part is that goeth down to the **b.**, 4421
1Sa 31:3 the **b.** went sore against Saul, 4421
2Sa 1:4 the people are fled from the **b.**, 4421
2Sa 1:25 fallen in the midst of the **b.**! 4421
2Sa 2:17 there was a very sore **b.** that day; 4421
2Sa 3:30 brother Asahel at Gibeon in the **b.** 4421
2Sa 10:8 put the **b.** in array at the entering 4421
2Sa 10:9 Joab saw that the front of the **b.** 4421
2Sa 10:13 unto the **b.** against the Syrians: 4421
2Sa 11:1 the time when kings go forth to **b.**,
2Sa 11:15 in the forefront of the hottest **b.**, 4421
2Sa 11:25 make thy **b.** more strong against 4421
2Sa 17:11 go to **b.** in thine own person. 7128
2Sa 18:6 **b.** was in the wood of Ephraim; 4421
2Sa 18:8 the **b.** was there scattered 4421
2Sa 19:3 steal away when they flee in **b.** 4421
2Sa 19:10 anointed over us, is dead in **b.** 4421

2Sa 21:17 go no more out with us to **b.**, 4421
2Sa 21:18 that there was again a **b.** with the 4421
2Sa 21:19 there was again a **b.** in Gob 4421
2Sa 21:20 And there was yet a **b.** in Gath, 4421
2Sa 22:40 girded me with strength to **b.** 4421
2Sa 23:9 gathered together to **b.**, and the 4421
1Ki 8:44 go out to **b.** against their enemy, 4421
1Ki 20:14 Who shall order the **b.**? And he 4421
1Ki 20:29 the seventh day the **b.** was joined: 4421
1Ki 20:39 went out into the midst of the **b.**; 4421
1Ki 22:4 Wilt thou go with me to **b.** 4421
1Ki 22:6 I go against Ramoth-gilead to **b.**, 4421
1Ki 22:15 go against Ramoth-gilead to **b.**, 4421
1Ki 22:30 enter into the **b.**; but put thou on 4421
1Ki 22:30 himself, and went into the **b.** 4421
1Ki 22:35 the **b.** increased that day: and the 4421
2Ki 3:7 go with me against Moab to **b.**? 4421
2Ki 3:26 the king of Moab saw that the **b.** 4421
1Ch 5:20 they cried to God in the **b.**, and he 4421
1Ch 7:11 fit to go out for war and **b.** 4421
1Ch 7:40 were apt to the war and to **b.** 4421
1Ch 10:3 the **b.** went sore against Saul, 4421
1Ch 11:13 were gathered together to **b.**, 4421
1Ch 12:8 men of war fit for the **b.**, that 4421
1Ch 12:19 Philistines against Saul to **b.** 4421
1Ch 12:33 Zebulun, such as went forth to **b.**, 6635
1Ch 12:36 of Asher, such as went forth to **b.**, 6635
1Ch 12:37 of instruments of war for the **b.**, 4421
1Ch 14:15 then thou shalt go out to **b.**: 4421
1Ch 19:7 from their cities, and came to **b.** 4421
1Ch 19:9 came out, and put the **b.** in array 4421
1Ch 19:10 Joab saw that the **b.** was set 4421
1Ch 19:14 before the Syrians unto the **b.**; 4421
1Ch 19:17 set the **b.** in array against them.
1Ch 19:17 David and put the **b.** in array 4421
1Ch 20:1 the time that kings go out to **b.**,
2Ch 13:3 Abijah set the **b.** in array with an 4421
2Ch 13:3 Jeroboam also set the **b.** in array 4421
2Ch 13:14 the **b.** was before and behind: 4421
2Ch 14:10 set the **b.** in array in the valley 4421
2Ch 18:5 we go to Ramoth-gilead to **b.**, 4421
2Ch 18:14 shall we go to Ramoth-gilead to **b.**, 4421
2Ch 18:29 myself, and will go to the **b.**; 4421
2Ch 18:29 himself, and they went to the **b.** 4421
2Ch 18:34 And the **b.** increased that day: 4421
2Ch 20:1 came against Jehoshaphat to **b.** 4421
2Ch 20:15 for the **b.** is not yours, but God's 4421
2Ch 20:17 shall not need to fight in this **b.**
2Ch 25:8 will go, do it, be strong for the **b.** 4421
2Ch 25:13 they should not go with him to **b.**, 4421
Job 15:24 him, as a king ready to the **b.** 3593
Job 38:23 against the day of **b.** and war? 7128
Job 39:25 he smelleth the **b.** afar off, 4421
Job 41:8 remember the **b.**, do no more. 4421
Ps 18:39 me with strength unto the **b.** 4421
Ps 24:8 mighty, the Lord mighty in **b.** 4421
Ps 55:18 my soul in peace from the **b.** 7128
Ps 76:3 shield, and the sword, and the **b.** 4421
Ps 78:9 turned back in the day of **b.** 7128
Ps 89:43 not made him to stand in the **b.** 4421
Ps 140:7 covered my head in the day of **b.** 5402
Pr 21:31 is prepared against the day of **b.** 4421
Ec 9:11 nor the **b.** to the strong, neither 4421
Isa 9:5 For every **b.** of the warrior is 5430
Isa 13:4 mustereth the host of the **b.** 4421
Isa 22:2 with the sword, nor dead in **b.** 4421
Isa 27:4 and thorns against me in **b.**? 4421
Isa 28:6 strength to them that turn the **b.** 4421
Isa 42:25 the strength of **b.**: and it hath set 4421
Jer 8:6 as the horse rusheth into the **b.** 4421
Jer 18:21 men be slain be the sword in **b.** 4421
Jer 46:3 and shield, and draw near to **b.** 4421
Jer 49:14 against her, and rise up to the **b.** 4421
Jer 50:22 A sound of **b.** is in the land, 4421
Jer 50:42 like a man to the **b.**, against thee, 4421
Jer 51:20 Thou art my **b.** axe and weapons 4661
Eze 7:14 none goeth to the **b.**: for my 4421
Eze 13:5 to stand in the **b.** in the day 4421
Da 11:20 neither in anger, nor in **b.** 4421
Da 11:25 stirred up to **b.** with a very great 4421
Hos 1:7 by bow, nor by sword, nor by **b.** 4421
Hos 2:18 the bow and the sword and the **b.** 4421
Hos 10:9 in Gibeah against the children 4421
Hos 10:14 spoiled Beth-arbel in the day of **b.** 4421
Joe 2:5 a strong people set in **b.** array 4421
Am 1:14 with shouting in the day of **b.** 4421
Ob 1 let us rise up against her in **b.** 4421
Zec 9:10 and the **b.** bow shall be cut off: 4421
Zec 10:3 them as his goodly horse in the **b.** 4421
Zec 10:4 out of him the **b.** bow, out of him 4421
Zec 10:5 down their enemies…in the **b.** 4421
Zec 14:2 nations against Jerusalem to **b.**; 4421
Zec 14:3 when he fought in the day of **b.** 7128
1Co 14:8 shall prepare himself to the **b.**? *4171*
Rev 9:7 horses prepared unto **b.**; and on *4171*
Rev 9:9 of many horses running to **b.** *4171*
Rev 16:14 to the **b.** of that great day of God *4171*
Rev 20:8 to gather them together to **b.**: *4171*

BATTLE-AXE See BATTLE and AX.

BATTLE-BOW See BATTLE and BOW.

BATTLEMENT See also BATTLEMENTS.
De 22:8 thou shalt make a **b.** for thy roof 4624

BATTLEMENTS
Jer 5:10 take away her **b.**; for they are 5189

BATTLES
1Sa 8:20 go out before us, and fight our **b.** 4421
1Sa 18:17 fight the Lord's **b.** For Saul 4421
1Sa 25:28 my lord fighteth the **b.** of the Lord, 4421
1Ch 26:27 spoils won in **b.** did they dedicate 4421
2Ch 32:8 and to fight our **b.** And the people 4421
Isa 30:32 and in **b.** of shaking will he fight 4421

BAVAI (bav'-a-i)
Ne 3:18 **B.** the son of Henadad, the ruler 942

BAY
Jos 15:2 the **b.** that looketh southward: 3956
Jos 15:5 the **b.** of the sea at the uttermost 3956
Jos 18:19 the north **b.** of the salt sea 3956
Ps 37:35 himself like a green **b.** tree 249
Zec 6:3 fourth chariot grisled and **b.** horses. 554
Zec 6:7 And the **b.** went forth, and sought 554

BAY-TREE See BAY and TREE.

BAZ See MAHER-SHALAL-HASH-BAZ.

BAZLITH (baz-'lith) See also BAZLUTH.
Ne 7:54 the children of **B.**, the children 1213

BAZLUTH (baz'-luth) See also BAZLITH.
Ezr 2:52 the children of **B.**, the children 1213

BDELLIUM (del'-le-um)
Ge 2:12 there is **b.** and the onyx stone 916
Nu 11:7 colour thereof as the colour of **b.** 916

BE See in the APPENDIX; also ALBEIT; AM; ARE; ART; BECOME; BEEN; BEING; HOWBEIT; IS; WAS; WERE; WERT.

BEACON
Isa 30:17 left as a **b.** upon the top of a 8650

BEALIAH (be-a-li'-ah)
1Ch 12:5 Eluzai, and Jerimoth, and **B.** 1183

BEALOTH (be'-a-loth) See also ALOTH.
Jos 15:24 Ziph, and Telem, and **B.** 1175

BEAM See also BEAMS.
Jg 16:14 went away with the pin of the **b.**, 708
1Sa 17:7 of his spear was like a weaver's **b.**; 4500
2Sa 21:19 whose spear was like a weaver's **b.** 4500
1Ki 7:6 the thick **b.** were before them. 5646
2Ki 6:2 take thence every man a **b.**, and 6982
2Ki 6:5 as one was felling a **b.**, the axe head 6982
1Ch 11:23 was a spear like a weaver's **b.** 4500
1Ch 20:5 spear staff was like a weaver's **b.** 4500
Hab 2:11 **b.** out of the timber shall answer 3714
Mt 7:3 **considerest not the b. that is in** *1385*
Mt 7:4 **behold, a b. is in thine own eye?** *1385*
Mt 7:5 **cast out b. out of thine own eye;** *1385*
Lu 6:41 **perceivest not the b. that is in** *1385*
Lu 6:42 **beholdest not the b. that is in** *1385*
Lu 6:42 **cast out first the b. out of thine** *1385*

BEAMS
1Ki 6:6 that the **b.** should not be fastened
1Ki 6:9 covered the house with **b.** and 1356
1Ki 6:36 stone, and a row of cedar **b.** 3773
1Ki 7:2 with cedar **b.** upon the pillars. 3773
1Ki 7:3 with cedar above upon the **b.**, 6763
1Ki 7:12 a row of cedar **b.**, both for the 3773
2Ch 3:7 the **b.**, the posts, and the walls 6982
Ne 2:8 give me timber to make **b.** for the 7136
Ne 3:3 who also laid the **b.** thereof, and 7136
Ne 3:6 they laid the **b.** thereof, and set up 7136
Ps 104:3 Who layeth the **b.** of his chambers 7136
Ca 1:17 The **b.** of our house are cedar, 6982

BEANS
2Sa 17:28 flour, and parched corn, and **b.** 6321
Eze 4:9 barley, and **b.**, and lentiles, 6321

BEAR See also BARE; BEAREST; BEARETH; BEARING; BEARS; FORBEAR.
Ge 4:13 is greater than I can **b.** 5375
Ge 13:6 the land was not able to **b.** them. 5375
Ge 16:11 art with child, and shalt **b.** a son. 3205
Ge 17:17 Sarah, that is ninety years old, **b.**? 3205
Ge 17:19 Sarah thy wife shall **b.** thee a son 3205
Ge 17:21 Sarah shall **b.** unto thee at this set 3205
Ge 18:13 Shall I of a surety **b.** a child, 3205
Ge 22:23 these eight Milcah did **b.** to Nahor, 3205
Ge 30:3 and she shall **b.** upon my knees, 3205
Ge 36:7 were strangers could not **b.** them 5375
Ge 43:9 then let me **b.** the blame forever: 2398
Ge 44:32 then I shall **b.** the blame to my 2398
Ge 49:15 and bowed his shoulder to **b.**, 5445
Ex 18:22 shall **b.** the burden with thee. 5375
Ex 20:16 Thou shalt not **b.** false witness. 6030
Ex 25:27 places of the staves to **b.** the table. 5375
Ex 27:7 the two sides of the altar, to **b.** it. 5375
Ex 28:12 and Aaron shall **b.** their names 5375
Ex 28:29 And Aaron shall **b.** the names 5375
Ex 28:30 and Aaron shall **b.** the judgment 5375
Ex 28:38 that Aaron may **b.** the iniquity 5375
Ex 28:43 that they **b.** not iniquity, and die: 5375
Ex 30:4 for the staves to **b.** it withal. 5375
Ex 37:5 the sides of the ark, to **b.** the ark. 5375
Ex 37:14 for the staves to **b.** the table. 5375
Ex 37:15 them with gold, to **b.** in the table. 5375
Ex 37:27 for the staves to **b.** it withal. 5375
Ex 38:7 sides of the altar, to **b.** it withal: 5375
Le 5:1 it, then he shall **b.** his iniquity. 5375
Le 5:17 guilty, and shall **b.** his iniquity. 5375
Le 7:18 eateth of it shall **b.** his iniquity. 5375
Le 10:17 **b.** the iniquity of the congregation, 5375
Le 12:5 But if she **b.** a maid child, 3205
Le 16:22 And the goat shall **b.** upon him 5375
Le 17:16 flesh; then he shall **b.** his iniquity. 5375
Le 19:8 every one that eateth it shall **b.** his 5375
Le 19:18 nor **b.** any grudge against the 5201
Le 20:17 nakedness; he shall **b.** his 5375
Le 20:19 they shall **b.** their iniquity. 5375
Le 20:20 they shall **b.** their sin; they shall 5375
Le 22:9 lest they **b.** sin for it, and die 5375
Le 22:16 Or suffer them to **b.** the iniquity 5375
Le 24:15 curseth his God shall **b.** his sin. 5375
Nu 1:50 they shall **b.** the tabernacle, and 5375
Nu 4:15 sons of Kohath shall come to **b.** it: 5375
Nu 4:25 And they shall **b.** the curtains of 5375
Nu 5:31 this woman shall **b.** her iniquity. 5375
Nu 7:9 should **b.** upon their shoulders. 5375
Nu 9:13 season, that man shall **b.** his sin. 5375
Nu 11:14 I am not able to **b.** all this people 5375
Nu 11:17 shall **b.** the burden of the people 5375
Nu 11:17 that thou **b.** it not thyself alone. 5375
Nu 14:27 how long shall I **b.** with this evil
Nu 14:33 years, and **b.** your whoredoms, 5375
Nu 14:34 shall ye **b.** your iniquities, even 5375
Nu 18:1 **b.** the iniquity of the sanctuary: 5375
Nu 18:1 **b.** the iniquity of your priesthood. 5375
Nu 18:22 congregation, lest they **b.** sin, and 5375
Nu 18:23 and they shall **b.** their iniquity: 5375
Nu 18:32 ye shall **b.** no sin by reason of it, 5375
Nu 30:15 them; then he shall **b.** her iniquity 5375
De 1:9 I am not able to **b.** you myself. 5375
De 1:12 I myself alone **b.** your cumbrance, 5375
De 1:31 as a man doth **b.** his son, in all 5375
De 5:20 Neither shalt thou **b.** false witness 6030
De 10:8 to **b.** the ark of the covenant of 5375
De 28:57 her children which she shall **b.** 3205
Jos 3:8 command the priests that **b.** the 5375
Jos 3:13 feet of the priests that **b.** the ark 5375
Jos 4:16 the priests that **b.** the ark of the 5375
Jos 6:4 seven priests shall **b.** before the 5375
Jos 6:6 let seven priests **b.** seven trumpets 5375
Jg 13:3 thou shalt conceive, and **b.** a son. 3205
Jg 13:5, 7 shalt conceive, and **b.** a son; 3205
Ru 1:12 to-night, and should also **b.** sons; 3205
1Sa 17:34 there came a lion, and a **b.**, 1677
1Sa 17:36 slew both the lion and the **b.** 1677
1Sa 17:37 out of the paw of the **b.**, he will 1677
2Sa 17:8 as a **b.** robbed of her whelps 1677

2Sa 18:19 and **b.** the king tidings, how that........ 1319
2Sa 18:20 Thou shalt not **b.** tidings this............ 1319
2Sa 18:20 thou shalt **b.** tidings another day: 1319
2Sa 18:20 thou shalt **b.** no tidings, because 1319
1Ki 3:21 it was not my son, which I did **b.**....... 3205
1Ki 21:10 before him, to **b.** witness against........ 5749
2Ki 18:14 thou puttest on me will I **b.**. 5375
2Ki 19:30 root downward, and **b.** fruit.............. 6213
1Ch 5:18 men able to **b.** buckler and sword,...... 5375
2Ch 2:2 ten thousand men to **b.** burdens,........ 5445
Es 1:22 every man should **b.** rule in his.......... 8323
Ps 75:3 dissolved: I **b.** up the pillars of 8505
Ps 89:50 how I do **b.** in my bosom the 5375
Ps 91:12 shall **b.** thee up in their hands, ... 5375
Pr 9:12 scornest, thou alone shalt **b.** it.......... 5375
Pr 12:24 The hand of the diligent shall **b.**.......... 4910
Pr 17:12 Let a **b.** robbed of her whelps 1677
Pr 18:14 but a wounded spirit who can **b.**? 5375
Pr 28:15 roaring lion, and a ranging **b.**;........... 1677
Pr 30:21 and for four which it cannot **b.**........... 5375
Ca 4:2 whereof every one **b.** twins, and........ 8382
Isa 1:14 unto me; I am weary to **b.**................ 5375
Isa 7:14 virgin shall conceive, and **b.** a son, ... 3205
Isa 11:7 the cow and the **b.** shall feed;........... 1677
Isa 37:31 downward, and **b.** fruit upward: 6213
Isa 46:4 I have made, and I will **b.**;............... 5375
Isa 46:7 They **b.** him upon the shoulder, ... 5375
Isa 52:11 ye clean, that **b.** the vessels of the..... 5375
Isa 53:11 for he shall **b.** their iniquities............ 5445
Isa 54:1 O barren, thou that didst not **b.**;........ 3205
Jer 5:31 the priests **b.** rule......................... 7287
Jer 10:19 this is a grief, and I must **b.** it............ 5375
Jer 17:21 **b.** no burden on the sabbath day, ... 5375
Jer 17:27 not to **b.** a burden, even entering....... 5375
Jer 29:6 they may **b.** sons and daughters:........ 3205
Jer 31:19 I did **b.** the reproach of my youth........ 5375
Jer 44:22 that the Lord could no longer **b.**, ... 5375
La 3:10 He was unto me as a **b.** lying in......... 1677
La 3:27 good for a man that he **b.** the yoke 5375
Eze 4:4 upon it thou shalt **b.** their iniquity....... 5375
Eze 4:5 so shalt thou **b.** the iniquity of the...... 5375
Eze 4:6 thou shalt **b.** the iniquity of the......... 5375
Eze 12:6 In their sight shalt thou **b.** it upon...... 5375
Eze 12:12 prince that is among them shall **b.**....... 5375
Eze 14:10 And they shall **b.** the punishment 5375
Eze 16:52 **b.** thine own shame for thy sins 5375
Eze 16:52 confounded also, and **b.** thy shame, ... 5375
Eze 16:54 thou mayest **b.** thine own shame,....... 5375
Eze 17:8 and that is might **b.** fruit,................ 5375
Eze 17:23 bring forth boughs, and **b.** fruit, ... 6213
Eze 18:19 doth not the son **b.** the iniquity.......... 5375
Eze 18:20 The son shall not **b.** the iniquity 5375
Eze 18:20 neither shall the father **b.** 5375
Eze 23:35 **b.** thou also thy lewdness and thy 5375
Eze 23:49 ye shall **b.** the sins of your idols: 5375
Eze 32:30 **b.** their shame with them that go 5375
Eze 34:29 neither **b.** the shame of the............... 5375
Eze 36:7 they shall **b.** their shame.................. 5375
Eze 36:15 neither shalt thou **b.** the reproach....... 5375
Eze 44:10 they shall even **b.** their iniquity........... 5375
Eze 44:12 and they shall **b.** their iniquity............ 5375
Eze 44:13 and they shall **b.** their shame,............ 5375
Eze 46:20 they **b.** them not out into the 3318
Da 2:39 which shall **b.** rule over all the........... 7981
Da 7:5 beast, a second, like to a **b.**,............. 1678
Ho 9:16 dried up, they shall **b.** no fruit: 6213
Ho 13:18 I will meet them as a **b.** that is.......... 1677
Am 5:19 from a lion, and a **b.** met him; 1677
Am 7:10 land is not able to **b.** all his words...... 3557
Mic 6:16 ye shall **b.** the reproach of my........... 5375
Mic 7:9 I will **b.** the indignation of the............ 5375
Zep 1:11 they that **b.** silver are cut off........... 5187
Hag 2:12 If one **b.** holy flesh in the skirt 5375
Zec 5:10 Whither do these **b.** the ephah? 3212
Zec 6:13 he shall **b.** the glory, and sit and......... 5375
Mt 3:11 whose shoes I am not worthy to **b.**...... *941*
Mt 4:6 their hands they shall **b.** thee up.......... *142*
Mt 19:18 **Thou shalt not b. false witness,**...... *5576*
Mt 27:32 him they compelled to **b.** his cross........ *142*
Mk 10:19 **Do not b. false witness, Defraud** ... *5576*
Mk 15:21 Alexander and Rufus, to **b.** his *142*
Lu 1:13 wife Elisabeth shall **b.** thee a son, ... *1080*
Lu 4:11 their hands they shall **b.** thee up,......... *142*
Lu 11:48 **Truly ye b. witness that ye allow** .. *3140*
Lu 13:9 **And if it b. fruit, well: and if not,**..*4160*
Lu 14:27 **whosoever doth not b. his cross,** *941*
Lu 18:7 **though he b. long with them?** *3114*
Lu 18:20 **Do not b. false witness, Honour**.... *5576*
Lu 23:26 that he might **b.** it after Jesus............ *5342*
Joh 1:7 to **b.** witness of the Light, that all...... *3140*
Joh 1:8 to **b.** witness of that Light. *3140*
Joh 2:8 **b. unto the governor of the feast**...*5342*
Joh 3:28 yourselves **b.** me witness, that I......... *3140*
Joh 5:31 **If I b. witness of myself, my**......... *3140*
Joh 5:36 **works that I do, b. witness of me**.. *3140*
Joh 8:14 **Though I b. record of myself,** *3140*
Joh 8:18 **I am one that b. witness of myself,** *3140*
Joh 10:25 **Father's name, they b. witness of..** *3140*
Joh 15:4 **the branch cannot b. fruit of itself,** *5342*
Joh 15:8 **that ye b. much fruit; so shall ye..** *5342*
Joh 15:27 **ye also shall b. witness, because ..** *3140*
Joh 16:12 **but ye cannot b. them now**............ *941*
Joh 18:23 **b. witness of the evil: but if well,..** *3140*
Joh 18:37 **I should b. witness unto the truth,** .*3140*
Ac 9:15 **to b. my name before the Gentiles,** ..*941*
Ac 15:10 our fathers nor we were able to **b.**? *941*
Ac 18:14 would that I should **b.** with you: *430*
Ac 22:5 doth **b.** me witness, and all the........... *3140*
Ac 23:11 **must thou b. witness also at Rome.***3140*
Ac 27:15 could not **b.** up in the wind,................ *503*
Ro 10:2 For I **b.** them record that they *3140*
Ro 13:9 Thou shalt not **b.** false witness, ... *5576*
Ro 15:1 to **b.** the infirmities of the weak, ... *941*
1Co 3:2 ye were not able to **b.** it, ...
1Co 10:13 that ye may be able to **b.** it. *5297*
1Co 15:49 also **b.** the image of the heavenly. *5409*
2Co 8:3 I **b.** record, yea, and beyond their...... *3140*
2Co 11:1 **b.** with me a little in my folly:............ *430*
2Co 11:1 and indeed **b.** with me...................... *430*
2Co 11:4 ye might well **b.** with him................... *430*
Ga 4:15 for I **b.** you record, that, if it had....... *3140*
Ga 5:10 shall **b.** his judgment, whosoever *941*
Ga 6:2 **B.** ye one another's burdens............... *941*
Ga 6:5 every man shall **b.** his own burden....... *941*
Ga 6:17 for I **b.** on my body the marks of......... *941*
Col 4:13 For I **b.** him reocrd, that he hath....... *3140*
1Ti 5:14 woman marry, **b.** children, ... *5041*
Heb 9:28 offered to **b.** the sins of many *399*
Jas 3:12 my brethren, **b.** olive berries? *4160*
1Jo 1:2 and **b.** witness and shew unto you...... *3140*
1Jo 5:7 three that **b.** record in heaven, ... *3140*
1Jo 5:8 three that **b.** witness in earth, the...... *3140*
3Jo 12 yea, and we also **b.** record;......................
Re 2:2 **canst not b. them which are evil:**.... *941*
Re 13:2 his feet were as the feet of a **b.**, ... *715*

BEARD See also BEARDS.

Le 13:29 Plague upon the head or the **b.**;......... 2206
Le 13:30 leprosy upon the head or **b.**. 2206
Le 14:9 head and his **b.** and his eyebrows, ... 2206
Le 19:27 thou mar the corners of thy **b.**. 2206
Le 21:5 shave off the corner of their **b.**,.......... 2206
1Sa 17:35 him by his **b.**, and smote him 2206
1Sa 21:13 his spittle fall down upon his **b.**........... 2206
2Sa 19:24 his feet, nor trimmed his **b.**,.............. 8222
2Sa 20:9 And Joab took Amasa by the **b.** 2206
Ezr 9:3 of my **b.**, and sat down astonied 2206
Ps 133:2 that ran down upon the **b.**, ... 2206
Ps 133:2 even Aaron's **b.**: that went down......... 2206
Isa 7:20 and it shall also consume the **b.**. 2206
Isa 15:2 be baldness, and every **b.** cut off. 2206
Jer 48:37 shall be bald and every **b.** clipped:...... 2206
Eze 5:1 upon thine head and upon thy **b.** 2206

BEARDS

2Sa 10:4 shaved off the one half of the **b.**, ... 2206
2Sa 10:5 at Jericho until your **b.** be grown,........ 2206
1Ch 19:5 Jericho until your **b.** be grown........... 2206
Jer 41:5 **b.** shaven, and their clothes rent,........ 2206

BEARER See ARMOURBEARER; BEARERS; CUPBEARER; STANDARDBEARER; TALEBEARER.

BEARERS

2Ch 2:18 of them to be **b.** of burdens, ... 5449
2Ch 34:13 they were over the **b.** of burdens,....... 5449
Ne 4:10 of the **b.** of burdens is decayed,.......... 5449

BEAREST

Jg 13:3 thou art barren and **b.** not: 3205
Ps 106:4 the favour that thou **b.** unto thy..............
Joh 8:13 Thou **b.** record of thyself; thy *3140*
Ro 11:18 thou **b.** not the root, but the root........ *941*
Ga 4:27 Rejoice, thou barren that **b.** not; *5088*

BEARETH See also FORBEARETH.

Le 11:25 whosoever **b.** ought of the................. 5375
Le 11:28 he that **b.** the carcase of them........... 5375
Le 11:40 he also that **b.** the carcase of it 5375
Le 15:10 and he that **b.** any of those things 5375
Nu 11:12 a nursing father **b.** the sucking........... 5375
De 25:6 the first born which she **b.** shall......... 3205
De 29:18 a root that **b.** gall and wormwood;...... 6509
De 29:23 is not sown, nor **b.**, nor any grass...... 6779
De 32:11 **b.** them on her wings: 5375
Job 16:8 rising up in me **b.** witness................ 6030
Job 24:21 entreateth the barren that **b.** not:....... 3205
Pr 25:18 A man that **b.** false witness............... 6030
Pr 29:2 but when the wicked **b.** rule,.............. 4910
Ca 6:6 every one **b.** twins, and there is 8382
Joe 2:22 tree that **b.** her fruit, the fig tree 5375
Mt 13:23 **also b. fruit, and bringeth forth,** ... *2592*
Joh 5:32 **another that b. witness of me:** *3140*
Joh 8:18 **that sent me b. witness of me.** *3140*
Joh 15:2 **branch in me that b. not fruit**....... *5342*
Joh 15:2 **branch that b. fruit, he purgeth it,** .*5342*
Ro 8:16 The Spirit itself **b.** witness with *4828*
Ro 13:4 for he **b.** not the sword in vain: *5409*
1Co 13:7 **B.** all things, believeth all things, ... *4722*
Heb 6:8 that which **b.** thorns and briers *1627*
1Jo 5:6 it is the Spirit that **b.** witness, ... *3140*

BEARING See also CHILDBEARING; FORBEARING.

Ge 1:29 given you every herb **b.** seed, ... 2232
Ge 16:2 Lord hath restrained me from **b.**......... 3205
Ge 29:35 his name Judah; and let **b.**. 3205
Ge 30:9 Leah saw that she had left **b.**, ... 3205
Ge 37:25 **b.** spicery and balm and myrrh,.......... 5375
Nu 10:17 set forward, **b.** the tabernacle............ 5375
Nu 10:21 set forward, **b.** the sanctuary: 5375
Jos 3:3 the priests of Levites **b.** it, ... 5375
Jos 3:14 priests **b.** the ark of the covenant........ 5375
Jos 6:8 seven priests **b.** the seven trumpets ... 5375
Jos 6:13 seven priests **b.** seven trumpets 5375
1Sa 17:7 one **b.** a shield went before him.......... 5375
2Sa 15:24 **b.** the ark of the covenant of God: 5375
Ps 126:6 **b.** precious seed, shall doubtless 5375
Mk 14:13 **a man b. a pitcher of water:**.......... *941*
Lu 22:10 **meet you, b. a pitcher of water;**...... *941*
Joh 19:17 **b.** his cross went forth *941*
Ro 2:15 conscience also **b.** witness, and.......... *4828*
Ro 9:1 conscience also **b.** me witness *4828*
2Co 4:10 Always **b.** about in the body the.......... *4064*
Heb 2:4 God also **b.** them witness both *4901*
Heb 13:13 without the camp, **b.** his reproach. *5342*

BEARS

2Ki 2:24 forth two she **b.** out of the wood, ... 1677
Isa 59:11 We roar all like **b.**, and mourn 1677

BEAST See also BEAST'S; BEASTS.

Ge 1:24 and **b.** of the earth after his kind:....... 2416
Ge 1:25 God made the **b.** of the earth............ 2416
Ge 1:30 And to ever **b.** of the earth,.............. 2416
Ge 2:19 God formed every **b.** of the field, ... 2416
Ge 2:20 every **b.** of the field; but for Adam..... 2416
Ge 3:1 subtil than any **b.** of the field............. 2416
Ge 3:14 above every **b.** of the field;................ 2416
Ge 6:7 man, and **b.**, and the creeping............. 929
Ge 7:2 Of every clean **b.** thou shalt take......... 929
Ge 7:14 every **b.** after his kind, and all the...... 2416
Ge 7:21 of **b.**, and of every creeping thing....... 2416
Ge 8:19 Every **b.**, every creeping thing, and.... 2416
Ge 8:20 clean **b.**, and of every clean fowl, ... 929
Ge 9:2 be upon every **b.** of the earth,........... 2416
Ge 9:5 hand of every **b.** will I require it, ... 2416
Ge 9:10 every **b.** of the earth with you;.......... 2416
Ge 9:10 to every **b.** of the earth. 2416
Ge 34:23 every **b.** of theirs be ours?................. 929
Ge 37:20 Some evil **b.** hath devoured him:......... 2416
Ge 37:33 an evil **b.** hath devoured him; 2416
Ex 8:17 became lice in man, and in **b.**;............ 929
Ex 8:18 were lice upon man, and upon **b.**. 929
Ex 9:9 blains upon man, and upon **b.**,............ 929
Ex 9:10 blains upon man, and upon **b.**............. 929
Ex 9:19 every man and **b.** which shall be.......... 929
Ex 9:22 man, and upon **b.**, and upon every....... 929
Ex 9:25 was in the field, both man and **b.**;........ 929
Ex 11:7 his tongue, against man or **b.**:............ 929
Ex 12:12 land of Egypt, both man and **b.**; 929
Ex 13:2 of man and of **b.**: it is mine. 929
Ex 13:12 cometh of a **b.** which thou hast; 929
Ex 13:15 of man, and the firstborn of **b.**;.......... 929
Ex 19:13 whether it be **b.** or man,.................... 929
Ex 21:34 them; and the dead **b.** shall be his..........

Ex	22:5	shall put in his **b.**, and shall feed........	1165
Ex	22:10	or an ox, or a sheep, or any **b.**,..........	929
Ex	22:19	lieth with a **b.** shall surely................	929
Ex	23:29	the **b.** of the field multiply against........	2416
Le	5:2	the carcase of an unclean **b.**,...........	2416
Le	7:21	unclean **b.**, or any abominable.............	929
Le	7:24	fat of the **b.** that dieth of itself...........	5038
Le	7:25	whosoever eateth the fat of the **b.**,......	929
Le	7:26	or of **b.**, in any of your dwellings.........	929
Le	11:26	every **b.** which divideth the hoof,........	929
Le	11:39	if any **b.**, of which ye may eat, die;......	929
Le	11:47	between the **b.** that may be eaten......	2416
Le	11:47	the **b.** that may not be eaten.............	2416
Le	17:13	hunteth and catcheth any **b.**............	2416
Le	18:23	Neither shalt thou lie with any **b.**.........	929
Le	18:23	shall any woman stand before a **b.**.......	929
Le	20:15	And if a man lie with a **b.**,................	929
Le	20:15	and ye shall slay the **b.**....................	929
Le	20:16	if a woman approach unto any **b.**,........	929
Le	20:16	kill the woman and the **b.**:................	929
Le	20:25	make your souls abominable by **b.**,......	929
Le	24:18	that killeth a **b.** shall make it........	5315,929
Le	24:18	**b.** for **b.**..	5315
Le	24:21	that killeth a **b.**, he shall restore it......	929
Le	25:7	cattle, and for the **b.** that are............	2416
Le	27:9	And if it be a **b.**, whereof men............	929
Le	27:10	if he shall at all change **b.** for **b.**.........	929
Le	27:11	if it be any unclean **b.**, of which..........	929
Le	27:11	present the **b.** before the priest:..........	929
Le	27:27	if it be an unclean **b.**,.......................	929
Le	27:28	of man and **b.**, and of the field..........	929
Nu	3:13	firstborn in Israel, both man and **b.**:.....	929
Nu	8:17	Israel are mine, both man and **b.**:........	929
Nu	31:26	man and of **b.**, thou, and Eleazar........	929
Nu	31:47	of man and of **b.**, and gave them........	929
De	4:17	likeness of any **b.**...on the earth,.........	929
De	14:6	And every **b.** that parteth the hoof,......	929
De	27:21	that lieth with any manner of **b.**........	929
Jg	20:48	the men of every city, as the **b.**,.........	929
2Ki	14:9	passed by a wild **b.** that was in........	2416
2Ch	25:18	passed by a wild **b.** that was in..........	2416
Ne	2:12	neither was there any **b.** with me,.......	929
Ne	2:12	save the **b.** that I rode upon...............	929
Ne	2:14	for the **b.** that was under me to pass....	929
Job	39:15	that the wild **b.** may break them.........	2416
Ps	36:6	thou preservest man and **b.**................	929
Ps	50:10	every **b.** of the forest is mine,...........	2416
Ps	73:22	I was as a **b.** before thee....................	929
Ps	80:13	wild **b.** of the field doth devour it.........	2123
Ps	104:11	give drink to every **b.** of the field:.......	2416
Ps	135:8	of Egypt, both of man and **b.**.............	929
Ps	147:9	He giveth to the **b.** his food,...............	929
Pr	12:10	regardeth the life of his **b.**:...............	929
Ec	3:19	hath no preeminence above a **b.**:.........	929
Ec	3:21	the spirit of the **b.** that goeth............	929
Isa	35:9	nor any ravenous **b.** shall go up..........	2416
Isa	43:20	The **b.** of the field shall honour...........	2416
Isa	46:1	they are a burden to the weary **b.**............	
Isa	63:14	As a **b.** goeth down into the valley,......	929
Jer	7:20	upon man, and upon **b.**, and upon.........	929
Jer	9:10	the fowl of the heavens and the **b.**........	929
Jer	21:6	of this city, both man and **b.**:.............	929
Jer	27:5	the **b.** that are upon the ground,..........	929
Jer	31:27	of man, and with the seed of **b.**...........	929
Jer	32:43	desolate without man or **b.**;..............	929
Jer	33:10	without man and without **b.**,...............	929
Jer	33:10	without inhabitant, and without **b.**,.......	929
Jer	33:12	without man and without **b.**,...............	929
Jer	36:29	to cease from thence man and **b.**?........	929
Jer	50:3	shall depart, both man and **b.**............	929
Jer	51:62	neither man nor **b.**, but that it shall......	929
Eze	14:13	will cut off man and **b.** from it:...........	929
Eze	14:17	so that I cut off man and **b.**................	929
Eze	14:19	to cut off from it man and **b.**:..............	929
Eze	14:21	the famine, and the noisome **b.**,.........	2416
Eze	14:21	to cut off from it man and **b.**?............	929
Eze	25:13	and will cut off man and **b.**................	929
Eze	29:8	cut off man and **b.** out of thee.............	929
Eze	29:11	nor foot of **b.** shall pass through it,......	929
Eze	34:8	meat to every **b.** of the field,............	2416
Eze	34:28	neither shall the **b.** of the land...........	2416
Eze	36:11	multiply upon you man and **b.**;............	929
Eze	39:17	to every **b.** of the field, Assemble.......	2416
Eze	44:31	or torn, whether it be fowl or **b.**..........	929
Da	7:5	And behold another **b.**, a second,.......	2423
Da	7:6	the **b.** had also four heads;................	2423
Da	7:7	behold a fourth **b.**, dreadful and.........	2423
Da	7:11	I beheld even till the **b.** was slain,......	2423
Da	7:19	know the truth of the fourth **b.**,.........	2423
Da	7:23	The fourth **b.** shall be the fourth........	2423
Ho	13:8	the wild **b.** shall tear them................	2416
Jon	3:7	Let neither man nor **b.**, herd nor.........	929
Jon	3:8	But let man and **b.** be covered...........	929
Mic	1:13	bind the chariot to the swift **b.**..........	7409
Zep	1:3	I will consume man and **b.**;................	929
Zec	8:10	no hire for man, nor any hire for **b.**;....	929
Lu	10:34	**and set him on his own b., and**.....	*2934*
Ac	28:4	the venomous **b.** hang on his hand,.....	*2342*
Ac	28:5	shook off the **b.** into the fire,............	*2342*
Heb	12:20	And if so much as a **b.** touch the.......	*2342*
Re	4:7	the first **b.** was like a lion,................	*2226*
Re	4:7	and the second **b.** like a calf,.............	*2226*
Re	4:7	third **b.** had a face as a man..............	*2226*
Re	4:7	and the fourth **b.** was like a..............	*2226*
Re	6:3	I heard the second **b.** say,.................	*2226*
Re	6:5	I heard the third **b.** say, Come..........	*2226*
Re	6:7	the voice of the fourth **b.** say,...........	*2226*
Re	11:7	the **b.** that ascendeth out of the.........	*2342*
Re	13:1	saw a **b.** rise up out of the sea,.........	*2342*
Re	13:2	the **b.** which I saw like.....................	*2342*
Re	13:3	the world wondered after the **b.**..........	*2342*
Re	13:4	power unto the **b.**: and they..............	*2342*
Re	13:4	worshipped the **b.**, saying,................	*2342*
Re	13:4	Who is like unto the **b.**?....................	*2342*
Re	13:11	I beheld another **b.** coming up...........	*2342*
Re	13:12	all the power of the first **b.** before......	*2342*
Re	13:12	therein to worship the first **b.**,...........	*2342*
Re	13:14	to do the sight of the **b.**;..................	*2342*
Re	13:14	should make an image to the **b.**,.........	*2342*
Re	13:15	unto the image of the **b.**, that the.......	*2342*
Re	13:15	image of the **b.** should both speak,......	*2342*
Re	13:15	worship the image of the **b.**.............	*2342*
Re	13:17	or the name of the **b.**, or the............	*2342*
Re	13:18	count the number of the **b.**;..............	*2342*
Re	14:9	If any man worship the **b.** and his.......	*2342*
Re	14:11	who worship the **b.** and his image.......	*2342*
Re	15:2	the victory over the **b.**, and over........	*2342*
Re	16:2	the mark of the **b.**, and upon them......	*2342*
Re	16:10	his vial upon the seat of the **b.**;..........	*2342*
Re	16:13	and out of the mouth of the **b.**,..........	*2342*
Re	17:3	upon a scarlet coloured **b.**,................	*2342*
Re	17:7	of the **b.** that carrieth her, which.......	*2342*
Re	17:8	The **b.** that thou sawest was..............	*2342*
Re	17:8	the **b.** that was, and is not,..............	*2342*
Re	17:11	And the **b.** that was and is not,.........	*2342*
Re	17:12	as kings one hour with the **b.**...........	*2342*
Re	17:13	power and strength unto the **b.**..........	*2342*
Re	17:16	which thou sawest upon the **b.**,..........	*2342*
Re	17:17	give their kingdom unto the **b.**,..........	*2342*
Re	19:19	And I saw the **b.**, and the kings.........	*2342*
Re	19:20	And the **b.** was taken,.......................	*2342*
Re	19:20	had received the mark of the **b.**,.........	*2342*
Re	20:4	had not worshipped the **b.**,................	*2342*
Re	20:10	where the **b.** and the false prophet......	*2342*

BEAST'S

Da	4:16	and let a **b.** heart be given unto.........	2423

BEASTS

Ge	7:2	of **b.** that are not clean by two,...........	929
Ge	7:8	Of clean **b.**, and of **b.** that are not.......	929
Ge	31:39	That which was torn of **b.** I.............	2966
Ge	36:6	and all his **b.**, and all his..................	929
Ge	45:17	lade your **b.**, and go, get you...........	1165
Ex	11:5	and all the firstborn of **b.**..................	929
Ex	22:31	flesh that is torn of **b.** in the field;......	2966
Ex	23:11	what they leave the **b.** of the field......	2416
Le	7:24	fat of that which is torn with **b.**,........	2966
Le	11:2	These are the **b.** which ye shall..........	2416
Le	11:2	among all the **b.** that are on...............	929
Le	11:3	cheweth the cud, among the **b.**,..........	929
Le	11:27	among all manner of **b.** that go..........	2416
Le	11:46	This is the law of the **b.**, and of.........	929
Le	17:15	or that which was torn with **b.**,..........	2966
Le	20:25	between clean **b.** and unclean,............	929
Le	22:8	or is torn with **b.**, he shall not eat......	2966
Le	26:6	I will rid evil **b.** out of the land,.........	2416
Le	26:22	I will also send wild **b.** among............	2416
Le	27:26	Only the firstling of the **b.**,..............	929
Nu	18:15	whether it be of men or **b.**,...............	929
Nu	18:15	the firstling of unclean **b.** shalt...........	929
Nu	20:8	congregation and their **b.** drink..........	1165
Nu	20:11	drank, and their **b.** also..................	1165
Nu	31:11	prey, both of men and of **b.**................	929
Nu	31:30	of all manner of **b.** and give...............	929
Nu	35:3	their goods, and for all their **b.**.........	2416
De	7:22	lest the **b.** of the field increase...........	2416
De	14:4	These are the **b.** which ye shall...........	929
De	14:6	cheweth the cud among the **b.**,...........	929
De	28:26	and unto the **b.** of the earth,.............	929
De	32:24	I will also send the teeth of **b.** upon.....	929
1Sa	17:44	of the air, and to the **b.** of the field......	929
1Sa	17:46	and to the wild **b.** of the earth;..........	2416
2Sa	21:10	nor the **b.** of the field by night...........	2416
1Ki	4:33	he spake also of **b.**, and of fowl,..........	929
1Ki	18:5	that we lose not all the **b.**.................	929
2Ki	3:17	and your cattle, and your **b.**................	929
2Ch	32:28	stalls for all manner of **b.**,...................	929
Ezr	1:4	with goods, and with **b.**, beside...........	929
Ezr	1:6	with goods, and with **b.**, and with........	929
Job	5:22	shalt thou be afraid of the **b.** of.........	2416
Job	5:23	and the **b.** of the field shall be at........	2416
Job	12:7	But ask now the **b.**, and they shall.......	929
Job	18:3	Wherefore are we counted as **b.**,.........	929
Job	35:11	teacheth us more than the **b.** of..........	929
Job	37:8	Then the **b.** go into dens, and...........	2416
Job	40:20	where all the **b.** of the field play........	2416
Ps	8:7	oxen, yea, and the **b.** of the field;........	929
Ps	49:12	he is like the **b.** that perish................	929
Ps	49:20	is like the **b.** that perish....................	929
Ps	50:11	the wild **b.** of the field are mine.........	2123
Ps	79:2	saints unto the **b.** of the earth...........	2416
Ps	104:20	all the **b.** of the forest do creep.........	2416
Ps	104:25	both small and great **b.**.....................	2416
Ps	148:10	**B.**, and all cattle; creeping things.......	2416
Pr	9:2	She hath killed her **b.**; she hath.........	2874
Pr	30:30	lion which is strongest among **b.**,..........	929
Ec	3:18	see that they themselves are **b.**..........	929
Ec	3:19	the sons of men befalleth **b.**;...............	929
Isa	1:11	the fat of fed **b.**; and I delight...........	4806
Isa	13:21	wild **b.** of the desert shall lie............	6728
Isa	13:22	wild **b.** of the island shall cry.............	338
Isa	18:6	and to the **b.** of the earth:..................	929
Isa	18:6	the **b.** of the earth shall winter...........	929
Isa	30:6	The burden of the beasts of the............	929
Isa	34:14	The wild **b.** of the desert shall...........	6728
Isa	34:14	with the wild **b.** of the island..............	338
Isa	40:16	nor the **b.** thereof sufficient for a.......	2416
Isa	46:1	their idols were upon the **b.**,.............	2416
Isa	56:9	ye **b.** of the field, come to devour,......	2416
Isa	56:9	all ye **b.** in the forest........................	2416
Isa	66:20	upon mules, and upon swift **b.**,...........	3753
Jer	7:33	and for the **b.** of the earth;................	929
Jer	12:4	the **b.** are consumed, and the birds;.....	929
Jer	12:9	assemble all the **b.** of the field,..........	2416
Jer	15:3	the **b.** of the earth, to devour.............	929
Jer	16:4	and for the **b.** of the earth..................	929
Jer	19:7	for the **b.** of the earth.......................	929
Jer	27:6	the **b.** of the field have I given him.....	2416
Jer	28:14	given him the **b.** of the field also.......	2416
Jer	34:20	heaven, and to the **b.** of the earth.......	929
Jer	50:39	Therefore the wild **b.** of the..............	6728
Jer	50:39	with the wild **b.** of the islands............	338
Eze	5:17	send upon you famine and evil **b.**,.......	2416
Eze	8:10	and abominable **b.**, and all the...........	929
Eze	14:15	cause noisome **b.** to pass through.......	2416
Eze	14:15	pass through because of the **b.**...........	2416
Eze	29:5	for meat to the **b.** of the field............	2416
Eze	31:6	under his branches did all the **b.** of.....	2416
Eze	31:13	all the **b.** of the field shall be upon......	2416
Eze	32:4	I will fill the **b.** of the whole earth......	2416
Eze	32:13	destroy also all the **b.** thereof............	929
Eze	32:13	nor the hoofs of **b.** trouble them..........	929
Eze	33:27	will I give to the **b.** to be devoured,...	2416
Eze	34:5	became meat to all the **b.** of the........	2416
Eze	34:25	the evil **b.** to cease out of the land;....	2416
Eze	38:20	and the **b.** of the field, and all...........	2416
Eze	39:4	and to the **b.** of the field, to be..........	2416
Da	2:38	the **b.** of the field and the fowls.........	2423
Da	4:12	the **b.** of the field had shadow............	2423
Da	4:14	let the **b.** get away from under it,......	2423
Da	4:15	let his portion be with the **b.**............	2423
Da	4:21	under which the **b.** of the field dwelt,..	2423
Da	4:23	let his portion be with the **b.** of.........	2423
Da	4:25	dwelling shall be with the **b.** of the.....	2423
Da	4:32	shall be with the **b.** of the field:.........	2423
Da	5:21	his heart was made like the **b.**,...........	2423
Da	7:3	four great **b.** came up from the sea,...	2423
Da	7:7	from all the **b.** that were before it;.....	2423
Da	7:12	concerning the rest of the **b.**,............	2423
Da	7:17	These great **b.**, which are four,.........	2423
Da	8:4	no **b.** might stand before him,............	2416

Ho 2:12 the **b.** of the field shall eat them. 2416
Ho 2:18 a covenant for them with the **b.** of 2416
Ho 4:3 with the **b.** of the field, and with 2416
Joe 1:18 How do the **b.** groan! the herds of 929
Joe 1:20 The **b.** of the field cry also 929
Joe 2:22 Be not afraid, ye **b.** of the field: 929
Am 5:22 the peace offerings of your fat **b.**. 4806
Mic 5:8 a lion among the **b.** of the forest, 929
Hab 2:17 the spoil of **b.**, which made them 929
Zep 2:14 of her, all the **b.** of the nations: 2416
Zep 2:15 a place for **b.** to lie down in! 2416
Zec 14:15 all the **b.** that shall be in these 929
Mk 1:13 was with the wild **b.**; and the *2342*
Ac 7:42 have ye offered to me slain **b.** *4968*
Ac 10:12 all manner of fourfooted **b.** *5074*
Ac 10:12 of the earth, and wild **b.**, *2342*
Ac 11:6 and saw fourfooted **b.** of the earth, *5074*
Ac 11:6 and wild **b.**, and creeping things, *2342*
Ac 23:24 And provide them **b.**, that they *2934*
Ro 1:23 fourfooted **b.**, and creeping things *5074*
1Co 15:32 I have fought with **b.** at Ephesus, *2341*
1Co 15:39 another flesh of **b.**, another of *2934*
Tit 1:12 alway liars, evil **b.**, slow bellies. *2342*
Heb 13:11 of those **b.**, whose blood is brought *2226*
Jas 3:7 Every kind of **b.**, and of birds, *2342*
2Pe 2:12 as natural brute **b.**, made to be *2226*
Jude 10 they know naturally, as brute **b.**, *2226*
Re 4:6 were four **b.** full of eyes *2226*
Re 4:8 And the four **b.** had each of them *2226*
Re 4:9 those **b.** give glory and honour *2226*
Re 5:6 of the throne and of the four **b.**, *2226*
Re 5:8 the four **b.** and four and twenty *2226*
Re 5:11 round about the throne and the **b.**, *2226*
Re 5:14 And the four **b.** said, Amen. *2226*
Re 6:1 one of the four **b.** saying, Come *2226*
Re 6:6 voice in the midst of the four **b.** *2226*
Re 6:8 death, and with the **b.** of the earth. *2342*
Re 7:11 about the elders and the four **b.**, *2226*
Re 14:3 before the four **b.**, and the elders: *2226*
Re 15:7 one of the four **b.** gave unto the *2226*
Re 18:13 and **b.**, and sheep, and horses, *2934*
Re 19:4 elders and the four **b.** fell down *2226*

BEAT See also BEATEN; BEATEST; BEATETH; BEATING.
Ex 30:36 shalt **b.** some of it very small, 7833
Ex 39:3 did **b.** the gold into thin plates, 7554
Nu 11:8 it in mills, or **b.** it in a mortar, 1743
De 25:3 and **b.** him above these with 5221
Jg 8:17 he **b.** down the tower of Penuel, 5422
Jg 9:45 and **b.** down the city, and sowed 5422
Jg 19:22 **b.** at the door, and spake to the 1849
Ru 2:17 and **b.** out that she had gleaned: 2251
2Sa 22:43 Then did I **b.** them as small as 7833
2Ki 3:25 they **b.** down the cities, and on 2040
2Ki 13:25 Three times did Joash **b.** him, 5221
2Ki 23:12 did the king **b.** down, and brake 5422
Ps 18:42 did I **b.** them small as the dust 7833
Ps 89:23 **b.** down his foes before his face, 3807
Pr 23:14 Thou shalt **b.** him with the rod, 5221
Isa 2:4 **b.** their swords into plowshares, 3807
Isa 3:15 ye **b.** my people to pieces, and 1792
Isa 27:12 Lord shall **b.** off from the channel 2251
Isa 41:15 and **b.** them small, and shalt make 1854
Joe 3:10 **B.** your plowshares into swords, 3807
Jon 4:8 the sun **b.** upon the head of Jonah, 5221
Mic 4:3 **b.** their swords into plowshares, 3807
Mic 4:13 shalt **b.** in pieces many people: 1854
Mt 7:25 **winds blew, and b. upon that** *4363*
Mt 7:27 **b. upon that house; and it fell:** *4350*
Mt 21:35 **took his servants, and b. one,** *1194*
Mk 4:37 and the waves **b.** into the ship, *1911*
Mk 12:3 **they caught him, and b. him,** *1194*
Lu 6:48 **stream b. vehemently upon that** *4366*
Lu 6:49 **against which the stream did b.** *4366*
Lu 12:45 **shall begin to b. the menservants** *5180*
Lu 20:10 **the husbandmen b. him, and** *1194*
Lu 20:11 **servant: and they b. him also,** *1194*
Ac 16:22 and commanded to **b.** them. *4463*
Ac 18:17 **b.** him before the judgment seat *5180*
Ac 22:19 and **b.** in every synagogue *1194*

BEATEN
Ex 5:14 had set over them, were **b.**, 5221
Ex 5:16 and, behold, thy servants are **b.**; 5221
Ex 25:18 of **b.** work shalt thou make them, 4749
Ex 25:31 of **b.** work shall the candlestick 4749
Ex 25:36 one **b.** work of pure gold. 4749
Ex 27:20 pure oil olive **b.** for the light, 3795
Ex 29:40 fourth part of an hin of **b.** oil; 3795
Ex 37:7 of gold, **b.** out of one piece 4749
Ex 37:17 **b.** work made he the candlestick; 4749
Ex 37:22 it was one **b.** work of pure gold. 4749
Le 2:14 even corn **b.** out of full ears. 1643
Le 2:16 of the **b.** corn thereof, and part 1643
Le 16:12 full of sweet incense **b.** small, 1851
Le 24:2 pure oil olive **b.** for the light, 3795
Nu 8:4 the candlestick was of **b.** gold, 4749
Nu 8:4 the flowers thereof, was **b.** work: 4749
Nu 28:5 fourth part of an hin of **b.** oil. 3795
De 25:2 the wicked man be worthy to be **b.**, 5221
De 25:2 and to be **b.** before his face, 5221
Jos 8:15 made as if they were **b.** before 5060
2Sa 2:17 and Abner was **b.**, and the men 5062
1Ki 10:16 two hundred targets of **b.** gold: 7820
1Ki 10:17 three hundred shields of **b.** gold; 7820
2Ch 2:10 measures of **b.** wheat, 4347
2Ch 9:15 two hundred targets of **b.** gold; 7820
2Ch 9:15 hundred shekels of **b.** gold 7820
2Ch 9:16 three hundred shields made he of **b.** 7820
2Ch 34:7 **b.** the graven images into powder, 3807
Pr 23:35 they have **b.** me, and I felt it not: 1986
Isa 27:9 chalkstones that are **b.** in sunder, 5310
Isa 28:27 the fitches are **b.** out with a staff, 2251
Isa 30:31 shall the Assyrian be **b.** down, 2865
Jer 46:5 and their mighty ones are **b.** down, 3807
Mic 1:7 images thereof shall be **b.** to pieces, 3807
Mk 13:9 **in the synagogues ye shall be b.** *1194*
Lu 12:47 **shall be b. with many stripes.** *1194*
Lu 12:48 **shall be b. with few stripes.** *1194*
Ac 5:40 called the apostles, and **b.** them, *1194*
Ac 16:37 have **b.** us openly uncondemned *1194*
2Co 11:25 Thrice was I **b.** with rods, once *4463*

BEATEST
De 24:20 When thou **b.** thine olive tree, 2251
Pr 23:13 if thou **b.** him with the rod, 5221

BEATETH
1Co 9:26 not as one that **b.** the air: *1194*

BEATING
1Sa 14:16 went on **b.** down one another. 1986
Mk 12:5 **others; b. some, and killing some** *1194*
Ac 21:32 the soldiers, they left **b.** of Paul. *5180*

BEAUTIES
Ps 110:3 in the **b.** of holiness from the 1926

BEAUTIFUL
Ge 29:17 Rachel was **b.** and well 3303,8389
De 21:11 among the captives a **b.** woman, 3303,8389
1Sa 16:12 withal of a **b.** countenance, 3303
1Sa 25:3 and of a **b.** countenance; 3303
2Sa 11:2 was very **b.** to look upon. 2896
Es 2:7 the maid was fair and **b.**; 2896,4758
Ps 48:2 **B.** for situation, the joy of the 3303
Ec 3:11 made every thing **b.** in his time: 3303
Ca 6:4 Thou art **b.**, O my love, 3303
Ca 7:1 How **b.** are thy feet with shoes, 3303
Isa 4:2 shall the branch of the Lord be **b.** 6643
Isa 52:1 put on thy **b.** garments, O 8597
Isa 52:7 How **b.** upon the mountains are 4998
Isa 64:11 Our holy and our **b.** house, 8597
Jer 13:20 was given thee, thy **b.** flock? 8597
Jer 48:17 strong staff broken, and the **b.** rod! 8597
Eze 16:12 a **b.** crown upon thine head. 8597
Eze 16:13 thou wast exceeding **b.**, and thou 3303
Eze 23:42 **b.** crowns upon their heads. 8597
Mt 23:27 **which indeed appear b. outward,** *5611*
Ac 3:2 the temple which is called **B.**, *5611*
Ac 3:10 sat for alms at the **B.** gate *5611*
Ro 10:15 How **b.** are the feet of them that *5611*

BEAUTIFY
Ezr 7:27 to **b.** the house of the Lord. 6286
Ps 149:4 he will **b.** the meek with salvation, 6286
Isa 60:13 to **b.** the place of my sanctuary; 6286

BEAUTY See also BEAUTIES.
Ex 28:2 thy brother, for glory and for **b.** 8597
Ex 28:40 for them, for glory and for **b.** 8597
2Sa 1:19 The **b.** of Israel is slain upon thy 6643
2Sa 14:25 praised as Absalom for his **b.** 3303
1Ch 16:29 the Lord in the **b.** of holiness. 1927
2Ch 3:6 house with precious stones for **b.** 8597
2Ch 20:21 should praise the **b.** of holiness, 1927
Es 1:11 the people and the princes her **b.** 3308
Job 40:10 array thyself with glory and **b.** 1926
Ps 27:4 to behold the **b.** of the Lord, 5278
Ps 29:2 the Lord in the **b.** of holiness. 1927
Ps 39:11 makest his **b.** to consume away 2530
Ps 45:11 the king greatly desire thy **b.** 3308
Ps 49:14 and their **b.** shall consume in the 6736
Ps 50:2 out of Zion, the perfection of **b.**, 3308
Ps 90:17 let the **b.** of the Lord our God 5278
Ps 96:6 and **b.** are in his sanctuary. 8597
Ps 96:9 the Lord in the **b.** of holiness: 1927
Pr 6:25 Lust not after her **b.** in thine 3308
Pr 20:29 **b.** of old men is the gray head. 1926
Pr 31:30 Favour is deceitful, and **b.** is vain: 3308
Isa 3:24 burning instead of **b.** 3308
Isa 13:19 the **b.** of the Chaldees' excellency, 8597
Isa 28:1 glorious **b.** is a fading flower, 8597
Isa 28:4 glorious **b.**, which is on the head 8597
Isa 28:5 of glory, and for a diadem of **b.**, 8597
Isa 33:17 eyes shall see the king in his **b.** 3308
Isa 44:13 according to the **b.** of a man; 8597
Isa 53:2 no **b.** that we should desire him. 4758
Isa 61:3 to give unto them **b.** for ashes, 6287
La 1:6 her **b.** is departed: her princes 1926
La 2:1 the **b.** of Israel, and remembered 8597
La 2:15 the perfection of **b.**, The joy of 3308
Eze 7:20 As for the **b.** of his ornament, 6643
Eze 16:14 among the heathen for thy **b.** 3308
Eze 16:15 thou didst trust in thine own **b.**, 3308
Eze 16:25 hast made thy **b.** to be abhorred, 3308
Eze 27:3 thou hast said, I am of perfect **b.**. 3308
Eze 27:4 thy builders have perfected thy **b.**. 3308
Eze 27:11 they have made thy **b.**. perfect. 3308
Eze 28:7 against the **b.** of thy wisdom, 3308
Eze 28:12 full of wisdom, and perfect in **b.**. 3308
Eze 28:17 was lifted up because of thy **b.**, 3308
Eze 31:8 God was like unto him in his **b.**. 3308
Eze 32:19 Whom dost thou pass in **b.**? 5276
Ho 14:6 his **b.** shall be as the olive tree, 1935
Zec 9:17 goodness, how great is his **b.**! 3308
Zec 11:7 the one I called **B.**, and the other 5278
Zec 11:10 I took my staff, even **B.**, and cut 5278

BEBAI (beb'-a-i)
Ezr 2:11 The children of **B.**, six hundred 893
Ezr 8:11 And of the sons of **B.** 893
Ezr 8:11 Zechariah the son of **B.**, 893
Ezr 10:28 the sons also of **B.**; Jehohanan, 893
Ne 7:16 The children of **B.**, six hundred 893
Ne 10:15 Bunni, Azgad, **B.**, 893

BECAME See also BECAMEST.
Ge 2:7 of life; and man **b.** a living soul. 1961
Ge 2:10 parted, and **b.** into four heads. 1961
Ge 6:4 the same **b.** mighty men which
Ge 19:26 and she **b.** a pillar of salt. 1961
Ge 20:12 my mother; and she **b.** my wife. 1961
Ge 21:20 in the wilderness, and **b.** an archer 1961
Ge 24:67 Rebekah, and she **b.** his wife; 1961
Ge 26:13 and grew until he **b.** very great: 1431
Ge 44:32 thy servant **b.** surety for the lad 6148
Ge 47:20 them: so the land **b.** Pharaoh's 1961
Ge 47:26 only, which **b.** not Pharaoh's. 1961
Ge 49:15 and **b.** a servant unto tribute. 1961
Ex 2:10 daughter, and he **b.** her son. 1961
Ex 4:3 it **b.** a serpent; and Moses fled 1961
Ex 4:4 and it **b.** a rod in his hand: 1961
Ex 7:10 his servants, and it **b.** a serpent. 1961
Ex 7:12 his rod, and they **b.** serpents: 1961
Ex 8:17 it **b.** lice in man, and in beast; 1961
Ex 8:17 all the dust of the land **b.** lice 1961
Ex 9:10 and it **b.** a boil breaking forth 1961
Ex 9:24 land of Egypt since it **b.** a nation. 1961
Ex 36:13 so it **b.** one tabernacle. 1961
Nu 12:10 Miriam **b.** leprous, white as
Nu 26:10 and fifty men: and they **b.** a sign. 1961
De 26:5 **b.** there a nation, great, mighty, 1961
Jos 7:5 hearts of the people melted, and **b.** 1961
Jos 14:14 therefore **b.** the inheritance 1961
Jos 24:32 and it **b.** the inheritance of the 1961
Jg 1:30 among them, and **b.** tributaries. 1961
Jg 1:33 and of Beth-anath **b.** tributaries. 1961
Jg 1:35 so that they **b.** tributaries. 1961
Jg 8:27 thing **b.** a snare unto Gideon, 1961
Jg 15:14 **b.** as flax that was burnt with fire, 1961
Jg 17:5 one of his sons, who **b.** his priest. 1961
Jg 17:12 and the young man **b.** his priest, 1961
Ru 4:16 laid it in her bosom, and **b.** nurse. 1961
1Sa 10:12 **b.** a proverb, Is Saul also among 1961
1Sa 16:21 and he **b.** his armourbearer. 1961

1Sa 18:29 **b.** David's enemy continually. 1961
1Sa 22:2 and he **b.** a captain over them: 1961
1Sa 25:37 and he **b.** as a stone. 1961
1Sa 25:42 messengers of David, and **b.** 1961
2Sa 2:25 and **b.** one troop, and stood on 1961
2Sa 4:4 he fell, and **b.** lame. And his 6452
2Sa 8:2 the Moabites **b.** David's servants, 1961
2Sa 8:6 the Syrians **b.** servants to David, 1961
2Sa 8:14 they of Edom **b.** David's servants. 1961
2Sa 11:27 she **b.** his wife, and bare him a son. 1961
1Ki 11:24 and **b.** captain over a band, when 1961
1Ki 12:30 And this thing **b.** a sin: for the 1961
1Ki 13:6 again, and **b.** as it was before. 1961
1Ki 13:33 and he **b.** one of the priests of the 1961
1Ki 13:34 this thing **b.** sin unto the house 1961
2Ki 17:3 and Hoshea **b.** his servant, 1961
2Ki 17:15 and **b.** vain, and went after 1891
2Ki 24:1 and Jehoiakim **b.** his servant 1961
1Ch 18:2 the Moabites **b.** David's servants, 1961
1Ch 18:6 the Syrians **b.** David's servants, 1961
1Ch 18:13 the Edomites **b.** David's servants. 1961
1Ch 19:19 with David, and **b.** his servants: 5647
2Ch 27:6 So Jotham **b.** mighty, because he 2388
Ne 9:25 and were filled, and **b.** fat, 8080
Es 8:17 people of the land **b.** Jews; 3054
Ps 69:11 my garment; and I **b.** a proverb 1961
Ps 83:10 perished at Endor: they **b.** as dung 1961
Ps 109:25 I **b.** also a reproach unto them: 1961
Jer 51:30 they **b.** as women: they have 1961
Eze 17:6 **b.** a spreading vine of low stature, 1961
Eze 17:6 **b.** a vine, and brought forth 1961
Eze 19:3 whelps: it **b.** a young lion, 1961
Eze 19:6 he **b.** a young lion, and learned 1961
Eze 23:10 she **b.** famous among women; 1961
Eze 31:5 and his branches **b.** long because 748
Eze 34:5 they **b.** meat to all the beasts 1961
Eze 34:8 **b.** a prey, and my flock **b.** 1961
Eze 36:4 are forsaken, which **b.** a prey 1961
Da 2:35 **b.** like the chaff of the summer 1934
Da 2:35 image **b.** a great mountain, 1934
Da 8:4 according to his will, and **b.** great. 1431
Da 10:15 toward the ground, and I **b.** dumb. 481
Ob 12 in the day that he **b.** a stranger; 5235
Mt 28:4 keepers did shake, and **b.** as dead *1096*
Mk 9:3 his raiment **b.** shining, exceeding *1096*
Ac 10:10 he **b.** very hungry, and would have *1096*
Ro 1:21 but **b.** vain in their imaginations, *3154*
Ro 1:22 to be wise, they **b.** fools, *3471*
Ro 6:18 **b.** the servants of righteousness. *1402*
1Co 9:20 unto the Jews I **b.** as a Jew, *1096*
1Co 9:22 To the weak **b.** I as weak. *1096*
1Co 13:11 when I **b.** a man, I put away *1096*
2Co 8:9 yet for your sakes he **b.** poor, *4433*
Php 2:8 and **b.** obedient unto death, even *1096*
1Th 1:6 ye **b.** followers of us, and of the *1096*
1Th 2:14 ye, brethren, **b.** followers of the *1096*
Heb 2:10 For it **b.** him, for whom are all *4241*
Heb 5:9 **b.** the author of eternal salvation *1096*
Heb 7:26 an high priest **b.** us, who is holy, *4241*
Heb 10:33 whilst ye **b.** companions of them *1096*
Heb 11:7 b. heir of the righteousness which *1096*
Re 6:12 sun **b.** black as sackcloth of hair, *1096*
Re 6:12 and the moon **b.** as blood; *1096*
Re 8:8 third part of the sea **b.** blood; *1096*
Re 8:11 of the waters **b.** wormwood; *1096,1519*
Re 16:3 it **b.** as the blood of a dead man: *1096*
Re 16:4 of waters; and they **b.** blood. *1096*

BECAMEST
1Ch 17:22 and thou, Lord, **b.** their God. 1961
Eze 16:8 and thou **b.** mine. 1961

BECAUSE
Ge 2:3 **b.** that in it he had rested 3588
Ge 2:23 called Woman, **b.** she was taken 3588
Ge 3:10 I was afraid, **b.** I was naked; 3588
Ge 3:14 **B.** thou hast done this, thou art 3588
Ge 3:17 he said, **B.** thou hast hearkened 3588
Ge 3:20 **B.** she was the mother of all living. 3588
Ge 5:29 **b.** of the ground which the Lord 4480
Ge 7:7 **b.** of the waters of the flood 6440
Ge 11:9 it is called Babel; **b.** the Lord did 3588
Ge 12:13 my soul shall live **b.** of thee. 1558
Ge 12:17 plagues **b.** of Sarai Abram's 5921,1697
Ge 16:11 his name Ishmael; **b.** the Lord 3588
Ge 18:20 the Lord said, **B.** the cry of Sodom 3588
Ge 18:20 Gomorrah is great, and **b.** their 3588
Ge 19:13 destroy this place, **b.** the cry of 3588
Ge 20:11 Abraham said, **B.** I thought, 3588
Ge 20:18 **b.** of Sarah Abraham's wife 5921,1697
Ge 21:11 Abraham's sight **b.** of his 2921,182
Ge 21:12 in thy sight **b.** of the lad, 5921
Ge 21:12 and **b.** of thy bondwoman; 5921
Ge 21:13 make a nation, **b.** he is thy seed 3588
Ge 21:25 reproved Abimelech **b.** of a 5921,182
Ge 21:31 **b.** there they sware both of them 3588
Ge 22:16 **b.** thou hast done this thing, 3282,834
Ge 22:18 **b.** thou hast obeyed my voice 6118,834
Ge 25:21 for his wife, **b.** she was barren: 3588
Ge 25:28 loved Esau, **b.** he did eat of his 3588
Ge 26:5 **B.** that Abraham obeyed my 6119
Ge 26:7 for Rebekah; **b.** she was fair 3588
Ge 26:9 **B.** I said, Lest I die for her. 3588
Ge 26:20 **b.** they strove with him. 3588
Ge 27:20 he said, **B.** the Lord thy God 3588
Ge 27:23 And he discerned him not, **b.** 3588
Ge 27:41 Esau hated Jacob **b.** of the 5921
Ge 27:46 weary of my life **b.** of the 6440
Ge 28:11 tarried there all night, **b.** the sun 3588
Ge 29:15 **B.** thou art my brother, 3588
Ge 29:33 And said, **B.** the Lord hath heard 3588
Ge 29:34 be joined unto me, **b.** I have born 3588
Ge 30:18 my hire, **b.** I have given my hand 834
Ge 30:20 dwell with me, **b.** I have born him 3588
Ge 31:30 be gone, **b.** thou sore longedst 3588
Ge 31:31 said to Laban, **B.** I was afraid: 3588
Ge 32:32 **b.** he touched the hollow of Jacob's 3588
Ge 33:11 **b.** God hath dealt graciously 3588
Ge 33:11 and **b.** I have enough. 3588
Ge 34:7 very wroth, **b.** he had wrought 3588
Ge 34:13 said, **B.** he had defiled Dinah 834
Ge 34:19 to do the thing, **b.** he had delight 3588
Ge 34:27 spoiled the city, **b.** they had 834
Ge 35:7 El-beth-el: **b.** there God appeared 3588
Ge 36:7 could not bear them **b.** of their 6440
Ge 37:3 **b.** he was the son of his old age 3588
Ge 38:15 an harlot; **b.** she had covered 3588
Ge 38:26 more righteous than I; **b.** that I 3588
Ge 39:9 **b.** thou art his wife: how then can 834
Ge 39:23 **b.** the Lord was with him, 834
Ge 41:32 **b.** the thing is established by God, 3588
Ge 41:57 to buy corn; **b.** that the famine 3588
Ge 43:18 afraid, **b.** they were brought 3588
Ge 43:18 **B.** of the money that was 5921,1697
Ge 43:32 **b.** the Egyptians might not eat 3588
Ge 46:30 seen thy face, **b.** thou art yet 3588
Ge 47:20 sold every man his field, **b.** the 3588
Ge 49:4 **b.** thou wentest up to thy 3588
Ex 1:12 were grieved **b.** of the children of 6440
Ex 1:19 **B.** the Hebrew women are not as 3588
Ex 1:21 **b.** the midwives feared God 3588
Ex 2:10 **B.** I drew him out of the water 3588
Ex 4:26 bloody husband thou art, **b.** of the
Ex 5:21 and judge; **b.** ye have made our 834
Ex 8:12 **b.** of the frogs which he had 5921,1697
Ex 9:11 not stand before Moses **b.** of the 6440
Ex 12:39 not leavened; **b.** they were 3588
Ex 13:8 **b.** of that which the Lord did 5668
Ex 14:11 said unto Moses, **B.** there were no 1115
Ex 17:7 **b.** of the chiding of the children 5921
Ex 17:7 and **b.** they tempted the Lord, 5921
Ex 17:16 he said, **B.** the Lord hath 3588
Ex 18:15 **B.** the people come unto me 3588
Ex 19:18 **b.** the Lord descended upon 6440,834
Ex 29:33 not eat thereof, **b.** they are holy. 3588
Ex 29:34 shall not be eaten, **b.** it is holy. 3588
Ex 32:35 plagued the people, **b.** they 5921,834
Ex 40:35 **b.** the cloud abode thereon, 3588
Le 6:4 it shall be, **b.** he hath sinned, 3588
Le 6:9 burnt offering, **b.** of the burning 5921
Le 10:13 **b.** it is thy due, and thy son's 3588
Le 11:4 as the camel, **b.** he cheweth the 3588
Le 11:5 and the coney, **b.** he cheweth the 3588
Le 11:6 and the hare, **b.** he cheweth the 3588
Le 14:48 the house clean, **b.** the plague 3588
Le 15:2 **b.** of his issue he is unclean
Le 16:16 **b.** of the uncleanness of the
Le 16:16 and **b.** of their transgressions
Le 19:8 shall bear his iniquity, **b.** he 3588
Le 19:20 not be put to death, **b.** she was not 3588
Le 20:3 **b.** he hath given of his seed 3588
Le 21:23 **b.** he hath a blemish; 3588
Le 22:7 **b.** it is his food 3588
Le 22:25 **b.** their corruption is in them 3588
Le 26:10 bring forth the old **b.** of the new. 6440
Le 26:35 it shall rest; **b.** it did not rest 854,834
Le 26:43 **b.**, even **b.** they despised my 3282
Le 26:43 judgments, and **b.** their soul
Nu 3:13 **B.** all the firstborn are mine; 3588
Nu 6:7 **b.** the consecration of his God 3588
Nu 6:12 shall be lost, **b.** his separation 3588
Nu 7:9 he gave none: **b.** the service 3588
Nu 9:13 **b.** he brought not the offering 3588
Nu 11:3 Taberah: **b.** the fire of the Lord 3588
Nu 11:14 this people alone, **b.** it is too 3588
Nu 11:20 **b.** that ye have despised the Lord 3282
Nu 11:34 Kibroth-hattaavah: **b.** there they 3588
Nu 12:1 against Moses **b.** of the 5921,182
Nu 13:24 **b.** of the cluster of grapes 5921,182
Nu 14:16 **B.** the Lord was not able to 1115
Nu 14:22 **B.** all those men which have 3588
Nu 14:24 **b.** he had another spirit with him, 6118
Nu 14:43 **b.** ye are turned away 3588,5921,3651
Nu 15:31 **B.** he hath despised the word 3588
Nu 15:34 put him in ward, **b.** it was not 3588
Nu 19:13 **b.** the water of separation 3588
Nu 19:20 **b.** he hath defiled the sanctuary 3588
Nu 20:12 unto Moses and Aaron, **B.** ye 3282
Nu 20:13 **b.** the children of Israel strove 834
Nu 20:24 **b.** ye rebelled against my 5921,834
Nu 21:4 much discouraged **b.** of the way.
Nu 22:3 of the people, **b.** they were many: 3588
Nu 22:3 **b.** of the children of Israel. 6640
Nu 22:22 God's anger was kindled **b.** he 3588
Nu 22:29 unto the ass, **B.** thou hast 3588
Nu 22:32 **b.** thy way is perverse before me: 3588
Nu 25:13 **b.** he was zealous for his God, 8478,834
Nu 26:62 **b.** there was no inheritance 3588
Nu 27:4 his family, **b.** he hath no son? 3588
Nu 30:5 forgive her, **b.** her father 3588
Nu 30:14 **b.** he held his peace at her 3588
Nu 32:11 **b.** they have not wholly followed 3588
Nu 32:17 **b.** of the inhabitants of the land 6440
Nu 32:19 **b.** our inheritance is fallen 3588
Nu 35:28 **B.** he should have remained 3588
De 1:27 and said, **B.** the Lord hated
De 1:36 **b.** he hath wholly followed the 3282,834
De 2:5 **b.** I have given Mount Seir 3588
De 2:9 for a possession; **b.** I have given 3588
De 2:19 any possession; **b.** I have given it 3588
De 2:25 and be in anguish **b.** of thee. 6440
De 4:3 the Lord did **b.** of Baal-peor:
De 4:37 And **b.** he loved thy fathers, 8478,3588
De 7:7 nor choose you, **b.** ye were more
De 7:8 But **b.** the Lord loved you, 3588
De 7:8 **b.** he would keep the oath which he
De 8:20 **b.** ye would not be obedient unto 6118
De 9:18 **b.** of all your sins which ye sinned, 5921
De 9:25 **b.** the Lord had said he would 3588
De 9:28 say, **B.** the Lord was not able to bring
De 9:28 **b.** he hated them, he hath brought
De 12:20 I will eat flesh, **b.** thy soul 3588
De 13:5 put to death; **b.** he hath spoken 3588
De 13:10 that he die; **b.** he hath sought to 3588
De 14:8 the swine, **b.** it divideth the hoof 3588
De 14:29 the Levite, (**b.** he hath no part 3588
De 15:2 **b.** it is called the Lord's release. 3588
De 15:10 **b.** that for this thing the Lord 3588
De 15:16 **b.** he loveth thee and thine house, 3588
De 15:16 **b.** he is well with thee; 3588
De 16:15 **b.** the Lord thy God shall bless 3588
De 18:12 and **b.** of these abominations 1558
De 19:6 **b.** the way is long, and slay him; 3588
De 20:3 neither be ye terrified **b.** of them; 6440
De 21:14 **b.** thou hast humbled her. 8478,834
De 22:19 **b.** he hath brought up an evil 3588
De 22:21 **b.** she hath wrought folly 3588
De 22:24 damsel, **b.** she cried not, 5921,1697,843
De 22:24 man, **b.** he hath humbled 5921,1697,843
De 22:29 his wife; **b.** he hath humbled 8478,834
De 23:4 **B.** they met you not 5921,1697,834
De 23:4 **b.** they hired against thee Balaam 834
De 23:5 blessing unto thee, **b.** the Lord 3588
De 23:7 **b.** thou wast a stranger 3588
De 24:1 no favour in his eyes, **b.** he hath 3588
De 27:20 **b.** he hath uncovered his 3588
De 28:20 **b.** of the wickedness of thy doings, 6440
De 28:45 destroyed; **b.** thou hearkenedst 3588
De 28:47 **B.** thou servedst not the Lord 8478,834
De 28:55 **b.** he hath nothing left him
De 28:62 **b.** thou wouldst not obey 3588
De 29:25 say, **B.** they have forsaken 5921, 834

De 31:17 **b.** our God is not among us?.......5921,3588
De 31:29 **b.** ye will do evil in the sight.......3588
De 32:3 **B.** I will publish the name.......3588
De 32:51 **b.** ye sanctified me not in the.......5921,834
De 32:19 abhorred them, **b.** of the provoking.......
De 32:47 vain thing for you; **b.** it is your.......3588
De 32:51 **B.** ye trespassed against me.......5921,834
De 33:21 part for himself, **b.** there, in a.......3588
Jos 2:9 inhabitants of the land faint **b.** of.......6440
Jos 2:11 more courage in any man, **b.** of.......6440
Jos 2:24 the country do faint **b.** of us.......6440
Jos 5:1 them any more, **b.** of the children.......6440
Jos 5:6 were consumed, **b.** they obeyed.......834
Jos 5:7 **b.** they had not circumcised.......3588
Jos 6:1 up **b.** of the children of Israel:.......6440
Jos 6:17 **b.** she hid the messengers.......3588
Jos 6:25 unto this day; **b.** she hid the.......3588
Jos 7:12 before their enemies, **b.** they were.......3588
Jos 7:15 **b.** he hath transgressed the.......3588
Jos 7:15 **b.** he hath wrought folly in Israel.......3588
Jos 9:9 thy servants are come **b.** of the.......
Jos 9:18 smote them not, **b.** the princes.......3588
Jos 9:20 be upon us, **b.** of the oath which.......5921
Jos 9:24 **B.** it was certainly told thy.......3588
Jos 9:24 sore afraid of our lives **b.** of you,.......6440
Jos 10:2 feared greatly, **b.** Gibeon was a.......3588
Jos 10:2 **b.** it was greater than Ai,.......3588
Jos 10:42 **b.** the Lord God...fought for Israel.......3588
Jos 11:6 Be not afraid **b.** of them:.......6440
Jos 14:9 for ever, **b.** thou hast wholly.......3588
Jos 14:14 unto this day, **b.** that he wholly.......3282
Jos 17:1 **b.** he was a man of war,.......3588
Jos 17:6 **B.** the daughters of Manasseh.......3588
Jos 20:5 **b.** he smote his neighbour.......3588
Jos 22:31 **b.** ye have not committed this.......834
Jos 23:3 done unto all these nations **b.** of.......6440
Jg 1:19 **b.** they had chariots.......3588
Jg 2:18 **b.** of their groanings by reason of.......6440
Jg 2:20 he said, **B.** that this people hath.......3282
Jg 3:12 against Israel, **b.** they had.......5921,3588
Jg 5:23 **b.** they came not to the help of the.......3588
Jg 6:2 against Israel: and **b.** of the.......6440
Jg 6:6 impoverished, **b.** of the Midianites;.......6440
Jg 6:7 cried unto the Lord **b.** of the.......5921,182
Jg 6:22 for **b.** I have seen an angel.......5921,3651
Jg 6:27 so it was, **b.** he feared his father's.......834
Jg 6:30 he may die: **b.** he hath cast down.......3588
Jg 6:30 and **b.** he hath cut down the grove.......3588
Jg 6:31 plead for himself, **b.** one hath cast.......3588
Jg 6:32 against him, **b.** he hath thrown.......3588
Jg 8:20 he feared, **b.** he was yet a youth.......3588
Jg 8:24 **b.** they were Ishmaelites.).......3588
Jg 9:18 **b.** he is your brother;).......3588
Jg 10:10 sinned against thee, both **b.** we.......3588
Jg 11:13 **B.** Israel took away my land,.......3588
Jg 12:4 smote Ephraim, **b.** they said,.......3588
Jg 13:22 surely die, **b.** we have seen God.......3588
Jg 14:17 told her, **b.** she lay sore upon him.......3588
Jg 15:6 **b.** he had taken his wife,.......3588
Jg 18:28 no deliverer, **b.** it was far.......3588
Jg 20:36 **b.** they trusted to the liers in wait.......3588
Jg 21:15 **b.** that the Lord had made a breach.......3588
Jg 21:22 **b.** we reserved not to each man.......3588
1Sa 1:6 make her fret, **b.** the Lord had.......3588
1Sa 1:20 **B.** I have asked him of the Lord.......3588
1Sa 2:1 **b.** I rejoice in thy salvation.......3588
1Sa 2:25 **b.** the Lord would slay them.......3588
1Sa 3:13 **b.** his sons made themselves.......3588
1Sa 4:21 **b.** the ark of God was taken,.......413
1Sa 4:21 and **b.** of her father in law.......413
1Sa 6:19 **b.** they had looked into the ark.......3588
1Sa 6:19 people lamented, **b.** the Lord had.......3588
1Sa 8:18 **b.** of your king which ye shall.......6440
1Sa 9:13 until he come, **b.** he doth bless.......3588
1Sa 9:16 my people, **b.** their cry is come.......3588
1Sa 10:1 it not **b.** the Lord hath anointed.......3588
1Sa 12:10 sinned, **b.** we have forsaken.......3588
1Sa 12:22 **b.** it hath pleased the Lord.......3588
1Sa 13:11 **B.** I saw that the people.......3588
1Sa 13:14 **b.** thou hast not kept.......3588
1Sa 14:29 enlightened, **b.** I tasted a little.......3588
1Sa 15:23 **B.** thou hast rejected the word.......3282
1Sa 15:24 thy words: **b.** I feared the people,.......3588
1Sa 16:7 **b.** I have refused him:.......3588
1Sa 17:32 no man's heart fail **b.** of him;.......5921
1Sa 18:3 **b.** he loved him as his own.......
1Sa 18:12 afraid of David, **b.** the Lord.......3588
1Sa 18:16 loved David, **b.** he went out.......3588
1Sa 19:4 **b.** he hath not sinned against thee,.......3588
1Sa 19:4 and **b.** his works have been.......3588
1Sa 20:17 swear again, **b.** he loved him.......
1Sa 20:18 missed, **b.** thy seat will be empty.......3588
1Sa 20:34 **b.** his father had done him shame.......3588
1Sa 21:8 with me, **b.** the king's business.......3588
1Sa 22:17 **b.** their hand also is with David,.......3588
1Sa 22:17 and **b.** they knew when he fled,.......3588
1Sa 24:5 smote him, **b.** he had cut off.......5921,834
1Sa 25:28 **b.** my lord fighteth the battles.......3588
1Sa 26:12 all asleep; **b.** a deep sleep from the.......3588
1Sa 26:16 worthy to die, **b.** ye have not kept.......834
1Sa 26:21 **b.** my soul was precious.......8478,834
1Sa 28:18 **b.** thou obeyedst not the voice of.......834
1Sa 28:20 **b.** of the words of Samuel:.......
1Sa 30:6 stoning him, **b.** the soul of all.......3588
1Sa 30:13 left me, **b.** three days agone I fell.......3588
1Sa 30:16 **b.** of all the great spoil.......
1Sa 30:22 said, **B.** they went not with us,.......3282
2Sa 1:9 **b.** my life is yet whole in me.......3588
2Sa 1:10 slew him, **b.** I was sure that he.......3588
2Sa 1:12 **b.** they were fallen by the sword.......3588
2Sa 2:6 **b.** ye have done this thing.......834
2Sa 3:11 a word again, **b.** he feared him.......
2Sa 3:30 **b.** he had slain their brother.......5921,834
2Sa 6:8 displeased, **b.** the Lord had.......5921,834
2Sa 6:12 **b.** of the ark of God.......5668
2Sa 8:10 bless him, **b.** he had fought.......5921,834
2Sa 10:5 **b.** the men were greatly.......3588
2Sa 12:6 **b.** he did this thing,.......6118,834
2Sa 12:6 **b.** he had no pity.......5921,834
2Sa 1:10 **b.** thou hast despised me,.......6118,3588
2Sa 1:14 **b.** by this deed thou hast given.......3588
2Sa 1:25 name Jedidiah, **b.** of the Lord.......5668
2Sa 13:22 **b.** he had forced his.......5921,1697,834
2Sa 14:15 it is **b.** the people have made me.......3588
2Sa 14:26 he polled it: **b.** the hair was heavy.......3588
2Sa 16:8 **b.** thou art a bloody man.......3588
2Sa 16:10 let him curse, **b.** the Lord hath said.......3588
2Sa 18:20 bear no tidings, **b.** the king's.......3588,5921
2Sa 19:21 **b.** he cursed the Lord's anointed?.......3588
2Sa 19:26 **b.** thy servant is lame.......3588
2Sa 19:42 **B.** the king is near of kin.......3588
2Sa 21:1 **b.** he slew the Gibeonites.......5921,834
2Sa 21:7 **b.** of the Lord's oath.......5921
2Sa 22:8 shook, **b.** he was wroth.......3588
2Sa 22:20 delivered me, **b.** he delighted in.......3588
2Sa 23:6 thrust away, **b.** they cannot be.......3588
1Ki 1:50 Adonijah feared **b.** of Solomon,.......6440
1Ki 2:7 I fled **b.** of Absalom thy brother.......6440
1Ki 2:26 **b.** thou bearest the ark of the Lord.......3588
1Ki 2:26 and **b.** thou hast been afflicted.......3588
1Ki 3:2 **b.** there was no house built.......3588
1Ki 3:11 **B.** thou hast asked this thing,.......3282
1Ki 3:19 died in the night; **b.** she overlaid.......834
1Ki 7:47 **b.** they were exceeding many:.......
1Ki 8:11 stand to minister **b.** of the cloud:.......6440
1Ki 8:33 **b.** they have sinned against thee,.......834
1Ki 8:35 no rain, **b.** they have sinned.......3588
1Ki 8:64 **b.** the brasen altar that was.......3588
1Ki 9:9 **B.** they forsook the Lord.......5921,834
1Ki 10:9 **B.** the Lord loved Israel for ever,.......
1Ki 11:9 **b.** his heart was turned.......3588
1Ki 11:33 **B.** that they have forsaken.......3282,834
1Ki 11:34 **b.** he kept my commandments.......834
1Ki 14:13 **b.** in him there is found some.......3282
1Ki 14:15 **b.** they have made their groves,.......834
1Ki 14:16 **b.** of the sins of Jeroboam, who.......1558
1Ki 15:5 **B.** David did that which was right.......834
1Ki 15:13 from being queen, **b.** she had made.......834
1Ki 15:30 **B.** of the sins of Jeroboam.......5921
1Ki 16:7 and **b.** he killed him.......834
1Ki 17:7 up, **b.** there had been no rain.......3588
1Ki 19:7 Arise and eat; **b.** the journey is too.......3588
1Ki 19:14 **b.** the children of Israel have.......3588
1Ki 20:28 **B.** the Syrians have said,.......3282,834
1Ki 20:36 **B.** thou hast not obeyed the.......3282,834
1Ki 20:42 **B.** thou hast let go out of thy.......3282
1Ki 21:2 garden of herbs, **b.** it is near.......3588
1Ki 21:4 displeased **b.** of the word which.......5921
1Ki 21:6 **B.** I snake unto Naboth.......3588
1Ki 21:20 found thee: **b.** thou hast sold.......3282
1Ki 21:29 **b.** he humbleth himself.......3282,3588
2Ki 1:3 Is it not **b.** there is not a God.......
2Ki 1:6 Is it not **b.** there is not a God in.......
2Ki 1:16 Is it not **b.** there is no God in Israel,.......
2Ki 1:17 king of Judah, **b.** he had no son.......3588
2Ki 5:1 honourable, **b.** by him the Lord.......3588
2Ki 8:12 answered, **B.** I know the evil that.......3588
2Ki 8:29 **b.** he was sick.......3588
2Ki 9:14 **b.** of Hazael king of Syria.......6440
2Ki 10:30 unto Jehu, **B.** thou hast done.......3282,834
2Ki 13:4 **b.** the king of Syria oppressed.......3588
2Ki 13:23 **b.** of his covenant with Abraham,.......4616
2Ki 15:16 **b.** they opened not to him,.......3588
2Ki 17:26 slay them, **b.** they know not.......834
2Ki 18:12 **B.** they obeyed not the voice.......3282,834
2Ki 19:28 **B.** thy rage against me.......3282
2Ki 21:11 **B.** Manasseh king of Judah.......3282,834
2Ki 21:15 **B.** they have done that.......3282,834
2Ki 22:7 into their hand, **b.** they dealt.......3588
2Ki 22:13 kindled against us, **b.** our.......3282,834
2Ki 22:17 **B.** they have forsaken me,.......8478,834
2Ki 22:19 **B.** thine heart was tender,.......3282
2Ki 23:26 against Judah, **b.** of all the.......5921
1Ch 1:19 Peleg; **b.** in his days the earth.......3588
1Ch 4:9 saying, **B.** I bare him with sorrow.......3588
1Ch 4:41 **b.** there was pasture there.......3588
1Ch 5:9 **b.** their cattle were multiplied.......3588
1Ch 5:20 intreated of them; **b.** they put.......3588
1Ch 5:22 many slain, **b.** the war was of God.......3588
1Ch 7:21 **b.** they came down to take.......3588
1Ch 7:23 Beriah, **b.** it went evil with his.......3588
1Ch 9:27 **b.** the charge was upon them,.......3588
1Ch 12:1 close **b.** of Saul the son of Kish:.......6440
1Ch 13:10 **b.** he put his hand to the ark:.......5921,834
1Ch 13:11 displeased, **b.** the Lord had made.......3588
1Ch 14:2 **b.** of his people Israel.......5668
1Ch 15:13 For **b.** ye did it not at the first,.......3588
1Ch 15:22 **b.** he was skilful.......3588
1Ch 16:33 **b.** he cometh to judge the earth.......3588
1Ch 16:41 thanks to the Lord, **b.** his mercy.......3588
1Ch 18:10 congratulate him, **b.** he had.......5921,834
1Ch 19:2 **b.** his father showed kindness.......3588
1Ch 21:8 **b.** I have done this thing:.......834
1Ch 21:30 **b.** of the sword of the angel.......6440
1Ch 22:8 unto my name, **b.** thou hast shed.......3588
1Ch 23:28 **B.** their office was to wait.......3588
1Ch 27:23 **b.** the Lord had said.......3588
1Ch 27:24 finished not, **b.** there fell wrath.......
1Ch 28:3 **b.** thou hast been a man of war,.......3588
1Ch 29:3 **b.** I have set my affection to the.......
1Ch 29:9 **b.** with perfect heart.......3588
2Ch 1:11 to Solomon, **B.** this was in.......3282,834
2Ch 2:11 **B.** the Lord hath loved his people,.......
2Ch 6:24 **b.** they have sinned against.......3588
2Ch 6:26 no rain, **b.** they have sinned.......3588
2Ch 7:2 **b.** the glory of the Lord.......3588
2Ch 7:6 praise the Lord, **b.** his mercy.......3588
2Ch 7:7 peace offerings, **b.** the brasen.......3588
2Ch 7:22 **B.** they forsook the Lord God.......3282,834
2Ch 8:11 **b.** the places are holy,.......3588
2Ch 9:8 **b.** thy God loved Israel,.......
2Ch 12:2 against Jerusalem, **b.** they had.......3588
2Ch 12:5 to Jerusalem **b.** of Shishak,.......6448
2Ch 12:14 did evil, **b.** he prepared not.......3588
2Ch 13:18 **b.** they relied upon the Lord.......3588
2Ch 14:6 **b.** the Lord had given him.......3588
2Ch 14:7 **b.** we have sought the Lord.......3588
2Ch 15:16 **b.** she had made an idol.......834
2Ch 16:7 **B.** thou hast relied on the king.......
2Ch 16:8 yet, because thou didst rely on.......
2Ch 16:10 rage with him **b.** of this thing.......5921
2Ch 17:3 **b.** he walked in the first.......3588
2Ch 20:37 **B.** thou hast joined thyself.......
2Ch 21:3 Jehoram; **b.** he was the firstborn.......3588
2Ch 21:7 **b.** of the covenant.......3282
2Ch 21:10 his hand; **b.** he had forsaken.......3588
2Ch 21:12 **B.** thou hast not walked.......8478,834
2Ch 22:6 in Jezreel **b.** of the wounds.......3588
2Ch 22:6 **b.** he was sick.......3588
2Ch 22:9 **B.**, said they, he is the son.......3588
2Ch 24:16 the kings, **b.** he had done good.......3588
2Ch 24:20 **b.** ye have forsaken the Lord,.......3588
2Ch 24:24 their hand, **b.** they had forsaken.......3588
2Ch 25:16 thee, **b.** thou hast done this,.......3588
2Ch 25:20 **b.** they sought after the gods.......3588
2Ch 26:20 to go out, **b.** the Lord had smitten.......3588
2Ch 27:6 became mighty, **b.** he prepared.......3588
2Ch 28:6 **b.** they had forsaken the Lord.......
2Ch 28:9 Behold, **b.** the Lord God.......
2Ch 28:19 brought Judah low **b.** of Ahaz.......5668
2Ch 28:23 he said, **B.** the gods of the kings.......3588

2Ch 30:3 at that time, **b.** the priests had... 3588
2Ch 34:21 poured out upon us, **b.** our... 3282,834
2Ch 34:25 **B.** they have forsaken me,... 8478,834
2Ch 34:27 **B.** thine heart was tender,... 3282
2Ch 35:14 for the priests: **b.** the priests... 3588
2Ch 36:15 **b.** he had compassion on his... 3588
Ezr 3:3 was upon them **b.** of the people...
Ezr 3:11 thanks unto the Lord; **b.** he is... 3588
Ezr 3:11 the Lord, **b.** the foundation... 5921
Ezr 4:14 Now **b.** we have... 3606,6903,1768
Ezr 8:22 **b.** we had spoken unto the king... 3588
Ezr 9:4 **b.** of the transgression of those... 5921
Ezr 9:15 cannot stand before thee **b.** of this... 5921
Ezr 10:6 he mourned **b.** of the transgression... 5921
Ezr 10:9 of God, trembling **b.** of this matter,... 5921
Ne 4:9 against them day and night, **b.** of... 6440
Ne 5:3 buy corn, **b.** of the dearth...
Ne 5:9 fear of our God, **b.** of the reproach...
Ne 5:15 So did not I, **b.** of the fear of God... 6440
Ne 5:18 **b.** the bondage was heavy upon... 3588
Ne 6:18 him, **b.** he was the son in law of... 3588
Ne 8:12 great mirth, **b.** they had... 3588
Ne 9:37 thou hast set over us **b.** of our...
Ne 9:38 And **b.** of all this we make...
Ne 13:2 **B.** they met not the children... 3588
Ne 13:29 **b.** they have defiled the... 5921
Es 1:15 **b.** she hath not performed... 5921,834
Es 8:7 upon the gallows, **b.** he laid... 5921,834
Es 9:3 helped the Jews; **b.** the fear of... 3588
Es 9:24 **B.** Haman the son of Hammedatha,... 3588
Job 3:10 **B.** it shut not up the doors... 3588
Job 6:20 were confounded **b.** they had... 3588
Job 8:9 **b.** our days upon earth are a shadow... 3588
Job 11:16 **B.** thou shalt forget thy misery,... 3588
Job 11:18 shalt be secure, **b.** there is hope;... 3588
Job 15:27 **B.** he covereth his face... 3588
Job 17:12 the light is short **b.** of darkness... 6440
Job 18:15 in his tabernacle, **b.** it is none...
Job 20:19 **B.** he hath oppressed... 3588
Job 20:19 **b.** he hath violently taken away...
Job 23:17 **B.** I was not cut off... 3588
Job 29:12 **B.** I delivered the poor that cried,... 3588
Job 30:11 **B.** he hath loosed my cord,... 3588
Job 31:25 I rejoiced **b.** my wealth was great,... 3588
Job 31:25 and **b.** mine hand had gotten much;... 3588
Job 32:1 answer Job, **b.** he was righteous... 3588
Job 32:2 his wrath kindled, **b.** he justified... 5921
Job 32:3 **b.** they had found no answer,... 5921,834
Job 32:4 Job had spoken, **b.** they were... 3588
Job 34:27 **B.** they turned back... 834,5921,3651
Job 34:36 unto the end **b.** of his answers... 5921
Job 35:12 **b.** of the pride of evil men... 6440
Job 35:15 But now, **b.** it is not so,... 3588
Job 36:18 **B.** there is wrath,... 3588
Job 38:21 thou it, **b.** thou wast then born?... 3588
Job 38:21 **b.** the number of thy days is...
Job 39:11 trust him, **b.** his strength... 3588
Job 39:17 **B.** God hath deprived her of... 3588
Ps 5:8 in thy righteousness **b.** of mine... 4616
Ps 5:11 shout for joy, **b.** thou defendest...
Ps 6:7 Mine eye is consumed **b.** of grief;...
Ps 6:7 it waxeth old **b.** of all mine...
Ps 7:6 lift up thyself **b.** of the rage...
Ps 8:2 strength **b.** of thine enemies,... 4616
Ps 13:6 **b.** he hath dealt bountifully... 3588
Ps 14:6 counsel of the poor, **b.** the Lord... 3588
Ps 16:8 **b.** he is at my right hand,... 3588
Ps 18:7 shaken, **b.** he was wroth... 3588
Ps 18:19 he delivered me, **b.** he delighted... 3588
Ps 27:11 plain path, **b.** of mine enemies... 4616
Ps 28:5 **B.** they regard not the works... 3588
Ps 28:6 Blessed be the Lord, **b.** he hath... 3588
Ps 31:10 my strength faileth **b.** of mine...
Ps 33:21 rejoice in him, **b.** we have... 3588
Ps 37:1 Fret not thyself **b.** of evil doers,...
Ps 37:7 fret not thyself **b.** of him who...
Ps 37:7 his way, **b.** of the man...
Ps 37:40 save them, **b.** they trust... 3588
Ps 38:3 **b.** of thine anger; neither is... 6440
Ps 38:3 any rest in my bones **b.** of my sin... 6440
Ps 38:5 corrupt **b.** of my foolishness... 6440
Ps 38:20 **b.** I follow the thing that good is... 8478
Ps 39:9 not my mouth; **b.** thou didst it... 3588
Ps 41:11 favourest me, **b.** mine enemy... 3588
Ps 42:9 go I mourning **b.** of the oppression...
Ps 43:2 mourning **b.** of the oppression...
Ps 44:3 **b.** thou hadst a favour unto them... 3588

Ps 45:4 **b.** of truth and meekness... 5921,1697
Ps 48:11 be glad, **b.** of thy judgments... 4616
Ps 52:9 forever, **b.** thou hast done it:... 3588
Ps 53:5 put them to shame, **b.** God... 3588
Ps 55:3 **B.** of the voice of the enemy,...
Ps 55:3 **b.** of the oppression of the wicked:... 6440
Ps 55:19 **B.** they have no change,... 834
Ps 59:9 **B.** of his strength will I wait...
Ps 60:4 may be displayed **b.** of the truth... 6440
Ps 60:8 triumph thou **b.** of me... 5921
Ps 63:3 **B.** thy loving kindness is better... 3588
Ps 63:7 **B.** thou hast been my help,... 3588
Ps 68:29 **B.** of thy temple at Jerusalem...
Ps 69:7 **B.** for thy sake I have borne... 3588
Ps 69:18 deliver me **b.** of mine enemies... 4616
Ps 78:22 **B.** they believed not in God,... 3588
Ps 86:17 **b.** thou, Lord, hast holpen me,... 3588
Ps 91:9 **B.** thou hast made the Lord,... 3588
Ps 91:14 **B.** he hath set his love upon me,... 3588
Ps 91:14 set him on high, **b.** he hath known... 3588
Ps 97:8 Judah rejoiced **b.** of thy... 4616
Ps 102:10 **B.** of thine indignation and thy... 6440
Ps 106:33 **B.** they provoked his spirit,... 3588
Ps 107:11 **B.** they rebelled against the... 3588
Ps 107:17 **b.** of their transgression,... 1870
Ps 107:17 **b.** of their iniquities, are afflicted...
Ps 107:26 their soul is melted **b.** of trouble...
Ps 107:30 glad **b.** they are quiet;... 3588
Ps 109:16 **B.** that he remembered not to... 3282
Ps 109:21 **b.** thy mercy is good,... 3588
Ps 116:1 **b.** he hath heard my voice... 3588
Ps 116:2 **B.** he hath inclined his ear... 3588
Ps 118:1 **b.** his mercy endureth for ever... 3588
Ps 119:53 taken hold upon me **b.** of the wicked...
Ps 119:56 I had, **b.** I kept thy precepts... 3588
Ps 119:62 give thanks unto thee **b.** of thy... 5921
Ps 119:74 **b.** I have hoped in thy word... 3588
Ps 119:100 than the ancients, **b.** I keep... 3588
Ps 119:136 down mine eyes, **b.** they keep... 5921
Ps 119:139 consumed me, **b.** mine enemies... 3588
Ps 119:158 was grieved; **b.** they kept not... 834
Ps 119:164 praise thee **b.** of thy righteous... 5921
Ps 122:9 **B.** of the house of the Lord... 4616
Pr 1:24 **B.** I have called, and ye refused;... 3282
Pr 21:7 destroy them; **b.** they refuse... 3588
Pr 22:22 Rob not the poor, **b.** he is poor:... 3588
Pr 24:13 eat honey, **b.** it is good;... 3588
Pr 24:19 Fret not thyself **b.** of evil men,...
Ec 2:17 I hated life; **b.** the work... 3588
Ec 2:18 **b.** I should leave it...
Ec 4:9 Two are better than one; **b.** they... 834
Ec 5:20 **b.** God answereth him in the joy... 3588
Ec 8:6 **B.** to every purpose there is... 3588
Ec 8:11 **B.** sentence against an evil work... 834
Ec 8:13 as a shadow; **b.** he feareth not... 834
Ec 8:15 mirth, **b.** a man hath no better... 834
Ec 8:17 **b.** though a man labor to seek it... 834
Ec 10:15 **b.** he knoweth not how to go... 834
Ec 12:3 grinders cease **b.** they are few,... 3588
Ec 12:5 shall fail: **b.** man goeth to his... 3588
Ec 12:9 moreover, **b.** the preacher was wise,...
Ca 1:3 **B.** of the savour of thy good...
Ca 1:6 not upon me, **b.** I am black,...
Ca 1:6 **b.** the sun hath looked upon me:...
Ca 3:8 upon his thigh **b.** of fear...
Isa 2:6 **b.** they be replenished... 3588
Isa 3:8 Judah is fallen: **b.** their tongue... 3588
Isa 3:16 **B.** the daughters of Zion... 3282,3588
Isa 5:13 into captivity, **b.** they have no...
Isa 5:24 **b.** they have cast away the law,... 3588
Isa 6:5 I am undone; **b.** I am a man... 3588
Isa 7:5 **B.** Syria, Ephraim, and the... 3282,3588
Isa 7:24 men come thither; **b.** all the land... 3588
Isa 8:20 it is **b.** there is no light... 834
Isa 10:27 destroyed **b.** of the anointing... 6440
Isa 14:20 with them in burial, **b.** thou hast... 3588
Isa 14:29 Palestina, **b.** the rod of him... 3588
Isa 15:1 **B.** in the night Ar of Moab... 3588
Isa 15:1 **b.** in the night Kir of Moab... 3588
Isa 17:9 left **b.** of the children of Israel:... 6440
Isa 17:10 **B.** thou hast forgotten the God... 3588
Isa 19:16 **b.** of the shaking of the hand... 6440
Isa 19:17 **b.** of the counsel of the Lord of... 6440
Isa 19:20 **b.** of the oppressors, and he shall... 6440
Isa 22:4 comfort me, **b.** of the spoiling... 5921
Isa 24:5 **b.** they have transgressed... 3588
Isa 26:3 **b.** he trusteth in thee... 3588

Isa 28:15 **B.** ye have said,... 3588
Isa 28:28 is bruised; **b.** he will not ever... 3588
Isa 30:12 **B.** ye despise this word,... 3282
Isa 31:1 **b.** they are many; and in... 3588
Isa 31:1 **b.** they are very strong;... 3588
Isa 32:14 **B.** the palaces shall be forsaken;... 3588
Isa 37:29 **B.** thy rage against me,... 3282
Isa 40:7 fadeth: **b.** the spirit of the Lord... 3588
Isa 43:20 **b.** I give waters in the wilderness,... 3588
Isa 48:4 **B.** I knew that thou art obstinate,...
Isa 49:7 shall worship, **b.** of the Lord... 4616
Isa 50:2 fish stinketh, **b.** there is no water,...
Isa 51:13 **b.** of the fury of the oppressor,... 6440
Isa 53:9 **b.** he had done no violence,... 5921
Isa 53:12 **b.** he hath poured out his... 8478,834
Isa 55:5 run unto thee **b.** of the Lord... 4616
Isa 60:5 be enlarged; **b.** the abundance... 3588
Isa 60:9 Holy One of Israel, **b.** he hath... 3588
Isa 61:1 **b.** the Lord hath anointed me... 3282
Isa 64:7 us, **b.** of our iniquities... 3027
Isa 65:12 down to the slaughter: **b.** when I... 3282
Isa 65:16 **b.** the former troubles are... 3588
Isa 65:16 forgotten, and **b.** they are hid... 3588
Isa 66:4 fears upon them; **b.** when I... 3282
Jer 2:35 **B.** I am innocent... 3588
Jer 2:35 plead with thee, **b.** thou sayest,... 5921
Jer 4:4 **b.** of the evil of your doings... 6440
Jer 4:17 **b.** she hath been rebellious... 3588
Jer 4:18 **b.** it is bitter, **b.** it reacheth... 3588
Jer 4:19 hold my peace, **b.** thou hast... 3588
Jer 4:28 **b.** I have spoken it,... 5921,3588
Jer 4:31 soul is wearied **b.** of murderers...
Jer 5:6 in pieces: **b.** their transgressions... 3588
Jer 5:14 **B.** ye speak this word, behold,... 3282
Jer 6:19 **b.** they have not... 3588,5921,1697
Jer 6:30 them, **b.** the Lord hath rejected... 3588
Jer 7:13 now, **b.** ye have done all these... 3282
Jer 8:14 gall to drink, **b.** we have sinned... 3588
Jer 8:19 daughter of my people **b.** of them...
Jer 9:10 lamentation, **b.** they are burned... 3588
Jer 9:13 saith, **B.** they have forsaken... 5921
Jer 9:19 confounded, **b.** we have forsaken... 3588
Jer 9:19 **b.** our dwellings have cast... 3588
Jer 10:5 be borne, **b.** they cannot go,... 3588
Jer 12:4 **b.** they said, He shall not see... 3588
Jer 12:11 made desolate, **b.** no man... 3588
Jer 12:13 **b.** of the fierce anger of the Lord...
Jer 13:17 **b.** the Lord's flock is carried... 3588
Jer 13:25 saith the Lord; **b.** thou hast... 834
Jer 14:4 **B.** the ground is chapt,... 5668
Jer 14:5 forsook it, **b.** there was no grass... 3588
Jer 14:6 did fail, **b.** there was no grass... 3588
Jer 14:16 **b.** of the famine and the sword;... 6440
Jer 15:4 **b.** of Manasseh the son of... 1558
Jer 15:17 I sat alone **b.** of thy hand:... 6440
Jer 16:11 say unto them, **B.** your fathers... 5921,834
Jer 16:18 sin doubled; **b.** they have defiled... 5921
Jer 17:13 **b.** they have forsaken the Lord,... 3588
Jer 18:15 **B.** my people hath forgotten... 3588
Jer 19:4 **B.** they have forsaken me,... 3282,834
Jer 19:8 hiss **b.** of all the plagues... 5921
Jer 19:13 Tophet, **b.** of all the houses... 3605
Jer 19:15 it, **b.** they have hardened... 3588
Jer 20:8 violence and spoil; **b.** the word... 3588
Jer 20:17 **B.** he slew me not... 834
Jer 21:12 **b.** of the evil of your doings... 6440
Jer 22:9 **B.** they have forsaken... 5921,834
Jer 22:15 reign, **b.** thou closest thyself... 3588
Jer 23:9 is broken **b.** of the prophets;...
Jer 23:9 **b.** of the Lord, and **b.** of the... 6440
Jer 23:10 **b.** of swearing the land mourneth;... 6440
Jer 23:38 **B.** ye say this word, The burden... 3282
Jer 25:8 **B.** ye have not heard... 3282,834
Jer 25:16 **b.** of the sword that I will send... 6440
Jer 25:27 **b.** of the sword which I will send... 6440
Jer 25:37 **b.** of the fierce anger of the Lord... 6440
Jer 25:38 **b.** of the fierceness of the oppressor,... 6440
Jer 25:38 and **b.** of his fierce anger... 6440
Jer 26:3 **b.** of the evil of their doings... 6440
Jer 28:16 shalt die, **b.** thou hast taught... 3588
Jer 29:15 **B.** ye have said,... 3588
Jer 29:19 **B.** they have not hearkened... 8478,834
Jer 29:23 **B.** they have committed... 3282,834
Jer 29:25 saying, **B.** thou hast sent... 3282,834
Jer 29:31 **B.** that Shemaiah hath... 3282,834
Jer 29:32 **b.** he hath taught rebellion... 3588
Jer 30:14, 15 **b.** thy sins were increased...

Book	Ref	Context	Strong's
Jer	30:17	**b.** they called thee an Outcast,	3588
Jer	31:15	comforted for her children, **b.** they	3588
Jer	31:19	even confounded, **b.** I did bear	3588
Jer	32:24	against it, **b.** of the sword,	6440
Jer	32:32	**B.** of all the evil of the children	5921
Jer	35:16	**B.** the sons of Jonadab	3588
Jer	35:17	against them: **b.** I have spoken	3282
Jer	35:18	**B.** ye have obeyed	3282,834
Jer	39:18	**b.** thou hast put thy trust in me,	3588
Jer	40:3	**b.** ye have sinned against	3588
Jer	41:9	**b.** of Gedaliah, was it which Asa	3027
Jer	41:18	**B.** of the Chaldeans: for they	6440
Jer	41:18	**b.** Ishmael the son of Nethaniah	3588
Jer	44:3	**B.** of their wickedness which they	6440
Jer	44:22	**b.** of the evil of your doings,	6440
Jer	44:22	and **b.** of the abominations	6440
Jer	44:23	**B.** ye have burned incense,	6440,834
Jer	44:23	and **b.** ye have sinned against	834
Jer	46:15	stood not, **b.** the Lord did	3588
Jer	46:21	did not stand, **b.** the day	3588
Jer	46:23	be searched; **b.** they are more	3588
Jer	47:4	**B.** of the day that cometh	5921
Jer	48:7	For **b.** thou hast trusted	3588,3282
Jer	48:36	**b.** the riches that he hath	5921,3651
Jer	48:42	being a people, **b.** he hath	3588,5921
Jer	48:45	of Heshbon **b.** of the force:	
Jer	50:7	not, **b.** they have sinned	8471,834
Jer	50:11	**B.** ye are glad, **b.** ye rejoiced,	3588
Jer	50:11	**b.** ye are grown fat as the heifer	3588
Jer	50:13	**B.** of the wrath of the Lord	
Jer	50:24	caught, **b.** thou hast striven	3588
Jer	51:11	destroy it; **b.** it is the vengeance	3588
Jer	51:51	are confounded, **b.** we have heard	3588
Jer	51:55	**B.** the Lord hath spoiled	3588
Jer	51:56	**B.** the spoiler is come	3588
La	1:3	gone into captivity **b.** of affliction,	
La	1:3	and **b.** of great servitude:	
La	1:4	do mourn, **b.** none come	
La	1:8	despise her, **b.** they have seen	3588
La	1:16	down with water, **b.** the comforter	3588
La	1:16	desolate, **b.** the enemy prevailed	3588
La	2:11	**b.** the children and the sucklings	
La	3:22	not consumed, **b.** his compassions	3588
La	3:28	keepeth silence, **b.** he hath borne	3588
La	3:51	affecteth mine heart **b.** of all	
La	5:9	**b.** of the sword of the wilderness.	6440
La	5:10	**b.** of the terrible famine.	6440
La	5:18	**B.** of the mountain of Zion,	5921
Eze	3:20	he shall die: **b.** thou hast not	3588
Eze	3:21	surely live, **b.** he is warned;	3588
Eze	5:7	**B.** ye multiplied more	3282
Eze	5:9	**b.** of all thine abominations,	3282
Eze	5:11	Surely, **b.** thou hast defiled	3282
Eze	6:9	captives, **b.** I am broken	834
Eze	7:19	**b.** it is the stumbling block	3588
Eze	12:19	**b.** of the violence of all them	
Eze	13:8	**B.** ye have spoken vanity, and	3282
Eze	13:10	**B.**, even **b.** they have seduced my	3282
Eze	13:22	**B.** with lies ye have made the	3282
Eze	14:5	**b.** they are all estranged	834
Eze	14:15	pass through **b.** of the beasts:	6440
Eze	15:8	desolate, **b.** they have committed	3282
Eze	16:15	the harlot **b.** of thy renown,	5921
Eze	16:28	**b.** thou wast unsatiable; yea,	1115
Eze	16:36	**B.** thy filthiness was poured	3282
Eze	16:43	**B.** thou hast not remembered	3282,834
Eze	16:63	**b.** of thy shame, when I am	6440
Eze	18:18	**b.** he cruelly oppressed,	3588
Eze	18:28	**B.** he considereth,	
Eze	20:16	**B.** they despised my judgments	3282
Eze	20:24	**B.** they had not executed	3282
Eze	21:7	For the tidings; **b.** it cometh:	3588
Eze	21:13	**B.** it is a trial,	3588
Eze	21:24	**B.** ye have made your iniquity	3282
Eze	21:24	do appear; **b.**, I say, ye are come	3282
Eze	21:28	to consume **b.** of the glittering:	4616
Eze	22:19	**B.** ye are all become dross,	3282
Eze	23:30	unto thee, **b.** thou hast gone	
Eze	23:30	and **b.** thou art polluted	5921,834
Eze	23:35	**B.** thou hast forgotten me,	3282
Eze	23:45	**b.** they are adulteresses,	3588
Eze	24:13	lewdness: **b.** I have purged thee,	3282
Eze	25:3	**B.** thou saidst, Aha,	3282
Eze	25:6	**B.** thou hast clapped thine hands	3282
Eze	25:8	**B.** that Moab and Seir do say,	3282
Eze	25:12	**B.** that Edom hath dealt	3282
Eze	25:15	**B.** the Philistines have dealt	3282
Eze	26:2	Son of man, **b.** that Tyrus	3282
Eze	28:2	**B.** thine heart is lifted up,	3282
Eze	28:5	heart is lifted up **b.** of thy riches:	
Eze	28:6	**B.** thou hast set thine heart	3282
Eze	28:17	was lifted up **b.** of thy beauty,	
Eze	29:6	am the Lord, **b.** they have been	3282
Eze	29:9	am the Lord: **b.** he hath said,	3282
Eze	29:20	served against it, **b.** they wrought	834
Eze	31:5	became long **b.** of the multitude	
Eze	31:10	**B.** thou hast lifted up thyself	3282,834
Eze	33:29	most desolate **b.** of all their	5921
Eze	34:5	scattered, **b.** there is no shepherd:	
Eze	34:8	surely **b.** my flock became	3282
Eze	34:8	**b.** there was no shepherd,	
Eze	34:21	**B.** ye have thrust with side	3282
Eze	35:5	**B.** thou hast had a perpetual	3282
Eze	35:10	**B.** thou hast said,	3282
Eze	35:15	of Israel, **b.** it was desolate,	5921,834
Eze	36:2	**B.** the enemy hath said	3282
Eze	36:3	**B.** they have made you desolate,	3282
Eze	36:6	and in my fury, **b.** ye have borne	3282
Eze	36:13	**B.** they say unto you,	3282
Eze	39:23	iniquity: **b.** they trespassed	5921,834
Eze	44:2	enter in by it; **b.** the Lord,	3588
Eze	44:7	**b.** of all your abominations.	413
Eze	44:12	**B.** they ministered unto them	3282,834
Eze	47:9	of fish, **b.** these waters shall	3588
Eze	47:12	**b.** their waters they issued	3588
Da	2:8	**b.** ye see the thing is	3606,6903,1768
Da	3:22	Therefore **b.** the king's	4481,1768
Da	3:29	**b.** there is no other God	3606,6903,1768
Da	4:9	**b.** I know that the spirit	1768
Da	6:3	**b.** an excellent spirit	3606,6903,1768
Da	6:23	upon him, **b.** he believed	1768
Da	7:11	**b.** of the voice of the great words	4481
Da	9:7	driven them, **b.** of their trespass	
Da	9:8	to our fathers, **b.** we have sinned	834
Da	9:11	**b.** we have sinned	3588
Da	9:16	**b.** for our sins,	3588
Da	11:35	**b.** it is yet for a time	3588,5750
Ho	4:1	of the land, **b.** there is no truth,	3588
Ho	4:6	knowledge, **b.** thou hast rejected	3588
Ho	4:10	increase: **b.** they have left	3588
Ho	4:13	and elms, **b.** the shadow	3588
Ho	4:19	ashamed **b.** of their sacrifices.	
Ho	5:1	is toward you, **b.** ye have been	3588
Ho	5:11	in judgment, **b.** he willingly	3588
Ho	7:13	destruction unto them! **b.** they	3588
Ho	8:1	**b.** they have transgressed	3282
Ho	8:11	**B.** Ephraim hath made	3588
Ho	9:6	they are gone **b.** of destruction:	
Ho	9:17	cast them away, **b.** they did not	3588
Ho	10:3	king **b.** we feared not the Lord,	3588
Ho	10:5	shall fear **b.** of the calves	
Ho	10:5	thereof, **b.** it is departed from it.	3588
Ho	10:13	**b.** thou didst trust in thy way,	3588
Ho	10:15	**b.** of your great wickedness:	6440
Ho	11:5	be his king, **b.** they refused	3588
Ho	11:6	them, **b.** of their own counsels	
Joe	1:5	of wine, **b.** of the new wine;	5921
Joe	1:11	**b.** the harvest of the field	3588
Joe	1:12	withered: **b.** joy is withered away	3588
Joe	1:18	perplexed, **b.** they have no pasture;	3588
Joe	2:20	come up, **b.** he hath done great	3588
Joe	3:5	**B.** ye have taken my silver	834
Joe	3:19	**b.** they have shed innocent blood	834
Am	1:3	**b.** they have threshed Gilead	5921
Am	1:6	**b.** they carried away captive the	5921
Am	1:9	**b.** they delivered up the whole	5921
Am	1:11	punishment thereof; **b.** he did	5921
Am	1:13	**b.** they have ripped up the women	5921
Am	2:1	**b.** he burned the bones of the king	5921
Am	2:4	**b.** they have despised the law	5921
Am	2:6	**b.** they sold the righteous	5921
Am	4:12	**b.** I will do this unto thee,	6118,3588
Jon	1:10	presence of the Lord, **b.** he had told	3588
Mic	2:1	practise it, **b.** it is in the power	3588
Mic	2:10	is not your rest: **b.** it is polluted,	5668
Mic	6:13	thee desolate **b.** of thy sins.	5921
Mic	7:9	**b.** I have sinned against him,	3588
Mic	7:13	be desolate **b.** of them that dwell	5921
Mic	7:17	and shall fear **b.** of thee.	
Mic	7:18	anger for ever, **b.** he delighteth	3588
Na	3:4	**B.** of the multitude of the	
Na	3:11	seek strength **b.** of the enemy.	
Hab	1:16	**b.** by them their portion is fat,	3588
Hab	2:3	wait for it; **b.** it will surely come,	3588
Hab	2:5	**b.** he transgresseth by wine,	3588
Hab	2:8	**b.** thou hast spoiled many nations,	3588
Hab	2:8	**b.** of men's blood, and for the violence	
Hab	2:17	them afraid, **b.** of men's blood,	
Zep	1:17	blind men, **b.** they have sinned	3588
Zep	2:10	pride, **b.** they have reproached	3588
Zep	3:11	haughty **b.** of my holy mountain	
Hag	1:9	**B.** of mine house that is waste,	3282
Zec	8:10	or came in **b.** of the affliction:	4480
Zec	9:8	about mine house **b.** of the army,	
Zec	9:8	**b.** of him that passeth by,	
Zec	9:8	and **b.** of him that returneth:	
Zec	10:2	troubled, **b.** there was no shepherd.	3588
Zec	10:5	fight, **b.** the Lord is with them,	3588
Zec	11:2	fallen; **b.** the mighty are spoiled:	834
Mal	2:2	**b.** ye do not lay it to heart.	3588
Mal	2:14	**B.** the Lord hath been	5921,3588
Mt	2:18	not be comforted, **b.** they are not.	*3754*
Mt	5:36	**b. thou canst not make one hair**	*3754*
Mt	7:14	**B. strait is the gate, and narrow**	*3754*
Mt	9:36	**b.** they fainted, and were	*3754*
Mt	11:20	were done, **b.** they repented not:	*3754*
Mt	11:25	**b. thou hast hid these things**	*3754*
Mt	12:41	**b. they repented at the**	*3754*
Mt	13:5	**b. they had no deepness of earth:**	*1223*
Mt	13:6	**b. they had no root, they withered**	*1223*
Mt	13:11	**B. it is given unto you to know**	*3754*
Mt	13:13	**b. they seeing see not;**	*3754*
Mt	13:21	**ariseth b. of the word,**	*1223*
Mt	13:58	works there **b.** of their unbelief.	*1223*
Mt	14:5	**b.** they counted him as a prophet.	*3754*
Mt	15:32	**b. they continue with me now**	*3754*
Mt	16:7	It is **b.** we have taken no bread.	*3754*
Mt	16:8	**b. ye have brought no bread?**	*3754*
Mt	17:20	unto them, **B. of your unbelief:**	*1223*
Mt	18:7	**unto the world b. of offences!**	*575*
Mt	18:32	**that debt, b. thou desiredst me:**	*1893*
Mt	19:8	**b. of the hardness of your hearts**	*4314*
Mt	20:7	**B. no man hath hired us,**	*3754*
Mt	20:15	**thine eye evil, b. I am good?**	*3754*
Mt	20:31	**b.** they should hold their peace:	*2443*
Mt	21:46	**b.** they took him for a prophet.	*1894*
Mt	23:29	**b. ye build the tombs of the**	*3754*
Mt	24:12	**b. iniquity shall abound, the**	*1223*
Mt	26:31	**be offended b. of me this night:**	*1722*
Mt	26:33	shall be offended **b.** of thee, yet	*1722*
Mt	27:6	**b.** it is the price of blood.	*1893*
Mt	27:19	this day in a dream **b.** of him.	*1223*
Mk	1:34	devils to speak, **b.** they knew him.	*3754*
Mk	3:9	wait on him **b.** of the multitude,	*1223*
Mk	3:30	**B.** they said, He hath an unclean	*3754*
Mk	4:5	**b. it had no depth of earth:**	*1223*
Mk	4:6	**b. it had no root, it withered away.**	*1223*
Mk	4:29	**sickle, b. the harvest is come.**	*3754*
Mk	5:4	**B.** that he had been often bound	*1223*
Mk	6:6	he marvelled **b.** of their unbelief.	*1223*
Mk	6:34	**b.** they were as sheep not having	*3754*
Mk	7:19	**B. it entereth not into his heart,**	*3754*
Mk	8:2	**b. they have now been with me**	*3754*
Mk	8:16	It is **b.** we have no bread.	*3754*
Mk	8:17	**reason ye, b. ye have no bread?**	*3754*
Mk	9:38	forbad him, **b.** he followeth not us.	*3754*
Mk	9:41	**b. ye belong to Christ, verily I say**	*3754*
Mk	11:18	**b.** all the people was astonished	*3754*
Mk	12:24	**err, b. ye know not the scriptures,**	
Mk	14:27	**be offended b. of me this night:**	*1722*
Mk	15:42	**b.** it was the preparation, that is,	*1893*
Mk	16:14	**b.** they believed not them which	*3754*
Lu	1:7	**b.** that Elisabeth was barren,	*2530*
Lu	1:20	**b.** thou believest not my	*473,3759*
Lu	2:4	(**b.** he was of the house and lineage	*1223*
Lu	2:7	**b.** there was no room for them in	*1360*
Lu	4:18	**b. he hath anointed me to**	*3739,1752*
Lu	5:19	bring him in **b.** of the multitude,	*1223*
Lu	8:6	**away, b. it lacked moisture.**	*1223*
Lu	8:30	**b.** many devils were entered into	*3754*
Lu	9:7	**b.** that it was said of some, that	*1223*
Lu	9:49	**b.** he followeth not with us.	*3754*
Lu	9:53	**b.** his face was as though	*3754*
Lu	10:20	**b. your names are written in**	*3754*
Lu	11:8	**give him, b. he is his friend,**	*1223*
Lu	11:8	**b. of his importunity he will rise**	*1223*
Lu	11:18	**b. ye say that I cast out**	*3754*
Lu	12:17	**b. I have no room where to**	*3754*
Lu	13:2	**b. they suffered such things?**	*3754*
Lu	13:14	**b.** that Jesus had healed on	*3754*
Lu	15:27	**b. he hath received him safe**	*3754*

Lu 16:8 **steward, b. he had done wisely:** 3754
Lu 17:9 **b. he did the things that were** 3754
Lu 18:5 **Yet b. this widow troubleth me,** 1223
Lu 19:3 **b.** he was little of stature. 3754
Lu 19:11 **b.** he was nigh to Jerusalem, 1223
Lu 19:11 **b.** they thought that the kingdom
Lu 19:17 **b. thou hast been faithful in a** 3754
Lu 19:21 **b. thou art an austere man: thou** 3754
Lu 19:31 **B. the Lord hath need of him.** 3754
Lu 19:44 **b. thou knewest not the time...** *473,3739*
Lu 23:8 **b.** he had heard many things of 1223
Joh 1:50 **B. I said unto thee, I saw thee** 3754
Joh 2:24 unto them, **b.** he knew all men, 1223
Joh 3:18 **b. he hath not believed in the** 3754
Joh 3:19 **b. their deeds were evil.** 1063
Joh 3:23 **b.** there was much water there: 3754
Joh 3:29 **b.** of the bridegroom's voice: 1223
Joh 4:41 more believed **b.** of his own word; 1223
Joh 4:42 we believe, not **b.** of the saying: 1223
Joh 5:16 **b.** he had done these things 3754
Joh 5:18 **b.** he not only had broken the 3754
Joh 5:27 **b. he is the Son of man.** 3754
Joh 5:30 **b. I seek not mine own will,** 3754
Joh 6:2 **b.** they saw his miracles which he 3754
Joh 6:26 **not b. ye saw the miracles, but** 3754
Joh 6:26 **b. ye did eat of the loaves,** 3754
Joh 6:41 **b.** he said, I am the bread which 3754
Joh 7:1 **b.** the Jews sought to kill him. 3754
Joh 7:7 **but me it hateth, b. I testify of** 3754
Joh 7:22 **(not b. it is of Moses, but of the** 3754
Joh 7:23 **are ye angry at me b. I have** 3754
Joh 7:30 **b.** his hour was not yet come. 3754
Joh 7:39 **b.** that Jesus was not yet glorified. 3754
Joh 7:43 a division among the people **b.** of 1223
Joh 8:22 **b.** he saith, Whither I go, ye 3754
Joh 8:37 **b. my word hath no place in you...** 3754
Joh 8:43 **b. ye cannot hear my word.** 3754
Joh 8:44 **b. there is no truth in him.** 3754
Joh 8:45 **And b. I tell you the truth,** 3754
Joh 8:47 **them not, b. ye are not of God.** 3754
Joh 9:16 **b.** he keepeth not the sabbath 3754
Joh 9:22 **b.** they feared the Jews: for the 3754
Joh 10:13 **fleeth, b. he is an hireling,** 3754
Joh 10:17 **b. I lay down my life, that I might.** 3754
Joh 10:26 **b. ye are not of my sheep, as** 1063
Joh 10:33 and **b.** that thou, being a man, 3754
Joh 10:36 **b. I said, I am the son of God?** 3754
Joh 11:9 **b. he seeth the light of this world.** 3754
Joh 11:10 **b. there is no light in him.** 3754
Joh 11:42 **b. of the people which stand by** 1223
Joh 12:6 but **b.** he was a thief, and had 3754
Joh 12:11 **B.** that by reason of him many 3754
Joh 12:30 **This voice came not b. of me,** 1223
Joh 12:39 **b.** that Esaias said again, 3754
Joh 12:42 **b.** of the Pharisees they did not 1223
Joh 13:29 **b.** Judas had the bag, that Jesus 1893
Joh 14:12 **b. I go unto my Father** 3754
Joh 14:17 **b. it seeth him not, neither** 3754
Joh 14:19 **b. I live, ye shall live also.** 3754
Joh 14:28 **b. I said, I go unto the Father:** 3754
Joh 15:19 **but b. ye are not of the world,** 3754
Joh 15:21 **b. they know not him that sent** 3754
Joh 15:27 **b. ye have been with me from** 3754
Joh 16:3 **b. they have not known the,** 3754
Joh 16:4 **beginning, b. I was with you.** 3754
Joh 16:6 **But b. I have said these things** 3754
Joh 16:9 **b. they believe not on me;** 3754
Joh 16:10 **b. I go to my Father, and ye see** 3754
Joh 16:11 **b. the prince of this world is** 3754
Joh 16:16 **see me, b. I go to the Father.** 3754
Joh 16:17 **B.** I go to the Father? 3754
Joh 16:21 **b. her hour is come: but as soon** 3754
Joh 16:27 **b. ye have loved me, and have** 3754
Joh 16:32 **b. the Father is with me.** 3754
Joh 17:14 **b. they are not of the world, even** 3754
Joh 19:7 **b.** he made himself the Son of God. 3754
Joh 19:31 **b.** it was the preparation, that the 1893
Joh 19:42 **b.** of the Jews' preparation, day; 1223
Joh 20:13 **B.** they have taken away my Lord, 3754
Joh 20:29 **Thomas, b. thou hast seen me,** 3754
Joh 21:17 Peter was grieved **b.** he said unto 3754
Ac 2:6 **b.** that every man heard them 3754
Ac 2:24 **b.** it was not possible that he 2530
Ac 2:27 **B.** thou wilt not leave my soul 3754
Ac 4:21 punish them, **b.** of the people: 1223
Ac 6:1 **b.** their widows were neglected. 3754
Ac 8:11 **b.** that of long time he had 1223
Ac 8:20 **b.** thou hast thought that the 3754
Ac 10:45 **b.** that on the Gentiles also 3754
Ac 12:3 And **b.** he saw it pleased the Jews,
Ac 12:20 **b.** their country was nourished 1223
Ac 12:23 smote him, **b.** he gave not God.... *473,3739*
Ac 13:27 **b.** they knew him not
Ac 14:12 Mercurius, **b.** he was the chief 1894
Ac 16:3 circumcised him **b.** of the Jews 1223
Ac 17:18 **b.** he preached unto them Jesus, 3754
Ac 17:31 **B.** he hath appointed a day, in 1360
Ac 18:2 **b.** that Claudius had commanded 1223
Ac 18:3 **b.** he was of the same craft, 1223
Ac 20:16 **b.** he would not spend the 3704
Ac 22:29 Roman, and **b.** he had bound him. 3754
Ac 22:30 the morrow, **b.** he would have
Ac 24:11 **B.** that thou mayest understand,
Ac 25:20 And **b.** I doubted of such
Ac 26:2 Agrippa, **b.** I shall answer
Ac 26:3 Especially **b.** I know thee
Ac 27:4 **b.** the winds were contrary. 1223
Ac 27:9 **b.** the fast was now already past, 1223
Ac 27:12 And **b.** the haven was not
Ac 28:2 **b.** of the present rain, 1223
Ac 28:2 and **b.** of the cold 1223
Ac 28:18 **b.** there was no cause of death in 1223
Ac 28:20 **b.** that for the hope of Israel 1063
Ro 1:19 **B.** that which may be known of 1360
Ro 1:21 **B.** that, when they knew God, 1360
Ro 3:2 chiefly, **b.** that unto them were 3754
Ro 4:15 **B.** the law worketh wrath: for 1063
Ro 5:5 **b.** the love of God is shed abroad 3754
Ro 6:15 **b.** we are not under the law, 3754
Ro 6:19 **b.** of the infirmity of your flesh: 1223
Ro 8:7 **B.** the carnal mind is enmity 1360
Ro 8:10 body is dead **b.** of sin; but the 1223
Ro 8:10 Spirit is life **b.** of righteousness 1223
Ro 8:21 **b.** the creature itself also shall be 3754
Ro 8:27 **b.** he maketh intercession for the 3754
Ro 9:7 Neither, **b.** they are the seed 3754
Ro 9:28 **b.** a short work will the Lord 3754
Ro 9:32 **B.** they sought it not by faith, 3754
Ro 11:20 Well; **b.** of unbelief they were
Ro 14:23 if he eat, **b.** he eateth not of faith: 3754
Ro 15:15 **b.** of the grace that is given to me 1223
1Co 1:25 **B.** the foolishness of God is wiser 3754
1Co 2:14 **b.** they are spiritually discerned. 3754
1Co 3:13 **b.** it shall be revealed by fire; 3754
1Co 6:7 **b.** ye go to law one with another. 3754
1Co 11:10 power on her head **b.** of the angels. 1223
1Co 12:15 **B.** I am not the hand, I am not of 3754
1Co 12:16 **B.** I am not the eye, I am not of 3754
1Co 15:9 **b.** I persecuted the church of God. 1360
1Co 15:15 **b.** we have testified of God that 3754
2Co 2:13 my spirit, **b.** I found not Titus
2Co 5:14 **b.** we thus judge,
2Co 7:13 **b.** his spirit was refreshed by you 3754
2Co 11:7 **b.** I have preached to you the 3754
2Co 11:11 Wherefore? **b.** I love you not? 3754
Ga 2:4 that **b.** of false brethren unawares 1223
Ga 2:11 **b.** he was to be blamed 3754
Ga 3:19 It was added **b.** of transgressions, 5484
Ga 4:6 And **b.** ye are sons, God hath 3754
Ga 4:16 your enemy, **b.** I tell you the truth?
Eph 4:18 **b.** of the blindness of their heart: 1223
Eph 5:6 for **b.** of these things cometh 1223
Eph 5:16 the time, **b.** the days are evil. 3754
Php 1:7 **b.** I have you in my heart; 1223
Php 2:26 **b.** that ye had heard that he 1360
Php 2:30 **B.** for the work of Christ he was 3754
Php 4:17 Not **b.** I desire a gift: but I desire 3754
1Th 2:8 **b.** ye were dear unto us 1360
1Th 2:9 night and day, **b.** we would not 4314
1Th 2:13 **b.**, when ye received the word 3754
1Th 4:6 **b.** that the Lord is the avenger 1360
2Th 1:3 **b.** that your faith groweth 3754
2Th 1:10 (**b.** our testimony among you was 3754
2Th 2:10 that perish; **b.** they received *473,3739*
2Th 2:13 **b.** God hath from the beginning 3754
2Th 3:9 Not **b.** we have not power, 3754
1Ti 1:13 **b.** I did it ignorantly in unbelief. 3754
1Ti 4:10 **b.** we trust in the living God, 3754
1Ti 5:12 **b.** they have cast off their first 3754
1Ti 6:2 despise them, **b.** they are brethren; 3754
1Ti 6:2 **b.** they are faithful and beloved, 3754
Phm 7 **b.** the bowels of the saints are 3754
Heb 3:19 could not enter in **b.** of unbelief. 1223
Heb 4:6 entered not in **b.** of unbelief: 1223
Heb 6:13 **b.** he could swear by no greater, 1893
Heb 7:23 many priests, **b.** they were not 1223
Heb 7:24 this man, **b.** he continueth 1223
Heb 8:9 **b.** they continued not in my 3754
Heb 10:2 **b.** that the worshippers once 1223
Heb 11:5 not found, **b.** God had translated 1360
Heb 11:11 **b.** she judged him faithful who 1893
Heb 11:23 **b.** they saw he was a proper 1360
Jas 1:10 **b.** as the flower of the grass 3754
Jas 4:2 ye have not, **b.** ye ask not. 1223
Jas 4:3 and receive not, **b.** ye ask amiss. 1360
1Pe 1:16 **B.** it is written, Be ye holy; 1360
1Pe 2:21 **b.** Christ also suffered us, leaving 3754
1Pe 5:8 **b.** your adversary the devil, as a 3754
1Jo 2:8 **b.** the darkness is past, and the 3754
1Jo 2:11 **b.** that darkness hath blinded his 3754
1Jo 2:12 **b.** your sins are forgiven 3754
1Jo 2:13 **b.** ye have known him that is 3754
1Jo 2:13 **b.** ye have overcome the wicked 3754
1Jo 2:13 **b.** ye have known the Father. 3754
1Jo 2:14 **b.** ye have known him that is from 3754
1Jo 2:14 young men, **b.** ye are strong, 3754
1Jo 2:21 **b.** ye know not the truth, 3754
1Jo 2:21 but **b.** ye know it, 3754
1Jo 3:1 us not, **b.** it knew him not. 3754
1Jo 3:9 cannot sin, **b.** he is born of God. 3754
1Jo 3:12 **B.** his own works were evil, and 3754
1Jo 3:14 **b.** we love the brethren. He that 3754
1Jo 3:16 **b.** he laid down his life for us: 3754
1Jo 3:22 **b.** we keep his commandments, 3754
1Jo 4:1 **b.** many false prophets are gone 3754
1Jo 4:4 **b.** greater is he that is in you, 3754
1Jo 4:9 **b.** that God sent his only begotten 3754
1Jo 4:13 **b.** he hath given us of his Spirit. 3754
1Jo 4:17 **b.** as he is, so are we in this world. 3754
1Jo 4:18 **b.** fear hath torment. He that 3754
1Jo 4:19 We love him, **b.** he first loved us. 3754
1Jo 5:6 beareth witness, **b.** the Spirit is 3754
1Jo 5:10 **b.** he believeth not the record 3754
3Jo 7 **B.** that for his name's sake 1063
Jude 16 in admiration **b.** of advantage. 5484
Re 1:7 shall wail **b.** of him. Even so, 1909
Re 2:4 **b. thou hast left thy first love.** 3754
Re 2:14 **b. thou hast there them that hold.** 3754
Re 2:20 **b. thou sufferest that woman** 3754
Re 3:10 **B. thou hast kept the word of my** 3754
Re 3:16 **So then b. thou art lukewarm,** 3754
Re 3:17 **B. thou sayest, I am rich,** 3754
Re 5:4 **b.** no man was found worthy to 3754
Re 8:11 **b.** they were made bitter. 3754
Re 11:10 **b.** these two prophets tormented 3754
Re 11:17 **b.** thou hast taken to thee 3754
Re 12:12 great wrath, **b.** he knoweth
Re 14:8 **b.** she made all the nations drink 3754
Re 16:5 **b.** thou hast judged thus. 3754
Re 16:11 **b.** of their pains and their sores, 1537
Re 16:21 **b.** of the plague of the hail; 1537

BECHER (be'-ker) See also BACHRITES.
Ge 46:21 Belah, and **B.**, and Ashbel, Gera, 1071
Nu 26:35 of **B.**, the family of the Bachrites: 1071
1Ch 7:6 Bela, and **B.**, and Jediael, three. 1071
1Ch 7:8 the sons of **B.**; Zemira, and Joash, 1071
1Ch 7:8 All these are the sons of **B.** 1071

BECHORATH (be-ko'-rath)
1Sa 9:1 Zeror, the son of **B.**, the son of 1064

BECKONED
Lu 1:22 he **b.** unto them, and remained 1269
Lu 5:7 they **b.** unto their partners 2656
Joh 13:24 Peter therefore **b.** to him, that 3506
Ac 19:33 Alexander **b.** with the hand, and 2678
Ac 21:40 **b.** with the hand unto the people 2678
Ac 24:10 after that the governor had **b.** 3506

BECKONING
Ac 12:17 **b.** unto them with the hand 2678
Ac 13:16 and **b.** with his hand, said 2678

BECOME See also BECAME; BECOMETH.
Ge 3:22 Behold, the man is **b.** as one of us, 1961
Ge 9:15 the waters shall no more **b.** a 1961
Ge 18:18 Abraham shall surely **b.** a great 1961
Ge 24:35 and he is **b.** great: and he hath 1431
Ge 32:10 and now I am **b.** two bands 1961
Ge 34:16 with you, and we will **b.** one 1961
Ge 37:20 We shall see what will **b.** of his 1961
Ge 48:19 he also shall **b.** a people, and he 1961
Ge 48:19 shall **b.** a multitude of nations. 1961

Ex 4:9 of the river shall **b.** blood upon 1961
Ex 7:9 and it shall **b.** a serpent 1961
Ex 7:19 water, that they may **b.** blood; 1961
Ex 8:16 that it may **b.** lice throughout all 1961
Ex 9:9 And it shall **b.** small dust in all 1961
Ex 15:2 and he is **b.** my salvation: he is 1961
Ex 15:6 **b.** glorious in power: thy right 142
Ex 23:29 lest the land **b.** desolate, and the 1961
Ex 32:1, 23 we wot not what is **b.** of him. 1961
Le 19:29 and the land **b.** full of wickedness. 4390
Nu 5:24 shall enter into her, and **b.** bitter
Nu 5:27 and **b.** bitter, and her belly shall
De 27:9 thou art **b.** the people of the Lord 1961
De 28:37 thou shalt **b.** an astonishment, 1961
Jos 9:13 **b.** old by reason of the very long 1086
Jg 16:17 and I shall **b.** weak, and be like 2470
1Sa 28:16 from thee, and is **b.** thine enemy? 1961
2Sa 7:24 and thou, Lord, art **b.** their God. 1961
1Ki 2:15 about, and is **b.** my brother's; 1961
1Ki 14:3 he shall tell thee what shall **b.** of 1961
2Ki 21:14 they shall **b.** a prey and a spoil 1961
2Ki 22:19 that they should **b.** a desolation 1961
Es 2:11 what should **b.** of her 6213
Job 7:5 skin is broken, and **b.** loathsome. 3988
Job 15:28 which are ready to **b.** heaps.
Job 21:7 do the wicked live, **b.** old, 6275
Job 30:19 and I am **b.** like dust and ashes. 4911
Job 30:21 Thou art **b.** cruel to me: with 2015
Ps 14:3 they are all together **b.** filthy: 444
Ps 28:1 I **b.** like them that go down into 4911
Ps 53:3 they are altogether **b.** filthy; 444
Ps 62:10 **b.** not vain in robbery: if riches 1891
Ps 69:8 I am **b.** a stranger unto my 1961
Ps 69:22 Let their table **b.** a snare before 1961
Ps 69:22 for their welfare, let it **b.** a trap.
Ps 79:4 **b.** a reproach to our neighbours, 1961
Ps 109:7 and let his prayer **b.** sin. 1961
Ps 118:14 and song, and is **b.** my salvation. 1961
Ps 118:21 heard me, and art **b.** my salvation. 1961
Ps 118:22 is **b.** the head stone of the corner. 1961
Ps 119:83 For I am **b.** like a bottle in the 1961
Pr 29:21 have him **b.** his son at the length 1961
Isa 1:21 the faithful city **b.** an harlot! 1961
Isa 1:22 Thy silver is **b.** dross, thy wine 1961
Isa 7:24 land shall **b.** briers and thorns. 1961
Isa 12:2 he also is **b.** my salvation. 1961
Isa 14:10 Art thou also **b.** weak as we? 2470
Isa 14:10 art thou **b.** like unto us? 4911
Isa 19:11 of Pharaoh is **b.** brutish: 1197
Isa 19:13 The princes of Zoan are **b.** fools, 2973
Isa 29:11 And the vision of all is **b.** unto 1961
Isa 34:9 thereof shall **b.** burning pitch. 1961
Isa 35:7 parched ground shall **b.** a pool, 1961
Isa 59:6 Their webs shall not **b.** garments, 1961
Isa 60:22 A little one shall **b.** a thousand, 1961
Jer 2:5 after vanity, and are **b.** vain? 1891
Jer 3:1 from him, and **b.** another man's, 1961
Jer 5:13 And the prophets shall **b.** wind, 1961
Jer 5:27 they are **b.** great, and waxen rich. 6238
Jer 7:11 **b.** a den of robbers in your eyes: 1961
Jer 10:21 the pastors are **b.** brutish, and 1197
Jer 22:5 this house shall **b.** a desolation 1961
Jer 26:18 and Jerusalem shall **b.** heaps, 1961
Jer 49:13 Bozrah shall **b.** a desolation, 1961
Jer 50:23 how is Babylon **b.** a desolation 1961
Jer 50:37 and they shall **b.** as women: 1961
Jer 51:37 And Babylon shall **b.** heaps, 1961
Jer 51:41 is Babylon **b.** an astonishment 1961
La 1:1 how is she **b.** as a widow! she 1961
La 1:1 provinces, how is she **b.** tributary! 1961
La 1:2 with her, they are **b.** her enemies. 1961
La 1:6 her princes are **b.** like harts that 1961
La 1:11 and consider; for I am **b.** vile. 1961
La 4:1 How is the gold **b.** dim! how is 6004
La 4:3 daughter of my people is **b.** cruel,
La 4:8 is withered, it is **b.** like a stick. 1961
Eze 22:4 Thou art **b.** guilty in thy blood 816
Eze 22:18 Israel is to me **b.** dross: all they 1961
Eze 22:19 Because ye are all **b.** dross, 1961
Eze 26:5 it shall **b.** a spoil to the nations. 1961
Eze 36:35 land that was desolate is **b.** like
Eze 36:35 and ruined cities are **b.** fenced,
Eze 37:17 they shall **b.** one in thine hand. 1961
Da 4:22 that art grown and **b.** strong: 8631
Da 9:16 people are **b.** a reproach to all
Da 11:23 come up, and shall **b.** strong 6105
Ho 12:8 Ephraim said, Yet I am **b.** rich, 6238
Ho 13:15 and his spring shall **b.** dry, and his
Ho 13:16 Samaria shall **b.** desolate; 816
Jon 4:5 see what would **b.** of the city. 1961
Mic 3:12 Jerusalem shall **b.** heaps, and 1961
Zep 1:13 their goods shall **b.** a booty, and 1961
Zep 2:15 is she **b.** a desolation, a place for 1961
Zec 4:7 Zerubbabel thou shalt **b.** a plain:
Mt 18:3 **converted, and b. as little children,** *1096*
Mt 21:42 **is b. the head of the corner.** *1096,1519*
Mk 1:17 **make you to b. fishers of men.** *1096*
Mk 12:10 **is b. the head of the corner:** *1096,1519*
Lu 20:17 **is b. the head of the corner?** *1096,1519*
Jon 1:12 he power to **b.** the sons of God, *1096*
Ac 4:11 is **b.** the head of the corner: *1096,1519*
Ac 7:40 we wot not what is **b.** of him. *1096*
Ac 12:18 the soldiers, what was **b.** of Peter. *1096*
Ro 3:12 they are together **b.** unprofitable; *889*
Ro 3:19 world may **b.** guilty before God. *1096*
Ro 4:18 he might **b.** the father of many *1096*
Ro 6:22 and **b.** servants to God, ye have *1402*
Ro 7:4 ye also are **b.** dead to the law *2289*
Ro 7:13 might **b.** exceeding sinful. *1096*
1Co 3:18 **b.** a fool, that he may be wise. *1096*
1Co 7:18 let him not **b.** uncircumcised. *1986*
1Co 8:9 **b.** a stumblingblock to them that *1096*
1Co 13:1 I am **b.** as sounding brass, or a *1096*
1Co 15:20 **b.** the firstfruits of them that slept. *1096*
2Co 5:17 behold, all things are **b.** new. *1096*
2Co 12:11 I am **b.** a fool in glorying; *1096*
Ga 4:16 Am I therefore **b.** your enemy, *1096*
Ga 5:4 Christ is **b.** of no effect unto you, *2673*
Ti 2:1 things which **b.** sound doctrine: *4241*
Phm 6 thy faith may **b.** effectual by *1096*
Heb 5:12 are **b.** such as have need of milk, *1096*
Jas 2:4 are **b.** judges of evil thoughts? *1096*
Jas 2:11 art **b.** a transgressor of the law. *1096*
Re 11:15 The kingdoms of this world are **b.** *1096*
Re 18:2 is **b.** the habitation of devils, and *1096*

BECOMETH
Ps 93:5 holiness **b.** thine house, O Lord, 4998
Pr 10:4 He **b.** poor that dealeth with a
Pr 17:7 Excellent speech **b.** not a fool: 5000
Pr 17:18 **b.** surety in the presence of his 6148
Ec 4:14 is born in his kingdom **b.** poor.
Mt 3:15 **for thus it b. us to fulfil all** *4241*
Mt 13:22 **the word, and he b. unfruitful.** *1096*
Mt 13:32 **among herbs, and b. a tree,** *1096*
Mk 4:19 **the word, and it b. unfruitful.** *1096*
Mk 4:32 **b. greater than all herbs,** *1096*
Ro 16:2 her in the Lord, as **b.** saints, *516*
Eph 5:3 named among you, as **b.** saints: *4241*
Php 1:27 be as it **b.** the gospel of Christ: *516*
1Ti 2:10 **b.** women professing godliness) *516*
Tit 2:3 be in behaviour as **b.** holiness, *2412*

BED See also BEDS; BEDCHAMBER; BEDSTEAD.
Ge 48:2 himself, and sat upon the **b.**. 4296
Ge 49:4 thou wentest up to thy father's **b.**; 4904
Ge 49:33 gathered up his feet into the **b.** 4296
Ex 8:3 bedchamber, and upon thy **b.**, 4296
Ex 21:18 he die not, but keepeth his **b.** 4904
Le 15:4 Every **b.**, whereon he lieth that 4904
Le 15:5 whosoever toucheth his **b.** shall 4904
Le 15:21 whosoever toucheth her **b.** shall 4904
Le 15:23 if it be on her **b.**, or on any 4904
Le 15:24 all the **b.** whereon he lieth shall be 4904
Le 15:26 Every **b.** whereon she lieth all the 4904
Le 15:26 her as the **b.** of her separation: 4904
1Sa 19:13 an image, and laid it in the **b.**, 4296
1Sa 19:15 Bring him up to me in the **b.**, 4296
1Sa 19:16 there was an image in the **b.**, 4296
1Sa 28:23 the earth, and sat upon the **b.**. 4296
2Sa 4:5 who lay on a **b.** at noon. 4904
2Sa 4:7 lay on his **b.** in his bedchamber, 4296
2Sa 4:11 in his own house upon his **b.**? 4904
2Sa 11:2 David arose from off his **b.**, 4904
2Sa 11:13 he went out to lie on his **b.** 4904
2Sa 13:5 Lay thee down on thy **b.**, and 4904
1Ki 1:47 king bowed himself upon the **b.** 4904
1Ki 17:19 and laid him upon his own **b.**. 4296
1Ki 21:4 he laid him down upon his **b.**, 4296
2Ki 1:4 that **b.** on which thou art gone up, 4296
2Ki 1:6 shalt not come down from that **b.** 4296
2Ki 1:16 shalt not come down off that **b.** 4296
2Ki 4:10 let us set for him there a **b.**, 4296
2Ki 4:21 him on the **b.** of the man of God, 4296
2Ki 4:32 was dead, and laid upon his **b.**. 4296
1Ch 5:1 he defiled his father's **b.**, his 3326
2Ch 16:14 laid him in the **b.** which was 4904
2Ch 24:25 slew him on his **b.**, and he died: 4296
Es 7:8 Haman was fallen upon the **b.** 4296
Job 7:13 My **b.** shall comfort me, my couch 6210
Job 17:13 made my **b.** in the darkness. 3326
Job 33:15 men, in slumberings upon the **b.**; 4904
Job 33:19 also with pain upon his **b.**, 4904
Ps 4:4 with your own heart upon your **b.**, 4904
Ps 6:6 the night make I my **b.** to swim; 4296
Ps 36:4 He deviseth mischief upon his **b.**; 4904
Ps 41:3 strengthen him upon the **b.** of 6210
Ps 41:3 make all his **b.** in his sickness, 4904
Ps 63:6 I remember thee upon my **b.**, 3326
Ps 132:3 my house, nor go up into my **b.**;. 6210,3326
Ps 139:8 if I make my **b.** in hell, behold, 3331
Pr 7:16 decked my **b.** with coverings 6210
Pr 7:17 perfumed my **b.** with myrrh, 4904
Pr 22:27 why should he take away thy **b.** 4904
Pr 26:14 So doth the slothful upon his **b.**. 4296
Ca 1:16 pleasant: also our **b.** is green. 6210
Ca 3:1 By night on my **b.** I sought him 4904
Ca 3:7 his **b.**, which is Solomon's; 4296
Ca 5:13 His cheeks are as a **b.** of spices, 6170
Isa 28:20 the **b.** is shorter than that a man 4702
Isa 57:7 mountain hast thou set thy **b.** 4904
Isa 57:8 thou hast enlarged thy **b.**, 4904
Isa 57:8 their **b.** where thou sawest it. 4904
Eze 23:17 came to her into the **b.** of love, 4904
Eze 23:41 And satest upon a stately **b.**, 4296
Eze 32:25 They have set her a **b.** in the 4904
Da 2:28 visions of thy head upon thy **b.**, 4903
Da 2:29 came into thy mind upon thy **b.**, 4903
Da 4:5 and the thoughts upon my **b.** 4903
Da 4:10 the visions of mine head in my **b.**; 4903
Da 4:13 the visions of my head upon my **b.**, 4903
Da 7:1 visions of his head upon his **b.** 4903
Am 3:12 in Samaria in the corner of a **b.**, 4296
Mt 9:2 sick of the palsy, lying on a **b.** *2825*
Mt 9:6 **take up thy b., and go unto thine.** *2825*
Mk 2:4 they let down the **b.** wherein *2895*
Mk 2:9 **Arise, and take up thy b.,** *2895*
Mk 2:11 **Arise, and take up thy b., and go** *2895*
Mk 2:12 he arose, took up the **b.**, and went *2895*
Mk 4:21 **under a bushel, or under a b.?** *2825*
Mk 7:30 and her daughter laid upon the **b.** *2825*
Lu 5:18 men brought in a **b.** a man which *2825*
Lu 8:16 **putteth it under a b.; but setteth** *2825*
Lu 11:7 **my children are with me in b.;** *2845*
Lu 17:34 **there shall be two men in one b.;** *2825*
Joh 5:8 **Rise, take up thy b., and walk.** *2895*
Joh 5:9 and took up his **b.**, and walked: *2895*
Joh 5:10 lawful for thee to carry thy **b.** *2895*
Joh 5:11 unto me, Take up thy **b.**, and walk. *2895*
Joh 5:12 Take up thy bed, and walk? *2895*
Ac 9:33 AEneas, which had kept his **b.** *2895*
Ac 9:34 arise, and make thy **b.**. And he *4766*
Heb 13:4 **b.** undefiled: but whoremongers *2845*
Re 2:22 **Behold, I will cast her into a b.,** *2825*

BEDAD (be'-dad)
Ge 36:35 and Hadad the son of **B.**, who 911
1Ch 1:46 Hadad the son of **B.**, which smote 911

BEDAN (be'-dan)
1Sa 12:11 the Lord sent Jerubbaal, and **B.**, 917
1Ch 7:17 sons of Ulam; **B.**. These were 917

BEDCHAMBER
Ex 8:3 into thy **b.**, and upon thy bed, 2315,4904
2Sa 4:7 he lay on his bed in his **b.**, 2315,4904
2Ki 6:12 that thou speakest in thy **b.** 2315,4904
2Ki 11:2 in the **b.** from Athalia, 2315,4296
2Ch 22:11 put him and his nurse in a **b.** 2315,4296
Ec 10:20 curse not the rich in thy **b.**; 2315,4296

BEDEIAH (be-de'-yah)
Ezr 10:35 Benaiah, **B.**, Chelluh, 912

BED'S
Ge 47:31 bowed himself upon the **b.** head. 4296

BEDS
2Sa 17:28 **b.**, and basons, and earthen 4904
Es 1:6 the **b.** were of gold and silver, 4296
Ps 149:5 let them sing aloud upon their **b.** 4904
Ca 6:2 to the **b.** of spices, to feed in 6170
Isa 57:2 they shall rest in their **b.**, each 4904
Ho 7:14 they howled upon their **b.** 4904
Am 6:4 That lie upon **b.** of ivory, 4296
Mic 2:1 and work evil upon their **b.**! 4904

Mk 6:55 and began to carry about in **b.**........... *2895*
Ac 5:15 and laid them on **b.** and couches, ... *2825*

BEDSTEAD
De 3:11 his **b.** was a **b.** of iron; 6210

BEE See also BEES.
Isa 7:18 and for the **b.** that is in the land......... 1682

BEELIADA (be-e-li'-ad-ah)
1Ch 14:7 Elishama, and **B.**, and Eliphalet.......... 1182

BEELZEBUB (be-el'-ze-bub) See also BAAL-ZEBUB.
Mt 10:25 **called the master of the house B.**,.. *954*
Mt 12:24 but by **B.** the prince of the devils......... *954*
Mt 12:27 **And if I by B. cast out devils,** *954*
Mk 3:22 said, He hath **B.**, and by the prince *954*
Lu 11:15 He casteth out devils through **B.**.......... *954*
Lu 11:18 **I cast out devils through B.**............ *954*
Lu 11:19 **And if I by B. cast out devils,** *954*

BEEN
Ge 13:3 place where his tent had **b.** at the...... 1961
Ge 26:8 when he had **b.** there a long time,...........
Ge 31:5 God of my father hath **b.** with me. 1961
Ge 31:38 twenty years have I **b.** with thee;............
Ge 31:41 have I **b.** twenty years in thy house:........
Ge 31:42 the fear of Isaac, had **b.** with me, ... 1961
Ge 38:26 She hath **b.** more righteous than ....
Ge 45:6 hath the famine **b.** in the land: ....
Ge 46:32 their trade hath **b.** to feed cattle; 1961
Ge 46:34 servants' trade hath **b.** about............ 1961
Ge 47:9 days of the years of my life **b.**.......... 1961
Ex 2:22 **b.** a stranger in a strange land........... 1961
Ex 9:18 such as hath not **b.** in Egypt 1961
Ex 14:12 had **b.** better for us to serve the.............
Ex 18:3 have **b.** an alien in a strange land: 1961
Ex 21:29 it hath **b.** testified to his owner,..............
Ex 34:10 such as have not **b.** done in all.................
Le 10:19 should it have **b.** accepted.........................
Le 13:7 he hath **b.** seen of the priest.....................
Nu 19:20 separation hath not **b.** sprinkled upon him;..
De 2:7 Lord thy God hath **b.** with thee; ....
De 4:32 there hath **b.** any such thing as.......... 1961
De 4:32 or hath **b.** heard like it?.............................
De 9:7 **b.** rebellious against the Lord. 1961
De 9:24 **b.** rebellious against the Lord from 1961
De 15:18 **b.** worth a double hired servant ....
De 21:3 which hath not **b.** wrought with,...............
De 31:27 **b.** rebellious against the Lord; 1961
Jos 7:7 would to God we had **b.** content, ...
Jos 9:4 as if they had **b.** ambassadors,....................
Jos 10:27 cave wherein they had **b.** hid,....................
Jos 23:9 no man hath **b.** able to stand......................
Jg 16:8 withs which had not **b.** dried, ...
Jg 16:17 for I have **b.** a Nazarite unto God............
Ru 2:11 It hath fully **b.** shewed me, ...
1Sa 1:13 Eli thought she had **b.** drunken. ....
1Sa 4:7 not **b.** such a thing heretofore. 1961
1Sa 4:9 Hebrews, as they have **b.** to you: ....
1Sa 4:17 hath **b.** also a great slaughter........... 1961
1Sa 9:24 hath it **b.** kept for thee.............................
1Sa 14:29 how mine eyes have **b.** enlightened,...........
1Sa 14:30 **b.** now a much greater slaughter..............
1Sa 14:38 wherein this sin hath **b.** this............ 1961
1Sa 15:21 should have **b.** utterly destroyed, ...
1Sa 18:19 daughter should have **b.** given...................
1Sa 19:4 have **b.** to thee-ward very good: ....
1Sa 20:13 as he hath **b.** with my father. 1961
1Sa 21:5 women have **b.** kept from us.....................
1Sa 25:28 evil hath not **b.** found in thee...................
1Sa 25:34 there had not **b.** left unto Nabal ....
1Sa 29:3 which hath **b.** with me these days, ... 1961
1Sa 29:6 Lord liveth, thou hast **b.** upright,.............
1Sa 29:8 so long as I have **b.** with thee 1961
2Sa 1:21 he had not **b.** anointed ....
2Sa 1:26 pleasant hast thou **b.** unto me:...................
2Sa 12:8 and if that had **b.** too little, I....................
2Sa 13:20 Amnon thy brother **b.** with thee? 1961
2Sa 13:32 this hath **b.** determined.................... 1961
2Sa 14:32 it had **b.** good for me...............................
2Sa 14:32 to have **b.** there still.................................
2Sa 15:34 as I have **b.** thy father's servant 1961
1Ki 1:37 As the Lord hath **b.** with my lord....... 1961
1Ki 2:26 because thou hast **b.** afflicted.....................
1Ki 14:8 hast not **b.** as my servant David, ... 1961
1Ki 16:31 as if it had **b.** a light thing for him ....
1Ki 17:7 because there had **b.** no rain in......... 1961
1Ki 19:10, 14 have **b.** very jealous for the Lord.........
2Ki 4:13 Behold, thou hast **b.** careful for us............
2Ki 20:12 he had heard that Hezekiah had **b.** sick......
1Ch 17:8 And I have **b.** with thee 1961
1Ch 28:3 thou hast **b.** a man of war,...........................
1Ch 29:25 majesty as had not **b.** on any king 1961
2Ch 1:12 kings have had that have **b.** before ....
2Ch 15:3 a long season Israel hath **b.** without..........
2Ch 23:9 shields, that had **b.** king David's,..............
Ezr 2:1 those which had **b.** carried away,...............
Ezr 4:18 hath **b.** plainly read before me. ....
Ezr 4:19 and search hath **b.** made,............................
Ezr 4:19 sedition have **b.** made therein. ....
Ezr 4:20 There have **b.** mighty kings also 1934
Ezr 5:16 now hath it **b.** in building, ...
Ezr 8:35 of those that had **b.** carried away, ...
Ezr 9:2 princes and rulers hath **b.** chief.......... 1961
Ezr 9:4 those that had **b.** carried away;.................
Ezr 9:7 our fathers have we **b.** in a great ....
Ezr 9:7 and our priests, **b.** delivered.......................
Ezr 9:8 grace hath **b.** showed from the Lord ....
Ezr 10:6 of them that had **b.** carried away..............
Ezr 10:8 those that had **b.** carried away...................
Ne 2:1 I had not **b.** beforetime sad in........... 1961
Ne 5:15 governors that had **b.** before me ....
Ne 7:6 of those that had **b.** carried away, ...
Ne 13:10 portions of the Levites had not **b.**............
Es 2:6 Who had **b.** carried away ....
Es 2:6 which had **b.** carried away..........................
Es 2:12 that she had **b.** twelve months,.......... 1961
Es 4:11 I have not **b.** called to come.....................
Es 6:3 honour and dignity hath **b.** done ....
Es 7:4 if we had **b.** sold for bondmen ....
Job 3:13 have lain still and **b.** quiet, ...
Job 3:13 have slept: then had I **b.** at rest...............
Job 3:16 untimely birth I had not **b.**; 1961
Job 10:19 I should have **b.** as though................ 1961
Job 10:19 as though I had not **b.**; 1961
Job 10:19 I should have **b.** carried from...................
Job 22:9 arms of the fatherless have **b.** broken. ......
Job 31:9 If mine heart have **b.** deceived..................
Job 31:27 my heart hath **b.** secretly enticed, ...
Job 38:17 Have the gates of death **b.** opened ....
Job 42:11 that had **b.** of his acquaintance ....
Ps 25:6 for they have **b.** ever of old. ....
Ps 27:9 thou hast **b.** my help: leave me.......... 1961
Ps 35:14 as though he had **b.** my friend ....
Ps 37:25 I have **b.** young, and now am old; 1961
Ps 42:3 My tears have **b.** my meat day and 1961
Ps 50:8 to have **b.** continually before, ...
Ps 50:18 hast **b.** partakers with adulterers. ....
Ps 59:16 hast **b.** my defence and refuge in 1961
Ps 60:1 thou hast **b.** displeased;...........................
Ps 61:3 thou hast **b.** a shelter for me,............ 1961
Ps 63:7 Because thou hast **b.** my help,............ 1961
Ps 69:22 which should have **b.** for their..................
Ps 71:6 by thee have I **b.** holden up ....
Ps 73:14 all the day long have I **b.** plagued, ... 1961
Ps 85:1 Lord, thou hast **b.** favourable unto............
Ps 89:38 hast **b.** wroth with thine anointed. ....
Ps 90:1 thou hast **b.** our dwelling place in 1961
Ps 94:17 Unless the Lord had **b.** my help...............
Ps 115:12 The Lord hath **b.** mindful of us: ....
Ps 119:54 Thy statutes have **b.** my songs........... 1961
Ps 119:71 good for me that I have **b.** afflicted;..........
Ps 119:92 Unless thy law had **b.** my delights, ...
Ps 124:1, 2 If it had not **b.** the Lord who.......... 1961
Ps 143:3 as those that have **b.** long dead................
Pr 7:26 many strong men have **b.** slain...................
Ec 1:9 The thing that hath **b.**, it is that.......... 1961
Ec 1:10 it hath **b.** already of old time, ... 1961
Ec 1:16 than all they that have **b.** before 1961
Ec 2:12 which hath **b.** already done.......................
Ec 3:15 that which hath **b.** is now; 1961
Ec 3:15 that which is to be hath already **b.**;..... 1961
Ec 4:3 which hath not yet **b.**,...................... 1961
Ec 4:16 of all that have **b.** before them:.......... 1961
Ec 6:10 which hath **b.** is named already, ... 1961
Isa 1:6 they have not **b.** closed, ...
Isa 1:9 we should have **b.** as Sodom, ... 1961
Isa 1:9 should have **b.** like unto Gomorrah. ....
Isa 5:4 What could have **b.** done more.................
Isa 17:10 hast not **b.** mindful of the rock of ....
Isa 23:16 harlot that hast **b.** forgotten; ....
Isa 25:4 hast **b.** a strength to the poor, ... 1961
Isa 26:17 so have we **b.** in thy sight, O Lord..... 1961
Isa 26:18 We have **b.** with child, ...
Isa 26:18 we have **b.** in pain,....................................
Isa 30:24 which hath **b.** winnowed ....
Isa 38:9 king of Judah, when he had **b.** sick, ...
Isa 39:1 he had heard that he had **b.** sick, ...
Isa 40:21 hath it not **b.** told you...........................
Isa 42:14 I have **b.** still, and refrained ....
Isa 43:4 thou hast **b.** honourable, and I ....
Isa 43:22 thou hast **b.** weary of me, O Israel. ....
Isa 48:18 then had thy peace **b.** as a river, ... 1961
Isa 48:19 Thy seed also had **b.** as the sand, ... 1961
Isa 48:19 name should not have **b.** cut off ....
Isa 49:21 these, where had they **b.**? ....
Isa 52:15 which had not **b.** told them ....
Isa 57:11 And of whom hast thou **b.** afraid ....
Isa 60:15 thou hast **b.** forsaken and hated, ... 1961
Isa 66:2 and all those things have **b.**,.............. 1961
Jer 2:31 Have I **b.** a wilderness unto Israel?..... 1961
Jer 3:2 where thou hast not **b.** lien with..............
Jer 3:3 the showers have **b.** withholden, ...
Jer 3:3 and there hath **b.** no latter rain; 1961
Jer 4:17 she hath **b.** rebellious against me,.............
Jer 15:9 she hath **b.** ashamed and confounded.........
Jer 20:17 mother might have **b.** my grave, ... 1961
Jer 22:21 **b.** thy manner since thy youth, ...
Jer 28:8 prophets that have **b.** before me 1961
Jer 32:31 city hath **b.** to me as a provocation..........
Jer 34:14 Hebrew, which hath **b.** sold unto thee; .....
Jer 42:18 and my fury hath **b.** poured.......................
Jer 43:5 whither they had **b.** driven, ...
Jer 44:18 and have **b.** consumed by the sword ....
Jer 48:11 hath not **b.** emptied from vessel to ....
Jer 48:11 Moab hath **b.** at ease from his youth, ...
Jer 50:6 My people hath been lost sheep: 1961
Jer 50:29 hath **b.** proud against the Lord, ...
Jer 51:5 For Israel hath not **b.** forsaken, ...
Jer 51:7 Babylon hath **b.** a golden cup in ....
Eze 2:5 hath **b.** a prophet among them. 1961
Eze 4:14 my soul had not **b.** polluted: ....
Eze 10:10 as if a wheel had **b.** in the midst 1961
Eze 11:17 where ye have **b.** scattered, and ....
Eze 16:31 hast not **b.** as an harlot, in that.......... 1961
Eze 20:41 wherein ye have **b.** scattered;....................
Eze 20:43 wherein ye have **b.** defiled; ....
Eze 22:13 blood which hath **b.** in the midst 1961
Eze 28:13 Thou hast **b.** in Eden the garden........ 1961
Eze 29:6 because they have **b.** a staff of reed ... 1961
Eze 33:33 that a prophet hath **b.** among them..... 1961
Eze 34:12 where they have **b.** scattered ....
Eze 38:8 which have **b.** always waste: 1961
Da 5:15 have **b.** brought in before me, ...
Da 9:12 whole heaven hath not **b.** done ....
Da 9:12 as hath **b.** done upon Jerusalem................
Hos 5:1 because ye have **b.** a snare on........... 1961
Hos 5:2 though I have **b.** a rebuker of....................
Joe 1:2 Hath this **b.** in your days,................ 1961
Joe 2:2 there hath not **b.** ever the like,........... 1961
Ob 16 be as though they had not **b.**............. 1961
Mic 5:2 goings forth have **b.** from of old, ...
Zep 3:19 they have **b.** put to shame........................
Zec 1:2 The Lord hath **b.** sore displeased ....
Mal 1:9 this hath **b.** by your means: 1961
Mal 2:9 but have **b.** partial in the law...................
Mal 2:14 the Lord hath **b.** witness between ....
Mal 3:13 Your words have **b.** stout against ....
Mt 1:6 that had **b.** the wife of Urias; ....
Mt 5:31 **It hath b. said,**.......................................
Mt 5:33 **heard that it hath b. said**........................
Mt 5:38 **that it hath b. said,**..................................
Mt 5:43 **have heard that it hath b. said,**...........
Mt 11:21 **had b. done in Tyre**...................................
Mt 11:23 **which have b. done in thee,** ....
Mt 11:23 **had b. done in Sodom,**.............................
Mt 13:35 which have **b.** kept secret.........................
Mt 23:30 **b. in the days of our fathers,** *2258*
Mt 23:30 **we would not have b. partakers**...... *2258*
Mt 25:21, 23 **thou hast b. faithful over a few** .*2258*
Mt 26:9 might have **b.** sold for much, ...
Mt 26:24 **it had b. good for that man** *2258*
Mt 26:24 **if he had not b. born.**............................
Mk 5:4 he had **b.** often bound.............................
Mk 5:4 chains had **b.** plucked asunder...................
Mk 5:18 he that had **b.** possessed..........................
Mk 6:49 they supposed he had **b.** a spirit, ... *1511*
Mk 8:2 **they have now b. with me three** *4357*
Mk 14:5 It might have **b.** sold ....
Mk 14:5 and have **b.** given to the poor...................
Mk 14:21 **if he had never b. born.**.........................
Mk 15:44 whether he had **b.** any while dead. ....
Mk 16:10 told them that had **b.** with him,.......... *1096*
Mk 16:11 and had **b.** seen of her, believed ....

Lu 1:4 wherein thou hast b. instructed
Lu 1:70 which have b. since the world
Lu 2:44 supposing him to have b. in the ... *1511*
Lu 4:16 where he had b. brought up:
Lu 7:10 the servant whole that had b. sick
Lu 8:2 which had b. healed of evil spirits
Lu 10:13 **mighty works had b. done**
Lu 10:13 **which have b. done in you,**
Lu 16:11 **ye have not b. faithful in the** ... *1096*
Lu 16:12 **And if ye have not b. faithful in** ... *1096*
Lu 19:17 **because thou hast b. faithful** ... *1096*
Lu 24:21 trusted that it had b. he which ... *2076*
Joh 5:6 that he had b. now a long time ... *2192*
Joh 9:18 that he had b. blind, and received ... *2258*
Joh 11:21, 32 if thou hadst b. here, my ... *2258*
Joh 11:39 for he hath b. dead four days ... *2076*
Joh 12:1 which had b. dead, whom he
Joh 12:38 arm of the Lord b. revealed?
Joh 14:9 **Have I b. so long time with you,** ... *1510*
Joh 15:27 **because ye have b. with me from** ... *2075*
Ac 1:16 must needs have b. fulfilled,
Ac 4:13 that they had b. with Jesus ... *2258*
Ac 4:16 miracle hath b. done by them
Ac 5:26 lest they should have b. stoned,
Ac 6:15 it had b. the face of an angel
Ac 7:52 ye have b. now the betrayers ... *1096*
Ac 9:18 from his eyes as it had b. scales:
Ac 10:11 as it had b. a great sheet knit
Ac 11:5 as it had b. a great sheet, let
Ac 13:1 which had b. brought up
Ac 13:46 should first have b. spoken
Ac 14:19 city, supposing he had b. dead
Ac 14:26 whence they had b. recommended
Ac 15:7 there had b. much disputing ... *1096*
Ac 16:27 that the prisoners had b. fled
Ac 19:21 After I have b. there, I must also ... *1096*
Ac 20:18 what manner I have b. with you ... *1096*
Ac 23:10 Paul should have b. pulled
Ac 23:27 and should have b. killed
Ac 24:10 that thou hast b. of many years ... *5607*
Ac 24:19 ought to have b. here before thee, ... *3918*
Ac 24:26 that money should have b. given
Ac 25:14 they had b. there many days, ... *1304*
Ac 26:32 This man might have b. set ... *1096*
Ro 6:5 For if we have b. planted
Ro 9:29 we have b. as Sodoma, ... *1096*
Ro 9:29 and b. made like unto Gomorrha
Ro 11:34 or who hath b. his counsellor? ... *1096*
Ro 15:22 I have b. much hindered
Ro 15:27 Gentiles have b. made partakers
Ro 16:2 hath b. a succourer of many, ... *1096*
1Co 1:11 it hath b. declared unto me of you,
1Co 12:13 and have b. all made to drink
2Co 11:6 but we have b. throughly made
2Co 11:21 as though we had b. weak
2Co 11:25 a night and a day I have been in ... *4160*
2Co 12:11 I ought to have b. commended
Gal 3:1 Christ had b. evidently set forth,
Gal 3:21 if there had b. a law given
Gal 3:21 should have b. by the law ... *2258*
Gal 3:27 as have b. baptized into Christ
Gal 4:15 if it had b. possible, ye would
Gal 5:13 ye have b. called unto liberty;
Eph 3:9 of the world had b. hid in God,
Eph 4:21 heard him, and have b. taught
Php 2:26 ye had heard that he had b. sick
Col 1:26 which hath b. hid from ages
Col 2:7 as ye have b. taught,
Col 4:11 which have b. a comfort unto me. ... *1096*
1Th 2:6 when we might have b.
2Th 2:15 which ye have b. taught,
1Ti 5:9 having b. the wife of one man, ... *1096*
2Ti 3:14 learned and hast b. assured of,
Tit 1:9 word as he hath b. taught,
Heb 8:7 first covenant had b. faultless, ... *2258*
Heb 8:7 no place have b. sought for the
Heb 11:15 if they had b. mindful,
Heb 13:9 them that hath b. occupied
Jas 3:7 and hath b. tamed of mankind:
Jas 5:5 pleasures on the earth, and b.
2Pe 2:21 For it had b. better for them ... *2258*
1Jo 2:19 for if they had b. of us, they ... *2258*
Re 5:6 stood a lamb as it had b. slain,
Re 17:2 of the earth have b. made drunk

BEER (be'-ur) See also BAALATH-BEER; BEER-ELIM; BEER-LAHAI-ROI; BEER-SHEBA.
Nu 21:16 from thence they went to B. ... 876
Jg 9:21 ran away, and fled, and went to B., ... 876

BEERA (be-e'-rah)
1Ch 7:37 Shilshah, and Ithran, and B. ... 878

BEERAH (be-e'-rah)
1Ch 5:6 B. his son, when Tilgath-pilneser ... 880

BEER-ELIM (be''-ur-e'-lim)
Isa 15:8 and the howling thereof unto B. ... 879

BEERI (be-e'-ri)
Ge 26:34 the daughter of B. the Hittite, ... 882
Ho 1:1 Hosea, the son of B., in the days ... 882

BEER-LAHAI-ROI (be'''-ur-la''-hahe-ro'-e)
Ge 16:14 Wherefore the well was called B.; ... 883

BEEROTH (be-e'-roth) See also BEEROTHITE.
De 10:6 took their journey from B. of ... 881
Jos 9:17 and B., and Kirjath-jearim ... 881
Jos 18:25 Gibeon, and Ramah, and B., ... 881
2Sa 4:2 B. also was reckoned to Benjamin: ... 881
Eze 2:25 Kirjath-arim, Chephirah, and B., ... 881
Neh 7:29 Kirjath-jearim, Chephirah, and B., ... 881

BEEROTHITE (be-er'-o-thite) See also BEEROTHITES; BEROTHITE.
2Sa 4:2 the sons of Rimmon a B., of the ... 886
2Sa 4:5 Rimmon the B., Rechab and ... 886
2Sa 4:9 brother, the sons of Rimmon the B., ... 886
2Sa 23:37 Nahari the B., armourbearer ... 886

BEEROTHITES (be-er'-o-thites)
2Sa 4:3 the B. fled to Gittaim, and were ... 886

BEER-SHEBA (be-ur'-she-bah)
Ge 21:14 wandered in the wilderness of B. ... 884
Ge 21:31 Wherefore he called that palce B.; ... 884
Ge 21:32 Thus they made a covenant at B. ... 884
Ge 21:33 Abraham planted a grove in B., ... 884
Ge 22:19 up and went together to B.; and ... 884
Ge 22:19 Abraham dwelt at B. ... 884
Ge 26:23 he went up from thence to B. ... 884
Ge 26:33 therefore the name of the city is B. ... 884
Ge 28:10 Jacob went out from B., and went ... 884
Ge 46:1 came to B., and offered sacrifices ... 884
Ge 46:5 rose up from B.: and the sons ... 884
Jos 15:28 Hazar-shual, and B., and ... 884
Jos 19:2 they had in their inheritance B., ... 884
Jg 20:1 as one man, from Dan even to B., ... 884
1Sa 3:20 all Israel from Dan even to B. ... 884
1Sa 8:2 they were judges in B. ... 884
2Sa 3:10 over Judah, from Dan even to B. ... 884
2Sa 17:11 from Dan even to B., as the sand ... 884
2Sa 24:2 of Israel, from Dan even to B., ... 884
2Sa 24:7 to the south of Judah even to B. ... 884
2Sa 24:15 from Dan even to B., seventy ... 884
1Ki 4:25 even to B., all the days of Solomon. ... 884
1Ki 19:3 went for his life, and came to B., ... 884
2Ki 12:1 his mother's name was Zibiah of B. ... 884
2Ki 23:8 from Geba to B., and brake down ... 884
1Ch 4:28 they dwelt at B., and Moladah, ... 884
1Ch 21:2 number Israel from B. even to Dan; ... 884
2Ch 19:4 people from B. to mount Ephraim, ... 884
2Ch 24:1 name also was Zibiah of B. ... 884
2Ch 30:5 all Israel, from B. even to Dan, ... 884
Ne 11:27 at B., and in the villages thereof, ... 884
Ne 11:30 from B. unto the valley of Hinnom ... 884
Am 5:5 into Gilgal, and pass not to B. ... 884
Am 8:14 manner of B. liveth; even they shall ... 884

BEES
De 1:44 you, as b. do, and destroyed you ... 1682
Jg 14:8 of b. and honey in the carcase ... 1682
Ps 118:12 They compassed me about like b.; ... 1682

BEESH-TERAH (be-esh'-te-rah) See also ASHTAROTH.
Jos 21:27 and B. with her suburbs; two ... 1203

BEETLE
Le 11:22 the b. after his kind, and the ... 2728

BEEVES
Le 22:19 blemish, of the b., of the sheep, ... 1241
Le 22:21 a freewill offering in b. or sheep, ... 1241
Nu 31:28 of persons, and of the b., ... 1241
Nu 31:30 of the persons, of the b., ... 1241
Nu 31:33 threescore and twelve thousand b. ... 1241
Nu 31:38 And the b. were thirty and six ... 1241
Nu 31:44 And thirty and six thousand b., ... 1241

BEFALL See also BEFALLEN; BEFALLETH; BEFELL.
Ge 42:4 peradventure mischief b. him ... 7122
Ge 42:38 if mischief b. him by the way ... 1241
Nu 44:29 mischief b. him, ye shall bring ... 7136
Nu 49:1 tell you that which shall b. you ... 7122
De 31:17 evils and troubles shall b. them; ... 4672
De 31:29 will b. you in the latter days; ... 7122
Ps 91:10 There shall be no evil b. thee, ... 579
Da 10:14 what shall b. thy people ... 7136
Ac 20:22 the things that shall b. me. ... *4876*

BEFALLEN
Le 10:19 and such things have b. me: ... 7122
Nu 20:14 travel that hath b. us: ... 4672
De 31:21 many evils and troubles are b. ... 4672
Jg 6:13 why then is all this b. us? ... 4672
1Sa 20:26 Something hath b. him, he is not ... 4745
Es 6:13 every thing that had b. him ... 7136
Mt 8:33 b. to the possessed of the devils ... *4876*

BEFALLETH
Ec 3:19 b. the sons of men b. beasts; ... 4745
Ec 3:19 even one thing b. them: ... 4745

BEFELL
Ge 42:29 told him all that b. unto them; ... 7136
Jos 2:23 told him all things that b. them: ... 4672
2Sa 19:7 evil that b. thee from thy youth ... 935
Mk 5:16 b. to him that was possessed ... *1096*
Ac 20:19 and temptations, which b. me by ... *4819*

BEFORE See also AFORE; BEFOREHAND; BEFORETIME.
Ge 2:5 b. it was in the earth, and every ... 2962
Ge 2:5 herb of the field b. it grew: ... 2962
Ge 6:11 earth also was corrupt b. God; ... 6440
Ge 6:13 flesh is come b. me; for the earth ... 6440
Ge 7:1 thee have I seen righteous b. me ... 6440
Ge 10:9 was a mighty hunter b. the Lord: ... 6440
Ge 10:9 the mighty hunter b. the Lord ... 6440
Ge 11:28 died b. his father Terah ... 5921,6440
Ge 12:15 saw her, and commended her b. ... 413
Ge 13:9 Is not the whole land b. thee? ... 6440
Ge 13:10 b. the Lord destroyed Sodom ... 6440
Ge 13:13 sinners b. the Lord exceedingly.
Ge 17:1 walk b. me, and be thou perfect. ... 6440
Ge 17:18 that Ishmael might live b. thee! ... 6440
Ge 18:8 and set it b. them; and he stood ... 6440
Ge 18:22 Abraham stood yet b. the Lord ... 6440
Ge 19:4 But b. they lay down, the men of ... 2962
Ge 19:13 great b. the face of the Lord; ... 854
Ge 19:27 where he stood b. the Lord: ... 854,6440
Ge 20:15 my land is b. thee: dwell where it ... 6440
Ge 23:3 stood up from b. his dead, ... 5921,6440
Ge 23:12 bowed down himself b. the ... 6440
Ge 23:17 Machpelah, which was b. Mamre, ... 6440
Ge 23:18 b. all that went in at the gate
Ge 23:19 field of Machpelah b. Mamre: ... 5921,6440
Ge 24:7 he shall send his angel b. thee, ... 6440
Ge 24:15 to pass, b. he had done speaking, ... 2962
Ge 24:33 there was set meat b. him to eat: ... 6440
Ge 24:40 The Lord, b. whom I walk, will send ... 6440
Ge 24:45 b. I had done speaking in mine ... 2962
Ge 24:51 Behold, Rebekah is b. thee, ... 6440
Ge 25:9 Hittite, which is b. Mamre; ... 5921,6440
Ge 25:18 that is b. Egypt, as thou goest ... 6440
Ge 27:4 my soul may bless thee b. I die ... 2962
Ge 27:7 bless thee b. the Lord b. my ... 6440
Ge 27:10 he may bless thee b. his death ... 6440
Ge 27:33 have eaten of all b. thou camest, ... 2962
Ge 29:26 give the younger b. the firstborn ... 6440
Ge 30:30 which thou hadst b. I came ... 6440
Ge 30:33 for my hire b. thy face;
Ge 30:38 pilled b. the flocks in the gutters ... 5227
Ge 30:39 the flocks conceived b. the rods, ... 413
Ge 30:41 the rods b. the eyes of the cattle
Ge 31:2 was not toward him as b. ... 8543,8032
Ge 31:5 it is not toward me as b.; ... 8543,8032
Ge 31:32 b. our brethren discern thou ... 5048
Ge 31:35 I cannot rise up b. thee; ... 6440
Ge 31:37 set it here b. my brethren ... 5048
Ge 32:3 sent messengers b. him to Esau ... 6440
Ge 32:16 Pass over b. me, and put a space ... 6440
Ge 32:17 and whose are these b. thee? ... 6440
Ge 32:20 with the present that goeth b. me, ... 6440
Ge 32:21 went the present over b. him: ... 5921,6440
Ge 33:3 he passed over b. them, and bowed ... 6440
Ge 33:12 and I will go b. thee ... 5048
Ge 33:14 thee, pass over b. his servant: ... 6440
Ge 33:14 as the cattle that goeth b. me ... 6440
Ge 33:18 and pitched his tent b. the city ... 854,6440
Ge 34:10 and the land shall be b. you; ... 6440

Ge 36:31 **b.** there reigned any king over the...... 6440
Ge 37:18 afar off, even **b.** he came near............2962
Ge 40:9 a vine was **b.** me;............................6440
Ge 41:43 cried **b.** him, Bow the knee:.............. 6440
Ge 41:46 stood **b.** Pharaoh king of Egypt...........6440
Ge 41:50 born two sons **b.** the years................2962
Ge 42:6 bowed down themselves **b.** him...............
Ge 42:24 and bound him **b.** their eyes....................
Ge 43:9 and set him **b.** thee, then let me.........6440
Ge 43:14 give you mercy **b.** the man,............... 6440
Ge 43:15 to Egypt, and stood **b.** Joseph............6440
Ge 43:33 And they sat **b.** him, the firstborn....... 6440
Ge 43:34 messes unto them from **b.** him:.......... 6440
Ge 44:14 they fell **b.** him on the ground............ 6440
Ge 45:1 Joseph could not refrain himself **b.**.............
Ge 45:5 did send me **b.** you to preserve.......... 6440
Ge 45:7 God sent me **b.** you to preserve.......... 6440
Ge 45:28 I will go and see him **b.** I die............. 2962
Ge 46:28 sent Judah **b.** him unto Joseph,........... 6440
Ge 47:6 The land of Egypt is **b.** thee;............. 6440
Ge 47:7 set him **b.** Pharaoh, and Jacob............ 6440
Ge 47:10 and went out **b.** Pharaoh................... 6440
Ge 47:19 shall we die **b.** thine eyes,........................
Ge 48:5 **b.** I came unto thee into Egypt,..........5704
Ge 48:15 said, God, **b.** whom my fathers...........6440
Ge 48:20 and he set Ephraim **b.** Manasseh........ 6440
Ge 49:8 shall bow down **b.** thee..........................
Ge 49:30 Machpelah, which is **b.** Mamre.... 5921,6440
Ge 50:13 of Ephron the Hittite, **b.** Mamre.. 5921,6440
Ge 50:16 father did command **b.** he died,...........6440
Ge 50:18 went and fell down **b.** his face;................
Ex 4:3 and Moses fled from **b.** it.................. 6440
Ex 4:21 do all those wonders **b.** Pharaoh,......... 6440
Ex 6:12 Moses spake **b.** the Lord, saying,....... 6440
Ex 6:30 Moses said **b.** the Lord, Behold,.........6440
Ex 7:9 thy rod, and cast it **b.** Pharaoh,.......... 6440
Ex 7:10 cast down his rod **b.** Pharaoh,............ 6440
Ex 7:10 and **b.** his servants,......................... 6440
Ex 8:20 morning, and stand **b.** Pharaoh;.......... 6440
Ex 8:26 of the Egyptians **b.** their eyes,....................
Ex 9:10 furnace and stood **b.** Pharaoh;............ 6440
Ex 9:11 magicians could not stand **b.** Moses..... 6440
Ex 9:13 morning, and stand **b.** Pharaoh,.......... 6440
Ex 10:1 shew these my signs **b.** him:..............7130
Ex 10:3 refuse to humble thyself **b.** me?..........6440
Ex 10:10 look to it; for evil is **b.** you................6440
Ex 10:14 **b.** them there were no such...............6440
Ex 11:10 did all these wonders **b.** Pharaoh:........6440
Ex 12:34 their dough **b.** it was leavened,...........2962
Ex 13:21 the Lord went **b.** them by day............6440
Ex 13:22 fire by night, from **b.** the people......... 6440
Ex 14:2 encamp **b.** Pi-hahiroth, between.......... 6440
Ex 14:2 **b.** it shall ye encamp by the sea..........5226
Ex 14:9 Pi-hahiroth, **b.** Baal-zephon................ 6440
Ex 14:19 angel of God, which went **b.** the......... 6440
Ex 14:19 pillar of cloud went from **b.** their......... 6440
Ex 16:9 Come near **b.** the Lord: for he............ 6440
Ex 16:33 lay it up **b.** the Lord, to be kept......... 6440
Ex 16:34 laid it up **b.** the Testimony, to be.........6440
Ex 17:5 Go on **b.** the people, and take............ 6440
Ex 17:6 I will stand **b.** thee there upon the....... 6440
Ex 18:12 bread with Moses' father-in-law **b.**.......6440
Ex 19:2 there Israel camped **b.** the mount........5048
Ex 19:7 and laid **b.** their faces...........................
Ex 20:3 shalt have no other gods **b.** me... 5921,6440
Ex 20:20 his fear may be **b.** your faces,............5921
Ex 21:1 judgments which thou shalt set **b.**........ 6440
Ex 22:9 parties shall come **b.** the judges;......... 5703
Ex 23:15 none shall appear **b.** me empty:.......... 6440
Ex 23:17 males shall appear **b.** the Lord...... 413,6440
Ex 23:20 I send an Angel **b.** thee to keep.... 413,6440
Ex 23:23 mine Angel shall go **b.** thee,......... 413,6440
Ex 23:27 I will send my fear **b.** thee, and.... 413,6440
Ex 23:28 I will send hornets **b.** thee, which.. 413,6440
Ex 23:28 and the Hittite, from **b.** thee,....... 413,6440
Ex 23:29 not drive them out from **b.** thee.... 413,6440
Ex 23:30 I will drive them out from **b.** thee,. 413,6440
Ex 23:31 thou shalt drive them out **b.** thee.. 413,6440
Ex 25:30 the table shewbread **b.** me alway........ 6440
Ex 27:21 without the vail, which is **b.** the..........5921
Ex 27:21 evening to morning **b.** the Lord:............ 6440
Ex 28:12 shall bear their names **b.** the Lord.......6440
Ex 28:25 of the ephod **b.** it................434,4136,6440
Ex 28:29 for a memorial **b.** the Lord................ 6440
Ex 28:30 when he goeth in **b.** the Lord:............6440
Ex 28:30 his heart **b.** the Lord continually.......... 6440
Ex 28:35 unto the holy place **b.** the Lord,......... 6440
Ex 28:38 they may be accepted **b.** the Lord.......6440
Ex 29:10 to be brought **b.** the tabernacle...........6440
Ex 29:11 kill the bullock **b.** the Lord,............... 6440
Ex 29:23 unleavened bread that is **b.** the.......... 6440
Ex 29:24 a wave offering **b.** the Lord............... 6440
Ex 29:25 for a sweet savour **b.** the Lord:........... 6440
Ex 29:26 a wave offering **b.** the Lord:.............. 6440
Ex 29:42 the congregation **b.** the Lord:.............6440
Ex 30:6 **b.** the vail that is by the ark of...........6440
Ex 30:6 the testimony, **b.** the mercy seat........ 6440
Ex 30:8 incense **b.** the Lord throughout...........6440
Ex 30:16 children of Israel **b.** the Lord,............ 6440
Ex 30:36 **b.** the testimony in the tabernacle....... 6440
Ex 32:1 make us gods, which shall go **b.** us;.....6440
Ex 32:5 he built an altar **b.** it; and Aaron......... 6440
Ex 32:23 shall go **b.** us: for as for this.............. 6440
Ex 32:34 behold, mine Angel shall go **b.** thee:.... 6440
Ex 33:2 I will send an angel **b.** thee;...............6440
Ex 33:19 my goodness pass **b.** thee, and.... 5921,6440
Ex 33:19 the name of the Lord **b.** thee;............ 6440
Ex 34:3 nor herds feed **b.** that mount........ 413,4136
Ex 34:6 the Lord passed by **b.** him,.........5921,6440
Ex 34:10 a covenant: **b.** all thy people.............. 5048
Ex 34:11 I drive out **b.** thee the Amorite,......... 6440
Ex 34:20 none shall appear **b.** me empty........... 6440
Ex 34:23 your menchildren appear **b.** the...........6440
Ex 34:24 I will cast out the nations **b.** thee,....... 6440
Ex 34:24 go up to appear **b.** the Lord......... 413,6440
Ex 34:34 when Moses went in **b.** the Lord........ 6440
Ex 39:18 of the ephod, **b.** it..............413,4136,6440
Ex 40:5 **b.** the ark of the testimony,...............6440
Ex 40:6 **b.** the door of the tabernacle.............6440
Ex 40:23 in order upon it **b.** the Lord;..............6440
Ex 40:25 he lighted the lamps **b.** the Lord;......... 6440
Ex 40:26 **b.** the vail:..6440
Le 1:3 of the congregation **b.** the Lord.......... 6440
Le 1:5 shall kill the bullock **b.** the Lord:........... 6440
Le 1:11 the altar northward **b.** the Lord:......... 6440
Le 3:1 it without blemish **b.** the Lord............ 6440
Le 3:7 shall he offer it **b.** the Lord............... 6440
Le 3:8 and kill it **b.** the tabernacle................ 6440
Le 3:12 then shall he offer it **b.** the Lord.......... 6440
Le 3:13 kill it **b.** the tabernacle.......................6440
Le 4:4 the congregation **b.** the Lord;..............6440
Le 4:4 kill the bullock **b.** the Lord................ 6440
Le 4:6 blood seven times **b.** the Lord,........... 6440
Le 4:6 **b.** the vail of the sanctuary................ 6440
Le 4:7 incense **b.** the Lord, which is in........... 6440
Le 4:14 bring him **b.** the tabernacle of the....... 6440
Le 4:15 head of the bullock **b.** the Lord:...........6440
Le 4:15 bullock shall be killed **b.** the Lord........6440
Le 4:17 sprinkle it seven times **b.** the Lord,..... 6440
Le 4:17 even **b.** the vail..............................6440
Le 4:18 the altar which is **b.** the Lord,............6440
Le 4:24 kill the burnt offering **b.** the Lord:.......6440
Le 6:7 an atonement for him **b.** the Lord:...... 6440
Le 6:14 offer it **b.** the Lord, **b.** the altar..........6440
Le 6:25 shall be killed **b.** the Lord:.................6440
Le 7:30 for a wave offering **b.** the Lord..........6440
Le 8:26 bread that was **b.** the Lord,............... 6440
Le 8:27 them for a wave offering **b.** the.......... 6440
Le 8:29 it for a wave offering **b.** the Lord:....... 6440
Le 9:2 blemish, and offer them **b.** the Lord.... 6440
Le 9:4 offerings, to sacrifice **b.** the Lord;....... 6440
Le 9:5 **b.** the tabernacle of the.............. 413,6440
Le 9:5 near and stood **b.** the Lord............... 6440
Le 9:21 for a wave offering **b.** the Lord;...........6440
Le 9:24 there came a fire out from **b.**.............. 6440
Le 10:1 offered strange fire **b.** the Lord,.......... 6440
Le 10:2 them, and they died **b.** the Lord.......... 6440
Le 10:3 **b.** all the people I will be........... 5921,6440
Le 10:4 near, carry your brethren from **b.**........ 6440
Le 10:15 for a wave offering **b.** the Lord;...........6440
Le 10:17 atonement for them **b.** the Lord?........ 6440
Le 10:19 their burnt offering **b.** the Lord;..........6440
Le 12:7 Who shall offer it **b.** the Lord,............6440
Le 14:11 clean, and those things, **b.** the Lord,... 6440
Le 14:12 for a wave offering **b.** the Lord:...........6440
Le 14:16 his finger seven times **b.** the Lord:......6440
Le 14:18 an atonement for him **b.** the Lord........ 6440
Le 14:23 of the congregation, **b.** the Lord........ 6440
Le 14:24 for a wave offering **b.** the Lord:...........6440
Le 14:27 left hand seven times **b.** the Lord:...... 6440
Le 14:29 an atonement for him **b.** the Lord....... 6440
Le 14:31 is to be cleansed **b.** the Lord............ 6440
Le 14:36 they empty the house, **b.** the priest.....2962
Le 15:14 come **b.** the Lord unto the door..........6440
Le 15:15 him **b.** the Lord for his issue..............6440
Le 15:30 an atonement for her **b.** the Lord........6440
Le 16:1 they offered **b.** the Lord, and died;......6440
Le 16:2 the vail **b.** the mercy seat,........... 413,6440
Le 16:7 present them **b.** the Lord at the......... 6440
Le 16:10 be presented alive **b.** the Lord,......... 6440
Le 16:12 from off the altar **b.** the Lord,............ 6440
Le 16:13 incense upon the fire **b.** the Lord,....... 6440
Le 16:14 eastward; and **b.** the mercy seat......... 6440
Le 16:15 seat, and **b.** the mercy seat:.............. 6440
Le 16:18 that is **b.** the Lord, and make.............6440
Le 16:30 from all your sins **b.** the Lord............. 6440
Le 17:4 **b.** the tabernacle of the.....................6440
Le 18:23 neither shall any woman stand **b.**........ 6440
Le 18:24 defiled which I cast out **b.** you:...........6440
Le 18:27 which were **b.** you, and the land.......... 6440
Le 18:28 the nations that were **b.** you.............. 6440
Le 18:30 which were committed **b.** you,.............6440
Le 19:14 put a stumblingblock **b.** the blind,........ 6440
Le 19:22 trespass offering **b.** the Lord for......... 6440
Le 19:32 shalt rise up **b.** the hoary head,.......... 6440
Le 20:23 nation, which I cast out **b.** you:.......... 6440
Le 23:11 wave the sheaf **b.** the Lord,...............6440
Le 23:20 for a wave offering **b.** the Lord,...........6440
Le 23:28 for you **b.** the Lord your God............. 6440
Le 23:40 rejoice **b.** the Lord your God.............. 6440
Le 24:3 morning **b.** the Lord continually:......... 6440
Le 24:4 pure candlestick **b.** the Lord.............. 6440
Le 24:6 upon the pure table **b.** the Lord..........6440
Le 24:8 in order **b.** the Lord continually,......... 6440
Le 26:7 they shall fall **b.** you by the sword.......6440
Le 26:8 your enemies shall fall **b.** you............ 6440
Le 26:17 ye shall be slain **b.** your enemies:....... 6440
Le 26:37 as it were **b.** a sword, when none........ 6440
Le 26:37 no power to stand **b.** your enemies..... 6440
Le 27:8 shall present himself **b.** the priest,.......6440
Le 27:11 present the beast **b.** the priest:.......... 6440
Nu 3:4 died **b.** the Lord, when they offered.... 6440
Nu 3:4 strange fire **b.** the Lord....................... 6440
Nu 3:6 present them **b.** Aaron the priest,........ 6440
Nu 3:7 **b.** the tabernacle of the.....................6440
Nu 3:38 **b.** the tabernacle toward the east,........ 6440
Nu 3:38 even **b.** the tabernacle of the............. 6440
Nu 5:16 near, and set her **b.** the Lord:............6440
Nu 5:18 set the woman **b.** the Lord, and........... 6440
Nu 5:25 wave the offering **b.** the Lord,............6440
Nu 5:30 the woman **b.** the Lord,.....................6440
Nu 6:12 days that were **b.** shall be lost,...........7223
Nu 6:16 priest shall bring them **b.** the Lord,..... 6440
Nu 6:20 for a wave offering **b.** the Lord:...........6440
Nu 7:3 brought their offering **b.** the Lord,........6440
Nu 7:3 brought them **b.** the tabernacle........... 6440
Nu 7:10 offered their offering **b.** the altar......... 6440
Nu 8:9 **b.** the tabernacle of the.....................6440
Nu 8:10 bring the Levites **b.** the Lord:.............6440
Nu 8:11 shall offer the Levites **b.** the Lord...... 6440
Nu 8:13 set the Levites **b.** Aaron, and **b.**..........6440
Nu 8:21 them as an offering **b.** the Lord;.......... 6440
Nu 8:22 congregation **b.** Aaron, and **b.** his.........6440
Nu 9:6 they came **b.** Moses and **b.** Aaron.......6440
Nu 10:9 **b.** the Lord your God, and ye shall......6440
Nu 10:10 memorial **b.** your God: I am the......... 6440
Nu 10:33 the Lord went **b.** them in the three..... 6440
Nu 10:35 let them that hate thee flee **b.** thee..... 6440
Nu 11:6 beside this manna, **b.** our eyes.............
Nu 11:20 and have wept **b.** him, saying,............ 6440
Nu 13:22 Hebron was built seven years **b.**.......... 6440
Nu 13:30 Caleb stilled the people **b.** Moses,........ 413
Nu 14:5 Aaron fell on their faces **b.** all............. 6440
Nu 14:10 of the congregation **b.** all the.................. 413
Nu 14:14 thou goest **b.** them, by day time......... 6440
Nu 14:37 died by the plague **b.** the Lord........... 6440
Nu 14:42 be not smitten **b.** your enemies.......... 6440
Nu 14:43 the Canaanites are there **b.** you,.......... 6440
Nu 15:15 shall the stranger be **b.** the Lord........ 6440
Nu 15:25 their sin offering **b.** the Lord for......... 6440
Nu 15:28 sinneth by ignorance **b.** the Lord,.........6440
Nu 16:2 they rose up **b.** Moses, with certain.... 6440
Nu 16:7 in them **b.** the Lord to morrow:...........6440
Nu 16:9 **b.** the congregation to minister........... 6440
Nu 16:16 **b.** the Lord, thou, and they,............... 6440
Nu 16:17 bring ye **b.** the Lord every man.......... 6440
Nu 16:38 for they offered them **b.** the Lord,....... 6440
Nu 16:40 near to offer incense **b.** the Lord;....... 6440
Nu 16:43 Moses and Aaron came **b.** the...... 413,6440
Nu 17:4 **b.** the testimony, where I will meet..... 6440
Nu 17:7 laid up the rods **b.** the Lord................6440

Nu 17:9 the rods from **b.** the Lord unto all....... 6440
Nu 17:10 again **b.** the testimony, to be kept....... 6440
Nu 18:2 minister **b.** the tabernacle of............. 6440
Nu 18:19 for ever **b.** the Lord unto thee.......... 6440
Nu 19:3 one shall slay her **b.** his face:............ 6440
Nu 19:4 blood directly **b.** the tabernacle.......... 6440
Nu 20:3 our brethren died **b.** the Lord!.......... 6440
Nu 20:8 speak ye unto the rock **b.** their eyes;.........
Nu 20:9 Moses took the rod from **b.** the.......... 6440
Nu 20:10 congregation together **b.**...rock,.... 413,6440
Nu 21:11 wilderness which is **b.** Moab,...... 5921,6440
Nu 22:32 thy way is perverse **b.** me:............. 5048
Nu 25:4 hang them up **b.** the Lord against.............
Nu 25:6 Who were weeping **b.** the door................
Nu 26:61 offered strange fire **b.** the Lord.......... 6440
Nu 27:2 And they stood **b.** Moses,................ 6440
Nu 27:2 and **b.** Eleazar the priest,................. 6440
Nu 27:2 and **b.** the princes.......................... 6440
Nu 27:5 brought their cause **b.** the Lord.......... 6440
Nu 27:14 sanctify me at the water **b.** their..............
Nu 27:17 Which may go out **b.** them,.............. 6440
Nu 27:17 and which may go in **b.** them,............ 6440
Nu 27:19 **b.** Eleazar the priest, and **b.** all.......... 6440
Nu 27:21 And he shall stand **b.** Eleazar the........ 6440
Nu 27:21 of Urim **b.** the Lord:........................ 6440
Nu 27:22 **b.** Eleazar the priest, and **b.** all.......... 6440
Nu 31:50 atonement for our souls **b.** the Lord.... 6440
Nu 31:54 children of Israel **b.** the Lord............ 6440
Nu 32:4 smote **b.** the congregation of Israel,..... 6440
Nu 32:17 **b.** the children of Israel, until we........ 6440
Nu 32:20 armed **b.** the Lord to war,................ 6440
Nu 32:21 over Jordan **b.** the Lord, until he........ 6440
Nu 32:21 driven out his enemies from **b.** him,..... 6440
Nu 32:22 the land be subdued **b.** the Lord:........ 6440
Nu 32:22 guiltless **b.** the Lord, and **b.** Israel;..........
Nu 32:22 be your possession **b.** the Lord......... 6440
Nu 32:27 **b.** the Lord to battle, as my lord......... 6440
Nu 32:29 to battle, **b.** the Lord,...................... 6440
Nu 32:29 the land shall be subdued **b.** you;........ 6440
Nu 32:32 pass over armed **b.** the Lord.............. 6440
Nu 33:7 **b.** Baal-zephon:......................... 5921,6440
Nu 33:7 and they pitched **b.** Migdol............... 6440
Nu 33:8 they departed from **b.** Pi-hahiroth,....... 6440
Nu 33:47 the mountains of Abarim, **b.** Nebo....... 6440
Nu 33:52 inhabitants of the land from **b.** you,..... 6440
Nu 33:55 the inhabitants of the land from **b.**....... 6440
Nu 35:12 until he stand **b.** the congregation........ 6440
Nu 36:1 and spake **b.** Moses, and **b.** the.......... 6440
De 1:8 I have set the land **b.** you:............... 6440
De 1:21 thy God hath set the land **b.** thee:....... 6440
De 1:22 We will send men **b.** us, and they....... 6440
De 1:30 your God which goeth **b.** you,............ 6440
De 1:30 did for you in Egypt **b.** your eyes;............
De 1:33 Who went in the way **b.** you,.............. 6440
De 1:38 son of Nun, which standeth **b.** thee,..... 6440
De 1:42 lest ye be smitten **b.** your enemies....... 6440
De 1:45 ye returned and wept **b.** the Lord;...... 6440
De 2:12 had destroyed them from **b.** them,....... 6440
De 2:21 the Lord destroyed them **b.** them;....... 6440
De 2:22 destroyed the Horims from **b.** them;.... 6440
De 2:31 to give Sihon and his land **b.** thee:...... 6440
De 2:33 Lord our God delivered him **b.** us;....... 6440
De 3:18 pass over armed **b.** your brethren....... 6440
De 3:28 he shall go over **b.** this people,........... 6440
De 4:8 this law, which I set **b.** you.............. 6440
De 4:10 thou stoodest **b.** the Lord thy God....... 6440
De 4:32 which were **b.** thee, since the day....... 6440
De 4:34 did for you in Egypt **b.** your eyes?...........
De 4:38 To drive out nations from **b.** thee....... 6440
De 4:44 Moses set **b.** the children of Israel:..... 6440
De 5:7 have none other gods **b.** me....... 5921,6440
De 6:19 all thine enemies from **b.** thee,........... 6440
De 6:22 all his household, **b.** our eyes:...................
De 6:25 **b.** the Lord our God, as he hath......... 6440
De 7:1 hath cast out many nations **b.** thee,..... 6440
De 7:2 God shall deliver them **b.** thee;........... 6440
De 7:22 put out those nations **b.** thee little....... 6440
De 7:24 no man be able to stand **b.** thee,......... 6440
De 8:20 the Lord destroyeth **b.** your face,..............
De 9:2 Who can stand **b.** the children of......... 6440
De 9:3 is he which goeth over **b.** thee;.......... 6440
De 9:3 shall bring them down **b.** thy face.............
De 9:4 cast them out from **b.** thee,................ 6440
De 9:4 drive them out from **b.** thee................ 6440
De 9:5 doth drive them out from **b.** thee,....... 6440
De 9:17 and brake them **b.** your eyes..................
De 9:18 And I fell down **b.** the Lord,.............. 6440
De 9:25 Thus I fell down **b.** the Lord.............. 6440
De 10:8 of the Lord, to stand **b.** the Lord....... 6440
De 10:11 take thy journey **b.** the people,........... 6440
De 11:23 all these nations from **b.** you,............. 6440
De 11:25 no man be able to stand **b.** you:.......... 6440
De 11:26 I set **b.** you this day a blessing.......... 6440
De 11:32 which I set **b.** you this day................ 6440
De 12:7 there ye shall eat **b.** the Lord............ 6440
De 12:12 And ye shall rejoice **b.** the Lord.......... 6440
De 12:18 thou must eat them **b.** the Lord.......... 6440
De 12:18 thou shalt rejoice **b.** the Lord.............. 6440
De 12:29 cut off the nations from **b.** thee,......... 6440
De 12:30 that they be destroyed from **b.** thee;... 6440
De 14:23 thou shalt eat **b.** the Lord thy God,..... 6440
De 14:26 thou shalt eat there **b.** the Lord.......... 6440
De 15:20 Thou shalt eat it **b.** the Lord............. 6440
De 16:11 thou shalt rejoice **b.** the Lord............ 6440
De 16:16 all thy males appear **b.** the Lord.... 854,6440
De 16:16 they shall not appear **b.** the Lord... 854,6440
De 17:12 to minister there **b.** the Lord.............. 854
De 17:18 that which is **b.** the priests................ 6440
De 18:7 which stand there **b.** the Lord........... 6440
De 18:12 drive them out from **b.** thee............... 6440
De 19:17 shall stand **b.** the Lord,..................... 6440
De 19:17 **b.** the priests and the judges,............. 6440
De 21:16 firstborn **b.** the son of the hated,........ 6440
De 22:6 a bird's nest chance to be **b.** thee....... 6440
De 22:17 cloth **b.** the elders of the city............ 6440
De 23:14 to give up thine enemies **b.** thee;........ 6440
De 24:4 that is abomination **b.** the Lord:.......... 6440
De 24:13 unto thee **b.** the Lord thy God.......... 6440
De 25:2 to be beaten **b.** his face,.........................
De 26:4 **b.** the altar of the Lord thy God......... 6440
De 26:5 shalt speak and say **b.** the Lord......... 6440
De 26:10 set it **b.** the Lord thy God,................ 6440
De 26:10 and worship **b.** the Lord thy God:........ 6440
De 26:13 shalt say **b.** the Lord thy God,........... 6440
De 27:7 and rejoice **b.** the Lord thy God......... 6440
De 28:7 thee to be smitten **b.** thy face:...................
De 28:7 and flee **b.** thee seven ways................ 6440
De 28:25 to be smitten **b.** thine enemies:.......... 6440
De 28:25 and flee seven ways **b.** them:.............. 6440
De 28:31 ox shall be slain **b.** thine eyes,..................
De 28:31 taken away from **b.** thy face,....................
De 28:66 life shall hang in doubt **b.** thee;........... 5048
De 29:2 all that the Lord did **b.** your eyes.............
De 29:10 all of you **b.** the Lord your God;......... 6440
De 29:15 this day **b.** the Lord our God,............. 6440
De 30:1 curse, which I have set **b.** thee,......... 6440
De 30:15 I have set **b.** thee this day................ 6440
De 30:19 I have set **b.** you life and death,......... 6440
De 31:3 he will go over **b.** thee, and he will..... 6440
De 31:3 destroy these nations from **b.** thee,...... 6440
De 31:3 Joshua, he shall go over **b.** thee,......... 6440
De 31:5 shall give them up **b.** your face,................
De 31:8 he it is that doth go **b.** thee;.............. 6440
De 31:11 is come to appear **b.** the Lord...... 854,6440
De 31:11 read this law **b.** all Israel................ 5048
De 31:21 now, **b.** I have brought them.............. 2962
De 32:52 thou shalt see the land **b.** thee;........... 5048
De 33:1 the children of Israel **b.** his death........ 6440
De 33:10 shall put incense **b.** thee, and............. 639
De 33:27 thrust out the enemy from **b.** thee;..... 6440
Jos 1:5 any man be able to stand **b.** thee........ 6440
Jos 1:14 ye shall pass **b.** your brethren............ 6440
Jos 2:8 And **b.** they were laid down,.............. 2962
Jos 3:1 lodged there **b.** they passed over........ 2962
Jos 3:6 and pass over **b.** the people............... 6440
Jos 3:6 covenant, and went **b.** the people........ 6440
Jos 3:10 without fail drive out from **b.** you........ 6440
Jos 3:11 the earth passeth over **b.** you............ 6440
Jos 3:14 of the covenant **b.** the people;............. 6440
Jos 4:5 Pass over **b.** the ark of the Lord......... 6440
Jos 4:7 **b.** the ark of the covenant.................. 6440
Jos 4:12 armed **b.** the children of Israel,........... 6440
Jos 4:13 passed over **b.** the Lord unto............. 6440
Jos 4:18 all his banks, as they did **b.**........ 8543,8032
Jos 4:23 the waters of Jordan from **b.** you,....... 6440
Jos 4:23 which he dried up from **b.** us,............ 6440
Jos 5:1 from **b.** the children of Israel,............. 6440
Jos 6:4 seven priests shall bear **b.** the ark....... 6440
Jos 6:5 up every man straight **b.** him............. 5048
Jos 6:6 horns **b.** the ark of the Lord............... 6440
Jos 6:7 pass on **b.** the ark of the Lord............ 6440
Jos 6:8 horns passed on **b.** the Lord,.............. 6440
Jos 6:9 the armed men went **b.** the priests...... 6440
Jos 6:13 rams' horns **b.** the ark of the Lord...... 6440
Jos 6:13 the armed men went **b.** them;............ 6440
Jos 6:20 every man straight **b.** him,................ 5048
Jos 6:26 Cursed be the man **b.** the Lord,......... 6440
Jos 7:4 they fled **b.** the men of Ai................. 6440
Jos 7:5 **b.** the gate even unto Shebarim,......... 6440
Jos 7:6 upon his face **b.** the ark..................... 6440
Jos 7:8 their backs **b.** their enemies!.............. 6440
Jos 7:12 could not stand **b.** their enemies,........ 6440
Jos 7:12 but turned their backs **b.** their........... 6440
Jos 7:13 canst not stand **b.** thine enemies,....... 6440
Jos 7:23 and laid them out **b.** the Lord............ 6440
Jos 8:5 first, that we will flee **b.** them,........... 6440
Jos 8:6 They flee **b.** us, as at the first:............ 6440
Jos 8:6 therefore we will flee **b.** them............ 6440
Jos 8:10 of Israel, **b.** the people to Ai.............. 6440
Jos 8:11 drew nigh, and came **b.** the city.......... 5048
Jos 8:14 a time appointed, **b.** the plain;............ 6440
Jos 8:15 made as if they were beaten **b.**........... 6440
Jos 8:33 and on that side **b.** the priests............ 5048
Jos 8:33 had commanded **b.**, that they............ 7223
Jos 8:35 which Joshua read not **b.** all.............. 5048
Jos 9:24 of the land from **b.** you,..................... 6440
Jos 10:5 and encamped **b.** Gibeon:.................. 5921
Jos 10:8 not a man of them stand **b.** thee......... 6440
Jos 10:10 Lord discomfited them **b.** Israel,......... 6440
Jos 10:11 as they fled from **b.** Israel,................ 6440
Jos 10:12 Amorites **b.** the children of Israel,....... 6440
Jos 10:14 no day like that **b.** it or after it,.......... 6440
Jos 11:6 deliver them up all slain **b.** Israel:....... 6440
Jos 13:3 Sihor, which is **b.** Egypt,............. 5921,6440
Jos 13:6 drive out from **b.** the children............. 6440
Jos 13:25 Aroer that is **b.** Rabbah;............ 5921,6440
Jos 14:15 of Hebron **b.** was Kirjath-arba;........... 6440
Jos 15:7 **b.** the going up to Adummim,.............. 5227
Jos 15:8 that lieth **b.** the valley.............. 5921,6440
Jos 15:15 of Debir **b.** was Kirjath-sepher............ 6440
Jos 17:4 came near **b.** Eleazar the priest,.......... 6440
Jos 17:4 and **b.** Joshua the son of Nun,............ 6440
Jos 17:4 and **b.** the princes,............................. 6440
Jos 17:7 that lieth **b.** Shechem;................ 5921,6440
Jos 18:1 the land was subdued **b.** them............ 6440
Jos 18:6 cast lots for you here **b.** the Lord........ 6440
Jos 18:8 for you **b.** the Lord in Shiloh............. 6440
Jos 18:10 for them in Shiloh **b.** the Lord:........... 6440
Jos 18:14 hill that lieth **b.** Beth-horon......... 5921,6440
Jos 18:16 **b.** the valley of the son of.......... 5921,6440
Jos 19:11 the river that is **b.** Jokneam;....... 5921,6440
Jos 19:46 the border **b.** Japho............................ 4136
Jos 19:51 by lot in Shiloh **b.** the Lord,............... 6440
Jos 20:6 he stand **b.** the congregation.............. 6440
Jos 20:9 he stood **b.** the congregation.............. 6440
Jos 21:44 of all their enemies **b.** them;.............. 6440
Jos 22:27 do the service of the Lord **b.** him........ 6440
Jos 22:29 Lord our God that is **b.** his................ 6440
Jos 23:5 shall expel them from **b.** you,............. 6440
Jos 23:9 Lord hath driven out from **b.** you........ 6440
Jos 23:9 hath been able to stand **b.** you........... 6440
Jos 23:13 any of these nations from **b.** you;........ 6440
Jos 24:1 they presented themselves **b.** God........ 6440
Jos 24:8 I destroyed them from **b.** you............ 6440
Jos 24:12 I sent the hornet **b.** you, which.......... 6440
Jos 24:12 drave them out from **b.** you,............... 6440
Jos 24:18 the Lord drave out from **b.** us.............. 6440
Jg 1:10 now the name of Hebron **b.** was.......... 6440
Jg 1:11 and the name of Debir **b.**.................. 6440
Jg 1:23 the name of the city **b.** was Luz.)........ 6440
Jg 2:3 not drive them out from **b.** you;.......... 6440
Jg 2:14 any longer stand **b.** their enemies........ 6440
Jg 2:21 drive out any from **b.** them of the........ 6440
Jg 3:2 such as **b.** knew nothing thereof;......... 6440
Jg 3:27 from the mount, and he **b.** them......... 6440
Jg 4:14 not the Lord gone out **b.** thee?........... 6440
Jg 4:15 the edge of the sword **b.** Barak;.......... 6440
Jg 4:23 Canaan **b.** the children of Israel.......... 6440
Jg 5:5 mountains melted from **b.** the............. 6440
Jg 5:5 even that Sinai from **b.** the Lord......... 6440
Jg 6:9 drave them out from **b.** you,............... 6440
Jg 6:18 my present, and set it **b.** thee............ 6440
Jg 7:24 take **b.** them the waters...............................
Jg 8:13 from battle **b.** the sun was up,........... 4608
Jg 8:28 Midian subdued **b.** the children........... 6440
Jg 9:39 Gaal went out **b.** the men of............. 6440
Jg 9:40 chased him and he fled **b.** him,........... 6440
Jg 11:9 the Lord deliver them **b.** me,............. 6440
Jg 11:11 Jephthah uttered all his words **b.**........ 6440
Jg 11:23 from **b.** his people Israel,.................. 6440
Jg 11:24 God shall drive out from **b.** us,........... 6440

Jg 11:33 subdued **b.** the children of Israel......6440
Jg 12:5 of Jordan **b.** the Ephraimites:..................
Jg 14:16 Sampson's wife wept **b.** him,..............5921
Jg 14:17 she wept **b.** him the seven days,........5921
Jg 14:18 seventh day **b.** the sun went down,......2962
Jg 16:3 of an hill that is **b.** Hebron..........5921,6440
Jg 16:20 as at other times **b.**, and shake.........6471
Jg 18:6 **b.** the Lord is your way wherein.........5227
Jg 18:21 cattle and the carriage **b.** them..........6440
Jg 20:23 and wept **b.** the Lord until even,..........6440
Jg 20:26 and sat there **b.** the Lord,..................6440
Jg 20:26 and peace offerings **b.** the Lord...........6440
Jg 20:28 Aaron, stood **b.** it in those days,)........6440
Jg 20:32 They are smitten down **b.** us,............6440
Jg 20:35 the Lord smote Benjamin **b.** Israel:.....6440
Jg 20:39 they are smitten down **b.** us,.............6440
Jg 20:42 turned their backs **b.** the men of.........6440
Jg 21:2 abode there till even **b.** God,.............6440
Ru 3:14 she rose up **b.** one could know...........2958
Ru 4:4 Buy it **b.** the inhabitants,......................5048
Ru 4:4 and **b.** the elders of my people...........5048
1Sa 1:12 continued praying **b.** the Lord,...........6440
1Sa 1:15 poured out my soul **b.** the Lord..........6440
1Sa 1:19 and worshipped **b.** the Lord,..............6440
1Sa 1:22 that he may appear **b.** the Lord,....854,6440
1Sa 2:11 the Lord **b.** Eli the priest............854,6440
1Sa 2:15 **b.** they burnt the fat, the priest's.........2962
1Sa 2:17 was very great **b.** the Lord..........854,6440
1Sa 2:18 Samuel ministered **b.** the............854,6440
1Sa 2:21 child Samuel grew **b.** the Lord............5973
1Sa 2:28 incense, to wear an ephod **b.** me?.......6440
1Sa 2:30 of thy father, should walk **b.** me.........6440
1Sa 2:35 he shall walk **b.** mine anointed............6440
1Sa 3:1 ministered unto the Lord **b.**....................6440
1Sa 4:2 was smitten **b.** the Philistines:.............6440
1Sa 4:3 us to day **b.** the Philistines?...............6440
1Sa 4:17 Israel is fled **b.** the Philistines,.........6440
1Sa 5:3 to the earth **b.** the ark of the Lord......6440
1Sa 5:4 ground **b.** the ark of the Lord;...........6440
1Sa 6:20 is able to stand **b.** this holy Lord.........6440
1Sa 7:6 drew water; and poured it out **b.**.........6440
1Sa 7:10 and they were smitten **b.** Israel...............
1Sa 8:11 some shall run **b.** his chariots.............6440
1Sa 8:20 may judge us, and go out **b.** us,.........6440
1Sa 9:12 He is; behold, he is **b.** you:...............6440
1Sa 9:13 find him, **b.** he go up to the high.........2962
1Sa 9:15 a day **b.** Saul came, saying,...............6440
1Sa 9:19 go up **b.** me unto the high place;..........6440
1Sa 9:24 and set it **b.** Saul. And Samuel.............6440
1Sa 9:24 is left! set it **b.** thee, and eat:...........6440
1Sa 9:27 Bid the servant pass on **b.** us,............6440
1Sa 10:5 and a pipe, and a harp, **b.** them;.........6440
1Sa 10:8 shalt go down **b.** me to Gilgal;............6440
1Sa 10:19 present yourselves **b.** the Lord..........6440
1Sa 10:25 book, and laid it up **b.** the Lord.........6440
1Sa 11:15 they made Saul king **b.** the Lord.........6440
1Sa 11:15 of peace offerings **b.** the Lord;...........6440
1Sa 12:2 the king walketh **b.** you: and I am.......6440
1Sa 12:2 I have walked **b.** you from my............6440
1Sa 12:3 witness against me **b.** the Lord,..........5048
1Sa 12:3 the Lord, and **b.** his anointed:.............5048
1Sa 12:7 may reason with you **b.** the Lord........6440
1Sa 12:16 the Lord will do **b.** your eyes...................
1Sa 14:13 him: and they fell **b.** Jonathan;.............6440
1Sa 14:21 the Philistines **b.** that time,..................865
1Sa 15:30 thee, **b.** the elders of my people,.........5048
1Sa 15:30 and **b.** Israel, and turn again..............5048
1Sa 15:33 hewed Agag in pieces **b.** the Lord,......6440
1Sa 16:6 the Lord's anointed is **b.** him..............5048
1Sa 16:8 made him pass **b.** Samuel....................6440
1Sa 16:10 made seven of his sons to pass **b.**.........6440
1Sa 16:16 thy servants, which are **b.** thee,.........6440
1Sa 16:21 came to Saul, and stood **b.** him:...........6440
1Sa 16:22 Let David, I pray thee, stand **b.** me;...6440
1Sa 17:7 one bearing a shield went **b.** him.........6440
1Sa 17:31 they rehearsed them **b.** Saul:...............6440
1Sa 17:41 that bare the shield went **b.** him.........6440
1Sa 17:57 brought him **b.** Saul with the head.......6440
1Sa 18:13 out and came in **b.** the people............6440
1Sa 18:16 he went out and came in **b.** them.........6440
1Sa 19:24 prophesied **b.** Samuel in like...............6440
1Sa 20:1 and came and said **b.** Jonathan,............6440
1Sa 20:1 what is my sin **b.** thy father,...............6440
1Sa 21:6 was taken from **b.** the Lord,...............6440
1Sa 21:7 that day, detained **b.** the Lord;............6440
1Sa 21:13 he changed his behaviour **b.** the,.........5869
1Sa 22:4 he brought them **b.** the king.........854,6440
1Sa 23:18 made a covenant **b.** the Lord:............6440
1Sa 23:24 arose and went to Ziph **b.** Saul:..........6440
1Sa 25:19 Go on **b.** me; behold, I come after......6440
1Sa 25:23 fell **b.** David on her face,......................639
1Sa 26:1 which is **b.** Jeshimon?..............5921,6440
1Sa 26:3 which is **b.** Jeshimon, by the.........5921,6440
1Sa 26:19 cursed be they **b.** the Lord;...............6440
1Sa 26:20 fall to the earth **b.** the face of the.......5048
1Sa 28:22 me set a morsel of bread **b.** thee;.......6440
1Sa 28:25 And she brought it **b.** Saul,.................6440
1Sa 28:25 and **b.** his servants;.............................6440
1Sa 30:20 they drave **b.** those other cattle,.........6440
1Sa 31:1 Israel fled from **b.** the Philistines,.........6440
2Sa 2:14 men now arise, and play **b.** us..............6440
2Sa 2:17 of Israel, **b.** the servants of David.......6440
2Sa 2:24 Ammah, that lieth **b.** Giah 5921,.........6440
2Sa 3:28 are guiltless **b.** the Lord......................5973
2Sa 3:31 sackcloth, and mourn **b.** Abner...........6440
2Sa 3:34 as a man falleth **b.** wicked men,..........6440
2Sa 5:3 with them in Hebron **b.** the Lord:.......6440
2Sa 5:20 forth upon mine enemies **b.** me,..........6440
2Sa 5:24 the Lord go out **b.** thee, to smite........6440
2Sa 6:4 and Ahio went **b.** the ark..................6440
2Sa 6:5 played **b.** the Lord on all manner.......6440
2Sa 6:14 David danced **b.** the Lord with all........6440
2Sa 6:16 leaping and dancing **b.** the Lord;.........6440
2Sa 6:17 and peace offerings **b.** the Lord..........6440
2Sa 6:21 It was **b.** the Lord, which chose.........6440
2Sa 6:21 which chose me **b.** thy father..................
2Sa 6:21 and **b.** all his house,...................................
2Sa 6:21 therefore will I play **b.** the Lord..........6440
2Sa 7:15 Saul, whom I put away **b.** thee...........6440
2Sa 7:16 be established forever **b.** thee:...........6440
2Sa 7:18 and sat **b.** the Lord, and he said,........6440
2Sa 7:23 for thy land, **b.** thy people,.................6440
2Sa 7:26 David be established **b.** thee...............6440
2Sa 7:29 it may continue for ever **b.** thee:.........6440
2Sa 10:6 that they stank **b.** David,..........................
2Sa 10:9 was against him **b.** and behind,...........6440
2Sa 10:13 the Syrians: and they fled **b.** him.........6440
2Sa 10:14 fled they also **b.** Abishai, and...............6440
2Sa 10:15 were smitten **b.** Israel, they................6440
2Sa 10:16 host of Hadarezer went **b.** them.........6440
2Sa 10:18 And the Syrians fled **b.** Israel;.............6440
2Sa 10:19 they were smitten **b.** Israel, they........6440
2Sa 11:13 he did eat and drink **b.** him;...............6440
2Sa 12:11 I will take thy wives **b.** thine eyes,..........
2Sa 12:12 I will do this thing **b.** all Israel,...........5048
2Sa 12:12 and **b.** the sun...................................5048
2Sa 12:20 they set bread **b.** him,..............................
2Sa 13:9 pan and poured them out **b.** him;.........6440
2Sa 14:33 face to the ground **b.** the king:............6440
2Sa 15:1 and fifty men to run **b.** him..................6440
2Sa 15:18 from Gath, passed...**b.** the king...5921,6440
2Sa 18:7 the people of Israel were slain **b.**.........6440
2Sa 18:28 upon his face **b.** the king,......................
2Sa 19:8 all the people came **b.** the king:...........6440
2Sa 19:13 captain of the host **b.** me...................6440
2Sa 19:17 went over Jordan **b.** the king..............6440
2Sa 19:18 fell down **b.** the king, as he was..........6440
2Sa 19:28 but dead men **b.** my lord the king............
2Sa 20:8 in Gibeon, Amasa went **b.** them...........6440
2Sa 21:9 them in the hill **b.** the Lord:...............6440
2Sa 22:13 Through the brightness **b.** him..............5048
2Sa 22:23 his judgments were **b.** me:..................5048
2Sa 22:24 I was also upright **b.** him,.........................
2Sa 24:13 wilt thou flee three months **b.**.............6440
2Sa 24:20 and bowed himself **b.** the king...................
1Ki 1:2 let her stand **b.** the king, and let.........6440
1Ki 1:5 and fifty men to run **b.** him..................6440
1Ki 1:23 he bowed himself **b.** the king with his........
1Ki 1:23 when he was come in **b.** the king,........6440
1Ki 1:25 behold, they eat and drink **b.** him,........6440
1Ki 1:28 king's presence, and stood **b.** the.........6440
1Ki 1:32 And they came **b.** the king..................6440
1Ki 2:4 heed to their way, to walk **b.** me.........6440
1Ki 2:26 the ark of the Lord God **b.** David........6440
1Ki 2:45 shall be established **b.** the Lord..........6440
1Ki 3:6 according as he walked **b.** thee............6440
1Ki 3:12 there was none like thee **b.** thee,........6440
1Ki 3:15 stood **b.** the ark of the covenant.........6440
1Ki 3:16 unto the king, and stood **b.** him...........6440
1Ki 3:22 Thus they spake **b.** the king...............6440
1Ki 3:24 they brought a sword **b.** the king.........6440
1Ki 6:3 **b.** the temple of the house,.........5921,6440
1Ki 6:3 was the breadth thereof **b.**..........5921,6440
1Ki 6:7 ready **b.** it was brought thither:...........4551
1Ki 6:17 the temple **b.** it, was forty cubits........3942
1Ki 6:21 **b.** the oracle; and he overlaid it..........6440
1Ki 7:6 the porch was **b.** them: and the...5921,6440
1Ki 7:6 and the thick beam were **b.** them.5921,6440
1Ki 7:49 left, **b.** the oracle, with the................6440
1Ki 8:5 **b.** the ark, sacrificing sheep and..........6440
1Ki 8:8 in the holy place **b.** the oracle,....5921,6440
1Ki 8:22 stood **b.** the altar of the Lord.............6440
1Ki 8:23 thy servants that walk **b.** thee.............6440
1Ki 8:25 that they walk **b.** me as thou..............6440
1Ki 8:25 hast walked **b.** me...............................6440
1Ki 8:28 servant prayeth **b.** thee to day:...........6440
1Ki 8:31 come **b.** thine altar in this house:.........6440
1Ki 8:33 people Israel be smitten down **b.**.........6440
1Ki 8:50 **b.** them who carried them captive,.......6440
1Ki 8:54 from **b.** the altar of the Lord,...............6440
1Ki 8:59 made supplication **b.** the Lord,..............6440
1Ki 8:62 Israel with him offered sacrifice **b.**........6440
1Ki 8:64 that was **b.** the house of the Lord:.......6440
1Ki 8:64 brasen altar that was **b.** the Lord.........6440
1Ki 8:65 **b.** the Lord our God, seven days.........6440
1Ki 9:3 that thou hast made **b.** me:..................6440
1Ki 9:4 if thou wilt walk **b.** me, as David.........6440
1Ki 9:6 statutes which I have set **b.** you,.........6440
1Ki 9:25 the altar that was **b.** the Lord..............6440
1Ki 10:8 which stand continually **b.** thee,..........6440
1Ki 11:7 the hill that is **b.** Jerusalem,........5921,6440
1Ki 11:36 a light alway **b.** me in Jerusalem,........6440
1Ki 12:6 men, that stood **b.** Solomon..........854,6440
1Ki 12:8 him, and which stood **b.** him:..............6440
1Ki 12:30 people went to worship **b.** the one,......6440
1Ki 13:6 again, and became as it was **b.**............7223
1Ki 14:9 evil above all that were **b.** thee:...........6440
1Ki 14:24 cast out **b.** the children of Israel.........6440
1Ki 15:3 father which he had done **b.** him:.........6440
1Ki 16:25 worse than all that were **b.** him...........6440
1Ki 16:30 above all that were **b.** him...................6440
1Ki 16:33 kings of Israel that were **b.** him.........6440
1Ki 17:1 of Israel liveth, **b.** whom I stand,..........6440
1Ki 17:3 Cherith, that is **b.** Jordan............5921,6440
1Ki 17:5 Cherith, that is **b.** Jordan............5921,6440
1Ki 18:15 liveth, **b.** whom I stand, I will............6440
1Ki 18:46 ran **b.** Ahab to the entrance................6440
1Ki 19:11 stand upon the mount **b.** the Lord.......6440
1Ki 19:11 in pieces the rocks **b.** the Lord;............6440
1Ki 19:19 with twelve yoke of oxen **b.** him,.........6440
1Ki 20:27 Israel pitched **b.** them like...................5048
1Ki 21:10 sons of Belial, **b.** him, to bear.............5048
1Ki 21:13 and sat **b.** him:.....................................5048
1Ki 21:26 cast out **b.** the children of Israel.........6440
1Ki 21:29 how Ahab humbleth himself **b.** me?......6440
1Ki 21:29 he humbleth himself **b.** me,..................6440
1Ki 22:10 the prophets prophesied **b.** them.........6440
1Ki 22:21 came forth a spirit, and stood **b.**..........6440
2Ki 1:13 and fell on his knees **b.** Elijah,............5048
2Ki 2:9 do for thee, **b.** I be taken away...........2962
2Ki 2:15 themselves to the ground **b.** him..............
2Ki 3:14 **b.** whom I stand, surely, were it.........6440
2Ki 3:24 so that they fled **b.** them:....................6440
2Ki 4:12 had called her, she stood **b.** him.........6440
2Ki 4:31 Gehazi passed on **b.** them, and laid......6440
2Ki 4:38 the prophets were sitting **b.** him:.........6440
2Ki 4:43 I set this **b.** an hundred men?.............6440
2Ki 4:44 So he set it **b.** them, and they.............6440
2Ki 5:15 and came, and stood **b.** him:...............6440
2Ki 5:16 the Lord liveth, **b.** whom I stand,........6440
2Ki 5:23 and they bare them **b.** him...................6440
2Ki 5:25 and stood **b.** his master.........................413
2Ki 6:22 set bread and water **b.** them,...............6440
2Ki 6:32 the king sent a man from **b.** him:..........6440
2Ki 8:9 and came and stood **b.** him, and............6440
2Ki 10:4 Behold, two kings stood not **b.** him:....6440
2Ki 11:18 the priest of Baal **b.** the altars...........6440
2Ki 14:12 was put to the worse **b.** Israel;...........6440
2Ki 15:10 and smote him **b.** the people,..............6905
2Ki 16:3 cast out from **b.** the children..............6440
2Ki 16:14 altar, which was **b.** the Lord,...............6440
2Ki 17:2 kings of Israel that were **b.** him...........6440
2Ki 17:8 out from **b.** the children of Israel,........6440
2Ki 17:11 the Lord carried away **b.** them;............6440
2Ki 18:5 Judah, nor any that were **b.** him.........6440
2Ki 18:22 Ye shall worship **b.** this altar in............6440
2Ki 19:14 Lord, and spread it **b.** the Lord..........6440
2Ki 19:15 Hezekiah prayed **b.** the Lord,...............6440
2Ki 19:26 corn blasted **b.** it be grown up.............6440
2Ki 19:32 nor come **b.** it with shield, nor...........6924
2Ki 20:3 I have walked **b.** thee in truth...............6440

2Ki 21:2 cast out **b.** the children of Israel. 6440
2Ki 21:9 destroyed **b.** the children of Israel. 6440
2Ki 21:11 Amorites did, which were **b.** him, 6440
2Ki 22:10 And Shaphan read it **b.** the king. 6440
2Ki 22:19 hast humbled thyself **b.** the Lord, 6440
2Ki 22:19 rent thy clothes, and wept **b.** me; 6440
2Ki 23:3 made a covenant **b.** the Lord, 6440
2Ki 23:13 that were **b.** Jerusalem, 5921,6440
2Ki 23:25 unto him was there no king **b.** him, 6440
2Ki 25:7 sons of Zedekiah **b.** his eyes.
2Ki 25:29 did eat bread continually **b.** him 6440
1Ch 1:43 of Edom **b.** any king reigned over 6440
1Ch 5:25 land whom God destroyed **b.** them. 6440
1Ch 6:32 they ministered **b.** the dwelling 6440
1Ch 10:1 Israel fled from **b.** the Philistines, 6440
1Ch 11:3 with them in Hebron **b.** the Lord; 6440
1Ch 11:13 people fled from **b.** the Philistines 6440
1Ch 13:8 David and all Israel played **b.** God 6440
1Ch 13:10 the ark: and there he died **b.** God. 6440
1Ch 14:15 God is gone forth **b.** thee to smite 6440
1Ch 15:24 the trumpets **b.** the ark of God: 6440
1Ch 16:1 and peace offerings **b.** God 6440
1Ch 16:4 to minister **b.** the ark of the Lord, 6440
1Ch 16:6 **b.** the ark of the covenant of God. 6440
1Ch 16:29 an offering, and come **b.** him: 6440
1Ch 16:30 Fear **b.** him, all the earth: the 6440
1Ch 16:37 there **b.** the ark of the covenant 6440
1Ch 16:37 to minister **b.** the ark continually, 6440
1Ch 16:39 **b.** the tabernacle of the Lord 6440
1Ch 17:8 off all thine enemies from **b.** thee, 6440
1Ch 17:13 it from him that was **b.** thee: 6440
1Ch 17:16 the king came and sat **b.** the Lord, 6440
1Ch 17:21 out nations from **b.** thy people, 6440
1Ch 17:24 thy servant be established **b.** thee. 6440
1Ch 17:25 found in his heart to pray **b.** thee. 6440
1Ch 17:27 that it may be **b.** thee for ever: 6440
1Ch 19:7 who came and pitched **b.** Medeba 6440
1Ch 19:9 the battle in array **b.** the gate
1Ch 19:10 was set against him **b.** and behind, 6440
1Ch 19:14 **b.** the Syrians unto the battle; 6440
1Ch 19:14 and they fled **b.** him. 6440
1Ch 19:15 likewise fled **b.** Abishai his brother, 6440
1Ch 19:16 put to the worse **b.** Israel, 6440
1Ch 19:16 host of Hadarezer went **b.** them 6440
1Ch 19:18 Syrians fled **b.** Israel; and David 6440
1Ch 19:19 put to the worse **b.** Israel, they 6440
1Ch 21:12 to be destroyed **b.** thy foes, while 6440
1Ch 21:30 not go **b.** it to enquire of God: 6440
1Ch 22:5 prepared abundantly **b.** his death. 6440
1Ch 22:18 the land is subdued **b.** the Lord, 6440
1Ch 22:18 and **b.** his people. 6440
1Ch 23:13 to burn incense **b.** the Lord, to 6440
1Ch 23:31 unto them continually **b.** the Lord: 6440
1Ch 24:2 and Abihu died **b.** their father, 6440
1Ch 24:6 wrote them **b.** the king, 6440
1Ch 24:6 and **b.** the chief of the fathers
1Ch 28:4 chose me **b.** all the house
1Ch 29:10 the Lord **b.** all the congregation: 5869
1Ch 29:15 strangers **b.** thee, and sojourners 6440
1Ch 29:22 And did eat and drink **b.** the Lord 6440
1Ch 29:25 been on any king **b.** him in Israel. 6440
2Ch 1:5 **b.** the tabernacle of the Lord: 6440
2Ch 1:6 to the brasen altar **b.** the Lord, 6440
2Ch 1:10 go out and come in **b.** this people: 6440
2Ch 1:12 have had that have been **b.** thee, 6440
2Ch 1:13 from **b.** the tabernacle of the 6440
2Ch 2:4 and to burn **b.** him sweet incense, 6440
2Ch 2:6 save only to burn sacrifice **b.** him? 6440
2Ch 3:15 he made **b.** the house two pillars 6440
2Ch 3:17 up the pillars **b.** the temple, 5921,6440
2Ch 4:20 after the manner **b.** the oracle, 6440
2Ch 5:6 assembled unto him **b.** the ark, 6440
2Ch 5:9 seen from the ark **b.** the oracle; 5921,6440
2Ch 6:12 he stood **b.** the altar of the Lord 6440
2Ch 6:13 down upon his knees **b.** all 5048
2Ch 6:14 thy servants, that walk **b.** thee 6440
2Ch 6:16 my law as thou hast walked **b.** me 6440
2Ch 6:19 which thy servant prayeth **b.** thee: 6440
2Ch 6:22 come **b.** thine altar in this house; 6440
2Ch 6:24 be put to the worse **b.** the enemy, 6440
2Ch 6:24 and make supplication **b.** thee 6440
2Ch 6:36 deliver them over **b.** their enemies, 6440
2Ch 7:4 offered sacrifices **b.** the Lord 6440
2Ch 7:6 priests sounded trumpets **b.** them, 5048
2Ch 7:7 was **b.** the house of the Lord: 6440
2Ch 7:17 if thou wilt walk **b.** me, as David 6440
2Ch 7:19 which I have set **b.** you, 6440
2Ch 8:12 which he had built **b.** the porch, 6440
2Ch 8:14 and minister **b.** the priests, 5048
2Ch 9:7 which stand continually **b.** thee, 6440
2Ch 9:11 and there were none such seen **b.** 6440
2Ch 10:6 men that had stood **b.** Solomon 6440
2Ch 10:8 up with him, that stood **b.** him 6440
2Ch 13:13 they were **b.** Judah, and the 6440
2Ch 13:14 the battle was **b.** and behind: 6440
2Ch 13:15 Jeroboam and all Israel **b.** Abijah 6440
2Ch 13:16 children of Israel fled **b.** Judah: 6440
2Ch 14:5 the kingdom was quiet **b.** him. 6440
2Ch 14:7 while the land is yet **b.** us; 6440
2Ch 14:12 the Lord smote the Ethiopians **b.** 6440
2Ch 14:12 Asa, and **b.** Judah; 6440
2Ch 14:13 they were destroyed **b.** the Lord, 6440
2Ch 14:13 and **b.** his host; 6440
2Ch 15:8 that was **b.** the porch of the Lord. 6440
2Ch 18:9 the prophets prophesied **b.** them. 6440
2Ch 18:20 and stood **b.** the Lord, and said, 6440
2Ch 19:2 wrath upon thee from **b.** the Lord. 6440
2Ch 19:11 the Levites shall be officers **b.** you. 6440
2Ch 20:5 **b.** the new court, 6440
2Ch 20:7 **b.** thy people Israel, and gavest 6440
2Ch 20:9 we stand **b.** this house, and in thy 6440
2Ch 20:13 and all Judah stood **b.** the Lord, 6440
2Ch 20:16 brook, **b.** the wilderness of Jeruel 6440
2Ch 20:18 of Jerusalem fell **b.** the Lord, 6440
2Ch 20:21 as they went out **b.** the army, 6440
2Ch 23:17 slew Mattan the priest of Baal **b.** 6440
2Ch 24:14 the rest of the money **b.** the king 6440
2Ch 25:8 shall make thee fall **b.** the enemy: 6440
2Ch 25:14 and bowed himself down **b.** them, 6440
2Ch 25:22 was put to the worse **b.** Israel, 6440
2Ch 26:19 forehead **b.** the priests in the 6440
2Ch 27:6 he prepared his ways **b.** the Lord 6440
2Ch 28:3 cast out **b.** the children of Israel. 6440
2Ch 28:9 he went out **b.** the host that came 6440
2Ch 28:14 **b.** the princes and all the 6440
2Ch 29:11 hath chosen you to stand **b.** him, 6440
2Ch 29:19 they are **b.** the altar of the Lord. 6440
2Ch 29:23 **b.** the king and the congregation, 6440
2Ch 30:9 **b.** them that lead them captive, 6440
2Ch 31:20 and truth **b.** the Lord his God. 6440
2Ch 32:12 Ye shall worship **b.** one altar, and 6440
2Ch 33:2 cast out **b.** the children of Israel. 6440
2Ch 33:7 which I have chosen **b.** all the
2Ch 33:9 destroyed **b.** the children of 6440
2Ch 33:12 himself greatly **b.** the God 854,6440
2Ch 33:19 graven images, **b.** he was humbled: 6440
2Ch 33:23 humbled not himself **b.** the Lord, 6440
2Ch 34:18 And Shaphan read it **b.** the king. 6440
2Ch 34:24 have read **b.** the king of Judah: 6440
2Ch 34:27 thou didst humble thyself **b.** God, 6440
2Ch 34:27 humbledst thyself **b.** me, and didst 6440
2Ch 34:27 rend thy clothes, and weep **b.** me; 6440
2Ch 34:31 and made a covenant **b.** the Lord, 6440
2Ch 36:12 humbled not himself **b.** Jeremiah 6440
Ezr 3:12 this house was laid **b.** their eyes, 6440
Ezr 4:18 us hath been plainly read **b.** me. 6925
Ezr 4:23 letter was read **b.** Rehum, 6925
Ezr 7:19 vessels...deliver thou **b.** the God 6925
Ezr 7:28 extended mercy unto me **b.** the 6440
Ezr 7:28 **b.** all the king's mighty princes. 6440
Ezr 8:21 might afflict ourselves **b.** our God, 6440
Ezr 8:29 weigh them **b.** the chief of the 6440
Ezr 9:15 we are **b.** thee in our trespasses: 6440
Ezr 9:15 for we cannot stand **b.** thee 6440
Ezr 10:1 himself down **b.** the house of God, 6440
Ezr 10:6 Ezra rose up from **b.** the house of 6440
Ne 1:4 and prayed **b.** the God of heaven, 6440
Ne 1:6 I pray **b.** thee now, day and night, 6440
Ne 2:1 the king, that wine was **b.** him: 6440
Ne 2:13 valley, even **b.** the dragon well, 413,6440
Ne 4:2 spake **b.** his brethren and the 6440
Ne 4:5 sin be blotted out from **b.** thee: 6440
Ne 4:5 to anger **b.** the builders. 5048
Ne 5:15 governors that had been **b.** me 6440
Ne 6:19 reported his good deeds **b.** me, 6440
Ne 8:1 street that was **b.** the water gate; 6440
Ne 8:2 law **b.** the congregation both of 6440
Ne 8:3 he read therein **b.** the street 6440
Ne 8:3 that was **b.** the water gate 6440
Ne 8:3 **b.** the men and the women, and 5048
Ne 9:8 foundest his heart faithful **b.** thee, 6440
Ne 9:11 thou didst divide the sea **b.** them, 6440
Ne 9:24 and thou subduedst **b.** them the 6440
Ne 9:28 rest, they did evil again **b.** thee: 6440
Ne 9:32 all the trouble seem little **b.** thee. 6440
Ne 9:35 land which thou gavest **b.** them, 6440
Ne 12:36 God, and Ezra the scribe **b.** them. 6440
Ne 13:4 And **b.** this, Eliashib the priest, 6440
Ne 13:19 began to be dark **b.** the sabbath, 6440
Es 1:3 princes of the provinces, being **b.** 6440
Es 1:11 bring Vashti the queen **b.** the king 6440
Es 1:16 Memucan answered **b.** the king 6440
Es 1:17 the queen to be brought in **b.** him, 6440
Es 1:19 That Vashti come no more **b.** king 6440
Es 2:11 walked every day **b.** the court 6440
Es 2:23 book of the chronicles **b.** the king. 6440
Es 3:7 the lot **b.** Haman from day to day, 6440
Es 4:2 And came even **b.** the king's gate: 6440
Es 4:6 which was **b.** the king's gate. 6440
Es 4:8 to make request **b.** him for her 6440
Es 6:1 And they were read **b.** the king. 6440
Es 6:9 and proclaim **b.** him, Thus shall 6440
Es 6:11 of the city, and proclaimed **b.** him, 6440
Es 6:13 **b.** whom thou hast begun to fall, 6440
Es 6:13 but shalt surely fall **b.** him. 6440
Es 7:6 afraid **b.** the king and the queen. 6440
Es 7:8 queen also **b.** me in the house? 5973
Es 7:9 chamberlains, said **b.** the king, 6440
Es 8:1 And Mordecai came **b.** the king; 6440
Es 8:3 Esther spake yet again **b.** the king, 6440
Es 8:4 Esther arose, and stood **b.** the 6440
Es 8:5 the thing seem right **b.** the king, 6440
Es 9:11 palace was brought **b.** the king. 6440
Es 9:25 when Esther came **b.** the king, 6440
Job 1:6 present themselves **b.** the Lord, 5921
Job 2:1 present themselves **b.** the Lord, 5921
Job 2:1 to present himself **b.** the Lord. 5921
Job 3:24 my sighing cometh **b.** I eat, and 6440
Job 4:15 Then a spirit passed **b.** my face; 5921
Job 4:16 an image was **b.** mine eyes, 5048
Job 4:19 dust, which are crushed **b.** the 6440
Job 8:12 it withereth **b.** any other herb. 6440
Job 8:16 He is green **b.** the sun, and his 6440
Job 10:21 **B.** I go whence I shall not return, 2962
Job 13:15 maintain mine own ways **b.** 413,6440
Job 13:16 an hypocrite shall not come **b.** him. 6440
Job 15:4 and restrainest prayer **b.** God. 6440
Job 15:7 or wast thou made **b.** the hills? 6440
Job 15:32 It shall be accomplished **b.** his 3808
Job 18:20 they that went **b.** were affrighted. 6931
Job 21:8 and their offspring **b.** their eyes.
Job 21:18 They are as stubble **b.** the wind, 6440
Job 21:33 as there are innumerable **b.** him. 6440
Job 23:4 I would order my cause **b.** him, 6440
Job 23:17 I was not cut off **b.** the darkness, 6440
Job 26:6 Hell is naked **b.** him, and 5048
Job 30:11 have also let loose the bridle **b.** me. 6440
Job 33:5 set thy words in order **b.** me, 6440
Job 35:14 judgment is **b.** him; therefore 6440
Job 41:10 who then is able to stand **b.** me? 6440
Job 41:22 sorrow is turned into joy **b.** him. 6440
Job 42:10 twice as much as he had **b.**
Job 42:11 had been of his acquaintance **b.**, 6440
Ps 5:8 make thy way straight **b.** my face.
Ps 16:8 set the Lord always **b.** me: 5048
Ps 18:6 and my cry came **b.** him, even 6440
Ps 18:12 brightness that was **b.** him 5048
Ps 18:22 his judgments were **b.** me, 5048
Ps 18:23 I was also upright **b.** him, 5973
Ps 18:42 small as the dust **b.** the 5921,6440
Ps 22:25 pay my vows **b.** them that fear 5048
Ps 22:27 the nations shall worship **b.** thee. 6440
Ps 22:29 down to the dust shall bow **b.** him: 6440
Ps 23:5 Thou preparest a table **b.** me in 6440
Ps 26:3 thy loving kindness is **b.** mine. 5048
Ps 31:19 that trust in thee **b.** the sons of 5048
Ps 31:22 I am cut off from **b.** thine eyes: 5048
Ps 34:*title* his behaviour **b.** Abimelech: 6440
Ps 35:5 Let them be as chaff **b.** the wind: 6440
Ps 36:1 no fear of God **b.** his eyes. 5048
Ps 38:9 Lord, all my desire is **b.** thee; 5048
Ps 38:17 my sorrow is continually **b.** me. 5048
Ps 39:1 while the wicked is **b.** me. 5048
Ps 39:5 mine age is nothing **b.** thee: 5048
Ps 39:13 I may recover strength **b.** I go 2962
Ps 41:12 settest me **b.** thy face for ever.
Ps 42:2 shall I come and appear **b.** God? 6440
Ps 44:15 confusion is continually **b.** me, 5048
Ps 50:3 a fire shall devour **b.** him, and it 6440
Ps 50:8 to have been continually **b.** me. 5048
Ps 50:21 set them in order **b.** thine eyes.

Ps 51:3 my sin is ever **b.** me. 5048
Ps 52:9 for it is good **b.** thy saints. 5048
Ps 54:3 they have not set God **b.** them. 5048
Ps 56:13 that I may walk **b.** God in the 6440
Ps 57:6 they have digged a pit **b.** me, 6440
Ps 58:9 **B.** your pots can feel the thorns, 2962
Ps 61:7 He shall abide **b.** God for ever: 6440
Ps 62:8 people, pour out your heart **b.** him: 6440
Ps 68:1 also that hate him flee **b.** him. 6440
Ps 68:2 as wax melteth **b.** the fire, so let 6440
Ps 68:3 let them rejoice **b.** God: yea, let 6440
Ps 68:4 his name Jah, and rejoice **b.** him. 6440
Ps 68:7 thou wentest forth **b.** thy people, 6440
Ps 68:25 The singers went **b.**, the players 6924
Ps 69:19 mine adversaries are all **b.** thee 5048
Ps 69:22 table become a snare **b.** them: 6440
Ps 72:9 the wilderness shall bow **b.** him; 6440
Ps 72:11 all kings shall fall down **b.** him,
Ps 73:22 I was a beast **b.** thee. 5973
Ps 78:55 cast out the heathen also **b.** them, 6440
Ps 79:11 sighing of the prisoner come **b.** thee; 6440
Ps 80:2 **B.** Ephraim and Benjamin and 6440
Ps 80:9 Thou preparedst room **b.** it, 6440
Ps 83:13 as the stubble **b.** the wind. 6440
Ps 84:7 of them in Zion appeareth **b.** God. 413
Ps 85:13 Righteousness shall go **b.** him: 6440
Ps 86:9 and worship **b.** thee, O Lord; 6440
Ps 86:14 have not set thee **b.** them. 5048
Ps 88:1 I have cried day and night **b.** thee: 5048
Ps 88:2 Let my prayer come **b.** thee: 6440
Ps 89:14 mercy and truth shall go **b.** thy
Ps 89:23 will beat down his foes **b.** his face,
Ps 89:36 his throne as the sun **b.** me 5048
Ps 90:2 **B.** the mountains were brought 2962
Ps 90:8 hast set our iniquities **b.** thee, 5048
Ps 95:2 Let us come **b.** his presence with 6924
Ps 95:6 us kneel **b.** the Lord our maker. 6440
Ps 96:6 Honour and majesty are **b.** him: 6440
Ps 96:9 fear **b.** him, all the earth. 6440
Ps 96:13 **B.** the Lord: for he cometh, for he 6440
Ps 97:3 A fire goeth **b.** him, and burneth 6440
Ps 98:6 make a joyful noise **b.** the Lord, 6440
Ps 98:9 **B.** the Lord; for he cometh 6440
Ps 100:2 come **b.** his presence with singing.
Ps 101:3 set no wicked thing **b.** mine eyes 5048
Ps 102:*title* poureth out his complaint **b.** the 6440
Ps 102:28 seed shall be established **b.** thee. 6440
Ps 105:17 He sent a man **b.** them, even 6440
Ps 106:23 Moses his chosen stood **b.** him 6440
Ps 109:15 them be **b.** the Lord continually, 5048
Ps 116:9 I will walk **b.** the Lord in the land 6440
Ps 119:30 thy judgments have I laid **b.** me.
Ps 119:46 of thy testimonies also **b.** kings, 5048
Ps 119:67 **B.** I was afflicted I went astray: 2962
Ps 119:168 all my ways are **b.** thee, 5048
Ps 119:169 Let my cry come near **b.** thee, 6440
Ps 119:170 Let my supplication come **b.** thee: 6440
Ps 138:1 **b.** the gods will I sing praise 5048
Ps 139:5 Thou hast beset me behind and **b.**, 6924
Ps 141:2 Let my prayer be set forth **b.** thee 6440
Ps 141:3 a watch, O Lord, **b.** my mouth
Ps 142:2 poured out my complaint **b.** him: 6440
Ps 142:2 I shewed **b.** him my trouble. 6440
Ps 147:17 who can stand **b.** his cold? 6440
Pr 4:25 eyelids look straight **b.** thee. 5048
Pr 5:21 ways of man are **b.** the eyes of 5227
Pr 8:22 of his way, **b.** his works of old. 6924
Pr 8:25 **B.** the mountains were settled, 2962
Pr 8:25 **b.** the hills was I brought forth: 6440
Pr 8:30 delight, rejoicing always **b.** him; 6440
Pr 14:19 The evil bow **b.** the good: and the 6440
Pr 15:11 and destruction are **b.** the Lord 5048
Pr 15:33 wisdom; and **b.** honour is humility. 6440
Pr 16:18 Pride goeth **b.** destruction, 6440
Pr 16:18 and an haughty spirit **b.** a fall 6440
Pr 17:14 off contention, **b.** it be meddled 6440
Pr 17:24 Wisdom is **b.** him that hath 854,6440
Pr 18:12 **B.** destruction the heart of man is 6440
Pr 18:12 and **b.** honour is humility. 6440
Pr 18:13 that answereth a matter **b.** he 2962
Pr 18:16 and bringeth him **b.** great men. 6440
Pr 22:29 he shall stand **b.** kings; 6440
Pr 22:29 he shall not stand **b.** mean men. 6440
Pr 23:1 consider diligently what is **b.** thee: 6440
Pr 25:5 Take away the wicked from **b.** the 6440
Pr 25:26 man falling down **b.** the wicked 6440
Pr 26:26 shewed **b.** the whole congregation.
Pr 27:4 but who is able to stand **b.** envy? 6440
Pr 30:7 deny me them not **b.** I die: 2962
Ec 1:10 of old time, which was **b.** us. 6440
Ec 1:16 all they that have been **b.** me 6440
Ec 2:7 all that were in Jerusalem **b.** me: 6440
Ec 2:9 more than all that were **b.** me 6440
Ec 2:26 to him that is good **b.** God. 6440
Ec 3:14 that men should fear **b.** him. 6440
Ec 4:16 of all that have been **b.** them: 6440
Ec 5:2 hasty to utter any thing **b.** God: 6440
Ec 5:6 neither say thou **b.** the angel, that 6440
Ec 6:8 knoweth to walk **b.** the living? 5048
Ec 7:17 shouldest thou die **b.** thy time? 3808
Ec 8:12 that fear God, which fear **b.** him: 6440
Ec 8:13 he feareth not **b.** God. 6440
Ec 9:1 or hatred by all that is **b.** them. 6440
Ca 8:12 vineyard, which is mine, is **b.** me: 6440
Isa 1:12 When ye come to appear **b.** me, 6440
Isa 1:16 of your doings from **b.** mine eyes; 5048
Isa 7:16 For **b.** the child shall know 2962
Isa 8:4 **b.** the child shall have knowledge 2962
Isa 8:4 taken away **b.** the king of Assyria 6440
Isa 9:3 they joy **b.** thee according to the 6440
Isa 9:12 Syrians **b.**, and the Philistines 6924
Isa 13:16 be dashed to pieces **b.** their eyes;
Isa 17:13 the chaff off the mountains **b.** the 6440
Isa 17:13 and like a rolling thing **b.** the 6440
Isa 17:14 **b.** the morning he is not 2962
Isa 23:18 them that dwell **b.** the Lord, to eat 6440
Isa 24:23 **b.** his ancients gloriously 5048
Isa 28:4 as the hasty fruit **b.** the summer; 2962
Isa 30:8 Now go, write it **b.** them 854
Isa 30:11 of Israel to cease from **b.** us. 6440
Isa 36:7 Ye shall worship **b.** this altar? 6440
Isa 37:14 Lord, and spread it **b.** the Lord. 6440
Isa 37:27 as corn blasted **b.** it be grown up. 6440
Isa 37:33 come **b.** it with shields, nor cast 6924
Isa 38:3 I have walked **b.** thee in truth 6440
Isa 40:10 with him, and his work **b.** him. 6440
Isa 40:17 all nations **b.** him are as nothing 5048
Isa 41:1 Keep silence **b.** me, 413
Isa 41:2 gave the nations **b.** him, 6440
Isa 42:9 **b.** they spring forth I tell you 2962
Isa 42:16 will make darkness light **b.** them, 6440
Isa 43:10 **b.** me there was no God 6440
Isa 43:13 **b.** the day was I am he;
Isa 45:1 to subdue nations **b.** him; and I 6440
Isa 45:1 open **b.** him the two leaved gates; 6440
Isa 45:2 I will go **b.** thee, and make the 6440
Isa 47:14 nor fire to sit **b.** it 5048
Isa 48:5 **b.** it came to pass I shewed 2962
Isa 48:7 even **b.** the day when thou 6440
Isa 48:19 cut off nor destroyed from **b.** me. 6440
Isa 49:16 thy walls are continually **b.** me 5048
Isa 52:12 will go **b.** you; and the God 6440
Isa 53:2 grow up **b.** him as a tender 6440
Isa 53:7 sheep **b.** her shearers is dumb, so 6440
Isa 55:12 the hills shall break forth **b.** you 6440
Isa 57:16 should fail **b.** me, and the souls 6440
Isa 58:8 thy righteousness, shall go **b.** thee; 6440
Isa 59:12 are multiplied **b.** thee, 5048
Isa 61:11 to spring forth **b.** all the nations. 5048
Isa 62:11 is with him and his work **b.** him. 6440
Isa 63:12 arm, dividing the water **b.** them, 6440
Isa 65:6 it is written **b.** me: I will not keep 6440
Isa 65:12 but did evil **b.** mine eyes, and did
Isa 65:24 that **b.** they call, I will answer; 2962
Isa 66:4 did evil **b.** mine eyes, and chose
Isa 66:7 **B.** she travailed, she brought 2962
Isa 66:7 **b.** her pain came, 2962
Isa 66:22 remain **b.** me,...so shall your seed 6440
Isa 66:23 all flesh come to worship **b.** me, 6440
Jer 1:5 **B.** I formed thee in the belly I 2962
Jer 1:5 and **b.** thou camest forth 2962
Jer 1:17 lest I confound thee **b.** them. 6440
Jer 2:22 is marked **b.** me, saith the Lord 6440
Jer 6:7 **b.** me continually is grief 5921,6440
Jer 6:21 lay stumblingblocks **b.** this people, 413
Jer 7:10 and stand **b.** me in this house, 6440
Jer 8:2 spread them **b.** the sun,
Jer 9:13 my law which I set **b.** them, 6440
Jer 13:16 **b.** he cause darkness, and 2962
Jer 13:16 **b.** your feet stumble 2962
Jer 15:1 Moses and Samuel stood **b.** me, 6440
Jer 15:9 to the sword **b.** their enemies, 6440
Jer 15:19 shalt stand **b.** me: and if thou 6440
Jer 17:16 of my lips was right **b.** thee. 5227,6440
Jer 18:17 with an east wind **b.** the enemy; 6440
Jer 18:20 I stood **b.** thee to speak good for 6440
Jer 18:23 let them be overthrown **b.** thee; 6440
Jer 19:7 fall by the sword **b.** their enemies, 6440
Jer 21:8 I set **b.** you the way of life, 6440
Jer 24:1 two baskets of figs were set **b.** the 6440
Jer 26:4 my law, which I have set **b.** you, 6440
Jer 28:8 prophets that have been **b.** me 6440
Jer 28:8 and **b.** thee of old prophesied 6440
Jer 29:21 he shall slay them **b.** your eyes;
Jer 30:20 shall be established **b.** me, 6440
Jer 31:36 ordinances depart from **b.** me, 6440
Jer 31:36 being a nation **b.** me for ever. 6440
Jer 32:12 **b.** all the Jews that sat in the 5869
Jer 32:13 charged Baruch **b.** them, saying, 5869
Jer 32:30 Judah have only done evil **b.** me 5869
Jer 32:31 should remove it from **b.** my face, 5921
Jer 33:9 an honour **b.** all the nations
Jer 33:18 the Levites want a man **b.** me 6440
Jer 33:24 should be no more a nation **b.** them. 6440
Jer 34:5 former kings which were **b.** thee, 6440
Jer 34:15 ye had made a covenant **b.** me 6440
Jer 34:18 which they had made **b.** me, 6440
Jer 35:5 I set **b.** the sons of the house 6440
Jer 35:19 not want a man to stand **b.** me 6440
Jer 36:7 their supplication **b.** the Lord, 6440
Jer 36:9 proclaimed a fast **b.** the Lord to all 6440
Jer 36:22 fire on the hearth burning **b.** him 6440
Jer 37:20 I pray thee, be accepted **b.** thee; 6440
Jer 38:10 out of the dungeon, **b.** he die. 2962
Jer 38:26 my supplication **b.** the king, 6440
Jer 39:6 Zedekiah in Riblah **b.** his eyes:
Jer 39:16 accomplished in that day **b.** thee. 6440
Jer 40:4 behold, all the land is **b.** thee: 6440
Jer 42:2 supplication be accepted **b.** thee, 6440
Jer 42:9 present your supplication **b.** him: 6440
Jer 44:10 statutes, that I set **b.** you and **b.** 6440
Jer 47:1 **b.** that Pharaoh smote Gaza 2962
Jer 49:19 shepherd that will stand **b.** me? 6440
Jer 49:37 to be dismayed **b.** their enemies, 6440
Jer 49:37 and **b.** them that seek their life: 6440
Jer 50:8 as the he goats **b.** the flocks. 6440
Jer 50:44 shepherd that will stand **b.** me? 6440
Jer 52:10 sons of Zedekiah **b.** his eyes:
Jer 52:33 did continually eat bread **b.** him 6440
La 1:5 gone into captivity **b.** the enemy. 6440
La 1:6 without strength **b.** the pursuer. 6440
La 1:22 all their wickedness come **b.** thee; 6440
La 2:3 right hand from **b.** the enemy, 6440
La 2:19 water **b.** the face of the Lord: 5227
La 3:35 man **b.** the face of the most High. 5048
Eze 2:10 he spread it **b.** me; and it was 6440
Eze 3:20 I lay a stumbling block **b.** him, 6440
Eze 4:1 thee a tile, and lay it **b.** thee, 6440
Eze 6:4 will cast down your slain men **b.** 6440
Eze 6:5 children of Israel **b.** their idols; 6440
Eze 8:1 the elders of Judah sat **b.** me, 6440
Eze 8:11 stood **b.** them seventy men of the 6440
Eze 9:6 men which were **b.** the house 6440
Eze 14:1 of Israel unto me, and sat **b.** me. 6440
Eze 14:3 their iniquity **b.** their face: 5227
Eze 14:4 his iniquity **b.** his face, and cometh 5227
Eze 14:7 his iniquity **b.** his face, 5227
Eze 16:18 oil and mine incense **b.** them. 6440
Eze 16:19 hast even set it **b.** them for a sweet 6440
Eze 16:50 committed abomination **b.** me: 6440
Eze 16:57 **B.** thy wickedness was discovered, 2962
Eze 20:1 inquire of the Lord, and sat **b.** me. 6440
Eze 20:9 not be polluted **b.** the heathen, 5869
Eze 20:14 that it should not be polluted **b.** 5869
Eze 20:41 sanctified in you **b.** the heathen 5869
Eze 21:6 with bitterness sigh **b.** their eyes.
Eze 22:30 stand in the gap **b.** me for the 6440
Eze 23:24 and I will set judgment **b.** them. 6440
Eze 23:41 bed, and a table prepared **b.** it, 6440
Eze 28:9 thou yet say **b.** him that slayeth 6440
Eze 28:17 I will lay thee **b.** kings, that they 6440
Eze 30:24 and he shall groan **b.** him with 6440
Eze 32:10 brandish my sword **b.** them; 5921,6440
Eze 33:31 they sit **b.** thee as my people, 6440
Eze 36:17 their way was **b.** me as the 6440
Eze 36:23 sanctified in you **b.** their eyes.
Eze 37:20 be in thine hand **b.** their eyes.
Eze 38:16 in thee, O Gog, **b.** their eyes.
Eze 40:12 space also **b.** the little chambers 6440
Eze 40:22 the arches thereof were **b.** them. 6440
Eze 40:26 the arches thereof were **b.** them: 6440

Eze 40:47 the altar that was **b.** the house. 6440
Eze 41:4 twenty cubits, **b.** the temple: 413,6440
Eze 41:12 **b.** the separate place at the end 413,6440
Eze 41:22 is the table that is **b.** the Lord. 6440
Eze 42:1 which was **b.** the building toward 5048
Eze 42:2 **B.** the length of an hundred 413,6440
Eze 42:4 And **b.** the chambers was a walk 6440
Eze 42:8 **b.** the temple was an hundred 5921,6440
Eze 42:11 And the way **b.** them was like 6440
Eze 42:12 directly **b.** the wall toward the east, 6440
Eze 42:13 which are **b.** the separate place, 413,6440
Eze 43:24 thou shalt offer them **b.** the Lord, 6440
Eze 44:3 sit in it to eat bread **b.** the Lord; 6440
Eze 44:4 of the north gate **b.** the house: 413,6440
Eze 44:11 shall stand **b.** them to minister 6440
Eze 44:12 they ministered unto them **b.** their 6440
Eze 44:15 they shall stand **b.** me to offer 6440
Eze 44:22 or a widow that had a priest **b.**
Eze 45:7 **b.** the oblation of the holy 413,6440
Eze 45:7 **b.** the possession of the city, 413,6440
Eze 46:3 gate **b.** the Lord in the sabbaths 6440
Eze 46:9 shall come **b.** the Lord in the 6440
Da 1:5 they might stand **b.** the king. 6440
Da 1:13 countenances be looked upon **b.** 6440
Da 1:18 them in **b.** Nebuchadnezzar. 6440
Da 1:19 therefore stood they **b.** the king. 6440
Da 2:2 they came and stood **b.** the king. 6440
Da 2:9 corrupt words to speak **b.** me, 6925
Da 2:10 Chaldeans answered **b.** the king, 6925
Da 2:11 other that can shew it **b.** the king, 6925
Da 2:24 bring me in **b.** the king, and I will 6925
Da 2:25 brought in Daniel **b.** the king 6925
Da 2:31 brightness was excellent, stood **b.** 6903
Da 2:36 interpretation thereof **b.** the king 6925
Da 3:3 and they stood **b.** the image 6903
Da 3:13 brought these men **b.** the king 6925
Da 4:6 the wise men of Babylon **b.** me, 6925
Da 4:7 and I told the dream **b.** them; 6925
Da 4:8 at...last Daniel came in **b.** me, 5922,6925
Da 4:8 and **b.** him I told the dream. 6925
Da 5:1 and drank wine **b.** the thousand. 6903
Da 5:13 Daniel brought in **b.** the king, 6925
Da 5:15 have been brought in **b.** me, 6925
Da 5:17 answered and said **b.** the king, 6925
Da 5:19 trembled and feared **b.** him: 4481,6925
Da 5:23 the vessels of his house **b.** thee, 6925
Da 6:10 and gave thanks **b.** his God, 6925
Da 6:11 making supplication **b.** his God. 6925
Da 6:12 and spake **b.** the king concerning 6925
Da 6:13 and said **b.** the king, That Daniel 6925
Da 6:18 of musick brought **b.** him; 6925
Da 6:22 **b.** him innocency was found in 6925
Da 6:22 and also **b.** thee, 6925
Da 6:26 and fear **b.** the God of Daniel: 4481,6925
Da 7:7 from all the beasts that were **b.** it; 6925
Da 7:8 **b.** whom there were three 6925
Da 7:10 and came forth from **b.** him: 6925
Da 7:10 times ten thousand stood **b.** him: 6925
Da 7:13 and they brought him near **b.** him 6925
Da 7:20 up, and **b.** whom three fell; 4481,6925
Da 8:3 there stood **b.** the river a ram 6440
Da 8:4 no beasts might stand **b.** him, 6440
Da 8:6 had seen standing **b.** the river, 6440
Da 8:7 power in the ram to stand **b.** him, 6440
Da 8:15 stood **b.** me as the appearance 5048
Da 9:10 his laws, which he set **b.** us by 6440
Da 9:13 prayer **b.** the Lord our God, 854,6440
Da 9:18 present our supplications **b.** thee 6440
Da 9:20 supplication **b.** the Lord my God 6440
Da 10:12 and to chasten thyself **b.** thy God, 6440
Da 10:16 and said unto him that stood **b.** me, 5048
Da 11:16 will, and none shall stand **b.** him: 6440
Da 11:22 they be overflown from **b.** him, 6440
Ho 7:2 them about; they are **b.** my face. 5048
Joe 1:16 Is not the meat cut off **b.** our eyes, 5048
Joe 2:3 A fire devoureth **b.** them; 6440
Joe 2:3 as the garden of Eden **b.** them, 6440
Joe 2:6 **B.** their face the people shall be
Joe 2:10 The earth shall quake **b.** them; 6440
Joe 2:11 Lord shall utter his voice **b.** his 6440
Joe 2:31 **b.** the great and the terrible day 6440
Am 1:1 two years **b.** the earthquake 6440
Am 2:9 destroyed I the Amorite **b.** them, 6440
Am 4:3 at that which is **b.** her; 5084
Am 9:4 go into captivity **b.** their enemies, 6440
Jon 1:2 their wickedness is come up **b.** me. 6440
Jon 4:2 Therefore I fled **b.** unto Tarshish 6924
Mic 1:4 as wax **b.** the fire, and as the 6440
Mic 2:13 The breaker is come up **b.** them: 6440
Mic 2:13 and their king shall pass **b.** them, 6440
Mic 6:1 contend thou **b.** the mountains, 854
Mic 6:4 I sent **b.** thee Moses, Aaron, and 6440
Mic 6:6 Wherewith shall I come **b.** the 6924
Mic 6:6 and bow myself **b.** the high God?
Mic 6:6 shall I come **b.** him with burnt 6924
Na 1:6 Who can stand **b.** his indignation? 6440
Na 2:1 in pieces is come up **b.** thy face: 5921
Hab 1:3 spoiling and violence are **b.** me: 5048
Hab 2:20 let all the earth keep silence **b.** 6440
Hab 3:5 **B.** him went the pestilence, and 6440
Zep 2:2 **B.** the decree bring forth, 2962
Zep 2:2 forth, **b.** the day pass as the chaff,
Zep 2:2 **b.** the fierce anger of the Lord 2962,3808
Zep 2:2 **b.** the day of the Lord's anger 2962,3808
Zep 3:20 turn back your captivity **b.** your
Hag 1:12 the people did fear **b.** the Lord. 6440
Hag 2:14 so is this nation **b.** me, saith the 6440
Hag 2:15 **b.** a stone was laid upon a stone 2962
Zec 2:13 Be silent, O all flesh, **b.** the Lord: 6440
Zec 3:1 standing **b.** the angel of the Lord, 6440
Zec 3:3 garments, and stood **b.** the angel. 6440
Zec 3:4 those that stood **b.** him, saying, 6440
Zec 3:8 and thy fellows that sit **b.** thee: 6440
Zec 3:9 stone that I have laid **b.** Joshua; 6440
Zec 4:7 **b.** Zerubbabel thou shalt become 6440
Zec 6:5 from standing **b.** the Lord 5921
Zec 7:2 their men, to pray **b.** the Lord, 854,6440
Zec 8:10 **b.** these days there was no hire 6440
Zec 8:21, 22 speedily to pray **b.** the Lord, 854,6440
Zec 12:8 the angel of the Lord **b.** them. 6440
Zec 14:4 the mount of Olives, which is **b.** 5921,6440
Zec 14:5 as ye fled from **b.** the earthquake 6440
Zec 14:20 shall be like the bowls **b.** the altar. 6440
Mal 2:5 me, and was afraid **b.** my name. 6440
Mal 2:9 and base **b.** all the people,
Mal 3:1 he shall prepare the way **b.** me: 6440
Mal 3:11 vine cast her fruit **b.** the time
Mal 3:14 mournfully **b.** the Lord of hosts? 6440
Mal 3:16 remembrance was written **b.** him 6440
Mal 4:5 **b.** the coming of the great and 6440
Mt 1:18 **b.** they came together, *4250,2228*
Mt 2:9 went **b.** them, till it came and *4254*
Mt 5:12 **the prophets which were b. you** *4253*
Mt 5:16 **Let your light so shine b. men,** *1715*
Mt 5:24 **Leave there thy gift b. the altar,** *1715*
Mt 6:1 **do not your alms b. men,** *1715*
Mt 6:2 **do not sound a trumpet b. thee,** *1715*
Mt 6:8 **ye have need of, b. ye ask him** *4253*
Mt 7:6 **cast ye your pearls b. swine,** *1715*
Mt 8:29 hither to torment us **b.** the time? *4253*
Mt 10:18 **b. governors and kings for my** *1909*
Mt 10:32 **shall confess me b. men, him will** *1715*
Mt 10:32 **I confess also b. my Father** *1715*
Mt 10:33 **shall deny me b. men,** *1715*
Mt 10:33 **him will I also deny b. my** *1715*
Mt 11:10 **I send my messenger b. thy face,** *4253*
Mt 11:10 **shall prepare thy way b. thee** *1715*
Mt 14:6 of Herodias danced **b.** them, *3319*
Mt 14:8 she, being **b.** instructed of her *4264*
Mt 14:22 to go **b.** him unto the other side, *4254*
Mt 17:2 was transfigured **b.** them: and his *1715*
Mt 21:9 the multitudes that went **b.**, *4254*
Mt 21:31 **go into the kingdom of God b. you** *4254*
Mt 24:25 **I have told you b.** *4280*
Mt 24:38 **in the days that were b. the flood** *4253*
Mt 25:32 **b. him shall be gathered all** *1715*
Mt 26:32 **I will go b. you into Galilee.** *4254*
Mt 26:34 **That this night, b. the cock crow,** *4250*
Mt 26:70 he denied **b.** them all, saying, *1715*
Mt 26:75 **B.** the cock crow, thou shalt deny *4250*
Mt 27:11 Jesus stood **b.** the governor: *1715*
Mt 27:24 washed his hands **b.** the multitude, *561*
Mt 27:29 and they bowed the knee **b.** him, *1715*
Mt 28:7 he goeth **b.** you into Galilee; *4254*
Mk 1:2 I send my messenger **b.** thy face, *4253*
Mk 1:2 shall prepare thy way **b.** thee. *1715*
Mk 1:35 rising up a great while **b.** day, *1773*
Mk 2:12 bed, and went forth **b.** them all; *1726*
Mk 3:11 they saw him, fell down **b.** him, *4363*
Mk 5:33 came and fell down **b.** him, *4363*
Mk 6:41 to his disciples to set **b.** them; *3908*
Mk 6:45 to go to the other side **b.** unto *4254*
Mk 8:6 to his disciples to set **b.** them; *3908*
Mk 8:6 they did set them **b.** the people. *3908*
Mk 8:7 commanded to set them also **b.** *3908*
Mk 9:2 and he was transfigured **b.** them. *1715*
Mk 10:32 Jesus went **b.** them: and they *4254*
Mk 11:9 And they that went **b.**, and they *4254*
Mk 13:9 **b. rulers and kings for my sake,** *1909*
Mk 14:28 **I will go b. you into Galilee.** *4254*
Mk 14:30 **b. the cock crow twice,** *4250, 2228*
Mk 14:72 **B.** the cock crow twice, thou shalt *4250*
Mk 15:42 that is, the day **b.** the sabbath, *4315*
Mk 16:7 that he goeth **b.** you into Galilee: *4254*
Lu 1:6 they were both righteous **b.** God, *1799*
Lu 1:8 **b.** God in the order of his course, *1725*
Lu 1:17 shall go **b.** him in the spirit and *1799*
Lu 1:75 In holiness and righteousness **b.** *1799*
Lu 1:76 shalt go **b.** the face of the Lord *4253*
Lu 2:21 **b.** he was conceived in the womb. *4253*
Lu 2:26 **b.** he had seen the Lord's *4250,2228*
Lu 2:31 **b.** the face of all people; *2596*
Lu 5:18 him in, and to lay him **b.** him. *1799*
Lu 5:19 his couch into the midst **b.** Jesus. *1715*
Lu 5:25 he rose up **b.** them, and took up *1799*
Lu 7:27 **I send my messenger b. thy face,** *4253*
Lu 7:27 **shall prepare thy way b. thee.** *1715*
Lu 8:28 and fell down **b.** him, and with a *4363*
Lu 8:47 and falling down **b.** him, *4363*
Lu 8:47 unto him **b.** all the people for *1799*
Lu 9:16 to set **b.** the multitude. *3908*
Lu 9:52 and sent messengers **b.** his face: *4253*
Lu 10:1 two and two **b.** his face into every *4253*
Lu 10:8 **such things as are set b. you:** *3908*
Lu 11:6 **and I have nothing to set b. him?** *3908*
Lu 11:38 he had not first washed **b.** dinner. *4253*
Lu 12:6 **one of them is forgotten b. God?** *1799*
Lu 12:8 **shall confess me b. men,** *1715*
Lu 12:8 **also confess b. the angels of God:** *1715*
Lu 12:9 **he that denieth me b. men shall** *1799*
Lu 12:9 **be denied b. the angels of God.** *1799*
Lu 14:2 there was a certain man **b.** him. *1715*
Lu 15:18 **against heaven, and b. thee,** *1799*
Lu 16:15 **which justify yourselves b. men;** *1799*
Lu 18:39 they which went **b.** rebuked him, *4254*
Lu 19:4 he ran **b.**, and climbed up *1715*
Lu 19:27 **bring hither, and slay them b. me.** *1715*
Lu 19:28 had thus spoken, he went **b.**, *1715*
Lu 20:26 his words **b.** the people: and they *1726*
Lu 21:12 **But b. all these, they shall lay** *4253*
Lu 21:12 **brought b. kings and rulers for** *1909*
Lu 21:14 **meditate b. what ye shall answer:** *4304*
Lu 21:36 **to stand b. the Son of man.** *1715*
Lu 22:15 **this passover with you b. I suffer:** *4253*
Lu 22:34 **b. that thou shalt thrice** *4250,2228*
Lu 22:47 one of the twelve, went **b.** them, *4281*
Lu 22:61 **B.** the cock crow, thou shalt *4250*
Lu 23:12 for **b.** they were at enmity *4391*
Lu 23:14 having examined him **b.** you, *1799*
Lu 23:53 wherein never man **b.** was laid. *3764*
Lu 24:19 word **b.** God and all the people: *1726*
Lu 24:43 did eat **b.** them. *1799*
Joh 1:15 after me is preferred **b.** me: *1709*
Joh 1:15 for he was **b.** me. *4413*
Joh 1:27 after me is preferred **b.** me, *1715*
Joh 1:30 a man which is preferred **b.** me; *1715*
Joh 1:30 for he was **b.** me. *4413*
Joh 3:48 **B. that Philip called thee, when** *4253*
Joh 3:28 but that I am sent **b.** him. *1715*
Joh 5:7 another steppeth down **b.** me. *4253*
Joh 6:62 **ascend up where he was b.?** *4386*
Joh 7:51 man, **b.** it hear him, *3362,4386*
Joh 8:58 **unto you, B. Abraham was, I am.** *4250*
Joh 9:8 they which **b.** had seen him *4386*
Joh 10:4 **he goeth b. them, and the sheep** *1715*
Joh 10:8 **that ever came b. me are thieves** *4253*
Joh 11:55 up to Jerusalem **b.** the passover, *4253*
Joh 12:1 Jesus six days **b.** the passover *4253*
Joh 12:37 done so many miracles **b.** them, *1715*
Joh 13:1 Now **b.** the feast of the passover, *4253*
Joh 13:19 **Now I tell you b. it come, that,** *4253*
Joh 14:29 **I have told you b. it come to pass,** *4250*
Joh 15:18 **hated me b. it hated you.** *4412*
Joh 17:5 **I had with thee b. the world.** *4253*
Joh 17:24 **b. the foundation of the world.** *4253*
Ac 1:16 by the mouth of David spake **b.** *4277*
Ac 2:20 **b.** that great and notable *4250,2228*
Ac 2:25 the Lord always **b.** my face, *1799*
Ac 2:31 He seeing this **b.** spake of the *4275*
Ac 3:18 which God **b.** had showed *4293*
Ac 3:20 which **b.** was preached unto you: *4296*

Ac 4:10 man stand here **b.** you whole. *1799*
Ac 4:28 counsel determined **b.** to be done *4309*
Ac 5:23 standing without **b.** the doors: *4253*
Ac 5:27 set them **b.** the counsel: and the *1722*
Ac 5:36 **b.** these days rose up Theudas, *4253*
Ac 6:6 Whom they set **b.** the apostles: *1799*
Ac 7:2 **b.** he dwelt in Charran, *4250,2228*
Ac 7:40 Make us gods to go **b.** us: for as *4313*
Ac 7:45 God drave out **b.** the face of our *575*
Ac 7:46 Who found favour **b.** God, *1799*
Ac 7:52 which shewed **b.** the coming *4293*
Ac 8:32 like a lamb dumb **b.** his shearer, *1726*
Ac 9:15 **to bear my name b. the Gentiles,** *1799*
Ac 10:4 come up for a memorial **b.** God. *1799*
Ac 10:17 stood **b.** the gate, *1909*
Ac 10:30 stood **b.** me in bright clothing, *1799*
Ac 10:33 are we all here present **b.** God *1799*
Ac 10:41 unto witnesses chosen **b.** of God, *4401*
Ac 12:6 and the keepers **b.** the door kept *4253*
Ac 12:14 told how Peter stood **b.** the gate *4253*
Ac 13:24 **b.** his coming the baptism *4253,4383*
Ac 14:13 Jupiter, which was **b.** their city, *4253*
Ac 16:29 and fell down **b.** Paul and Silas, *4363*
Ac 16:34 he set meat **b.** them, *3908*
Ac 17:26 hath determined the times **b.** *4384*
Ac 18:17 beat him **b.** the judgment seat. *1715*
Ac 19:9 that way **b.** the multitude, *1799*
Ac 19:19 burned them **b.** all men: and *1799*
Ac 20:5 going **b.** tarried for us at Troas *4281*
Ac 20:13 And we went **b.** to ship, and *4281*
Ac 21:29 (For they had seen **b.** with him *4308*
Ac 21:38 which **b.** these days madest *4253*
Ac 22:30 Paul down, and set him **b.** them *1519*
Ac 23:1 in all good conscience **b.** God
Ac 23:30 to say **b.** thee what they had *1909*
Ac 23:33 presented Paul also **b.** him.
Ac 24:19 to have been here **b.** thee, and *1909*
Ac 24:20 while I stood **b.** the council, *1909*
Ac 25:9 judge of these things **b.** me? *1909*
Ac 25:16 **b.** that he which is accused have *4250*
Ac 25:26 brought him forth **b.** you, *1909*
Ac 25:26 and specially **b.** thee, O king *1909*
Ac 26:2 for myself this day **b.** thee *1909*
Ac 26:26 **b.** whom also I speak freely: *4314*
Ac 27:24 thou must be brought **b.** Caesar: *3936*
Ro 2:13 of the law are just **b.** God, *3844*
Ro 3:9 **b.** proved both Jews and Gentiles, *4256*
Ro 3:18 no fear of God **b.** their eyes. *561*
Ro 3:19 world may become guilty **b.** God.
Ro 4:2 but not **b.** God. *4314*
Ro 4:17 **b.** him whom he believed, even *2713*
Ro 9:29 as Esaias said **b.**, Except the Lord *4280*
Ro 14:10 all stand **b.** the judgment seat *3936*
Ro 14:22 have it to thyself **b.** God. Happy *1799*
Ro 16:7 who also were in Christ **b.** me *4253*
1Co 2:7 God ordained **b.** the world unto *4253*
1Co 4:5 judge nothing **b.** the time, *4253*
1Co 6:1 go to law **b.** the unjust, *1909*
1Co 6:1 and not **b.** the saints? *1909*
1Co 6:6 and that **b.** the unbelievers *1909*
1Co 10:27 whatsoever is set **b.** you, eat, *3908*
1Co 11:21 taketh **b.** other his own supper: *4301*
2Co 1:15 was minded to come unto you **b.**, *4386*
2Co 5:10 **b.** the judgment seat of Christ; *1715*
2Co 7:3 I have said **b.**, that ye are in our *4280*
2Co 7:14 which I made **b.** Titus, is found *1909*
2Co 8:10 who have begun **b.**, not only to *4278*
2Co 8:24 and **b.** the churches, the *1519,4383*
2Co 9:5 that they would go **b.** unto you, *4281*
2Co 9:5 whereof ye had notice **b.**, that *4293*
2Co 12:19 we speak **b.** God in Christ: 2714
2Co 13:2 I told you **b.**, and foretell you, *4280*
Gal 1:9 As we said **b.**, so say I now again, *4280*
Gal 1:17 which were apostles **b.** me; *4253*
Gal 1:20 you, behold, **b.** God, I lie not. *1799*
Gal 2:12 **b.** that certain came from James, *4253*
Gal 2:14 I said unto Peter **b.** them all, *1715*
Gal 3:1 **b.** whose eyes Jesus Christ hath *2596*
Gal 3:8 **b.** the gospel unto Abraham, *4283*
Gal 3:17 that was confirmed **b.** of God *4300*
Gal 3:23 But **b.** faith came, *4253*
Gal 5:21 of the which I tell you **b.**, as I *4302*
Eph 1:4 us in him **b.** the foundation *4253*
Eph 1:4 and without blame **b.** him in love: *2714*
Eph 2:10 which God hath **b.** ordained that *4282*
Php 3:13 unto those things which are **b.**, *1715*
Col 1:5 heard **b.** in the word of the truth *4257*
Col 1:17 he is **b.** all things, and by him *4253*
1Th 2:2 after that we had suffered **b.**, *4310*
1Th 3:4 you **b.** that we should suffer *4302*
1Th 3:9 joy for your sakes **b.** our God; *1715*
1Th 3:13 unblameable in holiness **b.** God, *1715*
1Ti 1:13 Who was **b.** a blasphemer, and a *4386*
1Ti 1:18 to the prophecies which went **b.** *4254*
1Ti 5:4 that is good and acceptable **b.** *1799*
1Ti 5:19 but **b.** two or three witnesses, *1909*
1Ti 5:20 Them that sin rebuke **b.** all, *1799*
1Ti 5:21 I charge thee **b.** God, and the *1799*
1Ti 5:21 preferring one **b.** another, *4299*
1Ti 5:24 going **b.** to judgment; and some *4254*
1Ti 6:12 profession **b.** many witnesses. *1799*
1Ti 6:13 and **b.** Christ Jesus,
1Ti 6:13 **b.** Pontius Pilate witnessed *1909*
2Ti *subscr.* Paul was brought **b.** Nero the *3936*
2Ti 1:9 Christ Jesus **b.** the world began, *4253*
2Ti 2:14 charging them **b.** the Lord *1799*
2Ti 4:1 therefore **b.** God, and the Lord *1799*
2Ti 4:21 thy diligence to come **b.** winter. *4253*
Ti 1:2 promised **b.** the world began; *4253*
Heb 6:18 lay hold upon the hope set **b.** us: *4295*
Heb 7:18 of the commandment going **b.** *4254*
Heb 10:15 after that he had said **b.**, *4280*
Heb 11:5 **b.** his translation he had this *4253*
Heb 12:1 the race that is set **b.** us, *4295*
Heb 12:2 for the joy that was set **b.** him *4295*
Jas 1:27 **b.** God and the Father is this, *3844*
Jas 2:6 you **b.** the judgment seats? *1519*
Jas 5:9 the judge standeth **b.** the door. *4253*
1Pe 1:20 **b.** the foundation of the world, *4253*
2Pe 2:11 against them **b.** the Lord. *3844*
2Pe 3:2 which were spoken **b.** by the holy *4280*
2Pe 3:17 seeing ye know these things **b.**, *4267*
1Jo 2:28 be ashamed **b.** him at his coming. *575*
1Jo 3:19 shall assure our hearts **b.** him. *1715*
3Jo 6 of thy charity **b.** the church: *1799*
Jude 4 who were **b.** of old ordained to *4270*
Jude 17 were spoken **b.** of the apostles *4280*
Jude 24 faultless **b.** the presence of his *2714*
Re 1:4 spirits which are **b.** his throne; *1799*
Re 2:14 **a stumblingblock b. the children** *1799*
Re 3:2 **found thy works perfect b. God.** *1799*
Re 3:5 **b. my Father, and b. his angels.** *1799*
Re 3:8 **I have set b. thee an open door,** *1799*
Re 3:9 **to come and worship b. thy feet,** *1799*
Re 4:5 of fire burning **b.** the throne, *1799*
Re 4:6 **b.** the throne there was a sea *1799*
Re 4:6 beasts full of eyes **b.** and behind. *1715*
Re 4:10 elders fall down **b.** him that sat *1799*
Re 4:10 and cast their crowns **b.** the throne, *1799*
Re 5:8 elders fell down **b.** the Lamb, *1799*
Re 7:9 **b.** the throne, and **b.** the Lamb, *1799*
Re 7:11 fell **b.** the throne on their faces, *1799*
Re 7:15 are they **b.** throne of God, *1799*
Re 8:2 seven angels which stood **b.** God; *1799*
Re 8:3 altar which was **b.** the throne. *1799*
Re 8:4 ascended up **b.** God out of the *1799*
Re 9:13 golden altar which is **b.** God, *1799*
Re 10:11 prophesy again **b.** many peoples, *1909*
Re 11:4 standing **b.** the God of the earth. *1799*
Re 11:16 which sat **b.** God on their seats, *1799*
Re 12:4 the dragon stood **b.** the woman *1799*
Re 12:10 accused them **b.** our God day and *1799*
Re 13:12 power of the first beast **b.** him, *1799*
Re 14:3 **b.** the throne, and **b.** the four *1799*
Re 14:5 without fault **b.** the throne of God. *1799*
Re 15:4 shall come and worship **b.** thee; *1799*
Re 16:19 came in remembrance **b.** God, *1799*
Re 19:20 that wrought miracles **b.** him, *1799*
Re 20:12 small and great, stand **b.** God; *1799*
Re 22:8 **b.** the feet of the angel which *1715*

BEFOREHAND See also AFOREHAND.
Mk 13:11 **take no thought b. what ye shall** *4305*
2Co 9:5 and make up **b.** your bounty, *4294*
1Ti 5:24 Some men's sins are open **b.**, *4271*
1Ti 5:25 works of some are manifest **b.** *4271*
1Pe 1:11 testified **b.** the sufferings of Christ, *4303*

BEFORETIME See also AFORETIME.
De 2:12 The Horims also dwelt in Seir **b.**; 6440
Jos 11:10 for Hazor **b.** was the head of all 6440
Jos 20:5 and hated him not **b.**. 8543,8032
1Sa 9:9 (**B.** in Israel, when a man 6440
1Sa 9:9 a Prophet was **b.** called a Seer.) 6440
1Sa 10:11 when all that knew him **b.** 865,8032
2Sa 7:10 afflict them any more, or **b.** 7223
2Ki 13:5 dwelt in their tents, as **b.**. 8543,8032
Ne 2:1 Now I had not been **b.** sad
Isa 41:26 and **b.**, that we may say, He is 6440
Ac 8:9 called Simon, which **b.** in the same *4391*

BEG See also BEGGED; BEGGING.
Ps 109:10 be continually vagabonds, and **b.** 7592
Pr 20:4 therefore shall he **b.** in the harvest, 7592
Lu 16:3 **cannot dig; to b. I am ashamed.** *1871*

BEGAN
Ge 4:26 then **b.** men to call upon the name 2490
Ge 6:1 when men **b.** to multiply on the 2490
Ge 9:20 And Noah **b.** to be an husbandman, 2490
Ge 10:8 **b.** to be a mighty one in the earth. 2490
Ge 41:54 seven years of dearth **b.** to come, 2490
Ge 44:12 he searched, and **b.** at the eldest, 2490
Nu 25:1 people **b.** to commit whoredom 2490
De 1:5 **b.** Moses to declare this law, 2974
Jg 13:25 the Spirit of the Lord **b.** to move 2490
Jg 16:19 and she **b.** to afflict him, and his 2490
Jg 16:22 the hair of his head **b.** to grow 2490
Jg 19:25 when the day **b.** to spring, they 5927
Jg 20:31 they **b.** to smite of the people, 2490
Jg 20:39 Benjamin **b.** to smite and kill 2490
Jg 20:40 when the flame **b.** to arise up out 2490
1Sa 3:2 his eyes **b.** to wax dim, that he 2490
2Sa 2:10 old when he **b.** to reign over Israel,
2Sa 5:4 years old when he **b.** to reign,
1Ki 6:1 **b.** to build the house of the Lord
1Ki 14:21 when he **b.** to reign, and he
1Ki 15:25 son of Jeroboam **b.** to reign over
1Ki 15:33 **b.** Baasha the son of Ahijah to
1Ki 16:8 **b.** Elah the son of Baasha to reign
1Ki 16:11 when he **b.** to reign, as soon as
1Ki 16:23 **b.** Omri to reign over Israel,
1Ki 16:29 **b.** Ahab the son of Omri to reign
1Ki 22:41 on of Asa **b.** to reign over Judah
1Ki 22:42 when he **b.** to reign; and he
1Ki 22:51 the son of Ahab **b.** to reign over
2Ki 3:1 the son of Ahab **b.** to reign over
2Ki 8:16 king of Judah **b.** to reign.
2Ki 8:17 when he **b.** to reign; and he
2Ki 8:26 when he **b.** to reign; and he
2Ki 9:29 **b.** Ahaziah to reign over Judah.
2Ki 10:32 the Lord **b.** to cut Israel short: 2490
2Ki 11:21 Jehoash when he **b.** to reign.
2Ki 12:1 Jehoash **b.** to reign; and forty
2Ki 13:1 the son of Jehu **b.** to reign
2Ki 13:10 **b.** Jehoash the son of Jehoahaz
2Ki 14:2 when he **b.** to reign, and reigned
2Ki 14:23 Joash king of Israel **b.** to reign
2Ki 15:1 **b.** Azariah son of Amaziah king
2Ki 15:2 old was he when he **b.** to reign,
2Ki 15:13 the son of Jabesh **b.** to reign
2Ki 15:17 **b.** Menahem the son of Gadi to reign
2Ki 15:23 the son of Menahem **b.** to reign
2Ki 15:27 the son of Remaliah **b.** to reign
2Ki 15:32 **b.** Jotham the son of Uzziah king
2Ki 15:33 old was he when he **b.** to reign,
2Ki 15:37 In those days the Lord **b.** to send 2490
2Ki 16:1 Jotham king of Judah **b.** to reign.
2Ki 16:2 Ahaz when he **b.** to reign, and
2Ki 17:1 **b.** Hoshea the son of Elah to reign
2Ki 18:1 of Ahaz king of Judah **b.** to reign.
2Ki 18:2 when he **b.** to reign; and he
2Ki 21:1 years old when he **b.** to reign,
2Ki 21:19 twenty and two years old when he **b.**
2Ki 22:1 years old when he **b.** to reign,
2Ki 23:31 years old when he **b.** to reign,
2Ki 23:36 twenty and five years old when he **b.**
2Ki 24:8 years old when he **b.** to reign,
2Ki 24:18 twenty and one years old when he **b.**
2Ki 25:27 in the year that he **b.** to reign did
1Ch 1:10 **b.** to be mighty upon the earth. 2490
1Ch 27:24 the son of Zeruiah **b.** to number, 2490
2Ch 3:1 Solomon **b.** to build the house 2490
2Ch 3:2 And he **b.** to build in the second 2490
2Ch 12:13 years old when he **b.** to reign,
2Ch 13:1 **b.** Abijah to reign over Judah.
2Ch 20:22 when they **b.** to sing and to praise, 2490
2Ch 20:31 years old when he **b.** to reign,
2Ch 21:5 years old when he **b.** to reign,
2Ch 21:20 years old was he when he **b.** to
2Ch 22:2 was Ahaziah when he **b.** to reign,
2Ch 24:1 seven years old when he **b.** to reign,
2Ch 25:1 years old when he **b.** to reign,

2Ch 26:3 was Uzziah when he **b.** to reign, ...
2Ch 27:1 twenty and five years old when he **b.** ...
2Ch 27:8 years old when he **b.** to reign, ...
2Ch 28:1 years old when he **b.** to reign, ...
2Ch 29:1 Hezekiah **b.** to reign when he was ...
2Ch 29:17 Now they **b.** on the first day of ... 2490
2Ch 29:27 when the burnt offering **b.**, ... 2490
2Ch 29:27 the song of the Lord **b.** ... 2490
2Ch 31:7 they **b.** to lay the foundation of ... 2490
2Ch 31:10 Since the people **b.** to bring the ... 2490
2Ch 31:21 And in every work that he **b.** ... 2490
2Ch 33:1 twelve years old when he **b.** to ...
2Ch 33:21 years old when he **b.** to reign, ...
2Ch 34:1 eight years old when he **b.** to reign, ...
2Ch 34:3 **b.** to seek after the God of David ... 2490
2Ch 34:3 in the twelfth year he **b.** to purge ... 2490
2Ch 36:2 twenty and three years old when he **b.** ...
2Ch 36:5 twenty and five years old when he **b.** ...
2Ch 36:9 eight years old when he **b.** to reign, ...
2Ch 36:11 one and twenty years old when he **b.** ...
Ezr 3:6 **b.** they to offer burnt offerings ... 2490
Ezr 3:8 **b.** Zerubbabel the son of Shealtiel ... 2490
Ezr 5:2 and **b.** to build the house of God ... 8271
Ezr 7:9 of the first month **b.** he to go up ... 3246
Ne 4:7 that the breaches **b.** to be stopped, ... 2490
Ne 13:19 gates of Jerusalem **b.** to be dark ... 6751
Jer 52:1 years old when he **b.** to reign, ...
Eze 9:6 Then they **b.** at the ancient men ... 2490
Jon 3:4 Jonah **b.** to enter into the city ... 2490
Mt 4:17 Jesus **b.** to preach, and to say, ... *756*
Mt 11:7 Jesus **b.** to say unto the multitudes ... *756*
Mt 11:20 Then **b.** he to upbraid the cities ... *756*
Mt 12:1 **b.** to pluck the ears of corn, and to ... *756*
Mt 16:21 **b.** Jesus to shew unto his disciples, ... *756*
Mt 16:22 **b.** to rebuke him, saying, Be it far ... *756*
Mt 26:22 **b.** every one of them to say unto ... *756*
Mt 26:37 **b.** to be sorrowful and very heavy. ... *756*
Mt 26:74 Then **b.** he to curse and to swear, ... *756*
Mt 28:1 as it **b.** to dawn toward the first ... *2020*
Mk 1:45 **b.** to publish it much, and to ... *756*
Mk 2:23 his disciples **b.**, as they went, ... *756*
Mk 4:1 he **b.** again to teach by the sea side: ... *756*
Mk 5:17 they **b.** to pray him to depart ... *756*
Mk 5:20 **b.** to publish in Decapolis how great ... *756*
Mk 6:2 he **b.** to teach in the synagogue: ... *756*
Mk 6:7 **b.** to send them forth by two and ... *756*
Mk 6:34 he **b.** to teach them many things. ... *756*
Mk 6:55 **b.** to carry about in beds those ... *756*
Mk 8:11 **b.** to question with him, seeking ... *756*
Mk 8:31 he **b.** to teach them, that the Son of ... *756*
Mk 8:32 Peter took him, and **b.** to rebuke ... *756*
Mk 10:28 Then Peter **b.** to say unto him, ... *756*
Mk 10:32 **b.** to tell them what things should ... *756*
Mk 10:41 they **b.** to be much displeased ... *756*
Mk 10:47 he **b.** to cry out, and say, Jesus, ... *756*
Mk 11:15 **b.** to cast out them that sold and ... *756*
Mk 12:1 **b.** to speak unto them by parables. ... *756*
Mk 13:5 Jesus answering them **b.** to say, ... *756*
Mk 14:19 they **b.** to be sorrowful, and to ... *756*
Mk 14:33 **b.** to be sore amazed, and to be ... *756*
Mk 14:65 some **b.** to spit on him, and to cover ... *756*
Mk 14:69 **b.** to say to them that stood by, ... *756*
Mk 14:71 he **b.** to curse and to swear, saying, ... *756*
Mk 15:8 crying aloud, **b.** to desire him to do ... *756*
Mk 15:18 **b.** to salute him, Hail, king of the ... *756*
Lu 1:70 have been since the world **b.** ...
Lu 3:23 Jesus himself **b.** to be about thirty ... *756*
Lu 4:21 he **b.** to say unto them, **This day** ... *756*
Lu 5:7 the ships, so that they **b.** to sink ...
Lu 5:21 scribes and the Pharisees **b.** to ... *756*
Lu 7:15 he that was dead sat up, and **b.** to ... *756*
Lu 7:24 he **b.** to speak unto the people ... *756*
Lu 7:38 **b.** to wash his feet with tears, and ... *756*
Lu 7:49 **b.** to say within themselves, Who is ... *756*
Lu 9:12 when the day **b.** to wear away, then ... *756*
Lu 11:29 gathered thick together, he **b.** to ... *756*
Lu 11:53 scribes and the Pharisees **b.** to ... *756*
Lu 12:1 he **b.** to say unto his disciples first ... *756*
Lu 14:18 **with one consent b. to make excuse** *756*
Lu 14:30 **Saying, This man b. to build, and** ... *756*
Lu 15:14 **famine in that land, and he b. to be** *756*
Lu 15:24 **And they b. to be merry.** ... *756*
Lu 19:37 multitude of the disciples **b.** to ... *756*
Lu 19:45 **b.** to cast out them that sold ... *756*
Lu 20:9 Then **b.** he to speak to the people ... *756*
Lu 22:23 they **b.** to enquire among themselves ... *756*
Lu 23:2 they **b.** to accuse him, saying, ... *756*
Joh 4:52 when he **b.** to amend. And they ... *2192*
Joh 9:32 Since the world **b.** was it not heard ...
Joh 13:5 **b.** to wash the disciples' feet, and ... *756*
Ac 1:1 all that Jesus **b.** both to do and ... *756*
Ac 2:4 **b.** to speak with other tongues, as ... *756*
Ac 3:21 holy prophets since the world **b.** ...
Ac 8:35 **b.** at the same scripture, and ... *756*
Ac 10:37 **b.** from Galilee, after the baptism ... *756*
Ac 11:15 as I **b.** to speak, the Holy Ghost fell ... *756*
Ac 18:26 he **b.** to speak boldly in the ... *756*
Ac 24:2 Tertullus **b.** to accuse him, saying, ... *756*
Ac 27:35 when he had broken it, he **b.** to eat ... *756*
Ro 16:25 kept secret since the world **b.**, ...
2Ti 1:9 Christ Jesus before the world **b.**; ...
Tit 1:2 promised before the world **b.** ...
Heb 2:3 which at the first **b.** to be ... *746,2983*

BEGAT

Ge 4:18 Irad **b.** Mehujael: ... 3205
Ge 4:18 and Mehujael **b.** Methusael: ... 3205
Ge 4:18 and Methusael **b.** Lamech, ... 3205
Ge 5:3 and **b.** a son in his own likeness, ... 3205
Ge 5:4 and he **b.** sons and daughters: ... 3205
Ge 5:6 an hundred and five years, and **b.** ... 3205
Ge 5:7 Seth lived after he **b.** Enos eight ... 3205
Ge 5:7 and seven years, and **b.** sons and ... 3205
Ge 5:9 Enos lived ninety years, and **b.** ... 3205
Ge 5:10 Enos lived after he **b.** Cainan eight ... 3205
Ge 5:10 fifteen years, and **b.** sons and ... 3205
Ge 5:12 Cainan lived seventy years, and **b.** ... 3205
Ge 5:13 And Cainan lived after he **b.** ... 3205
Ge 5:13 forty years, and **b.** sons and ... 3205
Ge 5:15 lived sixty and five years and **b.** ... 3205
Ge 5:16 Mahalaleel lived after he **b.** Jared ... 3205
Ge 5:16 and thirty years, and **b.** sons and ... 3205
Ge 5:18 sixty and two years, and he **b.** ... 3205
Ge 5:19 And Jared lived after he **b.** Enoch ... 3205
Ge 5:19 hundred years, and **b.** sons and ... 3205
Ge 5:21 lived sixty and five years, and **b.** ... 3205
Ge 5:22 walked with God after he **b.** ... 3205
Ge 5:22 three hundred years, and **b.** sons ... 3205
Ge 5:25 eighty and seven years, and **b.** ... 3205
Ge 5:26 And Methuselah lived after he **b.** ... 3205
Ge 5:26 and two years, and **b.** sons and ... 3205
Ge 5:28 eighty and two years, and **b.** a son: ... 3205
Ge 5:30 And Lamech lived after he **b.** Noah ... 3205
Ge 5:30 and five years, and **b.** sons and ... 3205
Ge 5:32 Noah **b.** Shem, Ham, and Japheth ... 3205
Ge 6:10 Noah **b.** three sons, Shem, Ham, ... 3205
Ge 10:8 Cush **b.** Nimrod: he began to be ... 3205
Ge 10:13 Mizraim **b.** Ludim, and Anamim, ... 3205
Ge 10:15 Canaan **b.** Sidon his firstborn ... 3205
Ge 10:24 Arphaxad **b.** Salah; ... 3205
Ge 10:24 and Salah **b.** Eber ... 3205
Ge 10:26 Joktan **b.** Almodad, and Sheleph, ... 3205
Ge 11:10 and **b.** Arphaxad two years after ... 3205
Ge 11:11 Shem lived after he **b.** Arphaxad ... 3205
Ge 11:11 five hundred years, and **b.** sons and ... 3205
Ge 11:12 and thirty years, and **b.** Salah: ... 3205
Ge 11:13 Arphaxad lived after he **b.** Salah ... 3205
Ge 11:13 and three years, and **b.** sons and ... 3205
Ge 11:14 lived thirty years, and **b.** Eber; ... 3205
Ge 11:15 Salah lived after he **b.** Eber four ... 3205
Ge 11:15 hundred and three years, and **b.** ... 3205
Ge 11:16 four and thirty years, and **b.** Peleg: ... 3205
Ge 11:17 Eber lived after he **b.** Peleg four ... 3205
Ge 11:17 hundred and thirty years, and **b.** ... 3205
Ge 11:18 Peleg lived thirty years, and **b.** ... 3205
Ge 11:19 Peleg lived after he **b.** Reu two ... 3205
Ge 11:19 hundred and nine years and **b.** ... 3205
Ge 11:20 two and thirty years, and **b.** Serug: ... 3205
Ge 11:21 Reu lived after he **b.** Serug two ... 3205
Ge 11:21 hundred and seven years, and **b.** ... 3205
Ge 11:22 lived thirty years, and **b.** Nahor: ... 3205
Ge 11:23 Serug lived after he **b.** Nahor two ... 3205
Ge 11:23 Nahor two hundred years, and **b.** ... 3205
Ge 11:24 nine and twenty years, and **b.** ... 3205
Ge 11:25 Nahor lived after he **b.** Terah an ... 3205
Ge 11:25 and nineteen years, and **b.** sons ... 3205
Ge 11:26 Terah lived seventy years, and **b.** ... 3205
Ge 11:27 Terah **b.** Abram, Nahor, and ... 3205
Ge 11:27 Haran: and Haran **b.** Lot. ... 3205
Ge 22:23 Bethuel **b.** Rebekah: these eight ... 3205
Ge 25:3 Jokshan **b.** Sheba, and Dedan. ... 3205
Ge 25:19 Abraham **b.** Isaac: ... 3205
Le 25:45 with you, which they **b.** in your ... 3205
Nu 26:29 Machir **b.** Gilead: of Gilead come ... 3205
Nu 26:58 Kohath **b.** Amram. ... 3205
De 32:18 the Rock that **b.** thee thou art ... 3205
Jg 11:1 an harlot: and Gilead **b.** Jephthah. ... 3205
Ru 4:18 Pharez **b.** Hezron, ... 3205
Ru 4:19 Hezron **b.** Ram, and Ram **b.** ... 3205
Ru 4:20 Amminadab **b.** Nahshon, ... 3205
Ru 4:20 and Nahshon **b.** Salmon, ... 3205
Ru 4:21 Salmon **b.** Boaz, and Boaz **b.** Obed, ... 3205
Ru 4:22 Obed **b.** Jesse, and Jesse **b.** David. ... 3205
1Ch 1:10 Cush **b.** Nimrod: he began to be ... 3205
1Ch 1:11 Mizraim **b.** Ludim, and Anamim, ... 3205
1Ch 1:13 Canaan **b.** Zidon his firstborn, ... 3205
1Ch 1:18 Arphaxad **b.** Shelah, ... 3205
1Ch 1:18 and Shelah **b.** Eber. ... 3205
1Ch 1:20 Joktan **b.** Almodad, and Sheleph, ... 3205
1Ch 1:34 Abraham **b.** Isaac. The sons of ... 3205
1Ch 2:10 Ram **b.** Amminadab; ... 3205
1Ch 2:10 and Amminadab **b.** Nahshon, ... 3205
1Ch 2:11 Nahshon **b.** Salma, and Salma **b.** ... 3205
1Ch 2:12 Boaz **b.** Obed, and Obed **b.** Jesse, ... 3205
1Ch 2:13 Jesse **b.** his firstborn Eliab, ... 3205
1Ch 2:18 Caleb, the son of Hezron **b.** ... 3205
1Ch 2:20 Hur **b.** Uri, and Uri **b.** Bezaleel, ... 3205
1Ch 2:22 Segub **b.** Jair, who had three ... 3205
1Ch 2:36 Attai **b.** Nathan, and Nathan **b.** ... 3205
1Ch 2:37 Zabad **b.** Ephlal, and Ephlal **b.** ... 3205
1Ch 2:38 Obed **b.** Jehu, and Jehu **b.** Azariah, ... 3205
1Ch 2:39 Azariah **b.** Helez, and Helez **b.** ... 3205
1Ch 2:40 Eleasah **b.** Sisamai, and Sisamai **b.** ... 3205
1Ch 2:41 Shallum **b.** Jekamiah, ... 3205
1Ch 2:41 and Jekamiah **b.** Elishama, ... 3205
1Ch 2:44 Shema **b.** Raham, the father of ... 3205
1Ch 2:44 Jorkoam: and Rekem **b.** Shammai. ... 3205
1Ch 2:46 Haran **b.** Gazez. ... 3205
1Ch 4:2 Reaiah the son of Shobal **b.** Jahath; ... 3205
1Ch 4:2 and Jahath **b.** Ahumai, ... 3205
1Ch 4:8 Coz **b.** Anub, and Zobebah, ... 3205
1Ch 4:11 Chelub the brother of Shuah **b.** ... 3205
1Ch 4:12 Eshton **b.** Beth-rapha, and Paseah, ... 3205
1Ch 4:14 Meonothai **b.** Ophrah: ... 3205
1Ch 4:14 and Seraiah **b.** Joab, ... 3205
1Ch 6:4 Elezar **b.** Phinehas, ... 3205
1Ch 6:4 Phinehas **b.** Abishua, ... 3205
1Ch 6:5 And Abishua **b.** Bukki, ... 3205
1Ch 6:5 and Bukki **b.** Uzzi, ... 3205
1Ch 6:6 And Uzzi **b.** Zerahiah, ... 3205
1Ch 6:6 and Zerahiah **b.** Meraioth, ... 3205
1Ch 6:7 Meraioth **b.** Amariah, ... 3205
1Ch 6:7 and Amariah **b.** Ahitub, ... 3205
1Ch 6:8 And Ahitub **b.** Zadok ... 3205
1Ch 6:8 and Zadok **b.** Ahimaaz, ... 3205
1Ch 6:9 And Ahimaaz **b.** Azariah, ... 3205
1Ch 6:9 and Azariah **b.** Johanan, ... 3205
1Ch 6:10 And Johanan **b.** Azariah (he it is ... 3205
1Ch 6:11 And Azariah **b.** Amariah, ... 3205
1Ch 6:11 and Amariah **b.** Ahitub, ... 3205
1Ch 6:12 And Ahitub **b.** Zadok, ... 3205
1Ch 6:12 and Zadok **b.** Shallum, ... 3205
1Ch 6:13 And Shallum **b.** Hilkiah, ... 3205
1Ch 6:13 and Hilkiah **b.** Azariah, ... 3205
1Ch 6:14 And Azariah **b.** Seraiah, ... 3205
1Ch 6:14 and Seraiah **b.** Jehozadak, ... 3205
1Ch 7:32 Heber **b.** Japhlet, and Shomer, ... 3205
1Ch 8:1 Benjamin **b.** Belah his firstborn, ... 3205
1Ch 8:7 removed them, and **b.** Uzza, and ... 3205
1Ch 8:8 Shaharaim **b.** children in the ... 3205
1Ch 8:9 And he **b.** of Hodesh his wife, ... 3205
1Ch 8:11 of Hushim he **b.** Abitub, and ... 3205
1Ch 8:32 Mikloth **b.** Shimeah. And these ... 3205
1Ch 8:33 Ner **b.** Kish, and Kish **b.** Saul, ... 3205
1Ch 8:33 and Saul **b.** Jonathan, ... 3205
1Ch 8:34 Merib-baal **b.** Micah. ... 3205
1Ch 8:36 Ahaz **b.** Jehoadah; and ... 3205
1Ch 8:36 Jehoadad **b.** Alemeth, and ... 3205
1Ch 8:36 and Zimri **b.** Moza, ... 3205
1Ch 8:37 Moza **b.** Binea: Rapha was his son, ... 3205
1Ch 9:38 Mikloth **b.** Shimeam. And they also ... 3205
1Ch 9:39 Ner **b.** Kish; and Kish **b.** Saul; ... 3205
1Ch 9:39 and Saul **b.** Jonathan. ... 3205
1Ch 9:40 was Merib-baal: Merib-baal **b.** ... 3205
1Ch 9:42 Ahaz **b.** Jarah; and ... 3205
1Ch 9:42 Jarah **b.** Alemeth, and Azmaveth, ... 3205
1Ch 9:42 and Zimri **b.** Moza, ... 3205
1Ch 9:43 Moza **b.** Binea; and Rephaiah his ... 3205
1Ch 14:3 and David **b.** more sons and ... 3205
2Ch 11:21 and **b.** twenty and eight sons, ... 3205
2Ch 13:21 and **b.** twenty and two sons, ... 3205

2Ch 24:3 and he **b.** sons and daughters. 3205
Ne 12:10 Jeshua **b.** Joiakim, 3205
Ne 12:10 Joiakim also **b.** Eliashib, 3205
Ne 12:10 and Eliashib **b.** Joiada, 3205
Ne 12:11 Joiada **b.** Jonathan, 3205
Ne 12:11 and Jonathan **b.** Jaddua. 3205
Pr 23:22 unto thy father that **b.** thee, 3205
Jer 16:3 their fathers that **b.** them in this 3205
Da 11:6 brought her, and he that **b.** her, 3205
Zec 13:3 father and his mother that **b.** him 3205
Zec 13:3 father and his mother that **b.** him 3205
Mt 1:2 Abraham **b.** Isaac; *1080*
Mt 1:2 and Isaac **b.** Jacob; *1080*
Mt 1:2 and Jacob **b.** Judas. *1080*
Mt 1:3 Judas **b.** Phares and Zara of *1080*
Mt 1:3 and Phares **b.** Esrom; *1080*
Mt 1:3 and Esrom **b.** Aram; *1080*
Mt 1:4 Aram **b.** Aminadab; *1080*
Mt 1:4 and Aminadab **b.** Naasson: *1080*
Mt 1:4 and Naasson **b.** Salmon; *1080*
Mt 1:5 Salmon **b.** Booz of Rachab; *1080*
Mt 1:5 and Booz **b.** Obed of Ruth; *1080*
Mt 1:5 and Obed **b.** Jesse; *1080*
Mt 1:6 Jesse **b.** David the king; and *1080*
Mt 1:6 David the king **b.** Solomon *1080*
Mt 1:7 Solomon **b.** Roboam; *1080*
Mt 1:7 and Roboam **b.** Abia; *1080*
Mt 1:7 and Abia **b.** Asa; *1080*
Mt 1:8 Asa **b.** Josaphat; *1080*
Mt 1:8 and Josaphat **b.** Joram; *1080*
Mt 1:8 and Joram **b.** Ozias; *1080*
Mt 1:9 Ozias **b.** Joatham; *1080*
Mt 1:9 and Joatham **b.** Achaz: *1080*
Mt 1:9 and Achaz **b.** Ezekias; *1080*
Mt 1:10 Ezekias **b.** Manasses; *1080*
Mt 1:10 and Manasses **b.** Amon; *1080*
Mt 1:10 and Amon **b.** Josias; *1080*
Mt 1:11 Josias **b.** Jechonias and his *1080*
Mt 1:12 Jechonias **b.** Salathiel; *1080*
Mt 1:12 and Salathiel **b.** Zorobabel; *1080*
Mt 1:13 Zorobabel **b.** Abiud; *1080*
Mt 1:13 and Abiud **b.** Eliakim; *1080*
Mt 1:13 and Eliakim **b.** Azor; *1080*
Mt 1:14 Azor **b.** Sadoc; *1080*
Mt 1:14 and Sadoc **b.** Achim; *1080*
Mt 1:14 and Achim **b.** Eliud; *1080*
Mt 1:15 Eliud **b.** Eleazar; *1080*
Mt 1:15 and Eleazar **b.** Matthan; *1080*
Mt 1:15 and Matthan **b.** Jacob; *1080*
Mt 1:16 Jacob **b.** Joseph the husband of *1080*
Ac 7:8 Abraham **b.** Isaac, and circumcised *1080*
Ac 7:8 Isaac **b.** Jacob; and Jacob **b.** the
Ac 7:29 Madian, where he **b.** two sons. *1080*
Jas 1:18 own will **b.** he us with the word *616*
1Jo 5:1 every one that loveth him that **b.** *1080*

BEGET See also BEGAT; BEGETTEST; BEGETTETH; BEGOTTEN.
Ge 17:20 twelve princes shall he **b.**, 3205
De 4:25 When thou shalt **b.** children, 3205
De 28:41 Thou shalt **b.** sons and daughters, 3205
2Ki 20:18 which thou shalt **b.**, shall they 3205
Ec 6:3 If a man **b.** a hundred children, 3205
Isa 39:7 from thee, which thou shalt **b.**, 3205
Jer 29:6 Take ye wives, and **b.** sons and 3205
Eze 18:10 If he **b.** a son that is a robber, 3205
Eze 18:14 if he **b.** a son, that seeth all 3205
Eze 47:22 which shall **b.** children among you: 3205

BEGETTEST
Ge 48:6 issue, which thou **b.** after them, 3205
Isa 45:10 unto his father, What **b.** thou? 3205

BEGETTETH
Pr 17:21 He that **b.** a fool doeth it to his 3205
Pr 23:24 and he that **b.** a wise child shall 3205
Ec 5:14 he **b.** a son, and there is nothing 3205

BEGGAR
1Sa 2:8 up the **b.** from the dunghill, 34
Lu 16:20 **was a certain b. named Lazarus,** *4434*
Lu 16:22 **that the b. died, and was carried** *4434*

BEGGARLY
Ga 4:9 to the weak and **b.** elements, *4434*

BEGGED
Mt 27:58 Pilate, and **b.** the body of Jesus. *154*
Lu 23:52 Pilate, and **b.** the body of Jesus. *154*
Joh 9:8 Is not this he that sat and **b.**? *4319*

BEGGING
Ps 37:25 forsaken, nor his seed **b.** bread. 1245
Mk 10:46 sat by the highway side **b.**. *4319*
Lu 18:35 man sat by the wayside **b.** *4319*

BEGIN See also BEGAN; BEGINNEST; BEGINNING; BEGUN.
Ge 11:6 this they **b.** to do: and now 2490
De 2:24 **b.** to possess it, and contend 2490
De 2:25 will I **b.** to put the dread of thee 2490
De 2:31 his land before thee: **b.** to possess, 2490
De 16:9 **b.** to number the seven weeks 2490
Jos 3:7 This day will I **b.** to magnify thee 2490
Jg 10:18 What man is he that will **b.** 2490
Jg 13:5 he shall **b.** to deliver Israel 2490
1Sa 3:12 I **b.**, I will also make an end 2490
1Sa 22:15 Did I then **b.** to enquire of God 2490
2Ki 8:25 Jehoram king of Judah **b.** to reign.
Ne 11:17 to **b.** the thanksgiving in prayer: 8462
Jer 25:29 I **b.** to bring evil on the city 2490
Eze 9:6 and **b.** at my sanctuary. 2490
Mt 24:49 **b. to smite his fellowservants,** *756*
Lu 3:8 **b.** not to say within yourselves, *756*
Lu 12:45 **shall b. to beat the menservants** *756*
Lu 13:25 **ye b. to stand without, and to** *756*
Lu 13:26 **Then shall ye b. to say, We have** *756*
Lu 14:9 **thou b. with shame to take the** *756*
Lu 14:29 **behold it b. to mock him,** *756*
Lu 21:28 **these things b. to come to pass,** *756*
Lu 23:30 **they b. to say to the mountains,** *756*
2Co 3:1 Do we **b.** again to commend *756*
1Pe 4:17 must **b.** at the house of God: *756*
1Pe 4:17 and if it first **b.** at us, what shall
Re 10:7 he shall **b.** to sound, the mystery *3195*

BEGINNEST
De 16:9 from such time as thou **b.** to put 2490

BEGINNING See also BEGINNINGS.
Ge 1:1 In the **b.** God created the heaven 7225
Ge 10:10 the **b.** of his kingdom was Babel, 7225
Ge 13:3 his tent had been at the **b.**, 8462
Ge 41:21 still ill favoured, as at the **b.** 8462
Ge 49:3 might, and the **b.** of my strength, 7225
Ex 12:2 the **b.** of months: it shall be the 7218
De 11:12 the **b.** of the year even unto the 7225
De 21:17 for he is the **b.** of his strength; 7225
De 32:42 **b.** of revenges upon the enemy. 7218
Jg 7:19 in the **b.** of the middle watch; 7218
Ru 1:22 Beth-lehem in the **b.** of barley 8462
Ru 3:10 in the latter end than at the **b.**, 7223
2Sa 21:9 in the **b.** of barley harvest. 8462
2Sa 21:10 from the **b.** of harvest until water 8462
2Ki 17:25 was at the **b.** of their dwelling 8462
1Ch 17:9 them any more, as at the **b.**, 7223
Ezr 4:6 Ahasuerus, in the **b.** of his reign, 8462
Job 8:7 Though thy **b.** was small, yet thy 7225
Job 42:12 end of Job more than his **b.** 7225
Ps 111:10 of the Lord is the **b.** of wisdom: 7225
Ps 119:160 is true from the **b.**: and every 7218
Pr 1:7 the **b.** of knowledge: but fools 7225
Pr 8:22 possessed me in the **b.** of his 7225
Pr 8:23 up from everlasting, from the **b.**, 7218
Pr 9:10 fear of the Lord is the **b.** of 8462
Pr 17:14 The **b.** of strife is as when 7225
Pr 20:21 hastily at the **b.**; but the end 7223
Ec 3:11 that God maketh from the **b.** 7218
Ec 7:8 end of a thing than the **b.** thereof: 7225
Ec 10:13 The **b.** of the words of his mouth 8462
Isa 1:26 thy counsellors as at the **b.**: 8462
Isa 18:2 terrible from their **b.** hitherto; a 1931
Isa 18:7 a people terrible from their **b.** 1931
Isa 40:21 you from the **b.**? have ye not 7218
Isa 41:4 the generations from the **b.**? 7218
Isa 41:26 Who hath declared from the **b.**, 7218
Isa 46:10 Declaring the end from the **b.**, 7225
Isa 48:3 the former things from the **b.**: 227
Isa 48:5 I have even from the **b.** declared 227
Isa 48:7 now, and not from the **b.**; even 227
Isa 48:16 not spoken in secret from the **b.**; 7218
Isa 64:4 For since the **b.** of the world men 5769
Jer 17:12 glorious high throne from the **b.** 7223
Jer 26:1 the **b.** of the reign of 7225
Jer 27:1 the **b.** of the reign of Jehoiakim 7225
Jer 28:1 in the **b.** of the reign of Zedekiah 7225
Jer 49:34 Elam in the **b.** of the reign. 7225
La 2:19 in the **b.** of the watches pour out 7218
Eze 40:1 in the **b.** of the year of our 7218
Da 9:21 seen in the vision at the **b.**, 8462
Da 9:23 At the **b.** of my supplications 8462
Ho 1:2 The **b.** of the word of the Lord 8462
Am 7:1 poured grasshoppers in the **b.** of 8462
Mic 1:13 the **b.** of the sin to the daughter 7225
Mt 14:30 **b.** to sink, he cried, saying, *756*
Mt 19:4 **which made them at the b** *746*
Mt 19:8 **from the b. it was not so** *746*
Mt 20:8 **b. from the last unto the first** *756*
Mt 24:8 **these are the b. of sorrows** *746*
Mt 24:21 **since the b. of the world to this** *746*
Mk 1:1 The **b.** of the gospel of Jesus *746*
Mk 10:6 **from the b. of the creation** *746*
Mk 13:19 **such as was not from the b.** *746*
Lu 1:2 from the **b.** were eyewitnesses, *746*
Lu 23:5 **b.** from Galilee to this place. *756*
Lu 24:27 **b.** at Moses and all the prophets, *756*
Lu 24:47 **among all nations, b. at Jerusalem,** *756*
Joh 1:1 In the **b.** was the Word, and the *746*
Joh 1:2 The same was in the **b.** with God. *746*
Joh 2:10 man at the **b.** doth set forth *4412*
Joh 2:11 This **b.** of miracles did Jesus *746*
Joh 6:64 Jesus knew from the **b.** who *746*
Joh 8:9 **b.** at the eldest, even unto the last: *756*
Joh 8:25 **I said unto you from the b.** *746*
Joh 8:44 **was a murderer from the b.**, *746*
Joh 15:27 **ye have been with me from the b.** *746*
Joh 16:4 **not unto you at the b., because I** *746*
Ac 1:22 **B.** from the baptism of John, *756*
Ac 11:4 rehearsed the matter from the **b.** *756*
Ac 11:15 fell on them, as on us at the **b.** *746*
Ac 15:18 his works from the **b.** of the
Ac 26:5 Which knew me from the **b.**, *509*
Eph 3:9 which from the **b.** of the world
Php 4:15 that in the **b.** of the gospel. *746*
Col 1:18 who is the **b.**, the firstborn *746*
2Th 2:13 God hath from the **b.** chosen you. *746*
Heb 1:10 Thou, Lord, in the **b.** hast laid *746*
Heb 3:14 if we hold the **b.** of our confidence *746*
Heb 7:3 having neither **b.** of days, nor end *746*
2Pe 2:20 is worse with them than the **b.** *4413*
2Pe 3:4 were from the **b.** of the creation. *746*
1Jo 1:1 That which was from the **b.**, *746*
1Jo 2:7 which ye had from the **b.** *746*
1Jo 2:7 ye have heard from the **b.** *746*
1Jo 2:13 him that is from the **b.** *746*
1Jo 2:14 known him that is from the **b.** *746*
1Jo 2:24 which ye have heard from the **b.** *746*
1Jo 2:24 ye have heard from the **b.** *746*
1Jo 3:8 the devil sinneth from the **b.** *746*
1Jo 3:11 that ye heard from the **b.**, *746*
2Jo 5 which we had from the **b.**, *746*
2Jo 6 as ye have heard from the **b.**, *746*
Re 1:8 **the b. and the ending,** *746*
Re 3:14 **the b. of the creation of God;** *746*
Re 21:6 the **b.** and the end. I will *746*
Re 22:13 **Alpha and Omega, the b. and the** *746*

BEGINNINGS
Nu 10:10 and in the **b.** of yours months, 7218
Nu 28:11 And in the **b.** of your months 7218
Eze 36:11 better unto you than at your **b.** 7221
Mk 13:8 **these are the b. of sorrows** *746*

BEGOTTEN See also FIRSTBEGOTTEN.
Ge 5:4 days of Adam after he had **b.** Seth 3205
Le 18:11 **b.** of thy father, she is thy sister, 4138
Nu 11:12 I **b.** them, that thou shouldest 3205
De 23:8 The children that are **b.** of them 3205
Jg 8:30 and ten sons of his body **b.** 3318
Job 38:28 who hath **b.** the drops of dew? 3205
Ps 2:7 my son; this day have I **b.** thee. 3205
Isa 49:21 Who hath **b.** me these, seeing I 3205
Hos 5:7 for they have **b.** strange children: 3205
Joh 1:14 as of the only **b.** of the Father,) *3439*
Joh 1:18 the only **b.** Son, which is *3439*
Joh 3:16 **his only b. Son, that whosoever** *3439*
Joh 3:18 **name of the only b. Son of God.** *3439*
Ac 13:33 my Son, this day have I **b.** thee. *1080*
1Co 4:15 I have **b.** you through the gospel. *1080*
Phm 10 whom I have **b.** in my bonds: *1080*
Heb 1:5 my Son, this day have I **b.** thee? *1080*
Heb 5:5 my Son, to day have I **b.** thee. *1080*
Heb 11:17 offered up his only **b.** son, *3439*
1Pe 1:3 **b.** us again unto a lively hope *313*
1Jo 4:9 God sent his only **b.** Son *3439*
1Jo 5:1 loveth him also that is **b.** of him. *1080*

1Jo 5:18 but he that is **b.** of God keepeth...... *1080*
Re 1:5 first **b.** of the dead, and the prince...... *4416*

BEGUILE See also BEGUILED; BEGUILING.
Col 2:4 lest any man should **b.** you with...... *3884*
Col 2:18 Let no man **b.** you of your reward...... *2603*

BEGUILED
Ge 3:13 The serpent **b.** me, and I did eat...... 5377
Ge 29:25 wherefore then hast thou **b.** me?...... 7411
Nu 25:18 they have **b.** you in the matter of...... 5230
Jos 9:22 Wherefore have ye **b.** us, saying,...... 7411
2Co 11:3 as the serpent **b.** Eve through his...... *1818*

BEGUILING
2Pe 2:14 **b.** unstable souls: an heart they...... *1185*

BEGUN
Nu 16:46 from the Lord; the plague is **b.**...... 2490
Nu 16:47 plague was **b.** among the people:...... 2490
De 2:31 I have **b.** to give Sihon and his...... 2490
De 3:24 thou hast **b.** to shew thy servant...... 2490
Es 6:13 before whom thou hast **b.** to fall,...... 2490
Es 9:23 undertook to do as they had **b.**,...... 2490
Mt 18:24 **when he had b. to reckon, one was**...... *756*
2Co 8:6 that as he had **b.**, so he would also...... *4278*
2Co 8:10 who have **b.** before, not only to do,...... *4278*
Ga 3:3 having **b.** in the Spirit, are ye now...... *1728*
Php 1:6 that he which hath **b.** a good...... *1728*
1Ti 5:11 when they have **b.** to wax wanton...... *2691*

BEHALF
Ex 27:21 on the **b.** of the children of Israel...... 854
2Sa 3:12 messengers to David on his **b.**,...... 8478
2Ch 16:9 to shew himself strong in the **b.**...... 5973
Job 36:2 I have yet to speak on God's **b.**......
Da 11:18 but a prince for his own **b.** shall......
Ro 16:19 I am glad therefore on your **b.**...... *1909*
1Co 1:4 thank my God always on your **b.**,...... 4012
2Co 1:11 may be given by many on our **b.**...... 5228
2Co 5:12 you occasion to glory on our **b.**,...... *5228*
2Co 8:24 and of our boasting on your **b.**...... *5228*
2Co 9:3 you should be in vain in this **b.**;...... *3313*
Php 1:29 it is given in the **b.** of Christ,...... *5228*
1Pe 4:16 let him glorify God on this **b.**...... *3313*

BEHAVE See also BEHAVED; BEHAVETH.
De 32:27 lest their adversaries should **b.**...... 5234
1Ch 19:13 and let us **b.** ourselves valiantly...... 2388
Ps 101:2 I will **b.** myself wisely in a perfect...... 7919
Isa 3:5 the child shall **b.** himself proudly...... 7292
1Co 13:5 Doth not **b.** itself unseemly,...... *807*
1Ti 3:15 to **b.** thyself in the house of God,...... *390*

BEHAVED
1Sa 18:5 sent him, and **b.** himself wisely:...... 7919
1Sa 18:14 David **b.** himself wisely in all his...... 7919
1Sa 18:15 saw that he **b.** himself very wisely,...... 7919
1Sa 18:30 David **b.** himself more wisely than...... 7919
Ps 35:14 I **b.** myself as though he had been...... 1980
Ps 131:2 I have **b.** and quieted myself...... 7737
Mic 3:4 as they have **b.** themselves ill...... 7489
1Th 2:10 unblameably we **b.** ourselves...... *1096*
2Th 3:7 for we **b.** not ourselves disorderly...... *312*

BEHAVETH
1Co 7:36 think that he **b.** himself uncomely...... *807*

BEHAVIOUR
1Sa 21:13 he changed his **b.** before them,...... 2940
Ps 34:*title* when he changed his **b.** before...... 2940
1Ti 3:2 vigilant, sober, of good **b.**,...... *2887*
Tit 2:3 that they be in **b.** as becometh...... *2688*

BEHEADED
De 21:6 the heifer that is **b.** in the valley:...... 6202
2Sa 4:7 and slew him, and **b.** him,...... 5493,7218
Mt 14:10 he sent, and **b.** John in the prison,...... *607*
Mk 6:16 It is John, whom I **b.**...... *607*
Mk 6:27 he went and **b.** him in the prison...... *607*
Lu 9:9 Herod said, John have I **b.**;...... *607*
Re 20:4 the souls of them that were **b.**...... *3990*

BEHELD
Ge 12:14 the Egyptians **b.** the woman that...... 7200
Ge 13:10 and **b.** all the plain of Jordan,...... 7200
Ge 19:28 and **b.**, and, lo, the smoke of...... 7200
Ge 31:2 And Jacob **b.** the countenance...... 7200
Ge 48:8 And Israel **b.** Joseph's sons,...... 7200
Nu 21:9 when he **b.** the serpent of brass,...... 5027
Nu 23:21 He hath not **b.** iniquity in Jacob,...... 5027
Jg 16:27 men and women, that **b.**...... 7200
1Sa 26:5 and David **b.** the place where Saul...... 7200
1Ch 21:15 the Lord **b.**, and he repented him...... 7200
Job 31:26 If I **b.** the sun when it shined,...... 7200
Ps 119:158 I **b.** the transgressors, and was...... 7200
Ps 142:4 and **b.**, but there was no man...... 7200
Pr 7:7 And **b.** among the simple ones,...... 7200
Ec 8:17 Then I **b.** all the work of God,...... 7200
Isa 41:28 For I **b.**, and there was no man;...... 7200
Jer 4:23 I **b.** the earth, and, lo, it was...... 7200
Jer 4:24 I **b.** the mountains, and, lo, they...... 7200
Jer 4:25 I **b.**, and, lo, there was no man,...... 7200
Jer 4:26 I **b.**, and, lo, the fruitful place...... 7200
Jer 31:26 I awaked, and **b.**; and my sleep...... 7200
Eze 1:15 Now as I **b.** the living creatures,...... 7200
Eze 8:2 Then I **b.**, and lo a likeness as the...... 7200
Eze 37:8 when I **b.**, lo, the sinews and the...... 7200
Da 7:4 **b.** till the wings thereof were...... 2370,934
Da 7:6 **b.**, and lo another, like a leopard,...... 2370,934
Da 7:9 **b.** till the thrones were cast down, 2370,934
Da 7:11 I **b.** then because of the voice...... 2370,934
Da 7:11 I **b.** even till the beast was slain,...... 2370,934
Da 7:21 I **b.**, and the same horn made war. 2370,934
Hab 3:6 he **b.**, and drove asunder the...... 7200
Mt 19:26 **b.** them, and said unto them,...... *1689*
Mk 9:15 the people, when they **b.** him,...... *1492*
Mk 12:41 **b.** how the people cast money...... *2334*
Mk 15:47 mother of Joses **b.** where he was...... *2334*
Lu 10:18 **I b. Satan as lightning fall from**...... *2334*
Lu 19:41 **b.** the city, and wept over it,...... *1492*
Lu 20:17 **b.** them, and said, **What is this**...... *1689*
Lu 22:56 a certain maid **b.** him as he sat...... *1492*
Lu 23:55 **b.** the sepulchre, and how his...... *2300*
Lu 24:12 he **b.** the linen clothes laid by...... *991*
Joh 1:14 we **b.** his glory, the glory as of...... *2300*
Joh 1:42 when Jesus **b.** him, he said,...... *1689*
Ac 1:9 while they **b.**, he was taken up;...... *991*
Ac 17:23 passed by, and **b.** your devotions,...... *333*
Re 5:6 I **b.**, and, lo, in the midst of the...... *1492*
Re 5:11 I **b.**, and I heard the voice of...... *1492*
Re 6:5 And I **b.**, and lo a black horse;...... *1492*
Re 6:12 **b.** when he had opened the sixth...... *1492*
Re 7:9 After this I **b.**, and lo, a great...... *1492*
Re 8:13 I **b.**, and heard an angel flying...... *1492*
Re 11:12 and their enemies **b.** them...... *2334*
Re 13:11 I **b.** another beast coming up out...... *1492*

BEHEMOTH (be'-he-moth)
Job 40:15 Behold now **b.**, which I made...... 930

BEHIND
Ge 18:10 in the tent door, which was **b.** him...... 310
Ge 19:17 look not **b.** thee, neither stay thou...... 310
Ge 19:26 his wife looked back from **b.** him,...... 310
Ge 22:13 **b.** him a ram, caught in a thicket...... 310
Ge 32:18 and, behold, also he is **b.** us...... 310
Ge 32:20 Behold, thy serant Jacob is **b.** us...... 310
Ex 10:26 there shall not an hoof be left **b.**;......
Ex 11:5 the maidservant that is **b.** the mill;...... 310
Ex 14:19 removed and went **b.** them; and the...... 310
Ex 14:19 before their face, and stood **b.** them:...... 310
Le 25:51 If there be yet many years **b.**,......
Nu 3:23 pitch **b.** the tabernacle westward...... 310
De 25:18 even all that were feeble **b.** thee...... 310
Jos 8:2 lay thee an ambush for the city **b.**...... 310
Jos 8:4 **b.** the city: go not very far from...... 310
Jos 8:14 in ambush against him **b.** the city...... 310
Jos 8:20 when the men of Ai looked **b.** them,...... 310
Jg 18:12 behold, it is **b.** Kirjath-jearim...... 310
Jg 20:40 the Benjamites looked **b.** them,...... 310
1Sa 21:9 wrapped in a cloth **b.** the ephod:...... 310
1Sa 24:8 when Saul looked **b.** him, David...... 310
1Sa 30:9 those that were left **b.** stayed...... 3498
1Sa 30:10 for two hundred abode **b.**, which...... 5975
2Sa 1:7 when he looked **b.** him, he saw...... 310
2Sa 2:20 Then Abner looked **b.** him,...... 310
2Sa 2:23 the spear came out **b.** him; and he...... 310
2Sa 3:16 weeping **b.** her to Bahurim...... 310
2Sa 5:23 fetch a compass **b.** them, and come...... 310
2Sa 10:9 was against him before and **b.**,...... 268
2Sa 13:34 by the way of the hill side **b.** him...... 310
1Ki 10:19 top of the throne was round **b.**:...... 310
1Ki 14:9 and hast cast me **b.** thy back:...... 310
2Ki 6:32 sound of his master's feet **b.** him?...... 310
2Ki 9:18, 19 do with peace? turn thee **b.** me...... 310
2Ki 11:6 third part at the gate **b.** the guard:...... 310
1Ch 19:10 was set against him before and **b.**,...... 268
2Ch 13:13 an ambushment to come about **b.**...... 310
2Ch 13:13 the ambushment was **b.** them...... 310
2Ch 13:14 the battle was before and **b.**...... 268
Ne 4:13 in the lower places **b.** the wall...... 310
Ne 4:16 the rulers were **b.** all the house...... 310
Ne 9:26 cast thy law **b.** their backs, and slew...... 310
Ps 50:17 and castest my words **b.** thee...... 310
Ps 139:5 Thou hast beset me **b.** and before,...... 268
Ca 2:9 he standeth **b.** our wall, he looketh...... 310
Isa 9:12 before, and the Philistines **b.**;...... 268
Isa 30:21 Ears shall hear a word **b.**,...... 310
Isa 38:17 hast cast all my sins **b.** thy back...... 310
Isa 57:8 **B.** the doors also and the posts...... 310
Isa 66:17 **b.** one tree in the midst, eating...... 310
Eze 3:12 I heard **b.** me a voice of a great...... 310
Eze 23:35 and cast me **b.** thy back, therefore...... 310
Eze 41:15 separate place which was **b.** it,...... 310
Joe 2:3 and **b.** them a flame burneth:...... 310
Joe 2:3 and **b.** them a desolate wilderness;...... 310
Joe 2:14 leave a blessing **b.** him; even a...... 310
Zec 1:8 and **b.** him were there red horses,...... 310
Mt 9:20 came **b.** him, and touched the hem...... *3693*
Mt 16:23 **Get thee b. me, Satan: thou art**...... *3694*
Mk 5:27 came in the press **b.**, and touched...... *3693*
Mk 8:33 **Get thee b. me, Satan: for thou**...... *3694*
Mk 12:19 brother die, and leave his wife **b.**,...... *2641*
Lu 2:43 Jesus tarried **b.** in Jerusalem;...... *5278*
Lu 4:8 **Get thee b. me, Satan: for it is**...... *3694*
Lu 7:38 And stood at his feet **b.** him...... *3694*
Lu 8:44 Came **b.** him, and touched the...... *3693*
1Co 1:7 So that ye come **b.** in no gift;...... *5302*
2Co 11:5 I suppose I was not a whit **b.** the...... *5302*
2Co 12:11 for in nothing am I **b.** the very...... *5302*
Php 3:13 those things which are **b.**...... *3694*
Col 1:24 that which is **b.** of the afflictions...... *5303*
Re 1:10 and heard **b.** me a great voice...... *3694*
Re 4:6 beasts full of eyes before and **b.**...... *3693*

BEHOLD See also BEHELD; BEHOLDEST; BEHOLDETH; BEHOLDING.
Ge 1:29 God said, **B.**, I have given you...... 2009
Ge 1:31 had made, and, **b.**, it was very good...... 2009
Ge 3:22 **B.**, the man is become as one of...... 2005
Ge 4:14 **B.**, thou hast driven me out this...... 2005
Ge 6:12 the earth, and, **b.**, it was corrupt;...... 2009
Ge 6:13 **b.**, I will destroy them with the...... 2005
Ge 6:17 And, **b.**, I, even I, do bring a flood...... 2005
Ge 8:13 **b.**, the face of the ground was dry...... 2009
Ge 9:9 And I, **b.**, I establish my covenant...... 2005
Ge 11:6 the Lord said, **B.**, the people is...... 2005
Ge 12:11 **B.** now, I know that thou art...... 2009
Ge 12:19 therefore **b.** thy wife, take her,...... 2009
Ge 15:3 **B.**, to me thou hast given no seed:...... 2005
Ge 15:4 And, **b.**, the word of the Lord came...... 2009
Ge 15:17 the sun went down, **b.** a smoking...... 2009
Ge 16:2 **B.** now, the Lord hath restrained...... 2009
Ge 16:6 **B.**, thy maid is in thy hand; do to...... 2009
Ge 16:11 **B.**, thou art with child, and shalt...... 2009
Ge 16:14 **b.**, it is between Kadesh and Bered...... 2009
Ge 17:4 As for me, **b.**, my covenant is...... 2009
Ge 17:20 have heard thee: **B.**, I have blessed...... 2009
Ge 18:9 And he said, **B.**, in the tent...... 2009
Ge 18:27, 31 **B.** now, I have taken upon me...... 2009
Ge 19:2 **B.** now, my lords, turn in, I pray...... 2009
Ge 19:8 **B.** now, I have two daughters...... 2009
Ge 19:19 **B.** now, thy servant hath found...... 2009
Ge 19:20 **B.** now, this city is near to flee...... 2009
Ge 19:34 **B.**, I lay yesternight with my...... 2005
Ge 20:3 **B.**, thou art but a dead man,...... 2009
Ge 20:15 said, **B.**, my land is before thee:...... 2009
Ge 20:16 unto Sarah he said, **B.**, I have,...... 2009
Ge 20:16 **b.**, he is to thee a covering of the...... 2009
Ge 22:1 And he said, **B.**, here I am...... 2009
Ge 22:7 he said, **B.**, the fire and the wood:...... 2009
Ge 22:13 and **b.** behind him a ram caught in...... 2009
Ge 22:20 **B.**, Milcah, she hath also born...... 2009
Ge 24:13 **B.**, I stand here by the well...... 2009
Ge 24:15 that, **b.**, Rebekah came out, who was...... 2009
Ge 24:30 and, **b.**, he stood by the camels at...... 2009
Ge 24:43 **B.**, I stand by the well of water; and...... 2009
Ge 24:45 **b.**, Rebekah came forth with her...... 2009
Ge 24:51 **B.**, Rebekah is before thee, take...... 2009
Ge 24:63 and, **b.**, the camels were coming...... 2009
Ge 25:24 were fulfilled, **b.**, there were...... 2009
Ge 25:22 **B.**, I am at the point to die:...... 2009
Ge 26:8 **b.**, Isaac was sporting with...... 2009
Ge 26:9 **B.**, of a surety she is thy wife:...... 2009
Ge 27:1 he said unto him, **B.**, here I am...... 2009
Ge 27:2 And he said, **B.** now, I am...... 2009

Book	Ref	Context	No.
Ge	27:6	saying, **B.**, I heard thy father	2009
Ge	27:11	**B.**, Esau my brother is a	2005
Ge	27:36	and, **b.**, now he hath taken away	2009
Ge	27:37	**B.**, I have made him thy lord,	2005
Ge	27:39	**B.**, thy dwelling shall be the	2009
Ge	27:42	**B.**, thy brother Esau, as touching	2009
Ge	28:12	he dreamed, and **b.** a ladder set	2009
Ge	28:12	**b.** the angels of God ascending	2009
Ge	28:13	And, **b.**, the Lord stood above it,	2009
Ge	28:15	And, **b.**, I am with thee, and will	2009
Ge	29:2	he looked, and **b.** a well in the field,	2009
Ge	29:6	and, **b.**, Rachel his daughter	2009
Ge	29:25	in the morning, **b.**, it was Leah:	2009
Ge	30:3	she said, **B.** my maid Bilhah, go in	2009
Ge	30:34	**B.**, I would it might be according	2005
Ge	31:2	and, **b.**, it was not toward him as	2009
Ge	31:10	and, **b.**, the rams which leaped	2009
Ge	31:51	**B.** this heap, and **b.** this pillar,	2009
Ge	32:18	unto my lord Esau: and, **b.**, also	2009
Ge	32:20	**B.**, thy servant Jacob is behind us.	2009
Ge	33:1	and, **b.**, Esau came, and with him	2009
Ge	34:21	for the land, **b.** it is large enough	2009
Ge	37:7	For, **b.**, we were binding sheaves	2009
Ge	37:7	and, **b.**, your sheaves stood round	2009
Ge	37:9	**B.**, I have dreamed a dream more;	2009
Ge	37:9	and, **b.** the sun and the moon and	2009
Ge	37:15	**b.**, he was wandering in the field:	2009
Ge	37:19	another, **B.**, this dreamer cometh	2009
Ge	37:25	and, **b.**, a company of Ishmeelites	2009
Ge	37:29	and, **b.**, Joseph was not in the pit;	2009
Ge	38:13	**B.** thy father in law goeth up to	2009
Ge	38:23	**b.**, I sent this kid, and thou hast	2009
Ge	38:24	and also, **b.**, she is with child	2009
Ge	38:27	that, **b.**, twins were in her womb.	2009
Ge	38:29	**b.**, his brother came out: and she	2009
Ge	39:8	**B.**, my master wotteth not what	2005
Ge	40:6	and looked upon them, and, **b.**,	2009
Ge	40:9	In my dream, **b.**, a vine was before	2009
Ge	40:16	and, **b.** I had three white baskets	2009
Ge	41:1	that Pharaoh dreamed: and, **b.**,	2009
Ge	41:2	And, **b.**, there came up out of the	2009
Ge	41:3	And, **b.**, seven other kine came up	2009
Ge	41:5	and, **b.**, seven ears of corn came	2009
Ge	41:6	**b.**, seven thin ears and blasted	2009
Ge	41:7	Pharaoh awoke, and, **b.**, it was a	2009
Ge	41:17	In my dream, **b.**, I stood upon the	2005
Ge	41:18	**b.**, there came up out of the river	2009
Ge	41:19	**b.**, seven other kine came up after	2009
Ge	41:22	**b.**, seven ears came up in one stalk,	2009
Ge	41:23	**b.**, seven ears, withered, thin, and	2009
Ge	41:29	**B.**, there came seven years of great	2009
Ge	42:2	**B.**, I have heard that there is corn	2009
Ge	42:13	**b.**, the youngest is this day with	2009
Ge	42:22	**b.**, also his blood is required.	2009
Ge	42:27	for, **b.**, it was in his sack's mouth.	2009
Ge	42:35	**b.**, every man's bundle of money	2009
Ge	43:21	we opened our sacks, and, **b.**,	2009
Ge	44:8	**B.**, the money, which we found	2005
Ge	44:16	**b.**, we are my lord's servants,	2009
Ge	45:12	And, **b.**, your eyes see, and the	2009
Ge	47:1	**b.**, they are in the land of Goshen.	2009
Ge	47:23	**B.**, I have brought you this day	2009
Ge	48:1	**B.**, thy father is sick: and he took	2009
Ge	48:2	**B.**, thy son Joseph cometh unto	2009
Ge	48:4	**B.**, I will make thee fruitful, and	2005
Ge	48:21	**B.**, I die; but God shall be with	2009
Ge	50:18	they said, **B.**, we be thy servants.	2009
Ex	1:9	**B.**, the people of the children of	2009
Ex	2:6	the child: and **b.** the babe wept	2009
Ex	2:13	**b.**, two men of the Hebrews	2009
Ex	3:2	looked, and, **b.**, the bush burned	2009
Ex	3:9	**b.**, the cry of the children of Israel	2009
Ex	3:13	**B.**, when I come unto the children	2009
Ex	4:1	But, **b.**, they will not believe me,	2005
Ex	4:6	**b.**, his hand was leprous as snow.	2009
Ex	4:7	**b.**, it was turned again as his	2009
Ex	4:14	**b.**, he cometh forth to meet thee:	2009
Ex	4:23	**b.**, I will slay thy son, even thy	2009
Ex	5:5	**B.**, the people of the land now are	2005
Ex	5:16	and, **b.**, thy servants are beaten;	2009
Ex	6:12	**B.**, the children of Israel have	2005
Ex	6:30	Moses said before the Lord, **B.**,	2005
Ex	7:16	**b.**, hitherto thou wouldest not	2009
Ex	7:17	know that I am the Lord: **b.**,	2009
Ex	8:2	if thou refuse to let them go, **b.**, I	2009
Ex	8:21	thou wilt not let my people go, **b.**,	2005
Ex	8:29	**B.**, I go out from thee,	2009
Ex	9:3	**B.**, the hand of the Lord is upon thy	2009
Ex	9:7	**b.**, there was not one of the cattle	2009
Ex	9:18	**B.**, to morrow about this time	2005
Ex	10:4	let my peole go, **b.**, to morrow	2005
Ex	14:10	and, **b.**, the Egyptians marched	2009
Ex	14:17	And I, **b.**, I will harden	2005
Ex	16:4	**B.**, I will rain bread	2005
Ex	16:10	**b.**, the glory of the Lord	2009
Ex	16:14	**b.**, upon the face of the wilderness	2009
Ex	17:6	**B.**, I will stand before thee	2005
Ex	23:20	**B.**, I send an Angel before thee,	2009
Ex	24:8	**B.** the blood of the covenant,	2009
Ex	24:14	**b.**, Aaron and Hur are with you:	2009
Ex	31:6	**b.**, I have given with him Aholiab,	2009
Ex	32:9	and, **b.**, it is a stiffnecked people:	2009
Ex	32:34	**b.**, mine Angel shall go before thee:	2009
Ex	33:21	said, **B.**, there is a place by me,	2009
Ex	34:10	he said, **B.**, I make a covenant:	2009
Ex	34:11	**b.**, I drive out before thee the	2005
Ex	34:30	**b.**, the skin of his face shone;	2009
Ex	39:43	and, **b.**, they had done it as the Lord	2009
Le	10:16	and, **b.**, it was burnt:	2009
Le	10:18	**B.**, the blood of it was not brought	2005
Le	10:19	**B.**, this day have they offered	2005
Le	13:5	**b.**, if the plague in his sight	2009
Le	13:6	**b.**, if the plague be somewhat	2009
Le	13:8	**b.**, the scab spreadeth in the skin,	2009
Le	13:10	**b.**, if the rising be white	2009
Le	13:13	**b.**, if the leprosy have covered	2009
Le	13:17	**b.**, if the plague be turned	2009
Le	13:20	**b.**, it be in sight lower than	2009
Le	13:21	**b.**, there be no white hairs	2009
Le	13:25	**b.**, if the hair in the bright	2009
Le	13:26	**b.**, there be no white hair	2009
Le	13:30	**b.**, if it be in sight deeper	2009
Le	13:31	**b.**, it be not in sight deeper	2009
Le	13:32	**b.**, if the scall spread not,	2009
Le	13:34	**b.**, if the scall be not spread	2009
Le	13:36	**b.**, if the scall be spread	2009
Le	13:39	**b.**, if the bright spots in the skin	2009
Le	13:43	and, **b.**, if the rising of the sore be	2009
Le	13:53	**b.**, the plague be not spread	2009
Le	13:55	**b.**, if the plague have not changed	2009
Le	13:56	**b.**, the plague be somewhat	2009
Le	14:3	**b.**, if the plague of leprosy	2009
Le	14:37	**b.**, if the plague be in the walls	2009
Le	14:39,	44 **b.**, if the plague be spread	2009
Le	14:48	**b.**, the plague hath not spread	2009
Le	25:20	**b.**, we shall not sow,	2005
Nu	3:12	**b.**, I have taken the Levites	2009
Nu	12:8	similitude of the Lord shall he **b.**:	5027
Nu	12:10	**b.**, Miriam became leprous	2009
Nu	12:10	**b.**, she was leprous.	2009
Nu	16:42	**b.**, the cloud covered it	2009
Nu	16:47	**b.**, the plague was begun	2009
Nu	17:8	**b.**, the rod of Aaron for the house	2009
Nu	17:12	**B.**, we die, we perish,	2005
Nu	18:6	**b.**, I have taken your brethren	2009
Nu	18:8	**B.**, I . . . have given thee the charge	2009
Nu	18:21	**b.**, I have given the children	2009
Nu	20:16	**b.**, we are in Kadesh,	2009
Nu	22:5	**B.**, there is a people come out from	2009
Nu	22:5	**b.**, they cover the face of the earth,	2009
Nu	22:11	**B.**, there is a people come out	2009
Nu	22:32	**b.**, I went out to withstand	2009
Nu	23:9	him, and from the hills I **b.** him:	7789
Nu	23:11	**b.**, thou hast blessed them	2009
Nu	23:17	**b.**, he stood by his burnt	2009
Nu	23:20	**B.**, I have received commandment	2009
Nu	23:24	**B.**, the people shall rise up	2005
Nu	24:10	**b.**, thou hast altogether blessed	2009
Nu	24:14	**b.**, I go unto my people:	2005
Nu	24:17	I shall **b.** him, put not nigh:	7789
Nu	25:6	**b.**, one of the children of Israel	2009
Nu	25:12	**B.**, I give unto him my covenant	2005
Nu	31:16	**B.**, these caused the children	2005
Nu	32:1	**b.**, the place was a place	2009
Nu	32:14	**b.**, ye are risen up	2009
Nu	32:23	**b.**, ye have sinned	2009
De	1:8	**B.**, I have set the land before you:	7200
De	1:10	**b.**, ye are this day as the stars	2009
De	1:21	**B.**, the Lord thy God hath set	7200
De	2:24	**b.**, I have given into thine hand	7200
De	2:31	**B.**, I have begun to give Sihon	7200
De	3:11	**b.**, his bedstead was a bedstead	2009
De	3:27	and **b.** it with thine eyes:	7200
De	4:5	**B.**, I have taught you statutes	7200
De	5:24	**B.**, the Lord our God hath shewed	2005
De	9:13	and, **b.**, it is a stiffnecked people:	2009
De	9:16	I looked, and, **b.**, ye had sinned	2009
De	10:14	**B.**, the heaven and the heaven	2005
De	11:26	**B.**, I set before you this day a	7200
De	13:14	**b.** if it be truth,	2009
De	17:4	**b.** if it be true,	2009
De	19:18	**b.**, if the witness be a false	2009
De	26:10	**b.**, I have brought the firstfruits	2009
De	31:14	**B.** thy days approach	2005
De	31:16	**B.**, thou shalt sleep with thy	2009
De	31:27	**b.**, while I am yet alive	2005
De	32:49	and **b.** the land of Canaan, which	7200
Jos	2:2	**B.**, there came men in hither	2009
Jos	2:18	**B.**, when we come into the land,	2009
Jos	3:11	**B.**, the ark of the covenant	2009
Jos	5:13	**b.**, there stood a man	2009
Jos	7:21	**b.**, they are hid in the earth	2009
Jos	7:22	**b.**, it was hid in his tent,	2009
Jos	8:4	**B.**, ye shall lie in wait against the	7200
Jos	8:20	**b.**, the smoke of the city	2009
Jos	9:12	**b.**, it is dry,	2009
Jos	9:13	**b.**, they be rent:	2009
Jos	9:25	And now, **b.**, we are in thine hand:	2005
Jos	14:10	**b.**, the Lord hath kept me	2009
Jos	22:11	**B.**, the children of Reuben	2009
Jos	22:28	**B.** the pattern of the altar	7200
Jos	23:4	**B.**, I have divided unto you by lot	7200
Jos	23:14	And, **b.**, this day I am going	2009
Jos	24:27	**B.**, this stone shall be a witness	2009
Jg	1:2	**b.**, I have delivered the land	2009
Jg	3:24	**b.**, the doors of the parlour were	2009
Jg	3:25	and, **b.**, he opened not	2009
Jg	3:25	and, **b.**, their lord was fallen	2009
Jg	4:22	And, **b.**, as Barak pursued	2009
Jg	4:22	**b.**, Sisera lay dead,	2009
Jg	6:15	**b.**, my family is poor	2009
Jg	6:28	**b.**, the altar of Baal was cast	2009
Jg	6:37	**B.**, I will put a fleece of wool	2009
Jg	7:13	**b.**, there was a man	2009
Jg	7:13	**B.**, I dreamed a dream,	2009
Jg	7:17	and, **b.**, when I come	2009
Jg	8:15	said, **B.**, Zebah and Zalmunna	2009
Jg	9:31	saying, **B.**, Gaal the son of Obed	2009
Jg	9:31	**b.**, they fortify the city	2009
Jg	9:33	**b.**, when he and the people	2009
Jg	9:36	**B.**, there come people	2009
Jg	9:43	**b.**, the people were come	2009
Jg	11:34	**b.**, his daughter came out	2009
Jg	13:3	**B.** now, thou art barren,	2009
Jg	13:7	**B.**, thou shalt conceive,	2009
Jg	13:10	**B.**, the man hath appeared	2009
Jg	14:5	and, **b.**, a young lion roared	2009
Jg	14:8	**b.**, there was a swarm of bees	2009
Jg	14:16	**B.**, I have not told it	2009
Jg	16:10	**B.**, thou hast mocked me	2009
Jg	17:2	**b.**, the silver is with me;	2009
Jg	18:9	and, **b.**, it is very good:	2009
Jg	18:12	**b.**, it is behind Kirjath-jearim.	2009
Jg	19:9	**B.**, now the day draweth	2009
Jg	19:9	**b.**, the day groweth to an end,	2009
Jg	19:16	And, **b.**, there came an old man	2009
Jg	19:22	**b.**, the men of the city,	2009
Jg	19:24	**B.**, here is my daughter	2009
Jg	19:27	**b.**, the woman his concubine	2009
Jg	20:7	**B.**, ye are all children	2009
Jg	20:40	**b.**, the flame of the city	2009
Jg	21:8	**b.**, there came none to the camp	2009
Jg	21:9	**b.**, there were none of the	2009
Jg	21:19	**B.**, there is a feast of the Lord	2009
Jg	21:21	**b.**, if the daughters of Shiloh	2009
Ru	1:15	**B.**, thy sister in law	2009
Ru	2:4	**b.**, Boaz came from Beth-lehem	2009
Ru	3:2	**B.**, he winnoweth barley	2009
Ru	3:8	**b.**, a woman lay at his feet.	2009
Ru	4:1	**b.**, the kinsman of whom Boaz	2009
1Sa	2:31	**B.**, the days come, that I will cut	2009
1Sa	3:11	to Samuel, **B.**, I will do a thing in	2009
1Sa	5:3,4	**b.**, Dagon was fallen upon his	2009
1Sa	8:5	**B.**, thou art old,	2009
1Sa	9:6	**B.** now, there is in this city	2009
1Sa	9:7	**b.**, if we go, what shall we bring	2009
1Sa	9:8	**B.**, I have here at hand	2009
1Sa	9:12	He is; **b.**, he is before you:	2009
1Sa	9:14	**b.**, Samuel came out against	2009
1Sa	9:17	**B.** the man whom I spake	2009
1Sa	9:24	**B.** that which is left!	2009

1Sa 10:8 **b.**, I will come down unto thee, 2009
1Sa 10:10 **b.**, a company of prophets 2009
1Sa 10:11 **b.**, he prophesied among 2009
1Sa 10:22 **B.**, he hath hid himself 2009
1Sa 11:5 **b.**, Saul came after the herd 2009
1Sa 12:1 **B.**, I have hearkened unto your 2009
1Sa 12:2 **b.**, the king walketh before you: 2009
1Sa 12:2 **b.**, my sons are with you: 2009
1Sa 12:3 **B.**, here I am: witness against me 2009
1Sa 12:13 Now therefore **b.** the king 2009
1Sa 12:13 And, **b.**, the Lord hath set 2009
1Sa 13:10 **b.**, Samuel came; 2009
1Sa 14:7 **b.**, I am with thee according 2005
1Sa 14:8 **B.**, we will pass over unto these 2009
1Sa 14:11 **B.**, the Hebrews come forth 2009
1Sa 14:16 **b.**, the multitude melted 2009
1Sa 14:17 **b.**, Jonathan and his 2009
1Sa 14:20 **b.**, every man's sword 2009
1Sa 14:26 **b.**, the honey dropped; 2009
1Sa 14:33 **B.**, the people sin against 2009
1Sa 15:12 **b.**, he set him up a place, 2009
1Sa 15:22 **B.**, to obey is better than sacrifice, 2009
1Sa 16:11 and, **b.**, he keepeth the sheep. 2009
1Sa 16:15 **B.** now, an evil spirit from God 2009
1Sa 16:18 **B.**, I have seen a son of Jesse, the 2009
1Sa 17:23 **b.**, there came up the champion, 2009
1Sa 18:17 **B.** my elder daughter 2009
1Sa 18:22 **B.**, the king hath delight 2009
1Sa 19:16 **b.**, there was an image 2009
1Sa 19:19 **B.**, David is at Naioth in Ramah 2009
1Sa 19:22 **B.**, they be at Naioth in Ramah. 2009
1Sa 20:2 **b.**, my father will do nothing 2009
1Sa 20:5 **B.**, to morrow is the new moon, 2009
1Sa 20:12 **b.**, if there be good toward 2009
1Sa 20:21 And, **b.**, I will send a lad, 2009
1Sa 20:21 **B.**, the arrows are on this side 2009
1Sa 20:22 **B.**, the arrows are beyond 2009
1Sa 20:23 **b.**, the Lord be between 2009
1Sa 21:9 **b.**, it is here wrapped in a cloth 2009
1Sa 23:1 **B.**, the Philistines fight against 2009
1Sa 23:3 **B.**, we be afraid here 2009
1Sa 24:1 **B.**, David is in the wilderness 2009
1Sa 24:4 **B.**, the day of which the Lord said 2009
1Sa 24:4 **B.**, I will deliver thine enemy 2009
1Sa 24:9 **B.**, David seeketh thy hurt? 2009
1Sa 24:10 **B.**, this day thine eyes have seen 2009
1Sa 24:20 now, **b.**, I know well that 2009
1Sa 25:14 **B.**, David sent messengers 2009
1Sa 25:19 **b.**, I come after you. 2005
1Sa 25:20 and, **b.**, David and his men 2009
1Sa 25:36 **b.**, he held a feast in his 2009
1Sa 25:41 **B.**, let thine handmaid 2009
1Sa 26:7 **b.**, Saul lay sleeping within 2009
1Sa 26:21 **b.**, I have played the fool, 2009
1Sa 26:22 **B.** the king's spear! 2009
1Sa 26:24 **b.**, as thy life was much 2009
1Sa 28:7 **B.**, there is a woman 2009
1Sa 28:9 **B.**, thou knowest what Saul 2009
1Sa 28:21 **B.**, thine handmaid hath 2009
1Sa 30:3 **b.**, it was burned with fire; 2009
1Sa 30:16 **b.**, they were spread abroad 2009
1Sa 30:26 **B.** a present for you 2009
2Sa 1:2 **b.**, a man came out 2009
2Sa 1:6 **b.**, Saul leaned upon his spear 2009
2Sa 1:18 **b.**, it is written in the book 2009
2Sa 3:12 **b.**, my hand shall be with 2009
2Sa 3:22 **b.**, the servants of David 2009
2Sa 3:24 **b.**, Abner came unto thee; 2009
2Sa 4:8 **B.** the head of Ish-bosheth 2009
2Sa 4:10 **B.**, Saul is dead, 2009
2Sa 5:1 **B.**, we are thy bone and thy flesh. 2005
2Sa 9:4 **B.**, he is in the house 2009
2Sa 9:6 answered, **B.** thy servant! 2009
2Sa 12:11 **B.**, I will raise up evil 2005
2Sa 12:18 **B.**, while the child was yet alive, 2009
2Sa 13:24 **B.** now, thy servant hath 2009
2Sa 13:34 **b.**, there came much people 2009
2Sa 13:35 **B.**, the king's sons come; 2009
2Sa 13:36 **B.**, the king's sons came, 2009
2Sa 14:7 And, **b.**, the whole family 2009
2Sa 14:21 **B.** now, I have done this thing, 2009
2Sa 14:32 **B.**, I sent unto thee, 2009
2Sa 15:15 **B.**, thy servants are ready 2009
2Sa 15:26 **b.**, here am I, let him do 2005
2Sa 15:32 **b.**, Hushai, the Archite 2009
2Sa 15:36 **B.**, they have there with them 2009
2Sa 16:1 **b.**, Ziba, the servant of 2009
2Sa 16:3 **B.**, he abideth at Jerusalem: 2009
2Sa 16:4 **B.**, thine are all that pertained 2009
2Sa 16:5 **b.**, thence came out a man 2009
2Sa 16:8 **b.**, thou art taken in thy 2009
2Sa 16:11 **B.**, my son, which came 2009
2Sa 17:9 **B.**, he is hid now 2009
2Sa 18:10 and said, **B.**, I saw Absalom hanged 2009
2Sa 18:11 **b.**, thou sawest him, 2009
2Sa 18:24 and **b.** a man running 2009
2Sa 18:26 **B.** another man running 2009
2Sa 18:31 And, **b.**, Cushi came; 2009
2Sa 19:1 **B.**, the king weepeth 2009
2Sa 19:8 **B.**, the king doth sit 2009
2Sa 19:20 therefore, **b.**, I am come 2009
2Sa 19:37 But **b.** thy servant Chimham; 2009
2Sa 19:41 And, **b.**, all the men of Israel 2009
2Sa 20:21 **B.**, his head shall be thrown 2009
2Sa 24:22 **b.**, here be oxen for burnt 7200
1Ki 1:14 **B.**, while thou yet talkest 2009
1Ki 1:18 **b.**, Adonijah reigneth; 2009
1Ki 1:23 **B.** Nathan the prophet. 2009
1Ki 1:25 **b.**, they eat and drink 2009
1Ki 1:42 **b.**, Jonathan the son of Abiathar 2009
1Ki 1:51 **B.**, Adonijah feareth king 2009
1Ki 2:8 **b.**, thou hast with thee 2009
1Ki 2:29 **b.**, he is by the altar. 2009
1Ki 2:39 **B.**, thy servants be in Gath. 2009
1Ki 3:12 **B.**, I have done according 2009
1Ki 3:15 **b.**, it was a dream 2009
1Ki 3:21 **b.**, it was dead: 2009
1Ki 3:21 **b.**, it was not my son. 2009
1Ki 5:5 And, **b.**, I purpose to build 2005
1Ki 8:27 **b.** the heaven and heaven of 2009
1Ki 10:7 **b.**, the half was not told me: 2009
1Ki 11:22 **b.**, thou seekest to go 2009
1Ki 11:31 **B.**, I will rend the kingdom 2005
1Ki 12:28 **b.** thy gods, O Israel, 2009
1Ki 13:1 **b.**, there came a man of God 2009
1Ki 13:2 **B.**, a child shall be born 2009
1Ki 13:3 **B.**, the altar shall be rent, 2009
1Ki 13:25 **b.**, men passed by 2009
1Ki 14:2 **b.**, there is Ahijah 2009
1Ki 14:5 **B.**, the wife of Jeroboam 2009
1Ki 14:10 **b.**, I will bring evil upon 2005
1Ki 14:19 **b.**, they are written in the book 2009
1Ki 15:19 **b.**, I have sent unto thee 2009
1Ki 16:3 **B.**, I will take away the posterity 2005
1Ki 17:9 **b.**, I have commanded 2009
1Ki 17:10 **b.**, the widow woman was 2009
1Ki 17:12 **b.**, I am gathering two sticks, 2005
1Ki 18:7 **b.**, Elijah met him: 2009
1Ki 18:8, 11,14 **B.**, Elijah is here: 2009
1Ki 18:44 **B.**, there ariseth a little cloud 2009
1Ki 19:5 **b.**, then an angel touched 2009
1Ki 19:6 **b.**, there was a cake baken 2009
1Ki 19:9 **b.**, the word of the Lord came 2009
1Ki 19:11 And, **b.**, the Lord passed by, 2009
1Ki 19:13 **b.**, there came a voice 2009
1Ki 20:13 **b.**, there came a prophet 2009
1Ik 20:13 **b.**, I will deliver it 2005
1Ki 20:31 **B.**, now, we have heard 2009
1Ki 20:36 **b.**, as soon as thou art 2009
1Ki 20:39 **b.**, a man turned aside, 2009
1Ki 21:18 **b.**, he is in the vineyard 2009
1Ki 21:21 **B.**, I will bring evil upon thee, 2005
1Ki 22:13 **B.** now, the words of the prophet 2009
1Ki 22:23 **b.**, the Lord hath put a lying 2009
1Ki 22:25 **b.**, thou shalt see in that 2009
2Ki 1:9 **b.**, he sat on the top of an hill. 2009
2Ki 1:14 **B.**, there came fire down from 2009
2Ki 2:11 **b.**, there appeared a chariot 2009
2Ki 2:16 **B.** now, there be with thy servants 2009
2Ki 2:19 **B.**, I pray thee, the situation 2009
2Ki 3:20 **b.**, there came water by the way 2009
2Ki 4:9 **B.** now, I perceive that this 2009
2Ki 4:13 **B.**, thou hast been careful 2009
2Ki 4:25 **B.**, yonder is that Shunammite: 2009
2Ki 4:32 **b.**, the child was dead, 2009
2Ki 5:6 **b.**, I have therewith sent 2009
2Ki 5:11 **B.**, I thought, He will surely 2009
2Ki 5:15 **B.**, now I know that there is 2009
2Ki 5:20 **B.**, my master hath spared 2009
2Ki 5:22 **B.**, even now there be come 2009
2Ki 6:1 **B.** now, the place where 2009
2Ki 6:13 **B.**, he is in Dothan. 2009
2Ki 6:15 **b.**, an host compassed the city 2009
2Ki 6:17 **b.**, the mountain was full 2009
2Ki 6:20 **b.**, they were in the midst 2009
2Ki 6:25 **b.**, they besieged it. 2009
2Ki 6:30 **b.**, he had sackcloth within 2009
2Ki 6:33 **b.**, the messenger came down 2009
2Ki 6:33 **B.**, this evil is of the Lord; 2009
2Ki 7:2 **B.**, if the Lord would make 2009
2Ki 7:2 **B.**, thou shalt see it with thine 2009
2Ki 7:5 **b.**, there was no man there 2009
2Ki 7:10 **b.**, there was no man there, 2009
2Ki 7:13 (**b.**, they are as all the multitude 2009
2Ki 7:13 **b.**, I say they are even as all 2009
2Ki 7:19 Now, **b.**, if the Lord should make 2009
2Ki 7:19 **B.**, thou shalt see it 2009
2Ki 8:5 **b.**, the woman, whose son 2009
2Ki 9:5 **b.**, the captains of the host 2009
2Ki 10:4 **B.**, two kings stood not 2009
2Ki 10:9 **b.**, I conspired against my 2009
2Ki 11:14 when she looked, **b.**, the king stood 2009
2Ki 13:21 **b.**, they spied a band of men; 2009
2Ki 15:11, 15 **b.**, they are written in the book 2009
2Ki 15:26, 31 **b.**, they are written in the book 2009
2Ki 17:26 and, **b.**, they slay them, 2009
2Ki 18:21 **b.**, thou trustest upon the staff 2009
2Ki 19:7 **B.**, I will send a blast upon him, 2005
2Ki 19:9 **B.**, he is come out to fight 2009
2Ki 19:11 **B.**, thou hast heard what 2009
2Ki 19:35 **b.**, they were all dead corpses 2009
2Ki 20:5 **b.**, I will heal thee: 2005
2Ki 20:17 **B.**, the days come, that all 2009
2Ki 21:12 **B.**, I am bringing such evil 2009
2Ki 22:16 **B.**, I will bring evil upon 2005
2Ki 22:20 **B.** therefore, I will gather thee 2005
1Ch 9:1 **b.**, they were written in the book 2009
1Ch 11:1 **B.**, we are thy bone and thy flesh. 2009
1Ch 11:25 **B.**, he was honourable among 2009
1Ch 22:9 **B.**, a son shall be born to thee, 2009
1Ch 22:14 **b.**, in my trouble I have 2009
1Ch 28:21 **b.**, the courses of the priests 2009
1Ch 29:29 **b.**, they are written in the book 2009
2Ch 2:4 **B.**, I build an house 2009
2Ch 2:8 **b.**, my servants shall be 2009
2Ch 2:10 **b.**, I will give to thy servants, 2009
2Ch 6:18 **b.**, heaven and the heaven of 2009
2Ch 9:6 **b.**, the one half of the greatness 2009
2Ch 13:12 **b.**, God himself is with us 2009
2Ch 13:14 looked back, **b.**, the battle was 2009
2Ch 16:3 **b.**, I have sent thee silver 2009
2Ch 16:11 **b.**, the acts of Asa, 2009
2Ch 18:12 **B.**, the words of the prophets 2009
2Ch 18:22 **b.**, the Lord hath put a lying 2009
2Ch 18:24 **B.**, thou shalt see on that day 2009
2Ch 19:11 **b.**, Amariah the chief priest 2009
2Ch 20:2 **b.**, they be in Hazazon-tamar, 2009
2Ch 20:10 **b.**, the children of Ammon 2009
2Ch 20:11 **b.**, I say, how they reward us, 2009
2Ch 20:16 **b.**, they come up by the cliff 2009
2Ch 20:24 **b.**, they were dead bodies 2009
2Ch 20:34 **b.**, they are written in the book 2009
2Ch 21:14 **B.**, with a great plague will the 2009
2Ch 23:3 **B.**, the king's son shall reign, 2009
2Ch 23:13 and, **b.**, the king stood at his pillar 2009
2Ch 24:27 **b.**, they are written in the story 2009
2Ch 25:26 **b.**, are they not written in the 2009
2Ch 26:20 **b.**, he was leprous in his forehead 2009
2Ch 28:9 **B.**, because the Lord God of your 2009
2Ch 28:26 **b.**, they are written in the book 2009
2Ch 29:19 **b.**, they are before the altar 2009
2Ch 32:32 **b.**, they are written in the vision 2009
2Ch 33:18 **b.**, they are written in the book 2009
2Ch 33:19 **b.**, they are written among 2009
2Ch 34:24 **B.**, I will bring evil upon this 2005
2Ch 34:28 **B.**, I will gather thee to thy fathers 2005
2Ch 35:25 and, **b.**, they are written in the 2009
2Ch 35:27 **b.**, they are written in the book 2009
2Ch 36:8 **b.**, they are written in the book 2009
Ezr 9:15 **b.**, we are before thee in our 2005
Ne 9:36 **B.**, we are servants this day, 2009
Ne 9:36 **b.**, we are servants in it: 2009
Es 6:5 **B.**, Haman standeth 2009
Es 7:9 **B.** also, the gallows fifty cubits 2009
Es 8:7 **B.**, I have given Esther the house 2009
Job 1:12 **B.**, all that he hath is in thy 2009
Job 1:19 **b.**, there came a great wind 2009
Job 2:6 **B.**, he is in thine hand; 2009
Job 4:3 **B.**, thou hast instructed many, 2009
Job 4:18 **B.**, he put no trust in his 2005
Job 5:17 **B.**, happy is the man whom 2009

Job	8:19	**B.**, this is the joy of his way,	2005
Job	8:20	**B.**, God will not cast away	2005
Job	9:12	**B.**, he taketh away, who can hinder	2005
Job	12:14	**B.**, he breaketh down,	2005
Job	12:15	**B.**, he withholdeth the waters,	2005
Job	13:18	**B.** now, I have ordered my	2009
Job	15:15	**B.**, he putteth no trust in his	2005
Job	16:19	**b.**, my witness is in heaven,	2009
Job	19:7	**B.**, I cry out of wrong,	2005
Job	19:27	and mine eyes shall **b.**,	7200
Job	20:9	shall his place any more **b.** him.	7789
Job	21:27	**B.**, I know your thoughts,	2005
Job	22:12	and **b.** the height of the stars,	7200
Job	23:8	**B.**, I go forward,	2005
Job	23:9	but I cannot **b.** him, he hideth	2372
Job	24:5	**B.**, as wild asses in the desert	2005
Job	25:5	**B.** even to the moon,	2005
Job	27:12	**B.**, all ye yourselves have seen	2005
Job	28:28	**B.**, the fear of the Lord,	2005
Job	31:35	**b.**, my desire is,	2005
Job	32:11	**B.**, I waited for your words;	2005
Job	32:12	**b.**, there was none of you	2009
Job	32:19	**B.**, my belly is as wine	2009
Job	33:2	**B.**, now I have opened my mouth,	2009
Job	33:6	**B.**, I am according to thy wish	2005
Job	33:7	**B.**, my terror shall not make	2009
Job	33:10	**B.**, he findeth occasions	2005
Job	33:12	**B.**, in this thou art not just:	2005
Job	34:29	who then can **b.** him? whether it	7789
Job	35:5	and **b.** the clouds which are higher	7789
Job	36:5	**B.**, God is mighty,	2005
Job	36:22	**B.**, God exalteth by his power:	2005
Job	36:24	his work, which men **b.**	7891
Job	36:25	man may see it; man may **b.** it	5027
Job	36:26	**B.**, God is great, and we know	2005
Job	36:30	**B.**, he spreadeth his light	2005
Job	39:29	her eyes **b.** afar off.	5027
Job	40:4	**B.**, I am vile;	2005
Job	40:11	and **b.** every one that is proud,	7200
Job	40:15	**B.** now behemoth, which I made	2009
Job	40:23	**B.**, he drinketh up a river,	2005
Job	41:9	**B.**, the hope of him is in vain:	2005
Ps	7:14	**B.**, he travaileth with iniquity,	2009
Ps	11:4	his eyes **b.**, his eyelids try, the	2372
Ps	11:7	his countenance doth **b.** the	2372
Ps	17:2	let thine eyes **b.** the things that	2372
Ps	17:15	will **b.** thy face in righteousness:	2372
Ps	27:4	to **b.** the beauty of the Lord, and	2372
Ps	33:18	**B.**, the eye of the Lord is upon	2009
Ps	37:37	and **b.** the upright: for the end of	7200
Ps	39:5	**B.**, thou hast made my days	2009
Ps	46:8	come, **b.** the works of the Lord,	2372
Ps	51:5	**B.**, I was shapen in iniquity;	2005
Ps	51:6	**B.**, thou desirest truth in the	2005
Ps	54:4	**B.**, God is mine helper:	2009
Ps	59:4	awake to help me, and **b.**,	7200
Ps	59:7	**B.**, they belch out with their	2009
Ps	66:7	power forever; his eyes **b.** the	6822
Ps	73:12	**B.**, these are the ungodly,	2009
Ps	73:15	**B.**, I should offend against	2009
Ps	78:20	**B.**, he smote the rock,	2005
Ps	80:14	look down from heaven, and **b.**,	7200
Ps	84:9	**B.**, O God our shield, and look	7200
Ps	87:4	**B.** Philistia, and Tyre, with	2009
Ps	91:8	with thine eyes shalt thou **b.** and	5027
Ps	102:19	from heaven did the Lord **b.** the	5027
Ps	113:6	to **b.** the things that are in	7200
Ps	119:18	that I may **b.** wondrous things	5027
Ps	119:40	**B.**, I have longed after thy	2009
Ps	121:4	**B.**, he that keepeth Israel shall	2009
Ps	123:2	**B.**, as the eyes of servants look	2009
Ps	128:4	**B.**, that thus shall the man be	2009
Ps	133:1	**B.**, how good and how pleasant	2009
Ps	134:1	**B.**, bless ye the Lord, all ye	2009
Ps	139:8	**b.**, thou art there.	2009
Pr	1:23	**B.**, I will pour out my spirit unto	2009
Pr	7:10	**b.**, there met him a woman	2009
Pr	11:31	**B.**, the righteous shall be	2005
Pr	23:33	Thine eyes shall **b.** strange	7200
Pr	24:12	**B.**, we knew it not;	2005
Ec	1:14	**b.**, all is vanity and vexation of	2009
Ec	2:1	**b.**, this also is vanity.	2009
Ec	2:11	**b.**, all was vanity and vexation of	2009
Ec	2:12	I turned myself to **b.** wisdom,	7200
Ec	4:1	**B.** the tears of such as were	2009
Ec	5:18	**B.** that which I have seen: good	2009
Ec	7:27	**B.**, this have I found, saith the	7200
Ec	11:7	it is for the eyes to **b.** the sun:	7200
Ca	1:15	**B.**, thou art fair, my love;	2009
Ca	1:15	**b.**, thou art fair;	2009
Ca	1:16	**B.**, thou art fair, my beloved,	2009
Ca	2:8	**b.**, he cometh leaping upon the	2009
Ca	2:9	**b.**, he standeth behind our wall,	2009
Ca	3:7	**B.** his bed,	2009
Ca	3:11	and **b.** king Solomon with the	7200
Ca	4:1	**B.**, thou art fair, my love;	2009
Ca	4:1	**b.**, thou art fair;	2009
Isa	3:1	**B.**, the Lord, the Lord of hosts,	2009
Isa	5:7	but **b.** oppression;	2009
Isa	5:7	but **b.** a cry.	2009
Isa	5:26	**b.**, they shall come with speed	2009
Isa	5:30	**b.** darkness and sorrow,	2009
Isa	7:14	**B.**, a virgin shall conceive,	2009
Isa	8:7	**b.**, the Lord bringeth up	2009
Isa	8:18	**B.**, I and the children whom	2009
Isa	8:22	and **b.** trouble and darkness,	2009
Isa	10:33	**B.**, the Lord, the Lord of hosts,	2009
Isa	12:2	**B.**, God is my salvation;	2009
Isa	13:9	**B.**, the day of the Lord cometh,	2009
Isa	13:17	**B.**, I will stir up the Medes against	2005
Isa	17:1	**B.**, Damascus is taken	2009
Isa	17:14	and **b.** at eventide trouble;	2009
Isa	19:1	**B.**, the Lord rideth upon a swift	2009
Isa	20:6	**B.**, such is our expectation,	2009
Isa	21:9	**b.**, here cometh a chariot of men	2009
Isa	22:13	and **b.** joy and gladness,	2009
Isa	22:17	**B.**, the Lord will carry thee	2009
Isa	23:13	**B.**, the land of the Chaldeans;	2005
Isa	24:1	**B.**, the Lord maketh the earth	2009
Isa	26:10	will not **b.** the majesty of the	7200
Isa	26:21	**b.**, the Lord cometh out of his	2009
Isa	28:2	**B.**, the Lord hath a mighty and	2009
Isa	28:16	**B.**, I lay in Zion for a foundation	2005
Isa	29:8	**b.**, he eateth; but he awaketh,	2009
Isa	29:8	**b.**, he drinketh; but he awaketh,	2009
Isa	29:8	**b.**, he is faint, and his soul hath	2009
Isa	29:14	**b.**, I will proceed to do a marvelous	2005
Isa	30:27	**B.**, the name of the Lord cometh	2009
Isa	32:1	**B.**, a king shall reign in	2005
Isa	33:7	**B.**, their valiant ones shall cry	2005
Isa	33:17	they shall **b.** the land that is very	7200
Isa	34:5	**B.**, it shall come down upon	2009
Isa	35:4	**b.**, your God will come with	2009
Isa	37:7	**B.**, I will send a blast upon	2005
Isa	37:11	**B.**, thou hast heard what	2009
Isa	37:36	**b.**, they were all dead corpses.	2009
Isa	38:5	**B.**, I will add unto thy days	2005
Isa	38:8	**B.**, I will bring again the shadow	2005
Isa	38:11	I shall **b.** man no more with the	7200
Isa	38:17	**B.**, for peace I had great	2009
Isa	39:6	**B.**, the days come,	2009
Isa	40:9	**B.** your God!	2009
Isa	40:10	**B.**, the Lord God will come with	2009
Isa	40:10	**b.**, his reward is with him.	2009
Isa	40:15	**B.**, the nations as a drop of a	2005
Isa	40:15	**b.**, he taketh up the isles as a	2005
Isa	40:26	and **b.** who hath created these	7200
Isa	41:11	**B.**, all they that were incensed	2005
Isa	41:15	**B.**, I will make thee a new sharp	2009
Isa	41:23	be dismayed, and **b.** it together.	7200
Isa	41:24	**B.**, ye are of nothing, and your	2005
Isa	41:27	shall say to Zion, **B.**, **b.** them;	2009
Isa	41:29	**B.**, they are all vanity;	2005
Isa	42:1	**B.** my servant, whom I upheld;	2005
Isa	42:9	**B.**, the former things are come	2009
Isa	43:19	**B.**, I will do a new thing;	2009
Isa	44:11	**B.**, all his fellows shall be	2005
Isa	47:14	**B.**, they shall be as stubble;	2009
Isa	48:7	**B.**, I knew them.	2009
Isa	48:10	**B.**, I have refined thee,	2009
Isa	49:12	**B.**, these shall come from far:	2009
Isa	49:16	**B.**, I have graven thee upon	2005
Isa	49:18	thine eyes round about, and **b.**:	7200
Isa	49:21	**B.**, I was left alone;	2005
Isa	49:22	**B.**, I will lift up mine hand,	2009
Isa	50:1	**B.**, for your iniquities have	2005
Isa	50:2	**b.**, at my rebuke I dry up the	2005
Isa	50:9	**B.**, the Lord God will help me;	2005
Isa	50:11	**B.**, all ye that kindle a fire,	2005
Isa	51:22	**B.**, I have taken out of	2009
Isa	52:6	**b.**, it is I.	2009
Isa	52:13	**B.**, my servant shall deal	2009
Isa	54:11	**b.**, I will lay thy stones with	2009
Isa	54:15	**B.**, they shall surely gather	2005
Isa	54:16	**B.**, I have created the smith	2005
Isa	55:4	**B.**, I have given him for	2005
Isa	55:5	**B.**, thou shalt call a nation	2005
Isa	56:3	**B.**, I am a dry tree.	2005
Isa	58:3	**B.**, in the day of your fast	2005
Isa	58:4	**B.**, ye fast for strife and debate,	2005
Isa	59:1	**B.**, the Lord's hand is not	2005
Isa	59:9	But **b.** obscurity;	2009
Isa	60:2	**b.**, the darkness shall cover	2009
Isa	62:11	**B.**, the Lord hath proclaimed	2009
Isa	62:11	**B.**, thy salvation cometh:	2009
Isa	62:11	**b.**, his reward is with him,	2009
Isa	63:15	Look down from heaven, and **b.**	7200
Isa	64:5	**b.**, thou art wroth;	2005
Isa	64:9	**b.**, see, we beseech thee, we are all	2005
Isa	65:1	I said **B.** me, **b.** me, unto a	2009
Isa	65:6	**B.**, it is written before me:	2009
Isa	65:13	**B.**, my servants shall eat,	2009
Isa	65:13	**b.**, my servants shall drink,	2009
Isa	65:13	**b.**, my servants shall rejoice,	2009
Isa	65:14	**B.**, my servants shall sing for	2009
Isa	65:17	**B.**, I create new heavens and a new	2005
Isa	65:18	**b.**, I create Jerusalem a rejoicing,	2005
Isa	66:12	**B.**, I will extend peace to her	2005
Isa	66:15	**b.**, the Lord will come with fire,	2009
Jer	1:6	**B.**, I cannot speak:	2009
Jer	1:9	**B.**, I have put my words in thy	2009
Jer	1:18	**b.**, I have made thee this day	2009
Jer	2:35	**B.**, I will plead with thee,	2005
Jer	3:5	**B.**, thou hast spoken and done	2009
Jer	3:22	**B.**, we come unto thee;	2005
Jer	4:13	**b.**, he shall come up as clouds,	2009
Jer	4:16	**b.**, publish against Jerusalem,	2009
Jer	5:14	**b.**, I will make my words in	2005
Jer	6:10	**b.**, their ear is uncircumcised, and	2009
Jer	6:10	**b.**, the word of the Lord is unto	2009
Jer	6:19	**b.**, I will bring evil upon this	2009
Jer	6:21	**B.**, I will lay stumblingblocks	2005
Jer	6:22	**B.**, a people cometh from the	2009
Jer	7:8	**B.**, ye trust in lying words,	2009
Jer	7:11	**B.**, even I have seen it,	2009
Jer	7:20	**B.**, mine anger and my fury	2009
Jer	7:32	**b.**, the days come,	2009
Jer	8:15	and **b.** trouble!	2009
Jer	8:17	**b.**, I will send serpents,	2005
Jer	8:19	**B.** the voice of the cry of the	2009
Jer	9:7	**B.**, I will melt them, and try them;	2005
Jer	9:15	**B.**, I will feed them, even this	2005
Jer	9:25	**B.**, the days come, saith the Lord,	2009
Jer	10:18	**B.**, I will sling out the inhabitants	2005
Jer	10:22	**B.**, the noise of the bruit is come,	2009
Jer	11:11	**B.**, I will bring evil upon them,	2005
Jer	11:22	**B.**, I will punish them:	2005
Jer	12:14	**B.**, I will pluck them out of their	2005
Jer	13:7	**b.**, the girdle was marred,	2009
Jer	13:13	**B.**, I will fill all the inhabitants of	2005
Jer	13:20	Lift up your eyes, and **b.** them	7200
Jer	14:13	**b.**, the prophets say unto them,	2009
Jer	14:18	**B.** the slain with the sword!	2009
Jer	14:18	then **b.** them that are sick with	2009
Jer	14:19	and **b.** trouble!	2009
Jer	16:9	**B.**, I will cause to cease out of	2005
Jer	16:12	for, **b.**, ye walk every one after	2009
Jer	16:14	**b.**, the days come, saith the Lord,	2009
Jer	16:16	**B.**, I will send for many fishers,	2005
Jer	16:21	**b.**, I will this once cause them	2005
Jer	17:15	**B.**, they say unto me,	2009
Jer	18:3	and, **b.**, he wrought a work	2009
Jer	18:6	**B.**, as the clay is in the potter's	2009
Jer	18:11	**B.**, I frame evil against you,	2009
Jer	19:3	**B.**, I will bring evil upon this place,	2005
Jer	19:6	**b.**, the days come.	2009
Jer	19:15	**B.**, I will bring upon this city	2005
Jer	20:4	**B.**, I will make thee a terror to	2005
Jer	20:4	thine eyes shall **b.** it: and I will	7200
Jer	21:4	**B.**, I will turn back the weapons	2005
Jer	21:8	**B.**, I set before you the way	2005
Jer	21:13	**B.**, I am against thee,	2005
Jer	23:2	**b.**, I will visit upon you the evil	2005
Jer	23:5,	7 **B.**, the days come,	2009
Jer	23:15	**B.**, I will feed them…wormwood,	2005
Jer	23:19	**B.**, a whirlwind of the Lord	2009
Jer	23:30,	31 **B.**, I am against the prophets,	2005
Jer	23:32	**B.**, I am against them that	2005
Jer	23:39	**b.**, I, even I, will utterly forget	2005
Jer	24:1	**b.**, two baskets of figs were	2009

Jer	25:9	**B.**, I will send and take all	2005
Jer	25:32	**B.**, evil shall go forth from	2009
Jer	26:14	**b.**, I am in your hand:	2005
Jer	27:16	**B.**, the vessels of the Lord's house	2009
Jer	28:16	**B.**, I will cast thee from off	2005
Jer	29:17	**B.**, I will send upon them the	2005
Jer	29:21	**B.**, I will deliver them into the hand	2009
Jer	29:32	**B.**, I will furnish Shemaiah the	2005
Jer	29:32	neither shall he **b.** the good that	7200
Jer	30:18	**B.**, I will bring again the captivity	2005
Jer	30:23	**B.**, the whirlwind of the Lord	2009
Jer	31:8	**B.**, I will bring them from the north	2005
Jer	31:27,	31,38 **B.**, the days come,	2009
Jer	32:3	**B.**, I will give this city into	2005
Jer	32:4	and his eyes shall **b.** his eyes;	7200
Jer	32:7	**B.**, Hanameel the son of Shallum	2009
Jer	32:17	**b.**, thou hast made the heaven	2009
Jer	32:24	**B.**, the mounts, they are come	2009
Jer	32:24	**B.**, thou seest it.	2009
Jer	32:27	**B.**, I am the Lord,	2009
Jer	32:28	**B.**, I will give this city into	2005
Jer	32:37	**B.**, I will gather them out of	2005
Jer	33:6	**B.**, I will bring it health and	2005
Jer	33:14	**B.**, the days come,	2009
Jer	34:2	**B.**, I will give this city into the	2005
Jer	34:3	thine eyes shall **b.** the eyes of	7200
Jer	34:17	**B.**, I proclaim a liberty for you,	2005
Jer	34:22	**B.**, I will command,	2005
Jer	35:17	**B.**, I will bring upon Judah	2005
Jer	37:7	**B.**, Pharaoh's army,	2005
Jer	38:5	**B.**, he is in your hand:	2009
Jer	38:22	**B.**, all the women that are left	2009
Jer	39:16	**b.**, I will bring my words upon	2005
Jer	40:4	**b.**, I loose thee this day from the	2009
Jer	40:4	**b.**, all the land is before thee:	7200
Jer	40:10	**b.**, I will dwell at Mizpah,	2005
Jer	42:2	of many, as thine eyes do **b.** us)	7200
Jer	42:4	**b.**, I will pray unto the Lord	2005
Jer	43:10	**B.**, I will send and take	2005
Jer	44:2	**b.**, this day they are a desolation,	2009
Jer	44:11	**B.**, I will set my face against	2005
Jer	44:26	**B.**, I have sworn by my great	2005
Jer	44:27	**B.**, I will watch over them	2005
Jer	44:30	**B.**, I will give Pharaoh-hophra	2005
Jer	45:4	**B.**, that which I have built	2009
Jer	45:5	**b.**, I will bring evil upon all	2005
Jer	46:25	**B.**, I will punish the multitude	2005
Jer	46:27	**b.**, I will save thee from afar	2005
Jer	47:2	**B.**, waters rise up out of the	2009
Jer	48:12	**b.**, the days come,	2009
Jer	48:40	**B.**, he shall fly as an eagle,	2009
Jer	49:2	**b.**, the days come,	2009
Jer	49:5	**B.**, I will bring a fear upon thee,	2005
Jer	49:12	**B.**, they whose judgment was	2009
Jer	49:19	**B.**, he shall come up like a lion	2009
Jer	49:22	**B.**, he shall come up and fly	2009
Jer	49:35	**B.**, I will break the bow of Elam,	2005
Jer	50:12	**b.**, the hindermost of the nations	2009
Jer	50:18	**B.**, I will punish the king of	2005
Jer	50:31	**B.**, I am against thee,	2005
Jer	50:41	**B.**, a people shall come from the	2009
Jer	50:44	**B.**, he shall come up like a	2009
Jer	51:1	**B.**, I will raise up against	2005
Jer	51:25	**B.**, I am against thee,	2005
Jer	51:36	**B.**, I will plead thy cause,	2005
Jer	51:47	**b.**, the days come, that I will do	2009
Jer	51:52	**b.**, the days come, saith the Lord,	2009
La	1:9	O Lord, **b.** my affliction: for the	7200
La	1:12	**b.**, and see if there be any sorrow	5027
La	1:18	all people, and **b.** my sorrow:	7200
La	1:20	**B.**, O Lord: for I am in distress:	7200
La	2:20	**B.**, O Lord, and consider to whom	7200
La	3:50	Till the Lord look down, and **b.**	7200
La	3:63	**B.** their sitting down, and their	5027
La	5:1	consider, and **b.** our reproach.	7200
Eze	1:4	And I looked, and, **b.**, a whirlwind	2009
Eze	1:15	the living creatures, **b.**, one wheel	2009
Eze	2:9	And when I looked, **b.**, an hand	2009
Eze	3:8	**B.**, I have made thy face strong	2009
Eze	3:23	**b.**, the glory of the Lord stood there,	2009
Eze	3:25	**b.**, they shall put bands upon	2009
Eze	4:8	**b.**, I will lay bands upon	2009
Eze	4:14	**b.**, my soul hath not been	2009
Eze	4:16	**b.**, I will break the staff of bread	2005
Eze	5:8	**B.**, I, even I, am against	2005
Eze	6:3	**B.**, I, even I, will bring a sword	2005
Eze	7:5	an only evil, **b.**, is come.	2009
Eze	7:6	**b.**, it is come.	2009
Eze	7:10	**B.** the day, **b.**, it is come:	2009
Eze	8:4	**b.**, the glory of the God of Israel	2009
Eze	8:5	and **b.** northward at the gate	2009
Eze	8:7	**b.** a hole in the wall	2009
Eze	8:8	**b.** a door	2009
Eze	8:9	and **b.** the wicked abominations	
Eze	8:10	and **b.** every form of creeping	2009
Eze	8:14	**b.**, there sat women weeping	2009
Eze	8:16	**B.**, at the door of the temple	2009
Eze	9:2	and, **b.**, six men came from the	2009
Eze	9:11	and, **b.**, the man clothed with	2009
Eze	10:1	and, **b.**, in the firmament	2009
Eze	10:9	**b.** the four wheels by the	2009
Eze	11:1	and **b.** at the door of the gate	2009
Eze	12:27	**b.**, they of the house of Israel say,	2009
Eze	13:8	**b.**, I am against you,	2005
Eze	13:20	**B.**, I am against your pillows,	2005
Eze	14:22	**b.**, therein shall be left a	2009
Eze	14:22	**b.**, they shall come forth unto you,	2009
Eze	15:4	**B.**, it is cast into the fire for fuel;	2009
Eze	15:5	**B.**, when it was whole,	2009
Eze	16:8	**b.**, thy time was the time of love;	2009
Eze	16:27	**B.**, therefore I have stretched out	2009
Eze	16:37	**B.**, therefore I will gather all thy	2005
Eze	16:43	**b.**, therefore I also will recompense	1887
Eze	16:44	**B.**, every one that useth proverbs	2009
Eze	16:49	**B.**, this was the iniquity of thy	2009
Eze	17:7	**b.**, this vine did bend her	2009
Eze	17:10	**b.**, being planted,	2009
Eze	17:12	**B.**, the king of Babylon is come	2009
Eze	18:4	**B.**, all souls are mine;	2005
Eze	20:47	**B.**, I will kindle fire in thee,	2005
Eze	21:3	**B.**, I am against thee,	2005
Eze	21:7	**B.**, it cometh, and shall be brought	2009
Eze	22:6	**B.**, the princes of Israel,	2009
Eze	22:13	**B.**, therefore I have smitten	2009
Eze	22:19	**b.**, therefore I will gather you	2005
Eze	23:22	**B.**, I will raise up thy lovers	2005
Eze	23:28	**B.**, I will deliver thee into the	2005
Eze	24:16	**b.**, I take away from thee the	2005
Eze	24:21	**B.**, I will profane my sanctuary,	2005
Eze	25:4	**B.**, therefore I will deliver thee to	2005
Eze	25:7	**B.**, therefore I will stretch out	2005
Eze	25:8	**B.**, the house of Judah is like	2009
Eze	25:9	**b.**, I will open the side of Moab	2005
Eze	25:16	**B.**, I will stretch out mine	2005
Eze	26:3	**B.**, I am against thee,	2005
Eze	26:7	**B.**, I will bring upon Tyrus	2005
Eze	28:3	**B.**, thou art wiser than Daniel;	2009
Eze	28:7	**B.**, therefore I will bring strangers	2005
Eze	28:17	kings, that they may **b.** thee.	7200
Eze	28:18	the sight of all them that **b.** thee.	7200
Eze	28:22	**B.**, I am against thee,	2005
Eze	29:3	**B.**, I am against thee,	2005
Eze	29:8	**B.**, I will bring a sword upon	2005
Eze	29:10	**B.**, therefore I am against thee,	2005
Eze	29:19	**B.**, I will give the land of	2005
Eze	30:22	**B.**, I am against Pharaoh	2005
Eze	31:3	**B.**, the Assyrian was a cedar	2009
Eze	34:10	**B.**, I am against the shepherds;	2005
Eze	34:11	**B.**, I, even I, will both search my	2005
Eze	34:17	**B.**, I judge between cattle and	2005
Eze	34:20	**B.**, I, even I, will judge between	2005
Eze	35:3	**B.**, O mount Seir, I am against	2005
Eze	36:6	**B.**, I have spoken in my jealousy	2005
Eze	36:9	**b.**, I am for you, and I will	2005
Eze	37:2	**b.**, there were very many in	2009
Eze	37:5	**B.**, I will cause breath to enter	2009
Eze	37:7	and **b.** a shaking, and the bones	2009
Eze	37:11	**b.**, they say, Our bones are	2009
Eze	37:12	**B.**, O my people, I will open	2009
Eze	37:19	**B.**, I will take the stick of Joseph,	2009
Eze	37:21	**B.**, I will take the children	2009
Eze	38:3	**B.**, I am against thee,	2005
Eze	39:1	**B.**, I am against thee,	2005
Eze	39:8	**B.**, it is come, and it is done,	2009
Eze	40:3	**b.**, there was a man,	2009
Eze	40:4	Son of man, **b.** with thine eyes,	7200
Eze	40:5	and **b.** a wall on the outside	2009
Eze	40:24	and **b.** a gate toward the south:	2009
Eze	43:2	**b.**, the glory of the God of Israel	2009
Eze	43:5	**b.**, the glory of the Lord filled	2009
Eze	43:12	**B.**, this is the law of the house.	2009
Eze	44:4	and, **b.**, the glory of the Lord filled	2009
Eze	44:5	and **b.** with thine eyes, and hear	7200
Eze	46:19	**b.**, there was a place on the two	2009
Eze	46:21	**b.**, in every corner of the court	2009
Eze	47:1	**b.**, waters issued out from	2009
Eze	47:2	**b.**, there ran out waters	2009
Eze	47:7	**b.**, at the bank of the river	2009
Da	2:31	king, sawest, and **b.** a great image	431
Da	4:10	**b.** a tree in the midst of the earth,	431
Da	4:13	and, **b.**, a watcher and a holy	431
Da	7:2	**b.**, the four winds of the heaven	718
Da	7:5	And **b.** another beast, a second,	718
Da	7:7	and **b.** a fourth beast, dreadful and	718
Da	7:8	and, **b.**, there came up among	431
Da	7:8	and, **b.**, in this horn were eyes like	431
Da	7:13	and, **b.**, one like the Son of man	718
Da	8:3	**b.**, there stood before the river	2009
Da	8:5	**b.**, an he goat came from	2009
Da	8:15	**b.**, there stood before me	2009
Da	8:19	**B.**, I will make thee know	2005
Da	9:18	thine eyes, and **b.** our desolations,	7200
Da	10:5	**b.** a certain man clothed in linen,	2009
Da	10:10	**b.**, an hand touched me,	2009
Da	10:16	**b.**, one like the similitude of the	2009
Da	11:2	**b.**, there shall stand up yet three	2009
Da	12:5	and **b.**, there stood other two,	2009
Ho	2:6	**b.** I will hedge up thy way	2005
Ho	2:14	**b.**, I will allure her,	2009
Joe	2:19	**B.**, I will send you corn,	2005
Joe	3:1	For, **b.**, in those days, and in that	2009
Joe	3:7	**B.**, I will raise them out of	2005
Am	2:13	B, I am pressed under you,	2009
Am	3:9	and **b.** the great tumults in	7200
Am	6:11	For, **b.**, the Lord commandeth, and	2009
Am	6:14	**b.**, I will raise up against you,	2005
Am	7:1	**b.**, he formed grasshoppers	2009
Am	7:4	**b.**, the Lord God called to contend	2009
Am	7:7	**b.**, the Lord stood upon a wall	2009
Am	7:8	**B.**, I will set a plumbline	2005
Am	8:1	and **b.** a basket of summer fruit.	2009
Am	8:11	**B.**, the days come,	2009
Am	9:8	**B.**, the eyes of the Lord God	2009
Am	9:13	**B.**, the days come,	2009
Ob	2	**B.**, I have made thee small	2009
Mic	1:3	**b.**, the Lord cometh forth out of	2009
Mic	2:3	**B.**, against this family do I	2005
Mic	7:9	and I shall **b.** his righteousness.	7200
Mic	7:10	mine eyes shall **b.** her: now shall	7200
Na	1:15	**B.** upon the mountains the	2209
Na	2:13	**B.**, I am against thee,	2205
Na	3:5	**B.**, I am against thee,	2205
Na	3:13	**B.**, thy people in the midst of	2009
Hab	1:3	and cause me to **b.** grievance?	5027
Hab	1:5	**B.** ye among the heathen, and	7200
Hab	1:13	art of purer eyes than to **b.** evil,	7200
Hab	2:4	**B.**, his soul which is lifted up	2009
Hab	2:13	**B.**, is it not of the Lord of hosts	2009
Hab	2:19	**B.**, it is laid over with gold and	2009
Zep	3:19	**B.**, at that time I will undo all	2005
Zec	1:8	and **b.** a man riding upon	2009
Zec	1:11	**b.**, all the earth sitteth still,	2009
Zec	1:18	and **b.** four horns.	2009
Zec	2:1	and **b.** a man with a measuring	2009
Zec	2:3	**b.**, the angel that talked with me	2009
Zec	2:9	**b.**, I will shake mine hand upon	2005
Zec	3:4	**B.**, I have caused thine iniquity	7200
Zec	3:8	**b.**, I will bring forth my servant	2005
Zec	3:9	For **b.** the stone that I have laid	2009
Zec	3:9	**b.**, I will engrave the graving	2005
Zec	4:2	and **b.** a candlestick all of gold,	2005
Zec	5:1	and **b.** a flying roll.	2009
Zec	5:7	**b.**, there was lifted up a talent	2009
Zec	5:9	**b.**, there came out two women,	2009
Zec	6:1	**b.**, there came four chariots out	2009
Zec	6:8	**B.**, these that go towards the	7200
Zec	6:12	**B.**, the man whose name is The	2009
Zec	8:7	**B.**, I will save my people	2005
Zec	9:4	**B.**, the Lord will cast her out,	2009
Zec	9:9	**b.**, thy king cometh unto thee:	2009
Zec	12:2	**B.**, I will make Jerusalem a	2009
Zec	14:1	**B.**, the day of the Lord cometh,	2009
Mal	1:13	**B.**, what a weariness is it!	2009
Mal	2:3	**B.**, I will corrupt your seed,	2005
Mal	3:1	**B.**, I will send my messenger,	2005
Mal	3:1	**b.** he shall come,	2009
Mal	4:1	For, **b.**, the day cometh,	2009
Mal	4:5	**B.**, I will send you Elijah the	2009
Mt	1:20	**b.**, the angel of the Lord appeared	*2400*
Mt	1:23	**B.**, a virgin shall be with child,	*2400*

Mt 2:1 b. there came wise men from the... 2400
Mt 2:13 b., the angel of the Lord appeareth... 2400
Mt 2:19 was dead, b., an angel of the Lord... 2400
Mt 4:11 leaveth him, and, b., angels came... 2400
Mt 6:26 B. the fowls of the air: for they... 1689
Mt 7:4 b., a beam is in thine own eye?... 2400
Mt 8:2 And, b., there came a leper... 2400
Mt 8:24 b., there arose a great tempest... 2400
Mt 8:29 and, b., they cried out, saying,... 2400
Mt 8:32 b., the whole herd of swine ran... 2400
Mt 8:34 And, b., the whole city came out... 2400
Mt 9:2 And, b., they brought to him... 2400
Mt 9:3 And, b., certain of the scribes... 2400
Mt 9:10 b., many publicans and sinners... 2400
Mt 9:18 b., there came a certain ruler... 2400
Mt 9:20 b., a woman, which was diseased... 2400
Mt 9:32 b., they brought to him a dumb... 2400
Mt 10:16 B., I send you forth as sheep... 2400
Mt 11:8 b., they that wear soft clothing... 2400
Mt 11:10 B., I send my messenger before... 2400
Mt 11:19 B. a man gluttonous, and a... 2400
Mt 12:2 B., thy disciples do that which is... 2400
Mt 12:10 And, b., there was a man... 2400
Mt 12:18 B. my servant, whom I have... 2400
Mt 12:41 b., a greater than Jonas is here... 2400
Mt 12:42 b., a greater than Solomon is here. 2400
Mt 12:46 b., his mother and his brethren... 2400
Mt 12:47 B., thy mother and thy brethren... 2400
Mt 12:49 B., my mother and my brethren!... 2400
Mt 13:3 B., a sower went forth to sow;... 2400
Mt 15:22 b., a woman of Canaan came out... 2400
Mt 17:3 And, b., there appeared unto them... 2400
Mt 17:5 b., a bright cloud overshadowed... 2400
Mt 17:5 and b. a voice out of the cloud,... 2400
Mt 18:10 do always b. the face of my Father.. 991
Mt 19:16 b., one came and said unto him,... 2400
Mt 19:27 B., we have forsaken all, and... 2400
Mt 20:18 B., we go up to Jerusalem; and... 2400
Mt 20:30 And, b., two blind men sitting... 2400
Mt 21:5 B., thy King cometh unto thee,... 2400
Mt 22:4 B., I have prepared my dinner:... 2400
Mt 23:34 Wherefore, b., I send unto you... 2400
Mt 23:38 B., your house is left unto you... 2400
Mt 24:25 B., I have told you before... 2400
Mt 24:26 B., he is in the desert; go not... 2400
Mt 24:26 b., he is in the secret chambers;... 2400
Mt 25:6 B., the bridegroom cometh; go ye.. 2400
Mt 25:20 b., I have gained beside them... 2396
Mt 25:22 b., I have gained two other... 2396
Mt 26:45 b., the hour is at hand, and the... 2400
Mt 26:46 b., he is at hand that doth betray.. 2400
Mt 26:51 And, b., one of them which were... 2400
Mt 26:65 b., now ye have heard his... 2396
Mt 27:51 b., the veil of the temple was rent... 2400
Mt 28:2 b., there was a great earthquake:... 2400
Mt 28:7 and, b., he goeth before you into... 2400
Mt 28:9 b., Jesus met them, saying, All hail.. 2400
Mt 28:11 were going, b., some of the watch... 2400
Mt 1:2 B., I send my messenger before... 2400
Mt 2:24 B., why do they on the sabbath... 2396
Mt 3:32 B., thy mother and thy brethren... 2396
Mr 3:34 B. my mother and my brethren!... 2396
Mk 4:3 B., there went out a sower to sow:.. 2400
Mk 5:22 b., there cometh one of the rulers... 2400
Mk 10:33 saying, B., we go up to Jerusalem,.. 2400
Mk 11:21 b., the fig tree which thou... 2396
Mk 13:23 b., I have foretold you all things... 2400
Mk 14:41 b., the Son of man is betrayed... 2400
Mk 15:4 b. how many things they witness... 2396
Mk 15:35 heard it, said, B., he calleth Elias... 2400
Mk 16:6 b. the place where they laid him... 2396
Lu 1:20 And, b., thou shalt be dumb,... 2400
Lu 1:31 And, b., thou shalt conceive in thy... 2400
Lu 1:36 And, b., thy cousin Elisabeth, she... 2400
Lu 1:38 B. the handmaid of the Lord;... 2400
Lu 1:48 for, b., from henceforth all... 2400
Lu 2:10 for, b., I bring you good tidings of... 2400
Lu 2:25 b., there was a man in Jerusalem,... 2400
Lu 2:34 B., this child is set for the fall... 2400
Lu 2:48 b., thy father and I have sought... 2400
Lu 5:12 city, b. a man full of leprosy:... 2400
Lu 5:18 And, b., men brought in a bed... 2400
Lu 6:23 for, b., your reward is great... 2400
Lu 7:12 b., there was a dead man carried... 2400
Lu 7:25 B., they which are gorgeously... 2400
Lu 7:27 B., I send my messenger before... 2400
Lu 7:34 B. a gluttonous man, and a... 2400
Lu 7:37 And, b., a woman in the city,... 2400
Lu 8:41 And, b., there came a man named... 2400
Lu 9:30 And, b., there talked with him two... 2400
Lu 9:38 And, b., a man of the company... 2400
Lu 10:3 b., I send you forth as lambs... 2400
Lu 10:19 B., I give unto you power to tread. 2400
Lu 10:25 And, b., a certain lawyer stood up,... 2400
Lu 11:31 and, b., a greater than Solomon... 2400
Lu 11:32 and, b., a greater than Jonas... 2400
Lu 11:41 and, b., all things are clean... 2400
Lu 13:7 B. these three years I come... 2400
Lu 13:11 And, b., there was a woman which... 2400
Lu 13:30 And, b., there are last which shall. 2400
Lu 13:32 B., I cast out devils, and I do... 2400
Lu 13:35 B., your house is left unto you... 2400
Lu 14:2 And, b., there was a certain man... 2400
Lu 14:29 all that b. it begin to mock him,... 2334
Lu 17:21 for, b., the kingdom of God... 2400
Lu 18:31 B., we go up to Jerusalem, and all. 2400
Lu 19:2 And, b., there was a man named... 2400
Lu 19:8 B., Lord, the half of my goods... 2400
Lu 19:20 b., here is thy pound, which I have 2400
Lu 21:6 As for these things which ye b.,... 2334
Lu 21:29 B. the fig tree, and all the trees;... 1492
Lu 22:10 B., when ye are entered into the... 2400
Lu 22:21 b., the hand of him that betrayeth. 2400
Lu 22:31 b., Satan hath desired to have you, 2400
Lu 22:38 Lord, b., here are two swords... 2400
Lu 22:47 b. a multitude, and he that was... 2400
Lu 23:14 and, b., I, having examined him... 2400
Lu 23:29 For, b., the days are coming, in... 2400
Lu 23:50 And, b., there was a man named... 2400
Lu 24:4 b., two men stood by them in... 2400
Lu 24:13 b., two of them went that same... 2400
Lu 24:39 B. my hands and my feet, that it.. 1492
Lu 24:49 And, b., I send the promise of... 2400
Joh 1:29 B. the Lamb of God, which taketh... 2396
Joh 1:36 B. the Lamb of God!... 2396
Joh 1:47 B. an Israelite indeed, in whom... 2396
Joh 3:26 b., the same baptizeth, and all... 2396
Joh 4:35 b., I say unto you, Lift up your... 2400
Joh 5:14 B., thou art made whole: sin no... 2396
Joh 11:3 Lord, b., he whom thou lovest is... 2396
Joh 11:36 the Jews, B. how he loved him!... 2396
Joh 12:15 b., thy King cometh, sitting on an... 2400
Joh 12:19 b., the world is gone after him... 2396
Joh 16:32 B., the hour cometh, yea, is now.. 2400
Joh 17:24 that they may b. my glory, which. 2334
Joh 18:21 unto them: b. they know what I... 2396
Joh 19:4 B., I bring him forth to you, that... 2396
Joh 19:5 Pilate saith unto them, B. the... 2396
Joh 19:14 unto the Jews, B. your king!... 2396
Joh 19:26 unto his mother, Woman, b. thy... 2400
Joh 19:27 B. thy mother! And from that... 2396
Joh 20:27 hither thy finger, and b. my... 2396
Ac 1:10 b., two men stood by them in... 2400
Ac 2:7 B., are not all these which speak... 2400
Ac 4:29 now, Lord, b. their threatenings:... 1896
Ac 5:9 b., the feet of them which have... 2400
Ac 5:25 B., the men whom ye put in prison... 2400
Ac 5:28 and, b., ye have filled Jerusalem... 2400
Ac 7:31 and as he drew near to b. it,... 2657
Ac 7:32 Moses trembled and durst not b... 2657
Ac 7:56 B., I see the heavens opened,... 2400
Ac 8:27 and, b., a man of Ethiopia, an... 2400
Ac 9:10 And he said, B., I am here, Lord... 2400
Ac 9:11 Saul, of Tarsus: for, b., he... 2400
Ac 10:17 b., the men which were sent from... 2400
Ac 10:19 B., three men seek thee... 2400
Ac 10:21 B., I am he whom ye seek: what... 2400
Ac 10:30 and, b., a man stood before me in... 2400
Ac 11:11 And, b., immediately there were... 2400
Ac 12:7 And, b., the angel of the Lord... 2400
Ac 13:11 And now, b., the hand of the Lord... 2400
Ac 13:25 But, b., there cometh one after me,... 2400
Ac 13:41 B., ye despisers, and wonder,... 1492
Ac 16:1 and, b., a certain disciple was... 2400
Ac 20:22 And now, b., I go bound in the... 2400
Ac 20:25 b., I know that ye all,... 2400
Ro 2:17 B., thou art called a Jew, and... 2396
Ro 9:33 B., I lay in Sion a stumblingstone... 2400
Ro 11:22 B. therefore the goodness and... 1492
1Co 10:18 B. Israel after the flesh: are not... 991
1Co 15:51 B., I shew you a mystery; We... 2400
2Co 3:7 Israel could not stedfastly b. the... 816
2Co 5:17 b., all things are become new... 2400
2Co 6:2 b., now is the accepted time;... 2400
2Co 6:2 b., now is the day of salvation.)... 2400
2Co 6:9 and, b., we live; as chastened,... 2400
2Co 7:11 For b. this selfsame thing that ye... 2400
2Co 12:14 B., the third time I am ready to... 2400
Ga 1:20 unto you, b., before God, I lie not... 2400
Ga 5:2 B., I Paul say unto you, that if ye... 2396
Heb 2:13 B. I and the children which God... 2400
Heb 8:8 B., the days come, saith the Lord,... 2400
Jas 3:3 B., we put bits in the horses'... 2400
Jas 3:4 B. also the ships, which though... 2400
Jas 3:5 B., how great a matter a little fire... 2400
Jas 5:4 B., the hire of the labourers who... 2400
Jas 5:7 B., the husbandman waiteth for... 2400
Jas 5:9 b., the judge standeth before the... 2400
Jas 5:11 B., we count them happy which... 2400
1Pe 2:6 B., I lay in Sion a chief corner... 2400
1Pe 2:12 good works, which they shall b.,... 2029
1Pe 3:2 they b. your chaste conversation... 2029
1Jo 3:1 B., what manner of love the... 1492
Jude 14 B., the Lord cometh with ten... 2400
Re 1:7 B., he cometh with clouds; and... 2400
Re 1:18 and, b., I am alive for evermore,... 2400
Re 2:10 b., the devil shall cast some of you. 2400
Re 2:22 B., I will cast her into a bed, and. 2400
Re 3:8 b., I have set before thee an open.. 2400
Re 3:9 B., I will make them of the... 2400
Re 3:9 b., I will make them to come and.. 2400
Re 3:11 B., I come quickly: hold that... 2400
Re 3:20 B., I stand at the door and knock:. 2400
Re 4:1 and, b., a door was opened in... 2400
Re 4:2 and, b., a throne was set in heaven,... 2400
Re 5:5 b., the Lion of the tribe of Juda,... 2400
Re 6:2 And I saw, and b. a white horse:... 2400
Re 6:8 And I looked, and b. a pale horse:... 2400
Re 9:12 and, b., there come two woes more... 2400
Re 11:14 and, b., the third woe cometh... 2400
Re 12:3 and b. a great red dragon, having... 2400
Re 14:14 And I looked, and b. a white cloud,... 2400
Re 15:5 b., the temple of the tabernacle... 2400
Re 16:15 B., I come as a thief. Blessed... 2400
Re 17:8 when they b. the beast that was... 991
Re 19:11 opened, and b. a white horse;... 2400
Re 21:3 B., the tabernacle of God is with... 2400
Re 21:5 said, B., I make all things new... 2400
Re 22:7 B., I come quickly: blessed is he... 2400
Re 22:12 And, b., I come quickly; and my... 2400

BEHOLDEST

Ps 10:14 thou b. mischief and spite, to... 5027
Mt 7:3 why b. thou the mote that is in thy... 991
Lu 6:41 And why b. thou the mote that is... 991
Lu 6:42 when thou thyself b. not the beam... 991

BEHOLDETH

Job 24:18 b. not the way of the vineyards... 6437
Job 41:34 He b. all high things: he is a... 7200
Ps 33:13 heaven; he b. all the sons of men... 7200
Jas 1:24 For he b. himself, and goeth his... 2657

BEHOLDING

Ps 119:37 Turn away mine eyes from b... 7200
Pr 15:3 every place, b. the evil and the... 6822
Ec 5:11 the b. of them with their eyes?... 7200
Mt 27:55 women were there b. afar off,... 2334
Mk 10:21 Jesus b. him loved him, and said... 1689
Lu 23:35 the people stood b.. And the... 2334
Lu 23:48 b. the things which were done,... 2334
Lu 23:49 stood afar off b. these things,... 3708
Ac 4:14 b. the man which was healed... 991
Ac 8:13 b. the miracles and signs which... 2334
Ac 14:9 who stedfastly b. him and... 816
Ac 23:1 Paul, earnestly b. the council,... 816
2Co 3:18 b. as in a glass the glory of the... 2734
Col 2:5 joying and b. your order, and the... 991
Jas 1:23 like unto a man b. his natural... 2657

BEHOVED

Lu 24:46 thus it b. Christ to suffer, and... 1163
Heb 2:17 in all things it b. him to be made... 3784

BEING

Ge 18:12 I have pleasure, my lord b. old...
Ge 19:16 the Lord b. merciful unto him:...
Ge 21:4 Isaac b. eight days old, as God...
Ge 24:27 I b. in the way, the Lord led me...
Ge 34:30 and I b. few in number, they shall...
Ge 35:29 gathered unto his people, b. old...
Ge 37:2 Joseph, b. seventeen years old,...
Ge 50:26 So Joseph died, b. an hundred and...

Ex	12:34	their kneadingtroughs **b.** bound	
Ex	13:15	all that openeth the matrix, **b.**	
Ex	22:14	the owner thereof **b.** not with it,	
Ex	28:16	it shall **b.** doubled; a span	
Ex	32:18	of them that cry for **b.** overcome:	
Ex	39:9	a span the breadth thereof, **b.**	
Le	21:4	**b.** a chief man among his people	
Le	24:8	**b.** taken from the children of	
Nu	1:44	princes of Israel, **b.** twelve men:	
Nu	22:24	of the vineyards, a wall **b.** on the	
Nu	30:3	bond, **b.** in her father's house in	
Nu	30:16	**b.** yet in her youth in her father's	
Nu	31:32	And the booty, **b.** the rest of the	
Nu	32:38	Baal-meon, (their names **b.**	
De	3:13	and all Bashan, **b.** the kingdom	
De	17:8	**b.** matters of controversy within	
De	22:24	because she cried not, **b.** in the	
De	32:31	even our enemies themselves **b.**	
Jos	9:23	of you be freed from **b.** bondmen,	
Jos	21:10	of Aaron, **b.** of the family of the	
Jos	24:29	died, **b.** an hundred and ten years	
Jg	2:8	servant of the Lord died, **b.** an	
Jg	9:5	Jerubbaal, **b.** threescore and ten	
1Sa	2:18	ministered before the Lord, **b.** a	
1Sa	15:23	also rejected thee from **b.** king	
1Sa	15:26	hath rejected thee from **b.** king	
1Sa	26:13	a great space **b.** between them:	
2Sa	8:13	salt, **b.** eighteen thousand men	
2Sa	13:4	Why art thou, **b.** the king's son,	
2Sa	13:14	but **b.** stronger than she, forced	
2Sa	19:3	as people **b.** ashamed steal away	
2Sa	21:16	he **b.** girded with a new sword,	
1Ki	1:41	noise of the city, **b.** in an uproar?	
1Ki	2:27	thrust out Abiathar from **b.** priest	1961
1Ki	11:17	Hadad **b.** yet a little child,	
1Ki	15:13	her he removed from **b.** queen,	
1Ki	16:7	in **b.** like the house of Jeroboam;	1961
1Ki	20:15	of Israel, **b.** seven thousand	
2Ki	8:16	Jehosaphat **b.** then king of Judah,	
2Ki	10:6	king's sons, **b.** seventy persons,	
2Ki	12:11	gave the money, **b.** told, into the	
1Ch	9:19	fathers, **b.** over the host of the	
1Ch	24:6	household **b.** taken for Eleazar,	
2Ch	5:12	**b.** arrayed in white linen,	
2Ch	13:3	thousand chosen men, **b.** mighty	
2Ch	15:16	he removed her from **b.** queen,	
2Ch	21:20	and departed without **b.** desired	
2Ch	26:21	in a several house, **b.** a leper;	
Ezr	6:11	down from his house, and **b.**	
Ezr	10:19	and **b.** guilty, they offered a ram	
Ne	6:11	and who is there, that, **b.** as I am,	
Es	1:3	of the provinces, **b.** before him:	
Es	1:7	(the vessels **b.** diverse one from	
Es	3:15	out, **b.** hastened by the king's	
Es	8:14	**b.** hastened and pressed on by	
Job	4:7	who ever perished, **b.** innocent?	
Job	21:23	**b.** wholly at ease and quiet,	
Job	42:17	Job died, **b.** old and full of days,	
Ps	49:12	man **b.** in honour abideth not:	
Ps	65:6	the mountains; **b.** girded with	
Ps	69:4	would destroy me, **b.** mine enemies	
Ps	78:9	children of Ephraim, **b.** armed,	
Ps	78:38	But he, **b.** full of compassion,	
Ps	83:4	cut them off from **b.** a nation;	
Ps	104:33	to my God while I have my **b.**	5750
Ps	107:10	**b.** bound in affliction and iron;	
Ps	139:16	substance, yet **b.** unperfect;	
Ps	146:2	unto my God while I have any **b.**	5750
Pr	3:26	shall keep thy foot from **b.** taken	
Pr	29:1	that **b.** often reproved hardeneth	
Ca	3:8	hold swords, **b.** expert in war:	
Ca	3:10	midst thereof **b.** paved with love,	
Isa	3:26	and she **b.** desolate shall set	
Isa	17:1	is taken away from **b.** a city,	
Isa	40:13	**b.** his counseller hath taught him?	
Isa	65:20	**b.** a hundred years old shall be	
Jer	2:25	Withhold thy foot from **b.** unshod,	
Jer	12:11	**b.** desolate it mourneth unto me;	
Jer	17:16	not hastened from **b.** a pastor	
Jer	31:36	shall cease from **b.** a nation	1961
Jer	34:9	his maidservant **b.** a Hebrew	
Jer	40:1	taken him **b.** bound in chains	
Jer	48:2	us cut it off from **b.** a nation	
Jer	48:42	Moab shall be destroyed from **b.** a	
Eze	17:10	Yea, behold, **b.** planted, shall it	
Eze	23:42	voice of the multitude **b.** at ease	
Eze	47:8	which **b.** brought forth into the sea	
Eze	48:22	**b.** in the midst of that which is	
Da	3:27	king's counsellers, **b.** gathered	
Da	5:31	**b.** about threescore and two	
Da	6:10	and his windows **b.** open in his	
Da	8:22	Now that **b.** broken, whereas	
Da	9:21	**b.** caused to fly swiftly, touched	
Mt	1:19	Joseph her husband, **b.** a just	*5607*
Mt	1:23	Emmanuel, which **b.** interpreted	
Mt	1:24	Joseph **b.** raised from sleep did	
Mt	2:12	**b.** warned of God in a dream	
Mt	2:22	go thither: notwithstanding, **b.**	
Mt	7:11	**if ye then, b. evil, know**	*5607*
Mt	12:34	**ye, b. evil, speak good things**	*5607*
Mt	14:8	**b.** before instructed of her mother,	
Mk	3:5	with anger, **b.** grieved for the	
Mk	5:41	which is, **b.** interpreted,	
Mk	8:1	the multitude **b.** very great,	*5607*
Mk	9:33	**b.** in the house he asked them,	*1096*
Mk	14:3	**b.** in Bethany in the house of	*5607*
Mk	15:22	Golgotha, which is, **b.** interpreted,	
Mk	15:34	which is, **b.** interpreted, My God,	
Lu	1:74	that we, **b.** delivered out of the	
Lu	2:5	wife, **b.** great with child	*5607*
Lu	3:1	Pontius Pilate **b.** governor of	
Lu	3:1	Herod **b.** tetrarch of Galilee,	
Lu	3:2	and Caiaphas **b.** the high priest,	*1909*
Lu	3:19	**b.** reproved by him for Herodias	
Lu	3:21	that Jesus also **b.** baptized,	
Lu	3:23	thirty years of age, **b.** (as was	*5607*
Lu	4:1	Jesus **b.** full of the Holy Ghost	
Lu	4:2	**B.** forty days tempted of the devil	
Lu	4:15	taught in their synagogues, **b.**	
Lu	7:29	justified God, **b.** baptized with	
Lu	7:30	themselves, **b.** not baptized of	
Lu	8:25	And they **b.** afraid wondered,	
Lu	11:13	**If ye then, b. evil, know how to**	*5225*
Lu	13:16	**this woman, b. a daughter of**	*5607*
Lu	14:21	**master of the house b. angry said**	
Lu	16:23	**lift up his eyes, b. in torments,**	*5225*
Lu	20:36	**children of God, b. the children**	*5607*
Lu	21:12	**b. brought before kings and rulers**	
Lu	22:3	Iscariot, **b.** of the number	*5607*
Lu	22:44	And **b.** in an agony he prayed	*1096*
Joh	1:38	is to say, **b.** interpreted, Master,)	
Joh	1:41	which is, **b.** interpreted, the Christ	
Joh	4:6	Jesus therefore, **b.** wearied with	
Joh	4:9	How is it that thou, **b.** a Jew,	*5607*
Joh	5:13	a multitude **b.** in that place,	*5607*
Joh	6:71	betray him, **b.** one of the twelve,	*5607*
Joh	7:50	Jesus by night, **b.** one of them,)	*5607*
Joh	8:9	**b.** convicted by their own	
Joh	10:33	that thou, **b.** a man, makest	*5607*
Joh	11:49	Caiaphas, **b.** the high priest that	*5607*
Joh	11:51	but **b.** high priest that year,	*5607*
Joh	13:2	And supper **b.** ended, the devil	
Joh	14:25	**you, b. yet present with you**	
Joh	18:26	high priest, **b.** his kinsman	*5607*
Joh	19:38	Joseph of Arimathaea, **b.** a disciple	*5607*
Joh	20:19	evening, **b.** the first day of the week	
Joh	20:26	came Jesus, the doors **b.** shut,	
Ac	1:3	**b.** seen of them forty days,	
Ac	1:4	And, **b.** assembled together with	
Ac	2:23	**b.** delivered by the determinate	
Ac	2:30	Therefore **b.** a prophet, and	*5225*
Ac	2:33	Therefore **b.** by the right hand	
Ac	3:1	of prayer, **b.** the ninth hour	
Ac	4:2	**B.** grieved that they taught the	
Ac	4:23	And **b.** let go, they went to their	
Ac	4:36	(which is, **b.** interpreted, The son	
Ac	5:2	his wife also **b.** privy to it, and	
Ac	7:55	**b.** full of the Holy Ghost,	*5225*
Ac	13:4	**b.** sent forth by the Holy Ghost,	
Ac	13:12	**b.** astonished at the doctrine of	
Ac	14:8	in his feet, **b.** a cripple from	*5225*
Ac	15:3	And **b.** brought on their way	
Ac	15:21	**b.** read in the synagogues every	
Ac	15:25	good unto us, **b.** assembled with	
Ac	15:32	**b.** prophets also themselves,	*5607*
Ac	15:40	chose Silas, and departed, **b.**	
Ac	16:18	But Paul, **b.** grieved, turned and said	
Ac	16:20	These men, **b.** Jews, do	*5225*
Ac	16:21	neither to observe, **b.** Romans	*5605*
Ac	16:37	openly uncondemned, **b.** Romans,	*5225*
Ac	17:28	and move, and have our **b.**;	*2070*
Ac	18:25	and **b.** fervent in the spirit,	
Ac	19:40	there **b.** no cause whereby we	*5225*
Ac	20:9	**b.** fallen into a deep sleep:	
Ac	22:11	see for the glory of that light, **b.**	
Ac	26:11	and **b.** exceedingly mad against	
Ac	27:2	Macedonian of Thessalonica, **b.**	*5607*
Ac	27:18	And we **b.** exceedingly tossed	
Ro	1:20	**b.** understood by the things	
Ro	1:29	**B.** filled with all unrighteousness,	
Ro	2:18	**b.** instructed out of the law;	
Ro	3:21	**b.** witnessed by the law and the	
Ro	3:24	**B.** justified freely by his grace	
Ro	4:11	he had yet **b.** uncircumcised:	
Ro	4:12	he had **b.** yet uncircumcised	
Ro	4:19	And **b.** not weak in faith, he	
Ro	4:21	And **b.** fully persuaded that, what	
Ro	5:1	Therefore **b.** justified by faith	
Ro	5:9	then, **b.** now justified by his	
Ro	5:10	much more, **b.** reconciled,	
Ro	6:9	that Christ **b.** raised from the dead	
Ro	6:18	**B.** then made free from sin, ye	
Ro	6:22	But now **b.** made free from sin,	
Ro	7:6	**b.** dead wherein we were held;	
Ro	9:11	(For the children **b.** not yet born,	
Ro	10:3	**b.** ignorant of God's righteousness	
Ro	11:17	thou, **b.** a wild olive tree,	*5607*
Ro	12:5	So we, **b.** many, are one body	
Ro	15:16	**b.** sanctified by the Holy Ghost	
1Co	4:12	**b.** reviled, we bless;	
1Co	4:12	**b.** persecuted, we suffer it:	
1Co	4:13	**B.** defamed, we intreat: we are	
1Co	7:18	any man called **b.** circumcised?	
1Co	7:21	Art thou called **b.** a servant?	
1Co	7:22	**b.** a servant, is the Lord's	
1Co	7:22	**b.** free is Christ's servant	
1Co	8:7	conscience **b.** weak is defiled	*5607*
1Co	9:21	(**b.** not without law to God,	*5607*
1Co	10:17	we **b.** many are one bread,	
1Co	12:12	of that one body, **b.** many	*5607*
2Co	5:3	If so be that **b.** clothed we shall	
2Co	5:4	tabernacle do groan, **b.** burdened:	
2Co	8:17	**b.** more forward, of his own	*5225*
2Co	9:11	**B.** enriched in every thing to all	
2Co	10:1	but **b.** absent am bold toward	
2Co	11:9	myself from **b.** burdensome	
2Co	12:16	nevertheless, **b.** crafty, I caught	*5225*
2Co	13:2	and **b.** absent now I write to	
2Co	13:10	these things **b.** absent,	
2Co	13:10	lest **b.** present I should use	
Gal	1:14	**b.** more exceedingly zealous of	*5225*
Gal	2:3	who was with me, **b.** a Greek,	*5607*
Gal	2:14	if thou, **b.** a Jew, livest after	*5225*
Gal	3:13	the curse of the law, **b.** made	
Eph	1:11	inheritance, **b.** predestinated	
Eph	1:18	understanding **b.** enlightened;	
Eph	2:11	that ye **b.** in time past Gentiles	
Eph	2:12	**b.** aliens from the commonwealth	
Eph	2:20	Jesus Christ himself **b.** the chief	*5607*
Eph	3:17	**b.** rooted and grounded in love,	
Eph	4:18	**b.** alienated from the life of God	*5607*
Eph	4:19	Who **b.** past feeling have given	
Php	1:6	**B.** confident of this very thing,	
Php	1:11	**B.** filled with the fruits of	
Php	2:2	the same love, **b.** of one accord,	
Php	2:6	Who, **b.** in the form of God,	*5225*
Php	2:8	And **b.** found in fashion as a man,	
Php	3:10	**b.** made conformable unto his	
Col	1:10	**b.** fruitful in every good work,	
Col	2:2	might be comforted, **b.** knit	
Col	2:13	And you, **b.** dead in your sins	*5607*
1Th	2:8	So **b.** desirous of you, we were	
1Th	2:17	But we, brethren, **b.** taken from	
1Ti	2:14	but the woman **b.** deceived	
1Ti	3:6	novice, lest **b.** lifted up with	
1Ti	3:10	office of a deacon, **b.** found	*5607*
2Ti	1:4	**b.** mindful of thy tears, that I	
2Ti	3:13	worse, deceiving and **b.** deceived	
Tit	1:16	they deny him, **b.** abominable,	*5607*
Tit	3:7	That **b.** justified by his grace,	
Tit	3:11	sinneth, **b.** condemned of himself	*5607*
Phm	9	**b.** such a one as Paul the aged,	*5607*
Heb	1:3	Who **b.** the brightness of his glory,	
Heb	1:4	**B.** made so much better than	
Heb	2:18	**b.** tempted, he is able to succour	
Heb	4:1	fear, lest, a promise **b.** left	
Heb	4:2	not **b.** mixed with faith in them	
Heb	5:9	And **b.** made perfect, he became	
Heb	7:2	first **b.** by interpretation King	
Heb	7:12	For the priesthood **b.** changed,	
Heb	9:11	Christ **b.** come an high priest of	

Heb 11:4 and by it he **b.** dead yet speaketh.
Heb 11:7 Noah, **b.** warned of God of things.
Heb 11:37 and goatskins; **b.** destitute,
Heb 13:3 as **b.** yourselves also in the body. *5607*
Jas 1:25 he **b.** not a forgetful hearer, but *1096*
Jas 2:17 hath not works, is dead, **b.** alone.
1Pe 1:7 your faith, **b.** much more precious *1096*
1Pe 1:23 **B.** born again, not of corruptible
1Pe 2:8 stumble at the word, **b.** disobedient:
1Pe 2:24 that we, **b.** dead to sins, should live
1Pe 3:5 **b.** in subjection unto their own
1Pe 3:7 as **b.** heirs together of the grace of
1Pe 3:18 bring us to God, **b.** put to death
1Pe 3:22 **b.** made subject unto him
1Pe 5:3 as **b.** lords over God's heritage,
1Pe 5:3 but **b.** ensamples to the flock. *1096*
2Pe 3:6 was, **b.** overflowed with water,
2Pe 3:12 heavens **b.** on fire shall be dissolved,
2Pe 3:17 **b.** led away with the error
Re 1:12 **b.** turned, I saw seven golden
Re 12:2 And she **b.** with child cried, *2192*
Re 14:4 **b.** the firstfruits unto God and

BEKAH (be'-kah)
Ex 38:26 A **b.** for every man, that is, 1235

BEL (bel) See also BAAL.
Isa 46:1 **B.** boweth down. Nebo stoopeth, 1078
Jer 50:2 Babylon is taken, **B.** is confounded, 1078
Jer 51:44 I will punish **B.** in Babylon, and 1078

BELA (be'-lah) See also BELAH; BELAITES.
Ge 14:2 and the king of **B.**, which is Zoar. 1106
Ge 14:8 the king of **B.** (the same is Zoar;) 1106
Ge 36:32 And **B.** the son of Beor reigned in 1106
Ge 36:33 And **B.** died, and Jobab the son of 1106
Nu 26:38 of **B.**, the family of the Belaites: 1106
Nu 26:40 sons of **B.** were Ard and Naaman: 1106
1Ch 1:43 **B.** the son of Beor: and the name 1106
1Ch 1:44 And when **B.** was dead, Jobab the 1106
1Ch 5:8 And **B.** the son of Azaz, the son of 1106
1Ch 7:6 sons of Benjamin; **B.**, and Becher, 1106
1Ch 7:7 the sons of **B.**: Ezbon, and Uzzi, 1106
1Ch 8:1 Benjamin begat **B.** his firstborn, 1106
1Ch 8:3 sons of **B.** were, Addar, and Gera, 1106

BELAH (be'-lah) See also BELA.
Ge 46:21 sons of Benjamin were **B.**, and 1106

BELAITES (be'-lah-ites)
Nu 26:38 the family of the **B.**: of Ashbel, 1108

BELCH
Ps 59:7 they **b.** out with their mouth: 5042

BELIAL (be'-le-al)
De 13:13 the children of **B.**, are gone out 1100
Jg 19:22 certain sons of **B.**, beset the 1100
Jg 20:13 the children of **B.**, which are in 1100
1Sa 1:16 handmaid for a daughter of **B.** 1100
1Sa 2:12 the sons of Eli were sons of **B.**; 1100
1Sa 10:27 But the children of **B.** said, How 1100
1Sa 25:17 for he is such a son of **B.**, that a 1100
1Sa 25:25 pray thee, regard this man of **B.**, 1100
1Sa 30:22 men of **B.**, of those that went 1100
2Sa 16:7 man, and thou man of **B.** 1100
2Sa 20:1 there a man of **B.**, whose name 1100
2Sa 23:6 the sons of of **B.** shall be all of 1100
1Ki 21:10 set two men, sons of **B.**, before 1100
1Ki 21:13 came in two men, children of **B.**, 1100
1Ki 21:13 the men of **B.** witnessed against 1100
2Ch 13:7 him vain men, the children of **B.**, 1100
2Co 6:15 what concord hath Christ with **B.**? *955*

BELIED
Jer 5:12 They have **b.** the Lord, and said, 3584

BELIEF See also UNBELIEF.
2Th 2:13 of the Spirit and **b.** of the truth: *4102*

BELIEVE See also BELIEVED; BELIEVEST; BELIEVETH; BELIEVING.
Ex 4:1 they will not **b.** me, nor hearken 539
Ex 4:5 That they may **b.** that the Lord 539
Ex 4:8 if they will not **b.** thee, neither 539
Ex 4:8 that they will **b.** the voice of the 539
Ex 4:9 if they will not **b.** also these two 539
Ex 19:9 with thee, and **b.** thee for ever. 539
Nu 14:11 how long will it be ere they **b.** me, 539
De 1:32 ye did not **b.** the Lord your God, 539
2Ki 17:14 that did not **b.** in the Lord their 539
2Ch 20:20 **B.** in the Lord your God, so shall 539
2Ch 20:20 **b.** his prophets, so shall ye prosper 539
2Ch 32:15 on this manner, neither yet **b.** him: 539
Job 9:16 I not **b.** that he had hearkened 539
Job 39:12 Wilt thou **b.** him, that he will 539
Pr 26:25 When he speaketh fair, **b.** him not: 539
Isa 7:9 If ye will not **b.**, surely ye shall not 539
Isa 43:10 that ye may know and **b.** me, and 539
Jer 12:6 **b.** them not, though they speak 539
Hab 1:5 ye will not **b.**, though it be told 539
Mt 9:28 **B. ye that I am able to do this?** *4100*
Mt 18:6 **little ones which b. in me, it were** *4100*
Mt 21:25 Why did ye not then **b.** him? *4100*
Mt 21:32 **afterwards, that ye might b. him** *4100*
Mt 24:23 **here is Christ, or there, b. it not** *4100*
Mt 24:26 **in the secret chambers; b. it not** *4100*
Mt 27:42 and we will **b.** him *4100*
Mk 1:15 **repent ye, and b. the gospel** *4100,1722*
Mk 5:36 **Be not afraid, only b.** *4100*
Mk 9:23 **If thou canst b., all things are** *4100*
Mk 9:24 Lord, I **b.**; help thou mine *4100*
Mk 9:42 **little ones that b. in me,** *4100*
Mk 11:23 **but shall b. that those things** *4100*
Mk 11:24 **b. that ye receive them, and ye** *4100*
Mk 11:31 say, Why then did ye not **b.** him? 4100
Mk 13:21 **or, lo, he is there; b. him not:** *4100*
Mk 15:32 that we may see and **b.** And they *4100*
Mk 16:7 **signs shall follow them that b.;** *4100*
Lu 8:12 **lest they should b. and be saved** *4100*
Lu 8:13 **which for a while b., and in time** *4100*
Lu 8:50 **b. only, and she shall be made** *4100*
Lu 22:67 **ye will not b.** *4100*
Lu 24:25 **fools, and slow of heart to b.** *4100,1909*
Joh 1:7 all men through him might **b.** *4100*
Joh 1:12 even to them that **b.** on his name: *4100*
Joh 3:12 **and ye b. not,** *4100*
Joh 3:12 **how shall ye b., if I tell you of** *4100*
Joh 4:21 **Woman, b. me, the hour cometh,** *4100*
Joh 4:42 Now we **b.**, not because of thy *4100*
Joh 4:48 **signs and wonders, ye will not b.** *4100*
Joh 5:38 **whom he hath sent, him ye b. not** *4100*
Joh 5:44 **How can ye b., which receive** *4100*
Joh 5:47 **But if ye b. not his writings,** *4100*
Joh 5:47 **how shall ye b. my words?** *4100*
Joh 6:29 **ye b. on him whom he hath sent** *4100*
Joh 6:30 that we may see, and **b.** thee? *4100*
Joh 6:36 **ye also have seen me, and b. not,** *4100*
Joh 6:64 **there are some of you that b. not** *4100*
Joh 6:69 And we **b.** and are sure that thou *4100*
Joh 7:5 neither did his brethren **b.** in him. *4100*
Joh 7:39 which they that **b.** on him should *4100*
Joh 8:24 **if ye b. not that I am he, ye shall** *4100*
Joh 8:45 **I tell you the truth, ye b. me not** *4100*
Joh 8:46 **the truth, why do ye not b. me?** *4100*
Joh 9:18 the Jews did not **b.** concerning *4100*
Joh 9:35 **Dost thou b. on the Son of God?** *4100*
Joh 9:36 he, Lord, that I might **b.** on him? *4100*
Joh 9:38 Lord, I **b.** And he worshipped *4100*
Joh 10:26 **But ye b. not, because ye are not** *4100*
Joh 10:37 **the works of my Father, b. me not** *4100*
Joh 10:38 **though ye b. not me,** *4100*
Joh 10:38 **b. the works; that ye may know,** *4100*
Joh 10:38 **and b., that the Father** *4100*
Joh 11:15 **the intent ye may b.;** *4100*
Joh 11:27 I **b.** that thou art the Christ, the *4100*
Joh 11:40 **thou wouldest b., thou shouldest** *4100*
Joh 11:42 **by I said it, that they may b. that** *4100*
Joh 11:48 thus alone, all men will **b.** on him: *4100*
Joh 12:36 **b. in the light, that ye may be** *4100*
Joh 12:39 Therefore they could not **b.**, *4100*
Joh 12:47 **man hear my words, and b. not,** *4100*
Joh 13:19 **ye may b. that I am he** *4100*
Joh 14:1 **ye b. in God, b. also in me** *4100*
Joh 14:11 **B. me that I am in the Father,** *4100*
Joh 14:11 **else b. me for the very works'** *4100*
Joh 14:29 **it is come to pass, ye might b.** *4100*
Joh 16:9 **because they b. not on me;** *4100*
Joh 16:30 by this we **b.** that thou camest *4100*
Joh 16:31 answered them, **Do ye now b.?** *4100*
Joh 17:20 **for them also which shall b. on me** *4100*
Joh 17:21 **that the world may b. that thou** *4100*
Joh 19:35 he saith true, that ye might **b.** *4100*
Joh 20:25 my hand into his side, I will not **b.** *4100*
Joh 20:31 might **b.** that Jesus is the Christ, *4100*
Ac 8:37 I **b.** that Jesus Christ is the Son of *4100*
Ac 13:39 by him all that **b.** are justified *4100*
Ac 13:41 which ye shall in no wise **b.**, *4100*
Ac 15:7 hear the word of the gospel, and **b.** *4100*
Ac 15:11 But we **b.** that through the grace *4100*
Ac 16:31 **B.** on the Lord Jesus Christ, and *4100*
Ac 19:4 that they should **b.** on him which *4100*
Ac 21:20 of Jews there are which **b.**; *4100*
Ac 21:25 touching the Gentiles which **b.**, *4100*
Ac 27:25 for I **b.** God, that it shall be even *4100*
Ro 3:3 For what if some did not **b.**? *569*
Ro 3:22 unto all and upon all them that **b.** *4100*
Ro 4:11 be the father of all them that **b.**, *4100*
Ro 4:24 if we **b.** on him that raised up *4100*
Ro 6:8 we **b.** that we shall also live with *4100*
Ro 10:9 shalt **b.** in thine heart that God *4100*
Ro 10:14 not believed? and how shall they **b.** *4100*
Ro 15:31 them that do not **b.** in Judaea; *544*
1Co 1:21 preaching to save them that **b.** *4100*
1Co 10:27 If any of them that **b.** not bid you *571*
1Co 11:18 and I partly **b.** it. *4100*
1Co 14:22 not to them that **b.**, *4100*
1Co 14:22 but to them that **b.** not: *571*
1Co 14:22 serveth not for them that **b.** not, *571*
1Co 14:22 but for them which **b.** *4100*
2Co 4:4 minds of them which **b.** not, *571*
2Co 4:13 spoken; we also **b.**, and therefore *4100*
Ga 3:22 might be given to them that **b.** *4100*
Eph 1:19 to us-ward who **b.**, according to *4100*
Php 1:29 not only to **b.** on him, but also to *4100*
1Th 1:7 were ensamples to all that **b.** *4100*
1Th 2:10 ourselves among you that **b.** *4100*
1Th 2:13 worketh also in you that **b.** *4100*
1Th 4:14 if we **b.** that Jesus died and rose *4100*
2Th 1:10 be admired in all them that **b.** *4100*
2Th 2:11 delusion, that they should **b.** a lie: *4100*
1Ti 1:16 should hereafter **b.** on him to life *4100*
1Ti 4:3 them which **b.** and know the truth. *4103*
1Ti 4:10 all men, specially of those that **b.** *4103*
2Ti 2:13 If we **b.** not, yet he abideth *569*
Heb 10:39 of them that **b.** to the saving *4102*
Heb 11:6 must **b.** that he is, and that he is *4100*
Jas 2:19 the devils also **b.**, and tremble. *4100*
1Pe 1:21 Who by him do **b.** in God, that *4100*
1Pe 2:7 Unto you therefore which **b.** he is *4100*
1Jo 3:23 That we should **b.** on the name of *4100*
1Jo 4:1 Beloved, **b.** not every spirit, but *4100*
1Jo 5:13 unto you that **b.** on the name of *4100*
1Jo 5:13 ye may **b.** on the name of the Son *4100*

BELIEVED
Ge 15:6 And he **b.** in the Lord; and he 539
Ge 45:26 Jacob's heart fainted, for he **b.** 539
Ex 4:31 And the people **b.**: and when they 539
Ex 14:31 and **b.** the Lord, and his servant 539
Nu 20:12 Because ye **b.** me not, to sanctify 539
De 9:23 and ye **b.** him not, nor hearkened 539
1Sa 27:12 And Achish **b.** David, saying, He 539
1Ki 10:7 Howbeit I **b.** not the words, until 539
2Ch 9:6 Howbeit I **b.** not their words, until 539
Job 29:24 I laughed on them, they **b.** it not: 539
Ps 27:13 unless I had **b.** to see the goodness 539
Ps 78:22 Because they **b.** not in God, and 539
Ps 78:32 **b.** not for his wondrous works. 539
Ps 106:12 Then **b.** they his words; they sang 539
Ps 106:24 pleasant land they **b.** not his word: 539
Ps 116:10 I **b.**, therefore have I spoken: I 539
Ps 119:66 for I have **b.** thy commandments. 539
Isa 53:1 Who hath **b.** our report? and to 539
Jer 40:14 the son of Ahikam, **b.** them not. 539
La 4:12 of the world, would not have **b.** that 539
Da 6:23 upon him, because he **b.** in his 540
Jon 3:5 So the people of Nineveh **b.** God, 539
Mt 8:13 **and as thou hast b., so be it** *4100*
Mt 21:32 **and ye b. him not: but the** *4100*
Mt 21:32 **publicans and the harlots b. him:** *4100*
Mk 16:11 and had been seen of her, **b.** not. *569*
Mk 16:13 unto the residue: neither **b.** they *4100*
Mk 16:14 because they **b.** not them which *4100*
Lu 1:1 things which are most surely **b.** *4135*
Lu 1:45 blessed is she that **b.**: for there *4100*
Lu 20:5 say, Why then **b.** ye him not? *4100*
Lu 24:11 idle tales, and they **b.** them not. *569*
Lu 24:41 **while they yet b. not for joy, and** *569*
Joh 2:11 his disciples **b.** on him. *4100*
Joh 2:22 and they **b.** the scripture, and the *4100*
Joh 2:23 many **b.** in his name, when they *4100*
Joh 3:18 **already, because he hath not b.** *4100*
Joh 4:39 of the Samaritans of that city **b.** on *4100*
Joh 4:41 many more **b.** because of his own *4100*

Joh 4:50 the man b. the word that Jesus had.... 4100
Joh 4:53 himself b., and his whole house. 4100
Joh 5:46 had ye b. Moses, ... 4100
Joh 5:46 ye would have b. me..................... 4100
Joh 6:64 who they were that b. not, and who... 4100
Joh 7:31 And many of the people b. on him,..... 4100
Joh 7:48 or of the Pharisees b. on him?.......... 4100
Joh 8:30 spake these words, many b. on 4100
Joh 8:31 to those Jews which b. on him,.......... 4100
Joh 10:25 ye b. not: the works that I do 4100
Joh 10:42 And many b. on him there. 4100
Joh 11:45 things which Jesus did, b. on him....... 4100
Joh 12:11 of the Jews went away, and b. on 4100
Joh 12:37 before them, yet they b. not on him:.. 4100
Joh 12:38 Lord, who hath b. our report?........... 4100
Joh 12:42 chief rulers also many b. on him; 4100
Joh 16:27 have b. that I came out from God. .4100
Joh 17:8 and they have b. that thou didst.... 4100
Joh 20:8 the sepulchre, and he saw, and b.. 4100
Joh 20:29 thou hast b.: blessed are they........ 4100
Joh 20:29 have not seen, and yet have b.. 4100
Ac 2:44 And all that b. were together, ... 4100
Ac 4:4 of them which heard the word b.; 4100
Ac 4:32 of them that b. were of one heart 4100
Ac 8:12 But when they b. Philip preaching 4100
Ac 8:13 Then Simon himself b. also: 4100
Ac 9:26 and b. not that he was a disciple. 4100
Ac 9:42 Joppa; and many b. in the Lord............ 4100
Ac 10:45 they of the circumcision which b. 4103
Ac 11:17 who b. on the Lord Jesus Christ; 4100
Ac 11:21 a great number b., and turned........... 4100
Ac 13:12 when he saw what was done, b., ... 4100
Ac 13:48 as were ordained to eternal life b.. 4100
Ac 14:1 Jews and also of the Greeks b.. 4100
Ac 14:23 them to the Lord, on whom they b..... 4100
Ac 15:5 of the Pharisees which b., saying, ... 4100
Ac 16:1 which was a Jewess, and b.; 4103
Ac 17:4 And some of them b., and 3982
Ac 17:5 the Jews which b. not, moved............. 544
Ac 17:12 Therefore many of them b.; also........ 4100
Ac 17:34 certain men clave unto him, and b...... 4100
Ac 18:8 b. on the Lord with all his house;....... 4100
Ac 18:8 of the Corinthians hearing b., ... 4100
Ac 18:27 helped them much which had b. 4100
Ac 19:2 received the Holy Ghost since ye b.?.. 4100
Ac 19:9 divers were hardened, and b. not, ... 544
Ac 19:18 And many that b. came, and.............. 4100
Ac 22:19 every synagogue them that b. on 4100
Ac 27:11 the centurion b. the master and......... 3982
Ac 28:24 And some b. the things which 3982
Ac 28:24 were spoken, and some b. not..............
Ro 4:3 Abraham b. God, and it was........ 569,4100
Ro 4:17 before him whom he b., even God, ... 4100
Ro 4:18 who against hope b. in hope,............ 4100
Ro 10:14 on him in whom they have not b.?...... 4100
Ro 10:16 saith, Lord, who hath b. our report?... 4100
Ro 11:30 ye in times past have not b. God,......... 544
Ro 11:31 so have these also now not b.,........... 544
Ro 13:11 salvation nearer than when we b.. 4100
1Co 3:5 ministers by whom ye b., even as...... 4100
1Co 15:2 unless ye have b. in vain................. 4100
1Co 15:11 or they, so we preach, and so ye b.. .. 4100
2Co 4:13 I b., and therefore have I spoken;...... 4100
Ga 2:16 even we have b. in Jesus Christ,........ 4100
Ga 3:6 as Abraham b. God, and it was........... 4100
Eph 1:13 in whom also after that ye b.,........... 4100
2Th 1:10 our testimony among you was b.)......... 4100
2Th 2:12 who b. not the truth, but had........... 4100
1Ti 3:16 b. on in the world, received up into.... 4100
2Ti 1:12 I know whom I have b., and am 4100
Tit 3:8 that they which have b. in God.......... 4100
Heb 3:18 his rest, but to them that b. not? 544
Heb 4:3 which have b. do enter into rest, ... 4100
Heb 11:31 perished not with them that b. 544
Jas 2:23 Abraham b. God, and it was............... 4100
1Jo 4:16 we have known and b. the love 4100
Jude 5 destroyed them that b. not. 4100

BELIEVERS See also UNBELIEVERS.

Ac 5:14 And b. were the more added............... 4100
1Ti 4:12 be thou an example of the b., in 4103

BELIEVEST

Lu 1:20 because thou b. not my words,.......... 4100
Joh 1:50 thee under the fig tree, b. thou?.... 4100
Joh 11:26 in me shall never die. B. thou....... 4100
Joh 14:10 B. thou not that I am in the........ 4100
Ac 8:37 If thou b. with all thine heart,........... 4100
Ac 26:27 King Agrippa, b. thou the prophets? ... 4100
Ac 26:27 I know that thou b.. 4100
Jas 2:19 Thou b. that there is one God;.......... 4100

BELIEVETH

Job 15:22 He b. not that he shall return 539
Job 39:24 neither b. he that it is the sound 539
Pr 14:15 The simple b. every word: 539
Isa 28:16 he that b. shall not make haste. 539
Mk 9:23 are possible to him that b.. 4100
Mk 16:16 He that b. and is baptized shall...... 4100
Mk 16:16 he that b. not shall be damned. 569
Joh 3:15, 16 whosoever b. in him should 4100
Joh 3:18 He that b. on him is not 4100
Joh 3:18 but he that b. not is condemned.... 4100
Joh 3:36 He that b. on the Son hath 4100
Joh 3:36 that b. not the Son shall not see.......... 544
Joh 5:24 and b. on him that sent me,.......... 4100
Joh 6:35 he that b. on me shall never thirst. 4100
Joh 6:40 and b. on him, may have 4100
Joh 6:47 He that b. on me hath everlasting .. 4100
Joh 7:38 He that b. on me, as the scripture.. 4100
Joh 11:25 he that b. in me, though he were .. 4100
Joh 11:26 and b. in me shall never die.......... 4100
Joh 12:44 He that b. on me, b. not on me,.... 4100
Joh 12:46 that whosoever b. on me should 4100
Joh 14:12 He that b. on me, the works that I. 4100
Ac 10:43 whosoever b. in him shall receive....... 4100
Ro 1:16 unto salvation to every one that b.; 4100
Ro 3:26 justifier of him which b. in......... 1537,4102
Ro 4:5 but b. on him that justifieth the.......... 4100
Ro 9:33 whosoever b. on him shall not be....... 4100
Ro 10:4 righteousness to every one that b.. 4100
Ro 10:10 For with the heart man b. unto.......... 4100
Ro 10:11 Whosoever b. on him shall not be 4100
Ro 14:2 For one b. that he may eat all 4100
1Co 7:12 hath a wife, that b. not, and she.......... 571
1Co 7:13 hath an husband that b. not, and.......... 571
1Co 13:7 b. all things, hopeth all things. 4100
1Co 14:24 there come in one that b. not, or 571
2Co 6:15 hath he that b. with infidel?.............. 4103
1Ti 5:16 If any man or woman that b.............. 4103
1Pe 2:6 and he that b. on him shall not be...... 4100
1Jo 5:1 Whosoever b. that Jesus is the 4100
1Jo 5:5 he that b. that Jesus is the Son 4100
1Jo 5:10 He that b. on the Son of God: 4100
1Jo 5:10 he that b. not God hath made........... 4100
1Jo 5:10 because he b. not the record............ 4100

BELIEVING See also UNBELIEVING.

Mt 21:22 ye shall ask in prayer, b., ye shall.. 4100
Joh 20:27 and be not faithless, but b.......... 4103
Joh 20:31 and that b. ye might have life 4100
Ac 16:34 rejoiced, b. in God with all his.......... 4100
Ac 24:14 b. all things which are written 4100
Ro 15:13 you with all joy and peace in b.,........ 4100
1Ti 6:2 And they that have b. masters,.......... 4103
1Pe 1:8 yet b., ye rejoice with joy................ 4100

BELL See also BELLS.

Ex 28:34 b. and a pomegranate, ... 6472
Ex 28:34 a golden b. 6472
Ex 39:26 A b. and a pomegranate, a b. 6472

BELLIES

Tit 1:12 always liars, evil beasts, slow b.. 1064

BELLOW See also BELLOWS.

Jer 50:11 as the heifer at grass, and b. as......... 6670

BELLOWS

Jer 6:29 The b. are burned, the lead is........... 4647

BELLS

Ex 28:33 and b. of gold between them............ 6472
Ex 39:25 b. of pure gold, and put the b. 6472
Zec 14:20 there be upon the b. of the horses, ... 4698

BELLY See also BELLIES.

Ge 3:14 upon thy b. shalt thou go, and............ 1512
Le 11:42 goeth upon the b., and whatsoever..... 1512
Nu 5:21 thy thigh to rot, and thy b. to............. 990
Nu 5:22 to make thy b. to swell, and thy.......... 990
Nu 5:27 her b. shall swell, and her thigh 990
Nu 25:8 and the woman through her b. 6897
Jg 3:21 thrust it into his b. 990
Jg 3:22 not draw the dagger out of his b., ... 990
1Ki 7:20 over against the b. which was by......... 990
Job 3:11 ghost when I came out of the b.? 990
Job 15:2 and fill his b. with the east wind?......... 990
Job 15:35 vanity, and their b. prepareth............. 990
Job 20:15 God shall cast them out of his b.. 990
Job 20:20 shall not feel quietness in his b.,......... 990
Job 20:23 he is about to fill his b., God 990
Job 32:19 b. is as wine which hath no vent; 990
Job 40:16 his force is in the navel of his b.......... 990
Ps 17:14 whose b. thou fillest with thy hid......... 990
Ps 22:10 art my God from my mother's b.. 990
Ps 31:9 grief, yea, my soul and my b.. 990
Ps 44:25 to the dust, our b. cleaveth unto 990
Pr 13:25 but the b. of the wicked shall want. 990
Pr 18:8 the innermost parts of the b.. 990
Pr 18:20 A man's b. shall be satisfied with......... 990
Pr 20:27 all the inward parts of the b.............. 990
Pr 20:30 stripes the inward parts of the b.......... 990
Pr 26:22 into the innermost parts of the b.. 990
Ca 5:14 his b. is as bright ivory, overlaid........ 4578
Ca 7:2 thy b. is like an heap of wheat set........ 990
Isa 46:3 borne by me from the b., which 990
Jer 1:5 Before I formed thee in the b. I.......... 990
Jer 51:34 he hath filled his b. with my.............. 3770
Eze 3:3 cause thy b. to eat, and fill thy............ 990
Da 2:32 arms of silver, his b. and his............ 4577
Jon 1:17 in the b. of the fish three days 4578
Jon 2:1 Lord his God out of the fish's b.. 4578
Jon 2:2 out of the b. of hell cried I, and 990
Hab 3:16 my b. trembled; my lips quivered 990
Mt 12:40 three nights in the whale's b.;....... 2836
Mt 15:17 in at the mouth goeth into the b.,.. 2836
Mk 7:19 but into the b., and goeth out into .2836
Lu 15:16 he would fain have filled his b...... 2836
Joh 7:38 out of his b. shall flow rivers of.... 2836
Ro 16:18 Jesus Christ, but their own b.; 2836
1Co 6:13 Meats for the b., ... 2836
1Co 6:13 and the b. for meats:........................ 2836
Php 3:19 whose God is their b., and whose 2836
Re 10:9 it shall make thy b. bitter, but it 2836
Re 10:10 as I had eaten it, my b. was bitter. 2836

BELONG See also BELONGED; BELONGETH; BELONGEST; BELONGING.

Ge 40:8 Do not interpretations b. to God?...........
Le 27:24 the possession of the land did b.. ....
Nu 1:50 and over all things that b. to it: ....
De 29:29 The secret things b. unto the Lord...........
De 29:29 things which are revealed b. unto.............
Ps 47:9 shields of the earth b. unto God...............
Ps 68:20 the Lord b. the issues from death. ....
Pr 24:23 These things also b. to the wise. ....
Da 9:9 To the Lord our God b. mercies ....
Mk 9:41 because ye b. to Christ, verily I 1510
Lu 19:42 things which b. unto thy peace! ....
1Co 7:32 careth for the things that b. to................

BELONGED

Jos 17:8 b. to the children of Ephraim;..................
1Sa 21:7 the herdmen that b. to Saul. ....
1Ki 1:8 mighty men which b. to David, ...
1Ki 15:27 which b. to the Philistines;......................
1Ki 16:15 which b. to the Philistines.......................
2Ki 14:28 and Hamath, which b. to Judah, ...
1Ch 2:23 these b. to the sons of Machir..................
1Ch 13:6 Kirjath-jearim, which b. to Judah, ...
2Ch 26:23 the burial which b. to the kings;...............
Es 1:9 house which b. to king Ahasuerus ....
Es 2:9 things as b. to her, and seven........... 4490
Lu 23:7 he b. unto Herod's jurisdiction, ... 1510

BELONGEST

1Sa 30:13 unto him, To whom b. thou?..................

BELONGETH

Nu 8:24 This is it that b. unto the Levites:...........
De 32:35 To me b. vengeance, and ....
Jg 19:14 by Gibeah, which b. to Benjamin. ....
Jg 20:4 into Gibeah that b. to Benjamin,...............
1Sa 17:1 at Shochoh, which b. to Judah,..................
1Sa 30:14 the coast which b. to Judah, and ....
1Ki 17:9 Zarephath, which b. to Zidon, ...
1Ki 19:3 Beer-sheba, which b. to Judah, ...
2Ki 14:11 Beth-shemesh, which b. to Judah. ....
2Ch 25:21 Beth-shemesh, which b. to Judah. ....
Ezr 10:4 for this matter b. unto thee:......................
Ps 3:8 Salvation b. unto the Lord: thy ....
Ps 62:11 heard this; that power b. unto God. ....
Ps 62:12 unto thee, O Lord, b. mercy: for thou ......
Ps 94:1 O Lord God, to whom vengeance b.; ....
Ps 94:1 O God, to whom vengeance b., shew.........

Da 9:7 O Lord, righteousness **b.** unto thee,
Da 9:8 O Lord, to us **b.** confusion of face,
Heb 5:14 But strong meat **b.** to them that *1510*
Heb 10:30 Vengeance **b.** unto me, I will

BELONGING
Nu 7:9 service of the sanctuary **b.** unto
Ru 2:3 a part of the field **b.** unto Boaz
1Sa 6:18 of the Philistines **b.** to the five lords,
Pr 26:17 with strife **b.** not to him, is like
Lu 9:10 desert place **b.** to the city called

BELOVED See also BELOVED'S; WELL BELOVED.
De 21:15 wives, one **b.**, and another hated, 157
De 21:15 both the **b.** and the hated; 157
De 21:16 not make the son of the **b.** firstborn 157
De 33:12 The **b.** of the Lord shall dwell in 3039
Ne 13:26 was **b.** of his God, and God made 157
Ps 60:5 That thy **b.** may be delivered; 3039
Ps 108:6 That thy **b.** may be delivered: 3039
Ps 127:2 for so he giveth his **b.** sleep 3039
Pr 4:3 only **b.** in the sight of my mother
Ca 1:14 My **b.** is unto me as a cluster 1730
Ca 1:16 Behold, thou art fair, my **b.**, 157
Ca 2:3 so is my **b.** among the sons 1730
Ca 2:8 The voice of my **b.**! behold, he 1730
Ca 2:9 My **b.** is like a roe or a young hart: 1730
Ca 2:10 My **b.** spake, and said unto me, 1730
Ca 2:16 My **b.** is mine, and I am his: 1730
Ca 2:17 turn, my **b.**, and be thou like a roe 1730
Ca 4:16 **b.** come into his garden, and eat 1730
Ca 5:1 yea, drink abundantly, O **b.** 1730
Ca 5:2 the voice of my **b.** that knocketh, 1730
Ca 5:4 My **b.** put in his hand by the hole 1730
Ca 5:5 rose up to open to my **b.**; and my 1730
Ca 5:6 to my **b.**; but my **b.** had withdrawn 1730
Ca 5:8 if ye find my **b.**, that ye tell him, 1730
Ca 5:9 thy **b.** more than another **b.**, O thou 1730
Ca 5:9 **b.** more than another **b.**, that thou 1730
Ca 5:10 my **b.** is white and ruddy, the 1730
Ca 5:16 This is my **b.**, and this is my friend 1730
Ca 6:1 Whither is thy **b.** gone, O thou 1730
Ca 6:1 whither is thy **b.** turned aside? 1730
Ca 6:2 My **b.** is gone down into his garden, 1730
Ca 6:3 my beloved's, and my **b.** is mine: 1730
Ca 7:9 the best wine for my **b.** that goeth, 1730
Ca 7:11 come my **b.**, let us go forth 1730
Ca 7:13 I have laid up for thee, O my **b.**. 1730
Ca 8:5 the wilderness, leaning upon her **b.**? 1730
Ca 8:14 Make haste, my **b.**, and be thou like 1730
Isa 5:1 to my wellbeloved a song of my **b.** 1730
Jer 11:15 hath my **b.** to do in mine house, 3039
Jer 12:7 dearly **b.** of my soul into the hand 3033
Da 9:23 greatly **b.**: therefore understand 2530
Da 10:11 a man greatly **b.**, understand the 2530
Da 10:19 said, O man greatly **b.**, fear not: 2530
Ho 3:1 yet, love a woman **b.** of her friend, 157
Ho 9:16 even the **b.** fruit of their womb 4261
Mt 3:17 saying, This is my **b.** Son, in whom *27*
Mt 12:18 I have chosen; my **b.** in whom, *27*
Mt 17:5 which said, This is my **b.** Son, *27*
Mk 1:11 Thou art my **b.** Son, in whom *27*
Mk 9:7 saying, This is my **b.** Son: hear him *27*
Lu 3:22 which said, Thou art my **b.** Son; *27*
Lu 9:35 saying, This is my **b.** Son: hear *27*
Lu 20:13 **shall I do? I will send my b. son:** *27*
Ac 15:25 chosen men unto you with our **b.** *27*
Ro 1:7 To all that be in Rome, **b.** of God, *27*
Ro 9:25 and her **b.**, which was not **b.** *25*
Ro 11:28 touching the election, they are **b.** *27*
Ro 12:19 Dearly **b.**, avenge not yourselves, *27*
Ro 16:8 Greet Amplias my **b.** in the Lord. *27*
Ro 16:9 helper in Christ, and Stachys my **b.** *27*
Ro 16:12 Salute the **b.** Persis, which laboured *27*
1Co 4:14 but as my **b.** sons I warn you *27*
1Co 4:17 who is my **b.** son, and faithful in the *27*
1Co 10:14 my dearly **b.**, flee from idolatry *27*
1Co 15:58 Therefore, my **b.** brethren, be ye *27*
2Co 7:1 dearly **b.**, let us cleanse ourselves *27*
2Co 12:19 we do all things, dearly **b.**, for your *27*
Eph 1:6 he hath made us accepted in the **b.** *25*
Eph 6:21 a **b.** brother and faithful minister *27*
Php 2:12 Wherefore, my **b.**, as ye have *27*
Php 4:1 brethren dearly **b.** and longed for, *27*
Php 4:1 stand fast in the Lord, my dearly **b.** *27*
Col 3:12 as the elect of God, holy and **b.**, *25*
Col 4:7 declare unto you, who is a **b.** brother *27*
Col 4:9 Onesimus, a faithful and **b.** brother, *27*
Col 4:14 Luke, the **b.** physician, and Demas, *27*
1Th 1:4 Knowing, brethren **b.**, your election *25*
2Th 2:13 for you, brethren **b.** of the Lord, *25*
1Ti 6:2 because they are faithful and **b.**, *27*
2Ti 1:2 To Timothy, my dearly **b.** son: *27*
Phm 1 unto Philemon our dearly **b.**, and *27*
Phm 2 to our **b.** Apphia, and Archippus *27*
Phm 16 but above a servant, a brother **b.**, *27*
Heb 6:9 **b.**, we are persuaded better things *27*
Jas 1:16 Do not err, my **b.** brethren. *27*
Jas 1:19 Wherefore, my **b.** brethren, let every *27*
Jas 2:5 Hearken, my **b.** brethren, Hath not *27*
1Pe 2:11 **b.**, I beseech you as strangers *27*
1Pe 4:12 **B.**, think it not strange concerning *27*
2Pe 1:17 This is my **b.** Son, in whom I am *27*
2Pe 3:1 This second epistle, **b.**, I now write *27*
2Pe 3:8 But, **b.**, be not ignorant of this *27*
2Pe 3:14 Wherefore, **b.**, seeing that ye look *27*
2Pe 3:15 our **b.** brother Paul also according *27*
2Pe 3:17 Ye therefore, **b.**, seeing ye know *27*
1Jo 3:2 **B.**, now are we the sons of God, *27*
1Jo 3:21 **B.**, if our heart condemn us not, *27*
1Jo 4:1 **B.**, believe not every spirit, but try *27*
1Jo 4:7 **B.**, let us love one another: for love *27*
1Jo 4:11 **B.**, if God so loved us, we ought also *27*
3Jo 2 **B.**, I wish above all things that *27*
3Jo 5 **B.**, thou doest faithfully whatsoever *27*
3Jo 11 **B.**, follow not that which is evil, *27*
Jude 3 **B.**, when I gave all diligence to *27*
Jude 17 **b.**, remember ye the words which *27*
Jude 20 But ye, **b.**, building up yourselves *27*
Re 20:9 of the saints about, and the **b.** city: *25*

BELOVED'S
Ca 6:3 my **b.**, and my beloved is mine: 1730
Ca 7:10 I am my **b.**, and his desire is 1730

BELSHAZZAR (bel-shaz'-ar)
Da 5:1 **B.** the king made a great feast to 1113
Da 5:2 **B.**, whiles he tasted the wine, 1113
Da 5:9 was king **B.** greatly troubled, and 1113
Da 5:22 **B.**, hast not humbled thine heart, 1113
Da 5:29 **B.**, and they clothed Daniel 1113
Da 5:30 **B.**, the king of the Chaldeans slain. 1113
Da 7:1 **B.** king of Babylon Daniel had 1113
Da 8:1 **B.** a vision appeared unto me, 1113

BELTESHAZZAR (bel-te-shaz'-ar) See also DANIEL.
Da 1:7 gave unto Daniel the name of **B.**; 1095
Da 2:26 to Daniel, whose name was **B.**, 1096
Da 4:8 in before me, whose name was **B.**, 1096
Da 4:9 O **B.**, master of the magicians, 1096
Da 4:18 **B.**, declare the interpretation 1096
Da 4:19 whose name was **B.**, was astonied 1096
Da 4:19 and said, **B.**, let not the dream, 1096
Da 4:19 **B.** answered and said, My lord, 1096
Da 5:12 Daniel, whom the king named **B.** 1096
Da 10:1 Daniel, whose name was called **B.**; 1095

BEMOAN See also BEMOANED; BEMOANING.
Jer 15:5 who shall **b.** thee? or who shall go 5110
Jer 16:5 neither go to lament nor **b.** them: 5110
Jer 22:10 ye not for the dead, neither **b.** him: 5110
Jer 48:17 All ye that are about him, **b.** him; 5110
Na 3:7 is laid waste: who will **b.** her? 5110

BEMOANED
Job 42:11 and they **b.** him, and comforted 5110

BEMOANING
Jer 31:18 heard Ephraim **b.** himself thus; 5110

BEN (ben) See also BEN-AMMI; BEN-HADAD; BEN-HAIL; BEN-HANAN; BEN-ONI; BEN-ZOHETH.
1Ch 15:18 second degree, Zechariah, **B.**, and 1122

BEN-AMMI (ben-am'-mi)
Ge 19:38 bare a son, and called his name **B.** 1151

BENAIAH (ben-ay'-ah)
2Sa 8:18 And **B.** the son of Jehoiada was 1141
2Sa 20:23 and **B.** the son of Jehoiada was 1141
2Sa 23:20 **B.** the son of Jehoiada, the son of 1141
2Sa 23:22 These things did **B.** the son of 1141
2Sa 23:30 **B.** the Pirathonite, Hiddai of the 1141
1Ki 1:8 priest, and **B.** the son of Jehoiada, 1141
1Ki 1:10 Nathan the prophet, and **B.**, 1141
1Ki 1:26 and Zadok the priest, and **B.** the 1141
1Ki 1:32 and **B.** the son of Jehoiada. 1141
1Ki 1:36 **B.** the son of Jehoiada answered 1141
1Ki 1:38 and Nathan the prophet, and **B.** 1141
1Ki 1:44 **B.** the son of Jehoiada, and the 1141
1Ki 2:25 Solomon sent by the hand of **B.** 1141
1Ki 2:29 sent **B.** the son of Jehoiada, 1141
1Ki 2:30 And **B.** came to the tabernacle 1141
1Ki 2:30 **B.** brought the king word again, 1141
1Ki 2:34 **B.** the son of Jehoiada went up, 1141
1Ki 2:35 king put **B.** the son of Jehoiada 1141
1Ki 2:46 So the king commanded **B.** the son 1141
1Ki 4:4 **B.** the son of Jehoiada was over 1141
1Ch 4:36 and Adiel, and Jesimiel, and **B.**, 1141
1Ch 11:22 **B.** the son of Jehoiada, the son of 1141
1Ch 11:24 These things did **B.** the son of 1141
1Ch 11:31 of Benjamin, **B.** the Pirathonite, 1141
1Ch 15:18 Eliab, and **B.**, and Maaseiah, 1141
1Ch 15:20 and Eliab, and Maaseiah, and **B.**, 1141
1Ch 15:24 Zechariah, and **B.**, and Eliezer, 1141
1Ch 16:5 and Eliab, and **B.**, and Obed-edom: 1141
1Ch 16:6 **B.** also and Jahaziel the priests 1141
1Ch 18:17 And **B.** the son of Jehoiada was 1141
1Ch 27:5 for the third month was **B.** the son 1141
1Ch 27:6 This is that **B.**, who was mighty 1141
1Ch 27:14 month was **B.** the Pirathonite, 1141
1Ch 27:34 was Jehoiada the son of **B.**, 1141
2Ch 20:14 of Zechariah, the son of **B.**, the 1141
2Ch 31:13 Mahath, and **B.**, were overseers 1141
Ezr 10:25 Eleazar, and Malchijah, and **B.** 1141
Ezr 10:30 Chelal, **B.**, Maaseiah, Mattaniah, 1141
Ezr 10:35 **B.**, Bedeiah, Chelluh, 1141
Ezr 10:43 Zebina, Jadau, and Joel, **B.** 1141
Eze 11:1 and Pelatiah the son of **B.**, 1141
Eze 11:13 that Pelatiah the son of **B.** died. 1141

BENCHES
Eze 27:6 made thy **b.** of ivory, brought out 7175

BEND See also BENDETH; BENDING; BENT.
Ps 11:2 the wicked **b.** their bow, they 1869
Ps 64:3 **b.** their bows to shoot their 1869
Jer 9:3 they **b.** their tongues like their 1869
Jer 46:9 Lydians, that handle and **b.** the 1869
Jer 50:14 all ye that **b.** the bow, 1869
Jer 50:29 Babylon: all ye that **b.** the bow, 1869
Jer 51:3 bendeth let the archer **b.** his bow, 1869
Eze 17:7 vine did **b.** her roots toward him, 3719

BENDETH
Ps 58:7 he **b.** his bow to shoot his arrows, 1869
Jer 51:3 Against him that **b.** let the archer 1869

BENDING
Isa 60:14 thee shall come **b.** unto thee; 7817

BENE See BENE-BERAH; BENE-JAAKAN.

BENEATH
Ge 35:8 and she was buried **b.** Beth-el. 8478
Ex 20:4 or that is in the earth **b.**, or that 8478
Ex 26:24 they shall be coupled together **b.**, 4295
Ex 27:5 under the compass of the altar **b.**, 4295
Ex 28:33 And **b.** upon the hem of it thou
Ex 32:19 and brake them **b.** the mount. 8478
Ex 36:29 they were coupled **b.**, and coupled 4295
Ex 38:4 thereof, **b.** unto the midst of it. 4295
De 4:18 that is in the waters **b.** the earth: 8478
De 4:39 upon the earth **b.**: there is none 8478
De 5:8 or that is in the earth **b.**, 8478
De 5:8 or that is in the waters **b.** 8478
De 28:13 above only, thou shalt not be **b.**; 4295
De 33:13 and for the deep that coucheth **b.**, 8478
Jos 2:11 in heaven above, and in earth **b.**. 8478
Jg 7:8 the host of Midian was **b.** him 8478
1Ki 4:12 which is by Zartanah **b.** Jezreel, 8478
1Ki 7:29 and **b.** the lions and oxen were 8478
1Ki 8:23 in heaven above, or on earth **b.**, 8478
Job 18:16 His roots shall be dried up **b.**, and 8478
Pr 15:24 that he may depart from hell **b.**. 4295
Isa 14:9 Hell from **b.** is moved for thee to 8478
Isa 51:6 and look upon the earth **b.** 8478
Jer 31:37 of the earth searched out **b.**, 4295
Am 2:9 from above, and his roots from **b.**. 8478
Mk 14:66 And as Peter was **b.** in the palace, *2736*
Joh 8:23 **Ye are from b.; I am from above:** *2736*
Ac 2:19 and signs in the earth **b.**; blood, *2736*

BENE-BERAK (be''-ne-be'-rak)
Jos 19:45 Jehud, and **B.**, and Gath-rimmon, 1138

BENEFACTORS
Lu 22:25 **authority upon them are called b.** *2110*

BENEFIT See also BENEFITS.
2Ch 32:25 according to the **b.** done unto 1576
Jer 18:10 wherewith I said I would **b.** them. 3190
2Co 1:15 that ye might have a second **b.**; *5485*
1Ti 6:2 and beloved, partakers of the **b.** *2108*
Phm 14 that thy **b.** should not be as it *18*

BENEFITS
Ps 68:19 who daily loadeth us with **b.**,
Ps 103:2 and forget not all his **b.**: 1576
Ps 116:12 Lord for all his **b.** toward me? 8408

BENE-JAAKAN (be''-ne-ja'-a-kan)
Nu 33:31 from Moseroth, and pitched in **B.** 1142
Nu 33:32 removed from **B.**, and encamped 1142

BENEVOLENCE
1Co 7:3 render unto the wife due **b.** *2133*

BEN-HADAD (ben'-ha-dad)
1Ki 15:18 and king Asa sent them to **B.**, 1131
1Ki 15:20 So **B.** hearkened unto king Asa, 1131
1Ki 20:1 And **B.** the king of Syria gathered 1131
1Ki 20:2 said unto him, Thus saith **B.**, 1131
1Ki 20:5 Thus speaketh **B.**, saying, 1131
1Ki 20:9 unto the messengers of **B.**, Tell 1131
1Ki 20:10 And **B.** sent unto him, and said, 1131
1Ki 20:12 when **B.** heard this message,
1Ki 20:16 **B.** was drinking himself drunk 1130
1Ki 20:17 and **B.** sent out, and they told him, 1130
1Ki 20:20 and **B.** the king of Syria escaped 1130
1Ki 20:26 the year, that **B.** numbered the 1130
1Ki 20:30 And **B.** fled, and came into the city, 1130
1Ki 20:32 thy servant **B.** saith, I pray thee, 1130
1Ki 20:33 and they said, Thy brother **B.** 1130
1Ki 20:33 Then **B.** came forth to him;
1Ki 20:34 And **B.** said unto him,
2Ki 6:24 after this, that **B.** king of Syria 1130
2Ki 8:7 and **B.** the king of Syria was sick; 1130
2Ki 8:9 and said, Thy son **B.** king of Syria 1130
2Ki 13:3 the hand of **B.** the son of Hazael, 1130
2Ki 13:24 and **B.** his son reigned in his stead. 1130
2Ki 13:25 of the hand of **B.** the son of Hazael 1130
2Ch 16:2 and sent to **B.** king of Syria, that 1130
2Ch 16:4 And **B.** hearkened unto king Asa, 1130
Jer 49:27 shall consume the palaces of **B.** 1130
Am 1:4 shall devour the palaces of **B.** 1130

BEN-HAIL (ben-ha'-il)
2Ch 17:7 sent to his princes, even to **B.**, 1134

BEN-HANAN (ben-ha'-nan)
1Ch 4:20 Amnon, and Rinnah, **B.**, and 1135

BENINU (ben'-i-nu)
Ne 10:13 Hodijah, Bani, **B.** 1148

BENJAMIN (ben'-ja-min) See also BENJAMIN'S; BENJAMITE.
Ge 35:18 but his father called him **B.** 1144
Ge 35:24 sons of Rachel; Joseph, and **B.**: 1144
Ge 42:4 **B.**, Joseph's brother, Jacob sent 1144
Ge 42:36 and ye will take **B.** away: 1144
Ge 43:14 away your other brother, and **B.** 1144
Ge 43:15 money in their hand, and **B.**; 1144
Ge 43:16 Joseph saw **B.** with them, he said 1144
Ge 43:29 saw his brother **B.**, his mother's 1144
Ge 45:12 and the eyes of my brother **B.**, 1144
Ge 45:14 and wept; and **B.** wept upon 1144
Ge 45:22 But to **B.** he gave three hundred 1144
Ge 46:19 Jacob's wife; Joseph, and **B.** 1144
Ge 46:21 sons of **B.** were Belah, and Becher, 1144
Ge 49:27 **B.** shall ravin as a wolf: in the 1144
Ex 1:3 Issachar, Zebulun, and **B.**, 1144
Nu 1:11 Of **B.**; Abidan the son of Gideoni. 1144
Nu 1:36 Of the children of **B.**, by their 1144
Nu 1:37 even of the tribe of **B.**, were thirty 1144
Nu 2:22 Then the tribe of **B.**: 1144
Nu 2:22 the captain of the sons of **B.**, 1144
Nu 7:60 prince of the children of **B.**, offered: 1144
Nu 10:24 the children of **B.** was Abidan the 1144
Nu 13:9 Of the tribe of **B.**, Palti the son of 1144
Nu 26:38 The sons of **B.** after their families: 1144
Nu 26:41 **B.** after their families; and they 1144
Nu 34:21 Of the tribe of **B.**, Elidad the son 1144
De 27:12 and Issachar, and Joseph, and **B.**: 1144
De 33:12 And of **B.** he said, The beloved of 1144
Jos 18:11 children of **B.** came up according 1144
Jos 18:20 children of **B.**, by the coasts 1144
Jos 18:21 **B.** according to their families were 1144
Jos 18:28 inheritance of the children of **B.** 1144
Jos 21:4 of the tribe of **B.**, thirteen cities. 1144
Jos 21:17 of **B.**, Gibeon with her suburbs, 1144
Jg 1:21 **B.** did not drive out the Jebusites 1144
Jg 1:21 of **B.** in Jerusalem unto this day. 1144
Jg 5:14 after thee, **B.**, among thy people; 1144
Jg 10:9 against Judah, and against **B.**, 1144
Jg 19:14 by Gibeah, which belongeth to **B.** 1144
Jg 20:3 children of **B.** heard that the 1144
Jg 20:4 belongeth to **B.**, I and my 1144
Jg 20:10 come to Gibeah of **B.**, according to 1144
Jg 20:12 men through all the tribe of **B.**, 1144
Jg 20:13 **B.** would not hearken to the voice 1144
Jg 20:14 children of **B.** gathered themselves 1144
Jg 20:15 of **B.** were numbered at that time 1144
Jg 20:17 Israel, beside **B.**, were numbered 1144
Jg 20:18 against the children of **B.**? 1144
Jg 20:20 went out to battle against **B.**; 1144
Jg 20:21 of **B.** came forth out of Gibeah, 1144
Jg 20:23 of **B.** my brother? And the Lord 1144
Jg 20:24 near against the children of **B.** 1144
Jg 20:25 **B.** went forth against them out of 1144
Jg 20:28 against the children of **B.** my 1144
Jg 20:30 against the children of **B.** on the 1144
Jg 20:31 **B.** went out against the people, 1144
Jg 20:32 **B.** said, They are smitten down 1144
Jg 20:35 the Lord smote **B.** before Israel: 1144
Jg 20:36 So the children of **B.** saw that they 1144
Jg 20:39 in the battle, **B.** began to smite 1144
Jg 20:41 the men of **B.** were amazed: 1144
Jg 20:44 fell of **B.** eighteen thousand men; 1144
Jg 20:46 fell that day of **B.** were twenty and 1144
Jg 20:48 upon the children of **B.**, and smote 1144
Jg 21:1 give his daughter unto **B.** to wife. 1144
Jg 21:6 Israel repented them for **B.** their 1144
Jg 21:13 speak to the children of **B.** that 1144
Jg 21:14 And **B.** came again at that time; 1144
Jg 21:15 repented them for **B.**, because the 1144
Jg 21:16 women are destroyed out of **B.**? 1144
Jg 21:17 that be escaped of **B.**, that a tribe 1144
Jg 21:18 be he that giveth a wife to **B.** 1144
Jg 21:20 commanded the children of **B.** 1144
Jg 21:21 Shiloh, and go to the land of **B.** 1144
Jg 21:23 children of **B.** did so, and took 1144
1Sa 4:12 ran a man of **B.** out of the army, 1144
1Sa 9:1 a man of **B.**, whose name was Kish, 1144
1Sa 9:16 man out of the land of **B.**, and thou 1144
1Sa 9:21 the families of the tribe of **B.**? 1144
1Sa 10:2 in the border of **B.** of Zelzah; 1144
1Sa 10:20 near, the tribe of **B.** was taken. 1144
1Sa 10:21 tribe of **B.** to come near by their 1144
1Sa 13:2 with Jonathan in Gibeah of **B.**: 1144
1Sa 13:15 up from Gilgal unto Gibeah of **B.** 1144
1Sa 13:16 with them, abode in Gibeah of **B.**: 1144
1Sa 14:16 watchmen of Saul in Gibeah of **B.** 1144
2Sa 2:9 and over Ephraim, and over **B.**, 1144
2Sa 2:15 went over by number twelve of **B.**, 1144
2Sa 2:25 children of **B.** gathered themselves 1144
2Sa 2:31 of David had smitten of **B.**, and 1144
2Sa 3:19 Abner also spake in the ears of **B.**: 1144
2Sa 3:19 good to the whole house of **B.** 1144
2Sa 4:2 Beerothite, of the children of **B.**: 1144
2Sa 4:2 Beeroth also was reckoned to **B.**: 1144
2Sa 19:17 thousand men of **B.** with him, 1144
2Sa 21:14 in the country of **B.** in Zelah, 1144
2Sa 23:29 of Gibeah of the children of **B.**, 1144
1Ki 4:18 Shimei the son of Elah, in **B.**: 1144
1Ki 12:21 Judah, with the tribe of **B.**, an 1144
1Ki 12:23 unto all the house of Judah and **B.**, 1144
1Ki 15:22 Asa built with them Geba of **B.** 1144
1Ch 2:2 Dan, Joseph, and **B.**, Naphtali, 1144
1Ch 6:60 And out of the tribe of **B.**; Geba 1144
1Ch 6:65 children of **B.**, these cities, which 1144
1Ch 7:6 The sons of **B.**; Bela, and Becher, 1144
1Ch 7:10 Jeush, and **B.**, and Ehud, and 1144
1Ch 8:1 Now **B.** begat Bela his firstborn, 1144
1Ch 8:40 All these are of the sons of **B.** 1144
1Ch 9:3 children of **B.**, and of the children 1144
1Ch 9:7 And of the sons of **B.**; Sallu the 1144
1Ch 11:31 to the children of **B.**, Benaiah 1144
1Ch 12:2 even of Saul's brethren of **B.** 1144
1Ch 12:16 came of the children of **B.**, and 1144
1Ch 12:29 children of **B.**, the kindred of 1144
1Ch 21:6 But Levi and **B.** counted he not 1144
1Ch 27:21 of **B.**, Jaasiel the son of Abner: 1144
2Ch 11:1 house of Judah and **B.**, saying, 1144
2Ch 11:3 all Israel in Judah and **B.**, saying, 1144
2Ch 11:10 which are in Judah and in **B.** 1144
2Ch 11:12 having Judah and **B.** on his side. 1144
2Ch 11:23 all the countries of Judah and **B.**, 1144
2Ch 14:8 and out of **B.**, that bare shields 1144
2Ch 15:2 ye me, Asa, and all Judah and **B.**; 1144
2Ch 15:8 land of Judah and **B.**, and out of 1144
2Ch 15:9 gathered all Judah and **B.**, and 1144
2Ch 17:17 And of **B.**; Eliada a mighty man 1144
2Ch 25:5 throughout all Judah and **B.**: 1144
2Ch 31:1 the altars out of all Judah and **B.**, 1144
2Ch 34:9 and all Judah and **B.**; and they 1144
2Ch 34:32 were present in Jerusalem and **B.** 1144
Ezr 1:5 fathers of Judah and **B.**, and the 1144
Ezr 4:1 adversaries of Judah and **B.** heard 1144
Ezr 10:9 men of Judah and **B.** gathered 1144
Ezr 10:32 **B.**, Malluch, and Shemariah. 1144
Ne 3:23 After him repaired **B.**, and Hashub 1144
Ne 11:4 of Judah, and of the children of **B.** 1144
Ne 11:7 All these are the sons of **B.**; Sallu 1144
Ne 11:31 The children also of **B.** from Geba 1144
Ne 11:36 were divisions in Judah, and in **B.** 1144
Ne 12:34 Judah, and **B.**, and Shemaiah, 1144
Ps 68:27 There is little **B.** with their ruler, 1144
Ps 80:2 Before Ephraim and **B.** and 1144
Jer 1:1 in Anathoth in the land of **B.**: 1144
Jer 6:1 O ye children of **B.**, gather 1144
Jer 17:26 and from the land of **B.**, 1144
Jer 20:2 that were in the high gate of **B.**, 1144
Jer 32:8 which is in the country of **B.**: 1144
Jer 32:44 take witnesses in the land of **B.**, 1144
Jer 33:13 and in the land of **B.**, and in the 1144
Jer 37:12 to go into the land of **B.**, to 1144
Jer 37:13 was in the gate of **B.**, a captain of 1144
Jer 38:7 king then sitting in the gate of **B.**; 1144
Eze 48:22 of Judah and the border of **B.**, 1144
Eze 48:23 west side, **B.** shall have a portion 1144
Eze 48:24 by the border of **B.**, from the east 1144
Eze 48:32 one gate of Joseph, one gate of **B.**, 1144
Hos 5:8 at Beth-aven, after thee, O **B.** 1144
Ob 19 Samaria; and **B.** shall possess 1144
Ac 13:21 a man of the tribe of **B.**, by the *958*
Ro 11:1 of Abraham, of the tribe of **B.** *958*
Php 3:5 of the tribe of **B.**, an Hebrew of *958*
Re 7:8 Of the tribe of **B.** were sealed *958*

BENJAMIN'S (ben'-ja-mins)
Ge 43:34 but **B.** mess was five times so 1144
Ge 44:12 the cup was found in **b.** sack. 1144
Ge 45:14 he fell upon his brother **B.** neck, 1144
Zec 14:10 inhabited in her place, from **B.** 1144

BENJAMITE (ben'-ja-mite) See also BENJAMITES.
Jg 3:15 Ehud the son of Gera, a **B.**, a man 1145
1Sa 9:1 the son of Aphiah, a **B.**, a mighty 1145
1Sa 9:21 Am not I a **B.**, of the smallest of 1145
2Sa 16:11 much more now may this **B.** do it? 1145
2Sa 19:16 Shimei the son of Gera, a **B.**, 1145
2Sa 20:1 Sheba, the son of Bichri, a **B.**: 1145
1Ki 2:8 the son of Gera, a **B.** of Bahurim, 1145
Es 2:5 Shimei, the son of Kish, a **B.**; 1145
Ps 7:*title* the words of Cush the **B.** 1145

BENJAMITES (ben'-ja-mites)
Jg 19:16 but the men of the place were **B.** 1145
Jg 20:35 Israel destroyed of the **B.** that 1145
Jg 20:36 Israel gave place to the **B.**, 1145
Jg 20:40 pillars of smoke, the **B.** looked 1145
Jg 20:43 thus they inclosed the **B.** round 1145
1Sa 9:4 passed through the land of the **B.**, 1145
1Sa 22:7 Hear now, ye **B.**; will the son of 1145
1Ch 27:12 Abiezer the Anetothite, of the **B.**: 1145

BENO (be'-no)
1Ch 24:26 Mushi: the sons of Jaaziah; **B.** 1121
1Ch 24:27 **B.**, and Shoham, and Zaccar, and 1121

BENOB See ISBI-BENOB.

BEN-ONI (ben-o'-ni)
Ge 35:18 she called his name **B.**: but his 1126

BENOTH See ISHBI-BENOTH.

BENT
Ps 7:12 he hath **b.** his bow, and made it 1869
Ps 37:14 and have **b.** their bow, to cast 1869
Isa 5:28 all their bows **b.**, their horses' 1869
Isa 21:15 drawn sword, and from the **b.** bow, 1869
La 2:4 He hath **b.** his bow like an enemy: 1869
La 3:12 He hath **b.** his bow, and set me as 1869
Ho 11:7 my people are **b.** to backsliding 8511
Zec 9:13 When I have **b.** Judah for me, 1869

BEN-ZOHETH (ben-zo'-heth)
1Ch 4:20 sons of Ishi were, Zoheth, and **B.**...... 1132

BEON (be'-on)
Nu 32:3 and Shebam, and Nebo, and **B.**,......... 1194

BEOR (be'-or)
Ge 36:32 And Bela the son of **B.** reigned in...... 1160
Nu 22:5 Balaam the son of **B.** to Pethor, ... 1160
Nu 24:3 Balaam the son of **B.** hath said, ... 1160
Nu 24:15 the son of **B.** hath said, and the......... 1160
Nu 31:8 Balaam also the son of **B.** they.......... 1160
De 23:4 against thee Balaam the son of **B.**....... 1160
Jos 13:22 Balaam also the son of **B.**, the 1160
Jos 24:9 called Balaam the son of **B.** to.......... 1160
1Ch 1:43 Bela the son of **B.**: and the name....... 1160
Mic 6:5 Balaam the son of **B.** answered 1160

BERA (be'-rah)
Ge 14:2 these made war with **B.** king of......... 1298

BERACHAH (ber'-a-kah)
1Ch 12:3 Azmaveth; and **B.**, and Jehu the 1294
2Ch 20:26 themselves in the valley of **B.**; 1294
2Ch 20:26 was called, The valley of **B.**,.............. 1294

BERACHIAH (ber-a-ki'-ah) See also BERECHIAH.
1Ch 6:39 even Asaph the son of **B.**, the son..... 1296

BERAIAH (ber-a-i'-ah)
1Ch 8:21 Adaiah, and **B.**, and Shimrath, ... 1256

BEREA (be-re'-a)
Ac 17:10 Paul and Silas by night unto **B.**: *960*
Ac 17:13 was preached of Paul at **B.**, they......... *960*
Ac 20:4 him into Asia Sopater of **B.**; *960*

BEREAVE See also BEREAVED; BEREAVETH.
Ec 4:8 I labour and **b.** my soul of good?........ 2637
Jer 15:7 I will **b.** them of children, I will.......... 7921
Eze 5:17 beasts, and they shall **b.** thee: 7921
Eze 36:12 no more henceforth **b.** them of 7921
Eze 36:14 neither **b.** thy nations any.. 3782,(7921)7921
Ho 9:12 yet will I **b.** them, that there shall...... 7921

BEREAVED
Ge 42:36 Me have ye **b.** of my children:........... 7921
Ge 43:14 I be **b.** of my children, I am **b.**.......... 7921
Jer 18:21 wives be **b.** of their children,............ 7909
Eze 36:13 up men, and hast **b.** thy nations; 7921
Ho 13:8 as a bear that is **b.** of her whelps, ... 7909

BEREAVETH
La 1:20 abroad the sword **b.**, at home........... 7921

BERECHIAH (ber-e-ki'-ah) See also BERACHIAH.
1Ch 3:20 and Ohel, and **B.**, and Hasadiah, ... 1296
1Ch 9:16 **B.** the son of Asa, the son of............ 1296
1Ch 15:17 his brethren, Asaph the son of **B.**; 1296
1Ch 15:23 **B.** and Elkanah were doorkeepers...... 1296
2Ch 28:12 **B.** the son of Meshillemoth, and 1296
Ne 3:4 Meshullam the son of **B.**, the son 1296
Ne 3:30 son of **B.** over against his chamber..... 1296
Ne 6:18 of Meshullam the son of **B.**.............. 1296
Zec 1:1,7 the son of **B.**, the son of Iddo.......... 1296

BERED (be'-red)
Ge 16:14 it is between Kadesh and **B.**. 1260
1Ch 7:20 Shuthelah, and **B.** his son, and 1260

BERI (be'-ri) See also BERITES.
1Ch 7:36 Shual, and **B.**, and Imrah,................ 1275

BERIAH (be-ri'-ah) See also BERITES.
Ge 46:17 and **B.**, and Serah their sister: 1283
Ge 46:17 sons of **B.**; Heber, and Maechiel........ 1283
Nu 26:44 Jesuites: of **B.**, the family of the........ 1283
Nu 26:45 Of the sons of **B.**: of Heber, the........ 1283
1Ch 7:23 he called his name **B.**, because it 1283
1Ch 7:30 and **B.**, and Serah their sister. 1283
1Ch 7:31 sons of **B.**; Heber, and Malchiel,........ 1283
1Ch 8:13 **B.** also, and Shema, who were.......... 1283
1Ch 8:16 Ispah, and Joha, the sons of **B.**;......... 1283
1Ch 23:10 Jahath, Zina, and Jeush, and **B.**........ 1283
1Ch 23:11 Jeush and **B.** had not many sons; 1283

BERIITES (be-ri'-ites)
Nu 26:44 of Beriah, the family of the **B.**........... 1284

BERITES (be'-rites)
2Sa 20:14 to Beth-maachah, and all the **B.**......... 1276

BERITH (be'-rith) See also BAAL-BERITH.
Jg 9:46 hold of the house of the god **B.**......... 1286

BERNICE (bur-ni'-see)
Ac 25:13 and **B.** came unto Caesarea to *959*
Ac 25:23 come, and **B.**, with great pomp, ... *959*
Ac 26:30 **B.**, and they that sat with them: *959*

BERODACH-BALADAN (ber-o''-dak-bal'-ad-an) See also MERODACH-BALADAN.
2Ki 20:12 At that time **B.**, the son of.............. 1255

BEROEA See BEREA.

BEROTHAH (ber-o'-thah) See also BEROTHAI; BEROTHITE.
Eze 47:16 Hamath, **B.**, Sibraim,...................... 1268

BEROTHAI (ber'-o-thahee) See also BEROTHAH.
2Sa 8:8 and from **B.**, cities of Hadadezer, ... 1268

BEROTHITE (be'-ro-thite) See also BEEROTHITE.
1Ch 11:39 Naharai the **B.**, the armourbearer....... 1307

BERRIES
Isa 17:6 two or three **b.** in the top of the....... 1620
Jas 3:12 tree, by brethren, bear olive **b.**? *1636*

BERYL (ber'-il)
Ex 28:20 the fourth row a **b.**, and an onyx,....... 8658
Ex 39:13 a **b.**, an onyx, and a jasper: they........ 8658
Ca 5:14 are as gold rings set with the **b.** 8658
Eze 1:16 was like unto the colour of a **b.** 8658
Eze 10:9 was as the colour of a **b.** stone.......... 8658
Eze 28:13 topaz, and the diamond, the **b.**, ... 8658
Da 10:6 His body also was like the **b.**,............ 8658
Re 21:20 seventh, chrysolyte; the eighth, **b.**;...... *969*

BESAI (be'-sahee)
Ezr 2:49 of Paseah, the children of **B.**,............ 1153
Ne 7:52 of **B.**, the children of Meunim, ... 1153

BESEECH See also BESEECHING; BESOUGHT.
Ex 3:18 and now let us go, we **b.** thee,.......... 4994
Ex 33:18 I **b.** thee, shew me thy glory............ 4994
Nu 12:11 I **b.** thee, lay not the sin upon us,...... 4994
Nu 12:13 Heal her now, O God, I **b.** thee......... 4994
Nu 14:17 And now, I **b.** thee, let the power....... 4994
Nu 14:19 Pardon, I **b.** thee, the iniquity 4994
1Sa 23:11 I **b.** thee, tell thy servant. 4994
2Sa 13:24 let the king, I **b.** thee, and his.......... 4994
2Sa 16:4 I humbly **b.** thee that I may find..............
2Sa 24:10 and now I **b.** thee, O Lord, take 4994
2Ki 19:19 I **b.** thee, save thou us out of his....... 4994
2Ki 20:3 I **b.** thee, O Lord, remember now 577
1Ch 21:8 I **b.** thee, do away the iniquity.......... 4994
2Ch 6:40 Now, my God, let, I **b.** thee, ... 4994
Ne 1:5 And said, I **b.** thee, O Lord God 577
Ne 1:8 Remember, I **b.** thee, the word......... 4994
Ne 1:11 O Lord, I **b.** thee, let now thine ear..... 577
Job 10:9 Remember, I **b.** thee, that thou 4994
Job 42:4 Hear, I **b.** thee, and I will speak: 4994
Ps 80:14 Return, we **b.** thee, O God of hosts: .. 4994
Ps 116:4 O Lord, I **b.** thee, deliver my soul. 577
Ps 118:25 Save now, I **b.** thee, O Lord: 577
Ps 118:25 O Lord, I **b.** thee, send now............. 577
Ps 119:108 Accept, I **b.** thee, the freewill 4994
Isa 38:3 Remember now, O Lord, I **b.** thee, ... 577
Isa 64:9 we **b.** thee, we are all thy people....... 4994
Jer 38:4 We **b.** thee, let this man be put to 4994
Jer 38:20 Obey, I beseech thee, the voice of..... 4994
Jer 42:2 we **b.** thee, our supplication be.......... 4994
Da 1:12 Prove thy servants, I **b.** thee, ten...... 4994
Da 9:16 I **b.** thee, let thine anger and thy 4994
Am 7:2 God, forgive, I **b.** thee: by whom....... 4994
Am 7:5 O Lord God, cease, I **b.** thee: by......... 4994
Jon 1:14 We **b.** thee, O Lord, we **b.** thee, ... 577
Jon 4:3 take, I **b.** thee, my life from me: 4994
Mal 1:9 **b.** God that he...be gracious....... 2470,6440
Mk 7:32 **b.** him to put his hand upon him......... *3870*
Lu 8:28 high? I **b.** thee, torment me not......... *1189*
Lu 9:38 I **b.** thee, look upon my son:............ *1189*
Ac 21:39 I **b.** thee, suffer me to speak unto...... *1189*
Ac 26:3 I **b.** thee to hear me patiently............ *1189*
Ro 12:1 I **b.** you therefore, brethren, by......... *3870*
Ro 15:30 Now I **b.** you, brethren, for the *3870*
Ro 16:17 Now I **b.** you, brethren, mark *3870*
1Co 1:10 Now I **b.** you, brethren, by the *3870*
1Co 4:16 Wherefore I **b.** you, be ye followers ... *3870*
1Co 16:15 I **b.** you, brethren, (ye know the........ *3870*
2Co 2:8 Wherefore I **b.** you that ye would........ *3870*
2Co 5:20 as though God did **b.** you by us: *3870*
2Co 6:1 him, **b.** you also that ye receive......... *3870*
2Co 10:1 I Paul myself **b.** you by the............... *3870*
2Co 10:2 I **b.** you, that I may not be bold......... *1189*
Ga 4:12 Brethren, I **b.** you, be as I am: *1189*
Eph 4:1 **b.** you that ye walk worthy of the *3870*
Php 4:2 I **b.** Euodias, and **b.** Syntyche, ... *3870*
1Th 4:1 we **b.** you, brethren, and exhort *2065*
1Th 4:10 but we **b.** you, brethren, that ye........ *3870*
1Th 5:12 And we **b.** you, brethren, to know *2065*
2Th 2:1 Now we **b.** you, brethren, by the....... *2065*
Phm 9 for love's sake I rather **b.** thee, ... *3870*
Phm 10 I **b.** thee for my son Onesimus, ... *3870*
Heb 13:19 But I **b.** you the rather to do this,...... *3870*
Heb 13:22 I **b.** you, brethren, suffer the *3870*
1Pe 2:11 beloved, I **b.** you as strangers........... *3870*
2Jo 5 now I **b.** thee, lady, not as though...... *2065*

BESEECHING
Mt 8:5 unto him a centurion, **b.** him, ... *3870*
Mk 1:40 there came a leper to him, **b.** him, ... *3870*
Lu 7:3 **b.** him that he would come and.......... *2065*

BESET
Jg 19:22 Belial, **b.** the house round about,......... 5437
Jg 20:5 and **b.** the house round about............ 5437
Ps 22:12 of Bashan have **b.** me round............. 3803
Ps 139:5 hast **b.** me behind and before, ... 6696
Ho 7:2 own doings have **b.** them about;......... 5437
Heb 12:1 the sin which doth so easily **b.** us,...... *2139*

BESETH See PI-BESETH.

BESIDE See also BESIDES.
Ge 26:1 **b.** the first famine that was in............ 905
Ge 31:50 take other wives **b.** my daughters, ... 5921
Ex 12:37 that were men, **b.** children. 905
Ex 14:9 the sea, **b.** Pi-hahiroth, before........... 5921
Ex 29:12 blood **b.** the bottom of the altar.......... 413
Le 1:16 cast it **b.** the altar on the east part, ... 681
Le 6:10 he shall put them **b.** the altar............. 681
Le 9:17 **b.** the burnt sacrifice of the 905
Le 10:12 eat it without leaven **b.** the altar:......... 681
Le 18:18 **b.** the other in her life time.............. 5921
Le 23:38 **B.** the sabbaths of the Lord,............... 905
Le 23:38 and **b.** your gifts,.............................. 905
Le 23:38 and **b.** all your vows, ... 905
Le 23:38 and **b.** all your freewill offerings,.......... 905
Nu 5:8 **b.** the ram of the atonement, ... 905
Nu 5:20 lain with thee **b.** thine husband: 1107
Nu 6:21 **b.** that that his hand shall get:............. 905
Nu 11:6 at all, **b.** this manna, before our......... 1115
Nu 16:49 **b.** them that died about the 905
Nu 24:6 and as cedar trees **b.** the waters......... 5921
Nu 28:10 **b.** the continual burnt offering,........... 5921
Nu 28:15 shall be offered, **b.** the continual 5921
Nu 28:23 Ye shall offer these **b.** the burnt.......... 905
Nu 28:24 it shall be offered **b.** the continual....... 5921
Nu 28:31 shall offer them **b.** the continual.......... 905
Nu 29:6 **B.** the burnt offering of the month, ... 905
Nu 29:11 **b.** the sin offering of atonement,.......... 905
Nu 29:16 **b.** the continual burnt offering..................
Nu 29:19 **b.** the continual burnt offering..................
Nu 29:22 **b.** the continual burnt offering..................
Nu 29:25 **b.** the continual burnt offering..................
Nu 29:28 **b.** the continual burnt offering..................
Nu 29:31 **b.** the continual burnt offering..................
Nu 29:34 **b.** the continual burnt offering..................
Nu 29:34, 38 **b.** the continual burnt offering, ... 905
Nu 29:39 **b.** your vows, and your freewill........... 905
Nu 31:8 **b.** the rest of them that were............. 5921
De 3:5 **b.** unwalled towns a great many. 905
De 4:35 is God; there is none else **b.** him......... 905
De 11:30 Gilgal, **b.** the plains of Moreh? 681
De 18:8 to eat, **b.** that which cometh............... 905
De 19:9 more for thee, **b.** these three;............ 5921
De 29:1 the land of Moab, **b.** the covenant........ 905
Jos 3:16 city Adam, that is **B.** Zaretan: 6654
Jos 7:2 to Ai, which is **b.** Beth-aven, on 5973
Jos 12:9 of Ai, which is **b.** Beth-el, one;.......... 6654
Jos 13:4 Mearah that is **b.** the Sidonians,...............
Jos 17:5 **b.** the land of Gilead......................... 905
Jos 22:19 building you an altar **b.** the altar......... 1107
Jos 22:29 or for sacrifices, **b.** the altar of............ 905
Jg 6:37 it be dry upon all the earth **b.**...................
Jg 7:1 and pitched **b.** the well of Harod: 5921
Jg 8:26 shekels of gold; **b.** ornaments, ... 905
Jg 8:26 **b.** the chains that were about.............. 905
Jg 11:34 and she was his only child; **b.** her............
Jg 20:15 drew sword, **b.** the inhabitants 905
Jg 20:17 the men of Israel, **b.** Benjamin, ... 905
Jg 20:36 wait which they had set **b.** Gibeah. 413
Ru 2:14 she sat **b.** the reapers: and he........... 6654

Ru 4:4 there is none to redeem it **b.** thee; 2108
1Sa 2:2 for there is none **b.** thee: neither 1115
1Sa 4:1 battle, and pitched **b.** Ebenezer: 5921
1Sa 19:3 go out and stand **b.** my father 3027
2Sa 7:22 neither is there any God **b.** thee, 2108
2Sa 13:23 Baal-hazor, which is **b.** Ephraim: 5973
2Sa 15:2 stood **b.** the way of the gate: 5921,3027
2Sa 15:18 his servants passed on **b.** him; 5921,3027
1Ki 3:20 my son from **b.** me, while thine 681
1Ki 4:23 sheep, **b.** harts, and roebucks, 905
1Ki 5:16 **B.** the chief of Solomon's officers 905
1Ki 9:26 Ezion-geber, which is **b.** Eloth, 854
1Ki 10:13 asked, **b.** that which Solomon 905
1Ki 10:15 **B.** that he had of the merchantmen 905
1Ki 10:19 two lions stood **b.** the stays 681
1Ki 11:25 **b.** the mischief that Hadad did: 854
1Ki 13:31 lay my bones **b.** his bones: 681
2Ki 11:20 the sword **b.** the king's house
2Ki 12:9 set it **b.** the altar, on the right 681
2Ki 21:16 **b.** his sin wherewith he made 905
1Ch 3:9 sons of David, **b.** the sons 905
1Ch 17:20 neither is there any God **b.** 2108
2Ch 9:12 **b.** that which she had brought 905
2Ch 9:14 **B.** that which chapmen and 905
2Ch 17:19 waited on the king, **b.** those 905
2Ch 20:1 them other **b.** the Ammonites,
2Ch 26:19 Lord, from **b.** the incense altar. 5921
2Ch 31:16 **B.** their genealogy of males, 905
Ezr 1:4 beasts, **b.** the freewill offering 5973
Ezr 1:6 **b.** all that was willingly 905,5921
Ezr 2:65 **B.** their servants and their 905
Ne 5:15 wine, **b.** forty shekels of silver; 310
Ne 5:17 fifty of the Jews and rulers, **b.**
Ne 7:67 **B.** their manservants and their 905
Ne 8:4 **b.** him stood Mattithiah, and 681
Job 1:14 the asses feeding **b.** them: 5921,3027
Ps 23:2 leadeth me **b.** the still waters. 5921
Ps 73:25 upon earth that I desire **b.** thee. 5973
Ca 1:8 thy kids **b.** the shepherds' tents, 5921
Isa 26:13 our God, other lords **b.** thee 2108
Isa 32:20 Blessed are ye that sow **b.** all 5921
Isa 43:11 and **b.** me there is no saviour. 1107
Isa 44:6 and **b.** me there is no God. 1107
Isa 44:8 Is there a God **b.** me? yea, there 1107
Isa 45:5 else, there is no God **b.** me: 2108
Isa 45:6 west, that there is none **b.** me. 1107
Isa 45:21 no God else **b.** me; 1107
Isa 45:21 there is none **b.** me 2108
Isa 47:8 I am, and none else **b.** me; 657
Isa 47:10 I am, and none else **b.** me. 657
Isa 56:8 others to him, **b.** those that
Isa 64:4 the eye seen, O God, **b.** thee, 2108
Jer 36:21 princes which stood **b.** the king 5921
Eze 9:2 and stood **b.** the brasen altar. 681
Eze 10:6 went in, and stood **b.** the wheels. 681
Eze 10:16 turned not from **b.** them. 681
Eze 10:19 the wheels also were **b.** them, 5980
Eze 11:22 wings, and the wheels **b.** them; 5980
Eze 32:13 beasts thereof from **b.** the great 5921
Da 11:4 even for others **b.** those. 905
Ho 13:4 for there is no saviour **b.** me. 1115
Zep 2:15 there is none **b.** me: how is she 657
Mt 14:21 men, **b.** women and children. *5565*
Mt 15:38 **b.** women and children. *5565*
Mt 25:20 **I have gained b. them five** *1909*
Mt 25:22 **gained two other talents b. them** *1909*
Mk 3:21 for they said, He is **b.** himself. *1839*
Lu 16:26 **b. all this, between us and you** *1909*
Lu 24:21 and **b.** all this, to day *4862*
Ac 26:24 Paul, thou art **b.** thyself; *3105*
2Co 5:13 whether we be **b.** ourselves, *1839*
2Co 11:28 **B.** those things that are without *5565*
2Pe 1:5 And **b.** this, giving all *846*

BESIDES
Ge 19:12 Lot, Hast thou here any **b.**? 5750
Ge 46:26 **b.** Jacob's sons' wives, all the 905
Le 7:13 **B.** the cakes, he shall offer for 5921
1Ki 22:7 not here a prophet of the Lord **b.**, 5750
2Ch 18:6 here a prophet of the Lord **b.**, 5750
Jer 36:32 and there were added **b.** unto 5750
1Co 1:16 **b.**, I know not whether I *3063*
Phm 19 unto me even thine own self **b.** *4359*

BESIEGE See also BESIEGED.
De 20:12 thee, then thou shalt **b.** it: 6696
De 20:19 When thou shalt **b.** a city a long 6696
De 28:52 And he shall **b.** thee in all thy 6887
De 28:52 **b.** thee in all thy gates 6887
1Sa 23:8 to **b.** David and his men. 6696
1Ki 8:37 if their enemy **b.** them in the 6887
2Ki 24:11 city, and his servants did **b.** 6696
2Ch 6:28 if their enemies **b.** them in the 6696
Isa 21:2 Go up, O Elam: **b.**, O Media; 6696
Jer 21:4 the Chaldeans, which **b.** you 6696
Jer 21:9 to the Chaldeans that **b.** you, 6696

BESIEGED
2Sa 11:1 of Ammon, and **b.** Rabbah 6696
2Sa 20:15 And they came and **b.** him 6696
1Ki 16:17 with him, and they **b.** Tirzah. 6696
1Ki 20:1 and he went up and **b.** Samaria, 6696
2Ki 6:24 and went up, and **b.** Samaria. 6696
2Ki 6:25 and, behold, they **b.** it, until 6696
2Ki 16:5 they **b.** Ahaz, but could not 6696
2Ki 17:5 Samaria, and **b.** it three years. 6696
2Ki 18:9 came up against Samaria, and **b.** it 6696
2Ki 19:24 up all the rivers of **b.** places 4693
2Ki 24:10 and the city was **b.** 935,4692
2Ki 25:2 And the city was **b.** unto the 935,4692
1Ch 20:1 and came and **b.** Rabbah 6696
Ec 9:14 and **b.** it, and built great 5437
Isa 1:8 of cucumbers, as a **b.** city 5341
Isa 37:25 all the rivers of the **b.** places 4693
Jer 32:2 the king of Babylon's army **b.** 6696
Jer 37:5 the Chaldeans that **b.** Jerusalem 6696
Jer 39:1 against Jerusalem, and they **b.** it. 6696
Jer 52:5 city was **b.** unto the eleventh 935,4692
Eze 4:3 it shall be **b.**, and thou shalt 4692
Eze 6:12 he that remaineth and is **b.** shall 5341
Da 1:1 unto Jerusalem, and **b.** it. 6696

BESODEIAH (bes-o-di'-ah)
Ne 3:6 and Meshullam the son of **B.**; 1152

BESOM
Isa 14:23 it with the **b.** of destruction, 4292

BESOR (be'-sor)
1Sa 30:9 and came to the brook **B.**, 1308
1Sa 30:10 could not go over the brook **B.**, 1308
1Sa 30:21 also to abide at the brook **B.**: 1308

BESOUGHT
Ge 42:21 when he **b.** us, and we would not 2603
Ex 32:11 And Moses **b.** the Lord his God, 2470
De 3:23 And I **b.** the Lord at that time, 2603
2Sa 12:16 David therefore **b.** God for the 1245
1Ki 13:6 And the man of God **b.** the Lord, 2470
2Ki 1:13 knees before Elijah, and **b.** him, 2603
2Ki 13:4 And Jehoahaz **b.** the Lord, and 2470
2Ch 33:12 he **b.** the Lord his God, 2470
Ezr 8:23 fasted and **b.** our God for this: 1245
Es 8:3 and **b.** him with tears to put 2603
Jer 26:19 fear the Lord, and **b.** the Lord, 2470
Mt 8:31 the devils **b.** him, saying, If thou *3870*
Mt 8:34 they **b.** him that he would depart *3870*
Mt 14:36 And **b.** him that they might only *3870*
Mt 15:23 his disciples came and **b.** him, *2065*
Mt 18:29 **b. him, saying, Have patience** *3870*
Mk 5:10 And he **b.** him much that he *3870*
Mk 5:12 And all the devils **b.** him, saying, *3870*
Mk 5:23 And **b.** him greatly, saying, *3870*
Mk 6:56 streets, and **b.** him that they *3870*
Mk 7:26 and she **b.** him that he would *2065*
Mk 8:22 him, and **b.** him to touch him *3870*
Lu 4:38 and they **b.** him for her. *2065*
Lu 5:12 Jesus fell on his face, and **b.** *1189*
Lu 7:4 they **b.** him instantly, saying, *3870*
Lu 8:31 And they **b.** him that he would *3870*
Lu 8:32 and they **b.** him that he would *3870*
Lu 8:37 **b.** him to depart from them; *2065*
Lu 8:38 **b.** him that he might be with *1189*
Lu 8:41 **b.** him that he would come into *3870*
Lu 9:40 I **b.** thy disciples to cast him out; *1189*
Lu 11:37 certain Pharisee **b.** him to dine *2065*
Joh 4:40 they **b.** him that he would tarry *2065*
Joh 4:47 **b.** him that he would come down, *2065*
Joh 19:31 **b.** Pilate that their legs might *2065*
Joh 19:38 **b.** Pilate that he might take *2065*
Ac 13:42 the Gentiles **b.** that these words *3870*
Ac 16:15 she **b.** us, saying, If ye have *3870*
Ac 16:39 And they came and **b.** them, *3870*
Ac 21:12 **b.** him not to go up to Jerusalem *3870*
Ac 25:2 him against Paul, and **b.** him, *3870*
Ac 27:33 Paul **b.** them all to take meat, *3870*
2Co 12:8 I **b.** the Lord thrice, that it might *3870*
1Ti 1:3 As I **b.** thee to abide still at *3870*

BEST
Ge 43:11 take of the **b.** fruits in the land in 2173
Ge 47:6 in the **b.** of the land make thy 4315
Ge 47:11 Egypt, in the **b.** of the land, in the 4315
Ex 22:5 of the **b.** of his own field, and of 4315
Ex 22:5 the **b.** of his own vineyard, 4315
Nu 18:12 All the **b.** of the oil, 2459
Nu 18:12 and all the **b.** of the wine, 2459
Nu 18:29 of all the **b.** thereof, even the 2459
Nu 18:30 when ye have heaved the **b.** 2459
Nu 18:32 ye have heaved from it the **b.** of it: 2459
Nu 36:6 to whom they think **b.**; 2896
De 23:16 where it liketh him **b.**: thou 2896
1Sa 8:14 your oliveyards, even the **b.** of 2896
1Sa 15:9 the **b.** of the sheep, and of the 4315
1Sa 15:15 for the people spared the **b.** of the 4315
2Sa 18:4 What seemeth you **b.** I will do 3190
1Ki 10:18 and overlaid it with the **b.** gold. 6338
2Ki 10:3 Look even out the **b.** and meetest 2896
Es 2:9 her maids unto the **b.** place of the 2896
Ps 39:5 man at his **b.** state is altogether 5324
Ca 7:9 roof of thy mouth like the **b.** wine 2896
Eze 31:16 the choice and **b.** of Lebanon, 2896
Mic 7:4 the **b.** of them is as a brier: the 2896
Lu 15:22 Bring forth the **b.** robe, and put *4413*
1Co 12:31 but covet earnestly the **b.** gifts: *2909*

BESTEAD
Isa 8:21 shall pass through it, hardly **b.**

BESTIR
2Sa 5:24 then thou shalt **b.** thyself: for 2782

BESTOW See also BESTOWED.
Ex 32:29 he may **b.** upon you a blessing 5414
De 14:26 And thou shalt **b.** that money for 5414
2Ch 24:7 of the Lord did they **b.** upon 6213
Ezr 7:20 thou shalt have occasion to **b.**, 5415
Ezr 7:20 **b.** it out of the king's treasure 5415
Lu 12:17 **I have no more room where to b.** *4863*
Lu 12:18 **there will I b. all my fruits and my** *4863*
1Co 12:23 upon these we **b.** more abundant *4060*
1Co 13:3 And though I **b.** all my goods to *5595*

BESTOWED
1Ki 10:26 horsemen, whom he **b.** in the 3240
2Ki 5:24 their hand, and **b.** them in the 6485
2Ki 12:15 the money to be **b.** on workmen: 5414
1Ch 29:25 **b.** upon him such royal majesty 5414
2Ch 9:25 whom he **b.** in the chariot cities, 3240
Isa 63:7 to all that the Lord hath **b.** on us, 1580
Isa 63:7 he hath **b.** on them according 1580
Joh 4:38 **whereon ye b. no labour: other** *2872*
Ro 16:6 Mary, who **b.** much labour on us. *2872*
1Co 15:10 his grace which was **b.** upon me
2Co 1:11 that for the gift **b.** upon us by the
2Co 8:1 grace of God **b.** on the churches *1325*
Ga 4:11 lest I have **b.** upon you labour in *2872*
1Jo 3:1 of love the Father hath **b.** on us. *1325*

BETAH (be'-tah)
2Sa 8:8 And from **B.**, and from Berothai, 984

BETEN (be'-ten)
Jos 19:25 and Hali, and **B.**, and Achshaph, 991

BETH See also BETH-ANATH; BETH-ANOTH; BETHANY; BETH-ARABAH; BETH-ARAM; BETH-ARBEL; BETH-AVEN; BETH-AZMAVETH; BETH-BAAL-MEON; BETH-BARAH; BETH-BIREI; BETH-CAR; BETH-DAGON; BETH-DIB-LATHAIM; BETHEL; BETH-EMEK; BETHESDA; BETH-EZEL; BETH-GADER; BETH-GAMUL; BETH-HACCEREM; BETH-LEHEM; BETH-HARAN; BETH-HOGLAH; BETH-HORON; BETH-JESHIMOTH; BETH-LEBAOTH; BETH-MAACHAH; BETH-MARCABOTH; BETH-MEON; BETH-NIMZAH; BETH-PALET; BETH-PAZZEZ; BETH-PEOR; BETHPHAGE; BETH-RAPHA; BETH-REHOB; BETHSAIDA; BETH-SHAW; BETH-SHEMESH; BETH-SHITTAH; BETH-TAPPUAH; BETH-ZUR.
Ps 119:9 *title* [ב] **B.**

BETHABARA (beth-ab'-ar-ah) See also BETH-BARAH.
Joh 1:28 These things were done in **B.** *962*

BETH-ANATH (beth'-a-nath)
Jos 19:38 Harem, and **B.**, and 1043
Jg 1:33 nor the inhabitants of **B.**; but he 1043
Jg 1:33 Beth-shemesh, and of **B.** became 1043

BETH-ANOTH (beth'-a-noth)
Jos 15:59 Maarath, and **B.** and Eltekon; 1042

BETHANY (beth'-a-ny)
Mt 21:17 and went out of the city into **B.**; 963
Mt 26:6 Now when Jesus was in **B.**, in the *963*
Mk 11:1 unto Bethphage and **B.**, at the *963*
Mk 11:11 he went out unto **B.** with the *963*
Mk 11:12 when they were come from **B.**, he *963*
Mk 14:3 And being in **B.** in the house of *963*
Lu 19:29 come nigh to Bethphage and **B.** *963*
Lu 24:50 he led them out as far as to **B.**, *963*
Joh 11:1 named Lazarus, of **B.**, the town *963*
Joh 11:18 Now **B.** was nigh unto Jerusalem, *963*
Joh 12:1 before the passover came to **B.**, *963*

BETH-ARABAH (beth-ar'-ab-ah)
Jos 15:6 passed along by the north of **B.**; 1026
Jos 15:61 In the wilderness, **B.**, Middin, and 1026
Jos 18:22 **B.**, and Zemaraim, and Beth-el, 1026

BETH-ARAM (beth'-a-ram)
Jos 13:27 And in the valley, **B.**, and 1027

BETH-ARBEL (beth-ar'-bel)
Ho 10:14 Shalman spoiled **B.** in the day of 1009

BETH-AVEN (beth-a'-ven)
Jos 7:2 to Ai, which is beside **B.**, on the 1007
Jos 18:12 were at the wilderness of **B.** 1007
1Sa 13:5 in Michmash, eastward from **B.**. 1007
1Sa 14:23 and the battle passed over unto **B.**. 1007
Ho 4:15 neither go ye up to **B.**, nor swear, 1007
Ho 5:8 cry aloud at **B.**, after thee, O 1007
Ho 10:5 because of the calves of **B.**: 1007

BETH-AZMAVETH (beth-az'-maveth) See also AZMAVETH.
Ne 7:28 The men of **B.**, forty and two. 1041

BETH-BAAL-MEON (beth-ba''-al-me'-on) See also BAAL-MEON.
Jos 13:17 Dibon, and Bamoth-baal, and **B.**, 1010

BETH-BARAH (beth-ba'-rah) See also BETHABARA.
Jg 7:24 before them the waters unto **B.** 1012
Jg 7:24 and took the waters unto **B.** and 1012

BETH-BIREI (beth-bir-e-i) See also BETH-LEBAOTH.
1Ch 4:31 Hazar-susim, and at **B.**, and at 1011

BETH-CAR (beth'-car)
1Sa 7:11 them, until they came under **B.**. 1033

BETH-DAGON (beth-da'-gon)
Jos 15:41 And Gederoth, **B.**, and Naamah, 1016
Jos 19:27 toward the sunrising to **B.**, 1016

BETH-DIBLATHAIM (beth-dib-lath-a'-im)
Jer 48:22 and upon Nebo, and upon **B.**, 1015

BETH-EL (beth'-el) See also BETHELITE; EL-BETHEL; LUZ.
Ge 12:8 a mountain on the east of **B.**, 1008
Ge 12:8 pitched his tent, having **B.** on the 1008
Ge 13:3 from the south even to **B.**, 1008
Ge 13:3 beginning, between **B.** and Hai; 1008
Ge 28:19 called the name of that place **B.**: 1008
Ge 31:13 I am the God of **B.**, where thou 1008
Ge 35:1 unto Jacob, Arise, go up to **B.**, 1008
Ge 35:3 let us arise, and go up to **B.**; 1008
Ge 35:6 in the land of Canaan, that is, **B.**, 1008
Ge 35:8 she was buried beneath **B.** under 1008
Ge 35:15 where God spake with him, **B.**. 1008
Ge 35:16 they journeyed from **B.**; and 1008
Jos 7:2 Beth-aven, on the east side of **B.** 1008
Jos 8:9 and abode between **B.** and Ai, 1008
Jos 8:12 lie in ambush between **B.** and Ai, 1008
Jos 8:17 was not man left in Ai or **B.**, 1008
Jos 12:9 king of Ai, which is beside **B.** 1008
Jos 12:16 the king of **B.**, one; 1008
Jos 16:1 from Jericho throughout mount **B.**, 1008
Jos 16:2 And goeth out from **B.** to Luz, 1008
Jos 18:13 to the side of Luz, which is **B.**, 1008
Jos 18:22 Zemaraim, and **B.**, 1008
Jg 1:22 they also went up against **B.**: 1008
Jg 1:23 house of Joseph sent to descry **B.** 1008
Jg 4:5 between Ramah and **B.** in mount 1008
Jg 21:19 which is on the north side of **B.**, 1008
Jg 21:19 the highway that goeth up from **B.** 1008
1Sa 7:16 from year to year in circuit to **B.**, 1008
1Sa 10:3 three men going up to God to **B.** 1008
1Sa 13:2 in Michmash and in mount **B.**, 1008
1Sa 30:27 To them which were in **B.**, and 1008
1Ki 12:29 he set the one in **B.**, and the other 1008
1Ki 12:32 So did he in **B.**, sacrificing unto 1008
1Ki 12:32 and he placed in **B.** the priests of 1008
1Ki 12:33 altar which he had made in **B.** 1008
1Ki 13:1 by the word of the Lord unto **B.** 1008
1Ki 13:4 had cried against the altar in **B.**. 1008
1Ki 13:10 by the way that he came to **B.** 1008
1Ki 13:11 there dwelt an old prophet in **B.**; 1008
1Ki 13:11 of God had done that day in **B.** 1008
1Ki 13:32 the Lord against the altar in **B.** 1008
2Ki 2:2 for the Lord hath sent me to **B.**. 1008
2Ki 2:2 So they went down to **B.**. 1008
2Ki 2:3 of the prophets that were at **B.** 1008
2Ki 2:23 he went up from thence unto **B.** 1008
2Ki 10:29 the golden calves that were in **B.**, 1008
2Ki 17:28 came and dwelt in **B.**, and taught 1008
2Ki 23:4 carried the ashes of them unto **B.**. 1008
2Ki 23:15 Moreover the altar that was at **B.**. 1008
2Ki 23:17 hast done against the altar of **B.**. 1008
2Ki 23:19 all the acts that he had done in **B.** 1008
1Ch 7:28 **B.** and the towns thereof, and 1008
2Ch 13:19 **B.** with the towns thereof, and 1008
Ezr 2:28 men of **B.** and Ai, two hundred 1008
Ne 7:32 The men of **B.** and Ai, a hundred 1008
Ne 11:31 and Aija, and **B.**, and in their 1008
Jer 48:13 house of Israel was ashamed of **B.** 1008
Ho 10:15 So shall **B.** do unto you because 1008
Ho 12:4 he found him in **B.**, and there 1008
Am 3:14 I will also visit the altars of **B.** 1008
Am 4:4 Come to **B.**, and transgress; at 1008
Am 5:5 But seek not **B.**, nor enter into 1008
Am 5:5 captivity, and **B.** shall come to 1008
Am 5:6 there be one to quench it in **B.**. 1008
Am 7:10 Then Amaziah the priest of **B.** 1008
Am 7:13 prophesy not again any more at **B.** 1008

BETH-ELITE (beth'-el-ite)
1Ki 16:34 did Hiel the **B.** build Jericho: 1017

BETH-EMEK (beth-e'-mek)
Jos 19:27 toward the north side of **B.** 1025

BETHER (be'-thur)
Ca 2:17 hart upon the mountains of **B.** 1336

BETHESDA (beth-ez'-dah)
Joh 5:2 is called in the Hebrew tongue **B.**, *964*

BETH-EZEL (beth-e'-zel)
Mic 1:11 not forth in the mourning of **B.**; 1018

BETH-GADER (beth-ga'-der) See also GEDER.
1Ch 2:51 Hareph the father of **B.** 1013

BETH-GAMUL (beth-ga'-mul)
Jer 48:23 upon **B.**, and upon Beth-meon, 1014

BETH-HACCEREM (beth-hak'-se-rem)
Ne 3:14 Rechab, the ruler of part of **B.**; 1021
Jer 6:1 and set up a sign of fire in **B.**: 1021

BETH-HANAN See ELON-BETH-HANAN.

BETH-HARAN (beth-ha'-ran) See also ELON-BETH-HARAN.
Nu 32:36 Beth-nimrah, and **B.**, fenced 1028

BETH-HOGLA (beth-hog'-lah) See also BETH-HOGLAH.
Jos 15:6 went up to **B.**, and passed 1031

BETH-HOGLAH (beth-hog'-lah) See also BETH-HOGLA.
Jos 18:19 along to the side of **B.** northward: 1031
Jos 18:21 Jericho, and **B.**, and the valley of 1031

BETH-HORON (beth-ho'-ron)
Jos 10:10 the way that goeth up to **B.**, 1032
Jos 10:11 and were in the going down to **B.**, 1032
Jos 16:3 the coast of **B.** the nether, and 1032
Jos 16:5 Ataroth-addar, unto **B.** the upper; 1032
Jos 18:13 on the south side of the nether **B.**. 1032
Jos 18:14 hill that lieth before **B.** southward; 1032
Jos 21:22 **B.** with her suburbs; four cities. 1032
1Sa 13:18 company turned the way to **B.** 1032
1Ki 9:17 built Gezer, and **B.** the nether, 1032
1Ch 6:68 **B.** with her suburbs, 1032
1Ch 7:24 Sherah, who built **B.** the nether, 1032
2Ch 8:5 Also he built **B.** the upper, and 1032
2Ch 8:5 **B.** the nether, fenced cities, 1032
2Ch 25:13 from Samaria even unto **B.**, and 1032

BETHINK
1Ki 8:47 **b.** themselves in the 7725,413,3820
2Ch 6:37 **b.** themselves in the 7725,413,3820

BETH-JESIMOTH (beth-jes'-im-oth) See also BETH-JESHIMOTH.
Nu 33:49 from **B.** even unto Abel-shittim 1020

BETH-JESHIMOTH (beth-jesh'-im-oth) See also BETH-JESIMOTH.
Jos 12:3 sea on the east, the way to **B.**; 1020
Jos 13:20 Ashdoth-pisgah, and **B.**, 1020
Eze 25:9 of the country, **B.**, Baal-meon, 1020

BETH-LEBAOTH (beth-leb'-a-oth) See also BETH-BISEL
Jos 19:6 And **B.**, and Sharuhen; thirteen 1034

BETH-LEHEM (beth'-le-hem) See also BETH-LEHEM-ITE; BETH-LEHEM-JUDAH.
Ge 35:19 the way to Ephrath, which is **B.**. 1035
Ge 48:7 way of Ephrath; the same is **B.**. 1035
Jos 19:15 Shimron, and Idalah, and **B.**: 1035
Jg 12:8 after him Ibzan of **B.** judged Israel. 1035
Jg 12:10 died Ibzan, and was buried at **B.** 1035
Ru 1:19 two went until they came to **B.**. 1035
Ru 1:19 they were come to **B.**, that all 1035
Ru 1:22 came to **B.** in the beginning of 1035
Ru 2:4 Boaz came from **B.**, and said 1035
Ru 4:11 in Ephratah, and be famous in **B.** 1035
1Sa 16:4 and came to **B.**. And the elders 1035
1Sa 17:15 to feed his father's sheep at **B.** 1035
1Sa 20:6 that he might run to **B.** his city: 1035
1Sa 20:28 asked leave of me to go to **B.** 1035
2Sa 2:32 of his father, which was in **B.** 1035
2Sa 23:14 of the Philistines was then in **B.**. 1035
2Sa 23:15 the water of the well of **B.**, which 1035
2Sa 23:16 drew water out of the well of **B.**, 1035
2Sa 23:24 Elhanan the son of Dodo of **B.**, 1035
1Ch 2:51 the father of **B.**, Hareph the 1035
1Ch 2:54 Salma; **B.**, and the Netophathites, 1035
1Ch 4:4 of Ephratah, the father of **B.**. 1035
1Ch 11:16 Philistines' garrison was then at **B.**. 1035
1Ch 11:17 the well of **B.**, that is at the gate! 1035
1Ch 11:18 drew water out of the well of **B.**, 1035
1Ch 11:26 Elhanan the son of Dodo of **B.**, 1035
2Ch 11:6 He built even **B.**, and Etam, and 1035
Ezr 2:21 children of **B.**, an hundred twenty 1035
Ne 7:26 The men of **B.**, and Netophah, 1035
Jer 41:17 of Chimham, which is by **B.**, to go 1035
Mic 5:2 thou, **B.** Ephratah, though thou 1035
Mt 2:1 Jesus was born in **B.** of Judaea *965*
Mt 2:5 In **B.** of Judaea: for thus it is *965*
Mt 2:6 And thou **B.**, in the land of Juda, *965*
Mt 2:8 And he sent them to **B.**, and said, *965*
Mt 2:16 all the children that were in **B.**, *965*
Lu 2:4 city of David, which is called **B.**; *965*
Lu 2:15 Let us now go even unto **B.**, and see *965*
Joh 7:42 and out of the town of **B.**, where *965*

BETH-LEHEMITE (beth'-le-hem-ite)
1Sa 16:1 I will send thee to Jesse the **B.**, 1022
1Sa 16:18 I have seen a son of Jesse the **B.** 1022
1Sa 17:58 the son of thy servant Jesse the **B.**, 1022
2Sa 21:19 the son of Jaare-oregim, a **B.**, 1022

BETH-LEHEM-JUDAH (beth''-le-hem-ju'-dah)
Jg 17:7 there was a young man out of **B.** 1035
Jg 17:8 from **B.** to sojourn where he could 1035
Jg 17:9 I am a Levite of **B.**, and I 1035
Jg 19:1 to him a concubine out of **B.**. 1035
Jg 19:2 unto her father's house to **B.**, 1035
Jg 19:18 We are passing from **B.** toward 1035
Jg 19:18 and I went to **B.**, but I 1035
Ru 1:1 a certain man of **B.** went to 1035
Ru 1:2 and Chilion, Ephrathites of **B.** 1035
1Sa 17:12 son of that Ephrathite of **B.**, 1035

BETH-MAACHAH (beth-ma'-a-kah) See also ABEL-BETH-MAACHAH.
2Sa 20:14 unto Abel, and to **B.**, and all 1038
2Sa 20:15 and besieged him in Abel of **B.**, 1038

BETH-MARCABOTH (beth-mar'-cab-oth)
Jos 19:5 Ziklag, and **B.**, and Hazar-susah, 1024
1Ch 4:31 at **B.**, and Hazar-susim, and at 1024

BETH-MEON (beth-me'-on) See also BETH-BAAL-MEON.
Jer 48:23 upon Beth-gamul, and upon **B.**, 1010

BETH-NIMRAH (beth-nim'-rah) See also NIMRAH.
Nu 32:36 **B.**, and Beth-haran, fenced cities: 1039
Jos 13:27 in the valley, Beth-aram, and **B.**, 1039

BETH-PALET (beth-pa'-let) See also BETH-PELET.
Jos 15:27 and Heshmon, and **B.**, 1046

BETH-PAZZEZ (beth-paz'-zez)
Jos 19:21 and En-haddah, and **B.**; 1048

BETH-PEOR (beth-pe'-or)
De 3:29 in the valley over against **B.**. 1047
De 4:46 against **B.**, in the land of Sihon 1047
De 34:6 the land of Moab, over against **B.** 1047
Jos 13:20 And **B.**, and Ashdoth-pisgah, and 1047

BETHPAGE (beth'-fa-je)
Mt 21:1 were come to **B.**, unto the mount *967*
Mk 11:1 Jerusalem, unto **B.**, and Bethany, *967*
Lu 19:29 was come nigh to **B.** and Bethany, *967*

BETH-PHELET (beth'-fe-let) See also BETH-PALET.
Ne 11:26 and at Moladah, and at **B.**, 1046

BETH-RAPHA (beth'-ra-fah)
1Ch 4:12 And Eshton begat **B.**, and 1051

BETH-REHOB (beth'-re-hob)
Jg 18:28 was in the valley that lieth by **B.**. 1050
2Sa 10:6 sent and hired the Syrians of **B.**, 1050

BETHSAIDA (beth-sa'-dah)
Mt 11:21 **woe unto thee, B.! for if the** *966*
Mk 6:45 go to the other side before unto **B.**, *966*
Mk 8:22 And he cometh to **B.**; and they *966*
Lu 9:10 belonging to the city called **B.** *966*
Lu 10:13 **woe unto thee, B.! for if the mighty** *966*
Joh 1:44 Now Philip was of **B.**, the city of *966*
Joh 12:21 therefore to Philip, which was of **B.**. *966*

BETH-SHAN (beth'-shan) See also BETH-SHEAN.
1Sa 31:10 his body to the wall of **B.**. 1052
1Sa 31:12 of his sons from the wall of **B.**, 1052
2Sa 21:12 stolen them from the street of **B.**, 1052

BETH-SHEAN (beth-she'-an) See also BETH-SHAN.
Jos 17:11 **B.** and her towns, and Ibleam 1052
Jos 17:16 both they who are of **B.** and her 1052
Jg 1:27 drive out the inhabitants of **B.** 1052
1Ki 4:12 and all **B.**, which is by Zartanah 1052
1Ki 4:12 Jezreel, from **B.** to Abel-meholah, 1052
1Ch 7:29 children of Manasseh, **B.** and her 1052

BETH-SHEMESH (beth'-she-mesh) See also BETH-SHEMITE.
Jos 15:10 and went down to **B.**, and passed 1053
Jos 19:22 to Tabor, and Shahazimah, and **B.**; 1053
Jos 19:38 Horem, and Beth-anath, and **B.**; 1053
Jos 21:16 Juttah with her suburbs, and **B.**. 1053
Jg 1:33 drive out the inhabitants of **B.**, 1053
Jg 1:33 the inhabitants of **B.** and of 1053
1Sa 6:9 by the way of his own coast to **B.**, 1053
1Sa 6:12 the straight way to the way of **B.**, 1053
1Sa 6:12 after them unto the border of **B.** 1053
1Sa 6:13 they of **B.** were reaping their 1053
1Sa 6:15 the men of **B.** offered burnt 1053
1Sa 6:19 smote the men of **B.**, because they 1053
1Sa 6:20 And the men of **B.** said, Who is 1053
1Ki 4:9 Makaz, and in Shaalbim, and **B.**, 1053
2Ki 14:11 looked one another in the face at **B.**, 1053
2Ki 14:13 the son of Ahaziah, at **B.**, and 1053
1Ch 6:59 Ashan with her suburbs, and **B.** 1053
2Ch 25:21 Amaziah king of Judah, at **B.**, 1053
2Ch 25:23 the son of Jehoahaz, at **B.**, and 1053
2Ch 28:18 Judah, and had taken **B.**, and 1053
Jer 43:13 break also the images of **B.**, that is 1053

BETH-SHEMITE (beth'-shem-ite)
1Sa 6:14 the field of Joshua, a **B.**, and 1030
1Sa 6:18 day in the field of Joshua, the **B.** 1030

BETH-SHITTAH (beth-shit'-tah)
Jg 7:22 and the host fled to **B.** in 1029

BETH-TAPPUAH (beth-tap'-pu-ah)
Jos 15:53 And Janum, and **B.**, and Aphekah, 1054

BETHUEL (beth-u'-el) See also BETHUL.
Ge 22:22 and Pildash, and Jidlaph, and **B.**. 1328
Ge 22:23 And **B.** begat Rebekah: these 1328
Ge 24:15 who was born to **B.**, son of Milcah 1328
Ge 24:24 I am the daughter of **B.** the son of 1328
Ge 24:47 And she said, The daughter of **B.**, 1328
Ge 24:50 Then Laban and **B.** answered and 1328
Ge 25:20 daughter of **B.** the Syrian of 1328
Ge 28:2 to the house of **B.** thy mother's 1328
Ge 28:5 unto Laban, son of **B.** the Syrian, 1328
1Ch 4:30 And at **B.**, and at Hormah, and at 1328

BETHUL (beth'-ul) See also BETHUEL.
Jos 19:4 And Eltolad, and **B.**, and Hormah, 1329

BETH-ZUR (beth'-zur)
Jos 15:58 Halhul, **B.**, and Gedor, 1049
1Ch 2:45 and Maon was the father of **B.**. 1049
2Ch 11:7 And **B.**, and Shoco, and Adullam, 1049
Ne 3:16 the ruler of the half part of **B.**, 1049

BETIMES
Ge 26:31 and they rose up **b.** in the 7925
2Ch 36:15 rising up **b.**, and sending; 7925
Job 8:5 thou wouldest seek unto God **b.**, 7836
Job 24:5 rising **b.** for a prey: the 7836
Pr 13:24 loveth him chasteneth him **b.**. 7836

BETONIM (bet'-o-nim)
Jos 13:26 unto Ramath-mizpeh, and **B.**; 993

BETRAY See also BETRAYED; BETRAYEST; BETRAYETH; BEWRAY.
1Ch 12:17 but if ye be come to **b.** me to 7411
Mt 24:10 **and shall b. one another, and** *3860*
Mt 26:16 he sought opportunity to **b.** him. *3860*
Mt 26:21 **one of you shall b. me** *3860*
Mt 26:23 **in the dish, the same shall b. me** *3860*
Mt 26:46 **he is at hand that doth b. me** *3860*
Mk 13:12 **the brother shall b. the brother** *3860*
Mk 14:10 the chief priests, to **b.** him unto *3860*
Mk 14:11 he might conveniently **b.** him. *3860*
Mk 14:18 **eateth with me shall b. me.** *3860*
Lu 22:4 how he might **b.** him unto them. *3860*
Lu 22:6 sought opportunity to **b.** him. *3860*
Joh 6:64 not, and who should **b.** him. *3860*
Joh 6:71 he it was that should **b.** him, being *3860*
Joh 12:4 Simon's son, which should **b.** him, *3860*
Joh 13:2 Iscariot, Simon's son, to **b.** him; *3860*
Joh 13:11 For he knew who should **b.** him; *3860*
Joh 13:21 **you, that one of you shall b. me.** *3860*

BETRAYED
Mt 10:4 Judas Iscariot, who also **b.** him. *3860*
Mt 17:22 **The Son of man shall be b. into** *3860*
Mt 20:18 **The Son of man shall be b. unto** *3860*
Mt 26:2 **Son of man is b. to be crucified** *3860*
Mt 26:24 **by whom the Son of man is b.!** *3860*
Mt 26:25 Then Judas, which **b.** him, *3860*
Mt 26:45 **Son of man is b. into the hands of** *3860*
Mt 26:48 Now he that **b.** him gave them a *3860*
Mt 27:3 Then Judas, which had **b.** him, *3860*
Mt 27:4 I have sinned in that I have **b.** *3860*
Mk 3:19 Judas Iscariot, which also **b.** him: *3860*
Mk 14:21 **by whom the Son of man is b.!** *3860*
Mk 14:41 **Son of man is b. into the hands** *3860*
Mk 14:44 And he that **b.** him had given them *3860*
Lu 21:16 **And ye shall be b. both by** *3860*
Lu 22:22 **unto that man by whom he is b.!** *3860*
Joh 18:2 And Judas also, which **b.** him, *3860*
Joh 18:5 Judas also, which **b.** him, stood *3860*
1Co 11:23 night in which he was **b.** took *3860*

BETRAYERS
Ac 7:52 ye have been now the **b.** and *4273*

BETRAYEST
Lu 22:48 **b. thou the Son of man with a** *3860*

BETRAYETH See also BEWRAYETH.
Mk 14:42 **lo, he that b. me is at hand.** *3860*
Lu 22:21 **the hand of him that b. me is with** *3860*
Joh 21:20 Lord, which is he that **b.** thee? *3860*

BETROTH See also BETROTHED.
De 28:30 Thou shalt **b.** a wife, and another 781
Ho 2:19 And I will **b.** thee unto me for ever; 781
Ho 2:19 yea, I will **b.** thee unto me in 781
Ho 2:20 I will even **b.** thee unto me in 781

BETROTHED
Ex 21:8 who hath **b.** her to himself, 3259
Ex 21:9 And if he have **b.** her unto his 3259
Ex 22:16 maid that is not **b.**, and lie with 781
Le 19:20 that is a bondmaid, **b.** to an 2778
De 20:7 that hath **b.** a wife, and hath not 781
De 22:23 that is a virgin be **b.** unto an 781
De 22:25 But if a man find a **b.** damsel in the 781
De 22:27 the **b.** damsel cried, and there was 781
De 22:28 which is not **b.**, and lay hold on her, 781

BETTER See also BETTERED.
Ge 29:19 **b.** that I give her to thee, than 2896
Ex 14:12 been **b.** for us to serve the 2896
Nu 14:3 not **b.** for us to return into Egypt? 2896
Jg 8:2 the grapes of Ephraim **b.** than the 2896
Jg 9:2 Whether is **b.** for you, either that 2896
Jg 11:25 now art thou any thing **b.** than 2896
Jg 18:19 is it **b.** for thee to be a priest unto 2896
Ru 4:15 which is **b.** to thee than seven sons, 2896
1Sa 1:8 am not I **b.** to thee than ten sons? 2896
1Sa 15:22 Behold, to obey is **b.** than sacrifice, 2896
1Sa 15:28 neighbour of thine, that is **b.** than 2896
1Sa 27:1 nothing **b.** for me than that I 2896
2Sa 17:14 **b.** than the counsel of Ahithophel. 2896
2Sa 18:3 **b.** that thou succour us out of the 2896
1Ki 1:47 God make the name of Solomon **b.** 3190
1Ki 2:32 more righteous and **b.** than he, 2896
1Ki 19:4 for I am not **b.** than my fathers. 2896
1Ki 21:2 I will give thee for it a **b.** vineyard 2896
2Ki 5:12 **b.** than all the waters of Israel? 2896
2Ch 21:13 which were **b.** than thyself: 2896
Es 1:19 estate unto another that is **b.** than 2896
Ps 37:16 **b.** than the riches of many wicked. 2896
Ps 63:3 loving kindness is **b.** than life, my 2896
Ps 69:31 This also shall please the Lord **b.** 3190
Ps 84:10 a day in thy courts is **b.** than a 2896
Ps 118:8, 9 **b.** to trust in the Lord than to 2896
Ps 119:72 the law of thy mouth is **b.** unto me 2896
Pr 3:14 **b.** than the merchandise of silver, 2896
Pr 8:11 For wisdom is **b.** than rubies; 2896
Pr 8:19 My fruit is **b.** than gold, yea, 2896
Pr 12:9 is **b.** than he that honoureth 2896
Pr 15:16 **B.** is little with the fear of the 2896
Pr 15:17 **B.** is a dinner of herbs where love 2896
Pr 16:8 **B.** is a little with righteousness 2896
Pr 16:16 how much **b.** is it to get wisdom 2896
Pr 16:19 **B.** it is to be of an humble spirit 2896
Pr 16:32 slow to anger is **b.** than the mighty 2896
Pr 17:1 **B.** is a dry morsel, and quietness 2896
Pr 19:1 **B.** is the poor that walketh in his 2896
Pr 19:22 and a poor man is **b.** than a liar. 2896
Pr 21:9 **b.** to dwell in a corner of the 2896
Pr 21:19 **b.** to dwell in the wilderness, 2896
Pr 25:7 **b.** it is that it be said unto thee, 2896
Pr 25:24 It is **b.** to dwell in the corner 2896
Pr 27:5 Open rebuke is **b.** than secret love. 2896
Pr 27:10 **b.** is a neighbour that is near than 2896
Pr 28:6 **B.** is the poor that walketh in his 2896
Ec 2:24 nothing **b.** for a man, than that he 2896
Ec 3:22 I perceive that there is nothing **b.**, 2896
Ec 4:3 Yea, **b.** is he than both they, which 2896
Ec 4:6 **B.** is an handful with quietness, 2896
Ec 4:9 Two are **b.** than one; because they 2896
Ec 4:13 **B.** is a poor and a wise child than 2896
Ec 5:5 **B.** is it that thou shouldest not 2896
Ec 6:3 an untimely birth is **b.** than he. 2896
Ec 6:9 **B.** is the sight of the eyes than the 2896
Ec 6:11 what is man the **b.**? 3148
Ec 7:1 A good name is **b.** than 2896
Ec 7:2 **b.** to go to the house of mourning, 2896
Ec 7:3 Sorrow is **b.** than laughter: for by 2896
Ec 7:3 countenance the heart is made **b.**. 3190
Ec 7:5 **b.** to hear the rebuke of the wise, 2896
Ec 7:8 **B.** is the end of a thing than the 2896
Ec 7:8 spirit is **b.** than the proud in spirit. 2896
Ec 7:10 cause that the former days were **b.** 2896
Ec 8:15 hath no **b.** thing under the sun, 2896
Ec 9:4 a living dog is **b.** than a dead lion. 2896
Ec 9:16 said I, Wisdom is **b.** than strength: 2896
Ec 9:18 Wisdom is **b.** than weapons of war: 2896
Ec 10:11 and a babbler is no **b.**. 3504
Ca 1:2 for thy love is **b.** than wine. 2896
Ca 4:10 how much **b.** is thy love than wine! 2896
Isa 56:5 **b.** than of sons and of daughters: 2896
La 4:9 **b.** than they that be slain with 2896
Eze 36:11 will do **b.** unto you than at your 2896
Da 1:20 ten times **b.** than all the magicians 3027
Ho 2:7 then it was **b.** with me than now. 2896
Am 6:2 be they **b.** than these kingdoms? 2896
Jon 4:3, 8 it is **b.** for me to die than to live. 2896
Na 3:8 Art thou **b.** than populous No, 3190
Mt 6:26 **Are ye not much b. than they?** *1308*
Mt 12:12 **then is a man b. than a sheep?** *1308*
Mt 18:6 **it were b. for him that a millstone** *4851*
Mt 18:8, 9 **it is b. for thee to enter into life** *2570*
Mk 9:42 **is b. for him that a millstone** *2570, 3123*
Mk 9:43 **it is b. for thee to enter into life** *2570*
Mk 9:45 **it is b. for thee to enter halt** *2570*
Mk 9:47 **it is b. for thee to enter into the** *2570*
Lu 5:39 **for he saith, The old is b.** *5543*
Lu 12:24 **more are ye b. than the fowls?** *1308*
Lu 17:2 **were b. for him that a millstone** *3081*

Ro 3:9 What then? are we **b.** than they? *4284*
1Co 7:9 it is **b.** to marry than to burn. *2909*
1Co 7:38 her not in marriage doeth **b.**. *2573*
1Co 8:8 neither, if we eat, are we the **b.**; *4052*
1Co 9:15 it were **b.** for me to die, *2570,3123*
1Co 11:17 not for the **b.**, but for the worse. *2909*
Php 1:23 to be with Christ; which is far **b.** *2909*
Php 2:3 esteem other **b.** than themselves. *5242*
Heb 1:4 made so much **b.** than the angels, *2909*
Heb 6:9 we are persuaded **b.** things of you, *2909*
Heb 7:7 the less is blessed of the **b.**. *2909*
Heb 7:19 but the bringing in of a **b.** hope. *2909*
Heb 7:22 made a surety of a **b.** testament. *2909*
Heb 8:6 the mediator of a **b.** covenant, *2909*
Heb 8:6 was established upon **b.** promises. *2909*
Heb 9:23 with **b.** sacrifices than these. *2909*
Heb 10:34 in heaven a **b.** and an enduring *2909*
Heb 11:16 But now they desire a **b.** country, *2909*
Heb 11:35 they might obtain a **b.** resurrection: *2909*
Heb 11:40 provided some **b.** thing for us, *2909*
Heb 12:24 **b.** things than that of Abel. *2909*
1Pe 3:17 it is **b.**, if the will of God be so, *2909*
2Pe 2:21 For it had been **b.** for them not to *2909*

BETTERED
Mk 5:26 nothing **b.**, but rather grew worse, *5623*

BETWEEN See also BETWIXT.
Ge 3:15 enmity **b.** thee and the woman, 996
Ge 3:15 and **b.** thy seed and her seed; 996
Ge 9:12 covenant which I make **b.** me and 996
Ge 9:13 a covenant **b.** me and the earth. 996
Ge 9:15 covenant, which is **b.** me and you 996
Ge 9:16 covenant **b.** God and every living 996
Ge 9:17 which I have established **b.** me and 996
Ge 10:12 And Resen **b.** Nineveh, and Calah 996
Ge 13:3 the beginning, **b.** Beth-el and Hai; 996
Ge 13:7 there was a strife **b.** the herdmen 996
Ge 13:8 **b.** me and thee, and **b.** my 996
Ge 15:17 lamp that passed **b.** those pieces. 996
Ge 16:5 the Lord judge **b.** me and thee. 996
Ge 16:14 behold, it is **b.** Kadesh and Bered. 996
Ge 17:2 make my covenant **b.** me and thee, 996
Ge 17:7 establish my covenant **b.** me and 996
Ge 17:10 **b.** me and you and thy seed after 996
Ge 20:1 and dwelled **b.** Kadesh and Shur, 996
Ge 31:44 be for a witness **b.** me and thee. 996
Ge 31:48 said, This heap is a witness **b.** me 996
Ge 31:49 The Lord watch **b.** me and thee, 996
Ge 48:12 them out from **b.** his knees, 5973
Ge 49:10 nor a lawgiver from **b.** his feet, 996
Ge 49:14 is a strong ass couching down **b.** two 996
Ex 8:23 I will put a division **b.** my people 996
Ex 9:4 the Lord shall sever **b.** the cattle of 996
Ex 11:7 a difference **b.** the Egyptians and 996
Ex 13:9 and for a memorial **b.** thine eyes, 996
Ex 13:16 and for frontlets **b.** thine eyes: 996
Ex 14:2 **b.** Migdol and the sea, over against 996
Ex 14:20 came **b.** the camp of the Egyptians 996
Ex 16:1 the wilderness of Sin, which is **b.** 996
Ex 18:16 and I judge **b.** one another, 996
Ex 22:11 an oath of the Lord be **b.** them both, 996
Ex 25:22 from **b.** the two cherubim which 996
Ex 26:33 vail shall divide unto you **b.** the holy 996
Ex 28:33 bells of gold **b.** them round about: 8432
Ex 30:18 thou shalt put it **b.** the tabernacle 996
Ex 31:13 for it is a sign **b.** me and you 996
Ex 31:17 It is a sign **b.** me and the children of 996
Ex 39:25 put the bells **b.** the pomegranates 8432
Ex 39:25 round about **b.** the pomegranates; 8432
Ex 40:7 thou shalt set the laver **b.** the tent 996
Ex 40:30 laver **b.** the tent of the congregation 996
Le 10:10 that ye may put difference **b.** holy 996
Le 10:10 and **b.** unclean and clean: 996
Le 11:47 make a difference **b.** the unclean 996
Le 11:47 and **b.** the beast that may be eaten 996
Le 20:25 therefore put difference **b.** clean 996
Le 20:25 and unclean, and **b.** unclean fowls 996
Le 26:46 which the Lord made **b.** him and 996
Nu 7:89 from **b.** the two cherubim: 996
Nu 11:33 the flesh was yet **b.** their teeth, 996
Nu 13:23 and they bare it **b.** two upon a staff; 996
Nu 16:48 stood **b.** the dead and the living; 996
Nu 21:13 is the border of Moab, **b.** Moab 996
Nu 26:56 thereof be divided **b.** many and few. 996
Nu 30:16 **b.** a man and his wife, 996
Nu 30:16 **b.** the father and his daughter, 996
Nu 31:27 prey into two parts; **b.** them that 996
Nu 31:27 and **b.** all the congregation. 996
Nu 35:24 congregation shall judge **b.** the 996
De 1:1 plain over against the Red sea, **b.** 996
De 1:16 Hear the causes **b.** your brethren, 996
De 1:16 and judge righteously **b.** 996
De 1:39 had no knowledge **b.** good and evil,
De 5:5 (I stood **b.** the Lord and you at 996
De 6:8 shall be as frontlets **b.** thine eyes. 996
De 11:18 may be as frontlets **b.** your eyes. 996
De 14:1 baldness **b.** your eyes for the dead. 996
De 17:8 **b.** blood and blood, **b.** plea and plea, 996
De 17:8 and **b.** stroke and stroke, 996
De 19:17 men, **b.** whom the controversy is,
De 25:1 If there be a controversy **b.** men, 996
De 28:57 young one that cometh out from **b.** 996
De 33:12 he shall dwell **b.** his shoulders. 996
Jos 3:4 there shall be a space **b.** you and it, 996
Jos 8:9 to lie in ambush, and abode **b.** 996
Jos 8:11 there was a valley **b.** them and Ai. 996
Jos 8:12 to lie in ambush **b.** Beth-el and Ai, 996
Jos 18:11 coast of their lot came forth **b.** the 996
Jos 22:25 Lord hath made Jordan a border **b.** 996
Jos 22:27 But that it may be a witness **b.** us, 996
Jos 22:28 but it is a witness **b.** us and 996
Jos 22:34 witness **b.** us that the Lord is God. 996
Jos 24:7 darkness **b.** you and the Egyptians, 996
Jg 4:5 **b.** Ramah and Beth-el in mount 996
Jg 4:17 there was peace **b.** Jabin the king 996
Jg 9:23 God sent an evil spirit **b.** Abimelech 996
Jg 11:10 The Lord be witness **b.** us, if we do 996
Jg 11:27 the Judge be judge this day **b.** the 996
Jg 13:25 camp of Dan **b.** Zorah and Eshtaol. 996
Jg 15:4 firebrand in the midst **b.** two tails. 996
Jg 16:25 and they set him **b.** the pillars 996
Jg 16:31 and buried him **b.** Zorah and Eshtaol. 996
Jg 20:38 there was an appointed sign **b.** the 5973
1Sa 4:4 which dwelleth **b.** the cherubim:
1Sa 7:12 Samuel took a stone, and set it **b.** 996
1Sa 7:14 was peace **b.** Israel and the Amorites. 996
1Sa 14:4 And **b.** the passages, by which 996
1Sa 14:42 And Saul said, Cast lots **b.** me and 996
1Sa 17:1 pitched **b.** Shochoh and Azekah, 996
1Sa 17:3 and there was a valley **b.** them. 996
1Sa 17:6 a target of brass **b.** his shoulders. 996
1Sa 20:3 there is but a step **b.** me and death. 996
1Sa 20:23 the Lord be **b.** thee and me for ever. 996
1Sa 20:42 **b.** me and thee, and **b.** my seed 996
1Sa 24:12 The Lord judge **b.** me and thee, 996
1Sa 24:15 therefore be judge and judge **b.** 996
1Sa 26:13 a great space being **b.** them: 996
2Sa 3:1 was long war **b.** the house of Saul 996
2Sa 3:6 there was war **b.** the house of Saul 996
2Sa 6:2 that dwelleth **b.** the cherubim.
2Sa 18:9 up **b.** the heaven and the earth; 996
2Sa 18:24 And David sat **b.** the two gates: 996
2Sa 19:35 can I discern **b.** good and evil? 996
2Sa 21:7 the Lord's oath that was **b.** them, **b.** 996
1Ki 3:9 I may discern **b.** good and bad: 996
1Ki 5:12 peace **b.** Hiram and Solomon; 996
1Ki 7:28 the borders were **b.** the ledges: 996
1Ki 7:29 **b.** the ledges were lions, oxen, 996
1Ki 7:46 in the clay ground **b.** Succoth 996
1Ki 14:30 war **b.** Rehoboam and Jeroboam 996
1Ki 15:6 war **b.** Rehoboam and Jeroboam all 996
1Ki 15:7 was war **b.** Abijam and Jeroboam. 996
1Ki 15:16 was war **b.** Asa and Baasha king of 996
1Ki 15:19 There is a league **b.** me and thee, 996
1Ki 15:19 and **b.** my father and thy father: 996
1Ki 15:32 was war **b.** Asa and Baasha king of 996
1Ki 18:6 divided the land **b.** them to pass
1Ki 18:21 How long halt ye **b.** two opinions? 5921
1Ki 18:42 and put his face **b.** his knees, 996
1Ki 22:1 without war **b.** Syria and Israel. 996
1Ki 22:34 smote the king of Israel **b.** the joints 996
2Ki 9:24 and smote Jehoram **b.** his arms, 996
2Ki 11:17 made a covenant **b.** the Lord 996
2Ki 11:17 **b.** the king also and the people. 996
2Ki 16:14 from **b.** the altar and the house of 996
2Ki 19:15 God of Israel, which dwellest **b.** the
2Ki 25:4 the way of the gate **b.** two walls, 996
1Ch 13:6 that dwelleth **b.** the cherubim,
1Ch 21:16 angel of the Lord stand **b.** the earth 996
2Ch 4:17 in the clay ground **b.** Succoth and 996
2Ch 12:15 wars **b.** Rehoboam and Jeroboam
2Ch 13:2 And there was war **b.** Abijah and 996
2Ch 16:3 There is a league **b.** me and thee, 996
2Ch 16:3 was **b.** my father and thy father: 996
2Ch 18:33 and smote the king of Israel **b.** 996
2Ch 19:10 **b.** blood and blood, **b.** law and 996
2Ch 23:16 Jehoiada made a covenant **b.** him, 996
2Ch 23:16 and **b.** all the people. 996
2Ch 23:16 and **b.** the king, that they should 996
Ne 3:32 And **b.** the going up of the corner 996
Job 41:16 that no air can come **b.** them. 996
Ps 80:1 that dwellest **b.** the cherubim,
Ps 99:1 he sitteth **b.** the cherubim:
Pr 18:18 cease and parteth **b.** the mighty. 996
Isa 22:11 Ye made also a ditch **b.** the 996
Isa 37:16 God of Israel, that dwellest **b.**
Isa 59:2 **b.** you and your God, and your 996
Jer 7:5 **b.** a man and his neighbour; 996
Jer 34:18 and passed **b.** the parts thereof, 996
Jer 34:19 passed **b.** the parts of the calf; 996
Jer 42:5 faithful witness **b.** us, if we do 996
Jer 52:7 way of the gate **b.** the two walls, 996
La 1:3 persecutors overtook her **b.** the 996
Eze 4:3 a wall of iron **b.** thee and the city: 996
Eze 8:3 lifted me up **b.** the earth and the 996
Eze 8:16 **b.** the porch and the altar, 996
Eze 10:2 Go in **b.** the wheels, even under 996
Eze 10:2 coals of fire from **b.** the cherubim 996
Eze 10:6 fire from **b.** the wheels, from **b.** the 996
Eze 10:7 his hand from **b.** the cherubim 996
Eze 10:7 that was **b.** the cherubim, 996
Eze 18:8 executed true judgment **b.** man 996
Eze 20:12 to be a sign **b.** me and them, that 996
Eze 20:20 and they shall be a sign **b.** 996
Eze 22:26 difference **b.** the holy and profane, 996
Eze 22:26 they shewed difference **b.** the 996
Eze 34:17 I judge **b.** cattle and cattle, 996
Eze 34:17 **b.** the rams and the he goats.
Eze 34:20 will judge **b.** the fat cattle and 996
Eze 34:20 **b.** the lean cattle. 996
Eze 34:22 I will judge **b.** cattle and cattle. 996
Eze 40:7 and **b.** the little chambers were 996
Eze 41:10 **b.** the chambers was the wideness 996
Eze 41:18 so that a palmtree was **b.** a cherub 996
Eze 42:20 a separation **b.** the sanctuary 996
Eze 43:8 and the wall **b.** me and them, they 996
Eze 44:23 difference **b.** the holy and profane, 996
Eze 44:23 cause them to discern **b.** the 996
Eze 47:16 which is **b.** the border of Damascus 996
Eze 48:22 **b.** the border of Judah and the 996
Da 7:5 three ribs in the mouth of it **b.** the 997
Da 8:5 goat had a notable horn **b.** his eyes. 996
Da 8:16 a man's voice **b.** the banks of Ulai, 996
Da 8:21 the great horn that is **b.** his eyes 996
Da 11:45 the tabernacles of his palace **b.** 996
Ho 2:2 her adulteries from **b.** her breasts; 996
Joe 2:17 weep **b.** the porch and the altar, 996
Jon 4:11 persons that cannot discern **b.** 996
Zec 5:9 lifted up the ephah **b.** the earth 996
Zec 6:1 out from **b.** two mountains; 996
Zec 6:13 counsel of peace shall be **b.** them 996
Zec 9:7 his abominations from **b.** his teeth: 996
Zec 11:14 brotherhood **b.** Judah and Israel. 996
Mal 2:14 Lord hath been witness **b.** thee 996
Mal 3:18 shall ye return, and discern **b.** the 996
Mal 3:18 the wicked, **b.** him that serveth 996
Mt 18:15 **his fault b. thee and him alone:** *3342*
Mt 23:35 **b. the temple and the altar.** *3342*
Lu 11:51 **b. the altar and the temple:** *3342*
Lu 16:26 **b. us and you there is a great gulf** *3342*
Lu 23:12 were at enmity **b.** themselves. *4314*
Joh 3:25 **b.** some of John's disciples *1537,3326*
Ac 12:6 was sleeping **b.** two soldiers, *3342*
Ac 15:9 no difference **b.** us and them, *3342*
Ac 15:39 contention was so sharp **b.** them,
Ac 23:7 dissension **b.** the Pharisees and
Ac 26:31 they talked **b.** themselves, *4314*
Ro 1:24 dishonour their own bodies **b.** *1722*
Ro 10:12 there is no difference **b.** the Jew
1Co 6:5 able to judge **b.** his brethren? *303,3319*
1Co 7:34 There is difference also **b.** a wife *3307*
Eph 2:14 middle wall of partition **b.** us;
1Ti 2:5 one God, and one mediator **b.** God

BETWIXT See also BETWEEN.
Ge 17:11 token of the covenant **b.** me and 996
Ge 23:15 what is that **b.** me and thee? 996
Ge 26:28 an oath **b.** us, even **b.** us and thee, 996
Ge 30:36 And he set three days' journey **b.** 996
Ge 31:37 that they may judge **b.** us both. 996
Ge 31:50 God is witness **b.** me and thee. 996

Ge 31:51 which I have cast **b.** me and thee; 996
Ge 31:53 God of their father, judge **b.** us. 996
Ge 32:16 put a space **b.** drove and drove. 996
Job 9:33 is there any daysman **b.** us, that 996
Job 36:32 by the cloud that cometh **b.** 6293
Ca 1:13 he shall lie all night **b.** my breasts. 996
Isa 5:3 pray you, **b.** me and my vineyard. 996
Jer 39:4 the gate **b.** the two walls: and he 996
Php 1:23 I am in a strait **b.** two, having *1537*

BEULAH (be-u'-lah)
Isa 62:4 and thy land **B.**: for the Lord 1166

BEWAIL See also BEWAILED; BEWAILETH.
Le 10:6 the whole house of Israel, **b.** 1058
De 21:13 and **b.** her father and her mother 1058
Jg 11:37 and **b.** my virginity, I and my 1058
Isa 16:9 I will **b.** with the weeping 1058
2Co 12:21 and that I shall **b.** many which *3996*
Re 18:9 shall **b.** her, and lament for her, *2799*

BEWAILED
Jg 11:38 companions, and **b.** her virginity 1058
Lu 8:52 And all wept, and **b.** her: but he *2875*
Lu 23:27 which also **b.** and lamented *2875*

BEWAILETH
Jer 4:31 daughter of Zion, that **b.** herself, 3306

BEWARE
Ge 24:6 **B.** thou that thou bring not my 8104
Ex 23:21 **B.** of him, and obey his voice, 8104
De 6:12 Then **b.** lest thou forget the Lord, 8104
De 8:11 **B.** that thou forget not the Lord 8104
De 15:9 **B.** that there be not a thought in 8104
Jg 13:4 Now therefore **b.**, I pray thee, 8104
Jg 13:13 I said unto the woman let her **b.** 8104
2Sa 18:12 **B.** that none touch the young man 8104
2Ki 6:9 **B.** that thou pass not such a place; 8104
Job 36:18 Because there is wrath, **b.** lest
Pr 19:25 a scorner, and the simple will **b.** 6191
Isa 36:18 **B.** lest Hezekiah persuade you,
Mt 7:15 **B. of false prophets, which come** *4337*
Mt 10:17 **But b. of men: for they will** *4337*
Mt 16:6 **Take heed and b. of the leaven** *4337*
Mt 16:11 **that ye should b. of the leaven** *4337*
Mt 16:12 not **b.** of the leaven of bread, but *4337*
Mk 8:15 **Take heed, b. of the leaven of the** *991*
Mk 12:38 **B. of the scribes, which love to go** *991*
Lu 12:1 **B. ye of the leaven of the** *4337*
Lu 12:15 **heed, and b. of covetousness:** *5442*
Lu 20:46 **B. of the scribes, which desire** *4337*
Ac 13:40 **B.** therefore, lest that come *991*
Php 3:2 **B.** of dogs, **b.** of evilworkers, *991*
Php 3:2 **b.** of the concision. *991*
Col 2:8 **B.** lest any man spoil you *991*
2Pe 3:17 ye know these things before, **b.** *5442*

BEWITCHED
Ac 8:9 **b.** the people of Samaria, giving *1839*
Ac 8:11 he had **b.** them with sorceries. *1839*
Ga 3:1 foolish Galatians, who hath **b.** *940*

BEWRAY See also BETRAY; BEWRAYETH.
Isa 16:3 the outcasts; **b.** not him that 1540

BEWRAYETH See also BETRAYETH.
Pr 27:16 of his right hand, which **b.** itself. 7121
Pr 29:24 heareth cursing, and **b.** it not. 5046
Mt 26:73 for thy speech **b.** thee. *1212,4160*

BEYOND
Ge 35:21 spread his tent **b.** the tower of 1973
Ge 50:10 of Atad, which is **b.** Jordan, 5676
Ge 50:11 called Abel-Mizraim, which is **b.** 5676
Le 15:25 run **b.** the time of her separation; 5921
Nu 22:18 I cannot go **b.** the word of the 5674
Nu 24:13 go **b.** the commandment of the 5674
De 3:20 God hath given them **b.** Jordan: 5676
De 3:25 the good land that is **b.** Jordan, 5676
De 30:13 Neither is it **b.** the sea, that thou 5676
Jos 9:10 the Amorites, that were **b.** Jordan, 5676
Jos 13:8 Moses gave them, **b.** Jordan 5676
Jos 18:7 received their inheritance **b.** 5676
Jg 3:26 and passed **b.** the quarries, and 5674
Jg 5:17 Gilead abode **b.** Jordan: and why 5676
1Sa 20:22 the arrows are **b.** thee; go thy 1973
1Sa 20:36 lad ran, he shot an arrow **b.** him. 5674
1Sa 20:37 and said, Is not the arrow **b.** thee? 1973
2Sa 10:16 the Syrians that were **b.** the river: 5676
1Ki 4:12 even unto the place that is **b.** 5676
1Ki 14:15 shall scatter them **b.** the river, 5676
1Ch 19:16 the Syrians that were **b.** the river: 5676
2Ch 20:2 from **b.** the sea on this side Syria; 5676
Ezr 4:17 and unto the rest **b.** the river, 5675
Ezr 4:20 have ruled over all countries **b.** 5675
Ezr 6:6 therefore, Tatnai, governor **b.** the 5675
Ezr 6:6 which are **b.** the river, be ye far 5675
Ezr 6:8 even of the tribute **b.** the river, 5675
Ezr 7:21 treasurers which are **b.** the river, 5675
Ezr 7:25 the people that are **b.** the river, all 5675
Ne 2:7 to the governors **b.** the river, that 5676
Ne 2:9 came to the governors **b.** the river, 5676
Ne 12:38 **b.** the tower of the furnaces 5921
Isa 7:20 by them **b.** the river, by the king 5676
Isa 9:1 **b.** Jordan, in Galilee of the nations. 5676
Isa 18:1 which is **b.** the rivers of Ethiopia: 5676
Jer 22:19 and cast forth **b.** the gates of 1973
Jer 25:22 the isles which are **b.** the sea, 5676
Am 5:27 you to go into captivity **b.** 1973
Zep 3:10 From **b.** the rivers of Ethiopia 5676
Mt 4:15 the way of the sea, **b.** Jordan, *4008*
Mt 4:25 Judaea, and from **b.** Jordan. *4008*
Mt 19:1 the coasts of Judaea **b.** Jordan; *4008*
Mk 3:8 Idumaea, and from **b.** Jordan; *4008*
Mk 6:51 in themselves **b.** measure, *1537,4053*
Mk 7:37 And were **b.** measure astonished, *5249*
Joh 1:28 in Bethabara **b.** Jordan, where *4008*
Joh 3:26 he that was with thee **b.** Jordan, *4008*
Joh 10:40 went away again **b.** Jordan into *4008*
Ac 7:43 I will carry you away **b.** Babylon. *1900*
2Co 8:3 yea, and **b.** their power they *5228*
2Co 10:14 we stretch not ourselves **b.** our *5239*
2Co 10:16 the gospel in the regions **b.** you, *5238*
Gal 1:13 **b.** measure I persecuted *2596,5236*
1Th 4:6 no man go **b.** and defraud *5233*

BEZAI (be'-zahee)
Ezr 2:17 The children of **B.**, three 1209
Ne 7:23 children of **B.**, three hundred 1209
Ne 10:18 Hodijah, Hashum, **B.**, 1209

BEZALEEL (be-zal'-e-el)
Ex 31:2 I have called by name **B.** the son 1212
Ex 35:30 the Lord hath called by name **B.** 1212
Ex 36:1 Then wrought **B.** and Aholiab, 1212
Ex 36:2 Moses called **B.** and Aholiab, 1212
Ex 37:1 **B.** made the ark of shittim wood: 1212
Ex 38:22 **B.** the son of Uri, the son of Hur, 1212
1Ch 2:20 Hur begat Uri, and Uri begat **B.** 1212
2Ch 1:5 Moreover the brasen altar, that **B.** 1212
Ezr 10:30 Mattaniah, **B.**, and Binnui, and 1212

BEZEK (be'-zek) See also ADONI-BEZEK.
Jg 1:4 they slew of them in **B.** ten 966
Jg 1:5 And they found Adoni-bezek in **B.** 966
1Sa 11:8 And when he numbered them in **B.**, 966

BEZER (be'-zer)
De 4:43 Namely, **B.** in the wilderness, 1221
Jos 20:8 assigned **B.** in the wilderness 1221
Jos 21:36 Reuben, **B.** with her suburbs 1221
1Ch 6:78 **B.** in the wilderness with her 1221
1Ch 7:37 **B.**, and Hod, and Shamma, and 1221

BIBBER See WINEBIBBER.

BICHRI (bik'-ri)
2Sa 20:1 the son of **B.**, a Benjamite: 1075
2Sa 20:2 Sheba the son of **B.**: but the men 1075
2Sa 20:6 Sheba the son of **B.** do us more 1075
2Sa 20:7 pursue after Sheba the son of **B.** 1075
2Sa 20:10 pursued after Sheba the son of **B.** 1075
2Sa 20:13 pursue after Sheba the son of **B.** 1075
2Sa 20:21 Sheba the son of **B.** by name, 1075
2Sa 20:22 the head of Sheba the son of **B.**, 1075

BID See also BADE; BIDDEN; BIDDING; FORBID.
Nu 15:38 and **b.** them that they make them 559
Jos 6:10 until the day I **b.** you shout; 559
1Sa 9:27 **B.** the servant pass on before us. 559
2Sa 2:26 long shall it be then, ere thou **b.** 559
2Ki 4:24 riding for me, except I **b.** thee. 559
2Ki 5:13 if the prophet had **b.** thee do 1696
2Ki 10:5 will do all that thou shalt **b.** us; 559
Jo 3:2 the preaching that I **b.** thee. 1696
Zep 1:7 prepared a sacrifice, he hath **b.** 6942
Mt 14:28 **b.** me come unto thee on the *2753*
Mt 22:9 **ye shall find, b. to the marriage.** *2564*
Mt 23:3 **therefore whatsoever they b. you** *2036*
Lu 9:61 let me first go **b.** them farewell, *657*
Lu 10:40 **b.** her therefore that she help me. *2036*
Lu 14:12 **lest they also b. thee again, and** *479*
1Co 10:27 any of them that believe not **b.** *2564*
2Jo 10 house, neither **b.** him God speed: *3004*

BIDDEN See also FORBIDDEN.
1Sa 9:13 afterwards they eat that be **b.** 7121
1Sa 9:22 among them that were **b.**, which 7121
2Sa 16:11 for the Lord hath **b.** him. 559
Mt 1:24 angel of the Lord had **b.** him, *4367*
Mt 22:3 **to call them that were b.** *2564*
Mt 22:4 **Tell them which are b., Behold, I** *2564*
Mt 22:8 **which were b. were not worthy.** *2564*
Lu 7:39 the Pharisee which had **b.** him *2564*
Lu 14:7 a parable to those which were **b.**, *2564*
Lu 14:8 **When thou art b. of any man** *2564*
Lu 14:8 **man than thou be b. of him;** *2564*
Lu 14:10 **when thou art b., go and sit down** *2564*
Lu 14:17 **to say to them that were b.,** *2564*
Lu 14:24 **none of those men which were b.** *2564*

BIDDETH See also FORBIDDETH.
2Jo 11 For he that **b.** him God speed *3004*

BIDDING See also FORBIDDING.
1Sa 22:14 and goeth at thy **b.**, and is 4928

BIDKAR (bid'-kar)
2Ki 9:25 said Jehu to **B.** his captain, 920

BIER
2Sa 3:31 king David himself followed the **b.** 4296
Lu 7:14 And he came and touched the **b.** *4673*

BIGTHA (big'-thah)
Es 1:10 Harbona, **B.**, and Abagtha, 903

BIGTHAN (big'-than) See also BIGTHANA.
Es 2:21 king's chamberlains, **B.** and 904

BIGTHANA (big'-than-ah) See also BIGTHAN.
Es 6:2 Mordecai had told of **B.** and 904

BIGVAI (big'-vahee)
Ezr 2:2 Mizpar, **B.**, Rehum, Baanah. 902
Ezr 2:14 The children of **B.**, two thousand 902
Ezr 8:14 Of the sons also of **B.**; Uthai, and 902
Ne 7:7 Bilshan, Mispereth, **B.**, Nehum, 902
Ne 7:19 The children of **B.**, two thousand 902
Ne 10:16 Adonijah, **B.**, Adin, 902

BILDAD (bil'-dad)
Job 2:11 **B.** the Shuhite, and Zophar 1085
Job 8:1 Then answered **B.** the Shuhite, 1085
Job 18:1 **B.** the Shuhite, and said, 1085
Job 25:1 **B.** the Shuhite, and said, 1085
Job 42:9 Temanite and **B.** the Shuhite 1085

BILEAM (bil'-e-am) See also IBLEAM.
1Ch 6:70 suburbs, and **B.** with her suburbs, 1109

BILGAH (bil'-gah)
1Ch 24:14 The fifteenth to **B.**, the 1083
Ne 12:5 Miamin, Maadiah, **B.**, 1083
Ne 12:18 Of **B.**, Shammua; of Shemaiah. 1083

BILGAI (bil'-gahee)
Ne 10:8 Maaziah, **B.**, Shemaiah: these 1084

BILHAH (bil'-hah) See also BALAH.
Ge 29:29 **B.** his handmaid to be her 1090
Ge 30:3 Behold my maid **B.**, go in unto 1090
Ge 30:4 gave him **B.** her handmaid to 1090
Ge 30:5 And **B.** conceived, and bare 1090
Ge 30:7 And **B.** Rachel's maid conceived 1090
Ge 35:22 went and lay with **B.** his father's 1090
Ge 35:25 And the sons of **B.**, Rachel's 1090
Ge 37:2 the lad was with the sons of **B.**, 1090
Ge 46:25 These are the sons of **B.**, which 1090
1Ch 4:29 And at **B.**, and at Ezem, and at 1090
1Ch 7:13 and Shallum, the sons of **B.** 1090

BILHAN (bil'-han)
Ge 36:27 **B.**, and Zaavan, and Akan. 1092
1Ch 1:42 Ezer; **B.**, and Zavan, and Jakan. 1092
1Ch 7:10 The sons also of Jediael; **B.** 1092
1Ch 7:10 and the sons of **B.**; Jeush, 1092

BILL
De 24:1 write her a **b.** of divorcement, 5612
De 24:3 and write her a **b.** of divorcement, 5612
Isa 50:1 Where is the **b.** of your mother's 5612
Jer 3:8 and given her a **b.** of divorce; 5612

Mk 10:4 to write a **b.** of divorcement, ... *975*
Lu 16:6, 7 **he said unto him, Take thy b.,** ... *1121*

BILLOWS
Ps 42:7 all thy waves and thy **b.** are ... 1530
Jon 2:3 all thy **b.** and thy waves passed ... 4867

BILSHAN (bil'-shan)
Ezr 2:2 Reelaiah, Mordecai, **B.**, Mizpar, ... 1114
Ne 7:7 Nahamani, Mordecai, **B.**, ... 1114

BIMHAL (bim'-hal)
1Ch 7:33 Pasach, and **B.**, and Ashvath. ... 1118

BIND See also BINDETH; BINDING; BOUND.
Ex 28:28 they shall **b.** the breastplate ... 7405
Ex 39:21 And they did **b.** the breastplate ... 7405
Nu 30:2 swear an oath to **b.** his soul ... 631
Nu 30:3 Lord, and **b.** herself by a bond, ... 631
De 6:8 thou shalt **b.** them for a sign ... 7194
De 11:18 and **b.** them for a sign upon ... 7194
De 14:25 **b.** up the money in thine hand, ... 6887
Jos 2:18 thou shalt **b.** this line of scarlet ... 7194
Jg 15:10 To **b.** Samson are we come up ... 631
Jg 15:12 We are come down to **b.** thee, ... 631
Jg 15:13 but we will **b.** thee fast, and ... 631
Jg 16:5 that we may **b.** him to afflict him: ... 631
Jg 16:7 they **b.** me with seven green withs ... 631
Jg 16:11 If they **b.** me fast with new ropes ... 631
Job 31:36 and **b.** it as a crown to me ... 6029
Job 38:31 Canst thou **b.** the sweet ... 7194
Job 39:10 Canst thou **b.** the unicorn with ... 7194
Job 40:13 and **b.** their faces in secret. ... 2280
Job 41:5 or wilt thou **b.** him for thy ... 7194
Ps 105:22 To **b.** his princes at his pleasure; ... 631
Ps 118:27 **b.** the sacrifice with cords, even ... 631
Ps 149:8 To **b.** their kings with chains, ... 631
Pro 3:3 **b.** them about thy neck; write ... 7194
Pro 6:21 **B.** them continually upon thine ... 7194
Pro 7:3 **B.** them upon thy fingers, write ... 7194
Isa 8:16 **B.** up the testimony, seal the law ... 6887
Isa 49:18 and **b.** them on thee, as a bride ... 7194
Isa 61:1 to **b.** up the brokenhearted, ... 2280
Jer 51:63 thou shalt **b.** a stone to it, and ... 7164
Eze 3:25 and shall **b.** thee with them, and ... 631
Eze 5:3 and **b.** them in thy skirts. ... 6887
Eze 24:17 **b.** the tire of thine head upon ... 2280
Eze 30:21 to put a roller to **b.** it, to make ... 2280
Eze 34:16 **b.** up that which was broken, ... 2280
Da 3:20 were in his army to **b.** Shadrach, ... 3729
Ho 6:1 smitten, and he will **b.** us up. ... 2280
Ho 10:10 when they shall **b.** themselves ... 631
Mic 1:13 **b.** the chariot to the swift beast: ... 7573
Mt 12:29 **except he first b. the strong man?** ... *1210*
Mt 13:30 **b. them in bundles to burn them:** ... *1210*
Mt 16:19 **whatsoever thou shalt b. on earth** ... *1210*
Mt 18:18 **shall b. on earth shall be bound in** ... *1210*
Mt 22:13 **B. him hand and foot, and take** ... *1210*
Mt 23:4 **For they b. heavy burdens and** ... *1195*
Mk 3:27 **he will first b. the strong man;** ... *1210*
Mk 5:3 no man could **b.** him, no, not with ... *1210*
Ac 9:14 to **b.** all that call on thy name ... *1210*
Ac 12:8 thyself, and **b.** on thy sandals. ... *5265*
Ac 21:11 the Jews at Jerusalem **b.** the man ... *1210*

BINDETH
Job 5:18 for he maketh sore, and **b.** up: ... 2280
Job 26:8 He **b.** up the waters in his thick ... 6887
Job 28:11 **b.** the floods from overflowing; ... 2280
Job 30:18 it **b.** me about as the collar of my ... 247
Job 36:13 they cry not when he **b.** them ... 631
Ps 129:7 nor he that **b.** sheaves his bosom. ... 6014
Ps 147:3 in heart, and **b.** up their wounds. ... 2280
Pr 26:8 As he that **b.** a stone in a sling, ... 6887
Isa 30:26 that the Lord **b.** up the breach ... 2280

BINDING
Ge 37:7 For, behold, we were **b.** sheaves ... 481
Ge 49:11 **B.** his foal unto the vine, and his ... 631
Ex 28:32 it shall have a **b.** of woven work ... 8193
Nu 30:13 every **b.** oath to afflict the soul, ... 632
Ac 22:4 **b.** and delivering into prisons ... *1195*

BINEA (bin'-e-ah)
1Ch 8:37 Moza begat **B.**: Rapha was his ... 1150
1Ch 9:43 Moza begat **B.**; and Rephaiah ... 1150

BINNUI (bin'-nu-ee)
Ezr 8:33 Noadiah the son of **B.**, Levites; ... 1131
Ezr 10:30 Mattaniah, Bezaleel, and **B.**, and ... 1131
Ezr 10:38 And Bani, and **B.**, Shimei, ... 1131
Ne 3:24 After him repaired **B.** the son of ... 1131
Ne 7:15 The children of **B.**, six hundred ... 1131
Ne 10:9 the son of Azaniah, **B.** of the sons ... 1131
Ne 12:8 Moreover the Levites: Jeshua, **B.**, ... 1131

BIRD See also BIRD'S; BIRDS.
Ge 7:14 his kind, every **b.** of every sort. ... 6833
Le 14:6 As for the living **b.**, he shall take ... 6833
Le 14:6 the living **b.** in the blood of the **b.** ... 6833
Le 14:7 and shall let the living **b.** loose ... 6833
Le 14:51 and the scarlet, and the living **b.**, ... 6833
Le 14:51 them in the blood of the slain **b.**, ... 6833
Le 14:52 the house with the blood of the **b.**, ... 6833
Le 14:52 living **b.**, and with the cedar wood, ... 6833
Le 14:53 But he shall let go the living **b.** ... 6833
Job 41:5 thou play with him as with a **b.**? ... 6833
Ps 11:1 Flee as a **b.** to your mountain? ... 6833
Ps 124:7 **b.** out of the snare of the fowlers: ... 6833
Pr 1:17 spread in the sight of any **b.**. ... 1167,3671
Pr 6:5 a **b.** from the hand of the fowler. ... 6833
Pr 7:23 as a **b.** hasteth to the snare, and ... 6833
Pr 26:2 As the **b.** by wandering, as the ... 6833
Pr 27:8 As a **b.** that wandereth from ... 6833
Ec 10:20 **b.** of the air shall carry the voice, ... 5775
Ec 12:4 the voice of the **b.**, and all the ... 6833
Isa 16:2 wandering **b.** cast out of the nest, ... 5775
Isa 46:11 a ravenous **b.** from the east, ... 5861
Jer 12:9 heritage is unto me as a speckled **b.**, ... 5861
La 3:52 enemies chased me sore, like a **b.**, ... 6833
Ho 9:11 their glory shall fly away like a **b.**, ... 5775
Ho 11:11 shall tremble as a **b.** out of Egypt, ... 6833
Am 3:5 Can a **b.** fall in a snare upon the ... 6833
Re 18:2 of every unclean and hateful **b.**. ... *3732*

BIRD'S
De 22:6 **b.** nest chance to be before thee ... 6833

BIRDS See also BIRDS'.
Ge 15:10 another: but the **b.** divided he not. ... 6833
Ge 40:17 and the **b.** did eat them out of the ... 5775
Ge 40:19 **b.** shall eat thy flesh from off thee. ... 5775
Le 14:4 cleansed two **b.** alive and clean, ... 6833
Le 14:5 that one of the **b.** be killed ... 6833
Le 14:49 take to cleanse the house two **b.**, ... 6833
Le 14:50 and he shall kill the one of the **b.** ... 6833
De 14:11 Of all clean **b.** ye shall eat. ... 6833
2Sa 21:10 neither the **b.** of the air to rest ... 5775
Ps 104:17 Where the **b.** make their nests: ... 6833
Ec 9:12 and as the **b.** that are caught in ... 6833
Ca 2:12 time of the singing of **b.** is come, ...
Isa 31:5 As **b.** flying, so will the Lord of ... 6833
Jer 4:25 the **b.** of the heavens were fled. ... 5775
Jer 5:27 As a cage is full of **b.**, so are their ... 5775
Jer 12:4 beasts are consumed, and the **b.** ... 5775
Jer 12:9 as a speckled bird, the **b.** round ... 5861
Eze 39:4 give thee unto the ravenous **b.** ... 6833
Mt 8:20 **and the b. of the air have nests;** ... *4071*
Mt 13:32 **so that the b. of the air come** ... *4071*
Lu 9:58 **holes, and b. of the air have nests;** ... *4071*
Ro 1:23 like to corruptible man, and to **b.**, ... *4071*
1Co 15:39 of fishes, and another of **b.**. ... *4421*
Jas 3:7 every kind of beasts, and of **b.**, ... *4071*

BIRDS'
Da 4:33 and his nails like **b.** claws. ... 6853

BIREI See BETH-BIREI.

BIRSHA (bur'-shah)
Ge 14:2 and with **B.** king of Gomorrah, ... 1306

BIRTH See also BIRTHDAY; BIRTHRIGHT.
Ex 28:10 other stone, according to their **b.**. ... 8435
2Ki 19:3 for the children are come to the **b.**, ... 4866
Job 3:16 untimely **b.** I had not been; ... 5309
Ps 58:8 like the untimely **b.** of a woman, ... 5309
Ec 6:3 an untimely **b.** is better than he. ... 5309
Ec 7:1 of death than the day of one's **b.** ... 3205
Isa 37:3 the children are come to the **b.**, ... 4866
Isa 66:9 I bring to the **b.**, and not cause ... 7665
Eze 16:3 Thy **b.** and thy nativity is of the ... 4351
Ho 9:11 from the **b.**, and from the womb, ... 3205
Mt 1:18 the **b.** of Jesus Christ was on this ... *1083*
Lu 1:14 and many shall rejoice at his **b.**. ... *1083*
Joh 9:1 man which was blind from his **b.**. ... *1079*
Ga 4:19 I travail in **b.** again until Christ ... *5605*
Re 12:2 cried, travailing in **b.**, and pained ... *5605*

BIRTHDAY
Ge 40:20 which was Pharaoh's **b.**, ... 3117,3205
Mt 14:6 when Herod's **b.** was kept, the ... *1077*
Mk 6:21 Herod on his **b.** made a supper ... *1077*

BIRTHRIGHT
Ge 25:31 said, Sell me this day thy **b.** ... 1062
Ge 25:32 what profit shall this **b.** do to me? ... 1062
Ge 25:33 and he sold his **b.** unto Jacob ... 1062
Ge 25:34 way; thus Esau despised his **b.** ... 1062
Ge 27:36 he took away my **b.**; and, behold, ... 1062
Ge 43:33 the firstborn according to his **b.**, ... 1062
1Ch 5:1 his **b.** was given unto the sons ... 1062
1Ch 5:1 is not to be reckoned after the **b.** ... 1062
1Ch 5:2 ruler; but the **b.** was Joseph's:) ... 1062
Heb 12:16 for one morsel of meat sold his **b.** ... *4415*

BIRZAVITH (bur'-za-vith)
1Ch 7:31 Malchiel, who is the father of **B.** ... 1269

BISHLAM (bish'-lam)
Ezr 4:7 days of Artaxerxes, wrote **B.**, ... 1312

BISHOP See also BISHOPRICK; BISHOPS.
1Ti 3:1 If a man desire the office of a **b.**, ... *1984*
1Ti 3:2 A **b.** then must be blameless, the ... *1985*
2Ti *subscr.* Timotheus, ordained the first **b.** ... *1985*
Tit 1:7 For a **b.** must be blameless, as the ... *1985*
Tit *subscr.* Titus, ordained the first **b.** of ... *1985*
1Pe 2:25 Shepherd and **B.** of your souls ... *1985*

BISHOPRICK
Ac 1:20 therein: and his **b.** let another ... *1984*

BISHOPS
Php 1:1 Philippi, with the **b.** and deacons: ... *1985*

BIT See also BITS.
Nu 21:6 people, and they **b.** the people; ... 5391
Ps 32:9 be held in with **b.** and bridle, ... 4964
Am 5:19 on the wall, and a serpent **b.** him. ... 5391

BITE See also BACKBITE; BIT; BITETH; BITTEN.
Ec 10:8 an hedge, a serpent shall **b.** him. ... 5391
Ec 10:11 will **b.** without enchantment; ... 5391
Jer 8:17 be charmed, and they shall **b.** you, ... 5391
Am 9:3 the serpent, and he shall **b.** them: ... 5391
Mic 3:5 that **b.** with their teeth, and cry, ... 5391
Hab 2:7 up suddenly that shall **b.** thee, ... 5391
Ga 5:15 if ye **b.** and devour one another, ... *1148*

BITETH See also BACKBITETH.
Ge 49:17 the path, that **b.** the horse heels, ... 5391
Pr 23:32 it **b.** like a serpent, and stingeth ... 5391

BITHIAH (bith-i'-ah)
1Ch 4:18 the sons of **B.** the daughter of ... 1332

BITHRON (bith'-ron)
2Sa 2:29 went through all **B.**, and they ... 1338

BITHYNIA (bith-in'-e-ah)
Ac 16:7 Mysia, they assayed to go into **B.** ... *978*
1Pe 1:1 Galatia, Cappadocia, Asia, and **B.**, ... *978*

BITS
Jas 3:3 we put **b.** in the horses' mouths, ... *5469*

BITTEN See also HUNGERBITTEN.
Nu 21:8 every one that is **b.**, and when he ... 5391
Nu 21:9 if a serpent had **b.** any man, when ... 5391

BITTER
Ge 27:34 with a great and exceeding **b.** cry, ... 4751
Ex 1:14 made their lives **b.** with hard ... 4843
Ex 12:8 with **b.** herbs they shall eat it ... 4844
Ex 15:23 waters of Marah, for they were **b.** ... 4751
Nu 5:18 **b.** water that causeth the curse: ... 4751
Nu 5:19 be thou free from this **b.** water ... 4751
Nu 5:23 blot them out with the **b.** water: ... 4751
Nu 5:24 drink the **b.** water that causeth ... 4751
Nu 5:24 enter into her, and become **b.**. ... 4751
Nu 5:27 into her, and become **b.**, and her ... 4751
Nu 9:11 unleavened bread and **b.** herbs ... 4844
De 32:24 heat, and with **b.** destruction: ... 4815
De 32:32 of gall, their clusters are **b.** ... 4846
2Ki 14:26 of Israel, that it was very **b.** ... 4784
Es 4:1 cried with a loud and a **b.** cry; ... 4751
Job 3:20 and life unto the **b.** in soul; ... 4751
Job 13:26 thou writest **b.** things against me, ... 4846
Job 23:2 Even to day is my complaint **b.** ... 4805
Ps 64:3 to shoot their arrows, even **b.** ... 4751
Pr 5:4 her end is **b.** as wormwood, sharp ... 4751
Pr 27:7 to the hungry soul every **b.** thing ... 4751
Ec 7:26 more **b.** than death the woman, ... 4751
Isa 5:20 put **b.** for sweet, and sweet for **b.**! ... 4751

Isa 24:9 strong drink shall be **b.** to them 4843
Jer 2:19 it is an evil thing and **b.**, that thou 4751
Jer 4:18 is thy wickedness, because it is **b.**, 4751
Jer 6:26 an only son, most **b.** lamentation: 8563
Jer 31:15 in Ramah, lamentation, and **b.** 8563
Eze 27:31 bitterness of heart and **b.** wailing 4751
Am 8:10 and the end thereof as a **b.** day. 4751
Hab 1:6 Chaldeans, that **b.** and hasty 4751
Col 3:19 wives, and be not **b.** against them. *4087*
Jas 3:11 same place sweet water and **b.**? *4089*
Jas 3:14 If ye have **b.** envying and strife *4089*
Re 8:11 waters, because they were made **b.** *4087*
Re 10:9 it shall make thy belly **b.**, but it *4087*
Re 10:10 I had eaten it, my belly was **b.** *4087*

BITTERLY
Jg 5:23 curse ye **b.** the inhabitants thereof; 779
Ru 1:20 Almighty hath dealt very **b.** with 4843
Isa 22:4 I will weep **b.**, labor not to comfort 4843
Isa 33:7 of peace shall weep **b.** 4751
Eze 27:30 and shall cry **b.**, and shall cast up 4751
Ho 12:14 provoked him to anger most **b.**: 8563
Zep 1:14 the mighty man shall cry there **b.** 4751
Mt 26:75 And he went out, and wept **b.** *4090*
Lu 22:62 Peter went out, and wept **b.** *4090*

BITTERN
Isa 14:23 make it a possession for the **b.**, 7090
Isa 34:11 cormorant and the **b.** shall 7090
Zep 2:14 cormorant and the **b.** shall lodge 7090

BITTERNESS
1Sa 1:10 she was in **b.** of soul, and prayed 4751
1Sa 15:32 said, Surely the **b.** of death is past. 4751
2Sa 2:26 that it will be **b.** in the latter end? 4751
Job 7:11 I will complain in the **b.** of my 4751
Job 9:18 breath, but filleth me with **b.** 4472
Job 10:1 I will speak in the **b.** of my soul, 4751
Job 21:25 another dieth in the **b.** of his soul, 4751
Pr 14:10 The heart knoweth his own **b.**; 4751
Pr 17:25 father, and **b.** to her that bare 4470
Isa 38:15 my years in the **b.** of my soul. 4751
Isa 38:17 Behold, for peace I had great **b.**: 4843
La 1:4 are afflicted, and she is in **b.** 4843
La 3:15 He hath filled me with **b.**, 4844
Eze 3:14 took me away, and I went in **b.**, 4751
Eze 21:6 and with **b.** sigh before their eyes. 4814
Eze 27:31 they shall weep for thee with **b.** 4751
Zec 12:10 and shall be in **b.** for him, 4843
Zec 12:10 as one that is in **b.** 4843
Ac 8:23 thou art in the gall of **b.**, and in *4088*
Ro 3:14 mouth is full of cursing and **b.**: *4088*
Eph 4:31 Let all **b.**, and wrath, and anger, *4088*
Heb 12:15 lest any root of **b.** springing up *4088*

BIZJOTHJAH (biz-joth'-jah)
Jos 15:28 and Beer-sheba, and **B.**, 964

BIZTHA (biz'-thah)
Es 1:10 he commanded Mehuman, **B.**, 968

BLACK See BLACKER; BLACKISH.
Le 13:31 that there is no **b.** hair in it; 7838
Le 13:37 there is **b.** hair grown up therein; 7838
1Ki 18:45 heaven was **b.** with clouds and 6937
Es 1:6 of red, and blue, and white, and **b.**, 5508
Job 30:30 My skin is **b.** upon me, and my 7835
Pr 7:9 in the evening, in the **b.** and 380
Ca 1:5 I am **b.**, but comely, O ye 7838
Ca 1:6 not upon me, because I am **b.**, 7840
Ca 5:11 his locks are bushy, and **b.** as a 7838
Jer 4:28 and the heavens above be **b.**: 6937
Jer 8:21 I am **b.**; astonishment hath taken 6937
Jer 14:2 they are **b.** unto the ground; and 6937
La 5:10 Our skin was **b.** like an oven 3648
Zec 6:2 in the second chariot **b.** horses; 7838
Zec 6:6 The **b.** horses which are therein 7838
Mt 5:36 **not make one hair white or b.** *3189*
Re 6:5 And I beheld, and lo a **b.** horse; *3189*
Re 6:12 sun became **b.** as sackcloth of *3189*

BLACKER
La 4:8 Their visage is **b.** than a coal; 2821

BLACKISH
Job 6:16 Which are **b.** by reason of the ice, 6937

BLACKNESS
Job 3:5 let the **b.** of the day terrify it. 3650
Isa 50:3 I clothe the heavens with **b.**, 6940
Joe 2:6 pained: all faces shall gather **b.** 6289
Na 2:10 the faces of them all gather **b.** 6289
Heb 12:18 nor unto **b.**, and darkness, and *1105*
Jude 13 to whom is reserved the **b.** of *2217*

BLADE
Jg 3:22 the haft also went in after the **b.**; 3851
Jg 3:22 and the fat closed upon the **b.**, 3851
Job 31:22 arm fall from my shoulder **b.**, 7929
Mt 13:26 **But when the b. was sprung up,** *5528*
Mk 4:28 **first the b., then the ear, after** *5528*

BLAINS
Ex 9:9 be a boil breaking forth with **b.** 76
Ex 9:10 a boil breaking forth with **b.** 76

BLAME See also BLAMES; BLAMELESS; UNBLAMEABLE.
Ge 43:9 then let me bear the **b.** for ever: 2398
Ge 44:32 then I shall bear the **b.** to my 2398
2Co 8:20 that no man should **b.** us in this *3469*
Eph 1:4 be holy and without **b.** *299*

BLAMED
2Co 6:3 that the ministry be not **b.**: *3469*
Ga 2:11 the face, because he was to be **b.** *2607*

BLAMELESS
Ge 44:10 my servant; and ye shall be **b.** 5355
Jos 2:17 We will be **b.** of this thine oath 5355
Jg 15:3 Now shall I be more **b.** than the 5352
Mt 12:5 **profane the sabbath, and are b.?** *338*
Lu 1:6 and ordinances of the Lord **b.** *273*
1Co 1:8 that ye may be **b.** in the day of *410*
Php 2:15 that ye may be **b.** and harmless, *273*
Php 3:6 which is in the law, **b.** *273*
1Th 5:23 be preserved **b.** unto the coming *274*
1Ti 3:2 a bishop then must be **b.**, the *423*
1Ti 3:10 office of a deacon, being found **b.** *410*
1Ti 5:7 in charge, that they may be **b.** *423*
Tit 1:6 if any be **b.**, the husband of one *410*
Tit 1:7 For a bishop must be **b.**, as the *410*
2Pe 3:14 in peace, without spot, and **b.** 298

BLASPHEME See also BLASPHEMED; BLASPHEMEST; BLASPHEMETH; BLASPHEMING.
2Sa 12:14 the enemies of the Lord to **b.**, 5006
1Ki 21:10 Thou didst **b.** God and the king. 1288
1Ki 21:13 Naboth did **b.** God and the king. 1288
Ps 74:10 shall the enemy **b.** thy name for 5006
Mk 3:28 **wherewith soever they shall b.** *987*
Mk 3:29 **he that shall b. against the Holy** *987*
Ac 26:11 and compelled them to **b.**; *987*
1Ti 1:20 that they may learn not to **b.** *987*
Jas 2:7 Do not they **b.** that worthy name *987*
Re 13:6 to **b.** his name, and his tabernacle, *987*

BLASPHEMED
Le 24:11 Israelitish woman's son **b.** the 5344
2Ki 19:6 of the king of Assyria have **b.** me 1442
2Ki 19:22 hast thou reproached and **b.**? 1442
Ps 74:18 the foolish people have **b.** thy 5006
Isa 37:6 of the king of Assyria have **b.** me 1442
Isa 37:23 hast thou reproached and **b.**? 1442
Isa 52:5 name continually every day is **b.** 5006
Isa 65:7 upon the mountains, and **b.** me 2778
Eze 20:27 in this your fathers have **b.** me, 1442
Ac 18:6 they opposed themselves, and **b.**, *987*
Ro 2:24 the name of God is **b.** among the *987*
1Ti 6:1 God and his doctrine be not **b.** *987*
Tit 2:5 that the word of God be not **b.** *987*
Re 16:9 heat, and **b.** the name of God, *987*
Re 16:11 **b.** the God of heaven because of *987*
Re 16:21 men **b.** God because of the plague *987*

BLASPHEMER See also BLASPHEMERS.
1Ti 1:13 Who was before a **b.**, and a *989*

BLASPHEMERS
Ac 19:37 churches, nor yet **b.** of your *987*
2Ti 3:2 covetous, boasters, proud, **b.** *989*

BLASPHEMEST
Joh 10:36 **Thou b.; because I said, I am the** *987*

BLASPHEMETH
Le 24:16 he that **b.** the name of the Lord, 5344
Le 24:16 when he **b.** the name of the Lord, 5344
Ps 44:16 of him that reproacheth and **b.**; 1442
Mt 9:3 within themselves, This man **b.** *987*
Lu 12:10 **unto him that b. against the Holy** *987*

BLASPHEMIES
Eze 35:12 I have heard all thy **b.** which thou 5007
Mt 15:19 **thefts, false witness, b.:** *988*
Mk 2:7 Why doth this man thus speak **b.**? *988*
Mk 3:28 **b. wherewith soever they shall** *988*
Lu 5:21 Who is this which speaketh **b.**? *988*
Re 13:5 mouth speaking great things and **b.**; *988*

BLASPHEMING
Ac 13:45 by Paul, contradicting and **b.** *987*

BLASPHEMOUS
Ac 6:11 we have heard him speak **b.** words *989*
Ac 6:13 ceaseth not to speak **b.** words *989*

BLASPHEMOUSLY
Lu 22:65 things **b.** spake they against him. *987*

BLASPHEMY See also BLASPHEMIES.
2Ki 19:3 of trouble, and of rebuke, and **b.**: 5007
Isa 37:3 trouble, and of rebuke, and of **b.**: 5007
Mt 12:31 **All manner of sin and b. shall be** *988*
Mt 12:31 **the b. against the Holy Ghost** *988*
Mt 26:65 clothes, saying, He hath spoken **b.**; *987*
Mt 26:65 behold, now ye have heard his **b.** *988*
Mk 7:22 **an evil eye, b., pride, foolishness:** *988*
Mk 14:64 Ye have heard the **b.**: what think *988*
Joh 10:33 for **b.**; and because that thou, *988*
Col 3:8 anger, wrath, malice, **b.**, filthy *988*
Re 2:9 **I know the b. of them which say** *988*
Re 13:1 and upon his heads the name of **b.** *988*
Re 13:6 And he opened his mouth in **b.** *988*
Re 17:3 full of names of **b.**, having seven *988*

BLAST See also BLASTED; BLASTING.
Ex 15:8 And with the **b.** of thy nostrils 7307
Jos 6:5 when they make a long **b.** with the
2Sa 22:16 at the **b.** of the breath of his 5397
2Ki 19:7 I will send a **b.** upon him, and he 7307
Job 4:9 By the **b.** of God they perish, and 5397
Ps 18:15 at the **b.** of the breath of thy 5397
Isa 25:4 when the **b.** of the terrible ones 7307
Isa 37:7 I will send a **b.** upon him, and he 7307

BLASTED
Ge 41:6 seven thin ears and **b.** with the 7710
Ge 41:23 seven ears, withered, thin, and **b.** 7710
Ge 41:27 seven empty ears **b.** with the east 7710
2Ki 19:26 and as corn **b.** before it be grown 7711
Isa 37:27 and as corn **b.** before it be grown 7709

BLASTING
De 28:22 sword, and with **b.**, and with 7711
1Ki 8:37 famine, if there be pestilence, **b.**, 7711
2Ch 6:28 if there be **b.**, or mildew, locusts, 7711
Am 4:9 I have smitten you with **b.** and 7711
Hag 2:17 I smote you with **b.** and with 7711

BLASTUS (blas'tus)
Ac 12:20 and having made **B.** the king's *986*

BLAZE
Mk 1:45 and to **b.** abroad the matter *1310*

BLEATING See also BLEATINGS.
1Sa 15:14 What meaneth then this **b.** of the 6963

BLEATINGS
Jg 5:16 to hear the **b.** of the flocks? 8292

BLEMISH See also BLEMISHES.
Ex 12:5 Your lamb shall be without **b.**, a 8549
Ex 29:1 and two rams without **b.**, 8549
Le 1:3 let him offer a male without **b.**: 8549
Le 1:10 he shall bring it a male without **b.** 8549
Le 3:1 he shall offer it without **b.** before 8549
Le 3:6 he shall offer it without **b.** 8549
Le 4:3 a young bullock without **b.** unto 8549
Le 4:23 of the goats, a male without **b.**: 8549
Le 4:28 goats, a female without **b.**, for his 8549
Le 4:32 shall bring it a female without **b.** 8549
Le 5:15 a ram without **b.** out of the flocks, 8549
Le 5:18 he shall bring a ram without **b.** 8549
Le 6:6 a ram without **b.** out of the flock, 8549
Le 9:2 for a burnt offering without **b.**, and 8549
Le 9:3 of the first year, without **b.**, for a 8549
Le 14:10 shall take two he lambs without **b.**, 8549
Le 14:10 lamb of the first year without **b.**, 8549
Le 21:17 generations that hath any **b.**, 3971
Le 21:18 man he be that hath a **b.**, 3971
Le 21:20 or that hath a **b.** in his eye, or be 8400
Le 21:21 No man that hath a **b.** of the seed 3971
Le 21:21 he hath a **b.**; he shall not come 3971
Le 21:23 the altar, because he hath a **b.**; 3971

Le 22:19 your own will a male without **b.**, ... 8549
Le 22:20 whatsoever hath a **b.**, that shall 3971
Le 22:21 there shall be no **b.** therein. 3971
Le 23:12 An he lamb without **b.** of the first 8549
Le 23:18 seven lambs without **b.** of the first 8549
Le 24:19 and if a man cause a **b.** in his 3971
Le 24:20 as he hath caused a **b.** in a 3971
Nu 6:14 lamb of the first year without **b.** 8549
Nu 6:14 lamb of the first year without **b.** 8549
Nu 6:14 and one ram without **b.** for peace 8549
Nu 19:2 without spot, wherein is no **b.**, ... 3971
Nu 28:19 they shall be unto you without **b.**: 8549
Nu 28:31 (they shall be unto you without **b.**) 8549
Nu 29:2 lambs of the first year without **b.**: 8549
Nu 29:8 they shall be unto you without **b.**: 8549
Nu 29:13 year: they shall be without **b.**: 8549
Nu 29:20 lambs of the first year without **b.**; 8549
Nu 29:23, 29,32,36 the first year without **b.**: 8549
De 15:21 be any **b.** therein, as if it be lame, ... 3971
De 15:21 or blind, or have any ill **b.**, ... 3971
De 17:1 bullock, or sheep, wherein is **b.** 3971
2Sa 14:25 head there was no **b.** in him 3971
Eze 43:22 offer a kid of the goats without **b.** 8549
Eze 43:23 a young bullock without **b.**, and 8549
Eze 43:23 a ram out of the flock without **b.** 8549
Eze 43:25 a ram out of the flock, without **b.** 8549
Eze 45:18 take a young bullock without **b.**, ... 8549
Eze 45:23 seven rams without **b.** daily the 8549
Eze 46:4 six lambs without **b.**, ... 8549
Eze 46:4 and a ram without **b.**. 8549
Eze 46:6 a young bullock without **b.**, and 8549
Eze 46:6 a ram: they shall be without **b.** 8549
Eze 46:13 lamb of the first year without **b.**: 8549
Da 1:4 Children in whom was no **b.**, but 3971
Eph 5:27 it should be holy and without **b.** *299*
1Pe 1:19 as of a lamb without **b.** and without *299*

BLEMISHES

Le 22:25 corruption in them, and **b.** be in 3971
2Pe 2:13 Spots they are and **b.**, sporting *3470*

BLESS See also BLESSED; BLESSEST; BLESSETH; BLESSING.

Ge 12:2 and I will **b.** thee, and make thy 1288
Ge 12:3 And I will **b.** them that **b.** thee, ... 1288
Ge 17:16 And I will **b.** her, and give thee a 1288
Ge 17:16 son also of her: yea, I will **b.** her, ... 1288
Ge 22:17 in blessing I will **b.** thee, and in 1288
Ge 26:3 be with thee, and will **b.** thee: for 1288
Ge 26:24 for I am with thee, and will **b.** thee, ... 1288
Ge 27:4 that my soul may **b.** thee before I 1288
Ge 27:7 and **b.** thee before the Lord before 1288
Ge 27:10 he may eat, and that he may **b.** thee .. 1288
Ge 27:19 venison, that thy soul may **b.** me. 1288
Ge 27:25 venison, that my soul may **b.** thee. 1288
Ge 27:31 venison, that thy soul may **b.** me. 1288
Ge 27:34 **B.** me, even me also, O my father. 1288
Ge 27:38 **b.** me, even me also, O my father. 1288
Ge 28:3 God Almighty **b.** thee, and make 1288
Ge 32:26 let thee go, except thou **b.** me. 1288
Ge 48:9 thee, unto me, and I will **b.** them. 1288
Ge 48:16 me from all evil, **b.** the lads; 1288
Ge 48:20 In thee shall Israel **b.**, saying, God 1288
Ge 49:25 the Almighty, who shall **b.** thee 1288
Ex 12:32 said, and be gone; and **b.** me also. 1288
Ex 20:24 come unto thee, and I will **b.** thee. 1288
Ex 23:25 and he shall **b.** thy bread, and thy 1288
Nu 6:23 on this wise ye shall **b.** the children 1288
Nu 6:24 The Lord **b.** thee, and keep thee: 1288
Nu 6:27 children of Israel; and I will **b.** 1288
Nu 23:20 have received commandment to **b.** 1288
Nu 23:25 Neither curse them at all, nor **b.** 1288
Nu 24:1 it pleased the Lord to **b.** Israel, he 1288
De 1:11 and **b.** you, as he hath promised 1288
De 7:13 will love thee, and **b.** thee, and 1288
De 7:13 he will also **b.** the fruit of thy 1288
De 8:10 then thou shalt **b.** the Lord thy 1288
De 10:8 unto him, and to **b.** in his name, ... 1288
De 14:29 the Lord thy God may **b.** thee in all 1288
De 15:4 the Lord shall greatly **b.** thee in 1288
De 15:10 thy God shall **b.** thee in all thy 1288
De 15:18 thy God shall **b.** thee in all that 1288
De 16:15 the Lord thy God shall **b.** thee in 1288
De 21:5 unto him, and to **b.** in the name of 1288
De 23:20 the Lord thy God may **b.** thee in all 1288
De 24:13 sleep in his own raiment, and **b.** 1288
De 24:19 thy God may **b.** thee in all the work ... 1288
De 26:15 from heaven, and **b.** thy people 1288
De 27:12 upon mount Gerizim to **b.** the 1288
De 28:8 and he shall **b.** thee in the land 1288
De 28:12 and to **b.** all the work of thine 1288
De 29:19 that he **b.** himself in his heart, ... 1288
De 30:16 and the Lord thy God shall **b.** 1288
De 33:11 **B.**, Lord, his substance, and accept 1288
Jos 8:33 that they should **b.** the people of 1288
Jg 5:9 among the people. **B.** ye the Lord 1288
Ru 2:4 answered him, the Lord **b.** thee 1288
1Sa 9:13 because he doth **b.** the sacrifice; 1288
2Sa 6:20 Then David returned to **b.** his 1288
2Sa 7:29 let it please thee to **b.** the house of 1288
2Sa 8:10 to salute him, and to **b.** him, ... 1288
2Sa 21:3 that ye may **b.** the inheritance of 1288
1Ki 1:47 servants came to **b.** our lord king 1288
1Ch 4:10 Oh that thou wouldest **b.** me 1288
1Ch 16:43 house: and David returned to **b.** 1288
1Ch 17:27 to **b.** the house of thy servant, that 1288
1Ch 23:13 minister unto him, and to **b.** in his 1288
1Ch 29:20 the congregation, Now **b.** the Lord 1288
Ne 9:5 **b.** the Lord your God forever and 1288
Ps 5:12 For thou, Lord, wilt **b.** the 1288
Ps 16:7 I will **b.** the Lord, who hath given 1288
Ps 26:12 in the congregations will I **b.** the 1288
Ps 28:9 Save thy people, and **b.** thine 1288
Ps 29:11 the Lord will **b.** his people with 1288
Ps 34:1 I will **b.** the Lord at all times: his 1288
Ps 62:4 they **b.** with their mouth, but they 1288
Ps 63:4 Thus will I **b.** thee while I live: 1288
Ps 66:8 O **b.** our God, ye people, and make 1288
Ps 67:1 God be merciful unto us and **b.** us; 1288
Ps 67:6 God, even our own God, shall **b.** us. .. 1288
Ps 67:7 God shall **b.** us; and all the ends of 1288
Ps 68:26 **B.** ye God in the congregations, ... 1288
Ps 96:2 Sing unto the Lord, **b.** his name; 1288
Ps 100:4 be thankful unto him, and **b.** his 1288
Ps 103:1 **B.** the Lord, O my soul, and all 1288
Ps 103:1 that is within me, **b.** his holy ....
Ps 103:2 **B.** the Lord, O my soul, and 1288
Ps 103:20 **B.** the Lord, ye his angels, that 1288
Ps 103:21 **B.** ye the Lord, all ye his hosts; ye 1288
Ps 103:22 **B.** the Lord, all his works in all 1288
Ps 103:22 places of his dominion; **b.** the Lord, ... 1288
Ps 104:1 **B.** the Lord, O my soul. O Lord, ... 1288
Ps 104:35 **B.** thou the Lord, O my soul 1288
Ps 109:28 Let them curse, but **b.** thou: when 1288
Ps 115:12 he will **b.** us; he will **b.** the house 1288
Ps 115:12 of Israel; he will **b.** the house of 1288
Ps 115:13 He will **b.** them that fear the Lord, ... 1288
Ps 115:18 But we will **b.** the Lord from this 1288
Ps 128:5 The Lord shall **b.** thee out of Zion: 1288
Ps 129:8 upon you: we **b.** you in the name 1288
Ps 132:15 I will abundantly **b.** her provision: 1288
Ps 134:1 **b.** ye the Lord, all ye servants of 1288
Ps 134:2 in the sanctuary, and **b.** the Lord. 1288
Ps 134:3 heaven and earth **b.** thee out of 1288
Ps 135:19 **B.** the Lord, O house of Israel: 1288
Ps 135:19 **b.** the Lord, O house of Aaron: 1288
Ps 135:20 **B.** the Lord, O house of Levi: 1288
Ps 135:20 ye that fear the Lord, **b.** the Lord. 1288
Ps 145:1 and I will **b.** thy name for ever 1288
Ps 145:2 Every day will I **b.** thee; and I will 1288
Ps 145:10 Lord; and thy saints shall **b.** thee. 1288
Ps 145:21 and let all flesh **b.** his holy name 1288
Pr 30:11 and doth not **b.** their mother. 1288
Isa 19:25 Whom the Lord of hosts shall **b.**, ... 1288
Isa 65:16 shall **b.** himself in the God of truth; 1288
Jer 4:2 and the nations shall **b.** themselves 1288
Jer 31:23 The Lord **b.** thee, O habitation of 1288
Hag 2:19 forth: from this day will I **b.** you. 1288
Mt 5:44 **b. them that curse you, do good** *2127*
Lu 6:28 **B. them that curse you, and pray** .. *2127*
Ac 3:26 sent him to **b.** you, in turning *2127*
Ro 12:14 **B.** them which persecute you: **b.**, ... *2127*
1Co 4:12 being reviled, we **b.**; being *2127*
1Co 10:16 The cup of blessing which we **b.**, ... *2127*
1Co 14:16 Else, when thou shalt **b.** with the *2127*
Heb 6:14 Surely blessing I will **b.** thee, and *2127*
Jas 3:9 Therewith **b.** we God, even the *2127*

BLESSED

Ge 1:22 And God **b.** them, saying, ... 1288
Ge 1:28 God **b.** them, and God said unto 1288
Ge 2:3 And God **b.** the seventh day, and 1288
Ge 5:2 created he them; and **b.** them, ... 1288
Ge 9:1 And God **b.** Noah and his sons, ... 1288
Ge 9:26 **B.** be the Lord God of Shem; 1288
Ge 12:3 shall all families of the earth be **b.** 1288
Ge 14:19 And he **b.** him, and said, ... 1288
Ge 14:19 **B.** be Abram of the most high 1288
Ge 14:20 And **b.** the most high God, which 1288
Ge 17:20 Behold, I have **b.** him, and will 1288
Ge 18:18 the nations of the earth shall be **b.** 1288
Ge 22:18 all the nations of the earth be **b.**; 1288
Ge 24:1 and the Lord had **b.** Abraham in 1288
Ge 24:27 **B.** be the Lord God of my master 1288
Ge 24:31 Come in, thou **b.** of the Lord; 1288
Ge 24:35 Lord hath **b.** my master greatly; 1288
Ge 24:48 and **b.** the Lord God of my master 1288
Ge 24:60 And they **b.** Rebekah, and said unto 1288
Ge 25:11 Abraham, that God **b.** his son Isaac; ... 1288
Ge 26:4 the nations of the earth be **b.**; 1288
Ge 26:12 hundredfold: and the Lord **b.** him. 1288
Ge 26:29 thou art now the **b.** of the Lord. 1288
Ge 27:23 brother Esau's hands: so he **b.** him. 1288
Ge 27:27 and **b.** him, and said, See, the smell ... 1288
Ge 27:27 of a field which the Lord hath **b.**: 1288
Ge 27:29 and **b.** be he that blesseth thee. 1288
Ge 27:33 thou camest, and have **b.** him? 1288
Ge 27:33 yea, and he shall be **b.** 1288
Ge 27:41 wherewith his father **b.** him: 1288
Ge 28:1 Isaac called Jacob, and **b.** him, ... 1288
Ge 28:6 Esau saw that Isaac had **b.** Jacob, ... 1288
Ge 28:6 and that as he **b.** him he gave him 1288
Ge 28:14 all the families of the earth be **b.** 1288
Ge 30:13 for the daughters will call me **b.** 833
Ge 30:27 that the Lord hath **b.** me for thy 1288
Ge 30:30 and the Lord hath **b.** thee since my 1288
Ge 31:55 and **b.** them: and Laban departed, ... 1288
Ge 32:29 my name? And he **b.** him there 1288
Ge 35:9 out of Padan-aram, and **b.** him. 1288
Ge 39:5 the Lord **b.** the Egyptian's house 1288
Ge 47:7 Pharaoh: and Jacob **b.** Pharaoh. 1288
Ge 47:10 Jacob **b.** Pharaoh, and went out 1288
Ge 48:3 in the land of Canaan, and **b.** me, ... 1288
Ge 48:15 And he **b.** Joseph, and said, God, ... 1288
Ge 48:20 And he **b.** them that day, saying, ... 1288
Ge 49:28 spake unto them, and **b.** them; 1288
Ge 49:28 according to his blessing he **b.** them. .. 1288
Ex 18:10 Jethro said, **B.** be the Lord, ... 1288
Ex 20:11 the Lord **b.** the sabbath day, and 1288
Ex 39:43 they done it: and Moses **b.** them. 1288
Le 9:22 toward the people, and **b.** them, ... 1288
Le 9:23 and came out, and **b.** the people: 1288
Nu 22:6 that he whom thou blessest is **b.**, ... 1288
Nu 22:12 curse the people: for they are **b.** 1288
Nu 23:11 thou hast **b.** them altogether. 1288
Nu 23:20 he hath **b.**; and I cannot reverse it. 1288
Nu 24:9 **B.** is he that blesseth thee, and 1288
Nu 24:10 thou hast altogether **b.** them these 1288
De 2:7 the Lord thy God hath **b.** thee in 1288
De 7:14 Thou shalt be **b.** above all people: 1288
De 12:7 the Lord thy God hath **b.** thee. 1288
De 14:24 the Lord thy God hath **b.** thee: 1288
De 15:14 the Lord thy God hath **b.** thee 1288
De 16:10 the Lord thy God hath **b.** thee: 1288
De 28:3 **B.** shalt thou be in the city, ... 1288
De 28:3 and **b.** shalt thou be in the field. 1288
De 28:4 **B.** shall be the fruit of thy body, ... 1288
De 28:5 **B.** shall be thy basket and thy 1288
De 28:6 **B.** shalt thou be when thou comest 1288
De 28:6 and **b.** shalt thou be when thou 1288
De 33:1 Moses the man of God **b.** the 1288
De 33:13 **B.** of the Lord be his land, for 1288
De 33:20 **B.** be he that enlargeth Gad: he 1288
De 33:24 Let Asher be **b.** with children; 1288
Jos 14:13 And Joshua **b.** him, and gave unto 1288
Jos 17:14 forasmuch as the Lord hath **b.** me 1288
Jos 22:6 So Joshua **b.** them, and sent them 1288
Jos 22:7 unto their tents, then he **b.** them, ... 1288
Jos 22:33 and the children of Israel **b.** God, ... 1288
Jos 24:10 Balaam; therefore he **b.** you still: 1288
Jg 5:24 **B.** above women shall Jael the wife 1288
Jg 5:24 **b.** shall she be above women. 1288
Jg 13:24 child grew, and the Lord **b.** him. 1288
Jg 17:2 **B.** be thou of the Lord, my son. 1288
Ru 2:19 **b.** be he that did take knowledge 1288
Ru 2:20 **B.** be he of the Lord, who hath not 1288
Ru 3:10 **B.** be thou of the Lord, my 1288
Ru 4:14 **B.** be the Lord, which hath not 1288
1Sa 2:20 And Eli **b.** Elkanah and his wife, ... 1288
1Sa 15:13 **B.** be thou of the Lord: I have 1288
1Sa 23:21 **B.** be ye of the Lord; for ye have 1288
1Sa 25:32 **B.** be the Lord God of Israel, ... 1288
1Sa 25:33 And **b.** be thy advice, ... 1288

1Sa 25:33 and **b.** be thou, which hast kept........ 1288
1Sa 25:39 **B.** be the Lord, that hath pleaded...... 1288
1Sa 26:25 **B.** be thou, my son David: thou......... 1288
2Sa 2:5 **B.** be ye of the Lord, that ye have..... 1288
2Sa 6:11 and the Lord **b.** Obed-edom, and........ 1288
2Sa 6:12 The Lord hath **b.** the house of.......... 1288
2Sa 6:18 he **b.** the people in the name of the.... 1288
2Sa 7:29 house of thy servant be **b.** forever. 1288
2Sa 13:25 he would not go, but **b.** him............ 1288
2Sa 18:28 **B.** be the Lord thy God, which hath... 1288
2Sa 19:39 king kissed Barzillai, and **b.** him; 1288
2Sa 22:47 the Lord liveth; and **b.** be my rock;.... 1288
1Ki 1:48 **B.** be the Lord God of Israel,............. 1288
1Ki 2:45 and king Solomon shall be **b.**,............ 1288
1Ki 5:7 **B.** be the Lord this day, which............ 1288
1Ki 8:14 and **b.** all the congregation of 1288
1Ki 8:15 **B.** be the Lord God of Israel, which... 1288
1Ki 8:55 stood, and **b.** all the congregation....... 1288
1Ki 8:56 **B.** be the Lord, that hath given......... 1288
1Ki 8:66 and they **b.** the king, and went.......... 1288
1Ki 10:9 **B.** be the Lord thy God, which.......... 1288
1Ch 13:14 And the Lord **b.** the house of............ 1288
1Ch 16:2 he **b.** the people in the name of the.... 1288
1Ch 16:36 **B.** be the Lord God of Israel for......... 1288
1Ch 17:27 O Lord, and it shall be **b.** for ever. 1288
1Ch 26:5 the eighth: for God **b.** him............... 1288
1Ch 29:10 Wherefore David **b.** the Lord 1288
1Ch 29:10 **B.** be thou, Lord God of Israel our..... 1288
1Ch 29:20 all the congregation **b.** the Lord......... 1288
2Ch 2:12 **B.** be the Lord God of Israel, that 1288
2Ch 6:3 and **b.** the whole congregation of........ 1288
2Ch 6:4 **B.** be the Lord God of Israel, who..... 1288
2Ch 9:8 **B.** be the Lord thy God, which.......... 1288
2Ch 20:26 for there they **b.** the Lord: 1288
2Ch 30:27 Levites arose and **b.** the people: 1288
2Ch 31:8 they **b.** the Lord, and his people 1288
2Ch 31:10 for the Lord hath **b.** his people; 1288
Ezr 7:27 **B.** be the Lord God of our fathers, ... 1288
Ne 8:6 Ezra **b.** the Lord, the great God. 1288
Ne 9:5 and **b.** be thy glorious name, which..... 1288
Ne 11:2 And the people **b.** all the men, ... 1288
Job 1:10 hast **b.** the work of his hands, ... 1288
Job 1:21 **b.** be the name of the Lord.............. 1288
Job 29:11 the ear heard me, then it **b.** me; 833
Job 31:20 If his loins have not **b.** me, and if....... 1288
Job 42:12 So the Lord **b.** the latter end of......... 1288
Ps 1:1 **B.** is the man that walketh not............ 835
Ps 2:12 **B.** are all they that put their.............. 835
Ps 18:46 Lord liveth; and **b.** be my rock; 1288
Ps 21:6 hast made him most **b.** for ever: 1293
Ps 28:6 **B.** be the Lord, because he hath........ 1288
Ps 31:21 **B.** be the Lord: for he hath.............. 1288
Ps 32:1 **B.** is he whose transgression is........... 835
Ps 32:2 **B.** is the man unto whom the Lord...... 835
Ps 33:12 **B.** is the nation whose God is the........ 835
Ps 34:8 **b.** is the man that trusteth in him. 835
Ps 37:22 For such as be **b.** of him shall 1288
Ps 37:26 and lendeth; and his seed is **b.**. 1293
Ps 40:4 **B.** is that man that maketh the............ 835
Ps 41:1 **B.** is he that considereth the poor: 835
Ps 41:2 and he shall be **b.** upon the earth:........ 833
Ps 41:13 **B.** be the Lord God of Israel............ 1288
Ps 45:2 therefore God hath **b.** thee for ever.... 1288
Ps 49:18 while he lived he **b.** his soul: and 1288
Ps 65:4 **B.** is the man whom thou choosest, ... 835
Ps 66:20 **B.** be God, which hath not turned...... 1288
Ps 68:19 **B.** be the Lord, who daily loadeth...... 1288
Ps 68:35 power unto his people. **B.** be God...... 1288
Ps 72:17 sun: and men shall be **b.** in him: 1288
Ps 72:17 him: all nations shall call him **b.**. 833
Ps 72:18 **B.** be the Lord God, the God of........ 1288
Ps 72:19 **b.** be his glorious name for ever: 1288
Ps 84:4 **B.** are they that dwell in thy house:..... 835
Ps 84:5 **B.** is the man whose strength is in 835
Ps 84:12 **b.** is the man that trusteth in thee. 835
Ps 89:15 **B.** is the people that know the........... 835
Ps 89:52 **B.** be the Lord for evermore. 1288
Ps 94:12 **B.** is the man whom thou.................. 835
Ps 106:3 **B.** are they that keep judgment,.......... 835
Ps 106:48 **B.** be the Lord God of Israel from 1288
Ps 112:1 **B.** is the man that feareth the Lord, ... 835
Ps 112:2 of the upright shall be **b.**. 1288
Ps 113:2 **B.** be the name of the Lord from....... 1288
Ps 115:15 Ye are **b.** of the Lord which made...... 1288
Ps 118:26 **B.** be he that cometh in the name....... 1288
Ps 118:26 we have **b.** you out of the house of.... 1288
Ps 119:1 **B.** are the undefiled in the way, ... 835
Ps 119:2 **B.** are they that keep his.................. 835
Ps 119:12 **B.** art thou, O Lord: teach me 1288
Ps 124:6 **B.** be the Lord, who hath not........... 1288
Ps 128:1 **B.** is every one that feareth the 835
Ps 128:4 thus shall the man be **b.** that............ 1288
Ps 135:21 **B.** be the Lord out of Zion, which...... 1288
Ps 144:1 **B.** be the Lord my strength,............ 1288
Ps 147:13 he hath **b.** thy children within 1288
Pr 5:18 Let thy fountain be **b.**: and rejoice...... 1288
Pr 8:32 for **b.** are they that keep my ways. 835
Pr 8:34 **B.** is the man that heareth me, ... 835
Pr 10:7 The memory of the just is **b.**: but 1293
Pr 20:7 his children are **b.** after him.............. 835
Pr 20:21 the end thereof shall not be **b.**........... 1288
Pr 22:9 hath a bountiful eye shall be **b.**; 1288
Pr 31:28 children arise up, and call her **b.**;......... 833
Ec 10:17 **B.** art thou, O land, when thy............ 835
Ca 6:9 daughters saw her, and **b.** her; 833
Isa 19:25 **B.** be Egypt my people, ... 1288
Isa 30:18 **b.** are all they that wait for him. 835
Isa 32:20 **B.** are ye that sow beside all............. 835
Isa 51:2 I called him alone, and **b.** him, ... 1288
Isa 56:2 **B.** is the man that doeth this, ... 835
Isa 61:9 the seed which the Lord hath **b.**. 1288
Isa 65:23 the seed of the **b.** of the Lord, ... 1288
Isa 66:3 incense, as if he **b.** an idol. 1288
Jer 17:7 **B.** is the man that trusteth in the....... 1288
Jer 20:14 wherein my mother bare me be **b.**. 1288
Eze 3:12 **B.** be the glory of the Lord from 1288
Da 2:19 Then Daniel **b.** the God of heaven. 1289
Da 2:20 **B.** be the name of God forever.......... 1289
Da 3:28 **B.** be the God of Shadrach, ... 1289
Da 4:34 I **b.** the most High, and I praised 1289
Da 12:12 **B.** is he that waiteth, and cometh........ 835
Zec 11:5 that sell them say, **B.** be the Lord; 1288
Mal 3:12 And all nations shall call you **b.**............ 833
Mt 5:3 **B. are the poor in spirit:** *3107*
Mt 5:4 **B. are they that mourn: for they...** *3107*
Mt 5:5 **B. are the meek: for they shall .....** *3107*
Mt 5:6 **B. are they which do hunger and ..** *3107*
Mt 5:7 **B. are the merciful: for they shall.** *3107*
Mt 5:8 **B. are the pure in heart: for they..** *3107*
Mt 5:9 **B. are the peacemakers: for they...** *3107*
Mt 5:10 **B. are they which are persecuted ..** *3107*
Mt 5:11 **B. are ye, when men shall revile ...** *3107*
Mt 11:6 **And b. is he, whosoever shall not..** *3107*
Mt 13:16 **But b. are your eyes, for they see:** *3107*
Mt 14:19 he **b.**, and brake, and gave *2127*
Mt 16:17 said unto him, **B. art thou, Simon ...** *3107*
Mt 21:9 **B.** is he that cometh in the name....... *2127*
Mt 23:39 **B. is he that cometh in the name..** *2127*
Mt 24:46 **B. is that servant, whom his lord..** *3107*
Mt 25:34 **ye b. of my Father, inherit the .....** *2127*
Mt 26:26 **b.** it, and brake it, and gave it to *2127*
Mk 6:41 he looked up to heaven, and **b.**,......... *2127*
Mk 8:7 and he **b.**, and commanded to set....... *2127*
Mk 10:16 hands upon them, and **b.** them........... *2127*
Mk 11:9 **B.** is he that cometh in the name....... *2127*
Mk 11:10 **B.** be the kingdom of our father......... *2127*
Mk 14:22 and **b.**, and brake it, and gave to *2127*
Mk 14:61 thou the Christ, the Son of the **B.**? *2128*
Lu 1:28 thee: **b.** art thou among women, ... *2127*
Lu 1:42 **B.** art thou among women,................ *2127*
Lu 1:42 and **b.** is the fruit of thy womb. *2127*
Lu 1:45 **b.** is she that believed: for there........ *3107*
Lu 1:48 all generations shall call me **b.**. *3106*
Lu 1:68 **B.** be the Lord God of Israel;............ *2128*
Lu 2:28 him up in his arms, and **b.** God,......... *2127*
Lu 2:34 And Simeon **b.** them, and said........... *2127*
Lu 6:20 disciples, and said, **B. be ye poor:**..... *3107*
Lu 6:21 **B. are ye that hunger now: for ye.** *3107*
Lu 6:21 **B. are ye that weep now: for ye.....** *3107*
Lu 6:22 **B. are ye, when men shall hate.....** *3107*
Lu 7:23 **And b. is he, whosoever shall not........**
Lu 9:16 he **b.** them, and brake, and gave........ *2127*
Lu 10:23 **B. are the eyes which see the........** *3107*
Lu 11:27 **B.** is the womb that bare thee,........... *3107*
Lu 11:28 **Yea rather, b. are they that hear ..** *3107*
Lu 12:37 **B. are those servants, whom the ...** *3107*
Lu 12:38 **b. are those servants......................** *3107*
Lu 12:43 **B. is that servant, whom his lord..** *3107*
Lu 13:35 **B. is he that cometh in the name..** *2127*
Lu 14:14 **thou shalt be b.; for they cannot...** *3107*
Lu 14:15 **B.** is he that shall eat bread in.......... *3107*
Lu 19:38 **B.** be the king that cometh............... *2127*
Lu 23:29 **they shall say, B. are the barren,..** *3107*
Lu 24:30 took bread, and **b.** it, and brake,........ *2127*
Lu 24:50 he lifted up his hands, and **b.** them..... *2127*
Lu 24:51 while he **b.** them, he was parted........ *2127*
Joh 12:13 **B.** is the King of Israel that.............. *2127*
Joh 20:29 **b. are they that have not seen.......** *3107*
Ac 3:25 all the kindreds of the earth be **b.**. *1757*
Ac 20:35 **more b. to give than to receive.....** *3107*
Ro 1:25 the Creator, who is **b.** for ever.......... *2128*
Ro 4:7 **B.** are they whose iniquities are......... *3107*
Ro 4:8 **B.** is the man to whom the Lord........ *3107*
Ro 9:5 who is over all, God **b.** for ever......... *2128*
2Co 1:3 **B.** be God, even the Father of our..... *2128*
2Co 11:31 Jesus Christ, which is **b.** for............. *2128*
Ga 3:8 In thee shall all nations be **b.**............ *1757*
Ga 3:9 are **b.** with faithful Abraham............ *2127*
Eph 1:3 **B.** be the God and Father of our *2128*
Eph 1:3 **b.** us with all spiritual blessings.......... *2127*
1Ti 1:11 the glorious gospel of the **b.** God, ... *3107*
1Ti 6:15 **b.** and only Potentate, the King *3107*
Tit 2:13 Looking for that **b.** hope, and the....... *3107*
Heb 7:1 slaughter of the kings, and **b.** him; *2127*
Heb 7:6 **b.** him that had the promises............. *2127*
Heb 7:7 contradiction the less is **b.** of............ *2127*
Heb 11:20 By faith Isaac **b.** Jacob and Esau *2127*
Heb 11:21 Jacob, when he was a dying, **b.** *2127*
Jas 1:12 **B.** is the man that endureth.............. *3107*
Jas 1:25 this man shall be **b.** in his deed.......... *3107*
1Pe 1:3 **B.** be the God and Father of our *2128*
Re 1:3 **B.** is he that readeth, and they.......... *3107*
Re 14:13 **B.** are the dead which die in the......... *3107*
Re 16:15 **B.** is he that watcheth, and............... *3107*
Re 19:9 **B.** are they which are called.............. *3107*
Re 20:6 **B.** and holy is he that hath part *3107*
Re 22:7 **b.** is he that keepeth the sayings........ *3107*
Re 22:14 **B.** are they that do his *3107*

BLESSEDNESS

Ro 4:6 also describeth the **b.** of the man, ... *3108*
Ro 4:9 Cometh this **b.** then upon the............ *3108*
Ga 4:15 Where is then the **b.** ye spake of?...... *3108*

BLESSEST

Nu 22:6 that he, whom thou **b.** is blessed, ... 1288
1Ch 17:27 for thou **b.**, O Lord, and it shall....... 1288
Ps 65:10 it soft with showers: thou **b.** the........ 1288

BLESSETH

Ge 27:29 and blessed be he that **b.** thee........... 1288
Nu 24:9 Blessed is he that **b.** thee, and.......... 1288
De 15:6 the Lord thy God **b.** thee, as he........ 1288
Ps 10:3 **b.** the covetous, whom the Lord......... 1288
Ps 107:38 He **b.** them also, so that they are 1288
Pr 3:33 but he **b.** the habitation of the just...... 1288
Pr 27:14 that **b.** his friend with a loud voice,..... 1288
Isa 65:16 That he who **b.** himself in the earth.... 1288

BLESSING See also BLESSINGS.

Ge 12:2 great; and thou shalt be a **b.**: 1293
Ge 22:17 That in **b.** I will bless thee, and in........ 1288
Ge 27:12 a curse upon me, and not a **b.**.......... 1293
Ge 27:30 Isaac had made an end of **b.**.............. 1293
Ge 27:35 and hath taken away thy **b.**............... 1293
Ge 27:36 hath taken away my **b.**. And he 1293
Ge 27:36 Hast thou not reserved a **b.**.............. 1293
Ge 27:38 Hast thou but one **b.**, my father? 1293
Ge 27:41 because of the **b.** wherewith his......... 1293
Ge 28:4 and give thee the **b.** of Abraham, ... 1293
Ge 33:11 Take, I pray thee, my **b.** that is 1293
Ge 39:5 the **b.** of the Lord was upon all......... 1293
Ge 49:28 every one according to his **b.** he 1293
Ex 32:29 he may bestow upon you a **b.**............ 1293
Le 25:21 I will command my **b.** upon you 1293
De 11:26 you this day a **b.** and a curse; 1293
De 11:27 A **b.**, if ye obey the commandments.... 1293
De 11:29 thou shalt put the **b.** upon mount 1293
De 12:15 according to the **b.** of the Lord.......... 1293
De 16:17 according to the **b.** of the Lord.......... 1293
De 23:5 thy God turned the curse into a **b.** 1293
De 28:8 The Lord shall command the **b.** 1293
De 30:1 the **b.** and the curse, which I have 1293
De 30:19 life and death, **b.** and cursing:............ 1293
De 33:1 this is the **b.** wherewith Moses........... 1293
De 33:7 And this is the **b.** of Judah:......................
De 33:16 **b.** come upon the head of Joseph,............
De 33:23 and full with the **b.** of the Lord:.......... 1293
Jos 15:19 Who answereth, Give me a **b.**; 1293
Jg 1:15 Give me a **b.**: for thou hast given....... 1293
1Sa 25:27 now this **b.** with thine handmaid......... 1293
2Sa 7:29 and with thy **b.** let the house of......... 1293

2Ki 5:15 thee, take a **b.** of thy servant........... 1293
Ne 9:5 is exalted above all **b.** and praise........ 1293
Ne 13:2 God turned the curse into a **b.**. 1293
Job 29:13 **b.** of him that was ready to perish...... 1293
Ps 3:8 thy **b.** is upon thy people................. 1293
Ps 24:5 shall receive the **b.** from the Lord, ... 1293
Ps 109:17 as he delighted not in **b.**, so let it 1293
Ps 129:8 The **b.** of the Lord be upon you:....... 1293
Ps 133:3 there the Lord commanded the **b.**, ... 1293
Pr 10:22 The **b.** of the Lord, it maketh rich,..... 1293
Pr 11:11 By the **b.** of the upright the city is..... 1293
Pr 11:26 but **b.** shall be upon the head of......... 1293
Pr 24:25 a good **b.** shall come upon them.......... 1293
Isa 19:24 even a **b.** in the midst of the land:...... 1293
Isa 44:3 and my **b.** upon thine offspring:.......... 1293
Isa 65:8 Destroy it not; for a **b.** is in it:.......... 1293
Eze 34:26 places round about my hill a **b.**; 1293
Eze 34:26 there shall be showers of **b.**.............. 1293
Eze 44:30 that he may cause the **b.** to rest......... 1293
Joe 2:14 repent, and leave a **b.** behind him;...... 1293
Zec 8:13 I save you, and ye shall be a **b.**: 1293
Mal 3:10 pour you out a **b.**, that there shall...... 1293
Lu 24:53 in the temple, praising and **b.** God...... *2127*
Ro 15:29 the fulness of the **b.** of the gospel...... *2129*
1Co 10:16 The cup of **b.** which we bless,........... *2129*
Ga 3:14 the **b.** of Abraham might come........... *2129*
Heb 6:7 is dressed, receiveth **b.** from God: *2129*
Heb 6:14 Saying, Surely **b.** I will bless thee, ... *2129*
Heb 12:17 would have inherited the **b.**,.............. *2129*
Jas 3:10 mouth proceedeth **b.** and cursing........ *2129*
1Pe 3:9 but contrariwise **b.**;......................... *2129*
1Pe 3:9 that ye should inherit a **b.**.................. *2129*
Re 5:12 and honour, and glory, and **b.**............ *2129*
Re 5:13 **B.**, and honour, and glory,................ *2129*
Re 7:12 **B.**, and glory, and wisdom,................ *2129*

BLESSINGS
Ge 49:25 bless thee with **b.** of heaven above, ... 1293
Ge 49:25 **b.** of the deep that lieth under, ... 1293
Ge 49:25 **b.** of the breasts, and of the womb:.... 1293
Ge 49:26 The **b.** of thy father have prevailed..... 1293
Ge 49:26 above the **b.** of my progenitors.......... 1293
De 28:2 all these **b.** shall come on thee, ... 1293
Jos 8:34 the **b.** and cursings, according to........ 1293
Ps 21:3 preventest with the **b.** of goodness:.... 1293
Pr 10:6 **B.** are upon the head of the just: 1293
Pr 28:20 faithful man shall abound with **b.**:........ 1293
Mal 2:2 I will curse your **b.**: yea, I have.......... 1293
Eph 1:3 with all spiritual **b.** in heavenly........... *2129*

BLEW
Jos 6:8 Lord, and **b.** with the trumpets:......... 8628
Jos 6:9 priests that **b.** with the trumpets,....... 8628
Jos 6:13 went on continually, and **b.** with......... 8628
Jos 6:16 the priests **b.** with the trumpets,......... 8628
Jos 6:20 people shouted when the priests **b.**...... 8628
Jg 3:27 he **b.** a trumpet in the mountain......... 8628
Jg 6:34 upon Gideon, and he **b.** a trumpet: 8628
Jg 7:19 they **b.** the trumpets, and brake......... 8628
Jg 7:20 three companies **b.** the trumpets, ... 8628
Jg 7:22 three hundred **b.** the trumpets,............ 8628
1Sa 13:3 **b.** the trumpet throughout all the 8628
2Sa 2:28 So Joab **b.** a trumpet, and all............ 8628
2Sa 18:16 And Joab **b.** the trumpet, and the....... 8628
2Sa 20:1 and he **b.** a trumpet, and said,........... 8628
2Sa 20:22 And he **b.** a trumpet, and they 8628
1Ki 1:39 And they **b.** the trumpet; and all........ 8628
2Ki 9:13 of the stairs, and **b.** with trumpets, ... 8628
2Ki 11:14 rejoiced, and **b.** with trumpets: 8628
Mt 7:25 **winds b., and beat upon that**........ *4154*
Mt 7:27 **b., and beat upon that house;**........ *4154*
Joh 6:18 by reason of a great wind that **b.**. *4154*
Ac 27:13 south wind **b.** softly, supposing.......... *5285*
Ac 28:13 one day the south wind **b.**, and.......... *1920*

BLIND See also BLINDED; BLINDETH; BLINDFOLDED.
Ex 4:11 or deaf, or the seeing, or the **b.**?....... 5787
Le 19:14 a stumblingblock before the **b.**, ... 5787
Le 21:18 a **b.** man, or a lame, or he that.......... 5787
Le 22:22 **B.**, or broken, or maimed, or............ 5788
De 15:21 it be lame, or **b.**, or have any ill 5787
De 16:19 a gift doth **b.** the eyes of the wise,..... 5786
De 27:18 he that maketh the **b.** to wander........ 5787
De 28:29 **b.** gropeth in darkness, and thou......... 5787
1Sa 12:3 bribe to **b.** mine eyes therewith?........ 5956
2Sa 5:6 take away the **b.** and the lame 5787
2Sa 5:8 **b.**, that are hated of David's soul, ... 5787
2Sa 5:8 The **b.** and the lame shall not come.... 5787
Job 29:15 I was eyes to the **b.**, and feet was I... 5787
Ps 146:8 Lord openeth the eyes of the **b.**: 5787
Isa 29:18 the **b.** shall see out of obscurity,........ 5787
Isa 35:5 eyes of the **b.** shall be opened, ... 5787
Isa 42:7 open the **b.** eyes, to bring out the...... 5787
Isa 42:16 bring the **b.** by a way that they 5787
Isa 42:18 Hear, ye deaf; and look, ye **b.**, that.... 5787
Isa 42:19 Who is **b.**, but my servant? or deaf 5787
Isa 42:19 who is **b.** as he that is perfect, and 5787
Isa 42:19 **b.** as the Lord's servant?................. 5787
Isa 43:8 forth the **b.** people that have eyes,...... 5787
Isa 56:10 His watchmen are **b.**: they are all....... 5787
Isa 59:10 for the wall like the **b.**, and we.......... 5787
Jer 31:8 and with them the **b.** and the lame, ... 5787
La 4:14 wandered as **b.** men in the streets, ... 5787
Zep 1:17 walk like **b.** men, because they.......... 5787
Mal 1:8 the **b.** for sacrifice, is it not evil? 5787
Mt 9:27 two **b.** men followed him, crying, ... *5185*
Mt 9:28 the house, the **b.** men came to him: ... *5185*
Mt 11:5 **The b. receive their sight, and the.** *5185*
Mt 12:22 one possessed with a devil, **b.**, ... *5185*
Mt 12:22 that the **b.** and dumb both spake........ *5185*
Mt 15:14 **Let them alone: they be b.**............ *5185*
Mt 15:14 **leaders of the b.. And**................... *5185*
Mt 15:14 **if the b. lead the b.,**..................... *5185*
Mt 15:30 lame, **b.**, dumb, maimed, and many *5185*
Mt 15:31 lame to walk, and the **b.** to see: *5185*
Mt 20:30 And, behold, two **b.** men sitting by..... *5185*
Mt 21:14 the **b.** and the lame came to him........ *5185*
Mt 23:16 **Woe unto you, ye blind guides,**..... *5185*
Mt 23:17, **19 Ye fools and b.: for whether is**.. *5185*
Mt 23:24 **Ye b. guides, which strain at a**..... *5185*
Mt 23:26 **Thou b. Pharisee, cleanse first**...... *5185*
Mk 8:22 and they bring a **b.** man unto him,...... *5185*
Mk 8:23 he took the **b.** man by the hand, ... *5185*
Mk 10:46 **b.** Bartimaeus, the son of Timaeus, ... *5185*
Mk 10:49 they call the **b.** man, saying unto......... *5185*
Mk 10:51 The **b.** man said unto him, Lord,........ *5185*
Lu 4:18 **and recovering of sight to the b.,**.. *5185*
Lu 6:39 **Can the b. lead the b.?**.................. *5185*
Lu 7:21 many that were **b.** he gave sight.......... *5185*
Lu 7:22 **how that the b. see, the lame walk,***5185*
Lu 14:13 **the maimed, the lame, the b.:**........ *5185*
Lu 14:21 **maimed, and the halt, and the b..** . *5185*
Lu 18:35 a certain **b.** man sat by the way side... *5185*
Joh 5:3 **b.**, halt, withered, waiting for the....... *5185*
Joh 9:1 which was **b.** from his birth............. *5185*
Joh 9:2 his parents, that he was born **b.**? *5185*
Joh 9:6 anointed the eyes of the **b.** man......... *5185*
Joh 9:8 had seen him that he was **b.**, ... *5185*
Joh 9:13 him that aforetime was **b.**................. *5185*
Joh 9:17 They say unto the **b.** man again, ... *5185*
Joh 9:18 he had been **b.**, and received his........ *5185*
Joh 9:19 your son, who ye say was born **b.**? *5185*
Joh 9:20 and that he was born **b.**: *5185*
Joh 9:24 called they the man that was **b.**, ... *5185*
Joh 9:25 whereas I was **b.**, now I see............. *5185*
Joh 9:32 the eyes of one that was born **b.**. *5185*
Joh 9:39 **they which see might be made b.**... *5185*
Joh 9:40 and said unto him, Are we **b.** also?..... *5185*
Joh 9:41 **If ye were b., ye should have no**.... *5185*
Joh 10:21 a devil open the eyes of the **b.**?......... *5185*
Joh 11:37 opened the eyes of the **b.**, have........... *5185*
Ac 13:11 shalt be **b.**, not seeing the sun *5185*
Ro 2:19 thou thyself art a guide of the **b.**,....... *5185*
2Pe 1:9 he that lacketh these things is **b.**,....... *5185*
Re 3:17 **and poor, and b., and naked:** *5185*

BLINDED
Joh 12:40 He hath **b.** their eyes, and............... *5186*
Ro 11:7 obtained it, and the rest were **b.**......... *4456*
2Co 3:14 But their minds were **b.**: for until....... *4456*
2Co 4:4 of this world hath **b.** the minds *5186*
1Jo 2:11 that darkness hath **b.** his eyes. *5186*

BLINDETH
Ex 23:8 **b.** the wise, and perverteth the 5786

BINDFOLDED
Lu 22:64 And when they had **b.** him, they *4028*

BLINDNESS
Ge 19:11 at the door of the house with **b.**, ... 5575
De 28:28 smite thee with madness, and **b.**, ... 5788
2Ki 6:18 this people, I pray thee, with **b.**......... 5575
2Ki 6:18 And he smote them with **b.**............... 5575
Zec 12:4 every horse of the people with **b.**....... 5788
Ro 11:25 **b.** in part is happened to Israel, ... *4457*
Eph 4:18 because of the **b.** of their heart:........ *4457*

BLOCK See also STUMBLINGBLOCK.
Isa 57:14 take up the stumbling **b.** out of.......... 4383

BLOOD See also BLOODGUILTINESS; BLOODTHIRSTY.
Ge 4:10 of thy brother's **b.** crieth unto me 1818
Ge 4:11 thy brother's **b.** from thy hand;.......... 1818
Ge 9:4 thereof, which is the **b.** thereof,......... 1818
Ge 9:5 surely your **b.** of your lives will 1818
Ge 9:6 sheddeth man's **b.**,...his **b.** be shed: ... 1818
Ge 37:22 Shed no **b.**, but cast him into 1818
Ge 37:26 our brother, and conceal his **b.**? 1818
Ge 37:31 goats, and dipped the coat in the **b.**;... 1818
Ge 42:22 behold, also his **b.** is required........... 1818
Ge 49:11 and his clothes in the **b.** of grapes:..... 1818
Ex 4:9 become **b.** upon the dry land............. 1818
Ex 7:17 and they shall be turned to **b.**............ 1818
Ex 7:19 that they may become **b.**;.................. 1818
Ex 7:19 and that there may be **b.**.................. 1818
Ex 7:20 in the river were turned to **b.**............ 1818
Ex 7:21 **b.** throughout all the land of Egypt. 1818
Ex 12:7 shall take of the **b.**, and strike it 1818
Ex 12:13 the **b.** shall be to you for a token....... 1818
Ex 12:13 when I see the **b.**, I will pass over..... 1818
Ex 12:22 dip it in the **b.** that is in the bason, ... 1818
Ex 12:22 the **b.** that is in the bason;................ 1818
Ex 12:23 he seeth the **b.** upon the lintel,.......... 1818
Ex 22:2 shall no **b.** be shed for him. 1818
Ex 22:3 there shall be **b.** shed for him;........... 1818
Ex 23:18 not offer the **b.** of my sacrifice 1818
Ex 24:6 took half of the **b.** and put it 1818
Ex 24:6 half of the **b.** he sprinkled on............. 1818
Ex 24:8 Moses took the **b.**, and sprinkled 1818
Ex 24:8 Behold the **b.** of the covenant,........... 1818
Ex 29:12 thou shalt take the **b.** of................... 1818
Ex 29:12 pour all the **b.** beside the bottom 1818
Ex 29:16 shalt take his **b.** and sprinkle it 1818
Ex 29:20 kill the ram, and take of his **b.**,.......... 1818
Ex 29:20 sprinkle the **b.** upon the altar 1818
Ex 29:21 shalt take of the **b.** that is upon 1818
Ex 30:10 with the **b.** of the sin offering............ 1818
Ex 34:25 not offer the **b.** of my sacrifice 1818
Le 1:5 bring the **b.**, and sprinkle the **b.** 1818
Le 1:11 sprinkle his **b.** round about upon 1818
Le 1:15 the **b.** thereof shall be wrung out 1818
Le 3:2 sprinkle the **b.** upon the altar 1818
Le 3:8 sons shall sprinkle the **b.** thereof......... 1818
Le 3:13 Aaron shall sprinkle the **b.** thereof...... 1818
Le 3:17 that ye eat neither fat nor **b.**............ 1818
Le 4:5 shall take of the bullock's **b.**, and 1818
Le 4:6 dip his finger in the **b.**, and.............. 1818
Le 4:6 sprinkle of the **b.** seven times 1818
Le 4:7 some of the **b.** upon the horns........... 1818
Le 4:7 pour all the **b.** of the bullock 1818
Le 4:16 shall bring of the bullock's **b.**............ 1818
Le 4:17 dip his finger in some of the **b.**,......... 1818
Le 4:18 And he shall put some of the **b.**......... 1818
Le 4:18 pour out all the **b.** at the bottom........ 1818
Le 4:25 the priest shall take of the **b.** of......... 1818
Le 4:25 shall pour out his **b.** at the bottom...... 1818
Le 4:30 shall take of the **b.** thereof.............. 1818
Le 4:30 shall pour out all the **b.** thereof.......... 1818
Le 4:34 priest shall take of the **b.** of the......... 1818
Le 4:34 shall pour out all the **b.** thereof.......... 1818
Le 5:9 he shall sprinkle of the **b.** of the 1818
Le 5:9 the rest of the **b.** shall be wrung out... 1818
Le 6:27 is sprinkled of the **b.** thereof............. 1818
Le 6:30 whereof any of the **b.** is brought 1818
Le 7:2 the **b.** thereof shall he sprinkle 1818
Le 7:14 the priest's that sprinkleth the **b.** of.... 1818
Le 7:26 ye shall eat no manner of **b.**,............. 1818
Le 7:27 that eateth any manner of **b.**,............. 1818
Le 7:33 the **b.** of the peace offerings, ... 1818
Le 8:15 Moses took the **b.**, and put it upon..... 1818
Le 8:15 poured the **b.** at the bottom of the 1818
Le 8:19 Moses sprinkled the **b.** upon the......... 1818
Le 8:23 and Moses took of the **b.** of it, and 1818
Le 8:24 Moses put of the **b.** upon the tip of.... 1818
Le 8:24 the **b.** upon the altar round about. 1818
Le 8:30 the **b.** which was upon the altar, ... 1818
Le 9:9 brought the **b.** unto him: and he.......... 1818
Le 9:9 dipped his finger in the **b.**,............... 1818
Le 9:9 poured out the **b.** at the bottom of..... 1818
Le 9:12, 18 sons presented unto him the **b.**, ... 1818
Le 10:18 Behold, the **b.** of it was not brought ... 1818
Le 12:4 shall then continue in the **b.** of her 1818
Le 12:5 shall continue in the **b.** of her 1818
Le 12:7 cleansed from the issue of her **b.**. 1818

Book	Ref	Context	No.
Le	14:6	the living bird in the **b.** of the	1818
Le	14:14	the **b.** of the trespass offering,	1818
Le	14:17	upon the **b.** of the trespass offering:	1818
Le	14:25	some of the **b.** of the trespass	1818
Le	14:28	upon the place of the **b.** of the	1818
Le	14:51	dip them in the **b.** of the slain	1818
Le	14:52	the house with the **b.** of the bird,	1818
Le	15:19	her issue in her flesh be **b.**,	1818
Le	15:25	if a woman have an issue of her **b.**	1818
Le	16:14	shall take of the **b.** of the bullock,	1818
Le	16:14	shall he sprinkle of the **b.**	1818
Le	16:15	bring his **b.** within the vail,	1818
Le	16:15	and do with that **b.** as he did	1818
Le	16:15	with the **b.** of the bullock,	1818
Le	16:18	take of the **b.** of the bullock,	1818
Le	16:18	and of the **b.** of the goat,	1818
Le	16:19	And he shall sprinkle of the **b.**	1818
Le	16:27	whose **b.** was brought in to make	1818
Le	17:4	**b.** shall be imputed unto that man;	1818
Le	17:4	he hath shed **b.**; and that man	1818
Le	17:6	the priest shall sprinkle the **b.**	1818
Le	17:10	that eateth any manner of **b.**:	1818
Le	17:10	against that soul that eateth **b.**	1818
Le	17:11	the life of the flesh is in the **b.**:	1818
Le	17:11	the **b.** that maketh an atonement	1818
Le	17:12	No soul of you shall eat **b.**,	1818
Le	17:12	that sojourneth among you eat **b.**.	1818
Le	17:13	shall even pour out the **b.** thereof,	1818
Le	17:14	the **b.** of it is for the life thereof:	1818
Le	17:14	Ye shall eat the **b.** of no manner	1818
Le	17:14	the life of all flesh is the **b.** thereof:	1818
Le	19:16	against the **b.** of thy neighbour:	1818
Le	19:26	shall not eat anything with the **b.**:	1818
Le	20:9	his **b.** shall be upon him.	1818
Le	20:11	their **b.** shall be upon them.	1818
Le	20:12	wrought confusion; their **b.** shall	1818
Le	20:13	their **b.** shall be upon them.	1818
Le	20:16	put to death; their **b.** shall be	1818
Le	20:18	uncovered the fountain of her **b.**	1818
Le	20:27	their **b.** shall be upon them.	1818
Nu	18:17	thou shalt sprinkle their **b.** upon	1818
Nu	19:4	take of her **b.** with his finger,	1818
Nu	19:4	and sprinkle of her **b.**	1818
Nu	19:5	her skin, and her flesh, and her **b.**,	1818
Nu	23:24	prey, and drink the **b.** of the slain	1818
Nu	35:19	The revenger of **b.** himself shall	1818
Nu	35:21	the revenger of **b.** shall slay	1818
Nu	35:24	the slayer and the revenger of **b.**	1818
Nu	35:25	of the hand of the revenger of **b.**,	1818
Nu	35:27	And the revenger of **b.** find him	1818
Nu	35:27	the revenger of **b.** kill the slayer;	1818
Nu	35:27	he shall not be guilty of **b.**:	1818
Nu	35:33	for **b.** it defileth the land: and the	1818
Nu	35:33	cannot be cleansed of the **b.**	1818
Nu	35:33	but by the **b.** of him that shed it.	1818
De	12:16	Only ye shall not eat the **b.**;	1818
De	12:23	sure that thou eat not the **b.**	1818
De	12:23	for the **b.** is the life;	1818
De	12:27	the flesh, and the **b.**, upon the	1818
De	12:27	and the **b.** of thy sacrifices shall	1818
De	15:23	thou shalt not eat the **b.** thereof;	1818
De	17:8	between **b.** and **b.**, between plea	1818
De	19:6	Lest the avenger of the **b.** pursue	1818
De	19:10	That innocent **b.** be not shed in	1818
De	19:10	and so **b.** be upon thee.	1818
De	19:12	into the hand of the avenger of **b.**,	1818
De	19:13	of innocent **b.** from Israel,	1818
De	21:7	Our hands have not shed this **b.**,	1818
De	21:8	lay not innocent **b.** unto thy people	1818
De	21:8	And the **b.** shall be forgiven them	1818
De	21:9	put away the guilt of innocent **b.**	1818
De	22:8	that thou bring not **b.** upon	1818
De	32:14	drink the pure **b.** of the grape.	1818
De	32:42	make mine arrows drunk with **b.**,	1818
De	32:42	and that with the **b.** of the slain	1818
De	32:43	will avenge the **b.** of his servants,	1818
Jos	2:19	his **b.** shall be upon his head,	1818
Jos	2:19	his **b.** shall be on our head, if any	1818
Jos	20:3	refuge from the avenger of **b.**	1818
Jos	20:5	if the avenger of **b.** pursue after	1818
Jos	20:9	by the hand of the avenger of **b.**,	1818
Jg	9:24	their **b.** be laid upon Abimelech	1818
1Sa	14:32	people did eat them with the **b.**.	1818
1Sa	14:33	Lord, in that they eat with the **b.**	1818
1Sa	14:34	the Lord in eating with the **b.**	1818
1Sa	19:5	wilt thou sin against innocent **b.**,	1818
1Sa	25:26	thee from coming to shed **b.**,	1818
1Sa	25:31	either that thou hast shed **b.**	1818
1Sa	25:33	this day from coming to shed **b.**,	1818
1Sa	26:20	let not my **b.** fall to the earth	1818
2Sa	1:16	Thy **b.** be upon thy head;	1818
2Sa	1:22	From the **b.** of the slain,	1818
2Sa	3:27	that he died, for the **b.** of Asahel	1818
2Sa	3:28	from the **b.** of Abner the son	1818
2Sa	4:11	therefore now require his **b.**	1818
2Sa	14:11	the revengers of **b.** to destroy	1818
2Sa	16:8	all the **b.** of the house of Saul,	1818
2Sa	20:12	Amasa wallowed in **b.** in the	1818
2Sa	23:17	the **b.** of the men that went in	1818
1Ki	2:5	shed the **b.** of war in peace,	1818
1Ki	2:5	put the **b.** of war upon his girdle	1818
1Ki	2:9	thou down to the grave with **b.**,	1818
1Ki	2:31	take away the innocent **b.**, which	1818
1Ki	2:32	the Lord shall return his **b.**	1818
1Ki	2:33	Their **b.** shall therefore return	1818
1Ki	2:37	thy **b.** shall be upon thine own	1818
1Ki	18:28	lancets, till the **b.** gushed out	1818
1Ki	21:19	dogs licked the **b.** of Naboth	1818
1Ki	21:19	shall dogs lick thy **b.**,	1818
1Ki	22:35	and the **b.** ran out of the wound	1818
1Ki	22:38	and the dogs licked up his **b.**;	1818
2Ki	3:22	on the other side as red as **b.**	1818
2Ki	3:23	they said, This is **b.**: the kings	1818
2Ki	9:7	avenge the **b.** of my servants	1818
2Ki	9:7	and the **b.** of all the servants	1818
2Ki	9:26	seen yesterday the **b.** of Naboth,	1818
2Ki	9:26	and the **b.** of his sons,	1818
2Ki	9:33	and some of her **b.** was sprinkled	1818
2Ki	16:13	sprinkled the **b.** of his peace	1818
2Ki	16:15	all the **b.** of the burnt offering.	1818
2Ki	16:15	and all the **b.** of the sacrifice:	1818
2Ki	21:16	shed innocent **b.** very much,	1818
2Ki	24:4	for the innocent **b.** that he shed	1818
2Ki	24:4	filled Jerusalem with innocent **b.**	1818
1Ch	11:19	shall I drink the **b.** of these men	1818
1Ch	22:8	Thou hast shed **b.** abundantly,	1818
1Ch	22:8	thou hast shed much **b.** upon the	1818
1Ch	28:3	man of war, and hast shed **b.**.	1818
2Ch	19:10	between **b.** and **b.**, between law	1818
2Ch	24:25	conspired against him for the **b.**	1818
2Ch	29:22	the priests received the **b.**, and	1818
2Ch	29:22	sprinkled the **b.** upon the altar:	1818
2Ch	29:22	lambs, and they sprinkled the **b.**	1818
2Ch	29:24	reconciliation with their **b.** upon	1818
2Ch	30:16	the priests sprinkled the **b.**, which	1818
2Ch	35:11	the priests sprinkled the **b.** from	
Job	16:18	O earth, cover not thou my **b.**,	1818
Job	39:30	Her young ones also suck up **b.**	1818
Ps	9:12	he maketh inquisition for **b.**,	1818
Ps	16:4	their drink offerings of **b.** will I	1818
Ps	30:9	What profit is their in my **b.**, when	1818
Ps	50:13	of bulls, or drink the **b.** of goats?	1818
Ps	58:10	his feet in the **b.** of the wicked.	1818
Ps	68:23	dipped in the **b.** of thine enemies,	1818
Ps	72:14	precious shall their **b.** be in his	1818
Ps	78:44	had turned their rivers into **b.**;	1818
Ps	79:3	Their **b.** have they shed like water	1818
Ps	79:10	revenging of the **b.** of thy servants	1818
Ps	94:21	and condemn the innocent **b.**	1818
Ps	105:29	turned their waters into **b.**, and	1818
Ps	106:38	shed innocent **b.**, even	1818
Ps	106:38	even the **b.** of their sons	1818
Ps	106:38	the land was polluted with **b.**	1818
Pr	1:11	let us lay wait for **b.**, let us look	1818
Pr	1:16	evil, and make haste to shed **b.**.	1818
Pr	1:18	they lay wait for their own **b.**;	1818
Pr	6:17	and hands that shed innocent **b.**,	1818
Pr	12:6	to lie in wait for **b.**: but the mouth	1818
Pr	28:17	violence to the **b.** of any person	1818
Pr	30:33	of the nose bringeth forth **b.**:	1818
Isa	1:11	delight not in the **b.** of bullocks,	1818
Isa	1:15	hear: your hands are full of **b.**.	1818
Isa	4:4	have purged the **b.** of Jerusalem	1818
Isa	9:5	noise, and garments rolled in **b.**;	1818
Isa	15:9	of Dimon shall be full of **b.**:	1818
Isa	26:21	the earth also shall disclose her **b.**,	1818
Isa	33:15	his ears from hearing of **b.**,	1818
Isa	34:3	shall be melted with their **b.**	1818
Isa	34:6	sword of the Lord is filled with **b.**,	1818
Isa	34:6	with the **b.** of lambs and goats	1818
Isa	34:7	their land shall be soaked with **b.**,	1818
Isa	49:26	be drunken with their own **b.**,	1818
Isa	59:3	your hands are defiled with **b.**,	1818
Isa	59:7	make haste to shed innocent **b.**	1818
Isa	63:3	their **b.** shall be sprinkled upon	5332
Isa	66:3	as if he offered swine's **b.**; he that	1818
Jer	2:34	skirts is found the **b.** of the souls	1818
Jer	7:6	shed not innocent **b.** in this place,	1818
Jer	18:21	pour out their **b.** by the force	
Jer	19:4	this place with the **b.** of innocents;	1818
Jer	22:3	neither shed innocent **b.** in this	1818
Jer	22:17	and for to shed innocent **b.**, and	1818
Jer	26:15	shall surely bring innocent **b.** upon	1818
Jer	46:10	and made drunk with their **b.**	1818
Jer	48:10	keepeth back his sword from **b.**.	1818
Jer	51:35	and my **b.** upon the inhabitants of	1818
La	4:13	that have shed the **b.** of the just	1818
La	4:14	polluted themselves with **b.**, so	1818
Eze	3:18,	20 but his **b.** will I require at thine	1818
Eze	5:17	pestilence and **b.** shall pass	1818
Eze	9:9	the land is full of **b.**, and the city	1818
Eze	14:19	and pour out my fury upon it in **b.**,	1818
Eze	16:6	polluted in thine own **b.**, I said	1818
Eze	16:6	when thou wast in thy **b.**, Live;	1818
Eze	16:6	thee when thou wast in thy **b.**,	1818
Eze	16:9	washed away thy **b.** from thee, and	1818
Eze	16:22	bare, and wast polluted in thy **b.**	1818
Eze	16:36	and by the **b.** of thy children,	1818
Eze	16:38	that break wedlock and shed **b.**	1818
Eze	16:38	will give thee **b.** in fury and	1818
Eze	18:10	that is a robber, a shedder of **b.**,	1818
Eze	18:13	surely die; his **b.** shall be upon him	1818
Eze	19:10	Thy mother is like a vine in thy **b.**,	1818
Eze	21:32	thy **b.** shall be in the midst of the	1818
Eze	22:3	The city sheddeth **b.** in the midst of	1818
Eze	22:4	Thou art become guilty in thy **b.**	1818
Eze	22:6	in thee to their power to shed **b.**.	1818
Eze	22:9	are men that carry tales to shed **b.**	1818
Eze	22:12	have they taken gifts to shed **b.**;	1818
Eze	22:13	at thy **b.** which hath been in the	1818
Eze	22:27	to shed **b.**, and to destroy souls,	1818
Eze	23:37	and **b.** is in their hands, and with	1818
Eze	23:45	the manner of women that shed **b.**;	1818
Eze	23:45	are adulteresses, and **b.** is in their	1818
Eze	24:7	For her **b.** is in the midst of her;	1818
Eze	24:8	I have set her **b.** upon the top of a	1818
Eze	28:23	her pestilence, and **b.** into her	1818
Eze	32:6	I will also water with thy **b.** the	1818
Eze	33:4	his **b.** shall be upon his own head.	1818
Eze	33:5	warning; his **b.** shall be upon him.	1818
Eze	33:6	but his **b.** will I require at the	1818
Eze	33:8	but his **b.** will I require at thine	1818
Eze	33:25	Ye eat with the **b.**, and lift up your	1818
Eze	33:25	toward your idols, and shed **b.**	1818
Eze	35:5	shed the **b.** of the children of	
Eze	35:6	I will prepare thee unto **b.**,	1818
Eze	35:6	and **b.** shall pursue thee: sith	1818
Eze	35:6	thou hast not hated **b.**, even **b.** shall	1818
Eze	36:18	the **b.** that they had shed upon the	1818
Eze	38:22	him with pestilence and with **b.**;	1818
Eze	39:17	that ye may eat flesh, and drink **b.**.	1818
Eze	39:18	and drink the **b.** of the princes of	1818
Eze	39:19	and drink **b.** till ye be drunken, of	1818
Eze	43:18	thereon, and to sprinkle **b.** thereon	1818
Eze	43:20	thou shalt take of the **b.** thereof,	1818
Eze	44:7	my bread, the fat and the **b.**, and	1818
Eze	44:15	offer unto me the fat and the **b.**,	1818
Eze	45:19	the priest shall take of the **b.** of the	1818
Ho	1:4	I will avenge the **b.** of Jezreel upon	1818
Ho	4:2	they break out, and **b.** toucheth **b.**.	1818
Ho	6:8	iniquity, and is polluted with **b.**.	1818
Ho	12:14	therefore shall he leave his **b.** upon	1818
Joe	2:30	**b.**, and fire, and pillars of smoke	1818
Joe	2:31	darkness, and the moon into **b.**,	1818
Joe	3:19	they have shed innocent **b.** in their	1818
Joe	3:21	For I will cleanse their **b.** that I	1818
Jon	1:14	and lay not upon us innocent **b.**:	1818
Mic	3:10	They build up Zion with **b.**, and	1818
Mic	7:2	they all lie in wait for **b.**; they	1818
Hab	2:8	because of men's **b.**, and for the	1818
Hab	2:12	him that buildeth a town with **b.**,	1818
Hab	2:17	them afraid, because of men's **b.**,	1818
Zep	1:17	and their **b.** shall be poured out as	1818
Zec	9:7	I will take away his **b.** out of his	1818
Zec	9:11	by the **b.** of thy covenant I have	1818
Mt	9:20	diseased with an issue of **b.** twelve	*131*
Mt	16:17	**for flesh and b. hath not revealed**	*129*
Mt	23:30	**with them in the b. of the prophets**	*129*
Mt	23:35	**the righteous b. shed upon the**	*129*
Mt	23:35	**from the b. of righteous Abel**	*129*
Mt	23:35	**unto the b. of Zacharias son of**	*129*

Mt 26:28 **for this is my b. of the new**... *129*
Mt 27:4 I have betrayed the innocent **b.**... *129*
Mt 27:6 because it is the price of **b.**... *129*
Mt 27:8 was called, The field of **b.**, unto this... *129*
Mt 27:24 I am innocent of the **b.** of this just... *129*
Mt 27:25 His **b.** be on us, and on our children... *129*
Mk 5:25 which had an issue of **b.** twelve... *129*
Mk 5:29 the fountain of her **b.** was dried up;... *129*
Mk 14:24 **This is my b. of the new testament,**... *129*
Lu 8:43 having an issue of **b.** twelve years,... *129*
Lu 8:44 and immediately her issue of **b.**... *129*
Lu 11:50 **the b. of all the prophets, which**... *129*
Lu 11:51 **From the b. of Abel**... *129*
Lu 11:51 **unto the b. of Zacharias,**... *129*
Lu 13:1 whose **b.** Pilate had mingled with... *129*
Lu 22:20 **new testament in my b., which is**... *129*
Lu 22:44 great drops of **b.** falling down to... *129*
Joh 1:13 Which were born, not of **b.**, nor of... *129*
Joh 6:53 **Son of man, and drink his b., he**... *129*
Joh 6:54 **my flesh, and drinketh my b.,**... *129*
Joh 6:55 **is meat indeed, and my b. is drink**... *129*
Joh 6:56 **my flesh, and drinketh my b.,**... *129*
Joh 19:34 forthwith came there out **b.** and... *129*
Ac 1:19 that is to say, The field of **b.**... *129*
Ac 2:19 **b.**, and fire, and vapour of smoke:... *129*
Ac 2:20 into darkness, and the moon into **b.**,... *129*
Ac 5:28 intend to bring this man's **b.** upon... *129*
Ac 15:20 from things strangled, and from **b.**... *129*
Ac 15:29 offered to idols, and from **b.**, and... *129*
Ac 17:26 hath made of one **b.** all nations of... *129*
Ac 18:6 Your **b.** be upon your own heads; I... *129*
Ac 20:26 that I am pure from the **b.** of all... *129*
Ac 20:28 hath purchased with his own **b.**... *129*
Ac 21:25 from **b.**, and from strangled, and... *129*
Ac 22:20 the **b.** of thy martyr Stephen was... *129*
Ro 3:15 Their feet are swift to shed **b.**:... *129*
Ro 3:25 through faith in his **b.**, to declare... *129*
Ro 5:9 then, being now justified by his **b.**,... *129*
1Co 10:16 the communion of the **b.** of Christ?... *129*
1Co 11:25 **the new testament in my b.:**... *129*
1Co 11:27 of the body and **b.** of the Lord... *129*
1Co 15:50 that flesh and **b.** cannot inherit the... *129*
Ga 1:16 I conferred not with flesh and **b.**:... *129*
Eph 1:7 have redemption through his **b.**, the... *129*
Eph 2:13 are made nigh by the **b.** of Christ... *129*
Eph 6:12 wrestle not against flesh and **b.**... *129*
Col 1:14 redemption through his **b.**, even... *129*
Col 1:20 made peace through the **b.** of his... *129*
Heb 2:14 partakers of flesh and **b.**, he also... *129*
Heb 9:7 once every year, not without **b.**,... *129*
Heb 9:12 neither by the **b.** of goats and... *129*
Heb 9:12 calves, but by his own **b.** he... *129*
Heb 9:13 For it the **b.** of bulls and of goats,... *129*
Heb 9:14 How much more shall the **b.** of... *129*
Heb 9:18 testament was dedicated without **b.**... *129*
Heb 9:19 he took the **b.** of calves and of... *129*
Heb 9:20 Saying, this is the **b.** of the... *129*
Heb 9:21 sprinkled with **b.** both the... *129*
Heb 9:22 are by the law purged with **b.**; and... *129*
Heb 9:22 without shedding of **b.** is no... *130*
Heb 9:25 the holy place every year with **b.** of... *129*
Heb 10:4 that the **b.** of bulls and of goats... *129*
Heb 10:19 to enter into the holiest by the **b.** of... *129*
Heb 10:29 and hath counted the **b.** of the... *129*
Heb 11:28 passover, and the sprinkling of **b.**,... *129*
Heb 12:4 not yet resisted unto **b.**, striving... *129*
Heb 12:24 to the **b.** of sprinkling, that... *129*
Heb 13:11 those beasts, whose **b.** is brought... *129*
Heb 13:12 sanctify the people with his own **b.**,... *129*
Heb 13:20 through the **b.** of the everlasting... *129*
1Pe 1:2 sprinkling of the **b.** of Jesus Christ:... *129*
1Pe 1:19 with the precious **b.** of Christ, as of... *129*
1Jo 1:7 the **b.** of Jesus Christ his Son... *129*
1Jo 5:6 water and **b.**, even Jesus Christ;... *129*
1Jo 5:6 by water only, but by water and **b.**... *129*
1Jo 5:8 spirit, and the water, and the **b.**... *129*
Re 1:5 us from our sins in his own **b.**,... *129*
Re 5:9 redeemed us to God by thy **b.** out of... *129*
Re 6:10 thou not judge and avenge our **b.**... *129*
Re 6:12 of hair, and the moon became as **b.**;... *129*
Re 7:14 them white in the **b.** of the Lamb... *129*
Re 8:7 hail and fire mingled with **b.**, and... *129*
Re 8:8 third part of the sea became **b.**... *129*
Re 11:6 over waters to turn them to **b.**, and... *129*
Re 12:11 by the **b.** of the Lamb, and by the... *129*
Re 14:20 the city, and **b.** came out of the... *129*
Re 16:3 it became as the **b.** of a dead man:... *129*
Re 16:4 of waters; and they became **b.**... *129*
Re 16:6 shed the **b.** of saints and prophets,... *129*
Re 16:6 thou hast given them **b.** to drink;... *129*
Re 17:6 drunken with the **b.** of the saints,... *129*
Re 17:6 and with the **b.** of the martyrs of... *129*
Re 18:24 And in her was found the **b.** of... *129*
Re 19:2 avenged the **b.** of his servants at... *129*
Re 19:13 clothed with a vesture dipped in **b.**... *129*

BLOODGUILTINESS
Ps 51:14 Deliver me from **b.**, O God,... 1818

BLOODTHIRSTY
Pr 29:10 The **b.** hate the upright: but... 582,1818

BLOODY
Ex 4:25 Surely a **b.** husband art thou to... 1818
Ex 4:26 A **b.** husband thou art because of... 1818
2Sa 16:7 come out, thou **b.** man, and thou... 1818
2Sa 16:8 because thou art a **b.** man... 1818
2Sa 21:1 for Saul, and for his **b.** house,... 1818
Ps 5:6 Lord will abhor the **b.** and... 1818
Ps 26:9 with sinners, nor my life with **b.**... 1818
Ps 55:23 **b.** and deceitful men shall not... 1818
Ps 59:2 iniquity, and save me from **b.**... 1818
Ps 139:19 depart from me therefore, ye **b.**... 1818
Eze 7:23 the land is full of **b.** crimes, and... 1818
Eze 22:2 wilt thou judge the **b.** city? yea,... 1818
Eze 24:6 Woe to the **b.** city, to the pot... 1818
Eze 24:9 Woe to the **b.** city! I will even... 1818
Nah 3:1 Woe to the **b.** city! it is all full... 1818
Ac 28:8 lay sick of a fever and of a **b.** flux:... *1420*

BLOOMED See also BLOSSOMED.
Nu 17:8 and **b.** blossoms, and yielded... 6692

BLOSSOM See also BLOSSOMED; BLOSSOMS.
Nu 17:5 whom I shall choose, shall **b.**... 6524
Isa 5:24 and their **b.** shall go up as dust:... 6525
Isa 27:6 Israel shall **b.** and bud, and fill... 6692
Isa 35:1 shall rejoice, and **b.** as the rose... 6524
Isa 35:2 it shall **b.** abundantly, and rejoice... 6524
Hab 3:17 Although the fig tree shall not **b.**,... 6524

BLOSSOMED See also BLOOMED.
Eze 7:10 rod hath **b.**, pride hath budded... 6692

BLOSSOMS
Ge 40:10 it budded, and her **b.** shot forth;... 5322
Nu 17:8 and bloomed **b.**, and yielded... 6731

BLOT See also BLOTTED; BLOTTETH; BLOTTING.
Ex 32:32 **b.** me, I pray thee, out of thy book... 4229
Ex 32:33 him will I **b.** out of my book... 4229
Nu 5:23 and he shall **b.** them out with the... 4229
De 9:14 and **b.** out their name from under... 4229
De 25:19 **b.** out the remembrance of Amalek... 4229
De 29:20 the Lord shall **b.** out his name... 4229
2Ki 14:27 he would **b.** out the name of Israel... 4229
Job 31:7 if any **b.** hath cleaved to mine... 3971
Ps 51:1 mercies **b.** out my transgressions... 4229
Ps 51:9 sins, and **b.** out all mine iniquities... 4229
Pr 9:7 wicked man getteth himself a **b.**... 3971
Jer 18:23 neither **b.** out their sin from thy... 4229
Re 3:5 **I will not b. out his name out of**... *1813*

BLOTTED
Ne 4:5 let not their sin be **b.** out from... 4229
Ps 69:28 Let them be **b.** out of the book... 4229
Ps 109:13 following let their name be **b.** out... 4229
Ps 109:14 the sin of his mother be **b.** out... 4229
Isa 44:22 **b.** out, as a thick cloud, thy... 4229
Ac 3:19 your sins may be **b.** out, when... *1813*

BLOTTETH
Isa 43:25 he that **b.** out thy transgressions... 4229

BLOTTING
Col 2:14 **B.** out the handwriting of... *1813*

BLOW See also BLEW; BLOWETH; BLOWING; BLOWN.
Ex 15:10 Thou didst **b.** with thy wind, the... 5398
Nu 10:3 when they shall **b.** with them,... 8628
Nu 10:4 they **b.** but with one trumpet,... 8628
Nu 10:5 When ye **b.** an alarm, then the... 8628
Nu 10:6 When ye **b.** an alarm the second... 8628
Nu 10:6 they shall **b.** an alarm for their... 8628
Nu 10:7 ye shall **b.**, but ye shall not sound... 8628
Nu 10:8 Aaron, the priests, shall **b.** with... 8628
Nu 10:9 then ye shall **b.** an alarm with... 7321
Nu 10:10 ye shall **b.** with the trumpets over... 8628
Nu 31:6 the trumpets to **b.** in his hand... 8643
Jos 6:4 priests shall **b.** with the trumpets... 8628
Jg 7:18 When I **b.** with the trumpet, I... 8628
Jg 7:18 with me, then **b.** ye the trumpets... 8628
Jg 7:20 trumpets in their right hands to **b.**... 8628
1Ki 1:34 and **b.** ye with the trumpet, and... 8628
1Ch 15:24 did **b.** with the trumpets before... 2690
Ps 39:10 I am consumed by the **b.** of thine... 8409
Ps 78:26 He caused an east wind to **b.** in... 5265
Ps 81:3 **B.** up the trumpet in the new... 8628
Ps 147:18 he causeth his wind to **b.**, and... 5380
Ca 4:16 **b.** upon my garden, that the... 6315
Isa 40:24 he shall also **b.** upon them, and... 5398
Jer 4:5 **B.** ye the trumpet in the land:... 8628
Jer 6:1 **b.** the trumpet in Tekoa, and set... 8628
Jer 14:17 breach, with a very grievous **b.**... 4347
Jer 51:27 **b.** the trumpet among the nations,... 8628
Eze 21:31 I will **b.** against thee in the fire... 6315
Eze 22:20 to **b.** the fire upon it, to melt it;... 5301
Eze 22:21 I will gather you, and **b.** upon... 5301
Eze 33:3 upon the land, he **b.** the trumpet,... 8628
Eze 33:6 **b.** not the trumpet, and the... 8628
Ho 5:8 **B.** ye the cornet in Gibeah, and... 8628
Joe 2:1 **B.** ye the trumpet in Zion,... 8628
Joe 2:15 **B.** the trumpet in Zion, sanctify... 8628
Hag 1:9 brought it home, I did **b.** upon it... 5301
Zec 9:14 Lord God shall **b.** the trumpet,... 8628
Lu 12:55 **when ye see the south wind b.,**... *4154*
Re 7:1 wind should not **b.** on the earth,... *4154*

BLOWETH
Isa 18:3 when he **b.** a trumpet, hear ye... 8628
Isa 40:7 the spirit of the Lord **b.** upon it:... 5380
Isa 54:16 the smith that **b.** the coals in the... 5301
Joh 3:8 **the wind b. where it listeth,**... *4154*

BLOWING
Le 23:24 a memorial of **b.** of trumpets,... 8643
Nu 29:1 a day of **b.** the trumpets unto you,... 8643
Jos 6:9, 13 on and **b.** with the trumpets,... 8628

BLOWN
Job 20:26 a fire not **b.** shall consume him;... 5301
Isa 27:13 the great trumpet shall be **b.**,... 8628
Eze 7:14 They have **b.** the trumpet, even... 8628
Am 3:6 Shall a trumpet be **b.** in the city,... 8628

BLUE
Ex 25:4 And **b.**, and purple, and scarlet,... 8504
Ex 26:1 twined linen, and **b.**, and purple,... 8504
Ex 26:4 thou shalt make loops of **b.** upon... 8504
Ex 26:31 shalt make a vail of **b.**, and purple,... 8504
Ex 26:36 for the door of the tent, of **b.**,... 8504
Ex 27:16 an hanging of twenty cubits, of **b.**,... 8504
Ex 28:5 shall take gold, and **b.**, and purple,... 8504
Ex 28:6 make the ephod of gold, of **b.**,... 8504
Ex 28:8 even of gold, of **b.**, and purple,... 8504
Ex 28:15 thou shalt make it; of gold, of **b.**,... 8504
Ex 28:28 the ephod with a lace of **b.** that it... 8504
Ex 28:31 the robe of the ephod all of **b.**... 8504
Ex 28:33 shalt make pomegranates of **b.**,... 8504
Ex 28:37 thou shalt put it on a **b.** lace, that... 8504
Ex 35:6 And **b.**, and purple, and scarlet,... 8504
Ex 35:23 man with whom was found **b.**,... 8504
Ex 35:25 spun, both of **b.**, and of purple,... 8504
Ex 35:35 and of the embroiderer, in **b.**,... 8504
Ex 36:8 twined linen, and **b.**, and purple,... 8504
Ex 36:11 he made loops of **b.** on the edge... 8504
Ex 36:35 he made a vail of **b.**, and purple,... 8504
Ex 36:37 for the tabernacle door of **b.**,... 8504
Ex 38:18 the court was needlework, of **b.**,... 8504
Ex 38:23 embroiderer in **b.**, and in purple,... 8504
Ex 39:1 of the **b.**, and purple, and scarlet,... 8504
Ex 39:2 the ephod of gold, **b.**, and purple... 8504
Ex 39:3 it into wires, to work it in the **b.**,... 8504
Ex 39:5 thereof; of gold, **b.**, and purple,... 8504
Ex 39:8 of gold, **b.**, and purple, and scarlet,... 8504
Ex 39:21 the ephod with a lace of **b.**, that it... 8504
Ex 39:22 ephod of woven work, all of **b.**... 8504
Ex 39:24 of the robe pomegranates of **b.**,... 8504
Ex 39:29 twined linen, and **b.**, and purple,... 8504
Ex 39:31 they tied unto it a lace of **b.**, to... 8504
Nu 4:6 spread over it a cloth wholly of **b.**,... 8504
Nu 4:7 they shall spread a cloth of **b.**,... 8504
Nu 4:9 they shall take a cloth of **b.**, and... 8504
Nu 4:11 spread a cloth of **b.**, and cover it... 8504
Nu 4:12 and put them in a cloth of **b.**,... 8504
Nu 15:38 of the borders a ribband of **b.**... 8504
2Ch 2:7 in purple, and crimson, and **b.**,... 8504
2Ch 2:14 in **b.**, and in fine linen, and in... 8504

2Ch 3:14 he made the vail of **b.**, and purple, ... 8504
Es 1:6 white, green, and **b.**, hangings,.......... 8504
Es 1:6 **b.**, and white, and black, marble. 8336
Es 8:15 the king in royal apparel of **b.**........... 8504
Jer 10:9 **b.** and purple is their clothing: 8504
Eze 23:6 were clothed with **b.**, captains 8504
Eze 27:7 **b.** and purple from the isles 8504
Eze 27:24 in **b.** clothes, and broidered work, ... 8504

BLUENESS
Pr 20:30 **b.** of a wound cleanseth away........... 2250

BLUNT
Ec 10:10 If the iron be **b.**, and he do not 6949

BLUSH
Ezr 9:6 I am ashamed and **b.** to lift 3637
Jer 6:15 ashamed, neither could they **b.** 3637
Jer 8:12 neither could they **b.**: therefore 3637

BOANERGES (bo-an-er'-jees)
Mk 3:17 he surnamed them **B.**, which is, ... *993*

BOAR
Ps 80:13 **b.** out of the wood doth waste it, ... 2386

BOARD See also ABOARD; BOARDS.
Ex 26:16 cubits shall be the length of a **b.**, ... 7175
Ex 26:16 half shall be the breadth of one **b.** 7175
Ex 26:17 tenons shall there be in one **b.**, ... 7175
Ex 26:19 under one **b.** for his two tenons,......... 7175
Ex 26:19 two sockets under another **b.** for........ 7175
Ex 26:21, 25 two sockets under one **b.**, and 7175
Ex 26:21, 25 two sockets under another **b.**. 7175
Ex 36:21 **b.** was ten cubits, ... 7175
Ex 36:21 and the breadth of a **b.** one cubit 7175
Ex 36:22 One **b.** had two tenons, equally.......... 7175
Ex 36:24 two sockets under one **b.** for his........ 7175
Ex 36:24 two sockets under another **b.** for 7175
Ex 36:26 two sockets under one **b.**, and........... 7175
Ex 36:26 two sockets under another **b.**. 7175
Ex 36:30 of silver, under every **b.** two sockets.. 7175

BOARDS
Ex 26:15 shalt make **b.** for the tabernacle......... 7175
Ex 26:17 for all the **b.** of the tabernacle. 7175
Ex 26:18 make the **b.** for the tabernacle,........... 7175
Ex 26:18 twenty **b.** on the south side 7175
Ex 26:19 of silver under the twenty **b.**;............. 7175
Ex 26:20 north side there shall be twenty **b.**. 7175
Ex 26:22 westward thou shalt make six **b.**. 7175
Ex 26:23 two **b.** shalt thou make for the 7175
Ex 26:25 And they shall be eight **b.**, and 7175
Ex 26:26 for the **b.** of the one side of the......... 7175
Ex 26:27 five bars for the **b.** of the other 7175
Ex 26:27 five bars for the **b.** of the side of 7175
Ex 26:28 in the midst of the **b.** shall reach........ 7175
Ex 26:29 overlay the **b.** with gold, and make..... 7175
Ex 27:8 with **b.** shalt thou make it: as............ 3871
Ex 35:11 his **b.**, his bars, his pillars, and 7175
Ex 36:20 he made **b.** for the tabernacle of 7175
Ex 36:22 for all the **b.** of the tabernacle. 7175
Ex 36:23 he made **b.** for the tabernacle;........... 7175
Ex 36:23 twenty **b.** for the south side.............. 7175
Ex 36:24 he made under the twenty **b.**;............. 7175
Ex 36:25 north corner, he made twenty **b.**,........ 7175
Ex 36:27 westward he made six **b.**.................. 7175
Ex 36:28 two **b.** made he for the corners of...... 7175
Ex 36:30 and there were eight **b.**; and their...... 7175
Ex 36:31 for the **b.** of the one side of the.......... 7175
Ex 36:32 five bars for the **b.** of the other 7175
Ex 36:32 bars for the **b.** of the tabernacle,......... 7175
Ex 36:33 middle bar to shoot through the **b.** 7175
Ex 36:34 And he overlaid the **b.** with gold, ... 7175
Ex 38:7 made the altar hollow with **b.**. 3871
Ex 39:33 his furniture, his taches, his **b.**, ... 7175
Ex 40:18 set up the **b.** thereof, and put in......... 7175
Nu 3:36 the **b.** of the tabernacle, and the 7175
Nu 4:31 the **b.** of the tabernacle, and the 7175
1Ki 6:9 the house with beams and **b.** of......... 7713
1Ki 6:15 walls of the house within with **b.**......... 6763
1Ki 6:16 and the walls with **b.** of cedar:........... 6763
Ca 8:9 we will inclose her with **b.** of............. 3871
Eze 27:5 thy ship **b.** of fir trees of Senir: 3871
Ac 27:44 And the rest, some on **b.**, and............ *4548*

BOAST See also BOASTED; BOASTEST; BOASTETH; BOASTING.
1Ki 20:11 that girdeth on his harness **b.**............ 1984
2Ch 25:19 thine heart lifteth thee up to **b.**.......... 3513
Ps 34:2 My soul shall make her **b.** in the.......... 1984
Ps 44:8 In God we **b.** all the day long, ... 1984
Ps 49:6 trust in their wealth, and **b.** 1984
Ps 94:4 workers of iniquity **b.** themselves? 559
Ps 97:7 images, that **b.** themselves of............ 1984
Pr 27:1 **B.** not thyself of to morrow; for 1984
Isa 10:15 Shall the ax **b.** itself against him......... 6286
Isa 61:6 their glory shall ye **b.** yourselves........ 3235
Ro 2:17 law, and makest thy **b.** of God, ... *2744*
Ro 2:23 Thou that makest thy **b.** of the.......... *2744*
Ro 11:18 **B.** not against the branches. But........ *2620*
Ro 11:18 if thou **b.**, thou bearest not ....
2Co 9:2 for which I **b.** of you to them of......... *2744*
2Co 10:8 though I should **b.** somewhat............ *2744*
2Co 10:13 we will not **b.** of things without.......... *2744*
2Co 10:16 not to **b.** in another man's line........... *2744*
2Co 11:16 me, that I may **b.** myself a little.......... *2744*
Eph 2:9 of works, lest any man should **b.**......... *2744*

BOASTED
Eze 35:13 with your mouth ye have **b.** 1431
2Co 7:14 I have **b.** any thing to him of............ *2744*

BOASTERS
Ro 1:30 despiteful, proud, **b.**, inventors *213*
2Ti 3:2 covetous, **b.**, proud, blasphemers,......... *213*

BOASTEST
Ps 52:1 Why **b.** thou thyself in mischief, ... 1984

BOASTETH
Ps 10:3 wicked **b.** of his heart's desire, ... 1984
Pr 20:14 he is gone his way, then he **b.**. 1984
Pr 25:14 Whoso **b.** himself of a false gift.......... 1984
Jas 3:5 little member, and **b.** great *3166*

BOASTING See also BOASTINGS.
Ac 5:36 Theudas, **b.** himself to be................ *3004*
Ro 3:27 Where is **b.** then? It is excluded. *2746*
2Co 7:14 even so our **b.**, which I made............ *2746*
2Co 8:24 love, and of our **b.** on your behalf. *2746*
2Co 9:3 lest our **b.** of you should be in........... *2745*
2Co 9:4 in this same confident **b.**.................. *2746*
2Co 10:15 Not **b.** of things without our............. *2744*
2Co 11:10 no man shall stop me of this **b.**.......... *2746*
2Co 11:17 in this confidence of **b.**. *2746*

BOASTINGS
Jas 4:16 now ye rejoice in your **b.**: all *212*

BOAT See also BOATS.
2Sa 19:18 And there went over a ferry **b.**.......... 5679
Joh 6:22 that there was none other **b.** there,.... *4142*
Joh 6:22 with his disciples into the **b.**,........... *4142*
Ac 27:16 much work to come by the **b.**............ *4627*
Ac 27:30 when they had let down the **b.** *4627*
Ac 27:32 cut off the ropes of the **b.**, and.......... *4627*

BOATS
Joh 6:23 (Howbeit there came other **b.**............ *4142*

BOAZ (bo'-az) See also BOOZ.
Ru 2:1 Elimelech; and his name was **B.**......... 1162
Ru 2:3 of the field belonging unto **B.**, ... 1162
Ru 2:4 behold, **B.** came from Bethlehem, ... 1162
Ru 2:5 Then said **B.** unto his servant 1162
Ru 2:8 Then said **B.** unto Ruth, Hearest 1162
Ru 2:11 **B.** answered and said unto her, ... 1162
Ru 2:14 **B.** said unto her, At mealtime 1162
Ru 2:15 **B.** commanded his young men, ... 1162
Ru 2:19 with whom I wrought to day is **B.**. 1162
Ru 2:23 she kept fast by the maidens of **B.**...... 1162
Ru 3:2 now is not **B.** of our kindred, ... 1162
Ru 3:7 when **B.** had eaten and drunk,........... 1162
Ru 4:1 Then went **B.** up to the gate,............ 1162
Ru 4:1 behold, the kinsman of whom **B.**......... 1162
Ru 4:5 Then said **B.**, What day thou 1162
Ru 4:8 the kinsman said unto **B.**, Buy it......... 1162
Ru 4:9 And **B.** said unto the elders, and......... 1162
Ru 4:13 So **B.** took Ruth, and she was his 1162
Ru 4:21 Salmon begat **B.**, and **B.** begat.......... 1162
1Ki 7:21 and called the name thereof **B.**. 1162
1Ch 2:11 begat Salma, and Salma begat **B.**. 1162
1Ch 2:12 **B.** begat Obed, and Obed begat......... 1162
2Ch 3:17 the name of that on the left **B.**. 1162

BOCHERU (bok'-er-u)
1Ch 8:38 these, Azrikam, **B.**, and Ishmael,...... 1074
1Ch 9:44 **B.**, and Ishmael, and Sheariah, ... 1074

BOCHIM (bo'-kim)
Jg 2:1 came up from Gilgal to **B.**, and......... 1066
Jg 2:5 called the name of that place **B.**......... 1066

BODIES
Ge 47:18 lord, but our **b.**, and our lands:.......... 1472
1Sa 31:12 body of Saul and the **b.** of his........... 1472
1Ch 10:12 away the body of Saul, and the **b.** 1480
2Ch 20:24 they were dead **b.** fallen to the......... 6297
2Ch 20:25 riches with the dead **b.**, and............. 6297
Ne 9:37 they have dominion over our **b.**, ... 1472
Job 13:12 ashes, your **b.** to **b.** of clay............. 1354
Ps 79:2 The dead **b.** of thy servants have....... 5038
Ps 110:6 fill the places with the dead **b.**, ... 1472
Jer 31:40 the whole valley of the dead **b.**, ... 6297
Jer 33:5 the dead **b.** of men, whom I have....... 6297
Jer 34:20 and their dead **b.** shall be for............ 5038
Jer 41:9 the dead **b.** of the men, whom he 6297
Eze 1:11 another, and two covered their **b.**. 1472
Eze 1:23 covered on that side, their **b.**............ 1472
Da 3:27 upon whose **b.** the fire had no 1655
Da 3:28 and yielded their **b.**, that they 1655
Am 8:3 there shall be many dead **b.** in............ 6297
Mt 27:52 and many **b.** of the saints which.......... *4983*
Joh 19:31 the **b.** should not remain upon *4983*
Ro 1:24 to dishonour their own **b.** between *4983*
Ro 8:11 shall also quicken your mortal **b.** *4983*
Ro 12:1 that ye present your **b.** a living.......... *4983*
1Co 6:15 that your **b.** are the members of........ *4983*
1Co 15:40 also celestial **b.**, and **b.** terrestrial: *4983*
Eph 5:28 to love their wives as their own **b.**. *4983*
Heb 10:22 and our **b.** washed with pure............ *4983*
Heb 13:11 For the **b.** of those beasts, whose...... *4983*
Re 11:8 And their dead **b.** shall lie in the *4430*
Re 11:9 shall see their dead **b.** three days....... *4430*
Re 11:9 shall not suffer their dead **b.** to be...... *4430*

BODILY
Lu 3:22 Holy Ghost descended in a **b.**............ *4984*
2Co 10:10 but his **b.** presence is weak, and......... *4983*
Col 2:9 all the fulness of the Godhead **b.**. *4985*
1Ti 4:8 For **b.** exercise profiteth little:........... *4984*

BODY See also BODIES; BODY'S; BUSYBODY; SOMEBODY.
Ex 24:10 and as it were the **b.** of heaven in...... 6106
Le 21:11 any dead **b.**, nor defile himself........... 5315
Nu 6:6 Lord he shall come at no dead **b.**. 5315
Nu 9:6 defiled by the dead **b.** of a man.......... 5315
Nu 9:7 we are defiled by the dead **b.** of a...... 5315
Nu 9:10 unclean by reason of a dead **b.**, ... 5315
Nu 19:11 He that toucheth the dead **b.** of......... 5315
Nu 19:13 Whosoever toucheth the dead **b.** of..... 5315
Nu 19:16 or a dead **b.**, or a bone of a man, ... 5315
De 21:23 His **b.** shall not remain all................. 5038
De 28:4 Blessed shall be the fruit of thy **b.**, ... 990
De 28:11 in goods, in the fruit of thy **b.**,............ 990
De 28:18 Cursed shall be the fruit of thy **b.**,....... 990
De 28:53 shalt eat the fruit of thine own **b.**, ... 990
De 30:9 in the fruit of thy **b.**, and in the......... 990
Jg 8:30 threescore and ten sons of his **b.** 3409
1Sa 31:10 they fastened his **b.** to the wall of...... 1472
1Sa 31:12 took the **b.** of Saul and the bodies...... 1472
2Ki 8:5 he had restored a dead **b.** to life, ...
1Ch 10:12 took away the **b.** of Saul, and the....... 1480
Job 19:17 children's sake of mine own **b.**. 990
Job 19:26 worms destroy this **b.**, yet in ....
Job 20:25 drawn, and cometh out of the **b.**; 1465
Ps 132:11 fruit of thy **b.**, will I set upon............ 990
Pr 5:11 when thy flesh and thy **b.** are............ 7607
Isa 10:18 both soul and **b.**: and they shall 1320
Isa 26:19 with my dead **b.** shall they arise......... 5038
Isa 51:23 thou hast laid thy **b.** as the 1460
Jer 26:23 and cast his dead **b.** into the 5038
Jer 36:30 and his dead **b.** shall be cast out 5038
La 4:7 they were more ruddy in **b.** than........ 6106
Eze 10:12 And their whole **b.**, and their 1320
Da 4:33 his **b.** was wet with the dew of.......... 1655
Da 5:21 his **b.** was wet with the dew of.......... 1655
Da 7:11 and his **b.** destroyed, and given to....... 1655
Da 7:15 in my spirit in the midst of my **b.**, ... 5085
Da 10:6 His **b.** also was like the beryl, ... 1472
Mic 6:7 the fruit of my **b.** for the sin of.......... 990
Hag 2:13 unclean by a dead **b.** touch any......... 5315
Mt 5:29 **not that thy whole b. should be.....** *4983*
Mt 5:30 **that thy whole b. should be cast....** 4983
Mt 6:22 **The light of the b. is the eye: if....** *4983*
Mt 6:22 **thy whole b. shall be full of light..** *4983*
Mt 6:23 **thy whole b. shall be full of.........** *4983*
Mt 6:25 **nor yet for your b., what ye shall..** *4983*
Mt 6:25 **more than meat, and the b. than...** *4983*
Mt 10:28 **fear not them which kill the b., ...** *4983*

Mt 10:28 **able to destroy both soul and b. in** *4983*
Mt 14:12 came, and took up the **b.**, and *4983*
Mt 26:12 **poured this ointment on my b.,** *4983*
Mt 26:26 and said, **Take, eat; this is my b.** *4983*
Mt 27:58 begged the **b.** of Jesus. Then *4983*
Mt 27:58 Pilate commanded the **b.** to be *4983*
Mt 27:59 when Joseph had taken the **b.**, *4983*
Mk 5:29 and she felt in her **b.** that she was *4983*
Mk 14:8 **aforehand to anoint my b. to the** *4983*
Mk 14:22 and said, **Take, eat: this is my b.** *4983*
Mk 14:51 cloth cast about his naked **b.**; *4983*
Mk 15:43 unto Pilate, and craved the **b.** of *4983*
Mk 15:45 of the centurion, he gave the **b.** *4983*
Lu 11:34 **The light of the b. is the eye:** *4983*
Lu 11:34 **is single, thy whole b. also is full** *4983*
Lu 11:34 **evil, thy b. also is full of darkness.** *4983*
Lu 11:36 **If thy whole b. therefore be full of.** *4983*
Lu 12:4 **not afraid of them that kill the b.,** *4983*
Lu 12:22 **neither for the b., what ye shall** *4983*
Lu 12:23 **than meat, and the b. is more** *4983*
Lu 17:37 **Wheresoever, the b. is, thither will.** *4983*
Lu 22:19 **This is my b. which is given for** *4983*
Lu 23:52 unto Pilate, and begged the **b.** of *4983*
Lu 23:55 sepulchre, and how his **b.** was laid, *4983*
Lu 24:3 and found not the **b.** of the Lord *4983*
Lu 24:23 when they found not his **b.**, they *4983*
Joh 2:21 he spake of the temple of his **b.** *4983*
Joh 19:38 that he might take away the **b.** of *4983*
Joh 19:38 came therefore, and took the **b.** *4983*
Joh 19:40 Then took they the **b.** of Jesus, *4983*
Joh 20:12 the feet, where the **b.** of Jesus had *4983*
Ac 9:40 and turning him to the **b.** said, *4983*
Ac 19:12 So that from his **b.** were brought *5559*
Ro 4:19 he considered not his own **b.** now *4983*
Ro 6:6 the **b.** of sin might be destroyed, *4983*
Ro 6:12 reign in your mortal **b.**, that ye *4983*
Ro 7:4 dead to the law by the **b.** of Christ; *4983*
Ro 7:24 shall deliver me from the **b.** of this *4983*
Ro 8:10 the **b.** is dead because of sin: but *4983*
Ro 8:13 do mortify the deeds of the **b.**, ye *4983*
Ro 8:23 to wit, the redemption of our **b.** *4983*
Ro 12:4 we have many members in one **b.**, *4983*
Ro 12:5 being many, are one **b.** in Christ, *4983*
1Co 5:3 For I verily, as absent in **b.**, but *4983*
1Co 6:13 Now the **b.** is not for fornication, *4983*
1Co 6:13 and the Lord for the **b.**. *4983*
1Co 6:16 is joined to an harlot is one **b.**? *4983*
1Co 6:18 that a man doeth is without the **b.**; *4983*
1Co 6:18 sinneth against his own **b.** *4983*
1Co 6:19 your **b.** is the temple of the Holy *4983*
1Co 6:20 therefore glorify God in your **b.**, *4983*
1Co 7:4 wife hath not power of her own **b.**, *4983*
1Co 7:4 hath not power of his own **b.**, *4983*
1Co 7:34 she may be holy both in **b.** and in *4983*
1Co 9:27 But I keep under my **b.**, and bring *4983*
1Co 10:16 is it not the communion of the **b.** *4983*
1Co 10:17 many are one bread, and one **b.**; *4983*
1Co 11:24 **Take, eat: this is my b., which is** *4983*
1Co 11:27 shall be guilty of the **b.** and blood *4983*
1Co 11:29 not discerning the Lord's **b.**. *4983*
1Co 12:12 For as the **b.** is one, and hath many *4983*
1Co 12:12 the members of that one **b.**, being *4983*
1Co 12:12 are one **b.**; so also is Christ. *4983*
1Co 12:13 are we all baptized into one **b.**, *4983*
1Co 12:14 For the **b.** is not one member, but *4983*
1Co 12:15 I am not of the **b.**; is it *4983*
1Co 12:15 therefore not of the **b.**? *4983*
1Co 12:16 I am not of the **b.**; is it *4983*
1Co 12:16 therefore not of the **b.**? *4983*
1Co 12:17 If the whole **b.** were an eye, where *4983*
1Co 12:18 every one of them in the **b.**, as it *4983*
1Co 12:19 all one member, where were the **b.**? *4983*
1Co 12:20 many members, yet but one **b.** *4983*
1Co 12:22 those members of the **b.** which *4983*
1Co 12:23 And those members of the **b.** *4983*
1Co 12:24 but God hath tempered the **b.** *4983*
1Co 12:25 should be no schism in the **b.**; *4983*
1Co 12:27 Now ye are the **b.** of Christ, and *4983*
1Co 13:3 though I give my **b.** to be burned, *4983*
1Co 15:35 and with what **b.** do they come? *4983*
1Co 15:37 thou sowest not that **b.** that shall *4983*
1Co 15:38 But God giveth it a **b.** as it hath *4983*
1Co 15:38 him, and to every seed his own **b.**. *4983*
1Co 15:44 It is sown a natural **b.**; *4983*
1Co 15:44 it is raised a spiritual **b.** *4983*
1Co 15:44 There is a natural **b.**, *4983*
1Co 15:44 and there is a spiritual **b.** *4983*
2Co 4:10 bearing about in the **b.** the dying *4983*
2Co 4:10 might be made manifest in our **b.**. *4983*
2Co 5:6 whilst we are at home in the **b.**, we *4983*
2Co 5:8 rather to be absent from the **b.**, *4983*
2Co 5:10 receive the things done in his **b.**, *4983*
2Co 12:2 the **b.**, I cannot tell; *4983*
2Co 12:2 or whether out of the **b.**, *4983*
2Co 12:3 in the **b.**, or out of the **b.**, I cannot *4983*
Gal 6:17 I bear in my **b.** the marks of the *4983*
Eph 1:23 Which is his **b.**, the fulness of him *4983*
Eph 2:16 unto God in one **b.** by the cross, *4983*
Eph 3:6 fellow heirs, and of the same **b.**, *4954*
Eph 4:4 There is one **b.**, and one Spirit, *4983*
Eph 4:12 ministry, for the edifying of the **b.** *4983*
Eph 4:16 From whom the whole **b.** fitly *4983*
Eph 4:16 maketh increase of the **b.** unto *4983*
Eph 5:23 and he is the saviour of the **b.**. *4983*
Eph 5:30 For we are members of his **b.**, of *4983*
Php 1:20 Christ shall be magnified in my **b.**, *4983*
Php 3:21 Who shall change our vile **b.**, that *4983*
Php 3:21 like unto his glorious **b.**, according *4983*
Col 1:18 And he is the head of the **b.**, the *4983*
Col 1:22 In the **b.** of his flesh through *4983*
Col 2:11 putting off the **b.** of the sins of the *4983*
Col 2:17 of things to come; but the **b.** is of *4983*
Col 2:19 from which all the **b.** by joints and *4983*
Col 2:23 humility, and neglecting of the **b.**; *4983*
Col 3:15 which also ye are called in one **b.**; *4983*
1Th 5:23 and **b.** be preserved blameless *4983*
Heb 10:5 but a **b.** hast thou prepared me: *4983*
Heb 10:10 through the offering of the **b.** of *4983*
Heb 13:3 as being yourselves also in the **b.** *4983*
Jas 2:16 things which are needful to the **b.**; *4983*
Jas 2:26 as the **b.** without the spirit is dead, *4983*
Jas 3:2 able also to bridle the whole **b.** *4983*
Jas 3:3 and to turn about their whole **b.** *4983*
Jas 3:6 that it defileth the whole **b.**, and *4983*
1Pe 2:24 bare our sins in his own **b.** on the *4983*
Jude 9 he disputed about the **b.** of Moses, *4983*

BODY'S
Col 1:24 in my flesh for his **b.** sake, which *4983*

BOHAN (Bo'-han).
Jos 15:6 border went up to the stone of **b.** 932
Jos 18:17 and descended to the stone of **B.** 932

BOIL See also BOILED; BOILING; BOILS.
Ex 9:9 a **b.** breaking forth with blains 7822
Ex 9:10 and it became a **b.** breaking forth 7822
Ex 9:11 because of the boils; for the **b.** 7822
Le 8:31 **B.** the flesh at the door of the 1310
Le 13:18 in the skin thereof, was a **b.**, and 7822
Le 13:19 in the place of the **b.** there be a 7822
Le 13:20 of leprosy broken out of the **b.**. 7822
Le 13:23 it is a burning **b.**; and the priest 7822
2Ki 20:7 And they took and laid it on the **b.**, 7822
Job 41:31 He maketh the deep to **b.** like a 7570
Isa 38:21 lay it for a plaister upon the **b.**, 7822
Isa 64:2 the fire causeth the waters to **b.**, 1158
Eze 24:5 make it **b.** well, and let them 7570
Eze 46:20 the priests shall **b.** the trespass 1310
Eze 46:24 the places of them that **b.**, where 1310
Eze 46:24 the ministers of the house shall **b.** 1310

BOILED
1Ki 19:21 **b.** their flesh with the instruments 1310
2Ki 6:29 So we **b.** my son, and did eat him: 1310
Job 30:27 My bowels **b.**, and rested not: 7570

BOILING
Eze 46:23 and it was made with **b.** places 4018

BOILING-PLACES See BOILING and PLACES.

BOILS
Ex 9:11 before Moses because of the **b.**; 7822
Job 2:7 smote Job with sore **b.** from the 7822

BOISTEROUS
Mt 14:30 when he saw the wind **b.**, he was *2478*

BOLD See also EMBOLDENED.
Pr 28:1 but the righteous are **b.** as a lion. 982
Ac 13:46 Paul and Barnabas waxed **b.**, *3955*
Ro 10:20 Esaias is very **b.**, and saith, I was *662*
2Co 10:1 being absent am **b.** toward you: *2292*
2Co 10:2 that I may not be **b.** when I am *2292*
2Co 10:2 wherewith I think to be **b.** against *5111*
2Co 11:21 whereinsoever any is **b.**, (I speak *5111*
2Co 11:21 foolishly,) I am **b.** also. *5111*
Php 1:14 much more **b.** to speak the word *5111*
1Th 2:2 we were **b.** in our God to speak *3955*
Phm 8 I might be much **b.** in Christ *3954*

BOLDLY
Ge 34:25 came upon the city **b.**, and slew 983
Mk 15:43 and went in **b.** unto Pilate, and *5111*
Joh 7:26 But, lo, he speaketh **b.**, and they *3954*
Ac 9:27 he had preached **b.** at Damascus *3955*
Ac 9:29 spake **b.** in the name of the Lord *3955*
Ac 14:3 speaking **b.** in the Lord, which *3955*
Ac 18:26 to speak **b.** in the synagogue: *3955*
Ac 19:8 spake **b.** for the space of three *3955*
Ro 15:15 I have written the more **b.** unto *5112*
Eph 6:19 may open my mouth **b.**, to make *3954*
Eph 6:20 may speak **b.**, as I ought to speak. *3955*
Heb 4:16 Let us therefore come **b.** unto *3954*
Heb 13:6 So that we may **b.** say, The Lord *2292*

BOLDNESS
Ec 8:1 the **b.** of his face shall be changed. 5797
Ac 4:13 they saw the **b.** of Peter and John, *3954*
Ac 4:29 all **b.** they may speak thy word, *3954*
Ac 4:31 they spake the word of God with **b.** *3954*
2Co 7:4 Great is my **b.** of speech toward *3954*
Eph 3:12 In whom we have **b.** and access *3954*
Php 1:20 but that with all **b.**, as always, *3954*
1Ti 3:13 great **b.** in the faith which is in *3954*
Heb 10:19 **b.** to enter into the holiest by the *3954*
1Jo 4:17 have **b.** in the day of judgment: *3954*

BOLLED
Ex 9:31 in the ear, and the flax was **b.**. 1392

BOLSTER
1Sa 19:13, 16 pillow of goats' hair for his **b.**, 4763
1Sa 26:7 stuck in the ground at his **b.**; 4763
1Sa 26:11 the spear that is at his **b.**, and 4763
1Sa 26:12 the cruse of water from Saul's **b.**; 4763
1Sa 26:16 cruse of water that was at his **b.** 4763

BOLT See also BOLTED; THUNDERBOLTS.
2Sa 13:17 woman out from me, and **b.** the 5274

BOLTED
2Sa 13:18 out, and **b.** the door after her 5274

BOND See also BONDMAID; BONDMAN; BONDSERVANT; BONDSERVICE; BONDWOMAN; BOUND.
Nu 30:2 an oath to bind his soul with a **b.**; 632
Nu 30:3 bind herself by a **b.**, being in her 632
Nu 30:4 and her **b.** wherewith she hath 632
Nu 30:4 every **b.** wherewith she hath bound 632
Nu 30:10 bound her soul by a **b.** with an oath; 632
Nu 30:11 and every **b.** wherewith she bound 632
Nu 30:12 or concerning the **b.** of her soul, 632
Job 12:18 He looseth the **b.** of kings, and 4148
Eze 20:37 I will bring you into the **b.** of the 4562
Lu 13:16 **be loosed from this b. on the** *1199*
Ac 8:23 bitterness, and in the **b.** of *4886*
1Co 12:13 whether we be **b.** or free; and *1401*
Ga 3:28 there is neither **b.** nor free, there *1401*
Eph 4:3 of the Spirit in the **b.** of peace. *4886*
Eph 6:8 Lord, whether he be **b.** or free *1401*
Col 3:11 Barbarian, Scythian, **b.** nor free: *1401*
Col 3:14 which is the **b.** of perfectness. *4886*
Re 13:16 rich and poor, free and **b.**, to *1401*
Re 19:18 flesh of all men, both free and **b.**, *1401*

BONDAGE
Ex 1:14 their lives bitter with hard **b.**, 5656
Ex 2:23 sighed by reason of the **b.**, 5656
Ex 2:23 up unto God by reason of the **b.**. 5656
Ex 6:5 whom the Egyptians keep in **b.**; 5647
Ex 6:6 and I will rid you out of their **b.**, 5656
Ex 6:9 anguish of spirit, and for cruel **b.** 5656
Ex 13:3 out of the house of **b.**; for by 5650
Ex 13:14 from Egypt, from the house of **b.** 5650
Ex 20:2 of Egypt, out of the house of **b.** 5650
De 5:6 of Egypt, from the house of **b.**. 5650
De 6:12 of Egypt, from the house of **b.**. 5650
De 8:14 of Egypt, from the house of **b.**; 5650
De 13:5 you out of the house of **b.**, 5650
De 13:10 of Egypt, from the house of **b.**. 5650
De 26:6 us, and laid upon us hard **b.**: 5656
Jos 24:17 from the house of **b.**, and which 5650
Jg 6:8 you forth out of the house of **b.**; 5650
Ezr 9:8 give us a little reviving in our **b.** 5659
Ezr 9:9 hath not forsaken us in our **b.**, 5659
Ne 5:5 we bring into **b.** our sons and our 3533

Ne 5:5 our daughters are brought unto **b.** 3533
Ne 5:18 because the **b.** was heavy upon 5656
Ne 9:17 a captain to return to their **b.**: 5659
Isa 14:3 the hard **b.** wherein thou wast 5656
Joh 8:33 and were never in **b.** to any man: *1398*
Ac 7:6 they should bring them into **b.**, *1402*
Ac 7:7 to whom they shall be in **b.** will *1398*
Ro 8:15 received the spirit of **b.** again to *1397*
Ro 8:21 shall be delivered from the **b.** of *1397*
1Co 7:15 a sister is not under **b.** in such 1402
2Co 11:20 if a man bring you into **b.**, *2615*
Ga 2:4 that they might bring us into **b.**: *2615*
Ga 4:3 were in **b.** under the elements of *1402*
Ga 4:9 ye desire again to be in **b.**? *1398*
Ga 4:24 which gendereth to **b.**, which is *1397*
Ga 4:25 and is in **b.** with her children. *1398*
Ga 5:1 again with the yoke of **b.**. *1397*
Heb 2:15 all their lifetime subject to **b.**. *1397*
2Pe 2:19 of the same is he brought in **b.**. *1402*

BONDMAID See also BONDMAIDS.
Le 19:20 is a **b.**, betrothed to an husband, 8198
Ga 4:22 two sons, the one by a **b.**, the *3814*

BONDMAIDS
Le 25:44 Both thy bondmen, and thy **b.**, 519
Le 25:44 them shall ye buy bondmen and **b.**. 519

BONDMAN See also BONDMEN.
Ge 44:33 instead of the lad a **b.** to my lord; 5650
De 15:15 remember that thou wast a **b.** in 5650
De 16:12 remember that thou wast a **b.** in 5650
De 24:18 thou wast a **b.** in Egypt, and the 5650
De 24:22 a **b.** in the land of Egypt: 5650
Re 6:15 every **b.**, and every free man, hid *1401*

BONDMEN
Ge 43:18 and take us for **b.**, and our asses. 5650
Ge 44:9 and we also will be my lord's **b.**. 5650
Le 25:42 Egypt: they shall not be sold as **b.**. 5650
Le 25:44 Both thy **b.**, and thy bondmaids, 5650
Le 25:44 of them shall ye buy **b.** and 5650
Le 25:46 they shall be your **b.** for ever; 5647
Le 26:13 that ye should not be their **b.**; 5650
De 6:21 We were Pharaoh's **b.** in Egypt; 5650
De 7:8 you out of the house of **b.**, 5650
De 28:68 be sold unto your enemies for **b.** 5650
Jos 9:23 none of you be freed from being **b.**, 5650
1Ki 9:22 Israel did Solomon make no **b.**: 5650
2Ki 4:1 unto him my two sons to be **b.**. 5650
2Ch 28:10 of Judah and Jerusalem for **b.** 5650
Ezr 9:9 For we were **b.**; yet our God hath 5650
Es 7:4 But if we had been sold for **b.** 5650
Jer 34:13 of Egypt, out of the house of **b.**, 5650

BONDS
Nu 30:5 or of her **b.** wherewith she 632
Nu 30:7 and her **b.** wherewith she bound 632
Nu 30:14 or all her **b.**, which are upon her: 632
Ps 116:16 handmaid....hast loosed my **b.**. 4147
Jer 5:5 broken the yoke, and burst the **b.**. 4147
Jer 27:2 Make thee **b.** and yokes, and put 4147
Jer 30:8 burst thy **b.**, and strangers shall 4147
Na 1:13 and will burst thy **b.** in sunder. 4147
Ac 20:23 saying that **b.** and afflictions *1199*
Ac 23:29 charge worthy of death or of **b.**. *1199*
Ac 25:14 a certain man left in **b.** by Felix: *1198*
Ac 26:29 such as I am, except these **b.**. *1199*
Ac 26:31 nothing worthy of death or of **b.**. *1199*
Eph 6:20 which I am an ambassador in **b.**: *254*
Php 1:7 as both in my **b.**, and in the *1199*
Php 1:13 So that my **b.** in Christ are *1199*
Php 1:14 waxing confident by my **b.**, are *1199*
Php 1:16 to add affliction to my **b.**: *1199*
Col 4:3 for which I am also in **b.**: *1210*
Col 4:18 Remember my **b.**. Grace be with *1199*
2Ti 2:9 as an evil doer, even unto **b.**; *1199*
Phm 10 whom I have begotten in my **b.** *1199*
Phm 13 have ministered unto me in the **b.** *1199*
Heb 10:34 had compassion of me in my **b.**, *1199*
Heb 11:36 moreover of **b.** and imprisonment: *1199*
Heb 13:3 Remember them that are in **b.**, *1198*

BONDSERVANT
Le 25:39 compel him to serve as a **b.** 5656,5650

BONDSERVICE
1Ki 9:21 Solomon levy a tribute of **b.** 5647

BONDWOMAN See also BONDWOMEN.
Ge 21:10 Cast out this **b.** and her son: for 519
Ge 21:10 the son of this **b.** shall not be heir 519
Ge 21:12 because of thy **b.**; in all that Sarah 519
Ge 21:13 the son of the **b.** will I make a 519
Ga 4:23 he who was of the **b.** was born *3814*
Ga 4:30 Cast out the **b.** and her son: *3814*
Ga 4:30 for the son of the **b.** shall not be *3814*
Ga 4:31 children of the **b.**, but of the free. *3814*

BONDWOMEN
De 28:68 for bondmen and **b.**, and no man 8198
2Ch 28:10 for bondmen and **b.** unto you: 8198
Es 7:4 bondmen and **b.**, I had held my 8198

BONE See BONES; JAWBONE.
Ge 2:23 This is now **b.** of my bones, and 6106
Ge 29:14 thou art my **b.** and my flesh. 6106
Ex 12:46 neither shall ye break a **b.** thereof. 6106
Nu 9:12 nor break any **b.** of it: 6106
Nu 19:16 a dead body, or a **b.** of a man, 6106
Nu 19:18 him that touched a **b.**, or one slain, 6106
Jg 9:2 that I am your **b.** and your flesh. 6106
2Sa 5:1 Behold, we are thy **b.** and thy flesh. 6106
2Sa 19:13 Art thou not of my **b.**, and of my 6106
1Ch 11:1 Behold, we are thy **b.** and thy flesh. 6106
Job 2:5 touch his **b.** and his flesh, and he 6106
Job 19:20 My **b.** cleaveth to my skin and to 6106
Job 31:22 mine arm be broken from the **b.**. 7070
Ps 3:7 all mine enemies upon the cheek **b.**;
Pr 25:15 a soft tongue breaketh the **b.** 1634
Eze 37:7 bones came together, **b.** to his **b.**. 6106
Eze 39:15 when any seeth a man's **b.**, then 6106
Joh 19:36 A **b.** of him shall not be broken. *3747*

BONES
Ge 2:23 bone of my **b.**, and flesh of my 6106
Ge 50:25 shall carry up my **b.** from hence 6106
Ex 13:19 took the **b.** of Joseph with him: 6106
Ex 13:19 ye shall carry up my **b.** away hence 6106
Nu 24:8 break their **b.**, and pierce them 6106
Jos 24:32 **b.** of Joseph, which the children 6106
Jg 19:29 divided her, together with her **b.**, 6106
1Sa 31:13 took their **b.**, and buried them 6106
2Sa 19:12 ye are my **b.** and my flesh: 6106
2Sa 21:12 went and took the **b.** of Saul 6106
2Sa 21:12 and the **b.** of Jonathan 6106
2Sa 21:13 **b.** of Saul and the **b.** of Jonathan 6106
2Sa 21:13 the **b.** of them that were hanged. 6106
2Sa 21:14 the **b.** of Saul and Jonathan 6106
1Ki 13:2 men's **b.** shall be burnt upon thee. 6106
1Ki 13:31 buried; lay my **b.** beside his **b.** 6106
2Ki 13:21 and touched the **b.** of Elisha, 6106
2Ki 23:14 their places with the **b.** of men. 6106
2Ki 23:16 took the **b.** out of the sepulchres, 6106
2Ki 23:18 let no man move his **b.**. So they let 6106
2Ki 23:18 his **b.** alone, with the **b.** of the 6106
2Ki 23:20 men's **b.** upon them, and returned 6106
1Ch 10:12 buried their **b.** under the oak in 6106
2Ch 34:5 **b.** of the priests upon their altars, 6106
Job 4:14 which made all my **b.** to shake 6106
Job 10:11 fenced me with **b.** and sinews, 6106
Job 20:11 His **b.** are full of the sin of his 6106
Job 21:24 his **b.** are moistened with marrow. 6106
Job 30:17 My **b.** are pierced in me in the 6106
Job 30:30 and my **b.** are burned with heat. 6106
Job 33:19 of his **b.** with strong pain: 6106
Job 33:21 **b.** that were not seen stick out. 6106
Job 40:18 **b.** are as strong as pieces of 6106
Job 40:18 his **b.** are like bars of iron. 1634
Ps 6:2 heal me; for my **b.** are vexed. 6106
Ps 22:14 all my **b.** are out of joint: 6106
Ps 22:17 all my **b.**: they look and stare 6106
Ps 31:10 and my **b.** are consumed. 6106
Ps 32:3 **b.** waxed old through my roaring 6106
Ps 34:20 He keepeth all his **b.**: not one of 6106
Ps 35:10 All my **b.** shall say, Lord, who is 6106
Ps 38:3 neither is there any rest in my **b.** 6106
Ps 42:10 with a sword in my **b.**, 6106
Ps 51:8 the **b.** which thou hast broken 6106
Ps 53:5 God hath scattered the **b.** of him 6106
Ps 102:3 my **b.** are burned as an hearth 6106
Ps 102:5 my **b.** cleave to my skin. 6106
Ps 109:18 water, and like oil into his **b.** 6106
Ps 141:7 Our **b.** are scattered at the grave's 6106
Pr 3:8 thy navel, and marrow to thy **b.** 6106
Pr 12:4 is as rottenness in his **b.**. 6106
Pr 14:30 but envy the rottenness of the **b.**. 6106
Pr 15:30 a good report maketh the **b.** fat. 6106
Pr 16:24 to the soul and health to the **b.** 6106
Pr 17:22 a broken spirit drieth the **b.**. 1634
11:5 how the **b.** do grow in the womb 6106
Isa 38:13 lion, so will he break all my **b.** 6106
Isa 58:11 drought and make fat thy **b.**: 6106
Isa 66:14 and your **b.** shall flourish like an 6106
Jer 8:1 the **b.** of the kings of Judah, 6106
Jer 8:1 and the **b.** of his princes, 6106
Jer 8:1 and the **b.** of the priests, 6106
Jer 8:1 and the **b.** of the prophets, 6106
Jer 8:1 and the **b.** of the inhabitants 6106
Jer 20:9 as a burning fire shut up in my **b.**, 6106
Jer 23:9 all my **b.** shake; I am like a 6106
Jer 50:17 king of Babylon hath broken his **b.** 6106
La 1:13 he sent fire into my **b.**, and it 6106
La 3:4 made old; he hath broken my **b.**. 6106
La 4:8 their skin cleaveth to their **b.**; 6106
Eze 6:5 scatter your **b.** round about your 6106
Eze 24:4 fill it with the choice **b.**. 6106
Eze 24:5 burn also the **b.** under it, 6106
Eze 24:5 let them seethe the **b.** of it 6106
Eze 24:10 it well, and let the **b.** be burned 6106
Eze 32:27 iniquities shall be upon their **b.**, 6106
Eze 37:1 the valley which was full of **b.**, 6106
Eze 37:3 Son of man, can these **b.** live? 6106
Eze 37:4 upon these **b.**, and say unto them, 6106
Eze 37:4 O ye dry **b.**, hear the word 6106
Eze 37:5 saith the Lord God unto these **b.** 6106
Eze 37:7 **b.** came together bone to his bone. 6106
Eze 37:11 these **b.** are the whole house of 6106
Eze 37:11 Our **b.** are dried, and our hope is 6106
Da 6:24 and brake all their **b.** in pieces or 1635
Am 2:1 burned the **b.** of the king of Edom 6106
Am 6:10 to bring out the **b.** out of the house, 6106
Mic 3:2 their flesh from off their **b.**; 6106
Mic 3:3 they break their **b.**, and chop them 6106
Hab 3:16 rottenness entered into my **b.**, and 6106
Zep 3:3 gnaw not the **b.** till the morrow. 1033
Mt 23:27 **full of dead men's b., and of all** *3747*
Lu 24:39 **hath not flesh and b., as ye see** *3747*
Ac 3:7 feet and ancle **b.** received *4974*
Eph 5:30 body, of his flesh, and of his **b.** *3747*
Heb 11:22 commandment concerning his **b.**. *3747*

BONNETS
Ex 28:40 and **b.** shalt thou make for them. 4021
Ex 29:9 put the **b.** on them: and the 4021
Ex 39:28 goodly **b.** of fine linen, and linen 4021
Le 8:13 put **b.** upon them; as the Lord 4021
Isa 3:20 The **b.**, and the ornaments of the 6287
Eze 44:18 They shall have linen **b.** upon 6287

BOOK See also BOOKS.
Ge *general* *title* The First **B.** Of Moses, Called
Ge 5:1 This is the **b.** of the generations of 5612
Ex *general* *title* The Second **B.** Of Moses, Called
Ex 17:14 Write this for a memorial in a **b.**, 5612
Ex 24:7 he took the **b.** of the covenant, and 5612
Ex 32:32 blot me, I pray thee, out of thy **b.** 5612
Ex 32:33 me, him will I blot out of my **b.**. 5612
Le *general* *title* The Third **B.** Of Moses, Called
Nu 5:23 shall write these curses in a **b.**, 5612
Nu *general* *title* The Fourth **B.** Of Moses, Called
Nu 21:14 it is said in the **b.** of the wars of 5612
De *general* *title* The Fifth **B.** Of Moses, Called
De 17:18 him a copy of this law in a **b.** out 5612
De 28:58 this law that are written in this **b.**, 5612
De 28:61 which is not written in the **b.** of 5612
De 29:20 curses that are written in this **b.** 5612
De 29:21 that are written in this **b.** of the 5612
De 29:27 curses that are written in this **b.** 5612
De 30:10 statutes which are written in this **b.** 5612
De 31:24 the words of this law in a **b.**, 5612
De 31:26 Take this **b.** of the law and put it 5612
Jos *general* *title* The **B.** Of Joshua
Jos 1:8 This **b.** of the law shall not depart 5612
Jos 8:31 it is written in the **b.** of the law 5612
Jos 8:34 all that is written in the **b.** of the 5612
Jos 10:13 Is not this written in the **b.** of 5612
Jos 18:9 by cities into seven parts in a **b.**, 5612
Jos 23:6 all that is written in the **b.** of the 5612
Jos 24:26 wrote these words in the **b.** of the 5612
Jg *general* *title* The **B.** Of Judges
Ru *general* *title* The **B.** Of Ruth
1Sa *general* *title* The First **B.** Of Samuel
1Sa *general* *title* Called, The First **B.** Of The Kings
1Sa 10:25 wrote it in a **b.**, and laid it up 5612
2Sa *general* *title* The Second **B.** Of Samuel,
2Sa *general* *title* The Second **B.** Of The Kings
2Sa 1:18 behold, it is written in the **b.** of 5612
1Ki *general* *title* The First **B.** Of The Kings

1Ki *general* *title* The Third **B.** Of The Kings
1Ki 11:41 they not written in the **b.** of the 5612
1Ki 14:19 **b.** of the chronicles of...Israel? 5612
1Ki 14:29 **b.** of the chronicles of...Israel? 5612
1Ki 15:7, 23 **b.** of the chronicles of...Judah? 5612
1Ki 15:31 **b.** of the chronicles of...Israel? 5612
1Ki 16:5, 14,20,27 **b.** of the ...of Israel? 5612
1Ki 22:39 **b.** of the chronicles of...Israel? 5612
1Ki 22:45 **b.** of the chronicles of...Judah? 5612
2Ki *general* *title* The Second **B.** Of The Kings
2Ki *general* *title* The Fourth **B.** Of The Kings
2Ki 1:18 **b.** of the chronicles of...Israel? 5612
2Ki 8:23 **b.** of the chronicles of...Judah? 5612
2Ki 10:34 **b.** of the chronicles of...Israel? 5612
2Ki 12:19 **b.** of the chronicles of...Judah? 5612
2Ki 13:8 **b.** of the chronicles of...Israel? 5612
2Ki 13:12 are they not written in the **b.** of the ... 5612
2Ki 14:6 which is written in the **b.** of the law ... 5612
2Ki 14:15 **b.** of the chronicles of...Israel? 5612
2Ki 14:18 **b.** of the chronicles of...Judah? 5612
2Ki 14:28 **b.** of the chronicles of...Israel? 5612
2Ki 15:6 11,15,21,26,31,36 in the **b.** of the chronicles of the kings of Judah? 5612
2Ki 16:19 **b.** of the chronicles of...Judah? 5612
2Ki 20:20 **b.** of the chronicles of...Judah? 5612
2Ki 21:17, 25 **b.** of the chronicles of...Judah? 5612
2Ki 22:8 I have found the **b.** of the law in 5612
2Ki 22:8 Hilkiah gave the **b.** to Shaphan 5612
2Ki 22:10 the priest hath delivered me a **b.**. 5612
2Ki 22:11 king had heard the words of the **b.** 5612
2Ki 22:13 concerning the words of this **b.** 5612
2Ki 22:13 hearkened unto the words of this **b.**, 5612
2Ki 22:16 all the words of the **b.** which the 5612
2Ki 23:2 all the words of the **b.** of the 5612
2Ki 23:3 that were written in this **b.**. 5612
2Ki 23:21 written in the **b.** of this covenant. 5612
2Ki 23:24 law which were written in the **b.** 5612
2Ki 23:28 written in the **b.** of the chronicles 5612
2Ki 24:5 did, are they not written in the **b.** 5612
1Ch *general* *title* The First **B.** Of The Chronicles
1Ch 9:1 were written in the **b.** of the kings 5612
1Ch 29:29 behold, they are written in the **b.** 1697
1Ch 29:29 in the **b.** of Nathan the prophet, 1697
1Ch 29:29 and in the **b.** of Gad the seer, 1697
2Ch *general* *title* The Second **B.** Of The Chronicles
2Ch 9:29 in the **b.** of Nathan the prophet, 1697
2Ch 12:15 in the **b.** of Shemaiah the 1697
2Ch 16:11 are written in the **b.** of the kings 5612
2Ch 17:9 had the **b.** of the law of the Lord 5612
2Ch 20:34 in the **b.** of Jehu the son of 1697
2Ch 20:34 who is mentioned in the **b.** of the 5612
2Ch 24:27 in the story of the **b.** of the kings. 5612
2Ch 25:4 in the law in the **b.** of Moses, 5612
2Ch 25:26 in the **b.** of the kings of Judah and 5612
2Ch 27:7 they are written in the **b.** of the 5612
2Ch 28:26 in the **b.** of the kings of Judah and 5612
2Ch 32:32 in the **b.** of the kings of Judah and 5612
2Ch 33:18 written in the **b.** of the kings of 1697
2Ch 34:14 Hilkiah the priest found a **b.** of 5612
2Ch 34:15 I have found the **b.** of the law in 5612
2Ch 34:15 And Hilkiah delivered the **b.** to 5612
2Ch 34:16 Shaphan carried the **b.** to the king, 5612
2Ch 34:18 the priest hath given me a **b.**. 5612
2Ch 34:21 concerning the words of the **b.** 5612
2Ch 34:21 after all that is written in this **b.**. 5612
2Ch 34:24 curses that are written in the **b.** 5612
2Ch 34:30 all the words of the **b.** of the 5612
2Ch 34:31 which are written in this **b.**. 5612
2Ch 35:12 as it is written in the **b.** of Moses. 5612
2Ch 35:27 in the **b.** of the kings of Israel 5612
2Ch 36:8 they are written in the **b.** of the 5612
Ezr 4:15 search may be made in the **b.** of 5609
Ezr 4:15 so shalt thou find it in the **b.** of the 5609
Ezr 6:18 as it is written in the **b.** of Moses. 5609
Ne *general* *title* The **B.** Of Nehemiah
Ne 8:1 bring the **b.** of the law of Moses, 5612
Ne 8:3 people were attentive unto the **b.** 5612
Ne 8:5 And Ezra opened the **b.** in the 5612
Ne 8:8 they read in the **b.** in the law of 5612
Ne 8:18 last day, he read in the **b.** of the 5612
Ne 9:3 read in the **b.** of the law of the 5612
Ne 12:23 written in the **b.** of the chronicles, 5612
Ne 13:1 they read in the **b.** of Moses in the 5612
Es *general* *title* The **B.** Of Esther
Es 2:23 written in the **b.** of the chronicles 5612
Es 6:1 he commanded to bring the **b.** of 5612
Es 9:32 Purim; and it was written in the **b.** 5612
Es 10:2 in the **b.** of the chronicles of the 5612
Job *general* *title* The **B.** Of Job
Job 19:23 oh that they were printed in a **b.**! 5612
Job 31:35 mine adversary had written a **b.** 5612
Ps *general* *title* The **B.** of Psalms
Ps 40:7 in the volume of the **b.** it is 5612
Ps 56:8 thy bottle: are they not in thy **b.**? 5612
Ps 69:28 Let them be blotted out of the **b.** of 5612
Ps 139:16 in thy **b.** all my members were 5612
Isa *general* *title* The **B.** Of The Prophet Isaiah
Isa 29:11 the words of a **b.** that is sealed, 5612
Isa 29:12 And the **b.** is delivered to him that 5612
Isa 29:18 the deaf hear the words of the **b.**, 5612
Isa 30:8 and note it in a **b.**, that it may be 5612
Isa 34:16 Seek ye out of the **b.** of the Lord 5612
Jer *general* *title* The **B.** Of The Prophet Jeremiah
Jer 25:13 even all that is written in this **b.**, 5612
Jer 30:2 I have spoken unto thee in a **b.**. 5612
Jer 32:12 subscribed the **b.** of the purchase, 5612
Jer 36:2 Take thee a roll of a **b.**, and write 5612
Jer 36:4 unto him, upon a roll of a **b.** 5612
Jer 36:8 reading in the **b.** the words of the 5612
Jer 36:10 Then read Baruch in the **b.** the 5612
Jer 36:11 out of the **b.** all the words of the 5612
Jer 36:13 Baruch read the **b.** in the ears of 5612
Jer 36:18 I wrote them with ink in the **b.** 5612
Jer 36:32 all the words of the **b.** which 5612
Jer 45:1 he had written these words in a **b.** 5612
Jer 51:60 Jeremiah wrote in a **b.** all the evil 5612
Jer 51:63 made an end of reading this **b.**, 5612
Eze *general* *title* The **B.** Of The Prophet Ezekiel
Eze 2:9 and, lo, a roll of a **b.** was therein; 5612
Da *general* *title* The **B.** Of Daniel
Da 12:1 shall be found written in the **b.** 5612
Da 12:4 shut up the words, and seal the **b.**, 5612
Na 1:1 The **b.** of the vision of Nahum the 5612
Mal 3:16 and a **b.** of remembrance was 5612
Mt 1:1 The **b.** of the generation of Jesus *976*
Mk 12:26 **have ye not read in the b. of Moses,** *976*
Lu 3:4 As it is written in the **b.** of the *976*
Lu 4:17 delivered unto him the **b.** of the *975*
Lu 4:17 And when he had opened the **b.**, he *975*
Lu 4:20 he closed the **b.**, and he gave it *975*
Lu 20:42 **David himself saith in the b. of** *976*
Joh 20:30 which are not written in this **b.**: *975*
Ac 1:20 For it is written in the **b.** of *976*
Ac 7:42 as it is written in the **b.** of the *976*
Gal 3:10 things which are written in the **b.** *975*
Php 4:3 whose names are in the **b.** of life *976*
Heb 9:19 sprinkled both the **b.**, and all the *975*
Heb 10:7 (in the volume of the **b.** it is *975*
Re 1:11 **What thou seest, write in a b., and** *975*
Re 3:5 **blot out his name out of the b. of** *976*
Re 5:1 on the throne a **b.** written within *975*
Re 5:2 Who is worthy to open the **b.**, and *975*
Re 5:3 was able to open the **b.**, neither to *975*
Re 5:4 worthy to open and to read the **b.**, *975*
Re 5:5 hath prevailed to open the **b.**, and *975*
Re 5:7 he came and took the **b.** out of the *975*
Re 5:8 when he had taken the **b.**, the four *975*
Re 5:9 Thou art worthy to take the **b.**, and *975*
Re 10:2 he had in his hand a little **b.** open: *974*
Re 10:8 Go and take the little **b.** which *974*
Re 10:9 said unto him, Give me the little **b.** *974*
Re 10:10 I took the little **b.** out of the *974*
Re 13:8 not written in the **b.** of life of the *976*
Re 17:8 names were not written in the **b.** *976*
Re 20:12 and another **b.** was opened, *976*
Re 20:12 which is the **b.** of life: *976*
Re 20:15 was not found written in the **b.** *976*
Re 21:27 written in the Lamb's **b.** of life. *975*
Re 22:7 sayings of the prophecy of this **b.**. *975*
Re 22:9 which keep the sayings of this **b.**: *975*
Re 22:10 sayings of the prophecy of this **b.**: *975*
Re 22:18 words of the prophecy of this **b.**, *975*
Re 22:18 plagues that are written in this **b.**: *975*
Re 22:19 take away from the words of the **b.** *976*
Re 22:19 take away his part out of the **b.** of *976*
Re 22:19 things which are written in this **b.** *975*

BOOKS
Ec 12:12 making many **b.** there is no end; 5612
Da 7:10 judgment was set, and the **b.** 5609
Da 9:2 I Daniel understood by **b.** the 5612
Joh 21:25 could not contain the **b.** that *975*
Ac 19:19 brought their **b.** together, and *976*
2Ti 4:13 bring with thee, and the **b.**, but *975*
Re 20:12 the **b.** were opened: and another *975*
Re 20:12 which were written in the **b.**, *975*

BOOTH See also BOOTHS.
Job 27:18 and as a **b.** that the keeper 5521
Jon 4:5 and there made him a **b.**, and sat 5521

BOOTHS
Ge 33:17 made **b.** for his cattle: therefore 5521
Le 23:42 Ye shall dwell in **b.** seven days; 5521
Le 23:42 are Israelites born shall dwell in **b.**: 5521
Le 23:43 children of Israel do dwell in **b.**, 5521
Ne 8:14 children of Israel should dwell in **b.** 5521
Ne 8:15 branches of thick trees, to make **b.**, 5521
Ne 8:16 made themselves **b.**, every one 5521
Ne 8:17 again out of the captivity made **b.**, 5521
Ne 8:17 and sat under the **b.**: 5521

BOOTIES
Hab 2:7 thou shalt be for **b.** unto them? 4933

BOOTY See also BOOTIES.
Nu 31:32 the **b.**, being the rest of the prey 4455
Jer 49:32 their camels shall be a **b.**, and 957
Zep 1:13 their goods shall become a b., 4933

BOOZ (Bo'-oz). See also BOAZ.
Mt 1:5 And Salmon begat **B.** of Rachab; *1003*
Mt 1:5 and **B.** begat Obed of Ruth; *1003*
Lu 3:32 which was the son of **B.**, which *1003*

BORDER See also BORDERS.
Ge 10:19 the **b.** of the Canaanites was 1366
Ge 49:13 and his **b.** shall be unto Zidon. 3411
Ex 19:12 or touch the **b.** of it: whosoever 7097
Ex 25:25 make unto it a **b.** of an hand 4526
Ex 25:25 a golden crown to the **b.** thereof 4526
Ex 25:27 Over against the **b.** shall the 4526
Ex 28:26 breastplate in the **b.** thereof, 8193
Ex 37:12 made thereunto a **b.** of an hand 4526
Ex 37:12 a crown of gold for the **b.** thereof 4526
Ex 37:14 Over against the **b.** were the rings, 4526
Ex 39:19 **b.** of it, which was on the 8193
Nu 20:16 a city in the uttermost of thy **b.**: 1366
Nu 20:21 passage through his **b.**: 1366
Nu 21:13 for Arnon is the **b.** of Moab, 1366
Nu 21:15 and lieth upon the **b.** of Moab. 1366
Nu 21:23 Israel to pass through his **b.**: 1366
Nu 21:24 the **b.** of the children of Ammon 1366
Nu 22:36 which is in the **b.** of Arnon, 1366
Nu 33:44 in Ije-abarim, in the **b.** of Moab. 1366
Nu 34:3 and your south **b.** shall be 1366
Nu 34:4 And your **b.** shall turn from 1366
Nu 34:5 the **b.** shall fetch a compass from 1366
Nu 34:6 And as for the western **b.**, ye 1366
Nu 34:6 even have the great sea for a **b.**: 1366
Nu 34:6 this shall be your west **b.**. 1366
Nu 34:7 And this shall be your north **b.**: 1366
Nu 34:8 shall point out your **b.** unto the
Nu 34:8 the goings forth of the **b.** shall be 1366
Nu 34:9 the **b.** shall go on to Ziphron, 1366
Nu 34:9 this shall be your north **b.** 1366
Nu 34:10 ye shall point out your east **b.** 1366
Nu 34:11 the **b.** shall descend, and shall 1366
Nu 34:12 the **b.** shall go down to Jordan, 1366
Nu 35:26 the **b.** of the city of his refuge, 1366
De 3:16 the **b.** even unto the river Jabbok 1366
De 3:16 the **b.** of the children of Ammon; 1366
De 12:20 God shall enlarge thy **b.**, as he 1366
Jos 4:19 in the east **b.** of Jericho 7097
Jos 12:2 is the **b.** of the children of Ammon 1366
Jos 12:5 unto the **b.** of the Geshurites 1366
Jos 12:5 the **b.** of Sihon king of Heshbon. 1366
Jos 13:10 the **b.** of the children of Ammon; 1366
Jos 13:11 and the **b.** of the Geshurites and 1366
Jos 13:23 the **b.** of the children of Reuben 1366
Jos 13:23 Jordan, and the **b.** thereof. 1366
Jos 13:26 Mahanaim unto the **b.** of Debir; 1366
Jos 13:27 Jordan and his **b.**, even unto the 1366
Jos 15:1 to the **b.** of Edom the wilderness 1366
Jos 15:2 their south **b.** was from the shore 1366
Jos 15:5 And the east **b.** was the salt sea, 1366
Jos 15:5 And their **b.** in the north quarter 1366
Jos 15:6 the **b.** went up to Beth-hogla, 1366
Jos 15:6 **b.** went up to the stone of Bohan 1366
Jos 15:7 And the **b.** went up toward Debir 1366
Jos 15:7 the **b.** passed toward the waters of 1366
Jos 15:8 the **b.** went up by the valley of 1366
Jos 15:8 and the **b.** went up to the top of 1366
Jos 15:9 the **b.** was drawn from the top 1366

Jos 15:9 and the **b.** was drawn to Baalah, 1366
Jos 15:10 the **b.** compassed from Baalah 1366
Jos 15:11 **b.** went out unto the side of Ekron 1366
Jos 15:11 and the **b.** was drawn to Shicron, 1366
Jos 15:11 goings out of the **b.** were at the 1366
Jos 15:12 the west **b.** was to the great sea, 1366
Jos 15:47 the great sea, and the **b.** thereof 1366
Jos 16:5 the **b.** of the children of Ephraim 1366
Jos 16:5 even the **b.** of their inheritance 1366
Jos 16:6 And the **b.** went out toward the 1366
Jos 16:6 the **b.** went about eastward 1366
Jos 16:8 The **b.** went out from Tappuah 1366
Jos 17:7 **b.** went along on the right hand 1366
Jos 17:8 Tappuah on the **b.** of Manasseh 1366
Jos 17:10 the sea is his **b.**; and they met 1366
Jos 18:12 And their **b.** on the north side 1366
Jos 18:12 **b.** went up to the side of Jericho 1366
Jos 18:13 the **b.** went over from thence 1366
Jos 18:13 the **b.** descended to Ataroth-adar, 1366
Jos 18:14 the **b.** was drawn thence, and 1366
Jos 18:15 **b.** went out on the west, 1366
Jos 18:16 the **b.** came down to the end of 1366
Jos 18:19 **b.** passed along to the side of 1366
Jos 18:19 outgoings of the **b.** were at the 1366
Jos 18:20 Jordan was the **b.** of it on the 1379
Jos 19:10 the **b.** of their inheritance was 1366
Jos 19:11 their **b.** went up toward the sea, 1366
Jos 19:12 unto the **b.** of Chisloth-tabor, 1366
Jos 19:14 the **b.** compasseth it on the north 1366
Jos 19:18 their **b.** was toward Jezreel, 1366
Jos 19:22 outgoings of their **b.** were at 1366
Jos 19:25 their **b.** was Helkath, and Hali, 1366
Jos 19:46 Rakkon, with the **b.** before Japho. 1366
Jos 22:25 the Lord hath made Jordan a **b.** 1366
Jos 24:30 in the **b.** of his inheritance in 1366
Jg 2:9 in the **b.** of his inheritance in 1366
Jg 7:22 to the **b.** of Abel-meholah, 8193
Jg 11:18 within the **b.** of Moab: 1366
Jg 11:18 for Arnon was the **b.** of Moab. 1366
1Sa 6:12 them unto the **b.** of Beth-shemesh 1366
1Sa 10:2 in the **b.** of Benjamin at Zelzah; 1366
1Sa 13:18 the way of the **b.** that looketh to 1366
2Sa 8:3 to recover his **b.** at the river 3027
1Ki 4:21 and unto the **b.** of Egypt: 1366
2Ki 3:21 and upward, and stood in the **b.** 1366
2Ch 9:26 Philistines, and to the **b.** of Egypt. 1366
Ps 78:54 he brought them to the **b.** of his 1366
Pr 15:25 will establish the **b.** of the widow. 1366
Isa 19:19 at the **b.** thereof to the Lord. 1366
Isa 37:24 into the height of his **b.**, and the 7093
Jer 31:17 shall come again to their own **b.** 1366
Jer 50:26 from the utmost **b.**, open her 7093
Eze 11:10 will judge you in the **b.** of Israel; 1366
Eze 11:11 I will judge you in the **b.** of Israel: 1366
Eze 29:10 even unto the **b.** of Ethiopia. 1366
Eze 43:13 and the **b.** thereof by the edge 1366
Eze 43:17 and the **b.** about it shall be half 1366
Eze 43:20 and upon the **b.** round about: 1366
Eze 45:7 the west **b.** unto the east **b.** 1366
Eze 47:13 This shall be the **b.**, whereby ye 1366
Eze 47:15 this shall be the **b.** of the land 1366
Eze 47:16 between the **b.** of Damascus 1366
Eze 47:16 and the **b.** of Hamath; 1366
Eze 47:17 the **b.** from the sea shall be 1366
Eze 47:17 Hazar-enan, the **b.** of Damascus, 1366
Eze 47:17 northward, and the **b.** of Hamath 1366
Eze 47:18 from the **b.** unto the east sea. 1366
Eze 47:20 the great sea from the **b.**, till a 1366
Eze 48:1 the **b.** of Damascus northward, 1366
Eze 48:2 by the **b.** of Dan, from the east side 1366
Eze 48:3 the **b.** of Asher, from the east side 1366
Eze 48:4 **b.** of Naphtali, from the east side 1366
Eze 48:5 **b.** of Manasseh, from the east side 1366
Eze 48:6 **b.** of Ephraim, from the east side 1366
Eze 48:7 **b.** of Reuben, from the east side 1366
Eze 48:8 **b.** of Judah, from the east side 1366
Eze 48:12 by the **b.** of the Levites. 1366
Eze 48:13 against the **b.** of the priests 1366
Eze 48:21 the oblation toward the east **b.**, 1366
Eze 48:21 thousand toward the west **b.**, 1366
Eze 48:22 between the **b.** of Judah 1366
Eze 48:22 and the **b.** of Benjamin, 1366
Eze 48:24 **b.** of Benjamin, from the east side 1366
Eze 48:25 **b.** of Simeon, from the east side 1366
Eze 48:26 **b.** of Issachar, from the east side 1366
Eze 48:27 **b.** of Zebulun, from the east side 1366
Eze 48:28 **b.** of Gad, at the south side 1366
Eze 48:28 the **b.** shall be even from Tamar 1366
Joe 3:6 remove them far from their **b.** 1366
Am 1:13 that they might enlarge their **b.**: 1366
Am 6:2 or their **b.** greater than your **b.**? 1366
Am 6:7 have brought thee even to the **b.**: 1366
Ob 7 have brought thee even to the **b.**: 1366
Zep 2:8 themselves against their **b.** 1366
Zec 9:2 Hamath also shall **b.** thereby; 1379
Mal 1:4 The **b.** of wickedness, and, The 1366
Mal 1:5 magnified from the **b.** of Israel. 1366
Mk 6:56 were but the **b.** of his garment: *2899*
Lu 8:44 touched the **b.** of his garment; *2899*

BORDERS

Ge 23:17 in all the **b.** round about, were 1366
Ge 47:21 from one end of the **b.** of Egypt 1366
Ex 8:2 I will smite all thy **b.** with frogs: 1366
Ex 16:35 unto the **b.** of the land of Canaan. 7097
Ex 34:24 before thee, and enlarge thy **b.**: 1366
Nu 15:38 in the **b.** of their garments 3671
Nu 15:38 the fringe of the **b.** a ribband 3671
Nu 20:17 until we have passed thy **b.** 1366
Nu 21:22 until we be passed thy **b.** 1366
Nu 35:27 him without the **b.** of the city of 1366
Jos 11:2 and in the **b.** of Dor on the west, 5299
Jos 13:2 all the **b.** of the Philistines, 1552
Jos 13:3 unto the **b.** of Ekron northward, 1366
Jos 13:4 Aphek, to the **b.** of the Amorites: 1366
Jos 16:2 unto the **b.** of Archi to Ataroth, 1366
Jos 22:10 came unto the **b.** of Jordan, that 1552
Jos 22:11 the **b.** of Jordan, at the passage 1552
1Ki 7:28 they had **b.**, and 4526
1Ki 7:28 the **b.** were between the ledges: 4526
1Ki 7:29 on the **b.** that were between the 4526
1Ki 7:31 with their **b.**, foursquare 4526
1Ki 7:32 under the **b.** were four wheels; 4526
1Ki 7:35 the **b.** thereof were of the same. 4526
1Ki 7:36 **b.** thereof, he graved cherubim, 4526
2Ki 16:17 Ahaz cut off the **b.** of the bases, 4526
2Ki 18:8 the **b.** thereof, from the tower 1366
2Ki 19:23 into the lodgings of his **b.**, 7093
1Ch 5:16 suburbs of Sharon, upon their **b.** 8444
1Ch 7:29 **b.** of the children of Manasseh, 3027
Ps 74:17 hast set all the **b.** of the earth: 1367
Ps 147:14 maketh peace in thy **b.**, and filleth 1366
Ca 1:11 **b.** of gold with studs of silver. 8447
Isa 15:8 gone round about the **b.** of Moab; 1366
Isa 54:12 and all thy **b.** of pleasant stones. 1366
Isa 60:18 nor destruction within thy **b.**; 1366
Jer 15:13 all thy sins, even in all thy **b.** 1366
Jer 17:3 for sin, throughout all thy **b.** 1366
Eze 27:4 Thy **b.** are in the midst of the seas, 1366
Eze 45:1 holy in all the **b.** thereof round 1366
Mic 5:6 when he treadeth within our **b.** 1366
Mt 4:13 the **b.** of Zabulon and Nephthalim: *3725*
Mt 23:5 **enlarge the b. of their garments,** *2899*
Mk 7:24 into the **b.** of Tyre and Sidon, *3181*

BORE See also BARE; BORED.

Ex 21:6 master shall **b.** his ear through 7527
Job 41:2 **b.** his jaw through with a thorn? 5344

BORED

2Ki 12:9 and **b.** a hole in the lid of it, 5344

BORN See also BORNE; FIRSTBORN; FORBORN; NEWBORN.

Ge 4:18 And unto Enoch was **b.** Irad: 3205
Ge 4:26 to him also there was **b.** a son; 3205
Ge 6:1 and daughters were **b.** unto them, 3205
Ge 10:1 them were sons **b.** after the flood. 3205
Ge 10:21 even to him were children **b.** 3205
Ge 10:25 unto Eber were **b.** two sons: the 3205
Ge 14:14 **b.** in his own house, three 3211
Ge 15:3 one **b.** in my house is mine heir. 1121
Ge 17:12 he that is **b.** in the house, or 3211
Ge 17:13 He that is **b.** in thy house, and 3211
Ge 17:17 Shall a child be **b.** unto him that 3205
Ge 17:23 all that were **b.** in his house, 3211
Ge 17:27 men of his house, **b.** in the house, 3211
Ge 21:3 his son that was **b.** unto him, whom 3205
Ge 21:5 his son Isaac was **b.** unto him. 3205
Ge 21:7 I have **b.** him a son in his old age. 3205
Ge 21:9 which she had **b.** unto Abraham, 3205
Ge 22:20 she hath also **b.** children unto 3205
Ge 24:15 was **b.** to Bethuel, son of Milcah, 3205
Ge 29:34 because I have **b.** him three sons: 3205
Ge 30:20 I have **b.** him six sons: and she 3205
Ge 30:25 Rachel had **b.** Joseph, that Jacob 3205
Ge 31:43 children which they have **b.**? 3205
Ge 35:26 were **b.** to him in Padan-aram. 3205
Ge 36:5 **b.** unto him in the land of Canaan. 3205
Ge 41:50 And unto Joseph were **b.** two sons 3205
Ge 46:20 land of Egypt were **b.** Manasseh 3205
Ge 46:22 of Rachel, which were **b.** to Jacob: 3205
Ge 46:27 which were **b.** him in Egypt, were 3205
Ge 48:5 Manasseh, which were **b.** unto thee 3205
Ex 1:22 Every son that is **b.** ye shall cast 3209
Ex 12:19 be a stranger, or **b.** in the land. 249
Ex 12:48 be as one that is **b.** in the land. 249
Ex 21:4 have **b.** him sons or daughters; 3205
Le 12:2 and **b.** a man child, then she 3205
Le 12:7 law for her that hath **b.** a male 3205
Le 18:9 whether she be **b.** at home, 4138
Le 18:9 or **b.** abroad, 4138
Le 19:34 unto you as one **b.** among you, 249
Le 22:11 and he that is **b.** in his house: 3211
Le 23:42 all that are Israelites **b.** shall 249
Le 24:16 as he that is **b.** in the land, when 249
Nu 9:14 him that was **b.** in the land. 249
Nu 15:13 All that are **b.** of the country 249
Nu 15:29 him that is **b.** among the children 249
Nu 15:30 be **b.** in the land, or a stranger, 249
Nu 26:60 unto Aaron was **b.** Nadab and 3205
De 21:15 and they have **b.** him children, 3205
Jos 5:5 the people that were **b.** in the 3209
Jos 8:33 as he that was **b.** among them; 249
Jg 13:8 do unto the child that shall be **b.** 3205
Jg 18:29 father, who was **b.** unto Israel: 3205
Ru 4:15 than seven sons, hath **b.** him. 3205
Ru 4:17 There is a son **b.** to Naomi; 3205
1Sa 2:5 so that the barren hath **b.** seven; 3205
1Sa 4:20 Fear not, for thou hast **b.** a son. 3205
2Sa 3:2 unto David were sons **b.** in Hebron: 3205
2Sa 3:5 These were **b.** to David in Hebron. 3205
2Sa 5:13 sons and daughters **b.** to David. 3205
2Sa 5:14 names of those that were **b.** unto 3209
2Sa 12:14 the child also that is **b.** unto thee 3209
2Sa 14:27 Absalom there were **b.** three sons, 3205
2Sa 21:20 and he also was **b.** to the giant. 3205
2Sa 21:22 four were **b.** to the giant in Gath, 3205
1Ki 13:2 be **b.** unto the house of David, 3205
1Ch 1:19 And unto Eber were **b.** two sons: 3205
1Ch 2:3 which three were **b.** unto him of 3205
1Ch 2:9 of Hezron, that were **b.** unto him; 3205
1Ch 3:1 which were **b.** unto him in Hebron: 3205
1Ch 3:4 six were **b.** unto him in Hebron; 3205
1Ch 3:5 were **b.** unto him in Jerusalem; 3205
1Ch 7:21 of Gath that were **b.** in that land 3205
1Ch 20:8 were **b.** unto the giant in Gath; 3205
1Ch 22:9 a son shall be **b.** to thee, who shall 3205
1Ch 26:6 Shemaiah his son were sons **b.**, 3205
Ezr 10:3 such as are **b.** of them, according 3205
Job 1:2 here were **b.** unto him seven sons 3205
Job 3:3 the day perish wherein I was **b.**, 3205
Job 5:7 man is **b.** unto trouble, as the 3205
Job 11:12 man be **b.** like a wild ass's colt. 3205
Job 14:1 Man that is **b.** of a woman is of 3205
Job 15:7 Art thou the first man that was **b.**? 3205
Job 15:14 he which is **b.** of a woman, that he 3205
Job 25:4 he be clean that is **b.** of a woman? 3205
Job 38:21 thou it, because thou wast then **b.**? 3205
Ps 22:31 a people that shall be **b.**, that he 3205
Ps 58:3 go astray as soon as they be **b.**, 990
Ps 78:6 the children which should be **b.**; 3205
Ps 87:4 Ethiopia; this man was **b.** there. 3205
Ps 87:5 that man was **b.** in her: and the 3205
Ps 87:6 people, that this man was **b.** there, 3205
Pr 17:17 and a brother is **b.** for adversity 3205
Ec 2:7 and had servants **b.** in my house; 1121
Ec 3:2 A time to be **b.**, and a time to die; 3205
Ec 4:14 is **b.** in his kingdom becometh 3205
Isa 9:6 unto us a child is **b.**, unto us a son 3205
Isa 66:8 shall a nation be **b.** at once? for as 3205
Jer 16:3 daughters that are **b.** in this place, 3205
Jer 20:14 be the day wherein I was **b.**: 3205
Jer 20:15 A man child is **b.** unto thee; 3205
Jer 22:26 country, where ye were not **b.**; 3205
Eze 16:4 in the day thou wast **b.** thy 3205
Eze 16:5 in the day that thou wast **b.** 3205
Eze 47:22 shall be unto you as **b.** in the 249
Ho 2:3 her as in the day that she was **b.** 3205
Mt 1:16 of whom was **b.** Jesus, who is *1080*
Mt 2:1 when Jesus was **b.** in Bethlehem *1080*
Mt 2:2 is he that is **b.** King of the Jews? *5088*
Mt 2:4 of them where Christ should be **b.** *1080*

Mt 11:11 Among them that are **b.** of women 1084
Mt 19:12 so **b.** from their mother's womb: 1080
Mt 26:24 that man if he had not been **b.** 1080
Mk 14:21 that man if he had never been **b.** 1080
Lu 1:35 that holy thing which shall be **b.** 1080
Lu 2:11 For unto you is **b.** this day in the 5088
Lu 7:28 Among those that are **b.** of women 1084
Joh 1:13 Which were **b.**, not of blood, nor 1080
Joh 3:3 Except a man be **b.** again, he 1080
Joh 3:4 can a man be **b.** when he is old? 1080
Joh 3:4 into his mother's womb, and be **b.**? 1080
Joh 3:5 Except a man be **b.** of water and 1080
Joh 3:6 which is **b.** of the flesh is flesh; 1080
Joh 3:6 which is **b.** of the Spirit is spirit 1080
Joh 3:7 unto thee, Ye must be **b.** again 1080
Joh 3:8 every one that is **b.** of the Spirit 1080
Joh 8:41 We be not **b.** of fornication; we 1080
Joh 9:2 or his parents, that he was **b.** blind? 1080
Joh 9:19 your son, who ye say was **b.** blind? 1080
Joh 9:20 our son, and that he was **b.** blind: 1080
Joh 9:32 the eyes of one that was **b.** blind. 1080
Joh 9:34 Thou wast altogether **b.** in sins, 1080
Joh 16:21 joy that a man is **b.** into the world 1080
Joh 18:37 To this end was I **b.**, and for this 1080
Ac 2:8 own tongue, wherein we were **b.**? 1080
Ac 7:20 In which time Moses was **b.**, and 1080
Ac 18:2 Aquila, **b.** in Pontus, lately come 1085
Ac 18:24 named Apollos, **b.** at Alexandria, 1085
Ac 22:3 which am a Jew, **b.** in Tarsus, 1080
Ac 22:28 Paul said, But I was free **b.** 1080
Ro 9:11 (For the children being not yet **b.** 1080
1Co 15:8 also, as of one **b.** out of due time 1626
Ga 4:23 bondwoman was **b.** after the flesh; 1080
Ga 4:29 he that was **b.** after the flesh 1080
Ga 4:29 him that was **b.** after the Spirit,
Heb 11:23 By faith Moses, when he was **b.**, 1080
1Pe 1:23 **b.** again not of corruptible seed, 313
1Jo 2:29 doeth righteousness is **b.** of him 1080
1Jo 3:9 Whosoever is **b.** of God doth not 1080
1Jo 3:9 sin, because he is **b.** of God 1080
1Jo 4:7 every one that loveth is **b.** of God, 1080
1Jo 5:1 Jesus is the Christ is **b.** of God: 1080
1Jo 5:4 For whatsoever is **b.** of God 1080
1Jo 5:18 whosoever is **b.** of God sinneth not; 1080
Re 12:4 her child as soon as it was **b.** 5088

BORNE See also BORN.
Ex 25:14 the ark may be **b.** with them 5375
Ex 25:28 the table may be **b.** with them 5375
Jg 16:29 and on which it was **b.** up, 5564
Job 34:31 I have **b.** chastisement, I will not 5375
Ps 55:12 then I could have **b.** it: neither 5375
Ps 69:7 I have **b.** reproach; shame hath 5375
Isa 46:3 are **b.** by me from the belly, 6006
Isa 53:4 Surely he hath **b.** our griefs, 5375
Isa 66:12 ye shall be **b.** upon her sides, 5375
Jer 10:5 they must needs be **b.**, because 5375
Jer 15:9 that hath **b.** seven languisheth: 3205
Jer 15:10 thou hast **b.** me a man of strife 3205
La 3:28 because he hath **b.** it upon him 5190
La 5:7 and we have **b.** their iniquities 5445
Eze 16:20 daughters, whom thou hast **b.** 3205
Eze 16:58 Thou hast **b.** thy lewdness 5375
Eze 32:24, 25 yet have they **b.** their shame 5375
Eze 36:6 ye have **b.** the shame of the 5375
Eze 39:26 that they have **b.** their shame, 5375
Am 5:26 **b.** the tabernacle of your Moloch 5375
Mt 20:12 which have **b.** the burden and heat 941
Mt 23:4 burdens and grievous to be **b.**, 1418
Mk 2:3 the palsy, which was **b.** of four 142
Lu 11:46 with burdens grievous to be **b.**, 1418
Joh 5:37 hath sent me, hath **b.** witness of me
Joh 20:15 Sir, if thou have **b.** him hence, 941
Ac 21:35 that he was **b.** of the soldiers 941
1Co 15:49 have **b.** the image of the earthy 5409
3Jo 6 have **b.** witness of thy charity
Re 2:3 And hast **b.**, and hast patience, 941

BORROW See also BORROWED; BORROWETH.
Ex 3:22 woman shall **b.** of her neighbour, 7592
Ex 11:2 every man **b.** of his neighbour, 7592
Ex 22:14 **b.** ought of his neighbour, 7592
De 15:6 nations, but thou shalt not **b.**; 5670
De 28:12 nations, and thou shalt not **b.** 3867
2Ki 4:3 **b.** thee vessels abroad of all thy 7592
2Ki 4:3 even empty vessels; **b.** not a few
Mt 5:42 from him that would **b.** of thee 1155

BORROWED
Ex 12:35 they **b.** of the Egyptians jewels 7592
2Ki 6:5 Alas, master! for it was **b.** 7592
Ne 5:4 We have **b.** money for the king's 3867

BORROWER
Pr 22:7 the **b.** is servant to the lender 3867
Isa 24:2 so with the **b.**; as with the taker 3867

BORROWETH
Ps 37:21 The wicked **b.**, and payeth not 3867

BOSCATH (bos'-cath) See also BOSKETH.
2Ki 22:1 the daughter of Adaiah of **B.** 1218

BOSKETH See ISH-BOSKETH.

BOSOM
Ge 16:5 I have given my maid into thy **b.**; 2436
Ex 4:6 Put now thine hand into thy **b.** 2436
Ex 4:6 And he put his hand into his **b.**: 2436
Ex 4:7 Put thine hand into thy **b.** again. 2436
Ex 4:7 he put his hand into his **b.** again; 2436
Ex 4:7 and plucked it out of his **b.**, 2436
Nu 11:12 Carry them in thy **b.**, as a nursing 2436
De 13:6 or the wife of thy **b.**, or thy friend, 2436
De 28:54 toward the wife of his **b.**, 2436
De 28:56 evil toward the husband of her **b.**, 2436
Ru 4:16 laid it in her **b.**, and became nurse 2436
2Sa 12:3 lay in his **b.**, and was unto him 2436
2Sa 12:8 thy master's wives into thy **b.**, 2436
1Ki 1:2 let her lie in thy **b.**, that my lord 2436
1Ki 3:20 and laid it in her **b.**, and laid her 2436
1Ki 3:20 and laid her dead child in my **b.** 2436
1Ki 17:19 he took him out of her **b.**, 2436
Job 31:33 by hiding mine iniquity in my **b.**: 2243
Ps 35:13 prayer returned into mine own **b.** 2436
Ps 74:11 hand? pluck it out of thy **b.** 2436
Ps 79:12 sevenfold into their **b.** their 2436
Ps 89:50 I do bear in my **b.** the reproach of 2436
Ps 129:7 he that bindeth sheaves his **b.** 2683
Pr 5:20 and embrace the **b.** of a stranger? 2436
Pr 6:27 Can a man take fire in his **b.**, and 2436
Pr 17:23 man taketh a gift out of the **b.** to 2436
Pr 19:24 man hideth his hand in his **b.**, 6747
Pr 21:14 a reward in the **b.** strong wrath. 2436
Pr 26:15 slothful hideth his hand in his **b.**; 6747
Ec 7:9 anger resteth in the **b.** of fools. 2436
Isa 40:11 and carry them in his **b.**, and shall 2436
Isa 65:6 even recompense into their **b.**, 2436
Isa 65:7 their former work into their **b.** 2436
Jer 32:18 into the **b.** of their children after 2436
La 2:12 poured out into their mother's **b.** 2436
Mic 7:5 from her that lieth in thy **b.** 2436
Lu 6:38 shall men give into your **b.** 2859
Lu 16:22 by the angels into Abraham's **b.**: 2859
Lu 16:23 afar off, and Lazarus in his **b.** 2859
Joh 1:18 which is in the **b.** of the Father, 2859
Joh 13:23 leaning on Jesus' **b.** one of his 2859

BOSOR (bo'-sor)
2Pe 2:15 Balaam the son of **B.**, who loved 1007

BOSSES
Job 15:26 upon the thick **b.** of his bucklers: 1354

BOTCH
De 28:27 smite thee with the **b.** of Egypt, 7822
De 28:35 with a sore **b.** that cannot be 7822

BOTH
Ge 2:25 they were **b.** naked, the man and 8147
Ge 3:7 the eyes of them **b.** were opened, 8147
Ge 6:7 **b.** man, and beast, and the
Ge 7:21 upon the earth, **b.** of fowl, and of
Ge 7:23 upon the face of the ground, **b.**
Ge 8:17 all flesh, **b.** of fowl, and of cattle,
Ge 9:23 laid it upon **b.** their shoulders, 8147
Ge 19:4 **b.** old and young, all the people
Ge 19:11 with blindness, **b.** small and great:
Ge 19:36 **b.** the daughters of Lot with child 8147
Ge 21:27 **b.** of them made a covenant 8147
Ge 21:31 and there they sware **b.** of them 8147
Ge 22:6 they went **b.** of them together 8147
Ge 22:8 so they went **b.** of them together 8147
Ge 24:25 We have **b.** straw and provender 1571
Ge 24:44 **b.** drink thou and I will also draw
Ge 27:45 deprived also of you **b.** in one day? 8147
Ge 31:37 they may judge betwixt us **b.** 8147
Ge 36:24 children of Zibeon; **b.** Ajah, and
Ge 40:5 dreamed a dream **b.** of them, 8147
Ge 41:10 **b.** me and the chief baker:
Ge 42:35 when **b.** they and their father
Ge 43:8 live, and not die, **b.** we, and thou, 1571
Ge 44:9 it be found, **b.** let him die,
Ge 44:16 my lord's servants, **b.** we, and he 1571
Ge 46:34 now, **b.** we, and also our fathers: 1571
Ge 47:3 **b.** we, and also our fathers. 1571
Ge 47:19 we die before thine eyes, **b.** we 1571
Ge 48:13 Joseph took them **b.**, Ephraim in 8147
Ge 50:9 went up with him **b.** chariots 1571
Ex 5:14 making brick **b.** yesterday and to 1571
Ex 7:19 **b.** in vessels of wood, and in vessels
Ex 8:4 the frogs shall come up **b.** on thee,
Ex 9:25 all . . . in the field, **b.** man and beast;
Ex 12:12 firstborn . . . of Egypt, **b.** man and beast;
Ex 12:31 forth from among my people, **b.** 1571
Ex 13:2 **b.** of man and of beast: it is mine.
Ex 13:15 of Egypt, **b.** the firstborn of man,
Ex 18:18 surely wear away, **b.** thou, and 1571
Ex 22:9 the cause of **b.** parties shall come 8147
Ex 22:11 the Lord be between them **b.** 8147
Ex 26:24 thus shall it be for them **b.**; 8147
Ex 29:44 sanctify also **b.** Aaron and his
Ex 32:15 tables were written on **b.** their 8147
Ex 35:22 **b.** men and women, as many as
Ex 35:25 that which they had spun, **b.** of
Ex 35:34 may teach, **b.** he, and Aholiab,
Ex 36:29 thus he did to **b.** of them in 8147
Ex 36:29 of them in **b.** the corners. 8147
Ex 37:26 overlaid it with pure gold, **b.** the
Le 6:28 brasen pot, it shall be **b.** scoured,
Le 8:11 **b.** the laver and his foot,
Le 9:3 and a lamb, **b.** of the first year,
Le 15:18 shall **b.** bathe themselves in water,
Le 16:21 And Aaron shall lay **b.** his hands 8147
Le 17:15 he shall **b.** wash his clothes,
Le 20:11 **b.** of them shall surely be put to 8147
Le 20:12 daughter in law, **b.** of them shall 8147
Le 20:13 **b.** of them have committed an 8147
Le 20:14 burnt with fire, **b.** he and they;
Le 20:18 and **b.** of them shall be cut off 8147
Le 21:22 eat the bread of his God, **b.** of the
Le 22:28 kill it and her young **b.** in one
Le 25:41 shall he depart from thee, **b.** he
Le 25:44 **B.** thy bondmen, and thy
Le 25:54 go out in the year of jubilee, **b.**
Le 27:28 **b.** of man and beast, and of the
Le 27:33 then **b.** it and the change thereof
Nu 3:13 **b.** man and beast: mine shall they
Nu 5:3 **B.** male and female shall ye put
Nu 7:1 **b.** the altar and all the vessels
Nu 7:13 **b.** of them were full of fine flour 8147
Nu 7:19, 25,31,37,43,49,55,61,67,73,79, **b.** of them full of fine flour 8147
Nu 8:17 of Israel are mine, **b.** man and
Nu 9:14 ordinance, **b.** for the stranger,
Nu 12:5 Aaron and Miriam, and they **b.** 8147
Nu 15:15 One ordinance shall be **b.** for you
Nu 15:29 **b.** for him that is born among
Nu 16:11 For which cause **b.** thou and all
Nu 25:8 thrust **b.** of them through, 8147
Nu 27:21 his word they shall come in, **b.** he,
Nu 31:11 and all the prey, **b.** of mean and of
Nu 31:19 any slain, purify **b.** yourselves
Nu 31:26 prey that was taken, **b.** of man
Nu 31:28 of five hundred, **b.** of the persons,
Nu 31:47 portion of fifty, **b.** of man and
Nu 35:15 be a refuge, **b.** for the children
De 19:17 Then **b.** the men, between whom 8147
De 21:15 **b.** the beloved, and the hated;
De 22:22 then they shall **b.** of them die, 1571,8147
De 22:22 **b.** the man that lay with the
De 22:24 bring them **b.** out unto the gate 8147
De 23:18 for even **b.** these are abomination
De 30:19 life, that **b.** thou and thy seed
De 32:25 shall destroy **b.** the young man 1571
Jos 6:21 all that was in the city, **b.** man
Jos 8:25 fell that day, **b.** of men and women,
Jos 14:11 war, **b.** to go out, and to come in
Jos 17:16 **b.** they who are of Beth-shean
Jg 5:30 colours of needlework on **b.** sides,
Jg 6:5 for **b.** they and their camels were
Jg 8:22 Rule thou over us, **b.** thou, and 1571
Jg 10:10 against thee, **b.** because we have
Jg 15:5 and burnt up **b.** the shocks,
Jg 19:6 did eat and drink **b.** of them 8147
Jg 19:8 afternoon, and they did eat **b.** of 8147

Jg 19:19 there is **b.** straw and provender 1571
Ru 1:5 Mahlon and Chilion died also **b.** 8147
1Sa 2:26 was in favour **b.** with the Lord, 1571
1Sa 2:34 one day they shall die **b.** of them. 8147
1Sa 3:11 **b.** the ears of every one that 8147
1Sa 5:4 **b.** the palms of his hands were cut 8147
1Sa 5:9 smote the men of the city, **b.** small
1Sa 6:18 five lords, **b.** of fenced cities, and of
1Sa 9:26 they went out **b.** of them, he and 8147
1Sa 12:14 then shall **b.** ye and also the king 1571
1Sa 12:25 be consumed, **b.** ye and your king 1571
1Sa 14:11 **b.** of them discovered themselves
1Sa 15:3 spare them not; but slay **b.** man
1Sa 17:36 Thy servant slew **b.** the lion and 1571
1Sa 20:11 they went out **b.** of them into the 8174
1Sa 20:42 we have sworn **b.** of us in the name 8174
1Sa 22:19 **b.** men and women, children and
1Sa 25:6 Peace be **b.** to thee, and peace be
1Sa 25:16 wall unto us **b.** by night and day, 1571
1Sa 25:43 were also **b.** of them his wives. 8147
1Sa 26:25 thou shalt **b.** do great things, 1571
2Sa 8:18 the son of Jehoiada was over **b.**
2Sa 9:13 and was lame on **b.** his feet. 8147
2Sa 15:25 shew me **b.** it, and his habitation:
2Sa 16:23 of Ahithophel **b.** with David 1571
2Sa 17:18 went **b.** of them away quickly, 8147
1Ki 3:13 thou hast not asked, **b.** riches, 1571
1Ki 6:5 **b.** of the temple and of the oracle:
1Ki 6:15 **b.** the floor of the house, and the
1Ki 6:16 **b.** the floor and the walls with
1Ki 6:25 **b.** the cherubims were of one 8147
1Ki 7:12 **b.** for the inner court of the
1Ki 7:50 hinges of gold, **b.** for the doors
2Ki 2:11 parted them **b.** asunder; and 8147
2Ki 3:17 that ye may drink, **b.** ye, and your
2Ki 6:15 host compassed the city **b.** with
2Ki 17:41 served their graven images, **b.** 1571
2Ki 21:12 of it, **b.** his ears shall tingle 8147
2Ki 23:2 all the people, **b.** small and great:
2Ki 23:15 **b.** that altar and the high place 1571
2Ki 25:26 people, **b.** small and great, and the
1Ch 12:2 and could use **b.** the right hand
1Ch 12:15 **b.** toward the east, and toward
1Ch 15:12 sanctify yourselves, **b.** ye and
1Ch 16:3 one of Israel, **b.** man and woman,
1Ch 23:29 **B.** for the shewbread, and for
1Ch 24:3 distributed them, **b.** Zadok of the sons
1Ch 28:15 by weight, **b.** for the candlestick,
1Ch 29:12 **B.** riches and honour come of thee,
2Ch 20:25 abundance **b.** riches with the dead
2Ch 24:16 done good in Israel, **b.** toward
2Ch 25:21 face, **b.** he and Amaziah king
2Ch 26:10 cattle, **b.** in the low country,
2Ch 27:5 of Ammon pay unto him, **b.** the
2Ch 31:17 **B.** to the genealogy of the priests
2Ch 32:26 pride of his heart, **b.** he and the
Ezr 3:5 burnt offering, **b.** of the new
Ezr 6:9 have need of, **b.** young bullocks,
Ne 1:6 **b.** I and my father's house have
Ne 4:16 half of them held **b.** the spears,
Ne 8:2 congregation **b.** of men and
Ne 10:9 And the Levites: **b.** Jeshua the
Ne 12:27 gladness, **b.** with thanksgivings,
Ne 12:28 **b.** out of the plain country round
Ne 12:45 **b.** the singers and the porters
Es 1:5 the palace, **b.** unto great and small,
Es 1:20 husbands honour, **b.** to great and
Es 2:23 therefore they were **b.** hanged on 8147
Es 3:13 to perish, all Jews, **b.** young and
Es 8:11 them, **b.** little ones and women,
Es 9:20 the king Ahasuerus, **b.** nigh, and
Job 9:33 might lay his hand upon us **b.** 8147
Job 15:10 With us are **b.** the greyheaded 1571
Ps 4:8 I will **b.** lay me down in peace, 3162
Ps 49:2 **B.** low and high, rich and poor, 1571
Ps 58:9 whirlwind, **b.** living, and in his
Ps 64:6 **b.** the inward thought of every
Ps 76:6 O God of Jacob, **b.** the chariot
Ps 104:25 innumerable, **b.** small and great
Ps 115:13 that fear the Lord, **b.** small and
Ps 135:8 the firstborn of Egypt, **b.** of man
Ps 139:12 darkness and the light are **b.** alike
Ps 148:12 **B.** young men and maidens; old
Pr 17:15 they **b.** are abomination 8147
Pr 20:10 **b.** of them are alike abomination 8147
Pr 20:12 the Lord hath made even **b.** of them 8147
Pr 24:22 who knoweth the ruin of them **b.**? 8147
Pr 26:10 formed all things **b.** rewardeth
Pr 27:3 wrath is heavier than them **b.** 8147
Pr 29:13 the Lord lighteneth **b.** their eyes. 8147
Ec 4:3 better is he than **b.** they, which 8147
Ec 4:6 than **b.** the hands full with
Ec 8:5 a wise man's heart discerneth **b.**
Ec 11:6 whether they **b.** shall be alike 8147
Isa 1:31 they shall **b.** burn together, and 8147
Isa 7:16 shall be forsaken of **b.** her 8147
Isa 8:14 to **b.** the houses of Israel, for a gin 8147
Isa 10:18 fruitful field, **b.** soul and body:
Isa 13:9 Lord cometh, cruel **b.** with
Isa 18:5 he shall **b.** cut off the sprigs
Isa 31:3 **b.** he that helpeth shall fall, and he
Isa 38:15 What shall I say? he hath **b.**
Isa 44:12 with the tongs **b.** worketh it in
Jer 5:24 that giveth rain, **b.** the former and
Jer 9:10 **b.** the fowl of the heavens and the
Jer 14:18 yea, **b.** the prophet and the priest 1571
Jer 16:6 **B.** the great and the small shall
Jer 21:6 of this city, **b.** man and beast:
Jer 23:11 For **b.** prophet and priest are 1571
Jer 26:5 sent unto you, **b.** rising up early
Jer 28:8 prophesied **b.** against many
Jer 31:13 **b.** young men and old together
Jer 32:11 purchase, **b.** that which was
Jer 32:14 of the purchase, **b.** which is
Jer 36:16 were afraid **b.** one and other, and 413
Jer 44:25 wives have **b.** spoken with your
Jer 46:12 the mighty, and they are fallen **b.** 8147
Jer 50:3 they shall depart, **b.** man and
Jer 51:12 for the Lord hath **b.** devised and 1571
Jer 51:46 a rumor shall **b.** come one year,
La 3:26 good that a man should **b.** hope
Eze 9:6 young, **b.** maids, and little
Eze 14:22 that shall be brought forth, **b.** sons
Eze 15:4 the fire devoureth **b.** the ends of 8147
Eze 21:19 **b.** twain shall come forth out of
Eze 23:13 defiled, that they took **b.** one way, 8147
Eze 23:29 **b.** thy lewdness and thy whoredoms.
Eze 34:11 I, will **b.** search my sheep, and
Eze 39:9 **b.** the shields and the bucklers,
Eze 42:11 their goings out were **b.** according
Da 8:13 to give **b.** the sanctuary and the
Da 11:27 And **b.** these kings' hearts shall 8147
Mic 5:8 he go through, **b.** treadeth down
Mic 7:3 they may do evil with **b.** hands
Na 3:3 horseman lifeth up **b.** the bright
Zep 2:14 **b.** the cormorant and the bittern 1571
Zec 6:13 of peace shall be between them **b.** 8147
Zec 12:2 siege **b.** against Judah and 1571
Mt 9:17 **new bottles, and b. are preserved** *297*
Mt 10:28 **to destroy b. soul and body in** *2532*
Mt 12:22 blind and dumb **b.** spake and *2532*
Mt 13:30 **Let b. grow together until the** *297*
Mt 15:14 **blind, b. shall fall into the ditch** *297*
Mt 22:10 **many as they found, b. bad** *5037*
Mk 6:30 him all things, **b.** what they had *5037*
Mk 7:37 he maketh **b.** the deaf to hear, *5037*
Lu 1:6 they were **b.** righteous before God, *297*
Lu 1:7 they **b.** were now well stricken in *297*
Lu 2:46 doctors, **b.** hearing them and *2532*
Lu 5:7 they came, and filled **b.** the ships, *297*
Lu 5:36 **then b. the new maketh a rent,** *2532*
Lu 5:38 **into new bottles; and b. are** *297*
Lu 6:39 **shall they not b. fall into the ditch?** *297*
Lu 7:42 **to pay, he frankly forgave them b.,** *297*
Lu 21:16 **shall be betrayed b. by parents** *2532*
Lu 22:33 thee, **b.** into prison, and to death. *2532*
Joh 2:2 And **b.** Jesus was called, and his *2532*
Joh 4:36 **that b. he that soweth and he** *2532*
Joh 7:28 **Ye b. know me, and ye know** *2532*
Joh 9:37 **Thou hast b. seen him, and it is** *2532*
Joh 11:48 take away **b.** our place and nation *2532*
Joh 11:57 Now **b.** the chief priests and the *2532*
Joh 12:28 saying, I have **b.** glorified it, and *2532*
Joh 15:24 **they b. seen and hated b. me and** *2532*
Joh 20:4 So they ran **b.** together: and the *1417*
Ac 1:1 Jesus began **b.** to do and teach, *5037*
Ac 1:8 **b. in Jerusalem, and in all Judaea,** *5037*
Ac 1:13 **b.** Peter, and James, and John, *5037*
Ac 2:29 patriarch David, that he is **b.** *2532*
Ac 2:36 have crucified, **b.** Lord and Christ. *2532*
Ac 4:27 **b.** Herod, and Pontius Pilate, *5037*
Ac 5:14 to the Lord, multitudes **b.** of men *5037*
Ac 8:12 they were baptized, **b.** men and *5037*
Ac 8:38 and they went down **b.** into the *297*
Ac 8:38 **b.** Philip and the eunuch; and he *5037*
Ac 10:39 **b.** in the land of the Jews, and in *5037*
Ac 14:1 that they went **b.** together into
Ac 14:1 **b.** of the Jews and also of the *5037*
Ac 14:5 **b.** of the Gentiles, and also of the *5037*
Ac 19:10 Lord Jesus, **b.** Jews and Greeks *5037*
Ac 20:21 **b.** to the Jews, and also to the *5037*
Ac 21:12 **b.** we, and they of that place, *5037*
Ac 22:4 delivering into prisons **b.** men and *5037*
Ac 23:8 but the Pharisees confess **b.** *297*
Ac 24:15 of the dead, **b.** of the just and *5037*
Ac 25:24 **b.** at Jerusalem, and also here, *5037*
Ac 26:16 **a witness b. of these things which** *5037*
Ac 26:22 witnessing **b.** to small and great, *5037*
Ac 26:29 hear me this day, were **b.** *2532*
Ac 28:23 **b.** out of the law of Moses, and out *5037*
Ro 1:12 by the mutual faith **b.** of you and *5037*
Ro 1:14 **b.** to the Greeks, and to the *5037*
Ro 1:14 **b.** to the wise, and to the unwise. *5037*
Ro 3:9 **b.** Jews and Gentiles, that they *5037*
Ro 11:33 the riches **b.** of the wisdom and *2532*
Ro 14:9 For to this end Christ **b.** died, *2532*
Ro 14:9 be Lord **b.** of the dead and living. *2532*
1Co 1:2 Jesus Christ our Lord **b.** theirs *5037*
1Co 1:24 **b.** Jews and Greeks, Christ the *5037*
1Co 4:5 Lord come, who **b.** will bring to *2532*
1Co 4:11 we **b.** hunger, and thirst, and are *2532*
1Co 6:13 God shall destroy **b.** it and them. *2532*
1Co 6:14 And God hath **b.** raised up the *2532*
1Co 7:29 it remaineth, that **b.** they that *2532*
1Co 7:34 that she may be holy **b.** in body *2532*
2Co 9:10 to the sower **b.** minister bread *2532*
Eph 1:10 **b.** which are in heaven, and *5037*
Eph 2:14 our peace, who hath made **b.** one, *297*
Eph 2:16 he might reconcile **b.** unto God *297*
Eph 2:18 through him we **b.** have access *297*
Php 1:7 inasmuch as **b.** in my bonds, and *5037*
Php 2:13 God which worketh in you **b.** to *2532*
Php 4:9 things which ye have **b.** learned. *2532*
Php 4:12 I know **b.** how to be abased, and *2532*
Php 4:12 **b.** to be full and to be hungry, **b.** *2532*
1Th 2:15 Who **b.** killed the Lord Jesus, and *2532*
1Th 5:15 is good, **b.** among yourselves, *2532*
2Th 3:4 you, that ye **b.** do and will do the *2532*
1Ti 4:10 For therefore we **b.** labour and *2532*
1Ti 4:16 shalt **b.** save thyself, and them *2532*
Tit 1:9 able by sound doctrine **b.** to exhort *2532*
Phm 16 thee, **b.** in the flesh, and in the *2532*
Heb 2:4 **b.** with signs and wonders, and *5037*
Heb 2:11 For **b.** he that sanctifieth and they *5037*
Heb 5:1 that he may offer **b.** gifts and *5037*
Heb 5:14 exercised to discern **b.** good and *5037*
Heb 6:19 an anchor of the soul, **b.** sure and *5037*
Heb 9:9 offered **b.** gifts and sacrifices, *5037*
Heb 9:19 sprinkled **b.** the book, and all the *5037*
Heb 9:21 he sprinkled with blood **b.** the *2532*
Heb 10:33 **b.** by reproaches and afflictions; *5037*
Heb 11:21 blessed **b.** the sons of Joseph; *1538*
Jas 3:12 so can no fountain **b.** yield salt
2Pe 3:1 in **b.** which I stir up your pure
2Pe 3:18 To him be glory **b.** now and for *2532*
2Jo 9 he hath **b.** the Father and the Son *2532*
Jude 25 dominion and power, **b.** now and *2532*
Re 13:15 image of the beast should **b.** speak, *2532*
Re 13:16 And he causeth all, **b.** small and
Re 19:5 ye that fear him, **b.** small and
Re 19:18 all men, **b.** free and bond, *5037*
Re 19:18 **b.** small and great. *2532*
Re 19:20 These **b.** were cast alive into a *1417*

BOTTLE See also BOTTLES.
Ge 21:14 took bread, and a **b.** of water, 2573
Ge 21:15 the water was spent in the **b.**, and 2573
Ge 21:19 filled the **b.** with water, and gave 2573
Jg 4:19 she opened a **b.** of milk, and gave 4997
1Sa 1:24 one ephah of flour, and a **b.** of 5035
1Sa 10:3 another carrying a **b.** of wine: 5035
1Sa 16:20 and a **b.** of wine, and a kid, and 4997
2Sa 16:1 summer fruits, and a **b.** of wine, 5035
Ps 56:8 put thou my tears into thy **b.**: 4997
Ps 119:83 am become like a **b.** in the smoke; 4997
Jer 13:12 Every **b.** shall be filled with wine: 5035
Jer 13:12 not certainly know that every **b.** 5035
Jer 19:1 get a potter's earthen **b.**, and take 1228
Jer 19:10 Then shalt thou break the **b.** in 1228
Hab 2:15 that puttest thy **b.** to him, and 2573

BOTTLES
Jos 9:4 and wine **b.**, old, and rent, and 4997
Jos 9:13 these **b.** of wine, which we filled, 4997
1Sa 25:18 two **b.** of wine, and five sheep 5035
Job 32:19 it is ready to burst like new **b.** 178
Job 38:37 or who can stay the **b.** of heaven, 5035
Jer 48:12 his vessels, and break their **b.** 5035
Ho 7:5 have made him sick with **b.** of 2573
Mt 9:17 **put new wine into old b.:** *779*
Mt 9:17 **else the b. break, and the wine** *779*
Mt 9:17 **runneth out, and the b. perish:** *779*
Mt 9:17 **put new wine into new b.** *779*
Mk 2:22 **putteth new wine into old b.:** *779*
Mk 2:22 **new wine doth burst the b.,** *779*
Mk 2:22 **spilled, and the b. will be** *779*
Mk 2:22 **wine must be put into new b.,** *779*
Lu 5:37 **putteth new wine into old b.;** *779*
Lu 5:37 **new wine will burst the b., and** *779*
Lu 5:37 **spilled, and the b. shall perish.** *779*
Lu 5:38 **wine must be put into new b.;** *779*

BOTTOM See also BOTTOMLESS; BOTTOMS.
Ex 15:5 they sank into the **b.** as a stone 4688
Ex 29:12 blood beside the **b.** of the altar. 3247
Le 4:7 blood of the bullock at the **b.** of 3247
Le 4:18 blood at the **b.** of the altar of the 3247
Le 4:25 pour out his blood at the **b.** of the 3247
Le 4:30 thereof at the **b.** of the altar. 3247
Le 4:34 thereof at the **b.** of the altar; 3247
Le 5:9 blood shall be wrung out at the **b.** 3247
Le 8:15 the blood at the **b.** of the altar. 3247
Le 9:9 poured out the blood at the **b.** of 3247
Job 36:30 and covereth the **b.** of the sea, 8328
Ca 3:10 **b.** thereof of gold, the covering 7507
Eze 43:13 even the **b.** shall be a cubit, and 2436
Eze 43:14 And from the **b.** upon the ground 2436
Eze 43:17 and the **b.** thereof shall be a cubit 2436
Da 6:24 or ever they came at the **b.** of the 773
Am 9:3 in the **b.** of the sea, thence will I 7172
Zec 1:8 myrtle trees that were in the **b.**; 4699
Mt 27:51 from the top to the **b.**; and the *2736*
Mk 15:38 in twain from the top to the **b.** *2736*

BOTTOMS
Jon 2:6 I went down to the **b.** of the 7095

BOTTOMLESS
Re 9:1 was given the key of the **b.** pit. *12*
Re 9:2 And he opened the **b.** pit; *12*
Re 9:11 the angel of the **b.** pit, whose *12*
Re 11:7 that ascendeth out of the **b.** pit *12*
Re 17:8 and shall ascend out of the **b.** pit, *12*
Re 20:1 having the key of the **b.** pit and a *12*
Re 20:3 cast him into the **b.** pit, and shut *12*

BOUGH See also BOUGHS.
Ge 49:22 Joseph is a fruitful **b.**, 1121
Ge 49:22 even a fruitful **b.** by a well; 1121
Jg 9:48 and cut down a **b.** from the trees, 7754
Jg 9:49 cut down every man his **b.**, and 7754
Isa 10:33 the Lord of hosts, shall lop the **b.** 6288
Isa 17:6 the top of the uppermost **b.**, four 534
Isa 17:9 strong cities be as a forsaken **b.**, 2793

BOUGHS
Le 23:40 the **b.** of goodly trees, branches 6529
Le 23:40 and the **b.** of thick trees, and 6057
De 24:20 thou shalt not go over the **b.** 6288
2Sa 18:9 the thick **b.** of a great oak, and 7730
Job 14:9 will bud, and bring forth **b.** like 7105
Ps 80:10 and the **b.** thereof were like the 6057
Ps 80:11 She sent out her **b.** unto the sea, 7105
Ca 7:8 I will take hold of the **b.** thereof: 5577
Isa 27:11 When the **b.** thereof are 7105
Eze 17:23 it shall bring forth **b.**, and bear 6057
Eze 31:3 his top was among the thick **b.** 5688
Eze 31:5 his **b.** were multiplied, and his 5634
Eze 31:6 heaven made their nests in his **b.**, 5589
Eze 31:8 the fir trees were not like his **b.**, 5589
Eze 31:10 up this top among the thick **b.** ,5688
Eze 31:12 his **b.** are broken by all the rivers 6288
Eze 31:14 up their top among the thick **b.**, 5688
Da 4:12 of the heaven dwelt in the **b.** 6056

BOUGHT
Ge 17:12 or **b.** with money of any stranger, 4736
Ge 17:13 and he that is **b.** with thy money, 4736
Ge 17:23 all that were **b.** with his money, 4736
Ge 17:27 **b.** with money of the stranger, 4736
Ge 33:19 And he **b.** a parcel of a field, 7069
Ge 39:1 **b.** him of the hands of the 7069
Ge 47:14 for the corn which they **b.**: 7666
Ge 47:20 And Joseph **b.** all the land of 7069
Ge 47:22 Only the land of the priests **b.** he 7069
Ge 47:23 Behold, I have **b.** you this day and 7069
Ge 49:30 which Abraham **b.** with the field 7069
Ge 50:13 which Abraham **b.** with the field 7069
Ex 12:44 man's servant that is **b.** for 4736
Le 25:28 hand of him that hath **b.** it until 7069
Le 25:30 to him that **b.** it throughout his 7069
Le 25:50 him that **b.** him from the year 7069
Le 25:51 of the money that he was **b.** for 4736
Le 27:22 field which he hath **b.**, which is 4736
Le 27:24 unto him of whom it was **b.**, even 7069
De 32:6 he thy father that hath **b.** thee? 7069
Jos 24:32 which Jacob **b.** of the sons of 7069
Ru 4:9 that I have **b.** all that was 7069
2Sa 12:3 which he had **b.** and nourished up: 7069
2Sa 24:24 So David **b.** the threshingfloor and 7069
1Ki 16:24 And he **b.** the hill Samaria of 7069
Ne 5:16 of this wall, neither **b.** we any 7069
Isa 43:24 Thou hast **b.** me no sweet cane 7069
Jer 32:9 And I **b.** the field of Hanameel my 7069
Jer 32:43 And fields shall be **b.** in this land, 7069
Ho 3:2 So I **b.** her to me for fifteen pieces 3739
Mt 13:46 **and sold all that he had, and b. it.** *59*
Mt 21:12 sold and **b.** in the temple, and *59*
Mt 27:7 **b.** with them the potter's field, to *59*
Mk 11:15 cast out them that sold and **b.** in *59*
Mk 15:46 he **b.** fine linen, and took him *59*
Mk 16:1 had **b.** sweet spices, that they *59*
Lu 14:18 **I have b. a piece of ground, and I** *59*
Lu 14:19 **I have b. five yoke of oxen, and I go** *59*
Lu 17:28 **they did eat, they drank, they b.,** *59*
Lu 19:45 that sold therein, and them that **b.**; *59*
Ac 7:16 Abraham **b.** for a sum of money of *5608*
1Co 6:20 For ye are **b.** with a price: *59*
1Co 7:23 Ye are **b.** with a price; be not ye *59*
2Pe 2:1 denying the Lord that **b.** them, and *59*

BOUND See also BOUNDS.
Ge 22:9 and **b.** Isaac his son, and laid 6123
Ge 38:28 and **b.** upon his hand a scarlet 7194
Ge 39:20 where the king's prisoners were **b.**: 631
Ge 40:3 the place where Joseph was **b.** 631
Ge 40:5 Egypt, which were **b.** in the prison. 631
Ge 42:19 let one of your brethren be **b.** in 631
Ge 42:24 Simeon, and **b.** him before their 631
Ge 44:30 seeing that his life is **b.** up in the 7194
Ge 49:26 the utmost **b.** of the everlasting 8379
Ex 12:34 their kneadingtroughs being **b.** 6887
Le 8:7 and **b.** it unto him therewith. 640
Nu 19:15 vessels, which hath no covering **b.** 6616
Nu 30:4 her bond wherein she hath **b.** her 631
Nu 30:4 wherewith she hath **b.** her soul, 631
Nu 30:5 bonds wherewith she hath **b.** her 631
Nu 30:6 out of her lips, wherewith she **b.** 631
Nu 30:7 wherewith she **b.** her soul shall 631
Nu 30:8 wherewith she **b.** her soul, of none 631
Nu 30:9 have **b.** their souls, shall stand 631
Nu 30:10 house, or **b.** her soul by a bond 631
Nu 30:11 every bond wherewith she **b.** her 631
Jos 2:21 and she **b.** the scarlet line in the 7194
Jos 9:4 wine bottles, old, and rent, and **b.** 6887
Jg 15:13 they **b.** him with two new cords, 631
Jg 16:6 wherewith thou mightest be **b.** to 631
Jg 16:8 not been dried, and she **b.** him 631
Jg 16:10 thee, wherewith thou mightest be **b.** 631
Jg 16:12 new ropes, and **b.** him therewith 631
Jg 16:13 me wherewith thou mightest be **b.** 631
Jg 16:21 and **b.** him with fetters of brass; 631
1Sa 25:29 the soul of my lord shall be **b.** in 6887
2Sa 3:34 Thy hands were not **b.**, nor thy 631
2Ki 5:23 and **b.** two talents of silver in two 6887
2Ki 17:4 of Assyria shut him up, and **b.** him 631
2Ki 25:7 and **b.** him with fetters of brass, 631
2Ch 33:11 and **b.** him with fetters, and 631
2Ch 36:6 and **b.** him in fetters, to carry him 631
Job 36:8 if they be **b.** in fetters, and be 631
Job 38:20 to the **b.** thereof, and that thou 1366
Ps 68:6 bringeth out those which are **b.** 615
Ps 104:9 Thou hast set a **b.** that they may 1366
Ps 107:10 shadow of death, being **b.** in 615
Pr 22:15 Foolishness is **b.** in the heart of a 7194
Pr 30:4 who hath **b.** the waters in a 6887
Isa 1:6 have not been closed, neither **b.** 2280
Isa 22:3 they are **b.** by the archers: 631
Isa 22:3 all that are found in thee are **b.** 631
Isa 61:1 of the prison to them that are **b.**; 631
Jer 5:22 the **b.** of the sea by a perpetual 1366
Jer 30:13 thy cause, that thou mayest be **b.** 4205
Jer 39:7 and **b.** him with chains to carry 631
Jer 40:1 being **b.** in chains among all that 631
Jer 52:11 and the king of Babylon **b.** him 631
La 1:14 yoke of my transgressions is **b.** by 8244
Eze 27:24 apparel, **b.** with cords, and made 2280
Eze 30:21 it shall not be **b.** up to be healed, 2280
Eze 34:4 neither have ye **b.** up that which 2280
Da 3:21 Then these men were **b.** in their 3729
Da 3:23 fell down **b.** into the midst of the 3729
Da 3:24 Did not we cast three men **b.** into 3729
Ho 4:19 The wind hath **b.** her up in her 6887
Ho 5:10 them that remove the **b.**; 1366
Ho 7:15 I have **b.** and strengthened their 3256
Ho 13:12 The iniquity of Ephraim is **b.** up; 6887
Na 3:10 and all her great men were **b.** in 7576
Mt 14:3 laid hold on John, and **b.** him, *1210*
Mt 16:19 **on earth shall be b. in heaven;** *1210*
Mt 18:18 **on earth shall be b. in heaven;** *1210*
Mt 27:2 when they had **b.** him, they led him *1210*
Mk 5:4 had been often **b.** with fetters and *1210*
Mk 6:17 laid hold upon John, and **b.** him in *1210*
Mk 15:1 and **b.** Jesus, and carried him *1210*
Mk 15:7 Barabbas, which lay **b.** with them *1210*
Lu 8:29 he was kept **b.** with chains and in *1196*
Lu 10:34 **And went to him, and b. up his** *2611*
Lu 13:16 **whom Satan hath b., lo, these** *1210*
Joh 11:44 **b.** hand and foot with *1210*
Joh 11:44 his face was **b.** about with a *4019*
Joh 18:12 the Jews took Jesus and **b.** him, *1210*
Joh 18:24 Now Annas had sent him **b.** unto *1210*
Ac 9:2, 21 he might bring them **b.** unto *1210*
Ac 12:6 **b.** with two chains: and the *1210*
Ac 20:22 I go **b.** in the spirit unto *1210*
Ac 21:11 **b.** his own hands and feet, and *1210*
Ac 21:13 I am ready not to be **b.** only, but *1210*
Ac 21:33 commanded him to be **b.** with *1210*
Ac 22:5 **b.** unto Jerusalem, for to be *1210*
Ac 22:25 as they **b.** him with thongs, Paul *4385*
Ac 22:29 a Roman, and because he had **b.** *1210*
Ac 23:12 and **b.** themselves under a curse, *332*
Ac 23:14 **b.** ourselves under a great curse, *332*
Ac 23:21 have **b.** themselves with an oath, *332*
Ac 24:27 the Jews a pleasure, left Paul **b.** *1210*
Ac 28:20 hope of Israel I am **b.** with this *4029*
Ro 7:2 which hath an husband is **b.** by *1210*
1Co 7:27 Art thou **b.** unto a wife? seek not *1210*
1Co 7:39 The wife is **b.** by the law as long as *1210*
2Th 1:3 We are **b.** to thank God always *3784*
2Th 2:13 we are **b.** to give thanks alway *3784*
2Ti 2:9 but the word of God is not **b.** *1210*
Heb 13:3 them that are in bonds, as **b.** *4887*
Re 9:14 Loose the four angels which are **b.** *1210*
Re 20:2 Satan, and **b.** him a thousand *1210*

BOUNDS
Ex 19:12 thou shalt set **b.** unto the people 1379
Ex 19:23 Set **b.** about the mount, and 1379
Ex 23:31 set thy **b.** from the Red sea even 1366
De 32:8 he set the **b.** of the people 1367
Job 14:5 hast appointed his **b.** that he 2706
Job 26:10 waters with **b.**, until the day 2706
Isa 10:13 removed the **b.** of the people, 1367
Ac 17:26 and the **b.** of their habitation; *3734*

BOUNTIFUL
Pr 22:9 hath a **b.** eye shall be blessed; 2896
Isa 32:5 nor the churl said to be **b.** 7771

BOUNTIFULLY
Ps 13:6 he hath deal **b.** with me. 1580
Ps 116:7 the Lord hath dealt **b.** with thee. 1580
Ps 119:17 Deal **b.** with thy servant, that I 1580
Ps 142:7 thou shalt deal **b.** with me. 1580
2Co 9:6 which soweth **b.** shall reap also **b.** *2129*

BOUNTIFULNESS
2Co 9:11 thing to all **b.**, which causeth *572*

BOUNTY
1Ki 10:13 Solomon gave her of his royal **b.** 3027
2Co 9:5 your **b.**, whereof ye had notice *2129*
2Co 9:5 might be ready, as a matter of **b.**, *2129*

BOW See also BOWED; BOWETH; BOWING; BOWMEN; BOWS; BOWSHOT.
Ge 9:13 I do set my **b.** in the cloud, and it 7198

Ge 9:14 the **b.** shall be seen in the cloud: 7198
Ge 9:16 And the **b.** shall be in the cloud; 7198
Ge 27:3 thy weapons, thy quiver and thy **b.**,.... 7198
Ge 27:29 and nations **b.** down to thee: 7812
Ge 27:29 thy mother's sons **b.** down to thee: 7812
Ge 37:10 come to **b.** down ourselves to thee..... 7812
Ge 41:43 cried before him, **B.** the knee:............ 86
Ge 48:22 with my sword and with my **b.**. 7198
Ge 49:8 children shall **b.** down before thee. 7812
Ge 49:24 his **b.** abode in strength, and the........ 7198
Ex 11:8 and **b.** down themselves unto me, ... 7812
Ex 20:5 Thou shalt not **b.** down thyself 7812
Ex 23:24 Thou halt not **b.** down to their.......... 7812
Le 26:1 in your land, to **b.** down unto it: 7812
De 5:9 Thou shalt not **b.** down thyself 7812
Jos 23:7 nor **b.** yourselves unto them: 7812
Jos 24:12 with thy sword, nor with thy **b.**. 7198
Jg 2:19 them, and to **b.** down unto them; 7812
1Sa 18:4 and to his **b.**, and to his girdle. 7198
2Sa 1:18 of Judah the use of the **b.**: 7198
2Sa 1:22 the **b.** of Jonathan turned not back,..... 7198
2Sa 22:35 a **b.** of steel is broken by mine 7198
1Ki 22:34 certain man drew a **b.** at a venture,.... 7198
2Ki 5:18 **b.** myself in the house of Rimmon: 7812
2Ki 5:18 when I **b.** down myself in the 7812
2Ki 6:22 with thy sword and with thy **b.**?......... 7198
2Ki 9:24 drew a **b.** with his full strength, ... 7198
2Ki 13:15 said unto him, Take **b.** and arrows. 7198
2Ki 13:15 he took unto him **b.** and arrows. 7198
2Ki 13:16 Put thine hand upon the **b.**. And 7198
2Ki 17:35 other gods, nor **b.** yourselves to 7812
2Ki 19:16 Lord, **b.** down thine ear and............. 5186
1Ch 5:18 to shoot with **b.**, and skillful in.......... 7198
1Ch 12:2 arrows out of a **b.**, even of Saul's....... 7198
2Ch 17:17 armed men with **b.** and shield............ 7198
2Ch 18:33 certain man drew a **b.** at a venture,.... 7198
Job 20:24 the **b.** of steel shall strike him 7198
Job 29:20 my **b.** was renewed in my hand. 7198
Job 31:10 and let others **b.** down upon her. 3766
Job 39:3 They **b.** themselves, they bring 3766
Ps 7:12 bent his **b.**, and made it ready. 7198
Ps 11:2 bend their **b.**, they make ready.......... 7198
Ps 18:34 a **b.** of steel is broken by mine 7198
Ps 22:29 go down to the dust shall **b.**.............. 3766
Ps 31:2 **B.** down thine ear to me; deliver 5186
Ps 37:14 have bent their **b.**, to cast down 7198
Ps 44:6 I will not trust in my **b.**, neither 7198
Ps 46:9 he breaketh the **b.**, and cutteth.......... 7198
Ps 58:7 bendeth his **b.** to shoot his arrows,...........
Ps 72:9 wilderness shall **b.** before him;........... 3766
Ps 76:3 the arrows of the **b.**, the shield, ... 7198
Ps 78:57 turned aside like a deceitful **b.**.......... 7198
Ps 86:1 **B.** down thine ear, O Lord, hear 5186
Ps 95:6 let us worship and **b.** down:.............. 3766
Ps 144:5 **B.** thy heavens, O Lord, and 5186
Pr 5:1 **b.** thine ear to my understanding:....... 5186
Pr 14:19 The evil **b.** before the good; and......... 7817
Pr 22:17 **B.** down thine ear, and hear the 5186
Ec 12:3 strong men shall **b.** themselves, ... 5791
Isa 10:4 Without me they shall **b.** down 3766
Isa 21:15 sword, and from the bent **b.**, ... 7198
Isa 41:2 and as driven stubble to his **b.**.......... 7198
Isa 45:23 unto me every knee shall **b.**, every 3766
Isa 46:2 stoop, they **b.** down together; 3766
Isa 49:23 **b.** down to thee with their face........... 7812
Isa 51:23 **B.** down, that we may go over: 7812
Isa 58:5 **b.** down his head as a bulrush, ... 3721
Isa 60:14 shall **b.** themselves down at the 7812
Isa 65:12 all **b.** down to the slaughter:.............. 3766
Isa 66:19 Pul, and Lud, that draw the **b.**, ... 7198
Jer 6:23 shall lay hold on **b.** and spear; 7198
Jer 9:3 bend their tongues like their **b.**........... 7198
Jer 46:9 that handle and bend the **b.**.............. 7198
Jer 49:35 I will break the **b.** of Elam, the.......... 7198
Jer 50:14 all ye that bend the **b.**, shoot at.......... 7198
Jer 50:29 all ye that bend the **b.**, camp............. 7198
Jer 50:42 shall hold the **b.** and the lance: 7198
Jer 51:3 bend his **b.**, and against him.............. 7198
La 2:4 hath bent his **b.** like an enemy:.......... 7198
La 3:12 He hath bent his **b.**, and set me as..... 7198
Eze 1:28 As the appearance of the **b.** that is..... 7198
Eze 39:3 smite thy **b.** out of thy left hand, ... 7198
Ho 1:5 I will break the **b.** of Israel 7198
Ho 1:7 not save them by **b.**, nor by sword,.... 7198
Ho 2:18 and I will break the **b.** and the........... 7198
Ho 7:16 they are like a deceitful **b.**: 7198
Am 2:15 he stand that handleth the **b.**;........... 7198
Mic 6:6 **b.** myself before the high God? 3721
Hab 3:6 the perpetual hills did **b.**: 7817
Hab 3:9 Thy **b.** was made quite naked,........... 7198
Zec 9:10 and the battle **b.** shall be cut off:........ 7198
Zec 9:13 filled the **b.** with Ephraim, and........... 7198
Zec 10:4 out of him the battle **b.** out of 7198
Ro 11:10 and **b.** down their back alway. *4781*
Ro 14:11 every knee shall **b.** to me, and *2578*
Eph 3:14 I **b.** my knees unto the Father........... *2578*
Php 2:10 of Jesus every knee should **b.**,........... *2578*
Re 6:2 he that sat on him had a **b.**;.............. *5115*

BOWED

Ge 18:2 and **b.** himself toward the ground, ... 7812
Ge 19:1 **b.** himself with his face toward 7812
Ge 23:7 and **b.** himself to the people 7812
Ge 23:12 **b.** down himself before the people 7812
Ge 24:26 the man **b.** down his head, and 6915
Ge 24:48 **b.** down my head, and worshipped...... 6915
Ge 33:3 and **b.** himself to the ground.............. 7812
Ge 33:6 children, and they **b.** themselves. 7812
Ge 33:7 came near, and **b.** themselves: 7812
Ge 33:7 and Rachel, and they **b.** themselves. ... 7812
Ge 42:6 and **b.** down themselves before 7812
Ge 43:26 and **b.** themselves to him to the.......... 7812
Ge 43:28 And they **b.** down their heads,........... 6915
Ge 47:31 Israel **b.** himself upon the bed's 7812
Ge 48:12 **b.** himself with his face to the............ 7812
Ge 49:15 and **b.** his shoulder to bear, and......... 5186
Ex 4:31 **b.** their heads and worshipped. 6915
Ex 12:27 **b.** the head and worshipped. 6915
Ex 34:8 Moses made haste, and **b.** his head 6915
Nu 22:31 he **b.** down his head, and fell flat......... 6915
Nu 25:2 eat, and **b.** down to their gods............ 7812
Jos 23:16 gods, and **b.** yourselves to them; 7812
Jg 2:12 and **b.** themselves unto them, and...... 7812
Jg 2:17 and **b.** themselves unto them:............ 7812
Jg 5:27 he **b.**, he fell, he lay down:.............. 3766
Jg 5:27 at her feet he **b.**, he fell:................... 3766
Jg 5:27 where he **b.**, there he fell................. 3766
Jg 7:6 people **b.** down upon their knees.......... 3766
Jg 16:30 he **b.** himself with all his might; 5186
Ru 2:10 and **b.** herself to the ground, and 7812
1Sa 4:19 she **b.** herself and travailed: for 3766
1Sa 20:41 and **b.** himself three times: 7812
1Sa 24:8 face to the earth, and **b.** himself. 7812
1Sa 25:23 and **b.** herself to the ground,............. 7812
1Sa 25:41 **b.** herself on her face to the earth,..... 7812
1Sa 28:14 to the ground, and **b.** himself. 7812
2Sa 9:8 And he **b.** himself, and said,.............. 7812
2Sa 14:22 **b.** himself, and thanked the king:........ 7812
2Sa 14:33 the king, and **b.** himself on his face..... 7812
2Sa 18:21 And Cushi **b.** himself unto Joab, ... 7812
2Sa 19:14 And he **b.** the heart of all the men 5186
2Sa 22:10 He **b.** the heavens also, and.............. 5186
2Sa 24:20 **b.** himself before the king on his 7812
1Ki 1:16 Bath-sheba **b.**, and did obeisance........ 6915
1Ki 1:23 he **b.** himself before the king.............. 7812
1Ki 1:31 Bath-sheba **b.** with her face to the...... 6915
1Ki 1:47 the king **b.** himself upon the bed. 7812
1Ki 1:53 and **b.** himself to king Solomon: 7812
1Ki 2:19 to meet her, and **b.** himself unto........ 7812
1Ki 19:18 which have not **b.** unto Baal, ... 3766
2Ki 2:15 and **b.** themselves to the ground 7812
2Ki 4:37 and **b.** herself to the ground,............. 7812
1Ch 21:21 **b.** himself to David with his face 7812
1Ch 29:20 and **b.** down their heads, and 6915
2Ch 7:3 the house, they **b.** themselves........... 3766
2Ch 20:18 Jehoshaphat **b.** his head with his......... 6915
2Ch 25:14 **b.** down himself before them, and....... 7812
2Ch 29:29 present with him **b.** themselves 3766
2Ch 29:30 **b.** their heads and worshipped. 6915
Ne 8:6 **b.** their heads, and worshipped 6915
Es 3:2 **b.**, and reverenced Haman: 3766
Es 3:2 Mordecai **b.** not, nor did him............... 3766
Es 3:5 Haman saw that Mordecai **b.** not,........ 3766
Ps 18:9 He **b.** the heavens also, and.............. 5186
Ps 35:14 I **b.** down heavily, as one that 7817
Ps 38:6 **b.** down greatly; I go mourning........... 7817
Ps 44:25 our soul is **b.** down to the dust:.......... 7743
Ps 57:6 my soul is **b.** down: they have........... 3721
Ps 145:14 all those that be **b.** down................ 3721
Ps 146:8 raiseth them that are **b.** down: 3721
Isa 2:11 of men shall be **b.** down, ... 7817
Isa 2:17 loftiness of man shall be **b.** down,........ 7817
Isa 21:3 I was **b.** down at hearing of it;........... 5791
Mt 27:29 and they **b.** the knee before him, ... *1120*
Lu 13:11 was **b.** together, and could in no........ *4794*
Lu 24:5 afraid, and **b.** down their faces........... *2827*
Joh 19:30 **b.** his head, and gave up the ghost..... *2827*
Ro 11:4 have not **b.** the knee to the image...... *2578*

BOWELS

Ge 15:4 of thine own **b.** shall be thine 4578
Ge 25:23 shall be separated from thy **b.**; 4578
Ge 43:30 his **b.** did yearn upon his brother:....... 7358
Nu 5:22 the curse shall go into thy **b.**,........... 4578
2Sa 7:12 which shall proceed out of thy **b.**,....... 4578
2Sa 16:11 which came forth of my **b.**, ... 4578
2Sa 20:10 and shed out his **b.** to the ground,...... 4578
1Ki 3:26 her **b.** yearned upon her son, ... 7358
2Ch 21:15 of thy **b.**, until thy **b.** fall out by......... 4578
2Ch 21:18 the Lord smote him in his **b.** with 4578
2Ch 21:19 his **b.** fell out by reason of his 4578
2Ch 32:21 they that came forth of his own **b.**....... 4578
Job 20:14 his meat in his **b.** is turned, it is 4578
Job 30:27 My **b.** boiled, and rested not: 4578
Ps 22:14 it is melted in the midst of my **b.**. 4578
Ps 71:6 took me out of my mother's **b.**: 4578
Ps 109:18 into his **b.** like water, and like 7130
Ca 5:4 and my **b.** were moved for him.......... 4578
Isa 16:11 my **b.** shall sound like an harp for....... 4578
Isa 48:19 the offspring of thy **b.** like the 4578
Isa 49:1 from the **b.** of my mother hath 4578
Isa 63:15 the sounding of my **b.** and of thy......... 4578
Jer 4:19 My **b.**, my **b.**! I am pained at my....... 4578
Jer 31:20 my **b.** are troubled for him;............... 4578
La 1:20 my **b.** are troubled; mine heart 4578
La 2:11 my **b.** are troubled, my liver is 4578
Eze 3:3 and fill thy **b.** with this roll that......... 4578
Eze 7:19 their souls, neither fill their **b.**: 4578
Ac 1:18 and all his **b.** gushed out.................. *4698*
2Co 6:12 are straightened in your own **b.**. *4698*
Php 1:8 you all in the **b.** of Jesus Christ. *4698*
Php 2:1 Spirit, if any **b.** and mercies, ... *4698*
Col 3:12 **b.** of mercies, kindness. *4698*
Phm 7 the **b.** of the saints are refreshed....... *4698*
Phm 12 receive him, that is, mine own **b.**: *4698*
Phm 20 refresh my **b.** in the Lord................. *4698*
1Jo 3:17 shutteth up his **b.** of compassion *4698*

BOWETH

Jg 7:5 every one that **b.** down upon............. 3766
Isa 2:9 And the mean man **b.** down, ... 7817
Isa 46:1 Bel **b.** down, Nebo stoopeth,.............. 3766

BOWING

Ge 24:52 worshipped the Lord, **b.**.........................
Ps 17:11 have set their eyes **b.** down............. 5186
Ps 62:3 as a **b.** wall shall ye be, and as a........ 5186
Mk 15:19 **b.** their knees worshipped him. *5087*

BOWL See also BOWLS.

Nu 7:13, 19,25,31,37,43,49,55,61,67,73,79, one silver **b.** of seventy shekels,.............. 4219
Nu 7:85 and thirty shekels, each **b.** seventy:.... 4219
Jg 6:38 of the fleece, a **b.** full of water. 5602
Ec 12:6 or the golden **b.** be broken, ... 1543
Zec 4:2 with a **b.** upon the top of it, and his..... 1543
Zec 4:3 upon the right side of the **b.**,............. 1543

BOWLS

Ex 25:29 covers thereof, and **b.** thereof, ... 4518
Ex 25:31 his branches, his **b.**, his knops,........... 1375
Ex 25:33 Three **b.** made like unto almonds, ... 1375
Ex 25:33 three **b.** made like almonds in............ 1375
Ex 25:34 four **b.** made like unto almonds, ... 1375
Ex 37:16 his spoons, and his **b.**, and his........... 4518
Ex 37:17 his branch, his **b.**, his knops,............. 1375
Ex 37:19 Three **b.** made after the fashion.......... 1375
Ex 37:19 and three **b.** made like almonds.......... 1375
Ex 37:20 in the candlestick were four **b.**............ 1375
Nu 4:7 the spoons, and the **b.**, and............... 4518
Nu 7:84 twelve silver **b.**, twelve spoons.......... 4219
1Ki 7:41 the two **b.** of the chapiters that 1543
1Ki 7:41 the two **b.**, of the chapiters which....... 1543
1Ki 7:42 cover the two **b.** of the chapiters 1543
1Ki 7:50 And the **b.**, and the snuffers, ... 5592
2Ki 12:13 house of the Lord **b.** of silver,........... 5592
2Ki 25:15 firepans, and the **b.**, and such............ 4219
1Ch 28:17 for the fleshhooks, and the **b.**,............ 4219
Jer 52:18 the snuffers, and the **b.**, and the......... 4219
Jer 52:19 the firepans, and the **b.**, and the 4219
Am 6:6 That drink wine in **b.**, and anoint........ 4219
Zec 9:15 they shall be filled like **b.**, and as 4219
Zec 14:20 shall be like **b.** before the altar. 4219

BOWMEN
Jer 4:29 of the horsemen and **b.**; 7411,7198

BOWS
1Sa 2:4 **b.** of the mighty men are broken, 7198
1Ch 12:2 They were armed with **b.**, 7198
2Ch 14:8 bare shields and drew **b.**, 7198
2Ch 26:14 helmets, and habergeons, and **b.** 7198
Ne 4:13 swords, their spears, and their **b.** 7198
Ne 4:16 spears, the shields, and the **b.**, 7198
Ps 37:15 and their **b.** shall be broken. 7198
Ps 64:3 and bend their **b.** to shoot their
Ps 78:9 being armed, and carrying **b.**, 7198
Isa 5:28 all their **b.** bent, their horses 7198
Isa 7:24 With arrows and with **b.** shall 7198
Isa 13:18 Their **b.** also shall dash the young 7198
Jer 51:56 every one of their **b.** is broken: 7198
Eze 39:9 bucklers, the **b.** and the arrows. 7198

BOWSHOT
Ge 21:16 way off, as it were a **b.**: 2909,7198

BOX
2Ki 9:1 take this **b.** of oil in thine hand, 6378
2Ki 9:3 Then take the **b.** of oil, and pour 6378
Isa 41:19 pine, and the **b.** tree together: 8391
Isa 60:13 and the **b.** together, to beautify 8391
Mt 26:7 having an alabaster **b.** of very *211*
Mk 14:3 having an alabaster **b.** of *211*
Mk 14:3 she brake the **b.**, and poured it *211*
Lu 7:37 brought an alabaster **b.** of *211*

BOX-TREE See BOX and TREE.

BOY See also BOYS.
Joe 3:3 given a **b.** for an harlot, and 3206

BOYS
Ge 25:27 And the **b.** grew: and Esau was 5288
Zec 8:5 **b.** and girls playing in the streets 3206

BOZEZ (bo'-zez)
1Sa 14:4 and the name of the one was **B.**, 949

BOZKATH (boz'-kath) See also BOSCATH.
Jos 15:39 Lachish, and **B.**, and Eglon, 1218

BOZNAI See SHETHAR-BOZNAI.

BOZRAH (boz'-rah)
Ge 36:33 the son of Zerah of **B.** reigned 1224
1Ch 1:44 Jobab the son of Zerah of **B.**, 1224
Isa 34:6 the Lord hath a sacrifice in **B.**, 1224
Isa 63:1 with dyed garments from **B.**? 1224
Jer 48:24 And upon Kerioth, and upon **B.**, 1224
Jer 49:13 that **B.** shall become a desolation, 1224
Jer 49:22 and spread his wings over **B.**: 1224
Am 1:12 shall devour the palaces of **B.** 1224
Mic 2:12 them together as the sheep of **B.** 1224

BRACELET See also BRACELETS.
2Sa 1:10 and the **b.** that was on his arm, 685

BRACELETS
Ge 24:22 two **b.** for her hands of ten 6781
Ge 24:30 **b.** upon his sister's hands, 6781
Ge 24:47 and the **b.** upon her hands. 6781
Ge 38:18 Thy signet, and thy **b.**, and thy 6616
Ge 38:25 the signet, and **b.**, and staff. 6616
Ex 35:22 brought **b.**, and earrings, and 2397
Nu 31:50 jewels of gold, chains, and **b.**, 6781
Isa 3:19 The chains, and the **b.**, and the 8285
Eze 16:11 I put **b.** upon thy hands, 6781
Eze 23:42 **b.** upon their hands, and 6781

BRAIDED See BROIDED.

BRAKE See also BRAKEST.
Ex 9:25 **b.** every tree of the field. 7665
Ex 32:3 people **b.** off the golden earrings 6561
Ex 32:19 and **b.** them beneath the mount. 7665
De 9:17 and **b.** them before your eyes. 7665
Jg 7:19 the trumpets, and **b.** the pitchers 5310
Jg 7:20 the trumpets, and **b.** the pitchers, 7665
Jg 9:53 head, and all to **b.** his skull. 7533
Jg 16:9 And he **b.** the withs, as a thread 5423
Jg 16:12 he **b.** them from off his arms 5423
1Sa 4:18 and his neck **b.**, and he died: 7665
2Sa 23:16 three mighty men **b.** through 1234
1Ki 19:11 and **b.** in pieces the rocks before 7665
2Ki 10:27 they **b.** down the image of Baal, 5422
2Ki 10:27 and **b.** down the house of Baal, 5422
2Ki 11:18 house of Baal, and **b.** it down; 5422
2Ki 11:18 his images **b.** they in pieces 7665
2Ki 14:13 **b.** down the wall of Jerusalem 6555
2Ki 18:4 and **b.** the images, and cut down 7665
2Ki 18:4 **b.** in pieces the brasen serpent 3807
2Ki 23:7 And he **b.** down the houses of 5422
2Ki 23:8 and **b.** down the high places 5422
2Ki 23:12 and **b.** them down from thence, 7323
2Ki 23:14 And he **b.** in pieces the images, 7665
2Ki 23:15 the high place he **b.** down, and 5422
2Ki 25:10 **b.** down the walls of Jerusalem 5422
1Ch 11:18 And the three **b.** through the host 1234
2Ch 14:3 and **b.** down the images, and cut 7665
2Ch 21:17 and **b.** into it, and carried away 1234
2Ch 23:17 the house of Baal, and **b.** it down, 5422
2Ch 23:17 and **b.** his altars and his images 7665
2Ch 25:23 **b.** down the wall of Jerusalem 6555
2Ch 26:6 and **b.** down the wall of Gath, 6555
2Ch 31:1 and **b.** the images in pieces, 7665
2Ch 34:4 they **b.** down the altas of Baalim 5422
2Ch 34:4 images, he **b.** in pieces, 7665
2Ch 36:19 **b.** down the wall of Jerusalem 5422
Job 29:17 I **b.** the jaws of the wicked, 7665
Job 38:8 when it **b.** forth, as if it had 1518
Job 38:10 **b.** up for it my decreed place, 7665
Ps 76:3 **b.** he the arrows of the bow, 7665
Ps 105:16 he **b.** the whole staff of bread 7665
Ps 105:33 and **b.** the trees of their coasts. 7665
Ps 106:29 inventions: and the plague **b.** in 6555
Ps 107:14 and **b.** their bands in sunder. 5423
Jer 28:10 off...Jeremiah's neck, and **b.** it. 7665
Jer 31:32 my covenant they **b.**, although 6565
Jer 39:8 **b.** down the walls of Jerusalem. 5422
Jer 52:14 **b.** down all the walls of Jerusalem 5422
Jer 52:17 the Chaldeans **b.**, and carried 7665
Eze 17:16 whose covenant he **b.**, even with 6565
Da 2:1 and his sleep **b.** from him. 1961
Da 2:34 and clay, and **b.** them to pieces. 1855
Da 2:45 that it **b.** in pieces the iron, 1855
Da 6:24 and **b.** all their bones in pieces 1855
Da 7:7 it devoured and **b.** in pieces, 1855
Da 7:19 which devoured, **b.** in pieces, 1855
Da 8:7 the ram, and **b.** his two horns: 7665
Mt 14:19 he blessed, and **b.**, and gave *2806*
Mt 15:36 and gave thanks, and **b.** them, *2806*
Mt 26:26 bread, and blessed it, and **b.** *2806*
Mk 6:41 and **b.** the loaves, and gave them *2622*
Mk 8:6 and gave thanks, and **b.**, and *2806*
Mk 8:19 **When I b. the five loaves among** *2806*
Mk 14:3 and she **b.** the box, and poured *4937*
Mk 14:22 took bread, and blessed, and **b.** *2806*
Lu 5:6 of fishes: and their net **b.** *1284*
Lu 8:29 he **b.** the bands, and was *1284*
Lu 9:16 he blessed them, and **b.**, and *2622*
Lu 22:19 and gave thanks, and **b.** it, *2806*
Lu 24:30 and blessed it, and **b.**, and gave *2806*
Joh 19:32 and **b.** the legs of the first, and of *2608*
Joh 19:33 already, they **b.** not his legs: *2608*
1Co 11:24 he **b.** it, and said, **Take, eat:** *2806*

BRAKEST
Ex 34:1 the first tables, which thou **b.** 7665
De 10:2 the first tables which thou **b.**, 7665
Ps 74:13 thou **b.** the heads of the dragons 7665
Ps 74:14 Thou **b.** the heads of leviathan 7533
Eze 29:7 they leaned upon thee, thou **b.**, 7665

BRAMBLE See also BRAMBLES.
Jg 9:14 said all the trees unto the **b.**, 329
Jg 9:15 the **b.** said unto the trees, If in 329
Jg 9:15 let fire come out of the **b.**, and 329
Lu 6:44 **of a b. bush gather they grapes.** *942*

BRAMBLES
Isa 34:13 nettles and **b.** in the fortresses 2336

BRANCH See also BRANCHES.
Ex 25:33 in one **b.**; and three bowls made 7070
Ex 25:33 like almonds in the other **b.**, 7070
Ex 37:17 his shaft, and his **b.**, his bowls, 7070
Ex 37:19 fashion of the almonds in one **b.**, 7070
Ex 37:19 made like almonds in another **b.**, 7070
Nu 13:23 cut down from thence a **b.** with 2156
Job 8:16 **b.** shooteth forth in his garden. 3127
Job 14:7 tender **b.** thereof will not cease.
Job 15:32 and his **b.** shall not be green. 3712
Job 18:16 above shall his **b.** be cut off. 7105
Job 29:19 dew lay all night upon my **b.** 7105
Ps 80:15 the **b.** that thou madest strong 1121
Pr 11:28 righteous shall flourish as a **b.** 5929
Isa 4:2 day shall the **b.** of the Lord 6780
Isa 9:14 head and tail, **b.** and rush, 3712
Isa 11:1 **B.** shall grow out of his roots: 5342
Isa 14:19 like an abominable **b.**, and as the 5342
Isa 17:9 bough, and an uppermost **b.**, 534
Isa 19:15 the head or tail, **b.** or rush, may 3712
Isa 25:5 the **b.** of the terrible ones shall 2158
Isa 60:21 the **b.** of my planting, the work of 5342
Jer 23:5 raise unto David a righteous **B.**, 6780
Jer 33:15 at that time, will I cause the **B.** of 6780
Eze 8:17 and, lo, they put the **b.** to their 2156
Eze 15:2 a **b.** which is among the trees of 2156
Eze 17:3 and took the highest **b.** of the 6788
Eze 17:22 the highest **b.** of the high cedar. 6788
Da 11:7 out of a **b.** of her roots shall 5342
Zec 3:8 bring forth my servant the **B.** 6780
Zec 6:12 the man whose name is The **B.**: 6780
Mal 4:1 leave them neither root nor **b.** 6057
Mt 24:32 When his b. is yet tender, and *2798*
Mk 13:28 When her b. is yet tender, and *2798*
Joh 15:2 Every b. in me that beareth not *2814*
Joh 15:2 and every b. that beareth fruit,
Joh 15:4 As the b. cannot bear fruit of *2814*
Joh 15:6 he is cast forth as a b., and is *2814*

BRANCHES
Ge 40:10 And in the vine were three **b.**: 8299
Ge 40:12 The three **b.** are three days: 8299
Ge 49:22 a well; whose **b.** run over the 1121
Ex 25:31 his shaft, and his **b.**, his bowls, 7070
Ex 25:32 six **b.** shall come out of the sides 7070
Ex 25:32 three **b.** of the candlestick out of 7070
Ex 25:32 and three **b.** of the candlestick 7070
Ex 25:33 so in the six **b.** that come out of 7070
Ex 25:35 a knop under two **b.** of the same, 7070
Ex 25:35 and a knop under two **b.** of the 7070
Ex 25:35 a knop under two **b.** of the same, 7070
Ex 25:35 according to the six **b.** 7070
Ex 25:36 and their **b.** shall be of the same: 7070
Ex 37:18 six **b.** going out of the sides 7070
Ex 37:18 three **b.** of the candlestick out of 7070
Ex 37:18 three **b.** of the candlestick out of 7070
Ex 37:19 so throughout the six **b.** going out 7070
Ex 37:21 a knop under two **b.** of the same, 7070
Ex 37:21 a knop under two **b.** of the same, 7070
Ex 37:21 a knop under two **b.** of the same, 7070
Ex 37:21 according to the six **b.** going out of 7070
Ex 37:22 Their knops and their **b.** were of 7070
Le 23:40 **b.** of palm trees, and the boughs 3709
Ne 8:15 and fetch olive **b.**, and pine **b.**, 5929
Ne 8:15 and myrtle **b.**, and palm **b.**, 5929
Ne 8:15 and **b.** of thick trees, 5929
Job 15:30 the flame shall dry up his **b.**, and 3127
Ps 80:11 unto the sea, and her **b.** unto the 3127
Ps 104:12 which sing among the **b.** 6073
Isa 16:8 her **b.** are stretched out, they 7976
Isa 17:6 in the outmost fruitful **b.** thereof, 5585
Isa 18:5 take away and cut down the **b.** 5189
Isa 27:10 lie down, and consume the **b.** 5585
Jer 11:16 it, and the **b.** of it are broken. 1808
Eze 17:6 whose **b.** turned toward him, and 1808
Eze 17:6 brought forth **b.**, and shot forth 905
Eze 17:7 and shot forth her **b.** toward him, 1808
Eze 17:8 that it might bring forth **b.**, and 6057
Eze 17:23 the shadow of the **b.** thereof shall 1808
Eze 19:10 fruitful and full of **b.** by reason 6058
Eze 19:11 was exalted among the thick **b.**, 5688
Eze 19:11 with the multitude of her **b.** 1808
Eze 19:14 fire is gone out of a rod of her **b.**, 905
Eze 31:3 a cedar in Lebanon with fair **b.**, 6057
Eze 31:5 his **b.** became long because of the 6288
Eze 31:6 under his **b.** did all the beasts 6288
Eze 31:7 greatness, in the length of his **b.**: 1808
Eze 31:8 chestnut trees were not like his **b.**; 6288
Eze 31:9 fair by the multitude of his **b.**: 1808
Eze 31:12 in all the valleys his **b.** are fallen, 1808
Eze 31:13 of the field shall be upon his **b.**: 6288
Eze 36:8 ye shall shoot forth your **b.**, and 6057
Da 4:14 cut off his **b.**, shake off his leaves, 6056
Da 4:14 under it, and the fowls from his **b.**: 6056
Da 4:21 and upon whose **b.** the fowls of 6056
Ho 11:6 consume his **b.**, and devour them, 905
Ho 14:6 His **b.** shall spread, and his 3127
Joe 1:7 the **b.** thereof are made white. 8299
Na 2:2 out, and marred their vine **b.** 2156
Zec 4:12 these two olive **b.** which through 7641
Mt 13:32 come and lodge in the b. thereof. *2798*

Mt 21:8 others cut down **b.** from the trees,...... *2798*
Mk 4:32 **shooteth out great b.; so that**........ *2798*
Mk 11:8 others cut down **b.** off the trees, ... *4746*
Lu 13:19 **fowls of the air lodged in the b.**..... *2798*
Joh 12:13 Took **b.** of palm trees, and went *902*
Joh 15:5 **I am the vine, ye are the b.**.......... *2814*
Ro 11:16 if the root be holy so are the **b.**......... *2798*
Ro 11:17 if some of the **b.** be broken off, ... *2798*
Ro 11:18 Boast not against the **b.**. But if.......... *2798*
Ro 11:19 The **b.** were broken off, that I........... *2798*
Ro 11:21 if God spared not the natural **b.**, ... *2798*
Ro 11:24 these, which be the natural **b.**, be...... *2798*

BRAND See also BRANDS; FIREBRAND.
Zec 3:2 is not this a **b.** plucked out of the........ 181

BRANDISH
Eze 32:10 I shall **b.** my sword before them; 5774

BRANDS See also FIREBRANDS.
Jg 15:5 when he had set the **b.** on fire, he..... 3940

BRASEN
Ex 27:4 make four **b.** rings in the four............ 5178
Ex 35:16 burnt offering with his **b.** grate, ... 5178
Ex 38:4 he made for the altar a **b.** grate......... 5178
Ex 38:10 their **b.** sockets twenty; the............... 5178
Ex 38:30 and the **b.** altar, and the **b.** grate....... 5178
Ex 39:39 **b.** altar, and his grate of brass,.......... 5178
Le 6:28 sodden in a **b.** pot, it shall be both..... 5178
Nu 16:39 the priest took the **b.** censers, ... 5178
1Ki 4:13 great cities walls and **b.** bars:............ 5178
1Ki 7:30 every base had four **b.** wheels,........... 5178
1Ki 8:64 **b.** altar that was before the Lord 5178
1Ki 14:27 made in their stead **b.** shields,........... 5178
2Ki 16:14 he brought also the **b.** altar,.............. 5178
2Ki 16:15 the **b.** altar shall be for me to............ 5178
2Ki 16:17 down the sea from off the **b.** oxen...... 5178
2Ki 18:4 brake in pieces the **b.** serpent that..... 5178
2Ki 25:13 the **b.** sea that was in the house of..... 5178
1Ch 18:8 wherewith Solomon made the **b.** 5178
2Ch 1:5 Moreover the **b.** altar, that Bezaleel... 5178
2Ch 1:6 the **b.** altar before the Lord, which..... 5178
2Ch 6:13 Solomon had made a **b.** scaffold, ... 5178
2Ch 7:7 **b.** altar which Solomon had made 5178
Jer 1:18 an iron pillar, and **b.** walls................ 5178
Jer 15:20 unto this people a fenced **b.** wall: 5178
Jer 52:17 the **b.** sea that was in the house of..... 5178
Jer 52:20 twelve **b.** bulls that were under the.... 5178
Eze 9:2 and stood beside the **b.** altar. 5178
Mk 7:4 of cups, and pots, **b.** vessels, ... *5478*

BRASS
Ge 4:22 of every artificer in **b.** and iron: 5178
Ex 25:3 of them; gold, and silver, and **b.**, ... 5178
Ex 26:11 thou shalt make fifty taches of **b.**, ... 5178
Ex 26:37 cast five sockets of **b.** for them. 5178
Ex 27:2 and thou shalt overlay it with **b.**......... 5178
Ex 27:3 thereof thou shalt make of **b.**. 5178
Ex 27:4 for it a grate of network of **b.**;............ 5178
Ex 27:6 wood, and overlay them with **b.**. 5178
Ex 27:10 their twenty sockets shall be of **b.**;...... 5178
Ex 27:11 and their twenty sockets of **b.**; 5178
Ex 27:17 of silver, and their sockets of **b.**. 5178
Ex 27:18 twined linen, and their sockets of **b.**. .. 5178
Ex 27:19 the pins of the court, shall be of **b.**..... 5178
Ex 30:18 Thou shalt also make a laver of **b.**,..... 5178
Ex 30:18 and his foot also of **b.**,..................... 5178
Ex 31:4 in gold, and in silver, and in **b.**, ... 5178
Ex 35:5 the Lord; gold, and silver, and **b.**,....... 5178
Ex 35:24 an offering of silver and **b.**................ 5178
Ex 35:32 in gold, and in silver, and in **b.**, ... 5178
Ex 36:18 he made fifty taches of **b.** to couple.... 5178
Ex 36:38 but their five sockets were of **b.**. 5178
Ex 38:2 same: and he overlaid it with **b.**. 5178
Ex 38:3 the vessels thereof made he of **b.**. 5178
Ex 38:5 the four ends of the grate of **b.**, ... 5178
Ex 38:6 wood, and overlaid them with **b.**. 5178
Ex 38:8 he made the laver of **b.**,.................... 5178
Ex 38:8 and the foot of it of **b.**,..................... 5178
Ex 38:11 and their sockets of **b.** twenty; 5178
Ex 38:17 sockets for the pillars were of **b.**;....... 5178
Ex 38:19 four, and their sockets of **b.** four;....... 5178
Ex 38:20 court round about, were of **b.**............ 5178
Ex 38:29 And the **b.** of the offering was........... 5178
Ex 39:39 brasen altar, and his grate of **b.**. 5178
Le 26:19 as iron, and your earth as **b.**: 5154
Nu 21:9 Moses made a serpent of **b.**, and....... 5178
Nu 21:9 when he beheld the serpent of **b.**,...... 5178
Nu 31:22 the gold, and the silver, the **b.**, ... 5178
De 8:9 of whose hills thou mayest dig **b.**. 5178
De 28:23 that is over thy head shall be **b.**. 5178
De 33:25 Thy shoes shall be iron and **b.**;.......... 5178
Jos 6:19 vessels of **b.** and iron, are 5178
Jos 6:24 the vessels of **b.** and of iron, they...... 5178
Jos 22:8 with gold, and with **b.**, and with......... 5178
Jg 16:21 bound him with fetters of **b.**; and 5178
1Sa 17:5 had an helmet of **b.** upon his head, ... 5178
1Sa 17:5 was five thousand shekels of **b.**.......... 5178
1Sa 17:6 had greaves of **b.** upon his legs,......... 5178
1Sa 17:6 and a target of **b.** between his............ 5178
1Sa 17:38 an helmet of **b.** upon his head;........... 5178
2Sa 8:8 David took exceeding much **b.**. 5178
2Sa 8:10 vessels of gold, and vessels of **b.**: 5178
2Sa 21:16 three hundred shekels of **b.** in........... 5178
1Ki 7:14 a man of Tyre, a worker in **b.**: 5178
1Ki 7:14 cunning to work all works in **b.**. 5178
1Ki 7:15 he cast two pillars of **b.**, of............... 5178
1Ki 7:16 two chapiters of molten **b.**, to set 5178
1Ki 7:27 he made ten bases of **b.**; four............. 5178
1Ki 7:30 brasen wheels, and plates of **b.**:......... 5178
1Ki 7:38 Then made he ten lavers of **b.**:........... 5178
1Ki 7:45 of the Lord, were of bright **b.**. 5178
1Ki 7:47 the weight of the **b.** found out, ... 5178
2Ki 25:7 bound him with fetters of **b.**, and 5178
2Ki 25:13 pillars of **b.** that were in the house..... 5178
2Ki 25:13 carried the **b.** of them to Babylon........ 5178
2Ki 25:14 all the vessels of **b.** wherewith 5178
2Ki 25:16 **b.** of all these vessels was without 5178
2Ki 25:17 and the chapiter upon it was **b.**;.......... 5178
2Ki 25:17 the chapiter round about, all of **b.**:...... 5178
1Ch 15:19 to sound with cymbals of **b.**; 5178
1Ch 18:8 brought David very much **b.**,.............. 5178
1Ch 18:8 the pillars, and the vessels of **b.**. 5178
1Ch 18:10 vessels of gold and silver and **b.**. 5178
1Ch 22:3 **b.** in abundance without weight; 5178
1Ch 22:14 and of **b.** and iron without weight; 5178
1Ch 22:16 the gold, the silver, and the **b.**, ... 5178
1Ch 29:2 the **b.** for things of **b.**, the iron for..... 5178
1Ch 29:7 of **b.** eighteen thousand talents, ... 5178
2Ch 2:7 in silver, and in **b.**, and in iron,.......... 5178
2Ch 2:14 in gold, and in silver, and in **b.**, ... 5178
2Ch 4:1 made an altar of **b.**, twenty cubits 5178
2Ch 4:9 overlaid the doors of them with **b.**...... 5178
2Ch 4:16 house of the Lord, of bright **b.**. 5178
2Ch 4:18 the weight of the **b.** could not be 5178
2Ch 12:10 king Reobohan made shields of **b.**....... 5178
2Ch 24:12 also such as wrought iron and **b.**. 5178
Job 6:12 of stones? or is my flesh of **b.**?.......... 5153
Job 28:2 **b.** is molten out of the stone. 5154
Job 40:18 bones are as strong pieces of **b.**; 5154
Job 41:27 as straw, and **b.** as rotten wood......... 5154
Ps 107:16 he hath broken the gates of **b.**,........... 5178
Isa 45:2 break in pieces the gates of **b.**,.......... 5154
Isa 48:4 is an iron sinew, and thy brow **b.**,...... 5154
Isa 60:17 For **b.** I will bring gold, and for 5178
Isa 60:17 bring silver, and for wood **b.**, ... 5178
Jer 6:28 they are **b.** and iron; they are all........ 5178
Jer 52:17 Also the pillars of **b.** that were in....... 5178
Jer 52:17 and carried all the **b.** of them to......... 5178
Jer 52:18 of **b.** wherewith they ministered,........ 5178
Jer 52:20 the **b.** of all these vessels was........... 5178
Jer 52:22 a chapiter of **b.** was upon it; and........ 5178
Jer 52:22 the chapiters round about, all of **b.**. 5178
Eze 1:7 like the colour of burnished **b.**. 5178
Eze 22:18 all they are **b.**, and tin, and iron,......... 5178
Eze 22:20 they gather silver, and **b.**, and iron,.... 5178
Eze 24:11 that the **b.** of it may be hot, and......... 5178
Eze 27:13 persons of men and vessels of **b.** 5178
Eze 40:3 was like the appearance of **b.**, ... 5178
Da 2:32 his belly and his thighs of **b.**,............. 5174
Da 2:35 the clay, the **b.**, the silver, and.......... 5174
Da 2:39 another third kingdom of **b.**,.............. 5174
Da 2:45 the iron, the **b.**, the clay, the............ 5174
Da 4:15, 23 with a band of iron and **b.**,............. 5174
Da 5:4 gods of gold, and of silver, of **b.**, ... 5174
Da 5:23 the gods of silver, and gold, of **b.**,...... 5174
Da 7:19 were of iron, and his nails of **b.**; 5174
Da 10:6 feet like in colour to polished **b.**. 5178
Mic 4:13 I will make thy hoofs **b.**: and............. 5178
Zec 6:1 mountains were mountains of **b.**. 5178
Mt 10:9 **nor silver, nor b. in your purses,**... *5475*
1Co 13:1 I am become as sounding **b.**,.............. *5475*
Re 1:15 and his feet like unto fine **b.**, as......... *5474*
Re 2:18 **and his feet are like fine b**........... *5474*
Re 9:20 idols of gold, and silver, and **b.**,......... *5470*
Re 18:12 and of **b.**, and iron, and marble, ... *5475*

BRAVERY
Isa 3:18 **b.** of their tinkling ornaments............ 8597

BRAWLER See also BRAWLERS.
1Ti 3:3 patient, not a **b.**, not covetous; *269*

BRAWLERS
Tit 3:2 evil of no man, to be no **b.**, but.......... *269*

BRAWLING
Pr 21:9 with a **b.** woman in a wide house. 4090
Pr 25:24 with a **b.** woman in a wide house. 4090

BRAY See also BRAYED.
Job 6:5 Doth the wild ass **b.** when he............ 5101
Pr 27:22 shouldest **b.** a fool in a mortar........... 3806

BRAYED
Job 30:7 Among the bushes they **b.**; 5101

BRAZEN See BRASEN.

BREACH See also BREACHES; BREAKING.
Ge 38:29 this **b.** be upon thee: therefore 6556
Le 24:20 **B.** for **b.**, eye for eye, tooth for 7667
Nu 14:34 ye shall know my **b.** of promise. 8569
Jg 21:15 made a **b.** in the tribes of Israel......... 6556
2Sa 5:20 before me, as the **b.** of waters. 6556
2Sa 6:8 Lord had made a **b.** upon Uzzah:......... 6556
2Ki 12:5 wheresoever any **b.** shall be found......... 919
1Ch 13:11 Lord had made a **b.** upon Uzzah:........ 6556
1Ch 15:13 our God made a **b.** upon us,.............. 6555
Ne 6:1 there was no **b.** left therein;............. 6556
Job 16:14 He breaketh me with **b.** upon **b.**, ... 6556
Ps 106:23 chosen stood before him in the **b.**, ... 6556
Pr 15:4 therein is a **b.** in the spirit. 7667
Isa 7:6 let us make a **b.** therein for us, ... 1234
Isa 30:13 as a **b.** ready to fall, swelling out 6556
Isa 30:26 bindeth up the **b.** of his people, ... 7667
Isa 58:12 repairer of the **b.**, the restorer........... 6556
Jer 14:17 people is broken with a great **b.**,........ 7667
La 2:13 thy **b.** is great like the sea:............... 7667
Eze 26:10 into a city wherein is made a **b.**. 1234

BREACHES
Jg 5:17 seashore, and abode in his **b.**. 4664
1Ki 11:27 repaired the **b.** of the city of............. 6556
2Ki 12:5 them repair the **b.** of the house,.......... 919
2Ki 12:6 not repaired the **b.** of the house. 919
2Ki 12:7 repair ye not the **b.** of the house?........ 919
2Ki 12:7 deliver it for the **b.** of the house.......... 919
2Ki 12:8 to repair the **b.** of the house............... 919
2Ki 12:12 stone to repair the **b.** of the house....... 919
2Ki 22:5 Lord, to repair the **b.** of the house, ... 919
Ne 4:7 the **b.** began to be stopped, then 6555
Ps 60:2 heal the **b.** thereof; for it shaketh...... 7667
Isa 22:9 **b.** of the city of David, that they......... 1233
Am 4:3 And ye shall go out at the **b.**,............ 6556
Am 6:11 smite the great house with **b.**,........... 7447
Am 9:11 and close up the **b.** thereof; 6556

BREAD See also SHEWBREAD.
Ge 3:19 sweat of thy face shalt thou eat **b.**,..... 3899
Ge 14:18 Salem brought forth **b.** and wine: 3899
Ge 18:5 I will fetch a morsel of **b.**, ... 3899
Ge 19:3 and did bake unleavened **b.**, ...
Ge 21:14 and took **b.**, and a bottle of water, ... 3899
Ge 25:34 Jacob gave Esau **b.** and pottage 3899
Ge 27:17 gave the savoury meat and the **b.**, ... 3899
Ge 28:20 and will give me **b.** to eat,................ 3899
Ge 31:54 called his brethren to eat **b.**: 3899
Ge 31:54 and they did eat **b.**,.......................... 3899
Ge 37:25 they sat down to eat **b.**: and they 3899
Ge 39:6 save the **b.** which he did eat. 3899
Ge 41:54 all the land of Egypt there was **b.**. 3899
Ge 41:55 the people cried to Pharaoh for **b.**: 3899
Ge 43:25 they heard that they should eat **b.**...... 3899
Ge 43:31 himself, and said, Set on **b.**............... 3899
Ge 43:32 the Egyptians might not eat **b.**........... 3899
Ge 45:23 laden with corn and **b.** and meat 3899
Ge 47:12 with **b.**, according to their................. 3899
Ge 47:13 And there was no **b.** in all the land;.... 3899
Ge 47:15 unto Joseph, and said, Give us **b.**:...... 3899
Ge 47:17 Joseph gave them **b.** in exchange 3899
Ge 47:17 fed them with **b.** for all their cattle..... 3899
Ge 47:19 buy us and our land for **b.**, and we..... 3899
Ge 49:20 Out of Asher his **b.** shall be fat,......... 3899
Ex 2:20 call him, that he may eat **b.**. 3899
Ex 12:8 roast with fire, and unleavened **b.**;...........

Ex 12:15 shall ye eat unleavened **b.**;
Ex 12:15 whosoever eateth leavened **b.**
Ex 12:17 observe the feast of unleavened **b.**;
Ex 12:18 ye shall eat unleavened **b.**, until
Ex 12:20 shall ye eat unleavened **b.**
Ex 13:3 shall no leavened **b.** be eaten.
Ex 13:6 thou shalt eat unleavened **b.**,
Ex 13:7 Unleavened **b.** shall be eaten
Ex 13:7 there shall no leavened **b.** be seen
Ex 16:3 when we did eat **b.** to the full; 3899
Ex 16:4 I will rain **b.** from heaven for you; 3899
Ex 16:8 and in the morning **b.** to the full; 3899
Ex 16:12 morning ye shall be filled with **b.**; 3899
Ex 16:15 the **b.** which the Lord hath given 3899
Ex 16:22 they gathered twice as much **b.**, 3899
Ex 16:29 on the sixth day the **b.** of two days; 3899
Ex 16:32 the **b.** wherewith I have fed you 3899
Ex 18:12 to eat **b.** with Moses' father in law 3899
Ex 23:15 the feast of unleavened **b.**:
Ex 23:15 thou shalt eat unleavened **b.**
Ex 23:18 of my sacrifice with leavened **b.**;
Ex 23:25 shall bless thy **b.**, and thy water; 3899
Ex 29:2 And unleavened **b.**, and cakes 3899
Ex 29:23 loaf of **b.**, and one cake of oiled **b.**, 3899
Ex 29:23 basket of the unleavened **b.** that is
Ex 29:32 the **b.** that is in the basket, by the 3899
Ex 29:34 of the **b.**, remain until the morning, 3899
Ex 34:18 The feast of unleavened **b.** shalt
Ex 34:18 thou shalt eat unleavened **b.**,
Ex 34:28 he did neither eat **b.**, nor drink 3899
Ex 40:23 he set the **b.** in order upon it 3899
Le 6:16 with unleavened **b.** shall it be
Le 7:13 leavened **b.** with the sacrifice of 3899
Le 8:2 and a basket of unleavened **b.**;
Le 8:26 the basket of unleavened **b.**, that
Le 8:26 a cake of oiled **b.**, and one wafer,
Le 8:31 the **b.** that is in the basket of 3899
Le 8:32 of the **b.** shall ye burn with fire. 3899
Le 21:6 by fire, and the **b.** of their God, 3899
Le 21:8 for he offereth the **b.** of thy God: 3899
Le 21:17 approach to offer the **b.** of his God. 3899
Le 21:21 nigh to offer the **b.** of his God. 3899
Le 21:22 He shall eat the **b.** of his God, 3899
Le 22:25 the **b.** of your God of any of these; 3899
Le 23:6 the feast of unleavened **b.** unto
Le 23:6 ye must eat unleavened **b.**
Le 23:14 ye shall eat neither **b.**, nor 3899
Le 23:18 offer with the **b.** seven lambs 3899
Le 23:20 the **b.** of the firstfruits for a wave 3899
Le 24:7 may be on the **b.** for a memorial, 3899
Le 26:5 ye shall eat your **b.** to the full, 3899
Le 26:26 the staff of your **b.**, 3899
Le 26:26 ten women shall bake your **b.** 3899
Le 26:26 and they shall deliver you your **b.** 3899
Nu 4:7 the continual **b.** shall be thereon: 3899
Nu 6:15 a basket of unleavened **b.**, cakes
Nu 6:15 wafers of unleavened **b.** anointed
Nu 6:17 the basket of unleavened **b.**:
Nu 9:11 eat it with unleavened **b.** and bitter
Nu 14:9 they are **b.** for us: their defence 3899
Nu 15:19 when ye eat of the **b.** of the land, 3899
Nu 21:5 for there is no **b.**, neither is there 3899
Nu 21:5 our soul loatheth this light **b.**. 3899
Nu 28:2 my **b.** for my sacrifices made by 3899
Nu 28:17 shall unleavened **b.** be eaten.
De 8:3 man doth not live by **b.** only, 3899
De 8:9 A land wherein thou shalt eat **b.** 3899
De 9:9 I neither did eat **b.** nor drink 3899
De 9:18 I did neither eat **b.**, nor drink 3899
De 16:3 shalt eat no leavened **b.** with it;
De 16:3 shalt thou eat unleavened **b.**
De 16:3 even the **b.** of affliction; for thou 3899
De 16:4 there shall be no leavened **b.**
De 16:8 thou shalt eat unleavened **b.**:
De 16:16 the feast of unleavened **b.**, and in
De 23:4 they met you not with **b.** and with 3899
De 29:6 Ye have not eaten **b.**, neither have 3899
Jos 9:5 all the **b.** of their provision was 3899
Jos 9:12 This our **b.** we took hot for our 3899
Jg 7:13 and, lo, a cake of barley **b.** 3899
Jg 8:5 Give, I pray you, loaves of **b.** 3899
Jg 8:6 should give **b.** unto thine army? 3899
Jg 8:15 we should give **b.** unto thy men 3899
Jg 13:16 detain me, I will not eat of thy **b.**: 3899
Jg 19:5 thine heart with a morsel of **b.**, 3899
Jg 19:19 there is **b.** and wine also for me, 3899
Ru 1:6 visited his people in giving them **b.**. 3899
Ru 2:14 eat of the **b.**, and dip thy 3899
1Sa 2:5 hired out themselves for **b.**; 3899
1Sa 2:36 and a morsel of **b.**, and shall say, 3899
1Sa 2:36 that I may eat a piece of **b.** 3899
1Sa 9:7 the **b.** is spent in our vessels, 3899
1Sa 10:3 another carrying three loaves of **b.**, 3899
1Sa 10:4 and give thee two loaves of **b.**; 3899
1Sa 16:20 an ass laden with **b.**, and a bottle 3899
1Sa 21:3 give me five loaves of **b.** in mine 3899
1Sa 21:4 no common **b.** under mine hand, 3899
1Sa 21:4 but there is hallowed **b.**: 3899
1Sa 21:5 the **b.** is in a manner common,
1Sa 21:6 the priest gave him hallowed **b.**:
1Sa 21:6 **b.** there but the shewbread, 3899
1Sa 21:6 to put hot **b.** in the day when it 3899
1Sa 22:13 in that thou hast given him **b.**, 3899
1Sa 25:11 Shall I then take my **b.**, and my 3899
1Sa 28:20 he had eaten no **b.** all the day, 3899
1Sa 28:22 let me set a morsel of **b.** before 3899
1Sa 28:24 did bake unleavened **b.** thereof:
1Sa 30:11 to David, and gave him **b.**, and he 3899
1Sa 30:12 for he had eaten no **b.**, nor drunk 3899
2Sa 3:29 on the sword, or that lacketh **b.** 3899
2Sa 3:35 if I taste **b.**, or ought else, till the 3899
2Sa 6:19 to every one a cake of **b.**, and a 3899
2Sa 9:7 thou shalt eat **b.** at my table 3899
2Sa 9:10 thy master's son shall eat **b.** always 3899
2Sa 12:17 neither did he eat **b.** with them. 3899
2Sa 12:20 they set **b.** before him, and he did 3899
2Sa 12:21 dead, thou didst rise and eat **b.**. 3899
2Sa 16:1 two hundred loaves of **b.**, and an 3899
2Sa 16:2 **b.** and summer fruit for the young 3899
1Ki 13:8 neither will I eat **b.** nor drink 3899
1Ki 13:9 Eat no **b.**, nor drink water, nor 3899
1Ki 13:15 Come home with me, and eat **b.**. 3899
1Ki 13:16 neither will I eat **b.** nor drink 3899
1Ki 13:17 Thou shalt eat no **b.**, nor drink 3899
1Ki 13:18 he may eat **b.** and drink water. 3899
1Ki 13:19 went back with him, and did eat **b.** 3899
1Ki 13:22 hast eaten **b.** and drunk water in 3899
1Ki 13:22 Eat no **b.**, and drink no water; 3899
1Ki 13:23 after he had eaten **b.**, and after he 3899
1Ki 17:6 ravens brought him **b.** and flesh 3899
1Ki 17:6 and **b.** and flesh in the evening; 3899
1Ki 17:11 me, I pray thee, a morsel of **b.** 3899
1Ki 18:4 and fed them with **b.** and water.) 3899
1Ki 18:13 and fed them with **b.** and water? 3899
1Ki 21:4 away his face, and would eat no **b.**. 3899
1Ki 21:5 so sad that thou eatest no **b.**? 3899
1Ki 21:7 arise, and eat **b.**, and let thine 3899
1Ki 22:27 feed him with **b.** of affliction and 3899
2Ki 4:8 and she constrained him to eat **b.** 3899
2Ki 4:8 he turned in thither to eat **b.** 3899
2Ki 4:42 **b.** of the firstfruits, twenty loaves 3899
2Ki 6:22 set **b.** and water before them, that 3899
2Ki 18:32 a land of **b.** and vineyards, a land 3899
2Ki 23:9 they did eat of the unleavened **b.**
2Ki 25:3 there was no **b.** for the people of 3899
2Ki 25:29 he did eat **b.** continually before 3899
1Ch 12:40 **b.** on asses, and on camels, and 3899
1Ch 16:3 to every one a loaf of **b.**, and a 3899
2Ch 8:13 in the feast of unleavened **b.**, and
2Ch 18:26 feed him with **b.** of affliction and 3899
2Ch 30:13 the feast of unleavened **b.** in the
2Ch 30:21 feast of unleavened **b.** seven days
2Ch 35:17 feast of unleavened **b.** seven days.
Ezr 6:22 feast of unleavened **b.** seven days
Ezr 10:6 he did eat no **b.**, nor drink water: 3899
Ne 5:14 brethren have not eaten the **b.** of 3899
Ne 5:15 had taken of them **b.** and wine, 3899
Ne 5:18 the **b.** of the governor, because 3899
Ne 9:15 And gavest them **b.** from heaven 3899
Ne 13:2 not the children of Israel with **b.** 3899
Job 15:23 wandereth abroad for **b.**, saying, 3899
Job 22:7 thou hast withholden **b.** from the 3899
Job 27:14 shall not be satisfied with **b.** 3899
Job 28:5 for the earth, out of it cometh **b.**: 3899
Job 33:20 his life abhorreth **b.**, and his soul 3899
Job 42:11 and did eat **b.** with him in his 3899
Ps 14:4 up my people as they eat **b.**, and 3899
Ps 37:25 forsaken, nor his seed begging **b.**. 3899
Ps 41:9 which did eat of my **b.**, hath lifted 3899
Ps 53:4 eat up my people as they eat **b.**: 3899
Ps 78:20 he give **b.** also? can he provide 3899
Ps 80:5 feedest them with the **b.** of tears; 3899
Ps 102:4 grass; so that I forget to eat my **b.**. 3899
Ps 102:9 I have eaten ashes like **b.**, and 3899
Ps 104:15 and **b.** which strengtheneth man's 3899
Ps 105:16 he brake the whole staff of **b.** 3899
Ps 105:40 and satisfied them with the **b.** of 3899
Ps 109:10 and beg: let them seek their **b.** also
Ps 127:2 to eat the **b.** of sorrows: for so 3899
Ps 132:15 I will satisfy her poor with **b.**. 3899
Pr 4:17 they eat the **b.** of wickedness, and 3899
Pr 6:26 a man is brought to a piece of **b.**: 3899
Pr 9:5 Come, eat of my **b.**, and drink of 3899
Pr 9:17 are sweet, and **b.** eaten in secret is 3899
Pr 12:9 honoureth himself, and lacketh **b.**. 3899
Pr 12:11 his land shall be satisfied with **b.**: 3899
Pr 20:13 and thou shalt be satisfied with **b.**. 3899
Pr 20:17 **B.** of deceit is sweet to a man; 3899
Pr 22:9 for he giveth of his **b.** to the poor. 3899
Pr 23:6 the **b.** of him that hath an evil eye, 3899
Pr 25:21 enemy be hungry, give him **b.** to 3899
Pr 28:19 his land shall have plenty of **b.**: 3899
Pr 28:21 For a piece of **b.** that man will 3899
Pr 31:27 and eateth not the **b.** of idleness. 3899
Ec 9:7 eat thy **b.** with joy, and drink 3899
Ec 9:11 neither yet **b.** to the wise, nor 3899
Ec 11:1 Cast thy **b.** upon the waters: for 3899
Isa 3:1 the whole stay of **b.**, and the whole 3899
Isa 3:7 house is neither **b.** nor clothing: 3899
Isa 4:1 We will eat our own **b.**, and wear 3899
Isa 21:14 they prevented with their **b.** him 3899
Isa 28:28 **B.** corn is bruised; because he 3899
Isa 30:20 the **b.** of adversity, and the water 3899
Isa 30:23 and **b.** of the increase of the earth, 3899
Isa 33:16 of rocks: **b.** shall be given him; 3899
Isa 36:17 wine, a land of **b.** and vineyards. 3899
Isa 44:15 he kindleth it and baketh **b.**; yea, 3899
Isa 44:19 I have baked **b.** upon the coals 3899
Isa 51:14 pit, nor that his **b.** should fail. 3899
Isa 55:2 money for that which is not **b.**? 3899
Isa 55:10 seed to the sower, and **b.** to the 3899
Isa 58:7 to deal thy **b.** to the hungry, and 3899
Jer 5:17 eat up thine harvest, and thy **b.**, 3899
Jer 37:21 give him daily a piece of **b.** out of 3899
Jer 37:21 the bakers' street, until all the **b.** 3899
Jer 38:9 for there is no more **b.** in the city. 3899
Jer 41:1 they did eat **b.** together in Mizpah. 3899
Jer 42:14 nor have hunger of **b.**; and there 3899
Jer 52:6 there was no **b.** for the people of 3899
Jer 52:33 did continually eat **b.** before him. 3899
La 1:11 All her people sigh, they seek **b.**; 3899
La 4:4 the young children ask **b.**, and no 3899
La 5:6 Assyrians, to be satisfied with **b.** 3899
La 5:9 We gat our **b.** with the peril of 3899
Eze 4:9 make thee **b.** thereof, according 3899
Eze 4:13 their defiled **b.** among the Gentiles, 3899
Eze 4:15 thou shalt prepare thy **b.** 3899
Eze 4:16 I will break the staff of **b.** in 3899
Eze 4:16 and they shall eat **b.** by weight, 3899
Eze 4:17 That they may want **b.** and water, 3899
Eze 5:16 and will break your staff of **b.**: 3899
Eze 12:18 of man, eat thy **b.** with quaking, 3899
Eze 12:19 shall eat their **b.** with carefulness, 3899
Eze 13:19 of barley and for pieces of **b.**, 3899
Eze 14:13 will break the staff of the **b.** 3899
Eze 16:49 fulness of **b.**, and abundance of 3899
Eze 18:7 given his **b.** to the hungry, and 3899
Eze 18:16 hath given his **b.** to the hungry, 3899
Eze 24:17 thy lips, and eat not the **b.** of men. 3899
Eze 24:22 your lips, nor eat the **b.** of men. 3899
Eze 44:3 sit in it to eat **b.** before the Lord; 3899
Eze 44:7 when ye offer my **b.**, the fat and 3899
Eze 45:21 days; unleavened **b.** shall be eaten.
Da 10:3 I ate no pleasant **b.**, neither 3899
Ho 2:5 give me my **b.** and my water, 3899
Ho 9:4 unto them as the **b.** of mourners; 3899
Ho 9:4 their **b.** for their soul shall not 3899
Am 4:6 and want of **b.** in all your places: 3899
Am 7:12 and there eat **b.**, and prophesy 3899
Am 8:11 not a famine of **b.**, nor a thirst for 3899
Ob 7 they that eat thy **b.** laid a 3899
Hag 2:12 and with his skirt do touch **b.**, 3899
Mal 1:7 Ye offer polluted **b.** upon mine 3899
Mt 4:3 that these stones be made **b.**. *740*
Mt 4:4 **Man shall not live by b. alone,** *740*
Mt 6:11 **Give us this day our daily b.** *740*
Mt 7:9 **whom if his son ask b., will he** *740*
Mt 15:2 not their hands, when they eat **b.**. *740*
Mt 15:26 **not meet to take the children's b.,** *740*
Mt 15:33 should we have so much **b.** in *740*
Mt 16:5 they had forgotten to take **b.**. *740*

Mt	16:7	It is because we have taken no **b.**	*740*
Mt	16:8	**because ye have brought no b.?**	*740*
Mt	16:11	**not to you concerning b., that**	*740*
Mt	16:12	not beware of the leaven of **b.**, but	*740*
Mt	26:17	the feast of unleavened **b.** the	
Mt	26:26	Jesus took **b.**, and blessed it, and	*740*
Mk	3:20	could not so much as eat **b.**	*740*
Mk	6:8	no scrip, no **b.**, no money in their	*740*
Mk	6:36	villages, and buy themselves **b.**:	*740*
Mk	6:37	two hundred pennyworth of **b.**,	*740*
Mk	7:2	saw some of his disciples eat **b.**	*740*
Mk	7:5	but eat **b.** with unwashen hands?	*740*
Mk	7:27	**not meet to take the children's b.**,	*740*
Mk	8:4	satisfy these men with **b.** here in	*740*
Mk	8:14	disciples had forgotten to take **b.**,	*740*
Mk	8:16	saying, It is because we have no **b.**	*740*
Mk	8:17	**reason ye, because ye have no b.?**	*740*
Mk	14:1	the passover, and of unleavened **b.**:	
Mk	14:12	the first day of unleavened **b.**,	
Mk	14:22	Jesus took **b.**, and blessed, and	*740*
Lu	4:3	this stone that it be made **b.**	*740*
Lu	4:4	**man shall not live by b. alone, but**	*740*
Lu	7:33	**neither eating b. nor drinking**	*740*
Lu	9:3	**scrip, neither b., neither money;**	*740*
Lu	11:3	**Give us day by day our daily b.**	*740*
Lu	11:11	**If a son shall ask b. of any of you**	*740*
Lu	14:1	to eat **b.** on the sabboth day, that	*740*
Lu	14:15	he that shall eat **b.** in the kingdom	*740*
Lu	15:17	**servants of my father's have b.**	*740*
Lu	22:1	Now the feast of unleavened **b.** drew	
Lu	22:7	came the day of unleavened **b.**,	
Lu	22:19	he took **b.**, and gave thanks, and	*740*
Lu	24:30	he took **b.**, and blessed it, and	*740*
Lu	24:35	known of them in breaking of **b.**	*740*
Joh	6:5	**Whence shall we buy b., that these**	*740*
Joh	6:7	Two hundred pennyworth of **b.**	*740*
Joh	6:23	place where they did eat **b.**, after	*740*
Joh	6:31	He gave them **b.** from heaven to	*740*
Joh	6:32	**Moses gave you not that b. from**	*740*
Joh	6:32	**my Father giveth you the true b.**	*740*
Joh	6:33	**For the b. of God is he which**	*740*
Joh	6:34	Lord, evermore give us this **b.**	*740*
Joh	6:35	**I am the b. of life: he that cometh**	*740*
Joh	6:41	I am the **b.** which came down from	*740*
Joh	6:48	**I am that b. of life**	*740*
Joh	6:50	**This is the b. which cometh down**	*740*
Joh	6:51	**I am the living b. which came**	*740*
Joh	6:51	**if any man eat of this b., he shall**	*740*
Joh	6:51	**the b. that I will give is my flesh,**	*740*
Joh	6:58	**This is that b. which came down**	*740*
Joh	6:58	**he that eateth of this b. shall live**	*740*
Joh	13:18	**He that eateth b. with me hath**	*740*
Joh	21:9	there, and fish laid thereon, and **b.**	*740*
Joh	21:13	Jesus then cometh, and taketh **b.**	*740*
Ac	2:42	in breaking of **b.**, and in prayers.	*740*
Ac	2:46	breaking **b.** from house to house,	*740*
Ac	12:3	were the days of unleavened **b.**.)	
Ac	20:6	after the days of unleavened **b.**,	
Ac	20:7	came together to break **b.**, Paul	*740*
Ac	20:11	had broken **b.**, and eaten, and	*740*
Ac	27:35	he took **b.**, and gave thanks to God	*740*
1Co	5:8	unleavened **b.** of sincerity and	
1Co	10:16	The **b.** which we break, it is not	*740*
1Co	10:17	we being many are one **b.**, and	*740*
1Co	10:17	are all partakers of that one **b.**,	*740*
1Co	11:23	which he was betrayed took **b.**:	*740*
1Co	11:26	as ofter as ye eat this **b.**, and drink	*740*
1Co	11:27	whosoever shall eat this **b.**, and	*740*
1Co	11:28	so let him eat of that **b.**, and drink	*740*
2Co	9:10	minister **b.** for your food, and	*740*
2Th	3:8	Neither did we eat any man's **b.**	*740*
2Th	3:12	they work, and eat their own **b.**	*740*

BREADTH See also HANDBREADTH.

Ge	6:15	the **b.** of it fifty cubits, and the	7341
Ge	13:17	the length of it and in the **b.** of it;	7341
Ex	25:10	a cubit and a half the **b.** thereof,	7341
Ex	25:17	and a cubit and a half the **b.**	7341
Ex	25:23	a cubit the **b.** thereof, and a cubit	7341
Ex	25:25	border of an hand **b.** round	2948
Ex	26:2	and the **b.** of one curtain four	7341
Ex	26:8	shall be thirty cubits, and the **b.**	7341
Ex	26:16	cubit and a half shall be the **b.** of	7341
Ex	27:12	And for the **b.** of the court on the	7341
Ex	27:13	And the **b.** of the court on the	7341
Ex	27:18	and the **b.** fifty every where, and	7341
Ex	28:16	and a span shall be the **b.** thereof.	7341
Ex	30:2	a cubit the **b.** thereof; four	7341
Ex	36:9	and the **b.** of one curtain four	7341
Ex	36:15	four cubits was the **b.** of one	7341
Ex	36:21	the **b.** of a board one cubit and a	7341
Ex	37:1	a cubit and a half the **b.** of it, and	7341
Ex	37:6	and one cubit and a half the **b.**	7341
Ex	37:10	a cubit the **b.** thereof, and a cubit	7341
Ex	37:25	the **b.** of it a cubit; it was four	7341
Ex	38:1	five cubits the **b.** thereof; it was	7341
Ex	38:18	length, and the height in the **b.**	7341
Ex	39:9	thereof, and span the **b.** thereof,	7341
De	2:5	so much as a foot **b.**;	4096
De	3:11	four cubits the **b.** of it, after the	7341
Jg	20:16	could sling stones at an hair **b.**,	
1Ki	6:2	the **b.** thereof twenty cubits, and	7341
1Ki	6:3	according to the **b.** of the house;	7341
1Ki	6:3	the **b.** thereof before the house.	7341
1Ki	6:20	in length, and twenty cubits in **b.**,	7341
1Ki	7:2	the **b.** thereof fifty cubits, and the	7341
1Ki	7:6	fifty cubits, and the **b.** thereof	7341
1Ki	7:26	And it was an hand **b.** thick,	2947
1Ki	7:27	four cubits the **b.** thereof, and	7341
2Ch	3:3	threescore cubits, and the **b.**	7341
2Ch	3:4	the **b.** of the house, twenty cubits,	7341
2Ch	3:8	was according to the **b.** of the	7341
2Ch	3:8	twenty cubits, and the **b.** thereof	7341
2Ch	4:1	twenty cubits the **b.** thereof, and	7341
Ezr	6:3	and the **b.** thereof threescore	6613
Job	37:10	and the **b.** of the waters is	7341
Job	38:18	Hast thou perceived the **b.** of the	7338
Isa	8:8	shall fill the **b.** of thy land, O	7341
Eze	40:5	by the cubit and an hand **b.**:	2948
Eze	40:5	he measured the **b.** of the	7341
Eze	40:11	the **b.** of the entry of the gate, ten	7341
Eze	40:13	the **b.** was five and twenty cubits,	7341
Eze	40:19	the **b.** from the forefront of	7341
Eze	40:20	the length thereof and the **b.**	7341
Eze	40:21,	25,36 and the **b.** five and twenty	7341
Eze	40:48	and the **b.** of the gate was three	7341
Eze	40:49	twenty cubits, and the **b.** eleven	7341
Eze	41:1	other side, which was the **b.** of the	7341
Eze	41:2	And the **b.** of the door was ten	7341
Eze	41:2	forty cubits; and the **b.**, twenty	7341
Eze	41:3	and the **b.** of the door, seven	7341
Eze	41:4	and the **b.**, twenty cubits, before	7341
Eze	41:5	and the **b.** of every side chamber,	7341
Eze	41:7	therefore the **b.** of the house was	7341
Eze	41:11	and the **b.** of the place that was	7341
Eze	41:14	Also the **b.** of the face of the house	7341
Eze	42:2	north door, and the **b.** was fifty	7341
Eze	42:4	a walk of ten cubits **b.** inward,	7341
Eze	43:13	cubit is a cubit and an hand **b.**;	2948
Eze	43:13	and the **b.** a cubit, and the border	7341
Eze	43:14	shall be two cubits. and the **b.**	7341
Eze	43:14	shall be four cubits, and the **b.**	7341
Eze	45:1	and the **b.** shall be ten thousand	7341
Eze	45:2	five hundred in **b.**, square round	7341
Eze	45:3	and the **b.** of ten thousand: and	7341
Eze	45:5	the ten thousand of **b.**, shall also	7341
Eze	48:8	and twenty thousand reeds in **b.**,	7341
Eze	48:9	length, and of ten thousand in **b.**	7341
Eze	48:10	the west ten thousand in **b.**,	7341
Eze	48:10	the east ten thousand in **b.**,	7341
Eze	48:13	and ten thousand in **b.**: all the	7341
Eze	48:13	twenty thousand, and the **b.** ten	7341
Eze	48:15	in the **b.** over against the five	7341
Da	3:1	threescore cubits, and the **b.**	6613
Hab	1:6	through the **b.** of the land, to	4800
Zec	2:2	to see what is the **b.** thereof, and	7341
Zec	5:2	twenty cubits, and the **b.** thereof	7341
Eph	3:18	what is the **b.**, and length, and	*4114*
Re	20:9	they went up on the **b.** of the	*4114*
Re	21:16	the length is as large as the **b.**:	*4114*
Re	21:16	and the **b.** and the height of it are	*4114*

BREAK See also BRAKE; BREAKEST; BREAKETH; BREAKING; BROKEN.

Ge	19:9	even Lot, came near to **b.** the	7665
Ge	27:40	that thou shalt **b.** his yoke from	6561
Ex	12:46	neither shall ye **b.** a bone	7665
Ex	13:13	then thou shalt **b.** his neck: and	6202
Ex	19:21	lest they **b.** through unto the	2040
Ex	19:22	lest the Lord **b.** forth upon them.	6555
Ex	19:24	the people **b.** through to come up	2040
Ex	19:24	lest he **b.** forth upon them.	6555
Ex	22:6	If fire **b.** out, and catch in thorns,	3318
Ex	23:24	overthrow them, and quite **b.**	7665
Ex	32:2	**B.** off the golden earrings, which	6561
Ex	32:24	hath any gold, let them **b.** it off.	6561
Ex	34:13	**b.** their images, and cut down	7665
Ex	34:20	him not, then shalt thou **b.** his	6202
Le	11:33	shall be unclean; and ye shall **b.**	7665
Le	13:12	if a leprosy **b.** out abroad in the	6524
Le	14:43	and **b.** out in the house, after that	6524
Le	14:45	And he shall **b.** down the house,	5422
Le	26:15	but that ye **b.** my covenant:	6565
Le	26:19	I will **b.** the pride of your power;	7665
Le	26:44	to **b.** my covenant with them: for	6565
Nu	9:12	of it unto the morning, nor **b.**	7665
Nu	24:8	shall **b.** their bones, and pierce	1633
Nu	30:2	he shall not **b.** his word, he shall	2490
De	7:5	**b.** down their images, and cut	7665
De	12:3	and **b.** their pillars, and burn	7665
De	31:16	and **b.** my covenant which I have	6565
De	31:20	provoke me, and **b.** my covenant.	6565
Jg	2:1	I will never **b.** my covenant with	6565
Jg	8:9	again in peace, I will **b.** down this	5422
1Sa	25:10	servants now a days that **b.** away	6555
2Sa	2:32	they came to Hebron at **b.** of day.	215
1Ki	15:19	and **b.** thy league with Baasha	6565
2Ki	3:26	that drew swords, to **b.** through	1234
2Ki	25:13	did the Chaldees **b.** in pieces, and	7665
2Ch	16:3	go, **b.** thy league with Baasha	6565
Ezr	9:14	Should we again **b.** thy	6565
Ne	4:3	he shall even **b.** down their	6565
Job	13:25	Wilt thou **b.** a leaf driven to and	6206
Job	19:2	vex my soul, and **b.** me in pieces	1792
Job	34:24	He shall **b.** in pieces mighty	7489
Job	39:15	that the wild beast may **b.** them.	1758
Ps	2:3	Let us **b.** their bands asunder,	5423
Ps	2:9	Thou shalt **b.** them with a rod of	7489
Ps	10:15	**B.** thou the arm of the wicked	7665
Ps	58:6	**B.** their teeth, O God, in their	2040
Ps	58:6	**b.** out the great teeth of the	5422
Ps	72:4	shall **b.** in pieces the oppressor.	1792
Ps	74:6	But now they **b.** down the carved	1986
Ps	89:31	If they **b.** my statutes, and keep	2490
Ps	89:34	My covenant will I not **b.**, nor	2490
Ps	94:5	They **b.** in pieces thy people,	1792
Ps	141:5	shall not **b.** my head: forget my	5106
Ec	3:3	a time to **b.** down, and a time to	6555
Ca	2:17	Until the day **b.**, and the	6315
Ca	4:6	day **b.**, and the shadows flee	6315
Isa	5:5	and **b.** down the wall thereof,	6555
Isa	14:7	and is quiet: they **b.** forth into	6476
Isa	14:25	That I will **b.** the Assyrian in my	7665
Isa	28:24	doth he open and **b.** the clods of	7702
Isa	28:28	nor **b.** it with the wheel of his	2000
Isa	30:14	And he shall **b.** it as the breaking	7665
Isa	35:6	in the wilderness shall waters **b.**	1234
Isa	38:13	as a lion, so will he **b.** all my	7665
Isa	42:3	A bruised reed shall he not **b.**,	7665
Isa	44:23	**b.** forth into singing, ye	6476
Isa	45:2	I will **b.** in pieces the gates of	7665
Isa	49:13	and **b.** forth into singing, O	6476
Isa	52:9	**B.** forth into joy, sing together,	6476
Isa	54:1	**b.** forth into singing, and cry	6476
Isa	54:3	thou shalt **b.** forth on the right	6555
Isa	55:12	mountains and the hills shall **b.**	6476
Isa	58:6	go free, and that ye **b.** every yoke:	5423
Isa	58:8	Then shall thy light **b.** forth as	1234
Jer	1:14	an evil shall **b.** forth upon all the	6605
Jer	4:3	**B.** up your fallow ground, and	5214
Jer	14:21	remember, **b.** not thy covenant	6565
Jer	15:12	Shall iron **b.** the northern iron	7489
Jer	19:10	Then shalt thou **b.** the bottle in	7665
Jer	19:11	Even so will I **b.** this people and	7665
Jer	28:4	I will **b.** the yoke of the king of	7665
Jer	28:11	Even so will I **b.** the yoke of	7665
Jer	30:8	I will **b.** his yoke from off thy	7665
Jer	31:28	to pluck up, and to **b.** down.	5422
Jer	33:20	If ye can **b.** my covenant of the	6565
Jer	43:13	He shall **b.** also the images of	7665
Jer	45:4	which I have built will I **b.** down,	2040
Jer	48:12	empty his vessels, and **b.** their	5310
Jer	49:35	I will **b.** the bow of Elam, the	7665
Jer	51:20	for with thee will I **b.** in pieces	5310
Jer	51:21	And with thee will I **b.** in pieces	5310
Jer	51:21	rider; and with thee will I **b.** in	5310
Jer	51:22	With thee also will I **b.** in pieces	5310
Jer	51:22	and with thee will I **b.** in pieces old	5310
Jer	51:22	and with thee will I **b.** in pieces	5310
Jer	51:23	I will also **b.** in pieces with thee	5310
Jer	51:23	and with thee will I **b.** in pieces	5310

Jer 51:23 And with thee will I **b.** in pieces 5310
Eze 4:16 I will **b.** the staff of bread in 7665
Eze 5:16 and will **b.** your staff of bread: 7665
Eze 13:14 So will I **b.** down the wall that ye 2040
Eze 14:13 and will **b.** the staff of the bread 7665
Eze 16:38 women that **b.** wedlock and shed 5003
Eze 16:39 shall **b.** down thy high places: 5422
Eze 17:15 or shall he **b.** the covenant, and 6565
Eze 23:34 thou shalt **b.** the sherds thereof, 1633
Eze 26:4 Tyrus, and **b.** down her towers: 2040
Eze 26:9 he shall **b.** down thy towers: 5422
Eze 26:12 and they shall **b.** down thy walls, 2040
Eze 29:7 thou didst **b.**, and rend all their 7533
Eze 30:18 when I shall **b.** there the yokes of 7665
Eze 30:22 and will **b.** his arms, the strong 7665
Eze 30:24 but I will **b.** Pharaoh's arms, and 7665
Da 2:40 all these shall it **b.** in pieces 1854
Da 2:44 it shall **b.** in pieces and consume 1854
Da 4:27 **b.** off thy sins by righteousness, 6562
Da 7:23 shall tread it down, and **b.** it in 1854
Ho 1:5 that I will **b.** the bow of Israel in 7665
Ho 2:18 I will **b.** the bow and the sword 7665
Ho 4:2 they **b.** out, and blood toucheth 6555
Ho 10:2 he shall **b.** down their altars, he 6202
Ho 10:11 shall plow, and Jacob shall **b.** his 7702
Ho 10:12 mercy; **b.** up your fallow ground: 5214
Joe 2:7 and they shall not **b.** their ranks: 5670
Am 1:5 I will **b.** also the bar of Damascus, 7665
Am 5:6 lest he **b.** out like fire in the 6743
Mic 3:3 they **b.** their bones, and chop 6476
Na 1:13 now will I **b.** his yoke from off 7665
Zec 11:10 that I might **b.** my covenant 6565
Zec 11:14 that I might **b.** the brotherhood 6565
Mt 5:19 **shall b. one of these least** *3089*
Mt 6:19 **where thieves b. through and** *1358*
Mt 6:20 **where thieves do not b. through** *1358*
Mt 9:17 **else the bottles b., and the wine** *4486*
Mt 12:20 A bruised reed shall he not **b.**, *2608*
Ac 20:7 came together to **b.** bread, Paul *2806*
Ac 20:11 a long while, even to **b.** of day, *827*
Ac 21:13 What mean ye to weep and to **b.** *4919*
1Co 10:16 The bread which we **b.**, is it not *2806*
Ga 4:27 **b.** forth and cry, thou that *4486*

BREAKER See also COVENANTBREAKER; TRUCEBREAKERS.
Mic 2:13 The **b.** is come up before them: 6555
Ro 2:25 but if thou be a **b.** of the law, *3848*

BREAKEST
Ps 48:7 Thou **b.** the ships of Tarshish 7665

BREAKETH
Ge 32:26 he said, Let me go, for the day **b.** 5927
Job 9:17 he **b.** me with a tempest, and 7779
Job 12:14 Behold, he **b.** and it 2040
Job 16:14 He **b.** me with breach upon 6555
Job 28:4 The flood **b.** out from the 6555
Ps 29:5 The voice of the Lord **b.** the 7665
Ps 29:5 yea, the Lord **b.** the cedars 7665
Ps 46:9 he **b.** the bow, and cutteth the 7665
Ps 119:20 My soul **b.** for the longing that it 1638
Pr 25:15 and a soft tongue **b.** the bone 7665
Ec 10:8 whoso **b.** an hedge, a serpent 6555
Isa 59:5 is crushed **b.** out into a viper 1234
Jer 19:11 as one **b.** a potter's vessel, that 7665
Jer 23:29 like a hammer that **b.** the rock in 6327
La 4:4 ask bread, and no man **b.** it unto 6566
Da 2:40 forasmuch as iron **b.** in pieces 1855
Da 2:40 as iron that **b.** all these, shall it 7940

BREAKING See also BREACH; BREAKINGS.
Ge 32:24 a man with him until the **b.** of 5927
Ex 9:9 a boil **b.** forth with blains upon 6524
Ex 9:10 it became a boil **b.** forth with 6524
Ex 22:2 If a thief be found **b.** up, and be 4290
1Ch 14:11 like the **b.** forth of waters: 6556
Job 30:14 me as a wide **b.** in of waters: 6556
Ps 144:14 that thee be no **b.** in, nor going 6556
Isa 22:5 **b.** down the walls, and of crying 6979
Isa 30:13 whose **b.** cometh suddenly at an 7667
Isa 30:14 as the **b.** of the potters' vessel 7667
Eze 16:59 despised the oath in **b.** the 6565
Eze 17:18 by **b.** the covenant, when, lo, he 6565
Eze 21:6 with the **b.** of thy loins; and 7670
Ho 13:13 in the place of the **b.** forth of 4866
Lu 24:35 known of them in **b.** of bread. *2800*
Ac 2:42 in **b.** of bread, and in prayers. *2800*
Ac 2:46 and **b.** bread from house to house, *2806*
Ro 2:23 **b.** the law dishonourest thou *3847*

BREAKINGS
Job 41:25 by reason of **b.** they purify 7667

BREAST See also BREASTPLATE; BREASTS.
Ex 29:26 thou shalt take the **b.** of the 2373
Ex 29:27 sanctify the **b.** of the wave 2373
Le 7:30 the fat with the **b.**, it shall he 2373
Le 7:30 that the **b.** may be waved 2373
Le 7:31 but the **b.** shall be Aaron's and his 2373
Le 7:34 the wave **b.** and the heave 2373
Le 8:29 Moses took the **b.**, and waved it 2373
Le 10:14 the wave **b.** and heave shoulder 2373
Le 10:15 heave shoulder and the wave **b.** 2373
Nu 6:20 priest, with the wave **b.** and heave 2373
Nu 18:18 as the wave **b.** and as the right 2373
Job 24:9 pluck the fatherless from the **b.**, 7699
Isa 60:16 shalt suck the **b.** of kings; and 7699
La 4:3 the sea monsters draw out the **b.**, 7699
Da 2:32 his **b.** and his arms of silver, his 2306
Lu 18:13 **but smote upon his b., saying,** *4738*
Joh 13:25 He then lying on Jesus' **b.** saith *4738*
Joh 21:20 which also leaned on his **b.** at *4738*

BREASTPLATE See also BREASTPLATES.
Ex 25:7 be set in the ephod, and in the **b.** 2833
Ex 28:4 they shall make; a **b.**, and an 2833
Ex 28:15 shalt make the **b.** of judgment 2833
Ex 28:22 make upon the **b.** chains at the 2833
Ex 28:23 make upon the **b.** two rings of 2833
Ex 28:23 two rings on the two ends of the **b.** 2833
Ex 28:24 which are on the ends of the **b.** 2833
Ex 28:26 two ends of the **b.** in the border 2833
Ex 28:28 they shall bind the **b.** by the rings 2833
Ex 28:28 that the **b.** be not loosed from the 2833
Ex 28:29 the children of Israel in the **b.** of 2833
Ex 28:30 put in the **b.** of judgment the 2833
Ex 29:5 the ephod, and the **b.**, and gird 2833
Ex 35:9 set for the ephod, and for the **b.** 2833
Ex 35:27 set, for the ephod, and for the **b.**; 2833
Ex 39:8 he made the **b.** of cunning work, 2833
Ex 39:9 they made the **b.** double: 2833
Ex 39:15 upon the **b.** chains at the ends, 2833
Ex 39:16 rings in the two ends of the **b.** 2833
Ex 39:17 two rings on the ends of the **b.** 2833
Ex 39:19 put them on the two ends of the **b.**, 2833
Ex 39:21 bind the **b.** by his rings unto the 2833
Ex 39:21 that the **b.** might not be loosed 2833
Le 8:8 he put the **b.** upon him: 2833
Le 8:8 also he put in the **b.** the Urim 2833
Isa 59:17 put on righteousness as a **b.**, 8302
Eph 6:14 having on the **b.** of righteousness; *2382*
1Th 5:8 putting on the **b.** of faith and love; *2382*

BREASTPLATES
Re 9:9 **b.**, as it were **b.** of iron; *2382*
Re 9:17 **b.** of fire, and of jacinth, and *2382*

BREASTS
Ge 49:25 blessings of the **b.**, and of the 7699
Le 9:20 they put the fat upon the **b.**, and 2373
Le 9:21 the **b.** and the right shoulder 2373
Job 3:12 or why the **b.** that I should suck? 7699
Job 21:24 His **b.** are full of milk, and his 5845
Ps 22:9 when I was upon my mother's **b.** 7699
Pr 5:19 let her **b.** satisfy thee at all times; 1717
Ca 1:13 shall lie all night betwixt my **b.** 7699
Ca 4:5 Thy two **b.** are like two young roes 7699
Ca 7:3 thy two **b.** are like two young roes 7699
Ca 7:7 and thy **b.** to clusters of grapes. 7699
Ca 7:8 thy **b.** shall be as clusters of the 7699
Ca 8:1 that sucked the **b.** of my mother! 7699
Ca 8:8 little sister, and she hath no **b.**: 7699
Ca 8:10 and my **b.** like towers: then was 7699
Isa 28:9 the milk, and drawn from the **b.** 7699
Isa 66:11 satisfied with the **b.** of her 7699
Eze 16:7 thy **b.** are fashioned, and thine 7699
Eze 23:3 there were their **b.** pressed, and 7699
Eze 23:8 bruised the **b.** of her virginity, 1717
Eze 23:34 and pluck off thine own **b.**: 7699
Ho 2:2 adulteries from between her **b.**; 7699
Ho 9:14 miscarrying womb and dry **b.** 7699
Joe 2:16 and those that suck the **b.**: 7699
Na 2:7 of doves, tabering upon their **b.** 3824
Lu 23:48 smote their **b.**, and returned. *4738*
Re 15:6 their **b.** girded with golden girdles. *4738*

BREATH
Ge 2:7 into his nostrils the **b.** of life; 5397
Ge 6:17 wherein is the **b.** of life, from 7307
Ge 7:15 flesh, wherein is the **b.** of life 7307
Ge 7:22 in whose nostrils was the **b.** of life, 5397
2Sa 22:16 at the blast of the **b.** of his nostrils 7307
1Ki 17:17 that there was no **b.** left in him. 5397
Job 4:9 and by the **b.** of his nostrils are 7307
Job 9:18 will not suffer me to take my **b.** 7307
Job 12:10 and the **b.** of all mankind. 7307
Job 15:30 by the **b.** of his mouth shall he go 7307
Job 17:1 My **b.** is corrupt, my days are 7307
Job 19:17 My **b.** is strange to my wife, 7307
Job 27:3 while my **b.** is in me, and the 5397
Job 33:4 and the **b.** of the Almighty hath 5397
Job 34:14 unto himself his spirit and his **b.**; 5397
Job 37:10 By the **b.** of God frost is given: 5397
Job 41:21 His **b.** kindleth coals, and a flame 5315
Ps 18:15 the blast of the **b.** of thy nostrils 7307
Ps 33:6 the host of them by the **b.** of his 7307
Ps 104:29 thou takest away their **b.**, they 7307
Ps 135:17 neither is there any **b.** in their 7307
Ps 146:4 His **b.** goeth forth, he returneth 7307
Ps 150:6 every thing that hath **b.** praise 5397
Ec 3:19 yea, they have all one **b.**; so that 7307
Isa 2:22 from man, whose **b.** is in his 5397
Isa 11:4 and with the **b.** of his lips shall 7307
Isa 30:28 And his **b.**, as an overflowing 7307
Isa 30:33 the **b.** of the Lord, like a stream 5397
Isa 33:11 your **b.**, as fire, shall devour you. 7307
Isa 42:5 he that giveth **b.** unto the people 5397
Jer 10:14 falsehood, and there is no **b.** in 7307
Jer 51:17 falsehood, and there is no **b.** in 7307
La 4:20 **b.** of our nostrils, the anointed 7307
Eze 37:5 I will cause **b.** to enter into you, 7307
Eze 37:6 and put **b.** in you, and ye shall 7307
Eze 37:8 but there was no **b.** in them. 7307
Eze 37:9 the four winds, O **b.**, and breathe 7307
Eze 37:10 the **b.** came into them, and they 7307
Da 5:23 God in whose hand thy **b.** is, and 5396
Da 10:17 me, neither is there **b.** left in me. 5397
Hab 2:19 there is no **b.** at all in the midst 7307
Ac 17:25 he giveth to all life, and **b.**, and *4157*

BREATHE See also BREATHED; BREATHEST; BREATHING.
Jos 11:11 there was not any left to **b.**: and 5397
Jos 11:14 them, neither left they any to **b.** 5397
Ps 27:12 me, and such as **b.** out cruelty, 3307
Eze 37:9 and **b.** upon these slain, that 5301

BREATHED
Ge 2:7 and **b.** into his nostrils the breath 5301
Jos 10:40 utterly destroyed all that **b.**, as 5397
1Ki 15:29 left not to Jeroboam any that **b.**, 5397
Joh 20:22 said this, he **b.** on them, and said *1720*

BREATHETH
De 20:16 shalt save alive nothing that **b.**: 5397

BREATHING
La 3:56 hide not thine ear at my **b.**, at 7309
Ac 9:1 Saul, yet **b.** out threatenings and *1709*

BRED
Ex 16:20 morning, and it **b.** worms, and 7311

BREECHES
Ex 28:42 thou shalt make them linen **b.** to 4370
Ex 39:28 and linen **b.** of fine twined linen, 4370
Le 6:10 and his linen **b.** shall he put upon 4370
Le 16:4 and he shall have the linen **b.** upon 4370
Eze 44:18 and shall have linen **b.** upon their 4370

BREED See also BRED; BREEDING.
Ge 8:17 that they may **b.** abundantly in 8317
De 32:14 rams of the **b.** of Bashan, and 1121

BREEDING
Zep 2:9 the **b.** of nettles, and salt pits, 4476

BRETHREN See also BRETHREN'S; BROTHERS'.
Ge 9:22 his father, and told his two **b.** 251
Ge 9:25 of servants shall he be unto his **b.** 251
Ge 13:8 and thy herdmen; for we be **b.** 251
Ge 16:12 dwell in the presence of his **b.** 251
Ge 19:7 pray you, **b.**, do not so wickedly. 251
Ge 24:27 to the house of my master's **b.** 251
Ge 25:18 died in the presence of all his **b.** 251
Ge 27:29 be lord over thy **b.**, and let thy 251
Ge 27:37 all his **b.** have I given to him for 251
Ge 29:4 unto them, My **b.**, whence be ye? 251
Ge 31:23 he took his **b.** with him, and 251
Ge 31:25 Laban with his **b.** pitched in the 251
Ge 31:32 before our **b.** discern thou what 251

Book	Ref	Context	No.
Ge	31:37	it here before my **b.** and thy **b.**,	251
Ge	31:46	Jacob said unto his **b.**, Gather	251
Ge	31:54	called his **b.** to eat bread: and they	251
Ge	34:11	unto her father and unto her **b.**,	251
Ge	34:25	Simeon and Levi, Dinah's **b.**, took	251
Ge	37:2	feeding the flock with his **b.**; and	251
Ge	37:4	his **b.** saw that their father loved	251
Ge	37:4	him more than all his **b.**,	251
Ge	37:5	a dream, and he told it his **b.**:	251
Ge	37:8	his **b.** said to him, Shalt thou	251
Ge	37:9	another dream, and told it his **b.**,:	251
Ge	37:10	told it to his father, and to his **b.**:	251
Ge	37:10	Shall I and thy mother and thy **b.**	251
Ge	37:11	his **b.** envied him; but his father	251
Ge	37:12	his **b.** went to feed their father's	251
Ge	37:13	Do not thy **b.** feed the flock in	251
Ge	37:14	whether it be well with thy **b.**,	251
Ge	37:16	he said, I seek my **b.**: tell me, I pray	251
Ge	37:17	Joseph went after his **b.**, and found	251
Ge	37:23	when Joseph was come unto his **b.**,	251
Ge	37:26	Judah said unto his **b.**, What profit	251
Ge	37:27	our flesh: and his **b.** were content	251
Ge	37:30	he returned unto his **b.**, and said,	251
Ge	38:1	Judah went down from his **b.**, and	251
Ge	38:11	peradventure he die also, as his **b.**	251
Ge	42:3	Joseph's ten **b.** went down to buy	251
Ge	42:4	not with his **b.**; for he said, Lest	251
Ge	42:6	Joseph's **b.** came, and bowed	251
Ge	42:7	Joseph saw his **b.**, and he knew	251
Ge	42:8	Joseph knew his **b.**, but they knew	251
Ge	42:13	Thy servants are twelve **b.**, the	251
Ge	42:19	let one of your **b.** be bound in the	251
Ge	42:28	he said unto his **b.**, My money is	251
Ge	42:32	We be twelve **b.**, sons of our father;	251
Ge	42:33	leave one of your **b.** here with me,	251
Ge	44:14	Judah and his **b.** came to Joseph's	251
Ge	44:33	and let the lad go up with his **b.**.	251
Ge	45:1	made himself known unto his **b.**	251
Ge	45:3	Joseph said unto his **b.**, I am	251
Ge	45:3	And his **b.** could not answer him;	251
Ge	45:4	Joseph said unto his **b.**, Come	251
Ge	45:15	Moreover he kissed all his **b.**, and	251
Ge	45:15	after that his **b.** talked with him.	251
Ge	45:16	Joseph's **b.** are come: and it	251
Ge	45:17	Say unto thy **b.**, This do ye; lade	251
Ge	45:24	So he sent his **b.** away, and they	251
Ge	46:31	Joseph said unto his **b.**, and unto	251
Ge	46:31	My **b.**, and my father's house,	251
Ge	47:1	My father and my **b.**, and their	251
Ge	47:2	he took some of his **b.**, even five	251
Ge	47:3	Pharaoh said unto his **b.**, What is	251
Ge	47:5	saying, Thy father and thy **b.** are	251
Ge	47:6	make thy father and **b.** to dwell;	251
Ge	47:11	placed his father and his **b.**, and	251
Ge	47:12	nourished his father, and his **b.**,	251
Ge	48:6	the name of their **b.** in their	251
Ge	48:22	to thee one portion above thy **b.**,	251
Ge	49:5	Simeon and Levi are **b.**:	251
Ge	49:8	art he whom thy **b.** shall praise:	251
Ge	49:26	him that was separate from his **b.**.	251
Ge	50:8	the house of Joseph, and his **b.**,	251
Ge	50:14	returned into Egypt, he, and his **b.**,	251
Ge	50:15	when Joseph's **b.** saw that their	251
Ge	50:17	trespass of thy **b.**, and their sin	251
Ge	50:18	his **b.** also went and fell down	251
Ge	50:24	And Joseph said unto his **b.**,	251
Ex	1:6	And Joseph died, and all his **b.**,	251
Ex	2:11	that he went out unto his **b.**,	251
Ex	2:11	smiting an Hebrew, one of his **b.**.	251
Ex	4:18	unto my **b.** which are in Egypt,	251
Le	10:4	carry your **b.** from before the	251
Le	10:6	but let your **b.**, the whole house of	251
Le	21:10	the high priest among his **b.**,	251
Le	25:46	over your **b.** the children of Israel,	251
Le	25:48	one of his **b.** may redeem him:	251
Nu	8:26	with their **b.** in the tabernacle	251
Nu	16:10	thy **b.** the sons of Levi with thee:	251
Nu	18:2	thy **b.** also of the tribe of Levi,	251
Nu	18:6	I have taken your **b.** the Levites	251
Nu	20:3	when our **b.** died before the Lord!	251
Nu	25:6	brought unto his **b.** a Midianitish	251
Nu	27:4	possession among the **b.** of our	251
Nu	27:7	among their father's **b.**, and thou	251
Nu	27:9	give his inheritance unto his **b.**.	251
Nu	27:10	if he have no **b.**, then ye shall give	251
Nu	27:10	his inheritance unto his father's **b.**,	251
Nu	27:11	if his father have no **b.**, then ye	251
Nu	32:6	Shall your **b.** go to war, and shall	251
De	1:16	Hear the causes between your **b.**,	251
De	1:28	our **b.** have discouraged our heart,	251
De	2:4	pass through the coast of your **b.**	251
De	2:8	when we passed by from our **b.**	251
De	3:18	pass over armed before your **b.**	251
De	3:20	Lord have given rest unto your **b.**,	251
De	10:9	no part nor inheritance with his **b.**;	251
De	15:7	a poor man of one of thy **b.** within	251
De	17:15	from among thy **b.** shalt thou set	251
De	17:20	heart be not lifted up above his **b.**,	251
De	18:2	no inheritance among their **b.**:	251
De	18:7	as all his **b.** the Levites do, which	251
De	18:15	from the midst of thee, of thy **b.**,	251
De	18:18	a Prophet from among their **b.**,	251
De	24:7	any of his **b.** of the children of	251
De	24:14	whether he be of thy **b.**, or of	251
De	25:5	If **b.** dwell together, and one of	251
De	33:9	neither did he acknowledge his **b.**,	251
De	33:16	him that was separated from his **b.**.	251
De	33:24	let him be acceptable to his **b.**,	251
Jos	1:14	ye shall pass before your **b.** armed,	251
Jos	1:15	Until the Lord have given your **b.**	251
Jos	2:13	father, and my mother, and my **b.**,	251
Jos	2:18	and thy **b.**, and all thy father's	251
Jos	6:23	father, and her mother, and her **b.**,	251
Jos	14:8	Nevertheless my **b.** that went up	251
Jos	17:4	us an inheritance among our **b.**	251
Jos	17:4	among the **b.** of their father	251
Jos	22:3	Ye have not left your **b.** these many	251
Jos	22:4	God hath given rest unto your **b.**,	251
Jos	22:7	gave Joshua among their **b.** on	251
Jos	22:8	spoil of your enemies with your **b.**,	251
Jg	8:19	They were my **b.**, even the sons of	251
Jg	9:1	to Shechem unto his mother's **b.**,	251
Jg	9:3	his mother's **b.** spake of him in	251
Jg	9:5	slew his **b.** the sons of Jerubbaal,	251
Jg	9:24	aided him in the killing of his **b.**.	251
Jg	9:26	son of Ebed came with his **b.**,	251
Jg	9:31	and his **b.** be come to Shechem;	251
Jg	9:41	Zebul thrust out Gaal and his **b.**,	251
Jg	9:56	his father, in slaying his seventy **b.**:	251
Jg	11:3	Jepthah fled from his **b.**, and dwelt	251
Jg	14:3	among the daughters of thy **b.**,	251
Jg	16:31	Then his **b.** and all the house	251
Jg	18:8	they came unto their **b.** to Zorah	251
Jg	18:8	and their **b.** said unto them,	251
Jg	18:14	said unto their **b.**, Do ye know	251
Jg	19:23	said unto them, Nay, my **b.**, nay,	251
Jg	20:13	hearken to the voice of their **b.**	251
Jg	21:22	their **b.** come unto us to complain,	251
Ru	4:10	not cut off from among his **b.**,	251
1Sa	16:13	anointed him in the midst of his **b.**:	251
1Sa	17:17	Take now for thy **b.** an ephah of	251
1Sa	17:17	and run to the camp to thy **b.**;	251
1Sa	17:18	look how thy **b.** fare, and take their	251
1Sa	17:22	and came and saluted his **b.**.	251
1Sa	20:29	I pray thee, and see my **b.**,	251
1Sa	22:1	his **b.** and all his father's house	251
1Sa	30:23	Ye shall not do so, my **b.**, with that	251
2Sa	2:26	return from following their **b.**?	251
2Sa	3:8	to his **b.**, and to his friends,	251
2Sa	15:20	take back thy **b.**: mercy and truth	251
2Sa	19:12	Ye are my **b.**, ye are my bones	251
2Sa	19:41	Why have our **b.** the men of Judah	251
1Ki	1:9	called all his **b.** the king's sons,	251
1Ki	12:24	nor fight against your **b.** the	251
2Ki	9:2	him arise up from among his **b.**,	251
2Ki	10:13	Jehu met with the **b.** of Ahaziah	251
2Ki	10:13	We are the **b.** of Ahaziah; and we	251
2Ki	23:9	unleavened bread among their **b.**.	251
1Ch	4:9	was more honourable than his **b.**:	251
1Ch	4:27	but his **b.** had not many children,	251
1Ch	5:2	Judah prevailed above his **b.**,	251
1Ch	5:7	And his **b.** by their families,	251
1Ch	5:13	And their **b.** of the house of their	251
1Ch	6:44	And their **b.** the sons of Merari	251
1Ch	6:48	Their **b.** also the Levites were	251
1Ch	7:5	And their **b.** among all the families	251
1Ch	7:22	and his **b.** came to comfort him.	251
1Ch	8:32	dwelt with their **b.** in Jerusalem,	251
1Ch	9:6	sons of Zerah; Jeuel, and their **b.**,	251
1Ch	9:9	And their **b.**, according to their	251
1Ch	9:13	And their **b.**, heads of the house of	251
1Ch	9:17	Talmon, and Ahiman, and their **b.**:	251
1Ch	9:19	the son of Korah, and his **b.**,	251
1Ch	9:25	And their **b.**, which were in their	251
1Ch	9:32	other of their **b.**, of the sons of the	251
1Ch	9:38	And they also dwelt with their **b.** at	251
1Ch	9:38	Jerusalem, over against their **b.**.	251
1Ch	12:2	even of Saul's **b.** of Benjamin.	251
1Ch	12:32	**b.** were at their commandment.	251
1Ch	12:39	for their **b.** had prepared for them.	251
1Ch	13:2	let us send abroad unto our **b.**	251
1Ch	15:5	and his **b.** an hundred and twenty:	251
1Ch	15:6	and his **b.** two hundred and twenty:	251
1Ch	15:7	and his **b.** an hundred and thirty:	251
1Ch	15:8	the chief, and his **b.** two hundred:	251
1Ch	15:9	the chief, and his **b.** fourscore:	251
1Ch	15:10	and his **b.** an hundred and twelve	251
1Ch	15:12	both ye and your **b.**, that ye may	251
1Ch	15:16	appoint their **b.** to be the singers	251
1Ch	15:17	the son of Joel, and of his **b.**,	251
1Ch	15:17	of the sons of Merari their **b.**,	251
1Ch	15:18	with them their **b.** of the second	251
1Ch	16:7	into the hand of Asaph and his **b.**	251
1Ch	16:37	Asaph and his **b.**, to minister before	251
1Ch	16:38	Obed-edom with their **b.**,	251
1Ch	16:39	Zadok the priest, and his **b.**	251
1Ch	23:22	and their **b.** the sons of Kish	251
1Ch	23:32	charge of the sons of Aaron their **b.**,	251
1Ch	24:31	cast lots over against their **b.** the	251
1Ch	24:31	over against their younger **b.**.	251
1Ch	25:7	their **b.** that were instructed in	251
1Ch	25:9	with his **b.** and sons were twelve:	251
1Ch	25:10,	11,12,13,14,15,16,17,18,19,20,21,22,23, 24,25,26,27,28,29,30,31, his sons, and his **b.**, were twelve:	251
1Ch	26:7	whose **b.** were strong men, Elihu,	251
1Ch	26:8	they and their sons, and their **b.**,	251
1Ch	26:9	Meshelemiah had sons and **b.**,	251
1Ch	26:11	all the sons and **b.** of Hosah were	251
1Ch	26:25	And his **b.** by Eliezer; Rehabiah	251
1Ch	26:26	Shelomith and his **b.** were over	251
1Ch	26:28	the hand of Shelomith, and of his **b.**.	251
1Ch	26:30	Hashabiah and his **b.**, men of	251
1Ch	26:32	And his **b.**, men of valour, were	251
1Ch	27:18	Elihu, one of the **b.** of David:	251
1Ch	28:2	Hear me, my **b.**, and my people:	251
2Ch	5:12	with their sons and their **b.**, being	251
2Ch	11:4	go up, nor fight against your **b.**:	251
2Ch	11:22	chief, to be ruler among his **b.**:	251
2Ch	19:10	shall come to you of your **b.** that	251
2Ch	19:10	come upon you, and upon your **b.**:	251
2Ch	21:2	he had **b.** the sons of Jehoshaphat,	251
2Ch	21:4	slew all his **b.** with the sword,	251
2Ch	21:13	hast slain thy **b.** of thy father's	251
2Ch	22:8	the sons of the **b.** of Ahaziah,	251
2Ch	28:8	carried away captive of their **b.**	251
2Ch	28:11	ye have taken captive of your **b.**:	251
2Ch	28:15	the city of palm trees, to their **b.**:	251
2Ch	29:15	they gathered their **b.**, and	251
2Ch	29:34	their **b.** the Levites did help	251
2Ch	30:7	and like your **b.**, which trespassed	251
2Ch	30:9	your **b.** and your children shall	251
2Ch	31:15	to give to their **b.** by courses,	251
2Ch	35:5	families of the fathers of your **b.**	251
2Ch	35:6	prepare your **b.**, that they may	251
2Ch	35:9	Shemaiah and Nethaneel, his **b.**	251
2Ch	35:15	for their **b.** the Levites prepared	251
Ezr	3:2	his **b.** the priests, and Zerubabel	251
Ezr	3:2	the son of Shealtiel, and his **b.**,	251
Ezr	3:8	their **b.** the priests and the Levites,	251
Ezr	3:9	Jeshua with his sons and his **b.**,	251
Ezr	3:9	their sons and their **b.** the Levites.	251
Ezr	6:20	for their **b.** the priests, and for	251
Ezr	7:18	seem good to thee, and to thy **b.**,	252
Ezr	8:17	to his **b.** the Nethinims at the place	251
Ezr	8:18	with his sons and his **b.**,	251
Ezr	8:19	sons of Merari, his **b.** and their	251
Ezr	8:24	and ten of their **b.** with them,	251
Ezr	10:18	the son of Jozadak, and his **b.**;	251
Ne	1:2	That Hanani, one of my **b.**, came,	251
Ne	3:1	with his **b.** the priests, and they	251
Ne	3:18	After him repaired their **b.**,	251
Ne	4:2	he spake before his **b.** and the	251
Ne	4:14	fight for your **b.**, your sons, and	251
Ne	4:23	So neither I, nor my **b.**, nor my	251
Ne	5:1	wives against their **b.** the Jews.	251
Ne	5:5	our flesh is as the flesh of our **b.**,	251
Ne	5:8	have redeemed our **b.** the Jews,	251
Ne	5:8	and will ye even sell your **b.**?	251
Ne	5:10	I likewise, and my **b.**, and my	251
Ne	5:14	and my **b.** have not eaten the bread	251

Book	Ref	Context	No.
Ne	10:10	And their **b.**, Shebaniah, Hodijah,	251
Ne	10:29	They clave to their **b.**, their nobles,	251
Ne	11:12	And their **b.** that did the work of	251
Ne	11:13	And his **b.**, chief of the fathers,	251
Ne	11:14	And their **b.**, mighty men of valour,	251
Ne	11:17	Bakbukiah the second among his **b.**,	251
Ne	11:19	and their **b.** that kept the gates,	251
Ne	12:7	of their **b.** in the days of Jeshua.	251
Ne	12:8	the thanksgiving, he and his **b.**.	251
Ne	12:9	Bakbukiah and Unni, their **b.**,	251
Ne	12:24	with their **b.** over against them,	251
Ne	12:36	his **b.**, Shemaiah, and Azarael.	251
Ne	13:13	was to distribute unto their **b.**.	251
Es	10:3	accepted of the multitude of his **b.**.	251
Job	6:15	My **b.** have dealt deceitfully as a	251
Job	19:13	He hath put my **b.** far from me,	251
Job	42:11	came there unto him all his **b.**,	251
Job	42:15	them inheritance among their **b.**.	251
Ps	22:22	will declare thy name unto my **b.**:	251
Ps	69:8	become a stranger unto my **b.**,	251
Ps	122:8	For my **b.** and companions sakes,	251
Ps	133:1	is for **b.** to dwell together in unity!	251
Pr	6:19	he that soweth discord among **b.**.	251
Pr	17:2	of the inheritance among the **b.**.	251
Pr	19:7	All the **b.** of the poor do hate him:	251
Isa	66:5	Your **b.** that hated you, that cast	251
Isa	66:20	they shall bring all your **b.** for an	251
Jer	7:15	I have cast out all your **b.**,	251
Jer	12:6	For even thy **b.**, and the house of	251
Jer	29:16	of your **b.** that are not gone forth	251
Jer	35:3	son of Habaziniah, and his **b.**,	251
Jer	41:8	and slew them not among their **b.**.	251
Jer	49:10	and his **b.**, and his neighbours,	251
Eze	11:15	Son of man, thy **b.**, even thy	251
Eze	11:15	even thy **b.**, the men of thy kindred,	251
Ho	2:1	Say ye unto your **b.**, Ammi; and to	251
Ho	13:15	he be fruitful among his **b.**,	251
Mic	5:3	the remnant of his **b.** shall return.	251
Mt	1:2	and Jacob begat Judas and his **b.**;	*80*
Mt	1:11	Josias begat Jechonias and his **b.**.	*80*
Mt	4:18	by the sea of Galilee, saw two **b.**,	*80*
Mt	4:21	he saw other two **b.**, James the son	*80*
Mt	5:47	**if ye salute your b. only, what do ye**	*80*
Mt	12:46	his mother and his **b.** stood without.	*80*
Mt	12:47	thy mother and thy **b.** that stand	*80*
Mt	12:48	**my mother? and who are my b.?**	*80*
Mt	12:49	said, **Behold my mother and my b.!**	*80*
Mt	13:55	**b.**, James, and Joses, and Simon,	*80*
Mt	19:29	**b., or sisters, or father, or mother,**	*80*
Mt	20:24	with indignation against the two **b.**.	*80*
Mt	22:25	there were with us seven **b.**: and	*80*
Mt	23:8	**even Christ; and all ye are b**	*80*
Mt	25:40	**the least of these my b., ye have**	*80*
Mt	28:10	**tell my b. that they go into Galilee,**	*80*
Mk	3:31	came then his **b.** and his mother.	*80*
Mk	3:32	and thy **b.** without seek for thee.	*80*
Mk	3:33	**Who is my mother, or my b.?**	*80*
Mk	3:34	**Behold my mother and my b.!**	*80*
Mk	10:29	**left house, or b., or sisters,**	*80*
Mk	10:30	**and b., and sisters, and mothers,**	*80*
Mk	12:20	Now there were seven **b.**: and the	*80*
Lu	8:19	his mother, and his **b.**, and could	*80*
Lu	8:20	Thy mother and thy **b.** stand	*80*
Lu	8:21	**My mother and my b. are these**	*80*
Lu	14:12	**not thy friends, nor thy b., neither**	*80*
Lu	14:26	**children, and b., and sisters, yea,**	*80*
Lu	16:28	**I have five b.; that he may testify**	*80*
Lu	18:29	**parents, or b., or wife, or children,**	*80*
Lu	20:29	There were therefore seven **b.**:	*80*
Lu	21:16	**by parents, and b., and kinsfolks,**	*80*
Lu	22:32	**art converted, strengthen thy b**	*80*
Joh	2:12	his mother, and his **b.**, and his	*80*
Joh	7:3	His **b.** therefore said unto him,	*80*
Joh	7:5	neither did his **b.** believe in him.	*80*
Joh	7:10	But when his **b.** were gone up,	*80*
Joh	20:17	**go to my b., and say unto them,**	*80*
Joh	21:23	saying abroad among the **b.**,	*80*
Ac	1:14	mother of Jesus, and with his **b.**.	*80*
Ac	1:16	Men and **b.**, this scripture must	*80*
Ac	2:29	Men and **b.**, let me freely speak	*80*
Ac	2:37	Men and **b.**, what shall we do?	*80*
Ac	3:17	**b.**, I wot that through ignorance	*80*
Ac	3:22	unto you of your **b.**, like unto me;	*80*
Ac	6:3	Wherefore, **b.**, look ye out among	*80*
Ac	7:2	said, Men, **b.**, and fathers, hearken;	*80*
Ac	7:13	Joseph was made known to his **b.**;	*80*
Ac	7:23	visit his **b.** the children of Israel.	*80*
Ac	7:25	his **b.** would have understood	*80*
Ac	7:26	saying, Sirs, ye are **b.**; why do ye	*80*
Ac	7:37	unto you of your **b.**, like unto me;	*80*
Ac	9:30	Which when the **b.** knew, they	*80*
Ac	10:23	**b.** from Joppa accompanied him.	*80*
Ac	11:1	apostles and **b.** that were in Judaea	*80*
Ac	11:12	these six **b.** accompanied me,	*80*
Ac	11:29	send relief unto the **b.** which dwelt	*80*
Ac	12:17	things unto James, and to the **b.**.	*80*
Ac	13:15	saying, Ye men and **b.**, if ye have	*80*
Ac	13:26	Men and **b.**, children of the stock of	*80*
Ac	13:38	unto you therefore, men and **b.**,	*80*
Ac	14:2	minds evil affected against the **b.**.	*80*
Ac	15:1	from Judaea taught the **b.**,	*80*
Ac	15:3	caused great joy unto all the **b.**.	*80*
Ac	15:7	and said unto them, Men and **b.**,	*80*
Ac	15:13	Men and **b.**, hearken unto me:	*80*
Ac	15:22	and Silas, chief men among the **b.**:	*80*
Ac	15:23	The apostles and elders and **b.**	*80*
Ac	15:23	send greeting unto the **b.**	*80*
Ac	15:32	exhorted the **b.** with many words	*80*
Ac	15:33	peace from the **b.** unto the apostles.	*80*
Ac	15:36	and visit our **b.** in every city where	*80*
Ac	15:40	being recommended by the **b.** unto	*80*
Ac	16:2	**b.** that were at Lystra and Iconium.	*80*
Ac	16:40	and when they had seen the **b.**.	*80*
Ac	17:6	they drew Jason and certain **b.**	*80*
Ac	17:10	the **b.** immediately sent away Paul	*80*
Ac	17:14	the **b.** sent away Paul to go as it	*80*
Ac	18:18	took his leave of the **b.**, and sailed	*80*
Ac	18:27	**b.** wrote, exhorting the disciples	*80*
Ac	20:32	now, **b.**, I commend you to God.	*80*
Ac	21:7	saluted the **b.** and abode with them	*80*
Ac	21:17	the **b.** received us gladly.	*80*
Ac	22:1	Men, **b.**, and fathers, hear ye my	*80*
Ac	22:5	I received letters unto the **b.**	*80*
Ac	23:1	Men and **b.**, I have lived in all good	*80*
Ac	23:5	I wist not, **b.**, that he was the high	*80*
Ac	23:6	Men and **b.**, I am a Pharisee,	*80*
Ac	28:14	we found **b.**, and were desired to	*80*
Ac	28:15	when the **b.** heard of us, they came	*80*
Ac	28:17	Men and **b.**, though I have committed	*80*
Ac	28:21	any of the **b.** that came shewed or	*80*
Ro	1:13	you ignorant, **b.**, that oftentimes I	*80*
Ro	7:1	Know ye not, **b.**, (for I speak to them	*80*
Ro	7:4	my **b.**, ye also are become dead to	*80*
Ro	8:12	Therefore, **b.**, we are debtors,	*80*
Ro	8:29	be the firstborn among many **b.**.	*80*
Ro	9:3	accursed from Christ for my **b.**,	*80*
Ro	10:1	**B.**, my heart's desire and prayer to	*80*
Ro	11:25	not, **b.**, that ye should be ignorant	*80*
Ro	12:1	I beseech you therefore, **b.**, by the	*80*
Ro	15:14	persuaded of you, my **b.**, that ye	*80*
Ro	15:15	**b.**, I have written the more	*80*
Ro	15:30	Now I beseech you, **b.**, for the Lord	*80*
Ro	16:14	and the **b.** which are with them.	*80*
Ro	16:17	I beseech you, **b.**, mark them which	*80*
1Co	1:10	I beseech you, **b.**, by the name of	*80*
1Co	1:11	declared unto me of you, my **b.**,	*80*
1Co	1:26	ye see your calling, **b.**, how that not	*80*
1Co	2:1	I, **b.**, when I came to you, came not	*80*
1Co	3:1	I, **b.**, could not speak unto you as	*80*
1Co	4:6	these things, **b.**, I have in a figure	*80*
1Co	6:5	be able to judge between his **b.**?	*80*
1Co	6:8	and defraud, and that your **b.**.	*80*
1Co	7:24	**B.**, let every man, wherein he is	*80*
1Co	7:29	But this I say, **b.**, the time is short:	*80*
1Co	8:12	ye sin so against the **b.**, and wound	*80*
1Co	9:5	the **b.** of the Lord, and Cephas?	*80*
1Co	10:1	**b.**, I would not that ye should be	*80*
1Co	11:2	praise you, **b.**, that ye remember	*80*
1Co	11:33	Wherefore, my **b.**, when ye come	*80*
1Co	12:1	Now concerning spiritual gifts, **b.**,	*80*
1Co	14:6	**b.**, if I come unto you speaking	*80*
1Co	14:20	**B.**, be not children in	*80*
1Co	14:26	How is it then, **b.**? when ye come	*80*
1Co	14:39	Wherefore, **b.**, covert to prophesy,	*80*
1Co	15:1	Moreover, **b.**, I declare unto you	*80*
1Co	15:6	of above five hundred **b.** at once;	*80*
1Co	15:50	this I say, **b.**, that flesh and blood	*80*
1Co	15:58	Therefore, my beloved **b.**, be ye	*80*
1Co	16:11	me: for I look for him with the **b.**,	*80*
1Co	16:12	him to come unto you with the **b.**,	*80*
1Co	16:15	beseech you, **b.**, (ye know the house	*80*
1Co	16:20	All the **b.** greet you. Greet ye one	*80*
2Co	1:8	**b.**, have you ignorant of our trouble	*80*
2Co	8:1	Moreover, **b.**, we do you to wit of	*80*
2Co	8:23	or our **b.** be enquired of, they are	*80*
2Co	9:3	Yet have I sent the **b.**, lest our	*80*
2Co	9:5	necessary to exhort the **b.**, that	*80*
2Co	11:9	the **b.** which came from Macedonia	*80*
2Co	11:26	the sea, in perils among false **b.**;	*5569*
2Co	13:11	Finally, **b.**, farewell. Be perfect,	*80*
Ga	1:2	And all the **b.** which are with me,	*80*
Ga	1:11	I certify you, **b.**, that the gospel	*80*
Ga	2:4	that because of false **b.** unwares	*5569*
Ga	3:15	**B.**, I speak after the manner of men;	*80*
Ga	4:12	**B.**, I beseech you, be as I am; for I	*80*
Ga	4:28	Now we, **b.**, as Issac was, are the	*80*
Ga	4:31	So then, **b.**, we are not children of	*80*
Ga	5:11	I, **b.**, if I yet preach circumcision,	*80*
Ga	5:13	**b.**, ye have been called unto liberty;	*80*
Ga	6:1	**B.**, if a man be overtaken in a fault,	*80*
Ga	6:18	**B.**, the grace of out Lord Jesus	*80*
Eph	6:10	Finally, my **b.**, be strong in the	*80*
Eph	6:23	Peace be to the **b.**, and love with	*80*
Php	1:12	ye should understand, **b.**, and love with	*80*
Php	1:14	many of the **b.** in the Lord, waxing	*80*
Php	3:1	Finally, my **b.**, rejoice in the Lord.	*80*
Php	3:13	**B.**, I count not myself to have	*80*
Php	3:17	**B.**, be followers together of me,	*80*
Php	4:1	my **b.** dearly beloved and longed	*80*
Php	4:8	Finally, **b.**, whatsoever things are	*80*
Php	4:21	The **b.** which are with me greet you	*80*
Col	1:2	saints and faithful **b.** in Christ	*80*
Col	4:15	Salute the **b.** which are in Laodicea,	*80*
1Th	1:4	Knowing, **b.** beloved, your election	*80*
1Th	2:1	yourselves, **b.**, know our entrance	*80*
1Th	2:9	ye remember, **b.**, our labour and	*80*
1Th	2:14	For ye, **b.**, became followers of the	*80*
1Th	2:17	we, **b.**, being taken from you for a	*80*
1Th	3:7	Therefore, **b.**, we were comforted	*80*
1Th	4:1	we beseech you, **b.**, and exhort you	*80*
1Th	4:10	toward all the **b.** which are in all	*80*
1Th	4:10	we beseech you, **b.**, that ye increase	*80*
1Th	4:13	not have you to be ignorant, **b.**,	*80*
1Th	5:1	the times and the seasons, **b.**, ye	*80*
1Th	5:4	ye, **b.**, are not in darkness, that	*80*
1Th	5:12	we beseech you, **b.** to know them	*80*
1Th	5:14	we exhort you, **b.**, warn them that	*80*
1Th	5:25	**B.**, pray for us.	*80*
1Th	5:26	Greet all the **b.** with an holy kiss.	*80*
1Th	5:27	epistle be read unto all the holy **b.**.	*80*
2Th	1:3	thank God always for you, **b.**, as it	*80*
2Th	2:1	we beseech you, **b.**, by the coming	*80*
2Th	2:13	for you, **b.** beloved of the Lord,	*80*
2Th	2:15	Therefore, **b.**, stand fast, and hold	*80*
2Th	3:1	Finally, **b.**, pray for us, that the	*80*
2Th	3:6	we command you, **b.**, in the name	*80*
2Th	3:13	ye, **b.** be not weary in well doing.	*80*
1Ti	4:6	put the **b.** in remembrance of these	*80*
1Ti	5:1	father; and the younger men as **b.**;	*80*
1Ti	6:2	despite them, because they are **b.**;	*80*
2Ti	4:21	Linus, and Claudia, and all the **b.**.	*80*
Heb	2:11	he is not ashamed to call them **b.**,	*80*
Heb	2:12	I will declare thy name unto my **b.**,	*80*
Heb	2:17	made like unto his **b.**, that he	*80*
Heb	3:1	Wherefore, holy **b.**, partakers of	*80*
Heb	3:12	Take heed, **b.**, lest there be in any	*80*
Heb	7:5	that is, of their **b.**, though they	*80*
Heb	10:19	Having therefore, **b.**, boldness to	*80*
Heb	13:22	I beseech you, **b.**, suffer the word	*80*
Jas	1:2	My **b.**, count it all joy when ye fall	*80*
Jas	1:16	Do not err, my beloved **b.**.	*80*
Jas	1:19	Wherefore, my beloved **b.**, let every	*80*
Jas	2:1	My **b.**, have not the faith of our	*80*
Jas	2:5	Hearken, my beloved **b.**, Hath not	*80*
Jas	2:14	What doth it profit, my **b.**, though	*80*
Jas	3:1	My **b.**, be not many masters,	*80*
Jas	3:10	My **b.**, these things ought not so to	*80*
Jas	3:12	Can the fig tree, my **b.**, bear olive	*80*
Jas	4:11	Speak not evil one of another, **b.**.	*80*
Jas	5:7	Be patient therefore, **b.**, unto the	*80*
Jas	5:9	Grudge not one against another, **b.**	*80*
Jas	5:10	Take, my **b.**, the prophets, who	*80*
Jas	5:12	above all things, my **b.**, swear not	*80*
Jas	5:19	**B.**, if any of you do err from the	*80*
1Pe	1:22	unto unfeigned love of the **b.**, see	*5360*
1Pe	3:8	love as **b.**, be pitiful, be courteous:	*5361*
1Pe	5:9	accomplished in your **b.** that are	*81*
2Pe	1:10	the rather, **b.**, give diligence to	*80*
1Jo	2:7	**B.**, I write no new commandment	*80*
1Jo	3:13	Marvel not, my **b.**, if the world	*80*
1Jo	3:14	because we love the **b.**. He that	*80*

1Jo 3:16 to lay down our lives for the **b.** *80*
3Jo 3 when the **b.** came and testified of.......... *80*
3Jo 5 thou doest to the **b.**, and to *80*
3Jo 10 he himself receive the **b.**, and................ *80*
Re 6:11 fellowservants also and their **b.**, ... *80*
Re 12:10 the accuser of our **b.** is cast down,......... *80*
Re 19:10 of thy **b.** that have the testimony *80*
Re 22:9 of thy **b.** the prophets, and of them *80*

BRETHREN'S See also BROTHERS'.
De 20:8 lest his **b.** heart faint as well as.......... 251

BRIBE See also BRIBES.
1Sa 12:3 hand have I received any **b.** 3724
Am 5:12 they take a **b.**, and they turn aside....... 3724

BRIBERY
Job 15:34 consume the tabernacles of **b.** 7810

BRIBES
1Sa 8:3 aside after lucre, and took **b.**,............ 7810
Ps 26:10 and their right hand is full of **b.**,......... 7810
Isa 33:15 his hands from holding of **b.**. 7810

BRICK See also BRICKKILN; BRICKS.
Ge 11:3 Go to, let us make **b.**, and burn......... 3835
Ge 11:3 they had **b.** for stone, and slime......... 3843
Ex 1:14 in morter, and in **b.**, and in all.......... 3843
Ex 5:7 give the people straw to make **b.**, ... 3835
Ex 5:14 fulfilled your task in making **b.** 3835
Ex 5:16 and they say to us, Make **b.**: and........ 3843
Isa 65:3 burneth incense upon altars of **b.**;........ 3843

BRICKKILN
2Sa 12:31 made them pass through the **b.**:.......... 4404
Jer 43:9 the clay in the **b.**, which is at the....... 4404
Na 3:14 morter, make strong the **b.**.............. 4404

BRICKS
Ex 5:8 the tale of the **b.**, which they did 3843
Ex 5:18 yet shall ye deliver the tale of **b.**,........ 3843
Ex 5:19 from your **b.** of your daily task............ 3843
Isa 9:10 The **b.** are fallen down, but we will 3843

BRIDE See also BRIDECHAMBER; BRIDEGROOM.
Isa 49:18 bind them on thee, as a **b.** doeth. 3618
Isa 61:10 a **b.** adorneth herself with jewels........ 3618
Isa 62:5 bridegroom rejoiceth over the **b.**, ... 3618
Jer 2:32 maid forget her ornaments, or a **b.**........ 3618
Jer 7:34 bridegroom, and the voice of the **b.**: ... 3618
Jer 16:9 and the voice of the **b.**.................... 3618
Jer 25:10 the voice of the **b.**, the sound of........ 3618
Jer 33:11 the voice of the **b.**, the voice of.......... 3618
Joe 2:16 and the **b.** out of her closet.............. 3618
Joh 3:29 that hath the **b.** is the bridegroom: *3565*
Re 18:23 of the **b.** shall be heard no more *3565*
Re 21:2 prepared as a **b.** adorned for her........ *3565*
Re 21:9 shew thee the **b.**, the Lamb's wife. *3565*
Re 22:17 the Spirit and the **b.** say, Come. *3565*

BRIDECHAMBER
Mt 9:15 **Can the children of the b. mourn,** ..*3567*
Mk 2:19 **Can the children of the b. fast,** *3567*
Lu 5:34 **make the children of the b. fast,** ... *3567*

BRIDEGROOM See also BRIDEGROOM'S.
Ps 19:5 a **b.** coming out of his chamber, ... 2860
Isa 61:10 as a **b.** decketh himself with............. 2860
Isa 62:5 the **b.** rejoiceth over the bride, so....... 2860
Jer 7:34 the voice of the **b.** and the voice........ 2860
Jer 16:9 of gladness, the voice of the **b.**, ... 2860
Jer 25:10 the voice of the **b.**, and the voice....... 2860
Jer 33:11 the voice of the **b.**, and the voice....... 2860
Joe 2:16 let the **b.** go forth of his chamber,....... 2860
Mt 9:15 **as long as the b. is with them?** *3566*
Mt 9:15 **when the b. shall be taken from** *3566*
Mt 25:1 **and went forth to meet the b.** *3566*
Mt 25:5 **While the b. tarried, they all** *3566*
Mt 25:6 **Behold, the b. cometh; go ye out** ... *3566*
Mt 25:10 **they went to buy, the b. came;** *3566*
Mk 2:19 **while the b. is with them?** *3566*
Mk 2:19 **as long as they have the b.** *3566*
Mk 2:20 **when the b. shall be taken away** ... *3566*
Lu 5:34 **fast, while the b. is with them?** *3566*
Lu 5:35 **come, when the b. shall be taken** .. *3566*
Joh 2:9 governor of the feast called the **b.**, ... *3566*
Joh 3:29 that hath the bride is the **b.**: *3566*
Joh 3:29 but the friend of the **b.**, ... *3566*
Re 18:23 and the voice of the **b.** and of the *3566*

BRIDEGROOM'S
Joh 3:29 greatly because of the **b.** voice: *3566*

BRIDLE See also BRIDLES; BRIDLETH.
2Ki 19:28 my **b.** in thy lips, and I will turn......... 4964
Job 30:11 they have also let loose the **b.** 7448
Job 41:13 come to him with his double **b.**? 7448
Ps 32:9 must be held in with bit and **b.**, ... 7448
Ps 39:1 I will keep my mouth with a **b.**, ... 4269
Pr 26:3 a **b.** for the ass, and a rod for the 4964
Isa 30:28 be a **b.** in the jaws of the people, ... 7448
Isa 37:29 in thy nose, and my **b.** in thy lips, ... 4964
Jas 3:2 able also to **b.** the whole body. *5469*

BRIDLES
Re 14:20 even unto the horse **b.**, by the *5469*

BRIDLETH
Jas 1:26 **b.** not his tongue, but deceiveth......... *5468*

BRIEFLY
Ro 13:9 **b.** comprehended in this saying,........... *346*
1Pe 5:12 I have written **b.**, exhorting *1223,3641*

BRIER See also BRIERS.
Isa 55:13 instead of the **b.** shall come up 5636
Eze 28:24 shall be no more a pricking **b.**............ 5544
Mic 7:4 The best of them is as a **b.**: the 2312

BRIERS
Jg 8:7 of the wilderness and with **b.**. 1303
Jg 8:16 thorns of the wilderness, and **b.**,......... 1303
Isa 5:6 but there shall come up **b.** and 8068
Isa 7:23 it shall even be for **b.** and thorns. 8068
Isa 7:24 all the land shall become **b.** and 8068
Isa 7:25 come thither the fear of **b.** and........... 8068
Isa 9:18 it shall devour the **b.** and thorns, ... 8068
Isa 10:17 and devour his thorns and his **b.** 8068
Isa 27:4 who would set the **b.** and thorns 8068
Isa 32:13 shall come up thorns and **b.**; 8068
Eze 2:6 **b.** and thorns be with thee, and 5621
Heb 6:8 which beareth thorns and **b.**.............. *5146*

BRIGANDINE See also BRIGANDINES.
Jer 51:3 that lifteth himself up in his **b.**: 5630

BRIGANDINES
Jer 46:4 the spears, and put on the **b.**. 5630

BRIGHT
Le 13:2 a rising, a scab, or **b.** spot, and it........ 934
Le 13:4 If the **b.** spot be white in the skin......... 934
Le 13:19 or a **b.** spot, white, and somewhat 934
Le 13:23 if the **b.** spot stay in his place, and 934
Le 13:24 have a white **b.** spot, somewhat 934
Le 13:25 the hair in the **b.** spot be turned........... 934
Le 13:26 no white hair in the **b.** spot, and it 934
Le 13:28 if the **b.** spot stay in his place, and 934
Le 13:38 in the skin of their flesh **b.** spots, ... 934
Le 13:38 even white **b.** spots; 934
Le 13:39 the **b.** spots in the skin of their 934
Le 14:56 and for a scab, and for a **b.** spot: 934
1Ki 7:45 of the Lord, were of **b.** brass. 4803
2Ch 4:16 for the house of the Lord of **b.** 4838
Job 37:11 he scattereth his **b.** cloud: 216
Job 37:21 now men see not the **b.** light 925
Ca 5:14 his belly is as **b.** ivory overlaid 6247
Jer 51:11 Make **b.** the arrows; gather the 1305
Eze 1:13 and the fire was **b.**, and out of........... 5051
Eze 21:15 ah! it is made **b.**, it is wrapped........... 1300
Eze 21:21 he made his arrows **b.**, he 7043
Eze 27:19 **b.** iron, cassia, and calamus,............. 6219
Eze 32:8 All the **b.** lights of heaven will I.......... 3974
Na 3:3 both the **b.** sword and the 3851
Zec 10:1 so the Lord shall make **b.** clouds,........ 2385
Mt 17:5 behold, a **b.** cloud overshadowed *5460*
Lu 11:36 **as when the b. shining of a candle** .. *796*
Ac 10:30 stood before me in **b.** clothing, ... *2986*
Re 22:16 **and the b. and morning star** *2986*

BRIGHTNESS
2Sa 22:13 Through the **b.** before him were 5051
Job 31:26 shined, or the moon walking in **b.**;........ 3368
Ps 18:12 At the **b.** that was before him his......... 5051
Isa 59:9 for **b.**, but we walk in darkness. 5054
Isa 60:3 and kings to the **b.** of thy rising. 5051
Isa 60:19 neither for **b.** shall the moon give........ 5051
Isa 62:1 righteousness thereof go forth as **b.**...... 5051
Eze 1:4 and a **b.** was about it, and out of......... 5051
Eze 1:27 of fire, and it had **b.** round about......... 5051
Eze 1:28 the appearance of the **b.** round 5051
Eze 8:2 as the apearance of **b.**, as the............ 2096
Eze 10:4 the court was full of the **b.** of the....... 5051
Eze 28:7 wisdom, they shall defile thy **b.**.......... 3314
Eze 28:17 thy wisdom by reason of thy **b.**: 3314
Da 2:31 This great image, whose **b.** was......... 2122
Da 4:36 mine honour and **b.** returned 2122
Da 12:3 shall shine as the **b.** of the............... 2096
Am 5:20 even very dark, and no **b.** in it?......... 5051
Hab 3:4 And his **b.** was as the light; 5051
Ac 26:13 light from heaven, above the **b.** of...... *2987*
2Th 2:8 with the **b.** of his coming; *2015*
Heb 1:3 Who being the **b.** of his glory *541*

BRIM See also BRIMSTONE.
Jos 3:15 were dipped in the **b.** of the.............. 7097
1Ki 7:23 ten cubits from the one **b.** to the 8193
1Ki 7:24 under the **b.** of it round about............ 8193
1Ki 7:26 and the **b.** thereof was wrought 8193
1Ki 7:26 like the **b.** of a cup,........................... 8193
2Ch 4:2 from **b.** to **b.**, round in compass,........ 8193
2Ch 4:5 and the **b.** of it like the work............. 8193
2Ch 4:5 like the work of the **b.** of a cup, ... 8193
Joh 2:7 And they filled them up to the **b.**......... *507*

BRIMSTONE
Ge 19:24 Sodom and upon Gomorrah **b.** 1614
De 29:23 the whole land thereof is **b.**, and........ 1614
Job 18:15 **b.** shall be scattered upon his 1614
Ps 11:6 he shall rain snares, fire and **b.**,......... 1614
Isa 30:33 like a stream of **b.**, doth kindle it. 1614
Isa 34:9 the dust thereof into **b.**, and the 1614
Eze 38:22 and great hail stones, fire and **b.**. 1614
Lu 17:29 **fire and b. from heaven, and**......... *2303*
Re 9:17 of fire, and of jacinth, and **b.**, ... *2306*
Re 9:17 issued fire and smoke and **b.**. *2303*
Re 9:18 the smoke, and by the **b.**, which......... *2303*
Re 14:10 with fire and **b.** in the presence of....... *2303*
Re 19:20 a lake of fire burning with **b.**, ... *2303*
Re 20:10 the lake of fire and **b.**, where the........ *2303*
Re 21:8 lake which burneth with fire and **b.**: *2303*

BRING See also BRINGEST; BRINGETH; BRINGING; BROUGHT.
Ge 1:11 Let the earth **b.** forth grass, the 1876
Ge 1:20 the waters **b.** forth abundantly 8317
Ge 1:24 Let the earth **b.** forth the living 3318
Ge 3:16 in sorrow thou shalt **b.** forth.............. 3205
Ge 3:18 also and thistles shall it **b.** forth 6779
Ge 6:17 do **b.** a flood of waters upon the.......... 935
Ge 6:19 two of every sort shalt thou **b.** into...... 935
Ge 8:17 **B.** forth with thee every living............ 3318
Ge 9:7 **b.** forth abundantly in the earth.......... 8317
Ge 9:14 when I **b.** a cloud over the earth,....... 6049
Ge 18:16 went with them to **b.** them on the........ 7971
Ge 18:19 the Lord may **b.** upon Abraham........... 935
Ge 19:5 **b.** them out unto us, that we may 3318
Ge 19:8 let me, I pray thee, **b.** them out 3318
Ge 19:12 hast in the city, **b.** them out of............ 3318
Ge 24:5 must I needs **b.** thy son again.............. 7725
Ge 24:6 Beware thou that thou **b.** not my 7725
Ge 24:8 my oath: only **b.** not my son 7725
Ge 27:4 and **b.** it to me, that I may eat; 935
Ge 27:5 to hunt for venison, and to **b.** it. 935
Ge 27:7 **B.** me venison, and make me............... 935
Ge 27:10 And thou shalt **b.** it to thy father, ... 935
Ge 27:12 and I shall **b.** a curse upon me, and...... 935
Ge 27:25 **B.** it near to me, and I will eat of 5066
Ge 28:15 and will **b.** thee again into this 7725
Ge 37:14 well with the flocks; and **b.** me 7725
Ge 38:24 **B.** her forth, and let her be burnt. 3318
Ge 40:14 and **b.** me out of this house: 3318
Ge 41:32 and God will shortly **b.** it to pass. 6213
Ge 42:20 **b.** your youngest brother unto............ 935
Ge 42:34 And **b.** your youngest brother 935
Ge 42:37 Slay my two sons, if I **b.** him not......... 935
Ge 42:37 and I will **b.** him to thee again. 7725
Ge 42:38 then shall ye **b.** down my gray............ 3381
Ge 43:7 know that he would say, **B.** your 3381
Ge 43:9 if I **b.** him not unto thee, and set......... 935
Ge 43:16 **B.** these men home, and slay, and......... 935
Ge 44:21 **B.** him down unto me, that I may 3381
Ge 44:29 ye shall **b.** down my gray hairs 3381
Ge 44:31 and thy servants shall **b.** down........... 3381
Ge 44:32 If I **b.** him not unto thee, then I.......... 935
Ge 45:13 ye shall haste and **b.** down my............ 3381
Ge 45:19 and for your wives, and **b.** your 5375
Ge 46:4 and I will also surely **b.** thee up......... 5927
Ge 48:9 **B.** them, I pray thee, unto me, ... 3947
Ge 48:21 and **b.** you again unto the land of 7725
Ge 50:20 to **b.** to pass, as it is this day, to....... 6213
Ge 50:24 and **b.** you out of this land into 5927
Ex 3:8 and to **b.** them up out of that 5927

Book	Ref	Text	No.
Ex	3:10	that thou mayest **b.** forth my	3318
Ex	3:11	I should **b.** forth the children of	3318
Ex	3:17	I will **b.** you up out of the	5927
Ex	6:6	and I will **b.** you out from under	3318
Ex	6:8	And I will **b.** you in unto the land,	935
Ex	6:13	to **b.** the children of Israel out of	935
Ex	6:26	**B.** out the children of Israel from	3318
Ex	6:27	to **b.** out the children of Israel	3318
Ex	7:4	and **b.** forth mine armies. and my	3318
Ex	7:5	and **b.** out the children of Israel	3318
Ex	8:3	And the river shall **b.** forth	8317
Ex	8:18	enchantments to **b.** forth lice,	3318
Ex	10:4	to morrow will I **b.** the locusts	935
Ex	11:1	Yet will I **b.** one plague more upon	935
Ex	12:51	the Lord did **b.** the children of	3318
Ex	13:5	the Lord shall **b.** thee into the	935
Ex	13:11	shall be when the Lord shall **b.**	935
Ex	15:17	Thou shalt **b.** them in, and plant	935
Ex	16:5	prepare that which they **b.** in;	935
Ex	18:19	that thou mayest **b.** the causes	935
Ex	18:22	they shall **b.** unto thee, but	935
Ex	21:6	Then his master shall **b.** him	5066
Ex	21:6	the judges; he shall also **b.** him	5066
Ex	22:13	let him **b.** it for witness, and he	935
Ex	23:4	thou shalt surely **b.** it back to	7725
Ex	23:19	thou shalt **b.** into the house of the	935
Ex	23:20	and to **b.** thee into the place which	935
Ex	23:23	and **b.** thee in unto the Amorites,	935
Ex	25:2	that they **b.** me an offering:	3947
Ex	26:33	that thou mayest **b.** in thither	935
Ex	27:20	that they **b.** thee pure oil olive	3947
Ex	29:3	and **b.** them in the basket, with	7126
Ex	29:4	Aaron and his sons thou shalt **b.**	7126
Ex	29:8	thou shalt **b.** his sons, and put	7126
Ex	32:2	your daughters, and **b.** them unto	935
Ex	32:12	For mischief did he **b.** them out,	3318
Ex	33:12	**B.** up this people: and thou hast	5927
Ex	34:26	firstfruits of thy land thou shalt **b.**	935
Ex	35:5	let him **b.** it, an offering	935
Ex	35:29	made them willing to **b.** for all	935
Ex	36:5	The people **b.** much more than	935
Ex	40:4	And thou shalt **b.** in the table,	935
Ex	40:4	thou shalt **b.** in the candlestick,	935
Ex	40:12	And thou shalt **b.** Aaron and his	7126
Ex	40:14	thou shalt **b.** his sons, and	7126
Le	1:2	If any man of you **b.** an offering	7126
Le	1:2	unto the Lord, ye shall **b.** your	7126
Le	1:5	the priests, Aaron's sons, shall **b.**	7126
Le	1:10	he shall **b.** it a male without	7126
Le	1:13	and the priest shall **b.** it all, and	7126
Le	1:14	he shall **b.** his offering of turtle	7126
Le	1:15	And the priest shall **b.** it unto	7126
Le	2:2	And he shall **b.** it to Aaron's sons	935
Le	2:4	if thou **b.** an oblation of a meat	7126
Le	2:8	thou shalt **b.** the meat offering	935
Le	2:8	priest, he shall **b.** it unto the	5066
Le	2:11	meat offering, which ye shall **b.**	7126
Le	4:3	then let him **b.** for his sin,	7126
Le	4:4	And he shall **b.** the bullock unto	935
Le	4:5	and **b.** it to the tabernacle of the	935
Le	4:14	and **b.** him before the tabernacle	935
Le	4:16	priest that is anointed shall **b.** of	935
Le	4:23	he shall **b.** his offering, a kid of	935
Le	4:28	then he shall **b.** his offering, a	935
Le	4:32	if he **b.** a lamb for a sin offering,	935
Le	4:32	shall **b.** it a female without blemish	935
Le	5:6	And he shall **b.** his trespass	935
Le	5:7	if he be not able to **b.** a lamb,	5060
Le	5:7	then he shall **b.** for his trespass,	935
Le	5:8	he shall **b.** them unto the priest,	935
Le	5:11	not able to **b.** two turtledoves,	5381
Le	5:11	sinned shall **b.** for his offering	935
Le	5:12	Then shall he **b.** it to the priest,	935
Le	5:15	**b.** for his trespass unto the Lord	935
Le	5:18	And he shall **b.** a ram without	935
Le	6:6	he shall **b.** his trespass offering	935
Le	6:21	it is baken, thou shalt **b.** it in:	935
Le	7:29	shall **b.** his oblation unto the	935
Le	7:30	His own hands shall they **b.** the	935
Le	7:30	he **b.**, that the breast may be	935
Le	10:15	the wave breast shall they **b.**	935
Le	12:6	she shall **b.** a lamb of the first	935
Le	12:8	if she not be able to **b.** a lamb,	4672
Le	12:8	then she shall **b.** two turtles,	3947
Le	14:23	And he shall **b.** them on the	935
Le	15:29	and **b.** them unto the priest,	935
Le	16:9	And Aaron shall **b.** the goat	7126
Le	16:11	And Aaron shall **b.** the bullock	7126
Le	16:12	small, and **b.** it within the vail:	935
Le	16:15	and **b.** his blood within the vail,	935
Le	16:20	altar, he shall **b.** the live goat:	7126
Le	17:5	may **b.** their sacrifices, which	935
Le	17:5	even that they may **b.** them unto	935
Le	18:3	whether I **b.** you, shall ye not do:	935
Le	19:21	he shall **b.** his trespass offering	935
Le	20:22	whether I **b.** you to dwell therein,	935
Le	23:10	then ye shall **b.** a sheaf of the	935
Le	23:17	Ye shall **b.** out of your habitations	935
Le	24:2	that they **b.** unto thee pure oil	3947
Le	24:14	**B.** forth him that hath cursed	3318
Le	24:23	they should **b.** forth him that	3318
Le	25:21	and it shall **b.** forth fruit for three	6213
Le	26:10	and **b.** forth the old because of	3318
Le	26:21	I will **b.** seven times more	3254
Le	26:25	And I will **b.** a sword upon you,	935
Le	26:31	and **b.** your sanctuaries unto	8074
Le	26:32	**b.** the land into desolation:	8074
Le	27:9	**b.** an offering unto the Lord,	7126
Nu	3:6	**B.** the tribe of Levi near, and	7126
Nu	5:9	**b.** unto the priest, shall be his.	7126
Nu	5:15	**b.** his wife unto the priest,	935
Nu	5:15	and he shall **b.** her offering	935
Nu	5:16	And the priest shall **b.** her near,	7126
Nu	6:10	he shall **b.** two turtles, or two	935
Nu	6:12	and shall **b.** a lamb of the first	935
Nu	6:16	**b.** them before the Lord,	7126
Nu	8:9,	10 And thou shalt **b.** the Levites	7126
Nu	11:16	and **b.** them unto the tabernacle	3947
Nu	13:20	and **b.** of the fruit of the land.	3947
Nu	14:8	then he will **b.** us into the land,	935
Nu	14:16	was not able to **b.** this people	935
Nu	14:24	him will I **b.** into the land	935
Nu	14:31	them will I **b.** in, and they shall	935
Nu	14:37	that did **b.** up the evil report	3318
Nu	15:4	his offering into the Lord **b.**	7126
Nu	15:9	shall he **b.** with a bullock	7126
Nu	15:10	thou shalt **b.** for a drink offering	7126
Nu	15:18	into the land whither I **b.** you,	935
Nu	15:25	they shall **b.** their offering, a	935
Nu	15:27	then he shall **b.** a she goat of	7126
Nu	16:9	to **b.** you near to himself to do	7126
Nu	16:17	and **b.** ye before the Lord every	7126
Nu	17:10	**B.** Aaron's rod again before the	7725
Nu	18:2	**b.** thou with thee, that they may	7126
Nu	18:13	they shall **b.** unto the Lord,	935
Nu	18:15	which they **b.** unto the Lord,	7126
Nu	19:2	that they **b.** thee a red heifer	3947
Nu	19:3	**b.** her forth without the camp,	3318
Nu	20:5	to **b.** us in unto this evil place?	935
Nu	20:8	and thou shalt **b.** forth to them	3318
Nu	20:12	therefore ye shall not **b.** this	935
Nu	20:25	and **b.** them up unto mount Hor:	5927
Nu	22:8	I will **b.** you word again, as the	7725
Nu	23:27	I will **b.** thee unto another place;	3947
Nu	27:17	which may **b.** them in; that the	935
Nu	28:26	when ye **b.** a new meat offering	7126
Nu	32:5	and **b.** us not over Jordan.	5674
De	1:17	**b.** it unto me, and I will hear it	7126
De	1:22	and **b.** us word again by what	7725
De	4:38	to **b.** thee in, to give thee their	935
De	6:23	that he might **b.** us in, to give us	935
De	7:1	shall **b.** thee into the land	935
De	7:26	Neither shalt thou **b.** an	935
De	9:3	**b.** them down before thy face:	3665
De	9:28	to **b.** them into the land which	935
De	12:6	And thither ye shall **b.** your	935
De	12:11	thither ye shall **b.** all that I	935
De	14:28	thou shalt **b.** forth all the tithe	3318
De	17:5	Then shalt thou **b.** forth that man	3318
De	21:4	elders of that city shall **b.** down	2381
De	21:12	Then thou shalt **b.** her home	935
De	21:19	and **b.** him out unto the elders	3318
De	22:1	any case **b.** them again unto	7725
De	22:2	shalt **b.** it unto thine own house,	622
De	22:8	that thou **b.** not blood upon	7760
De	22:14	and **b.** up an evil name upon her,	3318
De	22:15	and **b.** forth the tokens of the	3318
De	22:21	Then they shall **b.** out the damsel	3318
De	22:24	Then ye shall **b.** them both out	3318
De	23:18	Thou shalt not **b.** the hire of a	935
De	24:11	shall **b.** out the pledge aboard	3318
De	26:2	which thou shalt **b.** of thy land	935
De	28:36	The Lord shall **b.** thee, and thy	3212
De	28:49	shall **b.** a nation against thee	5375
De	28:60	**b.** upon thee all the diseases	7725
De	28:61	them will the Lord **b.** upon thee,	5927
De	28:63	and to **b.** you to nought; and ye	8045
De	28:68	shall **b.** thee into Egypt again	7725
De	29:27	to **b.** upon it all the curses that	935
De	30:5	And the Lord thy God will **b.** thee	935
De	30:12	us to heaven, and **b.** it unto us,	3947
De	30:13	the sea for us, and **b.** it unto us,	3947
De	31:23	for thou shalt **b.** the children	935
De	33:7	and **b.** him unto his people:	935
Jos	2:3	**B.** forth the men that are come	3318
Jos	2:18	**b.** thy father, and thy mother,	622
Jos	6:22	and **b.** out thence the woman,	3318
Jos	10:22	and **b.** out those five kings	3318
Jos	18:6	and **b.** the description hither	935
Jos	23:15	so shall the Lord **b.** upon you	935
Jg	6:13	Did not the Lord **b.** us up	5927
Jg	6:18	and **b.** forth my present, and	3318
Jg	6:30	**B.** out thy son, that he may die:	3318
Jg	7:4	**b.** them down unto the water,	338
Jg	11:9	If ye **b.** me home again to fight	7725
Jg	19:3	unto her, and to **b.** her again,	7725
Jg	19:22	**B.** forth the man that came into	3318
Jg	19:24	I will **b.** out now, and humble ye	3318
Ru	3:15	**B.** the vail that thou hast upon	3051
1Sa	1:22	and then I will **b.** him, that he	935
1Sa	4:4	might **b.** from thence the ark	5375
1Sa	6:7	**b.** their calves home from them:	7725
1Sa	9:7	what shall we **b.** the man?	935
1Sa	9:7	not a present to **b.** to the man	935
1Sa	9:23	**B.** the portion which I gave thee,	5414
1Sa	11:12	**b.** the men, that we may put them	5414
1Sa	13:9	**B.** hither a burnt offering to me,	5066
1Sa	14:18	**B.** hither the ark of God. For the	5066
1Sa	14:34	**B.** me hither every man his ox,	5066
1Sa	15:32	**B.** ye hither to me Agag the king	5066
1Sa	16:17	well, and **b.** him to me.	935
1Sa	19:15	**B.** him up to me in the bed,	5927
1Sa	20:8	why shouldest thou **b.** me to thy	935
1Sa	23:9	priest, **B.** hither the ephod.	5066
1Sa	27:11	to **b.** tidings to Gath, saying,	935
1Sa	28:8	and **b.** me him up, whom I shall	5927
1Sa	28:11	Whom shall I **b.** up unto thee?	5927
1Sa	28:11	And he said, **B.** me up Samuel.	5927
1Sa	28:15	disquieted me, to **b.** me up?	5927
1Sa	30:7	**b.** me hither the ephod,	5066
1Sa	30:15	Canst thou **b.** me down to this	3381
1Sa	30:15	and I will **b.** thee down to this	3381
2Sa	2:3	were with him did David **b.** up,	5927
2Sa	3:12	to **b.** about all Israel unto thee,	5437
2Sa	3:13	except thou first **b.** Michal	935
2Sa	6:2	to **b.** up from thence the ark	5927
2Sa	9:10	and thou shalt **b.** in the fruits,	935
2Sa	12:23	can I **b.** him back again? I shall	7725
2Sa	13:10	**B.** the meat into the chamber,	935
2Sa	14:10	**b.** him to me, and he shall not	935
2Sa	14:21	**b.** the young man Absalom	7725
2Sa	15:8	shall **b.** me again indeed to	7725
2Sa	15:14	and **b.** evil upon us, and smite	5080
2Sa	15:25	he will **b.** me again, and shew	7725
2Sa	17:3	I will **b.** back all the people unto	7725
2Sa	17:13	then shall all Israel **b.** ropes	5375
2Sa	17:14	that the Lord might **b.** evil	935
2Sa	19:11	the last to **b.** the king back	7725
2Sa	19:12	the last to **b.** back the king?	7725
2Sa	22:28	that thou mayest **b.** them down,	8213
1Ki	1:33	and **b.** him down to Gihon:	3381
1Ki	2:9	head **b.** thou down to the grave	3381
1Ki	3:24	king said, **B.** me a sword.	3947
1Ki	5:9	My servants shall **b.** them down	3381
1Ki	8:1	that they might **b.** up the ark	5927
1Ki	8:4	priests and the Levites **b.** up	5927
1Ki	8:32	to **b.** his way upon his head;	5414
1Ki	8:34	and **b.** them again unto the land	7725
1Ki	10:29	did they **b.** them out by their	3318
1Ki	12:21	to **b.** the kingdom again to	7725
1Ki	13:18	**B.** him back with thee unto thine	7725
1Ki	14:10	I will **b.** evil upon the house of	935
1Ki	17:11	**B.** me, I pray thee, a morsel of	3947
1Ki	17:13	and **b.** it unto me, and after	3318
1Ki	20:33	Go ye, **b.** him. Then Ben-hadad	3947
1Ki	21:21	I will **b.** evil upon thee, and will	935
1Ki	21:29	I will not **b.** evil in his days:	935
1Ki	21:29	son's days will I **b.** evil upon his	935
2Ki	2:20	**B.** me a new cruse, and put salt	3947
2Ki	3:15	**b.** me a minstrel. And it came to	3947
2Ki	4:6	unto her son, **B.** me yet a vessel.	5066

Book	Ref	Context	No.
2Ki	4:41	Then **b.** meal. And he cast it	3947
2Ki	6:19	and I will **b.** you to the man	3212
2Ki	10:22	**B.** forth vestments for all the	3318
2Ki	12:4	**b.** into the house of the Lord,	935
2Ki	19:3	there is not strength to **b.** forth	3205
2Ki	22:16	I will **b.** evil upon this place,	935
2Ki	22:20	which I will **b.** upon this place	935
2Ki	23:4	to **b.** forth out of the temple	3318
1Ch	9:28	that they should **b.** them in	935,3318
1Ch	13:3	And let us **b.** again the ark of our	5437
1Ch	13:5	to **b.** the ark of God from	935
1Ch	13:6	to **b.** up thence the ark of God	5927
1Ch	13:12	How shall I **b.** the ark of God	935
1Ch	15:3	to **b.** up the ark of the Lord unto	5927
1Ch	15:12	that ye may **b.** up the ark of the	5927
1Ch	15:14	sanctified themselves to **b.** up the	5927
1Ch	15:25	to **b.** up the ark of the covenant of	5927
1Ch	16:29	**b.** an offering, and come before	5375
1Ch	21:2	and **b.** the number of them to me,	935
1Ch	21:12	what word I shall **b.** again	7725
1Ch	22:19	to **b.** the ark of the covenant of the	935
2Ch	2:16	and we will **b.** it to thee in floats	935
2Ch	5:2	to **b.** up the ark of the covenant	5927
2Ch	5:5	did the priests and the Levites **b.**	5927
2Ch	6:25	and **b.** them again unto the land	7725
2Ch	11:1	that he might **b.** the kingdom	7725
2Ch	24:6	required of the Levites to **b.** in	935
2Ch	24:9	to **b.** in to the Lord the collection	935
2Ch	24:19	to **b.** them again unto the Lord;	7725
2Ch	28:13	Ye shall not **b.** in the captives	935
2Ch	29:31	**b.** sacrifices and thank offerings	935
2Ch	31:10	Since the people began to **b.** the	935
2Ch	34:24	I will **b.** evil upon this place, and	935
2Ch	34:28	all the evil that I will **b.** upon this	935
Ezr	1:8	did Cyrus king of Persia **b.** forth	3318
Ezr	1:11	All these did Sheshbazzar **b.** up	5927
Ezr	3:7	to **b.** cedar trees from Lebanon to	935
Ezr	8:17	they should **b.** unto us ministers	935
Ezr	8:30	to **b.** them to Jerusalem unto the	935
Ne	1:9	and will **b.** them unto the place	935
Ne	5:5	we **b.** into bondage our sons and	3533
Ne	8:1	to **b.** the book of the law of Moses,	935
Ne	9:29	that thou mightest **b.** them again	7725
Ne	10:31	the people of the land **b.** ware	935
Ne	10:34	to **b.** it into the house of our God,	935
Ne	10:35	And to **b.** the firstfruits of our	935
Ne	10:36	to **b.** to the house of our God,	935
Ne	10:37	we should **b.** the firstfruits of our	935
Ne	10:38	the Levites shall **b.** up the tithe	5927
Ne	10:39	**b.** the offering of the corn, of the	935
Ne	11:1	**b.** one of ten to dwell in Jerusalem	935
Ne	12:27	to **b.** them to Jerusalem, to keep	935
Ne	13:18	and did not our God **b.** all this	935
Ne	13:18	**b.** more wrath upon Israel by	935
Es	1:11	To **b.** Vashti the queen before the	935
Es	3:9	business to **b.** it into the king's	935
Es	6:1	to **b.** the book of records of the	935
Es	6:9	**b.** him on horseback through	7392
Es	6:14	hasted to **b.** Haman unto the	935
Job	6:22	Did I say **B.** unto me? or, Give	3051
Job	10:9	and wilt thou **b.** me into dust	7725
Job	14:4	Who can **b.** a clean thing out of	5414
Job	14:9	will bud, and **b.** forth boughs	6213
Job	15:35	They conceive mischief, and **b.**	3205
Job	18:14	and it shall **b.** him to the king of	6805
Job	30:23	thou wilt **b.** me to death, and the	7725
Job	33:30	To **b.** back his soul from the pit	7725
Job	38:32	Canst thou **b.** forth Mazzaroth	3318
Job	39:1	when the wild goats of the rock **b.**	3205
Job	39:2	thou the time when they **b.**	3205
Job	39:3	They bow themselves, they **b.**	6398
Job	39:12	he will **b.** home thy seed, and	7725
Job	40:12	and **b.** him low; and tread down	3665
Job	40:20	the mountains **b.** him forth food,	5375
Ps	18:27	afflicted; but wilt **b.** down high	8213
Ps	25:17	O **b.** thou me out of my distress	3318
Ps	37:5	him; and he shall **b.** it to pass	6213
Ps	37:6	shall **b.** forth thy righteousness	3318
Ps	38:*title*	A Psalm of David, to **b.** to	2142
Ps	43:3	let them **b.** me unto thy holy hill,	935
Ps	55:23	thou, O God, shalt **b.** them down	3381
Ps	59:11	and **b.** them down, O Lord our	3381
Ps	60:9	Who will **b.** me into the strong	2986
Ps	68:22	I will **b.** again from Bashan,	7725
Ps	68:22	I will **b.** my people again	7725
Ps	68:29	Jerusalem shall kings **b.** presents	2986
Ps	70:*title*	A Psalm of David, to **b.** to	2142
Ps	71:20	**b.** me up again from the depths	5927
Ps	72:3	The mountains shall **b.** peace to	5375
Ps	72:10	Tarshish and of the isles shall **b.**	7725
Ps	76:11	all that be round about him **b.**	2986
Ps	81:2	and **b.** hither the timbrel, the	5414
Ps	92:14	They shall still **b.** forth fruit in	5107
Ps	94:23	And he shall **b.** upon them their	7725
Ps	96:8	**b.** an offering, and come into his	5375
Ps	104:14	that he may **b.** forth food out of	3318
Ps	108:10	Who will **b.** me into the strong	2986
Ps	142:7	**B.** my soul out of prison, that I	3318
Ps	143:11	sake **b.** my soul out of trouble	3318
Ps	144:13	our sheep may **b.** forth thousands	503
Pr	4:8	she shall **b.** thee to honour, when	3513
Pr	19:24	will not so much as **b.** it to his	7725
Pr	26:15	him to **b.** it again to his mouth	7725
Pr	27:1	knowest not what a day may **b.**	3205
Pr	29:8	Scornful men **b.** a city into a	6315
Pr	29:23	A man's pride shall **b.** him low:	8213
Ec	3:22	for who shall **b.** him to see what	935
Ec	11:9	God will **b.** thee into judgment	935
Ec	12:14	God shall **b.** every work into	935
Ca	8:2	I would lead thee, and **b.** thee	935
Ca	8:11	was to **b.** a thousand pieces of	935
Isa	1:13	**B.** no more vain oblations; incense	935
Isa	5:2	he looked that it should **b.** forth	6213
Isa	5:4	when I looked that it should **b.**	6213
Isa	7:17	The Lord shall **b.** upon thee, and	935
Isa	14:2	and **b.** them to their place: and	935
Isa	15:9	I will **b.** more upon Dimon, lions	7896
Isa	23:4	I travail not, nor **b.** forth	3205
Isa	23:4	up young men, nor **b.** up virgins	7311
Isa	23:9	to **b.** into contempt all the	7034
Isa	25:5	Thou shalt **b.** down the noise	3665
Isa	25:11	and he shall **b.** down their pride	8213
Isa	25:12	of thy walls shall he **b.** down,	7817
Isa	25:12	lay low, and **b.** to the ground,	5060
Isa	28:21	and **b.** to pass his act, his strange	5647
Isa	31:2	and will **b.** evil, and will not call	935
Isa	33:11	ye shall **b.** forth stubble: your	3205
Isa	37:3	and there is not strength to **b.**	3205
Isa	38:8	I will **b.** again the shadow of the	7725
Isa	41:21	**b.** forth your strong reasons,	5066
Isa	41:22	Let them **b.** them forth, and shew	5066
Isa	42:1	he shall **b.** forth judgment to the	3318
Isa	42:3	he shall **b.** forth judgment unto	3318
Isa	42:7	to **b.** out the prisoners from the	3318
Isa	42:16	And I will **b.** the blind by a way	3212
Isa	43:5	I will **b.** thy seed from the east,	935
Isa	43:6	**b.** my sons from far, and my	935
Isa	43:8	**B.** forth the blind people that	3318
Isa	43:9	let them **b.** forth their witnesses,	5414
Isa	45:8	and let them **b.** forth salvation,	6509
Isa	45:21	Tell ye, and **b.** them near; yea,	5066
Isa	46:8	**b.** it again to mind, O ye	7725
Isa	46:11	I will also **b.** it to pass; I have	935
Isa	46:13	I **b.** near my righteousness; it	7126
Isa	49:5	to **b.** Jacob again to him, Though	7725
Isa	49:22	and they shall **b.** thy sons in their	935
Isa	52:8	the Lord shall **b.** again Zion	7725
Isa	55:10	and maketh it **b.** forth and bud	3205
Isa	56:7	Even them will I **b.** to my holy	935
Isa	58:7	that thou **b.** the poor that are cast	935
Isa	59:4	they conceive mischief, and **b.**	3205
Isa	60:6	they shall **b.** gold and incense;	5375
Isa	60:9	to **b.** thy sons from far, their	935
Isa	60:11	that men may **b.** unto thee the	935
Isa	60:17	For brass I will **b.** gold,	935
Isa	60:17	and for iron I will **b.** silver,	935
Isa	63:6	and I will **b.** down their strength	3381
Isa	65:9	And I will **b.** forth a seed out of	3318
Isa	65:23	in vain, nor **b.** forth for trouble;	3205
Isa	66:4	will **b.** their fears upon them;	935
Isa	66:8	Shall the earth be made to **b.**	2342
Isa	66:9	Shall I **b.** to the birth,	7665
Isa	66:9	and not cause to **b.** forth?	3205
Isa	66:9	shall I cause to **b.** forth, and	3205
Isa	66:20	And they shall **b.** all your brethren	935
Isa	66:20	as the children of Israel **b.** an	935
Jer	3:14	family, and I will **b.** you to Zion:	935
Jer	4:6	for I will **b.** evil from the north,	935
Jer	5:15	I will **b.** a nation upon you from	935
Jer	6:19	I will **b.** evil upon this people,	935
Jer	8:1	they shall **b.** out the bones of the	3318
Jer	10:24	anger, lest thou **b.** me to nothing.	
Jer	11:8	therefore I will **b.** upon them all	935
Jer	11:11	I will **b.** evil upon them, which	935
Jer	11:23	for I will **b.** evil upon the men of	935
Jer	12:2	they grow, yea, they **b.** forth	6213
Jer	12:15	and will **b.** them again, every	7725
Jer	15:19	then will I **b.** thee again, and thou	7725
Jer	16:15	and I will **b.** them again into their	7725
Jer	17:18	**b.** upon them the day of evil, and	935
Jer	17:21	sabbath day, nor **b.** it in by the	935
Jer	17:24	to **b.** in no burden through the	935
Jer	18:22	when thou shalt **b.** a troop suddenly	935
Jer	19:3	I will **b.** evil upon this place, the	935
Jer	19:15	I will **b.** upon this city and upon all	935
Jer	23:3	and will **b.** them again to their	7725
Jer	23:12	for I will **b.** evil upon them, even	935
Jer	23:40	I will **b.** an everlasting reproach	5414
Jer	24:6	And will **b.** them again to this	7725
Jer	25:9	and will **b.** them against this	935
Jer	25:13	And I will **b.** upon that land all	935
Jer	25:29	I begin to **b.** evil on the city	
Jer	26:15	ye shall surely **b.** innocent blood	5414
Jer	27:11	But the nations that **b.** their neck	935
Jer	27:12	**B.** your necks under the yoke of	935
Jer	27:22	will I **b.** them up, and restore	5927
Jer	28:3	will I **b.** again into this place all	7725
Jer	28:4	will **b.** again to this place Jeconiah	7725
Jer	28:6	to **b.** again the vessels of the	7725
Jer	29:14	and I will **b.** you again into the	7725
Jer	30:3	that I will **b.** again the captivity	7725
Jer	30:18	I will **b.** again the captivity of	7725
Jer	31:8	I will **b.** them from the north	935
Jer	31:23	I shall **b.** again their captivity	7725
Jer	31:32	**b.** them out of the land of Egypt;	3318
Jer	32:37	and I will **b.** them again unto	7725
Jer	32:42	so will I **b.** unto them all the	935
Jer	33:6	I will **b.** it health and cure, and	4608
Jer	33:11	of them that shall **b.** the sacrifice	935
Jer	35:2	and **b.** them into the house of the	935
Jer	35:17	I will **b.** upon Judah and upon all	935
Jer	36:31	and I will **b.** upon them, and upon	935
Jer	38:23	they shall **b.** out all thy wives	4672
Jer	39:16	I will **b.** my words upon this city	935
Jer	41:5	**b.** them to the house of the Lord.	935
Jer	42:17	the evil that I will **b.** upon them.	935
Jer	45:5	I will **b.** evil upon all flesh, saith	935
Jer	48:44	for I will **b.** upon it, even upon	935
Jer	48:47	Yet will I **b.** again the captivity	7725
Jer	49:5	I will **b.** a fear upon thee, saith	935
Jer	49:6	I will **b.** again the captivity of	7725
Jer	49:8	I will **b.** the calamity of Esau	935
Jer	49:16	I will **b.** thee down from thence,	3381
Jer	49:32	I will **b.** their calamity from all	935
Jer	49:36	And upon Elam will I **b.** the four	935
Jer	49:37	and I will **b.** evil upon them, even	935
Jer	49:39	I will **b.** again the captivity of	7725
Jer	50:19	And I will **b.** Israel again to his	7725
Jer	51:40	I will **b.** them down like lambs to	3381
Jer	51:44	I will **b.** forth out of his mouth	3318
Jer	51:64	the evil that I will **b.** upon her:	935
La	1:21	thou wilt **b.** the day that thou hast	935
Eze	5:17	I will **b.** the sword upon thee.	935
Eze	6:3	will **b.** a sword upon you, and I	935
Eze	7:24	Wherefore I will **b.** the worst of	935
Eze	11:7	I will **b.** you forth out of the	3318
Eze	11:8	I will **b.** a sword upon you, saith	935
Eze	11:9	And I will **b.** you out of the midst	3318
Eze	12:4	Then shalt thou **b.** forth thy stuff	3318
Eze	12:13	and I will **b.** him to Babylon to the	935
Eze	13:14	and **b.** it down to the ground, so	5060
Eze	14:17	Or if I **b.** a sword upon that land,	935
Eze	16:40	They shall also **b.** up a company	5927
Eze	16:53	When I shall **b.** again their	7725
Eze	16:53	then will I **b.** again the captivity	
Eze	17:8	that might **b.** forth branches,	6213
Eze	17:20	and I will **b.** him to Babylon, and	935
Eze	17:23	and it shall **b.** forth boughs, and	5375
Eze	20:6	to **b.** them forth of the land of	3318
Eze	20:15	I would not **b.** them into the land	935
Eze	20:34	I will **b.** you out from the people,	3318
Eze	20:35	I will **b.** you into the wilderness	935
Eze	20:37	and I will **b.** you into the bond of	935
Eze	20:38	I will **b.** them forth out of the	3318
Eze	20:41	when I **b.** you out from the people,	3318
Eze	20:42	when I shall **b.** you into the land	935
Eze	21:29	to **b.** thee upon the necks of them	5414
Eze	23:22	and I will **b.** them against thee on	935
Eze	23:46	I will **b.** up a company upon	5927
Eze	24:6	**b.** it out piece by piece; let no lot	3318
Eze	26:7	**b.** upon Tyrus Nebuchadrezzar	935

Book	Ref	Context	No.
Eze	26:19	when I shall **b.** up the deep upon	5927
Eze	26:20	When I shall **b.** thee down with	3381
Eze	28:7	I will **b.** strangers upon thee, the	935
Eze	28:8	They shall **b.** thee down to the	3381
Eze	28:18	therefore will I **b.** forth a fire	3318
Eze	28:18	and I will **b.** thee to ashes upon	5414
Eze	29:4	I will **b.** thee up out of the midst	5927
Eze	29:8	I will **b.** a sword upon thee, and	935
Eze	29:14	And I will **b.** again the captivity	7725
Eze	31:6	did all the beast of the field **b.**	3205
Eze	32:3	and they shall **b.** thee up in my	5927
Eze	32:9	when I shall **b.** thy destruction	935
Eze	33:2	When I **b.** the sword upon a land,	935
Eze	34:13	will **b.** them out from the people,	3318
Eze	34:13	and will **b.** them to their own land,	935
Eze	34:16	and **b.** again that which was	7725
Eze	36:11	they shall increase and **b.** fruit:	6509
Eze	36:24	and will **b.** you into your own land.	935
Eze	37:6	and will **b.** up flesh upon you,	5927
Eze	37:12	your graves, and **b.** you into the	935
Eze	37:21	every side, and **b.** them into their	935
Eze	38:4	and I will **b.** thee forth, and all	3318
Eze	38:16	and I will **b.** thee against my land,	935
Eze	38:17	I would **b.** thee against them?	935
Eze	39:2	**b.** thee upon the mountains of	935
Eze	39:25	Now will I **b.** again the captivity	7725
Eze	47:12	it shall **b.** forth...fruit according	1069
Da	1:3	that he should **b.** certain of the	935
Da	1:18	he should **b.** them in, then the	935
Da	2:24	**b.** me in before the king, and I	5924
Da	3:13	his rage and fury commanded to **b.**	858
Da	4:6	made I a decree to **b.** in all the	5924
Da	5:2	commanded to **b.** the golden and	858
Da	5:7	The king cried aloud to **b.** in the	5924
Da	9:24	**b.** in everlasting righteousness,	935
Ho	2:14	and **b.** her into the wilderness,	1980
Ho	7:12	I will **b.** them down as the fowls	3381
Ho	9:12	Though they **b.** up their children,	1431
Ho	9:13	Ephraim shall **b.** forth his	3318
Ho	9:16	though they **b.** forth, yet will I	3205
Joe	3:1	I shall **b.** again the captivity of	7725
Joe	3:2	and will **b.** them down into the	3381
Am	3:11	and he shall **b.** down thy strength	3381
Am	4:1	masters, **B.**, and let us drink.	935
Am	4:4	and **b.** your sacrifices every	935
Am	6:10	to **b.** the bones out of the	3318
Am	8:10	and I will **b.** up sackcloth upon	5927
Am	9:2	heaven, thence will I **b.** them	3381
Am	9:14	And I will **b.** again the captivity	7725
Ob	3	Who shall **b.** me down to the	3381
Ob	4	thence will I **b.** thee down, saith	3381
Jon	1:13	the men rowed hard to **b.** it to	7725
Mic	1:15	Yet will I **b.** an heir unto thee,	935
Mic	4:10	and labour to **b.** forth, O daughter	1518
Mic	7:9	he will **b.** me forth to the light,	3318
Zep	1:17	And I will **b.** distress upon men,	
Zep	2:2	Before the decree **b.** forth,	3205
Zep	3:5	doth he **b.** his judgment to	5414
Zep	3:10	dispersed, shall **b.** mine offering.	2986
Zep	3:20	At that time will I **b.** you again,	935
Hag	1:6	and **b.** in little; yet eat, but ye	935
Hag	1:8	Go up to the mountain, and **b.** wood,	935
Zec	3:8	I will **b.** forth my servant the	935
Zec	4:7	he shall **b.** forth the headstone	3318
Zec	5:4	I will **b.** it forth, saith the Lord of	3318
Zec	8:8	And I will **b.** them, and they shall	935
Zec	10:6	and I will **b.** them again to place	7725
Zec	10:10	I will **b.** them again also out of	7725
Zec	10:10	I will **b.** them into the land of	935
Zec	13:9	And I will **b.** the third part	935
Mal	3:10	**B.** ye all the tithes into the	935
Mt	1:21	And she shall **b.** forth a son, and	*5088*
Mt	1:23	and shall **b.** forth a son, and they	*5088*
Mt	2:8	**b.** me word again, that I may	*518*
Mt	2:13	until I **b.** thee word: for Herod	*2036*
Mt	3:8	**B.** forth therefore fruits meet for	*4160*
Mt	5:23	**if thou b. thy gift to the altar,**	*4374*
Mt	7:18	**A good tree cannot b. forth evil**	*4160*
Mt	7:18	**a corrupt tree b. forth good fruit**	*4160*
Mt	14:18	He said, **B. them hither to me,**	*5342*
Mt	17:17	**suffer you? b. him hither to me.**	*5342*
Mt	21:2	**loose them, and b. them unto me.**	*71*
Mt	28:8	did run to **b.** his disciples word.	*518*
Mk	4:20	**b. forth fruit, some thirtyfold,**	*2592*
Mk	7:32	And they **b.** unto him one that	*5342*
Mk	8:22	and they **b.** a blind man unto him,	*5342*
Mk	9:19	**shall I suffer you? b. him unto me.**	*5342*
Mk	11:2	**never man sat; loose him, and b**	*71*
Mk	12:15	**tempt ye me? b. me a penny,**	*5342*
Mk	15:22	And they **b.** him unto the place	*5342*
Lu	1:31	and **b.** forth a son, and shall call	*5088*
Lu	2:10	I **b.** you good tidings of great joy,	*2097*
Lu	3:8	**B.** forth therefore fruits worthy	*4160*
Lu	5:18	sought means to **b.** him in, and to	*1533*
Lu	5:19	they might **b.** him in because of	*1533*
Lu	6:43	**neither doth a corrupt tree b**	*4160*
Lu	8:14	**pleasures of this life, and b. no**	*5062*
Lu	8:15	**keep it, and b. forth fruit with**	*2592*
Lu	9:41	**suffer you? B. thy son hither.**	*4317*
Lu	12:11	**when they b. you unto the**	*4374*
Lu	14:21	**b. in hither the poor, and the**	*1521*
Lu	15:22	**B. forth the best robe, and put it**	*1627*
Lu	15:23	**b. hither the fatted calf, and kill**	*5342*
Lu	19:27	**reign over them, b. hither, and**	*71*
Lu	19:30	**sat: loose him, and b. him hither.**	*71*
Joh	10:16	**this fold: them also I must b.,**	*71*
Joh	14:26	**shall teach you all things, and b.**	*5179*
Joh	15:2	**that it may b. forth more fruit**	*5342*
Joh	15:16	**that ye should go and b. forth**	*5342*
Joh	18:29	What accusation **b.** ye against	*5342*
Joh	19:4	Behold, I **b.** him forth to you,	*71*
Joh	21:10	**B. of the fish which ye have now**	*5342*
Ac	5:28	and intend to **b.** this man's blood	*1863*
Ac	7:6	they should **b.** them into bondage,	*1402*
Ac	9:2	he might **b.** them bound unto	*71*
Ac	9:21	he might **b.** them bound unto the	*71*
Ac	12:4	after Easter to **b.** him forth to the	*321*
Ac	17:5	and sought to **b.** them out to the	*71*
Ac	22:5	to **b.** them which were there bound	*71*
Ac	23:10	them, and to **b.** him into the castle.	*71*
Ac	23:15	**b.** him down unto you to morrow	*2609*
Ac	23:17	**B.** this young man unto the chief	*520*
Ac	23:18	to **b.** this young man unto thee,	*71*
Ac	23:20	that thou wouldest **b.** down Paul	*2609*
Ac	23:24	and **b.** him safe unto Felix the	*1295*
Ac	24:17	I came to **b.** alms to my nation,	*4160*
Ro	7:4	we should **b.** forth fruit unto God.	*2592*
Ro	7:5	to **b.** forth fruit unto death.	*2592*
Ro	10:6	(this is, to **b.** Christ down from	*2609*
Ro	10:7	to **b.** up Christ again from the	*321*
Ro	10:15	and **b.** glad tidings of good things!	*2097*
1Co	1:19	**b.** to nothing the understanding	*114*
1Co	1:28	to **b.** to nought things that are:	*2673*
1Co	4:5	who both will **b.** to light the	*5461*
1Co	4:17	**b.** you unto remembrance of my	*363*
1Co	9:27	under my body, and **b.** it into	*1396*
1Co	16:3	them will I send to **b.** your	*667*
1Co	16:6	ye may **b.** me on my journey	*4311*
2Co	11:20	if any man **b.** you unto bondage,	*2615*
Ga	2:4	they might **b.** us into bondage:	*2615*
Ga	3:24	schoolmaster to **b.** us unto Christ,	
Eph	6:4	**b.** them up in the nurture and	*1625*
1Th	4:14	in Jesus will God **b.** with him.	*71*
2Ti	4:11	Take Mark, and **b.** him with thee:	*71*
2Ti	4:13	**b.** with thee, and the books, but	*5342*
Tit	3:13	**B.** Zenas the lawyer and Apollos	*4311*
1Pe	3:18	that he might **b.** us to God, being	*4317*
2Pe	2:1	who privily shall **b.** in damnable	*3919*
2Pe	2:1	and **b.** upon themselves swift	*1863*
2Pe	2:11	**b.** not railing accusation against	*5342*
2Jo	10	and **b.** not this doctrine, receive	*5342*
3Jo	6	thou **b.** forward on their journey	*4311*
Jude	9	durst not **b.** against him a railing	*2018*
Re	21:24	do **b.** their glory and honour into	*5342*
Re	21:26	shall **b.** the glory and honour of	*5342*

BRINGERS

Book	Ref	Context	No.
2Ki	10:5	and the **b.** up of the children,	539

BRINGEST

Book	Ref	Context	No.
1Ki	1:42	art a valiant man, and **b.** good	1319
Job	14:3	**b.** me into judgment with thee?	935
Isa	40:9	O Zion, that **b.** good tidings, get	1319
Isa	40:9	O Jerusalem, that **b.** good	1319
Ac	17:20	thou **b.** certain strange things to	*1533*

BRINGETH

Book	Ref	Context	No.
Ex	6:7	**b.** you out from under the	3318
Le	11:45	I am the Lord that **b.** you up	5927
Le	17:4	**b.** it not unto the door of the	935
Le	17:9	**b.** it not unto the door of the	935
De	8:7	the Lord thy God **b.** thee into a	935
De	14:22	the field **b.** forth year by year.	3318
1Sa	2:6	he **b.** down to the grave,	3381
1Sa	2:6	to the grave, and **b.** up.	5927
1Sa	2:7	rich: he **b.** low, and lifteth up.	8213
2Sa	18:26	He also **b.** things.	1319
2Sa	22:48	and that **b.** down the people	3381
2Sa	22:49	And that **b.** me forth from mine	3318
Job	12:6	into whose hand God **b.**	935
Job	12:22	and **b.** out to light the shadow of	3318
Job	19:29	for wrath **b.** the punishments	
Job	28:11	that is hid **b.** he forth to light.	3318
Ps	1:3	**b.** forth his fruit in his season;	5414
Ps	14:7	when the Lord **b.** back the	7725
Ps	33:10	The Lord **b.** the counsel of the	6331
Ps	37:7	of the man who **b.** wicked	6213
Ps	53:6	When God **b.** back the captivity	7725
Ps	68:6	he **b.** out those which are bound	3318
Ps	107:28	he **b.** them out of their distresses.	3318
Ps	107:30	**b.** them unto their desired haven	5148
Ps	135:7	**b.** the wind out of his treasuries.	3318
Pr	10:31	The mouth of the just **b.** forth	5107
Pr	16:30	moving his lips he **b.** evil to pass.	3615
Pr	18:16	and **b.** him before great men.	5148
Pr	19:26	causeth shame, and **b.** reproach.	2659
Pr	20:26	and **b.** the wheel over them.	7725
Pr	21:27	he **b.** it with a wicked mind?	935
Pr	29:15	himself **b.** his mother to shame.	
Pr	29:21	He that delicately **b.** up his	6445
Pr	29:25	The fear of man **b.** a snare: but	5414
Pr	30:33	churning of milk **b.** forth butter,	3318
Pr	30:33	wringing of the nose **b.** forth	3318
Pr	30:33	forcing of wrath **b.** forth strife.	3318
Pr	31:14	ships; she **b.** her food from afar.	935
Ec	2:6	the wood that **b.** forth trees	6779
Isa	8:7	the Lord **b.** up upon them the	5927
Isa	26:5	he **b.** down them that dwell on	7817
Isa	26:5	ground; he **b.** it even to the dust.	5060
Isa	40:23	That **b.** the princes to nothing;	5414
Isa	40:26	that **b.** their host by numbers:	3318
Isa	41:27	to Jerusalem one that **b.** good	1319
Isa	43:17	Which **b.** forth the chariot and	3318
Isa	52:7	the feet of him that **b.** good	1319
Isa	52:7	peace; that **b.** good tidings	1319
Isa	54:16	**b.** forth an instrument for his	3318
Isa	61:11	as the earth **b.** forth her bud,	3318
Jer	4:31	her that **b.** forth her first child,	1069
Jer	10:13	and **b.** forth the wind out of his	3318
Jer	51:16	and **b.** forth the wind out of his	3318
Eze	29:16	which **b.** their iniquity to	2142
Ho	10:1	he **b.** forth fruit unto himself:	7737
Na	1:15	feet of him that **b.** good tidings,	1319
Hag	1:11	that which the ground **b.** forth,	3318
Mt	3:20	tree which **b.** not forth good fruit	*4160*
Mt	7:17	**good tree b. forth good fruit;**	*4160*
Mt	7:17	**but a corrupt tree b. forth evil**	*4160*
Mt	7:19	**tree that b. not forth good fruit is**	*4160*
Mt	12:35	**of the heart b. forth good things:**	*1544*
Mt	12:35	**evil treasure b. forth evil things**	*1544*
Mt	13:23	**and b. forth some an hundredfold,**	*4160*
Mt	13:52	**b. forth out of his treasure things**	*1544*
Mt	17:1	**b.** them up into an high mountain	*399*
Mk	4:28	**earth b. forth fruit of herself;**	*2592*
Lu	3:9	which **b.** not forth good fruit is	*4160*
Lu	6:43	**b. not forth corrupt fruit; neither**	*4160*
Lu	6:45	**b. forth that which is good;**	*4393*
Lu	6:45	**an evil b. forth that which is evil:**	*4393*
Joh	12:24	**if it die, it b. forth much fruit.**	*5342*
Joh	15:5	**the same b. forth much fruit:**	*5342*
Col	1:6	and **b.** forth fruit, as it doth also	*2592*
Tit	2:11	grace of God that **b.** salvation	*4992*
Heb	1:6	when he **b.** in the firstbegotton	*1521*
Heb	6:7	**b.** forth herbs meet for them by	*5088*
Jas	1:15	when lust hath conceived, it **b.**	*616*
Jas	1:15	when it is finished, **b.** forth death.	*5088*

BRINGING

Book	Ref	Context	No.
Ex	12:42	for **b.** them out from the land of	3318
Ex	36:6	people were restrained from **b.**	935
Nu	5:15	**b.** iniquity to remembrance.	2142
Nu	14:36	by **b.** up a slander upon the land,	3318
2Sa	19:10	speak ye not a word of **b.** the king	7725
2Sa	19:43	be first had in **b.** back our king?	7725
1Ki	10:22	**b.** gold, and silver, and ivory, and	5375
2Ki	21:12	am **b.** such evil upon Jerusalem	935
2Ch	9:21	the ships of Tarshish **b.** gold, and	5375
Ne	13:15	**b.** in sheaves, and lading asses;	935
Ps	126:6	rejoicing, **b.** his sheaves with him.	5375
Jer	17:26	**b.** burnt offerings, and sacrifices,	935
Jer	17:26	and **b.** sacrifices of praise unto the	935
Eze	20:9	**b.** them forth out of the land of	3318

Da 9:12 by **b.** upon us a great evil: 935
Mt 21:43 **a nation b. forth the fruits thereof.** *4160*
Mk 2:3 **b.** one sick of the palsy, which was *5342*
Lu 24:1 **b.** the spices which they had *5342*
Ac 5:16 unto Jerusalem, **b.** sick folks, and *5342*
Ro 7:23 **b.** me into captivity to the law of *163*
2Co 10:5 **b.** into captivity every thought to *163*
Heb 2:10 **b.** many sons unto glory, to make *71*
Heb 7:19 the **b.** in of a better hope did; *1898*
2Pe 2:5 **b.** in the flood upon the world *1863*

BRINK
Ge 41:3 kine upon the **b.** of the river. 8193
Ex 2:3 in the flags by the river's **b.**. 8193
Ex 7:15 stand by the river's **b.** against he 8193
De 2:36 is by the **b.** of the river Arnon, 8193
Jos 3:8 When ye are come to the **b.** of 7097
Eze 47:6 to return to the **b.** of the river. 8193

BROAD See also ABROAD; BROADER.
Ex 27:1 five cubits long, and five cubits **b.**; 7341
Nu 16:38 let them make them **b.** plates for 7555
Nu 16:39 and they were made **b.** plates for 7554
1Ki 6:6 chamber was five cubits **b.**, 7341
1Ki 6:6 and the middle was six cubits **b.**, 7341
1Ki 6:6 and the third was seven cubits **b.**: 7341
2Ch 6:13 five cubits long, and five cubits **b.**, 7341
Ne 3:8 Jerusalem unto the **b.** wall. 7342
Ne 12:38 furnaces even unto the **b.** wall; 7342
Job 36:16 out of the strait into a **b.** place, 7338
Ps 119:96 commandment is exceeding **b.**. 7342
Ca 3:2 in the streets, and in the **b.** ways. 7339
Isa 33:21 of **b.** rivers and streams; 7338,3027
Jer 5:1 seek in the **b.** places thereof, if ye 7339
Jer 51:58 The **b.** walls of Babylon shall be 7342
Eze 40:6 the gate, which was one reed **b.**; 7341
Eze 40:6 the other threshold...one reed **b.**. 7341
Eze 40:7 one reed long, and one reed **b.**; 7341
Eze 40:29 and five and twenty cubits **b.** 7341
Eze 40:30 cubits long, and five cubits **b.** 7341
Eze 40:33 and five and twenty cubits **b.** 7341
Eze 40:42 and a cubit and a half **b.**. and one 7341
Eze 40:43 hooks, an hand **b.**, fastened
Eze 40:47 and an hundred cubits **b.**; four 7341
Eze 41:1 six cubits **b.** on the one side, 7341
Eze 41:1 six cubits **b.** on the other side, 7341
Eze 41:12 the west was seventy cubits **b.**; 7341
Eze 42:11 long as they, and as **b.** as they: 7342
Eze 42:20 and five hundred **b.**, to make a 7341
Eze 43:16 twelve cubits long, twelve **b.**, 7341
Eze 43:17 cubits long and fourteen **b.** in the 7341
Eze 45:6 of the city five thousand **b.**, 7341
Eze 46:22 forty cubits long and thirty **b.**: 7341
Na 2:4 against another in the **b.** ways: 7339
Mt 7:13 **b. is the way, that leadeth to** *2149*
Mt 23:5 **they make b. their phylacteries,** *4115*

BROADER
Job 11:9 the earth, and **b.** them the sea. 7342

BROIDED See also BROIDERED.
1Ti 2:9 not with **b.** hair, of gold, or *4117*

BROIDERED
Ex 28:4 a **b.** coat, a mitre, and a girdle: 8665
Eze 16:10 I clothed thee also with **b.** work, 7553
Eze 16:13 fine linen, and silk, and **b.** work; 7553
Eze 16:18 tookest thy **b.** garments, and 7553
Eze 26:16 and put off their **b.** garments: 7553
Eze 27:7 linen with **b.** work from Egypt 7553
Eze 27:16 **b.** work, and fine linen, and coral, 7553
Eze 27:24 blue clothes, and **b.** work, and in 7553

BROILED
Lu 24:42 they gave him a piece of a **b.** fish, *3702*

BROKE See BRAKE.

BROKEN See also BROKENFOOTED; BROKENHANDED; BROKENHEARTED.
Ge 7:11 fountains of the great deep **b.** up, 1234
Ge 17:14 he hath **b.** my covenant. 6565
Ge 38:29 How hast thou **b.** forth? this 6555
Le 6:28 wherein it is sodden shall be **b.**: 7665
Le 11:35 they shall be **b.** down: for they 5422
Le 13:20 a plague of leprosy **b.** out of the 6524
Le 13:25 a leprosy **b.** out of the burning: 6524
Le 15:12 which hath the issue, shall be **b.**: 7665
Le 21:20 scabbed, or hath his stones **b.**; 4790
Le 22:22 Blind, or **b.**, or maimed, or having 7665
Le 22:24 bruised, or crushed, or **b.**, or cut; 5423
Le 26:13 I have **b.** the bands of your yoke, 7665
Le 26:26 I have **b.** the staff of your bread, 7665
Nu 15:31 and hath **b.** his commandment, 6565
Jg 5:22 Then were the horsehoofs **b.** by 1986
Jg 16:9 as a thread of tow is **b.** when it 5423
1Sa 2:4 bows of the mighty men are **b.**, 2844
1Sa 2:10 shall be **b.** to pieces; out of 2865
2Sa 5:20 hath **b.** forth upon mine enemies 6555
2Sa 22:35 a bow of steel is **b.** by mine arms. 5181
1Ki 18:30 altar of the Lord that was **b.** 2040
1Ki 22:48 the ships were **b.** at Ezion-geber. 7665
2Ki 11:6 the house, that it be not **b.** down. 4535
2Ki 25:4 And the city was **b.** up, and all 1234
1Ch 14:11 God hath **b.** in upon mine enemies 6555
2Ch 20:37 the Lord hath **b.** thy works. 6555
2Ch 20:37 And the ships were **b.**, that they 7665
2Ch 24:7 that wicked woman, had **b.** up 6555
2Ch 25:12 that they all were **b.** in pieces. 1234
2Ch 32:5 the wall that was **b.**, and raised 6555
2Ch 33:3 his father had **b.** down, and he 5422
2Ch 34:7 when he had **b.** down the altars 5422
Ne 1:3 wall of Jerusalem also is **b.** down, 6555
Ne 2:13 of Jerusalem. which were **b.** down, 6555
Job 4:10 teeth of the young lions, are **b.** 5421
Job 7:5 my skin is **b.**, and become 7280
Job 16:12 but he hath **b.** me asunder: 6565
Job 17:11 my purposes are **b.** off, even the 5423
Job 22:9 of the fatherless have been **b.**. 1792
Job 24:20 wickedness shall be **b.** as a tree. 7665
Job 31:22 mine arm be **b.** from the bone. 7665
Job 38:15 and the high arm shall be **b.** 7665
Ps 3:7 hast **b.** the teeth of the ungodly. 7665
Ps 18:34 a bow of steel is **b.** by mine arms. 5181
Ps 31:12 of mind: I am like a **b.** vessel. 6
Ps 34:18 unto them that are of a **b.** heart; 7665
Ps 34:20 his bones: not one of them is **b.**. 7665
Ps 37:15 and their bows shall be **b.** 7665
Ps 37:17 the arms of the wicked shall be **b.**; 7665
Ps 38:8 I am feeble and sore **b.**: I have 1794
Ps 44:19 Though thou hast sore **b.** us in 1794
Ps 51:8 the bones which thou hast **b.** may 1794
Ps 51:17 sacrifices of God are a **b.** spirit: 7665
Ps 51:17 a **b.** and a contrite heart, 7665
Ps 55:20 him: he hath **b.** his covenant. 2490
Ps 60:2 earth to tremble; thou hast **b.** it; 6480
Ps 69:20 Reproach hath **b.** my heart; 7665
Ps 80:12 thou then **b.** down her hedges, 6555
Ps 89:10 Thou hast **b.** Rahab in pieces, 1792
Ps 89:40 thou hast **b.** down all his hedges; 6555
Ps 107:16 he hath **b.** the gates of brass, 7665
Ps 109:16 might even slay the **b.** in heart. 5218
Ps 124:7 snare is **b.**, and we are escaped. 7665
Ps 147:3 He healeth the **b.** in heart, 7665
Pr 3:20 knowledge the depths are **b.** up, 1234
Pr 6:15 suddenly shall he be **b.** without 7665
Pr 15:13 sorrow of the heart the spirit is **b.**, 5218
Pr 17:22 but a **b.** spirit drieth the bones. 5218
Pr 24:31 stone wall thereof was **b.** down. 2040
Pr 25:19 is like a **b.** tooth, and a foot out 7465
Pr 25:28 is like a city that is **b.** down, 6555
Ec 4:12 a threefold cord is not quickly **b.**. 5423
Ec 12:6 or the golden bowl be **b.**, 7533
Ec 12:6 the pitcher be **b.** at the fountain, 7665
Ec 12:6 or the wheel **b.** at the cistern. 7533
Isa 5:27 the latchet of their shoes be **b.**; 5423
Isa 7:8 five years shall Ephraim be **b.**, 2844
Isa 8:9 people, and ye shall be **b.** in pieces; 2844
Isa 8:9 be **b.** in pieces; gird yourselves, 2844
Isa 8:9 and ye shall be **b.** in pieces. 2844
Isa 8:15 shall stumble, and fall, and be **b.**, 7665
Isa 9:4 hast **b.** the yoke of his burden, 2865
Isa 14:5 hath **b.** the staff of the wicked, 7665
Isa 14:29 rod of him that smote thee is **b.**: 7665
Isa 16:8 the heathen have **b.** down the 1986
Isa 19:10 they shall be **b.** in the purposes 1792
Isa 21:9 images of her gods he hath **b.** 7665
Isa 22:10 and the houses have ye **b.** down 5422
Isa 24:5 **b.** the everlasting covenant. 6565
Isa 24:10 The city of confusion is **b.** down: 7665
Isa 24:19 The earth is utterly **b.** down, 7489
Isa 27:11 withered, they shall be **b.** off; 7665
Isa 28:13 and fall backward, and be **b.**, 7665
Isa 30:14 potter's vessel that is **b.** in pieces; 3807
Isa 33:8 he hath **b.** the covenant, he hath 6565
Isa 33:20 any of the cords thereof be **b.**, 5423
Isa 36:6 staff of this **b.** reed, on Egypt; 7533
Jer 2:13 **b.** cisterns, that can hold no 7665
Jer 2:16 have **b.** the crown of thy head. 7462
Jer 2:20 I have **b.** thy yoke, and burst thy 7665
Jer 4:26 all the cities thereof were **b.** down 5422
Jer 5:5 have altogether **b.** the yoke, 7665
Jer 10:20 all my cords are **b.**: my children 5423
Jer 11:10 of Judah have **b.** my covenant 6565
Jer 11:16 it, and the branches of it are **b.**. 7489
Jer 14:17 virgin daughter of my people is **b.** 7665
Jer 22:28 man Coniah a despised **b.** idol? 5310
Jer 23:9 Mine heart within me is **b.** 7665
Jer 28:2 **b.** the yoke of the king of Babylon. 7665
Jer 28:12 had **b.** the yoke from off the neck 7665
Jer 28:13 Thou hast **b.** the yokes of wood; 7665
Jer 33:21 Then may also my covenant be **b.** 6565
Jer 37:11 The army of the Chaldeans was **b.** 5927
Jer 39:2 the month, the city was **b.** up. 1234
Jer 48:17 How is the strong staff **b.**, and 7665
Jer 48:20 for it is **b.** down: howl and cry; 2865
Jer 48:25 his arm is **b.**, saith the Lord. 7665
Jer 48:38 I have **b.** Moab like a vessel 7665
Jer 48:39 howl, saying, How is it **b.** down! 2865
Jer 50:2 Merodach is **b.** in pieces; her 2844
Jer 50:2 her images are **b.** in pieces. 2865
Jer 50:17 king of Babylon hath **b.** his bones 6105
Jer 50:23 whole earth cut asunder and **b.**! 7665
Jer 51:30 dwelling places; her bars are **b.**. 7665
Jer 51:56 every one of their bows is **b.**; 2865
Jer 51:58 of Babylon shall be utterly **b.**, 6209
Jer 52:7 Then the city was **b.** up, and all 1234
La 2:9 destroyed and **b.** her bars: 7665
La 3:4 made old; he hath **b.** my bones. 7665
La 3:16 **b.** my teeth with gravel stones, 1638
Eze 6:4 and your images shall be **b.**; 7665
Eze 6:6 and your idols may be **b.** and 7665
Eze 6:9 I am **b.** with their whorish heart, 7665
Eze 17:19 and my covenant that he hath **b.**, 6331
Eze 19:12 her strong rods were **b.** and 6561
Eze 26:2 **b.** that was the gates of the people: 7665
Eze 27:26 the east wind hath **b.** thee in the 7665
Eze 27:34 thou shalt be **b.** by the seas in 7665
Eze 30:4 her foundations shall be **b.** 2040
Eze 30:21 I have **b.** the arm of Pharaoh. 7665
Eze 30:22 strong, and that which was **b.**; 7665
Eze 31:12 and his boughs are **b.** by all the 7665
Eze 32:28 thou shalt be **b.** in the midst of 7665
Eze 34:4 ye bound up that which was **b.**, 7665
Eze 34:16 will bind up that which was **b.**, 7665
Eze 34:27 have **b.** the bands of their yoke, 7665
Eze 44:7 and they have **b.** my covenant 6565
Da 2:35 silver, and the gold, **b.** to pieces 1854
Da 2:42 be partly strong, and partly **b.**. 8406
Da 8:8 strong, the great horn was **b.**; 7665
Da 8:22 Now that being **b.**, whereas 7665
Da 8:25 but he shall be **b.** without hand. 7665
Da 11:4 his kingdom shall be **b.**, and shall 7665
Da 11:22 and shall be **b.**; yea, also the prince 7665
Ho 5:11 Ephraim is oppressed and **b.** 7533
Ho 8:6 Samaria shall be **b.** in pieces. 7616
Joe 1:17 the barns are **b.** down; for the 2040
Jon 1:4 that the ship was like to be **b.** 7665
Mic 2:13 they have **b.** up, and have passed 6555
Zec 11:11 And it was **b.** in that day; and so 6565
Zec 11:16 nor heal that that is **b.**, nor feed 7665
Mt 15:37 they took up of the **b.** meat that *2801*
Mt 21:44 **fall on this stone shall be b.:** *4917*
Mt 24:43 **suffered his house to be b. up** *1358*
Mk 2:4 when they had **b.** it up, they let *1846*
Mk 5:4 and the fetters **b.** in pieces: *4937*
Mk 8:8 they took up the **b.** meat that *2801*
Lu 12:39 **suffered his house to be b.** *1358*
Lu 20:18 **fall upon that stone shall be b.;** *4917*
Joh 5:18 he not only had **b.** the sabbath, *3089*
Joh 7:23 **law of Moses should not be b.;** *3089*
Joh 10:35 **and the scripture cannot be b.;** *3089*
Joh 19:31 that their legs might be **b.**, *2608*
Joh 19:36 A bone of him shall not be **b.**. *4937*
Joh 21:11 many, yet was not the net **b.**, *4977*
Ac 13:43 when the congregation was **b.** 3089
Ac 20:11 and had **b.** bread, and eaten, *2806*
Ac 27:35 when he had **b.** it, he began to *2806*
Ac 27:41 the hinder part was **b.** with the *3089*
Ac 27:44 some on **b.** pieces of the ship. *3089*
Ro 11:17 some of the branches be **b.** off, *1575*
Ro 11:19 The branches were **b.** off, that I *1575*
Ro 11:20 because of unbelief they were **b.** off, *1575*
1Co 11:24 **is my body, which is b. for you:** *2806*

Eph 2:14 hath **b.** down the middle wall... *3089*
Re 2:27 **of the potter shall they be b.**... *4937*

BROKENFOOTED
Le 21:19 Or a man that is **b.**,... 7667,7272

BROKENHANDED
Le 21:19 that is brokenfooted, or **b.**... 7667,3027

BROKENHEARTED
Isa 61:1 bind up the **b.**, to proclaim... 7665,3820
Lu 4:18 **hath sent me to heal the b.**,... *4937, 2588*

BROOD
Lu 13:34 **as a hen doth gather her b.**... *3555*

BROOK See also BROOKS.
Ge 32:23 and sent them over the **b.**,... 5158
Le 23:40 willows of the **b.**; and ye shall... 5158
Nu 13:23 they came unto the **b.** of Eschol,... 5158
Nu 13:24 The place was called the **b.**... 5158
De 2:13 you over the **b.** Zered... 5158
De 2:13 And we went over the **b.** Zered... 5158
De 2:14 until we were come over the **b.**... 5158
De 9:21 I cast the dust thereof into the **b.**... 5158
1Sa 17:40 five smooth stones out of the **b.**,... 5158
1Sa 30:9 and came to the **b.** Besor, where... 5158
1Sa 30:10 could not go over the **b.** Besor... 5158
1Sa 30:21 to abide at the **b.** Besor: and they... 5158
2Sa 15:23 himself passed over the **b.** Kidron,... 5158
2Sa 17:20 They be gone over the **b.** of water... 4323
1Ki 2:37 out and passest over the **b.** Kidron,... 5158
1Ki 15:13 and burnt it by the **b.** Kidron... 5158
1Ki 17:3 hide thyself by the **b.** Cherith,... 5158
1Ki 17:4 thou shalt drink of the **b.**;... 5158
1Ki 17:5 and dwelt by the **b.** Cherith, that... 5158
1Ki 17:6 evening; and he drank of the **b.**... 5158
1Ki 17:7 the **b.** dried up, because there... 5158
1Ki 18:40 brought them down to the **b.**... 5158
2Ki 23:6 unto the **b.** Kidron, and... 5158
2Ki 23:6 burned it at the **b.** Kidron... 5158
2Ki 23:12 dust of them into the **b.** Kidron... 5158
2Ch 15:16 and burnt it at the **b.** Kidron... 5158
2Ch 20:16 at the end of the **b.**, before... 5158
2Ch 29:16 abroad into the **b.** Kidron... 5158
2Ch 30:14 cast them into the **b.** Kidron... 5158
2Ch 32:4 the **b.** that ran through the midst... 5158
Ne 2:15 went I up in the night by the **b.**... 5158
Job 6:15 have dealt deceitfully as a **b.**,... 5158
Job 40:22 willows of the **b.** compass him... 5158
Ps 83:9 as to Jabin, at the **b.** of Kison:... 5158
Ps 110:7 He shall drink of the **b.** in the way:... 5158
Pr 18:4 of wisdom as a flowing **b.**... 5158
Isa 15:7 away to the **b.** of the willows... 5158
Jer 31:40 the fields unto the **b.** of Kidron,... 5158
Joh 18:1 over the **b.** Cedron. where was... *5493*

BROOKS
Nu 21:14 in the **b.** of Arnon,... 5158
Nu 21:15 the stream of the **b.** that goeth... 5158
De 8:7 good land, a land of **b.** of water,... 5158
2Sa 23:30 Hiddai of the **b.** of Gaash,... 5158
1Ki 18:5 and unto all **b.**: peradventure... 5158
1Ch 11:32 Hurai of the **b.** of Gaash,... 5158
Job 6:15 and as a stream of **b.** they pass... 5158
Job 20:17 the **b.** of honey and butter... 5158
Job 22:24 of Ophir as the stones of the **b.**... 5158
Ps 42:1 hart panteth after the water **b.**... 650
Isa 19:6 and the **b.** of defence shall be... 2975
Isa 19:7 the paper reeds by the **b.**,... 2975
Isa 19:7 by the mouth of the **b.**,... 2975
Isa 19:7 and everything sown by the **b.**,... 2975
Isa 19:8 they that cast angle into the **b.**... 2975

BROTH
Jg 6:19 and he put the **b.** in a pot, and... 4839
Jg 6:20 this rock, and pour out the **b.**... 4839
Isa 65:4 and **b.** of abominable things... 6564

BROTHER See also BRETHREN; BROTHERHOOD; BROTHER'S; BROTHERS'.
Ge 4:2 And she again bare his **b.** Abel... 251
Ge 4:8 And Cain talked with Abel his **b.**;... 251
Ge 4:8 Cain rose up against Abel his **b.**,... 251
Ge 4:9 Where is Abel thy **b.**?... 251
Ge 9:5 at the hand of every man's **b.**... 251
Ge 10:21 the **b.** of Japheth the elder, even... 251
Ge 14:13 **b.** of Eschol, and **b.** of Aner;... 251
Ge 14:14 Abram heard that his **b.** was taken... 251
Ge 14:16 also brought his **b.** Lot, and his... 251
Ge 20:5 she herself said, He is my **b.**:... 251
Ge 20:13 come, say of me, He is my **b.**... 251
Ge 20:16 Behold, I have given thy **b.**... 251
Ge 22:20 born children unto thy **b.** Nahor;... 251
Ge 22:21 Huz his firstborn, and Buz his **b.**,... 251
Ge 22:23 did bear of Nahor, Abraham's **b.**... 251
Ge 24:15 the wife of Nahor, Abraham's **b.**,... 251
Ge 24:29 Rebekah had a **b.**, and his name... 251
Ge 24:53 he gave also to her **b.** and to her... 251
Ge 24:55 her **b.** and her mother said, Let the... 251
Ge 25:26 after that came his **b.** out, and his... 251
Ge 27:6 thy father speak unto Esau thy **b.**,... 251
Ge 27:11 Esau my **b.** is a hairy man, and... 251
Ge 27:23 as his **b.** Esau's hands: so he... 251
Ge 27:30 Esau his **b.** came in from his... 251
Ge 27:35 Thy **b.** came with subtlty,... 251
Ge 27:40 thou live, and shalt serve thy **b.**;... 251
Ge 27:41 then will I slay my **b.** Jacob... 251
Ge 27:42 Behold, thy **b.** Esau, as touching... 251
Ge 27:43 flee thou to Laban my **b.** to Haran;... 251
Ge 28:2 daughters of Laban thy mother's **b.**... 251
Ge 28:5 the Syrian, the **b.** of Rebekah,... 251
Ge 29:10 daughter of Laban his mother's **b.**,... 251
Ge 29:10 sheep of Laban his mother's **b.**,... 251
Ge 29:10 the flock of Laban his mother's **b.**... 251
Ge 29:12 Rachel that he was her father's **b.**,... 251
Ge 29:15 Because thou art my **b.**,... 251
Ge 32:3 before him to Esau his **b.**... 251
Ge 32:6 We came to thy **b.** Esau, and also... 251
Ge 32:11 from the hand of my **b.**, from the... 251
Ge 32:13 hand a present for Esau his **b.**;... 251
Ge 32:17 When Esau my **b.** meeteth thee,... 251
Ge 33:3 until he came near to his **b.**... 251
Ge 33:9 Esau said, I have enough, my **b.**;... 251
Ge 35:1 from the face of Esau thy **b.**... 251
Ge 35:7 he fled from the face of his **b.**... 251
Ge 36:6 from the face of his **b.** Jacob... 251
Ge 37:26 is it if we slay our **b.**, and conceal... 251
Ge 37:27 for he is our **b.** and our flesh:... 251
Ge 38:8 her, and raise up seed to thy **b.**... 251
Ge 38:9 that he should give seed to his **b.**... 251
Ge 38:29 behold, his **b.** came out: and she... 251
Ge 38:30 afterward came out his **b.**, that... 251
Ge 42:4 But Benjamin, Joseph's **b.**,... 251
Ge 42:15 except your youngest **b.** come... 251
Ge 42:16 let him fetch your **b.**, and ye shall... 251
Ge 42:20 bring your youngest **b.** unto me;... 251
Ge 42:21 guilty concerning our **b.**, in that... 251
Ge 42:34 bring your youngest **b.** unto me:... 251
Ge 42:34 I deliver you your **b.**, and ye shall... 251
Ge 42:38 his **b.** is dead, and he is left alone:... 251
Ge 43:3 face, except your **b.** be with you... 251
Ge 43:4 If thou wilt send our **b.** with us, we... 251
Ge 43:5 face, except your **b.** be with you,... 251
Ge 43:6 the man whether ye had yet a **b.**?... 251
Ge 43:7 have ye another **b.**? and we told... 251
Ge 43:7 he would say, Bring your **b.** down?... 251
Ge 43:13 Take also your **b.**, and arise, and... 251
Ge 43:14 he may send away your other **b.**,... 251
Ge 43:29 saw his **b.** Benjamin, his mother's... 251
Ge 43:29 Is this your younger **b.**, of whom... 251
Ge 43:30 his bowels did yearn upon his **b.**;... 251
Ge 44:19 saying, Have ye a father, or a **b.**?... 251
Ge 44:20 and his **b.** is dead, and he alone is... 251
Ge 44:23 Except your youngest **b.** come... 251
Ge 44:26 if our youngest **b.** be with us, then... 251
Ge 44:26 except our youngest **b.** be with us... 251
Ge 45:4 he said, I am Joseph your **b.**, whom... 251
Ge 45:12 the eyes of my **b.** Benjamin, that... 251
Ge 45:14 fell upon his **b.** Benjamin's neck,... 251
Ge 48:19 younger **b.** shall be greater than he,... 251
Ex 4:14 Is not Aaron the Levite thy **b.**?... 251
Ex 7:1 Aaron thy **b.** shall be thy prophet... 251
Ex 7:2 thy **b.** shall speak unto Pharoah,... 251
Ex 28:1 take thou unto thee Aaron thy **b.**,... 251
Ex 28:2, 4 holy garments for Aaron thy **b.**,... 251
Ex 28:41 put them upon Aaron thy **b.**, and... 251
Ex 32:27 slay every man his **b.**, and every... 251
Ex 32:29 man upon his son, and upon his **b.**;... 251
Le 16:2 Speak unto Aaron thy **b.**, that he... 251
Le 18:14 the nakedness of thy father's **b.**,... 251
Le 19:17 Thou shalt not hate thy **b.** in thine... 251
Le 21:2 for his daughter, and for his **b.**,... 251
Le 25:25 If thy **b.** be waxen poor, and hath... 251
Le 25:25 he redeem that which his **b.** sold... 251
Le 25:35 if thy **b.** be waxen poor, and fallen... 251
Le 25:36 God; that thy **b.** may live with thee... 251
Le 25:39 if thy **b.** that dwelleth by thee be... 251
Le 25:47 **b.** that dwelleth by him wax poor,... 251
Nu 6:7 for his **b.**, or for his sister, when... 251
Nu 20:8 thou, and Aaron thy **b.**, and speak... 251
Nu 20:14 Thus saith thy **b.** Israel, Thou... 251
Nu 27:13 as Aaron thy **b.** was gathered,... 251
Nu 36:2 our **b.** unto his daughters... 251
De 1:16 between every man and his **b.**, and... 251
De 13:6 If thy **b.**, the son of thy mother, or... 251
De 15:2 of his neighbour, or of his **b.**;... 251
De 15:3 that which is thine with thy **b.**... 251
De 15:7 shut thine hand from thy poor **b.**:... 251
De 15:9 eye be evil against thy poor **b.**, and... 251
De 15:11 open thine hand wide unto thy **b.**,... 251
De 15:12 if thy **b.**, an Hebrew man, or an... 251
De 17:15 over thee, which is not thy **b.**... 251
De 19:18 hath testified falsely against his **b.**;... 251
De 19:19 thought to have done unto his **b.**:... 251
De 22:1 case bring them again unto thy **b.**... 251
De 22:2 of thy **b.** be not nigh unto thee, or if... 251
De 22:2 until thy **b.** seek after it, and thou... 251
De 23:7 and Edomite; for he is thy **b.**:... 251
De 23:19 not lend upon usury to thy **b.**;... 251
De 23:20 unto thy **b.** thou shalt not lend upon... 251
De 24:10 When thou dost lend thy **b.**... 7453
De 25:3 thy **b.** should seem vile unto thee... 251
De 25:5 husband's **b.** shall go in unto her,... 2993
De 25:5 the duty of an husband's **b.**... 2992
De 25:6 shall succeed in the name of his **b.**... 251
De 25:7 My husband's **b.** refuseth to raise... 2993
De 25:7 his **b.** a name in Israel, he will not... 251
De 25:7 the duty of my husband's **b.**... 2992
De 28:54 his eye shall be evil toward his **b.**,... 251
De 32:50 Aaron thy **b.** died in mount Hor,... 251
Jos 15:17 son of Kenaz, the **b.** of Caleb, took... 251
Jg 1:3 And Judah said unto Simeon his **b.**... 251
Jg 1:13 son of Kenaz, Caleb's younger **b.**,... 251
Jg 1:17 Judah went with Simeon his **b.**,... 251
Jg 3:9 son of Kenaz, Caleb's younger **b.**... 251
Jg 9:3 for they said, He is our **b.**... 251
Jg 9:18 Shechem, because he is your **b.**;... 251
Jg 9:21 there, for fear of Abimelech his **b.**... 251
Jg 9:24 upon Abimelech their **b.**, which... 251
Jg 20:23 the children of Benjamin my **b.**?... 251
Jg 20:28 of Benjamin my **b.**, or shall I cease?... 251
Jg 21:6 repented them for Benjamin their **b.**,... 251
Ru 4:3 which was our **b.** Elimelech's:... 251
1Sa 14:3 the son of Ahitub, I-chabod's **b.**,... 251
1Sa 17:28 Eliab his eldest **b.** heard when he... 251
1Sa 20:29 my **b.**, he hath commanded me to... 251
1Sa 26:6 the son of Zeruiah, **b.** to Joab,... 251
2Sa 1:26 distressed for thee, my **b.** Jonathan:... 251
2Sa 2:22 I hold up my face to Joab thy **b.**?... 251
2Sa 2:27 every one from following his **b.**... 251
2Sa 3:27 died, or the blood of Asahel his **b.**... 251
2Sa 3:30 Joab and Abishai his **b.** slew Abner,... 251
2Sa 3:30 because he had slain their **b.**... 251
2Sa 4:6 Rechab and Baanah his **b.** escaped... 251
2Sa 4:9 answered Rechab and Baanah his **b.**,... 251
2Sa 10:10 into the hand of Abishai his **b.**,... 251
2Sa 13:3 the son of Shimeah David's **b.**:... 251
2Sa 13:4 Tamar, my **b.** Absalom's sister... 251
2Sa 13:7 Go now to thy **b.** Amnon's house,... 251
2Sa 13:8 Tamar went to her **b.** Amnon's... 251
2Sa 13:10 into the chamber to Amnon her **b.**... 251
2Sa 13:12 she answered him, Nay, my **b.**, do... 251
2Sa 13:20 Absalom her **b.** said unto her, Hath... 251
2Sa 13:20 Amnon thy **b.** been with thee?... 251
2Sa 13:20 peace, my sister: he is thy **b.**;... 251
2Sa 13:20 desolate in her **b.** Absalom's house... 251
2Sa 13:22 Absalom spake unto his **b.** Amnon...
2Sa 13:26 thee, let my **b.** Amnon go with us... 251
2Sa 13:32 the son of Shimeah David's **b.**,... 251
2Sa 14:7 Deliver him that smote his **b.**, that... 251
2Sa 14:7 life of his **b.** whom he slew;... 251
2Sa 18:2 the son of Zeruiah, Joab's **b.**, and... 251
2Sa 20:9 said, Art thou in health, my **b.**?... 251
2Sa 20:10 Abishai his **b.** pursued after Sheba... 251
2Sa 21:19 slew the **b.** of Goliath the Gittite,...
2Sa 21:21 Shimeah the **b.** of David slew him... 251
2Sa 23:18 Abishai, the **b.** of Joab, the son of... 251
2Sa 23:24 Asahel the **b.** of Joab was one of... 251
1Ki 1:10 and Solomon his **b.**, he called not... 251
1Ki 2:7 I fled because of Absalom thy **b.**... 251
1Ki 2:21 be given to Adonijah thy **b.** to wife... 251
1Ki 2:22 for he is mine elder **b.**; even for... 251
1Ki 9:13 which thou hast given me, my **b.**?... 251
1Ki 13:30 over him, saying, Alas, my **b.**... 251

1Ki 20:32 said, Is he yet alive? he is my **b.** 251
1Ki 20:33 Thy **b.** Ben-hadad. Then he said, 251
2Ki 24:17 made Mattaniah his father's **b.** king 251
1Ch 2:32 sons of Jada the **b.** of Shammai; 251
1Ch 2:42 sons of Caleb the **b.** of Jerahmeel 251
1Ch 4:11 Chelub the **b.** of Shuah begat Mehir, 251
1Ch 6:39 And his **b.** Asaph, who stood on 251
1Ch 7:16 the name of his **b.** was Sheresh; 251
1Ch 7:35 the sons of his **b.** Helem; Zophah, 251
1Ch 8:39 the sons of Eshek his **b.** were, Ulam 251
1Ch 11:20 Abishai the **b.** of Joab, he was chief 251
1Ch 11:26 Asahel the **b.** of Joab, Elhanan 251
1Ch 11:38 Joel the **b.** of Nathan, Mibharthe 251
1Ch 11:45 Shimei, and Joha his **b.**, the Tizite, 251
1Ch 19:11 unto the hand of Abishai his **b.**, 251
1Ch 19:15 fled before Abishai his **b.**, and 251
1Ch 20:5 Jair slew Lahmi the **b.** of Goliath 251
1Ch 20:7 son of Shimea David's **b.** slew him. 251
1Ch 24:25 The **b.** of Michah was Isshiah: of 1730
1Ch 26:22 Zetham, and Joel his **b.**, which 251
1Ch 27:7 Asahel the **b.** of Joab, and Zebadiah 251
2Ch 31:12 and Shimei his **b.**, was the next, 251
2Ch 31:13 Cononiah and Shimei his **b.**, at the 251
2Ch 36:4 Eliakim his **b.** king over Judah 251
2Ch 36:4 Necho took Jehoahaz his **b.**, and 251
2Ch 36:10 Zedekiah his **b.** king over Judah 251
Ne 5:7 Ye exact usury, every one of his **b.**. 251
Ne 7:2 That I gave my **b.** Hanani, and 251
Job 22:6 hast taken a pledge from thy **b.** 251
Job 30:29 I am a **b.** to dragons, and a 251
Ps 35:14 though he had been my friend or **b.**: 251
Ps 49:7 can by any means redeem his **b.**, 251
Ps 50:20 sittest and speakest against thy **b.**; 251
Pr 17:17 times, and a **b.** is born for adversity 251
Pr 18:9 is **b.** to him that is a great waster 251
Pr 18:19 A **b.** offended is harder to be won 251
Pr 18:24 friend that sticketh closer than a **b.**. 251
Pr 27:10 that is near than a **b.** far off 251
Ec 4:8 yea, he hath neither child nor **b.**: 251
Ca 8:1 O that thou wert as my **b.**, that 251
Isa 3:6 a man shall take hold of his **b.** of 251
Isa 9:19 the fire: no man shall spare his **b.** 251
Isa 19:2 fight every one against his **b.**, and 251
Isa 41:6 every one said to his **b.**, Be of good 251
Jer 9:4 trust ye not in any **b.**: for 251
Jer 9:4 every **b.** will utterly supplant, 251
Jer 22:18 saying, Ah my **b.**! or, Ah sister! 251
Jer 23:35 every one to his **b.**, What hath the 251
Jer 31:34 every man his **b.**, saying, Know the 251
Jer 34:9 of them, to wit, of a Jew his **b.**. 251
Jer 34:14 ye go every man his **b.** an Hebrew, 251
Jer 34:17 liberty, every one to his **b.**, 251
Eze 18:18 spoiled his **b.** by violence, and did 251
Eze 33:30 every one to his **b.**, saying, Come, 251
Eze 38:21 man's sword shall be against his **b.** 251
Eze 44:25 for son, or for daughter, for **b.**, or 251
Ho 12:3 He took his **b.** by the heel in the 251
Am 1:11 because he did pursue his **b.** with 251
Ob 10 thy violence against thy **b.** Jacob, 251
Ob 12 have looked on the day of thy **b.** 251
Mic 7:2 hunt every man his **b.** with a net 251
Hag 2:22 every one by the sword of his **b.** 251
Zec 7:9 compassions every man to his **b.**: 251
Zec 7:10 evil against his **b.** in your heart. 251
Mal 1:2 Was not Esau Jacob's **b.**? saith 251
Mal 2:10 every man against his **b.**, 251
Mt 4:18 called Peter, and Andrew his **b.**, *80*
Mt 4:21 of Zebedee, and John his **b.**, *80*
Mt 5:22 **whosoever is angry with his b** *80*
Mt 5:22 **whosoever shall say to his b., Raca,** *80*
Mt 5:23 **thy b. hath ought against thee;** *80*
Mt 5:24 **first be reconciled to thy b., and** *80*
Mt 7:4 **wilt thou say to thy b., Let me** *80*
Mt 10:2 called Peter, and Andrew his **b.**; *80*
Mt 10:2 son of Zebedee, and John his **b.**; *80*
Mt 10:21 **b. shall deliver up the b. to death,** *80*
Mt 12:50 **the same is my b., and sister, and** *80*
Mt 14:3 Herodias' sake, his **b.** Phillip's wife. *80*
Mt 17:1 James, and John his **b.**, and *80*
Mt 18:15 **thy b. shall trespass against thee,** *80*
Mt 18:15 **hear thee, thou hast gained thy b** *80*
Mt 18:21 how oft shall my **b.** sin against me, *80*
Mt 18:35 **every one his b. their trespasses** *80*
Mt 22:24 his **b.** shall marry his wife, *80*
Mt 22:24 and raise up seed unto his **b.** *80*
Mt 22:25 no issue, left his wife unto his **b.**: *80*
Mk 1:16 saw Simon and Andrew his **b.** *80*
Mk 1:19 the son of Zebedee and John his **b.**, *80*
Mk 3:17 and John the **b.** of James; and he *80*
Mk 3:35 **will of God, the same is my b., and** *80*
Mk 5:37 James, and John the **b.** of James. *80*
Mk 6:3 son of Mary, the **b.** of James, and *80*
Mk 6:17 Herodias' sake, his **b.** Phillip's wife: *80*
Mk 12:19 If a man's **b.** die, and leave his wife *80*
Mk 12:19 that his **b.** should take his wife, *80*
Mk 12:19 and raise up seed unto his **b.** *80*
Mk 13:12 **the b. shall betray the b. to death,** *80*
Lu 3:1 and his **b.** Phillip tetrarch of Ituraea *80*
Lu 3:19 for Herodias his **b.** Phillip's wife, *80*
Lu 6:14 named Peter,)and Andrew his **b.**, *80*
Lu 6:16 And Judas the **b.** of James, and
Lu 6:42 **say to thy b., B., let me pull out the** *.80*
Lu 12:13 Master, speak to my **b.**, that he *80*
Lu 15:27 **said unto him, Thy b. is come;** *80*
Lu 15:32 **for this thy b. was dead, and is alive** *.80*
Lu 17:3 **If thy b. trespass against thee,** *80*
Lu 20:28 If any man's **b.** die, having a wife, *80*
Lu 20:28 that his **b.** should take his wife, *80*
Lu 20:28 and raise up seed unto his **b.** *80*
Joh 1:40 was Andrew, Simon Peter's **b.** *80*
Joh 1:41 findeth his own **b.** Simon, and saith *80*
Joh 6:8 Andrew, Simon Peter's **b.**, saith *80*
Joh 11:2 hair, whose **b.** Lazarus was sick.) *80*
Joh 11:19 to comfort them concerning their **b.**. *80*
Joh 11:21 hadst been here, my **b.** had not died. *80*
Joh 11:23 unto her, **Thy b. shall rise again** *80*
Joh 11:32 hadst been here, my **b.** had not died. *80*
Ac 1:13 Zelotes, and Judas the **b.** of James.
Ac 9:17 said, **B.** Saul, the Lord, even Jesus, *80*
Ac 12:2 he killed James the **b.** of John with *80*
Ac 21:20 Thou seest, **b.**, how many thousands *80*
Ac 22:14 unto me, **B.** Saul, receive thy sight. *80*
Ro 14:10 why dost thou judge thy **b.**? or why *80*
Ro 14:10 dost thou set at nought thy **b.**? *80*
Ro 14:15 if thy **b.** be grieved with thy meat, *80*
Ro 14:21 thing whereby thy **b.** stumbleth, *80*
Ro 16:23 city saluteth you, and Quartus a **b.**. *80*
1Co 1:1 will of God, and Sosthenes our **b.**, *80*
1Co 5:11 that is called a **b.** be a fornicator, *80*
1Co 6:6 **b.** goeth to law with **b.**, and that *80*
1Co 7:12 If any **b.** hath a wife that *80*
1Co 7:15 A **b.** or a sister is not under *80*
1Co 8:11 shall the weak **b.** perish, for *80*
1Co 8:13 meat make my **b.** to offend, *80*
1Co 8:13 lest I make my **b.** to offend. *80*
1Co 16:12 As touching our **b.** Apollos, *80*
2Co 1:1 will of God, and Timothy our **b.**, *80*
2Co 2:13 I found not Titus my **b.**: but *80*
2Co 8:18 have sent with him the **b.**, whose *80*
2Co 8:22 have sent with them our **b.**, *80*
2Co 12:18 Titus, and with him I sent a **b.**. *80*
Ga 1:19 none, save James the Lord's **b.** *80*
Eph 6:21 a beloved **b.** and faithful minister *80*
Php 2:25 send to you Epaphroditus, my **b.**, *80*
Col 1:1 will of God, and Timotheus our **b.**, *80*
Col 4:7 you, who is a beloved **b.**, and a *80*
Col 4:9 a faithful and beloved **b.**, who is *80*
1Th 3:2 sent Timotheus, our **b.**, and *80*
1Th 4:6 and defraud his **b.** in any matter: *80*
2Th 3:6 from every **b.** that walketh *80*
2Th 3:15 but admonish him as a **b.**. *80*
Phm 1 Timothy our **b.**; unto Philemon *80*
Phm 7 the saints are refreshed by thee, **b.**. *80*
Phm 16 above a servant, a **b.** beloved, *80*
Phm 20 Yea, **b.**, let me have *80*
Heb 8:11 neighbour, and every man his **b.**, *80*
Heb 13:23 Know ye that our **b.** Timothy *80*
Jas 1:9 Let the **b.** of low degree rejoice *80*
Jas 2:15 If a **b.** or sister be naked, and *80*
Jas 4:11 evil of his **b.**, and judgeth his **b.**, *80*
1Pe 5:12 a faithful **b.** unto you, as I suppose, *80*
2Pe 3:15 as our beloved **b.** Paul also *80*
1Jo 2:9 in the light, and hateth his **b.**, *80*
1Jo 2:10 He that loveth his **b.** abideth in the *80*
1Jo 2:11 he that hateth his **b.** is in darkness, *80*
1Jo 3:10 neither he that loveth not his **b.**. *80*
1Jo 3:12 wicked one, and slew his **b.**. *80*
1Jo 3:14 loveth not his **b.** abideth in death. *80*
1Jo 3:15 Whosever hateth his **b.** is a *80*
1Jo 3:17 seeth his **b.** have need, and *80*
1Jo 4:20 hateth his **b.**, he is a liar: for he *80*
1Jo 4:20 that loveth not his **b.** whom he *80*
1Jo 4:21 who loveth God, love his **b.** also. *80*
1Jo 5:16 any man see his **b.** sin a sin which *80*
Jude 1 of Jesus Christ, and **b.** of James, *80*
Re 1:9 I John who also am your **b.**, and *80*

BROTHERHOOD

Zec 11:14 the **b.** between Judah and Israel. 264
1Pe 2:17 Love the **b.**. Fear God. Honour *81*

BROTHERLY

Am 1:9 remembered not the **b.** covenant: 251
Ro 12:10 one to another with **b.** love; *5360*
1Th 4:9 But as touching **b.** love ye need *5360*
Heb 13:1 Let **b.** love continue. *5360*
2Pe 1:7 godliness **b.** kindness; and to **b.** *5360*

BROTHER'S

Ge 4:9 I know not: Am I my **b.** keeper? 251
Ge 4:10 the voice of thy **b.** blood crieth 251
Ge 4:11 her mouth to receive thy **b.** blood 251
Ge 4:21 And his **b.** name was Jubal: 251
Ge 10:25 and his **b.** name was Joktan. 251
Ge 12:5 Sarah his wife, and Lot his **b.** son, 251
Ge 14:12 And they took Lot, Abram's **b.** son, 251
Ge 24:48 to take my master's **b.** daughter 251
Ge 27:44 until thy **b.** fury turn away; 251
Ge 27:45 Until thy **b.** anger turn away 251
Ge 38:8 in unto thy **b.** wife, and marry her, 251
Ge 38:9 he went in unto his **b.** wife, that he 251
Le 18:16 the nakedness of thy **b.** wife: 251
Le 18:16 it is thy **b.** nakedness. 251
Le 20:21 if a man shall take his **b.** wife, 251
Le 20:21 hath uncovered his **b.** nakedness; 251
De 22:1 Thou shalt not see thy **b.** ox 251
De 22:3 with all lost thing of thy **b.**, 251
De 22:4 Thou shalt not see thy **b.** ass of 251
De 25:7 like not to take his **b.** wife, 2994
De 25:7 then let his **b.** wife go up to the 2994
De 25:9 Then shall his **b.** wife come unto 2994
De 25:9 will not build up his **b.** house 251
1Ki 2:15 turned about, and is become my **b.**: 251
1Ch 1:19 and his **b.** name was Joktan. 251
Job 1:13 drinking wine in their eldest **b.** 251
Job 1:18 wine in their eldest **b.** house: 251
Pr 27:10 neither go into thy **b.** house in 251
Mt 7:3 **the mote that is in thy b. eye,** *80*
Mt 7:5 **out the mote out of thy b. eye** *80*
Mk 6:18 lawful for thee to have thy **b.** wife, *80*
Lu 6:41 **mote that is in thy b. eye,** *80*
Lu 6:42 **out the mote that is in thy b. eye** *80*
Ro 14:13 an occasion to fall in his **b.** way. *80*
1Jo 3:12 were evil, and his **b.** righteous. *80*

BROTHERS' See also BRETHREN'S.

Nu 36:11 unto their father's **b.** sons: 1730

BROUGHT See also BROUGHTEST.

Ge 1:12 And the earth **b.** forth grass, 3318
Ge 1:21 the waters **b.** forth abundantly, 8317
Ge 2:19 and **b.** them unto Adam to see 935
Ge 2:22 and **b.** her unto the man. 935
Ge 4:3 that Cain **b.** of the fruit of the 935
Ge 4:4 he also **b.** of the firstlings of his 935
Ge 14:16 **b.** back all the goods, and also 7725
Ge 14:16 **b.** again his brother Lot, 7725
Ge 14:18 King of Salem **b.** forth bread and 3318
Ge 15:5 And he **b.** him forth abroad, and 3318
Ge 15:7 I am the Lord that **b.** thee out of 3318
Ge 19:16 and they **b.** him forth, and set him 3318
Ge 19:17 when they had **b.** them forth 3318
Ge 20:9 thou hast **b.** on me and on my 935
Ge 24:53 And the servant **b.** forth jewels 3318
Ge 24:67 And Isaac **b.** her into his mother 935
Ge 26:10 and thou shouldest have **b.** 935
Ge 27:14 and **b.** them to his mother: 935
Ge 27:20 the Lord thy God **b.** it to me. 7136
Ge 27:25 And he **b.** it near to him, and 5066
Ge 27:25 he **b.** him wine, and he drank 935
Ge 27:31 and **b.** it unto his father, and 935
Ge 27:33 hath taken venison, and **b.** it me, 935
Ge 29:13 and **b.** him to his house. 935
Ge 29:23 and **b.** her to him; and he went 935
Ge 30:14 and **b.** them unto his mother Leah. 935
Ge 30:39 and **b.** forth cattle ringstraked, 3205
Ge 31:39 I **b.** not unto thee; I bear the loss 935
Ge 33:11 I pray thee, my blessing that is **b.** 935
Ge 37:2 and Joesph **b.** unto his father 935
Ge 37:28 and they **b.** Joseph into Egypt. 935
Ge 37:32 and they **b.** it to their father; 935
Ge 38:25 When she was **b.** forth, she sent 3318
Ge 39:1 Joseph was **b.** down to Egypt; 3381

Ge 39:1 which had **b.** him down thither. 3381
Ge 39:14 he hath **b.** in an Hebrew unto us 935
Ge 39:17 which thou hast **b.** unto us, 935
Ge 40:10 thereof **b.** forth ripe grapes: 1310
Ge 41:14 **b.** him hastily out of the dungeon: 7323
Ge 41:47 the earth **b.** forth by handfuls. 6213
Ge 43:2 which they had **b.** out of Egypt, 935
Ge 43:12 the money that was **b.** again 7725
Ge 43:17 and the man **b.** the men into 935
Ge 43:18 they were **b.** into Joseph's house; 935
Ge 43:18 at the first time are we **b.** in; 935
Ge 43:21 have **b.** it again in our hand 7725
Ge 43:22 other money have we **b.** down 3381
Ge 43:23 And he **b.** Simeon out unto them 3318
Ge 43:24 **b.** the men into Joseph's house, 935
Ge 43:26 they **b.** him the present 935
Ge 44:8 we **b.** again unto thee out of the 7725
Ge 46:7 seed **b.** he with him into Egypt. 935
Ge 46:32 they have **b.** their flocks, and 935
Ge 47:7 And Joseph **b.** Jacob his father, 935
Ge 47:14 and Joseph **b.** the money into 935
Ge 47:17 they **b.** their cattle unto Joseph: 935
Ge 48:10 And he **b.** them near unto him; 5066
Ge 48:12 And Joseph **b.** them out from 3318
Ge 48:13 hand, and **b.** them near unto him 5066
Ge 50:23 were **b.** up upon Joseph's knees. 3205
Ex 2:10 **b.** him unto Pharaoh's daughter, 935
Ex 3:12 When thou hast **b.** forth the 3318
Ex 8:7 and **b.** up frogs upon the land 5927
Ex 8:12 the frogs which he had **b.** against 7760
Ex 9:19 be **b.** home, the hail shall come 622
Ex 10:8 And Moses and Aaron were **b.** 7725
Ex 10:13 the Lord **b.** an east wind upon 5090
Ex 10:13 the east wind **b.** the locusts. 5375
Ex 12:17 day have I **b.** your armies out 3318
Ex 12:39 the dough which they **b.** forth 3318
Ex 13:3 Lord **b.** you out from this place: 3318
Ex 13:9 hand hath the Lord **b.** thee out 3318
Ex 13:14 the Lord **b.** us out from Egypt, 3318
Ex 13:16 the Lord **b.** us forth out of Egypt. 3318
Ex 15:19 **b.** again the waters of the sea 7725
Ex 15:22 So Moses **b.** Israel from the Red 5265
Ex 15:26 I have **b.** upon the Egyptians: 7760
Ex 16:3 ye have **b.** us forth into this 3318
Ex 16:6 the Lord hath **b.** you out from 3318
Ex 16:32 when I **b.** you forth from 3318
Ex 17:3 thou hast **b.** us up out of Egypt. 5927
Ex 18:1 had **b.** Israel out of Egypt; 3318
Ex 18:26 the hard causes they **b.** unto 935
Ex 19:4 and **b.** you unto myself 935
Ex 19:17 And Moses **b.** forth the people 3318
Ex 20:2 have **b.** thee out of the land of 3318
Ex 22:8 master of the house shall be **b.** 7126
Ex 29:10 shalt cause a bullock to be **b.** 7126
Ex 29:46 that **b.** them forth out of the land 3318
Ex 32:1 the man that **b.** us up out of the 5927
Ex 32:3 ears, and **b.** them unto Aaron. 935
Ex 32:4 gods, O Israel, which **b.** thee up 5927
Ex 32:6 and **b.** peace offerings; and the 5066
Ex 32:8 Israel, which have **b.** thee up 5927
Ex 32:11 **b.** forth out of the land of Egypt 3318
Ex 32:21 hast **b.** so great a sin upon them? 935
Ex 32:23 the man that **b.** us up out of the 5927
Ex 33:1 thou hast **b.** up out of the land 5927
Ex 35:21 they **b.** the Lord's offering to the 935
Ex 35:22 **b.** bracelets, and earrings, and rings, 935
Ex 35:23 rams, and badgers' skins, **b.** them 935
Ex 35:24 **b.** the Lord's offering: and every 935
Ex 35:24 for any work of the service, **b.** it. 935
Ex 35:25 and **b.** that which they had spun, 935
Ex 35:27 the rulers **b.** onyx stones, and 935
Ex 35:29 Israel **b.** a willing offering 935
Ex 36:3 Israel had **b.** for the work of the 935
Ex 36:3 they **b.** yet unto him free offerings 935
Ex 39:33 And they **b.** the tabernacle unto 935
Ex 40:21 he **b.** the ark into the tabernacle, 935
Le 6:30 whereof any of the blood is **b.** into 935
Le 8:6 And Moses **b.** Aaron and his 7126
Le 8:13 And Moses **b.** Aaron's sons, and 7126
Le 8:14 And he **b.** the bullock for the sin 5066
Le 8:18 And he **b.** the ram for the 7126
Le 8:22 And he **b.** the other ram, the 7126
Le 8:24 And he **b.** Aaron's sons, and 7126
Le 9:5 And they **b.** that which Moses 3947
Le 9:9 And the sons of Aaron **b.** the 7126
Le 9:15 And he **b.** the people's offering, 7126
Le 9:16 And he **b.** the burnt offering, 7126
Le 9:17 And he **b.** the meat offering, 7126
Le 10:18 the blood of it was not **b.** in 935
Le 13:2 then he shall be **b.** unto Aaron 935
Le 13:9 in a man, then he shall be **b.** unto 935
Le 14:2 He shall be **b.** unto the priest: 935
Le 16:27 whose blood was **b.** in to make 935
Le 19:36 which **b.** you out of the land of 3318
Le 22:27 or a sheep, or a goat, is **b.** forth, 3205
Le 22:33 That **b.** you out of the land of 3318
Le 23:14 that ye have **b.** an offering unto 935
Le 23:15 the day that ye **b.** the sheaf of 935
Le 23:43 when I **b.** them out of the land of 3318
Le 24:11 And they **b.** him unto Moses: (and 935
Le 25:38 which **b.** you forth out of the land 3318
Le 25:42 which I **b.** forth out of the land of 3318
Le 25:55 whom I **b.** forth out of the land of 3318
Le 26:13 which **b.** you forth out of the land 3318
Le 26:41 and have **b.** them into the land of 935
Le 26:45 whom I **b.** forth out of the land 3318
Nu 6:13 he shall be **b.** unto the door of 935
Nu 7:3 And they **b.** their offering before 935
Nu 7:3 and they **b.** them before the 7126
Nu 9:13 he **b.** not the offering of the Lord 7126
Nu 11:13 and **b.** quails from the sea, and 1468
Nu 12:15 not till Miriam was **b.** in again. 622
Nu 13:23 and they **b.** of the pomegranates,
Nu 13:26 and **b.** back word unto them, and 7725
Nu 13:32 And they **b.** up an evil report of 3318
Nu 14:3 wherefore hath the Lord **b.** us 935
Nu 15:33 him gathering sticks **b.** him 7126
Nu 15:36 And all the congregation **b.** him 3318
Nu 15:41 which **b.** you out of the land of 3318
Nu 16:10 And he hath **b.** thee near to him, 7126
Nu 16:13 thou hast **b.** us up out of a land 5927
Nu 16:14 thou hast not **b.** us into a land 935
Nu 17:8 and **b.** forth buds, and bloomed 3318
Nu 17:9 And Moses **b.** out all the rods 3318
Nu 20:4 And why have ye **b.** up the 935
Nu 20:16 hath **b.** us forth out of Egypt: 3318
Nu 21:5 Wherefore have ye **b.** us up out 5927
Nu 22:41 and **b.** him up into the high 5927
Nu 23:7 Balak the king of Moab hath **b.** 5148
Nu 23:14 And he **b.** him into the field of 3947
Nu 23:22 God **b.** them out of Egypt; he 3318
Nu 23:28 And Balak **b.** Balaam unto the 3947
Nu 24:8 God **b.** him forth out of Egypt; 3318
Nu 25:6 and **b.** unto his brethren a 7126
Nu 27:5 And Moses **b.** their cause before 7126
Nu 31:12 And they **b.** the captives, and the 935
Nu 31:50 We have therefore **b.** an oblation 7126
Nu 31:54 and **b.** it into the tabernacle of 935
Nu 32:17 until we have **b.** them unto their 935
De 1:25 in their hands, and **b.** it down 3381
De 1:25 unto us. and **b.** us word again, 7725
De 1:27 he has **b.** us forth out of the land 3318
De 4:20 hath taken you, and **b.** you forth 3318
De 4:37 and **b.** thee out in his sight with 3318
De 5:6 which **b.** thee out of the land of 3318
De 5:15 the Lord thy God **b.** thee out 3318
De 6:10 Lord thy God shall have **b.** thee 935
De 6:12 which **b.** thee forth out of the 3318
De 6:21 and the Lord **b.** us out of Egypt 3318
De 6:23 he **b.** us out from thence, that he 3318
De 7:8 **b.** you out with a mighty hand, 3318
De 7:19 the Lord thy God **b.** thee out: 3318
De 8:14 which **b.** thee forth out of the land 3318
De 8:15 who **b.** thee forth water out of the 3318
De 9:4 hath **b.** me in to posses this land: 935
De 9:12 people which thou hast **b.** forth 3318
De 9:26 which thou hast **b.** forth out of 3318
De 9:28 he hath **b.** them out to slay them 3318
De 11:29 hath **b.** thee in unto the land 935
De 13:5 which **b.** you out of the land of 3318
De 13:10 which **b.** thee out of the land of 3318
De 16:1 the Lord thy God **b.** thee forth out 3318
De 20:1 God is with thee, which **b.** thee 5927
De 22:19 he hath **b.** up an evil name upon 3318
De 26:8 And the Lord **b.** us forth out of 3318
De 26:9 And he hath **b.** us into this place. 935
De 26:10 I have **b.** the firstfruits of the land, 935
De 26:13 I have **b.** away the hollowed 1197
De 29:25 when he **b.** them forth out of the 3318
De 31:20 For when I shall have **b.** them 935
De 31:21 before I have **b.** them into the land 935
De 33:14 precious fruits **b.** forth by the sun,
Jos 2:6 she had **b.** them up to the roof 5927
Jos 6:23 and **b.** out Rahab, and her father, 3318
Jos 6:23 they **b.** out all her kindred, and 3318
Jos 7:7 hast thou at all **b.** this people 5674
Jos 7:14 ye shall be **b.** according to your 7126
Jos 7:16 and **b.** Israel by their tribes; and 7126
Jos 7:17 And he **b.** the family of Judah; 7126
Jos 7:17 he **b.** the family of the Zarhites 7126
Jos 7:18 And he **b.** his household man by 7126
Jos 7:23 and **b.** them unto Joshua, and 935
Jos 7:24 and they **b.** them unto the valley 5927
Jos 8:23 took alive, and **b.** him to Joshua. 7126
Jos 10:23 and **b.** forth those five kings unto 3318
Jos 10:24 when they **b.** out those kings unto 3318
Jos 14:7 and I **b.** him word again as it was 7725
Jos 22:32 of Israel, and **b.** them word again. 7725
Jos 24:5 them: and afterward I **b.** you out. 3318
Jos 24:6 And I **b.** your fathers out of Egypt: 3318
Jos 24:7 and **b.** the sea upon them, and 935
Jos 24:8 And I **b.** you into the land of the 935
Jos 24:17 he it is that **b.** us up and our 5927
Jos 24:32 which the children of Israel **b.** up 5927
Jg 1:7 And they **b.** him to Jerusalem, 935
Jg 2:1 and have **b.** you unto the land 935
Jg 2:12 **b.** them out of the land of Egypt, 3318
Jg 3:17 he **b.** the present unto Eglon 7126
Jg 5:25 she **b.** forth butter in a lordly dish. 7126
Jg 6:8 I **b.** you up from Egypt, and 5927
Jg 6:8 **b.** you forth out of the house of 3318
Jg 6:19 **b.** it out unto him under the oak, 3318
Jg 7:5 So he **b.** down the people unto the 3381
Jg 7:25 and **b.** the heads of Oreb and Zeeb 935
Jg 11:35 thou hast **b.** me very low, and 3766
Jg 14:11 that they **b.** thirty companions to 3947
Jg 15:13 and **b.** him up from the rock 5927
Jg 16:8 the lords of the Philistines **b.** up 5927
Jg 16:18 her, and **b.** money in their hand. 5927
Jg 16:21 **b.** him down to Gaza, and bound 3381
Jg 16:31 and **b.** him up, and buried him 5927
Jg 18:3 unto him, Who **b.** thee hither? 935
Jg 19:3 **b.** him into her father's house: 935
Jg 19:21 So he **b.** him into his house, and 935
Jg 19:25 took his concubine, and **b.** her 3318
Jg 21:12 and they **b.** them unto the camp 935
Ru 1:21 the Lord hath **b.** me home again 7725
Ru 2:18 and she **b.** forth, and gave to her 3318
1Sa 1:24 and **b.** him unto the house of the 935
1Sa 1:25 a bullock, and **b.** the child to Eli. 935
1Sa 2:14 all that the fleshhook **b.** up the 5927
1Sa 2:19 and **b.** it to him from year to year, 5927
1Sa 5:1 and **b.** it from Eben-ezer unto 935
1Sa 5:2 they **b.** it into the house of Dagon, 935
1Sa 5:10 They have **b.** about the ark of the 5437
1Sa 6:21 Philistines have **b.** again the ark 7725
1Sa 7:1 **b.** it into the house of Abinadab 935
1Sa 8:8 that I **b.** them up out of Egypt 5927
1Sa 9:22 and **b.** them into the parlour, and 935
1Sa 10:18 I **b.** up Israel out of Egypt, and 5927
1Sa 10:27 him, and **b.** him no presents. 935
1Sa 12:6 that **b.** your fathers up out of the 5927
1Sa 12:8 **b.** forth your fathers out of Egypt, 3318
1Sa 14:34 the people **b.** every man his ox 5066
1Sa 15:15 Saul said, They have **b.** them from 935
1Sa 15:20 have **b.** Agag the king of Amalek, 935
1Sa 16:12 he sent, and **b.** him in. Now he 935
1Sa 17:54 and **b.** it to Jerusalem; but he put 935
1Sa 17:57 **b.** him before Saul with the head 935
1Sa 18:27 David **b.** their foreskins, and they 935
1Sa 19:7 And Jonathan **b.** David to Saul, 935
1Sa 20:8 **b.** thy servant into a covenant of 935
1Sa 21:8 I have neither **b.** my sword nor 3947
1Sa 21:14 then have ye **b.** him to me? 935
1Sa 21:15 **b.** this fellow to play the mad man 935
1Sa 22:4 he **b.** them before the king of 5148
1Sa 23:5 **b.** away their cattle, and smote 5090
1Sa 25:27 which thine handmaid hath **b.** 935
1Sa 25:35 which she had **b.** him, and said 935
1Sa 28:25 she **b.** it before Saul, and before 5066
1Sa 30:7 Abiathar **b.** thither the ephod to 5066
1Sa 30:11 **b.** him to David, and gave him 3947
1Sa 30:16 And when he had **b.** him down, 3381
2Sa 1:10 have **b.** them thither unto my Lord. 935
2Sa 2:8 and **b.** him over to Mahanaim; 5674
2Sa 3:22 **b.** in a great spoil with them: 935
2Sa 3:26 messengers after Abner, which **b.** 7725
2Sa 4:8 **b.** the head of Ish-bosheth unto 935
2Sa 4:10 thinking to have **b.** good tidings, 1319
2Sa 6:3,4 **b.** it out of the house of Abinadab 5375
2Sa 6:12 David went and **b.** up the ark 5927

Book	Ref	Context	Number
2Sa	6:15	**b.** up the ark of the Lord with	5927
2Sa	6:17	they **b.** in the ark of the Lord,	935
2Sa	7:6	I **b.** up the children of Israel out	5927
2Sa	7:18	that thou hast **b.** me hitherto?	935
2Sa	8:2	became David's servants, and **b.**	5375
2Sa	8:6	servants to David, and **b.** gifts	5375
2Sa	8:7	of Hadadezer, and **b.** them to	935
2Sa	8:10	Joram **b.** with him vessels of	1961
2Sa	10:16	and **b.** out the Syrians that were	3318
2Sa	12:30	he **b.** forth the spoil of the city in	3318
2Sa	12:31	And he **b.** forth the people that	3318
2Sa	13:10	and **b.** them into the chamber to	935
2Sa	13:11	when she had **b.** them unto him to	5066
2Sa	13:18	Then his servant **b.** her out, and	3318
2Sa	14:23	went to Geshur, and **b.** Absalom to	935
2Sa	17:28	**B.** beds, and basons, and earthen	5066
2Sa	19:41	and have **b.** the king, and his	5674
2Sa	21:8	whom she **b.** up for Adriel the son	3205
2Sa	21:13	And he **b.** up from thence the	5927
2Sa	22:20	He **b.** me forth also into a large	3318
2Sa	23:16	and **b.** it to David: nevertheless	935
1Ki	1:3	Shunammite, and **b.** her to the	935
1Ki	1:38	king David's mule, and **b.** him	3212
1Ki	1:53	and they **b.** him down from the	3381
1Ki	2:30	And Benaiah **b.** the king word	7725
1Ki	2:40	and **b.** his servants from Gath	935
1Ki	3:1	and **b.** her into the city of David,	935
1Ki	3:24	And they **b.** a sword before the	935
1Ki	4:21	they **b.** presents, and served	5066
1Ki	4:28	dromedaries **b.** they unto the	935
1Ki	5:17	and they **b.** great stones, costly	5265
1Ki	6:7	made ready before it was **b.**	4551
1Ki	7:51	And Solomon **b.** in the things	935
1Ki	8:4	And they **b.** up the ark of the	5927
1Ki	8:6	And the priests **b.** in the ark of	935
1Ki	8:16	the day that I **b.** forth my people	3318
1Ki	8:21	when he **b.** them out of the land	3318
1Ki	9:9	who **b.** forth their fathers out of	3318
1Ki	9:9	therefore hath the Lord **b.** upon	935
1Ki	9:28	twenty talents, and **b.** it to king	935
1Ki	10:11	that **b.** gold from Ophir,	5375
1Ki	10:11	**b.** in from Ophir great plenty	935
1Ki	10:25	they **b.** every man his present,	935
1Ki	10:28	And Solomon had horses **b.** out	4161
1Ki	12:28	gods, O Israel, which **b.** thee up	5927
1Ki	13:20	unto the prophet that **b.** him	7725
1Ki	13:23	the prophet whom he had **b.** back	7725
1Ki	13:26	And when the prophet that **b.** him	7725
1Ki	13:29	it upon the ass, and **b.** it back:	7725
1Ki	14:28	and **b.** them back into the guard	7725
1Ki	15:15	And he **b.** in the things which	935
1Ki	17:6	the ravens **b.** him bread and flesh	935
1Ki	17:20	hast thou also **b.** evil upon the	
1Ki	17:23	**b.** him down out of the chamber	3381
1Ki	18:40	and Elijah **b.** them down to the	3381
1Ki	20:9	the messengers departed, and **b.**	7725
1Ki	20:39	and **b.** a man unto me, and said,	935
1Ki	22:37	and was **b.** to Samaria; and they	935
2Ki	2:20	salt therein. And they **b.** it to	3947
2Ki	4:5	who **b.** the vessels to her; and	5066
2Ki	4:20	and **b.** him to his mother, he sat	935
2Ki	4:42	and **b.** the man of God bread of	935
2Ki	5:2	and had **b.** away captive out of	7617
2Ki	5:6	And he **b.** the letter to the king	935
2Ki	5:20	at his hands that which he **b.**:	935
2Ki	10:1	them that **b.** up Ahab's children,	539
2Ki	10:6	of the city, which **b.** them up	1431
2Ki	10:8	They have **b.** the heads of the	935
2Ki	10:22	And he **b.** them forth vestments	3318
2Ki	10:24	any of the men whom I have **b.**	935
2Ki	10:26	And they **b.** forth the images out	3318
2Ki	11:4	**b.** them to him into the house of	935
2Ki	11:12	And he **b.** forth the king's son,	3318
2Ki	11:19	and they **b.** down the king from	3381
2Ki	12:4	that is **b.** into the house of the	935
2Ki	12:9	money that was **b.** into the house	935
2Ki	12:13	that was **b.** into the house of the	935
2Ki	12:16	money was not **b.** into the house	935
2Ki	14:20	And they **b.** him on horses: and	5375
2Ki	16:14	And he **b.** also the brasen altar,	7126
2Ki	17:4	and **b.** no present to the king of	5927
2Ki	17:7	Lord their God, which had **b.**	5927
2Ki	17:24	And the king of Assyria **b.** men	935
2Ki	17:27	whom ye **b.** from thence; and let	1540
2Ki	17:36	But the Lord, who **b.** you up out	5927
2Ki	19:25	now have I **b.** it to pass, that	935
2Ki	20:11	and he **b.** the shadow ten degrees	7725
2Ki	20:20	and **b.** water into the city, are	935
2Ki	22:4	the silver which is **b.** into the house	935
2Ki	22:9	and **b.** the king word again, and	7725
2Ki	22:20	And they **b.** the king word again	7725
2Ki	23:6	And he **b.** out the grove from the	3318
2Ki	23:8	And he **b.** all the priests out of the	935
2Ki	23:30	and **b.** him to Jerusalem, and	935
2Ki	24:16	the king of Babylon **b.** captive to	935
2Ki	25:6	So they took the king, and **b.**	5927
2Ki	25:20	**b.** them to the king of Babylon	3212
1Ch	5:26	and **b.** them unto Halah, and	935
1Ch	10:12	and **b.** them to Jabesh, and buried	935
1Ch	11:18	and **b.** it to David; but David	935
1Ch	11:19	jeopardy of their lives they **b.** it	935
1Ch	12:40	**b.** bread on assess, and on camels,	935
1Ch	13:13	David **b.** not the ark home to	5493
1Ch	14:17	and the Lord **b.** the fear of him	5414
1Ch	15:28	Thus all Israel **b.** up the ark of	5927
1Ch	16:1	So they **b.** the ark of God, and set	935
1Ch	17:5	since the day that I **b.** up Israel	5927
1Ch	17:16	that thou hast **b.** me hitherto?	935
1Ch	18:2,6	David's servants, and **b.** gifts	5375
1Ch	18:7	servants of Hadarezer, and **b.** them	935
1Ch	18:8	**b.** David very much brass,	3947
1Ch	18:11	silver and the gold that he **b.**	5375
1Ch	20:2	he **b.** also exceeding much spoil	3318
1Ch	20:3	he **b.** out the people that were in	3318
1Ch	22:4	they of Tyre **b.** much cedar wood	935
2Ch	1:4	the ark of God had David **b.** up	5927
2Ch	1:16	And Solomon had horses **b.** out of	4161
2Ch	1:17	**b.** forth out of Egypt a chariot	3318
2Ch	1:17	and so **b.** they out horses for all	3318
2Ch	5:1	and Solomon **b.** in all the things	935
2Ch	5:5	And they **b.** up the ark, and the	5927
2Ch	5:7	And the priests **b.** in the ark of the	935
2Ch	6:5	Since the day that I **b.** forth my	3318
2Ch	7:22	of their fathers, which **b.** them	3318
2Ch	7:22	hath he **b.** all this evil upon them	935
2Ch	8:11	Solomon **b.** up the daughter of	5927
2Ch	8:18	gold, and **b.** them to king Solomon	935
2Ch	9:10	which **b.** gold from Ophir, **b.** algum	935
2Ch	9:12	which she had **b.** unto the king	935
2Ch	9:14	which chapmen and merchants **b.**	935
2Ch	9:14	**b.** gold and silver to Solomon	935
2Ch	9:24	they **b.** every man his present,	935
2Ch	9:28	And they **b.** unto Solomon horses	3318
2Ch	10:8	that were **b.** up with him, that	1431
2Ch	10:10	the young men that were **b.** up	1431
2Ch	12:11	and **b.** them again into the guard	7725
2Ch	13:18	the children of Israel were **b.**	3665
2Ch	15:11	of the spoil which they had **b.**	935
2Ch	15:18	And he **b.** into the house of God	935
2Ch	16:2	Then Asa **b.** out silver and gold	3318
2Ch	17:5	and all Judah **b.** to Jehoshaphat	5414
2Ch	17:11	the Philistines **b.** Jehoshaphat	935
2Ch	17:11	the Arabians **b.** him flocks, seven	935
2Ch	19:4	and **b.** them back unto the Lord	7725
2Ch	22:9	and **b.** him to Jehu: and when	935
2Ch	23:11	Then they **b.** out the king's son,	3318
2Ch	23:14	Then Jehoiada the priest **b.** out	3318
2Ch	23:20	and **b.** down the king from the	3381
2Ch	24:10	and **b.** in, and cast into the chest,	935
2Ch	24:11	at what time the chest was **b.** unto	935
2Ch	24:14	they **b.** the rest of the money	935
2Ch	25:12	and **b.** them unto the top of the	935
2Ch	25:14	that he **b.** the gods of the children	935
2Ch	25:23	and **b.** him to Jerusalem, and	935
2Ch	25:28	And they **b.** him upon horses, and	5375
2Ch	28:5	captives, and **b.** them to Damascus	935
2Ch	28:8	and **b.** the spoil to Samaria	935
2Ch	28:15	and **b.** them to Jericho, the	935
2Ch	28:19	the Lord **b.** Judah low because	3665
2Ch	28:27	they **b.** him not into the sepulchres	935
2Ch	29:4	And he **b.** in the priests and the	935
2Ch	29:16	and **b.** out all the uncleanness	3318
2Ch	29:21	And they **b.** seven bullocks, and	935
2Ch	29:23	And they **b.** forth the he goats	5066
2Ch	29:31	the congregation **b.** in sacrifices	935
2Ch	29:32	which the congregation **b.**, was	935
2Ch	30:15	and **b.** in the burnt offerings into	935
2Ch	31:5	children of Israel **b.** in abundance	935
2Ch	31:5	all things **b.** they in abundantly	935
2Ch	31:6	they also **b.** in the tithe of oxen	935
2Ch	31:12	And **b.** in the offerings and the	935
2Ch	32:23	many **b.** gifts unto the Lord to	935
2Ch	32:30	**b.** it straight down to the west	3474
2Ch	33:11	Wherefore the Lord **b.** upon them	935
2Ch	33:13	and **b.** him again to Jerusalem	7725
2Ch	34:9	the money that was **b.** into the	935
2Ch	34:14	they **b.** out the money	3318
2Ch	34:14	was **b.** into the	935
2Ch	34:16	**b.** the king word back again,	7725
2Ch	34:28	So they **b.** the king word again	7725
2Ch	35:24	and they **b.** him to Jerusalem,	3212
2Ch	36:10	and **b.** him to Babylon, with the	935
2Ch	36:17	Therefore he **b.** upon them the	5927
2Ch	36:18	all these he **b.** to Babylon	935
Ezr	1:7	the king **b.** forth the vessels of the	3318
Ezr	1:7	which Nebuchadnezzar had **b.**	3318
Ezr	1:11	were **b.** up from Babylon unto	5927
Ezr	4:2	of Assur, which **b.** us up hither	5927
Ezr	4:10	and noble Asnapper **b.** over, and	1541
Ezr	5:14	and **b.** them into the temple of	2987
Ezr	6:5	and **b.** unto Babylon, be restored,	2987
Ezr	6:5	and **b.** again unto the temple	1946
Ezr	8:18	they **b.** us a man of understanding,	935
Ne	4:15	and God had **b.** their counsel	6565
Ne	5:5	daughters are **b.** unto bondage	3533
Ne	8:2	And Ezra the priest **b.** the law	935
Ne	8:16	went forth, and **b.** them and made	935
Ne	9:18	This is thy God that **b.** thee up	5927
Ne	9:33	in all that is **b.** upon us; for	935
Ne	12:31	Then I **b.** up the princes of	5927
Ne	13:9	and thither **b.** I again the vessels	7725
Ne	13:12	Then **b.** all Judah the tithe of the	935
Ne	13:15	which they **b.** into Jerusalem	935
Ne	13:16	which **b.** fish, and all manner of	935
Ne	13:19	there should no burden be **b.** in	935
Es	1:17	Vashti the queen to be **b.** in before	935
Es	2:7	And he **b.** up Hadassah, that is,	539
Es	2:8	that Esther was **b.** also unto the	3947
Es	2:20	like as when she was **b.** up with	539
Es	6:8	Let the royal apparel be **b.** which	935
Es	6:11	**b.** him on horseback through	7392
Es	9:11	palace was **b.** before the king	935
Job	4:12	a thing was secretly **b.** to me,	1589
Job	10:18	Wherefore then hast thou **b.** me	3318
Job	14:21	and they are **b.** low, but he	6819
Job	21:30	they shall be **b.** forth to the day	2986
Job	21:32	Yet shall he be **b.** to the grave,	2986
Job	24:24	are gone and **b.** low; they are	4355
Job	31:18	he was **b.** up with me, as with a	1431
Job	42:11	evil the Lord had **b.** upon him:	935
Ps	7:14	mischief, and **b.** forth falsehood	3205
Ps	18:19	He **b.** me forth also into a large	3318
Ps	20:8	They are **b.** down and fallen:	3766
Ps	22:15	thou hast **b.** me into the dust	8239
Ps	30:3	thou hast **b.** up my soul from	5927
Ps	35:4	turned back and **b.** to confusion	2659
Ps	35:26	be ashamed and **b.** to confusion	2659
Ps	40:2	He **b.** me up also out of an	5927
Ps	45:14	She shall be **b.** unto the king	2986
Ps	45:14	that follow her shall be **b.** unto	935
Ps	45:15	and rejoicing shall they be **b.**:	2986
Ps	71:24	for they are **b.** unto shame,	2659
Ps	73:19	How are they **b.** into desolation,	
Ps	78:16	**b.** streams also out of the rock,	3318
Ps	78:26	his power he **b.** in the south wind	5090
Ps	78:54	And he **b.** them to the border of	935
Ps	78:71	he **b.** him to feed Jacob his people,	935
Ps	79:8	us: for we are **b.** very low	1809
Ps	80:8	Thou hast **b.** a vine out of Egypt:	5265
Ps	81:10	Lord thy God, which **b.** thee out	5927
Ps	85:1	**b.** back the captivity of Jacob	7725
Ps	89:40	hast **b.** his strong holds to ruin	7760
Ps	90:2	Before the mountains were **b.**	3205
Ps	105:30	**b.** forth frogs in abundance,	8317
Ps	105:37	He **b.** them forth also with silver	3318
Ps	105:40	and he **b.** quails, and satisfied	935
Ps	105:43	And he **b.** forth his people with	3318
Ps	106:42	and they were **b.** into subjection	3665
Ps	106:43	and were **b.** low for their iniquity	4355
Ps	107:12	Therefore he **b.** down their heart	3665
Ps	107:14	He **b.** them out of darkness and	3318
Ps	107:39	they are minished and **b.** low	7817
Ps	116:6	I was **b.** low, and he helped me	1809
Ps	136:11	**b.** out Israel from among them:	3318
Ps	142:6	for I am **b.** very low; deliver me	1809
Pr	6:26	a man is **b.** to a piece of bread:	
Pr	8:24	no depths, I was **b.** forth; when	2342
Pr	8:25	before the hills was I **b.** forth:	2342
Pr	8:30	as one **b.** up with him: and I	539
Ec	12:4	of music shall be **b.** low;	7817
Ca	1:4	the king hath **b.** me into his	935

Book	Ref	Context	No.
Ca	2:4	He **b.** me to the banqueting house,	935
Ca	3:4	**b.** him into my mother's house,	935
Ca	8:5	there thy mother **b.** thee forth:	2254
Ca	8:5	she **b.** thee forth that bare thee.	2254
Isa	1:2	nourished and **b.** up children.	7311
Isa	2:12	lifted up; and he shall be **b.** low:	8213
Isa	5:2	grapes, and it **b.** forth wild grapes.	6213
Isa	5:4	grapes, **b.** it forth wild grapes?	6213
Isa	5:15	the mean man shall be **b.** down,	7817
Isa	14:11	Thy pomp is **b.** down to the	3381
Isa	14:15	thou shalt be **b.** down to hell,	3381
Isa	15:1	is laid waste, and **b.** to silence;	1820
Isa	15:1	is laid waste, and **b.** to silence;	1820
Isa	18:7	shall the present be **b.** unto	2986
Isa	21:14	land of Tema **b.** water to him.	857
Isa	23:13	thereof; and he **b.** it to ruin.	7760
Isa	25:5	the terrible ones shall be **b.** low.	6030
Isa	26:18	have as it were **b.** forth wind;	3205
Isa	29:4	And thou shalt be **b.** down.	8213
Isa	29:20	the terrible one is **b.** to nought,	656
Isa	37:26	now have I **b.** it to pass, that thou	935
Isa	43:14	have **b.** down all their nobles,	3381
Isa	43:23	Thou hast not **b.** me the small	935
Isa	45:10	What hast thou **b.** forth?	2342
Isa	48:15	I have **b.** him, and he shall make	935
Isa	49:21	who hath **b.** up these? Behold,	1431
Isa	51:18	the sons whom she hath **b.** forth;	3205
Isa	51:18	the sons that she hath **b.** up.	1431
Isa	53:7	is **b.** as a lamb to the slaughter,	2986
Isa	59:16	therefore his arm **b.** salvation	3467
Isa	60:11	and that their kings may be **b.**.	5090
Isa	62:9	they that have **b.** it together	6908
Isa	63:5	mine own arm **b.** salvation unto	3467
Isa	63:11	Where is he that **b.** them up out	5927
Isa	66:7	Before she travailed, she **b.** forth;	3205
Isa	66:8	she **b.** forth her children.	3205
Jer	2:6	where is the Lord that **b.** us up	5927
Jer	2:7	**b.** you into a plentiful country,	935
Jer	2:27	Thou hast **b.** me forth: for they	3205
Jer	7:22	the day that I **b.** them out of the	3318
Jer	10:9	Silver spread into plates is **b.**	935
Jer	11:4	the day that I **b.** them forth out	3318
Jer	11:7	in the day that I **b.** them up	5927
Jer	11:19	ox that is **b.** to the slaughter;	2986
Jer	15:8	I have **b.** upon them against	935
Jer	16:14, 15	liveth, that **b.** up the children	5927
Jer	20:3	that Pashur **b.** forth Jeremiah	3318
Jer	20:15	man who **b.** tidings to my father,	1319
Jer	23:7, 8	The Lord liveth, which **b.** up	5927
Jer	24:1	and had **b.** them to Babylon.	935
Jer	26:23	and **b.** him unto Jehoiakim the	935
Jer	27:16	shortly be **b.** again from Babylon:	7725
Jer	32:21	And hast **b.** forth thy people	3318
Jer	32:42	Like as I have **b.** all this great	935
Jer	34:11	and **b.** them into subjection for	3533
Jer	34:13	the day that I **b.** them forth out	3318
Jer	34:16	and **b.** them into subjection,	3533
Jer	35:4	And I **b.** them into the house	935
Jer	37:14	and **b.** him to the princes.	935
Jer	38:22	**b.** forth to the king of Babylon's	3318
Jer	39:5	they **b.** him up to Nebuchadnezzar	5927
Jer	40:3	Now the Lord hath **b.** it, and done	935
Jer	41:16	whom he had **b.** again from	7725
Jer	44:2	all the evil that I have **b.** upon	935
Jer	50:25	and hath **b.** forth the weapons	3318
Jer	51:10	The Lord hath **b.** forth our	3318
Jer	52:26	**b.** them to the king of Babylon	3212
Jer	52:31	and **b.** him forth out of prison,	3218
La	2:2	hath **b.** them down to the ground:	5060
La	2:22	that I have swaddled and **b.** up	7235
La	3:2	led me, and **b.** me into darkness,	3212
La	4:5	they that were **b.** up in scarlet	539
Eze	8:3	and **b.** me in the visions of God	935
Eze	8:7	he **b.** me to the door of the court;	935
Eze	8:14	Then he **b.** me to the door of the	935
Eze	8:16	And he **b.** me into the inner court	935
Eze	11:1	and **b.** me unto the east gate	935
Eze	11:24	and **b.** me in a vision by the Spirit	935
Eze	12:7	I **b.** forth my stuff by day,	3318
Eze	12:7	I **b.** it forth in the twilight,	3318
Eze	14:22	remnant that shall be **b.** forth,	3318
Eze	14:22	the evil that I have **b.** upon	935
Eze	14:22	all that I have **b.** upon it.	935
Eze	17:6	a vine, and **b.** forth branches,	5375
Eze	17:24	I the Lord have **b.** down the high	8213
Eze	19:3	she **b.** up one of her whelps:	5927
Eze	19:4	and they **b.** him with chains	935
Eze	19:9	**b.** him to the king of Babylon:	935
Eze	19:9	they **b.** him into holds,	935
Eze	20:10	and **b.** them into the wilderness.	935
Eze	20:14	in whose sight I **b.** them out.	3318
Eze	20:22	in whose sight I **b.** them forth.	3318
Eze	20:28	I had **b.** them into the land,	935
Eze	21:7	cometh, and shall be **b.** to pass,	1961
Eze	23:8	her whoredoms **b.** from Egypt:	
Eze	23:27	whoredom **b.** from the land of	
Eze	23:42	the common sort were **b.**	935
Eze	27:6	**b.** out of the isles of Chittim.	
Eze	27:15	they **b.** thee for a present	7725
Eze	27:26	Thy rowers have **b.** thee into	935
Eze	29:5	thou shalt not be **b.** together,	622
Eze	30:11	shall be **b.** to destroy the land:	935
Eze	31:18	thou be **b.** down with the trees	3381
Eze	34:4	have ye **b.** again that which	7725
Eze	37:13	**b.** you up out of your graves,	5927
Eze	38:8	the land that is **b.** back from the	7725
Eze	38:8	it is **b.** forth out of the nations,	3318
Eze	39:27	**b.** them again from the people,	7725
Eze	40:1	was upon me, and **b.** me thither	935
Eze	40:2	In the visions of God **b.** he me	935
Eze	40:3	And he **b.** me thither, and	935
Eze	40:4	art thou **b.** hither: declare all	935
Eze	40:17	Then **b.** he me into the outward	935
Eze	40:24	that he **b.** me toward the south,	3212
Eze	40:28	And he **b.** me to the inner court	935
Eze	40:32	And he **b.** me into the inner court	935
Eze	40:35	And he **b.** me to the north gate,	935
Eze	40:48	And he **b.** me to the porch of the	935
Eze	40:49	cubits; and he **b.** me by the steps	935
Eze	41:1	Afterward he **b.** me to the temple,	935
Eze	42:1	Then he **b.** me forth into the	3318
Eze	42:1	and he **b.** me into the chamber	935
Eze	42:15	he **b.** me forth toward the gate	3318
Eze	43:1	Afterward he **b.** me to the gate	3212
Eze	43:5	and **b.** me into the inner court;	935
Eze	44:1	Then he **b.** me back the way of	7725
Eze	44:4	Then **b.** he me the way of the	935
Eze	44:7	that ye have **b.** into my sanctuary	935
Eze	46:19	After he **b.** me through the entry,	935
Eze	46:21	Then he **b.** me forth into the	3318
Eze	47:1	Afterward he **b.** me again unto	7725
Eze	47:2	Then **b.** he me out of the way of	3318
Eze	47:3	he **b.** me through the waters;	5674
Eze	47:4	and **b.** me through the waters;	5674
Eze	47:4	**b.** me through; the waters were	5674
Eze	47:6	**b.** me, and caused me to return	3212
Eze	47:8	**b.** forth into the sea, the waters	3318
Da	1:2	**b.** the vessels into the treasure	935
Da	1:9	God had **b.** Daniel into favour	5414
Da	1:18	then the prince of the eunuchs **b.**	935
Da	2:25	Then Arioch **b.** in Daniel	5954
Da	3:13	**b.** these men before the king.	858
Da	5:3	Then they **b.** the golden vessels	858
Da	5:13	was Daniel **b.** in before the king	5954
Da	5:13	king my father **b.** out of Jewry?	858
Da	5:15	been **b.** in before me, that they	5954
Da	5:23	and they have **b.** the vessels of	858
Da	6:16	and they **b.** Daniel, and cast him	858
Da	6:17	And a stone was **b.**, and laid	858
Da	6:18	**b.** before him: and his sleep	5954
Da	6:24	and they **b.** those men which	858
Da	7:13	and they **b.** him near before him.	7127
Da	9:14	upon the evil, and **b.** it upon us:	935
Da	9:15	that hast **b.** thy people forth out	3318
Da	11:6	and they that **b.** her, and he that	935
Ho	12:13	the Lord **b.** Israel out of Egypt,	5927
Am	2:10	I **b.** you up from the land of	5927
Am	3:1	I **b.** up from the land of Egypt,	5927
Am	9:7	Have not I **b.** up Israel out of the	5927
Ob	7	of thy confederacy have **b.** thee	7971
Jon	2:6	yet hast thou **b.** up my life	5927
Mic	5:3	which travaileth hath **b.** forth:	3205
Mic	6:4	I **b.** thee up out of the land of	5927
Na	2:7	she shall be **b.** up, and her maids	5927
Hag	1:9	and when ye **b.** it home, I did	935
Hag	2:19	the olive tree, hath not **b.** forth:	5375
Zec	10:11	of Assyria shall be **b.** down,	3381
Mal	1:13	and ye **b.** that which was torn,	935
Mal	1:13	thus ye **b.** an offering: should I	935
Mt	1:12	after they were **b.** to Babylon,	*3350*
Mt	1:25	**b.** forth her firstborn son:	*5088*
Mt	4:24	they **b.** unto him all sick people	*4374*
Mt	8:16	they **b.** unto him many that were	*4374*
Mt	9:2	**b.** to him a man sick of the palsy,	*4374*
Mt	9:32	they **b.** to him a dumb man	*4374*
Mt	10:18	**ye shall be b. before governors**	*71*
Mt	11:23	**heaven, shalt be b. down to hell:**	*2601*
Mt	12:22	Then was **b.** unto him one	*4374*
Mt	12:25	**is b. to desolation; and every city**	*2049*
Mt	13:8	**unto good ground, and b. forth**	*1325*
Mt	13:26	**and b. forth fruit, then appeared**	*4160*
Mt	14:11	his head was **b.** in a charger,	*5342*
Mt	14:11	and she **b.** it to her mother.	*5342*
Mt	14:35	and **b.** unto him all that were	*4374*
Mt	16:8	**because ye have b. no bread?**	*2989*
Mt	17:16	And I **b.** him to thy disciples,	*4374*
Mt	18:24	**one was b. unto him, which owed**	*4374*
Mt	19:13	these **b.** unto him little children	*4374*
Mt	21:7	And **b.** the ass, and the colt,	*71*
Mt	22:19	And they **b.** unto him a penny.	*4374*
Mt	25:20	**came and b. other five talents,**	*4374*
Mt	27:3	**b.** again the thirty pieces of	*654*
Mk	1:32	they **b.** unto him all that were	*5342*
Mk	4:8	**and b. forth, some thirty, and**	*5342*
Mk	4:21	**b. to be put under a bushel,**	*2064*
Mk	4:29	**when the fruit is b. forth,**	*3860*
Mk	6:27	commanded his head to be **b.**:	*5342*
Mk	6:28	And **b.** his head in a charger,	*5342*
Mk	9:17	I have **b.** unto thee my son,	*5342*
Mk	9:20	And they **b.** him unto him: and	*5342*
Mk	10:13	they **b.** young children to him,	*4374*
Mk	10:13	disciples rebuked those that **b.**	*4374*
Mk	11:7	And they **b.** the colt to Jesus,	*71*
Mk	12:16	And they **b.** it. And he saith,	*5342*
Mk	13:9	**ye shall be b. before rulers and**	*2476*
Lu	1:57	delivered; and she **b.** forth a son.	*1080*
Lu	2:7	she **b.** forth her firstborn son,	*5088*
Lu	2:22	they **b.** him to Jerusalem to	*321*
Lu	2:27	when the parents **b.** in the child	*1521*
Lu	3:5	mountain and hill shall be **b.** low;	*5013*
Lu	4:9	And he **b.** him to Jerusalem, and	*71*
Lu	4:16	Nazareth, where he had been **b.** up:	*5142*
Lu	4:40	divers diseases **b.** them unto him;	*71*
Lu	5:11	they had **b.** their ships to land,	*2609*
Lu	5:18	And, behold, men **b.** in a bed	*5342*
Lu	7:37	**b.** an alabaster box of ointment,	*2865*
Lu	10:34	**b. him to an inn, and took care**	*71*
Lu	11:17	**against itself is b. to desolation;**	*2049*
Lu	12:16	**of a certain rich man b. forth**	*2164*
Lu	18:15	they **b.** unto him also infants,	*4374*
Lu	18:40	commanded him to be **b.** unto him:	*71*
Lu	19:35	And they **b.** him to Jesus: and	*71*
Lu	21:12	**being b. before kings and rulers**	*71*
Lu	22:54	**b.** him into the high priest's	*1521*
Lu	23:14	Ye have **b.** this man unto me,	*4374*
Joh	1:42	And he **b.** him to Jesus. And	*71*
Joh	4:33	any man **b.** him ought to eat?	*5842*
Joh	7:45	Why have ye not **b.** him?	*71*
Joh	8:3	the scribes and Pharisees **b.**	*71*
Joh	9:13	They **b.** to the Pharisees him	*71*
Joh	18:16	kept the door, and **b.** in Peter,	*1521*
Joh	19:13	he **b.** Jesus forth, and sat down	*71*
Joh	19:39	**b.** a mixture of myrrh and aloes,	*5342*
Ac	4:34	and **b.** the prices of the things	*5342*
Ac	4:37	and **b.** the money, and laid it at	*5342*
Ac	5:2	and **b.** a certain part, and laid it	*5342*
Ac	5:15	**b.** forth the sick into the streets,	*1627*
Ac	5:19	**b.** them forth, and said,	*1806*
Ac	5:21	to the prison to have them **b.**	*71*
Ac	5:26	officers and **b.** them without	*71*
Ac	5:27	And when they had **b.** them,	*71*
Ac	5:36	scattered, and **b.** to nought.	*1096*
Ac	6:12	and caught him, and **b.** him	*71*
Ac	7:36	He **b.** them out, after that	*1806*
Ac	7:40	Moses, which **b.** us out of the	*1806*
Ac	7:45	**b.** in with Jesus into the	*1521*
Ac	9:8	hand, and **b.** him to Damascus.	*1521*
Ac	9:27	took him, and **b.** him to the	*71*
Ac	9:30	they **b.** him down to Caesarea,	*2609*
Ac	9:39	**b.** him into the upper chamber:	*321*
Ac	11:26	when he had found him, he **b.** him	*71*
Ac	12:6	Herod would have **b.** him forth,	*4254*
Ac	12:17	Lord had **b.** him out of the prison.	*1806*
Ac	13:1	which had been **b.** up with	*4939*
Ac	13:17	**b.** he them out of it.	*1806*
Ac	14:13	**b.** oxen and garlands unto the	*5342*
Ac	15:3	And being **b.** on their way by	*4311*
Ac	16:16	which **b.** her masters much gain	*3930*
Ac	16:20	And **b.** them to the magistrates,	*4317*
Ac	16:30	And **b.** them out, and said, Sirs,	*4254*
Ac	16:34	he had **b.** them into his house,	*321*

Ac 16:39 **b.** them out, and desired them *1806*
Ac 17:15 conducted Paul **b.** him unto Athens: *71*
Ac 17:19 him, and **b.** him unto Areopagus, *71*
Ac 18:12 against Paul, and **b.** him to the *71*
Ac 19:12 his body were **b.** unto the sick *2018*
Ac 19:19 **b.** their books together, and *4851*
Ac 19:24 **b.** no small gain unto the *3930*
Ac 19:37 **b.** hither these men, which are *71*
Ac 20:12 they **b.** the young man alive, and *71*
Ac 21:5 and they all **b.** us on our way, *4311*
Ac 21:16 **b.** with them one Mnason of *71*
Ac 21:28 **b.** Greeks also into the temple, *1521*
Ac 21:29 that Paul had **b.** into the temple.) *1521*
Ac 22:3 yet **b.** up in this city at the feet *397*
Ac 22:24 him to be **b.** into the castle, *71*
Ac 22:30 **b.** Paul down, and set him before *2609*
Ac 23:18 and **b.** him to the chief captain, *71*
Ac 23:28 I **b.** him forth into their council: *2609*
Ac 23:31 and **b.** him by night to Antipatris. *71*
Ac 25:6 seat commanded Paul to be **b.**. *71*
Ac 25:17 commanded the man to be **b.** forth. *71*
Ac 25:18 they **b.** none accusation of such *2018*
Ac 25:23 commandment Paul was **b.** forth. *71*
Ac 25:26 Wherefore I have **b.** him forth *4254*
Ac 27:24 thou must be **b.** before Caesar *3936*
Ro 15:24 to be **b.** on my way thitherward *4311*
1Co 6:12 not be **b.** under the power of any *1850*
1Co 15:54 then shall be **b.** to pass the *1096*
2Co 1:16 **b.** on my way toward Judaea. *4311*
Ga 2:4 false brethren unawares **b.** in, *3920*
1Th 3:6 **b.** us good tidings of your faith *2097*
1Ti 5:10 if she have **b.** up children, if she *5044*
1Ti 6:7 we **b.** nothing into this world, *1533*
2Ti 1:10 and hath **b.** life and immortality *5461*
2Ti *subscr.* when Paul was **b.** before Nero *3936*
Heb 13:11 **b.** into the sanctuary by the high *1533*
Heb 13:20 that **b.** again from the dead our *321*
Jas 5:18 and the earth **b.** forth her fruit. *985*
1Pe 1:13 be **b.** unto you at the revelation *5342*
2Pe 2:19 of the same is he **b.** in bondage. *1402*
Re 12:5 And she **b.** forth a man child, *5088*
Re 12:13 which **b.** forth the man child. *5088*

BROUGHTEST
Ex 32:7 thy people, which thou **b.** out of 5927
Nu 14:13 thou **b.** up this people in thy 5927
De 9:28 land whence thou **b.** us out say, 3318
De 9:29 which thou **b.** out by thy mighty 3318
2Sa 5:2 that leddest out and **b.** in Israel: 935
1Ki 8:51 thou **b.** forth out of Egypt, from 3318
1Ki 8:53 thou **b.** our fathers out of Egypt, 3318
1Ch 11:2 and **b.** in Israel: and the Lord 935
Ne 9:7 and **b.** him forth out of Ur of the 3318
Ne 9:15 **b.** forth water for them out of 3318
Ne 9:23 and **b.** them into the land, 935
Ps 66:11 thou **b.** us into the net; thou 935
Ps 66:12 thou **b.** us out into a wealthy place. 3318

BROW See also EYEBROW.
Isa 48:4 an iron sinew, and thy **b.** brass; 4696
Lu 4:29 and led him unto the **b.** of the hill *3790*

BROWN
Ge 30:32 the **b.** cattle among the sheep, 2345
Ge 30:33 **b.** among the sheep, that shall 2345
Ge 30:35 all the **b.** among the sheep, and 2345
Ge 30:40 all the **b.** in the flock of Laban; 2345

BRUISE See also BRUISED; BRUISES; BRUISING.
Ge 3:15 it shall **b.** thy head, 7779
Ge 3:15 and thou shalt **b.** his heel. 7779
Isa 28:28 cart, nor **b.** it with his horsemen. 1854
Isa 53:10 Yet it pleased the Lord to **b.** him; 1792
Jer 30:12 Thy **b.** is incurable, and thy 7667
Da 2:40 shall it break in pieces and **b.**. 7490
Na 3:19 no healing of thy **b.**; thy wound 7667
Ro 16:20 **b.** Satan under your feet shortly. *4937*

BRUISED
Le 22:24 unto the Lord that which is **b.**, 4600
2Ki 18:21 the staff of this **b.** reed, even 7533
Isa 28:28 Bread corn is **b.**; because he 1854
Isa 42:3 A **b.** reed shall he not break, and 7533
Isa 53:5 he was **b.** for our iniquities: the 1792
Eze 23:3 they **b.** the teats of their virginity 6213
Eze 23:8 **b.** the breasts of her virginity, 6213
Mt 12:20 A **b.** reed shall he not break, and *4937*
Lu 4:18 .. *2352*

BRUISES
Isa 1:6 and **b.**, and putrifying sores: 2250

BRUISING
Eze 23:21 in **b.** thy teats by the Egyptians 6213
Lu 9:39 **b.** him, hardly departeth from *4937*

BRUIT
Jer 10:22 the noise of the **b.** is come, and 8052
Na 3:19 that hear the **b.** of thee shall 8088

BRUTE
2Pe 2:12 these, as natural **b.** beasts, made *249*
Jude 10 know naturally, as **b.** beasts, in *249*

BRUTISH
Ps 49:10 the fool and the **b.** person perish, 1197
Ps 92:6 a **b.** man knoweth not; neither 1197
Ps 94:8 ye **b.** among the people: and ye 1197
Pr 12:1 but he that hateth reproof is **b.**. 1197
Pr 30:2 Surely I am more **b.** than any 1197
Isa 19:11 of Pharaoh is become **b.**: 1197
Jer 10:8 they are altogether **b.** and foolish: 1197
Jer 10:14 Every man is **b.** in his knowledge: 1197
Jer 10:21 the pastors are become **b.**, and 1197
Jer 51:17 Every man is **b.** by his knowledge; 1197
Eze 21:31 into the hand of **b.** men, and skilful 1197

BUCK See ROEBUCK.

BUCKET See also BUCKETS.
Isa 40:15 the nations are as a drop of a **b.**, 1805

BUCKETS
Nu 24:7 our the water out of his **b.**, and 1805

BUCKLER See also BUCKLERS.
2Sa 22:31 a **b.** to all them that trust in him. 4043
1Ch 5:18 men able to bear **b.** and sword, 4043
1Ch 12:8 that could handle shield and **b.**, 7420
Ps 18:2 my **b.**, and the horn of my 4043
Ps 18:30 he is a **b.** to all those that trust 4043
Ps 35:2 Take hold of shield and **b.**, and 6793
Ps 91:4 truth shall be thy shield and **b.**. 5507
Pr 2:7 a **b.** to them that walk uprightly. 4043
Jer 46:3 Order ye the **b.** and shield, and 4043
Eze 23:24 set against thee **b.** and shield 6793
Eze 26:8 and lift up the **b.** against thee. 6793

BUCKLERS
2Ch 23:9 spears, and **b.**, and shields, that 4043
Job 15:26 upon the thick bosses of his **b.**: 4043
Ca 4:4 there hang a thousand **b.**, all 4043
Eze 38:4 company with **b.** and shields, 6793
Eze 39:9 the shields and the **b.**, the bows 6793

BUD See also BUDDED; BUDS.
Job 14:9 the scent of water it will **b.**, and 6524
Job 38:27 to cause the **b.** of the tender herb 4161
Ps 132:17 I make the horn of David to **b.**: 6779
Ca 7:12 the pomegranates **b.** forth: there 5132
Isa 18:5 when the **b.** is perfect, and the 6525
Isa 27:6 Israel shall blossom and **b.**, and 6524
Isa 55:10 maketh it bring forth and **b.**, that 6779
Isa 61:11 the earth bringeth forth her **b.**, 6779
Eze 16:7 to multiply as the **b.** of the field, 6779
Eze 29:21 of the house of Israel to **b.** forth, 6779
Ho 8:7 the **b.** shall yield no meal: if so 6779

BUDDED
Ge 40:10 it was as though it **b.**, and her 6524
Nu 17:8 Aaron for the house of Levi was **b.**, 6524
Ca 6:11 and the pomegranates **b.**. 5132
Eze 7:10 hath blossomed, pride hath **b.**. 6524
Heb 9:4 Aaron's rod that **b.**, and the tables *985*

BUDS
Nu 17:8 was budded, and brought forth **b.**, 6525

BUFFET See also BUFFETED.
Mk 14:65 to cover his face, and to **b.** him *2852*
2Co 12:7 messenger of Satan to **b.** me, lest *2852*

BUFFETED
Mt 26:67 they spit in his face and **b.** him; *2852*
1Co 4:11 and are **b.**, and have no certain *2852*
1Pe 2:20 when ye be **b.** for your faults, ye *2852*

BUILD See also BUILDED; BUILDEST; BUILDETH; BUILDING; BUILT.
Ge 11:4 Go to, let us **b.** us a city and 1129
Ge 11:8 and they left off to **b.** the city. 1129
Ex 20:25 thou shalt not **b.** it of hewn stone: 1129
Nu 23:1, 29 **B.** me here seven altars, and 1129
Nu 32:16 We will **b.** sheepfolds here for our 1129
Nu 32:24 **B.** you cities for your little ones, 1129
De 20:20 and thou shalt **b.** bulwarks against 1129
De 25:9 will not **b.** up his brother's house. 1129
De 27:5 there shalt thou **b.** an altar unto 1129
De 27:6 Thou shalt **b.** the altar of the Lord 1129
De 28:30 thou shalt **b.** an house, and thou 1129
Jos 22:26 Let us now prepare to **b.** us an 1129
Jos 22:29 to **b.** an altar for burnt offerings, 1129
Jg 6:26 And **b.** an altar unto the Lord 1129
Ru 4:11 two did **b.** the house of Israel: 1129
1Sa 2:35 and I will **b.** him a sure house; 1129
2Sa 7:5 Shalt thou **b.** me an house for me 1129
2Sa 7:7 Why **b.** ye not me an house of 1129
2Sa 7:13 shall **b.** an house for my name, 1129
2Sa 7:27 saying, I will **b.** thee an house: 1129
2Sa 24:21 to **b.** an altar unto the Lord, that 1129
1Ki 2:36 **B.** thee an house in Jerusalem 1129
1Ki 5:3 my father could not **b.** an house 1129
1Ki 5:5 behold, I purpose to **b.** an house 1129
1Ki 5:5 shall **b.** an house unto my name. 1129
1Ki 5:18 timber and stones to **b.** the house. 1129
1Ki 6:1 that he began to **b.** the house of 1129
1Ki 8:16 tribes of Israel to **b.** an house, 1129
1Ki 8:17 David my father to **b.** an house 1129
1Ki 8:18 to **b.** an house unto my name, thou 1129
1Ki 8:19 thou shalt not **b.** the house; but 1129
1Ki 8:19 shall **b.** the house unto my name. 1129
1Ki 9:15 to **b.** the house of the Lord, and 1129
1Ki 9:19 which Solomon desired to **b.** in 1129
1Ki 9:24 built for her: then did he **b.** Millo. 1129
1Ki 11:7 Then did Solomon **b.** an high place 1129
1Ki 11:38 and **b.** thee a sure house, 1129
1Ki 16:34 did Hiel the Beth-elite **b.** Jericho: 1129
1Ch 14:1 carpenters, to **b.** him an house. 1129
1Ch 17:4 Thou shalt not **b.** me an house 1129
1Ch 17:10 the Lord will **b.** thee an house. 1129
1Ch 17:12 He shall **b.** me an house, and I will 1129
1Ch 17:25 that thou wilt **b.** him an house: 1129
1Ch 21:22 that I may **b.** an altar therein unto 1129
1Ch 22:2 stones to **b.** the house of God. 1129
1Ch 22:6 him to **b.** an house for the Lord 1129
1Ch 22:7 it was in my mind to **b.** an house 1129
1Ch 22:8 thou shalt not **b.** an house unto 1129
1Ch 22:10 shall **b.** an house for my name; 1129
1Ch 22:11 **b.** the house of the Lord thy God, 1129
1Ch 22:19 and **b.** the sanctuary of the Lord 1129
1Ch 28:2 in mine heart to **b.** an house of 1129
1Ch 28:3 Thou shalt not **b.** an house for my 1129
1Ch 28:6 shall **b.** my house and my courts, 1129
1Ch 28:10 to **b.** an house for the sanctuary: 1129
1Ch 29:16 to **b.** thee an house for thine holy 1129
1Ch 29:19 and to **b.** the palace, for the which 1129
2Ch 2:1 Solomon determined to **b.** an house 1129
2Ch 2:3 send him cedars to **b.** him an 1129
2Ch 2:4 Behold, I **b.** an house to the name 1129
2Ch 2:5 the house which I **b.** is great: for 1129
2Ch 2:6 who is able to **b.** him an house, 1129
2Ch 2:6 that I should **b.** him an house, 1129
2Ch 2:9 the house which I am about to **b.** 1129
2Ch 2:12 that might **b.** an house for the Lord, 1129
2Ch 3:1 Solomon began to **b.** the house 1129
2Ch 3:2 And he began to **b.** in the second 1129
2Ch 6:5 to **b.** an house in, that my name 1129
2Ch 6:7 David my father to **b.** an house 1129
2Ch 6:8 heart to **b.** an house for my name, 1129
2Ch 6:9 thou shalt not **b.** the house; but 1129
2Ch 6:9 he shall **b.** the house for my name. 1129
2Ch 8:6 desired to **b.** in Jerusalem, 1129
2Ch 14:7 Let us **b.** these cities, and make 1129
2Ch 35:3 son of David king of Israel did **b.**; 1129
2Ch 36:23 to **b.** him an house in Jerusalem, 1129
Ezr 1:2 to **b.** him an house at Jerusalem, 1129
Ezr 1:3 and **b.** the house of the Lord God 1129
Ezr 1:5 to **b.** the house of the Lord which 1129
Ezr 4:2 Let us **b.** with you: for we seek 1129
Ezr 4:3 to **b.** an house unto our God; 1129
Ezr 4:3 but we ourselves together will **b.** 1129
Ezr 5:2 and began to **b.** the house of God 1124
Ezr 5:3 Who hath commanded you to **b.** 1124
Ezr 5:9 commanded you to **b.** this house, 1124
Ezr 5:11 and **b.** the house that was builded 1124
Ezr 5:13 made a decree to **b.** this house of 1124
Ezr 5:17 was made of Cyrus the king to **b.** 1124
Ezr 6:7 the elders of the Jews **b.** this house. 1124
Ne 2:5 sepulchres, that I may **b.** it. 1129
Ne 2:17 let us **b.** up the wall of Jerusalem, 1129
Ne 2:18 Let us rise up and **b.**. So they 1129

Ne 2:20 we his servants will arise and **b.**: 1129
Ne 3:3 did the sons of Hassenaah **b.**, who 1129
Ne 4:3 Even that which they **b.**, if a fox 1129
Ne 4:10 that we are not able to **b.** the wall. 1129
Ps 28:5 destroy them, and not **b.** them up. 1129
Ps 51:18 **b.** thou the walls of Jerusalem. 1129
Ps 69:35 and will **b.** the cities of Judah: 1129
Ps 89:4 **b.** up thy throne to all generations. 1129
Ps 102:16 the Lord shall **b.** up Zion, he shall 1129
Ps 127:1 Except the Lord **b.** the house, they 1129
Ps 127:1 house, they labor in vain that **b.** it 1129
Ps 147:2 The Lord doth **b.** up Jerusalem: 1129
Pr 24:27 and afterwards **b.** thine house 1129
Ec 3:3 break down, and a time to **b.** up; 1129
Ca 8:9 will **b.** upon her a palace of silver: 1129
Isa 9:10 but we will **b.** with hewn stones: 1129
Isa 45:13 he shall **b.** my city, and he shall 1129
Isa 58:12 they that shall be of thee shall **b.** 1129
Isa 60:10 the sons of strangers shall **b.** up 1129
Isa 61:4 And they shall **b.** the old wastes, 1129
Isa 65:21 shall **b.** houses, and inhabit them; 1129
Isa 65:22 shall not **b.**, and another inhabit; 1129
Isa 66:1 where is the house that ye **b.** unto 1129
Jer 1:10 to throw down, to **b.**, and to plant 1129
Jer 18:9 concerning a kingdom, to **b.** and 1129
Jer 22:14 I will **b.** me a wide house and large 1129
Jer 24:6 I will **b.** them, and not pull them 1129
Jer 29:5, 28 **B.** ye houses, and dwell in them; 1129
Jer 31:4 Again I will **b.** thee, and thou shalt 1129
Jer 31:28 so will I watch over them, to **b.**, 1129
Jer 33:7 and will **b.** them, as at the first 1129
Jer 35:7 Neither shall ye **b.** house, nor sow 1129
Jer 35:9 Nor to **b.** houses for us to dwell in: 1129
Jer 42:10 then will I **b.** you, and not pull you 1129
Eze 4:2 and **b.** a fort against it, and cast a 1129
Eze 11:3 let us **b.** houses: this city is the 1129
Eze 21:22 to cast a mount, and to **b.** a fort. 1129
Eze 28:26 and shall **b.** houses, and plant 1129
Eze 36:36 that I the Lord **b.** the ruined 1129
Da 9:25 to restore and to **b.** Jerusalem 1129
Am 9:11 I will **b.** it as in the days of old: 1129
Am 9:14 and they shall **b.** the waste cities, 1129
Mic 3:10 They **b.** up Zion with blood, and 1129
Zep 1:13 they shall also **b.** houses, but not 1129
Hag 1:8 and **b.** the house; and I will take 1129
Zec 5:11 To **b.** it an house in the land of 1129
Zec 6:12 and he shall **b.** the temple of the 1129
Zec 6:13 Even he shall **b.** the temple of 1129
Zec 6:15 and **b.** in the temple of the Lord, 1129
Zec 9:3 Tyrus did **b.** herself a strong hold, 1129
Mal 1:4 return and **b.** the desolate places; 1129
Mal 1:4 shall **b.**, but I will throw down; 1129
Mt 16:18 **upon this rock I will b. my** *3618*
Mt 23:29 **because ye b. the tombs of the** *3618*
Mt 26:61 God, and to **b.** it in three days. *3618*
Mk 14:58 within three days I will **b.** another *3618*
Lu 11:47 **b. the sepulchres of the prophets,** *3618*
Lu 11:48 **them, and ye b. their sepulchres.** *3618*
Lu 12:18 **I will pull down my barns, and b.** *3618*
Lu 14:28 **intending to b. a tower, sitteth** *3618*
Lu 14:30 **This man began to b., and was not** *3618*
Ac 7:49 what house will ye **b.** me? saith *3618*
Ac 15:16 **b.** again the tabernacle of David, *456*
Ac 15:16 I will **b.** again the ruins thereof, *456*
Ac 20:32 to **b.** you up, and to give you an *2026*
Ro 15:20 lest I should **b.** upon another *3618*
1Co 3:12 Now if any man **b.** upon this *2026*
Ga 2:18 if I **b.** again the things which I *3618*

BUILDED See also BUILDEDST; BUILT.
Ge 4:17 and he **b.** a city, and called the 1129
Ge 8:20 Noah **b.** an altar unto the Lord; 1129
Ge 10:11 and **b.** Nineveh, and the city 1129
Ge 11:5 which the children of men **b.** 1129
Ge 12:7 there **b.** he an altar unto the Lord, 1129
Ge 12:8 and there he **b.** an altar unto the 1129
Ge 26:25 And he **b.** an altar there, and 1129
Ex 24:4 and **b.** an altar under the hill, 1129
Nu 32:38 unto the cities which they **b.**, 1129
Jos 22:16 in that ye have **b.** you an altar, 1129
1Ki 8:27 less this house that I have **b.**? 1129
1Ki 8:43 this house, which I have **b.**, is 1129
1Ki 15:22 thereof, wherewith Baasha had **b.**; 1129
2Ki 23:13 Solomon the king of Israel had **b.** 1129
1Ch 22:5 to be **b.** for the Lord must be 1129
Ezr 3:2 and **b.** the altar of the God of Israel, 1129
Ezr 4:1 children of the captivity **b.** the 1129
Ezr 4:13 if this city be **b.**, and the walls set 1124
Ezr 4:16 if this city be **b.** again, and the 1124
Ezr 4:21 and that this city be not **b.**, until 1124
Ezr 5:8 which is **b.** with great stones, 1124
Ezr 5:11 **b.** these many years ago, which 1124
Ezr 5:11 which a great king of Israel **b.** and 1124
Ezr 5:15 let the house of God be **b.** in this 1124
Ezr 6:3 Let the house be **b.**, the place 1124
Ezr 6:14 And the elders of the Jews **b.**, 1124
Ezr 6:14 And they **b.**, and finished it, 1124
Ne 3:1 and they **b.** the sheep gate; 1129
Ne 3:2 And next unto him **b.** the men 1129
Ne 3:2 And next to him **b.** Zaccur 1129
Ne 4:1 heard that we **b.** the wall, he was 1129
Ne 4:17 They which **b.** on the wall, and 1129
Ne 4:18 is girded by his side, and so **b.** 1129
Ne 6:1 heard that I had **b.** the wall, and 1129
Ne 7:4 and the houses were not **b.** 1129
Ne 12:29 the singers had **b.** them villages 1129
Job 20:19 away an house which he **b.** not; 1129
Ps 122:3 Jerusalem is **b.** as a city that is 1129
Pr 9:1 Wisdom hath **b.** her house, she 1129
Pr 24:3 Through wisdom is an house **b.**; 1129
Ec 2:4 I **b.** me houses; I planted me 1129
Ca 4:4 tower of David **b.** for an armoury, 1129
Jer 30:18 and the city shall be **b.** upon 1129
La 3:5 He hath **b.** against me, and 1129
Eze 36:10 and the wastes shall be **b.**: 1129
Eze 36:33 cities, and the wastes shall be **b.** 1129
Lu 17:28 **they sold, they planted, they b.;** *3618*
Eph 2:22 In whom ye also are **b.** together *4925*
Heb 3:3 as he who hath **b.** the house hath *2680*
Heb 3:4 every house is **b.** by some man; *2680*

BUILDEDST
De 6:10 goodly cities, which thou **b.** not, 1129

BUILDER See also BUILDERS; MASTERBUILDER.
Heb 11:10 whose **b.** and maker is God *5079*

BUILDERS
1Ki 5:18 Solomon's **b.** and Hiram's **b.** 1129
2Ki 12:11 to the carpenters and **b.**, that 1129
2Ki 22:6 Unto carpenters, and **b.**, and 1129
2Ch 34:11 to the artificers and **b.** gave they it, 1129
Ezr 3:10 when the **b.** laid the foundation 1129
Ne 4:5 thee to anger before the **b.** 1129
Ne 4:18 For the **b.**, every one had his 1129
Ps 118:22 the stone which the **b.** refused 1129
Eze 27:4 thy **b.** have perfected thy beauty. 1129
Mt 21:42 **The stone which the b. rejected,** *3618*
Mk 12:10 **The stone which the b. rejected** *3618*
Lu 20:17 **The stone which the b. rejected,** *3618*
Ac 4:11 which was set at nought of you **b.**, *3618*
1Pe 2:7 the stone which the **b.** disallowed, *3618*

BUILDEST
De 22:8 When thou **b.** a new house, 1129
Neh 6:6 which cause thou **b.** the wall, 1129
Eze 16:31 In that thou **b.** thine eminent 1129
Mt 27:40 temple and **b.** it in three days, *3618*
Mk 15:29 temple, and **b.** it in three days, *3618*

BUILDETH
Jos 6:26 and **b.** this city Jericho: he shall 1129
Job 27:18 he **b.** his house as a moth, and 1129
Pr 14:1 Every wise woman **b.** her house: 1129
Jer 22:13 Woe unto him that **b.** his house 1129
Ho 8:14 and **b.** temples; and Judah 1129
Am 9:6 that **b.** his stories in the heaven, 1129
Hab 2:12 Woe to him that **b.** a town with 1129
1Co 3:10 foundation, and another **b.** *2026*
1Co 3:10 take heed how he **b.** thereupon. *2026*

BUILDING See also BUILDINGS.
Jos 22:19 in **b.** you an altar beside the 1129
1Ki 3:1 made an end of **b.** his own house, 1129
1Ki 6:7 when it was in **b.**, was built of 1129
1Ki 6:7 in the house, while it was in **b.** 1129
1Ki 6:12 which thou art in **b.**, if thou wilt 1129
1Ki 6:38 So was he seven years in **b.** it. 1129
1Ki 7:1 Solomon was **b.** his own house 1129
1Ki 9:1 Solomon had finished the **b.** of 1129
1Ki 15:21 that he left off **b.** of Ramah, 1129
1Ch 28:2 and had made ready for the **b.**: 1129
2Ch 3:3 for the **b.** of the house of God. 1129
2Ch 16:5 that he left off **b.** of Ramah, 1129
2Ch 16:6 wherewith Baasha was **b.**; and 1129
Ezr 4:4 Judah, and troubled them in **b.**, 1129
Ezr 4:12 **b.** the rebellious and the bad 1124
Ezr 5:4 of the men that make this **b.**? 1147
Ezr 5:16 even until now hath it been in **b.**, 1124
Ezr 6:8 for the **b.** of this house of God: 1124
Ec 10:18 By much slothfulness the **b.** 4746
Eze 17:17 and **b.** forts, to cut off many 1129
Eze 40:5 the breadth of the **b.**, one reed; 1146
Eze 41:12 Now the **b.** that was before the 1146
Eze 41:12 broad; and the wall of the **b.** 1146
Eze 41:13 and the **b.**, with the walls thereof, 1140
Eze 41:15 the length of the **b.** over against 1146
Eze 42:1 before the **b.** toward the north. 1146
Eze 42:5 and than the middlemost of the **b.**, 1146
Eze 42:6 therefore the **b.** was straitened
Eze 42:10 place, and over against the **b.** 1146
Eze 46:23 there was a row of **b.** round about
Joh 2:20 was this temple in **b.**, and wilt *3618*
1Co 3:9 husbandry, ye are God's **b.** *3619*
2Co 5:1 we have a **b.** of God, an house *3619*
Eph 2:21 In whom all the **b.** fitly framed *3619*
Heb 9:11 that is to say, not of this **b.**; *2937*
Jude 20 **b.** up yourselves on your most *2026*
Re 21:18 the **b.** of the wall of it was of *1739*

BUILDINGS
Mt 24:1 to shew him the **b.** of the temple. *3619*
Mk 13:1 stones and what **b.** are here! *3619*
Mk 13:2 him, **Seest thou these great b.?** *3619*

BUILT See also BUILDED.
Ge 13:18 **b.** there an altar unto the Lord. 1129
Ge 22:9 and Abraham **b.** an altar there, 1129
Ge 33:17 and **b.** him an house, and made 1129
Ge 35:7 And he **b.** there an altar, 1129
Ex 1:11 **b.** for Pharaoh treasure cities, 1129
Ex 17:15 And Moses **b.** an altar, and called 1129
Ex 32:5 he **b.** an altar before it; and Aaron 1129
Nu 13:22 Hebron was **b.** seven years before 1129
Nu 21:27 let the city of Sihon be **b.** and 1129
Nu 23:14 and **b.** seven altars, and offered 1129
Nu 32:34 And the children of Gad **b.** Dibon, 1129
Nu 32:37 the children of Reuben **b.** Heshbon, 1129
De 8:12 and hast **b.** goodly houses, and 1129
De 13:16 for ever; it shall not be **b.** again. 1129
De 20:5 that hath **b.** a new house, and 1129
Jos 8:30 Joshua **b.** an altar unto the Lord 1129
Jos 19:50 Ephraim: and he **b.** the city, 1129
Jos 22:10 tribe of Manasseh **b.** there an altar 1129
Jos 22:11 **b.** an altar over against the land 1129
Jos 22:23 That we have **b.** us an altar to 1129
Jos 24:13 cities which ye **b.** not, and ye 1129
Jg 1:26 and **b.** a city, and called the name 1129
Jg 6:24 Then Gideon **b.** an altar there 1129
Jg 6:28 offered upon the altar that was **b.** 1129
Jg 18:28 And they **b.** a city, and dwelt 1129
Jg 21:4 and **b.** there an altar, and offered 1129
1Sa 7:17 there he **b.** an altar unto the Lord. 1129
1Sa 14:35 And Saul **b.** an altar unto the Lord: 1129
1Sa 14:35 same was the first altar that he **b.** 1129
2Sa 5:9 And David **b.** round about from 1129
2Sa 5:11 and they **b.** David an house. 1129
2Sa 24:25 And David **b.** there an altar unto 1129
1Ki 3:2 **b.** unto the name of the Lord, 1129
1Ki 6:2 the house which king Solomon **b.** 1129
1Ki 6:5 against the wall of the house he **b.** 1129
1Ki 6:7 was **b.** of stone made ready before 1129
1Ki 6:9 So he **b.** the house, and finished it; 1129
1Ki 6:10 And then he **b.** chambers against 1129
1Ki 6:14 So Solomon **b.** the house, and 1129
1Ki 6:15 And he **b.** the walls of the house 1129
1Ki 6:16 And he **b.** twenty cubits on the 1129
1Ki 6:16 with boards of cedar: he even **b.** 1129
1Ki 6:36 And he **b.** the inner court with 1129
1Ki 7:2 He **b.** also the house of the forest 1129
1Ki 8:13 I have surely **b.** thee an house to 1129
1Ki 8:20 promised, and have **b.** an house 1129
1Ki 8:44 house that I have **b.** for thy name: 1129
1Ki 8:48 and the house which I have **b.** 1129
1Ki 9:3 thou hast **b.**, to put my name 1129
1Ki 9:10 Solomon had **b.** the two houses, 1129
1Ki 9:17 And Solomon **b.** Gezer, and 1129
1Ki 9:24 house which Solomon had **b.** for 1129
1Ki 9:25 altar which he **b.** unto the Lord, 1129
1Ki 10:4 and the house that he had **b.**, 1129
1Ki 11:27 Solomon **b.** Millo, and repaired the 1129
1Ki 11:38 a sure house, as I **b.** for David, 1129
1Ki 12:25 Then Jeroboam **b.** Shechem in 1129
1Ki 12:25 out from thence, and **b.** Penuel. 1129
1Ki 14:23 they also **b.** them high places, 1129

1Ki 15:17 up against Judah, and **b.** Ramah, ... 1129
1Ki 15:22 and king Asa **b.** with them Geba 1129
1Ki 15:23 the cities which he **b.**, are they 1129
1Ki 16:24 and **b.** on the hill, and called.............. 1129
1Ki 16:24 the name of the city which he **b.**,........ 1129
1Ki 16:32 Baal, which he had **b.** in Samaria........ 1129
1Ki 18:32 And with the stones he **b.** an altar...... 1129
1Ki 22:39 made, and all the cities that he **b.**, ... 1129
2Ki 14:22 He **b.** Elath, and restored it to 1129
2Ki 15:35 He **b.** the higher gate of the house..... 1129
2Ki 16:11 And Urijah the priest **b.** an altar......... 1129
2Ki 16:18 that they had **b.** in the house, and...... 1129
2Ki 17:9 and they **b.** them high places in all...... 1129
2Ki 21:3 he **b.** up again the high places............ 1129
2Ki 21:4 And he **b.** altars in the house of......... 1129
2Ki 21:5 And he **b.** altars for all the host of...... 1129
2Ki 25:1 they **b.** forts against it round about..... 1129
1Ch 6:10 that Solomon **b.** in Jerusalem:)............ 1129
1Ch 6:32 until Solomon had **b.** the house of........ 1129
1Ch 7:24 who **b.** Beth-horon the nether, and..... 1129
1Ch 8:12 who **b.** Ono, and Lod, with the towns. 1129
1Ch 11:8 And he **b.** the city round about, ... 1129
1Ch 17:6 Why have ye not **b.** me an house....... 1129
1Ch 21:26 And David **b.** there an altar unto........ 1129
1Ch 22:19 the house that is to be **b.** to the 1129
2Ch 6:2 I have **b.** an house of habitation 1129
2Ch 6:10 and have **b.** the house for the name.... 1129
2Ch 6:18 less this house which I have **b.**! 1129
2Ch 6:33 this house which I have **b.** is called..... 1129
2Ch 6:34 which I have **b.** for thy name;............ 1129
2Ch 6:38 toward the house which I have **b.**........ 1129
2Ch 8:1 Solomon had **b.** the house of the......... 1129
2Ch 8:2 Solomon **b.** them, and caused the....... 1129
2Ch 8:4 he **b.** Tadmor in the wilderness, ... 1129
2Ch 8:4 store cities, which he **b.** in Hamath..... 1129
2Ch 8:5 Also he **b.** Beth-horon the upper, ... 1129
2Ch 8:11 house that he had **b.** for her:............. 1129
2Ch 8:12 which he had **b.** before the porch, ... 1129
2Ch 9:3 and the house that he had **b.**,............ 1129
2Ch 11:5 **b.** cities for defence in Judah, ... 1129
2Ch 11:6 He **b.** even Beth-lehem, and Etam,..... 1129
2Ch 14:6 And he **b.** fenced cities in Judah: 1129
2Ch 14:7 So they **b.** and prospered. 1129
2Ch 16:1 and **b.** Ramah, to the intent that 1129
2Ch 16:6 he **b.** therewith Geba and Mizpah....... 1129
2Ch 17:12 he **b.** in Judah castles, and cities 1129
2Ch 20:8 **b.** thee a sanctuary therein for thy 1129
2Ch 26:2 He **b.** Eloth, and restored it to 1129
2Ch 26:6 and **b.** cities about Ashdod, and 1129
2Ch 26:9 Uzziah **b.** towers in Jerusalem at........ 1129
2Ch 26:10 Also he **b.** towers in the desert, ... 1129
2Ch 27:3 He **b.** the high gate of the house of 1129
2Ch 27:3 and on the wall of Ophel he **b.**.......... 1129
2Ch 27:4 he **b.** cities in the mountains of.......... 1129
2Ch 27:4 and in the forests he **b.** castles.......... 1129
2Ch 32:5 and **b.** up all the wall that was........... 1129
2Ch 33:3 For he **b.** again the high places.......... 1129
2Ch 33:4 Also he **b.** altars in the house of 1129
2Ch 33:5 And he **b.** altars for all the host of...... 1129
2Ch 33:14 after this he **b.** a wall without the....... 1129
2Ch 33:15 all the altars that he had **b.** in the 1129
2Ch 33:19 places wherein he **b.** high places, ... 1129
Ne 3:13 they **b.** it, and set up the doors 1129
Ne 3:14 he **b.** it, and set up the doors............ 1129
Ne 3:15 he **b.** it, and covered it, and set up 1129
Ne 4:6 So **b.** we the wall; and all the wall...... 1129
Ne 7:1 when the wall was **b.**, and I had set ... 1129
Job 3:14 **b.** desolate places for themselves;...... 1129
Job 12:14 down, and it cannot be **b.** again: 1129
Job 22:23 thou shalt be **b.** up, thou shalt put...... 1129
Ps 78:69 **b.** his sanctuary like high palaces,....... 1129
Ps 89:2 Mercy shall be **b.** up for ever: thy...... 1129
Ec 9:14 and **b.** great bulwarks against it: 1129
Isa 5:2 and **b.** a tower in the midst of it, ... 1129
Isa 25:2 to be no city; it shall never be **b.**....... 1129
Isa 44:26 Ye shall be **b.**, and I will raise up....... 1129
Isa 44:28 Thou shalt be **b.**; and to the............. 1129
Jer 7:31 And they have **b.** the high places 1129
Jer 12:16 then shall they be **b.** in the midst....... 1129
Jer 19:5 They have **b.** also the high places....... 1129
Jer 31:4 thou shalt be **b.**, O virgin of Israel:..... 1129
Jer 31:38 the city shall be **b.** to the Lord.......... 1129
Jer 32:31 from the day that they **b.** it even 1129
Jer 32:35 And they **b.** the high places of Baal, ... 1129
Jer 45:4 which I have **b.** will I break down,...... 1129
Jer 52:4 and **b.** forts against it round about. 1129
Eze 13:10 one **b.** up a wall, and, lo, others 1129
Eze 16:24 also **b.** unto thee an eminent place,..... 1129
Eze 16:25 Thou hast **b.** thy high place at........... 1129
Eze 26:14 thou shalt be **b.** no more: for I the..... 1129
Da 4:30 I have **b.** for the house of the........... 1124
Da 9:25 the street shall be **b.** again,.............. 1129
Am 5:11 ye have **b.** houses of hewn stone, ... 1129
Mic 7:11 the day that thy walls are to be **b.**, ... 1129
Hag 1:2 that the Lord's house should be **b.**. 1129
Zec 1:16 my house shall be **b.** in it, saith......... 1129
Zec 8:9 laid, that the temple might be **b.**. 1129
Mt 7:24 **which b. his house upon a rock:**.... *3618*
Mt 7:26 **which b. his house upon the sand:**. *3618*
Mt 21:33 **winepress in it, and b. a tower,**..... *3618*
Mk 2:1 **and b. a tower, and let it out to**.... *3618*
Lu 4:29 whereon their city was **b.**, that.......... *3618*
Lu 6:48 **a man which b. an house, and**...... *3618*
Lu 6:49 **a man that...b. an house upon**...... *3618*
Lu 7:5 and he hath **b.** us a synagogue........... *3618*
Ac 7:47 But Solomon **b.** him an house............ *3618*
1Co 3:14 abide which he hath **b.** thereupon, ... *2026*
Eph 2:20 And are **b.** upon the foundation.......... *2026*
Col 2:7 Rooted and **b.** up in him, and *2026*
Heb 3:4 but he that **b.** all things is God. *2680*
1Pe 2:5 are **b.** up a spiritual house, ... *3618*

BUKKI (buk'-ki)
Nu 34:22 of Dan, **B.** the son of Jogli................ 1231
1Ch 6:5 Abishua begat **B.**, and **B.** begat......... 1231
1Ch 6:51 **B.** his son, Uzzi his son, Zerahiah...... 1231
Ezr 7:4 the son of Uzzi, the son of **B.**,............ 1231

BUKKIAH (buk-ki'-ah)
1Ch 25:4 **B.**, Mattaniah, Uzziel, Shebuel,.......... 1232
1Ch 25:13 The sixth to **B.**, he, his sons, and...... 1232

BUL (bul)
1Ki 6:38 in the month **B.**, which is the 945

BULL See also BULLS; BULRUSH.
Job 21:10 Their **b.** gendereth, and faileth........... 7794
Isa 51:20 as a wild **b.** in a net: they are 8377

BULLOCK See also BULLOCK'S; BULLOCKS.
Ex 29:1 Take one young **b.**, and two rams...... 6499
Ex 29:3 with the **b.** and the two rams. 6499
Ex 29:10 thou shalt cause a **b.** to be brought..... 6499
Ex 29:10 hands upon the head of the **b.**. 6499
Ex 29:11 shalt kill the **b.** before the Lord, ... 6499
Ex 29:12 take of the blood of the **b.**, and 6499
Ex 29:14 the flesh of the **b.**, and his skin, ... 6499
Ex 29:36 And thou shalt offer every day a **b.** 6499
Le 1:5 kill the **b.** before the Lord: 1121,1241
Le 4:3 a young **b.** without blemish unto......... 6499
Le 4:4 he shall bring the **b.** unto the door 6499
Le 4:4 the bullock's head, and kill the **b.** 6499
Le 4:7 the blood of the **b.** at the bottom 6499
Le 4:8 fat of the **b.** for the sin offering; 6499
Le 4:10 from the **b.** of the sacrifice of........... 7794
Le 4:11 skin of the **b.**, and all his flesh,.......... 6499
Le 4:12 Even the whole **b.** shall he carry.......... 6499
Le 4:14 congregation shall offer a young **b.**...... 6499
Le 4:15 upon the head of the **b.** before the 6499
Le 4:15 Lord: and the **b.** shall be killed 6499
Le 4:20 And he shall do with the **b.**............... 6499
Le 4:20 as he did with the **b.** for.................. 6499
Le 4:21 he shall carry forth the **b.** without 6499
Le 4:21 burn him as he burned the first **b.**:...... 6499
Le 8:2 a **b.** for the sin offering, and two........ 6499
Le 8:14 the **b.** for the sin offering: and........... 6499
Le 8:14 hands upon the head of the **b.** for....... 6499
Le 8:17 the **b.**, and his hide, his flesh, and...... 6499
Le 9:4 Also a **b.** and a ram for peace........... 7794
Le 9:18 He slew also the **b.** and the ram 7794
Le 9:19 the fat of the **b.** and the ram,............ 7794
Le 16:3 a young **b.** for a sin offering, and 6499
Le 16:6 shall offer his **b.** of the sin offering, ... 6499
Le 16:11 Aaron shall bring the **b.** of the........... 6499
Le 16:11 shall kill the **b.** of the sin offering....... 6499
Le 16:14 take of the blood of the **b.**, and 6499
Le 16:15 as he did with the blood of the **b.**,....... 6499
Le 16:18 and shall take of the blood of the **b.**,... 6499
Le 16:27 the **b.** for the sin offering, and........... 6499
Le 22:23 Either a **b.** or a lamb, that hath 7794
Le 22:27 When a **b.**, or a sheep, or a goat 7794
Le 23:18 and one young **b.**, and two rams: 6499
Nu 7:15, 21,27,33,39,45,51,57,63,69,75,81, One
young **b.**, one ram, one lamb............. 6499
Nu 8:8 Then let them take a young **b.** with.... 6499
Nu 8:8 another young **b.** shalt thou take 6499
Nu 15:8 when thou preparest a **b.** for...... 1121,1241
Nu 15:9 with a **b.** a meat offering of........ 1121,1241
Nu 15:11 Thus shall it be done for one **b.**, ... 7794
Nu 15:24 offer one young **b.** for a burnt 6499
Nu 23:2 offered on every altar a **b.** and a........ 6499
Nu 23:4 offered upon every altar a **b.** and 6499
Nu 23:14, 30 offered a **b.** and a ram on every 6499
Nu 28:12 mingled with oil, for one **b.**;.............. 6499
Nu 28:14 half an hin of wine unto a **b.**, and 6499
Nu 28:20 tenth deals shall ye offer for a **b.**, ... 6499
Nu 28:28 three tenth deals unto one **b.**, two 6499
Nu 29:2 one young **b.**, one ram, and seven...... 6499
Nu 29:3 three tenth deals for a **b.**, and two..... 6499
Nu 29:8 for a sweet savour; one young **b.**, ... 6499
Nu 29:9 three tenth deals to a **b.**, and two...... 6499
Nu 29:14 deals unto every **b.** of the thirteen 6499
Nu 29:36 one **b.**, one ram, seven lambs of........ 6499
Nu 29:37 for the **b.**, for the ram, and for the..... 6499
De 15:19 the firstling of thy **b.**, nor shear......... 7794
De 17:1 any **b.**, or sheep, wherein is.............. 7794
De 33:17 like the firstling of his **b.**, and his 7794
Jg 6:25 Take thy father's young **b.**,................ 6499
Jg 6:25 even the second **b.** of seven years 6499
Jg 6:26 and take the second **b.**, and offer 6499
Jg 6:28 the second **b.** was offered upon the 6499
1Sa 1:25 And they slew a **b.**, and brought 6499
1Ki 18:23 and let them choose one **b.** for 6499
1Ki 18:23 and I will dress the other **b.**,............. 6499
1Ki 18:25 Choose you one **b.** for yourselves, ... 6499
1Ki 18:26 they took the **b.** which was given....... 6499
1Ki 18:33 and cut the **b.** in pieces; and laid........ 6499
2Ch 13:9 consecrate himself with a young **b.** 6499
Ps 50:9 I will take no **b.** out of thy house, ... 6499
Ps 69:31 or **b.** that hath horns and hoofs.......... 6499
Isa 65:25 lion shall eat straw like the **b.**:........... 1241
Jer 31:18 a **b.** unaccustomed to the yoke: 5695
Eze 43:19 a young **b.** for a sin offering. 6499
Eze 43:21 take the **b.** also of the sin offering, ... 6499
Eze 43:22 as they did cleanse it with the **b.**. 6499
Eze 43:23 offer a young **b.** without blemish, ... 6499
Eze 43:25 they shall also prepare a young **b.**, ... 6499
Eze 45:18 take a young **b.** without blemish,........ 6499
Eze 45:22 for all the people of the land a **b.** 6499
Eze 45:24 an ephah for a **b.**, and an ephah......... 6499
Eze 46:6 a young **b.** without blemish, ... 6499
Eze 46:7 an ephah for a **b.**, and an ephah......... 6499
Eze 46:11 shall be an ephah to a **b.**, and an......... 6499

BULLOCK'S
Le 4:4 his hand upon the **b.** head,................ 6499
Le 4:5 shall take of the **b.** blood,.................. 6499
Le 4:16 anointed, shall bring of the **b.** 6499

BULLOCKS
Nu 7:87 were twelve **b.**, the rams twelve,........ 6499
Nu 7:88 were twenty and four **b.**, the rams 6499
Nu 8:12 upon the heads of the **b.**: 6499
Nu 23:29 prepare me here seven **b.** and........... 6499
Nu 28:11 unto the Lord; two young **b.**,............ 6499
Nu 28:19 two young **b.**, and one ram,............... 6499
Nu 28:27 unto the Lord; two young **b.**,............ 6499
Nu 29:13 thirteen young **b.**, two rams,............. 6499
Nu 29:14 every bullock of the thirteen **b.**,......... 6499
Nu 29:17 ye shall offer twelve young **b.**,........... 6499
Nu 29:18 their drink offerings for the **b.**, ... 6499
Nu 29:20 the third day eleven **b.**, two rams, ... 6499
Nu 29:21 for the **b.**, for the rams, and for 6499
Nu 29:23 on the fourth day ten **b.**, two rams,.... 6499
Nu 29:24 drink offerings for the **b.**, for the 6499
Nu 29:26 And on the fifth day nine **b.**, two 6499
Nu 29:27 offerings for the **b.**, for the rams,........ 6499
Nu 29:29 on the sixth day eight **b.**, two............ 6499
Nu 29:30 **b.**, for the rams, and for the lambs,.... 6499
Nu 29:32 And on the seventh day seven **b.**,...... 6499
Nu 29:33 and their drink offerings for the **b.**,..... 6499
1Sa 1:24 him up with her, with three **b.**,........... 6499
1Ki 18:23 them therefore give us two **b.**; 6499
1Ch 15:26 they offered seven **b.**, and seven 6499
1Ch 29:21 a thousand **b.**, a thousand rams,......... 6499
2Ch 29:21 they brought seven **b.**, and seven....... 6499
2Ch 29:22 they killed the **b.**, and the priests....... 1241
2Ch 29:32 threescore and ten **b.**, an hundred...... 1241
2Ch 30:24 thousand **b.** and seven thousand......... 6499
2Ch 30:24 to the congregation a thousand **b.**....... 6499
2Ch 35:7 three thousand **b.**: these were........... 1241
Ezr 6:9 both young **b.**, and rams, and............ 8450
Ezr 6:17 an hundred **b.**, two hundred rams,...... 8450

Ezr 7:17 buy speedily with this money **b.**, ... 8450
Ezr 8:35 twelve **b.** for all Israel, ninety........... 6499
Job 42:8 take unto you now seven **b.** and 6499
Ps 51:19 then shall they offer **b.** upon thine 6499
Ps 66:15 I will offer **b.** with goats................. 1241
Isa 1:11 I delight not in the blood of **b.**, ... 6499
Isa 34:7 and the **b.** with the bulls; and........... 6499
Jer 46:21 in the midst of her like fatted **b.**; 5695
Jer 50:27 Slay all her **b.**; let them go down 6499
Eze 39:18 of lambs, and of goats, of **b.**, all of...... 6499
Eze 45:23 seven **b.** and seven rams without 6499
Ho 12:11 they sacrifice **b.** in Gilgal; yea,........... 7794

BULLS
Ge 32:15 forty kine, and ten **b.**, twenty............ 6499
Ps 22:12 Many **b.** have compassed me:............ 6499
Ps 22:12 strong **b.** of Bashan have beset me...........
Ps 50:13 Will I eat the flesh of **b.**, or drink.......... 47
Ps 68:30 the multitude of the **b.**, with the 47
Isa 34:7 the bullocks with the **b.**; and their 47
Jer 50:11 heifer at grass, and bellow as **b.**; 47
Jer 52:20 and twelve brasen **b.** that were.......... 1241
Heb 9:13 if the blood of **b.** and of goats,........... *5022*
Heb 10:4 not possible that the blood of **b.**......... *5022*

BULRUSH See also BULRUSHES.
Isa 58:5 bow down his head as a **b.**, ... 100

BULRUSHES
Ex 2:3 took for him an ark of **b.**, ... 1573
Isa 18:2 in vessels of **b.** upon the waters, ... 1573

BULWARKS
De 20:20 shalt build **b.** against the city............ 4692
2Ch 26:15 be on the towers and upon the **b.**, ... 6438
Ps 48:13 Mark ye well her **b.**, consider her 2430
Ec 9:14 and built great **b.** against it: 4685
Isa 26:1 will God appoint for walls and **b.**. 2426

BUNAH (boo'-nah)
1Ch 2:25 Ram the firstborn, and **B.**, and............ 946

BUNCH See also BUNCHES.
Ex 12:22 ye shall take a **b.** of hyssop, and........... 92

BUNCHES
2Sa 16:1 an hundred **b.** of raisins, and an......... 6778
1Ch 12:40 cakes of figs, and **b.** of raisins, ... 6778
Isa 30:6 upon the **b.** of camels, to a............... 1707

BUNDLE See also BUNDLES.
Ge 42:35 every man's **b.** of money was in......... 6872
1Sa 25:29 bound in the **b.** of life with the.......... 6872
Ca 1:13 a **b.** of myrrh is my wellbeloved........... 6872
Ac 28:3 gathered a **b.** of sticks, and laid......... *4128*

BUNDLES
Ge 42:35 their father saw the **b.** of money, ... 6872
Mt 13:30 **bind them in b. to burn them:** *1197*

BUNNI (bun'-ni)
Ne 9:4 Shebaniah, **B.**, Sherebiah, Bani, ... 1137
Ne 10:15 **B.**, Azgad, Bebai, ... 1137
Ne 11:15 son of Hashabiah, the son of **B.**;......... 1137

BURDEN See also BURDENED; BURDENS; BURDENSOME.
Ex 18:22 they shall bear the **b.** with thee. ....
Ex 23:5 lying under his **b.**, and wouldest......... 4853
Nu 4:15 the **b.** of the sons of Kohath in the..... 4853
Nu 4:19 one to his service and to his **b.**:.......... 4853
Nu 4:31 And this is the charge of their **b.**, ... 4853
Nu 4:32 of the charge of their **b.**. 4853
Nu 4:47 service of the **b.** in the tabernacle 4853
Nu 4:49 according to his **b.**: thus were they...... 4853
Nu 11:11 the **b.** of all this people upon me?...... 4853
Nu 11:17 they shall bear the **b.** of the people 4853
De 1:12 and your **b.**, and your strife? 4853
2Sa 15:33 then thou shalt be a **b.** unto me: 4853
2Sa 19:35 should thy servant be yet a **b.**........... 4853
2Ki 5:17 servant two mules' **b.** of earth?........... 4853
2Ki 8:9 forty camels' **b.**, and came and 4853
2Ki 9:25 the Lord laid this **b.** upon him; 4853
2Ch 35:3 not be a **b.** upon your shoulders:......... 4853
Ne 13:19 there should no **b.** be brought in......... 4853
Job 7:20 so that I am a **b.** to myself?............... 4853
Ps 38:4 as an heavy **b.** they are too heavy...... 4853
Ps 55:22 Cast thy **b.** upon the Lord, and he 3053
Ps 81:6 removed his shoulder from the **b.**;....... 5449
Ec 12:5 and the grasshopper shall be a **b.**, ... 5445
Isa 9:4 broken the yoke of his **b.**, and the....... 5448
Isa 10:27 his **b.** shall be taken away from off 5448
Isa 13:1 The **b.** of Babylon, which Isaiah......... 4853
Isa 14:25 and his **b.** depart from off their.......... 5448
Isa 14:28 that king Ahaz died was this **b.**. 4853
Isa 15:1 The **b.** of Moab. Because in the......... 4853
Isa 17:1 The **b.** of Damascus. Behold, ... 4853
Isa 19:1 The **b.** of Egypt. Behold, the Lord 4853
Isa 21:1 The **b.** of the desert of the sea.......... 4853
Isa 21:11 The **b.** of Dumah. He calleth to 4853
Isa 21:13 The **b.** upon Arabia. In the forest....... 4853
Isa 22:1 The **b.** of the valley of vision............ 4853
Isa 22:25 fall; and the **b.** that was upon it 4853
Isa 23:1 The **b.** of Tyre. Howl, ye ships 4853
Isa 30:6 The **b.** of the beasts of the south:........ 4853
Isa 30:27 the **b.** thereof is heavy: his lips.......... 4858
Isa 46:1 they are a **b.** to the weary beast,........ 4853
Isa 46:2 they could not deliver the **b.**, but 4853
Jer 17:21 bear no **b.** on the sabbath day, ... 4853
Jer 17:22 Neither carry forth a **b.** out of.......... 4853
Jer 17:24 to bring in no **b.** through the gates 4853
Jer 17:27 not to bear a **b.**, even entering in at ... 4853
Jer 23:33 saying, What is the **b.** of the Lord? 4853
Jer 23:33 then say unto them, What **b.**? 4853
Jer 23:34 that shall say, The **b.** of the Lord,...... 4853
Jer 23:36 And the **b.** of the Lord shall ye.......... 4853
Jer 23:36 every man's word shall be his **b.**. 4853
Jer 23:38 ye say, The **b.** of the Lord; 4853
Jer 23:38 this word, The **b.** of the Lord, ... 4853
Jer 23:38 shall not say, The **b.** of the Lord; 4853
Eze 12:10 This **b.** concerneth the prince............ 4853
Ho 8:10 for the **b.** of the king of princes. 4853
Na 1:1 The **b.** of Nineveh. The book of........... 4853
Hab 1:1 **b.** which Habakkuk the prophet.......... 4853
Zep 3:18 whom the reproach of it was a **b.**........ 4864
Zec 9:1 The **b.** of the word of the Lord in........ 4853
Zec 12:1 The **b.** of the word of the Lord 4853
Zec 12:3 all that **b.** themselves with it............ 6006
Mal 1:1 The **b.** of the word of the Lord to......... 4853
Mt 11:30 **yoke is easy, and my b. is light.**..... *5413*
Mt 20:12 **which have borne the b. and heat** ... *922*
Ac 15:28 upon you no greater **b.** than these *922*
Ac 21:3 the ship was to unlade her **b.**. *1117*
2Co 12:16 I did not **b.** you: nevertheless,........... *2599*
Ga 6:5 every man shall bear his own **b.**......... *5413*
Re 2:24 **will put upon you none other b.**...... *922*

BURDENED
2Co 5:4 do groan, being **b.**: not for that.......... *916*
2Co 8:13 other men be eased, and ye **b.**: *2347*

BURDENS
Ge 49:14 crouching down between two **b.**: 4942
Ex 1:11 to afflict them with their **b.**. 5450
Ex 2:11 looked on their **b.**: and he spied......... 5450
Ex 5:4 their works? get you unto your **b.**. 5450
Ex 5:5 ye make them rest from their **b.**......... 5450
Ex 6:6 from under the **b.** of the Egyptians, ... 5450
Ex 6:7 bringeth you out from under the **b.**...... 5450
Nu 4:24 Gershonites, to serve, and for **b.**: 4853
Nu 4:27 the Gershonites, in all their **b.**, ... 4853
Nu 4:27 unto them in charge all their **b.**.......... 4853
1Ki 5:15 and ten thousand that bare **b.**, ... 5449
2Ch 2:2 ten thousand men to bear **b.**, ... 5449
2Ch 2:18 to be bearers of **b.**, and fourscore 5449
2Ch 24:27 the greatness of the **b.** laid upon......... 4853
2Ch 34:13 over the bearers of **b.**, and were 5449
Ne 4:10 The strength of the bearers of **b.**....... 5449
Ne 4:17 and they that bare **b.**, with those 5447
Ne 13:15 all manner of **b.**, which they.............. 4853
Isa 58:6 to undo the heavy **b.**, and to.............. 92
La 2:14 false **b.** and causes of banishment. 4864
Am 5:11 ye take from him **b.** of wheat: 4864
Mt 23:4 **For they bind heavy b. and**............. *5413*
Lu 11:46 **with b. grievous to be borne, and** .. *5413*
Lu 11:46 **ye yourselves touch not the b.**....... *5413*
Ga 6:2 Bear ye one another's **b.**, and............ *922*

BURDENSOME
Zec 12:3 will I make Jerusalem a **b.** stone 4614
2Co 11:9 kept myself from being **b.** unto.............. *4*
2Co 12:13 I myself was not **b.** to you? *2655*
2Co 12:14 I will not be **b.** to you: for I seek....... *2655*
1Th 2:6 we might have been **b.**, as the..... *1722,922*

BURIAL
2Ch 26:23 in the field of the **b.** which.............. 6900
Ec 6:3 good, and also that ye have no **b.**;...... 6900
Isa 14:20 not be joined with them in **b.**,............ 6900
Jer 22:19 with the **b.** of an ass, drawn and........ 6900
Mt 26:12 **my body, she did it for my b.**........ *1779*
Ac 8:2 men carried Stephen to his **b.**,................

BURIED
Ge 15:15 thou shalt be **b.** in a good old age. 6912
Ge 23:19 Abraham **b.** Sarah his wife in the........ 6912
Ge 25:9 his sons Isaac and Ishmael **b.** him......... 6912
Ge 25:10 there was Abraham **b.**, and Sarah....... 6912
Ge 35:8 nurse died, and she was **b.**............... 6912
Ge 35:19 Rachel died, and was **b.** in the........... 6912
Ge 35:29 his sons Esau and Jacob **b.** him.......... 6912
Ge 48:7 and I **b.** her there in the way of......... 6912
Ge 49:31 There they **b.** Abraham and Sarah....... 6912
Ge 49:31 there they **b.** Isaac and Rebekah 6912
Ge 49:31 and there I **b.** Leah. 6912
Ge 50:13 and **b.** him in the cave of the field 6912
Ge 50:14 after he had **b.** his father.................. 6912
Nu 11:34 because there they **b.** the people 6912
Nu 20:1 Miriam died there, and was **b.**........... 6912
Nu 33:4 For the Egyptians **b.** all their 6912
De 10:6 Aaron died, and there he was **b.**; 6912
De 34:6 And he **b.** him in a valley in the........ 6912
Jos 24:30 And they **b.** him in the border of......... 6912
Jos 24:32 **b.** they in Shechem, in a parcel........... 6912
Jos 24:33 and they **b.** him in a hill that 6912
Jg 2:9 And they **b.** him in the border of........ 6912
Jg 8:32 died in a good old age, and was **b.** 6912
Jg 10:2 and died, and was **b.** in Shamir. 6912
Jg 10:5 Jair died, and was **b.** in Camon. 6912
Jg 12:7 the Gileadite, and was **b.** in one of 6912
Jg 12:10 Ibzan, and was **b.** at Bethlehem. 6912
Jg 12:12 died, and was **b.** in Aijalon................ 6912
Jg 12:15 died, and was **b.** in Pirathon in 6912
Jg 16:31 **b.** him between Zorah and Eshtaol...... 6912
Ru 1:17 and there will I be **b.**: the Lord 6912
1Sa 25:1 and **b.** him in his house at Ramah....... 6912
1Sa 28:3 and **b.** him in Ramah, even in........... 6912
1Sa 31:13 **b.** them under a tree at Jabesh, ... 6912
2Sa 2:4 Jabesh-gilead were they that **b.**......... 6912
2Sa 2:5 even unto Saul, and have **b.** him. 6912
2Sa 2:32 and **b.** him in the sepulchre of his....... 6912
2Sa 3:32 And they **b.** Abner in Hebron: 6912
2Sa 4:12 head of Ish-bosheth, and **b.** it............ 6912
2Sa 17:23 and was **b.** in the sepulchre of his 6912
2Sa 19:37 be **b.** by the grave of my father..............
2Sa 21:14 and Jonathan his son **b.** they............... 6912
1Ki 2:10 slept with his fathers, and was **b.**....... 6912
1Ki 2:34 and he was **b.** in his own house 6912
1Ki 11:43 slept with his fathers, and was **b.**........ 6912
1Ki 13:31 after he had **b.** him, that he spake...... 6912
1Ki 13:31 wherein the man of God is **b.**;............ 6912
1Ki 14:18 And they **b.** him; and all Israel........... 6912
1Ki 14:31 slept with his fathers, and was **b.**....... 6912
1Ki 15:8 they **b.** him in the city of David: 6912
1Ki 15:24 slept with his fathers, and was **b.**....... 6912
1Ki 16:6, 28 with his fathers, and was **b.**........ 6912
1Ki 22:37 and they **b.** the king in Samaria.......... 6912
1Ki 22:50 slept with his fathers, and was **b.**....... 6912
2Ki 8:24 slept with his fathers, and was **b.**....... 6912
2Ki 9:28 and **b.** him in his sepulchre with......... 6912
2Ki 10:35 fathers: and they **b.** him in................ 6912
2Ki 12:21 and they **b.** him with his fathers......... 6912
2Ki 13:9 and they **b.** him in Samaria: and......... 6912
2Ki 13:13 and Joash was **b.** in Samaria with 6912
2Ki 13:20 And Elisha died, and they **b.** him........ 6912
2Ki 14:16 slept with his fathers, and was **b.**....... 6912
2Ki 14:20 and he was **b.** at Jerusalem with 6912
2Ki 15:7 and they **b.** him with his fathers......... 6912
2Ki 15:38 slept with his fathers, and was **b.**....... 6912
2Ki 16:20 slept with his fathers, and was **b.**....... 6912
2Ki 21:18 slept with his fathers, and was **b.**....... 6912
2Ki 21:26 And he was **b.** in his sepulchre........... 6912
2Ki 23:30 and **b.** him in his own sepulchre.......... 6912
1Ch 10:12 and **b.** their bones under the oak......... 6912
2Ch 9:31 and he was **b.** in the city of David...... 6912
2Ch 12:16 slept with his fathers, and was **b.**....... 6912
2Ch 14:1 they **b.** him in the city of David: 6912
2Ch 16:14 **b.** him in his own sepulchres, ... 6912
2Ch 21:1 slept with his fathers, and was **b.**....... 6912
2Ch 21:20 Howbeit they **b.** him in the city of...... 6912
2Ch 22:9 they had slain him, they **b.** him:......... 6912
2Ch 24:16 they **b.** him in the city of David 6912
2Ch 24:25 and they **b.** him in the city of David,... 6912
2Ch 24:25 they **b.** him not in the sepulchres 6912
2Ch 25:28 and **b.** him with his fathers in the....... 6912
2Ch 26:23 **b.** him with his fathers in the field...... 6912
2Ch 27:9 they **b.** him in the city of David: 6912

2Ch 28:27 and they **b.** him in the city, even ... 6912
2Ch 32:33 and they **b.** him in the chiefest of ... 6912
2Ch 33:20 and they **b.** him in his own house: ... 6912
2Ch 35:24 and was **b.** in one of the sepulchres ... 6912
Job 27:15 remain of him shall be **b.** in death: ... 6912
Ec 8:10 And so I saw the wicked **b.**, who ... 6912
Jer 8:2 shall not be gathered, nor be **b.**; ... 6912
Jer 16:4 lamented; neither shall they be **b.**; ... 6912
Jer 16:6 they shall not be **b.**, neither shall ... 6912
Jer 20:6 thou shalt die, and shalt be **b.** ... 6912
Jer 22:19 He shall be **b.** with the burial of an ... 6912
Jer 25:33 lamented, neither gathered, nor **b.**; ... 6912
Eze 39:15 till the buriers have **b.** it in the ... 6912
Mt 14:12 and **b.** it, and went and told Jesus. ... *2290*
Lu 16:22 **rich man also died, and was b.**; ... *2290*
Ac 2:29 he is both dead and **b.**, and his ... *2290*
Ac 5:6 and carried him out, and **b.** him. ... *2290*
Ac 5:9 the feet of them which have **b.** thy ... *2290*
Ac 5:10 carrying her forth, **b.** her by her ... *2290*
Ro 6:4 we are **b.** with him by baptism ... *4916*
1Co 15:4 And that he was **b.**, and that he ... *2290*
Col 2:12 **B.** with him in baptism, wherein ... *4916*

BURIERS
Eze 39:15 till the **b.** have buried it in the ... 6912

BURN See also BURNED; BURNETH; BURNING; BURNT.
Ge 11:3 let us make brick, and **b.** them ... 8313
Ge 44:18 let not thine anger **b.** against thy ... 2734
Ex 12:10 until the morning ye shall **b.** with ... 8313
Ex 27:20 light, to cause the lamp to **b.** ... 5927
Ex 29:13 them, and **b.** them upon the altar. ... 6999
Ex 29:14 his dung, shalt thou **b.** with fire ... 8313
Ex 29:18 And thou shalt **b.** the whole ram ... 6999
Ex 29:25 and **b.** them upon the altar for a ... 6999
Ex 29:34 then thou shalt **b.** the remainder ... 8313
Ex 30:1 make an altar to **b.** incense upon: ... 4729
Ex 30:7 And Aaron shall **b.** thereon sweet ... 6999
Ex 30:7 lamps, he shall **b.** incense upon it. ... 6999
Ex 30:8 at even, he shall **b.** incense upon ... 6999
Ex 30:20 to **b.** offering made by fire unto ... 6999
Le 1:9 the priest shall **b.** all on the altar, ... 6999
Le 1:13 and **b.** it upon the altar: it is a ... 6999
Le 1:15 **b.** it on the altar; and the blood ... 6999
Le 1:17 the priest shall **b.** it upon the altar, ... 6999
Le 2:2 the priest shall **b.** the memorial ... 6999
Le 2:9 and shall **b.** it upon the altar: ... 6999
Le 2:11 ye shall **b.** no leaven, nor any ... 6999
Le 2:16 the priest shall **b.** the memorial of ... 6999
Le 3:5 And Aaron's sons shall **b.** it on the ... 6999
Le 3:11 And the priest shall **b.** it upon the ... 6999
Le 3:16 And the priest shall **b.** them upon ... 6999
Le 4:10 and the priest shall **b.** them upon ... 6999
Le 4:12 are poured out, and **b.** him on the ... 8313
Le 4:19 from him, and **b.** it upon the altar. ... 6999
Le 4:21 bullock without the camp, and **b.** ... 8313
Le 4:26 he shall **b.** all his fat upon the ... 6999
Le 4:31 and the priest shall **b.** it upon the ... 6999
Le 4:35 and the priest shall **b.** them upon ... 6999
Le 5:12 and **b.** it on the altar, according ... 6999
Le 6:12 and the priest shall **b.** wood on it ... 1197
Le 6:12 and he shall **b.** thereon the fat ... 6999
Le 6:15 and shall **b.** it upon the altar ... 6999
Le 7:5 the priest shall **b.** them upon the ... 6999
Le 7:31 And the priest shall **b.** the fat ... 6999
Le 8:32 of the bread shall ye **b.** with fire. ... 8313
Le 13:52 He shall therefore **b.** that garment, ... 8313
Le 13:55 thou shalt **b.** it in the fire; ... 8313
Le 13:57 thou shalt **b.** that wherein the ... 8313
Le 16:25 offering shall he **b.** upon the altar. ... 6999
Le 16:27 and they shall **b.** in the fire their ... 8313
Le 17:6 and **b.** the fat for a sweet savour ... 6999
Le 24:2 cause the lamps to **b.** continually. ... 5927
Nu 5:26 and **b.** it upon the altar, and ... 6999
Nu 18:17 shalt **b.** their fat for an offering ... 6999
Nu 19:5 And one shall **b.** the heifer in his ... 8313
Nu 19:5 blood, with her dung, shall he **b.**: ... 8313
De 5:23 the mountain did **b.** with fire,) ... 1197
De 7:5 **b.** their graven images with fire. ... 8313
De 7:25 images of their gods shall ye **b.** ... 8313
De 12:3 **b.** their groves with fire; and ye ... 8313
De 13:16 and shalt **b.** with fire the city, ... 8313
De 32:22 and shall **b.** unto the lowest hell, ... 3344
Jos 11:6 and **b.** their chariots with fire. ... 8313
Jos 11:13 Hazor only; that did Joshua **b.**. ... 8313
Jg 9:52 the door of the tower to **b.** it ... 8313
Jg 12:1 we will **b.** thine house upon thee ... 8313
Jg 14:15 lest we **b.** thee and thy father's ... 8313
1Sa 2:16 Let them not fail to **b.** the fat ... 6999
1Sa 2:28 to **b.** incense, to wear an ephod ... 6999
1Ki 13:1 stood by the altar to **b.** incense. ... 6999
1Ki 13:2 the high places that **b.** incense ... 6999
2Ki 16:15 Upon the great altar **b.** the morning ... 6999
2Ki 18:4 children of Israel did **b.** incense ... 6699
2Ki 23:5 ordained to **b.** incense in the ... 6699
1Ch 23:13 to **b.** incense before the Lord, ... 6699
2Ch 2:4 to **b.** before him sweet incense, ... 6699
2Ch 2:6 save only to **b.** sacrifice before ... 6699
2Ch 4:20 that they should **b.** after the ... 1197
2Ch 13:11 And they **b.** unto the Lord ... 6999
2Ch 13:11 to **b.** every evening: for we keep ... 1197
2Ch 26:16 the temple of the Lord to **b.** ... 6999
2Ch 26:18 to **b.** incense unto the Lord, ... 6999
2Ch 26:18 that are consecrated to **b.** incense: ... 6999
2Ch 26:19 a censer in his hand to **b.** incense: ... 6999
2Ch 28:25 places to **b.** incense unto other ... 6999
2Ch 29:11 unto him, and **b.** incense. ... 6999
2Ch 32:12 altar, and **b.** incense upon it? ... 6999
Ne 10:34 to **b.** upon the altar of the Lord ... 1197
Ps 79:5 shall thy jealousy **b.** like fire? ... 1197
Ps 89:46 shall thy wrath **b.** like fire? ... 1197
Isa 1:31 and they shall both **b.** together, ... 1197
Isa 10:17 and it shall **b.** and devour his ... 1197
Isa 27:4 I would **b.** them together. ... 6702
Isa 40:16 Lebanon is not sufficient to **b.**, ... 1197
Isa 44:15 shall it be for a man to **b.**: for he ... 1197
Isa 47:14 the fire shall **b.** them; they shall ... 8313
Jer 4:4 and **b.** that none can quench it, ... 1197
Jer 7:9 and **b.** incense unto Baal, and ... 6999
Jer 7:20 and it shall **b.**, and shall not be ... 1197
Jer 7:31 **b.** their sons and their daughters ... 8313
Jer 11:13 altars to **b.** incense unto Baal. ... 6999
Jer 15:14 anger, which shall **b.** upon you. ... 3344
Jer 17:4 anger, which shall **b.** for ever. ... 3344
Jer 19:5 to **b.** their sons with fire for ... 8313
Jer 21:10 and he shall **b.** it with fire. ... 8313
Jer 21:12 and **b.** that none can quench it. ... 1197
Jer 32:29 and **b.** it with the houses, upon ... 8313
Jer 34:2 and he shall **b.** it with fire: ... 8313
Jer 34:5 so shall they **b.** odours for thee; ... 8313
Jer 34:22 and **b.** it with fire: and I will ... 8313
Jer 36:25 that he would not **b.** the roll: ... 8313
Jer 37:8 and take it, and **b.** it with fire. ... 8313
Jer 37:10 and **b.** this city with fire. ... 8313
Jer 38:18 and they shall **b.** it with fire, ... 8313
Jer 43:12 and he shall **b.** them, and carry ... 8313
Jer 43:13 the Egyptians shall he **b.** with fire. ... 8313
Jer 44:3 in that they went to **b.** incense, ... 6999
Jer 44:5 to **b.** no incense unto other gods. ... 6999
Jer 44:17 to **b.** incense unto the queen of ... 6999
Jer 44:18 since we left off to **b.** incense ... 6999
Jer 44:25 **b.** incense to the queen of heaven, ... 6999
Eze 5:2 Thou shalt **b.** with fire a third ... 1197
Eze 5:4 and **b.** them in the fire; for ... 8313
Eze 16:41 And they shall **b.** thine houses ... 8313
Eze 23:47 and **b.** up their houses with fire. ... 8313
Eze 24:5 **b.** also the bones under it, and ... 1754
Eze 24:11 may be hot, and may **b.**, and ... 2787
Eze 39:9 set on fire and **b.** the weapons, ... 5400
Eze 39:9 and they shall **b.** them with fire ... 1197
Eze 39:10 shall **b.** the weapons with fire: ... 1197
Eze 43:21 and he shall **b.** it in the appointed ... 8313
Ho 4:13 **b.** incense upon the hills, ... 6999
Na 2:13 and I will **b.** her chariots in the ... 1197
Hab 1:16 and **b.** incense unto their drag; ... 6999
Mal 4:1 that shall **b.** as an oven; and all ... 1197
Mal 4:1 and the day that cometh shall **b.** ... 3857
Mt 3:12 but he will **b.** up the chaff with ... *2618*
Mt 13:30 **bind them in bundles to b.** ... *2618*
Lu 1:9 his lot was to **b.** incense when ... *2370*
Lu 3:17 but the chaff he will **b.** with fire ... *2618*
Lu 24:32 Did not our heart **b.** within us, ... *2545*
1Co 7:9 it is better to marry than to **b.**. ... *4448*
2Co 11:29 who is offended, and I **b.** not? ... *4448*
Re 17:16 and **b.** her with fire. ... *2618*

BURNED See also BURNT.
Ex 3:2 the bush **b.** with fire, and the ... 1197
Le 4:21 him as he **b.** the first bullock: ... 8313
Le 8:16 and Moses **b.** it upon the altar. ... 6999
De 4:11 the mountain **b.** with fire unto ... 1197
De 9:15 and the mount **b.** with fire: ... 1197
Jos 7:25 and **b.** them with fire, after ... 8313
Jos 11:13 Israel **b.** none of them, save Hazor ... 8313
1Sa 30:1 Ziklag, and **b.** it with fire; ... 8313
1Sa 30:3 behold, it was **b.** with fire; and ... 8313
1Sa 30:14 Caleb; and we **b.** Ziklag with fire. ... 8313
2Sa 5:21 and David and his men **b.** them. ... 5375
2Sa 23:7 they shall be utterly **b.** with fire ... 8313
2Ki 10:26 the house of Baal, and **b.** them. ... 8313
2Ki 15:35 **b.** incense still in the high places. ... 6999
2Ki 22:17 have **b.** incense unto other gods, ... 6999
2Ki 23:4 he **b.** them without Jerusalem ... 8313
2Ki 23:5 also that **b.** incense unto Baal, ... 6999
2Ki 23:6 and **b.** it at the brook Kidron, ... 8313
2Ki 23:8 where the priest had **b.** incense, ... 6999
2Ki 23:11 and **b.** the chariots of the sun ... 8313
2Ki 23:15 brake down, and **b.** the high place ... 8313
2Ki 23:15 to powder, and **b.** the grove. ... 8313
2Ki 23:16 and **b.** them upon the altar, ... 8313
2Ki 23:20 and **b.** men's bones upon them, ... 8313
1Ch 14:12 and they were **b.** with fire. ... 8313
2Ch 25:14 them, **b.** incense unto them. ... 6999
2Ch 29:7 have not **b.** incense nor offered ... 6999
2Ch 34:25 have **b.** incense unto other gods, ... 6999
Ne 1:3 gates thereof are **b.** with fire ... 3341
Ne 2:17 and the gates thereof are **b.** with ... 3341
Ne 4:2 heaps of rubbish which are **b.**? ... 8313
Es 1:12 wroth, and his anger **b.** in him. ... 1197
Job 1:16 and hath **b.** up the sheep, ... 1197
Job 30:30 and my bones are **b.** with heat. ... 2787
Ps 39:3 while I was musing the fire **b.**: ... 1197
Ps 74:8 have **b.** up all the synagogues ... 8313
Ps 80:16 It is **b.** with fire, it is cut down: ... 8313
Ps 102:3 and my bones are **b.** as an hearth. ... 2787
Ps 106:18 the flame **b.** up the wicked ... 3857
Pr 6:27 and his clothes not be **b.**? ... 8313
Pr 6:28 hot coals, and his feet not be **b.**? ... 3554
Isa 1:7 your cities are **b.** with fire: your ... 8313
Isa 24:6 inhabitants of the earth are **b.** ... 2787
Isa 33:12 as thorns cut up shall they be **b.** ... 3341
Isa 42:25 and it **b.** him, yet he laid it not ... 1197
Isa 43:2 thou shalt not be **b.**; neither ... 3554
Isa 44:19 I have **b.** part of it in the fire; ... 8314
Isa 64:11 is **b.** up with fire: and all our ... 8316
Isa 65:7 **b.** incense upon the mountains, ... 6999
Jer 1:16 have **b.** incense unto other gods, ... 6999
Jer 2:15 cities are **b.** without inhabitant. ... 3341
Jer 6:29 The bellows are **b.**, the lead is ... 2787
Jer 9:10 they are **b.** up, so that none can ... 3341
Jer 9:12 the land perisheth and is **b.** up ... 3341
Jer 18:15 they have **b.** incense to vanity, ... 6999
Jer 19:4 **b.** incense in it unto other gods, ... 6999
Jer 19:13 they have **b.** incense unto all the ... 6999
Jer 36:27 after that the king had **b.** the roll. ... 8313
Jer 36:28 the king of Judah hath **b.**. ... 8313
Jer 36:29 Thou hast **b.** this roll, saying, ... 8313
Jer 36:32 Jehoiakim king of Judah had **b.** ... 8313
Jer 38:17 this city shall not be **b.** with fire; ... 8313
Jer 38:23 cause this city to be **b.** with fire. ... 8313
Jer 39:8 the Chaldeans **b.** the king's house, ... 8313
Jer 44:15 wives had **b.** incense unto other ... 6999
Jer 44:19 **b.** incense to the queen of heaven, ... 6999
Jer 44:21 that ye **b.** in the cities of Judah, ... 6999
Jer 44:23 Because ye have **b.** incense, and ... 6999
Jer 49:2 her daughters shall be **b.** with fire: ... 3341
Jer 51:30 they have **b.** her dwellingplaces; ... 3341
Jer 51:32 the reeds they have **b.** with fire, ... 8313
Jer 51:58 high gates shall be **b.** with fire ... 3341
Jer 52:13 And **b.** the house of the Lord, ... 8313
Jer 52:13 of the great men, **b.** he with fire: ... 8313
La 2:3 he **b.** against Jacob like a flaming ... 1197
Eze 15:4 of it, and the midst of it is **b.**. ... 2787
Eze 15:5 fire hath devoured it, and it is **b.**? ... 2787
Eze 20:47 the south to the north shall be **b.** ... 6866
Eze 24:10 it well, and let the bones be **b.**. ... 2787
Ho 2:13 wherein she **b.** incense to them, ... 6999
Ho 11:2 and **b.** incense to graven images. ... 6999
Joe 1:19 the flame hath **b.** all the trees of ... 3857
Am 2:1 **b.** the bones of the king of Edom ... 8313
Mic 1:7 the hires thereof shall be **b.** with ... 8313
Na 1:5 the earth is **b.** at his presence, ... 5375
Mt 13:40 **the tares are gathered and b. in** ... *2618*
Mt 22:7 **murderers, and b. up their city** ... *1714*
Joh 15:6 **into the fire, and they are b.** ... *2545*
Ac 19:19 and **b.** them before all men: and ... *2618*
Ro 1:27 **b.** in their lust one toward ... *1572*
1Co 3:15 If any man's work shall be **b.**, he ... *2618*
1Co 13:3 I give my body to be **b.**, and have ... *2545*
Heb 6:8 cursing, whose end is to be **b.** ... *2740*
Heb 12:18 and that **b.** with fire, nor unto ... *2545*
Heb 13:11 high priest for sin, are **b.** without ... *2618*

2Pe 3:10 works that are therein shall be **b.** *2618*
Re 1:15 as if they **b.** in a furnace; and his *4448*
Re 18:8 she shall be utterly **b.** with fire: *2618*

BURNETH
Le 13:24 that **b.** have a white bright spot. 4348
Le 16:28 And he that **b.** them shall wash 8313
Nu 19:8 And he that **b.** her shall wash his 8313
Ps 46:9 he **b.** the chariot in the fire. 8313
Ps 83:14 As the fire **b.** a wood, and as the 1197
Ps 97:3 A fire goeth before him, and **b.** up 3857
Isa 9:18 For wickedness **b.** as a fire: it shall 1197
Isa 44:16 He **b.** part thereof in the fire; 8313
Isa 62:1 thereof as a lamp that **b.**. 1197
Isa 64:2 As when the melting fire **b.**, the 6919
Isa 65:3 **b.** incense upon altars of brick; 6999
Isa 65:5 nose, a fire that **b.** all the day. 3344
Isa 66:3 he that **b.** incense, as if he 2142
Jer 48:35 and him that **b.** incense to his gods 6999
Ho 7:6 in the morning it **b.** as a flaming 1197
Joe 2:3 behind them a flame **b.**: the land 3857
Am 6:10 that **b.** him, to bring out the bones 5635
Re 21:8 in the lake which **b.** with fire and *2545*

BURNING See also BURNINGS.
Ge 15:17 a **b.** lamp that passed between 784
Ex 21:25 **B.** for **b.**, wound for wound, 3555
Le 6:9 because of the **b.** upon the altar 4169
Le 6:9 the fire of the altar shall be **b.** in 3344
Le 6:12 the fire upon the altar shall be **b.** 3344
Le 6:13 The fire shall ever be **b.** upon 3344
Le 10:6 **b.** which the Lord hath kindled. 8316
Le 13:23 it is a **b.** boil; and the priest 6867
Le 13:24 skin thereof there is a hot **b.**, 4348
Le 13:25 a leprosy broken out of the **b.**: 4348
Le 13:28 a rising of the **b.**, and the priest 4348
Le 13:28 it is an inflammation of the **b.**. 4348
Le 16:12 shall take a censer full of **b.** coals 784
Le 26:16 consumption, and the **b.** ague, 6920
Nu 16:37 take up the censers out of the **b.**, 8316
Nu 19:6 cast it into the midst of the **b.** of 8316
De 28:22 and with an extreme **b.**, and with 2746
De 29:23 brimstone, and salt, and **b.**, that 8316
De 32:24 devoured with **b.** heat, and with
2Ch 16:14 they made a very great **b.** for him. 8316
2Ch 21:19 his people made no **b.** for him. 8316
2Ch 21:19 like the **b.** of his fathers. 8316
Job 41:19 Out of his mouth go **b.** lamps, 3940
Ps 140:10 Let **b.** coals fall upon them: let 784
Pr 16:27 in his lips there is as a **b.** fire. 6867
Pr 26:21 As coals are to **b.** coals, and 1513
Pr 26:23 **B.** lips and a wicked heart are 1814
Isa 3:24 and **b.** instead of beauty. 3587
Isa 4:4 and by the spirit of **b.**. 1197
Isa 9:5 but this shall be with **b.** and fuel 8316
Isa 10:16 kindle a **b.** like the **b.** of a fire. 3350
Isa 30:27 **b.** with his anger, and the burden 1197
Isa 34:9 land thereof shall become **b.** pitch 1197
Jer 20:9 was in mine heart as a **b.** fire 1197
Jer 36:22 fire on the hearth **b.** before him. 1197
Jer 44:8 **b.** incense unto other gods in 6999
Eze 1:13 like **b.** coals of fire, and like the 1197
Da 3:6 into the midst of a **b.** fiery furnace. 3345
Da 3:11 should be cast into the midst of a **b.** 3345
Da 3:15 same hour into the midst of a **b.** 3345
Da 3:17 able to deliver us from the **b.** fiery 3345
Da 3:20 cast them into the **b.** fiery furnace. 3345
Da 3:21, 23 the midst of the **b.** fiery furnace. 3345
Da 3:26 to the mouth of the **b.** fiery furnace, 3345
Da 7:9 flame, and his wheels as **b.** fire. 1815
Da 7:11 and given to the **b.** flame. 3346
Am 4:11 firebrand plucked out of the **b.**: 8316
Hab 3:5 **b.** coals went forth at his feet. 7565
Lu 12:35 **girded about, and your lights b.**; *2545*
Joh 5:35 **He was a b. and a shining light**: *2545*
Jas 1:11 no sooner risen with a **b.** heat, *2742*
Re 4:5 lamps of fire **b.** before the throne, *2545*
Re 8:8 a great mountain **b.** with fire was *2545*
Re 8:10 **b.** as it were a lamp, and it fell *2545*
Re 18:9 they shall see the smoke of her **b.**, *4451*
Re 18:18 saw the smoke of her **b.**, saying, *4451*
Re 19:20 a lake of fire **b.** with brimstone. *2545*

BURNINGS
Isa 33:12 people shall be as the **b.** of lime: 4955
Isa 33:14 us shall dwell with everlasting **b.**? 4168
Jer 34:5 and with the **b.** of thy fathers. 4955

BURNISHED
Eze 1:7 like the colour of **b.** brass. 7044

BURNT See also BURNED.
Ge 8:20 offered **b.** offerings on the altar. 5930
Ge 22:2 offer him there for a **b.** offering 5930
Ge 22:3 clave the wood for the **b.** offering, 5930
Ge 22:6 took the wood of the **b.** offering, 5930
Ge 22:7 where is the lamb for a **b.** offering? 5930
Ge 22:8 himself a lamb for a **b.** offering: 5930
Ge 22:13 offered him up for a **b.** offering in 5930
Ge 38:24 Bring her forth, and let her be **b.** 8313
Ex 3:3 sight, why the bush is not **b.** 1197
Ex 10:25 **b.** offerings, that we may sacrifice 5930
Ex 18:12 father in law, took a **b.** offering 5930
Ex 20:24 sacrifice thereon thy **b.** offerings, 5930
Ex 24:5 of Israel, which offered **b.** offerings, 5930
Ex 29:18 it is a **b.** offering unto the Lord: 5930
Ex 29:25 upon the altar for a **b.** offering, 5930
Ex 29:42 continual **b.** offering throughout 5930
Ex 30:9 nor **b.** sacrifice, nor meat offering; 5930
Ex 30:28 of **b.** offering with all his vessels, 5930
Ex 31:9 of **b.** offering with all his furniture, 5930
Ex 32:6 offered **b.** offerings, and brought 5930
Ex 32:20 and **b.** it in the fire, and ground 8313
Ex 35:16 of **b.** offering, with his brasen 5930
Ex 38:1 he made the altar of **b.** offering 5930
Ex 40:6 shalt set the altar of the **b.** offering 5930
Ex 40:10 anoint the altar of the **b.** offering, 5930
Ex 40:27 And he **b.** sweet incense thereon; 6999
Ex 40:29 he put the altar of **b.** offering by 5930
Ex 40:29 and offered upon it the **b.** offering 5930
Le 1:3 If his offering be a **b.** sacrifice of 5930
Le 1:4 upon the head of the **b.** offering; 5930
Le 1:6 shall flay the **b.** offering, and cut 5930
Le 1:9 on the altar, to be a **b.** sacrifice, 5930
Le 1:10 or of the goats, for a **b.** sacrifice: 5930
Le 1:13 a **b.** sacrifice, an offering made by 5930
Le 1:14 the **b.** sacrifice for his offering to 5930
Le 1:17 it is a **b.** sacrifice, an offering 5930
Le 2:12 they shall not be **b.** on the altar 5927
Le 3:5 upon the **b.** sacrifice, which is 5930
Le 4:7 of the altar of the **b.** offering, 5930
Le 4:10 upon the altar of the **b.** offering. 5930
Le 4:12 are poured out shall he be **b.** 8313
Le 4:18 the altar of the **b.** offering, which 5930
Le 4:24 kill the **b.** offering before the Lord: 5930
Le 4:25 horns of the altar of **b.** offering, 5930
Le 4:25 bottom of the altar of **b.** offering. 5930
Le 4:29 in the place of the **b.** offering. 5930
Le 4:30 horns of the altar of **b.** offering, 5930
Le 4:33 where they kill the **b.** offering. 5930
Le 4:34 altar of **b.** offering, and shall pour 5930
Le 5:7 and the other for a **b.** offering. 5930
Le 5:10 offer the second for a **b.** offering, 5930
Le 6:9 the law of the **b.** offering: 5930
Le 6:9 It is the **b.** offering, because of 5930
Le 6:10 with the **b.** offering on the altar, 5930
Le 6:12 lay the **b.** offering in order upon it; 6999
Le 6:22 the Lord; it shall be wholly **b.**. 6999
Le 6:23 shall be wholly **b.**: it shall not 6999
Le 6:25 place where the **b.** offering is killed 5930
Le 6:30 eaten: it shall be **b.** in the fire. 8313
Le 7:2 where they kill the **b.** offering 5930
Le 7:8 offereth any man's **b.** offering, 5930
Le 7:8 himself the skin of the **b.** offering 5930
Le 7:17 the third day shall be **b.** with fire. 8313
Le 7:19 it shall be **b.** with fire: and as for 8313
Le 7:37 This is the law of the **b.** offering, 5930
Le 8:17 he **b.** with fire without the camp; 8313
Le 8:18 the ram for the **b.** offering: 5930
Le 8:20 **b.** the head, and the pieces, and 6999
Le 8:21 Moses **b.** the whole ram upon the 6999
Le 8:21 a **b.** sacrifice for a sweet savour, 5930
Le 8:28 from off their hands, and **b.** them 6999
Le 8:28 on the altar upon the **b.** offering: 5930
Le 9:2 a ram for a **b.** offering, without 5930
Le 9:3 without a blemish, for a **b.** offering; 5930
Le 9:7 sin offering, and thy **b.** offering, 5930
Le 9:10 sin offering, he **b.** upon the altar; 5930
Le 9:11 he **b.** with fire without the camp. 8313
Le 9:12 he slew the **b.** offering; and 5930
Le 9:13 presented the **b.** offering unto him, 5930
Le 9:13 and he **b.** them upon the altar. 6999
Le 9:14 inwards and the legs, and **b.** them 6999
Le 9:14 upon the **b.** offering on the 5930
Le 9:16 the **b.** offering, and offered it 5930
Le 9:17 and **b.** it upon the altar, 6999
Le 9:17 the **b.** sacrifice of the morning. 5930
Le 9:20 and he **b.** the fat upon the altar: 6999
Le 9:22 sin offering, and the **b.** offering, 5930
Le 9:24 upon the altar the **b.** offering 5930
Le 10:16 it was **b.**: and he was angry with 8313
Le 10:19 sin offering and their **b.** offering 5930
Le 12:6 of the first year for a **b.** offering, 5930
Le 12:8 the one for the **b.** offering, and the 5930
Le 13:52 leprosy; it shall be **b.** in the fire. 8313
Le 14:13 sin offering and the **b.** offering, in 5930
Le 14:19 he shall kill the **b.** offering: 5930
Le 14:20 the priest shall offer the **b.** offering 5930
Le 14:22 and the other a **b.** offering. 5930
Le 14:31 and the other for a **b.** offering, 5930
Le 15:15 and the other for a **b.** offering; 5930
Le 15:30 and the other for a **b.** offering. 5930
Le 16:3 a ram for a **b.** offering. 5930
Le 16:5 and one ram for a **b.** offering. 5930
Le 16:24 and offer his **b.** offering, and the 5930
Le 16:24 **b.** offering of the people, 5930
Le 17:8 offereth a **b.** offering or sacrifice, 5930
Le 19:6 it shall be **b.** in the fire. 8313
Le 20:14 they shall be **b.** with fire, both he 8313
Le 21:9 she shall be **b.** with fire. 8313
Le 22:18 unto the Lord for a **b.** offering; 5930
Le 23:12 for a **b.** offering unto the Lord. 5930
Le 23:18 a **b.** offering unto the Lord, 5930
Le 23:37 a **b.** offering, and a meat offering, 5930
Nu 6:11 the other for a **b.** offering, 5930
Nu 6:14 without blemish for a **b.** offering, 5930
Nu 6:16 sin offering, and his **b.** offering: 5930
Nu 7:15, 21,27,33,39,45,51,57,63,69,75,81 the first year, for a **b.** offering: 5930
Nu 7:87 the oxen for the **b.** offering 5930
Nu 8:12 for a **b.** offering, unto the Lord, 5930
Nu 10:10 over your **b.** offerings, and over 5930
Nu 11:1 fire of the Lord **b.** among them, 1197
Nu 11:3 the fire of the Lord **b.** among them. 1197
Nu 15:3 a **b.** offering, or a sacrifice 5930
Nu 15:5 with the **b.** offering or sacrifice, 5930
Nu 15:8 a bullock for a **b.** offering, 5930
Nu 15:24 one young bullock for a **b.** offering, 5930
Nu 16:39 they that were **b.** had offered; 8313
Nu 19:17 take of the ashes of the **b.** heifer 8316
Nu 23:3 Stand by thy **b.** offering, and I 5930
Nu 23:6 he stood by his **b.** sacrifice, 5930
Nu 23:15 Stand here by thy **b.** offering, 5930
Nu 23:17 he stood by his **b.** offering, and 5930
Nu 28:3 by day, for a continual **b.** offering. 5930
Nu 28:6 a continual **b.** offering, which was 5930
Nu 28:10 the **b.** offering of every Sabbath, 5930
Nu 28:10 beside the continual **b.** offering, 5930
Nu 28:11 ye shall offer a **b.** offering unto 5930
Nu 28:13 a **b.** offering of a sweet savour, 5930
Nu 28:14 the **b.** offering of every month 5930
Nu 28:15 the continual **b.** offering, and his 5930
Nu 28:19 for a **b.** offering unto the Lord; 5930
Nu 28:23 the **b.** offering in the morning, 5930
Nu 28:23 is for a continual **b.** offering. 5930
Nu 28:24 the continual **b.** offering, and his 5930
Nu 28:27 ye shall offer the **b.** offering for a 5930
Nu 28:31 beside the continual **b.** offering, 5930
Nu 29:2 ye shall offer a **b.** offering for a 5930
Nu 29:6 Beside the **b.** offering of the month, 5930
Nu 29:6 and the daily **b.** offering, 5930
Nu 29:8 a **b.** offering unto the Lord. 5930
Nu 29:11 and the continual **b.** offering, 5930
Nu 29:13 And ye shall offer a **b.** offering, 5930
Nu 29:16, 19,22,25,28,31,34 beside the continual **b.** offering 5930
Nu 29:36 ye shall offer a **b.** offering, 5930
Nu 29:38 **b.** offering, and his meat offering, 5930
Nu 29:39 for your **b.** offerings, and for your 5930
Nu 31:10 they **b.** all their cities wherein 8313
De 9:21 and **b.** it with fire, and stamped it, 8313
De 12:6 ye shall bring your **b.** offerings, 5930
De 12:11 **b.** offerings, and your sacrifices, 5930
De 12:13 thou offer not thy **b.** offerings 5930
De 12:14, 27 thou shalt offer thy **b.** offerings, 5930
De 12:31 daughters they have **b.** in the fire 8313
De 27:6 shalt offer **b.** offerings thereon 5930
De 32:24 They shall be **b.** with hunger, 4198
De 33:10 whole **b.** sacrifice upon thine altar 3632
Jos 6:24 they **b.** the city with fire, and 8313
Jos 7:15 the accursed thing shall be **b.** 8313
Jos 8:28 And Joshua **b.** Ai, and made it 8313

Jos 8:31 they offered thereon **b.** offerings 5930
Jos 11:9 and **b.** their chariots with fire. 8313
Jos 11:11 and he **b.** Hazor with fire. 8313
Jos 22:23 to offer thereon **b.** offering 5930
Jos 22:26 not for **b.** offering, nor for sacrifice: 5930
Jos 22:27 before him with our **b.** offerings, 5930
Jos 22:28 **b.** offerings, nor for sacrifices; 5930
Jos 22:29 to build an altar for **b.** offerings, 5930
Jg 6:26 and offer a **b.** sacrifice with the 5930
Jg 11:31 will offer it up for a **b.** offering. 5930
Jg 13:16 if thou wilt offer a **b.** offering, 5930
Jg 13:23 not have received a **b.** offering 5930
Jg 15:5 and **b.** up both the shocks, and 1197
Jg 15:6 **b.** her and her father with fire. 8313
Jg 15:14 as flax that was **b.** with fire, 1197
Jg 18:27 sword, and **b.** the city with fire 8313
Jg 20:26 and offered **b.** offerings and 5930
Jg 21:4 and offered **b.** offerings and 5930
1Sa 2:15 before they **b.** the fat, the priest's 6999
1Sa 6:14 a **b.** offering unto the Lord 5930
1Sa 6:15 Beth-shemesh offered **b.** offerings 5930
1Sa 7:9 a **b.** offering wholly unto the Lord: 5930
1Sa 7:10 **b.** offering, the Philistines drew 5930
1Sa 10:8 unto thee, to offer **b.** offerings, 5930
1Sa 13:9 Bring hither a **b.** offering to me. 5930
1Sa 13:9 And he offered the **b.** offering. 5930
1Sa 13:10 an end of offering the **b.** offering, 5930
1Sa 13:12 therefore, and offered a **b.** offering. 5930
1Sa 15:22 as great delight in **b.** offerings 5930
1Sa 31:12 Jabesh, and **b.** them there 8313
2Sa 6:17 and David offered **b.** offerings 5930
2Sa 6:18 an end of offering **b.** offerings 5930
2Sa 24:22 here be oxen for **b.** sacrifice, 5930
2Sa 24:24 neither will I offer **b.** offerings 5930
2Sa 24:25 the Lord, and offered **b.** offerings 5930
1Ki 3:3 and **b.** incense in high places. 6999
1Ki 3:4 a thousand **b.** offerings did 5930
1Ki 3:15 and offered up **b.** offerings, 5930
1Ki 8:64 there he offered **b.** offerings, 5930
1Ki 8:64 too little to receive the **b.** offerings. 5930
1Ki 9:16 and **b.** it with fire, and slain 8313
1Ki 9:25 did Solomon offer **b.** offerings 5930
1Ki 9:25 and he **b.** incense upon the altar 6999
1Ki 11:8 which **b.** incense and sacrificed 6999
1Ki 12:33 upon the altar, and **b.** incense. 6999
1Ki 13:2 bones shall be **b.** upon thee 8313
1Ki 15:13 her idol, and **b.** it by the brook 8313
1Ki 16:18 and **b.** the king's house over him 8313
1Ki 18:33 pour it on the **b.** sacrifice, and 5930
1Ki 18:38 fell, and consumed the **b.** sacrifice, 5930
1Ki 22:43 the people offered and **b.** incense 6999
2Ki 1:14 and **b.** up the two captains of 398
2Ki 3:27 and offered him for a **b.** offering 5930
2Ki 5:17 neither **b.** offering nor sacrifice 5930
2Ki 10:24 to offer sacrifices and **b.** offerings, 5930
2Ki 10:25 an end of offering the **b.** offering, 5930
2Ki 12:3 sacrificed and **b.** incense in the 6999
2Ki 14:4 **b.** incense on the high places 6999
2Ki 15:4 people sacrificed and **b.** incense 6999
2Ki 16:4 And he sacrificed and **b.** incense 6999
2Ki 16:13 And he **b.** [6999] his **b.** offering and 5930
2Ki 16:15 the morning **b.** offering, and the 5930
2Ki 16:15 the king's **b.** sacrifice, and his 5930
2Ki 16:15 the **b.** offering of all the people 5930
2Ki 16:15 the blood of the **b.** offering, 5930
2Ki 17:11 And there they **b.** incense in all 6999
2Ki 17:31 Sepharvites **b.** their children 8313
2Ki 25:9 And he **b.** the house of the Lord, 8313
2Ki 25:9 every great man's house **b.** he 8313
1Ch 6:49 the altar of the **b.** offering, and 5930
1Ch 16:1 they offered **b.** sacrifices and 5930
1Ch 16:2 end of offering the **b.** offerings 5930
1Ch 16:40 To offer **b.** offerings unto the Lord 5930
1Ch 16:40 the altar of the **b.** offering 5930
1Ch 21:23 the oxen also for **b.** offerings, 5930
1Ch 21:24 nor offer **b.** offerings without cost. 5930
1Ch 21:26 offered **b.** offerings and peace 5930
1Ch 21:26 by fire upon the altar of **b.** offering. 5930
1Ch 21:29 the altar of the **b.** offering, 5930
1Ch 22:1 is the altar of the **b.** offering 5930
1Ch 23:31 offer all **b.** sacrifices unto the Lord 5930
1Ch 29:21 offered **b.** offerings unto the Lord, 5930
2Ch 1:6 offered a thousand **b.** offerings 5930
2Ch 2:4 and for the **b.** offerings morning 5930
2Ch 4:6 as they offered for the **b.** offering 5930
2Ch 7:1 and consumed the **b.** offering 5930
2Ch 7:7 there he offered **b.** offerings, 5930
2Ch 7:7 to receive the **b.** offerings, 5930
2Ch 8:12 Solomon offered **b.** offerings 5930
2Ch 13:11 **b.** sacrifices and sweet incense: 5930
2Ch 15:16 and **b.** it at the brook Kidron. 8313
2Ch 23:18 the **b.** offerings of the Lord, as it 5930
2Ch 24:14 they offered **b.** offerings in the 5930
2Ch 28:3 he **b.** incense in the valley of the 6999
2Ch 28:3 and **b.** his children in the fire, 1197
2Ch 28:4 and **b.** incense in the high place, 6999
2Ch 29:7 nor offered **b.** offerings in the 5930
2Ch 29:18 the altar of **b.** offering, with all 5930
2Ch 29:24 the **b.** offering and the sin 5930
2Ch 29:27 offer the **b.** offering upon the altar 5930
2Ch 29:27 And when the **b.** offering began, 5930
2Ch 29:28 until the **b.** offering was finished 5930
2Ch 29:31 as were of a free heart **b.** offerings. 5930
2Ch 29:32 the number of the **b.** offerings, 5930
2Ch 29:32 for a **b.** offering to the Lord 5930
2Ch 29:34 could not flay all the **b.** offerings: 5930
2Ch 29:35 the **b.** offerings were in abundance, 5930
2Ch 29:35 drink offerings for every **b.** offering. 5930
2Ch 30:15 brought in the **b.** offerings unto 5930
2Ch 31:2 priests and Levites for **b.** offerings 5930
2Ch 31:3 his substance for the **b.** offerings, 5930
2Ch 31:3 morning and evening **b.** offerings, 5930
2Ch 31:3 the **b.** offerings for the sabbaths, 5930
2Ch 34:5 he **b.** the bones of the priests, 8313
2Ch 35:12 they removed the **b.** offerings, 5930
2Ch 35:14 in offering of **b.** offerings 5930
2Ch 35:16 to offer **b.** offerings upon the altar 5930
2Ch 36:19 And they **b.** the house of God, 8313
2Ch 36:19 and **b.** all the palaces thereof 8313
Ezr 3:2 to offer **b.** offerings thereon, 5930
Ezr 3:3 they offered **b.** offerings thereon 5930
Ezr 3:3 **b.** offerings morning and evening. 5930
Ezr 3:4 and offered the daily **b.** offerings 5930
Ezr 3:5 offered the continual **b.** offering, 5930
Ezr 3:6 to offer **b.** offerings unto the Lord. 5930
Ezr 6:9 for the **b.** offerings of the God of 5928
Ezr 8:35 **b.** offerings unto the God of Israel, 5930
Ezr 8:35 a **b.** offering unto the Lord 5930
Ne 10:33 and for the continual **b.** offering, 5930
Job 1:5 and offered **b.** offerings according 5930
Job 42:8 up for yourselves a **b.** offering; 5930
Ps 20:3 and accept thy **b.** sacrifice; 5930
Ps 40:6 **b.** offering and sin offering hast 5930
Ps 50:8 thy sacrifices or thy **b.** offerings, 5930
Ps 51:16 thou delightest not in **b.** offering. 5930
Ps 51:19 **b.** offering and whole **b.** offering: 5930
Ps 66:13 go into thy house with **b.** offerings: 5930
Ps 66:15 I will offer unto thee **b.** sacrifices 5930
Isa 1:11 I am full of the **b.** offerings of 5930
Isa 40:16 thereof sufficient for a **b.** offering. 5930
Isa 43:23 the small cattle of thy **b.** offerings; 5930
Isa 56:7 **b.** offerings and their sacrifices 5930
Isa 61:8 I hate robbery for **b.** offering; 5930
Jer 6:20 your **b.** offerings are not acceptable, 5930
Jer 7:21 Put your **b.** offerings unto your 5930
Jer 7:22 concerning **b.** offerings or 5930
Jer 14:12 when they offer **b.** offering and 5930
Jer 17:26 bringing **b.** offerings, and sacrifices, 5930
Jer 19:5 burn their sons with fire for **b.** 5930
Jer 33:18 before me to offer **b.** offerings, 5930
Jer 51:25 will make thee a **b.** mountain. 8316
Eze 40:38 they washed the **b.** offering. 5930
Eze 40:39 to slay thereon the **b.** offering 5930
Eze 40:42 of hewn stone for the **b.** offering, 5930
Eze 40:42 they slew the **b.** offering, and 5930
Eze 43:18 to offer **b.** offerings thereon, 5930
Eze 43:24 for a **b.** offering unto the Lord. 5930
Eze 43:27 priests shall make your **b.** offerings 5930
Eze 44:11 they shall slay the **b.** offering 5930
Eze 45:15 and for a **b.** offering, and for 5930
Eze 45:17 prince's part to give **b.** offerings, 5930
Eze 45:17 meat offering, and the **b.** offering, 5930
Eze 45:23 a **b.** offering to the Lord, seven 5930
Eze 45:25 according to the **b.** offering, 5930
Eze 46:2 priests shall prepare his **b.** offering 5930
Eze 46:4 And the **b.** offering that the prince 5930
Eze 46:12 prepare a voluntary **b.** offering 5930
Eze 46:12 he shall prepare his **b.** offering 5930
Eze 46:13 a **b.** offering unto the Lord of 5930
Eze 46:15 for a continual **b.** offering. 5930
Ho 6:6 of God more than **b.** offerings 5930
Am 5:22 ye offer me **b.** offerings and your 5930
Mic 6:6 come before him with **b.** offerings, 5930
Mk 12:33 more than all whole **b.** offerings *3646*
Heb 10:6 In **b.** offerings and sacrifices for *3646*
Heb 10:8 and **b.** offerings and offering for *3646*
Re 8:7 the third part of trees was **b.** up, *2618*
Re 8:7 and all green grass was **b.** up. *2618*

BURNT-OFFERING See BURNT and OFFERING.

BURNT-SACRIFICE See BURNT and SACRIFICE.

BURST See also BURSTING.
Job 32:19 it is ready to **b.** like new bottles. 1234
Pr 3:10 and thy presses shall **b.** out 6555
Jer 2:20 thy yoke, and **b.** thy bands; 5423
Jer 5:5 broken the yoke, and **b.** the bonds. 5423
Jer 30:8 and will **b.** thy bonds, and 5423
Na 1:13 and will **b.** thy bonds in sunder. 5423
Mk 2:22 **doth b. the bottles, and the wine** *4486*
Lu 5:37 **new wine will b. the bottles,** *4486*
Ac 1:18 he **b.** asunder in the midst, *2297*

BURSTING
Isa 30:14 shall not be found in the **b.** of it 4386

BURY See also BURIED; BURYING.
Ge 23:4 I may **b.** my dead out of my sight. 6912
Ge 23:6 of our sepulchres **b.** thy dead; 6912
Ge 23:6 but that thou mayest **b.** thy dead. 6912
Ge 23:8 mind that I should **b.** my dead 6912
Ge 23:11 people give I it thee; **b.** thy dead. 6912
Ge 23:13 me, and I will **b.** my dead there. 6912
Ge 23:15 and thee: **b.** therefore thy dead. 6912
Ge 47:29 **b.** me not, I pray thee, in Egypt: 6912
Ge 47:30 and **b.** me in their buryingplace. 6912
Ge 49:29 **b.** me with my fathers in the 6912
Ge 50:5 Canaan, there shalt thou **b.** me. 6912
Ge 50:5 and **b.** my father, and I will come 6912
Ge 50:6 Go up, and **b.** thy father, according 6912
Ge 50:7 Joseph went up to **b.** his father: 6912
Ge 50:14 went up with him to **b.** his father, 6912
De 21:23 shalt in any wise **b.** him that day; 6912
1Ki 2:31 and fall upon him, and **b.** him; 6912
1Ki 11:15 host was gone up to **b.** the slain, 6912
1Ki 13:29 the city, to mourn and to **b.** him. 6912
1Ki 13:31 When I am dead, then **b.** me in 6912
1Ki 14:13 shall mourn for him, and **b.** him: 6912
2Ki 9:10 and there shall be none to **b.** her. 6912
2Ki 9:34 and **b.** her: for she is the king's 6912
2Ki 9:35 they went to **b.** her: but they 6912
Ps 79:3 and there was none to **b.** them. 6912
Jer 7:32 for they shall **b.** in Tophet, 6912
Jer 14:16 they shall have none to **b.** them, 6912
Jer 19:11 they shall **b.** them in Tophet, 6912
Jer 19:11 till there be no place to **b.**. 6912
Eze 39:11 and there shall they **b.** Gog and 6912
Eze 39:13 all the people of the land shall **b.** 6912
Eze 39:14 to **b.** with the passengers those 6912
Ho 9:6 them up, Memphis shall **b.** them: 6912
Mt 8:21 me first to go and **b.** my father *2290*
Mt 8:22 **and let the dead b. their dead.** *2290*
Mt 27:7 potter's field, to **b.** strangers in. *5027*
Lu 9:59 me first to go and **b.** my father. *2290*
Lu 9:60 **Let the dead b. their dead:** *2290*
Joh 19:40 the manner of the Jews is to **b.**. *1779*

BURYING See also BURYINGPLACE.
2Ki 13:21 as they were **b.** a man, that, 6912
Eze 39:12 house of Israel be **b.** of them, 6912
Mk 14:8 **to anoint my body to the b.,** *1780*
Joh 12:7 **against the day of my b. hath she** *1780*

BURYINGPLACE
Ge 23:4 give me a possession of a **b.** 6913
Ge 23:9 possession of a **b.** amongst you. 6913
Ge 23:20 possession of a **b.** by the sons 6913
Ge 47:30 bury me in their **b.**. And he said, 6913
Ge 49:30 Hittite for a possession of a **b.** 6913
Ge 50:13 for a possession of a **b.** of Ephron 6913
Jg 16:31 in the **b.** of Manoah his father. 6913

BUSH See also BUSHES.
Ex 3:2 fire out of the midst of a **b.**: 5572
Ex 3:2 behold, the **b.** burned with fire, 5572
Ex 3:2 and the **b.** was not consumed. 5572
Ex 3:3 sight, why the **b.** is not burnt. 5572
Ex 3:4 him out of the midst of the **b.**, 5572
De 33:16 will of him that dwelt in the **b.**: 5572
Mk 12:26 **how in the b. God spake unto him** *942*
Lu 6:44 **of a bramble b. gather they grapes,** *942*
Lu 20:37 **even Moses shewed at the b.,** *942*
Ac 7:30 Lord in a flame of fire in a **b.** *942*
Ac 7:35 which appeared to him in the **b.**. *942*

BUSHEL
Mt 5:15 **a candle, and put it under a b.,**..... *3426*
Mk 4:21 **brought to be put under a b.,**........ *3426*
Lu 11:33 **neither under a b., but on a**.......... *3426*

BUSHES
Job 30:4 Who cut up mallows by the **b.**,.......... 7880
Job 30:7 Among the **b.** they brayed; under....... 7880
Isa 7:19 all thorns, and upon all **b.**................ 5097

BUSHY
Ca 5:11 his locks are **b.**, and black as a.......... 8534

BUSIED
2Ch 35:14 priests the sons of Aaron were **b.**...........

BUSINESS
Ge 39:11 went into the house to do his **b.**;....... 4399
De 24:5 shall he be charged with any **b.**;......... 1697
Jos 2:14 yours, if ye utter not this our **b.**......... 1697
Jos 2:20 if thou utter this our **b.**, then we....... 1697
Jg 18:7 and had no **b.** with any man............. 1697
Jg 18:28 they had no **b.** with any man;............ 1697
1Sa 20:19 when the **b.** was in hand,................ 4639
1Sa 21:2 hath commanded me a **b.**, and........... 1697
1Sa 21:2 man know anything of the **b.**............. 1697
1Sa 21:8 the king's **b.** required haste.............. 1697
1Ch 26:29 his sons were for the outward **b.**....... 4399
1Ch 26:30 westward in all the **b.** of the Lord,..... 4399
2Ch 13:10 the Levites wait upon their **b.**:.......... 4399
2Ch 17:13 much **b.** in the cities of Judah:........... 4399
2Ch 32:31 in the **b.** of the ambassadors of................
Ne 11:16 outward **b.** of the house of God............ 4399
Ne 11:22 over the **b.** of the house of God.......... 4399
Ne 13:30 Levites, every one in his **b.**;.............. 4399
Es 3:9 that have the charge of the **b.**,............ 4399
Ps 107:23 ships, that do **b.** in great waters;........ 4399
Pr 22:29 thou a man diligent in his **b.**?............ 4399
Ec 5:3 through the multitude of **b.**;............... 6045
Ec 8:16 the **b.** that is done upon the earth:...... 6045
Da 8:27 rose up, and did the king's **b.**;............ 4399
Lu 2:49 **must be about my father's b.?**..................
Ac 6:3 we may appoint over this **b.**................ *5532*
Ro 12:11 Not slothful in **b.**; fervent in............... *4710*
Ro 16:2 in whatsoever **b.** she hath need of.......... *4229*
1Th 4:11 to do your own **b.**, and to work............ *2398*

BUSY See also BUSIED; BUSYBODY.
1Ki 20:40 servant was **b.** here and there,.......... 6213

BUSYBODIES
2Th 3:11 working not at all, but are **b.**............ *4020*
1Ti 5:13 but tattlers also and **b.**, speaking........... *4021*

BUSYBODY See also BUSYBODIES.
1Pe 4:15 or as a **b.** in other men's matters......... *244*

BUT See in the APPENDIX; also SACKBUT.

BUTLER See also BUTLERS; BUTLERSHIP.
Ge 40:1 the **b.** of the king of Egypt and.......... 4945
Ge 40:5 the **b.** and the baker of the king of...... 4945
Ge 40:9 chief **b.** told his dream to Joseph,....... 4945
Ge 40:13 manner when thou wast his **b.**............ 4945
Ge 40:20 lifted up the head of the chief **b.**......... 4945
Ge 40:21 he restored the chief **b.** unto his......... 4945
Ge 40:23 Yet did not the chief **b.** remember....... 4945
Ge 41:9 spake the chief **b.** unto Pharaoh,......... 4945

BUTLERS
Ge 40:2 against the chief of the **b.**, and.......... 4945

BUTLERSHIP
Ge 40:21 the chief butler unto his **b.**............... 4945

BUTTER
Ge 18:8 he took **b.** and milk, and the calf......... 2529
De 32:14 **B.** of kine, and milk of sheep,............ 2529
Jg 5:25 brought forth **b.** in a lordly dish.......... 2529
2Sa 17:29 honey, and **b.**, and sheep, and............ 2529
Job 20:17 floods, the brooks of honey and **b.**....... 2529
Job 29:6 When I washed my steps with **b.**;........ 2529
Ps 55:21 his mouth were smoother than **b.**,....... 4260
Pr 30:33 of milk bringeth forth **b.**, and the........ 2529
Isa 7:15 **B.** and honey shall he eat, that he....... 2529
Isa 7:22 they shall give, he shall eat **b.**:........... 2529
Isa 7:22 for **b.** and honey shall every one.......... 2529

BUTTOCKS
2Sa 10:4 in the middle, even to their **b.**,........... 8357
1Ch 19:4 in the midst hard by their **b.**,............. 4667
Isa 20:4 with their **b.** uncovered, to the........... 8357

BUY See also BUYEST; BUYETH; BOUGHT.
Ge 41:57 Egypt to Joseph for to **b.** corn;........... 7666
Ge 42:2 **b.** for us from thence; that we............ 7666
Ge 42:3 went down to **b.** corn in Egypt............. 7666
Ge 42:5 the sons of Israel came to **b.** corn....... 7666
Ge 42:7 From the land of Canaan to **b.** food. ... 7666
Ge 42:10 to **b.** food are thy servants come. 7666
Ge 43:2 Go again, **b.** us a little food.............. 7666
Ge 43:4 we will go down and **b.** thee food:....... 7666
Ge 43:20 down at the first time to **b.** food:....... 7666
Ge 43:22 money have we brought...to **b.**............ 7666
Ge 44:25 Go again, and **b.** us a little food.......... 7666
Ge 47:19 **b.** us and our land for bread,............... 7069
Ex 21:2 If thou **b.** an Hebrew servant,............. 7069
Le 22:11 But if the priest **b.** any soul with......... 7069
Le 25:15 thou shalt **b.** of thy neighbour,........... 7069
Le 25:44 of them shall ye **b.** bondmen............... 7069
Le 25:45 of them shall ye **b.**, and of their.......... 7069
De 2:6 shall **b.** meat of them for money,......... 7666
De 2:6 ye shall also **b.** water of them for........ 3739
De 28:68 bondwomen, and no man shall **b.**......... 7069
Ru 4:4 **B.** it before the inhabitants,................ 7069
Ru 4:5 **b.** it also of Ruth the Moabitess,........... 7069
Ru 4:8 said unto Boaz, **B.** it for thee.............. 7069
2Sa 24:21 To **b.** the threshingfloor of thee to...... 7069
2Sa 24:24 will surely **b.** it of thee at a price:....... 7069
2Ki 12:12 to **b.** timber and hewed stone.............. 7069
2Ki 22:6 and to **b.** timber and hewn stone.......... 7069
1Ch 21:24 I will verily **b.** it for the full price:...... 7069
2Ch 34:11 to **b.** hewn stone, and timber for.......... 7069
Ezr 7:17 **b.** speedily with this money................ 7066
Ne 5:3 that we might **b.** corn, because............ 3947
Ne 10:31 not **b.** it of them on the sabbath,......... 3947
Pr 23:23 **B.** the truth, and sell it not;............... 7069
Isa 55:1 come ye, **b.**, and eat;.......................... 7666
Isa 55:1 yea, come, **b.** wine and milk.............. 7666
Jer 32:7 **B.** thee my field that is in................ 7069
Jer 32:7 of redemption is thine to **b.** it............ 7069
Jer 32:8 **B.** my field, I pray thee, that is in....... 7069
Jer 32:8 is thine; **b.** it for thyself..................... 7069
Jer 32:25 **B.** thee the field for money, and......... 7069
Jer 32:44 Men shall **b.** fields for money,............. 7069
Am 8:6 That we may **b.** the poor for silver...... 7069
Mt 14:15 villages, and **b.** themselves victuals........ *59*
Mt 25:9 **that sell, and b. for yourselves**........ *59*
Mt 25:10 **while they went to b., the**................ *59*
Mk 6:36 villages, and **b.** themselves bread:......... *59*
Mk 6:37 **b.** two hundred pennyworth of bread,..... *59*
Lu 9:13 go and **b.** meat for all this people.......... *59*
Lu 22:36 **let him sell his garment, and b. one**. *59*
Joh 4:8 away unto the city to **b.** meat.)............. *59*
Joh 6:5 **Whence shall we b. bread, that**........ *59*
Joh 13:29 **B.** those things that we have need........ *59*
1Co 7:30 they that **b.**, as though they............... *59*
Jas 4:13 and **b.** and sell, and get gain:............. *1710*
Re 3:18 **I counsel thee to b. of me gold**......... *59*
Re 13:17 that no man might **b.** or sell,............... *59*

BUYER
Pr 20:14 it is naught, saith the **b.**: but............. 7069
Isa 24:2 as with the **b.**, so with the seller;...... 7069
Eze 7:12 let not the **b.** rejoice, nor the seller..... 7069

BUYEST
Le 25:14 **b.** ought of thy neighbour's hand,....... 7069
Ru 4:5 What day thou **b.** the field of the......... 7069

BUYETH
Pr 31:16 She considereth a field, and **b.** it:........ 3947
Mt 13:44 **all that he hath, and b. that field**.... *59*
Re 18:11 for no man **b.** their merchandise........... *59*

BUZ (buz)
Ge 22:21 his firstborn, and **B.** his brother,......... 938
1Ch 5:14 the son of Jahdo, the son of **B.**;........... 938
Jer 25:23 Dedan, and Tema, and **B.**,.................... 938

BUZI (boo'-zi) See also BUZITE.
Eze 1:3 Ezekiel the priest, the son of **B.**,......... 941

BUZITE (boo'-zite)
Job 32:2 of Barachel the **B.**, of the kindred......... 940
Job 32:6 Elihu the son of Barachel the **B.**.......... 940

BY See in the APPENDIX; also BYWAYS; BYWORD; HEREBY; THEREBY; WHEREBY.

BY-AND-BY See BY and AND.

BYWAYS
Jg 5:6 travellers walked through **b.**........ 734,6128

BYWORD
De 28:37 a **b.**, among all nations whither.......... 8148
1Ki 9:7 and a **b.** among all people:................. 8148
2Ch 7:20 and a **b.** among all nations.................. 8148
Job 17:6 made me also a **b.** of the people;........ 4914
Job 30:9 their song, yea, I am their **b.**............ 4405
Ps 44:14 us a **b.** among the heathen,................ 4912

C.

CAB
2Ki 6:25 fourth part of a **c.** of dove's dung....... 6894

CABBON (cab'-bon)
Jos 15:40 **C.**, and Lahmam, and Kithlish,............ 3522

CABINS
Jer 37:16 into the **c.**, and Jeremiah.................. 2588

CABUL (ca'-bul)
Jos 19:27 goeth out to **C.** on the left hand,......... 3521
1Ki 9:13 he called them the land of **C.**.............. 3521

CAESAR (se'-zur) See also CAESAR'S.
Mt 22:17 to give tribute unto **C.**, or not?........... *2541*
Mt 22:21 **unto C. the things which are**......... *2541*
Mk 12:14 to give tribute to **C.**, or not?............. *2541*
Mk 12:17 **C. the things that are Caesar's,**..... *2541*
Lu 2:1 a decree from **C.** Augustus,............... *2541*
Lu 3:1 the reign of Tiberius **C.**, Pontius......... *2541*
Lu 20:22 to give tribute unto **C.**, or no?............ *2541*
Lu 20:25 **C. the things which be Caesar's,**... *2541*
Lu 23:2 forbidding to give tribute to **C.**,.......... *2541*
Joh 19:12 himself a king speaketh against **C.**...... *2541*
Joh 19:15 answered, We have no king but **C.**..... *2541*
Ac 11:28 pass in the days of Claudius **C.**.......... *2541*
Ac 17:7 contrary to the decrees of **C.**,............ *2541*
Ac 25:8 nor yet against **C.**, have I offended...... *2541*
Ac 25:11 unto them. I appeal unto **C.**............... *2541*
Ac 25:12 Hast thou appealed unto **C.**?.............. *2541*
Ac 25:12 unto **C.** shalt thou go.......................... *2541*
Ac 25:21 be kept till I might send him to **C.**..... *2541*
Ac 26:32 if he had not appealed unto **C.**.......... *2541*
Ac 27:24 thou must be brought before **C.**:......... *2541*
Ac 28:19 constrained to appeal unto **C.**;........... *2541*

CAESAR Augustus See CAESAR and AUGUSTUS.

CAESAREA (ses-a-re'-ah)
Mt 16:13 into the coasts of **C.** Philippi,............. *2542*
Mk 8:27 into the towns of **C.** Philippi:............... *2542*
Ac 8:40 all the cities, till he came to **C.**.......... *2542*
Ac 9:30 they brought him down to **C.**,............... *2542*
Ac 10:1 certain man in **C.** called Cornelius,...... *2542*
Ac 10:24 morrow after they entered into **C.**........ *2542*
Ac 11:11 I was, sent from **C.** unto me................ *2542*
Ac 12:19 went down from Judaea to **C.**,............. *2542*
Ac 18:22 he had landed at **C.**, and gone up,........ *2542*
Ac 21:8 came unto **C.**: and we entered.............. *2542*
Ac 21:16 of the disciples of **C.**, and brought........ *2542*
Ac 23:23 soldiers to go to **C.**,............................ *2542*
Ac 23:33 they came to **C.**, and delivered............. *2542*
Ac 25:1 ascended from **C.** to Jerusalem............. *2542*
Ac 25:4 that Paul should be kept at **C.**,............ *2542*
Ac 25:6 ten days, he went down into **C.**;........... *2542*
Ac 25:13 Bernice came into **C.** to salute.............. *2542*

CAESAREA-PHILIPPI See CAESAREA and PHILIPPI.

CAESAR'S (se'-zurs)
Mt 22:21 They say unto him, **C.**. Then............... *2541*
Mt 22:21 **Caesar the things which are C.;**..... *2541*
Mk 12:16 And they said unto him, **C.**................. *2541*
Mk 12:17 **to Caesar the things that are C.**..... *2541*
Lu 20:24 They answered and said, **C.**................ *2541*
Lu 20:25 **Caesar the things which be C.,**......... *2541*
Jo 19:12 thou art not **C.** friend: whosoever....... *2541*
Ac 25:10 I stand at **C.** judgment seat,............... *2541*
Php 4:22 they that are of **C.** household............... *2541*

CAGE
Jer 5:27 As a **c.** is full of birds, so are their..... 3619
Re 18:2 a **c.** of every unclean and hateful........ *5438*

CAIAPHAS (cah'-ya-fus)
Mt 26:3 high priest, who was called **C.**.......... *2533*
Mt 26:57 led him away to **C.** the high priest,..... *2533*
Lu 3:2 Annas and **C.** being the high............. *2533*
Joh 11:49 And one of them, named **C.**,............ *2533*
Joh 18:13 he was father in law to **C.**,............ *2533*
Joh 18:14 **C.** was he, which gave counsel to...... *2533*
Joh 18:24 Annas had sent him bound unto **C.**...... *2533*
Joh 18:28 Then led they Jesus from **C.** unto...... *2533*
Ac 4:6 Annas the high priest, and **C.**,........... *2533*

CAIN See also TUBAL-CAIN.
Ge 4:1 and she conceived, and bare **C.**,........ 7014
Ge 4:2 but **C.** was a tiller of the ground......... 7014
Ge 4:3 pass, that **C.** brought of the fruit........ 7014
Ge 4:5 unto **C.** and to his offering he had...... 7014
Ge 4:5 and **C.** was very wroth, and his......... 7014
Ge 4:6 And the Lord said unto **C.**, Why......... 7014
Ge 4:8 **C.** talked with Abel his brother:......... 7014
Ge 4:8 **C.** rose up against Abel his.............. 7014
Ge 4:9 And the Lord said unto **C.**, Where..... 7014
Ge 4:13 And **C.** said unto the Lord,............... 7014
Ge 4:15 Therefore whosoever slayeth **C.**,........ 7014
Ge 4:15 And the Lord set a mark upon **C.**,..... 7014
Ge 4:16 **C.** went out from the presence of...... 7014
Ge 4:17 And **C.** knew his wife; and she.......... 7014
Ge 4:24 If **C.** shall be avenged seven fold........ 7014
Ge 4:25 instead of Abel, whom **C.** slew.......... 7014
Jos 15:57 **C.**, Gibeah, and Timnah; ten cities..... 7014
Heb 11:4 a more excellent sacrifice than **C.**,...... *2535*
1Jo 3:12 Not as **C.**, who was of that wicked..... *2535*
Jude 11 gone in the way of **C.**, and ran......... *2535*

CAINAN (ca'-nun) See also KENAN.
Ge 5:9 lived ninety years, and begat **C.**:........ 7018
Ge 5:10 Enos lived after he begat **C.**.............. 7018
Ge 5:12 **C.** lived seventy years, and.............. 7018
Ge 5:13 **C.** lived after he begat..................... 7018
Ge 5:14 the days of **C.** were nine hundred...... 7018
Lu 3:36,37 Which was the son of **C.**,................ *2536*

CAKE See also CAKES.
Ex 29:23 and one **c.** of oiled bread, and one...... 2471
Le 8:26 he took one unleavened **c.**,.............. 2471
Le 8:26 and a **c.** of oiled bread,...................... 2471
Le 24:5 two tenth deals shall be in one **c.**....... 2471
Nu 6:19 unleavened **c.** out of the basket,........ 2471
Nu 15:20 Ye shall offer up a **c.** of the first........ 2471
Jg 7:13 a **c.** of barley bread tumbled into........ 6742
1Sa 30:12 gave him a piece of a **c.** of figs,........ 1690
2Sa 6:19 to every one a **c.** of bread, and a........ 2471
1Ki 17:12 I have not a **c.**, but an handful of....... 4580
1Ki 17:13 make me thereof a little **c.** first,........ 5692
1Ki 19:6 there was a **c.** baken on the coals,..... 5692
Hos 7:8 Ephraim is a **c.** not turned................ 5692

CAKES
Ge 18:6 it, and make **c.** upon the hearth......... 5692
Ex 12:39 baked unleavened **c.** of the dough....... 5692
Ex 29:2 bread, and **c.** unleavened.................. 2471
Le 2:4 unleavened **c.** of fine flour................. 2471
Le 7:12 unleavened **c.** mingled with oil,.......... 2471
Le 7:12 with oil, and **c.** mingled with oil,........ 2471
Le 7:13 Besides the **c.**, he shall offer for........ 2471
Le 24:5 bake twelve **c.** thereof: two tenth........ 2471
Nu 6:15 **c.** of fine flour mingled with oil,......... 2471
Nu 11:8 baked it in pans, and make **c.** of it:..... 5692
Jos 5:11 unleavened **c.**, and parched corn........ 4682
Jg 6:19 unleavened **c.** of an ephah of flour:..... 4682
Jg 6:20, 21 flesh and the unleavened **c.**........... 4682
1Sa 25:18 two hundred **c.** of figs, and laid.......... 1690
2Sa 13:6 make me a couple of **c.** in my sight,... 3834
2Sa 13:8 made **c.** in his sight,........................ 3823
2Sa 13:8 and did bake the **c.**............................ 3834
2Sa 13:10 and Tamar took the **c.** which she had.. 3834
1Ch 12:40 meal, **c.** of figs, and bunches of........ 1690
1Ch 23:29 for the unleavened **c.**, and................ 7550
Jer 7:18 make **c.** to the queen of heaven,........ 3561
Jer 44:19 we make her **c.** to worship her,......... 3561
Eze 4:12 And thou shalt eat it as barley **c.**,...... 5692

CALAH (ca'-lah)
Ge 10:11 and the city Rehoboth, and **C.**,.......... 3625
Ge 10:12 Resen between Nineveh and **C.**:........ 3625

CALAMITIES
Ps 57:1 refuge, until these **c.** be overpast....... 1942
Ps 141:5 prayer also shall be in their **c.**......... 7451
Pr 17:5 he that is glad at **c.** shall not be......... 343

CALAMITY See also CALAMITIES.
De 32:35 the day of their **c.** is at hand, and........ 343
2Sa 22:19 prevented me in the day of my **c.**:....... 343
Job 6:2 and my **c.** laid in the balances............ 1942
Job 30:13 they set forward my **c.**, they have...... 1942
Ps 18:18 prevented me in the day of my **c.**:....... 343
Pr 1:26 I also will laugh at your **c.**; I will......... 343
Pr 6:15 shall his **c.** come suddenly;.................. 343
Pr 19:13 foolish son is the **c.** of his father:....... 1942
Pr 24:22 For their **c.** shall rise suddenly;........... 343
Pr 27:10 brother's house in the day of thy **c.**:..... 343
Jer 18:17 the face, in the day of their **c.**.............. 343
Jer 46:21 the day of their **c.** was come upon....... 343
Jer 48:16 The **c.** of Moab is near to come,......... 343
Jer 49:8 will bring the **c.** of Esau upon him,...... 343
Jer 49:32 bring their **c.** from all sides thereof,..... 343
Eze 35:5 the sword in the time of their **c.**,........ 343
Ob 13 in the day of their **c.**; yea, thou............ 343
Ob 13 their affliction in the day of their **c.**,..... 343
Ob 13 substance in the day of their **c.**;.......... 343

CALAMUS (cal'-a-mus)
Ex 30:23 of sweet **c.** two hundred and fifth....... 7070
Ca 4:14 and saffron; **c.** and cinnamon,............ 7070
Eze 27:19 cassia, and **c.**, were in thy market...... 7070

CALCOL (cal'-col) See also CHALCOL.
1Ch 2:6 and Heman, and **C.** and Dara:........... 3633

CALDRON See also CALDRONS.
1Sa 2:14 the pan, or kettle, or **c.**, or pot;........ 7037
Job 41:20 as out of a seething pot or **c.**............. 100
Eze 11:3 city is the **c.**, and we be the flesh...... 5518
Eze 11:7 this city is the **c.**: but I will bring....... 5518
Eze 11:11 This city shall not be your **c.**,............ 5518
Mic 3:3 the pot, and as flesh within the **c.**...... 7037

CALDRONS
2Ch 35:13 sod they in pots, and in **c.**, and in...... 1731
Jer 52:18 The **c.** also, and the shovels,............ 5518
Jer 52:19 the **c.**, and the candlesticks,............. 5518

CALEB (ca'-leb) See also CALEB'S; CALEB-EPHRATAH; CHELLUBAL.
Nu 13:6 Judah, **C.** the son of Jephunneh.......... 3612
Nu 13:30 **C.** stilled the people before Moses,.... 3612
Nu 14:6 Joshua the son of Nun, and **C.** the...... 3612
Nu 14:24 But my servant **C.**, because he had.... 3612
Nu 14:30 to make you dwell therein, save **C.**.... 3612
Nu 14:38 Joshua, the son of Nun, and **C.** the..... 3612
Nu 26:65 was not left a man of them, save **C.**.... 3612
Nu 32:12 Save **C.** the son of Jephunneh............ 3612
Nu 34:19 Judah, **C.** the son of Jephunneh.......... 3612
De 1:36 Save **C.** the son of Jephunneh;........... 3612
Jos 14:6 **C.** the son of Jephunneh the............. 3612
Jos 14:13 blessed him, and gave unto **C.**........... 3612
Jos 14:14 became the inheritance of **C.**............. 3612
Jos 15:13 unto **C.** the son of Jephunneh he........ 3612
Jos 15:14 **C.** drove thence the three sons of...... 3612
Jos 15:16 And **C.** said, He that smiteth............ 3612
Jos 15:17 Kenaz, the brother of **C.**, took:......... 3612
Jos 15:18 **C.** said unto her, What wouldest........ 3612
Jos 21:12 villages thereof, gave they to **C.**........ 3612
Jg 1:12 And **C.** said, He that smiteth.............. 3612
Jg 1:14 **C.** said unto her, What wilt thou?......... 3612
Jg 1:15 And **C.** gave her the upper springs..... 3612
Jg 1:20 they gave Hebron unto **C.**, as............ 3612
1Sa 25:3 and he was of the house of **C.**............ 3612
1Sa 30:14 Judah, and upon the south of **C.**;........ 3612
1Ch 2:18 And **C.** the son of Hezron begat.......... 3612
1Ch 2:19 Azubah was dead, **C.** took unto......... 3612
1Ch 2:42 Now the sons of **C.** the brother of..... 3612
1Ch 2:49 and the daughter of **C.** was Achsa...... 3612
1Ch 2:50 These were the sons of **C.** the son.... 3612
1Ch 4:15 sons of **C.** the sons of Jephunneh;...... 3612
1Ch 6:56 villages thereof, they gave to **C.**........ 3612

CALEB-EPHRATAH (ca''-leb-ef'-ra-tah)
1Ch 2:24 after that Hezron was dead in **C.**,...... 3613

CALEB'S (ca'-lebs)
Jg 1:13 son of Kenaz, **C.** younger brother,...... 3612
Jg 3:9 son of Kenaz, **C.** younger brother...... 3612
1Ch 2:46 Ephah, **C.** concubine, bare Haran,...... 3612
1Ch 2:48 Maachah, **C.** concubine, bare............ 3612

CALF See also CALF'S; CALVES.
Ge 18:7 fetcht a **c.** tender and good,....... 1121,1241
Ge 18:8 the **c.** which he had dressed,........ 1121,1241
Ex 32:4 after he had made it a molten **c.**:....... 5695
Ex 32:8 they have made them a molten **c.**,....... 5695
Ex 32:19 he saw the **c.**, and the dancing:......... 5695
Ex 32:20 took the **c.** which they had made,....... 5695
Ex 32:24 fire, and there came out this **c.**.......... 5695
Ex 32:35 made the **c.**, which Aaron made......... 5695
Le 9:2 a young **c.** for a sin offering,............. 5695
Le 9:3 a **c.** and a lamb, both of the first........ 5695
Le 9:8 slew the **c.** of the sin offering,............ 5695
De 9:16 and had made you a molten **c.**:............ 5695
De 9:21 the **c.** which ye had made, and.......... 5695
1Sa 28:24 woman had a fat **c.** in the house;....... 5695
Ne 9:18 They had made them a molten **c.**,...... 5695
Job 21:10 cow calveth, and casteth not her **c.**.........
Ps 29:6 maketh them also to skip like a **c.**;..... 5695
Ps 106:19 They made a **c.** in Horeb, and.......... 5695
Isa 11:6 and the **c.** and the young lion and........ 5695
Isa 27:10 wilderness: there shall the **c.** feed,..... 5695
Jer 34:18 when they cut the **c.** in twain, and..... 5695
Jer 34:19 passed between the parts of the **c.**;.... 5695
Ho 8:5 Thy **c.**, O Samaria, hath cast thee...... 5695
Ho 8:6 the **c.** of Samaria shall be broken........ 5695
Lu 15:23 **bring hither the fatted c., and kill** *3448*
Lu 15:27 **thy father hath killed the fatted c.,** *3448*
Lu 15:30 **hast killed for him the fatted c.**.... *3448*
Ac 7:41 they made a **c.** in those days and....... *3447*
Re 4:7 the second beast like a **c.**, and the...... *3448*

CALF'S
Eze 1:7 feet was like the sole of a **c.** foot:...... 5695

CALKERS
Eze 27:9 thereof were in thee thy **c.**.......... 2388,919
Eze 27:27 mariners, and thy pilots, thy **c.**,... 2388,919

CALL See also CALLED; CALLEST; CALLETH; CALLING; RECALL.
Ge 2:19 to see what he would **c.** them:.......... 7121
Ge 4:26 began men to **c.** upon the name......... 7121
Ge 16:11 shalt **c.** his name Ishmael;................. 7121
Ge 17:15 thou shalt not **c.** her name Sarai,....... 7121
Ge 17:19 and thou shalt **c.** his name Isaac:........ 7121
Ge 24:57 We will **c.** the damsel, and enquire...... 7121
Ge 30:13 the daughters will **c.** me blessed:......... 833
Ge 46:33 when Pharaoh shall **c.** you, and.......... 7121
Ex 2:7 Shall I go and **c.** to thee a nurse........ 7121
Ex 2:20 **c.** him, that he may eat bread........... 7121
Ex 34:15 **c.** thee, and thou eat of his sacrifice; .. 7121
Nu 16:12 Moses sent to **c.** Dathan and............ 7121
Nu 22:5 of his people, to **c.** him, saying,......... 7121
Nu 22:20 If the men come to **c.** thee, rise......... 7121
Nu 22:37 earnestly send unto thee to **c.** thee?... 7121
De 2:11 but the Moabites **c.** them Emims......... 7121
De 2:20 Ammonites **c.** them Zamzummims;...... 7121
De 3:9 Hermon the Sidonians **c.** Sirion;......... 7121
De 3:9 and the Amorites **c.** it Shenir;).......... 7121
De 4:7 things that we **c.** upon him for?.......... 7121
De 4:26 I **c.** heaven and earth to witness........ 5749
De 25:8 the elders of his city shall **c.** him,....... 7121
De 30:1 thou shalt **c.** them to mind among...... 7725
De 30:19 I **c.** heaven and earth to record.......... 5749
De 31:14 **c.** Joshua, and present yourselves....... 7121
De 31:28 and **c.** heaven and earth to record....... 5749
De 33:19 **c.** the people unto the mountain;........ 7121
Jg 12:1 didst not **c.** us to go with thee?.......... 7121
Jg 16:25 **C.** for Samson, that he may make...... 7121
Jg 21:13 and to **c.** peaceably unto them........... 7121
Ru 1:20 **C.** me not Naomi, **c.** me Mara: for...... 7121
Ru 1:21 why then **c.** ye me Naomi, seeing...... 7121
1Sa 3:6 Here am I; for thou didst **c.** me.......... 7121
1Sa 3:8 for thou didst **c.** me. And Eli............. 7121
1Sa 3:9 if he **c.** thee, that thou shalt say,........ 7121
1Sa 12:17 I will **c.** unto the Lord, and he.......... 7121
1Sa 16:3 And **c.** Jesse to the sacrifice, and I...... 7121
1Sa 22:11 Then the king sent to **c.** Ahimelech.... 7121
2Sa 17:5 **C.** now Hushai the Archite also,......... 7121
2Sa 22:4 I will **c.** on the Lord, who is worthy... 7121
1Ki 1:28 **C.** me Bath-sheba. And she came......... 7121
1Ki 1:32 **C.** me Zadok the priest, and Nathan... 7121
1Ki 8:52 in all that they **c.** for unto thee........... 7121
1Ki 17:18 to **c.** my sin to remembrance, and....... 2142
1Ki 18:24 **c.** ye on the name of your gods,......... 7121
1Ki 18:24 I will **c.** on the name of the Lord:....... 7121
1Ki 18:25 and **c.** on the name of your gods,........ 7121
1Ki 22:13 messenger that was gone to **c.**............ 7121
2Ki 4:12 **C.** this Shunammite. And when he...... 7121

2Ki 4:15 And he said, C. her. And when he 7121
2Ki 4:36 and said, C. this Shunammite. 7121
2Ki 5:11 c. on the name of the Lord his 7121
2Ki 10:19 c. unto me all the prophets of Baal, ... 7121
1Ch 16:8 c. upon his name, make known his 7121
2Ch 18:12 messenger that went to c. Micaiah 7121
Job 5:1 C. now, if there be any that will 7121
Job 13:22 Then c. thou, and I will answer: 7121
Job 14:15 Thou shalt c., and I will answer 7121
Job 27:10 will he always c. upon God? 7121
Ps 4:1 Hear me when I c., O God of my 7121
Ps 4:3 the Lord will hear when I c. unto....... 7121
Ps 14:4 bread, and c. not upon the Lord. 7121
Ps 18:3 I will c. upon the Lord, who is 7121
Ps 20:9 let the king hear us when we c.......... 7121
Ps 49:11 c. their lands after their own names.... 7121
Ps 50:4 shall c. to the heavens from above, ... 7121
Ps 50:15 c. upon me in the day of trouble: 7121
Ps 55:16 I will c. upon God; and the Lord 7121
Ps 72:17 all nations shall c. him blessed............. 833
Ps 77:6 I c. to remembrance my song in 2142
Ps 80:18 and we will c. upon thy name. 7121
Ps 86:5 unto all them that c. upon thee. 7121
Ps 86:7 In the day of my trouble I will c. 7121
Ps 91:15 He shall c. upon me, and I will 7121
Ps 99:6 among them that c. upon his name; 7121
Ps 102:2 day when I c. answer me speedily...... 7121
Ps 105:1 c. upon his name: make known his 7121
Ps 116:2 therefore will I c. upon him as long 7121
Ps 116:13 and c. upon the name of the Lord. 7121
Ps 116:17 will c. upon the name of the Lord. 7121
Ps 145:18 unto all them that c. upon him, ... 7121
Ps 145:18 to all that c. upon him.......................... 7121
Pr 1:28 Then shall they c. upon me, but I 7121
Pr 7:4 c. understanding thy kinswoman:........ 7121
Pr 8:4 Unto thee, O men, I c.; and my 7121
Pr 9:15 To c. passengers who go right on 7121
Pr 31:28 arise up, and c. her blessed;............... 833
Isa 5:20 that c. evil good, and good evil; 559
Isa 7:14 and shall c. his name Immanuel.......... 7121
Isa 8:3 C. his name Maher-shalal-hash-baz. 7121
Isa 12:4 Praise the Lord, c. upon his name, ... 7121
Isa 22:12 Lord God of hosts c. to weeping, ... 7121
Isa 22:20 that I will c. my servant Eliakim 7121
Isa 31:2 will not c. back his words: but........... 5493
Isa 34:12 They shall c. the nobles thereof......... 7121
Isa 41:25 shall he c. upon my name: and 7121
Isa 44:5 c. himself by the name of Jacob; 7121
Isa 44:7 who, as I, shall c., and shall.............. 7121
Isa 45:3 the Lord, which c. thee by thy name, ..7121
Isa 48:2 they c. themselves of the holy city, ... 7121
Isa 48:13 when I c. unto them, they stand 7121
Isa 55:5 c. a nation that thou knowest not, ... 7121
Isa 55:6 c. ye upon him while he is near: 7121
Isa 58:5 wilt thou c. this a fast, and an 7121
Isa 58:9 thou c., and the Lord shall answer; 7121
Isa 58:13 and c. the sabbath a delight, the 7121
Isa 60:14 shall c. thee, The city of the Lord,..... 7121
Isa 60:18 thou shalt c. thy walls Salvation, ... 7121
Isa 61:6 c. you the Ministers of our God:........ 7121
Isa 62:12 they shall c. them, The holy people, ... 7121
Isa 65:15 c. his servants by another name:........ 7121
Isa 65:24 and before they c., I will answer;....... 7121
Jer 1:15 I will c. all the families of the 7121
Jer 3:17 c. Jerusalem the throne of the Lord;... 7121
Jer 3:19 Thou shalt c. me, My father: and....... 7121
Jer 6:30 Reprobate silver shall men c. 7121
Jer 7:27 thou shalt also c. unto them; but........ 7121
Jer 9:17 and c. for the mourning women, ... 7121
Jer 10:25 families that c. not on thy name: 7121
Jer 25:29 I will call for a sword upon all the....... 7121
Jer 29:12 Then shall ye c. upon me, and ye 7121
Jer 33:3 C. unto me, and I will answer 7121
Jer 50:29 C. together the archers against.......... 8085
Jer 51:27 c. together against her the............... 8085
La 2:15 city that men c. The perfection of........ 559
Eze 21:23 c. to remembrance the iniquity, ... 2142
Eze 36:29 and I will c. for the corn, and will 7121
Eze 38:21 And I will c. for a sword against 7121
Eze 39:11 shall c. it The valley of Hamon-gog..... 7121
Da 2:2 commanded to c. the magicians,.......... 7121
Ho 1:4 C. his name Jezreel; for yet a............ 7121
Ho 1:6 C. her name Lo-ruhamah: for I.......... 7121
Ho 1:9 C. his name Lo-ammi: for ye are 7121
Ho 2:16 thou shalt c. me Ishi;.......................... 7121
Ho 2:16 and shalt c. me no more Baali. 7121
Ho 7:11 they c. to Egypt, they go to Assyria... 7121
Joe 1:14 c. a solemn assembly, gather the 7121
Joe 2:15 a fast, c. a solemn assembly: 7121
Joe 2:32 whosoever shall c. on the name of...... 7121
Joe 2:32 remnant whom the Lord shall c.......... 7121
Am 5:16 and they shall c. the husbandman 7121
Jon 1:6 arise, c. upon thy God, if so be 7121
Zep 3:9 all c. upon the name of the Lord, ... 7121
Zec 3:10 ye c. every man his neighbour........... 7121
Zec 13:9 they shall c. on my name, and I.......... 7121
Mal 1:4 c. them, The border of wickedness,.... 7121
Mal 3:12 all nations shall c. you blessed:............ 833
Mal 3:15 now we c. the proud happy; yea,.......... 833
Mt 1:21 thou shalt c. his name Jesus:............. *2564*
Mt 1:23 shall call his name Emmanuel,............ *2564*
Mt 9:13 **I am not come to c. the righteous,**.*2564*
Mt 10:25 **shall they c. them of his household**.....
Mt 20:8 **C. the labourers, and give them**.... *2564*
Mt 22:3 **to c. them that were bidden**........... *2564*
Mt 22:43 **doth David in spirit c. him Lord,**.. *2564*
Mt 22:45 **If David then c. him Lord, how is.** *2564*
Mt 23:9 **And c. no man your father upon**... *2564*
Mk 2:17 **came not to c. the righteous, but**.. *2564*
Mk 10:49 they c. the blind man, saying unto...... *5455*
Mk 15:12 whom ye c. the King of the Jews?...... *3004*
Mk 15:16 and they c. together the whole *4779*
Lu 1:13 thou shalt c. his name John. *2564*
Lu 1:31 son, and shalt c. his name Jesus. *2564*
Lu 1:48 generations shall c. me blessed. *3106*
Lu 5:32 **I came not to c. the righteous,**..... *2564*
Lu 6:46 **And why c. ye me, Lord, Lord,**..... *2564*
Lu 14:12 **c. not thy friends, nor thy**............ *5455*
Lu 14:13 **when thou makest a feast, c. the**.. *2564*
Joh 4:16 **Go, c. thy husband, and come**....... *5455*
Joh 13:13 **Ye c. me Master and Lord: and ye**.*5455*
Joh 15:15 **Henceforth I c. you not servants;**.. *3004*
Ac 2:21 whosoever shall c. on the name of....... *1941*
Ac 2:39 many as the Lord our God shall c.. .... *4341*
Ac 9:14 to bind all that c. on thy name........... *1941*
Ac 10:5 to Joppa, and c. for one Simon *3343*
Ac 10:15 that c. not thou common. *2840*
Ac 10:28 I should not c. any man common........ *3004*
Ac 10:32 c. hither Simon, whose surname *3333*
Ac 11:9 that c. not thou common. *2840*
Ac 11:13 and c. for Simon, whose surname........ *3343*
Ac 19:13 c. over them which had evil *3687*
Ac 24:14 c. heresy, so worship I the God *3004*
Ac 24:25 season, I will c. for thee. *3333*
Ro 9:25 I will c. them my people which........... *2564*
Ro 10:12 rich unto all that c. upon him............ *1941*
Ro 10:13 whosoever shall c. upon the name *1941*
Ro 10:14 How then shall they c. on him in........ *1941*
1Co 1:2 in every place c. upon the name *1941*
2Co 1:23 I c. God for a record upon my........... *1941*
2Ti 1:5 When I c. to remembrance the........... *2983*
2Ti 2:22 with them that c. on the Lord *1941*
He 2:11 not ashamed to c. them brethren, ... *2564*
He 10:32 c. to remembrance the former days,...... *363*
Jas 5:14 c. for the elders of the church;........... *4341*
1Pe 1:17 And if ye c. on the Father, who......... *1941*

CALLED See also CALLEDST.

Ge *general* *title* First Book Of Moses, C. Genesis.......
Ge 1:5 And God c. the light Day,................ 7121
Ge 1:5 and the darkness he c. Night............ 7121
Ge 1:8 God c. the firmament Heaven............ 7121
Ge 1:10 and God c. the dry land Earth; 7121
Ge 1:10 together of the waters c. he Seas: 7121
Ge 2:19 Adam c. every living creature,........... 7121
Ge 2:23 she shall be c. Woman, because......... 7121
Ge 3:9 And the Lord God c. unto Adam, ... 7121
Ge 3:20 And Adam c. his wife's name Eve; 7121
Ge 4:17 c. the name of the city, after the 7121
Ge 4:25 and c. his name Seth: 7121
Ge 4:26 and he c. his name Enos: 7121
Ge 5:2 and c. their name Adam, ... 7121
Ge 5:3 his image; and c. his name Seth:........ 7121
Ge 5:29 And he c. his name Noah, ... 7121
Ge 11:9 therefore is the name of it c. Babel; ... 7121
Ge 12:8 and c. upon the name of the Lord. 7121
Ge 12:18 And Pharoah c. Abram, and said, ... 7121
Ge 13:4 Abram c. on the name of the Lord. 7121
Ge 16:13 And she c. the name of the Lord 7121
Ge 16:14 the well was c. Beer-lahai-roi; 7121
Ge 16:15 Abram c. his son's name, which......... 7121
Ge 17:5 thy name any more be c. Abram, ... 7121
Ge 19:5 And they c. unto Lot, and said 7121
Ge 19:22 the name of the city was c. Zoar........ 7121
Ge 19:37 and c. his name Moab:..................... 7121
Ge 19:38 and c. his name Ben-ammi:................. 7121
Ge 20:8 and c. all his servants, and told all...... 7121
Ge 20:9 Then Abimelech c. Abraham, and 7121
Ge 21:3 And Abraham c. the name of his 7121
Ge 21:12 in Isaac shall thy seed be c.. 7121
Ge 21:17 the angel of God c. to Hagar............ 7121
Ge 21:31 he c. that place Beer-sheba;............... 7121
Ge 21:33 c. there on the name of the Lord, ... 7121
Ge 22:11 angel of the Lord c. unto him out....... 7121
Ge 22:14 Abraham c. the name of that place 7121
Ge 22:15 angel of the Lord c. unto Abraham 7121
Ge 24:58 And they c. Rebekah, and said 7121
Ge 25:25 and they c. his name Esau. 7121
Ge 25:26 and his name was c. Jacob: 7121
Ge 25:30 therefore was his name c. Edom. 7121
Ge 26:9 And Abimelech c. Isaac, and said, ... 7121
Ge 26:18 he c. their names after the names 7121
Ge 26:18 by which his father had c. them. 7121
Ge 26:20 he c. the name of the well Esek; 7121
Ge 26:21 and he c. the name of it Sitnah. 7121
Ge 26:22 and he c. the name of it Rehoboth;..... 7121
Ge 26:25 and c. upon the name of the Lord, ... 7121
Ge 26:33 and he c. it Shebah: 7121
Ge 27:1 he c. Esau his eldest son, and........... 7121
Ge 27:42 she sent and c. Jacob........................ 7121
Ge 28:1 Isaac c. Jacob, and blessed him......... 7121
Ge 28:19 c. the name of that place Beth-el: 7121
Ge 28:19 the name of that city was c. Luz..............
Ge 29:32 and she c. his name Reuben:............. 7121
Ge 29:33 and she c. his name Simeon. 7121
Ge 29:34 therefore was his name c. Levi........... 7121
Ge 29:35 she c. his name Judah; 7121
Ge 30:6 therefore c. she his name Dan........... 7121
Ge 30:8 and she c. his name Naphtali. 7121
Ge 30:11 and she c. his name Gad. 7121
Ge 30:13 and she c. his name Asher................ 7121
Ge 30:18 and she c. his name Issachar. 7121
Ge 30:20 and she c. his name Zebulun. 7121
Ge 30:21 and c. her name Dinah..................... 7121
Ge 30:24 And she c. his name Joseph; 7121
Ge 31:4 Jacob sent and c. Rachel and Leah...... 7121
Ge 31:47 And Laban c. it Jegar-sahadutha: 7121
Ge 31:47 Jacob c. it Galeed............................ 7121
Ge 31:48 was the name of it c. Galeed;............ 7121
Ge 31:54 and c. his brethren to eat bread:........ 7121
Ge 32:2 and he c. the name of that place 7121
Ge 32:28 name shall be c. no more Jacob,.......... 559
Ge 32:30 c. the name of the place Peniel:......... 7121
Ge 33:17 name of the place is c. Succoth.......... 7121
Ge 33:20 and c. it El-elohe-Israel. 7121
Ge 35:7 and c. the place El-Beth-el:............... 7121
Ge 35:8 name of it was c. Allon-bachuth. 7121
Ge 35:10 shall not be c. any more Jacob,.......... 7121
Ge 35:10 and he c. his name Israel................. 7121
Ge 35:15 And Jacob c. the name of the place..... 7121
Ge 35:18 that she c. his name Ben-oni: 7121
Ge 35:18 his father c. him Benjamin. 7121
Ge 38:3 and he c. his name Er. 7121
Ge 38:4 and she c. his name Onan................. 7121
Ge 38:5 and c. his name Shelah:.................... 7121
Ge 38:29 therefore his name was c. Pharez........ 7121
Ge 38:30 and his name was c. Zarah................ 7121
Ge 39:14 she c. unto the men of her house,...... 7121
Ge 41:8 and c. for all the magicians................ 7121
Ge 41:14 Pharoah sent and c. Joseph, ... 7121
Ge 41:45 And Pharoah c. Joseph's name........... 7121
Ge 41:51 c. the name of the firstborn 7121
Ge 41:52 of the second c. he Ephraim: 7121
Ge 47:29 and he c. his son Joseph,................... 7121
Ge 48:6 c. after the name of their brethren 7121
Ge 49:1 And Jacob c. unto his sons,............... 7121
Ge 50:11 name of it was c. Abel-mizraim,......... 7121
Ex *general* *title* Second Book Of Moses, C. Exodus ....
Ex 1:18 king of Egypt c. for the midwives,....... 7121
Ex 2:8 went and c. the child's mother........... 7121
Ex 2:10 And she c. his name Moses: 7121
Ex 2:22 and he c. his name Gershom: 7121
Ex 3:4 God c. unto him out of the midst 7121
Ex 7:11 Pharoah also c. the wise men............ 7121
Ex 8:8 Pharoah c. for Moses and Aaron, ... 7121
Ex 8:25 c. for Moses and for Aaron,............... 7121
Ex 9:27 Pharoah sent, and c. for Moses 7121
Ex 10:16 Pharoah c. for Moses and Aaron 7121
Ex 10:24 And Pharoah c. unto Moses, ... 7121
Ex 12:21 Then Moses c. for all the elders 7121
Ex 12:31 And he c. for Moses and Aaron 7121

Book	Ref	Context	No.
Ex	15:23	the name of it was **c.** Marah.	7121
Ex	16:31	**c.** the name thereof Manna:	7121
Ex	17:7	**c.** the name of the place Massah,	7121
Ex	17:15	**c.** the name of it Jehovah-nissi:	7121
Ex	19:3	**c.** unto him out of the mountain,	7121
Ex	19:7	Moses came and **c.** for the elders	7121
Ex	19:20	and the Lord **c.** Moses up	7121
Ex	24:16	the seventh day he **c.** unto Moses	7121
Ex	31:2	I have **c.** by name Bazaleel	7121
Ex	33:7	and **c.** it the Tabernacle of the	7121
Ex	34:31	Moses **c.** unto them; and Aaron	7121
Ex	35:30	the Lord hath **c.** by name Bezaleel	7121
Ex	36:2	**c.** Bezaleel and Aholiab,	7121
Le	*general*	*title* Third Book Of Moses, **C.** Leviticus	
Le	1:1	And the Lord **c.** unto Moses,	7121
Le	9:1	Moses **c.** Aaron and his sons,	7121
Le	10:4	Moses **c.** Mishael and Elzaphan,	7121
Nu	*general*	*title* Book Of Moses, **C.** Numbers	
Nu	11:3	**c.** the name of the place Taberah:	7121
Nu	11:34	And he **c.** the name of that place	7121
Nu	12:5	and **c.** Aaron and Miriam:	7121
Nu	13:16	And Moses **c.** Oshea the son of Nun	7121
Nu	13:24	The place was **c.** the brook Eshcol,	7121
Nu	21:3	**c.** the name of the place Hormah.	7121
Nu	24:10	I **c.** thee to curse mine enemies,	7121
Nu	25:2	**c.** the people unto the sacrifices	7121
Nu	32:41	and **c.** them Havoth-jair.	7121
Nu	32:42	**c.** it Nobah, after his own name.	7121
De	*general*	*title* Book Of Moses, **C.** Deuteronomy	
De	3:13	which was **c.** the land of giants.	7121
De	3:14	and **c.** them after his own name,	7121
De	5:1	**c.** all Israel, and said unto them,	7121
De	15:2	because it is **c.** the Lord's release.	7121
De	25:10	And his name shall be **c.** in Israel,	7121
De	28:10	art **c.** by the name of the Lord;	7121
De	29:2	And Moses **c.** unto all Israel,	7121
De	31:7	And Moses **c.** unto Joshua,	7121
Jos	4:4	Then Joshua **c.** the twelve men,	7121
Jos	5:9	the name of the place is **c.** Gilgal	7121
Jos	6:6	the son of Nun **c.** the priests,	7121
Jos	7:26	place was **c.**, The valley of Achor,	7121
Jos	8:16	**c.** together to pursue after them:	2199
Jos	9:22	And Joshua **c.** for them,	7121
Jos	10:24	Joshua **c.** for all the men of Israel,	7121
Jos	19:47	**c.** Leshem, Dan, after the name	7121
Jos	22:1	Then Joshua **c.** the Reubenites,	7121
Jos	22:34	and the children of Gad **c.** the altar	7121
Jos	23:2	And Joshua **c.** for all Israel,	7121
Jos	24:1	and **c.** for the elders of Israel.	7121
Jos	24:9	sent and **c.** Balaam the son of Beor	7121
Jg	1:17	name of the city was **c.** Hormah.	7121
Jg	1:26	and **c.** the name thereof Luz:	7121
Jg	2:5	**c.** the name of that place Bochim:	7121
Jg	4:6	**c.** Barak the son of Abinoam	7121
Jg	4:10	Barak **c.** Zebulun and Naphtali	2199
Jg	6:24	and **c.** it Jehovah-shalom:	7121
Jg	6:32	on that day he **c.** him Jerubbaal,	7121
Jg	8:31	son, whose name he **c.** Abimelech.	7760
Jg	9:54	he **c.** hastily unto the young man	7121
Jg	10:4	cities, which are **c.** Havoth-jair	7121
Jg	12:2	I **c.** you, ye delivered me not	2199
Jg	13:24	and **c.** his name Samson:	7121
Jg	14:15	have ye **c.** us to take that we have?	7121
Jg	15:17	and **c.** that place Ramath-lehi.	7121
Jg	15:18	and **c.** on the Lord, and said,	7121
Jg	15:19	**c.** the name thereof En-hakkore,	7121
Jg	16:18	**c.** for the lords of the Philistines,	7121
Jg	16:19	and she **c.** for a man, and she	7121
Jg	16:25	**c.** for Samson out of the prison	7121
Jg	16:28	And Samson **c.** unto the Lord,	7121
Jg	18:12	they **c.** that place Mahaneh-dan	7121
Jg	18:29	they **c.** the name of the city Dan	7121
Ru	4:17	and they **c.** his name Obed:	7121
1Sa	*general*	*title* Otherwise **C.** The First Book	
1Sa	1:20	a son, and **c.** his name Samuel,	7121
1Sa	3:4	That the Lord **c.** Samuel:	7121
1Sa	3:5	he said, I **c.** not; lie down again.	7121
1Sa	3:6	the Lord **c.** yet again, Samuel.	7121
1Sa	3:6	I **c.** not, my son; lie down again.	7121
1Sa	3:8	Lord **c.** Samuel again the third	7121
1Sa	3:8	that the Lord had **c.** the child.	7121
1Sa	3:10	the Lord came, and stood, and **c.**	7121
1Sa	3:16	Then Eli **c.** Samuel, and said,	7121
1Sa	6:2	the Philistines **c.** for the priests	7121
1Sa	7:12	and **c.** the name of it Eben-ezer,	7121
1Sa	9:9	he that is now **c.** a Prophet was	
1Sa	9:9	beforetime **c.** a Seer	7121
1Sa	9:26	**c.** Saul to the top of the house,	7121
1Sa	10:17	And Samuel **c.** the people together	6817
1Sa	12:18	So Samuel **c.** unto the Lord;	7121
1Sa	13:4	were **c.** together after Saul,	6817
1Sa	16:5	and **c.** them to the sacrifice.	7121
1Sa	16:8	Then Jesse **c.** Abinadab, and	7121
1Sa	19:7	And Jonathan **c.** David, and	7121
1Sa	23:8	Saul **c.** all the people together	8085
1Sa	23:28	**c.** that place Sela-hammahlekoth.	
1Sa	28:15	I have **c.** thee, that thou mayest	7121
1Sa	29:6	Then Achish **c.** Davis, and said	7121
2Sa	*general*	*title* Otherwise **C.** The Second Book	
2Sa	1:7	he saw me, and **c.** unto me.	7121
2Sa	1:15	David **c.** one of the young men,	7121
2Sa	2:16	place was **c.** Helkath-hazzurim,	7121
2Sa	2:26	Then Abner **c.** to Joab, and said,	7121
2Sa	5:9	and **c.** it the city of David.	7121
2Sa	5:20	he **c.** the name of that place	7121
2Sa	6:2	whose name is **c.** by the name of	7121
2Sa	6:8	and he **c.** the name of the place	7121
2Sa	9:2	when they had **c.** him unto David,	7121
2Sa	9:9	king **c.** to Ziba, Saul's servant,	7121
2Sa	11:13	David had **c.** him, he did eat	7121
2Sa	12:24	and he **c.** his name Solomon:	7121
2Sa	12:25	and he **c.** his name Jedidiah,	7121
2Sa	12:28	and it be **c.** after my name.	7121
2Sa	13:17	Then he **c.** his servant that	7121
2Sa	14:33	he had **c.** for Absalom, he came	7121
2Sa	15:2	Absalom **c.** unto him, and said,	7121
2Sa	15:11	out of Jerusalem, that were **c.**;	7121
2Sa	18:18	**c.** the pillar after his own name:	7121
2Sa	18:18	and it is **c.** unto this day,	7121
2Sa	18:26	the watchman **c.** unto the porter,	7121
2Sa	18:28	Ahimaaz **c.**, and said unto the king,	7121
2Sa	21:2	And the king **c.** the Gibeonites,	7121
2Sa	22:7	In my distress I **c.** upon the Lord,	7121
1Ki	*general*	*title* Commonly **C.** The Third book	
1Ki	1:9	**c.** all his brethren the king's sons,	7121
1Ki	1:10	Solomon his brother, he **c.** not.	7121
1Ki	1:19	and hath **c.** all the sons of the king,	7121
1Ki	1:19	Solomon thy servant hath he not **c.**	7121
1Ki	1:25	and hath **c.** all the king's sons,	7121
1Ki	1:26	servant Solomon, hath he not **c.**	7121
1Ki	2:36	the king sent and **c.** for Shimei,	7121
1Ki	2:42	sent and **c.** for Shimei, and said	7121
1Ki	7:21	and **c.** the name thereof Jachin:	7121
1Ki	7:21	and **c.** the name thereof Boaz.	7121
1Ki	8:43	have builded, is **c.** by thy name.	7121
1Ki	9:13	And he **c.** them the land of Cabul	7121
1Ki	12:3	and **c.** him. And Jeroboam	7121
1Ki	12:20	and **c.** him unto the congregation,	7121
1Ki	16:24	and **c.** the name of the city	7121
1Ki	17:10	he **c.** to her, and said, Fetch me,	7121
1Ki	17:11	he **c.** to her, and said, Bring me,	7121
1Ki	18:3	And Ahab **c.** Obadiah, which was	7121
1Ki	18:26	and **c.** on the name of Baal	7121
1Ki	20:7	the king of Israel **c.** all the elders	7121
1Ki	22:9	the king of Israel **c.** an officer	7121
2Ki	*general*	*title* Commonly **C.** The Fourth Book	
2Ki	3:10	that the Lord hath **c.** these three	7121
2Ki	3:13	for the Lord hath **c.** these three	7121
2Ki	4:12	had **c.** her, she stood before him.	7121
2Ki	4:15	had **c.** her, she stood in the door.	7121
2Ki	4:22	And she **c.** unto her husband,	7121
2Ki	4:36	And he **c.** Gehazi, and said, Call	7121
2Ki	4:36	this Shunammite. So he **c.** her.	7121
2Ki	6:11	and he **c.** his servants, and said	7121
2Ki	7:10	they came and **c.** unto the porter	7121
2Ki	7:11	**c.** the porters; and they told	7121
2Ki	8:1	for the Lord hath **c.** for a famine;	7121
2Ki	9:1	the prophet **c.** one of the children	7121
2Ki	12:7	Jehoash **c.** for Jehoiada the priest,	7121
2Ki	14:7	and **c.** the name of it Joktheel.	7121
2Ki	18:4	and he **c.** it Nehushtan.	7121
2Ki	18:18	when they had **c.** to the king,	7121
1Ch	4:9	**c.** his name Jabez, saying,	7121
1Ch	4:10	And Jabez **c.** on the God of Israel,	7121
1Ch	6:65	which are **c.** by their names.	7121
1Ch	7:16	and she **c.** his name Peresh;	7121
1Ch	7:23	he **c.** his name Beriah, because	7121
1Ch	11:7	they **c.** it in the city of David.	7121
1Ch	13:6	cherubims, whose name is **c.** on it.	7121
1Ch	13:11	that place is **c.** Perez-uzza	7121
1Ch	14:11	they **c.** the name of that place	7121
1Ch	15:11	David **c.** for Zadok and Abiathar	7121
1Ch	21:26	and **c.** upon the Lord;	7121
1Ch	22:6	Then he **c.** for Solomon his son,	7121
2Ch	3:17	and **c.** the name of that on the	7121
2Ch	6:33	I have built is **c.** by thy name.	7121
2Ch	7:14	people, which are **c.** by thy name,	7121
2Ch	10:3	And they sent and **c.** him.	7121
2Ch	18:8	Israel **c.** for one of his officers,	7121
2Ch	20:26	the name of the same place was **c.**,	7121
2Ch	24:6	And the king **c.** for Jehoiada	7121
Ezr	2:61	and was **c.** after their name:	7121
Ne	5:12	Then I **c.** the priests, and took	7121
Ne	7:63	and was **c.** after their name.	7121
Es	2:14	that she were **c.** by name.	7121
Es	3:12	scribes **c.** on the thirteenth day	7121
Es	4:5	Then **c.** Esther for Hatach,	7121
Es	4:11	who is not **c.**, there is one law	7121
Es	4:11	I have not been **c.** to come in.	7121
Es	5:10	and **c.** for his friends, and	935
Es	8:9	king's scribes **c.** at that time	7121
Es	9:26	they **c.** these days Purim after	7121
Job	1:4	and **c.** for their three sisters to eat	7121
Job	9:16	I had **c.**, and he had answered me;	7121
Job	19:16	I **c.** my servant, and he gave me	7121
Job	42:14	**c.** the name of the first, Jemima;	7121
Ps	17:6	I have **c.** upon thee, for thou	7121
Ps	18:6	In my distress I **c.** upon the Lord,	7121
Ps	31:17	O Lord; for I have **c.** upon thee:	7121
Ps	50:1	Lord hath spoken and **c.** the earth	7121
Ps	53:4	they have not **c.** upon God	7121
Ps	79:6	kingdoms that have not **c.** upon	7121
Ps	88:9	Lord, I have **c.** daily upon thee,	7121
Ps	99:6	they **c.** upon the Lord, and he	7121
Ps	105:16	**c.** for a famine upon the land,	7121
Ps	116:4	**c.** I upon the name of the Lord;	7121
Ps	118:5	I **c.** upon the Lord in distress: the	7121
Pr	1:24	I have **c.**, and ye refused; I have	7121
Pr	16:21	wise in heart shall be **c.** prudent:	7121
Pr	24:8	be **c.** a mischievous person.	7121
Ca	5:6	**c.** him, but he gave me no answer.	7121
Isa	1:26	**c.**, The city of righteousness,	7121
Isa	4:1	only let us be **c.** by thy name,	7121
Isa	4:3	**c.** holy, even every one that is	559
Isa	9:6	his name shall be **c.** Wonderful,	7121
Isa	13:3	I have also **c.** my mighty ones	7121
Isa	19:18	be **c.**, The city of destruction,	559
Isa	31:4	multitude of shepherds is **c.** forth	7121
Isa	32:5	person shall be no more **c.** liberal,	7121
Isa	35:8	it shall be **c.** The way of holiness;	7121
Isa	41:2	man from the east, **c.** him	7121
Isa	41:9	**c.** thee from the chief men thereof,	7121
Isa	42:6	I the Lord have **c.** thee.	7121
Isa	43:1	I have **c.** thee by thy name;	7121
Isa	43:7	every one that is **c.** by my name:	7121
Isa	43:22	thou hast not **c.** upon me, O Jacob,	7121
Isa	45:4	I have even **c.** thee by thy name:	7121
Isa	47:1	thou shalt no more be **c.** tender	7121
Isa	47:5	be **c.**, The lady of kingdoms.	7121
Isa	48:1	which are **c.** by the name of Israel,	7121
Isa	48:8	and wast **c.** a transgressor	7121
Isa	48:12	O Jacob and Israel, my **c.**; I am he;	7121
Isa	48:15	yea, I have **c.** him: I have	7121
Isa	49:1	The Lord hath **c.** me from the	7121
Isa	50:2	I **c.**, was there none to answer?	7121
Isa	51:2	I **c.** him alone, and blessed him,	7121
Isa	54:5	of the whole earth shall be **c.**	7121
Isa	54:6	the Lord hath **c.** thee as a woman	7121
Isa	56:7	mine house shall be **c.** an house of	7121
Isa	58:12	and thou shalt be **c.**, The repairer	7121
Isa	61:3	might be **c.** trees of righteousness,	7121
Isa	62:2	thou shalt be **c.** by a new name,	7121
Isa	62:4	thou shalt be **c.** Hephzi-bah, and	7121
Isa	62:12	thou shalt be **c.**, Sought out,	7121
Isa	63:19	they were not **c.** by thy name.	7121
Isa	65:1	a nation that was not **c.** by my	7121
Isa	65:12	when I **c.**, ye did not answer;	7121
Isa	66:4	when I **c.**, none did answer;	7121
Jer	7:10	in this house, which is **c.** by my	7121
Jer	7:11	Is this house, which is **c.** by my	7121
Jer	7:13	I **c.** you, but ye answered not;	7121
Jer	7:14	this house, which is **c.** by my name,	7121
Jer	7:30	the house which is **c.** by my name,	7121
Jer	7:32	it shall no more be **c.** Tophet,	559
Jer	11:16	The Lord **c.** thy name. A green	7121
Jer	12:6	they have **c.** a multitude after	7121
Jer	14:9	we are **c.** by thy name; leave us	7121
Jer	15:16	I am **c.** by thy name, O Lord God	7121
Jer	19:6	place shall no more be **c.** Tophet,	7121
Jer	20:3	Lord hath not **c.** thy name Pashur,	7121
Jer	23:6	he shall be **c.**, The Lord our	7121

Jer 25:29 the city which is c. by my name, ... 7121
Jer 30:17 they c. thee an Outcast, saying, ... 7121
Jer 32:34 house, which is c. by my name, ... 7121
Jer 33:16 name wherewith she shall be c., ... 7121
Jer 34:15 house which is c. by my name: ... 7121
Jer 35:17 and I have c. unto them, but they ... 7121
Jer 36:4 Then Jeremiah c. Baruch the ... 7121
Jer 42:8 Then c. he Johanan the son of ... 7121
La 1:15 he hath c. an assembly against me ... 7121
La 1:19 I c. for my lovers, but they ... 7121
La 1:21 bring the day that thou hast c., ... 7121
La 2:22 Thou hast c. as in a solemn day ... 7121
La 3:55 I c. upon thy name, O Lord, ... 7121
La 3:57 in the day that I c. upon thee: ... 7121
Eze 9:3 he c. to the man clothed with linen, ... 7121
Eze 20:29 And the name thereof is c. Bamah ... 7121
Da 5:12 now let Daniel be c., and he will ... 7123
Da 8:16 which c., and said, Gabriel, make ... 7121
Da 9:18 the city which is c. by thy name; ... 7121
Da 9:19 thy people are c. by thy name. ... 7121
Da 10:1 whose name was c. Belteshazzar: ... 7121
Ho 11:1 c. my son out of Egypt. ... 7121
Ho 11:2 As they c. them, so they went ... 7121
Ho 11:7 though they c. them to the most ... 7121
Am 7:4 Lord God c. to contend by fire, ... 7121
Am 9:12 heathen, which are c. by my name, ... 7121
Hag 1:11 And I c. for a drought upon the ... 7121
Zec 8:3 Jerusalem shall be c. a city of ... 7121
Zec 11:7 the one I c. Beauty, ... 7121
Zec 11:7 and the other I c. Bands; ... 7121
Mt 1:16 born Jesus, who is c. Christ. ... 3004
Mt 1:25 and he c. his name Jesus. ... 2564
Mt 2:7 privily c. the wise men, enquired ... 2564
Mt 2:15 Out of Egypt have I c. my son. ... 2564
Mt 2:23 and dwelt in a city c. Nazareth: ... 3004
Mt 2:23 He shall be c. a Nazarene. ... 2564
Mt 4:18 Simon c. Peter, and Andrew his ... 3004
Mt 4:21 mending their nets; and he c. ... 2564
Mt 5:9 **shall be c. the children of God.** ... 2564
Mt 5:19 **he shall be c. the least in the** ... 2564
Mt 5:19 **the same shall be c. great in the** ... 2564
Mt 10:1 And when he had c. unto him his ... 4341
Mt 10:2 The first, Simon, who is c. Peter, ... 3004
Mt 10:25 **If they have c. the master of the** ... 2564
Mt 13:55 is not his mother c. Mary? and ... 3004
Mt 15:10 And he c. the multitude, and said ... 4341
Mt 15:32 Then Jesus c. his disciples unto ... 4341
Mt 18:2 Jesus c. a little child unto him, ... 4341
Mt 18:32 **after that he had c. him, said** ... 4341
Mt 20:16 **for many be c., but few chosen.** ... 2822
Mt 20:25 But Jesus c. them unto him, and ... 4341
Mt 20:32 Jesus stood still, and c. them, ... 5455
Mt 21:13 **My house shall be c. the house of** ... 2564
Mt 22:14 **many are c., but few are chosen.** ... 2822
Mt 23:7 **and to be c. of men, Rabbi, Rabbi.** ... 2564
Mt 23:8 **be not ye c. Rabbi: for one is your** ... 2564
Mt 23:10 **Neither be ye c. masters: for one** ... 2564
Mt 25:14 **c. his own servants, and delivered** ... 2564
Mt 26:3 high priest, who was c. Caiaphas, ... 3004
Mt 26:14 Then one of the twelve, c. Judas ... 3004
Mt 26:36 unto a place c. Gethsemane, and ... 3004
Mt 27:8 that field was c., The field of ... 2564
Mt 27:16 a notable prisoner, c. Baraabbas ... 3004
Mt 27:17 or Jesus which is c. Christ? ... 3004
Mt 27:22 do then with Jesus which is c. ... 3004
Mt 27:33 unto a place c. Golgotha, that is ... 3004
Mk 1:20 straightway he c. them: and they ... 2564
Mk 3:23 And he c. them unto him, and said ... 4341
Mk 6:7 And he c. unto him the twelve, ... 4341
Mk 7:14 when he had c. all the people unto ... 4341
Mk 8:1 Jesus c. his disciples unto him, ... 4341
Mk 8:34 when he had c. the people unto ... 4341
Mk 9:35 and c. the twelve, and saith unto ... 5455
Mk 10:42 But Jesus c. them to him, and ... 4341
Mk 10:49 and commanded him to be c. ... 5455
Mk 11:17 **My house shall be c. of all nations.** ... 2564
Mk 12:43 he c. unto him his disciples, and ... 4341
Mk 14:72 Peter c. to mind the word that ... 363
Mk 15:16 into the hall, c. Praetorium; ... 3739,2076
Lu 1:32 shall be c. the Son of the Highest: ... 2564
Lu 1:35 shall be c. the Son of God. ... 2564
Lu 1:36 with her, who was c. barren. ... 2564
Lu 1:59 and they c. him Zacharias, after ... 2564
Lu 1:60 Not so, but he shall be c. John. ... 2564
Lu 1:61 kindred that is c. by this name. ... 2564
Lu 1:62 father, how he would have him c. ... 2564
Lu 1:76 shalt be c. the prophet of the ... 2564
Lu 2:4 David, which is c. Bethlehem; ... 2564
Lu 2:21 his name was c. Jesus, which was ... 2564
Lu 2:23 shall be c. holy to the Lord;) ... 2564
Lu 6:13 he c. unto him his disciples: ... 4377
Lu 6:15 and Simon c. Zelotes, ... 2564
Lu 7:11 he went into a city c. Nain; ... 2564
Lu 8:2 Mary c. Magdalene, out of whom ... 2564
Lu 8:54 and c., saying, **Maid, arise.** ... 5455
Lu 9:1 c. his twelve disciples together, ... 4779
Lu 9:10 belonging to the city c. Bethsaida. ... 2564
Lu 10:39 she had a sister c. Mary, which ... 2564
Lu 13:12 he c. her to him, ... 4377
Lu 15:19 **no more worthy to be c. thy son:** ... 2564
Lu 15:21 **no more worthy to be c. thy son.** ... 2564
Lu 15:26 **he c. one of the servants, and** ... 4341
Lu 16:2 **And he c. him, and said unto** ... 5455
Lu 16:5 **So he c. every one of his lord's** ... 4341
Lu 18:16 But Jesus c. them unto him, ... 4341
Lu 19:13 **And he c. his ten servants, and** ... 2564
Lu 19:15 **these servants to be c. unto him,** ... 5455
Lu 19:29 the mount c. the mount of Olives, ... 2564
Lu 21:37 that is c. the mount of Olives. ... 2564
Lu 22:1 which is c. the Passover. ... 3004
Lu 22:25 **upon them are c. benefactors.** ... 2564
Lu 22:47 he that was c. Judas, one of the ... 3004
Lu 23:13 when he had c. together the ... 4779
Lu 23:33 to the place which is c. Calvary. ... 2564
Lu 24:13 to a village c. Emmaus, which ... 3686
Joh 1:42 **thou shalt be c. Cephas, which.** ... 2564
Joh 1:48 **Before that Philip c. thee, when** ... 5455
Joh 2:2 Jesus was c., and his disciples, ... 2564
Joh 2:9 governor of the feast c. the ... 5455
Joh 4:5 of Samaria, which is c. Sychar, ... 3004
Joh 4:25 Messias cometh, which is c. Christ: ... 3004
Joh 5:2 which is c. in the Hebrew tongue ... 1951
Joh 9:11 A man that is c. Jesus made clay. ... 3004
Joh 9:18 until they c. the parents of him ... 5455
Joh 9:24 Then again c. they the man that ... 5455
Joh 10:35 **If he c. them gods, unto whom** ... 2036
Joh 11:16 Thomas, which is c. Didymus, ... 3004
Joh 11:28 and c. Mary her sister secretly, ... 5455
Joh 11:54 into a city c. Ephraim, and there ... 3004
Joh 12:17 when he c. Lazarus out of his ... 5455
Joh 15:15 **but I have c. you friends;** ... 2046
Joh 18:33 c. Jesus, and said unto him, Art ... 5455
Joh 19:13 in a place that is c. the Pavement, ... 3004
Joh 19:17 a place c. the place of a skull, ... 3004
Joh 19:17 is c. in the Hebrew Golgotha: ... 3004
Joh 20:24 one of the twelve, c. Didymus, ... 3004
Joh 21:2 and Thomas c. Didymus, and ... 3004
Ac 1:12 from the mount c. Olivet, which ... 2564
Ac 1:19 insomuch as that field is c. in ... 2564
Ac 1:23 Joseph c. Barsabas, who was ... 2564
Ac 3:2 gate of the temple which is c. ... 3004
Ac 3:11 the porch that is c. Solomon's, ... 2564
Ac 4:18 they c. them, and commanded ... 2564
Ac 5:21 and c. the council together, and ... 4779
Ac 5:40 when they had c. the apostles, ... 4341
Ac 6:2 Then the twelve c. the multitude ... 4341
Ac 6:9 of the synagogue, which is c. ... 3004
Ac 7:14 and c. his father Jacob to him, ... 3333
Ac 8:9 a certain man, c. Simon, which ... 3686
Ac 9:11 **the street which is c. Straight,** ... 2564
Ac 9:11 **for one c. Saul, of Tarsus: for** ... 3686
Ac 9:21 them which c. on his name in ... 1941
Ac 9:36 by interpretation is c. Dorcas: ... 3004
Ac 9:41 when he had c. the saints and ... 5455
Ac 10:1 man in Caesarea c. Cornelius, ... 3686
Ac 10:1 of the band c. the Italian band, ... 2564
Ac 10:7 c. two of his household serevants, ... 5455
Ac 10:18 And c., and asked whether Simon, ... 5455
Ac 10:23 Then c. he them in, and lodged ... 1528
Ac 10:24 and had c. together his kinsmen ... 4779
Ac 11:26 the disciples were c. Christians ... 5537
Ac 13:1 and Simeon that was c. Niger, ... 2564
Ac 13:2 work whereunto I have c. them. ... 4341
Ac 13:7 who c. for Barnabas and Saul, ... 4341
Ac 13:9 Then Saul, (who also is c. Paul,) ... 4341
Ac 14:12 they c. Barnabas, Jupiter; and ... 2564
Ac 15:17 upon whom my name is c., ... 1941
Ac 16:10 that the Lord had c. us for to ... 4341
Ac 16:29 Then he c. for a light, and ... 154
Ac 19:25 Whom he c. together with the ... 4867
Ac 19:40 we are in danger to be c. in ... 1458
Ac 20:1 Paul c. unto him the disciples, ... 4341
Ac 20:17 and c. the elders of the church. ... 3333
Ac 23:6 I am c. in question. ... 2919
Ac 23:17 c. one of the centurions unto him, ... 4341
Ac 23:18 Paul the prisoner c. me unto him, ... 4341
Ac 23:23 he c. unto him two centurions, ... 4341
Ac 24:2 when he was c. forth, Tertullus ... 2564
Ac 24:21 I am c. in question by you this ... 2919
Ac 27:8 which is c. The fair havens; ... 2564
Ac 27:14 tempestuous wind, c. Euroclydon. ... 2564
Ac 27:16 a certain island which is c. Clauda, ... 2564
Ac 28:1 knew that the island was c. Melita ... 2564
Ac 28:17 Paul c. the chief of the Jews ... 4779
Ac 28:20 have I c. for you, to see you, ... 3870
Ro 1:1 c. to be an apostle, separated ... 2822
Ro 1:6 are ye also the c. of Jesus Christ: ... 2822
Ro 1:7 c. to be saints: grace to you ... 2822
Ro 2:17 Behold, thou are c. a Jew, and ... 2028
Ro 7:3 she shall be c. an adulteress: ... 5537
Ro 8:28 to them who are the c. according ... 2822
Ro 8:30 them he also c.: and whom he c. ... 2564
Ro 9:7 In Isaac shall thy seed be c. ... 2564
Ro 9:24 Even us, whom he hath c., not of ... 2564
Ro 9:26 there shall they be c. the children ... 2564
1Co 1:1 c. to be an apostle of Jesus Christ ... 2822
1Co 1:2 in Christ Jesus, c. to be saints, ... 2822
1Co 1:9 by whom ye were c. unto the ... 2564
1Co 1:24 But unto them which are c., both ... 2822
1Co 1:26 mighty, not many noble, are c.: ...
1Co 5:11 if any man that is c. a brother ... 3687
1Co 7:15 but God hath c. us to peace. ... 2564
1Co 7:17 as the Lord hath c. every one, so ... 2564
1Co 7:18 Is any man c. being circumcised? ... 2564
1Co 7:18 Is any c. in uncircumcision? let ... 2564
1Co 7:20 same calling wherein he was c. ... 2564
1Co 7:21 Art thou c. being a servant? care ... 2564
1Co 7:22 For he that is c. in the Lord, being ... 2564
1Co 7:22 he that is c., being free, is ... 2564
1Co 7:24 wherein he is c., therein abide ... 2564
1Co 8:5 though there be that are c. gods, ... 3004
1Co 15:9 am not meet to be c. an apostle, ... 2564
Ga 1:6 from him that c. you into the ... 2564
Ga 1:15 and c. me by his grace, ... 2564
Ga 5:13 ye have been c. unto liberty; ... 2564
Eph 2:11 c. Uncircumcision by ... 3004
Eph 2:11 that which is c. the Circumcision ... 3004
Eph 4:1 wherewith ye are c., ... 2564
Eph 4:4 even as ye are c. in one hope ... 2564
Col 3:15 to the which also ye are c. ... 2564
Col 4:11 Jesus, which is c. Justus, who are ... 3004
1Th 2:12 worthy of God, who hath c. you ... 2564
1Th 4:7 hath not c. us unto uncleanness, ... 2564
2Th 2:4 himself above all that is c. God, ... 3004
2Th 2:14 he c. you by our gospel, to the ... 2564
1Ti 6:12 life, whereunto thou art also c., ... 2564
1Ti 6:20 of science falsely so c. ... 5581
2Ti 1:9 and c. us with an holy calling, ... 2564
Heb 3:13 while it is c. To day; lest any ... 2564
Heb 5:4 but he that is c. of God, as was ... 2564
Heb 5:10 C. of God an high priest after ... 4316
Heb 7:11 not be c. after the order of Aaron? ... 3004
Heb 9:2 which is c. the sanctuary. ... 3004
Heb 9:3 tabernacle which is c. the Holiest ... 3004
Heb 9:15 are c. might receive the promise ... 2564
Heb 11:8 Abraham, when he was c. to go ... 2564
Heb 11:16 not ashamed to be c. their God: ... 1941
Heb 11:18 in Isaac shall thy seed be c.: ... 2564
Heb 11:24 refused to be c. the son of ... 3004
Jas 2:7 name by the which ye are c.? ... 1941
Jas 2:23 he was c. the Friend of God. ... 2564
1Pe 1:15 as he which hath c. you is holy ... 2564
1Pe 2:9 who hath c. you out of darkness ... 2564
1Pe 2:21 hereunto were ye c.: because ... 2564
1Pe 3:9 that ye are thereunto c., that ye ... 2564
1Pe 5:10 the God of all grace, who hath c. ... 2564
2Pe 1:3 of him that hath c. us to glory ... 2564
1Jo 3:1 we should be c. the sons of God: ... 2564
Jude 1 preserved in Jesus Christ, and c. ... 2822
Re 1:9 was in the isle that is c. Patmos, ... 2564
Re 8:11 name of the star is c. Wormwood: ... 3004
Re 11:8 spiritually is c. Sodom and Egypt, ... 2564
Re 12:9 serpent, c. the Devil, and Satan. ... 2564
Re 16:16 c. in the Hebrew tongue ... 2564
Re 17:14 they that are with him are c., ... 2822
Re 19:9 which are c. unto the marriage ... 2564
Re 19:11 him was c. Faithful and True, ... 2564
Re 19:13 his name is c. The Word of God. ... 2564

CALLEDST

Jg 8:1 that thou c. us not, when thou ... 7121

1Sa 3:5 for thou c. me. And he said, I.......... 7121
Ps 81:7 c. in trouble, and I delivered thee; 7121
Eze 23:21 Thus thou c. to remembrance the 6485

CALLEST
Mt 19:17 **Why c. thou me good? there is**...... *3004*
Mk 10:18 unto him, **Why c. thou me good?**.... *3004*
Lu 18:19 **Why c. thou my good? none is**...... *3004*

CALLETH
1Ki 8:43 that the stranger c. to thee for:......... 7121
2Ch 6:33 that the stranger c. to thee for;......... 7121
Job 12:4 c. upon God, and he answereth 7121
Ps 42:7 Deep c. unto deep at the noise.......... 7121
Ps 147:4 he c. them all by their names. 7121
Pro 18:6 and his mouth c. for strokes. 7121
Isa 21:11 He c. to me out of Seir, Watchman, ... 7121
Isa 40:26 he c. them all by names by the.......... 7121
Isa 59:4 None c. for justice, nor any 7121
Isa 64:7 there is none that c. upon thy 7121
Hos 7:7 there is none among them that c........ 7121
Am 5:8 that c. for the waters of the sea, ... 7121
Am 9:6 he that c. for the waters of the sea, ... 7121
Mt 27:47 that, said, This man c. for Elias......... *5455*
Mk 3:13 and c. unto him whom he would:.......... *4341*
Mk 10:49 of good comfort, rise; he c. thee......... *5455*
Mk 12:37 **therefore himself c. him Lord;**...... *3004*
Mk 15:35 heard it, said Behold, he c. Elias........ *5455*
Lu 15:6 **home, he c. together his friends**.... *4779*
Lu 15:9 **c. her friends and her neighbours**.. *4779*
Lu 20:37 **c. the Lord the God of Abraham,**.. *3004*
Lu 20:44 **David therefore c. him Lord, how**..*2564*
Joh 10:3 **and he c. his own sheep by name,**..*2564*
Joh 11:28 The Master is come, and c. for thee... *5455*
Ro 4:17 c. those things which be not as.......... *2564*
Ro 9:11 not of works, but of him that c.;)....... *2564*
1Co 12:3 c. Jesus accursed: and that no........... *3004*
Gal 5:8 cometh not of him that c. you. *2564*
1Th 5:24 Faithful is he that c. you, who........... *2564*
Re 2:20 **which c. herself a prophetess, to**... *3004*

CALLING
Nu 10:2 for the c. of the assembly, and for 4744
Isa 1:13 the c. of assemblies, I cannot............ 7121
Isa 41:4 c. the generations from the.............. 7121
Isa 46:11 C. a ravenous bird from the east,....... 7121
Eze 23:19 in c. to remembrance the days of....... 2142
Mt 11:16 **and c. unto their fellows,**............. *4377*
Mk 3:31 without, sent unto him, c. him........... *5455*
Mk 11:21 Peter c. to remembrance saith............ *363*
Mk 15:44 and c. unto him the centurion, he....... *4341*
Lu 7:19 And John c. unto him two of his......... *4341*
Lu 7:32 **c. one to another, and saying,**....... *4377*
Ac 7:59 stoned Stephen, c. upon God, and...... *1941*
Ac 22:16 sins, c. on the name of the Lord........ *1941*
Ro 11:29 gifts and c. of God are without *2821*
1Co 1:26 For ye see your c., brethren, how *2821*
1Co 7:20 abide in the same c. wherein he......... *2821*
Eph 1:18 what is the hope of his c., and........... *2821*
Eph 4:4 are called in one hope of your c.;....... *2821*
Php 3:14 for the prize of the high c. of............ *2821*
2Th 1:11 would count you worthy of this c.. ...... *2821*
2Ti 1:9 us, and called us with an holy c.. .... *2821*
Heb 3:1 partakers of the heavenly c., ... *2821*
1Pe 3:6 Even as Sara obeyed Abraham, c....... *2564*
2Pe 1:10 give diligence to make your c............ *2821*

CALM
Ps 107:29 He maketh the storm a c., so that 1827
Jon 1:11 unto thee, that the sea may be c. 8367
Jon 1:12 so shall the sea be c. unto you: 8367
Mt 8:26 the sea; and there was a great c........ *1055*
Mk 4:39 ceased, and there was a great c......... *1055*
Lu 8:24 they ceased, and there was a c......... *1055*

CALNEH (cal'-neh) See also CALNO; CANNEH.
Ge 10:10 and Erech, and Accad, and C., ... 3641
Am 6:2 Pass ye unto C., and see; and.......... 3641

CALNO (cal'-no) See also CALNEH.
Isa 10:9 Is not C. as Carchemish? is not......... 3641

CALVARY (cal'-va-ry)
Lu 23:33 which is called C., there they........... *2898*

CALVE See also CALVED; CALVETH.
Job 39:1 thou mark when the hinds do c.? 2342
Ps 29:9 the Lord maketh the hinds to c.......... 2342

CALVED
Jer 14:5 the hind also c. in the field, and......... 3205

CALVES
1Sa 6:7 bring their c. home from them:.......... 1121
1Sa 6:10 and shut up their c. at home: 1121
1Sa 14:32 took sheep, and oxen, and c., ... 1121,1242
1Ki 12:28 made two c. of gold, and said........... 5695
1Ki 12:32 unto the c. that he had made:............ 5695
2Ki 10:29 golden c. that were in Beth-el, ... 5695
2Ki 17:16 them molten images, even two c.,...... 5695
2Ch 11:15 and for the c. which he had made....... 5695
2Ch 13:8 there are with you golden c., which.... 5695
Ps 68:30 with the c. of the people, till............ 5695
Ho 10:5 shall fear because of the c. of............ 5697
Ho 13:2 the men that sacrifice kiss the c......... 5697
Ho 14:2 will we render the c. of our lips......... 6499
Am 6:4 the c. out of the midst of the stall;..... 5695
Mic 6:6 offerings, with c. of a year old? 5695
Mal 4:2 and grow up as c. of the stall. 5695
Heb 9:12 by the blood of goats and c., but........ *3448*
Heb 9:19 took the blood of c. and of goats,....... *3448*

CALVETH
Job 21:10 their cow c., and casteth not her 6403

CAME See also BECAME; CAMEST; OVERCAME.
Ge 4:3 c. to pass, that Cain brought of 1961
Ge 4:8 c. to pass, when they were in the...... 1961
Ge 6:1 c. to pass, when men began to.......... 1961
Ge 6:4 sons of God c. in unto the daughters.... 935
Ge 7:10 c. to pass after seven days, that 1961
Ge 8:6 it c. to pass at the end of forty.......... 1961
Ge 8:11 And the dove c. in to him in the.......... 935
Ge 8:13 it c. to pass in the six hundredth........ 1961
Ge 10:14 (out of whom c. Philistim,) and.......... 3318
Ge 11:2 it c. to pass, as they journeyed.......... 1961
Ge 11:5 the Lord c. down to see the city.......... 3381
Ge 11:31 and they c. unto Haran, and 935
Ge 12:5 and into the land of Canaan they c.. 935
Ge 12:11 it c. to pass, when he was come......... 1961
Ge 12:14 c. to pass, that, when Abram was...... 1961
Ge 13:18 c. and dwelt in the plain of Mamre,...... 935
Ge 14:1 c. to pass in the days of Amraphel 1961
Ge 14:5 fourteenth year c. Chedorlaomer,......... 935
Ge 14:7 and c. to En-mishpat, which is 935
Ge 14:13 there c. one that had escaped, ... 935
Ge 15:1 word of the Lord c. unto Abram 1961
Ge 15:4 the word of the Lord c. unto him, ...
Ge 15:11 when the fowls c. down upon the....... 3381
Ge 15:17 And it c. to pass, that, when the 1961
Ge 19:1 And there c. two angels to Sodom....... 935
Ge 19:5 Where are the men which c. in to........ 935
Ge 19:8 c. they under the shadow.................. 935
Ge 19:9 This one fellow c. in to sojourn 935
Ge 19:9 Lot, and c. near to break the door. 5066
Ge 19:17 c. to pass, when they had brought....... 1961
Ge 19:29 it c. to pass, when God destroyed...... 1961
Ge 19:34 c. to pass on the morrow, that the..... 1961
Ge 20:3 God c. to Abimelech in a dream 935
Ge 20:13 c. to pass when God caused me......... 1961
Ge 21:22 And it c. to pass at that time, that 1961
Ge 22:1 c. to pass after these things, that....... 1961
Ge 22:9 they c. to the place which God had...... 935
Ge 22:20 it c. to pass after these things, ... 1961
Ge 23:2 Abraham c. to mourn for Sarah, ... 935
Ge 24:15 it c. to pass, before he had done........ 1961
Ge 24:15 behold, Rebekah c. out, who was........ 3318
Ge 24:16 and filled her pitcher, and c. up. 5927
Ge 24:22 it c. to pass, as the camels had 1961
Ge 24:30 it c. to pass, when he saw the........... 1961
Ge 24:30 that he c. unto the man; and,.............. 935
Ge 24:32 And the man c. into the house: 935
Ge 24:42 And I c. this day unto the well,........... 935
Ge 24:45 Rebekah c. forth with her pitcher....... 3318
Ge 24:52 c. to pass, that when Abraham's 1961
Ge 24:62 Isaac c. from the way of the well.......... 935
Ge 25:11 it c. to pass after the death of........... 1961
Ge 25:25 And the first c. out red, all over 3318
Ge 25:26 after that c. his brother out,............. 3318
Ge 25:29 and Esau c. from the field, ... 935
Ge 26:8 And it c. to pass, when he had.......... 1961
Ge 26:32 And it c. to pass the same day, ... 1961
Ge 26:32 that Isaac's servants c., and told......... 935
Ge 27:1 And it c. to pass, that when Isaac 1961
Ge 27:18 And he c. unto his father and............. 935
Ge 27:27 And he c. near, and kissed him:......... 5066
Ge 27:30 And it c. to pass, as soon as............ 1961
Ge 27:30 that Esau his brother c. in from 935
Ge 27:35 Thy brother c. with subtilty,.............. 935
Ge 29:1 on his journey, and c. into the........... 3212
Ge 29:9 Rachel c. with her father's sheep: 935
Ge 29:10 And it c. to pass, when Jacob........... 1961
Ge 29:13 And it c. to pass, when Laban........... 1961
Ge 29:23 And it c. to pass in the evening, ... 1961
Ge 29:25 it c. to pass, that in the morning,....... 1961
Ge 30:16 And Jacob c. out of the field in............ 935
Ge 30:25 And it c. to pass, when Rachel.......... 1961
Ge 30:30 little which thou hadst before I c., ...
Ge 30:38 when the flocks c. to drink, ... 935
Ge 30:38 when they c. to drink........................ 935
Ge 30:41 And it c. to pass, whensoever 1961
Ge 31:10 And it c. to pass at the time that 1961
Ge 31:24 And God c. to Laban...in a dream........ 935
Ge 32:6 We c. to thy brother Esau, ... 935
Ge 32:13 took of that which c. to his hand 935
Ge 33:1 Esau c., and with him four hundred...... 935
Ge 33:3 until he c. near to his brother............ 5066
Ge 33:6 Then the handmaidens c. near, ... 5066
Ge 33:7 Leah also with her children c. near..... 5066
Ge 33:7 after c. Joseph near and Rachel,......... 5066
Ge 33:18 And Jacob c. to Shalem, a city of......... 935
Ge 33:18 when he c. from Padan-aram; 935
Ge 34:7 c. out of the field when they heard 935
Ge 34:20 And Hamor and Shechem his son c. 935
Ge 34:25 And it c. to pass on the third day,...... 1961
Ge 34:25 and c. upon the city boldly, ... 935
Ge 34:27 The sons of Jacob c. upon the slain, ... 935
Ge 35:6 So Jacob c. to Luz, which is in the....... 935
Ge 35:9 when he c. out of Padan-aram, and 935
Ge 35:17 it c. to pass, when she was in hard 1961
Ge 35:18 it c. to pass, as her soul was in......... 1961
Ge 35:22 And it c. to pass when Israel dwelt 1961
Ge 35:27 Jacob c. unto Isaac his father 935
Ge 36:16 dukes that c. of Eliphaz in the ....
Ge 36:17 these are the dukes that c. of Reuel.........
Ge 36:18 the dukes that c. of Aholibamah ....
Ge 36:29 the dukes that c. of the Horites; ....
Ge 36:30 these are the dukes that c. of Hori, ...
Ge 36:40 names of the dukes that c. of Esau,..........
Ge 37:14 Hebron, and he c. to Shechem. 935
Ge 37:18 before he c. near unto them,............. 7126
Ge 37:23 And it c. to pass, when Joseph........... 1961
Ge 37:25 a company of Ishmeelites c................. 935
Ge 38:1 it c. to pass at that time,.................. 1961
Ge 38:9 and it c. to pass, when he 1961
Ge 38:18 and c. in unto her, and she................. 935
Ge 38:24 it c. to pass about three months 1961
Ge 38:27 And it c. to pass in the time of.......... 1961
Ge 38:28 it c. to pass, when she travailed, ... 1961
Ge 38:28 thread, saying, This c. out first.......... 3318
Ge 38:29 And it c. to pass, as he drew back..... 1961
Ge 38:29 behold, his brother c. out: and........... 3318
Ge 38:30 afterward c. out his brother, ... 3318
Ge 39:5 And it c. to pass from the time.......... 1961
Ge 39:7 And it c. to pass after these things,.... 1961
Ge 39:10 And it c. to pass, as she spake.......... 1961
Ge 39:11 And it c. to pass about this time, ... 1961
Ge 39:13 And it c. to pass, when she saw........ 1961
Ge 39:14 he c. unto me to lie with me, ... 935
Ge 39:15 And it c. to pass, when he heard 1961
Ge 39:16 by her, until his lord c. home............. 935
Ge 39:17 us, c. in unto me to mock me: 935
Ge 39:18 And it c. to pass, as I lifted............. 1961
Ge 39:19 And it c. to pass, when his master..... 1961
Ge 40:1 it c. to pass after these things, ... 1961
Ge 40:6 And Joseph c. in unto them 935
Ge 40:20 And it c. to pass the third day,.......... 1961
Ge 41:1 And it c. to pass at the end of........... 1961
Ge 41:2 there c. up out of the river seven 5927
Ge 41:3 seven other kine c. up after them 5927
Ge 41:5 seven ears of corn c. up upon 5927
Ge 41:8 And it c. to pass in the morning......... 1961
Ge 41:13 And it c. to pass, as he interpreted 1961
Ge 41:14 raiment, and c. in unto Pharaoh.......... 935
Ge 41:18 there c. up out of the river seven...... 5927
Ge 41:19 seven other kine c. up after them, ... 5927
Ge 41:22 seven ears c. up in one stalk,........... 5927
Ge 41:27 ill favoured kine that c. up 5927
Ge 41:50 sons before the years of famine c.. 935
Ge 41:57 all countries c. into Egypt to 935
Ge 42:5 And the sons of Israel c. to buy.......... 935
Ge 42:6 and Joseph's brethren c., and............. 935
Ge 42:29 they c. unto Jacob their father,............ 935
Ge 42:35 And it c. to pass as they emptied....... 1961
Ge 43:2 And it c. to pass, when they had 1961
Ge 43:19 And they c. near to the steward 5066
Ge 43:20 we c. indeed down at the first........... 3381

Ge 43:21 And it **c.** to pass, when we....1961
Ge 43:21 when we **c.** to the inn, that we....935
Ge 43:25 against Joseph **c.** at noon: for they....935
Ge 43:26 And when Joseph **c.** home, they....935
Ge 44:14 And Judah and his brethren **c.**....935
Ge 44:18 Then Judah **c.** near unto him,....5066
Ge 44:24 And it **c.** to pass when we....1961
Ge 44:24 when we **c.** up unto thy servant....5927
Ge 45:4 And they **c.** near. And he said,....5066
Ge 45:25 and **c.** into the land of Canaan....935
Ge 46:1 and **c.** to Beer-sheba, and offered....935
Ge 46:6 and **c.** into Egypt, Jacob, and all....935
Ge 46:8 of the children of Israel, which **c.**....935
Ge 46:26 All the souls that **c.** with Jacob....935
Ge 46:26 which **c.** out of his loins,....3318
Ge 46:27 which **c.** into Egypt, were....935
Ge 46:28 they **c.** into the land of Goshen....935
Ge 47:1 Then Joseph **c.** and told Pharaoh,....935
Ge 47:15 the Egyptians **c.** unto Joseph,....935
Ge 47:18 they **c.** unto him the second year,....935
Ge 48:1 And it **c.** to pass after these....1961
Ge 48:5 before I **c.** unto thee into Egypt,....935
Ge 48:7 for me, when I **c.** from Padan,....935
Ge 50:10 And they **c.** to the threshingfloor....935
Ex 1:1 of Israel, which **c.** into Egypt;....935
Ex 1:1 and his household **c.** with Jacob....935
Ex 1:5 all the souls that **c.** out of the....3318
Ex 1:21 And it **c.** to pass, because the....1961
Ex 2:5 And the daughter of Pharaoh **c.**....3381
Ex 2:11 And it **c.** to pass in those days,....1961
Ex 2:16 and they **c.** and drew water,....935
Ex 2:17 And the shepherds **c.** and drove....935
Ex 2:18 And when they **c.** to Reuel their....935
Ex 2:23 And it **c.** to pass in process of....1961
Ex 2:23 and their cry **c.** up unto God....5927
Ex 3:1 and **c.** to the mountain of God,....935
Ex 4:24 And it **c.** to pass by the way in....1961
Ex 5:15 officers of the children of Israel **c.**....935
Ex 5:20 as they **c.** forth from Pharaoh:....3318
Ex 5:23 For since I **c.** to Pharaoh to speak....935
Ex 6:28 And it **c.** to pass on the day when....1961
Ex 8:6 and the frogs **c.** up, and covered....5927
Ex 8:24 and there **c.** a grievous swarm....935
Ex 10:3 And Moses and Aaron **c.** in unto....935
Ex 12:29 it **c.** to pass, that at midnight....1961
Ex 12:41 And it **c.** to pass at the end of the....1961
Ex 12:41 the selfsame day it **c.** to pass,....1961
Ex 12:51 And it **c.** to pass the selfsame day,....1961
Ex 13:3 ye **c.** out from Egypt, out of the....3318
Ex 13:4 **c.** ye out in the month Abib....3318
Ex 13:8 when I **c.** forth out of Egypt....3318
Ex 13:15, 17 it **c.** to pass, when Pharaoh....1961
Ex 14:20 And it **c.** between the camp of....935
Ex 14:20 the one **c.** not near the other....7126
Ex 14:24 it **c.** to pass, that in the morning....1961
Ex 14:28 that **c.** into the sea after them;....935
Ex 15:23 And when they **c.** to Marah,....935
Ex 15:27 And they **c.** to Elim, where were....935
Ex 16:1 Israel **c.** unto the wilderness of....935
Ex 16:10 And it **c.** to pass, as Aaron spake....1961
Ex 16:13 And it **c.** to pass, that at even....1961
Ex 16:13 that at even the quails **c.** up,....5927
Ex 16:22 **c.** to pass, that on the sixth day....1961
Ex 16:22 the rulers of the congregation **c.**....935
Ex 16:27 And it **c.** to pass, that there....1961
Ex 16:35 until they **c.** to a land inhabited;....935
Ex 16:35 until they **c.** unto the borders....935
Ex 17:8 Then **c.** Amalek, and fought with....935
Ex 17:11 And it **c.** to pass, when Moses....1961
Ex 18:5 Jethro, Moses' father in law, **c.**....935
Ex 18:7 welfare; and they **c.** into the tent....935
Ex 18:12 and Aaron **c.**, and all the elders....935
Ex 18:13 it **c.** to pass on the morrow,....1961
Ex 19:1 day **c.** they into the wilderness....935
Ex 19:7 Moses **c.** and called for the elders....935
Ex 19:16 And it **c.** to pass on the third day....1961
Ex 19:20 Lord **c.** down upon mount Sinai,....3381
Ex 21:3 If he **c.** in by himself, he shall....935
Ex 22:15 hired thing, it **c.** for his hire....935
Ex 24:3 And Moses **c.** and told the people....935
Ex 32:19 **c.** [1961] to pass, as soon as he **c.**....7126
Ex 32:24 fire, and there **c.** out this calf....3318
Ex 32:30 And it **c.** to pass on the morrow,....1961
Ex 33:7 **c.** to pass, that every one which....1961
Ex 33:8 And it **c.** to pass, when Moses....1961
Ex 33:9 And it **c.** to pass, as Moses entered....1961
Ex 34:29 And it **c.** to pass, when Moses....1961

Ex 34:29 Moses **c.** down from mount Sinai....3381
Ex 34:29 when he **c.** down from the mount,....3381
Ex 34:32 all the children of Israel **c.** nigh:....5066
Ex 34:34 took the vail off, until he **c.** out....3318
Ex 34:34 And he **c.** out, and spake unto....3318
Ex 35:21 And they **c.**, every one whose....935
Ex 35:22 And they **c.**, both men and women,....935
Ex 36:4 sanctuary, **c.** every man from his....935
Ex 40:17 it **c.** to pass in the first month....1961
Ex 40:32 when they **c.** near unto the altar,....7126
Le 9:1 it **c.** to pass, on the eighth day,....1961
Le 9:22 and **c.** down from offering of the....3381
Le 9:23 **c.** out, and blessed the people:....3318
Le 9:24 And there **c.** a fire out from before....3318
Nu 4:47 every one that **c.** to do the service....935
Nu 7:1 And it **c.** to pass on the day that....1961
Nu 9:6 **c.** before Moses and before Aaron....7126
Nu 10:11 it **c.** to pass on the twentieth day....1961
Nu 10:21 the tabernacle against they **c.**....935
Nu 10:35 And it **c.** to pass when the ark....1961
Nu 11:20 Why **c.** we forth out of Egypt?....3318
Nu 11:25 And the Lord **c.** down in a cloud,....3381
Nu 11:25 and it **c.** to pass, that, when the....1961
Nu 12:4 And they three **c.** out....3318
Nu 12:5 And the Lord **c.** down in the pillar....3381
Nu 12:5 Miriam: and they both **c.** forth....3318
Nu 13:22 the south, and **c.** unto Hebron;....935
Nu 13:23 they **c.** unto the brook of Eshcol,....935
Nu 13:26 they went and **c.** to Moses, and to....935
Nu 13:27 We **c.** unto the land whither thou....935
Nu 14:45 Amalekites **c.** down, and the....3381
Nu 16:27 Dathan and Abiram **c.** out, and....3318
Nu 16:31 And it **c.** to pass, as he had made....1961
Nu 16:35 there **c.** out a fire from the Lord,....3318
Nu 16:42 **c.** to pass, when the congregation....1961
Nu 16:43 And Moses and Aaron **c.** before....935
Nu 17:8 it **c.** to pass, that on the morrow....1961
Nu 19:2 and upon which never **c.** yoke....5927
Nu 20:1 Then **c.** the children of Israel, even....935
Nu 20:11 and the water **c.** out abundantly,....3318
Nu 20:20 And Edom **c.** out against him with....3318
Nu 20:22 Kadesh, and **c.** unto Mount Hor....935
Nu 20:28 Eleazar **c.** down from the mount....3381
Nu 21:1 heard tell that Israel **c.** by the way....935
Nu 21:7 Therefore the people **c.** to Moses,....935
Nu 21:9 and it **c.** to pass, that if a serpent....1961
Nu 21:23 and he **c.** to Jahaz, and fought....935
Nu 22:7 they **c.** unto Balaam, and spake....935
Nu 22:9 And God **c.** unto Balaam, and said,....935
Nu 22:16 And they **c.** to Balaam, and said to....935
Nu 22:20 And God **c.** unto Balaam at night,....935
Nu 22:39 and they **c.** unto Kirjath-huzoth,....935
Nu 22:41 And it **c.** to pass on the morrow,....1961
Nu 23:17 And when he **c.** to him, behold, he....935
Nu 24:2 the spirit of God **c.** upon him....1961
Nu 25:6 one of the children of Israel **c.**....935
Nu 26:1 And it **c.** to pass after the plague,....1961
Nu 27:1 **c.** the daughters of Zelophehad,....7126
Nu 31:14 hundreds, which **c.** from the battle....935
Nu 31:48 of hundreds, **c.** near unto Moses:....7126
Nu 32:2 Reuben **c.** and spake unto Moses,....935
Nu 32:11 none of the men that **c.** up out of....5927
Nu 32:16 they **c.** near unto him, and said,....5066
Nu 33:9 from Marah, and **c.** unto Elim:....935
Nu 36:1 of the sons of Joseph, **c.** near, and....7126
De 1:3 it **c.** to pass in the fortieth year,....1961
De 1:19 and we **c.** to Kadesh-barnea....935
De 1:22 And ye **c.** near unto me every one....7126
De 1:24 and **c.** unto the valley of Eshcol,....935
De 1:31 ye went, until ye **c.** into this place....935
De 1:44 **c.** out against you, and chased....3318
De 2:14 which we **c.** from Kadesh-barnea,....1980
De 2:16 it **c.** to pass, when all the men....1961
De 2:23 which **c.** forth out of Caphtor,....3318
De 2:32 Then Sihon **c.** out against us, he....3318
De 3:1 king of Bashan **c.** out against us,....3318
De 4:11 And ye **c.** near and stood under....7126
De 4:45 after they **c.** forth out of Egypt,....3318
De 5:23 **c.** to pass, when ye heard the voice....1961
De 5:23 that ye **c.** near unto me, even all....7126
De 9:7 until ye **c.** unto this place, ye have....935
De 9:11 **c.** to pass at the end of forty days....1961
De 9:15 So I turned and **c.** down from the....3381
De 10:5 I turned myself and **c.** down from....3381
De 11:5 until ye **c.** into this place;....935
De 11:10 from whence ye **c.** out, where....3318
De 22:14 took this woman, and when I **c.**....7126

De 23:4 when ye **c.** forth out of Egypt;....3318
De 29:7 And when ye **c.** unto this place,....935
De 29:7 Og the king of Bashan, **c.** out....3318
De 29:16 how we **c.** through the nations....5674
De 31:24 And it **c.** to pass, when Moses....1961
De 32:17 to new gods that **c.** newly up,....935
De 32:44 And Moses **c.** and spake all the....935
De 33:2 The Lord **c.** from Sinai, and....935
De 33:2 and he **c.** with ten thousands of....857
De 33:21 **c.** with the heads of the people, he....857
Jos 1:1 it **c.** to pass, that the Lord spake....1961
Jos 2:1 and **c.** into an harlot's house,....935
Jos 2:2 there **c.** men in hither to-night of....935
Jos 2:4 There **c.** men unto me, but I....935
Jos 2:5 it **c.** to pass about the time of....1961
Jos 2:8 **c.** up unto them upon the roof;....5927
Jos 2:10 when ye **c.** out of Egypt; and....3318
Jos 2:22 **c.** unto the mountain, and abode....935
Jos 2:23 and **c.** to Joshua the son of Nun,....935
Jos 3:1 **c.** to Jordan, he and all the....935
Jos 3:2 And it **c.** to pass after three....1961
Jos 3:14 And it **c.** to pass, when the people....1961
Jos 3:16 waters which **c.** down from....3381
Jos 3:16 those that **c.** down toward the sea....3381
Jos 4:1, 11 it **c.** to pass, when all the people....1961
Jos 4:18 it **c.** to pass, when the priests....1961
Jos 4:19 the people **c.** up out of Jordan on....5927
Jos 4:22 Israel **c.** over this Jordan on dry....5674
Jos 5:1 it **c.** to pass, when all the kings....1961
Jos 5:4 the people that **c.** out of Egypt,....3318
Jos 5:4 the way, after they **c.** out of Egypt....3318
Jos 5:5 all the people that **c.** out were....3318
Jos 5:5 as they **c.** forth out of Egypt,....3318
Jos 5:6 **c.** out of Egypt, were consumed,....3318
Jos 5:8 it **c.** to pass, when they had done....1961
Jos 5:13 And it **c.** to pass, when Joshua was....1961
Jos 6:1 none went out, and none **c.** in....935
Jos 6:8 **c.** to pass, when Joshua had....1961
Jos 6:9 the rereward **c.** after the ark,....1980
Jos 6:11 and they **c.** into the camp, and....935
Jos 6:13 the rereward **c.** after the ark of....1980
Jos 6:15 it **c.** to pass on the seventh day,....1961
Jos 6:16 it **c.** to pass, at the seventh time,....1961
Jos 6:20 **c.** to pass, when the people heard....1961
Jos 8:11 **c.** before the city, and pitched....935
Jos 8:14 it **c.** to pass, when the king of Ai....1961
Jos 8:24 And it **c.** to pass, when Israel....1961
Jos 9:1 it **c.** to pass, when all the kings....1961
Jos 9:12 we **c.** forth to go unto you; but....3318
Jos 9:16 it **c.** to pass, at the end of three....1961
Jos 9:17 **c.** unto their cities on the third....935
Jos 10:1 it **c.** to pass, when Adoni-zedec....1961
Jos 10:9 Joshua therefore **c.** unto them....935
Jos 10:11 And it **c.** to pass, as they fled....1961
Jos 10:20 And it **c.** to pass, when Joshua....1961
Jos 10:24 it **c.** to pass, when they brought....1961
Jos 10:24 they **c.** near, and put their feet....7126
Jos 10:27 And it **c.** to pass at the time of....1961
Jos 10:33 king of Gezer **c.** up to help....5927
Jos 11:1 **c.** to pass, when Jabin king of....1961
Jos 11:5 they **c.** and pitched together at....935
Jos 11:7 So Joshua **c.**, and all the people of....935
Jos 11:21 And at that time **c.** Joshua, and....935
Jos 14:6 Then the children of Judah **c.**....5066
Jos 15:18 And it **c.** to pass, as she....1961
Jos 15:18 as she **c.** unto him, that she....935
Jos 16:7 and **c.** to Jericho, and went out....6293
Jos 17:4 they **c.** near before Eleazar the....7126
Jos 17:13 it **c.** to pass, when the children of....1961
Jos 18:9 and **c.** again to Joshua to the host....935
Jos 18:11 the children of Benjamin **c.** up....5927
Jos 18:11 the coast of their lot **c.** forth....3318
Jos 18:16 And the border **c.** down to the....3381
Jos 19:1 the second lot **c.** forth to Simeon,....3318
Jos 19:10 And the third lot **c.** up for the....5927
Jos 19:17 And the fourth lot **c.** out to....3318
Jos 19:24 the fifth lot **c.** out for the tribe....3318
Jos 19:32 The sixth lot **c.** out to the children....3318
Jos 19:40 And the seventh lot **c.** out for the....3318
Jos 21:1 **c.** near the heads of the fathers....5066
Jos 21:4 the lot **c.** out for the families of....3318
Jos 21:45 the house of Israel; all **c.** to pass....935
Jos 22:10 And when they **c.** unto the borders....935
Jos 22:15 they **c.** unto the children of Reuben,....935
Jos 23:1 it **c.** to pass a long time after that....1961
Jos 24:6 and ye **c.** unto the sea; and the....935
Jos 24:11 and **c.** unto Jericho: and the men....935

Book	Ref	Context	No.
Jos	24:29	it **c.** to pass after these things,	1961
Jg	1:1	after the death of Joshua it **c.** to	1961
Jg	1:14	And it **c.** to pass, when she	1961
Jg	1:14	when she **c.** to him, that she	935
Jg	1:28	**c.** to pass, when Israel was strong,	1961
Jg	2:1	an angel of the Lord **c.** up from	5927
Jg	2:4	it **c.** to pass, when the angel of the	1961
Jg	2:19	**c.** to pass, when the judge was	1961
Jg	3:10	the Spirit of the Lord **c.** upon him,	1961
Jg	3:20	Ehud **c.** unto him; and he was	935
Jg	3:22	of his belly: and the dirt **c.** out.	3318
Jg	3:24	his servants **c.**; and when they	935
Jg	3:27	it **c.** to pass, when he was come,	1961
Jg	4:5	and the children of Israel **c.** up to	5927
Jg	4:22	Jael **c.** out to meet him, and said	3318
Jg	4:22	and when he **c.** into her tent,	935
Jg	5:14	out of Machir **c.** down governors,	3381
Jg	5:19	The kings **c.** and fought, then	935
Jg	5:23	because they **c.** not to the help of	935
Jg	6:3	that the Midianites **c.** up, and	5927
Jg	6:3	east, even they **c.** up against them;	5927
Jg	6:5	they **c.** up with their cattle and	5927
Jg	6:5	and they **c.** as grasshoppers.	935
Jg	6:7	it **c.** to pass, when the children of	1961
Jg	6:11	And there **c.** an angel of the Lord,	935
Jg	6:25	And it **c.** to pass the same night,	1961
Jg	6:34	Spirit of the Lord **c.** upon Gideon,	3847
Jg	6:35	and they **c.** up to meet them.	5927
Jg	7:9	And it **c.** to pass the same night,	1961
Jg	7:13	and **c.** unto a tent, and smote it	935
Jg	7:19	were with him, **c.** unto the outside	935
Jg	8:4	Gideon **c.** to Jordan, and passed	935
Jg	8:15	And he **c.** unto the men of Succoth,	935
Jg	8:33	it **c.** to pass, as soon as Gideon	1961
Jg	9:25	they robbed all that **c.** along that	5674
Jg	9:26	And Gaal the son of Ebed **c.** with	935
Jg	9:42	And it **c.** to pass on the morrow,	1961
Jg	9:52	And Abimelech **c.** unto the tower,	935
Jg	9:57	and upon them **c.** the curse of	935
Jg	11:4	**c.** to pass in process of time, that	1961
Jg	11:13	when they **c.** up out of Egypt.	5927
Jg	11:16	when Israel **c.** up from Egypt,	5927
Jg	11:16	the Red sea, and **c.** to Kadesh;	935
Jg	11:18	**c.** by the east side of the land of	935
Jg	11:18	**c.** not within the border of Moab:	935
Jg	11:29	Spirit of the Lord **c.** upon	1961
Jg	11:34	Jephthah **c.** to Mizpeh unto his	935
Jg	11:34	his daughter **c.** out to meet him	3318
Jg	11:35	it **c.** to pass, when he saw her,	1961
Jg	11:39	**c.** to pass at the end of two months,	1961
Jg	13:6	woman **c.** and told her husband,	935
Jg	13:6	A man of God **c.** unto me.	935
Jg	13:9	the angel of God **c.** again unto the	935
Jg	13:10	that **c.** unto me the other day.	935
Jg	13:11	**c.** to the man, and said unto him,	935
Jg	13:20	it **c.** to pass, when the flame went	1961
Jg	14:2	And he **c.** up, and told his father	5927
Jg	14:5	**c.** to the vineyards of Timnath:	935
Jg	14:6	Spirit of the Lord **c.** mightily	6743
Jg	14:9	and **c.** to his father and mother,	1980
Jg	14:11	it **c.** to pass, when they saw him,	1961
Jg	14:14	Out of the eater **c.** forth meat,	3318
Jg	14:14	out of the strong **c.** forth sweetness.	3318
Jg	14:15,	17 **c.** to pass on the seventh day,	1961
Jg	14:19	Spirit of the Lord **c.** upon him,	6743
Jg	15:1	it **c.** to pass, within a while after,	1961
Jg	15:6	the Philistines **c.** up, and burnt	5927
Jg	15:14	he **c.** unto Lehi, the Philistines	935
Jg	15:14	Spirit of the Lord **c.** mightily	6743,935
Jg	15:17	**c.** to pass, when he had made an	1961
Jg	15:19	there **c.** water thereout; and when	3318
Jg	15:19	spirit **c.** again, and he revived:	7725
Jg	16:4	it **c.** to pass afterward, that he	1961
Jg	16:5	lords of the Philistines **c.** up unto	5927
Jg	16:16	**c.** to pass, when she pressed him	1961
Jg	16:18	lords of the Philistines **c.** up unto	5927
Jg	16:25	it **c.** to pass, when their hearts	1961
Jg	16:31	the house of his father **c.** down,	3381
Jg	17:8	he **c.** to mount Ephraim to the	935
Jg	18:2	when they **c.** to mount Ephraim,	935
Jg	18:7	**c.** to Laish, and saw the people	935
Jg	18:8	they **c.** unto their brethren to Zorah	935
Jg	18:13	and **c.** unto the house of Micah.	935
Jg	18:15	**c.** to the house of the young man	935
Jg	18:17	**c.** in thither, and took the graven	935
Jg	18:27	and **c.** unto Laish, unto a people	935
Jg	19:1	And it **c.** to pass on those days,	1961
Jg	19:5	it **c.** to pass on the fourth day,	1961
Jg	19:10	and **c.** over against Jebus, which	935
Jg	19:16	there **c.** an old man from his work	935
Jg	19:22	the man that **c.** into thine house,	935
Jg	19:26	Then **c.** the woman in the dawning	935
Jg	19:30	day that the children of Israel **c.**	5927
Jg	20:4	I **c.** into Gibeah that belongeth to	935
Jg	20:21	the children of Benjamin **c.** forth	3318
Jg	20:24	And the children of Israel **c.** near	7126
Jg	20:26	**c.** unto the house of God, and wept,	935
Jg	20:33	**c.** forth out of their places even	1518
Jg	20:34	there **c.** against Gibeah ten	935
Jg	20:42	them which **c.** out of the cities	
Jg	20:48	all that **c.** to hand: also they set	4672
Jg	20:48	all the cities that they **c.** to	4672
Jg	21:2	the people **c.** to the house of God,	935
Jg	21:4	And it **c.** to pass on the morrow,	1961
Jg	21:5	**c.** not up with the congregation	5927
Jg	21:5	him that **c.** not up to the Lord	5927
Jg	21:8	**c.** not up to Mizpeh to the Lord?	5927
Jg	21:8	there **c.** none to the camp from	935
Jg	21:14	Benjamin **c.** again at that time;	7725
Ru	1:1	it **c.** to pass in the days when	1961
Ru	1:2	they **c.** into the country of Moab,	935
Ru	1:19	until they **c.** to Beth-lehem. And it	935
Ru	1:19	And it **c.** to pass, when they were	1961
Ru	1:22	until they **c.** to Beth-lehem in the	935
Ru	2:3	she went, and **c.**, and gleaned in	935
Ru	2:4	Boaz **c.** from Beth-lehem, and said	935
Ru	2:6	the Moabitish damsel that **c.** back	7725
Ru	2:7	among the sheaves: so she **c.**,	935
Ru	3:7	she **c.** softly, and uncovered his	935
Ru	3:8	it **c.** to pass at midnight, that the	1961
Ru	3:14	that a woman **c.** into the floor.	935
Ru	3:16	when she **c.** to her mother in law,	935
Ru	4:1	of whom Boaz spake **c.** by; unto	5674
1Sa	1:12	**c.** to pass, as she continued	1961
1Sa	1:19	and **c.** to their house to Ramah:	935
1Sa	1:20	it **c.** to pass, when the time was	1961
1Sa	2:13	sacrifice, the priest's servant **c.**,	935
1Sa	2:14	all the Israelites that **c.** thither.	935
1Sa	2:15	the priest's servant **c.**, and said	935
1Sa	2:19	when she **c.** up with her husband	5927
1Sa	2:27	there **c.** a man of God unto Eli,	935
1Sa	3:2	And it **c.** to pass at that time,	1961
1Sa	3:10	the Lord **c.**, and stood, and called	935
1Sa	4:1	the word of Samuel **c.** to all Israel.	1961
1Sa	4:5	ark of the covenant of the Lord **c.**	935
1Sa	4:12	and **c.** to Shiloh the same day with	935
1Sa	4:13	when he **c.**, lo, Eli sat upon a seat	935
1Sa	4:13	when the man **c.** into the city,	935
1Sa	4:14	the man **c.** in hastily, and told Eli.	935
1Sa	4:16	I am he that **c.** out of the army,	935
1Sa	4:18	**c.** to pass, when he made mention	1961
1Sa	4:19	for her pains **c.** upon her.	2015
1Sa	5:10	it **c.** to pass, as the ark of God	1961
1Sa	5:10	as the ark of God **c.** to Ekron,	935
1Sa	6:14	the cart **c.** into the field of Joshua,	935
1Sa	7:1	And the men of Kirjath-jearim **c.**,	935
1Sa	7:2	it **c.** to pass, while the ark abode	1961
1Sa	7:11	them, until they **c.** under Beth-car.	
1Sa	7:13	**c.** no more into the coast of Israel:	935
1Sa	8:1	**c.** to pass, when Samuel was old,	1961
1Sa	8:4	and **c.** to Samuel unto Ramah,	935
1Sa	9:12	for he **c.** to-day to the city; for	935
1Sa	9:14	Samuel **c.** out against them, for	3318
1Sa	9:15	a day before Saul **c.**, saying,	935
1Sa	9:26	**c.** to pass about the spring of the	1961
1Sa	10:19	all those signs **c.** to pass that day.	935
1Sa	10:10	when they **c.** thither to the hill,	935
1Sa	10:10	the Spirit of God **c.** upon him,	6743
1Sa	10:11	**c.** to pass, when all that knew	1961
1Sa	10:13	made an end of prophesying, he **c.**	935
1Sa	10:14	were no where, we **c.** to Samuel.	935
1Sa	11:1	Then Nahash the Ammonite **c.** up,	5927
1Sa	11:4	Then **c.** the messengers to Gibeah	935
1Sa	11:5	Saul **c.** after the herd out of the	935
1Sa	11:6	the Spirit of God **c.** upon Saul	6743
1Sa	11:7	and they **c.** out with one consent.	3318
1Sa	11:9	the messengers that **c.**, Thus shall	935
1Sa	11:9	the messengers **c.** and shewed it	935
1Sa	11:11	they **c.** into the midst of the	935
1Sa	11:11	and it **c.** to pass that they which	1961
1Sa	12:12	Ammon **c.** against you, ye said	935
1Sa	13:5	**c.** up and pitched in Michmash,	5927
1Sa	13:8	Samuel **c.** not to Gilgal; and the	935
1Sa	13:10	it **c.** to pass, that as soon as he	1961
1Sa	13:10	behold, Samuel **c.**; and Saul went	935
1Sa	13:17	the spoilers **c.** out of the camp	3318
1Sa	13:22	it **c.** to pass in the day of battle,	1961
1Sa	14:1	Now it **c.** to pass upon a day,	1961
1Sa	14:19	it **c.** to pass, while Saul talked	1961
1Sa	14:20	they **c.** to the battle: and, behold,	935
1Sa	14:25	all they of the land **c.** to a wood;	935
1Sa	15:2	way, when he **c.** up from Egypt.	5927
1Sa	15:5	And Saul **c.** to a city of Amalek,	935
1Sa	15:6	when they **c.** up out of Egypt.	5927
1Sa	15:10	**c.** the word of the Lord unto	1961
1Sa	15:12	Saul **c.** to Carmel, and, behold,	935
1Sa	15:13	Samuel **c.** to Saul: and Saul said	935
1Sa	15:32	And Agag **c.** unto him delicately.	1980
1Sa	15:35	Samuel **c.** no more to see Saul	
1Sa	16:4	spake, and **c.** to Beth-lehem.	935
1Sa	16:6	**c.** to pass, when they were come,	1961
1Sa	16:13	Spirit of the Lord **c.** upon David	6743
1Sa	16:21	David **c.** to Saul, and stood before	935
1Sa	16:23	it **c.** to pass, when the evil spirit	1961
1Sa	17:20	he **c.** to the trench, as the host	935
1Sa	17:22	and **c.** and saluted his brethren.	935
1Sa	17:23	there **c.** up the champion, the	5927
1Sa	17:34	and there **c.** a lion, and a bear,	935
1Sa	17:41	the Philistine **c.** on and drew	3212
1Sa	17:48	it **c.** to pass, when the Philistine	1961
1Sa	17:48	and **c.** and drew nigh to meet	3212
1Sa	18:1	**c.** to pass, when he had made	1961
1Sa	18:6	And it **c.** to pass as they	1961
1Sa	18:6	as they **c.**, when David was	935
1Sa	18:6	the women **c.** out of all cities	3318
1Sa	18:10	And it **c.** to pass on the morrow,	1961
1Sa	18:10	spirit from God **c.** upon Saul,	6473
1Sa	18:13	out and **c.** in before the people.	935
1Sa	18:16	he went out and **c.** in before them.	935
1Sa	18:19	**c.** to pass at the time when Merab	1961
1Sa	18:30	it **c.** to pass, after they went forth,	1961
1Sa	19:18	**c.** to Samuel to Ramah, and told	935
1Sa	19:22	**c.** to a great well that is in Sechu:	935
1Sa	19:23	until he **c.** to Naioth in Ramah.	935
1Sa	20:1	and **c.** and said before Jonathan,	935
1Sa	20:27	it **c.** to pass on the morrow,	1961
1Sa	20:35	And it **c.** to pass in the morning,	1961
1Sa	20:38	the arrows, and **c.** to his master.	935
1Sa	21:1	**c.** David to Nob to Ahimelech	935
1Sa	21:5	these three days, since I **c.** out,	3318
1Sa	22:5	and **c.** into the forest of Hareth.	935
1Sa	22:11	they **c.** all of them to the king.	935
1Sa	23:6	it **c.** to pass, when Abiathar	1961
1Sa	23:6	**c.** down with an ephod in his	3381
1Sa	23:19	Then **c.** up the Ziphites to Saul	5927
1Sa	23:25	wherefore he **c.** down into a rock,	3381
1Sa	23:27	there **c.** a messenger unto Saul,	935
1Sa	24:1	**c.** to pass, when Saul was	1961
1Sa	24:3	he **c.** to the sheepcotes by the way,	935
1Sa	24:5	**c.** to pass afterward, that David	1961
1Sa	24:16	And it **c.** to pass, when David	1961
1Sa	25:9	when David's young men **c.**. they	935
1Sa	25:12	went again, and **c.** and told him all	935
1Sa	25:20	**c.** down by the covert of the hill,	3381
1Sa	25:20	and his men **c.** down against her;	3381
1Sa	25:36	Abigail **c.** to Nabal; and, behold,	935
1Sa	25:37	But it **c.** to pass in the morning,	1916
1Sa	25:38	it **c.** to pass about ten days after,	1916
1Sa	26:1	And the Ziphites **c.** unto Saul to	935
1Sa	26:3	he saw that Saul **c.** after him into	935
1Sa	26:5	and **c.** to the place where Saul had	935
1Sa	26:7	David and Abishai **c.** to the people	935
1Sa	26:15	for there **c.** one of the people in to	935
1Sa	27:9	and returned, and **c.** to Achish.	935
1Sa	28:1	And it **c.** to pass in those days,	1961
1Sa	28:4	and **c.** and pitched in Shunem:	935
1Sa	28:8	they **c.** to the woman by night:	935
1Sa	28:21	And the woman **c.** unto Saul,	935
1Sa	30:1	And it **c.** to pass, when David	1961
1Sa	30:3	David and his men **c.** to the city,	935
1Sa	30:9	and **c.** to the brook Besor, where	935
1Sa	30:12	when he had eaten, his spirit **c.**	7725
1Sa	30:21	David **c.** to the two hundred men,	935
1Sa	30:21	when David **c.** near to the people,	5066
1Sa	30:23	the company that **c.** against us	935
1Sa	30:26	when David **c.** to Ziklag, he sent	935
1Sa	31:7	Philistines **c.** and dwelt in them.	935
1Sa	31:8	And it **c.** to pass on the morrow,	1691
1Sa	31:8	Philistines **c.** to strip the slain,	935
1Sa	31:12	**c.** to Jabesh, and burnt them.	935
2Sa	1:1	**c.** to pass after the death of Saul,	1961

2Sa 1:2 It **c.** even to pass on the third day, ... 1961
2Sa 1:2 a man **c.** out of the camp from Saul..... 935
2Sa 1:2 when he **c.** to David, that he fell to..... 935
2Sa 2:1 And it **c.** to pass after this, that........ 1961
2Sa 2:4 the men of Judah **c.**, and there.......... 935
2Sa 2:23 that the spear **c.** out behind............ 3318
2Sa 2:23 that as many as **c.** to the place.......... 935
2Sa 2:29 and they **c.** to Mahanaim.................. 935
2Sa 2:32 they **c.** to Hebron at break of day....... 935
2Sa 3:6 it **c.** to pass, while there was war 1961
2Sa 3:20 So Abner **c.** to David to Hebron,........ 935
2Sa 3:22 Joab **c.** from pursuing a troop,............ 935
2Sa 3:23 Abner the son of Ner **c.** to the king, ... 935
2Sa 3:24 Then Joab **c.** to the king, and said, ... 935
2Sa 3:24 behold, Abner **c.** unto thee; why is 935
2Sa 3:25 he **c.** to deceive thee, and to know 935
2Sa 3:35 all the people **c.** to cause David to 935
2Sa 4:4 when the tidings **c.** of Saul and.......... 935
2Sa 4:4 **c.** to pass, as she made haste to.......... 1961
2Sa 4:5 **c.** about the heat of the day to the....... 935
2Sa 4:6 And they **c.** thither into the midst....... 935
2Sa 4:7 For when they **c.** into the house,......... 935
2Sa 5:1 **c.** all the tribes of Israel to David 935
2Sa 5:3 the elders of Israel **c.** to the king 935
2Sa 5:17 Philistines **c.** up to seek David;.......... 5927
2Sa 5:18 Philistines also **c.** and spread.............. 935
2Sa 5:20 And David **c.** to Baal-perazim,............ 935
2Sa 5:22 Philistines **c.** up yet again, and.......... 5927
2Sa 6:6 they **c.** to Nachon's threshingfloor,....... 935
2Sa 6:16 the ark of the Lord **c.** into the city 935
2Sa 6:20 daughter of Saul **c.** out to meet 3318
2Sa 7:1 it **c.** to pass, when the king sat in 1961
2Sa 7:4 **c.** to pass that night, that the........... 1961
2Sa 7:4 word of the Lord **c.** unto Nathan,....... 1961
2Sa 8:1 **c.** to pass, that David smote the 1961
2Sa 8:5 Syrians of Damascus **c.** to succour....... 935
2Sa 10:1 And it **c.** to pass after this, that........ 1961
2Sa 10:2 David's servants **c.** into the land......... 935
2Sa 10:8 the children of Ammon **c.** out, ... 3318
2Sa 10:14 of Ammon, and **c.** to Jerusalem. 935
2Sa 10:16 and they **c.** to Helam; and Shobach 935
2Sa 10:17 over Jordan, and **c.** to Helam............. 935
2Sa 11:1 And it **c.** to pass, after the year.......... 1961
2Sa 11:2 it **c.** to pass in an evening tide,.......... 1961
2Sa 11:4 and she **c.** in unto him, and he lay 935
2Sa 11:14 And it **c.** to pass in the morning......... 1961
2Sa 11:16 it **c.** to pass, when Joab observed....... 1961
2Sa 11:22 and **c.** and shewed David all that 935
2Sa 11:22 and **c.** out unto us into the field, ... 3318
2Sa 12:1 he **c.** unto him, and said unto him, ... 935
2Sa 12:4 And there **c.** a traveller unto the 935
2Sa 12:18 it **c.** to pass on the seventh day,........ 1961
2Sa 12:20 and **c.** into the house of the Lord, ... 935
2Sa 12:20 then he **c.** to his own house; 935
2Sa 13:1 **c.** to pass after this, that Absalom...... 1961
2Sa 13:23 it **c.** to pass after two full years, ... 1961
2Sa 13:24 Absalom **c.** to the king, ... 935
2Sa 13:30 And it **c.** to pass, while they were........ 1961
2Sa 13:30 that tidings **c.** to David, saying, ... 935
2Sa 13:34 there **c.** much people by the way 1980
2Sa 13:36 it **c.** to pass, as soon as he had 1961
2Sa 13:36 behold, the king's sons **c.**;.................. 935
2Sa 14:31 and **c.** to Absalom unto his house, ... 935
2Sa 14:33 Joab **c.** to the king, and told him:......... 935
2Sa 14:33 called for Absalom, he **c.** to the........... 935
2Sa 15:1 **c.** to pass after this, that.................. 1961
2Sa 15:2 **c.** to the king for judgment,................ 935
2Sa 15:5 when any man **c.** nigh to him to.......... 7126
2Sa 15:6 all Israel that **c.** to the king for............ 935
2Sa 15:7 And it **c.** to pass after forty years, ... 1961
2Sa 15:13 there **c.** a messenger to David, ... 935
2Sa 15:18 six hundred men which **c.** after 935
2Sa 15:32 it **c.** to pass, that when David........... 1961
2Sa 15:32 Hushai the Archite **c.** to meet him...........
2Sa 15:37 Hushai David's friend **c.** into the.......... 935
2Sa 15:37 Absalom **c.** into Jerusalem. 935
2Sa 16:5 when king David **c.** to Bahurim, ... 935
2Sa 16:5 behold, thence **c.** out a man.............. 3318
2Sa 16:5 he **c.** forth, and cursed still as he....... 3318
2Sa 16:5 and cursed still as he **c.**. 3318
2Sa 16:11 my son, which **c.** forth of my 3318
2Sa 16:14 the people that were with him, **c.**......... 935
2Sa 16:15 the men of Israel, **c.** to Jerusalem,....... 935
2Sa 16:16 it **c.** to pass, when Hushai the........... 1961
2Sa 17:18 **c.** to a man's house in Bahurim, ... 935
2Sa 17:20 And when Absalom's servants **c.**.......... 935
2Sa 17:21 **c.** to pass, after they were 1961
2Sa 17:21 that they **c.** up out of the well, ... 5927
2Sa 17:24 Then David **c.** to Mahanaim................ 935
2Sa 17:27 And it **c.** to pass, when David 1961
2Sa 18:4 all the people **c.** out by hundreds 3318
2Sa 18:25 And he **c.** apace, and drew near......... 3212
2Sa 18:31 And, behold, Cushi **c.**; and Cushi......... 935
2Sa 19:5 Joab **c.** into the house to the king, ... 935
2Sa 19:8 all the people **c.** before the king: 935
2Sa 19:15 king returned, and **c.** to Jordan............ 935
2Sa 19:15 And Judah **c.** to Gilgal, ... 935
2Sa 19:16 **c.** down with the men of Judah 3381
2Sa 19:24 the son of Saul **c.** down to meet 3381
2Sa 19:24 until the day he **c.** again in peace......... 935
2Sa 19:25 And it **c.** to pass, when he was 1961
2Sa 19:31 Gileadite **c.** down from Rogelim, ... 3381
2Sa 19:41 all the men of Israel **c.** to the king, ... 935
2Sa 20:3 David **c.** to his house at Jerusalem; 935
2Sa 20:12 every one that **c.** by him stood still...... 935
2Sa 20:15 they **c.** and besieged him in Abel 935
2Sa 21:18 **c.** to pass after this, that there 1961
2Sa 22:10 bowed the heavens also, and **c.** 3381
2Sa 23:13 **c.** to David in the harvest time............ 935
2Sa 24:6 Then they **c.** to Gilead, and to the....... 935
2Sa 24:6 and they **c.** to Dan-jaan,.................... 935
2Sa 24:7 And **c.** to the stronghold of Tyre, ... 935
2Sa 24:8 all the land, they **c.** to Jerusalem 935
2Sa 24:11 the word of the Lord **c.** unto the 1961
2Sa 24:13 So Gad **c.** to David, and told him,........ 935
2Sa 24:18 And Gad **c.** that day to David,............. 935
1Ki 1:22 Nathan the prophet also **c.** in.............. 935
1Ki 1:28 And she **c.** into the king's presence,..... 935
1Ki 1:32 And they **c.** before the king................ 935
1Ki 1:40 all the people **c.** up after him,............ 5927
1Ki 1:42 Abiathar the priest **c.**: and................. 935
1Ki 1:47 the king's servants **c.** to bless our 935
1Ki 1:53 he **c.** and bowed himself to king......... 7126
1Ki 2:7 they **c.** to me when I fled because 935
1Ki 2:8 he **c.** down to meet me at Jordan, ... 3381
1Ki 2:13 son of Haggith **c.** to Bathsheba............ 935
1Ki 2:28 Then tidings **c.** to Joab: for Joab 935
1Ki 2:30 And Benaiah **c.** to the tabernacle 935
1Ki 2:39 **c.** to pass at the end of three............ 1961
1Ki 3:15 And he **c.** to Jerusalem, and stood 935
1Ki 3:16 Then **c.** there two women, that........... 935
1Ki 3:18 And it **c.** to pass the third day........... 1961
1Ki 4:27 that **c.** unto king Solomon's table,....... 7131
1Ki 4:34 And there **c.** of all people to hear 935
1Ki 5:7 it **c.** to pass, when Hiram heard......... 1961
1Ki 6:1 it **c.** to pass in the four hundred......... 1961
1Ki 6:11 word of the Lord **c.** to Solomon, ... 1961
1Ki 7:14 And he **c.** to king Solomon, ... 935
1Ki 8:3 And all the elders of Israel **c.**.............. 935
1Ki 8:9 they **c.** out of the land of Egypt. 3318
1Ki 8:10 **c.** to pass, when the priests were 1961
1Ki 9:1 And it **c.** to pass, when Solomon......... 1961
1Ki 9:10 **c.** to pass at the end of twenty.......... 1961
1Ki 9:12 And Hiram **c.** out from Tyre 3318
1Ki 9:24 Pharaoh's daughter **c.** up out of 5927
1Ki 9:28 And they **c.** to Ophir, and fetched........ 935
1Ki 10:1 **c.** to prove him with hard questions. 935
1Ki 10:2 And she **c.** to Jerusalem with a........... 935
1Ki 10:7 believed not the words, until I **c.**, ... 935
1Ki 10:10 **c.** no more such abundance of spices.... 935
1Ki 10:12 there **c.** no such almug trees, ... 935
1Ki 10:14 gold that **c.** to Solomon in one year...... 935
1Ki 10:22 once in three years **c.** the navy of 935
1Ki 10:29 And a chariot **c.** up and went out 5927
1Ki 11:4 **c.** to pass, when Solomon was old, ... 1961
1Ki 11:15 **c.** to pass, when David was in.......... 1961
1Ki 11:18 and **c.** to Paran: and they took........... 935
1Ki 11:18 out of Paran, and they **c.** to Egypt,...... 935
1Ki 11:29 it **c.** to pass at that time when.......... 1961
1Ki 12:2 And it **c.** to pass, when Jeroboam....... 1961
1Ki 12:3 all the congregation of Israel **c.**, ... 935
1Ki 12:12 Jeroboam and all the people **c.** to......... 935
1Ki 12:20 And it **c.** to pass, when all Israel....... 1961
1Ki 12:22 word of God **c.** unto Shemaiah............ 1961
1Ki 13:1 there **c.** a man of God out of Judah...... 935
1Ki 13:4 it **c.** to pass, when king Jeroboam 1961
1Ki 13:10 returned not by the way that he **c.** 935
1Ki 13:11 and his sons **c.** and told him all........... 935
1Ki 13:12 God went, which **c.** from Judah. 935
1Ki 13:20 **c.** to pass, as they sat at the table, ... 1961
1Ki 13:20 the word of the Lord **c.** unto the 1961
1Ki 13:21 that **c.** from Judah, saying, ... 935
1Ki 13:23 **c.** to pass, after he had eaten........... 1961
1Ki 13:25 and they **c.** and told it in the city........ 935
1Ki 13:29 and the old prophet **c.** to the city, ... 935
1Ki 13:31 **c.** to pass, after he had buried........... 1961
1Ki 14:4 and **c.** to the house of Ahijah............. 935
1Ki 14:6 as she **c.** in at the door, that he.......... 935
1Ki 14:17 and departed, and **c.** to Tirzah: 935
1Ki 14:17 **c.** to the threshold of the door, ... 935
1Ki 14:25 And it **c.** to pass in the fifth year 1961
1Ki 14:25 of Egypt **c.** up against Jerusalem: 5927
1Ki 15:21 it **c.** to pass, when Baasha heard......... 1961
1Ki 15:29 it **c.** to pass, when he reigned, ... 1961
1Ki 16:1 the word of the Lord **c.** to Jehu......... 1961
1Ki 16:7 Jehu the son of Hanani **c.** the............ 1961
1Ki 16:11 **c.** to pass, when he began to reign,.... 1961
1Ki 16:18 **c.** to pass, when Zimri saw that......... 1961
1Ki 16:31 **c.** to pass, as it it had been a light 1961
1Ki 17:2 the word of the Lord **c.** unto him,...... 1961
1Ki 17:7 And it **c.** to pass after a while, that 1961
1Ki 17:8 word of the Lord **c.** unto him, ... 1961
1Ki 17:10 when he **c.** to the gate of the city,....... 935
1Ki 17:17 it **c.** to pass after these things, ... 1961
1Ki 17:22 soul of the child **c.** into him again, ... 7725
1Ki 18:1 it **c.** to pass after many days, ... 1961
1Ki 18:1 the word of the Lord **c.** to Elijah......... 1961
1Ki 18:17 **c.** to pass, when Ahab saw Elijah, ... 1961
1Ki 18:21 And Elijah **c.** unto all the people,........ 5066
1Ki 18:27 it **c.** to pass at noon, that Elijah......... 1961
1Ki 18:29 **c.** to pass, when midday was past, ... 1961
1Ki 18:30 all the people **c.** near unto him. 5066
1Ki 18:31 word of the Lord **c.**, saying, Israel..... 1961
1Ki 18:36 And it **c.** to pass at the time of the 1961
1Ki 18:36 that Elijah the prophet **c.** near, ... 5066
1Ki 18:44 **c.** to pass at the seventh time, ... 1961
1Ki 18:45 it **c.** to pass in the mean while,.......... 1961
1Ki 19:3 and **c.** to Beer-sheba, which 935
1Ki 19:4 **c.** and sat down under a juniper........... 935
1Ki 19:7 the angel of the Lord **c.** again........... 7725
1Ki 19:9 And he **c.** thither unto a cave,............. 935
1Ki 19:9 behold, the word of the Lord **c.** to ....
1Ki 19:13 And, behold, there **c.** a voice unto him, 1961
1Ki 20:5 the messengers **c.** again, and said, ... 7725
1Ki 20:12 **c.** to pass, when Ben-hadad heard......... 1961
1Ki 20:13 there **c.** a prophet unto Ahab king...... 5066
1Ki 20:19 the princes of the provinces **c.**........... 3318
1Ki 20:22 the prophet **c.** to the king of Israel, ... 5066
1Ki 20:26 **c.** to pass at the return of the year, ... 1961
1Ki 20:28 there **c.** a man of God, and spake 5066
1Ki 20:30 Ben-hadad fled, and **c.** into the............ 935
1Ki 20:32 **c.** to the king of Israel, and said, ... 935
1Ki 20:33 Then Ben-hadad **c.** forth to him; 3318
1Ki 20:43 and displeased, and **c.** to Samaria......... 935
1Ki 21:1 it **c.** to pass after these things, ... 1961
1Ki 21:4 Ahab **c.** into his house heavy and........ 935
1Ki 21:5 But Jezebel his wife **c.** to him, and....... 935
1Ki 21:13 there **c.** in two men, children of.......... 935
1Ki 21:15 **c.** to pass, when Jezebel heard 1961
1Ki 21:16 And it **c.** to pass, when Ahab heard.... 1961
1Ki 21:17 word of the Lord **c.** to Elijah............. 1961
1Ki 21:27 And it **c.** to pass, when Ahab heard.... 1961
1Ki 21:28 the word of the Lord **c.** to Elijah........ 1961
1Ki 22:2 it **c.** to pass in the third year,............ 1961
1Ki 22:2 the king of Judah **c.** down................. 3381
1Ki 22:15 So he **c.** to the king. And the 935
1Ki 22:21 there **c.** forth a spirit, and stood 3318
1Ki 22:32, 33 it **c.** to pass, when the captains 1961
2Ki 1:6 There **c.** a man up to meet us, ... 5927
2Ki 1:7 manner of man was he which **c.**.......... 5927
2Ki 1:10 there **c.** down fire from heaven,......... 3381
2Ki 1:12 fire of God **c.** down from heaven,........ 3381
2Ki 1:13 **c.** and fell on his knees before............. 935
2Ki 1:14 there **c.** fire down from heaven,......... 3381
2Ki 2:1 **c.** to pass, when the Lord would......... 1961
2Ki 2:3 that were at Beth-el **c.** forth 3318
2Ki 2:4 leave thee. So they **c.** to Jericho. 935
2Ki 2:5 that were at Jericho **c.** to Elisha,........ 5066
2Ki 2:9 it **c.** to pass when they were............... 1961
2Ki 2:11 **c.** to pass, as they still went on, ... 1961
2Ki 2:15 they **c.** to meet him, and bowed.......... 935
2Ki 2:18 when they **c.** again to him, (for he...... 7725
2Ki 2:23 there **c.** forth little children out.......... 3318
2Ki 2:24 there **c.** forth two she bears out 3318
2Ki 3:5 it **c.** to pass, when Ahab was dead, ... 1961
2Ki 3:15 it **c.** to pass, when the minstrel 1961
2Ki 3:15 the hand of the Lord **c.** upon him. 1961
2Ki 3:20 **c.** to pass in the morning, when......... 1961
2Ki 3:20 there **c.** water by the way of Edom,..... 935
2Ki 3:24 when they **c.** to the camp of Israel,...... 935
2Ki 4:6 it **c.** to pass, when the vessels 1961

2Ki 4:7 Then she **c.** and told the man of.......... 935
2Ki 4:11 that he **c.** thither, and he turned.......... 935
2Ki 4:25 went, and **c.** unto the man of God....... 935
2Ki 4:25 it **c.** to pass, when the man of God.... 1961
2Ki 4:27 when she **c.** to the man of God to....... 935
2Ki 4:27 Gehazi **c.** near to thrust her away...... 5066
2Ki 4:38 Elisha **c.** again to Gilgal: and............ 7725
2Ki 4:39 **c.** and shred them into the pot............ 935
2Ki 4:40 it **c.** to pass, as they were eating....... 1961
2Ki 4:42 there **c.** a man from Baal-shalisha, ... 935
2Ki 5:7 it **c.** to pass, when the king of........... 1961
2Ki 5:9 So Naaman **c.** with his horses............. 935
2Ki 5:13 his servants **c.** near, and spake.......... 5066
2Ki 5:14 his flesh **c.** again like unto the.......... 7725
2Ki 5:15 and **c.**, and stood before him:............. 935
2Ki 5:24 And when he **c.** to the tower, he......... 935
2Ki 6:4 when they **c.** to Jordan, they cut......... 935
2Ki 6:14 they **c.** by night, and compassed.......... 935
2Ki 6:18 when they **c.** down to him, Elisha...... 3381
2Ki 6:20 it **c.** to pass, when they were come.... 1961
2Ki 6:23 the bands of Syria **c.** no more into....... 935
2Ki 6:24 **c.** to pass after this, that................. 1961
2Ki 6:30 it **c.** to pass, when the king heard...... 1961
2Ki 6:32 ere the messenger **c.** to him, he......... 935
2Ki 6:33 behold, the messenger **c.** down.......... 3381
2Ki 7:8 when these lepers **c.** to the............... 935
2Ki 7:8 **c.** again, and entered into................ 7725
2Ki 7:10 they **c.**, and called unto the porter....... 935
2Ki 7:10 We **c.** to the camp of the Syrians, ... 935
2Ki 7:17 when the king **c.** down to him. 3381
2Ki 7:18 it **c.** to pass as the man of God.......... 1961
2Ki 8:3 **c.** to pass at the seven years' end,..... 1961
2Ki 8:5 it **c.** to pass, as he was telling the...... 1961
2Ki 8:7 And Elisha **c.** to Damascus; and 935
2Ki 8:9 **c.** and stood before him, and said, ... 935
2Ki 8:14 and **c.** to his master; who said to......... 935
2Ki 8:15 it **c.** to pass on the morrow, that....... 1961
2Ki 9:5 when he **c.**, behold, the captains of...... 935
2Ki 9:11 Jehu **c.** forth to the servants of.......... 3318
2Ki 9:11 wherefore **c.** this mad fellow to........... 935
2Ki 9:17 spied the company of Jehu as he **c.**,..... 935
2Ki 9:18 The messenger **c.** to them, but he....... 935
2Ki 9:19 on horseback which **c.** to them,........... 935
2Ki 9:20 He **c.** even unto them, and cometh...... 935
2Ki 9:22 **c.** to pass, when Joram saw Jehu, ... 1961
2Ki 9:36 Wherefore they **c.** again, and told....... 7725
2Ki 10:7 And it **c.** to pass, when the letter...... 1961
2Ki 10:7 when the letter **c.** to them, ... 935
2Ki 10:8 And there **c.** a messenger, and told...... 935
2Ki 10:9 it **c.** to pass in the morning, that........ 1961
2Ki 10:12 and departed, and **c.** to Samaria......... 1980
2Ki 10:17 And when he **c.** to Samaria, he slew.... 935
2Ki 10:21 and all the worshippers of Baal **c.**, ... 935
2Ki 10:21 not a man left that **c.** not.................. 935
2Ki 10:21 And they **c.** into the house of Baal;...... 935
2Ki 10:25 it **c.** to pass, as soon as he had......... 1961
2Ki 11:9 and **c.** to Jehoiada the priest, ... 935
2Ki 11:13 she **c.** to the people into the temple.... 935
2Ki 11:16 way by the which the horses **c.**......... 3996
2Ki 11:19 and **c.** by the way of the gate of.......... 935
2Ki 12:10 scribe and the high priest **c.** up,......... 5927
2Ki 13:14 Joash the king of Israel **c.** down......... 3381
2Ki 13:21 it **c.** to pass, as they were burying..... 1961
2Ki 14:5 **c.** to pass, as soon as the kingdom..... 1961
2Ki 14:13 and **c.** to Jerusalem, and brake............ 935
2Ki 15:12 And so it **c.** to pass........................ 1961
2Ki 15:14 and **c.** to Samaria, and smote............. 935
2Ki 15:19 of Assyria **c.** against the land: 935
2Ki 15:29 **c.** Tiglath-pileser king of Assyria,......... 935
2Ki 16:5 son of Remaliah king of Israel **c.** 5927
2Ki 16:6 the Syrians **c.** to Elath, and dwelt........ 935
2Ki 16:11 against king Ahaz **c.** from Damascus..... 935
2Ki 17:3 Against him **c.** up Shalmaneser 5927
2Ki 17:5 Then the king of Assyria **c.** up 5927
2Ki 17:28 had carried away from Samaria **c.**. 935
2Ki 18:1 it **c.** to pass in the third year of......... 1961
2Ki 18:9 it **c.** to pass in the fourth year of....... 1961
2Ki 18:9 Shalmaneser king of Assyria **c.** up...... 5927
2Ki 18:17 and **c.** to Jerusalem. And when............ 935
2Ki 18:17 they were come up, they **c.** and.......... 935
2Ki 18:18 there **c.** out to them Eliakim the........ 3318
2Ki 18:37 Then **c.** Eliakim the son of Hilkiah. 935
2Ki 19:1 it **c.** to pass, when king Hezekiah........ 1961
2Ki 19:5 So the servants of king Hezekiah **c.** 935
2Ki 19:33 By the way that he **c.**, by the same..... 935
2Ki 19:35 **c.** to pass that night, that the............ 1961
2Ki 19:37 And it **c.** to pass, as he was.............. 1961
2Ki 20:1 prophet Isaiah the son of Amoz **c.**........ 935
2Ki 20:4 **c.** to pass, afore Isaiah was gone 1961
2Ki 20:4 word of the Lord **c.** to him, saying, ... 1961
2Ki 20:14 Then **c.** Isaiah the prophet unto........... 935
2Ki 20:14 from whence **c.** they unto thee? 935
2Ki 21:15 the day their fathers **c.** forth out........ 3318
2Ki 22:3 it **c.** to pass in the eighteenth year..... 1961
2Ki 22:9 Shaphan the scribe **c.** to the king,........ 935
2Ki 22:11 **c.** to pass, when the king had............ 1961
2Ki 23:9 the priests of the high places **c.**.......... 5927
2Ki 23:17 which **c.** from Judah, and.................... 935
2Ki 23:18 prophet that **c.** out of Samaria............. 935
2Ki 23:34 he **c.** to Egypt, and died there. 935
2Ki 24:1 king of Babylon **c.** up, and 5927
2Ki 24:3 **c.** this upon Judah, to remove............ 1961
2Ki 24:7 And the king of Egypt **c.** not............. 3318
2Ki 24:10 king of Babylon **c.** up against............. 5927
2Ki 24:11 Nebuchadnezzar king of Babylon **c.**........ 935
2Ki 24:20 **c.** to pass in Jerusalem and.............. 1961
2Ki 25:1 it **c.** to pass in the ninth year of......... 1961
2Ki 25:1 king of Babylon **c.**, he, and all............. 935
2Ki 25:8 king of Babylon, **c.** Nebuzar-adan, ... 935
2Ki 25:23 there **c.** to Gedaliah, to Mizpah, ... 935
2Ki 25:25 **c.** to pass in the seventh month.......... 1961
2Ki 25:25 **c.**, and ten men with him, and............. 935
2Ki 25:26 and **c.** to Egypt: for they were............ 935
2Ki 25:27 it **c.** to pass in the seven and............ 1961
1Ch 1:12 (of whom **c.** the Philistines,) and......... 3318
1Ch 2:53 of them **c.** the Zareathites, and........... 3318
1Ch 2:55 the Kenites that **c.** of Hemath, the....... 935
1Ch 4:41 And these written by name **c.** in.......... 935
1Ch 5:2 and of him **c.** the chief ruler; but.............
1Ch 7:21 because they **c.** down to take away 3381
1Ch 7:22 and his brethren **c.** to comfort him....... 935
1Ch 10:7 the Philistines **c.** and dwelt in.............. 935
1Ch 10:8 it **c.** to pass on the morrow, ... 1961
1Ch 10:8 when the Philistines **c.** to strip the....... 935
1Ch 11:3 Therefore **c.** all the elders of Israel...... 935
1Ch 12:1 these are they that **c.** to David............ 935
1Ch 12:16 And there **c.** of the children of............ 935
1Ch 12:18 the spirit **c.** upon Amasai, who 3847
1Ch 12:19 when he **c.** with the Philistines............ 935
1Ch 12:22 there **c.** to David to help him,............ 935
1Ch 12:23 **c.** to David to Hebron, to turn the........ 935
1Ch 12:38 **c.** with a perfect heart to Hebron, ... 935
1Ch 13:9 they **c.** unto the threshingfloor............ 935
1Ch 14:9 the Philistines **c.** and spread.............. 935
1Ch 14:11 So they **c.** up to Baal-perazim;............ 5927
1Ch 15:26 **c.** to pass, when God helped the........ 1961
1Ch 15:29 And it **c.** to pass, as the ark of the..... 1961
1Ch 15:29 ark of the covenant of the Lord **c.** 935
1Ch 17:1 it **c.** to pass, as David sat in his......... 1961
1Ch 17:3 And it **c.** to pass the same night, ... 1961
1Ch 17:3 that the word of God **c.** to Nathan,..... 1961
1Ch 17:16 And David the king **c.** and sat............ 935
1Ch 18:1 it **c.** to pass, that David smote the..... 1961
1Ch 18:5 Syrians of Damascus **c.** to help........... 935
1Ch 19:1 **c.** to pass after this, that Nahash 1961
1Ch 19:2 So the servants of David **c.** into 935
1Ch 19:7 who **c.** and pitched before Medeba....... 935
1Ch 19:7 from their cities, and **c.** to battle. 935
1Ch 19:9 the children of Ammon **c.** out, ... 3318
1Ch 19:15 city. Then Joab **c.** to Jerusalem. 935
1Ch 19:17 and **c.** upon them, and set the............ 935
1Ch 20:1 it **c.** to pass, that after the year......... 1961
1Ch 20:1 and **c.** and besieged Rabbah................ 935
1Ch 20:4 And it **c.** to pass after this, that......... 1961
1Ch 21:4 all Israel, and **c.** to Jerusalem.............. 935
1Ch 21:11 So Gad **c.** to David, and said unto........ 935
1Ch 21:21 And as David **c.** to Ornan, Ornan......... 935
1Ch 22:8 But the word of the Lord **c.** to me,.... 1961
1Ch 24:7 the first lot **c.** forth to Jehoiarib, ... 3318
1Ch 24:28 Mahli **c.** Eleazar, who had no son............
1Ch 25:9 the first lot **c.** forth for Asaph........... 3318
1Ch 26:14 lots; and his lot **c.** out northward. 3318
1Ch 26:16 Hosah the lot **c.** forth westward,..............
1Ch 27:1 which **c.** in and went out month........... 935
2Ch 1:13 Solomon **c.** from his journey to............ 935
2Ch 5:4 And all the elders of Israel **c.**;............ 935
2Ch 5:10 children of Israel, when they **c.** out 3318
2Ch 5:11 And it **c.** to pass, when the priests..... 1961
2Ch 5:13 It **c.** even to pass, as the trumpeters.. 1961
2Ch 7:1 the fire **c.** down from heaven, and....... 3381
2Ch 7:3 Israel saw how the fire **c.** down, ... 3381
2Ch 7:11 all that **c.** into Solomon's heart to 935
2Ch 8:1 it **c.** to pass at the end of twenty....... 1961
2Ch 9:1 she **c.** to prove Solomon with hard....... 935
2Ch 9:6 believed not their words, until I **c.**....... 935
2Ch 9:13 Now the weight of gold that **c.** to........ 935
2Ch 9:21 **c.** the ships of Tarshish bringing.......... 935
2Ch 10:2 And it **c.** to pass, when Jeroboam....... 1961
2Ch 10:3 So Jeroboam and all Israel **c.** and......... 935
2Ch 10:12 So Jeroboam and all the people **c.**......... 935
2Ch 11:2 word of the Lord **c.** to Shemaiah........ 1961
2Ch 11:14 and **c.** to Judah and Jerusalem:.......... 3212
2Ch 11:16 **c.** to Jerusalem, to sacrifice unto 935
2Ch 12:1 it **c.** to pass, when Rehoboam had...... 1961
2Ch 12:2 it **c.** to pass, that in the fifth year 1961
2Ch 12:2 Shishak king of Egypt **c.** up............... 5927
2Ch 12:3 that **c.** with him out of Egypt;............. 935
2Ch 12:4 to Judah, and **c.** to Jerusalem.............. 935
2Ch 12:5 Then **c.** Shemaiah, the prophet to........ 935
2Ch 12:7 word of the Lord **c.** to Shemaiah,....... 1961
2Ch 12:9 So Shishak king of Egypt **c.** up.......... 5927
2Ch 12:11 the guard **c.** and fetched them,............ 935
2Ch 13:15 of Judah shouted, it **c.** to pass, ... 1961
2Ch 14:9 there **c.** out against them Zerah......... 3318
2Ch 14:9 chariots; and **c.** unto Mareshah............ 935
2Ch 14:14 the fear of the Lord **c.** upon them: 1961
2Ch 15:1 the Spirit of God **c.** upon Azariah....... 1961
2Ch 15:5 nor to him that **c.** in, but great........... 935
2Ch 16:1 Baasha king of Israel **c.** up................ 5927
2Ch 16:5 it **c.** to pass, when Baasha heard........ 1961
2Ch 16:7 Hanani the seer **c.** to Asa king of........ 935
2Ch 18:20 Then there **c.** out a spirit, and.......... 3318
2Ch 18:23 the son of Chenaanah **c.** near, ... 5066
2Ch 18:31 it **c.** to pass, when the captains of...... 1961
2Ch 18:32 For it **c.** to pass, that, when the........ 1961
2Ch 20:1 **c.** to pass after this also, that the....... 1961
2Ch 20:1 Ammonites **c.** against Jehoshaphat........ 935
2Ch 20:2 **c.** some that told Jehoshaphat, ... 935
2Ch 20:4 of Judah they **c.** to seek the Lord. 935
2Ch 20:10 invade, when they **c.** out of the land,.... 935
2Ch 20:14 Asaph, **c.** the Spirit of the Lord......... 1961
2Ch 20:24 Judah **c.** toward the watch tower......... 935
2Ch 20:25 when Jehoshaphat and his people **c.**...... 935
2Ch 20:28 And they **c.** to Jerusalem with............. 935
2Ch 21:12 And there **c.** a writing to him from....... 935
2Ch 21:17 And they **c.** up into Judah, and 5927
2Ch 21:19 **c.** to pass that in process of time, ... 1961
2Ch 22:1 the band of men that **c.** with the 935
2Ch 22:8 **c.** to pass, that, when Jehu was......... 1961
2Ch 23:2 Israel, and they **c.** to Jerusalem........... 935
2Ch 23:12 and praising the king, she **c.** to 935
2Ch 23:20 they **c.** through the high gate into........ 935
2Ch 24:4 it **c.** to pass after this, that Joash....... 1961
2Ch 24:11 it **c.** to pass, that at what time 1961
2Ch 24:11 hight priest's officer **c.** and emptied...... 935
2Ch 24:17 **c.** the princes of Judah, and made 935
2Ch 24:18 **c.** upon Judah and Jerusalem............. 1961
2Ch 24:20 the Spirit of God **c.** upon Zechariah..... 3847
2Ch 24:23 it **c.** to pass at the end of the year,.... 1961
2Ch 24:23 host of Syria **c.** up against him:.......... 5927
2Ch 24:23 and they **c.** to Judah.......................... 935
2Ch 24:24 **c.** with a small company of men,........... 935
2Ch 25:3 it **c.** to pass, when the kingdom.......... 1961
2Ch 25:7 But there **c.** a man of God to him,....... 935
2Ch 25:14 it **c.** to pass, after that Amaziah......... 1961
2Ch 25:16 it **c.** to pass, as he talked with........... 1961
2Ch 25:20 would not hear; for it **c.** of......................
2Ch 28:9 went out before the host that **c.** to 935
2Ch 28:12 against them that **c.** from the war,....... 935
2Ch 28:20 Tilgath-pilneser king of Assyria **c.**........ 935
2Ch 29:15 sanctified themselves, and **c.**,.............. 935
2Ch 29:17 **c.** they to the porch of the Lord:......... 935
2Ch 30:11 themselves, and **c.** to Jerusalem. 935
2Ch 30:25 all the congregation that **c.** out of 935
2Ch 30:25 and the strangers that **c.**.................... 935
2Ch 30:27 their prayer **c.** up to his holy.............. 935
2Ch 31:5 as the commandment **c.** abroad, ... 6555
2Ch 31:8 Hezekiah and the princes **c.** and......... 935
2Ch 32:1 Sennacherib king of Assyria **c.**, and...... 935
2Ch 32:21 they that **c.** forth of his own bowels.... 3329
2Ch 32:26 the wrath of the Lord **c.** not upon........ 935
2Ch 34:9 And when they **c.** to Hilkiah the......... 935
2Ch 34:19 And it **c.** to pass, when the king........ 1961
2Ch 35:20 Necho king of Egypt **c.** up to fight...... 5927
2Ch 35:22 **c.** to fight in the valley of Megiddo....... 935
2Ch 36:6 **c.** up Nebuchadnezzar king of........... 5927
Ezr 2:1 and **c.** again unto Jerusalem and.......... 7725
Ezr 2:2 Which **c.** with Zerubbabel: Jeshua,........ 935
Ezr 2:68 they **c.** to the house of the Lord 935
Ezr 4:2 Then they **c.** to Zerubbabel, and........ 5066
Ezr 4:12 the Jews which **c.** up from thee 5559

Ezr 5:3 At the same time **c.** to them Tatni,.......858
Ezr 5:5 till the matter **c.** to Darius: and.......... 1946
Ezr 5:16 Then **c.** the same Sheshbazzar,............858
Ezr 7:8 **c.** to Jerusalem in the fifth month,........ 935
Ezr 7:9 **c.** he to Jerusalem, according to.......... 935
Ezr 8:32 And we **c.** to Jerusalem, and abode....... 935
Ezr 9:1 the princes **c.** to me, saying..............5066
Ezr 10:6 he **c.** thither, he did eat no bread,.........3212
Ne 1:1 it **c.** to pass in the month Chisleu,.......1961
Ne 1:2 Hanani, one of my brethren, **c.**, he....... 935
Ne 1:4 it **c.** to pass, when I heard these........ 1961
Ne 2:1 it **c.** to pass in the month Nisan.......... 1961
Ne 2:9 Then I **c.** to the governors beyond....... 935
Ne 2:11 So I **c.** to Jerusalem, and was there...... 935
Ne 4:1, 7 **c.** to pass, that when Sanballat,........1961
Ne 4:12 it **c.** to pass, that when the Jews........ 1961
Ne 4:12 the Jews which dwelt by them **c.**..........935
Ne 4:15 it **c.** to pass, when our enemies............1961
Ne 4:16 And it **c.** to pass from that time..........1961
Ne 5:17 beside those that **c.** unto us from......... 935
Ne 6:1 Now it **c.** to pass, when Sanballat,...... 1961
Ne 6:10 I **c.** unto the house of Shemaiah.......... 935
Ne 6:16 it **c.** to pass, that when all our............1961
Ne 6:17 the letters of Tobiah **c.** unto them........ 935
Ne 7:1 it **c.** to pass, when the wall was..........1961
Ne 7:5 the genealogy of them which **c.** up...... 5927
Ne 7:6 and **c.** again to Jerusalem and............ 7725
Ne 7:7 Who **c.** with Zerubbabel, Jeshua,.......... 935
Ne 7:73 when the seventh month **c.**, the......... 5060
Ne 13:3 **c.** to pass, when they had heard......... 1961
Ne 13:6 **c.** I unto the king, and after................ 935
Ne 13:7 I **c.** to Jerusalem, and understood.......... 935
Ne 13:19 it **c.** to pass, that when the gates........1961
Ne 13:21 **c.** they no more on the sabbath............935
Es 1:1 Now it **c.** to pass in the days of..........1961
Es 1:17 in before him, but she **c.** not............... 935
Es 2:8 So it **c.** to pass, when the king's.........1961
Es 2:13 Then thus **c.** every maiden unto.............935
Es 2:14 she **c.** in unto the king no more,.......... 935
Es 3:4 Now it **c.** to pass, when they............ 1961
Es 4:2 **c.** even before the king's gate:.............935
Es 4:3 commandment and his decree **c.**,......... 5060
Es 4:4 maids and her chamberlains **c.**...............935
Es 4:9 And Hatach **c.** and told Esther..............935
Es 5:1 it **c.** to pass on the third day.............1961
Es 5:5 So the king and Haman **c.** to the.......... 935
Es 5:10 and when he **c.** home, he sent............. 935
Es 6:6 So Haman **c.** in. And the king.............. 935
Es 6:12 Mordecai **c.** again to the king's.......... 7725
Es 6:14 **c.** the king's chamberlains,.................. 935
Es 7:1 king and Haman **c.** to banquet..............935
Es 8:1 Mordecai **c.** before the king;..................935
Es 8:17 commandment and his decree **c.**,......... 5060
Es 9:25 when Esther **c.** before the king,........... 935
Job 1:6 a day when the sons of God **c.**..............935
Job 1:6 and Satan **c.** also among them..............935
Job 1:14 there **c.** a messenger unto Job,............ 935
Job 1:16, 17,18 **c.** also another, and said,..............935
Job 1:19 there **c.** a great wind from the............. 935
Job 1:21 **c.** I out of my mother's womb,............3318
Job 2:1 a day when the sons of God **c.**..............935
Job 2:1 and Satan **c.** also among them..............935
Job 2:11 **c.** every one from his own place;..........935
Job 3:11 when I **c.** out of the belly?................ 3318
Job 3:26 was I quiet; yet trouble **c.**.................. 935
Job 4:14 Fear **c.** upon me, and trembling,......... 7122
Job 6:20 they **c.** thither, and were ashamed........ 935
Job 26:4 and whose spirit **c.** from thee?........... 3318
Job 29:13 was ready to perish **c.** upon me:.......... 935
Job 30:14 They **c.** upon me as a wide................. 857
Job 30:26 then evil **c.** unto me: and when I..........935
Job 30:26 waited for light, there **c.** darkness........ 935
Job 38:29 Out of whose womb **c.** the ice?............ 3318
Job 42:11 Then **c.** there unto him all his..............935
Ps 18:6 and my cry **c.** before him, even........... 935
Ps 18:9 the heavens also, and **c.** down: 3381
Ps 27:2 **c.** upon me to eat up my flesh,...........7126
Ps 51:*title* when Nathan the prophet **c.**................. 935
Ps 52:*title* when Doeg the Edomite **c.** and............ 935
Ps 54:*title* when the Ziphims **c.** and said...............935
Ps 78:21 anger also **c.** up against Israel;........... 5927
Ps 78:31 The wrath of God **c.** upon them,..........5927
Ps 88:17 They **c.** round about me daily...............5437
Ps 105:19 Until the time that his word **c.**:............ 935
Ps 105:23 Israel also **c.** into Egypt; and...............935
Ps 105:31 and there **c.** divers sorts of flies,...........935
Ps 105:34 He spake, and the locusts **c.**,.............. 935
Pr 7:15 Therefore **c.** I forth to meet thee,.......3318
Ec 5:15 he **c.** forth of his mother's.................3318
Ec 5:15 shall he return to go as he **c.**,.............. 935
Ec 5:16 in all points as he **c.**, so shall he go:..... 935
Ec 9:14 there **c.** a great king against it............. 935
Ca 4:2 which **c.** up from the washing:............5927
Isa 7:1 And it **c.** to pass in the day of............1961
Isa 11:16 in the days that he **c.** up out of.......... 5927
Isa 20:1 that Tartan **c.** unto Ashdod,................ 935
Isa 30:4 his ambassadors **c.** to Hanes.............. 5060
Isa 36:1 Now it **c.** to pass in the fourteenth......1961
Isa 36:1 Sennacherib king of Assyria **c.** up.........5927
Isa 36:3 Then **c.** forth unto him Eliakim,.......... 3318
Isa 36:22 Then **c.** Eliakim, the son of...............935
Isa 37:1 **c.** to pass, when king Hezekiah.......... 1961
Isa 37:5 servants of king Hezekiah **c.** to............ 935
Isa 37:34 By the way that he **c.**, by the same...... 935
Isa 37:38 **c.** to pass, as he was worshipping....... 1961
Isa 38:1 the son of Amoz **c.** unto him,.............. 935
Isa 38:4 Then **c.** the word of the Lord to.........1961
Isa 39:3 Then **c.** Isaiah the prophet unto.......... 935
Isa 39:3 from whence **c.** they unto thee?........... 935
Isa 41:5 were afraid, drew near, and **c.**............. 857
Isa 48:3 suddenly, and they **c.** to pass............. 935
Isa 48:5 before it **c.** to pass I shewed it............ 935
Isa 50:2 when I **c.**, was there no man?............. 935
Isa 66:7 before her pain **c.**, she was.................935
Jer 1:2 word of the Lord **c.** in the days.......... 1961
Jer 1:3 **c.** also in the day of Jehoiakim............1961
Jer 1:4 word of the Lord **c.** unto me,...............1961
Jer 1:11 the word of the Lord **c.** unto me.........1961
Jer 1:13 word of the Lord **c.** unto me the.........1961
Jer 2:1 word of the Lord **c.** to me,.................1961
Jer 3:9 it **c.** to pass through the lightness....... 1961
Jer 7:1 The word that **c.** to Jeremiah from...... 1961
Jer 7:25 day that your fathers **c.** forth............ 3318
Jer 7:31 neither **c.** it into my heart................ 5927
Jer 8:15 looked for peace, but no good **c.**;.............
Jer 11:1 The word that **c.** to Jeremiah............ 1961
Jer 13:3 And the word of the Lord **c.** unto...... 1961
Jer 13:6 it **c.** to pass after many days,............1961
Jer 13:8 the word of the Lord **c.** unto me,........1961
Jer 14:1 **c.** to Jeremiah concerning the............1961
Jer 14:3 they **c.** to the pits, and found no.......... 935
Jer 16:1 The word of the Lord **c.** also unto.......1961
Jer 17:16 that which **c.** out of my lips was.......... 4161
Jer 18:1 The word which **c.** to Jeremiah...........1961
Jer 18:5 Then the word of the Lord **c.** to.........1961
Jer 19:5 neither **c.** it into my mind:...................5927
Jer 19:14 Then **c.** Jeremiah from Tophet............ 935
Jer 20:3 And it **c.** to pass on the morrow,........ 1961
Jer 20:18 Wherefore **c.** I forth out of the...........3318
Jer 21:1 the word which **c.** unto Jeremiah.........1961
Jer 24:4 the word of the Lord **c.** unto me,........1961
Jer 25:1 The word that **c.** to Jeremiah............ 1961
Jer 26:1 Judah **c.** this word from the Lord,....... 1961
Jer 26:8 Now it **c.** to pass, when Jeremiah....... 1961
Jer 26:10 they **c.** up from the king's house.........5927
Jer 27:1 **c.** this word unto Jeremiah.................1961
Jer 28:1 And it **c.** to pass the same year,.......... 1961
Jer 28:12 word of the Lord **c.** unto Jeremiah...... 1961
Jer 29:30 Then **c.** the word of the Lord unto...... 1961
Jer 30:1 The word that **c.** to Jeremiah from...... 1961
Jer 32:1 The word that **c.** to Jeremiah from...... 1961
Jer 32:6 The word of the Lord **c.** unto me,.......1961
Jer 32:8 Hanameel mine uncle's son **c.** to............935
Jer 32:23 And they **c.** in, and possessed it;..........935
Jer 32:26 Then **c.** the word of the Lord unto...... 1961
Jer 32:35 neither **c.** it into my mind, that.......... 5927
Jer 33:1 word of the Lord **c.** unto Jeremiah...... 1961
Jer 33:19 word of the Lord **c.** unto Jeremiah,...... 1961
Jer 33:23 word of the Lord **c.** to Jeremiah,....... 1961
Jer 34:1 The word which **c.** unto Jeremiah........ 1961
Jer 34:8 This is the word that **c.** unto............ 1961
Jer 34:12 word of the Lord **c.** to Jeremiah......... 1961
Jer 35:1 The word which **c.** unto Jeremiah........1961
Jer 35:11 But it **c.** to pass, when..................... 1961
Jer 35:11 king of Babylon **c.** up into the land,..... 5927
Jer 35:12 Then **c.** the word of the Lord............ 1961
Jer 36:1 And it **c.** to pass in the fourth........... 1961
Jer 36:1 **c.** unto Jeremiah from the Lord,......... 1961
Jer 36:9 And it **c.** to pass in the fifth year........ 1961
Jer 36:9 to all the people that **c.** from the.......... 935
Jer 36:14 in his hand, and **c.** unto them.............. 935
Jer 36:16 Now it **c.** to pass when they had.........1961
Jer 36:23 it **c.** to pass, that when Jehudi........... 1961
Jer 36:27 word of the Lord **c.** to Jeremiah,........ 1961
Jer 37:4 Jeremiah **c.** in and went out..................935
Jer 37:6 Then **c.** the word of the Lord........... 1961
Jer 37:11 it **c.** to pass, that when the army........ 1961
Jer 38:27 **c.** all the princes unto Jeremiah,........... 935
Jer 39:1 **c.** Nebuchadrezzar king of Babylon........935
Jer 39:3 of the king of Babylon **c.** in,................ 935
Jer 39:4 it **c.** to pass, that when Zedekiah........ 1961
Jer 39:15 **c.** unto Jeremiah, while he was........... 1961
Jer 40:1 The word that **c.** to Jeremiah............ 1961
Jer 40:8 Then they **c.** to Gedaliah to..................935
Jer 40:12 and **c.** to the land of Judah, to............. 935
Jer 40:13 fields, **c.** to Gedaliah to Mizpah,.......... 935
Jer 41:1 it **c.** to pass in the seventh month,....... 1961
Jer 41:1 **c.** unto Gedaliah the son of Ahikam....... 935
Jer 41:4 it **c.** to pass the second day after........ 1961
Jer 41:5 there **c.** certain from Shechem,............ 935
Jer 41:6 and it **c.** to pass, as he met them,.........1961
Jer 41:7 when they **c.** into the midst of............. 935
Jer 41:13 now it **c.** to pass, that when all...........1961
Jer 42:1 even unto the greatest, **c.** near,......... 5066
Jer 42:7 And it **c.** to pass after ten days,......... 1961
Jer 42:7 that the word of the Lord **c.** unto........1961
Jer 43:1 it **c.** to pass, that when Jeremiah....... 1961
Jer 43:7 they **c.** into the land of Egypt:............ 935
Jer 43:7 the Lord: thus **c.** they even to..............935
Jer 43:8 Then **c.** the word of the Lord........... 1961
Jer 44:1 The word that **c.** to Jeremiah............ 1961
Jer 44:21 and **c.** it not into his mind?................ 5927
Jer 46:1 The word of the Lord which **c.** to....... 1961
Jer 47:1 word of the Lord that **c.** to................1961
Jer 49:34 of the Lord that **c.** to Jeremiah.......... 1961
Jer 52:3 anger of the Lord it **c.** to pass..............1961
Jer 52:4 it **c.** to pass in the ninth year of..........1961
Jer 52:4 Nebuchadrezzar king of Babylon **c.**,........935
Jer 52:12 **c.** Nebuzar-adan, captain of the............ 935
Jer 52:31 And it **c.** to pass in the seven............ 1961
La 1:9 end; therefore she **c.** down..................3381
Eze 1:1 it **c.** to pass in the thirtieth year......... 1961
Eze 1:3 word of the Lord **c.** expressly............ 1961
Eze 1:4 whirlwind **c.** out of the north,.............. 935
Eze 1:5 the midst thereof **c.** the likeness..............
Eze 3:15 Then I **c.** to them of the captivity.........935
Eze 3:16 it **c.** to pass at the end of seven......... 1961
Eze 3:16 of the Lord **c.** unto me, saying,.......... 1961
Eze 4:14 neither **c.** there abominable................ 935
Eze 6:1 the word of the Lord **c.** unto me,........1961
Eze 7:1 the word of the Lord **c.** unto me,........1961
Eze 8:1 And it **c.** to pass in the sixth...............1961
Eze 9:2 six men **c.** from the way of the............ 935
Eze 9:8 it **c.** to pass, while they were.............1961
Eze 10:6 it **c.** to pass, that when he had........... 1961
Eze 11:13 it **c.** to pass, when I prophesied,.........1961
Eze 11:14 the word of the Lord **c.** unto me,........1961
Eze 12:1 The word of the Lord also **c.** unto.......1961
Eze 12:8 in the morning **c.** the word of the.........1961
Eze 12:17 word of the Lord **c.** to me, saying,.......1961
Eze 12:21 word of the Lord **c.** unto me,..............1961
Eze 12:26 word of the Lord **c.** to me, saying,.......1961
Eze 13:1 word of the Lord **c.** unto me,..............1961
Eze 14:1 Then **c.** certain of the elders of............935
Eze 14:2 word of the Lord **c.** unto me,..............1961
Eze 14:12 word of the Lord **c.** again to me,......... 1961
Eze 15:1 word of the Lord **c.** unto me,..............1961
Eze 16:1 the word of the Lord **c.** unto me,........1961
Eze 16:23 **c.** to pass after all thy........................ 1961
Eze 17:1 word of the Lord **c.** unto me,..............1961
Eze 17:3 **c.** unto Lebanon, and took the............. 935
Eze 17:11 word of the Lord **c.** unto me..............1961
Eze 18:1 word of the Lord **c.** unto me again,..... 1961
Eze 20:1 it **c.** to pass in the seventh year,......... 1961
Eze 20:1 certain of the elders of Israel **c.**........... 935
Eze 20:2 Then **c.** the word of the Lord........... 1961
Eze 20:45 of the Lord **c.** unto me, saying,.......... 1961
Eze 21:1 word of the Lord **c.** unto me,..............1961
Eze 21:8 the word of the Lord **c.** unto me,........1961
Eze 21:18 word of the Lord **c.** unto me again,..... 1961
Eze 22:1 17,23 word of the Lord **c.** unto me,......1961
Eze 23:1 word of the Lord **c.** again unto me,..... 1961
Eze 23:17 And the Babylonians **c.** to her into........ 935
Eze 23:39 then they **c.** the same day into..............935
Eze 23:40 lo, they **c.**: for whom thou didst........... 935
Eze 24:1, 15,20 word of the Lord **c.** unto.......... 1961
Eze 25:1 word of the Lord **c.** again unto me,..... 1961
Eze 26:1 it **c.** to pass in the eleventh year,........1961
Eze 26:1 of the Lord **c.** unto me, saying,.......... 1961
Eze 27:1 word of the Lord **c.** again unto me,..... 1961

Eze 28:1 The word of the Lord **c.** again..........1961
Eze 28:11 Moreover the word of the Lord **c.**...... 1961
Eze 28:20 word of the Lord **c.** unto me,............1961
Eze 29:1 of the Lord **c.** unto me, saying,.......... 1961
Eze 29:17 And it **c.** to pass in the seven and.......1961
Eze 29:17 the word of the Lord **c.** unto me,........1961
Eze 30:1 word of the Lord **c.** again unto.......... 1961
Eze 30:20 it **c.** to pass in the eleventh year,........1961
Eze 30:20 the word of the Lord **c.** unto me,........1961
Eze 31:1 it **c.** to pass in the eleventh year,........1961
Eze 31:1 the word of the Lord **c.** unto me,........1961
Eze 32:1 it **c.** to pass in the twelfth year,..........1961
Eze 32:1 the word of the Lord **c.** unto me,........1961
Eze 32:17 **c.** to pass also in the twelfth year,...... 1961
Eze 32:17 of the Lord **c.** unto me, saying........... 1961
Eze 33:1 word of the Lord **c.** unto me,............1961
Eze 33:21 it **c.** to pass in the twelfth year of....... 1961
Eze 33:21 **c.** unto me, saying, The city is.......... 935
Eze 33:22 afore he that was escaped **c.**; and......... 935
Eze 33:22 until he **c.** to me in the morning;.......... 935
Eze 33:23 the word of the Lord **c.** unto me,........1961
Eze 34:1 the word of the Lord **c.** unto me,........1961
Eze 35:1 the word of the Lord **c.** unto me,........1961
Eze 36:16 the word of the Lord **c.** unto me,........1961
Eze 37:7 the bones **c.** together, bone to his.......7126
Eze 37:8 the sinews and the flesh **c.** up........... 5927
Eze 37:10 the breath **c.** into them, and they......... 935
Eze 37:15 The word of the Lord **c.** again...........1961
Eze 38:1 the word of the Lord **c.** unto me,........1961
Eze 40:6 Then **c.** he unto the gate which............935
Eze 43:2 the glory of the God of Israel **c.**............935
Eze 43:3 when I **c.** to destroy the city: and.........935
Eze 43:4 the glory of the Lord **c.** into the............935
Eze 46:9 whereby he **c.** in, but shall go forth.......935
Eze 47:1 the waters **c.** down from under...........3381
Da 1:1 **c.** Nebuchadnezzar king of...................935
Da 2:2 they **c.** and stood before the king......... 935
Da 2:29 O king, thy thoughts **c.** into thy.......... 5559
Da 3:8 at that time certain Chaldeans **c.**.......... 7127
Da 3:26 Nebuchadnezzar **c.** near to the........... 7127
Da 3:26 **c.** forth of the midst of the fire........... 5312
Da 4:7 Then **c.** in the magicians, the............ 5954
Da 4:8 But at the last Daniel **c.** in before....... 5954
Da 4:13 an holy one **c.** down from heaven;....... 5182
Da 4:28 All this **c.** upon the king.................... 4291
Da 5:5 In the same hour **c.** forth fingers........ 5312
Da 5:8 Then **c.** in all the king's wise men:...... 5954
Da 5:10 **c.** into the banquet house: and...........5954
Da 6:12 Then they **c.** near, and spake.............7127
Da 6:20 when he **c.** to the den, he cried..........7127
Da 6:24 they **c.** at the bottom of the den......... 4291
Da 7:3 great beasts **c.** up from the sea,......... 5559
Da 7:8 there **c.** up among them another......... 5559
Da 7:10 A fiery stream issued and **c.** forth....... 5312
Da 7:13 one like the Son of man **c.**........... 858,1934
Da 7:13 and to **c.** to the Ancient of days,.........4291
Da 7:16 I **c.** near unto one of them that...........7127
Da 7:20 and of the other which **c.** up,............ 5559
Da 7:22 Until the Ancient of days **c.**, and.......... 858
Da 7:22 time **c.** that the saints possessed........ 4291
Da 8:2 **c.** to pass, when I saw, that I........... 1961
Da 8:3 other, and the higher **c.** up last.......... 5927
Da 8:5 an he goat **c.** from the west on............935
Da 8:6 **c.** to the ram that had two horns..........935
Da 8:8 for it **c.** up four notable ones..............5927
Da 8:9 one of them **c.** forth a little horn,.........3318
Da 8:15 **c.** to pass, when I, even I Daniel,....... 1961
Da 8:17 So he **c.** near where I stood:...............935
Da 8:17 and when he **c.**, I was afraid,............. 935
Da 9:2 word of the Lord **c.** to Jeremiah......... 1961
Da 9:23 the commandment **c.** forth,................3318
Da 10:3 neither **c.** flesh nor wine in my.......... 935
Da 10:13 **c.** to help me; and I remained.............935
Da 10:18 there **c.** again and touched.......................
Ho 1:1 word of the Lord that **c.** unto.............1961
Ho 2:15 **c.** up out of the land of Egypt........... 5927
Joe 1:1 word of the Lord that **c.** to Joel.......... 1961
Am 6:1 to whom the house of Israel **c.**!........... 935
Am 7:2 it **c.** to pass, that when they had.........1961
Ob 5 If thieves **c.** to thee, if robbers........... 935
Ob 5 if the grapegatherers **c.** to thee,...........935
Jon 1:1 word of the Lord **c.** unto Jonah...........1961
Jon 1:6 So the shipmaster **c.** to him, and........ 7126
Jon 2:7 and my prayer **c.** in unto thee,.............935
Jon 3:1 word of the Lord **c.** unto Jonah..........1961
Jon 3:6 word **c.** unto the king of Nineveh,....... 5060
Jon 4:8 it **c.** to pass, when the sun did........... 1961
Jon 4:10 **c.** up in a night, and perished............ 1961
Mic 1:1 word of the Lord that **c.** to Micah....... 1961
Mic 1:11 inhabitant of Zaanah **c.** not forth..........3318
Mic 1:12 evil **c.** down from the Lord unto......... 3381
Hab 3:3 God **c.** from Teman, and the............... 935
Hab 3:14 they **c.** out as a whirlwind to......................
Zep 1:1 which **c.** unto Zephaniah the son......... 1961
Hag 1:1, 3 **c.** the word of the Lord by........... 1961
Hag 1:9 for much, and, lo, it **c.** to little;................
Hag 1:14 they **c.** and did work in the house.........935
Hag 2:1 **c.** the word of the Lord by the........... 1961
Hag 2:5 when ye **c.** out of Egypt, so my......... 3318
Hag 2:10 in the second year of Darius, **c.**.......... 1961
Hag 2:16 when one **c.** to an heap of twenty.........935
Hag 2:16 when one **c.** to the pressfat for to........ 935
Hag 2:20 word of the Lord **c.** unto Haggai......... 1961
Zec 1:1 year of Darius, **c.** the word of........... 1961
Zec 1:7 Darius, **c.** the word of the Lord.......... 1961
Zec 4:1 angel that talked with me **c.** again,...... 7725
Zec 4:8 the word of the Lord **c.** unto me,.........1961
Zec 5:9 there **c.** out two women, and the........ 3318
Zec 6:1 there **c.** four chariots out from........... 3318
Zec 6:9 And the word of the Lord **c.** unto........ 1961
Zec 7:1 And it **c.** to pass in the fourth year......1961
Zec 7:1 word of the Lord **c.** unto Zechariah..... 1961
Zec 7:4 Then **c.** the word of the Lord of......... 1961
Zec 7:8 word of the Lord **c.** unto Zechariah,..... 1961
Zec 7:12 therefore **c.** a great wrath from........... 1961
Zec 8:1 word of the Lord of hosts **c.** to me,..... 1961
Zec 8:10 to him that went out or **c.** in............... 935
Zec 8:18 word of the Lord of hosts **c.** unto....... 1961
Zec 10:4 Out of him **c.** forth the corner,........... 3318
Zec 14:16 which **c.** against Jerusalem shall...........935
Mt 1:18 before they **c.** together, she was........ *4905*
Mt 2:1 behold, there came wise men............. *3854*
Mt 2:9 till it **c.** and stood over where the....... *2064*
Mt 2:21 and **c.** into the land of Israel............. *2064*
Mt 2:23 he **c.** and dwelt in a city called........... *2064*
Mt 3:1 those days **c.** John the Baptist............*3854*
Mt 4:3 when the tempter **c.** to him,.............. *4334*
Mt 4:11 angels **c.** and ministered unto him....... *4334*
Mt 4:13 he **c.** and dwelt in Capernaum,........... *2064*
Mt 5:1 was set, his disciples **c.** unto him:........ *4334*
Mt 7:25, 27 **the floods c., and the winds**.......*2064*
Mt 7:28 it **c.** to pass, when Jesus had............ *1096*
Mt 8:2 there **c.** a leper and worshipped..........*2064*
Mt 8:5 there **c.** unto him a centurion,.............*4334*
Mt 8:19 a certain scribe **c.**, and said unto.........*4334*
Mt 8:25 his disciples **c.** to him, and awoke....... *4334*
Mt 8:34 whole city **c.** out to meet Jesus:......... *1831*
Mt 9:1 over, and **c.** into his own city.............*2064*
Mt 9:10 it **c.** to pass, as Jesus sat at meat........ *1096*
Mt 9:10 sinners **c.** and sat down with him........ *2064*
Mt 9:14 **c.** to him the disciples of John,........... *4334*
Mt 9:18 there **c.** a certain ruler, and...............*2064*
Mt 9:20 **c.** behind him, and touched the........... *4334*
Mt 9:23 when Jesus **c.** unto the ruler's............*2064*
Mt 9:28 the blind men **c.** to him: and Jesus...... *4334*
Mt 10:34 **I c. not to send peace, but a sword**.*2064*
Mt 11:1 it **c.** to pass, when Jesus had made......*1096*
Mt 11:18 **For John c. neither eating nor**.......*2064*
Mt 11:19 **The Son of man c. eating and**.......*2064*
Mt 12:42 **she c. from the uttermost parts**......*2064*
Mt 12:44 **from whence I c. out; and when**.....*1831*
Mt 13:4 **fowls c. and devoured them up:**.......*2064*
Mt 13:10 disciples **c.**, and said unto him,........... *4334*
Mt 13:25 **his enemy c. and sowed tares**.......... *2064*
Mt 13:27 **c. and said unto him, Sir, didst**......*4334*
Mt 13:36 his disciples **c.** unto him, saying,.......... *4334*
Mt 13:53 it **c.** to pass, that when Jesus had....... *1096*
Mt 14:12 disciples **c.**, and took up the body,....... *4334*
Mt 14:15 his disciples **c.** to him, saying,........... *4334*
Mt 14:33 **c.** and worshipped him, saying,............ *2064*
Mt 14:34 when they were gone over, they **c.**...... *2064*
Mt 15:1 Then **c.** to Jesus scribes and............. *4334*
Mt 15:12 Then **c.** his disciples, and said........... *4334*
Mt 15:22 a woman of Canaan **c.** out of the.........*1831*
Mt 15:23 his disciples **c.** and besought him,.........*4334*
Mt 15:25 Then **c.** she and worshipped him,.........*2064*
Mt 15:29 **c.** nigh unto the sea of Galilee;.......... *2064*
Mt 15:30 great multitudes **c.** unto him,............. *4334*
Mt 15:39 and **c.** into the coasts of Magdala........ *2064*
Mt 16:1 the Sadducees **c.**, and tempting......... *4334*
Mt 16:13 When Jesus **c.** into the coasts............ *2064*
Mt 17:7 Jesus **c.** and touched them, and......... *4334*
Mt 17:9 they **c.** down from the mountain,........ *2597*
Mt 17:14 there **c.** to him a certain man,............ *4334*
Mt 17:19 **c.** the disciples to Jesus apart,............*4334*
Mt 17:24 **c.** to Peter, and said, Doth not........... *4334*
Mt 18:1 time **c.** the disciples unto Jesus,.......... *4334*
Mt 18:21 Then **c.** Peter to him, and said,.......... *4334*
Mt 18:31 **and c. and told unto their lord**........*2064*
Mt 19:1 it **c.** to pass, that when Jesus had....... *1096*
Mt 19:1 and **c.** into the coasts of Judaea.......... *2064*
Mt 19:3 the Pharisees also **c.** unto him,.......... *4334*
Mt 19:16 And, behold, one **c.** and said unto....... *4334*
Mt 20:9 **when they c. that were hired**......... *2064*
Mt 20:10 **when the first c., they supposed**..... *2064*
Mt 20:20 Then **c.** to him the mother of............. *4334*
Mt 20:28 **c. not to be ministered unto,**.......... *2064*
Mt 21:14 the blind and the lame **c.** to him.......... *4334*
Mt 21:19 he **c.** to it, and found nothing............. *2064*
Mt 21:23 the elders of the people **c.** unto.......... *4334*
Mt 21:28 **and he c. to the first, and said,**........ *4334*
Mt 21:30 **And he c. to the second, and said**... *4334*
Mt 21:32 **For John c. unto you in the way**.... *2064*
Mt 22:11 **when the king c. in to see the**........ *1525*
Mt 22:23 same day **c.** to him the Sadducees,...... *4334*
Mt 24:1 and his disciples **c.** to him for to......... *4334*
Mt 24:3 Olives, the disciples **c.** unto him......... *4334*
Mt 24:39 **until the flood c., and took them**... *2064*
Mt 25:10 **went to buy, the bridegroom c.;**..... *2064*
Mt 25:11 **Afterward c. also the other**........... *2064*
Mt 25:20 **c. and brought other five talents,**... *4334*
Mt 25:22 **c. and said, Lord, thou deliveredst**. *4334*
Mt 25:24 **c. and said, Lord, I knew thee**........ *4334*
Mt 25:36 **in prison, and ye c. unto me**......... *2064*
Mt 25:39 **or in prison, and c. unto thee?**......... *2064*
Mt 26:1 it **c.** to pass, when Jesus had............ *1096*
Mt 26:7 There **c.** unto him a woman............... *4334*
Mt 26:17 the disciples **c.** to Jesus, saying,.......... *4334*
Mt 26:43 he **c.** and found them asleep............. *2064*
Mt 26:47 one of the twelve, **c.**, and with........... *2064*
Mt 26:49 he **c.** to Jesus, and said, Hail,............ *4334*
Mt 26:50 Then **c.** they, and laid hands on.......... *4334*
Mt 26:60 though many false witnesses **c.**,.......... *4334*
Mt 26:60 At the last **c.** two false witnesses,....... *4334*
Mt 26:69 a damsel **c.** unto him, saying,............. *4334*
Mt 26:73 **c.** unto him they that stood by............ *4334*
Mt 27:32 as they **c.** out, they found a man......... *1831*
Mt 27:53 **c.** out of the graves after his.............. *1831*
Mt 27:57 there **c.** a rich man of Arimathaea,....... *2064*
Mt 27:62 priests and Pharisees **c.** together........ *4863*
Mt 28:1 **c.** Mary Magdalene and the other........ *2064*
Mt 28:2 and **c.** and rolled back the stone.......... *4334*
Mt 28:9 they **c.** and held him by the feet,........ *4334*
Mt 28:11 **c.** into the city, and shewed unto........ *2064*
Mt 28:13 **c.** by night, and stole him away.......... *2064*
Mt 28:18 Jesus **c.** and spake unto them,............ *4334*
Mk 1:9 it **c.** to pass in those days, that........... *1096*
Mk 1:9 Jesus **c.** from Nazareth *2064*
Mk 1:11 And there **c.** a voice from heaven,....... *1096*
Mk 1:14 Jesus **c.** into Galilee, preaching........... *2064*
Mk 1:26 with a loud voice, he **c.** out of him....... *1831*
Mk 1:31 he **c.** and took her by the hand,.......... *4334*
Mk 1:38 **also: for therefore c. I forth**.......... *1831*
Mk 1:40 **c.** a leper to him, beseeching............. *2064*
Mk 1:45 they **c.** to him from every quarter....... *2064*
Mk 2:15 it **c.** to pass, that, as Jesus sat at........ *1096*
Mk 2:17 **I c. not to call the righteous, but**... *2064*
Mk 2:23 it **c.** to pass, that he went through...... *1096*
Mk 3:8 what great things he did, **c.** unto.......... *2064*
Mk 3:13 whom he would: and they **c.**................ *565*
Mk 3:22 And the scribes which **c.** down........... *2597*
Mk 3:31 There **c.** then his brethren and............ *2064*
Mk 4:4 **it c. to pass, as he sowed, some**...... *1096*
Mk 4:4 **and the fowls of the air c.**............. *2064*
Mk 5:1 they **c.** over unto the other side of...... *2064*
Mk 5:27 **c.** in the press behind, and touched..... *2064*
Mk 5:33 **c.** and fell down before him, and......... *2064*
Mk 5:35 **c.** from the ruler of the.................... *2064*
Mk 6:1 and **c.** into his own country; and......... *2064*
Mk 6:22 daughter of the said Herodias **c.**.......... *1525*
Mk 6:25 **c.** in straightway with haste unto......... *1525*
Mk 6:29 his disciples heard of it, they **c.**.......... *2064*
Mk 6:33 outwent them, and **c.** together............ *4905*
Mk 6:34 Jesus, when he **c.** out, saw much........ *1831*
Mk 6:35 his disciples **c.** unto him, and said,...... *4334*
Mk 6:53 when they had passed over, they **c.**...... *2064*
Mk 7:1 **c.** together unto him the Pharisees,...... *4863*
Mk 7:1 certain of the scribes, which **c.**........... *2064*
Mk 7:25 him, and **c.** and fell at his feet:........... *2064*
Mk 7:31 he **c.** unto the sea of Galilee,............ *2064*
Mk 8:3 **for divers of them c. from far**........ *2240*

Mk 8:10 c. into the parts of Dalmanutha. 2064
Mk 8:11 the Pharisees c. forth, and began 1831
Mk 9:7 a voice c. out of the cloud, saying, 2064
Mk 9:9 they c. down from the mountain, 2597
Mk 9:14 when he c. to his disciples, he 2064
Mk 9:21 **is it ago since this c. unto him?** 1096
Mk 9:25 the people c. running together, 1998
Mk 9:26 rent him sore, and c. out of him: 1831
Mk 9:33 And he c. to Capernaum: and 2064
Mk 10:2 the Pharisees c. to him, and asked 4334
Mk 10:17 there c. one running, and kneeled 4370
Mk 10:45 **c. not to be ministered unto, but** 2064
Mk 10:46 they c. to Jericho: and as he 2064
Mk 10:50 garment, rose, and c. to Jesus. 2064
Mk 11:1 when they c. nigh to Jerusalem, 1448
Mk 11:13 he c., if haply he might find 2064
Mk 11:13 thereon: and when he c. to it, 2064
Mk 12:28 And one of the scribes c., and 4334
Mk 12:42 There c. a certain poor widow, and 2064
Mk 14:3 c. a woman having an alabaster 2064
Mk 14:16 and c. into the city, and found as 2064
Mk 14:32 And they c. to a place which was 2064
Mk 15:41 many other women which c. up 4872
Mk 15:43 for the kingdom of God, c., 2064
Mk 16:2 they c. unto the sepulchre at the 2064
Lu 1:8 c. to pass, that while he executed 1096
Lu 1:22 when he c. out, he could not 1831
Lu 1:23 it c. to pass, that, as soon as the 1096
Lu 1:28 the angel c. in unto her, and said, 1525
Lu 1:41 c. to pass, that, when Elisabeth 1096
Lu 1:57 Now Elisabeth's full time c. that 4130
Lu 1:59 c. to pass, that on the eighth day 1096
Lu 1:59 they c. to circumcise the child; 2064
Lu 1:65 fear c. on all that dwelt round 1096
Lu 2:1 it c. to pass in those days, that 1096
Lu 2:9 the angel of the Lord c. upon 2186
Lu 2:15 it c. to pass, as the angels were 1096
Lu 2:16 they c. with haste, and found 2064
Lu 2:27 he c. by the Spirit into the temple: 2064
Lu 2:46 it c. to pass, that after three days 1096
Lu 2:51 c. to Nazareth, and was subject 2064
Lu 3:2 the word of God c. unto John the 1096
Lu 3:3 he c. into all the country about 2064
Lu 3:7 to the multitude that c. forth to 1607
Lu 3:12 c. also publicans to be baptized, 2064
Lu 3:21 it c. to pass, that Jesus also being 1096
Lu 3:22 a voice c. from heaven, which said, 1096
Lu 4:16 he c. to Nazareth, where he had 2064
Lu 4:31 c. down to Capernaum, a city of 2718
Lu 4:35 c. out of him, and hurt him not. 1831
Lu 4:41 devils also c. out of many, crying 1831
Lu 4:42 c. unto him, and stayed him, that 2064
Lu 5:1 c. to pass, that, as the people 1096
Lu 5:7 they c., and filled both the ships, 2064
Lu 5:12 it c. to pass, when he was in a 1096
Lu 5:15 great multitudes c. together to 4905
Lu 5:17 it c. to pass on a certain day, as 1096
Lu 5:32 **I c. not to call the righteous, but** 2064
Lu 6:1 c. to pass on the second sabbath 1096
Lu 6:6 it c. to pass also on another 1096
Lu 6:12 And it c. to pass in those days. 1096
Lu 6:17 he c. down with them, and stood 2597
Lu 6:17 which c. to hear him, and to be 2064
Lu 7:4 when they c. to Jesus, they 3854
Lu 7:11 it c. to pass the day after, that he 1096
Lu 7:12 when he c. nigh to the gate of the 1448
Lu 7:14 And he c. and touched the bier: 4334
Lu 7:16 And there c. a fear on all: and 2983
Lu 7:33 **For John the Baptist c. neither** 2064
Lu 7:45 **since the time I c. in hath not** 1525
Lu 8:1 it c. to pass afterward, that he 1096
Lu 8:19 c. to him his mother and his 3854
Lu 8:22 it c. to pass on a certain day, that 1096
Lu 8:23 there c. down a storm of wind on 2597
Lu 8:24 And they c. to him, and awoke him, 4334
Lu 8:35 c. to Jesus, and found the man, 2064
Lu 8:40 c. to pass, that, when Jesus was 1096
Lu 8:41 there c. a man named Jairus, and 2064
Lu 8:44 C. behind him, and touched the 4334
Lu 8:47 was not hid, she c. trembling, 2064
Lu 8:51 when he c. into the house, he 1525
Lu 8:55 her spirit c. again, and she arose 1994
Lu 9:12 then c. the twelve, and said unto 4334
Lu 9:18 c. to pass, as he was alone 1096
Lu 9:28 it c. to pass about an eight days 1096
Lu 9:33 it c. to pass, as they departed 1096
Lu 9:34 c. a cloud, and overshadowed 1096
Lu 9:35 there c. a voice out of the cloud, 1096
Lu 9:37 it c. to pass, that on the next day, 1096
Lu 9:51 c. to pass, when the time was come 1096
Lu 9:57 c. to pass, that, as they went in 1096
Lu 10:31 **by chance there c. down a certain** 2597
Lu 10:32 **c. and looked on him, and passed** 2064
Lu 10:33 **as he journeyed, c. where he was:** 2064
Lu 10:38 Now it c. to pass, as they went, 1096
Lu 10:40 and c. to him, and said, Lord, 2186
Lu 11:1 c. to pass, that, as he was praying 1096
Lu 11:14 it c. to pass, when the devil was 1096
Lu 11:24 **unto my house whence I c. out.** 1831
Lu 11:27 c. to pass, as he spake these 1096
Lu 11:31 **c. from the utmost parts of the** 2064
Lu 13:6 **he c. and sought fruit thereon,** 2064
Lu 13:31 The same day there c. certain of 4334
Lu 14:1 c. to pass, as he went into the 1096
Lu 14:21 **So that servant c., and shewed** 3854
Lu 15:17 **And when he c. to himself, he** 2064
Lu 15:20 **he arose, and c. to his father.** 2064
Lu 15:25 **c. and drew nigh to the house, he** 2064
Lu 15:28 **therefore c. his father out, and** 1831
Lu 16:21 **the dogs c. and licked his sores.** 2064
Lu 16:22 **it c. to pass that the beggar died,** 1096
Lu 17:11 it c. to pass, as he went to 1096
Lu 17:14 it c. to pass, that, as they went. 1096
Lu 17:27 and the flood c., and destroyed 2064
Lu 18:3 she c. unto him, saying, Avenge 2064
Lu 18:35 c. to pass, that as he was come 1096
Lu 19:5 when Jesus c. to the place, he 2064
Lu 19:6 And he made haste, and c. down, 2597
Lu 19:15 **it c. to pass, that when he was** 1096
Lu 19:16 **Then c. the first, saying, Lord,** 3854
Lu 19:18 **And the second c., saying, Lord,** 2064
Lu 19:20 **another c. saying, Lord, behold,** 2064
Lu 19:29 c. to pass, when he was come nigh 1096
Lu 20:1 c. to pass, that on one of those 1096
Lu 20:1 chief priests and the scribes c. 2186
Lu 20:27 c. to him certain of the Sadducees, 4334
Lu 21:38 And all the people c. early in the 3719
Lu 22:7 c. the day of unleavened bread, 2064
Lu 22:39 c. out, and went, as he was wont, 1831
Lu 22:66 priests and the scribes c. together, 4863
Lu 23:48 all the people that c. together to 4836
Lu 23:55 which c. with him from Galilee, 4905
Lu 24:1 very early in the morning, they c. 2064
Lu 24:4 it c. to pass, as they were much 1096
Lu 24:15 it c. to pass, that, while they 1096
Lu 24:23 found not his body, they c., saying, 2064
Lu 24:30 c. to pass, as he sat at meat with 1096
Lu 24:51 it c. to pass, while he blessed 1096
Joh 1:7 The same c. for a witness, to bear 2064
Joh 1:11 He c. unto his own, and his own 2064
Joh 1:17 grace and truth c. by Jesus Christ. 1096
Joh 1:39 They c. and saw where he dwelt, 2064
Joh 3:2 The same c. to Jesus by night, and 2064
Joh 3:13 **but he that c. down from heaven,** 2597
Joh 3:22 After these things c. Jesus and 2064
Joh 3:23 and they c., and were baptized. 3854
Joh 3:26 c. unto John, and said unto him, 2064
Joh 4:27 upon this c. his disciples, and 2064
Joh 4:30 out of the city, and c. unto him. 2064
Joh 4:46 So Jesus c. again into Cana of 2064
Joh 6:23 (Howbeit there c. other boats from 2064
Joh 6:24 shipping, and c. to Capernaum, 2064
Joh 6:38 **For I c. down from heaven, not to** 2597
Joh 6:41 I am the bread which c. down from 2597
Joh 6:42 I c. down from heaven? 2597
Joh 6:51 **bread which c. down from heaven:** 2597
Joh 6:58 **This is that bread which c. down** 2597
Joh 7:45 Then c. the officers to the chief 2064
Joh 7:50 (he that c. to Jesus by night, 2064
Joh 8:2 early in the morning he c. again 3854
Joh 8:2 the people c. unto him; 2064
Joh 8:14 **for I know whence I c., and** 2064
Joh 8:42 **I proceeded forth and c. from** 2240
Joh 8:42 **neither c. I of myself,** 2064
Joh 9:7 therefore, and washed, and c. 2064
Joh 10:8 **All that ever c. before me are** 2064
Joh 10:24 c. the Jews round about him, 2944
Joh 10:35 **unto whom the word of God c.,** 1096
Joh 11:17 Then when Jesus c., he found that 2064
Joh 11:19 many of the Jews c. to Martha 2064
Joh 11:29 arose quickly, and c. unto him. 2064
Joh 11:33 Jews also weeping which c. with 4905
Joh 11:44 he that was dead c. forth, bound 1831
Joh 11:45 of the Jews which c. to Mary, 2064
Joh 12:1 before the passover c. to Bethany, 2064
Joh 12:9 they c. not for Jesus' sake only, 2064
Joh 12:20 Greeks among them that c. up to 305
Joh 12:21 The same c. therefore to Philip, 4334
Joh 12:27 **for this cause c. I unto this hour.** 2064
Joh 12:28 Then c. there a voice from heaven. 2064
Joh 12:30 **This voice c. not because of me,** 1096
Joh 12:47 **for I c. not to judge the world,** 2064
Joh 16:27 **believed that I c. out from God.** 1831
Joh 16:28 **I c. forth from the Father, and am.** 1831
Joh 17:8 **that I c. out from thee, and they** 1831
Joh 18:37 **for this cause c. I into the world,** 2064
Joh 19:5 then c. Jesus forth, wearing the 1831
Joh 19:32 Then c. the soldiers, and 2064
Joh 19:33 But when they c. to Jesus, 2064
Joh 19:34 forthwith c. there out blood and 1831
Joh 19:38 He c. therefore, and took the body 2064
Joh 19:39 And there c. also Nicodemus, 2064
Joh 19:39 at the first c. to Jesus by night, 2064
Joh 20:3 disciple, and c. to the sepulchre. 2064
Joh 20:4 Peter, and c. first to the sepulchre. 2064
Joh 20:8 which c. first to the sepulchre, 2064
Joh 20:18 Mary Magdalene c. and told the 2064
Joh 20:19 c. Jesus and stood in the midst, 2064
Joh 20:24 was not with them when Jesus c. 2064
Joh 20:26 c. Jesus, the doors being shut, 2064
Joh 21:8 other disciples c. in a little ship; 2064
Ac 2:2 suddenly there c. a sound from 1096
Ac 2:6 multitude c. together and were 4905
Ac 2:43 And fear c. upon every soul: 1096
Ac 4:1 and the Sadducees, c. upon them, 2186
Ac 4:5 it c. to pass on the morrow, that 1096
Ac 5:5 great fear c. on all them that 1096
Ac 5:7 knowing what was done, c. in. 1525
Ac 5:10 young men c. in, and found 1525
Ac 5:11 great fear c. upon all the church, 1096
Ac 5:16 There c. also a multitude out of 4905
Ac 5:21 But the high priest c., and they 3854
Ac 5:22 But when the officers c., and found 3854
Ac 5:25 Then c. one and told them, saying 3854
Ac 6:12 c. upon him, and caught him, 2186
Ac 7:4 Then c. he out of the land of the 1831
Ac 7:11 c. a dearth over all the land of 2064
Ac 7:23 it c. into his heart to visit his 305
Ac 7:31 the voice of the Lord c. unto him, 1096
Ac 7:45 also our fathers that c. after 1237
Ac 8:7 c. out of many that were possessed 1831
Ac 8:36 they c. unto a certain water: 2064
Ac 8:40 the cities, till he c. to Caesarea. 2064
Ac 9:3 journeyed, he c. near Damascus: 1096
Ac 9:21 and c. hither for that intent, that 2064
Ac 9:32 it c. to pass, as Peter passed 1096
Ac 9:32 he c. down also to the saints 2718
Ac 9:37 it c. to pass in those days, that 1096
Ac 9:43 it c. to pass, that he tarried many 1096
Ac 10:13 there c. a voice to him, Rise, 1096
Ac 10:29 Therefore c. I unto you without 2064
Ac 10:45 as many as c. with Peter, because 4905
Ac 11:5 four corners; and it c. even to me: 2064
Ac 11:22 tidings of these things c. unto the 191
Ac 11:23 Who, when he c., and had seen 3854
Ac 11:26 it c. to pass, that a whole year 1096
Ac 11:27 c. prophets from Jerusalem unto 2718
Ac 11:28 which c. to pass in the days of 1096
Ac 12:7 angel of the Lord c. upon him, 2186
Ac 12:10 they c. unto the iron gate that 2064
Ac 12:12 c. to the house of Mary the mother 2064
Ac 12:13 a damsel c. to hearken, named 4334
Ac 12:20 they c. with one accord to him, 3918
Ac 13:13 they c. to Perga in Pamphylia: 2064
Ac 13:14 they c. to Antioch in Pisidia, 3854
Ac 13:31 of them which c. up with him 4872
Ac 13:44 c. almost the whole city together 4863
Ac 13:51 them, and c. unto Iconium. 2064
Ac 14:1 it c. to pass in Iconium, that they 1096
Ac 14:19 there c. thither certain Jews 1904
Ac 14:20 he rose up, and c. into the city: 1525
Ac 14:24 Pisidia, they c. to Pamphylia. 2064
Ac 15:1 men which c. down from Judaea 2718
Ac 15:6 apostles and elders c. together 4863
Ac 15:30 dismissed, they c. to Antioch: 2064
Ac 16:1 Then c. he to Derbe and Lystra: 2658
Ac 16:8 passing by Mysia c. down to Troas. 2597
Ac 16:11 we c. with a straight course to 2113
Ac 16:16 it c. to pass, as he went to prayer, 1096
Ac 16:18 And he c. out the same hour. 1881
Ac 16:29 and c. trembling, and fell down 1096

Ac 16:39 they **c.** and besought them, *2064*
Ac 17:1 they **c.** to Thessalonica, where *2064*
Ac 17:13 they **c.** thither also, and stirred up *2064*
Ac 18:1 from Athens, and **c.** to Corinth; *2064*
Ac 18:2 from Rome:) and **c.** unto them *4884*
Ac 18:19 he **c.** to Ephesus, and left them *2658*
Ac 18:24 mighty in the scriptures, **c.** to *2658*
Ac 19:1 it **c.** to pass, that, while Apollos *1096*
Ac 19:1 the upper coasts **c.** to Ephesus: *2064*
Ac 19:6 the Holy Ghost **c.** on them; *2064*
Ac 19:18 that believed **c.**, and confessed, *2064*
Ac 20:2 exhortation, he **c.** into Greece. *2064*
Ac 20:6 **c.** unto them to Troas in five days; *2064*
Ac 20:7 when the disciples **c.** together to *4868*
Ac 20:14 took him in, and **c.** to Mitylene. *2064*
Ac 20:15 **c.** the next day over against Chios; *2064*
Ac 20:15 and the next day we **c.** to Miletus. *2658*
Ac 20:18 first day that I **c.** into Asia, *1910*
Ac 21:1 it **c.** to pass, that after we were *1096*
Ac 21:1 we **c.** with a straight course unto *2064*
Ac 21:7 we **c.** to Ptolemais, and saluted *2658*
Ac 21:8 departed, and **c.** unto Caesarea: *2064*
Ac 21:10 there **c.** down from Judaea a *2718*
Ac 21:31 tidings **c.** unto the chief captain of *305*
Ac 21:33 Then the chief captain **c.** near, *1448*
Ac 21:35 when he **c.** upon the stairs, so it *1096*
Ac 22:6 it **c.** to pass, that, as I made my *1096*
Ac 22:11 with me, I **c.** into Damascus. *2064*
Ac 22:13 **C.** unto me, and stood, and said *2064*
Ac 22:17 And it **c.** to pass, that, when I *1096*
Ac 22:27 Then the chief captain **c.**, and *4884*
Ac 23:14 And they **c.** to the chief priests *4884*
Ac 23:27 **c.** I with an army, and rescued *2186*
Ac 23:33 Who, when they **c.** to Caesarea, *1525*
Ac 24:7 chief captain Lysias **c.** upon us, *3928*
Ac 24:17 I **c.** to bring alms to my nation, *3854*
Ac 24:24 Felix **c.** with his wife Drusilla, *3854*
Ac 24:27 Porcius Festus **c.** into Felix' *2983,1240*
Ac 25:7 the Jews which **c.** down from *2597*
Ac 25:13 Agrippa and Bernice **c.** unto *2658*
Ac 27:5 we **c.** to Myra, a city of Lycia. *2718*
Ac 27:8 hardly passing it, **c.** unto a place *2064*
Ac 27:44 so it **c.** to pass, that they escaped *1096*
Ac 28:3 **c.** a viper out of the heat, *1831*
Ac 28:8 it **c.** to pass, that the father of *1096*
Ac 28:9 in the island, **c.**, and were healed: *4334*
Ac 28:13 **c.** to Rhegium: and after one day *2658*
Ac 28:13 and we **c.** the next day to Puteoli: *2064*
Ac 28:15 they **c.** to meet us as far as Appii *1831*
Ac 28:16 when we **c.** to Rome, the *2064*
Ac 28:17 it **c.** to pass, that after three days *1096*
Ac 28:21 any of the brethren that **c.** *3854*
Ac 28:23 **c.** many to him into his lodging; *2240*
Ac 28:30 received all that **c.** in unto him, *1531*
Ro 5:18 one judgment **c.** upon all men to
Ro 5:18 the free gift **c.** upon all men unto
Ro 7:9 but when the commandment **c.**, *2064*
Ro 9:5 concerning the flesh Christ **c.**,
1Co 2:1 I, brethren, when I **c.** to you, *2064*
1Co 2:1 **c.** not with excellency of speech *2064*
1Co 14:36 **c.** the word of God out from you? *1831*
1Co 14:36 or **c.** it unto you only? *2658*
1Co 15:21 since by man **c.** death, by man **c.** also
2Co 1:8 trouble which **c.** to us in Asia, *1096*
2Co 1:23 I **c.** not as yet unto Corinth. *2064*
2Co 2:3 lest, when I **c.**, I should have *2064*
2Co 2:12 when I **c.** to Troas to preach *2064*
2Co 11:9 brethren which **c.** from Macedonia *2064*
Gal 1:21 I **c.** into the regions of Syria and *2064*
Gal 2:4 who **c.** in privily to spy out our *3922*
Gal 2:12 before that certain **c.** from James, *2064*
Gal 3:23 But before faith **c.**, we were kept *2064*
Eph 2:17 And **c.** and preached peace to you *2064*
1Th 1:5 our gospel **c.** not unto you in *1096*
1Th 3:4 even as it **c.** to pass, and ye know. *1096*
1Th 3:6 now when Timotheus **c.** from you *2064*
1Ti 1:15 Christ Jesus **c.** into the world to *2064*
2Ti 3:11 afflictions, which **c.** unto me at *1096*
Heb 3:16 not all that **c.** out of Egypt *1831*
Heb 11:15 from whence they **c.** out, they *1831*
2Pe 1:17 when there **c.** such a voice to him *5342*
2Pe 1:18 this voice which **c.** from heaven *5342*
2Pe 1:21 the prophecy **c.** not in old time *5342*
1Jo 5:6 he that **c.** by water and blood, *2064*
3Jo 3 the brethren **c.** and testified of the *2064*
Re 5:7 And he **c.** and took the book out *2064*
Re 7:13 in white robes? and whence **c.** *2064*
Re 7:14 These are they which **c.** out of *2064*
Re 8:3 angel **c.** and stood at the altar, *2064*
Re 8:4 smoke of the incense, which **c.**
Re 9:3 there **c.** out of the smoke locusts *1831*
Re 14:15 another angel **c.** out of the temple, *1831*
Re 14:17 And another angel **c.** out of the *1831*
Re 14:18 angel **c.** out from the altar, *1831*
Re 14:20 blood **c.** out of the winepress, *1831*
Re 15:6 seven angels **c.** out of the temple, *1831*
Re 16:17 **c.** a great voice out of the temle *1831*
Re 16:19 Babylon **c.** in remembrance *3415*
Re 17:1 there **c.** one of the seven angels *2064*
Re 19:5 And a voice **c.** out of the throne, *1881*
Re 20:9 and fire **c.** down from God out of *2597*
Re 21:9 **c.** unto me one of the seven angels *2064*

CAME TO PASS See CAME and PASS.

CAMEL See also CAMEL'S; CAMELS.

Ge 24:64 saw Isaac, she lighted off the **c.** 1581
Le 11:4 **c.**, because he cheweth the cud, 1581
De 14:7 the **c.**, and the hare, and the 1581
1Sa 15:3 suckling, ox and sheep, **c.** and ass 1581
Zec 14:15 of the mule, of the **c.**, 1581
Mt 19:24 **easier for a c. to go through the** *2574*
Mt 23:24 **at a gnat, and swallow a c** *2574*
Mk 10:25 **easier for a c. to go through the** *2574*
Lu 18:25 **easier for a c. to go through a** *2574*

CAMEL'S

Ge 31:34 put them in the **c.** furniture, and 1581
Mt 3:4 his raiment of **c.** hair, and a *2574*
Mk 1:6 clothed with **c.** hair, and with a *2574*

CAMELS See also CAMELS'.

Ge 12:16 and she asses, and **c.** 1581
Ge 24:10 took ten **c.** of the **c.** of his master, 1581
Ge 24:11 he made his **c.** to kneel down 1581
Ge 24:14 I will give thy **c.** drink also: let 1581
Ge 24:19 draw water for thy **c.** also, until 1581
Ge 24:20 water, and drew for all his **c.** 1581
Ge 24:22 as the **c.** had done drinking, that 1581
Ge 24:30 he stood by the **c.** at the well 1581
Ge 24:31 the house, and room for the **c.**, 1581
Ge 24:32 and he ungirded his **c.**, and gave 1581
Ge 24:32 and provender for the **c.**, 1581
Ge 24:35 maidservants, and **c.**, and asses. 1581
Ge 24:44 I will also draw for thy **c.**: let the 1581
Ge 24:46 I will give thy **c.** drink also: so I 1581
Ge 24:46 and she made the **c.** drink 1581
Ge 24:61 they rode upon the **c.**, and 1581
Ge 24:63 and, behold, the **c.** were coming. 1581
Ge 30:43 menservants, and **c.**, and asses. 1581
Ge 31:17 set his sons and his wives upon **c.**; 1581
Ge 32:7 herds, and the **c.**, into two bands; 1581
Ge 32:15 Thirty milch **c.** with their colts, 1581
Ge 37:25 came from Gilead with their **c.** 1581
Ex 9:3 upon the asses, upon the **c.**, upon 1581
Jg 6:5 both they and their **c.** were 1581
Jg 7:12 and their **c.** were without number, 1581
1Sa 27:9 the asses, and the **c.**, and the 1581
1Sa 30:17 young men, which rode upon **c.**, 1581
1Ki 10:2 with **c.** that bare spices, and very 1581
1Ch 5:21 cattle; of their **c.** fifty thousand, 1581
1Ch 12:40 bread on asses, and on **c.**, and on 1581
1Ch 27:30 Over the **c.** also was Obil the 1581
2Ch 9:1 company, and **c.** that bare spices, 1581
2Ch 14:15 carried away sheep and **c.** in 1581
Ezr 2:67 Their **c.**, four hundred thirty and 1581
Ne 7:69 **c.**, four hundred thirty and five: 1581
Es 8:10 **c.**, and young dromedaries: 327
Es 8:14 rode upon mules and **c.** went out, 327
Job 1:3 three thousand **c.**, and five 1581
Job 1:17 fell upon the **c.**, and have carried 1581
Job 42:12 six thousand **c.**, and a thousand 1581
Isa 21:7 of asses, and a chariot of **c.**; 1581
Isa 30:6 treasures upon the bunches of **c.** 1581
Isa 60:6 The multitude of **c.** shall cover 1581
Jer 49:29 and all their vessels, and their **c.**; 1581
Jer 49:32 And their **c.** shall be a booty, and 1581
Eze 25:5 make Rabbah a stable for **c.**, and 1581

CAMELS'

Jg 8:21 that were on their **c.** necks. 1581
Jg 8:26 chains that were about their **c.** 1581
2Ki 8:9 of Damascus, forty **c.** burden, 1581

CAMEST See also BECAMEST.

Ge 16:8 whence **c.** thou? and whither wilt 935
Ge 24:5 the land from whence thou **c.**? 3318
Ge 27:33 eaten of all before thou **c.**, and 935
Ex 23:15 in it thou **c.** out from Egypt: 3318
Ex 34:18 Abib thou **c.** out from Egypt. 3318
Nu 22:37 wherefore **c.** thou not unto me? 1980
De 2:37 children of Ammon thou **c.** not 7126
De 16:3 for thou **c.** forth out of the land of 3318
De 16:3 when thou **c.** forth out of the land 3318
De 16:6 season that thou **c.** forth out of 3318
1Sa 13:11 thou **c.** not within the days 935
1Sa 17:28 Why **c.** thou down hither? and 3381
2Sa 11:10 **C.** thou not from thy journey? 935
2Sa 15:20 Whereas thou **c.** but yesterday, 935
1Ki 13:9 by the same way that thou **c.** 1980
1Ki 13:14 man of God that **c.** from Judah? 935
1Ki 13:17 to go by the way that thou **c.** 1980
1Ki 13:22 But **c.** back, and hast eaten bread 7725
2Ki 19:28 back by the way by which thou **c.** 935
Ne 9:13 Thou **c.** down also upon mount 3381
Isa 37:29 back by the way by which thou **c.** 935
Isa 64:3 thou **c.** down, the mountains 3381
Jer 1:5 before thou **c.** forth out of the 3318
Eze 32:2 thou **c.** forth with thy rivers, and 1518
Mt 22:12 **Friend, how c. thou in hither** *1525*
Joh 6:25 him, Rabbi, when **c.** thou hither? *1096*
Joh 16:30 that thou **c.** forth from God. *1831*
Ac 9:17 in the way as thou **c.**, hath sent *2064*

CAMON (ca'-mon)

Jg 10:5 Jair died, and was buried in **C.** 7056

CAMP See also CAMPED; CAMPS; ENCAMP.

Ex 14:19 which went before the **c.** of Israel, 4264
Ex 14:20 between the **c.** of the Egyptians 4264
Ex 14:20 and the **c.** of Israel; 4264
Ex 16:13 quails came up, and covered the **c.**: 4264
Ex 19:16 people that was in the **c.** trembled 4264
Ex 19:17 all the people out of the **c.** to meet 4264
Ex 29:14 burn with fire without the **c.**: 4264
Ex 32:17 There is a noise of war in the **c.** 4264
Ex 32:19 as he came nigh unto the **c.**, that 4264
Ex 32:26 stood in the gate of the **c.**, and 4264
Ex 32:27 gate to gate throughout the **c.**, 4264
Ex 33:7 without the **c.**, afar off from the **c.**, 4264
Ex 33:7 which was without the **c.** 4264
Ex 33:11 he turned again into the **c.**: but 4264
Ex 36:6 proclaimed throughout the **c.** 4264
Le 4:12 he carry forth without the **c.** unto 4264
Le 4:21 forth the bullock without the **c.** 4264
Le 6:11 the ashes without the **c.** unto a 4264
Le 8:17 he burnt with fire without the **c.**; 4264
Le 9:11 he burnt with fire without the **c.** 4264
Le 10:4 before the sanctuary out of the **c.** 4264
Le 10:5 their coats out of the **c.**; as Moses 4264
Le 13:46 without the **c.** shall his habitation 4264
Le 14:3 shall go forth out of the **c.**; and 4264
Le 14:8 come into the **c.**, and shall tarry 4264
Le 16:26 and afterward come into the **c.** 4264
Le 16:27 carry forth without the **c.**; and 4264
Le 16:28 afterward he shall come into the **c.** 4264
Le 17:3 lamb, or goat, in the **c.**, or that 4264
Le 17:3 killeth it out of the **c.**, 4264
Le 24:10 strove together in the **c.**; 4264
Le 24:14 that hath cursed without the **c.**; 4264
Le 24:23 had cursed out of the **c.**, and 4264
Nu 1:52 every man by his own **c.**, and 4264
Nu 2:3 standard of the **c.** of Judah pitch 4264
Nu 2:9 All that were numbered in the **c.** 4264
Nu 2:10 the standard of the **c.** of Reuben 4264
Nu 2:16 All that were numbered in the **c.** 4264
Nu 2:17 with the **c.** of the Levites 4264
Nu 2:17 in the midst of the **c.**: 4264
Nu 2:18 standard of the **c.** of Ephraim 4264
Nu 2:24 that were numbered of the **c.** of 4264
Nu 2:25 The standard of the **c.** of Dan 4264
Nu 2:31 that were numbered in the **c.** of 4264
Nu 4:5 when the **c.** setteth forward, 4264
Nu 4:15 as the **c.** is to set forward; 4264
Nu 5:2 put out of the **c.** every leper, 4264
Nu 5:3 without the **c.** shall ye put them; 4264
Nu 5:4 and put them out without the **c.**: 4264
Nu 10:14 standard of the **c.** of the children 4264
Nu 10:18 standard of the **c.** of Reuben set 4264
Nu 10:22 **c.** of the children of Ephraim set 4264
Nu 10:25 the **c.** of the children of Dan set 4264
Nu 10:34 when they went out of the **c.** 4264
Nu 11:1 in the uttermost parts of the **c.** 4264
Nu 11:9 dew fell upon the **c.** in the night, 4264

Nu 11:26 remained two of the men in the **c.**, 4264
Nu 11:26 and they prophesied in the **c.**. 4264
Nu 11:27 and Medad do prophesy in the **c.**. 4264
Nu 11:30 Moses gat him into the **c.**, 4264
Nu 11:31 let them fall by the **c.**, as it were 4264
Nu 11:31 the other side, round about the **c.**, 4264
Nu 11:32 themselves round about the **c.**. 4264
Nu 12:14 let her be shut out from the **c.**. 4264
Nu 12:15 Miriam was shut out from the **c.**. 4264
Nu 14:44 Moses departed not out of the **c.**. 4264
Nu 15:35 him with stones without the **c.** 4264
Nu 15:36 brought him without the **c.**, and 4264
Nu 19:3 bring her forth without the **c.**, and 4264
Nu 19:7 afterward he shall come into the **c.**, 4264
Nu 19:9 without the **c.** in a clean place, 4264
Nu 31:12 unto the **c.** at the plains of Moab, 4264
Nu 31:13 forth to meet them without the **c.**. 4264
Nu 31:19 do ye abide without the **c.** seven 4264
Nu 31:24 afterward ye shall come into the **c.**. 4264
De 23:10 shall he go abroad out of the **c.**, 4264
De 23:10 he shall not come within the **c.**: 4264
De 23:11 he shall come into the **c.** again. 4264
De 23:12 have a place also without the **c.**, 4264
De 23:14 God walketh in the midst of thy **c.**, 4264
De 23:14 therefore shall thy **c.** be holy: 4264
De 29:11 thy stranger that is in thy **c.**, 4264
Jos 5:8 abode in their places in the **c.**, till 4264
Jos 6:11 into the **c.**, and lodged in the **c.**. 4264
Jos 6:14 returned into the **c.**: so they did 4264
Jos 6:18 make the **c.** of Israel a curse, and 4264
Jos 6:23 left them without the **c.** of Israel. 4264
Jos 9:6 to Joshua unto the **c.** at Gilgal, 4264
Jos 10:6 sent unto Joshua to the **c.** to Gilgal, 4264
Jos 10:15 and all Israel with him, unto the **c.** 4264
Jos 10:21 all the people returned to the **c.** to 4264
Jos 10:43 with him, unto the **c.** to Gilgal. 4264
Jg 7:17 I come to the outside of the **c.**, 4264
Jg 7:18 also on every side of all the **c.**, 4264
Jg 7:19 came unto the outside of the **c.** 4264
Jg 7:21 in his place round about the **c.**: 4264
Jg 13:25 him at times in the **c.** of Dan 4264
Jg 21:8 there came none to the **c.** from 4264
Jg 21:12 brought them unto the **c.** to Shiloh, 4264
1Sa 4:3 the people were come into the **c.**, 4264
1Sa 4:5 of the Lord came into the **c.**, 4264
1Sa 4:6 noise of this great shout in the **c.** 4264
1Sa 4:6 of the Lord was come into the **c.**. 4264
1Sa 4:7 they said, God is come into the **c.**. 4264
1Sa 13:17 out of the **c.** of the Philistines 4264
1Sa 14:21 went up with them into the **c.** 4264
1Sa 17:4 out of the **c.** of the Philistines, 4264
1Sa 17:17 run to the **c.** to thy brethren; 4264
1Sa 26:6 down with me to Saul to the **c.**? 4264
2Sa 1:2 a man came out of the **c.** from 4264
2Sa 1:3 Out of the **c.** of Israel am I 4264
1Ki 16:16 king over Israel that day in the **c.** 4264
2Ki 3:24 when they came to the **c.** of Israel, 4264
2Ki 6:8 and such a place shall be my **c.** 8466
2Ki 7:5 to go unto the **c.** of the Syrians: 4264
2Ki 7:5 to the uttermost part of the **c.** 4264
2Ki 7:7 even the **c.** as it was, and fled 4264
2Ki 7:8 to the uttermost part of the **c.**, 4264
2Ki 7:10 We came to the **c.** of the Syrians, 4264
2Ki 7:12 are they gone out of the **c.** to hide 4264
2Ki 19:35 smote in the **c.** of the Assyrians 4264
2Ch 22:1 came with the Arabians to the **c.** 4264
2Ch 32:21 the leaders and captains in the **c.** 4264
Ps 78:28 let it fall in the midst of their **c.**, 4264
Ps 106:16 They envied Moses also in the **c.**, 4264
Isa 29:3 And I will **c.** against thee round 2583
Isa 37:36 smote in the **c.** of the Assyrians 4264
Jer 50:29 **c.** against it round about; and 2583
Eze 4:2 set the **c.** also against it, and set 4264
Joe 2:11 for his **c.** is very great: for he is 4264
Na 3:17 **c.** in the hedges in the cold day, 2583
Heb 13:11 sin, are burned without the **c.**. *3925*
Heb 13:13 unto him without the **c.**, bearing *3925*
Re 20:9 compassed the **c.** of the saints *3925*

CAMPED
Ex 19:2 and there Israel **c.** before the 2583

CAMPHIRE
Ca 1:14 a cluster of **c.** in the vineyards 3724
Ca 4:13 **c.**, with spikenard, 3724

CAMPS
Nu 2:32 that were numbered of the **c.** 4264
Nu 5:3 that they defile not their **c.**, in 4264
Nu 10:2 for the journeying of the **c.**. 4264
Nu 10:5 then the **c.** that lie on the east 4264
Nu 10:6 then the **c.** that lie on the south 4264
Nu 10:25 the rereward of all the **c.** 4264
Am 4:10 the stink of your **c.** to come up 4264

CAN See also CANNOT; CANST.
Ge 4:13 punishment is greater than I **c.**
Ge 13:16 **c.** number the dust of the 3201
Ge 31:43 and what **c.** I do this day unto
Ge 39:9 then **c.** I do this great wickedness,
Ge 41:15 is none that **c.** interpret it:
Ge 41:38 **C.** we find such a one as this is)
Ge 44:1 as much as they **c.** carry, 3201
Ge 44:15 a man as I **c.** certainly divine?
Ex 4:14 I know that he **c.** speak well.
Ex 5:11 you straw where ye **c.** find it:
Le 14:30 pigeons such as he **c.** get;
Nu 23:10 Who **c.** count the dust of Jacob,
De 1:12 How **c.** I myself alone bear your
De 3:24 **c.** do according to thy works,
De 7:17 how **c.** I dispossess them? 3201
De 9:2 Who **c.** stand before the children
De 31:2 I **c.** no more go out and 3201
De 32:39 that **c.** deliver out of my hand
Jg 14:12 if ye **c.** certainly declare it me
1Sa 9:6 peradventure he **c.** shew us our
1Sa 16:2 Samuel said, How **c.** I go?
1Sa 16:17 me now a man that **c.** play well,
1Sa 18:8 and what **c.** he have more but
1Sa 26:9 **c.** stretch forth his hand against
1Sa 28:2 know what thy servant **c.** do.
2Sa 7:20 And what **c.** David say more unto
2Sa 12:22 Who **c.** tell whether God will
2Sa 12:23 **c.** I bring him back again? 3201
2Sa 14:19 none **c.** turn to the right hand
2Sa 15:36 me every thing that ye **c.** hear.
2Sa 19:35 **c.** I discern between good and evil?
2Sa 19:35 **c.** thy servant taste what I eat
2Sa 19:35 **c.** I hear any more the voice of
1Ki 5:6 not among us any that **c.** skill to hew
1Ch 17:18 What **c.** David speak more to thee
2Ch 1:10 who **c.** judge this thy people,
2Ch 2:7 and that **c.** skill to grave with the
2Ch 2:8 I know that thy servants **c.**
Es 8:6 **c.** I endure to see the evil 3201
Es 8:6 people? or how **c.** I endure to 3201
Job 3:22 when they **c.** find the grave?
Job 4:2 but who **c.** withhold himself 3201
Job 6:6 **C.** that which is unsavoury be
Job 8:11 **C.** the rush grow up without mire?
Job 8:11 **c.** the flag grow without water?
Job 9:12 taketh away, who **c.** hinder him?
Job 10:7 there is none that **c.** deliver out
Job 11:10 together, then who **c.** hinder him?
Job 12:14 man, and there **c.** be no opening.
Job 14:4 Who **c.** bring a clean thing out of
Job 15:3 wherewith he **c.** do no good?
Job 22:2 **C.** a man be profitable unto God,
Job 22:13 doth God know? **c.** he judge
Job 22:17 and what **c.** the Almighty do for
Job 23:13 one mind and who **c.** turn him?
Job 25:4 How then **c.** man be justified with
Job 25:4 how **c.** he be clean that is born of
Job 26:14 of his power who **c.** understand?
Job 34:29 who then **c.** make trouble?
Job 34:29 his face, who then **c.** behold him?
Job 36:23 or who **c.** say, Thou hast wrought
Job 36:26 neither **c.** the number of his
Job 36:29 **c.** any understand the spreadings
Job 38:37 **c.** number the clouds in wisdom?
Job 38:37 who **c.** stay the bottles of heaven,
Job 40:14 thine own right hand **c.** save thee.
Job 40:19 he that made him **c.** make his
Job 40:23 he trusteth that he **c.** draw
Job 41:13 Who **c.** discover the face of his
Job 41:13 who **c.** come to him with his double
Job 41:14 **c.** open the doors of his face?
Job 41:16 that no air **c.** come between
Job 42:2 that no thought **c.** be withholden
Ps 11:3 destroyed, what **c.** the righteous
Ps 19:12 Who **c.** understand his errors?
Ps 22:29 none **c.** keep alive his own soul.
Ps 40:5 they are more than **c.** be numbered.
Ps 49:7 None of them **c.** by any means
Ps 56:4 fear what flesh **c.** do unto me.
Ps 56:11 not be afraid what man **c.** do unto
Ps 58:9 Before your pots **c.** feel the thorns,
Ps 78:19 **C.** God furnish a table in 3201
Ps 78:20 **c.** he give bread also? 3201
Ps 78:20 **c.** he provide flesh 3201
Ps 89:6 who in the heaven **c.** be compared.
Ps 89:6 sons of the mighty **c.** be likened
Ps 106:2 Who **c.** utter the mighty acts
Ps 106:2 who **c.** shew forth all his praise?
Ps 118:6 fear: what **c.** man do unto me?
Ps 147:17 who **c.** stand before his cold?
Pr 6:27 **C.** a man take fire in his bosom,
Pr 6:28 **C.** one go upon hot coals, and his
Pr 18:14 but a wounded spirit who **c.** bear?
Pr 20:6 but a faithful man who **c.** find?
Pr 20:9 Who **c.** say, I have made my heart
Pr 20:24 how **c.** a man then understand
Pr 26:16 seven men that **c.** render a reason,
Pr 31:10 Who **c.** find a virtuous woman?
Ec 2:12 for what **c.** the man do that
Ec 2:25 For who **c.** eat,
Ec 2:25 or who else **c.** hasten hereunto,
Ec 3:11 no man **c.** find out the work
Ec 3:14 nothing **c.** be put to it, nor
Ec 4:11 but how **c.** one be warm alone?
Ec 6:12 for who **c.** tell a man what shall
Ec 7:13 who **c.** make that straight, 3201
Ec 7:24 who **c.** find it out
Ec 8:7 for who **c.** tell him when it shall
Ec 10:14 be after him, who **c.** tell him?
Ca 8:7 neither **c.** the floods drown it:
Isa 28:20 shorter than a man **c.** stretch
Isa 28:20 narrower than that he **c.** wrap
Isa 38:18 death **c.** not celebrate thee: they that
Isa 43:9 among them **c.** declare this,
Isa 43:13 that **c.** deliver out of my hand:
Isa 46:7 unto him, yet **c.** he not answer,
Isa 49:15 **C.** a woman forget her sucking
Isa 56:11 greedy dogs which **c.** never have 3045
Jer 2:13 cisterns, that **c.** hold no water.
Jer 2:24 occasion who **c.** turn her away?
Jer 2:28 if they **c.** save thee in the time of
Jer 2:32 **C.** a maid forget her ornaments,
Jer 4:4 and burn that none **c.** quench it,
Jer 5:1 if ye **c.** find a man, if there be any
Jer 5:22 yet **c.** they not prevail;
Jer 5:22 yet **c.** they not pass over it? 3201
Jer 9:10 so that none **c.** pass through them;
Jer 9:10 neither **c.** men hear the voice
Jer 13:23 **C.** the Ethiopian change his skin,
Jer 14:22 the Gentiles that **c.** cause rain?
Jer 14:22 or **c.** the heavens give showers?
Jer 17:9 desperately wicked; who **c.** know
Jer 21:12 and burn that none **c.** quench it,
Jer 23:24 **C.** any hide himself in secret
Jer 31:37 If heaven above **c.** be measured,
Jer 33:20 If ye **c.** break my covenant of the
Jer 38:5 king is not he that **c.** do 3201
Jer 47:7 How **c.** it be quiet, seeing the
La 2:13 like the sea: who **c.** heal thee?
Eze 22:14 **C.** thine heart endure, or **c.** thine
Eze 28:3 no secret that they **c.** hide from
Eze 33:32 **c.** play well on an instrument:
Eze 37:3 **c.** these bones live? And I
Da 2:9 know that ye **c.** shew me the
Da 2:10 upon the earth that **c.** shew the 3202
Da 2:11 none other that **c.** shew it before
Da 3:29 God that **c.** deliver after this 3202
Da 4:35 none **c.** stay his hand,
Da 10:17 **c.** the servant of this my lord 3201
Joe 2:11 terrible; and who **c.** abide it?
Am 3:3 **C.** two walk together, except
Am 3:5 **C.** a bird fall in a snare upon the
Am 3:8 hath spoken, who **c.** but prophesy?
Jon 3:9 Who **c.** tell if God will turn and
Mic 3:11 none evil **c.** come upon us.
Mic 5:8 in pieces, and none **c.** deliver.
Na 1:6 Who **c.** stand before his indignation?
Na 1:6 and who **c.** abide in the fierceness
Mt 6:24 **No man c. serve two masters:** *1410*
Mt 6:27 **Which of you by taking thought c.** *1410*
Mt 7:18 **neither c. a corrupt tree bring**
Mt 9:15 **C. the children of the** *1410*
Mt 12:29 **Or else how c. one enter into a** *1410*
Mt 12:34 **how c. ye, being evil, speak good** *1410*
Mt 16:3 **ye c. discern the face of the sky;** *1097*
Mt 16:3 **but c. ye not discern the signs of** *1410*

Mt 19:25 saying, Who then **c.** be saved? *1410*
Mt 23:33 **how c. ye escape the damnation**
Mt 27:65 way, make it as sure as ye **c.**. *1492*
Mk 2:7 who **c.** forgive sins but God only? *1410*
Mk 2:19 **C. the children of the** *1410*
Mk 3:23 **How c. Satan cast out Satan?** *1410*
Mk 3:27 **No man c. enter into a strong** *1410*
Mk 7:15 **entering into him c. defile him:** *1410*
Mk 8:4 From whence **c.** a man satisfy *1410*
Mk 9:3 no fuller on earth **c.** white them. *1410*
Mk 9:29 **This kind c. come forth by** *1410*
Mk 9:39 **name, that c. lightly speak evil** *1410*
Mk 10:26 themselves, Who then **c.** be saved? *1410*
Mk 10:38 **know not what ye ask: c. ye** *1410*
Mk 10:39 And they said unto him, We **c.**. *1410*
Lu 5:21 Who **c.** forgive sins, but God alone? *1410*
Lu 5:34 **C. ye make the children of the** *1410*
Lu 6:39 **C. the blind lead the blind?** *1410*
Lu 12:4 **have no more that they c. do.** *1410*
Lu 12:25 **thought c. add to his stature** *1410*
Lu 12:56 **ye c. discern the face of the sky** *1492*
Lu 16:13 **No servant c. serve two masters:** *1410*
Lu 16:26 **neither c. they pass to us, that** *1410*
Lu 18:26 it said, Who then **c.** be saved? *1410*
Lu 20:36 **Neither c. they die any more:** *1410*
Joh 1:46 **C.** there any good thing come out *1410*
Joh 3:2 for no man **c.** do these miracles *1410*
Joh 3:4 How **c.** a man be born when he is *1410*
Joh 3:4 **c.** he enter the second time into *1410*
Joh 3:9 unto him, How **c.** these things be? *1410*
Joh 3:27 A man **c.** receive nothing except it *1410*
Joh 5:19 **The Son c. do nothing of himself,** *1410*
Joh 5:30 **I c. of mine own self do nothing:** *1410*
Joh 5:44 **How c. ye believe, which received** *1410*
Joh 6:44 **No man c. come to me, except the** *1410*
Joh 6:52 How **c.** this man give us his flesh *1410*
Joh 6:60 an hard saying: who **c.** hear it? *1410*
Joh 6:65 **that no man c. come unto me,** *1410*
Joh 9:4 **cometh, when no man c. work.** *1410*
Joh 9:16 How **c.** a man that is a sinner do *1410*
Joh 10:21 **C.** a devil open the eyes of the *1410*
Joh 14:5 and how **c.** we know the way? *1410*
Joh 15:4 **no more c. ye, except ye abide in** *1410*
Joh 15:5 **for without me ye c. do nothing.** *1410*
Ac 8:31 How **c.** I, except some man should *1410*
Ac 10:47 **C.** any man forbid water, that *1410*
Ac 24:13 Neither **c.** they prove the things *1410*
Ro 8:7 law of God, neither indeed **c.** be. *1410*
Ro 8:31 If God be for us, who **c.** be against
1Co 2:14 neither **c.** he know them, for *1410*
1Co 3:11 other foundation **c.** no man lay *1410*
1Co 12:3 no man **c.** say that Jesus is the *1410*
2Co 13:8 we **c.** do nothing against the truth, *1410*
Php 4:13 I **c.** do all things through Christ *2480*
1Th 3:9 what thanks **c.** we render to God *1410*
1Ti 6:7 is certain we **c.** carry nothing out *1410*
1Ti 6:16 light which no man **c.** approach
1Ti 6:16 no man hath seen, nor **c.** see: *1410*
Heb 5:2 Who **c.** have compassion on the *1410*
Heb 10:1 very image of the things, **c.** never *1410*
Heb 10:11 the same sacrifices, which **c.** never *1410*
Jas 2:14 not works? **C.** faith save him? *1410*
Jas 3:8 But the tongue **c.** no man tame; *1410*
Jas 3:12 **C.** the fig tree, my brethren, bear *1410*
Jas 3:12 so **c.** no fountain both yield salt
1Jo 4:20 how **c.** he love God whom he *1410*
Re 3:8 **open door, and no man c. shut it:** *1410*
Re 9:20 neither **c.** see, nor hear, nor walk: *1410*

CANA (ca'-nah)
Joh 2:1 in **C.** of Galilee; and the mother *2580*
Joh 2:11 did Jesus in **C.** of Galilee, *2580*
Joh 4:46 Jesus came again into **C.** of *2580*
Joh 21:2 Nathanael of **C.** in Galilee. *2580*

CANAAN (ca'-na-an) See also CANAANITE.
Ge 9:18 and Ham is the father of **C.**. 3667
Ge 9:22 Ham, the father of **C.**, saw the 3667
Ge 9:25 And he said, Cursed be **C.**; 3667
Ge 9:26 God of Shem; and **C.** shall be his 3667
Ge 9:27 tents of Shem; and **C.** shall be his 3667
Ge 10:6 and Mizraim, and Phut, and **C.**. 3667
Ge 10:15 And **C.** begat Sidon his firstborn, 3667
Ge 11:31 Chaldees, to go into the land of **C.** 3667
Ge 12:5 forth to go into the land of **C.**; 3667
Ge 12:5 into the land of **C.** they came. 3667
Ge 13:12 Abram dwelt in the land of **C.**, 3667
Ge 16:3 dwelt ten years in the land of **C.**, 3667
Ge 17:8 the land of **C.**, for an everlasting 3667
Ge 23:2 same is Hebron in the land of **C.** 3667
Ge 23:19 same is Hebron in the land of **C.** 3667
Ge 28:1 take a wife of the daughters of **C.**. 3667
Ge 28:6 take a wife of the daughters of **C.**; 3667
Ge 28:8 daughters of **C.** pleased not Isaac 3667
Ge 31:18 Isaac his father in the land of **C.**. 3667
Ge 33:18 which is in the land of **C.**, 3667
Ge 35:6 to Luz, which is in the land of **C.**, 3667
Ge 36:2 his wives of the daughters of **C.**; 3667
Ge 36:5 born unto him in the land of **C.**. 3667
Ge 36:6 which he had got in the land of **C.**; 3667
Ge 37:1 was a stranger, in the land of **C.**. 3667
Ge 42:5 the famine was in the land of **C.**. 3667
Ge 42:7 From the land of **C.** to buy food. 3667
Ge 42:13 sons of one man in the land of **C.**; 3667
Ge 42:29 their father unto the land of **C.**, 3667
Ge 42:32 with our father in the land of **C.** 3667
Ge 44:8 unto thee out of the land of **C.** 3667
Ge 45:17 go, get you unto the land of **C.**; 3667
Ge 45:25 came into the land of **C.** unto 3667
Ge 46:6 they had gotten in the land of **C.**, 3667
Ge 46:12 Er and Onan died in the land of **C.**. 3667
Ge 46:31 which were in the land of **C.**, 3667
Ge 47:1 are come out of the land of **C.**; 3667
Ge 47:4 famine is sore in the land of **C.**: 3667
Ge 47:13 the land of **C.** fainted by reason 3667
Ge 47:14 of Egypt, and in the land of **C.**, 3667
Ge 47:15 in the land of **C.**, all the Egyptians 3667
Ge 48:3 at Luz in the land of **C.**, 3667
Ge 48:7 Rachel died by me in the land of **C.** 3667
Ge 49:30 is before Mamre, in the land of **C.**, 3667
Ge 50:5 digged for me in the land of **C.**, 3667
Ge 50:13 carried him into the land of **C.**, 3667
Ex 6:4 them, to give them the land of **C.**, 3667
Ex 15:15 inhabitants of **C.** shall melt away. 3667
Ex 16:35 unto the borders of the land of **C.**. 3667
Le 14:34 come into the land of **C.**, which 3667
Le 18:3 the doings of the land of **C.**, 3667
Le 25:38 to give you the land of **C.**, and 3667
Nu 13:2 they may search the land of **C.**, 3667
Nu 13:17 them to spy out the land of **C.**, 3667
Nu 26:19 Onan died in the land of **C.**. 3667
Nu 32:30 among you in the land of **C.**. 3667
Nu 32:32 before the Lord into the land of **C.**, 3667
Nu 33:40 in the south in the land of **C.**, 3667
Nu 33:51 over Jordan into the land of **C.**; 3667
Nu 34:2 When ye come into the land of **C.**; 3667
Nu 34:2 land of **C.** with the coasts thereof:) 3667
Nu 34:29 children of Israel in the land of **C.**. 3667
Nu 35:10 over Jordan into the land of **C.**, 3667
Nu 35:14 shall ye give in the land of **C.**, 3667
De 32:49 the land of **C.**, which I give 3667
Jos 5:12 the fruit of the land of **C.** that 3667
Jos 14:1 of Israel inherited the land of **C.**, 3667
Jos 21:2 at Shiloh in the land of **C.**, saying, 3667
Jos 22:9 Shiloh, which is in the land of **C.**, 3667
Jos 22:10 Jordan, that are in the land of **C.**, 3667
Jos 22:11 an altar over against the land of **C.**, 3667
Jos 22:32 unto the land of **C.**, to the children 3667
Jos 24:3 throughout all the land of **C.**, 3667
Jg 3:1 had not known all the wars of **C.**; 3667
Jg 4:2 the hand of Jabin the king of **C.**, 3667
Jg 4:23 on that day Jabin the king of **C.**, 3667
Jg 4:24 against Jabin the king of **C.**, 3667
Jg 4:24 had destroyed Jabin king of **C.**. 3667
Jg 5:19 fought the kings of **C.** in Taanach 3667
Jg 21:12 to Shiloh, which is in the land of **C.**. 3667
1Ch 1:8 Cush, and Mizraim, Put, and **C.** 3667
1Ch 1:13 And **C.** begat Zidon his firstborn, 3667
1Ch 16:18 Unto thee will I give the land of **C.**, 3667
Ps 105:11 Unto thee will I give the land of **C.**, 3667
Ps 106:38 they sacrificed unto the idols of **C.** 3667
Ps 135:11 and all the kingdoms of **C.** 3667
Isa 19:18 speak the language of **C.**, and 3667
Eze 16:3 thy nativity is of the land of **C.**; 3667
Eze 16:29 thy fornication in the land of **C.** 3667
Zep 2:5 O **C.**, the land of the Philistines, 3667
Mt 15:22 behold, a woman of **C.** came out *5478*

CANAANITE (ca'-na-an-ite) See also CANAANITES; CANAANITESS; CANAANITISH; ZELOTES.
Ge 12:6 And the **C.** was then in the land. 3669
Ge 13:7 the **C.** and the Perizzite dwelled 3669
Ge 38:2 certain **C.**, whose name was Shuah; 3669
Ex 23:28 shall drive out the Hivite, the **C.**, 3669
Ex 33:2 and I will drive out the **C.**, 3669
Ex 34:11 before thee the Amorite, and the **C.**, 3669
Nu 21:1 king Arad the **C.**, which dwelt in 3669
Nu 33:40 king Arad the **C.**, which dwelt in 3669
Jos 9:1 Hittite, and the Amorite, the **C.**, 3669
Jos 11:3 the **C.** on the east and on the west, 3669
Jos 13:3 which is counted to the **C.**: 3669
Zec 14:21 the **C.** in the house of the Lord 3669
Mt 10:4 Simon the **C.**, and Judas Iscariot, *2581*
Mk 3:18 Thaddaeus, and Simon the **C.**, *2581*

CANAANITES (ca'-na-an-ites)
Ge 10:18 families of the **C.** spread abroad 3669
Ge 10:19 border of the **C.** was from Sidon, 3669
Ge 15:21 And the Amorites, and the **C.**, 3669
Ge 24:3 my son of the daughters of the **C.**, 3669
Ge 24:37 my son of the daughters of the **C.**, 3669
Ge 34:30 among the **C.**, and the Perizzites: 3669
Ge 50:11 the **C.**, saw the mourning in the 3669
Ex 3:8 place of the **C.**, and the Hittites, 3669
Ex 3:17 land of the **C.**, and the Hittites, 3669
Ex 13:5, 11 thee into the land of the **C.**, 3669
Ex 23:23 **C.**, the Hivites, and the Jebusites; 3669
Nu 13:29 and the **C.** dwell by the sea, 3669
Nu 14:25 and the **C.** dwelt in the valley, 3669
Nu 14:43 the **C.** are there before you, 3669
Nu 14:45 the **C.** which dwelt in that hill, 3669
Nu 21:3 and delivered up the **C.**; and they 3669
De 1:7 sea side, to the land of the **C.** 3669
De 7:1 and the Amorites, and the **C.**, 3669
De 11:30 goeth down in the land of the **C.**, 3669
De 20:17 and the Amorites, the **C.**, 3669
Jos 3:10 drive out from before you the **C.**, 3669
Jos 5:1 the kings of the **C.**, which were 3669
Jos 7:9 the **C.** and all the inhabitants 3669
Jos 12:8 the Amorites, and the **C.**, 3669
Jos 13:4 the south, all the land of the **C.**, 3669
Jos 16:10 And they drove not out the **C.** 3669
Jos 16:10 the **C.** dwell among the Ephraimites 3669
Jos 17:12 the **C.** would dwell in that land. 3669
Jos 17:13 that they put the **C.** to tribute; 3669
Jos 17:16 all the **C.** that dwell in the land 3669
Jos 17:18 for thou shalt drive out the **C.**, 3669
Jos 24:11 and the Perizzites, and the **C.**, 3669
Jg 1:1 shall go up for us against the **C.** 3669
Jg 1:3 that we may fight against the **C.**: 3669
Jg 1:4 and the Lord delivered the **C.** 3669
Jg 1:5 slew the **C.** and the Perizzites. 3669
Jg 1:9 went down to fight against the **C.**, 3669
Jg 1:10 went against the **C.** that dwelt 3669
Jg 1:17 they slew the **C.** that inhabited 3669
Jg 1:27 the **C.** would dwell in that land. 3669
Jg 1:28 that they put the **C.** to tribute, 3669
Jg 1:29 did Ephraim drive out the **C.** 3669
Jg 1:29 the **C.** dwelt in Gezer among them. 3669
Jg 1:30 but the **C.** dwelt among them, 3669
Jg 1:32 the Asherites dwelt among the **C.**, 3669
Jg 1:33 but he dwelt among the **C.**, 3669
Jg 3:3 the Philistines, and all the **C.**, 3669
Jg 3:5 of Israel dwelt among the **C.**, 3669
2Sa 24:7 of the Hivites, and of the **C.**: 3669
1Ki 9:16 slain the **C.** that dwelt in the city, 3669
Ezr 9:1 their abominations, even of the **C.**, 3669
Ne 9:8 him to give the land of the **C.** 3669
Ne 9:24 inhabitants of the land, the **C.**, 3669
Ob 20 Israel shall possess that of the **C.** 3669

CANAANITESS (ca'-na-an-ite-ess)
1Ch 2:3 of the daughter of Shua the **C.**. 3669

CANAANITISH (ca'-na-an-i-tish)
Ge 46:10 Shaul the son of a **C.** woman. 3669
Ex 6:15 Shaul the son of a **C.** woman. 3669

CANDACE (can'-da-see)
Ac 8:27 under **C.** queen of the Ethiopians, *2582*

CANDLE See also CANDLES; CANDLESTICK.
Job 18:6 and his **c.** shall be put out. 5216
Job 21:17 is the **c.** of the wicked put out! 5216
Job 29:3 When his **c.** shined upon my 5216
Ps 18:28 For thou wilt light my **c.**: 5216
Pr 20:27 the **c.** of the Lord, searching 5216
Pr 24:20 **c.** of the wicked shall be put out. 5216
Pr 31:18 her **c.** goeth not out by night. 5216
Jer 25:10 and the light of the **c.**. 5216
Mt 5:15 **men light a c., and put it under** *3088*
Mk 4:21 **Is a c. brought to be put under** *3088*
Lu 8:16 **when he hath lighted a c.,** *3088*

Lu 11:33 when he hath lighted a c., ... 3088
Lu 11:36 the bright shining of a c. doth 3088
Lu 15:8 doth not light a c., and sweep 3088
Re 18:23 And the light of a c. shall shine.......... 3088
Re 22:5 they need no c., neither light of......... 3088

CANDLES

Zep 1:12 I will seach Jerusalem with c.. 5216

CANDLESTICK See also CANDLESTICKS.

Ex 25:31 thou shalt make a c. of pure gold: 4501
Ex 25:31 beaten work shall the c. be made: 4501
Ex 25:32 branches of the c. out of the one 4501
Ex 25:32 branches of the c. out of the other 4501
Ex 25:33 branches that come out of the c.......... 4501
Ex 25:34 And in the c. shall be four bowls......... 4501
Ex 25:35 branches that proceed out of the c.. ... 4501
Ex 26:35 the c. over against the table.............. 4501
Ex 30:27 the c. and his vessels, and the 4501
Ex 31:8 the pure c. with all his furniture,........ 4501
Ex 35:14 The c. also for the light, ... 4501
Ex 37:17 he made the c. of pure gold: 4501
Ex 37:17 of beaten work made he the c.; 4501
Ex 37:18 c. out of the one side thereof,........... 4501
Ex 37:18 and three branches of the c.............. 4501
Ex 37:19 six branches going out of the c.. 4501
Ex 37:20 And in the c. were four bowls 4501
Ex 39:37 The pure c., with the lamps.............. 4501
Ex 40:4 thou shalt bring in the c., ... 4501
Ex 40:24 he put the c. in the tent of the.......... 4501
Le 24:4 the lamps upon the pure c. 4501
Nu 3:31 c., and the altars, and the vessels 4501
Nu 4:9 and cover the c. of the light,............. 4501
Nu 8:2 give light over against the c.. 4501
Nu 8:3 over against the c., as the Lord......... 4501
Nu 8:4 work of the c. was of beaten gold, ... 4501
Nu 8:4 Moses, so he made the c.. 4501
2Ki 4:10 a table, a stool, and a c.:................. 4501
1Ch 28:15 by weight for every c., and for the..... 4501
1Ch 28:15 the c., and also for the lamps............ 4501
1Ch 28:15 according to the use of every c.......... 4501
2Ch 13:11 and the c. of gold with the lamps 4501
Da 5:5 and wrote over against the c............ 5043
Zec 4:2 a c. all of gold, with a bowl.............. 4501
Zec 4:11 upon the right side of the c............. 4501
Mt 5:15 but on a c.; and it giveth light 3087
Mk 4:21 abed? and not to be set on a c.? 3087
Lu 8:16 but setteth it on a c., that they 3087
Lu 11:33 but on a c., that they which 3087
Heb 9:2 wherein was the c., and the table,...... 3087
Re 2:5 remove thy c. out of his place, ... 3087

CANDLESTICKS

1Ki 7:49 the c. of pure gold, five on the........... 4501
1Ch 28:15 the weight for the c. of gold, and......... 4501
1Ch 28:15 and for the c. of silver by weight, ... 4501
2Ch 4:7 he made ten c. of gold according........ 4501
2Ch 4:20 the c. with their lamps, that they 4501
Jer 52:19 the c., and the spoons, and the 4501
Re 1:12 turned, I saw seven golden c.; 3087
Re 1:13 in the midst of the seven c. one 3087
Re 1:20 hand, and the seven golden c.. 3087
Re 1:20 the seven c. which thou sawest 3087
Re 2:1 the midst of the seven golden c.; ... 3087
Re 11:4 and the two c. standing before the 3087

CANE

Isa 43:24 Thou hast bought me no sweet c. 7070
Jer 6:20 Sheba, and the sweet c. from a far..... 7070

CANKER See also CANKERED; CANKERWORM.

2Ti 2:17 their word will eat as doth a c........... 1044

CANKERED

Jas 5:3 Your gold and silver is c.; and........... 2728

CANKERWORM

Joe 1:4 hath the c. eaten; 3218
Joe 1:4 and that which the c. hath left 3218
Joe 2:25 the c., and the caterpillar, and the...... 3218
Na 3:15 it shall eat thee up like the c.: 3218
Na 3:15 make thyself many as the c.,............. 3218
Na 3:16 the c. spoileth, and fleeth away.......... 3218

CANNEH (can'-neh) See also CALNEH.

Eze 27:23 C., and Eden, the merchants of......... 3656

CANNOT

Ge 19:19 I c. escape to the mountain,........ 3808,3201
Ge 19:22 I c. do any thing till thou be....... 3808,3201
Ge 24:50 we c. speak unto thee bad or..... 3808,3201
Ge 29:8 We c., until all the flocks be 3808,3201
Ge 31:35 I c. rise up before thee: for 3808,3201
Ge 32:12 the sand of the sea, which c. be 3808
Ge 34:14 We c. do this thing, to give 3808,3201
Ge 38:22 and said, I c. find her; and also.......... 3808
Ge 43:22 c. tell who put our money................. 3808
Ge 44:22 The lad c. leave his father: 3808,3201
Ge 44:26 c. go down: if our youngest 3808,3201
Ex 10:5 one c. be able to see the earth: 3808
Ex 19:23 people c. come up to mount....... 3808,3201
Le 14:21 be poor, and c. get so much;....... 369,3027
Nu 22:18 I c. go beyond the word of........ 3808,3201
Nu 23:20 he hath blessed; and I c. reverse 3808
Nu 24:13 I c. go beyond the 3808,3201
Nu 35:33 and the land c. be cleansed of............ 3308
De 28:35 a sore botch that c. be.............. 3808,3201
Jos 24:19 Ye c. serve the Lord: for he is... 3808,3201
Jg 11:35 mouth unto the Lord, and I c..... 3808,3201
Jg 14:13 if ye c. declare it me, then 3808,3201
Ru 4:6 I c. redeem it for myself, lest 3808,3201
Ru 4:6 my right to thyself; for I c......... 3808,3201
1Sa 12:21 things, which c. profit nor deliver: 3308
1Sa 17:39 I c. go with these; for I 3808
1Sa 17:55 As thy soul liveth, O king, I c. tell....... 518
1Sa 25:17 that a man c. speak to him. ....
2Sa 5:6 thinking, David c. come in hither........ 3808
2Sa 14:14 which c. be gathered up again: 3808
2Sa 23:6 they c. be taken with hands: 3808
1Ki 3:8 that c. be numbered nor counted........ 3808
1Ki 8:27 heaven of heavens c. contain............ 3808
1Ki 18:12 tell Ahab, and he c. find thee, ... 3808
2Ch 2:6 heaven of heavens c. contain him?....... 3808
2Ch 6:18 heaven of heavens c. contain............ 3808
2Ch 24:20 of the Lord, that ye c. prosper?......... 3808
Ezr 9:15 we c. stand before thee because 3808
Ne 6:3 so that I c. come down:...................... 369
Job 5:12 their hands c. perform their 3808,3201
Job 6:30 c. my taste discern perverse things?... 3808
Job 9:3 c. answer him one of a thousand. 3808
Job 12:14 c. be built again: he shutteth............ 3808
Job 14:5 appointed his bounds that he c........... 3808
Job 17:10 c. find one wise man among you 3808
Job 19:8 fenced up my way that I c. pass, ... 3808
Job 23:8 backward, but I c. perceive him: 3808
Job 23:9 doth work, but I c. behold him: 3808
Job 23:9 the right hand, that I c. see him: 3808
Job 28:15 It c. be gotten for gold, neither 3808
Job 28:16 It c. be valued with the gold of.......... 3808
Job 28:17 gold and the crystal c. equal it:.......... 3808
Job 31:31 of his flesh! we c. be satisfied. 3808
Job 33:21 that it c. be seen; and his bones 3808
Job 36:18 then a great ransom c. deliver........... 3808
Job 37:5 which we c. comprehend. 408
Job 37:19 we c. order our speech by reason 3808
Job 37:23 Almighty, we c. find him out: 3808
Job 41:17 stick together, that they c. be 3808
Job 41:23 in themselves; they c. be moved........ 1077
Job 41:26 him c. hold: the spear, the dart, ... 1097
Job 41:28 The arrow c. make him flee: 3808
Ps 40:5 they c. be reckoned up in order 408
Ps 77:4 I am so troubled that I c. speak......... 3808
Ps 88:8 I am shut up, and I c. come forth 3808
Ps 93:1 is stablished, that it c. be moved......... 1077
Ps 125:1 mount Zion, which c. be removed,...... 3808
Ps 139:6 for me; it is high, I c. attain....... 3808,3201
Pr 30:21 and for four which it c. bear:...... 3808,3201
Ec 1:8 man c. utter it: the eye is not.... 3808,3201
Ec 1:15 crooked c. be made straight:...... 3808,3201
Ec 1:15 that which is wanting c. be 3808,3201
Ec 8:17 man c. find out the work that..... 3808,3201
Ec 10:14 a man c. tell what shall be; 3045
Ca 8:7 Many waters c. quench love,...... 3808,3201
Isa 1:13 the calling of assemblies, I c. 3808,3201
Isa 29:11 and he saith, I c.; for it is 3808,3201
Isa 38:18 death [c.] celebrate thee: they that go.......
Isa 38:18 For the grave c. praise thee, ... 3808
Isa 38:18 go down into the pit c. hope for.......... 3808
Isa 44:18 shut their eyes, that they c. see: ....
Isa 44:18 and their hearts, that they c.................
Isa 44:20 that he c. deliver his soul, nor............. 3808
Isa 45:20 and pray unto a god that c. save. 3808
Isa 50:2 hand shortened at all, that it c. 3808
Isa 56:10 all dumb dogs, they c. bark;....... 3808,3201
Isa 56:11 shepherds that c. understand:..... 3808,3045
Isa 57:20 troubled sea, when it c. rest, ... 3808,3201
Isa 59:1 is not shortened, that it c. save; 3808
Isa 59:1 his ear heavy, that it c. hear: 3808
Isa 59:14 and equity c. enter.................... 3808,3201
Jer 1:6 Ah, Lord God! behold, I c. speak;....... 3808
Jer 4:19 noise in me; I c. hold my peace, ... 3808
Jer 5:22 perpetual decree, that it c. pass it:..... 3808
Jer 6:10 they c. hearken: behold,............ 3808,3201
Jer 7:8 trust in lying words, that c. profit....... 1115
Jer 10:5 needs be borne, because they c. go.... 3808
Jer 10:5 for they c. do evil, neither also.......... 3808
Jer 14:9 as a mighty man that c. 3808,3201
Jer 18:6 of Israel, c. I do with you as...... 3808,3201
Jer 19:11 vessel, that c. be made whole 3808,3201
Jer 24:3 that c. be eaten, they are so evil. 3808
Jer 24:8 evils figs, which c. be eaten, they 3808
Jer 29:17 them like vile figs, that c. be............ 3808
Jer 33:22 host of heaven c. be numbered,......... 3808
Jer 36:5 am shut up; I c. go into 3808,3201
Jer 46:23 Lord, though it c. be searched;.......... 3808
Jer 49:23 on the sea it c. be quiet............. 3808,3201
La 3:7 I c. get out: he hath made my........... 3808
La 4:18 that we c. go in our streets: 3808
Da 2:27 c. the wise men, the 3809,3202
Ho 1:10 sea, which c. be measured nor 3808
Jon 4:11 that c. discern between their............ 3808
Hab 2:5 and c. be satisfied, but gathereth 3808
Mt 5:14 city that is set on an hill c. ... 3756,1410
Mt 6:24 c. serve God and mammon..... 3756,1410
Mt 7:18 good tree c. bring forth evil ... 3756,1410
Mt 19:11 All men c. receive this saying, ... 3756
Mt 21:27 We c. tell. And he said unto 3756,1492
Mt 26:53 Thinkest thou that I c. now ... 3756,1410
Mt 27:42 saved others; himself he c......... 3756,1410
Mk 2:19 bridegroom with them, they c. 3756,1410
Mk 3:24 itself, that kingdom c. stand....3756,1410
Mk 3:25 itself, that house c. stand. 3756,1410
Mk 3:26 he c. stand, but hath an end.. 3756,1410
Mk 7:18 it c. defile him;.................... 3756,1410
Mk 11:33 c. tell, And Jesus answering........ 3756,1492
Mk 15:31 others; himself he c. save........... 3756,1410
Lu 11:7 in bed; I c. rise and give thee..3756,1410
Lu 13:33 it c. be that a prophet perish ..3756,1735
Lu 14:14 for they c. recompense thee: .. 3756,2192
Lu 14:20 wife, and therefore I c. come...3756,1410
Lu 14:26 life also, he c. be my disciple..3756,1410
Lu 14:27 after me, c. be my disciple..... 3756,1410
Lu 14:33 he hath, he c. be my disciple. .3756,1410
Lu 16:3 I c. dig; to beg I am ashamed.3756,2480
Lu 16:13 Ye c. serve God and mammon.3756,1410
Lu 16:26 pass from hence to you c.;..... 3361,1410
Joh 3:3 c. see the kingdom of God..... 3756,1410
Joh 3:5 c. enter into the kingdom of .. 3756,1410
Joh 7:7 world c. hate you; but me it .. 3756,1410
Joh 7:34, 36 I am, thither ye c. come.... 3756,1410
Joh 7:36 where I am, thither ye c. come?.............
Joh 8:14 ye c. tell whence I come, ... 3756,1492
Joh 8:21 whither I go, ye c. come......... 3756,1410
Joh 8:22 Whither I go, ye c. come. 3756,1410
Joh 8:43 because ye c. hear my word... 3756,1410
Joh 10:35 the scripture c. be broken; 3756,1410
Joh 13:33 Whither I go, ye c. come; so .. 3756,1410
Joh 13:37 why c. I follow thee now? I 3756,1410
Joh 14:17 whom the world c. receive, ... 3756,1410
Joh 15:4 As the branch c. bear fruit 3756,1410
Joh 16:12 but ye c. bear them now......... 3756,1410
Joh 16:18 we c. tell what he saith............. 3756,1492
Ac 4:16 Jerusalem; and we c. deny......... 3756,1410
Ac 4:20 we c. but speak the things......... 3756,1410
Ac 5:39 ye c. overthrow it lest; haply 3756,1410
Ac 15:1 of Moses, ye c. be saved. 3756,1410
Ac 19:36 these things c. be spoken against,......... 368
Ac 27:31 in the ship, ye c. be saved. 3756,1410
Ro 8:8 are in the flesh c. please God..... 3756,1410
Ro 8:26 groanings which c. be uttered. 215
1Co 7:9 But if they c. contain, let them.......... 3756
1Co 10:21 c. drink the cup of the Lord,...... 3756,1410
1Co 10:21 ye c. be partakers of the.......... 3756,1410
1Co 12:21 the eye c. say unto the hand, I... 3756,1410
1Co 15:50 flesh and blood c. inherit the...... 3756,1410
2Co 12:2 I c. tell; or whether out........... 3756,1492
2Co 12:2 of the body, I c. tell:................ 3756,1492
2Co 12:3 the body, I c. tell: God............. 3756,1492
Ga 3:17 c. disannul, that it should make.......... 3756
Ga 5:17 ye c. do the things that ye would. 3361
1Ti 5:25 that are otherwise c. be hid. 3756,1410
2Ti 2:13 abideth faithful: he c. deny......... 3756,1410
Tit 1:2 which God, that c. lie, promised.......... 893
Tit 2:8 speech, that c. be condemned; 176
Heb 4:15 priest which c. be touched......... 3361,1410

Heb 9:5 of which we **c.** now speak *3756,1410*
Heb 12:27 things which **c.** be shaken may *3361*
Heb 12:28 a kingdom which **c.** be moved, ... *761*
Jas 1:13 for God **c.** be tempted with evil,.......... *551*
Jas 4:2 desire to have, and **c.** obtain: *3756,1410*
2Pe 1:9 is blind, and **c.** see afar off, and......... *3467*
2Pe 2:14 that **c.** cease from sin; beguiling *180*
1Jo 3:9 he **c.** sin, because he is born...... *3756,1410*

CANST
Ge 41:15 that thou **c.** understand a dream to..........
Ex 33:20 And he said, Thou **c.** not see 3201
De 28:27 the itch, whereof thou **c.** not............ 3201
Jos 7:13 thou **c.** not stand before 3201
Jg 16:15 unto him, How **c.** thou say, I love ....
1Sa 30:15 David said to him, **C.** thou bring ....
2Ki 8:1 sojourn wheresover thou **c.** sojourn: ....
Ezr 7:16 silver and gold that thou **c.** find................
Job 11:7 **C.** thou by searching find out God?..........
Job 11:7 **c.** thou find out the Almighty unto ....
Job 11:8 is as high as heaven; what **c.** thou do? ......
Job 11:8 deeper than hell; what **c.** thou know? ....
Job 22:11 Or darkness, that thou **c.** not see;.............
Job 33:5 If thou **c.** answer me, set thy........... 3201
Job 38:31 **C.** thou bind the sweet influences of.........
Job 38:32 **C.** thou bring forth Mazzaroth in his ....
Job 38:32 or **c.** thou guide Arcturus with his ....
Job 38:33 **c.** thou set the dominion thereof in...........
Job 38:34 **C.** thou lift up thy voice to the clouds, ...
Job 38:35 **C.** thou send lightnings, that they............
Job 39:1 or **c.** thou mark when the hinds do............
Job 39:2 **C.** thou number the months that they.........
Job 39:10 **C.** thou bind the unicorn with his.............
Job 39:20 **C.** thou make him afraid as a..................
Job 40:9 or **c.** thou thunder with a voice ....
Job 41:1 **C.** thou draw out leviathan with an ....
Job 41:2 **C.** thou put an hook into his nose? ....
Job 41:7 **C.** thou fill his skin with barbed...............
Job 42:2 I know that thou **c.** do every............ 3201
Pr 3:15 and all the things thou **c.** desire are.........
Pr 5:6 ways are moveable, that thou **c.**................
Pr 30:4 is his son's name, if thou **c.** tell? ....
Isa 33:19 deeper speech than thou **c.** perceive; ....
Isa 33:19 tongue, that thou **c.** not understand ....
Jer 2:23 How **c.** thou say, I am not polluted, I ....
Jer 12:5 how **c.** thou contend with horses? ....
Eze 3:6 words thou **c.** not understand. ....
Da 5:16 that thou **c.** make interpretations,....... 3202
Da 5:16 doubts: now if thou **c.** read................ 3202
Hab 1:13 and **c.** not look on iniquity:................ 3201
Mt 5:36 **because thou c. not make** *1410*
Mt 8:2 thou **c.** make me clean..................... *1410*
Mk 1:40 If thou wilt, thou **c.** make me............ *1410*
Mk 9:22 but if thou **c.** do any thing, have *1410*
Mk 9:23 **If thou c. believe, all things are** *1410*
Lu 5:12 if thou wilt, thou **c.** make me clean..... *1410*
Lu 6:42 **how c. thou say to thy brother,**..... *1410*
Joh 3:8 **but c. not tell whence it cometh,**... *1492*
Joh 13:36 **Whither I go, thou c. not follow** ... *1410*
Ac 21:37 Who said, **C.** thou speak Greek?........ *1097*
Re 2:2 **and how thou c. not bear them** *1410*

CAPERNAUM (ca-pur'-na-um)
Mt 4:13 he came and dwelt in **C.**, which is...... *2584*
Mt 8:5 when Jesus was entered into **C.**,........ *2584*
Mt 11:23 **And thou, C., which art exalted** *2584*
Mt 17:24 were come to **C.**, they that............... *2584*
Mk 1:21 they went into **C.**; and straightway...... *2584*
Mk 2:1 he entered into **C.** after some days;.... *2584*
Mk 9:33 he came to **C.**: and being in the.......... *2584*
Lu 4:23 **have heard done in C., do also** *2584*
Lu 4:31 And came down to **C.**, a city of......... *2584*
Lu 7:1 of the people, he entered into **C.**....... *2584*
Lu 10:15 **And thou, C., which art exalted to** .*2584*
Joh 2:12 After this he went down to **C.**,.......... *2584*
Joh 4:46 whose son was sick at **C.**................ *2584*
Joh 6:17 and went over the sea toward **C.**....... *2584*
Joh 6:24 came to **C.**, seeking for Jesus............ *2584*
Joh 6:59 synagogue, as he taught in **C.**........... *2584*

CAPH (kaf)
Ps 119:81 *title* [כ] **C.**..

CAPHTHORIM (caf'-tho-rim) See also CAPHTORIM.
1Ch 1:12 came the Phillistines,) and **C.**............ 3732

CAPHTOR (caf'-tor) See also CAPHTORIM.
De 2:23 which came forth out of **C.**, ... 3731
Jer 47:4 the remnant of the country of **C.**......... 3731
Am 9:7 the Philistines from **C.**, and the 3731

CAPHTORIM (caf'-to-rim) See also CAPHTHORIM; CAPHTORIMS.
Ge 10:14 came Philistim,) and **C.**.................... 3732

CAPHTORIMS (caf'-to-rims) See also CAPHTORIM.
De 2:23 the **C.**, which came forth out of......... 3732

CAPITAL See CHAPITER.

CAPPADOCIA (cap-pa-do'-she-ah)
Ac 2:9 and **C.**, in Pontus, and Asia,............... *2587*
1Pe 1:1 Galatia, **C.**, Asia, and Bithynia, ... *2587*

CAPTAIN See also CAPTAINS.
Ge 21:22 **c.** of his host spake unto 8269
Ge 21:32 Phichol, the chief **c.** of his host,......... 8269
Ge 26:26 Phichol, the chief **c.** of his army......... 8269
Ge 37:36 Pharaoh's, and **c.** of the guard. 8269
Ge 39:1 **c.** of the guard, an Egyptian,............. 8269
Ge 40:3 the house of the **c.** of the guard,........ 8269
Ge 40:4 **c.** of the guard charged Joseph 8269
Ge 41:10 **c.** of the guard's house, both me......... 8269
Ge 41:12 Hebrew, servant to the **c.** of the........ 8269
Nu 2:3 be **c.** of the children of Judah............ 5387
Nu 2:5 be **c.** of the children of Issachar.......... 5387
Nu 2:7 be **c.** of the children of Zebulun. 5387
Nu 2:10 the **c.** of the children of Reuben.......... 5387
Nu 2:12 the **c.** of the children of Simeon 5387
Nu 2:14 the **c.** of the sons of Gad shall be....... 5387
Nu 2:18 the **c.** of the sons of Ephraim............ 5387
Nu 2:20 **c.** of the children of Manasseh............ 5387
Nu 2:22 the **c.** of the sons of Benjamin............ 5387
Nu 2:25 the **c.** of the children of Dan 5387
Nu 2:27 the **c.** of the children of Asher............ 5387
Nu 2:29 the **c.** of the children of Naphtali......... 5387
Nu 14:4 Let us make a **c.**, and let us 7218
Jos 5:14 but as **c.** of the host of the Lord......... 8269
Jos 5:15 **c.** of the Lord's host said unto........... 8269
Jg 4:2 the **c.** of whose host was Sisera,......... 8269
Jg 4:7 the **c.** of Jabin's army, with his 8269
Jg 11:6 and be our **c.**, that we may fight......... 7101
Jg 11:11 made him head and **c.** over them: 7101
1Sa 9:16 to be **c.** over my people Israel,.......... 5057
1Sa 10:1 thee to be **c.** over his inheritance?...... 5057
1Sa 12:9 **c.** of the host of Hazor, and into........ 8269
1Sa 13:14 to be **c.** over his people, because......... 5057
1Sa 14:50 the name of the **c.** of his host was 8269
1Sa 17:18 unto the **c.** of their thousand, ... 8269
1Sa 17:55 the **c.** of the host, Abner. whose 8269
1Sa 18:13 made him his **c.** over a thousand;....... 8269
1Sa 22:2 he became a **c.** over them; and........... 8269
1Sa 26:5 Abner the son of Ner, the **c.** of his 8269
2Sa 2:8 Abner the son of Ner, **c.** of Saul's...... 8269
2Sa 5:2 and thou shalt be a **c.** over Israel....... 5057
2Sa 5:8 soul, he shall be chief and **c.**..................
2Sa 10:16 Shobach, the **c.** of the host of............ 8269
2Sa 10:18 Shobach, the **c.** of their host, who...... 8269
2Sa 17:25 And Absalom made Amasa **c.** 5921
2Sa 19:13 **c.** of the host before me.................. 8269
2Sa 23:19 therefore he was their **c.**: howbeit...... 8269
2Sa 24:2 Joab the **c.** of the host, which was....... 8269
1Ki 1:19 Joab the **c.** of the host: but.............. 8269
1Ki 2:32 **c.** of the host of Israel, and Amasa..... 8269
1Ki 2:32 Jether, **c.** of the host of Judah. 8269
1Ki 11:15 Joab the **c.** of the host was gone up.... 8269
1Ki 11:21 Joab the **c.** of the host was dead,........ 8269
1Ki 11:24 became **c.** over a band, when............ 8269
1Ki 16:9 **c.** of half his chariots, conspired......... 8269
1Ki 16:16 Omri, the **c.** of the host, king over...... 8269
2Ki 1:9 unto him a **c.** of fifty with his fifty. 8269
2Ki 1:10 said to the **c.** of fifty, If I be a man 8269
2Ki 1:11 unto him another **c.** of fifty 8269
2Ki 1:13 a **c.** of the third fifty with his............ 8269
2Ki 1:13 And the third **c.** of fity went up, ... 8269
2Ki 4:13 the **c.** of the host? And she................ 8269
2Ki 5:1 **c.** of the host of the king of Syria,....... 8269
2Ki 9:5 I have an errand to thee, O **c.**........... 8269
2Ki 9:5 all us? And he said, To thee, O **c.**...... 8269
2Ki 9:25 Then said Jehu to Bidkah his **c.**, ... 7991
2Ki 15:25 Pekah, the son of Remaliah, a **c.**........ 7991
2Ki 18:24 one **c.** of the least of my master's 6346
2Ki 20:5 Hezekiah the **c.** of my people, ... 5057
2Ki 25:8 Nebuzar-adan, **c.** of the guard,........... 7227
2Ki 25:10 were with the **c.** of the guard 7227
2Ki 25:11 Nebuzar-adan the **c.** of the guard 7227
2Ki 25:12 But the **c.** of the guard left of the 7227
2Ki 25:15 in silver, the **c.** of the guard took....... 7227
2Ki 25:18 the **c.** of the guard took Seraiah......... 7227
2Ki 25:20 **c.** of the guard took these, and........... 7227
1Ch 11:6 first shall be the chief and **c.**............. 8269
1Ch 11:21 than the two; for he was their **c.** 8269
1Ch 11:42 a **c.** of the Reubenites, and............... 7218
1Ch 19:16 the **c.** of the host of Hadarezer.......... 8269
1Ch 19:18 killed Shophach the **c.** of the host....... 8269
1Ch 27:5 The third **c.** of the host for the.......... 8269
1Ch 27:7 The fourth **c.** for the fourth month..........
1Ch 27:8 fifth **c.** for the fifth month was........... 8269
1Ch 27:9 The sixth **c.** for the sixth month.............
1Ch 27:10 The seventh **c.** for the seventh...............
1Ch 27:11 The eighth **c.** for the eighth month ....
1Ch 27:12 The ninth **c.** for the ninth month ....
1Ch 27:13 The tenth **c.** for the tenth month.............
1Ch 27:14 The eleventh **c.** for the eleventh ....
1Ch 27:15 The twelfth **c.** for the twelfth ....
2Ch 13:12 himself is with us for our **c.**............. 7218
2Ch 17:15 Jehohanan the **c.**, and with him.......... 8269
Ne 9:17 in their rebellion appointed a **c.**.......... 7218
Isa 3:3 **c.** of fifty, and the honourable............ 8269
Isa 36:9 one **c.** of the least of my master's...... 6346
Jer 37:13 a **c.** of the ward was there................ 1167
Jer 39:9 the **c.** of the guard carried away 7227
Jer 39:10 the **c.** of the guard left of the poor ....
Jer 39:11 Nebuzar-adan, the **c.** of the guard, ... 7227
Jer 39:13 the **c.** of the guard sent, ... 7227
Jer 40:1 after that Nebuzar-adan the **c.** of......... 7227
Jer 40:2 **c.** of the guard took Jeremiah, ... 7227
Jer 40:5 the **c.** of the guard gave him 7227
Jer 41:10 Nebuzar-adan the **c.** of the guard 7227
Jer 43:6 person that Nebuzar-adan the **c.**......... 7227
Jer 51:27 appoint a **c.** against her; cause........... 2951
Jer 52:12 Nebuzar-adan, **c.** of the guard,............ 7227
Jer 52:14 that were with the **c.** of the guard,..... 7227
Jer 52:15 the **c.** of the guard carried away 7227
Jer 52:16 the **c.** of the guard left certain........... 7227
Jer 52:19 took the **c.** of the guard away............ 7227
Jer 52:24 the **c.** of the guard took Seraiah.......... 7227
Jer 52:26 Nebuzar-adan the **c.** of the guard 7227
Jer 52:30 the **c.** of the guard carried away 7227
Da 2:14 the **c.** of the king's guard, which......... 7229
Da 2:15 said to Arioch the king's **c.**, Why 7990
Joh 18:12 band and the **c.** and officers *5506*
Ac 4:1 and the **c.** of the temple, and the *4755*
Ac 5:24 and the **c.** of the temple and the *4755*
Ac 5:26 went the **c.** with the officers, ... *4755*
Ac 21:31 tidings came unto the chief **c.**............ *5506*
Ac 21:32 the chief **c.** and the soldiers, ... *5506*
Ac 21:33 Then the chief **c.** came near,.............. *5506*
Ac 21:37 he said unto the chief **c.**, May I.......... *5506*
Ac 22:24 The chief **c.** commanded him to *5506*
Ac 22:26 he went and told the chief **c.**,............ *5506*
Ac 22:27 Then the chief **c.** came, and said........ *5506*
Ac 22:28 And the chief **c.** answered. With a...... *5506*
Ac 22:29 the chief **c.** also was afraid, after........ *5506*
Ac 23:10 the chief **c.**, fearing lest Paul............ *5506*
Ac 23:15 signify to the chief **c.** that he............ *5506*
Ac 23:17 this young man unto the chief **c.** *5506*
Ac 23:18 and brought him to the chief **c.**,.......... *5506*
Ac 23:19 chief **c.** took him by the hand, ... *5506*
Ac 23:22 chief **c.** then let the young man.......... *5506*
Ac 24:7 But the chief **c.** Lysias came *5506*
Ac 24:22 When Lysias the chief **c.** shall *5506*
Ac 28:16 delivered the prisoners to the **c.** *4759*
Heb 2:10 make the **c.** of their salvation.............. *747*

CAPTAINS
Ex 14:7 and **c.** over every one of them. 7991
Ex 15:4 his chosen **c.** also are drowned.......... 7991
Nu 31:14 the **c.** over thousands, ... 8269
Nu 31:14 and **c.** over hundreds, ... 8269
Nu 31:48 the **c.** of thousands,........................ 8269
Nu 31:48 and **c.** of hundreds, ... 8269
Nu 31:52 of the **c.** of thousands, ... 8269
Nu 31:52 and of the **c.** of hundreds,................. 8269
Nu 31:54 **c.** of thousands and of hundreds, ... 8269
De 1:15 **c.** over thousands, ... 8269
De 1:15 and **c.** over hundreds....................... 8269
De 1:15 and **c.** over fifties,.......................... 8269
De 1:15 and **c.** over tens. 8269
De 20:9 **c.** of the armies to lead the................ 8269
De 29:10 your **c.** of your tribes, your.............. 7218
Jos 10:24 unto the **c.** of the men of war............ 7101
1Sa 8:12 **c.** over thousands, ... 8269
1Sa 8:12 and **c.** over fifties;......................... 8269
1Sa 22:7 make you all **c.** of thousands, ... 8269
1Sa 22:7 and **c.** of hundreds; 8269
2Sa 4:2 two men that were **c.** of bands: 8269

2Sa 18:1 **c.** of thousands 8269
2Sa 18:1 and **c.** of hundreds 8269
2Sa 18:5 the king gave all the **c.** charge 8269
2Sa 23:8 chief among the **c.**; the same 7991
2Sa 24:4 against the **c.** of the host 8269
2Sa 24:4 and the **c.** of the host went out 8269
1Ki 1:25 and the **c.** of the host, and 8269
1Ki 2:5 two **c.** of the hosts of Israel, unto 8269
1Ki 9:22 his princes, and his **c.**, and rulers 7991
1Ki 15:20 the **c.** of the hosts which he had 8269
1Ki 20:24 and put **c.** in their rooms: 6346
1Ki 22:31 thirty and two **c.** that had rule 8269
1Ki 22:32 the **c.** of the chariots saw 8269
1Ki 22:33 the **c.** of the chariots perceived 8269
2Ki 1:14 the two **c.** of the former fifties 8269
2Ki 8:21 the **c.** of the chariots: and the 8269
2Ki 9:5 the **c.** of the host were sitting; 8269
2Ki 10:25 said to the guard and to the **c.**, 7991
2Ki 10:25 guard and the **c.** cast them out, 7991
2Ki 11:4 with the **c.** and the guard, 3746
2Ki 11:9 the **c.** over the hundreds did 8269
2Ki 11:10 to the **c.** over hundreds did the 8269
2Ki 11:15 the **c.** of the hundreds, and 8269
2Ki 11:19 the **c.**, and the guard, and all 3746
2Ki 25:23 all the **c.** of the armies, 8269
2Ki 25:26 and the **c.** of the armies, 8269
1Ch 4:42 having for their **c.** Pelatiah, 7218
1Ch 11:11 chief of the **c.**: he lifted up 7991
1Ch 11:15 three of the thirty **c.** went down 7218
1Ch 12:14 the sons of Gad, **c.** of the host: 7218
1Ch 12:18 chief of the **c.**, and he said, 7991
1Ch 12:18 and made them **c.** of the band. 7218
1Ch 12:20 **c.** of the thousands that were 7218
1Ch 12:21 and were **c.** of the host 8269
1Ch 12:28 father's house twenty and two **c.** 8269
1Ch 12:34 of Naphtali a thousand **c.**, and 8269
1Ch 13:1 **c.** of thousands and hundreds, 8269
1Ch 15:25 and the **c.** over thousands, went 8269
1Ch 25:1 and the **c.** of the host separated 8269
1Ch 26:26 the **c.** over thousands and 8269
1Ch 26:26 hundreds, and the **c.** of the host, 8269
1Ch 27:1 **c.** of thousands and hundreds, 8269
1Ch 27:3 the chief of all the **c.** of the host 8269
1Ch 28:1 and the **c.** of the companies that 8269
1Ch 28:1 and the **c.** over the thousands, 8269
1Ch 28:1 and **c.** over the hundreds, 8269
1Ch 29:6 **c.** of thousands and of hundreds, 8269
2Ch 1:2 **c.** of thousands and of hundreds, 8269
2Ch 8:9 and chief of his **c.**, 7991
2Ch 8:9 and **c.** of his chariots 8269
2Ch 11:11 strong holds, and put **c.** in them, 5057
2Ch 16:4 the **c.** of his armies against the 8269
2Ch 17:14 the **c.** of thousands; Adnah the 8269
2Ch 18:30 Syria had commanded the **c.** of 8269
2Ch 18:31 when the **c.** of the chariots saw 8269
2Ch 18:32 the **c.** of the chariots perceived 8269
2Ch 21:9 and the **c.** of the chariots 8269
2Ch 23:1 took the **c.** of hundreds, Azariah 8269
2Ch 23:9 to the **c.** of hundreds spears, 8269
2Ch 23:14 the priest brought out the **c.** of 8269
2Ch 23:20 he took the **c.** of hundreds, and 8269
2Ch 25:5 **c.** over thousands, 8269
2Ch 25:5 and **c.** over hundreds, 8269
2Ch 26:11 Hananiah, one of the king's **c.** 8269
2Ch 32:6 set **c.** of war over the people, 8269
2Ch 32:21 the leaders and **c.** in the camp 8269
2Ch 33:11 the **c.** of the host of the king 8269
2Ch 33:14 **c.** of war in all the fenced cities 8269
Ne 2:9 king had sent **c.** of the army 8269
Job 39:25 the thunder of the **c.**, and the 8269
Jer 13:21 hast taught them to be **c.**, 441
Jer 40:7 Now when all the **c.** of the 8269
Jer 40:13 and all the **c.** of the forces that 8269
Jer 41:11, 13, 16 all the **c.** of the forces that 8269
Jer 42:1 Then all the **c.** of the forces, and 8269
Jer 42:8 all the **c.** of the forces which were 8269
Jer 43:4 all the **c.** of the forces, and all 8269
Jer 43:5 and all the **c.** of the forces, took 8269
Jer 51:23 will I break in pieces **c.** and 6346
Jer 51:28 the Medes, the **c.** thereof, and 6346
Jer 51:57 her **c.**, and her rulers, and her 6346
Eze 21:22 to appoint **c.**, to open the mouth 3733
Eze 23:6 **c.** and rulers, all of them 6346
Eze 23:12 **c.** and rulers clothed most 6346
Eze 23:23 desirable young men, **c.** and 6346
Da 3:2 and the **c.**, the judges, the 6347
Da 3:3 the governors, and **c.**, the judges, 6347
Da 3:27 **c.**, and the king's counsellers, 6347
Da 6:7 counsellers, and the **c.**, have 6347
Na 3:17 locusts, and thy **c.** as the great 2951
Mk 6:21 a supper to his lords, high **c.**, *5506*
Lu 22:4 with the chief priest and **c.**, *4755*
Lu 22:52 and **c.** of the temple, and the *4755*
Ac 25:23 with the chief **c.**, and principal *5506*
Re 6:15 the rich men, and the chief **c.**, *5506*
Re 19:18 of kings, and the flesh of **c.** *5506*

CAPTIVE See also CAPTIVES.

Ge 14:14 that his brother was taken **c.**, 7617
Ge 34:29 their wives took they **c.**, and 7617
Ex 12:29 the firstborn of the **c.** that was 7628
Nu 24:22 Asshur shall carry thee away **c.**. 7617
De 21:10 and thou hast taken them **c.**, 7617
Jg 5:12 and lead thy captivity **c.**, thou son 7617
1Ki 8:48 enmemies, which led them away **c.**, 7617
1Ki 8:50 who carried them **c.**, that they 7617
2Ki 5:2 and had brought away **c.** out of 7617
2Ki 6:22 those whom thou hast taken **c.** 7617
2Ki 15:29 and carried them **c.** to Assyria 1540
2Ki 16:9 and carried the people of it **c.** to 1540
2Ki 24:16 king of Babylon brought **c.** to 1473
1Ch 5:6 king of Assyria carried away **c.**: 1540
2Ch 6:37 whither they are carried **c.**, and 7617
2Ch 25:12 children of Judah carry away **c.**, 7617
2Ch 28:8 carried away **c.** of their brethren 7617
2Ch 28:11 again, which ye have taken **c.** 7617
2Ch 30:9 them that lead them **c.**, so that 7617
Ps 68:18 thou hast led captivity **c.**: thou 7617
Ps 137:3 that carried us away **c.** required 7617
Isa 49:21 am desolate, a **c.**, and removing 1473
Isa 49:24 the mighty, or the lawful **c.** 7628
Isa 51:14 The **c.** exile hasteneth that he 6808
Isa 52:2 thy neck, O **c.** daughter of Zion. 7628
Jer 1:3 carrying away of Jerusalem **c.** 1540
Jer 13:17 Lord's flock is carried away **c.**. 7617
Jer 13:19 shall be carried away **c.** all of it, 1540
Jer 13:19 it shall be wholly carried away **c.** 1540
Jer 20:4 and he shall carry them **c.** into 1540
Jer 22:12 they have led him **c.**, and shall 1540
Jer 24:1 had carried away **c.** Jeconiah the 1540
Jer 24:5 are carried away **c.** of Judah, 1546
Jer 27:20 he carried away **c.** Jeconiah the 1540
Jer 28:6 all that is carried away **c.**, from 1473
Jer 29:1 carried away **c.** from Jerusalem 1473
Jer 29:14 caused you to be carried away **c.**. 1540
Jer 39:9 carried away **c.** into Babylon the 1540
Jer 40:1 all that were carried away **c.** of 1546
Jer 40:1 which were carried away **c.** unto 1540
Jer 40:7 not carried away **c.** to Babylon; 1540
Jer 41:10 Then Ishmael carried away **c.** 7617
Jer 41:10 carried them away **c.**, and 7617
Jer 41:14 Ishmael had carried away **c.** from 7617
Jer 52:15 carried away **c.** certain of the 1540
Jer 52:27 Thus Judah was carried away **c.** 1540
Jer 52:28 Nebuchadrezzar carried away **c.** 1540
Jer 52:29 he carried away **c.** from Jerusalem 1540
Jer 52:30 carried away **c.** of the Jews seven 1540
Am 1:6 they carried away **c.** the whole 1540
Am 6:7 therefore now shall they go **c.** with 1540
Am 6:7 with the first that go **c.**, 1540
Am 7:11 Israel shall surely be led away **c.** 1540
Ob 11 the strangers carried away **c.** 7617
Na 2:7 Huzzab shall be led away **c.**, 1540
Lu 21:24 **shall be led away c. into all** *163*
Eph 4:8 upon high, he led captivity **c.**, and *162*
2Ti 2:26 who are taken **c.** by him at his *2221*
2Ti 3:6 lead **c.** silly women laden with *162*

CAPTIVES

Ge 31:26 away my daughters, as **c.** taken 7617
Nu 31:9 took all the women of Midian **c.**, 7617
Nu 31:12 they brought the **c.**, and the prey, 7628
Nu 31:19 purify both yourselves and your **c.** 7628
De 21:11 And seest among the **c.** a 7633
De 32:42 blood of the slain and of the **c.**, 7633
1Sa 30:2 And had taken the women **c.**, 7617
1Sa 30:3 their daughters, were taken **c.** 7617
1Sa 30:5 David's two wives were taken **c.**, 7617
1Ki 8:46 they carry them away **c.** unto 7617
1Ki 8:47 whither they were carried **c.**, 7617
1Ki 8:47 of them that carried them **c.**, 7617
2Ki 24:14 ten thousand **c.**, and all the 1540
2Ch 6:36 they carry them away **c.** unto a 7617
2Ch 6:38 they have carried them **c.**, and 7617
2Ch 28:5 a great multitude of them **c.**. 7633
2Ch 28:11 deliver the **c.** again, which ye 7633
2Ch 28:13 Ye shall not bring in the **c.** hither: 7633
2Ch 28:14 the armed men left the **c.** and the 7633
2Ch 28:15 by name rose up, and took the **c.**, 7633
2Ch 28:17 Judah, and carried away **c.** 7628
Ps 106:46 of all those that carried them **c.**. 7617
Isa 14:2 and they shall take them **c.** 7617
Isa 14:2 whose **c.** they were; and they shall 7617
Isa 20:4 the Ethiopians **c.**, young and old, 1546
Isa 45:13 and he shall let go my **c.**, not 1546
Isa 49:25 the **c.** of the mighty shall be 7628
Isa 61:1 to proclaim liberty to the **c.**, and 7628
Jer 28:4 with all the **c.** of Judah, that went 1546
Jer 29:1 which were carried away **c.**, 1473
Jer 29:4 all that are carried away **c.**, 1473
Jer 29:7 caused you to be carried away **c.**, 1540
Jer 43:3 death, and carry us away **c.** into 1540
Jer 43:12 and carry them away **c.**: and he 7617
Jer 48:46 thy sons are taken **c.**, and 7628
Jer 48:46 and thy daughters **c.** 7633
Jer 50:33 and all that took them **c.** held 7617
Eze 1:1 as I was among the **c.** by the 1473
Eze 6:9 they shall be carried **c.**, because 7617
Eze 16:53 captivity of thy **c.** in the midst of 7628
Da 2:25 found a man of the **c.** of 1123,1547
Da 11:8 shall also carry **c.** into Egypt 7628
Lu 4:18 **to preach deliverance to the c.** *164*

CAPTIVITY

Nu 21:29 and his daughters, into **c.** 7628
De 21:13 the raiment of her **c.** from off 7633
De 28:41 them; for they shall go into **c.**. 7628
De 30:3 the Lord thy God will turn thy **c.**, 7622
Jg 5:12 and lead thy **c.** captive, thou son 7628
Jg 18:30 Dan until the day of the **c.** of the 1546
2Ki 24:15 carried he into **c.** from Jerusalem 1473
2Ki 25:27 thirtieth year of the **c.** of 1546
1Ch 5:22 dwelt in their steads until the **c.** 1473
1Ch 6:15 And Jehozadak went into **c.**,
2Ch 6:37 the land of their **c.**, saying. We 7633
2Ch 6:38 in the land of their **c.**, whither 7633
2Ch 29:9 daughters and our wives are in **c.** 7628
Ezr 1:11 bring up with them of the **c.** that 1473
Ezr 2:1 that went up out of the **c.**, 7628
Ezr 3:8 that were come out of the **c.** unto 7628
Ezr 4:1 that the children of the **c.** 1473
Ezr 6:16 the rest of the children of the **c.**, 1547
Ezr 6:19 And the children of the **c.** kept 1473
Ezr 6:20 all the children of the **c.**, and for 1473
Ezr 6:21 were come again out of **c.**, and all 1473
Ezr 8:35 which were come out of the **c.**. 7628
Ezr 9:7 to the sword, to **c.**, and to a spoil, 7628
Ezr 10:7 all the children of the **c.**, that 1473
Ezr 10:16 the children of the **c.** did so. And 1473
Ne 1:2 escaped, which were left of the **c.**, 7628
Ne 1:3 remnant that are left of the **c.** 7628
Ne 4:4 them for a prey in the land of **c.** 7633
Ne 7:6 went up out of the **c.**, of those 7628
Ne 8:17 come again out of the **c.** made 7628
Es 2:6 from Jerusalem with the **c.**, 1473
Job 42:10 Lord turned the **c.** of Job when 7622
Ps 14:7 Lord bringeth back the **c.** of his 7622
Ps 53:6 God bringeth back the **c.** of his 7622
Ps 68:18 high, thou hast led **c.** captive: 7628
Ps 78:61 delivered his strength into **c.**, and 7628
Ps 85:1 brought back the **c.** of Jacob 7622
Ps 126:1 the Lord turned again the **c.** of 7622
Ps 126:4 Turn again our **c.**, O Lord, as the 7622
Isa 5:13 my people are gone into **c.**, 1540
Isa 22:17 thee away with a mighty **c.**, 2925
Isa 46:2 but themselves are gone into **c.**. 7628
Jer 15:2 such as are for the **c.**, to the **c.** 7628
Jer 20:6 in thine house, shall go into **c.** 7628
Jer 22:22 and thy lovers shall go into **c.** 7628
Jer 29:14 and I will turn away your **c.**, 7622
Jer 29:16 not gone forth with you into **c.**; 1473
Jer 29:20 word of the Lord, all ye of the **c.**, 1473
Jer 29:22 a curse by all the **c.** of Judah 1546
Jer 29:28 This **c.** is long: build ye houses,
Jer 29:31 Send to all them of the **c.**, saying, 1473
Jer 30:3 I will bring again the **c.** of my 7622
Jer 30:10 seed from the land of their **c.**: 7628
Jer 30:16 every one of them, shall go into **c.**; 7633
Jer 30:18 will bring again the **c.** of Jacob's 7622
Jer 31:23 when I shall bring again their **c.**; 7622
Jer 32:44 I will cause their **c.** to return, 7622
Jer 33:7 I will cause the **c.** of Judah and the 7622

Jer 33:7 and the **c.** of Israel to return, 7622
Jer 33:11 I will cause to return the **c.** of the 7622
Jer 33:26 I will cause their **c.** to return, and 7622
Jer 43:11 and such as are for **c.** to **c.**; 7628
Jer 46:19 furnish thyself to go into **c.**: 1473
Jer 46:27 seed from the land of their **c.**; 7633
Jer 48:7 Chemosh shall go forth into **c.** 1473
Jer 48:11 neither hath he gone into **c.**: 1473
Jer 48:47 Yet will I bring again the **c.** of 7622
Jer 49:3 their king shall go into **c.**, and 1473
Jer 49:6 I will bring again the **c.** of the 7622
Jer 49:39 I will bring again the **c.** of Elam, 7622
Jer 52:31 and thirtieth year of the **c.** of 1546
La 1:3 Judah is gone into **c.** because 1540
La 1:5 her children are gone into **c.** 7628
La 1:18 my young men are gone into **c.**. 7628
La 2:14 to turn away thy **c.**; but have 7622
La 4:22 more carry thee away into **c.**: 1540
Eze 1:2 fifth year of king Jehoiachin's **c.**, 1546
Eze 3:11 get thee to them of the **c.**, unto 1473
Eze 3:15 I came to them of the **c.** at 1473
Eze 11:24 God into Chaldea, to them of the **c.** 1473
Eze 11:25 Then I spake unto them of the **c.** 1473
Eze 12:4 as they that go forth into **c.**. 1473
Eze 12:7 as stuff for **c.**, and in the even 1473
Eze 12:11 they shall remove and go into **c.**. 7628
Eze 16:53 I shall bring again their **c.**, 7622
Eze 16:53 the **c.** of Sodom and her daughters, 7622
Eze 16:53 and the **c.** of Samaria and her 7622
Eze 16:53 the **c.** of thy captives in the midst 7622
Eze 25:3 Judah, when they went into **c.**; 1473
Eze 29:14 And I will bring again the **c.** of 7622
Eze 30:17 and these cities shall go into **c.**. 7628
Eze 30:18 her daughters shall go into **c.**. 7628
Eze 33:21 the twelfth year of our **c.**, in the 1546
Eze 39:23 Israel went into **c.** for their 1540
Eze 39:25 will I bring again the **c.** of Jacob, 7622
Eze 39:28 them to be led into **c.** among the 1473
Eze 40:1 year of our **c.**, in the beginning 1546
Da 5:13 art of the children of the **c.** of 1547
Da 6:13 which is of the children of the **c.** 1547
Da 11:33 the sword, and by flame, by **c.**, 7628
Ho 6:11 when I returned the **c.** of my 7622
Joe 3:1 shall bring again the **c.** of Judah, 7622
Am 1:5 people of Syria shall go into **c.** 1540
Am 1:6 carried away captive the whole **c.**, 1546
Am 1:9 they delivered up the whole **c.** to 1546
Am 1:15 their king shall go into **c.**, he 1473
Am 5:5 Gilgal shall surely go into **c.**, and 1540
Am 5:27 will I cause you to go into **c.** 1540
Am 7:17 Israel shall surely go into **c.** 1540
Am 9:4 though they go into **c.** before 7628
Am 9:14 I will bring again the **c.** of my 7622
Ob 20 And the **c.** of this host of the 1546
Ob 20 and the **c.** of Jerusalem, which 1546
Mic 1:16 for they are gone into **c.** from 1540
Na 3:10 she went into **c.**: her young 7628
Hab 1:9 they shall gather the **c.** as the 7628
Zep 2:7 them, and turn away their **c.**. 7622
Zep 3:20 when I turn back your **c.** before 7622
Zec 6:10 Take of them of the **c.**, even of 1473
Zec 14:2 of the city shall go forth into **c.**, 1473
Ro 7:23 bringing me into **c.** to the law of *163*
2Co 10:5 bringing into **c.** every thought to *163*
Eph 4:8 he led **c.** captive, and gave gifts *161*
Re 13:10 that leadeth into **c.** shall go into **c.**: *161*

CAR See BETH-CAR.

CARBUNCLE See also CARBUNCLES.
Ex 28:17 topaz, and a **c.**: this shall be the 1304
Ex 39:10 was a sardius, a topaz, and a **c.**: 1304
Eze 28:13 emerald, and the **c.**, and gold: 1304

CARBUNCLES
Isa 54:12 and thy gates of **c.**, and all thy 68,688

CARCAS (car'-cas)
Es 1:10 Abagtha, Zethar, and **C.**. 3752

CARCASE See also CARCASES.
Le 5:2 a **c.** of an unclean beast, 5038
Le 5:2 or a **c.** of unclean cattle, 5038
Le 5:2 the **c.** of unclean creeping things, 5038
Le 11:8 and their **c.** shall ye not touch; 5038
Le 11:24 whosoever toucheth the **c.** of them 5038
Le 11:25 beareth ought of the **c.** of them 5038
Le 11:27 whoso toucheth their **c.** shall be 5038
Le 11:28 he that beareth the **c.** of them 5038
Le 11:35 any part of their **c.** falleth 5038
Le 11:36 that which toucheth their **c.** shall 5038
Le 11:37 if any part of their **c.** fall upon any 5038
Le 11:38 any part of their **c.** fall thereon, 5038
Le 11:39 he that toucheth the **c.** thereof 5038
Le 11:40 he that eateth of the **c.** of it shall 5038
Le 11:40 he also that beareth the **c.** of it 5038
De 14:8 flesh, nor touch their dead **c.**. 5038
De 28:26 thy **c.** shall be meat unto all fowls 5038
Jos 8:29 they should take his **c.** down from 5038
Jg 14:8 aside to see the **c.** of the lion: 4658
Jg 14:8 and honey in the **c.** of the lion. 1472
Jg 14:9 honey out of the **c.** of the lion. 1472
1Ki 13:22 thy **c.** shall not come unto the 5038
1Ki 13:24 his **c.** was cast in the way, 5038
1Ki 13:24 the lion also stood by the **c.**. 5038
1Ki 13:25 and saw the **c.** cast in the way, 5038
1Ki 13:25 and the lion standing by the **c.**: 5038
1Ki 13:28 and found his **c.** cast in the way, 5038
1Ki 13:28 ass and the lion standing by the **c.**: 5038
1Ki 13:28 the lion had not eaten the **c.**, 5038
1Ki 13:29 prophet took up the **c.** of the man 5038
1Ki 13:30 he laid his **c.** in his own grave; 5038
2Ki 9:37 the **c.** of Jezebel shall be as dung 5038
Isa 14:19 as a **c.** trodden under feet. 6297
Mt 24:28 **For wheresoever the c. is, there** *4430*

CARCASES
Ge 15:11 the fowls came down upon the **c.**, 6297
Le 11:11 shall have their **c.** in abomination. 5038
Le 11:26 The **c.** of every beast which divideth
Le 26:30 cast your **c.** upon the **c.** of your 6297
Nu 14:29 Your **c.** shall fall in this wilderness; 6297
Nu 14:32 for you, your **c.**, they shall fall 6297
Nu 14:33 your **c.** be wasted in the wilderness 6297
1Sa 17:46 the **c.** of the host of the Philistines 6297
Isa 5:25 their **c.** were torn in the midst of 5038
Isa 34:3 stink shall come up out of their **c.**, 6297
Isa 66:24 upon the **c.** of the men that have 6297
Jer 7:33 the **c.** of this people shall be meat 5038
Jer 9:22 the **c.** of men shall fall as dung 5038
Jer 16:4 their **c.** shall be meat for the fowls 5038
Jer 16:18 with the **c.** of their detestable 5038
Jer 19:7 their **c.** will I give to be meat for 5038
Eze 6:5 dead **c.** of the children of Israel 6297
Eze 43:7 nor by the **c.** of their kings in 6297
Eze 43:9 the **c.** of their kings, far from me, 6297
Na 3:3 slain, and a great number of **c.**; 6297
Heb 3:17 whose **c.** fell in the wilderness? *2966*

CARCASS See CARCASE.

CARCHEMISH (car'-ke-mish) See also CHARCHEMISH.
Isa 10:9 Is not Calno as **C.**? is not Hamath 3751
Jer 46:2 was by the river Euphrates in **C.**, 3751

CARE See also CARED; CAREFUL; CARELESS; CARES; CAREST; CARETH; CARING.
1Sa 10:2 hath left the **c.** of the asses, 1697
2Sa 18:3 they will not **c.** for us; 7760,3820
2Sa 18:3 of us die, will they **c.** for us: 7760,3820
2Ki 4:13 been careful for us with all this **c.**; 2731
Jer 49:31 nation, that dwelleth without **c.**, 983
Eze 4:16 eat bread by weight, and with **c.**; 1674
Mt 13:22 **the c. of this world, and the** *3308*
Lu 10:34 **to an inn, and took c. of him** *1959*
Lu 10:35 **Take c. of him; and whatsoever** *1959*
Lu 10:40 Lord, dost thou not **c.** that my *3199*
1Co 7:21 being a servant? **c.** not for it; *3199*
1Co 9:9 Doth God take **c.** for oxen? *3199*
1Co 12:25 the same **c.** one for another. *3309*
2Co 7:12 or **c.** for you in the sight of God *4710*
2Co 8:16 earnest **c.** into the heart of Titus *4710*
2Co 11:28 daily, the **c.** of all the churches. *3308*
Php 2:20 will naturally **c.** for your state. *3309*
Php 4:10 your **c.** of me hath flourished *5426*
1Ti 3:5 shall he take **c.** of the church of *1959*
1Pe 5:7 Casting all your **c.** upon him; *3308*

CAREAH (ca-re'-ah) See also KAREAH.
2Ki 25:23 and Johanan the son of **C.**, 7143

CARED
Ps 142:4 failed me; no man **c.** for my soul. 1875
Joh 12:6 not that he **c.** for the poor; *3199*
Ac 18:17 Gallio **c.** for none of those things. *3199*

CAREFUL
2Ki 4:13 thou hast been **c.** for us with all 2729
Jer 17:8 not be **c.** in the year of drought, 1672
Da 3:16 we are not **c.** to answer thee in 2818
Lu 10:41 **Martha, thou art c. and troubled** *3309*
Php 4:6 Be **c.** for nothing; but in *3309*
Php 4:10 wherein ye were also **c.**, but ye *5426*
Tit 3:8 be **c.** to maintain good works. *5431*

CAREFULLY
De 15:5 Only if thou **c.** hearken unto the 8085
Mic 1:12 inhabitant of Maroth waited **c.** 2470
Php 2:28 sent him therefore the more **c.**, *4708*
Heb 12:17 though he sought it **c.** with tears. *1567*

CAREFULNESS
Eze 12:18 water with trembling and with **c.**; 1674
Eze 12:19 eat their bread with **c.**, and drink 1674
1Co 7:32 But I would have you without **c.** *275*
2Co 7:11 sort, what **c.** it wrought in you, *4710*

CARELESS
Jg 18:7 how they dwelt **c.**, after the 983
Isa 32:9 ye **c.** daughters; give ear unto my 982
Isa 32:10 ye be troubled, ye **c.** women: for 982
Isa 32:11 at ease; be troubled, ye **c.** ones: 982
Eze 30:9 to make the **C.** Ethiopians afraid, 983

CARELESSLY
Isa 47:8 that dwellest **c.**, that sayest in 983
Eze 39:6 and among them that dwell **c.** in 983
Zep 2:15 is the rejoicing city that dwelt **c.**, 983

CARES
Mk 4:19 **the c. of this world, and the** 3308
Lu 8:14 **are choked with c. and riches and** 3308
Lu 21:34 **and c. of this life, and so that day** 3308

CAREST
Mt 22:16 neither **c.** thou for any man: for 3199
Mk 4:38 Master, **c.** thou not that we perish? 3199
Mk 12:14 thou art true, and **c.** for no man: 3199

CARETH
De 11:12 which the Lord thy God **c.** for: 1875
Joh 10:13 **hireling, and c. not for the sheep.** *3199*
1Co 7:32 He that is unmarried **c.** for the *3309*
1Co 7:33 he that is married **c.** for the *3309*
1Co 7:34 unmarried woman **c.** for the *3309*
1Co 7:34 married **c.** for the things of the *3309*
1Pe 5:7 upon him, for he **c.** for you. *3199*

CARING
1Sa 9:5 lest my father leave **c.** for the asses,

CARMEL (car'-mel) See also CARMELITE.
Jos 12:22 the king of Jokneam of **C.**, one; 3760
Jos 15:55 Maon, **C.**, and Ziph, and Juttah, 3760
Jos 19:26 Misheal; and reacheth to **C.** 3760
1Sa 15:12 Samuel, saying, Saul came to **C.**, 3760
1Sa 25:2 whose possessions were in **C.**; 3760
1Sa 25:2 he was shearing his sheep in **C.**. 3760
1Sa 25:5 Get you up to **C.**, and go to Nabal, 3760
1Sa 25:7 them, all the while they were in **C.**. 3760
1Sa 25:40 of David were come to Abigail to **C.**, 3760
1Ki 18:19 to me all Israel unto mount **C.** 3760
1Ki 18:20 prophets together unto mount **C.**. 3760
1Ki 18:42 Elijah went up to the top of **C.**; 3760
2Ki 2:25 he went from thence to mount **C.**, 3760
2Ki 4:25 unto the man of God to mount **C.**. 3760
2Ki 19:23 and into the forest of his **C.**. 3760
2Ch 26:10 in the mountains, and in **C.**: 3760
Ca 7:5 Thine head upon thee is like **C.**, 3760
Isa 33:9 and **C.** shake off their fruits. 3760
Isa 35:2 the excellency of **C.** and Sharon, 3760
Isa 37:24 border, and the forests of his **C.**. 3760
Jer 46:18 and as **C.** by the sea, so shall he 3760
Jer 50:19 he shall feed on **C.** and Bashan, 3760
Am 1:2 shall mourn, and the top of **C.** 3760
Am 9:3 hide themselves in the top of **C.**, 3760
Mic 7:14 in the wood, in the midst of **C.**: 3760
Na 1:4 Bashan languisheth, and **C.**, and 3760

CARMELITE (car'-mel-ite) See also CARMELITESS.
1Sa 30:5 Abigail the wife of Nabal the **C.**. 3761
2Sa 2:2 and Abigail Nabal's wife the **C.**. 3761
2Sa 3:3 Abigail the wife of Nabal the **C.**; 3761
2Sa 23:35 Hezrai the **C.**, Paarai the Arbite, 3761
1Ch 11:37 Hezro the **C.**, Naarai the son of 3761

CARMELITESS (car'-mel-i-tess)
1Sa 27:3 and Abigail the **C.**, Nabal's wife. 3762
1Ch 3:1 second Daniel, of Abigail the **C.**: 3762

CARMI (car'-mi) See also CARMITES.
Ge 46:9 and Phallu, and Hezron, and **C.**. 3756

Ex 6:14 Hanoch, and Pallu, Hezro, and **C.**:...... 3756
Nu 26:6 Hezronites: of **C.**, the family of......... 3756
Jos 7:1 for Achan, the son of **C.**, the son...... 3756
Jos 7:18 by man; and Achan, the son of **C.**,..... 3756
1Ch 2:7 And the sons of **C.**; Achar, the.......... 3756
1Ch 4:1 of Judah; Pharez, Hezron, and **C.**,...... 3756
1Ch 5:3 Hanoch, and Pallu, Hezron, and **C.**..... 3756

CARMITES (car'-mites)
Nu 26:6 of Carmi, the family of the **C.**........... 3757

CARNAL
Ro 7:14 but I am **c.**, sold under sin............... *4559*
Ro 8:7 Because the **c.** mind is enmity.......... *4561*
Ro 15:27 to minister unto them in **c.** things,...... *4559*
1Co 3:1 but as unto **c.**, even as unto............. *4559*
1Co 3:3 For ye are yet **c.**: for whereas......... *4559*
1Co 3:3 are ye not **c.**, and walk as men?........ *4559*
1Co 3:4 I am of Apollos; are ye not **c.**?......... *4559*
1Co 9:11 if we shall reap your **c.** things?......... *4559*
2Co 10:4 weapons of our warfare are not **c.**,..... *4559*
Heb 7:16 the law of a **c.** commandment,............ *4559*
Heb 9:10 and **c.** ordinances, imposed on........... *4561*

CARNALLY
Le 18:20 thou shalt not lie **c.** with thy...... 7903,2233
Le 19:20 whosoever lieth **c.** with a.......... 7902,2233
Nu 5:13 And a man lie with her **c.**, and... 7902,2233
Ro 8:6 to be **c.** minded is death; but to......... *4561*

CARPENTER See also CARPENTER'S; CARPENTERS.
Isa 41:7 the **c.** encouraged the goldsmith,........ 2796
Isa 44:13 The **c.** stretched out his rule;..... 2796,6086
Mk 6:3 Is not this the **c.**, the son of............ *5045*

CARPENTER'S
Mt 13:55 Is not this the **c.** son? is not his........ *5045*

CARPENTERS
2Sa 5:11 **c.**, and masons: and they.......... 2796,6086
2Ki 12:11 they laid it out to the **c.** and............ 6086
2Ki 22:6 Unto **c.**, and builders, and................ 2796
1Ch 14:1 with masons and **c.**, to build....... 2796,6086
2Ch 24:12 and hired masons and **c.** to repair....... 2796
Ezr 3:7 unto the masons, and to the **c.**;......... 2796
Jer 24:1 with the **c.** and smiths, from............. 2796
Jer 29:2 and the **c.**, and the smiths,.............. 2796
Zec 1:20 And the Lord shewed me four **c.**........ 2796

CARPUS (car'-pus)
2Ti 4:13 cloak that I left at Troas with **c.**,....... *2591*

CARRIAGE See also CARRIAGES.
Jg 18:21 the cattle and the **c.** before them,...... 3520
1Sa 17:22 David left his **c.** in the hand............. 3627
1Sa 17:22 the hand of the keeper of the **c.**,......... 3627

CARRIAGES
Isa 10:28 Michmash he hath laid up his **c.**......... 3627
Isa 46:1 your **c.** were heavy loaden;............... 5385
Ac 21:15 we took up our **c.**, and went up.......... *643*

CARRIED
Ge 31:18 And he **c.** away all his cattle,............ 5090
Ge 31:26 and **c.** away my daughters,................ 5090
Ge 46:5 of Israel **c.** Jacob their father,........... 5375
Ge 50:13 For his sons **c.** him into the land........ 5375
Le 10:5 and **c.** them in their coats out of......... 5375
Jos 4:8 and **c.** them over with them............... 5674
Jg 16:3 **c.** them up to the top of an hill.......... 5927
1Sa 5:8 ark of the God of Israel be **c.**.......... 5437
1Sa 5:8 **c.** the ark of the God of Israel.......... 5437
1Sa 5:9 so, that, after they had **c.** it about,..... 5437
1Sa 30:2 or small, but **c.** them away,............. 5090
1Sa 30:18 the Amalekites had **c.** away:............. 3947
2Sa 6:10 David **c.** it aside into the house......... 5186
2Sa 15:29 and Abiathar **c.** the ark of God.......... 7725
1Ki 8:47 whither they were **c.** captives,............ 7617
1Ki 8:47 of them that **c.** hem captives,............ 7617
1Ki 8:50 before them who **c.** them captive,....... 7617
1Ki 17:19 and **c.** him up into a loft,.................. 5927
1Ki 21:13 **c.** him forth out of the city,............... 3318
2Ki 7:8 and **c.** thence silver, and gold,.......... 5375
2Ki 7:8 and **c.** thence also, and went............. 5375
2Ki 9:28 **c.** him in a chariot to Jerusalem,........ 7392
2Ki 15:29 and **c.** them captive to Assyria......... 1540
2Ki 16:9 and **c.** the people of it captive........... 1540
2Ki 17:6 and **c.** Israel away into Assyria,.......... 1540
2Ki 17:11 the Lord **c.** away before them;.......... 1540
2Ki 17:23 So was Israel **c.** away out of their...... 1540
2Ki 17:28 had **c.** away from Samaria................ 1540
2Ki 17:33 whom they **c.** away from thence........ 1540
2Ki 20:17 shall be **c.** unto Babylon:................ 5375
2Ki 23:4 **c.** the ashes of them unto Beth-el...... 5375
2Ki 23:30 his servants **c.** him in a chariot.......... 7392
2Ki 24:13 he **c.** out thence all the treasures........ 3318
2Ki 24:14 And he **c.** away all Jerusalem,............ 1540
2Ki 24:15 And he **c.** away Jehoiachin................ 1540
2Ki 24:15 those **c.** he into captivity from........... 1980
2Ki 25:7 of brass, and **c.** him to Babylon.......... 935
2Ki 25:13 **c.** the brass of them to Babylon.......... 5375
2Ki 25:21 So Judah was **c.** away....................... 1540
1Ch 5:6 king of Assyria **c.** away captive:......... 1540
1Ch 5:26 of Assyria, and he **c.** them away........ 1540
1Ch 6:15 when the Lord **c.** away Judah............ 1540
1Ch 9:1 were **c.** away to Babylon................... 1540
1Ch 13:7 And they **c.** the ark of God............... 7392
1Ch 13:13 but **c.** it aside into the house of......... 5186
2Ch 6:37 whither they are **c.** captive,............... 7617
2Ch 6:38 they have **c.** them captives,.............. 7617
2Ch 12:9 he **c.** away also the shields.............. 3947
2Ch 14:13 they **c.** away very much spoil........... 5375
2Ch 14:15 and **c.** away sheep and camels.......... 7617
2Ch 16:6 they **c.** away the stones of Ramah,...... 5375
2Ch 21:17 and **c.** away all the substance............ 7617
2Ch 24:11 it, and **c.** it to his place again........... 7725
2Ch 28:5 and they smote him, and **c.** away........ 7617
2Ch 28:8 **c.** away captive of their brethren........ 7617
2Ch 28:15 and **c.** all the feeble of them............. 5095
2Ch 28:17 Judah, and **c.** away captives.............. 7617
2Ch 33:11 fetters, and **c.** him to Babylon........... 3212
2Ch 34:16 Shaphan **c.** the book to the king,......... 935
2Ch 36:4 brother, and **c.** him to Egypt............... 935
2Ch 36:7 Nebuchadnezzar also **c.** of the............ 935
2Ch 36:20 sword **c.** he away to Babylon;............ 1473
Ezr 2:1 of those which had been **c.** away,....... 1540
Ezr 2:1 king of Babylon had **c.** away............. 1540
Ezr 5:12 **c.** the people away into Bablyon......... 1541
Ezr 8:35 those that had been **c.** away,............. 1473
Ezr 9:4 those that had been **c.** away;............. 1473
Ezr 10:6 them that had been **c.** away.............. 1473
Ezr 10:8 those that had been **c.** away............... 1473
Ne 7:6 of those that had been **c.** away,......... 1473
Ne 7:6 king of Babylon had **c.** away,............. 1540
Es 2:6 been **c.** away from Jerusalem............. 1540
Es 2:6 captivity which had been **c.** away......... 1540
Es 2:6 king of Babylon had **c.** away............. 1540
Job 1:17 and have **c.** them away, yea,.............. 3947
Job 5:13 of the froward is **c.** headlong............ 4116
Job 10:19 I should have been **c.** from the........... 2986
Ps 46:2 though the mountains be **c.** into......... 4131
Ps 106:46 those that **c.** them captives............... 7617
Ps 137:3 they that **c.** us away captive............. 7617
Isa 39:6 shall be **c.** to Babylon: nothing.......... 5375
Isa 46:3 are **c.** from the womb:...................... 5375
Isa 49:22 thy daughters shall be **c.** upon........... 5375
Isa 53:4 our grief, and **c.** our sorrows:........... 5445
Isa 63:9 and **c.** them all the days of old.......... 5375
Jer 13:17 Lord's flock is **c.** away captive........... 7617
Jer 13:19 shall be **c.** away captive all of........... 1540
Jer 13:19 shall be wholly **c.** away captive.......... 1540
Jer 24:1 had **c.** away captive Jeconiah............ 1540
Jer 24:5 them that are **c.** away captive............ 1546
Jer 27:20 he **c.** away captive Jeconiah the......... 1546
Jer 27:22 They shall be **c.** to Babylon,.............. 935
Jer 28:3 this place, and **c.** them to Babylon:...... 935
Jer 28:6 all that is **c.** away captive,................ 1473
Jer 29:1 which were **c.** away captives,............. 1473
Jer 29:1 Nebuchadnezzar had **c.** away........... 1540
Jer 29:4 all that are **c.** away captives,............. 1473
Jer 29:4 whom I have caused to be **c.** away..... 1540
Jer 29:7 caused you to be **c.** away captives,...... 1540
Jer 29:14 caused you to be **c.** away captive....... 1540
Jer 39:9 the guard **c.** away captive into........... 1540
Jer 40:1 **c.** away captive of Jerusalem............ 1546
Jer 40:1 which were **c.** away captive unto.......... 1540
Jer 40:7 that were not **c.** away captive............ 1540
Jer 41:10 Then Ishmael **c.** away captive........... 7617
Jer 41:10 **c.** them away captive, and............... 7617
Jer 41:14 Ishmael had **c.** away captive............. 7617
Jer 52:9 they took the king and **c.** him up......... 5927
Jer 52:11 and **c.** him to Babylon, and put............ 935
Jer 52:15 the captain of the guard **c.** away........ 1540
Jer 52:17 and **c.** all the brass of them to.......... 5375
Jer 52:27 Thus Judah was **c.** away captive......... 1540
Jer 52:28 whom Nebuchadrezzar **c.** away.......... 1540
Jer 52:29 Nebuchadrezzar he **c.** away......................
Jer 52:30 **c.** away captive of the Jews.....................
Eze 6:9 they shall be **c.** captives,................. 7617
Eze 17:4 and **c.** it into a land of traffick;........... 935
Eze 37:1 and **c.** me out in the spirit.............. 3318
Da 1:2 he **c.** into the land of Shinar................ 935
Da 2:35 and the wind **c.** them away,............. 5376
Ho 10:6 It shall be also **c.** unto Assyria........... 2986
Ho 12:1 and oil is **c.** into Egypt.................... 2986
Joe 3:5 have **c.** into your temples.................. 935
Am 1:6 because they **c.** away captive............ 1540
Ob 11 the strangers **c.** away captive............ 7617
Na 3:10 Yet was she **c.** away, she went.......... 1473
Mt 1:11 the time they were **c.** away............... *3350*
Mr 15:1 bound Jesus, and **c.** him away............ *667*
Lu 7:12 there was a dead man **c.** out,............ *1580*
Lu 16:22 **was c. by the angels into**............... *667*
Lu 24:51 them, and **c.** up into heaven............... *399*
Ac 3:2 from his mother's womb was **c.**........... *941*
Ac 5:6 up, and **c.** him out, and buried............ *1627*
Ac 7:16 And were **c.** over into Sychem,......... *3346*
Ac 8:2 **c.** Stephen to his burial,................... *4792*
Ac 21:34 him to be **c.** into the castle................. *71*
1Co 12:2 **c.** away unto these dumb idols,........... *520*
Ga 2:13 Barnabas also was **c.** away with......... *4879*
Eph 4:14 and **c.** about with every wind............ *4064*
Heb 13:9 Be not **c.** about with divers................ *4064*
2Pe 2:17 that are **c.** with a tempest;................ *4064*
Jude 12 without water, **c.** about of winds;....... *4064*
Re 12:15 her to be **c.** away of the flood............ *4216*
Re 17:3 So he **c.** me away in the spirit............ *667*
Re 21:10 **c.** me away in the spirit to a great....... *667*

CARRIEST
Ps 90:5 **c.** them away as with a flood;............ 2229

CARRIETH
Job 21:18 chaff that the storm **c.** away............. 1589
Job 27:21 The east wind **c.** him away,............... 5375
Re 17:7 and of the beast that **c.** her,............... *941*

CARRY See also CARRIED; CARRIEST; CARRIETH; CARRYING.
Ge 37:25 going to **c.** it down to Egypt............. 3381
Ge 42:19 go ye, **c.** corn for the famine of........... 935
Ge 43:11 and **c.** down the man a present,.......... 3381
Ge 43:12 sacks, **c.** it again in your hand;.......... 7725
Ge 44:1 as much as they can **c.**, and put.......... 5375
Ge 45:27 which Joseph had sent to **c.** him,........ 5375
Ge 46:5 which Pharaoh had sent to **c.** him....... 5375
Ge 47:30 and thou shalt **c.** me out of Egypt,....... 5375
Ge 50:25 shall **c.** up my bones from hence.......... 5927
Ex 12:46 thou shalt not **c.** forth aught of.......... 3318
Ex 13:19 ye shall **c.** up my bones away............. 5927
Ex 14:11 us, to **c.** us forth out of Egypt?.......... 3318
Ex 33:15 with me, **c.** us not up hence.............. 5927
Le 4:12 whole bullock shall he **c.** forth............ 3318
Le 4:21 And he shall **c.** forth the bullock......... 3318
Le 6:11 **c.** forth the ashes without the............ 3318
Le 10:4 **c.** your brethren from before the........ 5375
Le 14:45 and he shall **c.** them forth out of........ 3318
Le 16:27 shall one **c.** forth without the............ 3318
Nu 11:12 **C.** them in thy bosom, as a............... 5375
Nu 24:22 Asshur shall **c.** thee away captive....... 7617
De 14:24 so that thou art not able to **c.** it;........ 5375
De 28:38 Thou shalt **c.** much seed out.............. 3318
Jos 4:3 ye shall **c.** them over with you,.......... 5674
1Sa 17:18 And **c.** these ten cheeses unto............ 935
1Sa 20:40 him, Go, **c.** them to the city................ 935
2Sa 15:25 **C.** back the ark of God into the......... 7725
2Sa 19:18 to **c.** over the king's household,......... 5674
1Ki 8:46 **c.** them away captives unto the........... 7617
1Ki 18:12 the Spirit of the Lord shall **c.** thee...... 5375
1Ki 21:10 And then **c.** him out and stone............ 3318
1Ki 22:26 and **c.** him back unto Amon................ 7725
1Ki 22:34 Turn thine hand, and **c.** me out.......... 3318
2Ki 4:19 **C.** him to his mother....................... 5375
2Ki 9:2 and **c.** him to an inner chamber;.......... 935
2Ki 17:27 **C.** thither one of the priests............... 1980
2Ki 18:11 the king of Assyria did **c.** away.......... 1540
2Ki 25:11 the captain of the guard **c.** away........ 1540
1Ch 10:9 to **c.** tidings unto their idols, and......... 1319
1Ch 15:2 None ought to **c.** the ark of God......... 5375
1Ch 15:2 the Lord chosen to **c.** the ark............. 5375
1Ch 23:26 shall no more **c.** the tabernacle,......... 5375
2Ch 2:16 shalt **c.** it up to Jerusalem................. 5927
2Ch 6:36 enemies, and they **c.** them away......... 7617
2Ch 18:25 Micaiah, and **c.** him back to Amon....... 7725
2Ch 18:33 mayest **c.** me out of the host;............ 3318
2Ch 20:25 more than they could **c.** away;........... 4853

2Ch 25:12 the children of Judah **c.** away... 7617
2Ch 29:5 and **c.** forth the filthiness out of... 3318
2Ch 29:16 And the Levites took it, to **c.** it... 3318
2Ch 36:6 in fetters, to **c.** him to Babylon... 3212
Ezr 5:15 go, **c.** them into the temple that... 5182
Ezr 7:15 And to **c.** the silver and gold,... 2987
Job 15:12 Why doth thine heart **c.** thee... 3947
Ps 49:17 he shall **c.** nothing away: his glory... 3947
Ec 5:15 he may **c.** away in his hand... 3212
Ec 10:20 a bird of the air shall **c.** the voice... 3212
Isa 5:29 the prey, and shall **c.** it away... 6403
Isa 15:7 laid up, shall they **c.** away to the... 5375
Isa 22:17 the Lord will **c.** thee away with a... 2904
Isa 23:7 her own feet shall **c.** her afar off... 2986
Isa 30:6 they will **c.** their riches upon the... 5375
Isa 40:11 and **c.** them in his bosom, and... 5375
Isa 41:16 and the wind shall **c.** them away,... 5375
Isa 46:4 to hoar hairs will I **c.** you: I have... 5445
Isa 46:4 even I will **c.**, and will deliver you... 5445
Isa 46:7 **c.** him, and set him in his place,... 5445
Isa 57:13 the wind shall **c.** them all away;... 5375
Jer 17:22 Neither **c.** forth a burden out of... 3318
Jer 20:4 shall **c.** them captive into Babylon,... 1540
Jer 20:5 them, and **c.** them to Babylon... 935
Jer 39:7 with chains, to **c.** him to Babylon... 935
Jer 39:14 Shaphan, that he should **c.** him... 3318
Jer 43:3 **c.** us away captives into Babylon... 1540
Jer 43:12 and **c.** them away captives: and... 7617
La 4:22 he will no more **c.** thee away... 1540
Eze 12:5 their sight, and **c.** out thereby... 3318
Eze 12:6 and **c.** it forth in the twilight:... 3318
Eze 12:12 the wall to **c.** out thereby:... 3318
Eze 22:9 In thee are men that **c.** tales to... 7400
Eze 38:13 to **c.** away silver and gold, to... 5375
Da 11:8 And shall also **c.** captives into... 935
Mk 6:55 to **c.** about in beds those that... *4064*
Mk 11:16 any man should **c.** any vessel... *1808*
Lu 10:4 **C. neither purse, nor scrip, nor**... *941*
Joh 5:10 it is not lawful for thee to **c.** thy... *142*
Joh 21:18 **gird thee, and c. thee whither**... *5342*
Ac 5:9 at the door, and shall **c.** thee out... *1627*
Ac 7:43 **c.** you away beyond Babylon... *3351*
1Ti 6:7 is certain we can **c.** nothing out... *1627*

CARRYING See also MISCARRYING.
1Sa 10:3 one **c.** three kids, and another... 5375
1Sa 10:3 another **c.** three loaves of bread,... 5375
1Sa 10:3 and another **c.** a bottle of wine:... 5375
Ps 78:9 **c.** bows, turned back in the day... 7411
Jer 1:3 **c.** away of Jerusalem captive... 1540
Mt 1:17 from David until the **c.** away... *3350*
Mt 1:17 from the **c.** away into Babylon... *3350*
Ac 5:10 **c.** her forth, buried her by her... *1627*

CARSHENA (car-she'-nah)
Es 1:14 And the next unto him was **C.**,... 3771

CART
1Sa 6:7 Now therefore make a new **c.**,... 5699
1Sa 6:7 tie the kine to the **c.**, and bring... 5699
1Sa 6:8 the Lord, and lay it upon the **c.**;... 5699
1Sa 6:10 milch kine, and tied them to the **c.**,... 5699
1Sa 6:11 the ark of the Lord upon the **c.**,... 5699
1Sa 6:14 And the **c.** came into the field of... 5699
1Sa 6:14 they clave the wood of the **c.**, and... 5699
2Sa 6:3 set the ark of God upon a new **c.**,... 5699
2Sa 6:3 of Abinadab, drave the new **c.**... 5699
1Ch 13:7 carried the ark of God in a new **c.**... 5699
1Ch 13:7 and Uzza and Ahio drave the **c.**... 5699
Isa 5:18 and sin as it were with a **c.** rope:... 5699
Isa 28:27 neither is a **c.** wheel turned about... 5699
Isa 28:28 break it with the wheel of his **c.**,... 5699
Am 2:13 as a **c.** is pressed that if full of... 5699

CARVED
Jg 18:18 fetched the **c.** image, the ephod,... 6459
1Ki 6:18 the house within was **c.** with... 4734
1Ki 6:29 he **c.** all the walls of the house... 7049
1Ki 6:29 **c.** figures of cherubims and palm... 6603
1Ki 6:32 and he **c.** upon them carvings of... 7049
1Ki 6:35 And he **c.** thereon cherubims... 7049
1Ki 6:35 with gold fitted upon the **c.** work... 2707
2Ch 33:7 he set a **c.** image, the idol which... 6459
2Ch 33:22 sacrificed unto all the **c.** images... 6456
2Ch 34:3 the **c.** images, and the molten... 6456
2Ch 34:4 the groves, and the **c.** images,... 6456
Ps 74:6 now they break down the **c.** work... 6603
Pr 7:16 with **c.** works, with fine linen of... 2405

CARVING See also CARVINGS.
Ex 31:5 and in **c.** of timber, to work in all... 2799
Ex 35:33 and in **c.** of wood, to make any... 2799

CARVINGS
1Ki 6:32 **c.** of cherubims and palm trees... 4734

CASE See also CASES.
Ex 5:19 did see that they were in evil **c.**,...
De 19:4 this is the **c.** of the slayer, which... 1697
De 22:1 thou shalt in any **c.** bring them... 7725
De 24:13 In any **c.** thou shalt deliver him... 7725
Ps 144:15 that people, that is in such a **c.**:... 3602
Mt 5:20 **ye shall in no c. enter into the**... *3364*
Mt 19:10 If the **c.** of the man be so with his... *156*
Joh 5:6 a long time in that **c.**, he saith unto...

CASEMENT
Pr 7:6 I looked through my **c.**,... 822

CASES
1Co 7:15 is not under bondage in such **c.**...

CASIPHIA (cas-if'-e-ah)
Ezr 8:17 Iddo the chief at the place **C.**,... 3703
Ezr 8:17 the Nethinims, at the place **C.**,... 3703

CASLUHIM (cas'-loo-him)
Ge 10:14 and **C.**, (out of whom came... 3695
1Ch 1:12 and **C.**, (of whom came the... 3695

CASSIA
Ex 30:24 And of **c.** five hundred shekels,... 6916
Ps 45:8 smell of myrrh, and aloes, and **c.**,... 7102
Eze 27:19 bright iron, **c.**, and calamus,... 6916

CAST See also CASTAWAY; CASTEDST; CASTEST; CASTETH; CASTING; FORECAST; OUTCAST.
Ge 21:10 **C.** out this bondwoman and her... 1644
Ge 21:15 and she **c.** the child under one of... 7993
Ge 31:38 she goats have not **c.** their young,... 7921
Ge 31:51 behold this pillar, which I have **c.**... 3384
Ge 37:20 him, and **c.** him into some pit,... 7993
Ge 37:22 **c.** him into this pit that is in the... 7993
Ge 37:24 took him, and **c.** him into a pit:... 7993
Ge 39:7 master's wife **c.** her eyes upon... 5375
Ex 1:22 is born ye shall **c.** into the river... 7993
Ex 4:3 And he said, **C.** it on the ground... 7993
Ex 4:3 And he **c.** it on the ground,... 7993
Ex 4:25 and **c.** it at his feet, and said,... 5060
Ex 7:9 Take thy rod, and **c.** it before... 7993
Ex 7:10 and Aaron **c.** down his rod before... 7993
Ex 7:12 For they **c.** down every man his... 7993
Ex 10:19 locusts, and **c.** them into the Red... 8628
Ex 15:4 his host hath he **c.** into the sea:... 3384
Ex 15:25 when he had **c.** into the waters,... 7993
Ex 22:31 ye shall **c.** it to the dogs... 7993
Ex 23:26 shall nothing **c.** their young,... 7921
Ex 25:12 thou shalt **c.** four rings of gold... 3332
Ex 26:37 thou shalt **c.** five sockets of brass... 3332
Ex 32:19 he **c.** the tables out of his hands,... 7993
Ex 32:24 then I **c.** it into the fire, and... 7993
Ex 34:24 I will **c.** out the nations before... 3423
Ex 36:36 and he **c.** for them four sockets of... 3332
Ex 37:3, 13 he **c.** for it four rings of gold,... 3332
Ex 38:5 he **c.** four rings for the four ends... 3332
Ex 38:27 hundred talents of silver were **c.**... 3332
Le 1:16 and **c.** it beside the altar on the... 7993
Le 14:40 and they shall **c.** them into an... 7993
Le 16:8 Aaron shall **c.** lots upon the two... 5414
Le 18:24 nations are defiled which I **c.** out... 7971
Le 20:23 nation, which I **c.** out before you:... 7971
Le 26:30 and **c.** your carcases upon the... 5414
Le 26:44 I will not **c.** them away, neither... 3988
Nu 19:6 and **c.** it into the midst of the... 7993
Nu 35:22 or have **c.** upon him any thing... 7993
Nu 35:23 and **c.** it upon him, that he die,... 5307
De 6:19 To **c.** out all thine enemies from... 1920
De 7:1 hath **c.** out many nations before... 5394
De 9:4 Lord thy God hath **c.** them out... 1920
De 9:17 and **c.** them out of my two hands,... 7993
De 9:21 and I **c.** the dust thereof into the... 7993
De 28:40 for thine olive shall **c.** his fruit... 5394
De 29:28 and **c.** them into another land, as... 7993
Jos 8:29 and **c.** it at the entering of the... 7993
Jos 10:11 the Lord **c.** down great stones... 7993
Jos 10:27 and **c.** them into the cave... 7993
Jos 13:12 Moses smite, and **c.** them out... 3423
Jos 18:6 that I may **c.** lots for you here... 3384
Jos 18:8 that I may here **c.** lots for you... 7993
Jos 18:10 And Joshua **c.** lots for them... 7993
Jg 6:28 the altar of Baal was **c.** down,... 5422
Jg 6:30 he hath **c.** down the altar of Baal,... 5422
Jg 6:31 because one hath **c.** down his... 5422
Jg 8:25 and did **c.** therein every man the... 7993
Jg 9:53 a certain woman **c.** a piece of... 7993
Jg 15:17 that he **c.** away the jawbone out... 7993
1Sa 14:42 **C.** lots between me and Jonathan... 5307
1Sa 18:11 And Saul **c.** the javelin; for he... 2904
1Sa 20:33 And Saul **c.** a javelin at him to... 2904
2Sa 1:21 of the mighty is vilely **c.** away,... 1602
2Sa 11:21 did not a woman **c.** a piece of a... 7993
2Sa 16:6 And he **c.** stones at David, and at... 5619
2Sa 16:13 threw stones at him, and **c.** dust... 6080
2Sa 18:17 and **c.** him into a great pit in... 7993
2Sa 20:12 and **c.** a cloth upon him,... 7993
2Sa 20:15 **c.** up a bank against the city,... 8210
2Sa 20:22 Bichri, and **c.** it out to Joab... 7993
1Ki 7:15 For he **c.** two pillars of brass,... 6696
1Ki 7:24 knops were **c.** in two rows,... 3332
1Ki 7:24 in two rows, when it was **c.**... 3333
1Ki 7:46 plain of Jordan did the king **c.**... 3332
1Ki 9:7 name, will I **c.** out of my sight;... 7971
1Ki 13:24 his carcase was **c.** in the way,... 7993
1Ki 13:25 passed by, and saw the carcase **c.**... 7993
1Ki 13:28 he went and found his carcase **c.**... 7993
1Ki 14:9 and hast **c.** me behind thy back:... 7993
1Ki 14:24 the nations which the Lord **c.**... 3423
1Ki 18:42 **c.** himself down upon the earth,... 1457
1Ki 19:19 and **c.** his mantle upon him... 7993
1Ki 21:26 whom the Lord **c.** out before the... 3423
2Ki 2:16 and **c.** him upon some mountain... 7993
2Ki 2:21 and **c.** the salt in there, and said,... 7993
2Ki 3:25 **c.** every man his stone, and... 7993
2Ki 4:41 And he **c.** it into the pot;... 7993
2Ki 6:6 and **c.** it in thither; and the iron... 7993
2Ki 7:15 Syrians had **c.** away in their haste... 7993
2Ki 9:25 **c.** him in the portion of the field... 7993
2Ki 9:26 **c.** him into the plot of ground,... 7993
2Ki 10:25 and the captain **c.** them out,... 7993
2Ki 13:21 **c.** the man into the sepulchre... 7993
2Ki 13:23 neither **c.** he them from his... 7993
2Ki 16:3 whom the Lord **c.** out from... 3423
2Ki 17:8 **c.** out from before the children... 3423
2Ki 17:20 had **c.** them out of his sight... 7993
2Ki 19:18 have **c.** their gods into the fire:... 5414
2Ki 19:32 shield, nor **c.** a bank against it... 8210
2Ki 21:2 heathen, whom the Lord **c.** out... 3423
2Ki 23:6 and **c.** the powder thereof upon... 7993
2Ki 23:12 and **c.** the dust of them into the... 7993
2Ki 23:27 will **c.** off this city Jerusalem... 3988
2Ki 24:20 until he had **c.** them out from... 7993
1Ch 24:31 These likewise **c.** lots over... 5307
1Ch 25:8 And they **c.** lots, hard against... 5307
1Ch 26:13 And they **c.** lots, as well the small... 5307
1Ch 26:14 they **c.** lots; and his lot came out... 5307
1Ch 28:9 thou forsake him, he will **c.** thee... 2186
2Ch 4:3 rows of oxen were **c.**,... 3332
2Ch 4:3 when it was **c.**... 4166
2Ch 4:17 plain of Jordan did the king **c.**... 3332
2Ch 7:20 will I **c.** out of my sight, and... 7993
2Ch 11:14 and his sons had **c.** them off... 2186
2Ch 13:9 Have ye not **c.** out the priests... 5080
2Ch 20:11 to come to **c.** us out of thy... 1644
2Ch 24:10 in, and **c.** into the chest,... 7993
2Ch 25:8 power to help, and to **c.** down... 3782
2Ch 25:12 and **c.** them down from the top of... 7993
2Ch 26:14 and bows, and slings to **c.** stones...
2Ch 28:3 whom the Lord had **c.** out... 3423
2Ch 29:19 king Ahaz in his reign did **c.**... 2186
2Ch 30:14 and **c.** them into the brook... 7993
2Ch 33:2 whom the Lord had **c.** out before... 3423
2Ch 33:15 and **c.** them out of the city... 7993
Ne 1:9 there were of you **c.** out unto... 5080
Ne 6:16 they were much **c.** down in their... 5307
Ne 9:26 and **c.** thy law behind their backs,... 7993
Ne 10:34 we **c.** the lots among the priests,... 5307
Ne 11:1 the rest of the people also **c.** lots,... 5307
Ne 13:8 therefore I **c.** forth all the... 7993
Es 3:7 they **c.** Pur, that is, the lot,... 5307
Es 9:24 and had **c.** Pur, that is, the lot,... 5307
Job 8:4 and he have **c.** them away for their... 7971
Job 8:20 God will not **c.** away a perfect... 3988
Job 15:33 and shall **c.** off his flower as the... 7993
Job 18:7 his own counsel shall **c.** him down... 7993
Job 18:8 he is **c.** into a net by his own... 7971
Job 20:15 God shall **c.** them out of his belly... 3423
Job 20:23 God shall **c.** the fury of his wrath... 7971

Book	Ref.	Context	No.
Job	22:29	When men are c. down, then thou	8213
Job	27:22	For God shall c. upon him, and	7993
Job	29:24	my countenance they c. not down.	5307
Job	30:19	He hath c. me into the mire,	3384
Job	39:3	ones, they c. out their sorrows	7971
Job	40:11	C. abroad the rage of thy wrath:	6327
Job	41:9	shall not one be c. down even	2904
Ps	2:3	and c. away their cords from us.	7993
Ps	5:10	c. them out in the multitude	5080
Ps	17:13	disappoint him, c. him down:	3766
Ps	18:42	I did c. them out as the dirt	7324
Ps	22:10	I was c. upon thee from the womb:	7993
Ps	22:18	and c. lots upon my vesture.	5307
Ps	36:12	they are c. down, and shall not	1760
Ps	37:14	to c. down the poor and needy,	5307
Ps	37:24	he shall not be utterly c. down:	2904
Ps	42:5	Why art thou c. down, O my soul?	7817
Ps	42:6	my soul is c. down within me:	7817
Ps	42:11	Why are thou c. down, O my soul?	7817
Ps	43:2	why dost thou c. me off?	2186
Ps	43:5	Why art thou c. down, O my soul?	7817
Ps	44:2	the people, and c. them out.	7971
Ps	44:9	But thou hast c. off, and put us	2186
Ps	44:23	arise, c. us not off for ever.	2186
Ps	51:11	C. me not away from thy presence;	7993
Ps	55:3	they c. iniquity upon me, and in	4131
Ps	55:22	C. thy burden upon the Lord,	7993
Ps	56:7	in thine anger c. down the people,	3381
Ps	60:1	O God, thou hast c. us off, thou	2186
Ps	60:8	over Edom will I c. out my shoe:	7993
Ps	60:10	O God, which hadst c. us off?	2186
Ps	62:4	They only consult to c. him down	5080
Ps	71:9	C. me not off in the time of old	7993
Ps	74:1	hast thou c. us off for ever?	2186
Ps	74:7	have c. fire into thy sanctuary,	7971
Ps	76:6	the chariot and horse are c. into	7290
Ps	77:7	Will the Lord c. off for ever?	2186
Ps	78:49	He c. upon them the fierceness	7971
Ps	78:55	He c. out the heathen also	1644
Ps	80:8	thou hast c. out the heathen,	1644
Ps	89:38	thou hast c. off and abhorred,	2186
Ps	89:44	c. his throne down to the ground.	4048
Ps	94:14	Lord will not c. off his people,	5203
Ps	102:10	lifted me up, and c. me down.	7993
Ps	108:9	over Edom will I c. out my shoe;	7993
Ps	108:11	O God, who hast c. us off?	2186
Ps	140:10	let them be c. into the fire;	5307
Ps	144:6	C. forth lightning, and scatter	1299
Pr	1:14	C. in thy lot among us; let us all	5307
Pr	7:26	she hath c. down many wounded:	5307
Pr	16:33	The lot is c. into the lap; but	2904
Pr	22:10	C. out the scorner, and contention	1644
Ec	3:5	A time to c. away stones, and a	7993
Ec	3:6	and a time to c. away;	7993
Ec	11:1	C. thy bread upon the waters:	7971
Isa	2:20	a man shall c. his idols of silver,	7993
Isa	5:24	because they have c. away the	3988
Isa	6:13	when they c. their leaves:	7995
Isa	14:19	thou art c. out of thy grave	7993
Isa	16:2	wandering bird c. out of the nest,	7971
Isa	19:8	all they that c. angle into the	7993
Isa	25:7	the covering c. over all people,	3874
Isa	26:19	the earth shall c. out the dead.	5307
Isa	28:2	shall c. down to the earth with	3240
Isa	28:25	doth he not c. abroad the fitches,	6327
Isa	28:25	and c. in the principal wheat	7760
Isa	30:22	gold: thou shalt c. them away	2219
Isa	31:7	every man shall c. away his idols	3988
Isa	34:3	Their slain also shall be c. out,	7993
Isa	34:17	he hath c. the lot for them,	5307
Isa	37:19	have c. their gods into the fire:	5414
Isa	37:33	nor c. a bank against it.	8210
Isa	38:17	c. all my sins behind thy back	7993
Isa	41:9	chosen thee, and not c. thee away.	3988
Isa	57:14	C. ye up, c. ye up, prepare the	5549
Isa	57:20	whose waters c. up mire and	1644
Isa	58:7	poor that are c. out to thy house?	4788
Isa	62:10	c. up, c. up the highway;	5549
Isa	66:5	c. you out for my name's sake,	5077
Jer	6:6	c. a mount against Jerusalem:	8210
Jer	6:15	I visit them they shall be c. down,	3782
Jer	7:15	I will c. you out of my sight,	7993
Jer	7:15	I have c. out all your brethren,	7993
Jer	7:29	O Jerusalem, and c. it away,	7993
Jer	8:12	visitation, they shall be c. down,	3782
Jer	9:19	our dwellings have c. us out	7993
Jer	14:16	shall be c. out in the streets of	7993
Jer	15:1	people: c. them out of my sight,	7971
Jer	16:13	Therefore will I c. you out of	2904
Jer	18:15	in paths, in a way not c. up;	5549
Jer	22:7	cedars, and c. them into the fire.	
Jer	22:19	burial of an ass, drawn and c. forth	7993
Jer	22:26	And I will c. thee out, and thy	2904
Jer	22:28	wherefore are they c. out, he and	7993
Jer	22:28	and are c. into a land which	2904
Jer	23:39	your fathers, and c. you out of	
Jer	26:23	and c. his dead body into the	7993
Jer	28:16	will c. thee from off the face of	7971
Jer	31:37	also c. off all the seed of Israel	3988
Jer	33:24	he hath even c. them off?	3988
Jer	33:26	I will c. away the seed of Jacob,	3988
Jer	36:23	and c. it into the fire that was	7993
Jer	36:30	his dead body shall be c. out in	7993
Jer	38:6	and c. him into the dungeon	7993
Jer	38:9	whom they have c. into the	7993
Jer	38:11	took thence old c. clouts and old	5499
Jer	38:12	Put now these old c. clouts and	5499
Jer	41:7	and c. them into the midst of the	
Jer	41:9	Ishmael had c. all the dead	7993
Jer	41:14	from Mizpah c. about and	5437
Jer	50:26	c. her up as heaps, and destroy	5549
Jer	51:34	my delicates, he hath c. me out.	1740
Jer	51:63	and c. it into the midst of	7993
Jer	52:3	till he had c. them out from his	7993
La	2:1	c. down from heaven unto the	7993
La	2:7	The Lord hath c. off his altar, he	2186
La	2:10	they have c. up dust upon their	5927
La	3:31	the Lord will not c. off for ever:	2186
La	3:53	and c. a stone upon me.	3034
Eze	4:2	against it, and c. a mount against	8210
Eze	5:4	and c. them into the midst of the	7993
Eze	6:4	and I will c. down your slain	5307
Eze	7:19	They shall c. their silver in the	7993
Eze	11:16	I have c. them far off among the	7368
Eze	15:4	Behold, it is c. into the fire for	5414
Eze	16:5	but thou wast c. out in the open	7993
Eze	18:31	C. away from you all your	7993
Eze	19:12	in fury, she was c. down to the	7993
Eze	20:7	C. ye away every man the	7993
Eze	20:8	they did not every man c. away	7993
Eze	21:22	to c. a mount, and to build a fort.	8210
Eze	23:35	forgotten me, and c. me behind	7993
Eze	26:8	and c. a mount against thee,	8210
Eze	27:30	shall c. up dust upon their heads,	5927
Eze	28:16	therefore I will c. thee as profane	2490
Eze	28:17	I will c. thee to the ground, I will	7993
Eze	31:16	when I c. him down to hell with	3381
Eze	32:4	I will c. thee forth upon the open	2904
Eze	32:18	of Egypt, and c. them down, even	3381
Eze	36:5	to c. it out for a prey.	4054
Eze	43:24	and the priests shall c. salt upon	7993
Da	3:6	shall the same hour be c. into	7412
Da	3:11	he should be c. into the midst of	7412
Da	3:15	ye shall be c. the same hour into	7412
Da	3:20	and to c. them into the burning	7412
Da	3:21	and were c. into the midst of the	7412
Da	3:24	Did not we c. three men bound	7412
Da	6:7	he shall be c. into the den of lions.	7412
Da	6:12	shall be c. into the den of lions?	7412
Da	6:16	they brought Daniel, and c. him	7412
Da	6:24	they c. them into the den of lions,	7412
Da	7:9	till the thrones were c. down,	7412
Da	8:7	but he c. him down to the	7993
Da	8:10	and it c. down some of the host	5307
Da	8:11	the place of his sanctuary was c.	7993
Da	8:12	and it c. down the truth to the	7993
Da	11:12	and he shall c. down many ten	5307
Da	11:15	and c. up a mount, and take the	8210
Ho	8:3	Israel hath c. off the thing that	2186
Ho	8:5	Thy calf, O Samaria, hath c. thee	2186
Ho	9:17	My God will c. them away,	3988
Ho	14:5	and c. forth his roots as Lebanon.	5221
Joe	1:7	made it clean bare, and c. it away;	7993
Joe	3:3	they have c. lots for my people;	3032
Am	1:11	and did c. off all pity, and his	7843
Am	4:3	and ye shall c. them into the	7993
Am	8:3	they shall c. them forth with	7993
Am	8:8	and it shall be c. out and	1644
Ob	11	and c. lots upon Jerusalem,	3032
Jon	1:5	and c. forth the wares that were	2904
Jon	1:7	Come, and let us c. lots, that we	5307
Jon	1:7	So they c. lots, and the lot fell	5307
Jon	1:12	and c. me forth into the sea;	2904
Jon	1:15	and c. him forth into the sea:	2904
Jon	2:3	For thou hadst c. me into the	7993
Jon	2:4	I said, I am c. out of thy sight;	1644
Mic	2:5	none that shall c. a cord by lot	7993
Mic	2:9	women of my people have ye c.	1644
Mic	4:7	and her that was c. far off a	1972
Mic	7:19	and thou wilt c. all their sins	7993
Na	3:6	And I will c. abominable filth	7993
Na	3:10	they c. lots for her honourable	3032
Zep	3:15	thy judgments, he hath c. out	6437
Zec	1:21	C. out the horns of the Gentiles,	3034
Zec	5:8	And he c. it into the midst of the	7993
Zec	5:8	and he c. the weight of lead upon	7993
Zec	9:4	the Lord will c. her out, and he	3423
Zec	10:6	though I had not c. them off:	2186
Zec	11:13	C. it unto the potter: a goodly	7993
Zec	11:13	and c. them to the potter in the	7993
Mal	3:11	shall your vine c. her fruit before	7921
Mt	3:10	hewn down, and c. into the fire.	906
Mt	4:6	the Son of God, c. thyself down:	906
Mt	4:12	had heard that John was c. into	3860
Mt	5:13	good for nothing, but to be c. out,	906
Mt	5:25	to the officer, and thou be c. into	906
Mt	5:29	pluck it out, and c. it from thee:	906
Mt	5:29	thy whole body should be c. into	906
Mt	5:30	cut it off, and c. it from thee:	906
Mt	5:30	that thy whole body should be c.	906
Mt	6:30	and to morrow is c. into the oven.	906
Mt	7:5	first c. out the beam out of thine	1544
Mt	7:5	see clearly to c. out the mote out	1544
Mt	7:6	neither c. ye your pearls before	906
Mt	7:19	hewn down, and c. into the fire.	906
Mt	7:22	in thy name have c. out devils?	1544
Mt	8:12	shall be c. out into outer darkness;	1544
Mt	8:16	he c. out the spirits with his word,	1544
Mt	8:31	saying, If thou c. us out, suffer us	1544
Mt	9:33	when the devil was c. out, the	1544
Mt	10:1	unclean spirits, to c. them out,	1544
Mt	10:8	lepers, raise the dead, c. out devils:	1544
Mt	12:24	doth not c. out devils, but by	1544
Mt	12:26	if Satan c. out Satan, he is divided.	1544
Mt	12:27	And if I by Beelzebub c. out devils,	1544
Mt	12:27	do your children c. them out?	1544
Mt	12:28	if I c. out devils by the Spirit	1544
Mt	13:42	shall c. them into a furnace of fire:	906
Mt	13:47	like unto a net, that was c. into the	906
Mt	13:48	good into vessels, but c. the bad	906
Mt	13:50	shall c. them into the furnace of	906
Mt	15:17	and is c. out into the draught?	1544
Mt	15:26	children's bread, and to c. it to	906
Mt	15:30	and c. them down at Jesus' feet;	4496
Mt	17:19	Why could not we c. him out?	1544
Mt	17:27	go thou to the sea, and c. an hook,	906
Mt	18:8	cut them off, and c. them from	906
Mt	18:8	feet to be c. into everlasting fire	906
Mt	18:9	pluck it out, and c. it from thee:	906
Mt	18:9	having two eyes to be c. into hell	906
Mt	18:30	went and c. him into prison, till he.	906
Mt	21:12	c. out all that sold and bought	1544
Mt	21:21	and be thou c. into the sea;	906
Mt	21:39	they caught him, and c. him out	1544
Mt	22:13	and c. him into outer darkness;	1544
Mt	25:30	And c. ye the unprofitable servant.	1544
Mt	27:5	And he c. down the pieces of	4496
Mt	27:35	upon my vesture did they c. lots.	906
Mt	27:44	him, c. the same in his teeth	3679
Mk	1:34	and c. out many devils; and	1544
Mk	1:39	throughout all Galilee, and c. out	1544
Mk	3:15	sicknesses, and to c. out devils:	1544
Mk	3:23	How can Satan c. out Satan?	1544
Mk	4:26	a man should c. seed into the	906
Mk	6:13	they c. out many devils, and	1544
Mk	7:26	he would c. forth the devil out of	1544
Mk	7:27	children's bread, and to c. it unto	906
Mk	9:18	that they should c. him out;	1544
Mk	9:22	it hath c. him into the fire,	906
Mk	9:28	Why could not we c. him out?	1544
Mk	9:42	his neck, and he were c. into the	906
Mk	9:45	two feet to be c. into hell, into the	906
Mk	9:47	two eyes to be c. into hell fire:	906
Mk	11:7	and c. their garments on him;	1911
Mk	11:15	and began to c. out them that	1544
Mk	11:23	removed, and be thou c. into the	906
Mk	12:4	at him they c. stones, and	3036
Mk	12:8	killed him, and c. him out of the	1544
Mk	12:41	people c. money into the treasury:	906
Mk	12:41	and many that were rich c. in	906
Mk	12:43	this poor widow hath c. more in,	906

Mk 12:43 than all they which have c. into..... *906*
Mk 12:44 they did c. in of their abundance,... *906*
Mk 12:44 but she of her want did c. in all..... *906*
Mk 14:51 having a linen cloth c. about his......... *4016*
Mk 16:9 out of whom he had c. seven............ *1544*
Mk 16:17 In my name shall they c. out........ *1544*
Lu 1:29 c. in her mind what manner of........... *1260*
Lu 3:9 is hewn down, and c. into the fire......... *906*
Lu 4:9 Son of God, c. thyself down from........ *906*
Lu 4:29 that they might c. him down............. *2630*
Lu 6:22 shall reproach you, and c. out....... *1544*
Lu 6:42 c. out first the beam out of thine.. *1544*
Lu 9:25 and lose himself, or be c. away?.... *2210*
Lu 9:40 I besought thy disciples to c. him....... *1544*
Lu 11:18 ye say that I c. out devils through..*1544*
Lu 11:19 if I by Beelzebub c. out devils,...... *1544*
Lu 11:19 by whom do your sons c. them....... *1544*
Lu 11:20 if I with the finger of God c. out.. *1544*
Lu 12:5 hath power to c. into hell; yea, I... *1685*
Lu 12:28 and to morrow is c. into the oven;.. *906*
Lu 12:58 and the officer c. thee into prison... *906*
Lu 13:19 a man took, and c. into his garden; .*906*
Lu 13:32 Behold, I c. out devils, and I do.... *1544*
Lu 14:35 for the dunghill; but men c. it out.. *906*
Lu 17:2 about his neck, and he c. into....... *4496*
Lu 19:35 they c. their garments upon the......... *1977*
Lu 19:43 thine enemies shall c. a trench...... *4016*
Lu 19:45 began to c. out them that sold........... *1544*
Lu 20:12 wounded him also, and c. him out..*1544*
Lu 20:15 c. him out of the vineyard, and..... *1544*
Lu 21:3 this poor widow hath c. in more.... *906*
Lu 21:4 of their abundance c. in unto the.... *906*
Lu 21:4 but she of her penury hath c. in..... *906*
Lu 22:41 from them about a stone's c.,............ *1000*
Lu 23:19 for murder, was c. into prison............. *906*
Lu 23:25 and murder was c. into prison,............ *906*
Lu 23:34 parted his raiment, and c. lots............ *906*
Joh 3:24 John was not yet c. into prison............ *906*
Joh 6:37 to me I will in no wise c. out........ *1544*
Joh 8:7 let him first c. a stone at her......... *906*
Joh 8:59 took they up stones to c. at him:........ *906*
Joh 9:34 each us? And they c. him out............ *1544*
Joh 9:35 heard that they had c. him out;.......... *1544*
Joh 12:31 the prince of this world be c. out. ..*1544*
Joh 15:6 he is c. forth as a branch, and is.... *906*
Joh 15:6 c. them into the fire, and they are.. *906*
Joh 19:24 Let us not rend it, but c. lots for it,... *2975*
Joh 19:24 and for my vesture they did c. lots. *906*
Joh 21:6 C. the net on the right side of the .. *906*
Joh 21:6 They c. therefore, and now they......... *906*
Joh 21:7 and did c. himself into the sea............ *906*
Ac 7:19 they c. out their young............ *4160,1570*
Ac 7:21 when he was c. out, Pharaoh's.......... *1620*
Ac 7:58 c. him out of the city, and stoned....... *1544*
Ac 12:8 C. thy garment about thee, and......... *4016*
Ac 16:23 they c. them into prison, charging........ *906*
Ac 16:37 have c. us into prison; and now do....... *906*
Ac 22:23 they cried out, and c. off their........... *4496*
Ac 27:19 we c. out with our own hands the...... *4496*
Ac 27:26 we must be c. upon a certain............ *1601*
Ac 27:29 they c. four anchors out of the.......... *4496*
Ac 27:30 as though they would have c.......... *1614*
Ac 27:38 and c. out the wheat into the sea......... *1544*
Ac 27:43 should c. themselves first into the........ *641*
Ro 11:1 Hath God c. away his people?............ *683*
Ro 11:2 God hath not c. away his people.......... *683*
Ro 13:12 let us therefore c. off the works of...... *656*
1Co 7:35 not that I may c. a snare upon you,.... *1911*
2Co 4:9 but not forsaken; c. down, but........... *2598*
2Co 7:6 comforteth those that are c. down,..... *5011*
Ga 4:30 C. out the bondwoman and her.......... *1544*
1Ti 5:12 they have c. off their first faith.......... *114*
Heb 10:35 C. not away therefore your................ *577*
2Pe 2:4 but c. them down to hell, and............ *5020*
Re 2:10 the devil shall c. some of you into.. *906*
Re 2:14 Balac to c. a stumblingblock.......... *906*
Re 2:22 Behold, I will c. her into a bed,...... *906*
Re 4:10 and c. their crowns before the........... *906*
Re 8:5 c. it into the earth: and there were...... *906*
Re 8:7 they were c. upon the earth: and......... *906*
Re 8:8 burning with fire was c. into the.......... *906*
Re 12:4 stars of heaven, and did c. them to...... *906*
Re 12:9 the great dragon was c. out, that......... *906*
Re 12:9 he was c. out into the earth, ... *906*
Re 12:9 and his angels were c. out with........... *906*
Re 12:10 acuser of our brethren is c. down,...... *2598*
Re 12:13 dragon saw that he was c. unto........... *906*
Re 12:15 the serpent c. out of his mouth.......... *906*
Re 12:16 the dragon c. out of his mouth............ *906*
Re 14:19 c. it into the great winepress of.......... *906*
Re 18:19 they c. dust on their heads, and.......... *906*
Re 18:21 millstone, and c. it into the sea, ... *906*
Re 19:20 These both were c. alive into a.......... *906*
Re 20:3 c. him into the bottomless pit, and....... *906*
Re 20:10 was c. into the lake of fire and........... *906*
Re 20:14 death and hell were c. into the........... *906*
Re 20:15 was c. into the lake of fire. *906*

CASTAWAY
1Co 9:27 to others, I myself should be a c........... *96*

CASTEDST
Ps 73:18 c. them down into destruction. 5307

CASTEST
Job 15:4 thou c. off fear, and restrainest.......... 6565
Ps 50:17 instruction, and c. my words............. 7993
Ps 88:14 Lord, why c. thou off my soul?.......... 2186

CASTETH
Job 21:10 their cow calveth, and c. not her........ 7921
Ps 147:6 he c. the wicked down to the............ 8213
Ps 147:17 He c. forth his ice like morsels:........ 7993
Pr 10:3 but he c. away the substance of......... 1920
Pr 19:15 Slothfulness c. into a deep sleep; 5307
Pr 21:22 and c. down the strength of the.......... 3381
Pr 26:18 who c. firebrands, arrows, and 3384
Isa 40:19 with gold, and c. silver chains.......... 6884
Jer 6:7 As a fountain c. out her waters,......... 6979
Jer 6:7 so she c. out her wickedness: 6979
Mt 9:34 He c. out devils through the prince..... *1544*
Mk 3:22 prince of the devils c. he out devils. ... *1544*
Lu 11:15 He c. out devils through Beelzebub *1544*
1Jo 4:18 perfect love c. out fear: because.......... *906*
3Jo 10 and c. them out of the church. *1544*
Re 6:13 as a fig tree c. her untimely figs,......... *906*

CASTING
2Sa 8:2 c. them down to the ground;............ 7901
1Ki 7:37 all of them had one c., one.............. 4165
Ezr 10:1 c. himself down before the house....... 5307
Job 6:21 ye see my c. down, and are afraid........ 2866
Ps 74:7 sanctuary, have they defiled by c. ....
Ps 89:39 his crown by c. it to the ground...............
Eze 17:17 by c. up mounts, and building........... 8210
Mic 6:14 and thy c. down shall be in the.......... 3445
Mt 4:18 c. a net into the sea: for they were *906*
Mt 27:35 parted his garments, c. lots: that....... *906*
Mk 1:16 Andrew his brother c. a net into......... *906*
Mk 9:38 we saw one c. out devils in thy......... *1544*
Mk 10:50 he, c. away his garment, rose, and....... *577*
Mk 15:24 parted his garments, c. lots upon......... *906*
Lu 9:49 we saw one c. out devils in thy......... *1544*
Lu 11:14 he was c. out a devil, and it was........ *1544*
Lu 21:1 the rich men c. their gifts into the *906*
Lu 21:2 a certain poor widow c. in thither........ *906*
Ro 11:15 For if the c. away of them be the......... *580*
2Co 10:5 C. down imaginations, and every......... *2507*
1Pe 5:7 C. all your care upon him; for he *1977*

CASTLE See also CASTLES.
1Ch 11:5 David took the c. of Zion, which......... 4686
1Ch 11:7 David dwelt in the c.; therefore......... 4679
Pr 18:19 contentions are like the bars of a c.. 759
Ac 21:34 him to be carried into the c.............. *3925*
Ac 21:37 Paul was to be led into the c., he *3925*
Ac 22:24 to be brought into the c., and bade..... *3925*
Ac 23:10 and to bring him into the c.............. *3925*
Ac 23:16 he went and entered into the c.,......... *3925*
Ac 23:32 and returned to the c.:.................. *3925*

CASTLES
Ge 25:16 by their towns, and by their c.; 2918
Nu 31:10 they dwelt, and all their goodly c., ... 2918
1Ch 6:54 places throughout their c.................. 2918
1Ch 27:25 in the villages, and in the c.,............ 4026
2Ch 17:12 he built in Judah c., and cities............ 1003
2Ch 27:4 and in the forests he built c. and........ 1003

CASTOR (cas'-tor)
Ac 28:11 whose sign was C. and Pollux. *1359*

CATCH See also CATCHETH; CAUGHT.
Ex 22:6 If fire break out, and c. in................ 4672
Jg 21:21 and c. you every man his wife of....... 2414
1Ki 20:33 from him, and did hastily c. it:.......... 2480
2Ki 7:12 we shall c. them alive, and get 8610
Ps 10:9 in wait to c. the poor: he doth c........ 2414
Ps 35:8 let his net that he hath hid c............. 3920
Ps 109:11 Let the extortioner c. all that he........ 5367
Jer 5:26 snares; they set a trap, they c. 3920
Eze 19:3 it learned to c. the prey; it............... 2963
Eze 19:6 and learned to c. the prey, and.......... 2963
Hab 1:15 they c. them in their net, and............ 1641
Mk 12:13 of the Herodians, to c. him in his......... *64*
Lu 5:10 henceforth thou shalt c. men. *2221*
Lu 11:54 seeking to c. something out of his...... *2340*

CATCHETH
Le 17:13 which hunteth and c. any beast.......... 6679
Mt 13:19 cometh the wicked one, and c......... *726*
Joh 10:12 the wolf c. them, and scattereth..... *726*

CATERPILLAR See CATERPILLER.

CATERPILLER See also CATERPELLERS.
1Ki 8:37 if there be c.; if their enemy............. 2625
Ps 78:46 their increase unto the c., and........... 2625
Isa 33:4 the gathering of the c.: as the........... 2625
Joe 1:4 cankerworm hath left hath the c......... 2625
Joe 2:25 cankerworm, and the c., and the.......... 2625

CATERPILLERS
2Ch 6:28 mildew, locusts, or c.; if their 2625
Ps 105:34 the locusts came, and c., and 3218
Jer 51:14 fill thee with men, as with c.:............ 3218
Jer 51:27 horses to come up as the rough c.. 3218

CATTLE
Ge 1:24 c., and creeping thing, and beast......... 929
Ge 1:25 c. after their kind, and every thing....... 929
Ge 1:26 and over the c., and over all the 929
Ge 2:20 Adam gave names to all c., and to........ 929
Ge 3:14 thou art cursed above all c., and......... 929
Ge 4:20 in tents, and of such as have c.. 4735
Ge 6:20 c. after their kind, of every 929
Ge 7:14 all the c. after their kind, and every..... 929
Ge 7:21 of fowl, and of c., and of beast, and..... 929
Ge 7:23 both man, and c., and the creeping..... 929
Ge 8:1 all the c. that was with him in the........ 929
Ge 8:17 of fowl, and of c., and of every 929
Ge 9:10 of the fowl, of the c., and of every........ 929
Ge 13:2 Abram was very rich in c., in............ 4735
Ge 13:7 between the herdmen of Abram's c...... 4735
Ge 13:7 and the herdmen of Lot's c.:............. 4735
Ge 29:7 neither is it time that the c. should..... 4735
Ge 30:29 I have served thee, and how thy c. 4735
Ge 30:32 all the speckled and spotted c.......... 7716
Ge 30:32 and all the brown c. among the.......... 7716
Ge 30:39 and brought forth c. ringstraked,........ 6629
Ge 30:40 and put them not unto Laban's c.. 6629
Ge 30:41 the stronger c. did conceive, that......... 6629
Ge 30:41 the rods before the eyes of the c.......... 6629
Ge 30:42 when the c. were feeble, he put 6629
Ge 30:43 had much c., and maidservants, ... 6629
Ge 31:8 all the c. bare speckled: and if........... 6629
Ge 31:8 then bare all the c. ringstraked. 6629
Ge 31:9 the c. of your father, and given 4735
Ge 31:10 the time that the c. conceived, ... 6629
Ge 31:10 the rams which leaped upon the c. 6629
Ge 31:12 the rams which leap upon the c. 6629
Ge 31:18 carried away all his c., and all........... 4735
Ge 31:18 the c. of his getting, which he had....... 4735
Ge 31:41 and six years for thy c.: and 6629
Ge 31:43 and these c. are my c., and all.......... 6629
Ge 33:14 according as the c. that goeth............ 4399
Ge 33:17 house, and made booths for his c.:..... 4735
Ge 34:5 his sons were with his c. in the......... 4735
Ge 34:23 Shall not their c. and their............... 4735
Ge 36:6 his c., and all his beasts, and all......... 4735
Ge 36:7 bear them because of their c............. 4735
Ge 46:6 And they took their c., and their........ 4735
Ge 46:32 their trade hath been to feed c.;......... 4735
Ge 46:34 trade hath been about c. from our....... 4735
Ge 47:6 then make them rulers over my c.. 4735
Ge 47:16 Joseph said, Give your c.; and I......... 4735
Ge 47:16 will give you for your c.,.................. 4735
Ge 47:17 they brought their c. unto Joseph: 4735
Ge 47:17 and for the c. of the herds, and for 4735
Ge 47:17 bread for all their c. for that year....... 4735
Ge 47:18 hath our herds of c.; there is not......... 929
Ex 9:3 hand of the Lord is upon thy c. 4735
Ex 9:4 sever between the c. of Israel 4735
Ex 9:4 and the c. of Egypt: and there shall.... 4735
Ex 9:6 all the c. of Egypt died: 4735
Ex 9:6 but of the c. of the children of.......... 4735
Ex 9:7 not one of the c. of the Israelites....... 4735

Ex 9:19 now, and gather thy **c.**, and all 4735
Ex 9:20 his servants and his **c.** flee into the 4735
Ex 9:21 his servants and his **c.** in the field. 4735
Ex 10:26 Our **c.** also shall go with us; there 4735
Ex 12:29 and all the firstborn of **c.** 929
Ex 12:38 and herds, even very much **c.** 4735
Ex 17:3 kill us and our children and our **c.** 4735
Ex 20:10 thy maidservant, nor thy **c.**, nor 929
Ex 34:19 firstling among thy **c.**, whether 4735
Le 1:2 bring your offering of the **c.**, even 929
Le 5:2 or a carcase of unclean **c.**, or the 929
Le 19:19 Thou shalt not let thy **c.** gender 929
Le 25:7 And for thy **c.**, and for the beast 929
Le 26:22 and destroy your **c.**, and make you 929
Nu 3:41 the **c.** of the Levites, instead of all 929
Nu 3:41 all the firstlings among the **c.** of the 929
Nu 3:45 **c.** of the Levites instead of their **c.**: 929
Nu 20:4 that we and our **c.** should die 1165
Nu 20:19 I and my **c.** drink of thy water, 4735
Nu 31:9 the spoil of all their **c.**, and all 929
Nu 32:1 had a very great multitude of **c.**: 4735
Nu 32:1 the place was a place for **c.**; 4735
Nu 32:4 Israel, is a land for **c.**, 4735
Nu 32:4 and thy servants have **c.**; 4735
Nu 32:16 sheepfolds here for our **c.**, and 4735
Nu 32:26 and all our **c.**, shall be there in the 929
Nu 35:3 shall be for their **c.**, and for their 929
De 2:35 Only the **c.** we took for a prey 929
De 3:7 But all the **c.**, and the spoil of the 929
De 3:19 your little ones, and your **c.**, 4735
De 3:19 (for I know that ye have much **c.**,) 4735
De 5:14 nor any of thy **c.**, nor thy stranger 929
De 7:14 among you, or among your **c.** 929
De 11:15 send grass in thy fields for thy **c.**, 929
De 13:15 and the **c.** thereof, with the edge of 929
De 20:14 the little ones, and the **c.**, and all 929
De 28:4 the fruit of thy **c.**, the increase of 929
De 28:11 thy body, and in the fruit of thy **c.**, 929
De 28:51 he shall eat the fruit of thy **c.**, and 929
De 30:9 in the fruit of thy **c.**, and in the 929
Jos 1:14 your little ones, and your **c.**, shall 4735
Jos 8:2 and the **c.** thereof, shall ye take 929
Jos 8:27 Only the **c.** and the spoil of that 929
Jos 11:14 these cities, and the **c.**, the children 929
Jos 14:4 with their suburbs for their **c.** and 4735
Jos 21:2 the suburbs thereof for our **c.** 929
Jos 22:8 with very much **c.**, with silver, 4735
Jg 6:5 came up with their **c.**, and their 4735
Jg 18:21 the little ones and the **c.** and the 4735
1Sa 23:5 and brought away their **c.**, and 4735
1Sa 30:20 before those other **c.**, and said, 4735
1Ki 1:9 slew sheep and oxen and fat **c.** 4806
1Ki 1:19 hath slain oxen and fat **c.** and 4806
1Ki 1:25 fat **c.** in abundance, and hath 4806
2Ki 3:9 for the **c.** that followed them. 929
2Ki 3:17 ye, and your **c.**, and your beasts. 4735
1Ch 5:9 because their **c.** were multiplied in 4735
1Ch 5:21 they took away their **c.**; of their 929
1Ch 7:21 came down to take away their **c.** 929
2Ch 14:15 also the tents of **c.**, and carried 929
2Ch 26:10 for he had much **c.**, both in the 929
2Ch 35:8 small **c.**, and three hundred oxen.
2Ch 35:9 offerings five thousand small **c.**, and
Ne 9:37 over our bodies, and over our **c.**, 929
Ne 10:36 of our **c.**, as it is written in the 929
Job 36:33 the **c.** also concerning the vapour. 4735
Ps 50:10 the **c.** upon a thousand hills. 929
Ps 78:48 He gave up their **c.** also to the 1165
Ps 104:14 the grass to grow for the **c.**, and 929
Ps 107:38 and suffereth not their **c.** to decrease. 929
Ps 148:10 Beasts, and all **c.**; creeping 929
Ec 2:7 possessions of great and small **c.** 4735
Isa 7:25 for the treading of lesser **c.** 7716
Isa 30:23 thy **c.** feed in large pastures. 4735
Isa 43:23 small **c.** of thy burnt offerings; 7716
Isa 46:1 upon the beasts, and upon the **c.**: 929
Jer 9:10 can men hear the voice of the **c.**; 4735
Jer 49:32 multitude of their **c.** a spoil: and 4734
Eze 34:17 between **c.** and **c.**, between the 7716
Eze 34:20 I, will judge between the fat **c.** 7716
Eze 34:20 and between the lean **c.** 7716
Eze 34:22 I will judge between **c.** and **c.** 7716
Eze 38:12 nations, which have gotten **c.** and 4735
Eze 38:13 to take away **c.** and goods, 4735
Joe 1:18 the herds of **c.** are perplexed, 1241
Jon 4:11 left hand; and also much **c.**? 929
Hag 1:11 upon men, and upon **c.**, and upon 929
Zec 2:4 for the multitude of men and **c.** 929
Zec 13:5 to keep **c.** from my youth. 7069
Lu 17:7 **a servant plowing or feeding c.**, *4165*
Joh 4:12 and his children, and his **c.**? *2353*

CAUGHT

Ge 22:13 ram **c.** in a thicket by his horns: 270
Ge 39:12 And she **c.** him by his garment, 8610
Ex 4:4 put forth his hand, and **c.** it, 2388
Nu 31:32 which the men of war had **c.**, 962
Jg 1:6 pursued after him, and **c.** him, 270
Jg 8:14 And **c. a young man of the men** 3920
Jg 15:4 went and c. three hundred foxes, 3920
Jg 21:23 whom they **c.**: and they went 1497
1Sa 17:35 he arose against me, I **c.** him 2388
2Sa 2:16 And they **c.** every one his fellow 2388
2Sa 18:9 and his head **c.** hold of the oak, 2388
1Ki 1:50 and **c.** hold on the horns of the 2388
1Ki 1:51 he hath **c.** hold on the horns of 270
1Ki 2:28 and **c.** hold on the horns of the 2388
1Ki 11:30 And Ahijah **c.** the new garment 8610
2Ki 4:27 she **c.** him by the feet: but 2388
2Ch 22:9 sought Ahaziah: and they **c.** him, 3920
Pr 7:13 So she **c.** him, and kissed him, 2388
Ec 9:12 birds that are **c.** in the snare; 270
Jer 50:24 thou art found, and also **c.**, 8610
Mt 14:31 **c.** him, and said unto him, *1949*
Mt 21:39 **they c. him, and cast him out** *2983*
Mk 12:3 **And they c. him and beat him,** *2983*
Lu 8:29 For oftentimes it had **c.** him: *4884*
Joh 21:3 and that night they **c.** nothing. *4084*
Joh 21:10 **the fish which we have now c.** *4084*
Ac 6:12 **c.** him, and brought him to the *4884*
Ac 8:39 Spirit of the Lord **c.** away Philip, *726*
Ac 16:19 they **c.** Paul and Silas, and drew *1949*
Ac 19:29 **c.** Gaius and Aristarchus, men *4884*
Ac 26:21 the Jews **c.** me in the temple, *4815*
Ac 27:15 And when the ship was **c.**, *4884*
2Co 12:2 one **c.** up to the third heaven. *726*
2Co 12:4 he was **c.** up into paradise, *726*
2Co 12:16 being crafty, I **c.** you with guile. *2983*
1Th 4:17 shall be **c.** up together with *726*
Re 12:5 her child was **c.** up unto God, *726*

CAUL See also CAULS.

Ex 29:13 the **c.** that is above the liver, 3508
Ex 29:22 and the **c.** above the liver, 3508
Le 3:4 **c.** above the liver, with the kidneys, 3508
Le 3:10 and the **c.** above the liver, 3508
Le 3:15 **c.** above the liver, with the kidneys, 3508
Le 4:9 **c.** above the liver, with the kidneys, 3508
Le 7:4 and the **c.** that is above the liver, 3508
Le 8:16 and the **c.** above the liver, and 3508
Le 8:25 he **c.** above the liver, and the two 3508
Le 9:10 and the **c.** above the liver of the 3508
Le 9:19 and the **c.** above the liver: 3508
Ho 13:8 and will rend the **c.** of their heart, 5458

CAULS

Isa 3:18 about their feet, and their **c.**, 7636

CAUSE See also BECAUSE; CAUSED; CAUSES; CAUSEST; CAUSETH; CAUSING; CAUSELESS; CAUSEWAY.

Ge 7:4 I will **c.** it to rain upon the earth
Ge 45:1 **C.** every man to go out from me
Ex 8:5 and **c.** frogs to come up upon
Ex 9:16 And in very deed for this **c.** have I 5668
Ex 9:18 I will **c.** it to rain a very grievous
Ex 21:19 shall **c.** him to be thoroughly healed.
Ex 22:5 **c.** a field or vineyard to be eaten,
Ex 22:9 the **c.** of both parties shall come 1697
Ex 23:2 speak in a **c.** to decline after 7379
Ex 23:3 countenance a poor man in his **c.** 7379
Ex 23:6 the judgment of thy poor in his **c.** 7379
Ex 27:20 to **c.** the lamp to burn always.
Ex 29:10 shalt **c.** a bullock to be brought
Le 14:41 he shall **c.** the house to be scraped
Le 19:29 to **c.** her to be a whore; lest the
Le 24:2 the light, to **c.** the lamps to burn
Le 24:19 **c.** a blemish in his neighbor; 5414
Le 25:9 Then shalt thou **c.** the trumpet
Le 26:16 the eyes, and **c.** sorrow of heart:
Nu 5:24 he shall **c.** the woman to drink
Nu 5:26 shall **c.** the woman to drink the
Nu 16:5 and will **c.** him to come near
Nu 16:5 will he **c.** to come near unto him.
Nu 16:11 which **c.** both thou and all thy 3651
Nu 27:5 brought their **c.** before the Lord. 4941
Nu 27:7 and thou shalt **c.** the inheritance
Nu 27:8 then ye shall **c.** his inheritance
Nu 28:7 shalt thou **c.** the strong wine
Nu 35:30 any person to **c.** him to die.
De 1:17 the **c.** that is too hard for you, 1697
De 1:38 he shall **c.** Israel to inherit it.
De 3:28 he shall **c.** them to inherit the land
De 12:11 choose to **c.** his name to dwell
De 17:16 nor **c.** the people to return to Egypt,
De 24:4 thou shalt not **c.** the land to sin,
De 25:2 the judge shall **c.** him to lie down,
De 28:7 shall **c.** thine enemies that rise 5414
De 28:25 shall **c.** thee to be smitten before 5414
De 31:7 thou shalt **c.** them to inherit it.
Jos 5:4 the **c.** why Joshua did circumcise: 1697
Jos 20:4 his **c.** in the ears of the elders 1697
Jos 23:7 nor **c.** to swear by them,
1Sa 17:29 now done? Is there not a **c.**? 1697
1Sa 19:5 blood, to slay David without a **c.**? 2600
1Sa 24:15 plead my **c.**, and deliver me out 7379
1Sa 25:39 pleaded the **c.** of my reproach 7379
1Sa 28:9 for my life to **c.** me to die?
2Sa 3:35 to **c.** David to eat meat while it
2Sa 13:13 whither shall I **c.** my shame
2Sa 13:16 said unto him, There is no **c.**:
2Sa 15:4 suit or **c.** might come unto me, 4941
1Ki 1:33 and **c.** Solomon my son to ride
1Ki 5:9 **c.** them to be discharged there,
1Ki 8:31 laid upon him to **c.** him to swear,
1Ki 8:45 supplication, and maintain their **c.** 4941
1Ki 8:49 place, and maintain their **c.**, 4941
1Ki 8:59 maintain the **c.** of his servant, 4941
1Ki 8:59 and the **c.** of his people Israel 4941
1Ki 11:27 the **c.** that he lifted up his hand 1697
1Ki 12:15 the **c.** was from the Lord, 5438
2Ki 19:7 **c.** him to fall by the sword
1Ch 21:3 he be a **c.** of trespass to Israel?
2Ch 6:35 supplication, and maintain their **c.** 4941
2Ch 6:39 maintain their **c.**, and forgive 4941
2Ch 10:15 for the **c.** was of God, that the 5252
2Ch 19:10 And what **c.** soever shall come 7379
2Ch 32:20 And for this **c.** Hezekiah the
Ezr 4:15 which **c.** was this city destroyed
Ezr 4:21 to **c.** these men to cease,
Ezr 5:5 they could not **c.** them to cease,
Ne 4:11 slay them, and **c.** the work to cease.
Ne 6:6 for which **c.** thou buildest the wall,
Ne 13:26 did outlandish women **c.** to sin.
Es 3:13 and to **c.** to perish, all Jews,
Es 5:5 **C.** Haman to make haste,
Es 8:11 to slay, and to **c.** to perish, all the
Job 2:3 him, to destroy him without **c.** 2600
Job 5:8 unto God would I commit my **c.**: 1700
Job 6:24 and **c.** me to understand wherein
Job 9:17 multiplieth my wounds without **c.** 2600
Job 13:18 I have ordered my **c.**; I know 4941
Job 20:2 do my thoughts **c.** me to answer,
Job 23:4 I would order my **c.** before him, 4941
Job 24:7 They **c.** the naked to lodge
Job 24:10 They **c.** him to go naked
Job 29:16 and the **c.** which I knew not I 7379
Job 31:13 If I did despise the **c.** of my 4941
Job 34:11 **c.** every man to find according to
Job 34:28 So that they **c.** the cry of the
Job 38:26 To **c.** it to rain on the earth,
Job 38:27 and to **c.** the bud of the tender
Ps 7:4 delivered him that without **c.** is 7387
Ps 9:4 maintained my right and my **c.**; 1779
Ps 10:17 their heart, thou wilt **c.** thine ear
Ps 25:3 which transgress without **c.** 7387
Ps 35:1 Plead my **c.**, O Lord, with them
Ps 35:7 For without **c.** have they hid for 2600
Ps 35:7 in a pit, which without **c.** they 2600
Ps 35:19 the eye that hate me without a **c.** 2600
Ps 35:23 my judgment, even unto my **c.**, 7379
Ps 35:27 glad, that favour my righteous **c.**:
Ps 43:1 plead my **c.** against an ungodly 7379
Ps 67:1 bless us; and **c.** his face to shine
Ps 69:4 that hate me without a **c.** are 2600
Ps 71:2 and **c.** me to escape: incline
Ps 74:22 Arise, O God, plead thine own **c.**: 7379
Ps 76:8 Thou didst **c.** judgment to be
Ps 80:3 and **c.** thy face to shine; and we
Ps 80:7 of hosts, and **c.** thy face to shine;
Ps 80:9 and didst **c.** it to take deep root,
Ps 80:19 God of hosts, **c.** thy face to shine;
Ps 85:4 and **c.** thine anger toward us to
Ps 109:3 fought against me without a **c.** 2600

Ps 119:78 perversely with me without a **c.**: 8267
Ps 119:154 Plead my **c.**, and deliver me: 7379
Ps 119:161 persecuted me without a **c.**: 2600
Ps 140:12 Lord will maintain the **c.** of the 1779
Ps 143:8 **C.** me to hear thy lovingkindness
Ps 143:8 **c.** me to know the way wherein
Pr 1:11 for the innocent without **c.**: 2600
Pr 3:30 Strive not with a man without **c.**, 2600
Pr 4:16 away, unless they **c.** some to fall
Pr 8:21 That I may **c.** those that love me
Pr 18:17 He that is first in his own **c.** 7379
Pr 22:23 the Lord will plead their **c.**, and 7379
Pr 23:11 mighty; he shall plead their **c.** 7379
Pr 23:29 who hath wounds without **c.**? 2600
Pr 24:28 against thy neighbour without **c.**; 2600
Pr 25:9 Debate thy **c.** with thy neighbour 7379
Pr 29:7 The righteous considereth the **c.** 1779
Pr 31:8 dumb in the **c.** of all such as are 1779
Pr 31:9 and plead the **c.** of the poor and
Ec 2:20 to **c.** my heart to despair of all
Ec 5:6 Suffer not thy mouth to **c.** thy
Ec 7:10 What is the **c.** that the former 1961
Ec 10:1 **c.** the ointment of the apothecary
Ca 8:1 I would **c.** thee to drink of spiced
Ca 8:13 hearken to thy voice: **c.** me to
Isa 1:23 neither doth the **c.** of the widow 7379
Isa 3:12 they which lead thee **c.** thee to
Isa 9:16 leaders of this people **c.** them to
Isa 10:30 **c.** it to be heard unto Laish, O
Isa 13:10 moon shall not **c.** her light to
Isa 13:11 and I will **c.** the arrogancy of the
Isa 27:6 He shall **c.** them that come of
Isa 28:12 ye may **c.** the weary to rest;
Isa 30:11 **c.** the Holy One of Israel to cease
Isa 30:30 And the Lord shall **c.** his glorious
Isa 32:6 he will **c.** the drink of the thirsty
Isa 37:7 and I will **c.** him to fall by the
Isa 41:21 Produce your **c.**, saith the Lord; 7379
Isa 42:2 nor **c.** his voice to be heard in the
Isa 49:8 the earth, to **c.** to inherit the
Isa 51:22 thy God that pleadeth the **c.** of
Isa 52:4 oppressed them without **c.**. 657
Isa 58:14 and I will **c.** thee to ride upon
Isa 61:11 the Lord God will **c.** righteousness
Isa 66:9 to the birth, and not **c.** to bring
Isa 66:9 shall I **c.** to bring forth, and shut
Jer 3:12 and I will not **c.** mine anger to
Jer 5:28 judge not the **c.**, the **c.** of the 1779
Jer 7:3 and I will **c.** you to dwell in this
Jer 7:7 Then will I **c.** you to dwell in this
Jer 7:34 Then will I **c.** to cease from the
Jer 11:20 unto thee have I revealed my **c.**. 7379
Jer 13:16 before he **c.** darkness, and before
Jer 14:22 of the Gentiles that can **c.** rain?
Jer 15:4 And I will **c.** them to be removed 5414
Jer 15:11 **c.** the enemy to entreat thee well
Jer 16:9 Behold, I will **c.** to cease out of
Jer 16:21 I will this once **c.** them to know,
Jer 16:21 I will **c.** them to know mine hand
Jer 17:4 and I will **c.** thee to serve thine
Jer 18:2 and there I will **c.** thee to hear
Jer 19:7 and I will **c.** them to fall by the
Jer 19:9 And I will **c.** them to eat the flesh
Jer 20:12 unto thee have I opened my **c.**. 7379
Jer 22:16 He judged the **c.** of the poor and 1779
Jer 23:27 which think to **c.** my people to
Jer 23:32 and **c.** my people to err by their
Jer 25:15 and **c.** all the nations, to whom I
Jer 29:8 to your dreams which ye **c.** to be
Jer 30:3 and I will **c.** them to return to
Jer 30:13 none to plead thy **c.**, that thou 1779
Jer 30:21 and I will **c.** him to draw near,
Jer 31:2 when I went to **c.** him to rest.
Jer 31:9 I will **c.** them to walk by the
Jer 32:35 **c.** their sons and their daughters 4616
Jer 32:35 abomination, to **c.** Judah to sin.
Jer 32:37 this place, and I will **c.** them to
Jer 32:44 I will **c.** their captivity to return,
Jer 33:7 And I will **c.** the captivity of
Jer 33:11 I will **c.** to return the captivity of
Jer 33:15 **c.** the Branch of righteousness
Jer 33:26 I will **c.** their captivity to return,
Jer 34:22 the Lord, and **c.** them to return
Jer 36:29 and shall **c.** to cease from thence
Jer 37:20 that thou **c.** me not to return to
Jer 38:23 thou shalt **c.** this city to be
Jer 38:26 that he would not **c.** me to return
Jer 42:12 and **c.** you to return to your own
Jer 48:12 that shall **c.** him to wander, and
Jer 48:35 Moreover I will **c.** to cease in
Jer 49:2 that I will **c.** an alarm of war to
Jer 49:37 For I will **c.** Elam to be dismayed
Jer 50:9 I will raise and **c.** to come up
Jer 50:34 he shall throughly plead their **c.**, 7379
Jer 51:27 **c.** the horses to come up as the
Jer 51:36 I will plead thy **c.**,and take 7379
La 3:32 though he **c.** grief, yet will he
La 3:36 To subvert a man in his **c.**, the 7379
La 3:52 me sore, like a bird, without **c.** 2600
La 3:59 seen my wrong: judge thou my **c.**. 4941
Eze 3:3 **c.** thy belly to eat, and fill thy bowels
Eze 5:1 and **c.** it to pass upon thine head
Eze 5:13 I will **c.** my fury to rest upon
Eze 9:1 **C.** them that have charge over the
Eze 14:15 If I **c.** noisome beasts to pass through
Eze 14:23 that I have not done without **c.** all 2600
Eze 16:2 **c.** Jerusalem to know her
Eze 16:21 **c.** them to pass through the fire
Eze 16:41 and I will **c.** thee to cease from
Eze 20:4 **c.** them to know the abominations
Eze 20:37 I will **c.** you to pass under the rod,
Eze 21:17 and I will **c.** my fury to rest:
Eze 21:30 Shall I **c.** it to return into his sheath?
Eze 23:48 Thus will I **c.** lewdness to cease out of
Eze 24:8 That it might **c.** fury to come up to
Eze 24:26 to **c.** thee to hear it with thine ears?
Eze 25:7 and I will **c.** thee to perish out of the
Eze 26:3 and will **c.** many nations to come up
Eze 26:13 And I will **c.** the noise of thy songs to
Eze 26:17 inhabitants, which **c.** their terror 5414
Eze 27:30 shall **c.** their voice to be heard
Eze 29:4 I will **c.** the fish of thy rivers to stick
Eze 29:14 will **c.** them to return into the land
Eze 29:21 I **c.** the horn of the house of Israel
Eze 30:13 I will **c.** their image to cease out of
Eze 30:22 and I will **c.** the sword to fall out of
Eze 32:4 will **c.** all the fowls of the heaven to
Eze 32:12 will I **c.** thy multitude to fall, the
Eze 32:14 **c.** their rivers to run like oil, saith the
Eze 34:10 **c.** them to cease from feeding the
Eze 34:15 I will **c.** them to lie down, saith the
Eze 34:25 and will **c.** the evil beasts to cease out
Eze 34:26 I will **c.** the shower to come down in
Eze 36:12 Yea, I will **c.** men to walk upon
Eze 36:15 Neither will I **c.** men to hear in
Eze 36:15 neither shalt thou **c.** thy nations to fall
Eze 36:27 and **c.** you to walk in my statutes,
Eze 36:33 I will also **c.** you to dwell in the cities,
Eze 37:5 Behold, I will **c.** breath to enter into
Eze 37:12 open your graves, and **c.** you to come
Eze 39:2 will **c.** thee to come up from the
Eze 39:3 and will **c.** thine arrows to fall out of
Eze 44:23 and **c.** them to discern between the
Eze 44:30 he may **c.** the blessing to rest in
Da 2:12 For this **c.** the king 3606,6903,1836
Da 8:25 also he shall **c.** craft to prosper in
Da 9:17 and **c.** thy face to shine upon thy
Da 9:27 shall **c.** the sacrifice and the oblation
Da 11:18 shall **c.** the reproach offered by him
Da 11:18 his own reproch he shall **c.** it to cease;
Da 11:39 he shall **c.** them to rule over many,
Ho 1:4 will **c.** to cease the kingdom of the
Ho 2:11 I will also **c.** all her mirth to cease,
Joe 2:23 he will **c.** to come down for you the
Joe 3:11 **c.** thy mighty ones to come down,
Am 5:27 Therefore will I **c.** you to go into
Am 6:3 and **c.** the seat of violence to come
Am 8:9 I will **c.** the sun to go down at noon,
Jon 1:7 may know for whose **c.** this evil is 7945
Jon 1:8 for whose **c.** this evil is upon us? 834
Mic 7:9 until he plead my **c.**, and execute 7379
Hab 1:3 and **c.** me to behold grievance?
Zec 8:12 and I will **c.** the remnant of this
Zec 13:2 I will **c.** the prophets and the unclean
Mt 5:22 **with his brother without a c.** *1500*
Mt 5:32 **saving for the c. of fornication** *3056*
Mt 10:21 **and c. them to be put to death** *2289*
Mt 19:3 put away his wife for every **c.**? *156*
Mt 19:5 **For this c. shall a man leave** *1752*
Mk 10:7 **For this c. shall a man leave his** *1752*
Mk 13:12 **shall c. them to be put to death.** *2289*
Lu 8:47 for what **c.** she had touched him, *156*
Lu 21:16 **some of you shall they c. to be** *2289*
Lu 23:22 I have found no **c.** of death in him: *158*
Joh 12:18 For this **c.** the people also met him, *1223*
Joh 12:27 **for this c. came I unto this hour** *1223*
Joh 15:25 **law, They hated me without a c.** *1432*
Joh 18:37 **this c. came I into the world,**
Ac 10:21 what is the **c.** wherefore ye are *156*
Ac 13:28 though they found no **c.** of death *156*
Ac 19:40 there being no **c.** whereby we may *158*
Ac 23:28 when I would have known the **c.** *156*
Ac 25:14 Festus declared Paul's **c.** *3588,2596*
Ac 28:18 there was no **c.** of death in me *156*
Ac 28:20 For this **c.** therefore have I called *156*
Ro 1:26 For this **c.** God gave them *1223*
Ro 13:6 For for this **c.** pay ye tribute *1223*
Ro 15:9 For this **c.** I will confess to *1223*
Ro 15:22 For which **c.** also I have been *1352*
Ro 16:17 mark them which **c.** divisions *4160*
1Co 4:17 For this **c.** have I sent unto *1223*
1Co 11:10 For this **c.** ought the woman *1223*
1Co 11:30 For this **c.** many are weak *1223*
2Co 4:16 For which **c.** we faint not; but *1352*
2Co 5:13 we be sober, it is for your **c.**.
2Co 7:12 not for his **c.** that had done the *1752*
2Co 7:12 nor for his **c.** that suffered wrong, *1752*
Eph 3:1 For this **c.** I Paul, the prisoner of *5484*
Eph 3:14 For this **c.** I bow my knees unto *5484*
Eph 5:31 For this **c.** shall a man leave his *873*
Php 2:18 For the same **c.** also do ye joy, *846*
Col 1:9 For this **c.** we also, since *1223,5124*
Col 4:16 **c.** that it be read also in the *4160*
1Th 2:13 For this **c.** also thank we God *1223*
1Th 3:5 For this **c.**, when I could no longer *1223*
2Th 2:11 for this **c.** God shall send them *1223*
1Ti 1:16 Howbeit for this **c.** I obtained *1223*
2Ti 1:12 For the which **c.** I also suffer *156*
Tit 1:5 For this **c.** left I thee in Crete, *5484*
Heb 2:11 for which **c.** he is not ashamed to *156*
Heb 9:15 for this **c.** he is the mediator *1223*
1Pe 4:6 for this **c.** was the gospel
Re 12:15 he might **c.** her to be carried *4160*
Re 13:15 and **c.** that as many as would not *4160*

CAUSED

Ge 2:5 the Lord God had not **c.** it to rain
Ge 2:21 And the Lord God **c.** a deep sleep to
Ge 20:13 when God **c.** me to wander from my
Ge 41:52 God hath **c.** me to be fruitful
Ex 14:21 and the Lord **c.** the sea to go
Ex 36:6 and they **c.** it to be proclaimed
Le 24:20 as he hath **c.** a blemish in a man 5414
Nu 31:16 Behold, these **c.** the children of 1961
De 34:4 I have **c.** thee to see it with
Jg 16:19 she **c.** him to shave off the seven
1Sa 10:20 when Samuel had **c.** all the tribes
1Sa 10:21 When he had **c.** the tribe of Benjamin
1Sa 20:17 Jonathan **c.** David to swear again,
2Sa 7:11 and have **c.** thee to rest from all
1Ki 1:38 and **c.** Solomon to ride upon king
1Ki 1:44 and they have **c.** him to ride upon
1Ki 2:19 and **c.** a seat to be set for the king's
1Ki 20:33 he **c.** him to come up into the chariot
2Ki 17:17 And they **c.** their sons and their
2Ch 8:2 and **c.** the children of Israel to dwell
2Ch 13:13 Jeroboam **c.** an ambushment to come
2Ch 21:11 **c.** the inhabitants of Jerusalem
2Ch 33:6 he **c.** his children to pass through the
2Ch 34:32 And he **c.** all . . . to stand to it.
Ezr 6:12 God that hath **c.** his name to dwell
Ne 8:7 **c.** the people to understand the law:
Ne 8:8 and **c.** them to understand the
Es 5:14 and he **c.** the gallows to be made.
Job 29:13 I **c.** the widow's heart to sing for joy.
Job 31:16 have **c.** the eyes of the widow to fail;
Job 31:39 have **c.** the owners thereof to lose
Job 37:15 and **c.** the light of his cloud to
Job 38:12 **c.** the dayspring to know his place;
Ps 66:12 Thou hast **c.** men to ride over our
Ps 78:13 the sea, and **c.** them to pass through;
Ps 78:16 and **c.** waters to run down like rivers
Ps 78:26 He **c.** an east wind to blow
Ps 119:49 upon which thou hast **c.** me to
Pr 7:21 With her much fair speech she **c.**
Isa 19:14 and they have **c.** Egypt to err
Isa 43:23 I have not **c.** thee to serve with
Isa 48:21 he **c.** the waters to flow out of the rock
Isa 63:14 the Spirit of the Lord **c.** him to rest:
Jer 12:14 I have **c.** my people Israel to inherit;
Jer 13:11 so have I **c.** to cleave unto me

Jer 15:8 I have c. him to fall upon it
Jer 18:15 they have c. them to stumble in
Jer 23:13 and c. my people Israel to err.
Jer 23:22 had c. my people to hear my words,
Jer 29:4 whom I have c. to be carried away
Jer 29:7 I have c. you to be carried away
Jer 29:14 I c. you to be carried away captive.
Jer 29:31 him not, and he c. you to trust in a lie:
Jer 32:23 therefore thou hast c. all this evil to
Jer 34:11 c. the servants and the handmaids,
Jer 34:16 c. every man his servant, and every
Jer 48:4 little ones have c. a cry to be heard
Jer 48:33 I have c. wine to fail from the
Jer 50:6 shepherds have c. them to go astray,
Jer 51:49 As Babylon hath c. the slain
La 2:6 c. the solemn feasts and sabbaths to
La 2:17 he hath c. thine enemy to rejoice
La 3:13 He hath c. the arrows of his quiver
Eze 3:2 mouth, and he c. me to eat that roll.
Eze 16:7 I have c. thee to multiply as the 5414
Eze 20:10 Wherefore I c. them to go forth out of
Eze 20:26 in that they c. to pass through the fire
Eze 22:4 and thou hast c. thy days to draw near,
Eze 23:37 c. their sons, whom they bare unto me,
Eze 24:13 have c. my fury to rest upon thee,
Eze 29:18 king of Babylon c. his army to serve
Eze 31:15 down to the grave I c. a mourning:
Eze 31:15 and I c. Lebanon to mourn for him,
Eze 32:23 c. terror in the land of the living. 5414
Eze 32:24 which c. their terror in the land 5414
Eze 32:25 their terror was c. in the land 5414
Eze 32:26 they c. their terror in the land of 5414
Eze 32:32 I have c. my terror in the land 5414
Eze 37:2 And c. me to pass by them round
Eze 39:28 which c. them to be led into captivity
Eze 44:12 c. the house of Israel to fall into
Eze 46:21 and c. me to pass by the four corners
Eze 47:6 and c. me to return to the brink
Da 9:21 being c. to fly swiftly, touched me
Ho 4:12 hath c. them to err, and they have
Am 2:4 and their lies c. them to err, after the
Am 4:7 and I c. it to rain upon one city,
Am 4:7 c. it not to rain upon another city:
Jon 3:7 And he c. it to be proclaimed and
Zec 3:4 c. thine iniquity to pass from thee,
Mal 2:8 ye have c. many to stumble at the law;
Joh 11:37 eyes of the blind, have c. that *4160*
Ac 15:3 they c. great joy unto all the *4160*
2Co 2:5 if any have c. grief, he hath not *3076*

CAUSELESS

1Sa 25:31 that thou hast shed blood c., 2600
Pr 26:2 by flying, so the curse c. shall

CAUSES

Ex 18:19 that thou mayest bring the c. 1697
Ex 18:26 hard c. they brought unto Moses, 1697
De 1:16 Hear the c. between your brethren,
Jer 3:8 I saw, when for all the c. whereby 182
La 2:14 for thee false burdens and c. of
La 3:58 O Lord, thou hast pleaded the c. 7379
Ac 26:21 For these c. the Jews caught me *1752*

CAUSEST

Job 30:22 thou c. me to ride upon it, and
Ps 65:4 man whom thou choosest, and c. to

CAUSETH

Nu 5:18 the bitter water that c. the curse:
Nu 5:19 free from this bitter water that c.
Nu 5:22 this water that c. the curse shall go
Nu 5:24 the bitter water that c. the curse:
Nu 5:24 and the water that c. the curse
Nu 5:27 that the water that c. the curse shall
Job 12:24 c. them to wander in a wilderness
Job 20:3 my understanding c. me to answer.
Job 37:13 He c. it to come, whether for
Ps 104:14 He c. the grass to grow for the cattle,
Ps 107:40 c. them to wander in the wilderness,
Ps 135:7 He c. the vapours to ascent from the
Ps 147:18 he c. his wind to blow, and the
Pr 10:5 in harvest is a son that c. shame.
Pr 10:10 winketh with the eye c. sorrow: 5414
Pr 14:35 wrath is against him that c. shame.
Pr 17:2 have rule over a son that c. shame,
Pr 18:18 The lot c. contentions to cease,
Pr 19:26 a son that c. shame, and bringeth
Pr 19:27 hear the instruction that c. to err
Pr 28:10 c. the righteous to go astray in an
Isa 61:11 the garden c. the things that are
Isa 64:2 fire burneth, the fire c. the waters to
Jer 10:13 and he c. the vapours to ascend from
Jer 51:16 in the heavens; and he c. the vapours
Eze 26:3 as the sea c. his waves to come up.
Eze 44:18 gird themselves with anything that c.
Mt 5:32 **c. her to commit adultery: and** *4160*
2Co 2:14 c. us to triumph in Christ, and *2358*
2Co 9:11 c. through us thanksgiving to *2716*
Re 13:12 beast before him, and c. the *4160*
Re 13:16 he c. all, both small and great, *4160*

CAUSEWAY

1Ch 26:16 by the c. of the going up, ward 4546
1Ch 26:18 four at the c., and two at Parbar 4546

CAUSING

Ca 7:9 c. the lips of those that are asleep
Isa 30:28 in the jaws of the people, c. them to
Jer 29:10 in c. you to return to this place.
Jer 33:12 of shepherds, c. their flocks to lie

CAVE See also CAVES.

Ge 19:30 and he dwelt in a c., he and his two 4631
Ge 23:9 That he may give me the c. of 4631
Ge 23:11 the field give I thee, and the c. 4631
Ge 23:17 field, and the c. which was therein, 4631
Ge 23:19 in the c. of the field of Machpelah 4631
Ge 23:20 field, and the c. that is therein, 4631
Ge 25:9 buried him in the c. of Machpelah 4631
Ge 49:29 in the c. that is in the field of 4631
Ge 49:30 In the c. that is in the field of 4631
Ge 49:32 purchase of the field and of the c. 4631
Ge 50:13 buried him in the c. of the field 4631
Jos 10:16 hid themselves in a c. at 4631
Jos 10:17 five kings are found hid in a c. 4631
Jos 10:18 stones upon the mouth of the c., 4631
Jos 10:22 Open the mouth of the c., and 4631
Jos 10:22 five kings unto me out of the c. 4631
Jos 10:23 five kings unto him out of the c., 4631
Jos 10:27 cast them into the c. wherein they 4631
1Sa 22:1 and escaped to the c. Adullam: 4631
1Sa 24:3 where was a c.; and Saul went in 4631
1Sa 24:3 remained in the sides of the c. 4631
1Sa 24:7 Saul rose up out of the c., and 4631
1Sa 24:8 went out of the c., and cried after 4631
1Sa 24:10 to day into mine hand in the c.: 4631
2Sa 23:13 in the harvest time unto the c. 4631
1Ki 18:4 hid them by fifty in a c., and fed 4631
1Ki 18:13 Lord's prophets by fifty in a c., 4631
1Ki 19:9 he came thither unto a c., and 4631
1Ki 19:13 stood in the entering in of the c. 4631
1Ch 11:15 into the c. of Adullam; and the 4631
Ps 57:*title* he fled from Saul in the c. 4631
Ps 142:*title* A Prayer when he was in the c. 4631
Joh 11:38 It was a c., and a stone lay upon *4693*

CAVE'S

Jos 10:27 laid great stones in the c. 4631

CAVES

Jg 6:2 in the mountains, and c., and 4631
1Sa 13:6 people did hide themselves in c., 4631
Job 30:6 cliffs of the valleys, in c. of the 2356
Isa 2:19 into the c. of the earth, for fear 4247
Eze 33:27 in the forts and in the c. shall die 4631
Heb 11:38 mountains, and in dens and c. *3692*

CEASE See also CEASED; CEASETH; CEASING.

Ge 8:22 and day and night shall not c. 7673
Ex 9:29 the thunder shall c., neither shall 2308
Nu 8:25 years they shall c. waiting upon 7725
Nu 11:25 they prophesied, and did not c. 3254
Nu 17:5 and I will make to c. from me the 7918
De 15:11 For the poor shall never c. out of 2308
De 32:26 the remembrance of them to c. 7673
Jos 22:25 children make our children c. 7673
Jg 15:7 of you, and after that I will c. 2308
Jg 20:28 or shall I c.? And the Lord said, 2308
1Sa 7:8 C. not to cry unto the Lord our 2790
2Ch 16:5 of Ramah, and let his work c. 7673
Ezr 4:21 to cause these men to c., 989
Ezr 4:23 and made them to c. by force and 989
Ezr 5:5 they could not cause them to c., 989
Ne 4:11 them, and cause the work to c. 7673
Ne 6:3 why should the work c., whilst I 7673
Job 3:17 the wicked c. from troubling; 2308
Job 10:20 C. then, and let me alone, that I 2308
Job 14:7 tender branch thereof will not c. 2308
Ps 37:8 C. from anger, and forsake 7503
Ps 46:9 He maketh wars to c. unto the 7673
Ps 85:4 cause thine anger toward us to c. 6565
Ps 89:44 Thou hast made his glory to c., 7673
Pr 18:18 The lot causeth contentions to c., 7673
Pr 19:27 C., my son, to hear the instruction 2308
Pr 20:3 It is an honour for a man to c. 7674
Pr 22:10 yea, strife and reproach shall c. 7673
Pr 23:4 c. from thine own wisdom. 2308
Ec 12:3 and the grinder c. because they 988
Isa 1:16 before mine eyes; c. to do evil: 2308
Isa 2:22 C. ye from man, whose breath is 2308
Isa 10:25 and the indignation shall c., 3615
Isa 13:11 the arrogancy of the proud to c., 7673
Isa 16:10 their vintage shouting to c. 7673
Isa 17:3 The fortress also shall c. from 7673
Isa 21:2 sighing thereof have I made to c. 7673
Isa 30:11 cause the Holy One of Israel to c. 7673
Isa 33:1 when thou shalt c. to spoil, thou 8552
Jer 7:34 Then will I cause to c. from the 7673
Jer 14:17 and day, and let them not c.: 1820
Jer 16:9 I will cause to c. out of this place 7673
Jer 17:8 drought, neither shall c. from 4185
Jer 31:36 the seed of Israel also shall c. 7673
Jer 36:29 and shall cause to c. from thence 7673
Jer 48:35 I will cause to c. in Moab, saith 7673
La 2:18 let not the apple of thine eye c. 1826
Eze 6:6 your idols may be broken and c., 7673
Eze 7:24 the pomp of the strong to c.; 7673
Eze 12:23 I will make this proverb to c., 7673
Eze 16:41 and I will cause thee to c. from 7673
Eze 23:27 will I make thy lewdness to c. 7673
Eze 23:48 Thus will I cause lewdness to c. 7673
Eze 26:13 cause the noise of thy songs to c.; 7673
Eze 30:10 make the multitude of Egypt to c. 7673
Eze 30:13 I will cause their images to c., 7673
Eze 30:18 the pomp of her strength shall c. 7673
Eze 33:28 the pomp of her strength shall c.; 7673
Eze 34:10 and cause them to c. from feeding 7673
Eze 34:25 and will cause the evil beasts to c. 7673
Da 9:27 sacrifice and the oblation to c., 7673
Da 11:18 reproach offered by him to c.; 7673
Ho 1:4 and will cause to c. the kingdom 7673
Ho 2:11 will also cause all her mirth to c., 7673
Am 7:5 O Lord God, c., I beseech thee: 2308
Ac 13:10 wilt thou not c. to pervert the *3973*
1Co 13:8 there be tongues, they shall c.; *3973*
Eph 1:16 C. not to give thanks for you, *3973*
Col 1:9 do not c. to pray for you, and to *3973*
2Pe 2:14 that cannot c. from sin; beguiling *180*

CEASED

Ge 18:11 it c. to be with Sarah after the 2308
Ex 9:33 and the thunders and hail c., 2308
Ex 9:34 hail and the thunders were c., 2308
Jos 5:12 and the manna c. on the morrow 7673
Jg 2:19 c. not from their own doings, 5307
Jg 5:7 the villages c., they c. in Israel, 2308
1Sa 2:5 they that were hungry c.: so that 2308
1Sa 25:9 in the name of David, and c. 5117
Ezr 4:24 Then c. the work of the house of 989
Ezr 4:24 So it c. unto the second year 1934,989
Job 32:1 these three men c. to answer Job, 7673
Ps 35:15 they did tear me, and c. not: 1826
Ps 77:2 my sore ran in the night, and c. 6313
Isa 14:4 How hath the oppressor c.! 7673
Isa 14:4 the golden city c.! 7673
La 5:14 The elders have c. from the gate, 7673
La 5:15 The joy of our heart is c.; our 7673
Jon 1:15 and the sea c. from her raging 5975
Mt 14:32 come into the ship, the wind c. *2869*
Mk 4:39 the wind c., and there was a great *2869*
Mk 6:51 the wind c.: and they were sore *2869*
Lu 7:45 **came in hath not c. to kiss my** *1257*
Lu 8:24 they c., and there was a calm. *3973*
Lu 11:1 when he c., one of his disciples *3973*
Ac 5:42 they c. not to teach and preach *3973*
Ac 20:1 And after the uproar was c., Paul *3973*
Ac 20:31 I c. not to warn every one night *3973*
Ac 21:14 not be persuaded, we c., saying, *2270*
Ga 5:11 then is the offence of the cross c. *2673*
Heb 4:10 he also hath c. from his own *2664*
Heb 10:2 would they not have c. to be *3973*
1Pe 4:1 suffered in the flesh hath c. from *3973*

CEASETH

Ps 12:1 Help, Lord, for the godly man c.; 1584
Ps 49:8 is precious, and it c. for ever:) 2308
Pr 26:20 there is no talebearer, the strife c. 8367

Isa 16:4 the spoiler **c.**, the oppressors are 3615
Isa 24:8 The mirth of tabrets **c.**, the noise 7673
Isa 24:8 endeth, the joy of the harp **c.** 7673
Isa 33:8 lie waste, the wayfaring man **c.**: 7673
La 3:49 eye trickleth down, and **c.** not, 1820
Ho 7:4 who **c.** from raising after he hath 7673
Ac 6:13 This man **c.** not to speak *3973*

CEASING
1Sa 12:23 the Lord in **c.** to pray for you: 2308
Ac 12:5 prayer was made without **c.** of *1618*
Ro 1:9 that without **c.** I make mention of *89*
1Th 1:3 Remembering without **c.** your *89*
1Th 2:13 also thank we God without **c.**, *89*
1Th 5:17 Pray without **c.** *89*
2Ti 1:3 without **c.** I have remembrance *83*

CEDAR See also CEDARS.
Le 14:4 **c.** wood, and scarlet, and hyssop: 730
Le 14:6 the **c.** wood, and the scarlet, and 730
Le 14:49 two birds, and **c.** wood, and scarlet, 730
Le 14:51 he shall take the **c.** wood, and the 730
Le 14:52 the **c.** wood, and with the hyssop, 730
Nu 19:6 the priest shall take **c.** wood, 730
Nu 24:6 and as **c.** trees beside the waters. 730
2Sa 5:11 **c.** trees, and carpenters, and 730
2Sa 7:2 I dwell in an house of **c.**, but the 730
2Sa 7:7 build ye not me an house of **c.**? 730
1Ki 4:33 from the **c.** tree that is in Lebanon 730
1Ki 5:6 hew me **c.** trees out of Lebanon; 730
1Ki 5:8 concerning timber of **c.**, and 730
1Ki 5:10 Hiram gave Solomon **c.** trees and fir 730
1Ki 6:9 house with beams and boards of **c.** 730
1Ki 6:10 on the house with timber of **c.** 730
1Ki 6:15 the house within with boards of **c.**, 730
1Ki 6:16 and the walls with boards of **c.**: 730
1Ki 6:18 **c.** of the house within was caved 730
1Ki 6:18 was **c.**; there was not stone seen. 730
1Ki 6:20 covered the altar which was of **c.** 730
1Ki 6:36 hewed stone, and a row of **c.** beams. 730
1Ki 7:2 upon four rows of **c.** pillars, 730
1Ki 7:2 with **c.** beams upon the pillars. 730
1Ki 7:3 And it was covered with **c.** above 730
1Ki 7:7 covered with **c.** from one side of 730
1Ki 7:12 a row of **c.** beams, both for the inner 730
1Ki 9:11 furnished Solomon with **c.** trees 730
2Ki 14:9 sent to the **c.** that was in Lebanon, 730
2Ki 19:23 and will cut down the tall **c.** trees 730
1Ch 22:4 Also **c.** trees in abundance: for the 730
1Ch 22:4 they of Tyre brought much **c.** wood 730
2Ch 1:15 **c.** trees made he as the sycomore 730
2Ch 2:8 Send me also **c.** trees, fir trees, and 730
2Ch 9:27 in Jerusalem as stones, and **c.** 730
2Ch 25:18 was in Lebanon sent to the **c.** that 730
Ezr 3:7 to bring **c.** trees from Lebanon 730
Job 40:17 He moveth his tail like a **c.**: the 730
Ps 92:12 he shall grow like a **c.** in Lebanon. 730
Ca 1:17 The beams of our house are **c.**, 730
Ca 8:9 we will inclose her with boards of **c.** 730
Isa 41:19 plant in the wilderness the **c.**, the 730
Jer 22:14 cieled with **c.**, and painted with 730
Jer 22:15 thou closest thyself in **c.**? did not 730
Eze 17:3 took the highest branch of the **c.** 730
Eze 17:22 the highest branch of the high **c.**, 730
Eze 17:23 be a goodly **c.**: and under it shall 730
Eze 27:24 bound with cords, and made of **c.**, 729
Eze 31:3 the Assyrian was a **c.** in Lebanon 730
Zep 2:14 for he shall uncover the **c.** work. 731
Zec 11:2 for the **c.** is fallen; because the 730

CEDARS
Jg 9:15 and devour the **c.** of Lebanon. 730
1Ki 7:11 measures of hewed stones, and **c.** 730
1Ki 10:27 **c.** made he to be as the sycomore 730
1Ch 14:1 timber of **c.**, with masons and 730
1Ch 17:1 I dwell in an house of **c.**, but the 730
1Ch 17:6 ye not built me an house of **c.**? 730
2Ch 2:3 send him **c.** to build him an house 730
Ps 29:5 the Lord breaketh the **c.**; yea, 730
Ps 29:5 the Lord breaketh the **c.** of 730
Ps 80:10 thereof were like the goodly **c.** 730
Ps 104:16 **c.** of Lebanon, which he hath 730
Ps 148:9 all hills; fruitful trees, and all **c.**: 730
Ca 5:15 as Lebanon, excellent as the **c.**, 730
Isa 2:13 upon all the **c.** of Lebanon, that 730
Isa 9:10 but we will change them into **c.**, 730
Isa 14:8 the **c.** of Lebanon, saying, Since 730
Isa 37:24 cut down the tall **c.** thereof, and 730
Isa 44:14 He heweth him down **c.**, and taketh 730
Jer 22:7 shall cut down thy choice **c.**, and 730
Jer 22:23 that makest thy nest in the **c.**, how 730
Eze 27:5 they have taken **c.** from Lebanon to 730
Eze 31:8 The **c.** in the garden of God could 730
Am 2:9 like the height of the **c.**, and he 730
Zec 11:1 that the fire may devour thy **c.** 730

CEDAR-TREE See CEDAR and TREE.

CEDAR-WOOD See CEDAR and WOOD.

CEDRON (se'-drun) See also KIDRON.
Joh 18:1 over the brook **C.**, where was a *2748*

CEILED See CIELED.

CEILING See CIELING.

CELEBRATE
Le 23:32 even, shall ye **c.** your sabbath. 7673
Le 23:41 shall **c.** it in the seventh month. 2287
Isa 38:18 praise thee, death can not **c.** thee: 1984

CELESTIAL
1Co 15:40 There are also **c.** bodies, and *2032*
1Co 15:40 but the glory of the **c.** is one, *2032*

CELLARS
1Ch 27:27 for the wine **c.** was Zabdi the 214
1Ch 27:28 and over the **c.** of oil was Joash: 214

CENCHREA (sen'-kre-ah)
Ac 18:18 having shorn his head in **C.** *2747*
Ro 16:1 of the church which is at **C.** *2747*
Ro *subscr.* servant of the church at **C.**

CENSER See also CENSERS.
Le 10:1 took either of them his **c.**, and put 4289
Le 16:12 shall take a **c.** full of burning coals 4289
Nu 16:17 take every man his **c.**, and put 4289
Nu 16:17 before the Lord every man his **c.**, 4289
Nu 16:17 and Aaron, each of you his **c.** 4289
Nu 16:18 took every man his **c.**, and put fire 4289
Nu 16:46 Take a **c.**, and put fire therein 4289
2Ch 26:19 a **c.** in his hand to burn incense: 4730
Eze 8:11 with every man his **c.** in his hand; 4730
Heb 9:4 Which had the golden **c.**, and the *2369*
Re 8:3 at the altar, having a golden **c.**; *3031*
Re 8:5 took the **c.**, and filled it with fire *3031*

CENSERS
Nu 4:14 the **c.**, the fleshhooks, and the 4289
Nu 16:6 This do; Take you **c.**, Korah, and 4289
Nu 16:17 two hundred and fifty **c.**; thou 4289
Nu 16:37 take up the **c.** out of the burning, 4289
Nu 16:38 The **c.** of these sinners against their 4289
Nu 16:39 the priest took the brasen **c.**, 4289
1Ki 7:50 spoons, and the **c.** of pure gold; 4289
2Ch 4:22 spoons, and the **c.**, of pure gold: 4289

CENTURION (sen-too'-ree-un) See also CENTURION'S; CENTURIONS.
Mt 8:5 unto him a **c.**, beseeching him, *1543*
Mt 8:8 The **c.** answered and said, Lord, *1543*
Mt 8:13 Jesus said unto the **c.**, Go thy way; *1543*
Mt 27:54 **c.**, and they that were with him, *1543*
Mk 15:39 **c.**, which stood over against him, *2760*
Mk 15:44 calling unto him the **c.**, he asked *2760*
Mk 15:45 when he knew it of the **c.**, he gave *2760*
Lu 7:6 the **c.** sent friends to him, saying *1543*
Lu 23:47 when the **c.** saw what was done, *1543*
Ac 10:1 **c.** of the band called the Italian *1543*
Ac 10:22 they said, Cornelius the **c.**, a just *1543*
Ac 22:25 Paul said unto the **c.** that stood by, *1543*
Ac 22:26 When the **c.** heard that, he went *1543*
Ac 24:23 commanded a **c.** to keep Paul, *1543*
Ac 27:1 Julius, a **c.** of Augustus' band. *1543*
Ac 27:6 there the **c.** found a ship of *1543*
Ac 27:11 the **c.** believed the master and the *1543*
Ac 27:31 Paul said to the **c.** and to the *1543*
Ac 27:43 the **c.**, willing to save Paul, kept *1543*
Ac 28:16 the **c.** delivered the prisoners to *1543*

CENTURION'S (sen-too'-ree-uns)
Lu 7:2 a certain **c.** servant, who was dear *1543*

CENTURIONS (sen-too'-ree-uns)
Ac 21:32 immediately took soldiers and **c.**, *1543*
Ac 23:17 Paul called one of the **c.** unto him, *1543*
Ac 23:23 he called unto him two **c.**, saying, *1543*

CEPHAS (se'-fas) See also PETER.
Joh 1:42 thou shalt be called **C.**, which is *2786*
1Co 1:12 and I of Apollos; and I of **C.**; *2786*
1Co 3:22 Whether Paul, or Apollos, or **C.**, *2786*
1Co 9:5 as the brethren of the Lord, and **C.**? *2786*
1Co 15:5 he was seen of **C.**, then of the *2786*
Ga 2:9 And when James, **C.**, and John, *2786*

CEREMONIES
Nu 9:3 all the **c.** thereof, shall ye keep it. 4941

CERTAIN See also UNCERTAIN.
Ge 28:11 And he lighted upon a **c.** place,
Ge 37:15 And a **c.** man found him, and
Ge 38:1 turned in to a **c.** Adullamite, 376
Ge 38:2 there a daughter of a **c.** Canaanite, 376
Ex 16:4 gather a **c.** rate every day, that I 1697
Nu 9:6 there were **c.** men, who were
Nu 16:2 with **c.** of the children of Israel, 582
De 13:13 **C.** men, the children of Belial,
De 13:14 thing **c.**, that such abomination 3559
De 17:4 Behold, it be true, and the thing **c.**, 3559
De 25:2 to his fault, by a **c.** number.
Jg 9:53 a **c.** woman cast a piece of a 259
Jg 13:2 a **c.** man of Zorah, of the family of 259
Jg 19:1 there was a **c.** Levite sojourning 376
Jg 19:22 men of the city, **c.** sons of Belial, 582
Ru 1:1 And a **c.** man of Beth-lehem-judah
1Sa 1:1 a **c.** man of Ramathaim-zophim, 259
1Sa 21:7 a **c.** man of the servants of Saul 259
2Sa 18:10 a **c.** man saw it, and told Joab, 259
1Ki 2:37 thou shalt know for **c.** that thou 3045
1Ki 2:42 Know for a **c.**, on the day thou
1Ki 7:29 **c.** additions made of thin work.
1Ki 11:17 Hadad fled, he and **c.** Edomites 582
1Ki 20:35 **c.** man of the sons of the prophets 259
1Ki 22:34 And a **c.** man drew a bow at a
2Ki 4:1 Now there cried a **c.** woman of the 259
2Ki 8:6 unto her a **c.** officer, saying,
1Ch 9:28 And **c.** of them had the charge
1Ch 16:4 he appointed **c.** of the Levites to
1Ch 19:5 Then there went **c.**, and told David
2Ch 8:13 Even after a **c.** rate every day, 1697
2Ch 18:2 And after **c.** years he went down
2Ch 18:33 And a **c.** man drew a bow at a
2Ch 28:12 **c.** of the heads of the children of 582
Ezr 10:16 **c.** chief of the fathers, after the 582
Ne 1:2 came, he and **c.** men of Judah;
Ne 1:4 and wept, and mourned **c.** days,
Ne 11:4 And at Jerusalem dwelt **c.** of the
Ne 11:23 that a **c.** portion should be for
Ne 12:35 and **c.** of the priests' sons with
Ne 13:6 after **c.** days obtained I leave of
Ne 13:25 smote **c.** of them, and plucked off 582
Es 2:5 **c.** Jew whose name was Mordecai, 376
Es 3:8 There is a **c.** people scattered 259
Jer 26:15 for **c.**, that if ye put me to death, 3045
Jer 26:17 rose up **c.** of the elders of the land, 582
Jer 26:22 and **c.** men with him into Egypt,
Jer 41:5 there came **c.** from Shechem 582
Jer 52:15 away captive **c.** of the poor of the
Jer 52:16 of the guard left **c.** of the poor
Eze 14:1 came **c.** of the elders of Israel 582
Eze 20:1 **c.** of the elders of Israel came to 582
Da 1:3 bring **c.** of the children of Israel,
Da 2:45 and the dream is **c.**, and the 3330
Da 3:8 that time **c.** Chaldeans came near, 1400
Da 3:12 There are **c.** Jews whom thou hast 1400
Da 8:13 another saint said unto that **c.** 6422
Da 8:27 Daniel fainted, and was sick **c.** days;
Da 10:5 behold a **c.** man clothed in linen, 259
Da 11:13 come after **c.** years with a great 6256
Mt 8:19 a **c.** scribe came, and said unto *1520*
Mt 9:3 And, behold, **c.** of the scribes said *5100*
Mt 9:18 behold, there came a **c.** ruler,
Mt 12:38 Then **c.** of the scribes and of the *5100*
Mt 17:14 came to him a **c.** man, kneeling
Mt 18:23 heaven likened unto a **c.** king, *444*
Mt 20:20 and desiring a **c.** thing of him. *5100*
Mt 21:28 A **c.** man had two sons; and he
Mt 21:33 There was a **c.** householder, *444,5100*
Mt 22:2 of heaven is like unto a **c.** king, *444*
Mk 2:6 But there were **c.** of the scribes *5100*
Mk 5:25 a **c.** woman, which had an issue
Mk 5:35 **c.** which said, Thy daughter is
Mk 7:1 and **c.** of the scribes, which came *5100*
Mk 7:25 **c.** woman, whose young daughter
Mk 11:5 And **c.** of them that stood there *5100*
Mk 12:1 A **c.** man planted a vineyard,
Mk 12:13 send unto him **c.** of the Pharisees *5100*

Mk 12:42 there came a c. poor widow, and....... 1520
Mk 14:51 followed him a c. young man,............ 5100
Mk 14:57 And there arose c., and bear false...... 5100
Lu 1:5 a c. priest named Zacharias, of the..... 5100
Lu 5:12 when he was in a c. city, behold........ 1520
Lu 5:17 it came to pass on a c. day, as he...... 1520
Lu 6:2 And c. of the Pharisees said unto......... 5100
Lu 7:2 And a c. centurion's servant, who 5100
Lu 7:41 There was a c. creditor which had. 5100
Lu 8:2 c. women, which had been healed 5100
Lu 8:20 And it was told him by c. which...............
Lu 8:22 it came to pass on a c. day, that........ 1520
Lu 8:27 c. man, which had devils long time, ... 5100
Lu 9:57 a c. man said unto him, Lord, I 5100
Lu 10:25 a c. lawyer stood up, and tempted...... 5100
Lu 10:30 A c. man went down from 5100
Lu 10:31 came down a c. priest that way:...... 5100
Lu 10:33 a c. Samaritan, as he journeyed,... 5100
Lu 10:38 he entered into a c. village:.............. 5100
Lu 10:38 and a c. woman named Martha 5100
Lu 11:1 as he was praying in a c. place, ... 5100
Lu 11:27 a c. woman of the company lifted....... 5100
Lu 11:37 a c. Pharisee besought him to 5100
Lu 12:16 ground of a c. rich man brought ... 5100
Lu 13:6 A c. man had a fig tree planted..... 5100
Lu 13:31 there came c. of the Pharisees, ... 5100
Lu 14:2 there was a c. man before him 5100
Lu 14:16 A c. man made a great supper,...... 5100
Lu 15:11 A c. man had two sons:................ 5100
Lu 16:1 There was a c. rich man, which 5100
Lu 16:19 a c. rich man, which was clothed.. 5100
Lu 16:20 was a c. beggar named Lazarus,.... 5100
Lu 17:12 as he entered into a c. village,......... 5100
Lu 18:9 c. which trusted in themselves.......... 5100
Lu 18:18 And a c. ruler asked him, saying, ... 5100
Lu 18:35 a c. blind man sat by the wayside....... 5100
Lu 19:12 A c. nobleman went into a far 5100
Lu 20:9 A c. man planted a vineyard, ... 5100
Lu 20:27 came to him c. of the Sadducees........ 5100
Lu 20:39 c. of the scribes answering said, ... 5100
Lu 21:2 saw also a c. poor widow casting 5100
Lu 22:56 a c. maid beheld him as he sat......... 5100
Lu 23:19 for a c. sedition made in the city,....... 5100
Lu 24:1 prepared, and c. others with them...........
Lu 24:22 Yea, and c. women also of our 5100
Lu 24:24 c. of them which were with us 5100
Joh 4:46 there was a c. nobleman, whose 5100
Joh 5:4 angel went down at a c. season ....
Joh 5:5 And a c. man was there, which.......... 5100
Joh 11:1 Now a c. man was sick, named.......... 5100
Joh 12:20 there were c. Greeks among them 5100
Ac 3:2 And a c. man lame from his 5100
Ac 5:1 But a c. man named Ananias, ... 5100
Ac 5:2 brought a c. part, and laid it at......... 5100
Ac 6:9 there arose c. of the synagogue, ... 5100
Ac 8:9 there was a c. man, called Simon,....... 5100
Ac 8:36 way, they came unto a c. water;......... 5100
Ac 9:10 was a c. disciple at Damascus,........... 5100
Ac 9:19 Then was Saul c. days with the 5100
Ac 9:33 And there he found a c. man............ 5100
Ac 9:36 at Joppa a c. disciple named............ 5100
Ac 10:1 a c. man in Caesarea called............ 5100
Ac 10:11 a c. vessel descending unto him,....... 5100
Ac 10:23 and c. brethren from Joppa, ... 5100
Ac 10:48 prayed they him to tarry c. days........ 5100
Ac 11:5 A c. vessel descend, as it had been.... 5100
Ac 12:1 his hands to vex c. of the church. 5100
Ac 13:1 c. prophets and teachers; 5100
Ac 13:6 a c. sorcerer, a false prophet, ... 5100
Ac 14:8 And there sat a c. man at Lystra, ... 5100
Ac 14:19 And there came thither c. Jews...............
Ac 15:1 And c. men which came down 5100
Ac 15:2 Barnabas, and c. other of them,......... 5100
Ac 15:5 up c. of the sect of the Pharisees....... 5100
Ac 15:24 that c. which went out from us.......... 5100
Ac 16:1 a c. disciple was there, named........... 5100
Ac 16:1 Timotheus, the son of a c. woman,..... 5100
Ac 16:12 were in that city abiding c. days........ 5100
Ac 16:14 a c. woman named Lydia, a seller 5100
Ac 16:16 a c. damsel possessed with a spirit..... 5100
Ac 17:5 took unto them c. lewd fellows of....... 5100
Ac 17:6 they drew Jason and c. brethren 5100
Ac 17:18 c. philosophers of the Epicureans, ... 5100
Ac 17:20 thou bringest c. strange things........... 5100
Ac 17:28 c. also of your own poets have said.... 5100
Ac 17:34 c. men clave unto him, and............... 5100
Ac 18:2 a c. Jew named Aquila, born in......... 5100
Ac 18:7 entered into a c. man's house,........... 5100
Ac 18:24 And a c. Jew named Apollos, born........ 5100
Ac 19:1 Ephesus: and finding c. disciples, ... 5100
Ac 19:13 Then c. of the vagabond Jews, ... 5100
Ac 19:24 a c. man named Demetrius, a............ 5100
Ac 19:31 And c. of the chief of Asia, which....... 5100
Ac 20:9 a window a c. young man named........ 5100
Ac 21:10 a c. prophet, named Agabus............. 5100
Ac 21:16 also c. of the disciples of Caesarea, ...
Ac 23:12 c. of the Jews banded together, ... 5100
Ac 23:17 for he hath a c. thing to tell him. 5100
Ac 24:1 with a c. orator named Tertullus, ... 5100
Ac 24:18 Whereupon c. Jews from Asia............ 5100
Ac 24:24 And after c. days, when Felix............ 5100
Ac 25:13 c. days king Agrippa and Bernice 5100
Ac 25:14 is a c. man left in bonds by Felix: 5100
Ac 25:19 had c. questions against him of 5100
Ac 25:26 Of whom I have no c. thing to 804
Ac 27:1 Paul and c. other prisoners 5100
Ac 27:16 running under a c. island which.......... 5100
Ac 27:26 we must be cast upon a c. island. 5100
Ac 27:39 they discovered a c. creek................ 5100
Ro 15:26 a c. contribution for the poor............ 5100
1Co 4:11 and have no c. dwellingplace; 790
Ga 2:12 before that c. came from James, ... 5100
1Ti 6:7 it is c. we can carry nothing out. 1212
Heb 2:6 But one in a c. place testified,........... 4225
Heb 4:4 spake in a c. place of the seventh 4225
Heb 4:7 Again, he limiteth a c. day, saying...... 5100
Heb 10:27 c. fearful looking for of judgment 5100
Jude 4 For there are c. men crept in............. 5100

CERTAINLY See also UNCERTAINLY.
Ge 18:10 I will c. return unto thee 7725
Ge 26:28 We saw c. that the Lord was with...........
Ge 43:7 could we c. know that he would...............
Ge 44:15 such a man as I can c. divine? ....
Ge 50:15 will c. requite us all the evil ....
Ex 3:12 he said, C. I will be with thee; 3588
Ex 22:4 If the theft be c. found in his...................
Le 5:19 hath c. trespassed against the Lord. ....
Le 24:16 the congregation shall c. stone him: ....
Jos 9:24 Because it was c. told thy ....
Jg 14:12 if ye can c. declare it me within ....
1Sa 20:3 Thy father c. knoweth that I ....
1Sa 20:9 if I knew c. that evil were ....
1Sa 23:10 thy servant hath c. heard........................
1Sa 25:28 the Lord will c. make my lord a sure ....
1Ki 1:30 even so will I c. do this day.....................
2Ki 8:10 him, Thou mayest c. recover:....................
2Ch 18:27 If thou c. return in peace,........................
Pr 23:5 riches c. make themselves wings;.............
Jer 8:8 Lo, c. in vain made he it;.................... 403
Jer 13:12 Do we not c. know that every..................
Jer 25:28 Lord of hosts; Ye shall c. drink................
Jer 36:29 king of Babylon shall c. come ....
Jer 40:14 Dost thou c. know that Baalis...................
Jer 42:19 know c. that I have admonished you ....
Jer 42:22 Now therefore know c. that ye shall ....
Jer 44:17 we will c. do whatsoever thing goeth ....
La 2:16 c. this is the day that we looked........... 389
Da 11:10 one shall c. come, and overflow, ...
Da 11:13 c. come after certain years ....
Lu 23:47 C. this was a righteous man............. 3689

CERTAINTY
Jos 23:13 Know for a c. that the Lord your God.......
1Sa 23:23 come ye again to me with the c.,........ 3559
Pr 22:21 the c. of the words of truth; that 7189
Da 2:8 I know of c. that ye would gain 3330
Lu 1:4 know the c. of those things, ... 803
Ac 21:34 not know the c. for the tumult, ... 804
Ac 22:30 he would have known the c. 804

CERTIFIED
Ezr 4:14 have we sent and c. the king;............ 3046
Es 2:22 and Esther c. the king thereof in......... 559

CERTIFY See also CERTIFIED.
2Sa 15:28 come word from you to c. me. 5046
Ezr 4:16 We c. the king that, if this city.......... 3046
Ezr 5:10 asked their names also, to c. thee, ... 3046
Ezr 7:24 Also we c. you that touching any 3046
Ga 1:11 But I c. you, brethren, that the......... 1107

CESAR See CAESAR.

CESAREA See CAESAREA.

CHABOD See I-CHABOD.

CHAFED
2Sa 17:8 be c. in their minds, as a bear........... 4751

CHAFF
Job 21:18 c. that the storm carrieth away........... 4671
Ps 1:4 c. which the wind driveth away.......... 4671
Ps 35:5 Let them be as c. before the wind: 4671
Isa 5:24 and the flame consumeth the c., ... 2842
Isa 17:13 chased as the c. of the mountains....... 4671
Isa 29:5 the terrible ones shall be as c............ 4671
Isa 33:11 Ye shall conceive c., ye shall............. 2842
Isa 41:15 and shalt make the hills as c.............. 4671
Jer 23:28 What is the c. to the wheat? 8401
Da 2:35 like the c. of the summer 5784
Ho 13:3 as the c. that is driven with the......... 4671
Zep 2:2 before the day pass as the c.,........... 4671
Mt 3:12 burn up the c. with unquenchable......... 892
Lu 3:17 the c. he will burn with fire 892

CHAIN See also CHAINS.
Ge 41:42 put a gold c. about his neck; 7242
1Ki 7:17 wreaths of c. work, for the............... 8333
Ps 73:6 compasseth them about as a c.; 6059
Ca 4:9 eyes, with one c. of thy neck. 6060
La 3:7 he hath made my c. heavy................. 5178
Eze 7:23 Make a c.: for the land is full of......... 7569
Eze 16:11 thy hands, and a c. on thy neck. 7242
Da 5:7 have a c. of gold about his neck, ... 2002
Da 5:16 have a c. of gold about thy neck, ... 2002
Da 5:29 put a c. of gold about his neck,.......... 2002
Ac 28:20 of Israel I am bound with this c.......... 254
2Ti 1:16 and was not ashamed of my c. 254
Re 20:1 pit and a great c. in his hand. 254

CHAINS
Ex 28:14 two c. of pure gold at the ends;......... 8333
Ex 28:14 the wreathen c. to the ouches............ 8333
Ex 28:22 upon the breastplate c. at the ends..... 8331
Ex 28:24 thou shalt put the two wreathen c...... 5688
Ex 28:25 two ends of the two wreathen c. thou.......
Ex 39:15 upon the breastplate c. at the ends,.... 8333
Ex 39:17 c. of gold in the two rings 5688
Ex 39:18 the two wreathen c. they fastened...... 5688
Nu 31:50 of gold, c., and bracelets, rings, ... 685
Jg 8:26 c. that were about their camels'......... 6060
1Ki 6:21 made a partition by the c. of gold....... 7569
2Ch 3:5 and set thereon palm trees and c.. 8333
2Ch 3:16 And he made c., as in the oracle,....... 8333
2Ch 3:16 and put them on the c.. 8333
Ps 68:6 those which are bound with c. 3574
Ps 149:8 To bind their kings with c.,............... 2131
Pr 1:9 thy head, and c. about thy neck. 6060
Ca 1:10 jewels, thy neck with c. of gold. 2737
Isa 3:19 The c., and the bracelets, and the...... 5188
Isa 40:19 with gold, and casteth silver c.. 7569
Isa 45:14 in c. they shall come over,................ 2131
Jer 39:7 and bound him with c., to carry 5178
Jer 40:1 being bound in c. among all that 246
Jer 40:4 I loose thee this day from the c. 246
Jer 52:11 king of Babylon bound him in c., ... 5178
Eze 19:4 brought him with c. unto the land....... 2397
Eze 19:9 put him in ward in c., and................. 2397
Na 3:10 her great men were bound in c........... 2131
Mk 5:3 could bind him, no, not with c............ 254
Mk 5:4 ofter bound with fetters and c.,........... 254
Mk 5:4 the c. had been plucked asunder.......... 254
Lu 8:29 he was kept bound with c. and in 254
Ac 12:6 two soldiers, bound with two c.:.......... 254
Ac 12:7 And his c. fell off from his hands. 254
Ac 21:33 him to be bound with two c.;.............. 254
2Pe 2:4 delivered them into c. of darkness,..... 4577
Jude 6 hath reserved in everlasting c........... 1199

CHAIN-WORK See CHAIN and WORK.

CHALCEDONY (kal-sed'-o-nee)
Re 21:19 the third, a c.; the fourth, ... 5472

CHALCOL (kal'-kol) See also CALCOL.
1Ki 4:31 the Ezrahite, and Heman, and C., ... 3633

CHALDAEANS (kal-de'-uns) See also CHALDEANS.
Ac 7:4 out of the land of the C.,.................. 5466

CHALDEA (kal-de'-ah) See also BABYLON; CHALDEAN.
Jer 50:10 And C. shall be a spoil: all that.......... 3778
Jer 51:24 the inhabitants of C. all their evil........ 3778
Jer 51:35 blood upon the inhabitants of C.,......... 3778
Eze 11:24 vision by the Spirit of God into C.,...... 3778

Eze 16:29 in the land of Canaan unto **C.**; 3778
Eze 23:15 manner of the Babylonians of **C.**, ... 3778
Eze 23:16 messengers unto them into **C.** 3778

CHALDEAN (kal-de'-un) See also BABYLONIAN; CHALDEANS; CHALDEANS'.
Ezr 5:12 the **C.**, who destroyed this house, ... 3777
Da 2:10 any magician, or astrologer, or **C.** 3777

CHALDEANS (kal-de'-uns) See also BABYLONIANS; CHALDAEANS; CHALDEANS'; CHALDEES.
Job 1:17 The **C.** made out three bands, ... 3778
Isa 23:13 Behold the land of the **C.**; this 3778
Isa 43:14 nobles, and the **C.**, whose cry is in 3778
Isa 47:1 no throne, O daughter of the **C.** 3778
Isa 47:5 darkness, O daughter of the **C.**: 3778
Isa 48:14 and his arm shall be on the **C.** 3778
Isa 48:20 flee ye from the **C.**, with a voice of 3778
Jer 21:4 and against the **C.**, which besiege 3778
Jer 21:9 out, and falleth to the **C.** that 3778
Jer 22:25 and into the hand of the **C.** 3778
Jer 24:5 the land of the **C.** for their good. 3778
Jer 25:12 iniquity, and the land of the **C.**, ... 3778
Jer 32:4 escape out of the hand of the **C.**, ... 3778
Jer 32:5 though ye fight with the **C.**, ... 3778
Jer 32:24, 25 is given into the hand of the **C.**, ... 3778
Jer 32:28 this city into the hand of the **C.**, ... 3778
Jer 32:29 the **C.**, that fight against the city, ... 3778
Jer 32:43 is given into the hand of the **C.** 3778
Jer 33:5 They come to fight with the **C.**, ... 3778
Jer 35:11 for fear of the army of the **C.**, ... 3778
Jer 37:5 the **C.** that besieged Jerusalem 3778
Jer 37:8 the **C.** shall come again, and fight 3778
Jer 37:9 The **C.** shall surely depart from us: 3778
Jer 37:10 smitten the whole army of the **C.** 3778
Jer 37:11 the army of the **C.** was broken up 3778
Jer 37:13 saying, Thou fallest away to the **C.** 3778
Jer 37:14 is false: I fall not away to the **C.** 3778
Jer 38:2 goeth forth to the **C.** shall live. 3778
Jer 38:18 be given into the hand of the **C.**, ... 3778
Jer 38:19 the Jews that are fallen to the **C.**, ... 3778
Jer 38:23 wives and thy children to the **C.**: 3778
Jer 39:8 And the **C.** burned the king's house, ... 3778
Jer 40:9 saying, Fear not to serve the **C.**: 3778
Jer 40:10 dwell at Mizpah, to serve the **C.**, ... 3778
Jer 41:3 and the **C.** that were found there, ... 3778
Jer 41:18 Because of the **C.**: for they were 3778
Jer 43:3 deliver us into the hand of the **C.**, ... 3778
Jer 50:1 and against the land of the **C.** 3778
Jer 50:8 go forth out of the land of the **C.**, ... 3778
Jer 50:25 God of hosts in the land of the **C.** 3778
Jer 50:35 A sword is upon the **C.**, saith the 3778
Jer 50:45 purposed against the land of the **C.**: 3778
Jer 51:4 shall fall in the land of the **C.**, ... 3778
Jer 51:54 destruction from the land of the **C.**: 3778
Jer 52:7 **C.** were by the city round about:) 3778
Jer 52:8 of the **C.** pursued after the king, ... 3779
Jer 52:14 the **c.**, that were with the captain 3779
Jer 52:17 **C.** brake, and carried all the brass 3779
Eze 1:3 land of the **C.** by the river Chebar: 3779
Eze 12:13 Babylon to the land of the **C.**; 3779
Eze 23:14 images of the **C.** pourtrayed with 3779
Eze 23:23 The Babylonians, and all the **C.**, ... 3779
Da 1:4 learning and the tongue of the **C.** 3779
Da 2:2 **C.**, for to shew the king his dreams 3779
Da 2:4 Then spake the **C.** to the king 3779
Da 2:5 king answered and said to the **C.**, ... 3779
Da 2:10 **C.** answered before the king, ... 3779
Da 3:8 at that time certain **C.** came near, ... 3779
Da 4:7 magicians, the astrologers, the **C.**, ... 3779
Da 5:7 to bring in the astrologers, the **C.** 3779
Da 5:11 astrologers, **C.**, and soothsayers; 3779
Da 5:30 Belshazzar the king of the **C.** slain 3779
Da 9:1 king over the realm of the **C.**; 3778
Hab 1:6 For, lo, I raise up the **C.**, that 3778

CHALDEANS' (kal-de'-uns) See also CHALDEES.
Jer 39:5 the **C.** army pursued after them, ... 3778

CHALDEES (kal'-dees) See also CHALDEES'.
Ge 11:28 of his nativity, in Ur of the **C.** 3778
Ge 11:31 forth with them from Ur of the **C.**, ... 3778
Ge 15:7 brought thee out of Ur of the **C.**, ... 3778
2Ki 24:2 sent against him bands of the **C.**, ... 3778
2Ki 25:4 the **C.** were against the city round 3778
2Ki 25:5 of the **C.** pursued after the king, ... 3778
2Ki 25:10 And all the army of the **C.**, that 3778
2Ki 25:13 **C.** break in pieces, and carried 3778
2Ki 25:24 to be the servants of the **C.**: 3778
2Ki 25:25 Jews and the **C.** that were with 3778
2Ki 25:26 for they were afraid of the **C.** 3778
2Ch 36:17 upon them the king of the **C.**, ... 3778
Ne 9:7 him forth out of Ur of the **C.**, ... 3778

CHALDEES' (kal'-dees) See also CHALDEANS.
Isa 13:19 the beauty of the **C.** excellency, ... 3778

CHALKSTONES
Isa 27:9 of the altar as **c.** that are beaten 68,1615

CHALLENGETH
Ex 22:9 which another **c.** to be his, ... 559

CHAMBER See also BEDCHAMBER; CHAMBERING; CHAMBERLAIN; CHAMBERS; GUESTCHAMBER.
Ge 43:30 he entered into his **c.**, ... 2315
Jg 3:24 covereth his feet in his summer **c.** 2315
Jg 15:1 I will go in to my wife into the **c.** 2315
Jg 16:9 wait, abiding with her in the **c.** 2315
Jg 16:12 were liers in wait abiding in the **c.** 2315
2Sa 13:10 Bring the meat into the **c.**, that I 2315
2Sa 13:10 brought them into the **c.** to 2315
2Sa 18:33 the **c.** over the gate, and wept: 5944
1Ki 1:15 in unto the king into the **c.**: 2315
1Ki 6:6 The nethermost **c.** was five cubits 3326
1Ki 6:8 The door for the middle **c.** was 6763
1Ki 6:8 into the middle **c.**, and out of the ....
1Ki 14:28 them back into the guard **c.** 8372
1Ki 17:23 brought him down out of the **c.** 5944
1Ki 20:30 into the city, into an inner **c.** 2315
1Ki 22:25 when thou shalt go into an inner **c.** 2315
2Ki 1:2 through a lattice in his upper **c.** 5944
2Ki 4:10 Let us make a little **c.**, I pray thee, ... 5944
2Ki 4:11 he turned into the **c.**, and lay 5944
2Ki 9:2 and carry him to an inner **c.**; 2315
2Ki 23:11 the **c.** of Nathan-melech the 3957
2Ki 23:12 the upper **c.** of Ahaz, which the 5944
2Ch 12:11 them again into the guard **c.** 8372
2Ch 18:24 thou shalt go into an inner **c.** 2315
Ezr 10:6 **c.** of Johanan the son of Eliashib: 3957
Ne 3:30 Berechiah over against his **c.** 5393
Ne 13:4 of the **c.** of the house of our God, ... 3957
Ne 13:5 had prepared for him a great **c.**, ... 3957
Ne 13:7 a **c.** in the courts of the house 5393
Ne 13:8 stuff of Tobiah out of the **c.** 3957
Ps 19:5 bridegroom coming out of his **c.**, ... 2646
Ca 3:4 the **c.** of her that conceived me. 2315
Jer 35:4 the **c.** of the sons of Hanan, ... 3957
Jer 35:4 by the **c.** of the princes, which 3957
Jer 35:4 was above the **c.** of Maaseiah 3957
Jer 36:10 in the **c.** of Gemariah the son of 3957
Jer 36:12 king's house, into the scribe's **c.**: 3957
Jer 36:20 in the **c.** of Elishama the scribe, ... 3957
Jer 36:21 it out of Elishama the scribe's **c.** 3957
Eze 40:7 every little **c.** was one reed long, ... 8372
Eze 40:13 from the roof of one little **c.** to 8372
Eze 40:45 This **c.**, whose prospect is toward 3957
Eze 40:46 **c.** whose prospect is toward the 3957
Eze 41:5 and the breadth of every side **c.**, ... 6763
Eze 41:7 from the lowest **c.** to the highest ....
Eze 41:9 which was for the side **c.** without, ... 6763
Eze 42:1 into the **c.** that was over against 3957
Da 6:10 windows being open in his **c.** 5952
Joe 2:16 the bridegroom go forth of his **c.**, ... 2315
Ac 9:37 they laid her in an upper **c.** *5253*
Ac 9:39 they brought him into the upper **c.**: *5253*
Ac 20:8 were many lights in the upper **c.**, ... *5253*

CHAMBERING
Ro 13:13 not in **c.** and wantonness, nor in *2845*

CHAMBERLAIN See also CHAMBERLAINS.
2Ki 23:11 chamber of Nathan-melech the **c.**, ... 5631
Es 2:3 custody of Hege the king's **c.**, ... 5631
Es 2:14 of Shaashgaz, the king's **c.**, which 5631
Es 2:15 Hegai the king's **c.**, the keeper of 5631
Ac 12:20 Blastus the king's **c.** *1909,2846,3588*
Ro 16:23 Erastus the **c.** of the city saluteth *3623*

CHAMBERLAINS
Es 1:10 the seven **c.** that served in the 5631
Es 1:12 king's commandment by his **c.** 5631
Es 1:15 of the king Ahasuerus by the **c.**? 5631
Es 2:21 two of the king's **c.**, Bigthan and 5631
Es 4:4 maids and her **c.** came and told it 5631
Es 4:5 for Hatach, one of the king's **c.**, ... 5631
Es 6:2 two of the king's **c.**, the keepers of 5631
Es 6:14 came the king's **c.**, and hasted 5631
Es 7:9 Harbonah, one of the **c.**, said 5631

CHAMBERS
1Ki 6:5 built **c.** round about, against the 3326
1Ki 6:5 of the oracle: and he made **c.** 6763
1Ki 6:10 he built **c.** against all the house 3326
1Ch 9:26 were over the **c.** and treasuries 3957
1Ch 9:33 Levites, who remaining in the **c.** 3957
1Ch 23:28 in the courts, and in the **c.**, and in 3957
1Ch 28:11 and of the upper **c.** thereof, and 5944
1Ch 28:12 all the **c.** round about, of the 3957
2Ch 3:9 he overlaid the upper **c.** with gold, ... 5944
2Ch 31:11 to prepare **c.** in the house of the 3957
Ezr 8:29 the **c.** of the house of the Lord 3957
Ne 10:37 to the **c.** of the house of our God; 3957
Ne 10:38 the **c.**, into the treasure house. 3957
Ne 10:39 the **c.**, where are the vessels of the ... 3957
Ne 12:44 the **c.** for the treasures, for the 5393
Ne 13:9 and they cleansed the **c.**: 3957
Job 9:9 Pleiades, and the **c.** of the south. 2315
Ps 104:3 Who layeth the beams of his **c.** 5944
Ps 104:13 He watereth the hills from his **c.** 5944
Ps 105:30 abundance, in the **c.** of their 2315
Pr 7:27 going down to the **c.** of death. 2315
Pr 24:4 by knowledge shall the **c.** be filled 2315
Ca 1:4 king hath brought me into his **c.** 2315
Isa 26:20 people, enter thou into thy **c.**, and 2315
Jer 22:13 and his **c.** by wrong; 5944
Jer 22:14 a wide house and large **c.**, and 5944
Jer 35:2 into one of the **c.**, and give them 3957
Eze 8:12 man in the **c.** of his imagery? 2315
Eze 21:14 which entereth into their privy **c.** 2315
Eze 40:7 between the little **c.** were five 8372
Eze 40:10 the little **c.** of the gate eastward 8372
Eze 40:12 The space also before the little **c.** 8372
Eze 40:12 the little **c.** were six cubits on 8372
Eze 40:16 narrow windows to the little **c.**, ... 8372
Eze 40:17 there were **c.**, and a pavement 3957
Eze 40:17 thirty **c.** were upon the pavement 3957
Eze 40:21 And the little **c.** thereof were 8372
Eze 40:29 And the little **c.** thereof, and the 8372
Eze 40:33 the little **c.** thereof, and the posts 8372
Eze 40:36 The little **c.** thereof, the posts 8372
Eze 40:38 the **c.** and the entries thereof 3957
Eze 40:44 the **c.** of the singers in the inner 3957
Eze 41:6 the side **c.** were three, one over 6763
Eze 41:6 house for the side **c.** round about, ... 6763
Eze 41:7 upward to the side **c.**: for the 6763
Eze 41:8 the foundations of the side **c.** were 6763
Eze 41:9 the place of the side **c.** that were 6763
Eze 41:10 And between the **c.** was the 3957
Eze 41:11 the doors of the side **c.** were 6763
Eze 41:26 and upon the side **c.** of the house, ... 6763
Eze 42:4 before the **c.** was a walk of ten 3957
Eze 42:5 Now the upper **c.** were shorter: 3957
Eze 42:7 over against the **c.**, toward the 3957
Eze 42:7 court on the forepart of the **c.**, ... 3957
Eze 42:8 For the length of the **c.** that were 3957
Eze 42:9 from under these **c.** was the entry 3957
Eze 42:10 The **c.** were in the thickness of 3957
Eze 42:11 the appearance of the **c.** which 3957
Eze 42:12 according to the doors of the **c.** 3957
Eze 42:13 The north **c.** and the south **c.**, ... 3957
Eze 42:13 separate place, they be holy **c.**, ... 3957
Eze 44:19 in the holy **c.**, and they shall put 3957
Eze 45:5 for a possession for twenty **c.** 3957
Eze 46:19 into the holy **c.** of the priests, ... 3957
Mt 24:26 **behold, he is in the secret c.**; *5009*

CHAMELEON (ca-me'-le-un)
Le 11:30 ferret, and the **c.**, and the lizard, ... 3581

CHAMOIS (sham'-my)
De 14:5 and the wild ox, and the **c.** 2169

CHAMPAIGN (sham-pane')
De 11:30 in the **c.** over against Gilgal, ... 6160

CHAMPION
1Sa 17:4 went out a **c.** out of the camp 376,1143
1Sa 17:23 the **c.**, the Philistine of Gath, ... 376,1143
1Sa 17:51 when the Philistines saw their **c.** 1368

CHANAAN (ka'-na-un) See also CANAAN.
Ac 7:11 over all the land of Egypt and **C.**, ... *5477*
Ac 13:19 seven nations in the land of **C.**, ... *5477*

CHANCE See also CHANCETH.
De 22:6 If a bird's nest **c.** to be before thee 7122

1Sa 6:9 it was a **c.** that happened to us.......... 4745
2Sa 1:6 I happened by **c.** upon mount........... 7122
Ec 9:11 time and **c.** happeneth to them.......... 6294
Lu 10:31 **by c. there came down a certain**.... *4795*
1Co 15:37 grain, it may **c.** of wheat,................ *5177*

CHANCELLOR
Ezr 4:8 Rehum the **c.**, and Shimshai....... 1169,2942
Ezr 4:9 Then wrote Rehum the **c.**,........ 1169,2942
Ezr 4:17 an answer unto Rehum the **c.**,.... 1169,2942

CHANCETH
De 23:10 by reason of uncleanness that **c.**........ 4745

CHANGE See also CHANGEABLE; CHANGED; CHANGES; CHANGEST; CHANGETH; CHANGING; EXCHANGE.
Ge 35:2 be clean, and **c.** your garments:......... 2498
Le 27:10 nor **c.** it, a good for a bad, or a......... 4171
Le 27:10 and if he shall at all **c.**....................... 4171
Le 27:33 neither shall he **c.** it:........................ 4171
Le 27:33 and if he **c.** it at all,.......................... 4171
Le 27:33 and the **c.** thereof shall be holy;......... 8545
Jg 14:12, 13 and thirty **c.** of garments:............. 2487
Jg 14:19 gave **c.** of garments unto them.......... 2487
Job 14:14 time will I wait, till my **c.** come......... 2487
Job 17:12 They **c.** the night into day: and......... 7760
Ps 102:26 as a vesture shalt thou **c.** them,......... 2498
Pr 24:21 with them that are given to **c.**:........... 8138
Isa 9:10 but we will **c.** them into cedars.......... 2498
Jer 2:36 about so much to **c.** thy way?............ 8138
Jer 13:23 Can the Ethiopian **c.** his skin, or........ 2015
Da 7:25 and think to **c.** times and laws:........... 8133
Ho 4:7 will I **c.** their glory into shame........... 4171
Hab 1:11 Then shall his mind **c.**, and he........... 2498
Zec 3:4 clothe thee with **c.** of raiment............ 4254
Mal 3:6 I am the Lord, I **c.** not; therefore...... 8138
Ac 6:14 shall **c.** the customs which Moses........ *236*
Ro 1:26 their women did **c.** the natural............ *3337*
Ga 4:20 with you now, and to **c.** my voice;....... *236*
Php 3:21 Who shall **c.** our vile body, that it...... *3345*
Heb 7:12 of necessity a **c.** also of the law......... *3331*

CHANGEABLE See also UNCHANGEABLE.
Isa 3:22 The **c.** suits of apparel, and the......... 4254

CHANGED
Ge 31:7 and **c.** my wages ten times; but........ 2498
Ge 31:41 thou hast **c.** my wages ten times........ 2498
Ge 41:14 **c.** his raiment, and came in unto........ 2498
Le 13:16 turn again, and be **c.** unto white,........ 2015
Le 13:55 the plague have not **c.** his colour,....... 2015
Nu 32:38 (their names being **c.**,) and................ 5437
1Sa 21:13 he **c.** his behaviour before them,......... 8138
2Sa 12:20 **c.** his apparel, and came into the........ 2498
2Ki 24:17 and **c.** his name to Zedekiah.............. 5437
2Ki 25:29 **c.** his prison garments: and he........... 8132
Job 30:18 of my disease is my raiment **c.**;.......... 2664
Ps 34:*title* when he **c.** his behaviour.................... 8138
Ps 102:26 and they shall be **c.**:........................ 2498
Ps 106:20 Thus they **c.** their glory into the......... 4171
Ec 8:1 boldness of his face shall be **c.**............ 8132
Isa 24:5 have transgressed the laws, **c.** the...... 2498
Jer 2:11 Hath a nation **c.** their gods,.............. 4171
Jer 2:11 my people have **c.** their glory for........ 4171
Jer 48:11 in him, and his scent is not **c.**............. 4171
Jer 52:33 And **c.** his prison garments: and.......... 8138
La 4:1 how is the most fine gold **c.**!............... 8132
Eze 5:6 And she had **c.** my judgments............ 4171
Da 2:9 before me, till the time be **c.**.............. 8133
Da 3:19 the form of his visage was **c.**.............. 8133
Da 3:27 neither were their coats **c.**, nor.......... 8133
Da 3:28 and have **c.** the king's word, and......... 8133
Da 4:16 Let his heart be **c.** from man's, and..... 8133
Da 5:6 the king's countenance was **c.**, and..... 8133
Da 5:9 his countenance was **c.** in him,........... 8133
Da 5:10 nor let thy countenance be **c.**:............ 8133
Da 6:8 that it be not **c.**, according to the........ 8133
Da 6:15 the king establisheth may be **c.**............ 8133
Da 6:17 might not be **c.** concerning Daniel........ 8133
Da 7:28 my countenance **c.** in me: but I.......... 8133
Mic 2:4 hath **c.** the portion of my people:........ 4171
Ac 28:6 they **c.** their minds, and said that....... *3328*
Ro 1:23 **c.** the glory of the uncorruptible.......... *236*
Ro 1:25 Who **c.** the truth of God into a.......... *3337*
1Co 15:51 all sleep, but we shall all be **c.**,........... *236*
1Co 15:52 incorruptible, and we shall be **c.**.......... *236*
2Co 3:18 are **c.** into the same image from.......... *3339*
Heb 1:12 them up, and they shall be **c.**:............. *236*
Heb 7:12 priesthood being **c.**, there is made....... *3346*

CHANGERS See also CHANGERS'; MONEYCHANGERS.
Joh 2:14 doves, and the **c.** of money sitting:...... *2773*

CHANGERS'
Joh 2:15 poured out the **c.** money, and............ *2855*

CHANGES
Ge 45:22 he gave each man **c.** of raiment;........ 2487
Ge 45:22 of silver, and five **c.** of raiment.......... 2487
2Ki 5:5 of gold, and ten **c.** of raiment............ 2487
2Ki 5:22 of silver, and two **c.** of garments........ 2487
2Ki 5:23 two bags, with two **c.** of garments,...... 2487
Job 10:17 me; **c.** and war are against me........... 2487
Ps 55:19 Because they have no **c.**, therefore..... 2487

CHANGEST
Job 14:20 thou **c.** his countenance, and............ 8138

CHANGETH
Ps 15:4 to his own hurt, and **c.** not............... 4171
Da 2:21 he **c.** the times and the seasons:........ 8133

CHANGING
Ru 4:7 redeeming and concerning **c.**,............ 8545

CHANNEL See also CHANNELS.
Isa 27:12 from the **c.** of the river unto the........ 7641

CHANNELS
2Sa 22:16 the **c.** of the sea appeared, the........... 650
Ps 18:15 Then the **c.** of waters were seen,........ 650
Isa 8:7 he shall come up over all his **c.**,.......... 650

CHANT
Am 6:5 That **c.** to the sound of the viol,........ 6527

CHAPEL
Am 7:13 it is the king's **c.**, and it is the........... 4720

CHAPITER See also CHAPITERS.
1Ki 7:16 the height of the one **c.** was five........ 3805
1Ki 7:16 and the height of the other **c.**............ 3805
1Ki 7:17 seven for the one **c.**.......................... 3805
1Ki 7:17 and seven for the other **c.**................. 3805
1Ki 7:18 and so he did for the other **c.**............ 3805
1Ki 7:20 round about upon the other **c.**........... 3805
1Ki 7:31 the mouth of it within the **c.** and........ 3805
2Ki 25:17 and the **c.** upon it was brass:............. 3805
2Ki 25:17 the height of the **c.** three cubits;......... 3805
2Ki 25:17 the pomegranates upon the **c.**............ 3805
2Ch 3:15 the **c.** that was on the top of each...... 6858
Jer 52:22 And a **c.** of brass was upon it;............ 3805
Jer 52:22 and the height of one **c.** was five...... 3805

CHAPITERS
Ex 36:38 he overlaid their **c.** and their............ 7218
Ex 38:17 overlaying of their **c.** of silver;........... 7218
Ex 38:19 their **c.** and their fillets of silver......... 7218
Ex 38:28 overlaid their **c.**, and filleted.............. 7218
1Ki 7:16 he made two **c.** of molten brass,......... 3805
1Ki 7:17 the **c.** which were upon the top........... 3805
1Ki 7:18 the **c.** that were upon the top,............. 3805
1Ki 7:19 the **c.** that were upon the top of......... 3805
1Ki 7:20 And the **c.** upon the two pillars.......... 3805
1Ki 7:41 the two bowls of the **c.** that were....... 3805
1Ki 7:41 to cover the two bowls of the **c.**.......... 3805
1Ki 7:42 the two bowls of the **c.** that were....... 3805
2Ch 4:12 the **c.** which were on the top............. 3805
2Ch 4:12 cover the two pommels of the **c.**......... 3805
2Ch 4:13 **c.** which were upon the pillars............ 3805
Jer 52:22 and pomegranates upon the **c.**............ 3805

CHAPMEN
2Ch 9:14 **c.** and merchants brought............ 582,8446

CHAPPED See CHAPT.

CHAPT
Jer 14:4 Because the ground is **c.**, for............ 2865

CHARASHIM (car'-a-shim)
1Ch 4:14 of **C.**; for they were craftsmen........... 2798

CHARCHEMISH (car'-ke-mish) see also CARCHEMISH.
2Ch 35:20 to fight against **C.** by Euphrates:........ 3751

CHARGE See also CHARGEABLE; CHARGED; CHARGES; CHARGEST; CHARGING; OVERCHARGE.
Ge 26:5 obeyed my voice, and kept my **c.**,....... 4931
Ge 28:6 he blessed him he gave him a **c.**,........ 6680
Ex 6:13 gave them a **c.** unto the children........ 6680
Ex 19:21 **c.** the people, lest they break............ 5749
Le 8:35 keep the **c.** of the Lord, that ye......... 4931
Nu 1:53 Levites shall keep the **c.** of the.......... 4931
Nu 3:7 they shall keep his **c.**, and the........... 4931
Nu 3:7 **c.** of the whole congregation............. 4931
Nu 3:8 the **c.** of the children of Israel,........... 4931
Nu 3:25 And the **c.** of the sons of Gershon...... 4931
Nu 3:28 keeping the **c.** of the sanctuary.......... 4931
Nu 3:31 And their **c.** shall be the ark,............. 4931
Nu 3:32 that keep the **c.** of the sanctuary......... 4931
Nu 3:36 the custody and **c.** of the sons........... 4931
Nu 3:38 keeping the **c.** of the sanctuary for...... 4931
Nu 3:38 the **c.** of the children of Israel;.......... 4931
Nu 4:27 unto them in **c.** all their burdens......... 4931
Nu 4:28 their **c.** shall be under the hand of...... 4931
Nu 4:31 this is the **c.** of their burden,............. 4931
Nu 4:32 instruments of the **c.** of their burden... 4931
Nu 5:19 the priest shall **c.** her by an oath,....... 7650
Nu 5:21 the priest shall **c.** the woman............ 7650
Nu 8:26 congregation, to keep the **c.**, and........ 4931
Nu 8:26 the Levites touching their **c.**............... 4931
Nu 9:19 the children of Israel kept the **c.**......... 4931
Nu 9:23 they kept the **c.** of the Lord,.............. 4931
Nu 18:3 shall keep thy **c.**, and the **c.** of........... 4931
Nu 18:4 keep the **c.** of the tabernacle of.......... 4931
Nu 18:5 keep the **c.** of the sanctuary,............... 4931
Nu 18:5 and the **c.** of the altar:....................... 4931
Nu 18:8 I also have given thee the **c.** of.......... 4931
Nu 27:19 and give him a **c.** in their sight........... 6680
Nu 27:23 and gave him a **c.**, as the Lord............ 6680
Nu 31:30 keep the **c.** of the tabernacle of.......... 4931
Nu 31:47 kept the **c.** of the tabernacle of........... 4931
Nu 31:49 which are under our **c.**, and................ 3027
De 3:28 **c.** Joshua, and encourage him,............ 6680
De 11:1 keep his **c.**, and his statutes,.............. 4931
De 21:8 unto thy people of Israel's **c.**,.............. 7130
De 31:14 that I may give him a **c.**..................... 6680
De 31:23 gave Joshua the son of Nun a **c.**,........ 6680
Jos 22:3 kept the **c.** of the commandment.......... 4931
2Sa 14:8 I will give **c.** concerning thee............. 6680
2Sa 18:5 the king gave all the captains **c.**......... 6680
1Ki 2:3 keep the **c.** of the Lord thy God,......... 4931
1Ki 4:28 every man according to his **c.**............ 4941
1Ki 11:28 the **c.** of the house of Joseph............. 5447
2Ki 7:17 hand he leaned to have the **c.**............. 5921
1Ch 9:27 because the **c.** was upon them,........... 4931
1Ch 9:28 And certain of them had the **c.**............ 5921
1Ch 22:12 give thee **c.** concerning Israel,............ 6680
1Ch 23:32 the **c.** of the tabernacle of the............ 4931
1Ch 23:32 and the **c.** of the holy place,............... 4931
1Ch 23:32 and the **c.** of the sons of Aaron........... 4931
2Ch 13:11 for we keep the **c.** of the Lord............. 4931
2Ch 30:17 Levites had the **c.** of the killing........... 5921
Ne 7:2 the palace, **c.** over Jerusalem:............. 6680
Ne 10:32 to **c.** ourselves yearly with the............ 5414
Es 3:9 that have the **c.** of the business,......... 6213
Es 4:8 to **c.** her that she should go in............ 6680
Job 34:13 Who hath given him a **c.** over............ 6485
Ps 35:11 to my **c.** things that I knew not.......... 7592
Ps 91:11 shall give his angels **c.** over thee,........ 6680
Ca 2:7 I **c.** you, O ye daughters of................ 7650
Ca 3:5 I **c.** you, O ye daughters of................ 7650
Ca 5:8 I **c.** you, O daughters of.................... 7650
Ca 5:9 beloved, that thou dost so **c.** us?......... 7650
Ca 8:4 I **c.** you, O daughters of.................... 7650
Isa 10:6 of my wrath will I give him a **c.**,......... 6680
Jer 39:11 King of Babylon gave **c.** concerning..... 6680
Jer 47:7 the Lord had given it a **c.** against........ 6680
Jer 52:25 which had the **c.** of the men............... 6496
Eze 9:1 them that have **c.** over the city........... 6486
Eze 40:45 keepers of the **c.** of the house............ 4931
Eze 40:46 the keepers of the **c.** of the altar:........ 4931
Eze 44:8 kept the **c.** of mine holy things:.......... 4931
Eze 44:8 but ye have set keepers of my **c.**........ 4931
Eze 44:11 **c.** at the gates of the house,.............. 6486
Eze 44:14 keepers of the **c.** of the house,........... 4931
Eze 44:15 kept a **c.** of my sanctuary when........... 4931
Eze 44:16 me, and they shall keep my **c.**............ 4931
Eze 48:11 which have kept my **c.**, which............ 4931
Zec 3:7 keep my **c.**, then thou shalt also......... 4931
Mt 4:6 give his angels **c.** concerning............. *1781*
Mk 9:25 **I c. thee, come out of him, and**...... *2004*
Lu 4:10 shall give his angels **c.** over thee,........ *1781*
Ac 7:60 Lord, lay not this sin to their **c.**.......... *2476*
Ac 8:27 who had the **c.** of all her treasure,...... *1909*
Ac 16:24 Who, having received such a **c.**,............ *3852*
Ac 23:29 to have nothing laid to his **c.**.............. *1462*
Ro 8:33 shall lay anything to the **c.** of.... *1458, 2596*
1Co 9:18 the gospel of Christ without **c.**,............. *77*
1Th 5:27 I **c.** you by the Lord that this............. *3726*
1Ti 1:3 that thou mightest **c.** some that.......... *3853*

1Ti 1:18 This **c.** I commit unto thee, son... *3852*
1Ti 5:7 And these things give in **c.**, that... *3853*
1Ti 5:21 I **c.** thee before God, and the Lord... *1263*
1Ti 6:13 I give thee **c.** in the sight of God,... *3853*
1Ti 6:17 **C.** them that are rich in this world,... *3853*
2Ti 4:1 I **c.** thee therefore before God,... *1263*
2Ti 4:16 it may not be laid to their **c.**... *3049*

CHARGEABLE
2Sa 13:25 now go, lest we be **c.** unto thee... 3513
Ne 5:15 before me were **c.** unto the people,... 3513
2Co 11:9 I was **c.** to no man: for that... *2655*
1Th 2:9 not be **c.** unto any of you,... *1912*
2Th 3:8 that we might not be **c.** to any... *1912*

CHARGED See also CHARGEDST; OVERCHARGED.
Ge 26:11 And Abimelech **c.** all his people,... 6680
Ge 28:1 and **c.** him, and said unto him,... 6680
Ge 40:4 the captain of the guard **c.** Joseph... 6485
Ge 49:29 he **c.** them, and said unto them,... 6680
Ex 1:22 Pharaoh **c.** all his people, saying,... 6680
De 1:16 I **c.** your judges at that time,... 6680
De 24:5 be **c.** with any business:... 5674,5921
De 27:11 Moses **c.** the people the same day,... 6680
Jos 18:8 and Joshua **c.** them that went... 6680
Jos 22:5 Moses the servant of the Lord **c.**... 6680
Ru 2:9 have I not **c.** the young men... 6680
1Sa 14:27 father **c.** the people with the oath:... 7650
1Sa 14:28 straitly **c.** the people with an oath,... 7650
2Sa 11:19 And **c.** the messenger, saying,... 6680
2Sa 18:12 **c.** thee and Abishai and Ittai,... 6680
1Ki 2:1 he **c.** Solomon his son, saying,... 6680
1Ki 2:43 that I have **c.** thee with?... 6680
1Ki 13:9 For so was it **c.** me by the word... 6680
2Ki 17:15 the Lord had **c.** them, that they... 6680
2Ki 17:35 had made a covenant, and **c.** them,... 6680
1Ch 22:6 and **c.** him to build an house... 6680
1Ch 22:13 **c.** Moses with concerning Israel:... 6680
2Ch 19:9 **c.** them, saying, Thus shall ye do... 6680
2Ch 36:23 hath **c.** me to build him an house... 6485
Ezr 1:2 and he hath **c.** me to build him... 6485
Ne 13:19 **c.** that they should not be opened... 559
Es 2:10 Mordecai had **c.** her that she... 6680
Es 2:20 Mordecai had **c.** her: for Esther... 6680
Job 1:22 sinned not, nor **c.** God foolishly... 5414
Job 4:18 and his angels he **c.** with folly:... 7760
Jer 32:13 And I **c.** Baruch before them,... 6680
Jer 35:8 he hath **c.** us, to drink no wine... 6680
Mt 9:30 Jesus straitly **c.** them, saying,... *1690*
Mt 12:16 And **c.** them that they should not... *2008*
Mt 16:20 Then **c.** he his disciples that they... *1291*
Mt 17:9 Jesus **c.** them, saying, **Tell the**... *1781*
Mk 1:43 he straitly **c.** him, and forthwith... *1690*
Mk 3:12 straitly **c.** them that they should... *2008*
Mk 5:43 he **c.** them straitly that no man... *1291*
Mk 7:36 **c.** them that they should tell no... *1291*
Mk 7:36 but the more he **c.** them,... *1291*
Mk 8:15 he **c.** them, saying, **Take heed,**... *1291*
Mk 8:30 he **c.** them that they should tell... *2008*
Mk 9:9 **c.** them they should tell no man... *1291*
Mk 10:48 And many **c.** him that he should... *2008*
Lu 5:14 And he **c.** him to **tell no man:**... *3853*
Lu 8:56 but he **c.** them that they should... *3853*
Lu 9:21 straitly **c.** them, and commanded... *2008*
Ac 23:22 **c.** him, See thou tell no man... *3853*
1Th 2:11 **c.** every one of you, as a father... *3143*
1Ti 5:16 and let not the church be **c.**;... *916*

CHARGEDST
Ex 19:23 thou **c.** us, saying, Set bounds... 5749

CHARGER See also CHARGERS.
Nu 7:13 And his offering was one silver **c.**,... 7086
Nu 7:19 for his offering one silver **c.**,... 7086
Nu 7:25, 31,37,43,49,55,61,67,73,79,
His offering was one silver **c.**,... 7086
Nu 7:85 **c.** of silver weighing an hundred... 7086
Mt 14:8 here John Baptist's head in a **c.**... *4094*
Mt 14:11 was brought in a **c.**, and given to... *4094*
Mk 6:25 by and by in a **c.** the head of John... *4094*
Mk 6:28 brought his head in a **c.**, and gave... *4094*

CHARGERS
Nu 7:84 **c.** of silver, twelve silver bowls,... 7086
Ezr 1:9 thirty **c.** of gold, and a thousandnd... 105
Ezr 1:9 **c.** of silver, nine and twenty... 105

CHARGES
2Ch 8:14 the Levites to their **c.**, to praise... 4931
2Ch 31:16 service in their **c.** according to... 4931
2Ch 31:17 in their **c.** by their courses;... 4931
2Ch 35:2 And he set the priests in their **c.**,... 4931
Ac 21:24 **c.** with them, that they may shave... *1159*
1Co 9:7 warfare any time at his own **c.**?... *3800*

CHARGEST
2Sa 3:8 thou **c.** me to day with a fault... 6485

CHARGING
Ac 16:23 **c.** the jailor to keep them safely:... *3853*
2Ti 2:14 **c.** them before the Lord that they... *1263*

CHARIOT See also CHARIOTS.
Ge 41:43 made him to ride in the second **c.**... 4818
Ge 46:29 Joseph made ready his **c.**, and... 4818
Ex 14:6 ready his **c.**, and took his people... 7393
Ex 14:25 their **c.** wheels, that they drave... 4818
Jg 4:15 Sisera lighted down off his **c.**, and... 4818
Jg 5:28 Why is his **c.** so long in coming?... 7393
2Sa 8:4 David houghed all the **c.** horses,... 7393
1Ki 7:33 like the work of a **c.** wheel:... 4818
1Ki 10:29 **c.** came up and went out of Egypt... 4818
1Ki 12:18 speed to get him up to his **c.**,... 4818
1Ki 18:44 say unto Ahab, Prepare thy **c.**,...
1Ki 20:25 horse for horse, and **c.** for **c.**... 7393
1Ki 20:33 caused him to come up into the **c.**... 4818
1Ki 22:34 he said unto the driver of his **c.**,... 7395
1Ki 22:35 the king was stayed up in his **c.**... 4818
1Ki 22:35 wound into the midst of the **c.**,... 7393
1Ki 22:38 the **c.** in the pool of Samaria;... 7393
2Ki 2:11 appeared a **c.** of fire, and horses... 7393
2Ki 2:12 **c.** of Israel, and the horsemen... 7393
2Ki 5:9 with his horses and with his **c.**,... 7393
2Ki 5:21 down from the **c.** to meet him,... 4818
2Ki 5:26 again from his **c.** to meet thee?... 4818
2Ki 7:14 took therefore two **c.** horses;... 7393
2Ki 9:16 Jehu rode in a **c.**, and went to Jezreel;. 7393
2Ki 9:21 And his **c.** was made ready... 7393
2Ki 9:21 of Judah went out, each in his **c.**,... 7393
2Ki 9:24 heart, and he sunk down in his **c.**... 7393
2Ki 9:27 and said, Smite him also in the **c.**... 4818
2Ki 9:28 carried him in a **c.** to Jerusalem,...
2Ki 10:15 took him up to him into the **c.**... 4818
2Ki 10:16 So they made him ride in his **c.**... 7393
2Ki 13:14 **c.** of Israel, and the horsemen... 7393
2Ki 23:30 servants carried him in a **c.** dead...
1Ch 18:4 also houghed all the **c.** horses,... 7393
1Ch 28:18 **c.** of the cherubims, that spread... 4818
2Ch 1:14 which he placed in the **c.** cities,... 7393
2Ch 1:17 brought forth out of Egypt a **c.**... 4818
2Ch 8:6 all the **c.** cities, and the cities... 7393
2Ch 9:25 in the **c.** cities, and with the king... 7393
2Ch 10:18 speed to get him up to his **c.**,... 4818
2Ch 18:33 to his **c.** man, Turn thine hand,... 7395
2Ch 18:34 Israel stayed himself up in his **c.**... 4818
2Ch 35:24 therefore took him out of that **c.**,... 4818
2Ch 35:24 him in the second **c.** that he had;... 7393
Ps 46:9 he burneth the **c.** in the fire... 5699
Ps 76:6 the **c.** and horse are cast into... 7393
Ps 104:3 who maketh the clouds his **c.**:... 7398
Ca 3:9 King Solomon made himself a **c.**... 668
Isa 21:7 a **c.** with a couple of horsemen,... 7393
Isa 21:7 a **c.** of asses, and a **c.** of camels;... 7393
Isa 21:9 behold, here cometh a **c.** of men,... 7393
Isa 43:17 bringeth forth the **c.** and horse,... 7393
Jer 51:21 thee will I break in pieces the **c.**... 7393
Mic 1:13 bind the **c.** to the swift beast:... 4818
Zec 6:2 In the first **c.** were red horses;... 4818
Zec 6:2 and in the second **c.** black horses;... 4818
Zec 6:3 in the third **c.** white horses;... 4818
Zec 6:3 in the fourth **c.** grisled and bay... 4818
Zec 9:10 will cut off the **c.** from Ephraim,... 7393
Ac 8:28 and sitting in his **c.** read Esaias... *716*
Ac 8:29 Go near, and join thyself to this **c.**... *716*
Ac 8:38 he commanded the **c.** to stand still:... *716*

CHARIOT-CITIES See CHARIOT and CITIES.

CHARIOT-HORSES See CHARIOT and HORSES.

CHARIOT-MAN See CHARIOT and MAN.

CHARIOTS
Ge 50:9 there went up with him both **c.**... 7393
Ex 14:7 he took six hundred chosen **c.**,... 7393
Ex 14:7 and all the **c.** of Egypt,... 7393
Ex 14:9 **c.** of Pharaoh, and his horsemen,... 7393
Ex 14:17 upon all his host, upon his **c.**,... 7393
Ex 14:18 his **c.**, and upon his horsemen... 7393
Ex 14:23 even all Pharaoh's horses, his **c.**,... 7393
Ex 14:26 the Egyptians, upon their **c.**,... 7393
Ex 14:28 returned, and covered the **c.**,... 7393
Ex 15:4 Pharaoh's **c.** and his host hath he... 4818
Ex 15:19 of Pharaoh went in with his **c.**... 7393
De 11:4 unto their horses, and to their **c.**;... 7393
De 20:1 seest horses, and **c.**, and a people... 7393
Jos 11:4 with horses and **c.** very many... 7393
Jos 11:6 and burn their **c.** with fire... 4818
Jos 11:9 and burnt their **c.** with fire... 4818
Jos 17:16 have **c.** of iron, both they who are... 7393
Jos 17:18 have iron **c.**, and though they... 7393
Jos 24:6 **c.** and horsemen unto the Red sea... 7393
Jg 1:19 because they had **c.** of iron... 7393
Jg 4:3 he had nine hundred **c.** of iron;... 7393
Jg 4:7 Jabin's army, with his **c.** and his... 7393
Jg 4:13 Sisera gathered together all his **c.**,... 7393
Jg 4:13 even nine hundred **c.** of iron,... 7393
Jg 4:15 discomfited Sisera, and all his **c.**,... 7393
Jg 4:16 Barak pursued after the **c.**, and... 7393
Jg 5:28 why tarry the wheels of his **c.**?... 4818
1Sa 8:11 them for himself, for his **c.**,... 4818
1Sa 8:11 and some shall run before his **c.**... 4818
1Sa 8:12 war, and instruments of his **c.**... 7393
1Sa 13:5 with Israel, thirty thousand **c.**,... 7393
2Sa 1:6 **c.** and horsemen followed hard... 7393
2Sa 8:4 took from him a thousand **c.**,...
2Sa 8:4 of them for an hundred **c.**... 7393
2Sa 10:18 of seven hundred **c.** of the Syrians,... 7393
2Sa 15:1 prepared him **c.** and horses,... 4818
1Ki 1:5 prepared him **c.** and horsemen,... 7393
1Ki 4:26 stalls of horses for his **c.**,... 4817
1Ki 9:19 cities for his **c.**, and cities for his... 7393
1Ki 9:22 his captains, and rulers of his **c.**,... 7393
1Ki 10:26 Solomon gathered together **c.**... 7393
1Ki 10:26 a thousand and four hundred **c.**,... 7393
1Ki 10:26 he bestowed in the cities for **c.**,... 7393
1Ki 16:9 Zimri, captain of half his **c.**,... 7393
1Ki 20:1 with him, and horses, and **c.**:... 7393
1Ki 20:21 and **c.**, and slew the Syrians... 7393
1Ki 22:31 captains that had rule over his **c.**,... 7393
1Ki 22:32 captains of the **c.** saw Jehosaphat,... 7393
1Ki 22:33 the captains of the **c.** perceived... 7393
2Ki 6:14 sent he thither horses, and **c.**,... 7393
2Ki 6:15 the city both with horses and **c.**... 7393
2Ki 6:17 mountain was full of horses and **c.**... 7393
2Ki 7:6 noise of **c.**, and a noise of horses,... 7393
2Ki 8:21 went over to Zair, and all the **c.**... 7393
2Ki 8:21 of the **c.**: and the people fled... 7393
2Ki 10:2 there are with you **c.** and horses,... 7393
2Ki 13:7 but fifty horsemen, and ten **c.**,... 7393
2Ki 18:24 put thy trust on Egypt for **c.**... 7393
2Ki 19:23 the multitude of my **c.** I am come... 7393
2Ki 23:11 burned the **c.** of the sun with fire... 4818
1Ch 18:4 **c.**, and seven thousand horsemen,... 7393
1Ch 18:4 reserved of them an hundred **c.**... 7393
1Ch 19:6 hire them **c.** and horsemen out of... 7393
1Ch 19:7 hired thirty and two thousand **c.**,... 7393
1Ch 19:18 thousand men which fought in **c.**,... 7393
2Ch 1:14 gathered **c.** and horsemen:... 7393
2Ch 1:14 a thousand and four hundred **c.**,... 7393
2Ch 8:9 captains of his **c.** and horsemen... 7393
2Ch 9:25 thousand stalls for horses and **c.**,... 4818
2Ch 12:3 twelve hundred **c.**, and threescore... 7393
2Ch 14:9 and three hundred **c.**; and came... 4818
2Ch 16:8 with very many **c.** and horsemen?... 7393
2Ch 18:30 of the **c.** that were with him,... 7393
2Ch 18:31 when the captains of the **c.** saw... 7393
2Ch 18:32 the captains of the **c.** perceived... 7393
2Ch 21:9 princes, and all his **c.** with him:... 7393
2Ch 21:9 him in, and the captains of the **c.**... 7393
Ps 20:7 trust in **c.**, and some in horses:... 7393
Ps 68:17 **c.** of God are twenty thousand,... 7393
Ca 1:9 company of horses in Pharaoh's **c.**... 7393
Ca 6:12 my soul made me like the **c.** of... 4818
Isa 2:7 neither is there any end of their **c.**:... 4818
Isa 22:6 Elam bare the quiver with **c.** of... 7393
Isa 22:7 choicest valleys shall be full of **c.**,... 7393
Isa 22:18 **c.** of thy glory shall be the shame... 4818
Isa 31:1 trust in **c.**, because they are... 7393
Isa 36:9 and put thy trust on Egypt for **c.**... 7393
Isa 37:24 By the multitude of my **c.** am I... 7393
Isa 66:15 with his **c.** like a whirlwind, to... 4818
Isa 66:20 upon horses, and in **c.**, and in... 7393
Jer 4:13 his **c.** shall be as a whirlwind:... 4818
Jer 17:25 riding in **c.** and on horses, they,... 7393
Jer 22:4 David, riding in **c.** and on horses,... 7393
Jer 46:9 rage, ye **c.**; and let the mighty... 7393

Jer 47:3 the rushing of his **c.**, and at the......... 7393
Jer 50:37 upon their **c.**, and upon all the.......... 7393
Eze 23:24 come against thee with **c.**,................ 2021
Eze 26:7 with horses, and with **c.**, and............ 7393
Eze 26:10 of the wheels, and of the **c.**, when...... 7393
Eze 27:20 in precious clothes for **c.**................ 7396
Eze 39:20 with horses and **c.**, with mighty......... 7393
Da 11:40 with **c.**, and with horsemen, and......... 7393
Joe 2:5 Like the noise of **c.** on the tops of...... 4818
Mic 5:10 I will destroy thy **c.**........................ 4818
Na 2:3 **c.** shall be with flaming torches.......... 7393
Na 2:4 The **c.** shall rage in the streets,......... 7393
Na 2:13 I will burn her **c.** in the smoke,......... 7393
Na 3:2 horses, and of the jumping **c.**............. 4818
Hab 3:8 thine horses and thy **c.** of.................. 4818
Hag 2:22 I will overthrow the **c.**, and those....... 4818
Zec 6:1 came four **c.** out from between........... 4818
Re 9:9 as the sound of **c.** of many horses....... *716*
Re 18:13 and horses, and **c.**, and slaves,........... *4480*

CHARITABLY
Ro 14:15 meat, now walkest thou not **c.**..... *2596, 26*

CHARITY
1Cor 8:1 Knowledge puffeth up,but **c.**................. *26*
1Cor 13:1 of angels, and have not **c.**, I am............ *26*
1Cor 13:2 mountains, and have not **c.**,.................. *26*
1Cor 13:3 to be burned, and have not **c.**................ *26*
1Cor 13:4 **C.** suffereth long, and is kind;.............. *26*
1Cor 13:4 **c.** envieth not; **c.** vaunteth not.............. *26*
1Cor 13:8 **C.** never faileth: but whether................. *26*
1Cor 13:13 now abideth faith, hope, **c.**, these.......... *26*
1Cor 13:13 the greatest of these is **c.**...................... *26*
1Cor 14:1 Follow after **c.**, and desire..................... *26*
1Cor 16:14 all your things be done with **c.**.............. *26*
Col 3:14 above all these things put on **c.**,............ *26*
1Th 3:6 good tidings of your faith and **c.**,............ *26*
2Th 1:3 the **c.** of every one of you all.................. *26*
1Ti 1:5 commandment is **c.** out of a.................... *26*
1Ti 2:15 in faith and **c.** and holiness with............ *26*
1Ti 4:12 in conversation, in **c.**, in spirit, in.......... *26*
2Ti 2:22 follow righteousness, faith, **c.**,............... *26*
2Ti 3:10 faith, longsuffering, **c.**, patience,............ *26*
Tit 2:2 temperate, sound in faith, in **c.**,............. *26*
1Pe 4:8 fervent **c.** among yourselves:.................. *26*
1Pe 4:8 for **c.** shall cover the multitude.............. *26*
1Pe 5:14 ye one another with a kiss of **c.**............. *26*
2Pe 1:7 and to brotherly kindness **c.**................... *26*
3Jo 6 have borne witness of thy **c.**.................. *26*
Jude 12 spots in your feasts of **c.**, when............... *26*
Re 2:19 **I know thy works, and c., and**......... *26*

CHARMED
Jer 8:17 which will not be **c.**, and they............ 3908

CHARMER See also CHARMERS.
De 18:11 Or a **c.**, or a consulter with....... 2266,2267

CHARMERS
Ps 58:5 hearken to the voice of **c.**,................ 3907
Isa 19:3 seek to the idols, and to the **c.**,.......... 328

CHARMING
Ps 58:5 to the voice of charmers, **c.**....... 2266,2267

CHARRAN (car'-ran) See also HARAN.
Ac 7:2 before he dwelt in **C.**,..................... *5488*
Ac 7:4 and dwelt in **C.**: and from thence,...... *5488*

CHASE See also CHASES; CHASETH; CHASING.
Le 26:7 And ye shall **c.** your enemies, and...... 7291
Le 26:8 And five of you shall **c.** an hundred,.... 7291
Le 26:36 the sound of a shaken leaf shall **c.**...... 7291
De 32:30 How should one **c.** a thousand,.......... 7291
Jos 23:10 man of you shall **c.** a thousand:.......... 7291
Ps 35:5 and let the angel of the Lord **c.**.......... 1760

CHASED
De 1:44 came out against you, and **c.** you,....... 7291
Jos 7:5 for they **c.** them from before the......... 7291
Jos 8:24 the wilderness wherein they **c.**............ 7291
Jos 10:10 and **c.** them along the way that.......... 7291
Jos 11:8 and **c.** them unto great Zidon,............ 7291
Jg 9:40 And Abimelech **c.** him, and he............ 7291
Jg 20:43 **c.** them, and trode them down............ 7291
Ne 13:28 Horonite: therefore I **c.** him from........ 1272
Job 18:18 into darkness, and **c.** out of the.......... 5074
Job 20:8 he shall be **c.** away as a vision of........ 5074
Isa 13:14 it shall be as the **c.** roe, and as a........ 5080
Isa 17:13 and shall be **c.** as the chaff of the....... 7291
La 3:52 Mine enemies **c.** me sore, like a......... 6679

CHASETH
Pr 19:26 **c.** away his mother, is a son that....... 1272

CHASING
1Sa 17:53 of Israel returned from **c.** after.......... 1814

CHASTE
2Co 11:2 present you as a **c.** virgin to............... *53*
Tit 2:5 discreet, **c.**, keepers at home,.............. *53*
1Pe 3:2 they behold your **c.** conversation........... *53*

CHASTEN See also CHASTENED; CHASTENEST; CHASTENETH; CHASTENING; CHASTISE.
2Sa 7:14 I will **c.** him with the rod of men,....... 3198
Ps 6:1 neither **c.** me in thy hot.................... 3256
Ps 38:1 **c.** me in thy hot displeasure............... 3256
Pr 19:18 **C.** thy son while there is hope,.......... 3256
Da 10:12 and to **c.** thyself before thy God,......... 6031
Re 3:19 **many as I love, I rebuke and c.**...... *3811*

CHASTENED
De 21:18 when they have **c.** him, will not.......... 3256
Job 33:19 He is **c.** also with pain upon his.......... 3198
Ps 69:10 When I wept, and **c.** my soul..................
Ps 73:14 have I been plagued, and **c.** every...... 8433
Ps 118:18 The Lord hath **c.** me sore: but he...... 3256
1Co 11:32 we are **c.** of the Lord, that we.......... *3811*
2Co 6:9 as **c.**, and not killed;........................ *3811*
Heb 12:10 for a few days **c.** us after their own.... *3811*

CHASTENEST
Ps 94:12 Blessed is the man whom thou **c.**,....... 3256

CHASTENETH
De 8:5 as a man **c.** his son, so..................... 3256
De 8:5 the Lord thy God **c.** thee.................. 3256
Pr 13:24 he that loveth him **c.** him.................. 4148
Heb 12:6 For whom the Lord loveth he **c.**,........ *3811*
Heb 12:7 son is he whom the father **c.** not?...... *3811*

CHASTENING
Job 5:17 therefore despise not thou the **c.**....... 4148
Pr 3:11 despise not the **c.** of the Lord;.......... 4148
Isa 26:16 a prayer when thy **c.** was upon.......... 4148
Heb 12:5 despise not thou the **c.** of the........... *3809*
Heb 12:7 If ye endure **c.**, God dealeth with....... *3809*
Heb 12:11 Now no **c.** for the present............... *3809*

CHASTISE See also CHASTEN: CHASTISED; CHASTISETH.
Le 26:28 and I, even I, will **c.** you seven.......... 3256
De 22:18 city shall take that man and **c.**.......... 3256
1Ki 12:11 but I will **c.** you with scorpions.......... 3256
1Ki 12:14 with whips, but I will **c.** you with....... 3256
2Ch 10:11, 14 I will **c.** you with scorpions.................
Ho 7:12 I will **c.** them, as their..................... 3256
Ho 10:10 in my desire that I should **c.**.............. 3256
Lu 23:16 I will therefore **c.** him, and release...... *3811*
Lu 23:22 I will therefore **c.** him, and let him...... *3811*

CHASTISED
1Ki 12:11 my father hath **c.** you with whips,....... 3256
1Ki 12:14 my father also **c.** you with whips,........ 3256
2Ch 10:11 my father **c.** you with whips, but........ 3256
2Ch 10:14 will add thereto: my father **c.** you....... 3256
Jer 31:18 Thou hast **c.** me, and I was **c.**,.......... 3256

CHASTISEMENT
De 11:2 not seen the **c.** of the Lord your......... 4148
Job 34:31 I have borne **c.**, I will not offend..............
Isa 53:5 the **c.** of our peace was upon............ 4148
Jer 30:14 the **c.** of a cruel one, for the............. 4148
Heb 12:8 But if ye be without **c.**, whereof......... *3309*

CHASTISETH
Ps 94:10 He that **c.** the heathen, shall not........ 3256

CHATTER
Isa 38:14 so did I **c.**: I did mourn as a............. 6850

CHEBAR (ke'-bar)
Eze 1:1 the captives by the river of **C.**,.......... 3529
Eze 1:3 the Chaldeans by the river **C.**;........... 3529
Eze 3:15 that dwelt by the river of **C.**,............ 3529
Eze 3:23 which I saw by the river of **C.**............ 3529
Eze 10:15 that I saw by the river of **C.**.............. 3529
Eze 10:20 God of Israel by the river of **C.**;......... 3529
Eze 10:22 which I saw by the river of **C.**,........... 3529
Eze 43:3 vision that I saw by the river **C.**;........ 3529

CHECK
Job 20:3 heard the **c.** of my reproach,............. 4148

CHECKER
1Ki 7:17 nets of **c.** work, and wreaths of.......... 7639

CHECKER-WORK See CHECKER and WORK.

CHEDORLAOMER (ke''-dor-la'-o-mer)
Ge 14:1 **C.** king of Elam, and Tidal king......... 3540
Ge 14:4 Twelve years they served **C.**, and........ 3540
Ge 14:5 in the fourteenth year came **C.**,......... 3540
Ge 14:9 With **C.** the king of Elam, and........... 3540
Ge 14:17 his return from the slaughter of **C.**,..... 3540

CHEEK See also CHEEKS.
1Ki 22:24 and smote Micaiah on the **c.**, and........ 3895
2Ch 18:23 and smote Micaiah upon the **c.**,......... 3895
Job 16:10 they have smitten me upon the **c.**........ 3895
Ps 3:7 all mine enemies upon the **c.** bone;...... 3895
La 3:30 He giveth his **c.** to him that.............. 3895
Joe 1:6 hath the **c.** teeth of a great lion.......... 4973
Mic 5:1 Israel with a rod upon the **c.**.............. 3895
Mt 5:39 **smite thee upon thy right c.**,.......... *4600*
Lu 6:29 **smiteth thee on the one c.**............. *4600*

CHEEK-BONE See CHEEK and BONE.

CHEEKS
De 18:3 the shoulder, and the two **c.**,............ 3895
Ca 1:10 Thy **c.** are comely with rows of........... 3895
Ca 5:13 His **c.** are as a bed of spices, as......... 3895
Isa 50:6 and my **c.** to them that plucked.......... 3895
La 1:2 and her tears are on her **c.**................ 3895

CHEEK-TEETH See CHEEK and TEETH.

CHEER See also CHEERETH; CHEERFUL.
De 24:5 and shall **c.** up his wife which he........ 8055
Ec 11:9 and let thy heart **c.** thee in the.......... 3190
Mt 9:2 **be of good c.; thy sins be forgiven.** *2293*
Mt 14:27 **Be of good c.; it is I; be not afraid** *2293*
Mk 6:50 saith unto them, **Be of good c.; it**.... *2293*
Joh 16:33 **but be of good c.; I have overcome.** *2293*
Ac 23:11 **Be of good c., Paul: for as thou**.... *2293*
Ac 27:22 I exhort you to be of good **c.**: for...... *2114*
Ac 27:25 Wherefore, sirs, be of good **c.**............ *2114*
Ac 27:36 Then were they all of good **c.**,............ *2114*

CHEERETH
Jg 9:13 which **c.** God and man, and go to........ 8055

CHEERFUL
Pr 15:13 A merry heart maketh a **c.**.................. 3190
Zec 8:19 gladness. and **c.** feasts; therefore........ 2896
Zec 9:17 shall make the young men **c.**,............ 5107
2Co 9:7 for God loveth a **c.** giver.................. *2431*

CHEERFULLY
Ac 24:10 the more **c.** answer for myself:........... *2115*

CHEERFULNESS
Ro 12:8 he that sheweth mercy, with **c.**......... *2432*

CHEESE See also CHEESES.
2Sa 17:29 sheep, and **c.** of kine, for David,........ 8194
Job 10:10 as milk, and curdled me like **c.**?.......... 1385

CHEESES
1Sa 17:18 carry these ten **c.** unto the........ 2757,2461

CHELAL (ke'-lal)
Ezr 10:30 Adna, and **C.**, Benaiah, Maaseiah,...... 3636

CHELLUH (kel'-loo)
Ezr 10:35 Benaiah, Bedeiah, **C.**,...................... 3622

CHELUB (ke'-lub)
1Ch 4:11 And **C.** the brother of Shuah............. 3620
1Ch 27:26 the ground was Ezri the son of **C.**....... 3620

CHELUBAI (ke-loo'-bahee) See also CALEB.
1Ch 2:9 Jerahmeel, and Ram, and **C.**............... 3621

CHEMARIMS (kem'-a-rims)
Zep 1:4 name of the **C.** with the priests;......... 3649

CHEMOSH (ke'-mosh)
Nu 21:29 thou art undone, O people of **C.**:........ 3645
Jg 11:24 that which **C.** thy god giveth............. 3645
1Ki 11:7 Solomon build an high place for **C.**,..... 3645
1Ki 11:33 **C.** the god of the Moabites, and.......... 3645
2Ki 23:13 **C.** the abomination of the Moabites,.... 3645
Jer 48:7 and **C.** shall go forth into captivity...... 3645
Jer 48:13 Moab shall be ashamed of **C.**, as........ 3645
Jer 48:46 O Moab! the people of **C.** perisheth:... 3645

CHENAANAH (ke-na'-a-nah)
1Ki 22:11 **C.** made him horns of iron:................ 3668
1Ki 22:24 **C.** went near, and smote Micaiah....... 3668
1Ch 7:10 Benjamin, and Ehud, and **C.**,............. 3668

2Ch 18:10 **C.** had made him horns of iron, ... 3668
2Ch 18:23 Zedekiah the son of **C.** came near, ... 3668

CHENANI (ken'-a-ni)
Ne 9:4 Bani, and **C.**, and cried with.............. 3662

CHENANIAH (ken-a-ni'-ah) See also CONONIAH.
1Ch 15:22 And **C.**, chief of the Levites, was....... 3663
1Ch 15:27 and **C.** the master of the song........... 3663
1Ch 26:29 **C.** and his sons were for the............ 3663

CHEPHAR-HAAMMONAI (ke''-far-ha-am'-mo-nahee)
Jos 18:24 And **C.**, and Ophni, and Gaba;........... 3726

CHEPHIRAH (ke-fi'-rah)
Jos 9:17 their cities were Gibeon, and **C**, ... 3716
Jos 18:26 Mizpeh, and **C.**, and Mozah, ... 3716
Ezr 2:25 Kirjath-arim, **C.**, and Beeroth, ... 3716
Ne 7:29 of Kirjath-jearim, **C.**, and Beeroth, ... 3716

CHERAN (ke'-ran)
Ge 36:26 and Eshban, and Ithran, and **C.**,.......... 3763
1Ch 1:41 and Eshban, and Ithran, and **C**............ 3763

CHERETHIMS (ker'-e-thims) See also CHERETHITES.
Eze 25:16 I will cut off the **C.**, and destroy........ 3774

CHERETHITES (ker'-e-thites) See also CHERETHIMS.
1Sa 30:14 invasion upon the south of the **C.**. 3774
2Sa 8:18 both the **C.** and the Pelethites;........... 3774
2Sa 15:18 all the **C.**, and all the Pelethites,........ 3774
2Sa 20:7 and the **C.**, and the Pelethites, ... 3774
2Sa 20:23 was over the **C.** and over................. 3774
1Ki 1:38 and the **C.**, and the Pelethites, ... 3746
1Ki 1:44 and the **C.**, and the Pelethites, ... 3774
1Ch 18:17 was over the **C.** and Pelethites;......... 3774
Zep 2:5 the nation of the **C.**! the word of 3774

CHERISH See also CHERISHED.
1Ki 1:2 let her **c.** him, and let her lie in......... 5532

CHERISHED
1Ki 1:4 was very fair, and **c.** the king,........... 5532

CHERISHETH
Eph 5:29 but nourished and **c.** it, even............ *2282*
1Th 2:7 even as a nurse **c.** her children:......... *2282*

CHERITH (ke'-rith)
1Ki 17:3 and hide thyself by the brook **C.**, ... 3747
1Ki 17:5 went and dwelt by the brook **C.**,......... 3747

CHERUB (ke'-rub)
Ezr 2:59 up from Tel-melah, Tel-harsa, **C.**, ... 3743
Ne 7:61 from Tel-melah, Tel-haresha, **C.**. 3743

CHERUB (cher'-ub) See also CHERUBIMS.
Ex 25:19 one **c.** on the one end,..................... 3742
Ex 25:19 and the other **c.** on the other end: 3742
Ex 37:8 One **c.** on the end on this side, ... 3742
Ex 37:8 and another **c.** on the other............... 3742
2Sa 22:11 he rode upon a **c.**, and did fly:........... 3742
1Ki 6:24 the one wing of the **c.**, and five 3742
1Ki 6:24 cubits the other wing of the **c.**........... 3742
1Ki 6:25 the other **c.** was ten cubits: both 3742
1Ki 6:26 height of the one **c.** was ten cubits,.... 3742
1Ki 6:26 and so was it of the other **c.**. 3742
1Ki 6:27 of the other **c.** touched the wall; 3742
2Ch 3:11 one wing of the one **c.** was five ....
2Ch 3:11 to the wing of the other **c.**................ 3742
2Ch 3:12 one wing of the other **c.** was five....... 3742
2Ch 3:12 joining to the wing of the other **c.**. 3742
Ps 18:10 he rode upon a **c.**, and did fly:........... 3742
Eze 9:3 was gone up from the **c.**, ... 3742
Eze 10:2 under the **c.**, and fill thine hand 3742
Eze 10:4 went up from the **c.**, and stood........... 3742
Eze 10:7 one **c.** stretched forth his hand 3742
Eze 10:9 one wheel by one **c.**, and another....... 3742
Eze 10:9 another wheel by another **c.**.............. 3742
Eze 10:14 the first face was the face of a **c.**, ... 3742
Eze 28:14 Thou art the anointed **c.** that............ 3742
Eze 28:16 I will destroy thee, O covering **c.**,....... 3742
Eze 41:18 between a **c.** and a **c.**; and 3742
Eze 41:18 every **c.** had two faces;.................... 3742

CHERUBIMS (cher'-u-bims) See also CHERUBIMS'.
Ge 3:24 of the garden of Eden **C.**. and........... 3742
Ex 25:18 thou shalt make two **c.** of gold,.......... 3742
Ex 25:19 mercy seat shall ye make the **c.**.......... 3742
Ex 25:20 **c.** shall stretch forth their wings......... 3742
Ex 25:20 seat shall the faces of the **c.**............ 3742
Ex 25:22 between the two **c.** which are 3742
Ex 26:1 **c.** of cunning work shalt thou 3742
Ex 26:31 work: with **c.** shall it be made: 3742
Ex 36:8 **c.** of cunning work made he 3742
Ex 36:35 **c.** made he it of cunning work. 3742
Ex 37:7 he made two **c.** of gold, beaten.......... 3742
Ex 37:8 the mercy seat made he the **c.** 3742
Ex 37:9 the **c.** spread out their wings on 3742
Ex 37:9 seatward were the faces of the **c.**. 3742
Nu 7:89 from between the two **c.**.................. 3742
1Sa 4:4 which dwelleth between the **c.**............ 3742
2Sa 6:2 that dwelleth between the **c.** 3742
1Ki 6:23 oracle he made two **c.** of olive........... 3742
1Ki 6:25 the **c.** were of one measure and......... 3742
1Ki 6:27 set the **c.** within the inner house:........ 3742
1Ki 6:27 stretched forth the wings of the **c.**, ... 3742
1Ki 6:28 And he overlaid the **c.** with gold. 3742
1Ki 6:29 about with carved figures of **c.**........... 3742
1Ki 6:32 carvings of **c.** and palm trees............ 3742
1Ki 6:32 spread gold upon the **c.**, and upon....... 3742
1Ki 6:35 carved thereon **c.** and palm trees 3742
1Ki 7:29 ledges were lions, oxen, and **c.**........... 3742
1Ki 7:36 graved **c.**, lions, and palm trees, ... 3742
1Ki 8:6 even under the wings of the **c.**. 3742
1Ki 8:7 **c.** spread forth their two wings.......... 3742
1Ki 8:7 ark, and the **c.** covered the ark 3742
2Ki 19:15 which dwellest between the **c.**, ... 3742
1Ch 13:6 that dwelleth between the **c.**, ... 3742
1Ch 28:18 the chariot of the **c.**, that spread........ 3742
2Ch 3:7 gold; and graved **c.** on the walls......... 3742
2Ch 3:10 he made two **c.** of image work, ... 3742
2Ch 3:11 wings of the **c.** were twenty.............. 3742
2Ch 3:13 The wings of these **c.** spread 3742
2Ch 3:14 linen, and wrought **c.** thereon............ 3742
2Ch 5:7 even under the wings of the **c.** 3742
2Ch 5:8 the **c.** spread forth their wings........... 3742
2Ch 5:8 **c.** covered the ark and the staves 3742
Ps 80:1 that dwellest between the **c.**, ... 3742
Ps 99:1 he sitteth between the **c.**; let 3742
Isa 37:16 that dwellest between the **c.**. 3742
Eze 10:1 head of the **c.** there appeared............ 3742
Eze 10:2 coals of fire from between the **c.**,....... 3742
Eze 10:3 **c.** stood on the right side of the......... 3742
Eze 10:6 the wheels, from between the **c.**......... 3742
Eze 10:7 from between the **c.** unto the fire....... 3742
Eze 10:7 the fire that was between the **c.**, ... 3742
Eze 10:8 there appeared in the **c.** the form....... 3742
Eze 10:9 behold the four wheels by the **c.**, ... 3742
Eze 10:15 the **c.** were lifted up. This is the......... 3742
Eze 10:16 when the **c.** went, the wheels 3742
Eze 10:16 them: and when the **c.** lifted............. 3742
Eze 10:18 house, and stood over the **c.**............ 3742
Eze 10:19 the **c.** lifted up their wings, and 3742
Eze 10:20 and I knew that they were the **c.**........ 3742
Eze 11:22 the **c.** lift up their wings, and the 3742
Eze 41:18 was made with **c.** and palm trees, ... 3742
Eze 41:20 door were **c.** and palm trees 3742
Eze 41:25 **c.** and palm trees, like as were.......... 3742
Heb 9:5 **c.** of glory shadowing the................. *5502*

CHERUBIMS'
Eze 10:5 sound of the **c.** wings was heard 3742

CHESALON (kes'-a-lon)
Jos 15:10 of mount Jearim, which is **C.**. 3693

CHESED (ke'-sed)
Ge 22:22 And **C.**, and Hazo, and Pildash, ... 3777

CHESIL (ke'-sil)
Jos 15:30 And Eltolad, and **C.**, and Hormah, ... 3686

CHESNUT
Ge 30:37 and of the hazel and **c.** tree 6196
Eze 31:8 and the **c.** trees were not like 6196

CHESTNUT-TREE See CHESTNUT and TREE.

CHEST See also CHESTS.
2Ki 12:9 Jehoiada the priest took a **c.**, and......... 727
2Ki 12:10 much money in the **c.**, that the 727
2Ch 24:8 made a **c.**, and set it without at the 727
2Ch 24:10 cast into the **c.**, until they had........... 727
2Ch 24:11 **c.** was brought unto the king's 727
2Ch 24:11 came and emptied the **c.**, and took........ 727

CHESTNUT See CHESNUT.

CHESTS
Eze 27:24 in **c.** of rich apparel, bound with......... 1595

CHESULLOTH (ke-sul'-loth) See also CHISLOTH-TABOR.
Jos 19:18 was toward Jezreel, and **C.**.............. 3694

CHETH (khayth)
Ps 119:57 *title* [ח] **C.**..

CHEW See also CHEWED; CHEWETH.
Le 11:4 shall ye not eat of them that **c.**.......... 5927
De 14:7 of them that **c.** the cud, or of them 5927
De 14:7 **c.** the cud, but divide not the hoof;..... 5927

CHEWED
Nu 11:33 between their teeth, ere it was **c.**, ... 3772

CHEWETH
Le 11:3 and **c.** the cud, among the beasts, ... 5927
Le 11:4 he **c.** the cud, but divideth not the 5927
Le 11:5 the coney, because he **c.** the cud, ... 5927
Le 11:6 because he **c.** the cud, but divideth..... 5927
Le 11:7 he **c.** not the cud; he is unclean 1641
Le 11:26 not clovenfooted, nor **c.** the cud,......... 5927
De 14:6 and **c.** the cud among the beasts, ... 5927
De 14:8 yet **c.** not the cud, it is unclean ....

CHEZIB (ke'-zib) See also ACHZIB; CHOZEBA.
Ge 38:5 he was at **C.**, when she bare him....... 3580

CHICKENS
Mt 23:37 **as a hen gathereth her c. under** *3556*

CHID See CHODE.

CHIDE See also CHIDING; CHODE.
Ex 17:2 Wherefore the people did **c.** with 7378
Ex 17:2 Why **c.** ye with me? wherefore.......... 7378
Jg 8:1 they did **c.** with him sharply............. 7378
Ps 103:9 He will not always **c.**: neither will....... 7378

CHIDED See CHODE.

CHIDING
Ex 17:7 of the **c.** of the children of Israel,....... 7379

CHIDON (ki'- don) See also NACHON.
1Ch 13:9 unto the threshingfloor of **C.**, ... 3592

CHIEF See also CHIEFEST.
Ge 21:22 Phicol the **c.** captain of his host...............
Ge 21:32 Phichol the **c.** captain of his host, ...
Ge 26:26 Phichol the **c.** captain of his army. ....
Ge 40:2 against the **c.** of the butlers, ... 8269
Ge 40:2 and against the **c.** of the bakers. 8269
Ge 40:9 **c.** butler told his dream to Joseph,...... 8269
Ge 40:16 When the **c.** baker saw that the......... 8269
Ge 40:20 of the **c.** butler and of the **c.** baker..... 8269
Ge 40:21 he restored the **c.** butler unto his........ 8269
Ge 40:22 he hanged the **c.** baker: as Joseph...... 8269
Ge 40:23 Yet did not the **c.** butler remember 8269
Ge 41:9 spake the **c.** butler unto Pharaoh,....... 8269
Ge 41:10 house, both me and the **c.** baker:....... 8269
Le 21:4 a **c.** man among his people, to........... 1167
Nu 3:24 the **c.** of the house of the father 5387
Nu 3:30 the **c.** of the house of the father 5387
Nu 3:32 be **c.** over the **c.** of the Levites, ... 5387
Nu 3:35 And the **c.** of the house of the........... 5387
Nu 4:34 and the **c.** of the congregation 5387
Nu 4:46 and the **c.** of Israel numbered,........... 5387
Nu 25:14 prince of a **c.** house among the.............. 1
Nu 25:15 and of a **c.** house in Midian..................... 1
Nu 31:26 **c.** fathers of the congregation: 7218
Nu 32:28 the **c.** fathers of the tribes of the 7218
Nu 36:1 the **c.** fathers of the families of.......... 7218
Nu 36:1 **c.** fathers of the children of............... 7218
De 1:15 I took the **c.** of your tribes, wise 7218
De 33:15 for the **c.** things of the ancient........... 7218
Jos 22:14 **c.** house a prince throughout all.............. 1
Jg 20:2 **c.** of all the people, even of all.......... 6438
1Sa 14:38 Draw ye near thither, all the **c.** of...... 6438
1Sa 15:21 **c.** of the things which should............ 7225
2Sa 5:8 of David's soul, he shall be **c.**..................
2Sa 8:18 and David's sons were **c.** rulers. 3548
2Sa 20:26 was a **c.** ruler about David................ 3548
2Sa 23:8 **c.** among the captains; the same 7218
2Sa 23:13 three of the thirty **c.** went down, ... 7218
2Sa 23:18 of Zeruiah, was **c.** among three.......... 7218
1Ki 5:16 Beside the **c.** of Solomon's officers 8269
1Ki 8:1 **c.** of the fathers of the children......... 5387
1Ki 9:23 the **c.** of the officers that were 8269
1Ki 14:27 **c.** of the guard, which kept the.......... 8269
2Ki 25:18 guard took Seraiah the **c.** priest, ... 7218
1Ch 5:2 and of him came the **c.** ruler; 5057
1Ch 5:7 the **c.**, Jeiel, and Zechariah,.............. 7218
1Ch 5:12 Joel the **c.**, and Shapham the............. 7218
1Ch 5:15 **c.** of the house of their fathers. 7218
1Ch 7:3 Isheah, five: all of them **c.** men. 7218
1Ch 7:40 men of valour, **c.** of the princes. 7218
1Ch 8:28 by their generations, **c.** men. 7218

Book	Ref	Context	No.
1Ch	9:9	these men were **c.** of the fathers	7218
1Ch	9:17	brethren: Shallum was the **c.**;	7218
1Ch	9:26	four **c.** porters, were in their set	1368
1Ch	9:33	**c.** of the fathers of the Levites,	7218
1Ch	9:34	**c.** fathers of the Levites were	7218
1Ch	9:34	**c.** throughout their generations;	7218
1Ch	11:6	the Jebusites first shall be **c.**	7218
1Ch	11:6	Zeruiah went first up, and was **c.**.	7218
1Ch	11:10	**c.** of the mighty men whom David	7218
1Ch	11:11	Hachmonite, the **c.** of the captains:	7218
1Ch	11:20	of Joab, he was **c.** of the three:	7218
1Ch	12:3	The **c.** was Ahiezer, then Joash,	7218
1Ch	12:18	Amasai, who was **c.** of the captains,	7218
1Ch	15:5	the sons of Kohath; Uriel the **c.**,	8269
1Ch	15:6	the sons of Merari; Asaiah the **c.**,	8269
1Ch	15:7	the sons of Gershom; Joel the **c.**,	8269
1Ch	15:8	of Elizaphan; Shemaiah the **c.**,	8269
1Ch	15:9	the sons of Hebron; Eliel the **c.**,	8269
1Ch	15:10	sons of Uzziel; Amminadab the **c.**,	8269
1Ch	15:12	**c.** of the fathers of the Levites:	7218
1Ch	15:16	spake to the **c.** of the Levites	8269
1Ch	15:22	Chenaniah, **c.** of the Levites, was	8269
1Ch	16:5	Asaph the **c.**, and next to him	7218
1Ch	18:17	sons of David were **c.** about the	7223
1Ch	23:8	the **c.** was Jehiel, and Zetham,	7218
1Ch	23:9	the **c.** of the fathers of Laadan	7218
1Ch	23:11	Jahath was the **c.**, and Zizah the	7218
1Ch	23:16	of Gershom, Shebuel was the **c.**.	7218
1Ch	23:17	of Eliezer were, Rehabiah the **c.**.	7218
1Ch	23:18	sons of Izhar; Shelomith the **c.**.	7218
1Ch	23:24	**c.** of the fathers, as they were	7218
1Ch	24:4	more **c.** men found of the sons of	7218
1Ch	24:4	were sixteen **c.** men of the house	7218
1Ch	24:6	and before the **c.** of the fathers	7218
1Ch	24:31	**c.** of the fathers of the priests	7218
1Ch	26:10	Simri the **c.**, (for though he was	7218
1Ch	26:10	yet his father made him the **c.**;)	7218
1Ch	26:12	even among the **c.** men, having	7218
1Ch	26:21	**c.** fathers, even of Laadan the	7218
1Ch	26:26	the **c.** fathers, the captains over	7218
1Ch	26:31	Jerijah the **c.**, even among the	7218
1Ch	26:32	two thousand and seven hundred **c.**	7218
1Ch	27:1	the **c.** fathers and captains of	7218
1Ch	27:3	Of the children of Perez was the **c.**	7218
1Ch	27:5	Benaiah the son of Jehoiada, a **c.**	7218
1Ch	29:6	the **c.** of the fathers and princes	8269
1Ch	29:22	to be the **c.** governor, and Zadok	5057
2Ch	1:2	all Israel, the **c.** of the fathers.	7218
2Ch	5:2	**c.** of the fathers of the children	5387
2Ch	8:9	**c.** of his captains, and captains of	8269
2Ch	8:10	**c.** of king Solomon's officers,	8269
2Ch	11:22	**c.**, to be ruler among his brethren:	7218
2Ch	12:10	the **c.** of the guard, that kept the	8269
2Ch	17:14	Aduah the **c.**, and with him	8269
2Ch	19:8	of the **c.** of the fathers of Israel,	7218
2Ch	19:11	Amariah the **c.** priest is over you	7218
2Ch	23:2	the **c.** of the fathers of Israel,	7218
2Ch	24:6	king called for Jehoiada the **c.**,	7218
2Ch	26:12	**c.** of the fathes of the mighty	7218
2Ch	26:20	the **c.** priest, and all the priests,	7218
2Ch	31:10	Azariah the **c.** priest of the house	7218
2Ch	35:9	and Jozabad, **c.** of the Levites,	8269
2Ch	36:14	**c.** of the priests, and the people	8269
Ezr	1:5	the **c.** of the fathers of Judah	7218
Ezr	2:68	some of the **c.** of the fathers,	7218
Ezr	3:12	and **c.** of the fathers, who were	7218
Ezr	4:2	the **c.** of the fathers, and said	7218
Ezr	4:3	of the **c.** of the fathers of Israel,	7218
Ezr	5:10	men that were the **c.** of them	7217
Ezr	7:5	the son of Aaron the **c.** priest:	7218
Ezr	7:28	Israel **c.** men to go up with me	7218
Ezr	8:1	are now the **c.** of their fathers,	7218
Ezr	8:16	and for Meshullam, **c.** men;	7218
Ezr	8:17	Iddo the **c.** at the place Casiphia,	7218
Ezr	8:24	twelve of the **c.** of the priests,	8269
Ezr	8:29	**c.** of the priests and the Levites,	8269
Ezr	8:29	and **c.** of the fathers of Israel,	8269
Ezr	9:2	hath been **c.** in this trespass.	7223
Ezr	10:5	Ezra, and made the **c.** priests,	8269
Ezr	10:16	**c.** of the fathers, after the house	7218
Ne	7:70	some of the **c.** of the fathers	7218
Ne	7:71	the **c.** of the fathers gave to the	7218
Ne	8:13	**c.** of the fathers of all the people,	7218
Ne	10:14	The **c.** of the people; Parosh,	7218
Ne	11:3	the **c.** of the province that dwelt	7218
Ne	11:13	his brethren, **c.** of the fathers,	7218
Ne	11:16	of the **c.** of the Levites, had the	7218
Ne	12:7	These were the **c.** of the priests	7218
Ne	12:12	the **c.** of the fathers: of Seraiah,	7218
Ne	12:22	were recorded **c.** of the fathers:	7218
Ne	12:23	sons of Levi, the **c.** of the fathers,	7218
Ne	12:24	the **c.** of the Levites; Hashabiah,	7218
Ne	12:46	old there were **c.** of the singers,	7218
Job	12:24	the **c.** of the people of the earth,	7218
Job	29:25	I chose out their way, and sat **c.**,	7218
Job	40:19	the **c.** of the ways of God:	7225
Ps	4:*title*	To the **c.** Musician on Neginoth,	5329
Ps	5:*title*	the **c.** Musician upon Nehiloth,	5329
Ps	6:*title*	To the **c.** Musician on Neginoth	5329
Ps	8:*title*	To the **c.** Musician upon Gittith,	
Ps	9:*title*	**c.** Musician upon Muth-labben,	5329
Ps	11:*title*	**c.** Musician, A Psalm of David.	5329
Ps	12:*title*	the **c.** Musician upon Sheminith,	5329
Ps	13:*title*	**c.** Musician, A Psalm of David.	5329
Ps	14:*title*	**c.** Musician, A Psalm of David.	5329
Ps	18:*title*	**c.** Muscian, A Psalm of David.	5329
Ps	19:*title*	**c.** Musician, A Psalm of David.	5329
Ps	20:*title*	**c.** Musician, A Psalm of David.	5329
Ps	21:*title*	**c.** Musician, A Psalm of David.	5329
Ps	22:*title*	**c.** Musician upon Aijeleth	5329
Ps	31:*title*	**c.** Musician, A Psalm of David.	5329
Ps	36:*title*	**c.** Musician, A Psalm of David	5329
Ps	39:*title*	**c.** Musician, even to Jeduthun,	5329
Ps	40:*title*	**c.** Musician, A Psalm of David.	5329
Ps	41:*title*	**c.** Musician, A Psalm of David.	5329
Ps	42:*title*	the **c.** Musician, Maschil, for the	5329
Ps	44:*title*	To the **c.** Musician for the sons	5329
Ps	45:*title*	**c.** Musician upon Shoshannim,	5329
Ps	46:*title*	*To the* **c.** Musician for the sons	5329
Ps	47:*title*	*To the* **c.** Musician, A Psalm for	5329
Ps	49:*title*	To the **c.** Musician, A Psalm for	5329
Ps	51:*title*	**c.** Musician, A Psalm of David,	5329
Ps	52:*title*	**c.** Musician, Maschil, A Psalm of	5329
Ps	53:*title*	the **c.** Musician upon Mahalath,	5329
Ps	54:*title*	To the **c.** Musician on Neginoth,	5329
Ps	55:*title*	To the **c.** Musician on Neginoth,	5329
Ps	56:*title*	To the **c.** Musician upon	5329
Ps	57:*title*	To the **c.** Musician, Al-taschith,	5329
Ps	58:*title*	To the **c.** Musician, Al-taschith,	5329
Ps	59:*title*	To the **c.** Musician, Al-taschith,	5329
Ps	60:*title*	**c.** Musician upon Shushan-eduth,	5329
Ps	61:*title*	the **c.** Musician upon Neginah,	5329
Ps	62:*title*	To the **c.** Musician, to Jeduthun,	5329
Ps	64:*title*	**c.** Musician, A Psalm of David.	5329
Ps	65:*title*	**c.** Musician, A Psalm and Song	5329
Ps	66:*title*	**c.** Musician, A Song or Psalm.	5329
Ps	67:*title*	To the **c.** Musician on Neginoth,	5329
Ps	68:*title*	**c.** Musician, A Psalm or Song of	5329
Ps	69:*title*	**c.** Musician upon Shoshannim,	5329
Ps	70:*title*	**c.** Musician, A Psalm of David,	5329
Ps	75:*title*	To the **c.** Musician, Al-taschith,	5329
Ps	76:*title*	To the **c.** Musician on Neginoth,	5329
Ps	77:*title*	To the **c.** Musician, to Jeduthun,	5329
Ps	78:51	the **c.** of their strength in the	7225
Ps	80:*title*	To the **c.** Musician upon	5329
Ps	81:*title*	To the **c.** Musician upon Gittith,	5329
Ps	84:*title*	To the **c.** Musician upon Gittith,	5329
Ps	85:*title*	To the **c.** Musician, A Psalm for	5329
Ps	88:*title*	the **c.** Musician upon Mahalath	5329
Ps	105:36	land, the **c.** of all their strength.	7225
Ps	109:*title*	**c.** Musician, A Psalm of David.	5329
Ps	137:6	not Jerusalem above my **c.** joy.	7218
Ps	139:*title*	**c.** Musician, A Psalm of David.	5329
Ps	140:*title*	**c.** musician, A Psalm of David.	5329
Pr	1:21	in the **c.** place of concourse,	7218
Pr	16:28	a whisperer separateth **c.** friends.	441
Ca	4:14	and aloes, with all the **c.** spices:	7218
Isa	14:9	even all the **c.** ones of the earth;	6260
Isa	41:9	thee from the **c.** men thereof,	678
Jer	13:21	them to be captains, and as **c.**	7218
Jer	20:1	**c.** governor in the house of the	5057
Jer	31:7	among the **c.** of the nations:	7218
Jer	49:35	of Elam, the **c.** of their might.	7225
Jer	52:24	guard took Seraiah the **c.** priest,	7218
La	1:5	Her adversaries are the **c.**, her	7218
Eze	27:22	in thy fairs with **c.** of all spices,	7218
Eze	38:2	**c.** prince of Meshech and Tubal,	7218
Eze	38:3	I am against thee, O Gog, the **c.**	7218
Eze	39:1	**c.** prince of Meshech and Tubal:	7218
Da	2:48	and **c.** of the governors over all	7229
Da	10:13	lo, Michael, one of the **c.** princes,	7223
Da	11:41	the **c.** of the children of Ammon	7225
Am	6:1	which are named **c.** of the nations,	7225
Am	6:6	themselves with the **c.** ointments:	7225
Hab	3:19	to the **c.** singer on my stringed	5329
Mt	2:4	all the **c.** priests and scribes	*749*
Mt	16:21	elders and **c.** priests and scribes,	*749*
Mt	20:18	**be betrayed unto the c. priests**	*749*
Mt	20:27	**whosoever will be c. among you,**	*4413*
Mt	21:15	when the **c.** priests and scribes	*749*
Mt	21:23	the **c.** priests and the elders of the	*749*
Mt	21:45	the **c.** priests and Pharisees had	*749*
Mt	23:6	**the c. seats in the synagogues,**	*4410*
Mt	26:3	assembled together the **c.** priests,	*749*
Mt	26:14	Iscariot, went unto the **c.** priests,	*749*
Mt	26:47	from the **c.** priests and elders	*749*
Mt	26:59	Now the **c.** priests, and elders,	*749*
Mt	27:1	**c.** priests and elders of the people	*749*
Mt	27:3	silver to the **c.** priests and elders,	*749*
Mt	27:6	the **c.** priests took the silver pieces,	*749*
Mt	27:12	he was accused of the **c.** priests	*749*
Mt	27:20	the **c.** priests and elders persuaded	*749*
Mt	27:41	also the **c.** priests mocking him,	*749*
Mt	27:62	the **c.** priests and Pharisees came	*749*
Mt	28:11	shewed unto the **c.** priests all the	*749*
Mk	6:21	captains, and **c.** estates of Galilee;	*4413*
Mk	8:31	of the **c.** priests, and scribes,	*749*
Mk	10:33	**be delivered unto the c. priests,**	*749*
Mk	11:18	the scribes and **c.** priests heard it,	*749*
Mk	11:27	there come to him the **c.** priests,	*749*
Mk	12:39	**the c. seats in the synagogues,**	*4410*
Mk	14:1	the **c.** priests and the scribes	*749*
Mk	14:10	went unto the **c.** priests, to betray	*749*
Mk	14:43	from the **c.** priests and the scribes	*749*
Mk	14:53	all the **c.** priests and the elders	*749*
Mk	14:55	the **c.** priests and all the council	*749*
Mk	15:1	the **c.** priests held a consultation	*749*
Mk	15:3	**c.** priests accused him of many	*749*
Mk	15:10	the **c.** priests had delivered him for	*749*
Mk	15:11	the **c.** priests moved the people,	*749*
Mk	15:31	also the **c.** priests mocking said	*749*
Lu	9:22	**c. priests and scribes, and be slain,**	*749*
Lu	11:15	devils through Beelzebub the **c.**	*758*
Lu	14:1	house of one of the **c.** Pharisees	*758*
Lu	14:7	how they chose out the **c.** rooms;	*4411*
Lu	19:2	was the **c.** among the publicans,	*754*
Lu	19:47	the **c.** priests and the scribes	*749*
Lu	19:47	and the **c.** of the people sought	*4413*
Lu	20:1	the **c.** priests and the scribes came	*749*
Lu	20:19	the **c.** priests and the scribes the	*749*
Lu	20:46	**and the c. rooms at feasts;**	*4411*
Lu	22:2	the **c.** priests and scribes sought	*749*
Lu	22:4	communed with the **c.** priests	*749*
Lu	22:26	**that is c., as he that doth serve.**	*2283*
Lu	22:52	Jesus said unto the **c.** priests,	*749*
Lu	22:66	the **c.** priests and the scribes came	*749*
Lu	23:4	said Pilate to the **c.** priests and to	*749*
Lu	23:10	the **c.** priests and scribes stood	*749*
Lu	23:13	together the **c.** priests and the	*749*
Lu	23:23	of them and of the **c.** priests	*749*
Lu	24:20	how the **c.** priests and our rulers	*749*
Joh	7:32	the Pharisees and the **c.** priests	*749*
Joh	7:45	came the officers to the **c.** priests	*749*
Joh	11:47	the **c.** priests and the Pharisees	*749*
Joh	11:57	both the **c.** priests and the Pharisees	*749*
Joh	12:10	**c.** priests consulted that they might	*749*
Joh	12:42	Nevertheless among the **c.** rulers	*758*
Joh	18:3	from the **c.** priests and Pharisees,	*749*
Joh	18:35	Thine own nation and the **c.** priests	*749*
Joh	19:6	**c.** priests therefore and officers	*749*
Joh	19:15	The **c.** priests answered, We have	*749*
Joh	19:21	Then said the **c.** priests of the Jews	*749*
Ac	4:23	the **c.** priests and elders had said	*749*
Ac	5:24	the **c.** priests heard these things	*749*
Ac	9:14	authority from the **c.** priests to	*749*
Ac	9:21	them bound unto the **c.** priests?	*749*
Ac	13:50	and the **c.** men of the city,	*4413*
Ac	14:12	because he was the **c.** speaker.	*2288*
Ac	15:22	**c.** men among the brethren:	*2288*
Ac	16:12	**c.** city of that part of Macedonia,	*4413*
Ac	17:4	and of the **c.** women not a few.	*4413*
Ac	18:8	the **c.** ruler of the synagogues,	*752*
Ac	18:17	the **c.** ruler of the synagogue,	*752*
Ac	19:4	a Jew, and **c.** of the priests,	*749*
Ac	19:31	and certain of the **c.** of Asia,	*775*
Ac	21:31	unto the **c.** captain of the band,	*5506*
Ac	21:32	when they saw the **c.** captain and	*5506*
Ac	21:33	Then the **c.** captain came near,	*5506*
Ac	21:37	he said unto the **c.** captain, May	*5506*
Ac	22:24	The **c.** captain commanded him	*5506*
Ac	22:26	he went and told the **c.** captain,	*5506*

Ac	22:27	Then the **c.** captain came, and said	*5506*
Ac	22:28	And the **c.** captain answered, With	*5506*
Ac	22:29	and the **c.** captain also was afraid,	*5506*
Ac	22:30	commanded the **c.** priests and all	*749*
Ac	23:10	the **c.** captain, fearing lest Paul	*5506*
Ac	23:14	came to the **c.** priests and elders,	*749*
Ac	23:15	signify to the **c.** captain that he	*5506*
Ac	23:17	this young man to the **c.** captain:	*5506*
Ac	23:18	brought him to the **c.** captain,	*5506*
Ac	23:19	Then the **c.** captain took him by	*5506*
Ac	23:22	**the c. captain then let the young**	*5506*
Ac	24:7	But the **c.** captain Lysias came	*5506*
Ac	24:22	When Lysias the **c.** captain shall	*5506*
Ac	25:2	the **c.** of the Jews informed him	*4413*
Ac	25:15	the **c.** priests and the elders of	*749*
Ac	25:23	with the **c.** captains, and principal	*5506*
Ac	26:10	authority from the **c.** priests;	*749*
Ac	26:12	commission from the **c.** priests,	*749*
Ac	28:7	of the **c.** man of the island,	*4413*
Ac	28:17	Paul called the **c.** of the Jews	*4413*
Eph	2:20	himself being the **c.** corner stone;	*204*
1Ti	1:15	to save sinners; of whom I am **c.**	*4413*
1Pe	2:6	I lay in Sion a **c.** corner stone,	*204*
1Pe	5:4	when the **c.** Shepherd shall appear,	*750*
Re	6:15	**c.** captains, and the mighty men,	*5506*

CHIEFEST

1Sa	2:29	with the **c.** of all the offerings	7225
1Sa	9:22	in the **c.** place among them that	7218
1Sa	21:7	Edomite, the **c.** of the herdmen	47
2Ch	32:33	they buried him in the **c.** of the	4608
Ca	5:10	ruddy, the **c.** among ten thousand	1713
Mk	10:44	**the c., shall be servant of all.**	*4413*
2Co	11:5	behind the very **c.** apostles,	*5228,3029*
2Co	12:11	behind the very **c.** apostles,	*5228,3029*
1Ti	*subscr.*	which is the **c.** city	*3390*

CHIEFLY

Ro	3:2	**c.**, because that unto them were	*4412*
Php	4:22	**c.** they that are of Caesar's	*3122*
2Pe	2:10	**c.** them that walk after the flesh	*3122*

CHIEF-PRIEST See CHIEF and PRIEST.

CHILD See also CHILDBEARING; CHILDHOOD; CHILDLESS; CHILDREN; CHILD'S.

Ge	11:30	Sarai was barren; she had no **c.**	2056
Ge	16:11	her, Behold, thou art with **c.**,	2030
Ge	17:10	Every man **c.** among you shall	
Ge	17:12	every man **c.** in your generations,	
Ge	17:14	the uncircumcised man **c.** whose	
Ge	17:17	Shall a **c.** be born unto him that is an	
Ge	18:13	Shall I of a surety bear a **c.**	
Ge	19:36	both the daughters of Lot with **c.**	2029
Ge	21:8	the **c.** grew, and was weaned:	3206
Ge	21:14	and the **c.**, and sent her away:	3206
Ge	21:15	cast the **c.** under one of the shrubs.	3206
Ge	21:16	Let me not see the death of the **c.**	3206
Ge	37:30	The **c.** is not; and I, whither shall	3206
Ge	38:24	she is with **c.** by whoredom.	2030
Ge	38:25	am I with **c.**: and she said,	2030
Ge	42:22	Do not sin against the **c.**;	3206
Ge	44:20	and a **c.** of his old age, a little one;	3206
Ex	2:2	saw him that he was a goodly **c.**,	3206
Ex	2:3	and put the **c.** therein; and she	3206
Ex	2:6	had opened it, she saw the **c.**	3206
Ex	2:7	women, that she may nurse the **c.**	3206
Ex	2:9	Take this **c.** away, and nurse it	3206
Ex	2:9	the woman took the **c.**, and nursed	3206
Ex	2:10	And the **c.** grew, and she brought	3206
Ex	21:22	hurt a woman with **c.**, so that her	2030
Ex	22:22	afflict any widow, or fatherless **c.**	
Le	12:2	and born a man **c.**: then she shall	
Le	12:5	if she bear a maid **c.**, then she	
Le	22:13	and have no **c.**, and is returned	2233
Nu	11:12	father beareth the sucking **c.**,	
De	25:5	and have no **c.**, the wife of the	1121
Jg	11:34	she was his only **c.**; beside her he	3173
Jg	13:5	for the **c.** shall be a Nazarite unto	5288
Jg	13:7	the **c.** shall be Nazarite to God	5288
Jg	13:8	what we shall do unto the **c.** that	5288
Jg	13:12	How shall we order the **c.**, and	5288
Jg	13:24	and the **c.** grew, and the Lord	5288
Ru	4:16	Naomi took the **c.**, and laid it in	3206
1Sa	1:11	unto thine handmaid a man **c.**,	2233
1Sa	1:22	I will not go up until the **c.** be	5288
1Sa	1:24	in Shiloh: and the **c.** was young,	5288
1Sa	1:25	and brought the **c.** to Eli.	5288
1Sa	1:27	For this **c.** I prayed; and the	5288
1Sa	2:11	the **c.** did minister unto the Lord	5288
1Sa	2:18	before the Lord, being a **c.**,	5288
1Sa	2:21	**c.** Samuel grew before the Lord	5288
1Sa	2:26	And the **c.** Samuel grew on, and	5288
1Sa	3:1	And the **c.** Samuel ministered	5288
1Sa	3:8	that the Lord had called the **c.**	5288
1Sa	4:19	Phinehas' wife, was with **c.**, near	2030
1Sa	4:21	she named the **c.** I-chabod,	5288
2Sa	6:23	the daughter of Saul had no **c.**	3206
2Sa	11:5	told David, and said, I am with **c.**	2030
2Sa	12:14	the **c.** also that is born unto thee	1121
2Sa	12:15	And the Lord struck the **c.** that	3206
2Sa	12:16	therefore besought God for the **c.**;	5288
2Sa	12:18	the seventh day, that the **c.** died	3206
2Sa	12:18	to tell him that the **c.** was dead:	3206
2Sa	12:18	while the **c.** was yet alive, we	3206
2Sa	12:18	if we tell him that the **c.** is dead?	3206
2Sa	12:19	David perceived that the **c.** was	3206
2Sa	12:19	unto his servants, Is the **c.** dead?	3206
2Sa	12:21	thou didst fast and weep for the **c.**,	3206
2Sa	12:21	when the **c.** was dead, thou didst	3206
2Sa	12:22	While the **c.** was yet alive, I fasted	3206
2Sa	12:22	gracious to me, that the **c.** may live?	3206
1Ki	3:7	I am but a little **c.**: I know not	5288
1Ki	3:17	and I was delivered of a **c.** with her	3205
1Ki	3:19	this woman's **c.** died in the night;	1121
1Ki	3:20	and laid her dead **c.** in my bosom.	1121
1Ki	3:21	in the morning to give my **c.** suck.	1121
1Ki	3:25	Divide the living **c.** in two, and	3206
1Ki	3:26	the woman whose the living **c.** was	1121
1Ki	3:26	O my Lord, give her the living **c.**,	3205
1Ki	3:27	Give her the living **c.**, and in no	3205
1Ki	11:17	Egypt; Hadad being yet a little **c.**	5288
1Ki	13:2	a **c.** shall be born unto the house	1121
1Ki	14:3	what shall become of the **c.**	5288
1Ki	14:12	enter into the city, the **c.** shall die	3206
1Ki	14:17	threshold of the door, the **c.** died;	5288
1Ki	17:21	he stretched himself upon the **c.**	3206
1Ki	17:22	the soul of the **c.** came into him	3206
1Ki	17:23	Elijah took the **c.**, and brought	3206
2Ki	4:14	Verily she hath no **c.**, and her	1121
2Ki	4:18	when the **c.** was grown, it fell on	3206
2Ki	4:26	is it well with the **c.**? And she	3206
2Ki	4:29	my staff upon the face of the **c.**.	5288
2Ki	4:30	the mother of the **c.** said, As the	5288
2Ki	4:31	laid the staff on the face of the **c.**;	5288
2Ki	4:31	him, saying, The **c.** is not awaked.	5288
2Ki	4:32	the **c.** was dead and laid upon his	5288
2Ki	4:34	he went up, and lay upon the **c.**,	3206
2Ki	4:34	stretched himself upon the **c.**;	
2Ki	4:34	the flesh of the **c.** waxed warm.	3206
2Ki	4:35	the **c.** sneezed seven times,	5288
2Ki	4:35	and the **c.** opened his eyes.	5288
2Ki	5:14	like unto the flesh of a little **c.**,	5288
2Ki	8:12	and rip up their women with **c.**.	2030
2Ki	15:16	women therein that were with **c.**	2030
Job	3:3	said, There is a man **c.** conceived	
Ps	131:2	**c.** that is weaned of his mother:	
Ps	131:2	my soul is even as a weaned **c.**.	
Pr	20:11	a **c.** is known by his doings,	5288
Pr	22:6	Train up a **c.** in the way he	5288
Pr	22:15	is bound in the heart of a **c.**;	5288
Pr	23:13	Withhold not correction from the **c.**	5288
Pr	23:24	he that begetteth a wise **c.** shall	
Pr	29:15	but a **c.** left to himself bringeth	5288
Pr	29:21	his servant from a **c.** shall have	5290
Ec	4:8	he hath neither **c.** nor brother:	1121
Ec	4:13	Better is a poor and a wise **c.**	3206
Ec	4:15	the second **c.** that shall stand up	3206
Ec	10:16	O land, when thy king is a **c.**,	5288
Ec	11:5	in the womb of her that is with **c.**	4392
Isa	3:5	the **c.** shall behave himself	5288
Isa	7:16	before the **c.** shall know to refuse	5288
Isa	8:4	the **c.** shall have knowledge to cry,	5288
Isa	9:6	unto us a **c.** is born, unto us a	3206
Isa	10:19	shall be few, that a **c.** may write	5288
Isa	11:6	and a little **c.** shall lead them.	5288
Isa	11:8	the sucking **c.** shall play on the	
Isa	11:8	and the weaned **c.** shall put his	
Isa	26:17	Like as a woman with **c.**, that	2030
Isa	26:18	We have been with **c.**, we have	2029
Isa	49:15	a woman forget her sucking **c.**,	
Isa	54:1	that didst not travail with **c.**	
Isa	65:20	the **c.** shall die an hundred years	5288
Isa	66:7	she was delivered of a man **c.**.	
Jer	1:6	I cannot speak: for I am a **c.**.	5288
Jer	1:7	Say not, I am a **c.**: for thou shalt	5288
Jer	4:31	that bringeth forth her first **c.**,	
Jer	20:15	A man **c.** is born unto thee;	1121
Jer	30:6	a man doth travail with **c.**?	3205
Jer	31:8	the lame, the woman with **c.**	2030
Jer	31:8	and her that travaileth with **c.**	3205
Jer	31:20	dear son? Is he a pleasant **c.**?	3206
Jer	44:7	off from you man and woman, **c.**	5768
La	4:4	The tongue of the sucking **c.**	
Ho	11:1	When Israel was a **c.**, then I	5288
Ho	13:16	women with **c.** shall be ripped up.	2030
Am	1:13	have ripped up the women with **c.**	2030
Mt	1:18	with **c.** of the Holy Ghost.	*1722,1064,2192*
Mt	1:23	a virgin shall be with **c.**	*1722,1064,2192*
Mt	2:8	search diligently for the young **c.**;	*3813*
Mt	2:9	stood over where the young **c.** was.	*3813*
Mt	2:11	they saw the young **c.** with Mary	*3813*
Mt	2:13	Arise, and take the young **c.** and	*3813*
Mt	2:13	Herod will seek the young **c.** to	*3813*
Mt	2:14	took the young **c.** and his mother	*3813*
Mt	2:20	Arise, and take the young **c.** and	*3813*
Mt	2:21	took the young **c.** and his mother,	*3813*
Mt	10:21	**and the father the c.: and the**	*5043*
Mt	17:18	**c.** was cured from that very hour.	*3816*
Mt	18:2	And Jesus called a little **c.** unto	*3813*
Mt	18:4	**humble himself as this little c.,**	*3813*
Mt	18:5	**shall receive one such little c.**	*3813*
Mt	23:15	**twofold more the c. of hell than**	*5207*
Mt	24:19	**them that are with c.,**	*1722,1064,2192*
Mk	9:21	**unto him?** And he said, Of a **c.**.	*3812*
Mk	9:24	straightway the father of the **c.**	*3813*
Mk	9:36	And he took a **c.**, and set him in	*3813*
Mk	10:15	the kingdom of God as a little **c.**,	*3813*
Mk	13:17	them that are with **c.**,	*1722,1064,2192*
Lu	1:7	And they had no **c.**, because that	*5043*
Lu	1:59	they came to circumcise the **c.**;	*3813*
Lu	1:66	What manner of **c.** shall this be!	*3813*
Lu	1:76	And thou, **c.**, shalt be called the	*3813*
Lu	1:80	the **c.** grew, and waxed strong	*3813*
Lu	2:5	wife, being great with **c.**	*1471*
Lu	2:17	was told them concerning this **c.**	*3813*
Lu	2:21	for the circumcising of the **c.**,	*3813*
Lu	2:27	parents brought in the **c.** Jesus,	*3813*
Lu	2:34	Behold, this **c.** is set for the fall	
Lu	2:40	And the **c.** grew, and waxed strong	*3813*
Lu	2:43	the **c.** Jesus tarried behind	*3816*
Lu	9:38	my son: for he is mine only **c.**	*3439*
Lu	9:42	and healed the **c.**, and delivered	*3816*
Lu	9:47	their heart, took a **c.**, and set him	*3813*
Lu	9:48	**Whosoever shall receive this c.**	*3813*
Lu	18:17	**the kingdom of God as a little c.**	*3813*
Lu	21:23	**them that are with c.,**	*1722,1064,2192*
Joh	4:49	Sir, come down ere my **c.** die.	*3813*
Joh	16:21	**soon as she is delivered of the c.,**	*3813*
Ac	4:27	against thy holy **c.** Jesus, whom	*3816*
Ac	4:30	by the name of thy holy **c.** Jesus.	*3816*
Ac	7:5	him, when as yet he had no **c.**	*5043*
Ac	13:10	thou **c.** of the devil, thou enemy	*5207*
1Co	13:11	When I was a **c.**, I spake as a **c.**,	*3516*
1Co	13:11	I understood as a **c.**,	*3516*
1Co	13:11	I thought as a **c.**:	*3516*
Gal	4:1	the heir, as long as he is a **c.**,	*3516*
1Th	5:3	upon a woman with **c.**;	*1722,1064,2192*
2Ti	3:15	from a **c.** thou hast known the	*1025*
Heb	11:11	and was delivered of a **c.** when	*5088*
Heb	11:23	they saw he was a proper **c.**;	*3813*
Re	12:2	And she being with **c.**	*1722,1064,2192*
Re	12:4	to devour her **c.** as soon as it	*5043*
Re	12:5	she brought forth a man **c.**, who	*5207*
Re	12:5	her **c.** was caught up unto God,	*5043*
Re	12:13	which brought forth the man **c.**.	

CHILDBEARING

1Ti	2:15	she shall be saved in **c.**, if they	*5042*

CHILDHOOD

1Sa	12:2	walked before you from my **c.**	5271
Ec	11:10	evil from thy flesh: for **c.** and	3208

CHILDISH

1Co	13:11	a man, I put away **c.** things	*3516*

CHILDLESS

Ge	15:2	wilt thou give me, seeing I go **c.**,	6185
Le	20:20	bear their sins; they shall die **c.**	6185
Le	20:21	nakedness; they shall be **c.**	6185
1Sa	15:33	thy sword hath made women **c.**,	7921
1Sa	15:33	so shall thy mother be **c.**	7921
Jer	22:30	Write ye this man **c.**, a man that	6185
Lu	20:30	took her to wife, and he died **c.**.	*815*

CHILDREN See also CHILDREN'S.

Ge 3:16 sorrow thou shalt bring forth **c.**; 1121
Ge 6:4 and they bare **c.** to them, the same
Ge 10:21 **c.** of Eber, the brother of Japheth 1121
Ge 10:21 the elder, even to him were **c.** born.
Ge 10:22 **c.** of Shem; Elam, and Asshur, 1121
Ge 10:23 And the **c.** of Aram; Uz, and Hul, 1121
Ge 11:5 which the **c.** of men builded. 1121
Ge 16:1 Sarai Abram's wife bare him no **c.**
Ge 16:2 that I may obtain **c.** by her. 1129
Ge 18:19 he will command his **c.** and his 1121
Ge 19:38 the father of the **c.** of Ammon 1121
Ge 20:17 maidservants; and they bare **c.**.
Ge 21:7 Sarah should have given **c.** suck? 1121
Ge 22:20 also born **c.** unto thy brother 1121
Ge 23:5 **c.** of Heth answered Abraham, 1121
Ge 23:7 the land, even to the **c.** of Heth. 1121
Ge 23:10 dwelt among the **c.** of Heth: 1121
Ge 23:10 in the audience of the **c.** of Heth, 1121
Ge 23:18 in the presence of the **c.** of Heth, 1121
Ge 25:4 these were the **c.** of Keturah. 1121
Ge 25:22 **c.** struggled together within her; 1121
Ge 30:1 she bare Jacob no **c.**, Rachel
Ge 30:1 Give me **c.**, or else I die, 1121
Ge 30:3 that I may also have **c.** by her. 1129
Ge 30:26 Give me my wives and my **c.**, 3206
Ge 31:43 and these **c.** are my **c.**, and these 1121
Ge 31:43 their **c.** which they have born? 1121
Ge 32:11 me, and the mother with the **c.**. 1121
Ge 32:32 Therefore the **c.** of Israel eat not 1121
Ge 33:1 the **c.** unto Leah, and unto Rachel, 3206
Ge 33:2 handmaids and their **c.** foremost, 3206
Ge 33:2 and Leah, and her **c.** after, 3206
Ge 33:5 and saw the women and the **c.**; 3206
Ge 33:5 The **c.** which God hath graciously 3206
Ge 33:6 came near, they and their **c.**, 3206
Ge 33:7 Leah also with her **c.** came near, 3206
Ge 33:13 knoweth that the **c.** are tender, 3206
Ge 33:14 and the **c.** be able to endure, 3206
Ge 33:19 at the hand of the **c.** of Hamor, 1121
Ge 36:21 the **c.** of Seir in the land of Edom. 1121
Ge 36:22 **c.** of Lotan were Hori and Hemam; 1121
Ge 36:23 the **c.** of Shobal were these: Alvan, 1121
Ge 36:24 **c.** of Zibeon; both Ajah, and Anah: 1121
Ge 36:25 the **c.** of Anah were these; Dishon, 1121
Ge 36:26 **c.** of Dishon; Hemdan, and Eshban, 1121
Ge 36:27 **c.** of Ezer are these; Bilhan and 1121
Ge 36:28 **c.** of Dishan are these; Uz, and 1121
Ge 36:31 any king over the **c.** of Israel. 1121
Ge 37:3 loved Joseph more than all his **c.**, 1121
Ge 42:36 bereaved of my **c.**: Joseph is not,
Ge 43:14 If I be bereaved of my **c.**, I am
Ge 45:10 and thy **c.**, and thy children's **c.**, 1121
Ge 45:21 the **c.** of Israel did so: and Joseph 1121
Ge 46:8 the names of the **c.** of Israel, 1121
Ge 49:8 thy father's **c.** shall bow down 1121
Ge 49:32 therein was from the **c.** of Heth. 1121
Ge 50:23 saw Ephraim's **c.** of the third 1121
Ge 50:23 **c.** also of Machir the son of Manasseh. 1121
Ge 50:25 took an oath of the **c.** of Israel, 1121
Ex 1:1 are the names of the **c.** of Israel, 1121
Ex 1:7 And the **c.** of Israel were fruitful, 1121
Ex 1:9 people of the **c.** of Israel are more 1121
Ex 1:12 grieved because of the **c.** of Israel. 1121
Ex 1:13 the **c.** of Israel to serve with rigour: 1121
Ex 1:17 but saved the men **c.** alive. 3206
Ex 1:18 have saved the men **c.** alive? 3206
Ex 2:6 This is one of the Hebrews' **c.**. 3206
Ex 2:23 the **c.** of Israel sighed by reason 1121
Ex 2:25 God looked upon the **c.** of Israel, 1121
Ex 3:9 the cry of the **c.** of Israel is come 1121
Ex 3:10 the **c.** of Israel out of Egypt. 1121
Ex 3:11 I should bring forth the **c.** of Israel 1121
Ex 3:13 come unto the **c.** of Israel, 1121
Ex 3:14 thou say unto the **c.** of Israel, I AM 1121
Ex 3:15 thou say unto the **c.** of Israel, The 1121
Ex 4:29 all the elders of the **c.** of Israel: 1121
Ex 4:31 Lord had visited the **c.** of Israel, 1121
Ex 5:14 the officers of the **c.** of Israel, 1121
Ex 5:15 the **c.** of Israel came and cried 1121
Ex 5:19 And the officers of the **c.** of Israel 1121
Ex 6:5 the groaning of the **c.** of Israel, 1121
Ex 6:6 say unto the **c.** of Israel, I am the 1121
Ex 6:9 Moses spake so unto the **c.** of 1121
Ex 6:11 let the **c.** of Israel go out of his land. 1121
Ex 6:12 **c.** of Israel have not hearkened 1121
Ex 6:13 a charge unto the **c.** of Israel, 1121
Ex 6:13 to bring the **c.** of Israel out of the 1121
Ex 6:26 the **c.** of Israel from the land of 1121
Ex 6:27 out the **c.** of Israel from Egypt: 1121
Ex 7:2 send the **c.** of Israel out of his land. 1121
Ex 7:4 and my people the **c.** of Israel, out 1121
Ex 7:5 bring out the **c.** of Israel from 1121
Ex 9:6 cattle of the **c.** of Israel died not 1121
Ex 9:26 Goshen, where the **c.** of Israel were, 1121
Ex 9:35 would he let the **c.** of Israel go; 1121
Ex 10:20 would not let the **c.** of Israel go. 1121
Ex 10:23 all the **c.** of Israel had light in their 1121
Ex 11:7 against any of the **c.** of Israel shall 1121
Ex 11:10 would not let the **c.** of Israel go 1121
Ex 12:26 when your **c.** shall say unto you, 1121
Ex 12:27 over the houses of the **c.** of Israel. 1121
Ex 12:28 the **c.** of Israel went away, 1121
Ex 12:31 both ye and the **c.** of Israel; 1121
Ex 12:35 And the **c.** of Israel did according 1121
Ex 12:37 the **c.** of Israel journeyed from 1121
Ex 12:37 on foot that were men, beside **c.**. 2945
Ex 12:40 the sojourning of the **c.** of Israel, 1121
Ex 12:42 of all the **c.** of Israel in their 1121
Ex 12:50 Thus did all the **c.** of Israel; 1121
Ex 12:51 the Lord did bring the **c.** of Israel 1121
Ex 13:2 among the **c.** of Israel, both of 1121
Ex 13:13 the firstborn of man among thy **c.** 1121
Ex 13:15 the firstborn of my **c.** I redeem. 1121
Ex 13:18 the **c.** of Israel went up harnessed. 1121
Ex 13:19 had straitly sworn the **c.** of Israel, 1121
Ex 14:2 Speak unto the **c.** of Israel, that 1121
Ex 14:3 Pharaoh will say of the **c.** of Israel, 1121
Ex 14:8 pursued after the **c.** of Israel: and 1121
Ex 14:8 the **c.** of Israel went out with an 1121
Ex 14:10 the **c.** of Israel lifted up their eyes, 1121
Ex 14:10 **c.** of Israel cried out unto the Lord. 1121
Ex 14:15 **c.** of Israel, that they go forward: 1121
Ex 14:16 **c.** of Israel shall go on dry ground 1121
Ex 14:22 the **c.** of Israel went into the midst 1121
Ex 14:29 but the **c.** of Israel walked upon 1121
Ex 15:1 sang Moses and the **c.** of Israel this 1121
Ex 15:19 but the **c.** of Israel went on dry 1121
Ex 16:1 congregation of the **c.** of Israel 1121
Ex 16:2 the **c.** of Israel murmured against 1121
Ex 16:3 the **c.** of Israel said unto them, 1121
Ex 16:6 Aaron said unto all the **c.** of Israel, 1121
Ex 16:9 the **c.** of Israel, Come near before 1121
Ex 16:10 the **c.** of Israel, that they looked 1121
Ex 16:12 the murmurings of the **c.** of Israel: 1121
Ex 16:15 when the **c.** of Israel saw it, 1121
Ex 16:17 the **c.** of Israel did so, and gathered, 1121
Ex 16:35 And the **c.** of Israel did eat manna 1121
Ex 17:1 congregation of the **c.** of Israel 1121
Ex 17:3 kill us and our **c.** and our cattle 1121
Ex 17:7 the chiding of the **c.** of Israel, 1121
Ex 19:1 when the **c.** of Israel were gone 1121
Ex 19:3 and tell the **c.** of Israel; 1121
Ex 19:6 shalt speak unto the **c.** of Israel. 1121
Ex 20:5 the fathers upon the **c.** unto 1121
Ex 20:22 shalt say unto the **c.** of Israel, 1121
Ex 21:4 the wife and her **c.** shall be her 3206
Ex 21:5 my master, my wife, and my **c.**; 1121
Ex 22:24 widows, and your **c.** fatherless. 1121
Ex 24:5 sent young men of the **c.** of Israel, 1121
Ex 24:11 upon the nobles of the **c.** of Israel 1121
Ex 24:17 mount in the eyes of the **c.** of Israel. 1121
Ex 25:2 Speak unto the **c.** of Israel, that 1121
Ex 25:22 commandment unto the **c.** of Israel. 1121
Ex 27:20 shalt command the **c.** of Israel, 1121
Ex 27:21 on the behalf of the **c.** of Israel, 1121
Ex 28:1 among the **c.** of Israel, that he 1121
Ex 28:9 them the names of the **c.** of Israel: 1121
Ex 28:11 with the names of the **c.** of Israel: 1121
Ex 28:12 stones of memorial unto the **c.** of 1121
Ex 28:21 the **c.** of Israel, twelve, according 1121
Ex 28:29 the **c.** of Israel in the breastplate 1121
Ex 28:30 the judgment of the **c.** of Israel 1121
Ex 28:38 which the **c.** of Israel shall hallow 1121
Ex 29:28 for ever from the **c.** of Israel: 1121
Ex 29:28 offering from the **c.** of Israel 1121
Ex 29:43 I will meet with the **c.** of Israel, 1121
Ex 29:45 I will dwell among the **c.** of Israel, 1121
Ex 30:12 takest the sum of the **c.** of Israel 1121
Ex 30:16 atonement money of the **c.** of Israel, 1121
Ex 30:16 memorial unto the **c.** of Israel. 1121
Ex 30:31 speak unto the **c.** of Israel, saying, 1121
Ex 31:13 thou also unto the **c.** of Israel, 1121
Ex 31:16 **c.** of Israel shall keep the sabbath, 1121
Ex 31:17 between me and the **c.** of Israel. 1121
Ex 32:20 made the **c.** of Israel drink of it. 1121
Ex 32:28 the **c.** of Levi did according to 1121
Ex 33:5 Moses, Say unto the **c.** of Israel, 1121
Ex 33:6 **c.** of Israel stripped themselves 1121
Ex 34:7 the fathers upon the **c.**, and upon 1121
Ex 34:7 the children's **c.**, unto the third
Ex 34:23 shall all your men **c.** appear
Ex 34:30 all the **c.** of Israel saw Moses, 1121
Ex 34:32 all the **c.** of Israel came nigh: 1121
Ex 34:34 spake unto the **c.** of Israel that 1121
Ex 34:35 **c.** of Israel saw the face of Moses, 1121
Ex 35:1 of the **c.** of Israel together, and said 1121
Ex 35:4 congregation of the **c.** of Israel, 1121
Ex 35:20 the **c.** of Israel departed from the 1121
Ex 35:29 The **c.** of Israel brought a willing 1121
Ex 35:30 Moses said unto the **c.** of Israel, 1121
Ex 36:3 the **c.** of Israel had brought for 1121
Ex 39:6 graven, with the names of the **c.** of 1121
Ex 39:7 for a memorial to the **c.** of Israel; 1121
Ex 39:14 names of the **c.** of Israel, twelve, 1121
Ex 39:32 the **c.** of Israel did according to 1121
Ex 39:42 the **c.** of Israel made all the work. 1121
Ex 40:36 the **c.** of Israel went onward in all 1121
Le 1:2 Speak unto the **c.** of Israel, and say 1121
Le 4:2 Speak unto the **c.** of Israel, saying, 1121
Le 6:18 among the **c.** of Aaron shall eat 1121
Le 7:23 29 Speak unto the **c.** of Israel. 1121
Le 7:34 have I taken of the **c.** of Israel 1121
Le 7:34 ever from among the **c.** of Israel. 1121
Le 7:36 be given them of the **c.** of Israel, 1121
Le 7:38 he commanded the **c.** of Israel 1121
Le 9:3 the **c.** of Israel thou shalt speak, 1121
Le 10:11 ye may teach the **c.** of Israel all 1121
Le 10:14 peace offerings of the **c.** of Israel. 1121
Le 11:2 unto the **c.** of Israel, saying, These 1121
Le 12:2 unto the **c.** of Israel, saying, If a 1121
Le 15:2 Speak unto the **c.** of Israel, and say 1121
Le 15:31 shall ye separate the **c.** of Israel 1121
Le 16:5 congregation of the **c.** of Israel two 1121
Le 16:16 of the uncleanness of the **c.** of Israel, 1121
Le 16:19 from the uncleanness of the **c.** of 1121
Le 16:21 the iniquities of the **c.** of Israel, 1121
Le 16:34 an atonement for the **c.** of Israel 1121
Le 17:2 sons, and unto all the **c.** of Israel, 1121
Le 17:5 the **c.** of Israel may bring their 1121
Le 17:12 I said unto the **c.** of Israel, 1121
Le 17:13 whatsoever man there be of the **c.** 1121
Le 17:14 therefore I said unto the **c.** of 1121
Le 18:2 **c.** of Israel, and say unto them, I 1121
Le 19:2 **c.** of Israel, and say unto them, Ye 1121
Le 19:18 against the **c.** of thy people, 1121
Le 20:2 say to the **c.** of Israel, Whosoever 1121
Le 20:2 he be of the **c.** of Israel, or of the 1121
Le 21:24 sons, and unto all the **c.** of Israel. 1121
Le 22:2 the holy things of the **c.** of Israel, 1121
Le 22:3 **c.** of Israel hallow unto the Lord, 1121
Le 22:15 the holy things of the **c.** of Israel, 1121
Le 22:18 and unto all the the **c.** of Israel, 1121
Le 22:32 hallowed among the **c.** of Israel: 1121
Le 23:2, 10 unto the **c.** of Israel, and say 1121
Le 23:24, 34 Speak unto the **c.** of Israel, 1121
Le 23:43 the **c.** of Israel to dwell in booths, 1121
Le 23:44 Moses declared unto the **c.** of 1121
Le 24:2 the **c.** of Israel, that they bring 1121
Le 24:8 being taken from the **c.** of Israel 1121
Le 24:10 Egyptian, went out among the **c.** of 1121
Le 24:15 speak unto the **c.** of Israel, saying, 1121
Le 24:23 Moses spake to the **c.** of Israel, 1121
Le 24:23 the **c.** of Israel did as the Lord 1121
Le 25:2 Speak unto the **c.** of Israel, and say 1121
Le 25:33 their possession among the **c.** of 1121
Le 25:41 both he and his **c.** with him, and 1121
Le 25:45 **c.** of the strangers that do sojourn 1121
Le 25:46 inheritance for your **c.** after you, 1121
Le 25:46 over your brethren the **c.** of Israel, 1121
Le 25:54 both he, and his **c.** with him. 1121
Le 25:55 me the **c.** of Israel are servants; 1121
Le 26:22 which shall rob you of your **c.**,
Le 26:46 him and the **c.** of Israel in mount 1121
Le 27:2 **c.** of Israel, and say unto them, 1121
Le 27:34 for the **c.** of Israel in mount Sinai. 1121
Nu 1:2 congregation of the **c.** of Israel, 1121
Nu 1:10 Of the **c.** of Joseph: of Ephraim; 1121
Nu 1:20 **c.** of Reuben, Israel's eldest son, 1121
Nu 1:22 **c.** of Simeon, by their generatins, 1121
Nu 1:24 **c.** of Gad, by their generations, 1121

Book	Ref.	Context	No.
Nu	1:26	Of the **c.** of Judah, by their	1121
Nu	1:28	Of the **c.** of Issachar, by their	1121
Nu	1:30	Of the **c.** of Zebulun, by their	1121
Nu	1:32	Of the **c.** of Joseph, namely,	1121
Nu	1:32	Of the **c.** of Ephraim, by their	1121
Nu	1:34	Of the **c.** of Manasseh, by their	1121
Nu	1:36	Of the **c.** of Benjamin, by their	1121
Nu	1:38	Of the **c.** of Dan,	1121
Nu	1:40	Of the **c.** of Asher, by their	1121
Nu	1:42	Of the **c.** of Naphtali, throughout	1121
Nu	1:45	were numbered of the **c.** of Israel,	1121
Nu	1:49	of them among the **c.** of Israel:	1121
Nu	1:52	**c.** of Israel shall pitch their tents,	1121
Nu	1:53	upon the congregation of the **c.** of	1121
Nu	1:54	the **c.** of Israel did according to all	1121
Nu	2:2	man of the **c.** of Israel shall pitch	1121
Nu	2:3	shall be captain of the **c.** of Judah	1121
Nu	2:5	be captain of the **c.** of Issachar	1121
Nu	2:7	be captain of the **c.** of Zebulun	1121
Nu	2:10	and the captain of the **c.** of Reuben	1121
Nu	2:12	captain of the **c.** of Simeon shall be	1121
Nu	2:20	the captain of the **c.** of Manasseh	1121
Nu	2:25	captain of the **c.** of Dan shall be	1121
Nu	2:27	captain of the **c.** of Asher shall be	1121
Nu	2:29	the captain of the **c.** of Naphtali	1121
Nu	2:32	were numbered of the **c.** of Israel	1121
Nu	2:33	numbered among the **c.** of Israel;	1121
Nu	2:34	the **c.** of Israel did according to all	1121
Nu	3:4	and they had no **c.**: and Eleazar	1121
Nu	3:8	the charge of the **c.** of Israel, to do	1121
Nu	3:9	unto him out of the **c.** of Israel	1121
Nu	3:12	from among the **c.** of Israel instead	1121
Nu	3:12	the matrix among the **c.** of Israel:	1121
Nu	3:15	the **c.** of Levi after the house of	1121
Nu	3:38	for the charge of the **c.** of Israel;	1121
Nu	3:40	of the males of the **c.** of Israel	1121
Nu	3:41	firstborn among the **c.** of Israel;	1121
Nu	3:41	among the cattle of the **c.** of Israel	1121
Nu	3:42	firstborn among the **c.** of Israel	1121
Nu	3:45	firstborn among the **c.** of Israel,	1121
Nu	3:46	the firstborn of the **c.** of Israel,	1121
Nu	3:50	the **c.** of Israel took he the money;	1121
Nu	5:2	Command the **c.** of Israel, that they	1121
Nu	5:4	the **c.** of Israel did so, and put	1121
Nu	5:4	unto moses, so did the **c.** of Israel	1121
Nu	5:6	Speak unto the **c.** of Israel, When	1121
Nu	5:9	the holy things of the **c.** of Israel,	1121
Nu	5:12	unto the **c.** of Israel and say	1121
Nu	6:2	unto the **c.** of Israel, and say	1121
Nu	6:23	wise ye shall bless the **c.** of Israel,	1121
Nu	6:27	put my name upon the **c.** of Israel;	1121
Nu	7:24	prince of the **c.** of Zebulun, did	1121
Nu	7:30	prince of the **c.** of Reuben, did offer:	1121
Nu	7:36	prince of the **c.** of Simeon, did offer:	1121
Nu	7:42	prince of the **c.** of Gad, offered:	1121
Nu	7:48	prince of the **c.** of Ephraim, offered:	1121
Nu	7:54	prince of the **c.** of Manasseh:	1121
Nu	7:60	prince of the **c.** of Benjamin,	1121
Nu	7:66	prince of the **c.** of Dan, offered:	1121
Nu	7:72	prince of the **c.** of Asher, offered:	1121
Nu	7:78	prince of the **c.** of Naphtali, offered:	1121
Nu	8:6	the Levites from among the **c.** of	1121
Nu	8:9	whole assembly of the **c.** of Israel	1121
Nu	8:10	**c.** of Israel shall put their hands	1121
Nu	8:11	for an offering of the **c.** of Israel,	1121
Nu	8:14	the Levites from among the **c.** of	1121
Nu	8:16	me from among the **c.** of Israel;	1121
Nu	8:16	of the firstborn of all the **c.** of	1121
Nu	8:17	For all the firstborn of the **c.** of	1121
Nu	8:18	for all the firstborn of the **c.** of	1121
Nu	8:19	sons from among the **c.** of Israel,	1121
Nu	8:19	do the service of the **c.** of Israel in	1121
Nu	8:19	an atonement for the **c.** of Israel:	1121
Nu	8:19	no plague among the **c.** of Israel,	1121
Nu	8:19	when the **c.** of Israel come nigh	1121
Nu	8:20	congregation of the **c.** of Israel,	1121
Nu	8:20	so did the **c.** of Israel unto them	1121
Nu	9:2	**c.** of Israel also keep the passover	1121
Nu	9:4	Moses spake unto the **c.** of Israel,	1121
Nu	9:5	Moses, so did the **c.** of Israel	1121
Nu	9:7	season among the **c.** of Israel?	1121
Nu	9:10	unto the **c.** of Israel, saying, If any	1121
Nu	9:17	after that the **c.** of Israel journeyed:	1121
Nu	9:17	the **c.** of Israel pitched their tents	1121
Nu	9:18	the Lord the **c.** of Israel journeyed,	1121
Nu	9:19	then the **c.** of Israel kept the charge	1121
Nu	9:22	**c.** of Israel abode in their tents,	1121
Nu	10:12	**c.** of Israel took their journeys	1121
Nu	10:14	of the camp of the **c.** of Judah	1121
Nu	10:15	the tribe of the **c.** of Issachar was	1121
Nu	10:16	the tribe of the **c.** of Zebulun was	1121
Nu	10:19	the **c.** of Simeon was Shelumiel	1121
Nu	10:20	of the **c.** of Gad was Eliasaph the	1121
Nu	10:22	of the camp of the **c.** of Ephraim	1121
Nu	10:23	of the tribe of the **c.** of Manasseh	1121
Nu	10:24	of the tribe of the **c.** of Benjamin	1121
Nu	10:25	the camp of the **c.** of Dan set	1121
Nu	10:26	the tribe of the **c.** of Asher was	1121
Nu	10:27	tribe of the **c.** of Naphtali was	1121
Nu	10:28	these were the journeyings of the **c.**	1121
Nu	11:4	and the **c.** of Israel also wept	1121
Nu	13:2	which I give unto the **c.** of Israel:	1121
Nu	13:3	men were heads of the **c.** of Israel	1121
Nu	13:22	and Talmai, the **c.** of Anak, were	3211
Nu	13:24	which the **c.** of Israel cut down	1121
Nu	13:26	**c.** of Israel, unto the wilderness of	1121
Nu	13:28	moreover we saw the **c.** of Anak	3211
Nu	13:32	had searched unto the **c.** of Israel,	1121
Nu	14:2	**c.** of Israel murmured against	1121
Nu	14:3	our wives and our **c.** should be a	2945
Nu	14:5	congregation of the **c.** of Israel	1121
Nu	14:7	all the company of the **c.** of Israel,	1121
Nu	14:10	before all the **c.** of Israel	1121
Nu	14:18	iniquity of the fathers upon the **c.**	1121
Nu	14:27	heard the murmurings of the **c.** of	1121
Nu	14:33	**c.** shall wander in the wilderness	1121
Nu	14:39	sayings unto all the **c.** of Israel:	1121
Nu	15:2,	18 Speak unto the **c.** of Israel, and	1121
Nu	15:25,	26 congregation of the **c.** of Israel,	1121
Nu	15:29	that is born among the **c.** of Israel,	1121
Nu	15:32	**c.** of Israel were in the wilderness,	1121
Nu	15:38	Speak unto the **c.** of Israel, and say	1121
Nu	16:2	with certain of the **c.** of Israel,	1121
Nu	16:27	and their sons, and their little **c.**	2945
Nu	16:38	be a sign unto the **c.** of Israel	1121
Nu	16:40	To be a memorial unto the **c.** of	1121
Nu	16:41	all the congregation of the **c.** of	1121
Nu	17:2	Speak unto the **c.** of Israel, and take	1121
Nu	17:5	me the murmurings of the **c.** of	1121
Nu	17:6	spake unto the **c.** of Israel, and	1121
Nu	17:9	before the Lord unto all the **c.** of	1121
Nu	17:12	the **c.** of Israel spake unto Moses,	1121
Nu	18:5	any more upon the **c.** of Israel	1121
Nu	18:6	the Levites from among the **c.** of	1121
Nu	18:8	hallowed things of the **c.** of Israel;	1121
Nu	18:11	wave offering of the **c.** of Israel:	1121
Nu	18:19	the **c.** of Israel offer unto the Lord,	1121
Nu	18:20	inheritance among the **c.** of Israel	1121
Nu	18:21	behold, I have given the **c.** of Levi	1121
Nu	18:22	Neither must the **c.** of Israel	1121
Nu	18:23	among the **c.** of Israel they have no	1121
Nu	18:24	But the tithes of the **c.** of Israel,	1121
Nu	18:24	Among the **c.** of Israel they shall	1121
Nu	18:26	When ye take of the **c.** of Israel	1121
Nu	18:28	which ye receive of the **c.** of Israel;	1121
Nu	18:32	the holy things of the **c.** of Israel,	1121
Nu	19:2	Speak unto the **c.** of Israel, that they	1121
Nu	19:9	of the **c.** of Israel for a water of	1121
Nu	19:10	it shall be unto the **c.** of Israel,	1121
Nu	20:1	Then came the **c.** of Israel, even	1121
Nu	20:12	in the eyes of the **c.** of Israel,	1121
Nu	20:13	because the **c.** of Israel strove with	1121
Nu	20:19	the **c.** of Israel said unto him,	1121
Nu	20:22	And the **c.** of Israel, even the	1121
Nu	20:24	I have given unto the **c.** of Israel	1121
Nu	21:10	the **c.** of Israel set forward, and	1121
Nu	21:24	even unto the **c.** of Ammon: for	1121
Nu	21:24	the border of the **c.** of Ammon	1121
Nu	22:1	And the **c.** of Israel set forward,	1121
Nu	22:3	was distressed because of the **c.** of	1121
Nu	22:5	the land of the **c.** of his people,	1121
Nu	24:17	and destroy all the **c.** of Sheth	1121
Nu	25:6	one of the **c.** of Israel came and	1121
Nu	25:6	the **c.** of Israel, who were weeping	1121
Nu	25:8	plague was stayed from the **c.** of	1121
Nu	25:11	wrath away from the **c.** of Israel,	1121
Nu	25:11	I consumed not the **c.** of Israel	1121
Nu	25:13	an atonement for the **c.** of Israel	1121
Nu	26:2	the congregation of the **c.** of Israel,	1121
Nu	26:4	Moses and the **c.** of Israel, which	1121
Nu	26:5	**c.** of Reuben; Hanoch, of whom	1121
Nu	26:11	Notwithstanding the **c.** of Korah	1121
Nu	26:15	The **c.** of Gad after their families;	1121
Nu	26:18	are the families of the **c.** of Gad	1121
Nu	26:44	**c.** of Asher after their families:	1121
Nu	26:51	the numbered of the **c.** of Israel,	1121
Nu	26:62	numbered among the **c.** of Israel,	1121
Nu	26:62	given them among the **c.** of Israel	1121
Nu	26:63	the **c.** of Israel in the plains of Moab	1121
Nu	26:64	they numbered the **c.** of Israel in	1121
Nu	27:8	shalt speak unto the **c.** of Israel,	1121
Nu	27:11	**c.** of Israel a statute of judgment,	1121
Nu	27:12	I have given unto the **c.** of Israel	1121
Nu	27:20	the **c.** of Israel may be obedient	1121
Nu	27:21	and all the **c.** of Israel with him,	1121
Nu	28:2	Command the **c.** of Israel, and say	1121
Nu	29:40	And Moses told the **c.** of Israel	1121
Nu	30:1	concerning the **c.** of Israel, saying,	1121
Nu	31:2	Avenge the **c.** of Israel of the	1121
Nu	31:9	the **c.** of Israel took all the women	1121
Nu	31:12	unto the **c.** of Israel, unto the camp	1121
Nu	31:16	Behold, these caused the **c.** of	1121
Nu	31:18	But all the women **c.**, that have	2945
Nu	31:30,	42 And of the **c.** of Israel's half,	1121
Nu	31:47	even of the **c.** of Israel's half, Moses	1121
Nu	31:54	for a memorial for the **c.** of Israel	1121
Nu	32:1	Now the **c.** of Reuben and the	1121
Nu	32:1	and the **c.** of Gad had a very	1121
Nu	32:2	**c.** of Gad and the **c.** of Reuben came	1121
Nu	32:6	Moses said unto the **c.** of Gad and	1121
Nu	32:6	of Gad and to the **c.** of Reuben,	1121
Nu	32:7	the heart of the **c.** of Israel from	1121
Nu	32:9	the heart of the **c.** of Israel, that	1121
Nu	32:17	ready armed before the **c.** of Israel	1121
Nu	32:18	until the **c.** of Israel have inherited	1121
Nu	32:25	the **c.** of Gad and the **c.** of Reuben	1121
Nu	32:28	of the tribes of the **c.** of Israel:	1121
Nu	32:29	If the **c.** of Gad and the **c.** of Reuben	1121
Nu	32:31	the **c.** of Gad and the **c.** of Reuben	1121
Nu	32:33	even to the **c.** of Gad, and to the	1121
Nu	32:33	and to the **c.** of Reuben,	1121
Nu	32:34	And the **c.** of Gad built Dibon,	1121
Nu	32:37	the **c.** of Reuben built Heshbon,	1121
Nu	32:39	**c.** of Machir the son of Manasseh	1121
Nu	33:1	are the journeys of the **c.** of Israel	1121
Nu	33:3	the **c.** of Israel went out with an	1121
Nu	33:5	**c.** of Israel removed from Rameses,	1121
Nu	33:38	after the **c.** of Israel were come	1121
Nu	33:40	of the coming of the **c.** of Israel	1121
Nu	33:51	Speak unto the **c.** of Israel, and	1121
Nu	34:2	Command the **c.** of Israel, and	1121
Nu	34:13	Moses commanded the **c.** of Israel,	1121
Nu	34:14	for the tribe of the **c.** of Reuben	1121
Nu	34:14	and the tribe of the **c.** of Gad	1121
Nu	34:20	And of the tribe of the **c.** of Simeon,	1121
Nu	34:22	prince of the tribe of the **c.** of Dan,	1121
Nu	34:23	The prince of the **c.** of Joseph,	1121
Nu	34:23	of the tribe of the **c.** of Manasseh,	1121
Nu	34:24	of the tribe of the **c.** of Ephraim,	1121
Nu	34:25	of the tribe of the **c.** of Zebulun,	1121
Nu	34:26	of the tribe of the **c.** of Issachar,	1121
Nu	34:27	of the tribe of the **c.** of Asher,	1121
Nu	34:28	of the tribe of the **c.** of Naphtali,	1121
Nu	34:29	inheritance unto the **c.** of Israel	1121
Nu	35:2	Command the **c.** of Israel, that they	1121
Nu	35:8	the possession of the **c.** of Israel:	1121
Nu	35:10	Speak unto the **c.** of Israel, and	1121
Nu	35:15	a refuge, both for the **c.** of Israel,	1121
Nu	35:34	Lord dwell among the **c.** of Israel	1121
Nu	36:1	families of the **c.** of Gilead, the son	1121
Nu	36:1	chief fathers of the **c.** of Israel:	1121
Nu	36:2	for an inheritance by lot to the **c.** of	1121
Nu	36:3	the other tribes of the **c.** of Israel,	1121
Nu	36:4	the jubile of the **c.** of Israel shall	1121
Nu	36:5	Moses commanded the **c.** of Israel	1121
Nu	36:7	the inheritance of the **c.** of Israel	1121
Nu	36:7	every one of the **c.** of Israel shall	1121
Nu	36:8	any tribe of the **c.** of Israel, shall	1121
Nu	36:8	that the **c.** of Israel may enjoy	1121
Nu	36:9	the tribes of the **c.** of Israel shall	1121
Nu	36:13	hand of Moses unto the **c.** of Israel	1121
De	1:3	Moses spake unto the **c.** of Israel,	1121
De	1:36	and to his **c.**,because he hath	1121
De	1:39	and your **c.**, which in that day had	1121
De	2:4	your brethren the **c.** of Esau,	1121
De	2:8	from our brethren the **c.** of Esau,	1121
De	2:9	unto the **c.** of Lot for a possession	1121
De	2:12	the **c.** of Esau succeeded them,	1121
De	2:19	nigh over against the **c.** of Ammon,	1121
De	2:19	the land of the **c.** of Ammon any	1121
De	2:19	unto the **c.** of Lot for a possession	1121

De 2:22 As he did to the **c.** of Esau, which... 1121
De 2:29 the **c.** of Esau which dwell in Seir,... 1121
De 2:37 the **c.** of Ammon thou camest not,... 1121
De 3:6 men, women, and **c.**, of every city... 2945
De 3:11 in Rabbath of the **c.** of Ammon?... 1121
De 3:16 is the border of the **c.** of Ammon;... 1121
De 3:18 your brethren the **c.** of Israel, all... 1121
De 4:10 and that they may teach their **c.**... 1121
De 4:25 shalt beget **c.**, and children's **c.**,... 1121
De 4:40 with thee, and with thy **c.** after... 1121
De 4:44 Moses set before the **c.** of Israel:... 1121
De 4:45 Moses spake unto the **c.** of Israel,... 1121
De 4:46 whom Moses and the **c.** of Israel... 1121
De 5:9 iniquity of the fathers upon the **c.**... 1121
De 5:29 them, and with their **c.** for ever!... 1121
De 6:7 teach them diligently unto thy **c.**,... 1121
De 9:2 and tall, the **c.** of the Anakims,... 1121
De 9:2 can stand before the **c.** of Anak!... 1121
De 10:6 the **c.** of Israel took their journey... 1121
De 10:6 from Beeroth of the **c.** of Jaakan... 1121
De 11:2 for I speak not with your **c.** which... 1121
De 11:19 ye shall teach them your **c.**,... 1121
De 11:21 the days of your **c.**, in the land... 1121
De 12:25 thy **c.** after thee, when thou shalt... 1121
De 12:28 well with thee, and with thy **c.**... 1121
De 13:13 Certain men, the **c.** of Belial, are... 1121
De 14:1 are the **c.** of the Lord your God:... 1121
De 17:20 and his **c.**, in the midst of Israel... 1121
De 21:15 hated, and they have born him **c.**,... 1121
De 23:8 The **c.** that are begotten of them... 1121
De 24:7 of his brethren of the **c.** of Israel,... 1121
De 24:16 shall not be put to death for the **c.**,... 1121
De 24:16 neither shall the **c.** be put to death... 1121
De 28:54 remnant of his **c.** which he shall... 1121
De 28:55 flesh of his **c.** whom he shall eat:... 1121
De 28:57 toward her **c.** which she shall bear:... 1121
De 29:1 with the **c.** of Israel in the land... 1121
De 29:22 the generation to come of your **c.**... 1121
De 29:29 unto us and to our **c.** for ever,... 1121
De 30:2 thee this day, thou and thy **c.**... 1121
De 31:12 men, and women, and **c.**,... 2945
De 31:13 And that their **c.**, which have not... 1121
De 31:19 and teach it the **c.** of Israel:... 1121
De 31:19 for me against the **c.** of Israel... 1121
De 31:22 and taught it the **c.** of Israel... 1121
De 31:23 thou shalt ring the **c.** of Israel... 1121
De 32:5 their spot is not the spot of his **c.**... 1121
De 32:8 according to the number of the **c.**... 1121
De 32:20 generation, **c.** in whom is no faith... 1121
De 32:46 command your **c.** to observe to do,... 1121
De 32:49 which I give unto the **c.** of Israel... 1121
De 32:51 among the **c.** of Israel at the waters,... 1121
De 32:51 in the midst of the **c.** of Israel... 1121
De 32:52 land which I give the **c.** of Israel... 1121
De 33:1 blessed the **c.** of Israel before his... 1121
De 33:9 his brethren, nor knew his own **c.**... 1121
De 33:24 Let Asher be blessed with **c.**;... 1121
De 34:8 the **c.** of Israel wept for Moses... 1121
De 34:9 **c.** of Israel hearkened unto him,... 1121
Jos 1:2 to them, even to the **c.** of Israel... 1121
Jos 2:2 men in hither to night of the **c.** of... 1121
Jos 3:1 he and all the **c.** of Israel, and... 1121
Jos 3:9 Joshua said unto the **c.** of Israel,... 1121
Jos 4:4 he had prepared of the **c.** of Israel,... 1121
Jos 4:5 of the tribes of the **c.** of Israel:... 1121
Jos 4:6 your **c.** ask their fathers in time... 1121
Jos 4:7 a memorial unto the **c.** of Israel... 1121
Jos 4:8 the **c.** of Israel did so as Joshua... 1121
Jos 4:8 of the tribes of the **c.** of Israel,... 1121
Jos 4:12 And the **c.** of Reuben, and the... 1121
Jos 4:12 of Reuben, and the **c.** of Gad,... 1121
Jos 4:12 over armed before the **c.** of Israel,... 1121
Jos 4:21 he spake unto the **c.** of Israel,... 1121
Jos 4:21 saying, When your **c.** shall ask... 1121
Jos 4:22 ye shall let your **c.** know, saying,... 1121
Jos 5:1 Jordan from before the **c.** of Israel,... 1121
Jos 5:1 more, because of the **c.** of Israel... 1121
Jos 5:2 circumcise again the **c.** of Israel... 1121
Jos 5:3 circumcised the **c.** of Israel at the... 1121
Jos 5:6 the **c.** of Israel walked forty years... 1121
Jos 5:7 And their **c.**, whom he raised up... 1121
Jos 5:10 **c.** of Israel encamped in Gilgal,... 1121
Jos 5:12 neither had the **c.** of Israel manna... 1121
Jos 6:1 shut up because of the **c.** of Israel:... 1121
Jos 7:1 **c.** of Israel committed a trespass... 1121
Jos 7:1 kindled against the **c.** of Israel... 1121
Jos 7:12 the **c.** of Israel could not stand... 1121
Jos 7:23 unto all the **c.** of Israel, and laid... 1121
Jos 8:31 Lord commanded the **c.** of Israel,... 1121
Jos 8:32 in the presence of the **c.** of Israel... 1121
Jos 9:17 the **c.** of Israel journeyed, and... 1121
Jos 9:18 the **c.** of Israel smote them not,... 1121
Jos 9:26 out of the hand of the **c.** of Israel,... 1121
Jos 10:4 peace with Joshua and with the **c.**... 1121
Jos 10:11 the **c.** of Israel slew with the sword... 1121
Jos 10:12 Amorites before the **c.** of Israel,... 1121
Jos 10:20 the **c.** of Israel had made an end... 1121
Jos 10:21 against any of the **c.** of Israel... 1121
Jos 11:14 the **c.** of Israel took for a prey... 1121
Jos 11:19 made peace with the **c.** of Israel,... 1121
Jos 11:22 Anakims left in the land of the **c.**... 1121
Jos 12:1 which the **c.** of Israel smote,... 1121
Jos 12:2 the border of the **c.** of Ammon;... 1121
Jos 12:6 Lord and the **c.** of Israel smite:... 1121
Jos 12:7 Joshua and the **c.** of Israel smote... 1121
Jos 13:6 will I drive out from before the **c.**... 1121
Jos 13:10 the border of the **c.** of Ammon;... 1121
Jos 13:13 the **c.** of Israel expelled not the... 1121
Jos 13:15 the tribe of the **c.** of Reuben... 1121
Jos 13:22 soothsayer, did the **c.** of Israel slay... 1121
Jos 13:23 the border of the **c.** of Reuben... 1121
Jos 13:23 inheritance of the **c.** of Reuben... 1121
Jos 13:24 unto the **c.** of Gad according to... 1121
Jos 13:25 the land of the **c.** of Ammon,... 1121
Jos 13:28 the inheritance of the **c.** of Gad... 1121
Jos 13:29 half tribe of the **c.** of Manasseh... 1121
Jos 13:31 unto the **c.** of Machir the son of... 1121
Jos 13:31 the one half of the **c.** of Machir... 1121
Jos 14:1 which the **c.** of Israel inherited... 1121
Jos 14:1 of the tribes of the **c.** of Israel,... 1121
Jos 14:4 the **c.** of Joseph were two tribes,... 1121
Jos 14:5 Moses, so the **c.** of Israel did,... 1121
Jos 14:6 Then the **c.** of Judah came unto... 1121
Jos 14:10 while the **c.** of Israel wandered...
Jos 15:1 the tribe of the **c.** of Judah... 1121
Jos 15:12 the coast of the **c.** of Judah... 1121
Jos 15:13 gave a part among the **c.** of Judah,... 1121
Jos 15:14 and Talmai, the **c.** of Anak... 3211
Jos 15:20 inheritance of the ... **c.** of Judah... 1121
Jos 15:21 cities of the tribe of the **c.** of Judah... 1121
Jos 15:63 the **c.** of Judah could not drive... 1121
Jos 15:63 Jebusites dwell with the **c.** of Judah... 1121
Jos 16:1 the lot of the **c.** of Joseph fell... 1121
Jos 16:4 So the **c.** of Joseph, Manasseh... 1121
Jos 16:5 the border of the **c.** of Ephraim... 1121
Jos 16:8 of the tribe of the **c.** of Ephraim... 1121
Jos 16:9 separate cities for the **c.** of Ephraim... 1121
Jos 16:9 inheritance of the **c.** of Manasseh,... 1121
Jos 17:2 **c.** of Manasseh by their families;... 1121
Jos 17:2 for the **c.** of Abiezer,... 1121
Jos 17:2 and for the **c.** of Helek,... 1121
Jos 17:2 and for the **c.** of Asriel,... 1121
Jos 17:2 and for the **c.** of Shechem,... 1121
Jos 17:2 and for the **c.** of Hepher,... 1121
Jos 17:2 and for the **c.** of Shemida:... 1121
Jos 17:2 these were the male **c.** of Manasseh... 1121
Jos 17:8 belonged to the **c.** of Ephraim;... 1121
Jos 17:12 the **c.** of Manasseh could not drive... 1121
Jos 17:13 when the **c.** of Israel were waxen... 1121
Jos 17:14 **c.** of Joseph spake unto Joshua,... 1121
Jos 17:16 the **c.** of Joseph said, The hill... 1121
Jos 18:1 **c.** of Israel assembled together... 1121
Jos 18:2 remained among the **c.** of Israel... 1121
Jos 18:3 Joshua said unto the **c.** of Israel,... 1121
Jos 18:10 the land unto the **c.** of Israel... 1121
Jos 18:11 the tribe of the **c.** of Benjamin... 1121
Jos 18:11 between the **c.** of Judah and the... 1121
Jos 18:11 of Judah and the **c.** of Joseph... 1121
Jos 18:14 a city of the **c.** of Judah:... 1121
Jos 18:20 the **c.** of Benjamin, by the coasts... 1121
Jos 18:21 of the tribe of the **c.** of Benjamin... 1121
Jos 18:28 inheritance of the **c.** of Benjamin... 1121
Jos 19:1 **c.** of Simeon according to their... 1121
Jos 19:1 the inheritance of the **c.** of Judah... 1121
Jos 19:8 of the tribe of the **c.** of Simeon... 1121
Jos 19:9 the portion of the **c.** of Judah was... 1121
Jos 19:9 the inheritance of the **c.** of Simeon:... 1121
Jos 19:9 for the part of the **c.** of Judah was... 1121
Jos 19:9 therefore the **c.** of Simeon had... 1121
Jos 19:10 came up for the **c.** of Zebulun... 1121
Jos 19:16 inheritance of the **c.** of Zebulun... 1121
Jos 19:17 Issachar, for the **c.** of Issachar... 1121
Jos 19:23 the tribe of the **c.** of Issachar... 1121
Jos 19:24 the **c.** of Asher according to their... 1121
Jos 19:31 the tribe of the **c.** of Asher... 1121
Jos 19:32 came out to the **c.** of Naphtali,... 1121
Jos 19:32 even for the **c.** of Naphtali... 1121
Jos 19:39 the tribe of the **c.** of Naphtali... 1121
Jos 19:40 out for the tribe of the **c.** of Dan... 1121
Jos 19:47 the coast of the **c.** of Dan went out... 1121
Jos 19:47 **c.** of Dan went up to fight against... 1121
Jos 19:48 the **c.** of Dan according to their... 1121
Jos 19:49 **c.** of Israel gave an inheritance... 1121
Jos 19:51 of the tribes of the **c.** of Israel,... 1121
Jos 20:2 Speak to the **c.** of Israel, saying,... 1121
Jos 20:9 appointed for all the **c.** of Israel,... 1121
Jos 21:1 of the tribes of the **c.** of Israel;... 1121
Jos 21:3 **c.** of Israel gave unto the Levites... 1121
Jos 21:4 the **c.** of Aaron the priest, which... 1121
Jos 21:5 And the rest of the **c.** of Kohath... 1121
Jos 21:6 And the **c.** of Gershon had by lot... 1121
Jos 21:7 The **c.** of Merari by their families... 1121
Jos 21:8 the **c.** of Israel gave by lot unto... 1121
Jos 21:9 out of the tribe of the **c.** of Judah,... 1121
Jos 21:9 out of the tribe of the **c.** of Simeon,... 1121
Jos 21:10 Which the **c.** of Aaron, being of... 1121
Jos 21:10 of the **c.** of Levi, had: for theirs... 1121
Jos 21:13 Thus they gave to the **c.** of Aaron... 1121
Jos 21:19 the cities of the **c.** of Aaron,... 1121
Jos 21:20 families of the **c.** of Kohath, the... 1121
Jos 21:20 which remained of the **c.** of Kohath,... 1121
Jos 21:26 the **c.** of Kohath that remained... 1121
Jos 21:27 And unto the **c.** of Gershon, of the... 1121
Jos 21:34 families of the **c.** of Merari, the... 1121
Jos 21:40 the **c.** of Merari by their families,... 1121
Jos 21:41 the possession of the **c.** of Israel... 1121
Jos 22:9 And the **c.** of Reuben... 1121
Jos 22:9 and the **c.** of Gad and the half... 1121
Jos 22:9 and departed from the **c.** of Israel... 1121
Jos 22:10 the **c.** of Reuben and the **c.** of Gad... 1121
Jos 22:11 And the **c.** of Israel heard say,... 1121
Jos 22:11 Behold the **c.** of Reuben... 1121
Jos 22:11 and the **c.** of Gad and the half... 1121
Jos 22:11 at the passage of the **c.** of Israel... 1121
Jos 22:12 when the **c.** of Israel heard of it,... 1121
Jos 22:12 congregation of the **c.** of Israel... 1121
Jos 22:13 And the **c.** of Israel sent unto... 1121
Jos 22:13 sent unto the **c.** of Reuben,... 1121
Jos 22:13 of Reuben, and to the **c.** of Gad,... 1121
Jos 22:15 they came unto the **c.** of Reuben,... 1121
Jos 22:15 of Reuben, and to the **c.** of Gad,... 1121
Jos 22:21 Then the **c.** of Reuben and the... 1121
Jos 22:21 and the **c.** of Gad and the half... 1121
Jos 22:24 your **c.** might speak unto our **c.**,... 1121
Jos 22:25 ye **c.** of Reuben and **c.** of Gad; ye... 1121
Jos 22:25 so shall your **c.** make our **c.** cease... 1121
Jos 22:27 your **c.** may not say to our **c.** in time... 1121
Jos 22:30 that the **c.** of Reuben and the... 1121
Jos 22:30 of Reuben and the **c.** of Gad... 1121
Jos 22:30 and the **c.** of Manesseh spake,... 1121
Jos 22:31 priest said unto the **c.** of Reuben,... 1121
Jos 22:31 and to the **c.** of Gad,... 1121
Jos 22:31 and to the **c.** of Manesseh, This... 1121
Jos 22:31 ye have delivered the **c.** of Israel... 1121
Jos 22:32 returned from the **c.** of Reuben,... 1121
Jos 22:32 and from the **c.** of Gad,... 1121
Jos 22:32 to the **c.** of Israel, and brought... 1121
Jos 22:33 the thing pleased the **c.** of Israel;... 1121
Jos 22:33 and the **c.** of Israel blessed God,... 1121
Jos 22:33 the **c.** of Reuben and Gad dwelt... 1121
Jos 22:34 And the **c.** of Reuben and... 1121
Jos 22:34 the **c.** of Gad called the altar Ed:... 1121
Jos 24:4 Jacob and his **c.** went down into... 1121
Jos 24:32 which the **c.** of Israel brought up... 1121
Jos 24:32 the inheritance of the **c.** of Joseph... 1121
Jg 1:1 the **c.** of Israel asked the Lord,... 1121
Jg 1:8 Now the **c.** of Judah had fought... 1121
Jg 1:9 afterward the **c.** of Judah went... 1121
Jg 1:16 And the **c.** of the Kenite, Moses'... 1121
Jg 1:16 the **c.** of Judah into the wilderness... 1121
Jg 1:21 And the **c.** of Benjamin did not... 1121
Jg 1:21 dwell with the **c.** of Benjamin... 1121
Jg 1:34 the Amorites forced the **c.** of Dan... 1121
Jg 2:4 words unto all the **c.** of Israel,... 1121
Jg 2:6 the **c.** of Israel went every man... 1121
Jg 2:11 the **c.** of Israel did evil in the sight... 1121
Jg 3:2 the generations of the **c.** of Israel... 1121
Jg 3:5 the **c.** of Israel dwelt among the... 1121
Jg 3:7 And the **c.** of Israel did evil... 1121
Jg 3:8 and the **c.** of Israel served... 1121
Jg 3:9 And when the **c.** of Israel cried... 1121

Jg 3:9 up a deliverer to the **c.** of Israel......... 1121
Jg 3:12 the **c.** of Israel did evil again............. 1121
Jg 3:13 gathered unto him the **c.** of Ammon..... 1121
Jg 3:14 **c.** of Israel served Eglon the king....... 1121
Jg 3:15 **c.** of Israel cried unto the Lord,.......... 1121
Jg 3:15 the **c.** of Israel sent a present unto...... 1121
Jg 3:27 **c.** of Israel went down with him.......... 1121
Jg 4:1 the **c.** of Israel again did evil............ 1121
Jg 4:3 **c.** of Israel cried unto the Lord:.......... 1121
Jg 4:3 oppressed the **c.** of Israel.................. 1121
Jg 4:5 the **c.** of Israel came up to her........... 1121
Jg 4:6 men of the **c.** of Naphtali and of.......... 1121
Jg 4:6 and of the **c.** of Zebulun?.................. 1121
Jg 4:11 the **c.** of Hobab the father in law......... 1121
Jg 4:23 of Canaan before the **c.** of Israel......... 1121
Jg 4:24 hand of the **c.** of Israel prospered,...... 1121
Jg 6:1 **c.** of Israel did evil in the sight of........ 1121
Jg 6:2 **c.** of Israel made them the dens........... 1121
Jg 6:3 and the **c.** of the east, even they........ 1121
Jg 6:6 **c.** of Israel cried unto the Lord........... 1121
Jg 6:7 when the **c.** of Israel cried unto.......... 1121
Jg 6:8 sent a prophet unto the **c.** of Israel,.... 1121
Jg 6:33 and the **c.** of the east were gathered... 1121
Jg 7:12 the **c.** of the east lay along................ 1121
Jg 8:10 the hosts of the **c.** of the east:........... 1121
Jg 8:18 one resembled the **c.** of a king.......... 1121
Jg 8:28 subdued before the **c.** of Israel,.......... 1121
Jg 8:33 the **c.** of Israel turned again, and......... 1121
Jg 8:34 **c.** of Israel remembered not the......... 1121
Jg 10:6 the **c.** of Israel did evil again............. 1121
Jg 10:6 the gods of the **c.** of Ammon,............ 1121
Jg 10:7 the hands of the **c.** of Ammon........... 1121
Jg 10:8 and oppressed the **c.** of Israel:........... 1121
Jg 10:8 the **c.** of Israel that were on the......... 1121
Jg 10:9 **c.** of Ammon passed over Jordan......... 1121
Jg 10:10 the **c.** of Israel cried unto the Lord,..... 1121
Jg 10:11 Lord said unto the **c.** of Israel,.......... 1121
Jg 10:11 Amorites, from the **c.** of Ammon,....... 1121
Jg 10:15 the **c.** of Israel said unto the Lord,...... 1121
Jg 10:17 the **c.** of Ammon were gathered......... 1121
Jg 10:17 **c.** of Israel assembled themselves....... 1121
Jg 10:18 to fight against the **c.** of Ammon?........ 1121
Jg 11:4 that the **c.** of Ammon made war.......... 1121
Jg 11:5 the **c.** of Ammon made war against...... 1121
Jg 11:6 may fight with the **c.** of Ammon.......... 1121
Jg 11:8 and fight against the **c.** of Ammon,...... 1121
Jg 11:9 to fight against the **c.** of Ammon,........ 1121
Jg 11:12 king of the **c.** of Ammon, saying,........ 1121
Jg 11:13 king of the **c.** of Ammon answered...... 1121
Jg 11:14 unto the king of the **c.** of Ammon:....... 1121
Jg 11:15 nor the land of the **c.** of Ammon:........ 1121
Jg 11:27 **c.** of Israel and the **c.** of Ammon......... 1121
Jg 11:28 of the **c.** of Ammon hearkened not...... 1121
Jg 11:29 passed over unto the **c.** of Ammon...... 1121
Jg 11:30 the **c.** of Ammon into mine hands,........ 1121
Jg 11:31 in peace from the **c.** of Ammon,......... 1121
Jg 11:32 passed over unto the **c.** of Ammon...... 1121
Jg 11:33 Thus the **c.** of Ammon were subdued... 1121
Jg 11:33 before the **c.** of Israel....................... 1121
Jg 11:36 enemies, even of the **c.** of Ammon...... 1121
Jg 12:1 to fight against the **c.** of Ammon,........ 1121
Jg 12:2 great strife with the **c.** of Ammon;........ 1121
Jg 12:3 the **c.** of Ammon, and the Lord........ 1121
Jg 13:1 the **c.** of Israel did evil again............. 1121
Jg 14:16 a riddle unto the **c.** of my people,....... 1121
Jg 14:17 the riddle to the **c.** of her people........ 1121
Jg 18:2 the **c.** of Dan sent of their family........ 1121
Jg 18:16 were of the **c.** of Dan, stood by.......... 1121
Jg 18:22 and overtook the **c.** of Dan................ 1121
Jg 18:23 they cried unto the **c.** of Dan............ 1121
Jg 18:25 **c.** of Dan said unto him, Let not......... 1121
Jg 18:26 the **c.** of Dan went their way:........... 1121
Jg 18:30 the **c.** of Dan set up the graven........... 1121
Jg 19:12 that is not of the **c.** of Israel;............. 1121
Jg 19:30 the day that the **c.** of Israel came........ 1121
Jg 20:1 Then all the **c.** of Israel went out,....... 1121
Jg 20:3 the **c.** of Benjamin heard that the........ 1121
Jg 20:3 **c.** of Israel were gone up to Mizpeh.).. 1121
Jg 20:3 Then said the **c.** of Israel,................. 1121
Jg 20:7 Behold, ye are all **c.** of Israel;............ 1121
Jg 20:13 **c.** of Belial, which are in Gibeah,........ 1121
Jg 20:13 **c.** of Benjamin would not hearken......... 1121
Jg 20:13 of their brethren the **c.** of Israel:........ 1121
Jg 20:14 But the **c.** of Benjamin gathered......... 1121
Jg 20:14 to battle against the **c.** of Israel.......... 1121
Jg 20:15 the **c.** of Benjamin were numbered...... 1121
Jg 20:18 the **c.** of Israel arose, and went up...... 1121
Jg 20:18 battle against the **c.** of Benjamin?........ 1121
Jg 20:19 the **c.** of Israel rose up in the............ 1121
Jg 20:21 the **c.** of Benjamin came forth............ 1121
Jg 20:23 the **c.** of Israel went up and wept......... 1121
Jg 20:23 against the **c.** of Benjamin my............ 1121
Jg 20:24 the **c.** of Israel came near against........ 1121
Jg 20:24 the **c.** of Benjamin the second day,...... 1121
Jg 20:25 to the ground of the **c.** of Israel......... 1121
Jg 20:26 the **c.** of Israel, and all the people,...... 1121
Jg 20:27 **c.** of Israel enquired of the Lord,........ 1121
Jg 20:28 the **c.** of Benjamin my brother,........... 1121
Jg 20:30 **c.** of Israel went up against the.......... 1121
Jg 20:30 **c.** of Benjamin on the third day,.......... 1121
Jg 20:31 **c.** of Benjamin went out against.......... 1121
Jg 20:32 the **c.** of Benjamin said, They are....... 1121
Jg 20:32 the **c.** of Israel said, Let us flee,......... 1121
Jg 20:35 the **c.** of Israel destroyed of the......... 1121
Jg 20:36 So the **c.** of Benjamin saw that.......... 1121
Jg 20:48 again upon the **c.** of Benjamin,............ 1121
Jg 21:5 the **c.** of Israel said, Who is there....... 1121
Jg 21:6 the **c.** of Israel repented them for....... 1121
Jg 21:10 sword with the women and the **c.**........ 2945
Jg 21:13 to speak to the **c.** of Benjamin........... 1121
Jg 21:18 **c.** of Israel have sworn, saying,........... 1121
Jg 21:20 commanded the **c.** of Benjamin,.......... 1121
Jg 21:23 the **c.** of Benjamin did so, and........... 1121
Jg 21:24 the **c.** of Israel departed thence.......... 1121
1Sa 1:2 and Peninnah had **c.**,......................... 3206
1Sa 1:3 but Hannah had no **c.**......................... 3206
1Sa 2:5 hath many **c.** is waxed feeble............ 1121
1Sa 2:28 made by fire of the **c.** of Israel?.......... 1121
1Sa 7:4 **c.** of Israel did put away Baalim.......... 1121
1Sa 7:6 judged the **c.** of Israel in Mizpeh......... 1121
1Sa 7:7 Philistines heard that the **c.** of............ 1121
1Sa 7:7 And when the **c.** of Israel heard it,...... 1121
1Sa 7:8 the **c.** of Israel said to Samuel,........... 1121
1Sa 9:2 was not among the **c.** of Israel.......... 1121
1Sa 10:18 And said unto the **c.** of Israel,............ 1121
1Sa 10:27 the **c.** of Belial said, How shall........... 1121
1Sa 11:8 the **c.** of Israel were three hundred..... 1121
1Sa 12:12 the king of the **c.** of Ammon.............. 1121
1Sa 14:18 at that time with the **c.** of Israel........ 1121
1Sa 14:47 and against the **c.** of Ammon,............. 1121
1Sa 15:6 kindness to all the **c.** of Israel,........... 1121
1Sa 16:11 unto Jesse, Are here all thy **c.**?.......... 5288
1Sa 17:53 **c.** of Israel returned from chasing........ 1121
1Sa 22:19 and women, **c.** and sucklings,............. 5768
1Sa 26:19 the **c.** of men, cursed be they............ 1121
1Sa 30:22 to every man his wife and his **c.**,......... 1121
2Sa 1:18 bade them teach the **c.** of Judah.......... 1121
2Sa 2:25 the **c.** of Benjamin gathered............... 1121
2Sa 4:2 Beerothite, of the **c.** of Benjamin:....... 1121
2Sa 7:6 up the **c.** of Israel out of Egypt,......... 1121
2Sa 7:7 walked with all the **c.** of Israel........... 1121
2Sa 7:10 the **c.** of wickedness afflict them......... 1121
2Sa 7:14 with the stripes of the **c.** of men:........ 1121
2Sa 8:12 **c.** of Ammon, and of the Philistines,.... 1121
2Sa 10:1 the king of the **c.** of Ammon died,....... 1121
2Sa 10:2 into the land of the **c.** of Ammon......... 1121
2Sa 10:3 the **c.** of Ammon said unto Hanun....... 1121
2Sa 10:6 when the **c.** of Ammon saw that......... 1121
2Sa 10:6 the **c.** of Ammon sent and hired.......... 1121
2Sa 10:8 the **c.** of Ammon came out, and.......... 1121
2Sa 10:10 in array against the **c.** of Ammon........ 1121
2Sa 10:11 if the **c.** of Ammon be too strong......... 1121
2Sa 10:14 **c.** of Ammon saw that the Syrians....... 1121
2Sa 10:14 returned from the **c.** of Ammon,.......... 1121
2Sa 10:19 feared to help the **c.** of Ammon.......... 1121
2Sa 11:1 they destroyed the **c.** of Ammon,......... 1121
2Sa 12:3 together with him, and with his **c.**;....... 1121
2Sa 12:9 the sword of the **c.** of Ammon........... 1121
2Sa 12:26 Rabbah of the **c.** of Ammon,.............. 1121
2Sa 12:31 all the cities of the **c.** of Ammon......... 1121
2Sa 17:27 of Rabbah of the **c.** of Ammon,........... 1121
2Sa 21:2 were not of the **c.** of Israel,............... 1121
2Sa 21:2 **c.** of Israel had sworn unto them:....... 1121
2Sa 21:2 zeal to the **c.** of Israel and Judah.)....... 1121
2Sa 23:29 of Gibeah of the **c.** of Benjamin,........ 1121
1Ki 2:4 If thy **c.** take heed to their way,......... 1121
1Ki 4:30 the wisdom of all the **c.** of the east..... 1121
1Ki 6:1 the **c.** of Israel were come out of........ 1121
1Ki 6:13 I will dwell among the **c.** of Israel,...... 1121
1Ki 8:1 of the fathers of the **c.** of Israel,........ 1121
1Ki 8:9 a covenant with the **c.** of Israel,......... 1121
1Ki 8:25 that thy **c.** take heed to their way,....... 1121
1Ki 8:39 the hearts of all the **c.** of men;........... 1121
1Ki 8:63 and all the **c.** of Israel dedicated......... 1121
1Ki 9:6 from following me, ye or your **c.**,........ 1121
1Ki 9:20 which were not of the **c.** of Israel,...... 1121
1Ki 9:21 Their **c.** that were left after them in.... 1121
1Ki 9:21 in the land, whom the **c.** of Israel........ 1121
1Ki 9:22 the **c.** of Israel did Solomon make....... 1121
1Ki 11:2 Lord said unto the **c.** of Israel,........... 1121
1Ki 11:7 abomination of the **c.** of Ammon.......... 1121
1Ki 11:33 the god of the **c.** of Ammon,............. 1121
1Ki 12:17 But as for the **c.** of Israel which......... 1121
1Ki 12:24 your brethren the **c.** of Israel:............ 1121
1Ki 12:33 a feast unto the **c.** of Israel:.............. 1121
1Ki 14:24 cast out before the **c.** of Israel.......... 1121
1Ki 18:20 Ahab sent unto all the **c.** of Israel,...... 1121
1Ki 19:10 the **c.** of Israel have forsaken thy......... 1121
1Ki 19:14 because the **c.** of Israel have............. 1121
1Ki 20:3 thy wives also and thy **c.**, even the..... 1121
1Ki 20:5 thy gold, and thy wives, and thy **c.**;...... 1121
1Ki 20:7 me for my wives, and for my **c.**,......... 1121
1Ki 20:15 **c.** of Israel, being seven thousand,...... 1121
1Ki 20:27 the **c.** of Israel were numbered,.......... 1121
1Ki 20:27 **c.** of Israel pitched before them.......... 1121
1Ki 20:29 the **c.** of Israel slew of the Syrians...... 1121
1Ki 21:13 came in two men, **c.** of Belial,............ 1121
1Ki 21:26 cast out before the **c.** of Israel.......... 1121
2Ki 2:23 came forth little **c.** out of the city,........ 5288
2Ki 2:24 and tare forty and two **c.** of them........ 3206
2Ki 4:7 live thou and thy **c.** of the rest........... 1121
2Ki 8:12 wilt do unto the **c.** of Israel:............... 1121
2Ki 8:12 and wilt dash their **c.**, and rip............ 6768
2Ki 8:19 him alway a light, and to his **c.**,.......... 1121
2Ki 9:1 one of the **c.** of the prophets,............ 1121
2Ki 10:1 them that brought up Ahab's **c.**,................
2Ki 10:5 and the bringers up of the **c.**....................
2Ki 10:13 down to salute the **c.** of the king......... 1121
2Ki 10:13 and the **c.** of the queen..................... 1121
2Ki 10:30 thy **c.** of the fourth generation............ 1121
2Ki 13:5 the **c.** of Israel dwelt in their tents,..... 1121
2Ki 14:6 But the **c.** of the murderers he........... 1121
2Ki 14:6 shall not be put to death for the **c.**,...... 1121
2Ki 14:6 nor the **c.** be put to death for the....... 1121
2Ki 16:3 Lord cast out from before the **c.**.......... 1121
2Ki 17:7 that the **c.** of Israel had sinned.......... 1121
2Ki 17:8 the Lord cast out from before the **c.**..... 1121
2Ki 17:9 the **c.** of Israel did secretly those........ 1121
2Ki 17:22 **c.** of Israel walked in all the sins......... 1121
2Ki 17:24 Samaria instead of the **c.** of Israel:...... 1121
2Ki 17:31 Sepharvites burnt their **c.** in fire......... 1121
2Ki 17:34 Lord commanded the **c.** of Jacob,......... 1121
2Ki 17:41 their **c.**, and their children's **c.**:.......... 1121
2Ki 18:4 the **c.** of Israel did burn incense.......... 1121
2Ki 19:3 for the **c.** are come to the birth,.......... 1121
2Ki 19:12 and the **c.** of Eden which were in........ 1121
2Ki 21:2 cast out before the **c.** of Israel.......... 1121
2Ki 21:9 destroyed before the **c.** of Israel......... 1121
2Ki 23:6 the graves of the **c.** of the people....... 1121
2Ki 23:10 in the valley of the **c.** of Hinnom,........ 1121
2Ki 23:13 abomination of the **c.** of Ammon,......... 1121
2Ki 24:2 bands of the **c.** of Ammon, and........... 1121
1Ch 1:43 king reigned over the **c.** of Israel:....... 1121
1Ch 2:10 Nahshon, prince of the **c.** of Judah;...... 1121
1Ch 2:18 Caleb the son of Hezron begat **c.**..............
1Ch 2:30 Appaim; but Seled died without **c.**......... 1121
1Ch 2:31 And the **c.** of Sheshan; Ahlai............. 1121
1Ch 2:32 and Jether died without **c.**................. 1121
1Ch 4:27 his brethren had not many **c.**,............. 1121
1Ch 4:27 multiply, like to the **c.** of Judah.......... 1121
1Ch 5:11 And the **c.** of Gad dwelt over............. 1121
1Ch 5:14 These are the **c.** of Abihail the........... 1121
1Ch 5:23 **c.** of the half tribe of Manasseh.......... 1121
1Ch 6:3 **c.** of Amram; Aaron, and Moses,........ 1121
1Ch 6:33 are they that waited with their **c.**......... 1121
1Ch 6:64 the **c.** of Israel gave to the Levites...... 1121
1Ch 6:65 the tribe of the **c.** of Judah, and......... 1121
1Ch 6:65 of the tribe of the **c.** of Simeon,.......... 1121
1Ch 6:65 of the tribe of the **c.** of Benjamin,....... 1121
1Ch 6:77 Unto the rest of the **c.** of Merari........ 1121
1Ch 7:12 and Huppim, the **c.** of Ir, and........... 1121
1Ch 7:29 the borders of the **c.** of Manesseh,...... 1121
1Ch 7:29 dwelt the **c.** of Joseph the son of........ 1121
1Ch 7:33 These are the **c.** of Japhlet............. 1121
1Ch 7:40 All these were the **c.** of Asher,.......... 1121
1Ch 8:8 And Shaharaim begat **c.** in the..................
1Ch 9:3 dwelt of the **c.** of Judah,................... 1121
1Ch 9:3 and of the **c.** of Benjamin,.................. 1121
1Ch 9:3 and of the **c.** of Ephraim,................... 1121
1Ch 9:4 the **c.** of Pharez the son of Judah........ 1121
1Ch 9:18 in the companies of the **c.** of Levi....... 1121

Book	Ref	Context	No.
1Ch	9:23	and their **c.** had the oversight	1121
1Ch	11:31	Gibeah, that pertained to the **c.** of	1121
1Ch	12:16	there came of the **c.** of Benjamin	1121
1Ch	12:24	The **c.** of Judah that bare shield	1121
1Ch	12:25	Of the **c.** of Simeon, mighty men	1121
1Ch	12:26	Of the **c.** of Levi four thousand	1121
1Ch	12:29	And of the **c.** of Benjamin, the	1121
1Ch	12:30	the **c.** of Ephraim twenty thousand	1121
1Ch	12:32	of the **c.** of Issachar, which were	1121
1Ch	14:4	these are the names of his **c.**	3205
1Ch	15:4	David assembled the **c.** of Aaron,	1121
1Ch	15:15	the **c.** of the Levites bare the ark	1121
1Ch	16:13	ye **c.** of Jacob, his chosen ones	1121
1Ch	17:9	neither shall the **c.** of wickedness	1121
1Ch	18:11	Moab, and from the **c.** of Ammon,	1121
1Ch	19:1	king of the **c.** of Ammon died,	1121
1Ch	19:2	into the land of the **c.** of Ammon	1121
1Ch	19:3	the princes of the **c.** of Ammon	1121
1Ch	19:6	when the **c.** of Ammon saw that	1121
1Ch	19:6	the **c.** of Ammon sent a thousand	1121
1Ch	19:7	And the **c.** of Ammon gathered	1121
1Ch	19:9	the **c.** of Ammon came out, and put	1121
1Ch	19:11	in array against the **c.** of Ammon	1121
1Ch	19:12	if the **c.** of Ammon be too strong	1121
1Ch	19:15	**c.** of Ammon saw that the Syrians	1121
1Ch	19:19	the Syrians help the **c.** of Ammon	1121
1Ch	20:1	the country of the **c.** of Ammon,	1121
1Ch	20:3	all the cities of the **c.** of Ammon	1121
1Ch	20:4	that was of the **c.** of the giant:	3211
1Ch	24:2	before their father, and had no **c.**	1121
1Ch	26:10	Hosah, of the **c.** of Merari, had	1121
1Ch	27:1	the **c.** of Israel after their number,	1121
1Ch	27:3	Of the **c.** of Perez was the chief	1121
1Ch	27:10	the Pelonite, of the **c.** of Ephraim:	1121
1Ch	27:14	Pirathonite, of the **c.** of Ephraim:	1121
1Ch	27:20	Of the **c.** of Ephraim, Hoshea the	1121
1Ch	28:8	inheritance for your **c.** after you	1121
2Ch	5:2	of the fathers of the **c.** of Israel,	1121
2Ch	5:10	a covenant with the **c.** of Israel,	1121
2Ch	6:11	that he made with the **c.** of Israel	1121
2Ch	6:16	yet so that thy **c.** take heed to	1121
2Ch	6:30	knowest the hearts of the **c.** of men:)	1121
2Ch	7:3	all the **c.** of Israel saw how the fire	1121
2Ch	8:2	caused the **c.** of Israel to dwell	1121
2Ch	8:8	of their **c.**, who were left after	1121
2Ch	8:8	whom the **c.** of Israel consumed	1121
2Ch	8:9	of the **c.** of Israel did Solomon	1121
2Ch	10:17	as for the **c.** of Israel that dwelt	1121
2Ch	10:18	and the **c.** of Israel stoned him	1121
2Ch	11:19	Which bare him **c.**; Jeush, and	1121
2Ch	11:23	wisely, and dispersed of all his **c.**	1121
2Ch	13:7	unto him vain men, the **c.** of Belial,	1121
2Ch	13:12	O **c.** of Israel, fight ye not against	1121
2Ch	13:16	the **c.** of Israel fled before Judah:	1121
2Ch	13:18	the **c.** of Israel were brought	1121
2Ch	13:18	the **c.** of Judah prevailed, because	1121
2Ch	20:1	**c.** of Moab, and the **c.** of Ammon,	1121
2Ch	20:10	the **c.** of Ammon and Moab and	1121
2Ch	20:13	little ones, their wives, and their **c.**	1121
2Ch	20:19	of the **c.** of the Kohathites,	1121
2Ch	20:19	and of the **c.** of the Korhites,	1121
2Ch	20:22	against the **c.** of Ammon, Moab,	1121
2Ch	20:23	the **c.** of Ammon and Moab stood	1121
2Ch	21:14	people, and thy **c.**, and thy wives,	1121
2Ch	25:4	But he slew not their **c.**, but did	1121
2Ch	25:4	The fathers shall not die for the **c.**,	1121
2Ch	25:4	neither shall the **c.** die for the	1121
2Ch	25:7	to wit, with all the **c.** of Ephraim	1121
2Ch	25:11	of the **c.** of Seir ten thousand	1121
2Ch	25:12	the **c.** of Judah carry away captive,	1121
2Ch	25:14	brought the gods of the **c.** of Seir,	1121
2Ch	27:5	the **c.** of Ammon gave him the	1121
2Ch	27:5	So much did the **c.** of Ammon pay	1121
2Ch	28:3	burnt his **c.** in the fire, after the	1121
2Ch	28:3	had cast out before the **c.** of Israel	1121
2Ch	28:8	**c.** of Israel carried away captive	1121
2Ch	28:10	to keep under the **c.** of Judah	1121
2Ch	28:12	the heads of the **c.** of Ephraim,	1121
2Ch	30:6	Ye **c.** of Israel, turn again unto	1121
2Ch	30:9	your brethren and your **c.** shall	1121
2Ch	30:21	the **c.** of Israel that were present	1121
2Ch	31:1	Then all the **c.** of Israel returned,	1121
2Ch	31:5	**c.** of Israel brought in abundance	1121
2Ch	31:6	And concerning the **c.** of Israel	1121
2Ch	33:2	had cast out before the **c.** of Israel	1121
2Ch	33:6	caused his **c.** to pass through the	1121
2Ch	33:9	Lord had destroyed before the **c.** of	1121
2Ch	34:33	that pertained to the **c.** of Israel,	1121
2Ch	35:17	the **c.** of Israel that were present	1121
Ezr	2:1	Now these are the **c.** of the province	1121
Ezr	2:3	**c.** of Parosh, two thousand an	1121
Ezr	2:4	**c.** of Shephatiah, three hundred	1121
Ezr	2:5	**c.** of Arah, seven hundred seventy	1121
Ezr	2:6	The **c.** of Pahath-moab, of the	1121
Ezr	2:6	of the **c.** of Jeshua and Joab, two	1121
Ezr	2:7	The **c.** of Elam, a thousand two	1121
Ezr	2:8	The **c.** of Zattu, nine hundred forty	1121
Ezr	2:9	The **c.** of Zaccai, seven hundred and	1121
Ezr	2:10	The **c.** of Bani, six hundred forty	1121
Ezr	2:11	The **c.** of Bebai, six hundred twenty	1121
Ezr	2:12	The **c.** of Azgad, a thousand two	1121
Ezr	2:13	The **c.** of Adonikam, six hundred	1121
Ezr	2:14	The **c.** of Bigvai, two thousand fifty	1121
Ezr	2:15	The **c.** of Adin, four hundred fifty	1121
Ezr	2:16	The **c.** of Ater of Hezekiah, ninety	1121
Ezr	2:17	The **c.** of Bezai, three hundred	1121
Ezr	2:18	The **c.** of Jorah, an hundred and	1121
Ezr	2:19	The **c.** of Hashum, two hundred	1121
Ezr	2:20	The **c.** of Gibbar, ninety and five	1121
Ezr	2:21	The **c.** of Beth-lehem, an hundred	1121
Ezr	2:24	The **c.** of Azmaveth, forty and two	1121
Ezr	2:25	The **c.** of Kirjath-arim, Chephirah,	1121
Ezr	2:26	The **c.** of Ramah and Gaba, six	1121
Ezr	2:29	The **c.** of Nebo, fifty and two	1121
Ezr	2:30	The **c.** of Magbish, an hundred fifty	1121
Ezr	2:31	The **c.** of the other Elam, a thousand	1121
Ezr	2:32	The **c.** of Harim, three hundred and	1121
Ezr	2:33	The **c.** of Lod, Hadid, and Ono, seven.	1121
Ezr	2:34	The **c.** of Jericho, three hundred	1121
Ezr	2:35	The **c.** of Senaah, three thousand	1121
Ezr	2:36	The priests: the **c.** of Jedaiah, of	1121
Ezr	2:37	The **c.** of Immer, a thousand fifty	1121
Ezr	2:38	The **c.** of Pashur, a thousand two	1121
Ezr	2:39	The **c.** of Harim, a thousand and	1121
Ezr	2:40	the **c.** of Jeshua and Kadmiel,	1121
Ezr	2:40	of the **c.** of Hodaviah, seventy	1121
Ezr	2:41	The singers: the **c.** of Asaph, an	1121
Ezr	2:42	The **c.** of the porters: the	1121
Ezr	2:42	the **c.** of Shallum, the **c.** of Ater,	1121
Ezr	2:42	the **c.** of Talmon, the **c.** of Akkub,	1121
Ezr	2:42	the **c.** of Hatita, the **c.** of Shobai,	1121
Ezr	2:43	the **c.** of Ziha, the **c.** of Hasupha,	1121
Ezr	2:43	the **c.** of Tabbaoth, in all an	1121
Ezr	2:44	The **c.** of Keros, the **c.** of Siaha	1121
Ezr	2:44	the **c.** of Padon,	1121
Ezr	2:45	The **c.** of Lebanah,	1121
Ezr	2:45	the **c.** of Hagabah,	1121
Ezr	2:45	the **c.** of Akkub,	1121
Ezr	2:46	The **c.** of Hagab, the **c.** of Shalmai,	1121
Ezr	2:46	the **c.** of Hanan,	1121
Ezr	2:47	The **c.** of Giddel, the **c.** of Gahar,	1121
Ezr	2:47	the **c.** of Reaiah,	1121
Ezr	2:48	The **c.** of Rezin, the **c.** of Nekoda,	1121
Ezr	2:48	the **c.** of Gazzam,	1121
Ezr	2:49	The **c.** of Uzza, the **c.** of Paseah,	1121
Ezr	2:49	the **c.** of Besai,	1121
Ezr	2:50	The **c.** of Asnah, the **c.** of Mehunim,	1121
Ezr	2:50	the **c.** of Nephusim,	1121
Ezr	2:51	The **c.** of Bakbuk, the **c.** of Hakupha,	1121
Ezr	2:51	the **c.** of Harhur,	1121
Ezr	2:52	The **c.** of Bazluth, the **c.** of Mehida,	1121
Ezr	2:52	the **c.** of Harsha,	1121
Ezr	2:53	The **c.** of Barkos, the **c.** of Sisera,	1121
Ezr	2:53	the **c.** of Thamah,	1121
Ezr	2:54	The **c.** of Neziah, the **c.** of Hatipha	1121
Ezr	2:55	The **c.** of Solomon's servants:	1121
Ezr	2:55	the **c.** of Sotai, the **c.** of Sophereth,	1121
Ezr	2:55	the **c.** of Peruda,	1121
Ezr	2:56	The **c.** of Jaalah, the **c.** of Darkon,	1121
Ezr	2:56	the **c.** of Giddel,	1121
Ezr	2:57	The **c.** of Shephatiah,	1121
Ezr	2:57	the **c.** of Hattil,	1121
Ezr	2:57	the **c.** of Pochereth of Zebaim,	1121
Ezr	2:57	the **c.** of Ami	1121
Ezr	2:58	and the **c.** of Solomon's servants,	1121
Ezr	2:60	The **c.** of Delaiah, the **c.** of Tobiah,	1121
Ezr	2:60	the **c.** of Nekoda,	1121
Ezr	2:61	And of the **c.** of the priests:	1121
Ezr	2:61	the **c.** of Habaiah, the **c.** of Koz,	1121
Ezr	2:61	the **c.** of Barzillai;	1121
Ezr	3:1	and the **c.** of Israel were in the	1121
Ezr	4:1	heard that the **c.** of the captivity	1121
Ezr	6:16	And the **c.** of Israel, the priests,	1121
Ezr	6:16	the rest of the **c.** of the captivity,	1121
Ezr	6:19	the **c.** of the captivity kept the	1121
Ezr	6:20	for all the **c.** of the captivity, and	1121
Ezr	6:21	And the **c.** of Israel, which were	1121
Ezr	7:7	went up some of the **c.** of Israel,	1121
Ezr	8:35	**c.** of those that had been carried	1121
Ezr	9:12	an inheritance to your **c.** forever	1121
Ezr	10:1	of men and women and **c.**:	3206
Ezr	10:7	unto all the **c.** of the captivity,	1121
Ezr	10:16	the **c.** of the captivity did so	1121
Ezr	10:44	and wives by whom they had **c.**	1121
Ne	1:6	for the **c.** of Israel thy servants,	1121
Ne	1:6	confess the sins of the **c.** of Israel,	1121
Ne	2:10	seek the welfare of the **c.** of Israel	1121
Ne	5:5	our **c.** as their **c.**: and, lo, we bring	1121
Ne	7:6	These are the **c.** of the province,	1121
Ne	7:8	The **c.** of Parosh, two thousand	1121
Ne	7:9	The **c.** of Shephatiah, three	1121
Ne	7:10	The **c.** of Arah, six hundred fifty	1121
Ne	7:11	The **c.** of Pahath-moab, of the	1121
Ne	7:11	**c.** of Jeshua and Joab,	1121
Ne	7:12	The **c.** of Elam, a thousand two	1121
Ne	7:13	The **c.** of Zatu, eight hundred	1121
Ne	7:14	The **c.** of Zaccai, seven hundred	1121
Ne	7:15	The **c.** of Binnui, six hundred	1121
Ne	7:16	The **c.** of Bebai, six hundred	1121
Ne	7:17	The **c.** of Azgad, two thousand	1121
Ne	7:18	The **c.** of Adonikam, six hundred	1121
Ne	7:19	The **c.** of Bigvai, two thousand	1121
Ne	7:20	The **c.** of Adin, six hundred fifty	1121
Ne	7:21	The **c.** of Ater of Hezekiah, ninety	1121
Ne	7:22	The **c.** of Hashum, three hundred	1121
Ne	7:23	The **c.** of Bezai, three hundred	1121
Ne	7:24	The **c.** of Hariph, an hundred	1121
Ne	7:25	The **c.** of Gibeon, ninety and five	1121
Ne	7:34	The **c.** of the other Elam,	1121
Ne	7:35	The **c.** of Harim, three hundred	1121
Ne	7:36	The **c.** of Jericho, three hundred	1121
Ne	7:37	The **c.** of Lod, Hadid, and Ono,	1121
Ne	7:38	The **c.** of Senaah, three thousand	1121
Ne	7:39	the **c.** of Jedaiah, of the house of	1121
Ne	7:40	The **c.** of Immer, a thousand	1121
Ne	7:41	The **c.** of Pashur, a thousand	1121
Ne	7:42	The **c.** of Harim, a thousand	1121
Ne	7:43	The **c.** of Jeshua of Kadmiel, and	1121
Ne	7:43	of the **c.** of Hodevah, seventy and	1121
Ne	7:44	the **c.** of Asaph, an hundred forty	1121
Ne	7:45	the **c.** of Shallum, the **c.** of Ater,	1121
Ne	7:45	the **c.** of Talmon, the **c.** of Akkub,	1121
Ne	7:45	the **c.** of Hatita, the **c.** of Shobai,	1121
Ne	7:46	the **c.** of Ziha, the **c.** of Hashupha,	1121
Ne	7:46	the **c.** of Tabbaoth:	1121
Ne	7:47	The **c.** of Keros, the **c.** of Sia,	1121
Ne	7:47	the **c.** of Padon,	1121
Ne	7:48	The **c.** of Lebana, the **c.** of Hagaba,	1121
Ne	7:48	the **c.** of Shalmai,	1121
Ne	7:49	The **c.** of Hanan, the **c.** of Giddel,	1121
Ne	7:49	the **c.** of Gahar,	1121
Ne	7:50	The **c.** of Reaiah, the **c.** of Rezin,	1121
Ne	7:50	the **c.** of Nekoda,	1121
Ne	7:51	The **c.** of Gazzam, the **c.** of Uzza,	1121
Ne	7:51	the **c.** of Phaseah,	1121
Ne	7:52	The **c.** of Besai, the **c.** of Meunim,	1121
Ne	7:52	the **c.** of Nephishesim,	1121
Ne	7:53	The **c.** of Bakbuk, the **c.** of Hakupha,	1121
Ne	7:53	the **c.** of Harhur,	1121
Ne	7:54	The **c.** of Bazlith, the **c.** of Mehida,	1121
Ne	7:54	the **c.** of Harsha,	1121
Ne	7:55	The **c.** of Barkos, the **c.** of Sisera,	1121
Ne	7:55	the **c.** of Tamah,	1121
Ne	7:56	The **c.** of Neziah, the **c.** of Hatipha,	1121
Ne	7:57	The **c.** of Solomon's servants:	1121
Ne	7:57	the **c.** of Sotai, the **c.** of Sophereth,	1121
Ne	7:57	the **c.** of Perida,	1121
Ne	7:58	The **c.** of Jaala, the **c.** of Darkon,	1121
Ne	7:58	the **c.** of Giddel,	1121
Ne	7:59	The **c.** of Shephatiah,	1121
Ne	7:59	the **c.** of Hattil,	1121
Ne	7:59	the **c.** of Pochereth of Zebaim,	1121
Ne	7:59	the **c.** of Amon	1121
Ne	7:60	and the **c.** of Solomon's servants,	1121
Ne	7:62	The **c.** of Delaiah, the **c.** of Tobiah,	1121
Ne	7:62	the **c.** of Nekoda,	1121
Ne	7:63	the **c.** of Habaiah, the **c.** of Koz,	1121
Ne	7:63	the **c.** of Barzillai,	1121
Ne	7:73	the **c.** of Israel were in their cities,	1121
Ne	8:14	the **c.** of Israel should dwell in	1121
Ne	8:17	had not the **c.** of Israel done so	1121

Ne 9:1 the **c.** of Israel were assembled 1121
Ne 9:23 Their **c.** also multipliedst thou 1121
Ne 9:24 **c.** went in and possessed the land, 1121
Ne 10:39 the **c.** of Israel and the **c.** of Levi 1121
Ne 11:3 and the **c.** of Solomon's servants 1121
Ne 11:4 certain of the **c.** of Judah, and of the 1121
Ne 11:4 **c.** of Benjamin. Of the **c.** of Judah; 1121
Ne 11:4 of Mahalaleel, of the **c.** of Perez; 1121
Ne 11:24 the **c.** of Zerah the son of Judah, 1121
Ne 11:25 **c.** of Judah dwelt at Kirjath-arba, 1121
Ne 11:31 **c.** also of Benjamin from Geba 1121
Ne 12:43 the wives also and the **c.** rejoiced: 3206
Ne 12:47 them unto the **c.** of Aaron. 1121
Ne 13:2 they met not the **c.** of Israel 1121
Ne 13:16 sabbath unto the **c.** of Judah, 1121
Ne 13:24 their **c.** spake half in the speech 1121
Es 3:13 and old, little **c.** and women, 2945
Es 5:11 and the multitude of his **c.**, 1121
Job 5:4 His **c.** are far from safety, and 1121
Job 8:4 If thy **c.** have sinned against him, 1121
Job 17:5 even the eyes of his **c.** shall fail. 1121
Job 19:18 young **c.** despised me; I arose.
Job 20:10 his **c.** shall seek to please the poor, 1121
Job 21:11 like a flock, and their **c.** dance. 3206
Job 21:19 layeth up his iniquity for his **c.** 1121
Job 24:5 food for them and for their **c.**. 5288
Job 27:14 If his **c.** be multiplied, it is for 1121
Job 29:5 my **c.** were about me; 5288
Job 30:8 **c.** of fools, yea, **c.** of base men: 1121
Job 41:34 a king over all the **c.** of pride. 1121
Ps 11:4 his eyelids try, the **c.** of men. 1121
Ps 12:1 fail from among the **c.** of men. 1121
Ps 14:2 from heaven upon the **c.** of men, to 1121
Ps 17:14 are full of **c.**, and leave the rest 1121
Ps 21:10 seed from among the **c.** of men. 1121
Ps 34:11 Come, ye **c.**, hearken unto me: 1121
Ps 36:7 the **c.** of men put their trust 1121
Ps 45:2 art fairer than the **c.** of men: 1121
Ps 45:16 of thy fathers shall be thy **c.**, 1121
Ps 53:2 from heaven upon the **c.** of men, to 1121
Ps 66:5 in his doing toward the **c.** of men. 1121
Ps 69:8 and an alien unto my mother's **c.** 1121
Ps 72:4 he shall save the **c.** of the needy, 1121
Ps 73:15 against the generation of thy **c.** 1121
Ps 78:4 will not hide them from their **c.**. 1121
Ps 78:5 make them known to their **c.** 1121
Ps 78:6 the **c.** which should be born; 1121
Ps 78:6 and declare them to their **c.** 1121
Ps 78:9 The **c.** of Ephraim, being armed, 1121
Ps 82:6 of you are **c.** of the most High. 1121
Ps 83:8 they have holpen the **c.** of Lot 1121
Ps 89:30 If his **c.** forsake my law, and walk 1121
Ps 90:3 and sayest, Return, ye **c.** of men. 1121
Ps 90:16 and thy glory unto their **c.**. 1121
Ps 102:28 **c.** of thy servants shall continue, 1121
Ps 103:7 his acts unto the **c.** of Israel. 1121
Ps 103:13 Like as a father pitieth his **c.**, so 1121
Ps 103:17 righteousness unto children's **c.**; 1121
Ps 105:6 ye **c.** of Jacob his chosen. 1121
Ps 107:8, 15,21,31 works to the **c.** of men! 1121
Ps 109:9 Let his **c.** be fatherless, and his wife 1121
Ps 109:10 Let his **c.** be continually vagabonds, 1121
Ps 109:12 be any to favour his fatherless **c.**
Ps 113:9 and to be a joyful mother of **c.**. 1121
Ps 115:14 more and more, you and your **c.**. 1121
Ps 115:16 earth hath he given to the **c.** of men 1121
Ps 127:3 Lo, **c.** are an heritage of the Lord: 1121
Ps 127:4 so are the **c.** of the youth. 1121
Ps 128:3 thy **c.** like olive plants round about 1121
Ps 128:6 thou shalt see thy children's **c.**, 1121
Ps 132:12 If thy **c.** will keep my covenant 1121
Ps 132:12 **c.** shall also sit upon the throne 1121
Ps 137:7 **c.** of Edom in the day of Jerusalem; 1121
Ps 144:7 from the hand of strange **c.**; 1121
Ps 144:11 me from the hand of strange **c.**, 1121
Ps 147:13 he hath blessed thy **c.** within thee. 1121
Ps 148:12 and maidens; old men, and **c.** 5288
Ps 148:14 even of the **c.** of Israel, a people 1121
Ps 149:2 **c.** of Zion be joyful in their king. 1121
Pr 4:1 Hear, ye **c.**, the instruction of a 1121
Pr 5:7 Hear me now therefore, O ye **c.**, 1121
Pr 7:24 unto me now therefore, O ye **c.** 1121
Pr 8:32 hearken unto me, O ye **c.** 1121
Pr 13:22 an inheritance to his children's **c.** 1121
Pr 14:26 his **c.** shall have a place of refuge 1121
Pr 15:11 the hearts of the **c.** of men? 1121
Pr 17:6 Children's **c.** are the crown of old 1121
Pr 17:6 and the glory of **c.** are their fathers. 1121
Pr 20:7 his **c.** are blessed after him. 1121
Pr 31:28 her **c.** arise up and call her blessed; 1121
Ec 6:3 If a man beget an hundred **c.**,
Ca 1:6 mother's **c.** were angry with me; 1121
Isa 1:2 I have nourished and brought up **c.**, 1121
Isa 1:4 **c.** that are corrupters: they have 1121
Isa 2:6 themselves in the **c.** of strangers, 3206
Isa 3:4 I will give **c.** to be their princes, 5288
Isa 3:12 people, **c.** are their oppressors, 5768
Isa 8:18 **c.** whom the Lord hath given me 3206
Isa 11:14 the **c.** of Ammon shall obey them. 1121
Isa 13:16 **c.** also shall be dashed to pieces 5768
Isa 13:18 their eye shall not spare **c.**. 1121
Isa 14:21 Prepare slaughter for his **c.** for 1121
Isa 17:3 be as the glory of the **c.** of Israel, 1121
Isa 17:9 left because of the **c.** of Israel: 1121
Isa 21:17 the mighty men of the **c.** of Kedar, 1121
Isa 23:4 nor bring forth **c.**, neither do I
Isa 27:12 one by one, O ye **c.** of Israel. 1121
Isa 29:23 he seeth his **c.**, the work of mine 3206
Isa 30:1 the rebellious **c.**, saith the Lord, 1121
Isa 30:9 lying **c.**, that will not hear the 1121
Isa 31:6 **c.** of Israel have deeply revolted. 1121
Isa 37:3 for the **c.** are come to the birth, 1121
Isa 37:12 and the **c.** of Eden which were in 1121
Isa 38:19 the **c.** shall make known thy truth. 1121
Isa 47:8 neither shall I know the loss of **c.**
Isa 47:9 day, the loss of **c.**, and widowhood:
Isa 49:17 Thy **c.** shall make haste; thy 1121
Isa 49:20 The **c.** which thou shalt have, 1121
Isa 49:21 I have lost my **c.**, and am desolate,
Isa 49:25 and I will save thy **c.**. 1121
Isa 54:1 for more are the **c.** of the desolate 1121
Isa 54:1 than the **c.** of the married wife, 1121
Isa 54:13 thy **c.** shall be taught of the Lord; 1121
Isa 54:13 great shall be the peace of thy **c.**. 1121
Isa 57:4 are ye not **c.** of transgression, 3206
Isa 57:5 slaying **c.** in the valleys under the 3206
Isa 63:8 my people, **c.** that will not lie: 1121
Isa 66:8 travailed, she brought forth her **c.**. 1121
Isa 66:20 the **c.** of Israel bring an offering 1121
Jer 2:9 your children's **c.** will I plead. 1121
Jer 2:16 the **c.** of Noph and Tahapanes 1121
Jer 2:30 In vain have I smitten your **c.**; 1121
Jer 3:14 O backsliding **c.**, saith the Lord; 1121
Jer 3:19 shall I put thee among the **c.**, 1121
Jer 3:21 supplications of the **c.** of Israel: 1121
Jer 3:22 Return, ye backsliding **c.**, and I 1121
Jer 4:22 are sottish **c.**, and they have none 1121
Jer 5:7 thy **c.** have forsaken me, and sworn 1121
Jer 6:1 O ye **c.** of Benjamin, gather 1121
Jer 6:11 pour it out upon the **c.** abroad, 5768
Jer 7:18 **c.** gather wood, and the fathers 1121
Jer 7:30 **c.** of Judah have done evil in my 1121
Jer 9:21 to cut off the **c.** from without, and 5768
Jer 9:26 and Edom, and the **c.** of Ammon, 1121
Jer 10:20 my **c.** are gone forth of me, and 1121
Jer 15:7 will bereave them of **c.**, I will destroy
Jer 16:14 the **c.** of Israel out of the land of 1121
Jer 16:15 that brought up the **c.** of Israel 1121
Jer 17:2 their **c.** remember their altars 1121
Jer 17:19 in the gate of the **c.** of the people, 1121
Jer 18:21 deliver up their **c.** to the famine, 1121
Jer 18:21 wives be bereaved of their **c.**,
Jer 23:7 brought up the **c.** of Israel out of 1121
Jer 25:21 Moab, and the **c.** of Ammon, 1121
Jer 30:20 their **c.** also shall be as aforetime, 1121
Jer 31:15 Rahel weeping for her **c.** refused 1121
Jer 31:15 to be comforted for her **c.**, 1121
Jer 31:17 Lord, that thy **c.** shall come again 1121
Jer 32:18 the bosom of their **c.** after them: 1121
Jer 32:30 For the **c.** of Israel and the 1121
Jer 32:30 **c.** of Judah have done evil before 1121
Jer 32:30 **c.** of Israel have only provoked me 1121
Jer 32:32 **c.** of Israel and of the **c.** of Judah, 1121
Jer 32:39 them, and of their **c.** after them: 1121
Jer 38:23 wives and thy **c.** to the Chaldeans: 1121
Jer 40:7 men, and women, and **c.**, and of 2945
Jer 41:16 women, and the **c.**, and the eunuchs, 2945
Jer 43:6 and **c.**, and the king's daughters, 2945
Jer 47:3 shall not look back to their **c.** 1121
Jer 49:6 the captivity of the **c.** of Ammon, 1121
Jer 49:11 Leave thy fatherless **c.**, I will preserve
Jer 50:4 the **c.** of Israel shall come, 1121
Jer 50:4 they and the **c.** of Judah together 1121
Jer 50:33 The **c.** of Israel and the **c.** of Judah 1121
La 1:5 her **c.** are gone into captivity 5768
La 1:16 my **c.** are desolate, because the 1121
La 2:11 the **c.** and the sucklings swoon 5768
La 2:19 the life of thy young **c.**, that faint
La 2:20 their fruit, and **c.** of a span long? 5768
La 3:33 nor grieve the **c.** of men. 1121
La 4:4 young **c.** ask bread, and no man 5768
La 4:10 women have sodden their own **c.** 3206
La 5:13 and the **c.** fell under the wood. 5288
Eze 2:3 I send thee to the **c.** of Israel, 1121
Eze 2:4 are impudent **c.** and stiffhearted. 1121
Eze 3:11 captivity, unto the **c.** of thy people, 1121
Eze 4:13 **c.** of Israel eat their defiled bread 1121
Eze 6:5 dead carcases of the **c.** of Israel 1121
Eze 9:6 maids, and little **c.**, and women: 2945
Eze 16:21 hast slain my **c.**, and delivered 1121
Eze 16:36 blood of thy **c.**, which thou didst 1121
Eze 16:45 lotheth her husband and her **c.** 1121
Eze 16:45 lothed their husbands and their **c.** 1121
Eze 20:18 unto their **c.** in the wilderness, 1121
Eze 20:21 the **c.** rebelled against me: they 1121
Eze 23:39 had slain their **c.** to their idols, 1121
Eze 31:14 in the midst of the **c.** of men, 1121
Eze 33:2 man, speak to the **c.** of thy people, 1121
Eze 33:12 man, say unto the **c.** of thy people, 1121
Eze 33:17 Yet the **c.** of thy people say, The 1121
Eze 33:30 **c.** of thy people still are talking 1121
Eze 35:5 shed the blood of the **c.** of Israel 1121
Eze 37:16 the **c.** of Israel his companions: 1121
Eze 37:18 the **c.** of thy people shall speak 1121
Eze 37:21 take the **c.** of Israel from among 1121
Eze 37:25 their **c.**, and their children's **c.** 1121
Eze 43:7 in the midst of the **c.** of Israel 1121
Eze 44:9 any stranger that is among the **c.** 1121
Eze 44:15 **c.** of Israel went astray from me, 1121
Eze 47:22 shall beget the **c.** among you: 1121
Eze 47:22 country among the **c.** of Israel; 1121
Eze 48:11 when the **c.** of Israel went astray, 1121
Da 1:3 bring certain of the **c.** of Israel, 1121
Da 1:4 **C.** in whom was no blemish, but 3206
Da 1:6 **c.** of Judah, Daniel, Hananiah, 1121
Da 1:10 the **c.** which are of your sort? 3206
Da 1:13 countenance of the **c.** that eat 3206
Da 1:15 the **c.** which did eat the portion 3206
Da 1:17 for these four **c.**, God gave them 3206
Da 2:38 wheresoever the **c.** of men dwell, 1123
Da 5:13 which art of the **c.** of the captivity 1123
Da 6:13 Daniel, which is of the **c.** of the 1123
Da 6:24 the den of lions, them, their **c.**, 1123
Da 11:41 and the chief of the **c.** of Ammon. 1121
Da 12:1 standeth for the **c.** of thy people: 1121
Ho 1:2 and **c.** of whoredoms: 3206
Ho 1:10 number of the **c.** of Israel shall be 1121
Ho 1:11 the **c.** of Judah and the **c.** of Israel 1121
Ho 2:4 will not have mercy upon her **c.**; 1121
Ho 2:4 for they be the **c.** of whoredoms. 1121
Ho 3:1 toward the **c.** of Israel, who look to 1121
Ho 3:4 **c.** of Israel shall abide many days 1121
Ho 3:5 shall the **c.** of Israel return, 1121
Ho 4:1 word of the Lord, ye **c.** of Israel: 1121
Ho 4:6 I will also forget thy **c.** 1121
Ho 5:7 for they have begotten strange **c.** 1121
Ho 9:12 Though they bring up their **c.**, 1121
Ho 9:13 Ephraim shall bring forth his **c.** 1121
Ho 10:9 Gibeah against the **c.** of iniquity 1121
Ho 10:14 was dashed in pieces upon her **c.**. 1121
Ho 11:10 the **c.** shall tremble from the west 1121
Ho 13:13 place of the breaking forth of **c.**. 1121
Joe 1:3 Tell ye your **c.** of it, and 1121
Joe 1:3 let your **c.** tell their **c.**, 1121
Joe 1:3 and their **c.** another generation. 1121
Joe 2:16 gather the **c.**, and those that suck 5768
Joe 2:23 Be glad then, ye **c.** of Zion, and 1121
Joe 3:6 The **c.** also of Judah and the 1121
Joe 3:6 **c.** of Jerusalem have ye sold unto 1121
Joe 3:8 into the hand of the **c.** of Judah, 1121
Joe 3:16 the strength of the **c.** of Israel 1121
Joe 3:19 violence against the **c.** of Judah, 1121
Am 1:13 transgressions of the **c.** of Ammon, 1121
Am 2:11 not even thus, O ye **c.** of Israel? 1121
Am 3:1 spoken against you, O **c.** of Israel, 1121
Am 3:12 so shall the **c.** of Israel be taken 1121
Am 4:5 ye **c.** of Israel, saith the Lord God. 1121
Am 9:7 Are ye not as **c.** of the Ethiopians 1121
Am 9:7 unto me, O **c.** of Israel? 1121
Ob 12 have rejoiced over the **c.** of Judah 1121
Ob 20 host of the **c.** of Israel shall possess 1121

Mic 1:16 and poll thee for thy delicate c.; ... 1121
Mic 2:9 c. have ye taken away my glory ... 5768
Mic 5:3 shall return unto the c. of Israel ... 1121
Na 3:10 young c. also were dashed in pieces ... 5768
Zep 1:8 the princes, and the king's c., ... 1121
Zep 2:8 the revilings of the c. of Ammon, ... 1121
Zep 2:9 the c. of Ammon as Gomorrah, ... 1121
Zec 10:7 their c. shall see it, and be glad; ... 1121
Zec 10:9 they shall live with their c., and ... 1121
Mal 4:6 the heart of the fathers to the c., ... 1121
Mal 4:6 the heart of the c. to their fathers, ... 1121
Mt 2:16 and slew all the c. that were in ... *3816*
Mt 2:18 Rachel weeping for her c., and ... *5043*
Mt 3:9 to raise up c. unto Abraham ... *5043*
Mt 5:9 **they shall be called the c. of God** ... *5207*
Mt 5:45 **That ye may be the c. of your** ... *5207*
Mt 7:11 **to give good gifts unto your c.,** ... *5043*
Mt 8:12 **But the c. of the kingdom shall be** *5207*
Mt 9:15 **Can the c. of the bridechamber** ... *5207*
Mt 10:21 **and the c. shall rise up against** ... *5043*
Mt 11:16 **It is like unto c. sitting in the** ... *3808*
Mt 11:19 **But wisdom is justified of her c.** ... *5043*
Mt 12:27 **by whom do your c. cast them** ... *5207*
Mt 13:38 **seed are the c. of the kingdom;** ... *5207*
Mt 13:38 **tares are the c. of the wicked** ... *5207*
Mt 14:21 men, beside women and c. ... *3813*
Mt 15:38 men, beside women and c. ... *3813*
Mt 17:25 **of their own c., or of strangers?** ... *5207*
Mt 17:26 saith unto him, **Then are the c.** ... *5207*
Mt 18:3 **and become as little c., ye shall** ... *3813*
Mt 18:25 **be sold, and his wife, and c.,** ... *5043*
Mt 19:13 brought unto him little c., that ... *3813*
Mt 19:14 said, **Suffer little c., and forbid** ... *3813*
Mt 19:29 **or c., or lands, for my names's** ... *5043*
Mt 20:20 him the mother of Zebedee's c. ... *5207*
Mt 21:15 and the c. crying in the temple, ... *3816*
Mt 22:24 If a man die, having no c., his ... *5043*
Mt 23:31 **that ye are the c. of them which** ... *5207*
Mt 23:37 **would I have gathered thy c.** ... *5043*
Mt 27:9 they of the c. of Israel did value; ... *5207*
Mt 27:25 His blood be on us, and on our c.. ... *5043*
Mt 27:56 and his mother of Zebedee's c.. ... *5207*
Mk 2:19 **Can the c. of the bridechamber** ... *5207*
Mk 7:27 said unto her, **Let the c. first be** ... *5043*
Mk 9:37 **receive one of such c. in my** ... *3813*
Mk 10:13 And they brought young c. to ... *3813*
Mk 10:14 **Suffer the little c. to come unto** ... *3813*
Mk 10:24 **C., how hard is it for them that** ... *5043*
Mk 10:29 **or wife, or c., or lands, for my** ... *5043*
Mk 10:30 **mothers, and c., and lands, with** ... *5043*
Mk 12:19 and leave no c.. that his brother ... *5043*
Mk 13:12 **and c. shall rise up against their** ... *5043*
Lu 1:16 many of the c. of Israel shall he ... *5207*
Lu 1:17 the hearts of the fathers to the c., ... *5043*
Lu 3:8 to raise up c. unto Abraham ... *5043*
Lu 5:34 **Can ye make the c. of the** ... *5207*
Lu 6:35 **ye shall be the c. of the Highest:** ... *5207*
Lu 7:32 **like unto c. sitting in the** ... *3813*
Lu 7:35 **wisdom is justified of all her c.** ... *5043*
Lu 11:7 **my c. are with me in bed; I cannot** *3813*
Lu 11:13 **to give good gifts unto your c.** ... *5043*
Lu 13:34 **have gathered thy c. together, as** ... *5043*
Lu 14:26 **c., and brethren, and sisters, yea,** ... *5043*
Lu 16:8 **for the c. of this world are** ... *5207*
Lu 16:8 **wiser than the c. of light.** ... *5207*
Lu 18:16 **Suffer little c. to come unto me,** ... *3813*
Lu 18:29 **or wife, or c., for the kingdom of** ... *5043*
Lu 19:44 **and thy c. within thee; and they** ... *5043*
Lu 20:28 he died without c., that his ... *815*
Lu 20:29 took a wife, and died without c.. ... *815*
Lu 20:31 and they left no c., and died ... *5043*
Lu 20:34 **The c. of this world marry, and** ... *5207*
Lu 20:36 **and are the c. of God, being** ... *5207*
Lu 20:36 **the c. of the resurrection.** ... *5207*
Lu 23:28 **for yourselves, and for your c..** ... *5043*
Joh 4:12 drank thereof himself, and his c., ... *5207*
Joh 8:39 **If ye were Abraham's c., ye would** *5043*
Joh 11:52 c. of God that were scattered ... *5043*
Joh 12:36 **that ye may be the c. of light.** ... *5207*
Joh 13:33 **Little c., yet a little while I am** ... *5040*
Joh 21:5 Jesus saith unto them, **C., have ye** ... *3813*
Ac 2:39 is unto you, and to your c., ... *5043*
Ac 3:25 Ye are the c. of the prophets, ... *5207*
Ac 5:21 all the senate of the c. of Israel, ... *5207*
Ac 7:19 they cast out their young c., to ... *1025*
Ac 7:23 visit his brethren the c. of Israel ... *5207*
Ac 7:37 which said unto the c. of Israel, ... *5207*
Ac 9:15 **Gentiles, and kings, and the c. of** ... *5207*
Ac 10:36 God sent unto the c. of Israel, ... *5207*
Ac 13:26 c. of the stock of Abraham ... *5207*
Ac 13:33 fulfilled the same unto us their c., ... *5043*
Ac 21:5 on our way, with wives and c., ... *5043*
Ac 21:21 ought not to circumcise their c., ... *5043*
Ro 8:16 spirit, that we are the c. of God: ... *5043*
Ro 8:17 And if c., then heirs; heirs of God, ... *5043*
Ro 8:21 the glorious liberty of the c. of God ... *5043*
Ro 9:7 seed of Abraham, are they all c. ... *5043*
Ro 9:8 They which are the c. of the flesh, ... *5043*
Ro 9:8 these are not the c. of God: ... *5043*
Ro 9:8 the c. of the promise are counted ... *5043*
Ro 9:11 (For the c. being not yet born, ...
Ro 9:26 be called the c. of the living God ... *5207*
Ro 9:27 the number of the c. of Israel be ... *5207*
1Co 7:14 else were your c. unclean; but ... *5043*
1Co 14:20 be not c. in understanding, ... *3813*
1Co 14:20 howbeit in malice be ye c., but ... *3515*
2Co 3:7 so that the c. of Israel could not ... *5207*
2Co 3:13 that the c. of Israel could not ... *5207*
2Co 6:13 (I speak as unto my c.,) be ye also ... *5043*
2Co 12:14 the c. ought not to lay up for the ... *5043*
2Co 12:14 but the parents for the c. ... *5043*
Ga 3:7 the same are the c. of Abraham ... *5207*
Ga 3:26 ye are all the c. of God by faith ... *5207*
Ga 4:3 when we were c., were in ... *3516*
Ga 4:19 My little c., of whom I travail ... *5040*
Ga 4:25 and is in bondage with her c. ... *5043*
Ga 4:27 the desolate hath many more c. ... *5043*
Ga 4:28 as Isaac was, are the c. of promise. ... *5043*
Ga 4:31 we are not c. of the bondwoman, ... *5043*
Eph 1:5 us unto the adoption of c. by ... *5206*
Eph 2:2 worketh in the c. of disobedience: ... *5207*
Eph 2:3 were by nature the c. of wrath, ... *5043*
Eph 4:14 be no more c., tossed to and fro, ... *3516*
Eph 5:1 followers of God, as dear c.; ... *5043*
Eph 5:6 God upon the c. of disobedience. ... *5207*
Eph 5:8 in the Lord: walk as c. of light: ... *5043*
Eph 6:1 C., obey your parents in the Lord: ... *5043*
Eph 6:4 provoke not your c. to wrath, ... *5043*
Col 3:6 cometh on the c. of disobedience: ... *5207*
Col 3:20 C., obey your parents in all ... *5043*
Col 3:21 provoke not your c. to anger, ... *5043*
1Th 2:7 even as a nurse cherisheth her c. ... *5043*
1Th 2:11 as a father doth his c., ... *5043*
1Th 5:5 Ye are all the c. of light, ... *5207*
1Th 5:5 and the c. of the day: ... *5207*
1Ti 3:4 having his c. in subjection with ... *5043*
1Ti 3:12 ruling their c. and their own ... *5043*
1Ti 5:4 But if any widow have c. or ... *5043*
1Ti 5:10 if she have brought up c., if she ... *5044*
1Ti 5:14 younger women marry, bear c., ... *5041*
Tit 1:6 having faithful c., not accused of ... *5043*
Tit 2:4 their husbands, to love their c., ... *5388*
Heb 2:13 Behold I and the c. which God ... *3813*
Heb 2:14 then as the c. are partakers ... *3813*
Heb 11:22 of the departing of the c. of Israel; ... *5027*
Heb 12:5 speaketh unto you as unto c. ... *5027*
1Pet 1:14 As obedient c., not fashioning ... *5043*
2Pet 2:14 with covetous practices; cursed c. ... *5043*
1Jo 2:1 My little c., these things write I ... *5040*
1Jo 2:12 I write unto you, little c., because ... *5040*
1Jo 2:13 I write unto you, little c., because ... *3813*
1Jo 2:18 Little c., it is the last time: and ... *3813*
1Jo 2:28 And now, little c., abide in him; ... *5040*
1Jo 3:7 Little c., let no man deceive you: ... *5040*
1Jo 3:10 In this the c. of God are manifest, ... *5043*
1Jo 3:10 and the c. of the devil: ... *5043*
1Jo 3:18 My little c., let us not love in ... *5040*
1Jo 4:4 Ye are of God, little c., and have ... *5040*
1Jo 5:2 know that we love the c. of God, ... *5043*
1Jo 5:21 Little c., keep yourselves from ... *5040*
2Jo 1 unto the elect lady and her c., ... *5043*
2Jo 4 that I found of thy c. walking in ... *5043*
2Jo 1:13 The c. of thy elect sister greet ... *5043*
3Jo 4 joy I have to hear that my c. walk ... *5043*
Re 2:14 **before the c. of Israel, to eat** ... *5207*
Re 2:23 **And I will kill her c. with death;** ... *5043*
Re 7:4 of all the tribes of the c. of Israel ... *5207*
Re 21:12 the twelve tribes of the c. of Israel: ... *5207*

CHILDREN OF ISRAEL See CHILDREN and ISRAEL.

CHILDREN OF MEN See CHILDREN and MEN.

CHILDREN'S
Ge 31:16 father, that is ours, and our c. ... 1121
Ge 45:10 thy c. children, and thy flocks, and ... 1121
Ex 9:4 die of all that is the c. of Israel ... 1121
Ex 34:7 the c. children, unto the third ... 1121
De 4:25 begat children and c. children, ...
Jos 14:9 inheritance, and thy c. for ever, ... 1121
2Ki 17:41 children, and their c. children: ... 1121
Job 19:17 I entreated for the c. sake of ... 1121
Ps 103:17 righteousness unto c. children; ... 1121
Ps 128:6 see thy c. children, and peace ... 1121
Pr 13:22 leaveth an inheritance to his c. ... 1121
Pr 17:6 C. children are the crown of old men; . 1121
Jer 2:9 and with your c. children will ... 1121
Jer 31:29 and the c. teeth are set on edge. ... 1121
Eze 18:2 the c. teeth are set on edge? ... 1121
Eze 37:25 their c. children for ever: and my ... 1121
Mt 15:26 **It is not meet to take the c. bread,** *5043*
Mk 7:27 **it is not meet to take the c. bread,** *5043*
Mk 7:28 the table eat of the c. crumbs. ... *3813*

CHILD'S
Ex 2:8 went and called the c. mother. ... 3206
1Ki 17:21 let this c. soul come into him again. ... 3206
Job 33:25 flesh shall be fresher than a c. ... 5290
Mt 2:20 which sought the young c. life. ... *3813*

CHILEAB (kil'-e-ab) See also DANIEL.
2Sa 3:3 And his second, C., of Abigail the ... 3609

CHILION (kil'-e-on) See also CHILION'S.
Ru 1:2 of his two sons Mahlon and C., ... 3630
Ru 1:5 And Mahlon and C. died also ... 3630

CHILION'S (kil'-e-ons)
Ru 4:9 Elimelech's, and all that was C. ... 3630

CHILMAD (kil'-mad)
Eze 27:23 of Sheba, Asshur, and C., ... 3638

CHIMHAM (kim'-ham)
2Sa 19:37 But behold thy servant C.; let ... 3643
2Sa 19:38 the king answered, C. shall go ... 3643
2Sa 19:40 and C. went on with him: and all ... 3643
Jer 41:17 and dwelt in the habitation of C., ... 3643

CHIMNEY
Ho 13:3 and as the smoke out of the c. ... 699

CHINNERETH (kin'-ne-reth) See also CHINNEROTH; CINNEROTH; GENNESARET.
Nu 34:11 the side of the sea of C. eastward: ... 3672
Deu 3:17 C. even unto the sea of the plain, ... 3672
Jos 13:27 even unto the edge of the sea of C.. .. 3672
Jos 19:35 and Hammath, Rakkath, and C., ... 3672

CHINNEROTH (kin'-ne-roth) See also CHINNERETH.
Jos 11:2 and the plains south of C., ... 3672
Jos 12:3 from the plain to the sea of C. ... 3672

CHIOS (ki'-os)
Ac 20:15 the next day over against C.; ... *5508*

CHISLEU (kis'-lew)
Ne 1:1 month C., in the twentieth year, ... 3691
Zec 7:1 of the ninth month, even in C.; ... 3691

CHISLON (kis'-lon)
Nu 34:21 Benjamin, Elidad the son of C. ... 3692

CHISLOTH-TABOR (kis''-loth-ta'-bor) See also CHESULLOTH.
Jos 19:12 sunrising unto the border of C.. ... 3696

CHITTIM (kit'-tim) See also KITTIM.
Nu 24:24 shall come from the coast of C.. ... 3794
Isa 23:1 from the land of C. it is revealed ... 3794
Isa 23:12 pass over to C.; there also shalt ... 3794
Jer 2:10 For pass over the isles of C., ... 3794
Eze 27:6 brought out of the isles of C. ... 3794
Da 11:30 ships of C. shall come against him: ... 3794

CHIUN (ki'-un) See also REMPHAN.
Am 5:26 tabernacle of your Moloch and C. ... 3594

CHLOE (clo'-e)
1Co 1:11 which are of the house of C., ... *5514*

CHODE
Ge 31:36 was wroth, and c. with Laban: ... 7378
Nu 20:3 And the people c. with Moses, ... 7378

CHOICE See also CHOICEST.
Ge 23:6 c. of our sepulchres bury thy dead; ... 4005
Ge 49:11 his ass's colt unto the c. vine; ... 8321
De 12:11 your c. vows which ye vow unto ... 4005
1Sa 9:2 a c. young man, and a goodly: ... 970
2Sa 10:9 chose of all the c. men of Israel, ... 977

2Ki 3:19 fenced city, and every c. city, 4005
2Ki 19:23 and the c. fir trees thereof: 4005
1Ch 7:40 c. and mighty men of valour, 1305
1Ch 19:10 all the c. of Israel, and put them 970
2Ch 25:5 three hundred thousand c. men, 970
Ne 5:18 one ox and six c. sheep; also 1305
Pr 8:10 knowledge rather than c. gold. 977
Pr 8:19 and my revenue than c. silver. 977
Pr 10:20 tongue of the just is as c. silver: 977
Ca 6:9 is the c. one of her that bare her. 1249
Isa 37:24 the c. fir trees thereof: and I will 4005
Jer 22:7 shall cut down thy c. cedars, 4005
Eze 24:4 shoulder, fill it with the c. bones. 4005
Eze 24:5 Take the c. of the flock, and burn 4005
Eze 31:16 Eden, the c. and best of Lebanon, 4005
Ac 15:7 God made c. among us, that the *1586*

CHOICEST
Isa 5:2 planted it with the c. vine, 8321
Isa 22:7 c. valleys shall be full of chariots, 4005

CHOKE See also CHOKED.
Mt 13:22 **deceitfulness of riches, c. the** *4846*
Mk 4:19 **entering in, c. the word, and it** *4846*

CHOKED
Mt 13:7 **thorns sprung up, and c. them:** *638*
Mk 4:7 **c. it, and it yielded no fruit.** *4846*
Mk 5:13 and were c. in the sea. *4155*
Lu 8:7 **sprang up with it, and c. it** *638*
Lu 8:14 **and are c. with cares and riches** *4846*
Lu 8:33 place into the lake, and were c. *638*

CHOLER (col'-ur)
Da 8:7 was moved with c. against him. 4843
Da 11:11 the south shall be moved with c., 4843

CHOOSE See also CHOOSEST; CHOOSETH; CHOOSING; CHOSE; CHOSEN.
Ex 17:9 C. us out men, and go out, 977
Nu 16:7 the man whom the Lord doth c., 977
Nu 17:5 the man's rod, whom I shall c., 977
De 7:7 nor c. you, because ye were more 977
De 12:5 the Lord your God shall c. out 977
De 12:11 God shall c. to cause his name 977
De 12:14 the place which the Lord shall c., 977
De 12:18 which the Lord thy God shall c., 977
De 12:26 the place which the Lord shall c.: 977
De 14:23 the place which he shall c. to 977
De 14:24 which the Lord thy God shall c. 977
De 14:25 which the Lord thy God shall c.: 977
De 15:20 the place which the Lord shall c., 977
De 16:2 the place which the Lord shall c. 977
De 16:6 which the Lord thy God shall c. 977
De 16:7 which the Lord thy God shall c.: 977
De 16:15 the place which the Lord shall c.: 977
De 16:16 in the place which he shall c.; 977
De 17:8 which the Lord thy God shall c.; 977
De 17:10 which the Lord shall c. shall shew 977
De 17:15 whom the Lord thy God shall c. 977
De 18:6 the place which the Lord shall c.; 977
De 23:16 that place which he shall c. in one 977
De 26:2 God shall c. to place his name 977
De 30:19 therefore c. life, that both 977
De 31:11 in the place which he shall c., 977
Jos 9:27 in the place which he should c. 977
Jos 24:15 c. you this day whom ye will serve; 977
1Sa 2:28 did I c. him out of all the tribes 977
1Sa 17:8 c. you a man for you, and let 1262
2Sa 16:18 and all the men of Israel, c., 977
2Sa 17:1 Let me now c. out twelve thousand 977
2Sa 21:6 of Saul, whom the Lord did c. 972
2Sa 24:12 c. thee one of them, that I may do 977
1Ki 14:21 which the Lord did c. out of all 977
1Ki 18:23 and let them c. one bullock for 977
1Ki 18:25 C. you one bullock for yourselves, 977
1Ch 21:10 c. thee one of them, that I may 977
1Ch 21:11 Thus saith the Lord, C. thee 6901
Ne 9:7 the God, who didst c. Abram, 977
Job 9:14 and c. out my words to reason 977
Job 34:4 Let us c. to us judgment: let us 977
Job 34:33 thou refuse, or whether thou c.; 977
Ps 25:12 teach in the way that he shall c. 977
Ps 47:4 He shall c. our inheritance for us, 977
Pr 1:29 did not c. the fear of the Lord: 977
Pr 3:31 oppressor, and c. none of his ways. 977
Isa 7:15, 16 refuse the evil, and c. the good, 977
Isa 14:1 and will yet c. Israel, and set them 977
Isa 49:7 of Israel, and he shall c. thee. 977
Isa 56:4 and c. the things that please me, 977
Isa 65:12 c. that wherein I delighted not. 977
Isa 66:4 I also will c. their delusions, 977
Eze 21:19 c. thou a place, c. it at the head 1254
Zec 1:17 Zion, and shall yet c. Jerusalem. 977
Zec 2:12 and shall c. Jerusalem again. 977
Php 1:22 yet what I shall c. I wot not. *138*

CHOOSEST
Job 15:5 thou c. the tongue of the crafty. 977
Ps 65:4 Blessed is the man whom thou c., 977

CHOOSETH
Job 7:15 So that my soul c. strangling, 977
Isa 40:20 he hath no oblation c. a tree that 977
Isa 41:24 an abomination is he that c. you. 977

CHOOSING
Heb 11:25 C. rather to suffer affliction with *138*

CHOP
Mic 3:3 their bones, and c. them in pieces, 6566

CHOR-ASHAN (cor-a'-shan)
1Sa 30:30 and to them which were in C., 3565

CHORAZIN (co-ra'-zin)
Mt 11:21 **Woe unto thee, C.! woe unto** *5523*
Lu 10:13 **Woe unto thee, C.! woe unto** *5523*

CHOSE
Ge 6:2 them wives of all which they c.. 977
Ge 13:11 Lot c. him all the plain of Jordan; 977
Ex 18:25 Moses c. able men out of all Israel, 977
De 4:37 therefore he c. their seed after them, 977
De 10:15 and he c. their seed after them, 977
Jos 8:3 Joshua c. out thirty thousand 977
Jg 5:8 They c. new gods; then was war in 977
1Sa 13:2 Saul c. him three thousand men. 977
1Sa 17:40 and c. him five smooth stones out 977
2Sa 6:21 which c. me before thy father, 977
2Sa 10:9 behind, he c. of all the choice men 977
1Ki 8:16 I c. no city out of all the tribes of 977
1Ki 8:16 but I c. David to be over my people 977
1Ki 11:34 David my servant's sake whom I c., 977
1Ch 19:10 c. out of all the choice of Israel, 977
1Ch 28:4 the Lord God of Israel c. me before 977
2Ch 6:5 I c. no city among all the tribes 977
2Ch 6:5 neither c. I any man to be a ruler 977
Job 29:25 I c. out their way, and sat chief, 977
Ps 78:67 and c. not the tribe of Ephraim: 977
Ps 78:68 But c. the tribe of Judah, the 977
Ps 78:70 He c. David also his servant, 977
Isa 66:4 and c. that in which I delighted not. 977
Eze 20:5 In the day when I c. Israel, 977
Lu 6:13 of them he c. twelve, whom also *1586*
Lu 14:7 they c. out the chief rooms; saying *1586*
Ac 6:5 they c. Stephen, a man full of faith *1586*
Ac 13:17 c. our fathers, and exalted the *1586*
Ac 15:40 And Paul c. Silas, and departed, *1951*

CHOSEN
Ex 14:7 he took six hundred c. chariots, 970
Ex 15:4 his c. captains also are drowned 4005
Nu 16:5 even him whom he hath c. will 977
De 7:6 the Lord thy God hath c. thee to be 977
De 12:21 which the Lord thy God hath c. 977
De 14:2 the Lord hath c. thee to be a 977
De 16:11 the Lord thy God hath c. to place 977
De 18:5 For the Lord thy God hath c. him 977
De 21:5 Lord thy God hath c. to minister 977
Jos 24:22 that ye have c. you the Lord to 977
Jg 10:14 cry unto the gods which ye have c.; 977
Jg 20:15 numbered seven hundred c. men. 970
Jg 20:16 there were seven hundred c. men 970
Jg 20:34 ten thousand c. men out of all 970
1Sa 8:18 your king which ye shall have c. 977
1Sa 10:24 See ye him whom the Lord hath c., 977
1Sa 12:13 the king whom ye have c., and 977
1Sa 16:8, 9 neither hath the Lord c. this. 977
1Sa 16:10 Jesse, The Lord hath not c. these. 977
1Sa 20:30 that thou hast c. the son of Jesse 977
1Sa 24:2 Saul took three thousand c. men 970
1Sa 26:2 having three thousand c. men of 970
2Sa 6:1 together all the c. men of Israel, 970
1Ki 3:8 thy people which thu hast c., 977
1Ki 8:44 toward the city which thou hast c., 977
1Ki 8:48 the city which thou hast c., and the 977
1Ki 11:13 Jerusalem's sake which I have c. out of 977
1Ki 11:32 sake, the city which I have c. out of 977
1Ki 11:36 Jerusalem, the city which I have c. 977
1Ki 12:21 hundred and fourscore thousand c. 970
2Ki 21:7 which I have c. out of all tribes 977
2Ki 23:27 Jerusalem, which I have c., and the 977
1Ch 9:22 c. to be porters in the gates 1305
1Ch 15:2 them hath the Lord c. to carry the 977
1Ch 16:13 ye children of Jacob, his c. ones. 972
1Ch 16:41 the rest that were c., who were 1305
1Ch 28:4 he hath c. Judah to be the ruler: 977
1Ch 28:5 he hath c. Solomon my son to sit 977
1Ch 28:6 I have c. him to be my son, and I 977
1Ch 28:10 heed now; for the Lord hath c. thee 977
1Ch 29:1 whom alone God hath c., is yet 977
2Ch 6:6 But I have c. Jerusalem, that my 977
2Ch 6:6 and have c. David to be over my 977
2Ch 6:34 toward this city which thou hast c., 977
2Ch 6:38 toward the city which thou hast c., 977
2Ch 7:12 and have c. this place to myself for 977
2Ch 7:16 For now have I c. and sanctified 977
2Ch 11:1 fourscore thousand c. men which 970
2Ch 12:13 which the Lord had c. out of all 977
2Ch 13:3 four hundred thousand c. men: 970
2Ch 13:3 eight hundred thousand c. men, 970
2Ch 13:17 five hundred thousand c. men. 970
2Ch 29:11 Lord hath c. you to stand before 970
2Ch 33:7 which I have c. before all the tribes 970
Ne 1:9 the place that I have c. to set 970
Job 36:21 for this hast thou c. rather than 970
Ps 33:12 the people whom he hath c. for his 970
Ps 78:31 smote down the c. men of Israel. 970
Ps 89:3 I have made a covenant with my c., 972
Ps 89:19 exalted one c. out of the people. 970
Ps 105:6 servant, ye children of Jacob his c. 972
Ps 105:26 and Aaron whom he had c. 977
Ps 105:43 with joy, and his c. with gladness: 972
Ps 106:5 That I may see the good of thy c., 972
Ps 106:23 had not Moses his c. stood before 972
Ps 119:30 I have c. the way of truth: thy 977
Ps 119:173 help me; for I have c. thy precepts. 977
Ps 132:13 the Lord hath c. Zion; he hath 977
Ps 135:4 the Lord hath c. Jacob unto himself, 977
Pr 16:16 rather to be c. than silver! 977
Pr 22:1 A good name is rather to be c. 977
Isa 1:29 for the gardens that ye have c. 977
Isa 41:8 servant, Jacob whom I have c., 977
Isa 41:9 I have c. thee, and not cast thee 977
Isa 43:10 and my servant whom I have c. 977
Isa 43:20 to give drink to my people, my c. 972
Isa 44:1 Israel, whom I have c. 977
Isa 44:2 and thou, Jesurun, whom I have c. 977
Isa 48:10 c. thee in the furnace of affliction. 977
Isa 58:5 Is it such a fast that I have c.? 977
Isa 58:6 Is not this the fast that I have c.? 977
Isa 65:15 your name for a curse unto my c. 972
Isa 66:3 they have c. their own ways, and 977
Jer 8:3 death shall be c. rather than life 977
Jer 33:24 families which the Lord hath c., 977
Jer 48:15 and his c. young men are gone 4005
Jer 49:19 and who is a c. man, that I may 970
Jer 50:44 from her: and who is a c. man, 970
Eze 23:7 with all them that were the c. 4005
Da 11:15 neither his c. people, neither 4005
Hag 2:23 for I have c. thee, saith the Lord 977
Zec 3:2 the Lord that hath c. Jerusalem 977
Mt 12:18 my servant, whom I have c.; *140*
Mt 20:16 **for many be called, but few c.** *1588*
Mt 22:14 **many are called, but few are c.** *1588*
Mk 13:20 **the elect's sake, whom he hath c.,** *1586*
Lu 10:42 **Mary hath c. that good part** *1586*
Lu 23:35 if he be Christ, the c. of God. *1588*
Joh 6:70 **Have not I c. you twelve, and one** *1586*
Joh 13:18 **I know whom I have c.** *1586*
Joh 15:16 **Ye have not c. me,** *1586*
Joh 15:16 **but I have c. you, and** *1586*
Joh 15:19 **I have c. you out of the world,** *1586*
Ac 1:2 the apostles whom he had c. *1586*
Ac 1:24 whether of these two thou hast c., *1586*
Ac 9:15 **he is a c. vessel unto me, to bear** *1589*
Ac 10:41 unto witnesses c. before of God, *4401*
Ac 15:22 to send c. men of their own *1586*
Ac 15:25 to send c. men unto you with our *1586*
Ac 22:14 hath c. thee, that thou shouldest *4400*
Ro 16:13 Salute Rufus c. in the Lord, and *1588*
1Co 1:27 God hath c. the foolish things of *1586*
1Co 1:27 God hath c. the weak things of *1586*
1Co 1:28 which are despised, hath God c., *1586*

2Co 8:19 who was also **c.** of the churches *5500*
Eph 1:4 as he hath **c.** us in him before the...... *1586*
2Th 2:13 God hath from the beginning **c.** *138*
2Ti 2:4 he may please him who hath **c.**......... *4758*
Jas 2:5 Hath not God **c.** the poor of this....... *1586*
1Pe 2:4 but **c.** of God, and precious,............ *1588*
1Pe 2:9 ye are a **c.** generation, a royal.......... *1588*
Re 17:14 him are called, and **c.**, and faithful. *1588*

CHOZEBA (ko-ze'-bah) See also CHEZIB.
1Ch 4:22 and the men of **C.**, and Joash, ... 3578

CHRIST (krist) See also ANTICHRIST; CHRISTIAN; CHRIST'S; CHRISTS; JESUS; MESSIAH.
Mt 1:1 book of the generation of Jesus **C.**,..... *5547*
Mt 1:16 was born Jesus, who is called **C.**,....... *5547*
Mt 1:17 unto **C.** are fourteen generations........ *5547*
Mt 1:18 the birth of Jesus **C.** was on this........ *5547*
Mt 2:4 of them where **c.** should be born........ *5547*
Mt 11:2 heard in the prison the works of **C.**,... *5547*
Mt 16:16 Thou art the **c.**, the Son of the.......... *5547*
Mt 16:20 no man that he was Jesus the **C.**. *5547*
Mt 22:42 **What think ye of C.? whose son**........ *5547*
Mt 23:8 **one is your Master, even C.; and**... *5547*
Mt 23:10 **for one is your Master, even C.**..... *5547*
Mt 24:5 **my name, saying, I am C.; and**..... *5547*
Mt 24:23 **Lo, here is C., or there; believe it** ..*5547*
Mt 26:63 whether thou be the **C.**, the Son........ *5547*
Mt 26:68 Prophesy unto us, thou **C.**, Who is..... *5547*
Mt 27:17 or Jesus which is called **C.**?.............. *5547*
Mt 27:22 with Jesus which is called **C.**?........... *5547*
Mk 1:1 of the gospel of Jesus **C.**, ... *5547*
Mk 8:29 saith unto him, Thou art the **C.**........ *5547*
Mk 9:41 **because ye belong to C., verily I** ... *5547*
Mk 12:35 **How say the scribes that C. is the.** *5547*
Mk 13:6 **saying, I am C.; and shall**....................
Mk 13:21 **Lo, here is C.: or, lo, he is there;**.. *5547*
Mk 14:61 Art thou the **C.**, the Son of the *5547*
Mk 15:32 Let **C.** the King of Israel descend *5547*
Lu 2:11 a Saviour, which is **C.** the Lord. *5547*
Lu 2:26 before he had seen the Lord's **C.**....... *5547*
Lu 3:15 whether he were the **C.**, or not;........ *5547*
Lu 4:41 Thou art **C.** the Son of God. *5547*
Lu 4:41 for they knew that he was **C.**............ *5547*
Lu 9:20 answering said, The **C.** of God. *5547*
Lu 20:41 **say they that C. is David's son?**..... *5547*
Lu 21:8 **in my name, saying, I am C.; and**.......
Lu 22:67 Art thou the **C.**? tell us. And he *5547*
Lu 23:2 saying that he himself is **C.** a king....... *5547*
Lu 23:35 if he be **C.**, the chosen of God. *5547*
Lu 23:39 saying, If thou be **C.**, save thyself...... *5547*
Lu 24:26 **Ought not C. to have suffered**........ *5547*
Lu 24:46 **thus it behoved C. to suffer, and to** *5547*
Joh 1:17 grace and truth came by Jesus **C.**........ *5547*
Joh 1:20 but confessed, I am not the **C.**.......... *5547*
Joh 1:25 if thou be not that **C.**, nor Elias, ... *5547*
Joh 1:41 which is, being interpreted, the **C.**. *5547*
Joh 3:28 said, I am not the **C.**, but that I am.... *5547*
Joh 4:25 Messias cometh, which is called **C.**.... *5547*
Joh 4:29 that even I did: is not this the **C.**? *5547*
Joh 4:42 this is indeed the **C.**, the Saviour of.... *5547*
Joh 6:69 are sure that thou art that **C.**,........... *5547*
Joh 7:26 indeed that this is the very **C.**?.......... *5547*
Joh 7:27 when **C.** cometh, no man knoweth...... *5547*
Joh 7:31 When **C.** cometh, will he do more...... *5547*
Joh 7:41 Others said, This is the **C.**. But......... *5547*
Joh 7:41 Shall **C.** come out of Galilee?............ *5547*
Joh 7:42 **C.** cometh of the seed of David, and... *5547*
Joh 9:22 man did confess that he was **C.**, ... *5547*
Joh 10:24 If thou be the **C.**, tell us plainly. *5547*
Joh 11:27 I believe that thou art the **C.**,............ *5547*
Joh 12:34 the law that **C.** abideth for ever: *5547*
Joh 17:3 **Jesus C., whom thou hast sent**....... *5547*
Joh 20:31 might believe that Jesus is the **C.**,...... *5547*
Ac 2:30 raise up **C.** to sit on his throne;......... *5547*
Ac 2:31 spake of the resurrection of **C.**, ... *5547*
Ac 2:36 ye have crucified, both Lord and **C.**.... *5547*
Ac 2:38 in the name of Jesus **C.** for the.......... *5547*
Ac 3:6 In the name of Jesus **C.** of.................. *5547*
Ac 3:18 prophets, that **C.** should suffer, he *5547*
Ac 3:20 And he shall send Jesus **C.** which....... *5547*
Ac 4:10 that by the name of Jesus **C.** of......... *5547*
Ac 4:26 the Lord, and against his **C.**............. *5547*
Ac 5:42 to teach and preach Jesus **C.**............. *5547*
Ac 8:5 Samaria, and preached **C.** unto *5547*
Ac 8:12 and the name of Jesus **C.**, they were.. *5547*
Ac 8:37 that Jesus **C.** is the Son of God. *5547*
Ac 9:20 preached **C.** in the synagogues, ... *5547*
Ac 9:22 proving that this is very **C.**.............. *5547*
Ac 9:34 Jesus **C.** maketh thee whole:............. *5547*
Ac 10:36 peace by Jesus **C.**: (he is Lord of....... *5547*
Ac 11:17 believed on the Lord Jesus **C.**; *5547*
Ac 15:11 the grace of the Lord Jesus **C.** *5547*
Ac 15:26 for the name of our Lord Jesus **C.**...... *5547*
Ac 16:18 thee in the name of Jesus **C.** to......... *5547*
Ac 16:31 Believe on the Lord Jesus **C.**, and...... *5547*
Ac 17:3 **C.** must needs have suffered, and *5547*
Ac 17:3 whom I preach unto you, is **C.**. *5547*
Ac 18:5 to the Jews that Jesus was **C.**. *5547*
Ac 18:28 the scriptures that Jesus was **C.** *5547*
Ac 19:4 after him, that is, on **C.** Jesus. *5547*
Ac 20:21 faith toward our Lord Jesus **C.**. *5547*
Ac 24:24 him concerning the faith in **C.**............ *5547*
Ac 26:23 That **C.** should suffer, and that........... *5547*
Ac 28:31 which concern the Lord Jesus **C.**,........ *5547*
Ro 1:1 Paul, a servant of Jesus **C.**, called...... *5547*
Ro 1:3 Concerning his Son Jesus **C.** our *5547*
Ro 1:6 ye also the called of Jesus **C.** *5547*
Ro 1:7 our Father, and the Lord Jesus **C.**....... *5547*
Ro 1:8 I thank my God through Jesus **C.**........ *5547*
Ro 1:16 not ashamed of the gospel of **C.**......... *5547*
Ro 2:16 judge the secrets of men by Jesus **C.**... *5547*
Ro 3:22 is by faith of Jesus **C.** unto all........... *5547*
Ro 3:24 redemption that is in **C.** Jesus: *5547*
Ro 5:1 God through our Lord Jesus **C.**........... *5547*
Ro 5:6 in due time **C.** died for the ungodly. ... *5547*
Ro 5:8 were yet sinners, **C.** died for us. *5547*
Ro 5:11 through our Lord Jesus **C.**, by........... *5547*
Ro 5:15 which is by one man, Jesus **C.**,.......... *5547*
Ro 5:17 shall reign in life by one, Jesus **C.**.).... *5547*
Ro 5:21 eternal life by Jesus **C.** our Lord. *5547*
Ro 6:3 were baptized into Jesus **C.** were......... *5547*
Ro 6:4 as **C.** was raised up from the dead *5547*
Ro 6:8 if we be dead with **C.**, we believe...... *5547*
Ro 6:9 Knowing that **C.** being raised from *5547*
Ro 6:11 God, through Jesus **C.** our Lord......... *5547*
Ro 6:23 eternal life through Jesus **C.** our *5547*
Ro 7:4 dead to the law by the body of **C.**; *5547*
Ro 7:25 God through Jesus **C.** our Lord.......... *5547*
Ro 8:1 to them which are in **C.** Jesus, ... *5547*
Ro 8:2 Spirit of life in **C.** Jesus hath *5547*
Ro 8:9 any man have not the Spirit of **C.**,...... *5547*
Ro 8:10 if **C.** be in you, the body is dead........ *5547*
Ro 8:11 that raised up **C.** from the dead *5547*
Ro 8:17 of God, and joint-heirs with **C.**;.......... *5547*
Ro 8:34 It is **C.** that died, yea rather, that...... *5547*
Ro 8:35 separate us from the love of **C.**?........ *5547*
Ro 8:39 love of God, which is in **C.** Jesus *5547*
Ro 9:1 say the truth in **C.**, I lie not, my........ *5547*
Ro 9:3 accursed from **C.** for my brethren, ... *5547*
Ro 9:5 **C.** came, who is over all, God............ *5547*
Ro 10:4 **C.** is the end of the law for............... *5547*
Ro 10:6 (that is, to bring **C.** down from.......... *5547*
Ro 10:7 (that is, to bring up **C.** again from...... *5547*
Ro 12:5 being many, are one body in **C.**, ... *5547*
Ro 13:14 But put ye on the Lord Jesus **C.**,....... *5547*
Ro 14:9 **C.** both died, and rose, and revived,... *5547*
Ro 14:10 before the judgment seat of **C.**. *5547*
Ro 14:15 with thy meat, for whom **C.** died. *5547*
Ro 14:18 that in these things serveth **C.** is *5547*
Ro 15:3 For even **C.** pleased not himself;........ *5547*
Ro 15:5 another according to **C.** Jesus:........... *5547*
Ro 15:6 the Father of our Lord Jesus **C.**.......... *5547*
Ro 15:7 as **C.** also received us to the glory..... *5547*
Ro 15:8 Jesus **C.** was a minister of the........... *5547*
Ro 15:16 minister of Jesus **C.** to the Gentiles, ... *5547*
Ro 15:17 I may glory through Jesus **C.** in......... *5547*
Ro 15:18 things which **C.** hath not wrought........ *5547*
Ro 15:19 fully preached the gospel of **C.**. *5547*
Ro 15:20 not where **C.** was named, lest I.......... *5547*
Ro 15:29 the blessing of the gospel of **C.**. *5547*
Ro 16:3 Aquila my helpers in **C.** Jesus:........... *5547*
Ro 16:5 the firstfruits of Achaia unto **C.**.......... *5547*
Ro 16:7 who also were in **C.** before me........... *5547*
Ro 16:9 Urbane, our helper in **C.**, and............ *5547*
Ro 16:10 Salute Apelles approved in **C.**........... *5547*
Ro 16:16 The churches of **C.** salute you............ *5547*
Ro 16:18 such serve not our Lord Jesus **C.**,...... *5547*
Ro 16:20 of our Lord Jesus **C.** be with you....... *5547*
Ro 16:24 our Lord Jesus **C.** be with you all....... *5547*
Ro 16:25 and the preaching of Jesus **C.**,........... *5547*
Ro 16:27 wise, be glory through Jesus **C.**......... *5547*
1Co 1:1 apostle of Jesus **C.** through the will *5547*
1Co 1:2 them that are sanctified in **C.** Jesus, ... *5547*
1Co 1:2 call upon the name of Jesus **C.** *5547*
1Co 1:3 and from the Lord Jesus **C.**............... *5547*
1Co 1:4 which is given you by Jesus **C.**; *5547*
1Co 1:6 of **C.** was confirmed in you: *5547*
1Co 1:7 the coming of our Lord Jesus **C.**......... *5547*
1Co 1:8 in the day of our Lord Jesus **C.**. *5547*
1Co 1:9 of his Son Jesus **C.** our Lord............. *5547*
1Co 1:10 by the name of our Lord Jesus **C.**, ... *5547*
1Co 1:12 and I of Cephas; and I of **C.**.............. *5547*
1Co 1:13 Is **C.** divided? was Paul crucified........ *5547*
1Co 1:17 **C.** sent me not to baptize, but to....... *5547*
1Co 1:17 **C.** should be made of none effect. *5547*
1Co 1:23 But we preach **C.** crucified,............... *5547*
1Co 1:24 **C.** the power of God, and the............ *5547*
1Co 1:30 But of him are ye in **C.** Jesus, ... *5547*
1Co 2:2 save Jesus **C.**, and him crucified......... *5547*
1Co 2:16 But we have the mind of **C.**.............. *5547*
1Co 3:1 even as unto babes in **C.**.................. *5547*
1Co 3:11 that is laid, which is Jesus **C.**. *5547*
1Co 3:23 ye are Christ's; and **C.** is God's......... *5547*
1Co 4:1 ministers of **C.**, and stewards of *5547*
1Co 4:10 sake, but ye are wise in **C.**;.............. *5547*
1Co 4:15 ten thousand instructors in **C.**, yet *5547*
1Co 4:15 for in **C.** Jesus I have begotten.......... *5547*
1Co 4:17 of my ways which be in **C.**, ... *5547*
1Co 5:4 the name of our Lord Jesus **C.**. *5547*
1Co 5:4 the power of our Lord Jesus **C.**, ... *5547*
1Co 5:7 **C.** our passover is sacrificed for......... *5547*
1Co 6:15 bodies are the membes of **C.**? *5547*
1Co 6:15 I then take the members of **C.**, ... *5547*
1Co 8:6 Jesus **C.**, by whom are all things,....... *5547*
1Co 8:11 brother perish, for whom **C.** died?...... *5547*
1Co 8:12 conscience, ye sin against **C.**. *5547*
1Co 9:1 have I not seen Jesus **C.** our Lord?.... *5547*
1Co 9:12 we should hinder the gospel of **C.**. *5547*
1Co 9:18 the gospel of **C.** without charge, ... *5547*
1Co 9:21 under the law to **C.**,) that I might *5547*
1Co 10:4 and that rock was **C.**. *5547*
1Co 10:9 neither let us tempt **C.**, as some........ *5547*
1Co 10:16 communion of the blood of **C.**? *5547*
1Co 10:16 communion of the body of **C.**? *5547*
1Co 11:1 of me, even as I also am of **C.**. *5547*
1Co 11:3 that the head of every man is **C.**;........ *5547*
1Co 11:3 man; and the head of **C.** is God. *5547*
1Co 12:12 are one body: so also is **C.**. *5547*
1Co 12:27 are the body of **C.**, and members....... *5547*
1Co 15:3 **C.** died for our sins according to *5547*
1Co 15:12 if **C.** be preached that he rose........... *5547*
1Co 15:13 of the dead, then is **C.** not risen: *5547*
1Co 15:14 if **C.** be not risen, then is our........... *5547*
1Co 15:15 of God that he raised up **C.** *5547*
1Co 15:16 rise not, then is not **C.** raised: *5547*
1Co 15:17 **C.** be not raised, your faith is vain; *5547*
1Co 15:18 also which are fallen asleep in **C.**........ *5547*
1Co 15:19 this life only we have hope in **C.**, ... *5547*
1Co 15:20 now is **C.** risen from the dead, ... *5547*
1Co 15:22 in **C.** shall all be made alive............... *5547*
1Co 15:23 **C.** the firstfruits; afterward they *5547*
1Co 15:31 which I have in **C.** Jesus our Lord, ... *5547*
1Co 15:57 victory through our Lord Jesus **C.**. *5547*
1Co 16:22 man love not the Lord Jesus **C.**, ... *5547*
1Co 16:23 of our Lord Jesus **C.** be with you. *5547*
1Co 16:24 love be with you all in **C.** Jesus. *5547*
2Co 1:1 of Jesus **C.** by the will of God, ... *5547*
2Co 1:2 and from the Lord Jesus **C.**............... *5547*
2Co 1:3 the Father of our Lord Jesus **C.**,......... *5547*
2Co 1:5 sufferings of **C.** abound in us,............ *5547*
2Co 1:5 consolation also aboundeth by **C.**........ *5547*
2Co 1:19 **C.**, who was preached among you *5547*
2Co 1:21 stablisheth us with you in **C.**............. *5547*
2Co 2:10 forgave I it in the person of **C.**; *5547*
2Co 2:14 always causeth us to triumph in **C.**, ... *5547*
2Co 2:15 unto God a sweet savour of **C.**, ... *5547*
2Co 2:17 in the sight of God speak we in **C.**. *5547*
2Co 3:3 the epistle of **C.** ministered by us,....... *5547*
2Co 3:4 have we through **C.** to God-ward: *5547*
2Co 3:14 which vail is done away in **C.**. *5547*
2Co 4:4 light of the glorious gospel of **C.**, ... *5547*
2Co 4:5 ourselves, but **C.** Jesus the Lord;....... *5547*
2Co 4:6 glory of God in the face of Jesus **C.**...... *5547*
2Co 5:10 judgment seat of **C.**; that every *5547*
2Co 5:14 For the love of **C.** constraineth us;..... *5547*
2Co 5:16 we have known **C.** after the flesh,...... *5547*
2Co 5:17 if any man be in **C.**, he is a new........ *5547*
2Co 5:18 us to himself by Jesus **C.**, and hath *5547*

Book	Ref	Context	No.
2Co	5:19	God was in C., reconciling the	5547
2Co	5:20	we are ambassadors for C., as	5547
2Co	6:15	what concord hath C. with Belial?	5547
2Co	8:9	the grace of our Lord Jesus C.,	5547
2Co	8:23	the churches, and the glory of C..	5547
2Co	9:13	subjection unto the gospel of C.,	5547
2Co	10:1	meekness and gentleness of C.,	5547
2Co	10:5	thought to the obedience of C.;	5547
2Co	10:14	in preaching the gospel of C.	5547
2Co	11:2	you as a chaste virgin to C..	5547
2Co	11:3	from the simplicity that is in C.	5547
2Co	11:10	truth of C. is in me, no man shall	5547
2Co	11:13	themselves into the apostles of C..	5547
2Co	11:23	Are they ministers of C.? (I speak	5547
2Co	11:31	the Father of our Lord Jesus C.,	5547
2Co	12:2	a man in C. above fourteen years	5547
2Co	12:9	power of C. may rest upon me.	5547
2Co	12:19	we speak before God in C.: but	5547
2Co	13:3	seek a proof of C. speaking in me.	5547
2Co	13:5	Jesus C. is in you, except ye be	5547
2Co	13:14	grace of the Lord Jesus C., and	5547
Ga	1:1	neither by man, but by Jesus C.,	5547
Ga	1:3	and from our Lord Jesus C.,	5547
Ga	1:6	grace of C. unto another gospel:	5547
Ga	1:7	would pervert the gospel of C..	5547
Ga	1:10	should not be the servant of C..	5547
Ga	1:12	but by the revelation of Jesus C.	5547
Ga	1:22	of Judaea which were in C.	5547
Ga	2:4	in C. Jesus, that they might bring	5547
Ga	2:16	law, but by the faith of Jesus C.,	5547
Ga	2:16	we have believed in Jesus C.,	5547
Ga	2:16	be justified by the faith of C.,	5547
Ga	2:17	we seek to be justified by C.,	5547
Ga	2:17	is therefore C. the minister of sin?	5547
Ga	2:20	I am crucified with C.	5547
Ga	2:20	yet not I, but C. liveth in me:	5547
Ga	2:21	by the law, then C. is dead in vain.	5547
Ga	3:1	C. hath been evidently set forth,	5547
Ga	3:13	C. hath redeemed us from the	5547
Ga	3:14	on the Gentiles through Jesus C.;	5547
Ga	3:16	one, And to thy seed, which is C..	5547
Ga	3:17	confirmed before of God in C.,	5547
Ga	3:22	promise by faith of Jesus C.	5547
Ga	3:24	schoolmaster to bring us unto C.,	5547
Ga	3:26	of God by faith in C. Jesus.	5547
Ga	3:27	baptized into C. have put on C..	5547
Ga	3:28	for ye are all one in C. Jesus.	5547
Ga	4:7	then an heir of God through C.	5547
Ga	4:14	angel of God, even as C. Jesus.	5547
Ga	4:19	in birth again until C. be formed	5547
Ga	5:1	wherewith C. hath made us free,	5547
Ga	5:2	C. shall profit you nothing.	5547
Ga	5:4	C. is become of no effect unto you,	5547
Ga	5:6	in Jesus C. neither circumcision	5547
Ga	6:2	burdens, and so fulfil the law of C..	5547
Ga	6:12	persecution for the cross of C..	5547
Ga	6:14	cross of our Lord Jesus C., by	5547
Ga	6:15	in C. Jesus neither circumcision	5547
Ga	6:18	Lord Jesus C. be with your spirit.	5547
Eph	1:1	Paul, an apostle of Jesus C. by the	5547
Eph	1:1	and to the faithful in C. Jesus:	5547
Eph	1:2	and from the Lord Jesus C.	5547
Eph	1:3	Father of our Lord Jesus C., who	5547
Eph	1:3	in heavenly places in C.	5547
Eph	1:5	children by Jesus C. to himself,	5547
Eph	1:10	all things in C., both which are in	5547
Eph	1:12	his glory, who first trusted in C..	5547
Eph	1:17	God of our Lord Jesus C., the	5547
Eph	1:20	Which he wrought it C., when he	5547
Eph	2:5	quickened us together with C.,	5547
Eph	2:6	in heavenly places in C. Jesus	5547
Eph	2:7	toward us through C. Jesus.	5547
Eph	2:10	in C. Jesus unto good works,	5547
Eph	2:12	without C., being aliens from the	5547
Eph	2:13	now in C. Jesus, ye who sometimes	5547
Eph	2:13	are made nigh by the blood of C..	5547
Eph	2:20	C. himself being the chief corner	5547
Eph	3:1	prisoner of Jesus C. for you	5547
Eph	3:4	knowledge in the mystery of C.)	5547
Eph	3:6	his promise in C. by the gospel:	5547
Eph	3:8	the unsearchable riches of C.;	5547
Eph	3:9	created all things by Jesus C.	5547
Eph	3:11	which he purposed in C. Jesus	5547
Eph	3:14	Father of our Lord Jesus C.,	5547
Eph	3:17	C. may dwell in your hearts by	5547
Eph	3:19	the love of C., which passeth	5547
Eph	3:21	by C. Jesus throughout all ages,	5547
Eph	4:7	to the measure of the gift of C..	5547
Eph	4:12	for the edifying of the body of C.	5547
Eph	4:13	of the stature of the fulness of C.	5547
Eph	4:15	which is the head, even C.	5547
Eph	4:20	ye have not so learned C.;	5547
Eph	5:2	as C. also hath loved us, and hath	5547
Eph	5:5	in the kingdom of C. and of God.	5547
Eph	5:14	dead, and C. shall give thee light.	5547
Eph	5:20	in the name of our Lord Jesus C.;	5547
Eph	5:23	C. is the head of the church:	5547
Eph	5:24	as the church is subject unto C.,	5547
Eph	5:25	even as C. also loved the church,	5547
Eph	5:32	concerning C. and the church.	5547
Eph	6:5	of your heart, as unto C.;	5547
Eph	6:6	the servants of C., doing the will	5547
Eph	6:23	Father and the Lord Jesus C..	5547
Eph	6:24	our Lord Jesus C. in sincerity.	5547
Php	1:1	the servants of Jesus C., to all	5547
Php	1:1	to all the saints in C. Jesus	5547
Php	1:2	Father, and from the Lord Jesus C.	5547
Php	1:6	perform it until the day of Jesus C.	5547
Php	1:8	you all in the bowels of Jesus C..	5547
Php	1:10	without offence till the day of C.;	5547
Php	1:11	are by Jesus C., unto the glory	5547
Php	1:13	my bonds in C. are manifest in all	5547
Php	1:15	indeed preach C. even of envy and	5547
Php	1:16	The one preach C. of contention,	5547
Php	1:18	or in truth, C. is preached;	5547
Php	1:19	supply of the Spirit of Jesus C.,	5547
Php	1:20	C. shall be magnified in my body,	5547
Php	1:21	For me to live is C., and to die is	5547
Php	1:23	to depart, and to be with C.	5547
Php	1:26	may be more abundant in Jesus C.	5547
Php	1:27	as it becometh the gospel of C.	5547
Php	1:29	it is given in the behalf of C., not	5547
Php	2:1	be therefore any consolation in C.,	5547
Php	2:5	you, which was also in C. Jesus:	5547
Php	2:11	Jesus C. is Lord, to the glory of God..	5547
Php	2:16	I may rejoice in the day of C.,	5547
Php	2:30	for the work of C. he was nigh	5547
Php	3:3	rejoice in C. Jesus, and have no	5547
Php	3:7	those I counted loss for C..	5547
Php	3:8	knowledge of C. Jesus my Lord:	5547
Php	3:8	but dung, that I may win C.,	5547
Php	3:9	which is through the faith of C.,	5547
Php	3:12	I am apprehended of C. Jesus.	5547
Php	3:14	the high calling of God in C. Jesus.	5547
Php	3:18	are the enemies of the cross of C.	5547
Php	3:20	for the Saviour, the Lord Jesus C.	5547
Php	4:7	hearts and minds through C. Jesus.	5547
Php	4:13	C. which strengtheneth me.	5547
Php	4:19	to his riches in glory by C. Jesus.	5547
Php	4:21	Salute every saint in C. Jesus.	5547
Php	4:23	The grace of our Lord Jesus C. be	5547
Col	1:1	an apostle of Jesus C. by the will	5547
Col	1:2	saints and faithful brethren in C.	5547
Col	1:2	Father and the Lord Jesus C.	5547
Col	1:3	the Father of our Lord Jesus C.,	5547
Col	1:4	we heard of your faith in C. Jesus,	5547
Col	1:7	for you a faithful minister of C.;	5547
Col	1:24	the afflictions of C. in my flesh for	5547
Col	1:27	is C. in you, the hope of glory:	5547
Col	1:28	every man perfect in C. Jesus:	5547
Col	2:2	and of the Father, and of C.;	5547
Col	2:5	stedfastness of your faith in C..	5547
Col	2:6	therefore received C. Jesus the	5547
Col	2:8	of the world, and not after C.	5547
Col	2:11	flesh by the circumcision of C.	5547
Col	2:17	but the body is of C..	5547
Col	2:20	dead with C. from the rudiments	5547
Col	3:1	If ye then be risen with C.,	5547
Col	3:1	where C. sitteth on the right hand	5547
Col	3:3	your life is hid with C. in God.	5547
Col	3:4	C., who is our life, shall appear,	5547
Col	3:11	but C. is all, and in all.	5547
Col	3:13	as C. forgave you, so also do ye.	5547
Col	3:16	the word of C. dwell in you richly	5547
Col	3:24	for ye serve the Lord C..	5547
Col	4:3	speak the mystery of C., for which	5547
Col	4:12	a servant of C., saluteth you,	5547
1Th	1:1	Father and in the Lord Jesus C.	5547
1Th	1:1	Father, and the Lord Jesus C..	5547
1Th	1:3	hope in our Lord Jesus C., in	5547
1Th	2:6	burdensome, as the apostles of C.	5547
1Th	2:14	which in Judaea are in C. Jesus:	5547
1Th	2:19	our Lord Jesus C. at his coming?	5547
1Th	3:2	fellowlabourer in the gospel of C.,	5547
1Th	3:11	Lord Jesus C., direct our way	5547
1Th	3:13	the coming of our Lord Jesus C.	5547
1Th	4:16	the dead in C. shall rise first:	5547
1Th	5:9	salvation by our Lord Jesus C.,	5547
1Th	5:18	this is the will of God in C. Jesus	5547
1Th	5:23	the coming of our Lord Jesus C..	5547
1Th	5:28	The grace of our Lord Jesus C. be	5547
2Th	1:1	our Father and the Lord Jesus C.	5547
2Th	1:2	our Father and the Lord Jesus C.	5547
2Th	1:8	the gospel of our Lord Jesus C.	5547
2Th	1:12	the name of our Lord Jesus C.	5547
2Th	1:12	of our God and the Lord Jesus C..	5547
2Th	2:1	the coming of our Lord Jesus C.,	5547
2Th	2:2	as that the day of C. is at hand.	5547
2Th	2:14	the glory of our Lord Jesus C.	5547
2Th	2:16	Now our Lord Jesus C. himself,	5547
2Th	3:5	into the patient waiting for C.	5547
2Th	3:6	in the name of our Lord Jesus C.,	5547
2Th	3:12	and exhort by our Lord Jesus C.,	5547
2Th	3:18	The grace of our Lord Jesus C. be	5547
1Ti	1:1	Paul, an apostle of Jesus C. by the	5547
1Ti	1:1	our Saviour, and Lord Jesus C.,	5547
1Ti	1:2	our Father and Jesus C. our Lord.	5547
1Ti	1:12	thank C. Jesus our Lord, who hath	5547
1Ti	1:14	and love which is in C. Jesus.	5547
1Ti	1:15	that C. Jesus came into the world	5547
1Ti	1:16	first Jesus C. might shew forth	5547
1Ti	2:5	and men, the man C. Jesus;	5547
1Ti	2:7	speak the truth in C., and lie not;)	5547
1Ti	3:13	in the faith which is in C. Jesus.	5547
1Ti	4:6	be a good minister of Jesus C.,	5547
1Ti	5:11	begun to wax wanton against C.,	5547
1Ti	5:21	before God, and the Lord Jesus C.,	5547
1Ti	6:3	the words of our Lord Jesus C.,	5547
1Ti	6:13	C. Jesus, who before Pontius Pilate	5547
1Ti	6:14	appearing of our Lord Jesus C.	5547
2Ti	1:1	an apostle of Jesus C. by the will	5547
2Ti	1:1	promise of life which is in C. Jesus,	5547
2Ti	1:2	the Father and C. Jesus our Lord.	5547
2Ti	1:9	in C. Jesus before the world began,	5547
2Ti	1:10	appearing of our Saviour Jesus C.,	5547
2Ti	1:13	and love which is in C. Jesus.	5547
2Ti	2:1	in the grace that is in C. Jesus.	5547
2Ti	2:3	as a good soldier of Jesus C.	5547
2Ti	2:8	Remember that Jesus C. of the	5547
2Ti	2:10	is in C. Jesus with eternal glory.	5547
2Ti	2:19	that nameth the name of C.	5547
2Ti	3:12	live godly in C. Jesus shall suffer	5547
2Ti	3:15	through faith which is in C. Jesus.	5547
2Ti	4:1	Lord Jesus C., who shall judge	5547
2Ti	4:22	Lord Jesus C. be with thy spirit.	5547
Tit	1:1	an apostle of Jesus C., according to	5547
Tit	1:4	and the Lord Jesus C. our Saviour	5547
Tit	2:13	great God and our Saviour Jesus C.;	5547
Tit	3:6	through Jesus C. our Saviour;	5547
Phm	1	Paul, a prisoner of Jesus C.,	5547
Phm	3	our Father and the Lord Jesus C.	5547
Phm	6	thing which is in you in C. Jesus.	5547
Phm	8	be much bold in C. to enjoin thee	5547
Phm	9	now also a prisoner of Jesus C..	5547
Phm	23	my fellowprisoner in C. Jesus;	5547
Phm	25	grace of our Lord Jesus C. be with	5547
Heb	3:1	Priest of our profession, C. Jesus	5547
Heb	3:6	C. as a son over his own house;	5547
Heb	3:14	For we are made partakers of C.,	5547
Heb	5:5	also C. glorified not himself to be	5547
Heb	6:1	the principles of the doctrine of C.,	5547
Heb	9:11	But C. being come an high priest	5547
Heb	9:14	much more shall the blood of C.,	5547
Heb	9:24	C. is not entered in to the holy places.	5547
Heb	9:28	C. was once offered to bear the sins	5547
Heb	10:10	of the body of Jesus C. once for all.	5547
Heb	11:26	the reproach of C. greater riches	5547
Heb	13:8	Jesus C. the same yesterday, and	5547
Heb	13:21	in his sight, through Jesus C.;	5547
Jas	1:1	Lord Jesus C., to the twelve tribes	5547
Jas	2:1	faith of our Lord Jesus C., the Lord	5547
1Pe	1:1	Peter, an apostle of Jesus C., to	5547
1Pe	1:2	sprinkling of the blood of Jesus C.	5547
1Pe	1:3	and Father of our Lord Jesus C..	5547
1Pe	1:3	resurrection of Jesus C. from the	5547
1Pe	1:7	glory at the appearing of Jesus C.	5547
1Pe	1:11	the spirit of C. which was in them	5547
1Pe	1:11	beforehand the sufferings of C.,	5547
1Pe	1:13	you at the revelation of Jesus C.;	5547
1Pe	1:19	precious blood of C., as of a lamb	5547
1Pe	2:5	acceptable to God by Jesus C..	5547

1Pe 2:21 because C. also suffered for us, 5547
1Pe 3:16 your good conversation in C. 5547
1Pe 3:18 C. also hath once suffered for sins 5547
1Pe 3:21 by the resurrection of Jesus C. 5547
1Pe 4:1 Forasmuch then as C. hath suffered 5547
1Pe 4:11 may be glorified through Jesus C., 5547
1Pe 4:14 be reproached for the name of C., 5547
1Pe 5:1 a witness of the sufferings of C., 5547
1Pe 5:10 his eternal glory by C. Jesus, 5547
1Pe 5:14 with you all that are in C. Jesus 5547
2Pe 1:1 Peter, an apostle of Jesus C., to 5547
2Pe 1:1 of God and our Saviour Jesus C. 5547
2Pe 1:8 knowledge of our Lord Jesus C. 5547
2Pe 1:11 of our Lord and Saviour Jesus C. 5547
2Pe 1:14 as our Lord Jesus C. hath shewed 5547
2Pe 1:16 and coming of our Lord Jesus C., 5547
2Pe 2:20 of the Lord and Saviour Jesus C., 5547
2Pe 3:18 of our Lord and Saviour Jesus C. 5547
1Jo 1:3 Father, and with his Son Jesus C. 5547
1Jo 1:7 and the blood of Jesus C. his Son 5547
1Jo 2:1 the Father, Jesus C. the righteous: 5547
1Jo 2:22 that denieth that Jesus is the C.? 5547
1Jo 3:23 on the name of his son Jesus C., 5547
1Jo 4:2 that Jesus C. is come in the flesh 5547
1Jo 4:3 confesseth not that Jesus C. is 5547
1Jo 5:1 believeth that Jesus is the C. is 5547
1Jo 5:6 water and blood, even Jesus C.; 5547
1Jo 5:20 is true, even in his Son Jesus C. 5547
2Jo 3 Lord Jesus C., the son of the Father, 5547
2Jo 7 that Jesus C. is come in the flesh 5547
2Jo 9 abideth not in the doctrine of C., 5547
2Jo 9 that abideth in the doctrine of C., 5547
Jude 1 the servant of Jesus C., and brother 5547
Jude 1 preserved in Jesus C., and called: 5547
Jude 4 Lord God, and our Lord Jesus C. 5547
Jude 17 the apostles of our Lord Jesus C.; 5547
Jude 21 the mercy of our Lord Jesus C. 5547
Re 1:1 Revelation of Jesus C., which God 5547
Re 1:2 testimony of Jesus C., and of all 5547
Re 1:5 from Jesus C., who is the faithful 5547
Re 1:9 kingdom and patience of Jesus C., 5547
Re 1:9 and for the testimony of Jesus C. 5547
Re 11:15 of our Lord, and of his C.; 5547
Re 12:10 our God, and the power of his C. 5547
Re 12:17 have the testimony of Jesus C. 5547
Re 20:4 reigned with C. a thousand years. 5547
Re 20:6 shall be priests of God and of C., 5547
Re 22:21 Lord Jesus C. be with you all. 5547

CHRIST JESUS See CHRIST and JESUS.

CHRIST'S (krists)
Ro 15:30 for the Lord Jesus C. sake, and 5547
1Co 3:23 ye are C.; and Christ is God's. 5547
1Co 4:10 for C. sake, but ye are wise in 5547
1Co 7:22 is called, being free, is C. servant. 5547
1Co 15:23 fruits; afterward they that are C. 5547
2Co 2:12 C. gospel, and a door was opened 5547
2Co 5:20 in C. stead, be ye reconciled to 5547
2Co 10:7 man trust to himself that he is C., 5547
2Co 10:7 think this again, that, as he is C. 5547
2Co 10:7 even so are we C. 5547
2Co 12:10 in distresses for C. sake: 5547
Ga 3:29 if ye be C., then are ye Abraham's 5547
Ga 5:24 are C. have crucified the flesh 5547
Eph 4:32 God for C. sake hath forgiven 5547
Php 2:21 not the things which are Jesus C. 5547
1Pe 4:13 as ye are partakers of C. 5547

CHRISTS (krists)
Mt 24:24 For there shall arise false C., and 5580
Mk 13:22 For false C. and false prophets 5580

CHRISTIAN (kris'-tyan) See also CHRISTIANS.
Ac 26:28 thou persuadest me to be a C. 5546
1Pe 4:16 if any man suffer as a C., let him 5546

CHRISTIANS (kris'-tyans)
Ac 11:26 disciples were called C. first in 5546

CHRONICLES
1Ki 14:19 c. of the kings of Israel? 1697,3117
1Ki 14:29 c. of the kings of Judah? 1697,3117
1Ki 15:7, 23 c. of the kings of Judah? 1697,3117
1Ki 15:31 c. of the kings of Israel? 1697,3117
1Ki 16:5, 14,20,27 c. of ... Israel? 1697,3117
1Ki 22:39 c. of the kings of Israel? 1697,3117
1Ki 22:45 c. of the kings of Judah? 1697,3117
2Ki 1:18 c. of the kings of Israel? 1697,3117
2Ki 8:23 c. of the kings of Judah? 1697,3117
2Ki 10:34 c. of the kings of Israel? 1697,3117
2Ki 12:19 c. of the kings of Judah? 1697,3117
2Ki 13:8, 12 c. of the kings of Israel? 1697,3117
2Ki 14:15 c. of the kings of Israel? 1697,3117
2Ki 14:18 c. of the kings of Judah? 1697,3117
2Ki 14:28 c. of the kings of Israel? 1697,3117
2Ki 15:6 c. of the kings of Judah? 1697,3117
2Ki 15:11, 15,21,26,31 c. of...Israel? 1697,3117
2Ki 15:36 c. of the kings of Judah? 1697,3117
2Ki 16:19 c. of the kings of Judah?
2Ki 20:20 c. of the kings of Judah? 1697,3117
2Ki 21:17, 25 c. of the kings of Judah? 1697,3117
2Ki 23:28 c. of the kings of Judah? 1697,3117
2Ki 24:5 c. of the kings of Judah? 1697,3117
1Ch *general title* The First Book Of The C. 1697,3117
1Ch 27:24 c. of King David. 1697,3117
2Ch *general title* The Second Book Of The C. 1697,3117
Ne 12:23 book of the c. even until 1697,3117
Es 2:23 book of the c. before the king 1697,3117
Es 6:1 records of the c.; and they 1697,3117
Es 10:2 c. of the kings of Media and 1697,3117

CHRYSOLITE (criso'-lite)
Re 21:20 the seventh, c.; the eighth, beryl: 5555

CHRYSOPRASUS (cris'-o-pra-sus)
Re 21:20 the tenth, a c.; the eleventh, a 5556

CHUB (cub)
Eze 30:5 all the mingled people, and C. 3552

CHUN (kun)
1Ch 18:8 from Tibhath, and from C., cities 3560

CHURCH See also CHURCHES.
Mt 16:18 upon this rock I will build my c. 1577
Mt 18:17 tell it unto the c. 1577
Mt 18:17 but if he neglect to hear the c., 1577
Ac 2:47 the Lord added to the c. daily 1577
Ac 5:11 fear came upon all the c., and 1577
Ac 7:38 he, that was in the c. in the 1577
Ac 8:1 against the c. which was at 1577
Ac 8:3 he made havock of the c., 1577
Ac 11:22 the c. which was in Jerusalem: 1577
Ac 11:26 assembled themselves with the c. 1577
Ac 12:1 his hands to vex certain of the c. 1577
Ac 12:5 without ceasing of the c. unto God 1577
Ac 13:1 Now there were in the c. that was 1577
Ac 14:23 ordained them elders in every c., 1577
Ac 14:27 and had gathered the c. together, 1577
Ac 15:3 brought on their way by the c., 1577
Ac 15:4 they were received of the c., and of 1577
Ac 15:22 and elders, with the whole c., 1577
Ac 18:22 gone up, and saluted the c., he 1577
Ac 20:17 and called the elders of the c. 1577
Ac 20:28 overseers, to feed the c. of God, 1577
Ro 16:1 is a servant of the c. which is at 1577
Ro 16:5 greet the c. that is in their house 1577
Ro 16:23 mine host, and of the whole c., 1577
Ro *subscr.* by Phebe servant of the c. 1577
1Co 1:2 Unto the c. of God which is at 1577
1Co 4:17 I teach everywhere in every c. 1577
1Co 6:4 who are least esteemed in the c. 1577
1Co 10:32 Gentiles; nor to the c. of God: 1577
1Co 11:18 when ye come together in the c., 1577
1Co 11:22 or despise ye the c. of God, and 1577
1Co 12:28 God hath set some in the c., 1577
1Co 14:4 that prophesieth edifieth the c. 1577
1Co 14:5 interpret, that the c. may receive 1577
1Co 14:12 excel to the edifying of the c. 1577
1Co 14:19 in the c. I had rather speak five 1577
1Co 14:23 therefore the whole c. be come 1577
1Co 14:28 let him keep silence in the c.; 1577
1Co 14:35 for women to speak in the c. 1577
1Co 15:9 I persecuted the c. of God. 1577
1Co 16:19 with the c. that is in their house. 1577
2Co 1:1 unto the c. of God which is 1577
Ga 1:13 I persecuted the c. of God, and 1577
Eph 1:22 the head over all things to the c., 1577
Eph 3:10 might be known by the c. the 1577
Eph 3:21 glory in the c. by Christ Jesus 1577
Eph 5:23 Christ is the head of the c. 1577
Eph 5:24 Therefore as the c. is subject unto 1577
Eph 5:25 as Christ also loved the c., and 1577
Eph 5:27 present it to himself a glorious c., 1577
Eph 5:29 even as the Lord the c. 1577
Eph 5:32 concerning Christ and the c., 1577
Php 3:6 Concerning zeal, persecuting the c.; 1577
Php 4:15 no c. communicated with me 1577
Col 1:18 the head of the body, the c. 1577
Col 1:24 for his body's sake, which is the c. 1577
Col 4:15 and the c. which is in his house. 1577
Col 4:16 it be read also in the c. of the 1577
1Th 1:1 unto the c. of the Thessalonians 1577
2Th 1:1 unto the c. of the Thessalonians 1577
1Ti 3:5 take care of the c. of God?) 1577
1Ti 3:15 the c. of the living God, the pillar 1577
1Ti 5:16 let not the c. be charged; 1577
2Ti *subscr.* first bishop of the c. of the 1577
2Ti *subscr.* first bishop of the c. of the 1577
Phm 2 to the c. in thy house: 1577
Heb 2:12 in the midst of the c. will I sing 1577
Heb 12:23 general assembly and c. of the 1577
Jas 5:14 call for the elders of the c.; 1577
1Pe 5:13 The c. that is at Babylon, elected 1577
3Jo 6 of thy charity before the c. 1577
3Jo 9 I wrote unto the c.: but 1577
3Jo 10 and casteth them out of the c. 1577
Re 2:1 the angel of the c. of Ephesus 1577
Re 2:8 the angel of the c. in Smyrna 1577
Re 2:12 to the angel of the c. in Pergamos 1577
Re 2:18 the angel of the c. in Thyatira 1577
Re 3:1 the angel of the c. in Sardis write; 1577
Re 3:7 the angel of the c. in Philadelphia 1577
Re 3:14 angel of the c. of the Laodiceans 1577

CHURCHES
Ac 9:31 Then had the c. rest throughout 1577
Ac 15:41 and Cilicia, confirming the c. 1577
Ac 16:5 so were the c. established in the 1577
Ac 19:37 which are neither robbers of c., 2417
Ro 16:4 but also all the c. of the Gentiles. 1577
Ro 16:16 The c. of Christ salute you. 1577
1Co 7:17 And so ordain I in all c. 1577
1Co 11:16 custom, neither the c. of God. 1577
1Co 14:33 of peace, as in all c. of the saints. 1577
1Co 14:34 your women keep silence in the c. 1577
1Co 16:1 I have given orden to the c. of 1577
1Co 16:19 The c. of Asia salute you. 1577
2Co 8:1 bestowed on the c. of Macedonia; 1577
2Co 8:18 gospel throughout all the c.; 1577
2Co 8:19 was also chosen of the c. to travel 1577
2Co 8:23 they are the messengers of the c., 1577
2Co 8:24 ye to them, and before the c., 1577
2Co 11:8 I robbed other c., taking wages of 1577
2Co 11:28 me daily, the care of all the c. 1577
2Co 12:13 ye were inferior to other c., 1577
Ga 1:2 unto the c. of Galatia: 1577
Ga 1:22 unto the c. of Judaea which were 1577
1Th 2:14 became followers of the c. of God 1577
2Th 1:4 glory in you in the c. of God 1577
Re 1:4 John to the seven c. which are in 1577
Re 1:11 and send it unto the seven c. 1577
Re 1:20 are the angels of the seven c. 1577
Re 1:20 which thou sawest are the seven c. 1577
Re 2:7 what the Spirit saith unto the c.; 1577
Re 2:11 the Spirit saith unto the c.; He 1577
Re 2:17 the Spirit saith unto the c.; To 1577
Re 2:23 all the c. shall know that I am he 1577
Re 2:29 what the Spirit saith unto the c. 1577
Re 3:6, 13,22 the Spirit saith unto the c. 1577
Re 22:16 unto you these things in the c. 1577

CHURL
Isa 32:5 nor the c. said to be bountiful. 3596
Isa 32:7 The instruments also of the c. 3596

CHURLISH
1Sa 25:3 the man was c. and evil in his 7186

CHURNING
Pr 30:33 c. of milk bringeth forth butter, 4330

CHUSHAN-RISHATHAIM (cu''-shan-rish-a-tha'-im)
Jg 3:8 he sold them into the hand of C. 3573
Jg 3:8 of Israel served C. eight years. 3573
Jg 3:10 Lord delivered C. into his hand; 3573
Jg 3:10 and his hand prevailed against C. 3573

CHUZA (cu'-zah)
Lu 8:3 the wife of C. Herod's steward, 5529

CIELED
2Ch 3:5 greater house he c. with fir tree, 2645
Jer 22:14 it is c. with cedar, and painted 5603
Eze 41:16 door, c. with wood round about, 7824
Hag 1:4 to dwell in your c. houses, 5603

CIELING
1Ki 6:15 the house, and the walls of the c. 5604

CILICIA (sil-ish'-yah)
Ac 6:9 and of them of C. and of Asia, *2791*
Ac 15:23 in Antioch and Syria and C. *2791*
Ac 15:41 And he went through Syria and C., *2791*
Ac 21:39 am a Jew of Tarsus, a city in C., *2791*
Ac 22:3 born in Tarsus, a city in C., *2791*
Ac 23:34 he understood that he was of C.; *2791*
Ac 27:5 we had sailed over the sea of C. *2791*
Ga 1:21 into the region of Syria and C.; *2791*

CINNAMON
Ex 30:23 and of sweet c. half so much, 7076
Pr 7:17 my bed with myrrh, aloes, and c. 7076
Ca 4:14 calamus and c., with all trees of 7076
Re 18:13 c., and odours, and ointments, *2792*

CINNEROTH (sin'-ne-roth) See also CHINNEROTH.
1Ki 15:20 and all C., with all the land of 3672

CIRCLE
Isa 40:22 sitteth upon the c. of the earth, 2329

CIRCUIT See also CIRCUITS.
1Sa 7:16 he went from year to year in c. 5437
Job 22:14 he walketh in the c. of heaven. 2329
Ps 19:6 and his c. unto the ends of it: 8622

CIRCUITS
Ec 1:6 again according to his c. 5439

CIRCUMCISE See also CIRCUMCISED; CIRCUMCISING.
Ge 17:11 shall c. the flesh of your foreskin; 5243
De 10:16 C. therefore the foreskin of your 4135
De 30:6 And the Lord thy God will c. thine 4135
Jos 5:2 c. again the children of Israel the 4135
Jos 5:4 is the cause why Joshua did c. 4135
Jer 4:4 C. yourselves to the Lord, and take 4135
Lu 1:59 day they came to c. the child; *4059*
Joh 7:22 ye on the sabbath day c. a man. *4059*
Ac 15:5 That it was needful to c. them, *4059*
Ac 21:21 saying that they ought not to c. *4059*

CIRCUMCISED See also UNCIRCUMCISED.
Ge 17:10 man child among you shall be c. 4135
Ge 17:12 that is eight days old shall be c. 4135
Ge 17:13 must needs be c. 4135
Ge 17:14 whose flesh of his foreskin is not c., 4135
Ge 17:23 and c. the flesh of their foreskin 4135
Ge 17:24 was c. in the flesh of his foreskin. 4135
Ge 17:25 when he was c. in the flesh of his 4135
Ge 17:26 the selfsame day was Abraham c., 4135
Ge 17:27 the stranger, were c. with him. 4135
Ge 21:4 And Abraham c. his son Isaac 4135
Ge 34:15 that every male of you be c.; 4135
Ge 34:17 will not hearken unto us, to be c.; 4135
Ge 34:22 if every male among us be c., 4135
Ge 34:22 as they are c. 4135
Ge 34:24 and every male was c., all that 4135
Ex 12:44 when thou hast c. him, then shall 4135
Ex 12:48 let all his males be c., and then let 4135
Le 12:3 flesh of his foreskin shall be c. 4135
Jos 5:3 c. the children of Israel at the hill 4135
Jos 5:5 the people that came out were c. 4135
Jos 5:5 of Egypt, them they had not c. 4135
Jos 5:7 them Joshua c.: for they were 4135
Jos 5:7 they had not c. them by the way. 4135
Jer 9:25 all them which are c. with the 4135
Ac 7:8 Isaac, and c. him the eighth day; *4059*
Ac 15:1 be c. after the manner of Moses, *4059*
Ac 15:24 Ye must be c., and keep the law: *4059*
Ac 16:3 and took and c. him because of *4059*
Ro 4:11 believe, though they be not c.; *203*
1Co 7:18 Is any man called being c.? *4059*
1Co 7:18 let him not be c. *4059*
Ga 2:3 a Greek, was compelled to be c. *4059*
Ga 5:2 if ye be c., Christ shall profit you *4059*
Ga 5:3 again to every man that is c., *4059*
Ga 6:12 they constrain you to be c.; only *4059*
Ga 6:13 they themselves who are c. keep *4059*
Ga 6:13 desire to have you c., that they may *4059*
Php 3:5 C. the eighth day, of the stock of *4061*
Col 2:11 In whom also ye are c. with the *4059*

CIRCUMCISING
Jos 5:8 they had done c. all the people, 4135
Lu 2:21 accomplished for the c. of the *4059*

CIRCUMCISION See also UNCIRCUMCISION.
Ex 4:26 husband thou art, because of the c. 4139
Joh 7:22 Moses therefore gave unto you c.; *4061*
Joh 7:23 man on the sabbath day receive c., *4061*
Ac 7:8 he gave him the covenant of c. *4061*
Ac 10:45 they of the c. which believed *4061*
Ac 11:2 they that wee of the c. contended *4061*
Ro 2:25 For c. verily profiteth, if thou keep *4061*
Ro 2:25 thy c. is made uncircumcision. *4061*
Ro 2:26 uncircumcision be counted for c.? *4061*
Ro 2:27 the letter and c. dost transgress *4061*
Ro 2:28 is that c., which is outward in the *4061*
Ro 2:29 c. is that of the heart, in the spirit, *4061*
Ro 3:1 what profit is there of c.? *4061*
Ro 3:30 shall justify the c. by faith, and *4061*
Ro 4:9 blessedness then upon the c. only, *4061*
Ro 4:10 when he was in c., or in *4061*
Ro 4:10 Not in c., but in uncircumcision, *4061*
Ro 4:11 And he received the sign of c., *4061*
Ro 4:12 the father of c. to them who are not *4061*
Ro 4:12 them who are not of the c. only, *4061*
Ro 15:8 a minister of the c. for the truth *4061*
1Co 7:19 C. is nothing, and uncircumcision *4061*
Ga 2:7 gospel of the c. was unto Peter; *4061*
Ga 2:8 Peter to the apostleship of the c., *4061*
Ga 2:9 heathen, and they unto the c. *4061*
Ga 2:12 fearing them which were of the c. *4061*
Ga 5:6 neither c. availeth any thing, *4061*
Ga 5:11 if I yet preach c., why do I yet *4061*
Ga 6:15 neither c. availeth any thing, *4061*
Eph 2:11 C. in the flesh made by hands; *4061*
Php 3:3 For we are the c., which worship *4061*
Col 2:11 with the c. made without hands, *4061*
Col 2:11 sins of the flesh by the c. of Christ: *4061*
Col 3:11 c. nor uncircumcision, Barbarian, *4061*
Col 4:11 called Justus, who are of the c. *4061*
Tit 1:10 deceivers, specially they of the c. *4061*

CIRCUMSPECT
Ex 23:13 that I have said unto you be c. 8104

CIRCUMSPECTLY
Eph 5:15 that ye walk c., not as fools, *199*

CIS (sis) See also KISH.
Ac 13:21 Saul the son of C., a man of the *2797*

CISTERN See also CISTERNS.
2Ki 18:31 every one the waters of his c. 953
Pr 5:15 Drink waters out of thine own c., 953
Ec 12:6 or the wheel broken at the c. 953
Isa 36:16 every one the waters of his own c.; 953

CISTERNS
Jer 2:13 hewed them out c., broken c., 877

CITIES
Ge 13:12 Lot dwelled in the c. of the plain, 5892
Ge 19:25 overthrew those c., and all the plain, 5892
Ge 19:25 and all the inhabitants of the c., 5892
Ge 19:29 God destroyed the c. of the plain, 5892
Ge 19:29 overthrew the c. in which Lot dwelt. 5892
Ge 35:5 the terror of God was upon the c. 5892
Ge 41:35 let them keep food in the c. 5892
Ge 41:48 and laid up the food in the c. 5892
Ge 47:21 removed them to c. from one end 5892
Ex 1:11 built for Pharaoh treasure c., 5892
Le 25:32 Notwithstanding the c. of the 5892
Le 25:32 and the houses of the c. of their 5892
Le 25:33 houses of the c. of the Levites 5892
Le 25:34 the field of the suburbs of their c. 5892
Le 26:25 gathered together within your c., 5892
Le 26:31 I will make your c. waste, and 5892
Le 26:33 shall be desolate, and your c. waste. 5892
Nu 13:19 what c. they be that they dwell in, 5892
Nu 13:28 and the c. are walled, and very 5892
Nu 21:2 then I will utterly destroy their c. 5892
Nu 21:3 utterly destroyed them and their c. 5892
Nu 21:25 Israel took all these c.: and Israel 5892
Nu 21:25 dwelt in all the c. of the Amorites, 5892
Nu 31:10 burnt all their c. wherein they 5892
Nu 32:16 cattle, and c. for our little ones: 5892
Nu 32:17 ones shall dwell in the fenced c. 5892
Nu 32:24 Build you c. for your little ones, 5892
Nu 32:26 shall be there in the c. of Gilead: 5892
Nu 32:33 with the c. thereof in the coasts, 5892
Nu 32:33 the c. of the country round about. 5892
Nu 32:36 and Beth-haran, fenced c. 5892
Nu 32:38 unto the c. which they builded. 5892
Nu 35:2 of their possession c. to dwell in; 5892
Nu 35:2 unto the Levites suburbs for the c. 5892
Nu 35:3 the c. shall they have to dwell in; 5892
Nu 35:4 And the suburbs of the c., which 5892
Nu 35:5 be to them the suburbs of the c. 5892
Nu 35:6 among the c. which ye shall give 5892
Nu 35:6 there shall be six c. for refuge, 5892
Nu 35:6 them ye shall add forty and two c. 5892
Nu 35:7 all the c. which ye shall give to 5892
Nu 35:7 Levites shall be forty and eight c. 5892
Nu 35:8 And the c. which ye shall give 5892
Nu 35:8 give of his c. unto the Levites 5892
Nu 35:11 ye shall appoint you c. to be 5892
Nu 35:11 to be c. of refuge for you; 5892
Nu 35:12 they shall be unto you c. for refuge 5892
Nu 35:13 And of these c. which ye shall give 5892
Nu 35:13 six c. shall ye have for refuge. 5892
Nu 35:14 give three c. on this side Jordan, 5892
Nu 35:14 three c. shall ye give in the land 5892
Nu 35:14 which shall be c. of refuge. 5892
Nu 35:15 These six c. shall be a refuge, 5892
De 1:22 and into what c. we shall come. 5892
De 1:28 the c. are great and walled up 5892
De 2:34 took all his c. at that time, 5892
De 2:35 the spoil of the c. which we took. 5892
De 2:37 nor unto the c. in the mountains, 5892
De 3:4 we took all his c. at that time, 5892
De 3:4 took not from them, threescore c., 5892
De 3:5 All these c. were fenced with high 5892
De 3:7 spoil of the c., we took for a prey 5892
De 3:10 the c. of the plain, and all Gilead, 5892
De 3:10 c. of the kingdom of Og in Bashan. 5892
De 3:12 half mount Gilead, and the c. 5892
De 3:19 abide in your c. which I have given 5892
De 4:41 Then Moses severed three c. on 5892
De 4:42 that fleeing unto one of these c. he 5892
De 6:10 to give thee great and goodly c., 5892
De 9:1 c. great and fenced up to heaven, 5892
De 13:12 thou shalt hear say in one of thy c., 5892
De 19:1 and dwellest in their c., and in 5892
De 19:2 three c. for thee in the midst of 5892
De 19:5 he shall flee unto one of those c., 5892
De 19:7 Thou shalt separate three c. for 5892
De 19:9 then shalt thou add three c. more 5892
De 19:11 and fleeth into one of these c.; 5892
De 20:15 Thus shalt thou do unto all the c. 5892
De 20:15 are not of the c. of these nations, 5892
De 20:16 But of the c. of these people, which 5892
De 21:2 they shall measure unto the c. 5892
Jos 9:17 and came unto their c. on the third 5892
Jos 9:17 c. were Gibeon, and Chephirah, 5892
Jos 10:2 a great city, as one of the royal c., 5892
Jos 10:19 them not to enter into their c. 5892
Jos 10:20 of them entered into fenced c. 5892
Jos 10:37 all the c. thereof, and all the souls 5892
Jos 10:39 king thereof, and all the c. thereof; 5892
Jos 11:12 all the c. of those kings, and all the 5892
Jos 11:13 c. that stood still in their strength, 5892
Jos 11:14 all the spoil of these c., and the 5892
Jos 11:21 them utterly with their c. 5892
Jos 13:10 c. of Sihon king of the Amorites, 5892
Jos 13:17 Heshbon, and all her c. that are in 5892
Jos 13:21 all the c. of the plain, and all the 5892
Jos 13:23 families, the c. and the villages 5892
Jos 13:25 all the c. of Gilead, and half the 5892
Jos 13:28 families, the c., and their villages. 5892
Jos 13:30 which are in Bashan, threescore c. 5892
Jos 13:31 c. of the kingdom of Og in Bashan, 5892
Jos 14:4 c. to dwell in, with their suburbs 5892
Jos 14:12 that the c. were great and fenced: 5892
Jos 15:9 out to the c. of mount Ephron; 5892
Jos 15:21 uttermost c. of the tribe of the 5892
Jos 15:32 all the c. are twenty and nine, 5892
Jos 15:36 fourteen c. with their villages. 5892
Jos 15:41 sixteen c. with their villages. 5892
Jos 15:44 nine c. with their villages. 5892
Jos 15:51 eleven c. with their villages. 5892
Jos 15:54 nine c. with their villages; 5892
Jos 15:57 ten c. with their villages. 5892
Jos 15:59 six c. with their villages. 5892
Jos 15:60 two c. with their villages. 5892
Jos 15:62 six c. with their villages. 5892
Jos 16:9 separate c. for the children 5892
Jos 16:9 all the c. with their villages. 5892
Jos 17:9 these c. of Ephraim are among 5892
Jos 17:9 are among the c. of Manasseh; 5892
Jos 17:12 out the inhabitants of those c.; 5892
Jos 18:9 the land, and described it by c. 5892
Jos 18:21 c. of the tribe of the children of 5892
Jos 18:24 twelve c. with their villages: 5892
Jos 18:28 fourteen c. with their villages. 5892

Book	Ref.	Context	No.
Jos	19:6	thirteen **c.** with their villages:	5892
Jos	19:7	four **c.** and their villages:	5892
Jos	19:8	that were round about these **c.**	5892
Jos	19:15	twelve **c.** with their villages	5892
Jos	19:16	these **c.** with their villages	5892
Jos	19:22	sixteen **c.** with their villages	5892
Jos	19:23	the **c.** and their villages	5892
Jos	19:30	twenty and two **c.** with their	5892
Jos	19:31	these **c.** with their villages	5892
Jos	19:35	And the fenced **c.** are Ziddim, Zer,	5892
Jos	19:38	nineteen **c.** with their villages	5892
Jos	19:39	the **c.** and their villages	5892
Jos	19:48	these **c.** with their villages	5892
Jos	20:2	Appoint out for you **c.** of refuge,	5892
Jos	20:4	flee unto one of those **c.** shall stand	5892
Jos	20:9	**c.** appointed for all the children of	5892
Jos	21:2	to give us **c.** to dwell in, with the	5892
Jos	21:3	Lord, these **c.** and their suburbs	5892
Jos	21:4	the tribe of Benjamin, thirteen **c.**	5892
Jos	21:5	the half tribe of Manasseh, ten **c.**	5892
Jos	21:6	of Manasseh in Bashan, thirteen **c.**	5892
Jos	21:7	of the tribe of Zebulun, twelve **c.**	5892
Jos	21:8	by lot unto the Levites these **c.**	5892
Jos	21:9	these **c.** which are here mentioned	5892
Jos	21:16	nine **c.** out of those two tribes	5892
Jos	21:18	Almon with her suburbs; four **c.**	5892
Jos	21:19	All the **c.** of the children of Aaron,	5892
Jos	21:19	were thirteen **c.** with their suburbs	5892
Jos	21:20	they had the **c.** of their lot out of	5892
Jos	21:22,	24 with her suburbs; four **c.**	5892
Jos	21:25	with her suburbs; two **c.**	5892
Jos	21:26	All the **c.** were ten with their	5892
Jos	21:27	with her suburbs; two **c.**	5892
Jos	21:29	with her suburbs; four **c.**	5892
Jos	21:31	Rehob with her suburbs; four **c.**	5892
Jos	21:32	Kartan with her suburbs; three **c.**	5892
Jos	21:33	All the **c.** of the Gershonites were	5892
Jos	21:33	were thirteen **c.** with their suburbs	5892
Jos	21:35	Nahalal with her suburbs; four **c.**	5892
Jos	21:37	Mephaath with her suburbs; four **c.**	5892
Jos	21:39	Jazer with her suburbs; four **c.** in	5892
Jos	21:40	the **c.** for the children of Merari by	5892
Jos	21:40	Levites, were by their lot twelve **c.**	5892
Jos	21:41	All the **c.** of the Levites within the	5892
Jos	21:41	forty and eight **c.** with their	5892
Jos	21:42	These **c.** were every one with their	5892
Jos	21:42	about them: thus were all these **c.**	5892
Jos	24:13	**c.** which ye built not, and ye dwell	5892
Jg	10:4	they had thirty **c.**, which are called	5892
Jg	11:26	the **c.** that be along by the coasts	5892
Jg	11:33	come to Minnith, even twenty **c.**,	5892
Jg	12:7	buried in one of the **c.** of Gilead	5892
Jg	20:14	themselves together out of the **c.**	5892
Jg	20:15	numbered at that time out of the **c.**	5892
Jg	20:42	them which came out of the **c.**	5892
Jg	20:48	they set on fire all the **c.** that they	5892
Jg	21:23	repaired the **c.**, and dwelt in them	5892
1Sa	6:18	the number of all the **c.** of the	5892
1Sa	6:18	of fenced **c.**, and of country villages,	5892
1Sa	7:14	the **c.** which the Philistines had	5892
1Sa	18:6	women came out of all **c.** of Israel,	5892
1Sa	30:29	in the **c.** of the Jerahmeelites, and	5892
1Sa	30:29	which were in the **c.** of the Kenites,	5892
1Sa	31:7	dead, they forsook the **c.**, and fled;	5892
2Sa	2:1	go up into any of the **c.** of Judah?	5892
2Sa	2:3	and they dwelt in the **c.** of Hebron	5892
2Sa	8:8	and from Berothai, **c.** of Hadadezer,	5892
2Sa	10:12	people, and for the **c.** of our God:	5892
2Sa	12:31	the **c.** of the children of Ammon	5892
2Sa	20:6	he get him fenced **c.**, and escape	5892
2Sa	24:7	all the **c.** of the Hivites, and of the	5892
1Ki	4:13	threescore great **c.** with walls and	5892
1Ki	8:37	besiege them in the land of their **c.**;	8179
1Ki	9:11	Solomon gave Hiram twenty **c.** in	5892
1Ki	9:12	came out from Tyre to see the **c.**	5892
1Ki	9:13	What **c.** are these which thou hast	5892
1Ki	9:19	the **c.** of store that Solomon had,	5892
1Ki	9:19	and **c.** for his chariots,	5892
1Ki	9:19	and **c.** for his horsemen,	5892
1Ki	10:26	he bestowed in the **c.** for chariots,	5892
1Ki	12:17	Israel which dwelt in the **c.** of	5892
1Ki	13:32	high places which are in the **c.** of	5892
1Ki	15:20	he had against the **c.** of Israel,	5892
1Ki	15:23	he did, and the **c.** which he built,	5892
1Ki	20:34	The **c.**, which my father took from	5892
1Ki	22:39	all the **c.** that he built, are they	5892
2Ki	3:25	And they beat down the **c.**, and on	5892
2Ki	13:25	son of Hazael the **c.**, which he had	5892
2Ki	13:25	and recovered the **c.** of Israel	5892
2Ki	17:6	Gozan, and in the **c.** of the Medes	5892
2Ki	17:9	them high places in all their **c.**,	5892
2Ki	17:24	placed them in the **c.** of Samaria	5892
2Ki	17:24	Samaria, and dwelt in the **c.**	5892
2Ki	17:26	and placed in the **c.** of Samaria,	5892
2Ki	17:29	every nation in their **c.** wherein	5892
2Ki	18:11	and in the **c.** of the Medes:	5892
2Ki	18:13	come up against all the fenced **c.**	5892
2Ki	19:25	shouldest be to lay waste fenced **c.**	5892
2Ki	23:5	the high places in the **c.** of Judah,	5892
2Ki	23:8	all the priests out of the **c.** of Judah,	5892
2Ki	23:19	the high places that were in the **c.**	5892
1Ch	2:22	Jair, who had three and twenty **c.**	5892
1Ch	2:23	towns thereof, even threescore **c.**	5892
1Ch	4:31	These were their **c.** unto the reign	5892
1Ch	4:32	and Tochen, and Ashan, five **c.**	5892
1Ch	4:33	that were round about the same **c.**,	5892
1Ch	6:57	the sons of Aaron they gave the **c.**	5892
1Ch	6:60	All their **c.** throughout their	5892
1Ch	6:60	their families were thirteen **c.**	5892
1Ch	6:61	of the family of that tribe, were **c.**	5892
1Ch	6:61	tribe of Manasseh, by lot, ten **c.**	5892
1Ch	6:62	Manasseh in Bashan, thirteen **c.**	5892
1Ch	6:63	of the tribe of Zebulun, twelve **c.**	5892
1Ch	6:64	Israel gave to the Levites these **c.**	5892
1Ch	6:65	these **c.**, which are called by their	5892
1Ch	6:66	the sons of Kohath had **c.** of their	5892
1Ch	6:67	unto them, of the **c.** of refuge,	5892
1Ch	9:2	dwelt in their possessions in their **c.**	5892
1Ch	10:7	they forsook their **c.**, and fled:	5892
1Ch	13:2	Levites which are in their **c.** and	5892
1Ch	18:8	and from Chun, **c.** of Hadarezer,	5892
1Ch	19:7	themselves together from their **c.**,	5892
1Ch	19:13	people, and for the **c.** of our God:	5892
1Ch	20:3	so dealt David with all the **c.** of	5892
1Ch	27:25	the fields, in the **c.**, and in the	5892
2Ch	1:14	which he placed in the chariot **c.**,	5892
2Ch	6:28	besiege them in the **c.** of their	8179
2Ch	8:2	**c.** which Huram had restored	5892
2Ch	8:4	wilderness, and all the store **c.**,	5892
2Ch	8:5	fenced **c.**, with walls, gates, and	5892
2Ch	8:6	all the store **c.** that Solomon had,	5892
2Ch	8:6	and all the chariot **c.**,	5892
2Ch	8:6	and the **c.** of the horsemen,	5892
2Ch	9:25	he bestowed in the chariot **c.**, and	5892
2Ch	10:17	Israel that dwelt in the **c.** of Judah,	5892
2Ch	11:5	in Jerusalem, and built **c.** for	5892
2Ch	11:10	Judah and in Benjamin fenced **c.**	5892
2Ch	12:4	he took the fenced **c.** which	5892
2Ch	13:19	and took **c.** from him, Bethel with	5892
2Ch	14:5	out of all the **c.** of Judah the high	5892
2Ch	14:6	he built fenced **c.** in Judah: for	5892
2Ch	14:7	unto Judah, Let us build these **c.**,	5892
2Ch	14:14	they smote all the **c.** round about	5892
2Ch	14:14	them: and they spoiled all the **c.**;	5892
2Ch	15:8	**c.** which he had taken from mount	5892
2Ch	16:4	captains of his armies against the **c.**	5892
2Ch	16:4	and all the store **c.** of Naphtali	5892
2Ch	17:2	placed forces in all the fenced **c.** of	5892
2Ch	17:2	and in the **c.** of Ephraim, which	5892
2Ch	17:7	to teach in the **c.** of Judah	5892
2Ch	17:9	throughout all the **c.** of Judah,	5892
2Ch	17:12	in Judah castles, and **c.** of store	5892
2Ch	17:13	much business in the **c.** of Judah:	5892
2Ch	17:19	fenced **c.** throughout all Judah	5892
2Ch	19:5	fenced **c.** of Judah, city by city,	5892
2Ch	19:10	brethren that dwell in their **c.**,	5892
2Ch	20:4	out of all the **c.** of Judah they	5892
2Ch	21:3	things, with fenced **c.** in Judah:	5892
2Ch	23:2	the Levites out of all the **c.** of	5892
2Ch	24:5	Go out unto the **c.** of Judah and	5892
2Ch	25:13	fell upon the **c.** of Judah, from	5892
2Ch	26:6	and built **c.** about Ashdod,	5892
2Ch	27:4	he built **c.** in the mountains	5892
2Ch	28:18	invaded the **c.** of the low country,	5892
2Ch	31:1	went out to the **c.** of Judah,	5892
2Ch	31:1	his possession, into their own **c.**	5892
2Ch	31:6	Judah, that dwelt in the **c.** of	5892
2Ch	31:15	in the **c.** of the priests, in their	5892
2Ch	31:19	fields of the suburbs of their **c.**,	5892
2Ch	32:1	encamped against the fenced **c.**,	5892
2Ch	32:29	Moreover he provided him **c.**, and	5892
2Ch	33:14	war in all the fenced **c.** of Judah	5892
2Ch	34:6	so did he in the **c.** of Manasseh,	5892
Ezr	2:70	the Nethinims, dwelt in their **c.**,	5892
Ezr	2:70	and all Israel in their **c.**	5892
Ezr	3:1	children of Israel were in the **c.**,	5892
Ezr	4:10	and set in the **c.** of Samaria,	7141
Ezr	10:14	taken strange wives in our **c.**	5892
Ne	7:73	and all Israel, dwelt in their **c.**;	5892
Ne	7:73	children of Israel were in their **c.**	5892
Ne	8:15	and proclaim in all their **c.**,	5892
Ne	9:25	took strong **c.**, and fat land,	5892
Ne	10:37	tithes in all the **c.** of our tillage	5892
Ne	11:1	nine parts to dwell in other **c.**	5892
Ne	11:3	in the **c.** of Judah dwelt every one	5892
Ne	11:3	in his possesion in their **c.**,	5892
Ne	11:20	the **c.** of Judah, every one in his	5892
Ne	12:44	of the fields of the **c.** the portions	5892
Es	9:2	themselves together in their **c.**	5892
Job	15:28	he dwelleth in desolate **c.**, and in	5892
Ps	9:6	and thou hast destroyed **c.**; their	5892
Ps	69:35	and will build the **c.** of Judah:	5892
Isa	1:7	**c.** are burned with fire: your land,	5892
Isa	6:11	**c.** be wasted without inhabitant,	5892
Isa	14:17	and destroyed the **c.** thereof;	5892
Isa	14:21	fill the face of the world with **c.**	5892
Isa	17:2	The **c.** of Aroer are forsaken:	5892
Isa	17:9	strong **c.** be as a forsaken bough,	5892
Isa	19:18	five **c.** in the land of Egypt speak	5892
Isa	33:8	hath despised the **c.**, he regardeth	5892
Isa	36:1	all the defenced **c.** of Judah,	5892
Isa	37:26	be to lay waste defenced **c.**	5892
Isa	40:9	say unto the **c.** of Judah, Behold	5892
Isa	42:11	the wilderness and the **c.** thereof	5892
Isa	44:26	and to the **c.** of Judah, Ye shall be	5892
Isa	54:3	the desolate **c.** to be inhabited	5892
Isa	61:4	they shall repair the waste **c.**, the	5892
Isa	64:10	Thy holy **c.** are a wilderness,	5892
Jer	1:15	and against all the **c.** of Judah,	5892
Jer	2:15	**c.** are burned without inhabitant	5892
Jer	2:28	the number of thy **c.** are thy gods,	5892
Jer	4:5	and let us go into the defenced **c.**	5892
Jer	4:7	thy **c.** shall be laid waste, without	5892
Jer	4:16	their voice against the **c.** of Judah	5892
Jer	4:26	the **c.** thereof were broken down	5892
Jer	5:6	leopard shall watch over their **c.**	5892
Jer	5:17	shall impoverish thy fenced **c.**,	5892
Jer	7:17	what they do in the **c.** of Judah	5892
Jer	7:34	to cease from the **c.** of Judah,	5892
Jer	8:14	let us enter into the defenced **c.**,	5892
Jer	9:11	will make the **c.** of Judah desolate,	5892
Jer	10:22	to make the **c.** of Judah desolate,	5892
Jer	11:6	all these words in the **c.** of Judah,	5892
Jer	11:12	Then shall the **c.** of Judah and	5892
Jer	11:13	number of thy **c.** were thy gods,	5892
Jer	13:19	**c.** of the south shall be shut up,	5892
Jer	17:26	shall come from the **c.** of Judah	5892
Jer	20:16	the **c.** which the Lord overthrew,	5892
Jer	22:6	and **c.** which are not inhabited	5892
Jer	25:18	Jerusalem, and the **c.** of Judah,	5892
Jer	26:2	speak unto all the **c.** of Judah,	5892
Jer	31:21	turn again to these thy **c.**,	5892
Jer	31:23	of Judah and in the **c.** thereof,	5892
Jer	31:24	in Judah itself, and in all the **c.**	5892
Jer	32:44	Jerusalem, and in the **c.** of Judah,	5892
Jer	32:44	and in the **c.** of the mountains,	5892
Jer	32:44	and in the **c.** of the valley,	5892
Jer	32:44	and in the **c.** of the south:	5892
Jer	33:10	**c.** of Judah, and in the streets of	5892
Jer	33:12	**c.** thereof, shall be an habitation	5892
Jer	33:13	In the **c.** of the mountains, in the	5892
Jer	33:13	**c.** of the vale, and in the **c.** of the	5892
Jer	33:13	Jerusalem, and in the **c.** of Judah,	5892
Jer	34:1	and against all the **c.** thereof,	5892
Jer	34:7	and against all the **c.** of Judah	5892
Jer	34:7	Azekah: for these defenced **c.**	5892
Jer	34:7	remained of the **c.** of Judah	5892
Jer	34:22	make the **c.** of Judah a desolation	5892
Jer	36:6	all Judah that come out of their **c.**	5892
Jer	36:9	the **c.** of Judah unto Jerusalem	5892
Jer	40:5	governor over the **c.** of Judah,	5892
Jer	40:10	in your **c.** that ye have taken	5892
Jer	44:2	upon all the **c.** of Judah; and,	5892
Jer	44:6	and was kindled in the **c.** of Judah	5892
Jer	44:17	and our princes, in the **c.** of Judah,	5892
Jer	44:21	that ye burned in the **c.** of Judah,	5892
Jer	48:9	for the **c.** thereof shall be desolate,	5892
Jer	48:15	spoiled, and gone up out of her **c.**,	5892
Jer	48:24	all the **c.** of the land of Moab, far	5892
Jer	48:28	ye that dwell in Moab, leave the **c.**,	5892
Jer	49:1	and his people dwell in his **c.**?	5892

Jer 49:13 the **c.** thereof shall be perpetual 5892
Jer 49:18 and the neighbour **c.** thereof, 5892
Jer 50:32 I will kindle a fire in his **c.**, and it 5892
Jer 50:40 Gomorrah and the neighbour **c.**
Jer 51:43 **c.** are a desolation, a dry land, 5892
La 5:11 and the maids in the **c.** of Judah, 5892
Eze 6:6 the **c.** shall be laid waste, 5892
Eze 12:20 And the **c.** that are inhabited shall 5892
Eze 19:7 palaces, and he laid waste their **c.**; 5892
Eze 25:9 open the side of Moab from the **c.**, 5892
Eze 25:9 his **c.** which are on his frontiers, 5892
Eze 26:19 like the **c.** that are not inhabited; 5892
Eze 29:12 that are desolate, and her **c.** 5892
Eze 29:12 among the **c.** that are laid waste 5892
Eze 30:7 and her **c.** shall be in the midst 5892
Eze 30:7 of the **c.** that are wasted. 5892
Eze 30:17 and these **c.** shall go into captivity.
Eze 35:4 I will lay thy **c.** waste, and thou 5892
Eze 35:9 and thy **c.** shall not return: and 5892
Eze 36:4 and to the **c.** that are forsaken, 5892
Eze 36:10 the **c.** shall be inhabited, and the 5892
Eze 36:33 also cause you to dwell in the **c.**, 5892
Eze 36:35 ruined **c.** are become fenced, 5892
Eze 36:38 waste **c.** be filled with flocks of 5892
Eze 39:9 in the **c.** of Israel shall go forth, 5892
Da 11:15 and take the most fenced **c.** 5892
Ho 8:14 Judah hath multiplied fenced **c.** 5892
Ho 8:14 but I will send a fire upon his **c.**, 5892
Ho 11:6 the sword shall abide on his **c.**, 5892
Ho 13:10 that may save thee in all thy **c.**? 5892
Am 4:6 cleanness of teeth in all your **c.**, 5892
Am 4:8 three **c.** wandered unto one city, 5892
Am 9:14 they shall build the waste **c.**, and 5892
Ob 20 shall possess the **c.** of the south. 5892
Mic 5:11 I will cut off the **c.** of thy land, 5892
Mic 5:14 so will I destroy thy **c.** 5892
Mic 7:12 Assyria, and from the fortified **c.**, 5892
Zep 1:16 and alarm against the fenced **c.**, 5892
Zep 3:6 their **c.** are destroyed, so that 5892
Zec 1:12 Jerusalem and on the **c.** of Judah. 5892
Zec 1:17 My **c.** through prosperity shall yet 5892
Zec 7:7 in prosperity, and the **c.** thereof 5892
Zec 8:20 and the inhabitants of many **c.** 5892
Mt 9:35 Jesus went about all the **c.** and *4172*
Mt 10:23 **over the c. of Israel, till the Son** *4172*
Mt 11:1 to teach and to preach in their **c.** *4172*
Mt 11:20 Then began he to upbraid the **c.** *4172*
Mt 14:13 followed him on foot out of the **c.** *4172*
Mk 6:33 and ran afoot thither out of all **c.** *4172*
Mk 6:56 into villages, or **c.**, or country, *4172*
Lu 4:43 **kingdom of God to other c. also:** *4172*
Lu 13:22 went through the **c.** and villages *4172*
Lu 19:17 **have thou authority over ten c.** *4172*
Lu 19:19 **to him, Be thou also over five c.** *4172*
Ac 5:16 out of the **c.** round about *4172*
Ac 8:40 he preached in all the **c.**, till he *4172*
Ac 14:6 Lystra and Derbe, **c.** of Lycaonia, *4172*
Ac 16:4 through the **c.**, they delivered *4172*
Ac 26:11 them even unto strange **c.** *4172*
2Pe 2:6 **c.** of Sodom and Gomorrha into *4172*
Jude 7 Gomorrha, and the **c.** about them *4172*
Re 16:19 parts, and the **c.** of the nations *4172*

CITIZEN See also CITIZENS.
Lu 15:15 **himself to a c. of that country;** *4177*
Ac 21:39 in Cilicia, a **c.** of no mean city: *4177*

CITIZENS See also FELLOWCITIZENS.
Lu 19:14 **But his c. hated him, and sent a** *4177*

CITY See also CITIES.
Ge 4:17 and he builded a **c.**, and called 5892
Ge 4:17 called the name of the **c.**, after 5892
Ge 10:11 and the **c.** Rehoboth, and Calah, 5892
Ge 10:12 and Calah: the same is a great **c.** 5892
Ge 11:4 let us build us a **c.** and a tower, 5892
Ge 11:5 the Lord came down to see the **c.** 5892
Ge 11:8 and they left off to build the **c.** 5892
Ge 18:24 be fifty righteous within the **c.** 5892
Ge 18:26 Sodom fifty righteous within the **c.**, 5892
Ge 18:28 destroy all the **c.** for lack of five? 5892
Ge 19:4 of the **c.**, even the men of Sodom, 5892
Ge 19:12 whatsoever thou hast in the **c.**, 5892
Ge 19:14 for the Lord will destroy this **c.** 5892
Ge 19:15 consumed in the iniquity of the **c.** 5892
Ge 19:16 forth, and set him without the **c.** 5892
Ge 19:20 this **c.** is near to flee unto, and it 5892
Ge 19:21 I will not overthrow this **c.**, for the 5892
Ge 19:22 the name of the **c.** was called Zoar. 5892
Ge 23:10 in at the gate of his **c.**, saying, 5892
Ge 23:18 that went in at the gate of his **c.** 5892
Ge 24:10 Mesopotamia, unto the **c.** of Nahor 5892
Ge 24:11 to kneel down without the **c.** 5892
Ge 24:13 of the men of the **c.** come out 5892
Ge 26:33 the name of the **c.** is Beer-sheba 5892
Ge 28:19 name of that **c.** was called Luz 5892
Ge 33:18 Jacob came to Shalem, a **c.** of 5892
Ge 33:18 and pitched his tent before the **c.** 5892
Ge 34:20 came unto the gate of their **c.**, 5892
Ge 34:20 with the men of their **c.**, saying, 5892
Ge 34:24 that went out of the gate of his **c.**; 5892
Ge 34:24 that went out of the gate of his **c.**; 5892
Ge 34:25 **c.** boldly, and slew all the males 5892
Ge 34:27 upon the slain, and spoiled the **c.**, 5892
Ge 34:28 and that which was in the **c.**, 5892
Ge 35:27 **c.** of Arbah, which is Hebron, 7151
Ge 36:32 name of his **c.** was Dinhabah. 5892
Ge 36:35 the name of his **c.** was Avith. 5892
Ge 36:39 the name of his **c.** was Pau; and 5892
Ge 41:48 which was round about every **c.**, 5892
Ge 44:4 when they were gone out of the **c.**, 5892
Ge 44:13 his ass, and returned to the **c.** 5892
Ex 9:29 As soon as I am gone out of the **c.**, 5892
Ex 9:33 Moses went out of the **c.** from 5892
Le 14:40 an unclean place without the **c.** 5892
Le 14:41 that they scrape off without the **c.** 5892
Le 14:45 carry them forth out of the **c.** 5892
Le 14:53 let go the living bird out of the **c.** 5892
Le 25:29 a dwelling house in a walled **c.**, 5892
Le 25:30 the house that is in the walled **c.** 5892
Le 25:33 sold, and the **c.** of his possession, 5892
Nu 20:16 Kadesh, a **c.** in the uttermost of 5892
Nu 21:26 Heshbon was the **c.** of Sihon the 5892
Nu 21:27 **c.** of Sihon be built and prepared: 5892
Nu 21:28 a flame from the **c.** of Sihon: 7151
Nu 22:36 meet him unto a **c.** of Moab, 5892
Nu 24:19 him that remaineth of the **c.** 5892
Nu 35:4 the wall of the **c.** and outward a 5892
Nu 35:5 shall measure from without the **c.** 5892
Nu 35:5 the **c.** shall be in the midst: 5892
Nu 35:25 shall restore him to the **c.** 5892
Nu 35:26 the border of the **c.** of his refuge, 5892
Nu 35:27 him without the borders of the **c.** 5892
Nu 35:28 remained in the **c.** of his refuge 5892
Nu 35:32 that is fled to the **c.** of his refuge, 5892
De 2:34 and the little ones, of every **c.**, 5892
De 2:36 and from the **c.** that is by the 5892
De 2:36 there was not one **c.** too strong 7151
De 3:4 not a **c.** which we took not from 7151
De 3:6 women, and children, of every **c.** 5892
De 13:13 the inhabitants of their **c.**, saying, 5892
De 13:15 smite the inhabitants of that **c.** 5892
De 13:16 and shalt burn with fire the **c.**, 5892
De 19:12 elders of his **c.** shall send and fetch 5892
De 20:10 When thou comest nigh unto a **c.** 5892
De 20:14 and all that is in the **c.**, even all the 5892
De 20:19 When thou shalt besiege a **c.** a long 5892
De 20:20 shalt build bulwarks against the **c.** 5892
De 21:3 the **c.** which is next unto the slain 5892
De 21:3 even the elders of that **c.** shall take 5892
De 21:4 elders of that **c.** shall bring down 5892
De 21:6 all the elders of that **c.**, that are 5892
De 21:19 him out unto the elders of his **c.**, 5892
De 21:20 shall say unto the elders of his **c.**, 5892
De 21:21 all the men of his **c.** shall stone 5892
De 22:15 the elders of the **c.** in the gate: 5892
De 22:17 the cloth before the elders of the **c.** 5892
De 22:18 elders of that **c.** shall take that 5892
De 22:21 the men of her **c.** shall stone her 5892
De 22:23 and a man find her in the **c.**, 5892
De 22:24 both out unto the gate of that **c.**, 5892
De 22:24 she cried not, being in the **c.**; 5892
De 25:8 the elders of his **c.** shall call him, 5892
De 28:3 Blessed shalt thou be in the **c.**, 5892
De 28:16 Cursed shalt thou be in the **c.**, and 5892
De 34:3 of Jericho, the **c.** of palm 5892
Jos 3:16 far from the **c.** Adam, that is 5892
Jos 6:3 And ye shall compass the **c.**, all ye 5892
Jos 6:3 go round about the **c.** once. Thus 5892
Jos 6:4 seventh day ye shall compass the **c.** 5892
Jos 6:5 wall of the **c.** shall fall down flat, 5892
Jos 6:7 Pass on, and compass the **c.**, and 5892
Jos 6:11 ark of the Lord compassed the **c.** 5892
Jos 6:14 second day they compassed the **c.** 5892
Jos 6:15 compassed the **c.** after the same 5892
Jos 6:15 day they compassed the **c.** seven 5892
Jos 6:16 for the Lord hath given you the **c.** 5892
Jos 6:17 the **c.** shall be accursed, even it, 5892
Jos 6:20 people went up into the **c.**, every 5892
Jos 6:20 before him, and they took the **c.** 5892
Jos 6:21 destroyed all that was in the **c.**, 5892
Jos 6:24 And they burnt the **c.** with fire, 5892
Jos 6:26 that riseth up and buildeth this **c.** 5892
Jos 8:1 king of Ai, and his people, and his **c.**, 5892
Jos 8:2 lay thee an ambush for the **c.** behind 5892
Jos 8:4 lie in wait against the **c.**, 5892
Jos 8:4 even behind the **c.**: 5892
Jos 8:4 go not very far from the **c.**, 5892
Jos 8:5 with me, will approach unto the **c.** 5892
Jos 8:6 we have drawn them from the **c.**; 5892
Jos 8:7 the ambush, and seize upon the **c.** 5892
Jos 8:8 when ye have taken the **c.**, 5892
Jos 8:8 that ye shall set the **c.** on fire: 5892
Jos 8:11 drew nigh, and came before the **c.**, 5892
Jos 8:12 and Ai, on the west side of the **c.** 5892
Jos 8:13 host that was on the north of the **c.**, 5892
Jos 8:13 liers in wait on the west of the **c.**, 5892
Jos 8:14 the men of the **c.** went out against 5892
Jos 8:14 ambush against him behind the **c.** 5892
Jos 8:16 and were drawn away from the **c.** 5892
Jos 8:17 and they left the **c.** open, and 5892
Jos 8:18 he had in his hand toward the **c.** 5892
Jos 8:19 they entered into the **c.**, and took it, 5892
Jos 8:19 and hasted and set the **c.** on fire. 5892
Jos 8:20 the smoke of the **c.** ascended up to 5892
Jos 8:21 the ambush had taken the **c.**, and 5892
Jos 8:21 that the smoke of the **c.** ascended 5892
Jos 8:22 And the other issued out of the **c.** 5892
Jos 8:27 the spoil of that **c.** Israel took for 5892
Jos 8:29 the entering of the gate of the **c.**, 5892
Jos 10:2 Gibeon was a great **c.**, as one of 5892
Jos 11:19 not a **c.** that made peace with the 5892
Jos 13:9, 16 **c.** ... in the midst of the river, 5892
Jos 15:13 the **c.** of Arba the father of Anak, 7151
Jos 15:13 which **c.** is Hebron.
Jos 15:62 Nibshan, and the **c.** of Salt, 5892
Jos 18:14 Kirjath-jearim, a **c.** of the 5892
Jos 19:29 the strong **c.** Tyre; and the coast 5892
Jos 19:50 gave him the **c.** which he asked, 5892
Jos 19:50 he built the **c.**, and dwelt therein. 5892
Jos 20:4 at the entering of the gate of the **c.**, 5892
Jos 20:4 in the ears of the elders of that **c.**, 5892
Jos 20:4 shall take him into the **c.** unto them, 5892
Jos 20:6 shall dwell in that **c.**, until he stand 5892
Jos 20:6 return, and come unto his own **c.**, 5892
Jos 20:6 unto the **c.** from whence he fled. 5892
Jos 21:11 they gave them the **c.** of Arba 7151
Jos 21:11 which **c.** is Hebron, in the hill
Jos 21:12 fields of the **c.**, and the villages 5892
Jos 21:13, 21,27,32,38, **c.** of refuge...slayer; 5892
Jg 1:8 the sword, and set the **c.** on fire 5892
Jg 1:16 out of the **c.** of palm trees with 5892
Jg 1:17 name of the **c.** was called Hormah. 5892
Jg 1:23 the name of the **c.** before was Luz.) 5892
Jg 1:24 saw a man come forth out of the **c.**, 5892
Jg 1:24 the entrance into the **c.**, and we will 5892
Jg 1:25 them the entrance into the **c.**, 5892
Jg 1:25 they smote the **c.** with the edge of 5892
Jg 1:26 land of the Hittites and built a **c.**, 5892
Jg 3:13 and possessed the **c.** of palm trees. 5892
Jg 6:27 household, and the men of the **c.**, 5892
Jg 6:28 when the men of the **c.** arose early 5892
Jg 6:30 the men of the **c.** said unto Joash, 5892
Jg 8:16 And he took the elders of the **c.**, 5892
Jg 8:17 and slew the men of the **c.** 5892
Jg 8:27 ephod thereof, and put it in his **c.**, 5892
Jg 9:30 Zebul the ruler of the **c.** heard 5892
Jg 9:31 they fortify the **c.** against thee. 5892
Jg 9:33 rise early, and set upon the **c.** 5892
Jg 9:35 the entering of the gate of the **c.** 5892
Jg 9:43 were come forth out of the **c.**; 5892
Jg 9:44 in the entering of the gate of the **c.** 5892
Jg 9:45 Abimelech fought against the **c.** all 5892
Jg 9:45 that day; and he took the **c.**, 5892
Jg 9:45 and beat down the **c.** and sowed it 5892
Jg 9:51 was a strong tower within the **c.**, 5892
Jg 9:51 and women, and all they of the **c.**, 5892
Jg 14:18 the men of the **c.** said unto him on 5892
Jg 16:2 him all night in the gate of the **c.**, 5892
Jg 16:3 took the doors of the gate of the **c.**, 5892
Jg 17:8 the man departed out of the **c.** 5892
Jg 18:27 and burnt the **c.** with fire 5892

Jg 18:28 they built a **c.** and dwelt therein......... 5892
Jg 18:29 they called the name of the **c.** Dan,..... 5892
Jg 18:29 name of the **c.** was Laish at the first.... 5892
Jg 19:11 turn in into this **c.** of the Jebusites,..... 5892
Jg 19:12 hither into the **c.** of a stranger,.......... 5892
Jg 19:15 sat him down in a street of the **c.**....... 5892
Jg 19:17 man in the street of the **c.**................ 5892
Jg 19:22 men of the **c.**, certain sons of Belial,.... 5892
Jg 20:11 Israel were gathered against the **c.**,...... 5892
Jg 20:31 were drawn away from the **c.**; and...... 5892
Jg 20:32 them from the **c.** unto the highways.... 5892
Jg 20:37 smote all the **c.** with the edge of......... 5892
Jg 20:38 with smoke rise up out of the **c.**.......... 5892
Jg 20:40 began to arise up out of the **c.**............ 5892
Jg 20:40 the flame of the **c.** ascended up to....... 5892
Jg 20:48 as well the men of every **c.**, as the..... 5892
Ru 1:19 all the **c.** was moved about them,........ 5892
Ru 2:18 took it up, and went into the **c.**.......... 5892
Ru 3:11 the **c.** of my people doth know.......... 8179
Ru 3:15 on her: and she went into the **c.**......... 5892
Ru 4:2 took ten men of the elders of the **c.**,.... 5892
1Sa 1:3 this man went up out of his **c.**............ 5892
1Sa 4:13 when the man came into the **c.**,.......... 5892
1Sa 4:13 told it, all the **c.** cried out................ 5892
1Sa 5:9 hand of the Lord was against the **c.**...... 5892
1Sa 5:9 he smote the men of the **c.**,............... 5892
1Sa 5:11 destruction throughout all the **c.**;......... 5892
1Sa 5:12 cry of the **c.** went up to heaven,......... 5892
1Sa 8:22 Go ye every man unto his **c.**............... 5892
1Sa 9:6 there is in this **c.** a man of God,......... 5892
1Sa 9:10 the **c.** where the man of God was....... 5892
1Sa 9:11 as they went up the hill to the **c.**,........ 5892
1Sa 9:12 for he came to day to the **c.**; for......... 5892
1Sa 9:13 As soon as ye be come into the **c.**,...... 5892
1Sa 9:14 they went up into the **c.**: and............ 5892
1Sa 9:14 when they were come into the **c.**,....... 5892
1Sa 9:25 from the high place into the **c.**,........... 5892
1Sa 9:27 going down to the end of the **c.**,.......... 5892
1Sa 10:5 thou art come thither to the **c.**,......... 5892
1Sa 15:5 Saul came to a **c.** of Amalek, and........ 5892
1Sa 20:6 he might run to Beth-lehem his **c.**........ 5892
1Sa 20:29 family hath a sacrifice in the **c.**;.......... 5892
1Sa 20:40 him, Go, carry them to the **c.**............ 5892
1Sa 20:42 and Jonathan went into the **c.**............. 5892
1Sa 22:19 Nob, the **c.** of the priests, smote he.... 5892
1Sa 23:10 to destroy the **c.** for my sake............ 5892
1Sa 27:5 thy servant dwell in the royal **c.**.......... 5892
1Sa 28:3 him in Ramah, even in his own **c.**........ 5892
1Sa 30:3 David and his men came to the **c.**,........ 5892
2Sa 5:7 Zion: the same is the **c.** of David........ 5892
2Sa 5:9 fort, and called it the **c.** of David......... 5892
2Sa 6:10 unto him into the **c.** of David: but....... 5892
2Sa 6:12 the house of Obed-edom into the **c.**...... 5892
2Sa 6:16 ark of the Lord came into the **c.**.......... 5892
2Sa 10:3 to search the **c.**, and to spy it out,...... 5892
2Sa 10:14 and entered into the **c.** So Joab.......... 5892
2Sa 11:16 to pass, when Joab observed the **c.**,..... 5892
2Sa 11:17 the men of the **c.** went out, and......... 5892
2Sa 11:20 approached ye so nigh unto the **c.**....... 5892
2Sa 11:25 battle more strong against the **c.**......... 5892
2Sa 12:1 There were two men in one **c.**;.......... 5892
2Sa 12:26 of Ammon, and took the royal **c.**......... 5892
2Sa 12:27 and have taken the **c.** of waters.......... 5892
2Sa 12:28 encamp against the **c.**, and take it:....... 5892
2Sa 12:28 lest I take the **c.**, and it be called........ 5892
2Sa 12:30 he brought forth the spoil of the **c.**....... 5892
2Sa 15:2 Of what **c.** art thou? And he said,....... 5892
2Sa 15:12 David's counseller, from his **c.**,........... 5892
2Sa 15:14 smite the **c.** with the edge of the........ 5892
2Sa 15:24 had done passing out of the **c.**............ 5892
2Sa 15:25 back the ark of God into the **c.**............ 5892
2Sa 15:27 return into the **c.** in peace, and.......... 5892
2Sa 15:34 But if thou return to the **c.**, and say.... 5892
2Sa 15:37 David's friend came into the **c.**,.......... 5892
2Sa 17:13 if he be gotten into a **c.**, then shall...... 5892
2Sa 17:13 all Israel bring ropes to that **c.**,.......... 5892
2Sa 17:17 not be seen to come into the **c.**.......... 5892
2Sa 17:23 him home to his house, to his **c.**,......... 5892
2Sa 18:3 that thou succour us out of the **c.**......... 5892
2Sa 19:3 by stealth that day into the **c.**,.......... 5892
2Sa 19:37 die in mine own **c.**, and be buried....... 5892
2Sa 20:15 they cast up a bank against the **c.**,....... 5892
2Sa 20:16 cried a wise woman out of the **c.**,........ 5892
2Sa 20:19 to destroy a **c.** and a mother in.......... 5892
2Sa 20:21 and I will depart from the **c.**.............. 5892
2Sa 20:22 they retired from the **c.**, every man.... 5892
2Sa 24:5 on the right side of the **c.** that lieth..... 5892
1Ki 1:41 of the **c.** being in an uproar?............. 7151
1Ki 1:45 **c.** rang again. This is the noise........... 7151
1Ki 2:10 and was buried in the **c.** of David........ 5892
1Ki 3:1 brought her into the **c.** of David,......... 5892
1Ki 8:1 of the Lord out of the **c.** of David,....... 5892
1Ki 8:16 I chose no **c.** out of all the tribes........ 5892
1Ki 8:44 pray unto the Lord toward the **c.**......... 5892
1Ki 8:48 the **c.** which thou hast chosen,........... 5892
1Ki 9:16 the Canaanites that dwelt in the **c.**,..... 5892
1Ki 9:24 came up out of the **c.** of David............ 5892
1Ki 11:27 the breaches of the **c.** of David........... 5892
1Ki 11:32 sake, the **c.** which I have chosen........ 5892
1Ki 11:36 Jerusalem, the **c.** which I have........... 5892
1Ki 11:43 was buried in the **c.** of David his......... 5892
1Ki 13:25 they came and told it in the **c.**............ 5892
1Ki 13:29 the old prophet came to the **c.**, to....... 5892
1Ki 14:11 that dieth of Jeroboam in the **c.**.......... 5892
1Ki 14:12 when thy feet enter into the **c.**, the..... 5892
1Ki 14:21 the **c.** which the Lord did choose........ 5892
1Ki 14:31 buried with his fathers in the **c.** of....... 5892
1Ki 15:8 they buried him in the **c.** of David:...... 5892
1Ki 15:24 buried with his fathers in the **c.** of....... 5892
1Ki 16:4 Him that dieth of Baasha in the **c.**........ 5892
1Ki 16:18 when Zimri saw that the **c.** was.......... 5892
1Ki 16:24 called the name of the **c.** which he....... 5892
1Ki 17:10 when he came to the gate of the **c.**,..... 5892
1Ki 20:2 to Ahab king of Israel into the **c.**,........ 5892
1Ki 20:12 themselves in array against the **c.**........ 5892
1Ki 20:19 the provinces came out of the **c.**,......... 5892
1Ki 20:30 the rest fled to Aphek, into the **c.**;...... 5892
1Ki 20:30 Ben-hadad fled and came into the **c.**,... 5892
1Ki 21:8 to the nobles that were in his **c.**,......... 5892
1Ki 21:11 the men of his **c.**, even the elders....... 5892
1Ki 21:11 who were the inhabitants in his **c.**,....... 5892
1Ki 21:13 they carried him forth out of the **c.**,..... 5892
1Ki 21:24 Him that dieth of Ahab in the **c.**.......... 5892
1Ki 22:26 Amon the governor of the **c.**, and....... 5892
1Ki 22:36 saying, Every man to his **c.**, and......... 5892
1Ki 22:50 buried with his fathers in the **c.** of....... 5892
2Ki 2:19 the men of the **c.** said unto Elisha,...... 5892
2Ki 2:19 the situation of this **c.** is pleasant,....... 5892
2Ki 2:23 forth little children out of the **c.**,......... 5892
2Ki 3:19 ye shall smite every fenced **c.**,............ 5892
2Ki 3:19 and every choice **c.**,.......................... 5892
2Ki 6:14 by night, and compassed the **c.**............ 5892
2Ki 6:15 an host compassed the **c.** both........... 5892
2Ki 6:19 not the way, neither is this the **c.**........ 5892
2Ki 7:4 If we say, We will enter into the **c.**,.... 5892
2Ki 7:4 then the famine is in the **c.**,............... 5892
2Ki 7:10 and called unto the porter of the **c.**....... 5892
2Ki 7:12 When they come out of the **c.**, we...... 5892
2Ki 7:12 them alive, and get into the **c.**..................
2Ki 7:13 remain, which are left in the **c.**,........... 5892
2Ki 8:24 with his fathers in the **c.** of David:...... 5892
2Ki 9:15 go forth nor escape out of the **c.**.......... 5892
2Ki 9:28 with his fathers in the **c.** of David....... 5892
2Ki 10:2 chariots and horses, a fenced **c.**........... 5892
2Ki 10:5 he that was over the **c.**, the elders...... 5892
2Ki 10:6 the great men of the **c.**, which............ 5892
2Ki 10:25 went to the **c.** of the house of Baal..... 5892
2Ki 11:20 the land rejoiced, and the **c.** was in..... 5892
2Ki 12:21 with his fathers in the **c.** of David:...... 5892
2Ki 14:20 with his fathers in the **c.** of David,...... 5892
2Ki 15:7 with his fathers in the **c.** of David:...... 5892
2Ki 15:38 in the **c.** of David his father: and......... 5892
2Ki 16:20 with his fathers in the **c.** of David:...... 5892
2Ki 17:9 of the watchman to the fenced **c.**......... 5892
2Ki 18:8 of the watchman to the fenced **c.**......... 5892
2Ki 18:30 this **c.** shall not be delivered into......... 5892
2Ki 19:13 the king of the **c.** of Sepharvaim,........ 5892
2Ki 19:32 He shall not come into this **c.**,............ 5892
2Ki 19:33 and shall not come into this **c.**,............ 5892
2Ki 19:34 I will defend this **c.**, to save it,........... 5892
2Ki 20:6 I will deliver thee and this **c.** out......... 5892
2Ki 20:6 I will defend this **c.** for mine own......... 5892
2Ki 20:20 and brought water into the **c.**, are....... 5892
2Ki 23:8 of Joshua the governor of the **c.**,........ 5892
2Ki 23:8 left hand at the gate of the **c.**............. 5892
2Ki 23:17 And the men of the **c.** told him,.......... 5892
2Ki 23:27 and will cast off this **c.** Jerusalem........ 5892
2Ki 24:10 and the **c.** was besieged.................... 5892
2Ki 24:11 of Babylon came against the **c.**,........... 5892
2Ki 25:2 the **c.** was besieged unto the............. 5892
2Ki 25:3 the famine prevailed in the **c.**,............ 5892
2Ki 25:4 And the **c.** was broken up, and all....... 5892
2Ki 25:4 the Chaldees were against the **c.**......... 5892
2Ki 25:11 the people that were left in the **c.**,...... 5892
2Ki 25:19 out of the **c.** he took an officer that..... 5892
2Ki 25:19 which were found in the **c.**, and.......... 5892
2Ki 25:19 the land that were found in the **c.**........ 5892
1Ch 1:43 the name of his **c.** was Dinhabah......... 5892
1Ch 1:46 the name of his **c.** was Avith.............. 5892
1Ch 1:50 name of his **c.** was Pai; and his........... 5892
1Ch 6:56 the fields of the **c.**, and the villages..... 5892
1Ch 6:57 namely, Hebron, the **c.** of refuge,.............
1Ch 11:5 castle of Zion, which is the **c.** of......... 5892
1Ch 11:7 they called it the **c.** of David.............. 5892
1Ch 11:8 he built the **c.** round about, even........ 5892
1Ch 11:8 and Joab repaired the rest of the **c.**...... 5892
1Ch 13:13 home to himself to the **c.** of David,..... 5892
1Ch 15:1 David made him houses in the **c.** of..... 5892
1Ch 15:29 came to the **c.** of David, that............. 5892
1Ch 19:9 in array before the gate of the **c.**......... 5892
1Ch 19:15 his brother, and entered into the **c.**...... 5892
1Ch 20:2 exceeding much spoil out of the **c.**....... 5892
2Ch 5:2 of the Lord out of the **c.** of David,....... 5892
2Ch 6:5 I chose no **c.** among all the tribes....... 5892
2Ch 6:34 they pray unto thee toward this **c.**....... 5892
2Ch 6:38 and toward the **c.** which thou hast....... 5892
2Ch 8:11 of Pharaoh out of the **c.** of David........ 5892
2Ch 9:31 he was buried in the **c.** of David......... 5892
2Ch 11:12 in every several **c.** he put shields......... 5892
2Ch 11:23 Benjamin, unto every fenced **c.**............ 5892
2Ch 12:13 the **c.** which the Lord had chosen....... 5892
2Ch 12:16 and was buried in the **c.** of David:....... 5892
2Ch 14:1 they buried him in the **c.** of David:...... 5892
2Ch 15:6 was destroyed of nation, and **c.** of **c.**..... 5892
2Ch 16:14 made for himself in the **c.** of David,..... 5892
2Ch 18:25 to Amon the governor of the **c.**,.......... 5892
2Ch 19:5 the fenced cities of Judah, **c.** by **c.**,...... 5892
2Ch 21:1 with his fathers in the **c.** of David,...... 5892
2Ch 21:20 they buried him in the **c.** of David,...... 5892
2Ch 23:21 and the **c.** was quiet, after that........... 5892
2Ch 24:16 in the **c.** of David among the kings,...... 5892
2Ch 24:25 they buried him in the **c.** of David,...... 5892
2Ch 25:28 with his fathers in the **c.** of Judah........ 5892
2Ch 27:9 they buried him in the **c.** of David:...... 5892
2Ch 28:15 Jericho, the **c.** of palm trees,............. 5892
2Ch 28:25 in every several **c.** of Judah he........... 5892
2Ch 28:27 they buried him in the **c.**, even in....... 5892
2Ch 29:20 and gathered the rulers of the **c.**,........ 5892
2Ch 30:10 the posts passed from **c.** to **c.**............ 5892
2Ch 31:19 in every several **c.**, the men that........ 5892
2Ch 32:3 which were without the **c.**................. 5892
2Ch 32:5 repaired Millo in the **c.** of David,........ 5892
2Ch 32:6 in the street of the gate of the **c.**,....... 5892
2Ch 32:18 them; that they might take the **c.**......... 5892
2Ch 32:30 to the west side of the **c.** of David...... 5892
2Ch 33:14 built a wall without the **c.** of David,..... 5892
2Ch 33:15 and cast them out of the **c.**................ 5892
2Ch 34:8 Maaseiah the governor of the **c.**,......... 5892
Ezr 2:1 Judah, every one unto his **c.**;............. 5892
Ezr 4:12 the rebellious and the bad **c.**,............. 7149
Ezr 4:13 if this **c.** be builded, and the walls....... 7149
Ezr 4:15 know that this **c.** is a rebellious **c.**,...... 7149
Ezr 4:15 which cause was this **c.** destroyed....... 7149
Ezr 4:16 if this **c.** be builded again, and the....... 7149
Ezr 4:19 and it is found that this **c.** of old......... 7149
Ezr 4:21 and that this **c.** be not builded,........... 7149
Ezr 10:14 the elders of every **c.**, and the............ 5892
Ne 2:3 when the **c.**, the place of my father's... 5892
Ne 2:5 the **c.** of my father's sepulchres,.......... 5892
Ne 2:8 house, and for the wall of the **c.**,......... 5892
Ne 3:15 the stairs that go down from the **c.**...... 5892
Ne 7:4 the **c.** was large and great: but the...... 5892
Ne 7:6 to Judah, every one unto his **c.**;.......... 5892
Ne 11:1 to dwell in Jerusalem the holy **c.**,......... 5892
Ne 11:9 of Senuah was second over the **c.**........ 5892
Ne 11:18 the Levites in the holy **c.** were........... 5892
Ne 12:37 by the stairs of the **c.** of David,........... 5892
Ne 13:18 this evil upon us, and upon this **c.**?...... 5892
Es 3:15 but the **c.** Shushan was perplexed....... 5892
Es 4:1 went out into the midst of the **c.**,......... 5892
Es 4:6 unto the street of the **c.**, which.......... 5892
Es 6:9, 11 through the street of the **c.**,.......... 5892
Es 8:11 the Jews which were in every **c.**............ 5892
Es 8:15 and the **c.** of Shushan rejoiced............ 5892
Es 8:17 in every province, and in every **c.**,....... 5892
Es 9:28 every province, and every **c.**;............... 5892
Job 24:12 Men groan from out of the **c.**,............ 5892
Job 29:7 out to the gate through the **c.**,........... 7176
Job 39:7 scorneth the multitude of the **c.**,......... 7151
Ps 31:21 kindness in a strong **c.**........................ 5892
Ps 46:4 shall make glad the **c.** of God,............ 5892

Ps	48:1	the **c.** of our God, in the mountain	5892
Ps	48:2	north, the **c.** of the great King	7151
Ps	48:8	in the **c.** of the Lord of hosts,	5892
Ps	48:8	in the **c.** of our God:	5892
Ps	55:9	seen violence and strife in the **c.**	5892
Ps	59:6,	14 dog, and go round about the **c.**	5892
Ps	60:9	will bring me into the strong **c.**?	5892
Ps	72:16	they of the **c.** shall flourish like	5892
Ps	87:3	are spoken of thee, O **c.** of God	5892
Ps	101:8	doers from the **c.** of the Lord	5892
Ps	107:4	they found no **c.** to dwell in	5892
Ps	107:7	they might go to a **c.** of habitation	5892
Ps	107:36	may prepare a **c.** for habitation;	5892
Ps	108:10	will bring me into the strong **c.**?	5892
Ps	122:3	is builded as a **c.** that is compact	5892
Ps	127:1	except the Lord keep the **c.**,	5892
Pr	1:21	in the **c.** she uttereth her words,	5892
Pr	8:3	the gates, at the entry of the **c.**,	7176
Pr	9:3	upon the highest places of the **c.**,	7176
Pr	9:14	in the high places of the **c.**,	7176
Pr	10:15	rich man's wealth is his strong **c.**	7151
Pr	11:10	the righteous, the **c.** rejoiceth:	7151
Pr	11:11	of the upright the **c.** is exalted:	7176
Pr	16:32	spirit than he that taketh a **c.**	5892
Pr	18:11	rich man's wealth is his strong **c.**,	7151
Pr	18:19	harder to be won than a strong **c.**	7151
Pr	21:22	man scaleth the **c.** of the mighty,	5892
Pr	25:28	like a **c.** that is broken down,	5892
Pr	29:8	men bring a **c.** into a snare:	7151
Ec	7:19	mighty men which are in the **c.**	5892
Ec	8:10	they were forgotten in the **c.**	5892
Ec	9:14	There was a little **c.**, and few men	5892
Ec	9:15	he by his wisdom delivered the **c.**;	5892
Ec	10:15	knoweth not how to go to the **c.**	5892
Ca	3:2	will rise now, and go about the **c.**	5892
Ca	3:3	that go about the **c.** found me:	5892
Ca	5:7	that went about the **c.** found me,	5892
Isa	1:8	of cucumbers, as a besieged **c.**	5892
Isa	1:21	is the faithful **c.** become an harlot!	7151
Isa	1:26	be called, The **c.** of righteousness,	5892
Isa	1:26	of righteousness, the faithful **c.**	7151
Isa	14:4	the golden **c.** ceased!	4062
Isa	14:31	Howl, O gate; cry, O **c.**;	5892
Isa	17:1	is taken away from being a **c.**,	5892
Isa	19:2	against his neighbour; **c.** against **c.**,	5892
Isa	19:18	The **c.** of destruction	5892
Isa	22:2	of stirs, a tumultuous **c.**,	5892
Isa	22:2	a joyous **c.**: thy slain men	7151
Isa	22:9	the breaches of the **c.** of David,	5892
Isa	23:7	this your joyous **c.**, whose	
Isa	23:8	against Tyre, the crowning **c.**,	
Isa	23:11	against the merchant **c.**,	
Isa	23:16	Take an harp, go about the **c.**,	5892
Isa	24:10	**c.** of confusion is broken down:	7151
Isa	24:12	In the **c.** is left desolation,	5892
Isa	25:2	thou hast made of a **c.** an heap;	5892
Isa	25:2	of a defenced **c.** a ruin:	7151
Isa	25:2	a palace of strangers to be no **c.**;	5892
Isa	25:3	the **c.** of the terrible nations shall	7151
Isa	26:1	We have a strong **c.**; salvation	5892
Isa	26:5	the lofty **c.**, he layeth it low;	7151
Isa	27:10	the defenced **c.** shall be desolate,	5892
Isa	29:1	Ariel, the **c.** where David dwelt!	7151
Isa	32:13	houses of joy in the joyous **c.**	7151
Isa	32:14	multitude of the **c.** shall be left;	5892
Isa	32:19	the **c.** shall be low in a low place	5892
Isa	33:20	Zion, the **c.** of our solemnities:	7151
Isa	36:15	this **c.** shall not be delivered into	5892
Isa	37:13	the king of the **c.** of Sepharvaim,	5892
Isa	37:33	He shall not come into this **c.**, nor	5892
Isa	37:34	and shall not come into this **c.**, saith	5892
Isa	37:35	I will defend this **c.** to save it	5892
Isa	38:6	I will deliver thee and this **c.** out	5892
Isa	38:6	and I will defend this **c.**	5892
Isa	45:13	he shall build my city, and he	5892
Isa	48:2	they call themselves of the holy **c.**,	5892
Isa	52:1	O Jerualem, the holy **c.**	5892
Isa	60:14	call thee, The **c.** of the Lord,	5892
Isa	62:12	Sought out, A **c.** not forsaken	5892
Isa	66:6	A voice of noise from the **c.**,	5892
Jer	1:18	made thee this day a defenced **c.**,	5892
Jer	3:14	I will take you one of a **c.**,	5892
Jer	4:29	whole **c.** shall flee for the noise	5892
Jer	4:29	every **c.** shall be forsaken, and not	5892
Jer	6:6	this is the **c.** to be visited;	5892
Jer	8:16	the **c.**, and those that dwell therein	5892
Jer	14:18	if I enter into the **c.**, then behold	5892
Jer	15:8	suddenly, and terrors upon the **c.**,	5892
Jer	17:24	burden through the gates of this **c.**	5892
Jer	17:25	there enter into the gates of this **c.**	5892
Jer	17:25	and this **c.** shall remain for ever	5892
Jer	19:8	I will make this **c.** desolate, and an	5892
Jer	19:11	will I break this people and this **c.**,	5892
Jer	19:12	and even make this **c.** as Tophet:	5892
Jer	19:15	upon this **c.** and upon all her towns	5892
Jer	20:5	deliver all the strength of this **c.**,	5892
Jer	21:4	them into the midst of this **c.**	5892
Jer	21:6	will smite the inhabitants of this **c.**,	5892
Jer	21:7	left in this **c.** from the pestilence,	5892
Jer	21:9	He that abideth in this **c.** shall	5892
Jer	21:10	have set my face against this **c.**	5892
Jer	22:8	many nations shall pass by this **c.**,	5892
Jer	22:8	Lord done thus unto this great **c.**?	5892
Jer	23:39	you, and the **c.** that I gave you	5892
Jer	25:29	I begin to bring evil on the **c.**	5892
Jer	26:6	and will make this **c.** a curse to all	5892
Jer	26:9	this **c.** shall be desolate without	5892
Jer	26:11	he hath prophesied against this **c.**,	5892
Jer	26:12	this house and against this **c.**	5892
Jer	26:15	upon yourselves, and upon this **c.**,	5892
Jer	26:20	who prophesied against this **c.**	5892
Jer	27:17	should this **c.** be laid waste?	5892
Jer	27:19	the vessels that remain in this **c.**,	5892
Jer	29:7	And seek the peace of the **c.**	5892
Jer	29:16	the people that dwelleth in this **c.**,	5892
Jer	30:18	**c.** shall be builded upon her own	5892
Jer	31:38	the **c.** shall be built to the Lord	5892
Jer	32:3	this **c.** into the hand of the king	5892
Jer	32:24	mounts, they are come unto the **c.**	5892
Jer	32:24	and the **c.** is given into the hand of	5892
Jer	32:25	for the **c.** is given into the hand of	5892
Jer	32:28	I will give this **c.** into the hand of	5892
Jer	32:29	that fight against this **c.**,	5892
Jer	32:29	shall come and set fire on this **c.**,	5892
Jer	32:31	For this **c.** hath been to me as a	5892
Jer	32:36	concerning this **c.**, whereof ye say	5892
Jer	33:4	concerning the houses of this **c.**,	5892
Jer	33:5	I have hid my face from this **c.**	5892
Jer	34:2	I will give this **c.** into the hand of	5892
Jer	34:22	cause them to return to this **c.**;	5892
Jer	37:8	and fight against this **c.**, and take	5892
Jer	37:10	tent; and burn this **c.** with fire	5892
Jer	37:21	all the bread in the **c.** were spent	5892
Jer	38:2	that remaineth in this **c.** shall die	5892
Jer	38:3	This **c.** shall surely be given into	5892
Jer	38:4	men of war that remain in this **c.**,	5892
Jer	38:9	there is no more bread in the **c.**	5892
Jer	38:17	and this **c.** shall not be burned	5892
Jer	38:18	shall this **c.** be given into the hand	5892
Jer	38:23	shalt cause this **c.** to be burned	5892
Jer	39:2	of the month, the **c.** was broken up	5892
Jer	39:4	went forth out of the **c.** by night,	5892
Jer	39:9	the people that remained in the **c.**,	5892
Jer	39:16	will bring my words upon this **c.**	5892
Jer	41:7	they came into the midst of the **c.**,	5892
Jer	46:8	the **c.** and the inhabitants thereof	5892
Jer	47:2	**c.**, and them that dwell therein:	5892
Jer	48:8	spoiler shall come upon every **c.**,	5892
Jer	48:8	and no **c.** shall escape:	5892
Jer	49:25	is the **c.** of praise not left,	5892
Jer	49:25	the **c.** of my joy!	7151
Jer	51:31	king of Babylon that his **c.** is taken	5892
Jer	52:5	the **c.** was besieged unto the	5892
Jer	52:6	the famine was sore in the **c.**, so	5892
Jer	52:7	the **c.** was broken up, and all the	5892
Jer	52:7	went forth out of the **c.** by night	5892
Jer	52:7	were by the **c.** round about:)	5892
Jer	52:15	the people that remained in the **c.**,	5892
Jer	52:25	took also out of the **c.** an eunuch,	5892
Jer	52:25	which were found in the **c.**;	5892
Jer	52:25	were found in the midst of the **c.**	5892
La	1:1	How doth the **c.** sit solitary,	5892
La	1:19	elders gave up the ghost in the **c.**,	5892
La	2:11	swoon in the streets of the **c.**	7151
La	2:12	wounded in the streets of the **c.**,	5892
La	2:15	**c.** that men call The perfection	5892
La	3:51	of all the daughters of my **c.**	5892
Eze	4:1	thee, and pourtray upon it the **c.**	5892
Eze	4:3	of iron between thee and the **c.**	5892
Eze	5:2	a third part in the midst of the **c.**,	5892
Eze	7:15	and he that is in the **c.**, famine and	5892
Eze	7:23	and the **c.** is full of violence	5892
Eze	9:1	that have charge over the **c.**	5892
Eze	9:4	Go through the midst of the **c.**,	5892
Eze	9:5	Go ye after him through the **c.**,	5892
Eze	9:7	went forth, and slew in the **c.**	5892
Eze	9:9	and the **c.** full of perverseness:	5892
Eze	10:2	and scatter them over the **c.**	5892
Eze	11:2	and give wicked counsel in this **c.**	5892
Eze	11:3	this **c.** is the caldron, and we be the	
Eze	11:6	multiplied your slain in this **c.**,	5892
Eze	11:7	and this **c.** is the caldron: but I will	
Eze	11:11	This **c.** shall not be your caldron,	
Eze	11:23	up from the midst of the **c.**,	5892
Eze	11:23	which is on the east side of the **c.**	5892
Eze	17:4	he set it in a **c.** of merchants	5892
Eze	21:19	at the head of the way to the **c.**	5892
Eze	22:2	wilt thou judge the bloody **c.**?	5892
Eze	22:3	The **c.** sheddeth blood in the midst	5892
Eze	24:6	Woe to the bloody **c.**, to the pot	5892
Eze	24:9	Woe to the bloody **c.**! I will even	5892
Eze	26:10	enter into a **c.** wherein is made	5892
Eze	26:17	the renowned **c.**, which wast	5892
Eze	26:19	I shall make thee a desolate **c.**	5892
Eze	27:32	saying, What **c.** is like Tyrus,	
Eze	33:21	me, saying, The **c.** is smitten	5892
Eze	39:16	name of the **c.** shall be Hamonah	5892
Eze	40:1	year after that the **c.** was smitten,	5892
Eze	40:2	the frame of a **c.** on the south	5892
Eze	43:3	when I came to destroy the **c.**	5892
Eze	45:6	possession of the **c.** five thousand	5892
Eze	45:7	possession of the **c.**, before the	5892
Eze	45:7	before the possession of the **c.**	5892
Eze	48:15	place for the **c.**, for dwelling,	5892
Eze	48:15	**c.** shall be in the midst thereof	5892
Eze	48:17	suburbs of the **c.** shall be toward	5892
Eze	48:18	food unto them that serve the **c.**	5892
Eze	48:19	that serve the **c.** shall serve it	5892
Eze	48:20	with the possession of the **c.**	5892
Eze	48:21	and of the possession of the **c.**,	5892
Eze	48:22	from the possession of the **c.**,	5892
Eze	48:30	out of the **c.** on the north side,	5892
Eze	48:31	the gates of the **c.** shall be after	5892
Eze	48:35	name of the **c.** from that day shall	5892
Da	9:16	away from thy **c.** Jerusalem,	5892
Da	9:18	**c.** which is called by thy name:	5892
Da	9:19	thy **c.** and thy people are called by	5892
Da	9:24	thy people and upon thy holy **c.**,	5892
Da	9:26	destroy the **c.** and the sanctuary;	5892
Ho	6:8	is a **c.** of them that work inquity,	7151
Ho	11:9	and I will not enter into the **c.**	5892
Joe	2:9	shall run to and fro in the **c.**;	5892
Am	3:6	a trumpet be blown in the **c.**,	5892
Am	3:6	there be evil in a **c.**, and the Lord	5892
Am	4:7	I caused it to rain upon one **c.**,	5892
Am	4:7	it not to rain upon another **c.**	5892
Am	4:8	cities wandered unto one **c.**	5892
Am	5:3	**c.** that went out by a thousand	5892
Am	6:8	deliver up the **c.** with all that is	5892
Am	7:17	wife shall be an harlot in the **c.**,	5892
Jon	1:2	go to Nineveh, that great **c.**, and	5892
Jon	3:2	go unto Nineveh, that great **c.**,	5892
Jon	3:3	Nineveh was an exceeding great **c.**	5892
Jon	3:4	Jonah began to enter into the **c.**	5892
Jon	4:5	Jonah went out of the **c.**, and sat	5892
Jon	4:5	on the east side of the **c.**,	5892
Jon	4:5	see what would become of the **c.**	5892
Jon	4:11	not I spare Nineveh, that great **c.**,	5892
Mic	4:10	shalt thou go forth out of the **c.**,	7151
Mic	6:9	Lord's voice crieth unto the **c.**,	5892
Na	3:1	Woe to the bloody **c.**! it is all full	5892
Hab	2:8	the violence of the land, of the **c.**,	7151
Hab	2:12	and stablisheth a **c.** by iniquity!	7151
Hab	2:17	of the **c.**, and of all that dwell	7151
Zep	2:15	rejoicing **c.** that dwelt carelessly,	5892
Zep	3:1	and polluted, to the oppressing **c.**!	5892
Zec	8:3	shall be called a **c.** of truth;	5892
Zec	8:5	**c.** shall be full of boys and girls	5892
Zec	8:21	the inhabitants of one **c.** shall go to	
Zec	14:2	**c.** shall be taken, and the houses	5892
Zec	14:2	the **c.** shall go forth into captivity,	5892
Zec	14:2	shall not be cut off from the **c.**	5892
Mt	2:23	and dwelt in a **c.** called Nazareth:	*4172*
Mt	4:5	taketh him up into the holy **c.**,	*4172*
Mt	5:14	**A c. that is set on an hill cannot**	*4172*
Mt	5:35	**for it is the c. of the great King**	*4172*
Mt	8:33	and went their ways into the **c.**,	*4172*
Mt	8:34	whole **c.** came out to meet Jesus:	*4172*
Mt	9:1	over, and came into his own **c.**	*4172*
Mt	10:5	**c. of the Samaritans enter ye not:**	*4172*
Mt	10:11	**c. or town ye shall enter,**	*4172*

Mt 10:14 **ye depart out of that house or c.,** 4172
Mt 10:15 **day of judgment, than for that c.** 4172
Mt 10:23 **when they persecute you in this c.,** 4172
Mt 12:25 **c. or house divided against itself** 4172
Mt 21:10 all the c. was moved, saying, Who 4172
Mt 21:17 went out of the c. into Bethany; 4172
Mt 21:18 returned into the c., he hungered. 4172
Mt 22:7 **and burned up their c.** 4172
Mt 23:34 **and persecute them from c. to c.** 4172
Mt 26:18 **Go into the c. to such a man, and** 4172
Mt 27:53 went into the holy c., and appeared 4172
Mt 28:11 of the watch came into the c., 4172
Mk 1:33 all the c. was gathered together 4172
Mk 1:45 no more openly enter into the c., 4172
Mk 5:14 told it in the c., and in the country. 4172
Mk 6:11 **day of judgment, than for that c.** 4172
Mk 11:19 was come, he went out of the c. 4172
Mk 14:13 **Go ye into the c., and there shall** 4172
Mk 14:16 went forth, and came into the c., 4172
Lu 1:26 a c. of Galilee, named Nazareth, 4172
Lu 1:39 with haste, into a c. of Juda; 4172
Lu 2:3 taxed, every one into his own c. 4172
Lu 2:4 out of the c. of Nazareth, into 4172
Lu 2:4 Judaea, unto the c. of David, 4172
Lu 2:11 day in the c. of David a Saviour, 4172
Lu 2:39 Galilee, to their own c. Nazareth. 4172
Lu 4:26 **save unto Sarepta, a c. of Sidon,**
Lu 4:29 up, and thrust him out of the c., 4172
Lu 4:29 hill whereon their c. was built, 4172
Lu 4:31 to Capernaum, a c. of Galilee, 4172
Lu 5:12 was in a certain c., behold a man 4172
Lu 7:11 he went into a c. called Nain; 4172
Lu 7:12 he came nigh to the gate of the c., 4172
Lu 7:12 much people of the c. was with her. 4172
Lu 7:37 And, behold, a woman in the c., 4172
Lu 8:1 throughout every c. and village, 4172
Lu 8:4 were come to him out of every c., 4172
Lu 8:27 him out of the c. a certain man, 4172
Lu 8:34 and went and told it in the c. 4172
Lu 8:39 published throughout the whole c. 4172
Lu 9:5 **when ye go out of that c., shake** 4172
Lu 9:10 to the c. called Bethsaida. 4172
Lu 10:1 into every c. and place, whither 4172
Lu 10:8, 10 **whatsoever c. ye enter, and** 4172
Lu 10:11 **Even the very dust of your c.,** 4172
Lu 10:12 **day for Sodom, than for that c.** 4172
Lu 14:21 **into the streets and lanes of the c.,** 4172
Lu 18:2 **There was in a c. a judge, which** 4172
Lu 18:3 **And there was a widow in that c.;** 4172
Lu 19:41 beheld the c., and wept over it, 4172
Lu 22:10 **when ye are entered into the c.,** 4172
Lu 23:19 a certain sedition made in the c., 4172
Lu 23:51 of Arimathea, a c. of the Jews: 4172
Lu 24:49 **tarry ye in the c. of Jerusalem,** 4172
Joh 1:44 the c. of Andrew and Peter. 4172
Joh 4:5 Then cometh he to a c. of Samaria, 4172
Joh 4:8 gone away unto the c. to buy meat. 4172
Joh 4:28 went her way into the c., and saith 4172
Joh 4:30 Then they went out of the c., and 4172
Joh 4:39 the Samaritans of that c. believed 4172
Joh 11:54 into a c. called Ephraim, and 4172
Joh 19:20 was crucified was nigh to the c. 4172
Ac 7:58 And cast him out of the c., and 4172
Ac 8:5 went down to the c. of Samaria, 4172
Ac 8:8 And there was great joy in that c., 4172
Ac 8:9 in the same c. used sorcery and 4172
Ac 9:6 **Arise, and go into the c., and it** 4172
Ac 10:9 and drew nigh unto the c., 4172
Ac 11:5 I was in the c. of Joppa praying: 4172
Ac 12:10 iron gate that leadeth unto the c.; 4172
Ac 13:44 came almost the whole c. together 4172
Ac 13:50 and the chief men of the c., 4172
Ac 14:4 multitude of the c. was divided: 4172
Ac 14:13 Jupiter, which was before their c., 4172
Ac 14:19 drew him out of the c., supposing 4172
Ac 14:20 he rose up, and came into the c. 4172
Ac 14:21 preached the gospel to that c., 4172
Ac 15:21 In every c. them that preach him, 4172
Ac 15:36 and visit our brethren in every c. 4172
Ac 16:12 chief c. of that part of Macedonia, 4172
Ac 16:12 in that c. abiding certain days. 4172
Ac 16:13 went out of the c. by a river side, 4172
Ac 16:14 of purple, of the c. of Thyatira, 4172
Ac 16:20 do exceedingly trouble our c., 4172
Ac 16:39 them to depart out of the c. 4172
Ac 17:5 set all the c. on an uproar, 4172
Ac 17:6 unto the rulers of the c., crying, 4173
Ac 17:8 rulers of the c., when they heard 4173
Ac 17:16 the c. wholly given to idolatry. 4172
Ac 18:10 **for I have much people in this c.** 4172
Ac 19:29 whole c. was filled with confusion: 4172
Ac 19:35 how that the c. of the Ephesians 4172
Ac 20:23 Holy Ghost witnesseth in every c., 4172
Ac 21:5 till we were out of the c.: and we 4172
Ac 21:29 in the c. Trophimus an Ephesian, 4172
Ac 21:30 the c. was moved, and the people 4172
Ac 21:39 which am a Jew of Tarsus, a c. 4172
Ac 21:39 in Cilicia, a citizen of no mean c. 4172
Ac 22:3 am a Jew, born in Tarsus, a c.
Ac 22:3 Cilicia, yet brought up in this c. 4172
Ac 24:12 in the synagogues, nor in the c.: 4172
Ac 25:23 principal men of the c., at Festus' 4172
Ac 27:5 we came to Myra, a c. of Lycia.
Ac 27:8 whereunto was the c. of Lasea. 4172
Ro 16:23 Erastus the chamberlain of the c. 4172
2Co 11:26 in perils in the c., in perils in 4172
2Co 11:32 king kept the c. of the Damascenes 4172
2Co *subscr.* written from Philippi, a c.
1Ti *subscr.* is the chiefest c. of Phrygia 3390
Tit 1:5 ordain elders in every c., as I had 4172
Heb 11:10 For he looked for a c. which hath 4172
Heb 11:16 he hath prepared for them a c. 4172
Heb 12:22 c. of the living God, the heavenly 4172
Heb 13:14 have we no continuing c., but we 4172
Jas 4:13 go into such a c., and continue 4172
Re 3:12 **the name of the c. of my God,** 4172
Re 11:2 holy c. shall they tread under foot 4172
Re 11:8 lie in the street of the great c., 4172
Re 11:13 and the tenth part of the c. fell, 4172
Re 14:8 is fallen, is fallen, that great c., 4172
Re 14:20 was trodden without the c., 4172
Re 16:19 the great c. was divided into three 4172
Re 17:18 is that great c., which reigneth 4172
Re 18:10 great c. Babylon, that mighty c.! 4172
Re 18:16 that great c., that was clothed 4172
Re 18:18 What c. is like unto this great c.! 4172
Re 18:19 alas that great c., wherein were 4172
Re 18:21 great c. Babylon be thrown down, 4172
Re 20:9 saints about, and the beloved c. 4172
Re 21:2 saw the holy c., new Jerusalem, 4172
Re 21:10 and shewed me that great c., the 4172
Re 21:14 of the c. had twelve foundations, 4172
Re 21:15 a golden reed to measure the c., 4172
Re 21:16 And the c. lieth foursquare, and 4172
Re 21:16 he measured the c. with the reed, 4172
Re 21:18 the c. was pure gold, like unto 4172
Re 21:19 the foundations of the wall of the c. 4172
Re 21:21 the street of the c. was pure gold, 4172
Re 21:23 the c. had no need of the sun, 4172
Re 22:14 in through the gates into the c. 4172
Re 22:19 out of the holy c., and from the 4172

CLAD See also CLOTHED.
1Ki 11:29 c. himself with a new garment; 3680
Isa 59:17 and was c. with zeal as a cloke. 5844

CLAMOROUS
Pr 9:13 foolish woman is c.: she is simple, 1993

CLAMOUR
Eph 4:31 anger, and c., and evil speaking, 2906

CLAP See also CLAPPED; CLAPPETH.
Job 27:23 Men shall c. their hands at him, 5606
Ps 47:1 O c. your hands, all ye people; 8628
Ps 98:8 Let the floods c. their hands: let 4222
Isa 55:12 of the field shall c. their hands. 4222
La 2:15 pass by c. their hands at thee; 5606
Na 3:19 shall c. the hands over thee: 8628

CLAPPED
2Ki 11:12 and they c. their hands, and said, 5221
Eze 25:6 thou hast c. thine hands, and 4222

CLAPPETH
Job 34:37 he c. his hands among us, and 5606

CLAUDA (claw'-dah)
Ac 27:16 certain island which is called C., 2802

CLAUDIA (claw'-de-ah)
2Ti 4:21 and C., and all the brethren. 2803

CLAUDIUS (claw'-de-us-)
Ac 11:28 to pass in the days of C. Caesar. 2804
Ac 18:2 C. had commanded all Jews to 2804
Ac 23:26 C. Lysias unto the most excellent 2804

CLAVE
Ge 22:3 and c. the wood for the burnt 1234
Ge 34:3 And his soul c. unto Dinah the 1692
Nu 16:31 ground c. asunder that was under 1234
Jg 15:19 But God c. an hollow place that 1234
Ru 1:14 but Ruth c. unto her. 1692
1Sa 6:14 and they c. the wood of the cart, 1234
2Sa 20:2 men of Judah c. unto their king, 1692
2Sa 23:10 and his hand c. unto the sword: 1692
1Ki 11:2 Solomon c. unto these in love. 1692
2Ki 18:6 he c. to the Lord, and departed not 1692
Ne 10:29 They c. to their brethren, their 2388
Ps 78:15 He c. the rocks in the wilderness, 1234
Isa 48:21 he c. the rock also, and the 1234
Ac 17:34 men c. unto him, and believed: 2853

CLAWS
De 14:6 cleaveth the cleft into two c., and 6541
Da 4:33 feathers, and his nails like birds' c.
Zec 11:16 fat, and tear their c. in pieces. 6541

CLAY
1Ki 7:46 king cast them, in the c. ground 4568
2Ch 4:17 in the c. ground between Succoth 4568
Job 4:19 them that dwell in houses of c., 2563
Job 10:9 thou hast made me as the c.; and 2563
Job 13:12 ashes, your bodies to bodies of c. 2563
Job 27:16 and prepare raiment as the c.; 2563
Job 33:6 I also am formed out of the c. 2563
Job 38:14 It is turned as c. to the seal; and 2563
Ps 40:2 out of the miry c., and set my feet 2916
Isa 29:16 be esteemed as the potter's c. 2563
Isa 41:25 and as the potter treadeth c. 2916
Isa 45:9 c. say to him that fashioneth it, 2563
Isa 64:8 thou art our father; we are the c. 2563
Jer 18:4 that he made of c. was marred 2563
Jer 18:6 as the c. is in the potter's hand, so 2563
Jer 43:9 them in the c. in the brickkiln, 4423
Da 2:33 feet part of iron and part of c. 2635
Da 2:34 were of iron and c., and brake them 2635
Da 2:35 iron, the c., the brass, the silver 2635
Da 2:41 part of potter's c., and part of iron, 2635
Da 2:41 sawest the iron mixed with miry c. 2635
Da 2:42 were part of iron, and part of c., 2635
Da 2:43 sawest iron mixed with miry c., 2635
Da 2:43 even as iron is not mixed with c. 2635
Da 2:45 in pieces the iron, the brass, the c., 2635
Na 3:14 go into c., and tread the morter, 2916
Hab 2:6 that ladeth himself with thick c.! 5671
Joh 9:6 and made c. of the spittle, and he 4081
Joh 9:6 eyes of the blind man with the c., 4081
Joh 9:11 man that is called Jesus made c., 4081
Joh 9:14 when Jesus made the c., and 4081
Joh 9:15 He put c. upon mine eyes, and 4081
Ro 9:21 not the potter power over the c., 4081

CLEAN See also UNCLEAN.
Ge 7:2 Of every c. beast thou shalt take 2889
Ge 7:2 of beasts that are not c. by two, 2889
Ge 7:8 Of c. beasts, and of 2889
Ge 7:8 beasts that are not c., 2889
Ge 8:20 every c. beast, and of every c. fowl, 2889
Ge 35:2 be c., and change your garments: 2891
Le 4:12 a c. place where the ashes are 2889
Le 6:11 without the camp unto a c. place. 2889
Le 7:19 all that be c. shall eat thereof. 2889
Le 10:10 and between unclean and c.; 2889
Le 10:14 shoulder shall ye eat in a c. place; 2889
Le 11:36 is plenty of water, shall be c. 2889
Le 11:37 which is to be sown, it shall be c. 2889
Le 11:47 between the unclean and the c., 2889
Le 12:8 for her, and she shall be c. 2891
Le 13:6 the priest shall pronounce him c. 2891
Le 13:6 he shall wash his clothes, and be c. 2891
Le 13:13 he shall pronounce him c. that 2891
Le 13:13 it is all turned white: he is c. 2889
Le 13:17 the priest shall pronounce him c. 2891
Le 13:17 that hath the plague: he is c. 2889
Le 13:23 the priest shall pronounce him c. 2891
Le 13:28 the priest shall pronounce him c. 2891
Le 13:34 pronounce him c.: and he shall 2891
Le 13:34 wash his clothes, and be c. 2891
Le 13:37 the scall is healed, he is c. 2889
Le 13:37 the priest shall pronounce him c. 2891
Le 13:39 groweth in the skin; he is c. 2889
Le 13:40 he is bald; yet is he c. 2889
Le 13:41 he is forehead bald: yet is he c. 2889
Le 13:58 the second time, and shall be c. 2891

Le 13:59 to pronounce it c., or to pronounce 2891
Le 14:4 be cleansed two birds alive and c., 2889
Le 14:7 and shall pronounce him c., and 2891
Le 14:8 himself in water, that he may be c. 2891
Le 14:9 flesh in water, and he shall be c. 2891
Le 14:11 the priest that maketh him c. 2891
Le 14:11 the man that is to be made c., and 2891
Le 14:20 for him, and he shall be c. 2891
Le 14:48 priest shall pronounce the house c., 2891
Le 14:53 for the house: and it shall be c. 2891
Le 14:57 unclean, and when it is c.: this is 2889
Le 15:8 spit upon him that is c.; then he 2889
Le 15:13 in running water, and shall be c. 2891
Le 15:28 days, and after that she shall be c. 2891
Le 16:30 ye may be c. from all your sins 2891
Le 17:15 until the even: then shall he be c. 2891
Le 20:25 between c. beasts and unclean, 2889
Le 20:25 and between unclean fowls and c. 2889
Le 22:4 of the holy things, until he be c. 2891
Le 22:7 the sun is down, he shall be c. 2891
Le 23:22 thou shalt not make c. riddance 2891
Nu 5:28 woman be not defiled, but be c.; 2889
Nu 8:7 and so make themselves c. 2891
Nu 9:13 But the man that is c., and is not 2889
Nu 18:11 every one that is c. in thy house 2889
Nu 18:13 every one that is c. in thine house 2889
Nu 19:9 a man that is c. shall gather up 2889
Nu 19:9 up without the camp in a c. place, 2889
Nu 19:12 on the seventh day he shall be c. 2891
Nu 19:12 the seventh day he shall not be c. 2891
Nu 19:18 a c. person shall take hyssop, and 2889
Nu 19:19 and the c. person shall sprinkle 2889
Nu 19:19 himself in water, and shall be c. 2891
Nu 31:23 through the fire, and it shall be c. 2891
Nu 31:24 and ye shall be c., and afterward 2891
De 12:15 the unclean and the c. may eat 2889
De 12:22 the unclean and the c. shall eat of 2889
De 14:11 Of all c. birds ye shall eat 2889
De 14:20 But of all c. fowls ye may eat 2889
De 15:22 unclean and the c. person shall 2889
De 23:10 not c. by reason of uncleanness 2889
Jos 3:17 all the people were passed c. over 8552
Jos 4:1 people were c. passed over Jordan, 8552
Jos 4:11 people were c. passed over, that 8552
1Sa 20:26 he is not c.; surely he is not c. 2889
2Ki 5:10 again to thee, and thou shalt be c. 2891
2Ki 5:12 may I not wash in them, and be c.? 2891
2Ki 5:13 he saith to thee, Wash, and be c.? 2891
2Ki 5:14 of a little child, and he was c. 2891
2Ch 30:17 for every one that was not c., to 2889
Job 9:30 and make my hands never so c.; 2141
Job 11:4 doctrine is pure, and I am c. in 1249
Job 14:4 Who can bring a c. thing out of an 2889
Job 15:14 What is man, that he should be c.? 2135
Job 15:15 the heavens are not c. in his sight 2141
Job 17:9 and he that hath c. hands shall 2891
Job 25:4 or how can he be c. that is born 2135
Job 33:9 I am c. without transgression, I 2134
Ps 19:9 The fear of the Lord is c., 2889
Ps 24:4 He that hath c. hands, and a pure 5355
Ps 51:7 me with hyssop, and I shall be c. 2891
Ps 51:10 Create in me a c. heart, O God; 2889
Ps 73:1 even to such as are of a c. heart. 1249
Ps 77:8 Is his mercy c. gone for ever? 656
Pr 14:4 Where no oxen are, the crib is c. 1249
Pr 16:2 ways of a man are c. in his own 2134
Pr 20:9 can say, I have made my heart c., 2135
Ec 9:2 to the good and to the c., and to 2889
Isa 1:16 Wash you, make you c.; put away 2135
Isa 24:19 broken down, the earth is c. 6565
Isa 28:8 so that there is no place c.
Isa 30:24 that ear the ground shall eat c. 2548
Isa 52:11 be ye c., that bear the vessels of 1305
Isa 66:20 bring an offering in a c. vessel 2889
Jer 13:27 wilt thou not be made c.? 2891
Eze 22:26 between the unclean and the c., 2889
Eze 36:25 Then will I sprinkle c. water 2889
Eze 36:25 and ye shall be c.: from all your 2891
Eze 44:23 between the unclean and the c. 2889
Joe 1:7 he hath made it c. bare, and cast
Zec 11:17 his arm shall be c. dried up, and 2889
Mt 8:2 thou wilt, thou canst make me c. *2513*
Mt 8:3 him, saying, **I will; be thou c.** *2513*
Mt 23:25 **for ye make c. the outside of the** *2511*
Mt 23:26 **the outside of them may be c.** *2513*
Mt 27:59 the body, he wrapped it in a c. *2513*
Mk 1:40 wilt, thou canst make me c. *2511*
Mk 1:41 saith unto him, **I will; be thou c.** *2511*
Lu 5:12 thou wilt, thou canst make me c. *2511*
Lu 5:13 him, saying, **I will: be thou c.** *2511*
Lu 11:39 **Now do ye Pharisees make c.** *2511*
Lu 11:41 **behold, all things are c. unto you** *2513*
Joh 13:10 **but is c. every whit:** *2513*
Joh 13:10 **and ye are c., but not all** *2513*
Joh 13:11 therefore said he, Ye are not all c. *2513*
Joh 15:3 **Now ye are c. through the word** *2513*
Ac 18:6 upon your own heads; I am c. *2513*
2Pe 2:18 those that were c. escaped from *3689*
Re 19:8 arrayed in fine linen, c. and white *2513*
Re 19:14 clothed in fine linen, white and c. *2513*

CLEANNESS See also UNCLEANNESS.
2Sa 22:21 to the c. of my hands hath he 1252
2Sa 22:25 according to my c. in his eye sight. 1252
Ps 18:20 to the c. of my hands hath he 1252
Ps 18:24 the c. of my hands in his eyesight. 1252
Am 4:6 I also have given you c. of teeth 5356

CLEANSE See also CLEANSED; CLEANSETH; CLEANSING.
Ex 29:36 and thou shalt c. the altar, when 2398
Le 14:49 he shall take to c. the house two 2398
Le 14:52 And he shall c. the house with the 2398
Le 16:19 seven times, and c. it, and hallow 2891
Le 16:30 an atonement for you, to c. you, 2891
Nu 8:6 children of Israel, and c. them. 2891
Nu 8:7 shalt thou do unto them, to c. 2891
Nu 8:15 and thou shalt c. them, and offer 2891
Nu 8:21 an atonement for them to c. them. 2891
2Ch 29:15 of the Lord, to c. the house of the 2891
2Ch 29:16 house of the Lord, to c. it, 2891
Neh 13:22 the Levites that they should c. 2891
Ps 19:12 c. thou me from secret faults. 5352
Ps 51:2 mine iniquity, and c. me from my 5352
Ps 119:9 Wherewithal shall a young man c. 2135
Jer 4:11 people, not to fan, nor to c., 1305
Jer 33:8 And I will c. them from all their 2891
Eze 36:25 from all your idols, will I c. you 2891
Eze 37:23 they have sinned, and will c. them: 2891
Eze 39:12 of them, that they may c. the land. 2891
Eze 39:14 upon the face of the earth, to c. it: 2891
Eze 39:16 Thus shall they c. the land. 2891
Eze 43:20 thus shalt thou c. and purge it. 2398
Eze 43:22 and they shall c. the altar, 2398
Eze 43:22 as they did c. it with the bullock. 2398
Eze 45:18 blemish, and c. the sanctuary: 2398
Joe 3:21 For I will c. their blood that I 5352
Mt 10:8 **c. the lepers, raise the dead, cast** *2511*
Mt 23:26 **c. first that which is within the** *2511*
2Co 7:1 let us c. ourselves from all *2511*
Eph 5:26 That he might sanctify and c. it *2511*
Jas 4:8 C. your hands, ye sinners; and *2511*
1Jo 1:9 to c. us from all unrighteousness *2511*

CLEANSED
Le 11:32 until the even; so it shall be c. 2891
Le 12:7 and she shall be c. from 2891
Le 14:4 take for him that is to be c. two 2891
Le 14:7 upon him that is to be c. from the 2891
Le 14:8 he that is to be c. shall wash his 2891
Le 14:14, 17 right ear of him that is to be c., 2891
Le 14:18 the head of him that is to be c. 2891
Le 14:19 for him that is to be c. from his 2891
Le 14:25, 28 right ear of him that is to be c., 2891
Le 14:29 the head of him that is to be c., to 2891
Le 14:31 atonement for him that is to be c. 2891
Le 15:13 when he that hath an issue is c. 2891
Le 15:28 if she be c. of her issue, then she 2891
Nu 35:33 the land cannot be c. of the blood 3722
Jos 22:17 which we are not c. until this day 2891
2Ch 29:18 have c. all the house of the Lord, 2891
2Ch 30:18 not c. themselves, yet did they eat 2891
2Ch 30:19 though he be not c. according to
2Ch 34:5 their altars, and c. Judah and 2891
Ne 13:9 and they c. the chambers: 2891
Ne 13:30 Thus c. I them from all strangers, 2891
Job 35:3 I have, if I be c. from my sin?
Ps 73:13 Verily I have c. my heart in vain. 2135
Eze 22:24 Thou art the land that is not c. 2891
Eze 36:33 In the day that I shall have c. you 2891
Eze 44:26 after he is c., they shall reckon 2893
Da 8:14 then shall the sanctuary be c. 6663
Joe 3:21 their blood that I have not c. 5352
Mt 8:3 immediately his leprosy was c. *2511*
Mt 11:5 **lepers are c., and the deaf hear,** *2511*
Mk 1:42 departed from him and he was c. *2511*
Lu 4:27 **and none of them was c., saving** *2511*
Lu 7:22 **the lepers are c., the deaf hear,** *2511*
Lu 17:14 to pass, as they went, they were c. *2511*
Lu 17:17 **Were there not ten c.? but where** *2511*
Ac 10:15 What God hath c., that call not thou *2511*
Ac 11:9 What God hath c., that call not thou *2511*

CLEANSETH
Job 37:21 the wind passeth, and c. them. 2891
Pr 20:30 blueness of a wound c. away evil: 8562
1Jo 1:7 blood of Jesus Christ his Son c. us *2511*

CLEANSING
Le 13:7 been seen of the priest for his c., 2893
Le 13:35 much in the skin after his c.; 2893
Le 14:2 law of the leper in the day of his c. 2893
Le 14:23 them on the eighth day for his c. 2893
Le 14:32 get that which pertaineth to his c. 2893
Le 15:13 to himself seven days for his c., 2893
Nu 6:9 shave his head in the day of his c., 2893
Eze 43:23 When thou hast made an end of c. 2893
Mk 1:44 **and offer for thy c. those things** *2512*
Lu 5:14 **and offer for thy c., according as** *2512*

CLEAR See also CLEARER; CLEARING.
Ge 24:8 shalt be c. from this my oath: 5352
Ge 24:41 shalt thou be c. from this my oath, 5352
Ge 24:41 thou shalt be c. from my oath. 5355
Ge 44:16 or how shall we c. ourselves? 6663
Ex 34:7 will by no means c. the guilty; 5352
2Sa 23:4 the earth by c. shining after rain.
Ps 51:4 speakest, and be c. when thou 2135
Ca 6:10 fair as the moon, c. as the sun, 1249
Isa 18:4 like a c. heat upon herbs, and like 6703
Am 8:9 will darken the earth in the c. day: 216
Zec 14:6 the light shall not be c., nor dark 3368
2Co 7:11 approved yourselves to be c. in *53*
Re 21:11 like a jasper stone, c. as crystal; *2929*
Re 21:18 was pure gold, like unto c. glass. *2513*
Re 22:1 river of water of life, c. as crystal, *2986*

CLEARER
Job 11:17 age shall be c. than the noonday; 6965

CLEARING
Nu 14:18 no means c. the guilty, visiting 5352
2Co 7:11 in you, yea, what c. of yourselves, *627*

CLEARLY
Job 33:3 my lips shall utter knowledge c. 1305
Mt 7:5 **then shalt thou see c. to cast out** *1227*
Mk 8:25 restored, and saw every man c. *5081*
Lu 6:42 **then shalt thou see c. to pull out** *1227*
Ro 1:20 are c. seen, being understood by *2529*

CLEARNESS
Ex 24:10 were the body of heaven in his c. 2892

CLEAVE See also CLAVE; CLEAVED; CLEAVETH; CLEFT; CLOVEN.
Ge 2:24 shall c. unto his wife: and they 1692
Le 1:17 shall c. it with the wings thereof, 8156
De 4:4 But ye that did c. unto the Lord 1695
De 10:20 to him shalt thou c., and swear by 1692
De 11:22 in all his ways, and to c. unto him; 1692
De 13:4 shall serve him, and c. unto him. 1692
De 13:17 shall c. nought of the cursed thing 1692
De 28:21 make the pestilence c. unto thee, 1692
De 28:60 they shall c. unto thee. 1692
De 30:20 and that thou mayest c. unto him: 1692
Jos 22:5 to c. unto him and to serve him, 1692
Jos 23:8 But c. unto the Lord your God, as 1692
Jos 23:12 and c. unto the remnant of these 1692
2Ki 5:27 of Naaman shall c. unto thee, 1692
Job 38:38 and the clods c. fast together? 1692
Ps 74:15 c. the fountain and the flood: 1234
Ps 101:3 it shall not c. to me. 1692
Ps 102:5 groaning my bones c. to my skin 1692
Ps 137:6 tongue c. to the roof of my mouth; 1692
Isa 14:1 they shall c. to the house of Jacob. 5596
Jer 13:11 so have I caused to c. unto me the 1692
Eze 3:26 tongue c. to the roof of thy mouth, 1692
Da 2:43 they shall not c. one to another, 1693
Da 11:34 shall c. to them with flatteries. 3867
Hab 3:9 didst c. the earth with rivers. 1234
Zec 14:4 of Olives shall c. in the midst 1234
Mt 19:5 **c. to his wife: and they twain** *4347*
Mk 10:7 **and mother, and c. to his wife;** *4347*
Ac 11:23 they would c. unto the Lord. *4347*
Ro 12:9 c. to that which is good. *2853*

CLEAVED
2Ki 3:3 Nevertheless he **c.** unto the sins 1692
Job 29:10 tongue **c.** to the roof of their 1692
Job 31:7 if any blot hath **c.** to mine hands; 1692

CLEAVETH
De 14:6 and **c.** the cleft into two claws, 8157
Job 16:13 he **c.** my reins asunder, and doth 6398
Job 19:20 My bone **c.** to my skin and to my 1692
Ps 22:15 and my tongue **c.** to my jaws; 1692
Ps 41:8 disease, say they, **c.** fast unto him: 3332
Ps 44:25 our belly **c.** unto the earth. 1692
Ps 119:25 My soul **c.** unto the dust: quicken 1692
Ps 141:7 when one cutteth and **c.** wood 1234
Ec 10:9 that **c.** wood shall be endangered 1234
Jer 13:11 the girdle **c.** to the loins of a man, 1692
La 4:4 The tongue of the sucking child **c.** 1692
La 4:8 their skin **c.** to their bones; it is 6821
Lu 10:11 **dust of your city, which c. on us,** *2853*

CLEFT See also CLEFTS; CLIFT.
De 14:6 cleaveth the **c.** into two claws. 8156
Mic 1:4 the valleys shall be **c.**, as wax 1234

CLEFTS See also CLIFTS.
Ca 2:14 in the **c.** of the rock, in the secret 2288
Isa 2:21 To go into the **c.** of the rocks, 5366
Jer 49:16 thou that dwellest in the **c.** of the 2288
Am 6:11 and the little house with **c.** 1233
Ob 3 that dwellest in the **c.** of the rock, 2288

CLEMENCY
Ac 24:4 hear us of thy **c.** a few words *1932*

CLEMENT (clem'-ent)
Php 4:3 in the gospel, with **C.** also, and *2815*

CLEOPAS (cle'-o-pas) See also ALPHAEUS; CLEOPHAS.
Lu 24:18 one of them, whose name was **C.** *2810*

CLEOPHAS (cle'-o-fas) See also CLEOPAS.
Joh 19:25 Mary the wife of **C.**, and Mary *2832*

CLERK See TOWNCLERK.

CLIFF See also CLIFFS.
2Ch 20:16 they come up by the **c.** of Ziz; 4608

CLIFFS
Job 30:6 in the **c.** of the valleys, in caves 6178

CLIFT See also CLEFT.
Ex 33:22 put thee in a **c.** of the rock, 5366

CLIFTS See also CLEFTS.
Isa 57:5 under the **c.** of the rocks? 5585

CLIMB See also CLIMBED; CLIMBETH.
Jer 4:29 and **c.** up upon the rocks: 5927
Joe 2:7 shall **c.** the wall like men of war: 5927
Joe 2:9 they shall **c.** up upon the houses; 5927
Am 9:2 though they **c.** up to heaven, 5927

CLIMBED
1Sa 14:13 Jonathan **c.** up upon his hands 5927
Lu 19:4 **c.** up into a sycomore tree to see *305*

CLIMBETH
Joh 10:1 **c. up some other way, the same** *305*

CLIPPED
Jer 48:37 shall be bald, and every beard **c.** 1639

CLOAK See also CLOKE.

CLODS
Job 7:5 with worms and **c.** of dust; 1487
Job 21:33 The **c.** of the valley shall be sweet 7263
Job 38:38 and the **c.** cleave fast together? 7263
Isa 28:24 and break the **c.** of his ground? 7702
Ho 10:11 and Jacob shall break his **c.** 7702
Joe 1:17 seed is rotten under their **c.**, 4053

CLOKE
Isa 59:17 was clad with zeal as a **c.** 4598
Mt 5:40 **thy coat, let him have thy c. also** *2440*
Lu 6:29 **him that taketh away thy c** *2440*
Joh 15:22 **they have no c. for their sin** *4392*
1Th 2:5 nor a **c.** of covetousness; God is *4392*
2Ti 4:13 The **c.** that I left at Troas with *5341*
1Pe 2:16 liberty for a **c.** of maliciousness *1942*

CLOSE See also CLOSED; CLOSER; CLOSEST; DISCLOSES; INCLOSE.
Nu 5:13 of her husband, and be kept **c.**, 5956
2Sa 22:46 be afraid out of their **c.** places. 4526
1Ch 12:1 he yet kept himself **c.** because of 6113
Job 28:21 kept **c.** from the fowls of the air. 5641
Job 41:15 shut up together as with a **c.** seal. 6862
Ps 18:45 be afraid out of their **c.** places. 4526
Jer 42:16 **c.** after you there in Egypt; 1692
Da 8:7 saw him come **c.** unto the ram, 681
Am 9:11 and **c.** up the breaches thereof; 1443
Lu 9:36 And they kept it **c.**, and told no *4601*
Ac 27:13 thence, they sailed **c.** by Crete. *788*

CLOSED See also INCLOSED.
Ge 2:21 **c.** up the flesh instead thereof; 5462
Ge 20:18 the Lord had fast **c.** up all the 6113
Nu 16:33 and the earth **c.** upon them: 3680
Jg 3:22 and the fat **c.** upon the blade, 5462
Isa 1:6 they have not been **c.**, neither 2115
Isa 29:10 sleep, and hath **c.** your eyes: 6105
Da 12:9 the words are **c.** up and sealed 5640
Jon 2:5 the depth **c.** me round about, 5437
Mt 13:15 **their eyes they have c.; lest at** *2576*
Lu 4:20 **c.** the book, and he gave it again *4428*
Ac 28:27 their eyes have they **c.**; lest they *2576*

CLOSER
Pr 18:24 that sticketh **c.** than a brother.

CLOSEST
Jer 22:15 because thou **c.** thyself in cedar? 8474

CLOSET See also CLOSETS.
Joe 2:16 and the bride out of her **c.** 2646
Mt 6:6 **thou prayest, enter into thy c.,** *5009*

CLOSETS
Lu 12:3 **ye have spoken in the ear in c.** *5009*

CLOTH See also CLOTHS; SACKCLOTH.
Nu 4:6 spread over it a **c.** wholly of blue, 899
Nu 4:7 they shall spread a **c.** of blue, 899
Nu 4:8 spread upon them a **c.** of scarlet, 899
Nu 4:9 they shall take a **c.** of blue, 899
Nu 4:11 they shall spread a **c.** of blue, 899
Nu 4:12 put them in a **c.** of blue, and cover 899
Nu 4:13 and spread a purple **c.** thereon: 899
De 22:17 spread the **c.** before the elders 8071
1Sa 19:13 bolster, and covered it with a **c.** 899
1Sa 21:9 wrapped in a **c.** behind the ephod: 8071
2Sa 20:12 cast a **c.** upon him, when he saw 899
2Ki 8:15 he took a thick **c.**, and dipped it 4346
Isa 30:22 them away as a menstruous **c.**; 4346
Mt 9:16 **of new c. unto an old garment,** *4470*
Mt 27:59 wrapped it in a clean linen **c.**, *4616*
Mk 2:21 **of new c. on an old garment:** *4470*
Mk 14:51 linen **c.** cast about his naked body; *4616*
Mk 14:52 And he left the linen **c.**, and fled *4616*

CLOTHE See also CLOTHED; CLOTHES; CLOTHEST; CLOTHING.
Ex 40:14 his sons, and **c.** them with coats: 3847
Es 4:4 she sent raiment to **c.** Mordecai, 3847
Ps 132:16 also her priests with salvation: 3847
Ps 132:18 His enemies will I **c.** with shame: 3847
Pr 23:21 shall **c.** a man with rags. 3847
Isa 22:21 And I will **c.** him with thy robe, 3847
Isa 49:18 shalt surely **c.** thee with them all, 3847
Isa 50:3 I **c.** the heavens with blackness, 3847
Eze 26:16 **c.** themselves with trembling; 3847
Eze 34:3 ye **c.** you with the wool, ye kill them 3847
Hag 1:6 ye **c.** you, but there is none warm; 3847
Zec 3:4 **c.** thee with change of raiment 3847
Mt 6:30 **if God so c. the grass of the field,** *294*
Mt 6:30 **shall he not much more c. you,**
Lu 12:28 **If then God so c. the grass, which** *294*
Lu 12:28 **how much more will he c. you,**

CLOTHED See also CLAD; UNCLOTHED.
Ge 3:21 make coats of skins, and **c.** them. 3847
Le 8:7 and **c.** him with the robe, and put 3847
2Sa 1:24 over Saul, who **c.** you in scarlet, 3847
1Ch 15:27 was **c.** with a robe of fine linen, 3736
1Ch 21:16 the elders of Israel, who were **c.** 3680
2Ch 6:41 thy priests...be **c.** with salvation, 3847
2Ch 18:9 **c.** in their robes, and they sat 3847
2Ch 28:15 **c.** all that were naked among them, 3847
Es 4:2 the king's gate **c.** with sackcloth 3830
Job 7:5 My flesh is **c.** with worms and 3847
Job 8:22 hate thee shall be **c.** with shame; 3847
Job 10:11 hast **c.** me with skin and flesh, 3847
Job 29:14 on righteousness, and it **c.** me: 3847
Job 39:19 thou **c.** his neck with thunder? 3847
Ps 35:26 let them be **c.** with shame and 3847
Ps 65:13 The pastures are **c.** with flocks; 3847
Ps 93:1 he is **c.** with majesty; 3847
Ps 93:1 the Lord is **c.** with strength, 3847
Ps 104:1 art **c.** with honour and majesty. 3847
Ps 109:18 As he **c.** himself with cursing 3847
Ps 109:29 mine adversaries be **c.** with shame, 3847
Ps 132:9 priests be **c.** with righteousness; 3847
Pr 31:21 her household are **c.** with scarlet 3847
Isa 61:10 he hath **c.** me with the garments 3847
Eze 7:27 prince shall be **c.** with desolation, 3847
Eze 9:2 among them was **c.** with linen, 3847
Eze 9:3 called to the man **c.** with linen, 3847
Eze 9:11 And, behold, the man **c.** with linen, 3847
Eze 10:2 spake unto the man **c.** with linen, 3847
Eze 10:6 commanded the man **c.** with linen, 3847
Eze 10:7 of him that was **c.** with linen: 3847
Eze 16:10 **c.** thee also with broidered work, 3847
Eze 23:6 **c.** with blue, captains and rulers, 3847
Eze 23:12 and rulers **c.** most gorgeously, 3847
Eze 38:4 **c.** with all sorts of armour, 3847
Eze 44:17 shall be **c.** with linen garments; 3847
Da 5:7 shall be **c.** with scarlet, and have 3848
Da 5:16 thou shalt be **c.** with scarlet, 3848
Da 5:29 and they **c.** Daniel with scarlet, 3848
Da 10:5 behold a certain man **c.** in linen, 3847
Da 12:6 one said to the man **c.** in linen, 3847
Da 12:7 I heard the man **c.** in linen, 3847
Zep 1:8 as are **c.** with strange apparel 3847
Zec 3:3 Joshua was **c.** with filthy garments, 3847
Zec 3:5 head, and **c.** him with garments. 3847
Mt 6:31 **or, Wherewithal shall we be c.?** *4016*
Mt 11:8 **A man c. in soft raiment?** *294*
Mt 25:36 **Naked, and ye c. me: I was sick,** *4016*
Mt 25:38 **thee in? or naked, and c. thee?** *4016*
Mt 25:43 **naked and ye c. me not: sick,** *4016*
Mk 1:6 And John was **c.** with camel's hair. *1746*
Mk 5:15 and **c.**, and in his right mind: *2439*
Mk 15:17 **c.** him with purple, and platted *1746*
Mk 16:5 **c.** in a long white garment; *4016*
Lu 7:25 **see? A man c. in soft raiment?** *294*
Lu 8:35 at the feet of Jesus, **c.**, and in his *2439*
Lu 16:19 **was c. in purple and fine linen,** *1737*
2Co 5:2 earnestly desiring to be **c.** upon *1902*
2Co 5:3 being **c.** we shall not be found *1746*
2Co 5:4 would be unclothed, but **c.** upon, *1902*
1Pe 5:5 be **c.** with humility: for God *1463*
Re 1:13 **c.** with a garment down to the *1746*
Re 3:5 **shall be c. in white raiment;** *4016*
Re 3:18 **raiment, that thou mayest be c.,** *4016*
Re 4:4 sitting, **c.** in white raiment; *4016*
Re 7:9 **c.** with white robes, and palms in *4016*
Re 10:1 from heaven, **c.** with a cloud: *4016*
Re 11:3 threescore days, **c.** in sackcloth. *4016*
Re 12:1 a woman **c.** with the sun, and the *4016*
Re 15:6 **c.** in pure and white linen, and *1746*
Re 18:16 city, that was **c.** in fine linen, *4016*
Re 19:13 **c.** with a vesture dipped in blood: *4016*
Re 19:14 **c.** in fine linen, white and clean. *1746*

CLOTHES See also SACKCLOTHES.
Ge 37:29 in the pit; and he rent his **c.** 899
Ge 37:34 And Jacob rent his **c.**, and put 8071
Ge 44:13 Then they rent their **c.**, and 8071
Ge 49:11 in wine, and his **c.** in the blood 5497
Ex 12:34 being bound up in their **c.** upon 8071
Ex 19:10 let them wash their **c.**, 8071
Ex 19:14 people, and they washed their **c.** 8071
Le 10:6 your heads, neither rend your **c.**; 899
Le 11:25 shall wash his **c.**, and be unclean 899
Le 11:28 carcase of them shall wash his **c.**, 899
Le 11:40 carcase of it shall wash his **c.**, 899
Le 11:40 shall wash his **c.**, and be unclean 899
Le 13:6, 34 shall wash his **c.**, and be clean. 899
Le 13:45 **c.** shall be rent, and his head bare, 899
Le 14:8 wash his **c.**, and shave off all his hair, 899
Le 14:9 he shall wash his **c.**, also he shall 899
Le 14:47 lieth in the house shall wash his **c.**; 899
Le 14:47 eateth in the house shall wash his **c.** 899
Le 15:5, 6,7,8,10,11,13,21,22,27 wash his **c.**, 899
Le 16:26, 28 shall wash his **c.**, and bathe 899
Le 16:32 shall put on the linen **c.**, even 899
Le 17:15 he shall both wash his **c.**, and 899
Le 21:10 uncover his head, nor rend his **c.**; 899
Nu 8:7 let them wash their **c.**, and so make 899
Nu 8:21 purified, and they washed their **c.**; 899
Nu 14:6 that searched the land, rent their **c.** 899
Nu 19:7 Then the priest shall wash his **c.**, 899
Nu 19:8 that burneth her shall wash his **c.** 899
Nu 19:10 of the heifer shall wash his **c.**, 899

Nu 19:19 purify himself, and wash his **c.**, ... 899
Nu 19:21 of separation shall wash his **c.**; ... 899
Nu 31:24 wash your **c.** on the seventh day, ... 899
De 29:5 **c.** are not waxen old upon you, ... 8008
Jos 7:6 Joshua rent his **c.**, and fell to the ... 8071
Jg 11:35 that he rent his **c.**, and said, Alas, ... 899
1Sa 4:12 with his **c.** rent, and with earth ... 4055
1Sa 19:24 he stripped off his **c.** also, and ... 899
2Sa 1:2 camp from Saul with his **c.** rent, ... 899
2Sa 1:11 David took hold on his **c.**, and rent ... 899
2Sa 3:31 Rend your **c.**, and gird you with ... 899
2Sa 13:31 servants stood by with their **c.** rent. ... 899
2Sa 19:24 nor washed his **c.**, from the day the ... 899
1Ki 1:1 they covered him with **c.**, but he gat ... 899
1Ki 21:27 that he rent his **c.**, and put ... 899
2Ki 2:12 he took hold of his own **c.**, and ... 899
2Ki 5:7 that he rent his **c.**, and said, Am I ... 899
2Ki 5:8 the king of Israel had rent his **c.**, ... 899
2Ki 5:8 hast thou rent thy **c.**? let him come ... 899
2Ki 6:30 the woman, that he rent his **c.**; ... 899
2Ki 11:14 Athaliah rent her **c.**, and cried, ... 899
2Ki 18:37 to Hezekiah with their **c.** rent, ... 899
2Ki 19:1 rent his **c.**, and covered himself ... 899
2Ki 22:11 book of the law, that he rent his **c.** ... 899
2Ki 22:19 hast rent thy **c.**, and wept before ... 899
2Ch 23:13 Then Athaliah rent her **c.**, and said, ... 899
2Ch 34:19 words of the law, that he rent his **c.** ... 899
2Ch 34:27 before me, and didst rend thy **c.**, ... 899
Ne 4:23 none of us put off our **c.**, saving ... 899
Ne 9:21 their **c.** waxed not old, and their ... 8008
Es 4:1 Mordecai rent his **c.**, and put on ... 899
Job 9:31 and mine own **c.** shall abhor me. ... 8008
Pr 6:27 bosom, and his **c.** not be burned? ... 899
Isa 36:22 to Hezekiah with their **c.** rent, ... 899
Isa 37:1 heard it, that he rent his **c.**, ... 899
Jer 41:5 and their **c.** rent, and having cut ... 899
Eze 16:39 shall strip thee also of thy **c.**, ... 899
Eze 23:26 strip thee out of thy **c.**, and take ... 899
Eze 27:20 in precious **c.** for chariots ... 899
Eze 27:24 in blue **c.**, and broidered work, ... 1545
Am 2:8 lay themselves down upon **c.** laid ... 899
Mt 21:7 put on them their **c.**, and they ... *2440*
Mt 24:18 **field return back to take his c** ... *2440*
Mt 26:65 Then the high priest rent his **c.**, ... *2440*
Mk 5:28 If I may but touch his **c.**, I shall ... *2440*
Mk 5:30 and said, **Who touched my c.?** ... *2440*
Mk 14:63 Then the high priest rent his **c.**, ... *5509*
Mk 15:20 and put his own **c.** on him, ... *2440*
Lu 2:7 and wrapped him in swaddling **c.**, ... *4683*
Lu 2:12 the babe wrapped in swaddling **c.**, ... *4683*
Lu 8:27 and ware no **c.**, neither abode in ... *2440*
Lu 19:36 they spread their **c.** in the way. ... *2440*
Lu 24:12 the linen **c.** laid by themselves, ... *3608*
Joh 19:40 and wound it in linen **c.** with the ... *3608*
Joh 20:5 looking in, saw the linen **c.** lying; ... *3608*
Joh 20:6 and seeth the linen **c.** lie, ... *3608*
Joh 20:7 not lying with the linen **c.**, but ... *3608*
Ac 7:58 the witnesses laid down their **c.** ... *2440*
Ac 14:14 rent their **c.**, and ran in among ... *2440*
Ac 16:22 the magistrates rent off their **c.**, ... *2440*
Ac 22:23 cast off their **c.**, and threw dust ... *2440*

CLOTHEST
Jer 4:30 thou **c.** thyself with crimson, ... 3847

CLOTHING
Job 22:6 and stripped the naked of their **c.** ... 899
Job 24:7 the naked to lodge without **c.**, ... 3830
Job 24:10 cause him to go naked without **c.**, ... 3830
Job 31:19 seen any perish for want of **c.**, ... 3830
Ps 35:13 were sick, my **c.** was sackcloth: ... 3830
Ps 45:13 within; her **c.** is of wrought gold. ... 3830
Pr 27:26 lambs are for thy **c.**, and the goats ... 3830
Pr 31:22 her **c.** is silk and purple ... 3830
Pr 31:25 Strength and honour are her **c.**; ... 3830
Isa 3:6 Thou hast **c.**, be thou our ruler, ... 8071
Isa 3:7 my house is neither bread nor **c.** ... 8071
Isa 23:18 sufficiently, and for durable **c.** ... 4374
Isa 59:17 the garments of vengeance for **c.**, ... 8516
Jer 10:9 blue and purple is their **c.**: they ... 3830
Mt 7:15 **come to you in sheeps c., but** ... *1742*
Mt 11:8 **wear soft c. are in kings' houses** ...
Mk 12:38 **which love to go in long c., and** ... *4749*
Ac 10:30 stood before me in bright **c.**, ... *2066*
Jas 2:3 to him that weareth the gay **c.**, ... *2066*

CLOTHS
Ex 31:10 the **c.** of service, and the holy ... 899
Ex 35:19 The **c.** of service, to do service in ... 899
Ex 39:1 they made **c.** of service, to do ... 899
Ex 39:41 The **c.** of service to do service in ... 899

CLOUD See also CLOUDS.
Ge 9:13 I do set my bow in the **c.**, and it ... 6051
Ge 9:14 when I bring a **c.** over the earth, ... 6051
Ge 9:14 the bow shall be seen in the **c.** ... 6051
Ge 9:16 And the bow shall be in the **c.**; ... 6051
Ex 13:21 them by day in a pillar of a **c.**, ... 6051
Ex 13:22 took not away the pillar of the **c.** ... 6051
Ex 14:19 the **c.** went from before their face, ... 6051
Ex 14:20 it was a **c.** and darkness to them, ... 6051
Ex 14:24 the pillar of fire and of the **c.**, ... 6051
Ex 16:10 of the Lord appeared in the **c.** ... 6051
Ex 19:9 I come unto thee in a thick **c.**, ... 6051
Ex 19:16 and a thick **c.** upon the mount, ... 6051
Ex 24:15 a **c.** covered the mount. ... 6051
Ex 24:16 the **c.** covered it six days: and ... 6051
Ex 24:16 Moses out of the midst of the **c.** ... 6051
Ex 24:18 went into the midst of the **c.**, ... 6051
Ex 34:5 And the Lord descended in the **c.**, ... 6051
Ex 40:34 a **c.** covered the tent of the ... 6051
Ex 40:35 **c.** abode thereon, and the glory ... 6051
Ex 40:36 when the **c.** was taken up from ... 6051
Ex 40:37 But if the **c.** were not taken up, ... 6051
Ex 40:38 the **c.** of the Lord was upon the ... 6051
Le 16:2 in the **c.** upon the mercy seat ... 6051
Le 16:13 that the **c.** of the incense may ... 6051
Nu 9:15 the **c.** covered the tabernacle. ... 6051
Nu 9:16 the **c.** covered it by day, and the ... 6051
Nu 9:17 And when the **c.** was taken up ... 6051
Nu 9:17 in the place where the **c.** abode, ... 6051
Nu 9:18 as long as the **c.** abode upon the ... 6051
Nu 9:19 **c.** tarried long upon the tabernacle ... 6051
Nu 9:20 when the **c.** was a few days upon ... 6051
Nu 9:21 when the **c.** abode from even unto ... 6051
Nu 9:21 **c.** was taken up in the morning, ... 6051
Nu 9:21 by night that the **c.** was taken up, ... 6051
Nu 9:22 the **c.** tarried upon the tabernacle, ... 6051
Nu 10:11 that the **c.** was taken up ... 6051
Nu 10:12 the **c.** rested in the wilderness of ... 6051
Nu 10:34 the **c.** of the Lord was upon them ... 6051
Nu 11:25 And the Lord came down in a **c.**, ... 6051
Nu 12:5 came down in the pillar of the **c.**, ... 6051
Nu 12:10 And the **c.** departed from off the ... 6051
Nu 14:14 that thy **c.** standeth over them, ... 6051
Nu 14:14 by day time in a pillar of a **c.**, ... 6051
Nu 16:42 behold, the **c.** covered it, and the ... 6051
De 1:33 ye should go, and in a **c.** by day. ... 6051
De 5:22 the **c.**, and of the thick darkness, ... 6051
De 31:15 the tabernacle in a pillar of a **c.** ... 6051
De 31:15 and the pillar of the **c.** stood over ... 6051
1Ki 8:10 the **c.** filled the house of the Lord, ... 6051
1Ki 8:11 stand to minister because of the **c.** ... 6051
1Ki 18:44 ariseth a little **c.** out of the sea, ... 5645
2Ch 5:13 the house was filled with a **c.**, ... 6051
2Ch 5:14 to minister by reason of the **c.** ... 6051
Ne 9:19 the pillar of the **c.** departed not ... 6051
Job 3:5 let a **c.** dwell upon it; let the ... 6053
Job 7:9 **c.** is consumed and vanisheth away: ... 6051
Job 22:13 he judge through the dark **c.**? ... 6205
Job 26:8 the **c.** is not rent under them. ... 6051
Job 26:9 and spreadeth his **c.** upon it. ... 6051
Job 30:15 my welfare passeth away as a **c.** ... 5645
Job 36:32 by the **c.** that cometh betwixt. ...
Job 37:11 he wearieth the thick **c.** ... 5645
Job 37:11 he scattereth his bright **c.** ... 6051
Job 37:15 caused the light of his **c.** to shine? ... 6051
Job 38:9 made the **c.** the garment thereof, ... 6051
Ps 78:14 daytime also he led them with a **c.**, ... 6051
Ps 105:39 He spread a **c.** for a covering; and ... 6051
Pr 16:15 favour is as a **c.** of the latter rain. ... 5645
Isa 4:5 a **c.** and smoke by day, and the ... 6051
Isa 18:4 a **c.** of dew in the heat of harvest. ... 5645
Isa 19:1 the Lord rideth upon a swift **c.**, ... 5645
Isa 25:5 the heat with the shadow of a **c.** ... 5645
Isa 44:22 I have blotted out, as a thick **c.**, ... 5645
Isa 44:22 as a **c.**, thy sins: return unto me; ... 6051
Isa 60:8 Who are these that fly as a **c.**, ... 5645
La 2:1 the daughter of Zion with a **c.** ... 5743
La 3:44 hast covered thyself with a **c.**, ... 6051
Eze 1:4 a great **c.**, and a fire infolding itself, ... 6051
Eze 1:28 that is in the **c.** in the day of rain, ... 6051
Eze 8:11 and a thick **c.** of incense went up. ... 6051
Eze 10:3 and the **c.** filled the inner court. ... 6051
Eze 10:4 the house was filled with the **c.**, ... 6051
Eze 30:18 as for her, a **c.** shall cover her, ... 6051
Eze 32:7 I will cover the sun with a **c.**, and ... 6051
Eze 38:9 shalt be like a **c.** to cover the land, ... 6051
Eze 38:16 as a **c.** to cover the land; it shall ... 6051
Ho 6:4 your goodness is as a morning **c.**, ... 6051
Ho 13:3 they shall be as the morning **c.**, ... 6051
Mt 17:5 a bright **c.** overshadowed them: ... *3507*
Mt 17:5 and behold a voice out of the **c.**, ... *3507*
Mk 9:7 a **c.** that overshadowed them: ... *3507*
Mk 9:7 and a voice came out of the **c.**, ... *3507*
Lu 9:34 a **c.**, and overshadowed them: ... *3507*
Lu 9:34 as they entered into the **c.** ... *3507*
Lu 9:35 there came a voice out of the **c.**, ... *3507*
Lu 12:54 **ye see a c. rise out of the west** ... *3507*
Lu 21:27 **in a c. with power and great glory** ... *3507*
Ac 1:9 a **c.** received him out of their sight. ... *3507*
1Co 10:1 all our fathers were under the **c.**, ... *3507*
1Co 10:2 Moses in the **c.** and in the sea; ... *3507*
Heb 12:1 with so great a **c.** of witnesses, ... *3509*
Re 10:1 from heaven, clothed with a **c.** ... *3507*
Re 11:12 ascended up to heaven in a **c.**; ... *3507*
Re 14:14 and behold a white **c.**, and upon the ... *3507*
Re 14:14 upon the **c.** one sat like unto the Son ... *3507*
Re 14:15 to him that sat on the **c.**, Thrust ... *3507*
Re 14:16 sat on the **c.** thrust in his sickle ... *3507*

CLOUDS
De 4:11 darkness, **c.**, and thick darkness. ... 6051
Jg 5:4 the **c.** also dropped water. ... 5645
2Sa 22:12 waters, and thick **c.** of the skies, ... 5645
2Sa 23:4 even a morning without **c.**; ... 5645
1Ki 18:45 was black with **c.** and wind, ... 5645
Job 20:6 and his head reach unto the **c.**; ... 5645
Job 22:14 Thick **c.** are a covering to him, ... 5645
Job 26:8 up the waters in his thick **c.**; ... 5645
Job 35:5 **c.** which are higher than thou. ... 7834
Job 36:28 **c.** do drop and distil upon man ... 7834
Job 36:29 the spreadings of the **c.**, ... 5645
Job 36:32 With **c.** he covereth the light; ... 3709
Job 37:16 know the balancings of the **c.**, ... 5645
Job 37:21 bright light which is in the **c.** ... 7834
Job 38:34 thou lift up thy voice to the **c.**, ... 5645
Job 38:37 can number the **c.** in wisdom? ... 7834
Ps 18:11 waters and thick **c.** of the skies. ... 5645
Ps 18:12 before him his thick **c.** passed, ... 5645
Ps 36:5 faithfulness reacheth unto the **c.** ... 7834
Ps 57:10 and thy truth unto the **c.** ... 7834
Ps 68:34 and his strength is in the **c.** ... 7834
Ps 77:17 The **c.** poured out water: the ... 5645
Ps 78:23 commanded the **c.** from above, ... 7834
Ps 97:2 **C.** and darkness are round about ... 6051
Ps 104:3 who maketh the **c.** his chariot: ... 5645
Ps 108:4 thy truth reacheth into the **c.** ... 7834
Ps 147:8 Who covereth the heaven with **c.**, ... 5645
Pr 3:20 and the **c.** drop down the dew. ... 7834
Pr 8:28 When he established the **c.** above: ... 7834
Pr 25:14 is like **c.** and wind without rain. ... 5387
Ec 11:3 If the **c.** be full of rain, they empty ... 5645
Ec 11:4 regardeth the **c.** shall not reap. ... 5645
Ec 12:2 nor the **c.** return after the rain: ... 5645
Isa 5:6 I will also command the **c.** that ... 5645
Isa 14:14 ascend above the heights of the **c.**; ... 5645
Jer 4:13 he shall come up as **c.**, and his ... 6053
Da 7:13 of man came with the **c.** of heaven ... 6050
Joe 2:2 a day of **c.** and of thick darkness, ... 6051
Na 1:3 and the **c.** are the dust of his feet. ... 6051
Zep 1:15 a day of **c.** and thick darkness, ... 6051
Zec 10:1 the Lord shall make bright **c.**, ... 2385
Mt 24:30 **in the c. of heaven with power** ... *3507*
Mt 26:64 **and coming in the c. of heaven** ... *3507*
Mk 13:26 **the Son of man coming in the c** ... *3507*
Mk 14:62 **and coming in the c. of heaven** ... *3507*
1Th 4:17 up together with them in the **c.**, ... *3507*
2Pe 2:17 **c.** that are carried with a ... *3507*
Jude 12 **c.** they are without water, carried ... *3507*
Re 1:7 Behold he cometh with **c.**; and ... *3507*

CLOUDY
Ex 33:9 **c.** pillar descended, and stood ... 6051
Ex 33:10 the people saw the **c.** pillar stand ... 6051
Ne 9:12 them in the day by a **c.** pillar; ... 6051
Ps 99:7 spake unto them in the **c.** pillar: ... 6051
Eze 30:3 day of the Lord is near, a **c.** day; ... 6051
Eze 34:12 scattered in the **c.** and dark day. ... 6051

CLOUTED
Jos 9:5 old shoes and **c.** upon their feet, ... 2921

CLOUTS
Jer 38:11 old cast **c.** and old rotten rags, 5499
Jer 38:12 Put now these old cast **c.** and 5499

CLOVE See CLAVE.

CLOVEN See also CLOVENFOOTED.
De 14:7 or of them that divide the **c.** hoof; 8156
Ac 2:3 appeared unto them **c.** tongues *1266*

CLOVENFOOTED
Le 11:3 the hoof, and is **c.**, 8156,8157,6541
Le 11:7 the hoof, and be **c.**, 8156,8157,6541
Le 11:26 the hoof, and is not **c.**, 8156,8157,6541

CLUSTER See also CLUSTERS.
Nu 13:23 a branch with one **c.** of grapes, 811
Nu 13:24 the **c.** of grapes which the children 811
Ca 1:14 My beloved is unto me as a **c.** of 811
Isa 65:8 As the new wine is found in the **c.**, 811
Mic 7:1 there is no **c.** to eat: my soul 811

CLUSTERS
Ge 40:10 the **c.** thereof brought forth ripe 811
De 32:32 grapes of gall, their **c.** are bitter: 811
1Sa 25:18 and an hundred **c.** of raisins, 6778
1Sa 30:12 cake of figs, and two **c.** of raisins: 6778
Ca 7:7 and thy breasts to **c.** of grapes 811
Ca 7:8 breasts shall be as **c.** of the vine, 811
Re 14:18 the **c.** of the vine of the earth; *1009*

CNIDUS (ni'-dus)
Ac 27:7 scarce were come over against **C.**, *2834*

COAL See also COALS.
2Sa 14:7 so they shall quench my **c.** which 1513
Isa 6:6 having a live **c.** in his hand, 7531
Isa 47:14 there shall not be a **c.** to warm at, 1513
La 4:8 Their visage is blacker than a **c.**; 7815

COALS
Le 16:12 take a censer full of burning **c.** 1513
2Sa 22:9 devoured: **c.** were kindled by it. 1513
2Sa 22:13 before him were **c.** of fire 1513
1Ki 19:6 there was a cake baken on the **c.**, 7529
Job 41:21 His breath kindleth **c.**, and a 1513
Ps 18:8 devoured: **c.** were kindled by it. 1513
Ps 18:12 passed, hail stones and **c.** of fire. 1513
Ps 18:13 his voice; hail stones and **c.** of fire. 1513
Ps 120:4 of the mighty, with **c.** of juniper. 1513
Ps 140:10 let burning **c.** fall upon them: let 1513
Pr 6:28 Can one go upon hot **c.**, and his 1513
Pr 25:22 thou shalt heap **c.** of fire upon his 1513
Pr 26:21 As **c.** are to burning 6352
Pr 26:21 are to burning **c.**, and wood to 1513
Ca 8:6 the **c.** thereof are **c.** of fire, which 7565
Isa 44:12 the tongs both worked in the **c.**, 6352
Isa 44:19 baked bread upon the **c.** thereof; 1513
Isa 54:16 the smith that bloweth the **c.** 6352
Eze 1:13 was like burning **c.** of fire, 1513
Eze 10:2 and fill thine hand with **c.** of fire 1513
Eze 24:11 Then set it empty upon the **c.** 1513
Hab 3:5 and burning **c.** went forth at his 7565
Joh 18:18 who had made a fire of **c.**; for it *439*
Joh 21:9 they saw a fire of **c.** there, and fish *439*
Ro 12:20 thou shalt heap **c.** of fire on his *440*

COAST See also COASTS.
Ex 10:4 I bring the locusts into thy **c.** 1366
Nu 13:29 the sea, and by the **c.** of Jordan. 3027
Nu 20:23 by the **c.** of the land of Edom, 1366
Nu 22:36 Arnon, which is in the utmost **c.** 1366
Nu 24:24 shall come from the **c.** of Chittim, 3027
Nu 34:3 of Zin along by the **c.** of Edom, 3027
Nu 34:3 the outmost **c.** of the salt sea 7097
Nu 34:11 **c.** shall go down from Shepham 1366
De 2:4 through the **c.** of your brethren 1366
De 2:18 over through Ar, the **c.** of Moab, 1366
De 3:17 Jordan, and the **c.** thereof, 1366
De 11:24 uttermost sea shall your **c.** be. 1366
De 16:4 seen with thee in all thy **c.** seven 1366
De 19:8 the Lord thy God enlarge thy **c.**, 1366
Jos 1:4 down of the sun, shall be your **c.** 1366
Jos 12:4 And the **c.** of Og king of Bashan, 1366
Jos 12:23 The king of Dor in the **c.** of Dor, 5299
Jos 13:16 their **c.** was from Aroer, that is 1366
Jos 13:25 their **c.** was Jazer, and all the 1366
Jos 13:30 And their **c.** wsas from Mahanaim, 1366
Jos 15:1 uttermost part of the south **c.** 1366
Jos 15:4 out of that **c.** were at the sea: 1366
Jos 15:4 this shall be your south **c.** 1366
Jos 15:12 the great sea, and the **c.** thereof. 1366
Jos 15:12 is the **c.** of the children of Judah, 1366
Jos 15:21 toward the **c.** of Edom southward 1366
Jos 16:3 to the **c.** of Japhleti, unto the **c.** 1366
Jos 17:7 the **c.** of Manesseh was from 1366
Jos 17:9 And the **c.** descended unto the 1366
Jos 17:9 the **c.** of Manesseh also was on 1366
Jos 18:5 Judah shall abide in their **c.** on 1366
Jos 18:11 and the **c.** of their lot came forth 1366
Jos 18:19 of Jordan: this was the south **c.** 1366
Jos 19:22 the **c.** reacheth to Tabor, and 1366
Jos 19:29 the **c.** turneth to Ramah, and to 1366
Jos 19:29 and the **c.** turneth to Hosah; 1366
Jos 19:29 at the sea from the **c.** to Achzib: 2256
Jos 19:33 their **c.** was from Heleph, from 1366
Jos 19:34 then the **c.** turneth westward to 1366
Jos 19:41 the **c.** of the inheritance was 1366
Jos 19:47 the **c.** of the children of Dan went 1366
Jg 1:18 Gaza with the **c.** thereof, 1366
Jg 1:18 and Askelon with the **c.** thereof, 1366
Jg 1:18 and Ekron with the **c.** thereof. 1366
Jg 1:36 And the **c.** of the Amorites was 1366
Jg 11:20 not Israel to pass through his **c.** 1366
1Sa 6:9 by the way of his own **c.** to 1366
1Sa 7:13 no more into the **c.** of Israel: 1366
1Sa 27:1 any more in any **c.** of Israel: 1366
1Sa 30:14 the **c.** which belongeth to Judah,
2Ki 14:25 He restored the **c.** of Israel from 1366
1Ch 4:10 me indeed, and enlarge my **c.**, 1366
Eze 25:16 destroy the remnant of the sea **c.** 2348
Eze 47:16 which is by the **c.** of Hauran. 1366
Eze 48:1 the **c.** of the way of Hethlon, as 3027
Eze 48:1 northward, to the **c.** of Hamath; 3027
Zep 2:5 unto the inhabitants of the sea **c.**, 2256
Zep 2:6 the sea **c.** shall be dwellings and 2256
Zep 2:7 the **c.** shall be for the remnant of 2256
Mt 4:13 which is upon the sea **c.** *3864*
Lu 6:17 from the sea **c.** of Tyre and Sidon, *3882*

COASTS
Ex 10:14 and rested in all the **c.** of Egypt: 1366
Ex 10:19 one locust in all the **c.** of Egypt. 1366
Nu 21:13 out of the **c.** of the Amorites: 1366
Nu 32:33 with the cities thereof in the **c.**, 1367
Nu 34:2 the land of Canaan with the **c.** 1367
Nu 34:12 your land with the **c.** thereof 1367
De 3:14 of Argob unto the **c.** of Geshuri 1366
De 19:3 divide the **c.** of thy land, which 1366
De 28:40 olive trees throughout all thy **c.**, 1366
Jos 9:1 in all the **c.** of the great sea over 2348
Jos 18:5 Joseph shall abide in their **c.** on 1366
Jos 18:20 Benjamin by the **c.** thereof 1367
Jos 19:49 land for inheritance by their **c.**, 1367
Jg 11:22 all the **c.** of the Amorites, 1366
Jg 11:26 that be along by the **c.** of Arnon, 3027
Jg 18:2 five men from their **c.**, men of 7098
Jg 19:29 sent her into all the **c.** of Israel. 1366
1Sa 5:6 even Ashdod and the **c.** thereof. 1366
1Sa 7:14 and the **c.** thereof did Israel 1366
1Sa 11:3 unto all the **c.** of Israel: 1366
1Sa 11:7 throughout all the **c.** of Israel 1366
2Sa 21:5 in any of the **c.** of Israel, 1366
1Ki 1:3 throughout all the **c.** of Israel, 1366
2Ki 10:32 smote them in all the **c.** of Israel; 1366
2Ki 15:16 therein, and the **c.** thereof from 1366
1Ch 6:54 their castles in their **c.**, 1366
1Ch 6:66 had cities of their **c.** out of the 1366
1Ch 21:12 throughout all the **c.** of Israel. 1366
2Ch 11:13 resorted to him out of all their **c.** 1366
Ps 105:31 flies, and lice in all their **c.** 1366
Ps 105:33 brake the trees of their **c.** 1366
Jer 25:32 up from the **c.** of the earth. 3411
Jer 31:8 them from the **c.** of the earth, 3411
Jer 50:41 up from the **c.** of the earth. 3411
Eze 33:2 take a man of their **c.**, and set 7097
Joe 3:4 Zidon, and all the **c.** of Palestine? 1552
Mt 2:16 and in all the **c.** thereof, from *3725*
Mt 8:34 he would depart out of their **c.** *3725*
Mt 15:21 departed into the **c.** of Tyre and *3313*
Mt 15:22 out of the same **c.**, and cried *3725*
Mt 15:39 came into the **c.** of Magdala. *3725*
Mt 16:13 Jesus came into the **c.** of Caesarea *3313*
Mt 19:1 and came into the **c.** of Judea *3725*
Mk 5:17 pray him to depart out of their **c.** *3725*
Mk 7:31 departing from the **c.** of Tyre *3725*
Mk 7:31 the midst of the **c.** of Decapolis. *3725*
Mk 10:1 and cometh into the **c.** of Judea *3725*
Ac 13:50 and expelled them out of their **c.** *3725*
Ac 19:1 passed through the upper **c.** *3313*
Ac 26:20 throughout all the **c.** of Judea, *5561*
Ac 27:2 meaning to sail by the **c.** of Asia; *5117*

COAT See also COATS.
Ge 37:3 made him a **c.** of many colours. 3801
Ge 37:23 out of his **c.**, his **c.** of many colours 3801
Ge 37:31 they took Joseph's **c.**, and killed 3801
Ge 37:31 and dipped the **c.** in the blood; 3801
Ge 37:32 they sent the **c.** of many colours, 3801
Ge 37:32 whether it be thy son's **c.** or no. 3801
Ge 37:33 it, and said, It is my son's **c.**; 3801
Ex 28:4 and a broidered **c.**, a mitre, and 3801
Ex 28:39 embroider the **c.** of fine linen, 3801
Ex 29:5 put upon Aaron the **c.**, and the 3801
Le 8:7 he put upon him the **c.**, and 3801
Le 16:4 He shall put on the holy linen **c.**, 3801
1Sa 2:19 his mother made him a little **c.**, 4598
1Sa 17:5 he was armed with a **c.** of mail; 8302
1Sa 17:5 and the weight of the **c.** was 8302
1Sa 17:38 he armed him with a **c.** of mail. 8302
2Sa 15:32 came to meet him with his **c.** rent, 3801
Job 30:18 me about as the collar of my **c.** 3801
Ca 5:3 I have put off my **c.**; how shall I 3801
Mt 5:40 **at the law, and take away thy c.,** *5509*
Lu 6:29 **forbid not to take thy c. also.** *5509*
Joh 19:23 and also his **c.**: now the **c.** was *5509*
Joh 21:7 he girt his fisher's **c.** unto him, *1903*

COAT OF MAIL See COAT and MAIL.

COATS
Gen 3:21 did the Lord God make **c.** of skins, 3801
Ex 28:40 Aaron's sons thou shalt make **c.**, 3801
Ex 29:8 his sons, and put **c.** upon them. 3801
Ex 39:27 they made **c.** of fine linen of 3801
Ex 40:14 sons, and clothe them with **c.** 3801
Le 8:13 put **c.** upon them, and girded them 3801
Le 10:5 carried them in their **c.** out of the 3801
Da 3:21 bound in their **c.**, their hosen 5622
Da 3:27 neither were their **c.** changed, 5622
Mt 10:10 **neither two c., neither shoes,** *5509*
Mk 6:9 sandals; and not put on two **c.** *5509*
Lu 3:11 He that hath two **c.**, let him *5509*
Lu 9:3 **money; neither have two c. apiece.** *5509*
Ac 9:39 shewing the **c.** and garments which *5509*

COCK See also COCKCROWING; PEACOCKS.
Mt 26:34 **this night, before the c. crow, thou** *220*
Mt 26:74 and immediately the **c.** crew. *220*
Mt 26:75 Before the **c.** crow, thou shalt deny *220*
Mk 14:30 **before the c. crow twice, thou shalt** *220*
Mk 14:68 into the porch; and the **c.** crew. *220*
Mk 14:72 the second time the **c.** crew. *220*
Mk 14:72 said unto him, Before the **c.** crow *220*
Lu 22:34 **the c. shall not crow this day,** *220*
Lu 22:60 while he yet spake, the **c.** crew. *220*
Lu 22:61 Before the **c.** crow, thou shalt deny *220*
Joh 13:38 **The c. shall not crow, till thou hast** *220*
Joh 18:27 and immediately the **c.** crew. *220*

COCKATRICE See also COCKATRICE'; COCKATRICES.
Isa 14:29 shall come forth a **c.**, and his 6848

COCKATRICE'
Isa 11:8 shall put his hand on the **c.** den. 6848
Isa 59:5 They hatch **c.** eggs, and weave the 6848

COCKATRICES
Jer 8:17 I will send serpents, **c.**, among, 6848

COCKCROWING
Mk 13:35 **at midnight, or at the c., or in the** *219*

COCKLE
Job 31:40 instead of wheat, and **c.** instead of 890

COFFER
1Sa 6:8 a trespass offering, in a **c.** by the 712
1Sa 6:11 the **c.** with the mice of gold and 712
1Sa 6:15 and the **c.** that was with it, wherein 712

COFFIN
Ge 50:26 and he was put in a **c.** in Egypt. 727

COGITATIONS
Da 7:28 my **c.** much troubled me, and 7476

COL See COL-HOZEH.

COLD
Ge 8:22 and **c.** and heat, and summer 7120

Job 24:7 they have no covering in the **c.** 7135
Job 37:9 whirlwind: and **c.** out of the north. 7135
Ps 147:17 who can stand before his **c.**? 7135
Pr 20:4 will not plow by reason of the **c.**; 2779
Pr 25:13 As the **c.** of snow in the time of 6793
Pr 25:20 away a garment in **c.** weather, 7135
Pr 25:25 **c.** waters to a thirsty soul, so is 7119
Jer 18:14 shall the **c.** flowing waters that 7119
Na 3:17 camp in the hedges in the **c.** day, 7135
Mt 10:42 **these little ones a cup of c. water** *5593*
Mt 24:12 **the love of many shall wax c.** *5594*
Joh 18:18 made a fire of coals; for it was **c.**: *5592*
Ac 28:2 present rain, and because of the **c.** *5592*
2Co 11:27 in fastings often, in **c.** and *5592*
Re 3:15 **that thou art neither c. nor hot:** *5593*
Re 3:15 **I would thou wert c. or hot.** *5593*
Re 3:16 **and neither c. nor hot, I will spue** *5593*

COL-HOZEH (col-ho'-zeh)
Ne 3:15 repaired Shallum the son of **C.**, 3626
Ne 11:5 the son of Baruch, the son of **C.**, 3626

COLLAR See also COLLARS.
Job 30:18 me about as the **c.** of my coat. 6310

COLLARS
Jg 8:26 and **c.**, and purple raiment 5188

COLLECTION
2Ch 24:6 out of Jerusalem the **c.**, according 4864
2Ch 24:9 to the Lord the **c.** that Moses 4864
1Co 16:1 concerning the **c.** for the saints, *3048*

COLLEGE
2Ki 22:14 she dwelt in Jerusalem in the **c.**;) 4932
2Ch 34:22 she dwelt in Jerusalem in the **c.**:) 4932

COLLOPS
Job 15:27 maketh **c.** of fat on his flanks. 6371

COLONY
Ac 16:12 part of Macedonia, and a **c.** *2862*

COLOR See COLOUR.

COLOSSAE See COLOSSE.

COLOSSE (co-los'-see) See also COLOSSIANS.
Col 1:2 in Christ which are at **C.**: *2857*

COLOSSIANS (co-los'-yans)
Col *general title* The Epistle Of Paul … To … **C.** *2858*
Col *subscr.* Written from Rome to the **C.** *2858*

COLOUR See also COLOURED; COLOURS.
Le 13:55 plague have not changed his **c.**, 5869
Nu 11:7 **c.** thereof as the **c.** of bdellium. 5869
Pr 23:31 when it giveth his **c.** in the cup, 5869
Eze 1:4 midst thereof as the **c.** of amber, 5869
Eze 1:7 like the **c.** of burnished brass. 5869
Eze 1:16 was like unto the **c.** of a beryl: 5869
Eze 1:22 as the **c.** of the terrible crystal, 5869
Eze 1:27 And I saw as **c.** of amber, as 5869
Eze 8:2 of brightness, as the **c.** of amber 5869
Eze 10:9 wheels was as the **c.** of a beryl 5869
Da 10:6 feet like in **c.** to polished brass, 5869
Ac 27:30 under **c.** as though they would *4392*
Re 17:4 arrayed in purple and scarlet **c.**, *4392*

COLOURED
Re 17:3 sit upon a scarlet **c.** beast,

COLOURS
Ge 37:3 he made him a coat of many **c.** 6446
Ge 37:23 coat of many **c.** that was on him; 6446
Ge 37:32 And they sent the coat of many **c.**, 6446
Jg 5:30 to Sisera a prey of divers **c.**, 6648
Jg 5:30 a prey of divers **c.** of needlework, 6648
Jg 5:30 of divers **c.** of needlework on both 6648
2Sa 13:18 a garment of divers **c.** upon her: 6446
2Sa 13:19 rent her garment of divers **c.** 6446
1Ch 29:2 glistering stones, and of divers **c.**, 7553
Isa 54:11 I will lay thy stones with fair **c.**, 6320
Eze 16:16 thy high places with divers **c.**, 2921
Eze 17:3 of feathers, which had divers **c.**, 7553

COLT See also COLTS.
Ge 49:11 ass's **c.** unto the choice vine; 1121
Job 11:12 man be born like a wild ass's **c.** 5895
Zec 9:9 and upon a **c.** the foal of an ass. 5895
Mt 21:2 **find an ass tied, and a c. with her:** *4454*
Mt 21:5 an ass, and a **c.** the foal of an ass. *4454*
Mt 21:7 brought the ass, and the **c.**, and put *4454*
Mk 11:2 **ye shall find a c. tied, whereon** *4454*
Mk 11:4 and found the **c.** tied by the door *4454*
Mk 11:5 them, What do ye, loosing the **c.**? *4454*
Mk 11:7 brought the **c.** to Jesus, and cast *4454*
Lu 19:30 **entering ye shall find a c. tied,** *4454*
Lu 19:33 as they were loosing the **c.**, the *4454*
Lu 19:33 unto them, Why loose ye the **c.**? *4454*
Lu 19:35 cast their garments upon the **c.**, *4454*
Joh 12:15 king cometh, sitting on an ass's **c.** *4454*

COLTS
Ge 32:15 milch camels with their **c.**, forty 1121
Jg 10:4 sons that rode on thirty ass **c.**, 5895
Jg 12:14 rode on threescore and ten ass **c.** 5895

COMBS See HONEYCOMBS.

COME See also CAME; COMEST; COMETH; COMING; BECOME; OVERCOME.
Ge 4:14 it shall **c.** to pass, that every one 1961
Ge 6:13 end of all flesh is **c.** before me; 935
Ge 6:18 and thou shalt **c.** into the ark, thou, 935
Ge 6:20 two of every sort shall **c.** unto thee, 935
Ge 7:1 **C.** thou and all thy house into the 935
Ge 9:14 And it shall **c.** t pass, when I bring 1961
Ge 12:11 was **c.** near to enter into Egypt, 7126
Ge 12:12 therefore it shall **c.** to pass,
Ge 12:14 when Abram was **c.** into Egypt, 935
Ge 15:4 shall **c.** forth out of thine own 3318
Ge 15:14 they **c.** out with great substance. 3318
Ge 15:16 they shall **c.** hither again: for the 7725
Ge 17:6 thee, and kings shall **c.** out of thee. 3318
Ge 18:5 therefore are ye **c.** to your servant. 5674
Ge 18:21 the cry of it, which is **c.** unto me; 935
Ge 19:22 cannot do any thing till thou be **c.** 935
Ge 19:31 to **c.** in unto us after the manner 935
Ge 19:32 **C.**, let us make our father drink 3212
Ge 20:4 Abimelech had not **c.** near her: 7126
Ge 20:13 whither we shall **c.**, say of me, 935
Ge 22:5 and worship, and **c.** again to you. 7725
Ge 24:13 of the city **c.** out to draw water: 3318
Ge 24:14 And let it **c.** to pass, that the damsel 1961
Ge 24:31 **C.** in, thou blessed of the Lord; 935
Ge 24:43 **c.** to pass, that when the virgin 1961
Ge 26:27 Wherefore **c.** ye to me, seeing ye 935
Ge 27:21 **C.** near, I pray thee, that I may 5066
Ge 27:26 **C.** near now, and kiss me, my son. 5066
Ge 27:40 it shall **c.** to pass when thou shalt 1961
Ge 28:21 I **c.** again to my father's house 7725
Ge 30:16 Thou must **c.** in unto me; for 935
Ge 30:33 answer for me in time to **c.**, 4279
Ge 30:33 **c.** for my hire before thy face: 935
Ge 31:44 **c.** thou, let us make a covenant, 3212
Ge 32:8 If Esau **c.** to the one company, 935
Ge 32:11 him, lest he will **c.** and smite me, 935
Ge 33:14 until I **c.** unto my Lord unto Seir. 935
Ge 34:5 his peace until they were **c.** 935
Ge 35:11 kings shall **c.** out of thy loins; 3318
Ge 35:16 but a little way to **c.** to Ephrath: 935
Ge 37:10 mother and thy brethren indeed **c.** 935
Ge 37:13 **c.**, and I will send thee unto them. 3212
Ge 37:20 **C.** now therefore, and let us slay 3212
Ge 37:23 Joseph was **c.** unto his brethren, 935
Ge 37:27 **C.**, and let us sell him to the 3212
Ge 38:16 pray thee, let me **c.** in unto thee; 935
Ge 38:16 that thou mayest **c.** in unto me? 935
Ge 41:29 there **c.** seven years of great plenty 935
Ge 41:35 the food of those good years that **c.**, 935
Ge 41:54 seven years of dearth began to **c.**, 935
Ge 42:7 Whence **c.** ye? And they said, 935
Ge 42:9 the nakedness of the land ye are **c.** 935
Ge 42:10 but to buy food are thy servants **c.** 935
Ge 42:12 the nakedness of the land ye are **c.** 935
Ge 42:15 your youngest brother **c.** hither. 935
Ge 42:21 therefore is this distress **c.** upon us. 935
Ge 44:23 Except your youngest brother **c.** 3381
Ge 44:30 when I **c.** to thy servant my father, 935
Ge 44:31 It shall **c.** to pass, when he seeth 1961
Ge 44:34 the evil that shall **c.** on my father 4672
Ge 45:4 **C.** near to me, I pray you. And 5066
Ge 45:9 **c.** down unto me, tarry not: 3381
Ge 45:11 all that thou hast, **c.** to poverty
Ge 45:16 Joseph's brethren are **c.**: and it 935
Ge 45:18 and **c.** unto me: and I will give you 935
Ge 45:19 wives, and bring your father, and **c.** 935
Ge 46:31 My brethren,…are **c.** unto me; 935
Ge 46:33 it shall **c.** to pass, when Pharaoh 1961
Ge 47:1 they have, are **c.** out of the land 935
Ge 47:4 to sojourn in the land are we **c.**; 935
Ge 47:5 and thy brethren are **c.** unto thee: 935
Ge 47:24 it shall **c.** to pass in the increase 1961
Ge 48:7 a little way to **c.** unto Ephrath: 935
Ge 49:6 soul, **c.** not thou into their secret; 935
Ge 49:10 until Shiloh **c.**; and unto him shall 935
Ge 50:5 my father, and I will **c.** again. 7725
Ex 1:10 **C.** on, let us deal wisely with 3051
Ex 1:10 and it **c.** to pass, that, when there 1961
Ex 1:19 ere the midwives **c.** in unto them. 935
Ex 2:18 is it that ye are **c.** so soon to day? 935
Ex 3:8 And I am **c.** down to deliver them 3381
Ex 3:9 children of Israel is **c.** unto me: 935
Ex 3:10 **C.** now therefore, and I will send 3212
Ex 3:13 I **c.** unto the children of Israel, 935
Ex 3:18 **c.**, thou and the elders of Israel, 935
Ex 3:21 and it shall **c.** to pass, that, when 1961
Ex 4:8,9 **c.** to pass, if they will not believe 1961
Ex 7:15 by the river's brink against he **c.**; 7125
Ex 8:3 **c.** into thine house, and into thy 935
Ex 8:4 the frogs shall **c.** up both on thee, 5927
Ex 8:5 cause frogs to **c.** up upon the land 5927
Ex 9:19 the hail shall **c.** down upon them, 3381
Ex 10:12 they may **c.** up upon the land 5927
Ex 10:26 serve the Lord, until we **c.** thither. 935
Ex 11:8 these thy servants shall **c.** down 3381
Ex 12:23 not suffer the destroyer to **c.** in 935
Ex 12:25 And it shall **c.** to pass, when ye 1961
Ex 12:25 be **c.** to the land which the Lord 935
Ex 12:26 it shall **c.** to pass, when your 1961
Ex 12:48 then let him **c.** near and keep it; 7126
Ex 13:14 thy son asketh thee in time to **c.**, 4279
Ex 14:26 may **c.** again upon the Egyptians, 7725
Ex 16:5 And it shall **c.** to pass, that on 1961
Ex 16:9 **C.** near before the Lord: for he 7126
Ex 17:6 and there shall **c.** water out of it, 3318
Ex 18:6 father in law Jethro am **c.** unto 935
Ex 18:8 the travail that had **c.** upon them 4672
Ex 18:15 the people **c.** unto me to enquire 935
Ex 18:16 have a matter, they **c.** unto me; 935
Ex 19:2 and were **c.** to the desert of Sinai. 935
Ex 19:9 **c.** unto thee in a thick cloud, 935
Ex 19:11 third day the Lord will **c.** down 3381
Ex 19:13 they shall **c.** up to the mount 5927
Ex 19:15 third day: **c.** not at your wives. 5066
Ex 19:22 also, which **c.** near to the Lord, 5066
Ex 19:23 cannot **c.** up to mount Sinai: 5927
Ex 19:24 thou shalt **c.** up, thou, and Aaron 5927
Ex 19:24 through to **c.** up unto the Lord, 5927
Ex 20:20 for God is **c.** to prove you, and 935
Ex 20:24 I will **c.** unto thee, and I will bless 935
Ex 21:14 if a man **c.** presumptuously upon
Ex 22:9 parties shall **c.** before the judges; 935
Ex 22:27 and it shall **c.** to pass, when 1961
Ex 23:27 to whom thou shalt **c.**, and I will 935
Ex 24:1 **C.** up unto the Lord, thou, and 5927
Ex 24:2 Moses alone shall **c.** near the Lord: 5066
Ex 24:2 they shall not **c.** nigh; neither 5066
Ex 24:12 Lord said unto Moses, **C.** up to me 5927
Ex 24:14 until we **c.** again unto you: and, 7725
Ex 24:14 to do, let him **c.** unto them. 5066
Ex 25:32 shall **c.** out of the sides of it; 3318
Ex 25:33 the six branches that **c.** out of 3318
Ex 28:43 when they **c.** in unto the tabernacle 935
Ex 28:43 when they **c.** near unto the altar 5066
Ex 30:20 **c.** near to the altar to minister, 5066
Ex 32:1 to **c.** down out of the mount, 3381
Ex 32:26 Lord's side? let him **c.** unto me.
Ex 33:5 I will **c.** up into the midst of thee 5927
Ex 33:22 it shall **c.** to pass, while my glory 1961
Ex 34:2 and **c.** up in the morning unto 5927
Ex 34:3 And no man shall **c.** up with thee, 5927
Ex 34:30 they were afraid to **c.** nigh him. 5066
Ex 35:10 wise hearted among you shall **c.**, 935
Ex 36:2 him up to **c.** unto the work 7126
Le 4:23 hath sinned, **c.** to his knowledge; 3045
Le 4:28 hath sinned, **c.** to his knowledge: 3045
Le 10:3 sanctified in them that **c.** nigh 7138
Le 10:4 **C.** near, carry your brethren 7126
Le 10:6 wrath **c.** upon all the people:
Le 12:4 nor **c.** into the sanctuary, until 935
Le 13:16 he shall **c.** unto the priest; 935
Le 14:8 that he shall **c.** into the camp. 935
Le 14:34 ye be **c.** into the land of Canaan, 935
Le 14:35 he that owneth the house shall **c.** 935
Le 14:39 shall **c.** again the seventh day, 7725
Le 14:43 if the plague **c.** again, and break 7725
Le 14:44 Then the priest shall **c.** and look, 935

Le 14:48 priest shall **c.** in, and look upon it,........ 935
Le 15:14 and **c.** before the Lord unto the door..... 935
Le 16:2 that he **c.** not at all times into the......... 935
Le 16:3 shall Aaron **c.** into the holy place:......... 935
Le 16:17 until he **c.** out, and have made an........ 3318
Le 16:23 Aaron shall **c.** into the tabernacle......... 935
Le 16:24 put on his garments, and **c.** forth,........ 3318
Le 16:26 and afterward **c.** into the camp............ 935
Le 16:28 afterward he shall **c.** into the camp....... 935
Le 19:19 of linen and woollen **c.** upon thee........ 5927
Le 19:23 when ye shall **c.** into the land,........... 935
Le 21:21 shall **c.** nigh to offer the offering......... 5066
Le 21:21 shall not **c.** nigh to offer the bread....... 5066
Le 21:23 nor **c.** nigh unto the altar, because...... 5066
Le 23:10 When ye be **c.** into the land which........ 935
Le 25:2 **c.** into the land which I give you,......... 935
Le 25:22 **c.** in ye shall eat of the old store.......... 935
Le 25:25 if any of his kin **c.** to redeem it,........... 935
Nu 1:1 were **c.** out of the land of Egypt,........ 3318
Nu 4:5 setteth forward, Aaron shall **c.**,........... 935
Nu 4:15 sons of Kohath shall **c.** to bear it:........... 935
Nu 5:14 spirit of jealousy **c.** upon him,............ 5674
Nu 5:14 the spirit of jealousy **c.** upon him,....... 5674
Nu 5:27 it shall **c.** to pass, that if she............. 1961
Nu 6:5 shall no rasor **c.** upon his head:......... 5674
Nu 6:6 he shall **c.** at no dead body................ 935
Nu 8:19 when the children of Israel **c.** nigh....... 5066
Nu 9:1 after they were **c.** out of the land........ 3318
Nu 10:29 **c.** thou with us, and we will do........... 3212
Nu 11:17 I will **c.** down and talk with thee......... 3381
Nu 11:20 until it **c.** out at your nostrils,........... 3318
Nu 11:23 shall **c.** to pass unto thee or not......... 7136
Nu 12:4 **C.** out ye three unto the.................. 3318
Nu 13:21 Rehob, as men **c.** to Hamath.............. 935
Nu 13:33 sons of Anak, which **c.** of the giants:.........
Nu 14:30 ye shall not **c.** into the land............. 935
Nu 15:2 When ye be **c.** into the land of............. 935
Nu 15:18 When ye **c.** into the land whither I........ 935
Nu 16:5 cause him to **c.** near unto him:........... 7126
Nu 16:5 will he cause to **c.** near unto him........ 7126
Nu 16:12 which said, We will not **c.** up:........... 5927
Nu 16:14 of these men? we will not **c.** up.......... 5927
Nu 16:40 **c.** near to offer incense before........... 7126
Nu 17:5 **c.** to pass, that the man's rod,.......... 1961
Nu 18:3 they shall not **c.** nigh the vessels........ 7126
Nu 18:4 stranger shall not **c.** nigh unto you...... 7126
Nu 18:22 **c.** nigh the tabernacle of the............. 7126
Nu 19:7 he shall **c.** into the camp,................... 935
Nu 19:14 all that **c.** into the tent, and all............ 935
Nu 20:5 have ye made us to **c.** up.................. 5927
Nu 20:18 lest I **c.** out against thee with the........ 3318
Nu 21:8 it shall **c.** to pass, that every one........ 1961
Nu 21:27 **C.** into Heshbon, let the city of............ 935
Nu 22:5 is a people **c.** out from Egypt:............ 3318
Nu 22:6 **C.** now therefore, I pray thee,........... 3212
Nu 22:11 there is a people **c.** out of Egypt,........ 3318
Nu 22:11 **c.** now, curse me them;..................... 3212
Nu 22:14 Balaam refuseth to **c.** with us............ 1980
Nu 22:17 **c.** therefore, I pray thee, curse.......... 3212
Nu 22:20 If the men **c.** to call thee, rise up,........ 935
Nu 22:36 Balak heard that Balaam was **c.**,............ 935
Nu 22:38 Lo, I am **c.** unto thee: have I now........ 935
Nu 23:3 the Lord will **c.** to meet me: and........ 7136
Nu 23:7 **C.**, curse me Jacob, and **c.**, defy......... 3212
Nu 23:13 **C.**, I pray thee, with me unto............ 3212
Nu 23:27 **C.**, I pray thee, I will bring thee......... 3212
Nu 24:14 **c.** therefore, and I will advertise......... 3212
Nu 24:17 there shall **c.** a Star out of Jacob,........ 1869
Nu 24:19 Out of Jacob shall **c.** he that.............. 3381
Nu 24:24 shall **c.** from the coast of Chittim,.............
Nu 26:29 **c.** the family of the Gileadites..................
Nu 27:21 at his word they shall **c.** in, both.......... 935
Nu 31:24 ye shall **c.** into the camp..................... 935
Nu 33:38 the children of Israel were **c.**............ 3318
Nu 33:55 then it shall **c.** to pass, that those....... 1961
Nu 33:56 Moreover it shall **c.** to pass,............. 1961
Nu 34:2 ye **c.** into the land of Canaan;.............. 935
Nu 35:10 When ye be **c.** over Jordan into.......... 5674
Nu 35:26 if the slayer shall at any time **c.**.......... 3318
Nu 35:32 **c.** again to dwell in the land,.............. 7725
De 1:20 Ye are **c.** unto the mountain of the....... 935
De 1:22 into what cities we shall **c.**.................. 935
De 2:14 we were **c.** over the brook Zered,....... 5674
De 4:30 all these things are **c.** upon thee,........ 4672
De 4:46 they were **c.** forth out of Egypt:.......... 3318
De 6:20 thy son asketh thee in time to **c.**,........ 4279
De 7:12 Wherefore it shall **c.** to pass, if ye....... 1961
De 10:1 **c.** up unto me into the mount,............ 5927
De 11:13 And it shall **c.** to pass, if ye shall........ 1961
De 11:29 it shall **c.** to pass, when the Lord........ 1961
De 12:5 seek, and thither thou shalt **c.**.............. 935
De 12:9 For ye are not as yet **c.** to the rest...... 935
De 13:2 the sign or the wonder **c.** to pass,......... 935
De 14:29 shall **c.**, and shall eat and be................ 935
De 15:19 firstling males that **c.** of thy herd........ 3205
De 17:9 And thou shalt **c.** unto the priests......... 935
De 17:14 thou art **c.** unto the land which............. 935
De 18:6 if a Levite **c.** from any of thy gates....... 935
De 18:6 **c.** with all the desire of his mind........... 935
De 18:9 When thou art **c.** into the land............. 935
De 18:19 it shall **c.** to pass, that whosoever....... 1961
De 18:22 thing follow not, nor **c.** to pass,........... 935
De 20:2 ye are **c.** nigh unto the battle,........... 7126
De 21:2 and thy judges shall **c.** forth,.............. 3318
De 21:5 the sons of Levi shall **c.** near;............ 5066
De 23:10 he shall not **c.** within the camp:............ 935
De 23:11 he shall **c.** into the camp again............. 935
De 24:1 and it **c.** to pass that she find no......... 1961
De 24:9 ye were **c.** forth out of Egypt............ 3318
De 25:1 and they **c.** unto judgment,................ 5066
De 25:9 Then shall his brother's wife **c.**.......... 5066
De 25:17 ye were **c.** forth out of Egypt;............ 3318
De 26:1 when thou art **c.** in unto the land.......... 935
De 26:3 **c.** unto the country which the Lord....... 935
De 27:12 when ye are **c.** over Jordan;.............. 5674
De 28:1 **c.** to pass, if thou shalt hearken.......... 1961
De 28:2 these blessings shall **c.** on thee,.......... 935
De 28:7 shall **c.** out against thee one way,........ 3318
De 28:15 it shall **c.** to pass, if thou wilt not........ 1961
De 28:15 all these curses shall **c.** upon thee,....... 935
De 28:24 shall it **c.** down upon thee,................ 3381
De 28:43 and thou shalt **c.** down very low.......... 3381
De 28:45 all these curses shall **c.** upon thee,....... 935
De 28:52 high and fenced walls **c.** down,........... 3381
De 28:63 shall **c.** to pass, that as the Lord......... 1961
De 29:19 And it **c.** to pass, when he heareth...... 1961
De 29:22 So that the generation to **c.** of............ 314
De 29:22 that shall **c.** from a far land,............... 935
De 30:1 And it shall **c.** to pass, when.............. 1961
De 30:1 all these things are **c.** upon thee,.......... 935
De 31:2 can no more go out and **c.** in:.............. 935
De 31:11 When all Israel is **c.** to appear............ 935
De 31:17 Are not these evils **c.** upon us,........... 4672
De 31:21 shall **c.** to pass, when many evil.......... 1961
De 32:35 shall **c.** upon them make haste........... 6264
De 33:16 **c.** upon the head of Joseph,................ 935
Jos 2:3 forth the men that are **c.** to thee,......... 935
Jos 2:3 **c.** to search out all the country............ 935
Jos 2:18 Behold, when we **c.** into the land,........ 935
Jos 3:4 **c.** not near unto it, that ye may.......... 7126
Jos 3:8 ye are **c.** to the brink of the water........ 935
Jos 3:9 **C.** hither, and hear the words of.......... 5066
Jos 3:13 And it shall **c.** to pass, as soon as....... 1961
Jos 3:13 waters that **c.** down from above;......... 3381
Jos 3:15 as they that bare the ark were **c.**......... 935
Jos 4:6 ask their fathers in time to **c.**,............ 4279
Jos 4:16 that they **c.** up out of Jordan............... 5927
Jos 4:17 saying, **C.** ye up out of Jordan............ 5927
Jos 4:18 **c.** up out of the midst of Jordan,......... 5927
Jos 4:21 in time to **c.**, saying, What men.......... 4279
Jos 5:14 the host of the Lord am I now **c.**.......... 935
Jos 6:5 **c.** to pass, that when they make......... 1961
Jos 6:19 **c.** into the treasury of the Lord............ 935
Jos 7:14 which the Lord taketh shall **c.**............ 7126
Jos 7:14 which the Lord shall take shall **c.**......... 7126
Jos 8:5 and it shall **c.** to pass, when they........ 1961
Jos 8:5 **c.** out against us, as at the first,......... 3318
Jos 8:6 (For they will **c.** out after us) till......... 3318
Jos 9:6 We be **c.** from a far country: now......... 935
Jos 9:8 are ye? and from whence **c.** ye?........... 935
Jos 9:9 thy servants are **c.** because of the........ 935
Jos 10:4 **C.** up unto me, and help me, that......... 5927
Jos 10:6 **c.** up to us quickly, and save us,......... 5927
Jos 10:24 **C.** near, put your feet upon the.......... 7126
Jos 11:20 should **c.** against Israel in battle,......... 7122
Jos 14:11 war, both to go out, and to **c.** in.......... 935
Jos 18:4 and they shall **c.** again to me,............. 935
Jos 18:8 and describe it, and **c.** again to me,...... 7725
Jos 20:6 and **c.** unto his own city, and unto........ 935
Jos 22:24 In time to **c.** your children might......... 4279
Jos 22:27 say to our children in time to **c.**.......... 4279
Jos 22:28 to our generations in time to **c.**,......... 4279
Jos 23:7 ye **c.** not among these nations............ 935
Jos 23:14 all are **c.** to pass unto you, and not....... 935
Jos 23:15 Therefore it shall **c.** to pass, that........ 1961
Jos 23:15 as all good things are **c.** upon you,......... 935
Jg 1:3 **C.** up with me into my lot, that.......... 5927
Jg 1:24 the spies saw a man **c.** forth out......... 3318
Jg 1:34 would not suffer them to **c.** down......... 3381
Jg 3:27 when he was **c.**, that he blew a........... 935
Jg 4:20 man doth **c.** and enquire of thee,........... 935
Jg 4:22 **C.**, and I will shew thee the.............. 3212
Jg 6:4 till thou **c.** unto Gaza, and left no......... 935
Jg 6:18 pray thee, until I **c.** unto thee,............. 935
Jg 6:18 I will tarry until thou **c.** again............ 7725
Jg 7:13 And when Gideon was **c.**, behold,.......... 935
Jg 7:17 I **c.** to the outside of the camp,............. 935
Jg 7:24 **C.** down against the Midianites,.......... 3381
Jg 8:9 When I **c.** again in peace, I will........... 7725
Jg 9:10 tree, **C.** thou, and reign over us.......... 3212
Jg 9:12 vine, **C.** thou, and reign over us......... 3212
Jg 9:14 bramble, **C.** thou, and reign over us.... 3212
Jg 9:15 **c.** and put your trust in my................. 935
Jg 9:15 let fire **c.** out of the bramble, and........ 3318
Jg 9:20 let fire **c.** out from Abimelech,............ 3318
Jg 9:20 fire **c.** out from the men of Shechem,.... 3318
Jg 9:24 and ten sons of Jerubbaal might **c.**,........ 935
Jg 9:29 Increase thine army, and **c.** out.......... 3318
Jg 9:31 his brethren be **c.** to Shechem;............. 935
Jg 9:33 is with him **c.** out against thee,........... 3318
Jg 9:36 there **c.** people down from the top...... 3381
Jg 9:37 **c.** people down by the middle............ 3381
Jg 9:37 another company **c.** along by the.......... 935
Jg 9:43 were **c.** forth out of the city;............. 3318
Jg 11:6 **C.**, and be our captain, that we.......... 3212
Jg 11:7 why are ye **c.** unto me now when......... 935
Jg 11:12 thou art **c.** against me to fight in.......... 935
Jg 11:33 Aroer, even till thou **c.** to Minnith,....... 935
Jg 12:3 are ye **c.** up unto me this day,........... 5927
Jg 13:5 and no rasor shall **c.** on his head:......... 5927
Jg 13:8 which thou didst send **c.** again............ 935
Jg 13:12 said, Now let thy words **c.** to pass........ 935
Jg 13:17 that when thy sayings **c.** to pass we...... 935
Jg 15:10 Why are ye **c.** up against us? And....... 5927
Jg 15:10 To bind Samson are we **c.**................ 5927
Jg 15:12 We are **c.** down to bind thee, that....... 3381
Jg 16:2 saying, Samson is **c.** hither................. 935
Jg 16:17 There hath not **c.** a rasor upon............ 5927
Jg 16:18 **C.** up this once, for he hath............... 5927
Jg 18:10 ye shall **c.** unto a people secure,.......... 935
Jg 19:11 **C.**, I pray thee, and let us turn in....... 3212
Jg 19:13 **C.**, and let us draw near to one of....... 3212
Jg 19:23 that this man is **c.** into mine house,....... 935
Jg 19:29 And when he was **c.** into his house,...... 935
Jg 20:10 they **c.** to Gibeah of Benjamin,............. 935
Jg 20:41 saw that evil was **c.** upon them.......... 5060
Jg 21:3 why is this **c.** to pass in Israel,........... 1961
Jg 21:21 daughters of Shiloh **c.** out to dance...... 3318
Jg 21:21 then **c.** ye out of the vineyards, and.... 3318
Jg 21:22 brethren **c.** unto us to complain,........... 935
Ru 1:19 when they were **c.** to Beth-lehem,......... 935
Ru 2:11 art **c.** unto a people which thou.......... 1980
Ru 2:12 whose wings thou art **c.** to trust......... 935
Ru 2:14 At mealtime **c.** thou hither, and.......... 5060
Ru 4:3 Naomi, that is **c.** again out of the........ 7725
Ru 4:11 woman that is **c.** into thine house......... 935
1Sa 1:11 shall no rasor **c.** upon his head........... 5927
1Sa 1:20 when the time was **c.** about after........ 8622
1Sa 2:3 arrogancy **c.** out of your mouth:.......... 3318
1Sa 2:31 Behold, the days **c.**, that I will cut........ 935
1Sa 2:34 that shall **c.** upon thy two sons, on....... 935
1Sa 2:36 shall **c.** to pass, that every one........... 1961
1Sa 2:36 **c.** and crouch to him for a piece.......... 935
1Sa 4:3 the people were **c.** into the camp,......... 935
1Sa 4:6 of the Lord was **c.** into the camp.......... 935
1Sa 4:7 they said, God is **c.** into the camp......... 935
1Sa 5:5 nor any that **c.** into Dagon's house,....... 935
1Sa 6:7 on which there hath **c.** no yoke,......... 5927
1Sa 6:21 **c.** ye down, and fetch it up to you....... 3381
1Sa 9:5 when they were **c.** to the land of.......... 935
1Sa 9:5 **C.**, and let us return; lest my............ 3212
1Sa 9:9 spake **C.**, and let us go to the seer:.... 3212
1Sa 9:10 Well said; **c.**, let us go, So they.......... 3212
1Sa 9:13 As soon as ye be **c.** into the city,.......... 935
1Sa 9:13 the people will not eat until he **c.**,.......... 935
1Sa 9:14 and when they were **c.** into the city,...... 935
1Sa 9:16 because their cry is **c.** unto me........... 935
1Sa 9:25 they were **c.** down from the high......... 3381
1Sa 10:3 thou shalt **c.** to the plain of Tabor,......... 935
1Sa 10:5 that thou shalt **c.** to the hill of God,....... 935
1Sa 10:5 it shall **c.** to pass, when thou art......... 1961

1Sa 10:5 thou art **c.** thither to the city,, 835
1Sa 10:6 of the Lord will **c.** upon thee, 6743
1Sa 10:7 when these signs are **c.** unto thee, 935
1Sa 10:8 **c.** down unto thee, to offer burnt 3381
1Sa 10:8 till I **c.** to thee, and shew thee what 935
1Sa 10:11 that is **c.** unto the son of Kish? 1961
1Sa 10:20 to **c.** near, the tribe of Benjamin 7126
1Sa 10:21 to **c.** near by their families, the 7126
1Sa 10:22 if the man should yet **c.** thither. 935
1Sa 11:3 to save us, we will **c.** out to thee 3318
1Sa 11:10 To morrow we will **c.** out unto you, 3318
1Sa 11:14 **C.** and let us go to Gilgal, and 3212
1Sa 12:8 When Jacob was **c.** into Egypt, 935
1Sa 13:12 The Philistines will **c.** down now 3381
1Sa 14:1 **C.**, and let us go over to the 3212
1Sa 14:6 **C.**, and let us go over unto the 3212
1Sa 14:9 Tarry until we **c.** to you; then we 5060
1Sa 14:10 if they say thus, **C.** up unto us; 5927
1Sa 14:11 Hebrews **c.** forth out of the holes 3318
1Sa 14:12 **C.** up to us, and we will shew you 5927
1Sa 14:12 **C.** up after me: for the Lord hath 5927
1Sa 14:26 when the people were **c.** into the 935
1Sa 16:2 say, I am **c.** to sacrifice to the Lord. 935
1Sa 16:5 I am **c.** to sacrifice unto the Lord: 935
1Sa 16:5 and **c.** with me to the sacrifice. 935
1Sa 16:6 when they were **c.**, that he looked 935
1Sa 16:11 will not sit down till he **c.** hither. 935
1Sa 16:16 **c.** to pass, when the evil spirit 1961
1Sa 17:8 Why are ye **c.** out to set your 3318
1Sa 17:8 you, and let him **c.** down to me. 3381
1Sa 17:25 ye seen this man that is **c.** up? 5927
1Sa 17:25 surely to defy Israel is he **c.** up: 5927
1Sa 17:28 art **c.** down that thou mightest 3381
1Sa 17:44 **C.** to me, and I will give thy flesh 3212
1Sa 17:45 but I **c.** to thee in the name of the 935
1Sa 17:52 until thou **c.** to the valley, and to 935
1Sa 19:16 And when the messengers were **c.** 935
1Sa 20:9 were determined by my father to **c.** 935
1Sa 20:11 **C.**, and let us go out into the 3212
1Sa 20:19 **c.** to the place where thou didst 935
1Sa 20:21 then **c.** thou: for there is peace to 935
1Sa 20:24 when the new moon was **c.**, the 1961
1Sa 20:37 when the lad was **c.** to the place 935
1Sa 21:15 shall this fellow **c.** into my house? 935
1Sa 22:3 my mother, I pray thee, **c.** forth, 3318
1Sa 23:3 much more then if we **c.** to Keilah 3212
1Sa 23:7 told Saul that David was **c.** to 935
1Sa 23:10 that Saul seeketh to **c.** to Keilah, 935
1Sa 23:11 will Saul **c.** down, as thy servant 3381
1Sa 23:11 And the Lord said, He will **c.** down. 3381
1Sa 23:15 David saw that Saul was **c.** out to 3318
1Sa 23:20 Now therefore, O king, **c.** down 3381
1Sa 23:20 the desire of thy soul to **c.** down; 3381
1Sa 23:23 and **c.** ye again to me with the 7725
1Sa 23:23 **c.** to pass, if he be in the land, 1961
1Sa 23:27 Haste thee, and **c.**; for the 3212
1Sa 24:14 After whom is the king of Israel **c.** 3318
1Sa 25:8 we **c.** in a good day: give, I pray 935
1Sa 25:19 before me; behold, I **c.** after you. 935
1Sa 25:30 **c.** to pass, when the Lord shall 1961
1Sa 25:34 hadst hasted and **c.** to meet me, 935
1Sa 25:40 when the servants of David were **c.** 935
1Sa 26:4 and understood that Saul was **c.** in 935
1Sa 26:10 him; or his day shall **c.** to die; 935
1Sa 26:20 king of Israel is **c.** out to seek a 3318
1Sa 26:22 let one of the young men **c.** over 5674
1Sa 29:10 servants that are **c.** with thee: 935
1Sa 30:1 when David and his men were **c.** to 935
1Sa 31:4 lest these uncircumcised **c.** and 935
2Sa 1:9 me: for anguish is **c.** upon me, 270
2Sa 2:24 went down when they were **c.** to 935
2Sa 3:23 the host that was with him were **c.**, 935
2Sa 3:26 when Joab was **c.** out from David, 3318
2Sa 5:6 thou shalt not **c.** in hither: 935
2Sa 5:6 David cannot **c.** in hither. 935
2Sa 5:8 the lame shall not **c.** into the house 935
2Sa 5:13 of Jerusalem, after he was **c.** from 935
2Sa 5:23 and **c.** upon them over against the 935
2Sa 5:25 from Geba until thou **c.** to Gazer. 935
2Sa 6:9 How shall the ark of the Lord **c.** to 935
2Sa 7:19 house for a great while to **c.**.
2Sa 9:6 the son of Saul, was **c.** unto David, 935
2Sa 10:11 thee, then I will **c.** and help thee. 1980
2Sa 11:7 And when Uriah was **c.** unto him, 935
2Sa 12:4 the wayfaring man that was **c.** unto 935
2Sa 12:4 it for the man that was **c.** to him. 935
2Sa 13:5 let my sister Tamar **c.**, and give me 935
2Sa 13:6 when the king was **c.** to see him, 935
2Sa 13:6 I pray thee, let Tamar my sister **c.**, 935
2Sa 13:11 unto her, **C.** lie with me, my sister 935
2Sa 13:35 Behold, the king's sons **c.**: as thy 935
2Sa 14:3 And **c.** to the king, and speak on 935
2Sa 14:15 Now therefore that I am **c.** to speak 935
2Sa 14:29 but he would not **c.** to him: and 935
2Sa 14:29 the second time, he would not **c.** 935
2Sa 14:32 **C.** hither, that I may send thee to 935
2Sa 14:32 Wherefore am I **c.** from Geshur? it 935
2Sa 15:4 any suit or cause might **c.** unto me, 935
2Sa 15:28 until there **c.** word from you to 935
2Sa 15:32 that when David was **c.** to the top of 935
2Sa 16:7 **C.** out, **c.** out, thou bloody man 3318
2Sa 16:16 David's friend, was **c.** unto 935
2Sa 17:2 And I will **c.** upon him while he is 935
2Sa 17:6 when Hushai was **c.** to Absalom, 935
2Sa 17:9 and it will **c.** to pass, when some 1961
2Sa 17:12 So shall we **c.** upon him in some 935
2Sa 17:17 they might not be seen to **c.** into 935
2Sa 17:27 it came to pass, when David was **c.** 935
2Sa 19:11 all Israel is **c.** to the king, even to 935
2Sa 19:18 before the king, as he was **c.** over 5674
2Sa 19:20 I am **c.** the first this day of all the 935
2Sa 19:25 when he was **c.** to Jerusalem to 935
2Sa 19:30 as my lord the king is **c.** again in 935
2Sa 19:33 **C.** thou over with me, and I will 5674
2Sa 19:39 when the king was **c.** over, the 5674
2Sa 20:16 **C.** near hither, that I may speak 7126
2Sa 20:17 when he was **c.** near unto her, 7126
2Sa 24:13 Shall seven years of famine **c.** unto 935
2Sa 24:21 my lord the king **c.** to his servant? 935
1Ki 1:12 therefore **c.**, let me, I pray thee, 3212
1Ki 1:14 I also will **c.** in after thee, and 935
1Ki 1:21 **c.** to pass, when my lord the king 1961
1Ki 1:23 And when he was **c.** in before the 935
1Ki 1:35 Then ye shall **c.** up after him, 5927
1Ki 1:35 that he may **c.** and sit upon my 935
1Ki 1:42 **C.** in; for thou art a valiant man, 935
1Ki 1:45 are **c.** up from thence rejoicing, 5927
1Ki 2:30 Thus saith the king, **C.** forth. 3318
1Ki 2:41 Jerusalem to Gath, and was **c.** 7725
1Ki 3:7 I know not how to go out or **c.** in. 935
1Ki 6:1 the children of Israel were **c.** out 3318
1Ki 8:10 when the priests were **c.** out of the 3318
1Ki 8:19 thy son that shall **c.** forth out of 3318
1Ki 8:31 and the oath **c.** before thine altar 935
1Ki 8:42 when he shall **c.** and pray toward 935
1Ki 10:2 and when she was **c.** to Solomon, 935
1Ki 11:2 neither shall they **c.** in unto you: 935
1Ki 12:1 all Israel were **c.** to Shechem to 935
1Ki 12:5 yet for three days, then **c.** again 7725
1Ki 12:12 saying, **C.** to me again the third 7725
1Ki 12:20 heard that Jeroboam was **c.** again, 7725
1Ki 12:21 And when Rehoboam was **c.** to 935
1Ki 13:7 **C.** home with me, and refresh 935
1Ki 13:15 said unto him, **C.** home with me, 3212
1Ki 13:22 thy carcase shall not **c.** unto the 935
1Ki 13:32 Samaria, shall surely **c.** to pass. 1961
1Ki 14:6 **C.** in, thou wife of Jeroboam; 935
1Ki 14:13 of Jeroboam shall **c.** to the grave, 935
1Ki 15:17 to go out or **c.** in to Asa king of 935
1Ki 15:19 **c.** and break thy league with 3212
1Ki 17:18 art thou **c.** unto me to call my sin 935
1Ki 17:21 let this child's soul **c.** into him 7725
1Ki 18:12 **c.** to pass, as soon as I am gone 1961
1Ki 18:12 and so when I **c.** and tell Ahab, 935
1Ki 18:30 said unto all the people, **C.** near 5066
1Ki 19:17 **c.** to pass, that him that escapeth 1961
1Ki 20:17 There are men **c.** out of Samaria 3318
1Ki 20:18 Whether they be **c.** out for peace, 3318
1Ki 20:18 alive; or whether they be **c.** out 3318
1Ki 20:22 king of Syria will **c.** up against 5927
1Ki 20:33 whether anything would **c.** from
1Ki 20:33 he caused him to **c.** up into the 5927
1Ki 22:27 of affliction, until I **c.** in peace. 935
2Ki 1:4 **c.** down from that bed on which 3381
2Ki 1:6 thou shalt not **c.** down from that 3381
2Ki 1:9 God, the king hath said, **C.** down. 3381
2Ki 1:10 then let fire **c.** down from heaven. 3381
2Ki 1:11 the king said, **C.** down quickly. 3381
2Ki 1:12 let fire **c.** down from heaven, and 3381
2Ki 1:16 shalt not **c.** down off that bed 3381
2Ki 3:21 heard that the kings were **c.** up 5927
2Ki 4:1 **c.** to take unto him my two sons 935
2Ki 4:4 And when thou art **c.** in, thou 935
2Ki 4:22 to the man of God, and **c.** again. 7725
2Ki 4:32 when Elisha was **c.** into the house, 935
2Ki 4:36 And when she was **c.** in unto him, 935
2Ki 5:6 when this letter is **c.** unto thee, 935
2Ki 5:8 let him **c.** now to me, and 935
2Ki 5:10 and thy flesh shall **c.** again to thee, 7725
2Ki 5:11 He will surely **c.** out to me, 3318
2Ki 5:22 be **c.** to me from mount Ephraim 935
2Ki 6:9 thither the Syrians are **c.** down. 5185
2Ki 6:20 when they were **c.** into Samaria, 935
2Ki 7:4 Now therefore **c.**, and let us fall 3212
2Ki 7:5 they were **c.** to the uttermost part 935
2Ki 7:6 of the Egyptians, to **c.** upon us. 935
2Ki 7:9 some mischief will **c.** upon us: 4672
2Ki 7:9 **c.**, that we may go and tell the 3212
2Ki 7:12 When they **c.** out of the city, we 3318
2Ki 8:1 **c.** upon the land seven years. 935
2Ki 8:7 saying, The man of God is **c.** hither. 935
2Ki 9:16 Ahaziah king of Judah was **c.** 3381
2Ki 9:30 when Jehu was **c.** to Jezreel, 935
2Ki 9:34 And when he was **c.** in, he did eat 935
2Ki 10:6 **c.** to me to Jezreel by to morrow 935
2Ki 10:16 **C.** with me, and see my zeal 3212
2Ki 10:25 and slay them; let none **c.** forth. 3381
2Ki 11:9 that were to **c.** in on the sabbath, 935
2Ki 14:8 **C.**, let us look one another in the 3212
2Ki 16:7 **c.** up, and save me out of the hand 5927
2Ki 16:12 the king was **c.** from Damascus, 935
2Ki 18:13 did Sennacherib king of Assyria **c.** 5927
2Ki 18:17 And when they were **c.** up, they 5927
2Ki 18:25 Am I now **c.** up without the Lord 5927
2Ki 18:31 and **c.** out to me, and then eat ye 3318
2Ki 18:32 Until I **c.** and take you away to a 935
2Ki 19:3 the children are **c.** to the birth, 935
2Ki 19:9 he is **c.** out to fight against thee: 3318
2Ki 19:23 multitude of my chariots I am **c.** 5927
2Ki 19:28 thy tumult is **c.** up into mine ears, 5927
2Ki 19:32 He shall not **c.** into this city, 935
2Ki 19:32 nor **c.** before it with shield, 6923
2Ki 19:33 not **c.** into this city, saith the Lord. 935
2Ki 20:14 They are **c.** from a far country, 935
2Ki 20:17 Behold, the days **c.**, that all that 935
1Ch 9:25 to **c.** after seven days from time 935
1Ch 10:4 lest these uncircumcised **c.** 935
1Ch 11:5 David, Thou shalt not **c.** hither. 935
1Ch 12:17 **c.** peaceably unto me to help me, 935
1Ch 12:17 **c.** to betray me to mine enemies,
1Ch 12:31 name, to **c.** and make David king. 935
1Ch 14:14 and **c.** upon them over against 935
1Ch 16:29 **c.** before him: worship the Lord 935
1Ch 17:11 And it shall **c.** to pass, when thy 1961
1Ch 17:17 house for a great while to **c.**,
1Ch 19:3 are not his servants **c.** unto thee 935
1Ch 19:9 the kings that were **c.** were by 935
1Ch 24:19 to **c.** into the house of the Lord, 935
1Ch 29:12 Both riches and honour **c.** of thee,
1Ch 29:14 for all things **c.** of thee, and of
2Ch 1:10 out and **c.** in before this people: 935
2Ch 5:11 were **c.** out of the holy place: 3318
2Ch 6:9 but thy son which shall **c.** forth 3318
2Ch 6:22 and the oath **c.** before thine altar 935
2Ch 6:32 but is **c.** from a far country for 935
2Ch 6:32 if they **c.** and pray in this house; 935
2Ch 8:11 the ark of the Lord hath **c.** 935
2Ch 9:1 and when she was **c.** to Solomon, 935
2Ch 10:1 to Shechem were all Israel **c.** 935
2Ch 10:5 **C.** again unto me after three days. 7725
2Ch 10:12 **C.** again to me on the third day. 7725
2Ch 11:1 Rehoboam was **c.** to Jerusalem, 935
2Ch 13:13 caused an ambushment to **c.** 935
2Ch 16:1 let none go out or **c.** in to Asa 935
2Ch 18:14 And when he was **c.** to the king, 935
2Ch 19:10 what cause soever shall **c.** to you 935
2Ch 19:10 Lord, and so wrath **c.** upon you, 1961
2Ch 20:11 **c.** to cast us out of thy possession, 935
2Ch 20:16 they **c.** up by the cliff of Ziz; 5927
2Ch 20:22 they which were **c.** against Judah; 935
2Ch 22:7 for when he was **c.**, he went out 935
2Ch 23:6 But let none **c.** into the house of 935
2Ch 23:8 his men that were to **c.** in on the 935
2Ch 23:15 when she was **c.** to the entering 935
2Ch 25:10 the army that was **c.** to him out 935
2Ch 25:14 Amaziah was **c.** from the slaughter 935
2Ch 25:17 **C.**, let us see one another in the 3212
2Ch 28:17 Edomites had **c.** and smitten Judah, 935
2Ch 29:31 **c.** near and bring sacrifices and 5066
2Ch 30:1 that they should **c.** to the house 935
2Ch 30:5 should **c.** to keep the passover 935

2Ch 30:9 they shall **c.** again into this land: ... 7725
2Ch 32:2 saw that Sennacherib was **c.**, ... 935
2Ch 32:4 should the kings of Assyria **c.** ... 935
2Ch 32:21 when he was **c.** into the house ... 935
2Ch 35:21 I **c.** not against thee this day, ...
Ezr 3:1 when the seventh month was **c.**, ... 5060
Ezr 3:8 that were **c.** out of the captivity ... 935
Ezr 4:12 are **c.** unto Jerusalem, building ... 858
Ezr 6:21 of Israel, which were **c.** again out ... 7725
Ezr 8:35 which were **c.** out of the captivity ... 935
Ezr 9:13 after all that is **c.** upon us for ... 935
Ezr 10:8 would not **c.** within three days, ... 935
Ezr 10:14 **c.** at appointed times, and with ... 935
Ne 2:7 convey me over till I **c.** to Judah; ... 935
Ne 2:10 that there was **c.** a man to seek ... 935
Ne 2:17 **c.**, and let us build up the wall ... 3212
Ne 4:8 together to **c.** and to fight against ... 935
Ne 4:11 we **c.** in the midst among them, ... 935
Ne 6:2 **C.**, let us meet together in some ... 3212
Ne 6:3 work, so that I cannot **c.** down: ... 3381
Ne 6:3 whilst I leave it, and **c.** down to ... 3381
Ne 6:7 **C.** now therefore, and let us take ... 3212
Ne 6:10 for they will **c.** to slay thee; ... 935
Ne 6:10 yea, in the night will they **c.** ... 935
Ne 8:17 were **c.** again out of the captivity ... 7725
Ne 9:32 hath **c.** upon us, on our kings, ... 4672
Ne 13:1 not **c.** into the congregation ... 935
Ne 13:22 and that they should **c.** and keep ... 935
Es 1:12 Vashti refused to **c.** at the kings ... 935
Es 1:17 shall **c.** abroad unto all women. ... 3318
Es 1:19 Vashti **c.** no more before king ... 935
Es 2:12 when every maid's turn was **c.** ... 5060
Es 2:15 was **c.** to go in unto the king, ... 5060
Es 4:11 shall **c.** unto the king into the ... 935
Es 4:11 to **c.** in unto the king these thirty ... 935
Es 4:14 thou art **c.** to the kingdom ... 5060
Es 5:4 **c.** this day unto the banquet ... 935
Es 5:8 let the king and Haman **c.** to the ... 935
Es 5:12 the queen did let no man **c.** in. ... 935
Es 6:4 Haman was **c.** into the outward ... 935
Es 6:5 And the king said, Let him **c.** in. ... 935
Es 8:6 evil that shall **c.** unto my people? ... 4672
Es 9:26 and which had **c.** unto them, ... 5060
Job 2:11 heard of all this evil that was **c.** ...
Job 2:11 to **c.** to mourn with him and ... 935
Job 3:6 let it not **c.** into the number ... 935
Job 3:7 let no joyful voice **c.** therein. ... 935
Job 3:25 which I greatly feared is **c.** upon ... 857
Job 3:25 which I was afraid of is **c.** unto me. ... 935
Job 4:5 But now it is **c.** upon thee, and ... 935
Job 5:26 Thou shalt **c.** to thy grave in a ... 935
Job 7:9 down to the grave shall **c.** up no ... 5927
Job 8:22 of the wicked shall **c.** to nought. ...
Job 9:32 should **c.** together in judgment. ... 935
Job 13:13 speak, and let **c.** on me what will. ... 5674
Job 13:16 hypocrite shall not **c.** before him. ... 935
Job 14:14 time will I wait, till my change **c.** ... 935
Job 14:21 His sons **c.** to honour, and he ...
Job 15:21 the destroyer shall **c.** upon him. ... 935
Job 16:22 When a few years are **c.**, ... 857
Job 17:10 you all, do ye return, and **c.** now: ... 935
Job 18:20 They that **c.** after him shall be ...
Job 19:12 His troops **c.** together, and raise ... 935
Job 20:22 hand of the wicked shall **c.** upon ... 935
Job 22:21 thereby good shall **c.** unto thee. ... 935
Job 23:3 that I might **c.** even to his seat! ... 935
Job 23:10 tried me, I shall **c.** forth as gold ... 3318
Job 26:10 the day and night **c.** to an end. ...
Job 34:28 cry of the poor to **c.** unto him, ... 935
Job 37:13 He causeth it to **c.**, whether for ... 4672
Job 38:11 Hitherto shalt thou **c.**, but no ... 935
Job 41:13 who can **c.** to him with his double ... 935
Job 41:16 that no air can **c.** between them. ... 935
Ps 5:7 **c.** into thy house in the multitude ... 935
Ps 7:9 of the wicked **c.** to an end; ...
Ps 7:16 his violent dealing shall **c.** down ... 3381
Ps 9:6 destructions are **c.** to a perpetual ...
Ps 14:7 salvation of Israel were **c.** out ...
Ps 17:2 **c.** forth from thy presence; ... 3318
Ps 22:31 They shall **c.**, and shall declare ... 935
Ps 24:7,9 and the King of glory shall **c.** in ... 935
Ps 32:6 they shall not **c.** nigh unto him ... 5060
Ps 32:9 bridle, lest they **c.** near unto thee. ... 7126
Ps 34:11 **C.**, ye children, hearken unto me: ... 3212
Ps 35:8 Let destruction **c.** upon him ... 935
Ps 36:11 not the foot of pride **c.** against me, ... 935
Ps 40:7 Then said I, Lo, I **c.**: in the ... 935
Ps 41:6 if he **c.** to see me, he speaketh ... 935
Ps 42:2 shall I **c.** and appear before God? ... 935
Ps 44:17 All this is **c.** upon us; yet have we ... 935
Ps 46:8 **C.**, behold the works of the Lord, ... 3212
Ps 50:3 Our God shall **c.**, and shall not ... 935
Ps 52:*title* David is **c.** to the house of ... 935
Ps 53:6 salvation of Israel were **c.** out of Zion ...
Ps 55:5 and trembling are **c.** upon me, ... 935
Ps 65:2 prayer, unto thee shall all flesh **c.** ... 935
Ps 66:5 **C.** and see the works of God: ... 3212
Ps 66:16 **C.** and hear, all ye that fear God, ... 3212
Ps 68:31 Princes shall **c.** out of Egypt; ... 857
Ps 69:1 waters are **c.** in unto my soul. ... 935
Ps 69:2 I am **c.** into deep waters, where ... 935
Ps 69:27 them not **c.** into thy righteousness. ... 935
Ps 71:18 power to every one that is to **c.** ... 935
Ps 72:6 He shall **c.** down like rain upon ... 3381
Ps 78:4 shewing to the generation to **c.** ... 314
Ps 78:6 That the generation to **c.** might ... 314
Ps 79:1 O God, the heathen are **c.** into ... 935
Ps 79:11 Let the sighing of the prisoner **c.** ... 935
Ps 80:2 strength, and **c.** and save us. ... 3212
Ps 83:4 **C.**, and let us cut them off from ... 3212
Ps 86:9 whom thou hast made shall **c.** ... 935
Ps 88:2 Let my prayer **c.** before thee: ... 935
Ps 88:8 shut up, and I cannot **c.** forth. ... 3318
Ps 91:7 but it shall not **c.** nigh thee. ... 5066
Ps 91:10 neither shall any plague **c.** nigh ... 7126
Ps 95:1 O **c.**, let us sing unto the Lord: ... 3212
Ps 95:2 Let us **c.** before his presence ... 6923
Ps 95:6 O **c.**, let us worship and bow down: ... 935
Ps 96:8 offering, and **c.** into his courts ... 935
Ps 100:2 **c.** before his presence with singing ... 935
Ps 101:2 O when wilt thou **c.** unto me? ... 935
Ps 102:1 O Lord, and let my cry **c.** unto thee. ... 935
Ps 102:13 favour her, yea, the set time, is **c.** ... 935
Ps 102:18 be written for the generation to **c.** ... 314
Ps 109:17 cursing, so let it **c.** unto him: ... 935
Ps 109:18 it **c.** into his bowels like water, ... 935
Ps 119:41 Let thy mercies **c.** also unto me, ... 935
Ps 119:77 Let thy tender mercies **c.** unto me ... 935
Ps 119:169 Let my cry **c.** near before thee ... 7126
Ps 119:170 my supplication **c.** before thee: ... 935
Ps 126:6 doubtless **c.** again with rejoicing, ... 935
Ps 132:3 I will not **c.** into the tabernacle ... 935
Ps 144:5 thy heavens, O Lord, and **c.** down: ... 3381
Pr 1:11 **C.** with us, let us lay wait for ... 3212
Pr 3:28 thy neighbour, Go, and **c.** again, ... 7725
Pr 5:8 **c.** not nigh the door of her house: ... 7126
Pr 6:3 **c.** into the hand of thy friend; ... 935
Pr 6:11 So shall thy poverty **c.** as one that ... 935
Pr 6:15 Therefore shall his calamity **c.** ... 935
Pr 7:18 **C.**, let us take our fill of love until ... 3212
Pr 7:20 will **c.** home at the day appointed ... 935
Pr 9:5 **C.**, eat of my bread, and drink ... 3212
Pr 10:24 the wicked, it shall **c.** upon him: ... 935
Pr 11:27 mischief, it shall **c.** unto him. ... 935
Pr 12:13 the just shall **c.** out of trouble ... 3318
Pr 20:13 not sleep, lest thou **c.** to poverty; ...
Pr 22:16 the rich, shall surely **c.** to want ...
Pr 23:21 the glutton shall **c.** to poverty: ...
Pr 24:25 good blessing shall **c.** upon them ... 935
Pr 24:34 So shall thy poverty **c.** as one that ... 935
Pr 25:4 shall **c.** forth a vessel for the finer ... 3318
Pr 25:7 said unto thee, **C.** up hither; than ... 5927
Pr 26:2 the curse causeless shall not **c.** ... 935
Pr 28:22 that poverty shall **c.** upon him. ... 935
Pr 31:25 she shall rejoice in time to **c.** ... 314
Ec 1:7 place from whence the rivers **c.** ... 1980
Ec 1:11 remembrance of things that are to **c.** ... 314
Ec 1:11 with those that shall **c.** after ... 1961
Ec 1:16 Lo, I am **c.** to great estate, ...
Ec 2:16 the days to **c.** shall all be forgotten. ... 935
Ec 4:16 also that **c.** after shall not rejoice ... 314
Ec 7:18 he that feareth God shall **c.** forth ... 3318
Ec 8:10 had **c.** and gone from the place ... 935
Ec 9:2 All things **c.** alike to all: there is ...
Ec 12:1 while the evil days **c.** not, nor ... 935
Ca 2:10 love, my fair one, and **c.** away ... 3212
Ca 2:12 of the singing of birds is **c.**, ... 5060
Ca 2:13 love, my fair one, and **c.** away ... 3212
Ca 4:8 **C.** with me from Lebanon, ... 935
Ca 4:16 O north wind; and **c.**, thou south; ... 935
Ca 4:16 Let my beloved **c.** into his garden ... 935
Ca 5:1 I am **c.** into my garden, my sister, ... 935
Ca 7:11 **C.**, my beloved, let us go forth ... 3212
Isa 1:12 When ye **c.** to appear before me, ... 935
Isa 1:18 **C.** now, and let us reason ... 3212
Isa 1:23 doth the cause of the widow **c.** ... 935
Isa 2:2 And it shall **c.** to pass in the last ... 1961
Isa 2:3 **C.** ye, and let us go up to the ... 3212
Isa 2:5 O house of Jacob, **c.** ye, and let us ... 3212
Isa 3:24 it shall **c.** to pass, that instead of ... 1961
Isa 4:3 **c.** to pass, that he that is left in ... 1961
Isa 5:6 shall **c.** up briers and thorns: ... 5927
Isa 5:19 One of Israel draw nigh and **c.**, ... 935
Isa 5:26 behold, they shall **c.** with speed ... 935
Isa 7:7 stand, neither shall it **c.** to pass. ... 1961
Isa 7:17 house, days that have not **c.**, ... 935
Isa 7:18 shall **c.** to pass in that day, that ... 1961
Isa 7:19 And they shall **c.**, and shall rest ... 935
Isa 7:21 **c.** to pass in that day, that a man ... 1961
Isa 7:22 **c.** to pass, for the abundance of ... 1961
Isa 7:23 **c.** to pass in that day, that every ... 1961
Isa 7:24 and with bows shall men **c.** ... 935
Isa 7:25 not **c.** thither the fear of briers ... 935
Isa 8:7 shall **c.** up over all his channels, ... 5927
Isa 8:10 and it shall **c.** to nought; ...
Isa 8:21 shall **c.** to pass, that when they ... 1961
Isa 10:3 desolation which shall **c.** from far? ... 935
Isa 10:12 **c.** to pass, that when the Lord ... 1961
Isa 10:20 **c.** to pass in that day, that the ... 1961
Isa 10:27 **c.** to pass in that day, that his ... 1961
Isa 10:28 **c.** to Aiath, he is passed to Migron; ... 935
Isa 11:1 And there shall **c.** forth a rod out ... 3318
Isa 11:11 **c.** to pass in that day, that the ... 1961
Isa 13:5 They **c.** from a far country, from ... 935
Isa 13:6 it shall **c.** as a destruction from ... 935
Isa 13:22 her time is near to **c.**, and her days ... 935
Isa 14:3 **c.** to pass in the day that the Lord ... 1961
Isa 14:8 no feller is **c.** up against us. ... 5927
Isa 14:24 thought, so shall it **c.** to pass; ... 1961
Isa 14:29 of the serpent's root shall **c.** forth ... 3318
Isa 14:31 shall **c.** from the north a smoke ... 935
Isa 16:8 they are **c.** even unto Jazer, ... 5060
Isa 16:12 **c.** to pass, when it is seen that ... 1961
Isa 16:12 shall **c.** to his sanctuary to pray; ... 935
Isa 17:4 And in that day it shall **c.** to pass, ... 1961
Isa 19:1 cloud, and shall **c.** into Egypt: ... 935
Isa 19:23 the Assyrian shall **c.** into Egypt, ... 935
Isa 21:12 enquire, enquire ye: return, **c.** ... 857
Isa 22:7 shall **c.** to pass, that thy choicest ... 1961
Isa 22:20 And it shall **c.** to pass in that day, ... 1961
Isa 23:15 **c.** to pass in that day, that Tyre ... 1961
Isa 23:17 **c.** to pass after the end of seventy ... 1961
Isa 24:10 is shut up, that no man may **c.** in. ... 935
Isa 24:18 shall **c.** to pass that he who fleeth ... 1961
Isa 24:21 And it shall **c.** to pass in that day, ... 1961
Isa 26:20 **C.**, my people, enter thou into thy ... 3212
Isa 27:6 shall cause them that **c.** of Jacob ... 935
Isa 27:11 women **c.**, and set them on fire: ... 935
Isa 27:12 **c.** to pass in that day, that the ... 1961
Isa 27:13 And it shall **c.** to pass in that day, ... 1961
Isa 27:13 shall **c.** which were ready to perish ... 935
Isa 28:15 it shall not **c.** unto us: for we have ... 935
Isa 29:24 shall **c.** to understanding, ... 3045
Isa 30:6 whence **c.** the young and old lion, ...
Isa 30:8 the time to **c.** for ever and ever: ... 314
Isa 30:29 **c.** into the mountain of the Lord, ... 935
Isa 31:4 so shall the Lord of hosts **c.** down ... 3381
Isa 32:10 fail, the gathering shall not **c.** ... 935
Isa 32:13 of my people shall **c.** up thorns ... 5927
Isa 34:1 **C.** near, ye nations, to hear; and ... 7126
Isa 34:1 and all things that **c.** forth of it. ... 6631
Isa 34:3 shall **c.** up out of their carcases, ... 5927
Isa 34:5 it shall **c.** down upon Idumea, ... 3381
Isa 34:7 unicorns shall **c.** down with them, ... 3381
Isa 34:13 thorns shall **c.** up in her palaces, ... 5927
Isa 35:4 God will **c.** with vengeance, ... 935
Isa 35:4 he will **c.** and save you. ... 935
Isa 35:10 and **c.** to Zion with songs and ... 935
Isa 36:10 am I now **c.** up without the Lord ... 5927
Isa 36:16 **c.** out to me: and eat ye every one ... 3318
Isa 36:17 Until I **c.** and take you away to a ... 935
Isa 37:3 the children are **c.** to the birth, ... 935
Isa 37:9 is **c.** forth to make war with thee ... 3318
Isa 37:24 multitude of my chariots am I **c.** ... 5927
Isa 37:29 tumult, is **c.** up into mine ears, ... 5927
Isa 37:33 He shall not **c.** into this city, nor ... 935
Isa 37:33 nor **c.** before it with shields, ... 6923
Isa 37:34 not **c.** into this city, saith the Lord ... 935
Isa 39:3 are **c.** from a far country unto me, ... 935
Isa 39:6 Behold, the days **c.**, that all that is ... 935
Isa 40:10 Lord God will **c.** with strong hand, ... 935

Isa 41:1 **c.** near; then let them speak: 5066
Isa 41:1 us **c.** near together to judgment. 7126
Isa 41:22 declare us things for to **c.**. 935
Isa 41:23 things that are to **c.** hereafter, 857
Isa 41:25 the north, and he shall **c.** 857
Isa 41:25 **c.** upon princes as upon morter. 935
Isa 42:9 the former things are **c.** to pass, 935
Isa 42:23 hearken and hear for the time to **c.**?
Isa 44:7 are coming, and shall **c.**, 935
Isa 45:11 things to **c.** concerning my sons, 857
Isa 45:14 stature, shall **c.** over unto thee, 5674
Isa 45:14 be thine: they shall **c.** after thee; 3212
Isa 45:14 in chains they shall **c.** over, and 5674
Isa 45:20 Assemble yourselves and **c.**; 935
Isa 45:24 even to him shall men **c.**; 935
Isa 47:1 **C.** down, and sit in the dust, O 3381
Isa 47:9 these two things shall **c.** to thee 935
Isa 47:9 they shall **c.** upon thee in their 935
Isa 47:11 Therefore shall evil **c.** upon thee; 935
Isa 47:11 shall **c.** upon thee suddenly. 935
Isa 47:13 things that shall **c.** upon thee. 935
Isa 48:1 are **c.** forth out of the waters of 3318
Isa 48:16 **C.** ye near unto me, hear ye this: 7126
Isa 49:12 these shall **c.** from far: and, lo, 935
Isa 49:18 themselves together, and **c.** to thee. 935
Isa 50:8 let him **c.** near to me. 5066
Isa 51:11 and **c.** with singing unto Zion; 935
Isa 51:19 two things are **c.** unto thee; 7122
Isa 52:1 there shall no more **c.** into thee 935
Isa 54:14 for it shall not **c.** near thee. 7126
Isa 55:1 **c.** ye to the waters, and he that 3212
Isa 55:1 hath no money; **c.** ye, buy, and eat; 3212
Isa 55:1 yea, **c.**, buy wine and milk 3212
Isa 55:3 Incline your ear, and **c.** unto me: 3212
Isa 55:13 the thorn shall **c.** up the fir tree, 5927
Isa 55:13 and instead of the brier shall **c.** up 5927
Isa 56:1 for my salvation is near to **c.**. 935
Isa 56:9 ye beasts of the field, **c.** to devour, 857
Isa 56:12 **C.** ye, say they, I will fetch wine, 857
Isa 57:1 is taken away from the evil to **c.**.
Isa 59:19 the enemy shall **c.** in like a flood, 935
Isa 59:20 And the Redeemer shall **c.** to Zion, 935
Isa 60:1 Arise, shine; for thy light is **c.**, 935
Isa 60:3 the Gentiles shall **c.** to thy light. 1980
Isa 60:4 together, they **c.** to thee: 935
Isa 60:4 thy sons shall **c.** from far, and thy 935
Isa 60:5 forces of the Gentiles shall **c.** unto 935
Isa 60:6 all they from Sheba shall **c.**: they 935
Isa 60:7 they shall **c.** up with acceptance 5927
Isa 60:13 of Lebanon shall **c.** unto thee, 935
Isa 60:14 of them that afflicted thee shall **c.** 1980
Isa 63:4 and the year of my redeemed is **c.** 935
Isa 64:1 that thou wouldest **c.** down, that 3381
Isa 65:5 **c.** not near to me; for I am holier 5066
Isa 65:17 shall not be remembered, nor **c.** 5927
Isa 65:24 **c.** to pass, that before they call, 1961
Isa 66:15 behold, the Lord will **c.** with fire. 935
Isa 66:18 and their thoughts: it shall **c.**, 935
Isa 66:18 they shall **c.**, and see my glory. 935
Isa 66:23 And it shall **c.** to pass, that from 1961
Isa 66:23 all flesh **c.** to worship before me, 935
Jer 1:15 and they shall **c.**, and they shall 935
Jer 2:3 shall **c.** upon them, saith the Lord 935
Jer 2:31 we will **c.** no more unto thee? 935
Jer 3:16 **c.** to pass, when ye be multiplied 1961
Jer 9:16 neither shall it **c.** to mind: 5927
Jer 9:18 shall **c.** together out of the land 935
Jer 9:22 we **c.** unto thee; for thou art the 857
Jer 4:4 lest my fury **c.** forth like fire. 3318
Jer 4:7 lion is **c.** up from his thicket, 5927
Jer 4:9 it shall **c.** to pass at that day, 1961
Jer 4:12 from those places shall **c.** unto me: 935
Jer 4:13 he shall **c.** up as clouds, 5927
Jer 4:16 watchers **c.** from a far country. 935
Jer 5:12 neither shall evil **c.** upon us; 935
Jer 5:19 it shall **c.** to pass, when ye shall 1961
Jer 6:3 their flocks shall **c.** unto her; 935
Jer 6:26 spoiler shall suddenly **c.** upon us. 935
Jer 7:10 And **c.** and stand before me in this 935
Jer 7:32 behold, the days **c.**, saith the Lord 935
Jer 8:16 for they are **c.**, and have devoured 935
Jer 9:17 mourning women, that they may **c.**; 935
Jer 9:17 cunning women, that they may **c.** 935
Jer 9:21 death is **c.** up into our windows, 5927
Jer 9:25 Behold, the days **c.**, saith the Lord, 935
Jer 10:22 Behold, the noise of the bruit is **c.**, 935
Jer 12:9 **c.** ye, assemble all the beasts 3212
Jer 12:9 beasts of the field, **c.** to devour, 857
Jer 12:12 The spoilers are **c.** upon all high 935
Jer 12:15 it shall **c.** to pass, after that I have 1961
Jer 12:16 And it shall **c.** to pass, if they will 1961
Jer 13:18 your principalities shall **c.** down, 3381
Jer 13:20 them that **c.** from the north: 935
Jer 13:22 Wherefore **c.** these things upon 7122
Jer 15:2 **c.** to pass, if they say unto thee, 1961
Jer 16:10 And it shall **c.** to pass, when thou 1961
Jer 16:14 behold, the days **c.**, saith the Lord, 935
Jer 16:19 the Gentiles shall **c.** unto thee 935
Jer 17:15 word of the Lord? let it **c.** now. 935
Jer 17:19 whereby the kings of Judah **c.** in, 935
Jer 17:24 it shall **c.** to pass, if ye diligently 1961
Jer 17:26 And they shall **c.** from the cities 935
Jer 18:14 waters that **c.** from another place
Jer 18:18 **C.**, and let us devise devices 3212
Jer 18:18 **C.**, and let us smite him with the 3212
Jer 19:6 the days **c.**, saith the Lord, that 935
Jer 20:6 thou shalt **c.** to Babylon, and 935
Jer 21:13 Who shall **c.** down against us? 5181
Jer 22:23 thou be when pangs **c.** upon thee, 935
Jer 23:5 days **c.**, saith the Lord, that I will 935
Jer 23:7 days **c.**, saith the Lord, that they 935
Jer 23:17 No evil shall **c.** upon you. 935
Jer 25:3 word of the Lord hath **c.** unto me, 1961
Jer 25:12 **c.** to pass, when seventy years 1961
Jer 25:31 **c.** even to the ends of the earth; 935
Jer 26:2 **c.** to worship in the Lord's house, 935
Jer 27:3 **c.** to Jerusalem unto Zedekiah king 935
Jer 27:7 until the very time of his land **c.** 935
Jer 27:8 **c.** to pass, that the nation and 1961
Jer 28:9 of the prophet shall **c.** to pass, 935
Jer 30:3 For, lo, the days **c.**, saith the Lord, 935
Jer 30:8 For it shall **c.** to pass in that day, 1961
Jer 31:9 They shall **c.** with weeping, 935
Jer 31:12 Therefore they shall **c.** and sing 935
Jer 31:16 and they shall **c.** again from the 7725
Jer 31:17 shall **c.** again to their own border; 7725
Jer 31:27, 31,38 Behold, the days **c.**, saith 935
Jer 31:28 And it shall **c.** to pass, that like 1961
Jer 32:7 thine uncle shall **c.** unto thee, 935
Jer 32:23 hast caused all this evil to **c.** 7122
Jer 32:24 they are **c.** unto the city to take 935
Jer 32:24 thou hast spoken is **c.** to pass; 1961
Jer 32:29 shall **c.** and set fire on this city, 935
Jer 33:5 They **c.** to fight with the Chaldeans, 935
Jer 33:14 days **c.**, saith the Lord, that I will 935
Jer 35:11 **C.**, and let us go to Jerusalem for 935
Jer 36:6 all Judah that **c.** out of their cities. 935
Jer 36:14 in the ears of the people, and **c.**. 3212
Jer 36:29 king of Babylon shall certainly **c.** 935
Jer 37:5 Pharaoh's army was **c.** forth out 3318
Jer 37:7 Pharaoh's army, which is **c.** forth 3318
Jer 37:8 And the Chaldeans shall **c.** again, 7725
Jer 37:19 The king of Babylon shall not **c.** 935
Jer 38:25 and they **c.** unto thee, and say 935
Jer 40:3 therefore this thing is **c.** upon 1961
Jer 40:4 to **c.** with me into Babylon, 935
Jer 40:4 **c.**; and I will look well unto thee: 935
Jer 40:4 but if it seem ill unto thee to **c.** 935
Jer 40:10 the Chaldeans, which will **c.** unto us: 935
Jer 41:6 unto them, **C.** to Gedaliah the son 935
Jer 42:4 **c.** to pass, that whatsoever thing 1961
Jer 42:16 it shall **c.** to pass, that the sword, 1961
Jer 46:9 **C.** up, ye horses; and rage, ye 5927
Jer 46:9 let the mighty men **c.** forth; 3318
Jer 46:13 king of Babylon should **c.** and 935
Jer 46:18 as Carmel by the sea, so shall he **c.** 935
Jer 46:21 the day of their calamity was **c.** 935
Jer 46:22 **c.** against her with axes, as hewers 935
Jer 47:5 Baldness is **c.** upon Gaza; 935
Jer 48:2 **c.**, and let us cut it off from being 3212
Jer 48:8 And the spoiler shall **c.** upon 935
Jer 48:12 days **c.**, saith the Lord, that I will 935
Jer 48:16 The calamity of Moab is near to **c.**, 935
Jer 48:18 Dibon, **c.** down from thy glory, 3381
Jer 48:18 the spoiler of Moab shall **c.** upon 5927
Jer 48:21 judgment is **c.** upon the plain 935
Jer 48:45 fire shall **c.** forth out of Heshbon, 3318
Jer 49:2 behold, the days **c.**, saith the Lord, 935
Jer 49:4 her treasures, saying, Who shall **c.** 935
Jer 49:9 If grapegatherers **c.** to thee, 935
Jer 49:14 and **c.** against her, and rise up to 935
Jer 49:19 he shall **c.** up like a lion from the 5927
Jer 49:22 he shall **c.** up and fly as the eagle, 5927
Jer 49:36 the outcasts of Elam shall not **c.** 935
Jer 49:39 it shall **c.** to pass in the latter days, 1961
Jer 50:4 the children of Israel shall **c.**, they 935
Jer 50:5 **C.**, and let us join ourselves to the 935
Jer 50:9 I will raise and cause to **c.** up 5927
Jer 50:26 **C.** against her from the utmost 935
Jer 50:27 for their day is **c.**, the time of their 935
Jer 50:31 for thy day is **c.**, the time that I will 935
Jer 50:41 Behold, a people shall **c.** from the 935
Jer 50:44 he shall **c.** up like a lion from the 5927
Jer 51:10 **c.**, and let us declare in Zion the 935
Jer 51:13 thine end is **c.**, and the measure 935
Jer 51:27 cause the horses to **c.** up as the 5927
Jer 51:33 and the time of her harvest shall **c.** 935
Jer 51:42 The sea is **c.** up upon Babylon: 5927
Jer 51:46 a rumour shall both **c.** one year, 935
Jer 51:46 in another year shall **c.** a rumour,
Jer 51:47 behold, the days **c.**, that I will do 935
Jer 51:48 for the spoilers shall **c.** unto her 935
Jer 51:50 and let Jerusalem **c.** into your 5927
Jer 51:51 for strangers are **c.** into the 935
Jer 51:52 behold, the days **c.**, saith the Lord, 935
Jer 51:53 from me shall spoilers **c.** unto her, 935
Jer 51:56 Because the spoiler is **c.** upon her, 935
Jer 51:60 all the evil that should **c.** upon 935
La 1:4 none **c.** to the solemn feasts: 935
La 1:14 they are wreathed, and **c.** up upon 5927
La 1:22 Let all their wickedness **c.** before 935
La 3:47 Fear and a snare is **c.** upon us, 1961
La 4:18 days are fulfilled; for our end is **c.**. 935
La 5:1 what is **c.** upon us: consider, and 1961
Eze 5:4 thereof shall a fire **c.** forth into 3318
Eze 7:2 the end is **c.** upon the four corners 935
Eze 7:3 Now is the end **c.** upon thee, and
Eze 7:5 evil, an only evil, behold, is **c.** 935
Eze 7:6 An end is **c.**, the end is **c.**: it 935
Eze 7:6 for thee; behold, it is **c.** 935
Eze 7:7 **c.** unto thee, O thou that dwellest 935
Eze 7:7 the time is **c.**, the day of trouble is 935
Eze 7:10 Behold the day, behold, it is **c.** 935
Eze 7:12 The time is **c.**, the day draweth 935
Eze 7:26 Mischief shall **c.** upon mischief, 935
Eze 9:6 **c.** not near any man upon whom 5066
Eze 11:5 for I know the things that **c.** into 4609
Eze 11:16 the countries where they shall **c.** 935
Eze 11:18 And they shall **c.** thither, and they 935
Eze 12:16 among the heathen whither they **c.**; 935
Eze 12:25 that I shall speak shall **c.** to pass 6213
Eze 12:27 he seeth is for many days to **c.**,
Eze 13:18 the souls alive that **c.** unto you?
Eze 14:22 they shall **c.** forth unto you, and 3318
Eze 16:7 art **c.** to excellent ornaments; 935
Eze 16:16 the like things shall not **c.**, 935
Eze 16:33 that they may **c.** unto thee on 935
Eze 17:12 the king of Babylon is **c.** to 935
Eze 18:6 neither hath **c.** near to a 7126
Eze 20:3 Are ye **c.** to enquire of me? As I 935
Eze 21:19 of the king of Babylon may **c.** 935
Eze 21:19 both twain shall **c.** forth out of 3318
Eze 21:20 that the sword may **c.** to Rabbath 935
Eze 21:24 I say, that ye are **c.** to remembrance,
Eze 21:25 whose day is **c.**, when iniquity 935
Eze 21:27 until he **c.** whose right it is; and I 935
Eze 21:29 wicked, whose day is **c.**, when 935
Eze 22:3 that her time may **c.**, and maketh 935
Eze 22:4 to draw near, and art **c.** even unto 935
Eze 23:24 And they shall **c.** against thee 935
Eze 23:40 ye have sent for men to **c.** from far, 935
Eze 24:8 That it might cause fury to **c.** up 5927
Eze 24:14 it shall **c.** to pass, and I will do it; 835
Eze 24:26 escapeth in that day shall **c.** unto 835
Eze 26:3 will cause many nations to **c.** up 5927
Eze 26:3 the sea causeth his waves to **c.** up. 5927
Eze 26:16 princes of the sea shall **c.** down 3381
Eze 27:29 pilots of the sea, shall **c.** down from 3381
Eze 30:4 And the sword shall **c.** upon Egypt, 935
Eze 30:6 pride of her power shall **c.** down: 3381
Eze 30:9 great pain shall **c.** upon them, 1961
Eze 32:11 of the king of Babylon shall **c.** 935
Eze 33:3 If when he seeth the sword **c.** upon 935
Eze 33:4 if the sword **c.**, and take him away, 935
Eze 33:6 if the watchman see the sword **c.**, 935
Eze 33:6 if the sword **c.**, and take any 935
Eze 33:30 **C.**, I pray you, and hear what is 935
Eze 33:31 And they **c.** unto thee as the people 935
Eze 33:33 this cometh to pass, (lo, it will **c.**,) 935
Eze 34:26 I will cause the shower to **c.** down 3381

Eze 36:8 Israel; for they are at hand to c.. 935
Eze 37:9 C. from the four winds, O breath, ... 935
Eze 37:12 graves, and cause you to c. up 5927
Eze 38:8 thou shalt c. into the land that is 935
Eze 38:9 Thou shalt ascend and c. like 935
Eze 38:10 It shall also c. to pass, that at the...... 1961
Eze 38:10 same time shall things c. into thy 5927
Eze 38:13 Art thou c. to take a spoil? hast 935
Eze 38:15 And thou shalt c. from thy place 935
Eze 38:16 And thou shalt c. up against my......... 5927
Eze 38:18 And it shall c. to pass at the same 1961
Eze 38:18 time when Gog shall c. against the....... 935
Eze 38:18 that my fury shall c. up in my............. 5927
Eze 39:2 will cause thee to c. up from the........ 5927
Eze 39:8 Behold, it is c., and it is done,........... 935
Eze 39:11 And it shall c. to pass in that............ 1961
Eze 39:17 Assemble yourselves, and c.;.............. 935
Eze 40:46 the sons of Levi, which c. near to...... 7131
Eze 44:13 they shall not c. near unto me,........... 5066
Eze 44:13 nor to c. near to any of my holy......... 5066
Eze 44:15 they shall c. near to me to................ 7126
Eze 44:16 they shall c. near to my table, to 7126
Eze 44:17 it shall c. to pass, that when they 1961
Eze 44:17 no wool shall c. upon them, ... 5927
Eze 44:25 they shall c. at no dead person............ 935
Eze 45:4 which shall c. near to minister........... 7131
Eze 46:9 the people of the land shall c. 935
Eze 47:9 And it shall c. to pass, that every 1961
Eze 47:9 whithersoever the rivers shall c........... 935
Eze 47:9 because these waters shall c.............. 935
Eze 47:10 And it shall c. to pass, that the.......... 1961
Eze 47:20 the border, till a man c. over............. 935
Eze 47:22 And it shall c. to pass, that ye........... 1961
Eze 47:23 shall c. to pass, that in what tribe 1961
Da 2:29 what should c. to pass hereafter: 1934
Da 2:29 to thee what shall c. to pass. 1934
Da 2:45 to the king what shall c. to pass 1934
Da 3:2 to c. to the dedication of the............. 858
Da 3:26 of the most high God, c. forth, ... 5312
Da 3:26 forth, and c. hither. Then................. 858
Da 4:24 which is c. upon my lord the............. 4291
Da 8:7 I saw him c. close unto the ram,........ 5060
Da 8:23 when the transgressors are c. to the ....
Da 9:13 all this evil is c. upon us: yet............. 935
Da 9:22 I am now c. forth to give thee........... 3318
Da 9:23 I am c. to shew thee; for thou art 935
Da 9:26 people of the prince that shall c......... 935
Da 10:12 words were heard, and I am c. for....... 935
Da 10:14 Now I am c. to make thee 935
Da 10:20 knowest thou wherefore I c. unto 935
Da 10:20 lo, the prince of Grecia shall c.. 935
Da 11:6 shall c. to the king of the north to 935
Da 11:7 which shall c. with an army, ... 935
Da 11:9 So the king of the south shall c. 935
Da 11:10 and one shall certainly c., and............ 935
Da 11:11 and shall c. forth and fight with.......... 3318
Da 11:13 and shall certainly c. after certain......... 935
Da 11:15 So the king of the north shall c., ... 935
Da 11:21 but he shall c. in peaceably, and.......... 935
Da 11:23 for he shall c. up, and shall............... 5927
Da 11:29 he shall return, and c. toward the........ 935
Da 11:30 For the ships of Chittim shall c. 935
Da 11:40 king of the north shall c. against 8175
Da 11:45 yet he shall c. to his end, and............ 935
Ho 1:5 it shall c. to pass at that day, ... 1961
Ho 1:10 c. to pass, that in the place where 1961
Ho 1:11 they shall c. up out of the land: 5927
Ho 2:21 c. to pass in that day, I will hear, ... 1961
Ho 4:15 c. not ye unto Gilgal, neither go......... 935
Ho 6:1 C., and let us return unto the............ 3212
Ho 6:3 and he shall c. unto us as the rain, ... 935
Ho 8:1 He shall c. as an eagle against the...........
Ho 9:4 not c. into the house of the Lord......... 935
Ho 9:7 The days of visitation are c., ... 935
Ho 9:7 the days of recompence are c.; 935
Ho 10:8 thistle shall c. up on their altars; 5927
Ho 10:12 till he c. and rain righteousness 935
Ho 13:13 c. upon him: he is an unwise son;........ 935
Ho 13:15 an east wind shall c., the wind of......... 935
Ho 13:15 the wind of the Lord shall c. up........... 5927
Joe 1:6 a nation is c. up upon my land, ... 5927
Joe 1:13 c., lie all night in sackcloth, ye........... 935
Joe 1:15 from the Almighty shall it c.. 935
Joe 2:20 and his stink shall c. up,.................. 5927
Joe 2:20 and his ill savour shall c. up, ... 5927
Joe 2:23 cause to c. down for you the rain, ... 3381
Joe 2:28 And it shall c. to pass afterward,........ 1961
Joe 2:31 and the terrible day of the Lord c.. 635
Joe 2:32 c. to pass, that whosoever shall.......... 1961
Joe 3:9 of war draw near; let them c. up: 5927
Joe 3:11 Assemble yourselves, and c., all ye...... 935
Joe 3:11 cause thy mighty ones to c. down, ... 5181
Joe 3:12 c. up to the valley of Jehoshaphat:...... 5927
Joe 3:13 c., get you down; for the press is........ 935
Joe 3:18 And it shall c. to pass in that day,...... 1961
Joe 3:18 a fountain shall c. forth out of the....... 3318
Am 4:2 the days shall c. upon you, that he....... 935
Am 4:4 C. to Beth-el, and transgress; at 935
Am 4:10 the stink of your camps to c. up 5927
Am 5:5 and Beth-el shall c. to nought............ 1961
Am 5:9 shall c. against the fortress................. 935
Am 6:3 the seat of violence to c. near; 5066
Am 6:9 shall c. to pass, if there remain ten 1961
Am 8:2 is c. upon my people of Israel;............ 935
Am 8:9 And it shall c. to pass in that day,...... 1961
Am 8:11 days c., saith the Lord God, that.......... 935
Am 9:13 the days c., saith the Lord, that the..... 935
Ob 21 saviours shall c. up on mount 5927
Jon 1:2 wickedness is c. up before me........... 5927
Jon 1:7 C., and let us cast lots, that we......... 3212
Jon 4:6 and made it to c. up over Jonah, ... 5927
Mic 1:3 will c. down, and tread upon the 3381
Mic 1:9 for it is c. unto Judah; he is............... 935
Mic 1:9 is c. unto the gate of my people 5060
Mic 1:15 c. unto Adullam, the glory of 935
Mic 2:13 The breaker is c. up before them:...... 5927
Mic 3:11 none evil can c. upon us. 935
Mic 4:1 c. to pass, that the mountain of 1961
Mic 4:2 many nations shall c., and say, ... 1980
Mic 4:2 C., and let us go up to the 3212
Mic 4:8 unto thee shall it c., even the first....... 857
Mic 4:8 kingdom shall c. to the daughter.......... 935
Mic 5:2 out of thee shall he c. forth unto........ 3318
Mic 5:5 Assyrian shall c. into our land: 935
Mic 5:10 shall c. to pass in that day, saith........ 1961
Mic 6:6 Wherewith shall I c. before the........... 6923
Mic 6:6 c. before him with burnt offerings,...... 6923
Mic 7:12 c. even to thee from Assyria, ... 935
Na 1:11 There is one c. out of thee,............... 3318
Na 2:1 that dasheth in pieces is c. up 5927
Na 3:7 c. to pass, that all they that look....... 1961
Hab 1:8 their horsemen shall c. from far;.......... 935
Hab 1:9 They shall c. all for violence: 935
Hab 2:3 it will surely c., it will not tarry........... 935
Zep 1:8 c. to pass in the day of the Lord's...... 1961
Zep 1:10 it shall c. to pass in that day. 1961
Zep 1:12 And it shall c. to pass at that time...... 1961
Zep 2:2 of the Lord c. upon you, before 935
Zep 2:2 the day of the Lord's anger c.............. 935
Hag 1:2 The time is not c., the time that 935
Hag 2:7 the desire of all nations shall c. 935
Hag 2:22 and their riders shall c. down, ... 3381
Zec 1:21 Then said I, What c. these to do?........ 935
Zec 1:21 but these are c. to fray them, to.......... 935
Zec 2:6 Ho, ho, c. forth, and flee from the ....
Zec 2:10 I c., and I will dwell in the midst......... 935
Zec 6:10 c. from Babylon, and c. thou the 935
Zec 6:15 that are far off shall c. and build 935
Zec 6:15 And this shall c. to pass, if ye will...... 1961
Zec 7:13 it is c. to pass, that as he cried, ... 1961
Zec 8:13 c. to pass, that as ye were a curse 1961
Zec 8:20 shall yet c. to pass, that there shall..........
Zec 8:20 c. people, and the inhabitants.............. 935
Zec 8:22 people and strong nations shall c.......... 935
Zec 8:23 In those days it shall c. to pass,..............
Zec 11:2 forest of the vintage is c. down. 3381
Zec 12:9 it shall c. to pass in that day, that...... 1961
Zec 12:9 nations that c. against Jerusalem.......... 935
Zec 13:2 And it shall c. to pass in that day, ... 1961
Zec 13:3 And it shall c. to pass, that when........ 1961
Zec 13:4 And it shall c. to pass in that day, ... 1961
Zec 13:8 And it shall c. to pass, that in all........ 1961
Zec 14:5 my God shall c., and all the saints 935
Zec 14:6, 13 it shall c. to pass in that day,.......... 1961
Zec 14:7 but it shall c. to pass, that at 1961
Zec 14:16 And it shall c. to pass, that every 1961
Zec 14:17 will not c. up of all the families, ... 5927
Zec 14:18 of Egypt go not up, and c. not, ... 935
Zec 14:18, 19 that c. not up to keep the feast..... 5927
Zec 14:21 they that sacrifice shall c. and take...... 935
Mal 3:1 shall suddenly c. to his temple, ... 935
Mal 3:1 behold, he shall c., saith the Lord......... 935
Mal 3:5 I will c. near to you to judgment; 7126
Mal 4:6 lest I c. and smite the earth.............. 935
Mt 2:2 east, and are c. to worship him. *2064*
Mt 2:6 out of thee shall c. a Governor, ... *1831*
Mt 2:8 I may c. and worship him also............ *2064*
Mt 2:11 when they were c. into the house, ... *2064*
Mt 3:7 and Sadducees c. to his baptism,........ *2064*
Mt 3:7 to flee from the wrath to c.? *3195*
Mt 5:17 that I am c. to destroy the law,..... *2064*
Mt 5:17 I am not c. to destroy, but to....... *2064*
Mt 5:24 and then c. and offer thy gift........ *2064*
Mt 5:26 shalt by no means c. out thence,... *1831*
Mt 6:10 Thy kingdom c.. Thy will be done.. *2064*
Mt 7:15 c. to you in sheep's clothing,........ *2064*
Mt 8:1 was c. down from the mountain, ... *2597*
Mt 8:7 unto him, I will c. and heal him. *2064*
Mt 8:8 thou shouldest c. under my roof:........ *1525*
Mt 8:9 to another, C., and he cometh;.......... *2064*
Mt 8:11 shall c. from the east and west, ... *2240*
Mt 8:14 Jesus was c. into Peter's house, ... *2064*
Mt 8:16 When the even was c., they............. *1096*
Mt 8:28 when he was c. to the other side....... *2064*
Mt 8:29 art thou c. hither to torment us......... *2064*
Mt 8:32 when they were c. out, they went...... *1831*
Mt 9:13 I am not c. to call the righteous,.. *2064*
Mt 9:15 days will c., when the bridegroom..*2064*
Mt 9:18 c. and lay thy hand upon her, and *2064*
Mt 9:28 And when he was c. into the house, ... *2064*
Mt 10:12 ye c. into an house, salute it......... *1525*
Mt 10:13 worthy, let your peace c. upon it;.. *2064*
Mt 10:23 of Israel, till the Son of man be c..*2064*
Mt 10:34 I am c. to send peace on earth:..... *2064*
Mt 10:35 I am c. to set a man at variance... *2064*
Mt 11:3 Art thou he that should c., or do *2064*
Mt 11:14 is Elias, which was for to c.. .... *2064*
Mt 11:28 C. unto me, all ye that labour....... *1205*
Mt 12:28 kingdom of God is c. unto you....... *5348*
Mt 12:32 neither in the world to c.............. *3195*
Mt 12:44 when he is c., he findeth it empty,.*2064*
Mt 13:32 so that the birds of the air c......... *2064*
Mt 13:49 the angels shall c. forth, and........ *1831*
Mt 13:54 he was c. into his own country, ... *2064*
Mt 14:23 when the evening was c., he was........ *1096*
Mt 14:28 bid me c. unto thee on the water....... *2064*
Mt 14:29 And he said, C.. And when............... *2064*
Mt 14:29 Peter was c. down out of the ship,..... *2597*
Mt 14:32 when they were c. into the ship,........ *1684*
Mt 15:18 c. forth from the heart; and they.. *1831*
Mt 16:5 when his disciples were c. to the *2064*
Mt 16:24 If any man will c. after me,.......... *2064*
Mt 16:27 Son of man shall c. in the glory.... *2064*
Mt 17:10 scribes that Elias must first c.?.......... *2064*
Mt 17:11 Elias truly shall first c., and........ *2064*
Mt 17:12 unto you, That Elias is c. already,.*2064*
Mt 17:14 when they were c. to the multitude, ... *2064*
Mt 17:24 when they were c. to Capernaum,...... *2064*
Mt 17:25 when he was c. into the house, ... *1525*
Mt 18:7 must needs be that offences c.;..... *2064*
Mt 18:11 For the Son of man is c. to save... *2064*
Mt 19:14 forbid them not, to c. unto me:..... *2064*
Mt 19:21 in heaven: and c. and follow me.... *1204*
Mt 20:8 So when even was c., the lord of... *1096*
Mt 21:1 and were c. to Bethphage, unto.......... *2064*
Mt 21:10 when he was c. into Jerusalem, ... *1525*
Mt 21:23 when he was c. into the temple, ... *2064*
Mt 21:38 c., let us kill him, and let us seize.*1205*
Mt 22:3 wedding: and they would not c...... *2064*
Mt 22:4 ready: c. unto the marriage. *1205*
Mt 23:35 That upon you may c. all the........ *2064*
Mt 23:36 shall c. upon this generation......... *2240*
Mt 24:5 For many shall c. in my name,...... *2064*
Mt 24:6 all these things must c. to pass,.... *1096*
Mt 24:14 and then shall the end c.. .... *2240*
Mt 24:17 is on the housetop not c. down...... *2597*
Mt 24:42 not what hour your Lord doth c.... *2064*
Mt 24:43 what watch the thief would c.,...... *2064*
Mt 24:50 The lord of that servant shall c..... *2240*
Mt 25:31 When the Son of man shall c. in... *2064*
Mt 25:34 C., ye blessed of my Father,......... *1205*
Mt 26:20 Now when the even was c., he sat..... *1096*
Mt 26:50 Friend, wherefore art thou c.?...... *3918*
Mt 26:55 Are ye c. out as against a thief..... *1831*
Mt 27:1 When the morning was c., all the....... *1096*
Mt 27:33 when they were c. unto a place *2064*
Mt 27:40 of God, c. down from the cross. *2597*
Mt 27:42 let him now c. down from the cross,... *2597*
Mt 27:49 whether Elias will c. to save him........ *2064*
Mt 27:57 When the even was c., there *1096*
Mt 27:64 lest his disciples c. by night, ... *2064*

Mt 28:6 C., see the place where the Lord... 1205
Mt 28:14 if this c. to the governor's ears,... 191
Mk 1:17 C. ye after me, and I will make... 1205
Mk 1:24 art thou c. to destroy us? I know... 2064
Mk 1:25 thy peace, and c. out of him... 1831
Mk 1:29 when they were c. out of the... 1831
Mk 2:3 And they c. unto him, bringing... 2064
Mk 2:4 And when they could not c. nigh... 4331
Mk 2:18 they c. and say unto him, Why do... 2064
Mk 2:20 But the days will c., when the... 2064
Mk 4:22 but that it should c. abroad... 2064
Mk 4:29 sickle, because the harvest is c... 3936
Mk 4:35 same day, when the even was c... 1096
Mk 5:2 when he was c. out of the ship,... 1831
Mk 5:8 C. out of the man, thou unclean... 1831
Mk 5:15 And they c. to Jesus, and see him... 2064
Mk 5:18 when he was c. into the ship,... 1684
Mk 5:23 c. and lay thy hands on her,... 2064
Mk 5:39 when he was c. in, he saith unto... 1525
Mk 6:2 when the sabbath day was c.,... 1096
Mk 6:21 when a convenient day was c.,... 1096
Mk 6:31 C. ye yourselves apart into a... 1205
Mk 6:47 when even was c., the ship was in... 1096
Mk 6:54 when they were c. out of the ship,... 1831
Mk 7:4 And when they c. from the market,...
Mk 7:15 the things which c. out of him,... 1607
Mk 7:23 these evil things c. from within,... 1607
Mk 7:30 when she was c. to her house,... 565
Mk 8:34 Whosoever will c. after me, let... 2064
Mk 9:1 kingdom of God c. with power... 2064
Mk 9:11 scribes that Elias must first c.?... 2064
Mk 9:13 That Elias is indeed c., and they... 2064
Mk 9:25 I charge thee, c. out of him,... 1831
Mk 9:28 when he was c. into the house,... 1525
Mk 9:29 This kind can c. forth by nothing,. 1831
Mk 10:14 Suffer the little children to c.... 2064
Mk 10:21 c., take up the cross, and follow... 1204
Mk 10:30 in the world to c. eternal life... 2064
Mk 10:35 c. unto him, saying, Master, we... 4365
Mk 11:11 and now the eventide was c.,... 1511
Mk 11:12 when they were c. from Bethany,... 1831
Mk 11:15 And they c. to Jerusalem: and... 2064
Mk 11:19 when even was c., he went out... 1096
Mk 11:23 which he saith shall c. to pass;... 1096
Mk 11:27 And they c. again to Jerusalem:... 2064
Mk 11:27 there c. to him the chief priests,... 2064
Mk 12:7 is the heir; c., let us kill him,... 1205
Mk 12:9 c. and destroy the husbandmen,... 2064
Mk 12:14 And when they were c., they say... 2064
Mk 12:18 Then c. unto him the Sadducees,... 2064
Mk 13:6 For many shall c. in my name,... 2064
Mk 13:29 shall see these things c. to pass,... 1096
Mk 14:8 she is c. aforehand to anoint... 4301
Mk 14:41 it is enough, the hour is c.;... 2064
Mk 14:45 And as soon as he was c., he goeth... 2064
Mk 14:48 Are ye c. out, as against a thief,... 1831
Mk 15:30 Save thyself, and c. down from... 2597
Mk 15:33 when the sixth hour was c., there... 1096
Mk 15:36 Elias will c. to take him down... 2064
Mk 15:42 now when the even was c.,... 1096
Mk 16:1 they might c. and anoint him... 2064
Lu 1:35 Holy Ghost shall c. upon thee,... 1904
Lu 1:43 the mother of my Lord should c... 2064
Lu 2:15 this thing which is c. to pass,... 1096
Lu 3:7 to flee from the wrath to c.?... 3195
Lu 4:34 art thou c. to destroy us? I know... 2064
Lu 4:35 Hold thy peace, and c. out of him.. 1831
Lu 4:36 unclean spirits, and they c. out... 1831
Lu 5:7 that they should c. and help them... 2064
Lu 5:17 which were c. out of every town... 2064
Lu 5:35 But the days will c., when the... 2064
Lu 7:3 he would c. and heal his servant... 2064
Lu 7:7 I myself worthy to c. unto thee:... 2064
Lu 7:8 and to another, C., and he cometh;... 2064
Lu 7:19 Art thou he that should c.?... 2064
Lu 7:20 When the men were c. unto him,... 3854
Lu 7:20 Art thou he that should c.?... 2064
Lu 7:34 The Son of man is c. eating and... 2064
Lu 8:4 were c. to him out of every city,... 1975
Lu 8:17 not be known and c. abroad... 2064
Lu 8:19 could not c. at him for the press... 4940
Lu 8:29 spirit to c. out of the man... 1831
Lu 8:41 that he would c. into his house:... 1525
Lu 9:23 If any man will c. after me,... 2064
Lu 9:26 when he shall c. in his own glory,.. 2064
Lu 9:37 they were c. down from the hill,... 2718
Lu 9:51 when the time was c. that he... 4845
Lu 9:54 that we command fire to c. down... 2597
Lu 9:56 is not c. to destroy men's lives,... 2064
Lu 10:1 whither he himself would c... 2064
Lu 10:9 The kingdom of God is c. nigh... 1448
Lu 10:11 the kingdom of God is c. nigh... 1448
Lu 10:35 when I c. again, I will repay thee.. 1880
Lu 11:2 Thy kingdom c.. Thy will be... 2064
Lu 11:6 mine in his journey is c. to me,... 3854
Lu 11:20 kingdom of God is c. upon you... 5348
Lu 11:22 he shall c. upon him, and... 1904
Lu 11:33 which c. in may see the light... 1531
Lu 12:37 and will c. forth and serve them... 3928
Lu 12:38 if he shall c. in the second watch,. 2064
Lu 12:38 or c. in the third watch,... 2064
Lu 12:39 what hour the thief would c.,... 2064
Lu 12:46 The lord of that servant will c.... 2240
Lu 12:49 I am c. to send fire on the earth;.. 2064
Lu 12:51 Suppose ye that I am c. to give... 3854
Lu 13:7 I c. seeking fruit on this fig tree,.. 2064
Lu 13:14 them therefore c. and be healed,... 2064
Lu 13:29 they shall c. from the east, and... 2240
Lu 13:35 the time c. when we shall say,... 2240
Lu 14:9 that bade thee and him c. and... 2064
Lu 14:17 C.; for all things are now ready... 2064
Lu 14:20 a wife, and therefore I cannot c... 2064
Lu 14:23 compel them to c. in, that my... 1525
Lu 14:26 If any man c. to me, and hate not. 2064
Lu 14:27 bear his cross, and c. after me,... 2064
Lu 15:27 Thy brother is c.; and thy father... 2240
Lu 15:30 as soon as this thy son was c.,... 2064
Lu 16:26 that would c. from thence...
Lu 16:28 lest they also c. into this place... 2064
Lu 17:1 but that offences will c.: but woe.. 2064
Lu 17:1 unto him, through whom they c.!.. 2064
Lu 17:7 when he is c. from the field,... 1525
Lu 17:20 the kingdom of God should c.,... 2064
Lu 17:22 The days will c., when ye shall... 2064
Lu 17:31 let him not c. down to take it... 2597
Lu 18:16 little children to c. unto me,... 2064
Lu 18:22 in heaven: and c., follow me... 1204
Lu 18:30 in the world to c. life everlasting.. 2064
Lu 18:35 as he was c. nigh unto Jericho,... 1448
Lu 18:40 when he was c. near, he asked... 1448
Lu 19:5 make haste, and c. down; for... 2597
Lu 19:9 day is salvation c. to this house,... 1096
Lu 19:10 For the Son of man is c. to seek... 2064
Lu 19:13 said unto them, Occupy till I c.... 2064
Lu 19:29 he was c. nigh to Bethphage and... 1448
Lu 19:37 when he was c. nigh, even now... 1448
Lu 19:41 when he was c. near, he beheld... 1448
Lu 19:43 the days shall c. upon thee, that... 2240
Lu 20:14 is the heir: c., let us kill him,... 1205
Lu 20:16 c. and destroy these husbandmen,.. 2064
Lu 21:6 the days will c., in the which... 2064
Lu 21:7 these things shall c. to pass?... 1096
Lu 21:8 for many shall c. in my name,... 2064
Lu 21:9 these things must first c. to pass;.. 1096
Lu 21:28 these things begin to c. to pass,... 1096
Lu 21:31 ye see these things c. to pass,... 1096
Lu 21:34 that day c. upon you unawares... 2186
Lu 21:35 as a snare shall it c. on all them... 1904
Lu 21:36 these things that shall c. to pass,.. 1096
Lu 22:14 when the hour was c., he sat down,... 1096
Lu 22:18 the kingdom of God shall c... 2064
Lu 22:45 and was c. to his disciples, he... 2064
Lu 22:52 the elders, which were c. to him,... 3854
Lu 22:52 Be ye c. out, as against a thief,... 1831
Lu 23:33 when they were c. to the place,... 565
Lu 24:12 at that which was c. to pass... 1096
Lu 24:18 things which are c. to pass there... 1096
Joh 1:31 am I c. baptizing with water... 2064
Joh 1:39 He saith unto them, C. and see... 2064
Joh 1:46 good thing c. out of Nazareth?... 1511
Joh 1:46 Philip saith unto him, C. and see... 2064
Joh 2:4 with thee? mine hour is not yet c... 2240
Joh 3:2 thou art a teacher c. from God:... 2064
Joh 3:19 light is c. into the world, and men. 2064
Joh 3:26 baptizeth, and all men c. to him... 2064
Joh 4:15 not, neither c. hither to draw... 2064
Joh 4:16 call thy husband, and c. hither,... 2064
Joh 4:25 is called Christ: when he is c.,... 2064
Joh 4:29 C., see a man, which told me all... 1205
Joh 4:40 the Samaritans were c. unto him,... 2064
Joh 4:45 Then when he was c. into Galilee,... 2064
Joh 4:47 that Jesus was c. out of Judaea... 2240
Joh 4:47 would c. down, and heal his son:... 2597
Joh 4:49 Sir, c. down ere my child die... 2597
Joh 4:54 was c. out of Judaea into Galilee... 2064
Joh 5:14 lest a worse thing c. unto thee... 1096
Joh 5:24 shall not c. into condemnation;... 2064
Joh 5:29 And shall c. forth; they that have.. 1607
Joh 5:40 ye will not c. to me, that ye might. 2064
Joh 5:43 I am c. in my Father's name, and. 2064
Joh 5:43 another shall c. in his own name,. 2064
Joh 6:5 saw a great company c. unto him,... 2064
Joh 6:14 a truth that prophet that should c... 2064
Joh 6:15 would c. and take him by force,... 2064
Joh 6:16 And when even was now c., his... 1096
Joh 6:17 and Jesus was not c. to them... 2064
Joh 6:37 Father giveth me shall c. to me;... 2240
Joh 6:44 No man can c. to me, except the... 2064
Joh 6:65 c. unto me, except it were given... 2064
Joh 7:6 My time is not yet c.: but your... 3918
Joh 7:8 for my time is not yet full c... 4137
Joh 7:28 I am not c. of myself, but he that. 2064
Joh 7:30 because his hour was not yet c... 2064
Joh 7:34 where I am, thither ye cannot c... 2064
Joh 7:36 where I am, thither ye cannot c.?... 2064
Joh 7:37 let him c. unto me, and drink... 2064
Joh 7:41 Shall Christ c. out of Galilee?... 2064
Joh 8:14 ye cannot tell whence I c., and... 2064
Joh 8:20 him; for his hour was not yet c... 2064
Joh 8:21 sins: whither I go, ye cannot c... 2064
Joh 8:22 saith, Whither I go, ye cannot c... 2064
Joh 9:39 I am c. into this world, that they.. 2064
Joh 10:10 I am c. that they might have life,.. 2064
Joh 11:27 Son of God, which should c. into... 2064
Joh 11:28 Master is c., and calleth for thee... 3918
Joh 11:30 Jesus was not yet c. into the town,... 2064
Joh 11:32 Mary was c. where Jesus was,... 2064
Joh 11:34 said unto him, Lord, c. and see... 2064
Joh 11:43 a loud voice, Lazarus, c. forth... 1204
Joh 11:48 the Romans shall c. and take... 2064
Joh 11:56 that he will not c. to the feast?... 2064
Joh 12:12 people that were c. to the feast,... 2064
Joh 12:23 hour is c., that the Son of man... 2064
Joh 12:35 lest darkness c. upon you:... 2638
Joh 12:46 I am c. a light into the world,... 2064
Joh 13:1 Jesus knew that his hour was c... 2064
Joh 13:3 was c. from God, and went to God;... 1831
Joh 13:19 Now I tell you before it c., that,... 1096
Joh 13:19 when it is c. to pass, ye may... 1096
Joh 13:33 Whither I go, ye cannot c.; so... 2064
Joh 14:3 I will c. again, and receive you... 2064
Joh 14:18 you comfortless: I will c. to you... 2064
Joh 14:23 we will c. unto him, and make our. 2064
Joh 14:28 I go away, and c. again unto you.. 2064
Joh 14:29 c. to pass, that, when it is c. to... 1096
Joh 15:22 not c., and spoken unto them,... 2064
Joh 15:26 But when the Comforter is c.,... 2064
Joh 16:4 that when the time shall c., ye... 2064
Joh 16:7 Comforter will not c. unto you;... 2064
Joh 16:8 when he is c., he will reprove... 2064
Joh 16:13 when he, the Spirit of truth, is c.,.. 2064
Joh 16:13 he will shew you things to c... 2064
Joh 16:21 because her hour is c.: but as... 2064
Joh 16:28 Father, and am c. into the world:. 2064
Joh 16:32 cometh, yea, is now c., that ye... 2064
Joh 17:1 Father, the hour is c.; glorify thy. 2064
Joh 17:11 are in the world, and I c. to thee.. 2064
Joh 17:13 And now c. I to thee; and these... 2064
Joh 18:4 all things that should c. upon him,... 2064
Joh 21:4 when the morning was now c.,... 1096
Joh 21:9 then as they were c. to land,... 576
Joh 21:12 Jesus saith unto them, C. and dine... 1205
Joh 21:22, 23 he tarry till I c., what is that... 2064
Ac 1:6 they therefore were c. together,... 4905
Ac 1:8 the Holy Ghost is c. upon you:... 1904
Ac 1:11 shall so c. in like manner as ye... 2064
Ac 1:13 when they were c. in, they went... 1525
Ac 2:1 the day of Pentecost was fully c.,... 4845
Ac 2:17 And it shall c. to pass in the last... 1511
Ac 2:20 and notable day of the Lord c... 2064
Ac 2:21 it shall c. to pass, that whosoever... 1511
Ac 3:19 the times of refreshing shall c... 2064
Ac 3:23 shall c. to pass, that every soul,... 1511
Ac 5:38 be of men, it will c. to nought:... 2647
Ac 7:3 c. into the land which I shall... 1204
Ac 7:7 after that shall they c. forth, and... 1834
Ac 7:34 and am c. down to deliver them... 2597
Ac 7:34 c., I will send thee into Egypt... 1204
Ac 8:15 were c. down, prayed for them,... 2597
Ac 8:24 which ye have spoken c. upon me... 1904

Ac 8:27 **c.** to Jerusalem for to worship, 2064
Ac 8:31 he would **c.** up and sit with him. 305
Ac 8:39 they were **c.** up out of the water, 305
Ac 9:26 when Saul was **c.** to Jerusalem, 3854
Ac 9:38 he would not delay to **c.** to them. 1330
Ac 9:39 When he was **c.**, they brought 3854
Ac 10:4 **c.** up for a memorial before God. 305
Ac 10:21 is the cause wherefore ye are **c.**? 3918
Ac 10:27 many that were **c.** together. 4905
Ac 10:28 or **c.** unto one of another nation; 4334
Ac 10:33 hast well done that thou art **c.**. 3854
Ac 11:2 Peter was **c.** up to Jerusalem, 305
Ac 11:11 were three men already **c.** unto the 2186
Ac 11:20 when they were **c.** to Antioch, 1525
Ac 12:11 Peter was **c.** to himself, he said, 1096
Ac 13:40 lest that **c.** upon you, which is 1904
Ac 14:11 The gods are **c.** down to us in the 2597
Ac 14:27 And when they were **c.**, and had 3854
Ac 15:4 when they were **c.** to Jerusalem, 3854
Ac 16:7 After they were **c.** to Mysia, they 2064
Ac 16:9 saying, **C.** over into Macedonia, 1224
Ac 16:15 **c.** into my house, and abide there. 1525
Ac 16:18 of Jesus Christ to **c.** out of her. 1831
Ac 16:37 **c.** themselves and fetch us out. 2064
Ac 17:6 upside down are **c.** hither also; 3918
Ac 17:15 for to **c.** to him with all speed, 2064
Ac 18:2 lately **c.** from Italy, with his wife 2064
Ac 18:5 Silas and Timotheus were **c.** from 2718
Ac 18:27 who, when he was **c.**, helped them 3854
Ac 19:4 him which should **c.** after him, 2064
Ac 19:32 wherefore they were **c.** together. 4905
Ac 20:11 therefore was **c.** up again, the 305
Ac 20:18 And when they were **c.** to him, he 3854
Ac 21:11 when he was **c.** unto us, he took 2064
Ac 21:17 when we were **c.** to Jerusalem, 1096
Ac 21:22 multitude must needs **c.** together; 4905
Ac 21:22 for they will hear that thou art **c.**. 2064
Ac 22:6 my journey, and was **c.** nigh 1448
Ac 22:17 I was **c.** again to Jerusalem, even 5290
Ac 23:15 he **c.** near, are ready to kill him. 1448
Ac 23:35 when thine accusers are also **c.**. 3854
Ac 24:8 his accusers to **c.** unto thee: 2064
Ac 24:22 the chief captain shall **c.** down, 2597
Ac 24:23 to minister or **c.** unto him. 4334
Ac 24:25 judgment to **c.**, Felix. 3195,1511
Ac 25:1 Festus was **c.** into the province, 1910
Ac 25:7 And when he was **c.**, the Jews 3854
Ac 25:17 when they were **c.** hither, without 4905
Ac 25:23 when Agrippa was **c.**, and Bernice, 2064
Ac 26:7 God day and night, hope to **c.**. 2658
Ac 26:22 and Moses did say should **c.** 1096
Ac 27:7 were **c.** over against Cnidus, 1096
Ac 27:16 much work to **c.** by the boat: 4031,1096
Ac 27:27 when the fourteenth night was **c.**, 1096
Ac 28:6 no harm **c.** to him, they changed 1096
Ac 28:17 they were **c.** together, he said 4905
Ro 1:10 by the will of God to **c.** unto you. 2064
Ro 1:13 oftentimes I purposed to **c.** unto 2064
Ro 3:8 Let us do evil, that good may **c.**? 2064
Ro 3:23 For all have sinned, and **c.** short 5302
Ro 5:14 the figure of him that was to **c.**. 3195
Ro 8:38 things present, nor things to **c.**, 3195
Ro 9:9 At this time will I **c.**, and Sarah 2064
Ro 9:26 shall **c.** to pass, that in the place 1511
Ro 11:11 salvation is **c.** unto the Gentiles,
Ro 11:25 fulness of the Gentiles be **c.** in. 1525
Ro 11:26 shall **c.** out of Sion the Deliverer, 2240
Ro 15:23 these many years to **c.** unto you; 2064
Ro 15:24 journey into Spain, I will **c.** to: 2064
Ro 15:28 I will **c.** by you into Spain. 565
Ro 15:29 when I **c.** unto you, I shall **c.** in 2064
Ro 15:32 That I may **c.** unto you with joy 2064
Ro 16:19 obedience is **c.** abroad unto all men. 864
1Co 1:7 So that ye **c.** behind in no gift; 5302
1Co 2:6 of this world, that **c.** to nought: 2673
1Co 3:22 or things to **c.**; all are yours; 3195
1Co 4:5 the Lord **c.**, who both will bring 2064
1Co 4:18 as though I would not **c.** to you 2064
1Co 4:19 **c.** to you shortly, if the Lord will, 2064
1Co 4:21 shall I **c.** unto you with a rod, or 2064
1Co 7:5 **c.** together again, that Satan 4905
1Co 10:11 whom the ends of the world are **c.**. 2658
1Co 11:17 ye **c.** together not for the better, 4905
1Co 11:18 when ye **c.** together in the church, 4905
1Co 11:20 When ye **c.** together therefore 4905
1Co 11:26 shew the Lord's death till he **c.**. 2064
1Co 11:33 when ye **c.** together to eat, tarry 4905
1Co 11:34 **c.** not together unto condemnation. 4905
1Co 11:34 rest will I set in order when I **c.**. 2064
1Co 13:10 when that which is perfect is **c.**, 2064
1Co 14:6 if I **c.** unto you speaking with 2064
1Co 14:23 the whole church be **c.** together 4905
1Co 14:23 **c.** in those that are unlearned, 1525
1Co 14:24 there **c.** in one that believeth not, 1525
1Co 14:26 when ye **c.** together, every one of 4905
1Co 15:35 and with what body do they **c.**? 2064
1Co 16:2 there be no gatherings when I **c.**. 2064
1Co 16:3 And when I **c.**, whomsoever ye 3854
1Co 16:5 Now I will **c.** unto you, when I 2064
1Co 16:10 Now if Timotheus **c.**, see that he 2064
1Co 16:11 in peace, that he may **c.** unto me: 2064
1Co 16:12 I greatly desired him to **c.** unto 2064
1Co 16:12 but his will was not at all to **c.** at 2064
1Co 16:12 this time: but he will **c.** when he 2064
2Co 1:15 I was minded to **c.** unto you before, 2064
2Co 1:16 to **c.** again out of Macedonia unto 2064
2Co 2:1 that I would not **c.** again to you in 2064
2Co 6:17 **c.** out from among them, and be 1831
2Co 7:5 For when we were **c.** into 2064
2Co 9:4 haply if they of Macedonia **c.** with 2064
2Co 10:14 for we are **c.** as far as to you also 5348
2Co 12:1 I will **c.** to visions and revelations 2064
2Co 12:14 third time I am ready to **c.** to you: 2064
2Co 12:20 lest, when I **c.**, I shall not find you 2064
2Co 12:21 lest, when I **c.** again, my God will 2064
2Co 13:2 other, that, if I **c.** again, I will not 2064
Ga 2:11 But when Peter was **c.** to Antioch, 2064
Ga 2:12 but when they were **c.**, he 2064
Ga 2:21 for if righteousness **c.** by the law
Ga 3:14 blessing of Abraham might **c.** on 1096
Ga 3:19 till the seed should **c.** to whom 2064
Ga 3:25 But after that faith is **c.**, we are 2064
Ga 4:4 the fulness of the time was **c.**, 2064
Eph 1:21 but also in that which is to **c.** 3195
Eph 2:7 that in the ages to **c.** he might 1904
Eph 4:13 Till we all **c.** in the unity of the 2658
Php 1:27 that whether I **c.** and see you, or 2064
Php 2:24 Lord that I also myself shall **c.** 2064
Col 1:6 Which is **c.** unto you as it is in all 3918
Col 2:17 are a shadow of things to **c.**; 3195
Col 4:10 if he **c.** unto you, receive him;) 2064
1Th 1:10 delivered us from the wrath to **c.**. 2064
1Th 2:16 for the wrath is **c.** upon them to 5348
1Th 2:18 we would have **c.** unto you, even 2064
2Th 1:10 When he shall **c.** to be glorified in 2064
2Th 2:3 for that day shall not **c.**, except 2064
2Th 2:3 except there **c.** a falling away 2064
1Ti 2:4 **c.** unto the knowledge of the truth. 2064
1Ti 3:14 hoping to **c.** unto thee shortly: 2064
1Ti 4:8 now is, and of that which is to **c.**. 3195
1Ti 4:13 Till I **c.**, give attendance to 2064
1Ti 6:19 foundation against the time to **c.**, 3195
2Ti 3:1 last days perilous times shall **c.**. 1764
2Ti 3:7 never able to **c.** to the knowledge 2064
2Ti 4:3 the time will **c.** when they will not 1511
2Ti 4:9 Do thy diligence to **c.** shortly 2064
2Ti 4:21 Do thy diligence to **c.** before winter. 2064
Tit 3:12 be diligent to **c.** unto me to 2064
Heb 2:5 put in subjection the world to **c.** 3195
Heb 4:1 any of you should seem to **c.** short 5302
Heb 4:16 Let us therefore **c.** boldly unto 4334
Heb 6:5 and the powers of the world to **c.**, 3195
Heb 7:5 **c.** out of the loins of Abraham: 1831
Heb 7:25 that **c.** unto God by him, seeing 4334
Heb 8:8 Behold, the days **c.**, saith the 2064
Heb 9:11 But Christ being **c.** an high priest 3854
Heb 9:11 high priest of good things to **c.**, 3195
Heb 10:1 a shadow of good things to **c.**, 3195
Heb 10:7 Then said I, Lo, I **c.** (in the 2240
Heb 10:9 Then said he, Lo, I **c.** to do thy 2240
Heb 10:37 and he that shall **c.** will 2064
Heb 10:37 will **c.**, and will not tarry. 2240
Heb 11:20 Esau concerning things to **c.**. 3195
Heb 11:24 Moses, when he was **c.** to years, 1096
Heb 12:18 For ye are not **c.** unto the mount 4334
Heb 12:22 But ye are **c.** unto mount Sion, 4334
Heb 13:14 city, but we seek one to **c.**. 3195
Heb 13:23 with whom, if he **c.** shortly, I will 2064
Jas 2:2 if there **c.** unto your assembly a 1525
Jas 2:2 there **c.** in also a poor man in vile 1525
Jas 4:1 From whence **c.** wars and fightings
Jas 4:1 **c.** they not hence, even of your lusts
Jas 5:1 miseries that shall **c.** upon you. 1904
1Pe 1:10 the grace that should **c.** unto you:
1Pe 4:17 For the time is **c.** that judgment
2Pe 3:3 there shall **c.** in the last days 2064
2Pe 3:9 that all should **c.** to repentance. 5562
2Pe 3:10 But the day of the Lord will **c.** as 2240
1Jo 2:18 heard that antichrist shall **c.**, 2064
1Jo 4:2 that Jesus Christ is **c.** in the flesh 2064
1Jo 4:3 Christ is **c.** in the flesh is not of 2064
1Jo 4:3 ye have heard that it should **c.**; 2064
1Jo 5:20 know that the Son of God is **c.**, 2240
2Jo 7 confess not that Jesus Christ is **c.** 2064
2Jo 10 If there **c.** any unto you, and bring 2064
2Jo 12 I trust to **c.** unto you, and speak 2064
3Jo 10 Wherefore, if I **c.**, I will remember 2064
Re 1:1 which must shortly **c.** to pass; 1096
Re 1:4 and which was, and which is to **c.**; 2064
Re 1:8 and which was, and which is to **c.**, 2064
Re 2:5 or else I will **c.** unto thee quickly, 2064
Re 2:16 I will **c.** unto thee quickly, and 2064
Re 2:25 ye have already, hold fast till I **c.** 2240
Re 3:3 I will **c.** on thee as a thief, and 2240
Re 3:3 shalt not know what hour I will **c.** 2240
Re 3:9 behold, I will make them to **c.** 2240
Re 3:10 of temptation, which shall **c.** upon 2064
Re 3:11 Behold, I **c.** quickly: hold that 2064
Re 3:20 open the door, I will **c.** into him, 1525
Re 4:1 which said, **C.** up hither, and I 305
Re 4:8 which was, and is, and is to **c.**. 2064
Re 6:1 one of the four beasts saying, **C.** 2064
Re 6:3 I heard the second beast say, **C.** 2064
Re 6:5 the third beast say, **C.** and see. 2064
Re 6:7 the fourth beast say, **C.** and see. 2064
Re 6:17 the great day of his wrath is **c.**; 2064
Re 9:12 and, behold, there **c.** two woes 2064
Re 10:1 I saw another mighty angel **c.** 2597
Re 11:12 saying unto them, **C.** up hither. 305
Re 11:17 which art, and wast, and art to **c.**; 2064
Re 11:18 thy wrath is **c.**, and the time of 2064
Re 12:10 Now is **c.** salvation, and strength, 1096
Re 12:12 the devil is **c.** down unto you, 2597
Re 13:13 so that he maketh fire **c.** down 2597
Re 14:7 for the hour of his judgment is **c.** 2064
Re 14:15 the time is **c.** for thee to reap; for 2064
Re 15:4 all nations shall **c.** and worship 2240
Re 16:13 unclean spirits like frogs **c.** out
Re 16:15 I **c.** as a thief. Blessed is he that 2064
Re 17:1 **C.** hither; I will shew unto thee 1204
Re 17:10 the other is not yet **c.**; and when 2064
Re 18:1 I saw another angel **c.** down from 2597
Re 18:4 **C.** out of her, my people, that ye 1831
Re 18:8 Therefore shall her plagues **c.** in 2240
Re 18:10 in one hour is thy judgment **c.**. 2064
Re 18:17 so great riches is **c.** to nought. 2049
Re 19:7 the marriage of the Lamb is **c.**, 2064
Re 19:17 **C.** and gather yourselves together 1205
Re 20:1 I saw an angel **c.** down from 2597
Re 21:9 **C.** hither, I will shew thee the 1204
Re 22:7 Behold, I **c.** quickly: blessed is he 2064
Re 22:12 behold, I **c.** quickly; and my 2064
Re 22:17 the Spirit and the bride say, **C.** 2064
Re 22:17 And let him that heareth say, **C.** 2064
Re 22:17 And let him that is athirst **c.**. 2064
Re 22:20 Surely I **c.** quickly. Amen. 2064
Re 22:20 Even so, **c.**, Lord Jesus. 2064

COMELINESS

Isa 53:2 he hath no form nor **c.**; and when 1926
Eze 16:14 for it was perfect through my **c.**, 1926
Eze 27:10 they set forth thy **c.**. 1926
Da 10:8 for my **c.** was turned in me into 1935
1Co 12:23 parts have more abundant **c.**. 2157

COMELY See also UNCOMELY.

1Sa 16:18 in matters, and a **c.** person, 8389
Job 41:12 his power, nor his **c.** proportion. 2433
Ps 33:1 for praise is **c.** for the upright. 5000
Ps 147:1 for it is pleasant; and praise is **c.**. 5000
Pr 30:29 go well, yea, four are **c.** in going: 3190
Ec 5:18 it is good and **c.** for one to eat and 3303
Ca 1:5 I am black, but **c.**, O ye daughters 5000
Ca 1:10 Thy cheeks are **c.** with rows of 4998
Ca 2:14 voice, and thy countenance is **c.** 5000
Ca 4:3 thy speech is **c.**: thy temples are 5000
Ca 6:4 love, as Tirzah, **c.** as Jerusalem, 5000
Isa 4:2 earth shall be excellent and **c.** for 8597
Jer 6:2 daughter of Zion to a **c.** and 5000
1Co 7:35 you, but for that which is **c.**, 2158
1Co 11:13 is it **c.** that a woman pray unto 4241
1Co 12:24 For our **c.** parts have no need: but 2158

COMERS

Heb 10:1 continually make the c. thereunto 4334

COMEST

Ge 10:19 Sidon, as thou c. to Gerar, unto 935
Ge 13:10 of Egypt, as thou c. unto Zoar. 935
Ge 24:41 this my oath, when thou c. to my 935
De 2:19 And when thou c. nigh over 7126
De 20:10 When thou c. nigh unto a city to 7126
De 23:24 When thou c. into thy neighbour's 935
De 23:25 When thou c. into the standing corn 935
De 28:6 when thou c. in, and blessed shalt 935
De 28:19 when thou c. in, and cursed shalt 935
Jg 17:9 said unto him, Whence c. thou? 935
Jg 18:23 that thou c. with such a company? 2199
Jg 19:17 goest thou? and whence c. thou? 935
1Sa 15:7 thou c. to Shur, that is over against 935
1Sa 16:4 C. thou peaceably? 935
1Sa 17:43 Am I a dog, that thou c. to me 935
1Sa 17:45 Thou c. to me with a sword, and 935
2Sa 1:3 unto him, From whence c. thou? 935
2Sa 3:13 when thou c. to see my face 935
1Ki 2:13 she said, C. thou peaceably? And 935
1Ki 19:15 and when thou c., anoint Hazael to 935
2Ki 5:25 Elisha said unto him, Whence c.
2Ki 9:2 And when thou c. thither, look out 935
Job 1:7 said unto Satan, Whence c. thou? 935
Job 2:2 From whence c. thou? And Satan 935
Jer 51:61 When thou c. to Babylon, and shalt 935
Jon 1:8 and whence c. thou? What is thy 935
Mt 3:14 and c. thou to me? *2064*
Lu 23:42 remember me when thou c. into *2064*
2Ti 4:13 when thou c., bring with thee, and *2064*

COMETH See also BECOMETH; OVERCOMETH.

Ge 24:43 when the virgin c. forth to draw 3318
Ge 29:6 his daughter c. with the sheep. 935
Ge 30:11 And Leah said, A troop c.: and 935
Ge 32:6 he c. to meet thee, and four 1980
Ge 37:19 Behold, this dreamer c. 935
Ge 48:2 thy son Joseph c. unto thee: 935
Ex 4:14 he c. forth to meet thee: and when 3318
Ex 8:20 he c. forth to the water; and say 3318
Ex 13:12 every firstling that c. of a beast 7698
Ex 28:35 when he c. out, that he die not. 3318
Ex 29:30 when he c. into the tabernacle of 935
Le 11:34 on which such water c. shall be 935
Nu 1:51 the stranger that c. nigh shall be 7131
Nu 3:10, 38 stranger that c. nigh shall be 7131
Nu 5:30 the spirit of jealousy c. upon him, 5674
Nu 12:12 he c. out of his mother's womb. 3318
Nu 17:13 Whosoever c. any thing near unto 7131
Nu 18:7 the stranger that c. nigh shall be 7131
Nu 21:13 that c. out of the coasts of the 3318
Nu 26:5 Hanoch, of whom c. the family of
De 18:8 that which c. of the sale of his
De 23:11 when evening c. on, he shall wash 6437
De 23:13 and cover that which c. from thee; 6627
De 28:57 that c. out from between her feet. 3318
Jg 11:31 whatsoever c. forth of the doors 3318
Jg 13:14 eat of any thing that c. of the vine, 3318
1Sa 4:3 when it c. among us, it may save 935
1Sa 9:6 all that he saith c. surely to pass: 935
1Sa 11:7 Whosoever c. not forth after Saul 3318
1Sa 20:27 Wherefore c. not the son of Jesse 935
1Sa 20:29 he c. not unto the king's table 935
1Sa 25:8 whatsoever c. to thine hand unto 4672
1Sa 28:14 An old man c. up; and he is 5927
2Sa 13:5 and when thy father c. to see thee, 935
2Sa 18:27 good man, and c. with good tidings. 935
1Ki 8:41 but c. out of a far country for thy 935
1Ki 14:5 wife of Jeroboam c. to ask a thing 935
1Ki 14:5 when she c. in, that she shall feign 935
2Ki 4:10 when he c. to us, that he shall turn 935
2Ki 6:32 when the messenger c., shut the 935
2Ki 9:18 came to them, but he c. not again. 7725
2Ki 9:20 even unto them, and c. not again: 7725
2Ki 10:2 Now as soon as this letter c. to you, 935
2Ki 11:8 and he that c. within the ranges, let 935
2Ki 11:8 king as he goeth out and a he c. in. 935
2Ki 12:4 all the money that c. into any 5927
2Ki 12:9 on the right side as one c. into the 935
1Ch 16:33 because he c. to judge the earth 935
1Ch 29:16 thine holy name c. of thine hand,
2Ch 13:9 so that whosoever c. to consecrate 935
2Ch 20:2 There c. a great multitude against 935
2Ch 20:9 If, when evil c. upon us, as the 935
2Ch 20:12 this great company that c. against 935
2Ch 23:7 whosoever else c. into the house, 935
2Ch 23:7 be ye with the king when he c. in, 935
Job 3:21 long for death, but it c. not; and
Job 3:24 For my sighing c. before I eat, and 935
Job 5:6 affliction c. not forth of the dust, 3318
Job 5:21 be afraid of destruction when it c. 935
Job 5:26 a shock of corn c. in his season. 5927
Job 14:2 He c. forth like a flower, and is 3318
Job 14:18 the mountain falling c. to nought, 5034
Job 20:25 is drawn, and c. out of the body; 3318
Job 20:25 glittering sword c. out of his gall: 1980
Job 21:17 oft c. their destruction upon them! 935
Job 27:9 his cry when trouble c. upon him? 935
Job 28:5 for the earth, out of it c. bread: 3318
Job 28:20 Whence then c. wisdom? and 935
Job 36:32 by the cloud that c. betwixt. 6293
Job 37:9 Out of the south c. the whirlwind: 935
Job 37:22 Fair weather c. out of the north: 857
Ps 30:5 a night, but joy c. in the morning.
Ps 62:1 God: from him c. my salvation.
Ps 75:6 For promotion c. neither from the
Ps 78:39 passeth away, and c. not again. 7725
Ps 96:13 Lord: for he c., for he c. to judge 935
Ps 98:9 Lord; for he c. to judge the earth: 935
Ps 118:26 Blessed be he that c. in the name 935
Ps 121:1 the hills, from whence c. my help. 935
Ps 121:2 My help c. from the Lord, which
Pr 1:26 I will mock when your fear c.; 935
Pr 1:27 When your fear c. as desolation, 935
Pr 1:27 and your destruction c. as a 857
Pr 1:27 distress and anguish c. upon 935
Pr 2:6 out of his mouth c. knowledge and
Pr 3:25 desolation of the wicked, when it c. 935
Pr 11:2 When pride c., then c. shame: 935
Pr 11:8 and the wicked c. in his stead. 935
Pr 13:5 man is loathsome, and c. to shame.
Pr 13:10 by pride c. contention: but with 5414
Pr 13:12 but when the desire c., it is a tree 935
Pr 18:3 When the wicked c., then c. also 935
Pr 18:17 but his neighbour c. and searcheth 935
Pr 29:26 every man's judgment c. from the Lord.
Ec 1:4 another generation c.: but the earth
Ec 2:12 the man do that c. after the king?
Ec 4:14 For out of prison he c. to reign; 3318
Ec 5:3 a dream c. through the multitude 935
Ec 6:4 For he c. in with vanity, and 935
Ec 11:8 All that c. is vanity. 935
Ca 2:8 he c. leaping upon the mountains, 935
Ca 3:6 Who is this that c. out of the 5927
Ca 8:5 Who is this that c. up from the 5927
Isa 13:9 Behold, the day of the Lord c., 935
Isa 21:1 it c. from the desert, from a terrible 935
Isa 21:9 here c. a chariot of men, a couple 935
Isa 21:12 The morning c., and also the night: 857
Isa 24:18 and he that c. up out of the midst 5927
Isa 26:21 Lord c. out of his place to punish 3318
Isa 28:29 This also c. forth from the Lord 3318
Isa 30:13 whose breaking c. suddenly at an 935
Isa 30:27 the name of the Lord c. from far. 935
Isa 42:5 earth, and that which c. out of it; 6631
Isa 55:10 as the rain c. down, and the snow 3381
Isa 62:11 salvation c.; behold, his reward is 935
Isa 63:1 Who is this that c. from Edom, 935
Jer 6:20 To what purpose c. there to me 935
Jer 6:22 a people c. from the north country, 935
Jer 17:6 shall not see when good c.; but 935
Jer 17:8 shall not see when heat c., but her 935
Jer 18:14 Lebanon which c. from the rock 935
Jer 43:11 when he c., he shall smite the 935
Jer 46:7 Who is this that c. up as a flood, 5927
Jer 46:20 c.; it c. out of the north. 935
Jer 47:4 Because of the day that c. to spoil 935
Jer 50:3 there c. up a nation against her, 5927
Jer 51:54 A sound of a cry c. from Babylon, and
La 3:37 he that saith, and it c. to pass, 1961
Eze 4:12 with dung that c. out of man, 6627
Eze 7:25 destruction c.; and they shall seek 935
Eze 14:4 and c. to the prophet; I the Lord 935
Eze 14:4 will answer him that c. according 935
Eze 14:7 and c. to a prophet to enquire of 935
Eze 20:32 And that which c. into your mind 5927
Eze 21:7 For the tidings; because it c.: and 935
Eze 21:7 be weak as water: behold, it c., 935
Eze 24:24 and when this c., ye shall know 935
Eze 30:9 in the day of Egypt: for, lo, it c. 935
Eze 33:30 the word that c. forth from the 3318
Eze 33:31 as the people c., and they sit 935
Eze 33:33 And when this c. to pass, (lo, it will 935
Eze 47:9 shall live whither the river c. 935
Da 11:16 But he that c., against him shall do 935
Da 12:12 waiteth, and c. to the thousand 5060
Ho 7:1 and the thief c. in, and the troop 935
Joe 2:1 for the day of the Lord c., for it is 935
Mic 1:3 the Lord c. forth out of his place, 3318
Mic 5:6 when he c. into our land, and when 935
Mic 7:4 watchmen and thy visitation c.; 935
Hab 3:16 when he c. up unto the people, he 5927
Zec 9:9 thy King c. unto thee: he is just, 935
Zec 14:1 day of the Lord c., and thy spoil 935
Mal 4:1 the day c., that shall burn as an 935
Mal 4:1 the day that c. shall burn them up, 935
Mt 3:11 but he that c. after me is mightier *2064*
Mt 3:13 Then c. Jesus from Galilee to *3854*
Mt 5:37 **is more than these c. of evil,** *1511*
Mt 8:9 and to another, Come, and he c.; *2064*
Mt 13:19 **then c. the wicked one, and** *2064*
Mt 15:11 **that which c. out of the mouth,** *1607*
Mt 17:27 **take up the fish that first c. up;** *305*
Mt 18:7 **that man by whom the offence c.** *2064*
Mt 21:5 c. unto thee, meek, and sitting *2064*
Mt 21:9 Blessed is he that c. in the name of *2064*
Mt 21:40 **lord therefore of the vineyard c.,** *2064*
Mt 23:39 **Blessed is he that c. in the name** *2064*
Mt 24:27 **as the lightning c. out of the east,** *1831*
Mt 24:44 **as ye think not the Son of man c.** *2064*
Mt 24:46 **whom his lord when he c. shall** *2064*
Mt 25:6 **made, Behold, the bridegroom c.;** *2064*
Mt 25:13 **hour wherein the Son of man c.** *2064*
Mt 25:19 **the lord of those servants c., and** *2064*
Mt 26:36 Then c. Jesus with them unto a *2064*
Mt 26:40 And he c. unto the disciples, and *2064*
Mt 26:45 Then c. he to his disciples, and *2064*
Mk 1:7 There c. one mightier than I *2064*
Mk 3:20 the multitude c. together again, *4905*
Mk 4:15 **Satan c. immediately, and taketh** *2064*
Mk 5:22 there c. one of the rulers of the *2064*
Mk 5:38 he c. to the house of the ruler *2064*
Mk 6:48 he c. unto them, walking upon the *2064*
Mk 7:20 **That which c. out of the man,** *1607*
Mk 8:22 c. to Bethsaida; and they bring *2064*
Mk 8:38 **he c. in the glory of his Father** *2064*
Mk 9:12 **Elias verily c. first, and restoreth** *2064*
Mk 10:1 thence, and c. into the coasts *2064*
Mk 11:9 he that c. in the name of the Lord: *2064*
Mk 11:10 of our father David, that c. in the *2064*
Mk 13:35 **master of the house c., at even,** *2064*
Mk 14:17 the evening he c. with the twelve. *2064*
Mk 14:37 he c., and findeth them sleeping, *2064*
Mk 14:41 And he c. the third time, and saith *2064*
Mk 14:43 while he yet spake, c. Judas, one *3854*
Mk 14:66 there c. one of the maids of the *2064*
Lu 3:16 but one mightier than I c., *2064*
Lu 6:47 **c. to me, and heareth my sayings,** *2064*
Lu 7:8 and to another, Come, and he c.; *2064*
Lu 8:12 **then c. the devil, and taketh away** *2064*
Lu 8:49 spake, there c. one from the ruler *2064*
Lu 11:25 **when he c., he findeth it swept** *2064*
Lu 12:36 **When he c. and knocketh, they** *2064*
Lu 12:37 **the lord when he c. shall find** *2064*
Lu 12:40 **Son of man c. at an hour when** *2064*
Lu 12:43 **when he c. shall find so doing** *2064*
Lu 12:54 **There c. a shower; and so it is** *2064*
Lu 12:55 **will be heat; and it c. to pass** *1096*
Lu 13:35 **Blessed is he that c. in the name** *2064*
Lu 14:10 **he that bade thee c., he may say** *2064*
Lu 14:31 **meet him that c. against him with** *2064*
Lu 15:6 **he c. home, he calleth together** *2064*
Lu 17:20 **of God c. not with observation:** *2064*
Lu 18:8 **Son of man c., shall he find faith** *2064*
Lu 19:38 that c. in the name of the Lord: *2064*
Joh 1:9 every man that c. into the world. *2064*
Joh 1:15 c. after me is preferred before me: *2064*
Joh 1:30 me c. a man which is preferred *2064*
Joh 3:8 **canst not tell whence it c., and** *2064*
Joh 3:20 **c. to the light, lest his deeds** *2064*
Joh 3:21 **he that doeth truth c. to the light,** *2064*
Joh 3:31 He that c. from above is above all: *2064*
Joh 3:31 that c. from heaven is above all. *2064*
Joh 4:5 Then c. he to a city of Samaria, *2064*
Joh 4:7 There c. a woman of Samaria to *2064*
Joh 4:21 **the hour c., when ye shall neither** *2064*
Joh 4:23 **the hour c., and now is, when** *2064*
Joh 4:25 Messias c., which is called Christ: *2064*
Joh 4:35 **four months, and then c. harvest?** *2064*

Joh 5:44 not the honour that c. from God
Joh 6:33 bread of God is he which c. down.. 2597
Joh 6:35 that c. to me shall never hunger;.. 2064
Joh 6:37 c. to me I will in no wise cast out..2064
Joh 6:45 learned of the Father, c. unto me. .2064
Joh 6:50 bread which c. down from heaven, .2597
Joh 7:27 when Christ c., no man knoweth 2064
Joh 7:31 Christ c., will he do more miracles 2064
Joh 7:42 Christ c. of the seed of David, 2064
Joh 9:4 night c., when no man can work 2064
Joh 10:10 The thief c. not, but for to steal,
Joh 11:38 in himself c. to the grave 2064
Joh 12:13 that c. in the name of the Lord 2064
Joh 12:15 King c., sitting on an ass's colt 2064
Joh 12:22 Philip c. and telleth Andrew: and 2064
Joh 13:6 c. he to Simon Peter: and Peter 2064
Joh 14:6 c. unto the Father, but by me 2064
Joh 14:30 the prince of this world c., and 2064
Joh 15:25 But this c. to pass, that the word
Joh 16:2 the time c., that whosoever killeth.2064
Joh 16:25 time c., when I shall no more 2064
Joh 16:32 the hour c., yea, is now come, 2064
Joh 18:3 c. thither with lanterns and 2064
Joh 20:1 c. Mary Magdalene early, when it 2064
Joh 20:2 she runneth, and c. to Simon Peter, 2064
Joh 20:6 Then c. Simon Peter following 2064
Joh 21:13 Jesus then c., and taketh bread, 2064
Ac 10:32 when he c., shall speak unto thee. 3854
Ac 13:25 there c. one after me, whose shoes 2064
Ac 18:21 this feast that c. in Jerusalem: 2064
Ro 4:9 C. this blessedness then upon
Ro 10:17 So then faith c. by hearing, and
1Co 15:24 Then c. the end, when he shall
2Co 11:4 For if he that c. preacheth another 2064
2Co 11:28 that which c. upon me daily, 1999
Ga 5:8 This persuasion c. not of him
Eph 5:6 of these things c. the wrath of God 2064
Col 3:6 the wrath of God c. on the children 2064
1Th 5:2 the day of the Lord so c. as a thief 2064
1Th 5:3 sudden destruction c. upon them, 2186
1Ti 6:4 strifes of words, whereof c. envy, 1096
Heb 6:7 in the rain that c. oft upon it, 2064
Heb 10:5 when he c. into the world, he
Heb 11:6 for he that c. to God must believe 4334
Jas 1:17 c. down from the Father of lights, 2591
Jude 14 the Lord c. with ten thousands of 2064
Re 1:7 Behold, he c. with clouds; and 2064
Re 3:12 new Jerusalem, which c. down 2597
Re 11:14 behold, the third woe c. quickly. 2064
Re 17:10 when he c., he must continue a 2064

COME TO PASS See COME and PASS.

COMFORT See also COMFORTABLE; COMFORTED; COMFORTETH; COMFORTLESS; COMFORTS.
Ge 5:29 shall c. us concerning our work 5162
Ge 18:5 and c. ye your hearts; after that 5582
Ge 27:42 c. himself, purposing to kill thee. 5162
Ge 37:35 all his daughters rose up to c. him; 5162
Jg 19:5 C. thine heart with a morsel of 5582
Jg 19:8 said, C. thine heart, I pray thee 5582
2Sa 10:2 David sent to c. him by the hand 5162
1Ch 7:22 and his brethren came to c. him 5162
1Ch 19:2 David sent messengers to c. him 5162
1Ch 19:2 of Ammon to Hanun, to c. him. 5162
Job 2:11 to mourn with him and to c. him. 5162
Job 6:10 should I yet have c.; yea, I would 5165
Job 7:13 My bed shall c. me, my couch 5162
Job 9:27 my heaviness, and c. myself: 1082
Job 10:20 alone, that I may take c. a little, 1082
Job 21:34 How then c. ye me in vain, seeing 5162
Ps 23:4 thy rod and thy staff they c. me. 5162
Ps 71:21 and c. me on every side 5162
Ps 119:50 This is my c. in my affliction: for 5162
Ps 119:76 merciful kindness be for my c., 5162
Ps 119:82 saying, When wilt thou c. me? 5162
Ca 2:5 with flagons, c. me with apples: 7502
Isa 22:4 to c. me, because of the spoiling 5162
Isa 40:1 C. ye, c. ye my people, saith your 5162
Isa 51:3 the Lord shall c. Zion: 5162
Isa 51:3 he will c. all her waste places; 5162
Isa 51:19 by whom shall I c. in thee? 5162
Isa 57:6 Should I receive c. in these? 5162
Isa 61:2 to c. all that mourn; 5162
Isa 66:13 comforteth, so will I c. you; 5162
Jer 8:18 I would c. myself against sorrow, 4010
Jer 16:7 to c. them for the dead; neither 5162
Jer 31:13 into joy, and will c. them, 5162
La 1:2 none to c. her: all her friends 5162
La 1:17 is none to c. her: the Lord hath 5162
La 1:21 I sigh: there is none to c. me: 5162
La 2:13 I may c. thee, O virgin daughter 5162
Eze 14:23 And they shall c. you, when ye see 5162
Eze 16:54 in that thou art a c. unto them. 5162
Zec 1:17 and the Lord shall yet c. Zion, 5162
Zec 10:2 they c. in vain: therefore they 5162
Mt 9:22 Daughter, be of good c.; thy faith..2293
Mk 10:49 of good c., rise; he calleth thee 2293
Lu 8:48 Daughter, be of good c.; thy faith..2293
Joh 11:19 to Martha and Mary, to c. them 3888
Ac 9:31 and in the c. of the Holy Ghost 3874
Ro 15:4 patience and c. of the scriptures 3874
1Co 14:3 and exhortation, and c. 3889
2Co 1:3 of mercies, and the God of all c.; 3874
2Co 1:4 that we may be able to c. them 3870
2Co 1:4 by the c. wherewith we ourselves 3874
2Co 2:7 to forgive him, and c. him, lest 3870
2Co 7:4 I am filled with c., I am exceeding 3874
2Co 7:13 we were comforted in your c. 3874
2Co 13:11 Be perfect, be of good c., be of 3870
Eph 6:22 and that he might c. your hearts. 3870
Php 2:1 if any c. of love, if any fellowship 3890
Php 2:19 that I also may be of good c., 2174
Col 4:8 your estate, and c. your hearts; 3870
Col 4:11 which have been a c. unto me. 3931
1Th 3:2 to c. you concerning your faith: 3870
1Th 4:18 c. one another with these words. 3870
1Th 5:11 c. yourselves together, and edify 3870
1Th 5:14 c. the feebleminded, support the 3888
2Th 2:17 C. your hearts, and stablish you 3870

COMFORTABLE
2Sa 14:17 my lord the king shall now be c. 4496
Zec 1:13 with good words and c. words. 5150

COMFORTABLY
2Sa 19:7 speak c. unto thy servants: 5921,3820
2Ch 30:22 spake c. unto all the Levites 5921,3820
2Ch 32:6 spake c. to them, saying, 5921,3824
Isa 40:2 Speak ye c. to Jerusalem, 5921,3820
Ho 2:14 speak c. unto her 5921,3820

COMFORTED See also COMFORTEDST.
Ge 24:67 Isaac was c. after his mother's 5162
Ge 37:35 he refused to be c.; and he said, 5162
Ge 38:12 wife died; and Judah was c., 5162
Ge 50:21 And he c. them, and spake kindly 5162
Ru 2:13 for that thou hast c. me, and for 5162
2Sa 12:24 And David c. Bath-sheba his wife, 5162
2Sa 13:39 he was c. concerning Amnon, 5162
Job 42:11 they bemoaned him, and c. him 5162
Ps 77:2 not: my soul refused to be c. 5162
Ps 86:17 Lord, hast holpen me, and c. me. 5162
Ps 119:52 of old, O Lord; and have c. myself. 5162
Isa 49:13 the Lord hath c. his people, and 5162
Isa 52:9 the Lord hath c. his people, he 5162
Isa 54:11 tossed with tempest, and not c. 5162
Isa 66:13 ye shall be c. in Jerusalem. 5162
Jer 31:15 children refused to be c. for her 5162
Eze 5:13 rest upon them, and I will be c.: 5162
Eze 14:22 and ye shall be c. concerning 5162
Eze 31:16 shall be c. in the nether parts 5162
Eze 32:31 shall be c. over all his multitude, 5162
Mt 2:18 would not be c., because they 3870
Mt 5:4 that mourn: for they shall be c. 3870
Lu 16:25 but now he is c., and thou art 3870
Joh 11:31 in the house, and c. her, when 3888
Ac 16:40 the brethren, they c. them, and 3870
Ac 20:12 alive, and were not a little c. 3870
Ro 1:12 that I may be c. together with you. 4837
1Co 14:31 may learn, and all may be c. 3870
2Co 1:4 wherewith we ourselves are c. 3870
2Co 1:6 or whether we be c., it is for your 3870
2Co 7:6 down, c. us by the coming of Titus; 3870
2Co 7:7 wherewith he was c. in you, 3870
2Co 7:13 we were c. in your comfort: yea, 3870
Col 2:2 That their hearts might be c., 3870
1Th 2:11 ye know how we exhorted and c. 3888
1Th 3:7 we were c. over you in all our 3870

COMFORTEDST
Isa 12:1 is turned away, and thou c. me 5162

COMFORTER See also COMFORTERS
Ec 4:1 oppressed, and they have no c.; 5162
Ec 4:1 was power; but they had no c.
La 1:9 down wonderfully: she had no c. 5162
La 1:16 the c. that should relieve my soul 5162
Joh 14:16 and he shall give you another C.,. 3875
Joh 14:26 the C., which is the Holy Ghost, 3875
Joh 15:26 But when the C. is come, whom I. 3875
Joh 16:7 the C. will not come unto you; 3875

COMFORTERS
2Sa 10:3 that he hath sent c. unto thee? 5162
1Ch 19:3 he hath sent c. unto thee? are not 5162
Job 16:2 miserable c. are ye all 5162
Ps 69:20 none; and for c., but I found none. 5162
Na 3:7 whence shall I seek c. for thee? 5162

COMFORTETH
Job 29:25 as one that c. the mourners. 5162
Isa 51:12 I, even I, am he that c. you: 5162
Isa 66:13 As one whom his mother c., so will 5162
2Co 1:4 Who c. us in all our tribulation, 3870
2Co 7:6 that c. those that are cast down, 3870

COMFORTLESS
Joh 14:18 I will not leave you c.: I will 3737

COMFORTS
Ps 94:19 within me thy c. delight my soul. 8575
Isa 57:18 and restore c. unto him and to 5150

COMING See also COMINGS.
Ge 24:63 and, behold, the camels were c. 935
Ge 30:30 hath blessed thee since my c. 7272
Nu 22:16 hinder them from c. unto me: 1980
Nu 33:40 of the c. of the children of Israel. 935
Jg 5:28 Why is his chariot so long in c.? 935
1Sa 10:5 a company of prophets c. down 3381
1Sa 16:4 of the town trembled at his c., 7122
1Sa 22:9 saw the son of Jesse c. to Nob, 935
1Sa 25:26 witholden thee from c. to shed 935
1Sa 25:33 me this day from c. to shed blood, 935
1Sa 29:6 thy going out and thy c. in with me 935
1Sa 29:6 of thy c. unto me unto this day: 935
2Sa 3:25 know thy going out and thy c. in, 4126
2Sa 24:20 saw the king and his servants c. 5674
2Ki 10:15 son of Rechab c. to meet him:
2Ki 13:20 invaded the land at the c. in of the 935
2Ki 19:27 and thy going out, and thy c. in, 935
2Ch 22:7 was of God by c. to Joram: for 935
Ezr 3:8 in the second year of their c. unto 935
Ps 19:5 bridegroom c. out of his chamber, 3318
Ps 37:13 for he seeth that his day is c. 935
Ps 121:8 and thy c. in from this time forth, 935
Pr 8:3 city, at the c. in at the doors. 3996
Isa 14:9 to meet thee at thy c.: it stirreth 935
Isa 32:19 When it shall hail, c. down on 3381
Isa 37:28 and thy c. in, and thy rage against 935
Isa 44:7 and the things that are c., and 857
Jer 8:7 swallow observe the time of their c.; 935
Da 4:23 watcher and an holy one c. down 5182
Mic 7:15 According to the days of thy c. 3318
Hab 3:4 he had horns c. out of his hand:
Mal 3:2 who may abide the day of hs c.? 935
Mal 4:5 before the c. of the great and 935
Mt 8:28 devils, c. out of the tombs, 1831
Mt 16:28 the Son of man c. in his kingdom. .2064
Mt 24:3 what shall be the sign of the c., 3952
Mt 24:27 also the c. of the Son of man be. 3952
Mt 24:30 they shall see the Son of man c. 2064
Mt 24:37, 39 also the c. of the Son of man 3952
Mt 24:48 heart, My lord delayeth his c.; 2064
Mt 25:27 at my c. I should have received 2064
Mt 26:64 and c. in the clouds of heaven 2064
Mk 1:10 straightway c. up our of the water, 305
Mk 6:31 for there were many c. and going, 2064
Mk 13:26 the Son of man c. in the clouds 2064
Mk 13:36 c. suddenly he find you sleeping 2064
Mk 14:62 and c. in the clouds of heaven 2064
Mk 15:21 passed by, c. out of the country, 2064
Lu 2:38 she c. in that instant gave thanks 2186
Lu 9:42 And as he was yet a c., the devil 4334
Lu 12:45 My lord delayeth his c.; and 2064
Lu 18:5 by her continual c. she weary me. 2064
Lu 19:23 at my c. I might have required 2064
Lu 21:26 things which are c. on the earth: 1904
Lu 21:27 shall they see the Son of man c. 2064
Lu 23:26 a Cyrenian, c. out of the country. 2064
Lu 23:29 behold, the days are c., in which 2064
Lu 23:36 c. to him, and offering him 4334
Joh 1:27 c. after me is preferred before me, 2064
Joh 1:29 John seeth Jesus c. unto him, 2064
Joh 1:47 Jesus saw Nathanael c. to him, 2064

Joh 5:7 but while I am **c.**, another steppeth *2064*
Joh 5:25 **The hour is c., and now is, when ..** *2064*
Joh 5:28 **for the hour is c., in the which all** .*2064*
Joh 10:12 **seeth the wolf c., and leaveth thee** .*2064*
Joh 11:20 as she heard that Jesus was **c.**, ... *2064*
Joh 12:12 that Jesus was **c.** to Jerusalem,.......... *2064*
Ac 7:52 before of the **c.** of the Just One; *1660*
Ac 9:12 **a man named Ananias c. in,** *1525*
Ac 9:28 with them **c.** in and going out........... *1531*
Ac 10:3 an angel of God **c.** in to him,............ *1525*
Ac 10:25 as Peter was **c.** in, Cornelius met *1525*
Ac 13:24 had first preached before his **c.**.......... *1529*
Ac 17:10 Berea: who **c.** thither went into.......... *3854*
Ac 27:33 while the day was **c.** on, ... *3195, 1096*
Ro 15:22 much hindered from **c.** to you............ *2064*
1Co 1:7 waiting for the **c.** of our Lord............. *602*
1Co 15:23 they that are Christ's at his **c.**.............. *3952*
1Co 16:17 glad of the **c.** of Stephanus and.......... *3952*
2Co 7:6 comforted us by the **c.** of Titus; *3952*
2Co 7:7 And not by his **c.** only, but by the...... *3952*
2Co 13:1 This is the third time I am **c.** *2064*
Php 1:26 for me by my **c.** to you again. *3952*
1Th 2:19 our Lord Jesus Christ at his **c.**? *3952*
1Th 3:13 at the **c.** of our Lord Jesus Christ *3952*
1Th 4:15 remain unto the **c.** of the Lord *3952*
1Th 5:23 the **c.** of our Lord Jesus Christ. *3952*
2Th 2:1 by the **c.** of our Lord Jesus............... *3952*
2Th 2:8 with the brightness of his **c.**............ *3952*
2Th 2:9 him, whose **c.** is after the working *3952*
Jas 5:7 brethren, unto the **c.** of the Lord. *3952*
Jas 5:8 the **c.** of the Lord draweth nigh. *3952*
1Pe 2:4 To whom **c.**, as unto a living stone,.... *4334*
2Pe 1:16 power and **c.** of our Lord Jesus *3952*
2Pe 3:4 Where is the promise of his **c.**? *3952*
2Pe 3:12 unto the **c.** of the day of God,........... *3952*
1Jo 2:28 be ashamed before him at his **c.**.......... *3952*
Re 13:11 beast **c.** up out of the earth;............... *305*
Re 21:2 new Jerusalem, **c.** down from God...... *2597*

COMINGS

Eze 43:11 and the **c.** in thereof, and all 4126

COMMAND See also COMMANDED; COMMANDEST; COMMANDETH; COMMANDING; COMMANDMENT.

Ge 18:19 **c.** his children and his household 6680
Ge 27:8 according to that which I **c.** thee. 6680
Ge 50:16 Thy father did **c.** before he died,........ 6680
Ex 7:2 shalt speak all that I **c.** thee: 6680
Ex 8:27 Lord our God, as he shall **c.** us. 559
Ex 18:23 do this thing, and God **c.** thee 6680
Ex 27:20 And thou shalt **c.** the children of 6680
Ex 34:11 thou that which I **c.** thee this day:...... 6680
Le 6:9 **C.** Aaron and his sons, saying, ... 6680
Le 13:54 the priest shall **c.** that they wash 6680
Le 14:4 Then shall the priest **c.** to take.......... 6680
Le 14:5 priest shall **c.** that one of the birds 6680
Le 14:36 the priest shall **c.** that they empty....... 6680
Le 14:40 priest shall **c.** that they take away 6680
Le 24:2 **C.** the children of Israel that they....... 6680
Le 25:21 I will **c.** my blessing upon you 6680
Nu 5:2 **C.** the children of Israel, that they...... 6680
Nu 9:8 the Lord will **c.** concerning you. 6680
Nu 28:2 **C.** the children of Israel, and say 6680
Nu 34:2 **C.** the children of Israel, and say 6680
Nu 35:2 **C.** the children of Israel, that they give 6680
Nu 36:6 which the Lord doth **c.** concerning...... 6680
De 2:4 **c.** thou the people, saying, Ye are...... 6680
De 4:2 add unto the word which I **c.** you,...... 6680
De 4:2 of the Lord your God which I **c.** 6680
De 4:40 I **c.** thee this day, that it may go 6680
De 6:2 commandments, which I **c.** thee, ... 6680
De 6:6 words, which I **c.** thee this day,......... 6680
De 7:11 judgments which I **c.** thee this........... 6680
De 8:1 the commandments which I **c.** thee......... 6680
De 8:11 statutes, which I **c.** thee this day: 6680
De 10:13 and his statutes, which I **c.** thee 6680
De 11:8 the commandments which I **c.** you...... 6680
De 11:13 my commandments which I **c.**............ 6680
De 11:22 these commandments which I **c.**........... 6680
De 11:27 your God, which I **c.** you this day: 6680
De 11:28 the way which I **c.** you this day, ... 6680
De 12:11 shall ye bring all that I **c.** you;.......... 6680
De 12:14 thou shalt do all that I **c.** thee. 6680
De 12:28 all these words which I **c.** thee, ... 6680
De 12:32 What thing soever I **c.** you, ... 6680
De 13:18 his commandments which I **c.** thee 6680
De 15:5 these commandments which I **c.**......... 6680
De 15:11 therefore I **c.** thee, saying, Thou 6680
De 15:15 therefore I **c.** thee this thing to day.... 6680
De 18:18 unto them all that I shall **c.** him. 6680
De 19:7 Wherefore I **c.** thee, saying, Thou........ 6680
De 19:9 which I **c.** thee this day, to love the ... 6680
De 24:18, 22 I **c.** thee to do this thing. 6680
De 27:1 which I **c.** you this day..................... 6680
De 27:4 set up these stones, which I **c.** you.... 6680
De 27:10 statutes, which I **c.** thee this day. 6680
De 28:1 I **c.** thee this day, that the Lord 6680
De 28:8 Lord shall **c.** the blessing upon thee.... 6680
De 28:13 which I **c.** thee this day, to observe.... 6680
De 28:14 the words which I **c.** thee this day, ... 6680
De 28:15 statutues which I **c.** thee this day;...... 6680
De 30:2 all that I **c.** thee this day, thou and..... 6680
De 30:8 his commandments which I **c.** thee 6680
De 30:11 which I **c.** thee this day, it is not 6680
De 30:16 In that I **c.** thee this day to love 6680
De 32:46 shall **c.** your children to observe to..... 6680
Jos 1:11 **c.** the people, saying, Prepare you 6680
Jos 3:8 **c.** the priests that bear the ark 6680
Jos 4:3 **c.** ye them, saying, Take you hence ... 6680
Jos 4:16 **C.** the priests that bear the ark 6680
Jos 11:15 so did Moses **c.** Joshua, and so did..... 6680
1Sa 16:16 Let our lord now **c.** thy servants, ... 559
1Ki 5:6 **c.** thou that they hew me cedar 6680
1Ki 11:38 hearken unto all that I **c.** thee, ... 6680
2Ch 7:13 I **c.** the locusts to devour the land,..... 6680
Job 39:27 the eagle mount up at thy **c.**, ... 6310
Ps 42:8 Lord will **c.** his lovingkindness 6680
Ps 44:4 God: **c.** deliverances for Jacob. 6680
Isa 5:6 also **c.** the clouds that they rain 6680
Isa 45:11 the work of my hands **c.** ye me. 6680
Jer 1:7 I **c.** thee thou shalt speak. 6680
Jer 1:17 speak unto them all that I **c.** thee:...... 6680
Jer 11:4 according to all which I **c.** you: 6680
Jer 26:2 the words that I **c.** thee to speak........ 6680
Jer 27:4 And **c.** them to say unto their........... 6680
Jer 34:22 I will **c.**, saith the Lord, and cause 6680
La 1:10 whom thou didst **c.** that they............ 6680
Am 9:3 thence will I **c.** the serpent, and 6680
Am 9:4 thence will I **c.** the sword, and it 6680
Am 9:9 For, lo, I will **c.**, and I will sift 6680
Mt 4:3 **c.** that these stones be made bread. ... *2036*
Mt 19:7 Why did Moses then **c.** to give a *1781*
Mt 27:64 **C.** therefore that the sepulchre be....... *2753*
Mk 10:3 unto them, **What did Moses c. you?** . *1781*
Lu 4:3 **c.** this stone that it be made bread. *2036*
Lu 8:31 he would not **c.** them to go out *2004*
Lu 9:54 wilt thou that we **c.** fire to come......... *2036*
Joh 15:14 **if ye do whatsoever I c. you**.......... *1781*
Joh 15:17 **These things I c. you, that ye love** .*1781*
Ac 5:28 Did not we straitly **c.** you that ye....... *3853*
Ac 15:5 **c.** them to keep the law of Moses. *3853*
Ac 16:18 I **c.** thee in the name of Jesus *3853*
1Co 7:10 unto the married I **c.**, yet not I, ... *3853*
2Th 3:4 and will do the things which we **c.**........ *3853*
2Th 3:6 we **c.** you, brethren, in the name........ *3853*
2Th 3:12 that are such we **c.** and exhort............ *3853*
1Ti 4:11 These things **c.** and teach. *3853*

COMMANDED See also COMMANDEDST.

Ge 2:16 And the Lord God **c.** the man, ... 6680
Ge 3:11 the tree, whereof I **c.** thee that 6680
Ge 3:17 the tree, of which I **c.** thee, saying,.... 6680
Ge 6:22 all that God **c.** him, so did he. 6680
Ge 7:5 unto all that the Lord **c.** him. 6680
Ge 7:9 the female, as God had **c.** Noah. 6680
Ge 7:16 of all flesh, as God had **c.** him: 6680
Ge 12:20 Pharaoh **c.** his men concerning.......... 6680
Ge 21:4 eight days old, as God had **c.** him. 6680
Ge 32:4 And he **c.** them, saying, Thus shall..... 6680
Ge 32:17 And he **c.** the foremost, saying, ... 6680
Ge 32:19 so **c.** he the second, and the third, ... 6680
Ge 42:25 Then Joseph **c.** to fill their sacks, ... 6680
Ge 44:1 And he **c.** the steward of his house, ... 6680
Ge 45:19 Now thou art **c.**, this do ye;............ 6680
Ge 47:11 of Rameses, as Pharaoh had **c.** 6680
Ge 50:2 And Joseph **c.** his servants the 6680
Ge 50:12 unto him according as he **c.** them: 6680
Ex 1:17 not as the king of Egypt **c.** them,....... 1696
Ex 4:28 all the signs which he had **c.** him........ 6680
Ex 5:6 And Pharaoh **c.** the same day the....... 6680
Ex 7:6 as the Lord **c.** them, so did they......... 6680
Ex 7:10 Aaron did so as the Lord had **c.**......... 6680
Ex 7:20 and Aaron did so, as the Lord **c.**;....... 6680
Ex 12:28 and did as the Lord had **c.** Moses 6680
Ex 12:50 as the Lord **c.** Moses and Aaron,....... 6680
Ex 16:16 the Lord hath **c.**, Gather of it every ... 6680
Ex 16:34 As the Lord **c.** Moses, so Aaron laid .. 6680
Ex 19:7 these words which the Lord **c.** him..... 6680
Ex 23:15 as I **c.** thee, in the time appointed...... 6680
Ex 29:35 which I have **c.** thee: seven days 6680
Ex 31:6 all that I have **c.** thee; 6680
Ex 31:11 that I have **c.** thee shall they do. 6680
Ex 32:8 out of the way which I **c.** them:......... 6680
Ex 34:4 as the Lord had **c.** him, and took 6680
Ex 34:18 as I **c.** thee, in the time of the month. 6680
Ex 34:34 that which he was **c.**. 6680
Ex 35:1 words which the Lord hath **c.**,........... 6680
Ex 35:4 the thing which the Lord **c.**,............. 6680
Ex 35:10 make all that the Lord hath **c.**; 6680
Ex 35:29 which the Lord had **c.** to be made...... 6680
Ex 36:1 all that the Lord had **c.**. 6680
Ex 36:5 work, which the Lord **c.** to make. 6680
Ex 38:22 made all that the Lord **c.** Moses. 6680
Ex 39:1 for Aaron; as the Lord **c.** Moses........ 6680
Ex 39:5 twined linen; as the Lord **c.** Moses..... 6680
Ex 39:7 of Israel; as the Lord **c.** Moses. 6680
Ex 39:21 ephod; as the Lord **c.** Moses. 6680
Ex 39:26 to minister in; as the Lord **c.** Moses... 6680
Ex 39:29 needlework; as the Lord **c.** Moses. 6680
Ex 39:31 the mitre; as the Lord **c.** Moses. 6680
Ex 39:32 that the Lord **c.** Moses, so did they. .. 6680
Ex 39:42 all that the Lord **c.** Moses, so 6680
Ex 39:43 the Lord had **c.**, even so had they...... 6680
Ex 40:16 that the Lord **c.** him, so did he.......... 6680
Ex 40:19 upon it; as the Lord **c.** Moses. 6680
Ex 40:21 testimony; as the Lord **c.** Moses......... 6680
Ex 40:23 Lord; as the Lord had **c.** Moses. 6680
Ex 40:25 the Lord; as the Lord **c.** Moses......... 6680
Ex 40:27 thereon; as the Lord **c.** Moses. 6680
Ex 40:29 meat offering; as the Lord **c.**.............. 6680
Ex 40:32 they washed; as the Lord **c.** Moses.... 6680
Le 7:36 Which the Lord **c.** to be given them ... 6680
Le 7:38 the Lord **c.** Moses in mount Sinai,....... 6680
Le 7:38 in the day that he **c.** the children of.... 6680
Le 8:4 And Moses did as the Lord **c.** him; 6680
Le 8:5 thing which the Lord **c.** to be done..... 6680
Le 8:9 holy crown; as the Lord **c.** Moses...... 6680
Le 8:13 bonnets upon them; as the Lord **c.**..... 6680
Le 8:17 without the camp; as the Lord **c.** 6680
Le 8:21 unto the Lord; as the Lord **c.**............ 6680
Le 8:29 it was Moses' part; as the Lord **c.** 6680
Le 8:31 as I **c.**, saying, Aaron and his sons 6680
Le 8:34 the Lord hath **c.** to do, to make an..... 6680
Le 8:35 that ye die not: for so I am **c.**............ 6680
Le 8:36 which the Lord **c.** by the hand.......... 6680
Le 9:5 Moses **c.** before the tabernacle......... 6680
Le 9:6 the Lord **c.** that ye should do:.......... 6680
Le 9:7 for them; as the Lord **c.**.................. 6680
Le 9:10 upon the altar; as the Lord **c.** Moses. . 6680
Le 9:21 before the Lord; as Moses **c.**............ 6680
Le 10:1 the Lord, which he **c.** them not. 6680
Le 10:13 made by fire: for so I am **c.**............. 6680
Le 10:15 for ever; as the Lord hath **c.**............ 6680
Le 10:18 eaten it in the holy place, as I **c.**......... 6680
Le 16:34 And he did as the Lord **c.** Moses........ 6680
Le 17:2 the Lord hath **c.**, saying, ... 6680
Le 24:23 Israel did as the Lord **c.** Moses. 6680
Le 27:34 the Lord **c.** Moses for the children 6680
Nu 1:19 the Lord **c.** Moses, so he numbered.... 6680
Nu 1:54 according to all the the Lord **c.**........ 6680
Nu 2:33 of Israel: as the Lord **c.** Moses. 6680
Nu 2:34 all that the Lord **c.** Moses: so they 6680
Nu 3:16 of the Lord, as he was **c.** 6680
Nu 3:42 the Lord **c.** him, all the firstborn....... 6680
Nu 3:51 of the Lord, as the Lord **c.** Moses. 6680
Nu 4:49 of him, as the Lord **c.** Moses. 6680
Nu 8:3 candlestick, as the Lord **c.** Moses. 6680
Nu 8:20 that the Lord **c.** Moses concerning..... 6680
Nu 8:22 the Lord had **c.** Moses concerning...... 6680
Nu 9:5 Lord **c.** Moses, so did the children..... 6680
Nu 15:23 the Lord hath **c.** you by the hand....... 6680
Nu 15:23 the day that the Lord **c.** Moses, ... 6680
Nu 15:36 and he died; as the Lord **c.** Moses. 6680
Nu 16:47 Aaron took as Moses **c.**, and ran 1696
Nu 17:11 did so: as the Lord **c.** him, so did 6680
Nu 19:2 the Lord hath **c.**, saying, Speak 6680
Nu 20:9 before the Lord, as he **c.** him............ 6680
Nu 20:27 Moses did as the Lord **c.**: and they.... 6680
Nu 26:4 the Lord **c.** Moses and the children 6680
Nu 27:11 of judgment, as the Lord **c.** Moses..... 6680
Nu 27:22 And Moses did as the Lord **c.** him: 6680

Nu 27:23 gave him a charge, as the Lord **c.** 1696
Nu 29:40 according to all that the Lord **c.** 6680
Nu 30:1 the thing which the Lord hath **c.** 6680
Nu 30:16 the Lord **c.** Moses, between a man 6680
Nu 31:7 the Lord **c.** Moses; and they slew 6680
Nu 31:21 the law which the Lord **c.** Moses; 6680
Nu 31:31 the priest did as the Lord **c.** Moses 6680
Nu 31:41 the priest, as the Lord **c.** Moses 6680
Nu 31:47 of the Lord; as the Lord **c.** Moses. 6680
Nu 32:28 So concerning them Moses **c.** 6680
Nu 34:13 **c.** the children of Israel, saying, 6680
Nu 34:13 Lord **c.** to give unto the nine tribes, 6680
Nu 34:29 Lord **c.** to divide the inheritance 6680
Nu 36:2 Lord **c.** my lord to give the land 6680
Nu 36:2 my lord was **c.** by the Lord to give 6680
Nu 36:5 And Moses **c.** the children of 6680
Nu 36:10 as the Lord **c.** Moses, so did the 6680
Nu 36:13 the Lord **c.** by the hand of Moses 6680
De 1:18 I **c.** you at that time all the things 6680
De 1:19 as the Lord our God **c.** us; and we 6680
De 1:41 all that the Lord our God **c.** us. 6680
De 3:18 And I **c.** you at that time, 6680
De 3:21 And I **c.** Joshua at that time, 6680
De 4:5 even as the Lord my God **c.** me, 6680
De 4:13 which he **c.** you to perform, 6680
De 4:14 the Lord **c.** me at that time to 6680
De 5:12 it, as the Lord thy God hath **c.** 6680
De 5:15 the Lord thy God **c.** thee to keep 6680
De 5:16 the Lord thy God hath **c.** thee; 6680
De 5:32 the Lord your God hath **c.** you: 6680
De 5:33 which the Lord your God hath **c.** 6680
De 6:1 the Lord your God **c.** to teach 6680
De 6:17 statues, which he hath **c.** thee. 6680
De 6:20 the Lord our God hath **c.** you? 6680
De 6:24 And the Lord **c.** us to do all these 6680
De 6:25 the Lord our God, as he hath **c.** us. 6680
De 9:12 out of the way which I **c.** them; 6680
De 9:16 the way which the Lord had **c.** you. 6680
De 10:5 they be, as the Lord **c.** me. 6680
De 12:21 as I have **c.** thee, and thou shalt 6680
De 13:5 the Lord thy God **c.** thee to walk 6680
De 17:3 of heaven, which I have not **c.**; 6680
De 18:20 I have not **c.** him to speak, or that 6680
De 20:17 as the Lord thy God hath **c.** thee: 6680
De 24:8 as I **c.** them, so ye shall observe 6680
De 26:13 which thou hast **c.** me: I have not 6680
De 26:14 to all that thou hast **c.** me. 6680
De 26:16 the Lord thy God hath **c.** thee to 6680
De 27:1 **c.** the people, saying, Keep all the 6680
De 28:45 and his statutes which he **c.** thee: 6680
De 29:1 the Lord **c.** Moses to make with 6680
De 31:5 commandments which I have **c.** you 6680
De 31:10 And Moses **c.** them, saying, At the 6680
De 31:25 That Moses **c.** the Levites 6680
De 31:29 the way which I have **c.** you; and 6680
De 33:4 Moses **c.** us a law, even the 6680
De 34:9 and did as the Lord **c.** Moses. 6680
Jos 1:7 which Moses my servant **c.** thee: 6680
Jos 1:9 Have not I **c.** thee? Be strong 6680
Jos 1:10 Then Joshua **c.** the officers of the 6680
Jos 1:13 the servant of the Lord **c.** you, 6680
Jos 3:3 And they **c.** the people, saying, 6680
Jos 4:8 as Joshua **c.**, and took up twelve 6680
Jos 4:10 the Lord **c.** Joshua to speak unto 6680
Jos 4:10 according to all that Moses **c.** 6680
Jos 4:17 Joshua therefore **c.** the priests, 6680
Jos 6:10 Joshua had **c.** the people, saying, 6680
Jos 7:11 my covenant which I **c.** them: for 6680
Jos 8:4 And he **c.** them, saying, Behold, ye 6680
Jos 8:8 See, I have **c.** you. 6680
Jos 8:27 word of the Lord, which he **c.** 6680
Jos 8:29 Joshua **c.** that they should take 6680
Jos 8:31 the servant of the Lord **c.** the 6680
Jos 8:33 the servant of the Lord had **c.** 6680
Jos 8:35 all that Moses **c.**, which Joshua 6680
Jos 9:24 the Lord thy God **c.** his servant 6680
Jos 10:27 Joshua **c.**, and they took them 6680
Jos 10:40 as the Lord God of Israel **c.** 6680
Jos 11:12 Moses the servant of the Lord **c.** 6680
Jos 11:15 As the Lord **c.** Moses his servant, 6680
Jos 11:15 undone of all that the Lord **c.** 6680
Jos 11:20 destroy them, as the Lord **c.** Moses 6680
Jos 13:6 for an inheritance, as I have **c.** 6680
Jos 14:2 as the Lord **c.** by the hand of Moses, 6680
Jos 14:5 As the Lord **c.** Moses, so the 6680
Jos 17:4 The Lord **c.** Moses to give us an 6680
Jos 21:2 The Lord **c.** by the hand of Moses 6680
Jos 21:8 with their suburbs, as the Lord **c.** 6680
Jos 22:2 the servant of the Lord **c.** you, 6680
Jos 22:2 obeyed my voice in all that I **c.** you: 6680
Jos 23:16 which he **c.** you, and have gone 6680
Jg 2:20 my convenant which I **c.** their 6680
Jg 3:4 which he **c.** their fathers by the 6680
Jg 4:6 the Lord God of Israel **c.**, saying, 6680
Jg 13:14 all that I **c.** her let her observe 6680
Jg 21:10 and **c.** them, saying, Go and smite 6680
Jg 21:20 Therefore they **c.** the children of 6680
Ru 2:15 Boaz **c.** his young men, saying, 6680
1Sa 2:29 I have **c.** in my habitation; and 6680
1Sa 13:13 which he **c.** thee: for now would 6680
1Sa 13:14 and the Lord hath **c.** him to be 6680
1Sa 13:14 not kept that which the Lord **c.** 6680
1Sa 17:20 and went, as Jesse had **c.** him; 6680
1Sa 18:22 And Saul **c.** his servants, saying, 6680
1Sa 20:29 he hath **c.** me to be there: and 6680
1Sa 21:2 The king hath **c.** me a business, 6680
1Sa 21:2 I send thee, and what I have **c.** 6680
2Sa 4:12 And David **c.** his young men, and 6680
2Sa 5:25 David did so, as the Lord had **c.** 6680
2Sa 7:7 whom I **c.** to feed my people 6680
2Sa 7:11 the time that I **c.** judges to be over 6680
2Sa 9:11 my lord the king hath **c.** his 6680
2Sa 13:28 Now Absalom had **c.** his servants, 6680
2Sa 13:28 have not I **c.** you? be courageous 6680
2Sa 13:29 unto Amnon as Absalom had **c.** 6680
2Sa 18:5 And the king **c.** Joab and Abishai 6680
2Sa 21:14 they performed all that the king **c.** 6680
2Sa 24:19 of Gad, went up as the Lord **c.** 6680
1Ki 2:46 So the king **c.** Benaiah the son of 6680
1Ki 5:17 And the king **c.**, and they brought 6680
1Ki 8:58 his judgments, which he **c.** our 6680
1Ki 9:4 all that I have **c.** thee, and wilt 6680
1Ki 11:10 And had **c.** him concerning this 6680
1Ki 11:10 kept not that which the Lord **c.** 6680
1Ki 11:11 which I have **c.** thee, I will surely 6680
1Ki 13:21 which the Lord thy God **c.** thee, 6680
1Ki 15:5 any thing that he **c.** him all the 6680
1Ki 17:4 I have **c.** the ravens to feed thee 6680
1Ki 17:9 I have **c.** a widow woman there to 6680
1Ki 22:31 the king of Syria **c.** his thirty and 6680
2Ki 11:5 And he **c.** them, saying, This is the 6680
2Ki 11:9 Jehoiada the priest **c.**: and they 6680
2Ki 11:15 But Jehoiada the priest **c.** the 6680
2Ki 14:6 wherein the Lord **c.**, saying, The 6680
2Ki 16:15 And king Ahaz **c.** Urijah the priest, 6680
2Ki 16:16 according to all that king Ahaz **c.** 6680
2Ki 17:13 the law which I **c.** your fathers, 6680
2Ki 17:27 Then the king of Assyria **c.**, saying, 6680
2Ki 17:34 which the Lord **c.** the children of 6680
2Ki 18:6 which the Lord **c.** Moses. 6680
2Ki 18:12 Moses the servant of the Lord **c.**, 6680
2Ki 21:8 all that I have **c.** them, and 6680
2Ki 21:8 the law that my servant Moses **c.** 6680
2Ki 22:12 And the king **c.** Hilkiah the priest, 6680
2Ki 23:4 And the king **c.** Hilkiah the high 6680
2Ki 23:21 And the king **c.** all the people, 6680
1Ch 6:49 Moses the servant of God had **c.** 6680
1Ch 14:16 David therefore did as God **c.** him: 6680
1Ch 15:15 thereon, as Moses **c.** according to 6680
1Ch 16:15 which he **c.** to a thousand 6680
1Ch 16:40 of the Lord, which he **c.** Israel; 6680
1Ch 17:6 whom I **c.** to feed my people 6680
1Ch 17:10 I **c.** judges to be over my people 6680
1Ch 21:17 Is it not I that **c.** the people to be 559
1Ch 21:18 Then the angel of the Lord **c.** Gad 559
1Ch 21:27 And the Lord **c.** the angel; and he 559
1Ch 22:2 And David **c.** to gather together 559
1Ch 22:17 David also **c.** all the princes of 6680
1Ch 23:31 according to the order **c.** unto
1Ch 24:19 as the Lord God of Israel had **c.** 6680
2Ch 7:17 I have **c.** thee, and shalt observe 6680
2Ch 8:14 so had David the man of God **c.** 4687
2Ch 14:4 And **c.** Judah to seek the Lord God 559
2Ch 18:30 king of Syria had **c.** the captains 6680
2Ch 23:8 that Jehoiada the priest had **c.**, 6680
2Ch 25:4 Lord **c.**, saying, The fathers shall 6680
2Ch 29:21 And he **c.** the priests the sons of 559
2Ch 29:24 the king **c.** that the burnt offering 559
2Ch 29:27 And Hezekiah **c.** to offer the burnt 559
2Ch 29:30 king and the princes **c.** the Levites 559
2Ch 31:4 Moreover he **c.** the people that 559
2Ch 31:11 Hezekiah **c.** to prepare chambers 559
2Ch 32:12 **c.** Judah and Jerusalem, saying, 559
2Ch 33:8 to do all that I have **c.** them, 6680
2Ch 33:16 **c.** Judah to serve the Lord God of 559
2Ch 34:20 the king **c.** Hilkiah, and Ahikam 6680
2Ch 35:21 God **c.** me to make haste: forbear 559
Ezr 4:3 the king of Persia hath **c.** us. 6680
Ezr 4:19 And I **c.**, and search hath 7761,2942
Ezr 5:3 Who hath **c.** you to build 7761,2942
Ezr 5:9 Who **c.** you to build this 7761,2942
Ezr 7:23 Whatsoever is **c.** by the God 4480,2941
Ezr 9:11 Which thou hast **c.** by thy servants 6680
Ne 8:1 which the Lord had **c.** to Israel. 6680
Ne 8:14 the Lord had **c.** by Moses, that the 6680
Ne 13:5 which was **c.** to be given to the 4687
Ne 13:9 Then I **c.**, and they cleansed the 559
Ne 13:19 I **c.** that the gates should be shut, 559
Ne 13:22 And I **c.** the Levites that they should 559
Es 1:10 he **c.** Mehuman, Biztha, Harbona, 559
Es 1:17 king Ahasuerus **c.** Vashti the queen 559
Es 3:2 king had so **c.** concerning him. 6680
Es 3:12 Haman had **c.** unto the king's 6680
Es 4:13 Mordecai **c.** to answer Esther, 559
Es 4:17 according to all that Esther had **c.** 6680
Es 6:1 he **c.** to bring the book of records 559
Es 8:9 that Mordecai **c.** unto the Jews, 6680
Es 9:14 And the king **c.** it so to be done: 559
Es 9:25 he **c.** by letters that his wicked 559
Job 38:12 Hast thou **c.** the morning since 6680
Job 42:9 and did according as the Lord **c.** 1696
Ps 7:6 to the judgment that thou hast **c.** 6680
Ps 33:9 was done; he **c.**, and it stood fast. 6680
Ps 68:28 Thy God hath **c.** thy strength: 6680
Ps 78:5 he **c.** our fathers, that they should 6680
Ps 78:23 Though he had **c.** the clouds from 6680
Ps 105:8 forever, the word which he **c.** to a 6680
Ps 106:34 concerning whom the Lord **c.** 559
Ps 111:9 he hath **c.** his convenant for ever: 6680
Ps 119:4 hast **c.** us to keep thy precepts 6680
Ps 119:138 testimonies that thou hast **c.** are 6680
Ps 133:3 the Lord **c.** the blessing, even life 6680
Ps 148:5 for he **c.**, and they were created. 6680
Isa 13:3 I have **c.** my sanctified ones, I have 6680
Isa 34:16 my mouth it hath **c.**, and his spirit 6680
Isa 45:12 and all their host have I **c.** 6680
Isa 48:5 my molten image, hath **c.** them. 6680
Jer 7:22 **c.** them in the day that I brought 6680
Jer 7:23 But this thing **c.** I them, saying, 6680
Jer 7:23 the ways that I have **c.** you, that it 6680
Jer 7:31 I **c.** them not, neither came it into 6680
Jer 11:4 I **c.** your fathers in the day that I 6680
Jer 11:8 I **c.** them to do; but they did them 6680
Jer 13:5 it by Euphrates, as the Lord **c.** me 6680
Jer 13:6 from thence, which I **c.** thee to hide 6680
Jer 14:14 neither have I **c.** them, neither 6680
Jer 17:22 sabbath day, as I **c.** your fathers. 6680
Jer 19:5 offerings unto Baal, which I **c.** not, 6680
Jer 23:32 nor **c.** them: therefore they shall 6680
Jer 26:8 Lord had **c.** him to speak unto all 6680
Jer 29:23 I have not **c.** them; even I know, 6680
Jer 32:35 I **c.** them not, neither came it into 6680
Jer 35:6 of Rechab our father **c.** us, saying, 6680
Jer 35:10 all that Jonadab our father **c.** us. 6680
Jer 35:14 he **c.** his sons not to drink wine, 6680
Jer 35:16 of their father, which he **c.** them. 6680
Jer 35:18 all that he hath **c.** you: 6680
Jer 36:5 And Jeremiah **c.** Baruch, saying, 6680
Jer 36:8 Jeremiah the prophet **c.** him, 6680
Jer 36:26 the king **c.** Jerahmeel the son of 6680
Jer 37:21 Then Zedekiah the king **c.** that 6680
Jer 38:10 Then the king **c.** Ebed-melech the 6680
Jer 38:27 all these words that the king had **c.** 6680
Jer 50:21 to all that I have **c.** thee. 6680
Jer 51:59 Jeremiah the prophet **c.** Seraiah 6680
La 1:17 the Lord hath **c.** concerning Jacob, 6680
La 2:17 his word that he had **c.** in the days 6680
Eze 9:11 saying, I have done as thou hast **c.** 6680
Eze 10:6 when he had **c.** the man clothed 6680
Eze 12:7 And I did so as I was **c.**: I brought 6680
Eze 24:18 I did in the morning as I was **c.** 6680
Eze 37:7 I prophesied as I was **c.**: and as I 6680
Eze 37:10 I prophesied as he **c.** me, and the 6680
Da 2:2 the king **c.** to call the magicians, 559
Da 2:12 and **c.** to destroy all the wise men 560
Da 2:46 **c.** that they should offer an oblation 560
Da 3:4 To you it is **c.**, O people, nations, 560
Da 3:13 in his rage and fury **c.** 560
Da 3:19 he spake, and **c.** that they should 560
Da 3:20 And he **c.** the most mighty men 560
Da 4:26 whereas they **c.** to leave the stump 560

Da 5:2 c. to bring the golden and silver 560
Da 5:29 c. Belshazzar, and they clothed 560
Da 6:16 Then the king c., and they brought 560
Da 6:23 and c. that they should take Daniel 560
Da 6:24 And the king c., and they brought 560
Am 2:12 c. the prophets, saying, Prophesy 6680
Zec 1:6 I c. my servants the prophets, 6680
Mal 4:4 which I c. unto him in Horeb for 6680
Mt 8:4 offer the gift that Moses c., for a 4367
Mt 10:5 and c. them, saying, Go not into 3853
Mt 14:9 he c. it to be given her. 2753
Mt 14:19 he c. the multitude to sit down on 2753
Mt 15:4 For God c., saying, Honour thy 1781
Mt 15:35 he c. the multitude to sit down 2753
Mt 18:25 his lord c. him to be sold, and his 2753
Mt 21:6 went, and did as Jesus c. them, 4367
Mt 27:58 Pilate c. the body to be delivered. 2753
Mt 28:20 whatsoever I have c. you: and, lo, 1781
Mk 1:44 those things which Moses c., for 4367
Mk 5:43 c. that something should be given 2036
Mk 6:8 And c. them that they should 3853
Mk 6:27 and c. his head to be brought 2004
Mk 6:39 he c. them to make all sit down 2004
Mk 8:6 And he c. the people to sit down 3853
Mk 8:7 c. to set them also before them. 2036
Mk 10:49 stood still, and c. him to be called. 2036
Mk 11:6 even as Jesus had c.: and they let 1781
Mk 13:34 and c. the porter to watch. 1781
Lu 5:14 according as Moses c., for a 4367
Lu 8:29 (For he had c. the unclean spirit 3853
Lu 8:55 and he c. to give her meat 1299
Lu 9:21 and c. them to tell no man 3853
Lu 14:22 it is done as thou hast c., and yet 2004
Lu 17:9 he did the things that were c. him? 1299
Lu 17:10 those things which are c. you, say, 1299
Lu 18:40 c. him to be brought unto him: 2753
Lu 19:15 c. these servants to be called unto 2036
Joh 8:5 Now Moses in the law c. us, 1781
Ac 1:4 c. them that they should not 3853
Ac 4:15 when they had c. them to go aside 2753
Ac 4:18 and c. them not to speak at all nor 3853
Ac 5:34 c. to put the apostles forth a little 2753
Ac 5:40 they c. that they should not speak 3853
Ac 8:38 he c. the chariot to stand still: 2753
Ac 10:33 all things that are c. thee of God 4367
Ac 10:42 he c. us to preach unto the people, 3853
Ac 10:48 he c. them to be baptized in the 4367
Ac 12:19 c. that they should be put to 2753
Ac 13:47 the Lord c. us, saying, I have set 1781
Ac 16:22 their clothes, and c. to beat them 2753
Ac 18:2 Claudius had c. all Jews to depart 1299
Ac 21:33 and c. him to be bound with two 2753
Ac 21:34 he c. him to be carried into the 2753
Ac 22:24 chief captain c. him to be brought 2753
Ac 22:30 c. the chief priests and all their 2753
Ac 23:2 Ananias c. them that stood by him 2004
Ac 23:10 c. the soldiers to go down, and to 2753
Ac 23:31 the soldiers, as it was c. them, 1299
Ac 23:35 he c. him to be kept in Herod's 2753
Ac 24:23 he c. a centurion to keep Paul, 1299
Ac 25:6 seat c. Paul to be brought. 2753
Ac 25:17 and c. the man to be brought forth. 2753
Ac 25:21 c. him to be kept till I might send 2753
Ac 27:43 c. that they which could swim 2753
1Co 14:34 c. to be under obedience, as
2Co 4:6 For God, who c. the light to shine 2036
1Th 4:11 with your own hands, as we c. 3853
2Th 3:10 this we c. you, that if any would 3853
Heb 12:20 not endure that which was c., 1291
Re 9:4 was c. them that they should not 4483

COMMANDEDST

Ne 1:7 thou c. thy servant Moses. 6680
Ne 1:8 the word that thou c. thy servant 6680
Ne 9:14 c. them precepts, statutes, and laws, 6680
Jer 32:23 of all that thou c. them to do: 6680

COMMANDER

Isa 55:4 a leader and c. to the people. 6680

COMMANDEST

Jos 1:16 All that thou c. us we will do, 6680
Jos 1:18 thy word in all that thou c. him, 6680
Ac 23:3 and c. me to be smitten contrary 2753

COMMANDETH

Ex 16:32 is the thing which the Lord c., 6680
Nu 32:25 Thy servants will do as my lord c. 6680
Job 9:7 Which c. the sun, and it riseth not; 559
Job 36:10 c. that they return from iniquity. 559
Job 36:32 and c. it not to shine by the cloud 6680
Job 37:12 they may do whatsoever he c. 6680
Ps 107:25 For he c., and raiseth the stormy 559
La 3:37 to pass, when the Lord c. it not? 6680
Am 6:11 the Lord c., and he will smite 6680
Mk 1:27 c. he even the unclean spirits, 2004
Lu 4:36 power he c. the unclean spirits 2004
Lu 8:25 he c. even the winds and water, 2004
Ac 17:30 but now c. all men every where to 3853

COMMANDING

Ge 49:33 Jacob had made an end of c. his 6680
Mt 11:1 an end of c. his twelve disciples, 1299
Ac 24:8 C. his accusers to come unto 2753
1Ti 4:3 c. to abstain from meats, which

COMMANDMENT See also COMMANDMENTS.

Ge 45:21 according to the c. of Pharaoh, 6310
Ex 17:1 journeys, according to the c. of 6310
Ex 25:22 give thee in c. unto the children 6680
Ex 34:32 gave them in c. all that the Lord 6680
Ex 36:6 Moses gave c., and they caused 6680
Ex 38:21 was counted according to the c. 6310
Nu 3:39 numbered at the c. of the Lord, 6310
Nu 4:37 did number according to the c. of 6310
Nu 4:41 according to the c. of the Lord. 6310
Nu 4:49 According to the c. of the Lord they 6310
Nu 9:18 At the c. of the Lord the children 6310
Nu 9:18 Israel journeyed, and at the c. of 6310
Nu 9:20 the tabernacle; according to the c. 6310
Nu 9:20 the c. of the Lord they journeyed 6310
Nu 9:23 At the c. of the Lord they rested 6310
Nu 9:23 the c. of the Lord they journeyed: 6310
Nu 9:23 c. of the Lord by the hand of Moses 6310
Nu 10:13 their journey according to the c. of 6310
Nu 13:3 by the c. of the Lord sent them 6310
Nu 14:41 do ye transgress the c. of the Lord? 6310
Nu 15:31 hath broken his c., that soul shall 4687
Nu 23:20 Behold, I have received c. to bless:
Nu 24:13 c. of the Lord to do either good 6310
Nu 27:14 ye rebelled against my c. in the 6310
Nu 33:2 their journeys by the c. of the Lord: 6310
Nu 33:38 the c. of the Lord, and died there 6310
De 1:3 the Lord had given him in c. unto 6680
De 1:26 rebelled against the c. of the Lord 6310
De 1:43 against the c. of the Lord, and 6310
De 9:23 against the c. of the Lord your God, 6310
De 17:20 that he turn not aside from the c., 4687
De 30:11 For this c. which I command thee 4687
Jos 1:18 be that doth rebel against thy c., 6310
Jos 8:8 city on fire: according to the c. 1697
Jos 15:13 the c. of the Lord to Joshua, even 6310
Jos 17:4 according to the c. of the Lord, he 6310
Jos 21:3 at the c. of the Lord, these cities 6310
Jos 22:3 of the c. of the Lord your God. 4687
Jos 22:5 But take diligent heed to do the c. 4687
1Sa 12:14 and not rebel against the c. of the 6310
1Sa 12:15 but rebel against the c. of the Lord, 6310
1Sa 13:13 hast not kept the c. of the Lord 4687
1Sa 15:13 have performed the c. of the Lord 1697
1Sa 15:24 transgressed the c. of the Lord. 6310
2Sa 12:9 despised the c. of the Lord, to do 1697
1Ki 2:43 c. that I have charged thee with? 4687
1Ki 13:21 not kept the c. which the Lord 4687
2Ki 17:34 after the law and c. which the Lord 4687
2Ki 17:37 the law, and the c., which he wrote 4687
2Ki 18:36 king's c. was, saying, Answer him 4687
2Ki 23:35 according to the c. of Pharaoh: 6310
2Ki 24:3 c. of the Lord came this upon Judah, 6310
1Ch 12:32 all their brethren were at their c. 6310
1Ch 14:12 David gave a c., and they were 559
1Ch 28:21 people will be wholly at thy c. 1697
2Ch 8:13 according to the c. of Moses, 4687
2Ch 8:15 not from the c. of the king 4687
2Ch 14:4 and to do the law and the c. 4687
2Ch 19:10 between law and c., statutes and 4687
2Ch 24:6 according to the c. of Moses the
2Ch 24:8 at the king's c. they made a chest, 559
2Ch 24:21 at the c. of the king in the court 4687
2Ch 29:15 according to the c. of the king, by 4687
2Ch 29:25 to the c. of David, and of Gad the 4687
2Ch 29:25 the c. of the Lord by his prophets. 4687
2Ch 30:6 and Judah, and according to the c. 4687
2Ch 30:12 c. of the king and of the princes, 4687
2Ch 31:5 as soon as the c. came abroad, 1697
2Ch 31:13 at the c. of Hezekiah the king, 4662
2Ch 35:10 courses according to the king's c. 4687
2Ch 35:15 to the c. of David, and Asaph, 4687
2Ch 35:16 according to the c. of king Josiah 4687
Ezr 4:21 Give ye now c. to cause these men 2942
Ezr 4:21 until another c. shall be given 2941
Ezr 6:14 according to the c. of the God of 2941
Ezr 6:14 and according to the c. of Cyrus, 2942
Ezr 8:17 And I sent them with c. unto Iddo 3318
Ezr 10:3 that tremble at the c. of our God; 4687
Ne 11:23 the king's c. concerning them, 4687
Ne 12:24 the c. of David the man of God, 4687
Ne 12:45 the c. of David, and of Solomon 4687
Es 1:12 refused to come at the king's c. 1697
Es 1:15 she hath not performed the c. of 3982
Es 1:19 let there go a royal c. from him, 1697
Es 2:8 when the king's c. and his decree 1697
Es 2:20 for Esther did the c. of Mordecai, 3982
Es 3:3 transgressest thou the king's c.? 4687
Es 3:14 a c. to be given in every province 1881
Es 3:15 being hastened by the king's c., 1697
Es 4:3 the king's c. and his decree came, 1697
Es 4:5 and gave him a c. to Mordecai, 6680
Es 4:10 and gave him c. unto Mordecai; 6680
Es 8:13 the writing for a c. to be given 1881
Es 8:14 and pressed on by the king's c. 1697
Es 8:17 the king's c. and his decree came, 1697
Es 9:1 when th king's c. and his decree 1697
Job 23:12 gone back from the c. of his lips; 4687
Ps 19:8 c. of the Lord is pure, enlightening 4687
Ps 71:3 thou hast given c. to save me; 6680
Ps 119:96 but thy c. is exceeding broad. 4687
Ps 147:15 sendeth forth his c. upon earth: 565
Pr 6:20 keep thy father's c., and forsake 4687
Pr 6:23 c. is a lamp: and the law is light; 4687
Pr 8:29 the waters should not pass his c. 6310
Pr 13:13 feareth the c. shall be rewarded 4687
Pr 19:16 keepeth the c. keepeth his own 4687
Ec 8:2 counsel thee to keep the king's c., 6310
Ec 8:5 keepeth the c. shall feel no evil 4687
Isa 23:11 the Lord hath given a c. against 6680
Isa 36:21 not a word: for the king's c. was, 4687
Jer 35:14 none, but obey their father's c. 4687
Jer 35:16 performed the c. of their father, 4687
Jer 35:18 the c. of Jonadab your father, 4687
La 1:18 for I have rebelled against his c. 6310
Da 3:22 because the king's c. was urgent 4406
Da 9:23 the c. came forth, and I am come 1697
Da 9:25 the going forth of the c. to restore 1697
Ho 5:11 he willingly walked after the c. 6673
Na 1:14 Lord hath given a c. concerning 6680
Mal 2:1 O ye priests, this c. is for you. 4687
Mal 2:4 that I have sent this c. unto you, 4687
Mt 8:18 he gave c. to depart unto the 2753
Mt 15:3 Why do ye also transgress the c. 1785
Mt 15:6 made the c. of God of none effect 1785
Mt 22:36 which is the great c. in the law? 1785
Mt 22:38 This is the first and great c. 1785
Mk 7:8 laying aside the c. of God, ye hold 1785
Mk 7:9 Full well ye reject the c. of God, 1785
Mk 12:28 Which is the first c. of all? 1785
Mk 12:30 strength: this is the first c. 1785
Mk 12:31 there is none other c. greater than 1785
Lu 15:29 transgressed I at any time thy c. 1785
Lu 23:56 the sabbath day according to the c. 1785
Joh 10:18 This c. have I received of my 1785
Joh 11:57 the Pharisees had given a c., 1785
Joh 12:49 he gave me a c., what I should 1785
Joh 12:50 And I know that his c. is life 1785
Joh 13:34 A new c. I give unto you, That ye 1785
Joh 14:31 as the Father gave me c., even so 1781
Joh 15:12 This is my c., That ye love 1785
Ac 15:24 to whom we gave no such c. 1291
Ac 17:15 and receiving a c. unto Silas and 1785
Ac 23:30 gave c. to his accusers also to say 3853
Ac 25:23 at Festus' c. Paul was brought 2753
Ro 7:8 taking occasion by the c., wrought 1785
Ro 7:9 but when the c. came, sin revived 1785
Ro 7:10 And the c., which was ordained 1785
Ro 7:11 taking occasion by the c., deceived 1785
Ro 7:12 the c. holy, and just, and good. 1785
Ro 7:13 that sin by the c. might appear 1785
Ro 13:9 and if there be any other c., 1785
Ro 16:26 the c. of the everlasting God, 2003
1Co 7:6 this by permission, and not of c. 2003
1Co 7:25 I have no c. of the Lord: yet I give 2003
2Co 8:8 I speak not by c., but by occasion 2003
Eph 6:2 which is the first c. with promise; 1785

1Ti 1:1 by the **c.** of God our Saviour, *2003*
1Ti 1:5 Now the end of the **c.** is charity *3852*
1Ti 6:14 That thou keep this **c.** without *1785*
Tit 1:3 according to the **c.** of God our *2003*
Heb 7:5 priesthood, have a **c.** to take tithes *1785*
Heb 7:16 not after the law of a carnal **c.**, *1785*
Heb 7:18 disannulling of the **c.** going before *1785*
Heb 11:22 and gave **c.** concerning his bones. *1781*
Heb 11:23 were not afraid of the king's **c.** *1297*
2Pe 2:21 to turn from the holy **c.** delivered *1785*
2Pe 3:2 and of the **c.** of us the apostles of *1785*
1Jo 2:7 I write no new **c.** unto you, *1785*
1Jo 2:7 but an old **c.** which ye had from the *1785*
1Jo 2:7 The old **c.** is the word which ye *1785*
1Jo 2:8 Again, a new **c.** I write unto you, *1785*
1Jo 3:23 And this is his **c.**, That we should *1785*
1Jo 3:23 love one another, as he gave us **c.** *1785*
1Jo 4:21 And this **c.** have we from him, That *1785*
2Jo 4 have received a **c.** from the Father *1785*
2Jo 5 though I wrote a new **c.** unto thee, *1785*
2Jo 6 This is the **c.**, That, as ye have *1785*

COMMANDMENTS
Ge 26:5 my **c.**, my statutes, and my laws. 4687
Ex 15:26 and wilt give ear to his **c.**, and keep 4687
Ex 16:28 refuse ye to keep my **c.** and my 4687
Ex 20:6 them that love me, and keep my **c.** 4687
Ex 24:12 a law, and **c.** which I have written; 4687
Ex 34:28 words of the covenant, the ten **c.** 1697
Le 4:2 against any of the **c.** of the Lord 4687
Le 4:13 any the **c.** of the Lord concerning 4687
Le 4:22 ignorance against any of the **c.** 4687
Le 4:27 against any of the **c.** of the Lord 4687
Le 5:17 to be done by the **c.** of the Lord; 4687
Le 22:31 Therefore shall ye keep my **c.**, 4687
Le 26:3 and keep my **c.**, and do them; 4687
Le 26:14 and will not do all these **c.**; 4687
Le 26:15 that ye will not do all my **c.**, but 4687
Le 27:34 These are the **c.**, which the Lord 4687
Nu 15:22 all these **c.**, which the Lord hath 4687
Nu 15:39 remember all the **c.** of the Lord, 4687
Nu 15:40 do all my **c.**, and be holy unto your 4687
Nu 36:13 These are the **c.** and the judgments, 4687
De 4:2 ye may keep the **c.** of the Lord 4687
De 4:13 to perform, even ten **c.**: and he 1697
De 4:40 his statutes, and his **c.**, which I 4687
De 5:10 them that love me and keep my **c.** 4687
De 5:29 keep all my **c.** always, that it might 4687
De 5:31 all the **c.**, and the statutes, and 4687
De 6:1 Now these are the **c.**, the statutes, 4687
De 6:2 his statutes and his **c.**, which I 4687
De 6:17 keep the **c.** of the Lord your God, 4687
De 6:25 to do all these **c.** before the Lord 4687
De 7:9 and keep his **c.** to a thousand 4687
De 7:11 keep the **c.**, and the statutes, and 4687
De 8:1 All the **c.** which I command thee 4687
De 8:2 whether thou wouldest keep his **c.**, 4687
De 8:6 the **c.** of the Lord thy God, to walk 4687
De 8:11 keeping his **c.**, and his judgments, 4687
De 10:4 the ten **c.**, which the Lord spake 1697
De 10:13 To keep the **c.** of the Lord, and 4687
De 11:1 his judgments, and his **c.**, alway 4687
De 11:8 keep all the **c.** which I command 4687
De 11:13 my **c.** which I command you this 4687
De 11:22 shall diligently keep all these **c.** 4687
De 11:27 A blessing, if ye obey the **c.** of the 4687
De 11:28 if ye will not obey the **c.** of the Lord 4687
De 13:4 keep his **c.**, and obey his voice, and 4687
De 13:18 Lord thy God, to keep all his **c.** 4687
De 15:5 observe to do all these **c.** which I 4687
De 19:9 shalt keep all these **c.** to do them, 4687
De 26:13 to all thy **c.** which thou hast 4687
De 26:13 I have not transgressed thy **c.**, 4687
De 26:17 and his **c.**, and his judgments, and 4687
De 26:18 thou shouldest keep all his **c.**; 4687
De 27:1 Keep all the **c.** which I command 4687
De 27:10 and do his **c.**, and his statutes, 4687
De 28:1 to do all his **c.** which I command 4687
De 28:9 keep the **c.** of the Lord thy God, 4687
De 28:13 if that thou hearken unto the **c.** of 4687
De 28:15 to observe to do all his **c.** and his 4687
De 28:45 thy God, to keep his **c.** and his 4687
De 30:8 do all his **c.** which I command thee 4687
De 30:10 thy God, to keep his **c.** and his 4687
De 30:16 walk in his ways, and to keep his **c.** 4687
De 31:5 unto all the **c.** which I have 4687
Jos 22:5 and to keep his **c.**, and to cleave 4687
Jg 2:17 walked in, obeying the **c.** of the 4687
Jg 3:4 they would hearken unto the **c.** of 4687
1Sa 15:11 and hath not performed my **c.** 1697
1Ki 2:3 his statutes, and his **c.**, and his 4687
1Ki 3:14 to keep my statutes and my **c.**, as 4687
1Ki 6:12 and keep all my **c.** to walk in them; 4687
1Ki 8:58 to keep his **c.**, and his statutes, 4687
1Ki 8:61 and to keep his **c.**, as at this day. 4687
1Ki 9:6 keep my **c.** and my statutes which 4687
1Ki 11:34 he kept my **c.** and my statutes: 4687
1Ki 11:38 my statutes and my **c.**, as David my 4687
1Ki 14:8 David, who kept my **c.**, and who 4687
1Ki 18:18 ye have forsaken the **c.** of the Lord, 4687
2Ki 17:13 your evil ways, and keep my **c.** and 4687
2Ki 17:16 they left all the **c.** of the Lord 4687
2Ki 17:19 Judah kept not the **c.** of the Lord 4687
2Ki 18:6 but kept his **c.**, which the Lord 4687
2Ki 23:3 to keep his **c.** and his testimonies 4687
1Ch 28:7 if he be constant to do my **c.** 4687
1Ch 28:8 seek for all the **c.** of the Lord 4687
1Ch 29:19 son a perfect heart, to keep thy **c.**, 4687
2Ch 7:19 my statutes and my **c.**, which I 4687
2Ch 17:4 and walked in his **c.**, and not after 4687
2Ch 24:20 Why transgress ye the **c.** of the 4687
2Ch 31:21 and in the **c.**, to seek his God, he 4687
2Ch 34:31 after the Lord, and to keep his **c.**, 4687
Ezr 7:11 of the words of the **c.** of the Lord, 4687
Ezr 9:10 for we have forsaken thy **c.**, 4687
Ezr 9:14 break thy **c.**, and join in affinity 4687
Ne 1:5 that love him, and observe his **c.** 4687
Ne 1:7 and have not kept the **c.**, nor the 4687
Ne 1:9 and keep my **c.**, and do them: 4687
Ne 9:13 and true laws, good statutes and **c.** 4687
Ne 9:16 necks, and hearkened not to thy **c.**, 4687
Ne 9:29 and hearkened not unto thy **c.**, but 4687
Ne 9:34 nor hearkened unto thy **c.** and 4687
Ne 10:29 do all the **c.** of the Lord our God, 4687
Ps 78:7 works of God, but keep his **c.** 4687
Ps 89:31 my statutes, and keep not my **c.**; 4687
Ps 103:18 those that remember his **c.** to do 6490
Ps 103:20 do his **c.**, hearkening unto the 1697
Ps 111:7 judgment; all his **c.** are sure. 6490
Ps 111:10 have all they that do his **c.**
Ps 112:1 that delighteth greatly in his **c.** 4687
Ps 119:6 when I have respect unto all thy **c.** 4687
Ps 119:10 O let me not wander from thy **c.** 4687
Ps 119:19 hide not thy **c.** from me. 4687
Ps 119:21 cursed, which do err from thy **c.** 4687
Ps 119:32 I will run the way of thy **c.**, when 4687
Ps 119:35 Make me to go in the path of thy **c.**; 4687
Ps 119:47 I will delight myself in thy **c.**, 4687
Ps 119:48 hands also will I lift up unto thy **c.**, 4687
Ps 119:60 and delayed not to keep thy **c.** 4687
Ps 119:66 for I have believed thy **c.** 4687
Ps 119:73 that I may learn thy **c.** 4687
Ps 119:86 All thy **c.** are faithful: they 4687
Ps 119:98 Thou through thy **c.** hast made me 4687
Ps 119:115 For I will keep the **c.** of my God. 4687
Ps 119:127 I love thy **c.** above gold; yea, 4687
Ps 119:131 and panted: for I longed for thy **c.** 4687
Ps 119:143 yet thy **c.** are my delights 4687
Ps 119:151 O Lord; and all thy **c.** are truth. 4687
Ps 119:166 for thy salvation, and done thy **c.** 4687
Ps 119:172 for all thy **c.** are righteousness. 4687
Ps 119:176 servant; for I do not forget thy **c.** 4687
Pr 2:1 words, and hide my **c.** with thee; 4687
Pr 3:1 but let thine heart keep my **c.** 4687
Pr 4:4 my words: keep my **c.**, and live. 4687
Pr 7:1 and lay up my **c.** with thee 4687
Pr 7:2 Keep my **c.**, and live; and my law 4687
Pr 10:8 The wise in heart will receive **c.** 4687
Ec 12:13 Fear God, and keep his **c.**: for this 4687
Isa 48:18 thou hadst hearkened to my **c.**! 4687
Da 9:4 and to them that keep his **c.**; 4687
Am 2:4 and have not kept his **c.**, and 2706
Mt 5:19 **shall break one of these least c.,** *1785*
Mt 15:9 **teaching for doctrines the c. of** *1778*
Mt 19:17 **wilt enter into life, keep the c.** *1785*
Mt 22:40 **On these two c. hang all the law** *1785*
Mk 7:7 **teaching for doctrines the c. of** *1778*
Mk 10:19 **Thou knowest the c., Do not kill,** *1785*
Mk 12:29 **of all the c. is, Hear, O Israel;** *1785*
Lu 1:6 in all the **c.** and ordinances of the *1785*
Lu 18:20 **Thou knowest the c., Do not** *1785*
Joh 14:15 **If ye love me, keep my c.** *1785*
Joh 14:21 **He that hath my c., and keepeth** *1785*
Joh 15:10 **If ye keep my c., ye shall abide in** *1785*
Joh 15:10 **kept my Father's c., and abide in** *1785*
Ac 1:2 had given **c.** unto the apostles *1781*
1Co 7:19 but the keeping of the **c.** of God. *1785*
1Co 14:37 I write unto you are the **c.** of the *1785*
Eph 2:15 law of **c.** contained in ordinances; *1785*
Col 2:22 after the **c.** and doctrines of men? *1778*
Col 4:10 touching whom ye received **c.** *1785*
1Th 4:2 ye know what **c.** we gave you *3852*
Tit 1:14 Jewish fables, and **c.** of men, *1785*
1Jo 2:3 that we know him, if we keep his **c.** *1785*
1Jo 2:4 and keepeth not his **c.**, is a liar, *1785*
1Jo 3:22 because we keep his **c.**, and do those *1785*
1Jo 3:24 he that keepeth his **c.** dwelleth in *1785*
1Jo 5:2 when we love God, and keep his **c.** *1785*
1Jo 5:3 love of God, that we keep his **c.** *1785*
1Jo 5:3 and his **c.** are not grievous *1785*
2Jo 6 this is love, that we walk after his **c.** *1785*
Re 12:17 her seed, which keep the **c.** of God, *1785*
Re 14:12 here are that keep the **c.** of God, *1785*
Re 22:14 Blessed are they that do his **c.**, *1785*

COMMEND See also COMMENDED; COMMENDETH; COMMENDING.
Lu 23:46 **into thy hands I c. my spirit:** *3908*
Ac 20:32 brethren, I **c.** you to God, and to *3908*
Ro 3:5 But if our righteousness **c.** the *4921*
Ro 16:1 I **c.** unto you Phebe our sister, *4921*
2Co 3:1 Do we begin again to **c.** ourselves? *4921*
2Co 5:12 **c.** not ourselves again unto you *4921*
2Co 10:12 with some that **c.** themselves: *4921*

COMMENDATION
2Co 3:1 some others, epistles of **c.** to you, *4956*
2Co 3:1 or letters of **c.** from you? *4956*

COMMENDED
Ge 12:15 her, and **c.** her before Pharaoh: 1984
Pr 12:8 be **c.** according to his wisdom: 1984
Ec 8:15 Then I **c.** mirth, because a man 7623
Lu 16:8 **the lord c. the unjust steward,** *1867*
Ac 14:23 they **c.** them to the Lord, on whom *3908*
2Co 12:11 I ought to have been **c.** of you: *4921*

COMMENDETH
Ro 5:8 But God **c.** his love toward us, *4921*
1Co 8:8 But meat **c.** us not to God: *3936*
2Co 10:18 not he that **c.** himself is approved, *4921*
2Co 10:18 but whom the Lord **c.** *4921*

COMMENDING
2Co 4:2 truth **c.** ourselves to every man's *4921*

COMMISSION See also COMMISSIONS.
Ac 26:12 with authority and **c.** from the *2011*

COMMISSIONS
Ezr 8:36 And they delivered the king's **c.** 1881

COMMIT See also COMMITTED; COMMITTEST; COMMITTETH; COMMITTING.
Ex 20:14 Thou shalt not **c.** adultery 5003
Le 5:15 If a soul **c.** a trespass, and sin 4600
Le 5:17 and **c.** any of these things which 6213
Le 6:2 If a soul sin, and **c.** a trespass 4600
Le 18:26 and shall not **c.** any of these 6213
Le 18:29 whosoever shall **c.** any of these 6213
Le 18:29 the souls that **c.** them shall be 6213
Le 18:30 that ye **c.** not any one of these 6213
Le 20:5 to **c.** whoredom with Molech, 2181
Nu 5:6 When a man or woman shall **c.** 6213
Nu 5:6 any sin that men **c.**, to do a
Nu 5:12 and **c.** a trespass against him, 4600
Nu 25:1 the people began to **c.** whoredom 2181
Nu 31:16 to **c.** trespass against the Lord 4560
De 5:18 Neither shalt thou **c.** adultery. 5003
De 19:20 **c.** no more any such evil among 6213
Jos 22:20 the son of Zerah **c.** a trespass 4600
2Sa 7:14 If he **c.** iniquity, I will chasten 5753
2Ch 21:11 of Jerusalem to **c.** fornication, 2181
Job 5:8 unto God would I **c.** my cause: 7760
Job 34:10 from the Almighty, that he should **c.**
Ps 31:5 Into thine hand I **c.** my spirit: 6485
Ps 37:5 **C.** thy way unto the Lord; trust 1556
Pr 16:3 **C.** thy works unto the Lord, 1556
Pr 16:12 to kings to **c.** wickedness: for the 6213
Isa 22:21 **c.** thy government into his hand: 5414
Isa 23:17 and shall **c.** fornication with 2181
Jer 7:9 ye steal, murder, and **c.** adultery, 5003
Jer 9:5 weary themselves to **c.** iniquity 5753
Jer 23:14 they **c.** adultery, and walk in lies: 5003
Jer 37:21 should **c.** Jeremiah into the court 6485

Jer 44:7 Wherefore c. ye this great evil 6213
Eze 3:20 his righteousness, and c. iniquity, 6213
Eze 8:17 that they c. the abominations 6213
Eze 8:17 which they c. here? 6213
Eze 16:17 didst c. whoredom with them, 2181
Eze 16:34 followeth thee to c. whoredoms: 2181
Eze 16:43 thou shalt not c. this lewdness 6213
Eze 20:30 and c. ye whoredom after their 2181
Eze 22:9 midst of thee they c. lewdness. 6213
Eze 23:43 Will they now c. whoredoms with 2181
Eze 33:13 and c. iniquity, all his 6213
Ho 4:10 they shall c. whoredom, and 2181
Ho 4:13 daughters shall c. whoredom, 2181
Ho 4:13 your spouses shall c. adultery. 5003
Ho 4:14 when they c. whoredom, nor your 2181
Ho 4:14 spouses when they c. adultery: 5003
Ho 6:9 consent: for they c. lewdness. 6313
Ho 7:1 they c. falsehood; and the thief 6466
Mt 5:27 **Thou shalt not c. adultery:** *3431*
Mt 5:32 **causeth her to c. adultery:** *3429*
Mt 19:9 **is put away doth c. adultery.** *3429*
Mt 19:18 **Thou shalt not c. adultery,** *3431*
Mk 10:19 **Do not c. adultery,** *3431*
Lu 12:48 **did c. things worthy of stripes,** *4160*
Lu 16:11 **c. to your trust the true riches?** *4100*
Lu 18:20 **Do not c. adultery,** *3431*
Joh 2:24 Jesus did not c. himself unto *4100*
Ro 1:32 which c. such things are worthy *4238*
Ro 2:2 them which c. such things *4238*
Ro 2:22 a man should not c. adultery, *3431*
Ro 2:22 dost thou c. adultery? *3431*
Ro 2:22 idols, dost thou c. sacrilege? *2416*
Ro 13:9 Thou shalt not c. adultery, *3431*
1Co 10:8 Neither let us c. fornication, *4203*
1Ti 1:18 This charge I c. unto thee, *3908*
2Ti 2:2 the same c. thou to faithful men, *3908*
Jas 2:9 ye c. sin, and are convinced of the *2038*
Jas 2:11 that said, Do not c. adultery, *3431*
Jas 2:11 Now if thou c. no adultery, *3431*
1Pe 4:19 c. the keeping of their souls to *3908*
1Jo 3:9 is born of God doth not c. sin; *4160*
Re 2:14 **unto idols, and to c. fornication** *4203*
Re 2:20 **to c. fornication,and to eat things** *4203*
Re 2:22 **them that c. adultery with her** *3431*

COMMITTED
Ge 39:8 he hath c. all that he hath to my 5414
Ge 39:22 of the prison c. to Joseph's hand 5414
Le 4:35 for his sin that he hath c., it 2398
Le 5:7 his trespass, which he hath c., 2398
Le 18:30 which were c. before you, 6213
Le 20:13 of them have c. an abomination: 6213
Le 20:23 for they c. all these things, and 6213
Nu 15:24 be c. by ignorance without the 6213
De 17:5 or that woman, which have c. 6213
De 21:22 man have c. a sin worthy of death, 1961
Jos 7:1 children of Israel c. a trespass 4600
Jos 22:16 that ye have c. against the God 4600
Jos 22:31 c. this trespass against the Lord: 4600
Jg 20:6 c. lewdness and folly in Israel. 6213
1Ki 8:47 we have c. wickedness; 7561
1Ki 14:22 with their sins which they had c., 2398
1Ki 14:27 and c. them unto the hands of the 6485
1Ch 10:13 for his transgression which he c. 4600
2Ch 12:10 shields of brass, and c. them 6485
2Ch 34:16 All that was c. to thy servants 5414
Ps 106:6 we have c. iniquity, we have done 5753
Jer 2:13 For my people have c. two evils; 6213
Jer 3:8 backsliding Israel c. adultery 5003
Jer 3:9 and c. adultery with stones and 5003
Jer 5:7 then c. adultery, and assembled 5003
Jer 5:30 horrible thing is c. in the land; 1961
Jer 6:15 when they had c. abomination? 6213
Jer 8:12 they had c. abomination? nay, 6213
Jer 16:10 that we have c. against the Lord 2398
Jer 29:23 and have c. adultery with their 6213
Jer 29:23 they have c. villany in Israel, and 6213
Jer 39:14 and c. him unto Gedaliah the son 5414
Jer 40:7 c. unto him men, and women, 6485
Jer 41:10 of the guard had c. to Gedaliah 6485
Jer 44:3 wickedness which they have c. to 6213
Jer 44:9 which they have c. in the land 6213
Jer 44:22 abominations which ye have c.; 6213
Eze 6:9 the evils which they have c. in all 6213
Eze 15:8 have c. a trespass, saith the Lord 4600
Eze 16:26 c. fornication with the Egyptians 2181
Eze 16:50 and c. abomination before me: 6213
Eze 16:51 hath Samaria c. half of thy sins; 2398
Eze 16:52 c. more abominable than they: 8581
Eze 18:12 to the idols, hath c. abomination, 6213
Eze 18:21 from all his sins that he hath c., 6213
Eze 18:22 his trangressions that he hath c., 6213
Eze 18:27 his wickedness that he hath c., 6213
Eze 18:28 his transgressions that he hath c., 6213
Eze 20:27 have c. a trespass against me. 4600
Eze 20:43 for all your evils that ye have c. 6213
Eze 22:11 And one hath c. abomination with 6213
Eze 23:3 they c. whoredoms in Egypt: 2181
Eze 23:3 c. whoredoms in their youth: 2181
Eze 23:7 she c. her whoredoms with them, 5414
Eze 23:37 they have c. adultery, and blood 5003
Eze 23:37 their idols have they c. adultery, 5003
Eze 33:13 for his iniquity that he hath c., 6213
Eze 33:16 None of his sins that he hath c. 2398
Eze 33:29 abominations which they have c. 6213
Eze 43:8 abominations that they have c. 6213
Eze 44:13 abominations which they have c. 6213
Da 9:5 sinned, and have c. iniquity, 5753
Ho 1:2 land hath c. great whoredom, 2181
Ho 4:18 have c. whoredom continually: 2181
Mal 2:11 an abomination is c. in Israel 6213
Mt 5:28 **hath c. adultery with her already** *3431*
Mk 15:7 c. murder in the insurrection. *4160*
Lu 12:48 **to whom men have c. much, of** *3908*
Joh 5:22 **c. all judgment unto the Son:** *1325*
Ac 8:3 men and women c. them to prison *3860*
Ac 25:11 or have c. any thing worthy of *4238*
Ac 25:25 he had c. nothing worthy of death, *4238*
Ac 27:40 they c. themselves unto the sea, *1439*
Ac 28:17 c. nothing against the people, *4160*
Ro 3:2 them were c. the oracles of God. *4100*
1Co 9:17 a dispensation of the gospel is c. *4100*
1Co 10:8 fornication, as some of them c., *4203*
2Co 5:19 and hath c. unto us the word of *5087*
2Co 11:7 I c. an offence in abasing myself *4160*
2Co 12:21 lasciviousness which they have c. *4238*
Ga 2:7 uncircumcision was c. unto me, *4100*
1Ti 1:11 which was c. to my trust. *4100*
1Ti 6:20 keep that which is c. to thy trust. *3872*
2Ti 1:12 able to keep that which I have c. *3866*
2Ti 1:14 That good thing which was c. unto *3872*
Tit 1:3 preaching, which is c. unto me *4100*
Jas 5:15 if he have c. sins, they shall be *4160*
1Pe 2:23 but c. himself to him that judgeth *3860*
Jude 15 deeds which they have ungodly c., *764*
Re 17:2 of the earth have c. fornication, *4203*
Re 18:3 have c. fornication with her, and *4203*
Re 18:9 who have c. fornication and lived *4203*

COMMITTEST
Ho 5:3 O Ephraim, thou c. whoredom, 2181

COMMITTETH
Le 20:10 man that c. adultery with another 5003
Le 20:10 c. adultery with his neighbour's 5003
Ps 10:14 the poor c. himself unto thee; 5800
Pr 6:32 whoso c. adultery with a woman 5003
Eze 8:6 that the house of Israel c. here, 6213
Eze 16:32 But as a wife that c. adultery, 5003
Eze 18:24 c. iniquity, and doeth according 6213
Eze 18:26 and c. iniquity, and dieth in them; 6213
Eze 33:18 and c. iniquity, he shall even die 6213
Mt 5:32 **her that is divorced c. adultery** *3429*
Mt 19:9 **marry another, c. adultery: and** *3429*
Mk 10:11 **another, c. adultery against her** *3429*
Mk 10:12 **to another, she c. adultery:** *3429*
Lu 16:18 marrieth another c. adultery: *3431*
Lu 16:18 **from her husband c. adultery** *3431*
Joh 8:34 **c. sin is the servant of sin** *4160*
1Co 6:18 but he that c. fornication sinneth *4203*
1Jo 3:4 Whosoever c. sin transgresseth *4160*
1Jo 3:8 He that c. sin is of the devil; for *4160*

COMMITTING
Eze 33:15 without c. iniquity; he shall 6213
Ho 4:2 stealing, and c. adultery, they 5003

COMMODIOUS
Ac 27:12 the haven was not c. to winter in, *428*

COMMON See also COMMONWEALTH.
Le 4:27 c. people sin through ignorance, 776
Nu 16:29 If these men die the c. death of
1Sa 21:4 is no c. bread under mine hand, 2455
1Sa 21:5 and the bread is in a manner c., 2455
Ec 6:1 and it is c. among men: 7227
Jer 26:23 into the graves of the c. people. 1121
Jer 31:5 and shall eat them as c. things. 2490
Eze 23:42 men of the c. sort were brought 7230
Mt 27:27 took Jesus into the c. hall, and *4232*
Mk 12:37 the c. people heard him gladly. *4183*
Ac 2:44 and had all things c.; *2839*
Ac 4:32 but they had all things c. *2839*
Ac 5:18 put them in the c. prison. *1219*
Ac 10:14 any thing that is c. or unclean. *2839*
Ac 10:15 cleansed, that call not thou c. *2840*
Ac 10:28 not call any man c. or unclean. *2839*
Ac 11:8 for nothing c. or unclean hath at *2839*
Ac 11:9 cleansed, that call not thou c. *2839*
1Co 10:13 you but such as is c. to man: *442*
Tit 1:4 mine own son after the c. faith: *2839*
Jude 3 write unto you of the c. salvation, *2839*

COMMON HALL See COMMON and HALL.

COMMONLY
1Ki *general title* The Kings, C. Called, The Third
2Ki *general title* The Kings, C. Called, The Fourth
Mt 28:15 is c. reported among the Jews *1310*
1Co 5:1 It is reported c. that there is *3654*

COMMON PEOPLE See COMMON, and PEOPLE.

COMMONWEALTH
Eph 2:12 being aliens from the c. of Israel, *4174*

COMMOTION See also COMMOTIONS.
Jer 10:22 great c. out of the north country, 7494

COMMOTIONS
Lu 21:9 **ye shall hear of wars and c.,** *181*

COMMUNE See also COMMUNED; COMMUNING.
Ge 34:6 out unto Jacob to c. with him. 1696
Ex 25:22 and I will c. with thee from above 1696
1Sa 18:22 C. with David secretly, and say, 1696
1Sa 19:3 I will c. with my father of thee; 1696
Job 4:2 we assay to c. with thee, wilt thou 1697
Ps 4:4 c. with your own heart upon your 559
Ps 64:5 they c. of laying snares privily; 5608
Ps 77:6 I c. with mine own heart: and my 7878

COMMUNED
Ge 23:8 And he c. with them, saying, If it 1696
Ge 34:8 And Hamor c. with them, saying, 1696
Ge 34:20 and c. with the men of their city, 1696
Ge 42:24 and c. with them, and took from 1696
Ge 43:19 and they c. with him at the door 1696
Jg 9:1 and c. with them, and with all 1696
1Sa 9:25 Samuel c. with Saul upon the top 1696
1Sa 25:39 David sent and c. with Abigail, 1696
1Ki 10:2 she was come to Solomon, she c. 1696
2Ki 22:14 and they c. with her. 1696
2Ch 9:1 she was come to Solomon, she c. 1696
Ec 1:16 I c. with mine own heart, saying, 1696
Da 1:19 And the king c. with them; and 1696
Zec 1:14 that c. with me said unto me, 1696
Lu 6:11 c. one with another what they *1255*
Lu 22:4 and c. with the chief priests and *4814*
Lu 24:15 they c. together and reasoned, *3656*
Ac 24:26 him the oftener, and c. with him. *3656*

COMMUNICATE See also COMMUNICATED.
Ga 6:6 c. unto him that teacheth in all *2841*
Php 4:14 that ye did c. with my affliction. *4790*
1Ti 6:18 ready to distribute, willing to c.; *2843*
Heb 13:16 to do good and to c. forget not: *2842*

COMMUNICATED
Ga 2:2 c. unto them that gospel which I *394*
Php 4:15 church c. with me as concerning *2841*

COMMUNICATION See also COMMUNICATIONS.
2Sa 3:17 And Abner had c. with the elders 1697
2Ki 9:11 Ye know the man, and his c. 7879
Mt 5:37 **your c. be, Yea, yea; Nay, nay:** *3056*
Eph 4:29 Let no corrupt c. proceed out of *3056*
Col 3:8 filthy c. out of your mouth. *148*
Phm 6 The c. of thy faith may become *2842*

COMMUNICATIONS
Lu 24:17 **What manner of c. are these that** *3056*
1Co 15:33 evil c. corrupt good manners *3657*

COMMUNION
1Co 10:16 not the c. of the blood of Christ? *2842*
1Co 10:16 it not the c. of the body of Christ? *2842*
2Co 6:14 what c. hath light with darkness? *2842*
2Co 13:14 the c. of the Holy Ghost, be with *2842*

COMMUNING

Ge 18:33 as he had left c. with Abraham: 1696
Ex 31:18 he had made an end of c. with him 1696

COMPACT See also COMPACTED.

Ps 122:3 as a city that is c. together: 2266

COMPACTED

Eph 4:16 and c. by that which every joint *4822*

COMPANIED See also ACCOMPANIED.

Ac 1:21 these men which have c. with us *4905*

COMPANIES

Jg 7:16 three hundred men into three c., 7218
Jg 7:20 the three c. blew the trumpets, 7218
Jg 9:34 wait against Shechem in four c. 7218
Jg 9:43 divided them into three c., and 7218
Jg 9:44 other c. ran upon all the people 7218
1Sa 11:11 Saul put the people in three c.; 7218
1Sa 13:17 camp of the Philistines in three c.: 7218
2Ki 5:2 the Syrians had gone out by c., 1416
1Ch 9:18 they were porters in the c. of the 4264
1Ch 28:1 c. that ministered to the king by 4256
Ne 12:31 two great c. of them that gave thanks, 4256
Ne 12:40 So stood the two c. of them that gave 4256
Job 6:19 the c. of Sheba waited for them 1979
Isa 21:13 O ye travelling c. of Dedanim 736
Isa 57:13 criest, let thy c. deliver thee 736
Eze 26:7 with horsemen, and c., and much 6951
Mk 6:39 sat down by c. upon the green *4849*

COMPANION See COMPANIONS.

Ex 32:27 brother, and every man his c., 7453
Jg 14:20 Samson's wife was given to his c., 4828
Jg 15:2 I gave her to thy c.: is not her 4828
Jg 15:6 his wife, and given her to his c. 4828
1Ch 27:33 the Archite was the king's c.: 7453
Job 30:29 brother to dragons, and a c. to owls. 7453
Ps 119:63 am a c. of all them that fear thee, 2270
Pr 13:20 but a c. of fools shall be destroyed. 7462
Pr 28:7 but he that is a c. of riotous men 7462
Pr 28:24 the same is the c. of a destroyer. 2270
Mal 2:14 yet is she thy c., and the wife of 2278
Php 2:25 my brother, and c. in labour, *4904*
Re 1:9 and c. in tribulation, and in the *4791*

COMPANIONS See also COMPANIONS'.

Jg 11:38 she went with her c., and bewailed 7464
Jg 14:11 they brought thirty c. to be with 4828
Ezr 4:7 Tabeel, and the rest of their c., 3675
Ezr 4:9 the rest of their c.; the Dinaites, 3675
Ezr 4:17 the rest of their c. that dwell in 3675
Ezr 4:23 Shimshai the scribe, and their c., 3675
Ezr 5:3 Shethar-boznai, and their c. and 3675
Ezr 5:6 Shethar-boznai, and his c. the 3675
Ezr 6:6 Shethar-boznai, and your c. the 3675
Ezr 6:13 Shethar-boznai, and their c., 3675
Job 35:4 will answer thee, and thy c. with 7453
Job 41:6 Shall the c. make a banquet of 2271
Ps 45:14 the virgins her c. that follow her 7464
Ca 1:7 aside by the flocks of thy c.? 2270
Ca 8:13 the c. hearken to thy voice: 2270
Isa 1:23 are rebellious, and c. of thieves: 2270
Eze 37:16 and for the children of Israel his c. 2270
Eze 37:16 for all the house of Israel his c. 2270
Da 2:17 Mishael, and Azariah, his c. 2269
Ac 19:29 of Macedonia, Paul's c. in travel, *4898*
Heb 10:33 ye became c. of them that were so *2844*

COMPANIONS'

Ps 122:8 For my brethren and c. sakes, 7453

COMPANY See also ACCOMPANY; COMPANIED; COMPANIES.

Ge 32:8 If Esau come to the one c., 4264
Ge 32:8 then the other c. which is left 4264
Ge 32:21 himself lodged that night in the c. 4264
Ge 35:11 a c. of nations shall be of thee, 6951
Ge 37:25 a c. of Ishmeelites came from 736
Ge 50:9 and it was a very great c. 4264
Nu 14:7 they spake unto all the c. of the 5712
Nu 16:5 unto all his c., saying, Even 5712
Nu 16:6 you censers, Korah, and all his c.; 5712
Nu 16:11 thou and all thy c. are gathered 5712
Nu 16:16 and all thy c. before the Lord, 5712
Nu 16:40 he be not as Korah, and as his c. 5712
Nu 22:4 Now shall this c. lick up all that 6951
Nu 26:9 in the c. of Korah, when they 5712
Nu 26:10 when that c. died, what time the 5712
Nu 27:3 in the c. of them that gathered 5712
Nu 27:3 against the Lord in the c. of Korah; 5712
Jg 9:37 and another c. come along by the 7218
Jg 9:44 Abimelech, and the c. that was 7218
Jg 18:23 that thou comest with such a c.? 2199
1Sa 10:5 thou shalt meet a c. of prophets 2256
1Sa 10:10 behold, a c. of prophets met him; 2256
1Sa 13:17 one c. turned unto the way that 7218
1Sa 13:18 And another c. turned the way to 7218
1Sa 13:18 Beth-horon: and another c. turned 7218
1Sa 19:20 they saw the c. of the prophets 3862
1Sa 30:15 thou bring me down to this c.? 1416
1Sa 30:15 I will bring thee down to this c. 1416
1Sa 30:23 the c. that came against us into 1416
2Ki 5:15 he and all his c., and came, 4264
2Ki 9:17 he spied the c. of Jehu as he came, 8229
2Ki 9:17 and said, I see a c.. And Joram 8229
2Ch 9:1 with a very great c., and camels 2428
2Ch 20:12 have no might against this great c. 1995
2Ch 24:24 Syrians came with a small c. of 1995
Ne 12:38 And the other c. of them that
Job 16:7 thou hast made desolate all my c. 5712
Job 34:8 Which goeth in c. with the 2274
Ps 55:14 unto the house of God in c.. 7285
Ps 68:11 great was the c. of those that 6635
Ps 68:30 Rebuke the c. of spearmen, the 2416
Ps 106:17 and covered the c. of Abiram. 5712
Ps 106:18 And a fire was kindled in their c.; 5712
Pr 29:3 he that keepeth c. with harlots 7462
Ca 1:9 c. of horses in Pharaoh's chariots.
Ca 6:13 As it were the c. of two armies. 4246
Jer 31:8 a great c. shall return thither. 6951
Eze 16:40 They shall also bring up a c. 6951
Eze 17:17 with his mighty army and great c. 6951
Eze 23:46 I will bring up a c. upon them, 6951
Eze 23:47 And the c. shall stone them with 6951
Eze 27:6 the c. of the Ashurites have made 1323
Eze 27:27 in all thy c. which is in the midst 6951
Eze 27:34 all thy c. in the midst of thee shall 6951
Eze 32:3 my net over thee with a c. of many 6951
Eze 32:22 Asshur is there and all her c.: his 6951
Eze 32:23 and her c. is round about her 6951
Eze 38:4 great c. with bucklers and shields, 6951
Eze 38:7 all thy c. that are assembled unto 6951
Eze 38:13 hast thou gathered thy c. to take a 6951
Eze 38:15 horses, a great c., and a mighty 6951
Ho 6:9 c. of priests murder in the way 2267
Lu 2:44 him to have been in the c., went *4923*
Lu 5:29 c. of publicans and of others that *3793*
Lu 6:17 and the c. of his disciples, and a *3793*
Lu 6:22 **shall separate you from their c.,**
Lu 9:14 **them sit down by fifties in a c.** *2828*
Lu 9:38 a man of the c. cried out, saying, *3793*
Lu 11:27 certain woman of the c. lifted up *3793*
Lu 12:13 And one of the c. said unto him, *3793*
Lu 23:27 great c. of people, and of women, *4128*
Lu 24:22 certain women also of our c. made us
Joh 6:5 saw a great c. come unto him, *3793*
Ac 4:23 go, they went to their own c., *2398*
Ac 6:7 and a great c. of the priests were *3793*
Ac 10:28 is a Jew to keep c., or come unto *2853*
Ac 13:13 when Paul and his c. loosed *3588, 4012*
Ac 15:22 chosen men of their own c.
Ac 17:5 gathered a c., and set all the city *3792*
Ac 21:8 day we that were of Paul's c. *4012*
Ro 15:24 somewhat filled with your c.
1Co 5:9 epistle not to c. with fornicators: *4874*
1Co 5:11 written unto you not to keep c., *4874*
2Th 3:14 that man, and have no c. with him, *4874*
Heb 12:22 to an innumerable c. of angels, *3461*
Re 18:17 all the c. in ships, and sailors, *3658*

COMPARABLE

La 4:2 The precious sons of Zion, c. to 5537

COMPARE See also COMPARABLE; COMPARED; COMPARING.

Isa 40:18 what likeness will ye c. unto him? 6186
Isa 46:5 and c. me, that we may be like? 4911
Mk 4:30 **what comparison shall we c. it?** *3846*
2Co 10:12 or c. ourselves with some that *4793*

COMPARED

Ps 89:6 who in the heaven can be c. unto 6186
Pr 3:15 thou canst desire are not to be c. 7737
Pr 8:11 may be desired are not to be c. to 7737
Ca 1:9 I have c. thee, O my love, to a 1819
Ro 8:18 not worthy to be c. with the glory

COMPARING

1Co 2:13 c. spiritual things with spiritual *4793*
2Co 10:12 c. themselves among themselves, *4793*

COMPARISON

Jg 8:2 have I done now in c. of you?
Jg 8:3 what was I able to do in c. of you?
Hag 2:3 is it not in your eyes in c. of it as 3644
Mk 4:30 **or with what c. shall we compare** *3850*

COMPASS See also COMPASSED; COMPASSEST; COMPASSETH; COMPASSING.

Ex 27:5 put it under the c. of the altar 3749
Ex 38:4 under the c. thereof beneath unto 3749
Nu 21:4 way of the Red sea, to c. the land 5437
Nu 34:5 And the border shall fetch a c. 5437
Jos 6:3 And ye shall c. the city, all ye men 5437
Jos 6:4 ye shall c. the city seven times, 5437
Jos 6:7 Pass on, and c. the city, and let him 5437
Jos 15:3 and fetched a c. to Karkaa: 5437
2Sa 5:23 fetch a c. behind them, and come 5437
1Ki 7:15 line of twelve cubits did c. either 5437
1Ki 7:23 of thirty cubits did c. it round 5437
1Ki 7:35 was there a round c. of half a cubit 5439
2Ki 3:9 they fetched a c. of seven days' 5437
2Ki 11:8 And ye shall c. the king round 5362
2Ch 4:2 from brim to brim, round in c., 5439
2Ch 4:2 a line of thirty cubits did c. it 5437
2Ch 4:3 oven, which did c. it round about: 5437
2Ch 23:7 And the Levites shall c. the king 5362
Job 16:13 His archers c. me round about, 5437
Job 40:22 willows of the brook c. him about. 5437
Ps 5:12 with favour wilt thou c. him as 5849
Ps 7:7 congregation of the people c. thee 5437
Ps 17:9 from my deadly enemies, who c. 5362
Ps 26:6 so will I c. thine altar, O Lord: 5437
Ps 32:7 thou shalt c. me about with songs 5437
Ps 32:10 Lord, mercy shall c. him about. 5437
Ps 49:5 the iniquity of my heels shall c. me 5437
Ps 140:9 for the head of those that c. me 4524
Ps 142:7 the righteous shall c. me about; 3803
Pr 8:27 he set a c. upon the face of the 2329
Isa 44:13 and he marketh it out with the c., 4230
Isa 50:11 c. yourselves about with sparks: 247
Jer 31:22 earth, A woman shall c. a man. 5437
Jer 31:39 hill Gareb, and shall c. about to 5437
Jer 52:21 a fillet of twelve cubits did c. it; 5437
Hab 1:4 for the wicked doth c. about the 3803
Mt 23:15 **ye c. sea and land to make one** *4013*
Lu 19:43 **a trench about thee, and c. thee** *4033*
Ac 28:13 thence we fetched a c., and came *4022*

COMPASSED

Ge 19:4 c. the house round, both old and 5437
De 2:1 and we c. mount Seir many days 5437
De 2:3 Ye have c. this mountain long 5437
Jos 6:11 So the ark of the Lord c. the city, 5437
Jos 6:14 the second day they c. the city once, 5437
Jos 6:15 c. the city after the same manner 5437
Jos 6:15 on that day they c. the city seven 5437
Jos 15:10 And the border c. from Baalah 5437
Jos 18:14 and c. the corner of the sea 5437
Jg 11:18 and c. the land of Edom, and the 5437
Jg 16:2 And they c. him in, and laid wait 5437
1Sa 23:26 Saul and his men c. David and his 5849
2Sa 18:15 c. about and smote Absalom, 5437
2Sa 22:5 waves of death c. me, the floods 661
2Sa 22:6 The sorrows of hell c. me about; 5437
2Ki 6:14 they came by night, and c. the city 5362
2Ki 6:15 host c. the city both with horses 5437
2Ki 8:21 smote the Edomites which c. him 5437
2Ch 18:31 Therefore they c. about him to 5437
2Ch 21:9 smote the Edomites which c. him 5437
2Ch 33:14 and c. about Ophel, and raised it 5437
Job 19:6 and hath c. me with his net 5362
Job 26:10 hath c. the waters with bounds, 2328
Ps 17:11 They have now c. us in our steps: 5437
Ps 18:4 The sorrows of death c. me, and 661
Ps 18:5 The sorrows of hell c. me about: 5437
Ps 22:12 Many bulls have c. me: strong 5437
Ps 22:16 For dogs have c. me: the assembly 5437
Ps 40:12 innumerable evils have c. me 661
Ps 88:17 water; they c. me about together 5362
Ps 109:3 They c. me about also with words 5437
Ps 116:3 The sorrows of death c. me, and 661
Ps 118:10 All nations c. me about: but in 5437
Ps 118:11 c. me about; yea, they c. me about: 5437
Ps 118:12 They c. me about like bees; they 5437
La 3:5 me, and c. me with gall and travel 5362
Jon 2:3 the floods c. me about: all thy 5437
Jon 2:5 The waters c. me about, even to 661
Lu 21:20 **shall see Jerusalem c. with armies,** *2944*

Heb 5:2 himself also is **c.** with infirmity *4029*
Heb 11:30 they were **c.** about seven days. *2944*
Heb 12:1 are **c.** about with so great a cloud *4029*
Re 20:9 and **c.** the camp of the saints about, *2944*

COMPASSEST
Ps 139:3 Thou **c.** my path and my lying 2219

COMPASSETH
Ge 2:11 **c.** the whole land of Havilah, 5437
Ge 2:13 that **c.** the whole land of Ethiopia. 5437
Jos 19:14 the border **c.** it on the north side 5437
Ps 73:6 pride **c.** them about as a chain; 6059
Ho 11:12 Ephraim **c.** me about with lies, 37

COMPASSING
1Ki 7:24 were knops **c.** it, ten in a cubit, 5437
1Ki 7:24 **c.** the sea round about: the knops 5362
2Ch 4:3 **c.** the sea round about. Two rows 5362

COMPASSION See also COMPASSIONS.
Ex 2:6 And she had **c.** on him, and said, 2550
De 13:17 thee mercy, and have **c.** upon thee, 7355
De 30:3 captivity, and have **c.** upon thee, 7355
1Sa 23:21 of the Lord: for ye have **c.** on me. 2550
1Ki 8:50 **c.** before them who carried them 7356
1Ki 8:50 that they may have **c.** on them: 7355
2Ki 13:23 had **c.** on them, and had respect 7355
2Ch 30:9 children shall find **c.** before them 7356
2Ch 36:15 because he had **c.** on his people, 2550
2Ch 36:17 had no **c.** on young man or maiden, 2550
Ps 78:38 he, being full of **c.**, forgave their 7349
Ps 86:15 a God full of **c.**, and gracious, 7349
Ps 111:4 Lord is gracious and full of **c.**. 7349
Ps 112:4 and full of **c.** and righteous, 7349
Ps 145:8 Lord is gracious, and full of **c.**; 7349
Isa 49:15 she should not have **c.** on the son 7355
Jer 12:15 I will return, and have **c.** on them, 7355
La 3:32 will he have **c.** according to the 7355
Eze 16:5 to have **c.** upon thee; but thou 2550
Mic 7:19 he will have **c.** upon us; he will 7355
Mt 9:36 he was moved with **c.** on them, *4697*
Mt 14:14 was moved with **c.** toward them, *4697*
Mt 15:32 **have c. on the multitude,** *4697*
Mt 18:27 **moved with c., and loosed him,** *4697*
Mt 18:33 **have had c. on thy fellow servant,** *1653*
Mt 20:34 Jesus had **c.** on them, and touched *4697*
Mk 1:41 Jesus, moved with **c.**, put forth *4697*
Mk 5:19 **for thee, and hath had c. on thee.** *1653*
Mk 6:34 was moved with **c.** toward them *4697*
Mk 8:2 **have c. on the multitude, because** *4697*
Mk 9:22 have **c.** on us, and help us. *4697*
Lu 7:13 he had **c.** on her, and said unto her, *4697*
Lu 10:33 **he saw him, he had c. on him,** *4697*
Lu 15:20 **his father saw him, and had c.,** *4697*
Ro 9:15 will have **c.** on whom I will have **c.** *3627*
Heb 5:2 Who can have **c.** on the ignorant, *3356*
Heb 10:34 For ye had **c.** of me in my bonds, *4834*
1Pe 3:8 having **c.** one of another, love *4835*
1Jo 3:17 shutteth up his bowels of **c.** from him,
Jude 22 have **c.** making a difference: *1653*

COMPASSIONS
La 3:22 consumed, because his **c.** fail not. 7355
Zec 7:9 shew mercy and **c.** every man to 7356

COMPEL See also COMPELLED.
Le 25:39 thou shalt not **c.** him to serve as 5647
Es 1:8 none did **c.**: for so the king had 597
Mt 5:41 **shall c. thee to go a mile, go with** *29*
Mk 15:21 they **c.** one Simon a Cyrenian, who *29*
Lu 14:23 **c. them to come in, that my house** *315*

COMPELLED
1Sa 28:23 together with the woman, **c.** him; 6555
2Ch 21:11 fornication, and **c.** Judah thereto. 5080
Mt 27:32 him they **c.** to bear his cross. *29*
Ac 26:11 and **c.** them to blaspheme; and *315*
2Co 12:11 a fool in glorying; ye have **c.** me: *315*
Ga 2:3 a Greek, was **c.** to be circumcised: *315*

COMPELLEST
Ga 2:14 why **c.** thou the Gentiles to live *315*

COMPLAIN See also COMPLAINED; COMPLAINING.
Jg 21:22 come unto us to **c.**, that we will say 7378
Job 7:11 **c.** in the bitterness of my soul. 7878
Job 31:38 the furrows likewise thereof **c.**; 1058
La 3:39 Wherefore doth a living man **c.**, 596

COMPLAINED
Nu 11:1 when the people **c.**, it displeased 596
Ps 77:3 I **c.**, and my spirit was 7878

COMPLAINERS
Jude 16 are murmurers, **c.**, walking after *3202*

COMPLAINING
Ps 144:14 that there be no **c.** in our streets. 6682

COMPLAINT See also COMPLAINTS.
1Sa 1:16 abundance of my **c.** and grief have 7879
Job 7:13 my couch shall ease my **c.**; 7879
Job 9:27 I will forget my **c.**, I will leave off 7879
Job 10:1 I will leave my **c.** upon myself; 7879
Job 21:4 is my **c.** to man? And if it were so, 7879
Job 23:2 to day is my **c.** bitter: my stroke is 7879
Ps 55:2 I mourn in my **c.**, and make a 7879
Ps 102:*title* poureth out his **c.** before the Lord. 7879
Ps 142:2 I poured out my **c.** before him; 7879

COMPLAINTS
Ac 25:7 and grievous **c.** against Paul, *157*

COMPLETE
Le 23:15 seven sabbaths shall be **c.**: 8549
Col 2:10 are **c.** in him, which is the head *4137*
Col 4:12 perfect and **c.** in all the will of God. *4137*

COMPOSITION
Ex 30:32 any other like it, after the **c.** of it: 4971
Ex 30:37 according to the **c.** thereof: it shall 4971

COMPOUND See also COUMPOUNDETH.
Ex 30:25 an ointment **c.** after the art of the 4842

COMPOUNDETH
Ex 30:33 Whosoever **c.** any like it, or 7543

COMPREHEND See also COMPREHENDED.
Job 37:5 doeth he, which we cannot **c.**. 3045
Eph 3:18 able to **c.** with all saints what is *2638*

COMPREHENDED
Isa 40:12 and **c.** the dust of the earth in a 3557
Joh 1:5 and the darkness **c.** it not. *2638*
Ro 13:9 it is briefly **c.** in this saying, *346*

CONANIAH (co-na-ni'-ah) See also CONONIAH.
2Ch 35:9 **C.** also, and Shemaiah, and 3562

CONCEAL See also CONCEALED; CONCEALETH.
Ge 37:26 slay our brother, and **c.** his blood? 3680
De 13:8 neither shalt thou **c.** him: 3680
Job 27:11 is with the Almighty will I not **c.**. 3582
Job 41:12 I will not **c.** his parts, nor his 2790
Pr 25:2 It is the glory of God to **c.** a thing: 5641
Jer 50:2 publish and **c.** not: say, 3582

CONCEALED
Job 6:10 not **c.** the words of the Holy One. 3582
Ps 40:10 I have not **c.** thy lovingkindness 3582

CONCEALETH
Pr 11:13 is of a faithful spirit **c.** the matter. 3680
Pr 12:23 A prudent man **c.** knowledge: but 3680

CONCEIT See also CONCEITS.
Pr 18:11 and as an high wall in his own **c.** 4906
Pr 26:5 lest he be wise in his own **c.** 5869
Pr 26:12 thou a man wise in his own **c.**? 5869
Pr 26:16 The sluggard is wiser in his own **c.** 5869
Pr 28:11 The rich man is wise in his own **c.**; 5869

CONCEITS
Ro 11:25 be wise in your own **c.**; *3844, 1438*
Ro 12:16 Be not wise in your own **c.**. *3844, 1438*

CONCEIVE See also CONCEIVED; CONCEIVING.
Ge 30:38 should **c.** when they came to drink. 3179
Ge 30:41 cattle did **c.**, that Jacob laid 3179
Ge 30:41 that they might **c.** among the rods. 3179
Nu 5:28 shall be free, and shall **c.** seed. 2232
Jg 13:3 but thou shalt **c.**, and bear a son. 2029
Jg 13:5 lo, thou shalt **c.**, and bear a son; 2030
Jg 13:7 thou shalt **c.**, and bear a son; 2030
Job 15:35 They **c.** mischief, and bring forth 2029
Ps 51:5 and in sin did my mother **c.** me. 3179
Isa 7:14 a virgin shall **c.**, and bear a son 2030
Isa 33:11 shall **c.** chaff, ye shall bring forth 2029
Isa 59:4 **c.** mischief, and bring forth iniquity. 2029
Lu 1:31 thou shalt **c.** in thy womb, and *4815*
Heb 11:11 received strength to **c.** seed, *2602*

CONCEIVED
Ge 4:1 and she **c.**, and bare Cain, and 2029
Ge 4:17 and she **c.**, and bare Enoch: and 2029
Ge 16:4 went in unto Hagar, and she **c.**: 2029
Ge 16:4 when she saw that she had **c.**, her 2029
Ge 16:5 when she saw that she had **c.**, I 2029
Ge 21:2 Sarah **c.**, and bare Abraham a son 2029
Ge 25:21 and Rebekah his wife **c.**. 2029
Ge 29:32 And Leah **c.**, and bare a son, 2029
Ge 29:33, 34 she **c.** again, and bare a son; 2029
Ge 29:35 And she **c.** again, and bare a son: 2029
Ge 30:5 Bilhah **c.**, and bare Jacob a son. 2029
Ge 30:7 And Bilhah Rachel's maid **c.** again, 2029
Ge 30:17 she **c.**, and bare Jacob the fifth son. 2029
Ge 30:19 And Leah **c.** again, and bare Jacob 2029
Ge 30:23 And she **c.**, and bare a son; 2029
Ge 30:39 And the flocks **c.** before the rods, 3179
Ge 31:10 pass at the time that the cattle **c.**, 3179
Ge 38:3 And she **c.**, and bare a son; 2029
Ge 38:4 and she **c.** again, and bare a son; 2029
Ge 38:5 And she yet again **c.**, and bare 3254
Ge 38:18 in unto her, and she **c.** by him. 2029
Ex 2:2 the woman **c.**, and bare a son: 2029
Le 12:2 If a woman have **c.** seed, and 2232
Nu 11:12 Have I **c.** all this people? have I 2029
1Sa 1:20 after Hannah had **c.**, that she bare 2029
1Sa 2:21 that she **c.**, and bare three sons 2029
2Sa 11:5 And the woman **c.**, and sent and 2029
2Ki 4:17 And the woman **c.**, and bare a son 2029
1Ch 7:23 she **c.**, and bare a son, and he 2029
Job 3:3 was said, There is a man child **c.**. 2029
Ps 7:14 and hath **c.** mischief, and brought 2029
Ca 3:4 into the chamber of her that **c.** me. 2029
Isa 8:3 and she **c.**, and bare a son. 2029
Jer 49:30 hath **c.** a purpose against you. 2803
Ho 1:3 which **c.**, and bare him a son. 2029
Ho 1:6 she **c.** again, and bare a daughter. 2029
Ho 1:8 Loruhamah, she **c.**, and bare a son. 2029
Ho 2:5 harlot: she that **c.** them hath done. 2029
Mt 1:20 that which is **c.** in her is of the *1080*
Lu 1:24 his wife Elisabeth **c.**, and hid *4815*
Lu 1:36 hath also **c.** a son in her old age: *4815*
Lu 2:21 before he was **c.** in the womb. *4815*
Ac 5:4 why hast thou **c.** this thing in *5087*
Ro 9:10 when Rebecca also had **c.** *2845, 2192*
Jas 1:15 Then when lust hath **c.**, it bringeth *4815*

CONCEIVING
Isa 59:13 **c.** and uttering from the heart 2029

CONCEPTION
Ge 3:16 multiply thy sorrow and thy **c.**; 2032
Ru 4:13 the Lord gave her **c.**, and she bare 2032
Ho 9:11 from the womb, and from the **c.**. 2032

CONCERN See also CONCERNETH; CONCERNING.
Ac 28:31 things which **c.** the Lord Jesus *4012*
2Co 11:30 glory of the things which **c.** mine *4012*

CONCERNETH
Ps 138:8 that which **c.** me: thy mercy, 1157
Eze 12:10 This burden **c.** the prince in

CONCERNING
Ge 5:29 comfort us **c.** our work and toil
Ge 12:20 commanded his men **c.** him: 5921
Ge 19:21 accepted thee **c.** this thing also,
Ge 24:9 and sware to him **c.** that matter. 5921
Ge 26:32 **c.** the well which they had 5921,182
Ge 42:21 are verily guilty **c.** our brother, 5921
Ex 6:8 the land, **c.** the which I did swear
Ex 24:8 made with you **c.** all these words. 5921
Le 4:2 the Lord **c.** things which ought
Le 4:13, 22 **c.** things which should not be
Le 4:26 atonement for him as **c.** his sin,
Le 4:27 **c.** things which ought not to be
Le 5:6 atonement for him **c.** his sin.
Le 5:18 for him **c.** his ignorance 5921
Le 6:3 which was lost, and lieth **c.** it,
Le 6:18 **c.** the offerings of the Lord
Le 23:2 **C.** the feasts of the Lord,
Le 27:32 And **c.** the tithe of the herd,
Nu 8:20 Lord commanded Moses **c.** the
Nu 8:22 commanded Moses **c.** the Levites, 5921
Nu 9:8 the Lord will command **c.** you.
Nu 10:29 Lord hath spoken good **c.** Israel. 5921
Nu 14:30 the land, **c.** which I sware to
Nu 30:1 tribes **c.** the children of Israel.
Nu 30:12 out of her lips **c.** her vows,
Nu 30:12 or **c.** the bond of her soul,
Nu 32:28 So **c.** them Moses commanded

Nu 36:6 **c.** the daughters of Zelophehad
Jos 14:6 man of God **c.** me and thee in 5921,182
Jos 23:14 Lord your God spake **c.** you; 5921
Jg 15:3 Samson said **c.** them, Now shall
Jg 21:5 a great oath **c.** him that came not
Ru 4:7 **c.** redeeming and **c.** changing, 5921
1Sa 3:12 which I have spoken **c.** his house: 413
1Sa 25:30 good that he hath spoken **c.** thee, 5921
2Sa 3:8 to day with a fault **c.** this woman?
2Sa 7:25 **c.** thy servant, and **c.** his house, 5921
2Sa 11:18 David all the things **c.** the war:
2Sa 13:39 for he was comforted **c.** Amnon, 5921
2Sa 14:8 and I will give charge **c.** thee. 5921
2Sa 18:5 captains charge **c.** Absalom. 5921,1697
1Ki 2:4 his word which he spake **c.** me, 5921
1Ki 2:27 which he spake **c.** the house of Eli 5921
1Ki 5:8 will do all thy desire **c.** timber
1Ki 5:8 of cedar, and **c.** timber of fir.
1Ki 6:12 **C.** this house which thou art
1Ki 8:41 Moreover **c.** a stranger, that is 413
1Ki 10:1 **c.** the name of the Lord, she
1Ki 11:2 nations **c.** which the Lord said
1Ki 11:10 had commanded him **c.** this thing, 5921
1Ki 22:8 doth not prophesy good **c.** me, 5921
1Ki 22:18 would prophesy no good **c.** me, 5921
1Ki 22:23 Lord hath spoken evil **c.** thee. 5921
2Ki 10:10 Lord spake **c.** the house of Ahab: 5921
2Ki 17:15 **c.** whom the Lord hath charged
2Ki 19:21 that the Lord hath spoken **c.** him; 5921
2Ki 19:32 the Lord **c.** the king of Assyria, 413
2Ki 22:13 **c.** the words of this book that is 5921
2Ki 22:13 unto all that which is written **c.** us. 5921
1Ch 11:10 to the word of the Lord **c.** Israel. 5921
1Ch 17:23 that thou hast spoken **c.** thy servant 5921
1Ch 17:23 and **c.** his house to be established for 5921
1Ch 19:2 to comfort him **c.** his father. 5921
1Ch 22:12 and give thee charge **c.** Israel, 5921
1Ch 22:13 Lord charged Moses with **c.** Israel: 5921
1Ch 23:14 Now **c.** Moses the man of God,
1Ch 24:21 **C.** Rehabiah: of the sons of
1Ch 24:29 **C.** Kish: the son of Kish was
1Ch 26:1 **C.** the divisions of the porters:
1Ch 26:21 As **c.** the sons of Laadan; the
2Ch 6:32 Moreover **c.** the stranger, which 413
2Ch 8:15 **c.** any matter, or **c.** the treasures.
2Ch 12:15 of Iddo the seer **c.** genealogies?
2Ch 15:16 **c.** Maachah the mother of Asa
2Ch 24:27 Now **c.** his sons, and the greatness
2Ch 31:6 And **c.** the children of Israel
2Ch 31:9 and the Levites **c.** the heaps. 5921
2Ch 34:21 **c.** the words of the book that 5921
2Ch 34:26 God of Israel **c.** the words which
Ezr 5:5 answer by letter **c.** this matter. 5922
Ezr 5:17 pleasure to us **c.** this matter. 5922
Ezr 6:3 a decree **c.** the house of God
Ezr 7:14 enquire **c.** Judah and Jerusalem. 5922
Ezr 10:2 hope in Israel **c.** this thing. 5921
Ne 1:2 and I asked them **c.** the Jews 5921
Ne 1:2 of the captivity, and **c.** Jerusalem. 5921
Ne 9:23 them into the land, **c.** which thou
Ne 11:23 king's commandment **c.** them, 5921
Ne 11:24 in all matters **c.** the people.
Ne 13:14 Remember me, O my God, **c.** this, 5921
Ne 13:22 Remember me, O my God, **c.** this also,
Es 3:2 king had so commanded **c.** him.
Es 9:26 of that which they had seen **c.** this 5921
Job 36:33 noise thereof sheweth **c.** it, 5921
Job 36:33 the cattle also **c.** the vapour. 5921
Ps 7:*title* the Lord, **c.** the words of Cush 5921
Ps 17:4 **C.** the works of men, by the
Ps 73:8 speak wickedly **c.** oppression:
Ps 90:13 let it repent thee **c.** thy servants. 5921
Ps 106:34 not destroy the nations, **c.** whom
Ps 119:128 I esteem all thy precepts **c.** all things
Ps 119:152 **C.** thy testimonies, I have
Ps 135:14 repent himself **c.** his servants. 5921
Ec 1:13 search out by wisdom **c.** all things 5921
Ec 3:18 I said in mine heart **c.** the estate 5921
Ec 7:10 dost not enquire wisely **c.** this. 5921
Isa 1:1 of Amoz, which he saw **c.** Judah 5921
Isa 2:1 Amoz saw **c.** Judah and Jerusalem. 5921
Isa 8:1 write in it with a man's pen **c.**
Isa 16:13 Lord hath spoken **c.** Moab since 413
Isa 23:5 As at the report **c.** Egypt, so
Isa 29:22 Abraham, **c.** the house of Jacob, 413
Isa 30:7 therefore have I cried **c.** this,
Isa 37:9 he heard say **c.** Tirhakah king 5921
Isa 37:22 Lord hath spoken **c.** him; The 5921
Isa 37:33 Lord **c.** the king of Assyria, He 413
Isa 45:11 **c.** my sons, and **c.** the work of my 5921
Jer 7:22 **c.** burnt offerings or 5921,1697
Jer 14:1 to Jeremiah **c.** the dearth. 1697
Jer 14:15 saith the Lord **c.** the prophets 5921
Jer 16:3 **c.** the sons, and **c.** the daughters 5921
Jer 16:3 and **c.** their mothers that bare 5921
Jer 16:3 and **c.** their fathers that begat 5921
Jer 18:7, 9 **c.** a nation, and **c.** a kingdom, 5921
Jer 22:18 thus saith the Lord **c.** Jehoiakim 413
Jer 23:15 the Lord of hosts **c.** the prophets; 5921
Jer 25:1 came to Jeremiah **c.** all the people 5921
Jer 27:19 **c.** [413] the pillars, and **c.** the sea, 5921
Jer 27:19 **c.** the bases, and **c.** the residue 5921
Jer 27:21 **c.** the vessels that remain in the 5921
Jer 29:31 Thus saith the Lord **c.** Shemaiah 413
Jer 30:4 Lord spake **c.** Israel and **c.** Judah. 413
Jer 32:36 **c.** the city, whereof ye say, 413
Jer 33:4 of Israel, **c.** the houses of this city, 5921
Jer 33:4 and **c.** the houses of the kings 5921
Jer 39:11 gave charge **c.** Jeremiah to 5921
Jer 42:19 The Lord hath said **c.** you, 5921
Jer 44:1 **c.** all the Jews which dwell in 413
Jer 49:1 **C.** the Ammonites, thus saith
Jer 49:7 **C.** Edom, thus saith the Lord
Jer 49:23 **C.** Damascus. Hamath is
Jer 49:28 **C.** Kedar, and **c.** the kingdoms
Jer 52:21 And **c.** the pillars, the height
La 1:17 Lord hath commanded **c.** Jacob
Eze 13:16 which prophesy **c.** Jerusalem, 413
Eze 14:7 to enquire of him **c.** me;
Eze 14:22 **c.** the evil that I have brought 5921
Eze 14:22 **c.** all that I have brought upon 854
Eze 18:2 proverb **c.** the land of Israel, 5921
Eze 21:28 the Lord God **c.** the Ammonites, 413
Eze 21:28 and **c.** their reproach; 413
Eze 36:6 Prophesy therefore **c.** the land. 5921
Eze 44:5 I say into thee **c.** all the ordinances
Eze 45:14 **C.** the ordinance of oil,
Eze 47:14 **c.** the which I lifted up mine hand
Da 2:18 God of heaven **c.** this secret; 5922
Da 5:29 made a proclamation **c.** him, 5922
Da 6:4 against Daniel **c.** the kingdom; 6655
Da 6:5 against him **c.** the law of his God.
Da 6:12 the king **c.** the king's decree; 5922
Da 6:17 might not be changed **c.** Daniel.
Da 7:12 As **c.** the rest of the beasts,
Da 8:13 the vision **c.** the daily sacrifice,
Am 1:1 which he saw **c.** Israel in the 5921
Ob 1 saith the Lord God **c.** Edom;
Mic 1:1 **c.** Samaria and Jerusalem. 5921
Mic 3:5 saith the Lord **c.** the prophets 5921
Na 1:14 given a commandment **c.** thee, 5921
Hag 2:11 Ask now the priests **c.** the law,
Mt 4:6 give his angels charge **c.** thee: *4012*
Mt 11:7 to say unto the multitudes **c.** John, *4012*
Mt 16:11 I spake it not to you **c.** bread, *4012*
Mk 5:16 and also **c.** the swine. *4012*
Mk 7:17 disciples asked him **c.** the parable *4012*
Lu 2:17 which was told them **c.** this child. *4012*
Lu 7:24 to speak unto the people **c.** John, *4012*
Lu 18:31 by the prophets **c.** the Son of man
Lu 22:37 for the things **c.** me have an end *4012*
Lu 24:19 **C.** Jesus of Nazareth, which was *4012*
Lu 24:27 scriptures the things **c.** himself. *4012*
Lu 24:44 and in the psalms, **c.** me. *4012*
Joh 7:12 among the people **c.** him: *4012*
Joh 7:32 murmured such things **c.** him; *4012*
Joh 9:18 believe **c.** him, that he had been *4012*
Joh 11:19 to comfort them **c.** their brother. *4012*
Ac 1:16 **c.** Judas, which was guide to them. *4012*
Ac 2:25 David speaketh **c.** him, I foresaw *1519*
Ac 8:12 the things **c.** the kingdom of God, *4012*
Ac 13:34 And as **c.** that he raised him up *3754*
Ac 19:8 the things **c.** the kingdom of God. *4012*
Ac 19:39 any thing **c.** other matters, *4012*
Ac 21:24 whereof they were informed **c.** thee. *4012*
Ac 22:18 not receive thy testimony **c.** me. *4012*
Ac 23:15 something more perfectly **c.** him: *4012*
Ac 24:24 and heard him **c.** the faith in Christ. *4012*
Ac 25:16 for himself **c.** the crime laid against *4012*
Ac 28:21 received letters out of Judaea **c.** thee, *4012*
Ac 28:22 as **c.** this sect, we know that every *4012*
Ac 28:23 persuading them **c.** Jesus, both *4012*
Ro 1:3 **C.** his son Jesus Christ our Lord, *4012*
Ro 9:5 as **c.** the flesh Christ came, who *2596*
Ro 9:27 Esaias also crieth **c.** Israel, *5228*
Ro 11:28 As **c.** the gospel, they are enemies *2596*
Ro 16:19 which is good, and simple **c.** evil. *1519*
1Co 5:3 present, **c.** him that hath so done
1Co 7:1 Now **c.** the things whereof ye *4012*
1Co 7:25 Now **c.** virgins I have no *4012*
1Co 8:4 As **c.** therefore the eating of those *4012*
1Co 12:1 Now **c.** spiritual gifts, brethren, I *4012*
1Co 16:1 **c.** the collection for the saints, as I *4012*
2Co 8:23 and fellowhelper **c.** you: *1519*
2Co 11:21 I speak as **c.** reproach, as though *2596*
Eph 4:22 **c.** the former conversation the old *2596*
Eph 5:32 I speak **c.** Christ and the church. *1519*
Php 3:6 **C.** zeal, persecuting the church: *2596*
Php 4:15 with me as **c.** giving and *1519, 3056*
1Th 3:2 and to comfort you **c.** your faith: *4012*
1Th 4:13 **c.** them which are asleep, that ye *4012*
1Th 5:18 will of God in Christ Jesus **c.** you, *1519*
1Ti 1:19 **c.** faith have made shipwreck: *4012*
1Ti 6:21 professing have erred **c.** the faith. *4012*
2Ti 2:18 Who **c.** the truth have erred, *4012*
2Ti 3:8 minds, reprobate **c.** the faith. *4012*
Heb 7:14 Moses spake nothing **c.** priesthood. *4012*
Heb 11:20 blessed Jacob and Esau **c.** things *4012*
Heb 11:22 gave commandment **c.** his bones *4012*
1Pe 4:12 **c.** the fiery trial which is to try you, *4012*
2Pe 3:9 Lord is not slack **c.** his promise, *4314*
1Jo 2:26 have I written unto you **c.** them. *4012*

CONCISION
Php 3:2 of evil workers, beware of the **c.** *2699*

CONCLUDE See also CONCLUDED.
Ro 3:28 Therefore we **c.** that a man is *3049*

CONCLUDED
Ac 21:25 we have written and **c.** that they *2919*
Ro 11:32 For God hath **c.** them all in *4788*
Ga 3:22 the scripture hath **c.** all under *4788*

CONCLUSION
Ec 12:13 Let us hear the **c.** of the whole 5490

CONCORD
2Co 6:15 And what **c.** hath Christ with *4857*

CONCOURSE
Pr 1:21 She crieth in the chief place of **c.**, 1993
Ac 19:40 we may give an account of this **c.** *4963*

CONCUBINE See also CONCUBINES.
Ge 22:24 And his **c.**, whose name was 6370
Ge 35:22 Bilhah his father's **c.**: and Israel 6370
Ge 36:12 Timna was **c.** to Eliphaz Esau's son; 6370
Jg 8:31 And his **c.** that was in Shechem, 6370
Jg 19:1 who took to him a **c.** out of 6370
Jg 19:2 his **c.** played the whore against 6370
Jg 19:9 and his **c.**, and his servant, his 6370
Jg 19:10 his **c.** also was with him. 6370
Jg 19:24 my daughter a maiden, and his **c.**; 6370
Jg 19:25 so the man took his **c.**, and brought 6370
Jg 19:27 the woman his **c.** was fallen down 6370
Jg 19:29 laid hold on his **c.**, and divided her 6370
Jg 20:4 I and my **c.**, to lodge. 6370
Jg 20:5 my **c.** have they forced, that she is 6370
Jg 20:6 And I took my **c.**, and cut her in 6370
2Sa 3:7 And Saul had a **c.**, whose name was 6370
2Sa 3:7 thou gone in unto my father's **c.**? 6370
2Sa 21:11 the daughter of Aiah, the **c.** of Saul, 6370
1Ch 1:32 the sons of Keturah, Abraham's **c.**: 6370
1Ch 2:46 And Ephah, Caleb's **c.**, bare Haran, 6370
1Ch 2:48 Maachah, Caleb's **c.**, bare Sheber 6370
1Ch 7:14 his **c.** the Aramitess bare Machir 6370

CONCUBINES
Ge 25:6 the sons of the **c.**, which Abraham 6370
2Sa 5:13 David took him more **c.** and wives 6370
2Sa 15:16 ten women, which were **c.**, to keep 6370
2Sa 16:21 Go in unto thy father's **c.**, which 6370
2Sa 16:22 Absalom went in unto his father's **c.** 6370
2Sa 19:5 of thy wives, and the lives of thy **c.**; 6370
2Sa 20:3 the ten women his **c.**, whom he had 6370
1Ki 11:3 and three hundred **c.**: and his 6370
1Ch 3:9 beside the sons of the **c.**, and 6370
2Ch 11:21 above all his wives and his **c.**: 6370
2Ch 11:21 and threescore **c.**; and begat 6370
Es 2:14 chamberlain, which kept the **c.**: 6370
Ca 6:8 and fourscore **c.**, and virgins 6370
Ca 6:9 the queens and the **c.**, and they 6370
Da 5:2 his wives, and his **c.**, might drink 3904

Da 5:3 his wives, and his c., drank in them.... 3904
Da 5:23 and thy c., have drunk wine in 3904

CONCUPISCENCE
Ro 7:8 wrought in me all manner of c.. .... *1939*
Col 3:5 evil c., and covetousness, which *1939*
1Th 4:5 Not in the lust of c., even as the *1939*

CONDEMN See also CONDEMNED; CONDEMNEST, CONDEMNETH: CONDEMNING.
Ex 22:9 whom the judges shall c., he shall 7561
De 25:1 the righteous, and c. the wicked. 7561
Job 9:20 mine own mouth shall c. me:............ 7561
Job 10:2 Do not c. me; shew me wherefore 7561
Job 34:17 wilt thou c. him that is most just? 7561
Job 40:8 wilt thou c. me, that thou mayest....... 7561
Ps 37:33 in his hand, nor c. him when he is...... 7561
Ps 94:21 the righteous, and c. the innocent 7561
Ps 109:31 him from those that c. his soul. 8199
Pr 12:2 a man of wicked devices will he c........ 7561
Isa 50:9 who is he that shall c. me? lo, they 7561
Isa 54:17 in judgment thou shalt c.. This is 7561
Mt 12:41 and shall c. it: because they........... *2632*
Mt 12:42 and shall c. it: for she came from ... *2632*
Mt 20:18 they shall c. him to death,............ *2632*
Mk 10:33 they shall c. him to death, and *2632*
Lu 6:37 c. not, and ye shall not be *2613*
Lu 11:31 of this generation, and c. them: *2632*
Lu 11:32 with this generation, and shall c.... *2632*
Joh 3:17 Son into the world to c. the world.. *2919*
Joh 8:11 Neither do I c. thee: go, and sin..... *2632*
2Co 7:3 I speak not this to c. you: for I *2633*
1Jo 3:20 For if our heart c. us, God is............ *2607*
1Jo 3:21 if our heart c. us not, then have *2607*

CONDEMNATION
Lu 23:40 seeing thou art in the same c.?.......... *2917*
Joh 3:19 And this is the c., that light is *2920*
Joh 5:24 shall not come into c.; but is *2920*
Ro 5:16 for the judgment was by one to c.,....... *2631*
Ro 5:18 judgment came upon all men to c.; *2631*
Ro 8:1 now no c. to them which are in *2631*
1Co 11:34 ye come not together unto c.. .... *2917*
2Co 3:9 For if the administration of c. be......... *2633*
1Ti 3:6 he fall into the c. of the devil. *2917*
Jas 3:1 we shall receive the greater c.. .... *2917*
Jas 5:12 your way, nay; lest ye fall into c.. .... *5272*
Jude 4 before of old ordained to this c., ... *2917*

CONDEMNED
2Ch 36:3 and c. the land in an hundred 6064
Job 32:3 no answer, and yet had c. Job. 7561
Ps 109:7 be judged, let him be c.: 3318,7563
Am 2:8 drink the wine of the c. in the 6064
Mt 12:7 ye would not have c. the guiltless. .*2613*
Mt 12:37 and by thy words thou shalt be c.. .*2613*
Mt 27:3 when he saw that he was c.,............. *2632*
Mk 14:64 they all c. him to be guilty of death. ... *2632*
Lu 6:37 and ye shall not be c.: forgive, ... *2613*
Lu 24:20 delivered him to be c. to.......... *1519*, *2917*
Joh 3:18 believeth on him is not c.: but he .. *2919*
Joh 3:18 that believeth not is c. already, ... *2919*
Joh 8:10 hath no man c. thee?..................... *2632*
Ro 8:3 c. sin in the flesh:............................ *2632*
1Co 11:32 that we should not be c. with............. *2632*
Tit 2:8 Sound speech, that cannot be c.; *176*
Tit 3:11 and sinneth, being c. of himself. *843*
Heb 11:7 by the which he c. the world, and *2632*
Jas 5:6 Ye have c. and killed the just; *2613*
Jas 5:9 lest ye be c.: behold, the judge *2632*
2Pe 2:6 c. them with an overthrow................ *2632*

CONDEMNEST
Ro 2:1 judgest another, thou c. thyself;........... *2632*

CONDEMNETH
Job 15:6 Thine own mouth c. thee, and............ 7561
Pr 17:15 and he that c. the just, even they 7561
Ro 8:34 Who is he that c.? It is Christ *2632*
Ro 14:22 Happy is he that c. not himself *4314*

CONDEMNING
1Ki 8:32 c. the wicked, to bring his way.......... 7561
Ac 13:27 they have fulfilled them in c. him........ *2919*

CONDESCEND
Ro 12:16 but c. to men of low estate.............. *4879*

CONDITION See also CONDITIONS.
1Sa 11:2 On this c. will I make a covenant ....

CONDITIONS
Lu 14:32 and desireth c. of peace................ *4314*

CONDUCT See also CONDUCTED.
2Sa 19:15 king, to c. the king over Jordan. 5674
2Sa 14:31 the king, to c. him over Jordan. 7971
1Co 16:11 but c. him forth in peace, that he......... *4311*

CONDUCTED
2Sa 19:40 the people of Judah c. the king, ... 5674
Ac 17:15 c. Paul brought him unto Athens: *2525*

CONDUIT (con'-dit)
2Ki 18:17 stood by the c. of the upper pool, ... 8585
2Ki 20:20 he made a pool, and a c., and............ 8585
Isa 7:3 the end of the c. of the upper pool..... 8585
Isa 36:2 he stood by the c. of the upper pool... 8585

CONEY See also CONIES.
Le 11:5 c., because he cheweth the cud, ... 8227
De 14:7 camel, and the hare, and the c.: 8227

CONFECTION
Ex 30:35 c. after the art of the apothecary, ... 7545

CONFECTIONARIES
1Sa 8:13 take your daughters to be c., ... 7543

CONFEDERACY
Isa 8:12 Say ye not, A c., to all them to......... 7195
Isa 8:12 this people shall say, A c.; neither...... 7195
Ob 7 All the men of thy c. have brought 1285

CONFEDERATE
Ge 14:13 these were c. with Abram. 1167,1285
Ps 83:5 they are c. against thee: 1285,3772
Isa 7:2 Syria is c. with Ephraim. And............ 5117

CONFERENCE
Ga 2:6 in c. added nothing to me:................ *4323*

CONFERRED
1Ki 1:7 And he c. with Joab the son........ 1961,1697
Ac 4:15 they c. among themselves, ... *4820*
Ac 25:12 Then Festus, when he had c. with *4814*
Ga 1:16 I c. not with flesh and blood:............. *4323*

CONFESS See also CONFESSED; CONFESSETH; CONFESSING.
Le 5:5 he shall c. that he hath sinned........... 3034
Le 16:21 and c. over him all the iniquities........ 3034
Le 26:40 If they shall c. their iniquity, and........ 3034
Nu 5:7 c. their sin which they have done:...... 3034
1Ki 8:33 and c. thy name, and pray, and.......... 3034
1Ki 8:35 and c. thy name, and turn from 3034
2Ch 6:24 c. thy name, and pray and make 3034
2Ch 6:26 toward this place, and c. thy name, ... 3034
Ne 1:6 c. the sins of the children of Israel, ... 3034
Job 40:14 Then will I also c. unto thee that 3034
Ps 32:5 I will c. my transgressions unto 3034
Mt 10:32 shall c. me before men, him will ... *3670*
Mt 10:32 will I c. also before my Father..... *3670*
Lu 12:8 shall c. me before men, him.......... *3670*
Lu 12:8 shall the Son of man also c. *3670*
Joh 9:22 any man did c. that he was Christ, ... *3670*
Joh 12:42 the Pharisees they did not c. him, ... *3670*
Ac 23:8 but the Pharisees c. both................... *3670*
Ac 24:14 But this I c. unto thee, that after....... *3670*
Ro 10:9 c. with thy mouth the Lord Jesus, ... *3670*
Ro 14:11 and every tongue shall c. to God........ *1843*
Ro 15:9 c. to thee among the Gentiles, ... *1843*
Php 2:11 should c. that Jesus Christ is Lord,..... *1843*
Jas 5:16 C. your faults one to another, and...... *1843*
1Jo 1:9 If we c. our sins, he is faithful and *3670*
1Jo 4:15 c. that Jesus is the Son of God. *3670*
2Jo 7 who c. not that Jesus Christ is *3670*
Re 3:5 will c. his name before my Father, .*1843*

CONFESSED
Ezr 10:1 when he had c., weeping and 3034
Ne 9:2 stood and c. their sins, and the.......... 3034
Ne 9:3 another fourth part they c., and......... 3034
Joh 1:20 he c., and denied not; but................ *3670*
Joh 1:20 c., I am not the Christ...................... *3670*
Ac 19:18 and c., and showed their deeds.......... *1843*
Heb 11:13 and c. that they were strangers *3670*

CONFESSETH
Pr 28:13 c. and forsaketh them shall have 3034
1Jo 4:2 Every spirit that c. that Jesus............ *3670*
1Jo 4:3 every spirit that c. not that Jesus....... *3670*

CONFESSING
Da 9:20 praying, and c. my sin and the........... 3034
Mt 3:6 of him in Jordan, c. their sins. *1843*
Mk 1:5 in the river of Jordan, c. their sins. *1843*

CONFESSION
Jos 7:19 make c. unto him; and tell me 8426
2Ch 30:22 and making c. to the Lord God of 3034
Ezr 10:11 make c. unto the Lord God of........... 8426
Da 9:4 Lord my God, and made my c., ... 3034
Ro 10:10 mouth c. is made unto salvation; *3670*
1Ti 6:13 Pontius Pilate witnessed a good c.:...... *3671*

CONFIDENCE See also CONFIDENCES.
Jg 9:26 men of Shechem put their c. in........... 982
2Ki 18:19 c. is this wherein thou trustest? 986
Job 4:6 not this thy fear, thy c., thy hope, ... 3690
Job 18:14 His c. shall be rooted out of his......... 4009
Job 31:24 to the fine gold, Thou art my c.;........ 4009
Ps 65:5 the c. of all the ends of the earth,...... 4009
Ps 118:8 in the Lord than to put c. in man........ 982
Ps 118:9 the Lord than to put c. in princes. 982
Pr 3:26 the Lord shall be thy c., and............. 3689
Pr 14:26 the fear of the Lord is strong c.: 4009
Pr 21:22 the strength of the c. thereof. 4009
Pr 25:19 C. in an unfaithful man in time of 4009
Isa 30:15 and in c. shall be your strength: 985
Isa 36:4 c. is this wherein thou trustest? 986
Jer 48:13 was ashamed of Beth-el their c........... 4009
Eze 28:26 they shall dwell with c., when I........... 983
Eze 29:16 be no more the c. of the house 4009
Mic 7:5 a friend, put ye not c. in a guide: 982
Ac 28:31 with all c., no man forbidding *3954*
2Co 1:15 in this c. I was minded to come.......... *4006*
2Co 2:3 having c. in you all, that my joy *3982*
2Co 7:16 I have c. in you in all things. *2292*
2Co 8:22 the great c. which I have in you. *4006*
2Co 10:2 c., wherewith I think to be bold.......... *4006*
2Co 11:17 foolishly, in this c. of boasting. *5287*
Ga 5:10 have c. in you through the Lord,......... *3982*
Eph 3:12 and access with c. by the faith........... *4006*
Php 1:25 And having this c., I know that I........ *3982*
Php 3:3 and have no c. in the flesh................ *3982*
Php 3:4 might also have c. in the flesh. *4006*
2Th 3:4 have c. in the Lord touching you,........ *3982*
Phm 21 Having c. in thy obedience I wrote..... *3982*
Heb 3:6 if we hold fast the c. and the............. *3954*
Heb 3:14 if we hold the beginning of our c. *5287*
Heb 10:35 therefore your c., which hath *3954*
1Jo 2:28 we may have c., and not be................ *3954*
1Jo 3:21 then have we c. toward God. *3954*
1Jo 5:14 is the c. that we have in him,............. *3954*

CONFIDENCES
Jer 2:37 the Lord hath rejected thy c., and...... 4009

CONFIDENT
Ps 27:3 against me, in this will I be c.............. 982
Pr 14:16 but the fool rageth, and is c................ 982
Ro 2:19 c. that thou thyself art a guide........... *3982*
2Co 5:6 Therefore we are always c., ... *2292*
2Co 5:8 are c., I say, and willing rather.......... *2292*
2Co 9:4 in this same c. boasting..................... *5287*
Php 1:6 Being c. of this very thing, that......... *3982*
Php 1:14 waxing c. by my bonds, are much *3982*

CONFIDENTLY
Lu 22:59 another c. affirmed, saying, Of a *1340*

CONFIRM See also CONFIRMED; CONFIRMETH; CONFIRMING.
Ru 4:7 changing, for to c. all things;............. 6965
1Ki 1:14 in after thee, and c. thy words. 4390
2Ki 15:19 be with him to c. the kingdom........... 2388
Es 9:29 to c. this second letter of Purim. 6965
Es 9:31 To c. these days of Purim in their...... 6965
Ps 68:9 thou didst c. thine inheritance,........... 3559
Isa 35:3 and c. the feeble knees.......................553
Eze 13:6 hope that they would c. the word....... 6965
Da 9:27 And he shall c. the convenant............ 1396
Da 11:1 stood to c. and to strengthen him...... 2388
Ro 15:8 to c. the promises made unto the *950*
1Co 1:8 Who shall also c. you unto the end,...... *950*
2Co 2:8 would c. your love toward him.......... *2964*

CONFIRMATION
Php 1:7 in the defence and c. of the gospel,...... *951*
Heb 6:16 an oath for c. is to them an end of....... *951*

CONFIRMED
2Sa 7:24 thou hast c. to thyself thy people 3559
2Ki 14:5 the kingdom was c. in his hand, ... 2388
1Ch 14:2 Lord had c. him king over Israel, ... 3559

1Ch 16:17 And hath **c.** the same to Jacob.......... 5975
Es 9:32 Esther **c.** these matters of Purim;...... 6965
Ps 105:10 **c.** the same unto Jacob for a law,....... 5975
Da 9:12 And he hath **c.** his words, which........ 6965
Ac 15:32 with many words, and **c.** them........... *1991*
1Co 1:6 testimony of Christ was **c.** in you:...... *950*
Ga 3:15 a man's convenant, yet if it be **c.**,...... *2964*
Ga 3:17 that was **c.** before of God in Christ,.... *4300*
Heb 2:3 **c.** unto us by them that heard him;...... *950*
Heb 6:17 of his counsel, **c.** it by an oath:.......... *3315*

CONFIRMETH
Nu 30:14 he **c.** them, because he held his......... 6965
De 27:26 Cursed by he that **c.** not all the......... 6965
Isa 44:26 That **c.** the word of his servant,........ 6965

CONFIRMING
Mk 16:20 **c.** the word with signs following.......... *950*
Ac 14:22 **C.** the souls of the disciples, and........ *1991*
Ac 15:41 Syria and Cilicia, **c.** the churches........ *1991*

CONFISCATION
Ezr 7:26 **c.** of goods, or to imprisonment......... 6065

CONFLICT
Php 1:30 the same **c.** which ye saw in me,.......... *73*
Col 2:1 knew what great **c.** I have for you,........ *73*

CONFORMABLE
Php 3:10 being made **c.** unto his death;............ *4832*

CONFORMED
Ro 8:29 to be **c.** to the image of his Son,........ *4832*
Ro 12:2 And be not **c.** to this world: but......... *4964*

CONFOUND See also CONFOUNDED.
Ge 11:7 and there **c.** their language,............... 1101
Ge 11:9 the Lord did there **c.** the language...... 1101
Jer 1:17 faces, lest I **c.** thee before them.......... 2865
1Co 1:27 things of the world to **c.** the wise;...... *2617*
1Co 1:27 **c.** the things which are mighty;............ *2617*

CONFOUNDED
2Ki 19:26 they were dismayed and **c.**;................ 954
Job 6:20 were **c.** because they had hoped;......... 954
Ps 22:5 trusted in thee, and were not **c.**.......... 954
Ps 35:4 Let them be **c.** and put to shame.......... 954
Ps 40:14 Let them be ashamed and **c.**.............. 2659
Ps 69:6 let not those that seek thee be **c.**....... 3637
Ps 70:2 Let them be ashamed and **c.**.............. 2659
Ps 71:13 Let them be **c.** and consumed............. 954
Ps 71:24 for they are **c.**, for they are brought..... 954
Ps 83:17 Let them be **c.** and troubled for.......... 954
Ps 97:7 **C.** be all they that serve graven.......... 954
Ps 129:5 Let them all be **c.** and turned.............. 954
Isa 1:29 ye shall be **c.** for the gardens............ 2659
Isa 19:9 that weave networks, shall be **c.**......... 954
Isa 24:23 Then the moon shall be **c.**,................ 2659
Isa 37:27 they were dismayed and **c.**:................ 954
Isa 41:11 shall be ashamed and **c.**: they............ 3637
Isa 45:16 They shall be ashamed, and also **c.**,..... 3637
Isa 45:17 ye shall not be ashamed nor **c.**.......... 3637
Isa 50:7 me; therefore shall I not be **c.**:........... 3637
Isa 54:4 neither be thou **c.**; for thou shalt........ 3637
Jer 9:19 we are greatly **c.**, because we have...... 954
Jer 10:14 founder is **c.** by the graven image:...... 3001
Jer 14:3 they were ashamed and **c.**,............... 3637
Jer 15:9 she hath been ashamed and **c.**:........... 2659
Jer 17:18 them be **c.** that persecute me,............ 954
Jer 17:18 let not me be **c.**: let them be............. 954
Jer 22:22 then shalt thou be ashamed and **c.**....... 3637
Jer 31:19 I was ashamed, yea, even **c.**,............. 3637
Jer 46:24 daughter of Egypt shall be **c.**;............ 3001
Jer 48:1 Kiriathaim is **c.** and taken:................ 3001
Jer 48:1 Misgab is **c.** and dismayed................ 3001
Jer 48:20 Moab is **c.**; for it is broken down:....... 3001
Jer 49:23 Hamath is **c.**, and Arpad: for............... 954
Jer 50:2 Bel is **c.**, Merodach is broken............. 3001
Jer 50:2 her idols are **c.**, her images are.......... 3001
Jer 50:12 Your mother shall be sore **c.**;.............. 954
Jer 51:17 founder is **c.** by the graven image:...... 3001
Jer 51:47 her whole land shall be **c.**,................ 954
Jer 51:51 We are **c.**, because we have............... 954
Eze 16:52 be thou **c.** also, and bear thy shame,..... 954
Eze 16:54 and mayest be **c.** in all that thou......... 3637
Eze 16:63 thou mayest remember, and be **c.**,........ 954
Eze 36:32 be ashamed and **c.** for your own......... 3637
Mic 3:7 ashamed, and the diviners **c.**:............ 2659
Mic 7:16 The nations shall see and be **c.**........... 954
Zec 10:5 the riders on horses shall be **c.**.......... 3001
Ac 2:6 came together, and were **c.**,............. *4797*
Ac 9:22 and **c.** the Jews which dwelt at.......... *4797*
1Pe 2:6 believeth on him shall not be **c.**.......... *2617*

CONFUSED
Isa 9:5 of the warrior is with **c.** noise,.......... 7494
Ac 19:32 for the assembly was **c.**;................... *4797*

CONFUSION
Le 18:23 to lie down thereto: it is **c.**.............. 8397
Le 20:12 they have wrought **c.**; their blood....... 8397
1Sa 20:30 to thine own **c.**, and unto the **c.** of..... 1322
Ezr 9:7 and to **c.** of face, as it is this day....... 1322
Job 10:15 I am full of **c.**; therefore see............. 7036
Ps 35:4 be turned back and brought to **c.**........ 2659
Ps 35:26 be ashamed and brought to **c.**............ 2659
Ps 44:15 My **c.** is continually before me,........... 3639
Ps 70:2 and put to **c.**, that desire my hurt...... 3637
Ps 71:1 let me never be put to **c.**.................. 954
Ps 109:29 themselves with their own **c.**,............ 1322
Isa 24:10 The city of **c.** is broken down:........... 8414
Isa 30:3 in the shadow of Egypt your **c.**.......... 3639
Isa 34:11 stretch out upon it the line of **c.**,....... 8414
Isa 41:29 molten images are wind and **c.**........... 8414
Isa 45:16 they shall go to **c.** together that......... 3639
Isa 61:7 and for **c.** they shall rejoice.............. 3639
Jer 3:25 our **c.** covereth us: for we have.......... 3639
Jer 7:19 to the **c.** of their own faces?............. 1322
Jer 20:11 their everlasting **c.** shall never........... 3639
Da 9:7 but unto us **c.** of faces, as at this....... 1322
Da 9:8 Lord, to us belongeth **c.** of face,......... 1322
Ac 19:29 the whole city was filled with **c.**:........ *4799*
1Co 14:33 For God is not the author of **c.**,.......... *181*
Jas 3:16 there is **c.** and every evil work,.......... *181*

CONGEALED
Ex 15:8 the depths were **c.** in the heart of...... 7087

CONGRATULATE
1Ch 18:10 and to **c.** him, because he had........... 1288

CONGREGATION See also CONGREGATIONS.
Ex 12:3 Speak ye unto all the **c.** of Israel,....... 5712
Ex 12:6 whole assembly of the **c.** of Israel...... 5712
Ex 12:19 be cut off from the **c.** of Israel,......... 5712
Ex 12:47 All the **c.** of Israel shall keep it......... 5712
Ex 16:1 the **c.** of the children of Israel came.... 5712
Ex 16:2 And the whole **c.** of the children of..... 5712
Ex 16:9 Say unto all the **c.** of the children...... 5712
Ex 16:10 Aaron spake unto the whole **c.** of....... 5712
Ex 16:22 all the rulers of the **c.** came and........ 5712
Ex 17:1 all the **c.** of the children of Israel....... 5712
Ex 27:21 the tabernacle of the **c.** without.......... 4150
Ex 28:43 in unto the tabernacle of the **c.**,.......... 4150
Ex 29:4 door of the tabernacle of the **c.**,......... 4150
Ex 29:10 before the tabernacle of the **c.**:........... 4150
Ex 29:11 door of the tabernacle of the **c.**.......... 4150
Ex 29:30 into the tabernacle of the **c.** of........... 4150
Ex 29:32 door of the tabernacle of the **c.**.......... 4150
Ex 29:42 door of the tabernacle of the **c.** of....... 4150
Ex 29:44 sanctify the tabernacle of the **c.**,........ 4150
Ex 30:16 service of the tabernacle of the **c.**;..... 4150
Ex 30:18 between the tabernacle of the **c.**........ 4150
Ex 30:20 go into the tabernacle of the **c.**,......... 4150
Ex 30:26 anoint the tabernacle of the **c.**.......... 4150
Ex 30:36 in the tabernacle of the **c.**, where....... 4150
Ex 31:7 tabernacle of the **c.**, and the ark........ 4150
Ex 33:7 called it the Tabernacle of the **c.**........ 4150
Ex 33:7 out unto the tabernacle of the **c.**,....... 4150
Ex 34:31 all the rulers of the **c.** returned.......... 5712
Ex 35:1 And Moses gathered all the **c.** of the.. 5712
Ex 35:4 spake unto all the **c.** of the children.... 5712
Ex 35:20 **c.** of the children of Israel departed.... 5712
Ex 35:21 work of the tabernacle of the **c.**,......... 4150
Ex 38:8 door of the tabernacle of the **c.**.......... 4150
Ex 38:25 that were numbered of the **c.**............. 5712
Ex 38:30 door of the tabernacle of the **c.**,......... 4150
Ex 39:32 tabernacle of the tent of the **c.**.......... 4150
Ex 39:40 for the tent of the **c.**,..................... 4150
Ex 40:2, 6 tabernacle of the tent of the **c.**......... 4150
Ex 40:7 the tent of the **c.** and the altar,......... 4150
Ex 40:12 door of the tabernacle of the **c.**,......... 4150
Ex 40:22 the table in the tent of the **c.**,........... 4150
Ex 40:24 candlestick in the tent of the **c.**,........ 4150
Ex 40:26 the tent of the **c.** before the vail:........ 4150
Ex 40:29 tabernacle of the tent of the **c.**,......... 4150
Ex 40:30 the tent of the **c.** and the altar,......... 4150
Ex 40:32 they went into the tent of the **c.**,....... 4150
Ex 40:34 cloud covered the tent of the **c.**,........ 4150
Ex 40:35 to enter into the tent of the **c.**,......... 4150
Le 1:1 out of the tabernacle of the **c.**,.......... 4150
Le 1:3 the tabernacle of the **c.** before........... 4150
Le 1:5 door of the tabernacle of the **c.**.......... 4150
Le 3:2 door of the tabernacle of the **c.**:......... 4150
Le 3:8, 13 before the tabernacle of the **c.**:....... 4150
Le 4:4 tabernacle of the **c.** before the........... 4150
Le 4:5 it to the tabernacle of the **c.**:............. 4150
Le 4:7 is in the tabernacle of the **c.**;............. 4150
Le 4:7 door of the tabernacle of the **c.**.......... 4150
Le 4:13 And if the whole **c.** of Israel sin......... 5712
Le 4:14 the **c.** shall offer a young bullock........ 6951
Le 4:14 before the tabernacle of the **c.**.......... 4150
Le 4:15 And the elders of the **c.** shall lay........ 5712
Le 4:16 blood to the tabernacle of the **c.**:....... 4150
Le 4:18 that is in the tabernacle of the **c.**,...... 4150
Le 4:18 door of the tabernacle of the **c.**.......... 4150
Le 4:21 it is a sin offering for the **c.**.............. 6951
Le 6:16 tabernacle of the **c.** they shall eat....... 4150
Le 6:26 court of the tabernacle of the **c.**......... 4150
Le 6:30 into the tabernacle of the **c.** to.......... 4150
Le 8:3 gather thou all the **c.** together........... 5712
Le 8:3, 4 door of the tabernacle of the **c.**.......... 4150
Le 8:5 And Moses said unto the **c.**,.............. 5712
Le 8:31 door of the tabernacle of the **c.**:......... 4150
Le 8:33 tabernacle of the **c.** in seven days,...... 4150
Le 8:35 door of the tabernacle of the **c.**.......... 4150
Le 9:5 before the tabernacle of the **c.**;.......... 4150
Le 9:5 the **c.** drew near and stood before...... 5712
Le 9:23 went into the tabernacle of the **c.**,...... 4150
Le 10:7 door of the tabernacle of the **c.**,......... 4150
Le 10:9 go into the tabernacle of the **c.**,......... 4150
Le 10:17 the iniquity of the **c.**, to make........... 5712
Le 12:6 door of the tabernacle of the **c.**,......... 4150
Le 14:11 door of the tabernacle of the **c.**:......... 4150
Le 14:23 door of the tabernacle of the **c.**,......... 4150
Le 15:14 door of the tabernacle of the **c.**,......... 4150
Le 15:29 door of the tabernacle of the **c.**,......... 4150
Le 16:5 shall take of the **c.** of the children...... 5712
Le 16:7 door of the tabernacle of the **c.**.......... 4150
Le 16:16 he do for the tabernacle of the **c.**,...... 4150
Le 16:17 man in the tabernacle of the **c.**........... 4150
Le 16:17 and for all the **c.** of Israel................ 6951
Le 16:20 and the tabernacle of the **c.**,....................
Le 16:23 come into the tabernacle of the **c.**,...........
Le 16:33 for the tabernacle of the **c.**,....................
Le 16:33 and for all the people of the **c.**........... 6951
Le 17:4, 5, 6, 9 of the tabernacle of the **c.**,..... 4150
Le 19:2 Speak unto all the **c.** of the.............. 5712
Le 19:21 door of the tabernacle of the **c.**,......... 4150
Le 24:3 in the tabernacle of the **c.**, shall......... 4150
Le 24:14 and let all the **c.** stone him............... 5712
Le 24:16 the **c.** shall certainly stone him:......... 5712
Nu 1:1 Sinai, in the tabernacle of the **c.**,......... 4150
Nu 1:2 Take ye the sum of all the **c.**............ 5712
Nu 1:16 were the renowned of the **c.**,............ 5712
Nu 1:18 they assembed all the **c.** together....... 5712
Nu 1:53 there be no wrath upon the **c.**............ 5712
Nu 2:2 about the tabernacle of the **c.**............ 4150
Nu 2:17 the tabernacle of the **c.** shall set......... 4150
Nu 3:7 and the charge of the whole **c.**.......... 5712
Nu 3:7 before the tabernacle of the **c.**.......... 4150
Nu 3:8 of the tabernacle of the **c.**,................ 4150
Nu 3:25 in the tabernacle of the **c.**................ 4150
Nu 3:25 door of the tabernacle of the **c.**.......... 4150
Nu 3:38 before the tabernacle of the **c.**.......... 4150
Nu 4:3 work in the tabernacle of the **c.**.......... 4150
Nu 4:4 Kohath in the tabernacle of the **c.**,...... 4150
Nu 4:15 Kohath in the tabernacle of the **c.**....... 4150
Nu 4:23 work in the tabernacle of the **c.**.......... 4150
Nu 4:25 and the tabernacle of the **c.**,............... 4150
Nu 4:25 door of the tabernacle of the **c.**,......... 4150
Nu 4:28 in the tabernacle of the **c.**:................ 4150
Nu 4:30 work of the tabernacle of the **c.**.......... 4150
Nu 4:31 service in the tabernacle of the **c.**;..... 4150
Nu 4:33 service in the tabernacle of the **c.**,..... 4150
Nu 4:34 the chief of the **c.** numbered the........ 5712
Nu 4:35 work in the tabernacle of the **c.**:......... 4150
Nu 4:37 service in the tabernacle of the **c.**,..... 4150
Nu 4:39 work in the tabernacle of the **c.**,........ 4150
Nu 4:41 service in the tabernacle of the **c.**,..... 4150
Nu 4:43 work in the tabernacle of the **c.**,........ 4150
Nu 4:47 burden in the tabernacle of the **c.**,...... 4150
Nu 6:10, 13 door of the tabernacle of the **c.**:.... 4150
Nu 6:18 door of the tabernacle of the **c.**,......... 4150
Nu 7:5 service of the tabernacle of the **c.**;..... 4150
Nu 7:89 gone into the tabernacle of the **c.**...... 4150
Nu 8:9 before the tabernacle of the **c.**:......... 4150

Nu 8:15 service of the tabernacle of the **c.**: 4150
Nu 8:19 Israel in the tabernacle of the **c.**, ... 4150
Nu 8:20 all the **c.** of the children of Israel, ... 5712
Nu 8:22 service in the tabernacle of the **c.** 4150
Nu 8:24 service of the tabernacle of the **c.**: 4150
Nu 8:26 brethren in..tabernacle of the **c.**, ... 4150
Nu 10:3 door of the tabernacle of the **c.**.......... 4150
Nu 10:7 But when the **c.** is to be gathered...... 6951
Nu 11:16 them unto the tabernacle of the **c.**, ... 4150
Nu 12:4 three unto the tabernacle of the **c.**. 4150
Nu 13:26 all the **c.** of the children of Israel, ... 5712
Nu 13:26 and unto all the **c.**, and shewed 5712
Nu 14:1 And all the **c.** lifted up their voice, ... 5712
Nu 14:2 And the whole **c.** said unto them, ... 5712
Nu 14:5 assembly of the **c.** of the children....... 5712
Nu 14:10 all the **c.** bade stone them with.......... 5712
Nu 14:10 the tabernacle of the **c.** before all....... 4150
Nu 14:27 shall I bear with this evil **c.**,............. 5712
Nu 14:35 surely do it unto all this evil **c.**, ... 5712
Nu 14:36 made all the **c.** to murmur against 5712
Nu 15:15 shall be both for you of the **c.**, ... 6951
Nu 15:24 without the knowledge of the **c.**, ... 5712
Nu 15:24 that all the **c.** shall offer one young..... 5712
Nu 15:25 for the **c.** of the children of Israel,...... 5712
Nu 15:26 forgiven all the **c.** of the children........ 5712
Nu 15:33 and Aaron, and unto all the **c.**. 5712
Nu 15:35 the **c.** shall stone him with stones............
Nu 15:36 **c.** brought him without the camp, ... 5712
Nu 16:2 the assembly, famous in the **c.**, ... 4150
Nu 16:3 seeing all the **c.** are holy, every......... 5712
Nu 16:3 lift ye up yourselves above the **c.**........ 6951
Nu 16:9 separated you from the **c.** of Israel, ... 5712
Nu 16:9 to stand before the **c.** to minister...... 5712
Nu 16:18 door of the tabernacle of the **c.**.......... 4150
Nu 16:19 Korah gathered all the **c.** against........ 5712
Nu 16:19 door of the tabernacle of the **c.**:.......... 4150
Nu 16:19 the Lord appeared unto all the **c.**. 5712
Nu 16:21 yourselves from among this **c.**, ... 5712
Nu 16:22 thou be wroth with all the **c.**?............ 5712
Nu 16:24 Speak unto the **c.**, saying, Get you..... 5712
Nu 16:26 he spake unto the **c.**, saying, ... 5712
Nu 16:33 they perished from among the **c.**........ 6951
Nu 16:41 morrow all the **c.** of the children........ 5712
Nu 16:42 where the **c.** was gathered against...... 5712
Nu 16:42 toward the tabernacle of the **c.**: 4150
Nu 16:43 before the tabernacle of the **c.**........... 4150
Nu 16:45 Get you up from among this **c.**, ... 5712
Nu 16:46 go quickly unto the **c.**, and make......... 5712
Nu 16:47 and ran into the midst of the **c.**; 6951
Nu 16:50 door of the tabernacle of the **c.**:......... 4150
Nu 17:4 them up in the tabernacle of the **c.**...... 4150
Nu 18:4 charge of the tabernacle of the **c.**, ... 4150
Nu 18:6 service of the tabernacle of the **c.**. 4150
Nu 18:21 service of the tabernacle of the **c.**. 4150
Nu 18:22 come nigh the tabernacle of the **c.**,...... 4150
Nu 18:23 service of the tabernacle of the **c.**, ... 4150
Nu 18:31 service in the tabernacle of the **c.**. 4150
Nu 19:4 tabernacle of the **c.** seven times:........ 4150
Nu 19:9 for the **c.** of the children of Israel....... 5712
Nu 19:20 shall be cut off from among the **c.**, ... 6951
Nu 20:1 even the whole **c.**, into the desert........ 5712
Nu 20:2 And there was no water for the **c.**: 5712
Nu 20:4 have ye brought up the **c.** of the...... 6951
Nu 20:6 door of the tabernacle of the **c.**,.......... 4150
Nu 20:8 thou shalt give the **c.** and their.......... 5712
Nu 20:10 Moses and Aaron gathered the **c.**........ 6951
Nu 20:11 the **c.** drank, and their beasts............ 5712
Nu 20:12 ye shall not bring this **c.** into the........ 6951
Nu 20:22 even the whole **c.**, journeyed from 5712
Nu 20:27 mount Hor in the sight of all the **c.**...... 5712
Nu 20:29 when all the **c.** saw that Aaron 5712
Nu 25:6 in the sight of all the **c.** of the.......... 5712
Nu 25:6 door of the tabernacle of the **c.**.......... 4150
Nu 25:7 he rose up from among the **c.**, ... 5712
Nu 26:2 Take the sum of all the **c.** of the........ 5712
Nu 26:9 which were famous in the **c.**, who...... 5712
Nu 27:2 the princes and all the **c.**, ... 5712
Nu 27:2 door of the tabernacle of the **c.**,.......... 4150
Nu 27:14 in the strife of the **c.**, to sanctify........ 5712
Nu 27:16 set a man over the **c.**, ... 5712
Nu 27:17 the **c.** of the Lord be not as sheep..... 5712
Nu 27:19 and before all the **c.**; and give him...... 5712
Nu 27:20 the **c.** of the children of Israel may..... 5712
Nu 27:21 Israel with him, even all the **c.**. 5712
Nu 27:22 and before all the **c.**: 5712
Nu 31:12 unto the **c.** of the children of Israel,.... 5712
Nu 31:13 all the princes of the **c.**, went forth 5712
Nu 31:16 was a plague among the **c.** of the....... 5712
Nu 31:26 and the chief fathers of the **c.**:......... 5712
Nu 31:27 to battle, and between all the **c.**:......... 5712
Nu 31:43 half that pertained unto the **c.**............ 5712
Nu 31:54 unto the tabernacle of the **c.**, for a..... 4150
Nu 32:2 and unto the princes of the **c.**,............ 5712
Nu 32:4 before the **c.** of Israel, is a land for 5712
Nu 35:12 until he stand before the **c.** in............ 5712
Nu 35:24 **c.** shall judge between the slayer......... 5712
Nu 35:25 **c.** shall deliver the slayer out of......... 5712
Nu 35:25 the **c.** shall restore him to the city 5712
De 23:1, 2 shall not enter into the **c.** of the...... 6951
De 23:2 shall he not enter into the **c.** of the 6951
De 23:3 Moabite shall not enter into the **c.**....... 6951
De 23:3 shall they not enter into the **c.** of....... 6951
De 23:8 of them shall enter into the **c.** 6951
De 31:14 in the tabernacle of the **c.**,................. 4150
De 31:14 in the tabernacle of the **c.**................. 4150
De 31:30 spake in the ears of all the **c.** of......... 4150
De 33:4 even the inheritance of the **c.** of 6952
Jos 8:35 Joshua read not before all the **c.** 6951
Jos 9:15 the princes of the **c.** sware unto 5712
Jos 9:18 because the princes of the **c.** had....... 5712
Jos 9:18 all the **c.** murmured against the.......... 5712
Jos 9:19 all the princes said unto all the **c.**,...... 5712
Jos 9:21 drawers of water unto all the **c.**; 5712
Jos 9:27 drawers of water for the **c.**, and for.... 5712
Jos 18:1 whole **c.** of the children of Israel........ 5712
Jos 18:1 set up the tabernacle of the **c.**........... 4150
Jos 19:51 door of the tabernacle of the **c.**........... 4150
Jos 20:6 until he stand before the **c.** for 5712
Jos 20:9 until he stood before the **c.**................ 5712
Jos 22:12 **c.** of the children of Israel gathered 5712
Jos 22:16 Thus saith the whole **c.** of the Lord,... 5712
Jos 22:17 was a plague in the **c.** of the Lord,..... 5712
Jos 22:18 will be wroth with the whole **c.** of...... 5712
Jos 22:20 wrath fell on all the **c.** of Israel? 5712
Jos 22:30 the princes of the **c.** and heads of 5712
Jg 20:1 **c.** was gathered together as one 5712
Jg 21:5 came not up with the **c.** unto the 6951
Jg 21:10 **c.** sent thither twelve thousand.......... 5712
Jg 21:13 the whole **c.** sent some to speak......... 5712
Jg 21:16 elders of the **c.** said, How shall we..... 5712
1Sa 2:22 door of the tabernacle of the **c.**........... 4150
1Ki 8:4 the tabernacle of the **c.**, and all.......... 4150
1Ki 8:5 **c.** of Israel, that were assembled 5712
1Ki 8:14 blessed all the **c.** of Israel:............... 6951
1Ki 8:14 (and all the **c.** of Israel stood;)........... 6951
1Ki 8:22 in the presence of all the **c.** of........... 6951
1Ki 8:55 blessed all the **c.** of Israel with a........ 6951
1Ki 8:65 all Israel with him, a great **c.**,............ 6951
1Ki 12:3 Jeroboam and all the **c.** of Israel......... 6951
1Ki 12:20 sent and called him unto the **c.**,........... 5712
1Ch 6:32 place of the tabernacle of the **c.**.......... 4150
1Ch 9:21 door of the tabernacle of the **c.**........... 4150
1Ch 13:2 David said unto all the **c.** of 6951
1Ch 13:4 the **c.** said that they would do so: 6951
1Ch 23:32 charge of the tabernacle of the **c.**, ... 4150
1Ch 28:8 of all Israel the **c.** of the Lord, ... 6951
1Ch 29:1 the king said unto all the **c.**,.............. 6951
1Ch 29:10 blessed the Lord before all the **c.**:........ 6951
1Ch 29:20 David said to all the **c.**, Now bless 6951
1Ch 29:20 all the **c.** blessed the Lord God........... 6951
2Ch 1:3 Solomon, and all the **c.** with him, ... 6951
2Ch 1:3 there was the tabernacle of the **c.**....... 4150
2Ch 1:5 Solomon and the **c.** sought unto it. 6951
2Ch 1:6 was at the tabernacle at the **c.**, ... 4150
2Ch 1:13 before the tabernacle of the **c.**,........... 4150
2Ch 5:5 ark, and the tabernacle of the **c.**, ... 4150
2Ch 5:6 **c.** of Israel that were assembled 5712
2Ch 6:3 blessed the whole **c.** of Israel:........... 6951
2Ch 6:3 and all the **c.** of Israel stood. 6951
2Ch 6:12 the presence of all the **c.** of Israel,..... 6951
2Ch 6:13 upon his knees before all the **c.** of...... 6951
2Ch 7:8 Israel with him, a very great **c.**, ... 6951
2Ch 20:5 stood in the **c.** of Judah and 6951
2Ch 20:14 of the Lord in the midst of the **c.**;...... 6951
2Ch 23:3 all the **c.** made a covenant with.......... 6951
2Ch 24:6 and of the **c.** of Israel, for the 6951
2Ch 28:14 before the princes and all the **c.**......... 6951
2Ch 29:23 offering before the king and the **c.**;..... 6951
2Ch 29:28 all the **c.** worshipped, and the............ 6951
2Ch 29:31 the **c.** brought in sacrifices and 6951
2Ch 29:32 burnt offerings, which the **c.** brought, ..6951
2Ch 30:2 all the **c.** in Jerusalem, to keep 6951
2Ch 30:4 pleased the king and all the **c.**. 6951
2Ch 30:13 the second month, a very great **c.**...... 6951
2Ch 30:17 there were many in the **c.** that.......... 6951
2Ch 30:24 give to the **c.** a thousand bullocks....... 6951
2Ch 30:24 princes gave to the **c.** a thousand....... 6951
2Ch 30:25 all the **c.** of Judah, with the priests 6951
2Ch 30:25 all the **c.** that came out of Israel, ... 6951
2Ch 31:18 their daughters, through all the **c.**: 6951
Ezr 2:64 whole **c.** together was forty and two... 6951
Ezr 10:1 a very great **c.** of men and women..... 6951
Ezr 10:8 himself separated from the **c.** of......... 6951
Ezr 10:12 Then all the **c.** answered and said 6951
Ezr 10:14 now our rulers of all the **c.** stand, ... 6951
Ne 5:13 all the **c.** said, Amen, and praised....... 6951
Ne 7:66 whole **c.** together was forty and two... 6951
Ne 8:2 brought the law before the **c.** both 6951
Ne 8:17 all the **c.** of them that were come 6951
Ne 13:1 not come into the **c.** of God............. 6951
Job 15:34 **c.** of hypocrites shall be desolate,....... 5712
Job 30:28 I stood up, and I cried in the **c.**........ 6951
Ps 1:5 sinners in the **c.** of the righteous......... 5712
Ps 7:7 shall the **c.** of the people compass...... 5712
Ps 22:22 midst of the **c.** will I praise thee. 6951
Ps 22:25 shall be of thee in the great **c.**........... 6951
Ps 26:5 have hated the **c.** of evil doers; 6951
Ps 35:18 give thee thanks in the great **c.** 6951
Ps 40:9 righteousness in the great **c.**............. 6951
Ps 40:10 and thy truth from the great **c.**........... 6951
Ps 58:1 speak righteousness, O **c.**?................. 482
Ps 68:10 Thy **c.** hath dwelt therein: thou, ... 2416
Ps 74:2 Remember thy **c.**, which thou hast..... 5712
Ps 74:19 forget not the **c.** of thy poor 2416
Ps 75:2 When I shall receive the **c.** I will........ 4150
Ps 82:1 God standeth in the **c.** of the............ 5712
Ps 89:5 faithfulness also in the **c.** of the 6951
Ps 107:32 him also in the **c.** of the people,......... 6951
Ps 111:1 of the upright, and in the **c.**. 5712
Ps 149:1 and his praise in the **c.** of saints......... 6951
Pr 5:14 in all evil in the midst of the **c.**........... 6951
Pr 21:16 shall remain in the **c.** of the dead. 6951
Pr 26:26 be shewed before the whole **c.**.......... 6951
Isa 14:13 sit also upon the mount of the **c.**,........ 4150
Jer 6:18 know, O **c.**, what is among them. 5712
Jer 30:20 and their **c.** shall be established 5712
La 1:10 they should not enter into thy **c.**........ 6951
Ho 7:12 chastise them, as their **c.** hath........... 5712
Joe 2:16 Gather the people, sanctify the **c.**,...... 6951
Mic 2:5 a cord by lot in the **c.** of the Lord,..... 6951
Ac 13:43 Now when the **c.** was broken up,....... *4864*

CONGREGATIONS
Ps 26:12 in the **c.** will I bless the Lord. 4721
Ps 68:26 Bless ye God in the **c.**, even the 4721
Ps 74:4 roar in the midst of thy **c.**; 4150

CONIAH (co-ni'-ah) See also JEHOIACHIN.
Jer 22:24 though **C.** the son of Jehoiakim.......... 3659
Jer 22:28 this man **C.** a despised broken idol?.... 3659
Jer 37:1 son of Josiah reigned instead of **C.**...... 3659

CONIES
Ps 104:18 goats; and the rocks for the **c.**. 8227
Pr 30:26 The **c.** are but a feeble folk, yet 8227

CONONIAH (co-no-ni'-ah) See also CONANIAH.
2Ch 31:12 over which **C.** the Levite was ruler, ... 3562
2Ch 31:13 overseers under the hand of **C.** 3562

CONQUER See also CONQUERING.
Re 6:2 went forth conquering, and to **c.**. *3528*

CONQUERING
Re 6:2 he went forth **c.**, and to conquer........ *3528*

CONQUERORS
Ro 8:37 we are more than **c.** through him....... *5245*

CONSCIENCE See also CONSCIENCES.
Joh 8:9 being convicted by their own **c.**, ... *4893*
Ac 23:1 have lived in all good **c.** before God.... *4893*
Ac 24:16 to have always a **c.** void of offence..... *4893*
Ro 2:15 their **c.** also bearing witness, and....... *4893*
Ro 9:1 my **c.** also bearing me witness.......... *4893*
Ro 13:5 for wrath, but also for **c.** sake. *4893*
1Co 8:7 for some with **c.** of the idol unto......... *4893*
1Co 8:7 and their **c.** being weak is defiled. *4893*
1Co 8:10 shall not the **c.** of him which is weak .. *4893*
1Co 8:12 and wound their weak **c.**, ye sin *4893*
1Co 10:25 eat, asking no question for **c.** sake: *4893*
1Co 10:27 eat, asking no question for **c.** sake. *4893*
1Co 10:28 sake that showed it, and for **c.** sake: .. *4893*
1Co 10:29 **C.**, I say, not thine own, but of the.... *4893*
1Co 10:29 liberty judged of another man's **c.**? *4893*

2Co 1:12 is this, the testimony of our **c.**, ... *4893*
2Co 4:2 ourselves to every man's **c.** in the......... *4893*
1Ti 1:5 a good **c.**, and of faith unfeigned: *4893*
1Ti 1:19 Holding faith, and a good **c.**;............. *4893*
1Ti 3:9 mystery of the faith in a pure **c.**. *4893*
1Ti 4:2 their **c.** seared with a hot iron; *4893*
2Ti 1:3 from my forefathers with pure **c.**,....... *4893*
Tit 1:15 even their mind and **c.** is defiled. *4893*
Heb 9:9 perfect, as pertaining to the **c.**;........... *4893*
Heb 9:14 purge your **c.** from dead works.......... *4893*
Heb 10:2 should have had no more **c.** of sins..... *4893*
Heb 10:22 hearts sprinkled from an evil **c.**,......... *4893*
Heb 13:18 we trust we have a good **c.**, ... *4893*
1Pe 2:19 if a man for **c.** toward God endure...... *4893*
1Pe 3:16 Having a good **c.**; that whereas.......... *4893*
1Pe 3:21 answer of a good **c.** toward God.) *4893*

CONSCIENCES
2Co 5:11 also are made manifest in your **c.**....... *4893*

CONSECRATE See also CONSECRATED.
Ex 28:3 make Aaron's garments to **c.** him, ... 6942
Ex 28:41 anoint them, and **c.** them,.......... 4390,3027
Ex 29:9 shalt **c.** Aaron and his sons. 3027
Ex 29:33 to **c.** and to sanctify them: 3027
Ex 29:35 seven days shalt thou **c.** them. 3027
Ex 30:30 Aaron and his sons, and **c.** them, ... 6942
Ex 32:39 **C.** yourselves to day to the 4390,3027
Le 8:33 for seven days shall he **c.** you. 3027
Le 16:32 he shall **c.** to minister in.................. 3027
Nu 6:12 And he shall **c.** unto the Lord the........ 5144
1Ch 29:5 **c.** his service this day unto........ 4390,3027
2Ch 13:9 to **c.** himself with a young................. 3027
Eze 43:26 and they shall **c.** themselves............... 3027
Mic 4:13 and I will **c.** their gain unto the.......... 2763

CONSECRATED
Ex 29:29 anointed therein, and to be **c.**..... 4390,3027
Le 21:10 and that is **c.** to put on the.............. 3027
Nu 3:3 whom he **c.** to minister in the........... 3027
Jos 6:19 of brass and iron, are **c.** unto the....... 6944
Jg 17:5 and **c.** one of his sons,............. 4390,3027
Jg 17:12 And Micah **c.** the Levite;.................. 3027
1Ki 13:33 he **c.** him, and he became one............ 3027
2Ch 26:18 Aaron, that are **c.** to burn incense:...... 6942
2Ch 29:31 have **c.** yourselves unto the 4390,3027
2Ch 29:33 the **c.** things were six hundred 6942
2Ch 31:6 which were **c.** unto the Lord their...... 6942
Ezr 3:5 set feasts of the Lord that were **c.**,.... 6942
Heb 7:28 the Son, who is **c.** for evermore. *5048*
Heb 10:20 way, which he hath **c.** for us, ... *1457*

CONSECRATION See also CONSECRATIONS.
Ex 29:22 for it is a ram of **c.**: 4394
Ex 29:26 breast of the ram of Aaron's **c.**,......... 4394
Ex 29:27 of the ram of the **c.**, even of that....... 4394
Ex 29:31 thou shalt take the ram of the **c.**,....... 4394
Le 8:22 the other ram, the ram of **c.**: 4394
Le 8:29 of the ram of **c.** it was Moses' part; ... 4394
Le 8:33 until the days of your **c.** be at an 4394
Nu 6:7 because the **c.** of his God is upon....... 5145
Nu 6:9 he hath defiled the head of his **c.**; 5145

CONSECRATIONS
Ex 29:34 And if ought of the flesh of the **c.**, ... 4394
Le 7:37 and of the **c.**, and of the sacrifice....... 4394
Le 8:28 they were **c.** for a sweet savour: 4394
Le 8:31 bread that is in the basket of **c.**. 4394

CONSENT See also CONSENTED; CONSENTING.
Ge 34:15 But in this will we **c.** unto you: 225
Ge 34:22 Only herein will the men **c.** unto us...... 225
Ge 34:23 only let us **c.** unto them, and they 225
De 13:8 Thou shalt not **c.** unto him,................. 14
Jg 11:17 but he would not **c.**:.......................... 14
1Sa 11:7 and they came out with one **c.**. 376
1Ki 20:8 him, Hearken not unto him, nor **c.**. 14
Ps 83:5 consulted together with one **c.**:.......... 3820
Pr 1:10 if sinners entice thee, **c.** thou not......... 14
Ho 6:9 priests murder in the way by **c.**: 7926
Zep 3:9 the Lord, to serve him with one **c.**...... 7926
Lu 14:18 **with one c. began to make excuse.** ......
Ro 7:16 I **c.** unto the law that it is good. *4852*
1Co 7:5 except it be with **c.** for a time, ... *4859*
1Ti 6:3 and **c.** not to wholesome words, ... *4334*

CONSENTED See also CONSENTEDST.
2Ki 12:8 the priests **c.** to receive no more......... 225
Da 1:14 So he **c.** to them in this matter,......... 8085
Lu 23:51 same had not **c.** to the counsel and..... *4784*
Ac 18:20 longer time with them, he **c.** not;....... *1962*

CONSENTEDST
Ps 50:18 then thou **c.** with him, and hast 7521

CONSENTING
Ac 8:1 And Saul was **c.** unto his death. *4909*
Ac 22:20 standing by, and **c.** unto his death, ... *4909*

CONSIDER See also CONSIDERED; CONSIDEREST; CONSIDERETH CONSIDERING.
Ex 33:13 and **c.** that this nation is thy............. 7200
Le 13:13 Then the priest shall **c.**; and, ... 7200
De 4:39 Know therefore this day, and **c.**.......... 7725
De 8:5 Thou shalt also **c.** in thine heart,........ 3045
De 32:7 **c.** the years of many generations: 995
De 32:29 that they would **c.** their latter end!....... 995
Jg 18:14 now therefore **c.** what ye have to....... 3045
Jg 19:30 **c.** of it, take advice, and speak 7760
1Sa 12:24 for **c.** how great things he hath.......... 7200
1Sa 25:17 therefore know and **c.** what thou........ 7200
2Ki 5:7 wherefore **c.**, I pray you, and see 3045
Job 11:11 wickedness also; will he not then **c.** 995
Job 23:15 when I **c.**, I am afraid of him. 995
Job 34:27 and would not **c.** any of his ways. 7919
Job 37:14 and **c.** the wondrous works of God....... 995
Ps 5:1 O Lord, **c.** my meditation.................... 995
Ps 8:3 When I **c.** thy heavens, the work 7200
Ps 9:13 **c.** my trouble which I suffer of 7200
Ps 13:3 **C.** and hear me, O Lord my God: 5027
Ps 25:19 **C.** mine enemies; for they are 7200
Ps 37:10 thou shalt diligently **c.** his place, ... 995
Ps 45:10 Hearken, O daughter, and **c.**,............. 7200
Ps 48:13 well her bulwarks, **c.** her palaces; 6448
Ps 50:22 Now **c.** this, ye that forget God, ... 995
Ps 64:9 they shall wisely **c.** of his doing. 7919
Ps 119:95 I will **c.** thy testimonies. 995
Ps 119:153 **C.** mine affliction, and deliver me: 7200
Ps 119:159 **C.** how I love thy precepts: 7200
Pr 6:6 the ant, thou sluggard; **c.** her ways, ... 7200
Pr 23:1 **c.** diligently what is before thee:.......... 995
Pr 24:12 he that pondereth the heart **c.** it? 995
Ec 5:1 for they **c.** not that they do evil. 3045
Ec 7:13 **C.** the work of God: for who............. 7200
Ec 7:14 in the day of adversity **c.**: God also 7200
Isa 1:3 not know, my people doth not **c.**. 995
Isa 5:12 neither **c.** the operation of his............ 7200
Isa 14:16 narrowly look upon thee, and **c.** thee.... 995
Isa 18:4 I will **c.** in my dwelling place 5027
Isa 41:20 they may see, and know, and **c.**, ... 7760
Isa 41:22 that we may **c.** them, and.......... 7760,3820
Isa 43:18 neither **c.** the things of old. 995
Isa 52:15 they had not heard shall they **c.**. 995
Jer 2:10 and **c.** diligently, and see if there 995
Jer 9:17 **C.** ye, and call for the mourning 995
Jer 23:20 in the latter days ye shall **c.** it............ 995
Jer 30:24 in the latter days ye shall **c.** it............ 995
La 1:11 see, O Lord, and **c.**; for I am............ 5027
La 2:20 Behold, O Lord, and **c.** to whom........ 5027
La 5:1 **c.**, and behold our reproach. 5027
Eze 12:3 may be they will **c.**, though they........ 7200
Da 9:23 the matter, and **c.** the vision............... 995
Ho 7:2 they **c.** not in their hearts that I.......... 559
Hag 1:5, 7 hosts; **C.** your ways. 7760,3820,5921
Hag 2:15 **c.** from this day and upward,...... 7760,3820
Hag 2:18 **C.** now from this day and 3820
Hag 2:18 Lord's temple was laid, **c.** it.............. 3820
Mt 6:28 **C. the lilies of the field, how they**. *2648*
Lu 12:24 **C. the ravens: for they neither** *2657*
Lu 12:27 **C. the lilies how they grow: they**... *2657*
Joh 11:50 Nor **c.** that it is expedient for us,........ *1260*
Ac 15:6 came together for to **c.** of this.......... *1492*
2Ti 2:7 **C.** what I say; and the Lord give *3539*
Heb 3:1 **c.** the Apostle and High Priest........... *2657*
Heb 7:4 Now **c.** how great this man was,........ *2334*
Heb 10:24 let us **c.** one another to provoke *2657*
Heb 12:3 For **c.** him that endured such.............. *357*

CONSIDERED
1Ki 3:21 but when I had **c.** it in the morning, ... 995
1Ki 5:8 I have **c.** the things which thou.......... 8085
Job 1:8 Hast thou **c.** my servant Job, ... 7760,3820
Job 2:3 Hast thou **c.** my servant Job, ... 3820
Ps 31:7 thou hast **c.** my trouble; thou 7200
Ps 77:5 have **c.** the days of old, the years 2803
Pr 24:32 I saw, and **c.** it well: I looked..... 7896,3820
Ec 4:1 and **c.** all the oppressions that 7200
Ec 4:4 Again, I **c.** all travail, and every 7200
Ec 4:15 I **c.** all the living which walk............. 7200
Ec 9:1 I **c.** in my heart even to declare......... 5414
Da 7:8 I **c.** the horns, and, behold, there....... 7920
Mk 6:52 For they **c.** not the miracle of the *4920*
Ac 11:6 I **c.**, and saw fourfooted beasts.......... *2657*
Ac 12:12 And when he had **c.** the thing,........... *4894*
Ro 4:19 he **c.** not his own body now dead, ... *2657*

CONSIDEREST
Jer 33:24 **C.** thou not what this people have 7200
Mt 7:3 **but c. not the beam that is in** *2657*

CONSIDERETH
Ps 33:15 hearts alike; he **c.** all their works......... 995
Ps 41:1 Blessed is he that **c.** the poor: 7919
Pr 21:12 wisely **c.** the house of the wicked:...... 7919
Pr 28:22 **c.** not that poverty shall come 3045
Pr 29:7 The righteous **c.** the cause of the....... 3045
Pr 31:16 She **c.** a field, and buyeth it: 2161
Isa 44:19 none **c.** in his heart, neither is........... 7725
Eze 18:14 and **c.**, and doeth not such like, ... 7200
Eze 18:28 Because he **c.**, and turneth away........ 7200

CONSIDERING
Isa 57:1 none **c.** that the righteous is taken....... 995
Da 8:5 I was **c.**, behold, an he goat came 995
Ga 6:1 **c.** thyself, lest thou also be.............. *4648*
Heb 13:7 **c.** the end of their conversation. *333*

CONSIST See also CONSISTETH.
Col 1:17 things, and by him all things **c.**. *4921*

CONSISTETH
Lu 12:15 **man's life c. not in the abundance** .*2076*

CONSOLATION See also CONSOLATIONS.
Jer 16:7 give them the cup of **c.** to drink........ 8575
Lu 2:25 waiting for the **c.** of Israel: *3874*
Lu 6:24 **for ye have received your c.**. *3874*
Ac 4:36 being interpreted, The son of **c.**,)....... *3874*
Ac 15:31 had read, they rejoiced for the **c.**. *3874*
Ro 15:5 the God of patience and **c.** grant *3874*
2Co 1:5 in us, so our **c.** also aboundeth *3874*
2Co 1:6 it is for your **c.** and salvation,............ *3874*
2Co 1:6 we be comforted, it is for your **c.** *3874*
2Co 1:7 so shall ye be also of the **c.**. *3874*
2Co 7:7 but by the **c.** wherewith he was.......... *3874*
Php 2:1 any **c.** in Christ, if any comfort *3874*
2Th 2:16 given us everlasting **c.** and good *3874*
Phm 7 we have great joy and **c.** in thy *3874*
Heb 6:18 we might have a strong **c.**, who......... *3874*

CONSOLATIONS
Job 15:11 Are the **c.** of God small with thee? 8575
Job 21:2 my speech, and let this be your **c.**. 8575
Isa 66:11 satisfied with the breasts of her **c.**;..... 8575

CONSORTED
Ac 17:4 believed, and **c.** with Paul and *4345*

CONSPIRACY
2Sa 15:12 the **c.** was strong; for the people 7195
2Ki 12:20 servants arose, and made a **c.**, and..... 7195
2Ki 14:19 Now they made a **c.** against............. 7195
2Ki 15:15 acts of Shallum, and his **c.** 7195
2Ki 15:30 the son of Elah made a **c.**................. 7195
2Ki 17:4 the king of Assyria found **c.** in........... 7195
2Ch 25:27 they made a **c.** against him 7195
Jer 11:9 the Lord said unto me, A **c.** is........... 7195
Eze 22:25 There is a **c.** of her prophets in the.... 7195
Ac 23:13 than forty which had made this **c.**....... *4945*

CONSPIRATORS
2Sa 15:31 Ahithophel is among the **c.** with......... 7194

CONSPIRED
Ge 37:18 they **c.** against him to slay him. 5230
1Sa 22:8 all of you have **c.** against me, and 7194
1Sa 22:13 Why have ye **c.** against me, thou 7194
1Ki 15:27 **c.** against him; and Baasha smote....... 7194
1Ki 16:9 **c.** against him, as he was in Tirzah..... 7194
1Ki 16:16 Zimri hath **c.**, and hath also slain......... 7194
2Ki 9:14 Jehoshaphat the son of Nimshi **c.**....... 7194
2Ki 10:9 I **c.** against my master, and slew........ 7194
2Ki 15:10 And Shallum the son of Jabesh **c.** 7194
2Ki 15:25 **c.** against him, and smote him in......... 7194
2Ki 21:23 And the servants of Amon **c.**............ 7194
2Ki 21:24 that had **c.** against king Amon;............ 7194
2Ch 24:21 And they **c.** against him, and............ 7194
2Ch 24:25 his own servants **c.** against him for..... 7194
2Ch 24:26 And these are they that **c.** against...... 7194
2Ch 33:24 And his servants **c.** against him,......... 7194

2Ch 33:25 slew all them that had **c.** against 7194
Ne 4:8 **c.** all of them together to come 7194
Am 7:10 Amos hath **c.** against thee in the 7194

CONSTANT
1Ch 28:7 he be **c.** to do my commandments 2388

CONSTANTLY
Pr 21:28 man that heareth speaketh **c.** 5331
Ac 12:15 she **c.** affirmed that it was even *1340*
Tit 3:8 things I will that thou affirm **c.**, *1226*

CONSTELLATIONS
Isa 13:10 stars of heaven and the **c.** thereof 3685

CONSTRAIN See also CONSTRAINED; CONSTRAINETH.
Ga 6:12 they **c.** you to be circumcised; *315*

CONSTRAINED
2Ki 4:8 she **c.** him to eat bread. And so 2388
Mt 14:22 Jesus **c.** his disciples to get into a *315*
Mk 6:45 straightway he **c.** his disciples to *315*
Lu 24:29 But they **c.** him, saying, Abide *3849*
Ac 16:15 And she **c.** us. *3849*
Ac 28:19 I was **c.** to appeal unto Caesar; *315*

CONSTRAINETH
Job 32:18 the spirit within me **c.** me 6693
2Co 5:14 the love of Christ **c.** us; because *4912*

CONSTRAINT
1Pe 5:2 thereof, not by **c.**, but willingly; *317*

CONSULT See also CONSULTED; CONSULTETH.
Ps 62:4 They only **c.** to cast him down 3289

CONSULTATION
Mk 15:1 priests held a **c.** with the elders *4824*

CONSULTED
1Ki 12:6 Rehoboam **c.** with the old men, 3289
1Ki 12:8 and **c.** with the young men that 3289
1Ch 13:1 And David **c.** with the captains of 3289
2Ch 20:21 when he had **c.** with the people, 3289
Ne 5:7 Then I **c.** with myself, and I 4427
Ps 83:3 and **c.** against thy hidden ones. 3289
Ps 83:5 have **c.** together with one consent: 3289
Eze 21:21 he **c.** with images, he looked in 7592
Da 6:7 have **c.** together to establish a 3272
Mic 6:5 now what Balak, king of Moab **c.**, 3289
Hab 2:10 Thou hast **c.** shame to thy house 3289
Mt 26:4 **c.** that they might take Jesus by *4823*
Joh 12:10 the chief priests **c.** that they *1011*

CONSULTER
De 18:11 or a **c.** with familiar spirits, or a 7592

CONSULTETH
Lu 14:31 **c. whether he be able with ten** *1011*

CONSUME See also CONSUMED, CONSUMETH; CONSUMING.
Ge 41:30 and the famine shall **c.** the land; 3615
Ex 32:10 that I may **c.** them; and I will 3615
Ex 32:12 **c.** them from the face of the earth? 3615
Ex 33:3 people: lest I **c.** thee in the way. 3615
Ex 33:5 in a moment, and **c.** thee: therefore 3615
Le 26:16 that shall **c.** the eyes, and cause 3615
Nu 16:21 that I may **c.** them in a moment. 3615
Nu 16:45 that I may **c.** them as in a moment. 3615
De 5:25 this great fire will **c.** us: if we 398
De 7:16 And thou shalt **c.** all the people 398
De 7:22 thou mayest not **c.** them at once, 3615
De 28:38 for the locust shall **c.** it. 2628
De 28:42 of thy land shall the locust **c.** 3423
De 32:22 and shall **c.** the earth with her 398
Jos 24:20 turn and do you hurt, and **c.** you, 3615
1Sa 2:33 to **c.** thine eyes, and to grieve thine 3615
2Ki 1:10, 12 heaven, and **c.** thee and thy fifty. 398
Ne 9:31 thou didst not utterly **c.** them, 3615
Es 9:24 to **c.** them, and to destroy them; 2000
Job 15:34 shall **c.** the tabernacles of bribery. 398
Job 20:26 a fire not blown shall **c.** him; it 398
Job 24:19 and heat **c.** the snow waters: 1497
Ps 37:20 **c.**; into smoke shall they **c.** away. 3615
Ps 39:11 thou makest his beauty to **c.** away 4529
Ps 49:14 their beauty shall **c.** in the grave 1086
Ps 59:13 **C.** them in wrath, **c.** them, that 3615
Ps 78:33 their days did he **c.** in vanity, 3615
Isa 7:20 and it shall also **c.** the beard. 5595
Isa 10:18 shall **c.** the glory of his forest, 3615
Isa 27:10 down, and **c.** the branches thereof. 3615
Jer 8:13 surely **c.** them, saith the Lord: 5486
Jer 14:12 I will **c.** them by the sword, and 3615
Jer 49:27 shall **c.** the palaces of Ben-hadad. 398
Eze 4:17 and **c.** away for their iniquity. 4743
Eze 13:13 hailstones in my fury to **c.** it. 3615
Eze 20:13 them in the wilderness, to **c.** them. 3615
Eze 21:28 to **c.** because of the glittering: 398
Eze 22:15 will **c.** thy filthiness out of thee. 8552
Eze 24:10 kindle the fire, **c.** the flesh, and 8552
Eze 35:12 desolate, they are given us to **c.**, 402
Da 2:44 and **c.** all these kingdoms, and it 5487
Da 7:26 **c.** and to destroy it unto the end. 8046
Ho 11:6 and shall **c.** his branches, and 3615
Zep 1:2 **c.** all things from off the land, 5486
Zep 1:3 I will **c.** man and beast; 5486
Zep 1:3 I will **c.** the fowls of heaven, 5486
Zec 5:4 and shall **c.** it with the timber 3615
Zec 14:12 Their flesh shall **c.** away 4743
Zec 14:12 eyes shall **c.** away in their holes, 4743
Zec 14:12 and their tongue shall **c.** away in 4743
Lu 9:54 down from heaven, and **c.** them, *355*
2Th 2:8 the Lord shall **c.** with the spirit *355*
Jas 4:3 that ye may **c.** it upon your lusts. *1159*

CONSUMED
Ge 19:15 lest thou be **c.** in the iniquity of 5595
Ge 19:17 to the mountain, lest thou be **c.** 5595
Ge 31:40 in the day the drought **c.** me, and 398
Ex 3:2 with fire, and the bush was not **c.** 398
Ex 15:7 wrath, which **c.** them as stubble. 398
Ex 22:6 standing corn, or the field, be **c.** 398
Le 6:10 which the fire hath **c.** with the 398
Le 9:24 and **c.** upon the altar the burnt 398
Nu 11:1 and **c.** them that were in the 398
Nu 12:12 the flesh is half **c.** when he cometh 398
Nu 14:35 in this wilderness they shall be **c.** 8552
Nu 16:26 lest ye be **c.** in all their sins. 5595
Nu 16:35 **c.** the two hundred and fifty men 398
Nu 17:13 shall we be **c.** with dying? 8552
Nu 21:28 hath **c.** Ar of Moab, and the lords 398
Nu 25:11 I **c.** not the children of Israel in 3615
Nu 32:13 in the sight of the Lord, was **c.** 8552
De 2:15 among the host, until they were **c.** 8552
De 2:16 when all the men of war were **c.** 8552
De 28:21 he have **c.** thee from off the land, 3615
Jos 5:6 which came out of Egypt, were **c.** 8552
Jos 8:24 of the sword, until they were **c.**, 8552
Jos 10:20 great slaughter, till they were **c.**, 8552
Jg 6:21 and **c.** the flesh and the unleavened 398
1Sa 12:25 ye shall be **c.**, both ye and your 5595
1Sa 15:18 fight against them until they be **c.** 3615
2Sa 21:5 The man that **c.** us, and that 3615
2Sa 22:38 not again until I had **c.** them. 3615
2Sa 22:39 I have **c.** them, and wounded them, 3615
1Ki 18:38 and **c.** the burnt sacrifice, and the 398
1Ki 22:11 Syrians, until thou have **c.** them. 3615
2Ki 1:10 heaven, and **c.** him and his fifty. 398
2Ki 1:12 God came down from heaven, and **c.** 398
2Ki 7:13 of the Israelites that are **c.**:) 8552
2Ki 13:17 Syrians in Aphek, till thou have **c.** 3615
2Ki 13:19 smitten Syria till thou hadst **c.** it: 3615
2Ch 7:1 and **c.** the burnt offering and the 398
2Ch 8:8 whom the children of Israel **c.** not, 3615
2Ch 18:10 shalt push Syria until they be **c.** 3615
Ezr 9:14 till thou hadst **c.** us, so that 3615
Ne 2:3 the gates thereof are **c.** with fire? 398
Ne 2:13 the gates thereof were **c.** with fire. 398
Job 1:16 sheep, and the servants, and **c.** them; 398
Job 4:9 breath of his nostrils are they **c.** 3615
Job 6:17 hot, they are **c.** out of their place. 1846
Job 7:9 cloud is **c.** and vanisheth away: 3615
Job 19:27 though my reins be **c.** within me. 3615
Job 33:21 His flesh is **c.** away, that it cannot 3615
Ps 6:7 Mine eye is **c.** because of grief: 6244
Ps 18:37 did I turn again till they were **c.** 3615
Ps 31:9 mine eye is **c.** with grief, yea, 6244
Ps 31:10 iniquity, and my bones are **c.** 6244
Ps 39:10 I am **c.** by the blow of thine hand. 3615
Ps 71:13 Let them be confounded and **c.** 3615
Ps 73:19 they are utterly **c.** with terrors. 8552
Ps 78:63 The fire **c.** their young men; and 398
Ps 90:7 we are **c.** by thine anger, and 3615
Ps 102:3 For my days are **c.** like smoke, 3615
Ps 104:35 Let the sinners be **c.** out of the 8552
Ps 119:87 They had almost **c.** me upon 3615
Ps 119:139 My zeal hath **c.** me, because mine 6789
Pr 5:11 thy flesh and thy body are **c.**, 3615
Isa 1:28 that forsake the Lord shall be **c.** 3615
Isa 16:4 the oppressors are **c.** out of the 8552
Isa 29:20 scorner is **c.**, and all that watch 3615
Isa 64:7 **c.** us, because of our iniquities 4127
Isa 66:17 shall be **c.** together, saith the 5486
Jer 5:3 thou hast **c.** them, but they have 3615
Jer 6:29 the lead is **c.** of the fire; the 8552
Jer 9:16 after them, till I have **c.** them. 3615
Jer 10:25 devoured him, and **c.** him, and 3615
Jer 12:4 the beasts are **c.**, and the birds; 5595
Jer 14:15 famine shall those prophets be **c.** 8552
Jer 16:4 they shall be **c.** by the sword, and 3615
Jer 20:18 my days should be **c.** with shame? 3615
Jer 24:10 till they be **c.** from off the land 8552
Jer 27:8 until I have **c.** them by his hand. 8552
Jer 36:23 until all the roll was **c.** in the fire 8552
Jer 44:12 and they shall all be **c.**, and fall 8552
Jer 44:12 they shall even be **c.** by the sword 8552
Jer 44:18 have been **c.** by the sword and by 8552
Jer 44:27 are in the land of Egypt shall be **c.** 8552
Jer 49:37 after them, till I have **c.** them: 3615
La 2:22 brought up hath mine enemy **c.** 3615
La 3:22 Lord's mercies that we are not **c.**, 8552
Eze 5:12 with famine shall they be **c.** in the 3615
Eze 13:14 ye shall be **c.** in the midst thereof: 3615
Eze 19:12 and withered; the fire **c.** them. 398
Eze 22:31 I have **c.** them with the fire of my 3615
Eze 24:11 that the scum of it may be **c.** 8552
Eze 34:29 be no more **c.** with hunger in the 622
Eze 43:8 wherefore I have **c.** them in mine 398
Eze 47:12 shall the fruit thereof be **c.**: 8552
Da 11:16 which by his hand shall be **c.** 3615
Mal 3:6 ye sons of Jacob are not **c.** 3615
Ga 5:15 take heed that ye be not **c.** one of *355*

CONSUMETH
Job 13:28 he, as a rotten thing, **c.**, as a 1086
Job 22:20 the remnant of them the fire **c.** 398
Job 31:12 it is a fire that **c.** to destruction, 398
Isa 5:24 flame **c.** the chaff, so their root 7503

CONSUMING
De 4:24 the Lord thy God is a **c.** fire, 398
De 9:3 as a **c.** fire he shall destroy them, 398
Heb 12:29 For our God is a **c.** fire. *2654*

CONSUMMATION
Da 9:27 until the **c.**, and that determined 3617

CONSUMPTION
Le 26:16 terror, **c.**, and the burning ague, 7829
De 28:22 The Lord shall smite thee with a **c.**, 7829
Isa 10:22 the **c.** decreed shall overflow with 3631
Isa 10:23 God of hosts shall make a **c.**, 3617
Isa 28:22 a **c.**, even determined upon the 3617

CONTAIN See also CONTAINED; CONTAINETH; CONTAINING.
1Ki 8:27 heaven of heavens cannot **c.** thee; 3557
1Ki 18:32 great as would **c.** two measures of 1004
2Ch 2:6 heaven of heavens cannot **c.** him? 3557
2Ch 6:18 heaven of heavens cannot **c.** thee; 3557
Eze 45:11 that the bath may **c.** the tenth 5375
Joh 21:25 even the world itself could not **c.** *5562*
1Co 7:9 if they cannot **c.**, let them marry: *1467*

CONTAINED
1Ki 7:26 of lilies: it **c.** two thousand baths. 3557
1Ki 7:38 of brass: one laver **c.** forty baths: 3557
Ro 2:14 by nature the things **c.** in the law,
Eph 2:15 on commandments **c.** in ordinances;
1Pe 2:6 also it is **c.** in the scripture, *4023*

CONTAINETH
Eze 23:32 and had in derision: it **c.** much, 3557

CONTAINING
Joh 2:6 of the Jews, **c.** two or three firkins. *5562*

CONTEMN See also CONTEMNED; CONTEMNETH.
Ps 10:13 Wherefore doth the wicked **c.** God? 5006
Eze 21:13 what if the sword **c.** even the rod? 3988

CONTEMNED
Ps 15:4 In whose eyes a vile person is **c.**; 959
Ps 107:11 **c.** the council of the most High: 5006
Ca 8:7 for love, it would utterly be **c.** 936
Isa 16:14 and the glory of Moab shall be **c.**, 7034

CONTEMNETH
Eze 21:10 it **c.** the rod of my son, as every 3988

CONTEMPT See also CONTEMPTIBLE.
Es 1:18 shall there arise too much **c.** and 963
Job 12:21 He poureth **c.** upon princes, and 937

Job 31:34 or did the **c.** of families terrify me, ... 937
Ps 107:40 He poureth **c.** upon princes, and......... 937
Ps 119:22 Remove from me reproach and **c.**; 937
Ps 123:3 for we are exceedingly filled with **c.**. 937
Ps 123:4 at ease, and with the **c.** of the proud.... 937
Pr 18:3 wicked cometh, then cometh also **c.**, ... 937
Isa 23:9 to bring into **c.** all the honourable 7043
Da 12:2 some to shame and everlasting **c.**....... 1860

CONTEMPTIBLE

Mal 1:7 ye say. The table of the Lord is **c.**. 959
Mal 1:12 the fruit thereof, even his meat, is **c.**. .. 959
Mal 2:9 have I also made you **c.** and base 959
2Co 10:10 is weak, and his speech **c.**. *1848*

CONTEMPTUOUSLY

Ps 31:18 and **c.** against the righteous. 937

CONTEND See also CONTENDED; CONTENDEST; CONTENDETH; CONTENDING.

De 2:9 neither **c.** with them in battle: 1624
De 2:24 possess it, and **c.** with him in battle.... 1624
Job 9:3 If he will **c.** with him, he cannot......... 7378
Job 13:8 his person? will ye **c.** for God? 7378
Pr 28:4 such as keep the law **c.** with them. 1624
Ec 6:10 neither may he **c.** with him that......... 1777
Isa 49:25 I will **c.** with him that contendeth....... 7378
Isa 50:8 who will **c.** with me? let us stand 7378
Isa 57:16 I will not **c.** for ever, neither will I..... 7378
Jer 12:5 how canst thou **c.** with horses?.......... 8474
Jer 18:19 the voice of them that **c.** with me. 3401
Am 7:4 the Lord God called to **c.** by fire,....... 7378
Mic 6:1 **c.** thou before the mountains, and 7378
Jude 3 ye should earnestly **c.** for the faith *1864*

CONTENDED

Ne 13:11 Then **c.** I with the rulers, and.......... 7378
Ne 13:17 Then I **c.** with the nobles of Judah,..... 7378
Ne 13:25 I **c.** with them, and cursed them, ... 7378
Job 31:13 when they **c.** with me;...................... 7378
Isa 41:12 them, even them that **c.** with thee: 4695
Ac 11:2 of the circumcision **c.** with him, ... *1252*

CONTENDEST

Job 10:2 me wherefore thou **c.** with me.......... 7378

CONTENDETH

Job 40:2 Shall he that **c.** with the Almighty....... 7378
Pr 29:9 If a wise man **c.** with a foolish........... 8199
Isa 49:25 with him that **c.** with thee, and.......... 3401

CONTENDING

Jude 9 when **c.** with the devil he disputed *1252*

CONTENT

Ge 37:27 flesh. And his brethren were **c.**. 8085
Ex 2:21 And Moses was **c.** to dwell with 2974
Le 10:20 Moses heard that, he was **c.**....... 3190,5869
Jos 7:7 would to God we had been **c.**, and 2974
Jg 17:11 And the Levite was **c.** to dwell.......... 2974
Jg 19:6 Be **c.**, I pray thee, and tarry all.......... 2974
2Ki 5:23 Naaman said, Be **c.**, take two........... 2974
2Ki 6:3 one said, Be **c.**, I pray thee, and go ... 2974
Job 6:28 Now therefore be **c.**, look upon 2974
Pr 6:35 neither will he rest **c.**, though thou......... 14
Mk 15:15 Pilate, willing to **c.** the....... *2425,3588,4160*
Lu 3:14 and be **c.** with your wages. *714*
Php 4:11 state I am, therewith to be **c.**. *842*
1Ti 6:8 raiment let us be therewith **c.**. *714*
Heb 13:5 be **c.** with such things as ye have: *714*
3Jo 10 with malicious words: and not **c.**........... *714*

CONTENTION See CONTENTIONS.

Pr 13:10 by pride cometh **c.**: but with the........ 4683
Pr 17:14 leave off **c.**, before it be meddled....... 7379
Pr 18:6 A fool's lips enter into **c.**, and his........ 7379
Pr 22:10 out the scorner, and **c.** shall go out; ... 4066
Jer 15:10 a man of **c.** to the whole earth! 4066
Hab 1:3 there are that raise up strife and **c.**. ... 4066
Ac 15:39 And the **c.** was so sharp between....... *3948*
Php 1:16 The one preach Christ of **c.**, not........ *2052*
1Th 2:2 the gospel of God with much **c.**. *73*

CONTENTIONS

Pr 18:18 The lot causeth **c.** to cease, and 4079
Pr 18:19 and their **c.** are like the bars of a........ 4079
Pr 19:13 the **c.** of a wife are a continual.......... 4079
Pr 23:29 who hath **c.**? who hath babbling? 4079
1Co 1:11 that there are **c.** among you............. *2504*
Tit 3:9 genealogies, and **c.**, and strivings *2504*

CONTENTIOUS

Pr 21:29 with a **c.** and an angry woman. 4066
Pr 26:21 so is a **c.** man to kindle strife. 4066
Pr 27:15 rainy day and a **c.** woman are alike..... 4066
Ro 2:8 But unto them that are **c.**,......... *1537, 2052*
1Co 11:16 But if any man seem to be **c.**, ... *5380*

CONTENTMENT

1Ti 6:6 godliness with **c.** is great gain. *841*

CONTINENCE See INCONTINENCY.

CONTINUAL

Ex 29:42 a **c.** burnt offering throughout........... 8548
Nu 4:7 the **c.** bread shall be thereon: 8548
Nu 28:3 day by day, for a **c.** burnt offering. 8548
Nu 28:6 It is a **c.** burnt offering, which was 8548
Nu 28:10 the **c.** burnt offering, and his drink 8548
Nu 28:15 offered, beside the **c.** burnt offering, ... 8548
Nu 28:23 which is for a **c.** burnt offering........... 8548
Nu 28:24 offered beside the **c.** burnt offering, ... 8548
Nu 28:31 them beside the **c.** burnt offering, ... 8548
Nu 29:11 and the **c.** burnt offering, and the....... 8548
Nu 29:16 beside the **c.** burnt offering, his 8548
Nu 29:19, 22 beside the **c.** burnt offering, and 8548
Nu 29:25 beside the **c.** burnt offering, his 8548
Nu 29:28 beside the **c.** burnt offering, and 8548
Nu 29:31, 34 beside the **c.** burnt offering, his 8548
Nu 29:38 beside the **c.** burnt offering, and 8548
2Ki 25:30 his allowance was a **c.** allowance 8548
2Ch 2:4 for the **c.** shewbread, and for the....... 8548
Ezr 3:5 the **c.** burnt offering, both of the........ 8548
Ne 10:33 for the **c.** meat offering, ... 8548
Ne 10:33 and for the **c.** burnt offering, ... 8548
Pr 15:15 of a merry heart hath a **c.** feast. 8548
Pr 19:13 of a wife are a **c.** dropping. 2956
Pr 27:15 A **c.** dropping in a very rainy day 2956
Isa 14:6 wrath with a **c.** stroke, ... 1115,5627
Jer 48:5 **c.** weeping shall go up; for in ....
Jer 52:34 a **c.** diet given him of the king.......... 8548
Eze 39:14 sever out men of **c.** employment,....... 8548
Eze 46:15 morning for a **c.** burnt offering........... 8548
Lu 18:5 **lest by her c. coming** *1519,5056*
Ro 9:2 great heaviness and **c.** sorrow *88*

CONTINUALLY

Ge 6:5 of his heart was only evil **c.**....... 3605,3117
Ge 8:3 returned from off the earth **c.**:..... 1980,7725
Ge 8:5 decreased **c.** until the tenth month:..... 1980
Ex 28:29 a memorial before the Lord **c.**. 8548
Ex 28:30 upon his heart before the Lord **c.**........ 8548
Ex 29:38 of the first year day by day **c.** 8548
Le 24:2 to cause the lamps to burn **c.**. 8548
Le 24:3 the morning before the Lord **c.**:.......... 8548
Le 24:4 pure candlestick before the Lord **c.**...... 8548
Le 24:8 set it in order before the Lord **c.**, ... 8548
Jos 6:13 went on **c.**, and blew with the 1980
1Sa 18:29 became David's enemy **c.** 3605,3117
2Sa 9:7 shalt eat bread at my table **c.**. 8548
2Sa 9:13 he did eat **c.** at the king's table;......... 8548
2Sa 15:12 people increased **c.** with Absalom. 1980
2Sa 19:13 of the host before me **c.** 3605,3117
1Ki 10:8 which stand **c.** before thee,................ 8548
2Ki 4:9 of God, which passeth by us **c.**.............. 8548
2Ki 25:29 he did eat bread **c.** before him........... 8548
1Ch 16:6 with trumpets **c.** before the ark 8548
1Ch 16:11 his strength, seek his face **c.**............. 8548
1Ch 16:37 to minister before the ark **c.**, ... 8548
1Ch 16:40 the altar of the burnt offering **c.**......... 8548
1Ch 23:31 unto them, **c.** before the Lord: 8548
2Ch 9:7 which stand **c.** before thee,................ 8548
2Ch 12:15 Rehoboam and Jeroboam **c.**......... 3605,3117
2Ch 24:14 house of the Lord **c.** all the days......... 8548
Job 1:5 Thus did Job **c.** 3605,3117
Ps 34:1 praise shall **c.** be in my mouth. 8548
Ps 35:27 let them say **c.**, Let the Lord be......... 8548
Ps 38:17 and my sorrow is **c.** before me. 8548
Ps 40:11 and thy truth **c.** preserve me. 8548
Ps 40:16 salvation say **c.**, The Lord be............ 8548
Ps 42:3 and night, while they **c.** say 3605,3117
Ps 44:15 My confusion is **c.** before 3117
Ps 50:8 to have seen **c.** before me. 8548
Ps 52:1 goodness of God endureth **c.**....... 3605,3117
Ps 58:7 away as waters which run **c.**: ....
Ps 69:23 and make their loins **c.** to shake.......... 8548
Ps 70:4 say **c.**, Let God be magnified. 8548
Ps 71:3 whereunto I may **c.** resort: 8548
Ps 71:6 my praise shall be **c.** of thee. 8548
Ps 71:14 I will hope **c.**, and will yet praise 8548
Ps 72:15 also shall be made for him **c.**;............ 8548
Ps 73:23 Nevertheless I am **c.** with thee: 8548
Ps 74:23 rise up against thee increaseth **c.**. 8548
Ps 109:10 his children be **c.** vagabonds, ...
Ps 109:15 Let them be before the Lord **c.**, ... 8548
Ps 109:19 girdle wherewith he is girded **c.**. 8548
Ps 119:44 So shall I keep thy law **c.** for ever 8548
Ps 119:109 My soul is **c.** in my hand: 8548
Ps 119:117 have respect unto thy statutes **c.**. 8548
Ps 140:2 **c.** are they gathered together..... 3605,3117
Pr 6:14 he deviseth mischief **c.**; 6256
Pr 6:21 Bind them **c.** upon thine heart, ... 8548
Ec 1:6 it whirleth about **c.**, and the wind ....
Isa 21:8 I stand **c.** upon the watchtower.......... 8548
Isa 49:16 thy walls are **c.** before me. 8548
Isa 51:13 hast feared **c.** every day because 8548
Isa 52:5 name **c.** every day is blasphemed. 8548
Isa 58:11 And the Lord shall guide thee **c.**, ... 8548
Isa 60:11 thy gates shall be open **c.**; 8548
Isa 65:3 that provoketh me to anger **c.** 8548
Jer 6:7 before me **c.** is grief and wounds. 8548
Jer 33:18 and to do sacrifice **c.** 3605,3117
Jer 52:33 he did **c.** eat bread before him........... 8548
Eze 46:14 offering **c.** by a perpetual ordinance 8548
Da 6:16 Thy God whom thou servest **c.**, ... 8411
Da 6:20 is thy God, whom thou servest **c.**, ... 8411
Ho 4:18 they have committed whoredom **c.**: ....
Ho 12:6 and wait on thy God **c.**. 8548
Ob 16 so shall all the heathen drink **c.**,......... 8548
Na 3:19 hath not thy wickedness passed **c.**? 8548
Hab 1:17 not spare **c.** to slay the nations? 8548
Lu 24:53 And were **c.** in the temple. *1725*
Ac 6:4 will give ourselves **c.** to prayer, ... *4342*
Ac 10:7 of them that waited on him **c.**;............ *4342*
Ro 13:6 attending **c.** upon this very thing. *4342*
Heb 7:3 of God; abideth a priest **c.**......... *1519, 1336*
Heb 10:1 offered year by year **c.** make *1519, 1336*
Heb 13:15 the sacrifice of praise to God **c.**, ... *1275*

CONTINUANCE

De 28:59 great plagues, and of long **c.**,............... 539
De 28:59 and sore sicknesses, and of long **c.**. 539
Ps 139:16 which in **c.** were fashioned,............... 3117
Isa 64:5 in those is **c.**, and we shall be 5769
Ro 2:7 by patient **c.** in well doing seek.......... *5281*

CONTINUE See also CONTINUED; CONTINUETH; CONTINUING.

Ex 21:21 if he **c.** a day or two, he shall not 5975
Le 12:4 she shall then **c.** in the blood of......... 3427
Le 12:5 she shall **c.** in the blood of her.......... 3427
1Sa 12:14 **c.** following the Lord your God: 1961
1Sa 13:14 now thy kingdom shall not **c.**:............. 6965
2Sa 7:29 it may **c.** for ever before thee: 1961
1Ki 2:4 That the Lord may **c.** his word........... 6965
Job 15:29 neither shall his substance **c.**,............ 6965
Job 17:2 doth not mine eye **c.** in their............ 3885
Ps 36:10 **c.** thy lovingkindness unto them......... 4900
Ps 49:11 is, that their houses shall **c.** for ever,.........
Ps 102:28 children of thy servants shall **c.**......... 7931
Ps 119:91 They **c.** this day according to 5975
Isa 5:11 that **c.** until night, till wine 309
Jer 32:14 that they may **c.** many days. 5975
Da 11:8 shall **c.** more years than the king 5975
Mt 15:32 **they c. with me now three days,**.... *4357*
Joh 8:31 **If ye c. in my word, then are ye**.... *3306*
Joh 15:9 **I loved you: c. ye in my love**......... *3306*
Ac 13:43 them to **c.** in the grace of God. *1961*
Ac 14:22 exhorting them to **c.** in the faith,........ *1696*
Ac 26:22 I **c.** unto this day, witnessing *2476*
Ro 6:1 Shall we **c.** in sin, that grace *1961*
Ro 11:22 if thou **c.** in his goodness:................. *1961*
Gal 2:5 of the gospel might **c.** with you.......... *1265*
Php 1:25 I shall abide and **c.** with you all.......... *4839*
Col 1:23 If ye **c.** in the faith grounded............. *1961*
Col 4:2 **C.** in prayer, and watch in the........... *4342*
1Ti 2:15 if they **c.** in faith and charity.............. *3306*
1Ti 4:16 **c.** in them: for in doing this thou......... *1961*
2Ti 3:14 **c.** thou in the things which thou......... *3306*
Heb 7:23 suffered to **c.** by reason of death:......... *3887*
Heb 13:1 Let brotherly love **c.**. *3306*
Jas 4:13 and **c.** there a year, and buy, ... *4160*
2Pe 3:4 all things **c.** as they were from *1265*
1Jo 2:24 remain in you, ye also shall **c.** *3306*
Re 13:5 him to **c.** forty and two months.......... *4160*
Re 17:10 cometh, he must **c.** a short space....... *3306*

CONTINUED

Ge 40:4 and they **c.** a season in ward............ 1961

Jg 5:17 Asher **c.** on the seashore, 3427
Ru 1:2 country of Moab, and **c.** there. 1961
Ru 2:7 hath **c.** even from the morning 5975
1Sa 1:12 she **c.** praying before the Lord, 7235
2Sa 6:11 ark of the Lord **c.** in the house 3427
1Ki 22:1 they **c.** three years without war 3427
2Ch 29:28 this **c.** until the burnt offering
Ne 5:16 also I **c.** in the work of this wall, 2388
Job 27:1 Moreover Job **c.** his parable, and 3254
Job 29:1 Moreover Job **c.** his parable, and 3254
Ps 72:17 shall be **c.** as long as the sun: 5125
Da 1:21 And Daniel **c.** even unto the 1961
Lu 6:12 and **c.** all night in prayer to God. *1273*
Lu 22:28 **c. with me in my temptations** *1265*
Joh 2:12 they **c.** there not many days. *3306*
Joh 8:7 So when they **c.** asking him, *1961*
Joh 11:54 and there **c.** with his disciples. *1304*
Ac 1:14 all **c.** with one accord in prayer *4342*
Ac 2:42 they **c.** steadfastly in the apostles' *4342*
Ac 8:13 he **c.** with Philip, and wondered, *4342*
Ac 12:16 But Peter **c.** knocking, and when *1961*
Ac 15:35 Paul also and Barnabas **c.** in *1304*
Ac 18:11 **c.** there a year and six months, *2523*
Ac 19:10 **c.** by the space of two years; *1096*
Ac 20:7 and **c.** his speech until midnight. *3905*
Ac 27:38 **c.** fasting, having taken nothing. *1300*
Heb 8:9 they **c.** not in my covenant, *1696*
1Jo 2:19 would no doubt have **c.** with us: *3306*

CONTINUETH
Job 14:2 fleeth also as a shadow, and **c.** not. 5975
Ga 3:10 every one that **c.** not in all things *1696*
1Ti 5:5 **c.** in supplications and prayers *4357*
Heb 7:24 this man, because he **c.** ever, *3306*
Jas 1:25 law of liberty, and **c.** therein, *3887*

CONTINUING
Jer 30:23 a **c.** whirlwind: it shall fall with 1641
Ac 2:46 And they, **c.** daily with one accord *4342*
Ro 12:12 tribulations; **c.** instant in prayer; *4342*
Heb 13:14 here have we no **c.** city, but we *3306*

CONTRADICTING
Ac 13:45 were spoken by Paul, **c.** and *483*

CONTRADICTION
Heb 7:7 without all **c.** the less is blessed *485*
Heb 12:3 **c.** of sinners against himself, *485*

CONTRARIWISE
2Co 2:7 that **c.** ye ought rather to forgive *5121*
Ga 2:7 But **c.**, when they saw that the *5121*
1Pe 3:9 railing for railing: but **c.** blessing; *5121*

CONTRARY See also CONTRARIWISE.
Le 26:21 if ye walk **c.** unto me, and will 7147
Le 26:23 but will walk **c.** unto me; 7147
Le 26:24 Then will I also walk **c.** unto you, 7147
Le 26:27 but walk **c.** unto me; 7147
Le 26:28 I will walk **c.** unto you also in fury; 7147
Le 26:40 and that also they have walked **c.** 7147
Le 26:41 I also have walked **c.** unto them, 7147
Es 9:1 (though it was turned to the **c.**,
Eze 16:34 the **c.** is in thee from other women 2016
Eze 16:34 unto thee, therefore thou art **c.** 2016
Mt 14:24 for the wind was **c.** *1727*
Mk 6:48 for the wind was **c.** unto them: *1727*
Ac 17:7 these all do **c.** to the decrees of *561*
Ac 18:13 men to worship God **c.** to the law. *3844*
Ac 23:3 commandest me to be smitten **c.** to *3891*
Ac 26:9 many things **c.** to the name of *1727*
Ac 27:4 Cyprus, because the winds were **c.** *1727*
Ro 11:24 graffed **c.** to nature into a good *3844*
Ro 16:17 **c.** to the doctrine which ye have *3844*
Ga 5:17 these are **c.** the one to the other: *480*
Col 2:14 which was **c.** to us, and took it out *5227*
1Th 2:15 not God, and are **c.** to all men: *1727*
1Ti 1:10 thing that is **c.** to sound doctrine; *480*
Tit 2:8 is of the **c.** part may be ashamed, *1727*

CONTRIBUTION
Ro 15:26 to make a certain **c.** for the poor *2842*

CONTRITE
Ps 34:18 saveth such as be of a **c.** spirit. 1793
Ps 51:17 a broken and a **c.** heart, O God, 1794
Isa 57:15 also that is of a **c.** and humble 1793
Isa 57:15 to revive the heart of the **c.** ones. 1792
Isa 66:2 him that is poor and of a **c.** spirit, 5223

CONTROVERSIES
2Ch 19:8 judgment of the Lord, and for **c.**, 7379

CONTROVERSY See also CONTROVERSIES.
De 17:8 being matters of **c.** within thy 7379
De 19:17 the men, between whom the **c.** is, 7379
De 21:5 by their word shall every **c.** and 7379
De 25:1 If there be a **c.** between men, 7379
2Sa 15:2 any man that had a **c.** came to 7379
Isa 34:8 year of recompences for the **c.** of 7379
Jer 25:31 Lord hath a **c.** with the nations, 7379
Eze 44:24 in **c.** they shall stand in judgment; 7379
Ho 4:1 the Lord hath a **c.** with the, 7379
Ho 12:2 Lord hath also a **c.** with Judah 7379
Mic 6:2 Hear ye, O mountains, the Lord's **c.**, 7379
Mic 6:2 the Lord hath a **c.** with his people, 7379
1Ti 3:16 without **c.** great is the mystery *3672*

CONVENIENT
Pr 30:8 feed me with food **c.** for me: 2706
Jer 40:4 whither it seemeth good and **c.** 3477
Jer 40:5 go wheresoever it seemeth **c.** unto 3477
Mk 6:21 And when a **c.** day was come, *2121*
Ac 24:25 when I have a **c.** season, I will call *2540*
Ro 1:28 do those things which are not **c.**; *2520*
1Co 16:12 come when he shall have **c.** time. *2119*
Eph 5:4 nor jesting, which are not **c.**: *433*
Phm 8 to enjoin thee that which is **c.** *433*

CONVENIENTLY
Mk 14:11 he sought how he might **c.** betray *2122*

CONVERSANT
Jos 8:35 the strangers that were **c.** among 1980
1Sa 25:15 as long as we were **c.** with them. 1980

CONVERSATION
Ps 37:14 to slay such as be of upright **c.** 1870
Ps 50:23 him that ordereth his **c.** aright 1870
2Co 1:12 we have had our **c.** in the world, *390*
Ga 1:13 ye have heard of my **c.** in time *391*
Eph 2:3 we all had our **c.** in times past *390*
Eph 4:22 put off concerning the former **c.** *391*
Php 1:27 let your **c.** be as it becometh the *4176*
Php 3:20 our **c.** is in heaven; from whence *4175*
1Ti 4:12 in word, in **c.**, in charity, in spirit, *391*
Heb 13:5 your **c.** be without covetousness; *5158*
Heb 13:7 considering the end of their **c.** *391*
Jas 3:13 shew out of a good **c.** his works *391*
1Pe 1:15 so be ye holy in all manner of **c.**; *391*
1Pe 1:18 from your vain **c.** received by *391*
1Pe 2:12 Having your **c.** honest among *391*
1Pe 3:1 be won by the **c.** of the wives; *391*
1Pe 3:2 While they behold your chaste **c.** *391*
1Pe 3:16 falsely accuse your good **c.** in *391*
2Pe 2:7 with the filthy **c.** of the wicked: *391*
2Pe 3:11 be in all holy **c.** and godliness, *391*

CONVERSION
Ac 15:3 declaring the **c.** of the Gentiles: *1995*

CONVERT See also CONVERTED; CONVERTETH; CONVERTING; CONVERTS.
Isa 6:10 with their heart, and **c.**, and be 7725
Jas 5:19 from the truth, and one **c.** him; *1994*

CONVERTED
Ps 51:13 and sinners shall be **c.** unto thee. 7725
Isa 60:5 of the sea shall be **c.** unto thee, 2015
Mt 13:15 **and should be c., and I should** *1994*
Mt 18:3 **Except ye be c., and become as** *4762*
Mk 4:12 **they should be c., and their sins** *1994*
Lu 22:32 **and when thou art c., strengthen** *1994*
Joh 12:40 and be **c.**, and I should heal them. *1994*
Ac 3:19 Repent ye therefore, and be **c.**, *1994*
Ac 28:27 should be **c.**, and I should heal *1994*

CONVERTETH
Jas 5:20 he which **c.** the sinner from the *1994*

CONVERTING
Ps 19:7 of the Lord is perfect, **c.** the soul: 7725

CONVERTS
Isa 1:27 with judgment, and her **c.** with 7725

CONVEY See also CONVEYED.
1Ki 5:9 will **c.** them by sea in floats unto 7760
Ne 2:7 river, that they may **c.** me over 5674

CONVEYED
Joh 5:13 for Jesus had **c.** himself away, *1593*

CONVICTED
Joh 8:9 being **c.** by their own conscience, *1651*

CONVINCE See also CONVINCED; CONVINCETH.
Tit 1:9 exhort and to **c.** the gainsayers. *1651*
Jude 15 to **c.** all that are ungodly among *1827*

CONVINCED
Job 38:12 there was none of you that **c.** Job, 3198
Ac 18:28 For he mightily **c.** the Jews, *1246*
1Co 14:24 unlearned, he is **c.** of all, he is *1651*
Jas 2:9 **c.** of the law as transgressors *1651*

CONVINCETH
Joh 8:46 **Which of you c. me of sin?** *1651*

CONVOCATION See also CONVOCATIONS.
Ex 12:16 first day there shall be an holy **c.**, 4744
Ex 12:16 seventh day there shall be an holy **c.** 4744
Le 23:3 is the sabbath of rest, an holy **c.**; 4744
Le 23:7 first day ye shall have an holy **c.**: 4744
Le 23:8 in the seventh day is an holy **c.**: 4744
Le 23:21 that it may be an holy **c.** unto you: 4744
Le 23:24 of blowing of trumpets, an holy **c.** 4744
Le 23:27 of atonement: it shall be an holy **c.** 4744
Le 23:35 On the first day shall be an holy **c.**: 4744
Le 23:36 the eighth day shall be an holy **c.** 4744
Nu 28:18 In the first day shall be an holy **c.**; 4744
Nu 28:25 seventh day ye shall have an holy **c.**; 4744
Nu 28:26 be out, ye shall have an holy **c.**; 4744
Nu 29:1 the month, ye shall have an holy **c.**; 4744
Nu 29:7 of this seventh month an holy **c.**; 4744
Nu 29:12 month ye shall have an holy **c.**; 4744

CONVOCATIONS
Le 23:2 ye shall proclaim to be holy **c.**, 4744
Le 23:4 the feasts of the Lord, even holy **c.**, 4744
Le 23:37 ye shall proclaim to be holy **c.**, to 4744

COOK See also COOKS.
1Sa 9:23 Samuel said unto the **c.**, Bring the 2876
1Sa 9:24 And the **c.** took up the shoulder, 2876

COOKS
1Sa 8:13 to be confectionaries, and to be **c.**, 2876

COOL
Ge 3:8 in the garden in the **c.** of the day; 7307
Lu 16:24 **finger in water, and c. my tongue;** *2711*

COOS (co'-os)
Ac 21:1 with a straight course unto **C.**, *2972*

COPIED
Pr 25:1 Hezekiah king of Judah **c.** out. 6275

COPING
1Ki 7:9 from the foundation unto the **c.**, 2947

COPPER See also COPPERSMITH.
Ezr 8:27 two vessels of fine **c.**, precious as 5178

COPPERSMITH
2Ti 4:14 Alexander the **c.** did me much *5471*

COPULATION
Le 15:16 if any man's seed of **c.** go out 7902
Le 15:17 whereon is the seed of **c.**, shall be 7902
Le 15:18 whom man shall lie with seed of **c.**, 7902

COPY See also COPIED.
De 17:18 he shall write him a **c.** of this law 4932
Jos 8:32 a **c.** of the law of Moses, which he 4932
Ezr 4:11 This is the **c.** of the letter that 6573
Ezr 4:23 when the **c.** of king Artaxerxes' 6573
Ezr 5:6 The **c.** of the letter that Tatnai, 6573
Ezr 7:11 Now this is the **c.** of the letter that 6573
Es 3:14 The **c.** of the writing for a 6572
Es 4:8 the **c.** of the writing of the decree 6572
Es 8:13 The **c.** of the writing for a 6572

COR
Eze 45:14 tenth part of a bath out of the **c.**, 3734

CORAL
Job 28:18 No mention shall be made of **c.**, 7215
Eze 27:16 and fine linen, and **c.**, and agate 7215

CORBAN (cor'-ban)
Mk 7:11 **It is C., that is to say, a gift,** *2878*

CORD See also ACCORD; CORDS; DISCORD; RECORD.
Jos 2:15 down by a **c.** through the window: 2256
Job 30:11 hath loosed my **c.**, and afflicted 3499
Job 41:1 or his tongue with a **c.** which 2256

Ec 4:12 threefold c. is not quickly broken. 2339
Ec 12:6 Or ever the silver c. be loosed, or..... 2256
Mic 2:5 cast a c. by lot in the congregation..... 2256

CORDS
Ex 35:18 the pins of the court, and their c.,....... 4340
Ex 39:40 his c., and his pins, and all the 4340
Nu 3:26 c. of it for all the service thereof. 4340
Nu 3:37 sockets, their pins, and their c.. 4340
Nu 4:26 their c., and all the instruments of...... 4340
Nu 4:32 their pins, and their c., with all.......... 4340
Jg 15:13 they bound him with two new c., ... 5688
Jg 15:14 the c. that were upon his arms.......... 5688
Es 1:6 fastened with c. of fine linen and......... 2256
Job 36:8 and be holden in c. of affliction; 2256
Ps 2:3 and cast away their c. from us........... 5688
Ps 118:27 with c., even unto the horns 5688
Ps 129:4 cut asunder the c. of the wicked. 5688
Ps 140:5 have hid a snare for me, and c.; 2256
Pr 5:22 be holden with the c. of his sins. 2256
Isa 5:18 that draw iniquity with c. of vanity,..... 2256
Isa 33:20 any of the c. thereof be broken. 2256
Isa 54:2 lengthen thy c., and strengthen.......... 4340
Jer 10:20 is spoiled, all my c. are broken: 4340
Jer 38:6 they let down Jeremiah with c.......... 2256
Jer 38:11 them down by c. into the dungeon...... 2256
Jer 38:12 under thine armholes under the c.. 2256
Jer 38:13 they drew up Jeremiah with c.,.......... 2256
Eze 27:24 of rich apparel, bound with c., ... 2256
Ho 11:4 I drew them with c. of a man, with 2256
Joh 2:15 he had made a scourge of small c.,..... *4979*

CORE (co'-ree) See also KORAH.
Jude 11 perished in the gainsaying of C.. .... *2879*

CORIANDER
Ex 16:31 and it was like c. seed, white;........... 1407
Nu 11:7 And the manna was as c. seed, and.... 1407

CORINTH (cor'-inth) See also CORINTHIANS; CORINTHUS.
Ac 18:1 from Athens, and came to C.; *2882*
Ac 19:1 while Apollos was at C., Paul............ *2882*
1Co 1:2 the church of God which is at C., to... *2882*
2Co 1:1 church of God which is at C., with *2882*
2Co 1:23 spare you I came not as yet unto C.... *2882*
2Ti 4:20 Erastus abode at C.: but *2882*

CORINTHIANS (co-rin'-the-uns)
Ac 18:8 many of the C. hearing believed,........ *2881*
1Co *general title* First Epistle Of Paul...To...C. *2881*
1Co *subscr.* The first epistle to the C. was........... *2881*
2Co *general title* Second Epistle...Paul...To...C...... *2881*
2Co 6:11 O ye C., our mouth is open unto *2881*
2Co *subscr.* The second epistle to the C. was....... *2881*

CORINTHUS (co-rin'-thus) See also CORINTH.
Ro *subscr.* Written to the Romans from C., ... *2882*

CORMORANT
Le 11:17 the little owl, and the c., and the 7994
De 14:17 and the gier eagle, and the c.,........ 7994
Isa 34:11 c. and the bittern shall possess.......... 6893
Zep 2:14 the c. and the bittern shall lodge........ 6893

CORN See also CORNFLOOR.
Ge 27:28 earth, and plenty of c. and wine:........ 1715
Ge 27:37 c. and wine have I sustained him:....... 1715
Ge 41:5 seven ears of c. came up upon ....
Ge 41:35 and lay up c. under the hand of 1250
Ge 41:49 Joseph gathered c. as the sand 1250
Ge 41:57 into Egypt to Joseph for to buy c.; ....
Ge 42:1 saw that there was c. in Egypt, ... 7668
Ge 42:2 heard that there is c. in Egypt:.......... 7668
Ge 42:3 went down to buy c. in Egypt. 1250
Ge 42:5 the sons of Israel came to buy c. ....
Ge 42:19 c. for the famine of your houses: 7668
Ge 42:25 to fill their sacks with c., and to 1250
Ge 42:26 laded their asses with the c., ... 7668
Ge 43:2 the c. which they had brought 7668
Ge 44:2 and his c. money. And he did............ 7668
Ge 45:23 ten she asses laden with c. and 1250
Ge 47:14 the c. which they had bought: 7668
Ex 22:6 so that the stacks of c., ...
Ex 22:6 or the standing c., or the field,.......... 7054
Le 2:14 of the firstfruits green ears of c. ....
Le 2:14 even c. beaten out of full ears. 1643
Le 2:16 part of the beaten c. thereof, and........ 1643
Le 23:14 eat neither bread, nor parched c., ...
Nu 18:27 the c. of the threshingfloor,.............. 1715
De 7:13 of thy land, thy c., and thy wine, ... 1715
De 11:14 gather in thy c., and thy wine, ... 1715
De 12:17 the tithe of thy c., or of thy wine,...... 1715
De 14:23 the tithe of thy c., of thy wine. 1715
De 16:9 to put the sickle to the c.. 7054
De 16:13 that thou hast gathered in thy c., ... 1637
De 18:4 also of thy c., of thy wine................ 1715
De 23:25 the standing c. of thy neighbour, ... 7054
De 23:25 unto thy neighbour's standing c.......... 7054
De 25:4 ox when he treadeth out the c.................
De 28:51 leave thee either c., wine, or oil, ... 1715
De 33:28 be upon a land of c. and wine;........... 1715
Jos 5:11 did eat of the old c. of the land.......... 5669
Jos 5:11 parched c. in the selfsame day.................
Jos 5:12 eaten of the old c. of the land;.......... 5669
Jg 15:5 the standing c. of the Philistines,........ 7054
Jg 15:5 shocks, and also the standing c.,........ 7054
Ru 2:2 glean ears of c. after him in ....
Ru 2:14 he reached her parched c., and................
Ru 3:7 down at the end of the heap of c.: 6194
1Sa 17:17 an ephah of this parched c., and..............
1Sa 25:18 five measures of parched c., and.............
2Sa 17:19 and spread ground c. thereon; 7383
2Sa 17:28 and parched c., and beans, and................
2Ki 4:42 and full ears of c. in the husk 3759
2Ki 18:32 a land of c. and wine, a land of.......... 1715
2Ki 19:26 and as c. blasted before it be grown up.....
2Ch 31:5 in abundance the firstfruits of c., ... 1715
2Ch 32:28 for the increase of c., and wine, ... 1715
Ne 5:2 therefore we take up c. for them, ... 1715
Ne 5:3 buy c., because of the dearth. 1715
Ne 5:10 exact of them money and c.: 1715
Ne 5:11 of the c., the wine, and the oil, ... 1715
Ne 10:39 offering of the c., of the new wine, ... 1715
Ne 13:5 vessels, and the tithes of the c., ... 1715
Ne 13:12 all Judah the tithe of the c. and.......... 1715
Job 5:26 age, like as a shock of c. cometh ....
Job 24:6 reap every one his c. in the field:........ 1098
Job 24:24 off as the tops of the ears of c.. ....
Job 39:4 grow up with c.; they go forth,.......... 1250
Ps 4:7 than in the time that their c. and........ 1715
Ps 65:9 thou preparest them c., when........... 1715
Ps 65:13 also are covered over with c.; 1250
Ps 72:16 be an handful of c. in the earth.......... 1250
Ps 78:24 given them of the c. of heaven. 1715
Pr 11:26 He that withholdeth c., the 1250
Isa 17:5 the harvestman gathereth the c.,......... 7054
Isa 21:10 threshing, and the c. of my floor: 1121
Isa 28:28 Bread c. is bruised; because he ....
Isa 36:17 own land, a land of c. and wine,......... 1715
Isa 37:27 as c. blasted before it be grown up..........
Isa 62:8 no more give they c. to be meat........ 1715
La 2:12 mothers, Where is c. and wine?......... 1715
Eze 36:29 call for the c., and will increase it,...... 1715
Ho 2:8 I gave her c., and wine, and oil, ... 1715
Ho 2:9 and take away my c. in the time 1715
Ho 2:22 the earth shall hear the c., and.......... 1715
Ho 7:14 assemble themselves for c. and.......... 1715
Ho 10:11 and loveth to tread out the c.; ....
Ho 14:7 they shall revive as the c., and.......... 1715
Joe 1:10 the c. is wasted: the new wine is....... 1715
Joe 1:17 down; for the c. is withered............. 1715
Joe 2:19 I will send you c., and wine, and........ 1715
Am 8:5 be gone, that we may sell c.?............ 7668
Am 9:9 like as c. is sifted in a sieve, ...
Hag 1:11 the mountains, and upon the c., ... 1715
Zec 9:17 c. shall make the young men 1715
Mt 12:1 the sabbath day through the c.; *4702*
Mt 12:1 and began to pluck the ears of c., ... *4719*
Mk 2:23 that he went through the c. fields...... *4702*
Mk 2:23 they went to pluck the ears of c.. ...... *4719*
Mk 4:28 **after that the full c. in the ear** *4621*
Lu 6:1 that he went through the c. fields;...... *4702*
Lu 6:1 disciples plucked the ears of c., ... *4719*
Joh 12:24 **Except a c. of wheat fall into the** .. *2848*
Ac 7:12 heard that there was c. in Egypt,....... *4621*
1Co 9:9 of the ox that treadeth out the c.. ....
1Ti 5:18 muzzle the ox that treadeth out the c........

CORNELIUS (cor-ne'-le-us)
Ac 10:1 C., a centurion of the band *2883*
Ac 10:3 to him, and saying unto him, C.. .... *2883*
Ac 10:7 which spake unto C. was departed,..... *2883*
Ac 10:17 the men which were sent from C. *2883*
Ac 10:21 which were sent unto him from C.; *2883*
Ac 10:22 said, C. the centurion, a just man,..... *2883*
Ac 10:24 C. waited for them, and had called *2883*
Ac 10:25 C. met him, and fell down at his *2883*
Ac 10:30 C. said, Four days ago I was fasting... *2883*
Ac 10:31 C., thy prayer is heard, and thine *2883*

CORNER See also CORNERS.
Ex 36:25 north c., he made twenty boards,....... 6285
Le 21:5 shave off the c. of their beard, ... 6285
Jos 18:14 the c. of the sea southward, from 6285
2Ki 11:11 from the right c. of the temple 3802
2Ki 11:11 to the left c. of the temple,.............. 3802
2Ki 14:13 gate of Ephraim unto the c. gate,....... 6438
2Ch 25:23 gate of Ephraim to the c. gate,......... 6437
2Ch 26:9 towers in Jerusalem at the c. gate, ... 6438
2Ch 28:24 altars in every c. of Jerusalem. 6438
Ne 3:24 of the wall, even unto the c.. 6438
Ne 3:31 and to the going up of the c.............. 6438
Ne 3:32 between the going up of the c. 6438
Job 38:6 or who laid the c. stone thereof;......... 6438
Ps 118:22 become the head stone of the c.. 6438
Ps 144:12 daughters may be as c. stones,.......... 2106
Pr 7:8 through the street near her c.; 6438
Pr 7:12 and lieth in wait at every c..) 6438
Pr 21:9 to dwell in a c. of the housetop, ... 6438
Pr 25:24 to dwell in the c. of the housetop,...... 6438
Isa 28:16 precious c. stone, a sure foundation:... 6438
Isa 30:20 thy teachers be removed into a c. 3671
Jer 31:38 Hananeel unto the gate of the c. 6438
Jer 31:40 unto the c. of the horse gate............. 6438
Jer 48:45 shall devour the c. of Moab, and........ 6285
Jer 51:26 not take of thee a stone for a c.. 6438
Eze 46:21 behold, in every c. the court............. 4742
Am 3:12 in Samaria in the c. of a bed, ... 6285
Zec 10:4 Out of him came forth the c.,............ 6438
Zec 14:10 the c. gate, and from the tower.......... 6434
Mt 21:42 **same is become the head of the c.:** .*1137*
Mk 12:10 **is become the head of the c.:** *1137*
Lu 20:17 **same is become the head of the c.?** .*1137*
Ac 4:11 which is become the head of the c...... *1137*
Ac 26:26 for this thing was not done in a c.. ..... *1137*
Eph 2:20 Christ himself being the chief c. *204*
1Pe 2:6 I lay in Sion a chief c. stone, elect, ... *204*
1Pe 2:7 same is made the head of the c., ... *1137*

CORNER-GATE See CORNER and GATE.

CORNERS
Ex 25:12 put them in the four c. thereof; 6471
Ex 25:26 the rings in the four c. that are 6285
Ex 26:23 make for the c. of the tabernacle 4742
Ex 26:24 both; they shall be for the two c.. 4742
Ex 27:2 horns of it upon the four c. thereof:.... 6438
Ex 27:4 brasen rings in the four c. thereof. 7098
Ex 30:4 by the two c. thereof, upon the 6763
Ex 36:28 made he for the c. of the tabernacle ... 4742
Ex 36:29 did to both of them in both the c.. 4742
Ex 37:3 gold, to be set by the four c. of it;..... 6471
Ex 37:13 put the rings upon the four c. that...... 6285
Ex 37:27 by the two c. of it, upon the two 6763
Ex 38:2 horns thereof on the four c. of it;....... 6438
Le 19:9 not wholly reap the c. of thy field,...... 6285
Le 19:27 shall not round the c. of your heads,... 6285
Le 19:27 shalt thou mar the c. of thy beard. 6285
Le 23:22 riddance of the c. of thy field............ 6285
Nu 24:17 and shall smite the c. of Moab,.......... 6285
De 32:26 said, I would scatter them into c.,...... 6284
1Ki 7:30 four c. thereof had undersetters:........ 6471
1Ki 7:34 to the four c. of one base: and the 6438
Ne 9:22 and didst divide them into c.: 6285
Job 1:19 smote the four c. of the house, ... 6438
Isa 11:12 from the four c. of the earth. 3671
Jer 9:26 are in the utmost c., that dwell.......... 6285
Jer 25:23 all that are in the utmost c.,.............. 6285
Jer 49:32 them that are in the utmost c.;........... 6285
Eze 7:2 come upon the four c. of the land....... 3671
Eze 41:22 and the c. thereof, and the length 4740
Eze 43:20 and on the four c. of the settle, ... 6438
Eze 45:19 upon the four c. of the settle of the.... 6438
Eze 46:21 to pass by the four c. of the court;..... 4742
Eze 46:22 In the four c. of the court there......... 4742
Eze 46:22 these four c. were of one measure. 7106
Zec 9:15 bowls, and as the c. of the altar.......... 2106
Mt 6:5 **in the c. of the streets, that they**... *1137*
Ac 10:11 knit at the four c., and let down.......... *746*
Ac 11:5 let down from heaven by four c.;......... *746*
Re 7:1 standing on the four c. of the earth, ... *1137*

CORNER-STONE See CORNER and STONE.

CORNET See also CORNETS.
1Ch 15:28 with sound of the c., and with........... 7782
Ps 98:6 With trumpets and sound of c. 7782
Da 3:5 ye hear the sound of the c., flute, ... 7162
Da 3:7 people heard the sound of the c., ... 7162

Da 3:10 that shall hear the sound of the **c.**, 7162
Da 3:15 ye hear the sound of the **c.** flute, 7162
Ho 5:8 Blow ye the **c.** in Gilbeah, and the 7782

CORNETS
2Sa 6:5 on timbrels, and on **c.**, and on 4517
2Ch 15:14 and with trumpets, and with **c.** 7782

CORNFLOOR
Ho 9:1 loved a reward upon every **c.** 1637,1715

CORPSE See also CORPSES.
Mk 6:29 they came and took up his **c.**, *4430*

CORPSES
2Ki 19:35 behold, they were all dead **c.** 6297
Isa 37:36 behold, they were all dead **c.** 6297
Na 3:3 **c.**; they stumble upon their **c.**: 1472

CORRECT See also CORRECTED; CORRECTETH.
Ps 39:11 thou with rebukes dost **c.** man 3256
Ps 94:10 the heathen, shall not he **c.**? 3198
Pr 29:17 **C.** thy son, and he shall give thee 3256
Jer 2:19 thine own wickedness shall **c.** thee, 3256
Jer 10:24 O Lord, **c.** me, but with judgment; 3256
Jer 30:11 I will **c.** thee in measure, and will 3256
Jer 46:28 but **c.** thee in measure; yet will I 3256

CORRECTED
Pr 29:19 A servant will not be **c.** by words: 3256
Heb 12:9 fathers of our flesh which **c.** us, *3810*

CORRECTETH
Job 5:17 happy is the man whom God **c.**: 3198
Pr 3:12 For whom the Lord loveth he **c.**; 3198

CORRECTION
Job 37:13 whether for **c.**, or for his land, 7626
Pr 3:11 neither be weary of his **c.**: 8433
Pr 7:22 as a fool to the **c.** of the stocks; 4148
Pr 15:10 **C.** is grievous unto him that 4148
Pr 22:15 rod of **c.** shall drive it far from him 4148
Pr 23:13 Withhold not **c.** from the child: 4148
Jer 2:30 they received no **c.** your own 4148
Jer 5:3 they have refused to receive **c.**: 4148
Jer 7:28 nor receiveth **c.**: truth is perished, 4148
Hab 1:12 thou hast established them for **c.** 3198
Zep 3:2 she received not **c.**; she trusted 4148
2Ti 3:16 for reproof, for **c.**, for instruction *1882*

CORRUPT See also CORRUPTED; CORRUPTETH; CORRUPTIBLE; CORRUPTING.
Ge 6:11 The earth also was **c.** before God, 7843
Ge 6:12 it was **c.**; for all flesh had corrupted 7843
De 4:16 Lest ye **c.** yourselves, and make you 7843
De 4:25 and shall **c.** yourselves, and make a 7843
De 31:29 ye will utterly **c.** yourselves, 7843
Job 17:1 breath is **c.**, my days are extinct, 2254
Ps 14:1 They are **c.**, they have done 7843
Ps 38:5 My wounds stink and are **c.** 4743
Ps 53:1 **C.** are they, and have done 7843
Ps 73:8 They are **c.**, and speak wickedly 4167
Pr 25:26 troubled fountain, and a **c.** spring. 7843
Eze 20:44 according to your **c.** doings, O ye 7843
Eze 23:11 was more **c.** in her inordinate love 7843
Da 2:9 have prepared lying and **c.** words 7844
Da 11:32 shall he **c.** by flatteries: but the 2610
Mal 1:14 sacrificeth unto the Lord a **c.** 7843
Mal 2:3 I will **c.** your seed, and spread 1605
Mt 6:19 **where moth and rust doth c., and** *853*
Mt 6:20 **neither moth nor dust doth c.,** *853*
Mt 7:17 **a c. tree bringeth forth evil fruit** *4550*
Mt 7:18 **neither can a c. tree bring forth** *4550*
Mt 12:33 **make the tree c., and his fruit c.:** *4550*
Lu 6:43 **tree bringeth not forth c. fruit;** *4550*
Lu 6:43 **neither doth a c. tree bring forth** *4550*
1Co 15:33 evil communications **c.** good *5351*
2Co 2:17 many, which **c.** the word of God: *2585*
Eph 4:22 old man, which is **c.** according to *5351*
Eph 4:29 Let no **c.** communication proceed *4550*
1Ti 6:5 disputings of men of **c.** minds, *1311*
2Ti 3:8 men of **c.** minds, reprobate *2704*
Jude 10 those things they **c.** themselves. *5351*
Re 19:2 which did **c.** the earth with her *5351*

CORRUPTED
Ge 6:12 flesh had **c.** his way upon the earth. 7843
Ex 8:24 land was **c.** by reason of the swarm 7843
Ex 32:7 out of Egypt, have **c.** themselves: 7843
De 9:12 out of Egypt have **c.** themselves; 7843
De 32:5 They have **c.** themselves, their 7843
Jg 2:19 **c.** themselves more than their 7843
Eze 16:47 wast **c.** more than they in all thy 7843
Eze 28:17 thou hast **c.** thy wisdom by reason 7843
Ho 9:9 They have deeply **c.** themselves, 7843
Zep 3:7 rose early, and **c.** all their doings. 7843
Mal 2:8 ye have **c.** the covenant of Levi, 7843
2Co 7:2 we have **c.** no man, we have *5351*
2Co 11:3 your minds should be **c.** from the *5351*
Jas 5:2 Your riches are **c.**, and your *4595*

CORRUPTERS
Isa 1:4 children that are **c.**: they have 7843
Jer 6:28 brass and iron; they are all **c.** 7843

CORRUPTETH
Lu 12:33 **approacheth, neither moth c.** *1311*

CORRUPTIBLE See also INCORRUPTIBLE.
Ro 1:23 into an image made like to **c.** man, *5349*
1Co 9:25 they do it to obtain a **c.** crown; *5349*
1Co 15:53 this **c.** must put on incorruption, *5349*
1Co 15:54 So when this **c.** shall have put on *5349*
1Pe 1:18 were not redeemed with **c.** things, *5349*
1Pe 1:23 not of **c.** seed, but of incorruptible, *5349*
1Pe 3:4 in that which is not **c.**, even the *862*

CORRUPTING
Da 11:17 the daughter of women, **c.** her: 7843

CORRUPTION See also INCORRUPTION.
Le 22:25 their **c.** is in them, and blemishes 4893
2Ki 23:13 the right hand of the mount of **c.**, 4889
Job 17:14 said to **c.**, Thou art my father: 7845
Ps 16:10 suffer thine Holy One to see **c.** 7845
Ps 49:9 still live for ever, and not see **c.** 7845
Isa 38:17 delivered it from the pit of **c.**: 1097
Da 10:8 was turned in me into **c.**, and I 4889
Jon 2:6 thou brought up my life from **c.** 7845
Ac 2:27 suffer thine Holy One to see **c.** *1312*
Ac 2:31 in hell, neither his flesh did see **c.** *1312*
Ac 13:34 to return to **c.**, he said on this wise, *1312*
Ac 13:35 not suffer thine Holy One to see **c.** *1312*
Ac 13:36 laid unto his fathers, and saw **c.** *1312*
Ac 13:37 whom God raised again, saw no **c.** *1312*
Ro 8:21 delivered from the bondage of **c.** *5356*
1Co 15:42 It is sown in **c.**; it is raised in *5356*
1Co 15:50 neither doth **c.** inherit incorruption. *5356*
Ga 6:8 shall of the flesh reap **c.**; but he *5356*
2Pe 1:4 escaped the **c.** that is in the world *5356*
2Pe 2:12 utterly perish in their own **c.**; *5356*
2Pe 2:19 themselves are the servants of **c.**: *5356*

CORRUPTLY
2Ch 27:2 And the people did yet **c.** 7843
Ne 1:7 We have dealt very **c.** against thee, 2254

COSAM (co'-sam)
Lu 3:28 Addi, which was the son of **C.**, *2973*

COST See COSTLY.
2Sa 19:42 have we eaten at all of the king's **c.**?
2Sa 24:24 of that which doth **c.** me nothing. 2600
1Ch 21:24 nor offer burnt offerings without **c.** 2600
Lu 14:28 **down first, and counteth the c.,** *1160*

COSTLINESS
Re 18:19 ships in the sea by reason of her **c.**! *5094*

COSTLY
1Ki 5:17 **c.** stones, and hewed stones, 3368
1Ki 7:9 All these were of **c.** stones, 3368
1Ki 7:10 the foundation was of **c.** stones, 3368
1Ki 7:11 And above were **c.** stones, after the 3368
Joh 12:3 of ointment of spikenard, very **c.**, *4186*
1Ti 2:9 or gold, or pearls, or **c.** array: *4185*

COTES See also SHEEPCOTES.
2Ch 32:28 of beasts, and **c.** for flocks. 220

COTTAGE See also COTTAGES.
Isa 1:8 daughter of Zion is left as a **c.** in 5521
Isa 24:20 and shall be removed like a **c.**: 4412

COTTAGES
Zep 2:6 **c.** for shepherds, and folds for 3741

COUCH See also COUCHED; COUCHES; COUCHETH; COUCHING.
Ge 49:4 thou it: he went up to my **c.** 3326
Job 7:13 my **c.** shall ease my complaint; 4904
Job 38:40 When they **c.** in their dens, and 7742
Ps 6:6 I water my **c.** with my tears. 6210
Am 3:12 of a bed, and in Damascus in a **c.** 6210
Lu 5:19 through the tiling with his **c.** into *2826*
Lu 5:24 **take up thy c., and go unto thine** *2826*

COUCHED
Ge 49:9 he **c.** as a lion, and as an old lion; 7257
Nu 24:9 He **c.**, he lay down as a lion, and 3766

COUCHES
Am 6:4 stretch themselves upon their **c.**, 6210
Ac 5:15 and laid them on beds and **c.**, *2895*

COUCHETH
De 33:13 and for the deep that **c.** beneath, 7257

COUCHING See also COUCHINGPLACE.
Ge 49:14 Issachar is a strong ass **c.** down 7257

COUCHINGPLACE
Eze 25:5 and the Ammonites a **c.** for flocks: 4769

COULD See also COULDEST.
Ge 13:6 so that they **c.** not dwell together. 3201
Ge 27:1 his eyes were dim, so that he **c.** not see,
Ge 36:7 were strangers **c.** not bear them 3201
Ge 37:4 they hated him, and **c.** not speak 3201
Ge 41:8 there was none that **c.** interpret them
Ge 41:21 it **c.** not be known that they had
Ge 41:24 there was none that **c.** declare it to me.
Ge 43:7 **c.** we certainly know that he
Ge 45:1 Then Joseph **c.** not refrain himself 3201
Ge 45:3 his brethren **c.** not answer him; 3201
Ge 48:10 dim for age so that he **c.** not see. 3201
Ex 2:3 when she **c.** not longer hide him, 3201
Ex 7:21 and the Egyptians **c.** not drink of 3201
Ex 7:24 for they **c.** not drink of the water of 3201
Ex 8:18 bring forth lice, but they **c.** not. 3201
Ex 9:11 magicians **c.** not stand before Moses 3201
Ex 12:39 out of Egypt, and **c.** not tarry, 3201
Ex 15:23 **c.** not drink of the waters of Marah. 3201
Nu 9:6 **c.** not keep the passover on that 3201
Jos 7:12 the children of Israel **c.** not stand 3201
Jos 15:63 of Judah **c.** not drive them out: 3201
Jos 17:12 children of Manasseh **c.** not drive 3201
Jg 1:19 **c.** not drive out the inhabitants of the
Jg 2:14 that they **c.** not any longer stand 3201
Jg 3:22 that he **c.** not draw the dagger out
Jg 6:27 of the city, that he **c.** not do it by day,
Jg 12:6 he **c.** not frame to pronounce it right.
Jg 14:14 they **c.** not in three days expound 3201
Jg 17:8 to sojourn where he **c.** find a place:
Jg 20:16 one **c.** sling stones at an hair breadth,
Ru 3:14 rose up before one **c.** known another.
1Sa 3:2 to wax dim, that he **c.** not see; 3201
1Sa 4:15 eyes were dim, that he **c.** not see. 3201
1Sa 10:21 they sought him, he **c.** not be found.
1Sa 23:13 and went whithersoever they **c.** go.
1Sa 30:10 they **c.** not go over the brook Besor.
1Sa 30:21 so faint that they **c.** not follow David,
2Sa 1:10 I was sure that he **c.** not live after that
2Sa 3:11 he **c.** not answer Abner a word 3201
2Sa 17:20 had sought and **c.** not find them,
2Sa 22:39 wounded them, that they **c.** not
1Ki 5:3 David my father **c.** not build an 3201
1Ki 8:5 oxen, that **c.** not be told nor numbered
1Ki 8:11 priests **c.** not stand to minister 3201
1Ki 13:4 he **c.** not pull it in again to him. 3201
1Ki 14:4 But Ahijah **c.** not see; for his eyes 3201
2Ki 3:26 the king of Edom; but they **c.** not. 3201
2Ki 4:40 And they **c.** not eat thereof. 3201
2Ki 16:5 besieged Ahaz, but **c.** not overcome 3201
1Ch 12:2 and **c.** use both the right hand and the
1Ch 12:8 for the battle, that **c.** handle shield and
1Ch 12:33 which **c.** keep rank; they were not of
1Ch 12:38 All these men of war, that **c.** keep rank,
1Ch 21:30 But David **c.** not go before it to 3201
2Ch 4:18 weight of the brass **c.** not be found out.
2Ch 5:6 which **c.** not be told nor numbered for
2Ch 5:14 priests **c.** not stand to minister by 3201
2Ch 7:2 priests **c.** not enter into the house 3201
2Ch 13:7 tenderhearted, and **c.** not withstand
2Ch 14:13 that they **c.** not recover themselves;
2Ch 20:25 more than they **c.** carry away: and
2Ch 25:5 war, that **c.** handle spear and shield.
2Ch 25:15 **c.** not deliver their own people
2Ch 29:34 **c.** not flay all the burnt offerings: 3201
2Ch 30:3 For they **c.** not keep it at that time, 3201
2Ch 32:14 **c.** deliver his people out of mine 3201
2Ch 34:12 all that **c.** skill of instruments
Ezr 2:59 **c.** not show their father's house, 3201
Ezr 3:13 the people **c.** not discern the noise of
Ezr 5:5 they **c.** not cause them to cease,
Ne 7:61 **c.** not show their father's house, 3201
Ne 8:2 all that **c.** hear with understanding,
Ne 8:3 and those that **c.** understand; and
Ne 13:24 **c.** not speak in the Jews' language, 5234

Es 6:1 that night **c.** not the king sleep, 5074
Es 7:4 the enemy **c.** not countervail the king's
Es 9:2 no man **c.** withstand them; for the fear
Job 4:16 It stood still, but I **c.** not discern the
Job 16:4 I also **c.** speak as ye do; if your souls
Job 16:4 **c.** heap up words against you,
Job 31:23 his highness I **c.** not endure. 3201
Ps 37:36 I sought him, but he **c.** not be found.
Ps 55:12 then I **c.** have borne it: neither was
Ps 73:7 they have more than heart **c.** wish.
Ps 78:44 their floods, that they **c.** not drink.
Ca 5:6 I sought him, but I **c.** not find him;
Isa 5:4 **c.** have been done more to my vineyard, ...
Isa 7:1 but **c.** not prevail against it. 3201
Isa 30:5 of a people that **c.** not profit
Isa 33:23 **c.** not well strength their mast,
Isa 33:23 they **c.** not spread the sail:
Isa 41:28 asked of them, **c.** answer a word.
Isa 46:2 they **c.** not deliver the burden, 3201
Jer 6:15 ashamed, neither **c.** they blush: 3045
Jer 8:12 ashamed, neither **c.** they blush: 3045
Jer 15:1 my mind **c.** not be toward this people:
Jer 20:9 with forbearing, and I **c.** not stay. 3201
Jer 24:2 **c.** not be eaten, they were so bad.
Jer 44:22 So that the Lord **c.** no longer bear, 3201
La 4:14 men **c.** not touch their garments. 3201
La 4:17 for a nation that **c.** not save us.
Eze 31:8 in the garden of God **c.** not hide him:
Eze 47:5 a river that I **c.** not pass over: 3201
Eze 47:5 a river that **c.** not be passed over.
Da 5:8 but they **c.** not read the writing, 3546
Da 5:15 they **c.** not shew the interpretation 3546
Da 6:4 but they **c.** find none occasion, nor 3202
Da 8:4 any that **c.** deliver out of his hand;
Da 8:7 none that **c.** deliver the ram out of his
Ho 5:13 **c.** he not heal you, nor cure you 3201
Jon 1:13 they **c.** not: for the sea wrought, 3201
Mt 17:16 and they **c.** not cure him. *1410*
Mt 17:19 Why **c.** not we cast him out? *1410*
Mt 26:40 **What, c. ye not watch with me** *2480*
Mt 27:24 When Pilate saw that he **c.** prevail
Mk 1:45 insomuch that Jesus **c.** no more *1410*
Mk 2:4 And when they **c.** not come nigh *1410*
Mk 3:20 that **c.** not so much as eat bread. *1410*
Mk 5:3 and no man **c.** bind him, no, not *1410*
Mk 5:4 neither **c.** any man tame him. *2480*
Mk 6:5 he **c.** there do no mighty work, *1410*
Mk 6:19 have killed him; but she **c.** not: *1410*
Mk 7:24 man know it: but he **c.** not be hid. *1410*
Mk 9:18 cast him out; and they **c.** not *2489*
Mk 9:28 privately, Why **c.** not we cast him *1410*
Mk 14:8 **She hath done what she c.: she is** *2192*
Lu 1:22 he came out, he **c.** not speak unto *1410*
Lu 5:19 And when they **c.** not find by what
Lu 6:48 **that house, and c. not shake it:** *2480*
Lu 8:19 and **c.** not come to him for the *1410*
Lu 8:43 physicians, neither **c.** be healed *2480*
Lu 9:40 cast him out; and they **c.** not *1410*
Lu 13:11 and **c.** in no wise lift up herself *1410*
Lu 14:6 And they **c.** not answer him again *2480*
Lu 19:3 who he was; and **c.** not for the *1410*
Lu 19:48 And **c.** not find what they might do:
Lu 20:7 that they **c.** not tell whence it *5342*
Lu 20:26 And they **c.** not take hold of his *2480*
Joh 9:33 were not of God, he **c.** do nothing *1410*
Joh 11:37 **C.** not this man, which opened the *1410*
Joh 12:39 Therefore they **c.** not believe, *1410*
Joh 21:25 even the word itself **c.** not contain
Ac 4:14 they **c.** say nothing against it *2192*
Ac 11:17 what was I, that I **c.** withstand *1415*
Ac 13:39 from which ye **c.** not be justified *1410*
Ac 21:34 and when he **c.** not know the *1410*
Ac 22:11 And when I **c.** not see for the
Ac 25:7 Paul, which they **c.** not prove *2480*
Ac 27:15 and **c.** not bear up into the wind, *1410*
Ac 27:43 that they which **c.** swim should *1410*
Ro 8:3 For what the law **c.** not do, *102*
Ro 9:3 For I **c.** wish that myself were
1Co 3:1 And I, brethren, **c.** not speak unto *1410*
1Co 13:2 all faith, so that I **c.** remove
2Co 3:7 Israel **c.** not stedfastly behold *1410*
2Co 3:13 Israel **c.** not stedfastly look to
2Co 11:1 Would to God ye **c.** bear with me
Ga 3:21 a law given which **c.** have given *1410*
1Th 3:1 when we **c.** no longer forbear,
1Th 3:5 cause, when I **c.** no longer forbear,
Heb 3:19 So we see that they **c.** not enter *1410*
Heb 6:13 because he **c.** swear by no greater, *2192*
Heb 9:9 and sacrifices, that **c.** not make *1410*
Heb 12:20 (For they **c.** not endure that which
Re 7:9 great multitude, which no man **c.** *1410*
Re 14:3 and no man **c.** learn that song but *1410*

COULDEST
Jer 3:5 and done evil things as thou **c.** 3201
Eze 16:28 and yet **c.** not be satisfied.
Da 2:47 seeing thou **c.** reveal this secret. 3202
Mk 14:37 **c. not thou watch one hour?** *2480*
Joh 19:11 **Thou c. have no power at all**

COULTER See also COULTERS.
1Sa 13:20 every man his share, and his **c.**, 855

COULTERS
1Sa 13:21 and for the **c.**, and for the forks, 855

COUNCIL See also COUNCILS.
Ps 68:27 princes of Judah and their **c.**, 7277
Mt 5:22 **Raca, shall be in danger of the c.:** *4892*
Mt 12:14 Pharisees went out, and held a **c.** *4824*
Mt 26:59 and elders, and all the **c.**, sought *4892*
Mk 14:55 chief priests and all the **c.** sought *4892*
Mk 15:1 and scribes and the whole **c.**, and *4892*
Lu 22:66 and led him into their **c.**, saying, *4892*
Joh 11:47 chief priests and the Pharisees a **c.**, *4892*
Ac 4:15 to go aside out of the **c.**, they *4892*
Ac 5:21 and called the **c.** together, and all *4892*
Ac 5:27 they set them before the **c.**: *4892*
Ac 5:34 Then stood there up one in the **c.**, *4892*
Ac 5:41 from the presence of the **c.**, *4892*
Ac 6:12 him, and brought him to the **c.**, *4892*
Ac 6:15 And all that sat in the **c.**, looking *4892*
Ac 22:30 and all their **c.** to appear, and *4892*
Ac 23:1 Paul, earnestly beholding the **c.**, *4892*
Ac 23:6 he cried out in the **c.**, Men and *4892*
Ac 23:15 Now therefore ye with the **c.** signify *4892*
Ac 23:20 down Paul to morrow into the **c.**, *4892*
Ac 23:28 I brought him forth into their **c.**: *4892*
Ac 24:20 while I stood before the **c.**, *4892*
Ac 25:12 he had conferred with the **c.**, *4824*

COUNCILS
Mt 10:17 **they will deliver you up to the c.,** *4894*
Mk 13:9 **they shall deliver you up to c.;** *4894*

COUNSEL See also COUNSELLED; COUNSELS.
Ex 18:19 I will give thee **c.**, and God shall 3289
Nu 27:21 the priest, who shall ask **c.**, for
Nu 31:16 through the **c.** of Balaam, to 1697
De 32:28 For they are a nation void of **c.**, 6098
Jos 9:14 and asked not **c.** at the mouth of
Jg 18:5 Ask **c.**, we pray thee, of God,
Jg 20:7 give here you advice and **c.** 6098
Jg 20:18 and asked **c.** of God, and said,
Jg 20:23 and asked **c.** of the Lord, saying,
1Sa 14:37 And Saul asked **c.** of God, Shall I
2Sa 15:31 turn the **c.** of Ahithophel into 6098
2Sa 15:34 for me defeat the **c.** of Ahithophel. 6098
2Sa 16:20 Give **c.** among you what we shall 6098
2Sa 16:23 And the **c.** of Ahithophel, which he 6098
2Sa 16:23 so was all the **c.** of Ahithophel both 6098
2Sa 17:7 The **c.** that Ahithophel hath given 6098
2Sa 17:11 I **c.** that all Israel be generally 3289
2Sa 17:14 The **c.** of Hushai the Archite 6098
2Sa 17:14 is better than the **c.** of Ahithophel. 6098
2Sa 17:14 to defeat the good **c.** of Ahithophel, 6098
2Sa 17:15 Thus and thus did Ahithophel **c.** 3289
2Sa 17:23 saw that his **c.** was not followed, 6098
2Sa 20:18 They shall surely ask **c.** at Abel:
1Ki 1:12 let me, I pray thee, give thee **c.**, 6098
1Ki 12:8 he forsook the **c.** of the old men, 6098
1Ki 12:9 What **c.** give ye that we may 3289
1Ki 12:13 forsook the old men's **c.** that they 6098
1Ki 12:14 to them after the **c.** of the young 6098
1Ki 12:28 Whereupon the king took **c.**, and 3289
2Ki 6:8 and took **c.** with his servants, 3289
2Ki 18:20 I have **c.** and strength for the war 6098
1Ch 10:13 asking **c.** of one that had a familiar
2Ch 10:6 Rehoboam took **c.** with the old 3289
2Ch 10:6 What **c.** give ye me to return 3289
2Ch 10:8 forsook the **c.** which the old men 6098
2Ch 10:8 and took **c.** with the young men 3289
2Ch 10:13 forsook the **c.** of the old men, 6098
2Ch 22:5 He walked also after their **c.**, and 6098
2Ch 25:16 Art thou made of the king's **c.**? 3289
2Ch 25:16 hast not hearkened unto my **c.** 6098
2Ch 30:2 For the king had taken **c.**, and 3289
2Ch 30:23 whole assembly took **c.** to keep 3289
2Ch 32:3 He took **c.** with his princes and 3289
Ezr 10:3 according to the **c.** of my lord, 6098
Ezr 10:8 according to the **c.** of the princes 6098
Ne 4:15 God had brought their **c.** to nought, 6098
Ne 6:7 and let us take **c.** together. 3289
Job 5:13 the **c.** of the froward is carried 6098
Job 10:3 shine upon the **c.** of the wicked? 6098
Job 12:13 strength, he hath **c.** and 6098
Job 18:7 and his own **c.** shall cast him down. 6098
Job 21:16 the **c.** of the wicked is far from me. 6098
Job 22:18 but the **c.** of the wicked is far from 6098
Job 29:21 waited, and kept silence at my **c.** 6098
Job 38:2 Who is this that darkeneth **c.** by 6098
Job 42:3 Who is he that hideth **c.** without 6098
Ps 1:1 walketh not in the **c.** of the ungodly, 6098
Ps 2:2 the rulers take **c.** together, 3245
Ps 13:2 How long shall I take **c.** in my 6098
Ps 14:6 Ye have shamed the **c.** of the poor, 6098
Ps 16:7 the Lord, who hath given me **c.** 3289
Ps 20:4 own heart, and fulfil all thy **c.** 6098
Ps 31:13 while they took **c.** together 3245
Ps 33:10 The Lord bringeth the **c.** of the 6098
Ps 33:11 The **c.** of the Lord standeth for 6098
Ps 55:14 We took sweet **c.** together, and 5475
Ps 64:2 Hide me from the secret **c.** of the 5475
Ps 71:10 that lay wait for my soul take **c.** 3289
Ps 73:24 Thou shalt guide me with thy **c.**, 6098
Ps 83:3 They have taken crafty **c.** against 5475
Ps 106:13 works; they waited not for his **c.**: 6098
Ps 106:43 they provoked him with their **c.**, 6098
Ps 107:11 contemned the **c.** of the most High, 6098
Pr 1:25 ye have set at nought all my **c.**, 6098
Pr 1:30 They would none of my **c.**: 6098
Pr 8:14 **C.** is mine, and sound wisdom: 6098
Pr 11:14 Where no **c.** is, the people fall: 8458
Pr 12:15 that hearkeneth unto **c.** is wise. 6098
Pr 15:22 Without **c.** purposes are 5475
Pr 19:20 Hear **c.**, and receive instruction, 6098
Pr 19:21 nevertheless the **c.** of the Lord, 6098
Pr 20:5 **C.** in the heart of man is like deep 6098
Pr 20:18 Every purpose is established by **c.**: 6098
Pr 21:30 nor **c.** against the Lord. 6098
Pr 24:6 wise **c.** thou shalt make thy war: 8458
Pr 27:9 of a man's friend by hearty **c.** 6098
Ec 8:2 I **c.** thee to keep the king's
Isa 5:19 the **c.** of the Holy One of Israel 6098
Isa 7:5 have taken evil **c.** against thee, 3289
Isa 8:10 Take **c.** together, and it shall 6098
Isa 11:2 the spirit of **c.** and might, 6098
Isa 16:3 Take **c.**, execute judgment; make 6098
Isa 19:3 and I will destroy the **c.** thereof: 6098
Isa 19:11 the **c.** of the wise counsellers 6098
Isa 19:17 because of the **c.** of the Lord of 6098
Isa 23:8 hath taken this **c.** against Tyre, 3289
Isa 28:29 which is wonderful in **c.**, 6098
Isa 29:15 hide their **c.** from the Lord, 6098
Isa 30:1 Lord, that take **c.**, but not of me; 6098
Isa 36:5 I have **c.** and strength for war: 6098
Isa 40:14 With whom took he **c.**, and who 3289
Isa 44:26 the **c.** of his messengers; 6098
Isa 45:21 let them take **c.** together: 3289
Isa 46:10 My **c.** shall stand, and I will do 6098
Isa 46:11 the man that executeth my **c.** 6098
Jer 18:18 nor **c.** from the wise, nor the word 6098
Jer 18:23 thou knowest all their **c.** against 6098
Jer 19:7 I will make void the **c.** of Judah 6098
Jer 23:18 hath stood in the **c.** of the Lord, 5475
Jer 23:22 if they had stood in my **c.**, 5475
Jer 32:19 Great in **c.**, and mighty in work: 6098
Jer 38:15 if I give thee **c.**, wilt thou not 3289
Jer 49:7 is **c.** perished from the prudent? 6098
Jer 49:20 hear the **c.** of the Lord, that he 6098
Jer 49:30 hath taken **c.** against you, 6098
Jer 50:45 hear ye the **c.** of the Lord, 6098
Eze 7:26 priest, and **c.** from the ancients. 6098
Eze 11:2 and give wicked **c.** in this city: 6098
Da 2:14 answered with **c.** and wisdom 5843
Da 4:27 let my **c.** be acceptable unto thee, 4431
Ho 4:12 My people ask **c.** at their stocks,
Ho 10:6 shall be ashamed of his own **c.** 6098
Mic 4:12 neither understand they his **c.**: 6098
Zec 6:13 **c.** of peace shall be between them 6098
Mt 22:15 took **c.** how they might entangle *4824*
Mt 27:1 and elders of the people took **c.** *4824*
Mt 27:7 And they took **c.**, and bought *4824*
Mt 28:12 and had taken **c.**, they gave large *4824*
Mk 3:6 took **c.** with the Herodians *4824*

Lu 7:30 lawyers rejected the **c.** of God *1012*
Lu 23:51 consented to the **c.** and deed of *1012*
Joh 11:53 they took **c.** together for to put *4823*
Joh 18:14 was he which gave **c.** to the Jews, *4823*
Ac 2:23 determinate **c.** and foreknowledge *1012*
Ac 4:28 thy hand and thy **c.** determined *1012*
Ac 5:33 heart, and took **c.** to slay them *1011*
Ac 5:38 this **c.** or this work be of men, *1012*
Ac 9:23 the Jews took **c.** to kill him: *4823*
Ac 20:27 declare unto you all the **c.** of God. *1012*
Ac 27:42 soldiers' **c.** was to kill the prisoners, *1012*
Eph 1:11 after the **c.** of his own will: *1012*
Heb 6:17 the immutability of his **c.**, *1012*
Re 3:18 **I c. thee to buy of me gold** *4823*

COUNSELLED

2Sa 16:23 which he **c.** in those days, was as if 3289
2Sa 17:15 and thus and thus have I **c.** 3289
2Sa 17:21 hath Ahithophel **c.** against you 3289
Job 26:3 How hast thou **c.** him that hath 3289

COUNSELLER See also COUNSELLERS; COUNSELLOR.
[*Most editions have uniformly* COUNSELLOR *and* COUNSELLORS.]

2Sa 15:12 David's **c.**, from his city, even 3289
1Ch 26:14 for Zechariah his son, a wise **c.**, 3289
1Ch 27:32 Jonathan David's uncle was a **c.**, 3289
1Ch 27:33 Ahithophel was the king's **c.**: 3289
2Ch 22:3 mother was his **c.** to do wickedly. 3289
Isa 3:3 the **c.**, and the cunning artificer, 3289
Isa 9:6 shall be called Wonderful, **C.**, 3289
Isa 40:13 Who being his **c.** hath taught him: 6098
Isa 41:28 there was no **c.**, that, when I asked 3289
Mic 4:9 is thy **c.** perished? for pangs have 3289
Na 1:11 against the Lord, a wicked **c.** 3289

COUNSELLERS

2Ch 22:4 they were his **c.** after the death 3289
Ezr 4:5 hired **c.** against them, to frustrate 3289
Ezr 7:14 of the king, and of his seven **c.**, 3272
Ezr 7:15 king and his **c.** have freely offered 3272
Ezr 7:28 me before the king, and his **c.**, 3289
Ezr 8:25 which the king, and his **c.**, 3289
Job 3:14 With kings and **c.** of the earth, 3289
Job 12:17 He leadeth **c.** away spoiled, 3289
Ps 119:24 also are my delight and my **c.** 6098
Pr 11:14 multitude of **c.** there is safety 3289
Pr 12:20 but to the **c.** of peace is joy 3289
Pr 15:22 in the multitude of **c.** they are 3289
Pr 24:6 multitude of **c.** there is safety 3289
Isa 1:26 and thy **c.** as at the beginning: 3289
Isa 19:11 counsel of the wise **c.** of Pharaoh 3289
Da 3:2,3 treasures, the **c.**, the sheriffs, 1884
Da 3:24 said unto his **c.**, Did not we cast 1907
Da 3:27 king's **c.**, being gathered together, 1907
Da 4:36 **c.** and my lords sought unto me; 1907
Da 6:7 **c.**, and the captains, have consulted 1907

COUNSELLOR See also COUNSELLER.

Mk 15:43 of Arimathaea, an honourable **c.**, *1010*
Lu 23:50 was a man named Joseph, a **c.**; *1010*
Ro 11:34 or who hath been his **c.**? *4825*

COUNSELS

Job 37:12 turned round about by his **c.**: 8458
Ps 5:10 let them fall by their own **c.**; 4156
Ps 81:12 and they walked in their own **c.** 4156
Pr 1:5 shall attain unto wise **c.**: 8458
Pr 12:5 the **c.** of the wicked are deceit 8458
Pr 22:20 things in **c.** and knowledge, 4156
Isa 25:1 thy **c.** of old are faithfulness 6098
Isa 47:13 in the multitude of thy **c.** 6098
Jer 7:24 in the **c.** and in the imagination 4156
Ho 11:6 them, because of their own **c.** 4156
Mic 6:16 ye walk in their **c.**; that I should 4156
1Co 4:5 manifest the **c.** of the hearts: *1012*

COUNT See also ACCOUNT; COUNTED; COUNTETH; COUNTING; RECOUNT.

Ex 12:4 shall make your **c.** for the lamb 3699
Le 19:23 **c.** the fruit thereof as uncircumcised:
Le 23:15 **c.** unto you from the morrow 5608
Le 25:27 **c.** the years of the sale thereof, 2803
Le 25:52 then he shall **c.** with him, 2803
Nu 23:10 Who can **c.** the dust of Jacob, 4487
1Sa 1:16 **C.** not thine handmaid for a 5414
Job 19:15 my maids, **c.** me for a stranger: 2803
Job 31:4 see my ways, and **c.** all my steps? 5608
Ps 87:6 The Lord shall **c.**, when he writeth 5608
Ps 139:18 If I should **c.** them, they are 5608
Ps 139:22 I **c.** them mine enemies 1961
Mic 6:11 Shall I **c.** them pure with the
Ac 20:24 neither **c.** I my life dear unto *2192*
Php 3:8 I **c.** all things but loss for the *2233*
Php 3:8 do **c.** them but dung, that I may *2233*
Php 3:13 Brethren, I **c.** not myself to have *3049*
2Th 1:11 God would **c.** you worthy of this *515*
2Th 3:15 **c.** him not as an enemy, but *2233*
1Ti 6:1 **c.** their own masters worthy of *2233*
Phm 17 If thou **c.** me therefore a partner, *2192*
Jas 1:2 **c.** it all joy when ye fall into *2233*
Jas 5:11 we **c.** them happy which endure *3106*
2Pe 2:13 as they that **c.** it pleasure to riot *2233*
2Pe 3:9 as some men **c.** slackness; but is *2233*
Re 13:18 hath understanding **c.** the number *5585*

COUNTED

Ge 15:6 he **c.** it to him for righteousness. 2803
Ge 30:33 that shall be **c.** stolen with me.
Ge 31:15 Are we not **c.** of him strangers? 2803
Ex 38:21 as it was **c.**, according to the 6485
Le 25:31 shall be **c.** as the fields of the 2803
Nu 18:30 it shall be **c.** unto the Levites 2803
Jos 13:3 is **c.** to the Canaanite: five lords 2803
1Ki 1:21 son Solomon shall be **c.** offenders.
1Ki 3:8 be numbered nor **c.** for multitude. 5608
1Ch 21:6 But Levi and Benjamin **c.** he not 6485
1Ch 23:24 they were **c.** by number of names 6485
Ne 13:13 they were **c.** faithful, and their 2803
Job 18:3 Wherefore are we **c.** as beasts, 2803
Job 41:29 Darts are **c.** as stubble: he 2803
Ps 44:22 we are **c.** as sheep for the slaughter 2803
Ps 88:4 I am **c.** with them that go down 2803
Ps 106:31 was **c.** unto him for righteousness 2803
Pr 17:28 he holdeth his peace, is **c.** wise: 2803
Pr 27:14 it shall be **c.** a curse to him. 2803
Isa 5:28 horses' hoofs shall be **c.** like flint, 2803
Isa 32:15 the fruitful field be **c.** for a forest. 2803
Isa 33:18 where is he that **c.** the towers? 5608
Isa 40:15 are **c.** as the small dust of the 2803
Isa 40:17 are **c.** to him less than nothing, 2803
Ho 8:12 they were **c.** as a strange thing. 2803
Mt 14:5 because they **c.** him as a prophet *2192*
Mk 11:32 men **c.** John, that he was a prophet. *2192*
Ac 5:41 that they were **c.** worthy to suffer *2661*
Ac 19:19 they **c.** the price of them, and found *4860*
Ro 2:26 shall not his uncircumcision be **c.** *3049*
Ro 4:3 **c.** unto him for righteousness. *3049*
Ro 4:5 his faith is **c.** for righteousness *3049*
Ro 9:8 of the promise are **c.** for the seed. *3049*
Php 3:7 gain to me, those I **c.** loss for *2233*
2Th 1:5 may be **c.** worthy of the kingdom *2661*
1Ti 1:12 that he **c.** me faithful, putting me *2233*
1Ti 5:17 well be **c.** worthy of double honour, *515*
Heb 3:3 was **c.** worthy of more glory than *515*
Heb 7:6 whose descent is not **c.** from them, *1075*
Heb 10:29 hath **c.** the blood of the covenant, *2233*

COUNTENANCE See also COUNTENANCES.

Ge 4:5 Cain was very wroth, and his **c.** fell 6440
Ge 4:6 why is thy **c.** fallen? 6440
Ge 31:2 Jacob beheld the **c.** of Laban, 6440
Ge 31:5 I see your father's **c.**, that it is 6440
Ex 23:3 Neither shalt thou **c.** a poor man 1921
Nu 6:26 The Lord lift up his **c.** upon thee, 6440
De 28:50 nation of fierce **c.**, which shall not 6440
Jg 13:6 his **c.** was like the **c.** of an angel 4758
1Sa 1:18 eat, and her **c.** was no more sad 6440
1Sa 16:7 Look not on his **c.**, or on the 4758
1Sa 16:12 of a beautiful **c.**, and goodly 5869
1Sa 17:42 youth, and ruddy, and of a fair **c.** 4758
1Sa 25:3 and of a beautiful **c.**: 8389
2Sa 14:27 she was a woman of a fair **c.** 4758
2Ki 8:11 And he settled his **c.** stedfastly, 6440
Ne 2:2 Why is thy **c.** sad, seeing thou art 6440
Ne 2:3 why should not thy **c.** be sad, 6440
Job 14:20 thou changest his **c.**, and sendest 6440
Job 29:24 light of my **c.** they cast not down 6440
Ps 4:6 lift thou up the light of thy **c.** 6440
Ps 10:4 through the pride of his **c.**, 639
Ps 11:7 his **c.** doth behold the upright 6440
Ps 21:6 him exceeding glad with thy **c.** 6440
Ps 42:5 praise him for the help of his **c.** 6440
Ps 42:11 health of my **c.**, and my God 6440
Ps 43:5 health of my **c.**, and my God 6440
Ps 44:3 light of thy **c.**, because thou hadst 6440
Ps 80:16 they perish at the rebuke of thy **c.** 6440
Ps 89:15 walk, O Lord, in the light of **c.**: 6440
Ps 90:8 secret sins in the light of thy **c.** 6440
Pr 15:13 merry heart maketh a cheerful **c.**: 6440
Pr 16:15 the light of the king's **c.** is life; 6440
Pr 25:23 an angry **c.** a backbiting tongue 6440
Pr 27:17 sharpeneth the **c.** of his friend 6440
Ec 7:3 by the sadness of the **c.** the heart 6440
Ca 2:14 let me see thy **c.**, let me hear 4758
Ca 2:14 is thy voice, and thy **c.** is comely 4758
Ca 5:15 his **c.** is as Lebanon, excellent as 4758
Isa 3:9 The shew of their **c.** doth witness 6440
Eze 27:35 they shall be troubled in their **c.** 6440
Da 1:13 and the **c.** of the children that 4758
Da 5:6 the king's **c.** was changed, and 2122
Da 5:9 his **c.** was changed in him, and 2122
Da 5:10 nor let thy **c.** be changed: 2122
Da 7:28 and my **c.** changed in me: but I 2122
Da 8:23 a king of fierce **c.**, and 6440
Mt 6:16 **the hypocrites, of a sad c.** *4659*
Mt 28:3 His **c.** was like lightning, and his *2397*
Lu 9:29 his **c.** was altered, and *4383*
Ac 2:28 make me full of joy with thy **c.** *4383*
2Co 3:7 of Moses for the glory of his **c.**; *4383*
Re 1:16 and his **c.** was as the sun shineth *3799*

COUNTENANCES

Da 1:13 Then let our **c.** be looked upon 4758
Da 1:15 their **c.** appeared fairer and 4758

COUNTERVAIL

Es 7:4 the enemy could not **c.** the king's 7737

COUNTETH

Job 19:11 he **c.** me unto him as one of his 2803
Job 33:10 he **c.** me for his enemy, 2803
Lu 14:28 **and c. the cost, whether he hath** *5585*

COUNTING

Ec 7:27 saith the preacher, **c.** one by one,

COUNTRIES

Ge 10:20 after their tongues, in their **c.**, 776
Ge 26:3 give all these **c.**, and I will 776
Ge 26:4 give unto thy seed all these **c.**; 776
Ge 41:57 all **c.** came into Egypt to Joseph 776
Jos 13:32 These are the **c.** which Moses did
Jos 14:1 And these are the **c.** which the
Jos 17:11 and her towns, even three **c.** 5316
2Ki 18:35 gods of the **c.**, that have delivered 776
1Ch 22:5 and of glory throughout all **c.**: 776
1Ch 29:30 over all the kingdoms of the **c.** 776
2Ch 11:23 all the **c.** of Judah and Benjamin, 776
2Ch 12:8 service of the kingdoms of the **c.** 776
2Ch 15:5 upon all the inhabitants of the **c.** 776
2Ch 20:29 on all the kingdoms of those **c.**, 776
2Ch 34:33 out of all the **c.** that pertained 776
Ezr 3:3 because of the people of those **c.** 776
Ezr 4:20 over all **c.** beyond the river;
Ps 110:6 wound the heads over many **c.** 776
Isa 8:9 and give ear, all ye of far **c.** 776
Isa 37:18 waste all the nations, and their **c.**, 776
Jer 23:3 my flock out of all **c.** whither I have 776
Jer 23:8 from all **c.** whither I had driven 776
Jer 28:8 prophesied both against many **c.**, 776
Jer 32:37 will gather them out of all **c.**, 776
Jer 40:11 that were in all the **c.**, heard that 776
Eze 5:5 the nations and **c.** that are round 776
Eze 5:6 more than the **c.** that are round 776
Eze 6:8 be scattered throughout the **c.** 776
Eze 11:16 have scattered them among the **c.**, 776
Eze 11:16 them as a little sanctuary in the **c.** 776
Eze 11:17 assemble you out of the **c.** where 776
Eze 12:15 and disperse them in the **c.** 776
Eze 20:23 and disperse them through the **c.**; 776
Eze 20:32 heathen, as the families of the **c.**, 776
Eze 20:34 gather you out of the **c.** wherein 776
Eze 20:41 **c.** wherein ye have been scattered: 776
Eze 22:4 and a mocking to all **c.** 776
Eze 22:15 disperse thee in the **c.**, and will 776
Eze 25:7 cause thee to perish out of the **c.**: 776
Eze 29:12 midst of the **c.** that are desolate, 776
Eze 29:12 will disperse them through the **c.** 776
Eze 30:7 midst of the **c.** that are desolate, 776
Eze 30:23 disperse them through the **c.** 776
Eze 30:26 and disperse them through the **c.**; 776
Eze 32:9 the **c.** which thou hast not known. 776
Eze 34:13 and gather them from the **c.**, 776
Eze 35:10 and these two **c.** shall be mine, 776
Eze 36:19 were dispersed through the **c.** 776

Eze 36:24 gather you out of all **c.**, and will.......... 776
Da 9:7 all the **c.** whither thou hast driven........ 776
Da 11:40 he shall enter in the **c.**, and shall......... 776
Da 11:41 many **c.** shall be overthrown:..................
Da 11:42 forth his hand also upon the **c.**: 776
Zec 10:9 they shall remember me in far **c.**;............
Lu 21:21 that are in the **c.** enter thereinto... *5561*

COUNTRY See also COUNTRIES; COUNTRYMEN.
Ge 12:1 Get thee out of thy **c.**, and from thy.... 776
Ge 14:7 smote all the **c.** of the Amalekites, ... 7704
Ge 19:28 the smoke of the **c.** went up as.......... 776
Ge 20:1 toward the south **c.**, and dwelled........ 776
Ge 24:4 thou shalt go unto my **c.**, and to.......... 776
Ge 24:62 for he dwelt in the south **c.**. 776
Ge 25:6 lived, eastward, unto the east **c.**........... 776
Ge 29:26 It must not be so done in our **c.**, ... 4725
Ge 30:25 mine own place, and to my **c.**............... 776
Ge 32:3 the land of Seir, the **c.** of Edom......... 7704
Ge 32:9 Return unto thy **c.**, and to thy 776
Ge 34:2 Hivite, prince of the **c.**, saw her.......... 776
Ge 36:6 went into the **c.** from the face of......... 776
Ge 42:30 and took us for spies of the **c.**. 776
Ge 42:33 man, the lord of the **c.**, said unto 776
Ge 47:27 of Egypt, in the **c.** of Goshen;............. 776
Le 16:29 whether it be one of your own **c.**, ... 249
Le 17:15 whether it be one of your own **c.**, ... 249
Le 24:22 stranger, as for one of your own **c.**:...... 249
Le 25:31 be counted as the fields of the **c.**:........ 776
Nu 15:13 All that are born of the **c.** shall do 249
Nu 20:17 pass, I pray thee, through thy **c.**: 776
Nu 21:20 **c.** of Moab, to the top of Pisgah, ... 7704
Nu 32:4 the **c.** which the Lord smote............... 776
Nu 32:33 the cities of the **c.** round about. 776
De 3:14 Manasseh took all the **c.** of Argob...... 2256
De 4:43 in the plain **c.**, of the Reubenites; 776
De 26:3 come unto the **c.** which the Lord......... 776
Jos 2:2 of Israel to search out the **c.**. 776
Jos 2:3 be come to search out all the **c.**. 776
Jos 2:24 the inhabitants of the **c.** do faint 776
Jos 6:22 men that had spied out the **c.**, ... 776
Jos 6:27 was noised throughout all the **c.**. 776
Jos 7:2 Go up and view the **c.**. And the 776
Jos 9:6 We be come from a far **c.**: now........... 776
Jos 9:9 From a very far **c.** thy servants are 776
Jos 9:11 inhabitants of our **c.** spake to us, ... 776
Jos 10:40 Joshua smote all the **c.** of the hills, ... 776
Jos 10:41 and all the **c.** of Goshen, even unto...... 776
Jos 11:16 all the south **c.**, and all the land ....
Jos 12:7 the kings of the **c.** which Joshua 776
Jos 12:8 and in the south **c.**; the Hittites, ...
Jos 13:6 of the hill **c.** from Lebanon......................
Jos 13:21 of Sihon, dwelling in the **c.**. 776
Jos 17:15 then get thee up to the wood **c.**,...............
Jos 19:51 made an end of dividing the **c.**............... 776
Jos 21:11 Hebron, in the hill **c.** of Judah...................
Jos 22:9 to go unto the **c.** of Gilead, to the 776
Jg 8:28 **c.** was in quietness forty years............ 776
Jg 11:21 Amorites, the inhabitants of that **c.**. 776
Jg 12:12 in Aijalon in the **c.** of Zebulun............. 776
Jg 16:24 the destroyer of our **c.**, which slew...... 776
Jg 18:14 that went to spy out the **c.** of Laish, ... 776
Jg 20:6 the **c.** of the inheritance of Israel: 7704
Ru 1:1 to sojourn in the **c.** of Moab, he, ... 7704
Ru 1:2 And they came into the **c.** of Moab,...... 7704
Ru 1:6 might return from the **c.** of Moab:...... 7704
Ru 1:6 for she had heard in the **c.** of Moab.... 7704
Ru 1:22 returned out of the **c.** of Moab: 7704
Ru 2:6 with Naomi out of the **c.** of Moab:....... 7704
Ru 4:3 come again out of the **c.** of Moab,...... 7704
1Sa 6:1 **c.** of the Philistines seven months 7704
1Sa 6:18 of fenced cities, and of **c.** villages, ... 6521
1Sa 14:21 the camp from the **c.** round about.............
1Sa 27:5 me a place in some town in the **c.**,...... 7704
1Sa 27:7 the time that David dwelt in the **c.** 7704
1Sa 27:11 dwelleth in the **c.** of the Philistines. 7704
2Sa 15:23 all the **c.** wept with a loud voice. 776
2Sa 18:8 scattered over the face of all the **c.**:..... 776
2Sa 21:14 in the **c.** of Benjamin in Zelah,............ 776
1Ki 4:19 the son of Uri was in the **c.** of............ 776
1Ki 4:19 Gilead, in the **c.** of Sihon king............ 776
1Ki 4:30 the children of the east **c.**, and all ....
1Ki 8:41 out of a far **c.** for thy name's sake; 776
1Ki 10:13 turned and went to her own **c.**,............. 776
1Ki 10:15 and of the governors of the **c.**............. 776
1Ki 11:21 that I may go to mine own **c.**,............... 776
1Ki 11:22 thou seekest to go to thine own **c.**? 776
1Ki 20:27 but the Syrians filled the **c.**.................. 776
1Ki 22:36 and every man to his own **c.**................ 776
2Ki 3:20 and the **c.** was filled with water........... 776
2Ki 3:24 the Moabites, even in their **c.**.................
2Ki 18:35 delivered their **c.** out of mine hand,...... 776
2Ki 20:14 They are come from a far **c.**, even 776
1Ch 8:8 begat children in the **c.** of Moab,......... 7704
1Ch 20:1 the **c.** of the children of Ammon, ... 776
2Ch 6:32 a far **c.** for thy great name's sake, ... 776
2Ch 9:14 governors of the **c.** brought gold.......... 776
2Ch 26:10 in the low **c.**, and in the plains:.................
2Ch 28:18 invaded the cities of the low **c.**, ...
2Ch 30:10 the **c.** of Ephraim and Manasseh.......... 776
Ne 12:28 plain **c.** round about Jerusalem, ...
Pr 25:25 soul, so is good news from a far **c.**..... 776
Isa 1:7 Your **c.** is desolate, your cities are....... 776
Isa 13:5 They come from a far **c.**, from the....... 776
Isa 22:18 toss thee like a ball into a large **c.**: 776
Isa 39:3 are come from a far **c.** unto me,......... 776
Isa 46:11 executeth my counsel from a far **c.**: 776
Jer 2:7 I brought you into a plentiful **c.**, ... 776
Jer 4:16 watchers come from a far **c.**, and 776
Jer 6:20 and the sweet cane from a far **c.**?........ 776
Jer 6:22 a people cometh from the north **c.**. 776
Jer 8:19 them that dwell in a far **c.**:................ 776
Jer 10:22 great commotion out of the north **c.**, ... 776
Jer 22:10 no more, nor see his native **c.**. 776
Jer 22:26 another **c.** where ye were not born; 776
Jer 23:8 out of the north **c.**, and from all 776
Jer 31:8 I will bring them from the north **c.**,....... 776
Jer 32:8 which is in the **c.** of Benjamin: 776
Jer 44:1 Noph, and in the **c.** of Pathros, ... 776
Jer 46:10 hath a sacrifice in the north **c.** by 776
Jer 47:4 the remnant of the **c.** of Caphtor. 339
Jer 48:21 upon the plain **c.**; upon Holon, ... 776
Jer 50:9 great nations from the north **c.**:........... 776
Jer 51:9 let us go every one into his own **c.**:..... 776
Eze 20:38 out of the **c.** where they sojourn, ... 776
Eze 20:42 into the **c.** for the which I lifted up 776
Eze 25:9 the glory of the **c.** Beth-jeshimoth,....... 776
Eze 32:15 and the **c.** shall be destitute of............ 776
Eze 34:13 in all the inhabited places of the **c.**. 776
Eze 47:8 issue out toward the east **c.**,............. 1552
Eze 47:22 be unto you as born in the **c.**............ 249
Ho 12:12 Jacob fled into the **c.** of Syria, ... 7704
Jon 1:8 what is thy **c.**? and of what people....... 776
Jon 4:2 saying, when I was yet in my **c.**? 127
Zec 6:6 go forth into the north **c.**; and the 776
Zec 6:6 go forth toward the south **c.**............... 776
Zec 6:8 that go toward the north **c.** have 776
Zec 6:8 quieted my spirit in the north **c.**. 776
Zec 8:7 save my people from the east **c.**,.......... 776
Zec 8:7 and from the west **c.**;......................... 776
Mt 2:12 into their own **c.** another way............ *5561*
Mt 8:28 side into the **c.** of the Gergesenes,..... *5561*
Mt 9:31 abroad his fame in all that **c.**. *1093*
Mt 13:54 he was come into his own **c.**, he........ *3968*
Mt 13:57 without honour, save in his own **c.**,*3968*
Mt 14:35 all that **c.** round about, and *4066*
Mt 21:33 and went into a far **c.**:.................... *589*
Mt 25:14 a man travelling into a far **c.**, who. *589*
Mk 5:1 into the **c.** of the Gadarenes............. *5561*
Mk 5:10 not send them away out of the **c.**........ *5561*
Mk 5:14 told it in the city, and in the **c.**........... *68*
Mk 6:1 and came into his own **c.**; and *3968*
Mk 6:4 without honour, but in his own **c.**,.*3968*
Mk 6:36 go into the **c.** round about, and into....... *68*
Mk 6:56 into villages, or cities, or **c.**, ... *68*
Mk 12:1 husbandmen, and went into a far **c.**..*589*
Mk 15:21 coming out of the **c.**, the father of.......... *68*
Mk 16:12 they walked, and went into the **c.**. *68*
Lu 1:39 and went into the hill **c.** with haste,..........
Lu 1:65 throughout all the hill **c.** of Judaea............
Lu 2:8 were in the same **c.** shepherds *5561*
Lu 3:3 into all the **c.** about Jordan,............... *4066*
Lu 4:23 Capernaum, do also here in thy **c.**..*3968*
Lu 4:24 prophet is accepted in his own **c.**... *3968*
Lu 4:37 every place of the **c.** round about....... *4066*
Lu 8:26 at the **c.** of the Gadarenes, which........ *5561*
Lu 8:34 and told it in the city and in the **c.**.......... *68*
Lu 8:37 **c.** of the Gadarenes round about *4066*
Lu 9:12 may go into the towns and **c.** round....... *68*
Lu 15:13 took his journey into a far **c.**, and..*5561*
Lu 15:15 himself to a citizen of that **c.**;......... *5561*
Lu 19:12 went into a far **c.** to receive for *5561*
Lu 20:9 went into a far **c.** for a long time... *589*
Lu 23:26 a Cyrenian, coming out of the **c.**, ... *68*
Joh 4:44 hath no honour in his own **c.**............ *3968*
Joh 11:54 unto a **c.** near to the wilderness,........ *5561*
Joh 11:55 went out of the **c.** up to Jerusalem *5561*
Ac 4:36 a Levite, and of the **c.** of Cyprus, ... *1085*
Ac 7:3 Get the out of thy **c.**, and from *1093*
Ac 12:20 **c.** was nourished by the king's **c.**. *5561*
Ac 13:7 deputy of the **c.**, Sergius Paulus,.............
Ac 18:23 all the **c.** of Galatia and Phrygia *5561*
Ac 27:27 that they drew near to some **c.**; *5561*
Heb 11:9 of promise, as in a strange **c.**, ...
Heb 11:14 declare plainly that they seek a **c.**. *3968*
Heb 11:15 mindful of that **c.** from whence................
Heb 11:16 But now they desire a better **c.**..............

COUNTRYMEN
2Co 11:26 in perils by mine own **c.**, in perils *1085*
1Th 2:14 suffered like things of your own **c.**,..... *4853*

COUPLE See also COUPLED; COUPLETH; COUPLING.
Ex 26:6 and **c.** the curtains together with........ 2266
Ex 26:9 **c.** five curtains by themselves,........... 2266
Ex 26:11 and **c.** the tent together, that it 2266
Ex 36:18 of brass to **c.** the tent together,.......... 2266
Ex 39:4 shoulderpieces for it, to **c.** it 2266
Jg 19:3 servant with him, and a **c.** of asses:.... 6776
2Sa 13:6 make me a **c.** of cakes in my sight, ... 8147
2Sa 16:1 him, with a **c.** of asses saddled 6776
Isa 21:7 a chariot with a **c.** of horsemen.......... 6776
Isa 21:9 of men, with a **c.** of horsemen........... 6776

COUPLED
Ex 26:3 five curtains shall be **c.** together 2266
Ex 26:3 **c.** one to another. 2266
Ex 26:24 they shall be **c.** together beneath, ... 8382
Ex 26:24 they shall be **c.** together above 8535
Ex 36:10 And he **c.** the five curtains one.......... 2266
Ex 36:10 five curtains he **c.** one unto another.... 2266
Ex 36:13 and **c.** the curtains one unto.............. 2266
Ex 36:16 And he **c.** five curtains by................ 2266
Ex 36:29 And they were **c.** beneath,................. 8382
Ex 36:29 **c.** together at the head thereof, ... 8535
Ex 39:4 by the two edges was it **c.** 2266
1Pe 3:2 chaste conversation **c.** with fear. ....

COUPLETH
Ex 26:10 the edge of the curtain which **c.**.......... 2279
Ex 36:17 of the curtain which **c.** the second. 2279

COUPLING See also COUPLINGS.
Ex 26:4 from the selvedge in the **c.**;.............. 2279
Ex 26:4 curtain, in the **c.** of the second. 4225
Ex 26:5 that is in the **c.** of the second;........... 4225
Ex 26:10 curtain that is outmost in the **c.**.......... 2279
Ex 28:27 over against the other **c.** thereof,........ 4225
Ex 36:11 from the selvedge in the **c.**:.............. 4225
Ex 36:11 side of another curtain, in the **c.** 4225
Ex 36:12 which was in the **c.** of the second: 4225
Ex 36:17 edge of the curtain in the **c.**,............. 4225
Ex 39:20 over against the other **c.** thereof,........ 4225

COUPLINGS
2Ch 34:11 buy hewn stone, and timber for **c.**,...... 4226

COURAGE See also DISCOURAGE; ENCOURAGE.
Nu 13:20 And be ye of good **c.**, and bring......... 2388
De 31:6 Be strong and of a good **c.**, fear not..... 553
De 31:7, 23 Be strong and of a good **c.**: for....... 553
Jos 1:6 Be strong and of a good **c.**: for unto 553
Jos 1:9 Be strong and of a good **c.**; be not 553
Jos 1:18 only be strong and of a good **c.**. 553
Jos 2:11 did there remain any more **c.** 7307
Jos 10:25 be strong and of good **c.**: for thus......... 553
2Sa 10:12 Be of good **c.**, and let us play the 2388
1Ch 19:13 Be of good **c.**, and let us behave........ 2388
1Ch 22:13 be strong, and of good **c.**; dread not, ... 553
1Ch 28:20 Be strong and of good **c.**, and do it:..... 553
2Ch 15:8 Oded the prophet, he took **c.**, and....... 2388
Ezr 10:4 with thee: be of good **c.**, and do it. 2388
Ps 27:14 Wait on the Lord: be of good **c.**,........ 2388
Ps 31:24 Be of good **c.**, and he shall............... 2388
Isa 41:6 said to his brother, Be of good **c.**........ 2388
Da 11:25 shall stir up his power and his **c.**........ 3824
Ac 28:15 saw, he thanked God, and took **c.**. *2294*

COURAGEOUS
Jos 1:7 Only be thou strong and very **c.**,......... 553
Jos 23:6 Be ye therefore very **c.** to keep 2388
2Sa 13:28 I commanded you? be **c.**, and be........ 2388
2Ch 32:7 Be strong and **c.**, be not afraid............ 553
Am 2:16 And he that is **c.** among the 533,3820

COURAGEOUSLY
2Ch 19:11 Deal **c.**, and the Lord shall be 2388

COURSE See also CONCOURSE; COURSES; WATERCOURSE.
1Ch 27:1 of every **c.** were twenty and four 4256
1Ch 27:2 Over the first **c.** for the first month 4256
1Ch 27:2 in his **c.** were twenty and four 4256
1Ch 27:4 over the **c.** of the second month 4256
1Ch 27:4 and of his **c.** was Mikloth also the 4256
1Ch 27:4 in his **c.** likewise were twenty and 4256
1Ch 27:5 and in his **c.** were twenty and four 4256
1Ch 27:6 and in his **c.** was Ammizabad his 4256
1Ch 27:7, 8, 9, 10, 11, 12, 13, 14, 15 and in his **c.** were twenty and four thousand 4256
1Ch 28:1 that ministered to the king by **c.**, 4256
2Ch 5:11 and did not then wait by **c.**: 4256
Ezr 3:11 And they sang together by **c.** in
Ps 82:5 of the earth are out of **c.** 4131
Jer 8:6 every one turned to his **c.**, as the 4794
Jer 23:10 their **c.** is evil, and their force is 4794
Lu 1:5 Zacharias, of the **c.** of Abia: *2183*
Lu 1:8 before God in the order of his **c.**, *2183*
Ac 13:25 as John fulfilled his **c.**, he said, *1408*
Ac 16:11 we came with a straight **c.** to *2113*
Ac 20:24 that I might finish my **c.** with joy, *1408*
Ac 21:1 we came with a straight **c.** unto *4144*
Ac 21:7 when we had finished our **c.** from *4144*
1Co 14:27 three, and that by **c.**; and let one *3313*
Eph 2:2 according to the **c.** of this world, *165*
2Th 3:1 word of the Lord may have free **c.**, *5143*
2Ti 4:7 I have finished my **c.**, I have kept *1408*
Jas 3:6 setteth on fire the **c.** of nature; *5164*

COURSES
Jg 5:20 stars in their **c.** fought against 4546
1Ki 5:14 ten thousand a month by **c.**: a 2487
1Ch 23:6 divided them into **c.** among the 4256
1Ch 27:1 the king in any matter of the **c.**, 4256
1Ch 28:13 Also for the **c.** of the priests and 4256
1Ch 28:21 behold, the **c.** of the priests and the 4256
2Ch 8:14 the **c.** of the priests to their service, 4256
2Ch 8:14 the porters also by their **c.** at every 4256
2Ch 23:8 the priest dismissed not the **c.** 4256
2Ch 31:2 appointed the **c.** of the priests and 4256
2Ch 31:2 and the Levites after their **c.**, 4256
2Ch 31:15 to give to their brethren by **c.**, as 4256
2Ch 31:16 their charges according to their **c.**; 4256
2Ch 31:17 in their charges by their **c.**; 4256
2Ch 35:4 fathers, after your **c.**, according to 4256
2Ch 35:10 the Levites in their **c.**, according to 4256
Ezr 6:18 and the Levites in their **c.**, for the 4255
Isa 44:4 as willows by the water **c.** 2988

COURT See also COURTS.
Ex 27:9 thou shalt make the **c.** of the 2691
Ex 27:9 hangings for the **c.** of fine twined 2691
Ex 27:12 the breadth of the **c.** on the west 2691
Ex 27:13 the breadth of the **c.** on the east 2691
Ex 27:16 for the gate of the **c.** shall be an 2691
Ex 27:17 the pillars round about the **c.** shall 2691
Ex 27:18 The length of the **c.** shall be an 2691
Ex 27:19 all the pins of the **c.**, shall be of 2691
Ex 35:17 The hangings of the **c.**, his pillars, 2691
Ex 35:17 the hanging for the door of the **c.**, 2691
Ex 35:18 the pins of the **c.**, and their cords, 2691
Ex 38:9 he made the **c.**: on the south side 2691
Ex 38:9 the hangings of the **c.** were of fine 2691
Ex 38:15 And for the other side of the **c.** 2691
Ex 38:16 All the hangings of the **c.** round 2691
Ex 38:17 and all the pillars of the **c.** were 2691
Ex 38:18 the hanging for the gate of the **c.** 2691
Ex 38:18 answerable to the hangings of the **c.** 2691
Ex 38:20 and of the **c.** round about, were of 2691
Ex 38:31 the sockets of the **c.** round about, 2691
Ex 38:31 and the sockets of the **c.** gate, 2691
Ex 38:31 all the pins of the **c.** round about 2691
Ex 39:40 The hangings of the **c.**, his pillars, 2691
Ex 39:40 the hanging for the **c.** gate, his 2691
Ex 40:8 thou shalt set up the **c.** round 2691
Ex 40:8 hang up the hanging at the **c.** gate 2691
Ex 40:33 he reared up the **c.** round about 2691
Ex 40:33 set up the hanging of the **c.** gate 2691
Le 6:16 place; in the **c.** of the tabernacle 2691
Le 6:26 be eaten, in the **c.** of the tabernacle 2691
Nu 3:26 the hangings of the **c.**, and the 2691
Nu 3:26 curtain for the door of the **c.**, 2691
Nu 3:37 And the pillars of the **c.** round 2691
Nu 4:26 And the hangings of the **c.**, and the 2691
Nu 4:26 the door of the gate of the **c.**, 2691
Nu 4:32 the pillars of the **c.** round about, 2691
2Sa 17:18 which had a well in his **c.**; whither 2691
1Ki 6:36 he built the inner **c.** with three 2691
1Ki 7:8 another **c.** within the porch, which 2691
1Ki 7:9 on the outside toward the great **c.** 2691
1Ki 7:12 And the great **c.** round about was 2691
1Ki 7:12 both for the inner **c.** of the house 2691
1Ki 8:64 hallow the middle of the **c.** that 2691
2Ki 20:4 was gone out into the middle **c.**, 5892
2Ch 4:9 he made the **c.** of the priests, 2691
2Ch 4:9 and the great **c.**, 5835
2Ch 4:9 and doors for the **c.**, 2691
2Ch 6:13 and had set it in the midst of the **c.**: 2691
2Ch 7:7 hallowed the middle of the **c.** that 2691
2Ch 20:5 house of the Lord, before the new **c.**, 2691
2Ch 24:21 in the **c.** of the house of the Lord. 2691
2Ch 29:16 into the **c.** of the house of the Lord 2691
Ne 3:25 that was by the **c.** of the prison. 2691
Es 1:5 in the **c.** of the garden of the king's 2691
Es 2:11 before the **c.** of the women's house, 2691
Es 4:11 unto the king into the inner **c.**, 2691
Es 5:1 stood in the inner **c.** of the king's 2691
Es 5:2 Esther the queen standing in the **c.**, 2691
Es 6:4 the king said, Who is in the **c.**? 2691
Es 6:4 into the outward **c.** of the king's 2691
Es 6:5 Behold, Haman standeth in the **c.** 2691
Isa 34:13 of dragons, and a **c.** for owls 2681
Jer 19:14 he stood in the **c.** of the Lord's 2691
Jer 26:2 Stand in the **c.** of the Lord's house, 2691
Jer 32:2 was shut up in the **c.** of the prison, 2691
Jer 32:8 came to me in the **c.** of the prison. 2691
Jer 32:12 Jews that sat in the **c.** of the prison 2691
Jer 33:1 yet shut up in the **c.** of the prison, 2691
Jer 36:10 in the higher **c.**, at the entry of the 2691
Jer 36:20 they went in to the king into the **c.**, 2691
Jer 37:21 Jeremiah into the **c.** of the prison, 2691
Jer 37:21 remained in the **c.** of the prison. 2691
Jer 38:6 that was in the **c.** of the prison: 2691
Jer 38:13 remained in the **c.** of the prison. 2691
Jer 38:28 abode in the **c.** of the prison until 2691
Jer 39:14 Jeremiah out of the **c.** of the prison, 2691
Jer 39:15 shut up in the **c.** of the prison, 2691
Eze 8:7 brought me to the door of the **c.**; 2691
Eze 8:16 brought me into the inner **c.** of the 2691
Eze 10:3 and the cloud filled the inner **c.** 2691
Eze 10:4 the **c.** was full of the brightness 2691
Eze 10:5 was heard even to the outer **c.**, 2691
Eze 40:14 unto the post of the **c.** round about 2691
Eze 40:17 brought he me into the outer **c.**, 2691
Eze 40:17 a pavement made for the **c.** round 2691
Eze 40:19 forefront of the inner **c.** without, 2691
Eze 40:20 gate of the outward **c.** that looked 2691
Eze 40:23 the gate of the inner **c.** was over 2691
Eze 40:27 a gate in the inner **c.** toward 2691
Eze 40:28 he brought me to the inner **c.** 2691
Eze 40:31 thereof were toward the utter **c.**; 2691
Eze 40:32 he brought me into the inner **c.** 2691
Eze 40:34 were toward the outward **c.**; 2691
Eze 40:37 thereof were toward the utter **c.**; 2691
Eze 40:44 the singers in the inner **c.**, which 2691
Eze 40:47 measured the **c.**, an hundred cubits 2691
Eze 41:15 temple, and the porches of the **c.**; 2691
Eze 42:1 brought me forth into the utter **c.**, 2691
Eze 42:3 cubits which were for the inner **c.**, 2691
Eze 42:3 which was for the utter **c.**, 2691
Eze 42:7 toward the utter **c.** on the forepart 2691
Eze 42:8 chambers that were in the utter **c.** 2691
Eze 42:9 goeth into them from the utter **c.** 2691
Eze 42:10 the thickness of the wall of the **c.** 2691
Eze 42:14 the holy place into the utter **c.**, 2691
Eze 43:5 and brought me into the inner **c.**, 2691
Eze 44:17 enter in at the gates of the inner **c.**, 2691
Eze 44:17 minister in the gates of the inner **c.**, 2691
Eze 44:19 they go forth into the utter **c.**, 2691
Eze 44:19 even into the utter **c.** to the people, 2691
Eze 44:21 when they enter into the inner **c.** 2691
Eze 44:27 unto the inner **c.**, to minister 2691
Eze 45:19 posts of the gate of the inner **c.** 2691
Eze 46:1 gate of the inner **c.** that looketh 2691
Eze 46:20 bear them not out into the utter **c.**, 2691
Eze 46:21 brought me forth into the utter **c.**, 2691
Eze 46:21 me to pass by the corners of the **c.**; 2691
Eze 46:21 corner of the **c.** there was a **c.** 2691
Eze 46:22 corners of the **c.** there were courts 2691
Am 7:13 chapel, and it is the king's **c.** 1004
Re 11:2 the **c.** which is without the temple *833*

COURTEOUS
1Pe 3:8 as brethren, be pitiful, be **c.**: *5391*

COURTEOUSLY
Ac 27:3 Julius **c.** entreated Paul, *5364*
Ac 28:7 us, and lodged us three days **c.** *5390*

COURTS
2Ki 21:5 two **c.** of the house of the Lord. 2691
2Ki 23:12 Manasseh had made in the two **c.** 2691
1Ch 23:28 in the **c.**, and in the chambers, 2691
1Ch 28:6 he shall build my house and my **c.**: 2691
1Ch 28:12 of the **c.** of the house of the Lord, 2691
2Ch 23:5 all the people shall be in the **c.** of 2691
2Ch 33:5 two **c.** of the house of the Lord. 2691
Ne 8:16 roof of his house, and in their **c.**, 2691
Ne 8:16 and in the **c.** of the house of God, 2691
Ne 13:7 preparing him a chamber in the **c.** 2691
Ps 65:4 thee, that he may dwell in thy **c.**: 2691
Ps 84:2 even fainteth for the **c.** of the Lord: 2691
Ps 84:10 For a day in thy **c.** is better than 2691
Ps 92:13 shall flourish in the **c.** of our God. 2691
Ps 96:8 an offering, and come into his **c.** 2691
Ps 100:4 into his **c.** with praise: be thankful 2691
Ps 116:19 In the **c.** of the Lord's house, 2691
Ps 135:2 in the **c.** of the house of our God. 2691
Isa 1:12 this at your hand, to tread my **c.**? 2691
Isa 62:9 drink it in the **c.** of my holiness. 2691
Eze 9:7 and fill the **c.** with the slain: 2691
Eze 42:6 not pillars as the pillars of the **c.**: 2691
Eze 46:22 were **c.** joined of forty cubits long 2691
Zec 3:7 and shalt also keep my **c.**, and I will 2691
Lu 7:25 **live delicately, are in the king's c.**

COUSIN See also COUSINS.
Lu 1:36 And, behold, thy **c.** Elizabeth, *4773*

COUSINS
Lu 1:58 her neighbours and her **c.** heard *4773*

COVENANT See also COVENANTBREAKERS; COVENANTED; COVENANTS.
Ge 6:18 with thee will I establish my **c.**; 1285
Ge 9:9 behold, I establish my **c.** with you, 1285
Ge 9:11 I will establish my **c.** with you; 1285
Ge 9:12 This is the token of the **c.** which 1285
Ge 9:13 shall be for a token of a **c.** between 1285
Ge 9:15 I will remember my **c.**, which is 1285
Ge 9:16 the everlasting **c.** between God 1285
Ge 9:17 This is the token of the **c.**, which 1285
Ge 15:18 the Lord made a **c.** with Abram, 1285
Ge 17:2 I will make my **c.** between me and 1285
Ge 17:4 for me, behold, my **c.** is with thee, 1285
Ge 17:7 I will establish my **c.** between me 1285
Ge 17:7 for an everlasting **c.**, to be a God 1285
Ge 17:9 Thou shalt keep my **c.** therefore. 1285
Ge 17:10 This is my **c.**, which ye shall keep, 1285
Ge 17:11 a token of the **c.** betwixt me and 1285
Ge 17:13 and my **c.** shall be in your flesh 1285
Ge 17:13 in your flesh for an everlasting **c.** 1285
Ge 17:14 his people; he hath broken my **c.** 1285
Ge 17:19 I will establish my **c.** with him 1285
Ge 17:19 with him for an everlasting **c.**, 1285
Ge 17:21 my **c.** will I establish with Isaac, 1285
Ge 21:27 and both of them made a **c.** 1285
Ge 21:32 Thus they made a **c.** at Beer-sheba: 1285
Ge 26:28 and let us make a **c.** with thee; 1285
Ge 31:44 let us make a **c.**, I and thou; 1285
Ex 2:24 God remembered his **c.** with 1285
Ex 6:4 I have also established my **c.** with 1285
Ex 6:5 and I have remembered my **c.** 1285
Ex 19:5 and keep my **c.**, then ye shall be 1285
Ex 23:32 Thou shalt make no **c.** with them, 1285
Ex 24:7 And he took the book of the **c.**, 1285
Ex 24:8 Behold, the blood of the **c.**, which 1285
Ex 31:16 generations, for a perpetual **c.** 1285
Ex 34:10 Behold, I make a **c.**: before all 1285
Ex 34:12 lest thou make a **c.** with the 1285
Ex 34:15 Lest thou make a **c.** with the 1285
Ex 34:27 of these words I have made a **c.** 1285
Ex 34:28 upon the tables the words of the **c.**, 1285
Le 2:13 the salt of the **c.** of thy God to be 1285
Le 24:8 of Israel by an everlasting **c.** 1285
Le 26:9 and establish my **c.** with you. 1285
Le 26:15 but that ye break my **c.**: 1285
Le 26:25 shall avenge the quarrel of my **c.**: 1285
Le 26:42 will I remember my **c.** with Jacob, 1285
Le 26:42 and also my **c.** with Isaac, 1285
Le 26:42 and also my **c.** with Abraham 1285

Le 26:44 and to break my **c.** with them: for...... 1285
Le 26:45 remember the **c.** of their ancestors,..... 1285
Nu 10:33 the ark of the **c.** of the Lord went....... 1285
Nu 14:44 the ark of the **c.** of the Lord, and 1285
Nu 18:19 it is a **c.** of salt for ever before the 1285
Nu 25:12 I give unto him my **c.** of peace: 1285
Nu 25:13 the **c.** of an everlasting priesthood;..... 1285
De 4:13 And he declared unto you his **c.**,........ 1285
De 4:23 lest ye forget the **c.** of the Lord 1285
De 4:31 nor forget the **c.** of thy fathers 1285
De 5:2 Lord our God made a **c.** with us in..... 1285
De 5:3 The Lord made not this **c.** with our.... 1285
De 7:2 thou shalt make no **c.** with them, ... 1285
De 7:9 keepeth **c.** and mercy with them........ 1285
De 7:12 God shall keep unto thee the **c.** and.... 1285
De 8:18 that he may establish his **c.** which 1285
De 9:9 the tables of the **c.** which the Lord..... 1285
De 9:11 stone, even the tables of the **c.**. 1285
De 9:15 the two tables of the **c.** were in my.... 1285
De 10:8 to bear the ark of the **c.** of the Lord... 1285
De 17:2 in transgressing his **c.**,..................... 1285
De 29:1 These are the words of the **c.**,.......... 1285
De 29:1 the **c.** which he made with them 1285
De 29:9 Keep therefore the words of this **c.**,... 1285
De 29:12 That thou shouldest enter into **c.** 1285
De 29:14 with you only do I make this **c.** 1285
De 29:21 curses of the **c.** that are written 1285
De 29:25 have forsaken the **c.** of the Lord........ 1285
De 31:9 which bare the ark of the **c.** of the..... 1285
De 31:16 break my **c.** which I have made 1285
De 31:20 and provoke me, and break my **c.**. 1285
De 31:25 which bare the ark of the **c.** of the..... 1285
De 31:26 in the side of the ark of the **c.** of....... 1285
De 33:9 thy word, and kept thy **c.**.................. 1285
Jos 3:3 When ye see the ark of the **c.** of 1285
Jos 3:6 Take up the ark of the **c.**, and pass.... 1285
Jos 3:6 they took up the ark of the **c.**, ... 1285
Jos 3:8 that bear the ark of the **c.**, saying, ... 1285
Jos 3:11 the ark of the **c.** of the Lord of the 1285
Jos 3:14 bearing the ark of the **c.** before the.... 1285
Jos 3:17 priests that bare the ark of the **c.** 1285
Jos 4:7 cut off before the ark of the **c.** of....... 1285
Jos 4:9 which bare the ark of the **c.** stood:...... 1285
Jos 4:18 bare the ark of the **c.** of the Lord 1285
Jos 6:6 Take up the ark of the **c.**, ... 1285
Jos 6:8 and the ark of the **c.** of the Lord 1285
Jos 7:11 also transgressed my **c.** which I......... 1285
Jos 7:15 he hath transgressed the **c.** of the...... 1285
Jos 8:33 which bare the ark of the **c.** of.......... 1285
Jos 23:16 When ye have transgressed the **c.**....... 1285
Jos 24:25 Joshua made a **c.** with the people 1285
Jg 2:1 I will never break my **c.** with you........ 1285
Jg 2:20 people hath transgressed my **c.**.......... 1285
Jg 20:27 the ark of the **c.** of God was there 1285
1Sa 4:3 Let us fetch the ark of the **c.** of the ... 1285
1Sa 4:4 from thence the ark of the **c.** of the.... 1285
1Sa 4:4 there with the ark of the **c.** of God..... 1285
1Sa 4:5 the ark of the **c.** of the Lord came 1285
1Sa 11:1 Make a **c.** with us, and we will.......... 1285
1Sa 11:2 condition will I make a **c.** with you,...........
1Sa 18:3 Jonathan and David made a **c.**,........... 1285
1Sa 20:8 brought thy servant into a **c.** of the.... 1285
1Sa 20:16 Jonathan made a **c.** with the house...........
1Sa 23:18 two made a **c.** before the Lord: 1285
2Sa 15:24 bearing the ark of the **c.** of God:........ 1285
2Sa 23:5 made with me an everlasting **c.**,......... 1285
1Ki 3:15 and stood before the ark of the **c.**, ... 1285
1Ki 6:19 there the ark of the **c.** of the Lord. 1285
1Ki 8:1 might bring up the ark of the **c.** of 1285
1Ki 8:6 brought in the ark of the **c.** of the...... 1285
1Ki 8:9 When the Lord made a **c.** with the ....
1Ki 8:21 wherein is the **c.** of the Lord,........... 1285
1Ki 8:23 who keepest **c.** and mercy with 1285
1Ki 11:11 thou hast not kept my **c.** and my 1285
1Ki 19:10, 14 of Israel have forsaken thy **c.**, ... 1285
1Ki 20:34 send thee away with this **c.**.............. 1285
1Ki 20:34 So he made a **c.** with him, ... 1285
2Ki 11:4 and made a **c.** with them, and took...... 1285
2Ki 11:17 Jehoiada made a **c.** between the......... 1285
2Ki 13:23 because of his **c.** with Abraham,......... 1285
2Ki 17:15 **c.** that he made with their fathers, ... 1285
2Ki 17:35 With whom the Lord had made a **c.**.. ... 1285
2Ki 17:38 the **c.** that I have made with you 1285
2Ki 18:12 but transgressed his **c.**, and all 1285
2Ki 23:2 words of the book of the **c.** which 1285
2Ki 23:3 made a **c.** before the Lord, to walk 1285
2Ki 23:3 words of this **c.** that were written...... 1285
2Ki 23:3 And all the people stood to the **c.**. 1285
2Ki 23:21 it is written in the book of this **c.**....... 1285
1Ch 11:3 David made a **c.** with them in............ 1285
1Ch 15:25 went to bring up the ark of the **c.** 1285
1Ch 15:26 Levites that bare the ark of the **c.**..... 1285
1Ch 15:28 Israel brought up the ark of the **c.**...... 1285
1Ch 15:29 the ark of the **c.** of the Lord came 1285
1Ch 16:6 before the ark of the **c.** of God......... 1285
1Ch 16:15 Be ye mindful always of his **c.**; 1285
1Ch 16:16 Even of the **c.** which he made 1285
1Ch 16:17 to Israel for an everlasting **c.**, ... 1285
1Ch 16:37 before the ark of the **c.** of the Lord.... 1285
1Ch 17:1 but the ark of the **c.** of the Lord......... 1285
1Ch 22:19 bring the ark of the **c.** of the Lord, ... 1285
1Ch 28:2 house of rest for the ark of the **c.**...... 1285
1Ch 28:18 and covered the ark of the **c.** of...............
2Ch 5:2 the ark of the **c.** of the Lord out........ 1285
2Ch 5:7 brought in the ark of the **c.** of 1285
2Ch 5:10 when the Lord made a **c.** with.................
2Ch 6:11 wherein is the **c.** of the Lord,............ 1285
2Ch 6:14 which keepest **c.**, and shewest 1285
2Ch 13:5 and to his sons by a **c.** of salt? 1285
2Ch 15:12 into a **c.** to seek the Lord................ 1285
2Ch 21:7 because of the **c.** that he had made 1285
2Ch 23:1 son of Zichri, into **c.** with him........... 1285
2Ch 23:3 congregation made a **c.** with the......... 1285
2Ch 23:16 Jehoiada made a **c.** between him, ... 1285
2Ch 29:10 a **c.** with the Lord God of Israel, ... 1285
2Ch 34:30 the book of the **c.** that was found....... 1285
2Ch 34:31 made a **c.** before the Lord, ... 1285
2Ch 34:31 to perform the words of the **c.** 1285
2Ch 34:32 did according to the **c.** of God, ... 1285
Ezr 10:3 let us make a **c.** with our God............ 1285
Ne 1:5 that keepeth **c.** and mercy for them.... 1285
Ne 9:8 madest a **c.** with him to give the land.. 1285
Ne 9:32 God, who keepest **c.** and mercy,......... 1285
Ne 9:38 we make a sure **c.**, and write.................
Ne 13:29 and the **c.** of the priesthood, and......... 1285
Job 31:1 I made a **c.** with mine eyes; why 1285
Job 41:4 Will he make a **c.** with thee? 1285
Ps 25:10 as keep his **c.** and his testimonies. 1285
Ps 25:14 and he will shew them his **c.**............. 1285
Ps 44:17 have we dealt falsely in thy **c.**. 1285
Ps 50:5 made a **c.** with me by sacrifice. 1285
Ps 50:16 shouldest take my **c.** in thy mouth? 1285
Ps 55:20 with him: he hath broken his **c.**. 1285
Ps 74:20 have respect unto the **c.**: for............. 1285
Ps 78:10 They kept not the **c.** of God, and....... 1285
Ps 78:37 neither were they stedfast in his **c.**..... 1285
Ps 89:3 I have made a **c.** with my chosen, ... 1285
Ps 89:28 my **c.** shall stand fast with him. 1285
Ps 89:34 My **c.** will I not break, nor alter 1285
Ps 89:39 made void the **c.** of thy servant; 1285
Ps 103:18 To such as keep his **c.**, and to those .. 1285
Ps 105:8 hath remembered his **c.** for ever, ... 1285
Ps 105:9 Which **c.** he made with Abraham, ... 1285
Ps 105:10 and to Israel for an everlasting **c.**:...... 1285
Ps 106:45 he remembered for them his **c.**,......... 1285
Ps 111:5 he will ever be mindful of his **c.**. 1285
Ps 111:9 he hath commanded his **c.** for ever:.... 1285
Ps 132:12 If thy children will keep my **c.** and...... 1285
Pr 2:17 and forgetteth the **c.** of her God. 1285
Isa 24:5 ordinance, broken the everlasting **c.**.... 1285
Isa 28:15 We have made a **c.** with death, and.... 1285
Isa 28:18 **c.** with death shall be disannulled,....... 1285
Isa 33:8 he hath broken the **c.**, he hath 1285
Isa 42:6 give thee for a **c.** of the people, for.... 1285
Isa 49:8 give thee for a **c.** of the people, to..... 1285
Isa 54:10 neither shall the **c.** of my peace be..... 1285
Isa 55:3 make an everlasting **c.** with you, ... 1285
Isa 56:4 please me, and take hold of my **c.**: 1285
Isa 56:6 and taketh hold of my **c.**; 1285
Isa 57:8 and made thee a **c.** with them; ....
Isa 59:21 As for me, this is my **c.** with them,.... 1285
Isa 61:8 make an everlasting **c.** with them. 1285
Jer 3:16 The ark of the **c.** of the Lord: 1285
Jer 11:2 Hear ye the words of this **c.**, and........ 1285
Jer 11:3 obeyeth not the words of this **c.**, ... 1285
Jer 11:6 Hear ye the words of this **c.**, and do .. 1285
Jer 11:8 upon them all the words of this **c.**, ... 1285
Jer 11:10 of Judah having broken my **c.** 1285
Jer 14:21 remember, break not thy **c.** with us.... 1285
Jer 22:9 Because they have forsaken the **c.** 1285
Jer 31:31 will make a new **c.** with the house...... 1285
Jer 31:32 Not according to the **c.** that I made.... 1285
Jer 31:32 which my **c.** they brake, although I..... 1285
Jer 31:33 shall be the **c.** that I will make........... 1285
Jer 32:40 I will make an everlasting **c.** with....... 1285
Jer 33:20 If ye can break my **c.** of the day........ 1285
Jer 33:20 and my **c.** of the night, ... 1285
Jer 33:21 also my **c.** be broken with David........ 1285
Jer 33:25 If my **c.** be not with day and night,..... 1285
Jer 34:8 had made a **c.** with all the people 1285
Jer 34:10 which had entered into the **c.**, ... 1285
Jer 34:13 a **c.** with your fathers in the day 1285
Jer 34:15 made a **c.** before me in the house 1285
Jer 34:18 men that have transgressed my **c.**,..... 1285
Jer 34:18 not performed the words of the **c.**...... 1285
Jer 50:5 to the Lord in a perpetual **c.** that....... 1285
Eze 16:8 and entered into a **c.** with thee, saith.. 1285
Eze 16:59 despised the oath in breaking the **c.**.... 1285
Eze 16:60 I will remember my **c.** with thee in..... 1285
Eze 16:60 establish unto thee an everlasting **c.**..... 1285
Eze 16:61 for daughters, but not by thy **c.**. 1285
Eze 16:62 I will establish my **c.** with thee; 1285
Eze 17:13 and made a **c.** with him, and hath....... 1285
Eze 17:14 by keeping of his **c.** it might stand...... 1285
Eze 17:15 he break the **c.**, and be delivered?...... 1285
Eze 17:16 whose **c.** he brake, even with him....... 1285
Eze 17:18 despised the oath by breaking the **c.**,.. 1285
Eze 17:19 and my **c.** that he hath broken,.......... 1285
Eze 20:37 bring you into the bond of the **c.**:....... 1285
Eze 34:25 will make with them a **c.** of peace, ... 1285
Eze 27:26 will make a **c.** of peace with them: 1285
Eze 27:26 shall be an everlasting **c.** with them: ... 1285
Eze 44:7 they have broken my **c.** because 1285
Da 9:4 keeping the **c.** and mercy to them...... 1285
Da 9:27 he shall confirm the **c.** with many....... 1285
Da 11:22 yea, also the prince of the **c.**............ 1285
Da 11:28 heart shall be against the holy **c.**; 1285
Da 11:30 indignation against the holy **c.**: 1285
Da 11:30 with them that forsake the holy **c.**. 1285
Da 11:32 such as do wickedly against the **c.**........ 1285
Ho 2:18 in that day will I make a **c.** for them... 1285
Ho 6:7 like men have transgressed the **c.**: 1285
Ho 8:1 they have transgressed my **c.**,........... 1285
Ho 10:4 swearing falsely in making a **c.**:.......... 1285
Ho 12:1 do make a **c.** with the Assyrians, ... 1285
Am 1:9 remembered not the brotherly **c.**:........ 1285
Zec 9:11 by the blood of thy **c.** I have sent 1285
Zec 11:10 that I might break my **c.** which I......... 1285
Mal 2:4 that my **c.** might be with Levi, ... 1285
Mal 2:5 My **c.** was with him of life and........... 1285
Mal 2:8 ye have corrupted the **c.** of Levi, ... 1285
Mal 2:10 by profaning the **c.** of our fathers?...... 1285
Mal 2:14 companion, and the wife of thy **c.**. 1285
Mal 3:1 the messenger of the **c.**, whom ye 1285
Lu 1:72 to remember his holy **c.**; *1242*
Ac 3:25 **c.** which God made with our fathers,... *1242*
Ac 7:8 And he gave him the **c.** of *1242*
Ro 11:27 this is my **c.** unto them, when I shall.. *1242*
Ga 3:15 Though it be but a man's **c.**, ... *1242*
Ga 3:17 the **c.**, that was confirmed before....... *1242*
Heb 8:6 he is the mediator of a better **c.**, ... *1242*
Heb 8:7 if that first **c.** had been faultless, ...
Heb 8:8 will make a new **c.** with the house...... *1242*
Heb 8:9 Not according to the **c.** that I made.... *1242*
Heb 8:9 they continued not in my **c.**, and....... *1242*
Heb 8:10 this is the **c.** that I will make with...... *1242*
Heb 8:13 In that he saith, A new **c.**, he ....
Heb 9:1 Then verily the first **c.** had also ....
Heb 9:4 the ark of the **c.** overlaid round *1242*
Heb 9:4 and the tables of the **c.**; *1242*
Heb 10:16 This is the **c.** that I will make with..... *1242*
Heb 10:29 the blood of the **c.**, wherewith he....... *1242*
Heb 12:24 Jesus the mediator of the new **c.**,........ *1242*
Heb 13:20 the blood of the everlasting **c.**, ... *1242*

COVENANTBREAKERS
Ro 1:31 **c.**, without natural affection. *802*

COVENANTED
2Ch 7:18 as I have **c.** with David thy father 3772
Hag 2:5 I **c.** with you when ye came out of..... 3772
Mt 26:15 they **c.** with him for thirty pieces *2476*
Lu 22:5 glad, and **c.** to give him money. *4934*

COVENANTS
Ro 9:4 glory, and the **c.**, and the giving *1242*
Ga 4:24 for these are the two **c.**; the one *1242*
Eph 2:12 strangers from the **c.** of promise, ... *1242*

COVER See also COVERED; COVERETH; COVERING; DISCOVER; RECOVER; UNCOVER.
Ex 10:5 they shall **c.** the face of the earth,...... 3680

Ex 21:33 a man shall dig a pit, and not **c.** it, 3680
Ex 25:29 and bowls thereof, to **c.** withal: of 5258
Ex 26:13 side and on that side, to **c.** it. 3680
Ex 28:42 breeches to **c.** their nakedness; 3680
Ex 33:22 and will **c.** thee with my hand while 5526
Ex 37:16 bowls, and his covers to **c.** withal, 5258
Ex 40:3 and **c.** the ark with the vail. 5526
Le 13:12 the leprosy **c.** all the skin of him 3680
Le 16:13 the incense may **c.** the mercy seat 3680
Le 17:13 blood thereof, and **c.** it with dust. 3680
Nu 4:5 **c.** the ark of testimony with it: 3680
Nu 4:7 the bowls, and covers to **c.** withal: 5258
Nu 4:8 and **c.** the same with a covering 3680
Nu 4:9 and **c.** the candlestick of the light, 3680
Nu 4:11 and **c.** it with a covering of badgers' 3680
Nu 4:12 **c.** them with a covering of badgers' 3680
Nu 22:5 they **c.** the face of the earth, and 3680
De 23:13 and **c.** that which cometh from thee: 3680
De 33:12 Lord shall **c.** him all the day 2645
1Sa 24:3 Saul went in to **c.** his feet: and 5526
1Ki 7:18 to **c.** the chapiters that were upon 3680
1Ki 7:41 two networks, to **c.** the two bowls of 3680
1Ki 7:42 to **c.** the two bowls of the chapiters 3680
2Ch 4:12 two wreaths to **c.** the two pommels 3680
2Ch 4:13 each wreath, to **c.** the two pommels 3680
Ne 4:5 And **c.** not their iniquity, and let 3680
Job 16:18 **c.** not thou my blood, and let my 3680
Job 21:26 and the worms shall **c.** them. 3680
Job 22:11 and abundance of waters **c.** thee. 3680
Job 38:34 abundance of waters may **c.** thee? 3680
Job 40:22 trees **c.** him with their shadow; 5526
Ps 91:4 He shall **c.** thee with his feathers, 5526
Ps 104:9 they turn not again to **c.** the earth 3680
Ps 109:29 them **c.** themselves with their own 5844
Ps 139:11 Surely the darkness shall **c.** me; 7779
Ps 140:9 mischief of their own lips **c.** them. 3680
Isa 11:9 the Lord, as the waters **c.** the sea. 3680
Isa 14:11 under thee, and the worms **c.** thee. 4374
Isa 22:17 captivity, and will surely **c.** thee. 5844
Isa 26:21 and shall no more **c.** her slain. 3680
Isa 30:1 that **c.** with a covering, but not 5258
Isa 58:7 seest the naked, that thou **c.** him; 3680
Isa 59:6 neither shall they **c.** themselves 3680
Isa 60:2 darkness shall **c.** the earth, and 3680
Isa 60:6 multitude of camels shall **c.** thee. 3680
Jer 46:8 I will go up, and will **c.** the earth; 3680
Eze 7:18 and horror shall **c.** them; 3680
Eze 12:6 thou shalt **c.** thy face, that thou 3680
Eze 12:12 he shall **c.** his face, that he see not 3680
Eze 24:7 the ground, to **c.** it with dust; 3680
Eze 24:17 and **c.** not thy lips, and eat not the 5844
Eze 24:22 ye shall not **c.** your lips, nor eat 5844
Eze 26:10 his horses their dust shall **c.** thee: 3680
Eze 26:19 and great waters shall **c.** thee; 3680
Eze 30:18 a cloud shall **c.** her, and her 3680
Eze 32:7 I will **c.** the heaven, and make the 3680
Eze 32:7 I will **c.** the sun with a cloud, 3680
Eze 37:6 and **c.** you with skin, and put 7159
Eze 38:9 like a cloud to **c.** the land, thou, 3680
Eze 38:16 as a cloud to **c.** the land; it shall 3680
Ho 2:9 flax given to **c.** her nakedness. 3680
Ho 10:8 shall say to the mountains, **C.** us; 3680
Ob 10 shame shall **c.** thee, and thou shalt 3680
Mic 3:7 yea, they shall all **c.** their lips; 5844
Mic 7:10 and shame shall **c.** her which said 3680
Hab 2:14 glory of the Lord, as the waters **c.** 3680
Hab 2:17 violence of Lebanon shall **c.** thee, 3680
Mk 14:65 spit on him, and to **c.** his face, *4028*
Lu 23:30 **Fall on us; and to the hills, C. us** *2572*
1Co 11:7 For a man indeed ought not to **c.** *2619*
1Pe 4:8 charity shall **c.** the multitude of *2572*

COVERED See also COVEREDST; DISCOVERED; RECOVERED; UNCOVERED.

Ge 7:19 under the whole heaven, were **c.** 3680
Ge 7:20 and the mountains were **c.** 3680
Ge 9:23 **c.** the nakedness of their father; 3680
Ge 24:65 she took a vail, and **c.** herself 3680
Ge 38:14 and **c.** her with a vail, and wrapped 3680
Ge 38:15 because she had **c.** her face. 3680
Ex 8:6 the frogs came up, and **c.** the land 3680
Ex 10:15 For they **c.** the face of the whole 3680
Ex 14:28 waters returned, and **c.** the chariots 3680
Ex 15:5 depths have **c.** them: they sank 3680
Ex 15:10 the sea **c.** them: they sank as lead 3680
Ex 16:13 quails came up, and **c.** the camp: 3680
Ex 24:15 and a cloud **c.** the mount. 3680
Ex 24:16 and the cloud **c.** it six days: 3680
Ex 37:9 and **c.** with their wings over the 5526
Ex 40:21 and **c.** the ark of the testimony; 5526
Ex 40:34 Then a cloud **c.** the tent of the 3680
Le 13:13 if the leprosy have **c.** all his flesh, 3680
Nu 4:20 when the holy things are **c.**, 1104
Nu 7:3 six **c.** wagons, and twelve oxen; 6632
Nu 9:15 cloud **c.** the tabernacle, namely, 3680
Nu 9:16 the cloud **c.** it by day, and the 3680
Nu 16:42 the cloud **c.** it, and the glory of 3680
De 32:15 thick, thou art **c.** with fatness; 3780
Jos 24:7 the sea upon them, and **c.** them; 3680
Jg 4:18 she **c.** him with a mantle. 3680
Jg 4:19 and give him drink, and **c.** him. 3680
1Sa 19:13 for his bolster, and **c.** it with a 3680
1Sa 28:14 and he is **c.** with a mantle. 5844
2Sa 15:30 had his head **c.**, and he went 2645
2Sa 15:30 **c.** every man his head, and they 2645
2Sa 19:4 the king **c.** his face, and the king 3813
1Ki 1:1 and they **c.** him with clothes, 3680
1Ki 6:9 and **c.** the house with beams and 5603
1Ki 6:15 he **c.** them on the inside with 6823
1Ki 6:15 and **c.** the floor of the house with 6823
1Ki 6:20 and so **c.** the altar which was of 6823
1Ki 6:35 and **c.** them with gold fitted upon 6823
1Ki 7:3 And it was **c.** with cedar above 5603
1Ki 7:7 and it was **c.** with cedar from one 5603
1Ki 8:7 and the cherubims **c.** the ark and 5526
2Ki 19:1 and **c.** himself with sackcloth, 3680
2Ki 19:2 of the priests, **c.** with sackcloth, 3680
1Ch 28:18 and **c.** the ark of the covenant 5526
2Ch 5:8 and the cherubims **c.** the ark and 3680
Ne 3:15 he built it, and **c.** it, and set up 2926
Es 6:12 mourning, and having his head **c.** 2645
Es 7:8 mouth, they **c.** Haman's face. 2645
Job 23:17 neither hath he **c.** the darkness 3680
Job 31:33 If I **c.** my transgressions as Adam, 3680
Ps 32:1 is forgiven, whose sin is **c.** 3680
Ps 44:15 the shame of my face hath **c.** me. 3680
Ps 44:19 and **c.** us with the shadow of death 3680
Ps 65:13 valleys also are **c.** over with corn; 5848
Ps 68:13 the wings of a dove **c.** with silver, 2645
Ps 69:7 reproach; shame hath **c.** my face. 3680
Ps 71:13 let them be **c.** with reproach and 5844
Ps 80:10 The hills were **c.** with the shadow 3680
Ps 85:2 people, thou hast **c.** all their sin. 3680
Ps 89:45 thou hast **c.** him with shame. 5844
Ps 106:11 And the waters **c.** their enemies: 3680
Ps 106:17 and **c.** the company of Abiram. 3680
Ps 139:13 thou hast **c.** me in my mother's 5526
Ps 140:7 thou hast **c.** my head in the day 5526
Pr 24:31 nettles had **c.** the face thereof, 3680
Pr 26:23 a potsherd **c.** with silver dross 6823
Pr 26:26 Whose hatred is **c.** by deceit, 3680
Ec 6:4 his name shall be **c.** with darkness 3680
Isa 6:2 with twain he **c.** his face, 3680
Isa 6:2 and with twain he **c.** his feet, 3680
Isa 29:10 your rulers, the seers hath he **c.** 3680
Isa 37:1 and **c.** himself with sackcloth, 3680
Isa 37:2 of the priests **c.** with sackcloth, 3680
Isa 51:16 I have **c.** thee in the shadow of mine 3680
Isa 61:10 he hath **c.** me with the robe of 3271
Jer 14:3 confounded, and **c.** their heads 2645
Jer 14:4 ashamed, they **c.** their heads. 2645
Jer 51:42 she is **c.** with the multitude of the 3680
Jer 51:51 shame hath **c.** our faces: for 3680
La 2:1 Lord **c.** the daughter of Zion with 5743
La 3:16 stones, he hath **c.** me with ashes. 3728
La 3:43 Thou hast **c.** with anger, and 5526
La 3:44 Thou hast **c.** thyself with a cloud, 5526
Eze 1:11 and two **c.** their bodies. 3680
Eze 1:23 had two, which **c.** on this side, and 3680
Eze 1:23 had two, which **c.** on that side, their 3680
Eze 16:8 over thee, and **c.** thy nakedness: 3680
Eze 16:10 fine linen, and I **c.** thee with silk. 3680
Eze 18:7 hath **c.** the naked with a garment; 3680
Eze 18:16 hath **c.** the naked with a garment, 3680
Eze 24:8 of a rock, that it should not be **c.** 3680
Eze 27:7 Elishah was that which **c.** thee. 4374
Eze 31:15 I **c.** the deep for him, and I 3680
Eze 37:8 them, and the skin **c.** them above: 7159
Eze 41:16 and the windows were **c.**; 3680
Jon 3:6 and **c.** him with sackcloth, and sat 3680
Jon 3:8 man and beast be **c.** with sackcloth, 3680
Hab 3:3 His glory **c.** the heavens, and the 3680
Mt 8:24 the ship was **c.** with the waves: *2572*
Mt 10:26 **there is nothing c., that shall not** *2572*
Lu 12:2 **there is nothing c., that shall not** *4780*
Ro 4:7 forgiven, and whose sins are **c.** *1943*
1Co 11:4 having his head **c.**, dishonoureth *2596*
1Co 11:6 the woman be not **c.**, let her also *2619*
1Co 11:6 shorn or shaven, let her be **c.** *2619*

COVEREDST

Ps 104:6 Thou **c.** it with the deep as with a 3680
Eze 16:18 broidered garments, and **c.** them:

COVEREST

De 22:12 vesture, wherewith thou **c.** thyself 3680
Ps 104:2 Who **c.** thyself with light as with 5844

COVERETH See also UNCOVERETH.

Ex 29:13 all the fat that **c.** the inwards, 3680
Ex 29:22 and the fat that **c.** the inwards, 3680
Le 3:3, 9, 14 the fat that **c.** the inwards, 3680
Le 4:8 the fat that **c.** the inwards, 3680
Le 7:3 and the fat that **c.** the inwards, 3680
Le 9:19 and that which **c.** the inwards, 4374
Nu 22:11 which **c.** the face of the earth: 3680
Jg 3:24 he **c.** his feet in his summer 5526
Job 9:24 he **c.** the faces of the judges 4374
Job 15:27 Because he **c.** his face with his 3680
Job 36:30 it, and **c.** the bottom of the sea. 3680
Job 36:32 With clouds he **c.** the light; 3680
Ps 73:6 violence **c.** them as a garment. 5848
Ps 109:19 him as the garment which **c.** him, 5844
Ps 147:8 Who **c.** the heaven with clouds, 3680
Pr 10:6, 11 but violence **c.** the mouth of the 3680
Pr 10:12 up strifes: but love **c.** all sins. 3680
Pr 12:16 but a prudent man **c.** shame. 3680
Pr 17:9 He that **c.** a transgression seeketh 3680
Pr 28:13 that **c.** his sins shall not prosper: 3680
Jer 3:25 and our confusion **c.** us: for we 3680
Eze 28:14 art the anointed cherub that **c.**; 5526
Mal 2:16 one **c.** violence with his garment, 3680
Lu 8:16 **a candle, c. it with a vessel,** *2572*

COVERING See also COVERINGS; DISCOVERING; RECOVERING.

Ge 8:13 Noah removed the **c.** of the ark, 4372
Ge 20:16 he is to thee a **c.** of the eyes, unto 3682
Ex 22:27 For that is his **c.** only, it is his 3682
Ex 25:20 **c.** the mercy seat with their wings, 5526
Ex 26:7 to be a **c.** upon the tabernacle: 168
Ex 26:14 a **c.** for the tent of rams' skins, 4372
Ex 26:14 and a **c.** above of badgers' skins. 4372
Ex 35:11 tabernacle, his tent, and his **c.**, 4372
Ex 35:12 mercy seat, and the vail of the **c.**, 4539
Ex 36:19 a **c.** for the tent of rams' skins 4372
Ex 36:19 a **c.** of badgers' skins above that. 4372
Ex 39:34 the **c.** of rams' skins dyed red, 4372
Ex 39:34 and the **c.** of badgers' skins. 4372
Ex 39:34 and the vail of the **c.**, 4539
Ex 40:19 the **c.** of the tent above upon it; 4372
Ex 40:21 set up the vail of the **c.**, and 4539
Le 13:45 shall put a **c.** upon his upper lip, 5844
Nu 3:25 the tent, the **c.** thereof, and the 4372
Nu 4:5 they shall take down the **c.** vail, 4539
Nu 4:6 the **c.** of badgers' skins, and 3681
Nu 4:8 same with a **c.** of badgers' skins, 4372
Nu 4:10 within a **c.** of badgers' skins, 4372
Nu 4:11 cover it with a **c.** of badgers' skins, 4372
Nu 4:12 them with a **c.** of badgers' skins, 4372
Nu 4:14 upon it a **c.** of badgers' skins, and 3681
Nu 4:15 made an end of **c.** the sanctuary, 3680
Nu 4:25 his **c.**, and the **c.** of the badgers' 4372
Nu 16:38, 39 plates for a **c.** of the altar: 6826
Nu 19:15 no **c.** bound upon it, is unclean. 6781
2Sa 17:19 spread a **c.** over the well's mouth, 4539
Job 22:14 Thick clouds are a **c.** to him, that 5643
Job 24:7 that they have no **c.** in the cold. 3682
Job 26:6 him, and destruction hath no **c.** 3682
Job 31:19 clothing, or any poor without **c.**; 3682
Ps 105:39 He spread a cloud for a **c.**; and 4539
Ca 3:10 the **c.** of it of purple, the midst 4817
Isa 22:8 he discovered the **c.** of Judah, 4539
Isa 25:7 face of the **c.** cast over all people, 3875
Isa 28:20 and the **c.** narrower than that he 4541
Isa 30:1 that cover with a **c.**, but not of 4541
Isa 30:22 **c.** of thy graven images of silver, 6826
Isa 50:3 and I make sackcloth their **c.** 3682
Eze 28:13 every precious stone was thy **c.**, 4540
Eze 28:16 I will destroy thee, O **c.** cherub, 5526
Mal 2:13 **c.** the altar of the Lord with tears, 3680
1Co 11:15 for her hair is given her for a **c.** *4018*

COVERINGS
Pr 7:16 decked my bed with **c.** of tapestry,...... 4765
Pr 31:22 She maketh herself **c.** of tapestry;...... 4765

COVERS
Ex 25:29 and **c.** thereof, and bowls thereof,...... 7184
Ex 37:16 and his **c.** to cover withal, or pure...... 7184
Nu 4:7 the bowls, and **c.** to cover withal: 7184

COVERT
1Sa 25:20 came down by the **c.** of the hill,......... 5643
2Ki 16:18 **c.** for the sabbath that they had......... 4329
Job 38:40 and abide in the **c.** to lie in wait? 5521
Job 40:21 in the **c.** of the reed, and fens........... 5643
Ps 61:4 I will trust in the **c.** of thy wings,....... 5643
Isa 4:16 a **c.** from storm and from rain............ 5643
Isa 16:4 be thou a **c.** to them from the face..... 5643
Isa 32:2 wind, and a **c.** from the tempest; 5643
Jer 25:38 hath forsaken his **c.**, as the lion: 5520

COVET See also COVETED; COVETETH.
Ex 20:17 shalt not **c.** thy neighbour's house, ... 2530
Ex 20:17 shalt not **c.** thy neighbour's wife,........ 2530
De 5:21 shalt thou **c.** thy neighbour's house, ... 183
Mic 2:2 And they **c.** fields, and take them....... 2530
Ro 7:7 law had said, Thou shalt not **c.**. *1937*
Ro 13:9 Thou shalt not **c.**; and if there be....... *1937*
1Co 12:31 But **c.** earnestly the best gifts: *2206*
1Co 14:39 **c.** to prophesy, and forbid not to........ *2206*

COVETED
Jos 7:21 then I **c.** them, and took them;.......... 2530
Ac 20:33 I have **c.** no man's silver, or gold,...... *1937*
1Ti 6:10 while some **c.** after, they have........... *3713*

COVETETH
Pr 21:26 He **c.** greedily all the day long:............ 183
Hab 2:9 him that **c.** an evil covetousness......... 1214

COVETOUS See also COVETOUSNESS.
Ps 10:3 blesseth the **c.**, whom the Lord......... 1214
Lu 16:14 the Pharisees also, who were **c.**, ... *5366*
1Co 5:10 or with the **c.**, or extortioners, or...... *4123*
1Co 5:11 or **c.**, or an idolator, or a railer, or..... *4123*
1Co 6:10 nor **c.**, nor drunkards, nor revilers, ... *4123*
Eph 5:5 nor **c.** man, who is an idolater, ... *4123*
1Ti 3:3 patient, not a brawler, not **c.**; *866*
2Ti 3:2 lovers of their own selves, **c.**, ... *5366*
2Pe 2:14 have exercised with **c.** practices;........ *4124*

COVETOUSNESS
Ex 18:21 fear God, men of truth, hating **c.**; 1215
Ps 119:36 thy testimonies, and not to **c.**,........... 1215
Pr 28:16 hateth **c.** shall prolong his days.......... 1215
Isa 57:17 the iniquity of his **c.** was I wroth,........ 1215
Jer 6:13 them every one is given to **c.**; and..... 1215
Jer 8:10 the greatest is given to **c.**, from 1215
Jer 22:17 are not but for **c.**, and for to shed...... 1215
Jer 51:13 is come, and the measure of thy **c.**,..... 1215
Eze 33:31 their heart goeth after their **c.**............ 1215
Hab 2:9 coveteth an evil **c.** to his house, ... 1215
Mk 7:22 **Thefts, c., wickedness, deceit,**....... *4124*
Lu 12:15 **Take heed, and beware of c.:**........ *4124*
Ro 1:29 wickedness, **c.**, maliciousness;........... *4124*
2Co 9:5 of bounty, and not as of **c.**............... *4124*
Eph 5:3 all uncleanness, or **c.**, let it not be *4124*
Col 3:5 and **c.**, which is idolatry:.................. *4124*
1Th 2:5 as ye know, nor a cloke of **c.**;........... *4124*
Heb 13:5 your conversation be without **c.**;.......... *866*
2Pe 2:3 through **c.** shall they with feigned....... *4124*

COW See also COW'S; KINE.
Le 22:28 And whether it be **c.** or ewe, ye........ 7794
Nu 18:17 But the firstling of a **c.**, or the........... 7794
Job 21:10 their **c.** calveth, and casteth not......... 6510
Isa 7:21 man shall nourish a young **c.**, ... 5697
Isa 11:7 And the **c.** and the bear shall feed;..... 6510
Am 4:3 every **c.** at that which is before her;.........

COW'S
Eze 4:15 me, Lo, I have given thee **c.** dung 1241

COZ (coz)
1Ch 4:8 And **C.** begat Anub, and Zobebah, ... 6976

COZBI (coz'-bi)
Nu 25:15 woman that was slain was **C.** 3579
Nu 25:18 of Peor, and in the matter of **C.** 3579

CRACKLING
Ec 7:6 as the **c.** of thorns under a pot, ... 6963

CRACKNELS
1Ki 14:3 take with thee ten loaves and **c.**, ... 5350

CRAFT See also CRAFTSMAN; WITCHCRAFT.
Da 8:25 cause **c.** to prosper in his hand; 4820
Mk 14:1 how they might take him by **c.**, ... *1388*
Ac 18:3 because he was of the same **c.**, ... *3673*
Ac 19:25 by this **c.** we have our wealth. *2039*
Ac 19:27 not only this our **c.** is in danger......... *3313*
Re 18:22 craftsman, of whatsoever **c.** he be,..... *5078*

CRAFTINESS
Job 5:13 taketh the wise in their own **c.**: 6193
Lu 20:23 But he perceived their **c.**, and........... *3834*
1Co 3:19 He taketh the wise in their own **c.**. *3834*
2Co 4:2 not walking in **c.**, nor handling the...... *3834*
Eph 4:14 the sleight of men, and cunning, **c.**..... *3834*

CRAFTSMAN See also CRAFTSMEN.
De 27:15 the work of the hands of the **c.**, ... 2796
Re 18:22 no **c.**, of whatsoever craft he be, ... *5079*

CRAFTSMEN
2Ki 24:14 and all the **c.** and smiths: none 2796
2Ki 24:16 and **c.** and smiths a thousand, all........ 2796
1Ch 4:14 of Charashim; for they were **c.**. 2796
Ne 11:35 Lod, and Ono, the valley of **c.**. 2796
Ho 13:2 all of it the work of the **c.** 2796
Ac 19:24 brought no small gain unto the **c.**; *5079*
Ac 19:38 and the **c.** which are with him, ... *5079*

CRAFTY
Job 5:12 disappointeth the devices of the **c.**,..... 6175
Job 15:5 thou choosest the tongue of the **c.**. 6175
Ps 83:3 They have taken **c.** counsel against..... 6191
2Co 12:16 being **c.**, I caught you with guile. *3835*

CRAG
Job 39:28 upon the **c.** of the rock, and the 8127

CRANE
Isa 38:14 a **c.** or a swallow, so did I chatter:..... 5483
Jer 8:7 the **c.**, and the swallow observe......... 5483

CRASHING
Zep 1:10 and a great **c.** from the hills............. 7667

CRAVED
Mk 15:43 Pilate, and **c.** the body of Jesus. *154*

CRAVETH
Pr 16:26 for his mouth **c.** it of him, ... 404

CREATE See also CREATED; CREATETH.
Ps 51:10 **C.** in me a clean heart, O God; 1254
Isa 4:5 Lord will **c.** upon every dwelling 1254
Isa 45:7 I form the light, and **c.** darkness: 1254
Isa 45:7 I make peace, and **c.** evil:................. 1254
Isa 57:19 I **c.** the fruit of the lips; Peace, ... 1254
Isa 65:17 I **c.** new heavens and a new earth:..... 1254
Isa 65:18 rejoice for ever in that which I **c.**:...... 1254
Isa 65:18 behold, I **c.** Jerusalem a rejoicing,....... 1254

CREATED
Ge 1:1 God **c.** the heaven and the earth. 1254
Ge 1:21 And God **c.** great whales, and every... 1254
Ge 1:27 So God **c.** man in his own image, ... 1254
Ge 1:27 in the image of God **c.** he him; 1254
Ge 1:27 male and female **c.** he them. 1254
Ge 2:3 his work which God **c.** and made........ 1254
Ge 2:4 and of the earth, when they were **c.**,.. 1254
Ge 5:1 In the day that God **c.** man, in the 1254
Ge 5:2 Male and female **c.** he them; and 1254
Ge 5:2 in the day when they were **c.**............ 1254
Ge 6:7 I will destroy man whom I have **c.** 1254
De 4:32 that God **c.** man upon the earth, ... 1254
Ps 89:12 and the south thou hast **c.** them:........ 1254
Ps 102:18 the people which shall be **c.** shall 1254
Ps 104:30 sendest forth thy spirit, they are **c.** 1254
Ps 148:5 he commanded, and they were **c.**. 1254
Isa 40:26 behold who hath **c.** these things, ... 1254
Isa 41:20 the Holy One of Israel hath **c.** it. 1254
Isa 42:5 he that **c.** the heavens, and............... 1254
Isa 43:1 thus saith the Lord that **c.** thee, ... 1254
Isa 43:7 I have **c.** him for my glory, I have...... 1254
Isa 45:8 I the Lord have **c.** it........................ 1254
Isa 45:12 made the earth, and **c.** man upon it: ... 1254
Isa 45:18 the Lord that **c.** the heavens; God....... 1254
Isa 45:18 he **c.** it not in vain, he formed it to 1254
Isa 48:7 They are **c.** now, and not from the..... 1254
Isa 54:16 **c.** the smith that bloweth the coals..... 1254
Isa 54:16 I have **c.** the waster to destroy. 1254
Jer 31:22 hath **c.** a new thing in the earth, ... 1254
Eze 21:30 in the place where thou wast **c.**, ... 1254
Eze 28:13 thee in the day that thou wast **c.**. 1254
Eze 28:15 from the day that thou wast **c.**, till 1254
Mal 2:10 hath not one God **c.** us? why do we ... 1254
Mk 13:19 **which God c. unto this time,**........ *2936*
1Co 11:9 was the man **c.** for the woman; but *2936*
Eph 2:10 **c.** in Christ Jesus unto good works, ... *2936*
Eph 3:9 in God, who **c.** all things by Jesus *2936*
Eph 4:24 after God is **c.** in righteousness *2936*
Col 1:16 by him were things **c.**, that are in *2936*
Col 1:16 all things were **c.** by him, and for....... *2936*
Col 3:10 after the image of him that **c.** him: *2936*
1Ti 4:3 which God hath **c.** to be received....... *2936*
Re 4:11 for thou hast **c.** all things, and for *2936*
Re 4:11 thy pleasure they are and were **c.**. *2936*
Re 10:6 who **c.** heaven, and the things that..... *2936*

CREATETH
Am 4:13 and **c.** the wind, and declareth........... 1254

CREATION
Mk 10:6 **But from the beginning of the c.**... *2937*
Mk 13:19 **not from the beginning of the c.** ... *2937*
Ro 1:20 from the **c.** of the world are clearly *2937*
Ro 8:22 that the whole **c.** groaneth and *2937*
2Pe 3:4 were from the beginning of the **c.** *2937*
Re 3:14 **the beginning of the c. of God;**..... *2937*

CREATOR
Ec 12:1 Remember now thy **C.** in the days 1254
Isa 40:28 the **C.** of the ends of the earth, ... 1254
Isa 43:15 your Holy One, the **c.** of Israel, ... 1254
Ro 1:25 more than the **C.**, who is blessed....... *2936*
1Pe 4:19 well doing, as unto a faithful **C.**,......... *2939*

CREATURE See also CREATURES.
Ge 1:20 the moving **c.** that hath life, and......... 8318
Ge 1:21 every living **c.** that moveth, which...... 5315
Ge 1:24 the earth bring forth the living **c.** 5315
Ge 2:19 called every living **c.**, that was the 5315
Ge 9:10 every living **c.** that is with you, of...... 5315
Ge 9:12 me and you and every living **c.**........... 5315
Ge 9:15 and every living **c.** of all flesh;........... 5315
Ge 9:16 between God and every living **c.**......... 5315
Le 11:46 every living **c.** that moveth in the....... 5315
Le 11:46 every **c.** that creepeth upon the......... 5315
Eze 1:20, 21 spirit of the living **c.** was in the 2416
Eze 1:22 upon the heads of the living **c.**........... 2416
Eze 10:15 This is the living **c.** that I saw by....... 2416
Eze 10:17 spirit of the living **c.** was in them. 2416
Eze 10:20 This is the living **c.** that I saw by........ 2416
Mk 16:15 **and preach the gospel to every c.**. *2937*
Ro 1:25 and served the **c.** more than the *2937*
Ro 8:19 the earnest expectation of the **c.**......... *2937*
Ro 8:20 For the **c.** was made subject to *2937*
Ro 8:21 Because the **c.** itself also shall be....... *2937*
Ro 8:39 nor any other **c.**, shall be able to *2937*
2Co 5:17 he is a new **c.**; old things are........... *2937*
Ga 6:15 uncircumcision, but a new **c.**. *2937*
Col 1:15 God, the firstborn of every **c.**:........... *2937*
Col 1:23 which was preached to every **c.**......... *2937*
1Ti 4:4 For every **c.** of God is good and........ *2938*
Heb 4:13 Neither is there any **c.** that is not *2937*
Re 5:13 And every **c.** which is in heaven, ... *2938*

CREATURES
Isa 13:21 houses shall be full of doleful **c.**;.......... 255
Eze 1:5 came the likeness of four living **c.**. 2416
Eze 1:13 the likeness of the living **c.**, their....... 2416
Eze 1:13 up and down among the living **c.**;....... 2416
Eze 1:14 And the living **c.** ran and returned...... 2416
Eze 1:15 Now as I beheld the living **c.**,............ 2416
Eze 1:15 upon the earth by the living **c.**,.......... 2416
Eze 1:19 when the living **c.** went, the wheels.... 2416
Eze 1:19 and when the living **c.** were lifted....... 2416
Eze 3:13 noise of the wings of the living **c.**........ 2416
Jas 1:18 be a kind of firstfruits of his **c.**. *2938*
Re 8:9 third part of the **c.** which were in....... *2938*

CREDIBLE See INCREDIBLE.

CREDITOR See CREDITORS.
De 15:2 Every **c.** that lendeth 1167, 4874,3027
2Ki 4:1 and the **c.** is come to take unto 5383
Lu 7:41 **There was a certain c. which had** ..*1157*

CREDITORS
Isa 50:1 which of my **c.** is it to whom I........... 5383

CREEK
Ac 27:39 they discovered a certain **c.** with........ *2859*

CREEP See also CREEPETH; CREEPING; CREPT.
Le 11:20 All fowls that **c.**, going upon all.......... 8318
Le 11:29 the creeping things that **c.** upon......... 8317
Le 11:31 unclean to you among all that **c.**:......... 8318
Le 11:42 all creeping things that **c.** upon 8317

Ps 104:20 the beasts of the forest do **c.** forth..... 7430
Eze 38:20 and all creeping things that **c.**........... 7430
2Ti 3:6 are they which **c.** into houses,... *1744, 1519*

CREEPETH
Ge 1:25 and every thing that **c.** upon the........ 7431
Ge 1:26 every creeping thing that **c.** upon....... 7430
Ge 1:30 to every thing that **c.** upon the.......... 7430
Ge 7:8 and of every thing that **c.** upon the..... 7430
Ge 7:14 and every creeping thing that **c.**.......... 7430
Ge 7:21 and of every creeping thing that **c.**..... 8317
Ge 8:17 and of every creeping thing that **c.**..... 7430
Ge 8:19 fowl, and whatsoever **c.** upon the....... 7430
Le 11:41 every creeping thing that **c.** upon....... 8317
Le 11:43 with any creeping thing that **c.**,.......... 8317
Le 11:44 manner of creeping thing that **c.**.......... 7430
Le 11:46 of every creature that **c.** upon the...... 8317
Le 20:25 manner of living thing that **c.** on......... 7430
De 4:18 The likeness of any thing that **c.**........ 7430

CREEPING
Ge 1:24 cattle, and **c.** thing, and beast of........ 7431
Ge 1:26 over every **c.** thing that creepeth....... 7431
Ge 6:7 the **c.** thing, and the fowls of the....... 7431
Ge 6:20 every **c.** thing of the earth after......... 7431
Ge 7:14 and every **c.** thing that creepeth......... 7431
Ge 7:21 and of beast, and of every **c.** thing..... 8318
Ge 7:23 the **c.** things, and the fowl of the....... 7431
Ge 8:17 of every **c.** thing that creepeth.......... 7431
Ge 8:19 Every beast, every **c.** thing, and........ 7431
Le 5:2 carcase of unclean **c.** things, and........ 8318
Le 11:21 every flying **c.** thing that goeth.......... 8318
Le 11:23 all other flying **c.** things, which.......... 8318
Le 11:29 among the **c.** things that creep.......... 8318
Le 11:41 every **c.** thing that creepeth upon........ 8318
Le 11:42 hath more feet among all **c.** things...... 8318
Le 11:43 abominable with any **c.** thing that....... 8318
Le 11:44 with any manner of **c.** thing that........ 8318
Le 22:5 whosoever toucheth any **c.** thing,....... 8318
De 14:19 every **c.** thing that flieth is unclean..... 8318
1Ki 4:33 of fowl, and of **c.** things, and of......... 7431
Ps 104:25 things **c.** innumerable, both small........ 7431
Ps 148:10 **c.** things, and flying fowl:................. 7431
Eze 8:10 and behold every form of **c.** things,.... 7431
Eze 38:20 field, and all **c.** things that creep........ 7431
Ho 2:18 with the **c.** things of the ground:......... 7431
Hab 1:14 as the **c.** things, that have no ruler...... 7431
Ac 10:12 and wild beasts, and **c.** things, and..... *2062*
Ac 11:6 and wild beasts, and **c.** things, and..... *2062*
Ro 1:23 fourfooted beasts, and **c.** things......... *2062*

CREPT
Jude 4 For there are certain men **c.** in.......... *3921*

CRESCENS (cres'-sens)
2Ti 4:10 **C.** to Galatia, Titus unto.................. *2913*

CRETANS See CRETES; CRETIANS.

CRETE (creet) See also CRETES.
Ac 27:7 suffering us, we sailed under **C.**,........ *2914*
Ac 27:12 which is an haven of **C.**, and lieth....... *2914*
Ac 27:13 thence, they sailed close by **C.**.......... *2914*
Ac 27:21 me, and not have loosed from **C.**,....... *2914*
Tit 1:5 For this cause left I thee in C.,.......... *2914*

CRETES (creets) See also CRETIANS.
Ac 2:11 **C.** and Arabians, we do hear............ *2912*

CRETIANS (cre'-shuns) See also CRETES.
Tit 1:12 The **C.** are always liars, evil............ *2912*
Tit *subscr* bishop of the church of the **C.**........... *2912*

CREW
Mt 26:74 And immediately the cock **c.**............. *5455*
Mk 14:68 out into the porch; and the cock **c.**..... *5455*
Mk 14:72 And the second time the cock **c.**........ *5455*
Lu 22:60 while he yet spake, the cock **c.**......... *5455*
Joh 18:27 again: and immediately the cock **c.**....... *5455*

CRIB
Job 39:9 to serve thee, or abide by thy **c.**?......... 18
Pr 14:4 Where no oxen are, the **c.** is clean:....... 18
Isa 1:3 owner, and the ass his master's **c.**:....... 18

CRIED
Ge 27:34 he **c.** with a great and exceeding........ 6817
Ge 39:14 me, and I **c.** with a loud voice:.......... 7121
Ge 39:15 that I lifted up my voice and **c.**,.......... 7121
Ge 39:18 as I lifted up my voice and **c.**, that..... 7121
Ge 41:43 they **c.** before him, Bow the knee:..... 7121
Ge 41:55 people **c.** to Pharaoh for bread:.......... 6817
Ge 45:1 and he **c.**, Cause every man to go...... 7121
Ex 2:23 and they **c.**, and their cry came up..... 2199
Ex 5:15 the children of Israel came and **c.**........ 6817
Ex 8:12 Moses **c.** unto the Lord because of..... 6817
Ex 14:10 and the children of Israel **c.** out......... 6817
Ex 15:25 And he **c.** unto the Lord; and the........ 6817
Ex 17:4 And Moses **c.** unto the Lord, saying,.. 6817
Nu 11:2 And the people **c.** unto Moses;.......... 6817
Nu 12:13 And Moses **c.** unto the Lord, saying,.. 6817
Nu 14:1 lifted up their voice, and **c.**;.............. 5414
Nu 20:16 And when we **c.** unto the Lord,......... 6817
De 22:24 the damsel, because she **c.** not,......... 6817
De 22:27 the betrothed damsel **c.**, and there..... 6817
De 26:7 And when we **c.** unto the Lord God.... 6817
Jos 24:7 And when they **c.** unto the Lord,....... 6817
Jg 3:9 And when the children of Israel **c.**...... 2199
Jg 3:15 But when the children of Israel **c.**....... 2199
Jg 4:3 And the children of Israel **c.** unto........ 6817
Jg 5:28 and **c.** through the lattice,................. 2980
Jg 6:6 and the children of Israel **c.** unto........ 2199
Jg 6:7 when the children of Israel **c.** unto..... 2199
Jg 7:20 they **c.**, The sword of the Lord,......... 7121
Jg 7:21 all the host ran, and **c.**, and fled......... 7321
Jg 9:7 and lifted up his voice, and **c.**,........... 7121
Jg 10:10 and the children of Israel **c.** unto........ 2199
Jg 10:12 and ye **c.** to me, and I delivered........ 6817
Jg 18:23 they **c.** unto the children of Dan......... 7121
1Sa 4:13 and told it, all the city **c.** out............ 2199
1Sa 5:10 that the Ekronites **c.** out, saying,....... 2199
1Sa 7:9 and Samuel **c.** unto the Lord for........ 2199
1Sa 12:8 and your fathers **c.** unto the Lord,....... 2199
1Sa 12:10 they **c.** unto the Lord, and said,......... 2199
1Sa 15:11 and he **c.** unto the Lord all night......... 2199
1Sa 17:8 and **c.** unto the armies of Israel.......... 7121
1Sa 20:37 Jonathan **c.** after the lad, and said....... 7121
1Sa 20:38 Jonathan **c.** after the lad, make.......... 7121
1Sa 24:8 out of the cave, and **c.** after Saul,....... 7121
1Sa 26:14 And David **c.** to the people, and to..... 7121
1Sa 28:12 woman saw Samuel, she **c.** with a...... 2199
2Sa 18:25 watchman **c.**, and told the king.......... 7121
2Sa 19:4 and the king **c.** with a loud voice,....... 2199
2Sa 20:16 Then **c.** a wise woman out of the....... 7121
2Sa 22:7 and **c.** to my God: and he did hear..... 7121
1Ki 13:2 he **c.** against the altar in the word...... 7121
1Ki 13:4 had **c.** against the altar in Beth-el,...... 7121
1Ki 13:21 And he **c.** unto the man of God.......... 7121
1Ki 13:32 which he **c.** by the word of the Lord... 7121
1Ki 17:20 he **c.** unto the Lord, and said,............ 7121
1Ki 17:21 the child three times, and **c.** unto....... 7121
1Ki 18:28 they **c.** aloud, and cut themselves....... 7121
1Ki 20:39 he **c.** unto the king: and he said,....... 6817
1Ki 22:32 against him: and Jehoshaphat **c.**......... 2199
2Ki 2:12 and he **c.**, My father, my father,......... 6817
2Ki 4:1 Now there **c.** a certain woman of....... 6817
2Ki 4:40 they **c.** out, and said, O thou man...... 6817
2Ki 6:5 and he **c.**, and said, Alas, master!...... 6817
2Ki 6:26 there **c.** a woman unto him, saying,.... 6817
2Ki 8:5 **c.** to the king for her house and........ 6817
2Ki 11:14 Athaliah rent her clothes, and **c.**,....... 7121
2Ki 18:28 Then Rab-shakeh stood and **c.** with.... 7121
2Ki 20:11 And Isaiah the prophet **c.** unto the..... 7121
1Ch 5:20 they **c.** to God in the battle, and he.... 2199
2Ch 13:14 and they **c.** unto the Lord, and the..... 6817
2Ch 14:11 And Asa **c.** unto the Lord his God,..... 7121
2Ch 18:31 Jehoshaphat **c.** out, and the Lord........ 2199
2Ch 32:18 Then they **c.** with a loud voice in....... 7121
2Ch 32:20 the son of Amoz, prayed and **c.** to..... 2199
Ne 9:4 and **c.** with a loud voice unto the....... 2199
Ne 9:27 they **c.** unto thee, thou heardest........ 6817
Ne 9:28 when they returned, and **c.** unto........ 2199
Es 4:1 and **c.** with a loud and a bitter cry;..... 2199
Job 29:12 I delivered the poor that **c.**,............. 7768
Job 30:5 **c.** after them as after a thief;).......... 7321
Job 30:28 up, and I **c.** in the congregation.......... 7768
Ps 3:4 I **c.** unto the Lord with my voice,....... 7121
Ps 18:6 and **c.** unto my God: he heard........... 7768
Ps 18:41 They **c.**, but there was none to......... 7768
Ps 22:5 They **c.** unto thee, and were............ 2199
Ps 22:24 when he **c.** unto him, he heard.......... 7768
Ps 30:2 O Lord my God, I **c.** unto thee,......... 7768
Ps 30:8 I **c.** to thee, O Lord; and unto the..... 7121
Ps 31:22 supplications when I **c.** unto thee........ 7768
Ps 34:6 This poor man **c.**, and the Lord......... 7121
Ps 66:17 I **c.** unto him with my mouth,............ 7121
Ps 77:1 I **c.** unto God with my voice,............. 6817
Ps 88:1 I have **c.** day and night before thee:... 6817
Ps 88:13 unto thee have I **c.**, O Lord; and........ 7768
Ps 107:6 Then they **c.** unto the Lord in........... 6817
Ps 107:13 Then they **c.** unto the Lord in........... 2199
Ps 119:145 I **c.** with my whole heart;................. 7121
Ps 119:146 I **c.** unto thee; save me, and I........... 7121
Ps 119:147 dawning of the morning, and **c.**:......... 7768
Ps 120:1 In my distress I **c.** unto the Lord....... 7121
Ps 130:1 Out of the depths have I **c.** unto........ 7121
Ps 138:3 day when I **c.** thou answeredst.......... 7121
Ps 142:1 I **c.** unto the Lord with my voice;...... 2199
Ps 142:5 I **c.** unto thee, O Lord: I said,........... 2199
Isa 6:3 And one **c.** unto another, and said,..... 7121
Isa 6:4 moved at the voice of him that **c.**,...... 7121
Isa 21:8 And he **c.**, A lion: My lord,............... 7121
Isa 30:7 therefore have I **c.** concerning........... 7121
Isa 36:18 Then Rabshakeh stood, and **c.** with.... 7121
Jer 4:20 Destruction upon destruction is **c.**;..... 7121
Jer 20:8 For since I spake, I **c.** out,............... 2199
Jer 20:8 I **c.** violence and spoil;..................... 7121
La 2:18 Their heart **c.** unto the Lord,............ 6817
La 4:15 they **c.** unto them, Depart ye;........... 7121
Eze 9:1 He **c.** also in mine ears with a loud..... 7121
Eze 9:8 I fell upon my face, and **c.**,............... 2199
Eze 10:13 As for the wheels, it was **c.** unto....... 7121
Eze 11:13 fell I down upon my face, and **c.**......... 2199
Da 3:4 Then an herald **c.** aloud, To you........ 7123
Da 4:14 He **c.** aloud, and said thus,............... 7123
Da 5:7 The king **c.** aloud to bring in the........ 7123
Da 6:20 he **c.** with a lamentable voice unto...... 2200
Ho 7:14 And they have not **c.** unto me........... 2199
Jon 1:5 and **c.** every man unto his god,.......... 2199
Jon 1:14 they **c.** unto the Lord, and said,......... 7121
Jon 2:2 And said, I **c.** by reason of mine......... 7121
Jon 2:2 out of the belly of hell **c.** I, and........ 7768
Jon 3:4 he **c.**, and said, Yet forty days, and.... 7121
Zec 1:4 former prophets have **c.**, saying,........ 7121
Zec 6:8 Then **c.** he unto me, and spake.......... 2199
Zec 7:7 the Lord hath **c.** by the former.......... 7121
Zec 7:13 as he **c.**, and they would not hear;..... 7121
Zec 7:13 so they **c.**, and I would not hear,....... 7121
Mt 8:29 behold, they **c.** out, saying,.............. *2896*
Mt 14:26 is a spirit; and they **c.** out for fear...... *2896*
Mt 14:30 beginning to sink, he **c.**, saying,......... *2896*
Mt 15:22 **c.** unto him, saying, Have mercy.......... *2905*
Mt 20:30 **c.** out, saying, Have mercy on us,...... *2896*
Mt 20:31 but they **c.** the more, saying,............ *2896*
Mt 21:9 **c.**, saying, Hosanna to the son of....... *2896*
Mt 27:23 But they **c.** out the more, saying,....... *2896*
Mt 27:46 Jesus **c.** with a loud voice, saying,....... *310*
Mt 27:50 Jesus, when he had **c.** again with....... *2896*
Mk 1:23 with an unclean spirit; and he **c.**.......... *349*
Mk 1:26 torn him, and **c.** with a loud voice,..... *2896*
Mk 3:11 **c.**, saying, Thou art the Son of God.... *2896*
Mk 5:7 **c.** with a loud voice, and said,........... *2896*
Mk 6:49 it had been a spirit, and **c.** out:........... *349*
Mk 9:24 **c.** out, and said with tears, Lord,....... *2896*
Mk 9:26 the spirit **c.**, and rent him sore,......... *2896*
Mk 10:48 but he **c.** the more a great deal,......... *2896*
Mk 11:9 and they that followed, **c.**, saying,...... *2896*
Mk 15:13 they **c.** out again, Crucify him........... *2896*
Mk 15:14 they **c.** out the more exceedingly,...... *2896*
Mk 15:34 hour Jesus **c.** with a loud voice,........... *994*
Mk 15:37 And Jesus **c.** with a loud voice,........... *863*
Mk 15:39 saw that he so **c.** out, and gave......... *2896*
Lu 4:33 unclean devil, and **c.** out with a........... *349*
Lu 8:8 he had said these things, he **c.**,......... *5455*
Lu 8:28 When he saw Jesus, he **c.** out, and...... *349*
Lu 9:38 a man of the company **c.** out,.............. *310*
Lu 16:24 **he c. and said, Father Abraham,**... *5455*
Lu 18:38 he **c.**, saying, Jesus, thou son of.......... *994*
Lu 18:39 he **c.** so much the more, Thou son..... *2896*
Lu 23:18 they **c.** out all at once, saying,........... *349*
Lu 23:21 But they **c.**, saying, Crucify him,......... *2019*
Lu 23:46 when Jesus had **c.** with a loud........... *5455*
Joh 1:15 and **c.**, saying, This was he of........... *2896*
Joh 7:28 Then **c.** Jesus in the temple as he...... *2896*
Joh 7:37 Jesus stood and **c.**, saying, **If any**..... *2896*
Joh 11:43 he **c.** with a loud voice, **Lazarus,**..... *2905*
Joh 12:13 to meet him, and **c.**, **He that**........... *2905*
Joh 18:40 Then **c.** they all again, saying,........... *2905*
Joh 19:6 saw him, they **c.** out, saying,.............. *2905*
Joh 19:12 the Jews **c.** out, saying, If thou.......... *2896*
Joh 19:15 they **c.** out, Away with him,............... *2905*
Ac 7:57 they **c.** out with a loud voice,............. *2896*
Ac 7:60 and **c.** with a loud voice, Lord,........... *2896*
Ac 16:17 and **c.**, saying, These men are the..... *2896*
Ac 16:28 Paul **c.** with a loud voice, saying,....... *5455*
Ac 19:28 and **c.** out, saying, Great is Diana....... *2896*
Ac 19:32 Some therefore **c.** one thing, and....... *2896*
Ac 19:34 **c.** out, Great is Diana of the............. *2896*

Ac 21:34 some **c.** one thing, some another,........ *994*
Ac 22:23 And as they **c.** out, and cast off........ *2905*
Ac 22:24 he might know wherefore they **c.**........ *2019*
Ac 23:6 he **c.** out in the council, Men and....... *2896*
Ac 24:21 I **c.** standing among them, ... *2896*
Re 6:10 they **c.** with a loud voice, saying, ... *2896*
Re 7:2 and he **c.** with a loud voice to the *2896*
Re 7:10 And **c.** with a loud voice, saying,........ *2896*
Re 10:3 And **c.** with a loud voice, as when...... *2896*
Re 10:3 when he had **c.**, seven thunders......... *2896*
Re 12:2 And she being with child **c.**, ... *2896*
Re 14:18 **c.** with a loud cry to him that had *5455*
Re 18:2 And he **c.** mightily with a strong *2896*
Re 18:18 And **c.** when they saw the smoke....... *2896*
Re 18:19 and **c.**, weeping and wailing,............ *2896*
Re 19:17 and he **c.** with a loud voice, ... *2896*

CRIES
Jas 5:4 the **c.** of them which have reaped........ *995*

CRIEST
Ex 14:15 Wherefore **c.** thou unto me?............. 6817
1Sa 26:14 Who art thou that **c.** to the king? 7121
Pr 2:3 Yea, if thou **c.** after knowledge, ... 7121
Isa 57:13 When thou **c.**, let thy companies.......... 2199
Jer 30:15 Why **c.** thou for thine affliction? 2199

CRIETH
Ge 4:10 the voice of thy brother's blood **c.**........ 6817
Ex 22:27 he **c.** unto me, that I will hear;.......... 6817
Job 24:12 the soul of the wounded **c.** out: 7768
Ps 72:12 shall deliver the needy when he **c.**;....... 7768
Ps 84:2 my heart and my flesh **c.** out for........ 7442
Pr 1:20 Wisdom **c.** without; she uttereth.......... 7442
Pr 1:21 **c.** in the chief place of concourse, ... 7121
Pr 8:3 She **c.** at the gates, at the entry......... 7442
Pr 9:3 she **c.** upon the highest places of 7121
Isa 26:17 in pain, and **c.** out in her pangs;......... 2199
Isa 40:3 of him that **c.** in the wilderness,........ 7121
Jer 12:8 it **c.** out against me:..................... 5414,6963
Mic 6:9 The Lord's voice **c.** unto the city, ... 7121
Mt 15:23 for she **c.** after us.......................... *2896*
Lu 9:39 him, and he suddenly **c.** out;.............. *2896*
Ro 9:27 Esaias also **c.** concerning Israel,.......... *2896*
Jas 5:4 is of you kept back by fraud, **c.**: *2896*

CRIME See also CRIMES.
Job 31:11 For this is an heinous **c.**; yea, ... 2154
Ac 25:16 concerning the **c.** laid against him. *1462*

CRIMES
Eze 7:23 for the land is full of bloody c, ... 4941
Ac 25:27 signify the **c.** laid against him. *156*

CRIMSON
2Ch 2:7 in purple, and **c.**, and blue, ... 3758
2Ch 2:14 blue, and in fine linen, and in **c.**; 3758
2Ch 3:14 purple, and **c.**, and fine linen, ... 3758
Isa 1:18 though they be red like **c.**,................. 8438
Jer 4:30 thou clothest thyself with **c.**, ... 8144

CRIPPLE
Ac 14:8 a **c.** from his mother's womb,............. *5560*

CRISPING
Isa 3:22 the wimples, and the **c.** pins, ... 2754

CRISPING-PINS See CRISPING and PINS.

CRISPUS (cris'-pus)
Ac 18:8 And **C.**, the chief ruler of the............ *2921*
1Co 1:14 I baptized none of you, but **C.** and *2921*

CROOKBACKT
Le 21:20 Or **c.**, or a dwarf, or that hath a........ 1384

CROOKED
De 32:5 are a perverse and **c.** generation. 6618
Job 26:13 hand hath formed the **c.** serpent. 1281
Ps 125:5 turn aside unto their **c.** ways,............ 6128
Pr 2:15 Whose ways are **c.**, and they 6141
Ec 1:15 is **c.** cannot be made straight:............ 5791
Ec 7:13 straight, which he hath made **c.**? 5791
Isa 27:1 even leviathan that **c.** serpent;........... 6129
Isa 40:4 and the **c.** shall be made straight,....... 6121
Isa 42:16 them, and **c.** things straight. 4625
Isa 45:2 and make the **c.** places straight:......... 1921
Isa 59:8 they have made them **c.** paths:........... 6140
La 3:9 he hath made my paths **c.**.................. 5753
Lu 3:5 the **c.** shall be made straight, ... *4646*
Php 2:15 midst of a **c.** and perverse nation, ... *4646*

CROP See also CROPPED.
Le 1:16 pluck away his **c.** with his feathers, ... 4760
Eze 17:22 I will **c.** off from the top of his........... 6998

CROPPED
Eze 17:4 **c.** off the top of his young twigs, ... 6998

CROSS See also CROSSWAY.
Mt 10:38 **And he that taketh not his c.**,....... *4716*
Mt 16:24 **deny himself, and take up his c.**,.. *4716*
Mt 27:32 him they compelled to bear his **c.**....... *4716*
Mt 27:40 Son of God, come down from the **c.**.. *4716*
Mt 27:42 let him now come down from the **c.**,... *4716*
Mk 8:34 **deny himself, and take up his c.**,.. *4716*
Mk 10:21 **take up the c., and follow me.** *4716*
Mk 15:21 and Rufus, to bear his **c.**.................. *4716*
Mk 15:30 and come down from the **c.**............... *4716*
Mk 15:32 descend now from the **c.**, that we *4716*
Lu 9:23 **himself, and take up his c. daily**,.. *4716*
Lu 14:27 **whosoever doth not bear his c.**,..... *4716*
Lu 23:26 and on him they laid the **c.**, that *4716*
Joh 19:17 And he bearing his **c.** went forth........ *4716*
Joh 19:19 wrote a title, and put it on the **c.**...... *4716*
Joh 19:25 stood by the **c.** of Jesus his mother, ... *4716*
Joh 19:31 should not remain upon the **c.** on *4716*
1Co 1:17 lest the **c.** of Christ should be made ... *4716*
1Co 1:18 the preaching of the **c.** is to them *4716*
Ga 5:11 then is the offence of the **c.** ceased. ... *4716*
Ga 6:12 should suffer persecution for the **c.**..... *4716*
Ga 6:14 save in the **c.** of our Lord Jesus......... *4716*
Eph 2:16 unto God in one body by the **c.**, ... *4716*
Php 2:8 death, even the death of the **c.**.......... *4716*
Php 3:18 are the enemies of the **c.** of Christ: *4716*
Col 1:20 peace through the blood of his **c.**, ... *4716*
Col 2:14 out of the way, nailing it to his **c.**;...... *4716*
Heb 12:2 endured the **c.**, despising the shame. .. *4716*

CROSSWAY
Ob 14 shouldest thou have stood in the **c.**,.... 6563

CROUCH See also CROUCHETH.
1Sa 2:36 **c.** to him for a piece of silver 7812

CROUCHETH
Ps 10:10 He **c.**, and humbleth himself,............. 1794

CROW See also COCKCROWING; CREW.
Mt 26:34 **this night, before the cock c.**,....... *5455*
Mt 26:75 Before the cock **c.**, thou shalt deny *5455*
Mk 14:30 **before the cock c. twice, thou**....... *5455*
Mk 14:72 him, Before the **c.** crow twice, thou ... *5455*
Lu 22:34 **the cock shall not c. this day**,...... *5455*
Lu 22:61 him, Before the cock **c.**, thou shalt..... *5455*
Joh 13:38 **The cock shall not c., till thou**..... *5455*

CROWN See also CROWNED; CROWNEST; CROWNETH; CROWNING; CROWNS.
Ge 49:26 and on the **c.** of the head of him 6936
Ex 25:11 make upon it a **c.** of gold round 2213
Ex 25:24 and make thereto a **c.** of gold........... 2213
Ex 25:25 make a golden **c.** to the border........... 2213
Ex 29:6 put the holy **c.** upon the mitre. 5145
Ex 30:3 shalt make unto it a **c.** of gold 2213
Ex 30:4 thou make to it under the **c.** of it, ... 2213
Ex 37:2 and made a **c.** of gold to it round 2213
Ex 37:11 and made thereunto a **c.** of gold.......... 2213
Ex 37:12 made a **c.** of gold for the border 2213
Ex 37:26 also he made unto it a **c.** of gold.......... 2213
Ex 37:27 of gold for it under the **c.** thereof,...... 2213
Ex 39:30 they made the plate of the holy **c.**....... 5145
Le 8:9 put the golden plate, the holy **c.** 5145
Le 21:12 **c.** of the anointing oil of his God 5145
De 33:20 the arm with the **c.** of the head. 6936
2Sa 1:10 took the **c.** that was upon his head, ... 5145
2Sa 12:30 And he took their king's **c.** from 5850
2Sa 14:25 his foot even to the **c.** of his head 6936
2Ki 11:12 and put the **c.** upon him, ... 5145
1Ch 20:2 David took the **c.** of their king........... 5850
2Ch 23:11 son, and put upon him the **c.**,............ 5145
Es 1:11 queen before the king with the **c.**........ 3804
Es 2:17 he set the royal **c.** upon her head,....... 3804
Es 6:8 **c.** royal which is set upon his head. 3804
Es 8:15 and with a great **c.** of gold.,.............. 5850
Job 2:7 the sole of his foot unto his **c.**............ 6936
Job 19:9 and taken the **c.** from my head. 5850
Job 31:36 and bind it as a **c.** to me. 5850
Ps 21:3 a **c.** of pure gold on his head............. 5850
Ps 89:39 hast profaned his **c.** by casting it......... 5145
Ps 132:18 upon himself shall his **c.** flourish. 5145
Pr 4:9 a **c.** of glory shall she deliver to.......... 5850
Pr 12:4 woman is a **c.** to her husband:........... 5850
Pr 14:24 The **c.** of the wise is their riches: 5850
Pr 16:31 The hoary head is a **c.** of glory............ 5850
Pr 17:6 Children's children are the **c.** of 5850
Pr 27:24 the **c.** endure to every generation? 5145
Ca 3:11 behold king Solomon with the **c.**......... 5850
Isa 3:17 Lord will smite with a scab the **c.** 6936
Isa 28:1 the **c.** of pride, to the drunkards 5850
Isa 28:3 The **c.** of pride, the drunkards of 5850
Isa 28:5 Lord of hosts be for a **c.** of glory, ... 5850
Isa 62:3 Thou shalt also be a **c.** of glory 5850
Jer 2:16 have broken the **c.** of thy head. 6936
Jer 13:18 down, even the **c.** of your glory........... 5850
Jer 48:45 **c.** of the head of the tumultuous 6936
La 5:16 The **c.** is fallen from our head: 5850
Eze 16:12 and a beautiful **c.** upon thine head....... 5850
Eze 21:26 the diadem, and take off the **c.**: 5850
Zec 9:16 shall be as the stones of a **c.**,............ 5145
Mt 27:29 they had platted a **c.** of thorns,.......... *4735*
Mk 15:17 and platted a **c.** of thorns,................. *4735*
Joh 19:2 the soldiers platted a **c.** of thorns,...... *4735*
Joh 19:5 wearing the **c.** of thorns, and the *4735*
1Co 9:25 to obtain a corruptible **c.**; but we *4735*
Php 4:1 and longed for, my joy and **c.**, ... *4735*
1Th 2:19 hope, or joy, or **c.** of rejoicing?.......... *4735*
2Ti 4:8 up for me a **c.** of righteousness, ... *4735*
Jas 1:12 he shall receive the **c.** of life, ... *4735*
1Pe 5:4 a **c.** of glory that fadeth not away....... *4735*
Re 2:10 **and I will give thee a c. of life**....... *4735*
Re 3:11 **thou hast, that no man take thy c.** *4735*
Re 6:2 and a **c.** was given unto him:............. *4735*
Re 12:1 upon her head a **c.** of twelve stars: *4735*
Re 14:14 having on his head a golden **c.**,.......... *4735*

CROWNED See also CROWNEDST.
Ps 8:5 **c.** him with glory and honour.............. 5849
Pr 14:18 prudent are **c.** with knowledge............ 3803
Ca 3:11 wherewith his mother **c.** him in.......... 5849
Na 3:17 Thy **c.** are as the locusts, and thy...... 4502
2Ti 2:5 yet is he not **c.**, except he strive *4737*
Heb 2:9 death, **c.** with glory and honour; *4737*

CROWNEDST
Heb 2:7 thou **c.** him with glory and honour,..... *4737*

CROWNEST
Ps 65:11 **c.** the year with thy goodness; 5849

CROWNETH
Ps 103:4 who **c.** thee with lovingkindness......... 5849

CROWNING
Isa 23:8 counsel against Tyre, the **c.** city, ... 5849

CROWNS
Eze 23:42 and beautiful **c.** upon their heads. 5850
Zec 6:11 take silver and gold, and make **c.**, ... 5850
Zec 6:14 And the **c.** shall be to Helem,............ 5850
Re 4:4 they had on their heads **c.** of gold *4735*
Re 4:10 and cast their **c.** before the throne, ... *4735*
Re 9:7 heads were as it were **c.** like gold,..... *4735*
Re 12:3 and seven **c.** upon his heads. *1238*
Re 13:1 and upon his horns ten **c.**, and........... *1238*
Re 19:12 and on his head were many **c.**; *1238*

CRUCIFIED
Mt 26:2 **Son of man is betrayed to be c.**..... *4717*
Mt 27:22 all say unto him, Let him be **c.**.......... *4717*
Mt 27:23 out the more, saying, Let him be **c.** .. *4717*
Mt 27:26 he delivered him to be **c.**.................. *4717*
Mt 27:35 And they **c.** him, and parted his......... *4717*
Mt 27:38 were there two thieves **c.** with him, ... *4717*
Mt 27:44 also, which were **c.** with him,............ *4957*
Mt 28:5 that ye seek Jesus, which was **c.** *4717*
Mk 15:15 when he had scourged him, to be **c.** .. *4717*
Mk 15:24 when they had **c.** him, they parted *4717*
Mk 15:25 was the third hour, and they **c.** him.... *4717*
Mk 15:32 that were **c.** with him reviled him....... *4957*
Mk 16:6 Jesus of Nazareth, which was **c.**:........ *4717*
Lu 23:23 requiring that he might be **c.**............ *4717*
Lu 23:33 called Calvary, there they **c.** him,........ *4717*
Lu 24:7 and be **c.**, and the third day rise *4717*
Lu 24:20 to death, and have **c.** him. *4717*
Joh 19:16 him therefore unto them to be **c.** *4717*
Joh 19:18 Where they **c.** him, and two others *4717*
Joh 19:20 place where Jesus was **c.** was nigh *4717*
Joh 19:23 soldiers, when they had **c.** Jesus, ... *4717*
Joh 19:32 the other which was **c.** with him. *4957*
Joh 19:41 Now in the place where he was **c.**....... *4717*
Ac 2:23 wicked hands have **c.** and slain: *4362*
Ac 2:36 same Jesus, whom ye have **c.**, ... *4717*
Ac 4:10 Christ of Nazareth, whom ye **c.**, ... *4717*
Ro 6:6 that our old man is **c.** with him,......... *4957*
1Co 1:13 was Paul **c.** for you? or were ye *4717*
1Co 1:23 we preach Christ **c.**, unto the Jews..... *4717*
1Co 2:2 you, save Jesus Christ, and him **c.** *4717*

1Co 2:8 would not have **c.** the Lord of glory.... *4717*
2Co 13:4 he was **c.** through weakness, ... *4717*
Ga 2:20 I am **c.** with Christ: nevertheless *4957*
Ga 3:1 evidently set forth, **c.** among you?...... *4717*
Ga 5:24 have **c.** the flesh with the affections.... *4717*
Ga 6:14 by whom the world is **c.** unto me,...... *4717*
Re 11:8 Egypt, where also our Lord was **c.**..... *4717*

CRUCIFY See also CRUCIFIED.
Mt 20:19 **and to scourge, and to c. him:** *4717*
Mt 23:34 **some of them, ye shall kill and c.;** .*4717*
Mt 27:31 and led him away to **c.** him. *4717*
Mk 15:13 they cried out again, **C.** him. *4717*
Mk 15:14 out the more exceedingly, **C.** him. *4717*
Mk 15:20 and led him out to **c.** him. 4717
Mk 15:27 And with him they **c.** two thieves;...... 4717
Lu 23:21 they cried, saying, **C.** him, **c.** him. 4717
Joh 19:6 cried out, saying, **C.** him, **c.** him....... 4717
Joh 19:6 Take ye him, and **c.** him: for I find..... 4717
Joh 19:10 not that I have power to **c.** thee, ... 4717
Joh 19:15 away with him, **c.** him, Pilate saith..... 4717
Joh 19:15 Shall I **c.** your King? The chief 4717
Heb 6:6 they **c.** to themselves the Son of God... *388*

CRUEL
Ge 49:7 and their wrath, for it was **c.**:........... 7185
Ex 6:9 of spirit, and for **c.** bondage. 7185
De 32:33 dragons, and the **c.** venom of asps....... 393
Job 30:21 Thou art become **c.** to me: with thy...... 393
Ps 25:19 and they hate me with **c.** hatred. 2555
Ps 71:4 of the unrighteous and **c.** man. 2556
Pr 5:9 others, and thy years unto the **c.**:........ 394
Pr 11:17 he that is **c.** troubleth his own flesh. 394
Pr 12:10 tender mercies of the wicked are **c.**. 394
Pr 17:11 a **c.** messenger shall be sent against..... 394
Pr 27:4 is **c.**, and anger is outrageous; 395
Ca 8:6 jealousy is **c.** as the grave: the coals.........
Isa 13:9 Lord cometh, **c.** both with wrath 394
Isa 19:4 over into the hand of a **c.** lord; 7186
Jer 6:23 they are **c.**, and have no mercy; 394
Jer 30:14 the chastisement of a **c.** one, for 394
Jer 50:42 they are **c.**, and will not shew mercy:... 394
La 4:3 daughter of my people is become **c.**, ... 393
Heb 11:36 others had trial of **c.** mockings................

CRUELLY
Eze 18:18 father, because he **c.** oppressed, ... 6233

CRUELTY
Ge 49:5 instruments of **c.** are in their............ 2555
Jg 9:24 the **c.** done to the threescore and 2555
Ps 27:12 against me, and breathe out **c.**............ 2555
Ps 74:20 are full of the habitations of **c.**. 2555
Eze 34:4 and with **c.** have ye ruled them.......... 6531

CRUMBS
Mt 15:27 dogs eat of the **c.** which fall from *5589*
Mk 7:28 the table eat of the children's **c.**......... *5589*
Lu 16:21 **to be fed with the c. which fell** *5589*

CRUSE
1Sa 26:11 and the **c.** of water, and let us go. 6835
1Sa 26:12 the **c.** of water from Saul's bolster;..... 6835
1Sa 26:16 and the **c.** of water that was at his 6835
1Ki 14:3 and a **c.** of honey, and go to him:....... 1228
1Ki 17:12 in a barrel, and a little oil in a **c.**: 6835
1Ki 17:14 waste, neither shall the **c.** of oil fail, ... 6835
1Ki 17:16 not, neither did the **c.** of oil fail, ... 6835
1Ki 19:6 and a **c.** of water at his head. 6835
2Ki 2:20 Bring me a new **c.**, and put salt......... 6746

CRUSH See also CRUSHED.
Job 39:15 that the foot may **c.** them, or that...... 2115
La 1:15 against me to **c.** my young men: 7665
La 3:34 **c.** under his feet all the prisoners....... 1792
Am 4:1 which **c.** the needy, which say to 7533

CRUSHED
Le 22:24 bruised, or **c.**, or broken, or cut: 3807
Nu 22:25 **c.** Balaam's foot against the wall:........ 3905
De 28:33 be only oppressed and **c.** alway:.......... 7533
Job 4:19 which are **c.** before the moth? 1792
Job 5:4 they are **c.** in the gate, neither is....... 1792
Isa 59:5 is **c.** breaketh out into a viper. 2116
Jer 51:34 he hath **c.** me, he hath made me........ 2000

CRY See also CRIED; CRIES; CRIEST; CRIETH; CRYING.
Ge 18:20 **c.** of Sodom and Gomorrah is 2201
Ge 18:21 altogether according to the **c.** of it,..... 6818
Ge 19:13 the **c.** of them is waxen great............ 6818
Ge 27:34 a great and exceeding bitter **c.**, ... 6818
Ex 2:23 their **c.** came up unto God by............ 7775
Ex 3:7 and have heard their **c.** by reason 6818
Ex 3:9 **c.** of the children of Israel is come 6818
Ex 5:8 they **c.**, saying, Let us go and.......... 6817
Ex 11:6 shall be great **c.** throughout all.......... 6818
Ex 12:30 there was a great **c.** in Egypt;........... 6818
Ex 22:23 and they **c.** at all unto me,................ 6817
Ex 22:23 I will surely hear their **c.**;................. 6818
Ex 32:18 is it the voice of them that **c.**............ 6030
Le 13:45 and shall **c.**, Unclean, unclean. 7121
Nu 16:34 about them fled at, the **c.** of them: 6963
De 15:9 he **c.** unto the Lord against thee, ... 7121
De 24:15 he **c.** against thee unto the Lord, ... 7121
Jg 10:14 Go and **c.** unto the gods which ye 2199
1Sa 5:12 **c.** of the city went up to heaven. 7775
1Sa 7:8 Cease not to **c.** unto the Lord our...... 2199
1Sa 8:18 And ye shall **c.** out in that day........... 2199
1Sa 9:16 because their **c.** is come unto me. 6818
2Sa 19:28 have I yet to **c.** any more unto the..... 2199
2Sa 22:7 and my **c.** did enter into his ears........ 7775
1Ki 8:28 unto the **c.** and to the prayer, ... 7440
1Ki 18:27 **C.** aloud: for he is a god; either......... 7121
2Ki 8:3 she went forth to **c.** unto the king....... 6817
2Ch 6:19 to hearken unto the **c.** and the 7440
2Ch 13:12 sounding trumpets to **c.** alarm 7321
2Ch 20:9 and **c.** unto thee in our affliction,........ 2199
Ne 5:1 there was a great **c.** of the people...... 6818
Ne 5:6 I heard their **c.** and these words. 2201
Ne 9:9 heardest their **c.** by the Red sea;........ 2201
Es 4:1 cried with a loud and a bitter **c.**; 2201
Es 9:31 matters of the fastings and their **c.**. 2201
Job 16:18 and let my **c.** have no place. 2201
Job 19:7 I **c.** out of wrong, but I am not.......... 6817
Job 19:7 I **c.** aloud, but there is no.................. 7768
Job 27:9 Will God hear his **c.** when trouble 6818
Job 30:20 I **c.** unto thee, and thou dost not 7768
Job 30:24 though they **c.** in his destruction. 7769
Job 31:38 If my land **c.** against me, or............. 2199
Job 34:28 **c.** of the poor to come unto him, ... 6818
Job 34:28 and he heareth the **c.** of the............. 6818
Job 35:9 they make the oppressed to **c.**: 2199
Job 35:9 they **c.** out by reason of the arm........ 7768
Job 35:12 they **c.**, but none giveth answer,........ 6817
Job 36:13 they **c.** not when he bindeth them. 7768
Job 38:41 when his young ones **c.** unto God,...... 7768
Ps 5:2 unto the voice of my **c.**, my King,...... 7773
Ps 9:12 forgetteth not the **c.** of the humble..... 6818
Ps 17:1 attend unto my **c.**, give ear unto 7440
Ps 18:6 and my **c.** came before him, even........ 7775
Ps 22:2 O my God, I **c.** in the daytime, ... 7121
Ps 27:7 Hear, O Lord, when I **c.** with my 7121
Ps 28:1 Unto thee will I **c.**, O Lord my.......... 7121
Ps 28:2 when I **c.** unto thee, when I lift 7768
Ps 34:15 his ears are open unto their **c.**........... 7775
Ps 34:17 The righteous **c.**, and the Lord.......... 6817
Ps 39:12 and give ear unto my **c.**; hold not....... 7775
Ps 40:1 inclined unto me, and heard my **c.**...... 7775
Ps 55:17 at noon; will I pray, and **c.** aloud:........ 1993
Ps 56:9 I **c.** unto thee, then shall mine........... 7121
Ps 57:2 I will **c.** unto God most high; unto...... 7121
Ps 61:1 Hear my **c.**, O God; attend unto 7440
Ps 61:2 of the earth will I **c.** unto thee,.......... 7121
Ps 86:3 O Lord: for I **c.** unto thee daily. 7121
Ps 88:2 incline thine ear unto my **c.**;............. 7440
Ps 89:26 He shall **c.** unto me, Thou art my 7121
Ps 102:1 and let my **c.** come unto thee........... 7775
Ps 106:44 affliction, when he heard their **c.**: 7440
Ps 107:19 **c.** unto the Lord in their trouble, ... 2199
Ps 107:28 **c.** unto the Lord in their trouble, ... 6817
Ps 119:169 Let my **c.** come near before thee, ... 7440
Ps 141:1 Lord, I **c.** unto thee: make haste 7121
Ps 141:1 my voice, when I **c.** unto thee........... 7121
Ps 142:6 Attend unto my **c.**; for I am.............. 7440
Ps 145:19 hear their **c.**, and will save them. 7775
Ps 147:9 and to the young ravens which **c.**....... 7121
Pr 8:1 Doth not wisdom **c.**? and................... 7121
Pr 21:13 his ears at the **c.** of the poor,............ 2201
Pr 21:13 he also shall **c.** himself, ... 7121
Ec 9:17 **c.** of him that ruleth among fools........ 2201
Isa 5:7 for righteousness, but behold a **c.**....... 6818
Isa 8:4 child shall have knowledge to **c.**, ... 7121
Isa 12:6 **C.** out and shout, thou inhabitant........ 6670
Isa 13:22 wild beasts of the islands shall **c.**........ 6030
Isa 14:31 Howl, O gate; **c.**, O city; thou,.......... 2199
Isa 15:4 Heshbon shall **c.**, and Elealeh: 2199
Isa 15:4 soldiers of Moab shall **c.** out; 7321
Isa 15:5 My heart shall **c.** out for Moab; 2199
Isa 15:5 shall raise up a **c.** of destruction......... 2201
Isa 15:8 For the **c.** is gone round about the..... 2201
Isa 19:20 shall **c.** unto the Lord because of 6817
Isa 24:14 they shall **c.** aloud from the sea. 6670
Isa 29:9 and wonder; **c.** ye out, and **c.**: 8173
Isa 30:19 unto thee at the voice of thy **c.**; 2201
Isa 33:7 their valiant ones shall **c.** without: 6817
Isa 34:14 the satyr shall **c.** to his fellow;.......... 7121
Isa 40:2 and **c.** unto her, that her warfare is.... 7121
Isa 40:6 The voice said, **C.**. 7121
Isa 40:6 And he said, what shall I **c.**? 7121
Isa 42:2 He shall not **c.**, nor lift up, nor.......... 6817
Isa 42:13 he shall **c.**, yea, roar; he shall 7321
Isa 42:14 will I **c.** like a travailing woman;......... 6463
Isa 43:14 the Chaldeans, whose **c.** is in the....... 7440
Isa 46:7 yea, one shall **c.** unto him, yet 6817
Isa 54:1 forth into singing, and **c.** aloud,.......... 6670
Isa 58:1 **C.** aloud, spare not, lift up thy.......... 7121
Isa 58:9 thou shalt **c.**, and he shall say, ... 7768
Isa 65:14 ye shall **c.** for sorrow of heart, ... 6817
Jer 2:2 and **c.** in the ears of Jerusalem, ... 7121
Jer 3:4 thou not from this time **c.** unto me, ... 7121
Jer 4:5 in the land: **c.**, gather together, ... 7121
Jer 7:16 lift up **c.** nor prayer for them,............ 7440
Jer 8:19 **c.** of the daughter of my people 7775
Jer 11:11 though they shall **c.** unto me, ... 2199
Jer 11:12 go, and **c.** unto the gods unto............ 2199
Jer 11:14 lift up a **c.** or prayer for them:........... 7440
Jer 11:14 the time that they **c.** unto me for........ 7121
Jer 14:2 the **c.** of Jerusalem is gone up. 6682
Jer 14:12 they fast, I will not hear their **c.**; 7440
Jer 18:22 a **c.** be heard from their houses, ... 2201
Jer 20:16 let him hear the **c.** in the morning, ... 2201
Jer 22:20 Go up to Lebanon, and **c.**; and lift....... 6817
Jer 22:20 up thy voice in Bashan, and **c.** from.... 6817
Jer 25:34 Howl, ye shepherds, and **c.**; and........ 2199
Jer 25:36 A voice of the **c.** of the shepherds,..... 6818
Jer 31:6 shall **c.**, Arise ye, and let us go 7121
Jer 46:12 and thy **c.** hath filled the land: 6682
Jer 46:17 They did **c.** there, Pharoah king.......... 7121
Jer 47:2 then the men shall **c.**, and all the 2199
Jer 48:4 her little ones have caused a **c.**........... 2201
Jer 48:5 have heard a **c.** of destruction. 6818
Jer 48:20 it is broken down: howl and **c.**;........... 2199
Jer 48:31 I will **c.** out for all Moab; mine 2199
Jer 48:34 **c.** of Heshbon even unto Elealeh, ... 2201
Jer 49:3 **c.**, ye daughters of Rabbah, gird 6817
Jer 49:21 at the **c.** the noise thereof was.......... 6818
Jer 49:29 they shall **c.** unto them, Fear is......... 7121
Jer 50:46 **c.** is heard among the nations............ 2201
Jer 51:54 sound of a **c.** cometh from Babylon,.... 2201
La 2:19 Arise, **c.** out in the night: in the 7442
La 3:8 Also when I **c.** and shout, he............. 2199
La 3:56 ear at my breathing, at my **c.**.............. 7775
Eze 8:18 though they **c.** in mine ears with........ 7121
Eze 9:4 that **c.** for all the abominations 602
Eze 21:12 **C.** and howl, son of man: for it.......... 2199
Eze 24:17 Forbear to **c.**, make no mourning......... 602
Eze 26:15 wounded **c.**, when the slaughter 602
Eze 27:28 the sound of the **c.** of thy pilots......... 2201
Eze 27:30 and shall **c.** bitterly, and shall cast...... 2199
Ho 5:8 Ramah: **c.** aloud at Beth-aven,........... 7321
Ho 8:2 Israel shall **c.** unto me, My God,....... 2199
Joe 1:14 and **c.** unto the Lord, ... 2199
Joe 1:19 O Lord, to thee will I **c.**: for the........ 7121
Joe 1:20 beasts of the field **c.** also unto........... 6165
Am 3:4 young lion **c.** out of his den,....... 5414,6963
Jon 1:2 that great city, and **c.** against it; 7121
Jon 3:8 and **c.** mightily unto God: 7121
Mic 3:4 Then shall they **c.** unto the Lord,....... 2199
Mic 3:5 with their teeth, and **c.**, Peace: 7121
Mic 4:9 why dost thou **c.** out aloud: is 7321
Na 2:8 Stand, stand, shall they **c.**; but none.........
Hab 1:2 O Lord, how long shall I **c.**, and 7768
Hab 1:2 **c.** out unto thee of violence, and........ 2199
Hab 2:11 the stone shall **c.** out of the wall, ... 2199
Zep 1:10 noise of a **c.** from the fish gate, ... 6818
Zep 1:14 mighty man shall **c.** there bitterly. 6873
Zec 1:14 **C.** thou, saying, Thus saith the.......... 7121
Zec 1:17 **C.** yet, saying, Thus saith the Lord.... 7121
Mt 12:19 He shall not strive, nor **c.**;.................. *2905*
Mt 25:6 **at midnight there was a c. made,**.. *2906*
Mk 10:47 he began to **c.** out, and say, Jesus,...... *2896*
Lu 18:7 **own elect, which c. day and night**... *994*
Lu 19:40 **stones would immediately c. out,** .. *2896*
Ac 23:9 And there arose a great **c.**: and......... *2906*
Ro 8:15 whereby we **c.**, Abba, Father. *2896*
Ga 4:27 and **c.** thou that travailest not: *994*

Re 14:18 and cried with a loud **c.** to him *2906*

CRYING

1Sa 4:14 Eli heard the noise of the **c.**,............ 6818
2Sa 13:19 hand on her head, and went on **c.**. 2201
Job 39:7 regardeth he the **c.** of the driver........ 8663
Ps 69:3 I am weary of my **c.**: my throat......... 7121
Pr 19:18 let not thy soul spare for his **c.**.......... 4191
Pr 30:15 hath two daughters, **c.**, Give, give............
Isa 22:5 walls, and of **c.** to the mountains........ 7771
Isa 24:11 is a **c.** for wine in the streets;........... 6682
Isa 65:19 heard in her, nor the voice of **c.**. 2201
Jer 48:3 of **c.** shall be from Horonaim, ... 6818
Zec 4:7 thereof with shoutings, **c.**, Grace, ...
Mal 2:13 with weeping, and with **c.** out, ... 603
Mt 3:3 voice of one **c.** in the wilderness, ... *994*
Mt 9:27 **c.**, and saying, Thou son of David, ... *2896*
Mt 21:15 and the children **c.** in the temple, ... *2896*
Mk 1:3 voice of one **c.** in the wilderness, ... *994*
Mk 5:5 and in the tombs, **c.**, and cutting........ *2896*
Mk 15:8 the multitude **c.** aloud began to *310*
Lu 3:4 voice of one **c.** in the wilderness, ... *994*
Lu 4:41 out of many, **c.** out, and saying,......... *2896*
Joh 1:23 the voice of one **c.** in the wilderness, ... *994*
Ac 8:7 unclean spirits, **c.** with loud voice, ... *994*
Ac 14:14 ran in among the people, **c.** out, ... *2896*
Ac 17:6 unto the rulers of the city, **c.**.............. *994*
Ac 21:28 **C.** out, Men of Israel, help: This *2896*
Ac 21:36 followed after, **c.**, Away with him. *2896*
Ac 25:24 **c.** that he ought not to live any.......... *1916*
Ga 4:6 into your hearts, **c.**, Abba, Father. *2896*
Heb 5:7 with strong **c.** and tears unto him....... *2906*
Re 14:15 **c.** with a loud voice to him that *2896*
Re 21:4 neither sorrow, nor **c.**, neither *2906*

CRYSTAL

Job 28:17 The gold and the **c.** cannot equal........ 2137
Eze 1:22 as the colour of the terrible **c.**,.......... 7140
Re 4:6 was a sea of glass like unto **c.**: *2930*
Re 21:11 like a jasper stone, clear as **c.**; *2929*
Re 22:1 river of water of life, clear as **c.**. *2930*

CUBIT See also CUBITS.

Ge 6:16 a **c.** shalt thou finish it above; 520
Ex 25:10 a **c.** and a half the breadth thereof, ... 520
Ex 25:10 a **c.** and a half the height thereof. 520
Ex 25:17 a **c.** and a half the breadth thereof. 520
Ex 25:23 and a **c.** the breadth thereof, and......... 520
Ex 25:23 a **c.** and a half the height thereof. 520
Ex 26:13 And a **c.** on the one side,..................... 520
Ex 26:13 and a **c.** on the other side of that......... 520
Ex 26:16 a **c.** and a half shall be the breadth....... 520
Ex 30:2 A **c.** shall be the length thereof, and..... 520
Ex 30:2 a **c.** the breadth thereof; foursquare 520
Ex 36:21 and the breadth of a board one **c.**........ 520
Ex 37:1 and a **c.** and a half the breadth of it,..... 520
Ex 37:1 and a **c.** and a half the height of it: 520
Ex 37:6 one **c.** and a half the breadth thereof, ... 520
Ex 37:10 and a **c.** the breadth thereof, ... 520
Ex 37:10 a **c.** and a half the height thereof. 520
Ex 37:25 the length of it was a **c.**,.................... 520
Ex 37:25 and the breadth of it a **c.**; 520
De 3:11 breadth of it, after the **c.** of a man....... 520
Jg 3:16 had two edges, of a **c.** length; 1574
1Ki 7:24 knops compassing it, ten in a **c.**, ... 520
1Ki 7:31 the chapiter and above was a **c.**: 520
1Ki 7:31 work of the base, a **c.** and an half:....... 520
1Ki 7:32 a wheel was a **c.** and half a **c.**............ 520
1Ki 7:35 a round compass of half a **c.** high:........ 520
2Ch 4:3 ten in a **c.**, compassing the sea 520
Eze 40:5 six cubits long by the **c.** and an hand.... 520
Eze 40:12 one **c.** on this side,............................. 520
Eze 40:12 the space was one **c.** on that side: 520
Eze 40:42 of a **c.** and an half long, ... 520
Eze 40:42 and a **c.** and an half broad, ... 520
Eze 40:42 and one **c.** high: 520
Eze 42:4 breadth inward, a way of one **c.**; 520
Eze 43:13 The **c.** is a **c.** and an hand breadth;...... 520
Eze 43:13 even the bottom shall be a **c.**.............. 520
Eze 43:13 and the breadth a **c.**,........................... 520
Eze 43:14 two cubits, and the breadth one **c.**; 520
Eze 43:14 four cubits, and the breadth one **c.**........ 520
Eze 43:17 border about it shall be half a **c.**; 520
Eze 43:17 bottom thereof shall be a **c.** about;....... 520
Mt 6:27 **can add one c. unto his stature?**.... *4083*
Lu 12:25 **can add to his stature one c.?**....... *4083*

CUBITS

Ge 6:15 the ark shall be three hundred **c.**,........ 520
Ge 6:15 the breadth of it fifty **c.**, ... 520
Ge 6:15 and the height of it thirty **c.**................ 520
Ge 7:20 Fifteen **c.** upward did the waters 520
Ex 25:10, 17 two **c.** and a half shall be the.......... 520
Ex 25:23 two **c.** shall be the length thereof, ... 520
Ex 26:2 curtain shall be eight and twenty **c.**, ... 520
Ex 26:2 the breadth of one curtain four **c.**: 520
Ex 26:8 of one curtain shall be thirty **c.**, and..... 520
Ex 26:8 the breadth of one curtain four **c.**: 520
Ex 26:16 Ten **c.** shall be the length of a 520
Ex 27:1 wood, five **c.** long, and five **c.** broad; ... 520
Ex 27:1 the height thereof shall be three **c.**. 520
Ex 27:9 fine twined linen of an hundred **c.** 520
Ex 27:11 be hangings of an hundred **c.** long,...........
Ex 27:12 side shall be hangings of fifty **c.**:.......... 520
Ex 27:13 east side eastward shall be fifty **c.**. 520
Ex 27:14 side of the gate shall be fifteen **c.**: 520
Ex 27:15 side shall be hangings fifteen **c.**:...............
Ex 27:16 shall be an hanging of twenty **c.**, ... 520
Ex 27:18 of the court shall be an hundred **c.**,...... 520
Ex 27:18 and the height five **c.** of fine twined 520
Ex 30:2 two **c.** shall be the height thereof; 520
Ex 36:9 one curtain was twenty and eight **c.**, ... 520
Ex 36:9 the breadth of one curtain four **c.**: 520
Ex 36:15 length of one curtain was thirty **c.**,....... 520
Ex 36:15 and four **c.** was the breadth of one....... 520
Ex 36:21 The length of a board was ten **c.**,......... 520
Ex 37:1 two **c.** and a half was the length of 520
Ex 37:6 **c.** and a half was the length thereof,..... 520
Ex 37:10 two **c.** was the length thereof, and....... 520
Ex 37:25 and two **c.** was the height of it; the 520
Ex 38:1 five **c.** was the length thereof, ... 520
Ex 38:1 and five **c.** the breadth thereof; 520
Ex 38:1 and three **c.** the height thereof............ 520
Ex 38:9 of fine twined linen, an hundred **c.**: 520
Ex 38:11 the hangings were an hundred **c.**, ... 520
Ex 38:12 side were hangings of fifty **c.**, ... 520
Ex 38:13 for the east side eastward fifty **c.**. 520
Ex 38:14 one side of the gate were fifteen **c.**;..... 520
Ex 38:15 hand, were hangings of fifteen **c.**; 520
Ex 38:18 twenty **c.** was the length, and the......... 520
Ex 38:18 the breadth was five **c.**, answerable...... 520
Nu 11:31 and as it were two **c.** high upon the 520
Nu 35:4 and outward a thousand **c.** round 520
Nu 35:5 east side two thousand **c.**,.................. 520
Nu 35:5 the south side two thousand **c.**,............ 520
Nu 35:5 the west side two thousand **c.**,............. 520
Nu 35:5 on the north side two thousand **c.**;....... 520
De 3:11 nine **c.** was the length thereof,............ 520
De 3:11 and four **c.** the breadth of it,............... 520
Jos 3:4 about two thousand **c.** by measure: 520
1Sa 17:4 whose height was six **c.** and a span........ 520
1Ki 6:2 the length thereof was threescore **c.**, ... 520
1Ki 6:2 the breadth thereof twenty **c.**, ...
1Ki 6:2 and the height thereof thirty **c.**............ 520
1Ki 6:3 twenty **c.** was the length thereof, ... 520
1Ki 6:3 and ten **c.** was the breadth thereof....... 520
1Ki 6:6 nethermost chamber was five **c.** 520
1Ki 6:6 and the middle was six **c.** broad, ... 520
1Ki 6:6 and the third was seven **c.** broad: 520
1Ki 6:10 against all the house, five **c.** high: 520
1Ki 6:16 he build twenty **c.** on the sides of........ 520
1Ki 6:17 temple before it, was forty **c.** long. 520
1Ki 6:20 forepart was twenty **c.** in length, ... 520
1Ki 6:20 and twenty **c.** in breadth, ... 520
1Ki 6:20 and twenty **c.** in the height thereof. 520
1Ki 6:23 cherubims of olive tree, each ten **c.** 520
1Ki 6:24 **c.** was the one wing of the cherub, ... 520
1Ki 6:24 five **c.** the other wing of the cherub: 520
1Ki 6:24 part of the other were ten **c.**. 520
1Ki 6:25 And the other cherub was ten **c.**: 520
1Ki 6:26 height of the one cherub was ten **c.**, ... 520
1Ki 7:2 the length thereof was an hundred **c.**,... 520
1Ki 7:2 and the breadth thereof fifty **c.**,.......... 520
1Ki 7:2 and the height thereof thirty **c.**,........... 520
1Ki 7:6 the length thereof was fifty **c.**, ... 520
1Ki 7:6 and the breadth thereof thirty **c.**:.......... 520
1Ki 7:10 stones of ten **c.**, and stones of eight **c.**. .520
1Ki 7:15 of brass, of eighteen **c.** high apiece: 520
1Ki 7:15 line of twelve **c.** did compass either...... 520
1Ki 7:16 one chapiter was five **c.**, and the 520
1Ki 7:16 of the other chapiter was five **c.**: 520
1Ki 7:19 of lily work in the porch, four **c.**.......... 520
1Ki 7:23 a molten sea, ten **c.** from the one........ 520
1Ki 7:23 and his height was five **c.**: and 520
1Ki 7:23 a line of thirty **c.** did compass it 520
1Ki 7:27 four **c.** was the length of one base, ... 520
1Ki 7:27 and four **c.** the breadth thereof,........... 520
1Ki 7:27 and three **c.** the height of it............... 520
1Ki 7:38 every laver was four **c.**: and upon........ 520
2Ki 14:13 the corner gate, four hundred **c.**. 520
2Ki 25:17 one pillar was eighteen **c.**, and the....... 520
2Ki 25:17 the height of the chapiter three **c.**;....... 520
1Ch 11:23 a man of great stature, five **c.** high; 520
2Ch 3:3 The length, by **c.** after the first........... 520
2Ch 3:3 measure was threescore **c.**,................ 520
2Ch 3:3 and the breadth twenty **c.**. 520
2Ch 3:4 the breadth of the house, twenty **c.**, ... 520
2Ch 3:8 length whereof was twenty **c.**, ... 520
2Ch 3:8 and the breadth thereof twenty **c.**: 520
2Ch 3:11 the cherubims were twenty **c.** long: 520
2Ch 3:11 wing of the one cherub was five **c.**,...... 520
2Ch 3:11 the other wing was likewise five **c.**, ... 520
2Ch 3:12 wing of the other cherub was five **c.**, ... 520
2Ch 3:12 the other wing was five **c.** also,........... 520
2Ch 3:13 spread themselves forth twenty **c.**: 520
2Ch 3:15 house two pillars of thirty and five **c.**..... 520
2Ch 3:15 the top of each of them was five **c.**. 520
2Ch 4:1 twenty **c.** the length thereof, ... 520
2Ch 4:1 and twenty **c.** the breadth thereof,........ 520
2Ch 4:1 and ten **c.** the height thereof............... 520
2Ch 4:2 a molten sea of ten **c.** from brim to...... 520
2Ch 4:2 brim, round in compass, and five **c.**....... 520
2Ch 4:2 a line of thirty **c.** did compass 520
2Ch 6:13 a brasen scaffold, of five **c.** long, ... 520
2Ch 6:13 and five **c.** broad, and three **c.** high,..... 520
2Ch 25:23 to the corner gate, four hundred **c.**. 520
Ezr 6:3 the height thereof threescore **c.**, ... 521
Ezr 6:3 the breadth thereof threescore **c.**;......... 521
Neh 3:13 and a thousand **c.** on the wall unto....... 520
Es 5:14 Let a gallows be made of fifty **c.** 520
Es 7:9 Behold also, the gallows fifty **c.** high,.... 520
Jer 52:21 height of one pillar was eighteen **c.**; 520
Jer 52:21 and a fillet of twelve **c.** did compass..... 520
Jer 52:22 height of one chapiter was five **c.**, ... 520
Eze 40:5 a measuring reed of six **c.** long by 520
Eze 40:7 the little chambers were five **c.**; 520
Eze 40:9 the porch of the gate, eight **c.**;............ 520
Eze 40:9 and the posts thereof, two **c.**;............. 520
Eze 40:11 the entry of the gate, ten **c.**; and 520
Eze 40:11 the length of the gate, thirteen **c.**. 520
Eze 40:12 chambers were six **c.** on this side, ... 520
Eze 40:12 and six **c.** on that side........................ 520
Eze 40:13 breadth was five and twenty **c.**, door.... 520
Eze 40:14 He made also posts of threescore **c.**,.... 520
Eze 40:15 porch of the inner gate were fifty **c.**..... 520
Eze 40:19 without, an hundred **c.** eastward and 520
Eze 40:21 the length thereof was fifty **c.**, ... 520
Eze 40:21 and the breadth five and twenty **c.**. 520
Eze 40:23 from gate to gate an hundred **c.**. 520
Eze 40:25 the length was fifty **c.**, and the............ 520
Eze 40:25 breadth five and twenty **c.**.................. 520
Eze 40:27 gate toward the south an hundred **c.**. ... 520
Eze 40:29 it was fifty **c.** long, and....................... 520
Eze 40:29 and five and twenty **c.** broad............... 520
Eze 40:30 about were five and twenty **c.** long, ... 520
Eze 40:30 and five **c.** broad. 520
Eze 40:33 it was fifty **c.** long, ... 520
Eze 40:33 and five and twenty **c.** broad............... 520
Eze 40:36 the length was fifty **c.**, and the............ 520
Eze 40:36 breadth five and twenty **c.**.................. 520
Eze 40:47 an hundred **c.** long, and 520
Eze 40:47 an hundred **c.** broad, four square; 520
Eze 40:48 post of the porch, five **c.** on this side, .. 520
Eze 40:48 and five **c.** on that side:...................... 520
Eze 40:48 of the gate was three **c.** on this side, ... 520
Eze 40:48 and three **c.** on that side.................... 520
Eze 40:49 length of the porch was twenty **c.**,....... 520
Eze 40:49 and the breadth eleven **c.**;.................. 520
Eze 41:1 posts, six **c.** broad on the one side, ... 520
Eze 41:1 and six **c.** broad on the other side,....... 520
Eze 41:2 breadth of the door was ten **c.**; 520
Eze 41:2 sides of the door were five **c.** on the.... 520
Eze 41:2 side, and five **c.** on the other side:....... 520
Eze 41:2 the length thereof, forty **c.**: 520
Eze 41:2 and the breadth, twenty **c.**. 520
Eze 41:3 door two **c.**; and the door, six **c.**; 520
Eze 41:3 the breadth of the door, seven **c.**. 520
Eze 41:4 the length thereof, twenty **c.**; 520
Eze 41:4 and the breadth, twenty **c.**. 520
Eze 41:5 the wall of the house, six **c.**; 520
Eze 41:5 of every side chamber, four **c.**, ... 520
Eze 41:8 were a full reed of six great **c.**.............. 520
Eze 41:9 side chamber without, was five **c.**: 520

Eze 41:10 was the wideness of twenty **c.** round.... 520
Eze 41:11 place that was left was five **c.** round..... 520
Eze 41:12 the west was seventy **c.** broad;........... 520
Eze 41:12 was five **c.** thick round about,............. 520
Eze 41:12 and the length thereof ninety **c.**.......... 520
Eze 41:13 the house an hundred **c.** long; and 520
Eze 41:13 walls thereof, an hundred **c.** long;........ 520
Eze 41:14 place toward the east, an hundred **c.**.... 520
Eze 41:15 the other side, an hundred **c.**, with 520
Eze 41:22 altar of wood was three **c.** high,.......... 520
Eze 41:22 and the length thereof two **c.**;............ 520
Eze 42:2 Before the length of an hundred **c.**....... 520
Eze 42:2 door, and the breadth was fifty **c.**........ 520
Eze 42:3 Over against the twenty **c.** which............
Eze 42:4 a walk of ten **c.** breadth inward,.......... 520
Eze 42:7 the length thereof was fifty **c.**............ 520
Eze 42:8 were in the utter court was fifty **c.**:..... 520
Eze 42:8 the temple were an hundred **c.**.............. 520
Eze 43:13 measures of the altar after the **c.**:........ 520
Eze 43:14 to the lower settle shall be two **c.**,...... 520
Eze 43:14 the greater settle shall be four **c.**,........ 520
Eze 43:15 the altar shall be four **c.**; and from....... 520
Eze 43:16 the altar shall be twelve **c.** long,..............
Eze 43:17 the settle shall be fourteen **c.** long............
Eze 45:2 fifty **c.** round about for the suburbs...... 520
Eze 46:22 were courts joined of forty **c.** long............
Eze 47:3 he measured a thousand **c.**, and 520
Da 3:1 whose height was threescore **c.**,........... 521
Da 3:1 and the breadth thereof six **c.**:............ 521
Zec 5:2 the length thereof is twenty **c.**,........... 520
Zec 5:2 and the breadth thereof ten **c.**............. 520
Joh 21:8 but as it were two hundred **c.**,)......... *4088*
Re 21:17 an hundred and forty and four **c.**,....... *4088*

CUCKOW
Le 11:16 the night hawk, and the **c.**, and 7828
De 14:15 the night hawk, and the **c.**, and 7828

CUCUMBERS
Nu 11:5 freely; the **c.**, and the melons,........... 7180
Isa 1:8 as a lodge in a garden of **c.**,............. 4750

CUD
Le 11:3 cheweth the **c.**, among the beasts,..... 1625
Le 11:4 of them that chew the **c.**, or of.......... 1625
Le 11:4, 5,6 because he cheweth the **c.**, but.... 1625
Le 11:7 yet he cheweth not the **c.**; he is......... 1625
Le 11:26 nor cheweth the **c.**, are unclean......... 1625
De 14:6 cheweth the **c.** among the beasts,...... 1625
De 14:7 of them that chew the **c.**, or of.......... 1625
De 14:7 for they chew the **c.**, but divide......... 1625
De 14:8 yet cheweth not the **c.**, it is............. 1625

CUMBERED
Lu 10:40 But Martha was **c.** about much.......... *4049*

CUMBERETH
Lu 13:7 **cut it down; why c. it the ground?**..*2673*

CUMBRANCE
De 1:12 can I myself alone bear your **c.**,......... 2960

CUMI (coo'-mi)
Mk 5:41 unto her, **Talitha c.**; which is,.......... *2891*

CUMMIN
Isa 28:25 and scatter the **c.**, and cast in the...... 3646
Isa 28:27 wheel turned about upon the **c.**;........... 3646
Isa 28:27 with a staff, and the **c.** with a rod....... 3646
Mt 23:23 **pay tithe of mint and anise and c.**,.*2951*

CUNNING
Ge 25:27 Esau was a **c.** hunter, a man of......... 3045
Ex 26:1 cherubims of **c.** work shalt thou......... 2803
Ex 26:31 and fine twined linen of **c.** work:........ 2803
Ex 28:6 fine twined linen, with **c.** work........... 2803
Ex 28:15 breastplate of judgment with **c.**........... 2803
Ex 31:4 devise **c.** works, to work in gold,........ 4284
Ex 35:33 to make any manner of **c.** work........... 4284
Ex 35:35 and of the **c.** workman, and of the......... 2803
Ex 35:35 and of those that devise **c.** work.......... 4284
Ex 36:8 cherubims of **c.** work made he........... 2803
Ex 36:35 cherubims made he it of **c.** work......... 2803
Ex 38:23 an engraver and a **c.** workman,........... 2803
Ex 39:3 in the fine linen, with **c.** work........... 2803
Ex 39:8 the breastplate of **c.** work, like.......... 2803
1Sa 16:16 seek out a man, who is a **c.** player..... 3045
1Sa 16:18 that is **c.** in playing, and a mighty....... 3045
1Ki 7:14 **c.** to work all works in brass............ 1847
1Ch 22:15 **c.** men for every manner of work....... 2450
1Ch 25:7 all that were **c.**, was two hundred........ 995
2Ch 2:7 **c.** to work in gold, and in silver,........ 2450
2Ch 2:7 skill to grave with **c.** the men that....... 2450
2Ch 2:13 now I have sent a **c.** man, endued....... 2450
2Ch 2:14 be put to him, with thy **c.**, men,......... 2450
2Ch 2:14 and with the **c.** men of my lord........... 2450
2Ch 26:15 engines, invented by **c.** men, to be..... 2803
Ps 137:5 let my right hand forget her **c.**..................
Ca 7:1 of the hands of a **c.** workman............. 542
Isa 3:3 counseller, and the **c.** artificer,........... 2450
Isa 40:20 seeketh unto a him **c.** workman.......... 2450
Jer 9:17 may come; and send for **c.** women,..... 2450
Jer 10:9 they are all the work of **c.** men.......... 2450
Da 1:4 and **c.** in knowledge, and.................. 3045
Eph 4:14 sleight of men, and **c.** craftiness..............

CUNNINGLY
2Pe 1:16 have not followed **c.** devised fables,..........

CUP See also CUPBEARER; CUPS.
Ge 40:11 and Pharaoh's **c.** was in my hand:....... 3563
Ge 40:11 pressed them into Pharaoh's **c.**,.......... 3563
Ge 40:11 I gave the **c.** into Pharaoh's hand....... 3563
Ge 40:13 deliver Pharaoh's **c.** into his hand,...... 3563
Ge 40:21 he gave the **c.** into Pharaoh's hand:.... 3563
Ge 44:2 And put my **c.**, the silver **c.**, in the.... 1375
Ge 44:12 **c.** was found in Benjamin's sack.......... 1375
Ge 44:16 he also with whom the **c.** is found........ 1375
Ge 44:17 man in whose hand the **c.** is found,..... 1375
2Sa 12:3 and drank of his own **c.**, and lay......... 3563
1Ki 7:26 was wrought like the brim of a **c.**,....... 3563
2Ch 4:5 like the work of the brim of a **c.**,........ 3563
Ps 11:6 this shall be the portion of their **c.**....... 3563
Ps 16:5 of mine inheritance and of my **c.**:......... 3563
Ps 23:5 head with oil; my **c.** runneth over........ 3563
Ps 73:10 and waters of a full **c.** are wrung out.........
Ps 75:8 hand of the Lord there is a **c.**,............ 3563
Ps 116:13 I will take the **c.** of salvation, and........ 3563
Pr 23:31 when it giveth his colour in the **c.**,...... 3599
Isa 51:17 of the Lord the **c.** of his fury;............ 3563
Isa 51:17 the dregs of the **c.** of trembling,......... 3563
Isa 51:22 of thine hand the **c.** of trembling......... 3563
Isa 51:22 even the dregs of the **c.** of my fury;... 3563
Jer 16:7 the **c.** of consolation to drink for......... 3563
Jer 25:15 the wine **c.** of this fury at my hand,.... 3563
Jer 25:17 took I the **c.** at the Lord's hand,......... 3563
Jer 25:28 take the **c.** at thine hand to drink,....... 3563
Jer 49:12 judgment was not to drink of the **c.**...... 3563
Jer 51:7 Babylon hath been a golden **c.** in......... 3563
La 4:21 the **c.** also shall pass through unto........ 3563
Eze 23:31 will I give her **c.** into thine hand......... 3563
Eze 23:32 of thy sister's **c.** deep and large:......... 3563
Eze 23:33 **c.** of astonishment and desolation,....... 3563
Eze 23:33 with the **c.** of thy sister Samaria......... 3563
Hab 2:16 **c.** of the Lord's right hand shall be...... 3563
Zec 12:2 make Jerusalem a **c.** of trembling........ 5592
Mt 10:42 **c. of cold water only in the name**.. *4221*
Mt 20:22 **drink of the c. that I shall drink**.. *4221*
Mt 20:23 **Ye shall drink indeed of my c.**,..... *4221*
Mt 23:25 **outside of the c. and of the platter**,*4221*
Mt 23:26 **first that which is within the c.** *4221*
Mt 26:27 he took the **c.**, and gave thanks,......... *4221*
Mt 26:39 **possible, let this c. pass from me**:.. *4221*
Mt 26:42 **c. may not pass away from me**,..... *4221*
Mk 9:41 **give you a c. of water to drink**....... *4221*
Mk 10:38 **ye drink of the c. that I drink of?**. *4221*
Mk 10:39 **indeed drink of the c. that I drink**..*4221*
Mk 14:23 And he took the **c.**, and when he....... *4221*
Mk 14:36 **take away this c. from me**:........... *4221*
Lu 11:39 **make clean the outside of the c.**.... *4221*
Lu 22:17 he took the **c.**, and gave thanks,......... *4221*
Lu 22:20 Likewise also the **c.** after supper,........ *4221*
Lu 22:20 **This c. is the new testament in my**.*4221*
Lu 22:42 **if thou be willing, remove this c.**... *4221*
Joh 18:11 **c. which my Father hath given me**,*4221*
1Co 10:16 The **c.** of blessing which we bless,..... *4221*
1Co 10:21 Ye cannot drink the **c.** of the Lord,.... *4221*
1Co 10:21 and the **c.** of devils:......................... *4221*
1Co 11:25 same manner also he took the **c.**,........ *4221*
1Co 11:25 **This c. is the new testament in my**.*4221*
1Co 11:26 and drink this **c.**, ye do show.............. *4221*
1Co 11:27 drink this **c.** of the Lord, unworthily,.. *4221*
1Co 11:28 of that bread, and drink of that **c.**........ *4221*
Re 14:10 into the **c.** of his indignation;............. *4221*
Re 16:19 the **c.** of the wine of the fierceness.... *4221*
Re 17:4 having a golden **c.** in her hand full...... *4221*
Re 18:6 in the **c.** which she hath filled, fill....... *4221*

CUPBEARER See also CUPBEARERS.
Ne 1:11 For I was the king's **c.**.................... 4945

CUPBEARERS
1KI 10:5 their apparel, and his **c.**, and his......... 4945
2Ch 9:4 their apparel; his **c.** also, and their..... 4945

CUPS
1Ch 28:17 and the bowls, and the **c.**:................ 7184
Isa 22:24 from the vessels of **c.** even to all.......... 101
Jer 35:5 pots full of wine, and **c.**, and I........... 3563
Jer 52:19 and the spoons, and the **c.**; that.......... 4518
Mk 7:4 as the washing of **c.**, and pots,........... *4221*
Mk 7:8 **as the washing of pots and c.**:......... *4221*

CURDLED
Job 10:10 as milk, and **c.** me like cheese?......... 7087

CURE See also CURED; CURES; INCURABLE; PROCURE.
Jer 33:6 I will bring it health and **c.**,............... 4832
Jer 33:6 and I will **c.** them, and will reveal........ 7495
Ho 5:13 you, nor **c.** you of your wound........... 1455
Mt 17:16 and they could not **c.** him................ *2323*
Lu 9:1 over all devils, and to **c.** diseases....... *2323*

CURED
Jer 46:11 for thou shalt not be **c.**.................... 8585
Mt 17:18 child was **c.** from that very hour........ *2323*
Lu 7:21 he **c.** many of their infirmities and....... *2323*
Joh 5:10 said unto him that was **c.**, It is the....... *2323*

CURES
Lu 13:32 **and I do c. to day and to morrow**,..*2392*

CURIOUS
Ex 28:8 And the **c.** girdle of the ephod,...............
Ex 28:27, 28 above the **c.** girdle of the....................
Ex 29:5 with the **c.** girdle of the ephod:...............
Ex 35:32 devise **c.** works, to work in gold,....... 4284
Ex 39:5 And the **c.** girdle of his ephod,...............
Ex 39:20, 21 above the **c.** girdle of the....................
Le 8:7 with the **c.** girdle of the ephod,...............
Ac 19:19 used **c.** arts brought their books........ *4021*

CURIOUSLY
Ps 139:15 **c.** wrought in the lowest parts........... 7551

CURRENT
Ge 23:16 **c.** money with the merchant............. 5674

CURSE See also CURSED; CURSES; CURSEST; CURSETH; CURSING.
Ge 8:21 I will not again **c.** the ground any....... 7043
Ge 12:3 and **c.** him that curseth thee: and in..... 779
Ge 27:12 I shall bring a **c.** upon me, and not..... 7045
Ge 27:13 Upon me be thy **c.**, my son:.............. 7045
Ex 22:28 gods, nor **c.** the ruler of thy people...... 779
Le 19:14 Thou shalt not **c.** the deaf, nor.......... 7043
Nu 5:18, 19 bitter water that causeth the **c.**:...... 779
Nu 5:21 Lord make thee a **c.** and an oath.......... 423
Nu 5:22 water that causeth the **c.** shall go........ 779
Nu 5:24 bitter water that causeth the **c.**:......... 779
Nu 5:24, 27 water that causeth the **c.** shall........ 779
Nu 5:27 woman shall be a **c.** among her........... 423
Nu 22:6 I pray thee, **c.** me this people;............ 779
Nu 22:11 come now, **c.** me them;................... 6895
Nu 22:12 shalt not **c.** the people: for they.......... 779
Nu 22:17 I pray thee, **c.** me this people........... 6895
Nu 23:7 Come, **c.** me Jacob, and come,............ 779
Nu 23:8 How shall I **c.**, whom God hath not..... 5344
Nu 23:11 I took thee to **c.** mine enemies,.......... 6895
Nu 23:13 all: and **c.** me them from thence......... 6895
Nu 23:25 **c.** them at all, nor bless them at all.... 6895
Nu 23:27 mayest **c.** me them from thence.......... 6895
Nu 24:10 I called thee to **c.** mine enemies,........ 6895
De 11:26 you this day a blessing and a **c.**;......... 7045
De 11:28 a **c.**, if ye will not obey the............... 7045
De 11:29 and the **c.** upon mount Ebal............... 7045
De 23:4 Pethor of Mesopotamia, to **c.** thee...... 7043
De 23:5 God turned the **c.** into a blessing........ 7045
De 27:13 shall stand upon mount Ebal to **c.**;........ 7045
De 29:19 he heareth the words of this **c.**,.......... 423
De 30:1 the blessing and the **c.**, which I.......... 7045
Jos 6:18 and make the camp of Israel a **c.**,....... 2764
Jos 24:9 Balaam the son of Beor to **c.** you:...... 7043
Jg 5:23 **C.** ye Meroz, said the angel................ 779
Jg 5:23 **c.** ye bitterly the inhabitants............... 779
Jg 9:57 upon them came the **c.** of Jotham....... 7045
2Sa 16:9 should this dead dog **c.** my lord.......... 7043
2Sa 16:10 let him **c.**, because the Lord hath........ 7043
2Sa 16:10 Lord hath said unto him, **C.** David....... 7043
2Sa 16:11 let him alone, and let him **c.**: for......... 7043
1Ki 2:8 a grievous **c.** in the day when I.......... 7045
2Ki 22:19 should become a desolation and a **c.**,... 7045
Ne 10:29 entered into a **c.**, and into an oath,...... 423

Ne 13:2 against them, that he should **c.** 7043
Ne 13:2 God turned the **c.** into a blessing. 7045
Job 1:11 and he will **c.** thee to thy face. 1288
Job 2:5 and he will **c.** thee to thy face. 1288
Job 2:9 **c.** God, and die. 1288
Job 3:8 Let them **c.** it that 5344
Job 3:8 that **c.** the day, who are 779
Job 31:30 to sin by wishing a **c.** to his soul. 423
Ps 62:4 their mouth, but they **c.** inwardly. 7043
Ps 109:28 Let them **c.**, but bless thou: 7043
Pr 3:33 The **c.** of the Lord is in the house 3994
Pr 11:26 corn, the people shall **c.** him: but 5344
Pr 24:24 him shall the people **c.**, nations 5344
Pr 26:2 the **c.** causeless shall not come. 7045
Pr 27:14 morning, it shall be counted a **c.** 7045
Pr 28:27 his eyes shall have many a **c.**. 3994
Pr 30:10 lest he **c.** thee, and thou be found 7043
Ec 7:21 lest thou hear thy servant **c.** thee: 7043
Ec 10:20 **C.** not the king, no not in thy 7043
Ec 10:20 **c.** not the rich in thy bedchamber: 7043
Isa 8:21 and **c.** their king and their God, 7043
Isa 24:6 hath the **c.** devoured the earth, 423
Isa 34:5 and upon the people of my **c.**, to 2764
Isa 43:28 given Jacob to the **c.**, and Israel 2764
Isa 65:15 ye shall leave your name for a **c.** 7621
Jer 15:10 every one of them doth **c.** me. 7043
Jer 24:9 and a proverb, a taunt and a **c.**, 7045
Jer 25:18 astonishment, an hissing, and a **c.**; 7045
Jer 26:6 will make this city a **c.** to all the 7045
Jer 29:18 to be a **c.**, and an astonishment, 423
Jer 29:22 them shall be taken up a **c.** by all 7045
Jer 42:18 an astonishment, and a **c.**, and a 7045
Jer 44:8 ye might be a **c.** and a reproach 7045
Jer 44:12 an astonishment, and a **c.**, and a 7045
Jer 44:22 astonishment, and a **c.**, without an 7045
Jer 49:13 a reproach, a waste, and a **c.**; and 7045
La 3:65 sorrow of heart, thy **c.** unto them. 8381
Da 9:11 the **c.** is poured upon us, and the 423
Zec 5:3 is the **c.** that goeth forth over the 423
Zec 8:13 ye were a **c.** among the heathen. 7045
Mal 2:2 I will even send a **c.** upon you. 3994
Mal 2:2 and I will **c.** your blessings: 779
Mal 3:9 are cursed with a **c.**: for ye have 3994
Mal 4:6 come and smite the earth with a **c.** 2764
Mt 5:44 **bless them that c. you, do good to** *2672*
Mt 26:74 Then began he to **c.** and to swear, *2653*
Mk 14:71 But he began to **c.** and to swear, *332*
Lu 6:28 **Bless them that c. you, and pray** *2672*
Ac 23:12 and bound themselves under a **c.**, *332*
Ac 23:14 bound ourselves under a great **c.**, *332*
Ro 12:14 persecute you: bless, and **c.** not. *2672*
Ga 3:10 works of the law are under the **c.**: *2671*
Ga 3:13 redeemed us from the **c.** of the *2671*
Ga 3:13 law, being made a **c.** for us: *2671*
Jas 3:9 therewith **c.** we men, which are *2672*
Re 22:3 there shall be no more **c.**: but the *2652*

CURSED See also ACCURSED; CURSEDST.
Ge 3:14 thou art **c.** above all cattle, and 779
Ge 3:17 **c.** is the ground for thy sake; in 779
Ge 4:11 now art thou **c.** from the earth, 779
Ge 5:29 ground which the Lord hath **c.**. 779
Ge 9:25 he said, **C.** be Canaan; a servant of 779
Ge 27:29 **c.** be every one that curseth thee, 779
Ge 49:7 **C.** be their anger, for it was fierce; 779
Le 20:9 hath **c.** his father or his mother; 7043
Le 24:11 the name of the Lord, and **c.** 7043
Le 24:14 forth him that hath **c.** without the 7043
Le 24:23 forth him that had **c.** out of the 7043
Nu 22:6 and he whom thou cursest is **c.**. 779
Nu 23:8 I curse, whom God hath not **c.**? 6895
Nu 24:9 and **c.** is he that curseth thee. 779
De 7:26 lest thou be a **c.** thing like it: 2764
De 7:26 abhor it; for it is a **c.** thing. 2764
De 13:17 cleave nought of the **c.** thing to 2764
De 27:15 **C.** be the man that maketh any 779
De 27:16 **C.** be he that setteth light by his 779
De 27:17 **C.** be he that removeth his 779
De 27:18 **C.** be he that maketh the blind to 779
De 27:19 **C.** be he that perverteth the 779
De 27:20 **C.** be he that lieth with his father's 779
De 27:21 **C.** be he that lieth with any manner 779
De 27:22 **C.** be he that lieth with his sister, 779
De 27:23 **C.** be he that lieth with his mother 779
De 27:24 **C.** be he that smiteth his neighbour 779
De 27:25 **C.** be he that taketh reward to slay 779
De 27:26 **C.** be he that confirmeth not all the 779
De 28:16 **C.** shalt thou be in the city, 779
De 28:16 and **c.** shalt thou be in the field. 779
De 28:17 **C.** shall be thy basket and thy store. 779
De 28:18 **C.** shall be the fruit of thy body, 779
De 28:19 **C.** shalt thou be when thou comest 779
De 28:19 **c.** shalt thou be when thou goest 779
Jos 6:26 **C.** be the man before the Lord, that 779
Jos 9:23 therefore ye are **c.**, and there shall 779
Jg 9:27 eat and drink, and **c.** Abimelech. 7043
Jg 21:18 **C.** be he that giveth a wife to 779
1Sa 14:24, 28 **C.** be the man that eateth any 779
1Sa 17:43 Philistine **c.** David by his gods: 7043
1Sa 26:19 of men, **c.** be they before the Lord; 779
2Sa 16:5 came forth, and **c.** still as he came. 7043
2Sa 16:7 said Shimei when he **c.**, Come out, 7043
2Sa 16:13 and **c.** as he went, and threw stones 7043
2Sa 19:21 because he **c.** the Lord's anointed? 7043
1Ki 2:8 which **c.** me with a grievous curse 7043
2Ki 2:24 **c.** them in the name of the Lord. 7043
2Ki 9:34 now this **c.** woman, and bury her: 779
Ne 13:25 contended with them, and **c.** them, 7043
Job 1:5 sinned, and **c.** God in their hearts. 1288
Job 3:1 Job his mouth, and **c.** his day. 7043
Job 5:3 but suddenly I **c.** his habitation. 5344
Job 24:18 their portion is **c.** in the earth: he 7043
Ps 37:22 they that be **c.** of him shall be cut 7043
Ps 119:21 hast rebuked the proud that are **c.**, 779
Ec 7:22 thyself likewise hast **c.** others. 7043
Jer 11:3 **C.** be the man that obeyeth not the 779
Jer 17:5 **C.** be the man that trusteth in man, 779
Jer 20:14 **C.** be the day wherein I was born: 779
Jer 20:15 **C.** be the man who brought tidings 779
Jer 48:10 **C.** be he that doeth the work 779
Jer 48:10 **c.** be he that keepeth back his 779
Mal 1:14 **c.** be the deceiver, which hath in 779
Mal 2:2 yea, I have **c.** them already, because 779
Mal 3:9 Ye are **c.** with a curse: for ye have 779
Mt 25:41 **Depart from me, ye c., into** *2672*
Joh 7:49 who knoweth not the law are **c.** *1944*
Ga 3:10 **C.** is every one that continueth *1944*
Ga 3:13 **C.** is every one that hangeth on a *1944*
2Pe 2:14 covetous practices; **c.** children: *2671*

CURSEDST
Jg 17:2 about which thou **c.**, and spakest 422
Mk 11:21 behold, the fig tree which thou **c.** *2672*

CURSES
Nu 5:23 the priest shall write these **c.** in 423
De 28:15, 45 these **c.** shall come upon thee, 7045
De 29:20 all the **c.** that are written in this 423
De 29:21 according to all the **c.** of the 423
De 29:27 to bring upon it all the **c.** that are 7045
De 30:7 put all these **c.** upon thine enemies, 423
2Ch 34:24 all the **c.** that are written in the 423

CURSEST
Nu 22:6 and he whom thou **c.** is cursed. 779

CURSETH
Ge 12:3 and curse him that **c.** thee: and in 7043
Ge 27:29 cursed be every one that **c.** thee, 779
Ex 21:17 And he that **c.** his father, or his 7043
Le 20:9 every one that **c.** his father or his 7043
Le 24:15 Whosoever **c.** his God shall bear 7043
Nu 24:9 thee, and cursed is he that **c.** thee. 779
Pr 20:20 Whoso **c.** his father or his mother, 7043
Pr 30:11 There is a generation that **c.** their 7043
Mt 15:4 **He that c. father or mother, let** *2551*
Mk 7:10 **Whoso c. father or mother, let** *2551*

CURSING See also CURSINGS.
Nu 5:21 the woman with an oath of **c.**, 423
De 28:20 The Lord shall send upon thee **c.**, 3994
De 30:19 life and death, blessing and **c.**: 7045
2Sa 16:12 will requite me good for his **c.** 7045
Ps 10:7 His mouth is full of **c.** and deceit 423
Ps 59:12 for **c.** and lying which they speak. 423
Ps 109:17 As he loved **c.**, so let it come unto 7045
Ps 109:18 he clothed himself with **c.** like as 7045
Pr 29:24 he heareth **c.**, and bewrayeth it 423
Ro 3:14 Whose mouth is full of **c.** and *685*
Heb 6:8 nigh unto **c.**; whose end is to be *2671*
Jas 3:10 mouth proceedeth blessing and **c.**. *2671*

CURSINGS
Jos 8:34 of the law, the blessings and **c.**, 7045

CURTAIN See also CURTAINS.
Ex 26:2 The length of one **c.** shall be eight 3407
Ex 26:2 the breadth of one **c.** four cubits; 3407
Ex 26:4 upon the edge of the one **c.** from 3407
Ex 26:4 in the uttermost edge of another **c.**, 3407
Ex 26:5 loops shalt thou make in the one **c.**, 3407
Ex 26:5 the edge of the **c.** that is in the 3407
Ex 26:8 length of one **c.** shall be thirty 3407
Ex 26:8 breadth of one **c.** four cubits; and 3407
Ex 26:9 double the sixth **c.** in the forefront 3407
Ex 26:10 edge of the one **c.** that is outmost 3407
Ex 26:10 fifty loops in the edge of the **c.** 3407
Ex 26:12 the half **c.** that remaineth, shall 3407
Ex 36:9 The length of one **c.** was twenty 3407
Ex 36:9 the breadth of one **c.** four cubits: 3407
Ex 36:11 loops of blue on the edge of one **c.** 3407
Ex 36:11 the uttermost side of another **c.**, 3407
Ex 36:12 Fifty loops made he in one **c.**, and 3407
Ex 36:12 the edge of the **c.** which was 3407
Ex 36:12 the loops held one **c.** to another.
Ex 36:15 length of one **c.** was thirty cubits, 3407
Ex 36:15 cubits was the breadth of one **c.**: 3407
Ex 36:17 upon the uttermost edge of the **c.** 3407
Ex 36:17 made he upon the edge of the **c.**, 3407
Nu 3:26 the **c.** for the door of the court, 4539
Ps 104:2 out the heavens like a **c.**: 3407
Isa 40:22 stretcheth out the heavens as a **c.**, 1852

CURTAINS
Ex 26:1 ten **c.** of fine twined linen, and 3407
Ex 26:2 every one of the **c.** shall have one 3407
Ex 26:3 five **c.** shall be coupled together 3407
Ex 26:3 other five **c.** shall be coupled one to 3407
Ex 26:6 couple the **c.** together with the 3407
Ex 26:7 thou shalt make **c.** of goats' hair 3407
Ex 26:7 eleven **c.** shalt thou make. 3407
Ex 26:8 the eleven **c.** shall be all of one 3407
Ex 26:9 thou shalt couple five **c.** by 3407
Ex 26:9 and six **c.** by themselves, and shalt 3407
Ex 26:12 remaineth of the **c.** of the tent, 3407
Ex 26:13 in the length of the **c.** of the tent, 3407
Ex 36:8 ten **c.** of fine twined linen, and blue 3407
Ex 36:9 the **c.** were all of one size. 3407
Ex 36:10 he coupled the five **c.** one unto 3407
Ex 36:10 the other five **c.** he coupled one 3407
Ex 36:13 coupled the **c.** one unto another 3407
Ex 36:14 made **c.** of goats' hair for the tent 3407
Ex 36:14 eleven **c.** he made them. 3407
Ex 36:15 the eleven **c.** were of one size. 3407
Ex 36:16 five **c.** by themselves, and six **c.** by 3407
Nu 4:25 shall bear the **c.** of the tabernacle, 3407
2Sa 7:2 the ark of God dwelleth within **c.**. 3407
1Ch 17:1 of the Lord remaineth under **c.**. 3407
Ca 1:5 of Kedar, as the **c.** of Solomon. 3407
Isa 54:2 and let them stretch forth the **c.** of 3407
Jer 4:20 spoiled, and my **c.** in a moment. 3407
Jer 10:20 and to set up my **c.** 3407
Jer 49:29 shall take to themselves their **c.**, 3407
Hab 3:7 the **c.** of the land of Midian did 3407

CUSH (*cush*) See also ETHIOPIA.
Ge 10:6 the sons of Ham; **C.**, and Mizraim, 3568
Ge 10:7 the sons of **C.**; Seba, and Havilah, 3568
Ge 10:8 **C.** begat Nimrod: he began to be 3568
1Ch 1:8 sons of Ham; **C.**, and Mizraim, 3568
1Ch 1:9 the sons of **C.**; Seba, and Havilah, 3568
1Ch 1:10 **C.** begat Nimrod: he began to be 3568
Ps 7:*title* the words of **C.** the Benjamite. 3568
Isa 11:11 from Pathros, and from **C.**, and 3568

CUSHAN (*cu'-shan*) See also CHUSHAN-RISHATHAIM.
Hab 3:7 I saw the tents of **C.** in affliction: 3572

CUSHI (*cu'-shi*)
2Sa 18:21 said Joab to **C.**, Go tell the king 3569
2Sa 18:21 And **C.** bowed himself unto Joab, 3569
2Sa 18:22 I pray thee, also run after **C.**. 3569
2Sa 18:23 way of the plain, and overran **C.**. 3569
2Sa 18:31 And, behold, **C.** came; and **C.** said, 3569
2Sa 18:32 said unto **C.**, Is the young man 3569
2Sa 18:32 **C.** answered, The enemies of my 3569
Jer 36:14 the son of **C.**, unto Baruch, saying, 3569
Zep 1:1 unto Zephaniah the son of **C.** 3569

CUSTODY
Nu 3:36 under the **c.** and charge of the 6486
Es 2:3 the women, unto the **c.** of Hege the 3027
Es 2:8 the palace, to the **c.** of Hegai, that 3027
Es 2:8 the king's house, to the **c.** of Hegai, 3027
Es 2:14 the women, to the **c.** of Shaashgaz, 3027

CUSTOM See also ACCUSTOM; CUSTOMS.
Ge 31:35 for the **c.** of women is upon me........ 1870
Jg 11:39 And it was a **c.** in Israel.................. 2706
1Sa 2:13 priest's **c.** with the people was, ... 4941
Ezr 3:4 according to the **c.**, as the duty 4941
Ezr 4:13 they not pay toll, tribute, and **c.**, ... 1983
Ezr 4:20 and toll, tribute, and **c.**, was paid....... 1983
Ezr 7:24 toll, tribute, or **c.**, upon them........... 1983
Jer 32:11 sealed according to the law and **c.** 2706
Mt 9:9 sitting at the receipt of **c.**: *5058*
Mt 17:25 **of the earth take c. or tribute?**...... *5056*
Mk 2:14 sitting at the receipt of **c.**, ... *5058*
Lu 1:9 to the **c.** of the priest's office, his *1485*
Lu 2:27 do for him after the **c.** of the law, ... *1480*
Lu 2:42 Jerusalem after the **c.** of the feast. *1485*
Lu 4:16 as his **c.** was, he went into........ *3588,1486*
Lu 5:27 Levi, sitting at the receipt of **c.**: *5058*
Joh 18:39 ye have a **c.**, that I should release *4914*
Ro 13:7 is due; **c.** to whom **c.**; fear to whom... *5056*
1Co 11:16 we have no such **c.**, neither the......... *4914*

CUSTOMS
Le 18:30 any one of these abominable **c.**, ... 2708
Jer 10:3 the **c.** of the people are vain: 2708
Ac 6:14 the **c.** which Moses delivered us. *1485*
Ac 16:21 teach **c.** which are not lawful for us *1485*
Ac 21:21 neither to walk after the **c.**. *1485*
Ac 26:3 to be expert in all **c.** and questions..... *1485*
Ac 28:17 the people, or **c.** of our fathers,......... *1485*

CUT See also CUTTEST; CUTTETH; CUTTING.
Ge 9:11 neither shall all flesh be **c.** off any 3772
Ge 17:14 shall be **c.** off from his people;........... 3772
Ex 4:25 and **c.** off the foreskin of her son, ... 3772
Ex 9:15 shalt be **c.** off from the earth............. 3582
Ex 12:15 soul shall be **c.** off from Israel. 3772
Ex 12:19 be **c.** off from the congregation.......... 3772
Ex 23:23 Jebusites; and I will **c.** them off. 3582
Ex 29:17 thou shalt **c.** the ram in pieces,.......... 5408
Ex 30:33, 38 even be **c.** off from his people. 3772
Ex 31:14 that soul shall be **c.** off from among.... 3772
Ex 34:13 images, and **c.** down their groves: 3772
Ex 39:3 and **c.** it into wires, to work it in 7112
Le 1:6 offering, and **c.** it into his pieces. 5408
Le 1:12 And he shall **c.** it into his pieces, ... 5408
Le 7:20, 21 even that soul shall be **c.** off......... 3772
Le 7:25 the soul that eateth it shall be **c.** off 3772
Le 7:27 even that soul shall be **c.** off from 3772
Le 8:20 And he **c.** the ram into pieces; 5408
Le 17:4 and that man shall be **c.** off from........ 3772
Le 17:9 even that man shall be **c.** off from 3772
Le 17:10 **c.** him off from among his people. 3772
Le 17:14 whosoever eateth it shall be **c.** off. 3772
Le 18:29 that commit them shall be **c.** off......... 3772
Le 19:8 and that soul shall be **c.** off from......... 3772
Le 20:3 **c.** him off from among his people; 3772
Le 20:5 and will **c.** him off, and all that go 3772
Le 20:6 and will **c.** him off from among........... 3772
Le 20:17 **c.** off in the sight of their people:....... 3772
Le 20:18 and both of them shall be **c.** off 3772
Le 22:3 shall be **c.** off from my presence: 3772
Le 22:24 or crushed, or broken, or **c.**; 3772
Le 23:29 day, he shall be **c.** off from among...... 3772
Le 26:30 places, and **c.** down your images, ... 3772
Nu 4:18 **C.** ye not off the tribe of the families .. 3772
Nu 9:13 even the same soul shall be **c.** off 3772
Nu 13:23 and **c.** down from thence a branch...... 3772
Nu 13:24 the children of Israel **c.** down from 3772
Nu 15:30 that soul shall be **c.** off from among 3772
Nu 15:31 that soul shall utterly be **c.** off; 3772
Nu 19:13 that soul shall be **c.** off from Israel: 3772
Nu 19:20 that soul shall be **c.** off from among.... 3772
De 7:5 **c.** down their groves, and burn.......... 1438
De 12:29 thy God shall **c.** off the nations.......... 3772
De 14:1 ye shall not **c.** yourselves, nor........... 1413
De 19:1 thy God hath **c.** off the nations, ... 3772
De 19:5 with the axe to **c.** down the tree,....... 3772
De 20:19 and thou shalt not **c.** them down........ 3772
De 20:20 shalt destroy and **c.** them down; 3772
De 23:1 or hath his privy member **c.** off, ... 3772
De 25:12 Then thou shalt **c.** off her hand,......... 7112
Jos 3:13 the waters of Jordan shall be **c.** off..... 3772
Jos 3:16 salt sea, failed, and were **c.** off: 3772
Jos 4:7 of Jordan were **c.** off before the ark.... 3772
Jos 4:7 the waters of Jordan were **c.** off: 3772
Jos 7:9 and **c.** off our name from the earth:.... 3772
Jos 11:21 and **c.** off the Anakims from the......... 3772

Jos 17:15 and **c.** down for thyself there in......... 1254
Jos 17:18 a wood, and thou shalt **c.** it down:....... 1254
Jos 23:4 all the nations that I have **c.** off......... 3772
Jg 1:6 **c.** off his thumbs and his great toes, ... 7112
Jg 1:7 thumbs and their great toes **c.** off, ... 7112
Jg 6:25 **c.** down the grove that is by it: 3772
Jg 6:26 the grove which thou shalt **c.** down. ... 3772
Jg 6:28 grove was **c.** down that was by it,...... 3772
Jg 6:30 because he hath **c.** down the grove..... 3772
Jg 9:48 **c.** down a bough from the trees, ... 3772
Jg 9:49 **c.** down every man his bough, ... 3772
Jg 20:6 and **c.** her in pieces, and sent her 5408
Jg 21:6 There is one tribe **c.** off from Israel.... 1438
Ru 4:10 the name of the dead be not **c.** off 3772
1Sa 2:31 that I will **c.** off thine arm, and.......... 1438
1Sa 2:33 I shall not **c.** off from mine altar,........ 3772
1Sa 5:4 the palms of his hands were **c.** off...... 3772
1Sa 17:51 him, and **c.** off his head therewith. 3772
1Sa 20:15 thou shalt not **c.** off thy kindness 3772
1Sa 20:15 the Lord hath **c.** off the enemies........ 3772
1Sa 24:4 and **c.** off the skirt of Saul's robe 3772
1Sa 24:5 because he had **c.** off Saul's skirt. 3772
1Sa 24:11 that I **c.** off the skirt of thy robe,....... 3772
1Sa 24:21 thou wilt not **c.** off my seed after....... 3772
1Sa 28:9 he hath **c.** off those that have........... 3772
1Sa 31:9 they **c.** off his head, and stripped 3772
2Sa 4:12 **c.** off their hands and their feet,......... 7112
2Sa 7:9 and have **c.** off all thine enemies 3772
2Sa 10:4 and **c.** off their garments in the.......... 3772
2Sa 20:22 And they **c.** off the head of Sheba 3772
1Ki 9:7 will I **c.** off Israel out of the land........ 3772
1Ki 11:16 until he had **c.** off every male............ 3772
1Ki 13:34 even to **c.** it off, and to destroy it...... 3582
1Ki 14:10 will **c.** off from Jeroboam him 3772
1Ki 14:14 shall **c.** off the house of Jeroboam....... 3772
1Ki 18:4 when Jezebel **c.** off the prophets of..... 3772
1Ki 18:23 **c.** it in pieces, and lay it on wood,...... 5408
1Ki 18:28 cried aloud, and **c.** themselves........... 1413
1Ki 18:33 **c.** the bullock in pieces, and laid......... 5408
1Ki 21:21 and will **c.** off from Ahab him that 3772
2Ki 6:4 they came to Jordan, they **c.** down..... 1504
2Ki 6:6 he **c.** down a stick, and cast it in 7094
2Ki 9:8 and I will **c.** off from Ahab him 3772
2Ki 10:32 the Lord began to **c.** Israel short: 7096
2Ki 16:17 And king Ahaz **c.** off the borders........ 7112
2Ki 18:4 **c.** down the groves, and brake 3772
2Ki 18:16 Hezekiah **c.** off the gold from the....... 7112
2Ki 19:23 will **c.** down the tall cedar trees......... 3772
2Ki 23:14 and **c.** down the groves, and filled...... 3772
2Ki 24:13 **c.** in pieces all the vessels of gold 7112
1Ch 17:8 and have **c.** off all thine enemies 3772
1Ch 19:4 and **c.** off their garments in the.......... 3772
1Ch 20:3 and **c.** them with saws, and with........ 7787
2Ch 2:8 skill to **c.** timber in Lebanon;............ 3772
2Ch 2:10 servants, the hewers that **c.** timber, ... 3772
2Ch 2:16 we will **c.** wood out of Lebanon, ... 3772
2Ch 14:3 images, and **c.** down the groves:........ 1438
2Ch 15:16 Asa **c.** down her idol, and stamped..... 3772
2Ch 22:7 anointed to **c.** off the house of Ahab. .. 3772
2Ch 26:21 **c.** off from the house of the Lord:...... 1504
2Ch 28:24 and **c.** in pieces the vessels of........... 7112
2Ch 31:1 and **c.** down the groves, and............. 1438
2Ch 32:21 Lord sent an angel, which **c.** off all..... 3582
2Ch 34:4 on high above them, he **c.** down; 1438
2Ch 34:7 **c.** down all the idols throughout 1438
Job 4:7 where were the righteous **c.** off?........ 3582
Job 6:9 loose his hand, and **c.** me off!............ 1214
Job 8:12 in his greenness, and not **c.** down, ... 6998
Job 8:14 Whose hope shall be **c.** off, and 6990
Job 11:10 If he **c.** off, and shut up, or 2498
Job 14:2 flower, and is **c.** down: he fleeth........ 5243
Job 14:7 is hope of a tree, if it be **c.** down,...... 3772
Job 18:16 above shall his branch be **c.** off. 5243
Job 21:21 his months is **c.** off in the midst? 2686
Job 22:16 Which were **c.** down out of time, ... 7059
Job 22:20 our substance is not **c.** down, but....... 3582
Job 23:17 was not **c.** off before the darkness,..... 6780
Job 24:24 and **c.** off as the tops of the ears 5243
Job 30:4 Who **c.** up mallows by the bushes. 6998
Job 36:20 people are **c.** off in their place. 5927
Ps 12:3 Lord shall **c.** off all flattering lips, ... 3772
Ps 31:22 I am **c.** off from before thine eyes: 1629
Ps 34:16 to **c.** off the remembrance of them...... 3772
Ps 37:2 they shall soon be **c.** down like 5243
Ps 37:9 evildoers shall be **c.** off: but those...... 3772
Ps 37:22 be cursed of him shall be **c.** off......... 3772
Ps 37:28 seed of the wicked shall be **c.** off. 3772

Ps 37:34 when the wicked are **c.** off, thou........ 3772
Ps 37:38 the end of the wicked shall be **c.** off. .. 3772
Ps 54:5 enemies: **c.** them off in thy truth........ 6789
Ps 58:7 let them be as **c.** in pieces............... 4135
Ps 75:10 of the wicked also will I **c.** off;........... 1438
Ps 76:12 He shall **c.** off the spirit of princes:..... 1219
Ps 80:16 It is burned with fire, it is **c.** down: 3683
Ps 83:4 Come, and let us **c.** them off from...... 3582
Ps 88:5 and they are **c.** off from thy hand....... 1504
Ps 88:16 thy terrors have **c.** me off. 6789
Ps 90:6 it is **c.** down, and withereth. 4135
Ps 90:10 it is soon **c.** off, and we fly away. 1504
Ps 94:23 **c.** them off in their own wickedness.... 6789
Ps 94:23 the Lord our God shall **c.** them off. 6789
Ps 101:5 his neighbour, him will I **c.** off: 6789
Ps 101:8 that I may **c.** off all wicked doers 3772
Ps 107:16 and **c.** the bars of iron in sunder. 1438
Ps 109:13 Let his posterity be **c.** off; and in...... 3772
Ps 109:15 he may **c.** off the memory of them 3772
Ps 129:4 **c.** asunder the cords of the wicked. 7112
Ps 143:12 of thy mercy **c.** off mine enemies, ... 6789
Pr 2:22 shall be **c.** off from the earth,............ 3772
Pr 10:31 the froward tongue shall be **c.** out. 3772
Pr 23:18 thine expectation shall not be **c.** off..... 3772
Pr 24:14 thy expectation shall not be **c.** off. 3772
Isa 9:10 the sycomores are **c.** down, but we.... 1438
Isa 9:14 Lord will **c.** off from Israel head......... 3772
Isa 10:7 destroy and **c.** off nations not a few. ... 3772
Isa 10:34 And he shall **c.** down the thickets 5362
Isa 11:13 adversaries of Judah shall be **c.** off:..... 3772
Isa 14:12 art thou **c.** down to the ground, ... 1438
Isa 14:22 and **c.** off from Babylon the name,...... 3772
Isa 15:2 be baldness, and every beard **c.** off. ... 1438
Isa 18:5 both **c.** off the sprigs with pruning...... 3772
Isa 18:5 away and **c.** down the branches. 8456
Isa 22:25 removed, and be **c.** down, and fall;..... 1438
Isa 22:25 that was upon it shall be **c.** off:.......... 3772
Isa 29:20 that watch for iniquity are **c.** off: 3772
Isa 33:12 thorns **c.** up shall they be burned....... 3683
Isa 37:24 **c.** down the tall cedars thereof, ... 3772
Isa 38:12 have **c.** off like a weaver my life: 7088
Isa 38:12 **c.** me off with pining sickness:............ 1214
Isa 45:2 and **c.** in sunder the bars of iron: 1438
Isa 48:9 for thee, that I **c.** thee not off. 3772
Isa 48:19 name should not have been **c.** off....... 3772
Isa 51:9 Art thou not it that hath **c.** Rahab, ... 2672
Isa 53:8 **c.** off out of the land of the living: 1504
Isa 55:13 sign that shall not be **c.** off. 3772
Isa 56:5 name, that shall not be **c.** off............. 3772
Isa 66:3 lamb, as if he **c.** off a dog's neck;.............
Jer 7:28 and is **c.** off from their mouth............ 3772
Jer 7:29 **C.** off thine hair, O Jerusalem,........... 1494
Jer 9:21 to **c.** off the children from without, ... 3772
Jer 11:19 and let us **c.** him off from the land...... 3772
Jer 16:6 nor **c.** themselves, nor make............. 1413
Jer 22:7 shall **c.** down thy choice cedars,......... 3772
Jer 25:37 peaceable habitations are **c.** down....... 1826
Jer 34:18 **c.** the calf in twain, and passed.......... 3772
Jer 36:23 he **c.** it with the penknife, and........... 7167
Jer 41:5 and having **c.** themselves, with 1413
Jer 44:7 **c.** off from you man and woman, ... 3772
Jer 44:8 that ye might **c.** yourselves off, ... 3772
Jer 44:11 you for evil, and to **c.** off all Judah...... 3772
Jer 46:23 They shall **c.** down her forest,........... 3772
Jer 47:4 **c.** off from Tyrus and Zidon every...... 3772
Jer 47:5 Ashkelon is **c.** off with the............... 1820
Jer 47:5 how long wilt thou **c.** thyself? 1413
Jer 48:2 let us **c.** it off from being a nation. 3772
Jer 48:2 thou shalt be **c.** down, O Madmen;..... 1826
Jer 48:25 The horn of Moab is **c.** off, and......... 1438
Jer 49:26 men of war shall be **c.** off in that 1826
Jer 50:16 **C.** off the sower from Babylon,.......... 3772
Jer 50:23 the hammer of the whole earth **c.** 1438
Jer 50:30 of war shall be **c.** off in that day, ... 1826
Jer 51:6 soul: be not **c.** off in her iniquity; 1826
Jer 51:62 against this place, to **c.** it off, ... 3772
La 2:3 He hath **c.** off in his fierce anger........ 1438
La 3:53 have **c.** off my life in the dungeon, ... 6789
La 3:54 then I said, I am **c.** off..................... 1504
Eze 6:6 and your images may be **c.** down, ... 1438
Eze 14:8 **c.** him off from the midst of my......... 3772
Eze 14:13 will **c.** off man and beast from it:........ 3772
Eze 14:17 that I **c.** off man and beast from it:..... 3772
Eze 14:19 to **c.** off from it man and beast: 3772
Eze 14:21 to **c.** off from it man and beast?......... 3772
Eze 16:4 thy navel was not **c.**, neither wast...... 3772
Eze 17:9 and **c.** off the fruit thereof, that it 7082

Eze 17:17 forts, to **c.** off many persons: 3772
Eze 21:3 will **c.** off from thee the righteous 3772
Eze 21:4 I will **c.** off from thee the righteous 3772
Eze 25:7 I will **c.** thee off from the people, 3772
Eze 25:13 will **c.** off man and beast from it; 3772
Eze 25:16 and I will **c.** off the Cherethims, 3772
Eze 29:8 and **c.** off man and beast out of thee 3772
Eze 30:15 I will **c.** off the multitude of No. 3772
Eze 31:12 of the nations, have **c.** him off, 3772
Eze 35:7 **c.** off from it him that passeth out 3772
Eze 37:11 is lost: we are **c.** off for our parts. 1504
Eze 39:10 out of the field, neither **c.** down 2404
Da 2:5 ye shall be **c.** in pieces, and your 5648
Da 2:34 a stone was **c.** out without hands, 1505
Da 2:45 stone was **c.** out of the mountain 1505
Da 3:29 shall be **c.** in pieces, and their 5648
Da 4:14 and **c.** off his branches, shake off 7113
Da 9:26 shall Messiah be **c.** off, but not for 3772
Ho 8:4 them idols, that they may be **c.** off. 3772
Ho 10:7 her king is **c.** off as the foam upon 1820
Ho 10:15 the king of Israel utterly be **c.** off. 1820
Joe 1:5 for it is **c.** off from your mouth. 3772
Joe 1:9 the drink offering is **c.** off from the 3772
Joe 1:16 not the meat **c.** off before our eyes, 3772
Am 1:5 and **c.** off the inhabitants from the 3772
Am 1:8 **c.** off the inhabitant from Ashdod, 3772
Am 2:3 **c.** off the judge from the midst 3772
Am 3:14 horns of the altar shall be **c.** off, 1438
Am 9:1 **c.** them in the head, all of them; 1214
Ob 5 (how art thou **c.** off!) would 1820
Ob 9 Esau may be **c.** off by slaughter. 3772
Ob 10 and thou shalt be **c.** off for ever. 3772
Ob 14 **c.** off those of his that did escape; 3772
Mic 5:9 all thine enemies shall be **c.** off. 3772
Mic 5:10 I will **c.** off thy horses out of the 3772
Mic 5:11 I will **c.** off the cities of thy land, 3772
Mic 5:12 **c.** off witchcrafts out of thine hand; 3772
Mic 5:13 Thy graven images also will I **c.** off, 3772
Na 1:12 shall they be **c.** down, when he 1494
Na 1:14 will I **c.** off the graven image and 3772
Na 1:15 through thee; he is utterly **c.** off. 3772
Na 2:13 I will **c.** off thy prey from the earth, 3772
Na 3:15 the sword shall **c.** thee off, it shall 3772
Hab 3:17 flock shall be **c.** off from the fold, 1504
Zep 1:3 I will **c.** off man from off the land, 3772
Zep 1:4 **c.** off the remnant of Baal from 3772
Zep 1:11 the merchant people are **c.** down; 1820
Zep 1:11 all they that bear silver are **c.** off. 3772
Zep 3:6 I have **c.** off the nations: their 3772
Zep 3:7 their dwelling should not be **c.** off, 3772
Zec 5:3 every one that stealeth shall be **c.** 5352
Zec 5:3 every one that sweareth shall be **c.** 5352
Zec 9:6 **c.** off the pride of the Philistines. 3772
Zec 9:10 **c.** off the chariot from Ephraim, 3772
Zec 9:10 and the battle bow shall be **c.** off: 3772
Zec 11:8 Three shepherds also I **c.** off in 3582
Zec 11:9 and that that is to be **c.** off, 3582
Zec 11:9 let it be **c.** off; 3582
Zec 11:10 even Beauty, and **c.** it asunder, 1438
Zec 11:14 Then I **c.** asunder mine other staff, 1438
Zec 11:16 those that be **c.** off, neither shall 3582
Zec 12:3 with it shall be **c.** in pieces, 8295
Zec 13:2 will **c.** off the name of the idols 3772
Zec 13:8 therein shall be **c.** off and die; 3772
Zec 14:2 of the people shall not be **c.** off 3772
Mal 2:12 The Lord will **c.** off the man that 3772
Mt 5:30 **c. it off, and cast it from thee;** *1581*
Mt 18:8 **c. them off, and cast them from** *1581*
Mt 21:8 **c.** down branches from the trees, *2875*
Mt 24:51 **shall c. him asunder, and appoint** *1371*
Mk 9:43 **if thy hand offend thee, c. it off:** *609*
Mk 9:45 **if thy foot offend thee, c. it off:** *609*
Mk 11:8 **c.** down branches of the trees, *2875*
Mk 14:47 the high priest, and **c.** off his ear. *851*
Lu 12:46 **will c. him in sunder, and will** *1371*
Lu 13:7 **c. it down; why cumbereth it the** *1581*
Lu 13:9 **after that thou shalt c. it down** *1581*
Lu 22:50 priest, and **c.** off his right ear. *851*
Joh 18:10 servant, and **c.** off his right ear. *609*
Joh 18:26 kinsman whose ear Peter **c.** off, *609*
Ac 5:33 that, they were **c.** to the heart, *1282*
Ac 7:54 they were **c.** to the heart, and they *1282*
Ac 27:32 soldiers **c.** off the ropes of the boat, *609*
Ro 9:28 and **c.** it short in righteousness: *4932*
Ro 11:22 otherwise thou also shalt be **c.** off. *1581*
Ro 11:24 thou wert **c.** out of the olive tree *1581*
2Co 11:12 I may **c.** off occasion from them *1581*
Ga 5:12 were even **c.** off which trouble you. *609*

CUTH (cuth) See also CUTHAH.
2Ki 17:30 and the men of **C.** made Nergal, 3575

CUTHAH (cu'-thah) See also CUTH.
2Ki 17:24 men from Babylon, and from **C.** 3575

CUTTEST
De 24:19 thou **c.** down thine harvest in 7114

CUTTETH
Job 28:10 **c.** out rivers among the rocks; 1234
Ps 46:9 bow, and **c.** the spear in sunder; 7112
Ps 141:7 when one **c.** and cleaveth wood 6398
Pr 26:6 hand of the fool **c.** off the feet, 7096
Jer 10:3 for one **c.** a tree out of the forest, 3772
Jer 22:14 and **c.** him out windows; 7167

CUTTING See also CUTTINGS.
Ex 31:5 And in **c.** of stones, to set them, 2799
Ex 35:33 And in the **c.** of stones, to set them, 2799
Isa 38:10 I said in the **c.** off of my days, 1824
Hab 2:10 thy house by **c.** off many people, 7096
Mk 5:5 crying, and **c.** himself with stones. *2629*

CUTTINGS
Le 19:28 not make any **c.** in your flesh for 8296
Le 21:5 nor make any **c.** in their flesh. 8296
Jer 48:37 upon all the hands shall be **c.**, 1417

CYMBAL See also CYMBALS.
1Co 13:1 sounding brass, or a tinkling **c.** *2950*

CYMBALS
2Sa 6:5 and on cornets, and on **c.** 6767
1Ch 13:8 with timbrels, and with **c.**, 4700
1Ch 15:16 psalteries and harps and **c.**, 4700
1Ch 15:19 to sound with **c.** of brass; 4700
1Ch 15:28 with trumpets, and with **c.**, 4700
1Ch 16:5 but Asaph made a sound with **c.**; 4700
1Ch 16:42 with trumpets and **c.** for those 4700
1Ch 25:1 harps, with psalteries, and with **c.**: 4700
1Ch 25:6 with **c.**, psalteries, and harps, 4700
2Ch 5:12 having **c.** and psalteries and harps, 4700
2Ch 5:13 trumpets and **c.** and instruments 4700
2Ch 29:25 the Lord with **c.**, with psalteries, 4700
Ezr 3:10 the sons of Asaph with **c.**, to praise 4700
Ne 12:27 with singing, with **c.**, psalteries, 4700
Ps 150:5 Praise him upon the loud **c.**: 6767
Ps 150:5 him upon the high sounding **c.** 6767

CYPRESS
Isa 44:14 and taketh the **c.** and the oak. 8645

CYPRUS (si'-prus)
Ac 4:36 Levite, and the country of **C.**, *2954*
Ac 11:19 and **C.**, and Antioch, preaching *2954*
Ac 11:20 them were men of **C.** and Cyrene, *2954*
Ac 13:4 and from thence they sailed to **C.** *2954*
Ac 15:39 took Mark, and sailed unto **C.**; *2954*
Ac 21:3 when we had discovered **C.**, we left *2954*
Ac 21:16 with them one Mnason of **C.**, *2954*
Ac 27:4 we sailed under **C.**, because the *2954*

CYRENE (si-re'-ne) See also CYRENIAN.
Mt 27:32 a man of **C.**, Simon by name: *2957*
Ac 2:10 of Libya about **C.**, and strangers *2957*
Ac 11:20 were men of Cyprus and **C.**, which *2957*
Ac 13:1 and Lucius of **C.**, and Manaen, *2957*

CYRENIAN (si-re'-ne-an) See also CYRENIANS.
Mk 15:21 compel one Simon a **C.**, who *2956*
Lu 23:26 laid hold upon one Simon, a **C.**, *2956*

CYRENIANS (si-re'-ne-ans)
Ac 6:9 of the Libertines, and **C.**, and *2956*

CYRENIUS (si-re'-ne-us)
Lu 2:2 when **C.** was governor of Syria.) *2958*

CYRUS (si'-rus)
2Ch 36:22 the first year of **C.** king of Persia, 3566
2Ch 36:22 the Lord stirred up the spirit of **C.** 3566
2Ch 36:23 Thus saith **C.** king of Persia, 3566
Ezr 1:1 the first year of **C.** king of Persia, 3566
Ezr 1:1 the Lord stirred up the spirit of **C.** 3566
Ezr 1:2 Thus saith **C.** king of Persia, 3566
Ezr 1:7 **C.** the king brought forth the 3566
Ezr 1:8 those did **C.** king of Persia bring 3566
Ezr 3:7 to the grant that they had of **C.** 3566
Ezr 4:3 as king **C.** the king of Persia hath 3566
Ezr 4:5 all the days of **C.** king of Persia, 3566
Ezr 5:13 first year of **C.** the king of Babylon 3567
Ezr 5:13 the same king **C.** made a decree 3567
Ezr 5:14 those did **C.** the king take out of 3567
Ezr 5:17 was made of **C.** the king to build 3567
Ezr 6:3 year of **C.** the king the same **C.** 3567
Ezr 6:14 to the commandment of **C.**, 3567
Isa 44:28 saith of **C.**, He is my shepherd, 3566
Isa 45:1 the Lord to his anointed, to **C.**, 3566
Da 1:21 even unto the first year of king **C.** 3566
Da 6:28 and in the reign of **C.** the Persian. 3567
Da 10:1 the third year of **C.** king of Persia 3566

D.

DABAREH (dab'-a-reh) See also DABARETH.
Jos 21:28 **D.** with her suburbs, 1705

DABBASHETH (dab'-ba-sheth)
Jos 19:11 and reached to **D.**, and reached 1708

DABERATH (dab'-e-rath) See also DABASEH.
Jos 19:12 and then goeth out to **D.**, 1705
1Ch 6:72 **D.** with her suburbs, 1705

DAGGER
Jg 3:16 Ehud made him a **d.** which had two 2719
Jg 3:21 took the **d.** from his right thigh, 2719
Jg 3:22 he could not draw the **d.** out 2719

DAGON See also BETH-DAGON; DAGON'S.
Jg 16:23 great sacrifice unto **D.** their god, 1712
1Sa 5:2 brought it into the house of **D.**, 1712
1Sa 5:2 and set it by **D.** 1712
1Sa 5:3 behold, **D.** was fallen upon his face 1712
1Sa 5:3 took **D.**, and set him in his place 1712
1Sa 5:4 behold, **D.** was fallen upon his face 1712
1Sa 5:4 the head of **D.** and both the palms 1712
1Sa 5:4 the stump of **D.** was left to him. 1712
1Sa 5:5 neither the priests of **D.**, nor any 1712
1Sa 5:5 house, tread on the threshold of **D.** 1712
1Sa 5:7 is sore upon us, and upon **D.** 1712
1Ch 10:10 his head in the temple of **D.** 1712

DAGON'S
1Sa 5:5 any that come into **D.** house, 1712

DAILY
Ex 5:13 Fulfill your works, your **d.** tasks, 3117
Ex 5:19 your bricks of your **d.** tasks. 3117
Ex 16:5 twice as much as they gather **d.** 3117
Nu 4:16 the **d.** meat offering and the 8548
Nu 28:24 this manner ye shall offer **d.**, 3117
Nu 29:6 **d.** burnt offering and his meat 8548
Jg 16:16 pressed him **d.** with her words, 3117
2Ki 25:30 a **d.** rate for every day, 3117
2Ch 31:16 his **d.** portion for their service 3117
Ezr 3:4 the **d.** burnt offerings by number 3117
Ne 5:18 prepared for me **d.** was one 3117,259
Es 3:4 when they spake **d.** unto him, 3117
Ps 13:2 having sorrow in my heart **d.**? 3119
Ps 42:10 while they say **d.** unto me. 3605,3117
Ps 56:1 he fighting **d.** oppresseth me. 3117
Ps 56:2 enemies would **d.** swallow me 3605,3117
Ps 61:8 I may **d.** perform my vows. 3117
Ps 68:19 who **d.** loadeth us with benefits, 3117
Ps 72:15 and **d.** shall he be praised. 3605,3117
Ps 74:22 foolish...reproacheth thee **d.** 3605,3117
Ps 86:3 O Lord for I cry unto thee **d.** 3605,3117
Ps 88:9 Lord, I...called **d.** upon thee, 3605,3117
Ps 88:17 They came round about me **d.** 3605,3117
Pr 8:30 and I was **d.** his delight, 3117
Pr 8:34 watching **d.** at my gates, 3117
Isa 58:2 Yet they seek me **d.**, and delight 3117
Jer 7:25 **d.** rising up early and sending 3117

Jer 20:7 I am in derision **d.**, every one 3605,3117
Jer 20:8 unto me and a derision, **d.**........ 3605,3117
Jer 37:21 **d.** a piece of bread out of the 3117
Eze 30:16 Noph shall have distresses **d.**. 3119
Eze 45:23 without blemish **d.** the seven days;..... 3117
Eze 45:23 and a kid of the goats **d.** 3117
Eze 46:13 shalt **d.** prepare a burnt offering......... 3117
Da 1:5 appointed them a **d.** provision.............. 3117
Da 8:11 the **d.** sacrifice was taken away,......... 8548
Da 8:12 given him against the **d.** sacrifice........ 8548
Da 8:13 vision concerning the **d.** sacrifice, ... 8548
Da 11:31 shall take away the **d.** sacrifice, ... 8548
Da 12:11 **d.** sacrifice shall be taken away,......... 8548
Ho 12:1 **d.** increaseth lies and............... 3605,3117
Mt 6:11 **Give us this day our d. bread**........ *1967*
Mt 26:55 **I sat d. with you teaching**.... *2596, 2250*
Mk 14:49 **d. with you in the temple**..... *2596, 2250*
Lu 9:23 **and take up his cross d.**,...... *2596, 2250*
Lu 11:3 **us day by day our d. bread**. *1967*
Lu 19:47 he taught **d.** in the temple. *2596, 2250*
Lu 22:53 **d. with you in the temple**,.... *2596, 2250*
Ac 2:46 continuing **d.** with one accord.... *2596, 2250*
Ac 2:47 Lord added to the church **d.** *2596, 2250*
Ac 3:2 whom they laid **d.** at the gate.... *2596, 2250*
Ac 5:42 And **d.** in the temple, and in..... *3956, 2250*
Ac 6:1 neglected in the **d.** ministration. *2522*
Ac 16:5 increased in number **d.**. *2596, 2250*
Ac 17:11 searched the scriptures **d.**, ... *2596, 2250*
Ac 17:17 the market **d.** with them.. *2596, 3956, 2250*
Ac 19:9 disputing **d.** in the school.......... *2596, 2250*
1Co 15:31 Jesus our Lord, I die **d.**. *2596, 2250*
2Co 11:28 which cometh upon me **d.**,........ *2596, 2250*
Heb 3:13 exhort one another **d.**,...... *2596, 1538, 2250*
Heb 7:27 Who needeth not **d.**, as *2596, 2250*
Heb 10:11 priest standeth **d.** ministering.... *2596, 2250*
Jas 2:15 naked, and destitute of **d.** food, ... *2184*

DAINTIES
Ge 49:20 fat, and he shall yield royal **d.**............ 4574
Ps 141:4 and let me not eat of their **d.**. 4516
Pr 23:3 not desirous of his **d.**: for they 4303

DAINTY See also DAINTIES.
Job 33:20 abhorreth bread, and his soul **d.**......... 8378
Pr 23:6 neither desire thou his **d.** meats:........ 4303
Re 18:14 things which were **d.** and goodly *3045*

DALAIAH (dal-a-i'-ah) See also DELAIAH.
1Ch 3:24 Johanan, and **D.**, and Anani, ... 1806

DALE
Ge 14:17 of Shaveh, which is the king's **d.**. 6010
2Sa 18:18 a pillar, which is in the king's **d.**:......... 6010

DALETH (daw'-leth)
Ps 119:25 *title* [ד] **D.**...

DALMANUTHA (dal-ma-nu'-thah)
Mk 8:10 and came into the parts of **D.**........... *1148*

DALMATIA (dal-ma'-she-ah)
2Ti 4:10 Crescens to Galatia, Titus unto **D.**. *1149*

DALPHON (dal'-fon)
Es 9:7 Parshandatha, and **D.**, and 1813

DAM
Ex 22:30 seven days it shall be with his **d.**; 517
Le 22:27 shall be seven days under the **d.**; 517
De 22:6 and the **d.** sitting upon the young,......... 517
De 22:6 shalt not take the **d.** with the............. 517
De 22:7 thou shalt in any wise let the **d.** go, ... 517

DAMAGE See also ENDAMAGE.
Ezr 4:22 why should **d.** grow to the hurt 2257
Es 7:4 not countervail the king's **d.**. 5143
Pr 26:6 off the feet, and drinketh **d.**. 2555
Da 6:2 and the king should have no **d.**. 5142
Ac 27:10 will be with hurt and much **d.**, ... *2209*
2Co 7:9 that ye might receive **d.** by us in *2210*

DAMARIS (dam'-a-ris)
Ac 17:34 and a woman named **D.**, and *1152*

DAMASCENES (dam-as-senes')
2Co 11:32 the king kept the city of the **D.** *1159*

DAMASCUS (da-mas'-cus) See also DAMASCENES; SYRIA-DAMASCUS.
Ge 14:15 which is on the left hand of **D.**. 1834
Ge 15:2 of my house is this Eliezer of **D.**? 1834
2Sa 8:5 when the Syrians of **D.** came to......... 1834
2Sa 8:6 David put garrisons in Syria of **D.**: 1834
1Ki 11:24 they went to **D.**, and dwelt therein,.... 1834
1Ki 11:24 and reigned in **D.**.......................... 1834
1Ki 15:18 king of Syria, that dwelt at **D.**, ... 1834
1Ki 19:15 on thy way to the wilderness of **D.**:..... 1834
1Ki 20:34 shalt make streets for thee in **D.**, ... 1834
2Ki 5:12 Abana and Pharpar, rivers of **D.**,........ 1834
2Ki 8:7 Elisha came to **D.**; and Ben-hadad 1834
2Ki 8:9 even of every good thing of **D.**, ... 1834
2Ki 14:28 how he recovered **D.**, and Hamath, ... 1834
2Ki 16:9 king of Assyria went up against **D.**, ... 1834
2Ki 16:10 king Ahaz went to **D.** to meet 1834
2Ki 16:10 and saw an altar that was at **D.**: 1834
2Ki 16:11 that king Ahaz had sent from **D.**: 1834
2Ki 16:11 against king Ahaz came from **D.**......... 1834
2Ki 16:12 when the king was come from **D.**,...... 1834
1Ch 18:5 when the Syrians of **D.** came to.......... 1834
2Ch 16:2 king of Syria, that dwelt at **D.**, ... 1834
2Ch 24:23 spoil of them unto the king of **D.**. 1834
2Ch 28:5 captives, and brought them to **D.**. 1834
2Ch 28:23 he sacrificed unto the gods of **D.**,........ 1834
Ca 7:4 Lebanon which looketh toward **D.**....... 1834
Isa 7:8 the head of Syria is **D.**,................... 1834
Isa 7:8 and the head of **D.** is Rezin;............... 1834
Isa 8:4 the riches of **D.** and the spoil of......... 1834
Isa 10:9 is not Samaria as **D.**?........................ 1834
Isa 17:1 The burden of **D.**. Behold,.................. 1834
Isa 17:1 **D.** is taken away from being a city, ... 1834
Isa 17:3 and the kingdom from **D.**, and the...... 1834
Jer 49:23 Concerning **D.**. Hamath is................ 1834
Jer 49:24 **D.** is waxed feeble, and turneth......... 1834
Jer 49:27 I will kindle a fire in the wall of **D.**, ... 1834
Eze 27:18 **D.** was thy merchant in the.............. 1834
Eze 47:16 which is between the border of **D.** 1834
Eze 47:17 the border of **D.**, and the north 1834
Eze 47:18 and from **D.**, and from Gilead,........... 1834
Eze 48:1 the border of **D.** northward, to the..... 1834
Am 1:3 For three transgressions of **D.**,........... 1834
Am 1:5 I will break also the bar of **D.**,........... 1834
Am 3:12 and in **D.** in a couch. 1833
Am 5:27 to go into captivity beyond **D.**, ... 1834
Zec 9:1 and **D.** shall be the rest thereof: 1834
Ac 9:2 And desired of him letters to **D.** *1154*
Ac 9:3 as he journeyed, he came near **D.**: *1154*
Ac 9:8 the hand, and brought him into **D.**. *1154*
Ac 9:10 there was a certain disciple at **D.**, ... *1154*
Ac 9:19 with the disciples which were at **D.**. ... *1154*
Ac 9:22 the Jews which dwelt at **D.**,............... *1154*
Ac 9:27 how he had preached boldly at **D.** *1154*
Ac 22:5 and went to **D.**, to bring them........... *1154*
Ac 22:6 and was come nigh unto **D.**............... *1154*
Ac 22:10 **Arise, and go into D.; and there it**. *1154*
Ac 22:11 that were with me, I came into **D.**. *1154*
Ac 26:12 Whereupon as I went to **D.** with......... *1154*
Ac 26:20 But shewed first unto them of **D.**,...... *1154*
2Co 11:32 In **D.** the governor under Aretas........ *1154*
Ga 1:17 Arabia, and returned again unto **D.**. *1154*

DAMMIN (dam'-mim) See also EPHES-DAMMIM; PASDAMMIM.

DAMNABLE
2Pe 2:1 privily shall bring in **d.** heresies, ... *684*

DAMNATION
Mt 23:14 **ye shall receive the greater d.**...... *2917*
Mt 23:33 **how can ye escape the d. of hell?**.. *2920*
Mk 3:29 **but is in danger of eternal d.**:....... *2920*
Mk 12:40 **these shall receive greater d.**......... *2917*
Lu 20:47 **the same shall receive greater d.**... *2917*
Joh 5:29 **unto the resurrection of d.**............ *2920*
Ro 3:8 good may come? whose **d.** is just....... *2917*
Ro 13:2 shall receive to themselves **d.**............ *2917*
1Co 11:29 eateth and drinketh **d.** to himself,....... *2917*
1Ti 5:12 Having **d.**, because they have cast...... *2917*
2Pe 2:3 not, and their **d.** slumbereth not. *684*

DAMNED
Mk 16:16 **he that believeth not shall be d.**.... *2632*
Ro 14:23 he that doubteth is **d.** if he eat, ... *2632*
2Th 2:12 That they all might be **d.** who........... *2919*

DAMSEL See also DAMSEL'S; DAMSELS.
Ge 24:14 the **d.** to whom I shall say,............... 5291
Ge 24:16 And the **d.** was very fair to look 5291
Ge 24:28 And the **d.** ran, and told them of........ 5291
Ge 24:55 Let the **d.** abide with us a few........... 5291
Ge 24:57 We will call the **d.**, and enquire.......... 5291
Ge 34:3 and he loved the **d.**, and.................. 5291
Ge 34:3 spake kindly unto the **d.**..................... 5291
Ge 34:4 saying, Get me this **d.** to wife. 3207
Ge 34:12 unto me: but give me the **d.** to.......... 5291
De 22:15 father of the **d.**, and her mother, ... 5291
De 22:19 unto the father of the **d.**, because 5291
De 22:20 of virginity be not found for the **d.**:..... 5291
De 22:21 they shall bring out the **d.** to the........ 5291
De 22:23 a **d.** that is a virgin be betrothed........ 5291
De 22:24 the **d.**, because she cried not, ... 5291
De 22:25 if a man find a betrothed **d.** in the 5291
De 22:26 unto the **d.** thou shalt do nothing;....... 5291
De 22:26 there is in the **d.** no sin 5291
De 22:27 the betrothed **d.** cried, and there 5291
De 22:28 If a man find a **d.** that is a virgin,....... 5291
Jg 5:30 to every man a **d.** or two; 7356
Jg 19:3 the father of the **d.** saw him,............... 5291
Ru 2:5 over the reapers, Whose **d.** is this? 5291
Ru 2:6 It is the Moabitish **d.** that came 5291
1Ki 1:3 So they sought for a fair **d.**................ 5291
1Ki 1:4 And the **d.** was very fair, ... 5291
Mt 14:11 in a charger, and given to the **d.**: *2877*
Mt 26:69 and a **d.** came unto him, saying,......... *3814*
Mk 5:39 **the d. is not dead, but sleepeth**. *3813*
Mk 5:40 father and the mother of the **d.**,......... *3813*
Mk 5:40 and entereth in where the **d.** was....... *3813*
Mk 5:41 he took the **d.** by the hand, ... *3813*
Mk 5:41 interpreted, **D.**, I say unto thee. *2877*
Mk 5:42 the **d.** arose, and walked, for she....... *2877*
Mk 6:22 the king said unto the **d.**, Ask of......... *2877*
Mk 6:28 and gave it to the **d.**: and................. *2877*
Mk 6:28 the **d.** gave it to her mother............... *2877*
Joh 18:17 Then saith the **d.** that kept the.......... *3814*
Ac 12:13 a **d.** came to hearken, named *3814*
Ac 16:16 a certain **d.** possessed with a *3814*

DAMSEL'S
De 22:15 bring forth the tokens of the **d.**.......... 5291
De 22:16 And the **d.** father shall say unto 5291
De 22:29 shall give unto the **d.** father fifty 5291
Jg 19:4 the **d.** father, retained him; and 5291
Jg 19:5 **d.** father said unto his son in law,....... 5291
Jg 19:6 the **d.** father had said unto the........... 5291
Jg 19:8 and the **d.** father said, Comfort.......... 5291
Jg 19:9 his father in law, the **d.** father, ... 5291

DAMSELS
Ge 24:61 Rebekah arose, and her **d.**, and 5291
1Sa 25:42 with five **d.** of hers that went............ 5291
Ps 68:25 were the **d.** playing with timbrels. 5959

DAN (dan) See also DANITES; DAN-JAAN; LAISH; MAHANEH-DAN.
Ge 14:14 and pursued them unto **D.**. 1835
Ge 30:6 therefore called she his name **D.**........ 1835
Ge 35:25 of Bilhah, Rachel's handmaid: **D.**, ... 1835
Ge 46:23 And the sons of **D.**; Hushim.............. 1835
Ge 49:16 **D.** shall judge his people, as one of 1835
Ge 49:17 **D.** shall be a serpent by the way, ... 1835
Ex 1:4 **D.**, and Naphtali, Gad, and Asher....... 1835
Ex 31:6 of Ahisamach, of the tribe of **D.**:......... 1835
Ex 35:34 Ahisamach, of the tribe of **D.**. 1835
Ex 38:23 of the tribe of **D.**, an engraver, ... 1835
Le 24:11 of Dibri, of the tribe of **D.**:)............. 1835
Nu 1:12 Of **D.**; Ahiezer the son of.................. 1835
Nu 1:38 children of **D.**, by their generations,.... 1835
Nu 1:39 of them, even of the tribe of **D.**,......... 1835
Nu 2:25 The standard of the camp of **D.**......... 1835
Nu 2:25 the captain of the children of **D.**......... 1835
Nu 2:31 were numbered in the camp of **D.**....... 1835
Nu 7:66 prince of the children of **D.**, ... 1835
Nu 10:25 of the camp of the children of **D.** 1835
Nu 13:12 the tribe of **D.**, Ammiel the son of 1835
Nu 26:42 the sons of **D.** after their families: 1835
Nu 26:42 families of **D.** after their families 1835
Nu 34:22 of the tribe of the children of **D.**, ... 1835
De 27:13 Gad, and Asher, and Zebulun, **D.**, ... 1835
De 33:22 of **D.** he said, **D.** is a lion's whelp: 1835
De 34:1 all the land of Gilead, unto **D.**,........... 1835
Jos 19:40 for the tribe of the children of **D.**........ 1835
Jos 19:47 of the children of **D.** went out 1835
Jos 19:47 the children of **D.** went up to fight 1835
Jos 19:47 and called Leshem, **D.**, after 1835
Jos 19:47 the name of **D.** their father. 1835
Jos 19:48 of the tribe of the children of **D.**. 1835
Jos 21:5 and out of the tribe of **D.**, and out 1835
Jos 21:23 of the tribe of **D.**, Eltekeh with her 1835
Jg 1:34 Amorites forced the children of **D.**...... 1835
Jg 5:17 and why did **D.** remain in ships? 1835
Jg 13:25 him at times in the camp of **D.**.......... 1835
Jg 18:2 children of **D.** sent of their family....... 1835
Jg 18:16 which were of the children of **D.**,....... 1835
Jg 18:22 and overtook the children of **D.**. 1835

Jg 18:23 they cried unto the children of **D.**....... 1835
Jg 18:25 the children of **D.** said unto him,........ 1835
Jg 18:26 the children of **D.** went their way:....... 1835
Jg 18:29 they called the name of the city **D.**,..... 1835
Jg 18:29 after the name of **D.** their father,....... 1835
Jg 18:30 children of **D.** set up the graven........ 1835
Jg 18:30 sons were priests to the tribe of **D.**.... 1835
Jg 20:1 man, from **D.** even to Beer-sheba,..... 1835
1Sa 3:20 Israel from **D.** even to Beer-sheba..... 1835
2Sa 3:10 Judah, from **D.** even to Beer-sheba..... 1835
2Sa 17:11 thee, from **D.** even to Beer-sheba,..... 1835
2Sa 24:2 Israel, from **D.** even to Beer-sheba,... 1835
2Sa 24:15 people from **D.** even to Beer-sheba..... 1835
1Ki 4:25 fig tree, from **D.** even to Beer-sheba,..1835
1Ki 12:29 Bethel, and the other put he in **D.**..... 1835
1Ki 12:30 before the one, even unto **D.**........... 1835
1Ki 15:20 and **D.**, and Abel-beth-maachah,......... 1835
2Ki 10:29 in Beth-el, and that were in **D.**......... 1835
1Ch 2:2 **D.**, Joseph, and Benjamin,................ 1835
1Ch 21:2 Israel from Beer-sheba even to **D.**;..... 1835
1Ch 27:22 Of **D.**, Azareel the son of Jeroham...... 1835
2Ch 2:14 a woman of the daughters, of **D.**,........ 1835
2Ch 16:4 smote Ijon, and **D.**, and Abel-maim,..... 1835
2Ch 30:5 Israel, from Beer-sheba even to **D.**,.... 1835
Jer 4:15 For a voice declareth from **D.**, and..... 1835
Jer 8:16 of his horses was heard from **D.**:....... 1835
Eze 27:19 **D.** also and Javan going to and.......... 1835
Eze 48:1 east and west; a portion for **D.**......... 1835
Eze 48:2 the border of **D.**, from the east side... 1835
Eze 48:32 gate of Benjamin, one gate of **D.**........ 1835
Am 8:14 and say, Thy god, O **D.**, liveth;......... 1835

DANCE See also DANCED; DANCES; DANCING.
Jg 21:21 of Shiloh come out to **d.** in dances,..... 2342
Job 21:11 like a flock, and their children **d.**..... 7540
Ps 149:3 praise his name in the **d.**: let.......... 4234
Ps 150:4 Praise him with the timbrel and **d.**:..... 4234
Ec 3:4 a time to mourn, and a time to **d.**;..... 7540
Isa 13:21 there, and satyrs shall **d.** there......... 7540
Jer 31:13 shall the virgin rejoice in the **d.**,........ 4234
La 5:15 our **d.** is turned into mourning........... 4234

DANCED
Jg 21:23 to their number, of them that **d.**,....... 2342
2Sa 6:14 David **d.** before the Lord with all....... 3769
Mt 11:17 **unto you, and ye have not d.**;....... *3738*
Mt 14:6 the daughter of Herodias **d.** before..... *3738*
Mk 6:22 the said Herodias came in, and **d.**,....... *3738*
Lu 7:32 **unto you, and ye have not d.**;....... *3738*

DANCES
Ex 15:20 her with timbrels and with **d.**........... 4246
Jg 11:34 him with timbrels and with **d.**:.......... 4246
Jg 21:21 of Shiloh come out to dance in **d.**,....... 4246
1Sa 21:11 sing one to another of him in **d.**,....... 4246
1Sa 29:5 they sang one to another in **d.**,......... 4246
Jer 31:4 shalt go forth in the **d.** of them................

DANCING
Ex 32:19 that he saw the calf, and the **d.**.......... 4246
1Sa 18:6 singing and **d.**, to meet king Saul,...... 4246
1Sa 30:16 eating and drinking, and **d.**,.............. 2287
2Sa 6:16 saw king David leaping and **d.**............ 3769
1Ch 15:29 saw king David **d.** and playing:........... 7540
Ps 30:11 for me my mourning into **d.**:............. 4234
Lu 15:25 **the house, he heard musick and d.** *5525*

DANDLED
Isa 66:12 and be **d.** upon her knees................. 8173

DANGER See also ENDANGER.
Mt 5:21, 22 **shall be in d. of the judgment:**.. *1777*
Mt 5:22 **shall be in d. of the council: but**... *1777*
Mt 5:22 **fool, shall be in d. of hell fire**...... *1777*
Mk 3:29 **is in d. of eternal damnation:**........ *1777*
Ac 19:27 not only this our craft is in **d.**........... *2798*
Ac 19:40 we are in **d.** to be called in question... *2798*

DANGEROUS
Ac 27:9 when sailing was now **d.**,................. *2000*

DANIEL See also BELTESHAZZAR.
1Ch 3:1 **D.**, of Abigail the Carmelitess:.......... 1840
Ezr 8:2 of the sons of Ithamar; **D.**: of the....... 1840
Ne 10:6 **D.**, Ginnethon, Baruch,.................... 1840
Eze 14:14 three men, Noah, **D.**, and Job,........... 1840
Eze 14:20 Noah, **D.**, and Job were in it,............. 1840
Eze 28:3 Behold, thou art wiser than **D.**;.......... 1840
Da *general title* The Book of **D.**........................ 1840
Da 1:6 children of Judah, **D.**, Hananiah,......... 1840
Da 1:7 for he gave unto **D.** the name of......... 1840
Da 1:8 But **D.** purposed in his heart that....... 1840
Da 1:9 God had brought **D.** into favour......... 1840
Da 1:10 prince of the eunuchs said unto **D.**,..... 1840
Da 1:11 said **D.** to Melzar, whom the prince.... 1840
Da 1:11 of the eunuchs had set over **D.**,.......... 1840
Da 1:17 **D.** had understanding in all visions...... 1840
Da 1:19 them all was found none like **D.**,........ 1840
Da 1:21 **D.** continued even unto the first......... 1840
Da 2:13 they sought **D.** and his fellows........... 1841
Da 2:14 Then **D.** answered with counsel......... 1841
Da 2:15 made the thing known to **D.**.............. 1841
Da 2:16 Then **D.** went in, and desired of the... 1841
Da 2:17 Then **D.** went to his house, and......... 1841
Da 2:18 that **D.** and his fellows should not....... 1841
Da 2:19 was the secret revealed unto **D.**......... 1841
Da 2:19 Then **D.** blessed the God of heaven,... 1841
Da 2:20 **D.** answered and said, Blessed be...... 1841
Da 2:24 Therefore **D.** went in unto Arioch,..... 1841
Da 2:25 Then Arioch brought in **D.** before....... 1841
Da 2:26 The king answered and said to **D.**,...... 1841
Da 2:27 **D.** answered in the presence of the.... 1841
Da 2:46 upon his face, and worshipped **D.**,...... 1841
Da 2:47 king answered unto **D.**, and said,....... 1841
Da 2:48 the king made **D.** a great man,.......... 1841
Da 2:49 Then **D.** requested of the king, and.... 1841
Da 2:49 but **D.** sat in the gate of the king....... 1841
Da 4:8 at the last **D.** came in before me,....... 1841
Da 4:19 **D.**, whose name was Belteshazzar,...... 1841
Da 5:12 in the same **D.**, whom the king.......... 1841
Da 5:12 now let **D.** be called, and he will........ 1841
Da 5:13 was **D.** brought in before the king...... 1841
Da 5:13 the king spake and said unto **D.**,........ 1841
Da 5:13 Art thou that **D.**, which art of........... 1841
Da 5:17 Then **D.** answered and said before..... 1841
Da 5:29 and they clothed **D.** with scarlet,........ 1841
Da 6:2 presidents; of whom **D.** was first:....... 1841
Da 6:3 Then this **D.** was preferred above...... 1841
Da 6:4 sought to find occasion against **D.**........ 1841
Da 6:5 find any occasion against this **D.**,........ 1841
Da 6:10 when **D.** knew that the writing was.... 1841
Da 6:11 and found **D.** praying and making........ 1841
Da 6:13 **D.**, which is of the children of the...... 1841
Da 6:14 set his heart on **D.** to deliver him:..... 1841
Da 6:16 and they brought **D.**, and cast him...... 1841
Da 6:16 the king spake and said unto **D.**,........ 1841
Da 6:17 not be changed concerning **D.**............ 1841
Da 6:20 with a lamentable voice unto **D.**:........ 1841
Da 6:20 and the king spake and said to **D.**,..... 1841
Da 6:20 O **D.**, servant of the living God,......... 1841
Da 6:21 Then said **D.** unto the king, O king,... 1841
Da 6:23 that they should take **D.** up out of...... 1841
Da 6:23 the den. So **D.** was taken up............. 1841
Da 6:24 those men which had accused **D.**,........ 1841
Da 6:26 and fear before the God of **D.**:........... 1841
Da 6:27 hath delivered **D.** from the power....... 1841
Da 6:28 **D.** prospered in the reign of Darius,... 1841
Da 7:1 **D.** had a dream and visions of........... 1841
Da 7:2 **D.** spake and said, I saw in my.......... 1841
Da 7:15 I **D.** was grieved in my spirit............. 1841
Da 7:28 As for me **D.**, my cogitations much.... 1841
Da 8:1 unto me, even unto me **D.**,................ 1840
Da 8:15 it came to pass, when I, even I **D.**,..... 1840
Da 8:27 And I **D.** fainted, and was sick........... 1840
Da 9:2 In the first year of his reign I **D.**....... 1840
Da 9:22 and said, O **D.**, I am now come forth.. 1840
Da 10:1 a thing was revealed unto **D.**,............ 1840
Da 10:2 In those days I **D.** was mourning........ 1840
Da 10:7 And I **D.** alone saw the vision:.......... 1840
Da 10:11 he said unto me, O **D.**, a man............ 1840
Da 10:12 Then said he unto me, Fear not, **D.**:.. 1840
Da 12:4 But thou, O **D.**, shut up the words,..... 1840
Da 12:5 **D.** looked, and behold, there stood..... 1840
Da 12:9 And he said, Go thy way, **D.**:............. 1840
Mt 24:15 **spoken of by D. the prophet,**........ *1158*
Mk 13:14 **spoken of by D. the prophet,**........ *1158*

DANITES (dan'-ites)
Jg 13:2 of Zorah, of the family of the **D.**,....... 1839
Jg 18:1 the tribe of the **D.** sought them......... 1839
Jg 18:11 from thence of the family of the **D.**,.... 1839
1Ch 12:35 And of the **D.** expert in war............. 1839

DAN-JAAN (dan-ja'-an)
2Sa 24:6 they came to **D.**, and about to........... 1842

DANNAH (dan'-nah)
Jos 15:49 **D.**, and Kirjath-sannah, which is......... 1837

DARA (da'-rah) See also DARDA.
1Ch 2:6 and Heman, and Calcol, and **D.**:......... 1873

DARDA (dar'-dah) See also DARA.
1Ki 4:31 Chalcol, and **D.**, the son of Mahol:..... 1862

DARE See also DURST.
Job 41:10 None is so fierce that **d.** stir him............
Ro 5:7 man some would even **d.** to die......... 5111
Ro 15:18 For I will not **d.** to speak of.............. 5111
1Co 6:1 **D.** any of you, having a matter.......... 5111
2Co 10:12 For we **d.** not make ourselves........... 5111

DARIUS (da-ri'-us)
Ezr 4:5 until the reign of **D.** king of............... 1867
Ezr 4:24 the second year of the reign of **D.**........ 1868
Ezr 5:5 till the matter came to **D.**: and then.... 1868
Ezr 5:6 this side of the river, sent unto **D.**..... 1868
Ezr 5:7 thus; Unto **D.** the king, all peace....... 1868
Ezr 6:1 Then **D.** the king made a decree,........ 1868
Ezr 6:12 I **D.** have made a decree; let it be..... 1868
Ezr 6:13 to that which **D.** the king had sent,.... 1868
Ezr 6:14 the commandment of Cyrus, and **D.**,... 1868
Ezr 6:15 the sixth year of the reign of **D.**........ 1868
Ne 12:22 also the priests, to the reign of **D.**..... 1867
Da 5:81 **D.** the Median took the kingdom,........ 1868
Da 6:1 It pleased **D.** to set over the............. 1868
Da 6:6 thus unto him, King **D.**, live forever... 1868
Da 6:9 Wherefore king **D.** signed the............ 1868
Da 6:25 Then king **D.** wrote unto all people,.... 1868
Da 6:28 Daniel prospered in the reign of **D.**,.... 1868
Da 9:1 year of **D.** the son of Ahasuerus,........ 1867
Da 11:1 I in the first year of **D.** the Mede,..... 1867
Hag 1:1 In the second year of **D.** the king,....... 1867
Hag 1:15 in the second year of **D.** the king....... 1867
Hag 2:10 month, in the second year of **D.**,........ 1867
Zec 1:1 month, in the second year of **D.**,........ 1867
Zec 1:7 Sebat, in the second year of **D.**,......... 1867
Zec 7:1 in the fourth year of king **D.**,............ 1867

DARK See also DARKISH.
Ge 15:17 the sun went down, and it was **d.**,..... 5939
Le 13:6 if the plague be somewhat **d.**,............ 3544
Le 13:21 the skin, but be somewhat **d.**;............ 3544
Le 13:26 other skin, but be somewhat **d.**;......... 3544
Le 13:28 the skin, but it be somewhat **d.**;......... 3544
Le 13:56 the plague be somewhat **d.** after......... 3544
Nu 12:8 apparently, and not in **d.** speeches;..... 2420
Jos 2:5 when it was **d.**, that the men went..... 2822
2Sa 22:12 round about him, **d.** waters,.............. 2841
Ne 13:19 gates of Jerusalem began to be **d.**....... 6751
Job 3:9 stars of the twilight thereof be **d.**;...... 2821
Job 12:25 grope in the **d.** without light,............. 2822
Job 18:6 light shall be **d.** in his tabernacle,....... 2821
Job 22:13 he judge through the **d.** cloud?........... 6205
Job 24:16 In the **d.** they dig through houses,....... 2822
Ps 18:11 round about him were **d.** waters......... 2824
Ps 35:6 Let their way be **d.** and slippery:........ 2822
Ps 49:4 open my **d.** saying upon the harp........ 2420
Ps 74:20 the **d.** places of the earth are full....... 4285
Ps 78:2 I will utter **d.** sayings of old:............ 2420
Ps 88:12 thy wonders be known in the **d.**?........ 2822
Ps 105:28 He sent darkness, and made it **d.**;...... 2821
Pr 1:6 of the wise, and their **d.** sayings,........ 2420
Pr 7:9 evening, in the black and **d.** night:....... 653
Isa 29:15 their works are in the **d.**, and they..... 4285
Isa 45:19 secret, in a **d.** place of the earth:....... 2822
Jer 13:16 stumble upon the **d.** mountains,.......... 5399
La 3:6 He hath sent me in **d.** places,............. 4285
Eze 8:12 the house of Israel do in the **d.**,.......... 2822
Eze 32:7 and make the stars thereof **d.**;............ 6937
Eze 32:8 of heaven will I make **d.** over thee,..... 6937
Eze 34:12 scattered in the cloudy and **d.** day...... 6205
Da 8:23 and understanding **d.** sentences,.......... 2420
Joe 2:10 the sun and the moon shall be **d.**,....... 6937
Am 5:8 maketh the day **d.** with night:............. 2821
Am 5:20 very **d.**, and no brightness in it?.......... 651
Mic 3:6 and it shall be **d.** unto you, that.......... 2821
Mic 3:6 and the day shall be **d.** over them....... 6937
Zec 14:6 light shall not be clear, nor **d.**:.......... 7087
Lu 11:36 **full of light, having no part d.,**....... *4652*
Joh 6:17 And it was now **d.**, and Jesus was...... *4653*
Joh 20:1 Magdalene early, when it was yet **d.**,.. *4653*
2Pe 1:19 light that shineth in a **d.** place,........... *850*

DARKEN See also DARKENED; DARKENETH.
Am 8:9 will **d.** the earth the clear day:........... 2821

DARKENED
Ex 10:15 earth, so that the land was **d.**;........... 2821
Ps 69:23 Let their eyes be **d.**, that they see..... 2821
Ec 12:2 stars, be not **d.**, nor the clouds.......... 2821

Ec 12:3 that look out of the windows be **d.**, 2821
Isa 5:30 light is **d.** in the heavens thereof. 2821
Isa 9:19 the Lord of hosts is the land **d.**, 6272
Isa 13:10 sun shall be **d.** in his going forth, 2821
Isa 24:11 all joy is **d.**, the mirth of the 6150
Eze 30:18 shall be **d.**, when I shall break 2821
Joe 3:15 sun and the moon shall be **d.**, 6937
Zec 11:17 his right eye shall be utterly **d.** 3543
Mt 24:29 **of those days shall the sun be d.,** *4654*
Mk 13:24 **the sun shall be d., and the moon** *4654*
Lu 23:45 And the sun was **d.**, and the veil *4654*
Ro 1:21 and their foolish heart was **d.**. *4654*
Ro 11:10 Let their eyes be **d.**, that they may *4654*
Eph 4:18 Having the understanding **d.**, *4654*
Re 8:12 so as the third part of them was **d.**, *4654*
Re 9:2 and the sun and the air were **d.** *4654*

DARKENETH
Job 38:2 Who is this that **d.** counsel by 2821

DARKISH
Le 13:39 skin of their flesh be **d.** white: 3544

DARKLY
1Co 13:12 we see through a glass, **d.**; *1722,135*

DARKNESS
Ge 1:2 **d.** was upon the face of the deep. 2822
Ge 1:4 God divided the light from the **d.**. 2822
Ge 1:5 Day, and the **d.** he called Night. 2822
Ge 1:18 and to divide the light from the **d.**: 2822
Ge 15:12 horror of great **d.** fell upon him. 2825
Ex 10:21 may be **d.** over the land of Egypt, 2822
Ex 10:21 even **d.** which may be felt. 2822
Ex 10:22 there was a thick **d.** in all the land. 2822
Ex 14:20 it was a cloud and **d.** to them, 2822
Ex 20:21 drew near unto the thick **d.** 6205
De 4:11 unto the midst of heaven, with **d.**, 2822
De 4:11 clouds, and thick **d.**. 6205
De 5:22 the cloud, and of the thick **d.**, with 6205
De 5:23 voice out of the midst of the **d.**, 2822
De 28:29 as the blind gropeth in **d.**, 653
Jos 24:7 **d.** between you and the Egyptians, 3990
1Sa 2:9 the wicked shall be silent in **d.**; 2822
2Sa 22:10 and **d.** was under his feet. 6205
2Sa 22:12 he made **d.** pavilions round about 2822
2Sa 22:29 and the Lord will lighten my **d.**. 2822
1Ki 8:12 he would dwell in the thick **d.** 6205
2Ch 6:1 he would dwell in the thick **d.** 6205
Job 3:4 Let that day be **d.**; let not God 2822
Job 3:5 Let **d.** and the shadow of death 2822
Job 3:6 for that night, let **d.** seize upon it; 652
Job 5:14 meet with **d.** in the day time. 2822
Job 10:21 Even to the land of **d.**, and the 2822
Job 10:22 A land of **d.**, as 5890
Job 10:22 as **d.** itself; and of the shadow 652
Job 10:22 and where the light is as **d.**. 652
Job 12:22 discovereth deep things out of **d.**, 2822
Job 15:22 that he shall return out of **d.**, 2822
Job 15:23 knoweth that the day of **d.** is ready 2822
Job 15:30 He shall not depart out of **d.**; 2822
Job 17:12 the light is short because of **d.** 2822
Job 17:13 I have made my bed in the **d.**. 2822
Job 18:18 be driven from light into **d.**, and 2822
Job 19:8 he hath set **d.** in my paths. 2822
Job 20:26 **d.** shall be hid in his secret places: 2822
Job 22:11 Or **d.**, that thou canst not see; 2822
Job 23:17 I was not cut off before the **d.**, 2822
Job 23:17 neither hath he covered the **d.**, 652
Job 28:3 He setteth an end to **d.**, and 2822
Job 28:3 the stones of **d.**, and the 652
Job 29:3 by his light I walked through **d.**; 2822
Job 30:26 I waited for light, there came **d.**. 652
Job 34:22 There is no **d.**, nor shadow of 2822
Job 37:19 order our speech by reason of **d.** 2822
Job 38:9 thick **d.** a swaddlingband for it, 6205
Job 38:19 and as for **d.**, where is the place 2822
Ps 18:9 and **d.** was under his feet. 6205
Ps 18:11 He made **d.** his secret place; 2822
Ps 18:28 my God will enlighten my **d.**. 2822
Ps 82:5 understand; they walk on in **d.**: 2825
Ps 88:6 lowest pit, in **d.**, in the deeps 4285
Ps 88:18 me, and mine acquaintance into **d.**. 4285
Ps 91:6 the pestilence that walketh in **d.**; 652
Ps 97:2 and **d.** are round about him: 6205
Ps 104:20 Thou makest **d.**, and it is night: 2822
Ps 105:28 He sent **d.**, and made it dark; 2822
Ps 107:10 Such as sit in **d.** and in the shadow 2822
Ps 107:14 He brought them out of **d.** and the 2822
Ps 112:4 upright there ariseth light in the **d.**: 2822
Ps 139:11 I say, Surely the **d.** shall cover me; 2822
Ps 139:12 Yea, the **d.** hideth not from thee; 2822
Ps 139:12 **d.** and the light are both alike to 2825
Ps 143:3 he hath made me to dwell in **d.**, 4285
Pr 2:13 to walk in the ways of **d.**; 2822
Pr 4:19 The way of the wicked is as **d.** 653
Pr 20:20 shall be put out in obscure **d.** 2822
Ec 2:13 folly, as far as light excelleth **d.**. 2822
Ec 2:14 head; but the fool walketh in **d.**: 2822
Ec 5:17 All his days also he eateth in **d.**, 2822
Ec 6:4 vanity, and departeth in **d.**, and 2822
Ec 6:4 his name shall be covered with **d.** 2822
Ec 11:8 let him remember the days of **d.**; 2822
Isa 5:20 put **d.** for light, and light for **d.**; 2822
Isa 5:30 behold **d.** and sorrow, and the light 2822
Isa 8:22 behold trouble and **d.**, dimness of 2825
Isa 8:22 and they shall be driven to **d.**. 653
Isa 9:2 The people that walked in **d.** have 2822
Isa 29:18 out of obscurity, and out of **d.**. 2822
Isa 42:7 them that sit in **d.** out of the prison 2822
Isa 42:16 I will make **d.** light before them, 4285
Isa 45:3 I will give thee the treasures of **d.**, 2822
Isa 45:7 I form the light, and create **d.**: 2822
Isa 47:5 Sit thou silent, and get thee into **d.**, 2822
Isa 49:9 to them that are in **d.**, Shew 2822
Isa 50:10 walketh in **d.**, and hath no light? 2825
Isa 58:10 and thy **d.** be as the noon day: 653
Isa 59:9 for brightness, but we walk in **d.**. 653
Isa 60:2 the **d.** shall cover the earth, 2822
Isa 60:2 and gross **d.** the people: 6205
Jer 2:31 unto Israel? a land of **d.**? 3991
Jer 13:16 before he cause **d.**, and before 2821
Jer 13:16 of death, and make it gross **d.**. 6205
Jer 23:12 as slippery ways in the **d.**: 653
La 3:2 led me, and brought me into **d.**, 2822
Eze 32:8 over thee, and set **d.** upon thy land, 2822
Da 2:22 he knoweth what is in the **d.**, 2816
Joe 2:2 A day of **d.** and of gloominess, 2822
Joe 2:2 a day of clouds and of thick **d.**, 6205
Joe 2:31 The sun shall be turned into **d.**, 2822
Am 4:13 that maketh the morning **d.**, and 5890
Am 5:18 the day of the Lord is **d.**, and not 2822
Am 5:20 shall not the day of the Lord be **d.**, 2822
Mic 7:8 I sit in **d.**, the Lord shall be a light 2822
Na 1:8 and **d.** shall pursue his enemies. 2822
Zep 1:15 a day of **d.** and gloominess, 2822
Zep 1:15 a day of clouds and thick **d.** 6205
Mt 4:16 The people which sat in **d.** saw *4655*
Mt 6:23 **thy whole body shall be full of d.** *4652*
Mt 6:23 **in thee be d., how great is that d.!** *4655*
Mt 8:12 **shall be cast out into outer d.:** *4655*
Mt 10:27 **What I tell you in d., that speak** *4653*
Mt 22:13 **away, and cast him into outer d.;** *4655*
Mt 25:30 **unprofitable servant into outer d.:** *4655*
Mt 27:45 there was **d.** over all the land *4655*
Mk 15:33 there was **d.** over the whole land *4655*
Lu 1:79 To give light to them that sit in **d.** *4655*
Lu 11:34 **is evil, thy body also is full of d.** *4652*
Lu 11:35 **light which is in thee be not d.** *4655*
Lu 12:3 **whatsoever ye have spoken in d.** *4658*
Lu 22:53 **is your hour, and the power of d.** *4655*
Lu 23:44 there was a **d.** over all the earth *4655*
Joh 1:5 And the light shineth in **d.**; and *4653*
Joh 1:5 and the **d.** comprehended it not. *4653*
Joh 3:19 **men loved d. rather than light,** *4655*
Joh 8:12 **followeth me shall not walk in d.,** *4653*
Joh 12:35 **for light, lest d. come upon you:** *4653*
Joh 12:35 **for he that walketh in d. knoweth.** *4653*
Joh 12:46 **on me should not abide in d.** *4653*
Ac 2:20 The sun shall be turned into **d.**, *4655*
Ac 13:11 there fell on him a mist and a **d.**; *4655*
Ac 26:18 **to turn them from d. to light,** *4655*
Ro 2:19 a light of them which are in **d.**, *4655*
Ro 13:12 cast off the works of **d.**, and let us *4655*
1Co 4:5 to light the hidden things of **d.**, *4655*
2Co 4:6 the light to shine out of **d.**, hath *4655*
2Co 6:14 communion hath light with **d.**? *4655*
Eph 5:8 ye were sometimes **d.**, but now are *4655*
Eph 5:11 with the unfruitful works of **d.**, *4655*
Eph 6:12 the rulers of the **d.** of this world, *4655*
Col 1:13 delivered us from the power of **d.**, *4655*
1Th 5:4 But ye, brethren, are not in **d.**, *4655*
1Th 5:5 we are not of the night, not of **d.**. *4655*
Heb 12:18 nor unto blackness, and **d.**, and *4655*
1Pe 2:9 hath called you out of **d.** into his *4655*
2Pe 2:4 delivered them into chains of **d.**, *2217*
2Pe 2:17 the mist of **d.** is reserved for ever. *4655*
1Jo 1:5 light, and in him is no **d.** at all. *4653*
1Jo 1:6 and walk in **d.**, we lie, and do not *4655*
1Jo 2:8 because the **d.** is past, and the *4653*
1Jo 2:9 brother, is in **d.** even until now. *4653*
1Jo 2:11 is in **d.**, and walketh in **d.**, and *4653*
1Jo 2:11 goeth, because that **d.** hath blinded *4653*
Jude 6 in everlasting chains under **d.** *2217*
Jude 13 the blackness of **d.** for ever. *4655*
Re 16:10 and his kingdom was full of **d.**; *4656*

DARKON (dar'-kon)
Ezr 2:56 of Jaalah, the children of **D.**, the 1874
Ne 7:58 of Jaala, the children of **D.**, the 1874

DARLING
Ps 22:20 my **d.** from the power of the dog. 3173
Ps 35:17 my **d.** from the lions. 3173

DART See also DARTS.
Job 41:26 spear, the **d.**, nor the habergeon. 4551
Pr 7:23 Till a **d.** strike through his liver; 2671
Heb 12:20 or thrust through with a **d.**: *1002*

DARTS
2Sa 18:14 he took three **d.** in his hand, 7626
2Ch 32:5 **d.** and shields in abundance. 7973
Job 41:29 **D.** are counted as stubble: he 8455
Eph 6:16 all the fiery **d.** of the wicked. *956*

DASH See also DASHED; DASHETH.
2Ki 8:12 wilt **d.** their children, and rip up 7376
Ps 2:9 thou shalt **d.** them in pieces like 5310
Ps 91:12 thou **d.** thy foot against a stone. 5062
Isa 13:18 shall **d.** the young men to pieces; 7376
Jer 13:14 **d.** them one against another, 5310
Mt 4:6 thou **d.** thy foot against a stone. *4350*
Lu 4:11 thou **d.** thy foot against a stone. *4350*

DASHED
Ex 15:6 hand, O Lord, hath **d.** in pieces 7492
Isa 13:16 children also shall be **d.** to pieces 7376
Ho 10:14 the mother was **d.** in pieces upon 7376
Ho 13:16 their infants shall be **d.** in pieces, 7376
Na 3:10 children also were **d.** in pieces 7376

DASHETH
Ps 137:9 that taketh and **d.** thy little ones 5310
Na 2:1 He that **d.** in pieces is come 6327

DATHAN (da'-than)
Nu 16:1 **D.** and Abiram, the sons of Eliab, 1885
Nu 16:12 Moses sent to call **D.** and Abiram, 1885
Nu 16:24 of Korah, **D.**, and Abiram. 1885
Nu 16:25 Moses rose up and went unto **D.** 1885
Nu 16:27 from the tabernacle of Korah, **D.**, 1885
Nu 16:27 side: and **D.** and Abiram came out, 1885
Nu 26:9 Nemuel, and **D.**, and Abiram. 1885
Nu 26:9 This is that **D.** and Abiram, which 1885
De 11:6 what he did unto **D.** and Abiram, 1885
Ps 106:17 earth opened and swallowed up **D.**, 1885

DAUB See also DAUBED; DAUBING.
Eze 13:11 **d.** it with untempered morter, 2902

DAUBED
Ex 2:3 it with slime and with pitch, 2560
Eze 13:10 **d.** it with untempered morter: 2902
Eze 13:12 daubing wherewith ye have **d.** it? 2902
Eze 13:14 down the wall that ye had **d.** 2902
Eze 13:15 have **d.** it with untempered morter, 2902
Eze 13:15 no more, neither they that **d.** it; 2902
Eze 22:28 And her prophets have **d.** them 2902

DAUBING
Eze 13:12 Where is the **d.** wherewith ye 2915

DAUGHTER See also DAUGHTER'S; DAUGHTERS.
Ge 11:29 Milcah, the **d.** of Haran, the 1323
Ge 11:31 and Sarai his **d.** in law, his son 3618
Ge 20:12 she is the **d.** of my father, 1328
Ge 20:12 but not the **d.** of my mother; 1328
Ge 24:23 Whose **d.** art thou; tell me, I pray. 1328
Ge 24:24 **d.** of Bethuel the son of Milcah, 1328
Ge 24:47 Whose **d.** art thou? And she said, 1328
Ge 24:47 The **d.** of Bethuel, Nahor's son, 1328
Ge 24:48 master's brother's **d.** unto his son. 1328
Ge 25:20 the **d.** of Bethuel the Syrian of 1328
Ge 26:34 Judith the **d.** of Berri the Hittite, 1328
Ge 26:34 and Bashemath the **d.** of Elon the 1328
Ge 28:9 Mahalath the **d.** of Ishmael 1328
Ge 29:6 his **d.** cometh with the sheep. 1328

Ge 29:10 Jacob saw Rachel the **d.** of Laban....... 1328
Ge 29:18 years for Rachel thy younger **d.**........ 1328
Ge 29:23 took Leah his **d.**, and brought her...... 1328
Ge 29:24 gave unto his **d.** Leah Zilpah his......... 1328
Ge 29:28 gave him Rachel his **d.** to wife also..... 1328
Ge 29:29 Laban gave to Rachel his **d.**............. 1328
Ge 30:21 afterwards she bare a **d.**, and............ 1328
Ge 34:1 And Dinah the **d.** of Leah,................ 1328
Ge 34:3 clave unto Dinah the **d.** of Jacob,........ 1328
Ge 34:5 that he had defiled Dinah his **d.**:........ 1328
Ge 34:7 Israel in lying with Jacob's **d.**;............ 1328
Ge 34:8 son Shechem longeth for your **d.**:.......... 1328
Ge 34:17 then will we take our **d.**, and we........ 1328
Ge 34:19 he had delight in Jacob's **d.**:.............. 1328
Ge 36:2 the **d.** of Elon the Hittite,................. 1328
Ge 36:2 **d.** of Anah the **d.** of Zibeon the......... 1328
Ge 36:3 Bashemath Ishmael's **d.**, sister of....... 1328
Ge 36:14 Aholibamah the **d.** of Anah.................. 1328
Ge 36:14 the **d.** of Zibeon, Esau's wife............ 1328
Ge 36:18 the **d.** of Anah, Esau's wife.............. 1328
Ge 36:25 and Aholibamah the **d.** of Anah.......... 1328
Ge 36:39 the **d.** of Matred, the **d.** of Mezahab... 1328
Ge 38:2 there a **d.** of a certain Canaanite,....... 1328
Ge 38:11 said Judah to Tamar his **d.** in law,...... 3618
Ge 38:12 the **d.** of Shuah Judah's wife died;....... 1323
Ge 38:16 not that she was his **d.** in law.).......... 3618
Ge 38:24 Tamar thy **d.** in law hath played......... 3618
Ge 41:45 gave him to wife Asenath the **d.** of..... 1323
Ge 41:50 Asenath the **d.** of Poti-pherah........... 1323
Ge 46:15 with his **d.** Dinah: all the souls of....... 1323
Ge 46:18 whom Laban gave to Leah his **d.**,........ 1323
Ge 46:20 Asenath the **d.** of Poti-pherah........... 1323
Ge 46:25 Laban gave unto Rachel his **d.**,.......... 1323
Ex 1:16 but if it be a **d.**, then she shall live..... 1323
Ex 1:22 every **d.** ye shall save alive............... 1323
Ex 2:1 took to wife a **d.** of Levi.................. 1323
Ex 2:5 And the **d.** of Pharaoh came down...... 1323
Ex 2:7 said his sister to Pharaoh's **d.**,........... 1323
Ex 2:8 And Pharaoh's **d.** said to her, Go....... 1323
Ex 2:9 Pharaoh's **d.** said unto her, Take........ 1323
Ex 2:10 she brought him unto Pharaoh's **d.**,..... 1323
Ex 2:21 he gave Moses Zipporah his **d.**.......... 1323
Ex 6:23 Elisheba, **d.** of Amminadab, sister....... 1323
Ex 20:10 thou, nor thy son, nor thy **d.**,............ 1323
Ex 21:7 man sell his **d.** to be a maidservant,.... 1323
Ex 21:31 a son, or have gored a **d.**,................ 1323
Le 12:6 or for a **d.**, she shall bring................ 1323
Le 18:9 **d.** of thy father, or **d.** of thy mother,.. 1323
Le 18:10 The nakedness of thy son's **d.**,.......... 1323
Le 18:10 or of thy daughter's **d.**,.................... 1323
Le 18:11 nakedness of thy father's wife's **d.**,..... 1323
Le 18:15 the nakedness of thy **d.** in law:.......... 3618
Le 18:17 nakedness of a woman and her **d.**,...... 1323
Le 18:17 shalt thou take her son's **d.**,............. 1323
Le 18:17 or her daughter's **d.**,........................ 1323
Le 19:29 Do not prostitute thy **d.**, to cause...... 1323
Le 20:12 if a man lie with his **d.** in law,.......... 3618
Le 20:17 take his sister, his father's **d.**,.......... 1323
Le 20:17 or his mother's **d.**,.......................... 1323
Le 21:2 for his son, and for his **d.**, and for...... 1323
Le 21:9 **d.** of any priest, if she profane........... 1323
Le 22:12 if the priest's **d.** also be married........ 1323
Le 22:13 But if the priest's **d.** be a widow,....... 1323
Le 24:11 was Shelomith, the **d.** of Dibri,.......... 1323
Nu 25:15 slain was Cozbi, the **d.** of Zur;........... 1323
Nu 25:18 Cozbi, the **d.** of a prince of Midian,.... 1323
Nu 26:46 of the **d.** of Asher was Sarah............. 1323
Nu 26:59 wife was Jochebed, the **d.** of Levi,..... 1323
Nu 27:8 his inheritance to pass unto his **d.**..... 1323
Nu 27:9 if he have no **d.**, then he shall give..... 1323
Nu 30:16 between his father and his **d.**,........... 1323
Nu 36:8 every **d.**, that possesseth an............ 1323
De 5:14 work, thou, nor thy son, nor thy **d.**,.... 1323
De 7:3 **d.** thou shalt not give unto his son,..... 1323
De 7:3 **d.** shalt thou take unto thy son......... 1323
De 12:18 thou, and thy son, and thy **d.**,........... 1323
De 13:6 thy mother, or thy son, or thy **d.**,...... 1323
De 16:11 thy **d.**, and thy manservant, and......... 1323
De 16:14 thou, and thy son, and thy **d.**,........... 1323
De 18:10 his son or his **d.** to pass through........ 1323
De 22:16 I gave my **d.** unto this man to wife,.... 1323
De 22:17 I found not thy **d.** a maid; and yet...... 1323
De 27:22 the **d.** of his father, or the **d.** of his.... 1323
De 28:56 toward her son, and toward her **d.**,.... 1323
Jos 15:16 will I give Achsah my **d.** to wife......... 1323
Jos 15:17 he gave him Achsah his **d.** to wife..... 1323

Jg 1:12 will I give Achsah my **d.** to wife......... 1323
Jg 1:13 he gave him Achsah his **d.** to wife...... 1323
Jg 11:34 his **d.** came out to meet him............. 1323
Jg 11:34 her he had neither son nor **d.**............ 1323
Jg 11:35 Alas, my **d.**! thou hast brought me..... 1323
Jg 11:40 yearly to lament the **d.** of Jephthah..... 1323
Jg 19:24 Behold, here is my **d.** a maiden,......... 1323
Jg 21:1 any of us give his **d.** unto Benjamin.... 1323
Ru 1:22 the Moabitess, her **d.** in law, with...... 3618
Ru 2:2 she said unto her, Go, my **d.**........... 1323
Ru 2:8 unto Ruth, Hearest thou not, my **d.**?.. 1323
Ru 2:20 Naomi said unto her **d.** in law,........... 3618
Ru 2:22 Naomi said unto Ruth her **d.** in law,.... 3618
Ru 2:22 It is good, my **d.**, that thou go.......... 1323
Ru 3:1 My **d.**, shall I not seek rest for thee,.. 1323
Ru 3:10 Blessed be thou of the Lord, my **d.**:... 1323
Ru 3:11 And now, my **d.**, fear not; I will do.... 1323
Ru 3:16 Who art thou, my **d.**? And she told..... 1323
Ru 3:18 Then said she, Sit still, my **d.**,.......... 1323
Ru 4:15 thy **d.** in law, which loveth thee,........ 3618
1Sa 1:16 thine handmaid for a **d.** of Belial:........ 1323
1Sa 4:19 And his **d.** in law, Phinehas' wife........ 3618
1Sa 14:50 was Ahinoam, the **d.** of Ahimaaz:....... 1323
1Sa 17:25 riches, and will give him his **d.**,......... 1323
1Sa 18:17 Behold my elder **d.** Merab, her will.... 1323
1Sa 18:19 Saul's **d.** should have been given........ 1323
1Sa 18:20 And Michal Saul's **d.** loved David:....... 1323
1Sa 18:27 gave him Michal his **d.** to wife........... 1323
1Sa 18:28 that Michal Saul's **d.** loved him.......... 1323
1Sa 25:44 But Saul had given Michal his **d.**........ 1323
2Sa 3:3 Maacah the **d.** of Talmai king of......... 1323
2Sa 3:7 name was Rizpah, the **d.** of Aiah:....... 1323
2Sa 3:13 thou first bring Michal Saul's **d.**,........ 1323
2Sa 6:16 Michal Saul's **d.** looked through a....... 1323
2Sa 6:20 And Michal the **d.** of Saul come out.... 1323
2Sa 6:23 Michal the **d.** of Saul had no child....... 1323
2Sa 11:3 this Bath-sheba, the **d.** of Eliam,........ 1323
2Sa 12:3 bosom, and was unto him as a **d.**........ 1323
2Sa 14:27 three sons, and one **d.**, whose name... 1323
2Sa 17:25 went in to Abigail the **d.** of Nahash,.... 1323
2Sa 21:8 the **d.** of Aiah, whom she bare unto.... 1323
2Sa 21:8 five sons of Michal the **d.** of Saul,...... 1323
2Sa 21:10 the **d.** of Aiah took sackcloth, and...... 1323
2Sa 21:11 David what Rizpah the **d.** of Aiah,...... 1323
1Ki 3:1 took Pharaoh's **d.**, and brought her..... 1323
1Ki 4:11 Taphath the **d.** of Solomon to wife:..... 1323
1Ki 4:15 took Basmath the **d.** of Solomon to..... 1323
1Ki 7:8 also an house for Pharaoh's **d.**,.......... 1323
1Ki 9:16 given it for a present unto his **d.**,...... 1323
1Ki 9:24 Pharaoh's **d.** came up out of the......... 1323
1Ki 11:1 together with the **d.** of Pharaoh,........ 1323
1Ki 15:2, 10 Maachah, the **d.** of Abishalom........ 1323
1Ki 16:31 to wife Jezebel the **d.** of Ethbaal....... 1323
1Ki 22:42 name was Azubah the **d.** of Shilhi....... 1323
2Ki 8:18 for the **d.** of Ahab was his wife:......... 1323
2Ki 8:26 the **d.** of Omri king of Israel............. 1323
2Ki 9:34 bury her for she is a king's **d.**.......... 1323
2Ki 11:2 Jehosheba the **d.** of king Joram,......... 1323
2Ki 14:9 Give thy **d.** to my son to wife:.......... 1323
2Ki 15:33 name was Jerusha the, **d.** of Zadok..... 1323
2Ki 18:2 also was Abi, the **d.** of Zachariah....... 1323
2Ki 19:21 virgin the **d.** of Zion hath despised...... 1323
2Ki 19:21 the **d.** of Jerusalem hath shaken.......... 1323
2Ki 21:19 Meshullemeth, the **d.** of Haruz of....... 1323
2Ki 22:1 Jedidah, the **d.** of Adiah of................ 1323
2Ki 23:10 or his **d.** to pass through the fire....... 1323
2Ki 23:31 Hamutal, the **d.** of Jeremiah of........... 1323
2Ki 23:36 Zebudah, the **d.** of Pedaiah of............ 1323
2Ki 24:8 Nehushta, the **d.** of Elnathan of.......... 1323
2Ki 24:18 Hamutal, the **d.** of Jeremiah of........... 1323
1Ch 1:50 the **d.** of Matred, the **d.** of Mezahab... 1323
1Ch 2:3 of the **d.** of Shua the Canaanitess....... 1323
1Ch 2:4 Tamar his **d.** in law bare him............. 3618
1Ch 2:21 Hezron went in to the **d.** of Machir.... 1323
1Ch 2:35 Sheshan gave his **d.** to Jarha his......... 1323
1Ch 2:49 and the **d.** of Caleb was Achsa........... 1323
1Ch 3:2 son of Maachah the **d.** of Talmai......... 1323
1Ch 3:5 of Bath-shua the **d.** of Ammiel:.......... 1323
1Ch 4:18 the **d.** of Pharaoh, which Mered.......... 1323
1Ch 7:24 (And his **d.** was Sherah, who built...... 1323
1Ch 15:29 Michal the **d.** of Saul looking out at..... 1323
2Ch 8:11 Solomon brought up the **d.** of............ 1323
2Ch 11:18 Mahalath the **d.** of Jerimoth the......... 1121
2Ch 11:18 Abihail the **d.** of Eliab..................... 1323
2Ch 11:20 took Maachah the **d.** of Absalom;........ 1323
2Ch 11:21 the **d.** of Absalom above all his.......... 1323
2Ch 13:2 Michaiah the **d.** of Uriel of Gibeah...... 1323

2Ch 20:31 was Azubah the **d.** of Shilhi............... 1323
2Ch 21:6 he had the **d.** of Ahab to wife:........... 1323
2Ch 22:2 also was Athaliah the **d.** of Omri,....... 1323
2Ch 22:11 Jehoshabeath, the **d.** of the king,..............
2Ch 22:11 So Jehoshabeath, the **d.** of king.......... 1323
2Ch 25:18 Give thy **d.** to my son to wife:........... 1323
2Ch 27:1 also was Jerushah, the **d.** of Zadok..... 1323
2Ch 29:1 was Abijah, the **d.** of Zechariah......... 1323
Ne 6:18 had taken the **d.** of Meshullam........... 1323
Es 2:7 that is, Esther, his uncle's **d.**:........... 1323
Es 2:7 were dead, took for his own **d.**........... 1323
Es 2:15 Esther, the **d.** of Abihail the uncle...... 1323
Es 2:15 who had taken her for his **d.**,............. 1323
Es 9:29 Esther the queen, the **d.** of Abihail,.... 1323
Ps 9:14 in the gates of the **d.** of Zion:............ 1323
Ps 45:10 Hearken, O **d.**, and consider, and....... 1323
Ps 45:12 And the **d.** of Tyre shall be there........ 1323
Ps 45:13 The king's **d.** is all glorious within:..... 1323
Ps 137:8 O **d.** of Babylon, who art to be.......... 1323
Ca 7:1 O prince's **d.**! the joints of thy........... 1323
Isa 1:8 the **d.** of Zion is left as a cottage....... 1323
Isa 10:30 Lift up thy voice, O **d.** of Gallim:....... 1323
Isa 10:32 against the mount of the **d.** of Zion..... 1004
Isa 16:1 unto the mount of the **d.** of Zion........ 1323
Isa 22:4 the spoiling of the **d.** of my people..... 1323
Isa 23:10 **d.** of Tarshish: there is no more........ 1323
Isa 23:12 thou oppressed virgin, **d.** of Zidon:..... 1323
Isa 37:22 virgin, the **d.** of Zion, hath despised.... 1323
Isa 37:22 the **d.** of Jerusalem hath shaken......... 1323
Isa 47:1 O virgin **d.** of Babylon, sit on the....... 1323
Isa 47:1 no throne, O **d.** of the Chaldeans:...... 1323
Isa 47:5 darkness, O **d.** of the Chaldeans:....... 1323
Isa 52:2 of thy neck, O captive **d.** of Zion......... 1323
Isa 62:11 Say ye to the **d.** of Zion,.................. 1323
Jer 4:11 wilderness toward the **d.** of my.......... 1323
Jer 4:31 the voice of the **d.** of Zion,............... 1323
Jer 6:2 I have likened the **d.** of Zion............ 1323
Jer 6:14 the hurt of the **d.** of my people................
Jer 6:23 war against thee, O **d.** of Zion........... 1323
Jer 6:26 O **d.** of my people, gird thee............. 1323
Jer 8:11 hurt of the **d.** of my people slightly,.... 1323
Jer 8:19 the cry of the **d.** of my people........... 1323
Jer 8:21 the hurt of the **d.** of my people.......... 1323
Jer 8:22 the health of the **d.** of my people....... 1323
Jer 9:1 the slain of the **d.** of my people!........ 1323
Jer 9:7 I do for the **d.** of my people?............ 1323
Jer 14:17 for the virgin **d.** of my people is......... 1323
Jer 31:22 go about, O thou backsliding **d.**?........ 1323
Jer 46:11 balm, O virgin, the **d.** of Egypt:......... 1323
Jer 46:19 O thou **d.** dwelling in Egypt,............. 1323
Jer 46:24 **d.** of Egypt shall be confounded;........ 1323
Jer 48:18 Thou **d.** that dost inhabit Dibon,......... 1323
Jer 49:4 O backsliding **d.**? that trusted........... 1323
Jer 50:42 against thee, O **d.** of Babylon............ 1323
Jer 51:33 The **d.** of Babylon is like a................ 1323
Jer 52:1 the **d.** of Jeremiah of Libnah.............. 1323
La 1:6 from the **d.** of Zion all her beauty....... 1323
La 1:15 the virgin, the **d.** of Judah,................ 1323
La 2:1 the Lord covered the **d.** of Zion.......... 1323
La 2:2 strongholds of the **d.** of Judah;........... 1323
La 2:4 the tabernacle of the **d.** of Zion:......... 1323
La 2:5 hath increased in the **d.** of Judah........ 1323
La 2:8 destroy the wall of the **d.** of Zion:...... 1323
La 2:10 The elders of the **d.** of Zion sit.......... 1323
La 2:11 destruction of the **d.** of my people;..... 1323
La 2:13 liken to thee, O **d.** of Jerusalem?........ 1323
La 2:13 comfort thee, O virgin **d.** of Zion?...... 1323
La 2:15 their head at the **d.** of Jerusalem,....... 1323
La 2:18 O wall of the **d.** of Zion, let tears....... 1323
La 3:48 destruction of the **d.** of my people...... 1323
La 4:3 the **d.** of my people is become cruel,.. 1323
La 4:6 the iniquity of the **d.** of my people...... 1323
La 4:10 destruction of the **d.** of my people...... 1323
La 4:21 and be glad, O **d.** of Edom,............... 1323
La 4:22 is accomplished, O **d.** of Zion;........... 1323
La 4:22 O **d.** of Edom; he will discover thy..... 1323
Eze 14:20 shall deliver neither son nor **d.**;......... 1323
Eze 16:44 As is the mother, so is her **d.**............ 1323
Eze 16:45 Thou art thy mother's **d.**, that........... 1323
Eze 22:11 hath lewdly defiled his **d.** in law;........ 3618
Eze 22:11 humbled his sister, his father's **d.**....... 1323
Eze 44:25 for son, or for **d.**, for brother,........... 1323
Da 11:6 for the king's **d.** of the south............ 1323
Da 11:17 shall give him the **d.** of women,.......... 1323
Ho 1:3 took Gomer the **d.** of Diblaim;........... 1323
Ho 1:6 conceived again, and bare a **d.**,.......... 1323
Mic 1:13 of the sin to the **d.** of Zion:............... 1323

Mic	4:8	the strong hold of the d. of Zion,	1323
Mic	4:8	shall come to the d. of Jerusalem.	1323
Mic	4:10	O d. of Zion, like a woman in travail:	1323
Mic	4:13	Arise and thresh, O d. of Zion:	1323
Mic	5:1	thyself in troops, O d. of troops:	1323
Mic	7:6	d. riseth up against her mother,	1323
Mic	7:6	d. in law against her mother in	3618
Zep	3:10	even the d. of my dispersed, shall	1323
Zep	3:14	Sing, O d. of Zion; shout, O Israel;	1323
Zep	3:14	all the heart, O d. of Jerusalem.	1323
Zec	2:7	dwellest with the d. of Babylon.	1323
Zec	2:10	Sing and rejoice, O d. of Zion:	1323
Zec	9:9	Rejoice greatly, O d. of Zion;	1323
Zec	9:9	shout, O d. of Jerusalem:	1323
Mal	2:11	hath married the d. of a strange god	1323
Mt	9:18	My d. is even now dead: but	*2364*
Mt	9:22	**D., be of good comfort; thy faith**	*2364*
Mt	10:35	**and the d. against her mother,**	*2364*
Mt	10:35	**and the d. in law against her**	*3565*
Mt	10:37	**loveth son or d. more than me**	*2364*
Mt	14:6	the d. of Herodias danced before	*2364*
Mt	15:22	my d. is grievously vexed with a	*2364*
Mt	15:28	And her d. was made whole from	*2364*
Mt	21:5	Tell ye the d. of Sion, Behold	*2364*
Mk	5:23	little d. lieth at the point of death:	*2365*
Mk	5:34	**D., thy faith hath made thee**	*2364*
Mk	5:35	Thy d. is dead: why troublest thou	*2364*
Mk	6:22	the d. of the said Herodias came	*2364*
Mk	7:25	young d. had an unclean spirit,	*2365*
Mk	7:26	cast forth the devil out of her d.	*2364*
Mk	7:29	**the devil is gone out of thy d.**	*2364*
Mk	7:30	and her d. laid upon the bed	*2364*
Lu	2:36	the d. of Phanuel, of the tribe of	*2364*
Lu	8:42	he had one only d., about twelve	*2364*
Lu	8:48	**D., be of good comfort: thy faith**	*2364*
Lu	8:49	Thy d. is dead; trouble not the	*2364*
Lu	12:53	**against the d., and the d. against**	*2364*
Lu	12:53	**d. in law, and the d. in law against**	*3565*
Lu	13:16	**a d. of Abraham, whom Satan**	*2364*
Joh	12:15	Fear not, d. of Sion: behold, thy	*2364*
Ac	7:21	Pharaoh's d. took him up and	*2364*
Heb	11:24	be called the son of Pharaoh's d.;	*2364*

DAUGHTER-IN-LAW See DAUGHTER and LAW.

DAUGHTER'S

Le	18:10	daughter, or thy d. daughter,	1323
Le	18:17	or her d. daughter, to uncover her	1323
De	22:17	are the tokens of my d. virginity.	1323

DAUGHTERS

Ge	5:4	years: and he begat sons and d.	1121
Ge	5:7,	10,13,16,19,22,26,30 sons and d.	1121
Ge	6:1	earth, and d. were born unto them.	1121
Ge	6:2	the sons of God saw the d. of men.	1121
Ge	6:4	came in unto the d. of men, and they	1121
Ge	11:11,	13,15,17,19,21,23,25 begat sons and d.	1121
Ge	19:8	have two d. which have not known	1121
Ge	19:12	in law, and thy sons, and thy d.,	1121
Ge	19:14	sons in law, which married his d.,	1121
Ge	19:15	and thy two d., which are here;	1121
Ge	19:16	and upon the hand of his two d.;	1121
Ge	19:30	in the mountain, and his two d.	1121
Ge	19:30	dwelt in a cave, he and his two d.,	1121
Ge	19:36	Thus were both the d. of Lot with	1121
Ge	24:3	my son of the d. of the Canaanites,	1121
Ge	24:13	and the d. of the men of the city	1121
Ge	24:37	d. of the Canaanites, in whose land	1121
Ge	27:46	my life because of the d. of Heth:	1121
Ge	27:46	Jacob take a wife of the d. of Heth,	1121
Ge	27:46	these which are of the d. of the land,	1121
Ge	28:1	not take a wife of the d. of Canaan.	1121
Ge	28:2	d. of Laban thy mother's brother.	1121
Ge	28:6	not take a wife of the d. of Canaan;	1121
Ge	28:8	Esau seeing that the d. of Canaan	1121
Ge	29:16	Laban had two d.: the name of the	1121
Ge	30:13	for the d. will call me blessed:	1121
Ge	31:26	carried away my d., as captives	1121
Ge	31:28	me to kiss my sons and my d.?	1121
Ge	31:31	take by force thy d. from me.	1121
Ge	31:41	thee fourteen years for thy two d.,	1121
Ge	31:43	These d. are my d., and these	1121
Ge	31:43	can I do this day unto these my d.,	1121
Ge	31:50	If thou shalt afflict my d., or if thou	1121
Ge	31:50	shalt take other wives beside my d.,	1121
Ge	31:55	and kissed his sons and his d.,	1121
Ge	34:1	went out to see the d. of the land,	1121
Ge	34:9	and give your d. unto us, and take	1121
Ge	34:9	and take our d. unto you.	1121
Ge	34:16	Then we will give our d. unto you,	1121
Ge	34:16	and we will take your d. unto us,	1121
Ge	34:21	let us take their d. to us for wives,	1121
Ge	34:21	and let us give them our d.	1121
Ge	36:2	wives of the d. of Canaan; Adah	1121
Ge	36:6	his wives, and his sons, and his d.,	1121
Ge	37:35	and his d. rose up to comfort	1121
Ge	46:7	his d., and his sons' d., and all	1121
Ge	46:15	and his d. were thirty and three.	1121
Ex	2:16	the priest of Midian had seven d.:	1121
Ex	2:20	And he said unto his d., And where	1121
Ex	3:22	upon your sons, and upon your d.;	1121
Ex	6:25	took him one of the d. of Putiel to	1121
Ex	10:9	with our sons and with our d.,	1121
Ex	21:4	she have born him sons or d.;	1121
Ex	21:9	with her after the manner of d.	1121
Ex	32:2	wives, of your sons, and of your d.,	1121
Ex	34:16	take of their d. unto thy sons,	1121
Ex	34:16	and their d. go a whoring after	1121
Le	10:14	and thy sons, and thy d. with thee:	1121
Le	26:29	the flesh of your d. shall ye eat.	1121
Nu	18:11	to thy sons and to thy d. with thee,	1121
Nu	18:19	and thy sons and thy d. with thee,	1121
Nu	21:29	and his d., into captivity unto Sihon	1121
Nu	25:1	whoredom with the d. of Moab.	1121
Nu	26:33	Hepner had no sons, but d.: and	1121
Nu	26:33	names of the d. of Zelophehad were	1121
Nu	27:1	Then came the d. of Zelophehad,	1121
Nu	27:1	these are the names of his d.;	1121
Nu	27:7	The d. of Zelophehad speak right:	1121
Nu	36:2	Zelophehad our brother unto his d.	1121
Nu	36:6	concerning the d. of Zelophehad,	1121
Nu	36:10	so did the d. of Zelophehad:	1121
Nu	36:11	the d. of Zelophehad, were married	1121
De	12:12	ye, and your sons, and your d.,	1121
De	12:31	sons and their d. they have burnt	1121
De	23:17	be no whore of the d. of Israel,	1121
De	28:32	Thy sons and thy d. shall be given	1121
De	28:41	Thou shalt beget sons and d., but	1121
De	28:53	the flesh of thy sons and of thy d.,	1121
De	32:19	provoking of his sons, and of his d.	1121
Jos	7:24	of gold, and his sons, and his d.,	1121
Jos	17:3	had no sons, but d.: and these	1121
Jos	17:3	and these are the names of his d.,	1121
Jos	17:6	Because the d. of Manasseh had an	1121
Jg	3:6	they took their d. to be their wives,	1121
Jg	3:6	and gave their d. to their sons,	1121
Jg	11:40	d. of Israel went yearly to lament	1121
Jg	12:9	he had thirty sons, and thirty d.,	1121
Jg	12:9	thirty d. from abroad for his sons.	1121
Jg	14:1,2	of the d. of the Philistines:	1121
Jg	14:3	among the d. of thy brethren, or	1121
Jg	21:7	give them of our d. to wives?	1121
Jg	21:18	may not give them wives of our d.:	1121
Jg	21:21	the d. of Shiloh come out to dance	1121
Jg	21:21	man his wife of the d. of Shiloh,	1121
Ru	1:6	she arose with her d. in law,	3618
Ru	1:7	her two d. in law with her;	3618
Ru	1:8	Naomi said unto her two d. in law,	3618
Ru	1:11	my d.: why will ye go with me?	1121
Ru	1:12	Turn again, my d., go your way;	1121
Ru	1:13	nay, my d.; for it grieveth me	1121
1Sa	1:4	to all her sons and her d., portions:	1121
1Sa	2:21	and bare three sons and two d.	1121
1Sa	8:13	And he will take your d. to be	1121
1Sa	14:49	names of his two d. were these;	1121
1Sa	30:3	their sons, and their d., were taken	1121
1Sa	30:6	man for his sons and for his d.:	1121
1Sa	30:19	neither sons nor d., neither spoil,	1121
2Sa	1:20	lest the d. of the Philistines rejoice,	1121
2Sa	1:20	d. of the uncircumcised triumph.	1121
2Sa	1:24	Ye d. of Israel, weep over Saul,	1121
2Sa	5:13	were yet sons and d. born to David.	1121
2Sa	13:18	with such robes were the king's d.	1121
2Sa	19:5	the lives of thy sons and of thy d.,	1121
2Ki	17:17	their d. to pass through the fire,	1121
1Ch	2:34	Sheshon had no sons, but d.	1121
1Ch	4:27	Shimei had sixteen sons and six d.;	1121
1Ch	7:15	and Zelophehad had d.	1121
1Ch	14:3	and David begat more sons and d.	1121
1Ch	23:22	dies, and had no sons, but d.:	1121
1Ch	25:5	Heman fourteen sons and three d.	1121
2Ch	2:14	son of a woman of the d. of Dan,	1121
2Ch	11:21	and eight sons, and threescore d.)	1121
2Ch	13:21	twenty and two sons, and sixteen d.	1121
2Ch	24:3	wives; and he begat sons and d.	1121
2Ch	28:8	women, sons, and d., and took also	1121
2Ch	29:9	our sons and our d. and our wives	1121
2Ch	31:18	their sons, and their d., through all	1121
Ezr	2:61	of the d. of Barzillai the Gileadite,	1121
Ezr	9:2	taken of their d. for themselves,	1121
Ezr	9:12	give not your d. unto their sons,	1121
Ezr	9:12	neither take their d. unto your sons,	1121
Ne	3:12	part of Jerusalem, he and his d.	1121
Ne	4:14	your sons, and your d., your wives,	1121
Ne	5:2	our sons, and our d., are many:	1121
Ne	5:5	our sons and our d. to be servants,	1121
Ne	5:5	our d. are brought unto bondage	1121
Ne	7:63	which took one of the d. of Barzillai,	1121
Ne	10:28	their sons, and their d., every one	1121
Ne	10:30	our d. unto the people of the land,	1121
Ne	10:30	nor take their d. for our sons:	1121
Ne	13:25	not give your d. unto their sons,	1121
Ne	13:25	nor take their d. unto your sons,	1121
Job	1:2	unto him seven sons and three d.	1121
Job	1:13	his sons and his d. were eating and	1121
Job	1:18	Thy sons and thy d. were eating	1121
Job	42:13	had also seven sons and three d.	1121
Job	42:15	found so fair as the d. of Job:	1121
Ps	45:9	Kings' d. were among thy	1121
Ps	48:11	let the d. of Judah be glad,	1121
Ps	97:8	the d. of Judah rejoiced because of	1121
Ps	106:37	sacrificed their sons and their d.	1121
Ps	106:38	blood of their sons and of their d.,	1121
Ps	144:12	that our d. may be as corner stones,	1121
Pr	30:15	horseleach hath two d., crying,	1121
Pr	31:29	Many d. have done virtuously, but	1121
Ec	12:4	d. of musick shall be brought low;	1121
Ca	1:5	O ye d. of Jerusalem, as the tents	1121
Ca	2:2	so is my love among the d.	1121
Ca	2:7	I charge you, O ye d. of Jerusalem,	1121
Ca	3:5	I charge you, O ye d. of Jerusalem,	1121
Ca	3:10	with love, for the d. of Jerusalem.	1121
Ca	3:11	Go forth, O ye d. of Zion, and	1121
Ca	5:8	I charge you, O d. of Jerusalem,	1121
Ca	5:16	is my friend, O d. of Jerusalem.	1121
Ca	6:9	The d. saw her, and blessed her;	1121
Ca	8:4	I charge you, O d. of Jerusalem,	1121
Isa	3:16	Because the d. of Zion are haughty,	1121
Isa	3:17	crown of the head of the d. of Zion,	1121
Isa	4:4	away the filth of the d. of Zion,	1121
Isa	16:2	the d. of Moab shall be at the fords	1121
Isa	32:9	hear my voice, ye careless d.;	1121
Isa	43:6	and my d. from the ends of the earth;	1121
Isa	49:22	thy d. shall be carried upon their	1121
Isa	56:5	name better than of sons and of d.:	1121
Isa	60:4	thy d. shall be nursed at thy side.	1121
Jer	3:24	their herds, their sons and their d.	1121
Jer	5:17	which thy sons and thy d. should eat:	1121
Jer	7:31	their sons and their d. in the fire;	1121
Jer	9:20	teach your d. wailing, and every	1121
Jer	11:22	and their d. shall die by famine:	1121
Jer	14:16	wives, nor their sons, nor their d.:	1121
Jer	16:2	neither shalt thou have sons or d.	1121
Jer	16:3	concerning the d. that are born in	1121
Jer	19:9	flesh of their d., and they shall eat	1121
Jer	29:6	beget sons and d.; and take wives	1121
Jer	29:6	and give your d. to husbands,	1121
Jer	29:6	that they may bear sons and d.;	1121
Jer	32:35	their d. to pass through the fire	1121
Jer	35:8	our wives, our sons, nor our d.;	1121
Jer	41:10	the king's d., and all the people	1121
Jer	43:6	and the king's d., and every person	1121
Jer	48:46	taken captives, and thy d. captives.	1121
Jer	49:2	her d. shall be burned with fire:	1121
Jer	49:3	cry, ye d. of Rabbah, gird you with	1121
La	3:51	because of all the d. of my city.	1121
Eze	13:17	against the d. of thy people, which	1121
Eze	14:16	deliver neither sons nor d.; they	1121
Eze	14:18	deliver neither sons nor d., but they	1121
Eze	14:22	both sons and d.: behold, they shall	1121
Eze	16:20	thou hast taken thy sons and thy d.,	1121
Eze	16:27	the d. of the Philistines, which are	1121
Eze	16:46	Samaria, she and her d. that dwell	1121
Eze	16:46	thy right hand, is Sodom and her d.	1121
Eze	16:48	hast not done, she nor her d., as	1121
Eze	16:48	thou hast done, thou and thy d.	1121
Eze	16:49	idleness was in her and in her d.,	1121
Eze	16:53	the captivity of Sodom and her d.,	1121
Eze	16:53	the captivity of Samaria and her d.,	1121
Eze	16:55	When thy sisters, Sodom and her d.,	1121
Eze	16:55	Samaria and her d., shall return	1121

Eze 16:55 then thou and thy **d.** shall return........ 1121
Eze 16:57 of thy reproach of the **d.** of Syria,...... 1121
Eze 16:57 about her, the **d.** of the Philistines,...... 1121
Eze 16:61 I will give them unto thee for **d.**,....... 1121
Eze 23:2 two women, the **d.** of one mother:..... 1121
Eze 23:4 mine, and they bare sons and **d.**...... 1121
Eze 23:10 they took her sons and her **d.**, and..... 1121
Eze 23:25 they shall take thy sons and thy **d.**;.... 1121
Eze 23:47 shall slay their sons and their **d.**,........ 1121
Eze 24:21 your sons and your **d.** whom ye......... 1121
Eze 24:25 their minds, their sons and their **d.**,.... 1121
Eze 26:6 And her **d.** which are in the field........ 1121
Eze 26:8 He shall slay with the sword thy **d.**.... 1121
Eze 30:18 and her **d.** shall go into captivity........ 1121
Eze 32:16 the **d.** of the nations shall lament........ 1121
Eze 32:18 and the **d.** of the famous nations,....... 1121
Ho 4:13 your **d.** shall commit whoredom,........ 1121
Ho 4:14 I will not punish your **d.** when they.... 1121
Joe 2:28 sons and your **d.** shall prophesy,........ 1121
Joe 3:8 I will sell your sons and **d.** into the..... 1121
Am 7:17 and thy **d.** shall fall by the sword,...... 1121
Lu 1:5 his wife was of the **d.** of Aaron,......... *2364*
Lu 23:28 **D. of Jerusalem, weep not for me,**. *2364*
Ac 2:17 sons and your **d.** shall prophesy,......... *2364*
Ac 21:9 four **d.**, virgins, which did prophesy.... *2364*
2Co 6:18 ye shall be my sons and **d.**, saith....... *2364*
1Pe 3:6 whose **d.** ye are, as long as ye do...... *5043*

DAVID See also DAVID'S.
Ru 4:17 father of Jesse, the father of **D.**......... 1732
Ru 4:22 begat Jesse, and Jesse begat **D.**......... 1732
1Sa 16:13 the Spirit of the Lord came upon **D.**... 1732
1Sa 16:19 Send me **D.** thy son, which is with.... 1732
1Sa 16:20 sent them by **D.** his son unto Saul...... 1732
1Sa 16:21 **D.** came to Saul, and stood before...... 1732
1Sa 16:22 Let **D.**, I pray thee, stand before....... 1732
1Sa 16:23 **D.** took a harp, and played with his.... 1732
1Sa 17:12 Now **D.** was the son of that............ 1732
1Sa 17:14 **D.** was the youngest: and the three.... 1732
1Sa 17:15 **D.** went and returned from Saul........ 1732
1Sa 17:17 Jesse said unto **D.** his son, Take........ 1732
1Sa 17:20 **D.** rose up early in the morning,........ 1732
1Sa 17:22 **D.** left his carriage in the hand of....... 1732
1Sa 17:23 same words: and **D.** heard them........ 1732
1Sa 17:26 **D.** spake to the men that stood by..... 1732
1Sa 17:28 anger was kindled against **D.**,........... 1732
1Sa 17:29 **D.** said, What have I now done?......... 1732
1Sa 17:31 words were heard which **D.** spake,..... 1732
1Sa 17:32 **D.** said to Saul, Let no man's heart.... 1732
1Sa 17:33 Saul said to **D.**, Thou art not able...... 1732
1Sa 17:34 **D.** said unto Saul, Thy servant......... 1732
1Sa 17:37 **D.** said moreover, The Lord that....... 1732
1Sa 17:37 Saul said unto **D.**, Go, and the.......... 1732
1Sa 17:38 Saul armed **D.** with his armour,......... 1732
1Sa 17:39 **D.** girded his sword upon his............ 1732
1Sa 17:39 **D.** said unto Saul, I cannot go.......... 1732
1Sa 17:39 And **D.** put them off him................. 1732
1Sa 17:41 came on and drew near unto **D.**;........ 1732
1Sa 17:42 looked about, and saw **D.**,............... 1732
1Sa 17:43 the Philistine said unto **D.**, Am I a..... 1732
1Sa 17:43 Philistine cursed **D.** by his gods......... 1732
1Sa 17:44 the Philistine said to **D.**, Come to...... 1732
1Sa 17:45 Then said **D.** to the Philistine,.......... 1732
1Sa 17:48 and came and drew nigh to meet **D.**,.. 1732
1Sa 17:48 that **D.** hasted and ran toward the...... 1732
1Sa 17:49 **D.** put his hand in his bag, and......... 1732
1Sa 17:50 So **D.** prevailed over the Philistine...... 1732
1Sa 17:50 was no sword in the hand of **D.**......... 1732
1Sa 17:51 Therefore **D.** ran, and stood upon...... 1732
1Sa 17:54 **D.** took the head of the Philistine,...... 1732
1Sa 17:55 when Saul saw **D.** go forth against,..... 1732
1Sa 17:57 as **D.** returned from the slaughter....... 1732
1Sa 17:58 **D.** answered, I am the son of thy...... 1732
1Sa 18:1 was knit with the soul of **D.**, and....... 1732
1Sa 18:3 Jonathan and **D.** made a covenant,...... 1732
1Sa 18:4 and gave it to **D.**, and his garments,... 1732
1Sa 18:5 **D.** went out whithersoever Saul......... 1732
1Sa 18:6 when **D.** was returned from the......... 1732
1Sa 18:7 slain his thousands, and **D.** his ten...... 1732
1Sa 18:8 They have ascribed unto **D.** ten......... 1732
1Sa 18:9 Saul eyed **D.** from that day and......... 1732
1Sa 18:10 and **D.** played with his hand, as at....... 1732
1Sa 18:11 I will smite **D.** even to the wall......... 1732
1Sa 18:11 And **D.** avoided out of his presence.... 1732
1Sa 18:12 Saul was afraid of **D.**, because the...... 1732
1Sa 18:14 **D.** behaved himself wisely in all......... 1732
1Sa 18:16 But all Israel and Judah loved **D.**,....... 1732
1Sa 18:17 Saul said to **D.**, Behold my elder........ 1732
1Sa 18:18 **D.** said unto Saul, Who am I? and...... 1732
1Sa 18:19 should have been given to **D.**, that..... 1732
1Sa 18:20 Michal Saul's daughter loved **D.**:........ 1732
1Sa 18:21 Wherefore Saul said to **D.**, Thou........ 1732
1Sa 18:22 Commune with **D.** secretly, and say,... 1732
1Sa 18:23 spake these words in the ears of **D.**.. 1732
1Sa 18:23 And **D.** said, Seemeth it to you a....... 1732
1Sa 18:24 On this manner spake **D.**................. 1732
1Sa 18:25 Thus shall ye say to **D.**, The king...... 1732
1Sa 18:25 Saul thought to make **D.** fall by the.... 1732
1Sa 18:26 when his servants told **D.** these......... 1732
1Sa 18:26 it pleased **D.** well to be the king's...... 1732
1Sa 18:27 Wherefore **D.** arose and went, he...... 1732
1Sa 18:27 **D.** brought their foreskins, and.......... 1732
1Sa 18:28 knew that the Lord was with **D.**,........ 1732
1Sa 18:29 Saul was yet the more afraid of **D.**;.... 1732
1Sa 18:30 **D.** behaved himself more wisely......... 1732
1Sa 19:1 servants, that they should kill **D.**........ 1732
1Sa 19:2 Saul's son delighted much in **D.**:........ 1732
1Sa 19:2 Jonathan told **D.**, saying, Saul my....... 1732
1Sa 19:4 Jonathan spake good of **D.** unto......... 1732
1Sa 19:4 sin against his servant, against **D.**;..... 1732
1Sa 19:5 against innocent blood, to slay **D.**........ 1732
1Sa 19:7 Jonathan called **D.**, and Jonathan......... 1732
1Sa 19:7 Jonathan brought **D.** to Saul, and........ 1732
1Sa 19:8 and **D.** went out, and fought with........ 1732
1Sa 19:9 hand: and **D.** played with his hand...... 1732
1Sa 19:10 Saul sought to smite **D.** even to the... 1732
1Sa 19:10 and **D.** fled, and escaped that night..... 1732
1Sa 19:12 So Michal let **D.** down through a......... 1732
1Sa 19:14 Saul sent messengers to take **D.**,......... 1732
1Sa 19:15 the messengers again to see **D.**,......... 1732
1Sa 19:18 So **D.** fled, and escaped, and came..... 1732
1Sa 19:19 Behold, **D.** is at Naioth in Ramah....... 1732
1Sa 19:20 Saul sent messengers to take **D.**:........ 1732
1Sa 19:22 said, Where are Samuel and **D.**?........ 1732
1Sa 20:1 **D.** fled from Naioth in Ramah, and..... 1732
1Sa 20:3 **D.** sware moreover, and said, Thy..... 1732
1Sa 20:4 Then said Jonathan unto **D.**,............... 1732
1Sa 20:5 **D.** said unto Jonathan, Behold,......... 1732
1Sa 20:6 **D.** earnestly asked leave of me that.... 1732
1Sa 20:10 Then said **D.** to Jonathan, Who.......... 1732
1Sa 20:11 Jonathan said unto **D.**, Come, and...... 1732
1Sa 20:12 Jonathan said unto **D.**, O Lord God..... 1732
1Sa 20:12 if there be good toward **D.**, and I........ 1732
1Sa 20:15 Lord hath cut off the enemies of **D.**..... 1732
1Sa 20:16 a covenant with the house of **D.**,....... 1732
1Sa 20:17 Jonathan cause **D.** to swear again,...... 1732
1Sa 20:18 Jonathan said to **D.**, To morrow......... 1732
1Sa 20:24 So **D.** hid himself in the field: and...... 1732
1Sa 20:28 And Jonathan answered Saul, **D.**........ 1732
1Sa 20:33 determined of his father to slay **D.**..... 1732
1Sa 20:34 for he was grieved for **D.**, because..... 1732
1Sa 20:35 at the time appointed with **D.**, and..... 1732
1Sa 20:39 only Jonathan and **D.** knew the.......... 1732
1Sa 20:41 **D.** arose out of a place toward the..... 1732
1Sa 20:41 with another, until **D.** exceeded......... 1732
1Sa 20:42 Jonathan said to **D.**, Go in peace,....... 1732
1Sa 21:1 Then came **D.** to Nob to Ahimelech.... 1732
1Sa 21:1 was afraid at the meeting of **D.**,......... 1732
1Sa 21:2 **D.** said unto Ahimelech the priest,...... 1732
1Sa 21:4 the priest answered **D.**, and said,....... 1732
1Sa 21:5 **D.** answered the priest, and said........ 1732
1Sa 21:8 **D.** said unto Ahimelech, And is.......... 1732
1Sa 21:9 **D.** said, There is none like that;........ 1732
1Sa 21:10 **D.** arose, and fled that day for fear..... 1732
1Sa 21:11 Is not this **D.** the king of the land?..... 1732
1Sa 21:11 slain his thousands, and **D.** his ten...... 1732
1Sa 21:12 **D.** laid up these words in his heart,.... 1732
1Sa 22:1 **D.** therefore departed thence, and...... 1732
1Sa 22:3 **D.** went thence to Mizpeh of Moab:.... 1732
1Sa 22:4 the while that **D.** was in the hold....... 1732
1Sa 22:5 the prophet Gad said unto **D.**,........... 1732
1Sa 22:5 Then **D.** departed, and came into........ 1732
1Sa 22:6 Saul heard that **D.** was discovered,...... 1732
1Sa 22:14 among all thy servants as **D.**,........... 1732
1Sa 22:17 because their hand also is with **D.**,..... 1732
1Sa 22:20 Abiathar, escaped, and fled after **D.**.... 1732
1Sa 22:21 Abiathar shewed **D.** that Saul had....... 1732
1Sa 22:22 **D.** said unto Abiathar, I knew it......... 1732
1Sa 23:1 Then they told **D.**, saying, Behold,..... 1732
1Sa 23:2 Therefore **D.** enquired of the Lord,.... 1732
1Sa 23:2 the Lord said unto **D.**, Go, and......... 1732
1Sa 23:4 **D.** enquired of the Lord yet again...... 1732
1Sa 23:5 So **D.** and his men went to Keilah,..... 1732
1Sa 23:5 **D.** saved the inhabitants of Keilah...... 1732
1Sa 23:6 the son of Ahimelech fled to **D.**......... 1732
1Sa 23:7 it was told Saul that **D.** was come...... 1732
1Sa 23:8 to Keilah, to besiege **D.** and his......... 1732
1Sa 23:9 **D.** knew that Saul secretly practised... 1732
1Sa 23:10 Then said **D.**, O Lord God of Israel,... 1732
1Sa 23:12 Then said **D.**, Will the men of........... 1732
1Sa 23:13 Then **D.** and his men, which were...... 1732
1Sa 23:13 was told Saul that **D.** was escaped...... 1732
1Sa 23:14 **D.** abode in the wilderness in............ 1732
1Sa 23:15 **D.** saw that Saul was come out to...... 1732
1Sa 23:15 **D.** was in the wilderness of Ziph........ 1732
1Sa 23:16 arose, and went to **D.** into the wood,.. 1732
1Sa 23:18 and **D.** abode in the wood, and.......... 1732
1Sa 23:19 Doth not **D.** hide himself with us........ 1732
1Sa 23:24 but **D.** and his men were in the......... 1732
1Sa 23:25 they told **D.**: wherefore he came........ 1732
1Sa 23:25 Pursued after **D.** in the wilderness...... 1732
1Sa 23:26 and **D.** and his men on that side of..... 1732
1Sa 23:26 and **D.** made haste to get away......... 1732
1Sa 23:26 Saul and his men compassed **D.**......... 1732
1Sa 23:28 returned from pursuing after **D.**,........ 1732
1Sa 23:29 **D.** went up from thence, and dwelt.... 1732
1Sa 24:1 **D.** is in the wilderness of En-gedi...... 1732
1Sa 24:2 and went to seek **D.** and his men....... 1732
1Sa 24:3 **D.** and his men remained in the......... 1732
1Sa 24:4 the men of **D.** said unto him,............ 1732
1Sa 24:4 **D.** arose, and cut off the skirt of........ 1732
1Sa 24:7 So **D.** stayed his servants with.......... 1732
1Sa 24:8 **D.** also arose afterward, and went...... 1732
1Sa 24:8 **D.** stooped with his face to the.......... 1732
1Sa 24:9 **D.** said to Saul, Wherefore hearest..... 1732
1Sa 24:9 saying, Behold, **D.** seeketh thy......... 1732
1Sa 24:16 when **D.** had made an end of............ 1732
1Sa 24:16 said, Is this thy voice, my son **D.**?..... 1732
1Sa 24:17 he said to **D.**, Thou are more............ 1732
1Sa 24:22 And **D.** sware unto Saul. And Saul...... 1732
1Sa 24:22 but **D.** and his men gat them up........ 1732
1Sa 25:1 **D.** arose, and went down to the........ 1732
1Sa 25:4 **D.** heard in the wilderness that.......... 1732
1Sa 25:5 And **D.** sent out ten young men,........ 1732
1Sa 25:5 and **D.** said unto the ten young.......... 1732
1Sa 25:8 unto thy servants, and to thy son **D.**...1732
1Sa 25:9 words in the name of **D.**, and ceased.. 1732
1Sa 25:10 Who is **D.**? and who is the son of...... 1732
1Sa 25:13 **D.** said unto his men, Gird ye on...... 1732
1Sa 25:13 and **D.** also girded on his sword:........ 1732
1Sa 25:13 went up after **D.** about four hundred... 1732
1Sa 25:14 **D.** sent messengers out of the.......... 1732
1Sa 25:20 **D.** and his men came down against..... 1732
1Sa 25:21 **D.** had said, Surely in vain have I....... 1732
1Sa 25:22 also do God unto the enemies of **D.**,.... 1732
1Sa 25:23 when Abigail saw **D.**, she hasted,....... 1732
1Sa 25:23 lighted off the ass, and fell before **D.**.. 1732
1Sa 25:32 **D.** said to Abigail, Blessed be the...... 1732
1Sa 25:35 So **D.** received of her hand that......... 1732
1Sa 25:39 when **D.** heard that Nabal was dead,... 1732
1Sa 25:39 And **D.** sent and communed with........ 1732
1Sa 25:40 when the servants of **D.** were come... 1732
1Sa 25:40 **D.** sent us unto thee, to take thee..... 1732
1Sa 25:42 went after the messengers of **D.**,........ 1732
1Sa 25:43 **D.** also took Ahinoam of Jezreel;........ 1732
1Sa 26:1 Doth not **D.** hide himself in the.......... 1732
1Sa 26:2 to seek **D.** in the wilderness of Ziph... 1732
1Sa 26:3 But **D.** abode in the wilderness, and... 1732
1Sa 26:4 **D.** therefore sent out spies, and......... 1732
1Sa 26:5 **D.** arose, and came to the place........ 1732
1Sa 26:5 **D.** beheld the place where Saul lay,.... 1732
1Sa 26:6 Then answered **D.** and said to........... 1732
1Sa 26:7 **D.** and Abishai came to the people..... 1732
1Sa 26:8 Then said Abishai to **D.**, God hath...... 1732
1Sa 26:9 **D.** said to Abishai, Destroy him not:.... 1732
1Sa 26:10 **D.** said furthermore, As the Lord....... 1732
1Sa 26:12 So **D.** took the spear and the cruse.... 1732
1Sa 26:13 Then **D.** went over to the other side,..1732
1Sa 26:14 **D.** cried to the people, and to Abner.. 1732
1Sa 26:15 **D.** said to Abner, Art not thou a........ 1732
1Sa 26:17 Is this thy voice, my son **D.**?............ 1732
1Sa 26:17 And **D.** said, It is my voice, my lord,.. 1732
1Sa 26:21 I have sinned: return, my son **D.**;...... 1732
1Sa 26:22 **D.** answered and said, Behold the...... 1732
1Sa 26:25 Then Saul said to **D.**,..................... 1732
1Sa 26:25 Blessed to thou, my son **D.**:............. 1732
1Sa 26:25 So **D.** went on his way, and Saul....... 1732
1Sa 27:1 **D.** said in his heart, I shall now......... 1732
1Sa 27:2 **D.** arose, and he passed over with..... 1732
1Sa 27:3 **D.** dwelt with Achish at Gath,........... 1732
1Sa 27:3 even **D.** with his two wives,.............. 1732

1Sa 27:4 it was told Saul that **D.** was fled to..... 1732
1Sa 27:5 **D.** said unto Achish, If I have now..... 1732
1Sa 27:7 And the time that **D.** dwelt in the 1732
1Sa 27:8 **D.** and his men went up, and............ 1732
1Sa 27:9 **D.** smote the land and left neither...... 1732
1Sa 27:10 **D.** said, Against the south of Judah,.... 1732
1Sa 27:11 **D.** saved neither man nor woman....... 1732
1Sa 27:11 So did **D.**, and so will be his............ 1732
1Sa 27:12 Achish believed **D.**, saying, He hath.... 1732
1Sa 28:1 Achish said unto **D.**, Know thou......... 1732
1Sa 28:2 **D.** said to Achish, Surely thou.......... 1732
1Sa 28:2 Achish said to **D.**, Therefore will I 1732
1Sa 28:17 given it to thy neighbor, even to **D.**:... 1732
1Sa 29:2 **D.** and his men passed on in the........ 1732
1Sa 29:3 Is not this **D.**, the servant of Saul...... 1732
1Sa 29:5 Is not this **D.**, of whom they sang...... 1732
1Sa 29:5 slew his thousands, and **D.** his ten 1732
1Sa 29:6 Then Achish called **D.**, and said......... 1732
1Sa 29:8 **D.** said unto Achish, But what.......... 1732
1Sa 29:9 Achish answered and said to **D.**, I....... 1732
1Sa 29:11 So **D.** and his men rose up early........ 1732
1Sa 30:1 when **D.** and his men were come to ... 1732
1Sa 30:3 So **D.** and his men came to the 1732
1Sa 30:4 Then **D.** and the people that were...... 1732
1Sa 30:6 **D.** was greatly distressed; for the 1732
1Sa 30:6 **D.** encouraged himself in the Lord...... 1732
1Sa 30:7 **D.** said to Abiathar the priest, ... 1732
1Sa 30:7 brought thither the ephod to **D.**.......... 1732
1Sa 30:8 **D.** enquired at the Lord, saying, ... 1732
1Sa 30:9 So **D.** went, he and the six hundred ... 1732
1Sa 30:10 **D.** pursued, he and four hundred........ 1732
1Sa 30:11 and brought him to **D.**, and gave........ 1732
1Sa 30:13 And **D.** said unto him, To whom 1732
1Sa 30:15 **D.** said to him, Canst thou bring........ 1732
1Sa 30:17 **D.** smote them from the twilight 1732
1Sa 30:18 **D.** recovered all that the 1732
1Sa 30:18 and **D.** rescued his two wives........... 1732
1Sa 30:19 taken to them: **D.** recovered all. 1732
1Sa 30:20 **D.** took all the flocks and the herds 1732
1Sa 30:21 **D.** came to the two hundred men,...... 1732
1Sa 30:21 faint that they could not follow **D.**, ... 1732
1Sa 30:21 and they went forth to meet **D.**, ... 1732
1Sa 30:21 when **D.** came near to the people,...... 1732
1Sa 30:22 Belial, of those that went with **D.**,....... 1732
1Sa 30:23 Then said **D.**, Ye shall not do so,....... 1732
1Sa 30:26 when **D.** came to Ziklag, he sent of.... 1732
1Sa 30:31 where **D.** himself and his men were..... 1732
2Sa 1:1 **D.** was returned from the slaughter.... 1732
2Sa 1:1 **D.** had abode two days in Ziklag; 1732
2Sa 1:2 And so it was, when he came to **D.**,... 1732
2Sa 1:3 **D.** said unto him, From whence......... 1732
2Sa 1:4 **D.** said unto him, How went the........ 1732
2Sa 1:5 **D.** said unto the young man that........ 1732
2Sa 1:11 Then **D.** took hold on his clothes, ... 1732
2Sa 1:13 **D.** said unto the young man that........ 1732
2Sa 1:14 **D.** said unto him, How wast thou....... 1732
2Sa 1:15 **D.** called one of the young men, ... 1732
2Sa 1:16 **D.** said unto him, Thy blood be 1732
2Sa 1:17 **D.** lamented with this lamentation....... 1732
2Sa 2:1 **D.** enquired of the Lord, saying, ... 1732
2Sa 2:1 **D.** said, Whither shall I go up? 1732
2Sa 2:2 **D.** went up thither, and his two.......... 1732
2Sa 2:3 were with him did **D.** bring up,.......... 1732
2Sa 2:4 And there they anointed **D.** king 1732
2Sa 2:4 they told **D.**, saying, That the men..... 1732
2Sa 2:5 **D.** sent messengers unto the men...... 1732
2Sa 2:10 the house of Judah followed **D.**.......... 1732
2Sa 2:11 time that **D.** was king in Hebron 1732
2Sa 2:13 of Zeruiah, and the servants of **D.**, ... 1732
2Sa 2:15 and twelve of the servants of **D.**, ... 1732
2Sa 2:17 Israel, before the servants of **D.**, ... 1732
2Sa 2:31 the servants of **D.** had smitten of........ 1732
2Sa 3:1 house of Saul and the house of **D.**: 1732
2Sa 3:1 **D.** waxed stronger and stronger,........ 1732
2Sa 3:2 unto **D.** were sons born in Hebron: 1732
2Sa 3:5 These were born to **D.** in Hebron. 1732
2Sa 3:6 house of Saul and the house of **D.**,..... 1732
2Sa 3:8 delivered thee into the hand of **D.**, ... 1732
2Sa 3:9 as the Lord hath sworn to **D.**, even.... 1732
2Sa 3:10 set up the throne of **D.** over Israel..... 1732
2Sa 3:12 sent messengers to **D.** on his behalf, .. 1732
2Sa 3:14 **D.** sent messengers to Ish-bosheth..... 1732
2Sa 3:17 Ye sought for **D.** in times past to....... 1732
2Sa 3:18 for the Lord hath spoken of **D.**, ... 1732
2Sa 3:18 By the hand of my servant **D.** I will.... 1732
2Sa 3:19 went also to speak in the ears of **D.** ... 1732
2Sa 3:20 So Abner came to **D.** to Hebron, ... 1732

2Sa 3:20 So Abner came to **D.** to Hebron, ... 1732
2Sa 3:20 **D.** made Abner and the men that........ 1732
2Sa 3:21 Abner said unto **D.**, I will arise and 1732
2Sa 3:21 **D.** sent Abner away; and he went...... 1732
2Sa 3:22 the servants of **D.** and Joab came....... 1732
2Sa 3:22 Abner was not with **D.** in Hebron;...... 1732
2Sa 3:26 when Joab was come out from **D.**,...... 1732
2Sa 3:26 well of Sirah: but **D.** knew it not........ 1732
2Sa 3:28 afterward when **D.** heard it, he said,... 1732
2Sa 3:31 And **D.** said to Joab, and to all the 1732
2Sa 3:31 king **D.** himself followed the bier. 1732
2Sa 3:35 people came to cause **D.** to eat 1732
2Sa 3:35 while it was yet day, **D.** sware, ... 1732
2Sa 4:8 the head of Ish-bosheth unto **D.**......... 1732
2Sa 4:9 And **D.** answered Rechab and........... 1732
2Sa 4:12 **D.** commanded his young men, and..... 1732
2Sa 5:1 came all the tribes of Israel to **D.**........ 1732
2Sa 5:3 king **D.** made a league with them 1732
2Sa 5:3 they anointed **D.** king over Israel. 1732
2Sa 5:4 **D.** was thirty years old when he 1732
2Sa 5:6 spake unto **D.**, saying, Except thou 1732
2Sa 5:6 thinking, **D.** cannot come in hither...... 1732
2Sa 5:7 **D.** took the strong hold of Zion:......... 1732
2Sa 5:7 the same is the city of **D.**................. 1732
2Sa 5:8 **D.** said on that day, Whosoever......... 1732
2Sa 5:9 So **D.** dwelt in the fort,.................... 1732
2Sa 5:9 and called it the city of **D.**................ 1732
2Sa 5:9 **D.** built round about from Millo.......... 1732
2Sa 5:10 **D.** went on, and grew great,............. 1732
2Sa 5:11 king of Tyre sent messengers to **D.**, .. 1732
2Sa 5:11 and they built **D.** an house................ 1732
2Sa 5:12 **D.** perceived that the Lord had.......... 1732
2Sa 5:13 **D.** took him more concubines and....... 1732
2Sa 5:13 yet sons and daughters born to **D.**. 1732
2Sa 5:17 had anointed **D.** king over Israel, ... 1732
2Sa 5:17 Philistines came up to seek **D.**;.......... 1732
2Sa 5:17 and **D.** heard of it, and went............. 1732
2Sa 5:19 **D.** enquired of the Lord, saying, ... 1732
2Sa 5:19 the Lord said unto **D.**, Go up: 1732
2Sa 5:20 And **D.** came to Baal-perazim, ... 1732
2Sa 5:20 and **D.** smote them there, ... 1732
2Sa 5:21 and **D.** and his men burned them. 1732
2Sa 5:23 when **D.** enquired of the Lord, he 1732
2Sa 5:25 And **D.** did so, as the Lord had 1732
2Sa 6:1 **D.** gathered together all the chosen.... 1732
2Sa 6:2 **D.** arose, and went with all the.......... 1732
2Sa 6:5 And **D.** and all the house of Israel...... 1732
2Sa 6:8 **D.** was displeased, because the.......... 1732
2Sa 6:9 **D.** was afraid of the Lord that day,..... 1732
2Sa 6:10 **D.** would not remove the ark of the.... 1732
2Sa 6:10 Lord unto him in the city of **D.**:......... 1732
2Sa 6:10 but **D.** carried it aside into the........... 1732
2Sa 6:12 was told king **D.**, saying, The Lord 1732
2Sa 6:12 So **D.** went and brought up the ark 1732
2Sa 6:12 into the city of **D.** with gladness. 1732
2Sa 6:14 **D.** danced before the Lord with all..... 1732
2Sa 6:14 and **D.** was girded with a linen 1732
2Sa 6:15 So **D.** and all the house of Israel........ 1732
2Sa 6:16 the Lord came into the city of **D.**....... 1732
2Sa 6:16 saw king **D.** leaping and dancing......... 1732
2Sa 6:17 tabernacle that **D.** had pitched for....... 1732
2Sa 6:17 and **D.** offered burnt offerings............ 1732
2Sa 6:18 as **D.** had made an end of offering...... 1732
2Sa 6:20 **D.** returned to bless his household. 1732
2Sa 6:20 daughter of Saul came to meet **D.**, ... 1732
2Sa 6:21 **D.** said unto Michal, It was before...... 1732
2Sa 7:5 Go and tell my servant **D.**, Thus......... 1732
2Sa 7:8 shalt thou say unto my servant **D.**,..... 1732
2Sa 7:17 so did Nathan speak unto **D.**. 1732
2Sa 7:18 Then went king **D.** in, and sat........... 1732
2Sa 7:20 what can **D.** say more unto thee?....... 1732
2Sa 7:26 of thy servant **D.** be established......... 1732
2Sa 8:1 **D.** smote the Philistines, and............ 1732
2Sa 8:1 **D.** took Metheg-ammah out of the...... 1732
2Sa 8:3 **D.** smote also Hadadezer, the son....... 1732
2Sa 8:4 **D.** took from him a thousand............. 1732
2Sa 8:4 **D.** houghed all the chariot horses, ... 1732
2Sa 8:5 **D.** slew of the Syrians two and.......... 1732
2Sa 8:6 **D.** put garrisons in Syria of............... 1732
2Sa 8:6 the Syrians became servants to **D.**, ... 1732
2Sa 8:6 preserved **D.** whithersoever he.......... 1732
2Sa 8:7 **D.** took the shields of gold that.......... 1732
2Sa 8:8 king **D.** took exceeding much brass..... 1732
2Sa 8:9 Toi king of Hamath heard that **D.**........ 1732
2Sa 8:10 sent Joram his son unto king **D.**,........ 1732
2Sa 8:11 Which also king **D.** did dedicate 1732
2Sa 8:13 **D.** gat him a name when he............. 1732

2Sa 8:14 And the Lord preserved **D.**.............. 1732
2Sa 8:15 And **D.** reigned over all Israel; 1732
2Sa 8:15 **D.** executed judgment and justice 1732
2Sa 9:1 **D.** said, Is there yet any that is left.... 1732
2Sa 9:2 when they had called him unto **D.**, ... 1732
2Sa 9:5 Then king **D.** sent, and fetched.......... 1732
2Sa 9:6 come unto **D.**, he fell on his face, ... 1732
2Sa 9:6 And **D.** said, Mephibosheth. 1732
2Sa 9:7 **D.** said unto him, Fear not: for I........ 1732
2Sa 10:2 Then said **D.**, I will shew kindness..... 1732
2Sa 10:2 **D.** sent to comfort him by the hand.... 1732
2Sa 10:3 that **D.** doth honour thy father,.......... 1732
2Sa 10:3 hath not **D.** rather sent his servants ... 1732
2Sa 10:5 When they told it unto **D.**, he sent..... 1732
2Sa 10:6 saw that they stank before **D.**, ... 1732
2Sa 10:7 when **D.** heard of it, he sent Joab, ... 1732
2Sa 10:17 was told **D.**, he gathered all Israel...... 1732
2Sa 10:17 set themselves in array against **D.**,..... 1732
2Sa 10:18 **D.** slew the men of seven hundred..... 1732
2Sa 11:1 **D.** sent Joab, and all his servants 1732
2Sa 11:1 But **D.** tarried still at Jerusalem. 1732
2Sa 11:2 that **D.** arose from off his bed, and..... 1732
2Sa 11:3 **D.** sent and enquired after the.......... 1732
2Sa 11:4 **D.** sent messengers, and took her;..... 1732
2Sa 11:5 conceived, and sent and told **D.**, ... 1732
2Sa 11:6 **D.** sent to Joab, saying, Send me....... 1732
2Sa 11:6 And Joab sent Uriah to **D.**............... 1732
2Sa 11:7 **D.** demanded of him how Joab did, ... 1732
2Sa 11:8 **D.** said to Uriah, Go down to thy....... 1732
2Sa 11:10 had told **D.**, saying, Uriah went 1732
2Sa 11:10 **D.** said unto Uriah, camest thou......... 1732
2Sa 11:11 Uriah said unto **D.**, The ark, and 1732
2Sa 11:12 And **D.** said to Uriah, Tarry here....... 1732
2Sa 11:13 when **D.** had called him, he did eat..... 1732
2Sa 11:14 **D.** wrote a letter to Joab, and sent..... 1732
2Sa 11:17 of the people of the servants of **D.**;..... 1732
2Sa 11:18 Joab sent and told **D.** all the things..... 1732
2Sa 11:22 come and shewed **D.** all that Joab........ 1732
2Sa 11:23 messenger said unto **D.**, Surely the.... 1732
2Sa 11:25 Then **D.** said unto the messenger,...... 1732
2Sa 11:27 the mourning was passed, **D.** sent...... 1732
2Sa 11:27 thing that **D.** had done displeased....... 1732
2Sa 12:1 the Lord sent Nathan unto **D.**. 1732
2Sa 12:7 Nathan said to **D.**, Thou art the......... 1732
2Sa 12:13 **D.** said unto Nathan, I have sinned..... 1732
2Sa 12:13 Nathan said unto **D.**, The Lord.......... 1732
2Sa 12:15 that Uriah's wife bare unto **D.**, ... 1732
2Sa 12:16 **D.** therefore besought God for the 1732
2Sa 12:16 and **D.** fasted, and went in,............... 1732
2Sa 12:18 servants of **D.** feared to tell him 1732
2Sa 12:19 **D.** saw that his servants whispered, ... 1732
2Sa 12:19 **D.** perceived that the child was.......... 1732
2Sa 12:19 **D.** said unto his servants, Is the 1732
2Sa 12:20 Then **D.** arose from the earth, and..... 1732
2Sa 12:24 **D.** comforted Bath-sheba his wife,...... 1732
2Sa 12:27 Joab sent messengers to **D.**, and....... 1732
2Sa 12:29 **D.** gathered all the people together,.... 1732
2Sa 12:31 So **D.** and all the people returned....... 1732
2Sa 13:1 Absalom the son of **D.** had a fair........ 1732
2Sa 13:1 Amnon the son of **D.** loved her.......... 1732
2Sa 13:7 Then **D.** sent home to Tamar,........... 1732
2Sa 13:21 king **D.** heard of all these things, ... 1732
2Sa 13:30 came to **D.**, saying, Absalom hath...... 1732
2Sa 13:37 **D.** mourned for his son every day. ....
2Sa 13:39 the soul of king **D.** longed to go......... 1732
2Sa 15:13 came a messenger to **D.**, saying, ... 1732
2Sa 15:14 **D.** said unto all his servants that........ 1732
2Sa 15:22 **D.** said to Ittai, Go and pass over. 1732
2Sa 15:30 **D.** went up by the ascent of mount 1732
2Sa 15:31 told **D.**, saying, Ahithophel is among... 1732
2Sa 15:31 **D.** said, O Lord, I pray thee, turn...... 1732
2Sa 15:32 when **D.** was come up to the top of.... 1732
2Sa 15:33 Unto whom **D.** said, If thou passest.... 1732
2Sa 16:1 when **D.** was a little past the top of.... 1732
2Sa 16:5 when king **D.** came to Bahurim,......... 1732
2Sa 16:6 And he cast stones at **D.**, and........... 1732
2Sa 16:6 at all the servants of king **D.**:............ 1732
2Sa 16:10 Lord hath said unto him, Curse **D.**. 1732
2Sa 16:11 **D.** said to Abishai, and to all his 1732
2Sa 16:13 as **D.** and his men went by the way,... 1732
2Sa 16:23 of Ahithophel both with **D.** and.......... 1732
2Sa 17:1 I will arise and pursue after **D.**.......... 1732
2Sa 17:16 and tell **D.**, saying, Lodge not this...... 1732
2Sa 17:17 and they went and told king **D.**.......... 1732
2Sa 17:21 and told king **D.**, and said unto.......... 1732
2Sa 17:21 said unto **D.**, Arise, and pass quickly .. 1732
2Sa 17:22 Then **D.** arose, and all the people 1732

Ref	Context	No.
2Sa 17:24	**D.** came to Mahanaim. And Absalom...	1732
2Sa 17:27	when **D.** was come to Mahanaim,	1732
2Sa 17:29	sheep, and cheese of kine, for **D.**	1732
2Sa 18:1	**D.** numbered the people that were	1732
2Sa 18:2	**D.** sent forth a third part of the	1732
2Sa 18:7	slain before the servants of **D.**,	1732
2Sa 18:9	Absalom met the servants of **D.**	1732
2Sa 18:24	**D.** sat between the two gates: and	1732
2Sa 19:11	**D.** sent to Zadok and to Abiathar	1732
2Sa 19:16	the men of Judah to meet king **D.**.	1732
2Sa 19:22	**D.** said, What have I to do with	1732
2Sa 19:43	have also more right in **D.** than ye:	1732
2Sa 20:1	We have no part in **D.**, neither	1732
2Sa 20:2	man of Israel went up from after **D.**,	1732
2Sa 20:3	**D.** came to his house at Jerusalem;	1732
2Sa 20:6	**D.** said to Abishai, Now shall Sheba	1732
2Sa 20:11	favoureth Joab, and he that is for **D.**,	1732
2Sa 20:21	against the king, even against **D.**:	1732
2Sa 20:26	Jairite was a chief ruler about **D.**	1732
2Sa 21:1	was a famine in the days of **D.**,	1732
2Sa 21:1	and **D.** enquired of the Lord. And	1732
2Sa 21:3	**D.** said unto the Gibeonites, What	1732
2Sa 21:7	**D.** and Jonathan the son of Saul.	1732
2Sa 21:11	it was told **D.** what Rizpah the	1732
2Sa 21:12	**D.** went and took the bones of Saul	1732
2Sa 21:15	**D.** went down, and his servants	1732
2Sa 21:15	Philistines: and **D.** waxed faint,	1732
2Sa 21:16	new sword, thought to have slain **D.**	1732
2Sa 21:17	the men of **D.** sware unto him,	1732
2Sa 21:21	the brother of **D.** slew him.	1732
2Sa 21:22	and fell by the hand of **D.**, and by	1732
2Sa 22:1	**D.** spake unto the Lord the words	1732
2Sa 22:51	mercy to his anointed, unto **D.**,	1732
2Sa 23:1	these be the last words of **D.**	1732
2Sa 23:1	**D.** the son of Jesse said, and the	1732
2Sa 23:8	of the mighty men whom **D.** had:	1732
2Sa 23:9	of the three mighty men with **D.**	1732
2Sa 23:13	came to **D.** in the harvest time	1732
2Sa 23:14	**D.** was then in an hold, and the	1732
2Sa 23:15	**D.** longed, and said, Oh that one	1732
2Sa 23:16	and took it, and brought it to **D.**,	1732
2Sa 23:23	And **D.** set him over his guard,	1732
2Sa 24:1	he moved **D.** against them to say,	1732
2Sa 24:10	**D.** said unto the Lord, I have	1732
2Sa 24:11	when **D.** was up in the morning,	1732
2Sa 24:12	Go and say unto **D.**, Thus saith the	1732
2Sa 24:13	So Gad came to **D.**, and told him,	1732
2Sa 24:14	**D.** said unto Gad, I am in a great	1732
2Sa 24:17	**D.** spake unto the Lord when he	1732
2Sa 24:18	Gad came that day to **D.**, and said	1732
2Sa 24:19	**D.**, according to the saying of Gad,	1732
2Sa 24:21	**D.** said, To buy the threshingfloor	1732
2Sa 24:22	Araunah said unto **D.**, Let my lord	1732
2Sa 24:24	So **D.** bought the threshingfloor	1732
2Sa 24:25	**D.** built there an altar unto the	1732
1Ki 1:1	Now king **D.** was old and stricken	1732
1Ki 1:8	mighty men which belonged to **D.**.	1732
1Ki 1:11	and **D.** our lord knoweth it not?	1732
1Ki 1:13	Go and get thee in unto king **D.**,	1732
1Ki 1:28	Then king **D.** answered and said,	1732
1Ki 1:31	Let my lord king **D.** live for ever.	1732
1Ki 1:32	**D.** said, Call me Zadok the priest,	1732
1Ki 1:37	than the throne of my Lord king **D.**	1732
1Ki 1:43	king **D.** hath made Solomon king.	1732
1Ki 1:47	came to bless our lord king **D.**,	1732
1Ki 2:1	of **D.** drew night that he should die;	1732
1Ki 2:10	So **D.** slept with his fathers,	1732
1Ki 2:10	and was buried in the city of **D.**	1732
1Ki 2:11	the days that **D.** reigned over Israel	1732
1Ki 2:12	sat Solomon upon the throne of **D.**	1732
1Ki 2:24	and set me on the throne of **D.**	1732
1Ki 2:26	the ark of the Lord God before **D.**	1732
1Ki 2:32	my father **D.** not knowing thereof,	1732
1Ki 2:33	but upon **D.**, and upon his seed,	1732
1Ki 2:44	that thou didst to **D.** my father:	1732
1Ki 2:45	throne of **D.** shall be established	1732
1Ki 3:1	and brought her into the city of **D.**,	1732
1Ki 3:3	in the statutes of **D.** his father:	1732
1Ki 3:6	hast shewed unto thy servant **D.**	1732
1Ki 3:7	made thy servant king instead of **D.**	1732
1Ki 3:14	as thy father **D.** did walk, then I	1732
1Ki 5:1	for Hiram was ever a lover of **D.**	1732
1Ki 5:3	Thou knowest how that **D.** my	1732
1Ki 5:5	the Lord spake unto **D.** my father,	1732
1Ki 5:7	hath given unto **D.** a wise son	1732
1Ki 6:12	which I spake unto **D.** thy father:	1732
1Ki 7:51	which **D.** his father had dedicated;	1732
1Ki 8:1	out of the city of **D.**, which is Zion.	1732
1Ki 8:15	which spake with his mouth unto **D.**	1732
1Ki 8:16	but I chose **D.** to be over my people	1732
1Ki 8:17	it was in the heart of **D.** my father	1732
1Ki 8:18	the Lord said unto **D.** my father,	1732
1Ki 8:20	I am risen up in the room of **D.**	1732
1Ki 8:24	Who has kept with thy servant **D.**	1732
1Ki 8:25	keep with thy servant **D.** my father	1732
1Ki 8:26	thou spakest unto thy servant **D.**	1732
1Ki 8:66	that the Lord had done for **D.** his	1732
1Ki 9:4	**D.** thy father walked, in integrity	1732
1Ki 9:5	I promised to **D.** thy father, saying,	1732
1Ki 9:24	came up out of the city of **D.** unto	1732
1Ki 11:4	as was the heart of **D.** his father	1732
1Ki 11:6	not fully after the Lord, as did **D.**	1732
1Ki 11:12	not do it for **D.** thy father's sake:	1732
1Ki 11:13	to thy son for **D.** my servant's sake,	1732
1Ki 11:15	to pass, when **D.** was in Edom,	1732
1Ki 11:21	Hadad heard in Egypt that **D.** slept	1732
1Ki 11:24	when **D.** slew them of Zobah:	1732
1Ki 11:27	the breaches of the city of **D.**	1732
1Ki 11:33	my judgments, as did **D.** his father	1732
1Ki 11:34	**D.** my servant's sake, whom I chose,	
1Ki 11:36	**D.** my servant may have a light	1732
1Ki 11:38	commandments, as **D.** my servant	1732
1Ki 11:38	thee a sure house, as I built for **D.**,	1732
1Ki 11:39	I will for this afflict the seed of **D.**,	1732
1Ki 11:43	buried in the city of **D.** his father:	1732
1Ki 12:16	What portion have we in **D.**?	1732
1Ki 12:16	now see to thine own house, **D.**.	1732
1Ki 12:19	rebelled against the house of **D.**	1732
1Ki 12:20	none that followed the house of **D.**,	1732
1Ki 12:26	kingdom return to the house of **D.**:	1732
1Ki 13:2	shall be born unto the house of **D.**,	1732
1Ki 14:8	kingdom away from the house of **D.**,	1732
1Ki 14:8	hast not been as my servant **D.**,	1732
1Ki 14:31	with his fathers in the city of **D.**.	1732
1Ki 15:3	Lord his God, as the heart of **D.**	1732
1Ki 15:5	**D.** did that which was right in the	1732
1Ki 15:8	they buried him in the city of **D.**	1732
1Ki 15:11	in the eyes of the Lord, as did **D.**	1732
1Ki 15:24	of **D.** his father: and Jehoshaphat	1732
1Ki 22:50	fathers in the city of **D.** his father:	1732
2Ki 8:19	Judah for **D.** his servant's sake.	1732
2Ki 8:24	with his fathers in the city of **D.**:	1732
2Ki 9:28	with his fathers in the city of **D.**.	1732
2Ki 12:21	with his fathers in the city of **D.**:	1732
2Ki 14:3	yet not like **D.** his father: he did	1732
2Ki 14:20	with his fathers in the city of **D.**.	1732
2Ki 15:7	with his fathers in the city of **D.**:	1732
2Ki 15:38	fathers in the city of **D.** his father	1732
2Ki 16:2	Lord his God, like **D.** his father.	1732
2Ki 16:20	with his fathers in the city of **D.**:	1732
2Ki 17:21	rent Israel from the house of **D.**;	1732
2Ki 18:3	according to all that **D.** his father	1732
2Ki 20:5	Thus saith the Lord, the God of **D.**	1732
2Ki 21:7	house, of which the Lord said to **D.**,	1732
2Ki 22:2	and walked in all the way of **D.**	1732
1Ch 2:15	Ozem the sixth, **D.** the seventh	1732
1Ch 3:1	these were the sons of **D.**, which	1732
1Ch 3:9	These were all the sons of **D.**,	1732
1Ch 4:31	their cities unto the reign of **D.**.	1732
1Ch 6:31	**D.** set over the service of song	1732
1Ch 7:2	whose number was in the days of **D.**.	1732
1Ch 9:22	**D.** and Samuel the seer did ordain	1732
1Ch 10:14	and turned the kingdom unto **D.**	1732
1Ch 11:1	Israel gathered themselves to **D.**	1732
1Ch 11:3	and **D.** made a covenant with them	1732
1Ch 11:3	they anointed **D.** king over Israel,	1732
1Ch 11:4	**D.** and all Israel went to Jerusalem,	1732
1Ch 11:5	the inhabitants of Jebus said to **D.**,	1732
1Ch 11:5	Nevertheless **D.** took the castle	1732
1Ch 11:5	of Zion, which is the city of **D.**.	1732
1Ch 11:6	**D.** said, Whosoever smiteth the	1732
1Ch 11:7	**D.** dwelt in the castle; therefore	1732
1Ch 11:7	they called it the city of **D.**.	1732
1Ch 11:9	So **D.** waxed greater and greater:	1732
1Ch 11:10	chief of the mighty men whom **D.**	1732
1Ch 11:11	number of the mighty men whom **D.**	
1Ch 11:13	He was with **D.** at Pas-dammim,	1732
1Ch 11:15	went down to the rock to **D.**,	1732
1Ch 11:16	**D.** was then in the hold, and the	1732
1Ch 11:17	**D.** longed, and said, Oh that one	1732
1Ch 11:18	and took it, and brought it to **D.**:	1732
1Ch 11:18	but **D.** would not drink of it,	1732
1Ch 11:25	and **D.** set him over his guard.	1732
1Ch 12:1	they that came to **D.** to Ziklag,	1732
1Ch 12:8	there separated themselves unto **D.**	1732
1Ch 12:16	and Judah to the hold unto **D.**	1732
1Ch 12:17	**D.** went out to meet them, and	1732
1Ch 12:18	Thine are we, **D.**, and on thy side,	1732
1Ch 12:18	**D.** received them, and made them	1732
1Ch 12:19	there fell some of Manasseh to **D.**,	1732
1Ch 12:21	**D.** against the band of the rovers:	1732
1Ch 12:22	day there came to **D.** to help him,	1732
1Ch 12:23	came to **D.** to Hebron, to turn the	1732
1Ch 12:31	name, to come and make **D.** king.	1732
1Ch 12:38	to make **D.** king over all Israel:	1732
1Ch 12:38	were of one heart to make **D.** king.	1732
1Ch 12:39	there they were with **D.** three days,	1732
1Ch 13:1	**D.** consulted with the captains of	1732
1Ch 13:2	**D.** said unto all the congregation	1732
1Ch 13:5	So **D.** gathered all Israel together,	1732
1Ch 13:6	**D.** went up, and all Israel, to	1732
1Ch 13:8	**D.** and all Israel played before God	1732
1Ch 13:11	**D.** was displeased, because the	1732
1Ch 13:12	**D.** was afraid of God that day,	1732
1Ch 13:13	So **D.** brought not the ark home	1732
1Ch 13:13	to himself to the city of **D.**,	1732
1Ch 14:1	king of Tyre sent messengers to **D.**,	1732
1Ch 14:2	**D.** perceived that the Lord had	1732
1Ch 14:3	**D.** took more wives at Jerusalem:	1732
1Ch 14:3	**D.** begat more sons and daughters.	1732
1Ch 14:8	when the Philistines heard that **D.**	1732
1Ch 14:8	the Philistines went up to seek **D.**	1732
1Ch 14:8	And **D.** heard of it, and went out	1732
1Ch 14:10	**D.** enquired of God, saying, Shall I	1732
1Ch 14:11	and **D.** smote them there. Then	1732
1Ch 14:11	**D.** said, God hath broken in upon	1732
1Ch 14:12	**D.** gave a commandment, and they	1732
1Ch 14:14	Therefore **D.** enquired again of God;	1732
1Ch 14:16	**D.** therefore did as God commanded	1732
1Ch 14:17	fame of **D.** went out into all lands;	1732
1Ch 15:1	**D.** made him houses in the city	
1Ch 15:1	houses in the city of **D.**,	1732
1Ch 15:2	Then **D.** said, None ought to carry	1732
1Ch 15:3	**D.** gathered all Israel together to	1732
1Ch 15:4	**D.** assembled the children of Aaron,	1732
1Ch 15:11	**D.** called for Zadok and Abiathar	1732
1Ch 15:16	**D.** spake to the chief of the Levites	1732
1Ch 15:25	So **D.**, and the elders of Israel, and	1732
1Ch 15:27	**D.** was clothed with a robe of fine	1732
1Ch 15:27	**D.** also had upon him an ephod of	1732
1Ch 15:29	came to the city of **D.**, that Michal	1732
1Ch 15:29	at a window saw king **D.** dancing	1732
1Ch 16:1	the tent that **D.** had pitched for it:	1732
1Ch 16:2	**D.** had made an end of offering	1732
1Ch 16:7	day **D.** delivered first this psalm	1732
1Ch 16:43	**D.** returned to bless his house	1732
1Ch 17:1	to pass, as **D.** sat in his house,	1732
1Ch 17:1	that **D.** said to Nathan the prophet,	1732
1Ch 17:2	Nathan said unto **D.**, Do all that is	1732
1Ch 17:4	Go and tell **D.** my servant, Thus	1732
1Ch 17:7	shalt thou say unto my servant **D.**,	1732
1Ch 17:15	so did Nathan speak unto **D.**.	1732
1Ch 17:16	**D.** the king came and sat before	1732
1Ch 17:18	What can **D.** speak more to thee	1732
1Ch 17:24	let the house of **D.** thy servant be	1732
1Ch 18:1	pass, that **D.** smote the Philistines,	1732
1Ch 18:3	**D.** smote Hadarezer king of Zobah	1732
1Ch 18:4	**D.** took from his a thousand	1732
1Ch 18:4	**D.** also houghed all the chariot	1732
1Ch 18:5	**D.** slew of the Syrians two and	1732
1Ch 18:6	**D.** put garrisons in	1732
1Ch 18:6	Thus the Lord preserved **D.**	1732
1Ch 18:7	**D.** took the shields of gold that	1732
1Ch 18:8	brought **D.** very much brass,	1732
1Ch 18:9	Tou king of Hamath heard how **D.**	1732
1Ch 18:10	sent Hadoram his son to king **D.**,	1732
1Ch 18:11	king **D.** dedicated unto the Lord,	1732
1Ch 18:13	Thus the Lord preserved **D.**	1732
1Ch 18:14	So **D.** reigned over all Israel, and	1732
1Ch 18:17	of **D.** were chief about the king.	1732
1Ch 19:2	**D.** said, I will shew kindness unto	1732
1Ch 19:2	**D.** sent messengers to comfort	1732
1Ch 19:2	servants of **D.** came into the land	1732
1Ch 19:3	Thinkest thou that **D.** doth honour	1732
1Ch 19:5	told **D.** how the men were served.	1732
1Ch 19:6	had made themselves odious to **D.**,	1732
1Ch 19:8	when **D.** heard of it, he sent Joab,	1732
1Ch 19:17	And it was told **D.**; and he gathered	1732
1Ch 19:17	**D.** had put the battle in array	1732
1Ch 19:18	**D.** slew of the Syrians seven	1732
1Ch 19:19	they made peace with **D.**, and	1732

Book	Ref	Context	No.
1Ch	20:1	But **D.** tarried at Jerusalem. And	1732
1Ch	20:2	**D.** took the crown of their king	1732
1Ch	20:3	Even so dealt **D.** with all the cities	1732
1Ch	20:3	**D.** and all the people returned to	1732
1Ch	20:8	and they fell by the hand of **D.**, and	1732
1Ch	21:1	and provoked **D.** to number Israel	1732
1Ch	21:2	**D.** said to Joab, and to the rulers of	1732
1Ch	21:5	of the number of people unto **D.**	1732
1Ch	21:8	**D.** said unto God, I have sinned	1732
1Ch	21:10	Go and tell **D.**, saying, Thus saith	1732
1Ch	21:11	Gad came to **D.**, and said unto him,	1732
1Ch	21:13	**D.** said unto Gad, I am in a great	1732
1Ch	21:16	**D.** lifted up his eyes, and saw the	1732
1Ch	21:16	Then **D.** and the elders of Israel,	1732
1Ch	21:17	**D.** said unto God, Is it not I that	1732
1Ch	21:18	Lord commanded Gad to say to **D.**	1732
1Ch	21:18	that **D.** should go up, and set up	1732
1Ch	21:19	**D.** went up at the saying of Gad,	1732
1Ch	21:21	as **D.** came to Ornan, Ornan looked	1732
1Ch	21:21	and saw **D.**, and went out of the	1732
1Ch	21:21	bowed himself to **D.** with his face	1732
1Ch	21:22	Then **D.** said to Ornan, Grant me	1732
1Ch	21:23	Ornan said unto **D.**, Take it to thee,	1732
1Ch	21:24	king **D.** said to Ornan, Nay; but I	1732
1Ch	21:25	So **D.** gave to Ornan for the place	1732
1Ch	21:26	**D.** built there an altar unto the	1732
1Ch	21:28	time when **D.** saw that the Lord	1732
1Ch	21:30	**D.** could not go before it to enquire	1732
1Ch	22:1	Then **D.** said, This is the house of	1732
1Ch	22:2	**D.** commanded to gather together	1732
1Ch	22:3	**D.** prepared iron in abundance for	1732
1Ch	22:4	brought much cedar wood to **D.**	1732
1Ch	22:5	**D.** said, Solomon my son is young	1732
1Ch	22:5	So **D.** prepared abundantly before	1732
1Ch	22:7	**D.** said to Solomon, My son, as for	1732
1Ch	22:17	**D.** also commanded all the princes	1732
1Ch	23:1	when **D.** was old and full of days,	1732
1Ch	23:5	I made, said **D.** to praise therewith	
1Ch	23:6	**D.** divided them into courses	1732
1Ch	23:25	For **D.** said, The Lord God of Israel	1732
1Ch	23:27	last words of **D.** the Levites were	1732
1Ch	24:3	**D.** distributed them, both Zadok of	1732
1Ch	24:31	sons of Aaron in the presence of **D.**	1732
1Ch	25:1	Moreover **D.** and the captains of	1732
1Ch	26:26	**D.** the king, and the chief fathers,	1732
1Ch	26:31	the fortieth year of the reign of **D.**	1732
1Ch	26:32	**D.** made rulers over the Reubenites,	1732
1Ch	27:18	Elihu, one of the brethren of **D.**:	1732
1Ch	27:23	**D.** took not the number of them	1732
1Ch	27:24	of the chronicles of king **D.**	1732
1Ch	28:1	**D.** assembled all the princes of	1732
1Ch	28:2	**D.** the king stood up upon his feet,	1732
1Ch	28:11	Then **D.** gave to Solomon his son	1732
1Ch	28:19	All this, said **D.**, the Lord made me	
1Ch	28:20	**D.** said to Solomon his son, Be	1732
1Ch	29:1	Furthermore **D.** the king said unto	1732
1Ch	29:9	**D.** the king also rejoiced with great	1732
1Ch	29:10	**D.** blessed the Lord before all the	1732
1Ch	29:10	**D.** said, Blessed be thou, Lord God	1732
1Ch	29:20	**D.** said to all the congregation,	1732
1Ch	29:22	the son of **D.** king the second time,	1732
1Ch	29:23	as king instead of **D.** his father, and	1732
1Ch	29:24	all the sons likewise of king **D.**,	1732
1Ch	29:26	Thus **D.** the son of Jesse reigned	1732
1Ch	29:29	acts of **D.** the king, first and last,	1732
2Ch	1:1	And Solomon the son of **D.** was	1732
2Ch	1:4	ark of God had **D.** brought up from	1732
2Ch	1:4	the place which **D.** had prepared	1732
2Ch	1:8	hast shewed great mercy unto **D.**	1732
2Ch	1:9	let thy promise unto **D.** my father	1732
2Ch	2:3	thou didst deal with **D.** my father,	1732
2Ch	2:7	whom **D.** my father did provide	1732
2Ch	2:12	hath given to **D.** the king a wise son,	1732
2Ch	2:14	with the cunning men of my lord **D.**	1732
2Ch	2:17	**D.** his father had numbered them;	1732
2Ch	3:1	Lord appeared unto **D.** his father,	1732
2Ch	3:1	the place that **D.** had prepared	1732
2Ch	5:1	brought in all the things that **D.** his	1732
2Ch	5:2	out of the city of **D.**, which is Zion	1732
2Ch	6:4	with his mouth to my father **D.**,	1732
2Ch	6:6	and have chosen **D.** to be over my	1732
2Ch	6:7	it was in the heart of **D.** my father	1732
2Ch	6:8	But the Lord said to **D.** my father	1732
2Ch	6:10	I am risen up in the room of **D.**	1732
2Ch	6:15	which hast kept with thy servant **D.**	1732
2Ch	6:16	keep with thy servant **D.** my father	1732
2Ch	6:17	hast spoken unto thy servant **D.**	1732
2Ch	6:42	remember the mercies of **D.** thy	1732
2Ch	7:6	which **D.** the king had made to	1732
2Ch	7:6	when **D.** praised by their ministry;	1732
2Ch	7:10	that the Lord had shewed unto **D.**,	1732
2Ch	7:17	as **D.** thy father walked, and do	1732
2Ch	7:18	as I have covenanted with **D.** thy	1732
2Ch	8:11	out of the city of **D.** unto the house	1732
2Ch	8:11	shall not dwell in the house of **D.**	1732
2Ch	8:14	according to the order of **D.** his	1732
2Ch	8:14	had **D.** the man of God commanded	1732
2Ch	9:31	he was buried in the city of **D.** his	1732
2Ch	10:16	What portion have we in **D.**? and	1732
2Ch	10:16	now, **D.**, see to thine own house	1732
2Ch	10:19	rebelled against the house of **D.**	1732
2Ch	11:17	years they walked in the way of **D.**	1732
2Ch	11:18	daughter of Jerimoth the son of **D.**	1732
2Ch	12:16	and was buried in the city of **D.**:	1732
2Ch	13:5	kingdom over Israel to **D.** forever,	1732
2Ch	13:6	servant of Solomon the son of **D.**,	1732
2Ch	13:8	in the hand of the sons of **D.**;	1732
2Ch	14:1	they buried him in the city of **D.**:	1732
2Ch	16:14	made for himself in the city of **D.**,	1732
2Ch	17:3	in the first ways of his father **D.**,	1732
2Ch	21:1	with his fathers in the city of **D.**	1732
2Ch	21:7	would not destroy the house of **D.**,	1732
2Ch	21:7	covenant that he had made with **D.**,	1732
2Ch	21:12	saith the Lord God of **D.** thy father,	1732
2Ch	21:20	they buried him in the city of **D.**,	1732
2Ch	23:3	Lord hath said of the sons of **D.**	1732
2Ch	23:18	whom **D.** had distributed in the	1732
2Ch	23:18	singing, as it was ordained by **D.**	1732
2Ch	24:16	in the city of **D.** among the kings,	1732
2Ch	24:25	in the city of **D.**, but they buried	1732
2Ch	27:9	they buried him in the city of **D.**:	1732
2Ch	28:1	of the Lord, like **D.** his father:	1732
2Ch	29:2	according to all that **D.** his father	1732
2Ch	29:25	to the commandment of **D.**, and of	1732
2Ch	29:26	stood with the instruments of **D.**,	1732
2Ch	29:27	the instruments ordained by **D.**	1732
2Ch	29:30	with the words of **D.**, and of Asaph	1732
2Ch	30:26	the time of Solomon the son of **D.**	1732
2Ch	32:5	repaired Millo in the city of **D.**,	1732
2Ch	32:30	to the west side of the city of **D.**	1732
2Ch	32:33	of the sepulchres of the sons of **D.**:	1732
2Ch	33:7	God had said to **D.** and to Solomon	1732
2Ch	33:14	built a wall without the city of **D.**,	1732
2Ch	34:2	walked in the ways of **D.** his father,	1732
2Ch	34:3	began to seek after the God of **D.**	1732
2Ch	35:3	house which Solomon the son of **D.**	1732
2Ch	35:4	according to the writing of **D.**	1732
2Ch	35:15	to the commandment of **D.**, and of	1732
Ezr	3:10	after the ordinance of **D.** king of	1732
Ezr	8:2	of the sons of **D.**; Hattush	1732
Ezr	8:20	of the Nethinims, whom **D.** and	1732
Ne	3:15	that go down from the city of **D.**	1732
Ne	3:16	over against the sepulchres of **D.**,	1732
Ne	12:24	to the commandment of **D.** the man	1732
Ne	12:36	with the musical instruments of **D.**	1732
Ne	12:37	up by the stairs of the city of **D.**,	1732
Ne	12:37	above the house of **D.**, even unto	1732
Ne	12:45	to the commandment of **D.**, and of	1732
Ne	12:46	For in the days of **D.** and Asaph of	1732
Ps	3:*title*	A Psalm of **D.**, when he fled from	1732
Ps	4:*title*	on Neginoth, A Psalm of **D.**	1732
Ps	5:*title*	upon Nehiloth, A Psalm of **D.**	1732
Ps	6:*title*	upon Sheminith, A Psalm of **D.**	1732
Ps	7:*title*	Shiggaion of **D.**, which he sang	1732
Ps	8:*title*	upon Gittith, A Psalm of **D.**	1732
Ps	9:*title*	upon Muth-labben, A Psalm of **D.**	1732
Ps	11:*title*	chief Musician, A Psalm of **D.**	1732
Ps	12:*title*	upon Sheminith, A Psalm of **D.**	1732
Ps	13:*title*	chief Musician, A Psalm of **D.**	1732
Ps	14:*title*	chief Musician, A Psalm of **D.**	1732
Ps	15:*title*	A Psalm of **D.**	1732
Ps	16:*title*	Michtam of **D.**	1732
Ps	17:*title*	A Prayer of **D.**	1732
Ps	18:*title*	A Psalm of **D.**, the servant of the	1732
Ps	18:50	to **D.**, and to his seed forevermore	1732
Ps	19:*title*	chief Musician, A Psalm of **D.**	1732
Ps	20:*title*	chief Musician, A Psalm of **D.**	1732
Ps	21:*title*	chief Musician, A Psalm of **D.**	1732
Ps	22:*title*	Aijeleth Shahar, A Psalm of **D.**	1732
Ps	23:*title*	A Psalm of **D.**	1732
Ps	24:*title*	A Psalm of **D.**	1732
Ps	25:*title*	A Psalm of **D.**	1732
Ps	26:*title*	A Psalm of **D.**	1732
Ps	27:*title*	A Psalm of **D.**	1732
Ps	28:*title*	A Psalm of **D.**	1732
Ps	29:*title*	A Psalm of **D.**	1732
Ps	30:*title*	the dedication of the house of **D.**	1732
Ps	31:*title*	chief Musician, A Psalm of **D.**	1732
Ps	32:*title*	A Psalm of **D.**, Maschil	1732
Ps	34:*title*	A Psalm of **D.**, when he changed	1732
Ps	35:*title*	A Psalm of **D.**	1732
Ps	36:*title*	A Psalm of **D.** the servant of the	1732
Ps	37:*title*	A Psalm of **D.**	1732
Ps	38:*title*	A Psalm of **D.**, to bring to	1732
Ps	39:*title*	even to Jeduthun, A Psalm of **D.**	1732
Ps	40:*title*	chief Musician, A Psalm of **D.**	1732
Ps	41:*title*	chief Musician, A Psalm of **D.**	1732
Ps	51:*title*	A Psalm of **D.**, when Nathan, the	1732
Ps	52:*title*	A Psalm of **D.**, when Doeg the	1732
Ps	52:*title*	**D.** is come to the house of	1732
Ps	53:*title*	Mahalath, Maschil, A Psalm of **D.**	1732
Ps	54:*title*	A Psalm of **D.**, when the Ziphims	1732
Ps	54:*title*	said to Saul, Doth not **D.** hide	1732
Ps	55:*title*	Neginoth, Maschil, A Psalm of **D.**	1732
Ps	56:*title*	Michtam of **D.**, when the	1732
Ps	57:*title*	Michtam of **D.**, when he fled from	1732
Ps	58:*title*	Al-taschith, Michtam of **D.**	1732
Ps	59:*title*	Michtam of **D.**; when Saul sent,	1732
Ps	60:*title*	Michtam of **D.**, to teach; when he	1732
Ps	61:*title*	upon Neginah, A Psalm of **D.**	1732
Ps	62:*title*	to Jeduthun, A Psalm of **D.**	1732
Ps	63:*title*	A Psalm of **D.**, when he was in the	1732
Ps	64:*title*	chief Musician, A Psalm of **D.**	1732
Ps	65:*title*	Musician, A Psalm and Song of **D.**	1732
Ps	68:*title*	Musician, A Psalm or Song of **D.**	1732
Ps	69:*title*	upon Shoshannim, A Psalm of **D.**	1732
Ps	70:*title*	A Psalm of **D.**, to bring to	1732
Ps	72:20	The prayers of **D.** the son of Jesse	1732
Ps	78:70	He chose **D.** also his servant, and	1732
Ps	86:*title*	A Prayer of **D.**	1732
Ps	89:3	I have sworn unto **D.** my servant,	1732
Ps	89:20	I have found **D.** my servant; with	1732
Ps	89:35	that I will not lie unto **D.**	1732
Ps	89:49	which thou swearest unto **D.** in	1732
Ps	101:*title*	A Psalm of **D.**	1732
Ps	103:*title*	A Psalm of **D.**	1732
Ps	108:*title*	A Song or Psalm of **D.**	1732
Ps	109:*title*	chief Musician, A Psalm of **D.**,	1732
Ps	110:*title*	A Psalm of **D.**	1732
Ps	122:*title*	A Song of degrees of **D.**	1732
Ps	122:5	the thrones of the house of **D.**	1732
Ps	124:*title*	A Song of degrees of **D.**,	1732
Ps	131:*title*	A Song of degrees of **D.**	1732
Ps	132:1	Lord, remember **D.**, and all his	1732
Ps	132:11	Lord hath sworn in truth unto **D.**;	1732
Ps	132:17	There will I make the horn of **D.**	1732
Ps	133:*title*	A Song of degrees of **D.**	1732
Ps	138:*title*	A Psalm of **D.**	1732
Ps	139:*title*	chief Musician, A Psalm of **D.**	1732
Ps	140:*title*	chief Musician, A Psalm of **D.**	1732
Ps	141:*title*	A Psalm of **D.**	1732
Ps	142:*title*	Maschil of **D.**; A Prayer when he	1732
Ps	143:*title*	A Psalm of **D.**	1732
Ps	144:*title*	A Psalm of **D.**	1732
Ps	144:10	who delivereth **D.** his servant from	1732
Pr	1:1	Proverbs of Solomon, the son of **D.**,	1732
Ec	1:1	words of the Preacher, the son of **D.**,	1732
Ca	4:4	Thy neck is like the tower of **D.**	1732
Isa	7:2	it was told the house of **D.**, saying,	1732
Isa	7:13	said, Hear ye now, O house of **D.**;	1732
Isa	9:7	upon the throne of **D.**, and upon	1732
Isa	16:5	in truth in the tabernacle of **D.**,	1732
Isa	22:9	the breaches of the city of **D.**,	1732
Isa	22:22	key of the house of **D.** will I lay	1732
Isa	29:1	to Ariel, the city where **D.** dwelt!	1732
Isa	38:5	the Lord, the God of **D.** thy father,	1732
Isa	55:3	even the sure mercies of **D.**	1732
Jer	17:25	sitting upon the throne of **D.**,	1732
Jer	21:12	O house of **D.**, thus saith the Lord;	1732
Jer	22:2	that sittest upon the throne of **D.**,	1732
Jer	22:4	kings sitting upon the throne of **D.**,	1732
Jer	22:30	sitting upon the throne of **D.**, and	1732
Jer	23:5	raise unto **D.** a righteous Branch,	1732
Jer	29:16	that sitteth upon the throne of **D.**,	1732
Jer	30:9	**D.** their king, whom I will raise up	1732
Jer	33:15	righteousness to grow up unto **D.**;	1732
Jer	33:17	**D.** shall never want a man to sit	1732
Jer	33:21	my covenant be broken with **D.**	1732
Jer	33:22	so will I multiply the seed of **D.**	1732
Jer	33:26	seed of Jacob, and **D.** my servant,	1732
Jer	36:30	none to sit upon the throne of **D.**:	1732

Eze 34:23 feed them, even my servant **D.**; 1732
Eze 34:24 servant **D.** a prince among them; 1732
Eze 37:24 **D.** my servant shall be king over 1732
Eze 37:25 my servant **D.** shall be their prince..... 1732
Ho 3:5 Lord their God, and **D.** their king;...... 1732
Am 6:5 instruments of musick, like **D.**; 1732
Am 9:11 will I raise up the tabernacle of **D.** 1732
Zec 12:7 that the glory of the house of **D.**........ 1732
Zec 12:8 them at that day shall be as **D.**;......... 1732
Zec 12:8 the house of **D.** shall be as God,........ 1732
Zec 12:10 I will pour upon the house of **D.**, ... 1732
Zec 12:12 the family of the house of **D.** apart. 1732
Zec 13:1 fountain opened to the house of **D.**..... 1732
Mt 1:1 son of **D.**, the son of Abraham. *1138*
Mt 1:6 Jesse begat **D.** the king; and **D.**........ *1138*
Mt 1:17 generations from Abraham to **D.** *1138*
Mt 1:17 **D.** until the carrying away into.......... *1138*
Mt 1:20 Joseph, thou son of **D.**, fear not to..... *1138*
Mt 9:27 Thou son of **D.**, have mercy on us. *1138*
Mt 12:3 **have ye not read what D. did,** *1138*
Mt 12:23 said, Is not this the son of **D.**? *1138*
Mt 15:22 Lord, thou son of **D.**; my daughter..... *1138*
Mt 20:30, 31 on us, O Lord, thou son of **D.**. *1138*
Mt 21:9 Hosanna to the son of **D.**: Blessed..... *1138*
Mt 21:15 Hosanna to the son of **D.**; they.......... *1138*
Mt 22:42 They say unto him, The son of **D.**.. .... *1138*
Mt 22:43 **How then doth D. in spirit call** *1138*
Mt 22:45 **If D. then call him Lord, how is** ... *1138*
Mk 2:25 **Have ye never read what D. did,** ... *1138*
Mk 10:47 Jesus, thou son of **D.**, have mercy *1138*
Mk 10:48 Thou son of **D.**, have mercy on me. ... *1138*
Mk 11:10 of our father **D.**, that cometh in......... *1138*
Mk 12:35 **that Christ is the son of D.?** *1138*
Mk 12:36 **D. himself said by the Holy Ghost,** .*1138*
Mk 12:37 **D. therefore himself calleth him** ... *1138*
Lu 1:27 was Joseph, of the house of **D.**;......... *1138*
Lu 1:32 him the throne of his father **D.**: *1138*
Lu 1:69 in the house of his servant **D.**; *1138*
Lu 2:4 unto the city of **D.**, which is called *1138*
Lu 2:4 was of the house and lineage of **D.**:)... *1138*
Lu 2:11 is born this day in the city of **D.** *1138*
Lu 3:31 Nathan, which was the son of **D.**, ... *1138*
Lu 6:3 **what D. did, when himself was an.** *1138*
Lu 18:38 Jesus, thou son of **D.**, have mercy *1138*
Lu 18:39 Thou son of **D.**, have mercy on me. *1138*
Lu 20:42 **And D. himself saith in the book...** *1138*
Lu 20:44 **D. therefore calleth him Lord, how** *1138*
Joh 7:42 Christ cometh of the seed of , ... *1138*
Joh 7:42 town of Bethlehem, where **D.** was?.... *1138*
Ac 1:16 the Holy Ghost by the mouth of **D.** *1138*
Ac 2:25 For **D.** speaketh concerning him,......... *1138*
Ac 2:29 speak unto you of the patriarch **D.**, ... *1138*
Ac 2:34 **D.** is not ascended into the heavens:... *1138*
Ac 4:25 Who by the mouth of thy servant **D.**... *1138*
Ac 7:45 of our fathers, unto the days of **D.**; *1138*
Ac 13:22 up unto them **D.** to be their king; *1138*
Ac 13:22 I have found **D.** the son of Jesse, ... *1138*
Ac 13:34 give you the sure mercies of **D.**......... *1138*
Ac 13:36 For **D.**, after he had served his own... *1138*
Ac 15:16 build again the tabernacle of **D.**,......... *1138*
Ro 1:3 which was made of the seed of **D.**....... *1138*
Ro 4:6 **D.** also describeth the blessedness *1138*
Ro 11:9 **D.** saith, Let their table be made *1138*
2Ti 2:8 Jesus Christ of the seed off **D.** *1138*
Heb 4:7 limiteth a certain day, saying in **D.**, ... *1138*
Heb 11:32 **D.** also, and Samuel, and of the......... *1138*
Re 3:7 **he that hath the key of D., he that** *1138*
Re 5:5 Root of **D.**, hath prevailed to open *1138*
Re 22:16 **the root and the offspring of D.,** ... *1138*

DAVID'S

1Sa 18:29 became **D.** enemy continually. 1732
1Sa 19:11 sent messengers unto **D.** house, ... 1732
1Sa 19:11 Michal **D.** wife told him, saying,......... 1732
1Sa 20:16 require it at the hand of **D.** enemies. .. 1732
1Sa 20:25 side, and **D.** place was empty:.......... 1732
1Sa 20:27 month, that **D.** place was empty: 1732
1Sa 23:3 And **D.** men said unto him, Behold, ... 1732
1Sa 24:5 afterward, that **D.** heart smote him,.... 1732
1Sa 25:9 when **D.** young men came, they......... 1732
1Sa 25:10 and Nabal answered **D.** servants, ...
1Sa 25:12 So **D.** young men turned their way,.... 1732
1Sa 25:44 **D.** wife, to Phalti the son of Laish,..... 1732
1Sa 26:17 Saul knew **D.** voice, and said, Is 1732
1Sa 30:5 **D.** two wives were taken captives, ... 1732
1Sa 30:20 cattle, and said, this is **D.** spoil......... 1732
2Sa 2:30 lacked of **D.** servants, nineteen.......... 1732
2Sa 3:5 sixth, Ithream, by Eglah **D.** wife........ 1732
2Sa 5:8 the blind that are hated of **D.** soul,..... 1732
2Sa 8:2 the Moabites became **D.** servants,....... 1732
2Sa 8:14 they of Edom became **D.** servants...... 1732
2Sa 8:18 and **D.** sons were chief rulers........... 1732
2Sa 10:2 **D.** servants came into the land of....... 1732
2Sa 10:4 **D.** servants, and shaved off the one.... 1732
2Sa 12:5 **D.** anger was greatly kindled............ 1732
2Sa 12:30 stones: and it was set on **D.** head. 1732
2Sa 13:3 son of Shimeah **D.** brother: and 1732
2Sa 13:32 of Shimeah **D.** brother, answered....... 1732
2Sa 15:12 the Gilonite, **D.** counseller, from........ 1732
2Sa 15:37 So Hushai **D.** friend came into the...... 1732
2Sa 16:16 Hushai the Archite, **D.** friend, ... 1732
2Sa 19:41 all **D.** men with him, over Jordan? 1732
2Sa 24:10 **D.** heart smote him after that he........ 1732
2Sa 24:11 unto the prophet Gad, **D.** seer, ... 1732
1Ki 1:38 Solomon to ride upon king **D.** mule,.... 1732
1Ki 11:32 one tribe for my servant **D.** sake, ... 1732
1Ki 15:4 for **D.** sake did the Lord his God 1732
2Ki 11:10 give king **D.** spears and shields,......... 1732
2Ki 19:34 sake, and for my servant **D.** sake....... 1732
2Ki 20:6 sake, and for my servant **D.** sake....... 1732
1Ch 18:2 the Moabites became **D.** servants,...... 1732
1Ch 18:6 the Syrians became **D.** servants, ... 1732
1Ch 18:13 the Edomites became **D.** servants. 1732
1Ch 19:4 Wherefore Hanun took **D.** servants..... 1732
1Ch 20:2 in it: and it was set upon **D.** head: 1732
1Ch 20:7 of Shimea **D.** brother slew him. 1732
1Ch 21:9 the Lord spake unto Gad, **D.** seer,..... 1732
1Ch 27:31 the substance which was king **D.**........ 1732
1Ch 27:32 **D.** uncle was a counseller, ... 1732
2Ch 23:9 and shields, that had been king **D.**,..... 1732
Ps 132:10 For thy servant **D.** sake turn not 1732
Ps 145:*title* **D.** Psalm of praise. 1732
Isa 37:35 sake, and for my servant **D.** sake....... 1732
Jer 13:13 kings that sit upon **D.** throne,............ 1732
Lu 20:41 **say they that Christ is D. son?** *1138*

DAWN See also DAWNING.

Mt 28:1 began to **d.** toward the first day......... *2020*
2Pe 1:19 until the day **d.**, and the day star *1306*

DAWNING

Jos 6:15 rose early about the **d.** of the day, ... 5927
Jg 19:26 the woman in the **d.** of the day,......... 6437
Job 3:9 neither let it see the **d.** of the day:..... 6079
Job 7:4 to and fro unto the **d.** of the day......... 5399
Ps 119:147 prevented the **d.** of the morning,........ 5399

DAY See also DAY'S; DAYS; DAYSMAN; DAYSPRING; DAYTIME; HOLYDAY; MIDDAY; NOONDAY; YESTERDAY.

Ge 1:5 God called the light **D.**, and the......... 3117
Ge 1:5 and the morning were the first **d.**......... 3117
Ge 1:8 and the morning were the second **d.**.. 3117
Ge 1:13 and the morning were the third **d.**..... 3117
Ge 1:14 to divide the **d.** from the night;.......... 3117
Ge 1:16 the greater light to rule the **d.**,.......... 3117
Ge 1:18 rule over the **d.** and over the night,.... 3117
Ge 1:19 and the morning were the fourth **d.**.. .. 3117
Ge 1:23 and the morning were the fifth **d.**.. 3117
Ge 1:31 and the morning were the sixth **d.**...... 3117
Ge 2:2 the seventh **d.** God ended his work 3117
Ge 2:2 and he rested on the seventh **d.** 3117
Ge 2:3 God blessed the seventh **d.**, and 3117
Ge 2:4 in the **d.** that the Lord God made....... 3117
Ge 2:17 in the **d.** that thou eatest thereof 3117
Ge 3:5 in the **d.** ye eat thereof, then your 3117
Ge 3:8 the garden in the cool of the **d.**: 3117
Ge 4:14 thou hast driven me out this **d.**.......... 3117
Ge 5:1 In the **d.** that God created man,......... 3117
Ge 5:2 in the **d.** when they were created....... 3117
Ge 7:11 the seventeenth **d.** of the month, ... 3117
Ge 7:11 the same **d.** were all the fountains...... 3117
Ge 7:13 In the selfsame **d.** entered Noah, ... 3117
Ge 8:4 on the seventeenth **d.** of the month, ... 3117
Ge 8:5 on the first *d.* of the month,....................
Ge 8:13 the first **d.** of the month........................
Ge 8:14 seven and twentieth **d.** of the month,.. 3117
Ge 8:22 and **d.** and night shall not cease. 3117
Ge 15:18 same **d.** the Lord made a covenant....... 3117
Ge 17:23 the selfsame **d.**, as God has said........ 3117
Ge 17:26 **d.** was Abraham circumcised, ... 3117
Ge 18:1 the tent door in the heat of the **d.**;..... 3117
Ge 19:37 father of the Moabites unto this **d.**.. ... 3117
Ge 19:38 children of Ammon unto this **d.**.. 3117
Ge 21:8 made a great feast the same **d.**.......... 3117
Ge 21:26 neither yet heard I of it, but to **d.**...... 3117
Ge 22:4 third **d.** Abraham lifted up his eyes, ... 3117
Ge 22:14 as it is said to this **d.**, In the mount.... 3117
Ge 24:12 send me good speed this **d.**, and........ 3117
Ge 24:42 I came this **d.** unto the well, and......... 3117
Ge 25:31 said, Sell me this **d.** thy birthright. 3117
Ge 25:33 Swear to me this **d.**; and he sware..... 3117
Ge 26:32 it came to pass the same **d.**, that....... 3117
Ge 26:33 the city is Beer-sheba unto this **d.**...... 3117
Ge 27:2 I know not the **d.** of my death:.......... 3117
Ge 27:45 deprived also of you both in one **d.**? ... 3117
Ge 29:7 it is yet high **d.**, neither is it time 3117
Ge 30:32 will pass through all thy flock to **d.**, ... 3117
Ge 30:35 he removed that **d.** the he goats........ 3117
Ge 31:22 it was told Laban on the third **d.**........ 3117
Ge 31:39 whether stolen by **d.**, or stolen by...... 3117
Ge 31:40 the **d.** the drought consumed me,........ 3117
Ge 31:43 this **d.** unto these my daughters,......... 3117
Ge 31:48 between me and thee this **d.**............. 3117
Ge 32:24 him until the breaking of the **d.**.......... 7837
Ge 32:26 Let me go, for the **d.** breaketh. 7837
Ge 32:32 hollow of the thigh, unto this **d.**: 3117
Ge 33:13 men should overdrive them one **d.**,..... 3117
Ge 33:16 Esau returned that **d.** on his way 3117
Ge 34:25 it came to pass on the third **d.**, ... 3117
Ge 35:3 answered me in the **d.** of my distress, .3117
Ge 35:20 pillar of Rachel's grave unto this **d.**..... 3117
Ge 39:10 as she spake to Joseph **d.** by **d.**,........ 3117
Ge 40:7 Wherefore look ye so sadly to **d.**? 3117
Ge 40:20 it came to pass the third **d.**, which 3117
Ge 41:9 I do remember my faults this **d.**:......... 3117
Ge 42:13 youngest is this **d.** with our father,..... 3117
Ge 42:18 Joseph said unto them the third **d.**,..... 3117
Ge 42:32 youngest is this **d.** with our father...... 3117
Ge 47:23 bought you this **d.** and your land......... 3117
Ge 47:26 over the land of Egypt unto this **d.**.. ... 3117
Ge 48:15 fed me all my life long unto this **d.**, ... 3117
Ge 48:20 he blessed them that **d.**, saying, ... 3117
Ge 50:20 as it is this **d.**, to save much people ... 3117
Ex 2:13 he went out the second **d.**, behold,..... 3117
Ex 2:18 it that ye are come so soon to **d.**?...... 3117
Ex 5:6 Pharaoh commanded the same **d.** 3117
Ex 5:14 yesterday and to **d.**, as heretofore? 3117
Ex 6:28 the **d.** when the Lord spake unto 3117
Ex 8:22 I will sever in that **d.** the land of........ 3117
Ex 10:6 have seen, since the **d.** that they 3117
Ex 10:6 were upon the earth unto this **d.**........ 3117
Ex 10:13 east wind upon the land all that **d.**, ... 3117
Ex 10:28 in that **d.** thou seest my face thou...... 3117
Ex 12:3 In the tenth **d.** of this month..................
Ex 12:6 fourteenth **d.** of the same month: 3117
Ex 12:14 **d.** shall be unto you for a memorial;.... 3117
Ex 12:15 first **d.** ye shall put away leaven......... 3117
Ex 12:15 the first **d.** until the seventh **d.**,......... 3117
Ex 12:16 in the first **d.** there shall be an holy.... 3117
Ex 12:16 the seventh **d.** there shall be an......... 3117
Ex 12:17 in this selfsame **d.** have I brought....... 3117
Ex 12:17 observe this **d.** in your generations..... 3117
Ex 12:18 fourteenth **d.** of the month at even, ... 3117
Ex 12:18 one and twentieth **d.** of the month..... 3117
Ex 12:41 the selfsame **d.** it came to pass,......... 3117
Ex 12:51 it came to pass the selfsame **d.**,......... 3117
Ex 13:3 Remember this **d.**, in which ye 3117
Ex 13:4 This **d.** came ye out in the month 3117
Ex 13:6 and in the seventh **d.** shall be a 3117
Ex 13:8 thou shalt shew thy son in that **d.**, ... 3117
Ex 13:21 the Lord went before them by **d.**....... 3119
Ex 13:21 them light; to go by **d.** and night:........ 3119
Ex 13:22 the pillar of the cloud by **d.**, nor 3119
Ex 14:13 which he will shew to you to **d.**: 3117
Ex 14:13 Egyptians whom ye have seen to **d.**,... 3117
Ex 14:30 the Lord saved Israel that **d.** out of.... 3117
Ex 16:1 the fifteenth **d.** of the second month ... 3117
Ex 16:4 gather a certain rate every **d.**, that..... 3117
Ex 16:5 on the sixth **d.** they shall prepare 3117
Ex 16:22 on the sixth **d.** they gathered twice 3117
Ex 16:23 bake that which ye will bake to **d.**, ...
Ex 16:25 that to **d.**; for to **d.** is a sabbath.......... 3117
Ex 16:25 to **d.** ye shall not find it in the.......... 3117
Ex 16:26 but on the seventh **d.**, which is the 3117
Ex 16:27 on the seventh **d.** for to gather,......... 3117
Ex 16:29 he giveth you on the sixth **d.** the 3117
Ex 16:29 out of his place on the seventh **d.**.. 3117
Ex 16:30 the people rested on the seventh **d.**.... 3117
Ex 19:1 the same **d.** came they into the 3117
Ex 19:10 sanctify them to **d.** and to morrow...... 3117
Ex 19:11 be ready against the third **d.**: for........ 3117
Ex 19:11 the third **d.** the Lord will come.......... 3117
Ex 19:15 Be ready against the third **d.**: come.... 3117

Ex 19:16 it came to pass on the third **d.** in........3117
Ex 20:8 Remember the sabbath **d.**, to keep......3117
Ex 20:10 But the seventh **d.** is the sabbath........3117
Ex 20:11 rested the seventh **d.**: wherefore........3117
Ex 20:11 the Lord blessed the sabbath **d.**,..........3117
Ex 21:21 if he continue a **d.** or two he shall.......3117
Ex 22:30 on the eighth **d.** thou shalt give it........3117
Ex 23:12 the seventh **d.** thou shalt rest: that.....3117
Ex 24:16 and the seventh **d.** he called unto........3117
Ex 29:36 thou shalt offer every **d.** a bullock.......3117
Ex 29:38 two lambs of the first year **d.** by **d.**.....3117
Ex 31:15 doeth any work in the sabbath **d.**.........3117
Ex 31:17 and on the seventh **d.** he rested,.........3117
Ex 32:28 there fell of the people that **d.**............3117
Ex 32:29 Consecrate yourselves to **d.** to the......3117
Ex 32:29 bestow upon you a blessing this **d.**.......3117
Ex 32:34 nevertheless in the **d.** when I visit......3117
Ex 34:11 that which I command thee this **d.**:.......3117
Ex 34:21 but on the seventh **d.** thou shalt.........3117
Ex 35:2 but on the seventh **d.** there shall be....3117
Ex 35:2 to you an holy **d.**, a sabbath of................
Ex 35:3 habitations upon the sabbath **d.**...........3117
Ex 40:2 On the first **d.** of the first month..........3117
Ex 40:17 second year, on the first **d.** of the............
Ex 40:37 they journeyed not till the **d.** that........3117
Ex 40:38 was upon the tabernacle by **d.**,...........3119
Le 6:5 in the **d.** of his trespass offering.........3119
Le 6:20 Lord in the **d.** when he is anointed;......3119
Le 7:15 eaten the same **d.** that it is offered;.....3119
Le 7:16 the same **d.** that he offereth his..........3119
Le 7:17 the sacrifice on the third **d.** shall be.....3119
Le 7:18 be eaten at all on the third **d.**,...........3119
Le 7:35 in the **d.** when he presented them.......3119
Le 7:36 in the **d.** that he anointed them,..........3119
Le 7:38 in the **d.** that he commanded the.........3119
Le 8:34 As he hath done this **d.**, so the..........3117
Le 8:35 **d.** and night seven days, and keep.........3119
Le 9:1 it came to pass on the eighth **d.**,........3117
Le 9:4 to **d.** the Lord will appear unto you.....3117
Le 10:19 this **d.** have they offered their sin.......3117
Le 10:19 I had eaten the sin offering to **d.**,.........3117
Le 12:3 And in the eighth **d.** the flesh of.........3117
Le 13:5 shall look on him the seventh **d.**:.........3117
Le 13:6 look on him again the seventh **d.**:........3117
Le 13:27 shall look upon him the seventh **d.**:.....3117
Le 13:32, 34 in the seventh **d.** the priest shall.....3117
Le 13:51 on the plague on the seventh **d.**:.........3117
Le 14:2 the leper in the **d.** of his cleansing:.......3117
Le 14:9 it shall be on the seventh **d.**, that........3117
Le 14:10 And on the eighth **d.** he shall take.......3117
Le 14:23 shall bring them on the eighth **d.**..........3117
Le 14:39 shall come again the seventh **d.**,.........3117
Le 15:14 And on the eighth **d.** he shall take.......3117
Le 15:29 And on the eighth **d.** she shall take......3117
Le 16:29 on the tenth **d.** of the month, ye.........3117
Le 16:30 in that **d.** shall the priest make an.......3117
Le 19:6 it shall be eaten the same **d.** ye..........3117
Le 19:6 if ought remain until the third **d.**,.........3117
Le 19:7 if it be eaten at all on the third **d.**,.......3117
Le 22:27 from the eighth **d.** and thenceforth......3117
Le 22:28 it and her young both in one **d.**............3117
Le 22:30 On the same **d.** it shall be eaten up;.....3117
Le 23:3 but the seventh **d.** is the sabbath of.....3117
Le 23:5 In the fourteenth **d.** of the first................
Le 23:6 the fifteenth **d.** of the same month......3117
Le 23:7 In the first **d.** ye shall have an holy......3117
Le 23:8 seventh **d.** is an holy convocation.......3117
Le 23:12 ye shall offer that **d.** when ye wave.....3117
Le 23:14 until the selfsame **d.** that ye have........3117
Le 23:15 from the **d.** that ye brought the..........3117
Le 23:21 shall proclaim on the selfsame **d.**,.........3117
Le 23:24 seventh month in the first **d.** of the.....3117
Le 23:27 Also on the tenth **d.** of this seventh...........
Le 23:27 there shall be a **d.** of atonement:.........3117
Le 23:28 ye shall do no work in that same **d.**:.....3117
Le 23:28 for it is a **d.** of atonement,................3117
Le 23:29 not be afflicted in that same **d.**,..........3117
Le 23:30 doeth any work in that same **d.**,.........3117
Le 23:32 in the ninth **d.** of the month at even,.........
Le 23:34 The fifteenth **d.** of this seventh...........3117
Le 23:35 On the first **d.** shall be an holy...........3117
Le 23:36 on the eighty **d.** shall be an holy.........3117
Le 23:37 every thing upon his **d.**:.....................3117
Le 23:39 in the fifteenth **d.** of the seventh.........3117
Le 23:39 on the first **d.** shall be a sabbath,........3117
Le 23:39 on the eighth **d.** shall be a sabbath......3117
Le 23:40 ye shall take you on the first **d.**..........3117
Le 25:9 the jubile to sound on the tenth **d.**.............
Le 25:9 in the **d.** of atonement shall ye...........3117
Le 27:23 give thine estimation in that **d.**,..........3117
Nu 1:1,18 on the first **d.** of the second month,...........
Nu 3:1 in the **d.** that the Lord spake with.......3117
Nu 3:13 the **d.** that I smote all the firstborn......3117
Nu 6:9 his head in the **d.** of his cleansing,.......3117
Nu 6:9 on the seventh **d.** shall he shave it......3117
Nu 6:10 And on the eighth **d.** he shall bring......3117
Nu 6:11 shall hallow his head that same **d.**........3117
Nu 7:1 to pass on the **d.** that Moses............3117
Nu 7:10 in the **d.** that it was anointed, even.....3117
Nu 7:11 each prince on his **d.**, for the............3117
Nu 7:12 offered his offering the first **d.**...........3117
Nu 7:18 On the second **d.** Nethaneel the son....3117
Nu 7:24 On the third **d.** Eliab the son of..........3117
Nu 7:30 On the fourth **d.** Elizur the son of.......3117
Nu 7:36 On the fifth **d.** Shelumiel the son of.....3117
Nu 7:42 On the sixth **d.** Eliasaph the son of......3117
Nu 7:48 On the seventh **d.** Elishama the son....3117
Nu 7:54 On the eighth **d.** offered Gamaliel........3117
Nu 7:60 On the ninth **d.** Abidan the son of.......3117
Nu 7:66 On the tenth **d.** Ahiezer the son of.......3117
Nu 7:72 On the eleventh **d.** Pagiel the son of....3117
Nu 7:78 On the twelfth **d.** Ahira the son of.......3117
Nu 7:84 in the **d.** when it was anointed,...........3117
Nu 8:17 on the **d.** that I smote every...............3117
Nu 9:3 In the fourteenth **d.** of this month,.......3117
Nu 9:5 the fourteenth **d.** of the first month.....3117
Nu 9:6 not keep the passover on that **d.**:.......3117
Nu 9:6 Moses and before Aaron on that **d.**:.....3117
Nu 9:11 The fourteenth **d.** of the second..........3117
Nu 9:15 And on the **d.** that the tabernacle........3117
Nu 9:16 alway: the cloud covered it by **d.**,.............
Nu 9:21 whether it was by **d.** or by night.........3119
Nu 10:10 Also in the **d.** of your gladness,..........3117
Nu 10:11 the twentieth **d.** of the second.................
Nu 10:34 of the Lord was upon them by **d.**,.........3119
Nu 11:19 Ye shall not eat one **d.**, nor two........3117
Nu 11:32 the people stood up all that **d.**, and......3117
Nu 11:32 all that night, and all the next **d.**,.........3117
Nu 14:14 by **d.** time in a pillar of a cloud,..........3119
Nu 14:34 each **d.** for a year, shall ye bear..........3117
Nu 15:23 the **d.** that the Lord commanded.........3117
Nu 15:32 gathered sticks upon the sabbath **d.**......3117
Nu 19:12 himself with it on the third **d.**,............3117
Nu 19:12 and on the seventh **d.** he shall be........3117
Nu 19:12 he purify not himself the third **d.**,.........3117
Nu 19:12 the seventh **d.** he shall not be...........3117
Nu 19:19 upon the unclean on the third **d.**,.........3117
Nu 19:19 and on the seventh **d.**: and on the.......3117
Nu 19:19 seventh **d.** he shall purify himself,.......3117
Nu 22:30 since I was thine unto this **d.**?............3117
Nu 25:18 the **d.** of the plague for Peor's sake.....3117
Nu 28:3 without spot **d.** by **d.**, for a...............3117
Nu 28:9 And on the sabbath **d.** two lambs of.....3117
Nu 28:16 in the fourteenth **d.** of the first...........3117
Nu 28:17 in the fifteenth **d.** of this month..........3117
Nu 28:18 In the first **d.** shall be an holy............3117
Nu 28:25 And on the seventh **d.** ye shall...........3117
Nu 28:26 Also in the **d.** of the first fruits,..........3117
Nu 29:1 On the first **d.** of the month,..................
Nu 29:1 it is a **d.** of blowing the trumpets........3117
Nu 29:7 on the tenth **d.** of this seventh.................
Nu 29:12 the fifteenth **d.** of the seventh...........3117
Nu 29:17 And on the second **d.** ye shall offer.....3117
Nu 29:20 And on the third **d.** eleven bullocks,....3117
Nu 29:23 And on the fourth **d.** ten bullocks,.....3117
Nu 29:26 And on the fifth **d.** nine bullocks,........3117
Nu 29:29 And on the sixth **d.** eight bullocks,......3117
Nu 29:32 And on the seventh **d.** seven............3117
Nu 29:35 On the eighth **d.** ye shall have a.........3117
Nu 30:5 her in the **d.** that he heareth;............3117
Nu 30:7 at her in the **d.** that he heard it:.........3117
Nu 30:8 her on the **d.** that he heard it;............3117
Nu 30:12 void on the **d.** he heard them;.............3117
Nu 30:14 hold his peace at her from **d.** to **d.**;.....3117
Nu 30:14 at her in the **d.** that he heard them.....3117
Nu 31:19 and your captives on the third **d.**,........3117
Nu 31:19 and on the seventh **d.**.......................3117
Nu 31:24 wash your clothes on the seventh **d.**,...3117
Nu 33:3 the fifteenth **d.** of the first month;.......3117
Nu 33:38 Egypt, in the first **d.** of the fifth..............
De 1:3 on the first **d.** of the month, that.............
De 1:10 are this **d.** as the stars of heaven........3117
De 1:33 should go, and in a cloud by **d.**...........3119
De 1:39 which in that **d.** had no knowledge.......3117
De 2:18 Ar, the coast of Moab, this **d.**:...........3117
De 2:22 in their stead even unto this **d.**:..........3117
De 2:25 This **d.** will I begin to put the dread....3117
De 2:30 thy hand, as appeareth this **d.**............3117
De 3:14 Bashan-havoth-jair, unto this **d.**...........3117
De 4:4 are alive every one of you this **d.**.........3117
De 4:8 which I set before you this **d.**?...........3117
De 4:10 the **d.** that thou stoodest before..........3117
De 4:15 on the **d.** that the Lord spake unto......3117
De 4:20 of inheritance, as ye are this **d.**..........3117
De 4:26 earth to witness against you this **d.**,.....3117
De 4:32 since the **d.** that God created man.......3117
De 4:38 for an inheritance, as it is this **d.**.........3117
De 4:39 Know therefore this **d.**, and..............3117
De 4:40 which I command thee this **d.**, that......3117
De 5:1 which I speak in your ears this **d.**,.......3117
De 5:3 who are all of us here alive this **d.**.......3117
De 5:12 Keep the sabbath **d.** to sanctify it,.......3117
De 5:14 But the seventh **d.** is the sabbath........3117
De 5:15 thee to keep the sabbath **d.**...............3117
De 5:24 we have seen this **d.** that God doth.....3117
De 6:6 which I command thee this **d.**,............3117
De 6:24 preserve us alive, as it is at this **d.**.....3117
De 7:11 command thee this **d.**, to do them.......3117
De 8:1 this **d.** shall ye observe to do, that......3117
De 8:11 which I command thee this **d.**:............3117
De 8:18 unto thy fathers, as, it is this **d.**.........3117
De 8:19 testify against you this **d.** that ye........3117
De 9:1 art to pass over Jordan this **d.**,..........3117
De 9:3 Understand therefore this **d.**, that.......3117
De 9:7 the **d.** that thou didst depart out.........3117
De 9:10 the fire in the **d.** of the assembly........3117
De 9:24 Lord from the **d.** that I knew you.........3117
De 10:4 of the fire in the **d.** of the assembly:....3117
De 10:8 to bless in his name, unto this **d.**.........3117
De 10:13 command thee this **d.** for thy good?.....3117
De 10:15 above all people, as it is this **d.**..........3117
De 11:2 And know ye this **d.**: for I speak not...3117
De 11:4 hath destroyed them unto this **d.**;.........3117
De 11:8 command you this **d.**, that ye may.......3117
De 11:13 command you this **d.**, to love the........3117
De 11:26 I set before you this **d.** a blessing.......3117
De 11:27 God, which I command you this **d.**:.....3117
De 11:28 I command you this **d.**, to go after......3117
De 11:32 which I set before you this **d.**............3117
De 12:8 the things that we do here this **d.**,.......3117
De 13:18 command thee this **d.**, to do that........3117
De 15:5 which I command thee this **d.**.............3117
De 15:15 I command thee this thing to **d.**...........3117
De 16:3 mayest remember the **d.** when...........3117
De 16:4 sacrificedst the first **d.** at even,..........3117
De 16:8 the seventh **d.** shall be a solemn.........3117
De 18:16 in the **d.** of the assembly, saying,.........3117
De 19:9 command thee this **d.**, to love the.......3117
De 20:3 ye approach this **d.** unto battle...........3117
De 21:23 shalt in any wise bury him that **d.**;......3117
De 24:15 his **d.** thou shalt give him his hire,........3117
De 26:3 I profess this **d.** unto the Lord............3117
De 26:16 This **d.** the Lord thy God hath...........3117
De 26:17 the Lord this **d.** to be thy God,..........3117
De 26:18 Lord hath avouched thee this **d.** to......3117
De 27:1 which I command you this **d.**...............3117
De 27:2 on the **d.** when ye shall pass over.......3117
De 27:4 which I command you this **d.**, in.........3117
De 27:9 **d.** thou art become the people of........3117
De 27:10 which I command thee this **d.**.............3117
De 27:11 charged his people the same **d.**,...........3117
De 28:1 thee this **d.**, that the Lord thy God,.....3117
De 28:13 I command thee this **d.**, to observe.....3117
De 28:14 I command thee this **d.**, to the...........3117
De 28:15 which I command thee this **d.**;.............3117
De 28:32 longing for them all the **d.** long:..........3117
De 28:66 thou shalt fear **d.** and night, and.........3119
De 29:4 and ears to hear, unto this **d.**.............3117
De 29:10 Ye stand this **d.** all of you before........3117
De 29:12 thy God maketh with thee this **d.**:.......3117
De 29:13 That he may establish thee to **d.**..........3117
De 29:15 that standeth here with us this **d.**.........3117
De 29:15 that is not here with us this **d.**:..........3117
De 29:18 whose heart turneth away this **d.**.........3117
De 29:28 into another land, as it is this **d.**.........3117
De 30:2 I command thee this **d.**, thou and........3117
De 30:8 which I command thee this **d.**..............3117
De 30:11 I command thee this **d.**, it is not.........3117
De 30:15 I have set before thee this **d.** life.........3117
De 30:16 this **d.** to love the Lord thy God,.........3117
De 30:18 I denounce unto you this **d.**, that ye....3117

De 30:19 heaven and earth to record this **d.**...3117
De 31:2 and twenty years old this **d.**;...3117
De 31:17 kindled against them in that **d.**,...3117
De 31:17 so that they will say in that **d.**,...3117
De 31:18 I will surely hide my face in that **d.**...3117
De 31:22 wrote this song the same **d.**,...3117
De 31:27 I am yet alive with you this **d.**,...3117
De 32:35 the **d.** of their calamity is at hand,...3117
De 32:46 I testify among you this **d.**, which...3117
De 32:48 spake unto Moses that selfsame **d.**,...3117
De 33:12 shall cover him all the **d.** long,...3117
De 34:6 of his sepulchre unto this **d.**...3117
Jos 1:8 meditate therein **d.** and night,...3119
Jos 3:7 **d.** will I begin to magnify thee...3117
Jos 4:9 and they are there unto this **d.**...3117
Jos 4:14 that **d.** the Lord magnified Joshua...3117
Jos 4:19 on the tenth **d.** of the first month,...
Jos 5:9 This **d.** have I rolled away the...3117
Jos 5:9 place is called Gilgal unto this **d.**...3117
Jos 5:10 on the fourteenth **d.** of the month...3117
Jos 5:11 parched corn in the selfsame **d.**...3117
Jos 6:4 and the seventh **d.** ye shall compass...3117
Jos 6:10 mouth, until the **d.** I bid you shout;...3117
Jos 6:14 the second **d.** they compassed the...3117
Jos 6:15 it came to pass on the seventh **d.**,...3117
Jos 6:15 about the dawning of the **d.**,...7837
Jos 6:15 that **d.** they compassed the city...3117
Jos 6:25 even unto this **d.**; because she hid...3117
Jos 7:25 the Lord shall trouble thee this **d.**...3117
Jos 7:26 a great heap of stones unto this **d.**...3117
Jos 7:26 The valley of Achor, unto this **d.**...3117
Jos 8:25 all that fell that **d.**, both of men...3117
Jos 8:28 ever, even a desolation unto this **d.**...3117
Jos 8:29 stones, that remaineth unto this **d.**...3117
Jos 9:12 on the **d.** we came forth to go unto...3117
Jos 9:17 unto their cities on the third **d.**...3117
Jos 9:27 Joshua made them that **d.** hewers...3117
Jos 9:27 of the Lord, even unto this **d.**,...3117
Jos 10:12 in the **d.** when the Lord delivered...3117
Jos 10:13 not to go down about a whole **d.**...3117
Jos 10:14 no **d.** like that before it or after it,...3117
Jos 10:27 which remain until this very **d.**...3117
Jos 10:28 that **d.** Joshua took Makkedah,...3117
Jos 10:32 it on the second **d.**, and smote it...3117
Jos 10:35 they took it on that **d.**, and smote it...3117
Jos 10:35 therein he utterly destroyed that **d.**,...3117
Jos 13:13 among the Israelites until this **d.**...3117
Jos 14:9 Moses sware on that **d.**, saying,...3117
Jos 14:10 this **d.** fourscore and five years old...3117
Jos 14:11 **d.** as I was in the **d.** that Moses sent..3117
Jos 14:12 the Lord spake in that **d.**;...3117
Jos 14:12 for thou heardest in that **d.**...3117
Jos 14:14 unto this **d.**, because that he wholly...3117
Jos 15:63 of Judah at Jerusalem unto this **d.**...3117
Jos 16:10 this **d.**, and serve under tribute...3117
Jos 22:3 these many days unto this **d.**,...3117
Jos 22:16 to turn away this **d.** from following...3117
Jos 22:16 rebel this **d.** against the Lord...3117
Jos 22:17 we are not cleansed until this **d.**,...3117
Jos 22:18 ye must turn away this **d.** from...3117
Jos 22:18 and it will be, seeing ye rebel to **d.**...3117
Jos 22:22 the Lord, (save us not this **d.**,)...3117
Jos 22:29 this **d.** from following the Lord,...3117
Jos 22:31 This **d.** we perceive that the Lord...3117
Jos 23:8 as ye have done unto this **d.**...3117
Jos 23:9 stand before you unto this **d.**...3117
Jos 23:14 this **d.** I am going the way of all...3117
Jos 24:15 choose you this **d.** whom ye will...3117
Jos 24:25 a covenant with the people that **d.**,...3117
Jg 1:21 in Jerusalem unto this **d.**,...3117
Jg 1:26 is the name thereof unto this **d.**...3117
Jg 3:30 So Moab was subdued that **d.**...3117
Jg 4:14 this is the **d.** in which the Lord...3117
Jg 4:23 God subdued on that **d.** Jabin the...3117
Jg 5:1 son of Abinoam on that **d.**, saying,...3117
Jg 6:24 unto this **d.** it is yet in Ophrah...3117
Jg 6:27 could not do it by **d.**, that he did...3119
Jg 6:32 that **d.** he called him Jerubbaal,...3117
Jg 9:18 against my father's house this **d.**,...3117
Jg 9:19 his house this **d.**, then rejoice ye...3117
Jg 9:45 fought against the city all that **d.**;...3117
Jg 10:4 are called Havoth-jair unto this **d.**,...3117
Jg 10:15 us only, we pray thee, this **d.**...3117
Jg 11:27 the Judge be judge this **d.** between...3117
Jg 12:3 are ye come up unto me this **d.**,...3117
Jg 13:7 the womb to the **d.** of his death...3117
Jg 13:10 that came unto me the other **d.**...3117
Jg 14:15 the seventh **d.**, that they said unto...3117
Jg 14:17 it came to pass on the seventh **d.**,...3117
Jg 14:18 said unto him on the seventh **d.**...3117
Jg 15:19 which is in Lehi unto this **d.**...3117
Jg 16:2 when it is **d.**, we shall kill him...1242
Jg 18:1 that **d.** all their inheritance had...3117
Jg 18:12 Mahaneh-dan unto this **d.**: behold,...3117
Jg 18:30 the **d.** of the captivity of the land...3117
Jg 19:5 it came to pass on the fourth **d.**,...3117
Jg 19:8 morning on the fifth **d.** to depart:...3117
Jg 19:9 the **d.** draweth toward evening, I...3117
Jg 19:9 behold, the **d.** groweth to an end,...3117
Jg 19:11 **d.** was far spent; and the servant...3117
Jg 19:25 when the **d.** began to spring, they...7837
Jg 19:26 dawning of the **d.**, and fell down...1242
Jg 19:30 the **d.** that the children of Israel...3117
Jg 19:30 of the land of Egypt unto this **d.**:...3117
Jg 20:21 **d.** twenty and two thousand men...3117
Jg 20:22 put themselves in array the first **d.**...3117
Jg 20:24 children of Benjamin the second **d.**...3117
Jg 20:25 them but of Gibeah the second **d.**,...3117
Jg 20:26 fasted that **d.** until even, and...3117
Jg 20:30 of Benjamin on the third **d.**,...3117
Jg 20:35 that **d.** twenty and five thousand...3117
Jg 20:46 all which fell that **d.** of Benjamin...3117
Jg 21:3 should be to **d.** one tribe lacking...3117
Jg 21:6 one tribe cut off from Israel this **d.**...3117
Ru 2:19 Where hast thou gleaned to **d.**?...3117
Ru 2:19 name with whom I wrought to **d.** is...3117
Ru 3:18 he hath finished the thing this **d.**:...3117
Ru 4:5 What **d.** thou buyest the field of...3117
Ru 4:9 witnesses this **d.**, that I have...3117
Ru 4:10 this place: ye are witnesses this **d.**...3117
Ru 4:14 which hath not left thee this **d.**...3117
1Sa 2:34 one **d.** they shall die both of them...3117
1Sa 3:12 In that **d.** I will perform against Eli...3117
1Sa 4:3 the Lord smitten us to **d.** before the...3117
1Sa 4:12 came to Shiloh the same **d.** with his...3117
1Sa 4:16 I fled to **d.** out of the army...3117
1Sa 5:5 of Dagon in Ashdod unto this **d.**...3117
1Sa 6:15 sacrifices the same **d.** unto the Lord...3117
1Sa 6:16 they returned to Ekron the same **d.**...3117
1Sa 6:18 unto this **d.** in the field of Joshua,...3117
1Sa 7:6 and fasted on that **d.**,...3117
1Sa 7:10 a great thunder on that **d.**...3117
1Sa 8:8 since the **d.** that I brought them up...3117
1Sa 8:8 out of Egypt even unto this **d.**,...3117
1Sa 8:18 ye shall cry out in that **d.** because...3117
1Sa 8:18 Lord will not hear you in that **d.**...3117
1Sa 9:12 he came to **d.** to the city; for there...3117
1Sa 9:12 a sacrifice of the people to **d.**...3117
1Sa 9:15 in his ear a **d.** before Saul came,...3117
1Sa 9:19 ye shall eat with me to **d.**,...3117
1Sa 9:24 Saul did eat with Samuel that **d.**...3117
1Sa 9:26 about the spring of the **d.**, that...7837
1Sa 10:2 art departed from me to **d.**, then...3117
1Sa 10:9 those signs came to pass that **d.**...3117
1Sa 10:19 ye have this **d.** rejected your God,...3117
1Sa 11:11 Ammonites until the heat of the **d.**:...3117
1Sa 11:13 not a man be put to death this **d.**:...3117
1Sa 11:13 for to **d.** the Lord hath wrought...3117
1Sa 12:2 you from my childhood unto this **d.**...3117
1Sa 12:5 his anointed is witness this **d.**, that...3117
1Sa 12:17 Is it not wheat harvest to **d.**?...3117
1Sa 12:18 Lord sent thunder and rain that **d.**:...3117
1Sa 13:22 it came to pass in the **d.** of battle,...3117
1Sa 14:1 it came to pass upon a **d.**,...3117
1Sa 14:23 the Lord saved Israel that **d.**:...3117
1Sa 14:24 of Israel were distressed that **d.**:...3117
1Sa 14:28 man that eateth any food this **d.**...3117
1Sa 14:30 the people had eateth any food this **d.**..3117
1Sa 14:31 they smote the Philistines that **d.**...3117
1Sa 14:33 roll a great stone unto me this **d.**...3117
1Sa 14:37 he answered him not that **d.**...3117
1Sa 14:38 wherein this sin hath been this **d.**...3117
1Sa 14:45 he hath wrought with God this **d.**...3117
1Sa 15:28 kingdom of Israel from thee this **d.**,...3117
1Sa 15:35 to see Saul until the **d.** of his death:...3117
1Sa 16:13 upon David from the **d.** forward...3117
1Sa 17:10 I defy the armies of Israel this **d.**;...3117
1Sa 17:46 This **d.** will the Lord deliver thee...3117
1Sa 17:46 this **d.** unto the fowls of the air,...3117
1Sa 18:2 Saul took him that **d.**, and would...3117
1Sa 18:9 Saul eyed David from that **d.** and...3117
1Sa 18:21 Thou shalt this **d.** be my son in law...3117
1Sa 19:24 lay down naked all that **d.** and all...3117
1Sa 20:5 in the field unto the third **d.** at even...
1Sa 20:12 to morrow any time, or the third **d.**,...
1Sa 20:26 Saul spake not any thing that **d.**:...3117
1Sa 20:27 was the second **d.** of the month,...
1Sa 20:27 neither yesterday, nor to **d.**?...3117
1Sa 20:34 meat the second **d.** of the month,...3117
1Sa 21:5 though it were sanctified this **d.**...3117
1Sa 21:6 in the **d.** when it was taken away...3117
1Sa 21:7 servants of Saul was there that **d.**,...3117
1Sa 21:10 fled that **d.** for fear of Saul,...3117
1Sa 22:8, 13 me, to lie in wait, as at this **d.**?...3117
1Sa 22:18 slew on that **d.** fourscore and five...3117
1Sa 22:22 I knew it that **d.**, when Doeg the...3117
1Sa 23:14 Saul sought him every **d.**, but God...3117
1Sa 24:4 Behold the **d.** of which the Lord...3117
1Sa 24:10 this **d.** thine eyes have seen how...3117
1Sa 24:10 the Lord had delivered thee to **d.**...3117
1Sa 24:18 thou hast shewed this **d.** how that...3117
1Sa 24:19 that thou hast done unto me this **d.**...3117
1Sa 25:8 we come in a good **d.**: give, I pray...3117
1Sa 25:16 both by night and **d.**, all the while...3119
1Sa 25:32 sent thee this **d.** to meet me:...3117
1Sa 25:33 which hast kept me this **d.** from...3117
1Sa 26:8 enemy into thine hand this **d.**:...3117
1Sa 26:10 his **d.** shall come to die;...3117
1Sa 26:19 they have driven me out this **d.**...3117
1Sa 26:21 was precious in thine eyes this **d.**:...3117
1Sa 26:23 delivered thee into my hand to **d.**,...3117
1Sa 26:24 thy life was much set by this **d.**...3117
1Sa 27:1 I shall now perish one **d.** by the...3117
1Sa 27:6 Achish gave him Ziklag that **d.**:...3117
1Sa 27:6 the kings of Judah unto this **d.**...3117
1Sa 27:10 Whither have ye made a road to **d.**?...3117
1Sa 28:18 done this thing unto thee this **d.**...3117
1Sa 28:20 he had eaten no bread all the **d.**,...3117
1Sa 29:3 since he fell unto me unto this **d.**?...3117
1Sa 29:6 **d.** of thy coming...unto this **d.**:...3117
1Sa 29:8 I have been with thee unto this **d.**,...3117
1Sa 30:1 were come to Ziklag on the third **d.**,...3117
1Sa 30:17 unto the evening of the next **d.**:...4283
1Sa 30:25 it was so from that **d.** forward,...3117
1Sa 30:25 an ordinance for Israel unto this **d.**...3117
1Sa 31:6 all his men, that same **d.** together...3117
2Sa 1:2 came even to pass on the third **d.**,...3117
2Sa 2:17 was a very sore battle that **d.**;...3117
2Sa 2:32 they came to Hebron at break of **d.**...215
2Sa 3:8 shew kindness this **d.** unto the...3117
2Sa 3:8 thou chargest me to **d.** with a fault...3117
2Sa 3:35 eat meat while it was yet **d.**,...3117
2Sa 3:37 all Israel understood that **d.** that it...3117
2Sa 3:38 great man fallen this **d.** in Israel?...3117
2Sa 3:39 I am this **d.** weak, though anointed...3117
2Sa 4:3 were sojourners there until this **d.**.)...3117
2Sa 4:5 about the heat of the **d.** to the...3117
2Sa 4:8 avenged my lord the king this **d.**...3117
2Sa 5:8 David said on that **d.**, Whosoever...3117
2Sa 6:8 of the place Perez-uzzah to this **d.**...3117
2Sa 6:9 was afraid of the Lord that **d.**,...3117
2Sa 6:20 glorious was the king of Israel to **d.**,...3117
2Sa 6:20 who uncovered himself to **d.**...3117
2Sa 6:23 no child unto the **d.** of her death...3117
2Sa 7:6 even to this **d.**, but have walked in...3117
2Sa 11:12 Tarry here to **d.** also, and to...3117
2Sa 11:12 Uriah abode in Jerusalem that **d.**,...3117
2Sa 12:18 it came to pass on the seventh **d.**,...3117
2Sa 13:4 the king's son, lean from **d.** to **d.**?...1242
2Sa 13:32 from the **d.** that he forced his sister...3117
2Sa 13:37 David mourned for his son every **d.**...3117
2Sa 14:22 **d.** thy servant knoweth that I have...3117
2Sa 15:20 should I this **d.** make thee go up...3117
2Sa 16:3 To **d.** shall the house of Israel...3117
2Sa 16:12 me good for his cursing this **d.**...3117
2Sa 18:7 was there a great slaughter that **d.**...3117
2Sa 18:8 wood devoured more people that **d.**...3117
2Sa 18:18 unto this **d.**, Absalom's place...3117
2Sa 18:20 Thou shalt not bear tidings this **d.**,...3117
2Sa 18:20 thou shalt bear tidings another **d.**:...3117
2Sa 18:20 this **d.** thou shalt bear no tidings,...3117
2Sa 18:31 the Lord hath avenged thee this **d.**...3117
2Sa 19:2 the victory that **d.** was turned into...3117
2Sa 19:2 for the people heard say that **d.**...3117
2Sa 19:3 people gat them by stealth that **d.**...3117
2Sa 19:5 shamed this **d.** the faces of all thy...3117
2Sa 19:5 which this **d.** have saved thy life,...3117
2Sa 19:6 thou hast declared this **d.**, that...3117
2Sa 19:6 this **d.** I perceive, that if Absalom...3117
2Sa 19:6 lived, and all we had died this **d.**,...3117
2Sa 19:19 the **d.** that my lord the king went...3117

Book	Ref	Text	No.
2Sa	19:20	I am come the first this **d.**	3117
2Sa	19:22	ye should this **d.** be adversaries	3117
2Sa	19:22	put to death this **d.** in Israel? for do	3117
2Sa	19:22	not I know that I am this **d.** king	3117
2Sa	19:24	from the **d.** the king departed until	3117
2Sa	19:24	the **d.** he came again in peace.	3117
2Sa	19:35	I am this **d.** fourscore years old:	3117
2Sa	20:3	shut up unto the **d.** of their death,	3117
2Sa	21:10	of the air to rest on them by **d.**,	3119
2Sa	22:1	the **d.** that the Lord had delivered	3117
2Sa	22:19	me in the **d.** of my calamity:	3117
2Sa	23:10	wrought a great victory that **d.**;	3117
2Sa	24:18	Gad came that **d.** to David, and	3117
1Ki	1:25	gone down this **d.**, and hath slain	3117
1Ki	1:30	so will I certainly do this **d.**	3117
1Ki	1:48	one to sit on my throne this **d.**,	3117
1Ki	1:51	king Solomon swear unto me to **d.**	3117
1Ki	2:8	the **d.** when I went to Mahanaim:	3117
1Ki	2:24	shall be put to death this **d.**.	3117
1Ki	2:37	the **d.** thou goest out, and passest	3117
1Ki	2:42	the **d.** thou goest out, and walkest	3117
1Ki	3:6	to sit on his throne, as it is this **d.**.	3117
1Ki	3:18	came to pass the third **d.** after that	3117
1Ki	4:22	Solomon's provision for one **d.** was	3117
1Ki	5:7	Blessed be the Lord this **d.**, which	3117
1Ki	8:8	and there they are unto this **d.**.	3117
1Ki	8:16	Since the **d.** that I brought forth	3117
1Ki	8:24	with thine hand, as it is this **d.**.	3117
1Ki	8:28	servant prayeth before thee to **d.**:	3117
1Ki	8:29	toward this house night and **d.**,	3117
1Ki	8:59	the Lord our God **d.** and night,	3119
1Ki	8:61	his commandments, as at this **d.**.	3117
1Ki	8:64	The same **d.** did the king hallow	3117
1Ki	8:66	eighth **d.** he sent the people away:	3117
1Ki	9:13	the land of Cabul unto this **d.**.	3117
1Ki	9:21	tribute of bondservice unto this **d.**.	3117
1Ki	10:12	trees, nor were seen unto this **d.**.	3117
1Ki	12:7	servant unto this people this **d.**,	3117
1Ki	12:12	came to Rehoboam the third **d.**,	3117
1Ki	12:12	Come to me again the third **d.**.	3117
1Ki	12:19	the house of David unto this **d.**.	3117
1Ki	12:32	the fifteenth **d.** of the month, like	3117
1Ki	12:33	fifteenth **d.** of the eighth month,	3117
1Ki	13:3	he gave a sign the same **d.**,	3117
1Ki	13:11	the man of God had done that **d.**	3117
1Ki	14:14	off the house of Jeroboam that **d.**:	3117
1Ki	16:16	over Israel that **d.** in the camp.	3117
1Ki	17:14	**d.** that the Lord sendeth rain	3117
1Ki	18:15	surely shew thyself unto him to **d.**	3117
1Ki	18:36	known this **d.** that thou art God	3117
1Ki	20:13	deliver it into thine hand this **d.**;	3117
1Ki	20:29	seventh **d.** the battle was joined:	3117
1Ki	20:29	thousand footmen in one **d.**.	3117
1Ki	22:5	at the word of the Lord to **d.**.	3117
1Ki	22:25	thou shalt see in that **d.**, when thou	3117
1Ki	22:35	the battle increased that **d.**: and	3117
2Ki	2:3, 5	thy master from thy head to **d.**?	3117
2Ki	2:22	the waters were healed unto this **d.**	3117
2Ki	4:8	it fell on a **d.**, that Elisha passed to	3117
2Ki	4:11	it fell on a **d.**, that he came thither,	3117
2Ki	4:18	it fell on a **d.**, that he went out	3117
2Ki	4:23	Wherefore wilt thou go to him to **d.**?	3117
2Ki	6:28	thy son, that we may eat him to **d.**,	3117
2Ki	6:29	I said unto her on the next **d.**,	3117
2Ki	6:31	Shaphat shall stand on him this **d.**	3117
2Ki	7:9	this **d.** is a **d.** of good tidings,	3117
2Ki	8:6	since the **d.** that she left the land,	3117
2Ki	8:22	the hand of Judah unto this **d.**	3117
2Ki	10:27	it a draught house unto this **d.**	3117
2Ki	14:7	name of it Joktheel unto this **d.**	3117
2Ki	15:5	was a leper unto the **d.** of his death,	3117
2Ki	16:6	Elath, and dwelt there unto this **d.**.	3117
2Ki	17:23	own land to Assyria unto this **d.**	3117
2Ki	17:34	this **d.** they do after the former	3117
2Ki	17:41	fathers, so do they unto this **d.**	3117
2Ki	19:3	This **d.** is a **d.** of trouble,	3117
2Ki	20:5	on the third **d.** thou shalt go up	3117
2Ki	20:8	the house of the Lord the third **d.**?	3117
2Ki	20:17	laid up in store unto this **d.**,	3117
2Ki	21:15	the **d.** their fathers came forth out	3117
2Ki	21:15	of Egypt, even unto this **d.**.	3117
2Ki	25:1	month, in the tenth **d.** of the month,	
2Ki	25:3	**d.** of the fourth month of famine	
2Ki	25:8	on the seventh **d.** of the month	
2Ki	25:27	seven and twentieth **d.** of the month.	
2Ki	25:30	daily rate for every **d.**, all the days	3117
1Ch	4:41	destroyed them utterly unto this **d.**,	3117
1Ch	4:43	and dwelt there unto this **d.**.	3117
1Ch	5:26	to the river Gozan, unto this **d.**.	3117
1Ch	9:33	in that work **d.** and night.	3119
1Ch	11:22	slew a lion in a pit in a snowy **d.**	3117
1Ch	12:22	**d.** by **d.** there came to David to	3117
1Ch	13:11	place is called Perez-uzza to this **d.**.	3117
1Ch	13:12	David was afraid of God that **d.**,	3117
1Ch	16:7	**d.** David delivered first this psalm	3117
1Ch	16:23	forth from **d.** to **d.** his salvation.	3117
1Ch	17:5	dwelt in an house since the **d.** that	3117
1Ch	17:5	I brought up Israel unto this **d.**;	3117
1Ch	26:17	Levites northward four a **d.**,	3117
1Ch	26:17	southward four a **d.**, and toward	3117
1Ch	28:7	and my judgments, as at this **d.**.	3117
1Ch	29:5	his service this **d.** unto the Lord?	3117
1Ch	29:21	on the morrow after that **d.**, even a	3117
1Ch	29:22	drink before the Lord on that **d.**	3117
2Ch	3:2	began to build in the second **d.** of	
2Ch	5:9	And there it is unto this **d.**.	3117
2Ch	6:5	since the **d.** that I brought forth	3117
2Ch	6:15	with thine hand, as it is this **d.**.	3117
2Ch	6:20	open upon this house **d.** and night,	3119
2Ch	7:9	**d.** they made a solemn assembly:	3117
2Ch	7:10	And on the three and twentieth **d.**	3117
2Ch	8:8	make to pay tribute until this **d.**	3117
2Ch	8:13	Even after a certain rate every **d.**,	3117
2Ch	8:14	as the duty of every **d.** required:	3117
2Ch	8:16	**d.** of the foundation of the house of	3117
2Ch	10:12	came to Rehoboam on the third **d.**,	3117
2Ch	10:12	Come again to me on the third **d.**	3117
2Ch	10:19	the house of David unto this **d.**	3117
2Ch	18:4	at the word of the Lord to **d.**.	3117
2Ch	18:24	thou shalt see on that **d.** when	3117
2Ch	18:34	battle increased that **d.**: howbeit	3117
2Ch	20:26	on the fourth **d.** they assembled	3117
2Ch	20:26	valley of Berachah, unto this **d.**	3117
2Ch	21:10	the hand of Judah unto this **d.**.	3117
2Ch	21:15	by reason of the sickness **d.** by **d.**	3117
2Ch	24:11	they did **d.** by **d.**, and gathered	3117
2Ch	26:21	the **d.** of his death, and dwelt in a	3117
2Ch	28:6	twenty thousand in one **d.**, which	3117
2Ch	29:17	on the first **d.** of the first month	
2Ch	29:17	and on the eighth **d.** of the month	
2Ch	29:17	in the sixteenth **d.** of the first month	
2Ch	30:15	fourteenth **d.** of the second month:	
2Ch	30:21	priests praised the Lord **d.** by **d.**,	3117
2Ch	35:1	the fourteenth **d.** of the first month.	
2Ch	35:16	Lord was prepared the same **d.**,	3117
2Ch	35:21	I come not against thee this **d.**,	3117
2Ch	35:25	their lamentations to this **d.**, and	3117
Ezr	3:4	as the duty of every **d.** required;	3117
Ezr	3:6	the first **d.** of the seventh month	3117
Ezr	6:9	let it be given them **d.** by **d.**	3118
Ezr	6:15	finished on the third **d.** of the month	3118
Ezr	6:19	the fourteenth **d.** of the first month.	
Ezr	7:9	upon the first **d.** of the first month	
Ezr	7:9	on the first **d.** of the fifth month	
Ezr	8:31	river of Ahava on the twelfth **d.** of	
Ezr	8:33	fourth **d.** was the silver and the	3117
Ezr	9:7	a great trespass unto this **d.**; and	3117
Ezr	9:7	to confusion of face, as it is this **d.**.	3117
Ezr	9:15	remain yet escaped, as it is this **d.**:	3117
Ezr	10:9	on the twentieth **d.** of the month;	
Ezr	10:13	work of one **d.** or two: for we are	3117
Ezr	10:16	in the first **d.** of the tenth month	3117
Ezr	10:17	by the first **d.** of the first month.	3117
Ne	1:6	pray before thee now, **d.** and night,	3119
Ne	1:11	I pray thee, thy servant this **d.**,	3117
Ne	4:2	will they make an end in a **d.**?	3117
Ne	4:9	watch against them **d.** and night,	3119
Ne	4:22	guard to us, and labour on the **d.**.	3117
Ne	5:11	I pray you, to them, even this **d.**,	3117
Ne	6:15	twenty and fifth **d.** of the month	
Ne	8:2	the first **d.** of the seventh month	3117
Ne	8:9	**d.** is holy unto the Lord your God;	3117
Ne	8:10	this **d.** is holy unto our Lord:	3117
Ne	8:11	Hold your peace, for the **d.** is holy;	3117
Ne	8:13	And on the second **d.** were gathered	3117
Ne	8:17	**d.** had not the children of Israel	3117
Ne	8:18	Also **d.** by **d.**, from the first	3117
Ne	8:18	**d.** unto the last **d.**,	3117
Ne	8:18	and on the eighth **d.** was a solemn	3117
Ne	9:1	Now in the twenty and fourth **d.**	3117
Ne	9:3	one fourth part of the **d.**;	3117
Ne	9:10	get thee a name, as it is this **d.**.	3117
Ne	9:12	them in the **d.** by a cloudy pillar;	3119
Ne	9:19	departed not from them by **d.**,	3119
Ne	9:32	the kings of Assyria unto this **d.**.	3117
Ne	9:36	Behold, we are servants this **d.**,	3117
Ne	10:31	victuals on the sabbath **d.** to sell,	3117
Ne	10:31	on the sabbath, or on the holy **d.**:	3117
Ne	11:23	for the singers, due for every **d.**.	3117
Ne	12:43	that **d.** they offered great sacrifices,	3117
Ne	12:47	the porters, every **d.** his portion:	3117
Ne	13:1	On that **d.** they read in the book	3117
Ne	13:15	into Jerusalem on the sabbath **d.**:	3117
Ne	13:15	in the **d.** wherein they sold victuals	3117
Ne	13:17	ye do, and profane the sabbath **d.**?	3117
Ne	13:19	be brought in on the sabbath **d.**.	3117
Ne	13:22	gates, to sanctify the sabbath **d.**.	3117
Es	1:10	**d.**, when the heart of the king	3117
Es	1:18	of Persia and Media say this **d.**	3117
Es	2:11	Mordecai walked every **d.** before	3117
Es	3:7	**d.** to **d.**, and from month to month,	3117
Es	3:12	thirteenth **d.** of the first month,	3117
Es	3:13	one **d.**, even upon the thirteenth **d.**	3117
Es	3:14	should be ready against that **d.**.	3117
Es	4:16	nor drink three days, night or **d.**:	3117
Es	5:1	it came to pass on the third **d.**,	3117
Es	5:4	the king and Haman come this **d.**	3117
Es	5:9	Then went Haman forth that **d.**	3117
Es	7:2	again unto Esther on the second **d.**	3117
Es	8:1	On that **d.** did the king Ahasuerus	3117
Es	8:9	the three and twentieth **d.** thereof:	
Es	8:12	Upon one **d.** in all the provinces	3117
Es	8:12	upon the thirteenth **d.** of the twelfth	
Es	8:13	should be ready against that **d.**	3117
Es	8:17	gladness, a feast and a good **d.**.	3117
Es	9:1	on the thirteenth **d.** of the same,	3117
Es	9:1	the **d.** that the enemies of the Jews	3117
Es	9:11	On that **d.** the number of those that	3117
Es	9:15	together on the fourteenth **d.**	3117
Es	9:17	On the thirteenth **d.** of the month	3117
Es	9:17	on the fourteenth **d.** of the same	
Es	9:17	and made it a **d.** of feasting and	3117
Es	9:18	on the thirteenth **d.** thereof,	
Es	9:18	the fifteenth **d.** of the same they	
Es	9:18	made it a **d.** of feasting and	3117
Es	9:19	the fourteenth **d.** of the month Adar,	3117
Es	9:19	month Adar a **d.** of gladness and	
Es	9:19	and feasting, and a good **d.**,	3117
Es	9:21	the fourteenth **d.** of the month Adar,	3117
Es	9:21	and the fifteenth **d.** of the same,	3117
Es	9:22	from mourning into a good **d.**: that	3117
Job	1:4	in their houses, every one his **d.**;	3117
Job	1:6	Now there was a **d.** when the sons of	3117
Job	1:13	there was a **d.** when his sons and	3117
Job	2:1	Again there was a **d.** when the sons	3117
Job	3:1	Job his mouth, and cursed his **d.**.	3117
Job	3:3	Let the **d.** perish wherein I was	3117
Job	3:4	Let that **d.** be darkness; let not	3117
Job	3:5	let the blackness of the **d.** terrify it.	3117
Job	3:8	Let them curse it that curse the **d.**,	3117
Job	3:9	let it see the dawning of the **d.**:	7837
Job	7:4	and fro unto the dawning of the **d.**	5399
Job	14:6	accomplish, as an hireling, his **d.**.	3117
Job	15:23	the **d.** of darkness is ready at his	3117
Job	17:12	They change the night into **d.**: the	3117
Job	18:20	shall be astonished at his **d.**, as they	3117
Job	19:25	stand at the latter **d.** upon the	
Job	20:28	flow away the **d.** of his wrath.	3117
Job	21:30	to the **d.** of destruction? they shall	3117
Job	21:30	brought forth to the **d.** of wrath.	3117
Job	23:2	Even to **d.** is my complaint bitter:	3117
Job	26:10	until the **d.** and night come to an	216
Job	38:23	against the **d.** of battle and war?	3117
Ps	1:2	in his law doth he meditate **d.** and	3119
Ps	2:7	Son; this **d.** have I begotten thee.	3117
Ps	7:11	angry with the wicked every **d.**	3117
Ps	18:*title*	in the **d.** that the Lord delivered	3117
Ps	18:18	in the **d.** of my calamity: but the	3117
Ps	19:2	**D.** unto **d.** uttereth speech, and	3117
Ps	20:1	Lord hear thee in the **d.** of trouble;	3117
Ps	25:5	on thee do I wait all the **d.**	3117
Ps	32:3	through my roaring all the **d.** long.	3117
Ps	32:4	**d.** and night thy hand was heavy	3119
Ps	35:28	of thy praise all the **d.** long.	3117
Ps	37:13	for he seeth that his **d.** is coming.	3117
Ps	38:6	I go mourning all the **d.** long.	3117
Ps	38:12	and imagine deceits all the **d.** long.	3117
Ps	42:3	My tears have been my meat **d.**	3119
Ps	44:8	In God we boast all the **d.** long,	3117
Ps	44:22	For thy sake are we killed all the **d.**	3117
Ps	50:15	call upon me in the **d.** of trouble:	3117

Ps	55:10	**D.** and night they go about it upon	3119
Ps	56:5	Every **d.** they wrest my words:	3117
Ps	59:16	and refuge in the **d.** of my trouble.	3117
Ps	71:8	and with thy honour all the **d.**,	3117
Ps	71:15	and thy salvation all the **d.**;	3117
Ps	71:24	thy righteousness all the **d.** long:	3117
Ps	73:14	all the **d.** long have I been plagued,	3117
Ps	74:16	The **d.** is thine, the night also is	3117
Ps	77:2	in the **d.** of my trouble I sought the	3117
Ps	78:9	turned back in the **d.** of battle.	3117
Ps	78:42	the **d.** when he delivered them from	3117
Ps	81:3	appointed, on our solemn feast **d.**	3117
Ps	84:10	a **d.** in thy courts is better than a	3117
Ps	86:7	the **d.** of my trouble I will call upon	3117
Ps	88:1	have cried **d.** and night before thee:	3117
Ps	89:16	name shall they rejoice all the **d.**:	3117
Ps	91:5	for the arrow that flieth by **d.**;	3119
Ps	92:*title*	Psalm or Song for the sabbath **d.**.	3117
Ps	95:7	To **d.** if ye will hear his voice,	3117
Ps	95:8	in the **d.** of temptation in the	3117
Ps	96:2	forth his salvation from **d.** to **d.**.	3117
Ps	102:2	in the **d.** when I am in trouble;	3117
Ps	102:2	in the **d.** when I call answer me	3117
Ps	102:8	enemies reproach me all the **d.**;	3117
Ps	110:3	be willing in the **d.** of thy power,	3117
Ps	110:5	through kings in the **d.** of his wrath.	3117
Ps	118:24	This is the **d.** which the Lord hath	3117
Ps	119:91	They continue this **d.** according to	3117
Ps	119:97	it is my meditation all the **d.**	3117
Ps	119:164	Seven times a **d.** do I praise thee	3117
Ps	121:6	The sun shall not smite thee by **d.**,	3119
Ps	136:8	The sun to rule by **d.**: for his	3117
Ps	137:7	of Edom in the **d.** of Jerusalem;	3117
Ps	138:3	In the **d.** when I cried thou	3117
Ps	139:12	the night shineth as the **d.**: the	3117
Ps	140:7	hast covered my head in the **d.** of	3117
Ps	145:2	Every **d.** will I bless thee;	3117
Ps	146:4	in that very **d.** his thoughts perish.	3117
Pr	4:18	more and more unto the perfect **d.**	3117
Pr	6:34	not spare in the **d.** of vengeance.	3117
Pr	7:14	this **d.** have I payed my vows.	3117
Pr	7:20	come home at the **d.** appointed.	3117
Pr	11:4	Riches profit not in the **d.** of wrath:	3117
Pr	16:4	the wicked for the **d.** of evil.	3117
Pr	21:26	He coveteth greedily all the **d.** long:	3117
Pr	21:31	horse is prepared against the **d.**	3117
Pr	22:19	I have made known to thee this **d.**,	3117
Pr	23:17	the fear of the Lord all the **d.** long.	3117
Pr	24:10	If thou faint in the **d.** of adversity,	3117
Pr	27:1	for thou knowest not what a **d.** may	3117
Pr	27:10	house in the **d.** of thy calamity:	3117
Pr	27:15	dropping in a very rainy **d.** and a	3117
Ec	7:1	the **d.** of death than the **d.** of one's	3117
Ec	7:14	In the **d.** of prosperity be joyful,	3117
Ec	7:14	but in the **d.** of adversity consider:	3117
Ec	8:8	hath he power in the **d.** of death:	3117
Ec	8:16	there is that neither **d.** nor night	3117
Ec	12:3	In the **d.** when the keepers of the	3117
Ca	2:17	Until the **d.** break, and the shadows	3117
Ca	3:11	in the **d.** of his espousals, and in	3117
Ca	3:11	the **d.** of the gladness of his heart.	3117
Ca	4:6	Until the **d.** break, and the shadows	3117
Ca	8:8	in the **d.** when she shall be spoken.	3117
Isa	2:11	alone shall be exalted in that **d.**	3117
Isa	2:12	the **d.** of the Lord of hosts shall be	3117
Isa	2:17	alone shall be exalted in that **d.**	3117
Isa	2:20	In that **d.** a man shall cast his idols	3117
Isa	3:7	In that **d.** shall he swear, saying, I	3117
Isa	3:18	In that **d.** the Lord will take away	3117
Isa	4:1	In that **d.** seven women shall take	3117
Isa	4:2	In that **d.** shall the branch of the	3117
Isa	4:5	a cloud and smoke by **d.**, and the	3119
Isa	5:30	in that **d.** they shall roar against	3117
Isa	7:17	from the **d.** that Ephraim departed	3117
Isa	7:18	to pass in that **d.**, that the Lord	3117
Isa	7:20	In the same **d.** shall the Lord shave	3117
Isa	7:21	to pass in that **d.**, that a man shall	3117
Isa	7:23	to pass in that **d.**, that every place	3117
Isa	9:4	oppressor, as in the **d.** of Midian	3117
Isa	9:14	tail, branch and rush, in one **d.**,	3117
Isa	10:3	will ye do in the **d.** of visitation,	3117
Isa	10:17	his thorns and his briers in one **d.**;	3117
Isa	10:20	to pass in that **d.**, that the remnant	3117
Isa	10:27	to pass in that **d.**, that his burden	3117
Isa	10:32	yet shall he remain at Nob that **d.**:	3117
Isa	11:10	in that **d.** there shall be a root of	3117
Isa	11:11	to pass in that **d.**, that the Lord	3117
Isa	11:16	in the **d.** that he came up out of the	3117
Isa	12:1	in that **d.** thou shalt say, O Lord, I	3117
Isa	12:4	And in that **d.** shall ye say, Praise	3117
Isa	13:6	the **d.** of the Lord is at hand;	3117
Isa	13:9	the **d.** of the Lord cometh, cruel	3117
Isa	13:13	and in the **d.** of his fierce anger.	3117
Isa	14:3	to pass in the **d.** that the Lord	3117
Isa	17:4	in that **d.** it shall come to pass, that	3117
Isa	17:7	At that **d.** shall a man look to his	3117
Isa	17:9	In that **d.** shall his strong cities be	3117
Isa	17:11	In the **d.** shalt thou make thy plant	3117
Isa	17:11	in the **d.** of grief and of desperate	3117
Isa	19:16	In that **d.** shall Egypt be like unto	3117
Isa	19:18	In that **d.** shall five cities in the	3117
Isa	19:19	In that **d.** shall there be an altar to	3117
Isa	19:21	shall know the Lord in that **d.**,	3117
Isa	19:23	In that **d.** shall there be a highway	3117
Isa	19:24	In that **d.** shall Israel be the third	3117
Isa	20:6	isle shall say in that **d.**, Behold,	3117
Isa	22:5	it is a **d.** of trouble, and of treading	3117
Isa	22:8	thou didst look in that **d.** to the	3117
Isa	22:12	in that **d.** did the Lord God of	3117
Isa	22:20	to pass in that **d.**, that I will call	3117
Isa	22:25	In that **d.**, saith the Lord of hosts,	3117
Isa	23:15	to pass in that **d.**, that Tyre shall	3117
Isa	24:21	to pass in that **d.**, that the Lord	3117
Isa	25:9	it shall be said in that **d.**, Lo, this	3117
Isa	26:1	In that **d.** shall this song be sung	3117
Isa	27:1	In that **d.** the Lord with his sore	3117
Isa	27:2	In that **d.** sing ye unto her, A	3117
Isa	27:3	it, I will keep it night and **d.**	3117
Isa	27:8	wind in the **d.** of the east wind	3117
Isa	27:12	to pass in that **d.**, that the Lord	3117
Isa	27:13	to pass in that **d.**, that the great	3117
Isa	28:5	In that **d.** shall the Lord of hosts	3117
Isa	28:19	shall it pass over, by **d.** and by	3117
Isa	28:24	Doth the plowman plow all **d.** to	3117
Isa	29:18	in the **d.** shall the deaf hear the	3117
Isa	30:23	in the **d.** shall thy cattle feed in	3117
Isa	30:25	in the **d.** of the great slaughter,	3117
Isa	30:26	in the **d.** that the Lord bindeth up	3117
Isa	31:7	in that **d.** every man shall cast	3117
Isa	34:8	is the **d.** of the Lord's vengeance,	3117
Isa	34:10	not be quenched night nor **d.**;	3119
Isa	37:3	This **d.** is a **d.** of trouble,	3117
Isa	38:12,	13 from **d.** even to night wilt thou	3117
Isa	38:19	he shall praise thee, as I do this **d.**:	3117
Isa	39:6	have laid up in store until this **d.**,	3117
Isa	43:13	before the **d.** was I am he;	3117
Isa	47:9	come to thee in a moment in one **d.**,	3117
Isa	48:7	before the **d.** when thou heardest	3117
Isa	49:8	and in a **d.** of salvation have I	3117
Isa	51:13	hast feared continually every **d.**	3117
Isa	52:5	continually every **d.** is blasphemed.	3117
Isa	52:6	they shall know in that **d.** that I	3117
Isa	56:12	to morrow shall be as this **d.**,	3117
Isa	58:3	in the **d.** of your fast ye find	3117
Isa	58:4	ye shall not fast as ye do this **d.**,	3117
Isa	58:5	a **d.** for a man to afflict his soul?	3117
Isa	58:5	and an acceptable **d.** to the Lord?	3117
Isa	58:10	thy darkness be as the noon **d.**:	
Isa	58:13	doing thy pleasure on my holy **d.**;	3117
Isa	59:10	We stumble at noon **d.** as in the	
Isa	60:11	they shall not be shut **d.** nor night;	3119
Isa	60:19	shall be no more thy light by **d.**;	3119
Isa	61:2	the **d.** of vengeance of our God;	3117
Isa	62:6	never hold their peace **d.** nor night;	3117
Isa	63:4	the **d.** of vengeance is in mine	3117
Isa	65:2	have spread out my hands all the **d.**	3117
Isa	65:5	a fire that burneth all the **d.**.	3117
Isa	66:8	be made to bring forth in one **d.**?	3117
Jer	1:10	I have this **d.** set thee over the	3117
Jer	1:18	I have made thee this **d.** a defenced	3117
Jer	3:25	from our youth even unto this **d.**,	3117
Jer	4:9	it shall come to pass at that **d.**,	3117
Jer	6:4	the **d.** goeth away, for the shadows	3117
Jer	7:22	in the **d.** that I brought them out	3117
Jer	7:25	Since the **d.** that your fathers came	3117
Jer	7:25	of the land of Egypt unto this **d.**	3117
Jer	9:1	that I might weep **d.** and night for	3119
Jer	11:4	in the **d.** that I brought them	3117
Jer	11:5	milk and honey, as it is this **d.**	3117
Jer	11:7	in the **d.** that I brought them up	3117
Jer	11:7	in the land of Egypt even unto this **d.**,	3117
Jer	12:3	prepare them for the **d.** of slaughter.	3117
Jer	14:17	run down with tears night and **d.**,	3119
Jer	15:9	is gone down while it was yet **d.**:	3119
Jer	16:13	there shall ye serve other gods **d.**	3119
Jer	16:19	my refuge in the **d.** of affliction,	3117
Jer	17:16	have I desired the woeful **d.**;	3117
Jer	17:17	thou art my hope in the **d.** of evil.	3117
Jer	17:18	bring upon them the **d.** of evil,	3117
Jer	17:21	bear no burden on the sabbath **d.**,	3117
Jer	17:22	of your houses on the sabbath **d.**,	3117
Jer	17:22	work, but hallow ye the sabbath **d.**,	3117
Jer	17:24	gates of this city on the sabbath **d.**,	3117
Jer	17:24	hallow the sabbath **d.**, to do no	3117
Jer	17:27	hallow the sabbath **d.**, and not to	3117
Jer	17:27	of Jerusalem on the sabbath **d.**;	3117
Jer	18:17	the face, in the **d.** of their calamity.	3117
Jer	20:14	Cursed be the **d.** wherein I was	3117
Jer	20:14	let not the **d.** wherein my mother	3117
Jer	25:3	even unto this **d.**, that is the three	3117
Jer	25:18	and a curse; as it is this **d.**;	3117
Jer	25:33	slain of the Lord shall be at that **d.**	3117
Jer	27:22	until the **d.** that I visit them,	3117
Jer	30:7	Alas! for that **d.** is great, so that	3117
Jer	30:8	come to pass in that **d.**, saith the	3117
Jer	31:6	For there shall be a **d.**, that the	3117
Jer	31:32	in the **d.** that I took them by the	3117
Jer	31:35	giveth the sun for a light by **d.**,	3119
Jer	32:20	even unto this **d.**, and in Israel,	3119
Jer	32:20	made thee a name, as at this **d.**;	3119
Jer	32:31	**d.** that they built it even unto this **d.**;	3119
Jer	33:20	break my covenant of the **d.**,	3117
Jer	33:20	there should not be **d.** and night	3119
Jer	33:25	covenant be not with **d.** and night,	3119
Jer	34:13	the **d.** that I brought them forth	3117
Jer	35:14	unto this **d.** they drink none, but	3117
Jer	36:2	from the **d.** I spake unto thee,	3117
Jer	36:2	days of Josiah, even unto this **d.**.	3117
Jer	36:6	Lord's house upon the fasting **d.**:	3117
Jer	36:30	body shall be cast out in the **d.**	3117
Jer	38:28	the **d.** that Jerusalem was taken:	3117
Jer	39:2	the ninth **d.** of the month, the city was	
Jer	39:16	accomplished in that **d.** before thee.	3117
Jer	39:17	I will deliver thee in that **d.**,	3117
Jer	40:4	I loose thee this **d.** from the chains	3117
Jer	41:4	**d.** after he had slain Gedaliah,	3117
Jer	42:19	that I have admonished you this **d.**.	3117
Jer	42:21	I have this **d.** declared it to you;	3117
Jer	44:2	this **d.** they are a desolation,	3117
Jer	44:6	wasted and desolate, as at this **d.**	3117
Jer	44:10	not humbled even unto this **d.**,	3117
Jer	44:22	without an inhabitant, as at this **d.**	3117
Jer	44:23	happened unto you, as at this **d.**.	3117
Jer	46:10	For this is the **d.** of the Lord God	3117
Jer	46:10	of hosts, a **d.** of vengeance,	3117
Jer	46:21	**d.** of their calamity was come upon	3117
Jer	47:4	the **d.** that cometh to spoil all the	3117
Jer	48:41	men's hearts in Moab at that **d.**	3117
Jer	49:22	at that **d.** shall the heart of the	3117
Jer	49:26	shall be cut off in that **d.**,	3117
Jer	50:27	their **d.** is come, the time of their	3117
Jer	50:30	of war shall be cut off in that **d.**,	3117
Jer	50:31	thy **d.** is come, the time that I will	3117
Jer	51:2	in the **d.** of trouble they shall be	3117
Jer	52:4	month, in the tenth **d.** of the month,	
Jer	52:6	ninth day of the month, the famine	
Jer	52:11	in prison till the **d.** of his death.	3117
Jer	52:12	in the tenth **d.** of the month, which	
Jer	52:31	in the five and twentieth **d.** of the	
Jer	52:34	every **d.** a portion until the **d.** of	3117
La	1:12	me in the **d.** of his fierce anger.	3117
La	1:13	me desolate and faint all the **d.**.	3117
La	1:21	bring the **d.** that thou hast called	3117
La	2:1	his footstool in the **d.** of his anger!	3117
La	2:7	as in the **d.** of a solemn feast.	3117
La	2:16	this is the **d.** that we looked for;	3117
La	2:18	down like a river **d.** and night:	3119
La	2:21	thou hast slain them in the **d.** of	3117
La	2:22	solemn **d.** my terrors round about,	3117
La	2:22	so that in the **d.** of the Lord's anger	3117
La	3:3	his hand against me all the **d.**	3117
La	3:14	people; and their song all the **d.**	3117
La	3:57	Thou drewest near in the **d.** that I	3117
La	3:62	their device against me all the **d.**	3117
Eze	1:1	in the fifth **d.** of the month, as I was	
Eze	1:2	In the fifth **d.** of the month, which	
Eze	1:28	is in the cloud in the **d.** of rain,	3117
Eze	2:3	against me, even unto this very **d.**.	3117
Eze	4:6	appointed thee each **d.** for a year.	3117
Eze	4:10	be by weight, twenty shekels a **d.**:	3117
Eze	7:7	the **d.** of trouble is near, and not	3117

Eze 7:10 Behold, the **d.**, behold, it is come: 3117
Eze 7:12 is come, the **d.** draweth near: 3117
Eze 7:19 in the **d.** of the wrath of the Lord: 3117
Eze 8:1 in the fifth **d.** of the month, as I
Eze 12:3 and remove by **d.** in their sight; 3119
Eze 12:4 forth thy stuff by **d.** in their sight, 3119
Eze 12:7 I brought forth my stuff by **d.** 3119
Eze 13:5 the battle in the **d.** of the Lord 3117
Eze 16:4 in the **d.** thou wast born thy navel 3117
Eze 16:5 in the **d.** that thou wast born 3117
Eze 16:56 by thy mouth in the **d.** of thy pride, 3117
Eze 20:1 the tenth **d.** of the month, that
Eze 20:5 In the **d.** when I chose Israel, 3117
Eze 20:6 In the **d.** that I lifted up mine hand 3117
Eze 20:29 is called Bamah unto this **d.** 3117
Eze 20:31 all your idols, even unto this **d.**: 3117
Eze 21:25 prince of Israel, whose **d.** is come, 3117
Eze 21:29 of the wicked, whose **d.** is come, 3117
Eze 22:24 rained upon in the **d.** of indignation 3117
Eze 23:38 defiled my sanctuary in the same **d.**, 3117
Eze 23:39 came the same **d.** into my sanctuary 3117
Eze 24:1 month, in the tenth **d.** of the month,
Eze 24:2 write thee the name of the **d.**, 3117
Eze 24:2 even of this same **d.**: 3117
Eze 24:2 against Jerusalem this same **d.** 3117
Eze 24:25 in the **d.** when I take from them 3117
Eze 24:26 in that **d.** shall come unto thee, 3117
Eze 24:27 that **d.** shall thy mouth be opened 3117
Eze 26:1 year, in the first **d.** of the month,
Eze 26:18 isles tremble in the **d.** of thy fall; 3117
Eze 27:27 of the seas in the **d.** of thy ruin 3117
Eze 28:13 in the **d.** that thou wast created 3117
Eze 28:15 from the **d.** that thou wast created, 3117
Eze 29:1 in the twelfth **d.** of the month, the
Eze 29:17 in the first **d.** of the month, the word
Eze 29:21 In that **d.** will I cause the horn of 3117
Eze 30:2 Howl ye, Woe worth the **d.**! 3117
Eze 30:3 For the **d.** is near, even the **d.** of 3117
Eze 30:3 the Lord is near, a cloudy **d.**; 3117
Eze 30:9 In that **d.** shall messengers go forth 3117
Eze 30:9 upon them, as in the **d.** of Egypt: 3117
Eze 30:18 the **d.** shall be darkened, when I 3117
Eze 30:20 in the seventh **d.** of the month, that
Eze 31:1 the first **d.** of the month, that the
Eze 31:15 In the **d.** when he went down to 3117
Eze 32:1 first **d.** of the month, that the word
Eze 32:10 his own life, in the **d.** of thy fall 3117
Eze 32:17 in the fifteenth **d.** of the month
Eze 33:12 in the **d.** of his transgression: 3117
Eze 33:12 in the **d.** that he turneth from his 3117
Eze 33:12 in the **d.** that he sinneth 3117
Eze 33:21 in the fifth **d.** of the month, that one
Eze 34:12 the **d.** that he is among his sheep 3117
Eze 34:12 scattered in the cloudy and dark **d.** 3117
Eze 36:33 In the **d.** that I shall have cleansed 3117
Eze 38:14 In that **d.** when my people of Israel 3117
Eze 38:19 in that **d.** there shall be a great 3117
Eze 39:8 this is the **d.** whereof I have spoken 3117
Eze 39:11 to pass in that **d.**, that I will 3117
Eze 39:13 the **d.** that I shall be glorified, 3117
Eze 39:22 their God from that **d.** and forward 3117
Eze 40:1 in the tenth **d.** of the month,
Eze 40:1 in the selfsame **d.** the hand of the 3117
Eze 43:18 in the **d.** when they shall make it 3117
Eze 43:22 the second **d.** thou shalt offer a kid 3117
Eze 43:25 every **d.** a goat for a sin offering: 3117
Eze 43:27 upon the eighth **d.**, and so forward, 3117
Eze 44:27 **d.** that he goeth into the sanctuary, 3117
Eze 45:18 the first month, in the first **d.** of the
Eze 45:20 And so shalt thou do the seventh **d.**
Eze 45:21 the fourteenth **d.** of the month, 3117
Eze 45:22 upon that **d.** shall the prince 3117
Eze 45:25 the fifteenth **d.** of the month, 3117
Eze 46:1 in the **d.** of the new moon it shall 3117
Eze 46:4 in the sabbath **d.** shall be six lambs 3117
Eze 46:6 the day of the new moon it shall be 3117
Eze 46:12 as he did on the sabbath **d.**: then 3117
Eze 48:35 of the city from that **d.** shall be, 3117
Da 6:10 upon his knees three times a **d.**, 3118
Da 6:13 maketh his petition three times a **d.** 3118
Da 9:7 confusion of faces, as at this **d.**; 3117
Da 9:15 gotten thee renown, as at this **d.**; 3117
Da 10:4 And in the four and twentieth **d.** 3117
Da 10:12 from the first **d.** that thou didst set 3117
Ho 1:5 it shall come to pass at that **d.**, 3117
Ho 1:11 great shall be the **d.** of Jezreel 3117
Ho 2:3 as in the **d.** that she was born, 3117
Ho 2:15 as in the **d.** when she came up out 3117
Ho 2:16 shall be at that **d.**, saith the Lord, 3117
Ho 2:18 in that **d.** will I make a covenant 3117
Ho 2:21 it shall come to pass in that **d.**, 3117
Ho 4:5 Therefore shalt thou fall in the **d.**, 3117
Ho 5:9 Ephraim shall be desolate in the **d.** 3117
Ho 6:2 in the third **d.** he will raise us up, 3117
Ho 7:5 in the **d.** of our king the princes 3117
Ho 9:5 What will ye do in the solemn **d.**, 3117
Ho 9:5 in the **d.** of the feast of the Lord? 3117
Ho 10:14 Beth-arbel in the **d.** of the battle: 3117
Joe 1:15 for the **d.**! for the **d.** of the Lord 3117
Joe 2:1 the **d.** of the Lord cometh, for it is 3117
Joe 2:2 A **d.** of darkness and of gloominess, 3117
Joe 2:2 **d.** of clouds and of thick darkness, 3117
Joe 2:11 the **d.** of the Lord is great and very 3117
Joe 2:31 and the terrible **d.** of the Lord come 3117
Joe 3:14 **d.** of the Lord is near in the valley 3117
Joe 3:18 it shall come to pass in that **d.**, 3117
Am 1:14 in the **d.** of battle, with a tempest 3117
Am 1:14 in the **d.** of the whirlwind: 3117
Am 2:16 shall flee away naked in that **d.** 3117
Am 3:14 in the **d.** that I shall visit the 3117
Am 5:8 and maketh the **d.** dark with night: 3117
Am 5:18 you that desire the **d.** of the Lord! 3117
Am 5:18 the **d.** of the Lord is darkness, 3117
Am 5:20 not the **d.** of the Lord be darkness, 3117
Am 6:3 Ye that put far away the evil **d.** 3117
Am 8:3 temple shall be howlings in that **d.**, 3117
Am 8:9 it shall come to pass in that **d.**, 3117
Am 8:9 darken the earth in the clear **d.**: 3117
Am 8:10 the end thereof as a bitter **d.** 3117
Am 8:13 In that **d.** shall the fair virgins 3117
Am 9:11 In that **d.** will I raise up the 3117
Ob 8 shall I not in that **d.**, saith the Lord, 3117
Ob 11 in the **d.** that thou stoodest on the 3117
Ob 11 in the **d.** that the strangers 3117
Ob 12 **d.** of thy brother in the **d.** that he 3117
Ob 12 in the **d.** of their destruction; 3117
Ob 12 spoken proudly in the **d.** of distress 3117
Ob 13 people in the **d.** of their calamity; 3117
Ob 13 affliction in the **d.** of their calamity, 3117
Ob 13 in the **d.** of their calamity; 3117
Ob 14 did remain in the **d.** of distress 3117
Ob 15 the **d.** of the Lord is near upon all 3117
Jon 4:7 the morning rose the next **d.** 4283
Mic 2:4 In that **d.** shall one take up 3117
Mic 3:6 the **d.** shall be dark over them 3117
Mic 4:6 In that **d.**, saith the Lord, will I 3117
Mic 5:10 it shall come to pass in that **d.**, 3117
Mic 7:4 the **d.** of thy watchmen and thy 3117
Mic 7:11 **d.** that thy walls are to be built, 3117
Mic 7:11 **d.** shall the decree be far removed 3117
Mic 7:12 In that **d.** also he shall come 3117
Na 1:7 a strong hold in the **d.** of trouble; 3117
Na 2:3 in the **d.** of his preparation, and 3117
Na 3:17 camp in the hedges in the cold **d.**, 3117
Hab 3:16 I might rest in the **d.** of trouble: 3117
Zep 1:7 the **d.** of the Lord is at hand: 3117
Zep 1:8 come to pass in the **d.** of the Lord's 3117
Zep 1:9 In the same **d.** also will I punish 3117
Zep 1:10 it shall come to pass in that **d.**, 3117
Zep 1:14 The great **d.** of the Lord is near, 3117
Zep 1:14 the voice of the **d.** of the Lord: 3117
Zep 1:15 That **d.** is a **d.** of wrath, 3117
Zep 1:15 a **d.** of trouble and distress 3117
Zep 1:15 a **d.** of wasteness and desolation, 3117
Zep 1:15 a **d.** of darkness and gloominess, 3117
Zep 1:15 a **d.** of clouds and thick darkness, 3117
Zep 1:16 A **d.** of the trumpet and alarm 3117
Zep 1:18 in the **d.** of the Lord's wrath; 3117
Zep 2:2 before the **d.** pass as the chaff, 3117
Zep 2:2 before the **d.** of the Lord's anger 3117
Zep 2:3 hid in the **d.** of the Lord's anger 3117
Zep 2:4 drive out Ashdod at the noon **d.**,
Zep 3:8 the **d.** that I rise up to the prey: 3117
Zep 3:11 that **d.** shalt thou not be ashamed 3117
Zep 3:16 that **d.** it shall be said to Jerusalem, 3117
Hag 1:1 in the first **d.** of the month, came 3117
Hag 1:15 In the four and twentieth **d.** of the 3117
Hag 2:1 one and twentieth **d.** of the month,
Hag 2:10 In the four and twentieth **d.** of the
Hag 2:15 consider from this **d.** and upward, 3117
Hag 2:18 now from this **d.** and upward, 3117
Hag 2:18 four and twentieth **d.** of the ninth 3117
Hag 2:18 from the **d.** that the foundation of 3117
Hag 2:19 from this **d.** will I bless you 3117
Hag 2:20 four and twentieth **d.** of the month,
Hag 2:23 In that **d.**, saith the Lord of hosts, 3117
Zec 1:7 the four and twentieth **d.** of the 3117
Zec 2:11 be joined to the Lord in that **d.**, 3117
Zec 3:9 the iniquity of the land in one **d.** 3117
Zec 3:10 In that **d.**, saith the Lord of hosts, 3117
Zec 4:10 despised the **d.** of small things? 3117
Zec 6:10 come thou the same **d.**, and go 3117
Zec 7:1 the fourth **d.** of the ninth month,
Zec 8:9 in the **d.** that the foundation of 3117
Zec 9:12 even to **d.** do I declare that I will 3117
Zec 9:16 their God shall save them in that **d.** 3117
Zec 11:11 And it was broken in that **d.**: and 3117
Zec 12:3 in that **d.** will I make Jerusalem 3117
Zec 12:4 that **d.**, saith the Lord, I will smite 3117
Zec 12:6 that **d.** will I make the governors 3117
Zec 12:8 that **d.** shall the Lord defend the 3117
Zec 12:8 he that is feeble...at that **d.** 3117
Zec 12:9 it shall come to pass in that **d.**, 3117
Zec 12:11 in that **d.** shall there be a great 3117
Zec 13:1 In that **d.** there shall be a fountain 3117
Zec 13:2 it shall come to pass in that **d.**, 3117
Zec 13:4 in that **d.**, that the prophets shall 3117
Zec 14:1 **d.** of the Lord cometh, and thy 3117
Zec 14:3 when he fought in the **d.** of battle 3117
Zec 14:4 his feet shall stand in that **d.** 3117
Zec 14:6 it shall come to pass in that **d.**, 3117
Zec 14:7 be one **d.** which shall be known 3117
Zec 14:7 to the Lord, not **d.**, nor night: 3117
Zec 14:8 be in that **d.**, that living waters 3117
Zec 14:9 in that **d.** shall there be one Lord, 3117
Zec 14:13 it shall come to pass in that **d.**, 3117
Zec 14:20 In that **d.** shall there be upon the 3117
Zec 14:21 in that **d.** there shall be no more 3117
Mal 3:2 who may abide the **d.** of his coming? 3117
Mal 3:17 that **d.** when I make up my jewels; 3117
Mal 4:1 the **d.** cometh, that shall burn as an 3117
Mal 4:1 and the **d.** that cometh shall burn 3117
Mal 4:3 in the **d.** that I shall do this, 3117
Mal 4:5 great and dreadful **d.** of the Lord: 3117
Mt 6:11 **Give us this d. our daily bread** *4594*
Mt 6:30 **grass of the field, which to d. is,** *4594*
Mt 6:34 **Sufficient unto this d. is the evil** *2250*
Mt 7:22 **Many will say to me in that d.** *2250*
Mt 10:15 **in the d. of judgment, than for** *2250*
Mt 11:22 **for Tyre and Sidon at the d. of** *2250*
Mt 11:23 **would have remained until this d.** *4594*
Mt 11:24 **of Sodom in the d. of judgment,** *2250*
Mt 12:1 Jesus went on the sabbath **d.**
Mt 12:2 lawful to do upon the sabbath **d.**
Mt 12:8 **is Lord even of the sabbath d.**
Mt 12:11 **fall into a pit on the sabbath d.,**
Mt 12:36 **thereof in the d. of judgment** *2250*
Mt 13:1 The same **d.** went Jesus out of *2250*
Mt 16:3 **It will be foul weather to d.: for** *4594*
Mt 16:21 and be raised again the third **d.** *2250*
Mt 17:23 **third d. he shall be raised again** *2250*
Mt 20:2 **with the laborers for a penny a d.,** *2250*
Mt 20:6 **Why stand ye here all the d. idle?** *2250*
Mt 20:12 **the burden and heat of the d.** *2250*
Mt 20:19 **the third d. he shall rise again** *2250*
Mt 21:28 **Son, go work to d. in my vineyard.** *4594*
Mt 22:23 **d.** came to him the Sadducees, *2250*
Mt 22:46 any man from that **d.** forth ask *2250*
Mt 24:20 **winter, neither on the sabbath d.:**
Mt 24:36 **d. and hour knoweth no man,** *2250*
Mt 24:38 **until the d. that Noe entered into** *2250*
Mt 24:50 **a d. when he looketh not for him,** *2250*
Mt 25:13 **know neither the d. nor the hour** *2250*
Mt 26:5 But they said, not on the feast **d.**,
Mt 26:17 the first **d.** of the feast of unleavened
Mt 26:29 **d. when I drink it new with you** *2250*
Mt 27:8 The field of blood, unto this **d.** *4594*
Mt 27:19 suffered many things this **d.** in a *4594*
Mt 27:62 Now the next **d.**, that followed *1887*
Mt 27:62 the **d.** of the preparation,
Mt 27:64 be made sure until the third **d.**, *2250*
Mt 28:1 began to dawn toward the first **d.**
Mt 28:15 among the Jews until this **d.** *4594*
Mk 1:21 on the sabbath **d.** he entered into
Mk 1:35 rising up a great while before **d.**, 1773
Mk 2:23 the corn fields on the sabbath **d.**;
Mk 2:24 why do they on the sabbath **d.**
Mk 3:2 would heal him on the sabbath **d.**;
Mk 4:27 **sleep, and rise night and d., and** *2250*
Mk 4:35 same **d.**, when the even was come, *2250*
Mk 5:5 And always, night and **d.**, he was *2250*

Mk	6:2	when the sabbath d. was come,	
Mk	6:11	Gomorrha in the d. of judgment,	2250
Mk	6:21	when a convenient d. was come,	2250
Mk	6:35	And when the d. was now far spent,	5610
Mk	9:31	killed, he shall rise the third d.	2250
Mk	10:34	the third d. he shall rise again.	2250
Mk	13:32	of that d. and that hour knoweth	2250
Mk	14:2	But they said, Not on the feast d.,	
Mk	14:12	the first d. of unleavened bread,	2250
Mk	14:25	until that d. that I drink it new	2250
Mk	14:30	That this d., even in this night,	4594
Mk	15:42	that is, the d. before the sabbath,	
Mk	16:2	first d. of the week, they came unto	
Mk	16:9	risen early the first d. of the week,	
Lu	1:20	not able to speak, until the d. that	2250
Lu	1:59	eighth d. they came to circumcise	2250
Lu	1:80	deserts till the d. of his shewing	2250
Lu	2:11	unto you is born this d. in the city	4594
Lu	2:37	fastings and prayers night and d.	2250
Lu	4:16	the synagogue on the sabbath d.,	2250
Lu	4:21	This d. is this scripture fulfilled	4594
Lu	4:42	And when it was d., he departed	2250
Lu	5:17	a certain d. he was teaching,	2250
Lu	5:26	We have seen strange things to d.	4594
Lu	6:7	he would heal on the sabbath d.;	
Lu	6:13	when it was d., he called	2250
Lu	6:23	Rejoice ye in that d., and leap for	2250
Lu	7:11	the d. after, that he went into a	2250
Lu	8:22	it came to pass on a certain d.,	2250
Lu	9:12	when the d. began to wear away,	2250
Lu	9:22	slain, and be raised the third d.	2250
Lu	9:37	that on the next d., when they	2250
Lu	10:12	tolerable in that d. for Sodom,	2250
Lu	11:3	d. by d. our daily bread.	3588, 2596, 2250
Lu	12:28	grass, which is to d. in the field	4594
Lu	12:46	d. when he looketh not for him,	2250
Lu	13:14	healed on the sabbath d., and	
Lu	13:14	healed, and not on the sabbath d.	2250
Lu	13:16	from this bond on the sabbath d.?	2250
Lu	13:31	The same d. there came certain	2250
Lu	13:32	I do cures to d. and to morrow,	4594
Lu	13:32	the third d. I shall be perfected	
Lu	13:33	Nevertheless I must walk to d.,	4594
Lu	13:33	and the d. following: for it cannot	
Lu	14:1	to eat bread on the sabbath d.,	
Lu	14:3	lawful to heal on the sabbath d.?	
Lu	14:5	pull him out on the sabbath d.?	2250
Lu	16:19	fared sumptuously every d.:	2250
Lu	17:4	seven times in a d., and seven	2250
Lu	17:4	times in a d. turn again to thee,	2250
Lu	17:24	also the Son of man be in his d.	2250
Lu	17:27	d. that Noe entered into the ark,	2250
Lu	17:29	d. that Lot went out of Sodom	2250
Lu	17:30	d. when the Son of man is	2250
Lu	17:31	In that d., he which shall be upon	2250
Lu	18:7	which cry d. and night unto him,	2250
Lu	18:33	the third d. he shall rise again.	2250
Lu	19:5	to d. I must abide at thy house.	4594
Lu	19:9	d. is salvation come to this house,	4594
Lu	19:42	at least in this thy d., the things	2250
Lu	21:34	that d. come upon you unawares	2250
Lu	21:37	And in the d. time he was teaching	2250
Lu	22:7	came the d. of unleavened bread,	2250
Lu	22:34	the cock shall not crow this d.,	4594
Lu	22:66	as soon as it was d., the elders	2250
Lu	23:12	the same d. Pilate and Herod were	2250
Lu	23:43	I say unto thee, To d. shalt thou	4594
Lu	23:54	that d. was the preparation, and	2250
Lu	23:56	rested the sabbath d. according to	
Lu	24:1	Now upon the first d. of the week,	
Lu	24:7	and the third d. rise again.	2250
Lu	24:13	them went that same d. to a village	2250
Lu	24:21	and beside all this, to d. is	4594
Lu	24:21	is the third d. since these things	2250
Lu	24:29	evening, and the d. is far spent.	2250
Lu	24:46	rise from the dead the third d.:	2250
Joh	1:29	next d. John seeth Jesus coming	1887
Joh	1:35	the next d. after John stood, and	1887
Joh	1:39	abode with him that d.: for it	2250
Joh	1:43	d. following Jesus would go forth	1887
Joh	2:1	the third d. there was a marriage	2250
Joh	2:23	at the passover, in the feast d.,	
Joh	5:9	on the same d. was the sabbath.	2250
Joh	5:10	is the sabbath d.: it is not lawful	
Joh	5:16	these things on the sabbath d.	
Joh	6:22	The d. following, when the people	1887
Joh	6:39	raise it up again at the last d.	2250
Joh	6:40,	44, 54 raise him up at the last d.	2250
Joh	7:22	ye on the sabbath d. circumcise a	
Joh	7:23	If a man on the sabbath d. receive	
Joh	7:23	whit whole on the sabbath d.?	
Joh	7:37	In the last d., that great	2250
Joh	7:37	that great d. of the feast, Jesus	
Joh	8:56	Abraham rejoiced to see my d.:	2250
Joh	9:4	him that sent me, while it is d.:	2250
Joh	9:14	And it was the sabbath d. when	
Joh	9:16	he keepeth not the sabbath d.	
Joh	11:9	there not twelve hours in the d.?	2250
Joh	11:9	If any man walk in the d.,	2250
Joh	11:24	in the resurrection at the last d.	2250
Joh	11:53	Then from that d. forth they took	2250
Joh	12:7	against the d. of my burying hath	2250
Joh	12:12	On the next d. much people that	1887
Joh	12:48	same shall judge him in the last d.	2250
Joh	14:20	At that d. ye shall know that I	2250
Joh	16:23	in that d. ye shall ask me nothing.	2250
Joh	16:26	that d. ye shall ask in my name:	2250
Joh	19:31	upon the cross on the sabbath d.,	
Joh	19:31	(for that sabbath d. was an high	
Joh	19:31	was an high d.) besought	
Joh	19:42	of the Jews' preparation d.;	
Joh	20:1	The first d. of the week cometh	
Joh	20:19	the same d. at evening, being the	2250
Joh	20:19	first d. of the week, when the doors	2250
Ac	1:2	Until the d. in which he was taken	2250
Ac	1:22	John, unto that same d. that he was	2250
Ac	2:1	the d. of Pentecost was fully come,	2250
Ac	2:15	it is but the third hour of the d.	2250
Ac	2:20	before that great and notable d. of	2250
Ac	2:29	sepulchre is with us unto this d.	2250
Ac	2:41	the same d. there were added unto	2250
Ac	4:3	put them in hold unto the next d.:	839
Ac	4:9	If we this d. be examined of the	4594
Ac	7:8	and circumcised him the eighth d.;	2250
Ac	7:26	And the next d. he shewed himself	2250
Ac	9:24	watched the gates d. and night to	2250
Ac	10:3	the ninth hour of the d. an angel of	2250
Ac	10:40	Him God raised up the third d.,	2250
Ac	12:18	Now as soon as it was d., there was	2250
Ac	12:21	And upon a set d. Herod, arrayed in	2250
Ac	13:14	the synagogue on the sabbath d.,	2250
Ac	13:27	which are read every sabbath d.,	
Ac	13:33	Son, this d. have I begotten thee.	4594
Ac	13:44	And the next sabbath d. came	
Ac	14:20	the next d. he departed with	1887
Ac	15:21	the synagogues every sabbath d.	
Ac	16:11	Samothracia, and the next d. to	
Ac	16:35	when it was d., the magistrates	2250
Ac	17:31	Because he hath appointed a d., in	2250
Ac	20:7	And upon the first d. of the week,	
Ac	20:11	a long while, even till break of d.,	827
Ac	20:15	next d. over against Chios; and	
Ac	20:15	the next d. we arrived at Samos,	
Ac	20:15	and the next d. we came to Miletus.	
Ac	20:16	at Jerusalem the d. of Pentecost.	2250
Ac	20:18	from the first d. that I came into	2250
Ac	20:26	I take you to record this d.,	4594
Ac	20:31	warn every one night and d. with	2250
Ac	21:1	and the d. following unto Rhodes,	
Ac	21:7	and abode with them one d.	2250
Ac	21:8	the next d. we that were of Paul's	
Ac	21:18	And the d. following Paul went	
Ac	21:26	and the next d. purifying himself	2250
Ac	22:3	toward God, as ye all are this d.	4594
Ac	23:1	conscience before God until this d.	2250
Ac	23:12	And when it was d., certain of the	2250
Ac	24:21	called in question by you this d.	4594
Ac	25:6	and the next d. sitting on the	1887
Ac	26:2	I shall answer for myself this d.	4594
Ac	26:7	serving God d. and night, hope to	2250
Ac	26:22	I continue unto this d., witnessing	2250
Ac	26:29	but also all that hear me this d.,	4594
Ac	27:3	And the next d. we touched at Sidon.	
Ac	27:18	the next d. they lightened the ship;	
Ac	27:19	And the third d. we cast out with	
Ac	27:29	stern, and wished for the d.	2250
Ac	27:33	while the d. was coming on,	2250
Ac	27:33	to take meat, saying, This d. is	4594
Ac	27:33	is the fourteenth d. that ye have	2250
Ac	27:39	And when it was d., they knew not	2250
Ac	28:13	after one d. the south wind blew,	2250
Ac	28:16	we came the next d. to Puteoli:	
Ac	28:23	when they had appointed him a d.,	2250
Ro	2:5	the d. of wrath and revelation	2250
Ro	2:16	In the d. when God shall judge	2250
Ro	8:36	we are killed all the d. long;	2250
Ro	10:21	All d. long I have stretched forth	2250
Ro	11:8	not hear;) unto this d.	2250
Ro	13:12	the d. is at hand: let us therefore	2250
Ro	13:13	Let us walk honestly, as in the d.;	2250
Ro	14:5	esteemeth one d. above another:	2250
Ro	14:5	another esteemeth every d. alike.	2250
Ro	14:6	that regardeth the d., regardeth	2250
Ro	14:6	and he that regardeth not the d.,	2250
1Co	1:8	in the d. of our Lord Jesus Christ.	2250
1Co	3:13	for the d. shall declare it, because	2250
1Co	4:13	of all things unto his d.	737
1Co	5:5	saved in the d. of the Lord Jesus.	2250
1Co	10:8	one d. three and twenty thousand.	2250
1Co	15:4	he rose again the third d. according	2250
1Co	16:2	Upon the first d. of the week let	
2Co	1:14	ours in the d. of the Lord Jesus.	2250
2Co	3:14	for until this d. remaineth	4594
2Co	3:15	unto this d., when Moses is read,	4594
2Co	4:16	inward man is renewed d. by d.	2250
2Co	6:2	d. of salvation have I succoured	2250
2Co	6:2	behold, now is the d. of salvation.)	2250
2Co	11:25	a night and a d. I have been in the	3574
Eph	4:30	sealed unto the d. of redemption.	2250
Eph	6:13	to withstand in the evil d., and	2250
Php	1:5	gospel from the first d. until now:	2250
Php	1:6	it until the d. of Jesus Christ:	2250
Php	1:10	without offence till the d. of Christ;	2250
Php	2:16	I may rejoice in the d. of Christ,	2250
Php	3:5	Circumcised the eighth d., of the	2250
Col	1:6	since the d. ye heard of it, and	2250
Col	1:9	we also, since the d. we heard it,	2250
1Th	2:9	for labouring night and d., because	2250
1Th	3:10	Night and d. praying exceedingly	2250
1Th	5:2	d. of the Lord so cometh as a thief	2250
1Th	5:4	that that d. should overtake you.	2250
1Th	5:5	of light, and the children of the d.:	2250
1Th	5:8	But let us, who are of the d.,	2250
2Th	1:10	among you was believed) in that d.	2250
2Th	2:2	as that the d. of Christ is at hand.	2250
2Th	2:3	for that d. shall not come, except	
2Th	3:8	labour and travail night and d.,	2250
1Ti	5:5	and prayers night and d.	2250
2Ti	1:3	thee in my prayers night and d.;	2250
2Ti	1:12	committed unto him against that d.	2250
2Ti	1:18	find mercy of the Lord in that d.:	2250
2Ti	4:8	judge, shall give me at that d.:	2250
Heb	1:5	this d. have I begotten thee?	4594
Heb	3:7	saith, To d. if ye will hear his voice,	4594
Heb	3:8	d. of temptation in the wilderness:	2250
Heb	3:13	while it is called To d.; lest any of	4594
Heb	3:15	While it is said, To d. if ye will hear	4594
Heb	4:4	in a certain place of the seventh d.	
Heb	4:4	And God did rest the seventh d.	2250
Heb	4:7	Again, he limiteth a certain d.,	2250
Heb	4:7	To d., after so long a time,	4594
Heb	4:7	To d., if ye will hear his voice,	4594
Heb	4:8	have spoken of another d.	2250
Heb	5:5	my Son, to d. have I begotten thee.	4594
Heb	8:9	d. when I took them by the hand	2250
Heb	10:25	as ye see the d. approaching.	2250
Heb	13:8	yesterday, and to d., and for ever.	4594
Jas	4:13	ye that say, To d. or to morrow we	4594
Jas	5:5	hearts, as in a d. of slaughter.	2250
1Pe	2:12	glorify God in the d. of visitation.	2250
2Pe	1:19	in a dark place, until the d. dawn,	2250
2Pe	1:19	the d. star arise in your hearts:	5459
2Pe	2:8	his righteous soul from d. to d.	2250
2Pe	2:9	the d. of judgment to be punished:	2250
2Pe	2:13	in pleasure to riot in the d. time.	2250
2Pe	3:7	against the d. of judgment and	2250
2Pe	3:8	d. is with the Lord as a thousand	2250
2Pe	3:8	and a thousand years as one d.	2250
2Pe	3:10	But the d. of the Lord will come	2250
2Pe	3:12	unto the coming of the d. of God,	2250
1Jo	4:17	boldness in the d. of judgment:	2250
Jude	6	unto the judgment of the great d.	2250
Re	1:10	I was in the Spirit on the Lord's d.	2250
Re	4:8	and they rest not d. and night,	2250
Re	6:17	the great d. of his wrath is come;	2250
Re	7:15	him d. and night in his temple:	2250
Re	8:12	d. shone not for a third part of it,	2250
Re	9:15	for an hour, and a d., and a month,	2250
Re	12:10	them before our God d. and night.	2250
Re	14:11	and they have no rest d. nor night,	2250
Re	16:14	of that great d. of God Almighty.	2250

Book	Ref.	Context	No.
Re	18:8	shall her plagues come in one **d.**,	*2250*
Re	20:10	**d.** and night for ever and ever.	*2250*
Re	21:25	shall not be shut at all by **d.**:	*2250*

DAY'S

Book	Ref.	Context	No.
Nu	11:31	it were a **d.** journey on this side,	3117
Nu	11:31	were a **d.** journey on the other side,	3117
1Ki	19:4	he himself went a **d.** journey	3117
1Ch	16:37	continually, as every **d.** work	3117
Es	9:13	according unto this **d.** decree, and	3117
Jon	3:4	a **d.** journey, and he cried, and said,	3117
Lu	2:44	a **d.** journey; and they sought	*2250*
Ac	1:12	Jerusalem a sabbath **d.** journey	
Ac	19:40	in question for this **d.** uproar,	*4594*

DAYS

Book	Ref.	Context	No.
Ge	1:14	for seasons, and for **d.**, and years:	3117
Ge	3:14	shalt thou eat all the **d.** of thy life:	3117
Ge	3:17	eat of it all the **d.** of thy life;	3117
Ge	5:4	**d.** of Adam after he had begotten	3117
Ge	5:5	the **d.** that Adam lived were nine	3117
Ge	5:8	the **d.** of Seth were nine hundred	3117
Ge	5:11	the **d.** of Enos were nine hundred	3117
Ge	5:14	**d.** of Cainan were nine hundred	3117
Ge	5:17	**d.** of Mahalaleel were eight hundred	3117
Ge	5:20	the **d.** of Jared were nine hundred	3117
Ge	5:23	the **d.** of Enoch were three hundred	3117
Ge	5:27	**d.** of Methuselah were nine hundred	3117
Ge	5:31	**d.** of Lamech were seven hundred	3117
Ge	6:3	**d.** shall be an hundred and twenty	3117
Ge	6:4	giants in the earth in those **d.**;	3117
Ge	7:4	For yet seven **d.**, and I will cause it	3117
Ge	7:4	to rain upon the earth forty **d.**	3117
Ge	7:10	it came to pass after seven **d.**,	3117
Ge	7:12	the rain was upon the earth forty **d.**	3117
Ge	7:17	flood was forty **d.** upon the earth;	3117
Ge	7:24	the earth an hundred and fifty **d.**	3117
Ge	8:3	the end of the hundred and fifty **d.**	3117
Ge	8:6	at the end of forty **d.**, that Noah	3117
Ge	8:10,	12 he stayed yet other seven **d.**;	3117
Ge	9:29	the **d.** of Noah were nine hundred	3117
Ge	10:25	in his **d.** was the earth divided;	3117
Ge	11:32	**d.** of Terah were two hundred and	3117
Ge	14:1	to pass in the **d.** of Amraphel	3117
Ge	17:12	he that is eight **d.** old shall be	3117
Ge	21:4	being eight **d.** old, as God had	3117
Ge	21:34	in the Philistines' land many **d.**	3117
Ge	24:55	the damsel abide with us a few **d.**,	3117
Ge	25:7	the **d.** of the years of Abraham's	3117
Ge	25:24	her **d.** to be delivered were fulfilled,	3117
Ge	26:1	that was in the **d.** of Abraham.	3117
Ge	26:15	servants had digged in the **d.**	3117
Ge	26:18	in the **d.** of Abraham his father;	3117
Ge	27:41	The **d.** of mourning for my father	3117
Ge	27:44	him a few **d.**, until thy brother's	3117
Ge	29:20	they seemed unto him but a few **d.**,	3117
Ge	29:21	my **d.** are fulfilled, that I may go	3117
Ge	30:14	in the **d.** of wheat harvest, and	3117
Ge	35:28	the **d.** of Isaac were an hundred	3117
Ge	35:29	his people, being old and full of **d.**:	3117
Ge	37:34	and mourned for his son many **d.**	3117
Ge	40:12	The three branches are three **d.**:	3117
Ge	40:13	Yet within three **d.** shall Pharaoh	3117
Ge	40:18	The three baskets are three **d.**:	3117
Ge	40:19	within three **d.** shall Pharaoh lift	3117
Ge	42:17	all together into ward three **d.**	3117
Ge	47:9	**d.** of the years of my pilgrimage	3117
Ge	47:9	and evil have the **d.** of the years of	3117
Ge	47:9	and have not attained unto the **d.**	3117
Ge	47:9	in the **d.** of their pilgrimage.	3117
Ge	49:1	which shall befall you in the last **d.**	3117
Ge	50:3	forty **d.** were fulfilled for him; for	3117
Ge	50:3	**d.** of those which are embalmed:	3117
Ge	50:3	for him threescore and ten **d.**	3117
Ge	50:4	the **d.** of his mourning were past,	3117
Ge	50:10	a mourning for his father seven **d.**	3117
Ex	2:11	And it came to pass in those **d.**,	3117
Ex	7:25	seven **d.** were fulfilled, after that	3117
Ex	10:22	in all the land of Egypt three **d.**:	3117
Ex	10:23	any from his place for three **d.**:	3117
Ex	12:15	**d.** shall ye eat unleavened bread;	3117
Ex	12:19	Seven **d.** shall there be no leaven	3117
Ex	13:6	**d.** thou shalt eat unleavened bread,	3117
Ex	13:7	bread shall be eaten seven **d.**;	3117
Ex	15:22	went three **d.** in the wilderness,	3117
Ex	16:26	Six **d.** ye shall gather it;	3117
Ex	16:29	the sixth day the bread of two **d.**;	3117
Ex	20:9	Six **d.** shalt thou labour, and do all	3117
Ex	20:11	**d.** the Lord made heaven and earth,	3117
Ex	20:12	thy **d.** may be long upon the land	3117
Ex	22:30	seven **d.** it shall be with his dam;	3117
Ex	23:12	Six **d.** thou shalt do thy work,	3117
Ex	23:15	eat unleavened bread seven **d.**,	3117
Ex	23:26	the number of thy **d.** I will fulfil.	3117
Ex	24:16	the cloud covered it six **d.**: and the	3117
Ex	24:18	Moses was in the mount forty **d.**	3117
Ex	29:30	shall put them on seven **d.**, when	3117
Ex	29:35	**d.** shalt thou consecrate them.	3117
Ex	29:37	Seven **d.** thou shalt make an	3117
Ex	31:15	Six **d.** may work be done; but in	3117
Ex	31:17	in six **d.** the Lord made heaven and	3117
Ex	34:18	Seven **d.** thou shalt eat unleavened	3117
Ex	34:21	Six **d.** thou shalt work, but on the	3117
Ex	34:28	he was there with the Lord forty **d.**	3117
Ex	35:2	Six **d.** shall work be done, but on	3117
Le	8:33	in seven **d.**, until the **d.** of your	3117
Le	8:33	seven **d.** shall he consecrate you.	3117
Le	8:35	congregation day and night seven **d.**,	3117
Le	12:2	she shall be unclean seven **d.**;	3117
Le	12:2	according to the **d.** of the separation	3117
Le	12:4	her purifying three and thirty **d.**;	3117
Le	12:4	the **d.** of her purifying be fulfilled.	3117
Le	12:5	her purifying threescore and six **d.**	3117
Le	12:6	the **d.** of her purifying are fulfilled,	3117
Le	13:4	him that hath the plague seven **d.**:	3117
Le	13:5	shall shut him up seven **d.** more:	3117
Le	13:21,	26 shall shut him up seven **d.**:	3117
Le	13:31	the plague of the scall seven **d.**:	3117
Le	13:33	up him that hath the scall seven **d.**	3117
Le	13:46	All the **d.** wherein the plague shall	3117
Le	13:50	up it that hath the plague seven **d.**:	3117
Le	13:54	he shall shut it up seven **d.** more:	3117
Le	14:8	abroad out of his tent seven **d.**	3117
Le	14:38	and shut up the house seven **d.**:	3117
Le	15:13	he shall number to himself seven **d.**	3117
Le	15:19	she shall be put apart seven **d.**:	3117
Le	15:24	he shall be unclean seven **d.**; and	3117
Le	15:25	many **d.** out of the time of her	3117
Le	15:25	**d.** of the issue of her uncleanness	3117
Le	15:25	shall be as the **d.** of her separation:	3117
Le	15:26	she lieth all the **d.** of her issue	3117
Le	15:28	shall number of herself seven **d.**,	3117
Le	22:27	it shall be seven **d.** under the dam;	3117
Le	23:3	Six **d.** shall work be done: but the	3117
Le	23:6	seven **d.** ye must eat unleavened	3117
Le	23:8	made by fire unto the Lord seven **d.**:	3117
Le	23:16	sabbath shall ye number fifty **d.**;	3117
Le	23:34	tabernacles for seven **d.** unto the	3117
Le	23:36	Seven **d.** ye shall offer an offering	3117
Le	23:39	a feast unto the Lord seven **d.**:	3117
Le	23:40	before the Lord your God seven **d.**	3117
Le	23:41	unto the Lord seven **d.** in the year.	3117
Le	23:42	Ye shall dwell in booths seven **d.**;	3117
Nu	6:4	All the **d.** of his separation shall he	3117
Nu	6:5	the **d.** of the vow of his separation	3117
Nu	6:5	his head: until the **d.** be fulfilled,	3117
Nu	6:6	the **d.** that he separateth himself	3117
Nu	6:8	All the **d.** of his separation he is	3117
Nu	6:12	the **d.** of his separation, and shall	3117
Nu	6:12	the **d.** that were before shall be lost,	3117
Nu	6:13	**d.** of his separation are fulfilled:	3117
Nu	9:19	upon the tabernacle many **d.**, then	3117
Nu	9:20	when the cloud was a few **d.**	3117
Nu	9:22	whether it were two **d.**, or a month,	3117
Nu	10:10	and in your solemn **d.**, and in the	
Nu	11:19	shall not eat one day nor two **d.**,	3117
Nu	11:19	five **d.**, neither ten **d.**, nor twenty **d.**;	3117
Nu	12:14	she not be ashamed seven **d.**?	3117
Nu	12:14	shut out from the camp seven **d.**,	3117
Nu	12:15	shut out from the camp seven **d.**:	3117
Nu	13:25	searching of the land after forty **d.**	3117
Nu	14:34	After the number of the **d.** in	3117
Nu	14:34	even forty **d.**, each day for a year,	3117
Nu	19:11	any man shall be unclean seven **d.**	3117
Nu	19:14	the tent, shall be unclean seven **d.**	3117
Nu	19:16	a grave, shall be unclean seven **d.**	3117
Nu	20:29	they mourned for Aaron thirty **d.**,	3117
Nu	24:14	do to thy people in the latter **d.**	3117
Nu	28:17	seven **d.** shall unleavened bread be	3117
Nu	28:24	daily, throughout the seven **d.**,	3117
Nu	29:12	a feast unto the Lord seven **d.**:	3117
Nu	31:19	abide without the camp seven **d.**:	3117
De	1:46	ye abode in Kadesh many **d.**,	3117
De	1:46	according unto the **d.** that ye abode	3117
De	2:1	we compassed mount Seir many **d.**	3117
De	4:9	from thy heart all the **d.** of thy life:	3117
De	4:10	fear me all the **d.** that they shall live	3117
De	4:26	shall not prolong your **d.** upon it,	3117
De	4:30	even in the latter **d.**, if thou turn	3117
De	4:32	ask now of the **d.** that are past,	3117
De	4:40	prolong thy **d.** upon the earth,	3117
De	5:13	Six **d.** thou shalt labour, and do all	3117
De	5:16	that thy **d.** may be prolonged, and	3117
De	5:33	that ye may prolong your **d.** in the	3117
De	6:2	all the **d.** of thy life; and that thy **d.**	3117
De	9:9	I abode in the mount forty **d.**	3117
De	9:11	at the end of forty **d.** and forty	3117
De	9:18	the Lord, as at the first, forty **d.**	3117
De	9:25	I fell down before the Lord forty **d.**	3117
De	10:10	according to the first time, forty **d.**	3117
De	11:9	that ye may prolong your **d.** in the	3117
De	11:21	That your **d.** may be multiplied,	3117
De	11:21	and the **d.** of your children,	3117
De	11:21	give them, as the **d.** of heaven	3117
De	12:1	all the **d.** that ye live upon the	3117
De	16:3	seven **d.** shalt thou eat unleavened	3117
De	16:3	of Egypt all the **d.** of thy life.	3117
De	16:4	with thee in all thy coast seven **d.**;	3117
De	16:8	Six **d.** thou shalt eat unleavened	3117
De	16:13	the feast of tabernacles seven **d.**,	3117
De	16:15	Seven **d.** shalt thou keep a solemn	3117
De	17:9	the judge that shall be in those **d.**,	3117
De	17:19	read therein all the **d.** of his life:	3117
De	17:20	that he may prolong his **d.** in his	3117
De	19:17	judges, which shall be in those **d.**;	3117
De	22:7	that thou mayest prolong thy **d.**	3117
De	22:19,	29 may not put her away all his **d.**	3117
De	23:6	their prosperity all thy **d.** for ever.	3117
De	25:15	that thy **d.** may be lengthened in	3117
De	26:3	the priest that shall be in those **d.**,	3117
De	30:18	ye shall not prolong your **d.** upon	3117
De	30:20	is thy life, and the length of thy **d.**:	3117
De	31:14	thy **d.** approach that thou must die:	3117
De	31:29	evil will befall you in the latter **d.**;	3117
De	32:7	Remember the **d.** of old, consider	3117
De	32:47	ye shall prolong your **d.** in the land,	3117
De	33:25	and as thy **d.**, so shall thy strength	3117
De	34:8	in the plains of Moab thirty **d.**:	3117
De	34:8	so the **d.** of weeping and mourning	3117
Jos	1:5	before thee all the **d.** of thy life:	3117
Jos	1:11	within three **d.** ye shall pass over	3117
Jos	2:16	hide yourselves there three **d.**	3117
Jos	2:22	mountain and abode there three **d.**,	3117
Jos	3:2	it came to pass after three **d.**,	3117
Jos	4:14	feared Moses, all the **d.** of his life.	3117
Jos	6:3	once. Thus shalt thou do six **d.**	3117
Jos	6:14	the camp: so they did six **d.**	3117
Jos	9:16	the end of three **d.** after they had	3117
Jos	20:6	priest that shall be in those **d.**:	3117
Jos	22:3	left your brethren these many **d.**	3117
Jos	24:31	Israel served the Lord all the **d.** of	3117
Jos	24:31	Joshua, and all the **d.** of the elders	3117
Jg	2:7	people served the Lord all the **d.** of	3117
Jg	2:7	Joshua, and all the **d.** of the elders	3117
Jg	2:18	their enemies all the **d.** of the judge:	3117
Jg	5:6	In the **d.** of Shamgar the son of	3117
Jg	5:6	Anath, in the **d.** of Jael,	3117
Jg	8:28	forty years in the **d.** of Gideon.	3117
Jg	11:40	of Jephthah the Gileadite four **d.**	3117
Jg	14:12	the seven **d.** of the feast, and find it	3117
Jg	14:14	they could not in three **d.** expound	3117
Jg	14:17	she wept before him the seven **d.**,	3117
Jg	15:20	**d.** of the Philistines twenty years.	3117
Jg	17:6	In those **d.** there was no king in	3117
Jg	18:1	those **d.** there was no king in Israel:	3117
Jg	18:1	in those **d.** the tribe of the Danites	3117
Jg	19:1	it came to pass in those **d.**, when	3117
Jg	19:4	he abode with him three **d.**: so	3117
Jg	20:27	of God was there in those **d.**,	3117
Jg	20:28	stood before it in those **d.**), saying,	3117
Jg	21:25	those **d.** there was no king in Israel:	3117
Ru	1:1	in the **d.** when the judges ruled,	3117
1Sa	1:11	unto the Lord all the **d.** of his life,	3117
1Sa	2:31	**d.** come, that I will cut off thine	3117
1Sa	3:1	the Lord was precious in those **d.**;	3117
1Sa	7:13	against the Philistines all the **d.** of	3117
1Sa	7:15	Samuel judged Israel all the **d.** of	3117
1Sa	9:20	thine asses that were lost three **d.**	3117
1Sa	10:8	**d.** shalt thou tarry, till I come	3117
1Sa	13:8	he tarried seven **d.**, according to	3117
1Sa	13:11	thou camest not within the **d.**	3117
1Sa	14:52	against the Philistines all the **d.** of	3117

1Sa 17:12 an old man in the **d.** of Saul. 3117
1Sa 17:16 and presented himself forty **d.** 3117
1Sa 18:26 law: and the **d.** were not expired. 3117
1Sa 20:19 when thou hast staid three **d.**
1Sa 21:5 kept from us about these three **d.**, 8543
1Sa 25:10 there be many servants now a **d.** 3117
1Sa 25:28 not been found in thee all thy **d.** 3117
1Sa 25:38 it came to pass about ten **d.** after, 3117
1Sa 28:1 it came to pass in those **d.**, that the 3117
1Sa 29:3 which hath been with me these **d.**, 3117
1Sa 30:12 nor drunk any water, three **d.** and 3117
1Sa 30:13 because three **d.** agone I fell sick.
1Sa 31:13 at Jabesh, and fasted seven **d.** 3117
2Sa 1:1 David had abode two **d.** in Ziklag; 3117
2Sa 7:12 when thy **d.** be fulfilled, and thou 3117
2Sa 16:23 which he counselled in those **d.**, 3117
2Sa 20:4 the men of Judah within three **d.**, 3117
2Sa 21:1 was a famine in the **d.** of David 3117
2Sa 21:9 the **d.** [3117] of harvest, in the first **d.**,
2Sa 24:8 end of nine months and twenty **d.** 3117
1Ki 2:1 the **d.** of David drew nigh that he 3117
1Ki 2:11 And the **d.** that David reigned over 3117
1Ki 2:38 Shimei dwelt in Jerusalem many **d.** 3117
1Ki 3:2 the name of the Lord, until those **d.** 3117
1Ki 3:13 the kings like unto thee all thy **d.** 3117
1Ki 3:14 walk, then I will lengthen thy **d.** 3117
1Ki 4:21 served Solomon all the **d.** of his life. 3117
1Ki 4:25 Beer-sheba, all the **d.** of Solomon. 3117
1Ki 8:40 fear thee all the **d.** that they live 3117
1Ki 8:65 **d.** and seven **d.**, even fourteen **d.** 3117
1Ki 10:21 nothing accounted of in the **d.** of 3117
1Ki 11:12 in thy **d.** I will not do it for David 3117
1Ki 11:25 to Israel all the **d.** of Solomon, 3117
1Ki 11:34 him prince all the **d.** of his life 3117
1Ki 12:5 Depart yet for three **d.**, then come 3117
1Ki 14:20 the **d.** which Jeroboam reigned 3117
1Ki 14:30 and Jeroboam all their **d.** 3117
1Ki 15:5 commanded him all the **d.** of his 3117
1Ki 15:6 and Jeroboam all the **d.** of his life. 3117
1Ki 15:14 perfect with the Lord all his **d.** 3117
1Ki 15:16, 32 Baasha king of Israel all their **d.** 3117
1Ki 16:15 did Zimri reign seven **d.** in Tirzah. 3117
1Ki 16:34 In his **d.** did Hiel the Beth-elite 3117
1Ki 17:15 and her house, did eat many **d.** 3117
1Ki 18:1 it came to pass after many **d.**, 3117
1Ki 19:8 the strength of that meat forty **d.** 3117
1Ki 20:29 one over against the other seven **d.** 3117
1Ki 21:29 evil in his **d.**: but in his son's **d.** 3117
1Ki 22:46 which remained in the **d.** of his 3117
2Ki 2:17 sought three **d.**, but found him not. 3117
2Ki 8:20 In his **d.** Edom revolted from 3117
2Ki 10:32 In those **d.** the Lord began to cut 3117
2Ki 12:2 **d.** wherein Jehoiada the priest 3117
2Ki 13:3 the son of Hazael, all their **d.** 3117
2Ki 13:22 oppressed Israel all the **d.** of 3117
2Ki 15:18 he departed not all his **d.** from the 3117
2Ki 15:29 In the **d.** of Pekah king of Israel 3117
2Ki 15:37 In those **d.** the Lord began to send 3117
2Ki 18:4 unto those **d.** the children of Israel 3117
2Ki 20:1 In those **d.** was Hezekiah sick 3117
2Ki 20:6 I will add unto thy **d.** fifteen years; 3117
2Ki 20:17 Behold, the **d.** come, that all that is 3117
2Ki 20:19 if peace and truth be in my **d.**? 3117
2Ki 23:22 from the **d.** of the judges that 3117
2Ki 23:22 Israel, nor in all the **d.** of the kings 3117
2Ki 23:29 In his **d.** Pharaoh-nechoh king of 3117
2Ki 24:1 In his **d.** Nebuchadnezzar king of 3117
2Ki 25:29 continually before him all the **d.** of 3117
2Ki 25:30 for every day, all the **d.** of his life. 3117
1Ch 1:19 because in his **d.** the earth was 3117
1Ch 4:41 the **d.** of Hezekiah king of Judah, 3117
1Ch 5:10 in the **d.** of Saul they made war 3117
1Ch 5:17 In the **d.** of Jotham king of Judah, 3117
1Ch 5:17 in the **d.** of Jeroboam king of Israel. 3117
1Ch 7:2 number was in the **d.** of David 3117
1Ch 7:22 their father mourned many **d.**, and 3117
1Ch 9:25 and were to come after seven **d.** 3117
1Ch 10:12 oak in Jabesh, and fasted seven **d.** 3117
1Ch 12:39 they were with David three **d.**, 3117
1Ch 13:3 enquired not at it in the **d.** of Saul. 3117
1Ch 17:11 when thy **d.**: be expired that thou 3117
1Ch 21:12 else three **d.** the sword of the Lord, 3117
1Ch 22:9 and quietness unto Israel in his **d.** 3117
1Ch 23:1 when David was old and full of **d.**, 3117
1Ch 29:15 our **d.** on the earth are as a shadow, 3117
1Ch 29:28 age, full of **d.**, riches, and honour: 3117
2Ch 7:8 Solomon kept the feast seven **d.**, 3117
2Ch 7:9 seven **d.**, and the feast seven **d.** 3117
2Ch 9:20 accounted of in the **d.** of Solomon. 3117
2Ch 10:5 Come again unto me after three **d.** 3117
2Ch 13:20 recover strength again in the **d.** of 3117
2Ch 14:1 In his **d.** the land was quiet 3117
2Ch 15:17 heart of Asa was perfect all his **d.** 3117
2Ch 20:25 three **d.** in gathering of the spoil, 3117
2Ch 21:8 In his **d.** the Edomites revolted 3117
2Ch 24:2 in the sight of the Lord all the **d.** 3117
2Ch 24:14 continually all the **d.** of Jehoiada. 3117
2Ch 24:15 was full of **d.** when he died; 3117
2Ch 26:5 sought God in the **d.** of Zechariah, 3117
2Ch 29:17 the house of the Lord in eight **d.**; 3117
2Ch 30:21 feast of unleavened bread seven **d.** 3117
2Ch 30:22 eat throughout the feast seven **d.**, 3117
2Ch 30:23 took counsel to keep other seven **d.**: 3117
2Ch 30:23 and they kept other seven **d.** 3117
2Ch 32:24 In those **d.** Hezekiah was sick to 3117
2Ch 32:26 upon them in the **d.** of Hezekiah. 3117
2Ch 34:33 all his **d.** they departed not from 3117
2Ch 35:17 feast of unleavened bread seven **d.** 3117
2Ch 35:18 from the **d.** of Samuel the prophet; 3117
2Ch 36:9 reigned three months and ten **d.** 3117
Ezr 4:2 him since the **d.** of Esar-haddon 3117
Ezr 4:5 their purpose, all the **d.** of Cyrus 3117
Ezr 4:7 **d.** of Artaxerxes wrote Bishlam, 3117
Ezr 6:22 feast of unleavened bread seven **d.** 3117
Ezr 8:15 there abode we in tents three **d.**: 3117
Ezr 8:32 and abode there three **d.** 3117
Ezr 9:7 **d.** of our fathers have we been 3117
Ezr 10:8 would not come within three **d.**, 3117
Ezr 10:9 unto Jerusalem within three **d.** 3117
Ne 1:4 wept, and mourned certain **d.**, 3117
Ne 2:11 Jerusalem, and was there three **d.** 3117
Ne 5:18 in ten **d.** store of all sorts of wine: 3117
Ne 6:15 month Elul, in fifty and two **d.** 3117
Ne 6:17 in those **d.** the nobles of Judah 3117
Ne 8:17 since the **d.** of Jeshua the son of 3117
Ne 8:18 they kept the feast seven days; 3117
Ne 12:7 their brethren in the **d.** of Jeshua. 3117
Ne 12:12 in the **d.** of Joiakim were priests, 3117
Ne 12:22 The Levites in the **d.** of Eliashib, 3117
Ne 12:23 until the **d.** of Johanan the son of 3117
Ne 12:26 These were in the **d.** of Joiakim 3117
Ne 12:26 the **d.** of Nehemiah the governor, 3117
Ne 12:46 in the **d.** of David and Asaph of old. 3117
Ne 12:47 in the **d.** of Zerubbabel, 3117
Ne 12:47 and in the **d.** of Nehemiah, 3117
Ne 13:6 after certain **d.** obtained I leave of 3117
Ne 13:15 In those **d.** saw I in Judah some 3117
Ne 13:23 In those **d.** also saw I Jews that 3117
Es 1:1 to pass in the **d.** of Ahasuerus, 3117
Es 1:2 That in those **d.**, when the king 3117
Es 1:4 excellent majesty many **d.**, even 3117
Es 1:4 an hundred and fourscore **d.** 3117
Es 1:5 when these **d.** were expired, the 3117
Es 1:5 both unto great and small, seven **d.**, 3117
Es 2:12 so were the **d.** of their purifications 3117
Es 2:21 In those **d.**, while Mordecai sat in 3117
Es 4:11 in unto the king these thirty **d.** 3117
Es 4:16 neither eat nor drink three **d.**, 3117
Es 9:22 As the **d.** wherein the Jews rested 3117
Es 9:22 should make them **d.** of feasting 3117
Es 9:26 they called these **d.** Purim after 3117
Es 9:27 that they would keep these two **d.** 3117
Es 9:28 these **d.** should be remembered 3117
Es 9:28 these **d.** of Purim should not fail 3117
Es 9:31 confirm these **d.** of Purim in their 3117
Job 1:5 the **d.** of their feasting were gone 3117
Job 2:13 with him upon the ground seven **d.** 3117
Job 3:6 be joined unto the **d.** of the year. 3117
Job 7:1 **d.** also like the **d.** of an hireling? 3117
Job 7:6 My **d.** are swifter than a weaver's 3117
Job 7:16 me alone; for my **d.** are vanity. 3117
Job 8:9 our **d.** upon earth are a shadow:) 3117
Job 9:25 Now my **d.** are swifter than a post: 3117
Job 10:5 Are thy **d.** as the **d.** of man? 3117
Job 10:5 are thy years as man's **d.**, 3117
Job 10:20 Are not my **d.** few? cease then, 3117
Job 12:12 in length of **d.** understanding. 3117
Job 14:1 born of a woman is of few **d.**, 3117
Job 14:5 Seeing his **d.** are determined, the 3117
Job 14:14 all the **d.** of my appointed time 3117
Job 15:20 man travaileth with pain all his **d.**, 3117
Job 17:1 my **d.** are extinct, the graves are 3117
Job 17:11 My **d.** are past, my purposes are 3117
Job 21:13 They spend their **d.** in wealth, and 3117
Job 24:1 they that know him not see his **d.**? 3117
Job 29:2 in the **d.** when God preserved me; 3117
Job 29:4 As I was in the **d.** of my youth, 3117
Job 29:18 I shall mutiply my **d.** as the sand 3117
Job 30:16 the **d.** of affliction have taken hold 3117
Job 30:27 the **d.** of affliction prevented me 3117
Job 32:7 **D.** should speak, and multitude 3117
Job 33:25 shall return to the **d.** of his youth: 3117
Job 36:11 shall spend their **d.** in prosperity, 3117
Job 38:12 the morning since thy **d.**; 3117
Job 38:21 the number of thy d is great? 3117
Job 42:17 Job died, being old and full of **d.** 3117
Ps 21:4 length of **d.** for ever and ever. 3117
Ps 23:6 shall follow me all the **d.** of my life: 3117
Ps 27:4 of the Lord all the **d.** of my life, 3117
Ps 34:12 loveth many **d.**, that he may see 3117
Ps 37:18 The Lord knoweth the **d.** of the 3117
Ps 37:19 **d.** of famine they shall be satisfied. 3117
Ps 39:4 the measure of my **d.**, what it is; 3117
Ps 39:5 made my **d.** as an hand breadth; 3117
Ps 44:1 what work thou didst in their **d.**, 3117
Ps 49:5 should I fear in the **d.** of evil, 3117
Ps 55:23 shall not live out half their **d.**; 3117
Ps 72:7 his **d.** shall the righteous flourish; 3117
Ps 77:5 I have considered the **d.** of old, 3117
Ps 78:33 their **d.** did he consume in vanity, 3117
Ps 89:29 his throne as the **d.** of heaven. 3117
Ps 89:45 **d.** of his youth hast thou shortened: 3117
Ps 90:9 **d.** are passed away in thy wrath: 3117
Ps 90:10 The **d.** of our years are threescore 3117
Ps 90:12 So teach us to number our **d.**, 3117
Ps 90:14 may rejoice and be glad all our **d.** 3117
Ps 90:15 **d.** wherein thou hast afflicted us, 3117
Ps 94:13 him rest from the **d.** of adversity, 3117
Ps 102:3 my **d.** are consumed like smoke, 3117
Ps 102:11 **d.** are like a shadow that declineth; 3117
Ps 102:23 in the way, he shortened my **d.** 3117
Ps 102:24 me not away in the midst of my **d.**: 3117
Ps 103:15 As for man, his **d.** are as grass: 3117
Ps 109:8 Let his **d.** be few; and let another 3117
Ps 119:84 many are the **d.** of thy servant? 3117
Ps 128:5 of Jerusalem all the **d.** of thy life. 3117
Ps 143:5 I remember the **d.** of old; 3117
Ps 144:4 his **d.** are as a shadow that passeth 3117
Pr 3:2 For length of **d.**, and long life, 3117
Pr 3:16 Length of **d.** is in her right hand; 3117
Pr 9:11 by me thy **d.** shall be multiplied, 3117
Pr 10:27 The fear of the Lord prolongeth **d.**: 3117
Pr 15:15 All the **d.** of the afflicted are evil: 3117
Pr 28:16 covetousness shall prolong his **d.** 3117
Pr 31:12 and not evil all the **d.** of her life. 3117
Ec 2:3 heaven all the **d.** of their life. 3117
Ec 2:16 **d.** to come shall all be forgotten. 3117
Ec 2:23 all his **d.** are sorrows, and his 3117
Ec 5:17 his **d.** also he eateth in darkness, 3117
Ec 5:18 all the **d.** of his life, which God 3117
Ec 5:20 much remember the **d.** of his life; 3117
Ec 6:3 the **d.** of his years be many, 3117
Ec 6:12 all the **d.** of his vain life which he 3117
Ec 7:10 former **d.** were better than these? 3117
Ec 7:15 In the **d.** of my vanity: there is a 3117
Ec 8:12 times, and his **d.** be prolonged, yet
Ec 8:13 neither shall he prolong his **d.**, 3117
Ec 8:15 **d.** of his life, which God giveth 3117
Ec 9:9 the **d.** of the life of thy vanity, 3117
Ec 9:9 sun, all the **d.** of thy vanity: 3117
Ec 11:1 thou shalt find it after many **d.** 3117
Ec 11:8 him remember the **d.** of darkness; 3117
Ec 11:9 cheer thee in the **d.** of thy youth, 3117
Ec 12:1 now thy Creator in the **d.** of thy 3117
Ec 12:1 youth, while the evil **d.** come not, 3117
Isa 1:1 in the **d.** of Uzziah, Jotham, Ahaz, 3117
Isa 2:2 it shall come to pass in the last **d.**, 3117
Isa 7:1 it came to pas in the **d.** of Ahaz 3117
Isa 7:17 **d.** that have not come, from the day 3117
Isa 13:22 and her **d.** shall not be prolonged. 3117
Isa 23:7 whose antiquity is of ancient **d.**? 3117
Isa 23:15 according to the **d.** of one king: 3117
Isa 24:22 after many **d.** shall they be visited. 3117
Isa 30:26 sevenfold, as the light of seven **d.**, 3117
Isa 32:10 Many **d.** and years shall ye be 3117
Isa 38:1 In those **d.** was Hezekiah sick unto 3117
Isa 38:5 I will add unto thy **d.** fifteen years. 3117
Isa 38:10 I said in the cutting off of my **d.**, 3117
Isa 38:20 all the **d.** of our life in the house of 3117
Isa 39:6 Behold, the **d.** come, that all that 3117
Isa 39:8 shall be peace and truth in my **d.** 3117

Book	Ref	Context	No.
Isa	51:9	awake, as in the ancient **d.**, in the......	3117
Isa	53:10	he shall also prolong his **d.**, and.........	3117
Isa	60:20	**d.** of thy mourning shall be ended.......	3117
Isa	63:9	and carried them all the **d.** of old........	3117
Isa	63:11	he remembered the **d.** of old,............	3117
Isa	65:20	thence an infant of **d.**, nor an old........	3117
Isa	65:20	man that hath not filled his **d.**:...........	3117
Isa	65:22	as the **d.** of a tree are the **d.** of my.....	3117
Jer	1:2	in the **d.** of Josiah the son of.............	3117
Jer	1:3	in the **d.** of Jehoiakim the son of.........	3117
Jer	2:32	forgotten me **d.** without number.........	3117
Jer	3:6	me in the **d.** of Josiah the king,...........	3117
Jer	3:16	in those **d.**, saith the Lord, they.........	3117
Jer	3:18	In those **d.** the house of Judah...........	3117
Jer	5:18	in those **d.**, saith the Lord, I will........	3117
Jer	6:11	the aged with him that is full of **d.**.......	3117
Jer	7:32	behold, the **d.** come, saith the Lord,....	3117
Jer	9:25	**d.** come, saith the Lord, that I will......	3117
Jer	13:6	it came to pass after many **d.**,............	3117
Jer	16:9	and in your **d.**, the voice of mirth,.......	3117
Jer	16:14	the **d.** come, saith the Lord, that it.....	3117
Jer	17:11	leave them in the midst of his **d.**,........	3117
Jer	19:6	the **d.** come, saith the Lord, that........	3117
Jer	20:18	**d.** should be consumed with shame?....	3117
Jer	22:30	that shall not prosper in his **d.**:..........	3117
Jer	23:5	Behold, the **d.** come, saith the Lord,...	3117
Jer	23:6	In his **d.** Judah shall be saved,...........	3117
Jer	23:7	the **d.** come, saith the Lord, that........	3117
Jer	23:20	in the latter **d.** ye shall consider it.......	3117
Jer	25:34	the **d.** of your slaughter and of your.....	3117
Jer	26:18	the **d.** of Hezekiah king of Judah,........	3117
Jer	30:3	the **d.** come, saith the Lord, that I......	3117
Jer	30:24	in the latter **d.** ye shall consider it......	3117
Jer	31:27	Behold, the **d.** come, saith the Lord,...	3117
Jer	31:29	In those **d.** they shall say no more,.....	3117
Jer	31:31	the **d.** come, saith the Lord, that I......	3117
Jer	31:33	After those **d.**, saith the Lord, I will....	3117
Jer	31:38	the **d.** come, saith the Lord, that........	3117
Jer	32:14	that they may continue many **d.**..........	3117
Jer	33:14	the **d.** come, saith the Lord, that I......	3117
Jer	33:15	In those **d.**, and at that time,............	3117
Jer	33:16	In those **d.** shall Judah be saved,.........	3117
Jer	35:1	**d.** of Jehoiakim the son of Josiah.......	3117
Jer	35:7	all your **d.** ye shall dwell in tents;........	3117
Jer	35:7	that ye may live many **d.** in the..........	3117
Jer	35:8	us, to drink no wine all our **d.**,...........	3117
Jer	36:2	from the **d.** of Josiah, even unto.........	3117
Jer	37:16	had remained there many **d.**;..............	3117
Jer	42:7	it came to pass after ten **d.**,.............	3117
Jer	46:26	as in the **d.** of old, saith the Lord........	3117
Jer	48:12	the **d.** come, saith the Lord, that I......	3117
Jer	48:47	in the latter **d.**, saith the Lord...........	3117
Jer	49:2	the **d.** come, saith the Lord, that I......	3117
Jer	49:39	shall come to pass in the latter **d.**,.......	3117
Jer	50:4,	20 In those **d.**, and in that time,.........	3117
Jer	51:47	Therefore, behold, the **d.** come, that...	3117
Jer	51:52	Wherefore, behold, the **d.** come,.........	3117
Jer	52:33	before him all the **d.** of his life...........	3117
Jer	52:34	his death, all the **d.** of his life............	3117
La	1:7	in the **d.** of her affliction and of her.....	3117
La	1:7	that she had in the **d.** of old,.............	3117
La	2:17	he had commanded in the **d.** of old:.....	3117
La	4:18	end is near, our **d.** are fulfilled;..........	3117
La	5:21	be turned; renew our **d.** as of old........	3117
Eze	3:15	astonished among them seven **d.**..........	3117
Eze	3:16	came to pass at the end of seven **d.**,....	3117
Eze	4:4	according to the number of the **d.**........	3117
Eze	4:5	according to the number of the **d.**,.......	3117
Eze	4:5	three hundred and ninety **d.**: so..........	3117
Eze	4:6	of the house of Judah forty **d.**:............	3117
Eze	4:8	thou hast ended the **d.** of thy siege.....	3117
Eze	4:9	the **d.** that thou shalt lie upon thy.......	3117
Eze	4:9	side, three hundred and ninety **d.**........	3117
Eze	5:2	when the **d.** of the siege are fulfilled:...	3117
Eze	12:22	The **d.** are prolonged, and every.........	3117
Eze	12:23	The **d.** are at hand, and the effect.......	3117
Eze	12:25	in your **d.**, O rebellious house, will......	3117
Eze	12:27	**d.** to come, and he prophesieth..........	3117
Eze	16:22	the **d.** of thy youth, when thou wast....	3117
Eze	16:43	the **d.** of thy youth, but hast fretted....	3117
Eze	16:60	with thee in the **d.** of thy youth,.........	3117
Eze	22:4	hast caused thy **d.** to draw near,.........	3117
Eze	22:14	in the **d.** that I shall deal with thee?....	3117
Eze	23:19	to remembrance the **d.** of her youth,...	3117
Eze	38:8	After many **d.** thou shalt be visited:.....	3117
Eze	38:16	it shall be in the latter **d.**, and I..........	3117
Eze	38:17	which prophesied in those **d.**..............	3117
Eze	43:25	Seven **d.** shalt thou prepare every........	3117
Eze	43:26	Seven **d.** shall they purge the altar......	3117
Eze	43:27	when these **d.** are expired, it shall......	3117
Eze	44:26	shall reckon unto him seven **d.**...........	3117
Eze	45:21	a feast of seven **d.**; unleavened..........	3117
Eze	45:23	seven **d.** of the feast he shall............	3117
Eze	45:23	without blemish daily the seven **d.**;.......	3117
Eze	45:25	the feast of the seven **d.**, according.....	3117
Eze	46:1	six working **d.**; but on the sabbath......	3117
Da	1:12	thy servants, I beseech thee, ten **d.**;...	3117
Da	1:14	matter, and proved them ten **d.**..........	3117
Da	1:15	end of ten **d.** their countenances.........	3117
Da	1:18	at the end of the **d.** that the king........	3117
Da	2:28	what shall be in the latter **d.**............	3118
Da	2:44	And in the **d.** of these kings..............	3118
Da	4:34	the end of the **d.** I Nebuchadnezzar.....	3118
Da	5:11	and in the **d.** of thy father................	3118
Da	6:7	of any God or man for thirty **d.**,.........	3118
Da	6:12	of any God or man within thirty **d.**,.....	3118
Da	7:9	and the Ancient of **d.** did sit,..............	3118
Da	7:13	and came to the Ancient of **d.**,...........	3118
Da	7:22	Until the Ancient of **d.** came, and........	3118
Da	8:14	and three hundred **d.**;................	6153,1242
Da	8:26	for it shall be for many **d.**..............	3117
Da	8:27	fainted, and was sick certain **d.**;.........	3117
Da	10:2	In those **d.** I Daniel was mourning.......	3117
Da	10:13	withstood me one and twenty **d.**:.........	3117
Da	10:14	befall thy people in the latter **d.**:.........	3117
Da	10:14	for yet the vision is for many **d.**..........	3117
Da	11:20	within few **d.** he shall be destroyed,....	3117
Da	11:33	by captivity, and by spoil, many **d.**......	3117
Da	12:11	thousand two hundred and ninety **d.**.....	3117
Da	12:12	hundred and five and thirty **d.**...........	3117
Da	12:13	stand in thy lot at the end of the **d.**.....	3117
Ho	1:1	in the **d.** of Uzziah, Jotham, Ahaz,.......	3117
Ho	1:1	Judah, and in the **d.** of Jeroboam.........	3117
Ho	2:11	her feast **d.**, her new moons,..................	
Ho	2:13	I will visit upon her the **d.** of............	3117
Ho	2:15	as in the **d.** of her youth, and as in......	3117
Ho	3:3	Thou shalt abide for me many **d.**;.........	3117
Ho	3:4	of Israel shall abide many **d.**...............	3117
Ho	3:5	and his goodness in the latter **d.**.........	3117
Ho	6:2	After two **d.** will he revive us:...........	3117
Ho	9:7	The **d.** of visitation are come,............	3117
Ho	9:7	the **d.** of recompence are come;..........	3117
Ho	9:9	as in the **d.** of Gibeah: therefore he.....	3117
Ho	10:9	hast sinned from the **d.** of Gibeah:......	3117
Ho	12:9	as in the **d.** of the solemn feast.........	3117
Joe	1:2	in your **d.**, or even in the **d.** of your....	3117
Joe	2:29	those **d.** will I pour out my spirit.........	3117
Joe	3:1	behold, in those **d.**, and in that..........	3117
Am	1:1	in the **d.** of Uzziah king of Judah,........	3117
Am	1:1	in the **d.** of Jeroboam the son of.........	3117
Am	4:2	the **d.** shall come upon you, that he.....	3117
Am	5:21	I hate, I despise your feast **d.**,.................	
Am	8:11	the **d.** come, saith the Lord God,........	3117
Am	9:11	I will build it as in the **d.** of old:.........	3117
Am	9:13	the **d.** come, saith the Lord, that........	3117
Jon	1:17	was in the belly of the fish three **d.**......	3117
Jon	3:4	Yet forty **d.**, and Nineveh shall be.......	3117
Mic	1:1	in the **d.** of Jotham, Ahaz, and...........	3117
Mic	4:1	in the last **d.** it shall come to pass,......	3117
Mic	7:14	and Gilead, as in the **d.** of old..........	3117
Mic	7:15	According to the **d.** of thy coming.......	3117
Mic	7:20	unto our fathers from the **d.** of old......	3117
Hab	1:5	I will work a work in your **d.**.............	3117
Zep	1:1	in the **d.** of Josiah the son of.............	3117
Hag	2:16	Since those **d.** were, when one............	
Zec	8:6	remnant of this people in these **d.**,.......	3117
Zec	8:9	ye that hear in these **d.** these words....	3117
Zec	8:10	before these **d.** there was no hire.......	3117
Zec	8:11	this people as in the former **d.**,..........	3117
Zec	8:15	have I thought in these **d.** to do..........	3117
Zec	8:23	In those **d.** it shall come to pass,.........	3117
Zec	14:5	in the **d.** of Uzziah king of Judah:........	3117
Mal	3:4	unto the Lord, as in the **d.** of old,.......	3117
Mal	3:7	from the **d.** of your fathers ye are.......	3117
Mt	2:1	in the **d.** of Herod the king,.............	*2250*
Mt	3:1	In those **d.** came John the Baptist,......	*2250*
Mt	4:2	when he had fasted forty **d.**...............	*2250*
Mt	9:15	**but the d. will come, when the**.......	*2250*
Mt	11:12	**from the d. of John the Baptist**......	*2250*
Mt	12:5	**on the sabbath d. the priests in**.........	
Mt	12:10	it lawful to heal on the sabbath **d.**?...........	
Mt	12:12	**lawful to do well on the sabbath d.**......	
Mt	12:40	**Jonas was three d. and three**.........	*2250*
Mt	12:40	**three d. and three nights in the**.....	*2250*
Mt	15:32	**continue with me now three d.,**......	*2250*
Mt	17:1	And after six **d.** Jesus taketh Peter,......	*2250*
Mt	23:30	**If we had been in the d. of our**......	*2250*
Mt	24:19	**to them that give suck in those d.!**	*2250*
Mt	24:22	**except those d. should be**...............	*2250*
Mt	24:22	**sake those d. shall be shortened**.....	*2250*
Mt	24:29	**After the tribulation of those d.**.....	*2250*
Mt	24:37	**But as the d. of Noe were,**.............	*2250*
Mt	24:38	**For as in the d. that were before**....	*2250*
Mt	26:2	**after two d. is the feast of the**.......	*2250*
Mt	26:61	and to build it in three **d.**..................	*2250*
Mt	27:40	and buildest it in three **d.**, save..........	*2250*
Mt	27:63	After three **d.** I will rise again..........	*2250*
Mk	1:9	in those **d.**, that Jesus came from........	*2250*
Mk	1:13	there in the wilderness forty **d.**,.........	*2250*
Mk	2:1	into Capernaum after some **d.**;...........	*2250*
Mk	2:20	**But the d. will come, when the**......	*2250*
Mk	2:20	**then shall they fast in those d.**......	*2250*
Mk	2:26	**of God in the d. of Abiathar**.........	*1909*
Mk	3:4	**to do good on the sabbath d., or**..........	
Mk	8:1	In those **d.** the multitude being..........	*2250*
Mk	8:2	**have now been with me three d.**.....	*2250*
Mk	8:31	killed, and after three **d.** rise again......	*2250*
Mk	9:2	after six **d.** Jesus taketh with him........	*2250*
Mk	13:17	**to them that give suck in those d.!**	*2250*
Mk	13:19	**For in those d. shall be affliction,**	*2250*
Mk	13:20	**had shortened those d., no flesh**.....	*2250*
Mk	13:20	**chosen, he hath shortened the d.**.....	*2250*
Mk	13:24	**in those d., after that tribulation**...	*2250*
Mk	14:1	After two **d.** was the feast of the........	*2250*
Mk	14:58	within three **d.** I will build another.......	*2250*
Mk	15:29	temple, and buildest it in three **d.**,.......	*2250*
Lu	1:5	There was in the **d.** of Herod,............	*2250*
Lu	1:23	soon as the **d.** of his ministration.........	*2250*
Lu	1:24	after those **d.** his wife Elisabeth..........	*2250*
Lu	1:25	in the **d.** wherein he looked on me,.....	*2250*
Lu	1:39	Mary arose in those **d.**, and went........	*2250*
Lu	1:75	before him, all the **d.** of our life..........	*2250*
Lu	2:1	in those **d.**, that there went out a.......	*2250*
Lu	2:6	the **d.** were accomplished that she.......	*2250*
Lu	2:21	eight **d.** were accomplished for the......	*2250*
Lu	2:22	when the **d.** of her purification............	*2250*
Lu	2:43	when they had fulfilled the **d.**,............	*2250*
Lu	2:46	that after three **d.** they found him.......	*2250*
Lu	4:2	forty **d.** tempted of the devil. And.......	*2250*
Lu	4:2	in those **d.** he did eat nothing:............	*2250*
Lu	4:25	**were in Israel in the d. of Elias,**....	*2250*
Lu	4:31	taught them on the sabbath **d.**.................	
Lu	5:35	**But the d. will come, when the**......	*2250*
Lu	5:35	**then shall they fast in those d.**......	*2250*
Lu	6:2	not lawful to do on the sabbath **d.**?...........	
Lu	6:9	**lawful on the sabbath d. to do good,**.....	
Lu	6:12	it came to pas in those **d.**, that he.........	*2250*
Lu	9:28	about an eight **d.** after these..............	*2250*
Lu	9:36	told no man in those **d.** any of those....	*2250*
Lu	13:14	There are six **d.** in which men............	*2250*
Lu	15:13	**not many d. after the younger son**	*2250*
Lu	17:22	**The d. will come, when ye shall**......	*2250*
Lu	17:22	**to see one of the d. of the Son of**...	*2250*
Lu	17:26	**as it was in the d. of Noe, so shall**	*2250*
Lu	17:26	**be also in the d. of the Son of**........	*2250*
Lu	17:28	**as it was in the d. of Lot;**...............	*2250*
Lu	19:43	**For the d. shall come upon thee**.....	*2250*
Lu	20:1	on one of those **d.**, as he taught.........	*2250*
Lu	21:6	**the d. will come, in the which**.......	*2250*
Lu	21:22	**For these be the d. of vengeance,**...	*2250*
Lu	21:23	**that give suck, in these d.!**............	*2250*
Lu	23:29	**behold, the d. are coming, in the**...	*2250*
Lu	24:18	come to pass there in these **d.**?..........	*2250*
Joh	2:12	they continued there not many **d.**.........	*2250*
Joh	2:19	**in three d. I will raise it up**...........	*2250*
Joh	2:20	wilt thou rear it up in three **d.**?..........	*2250*
Joh	4:40	and he abode there two **d.**.................	*2250*
Joh	4:43	after two **d.** he departed thence,.........	*2250*
Joh	11:6	abode two **d.** still in the same place.....	*2250*
Joh	11:17	he had lain in the grave four **d.**...........	*2250*
Joh	11:39	for he hath been dead four **d.**............	*5066*
Joh	12:1	Jesus six **d.** before the passover..........	*2250*
Joh	20:26	after eight **d.** again his disciples..........	*2250*
Ac	1:3	being seen of them forty **d.**, and.........	*2250*
Ac	1:5	**the Holy Ghost not many d. hence.**	*2250*
Ac	1:15	And in those **d.** Peter stood up...........	*2250*
Ac	2:17	it shall come to pass in the last **d.**,.......	*2250*
Ac	2:18	pour out in those **d.** of my Spirit;........	*2250*
Ac	3:24	have likewise foretold of these **d.**........	*2250*
Ac	5:36	before these **d.** rose up Theudas,.........	*2250*
Ac	5:37	in the **d.** of the taxing, and drew.........	*2250*

Ac 6:1 And in those **d.**, when the number *2250*
Ac 7:41 they made a calf in those **d.**, *2250*
Ac 7:45 our fathers, unto the **d.** of David; *2250*
Ac 9:9 And he was three **d.** without sight, *2250*
Ac 9:19 Saul certain **d.** with the disciples *2250*
Ac 9:23 **d.** were fulfilled, the Jews took *2250*
Ac 9:37 came to pass in those **d.**, that she *2250*
Ac 9:43 tarried many **d.** in Joppa with one *2250*
Ac 10:30 Four **d.** ago I was fasting until this *2250*
Ac 10:48 prayed they him to tarry certain **d.**. *2250*
Ac 11:27 And in these **d.** came prophets *2250*
Ac 11:28 pass in the **d.** of Claudius Caesar. *1909*
Ac 12:3 were the **d.** of unleavened bread. *2250*
Ac 13:31 he was seen many **d.** of them *2250*
Ac 13:41 for I work a work in your **d.**, *2250*
Ac 15:36 some **d.** after Paul said unto *2250*
Ac 16:12 in that city abiding certain **d.**. *2250*
Ac 16:18 this did she many **d.**. But Paul, *2250*
Ac 17:2 three sabbath **d.** reasoned with them
Ac 20:6 Phillippi after the **d.** of unleavened *2250*
Ac 20:6 five **d.**; where we abode seven **d.** *2250*
Ac 21:4 we tarried there seven **d.**: who said *2250*
Ac 21:5 we had accomplished those **d.**, *2250*
Ac 21:10 And as we tarried there many **d.**, *2250*
Ac 21:15 And after those **d.** we took up our *2250*
Ac 21:26 the accomplishment of the **d.** of *2250*
Ac 21:27 the seven **d.** were almost ended, *2250*
Ac 21:38 Egyptian, which before these **d.** *2250*
Ac 24:1 And after five **d.** Ananias the high *2250*
Ac 24:11 there are yet but twelve **d.** since I *2250*
Ac 24:24 after certain **d.**, when Felix came *2250*
Ac 25:1 three **d.** he ascended from Caesarea *2250*
Ac 25:6 among them more than ten **d.**, *2250*
Ac 25:13 And after certain **d.** king Agripa *2250*
Ac 25:14 when they had been there many **d.**, *2250*
Ac 27:7 when we had sailed slowly many **d.**, *2250*
Ac 27:20 sun nor stars in many **d.** apeared, *2250*
Ac 28:7 and lodged us three **d.** courteously. *2250*
Ac 28:12 Syracuse, we tarried there three **d.**. *2250*
Ac 28:14 desired to tarry with them seven **d.**: *2250*
Ac 28:17 after three **d.** Paul called the chief *2250*
Ga 1:18 and abode with him fifteen **d.**. *2250*
Ga 4:10 Ye observe **d.**, and months, *2250*
Eph 5:16 the time, because the **d.** are evil. *2250*
Col 2:16 the new moon, or of the sabbath **d.**.
2Ti 3:1 last **d.** perilous times shall come *2250*
Heb 1:2 in these last **d.** spoken unto us *2250*
Heb 5:7 Who in the **d.** of his flesh, when *2250*
Heb 7:3 beginning of **d.**, nor end of life; *2250*
Heb 8:8 Behold, the **d.** come, saith the Lord, *2250*
Heb 8:10 the house of Israel after those **d.**, *2250*
Heb 10:16 will make with them after those **d.**, *2250*
Heb 10:32 call to remembrance the former **d.**, *2250*
Heb 11:30 were compassed about seven **d.**. *2250*
Heb 12:10 they verily for a few **d.** chastened *2250*
Jas 5:3 treasure together for the last **d.**. *2250*
1Pe 3:10 that will love life, and see good **d.**, *2250*
1Pe 3:20 of God waited in the **d.** of Noah, *2250*
2Pe 3:3 shall come in the last **d.** scoffers, *2250*
Re 2:10 **ye shall have tribulation ten d.:** *2250*
Re 2:13 **in those d. wherein Antipas was** *2250*
Re 9:6 in those **d.** shall men seek death, *2250*
Re 10:7 But in the **d.** of the voice of the *2250*
Re 11:3 two hundred and threescore **d.**, *2250*
Re 11:6 rain not in the **d.** of their prophecy: *2250*
Re 11:9 dead bodies three **d.** and a half, *2250*
Re 11:11 three **d.** and a half the Spirit of life *2250*
Re 12:6 two hundred and threescore **d.**. *2250*

DAYS'

Ge 30:36 three **d.** journey betwixt himself 3117
Ge 31:23 pursued after him seven **d.** journey; 3117
Ex 3:18 we beseech thee, three **d.** journey 3117
Ex 5:3 we pray thee, three **d.** journey into 3117
Ex 8:27 **d.** journey into the wilderness, 3117
Nu 10:33 of the Lord three **d.** journey: 3117
Nu 10:33 them in the three **d.** journey: 3117
Nu 33:8 three **d.** journey in the wilderness 3117
De 1:2 are eleven **d.** journey from Horeb 3117
1Sa 11:3 Give us seven **d.** respite, that we 3117
2Sa 24:13 three **d.** pestilence in thy land? 3117
2Ki 3:9 a compass of seven **d.** journey: 3117
Jon 3:3 great city of three **d.** journey. 3117

DAYSMAN

Job 9:33 Neither is there any **d.** betwixt us, 3198

DAYSPRING

Job 38:12 caused the **d.** to know his place; 7837
Lu 1:78 **d.** from on high hath visited us, *395*

DAYSTAR See DAY and STAR.

DAYTIME See also DAY and TIME.

Job 5:14 They meet with darkness in the **d.**, 3119
Job 24:16 marked for themselves in the **d.**: 3119
Ps 22:2 O my God, I cry in the **d.**, but thou 3119
Ps 42:8 his lovingkindness in the **d.**, and in 3119
Ps 78:14 **d.** also he led them with a cloud, 3119
Isa 4:6 a shadow in the **d.** from the heat, 3119
Isa 21:8 upon the watchtower in the **d.**, 3119

DEACON See also DEACONS.

1Ti 3:10 let them use the office of a **d.**, *1247*
1Ti 3:13 that have used the office of a **d.**, *1247*

DEACONS

Php 1:1 Philippi, with the bishops and **d.**: *1249*
1Ti 3:8 Likewise must the **d.** be grave, *1249*
1Ti 3:12 the **d.** be the husbands of one wife, *1249*

DEAD

Ge 20:3 art but a **d.** man, for the woman 4191
Ge 23:3 stood up from before his **d.**, 4191
Ge 23:4 that I may bury my **d.** out of my 4191
Ge 23:6 of our sepulchres bury thy **d.**; 4191
Ge 23:6 but that thou mayest bury thy **d.** 4191
Ge 23:8 that I should bury my **d.** out of my 4191
Ge 23:11 people give I it thee: bury thy **d.**. 4191
Ge 23:13 and I will bury my **d.** there. 4191
Ge 23:15 me and thee? bury therefore thy **d.**. 4191
Ge 42:38 for his brother is **d.**, and he is 4191
Ge 44:20 and his brother is **d.**, and he alone 4191
Ge 50:15 that their father was **d.**, they said, 4191
Ex 4:19 men are **d.** which sought thy life. 4191
Ex 9:7 one of the cattle of the Israelites **d.**. 4191
Ex 12:30 a house where there was not one **d.**. 4191
Ex 12:33 for they said, We be all **d.** men. 4191
Ex 14:30 Israel saw the Egyptians **d.** upon 4191
Ex 21:34 and the **d.** beast shall be his 4191
Ex 21:35 the **d.** ox also they shall divide. 4191
Ex 21:36 and the **d.** shall be his own. 4191
Le 11:31 when they be **d.**, shall be unclean 4194
Le 11:32 when they are **d.**, doth fall, it shall 4194
Le 19:28 cuttings in your flesh for the **d.**, 5315
Le 21:1 shall none be defiled for the **d.** 5315
Le 21:11 shall he go in to any **d.** body, 4191
Le 22:4 thing that is unclean by the **d.**, 5315
Nu 5:2 whosoever is defiled by the **d.**: 5315
Nu 6:6 he shall come at no **d.** body. 4191
Nu 6:11 him, for that he sinned by the **d.**, 5315
Nu 9:6, 7 defiled by the **d.** body of a man, 5315
Nu 9:10 unclean by the reason of a **d.** body, 5315
Nu 12:12 Let her not be as one **d.**, 4191
Nu 16:48 stood between the **d.** and the living; 4191
Nu 19:11 He that toucheth the **d.** body of any 4191
Nu 19:13 Whosoever toucheth the **d.** body 4191
Nu 19:13 of any man that is **d.**, and 4191
Nu 19:16 or a **d.** body, or a bone of a man, 4191
Nu 19:18 or one slain, or one **d.**, or a grave: 4191
Nu 20:29 that Aaron was **d.**, they mourned 1478
De 2:16 men of war were consumed and **d.** 4191
De 14:1 between your eyes for the **d.**. 4191
De 14:8 flesh, nor touch their **d.** carcass. 5038
De 25:5 the wife of the **d.** shall not marry 4191
De 25:6 the name of his brother which is **d.**, 4191
De 26:14 nor given ought thereof for the **d.**: 4191
Jos 1:2 Moses my servant is **d.**; now 4191
Jg 2:19 the judge was **d.**, that they returned, 4191
Jg 3:25 their lord was fallen down **d.** 4191
Jg 4:1 of the Lord, when Ehud was **d.**. 4191
Jg 4:22 into her tent, behold, Sisera lay **d.**, 4191
Jg 5:27 he bowed, there he fell down **d.**. 7703
Jg 8:33 as soon as Gideon was **d.**, that the 4191
Jg 9:55 Israel saw that Abimelech was **d.**, 4191
Jg 16:30 the **d.** which he slew at his death 4191
Jg 20:5 have they forced, that she is **d.**. 4191
Ru 1:8 as ye have dealt with the **d.**, 4191
Ru 2:20 to the living and to the **d.**. 4191
Ru 4:5 the **d.**, to raise up the name of the **d.** 4191
Ru 4:10 name of the **d.** upon his inheritance, 4191
Ru 4:10 the name of the **d.** be not cut off 4191
1Sa 4:17 Hophni and Phinehas, are **d.**, and 4191
1Sa 4:19 in law and her husband were **d.**, 4191
1Sa 17:51 saw their champion was **d.**, they 4191
1Sa 24:14 after a **d.** dog, after a flea 4191
1Sa 25:39 David heard that Nabal was **d.**, 4191
1Sa 28:3 Now Samuel was **d.**, and all Israel 4191
1Sa 31:5 armourbearer saw that Saul was **d.**, 4191
1Sa 31:7 Saul and his sons were **d.**, they 4191
2Sa 1:4 the people also are fallen and **d.**; 4191
2Sa 1:4 Saul and Jonathan his son are **d.** 4191
2Sa 1:5 Saul and Jonathan his son be **d.**? 4191
2Sa 2:7 your master Saul is **d.**, and also the 4191
2Sa 4:1 Abner was **d.** in Hebron, his hands 4191
2Sa 4:10 Saul is **d.**, thinking to have brought 4191
2Sa 9:8 such a **d.** dog as I am? 4191
2Sa 11:21 Thy servant Uriah the Hittite is **d.** 4191
2Sa 11:24 some of the king's servants be **d.**, 4191
2Sa 11:24 Uriah the Hittite is **d.** also, 4191
2Sa 11:26 Uriah her husband was **d.**, she 4191
2Sa 12:18 to tell him that the child was **d.**: 4191
2Sa 12:18 if we tell him that the child is **d.**? 4191
2Sa 12:19 perceived that the child was **d.**: 4191
2Sa 12:19 unto his servants, Is the child **d.**? 4191
2Sa 12:19 And they said, He is **d.**. 4191
2Sa 12:21 the child was **d.**, thou didst rise 4191
2Sa 12:23 he is **d.**, wheefore should I fast? 4191
2Sa 13:32 Amnon only is **d.**: for by the 4191
2Sa 13:33 that all the king's sons are **d.**: 4191
2Sa 13:33 for Amnon only is **d.**. 4191
2Sa 13:39 Amnon, seeing he was **d.**. 4191
2Sa 14:2 a long time mourned for the **d.**: 4191
2Sa 14:5 woman, and mine husband is **d.**. 4191
2Sa 16:9 this **d.** dog curse my lord the king? 4191
2Sa 18:20 because the king's son is **d.**. 4191
2Sa 19:10 we anointed over us, is **d.** in batte. 4191
2Sa 19:28 my father's house were but **d.** men 4194
1Ki 3:20 laid her **d.** child in my bosom. 4191
1Ki 3:21 my child suck, behold, it was **d.**; 4191
1Ki 3:22 the **d.** is thy son. And this said, 4191
1Ki 3:22 No; but the **d.** is thy son, and 4191
1Ki 3:23 and thy son is the **d.**: and the other 4191
1Ki 3:23 saith, Nay; but thy son is the **d.**, 4191
1Ki 11:21 Joab the captain of the host was **d.**, 4191
1Ki 13:31 When I am **d.**, then bury me in the 4191
1Ki 21:14 saying, Naboth is stoned, and is **d.** 4191
1Ki 21:15 that Naboth was stoned, and was **d.**, 4191
1Ki 21:15 for Naboth is not alive, but **d.**. 4191
1Ki 21:16 Ahab heard that Naboth was **d.**, 4191
2Ki 3:5 when Ahab was **d.**, that the king 4194
2Ki 4:1 Thy servant my husband is **d.**; and 4191
2Ki 4:32 child was **d.**, and laid upon his bed. 4191
2Ki 8:5 he had restored a **d.** body to life, 4191
2Ki 11:1 of Ahaziah saw that her son was **d.**, 4191
2Ki 19:35 morning, behold, they were all **d.** 4191
2Ki 23:30 servants carried him in a chariot **d.** 4191
1Ch 1:44 when Bela was **d.**, Jobab the son 4191
1Ch 1:45 And when Jobab was **d.**, Husham 4191
1Ch 1:46 when Husham was **d.**, Hadad 4191
1Ch 1:47 And when Hadad was **d.**, Samlah 4191
1Ch 1:48 And when Samlah was **d.**, Shaul 4191
1Ch 1:49 when Shaul was **d.**, Baal-hanan 4191
1Ch 1:50 And when Baal-hanan was **d.**, 4191
1Ch 2:19 And when Azubah was **d.**, Caleb 4191
1Ch 2:24 after that Hezron was **d.** in 4194
1Ch 10:5 saw that Saul was **d.**, he fell 4191
1Ch 10:7 Saul and his sons were **d.**, then 4191
2Ch 20:24 they were **d.** bodies fallen to the 6297
2Ch 20:25 riches with the **d.** bodies, and 6297
2Ch 22:10 Ahaziah saw that her son was **d.**. 4191
Es 2:7 her father and mother were **d.**, 4194
Job 1:19 the young men, and they are **d.**; 4191
Job 26:5 **D.** things are formed from under 7496
Ps 31:12 I am forgotten as a **d.** man 4191
Ps 76:6 and horse are cast into a **d.** sleep.
Ps 79:2 The **d.** bodies of thy servants 5038
Ps 88:5 Free among the **d.**, like the slain 4191
Ps 88:10 Wilt thou shew wonders to the **d.**? 4191
Ps 88:10 shall the **d.** arise and praise thee? 7496
Ps 106:28 and ate the sacrifices of the **d.** 4191
Ps 110:6 fill the places with the **d.** bodies; 1472
Ps 115:17 The **d.** praise not the Lord, 4191
Ps 143:3 as those that have been long **d.**. 4191
Pr 2:18 death, and her paths unto the **d.**. 7496
Pr 9:18 knoweth not that the **d.** are there; 7496
Pr 21:16 in the congregation of the **d.**. 7496
Ec 4:2 praised the **d.** which are already **d.** 4191
Ec 9:3 and after that they go to the **d.**. 4191
Ec 9:4 a living dog is better than a **d.** lion. 4191
Ec 9:5 but the **d.** know not any thing, 4191
Ec 10:1 **D.** flies cause the ointment of the 4194
Isa 8:19 their God? for the living to the **d.**? 4191
Isa 14:9 it stirreth up the **d.** for thee, 7496

Isa 22:2 slain with the sword, not **d.** in.......... 4191
Isa 26:14 They are **d.**, they shall not live;......... 4191
Isa 26:19 Thy **d.** men shall live, together......... 4191
Isa 26:19 with my **d.** body shall they arise. 5038
Isa 26:19 the earth shall cast out the **d.**........... 7496
Isa 37:36 behold, they were all **d.** corpses. 4191
Isa 59:10 are in desolate places as **d.** men 4191
Jer 16:7 to comfort them for the **d.**;............... 4191
Jer 22:10 Weep ye not for the **d.**, neither......... 4191
Jer 26:23 cast his **d.** body into the graves......... 5038
Jer 31:40 the whole valley of the **d.** bodies,....... 6297
Jer 33:5 fill them with the **d.** bodies of men, ... 6297
Jer 34:20 their **d.** bodies shall be for meat......... 5038
Jer 36:30 and his **d.** body shall be cast out........ 5038
Jer 41:9 cast all the **d.** bodies of the men, ... 6297
La 3:6 as they that be **d.** of old.................. 4191
Eze 6:5 And I will lay the **d.** carcasses................
Eze 24:17 make no mourning for the **d.**,............ 4191
Eze 44:25 they shall come at no **d.** person......... 4191
Eze 44:31 any thing that is **d.** of itself, or......... 5038
Am 8:3 there shall be many **d.** bodies........... 6297
Hag 2:13 unclean by a **d.** body touch any of...........
Mt 2:19 But when Herod was **d.**, behold,......... *5053*
Mt 2:20 for they are **d.** which sought the........ *2348*
Mt 8:22 **me; and let the d. bury their d.**........ *3498*
Mt 9:18 My daughter is even now **d.**: but....... *5053*
Mt 9:24 **for the maid is not d., but sleepeth**..*599*
Mt 10:8 **lepers, raise the d., cast out**.......... *3498*
Mt 11:5 **the d. are raised up, and the poor** ..*3498*
Mt 14:2 Baptist; he is risen from the **d.**;......... *3498*
Mt 17:9 **of man be risen again from the d.**. *3498*
Mt 22:31 **touching the resurrection of the d.**, *3498*
Mt 22:32 **God is not the God of the d., but** .. *3498*
Mt 23:27 **within full of d. men's bones, and** ..*3498*
Mt 27:64 He is risen from the **d.**: so the last *3498*
Mt 28:4 did shake, and became as **d.** men........ *3498*
Mt 28:7 that he is risen from the **d.**;.............. *3498*
Mk 5:35 which said, Thy daughter is **d.**: *599*
Mk 5:39 **the damsel is not d., but sleepeth**.... *599*
Mk 6:14 the Baptist was risen from the **d.**,...... *3498*
Mk 6:16 beheaded: he is risen from the **d.**........ *3498*
Mk 9:9 Son of man were risen from the **d.**..... *3498*
Mk 9:10 what the rising from the **d.** should...... *3498*
Mk 9:26 out of him: and he was as one **d.**; *3498*
Mk 9:26 insomuch that many said, He is **d.**. *599*
Mk 12:25 **when they shall rise from the d.**,.... *3498*
Mk 12:26 **as touching the d., that they rise:** . *3498*
Mk 12:27 **He is not the God of the d.**, ... *3498*
Mk 15:44 marvelled if he were already **d.**:........ *2348*
Mk 15:44 whether he had been any while **d.**........ *599*
Lu 7:12 there was a **d.** man carried out,......... *2348*
Lu 7:15 And he that was **d.** sat up, ... *3498*
Lu 7:22 **the deaf hear, the d. are raised**..... *3498*
Lu 8:49 Thy daughter is **d.**; trouble not.......... *2348*
Lu 8:52 **not; she is not d., but sleepeth**......... *599*
Lu 8:53 to scorn, knowing that she was **d.** *599*
Lu 9:7 that John was risen from the **d.**; *3498*
Lu 9:60 unto him, **Let the d. bury the d.**: *3498*
Lu 10:30 **and departed, leaving him half d.**:.. *2258*
Lu 15:24 **For this my son was d., and is**....... *3498*
Lu 15:32 **for this thy brother was d., and is** . *3498*
Lu 16:30 **if one went unto them from the d.**, *3498*
Lu 16:31 **though one rose from the d.**.......... *3498*
Lu 20:35 **and the resurrection from the d.**, .. *3498*
Lu 20:37 **Now that the d. are raised, even**.... *3498*
Lu 20:38 **For he is not a God of the d.**, ... *3498*
Lu 24:5 seek ye the living among the **d.**?........ *3498*
Lu 24:46 **to rise from the d. the third day**:... *3498*
Joh 2:22 therefore he was risen from the **d.**,..... *3498*
Joh 5:21 **as the Father raiseth up the d.**,..... *3498*
Joh 5:25 **when the d. shall hear the voice**.... *3498*
Joh 6:49 **in the wilderness, and are d.** *599*
Joh 6:58 **fathers did eat manna, and are d.**: .. *599*
Joh 8:52 Abraham is **d.**, and the prophets;......... *599*
Joh 8:53 Abraham, which is **d.**?....................... *599*
Joh 8:53 and the prophets are **d.**: *599*
Joh 11:14 unto them plainly, **Lazarus is d**.......... *599*
Joh 11:25 **though he were d., yet shall he live**: *599*
Joh 11:39 the sister of him that was **d.**, ... *2348*
Joh 11:39 for he hath been **d.** four days. ....
Joh 11:41 the place where the **d.** was laid. *2348*
Joh 11:44 And he that was **d.** came forth, ... *2348*
Joh 12:1 Lazarus was which had been **d.**.......... *2348*
Joh 12:1 **d.** whom he raised from the **d.**,......... *3498*
Joh 12:9 whom he had raised from the **d.**. *3498*
Joh 12:17 him from the **d.**, bare record............. *3498*
Joh 19:33 that he was **d.** already,they brake....... *2348*
Joh 20:9 he must rise again from the **d.**........... *3498*
Joh 21:14 after that he was risen from the **d.**..... *3498*
Ac 2:29 that he is both **d.** and buried,........... *5053*
Ac 3:15 God hath raised from the **d.**;.............. *3498*
Ac 4:2 Jesus the resurrection from the **d.**........ *3498*
Ac 4:10 whom God raised from the **d.**, even.... *3498*
Ac 5:10 men came in and found her **d.**, ... *3498*
Ac 7:4 thence, when his father was **d.**, he *599*
Ac 10:41 with him after he rose from the **d.**. *3498*
Ac 10:42 to be the Judge of quick and **d.**......... *3498*
Ac 13:30 But God raised him from the **d.**:........ *3498*
Ac 13:34 that he raised him up from the **d.**,...... *3498*
Ac 14:19 city, supposing he had been **d.**.......... *2348*
Ac 17:3 and risen again from the **d.**; *3498*
Ac 17:31 he hath raised him from the **d.**. *3498*
Ac 17:32 heard of the resurrection of the **d.**,..... *3498*
Ac 20:9 the third loft, and was taken up **d.**...... *3498*
Ac 23:6 the hope and resurrection of the **d.**..... *3498*
Ac 24:15 shall be a resurrection of the **d.**, ... *3498*
Ac 24:21 Touching the resurrection of the **d.**...... *3498*
Ac 25:19 of one Jesus, which was **d.**, whom...... *2348*
Ac 26:8 you, that God should raise the **d.**?....... *3498*
Ac 26:23 first that should rise from the **d.**, ... *3498*
Ac 28:6 or fallen down **d.** suddenly: but.......... *3498*
Ro 1:4 by the ressurrection from the **d.**: *3498*
Ro 4:17 God, who quickeneth the **d.**, ... *3498*
Ro 4:19 not his own body now **d.**,................. *3499*
Ro 4:24 Jesus our Lord from the **d.**; Who *3498*
Ro 5:15 the offence of one many be **d.**,............ *599*
Ro 6:2 How shall we, that are **d.** to sin, ... *599*
Ro 6:4 Christ was raised up from the **d.**........ *3498*
Ro 6:7 For he that is **d.** is freed from sin........ *599*
Ro 6:8 if we be **d.** with Christ, we believe *599*
Ro 6:9 raised from the **d.** dieth no more:....... *3498*
Ro 6:11 to be **d.** indeed unto sin, but alive....... *3498*
Ro 6:13 as those that are alive from the **d.**,...... *3498*
Ro 7:2 if the husband be **d.**, she is loosed...... *599*
Ro 7:3 if her husband be **d.**, she is free.......... *599*
Ro 7:4 ye also are become **d.** to the law *2289*
Ro 7:4 to him who is raised from the **d.**. *3498*
Ro 7:6 being **d.** wherein we were held; *599*
Ro 7:8 For without the law sin was **d.**. *3498*
Ro 8:10 the body is **d.** because of sin;........... *3498*
Ro 8:11 up Jesus from the **d.** dwell in you,....... *3498*
Ro 8:11 that raised up Christ from the **d.**......... *3498*
Ro 10:7 bring up Christ again from the **d.**. *3498*
Ro 10:9 hath raised him from the **d.**, thou....... *3498*
Ro 11:15 of them be, but life from the **d.**?........ *3498*
Ro 14:9 be Lord both of the **d.** and living....... *3498*
1Co 7:39 but if her husband be **d.**, she is at....... *2837*
1Co 15:12 preached that he rose from the **d.**, ... *3498*
1Co 15:12 there is no resurrection of the **d.**?...... *3498*
1Co 15:13 if there be no resurrection of the **d.**,.... *3498*
1Co 15:15 if so be that the **d.** rise not............. *3498*
1Co 15:16 For if the **d.** rise not, then is not *3498*
1Co 15:20 now is Christ risen from the **d.**,.......... *3498*
1Co 15:21 came also the resurrection of the **d.**..... *3498*
1Co 15:29 which are baptized for the **d.**,............ *3498*
1Co 15:29 if the **d.** rise not at all? why are......... *3498*
1Co 15:29 they then baptized for the **d.**?........... *3498*
1Co 15:32 it me, if the **d.** rise not?.................... *3498*
1Co 15:35 How are the **d.** raised up? and with.... *3498*
1Co 15:42 also is the resurrection of the **d.**. *3498*
1Co 15:52 the **d.** shall be raised incorruptible, ... *3498*
2Co 1:9 but in God which raiseth the **d.**:......... *3498*
2Co 5:14 one died for all, then were all **d.**:........ *599*
Ga 1:1 who raised him from the **d.**;.............. *3498*
Ga 2:19 I through the law am **d.** to the........... *599*
Ga 2:21 the law, then Christ is **d.** in vain. *599*
Eph 1:20 when he raised him from the **d.**, ... *3498*
Eph 2:1 were **d.** in trespasses and sins;.......... *3498*
Eph 2:5 when we were **d.** in sins, hath.......... *3498*
Eph 5:14 and arise from the **d.**, and Christ *3498*
Php 3:11 unto the resurrection of the **d.**.......... *3498*
Col 1:18 the firstborn from the **d.**;................ *3498*
Col 2:12 who hath raised him from the **d.**. *3498*
Col 2:13 And you, being **d.** in your sins.......... *3498*
Col 2:20 if ye be **d.** with Christ from the........... *599*
Col 3:3 For ye are **d.**, and your life is hid....... *599*
1Th 1:10 whom he raised from the **d.**, even....... *3498*
1Th 4:16 the **d.** in Christ shall rise first:.......... *3498*
1Ti 5:6 in pleasure is **d.** while she liveth. *2348*
2Ti 2:8 of David was raised from the **d.**......... *3498*
2Ti 2:11 For if we be **d.** with him, we shall...... *4880*
2Ti 4:1 shall judge the quick and the **d.**.......... *3498*
Heb 6:1 repentance from **d.** works, and of....... *3498*
Heb 6:2 and of resurrection of the **d.**, and....... *3498*
Heb 9:14 your conscience from **d.** works to....... *3498*
Heb 9:17 of force after men are **d.**: *3498*
Heb 11:4 by it he being **d.** yet speaketh............ *599*
Heb 11:12 even of one, and him as good as **d.**, ... *3499*
Heb 11:19 to raise him up, even from the **d.**; *3498*
Heb 11:35 received their **d.** raised to life........... *3498*
Heb 13:20 brought again from the **d.** our Lord..... *3498*
Jas 2:17 hath not works, is **d.**, being alone. *3498*
Jas 2:20 that faith without works is **d.**? *3498*
Jas 2:26 the body without the spirit is **d.**,......... *3498*
Jas 2:26 so faith without works is **d.** also........ *3498*
1Pe 1:3 of Jesus Christ from the **d.**, ... *3498*
1Pe 1:21 that raised him up from the **d.**, and *3498*
1Pe 2:24 that we, being **d.** to sins, should.......... *581*
1Pe 4:5 to judge the quick and the **d.**............ *3498*
1Pe 4:6 preached also to them that are **d.**,....... *3498*
Jude 12 without fruit, twice **d.**, plucked............ *599*
Re 1:5 the first begotten of the **d.**, and......... *3498*
Re 1:17 saw him, I fell at his feet as **d.**. *3498*
Re 1:18 **I am he that liveth, and was d.**; *3498*
Re 2:8 **last, which was d., and is alive**; *3498*
Re 3:1 **a name that thou livest, and art d.**..*3498*
Re 11:8 **d.** bodies shall lie in the streets *4430*
Re 11:9 shall see their **d.** bodies three days..... *4430*
Re 11:9 shall not suffer their **d.** bodies to........ *4430*
Re 11:18 time of the **d.**, that they should *3498*
Re 14:13 Blessed are the **d.** which die in the..... *3498*
Re 16:3 became as the blood of a **d.** man:....... *3498*
Re 20:5 the rest of the **d.** lived not again........ *3498*
Re 20:12 And I saw the **d.**, small and great, ... *3498*
Re 20:12 and the **d.** were judged out of............ *3498*
Re 20:13 gave up the **d.** which were in it, ... *3498*
Re 20:13 death and hell delivered up the **d.**........ *3498*

DEADLY

1Sa 5:11 was a **d.** destruction throughout......... 4194
Ps 17:9 my **d.** enemies, who compass me....... 5315
Eze 30:24 groanings of a **d.** wounded man..............
Mk 16:18 **and if they drink any d. thing**,...... *2286*
Jas 3:8 an unruly evil, full of **d.** poison.......... *2287*
Re 13:3 **d.** wound was healed; and all........... *2288*
Re 13:12 whose **d.** wound was healed............. *2288*

DEADNESS

Ro 4:19 yet the **d.** of Sarah's womb............... *3500*

DEAF

Ex 4:11 who maketh the dumb, or **d.**, or 2795
Le 19:14 Thou shalt not curse the **d.**, nor 2795
Ps 38:13 But I, as a **d.** man, heard not;........... 2795
Ps 58:4 the **d.** adder that stoppeth her ear;..... 2795
Isa 29:18 in that day shall the **d.** hear 2795
Isa 35:5 ears of the **d.** shall be unstopped........ 2795
Isa 42:18 Hear, ye **d.**; and look, ye blind, ... 2795
Isa 42:19 **d.**, as my messenger that I sent? 2795
Isa 43:8 eyes, and the **d.** that have ears. 2795
Mic 7:16 their mouth, their ears shall be **d.**. 2790
Mt 11:5 **and the d. hear, the dead are** *2974*
Mk 7:32 was **d.**, and had an impediment *2974*
Mk 7:37 he maketh both the **d.** to hear, and *2974*
Mk 9:25 **Thou dumb and d. spirit, I charge** . *2974*
Lu 7:22 **the d. hear, the dead are raised**,.... *2974*

DEAL See also DEALEST; DEALETH; DEALING; DEALS; DEALT.

Ge 19:9 now will we **d.** worse with thee, ...
Ge 21:23 thou wilt not **d.** falsely with me,..............
Ge 24:49 if ye will **d.** kindly and truly with........ 6213
Ge 32:9 and I will **d.** well with thee: ....
Ge 34:31 Should he **d.** with our sister as.......... 6213
Ge 47:29 and **d.** kindly and truly with me;......... 6213
Ex 1:10 let us **d.** wisely with them; lest................
Ex 8:29 let not Pharaoh **d.** deceitfully any..............
Ex 21:9 **d.** with her after the manner............. 6213
Ex 23:11 thou shalt **d.** with thy vineyard, ... 6213
Ex 29:40 the one lamb a tenth **d.** of flour ....
Le 14:21 and one tenth **d.** of fine flour..................
Le 19:11 shall not steal, neither **d.** falsely,............
Nu 11:15 if thou **d.** thus with me, kill me,......... 6213
Nu 15:4 a tenth **d.** of flour mingled with...............
Nu 28:13 And a several tenth **d.** of flour................
Nu 28:21 several tenth **d.** shalt thou offer..............
Nu 28:29 several tenth **d.** unto one lamb................
Nu 29:4 And one tenth **d.** for one lamb,...............
Nu 29:10 A several tenth **d.** for one lamb, ...
Nu 29:15 a several tenth **d.** to each lamb................
De 7:5 shall ye **d.** with them; ye shall........... 6213
Jos 2:14 will **d.** kindly and truly with thee. 6213
Ru 1:8 the Lord **d.** kindly with you, as ye...... 6213
1Sa 20:8 shalt **d.** kindly with thy servant; 6213

2Sa 18:5 **D.** gently for my sake with the
2Ch 2:3 didst **d.** with David my father, 6213
2Ch 2:3 dwell therein, even so **d.** with me
2Ch 19:11 **D.** courageously, and the Lord 6213
Job 42:8 lest I **d.** with you after your folly, 6213
Ps 75:4 **D.** not foolishly: and to the
Ps 105:25 to **d.** subtilly with his servants.
Ps 119:17 **D.** bountifully with thy servant, 1580
Ps 119:124 **D.** with thy servant according 6213
Ps 142:7 thou shalt **d.** bountifully with me, 1580
Pr 12:22 they that **d.** truly are his delight 6213
Isa 26:10 of uprightness will he **d.** unjustly,
Isa 33:1 an end to **d.** treacherously,
Isa 33:1 shall **d.** treacherously with thee.
Isa 48:8 wouldst **d.** very treacherously,
Isa 52:13 my servant shall **d.** prudently,
Isa 58:7 to **d.** thy bread to the hungry, 6536
Jer 12:1 happy that **d.** very treacherously?
Jer 18:23 **d.** thus with them in the time of 6213
Jer 21:2 Lord will **d.** with us according to 6213
Eze 8:18 Therefore will I also **d.** in fury: 6213
Eze 16:59 **d.** with thee as thou hast done 6213
Eze 18:9 kept my judgments, to **d.** truly; 6213
Eze 22:14 the days that I shall **d.** with thee? 6213
Eze 23:25 they shall **d.** furiously with thee: 6213
Eze 23:29 they shall **d.** with thee hatefully, 6213
Eze 31:11 he shall surely **d.** with him: 6213
Da 1:13 thou seest, **d.** with thy servants 6213
Da 11:7 and shall **d.** against them, and 6213
Hab 1:13 upon them that **d.** treacherously,
Mal 2:10 why do we **d.** treacherously every
Mal 2:15 let none **d.** treacherously against
Mal 2:16 spirit, that ye **d.** not treacherously.
Mk 7:36 so much the more a great **d.** *4054*
Mk 10:48 he cried the more a great **d.**

DEALER See also DEALERS.
Isa 21:2 the treacherous **d.** dealeth

DEALERS
Isa 24:16 the treacherous **d.** have dealt
Isa 24:16 yea, the treacherous **d.** have dealt very

DEALEST
Ex 5:15 **d.** thou thus with thy servants? 6213
Isa 33:1 **d.** treacherously, and they dealt

DEALETH
Jg 18:4 **d.** Micah with me, and hath 6213
1Sa 23:22 told me that he **d.** very subtilly.
Pr 10:4 He becometh poor that **d.** with 6213
Pr 13:16 prudent man **d.** with knowledge: 6213
Pr 14:17 He that is soon angry **d.** foolishly: 6213
Pr 21:24 his name, who **d.** in proud wrath. 6213
Isa 21:2 treacherous dealer **d.** treacherously; 6213
Jer 6:13 the priest every one **d.** falsely. 6213
Jer 8:10 unto the priest every one **d.** falsely. 6213
Heb 12:7 God **d.** with you as with sons; *4374*

DEALING See also DEALINGS.
Ps 7:16 his violent **d.** shall come down

DEALINGS
1Sa 2:23 of your evil **d.** by all this people 1697
Joh 4:9 have no **d.** with the Samaritans, *4798*

DEALS
Le 14:10 three tenth **d.** of fine flour for
Le 23:13 two tenth **d.** of fine flour mingled
Le 23:17 two wave loaves of two tenth **d.**:
Le 24:5 two tenth **d.** shall be in one cake
Nu 15:6 two tenth **d.** of flour mingled
Nu 15:9 three tenth **d.** of flour mingled
Nu 28:9 and two tenth **d.** of flour for a
Nu 28:12 three tenth **d.** of flour for a meat
Nu 28:12 two tenth **d.** of flour for a meat
Nu 28:20 three tenth **d.** shall ye offer for a
Nu 28:20 and two tenth **d.** for a ram;
Nu 28:28 three tenth **d.** unto one bullock,
Nu 28:28 two tenth **d.** unto one ram,
Nu 29:3 three tenth **d.** for a bullock,
Nu 29:3 and two tenth **d.** for a ram,
Nu 29:9 three tenth **d.** to a bullock,
Nu 29:9 and two tenth **d.** to one ram,
Nu 29:14 three tenth **d.** unto every bullock
Nu 29:14 two tenth **d.** to each ram

DEALT
Ge 16:6 when Sarai **d.** hardly with her
Ge 33:11 God hath **d.** graciously with me,
Ge 43:6 Wherefore **d.** ye so ill with me,
Ex 1:20 God **d.** well with the midwives:
Ex 14:11 wherefore hast thou **d.** thus with 6213
Ex 18:11 the thing wherein they **d.** proudly
Ex 21:8 seeing he hath **d.** deceitfully with
Jg 9:16 if ye have **d.** well with Jerubbaal 6213
Jg 9:19 ye then have **d.** truly and sincerely 6213
Jg 9:23 men of Shechem **d.** treacherously
Ru 1:8 as ye have **d.** with the dead, 6213
Ru 1:20 the Almighty hath **d.** very bitterly
1Sa 24:18 thou hast **d.** well with me: for as 6213
1Sa 25:31 when the Lord shall have **d.** well
2Sa 6:19 And he **d.** among all the people, 2505
2Ki 12:15 workmen: for they **d.** faithfully. 6213
2Ki 21:6 and **d.** with familiar spirits and 6213
2Ki 22:7 hand, because they **d.** faithfully. 6213
1Ch 16:3 And he **d.** to every one of Israel, 2505
1Ch 20:3 so **d.** David with all the cities 6213
2Ch 6:37 done amiss, and have **d.** wickedly;
2Ch 11:23 And he **d.** wisely, and dispersed of
2Ch 33:6 **d.** with a familiar spirit, and with 6213
Ne 1:7 **d.** very corruptly against thee,
Ne 9:10 that they **d.** proudly against them.
Ne 9:16 they and our fathers **d.** proudly
Ne 9:29 yet they **d.** proudly and hearkened
Job 6:15 My brethren have **d.** deceitfully as
Ps 13:6 he hath **d.** bountifully with me. 1580
Ps 44:17 have we **d.** falsely in thy covenant.
Ps 78:57 **d.** unfaithfully like their fathers:
Ps 103:10 hath not **d.** with us after our sins; 6213
Ps 116:7 hath **d.** bountifully with thee. 1580
Ps 119:65 hast **d.** well with thy servant, 6213
Ps 119:78 for they **d.** perversely with me
Ps 147:20 He hath not **d.** so with any nation: 6213
Isa 24:16 dealers have **d.** treacherously; yea,
Isa 24:16 have **d.** very treacherously.
Isa 33:1 **d.** not treacherously with thee!
Jer 3:20 have ye **d.** treacherously with me,
Jer 5:11 **d.** very treacherously against me,
Jer 12:6 have **d.** treacherously with thee;
La 1:2 have **d.** treacherously with her,
Eze 22:7 of thee have they **d.** by oppression 6213
Eze 25:12 **d.** against the house of Judah 6213
Eze 25:15 the Philistines have **d.** by revenge, 6213
Ho 5:7 **d.** treacherously against the Lord:
Ho 6:7 have **d.** treacherously against me.
Joe 2:26 your God that hath **d.** wondrously 6213
Zec 1:6 our doings, so hath he **d.** with us. 6213
Mal 2:11 Judah hath **d.** treacherously, and
Mal 2:14 hast **d.** treacherouly; yet is she
Lu 1:25 Thus hath the Lord **d.** with me *4160*
Lu 2:48 why hast thou thus **d.** with us? *4160*
Ac 7:19 The same **d.** subtilly with our *2686*
Ac 25:24 the Jews have **d.** with me, both *1793*
Ro 12:3 as God hath **d.** to every man *3307*

DEAR
Jer 31:20 Is Ephraim my **d.** son? is he a 3357
Lu 7:2 who was **d.** unto him, was sick, *1784*
Ac 20:24 count I my life **d.** unto myself, *5093*
Eph 5:1 followers of God, as **d.** children; *27*
Col 1:7 our **d.** fellowservant, who is *27*
Col 1:13 into the kingdom of his **d.** Son: *26*
1Th 2:8 souls, because ye were **d.** unto us. *27*

DEARLY
Jer 12:7 the **d.** beloved of my soul
Ro 12:19 **D.** beloved, avenge not
1Co 10:14 Wherefore, my **d.** beloved, flee
2Co 7:1 these promises **d.** beloved, let us
2Co 12:19 do all things **d.** beloved for
Php 4:1 my brethren **d.** beloved and longed
Php 4:1 fast in the Lord, my **d.** beloved.
2Ti 1:2 To Timothy my **d.** beloved son:
Phm 1 unto Philemon our **d.** beloved
1Pe 2:11 **D.** beloved, I beseech you as

DEARTH
Ge 41:54 seven years of **d.** began to come, 7458
Ge 41:54 said, and the **d.** was in all lands; 7458
2Ki 4:38 and there was a **d.** in the land; 7458
2Ch 6:28 If there be **d.** in the land, 7458
Ne 5:3 might buy corn, because of the **d.** 7458
Jer 14:1 to Jeremiah concerning the **d.** 1226
Ac 7:11 there came a **d.** over all the land *3042*
Ac 11:28 be great **d.** throughout all the *3042*

DEATH See also DEATHS.
Ge 21:16 Let me not see the **d.** of the child. 4194
Ge 24:67 was comforted after his mother's **d.**
Ge 25:11 after the **d.** of Abraham, that God 4194
Ge 26:11 his wife shall surely be put to **d.** 4191
Ge 26:18 after the **d.** of Abraham: and he 4194
Ge 27:2 I know not the day of my **d.**: 4194
Ge 27:7 before the Lord before my **d.** 4194
Ge 27:10 he may bless thee before his **d.** 4194
Ex 10:17 take away from me this **d.** only 4194
Ex 19:12 mount shall be surely put to **d.**: 4191
Ex 21:12 he die shall be surely put to **d.**: 4191
Ex 21:15 his mother, shall be surely put to **d.** 4191
Ex 21:16 hand, he shall surely be put to **d.** 4191
Ex 21:17 his mother shall surely be put to **d.** 4191
Ex 21:29 his owner also shall be put to **d.** 4191
Ex 22:19 a beast shall surely be put to **d.** 4191
Ex 31:14 defileth it shall surely be put to **d.**: 4191
Ex 31:15 day, he shall surely be put to **d.** 4191
Ex 35:2 work therein shall be put to **d.** 4191
Le 16:1 after the **d.** of the two sons of 4194
Le 19:20 they shall not be put to **d.**, because 4191
Le 20:2 he shall surely be put to **d.**: the 4191
Le 20:9 shall be surely put to **d.**: he hath 4191
Le 20:10 adulteress shall surely be put to **d.** 4191
Le 20:11, 12 them shall surely be put to **d.**; 4191
Le 20:13 they shall surely be put to **d.**; their 4191
Le 20:15 he shall surely be put to **d.**: and ye 4191
Le 20:16 they shall surely be put to **d.**; their 4191
Le 20:27 a wizard, shall surely be put to **d.**: 4191
Le 24:16 he shall surely be put to **d.**, and all 4191
Le 24:16 of the Lord, shall be put to **d.** 4191
Le 24:17 any man shall surely be put to **d.** 4191
Le 24:21 a man, he shall be put to **d.** 4191
Le 27:29 but shall surely be put to **d.** 4191
Nu 1:51 that cometh nigh shall be put to **d.** 4191
Nu 3:10, 38 cometh nigh shall be put to **d.** 4191
Nu 15:35 The man shall be surely put to **d.**: 4191
Nu 16:29 these men die the common **d.** of all 4194
Nu 18:7 that cometh nigh shall be put to **d.** 4191
Nu 23:10 Let me die the **d.** of the righteous, 4194
Nu 35:16, 17,18 murderer...be put to **d.** 4191
Nu 35:21 smote him shall surely be put to **d.**: 4191
Nu 35:25 unto the **d.** of the high priest, 4194
Nu 35:28 until the **d.** of the high priest: 4194
Nu 35:28 but after the **d.** of the high priest 4194
Nu 35:30 the murderer shall be put to **d.** by 7523
Nu 35:31 a murderer, which is guilty of **d.** 4191
Nu 35:31 but he shall surely be put to **d.** 4191
Nu 35:32 land, until the **d.** of the priest. 4194
De 13:5 of dreams, shall be put to **d.**; 4191
De 13:9 be first upon him to put him to **d.**, 4191
De 17:6 shall he that is worthy of **d.** be 4191
De 17:6 be put to **d.**; but at the mouth of 4191
De 17:6 witness he shall not be put to **d.** 4191
De 17:7 upon him to put him to **d.**, and 4191
De 19:6 whereas he was not worthy of **d.**, 4194
De 21:22 committed a sin worthy of **d.**, 4194
De 21:22 and he be to be put to **d.**, 4191
De 22:26 in the damsel no sin worthy of **d.**: 4194
De 24:16 The fathers shall not be put to **d.** 4191
De 24:16 the children be put to **d.** for the 4191
De 24:16 shall be put to **d.** for his own sin 4191
De 30:15 life and good, and **d.** and evil; 4194
De 30:19 I have set before you life and **d.**, 4194
De 31:27 how much more after my **d.**? 4194
De 31:29 I know that after my **d.** ye will 4194
De 33:1 the children of Israel before his **d.** 4194
Jos 1:1 after the **d.** of Moses the servant of 4194
Jos 1:18 he shall be put to **d.**; only be 4191
Jos 2:13 have, and deliver our lives from **d.** 4194
Jos 20:6 until the **d.** of the high priest. 4194
Jg 1:1 after the **d.** of Joshua it came to 4194
Jg 5:18 jeoparded their lives unto the **d.** 4191
Jg 6:31 let him be put to **d.** whilst it is yet 4191
Jg 13:7 the womb to the day of his **d.** 4194
Jg 16:16 his soul was vexed unto **d.**; 4191
Jg 16:30 the dead which he slew at his **d.** 4194
Jg 20:13 that we may put them to **d.**, and 4191
Jg 21:5 saying, He shall surely be put to **d.** 4191
Ru 1:17 if ought but **d.** art thee and me 4194
Ru 2:11 since the **d.** of thine husband: 4194
1Sa 4:20 about the time of her **d.** the women 4191
1Sa 11:12 men, that we may put them to **d.** 4191
1Sa 11:13 There shall not a man be put to **d.** 4191
1Sa 15:32 Surely the bitterness of **d.** is past 4194
1Sa 15:35 to see Saul until the day of his **d.**: 4194
1Sa 20:3 but a step between me and **d.** 4194
1Sa 22:22 I have occasioned the **d.** of all the
2Sa 1:1 came to pass after the **d.** of Saul, 4194
2Sa 1:23 in their **d.** they were not divided: 4194

Book	Ref	Context	No.
2Sa	6:23	had no child unto the day of her **d.**	4194
2Sa	8:2	two lines measured he to put to **d.**,	4191
2Sa	15:21	whether in **d.** or life, even there	4194
2Sa	19:21	shall not Shimei be put to **d.** for	4191
2Sa	19:22	shall there any man be put to **d.**	4191
2Sa	20:3	shut up unto the day of their **d.**,	4191
2Sa	21:9	and were put to **d.** in the days of	4191
2Sa	22:5	When the waves of **d.** compassed	4194
2Sa	22:6	the snares of **d.** prevented me;	4194
1Ki	2:8	I will not put thee to **d.** with the	4191
1Ki	2:24	Adonijah shall be put to **d.** this day	4191
1Ki	2:26	thou art worthy of **d.**: but	4194
1Ki	2:26	not at this time put thee to **d.**,	4191
1Ki	11:40	in Egypt until the **d.** of Solomon	4194
2Ki	1:1	against Israel after the **d.** of Ahab	4194
2Ki	2:21	thence any more **d.** or barren land	4194
2Ki	4:40	man of God, there is **d.** in the pot	4194
2Ki	14:6	fathers shall not be put to **d.** for	4191
2Ki	14:6	nor the children be put to **d.**	4191
2Ki	14:6	but every man shall be put to **d.**	4191
2Ki	14:17	after the **d.** of Jehoash son of	4194
2Ki	15:5	a leper unto the day of his **d.**,	4194
2Ki	20:1	days was Hezekiah sick unto **d.**	4191
1Ch	22:5	prepared abundantly before his **d.**	4194
2Ch	15:13	God of Israel should be put to **d.**,	4191
2Ch	22:4	after the **d.** of his father to his	4194
2Ch	23:7	the house, he shall be put to **d.**:	4191
2Ch	24:17	after the **d.** of Jehoiada came the	4194
2Ch	25:25	after the **d.** of Joash son of	4194
2Ch	26:21	a leper unto the day of his **d.**,	4194
2Ch	32:24	Hezekiah was sick to the **d.**, and	4191
2Ch	32:33	did him honour at his **d.**	4194
Ezr	7:26	whether it be unto **d.**, or to	4193
Es	4:11	one law of his to put him to **d.**,	4191
Job	3:5	Let darkness and the shadow of **d.**	6757
Job	3:21	long for **d.**, but it cometh not;	4194
Job	5:20	he shall redeem thee from **d.**:	4194
Job	7:15	and **d.** rather than my life	4194
Job	10:21	of darkness and the shadow of **d.**;	6757
Job	10:22	itself; and of the shadow of **d.**,	6757
Job	12:22	out to light the shadow of **d.**	6757
Job	16:16	on my eyelids is the shadow of **d.**;	6757
Job	18:13	firstborn of **d.** shall devour his	4194
Job	24:17	to them even as the shadow of **d.**:	6757
Job	24:17	the terrors of the shadow of **d.**	6757
Job	27:15	of him shall be buried in **d.**:	4194
Job	28:3	of darkness, and the shadow of **d.**	6757
Job	28:22	Destruction and **d.** say, We have	4194
Job	30:23	thou wilt bring me to **d.**, and to the	4194
Job	34:22	is no darkness, nor shadow of **d.**,	6757
Job	38:17	Have the gates of **d.** been opened	4194
Job	38:17	the doors of the shadow of **d.**?	6757
Ps	6:5	in **d.** there is no remembrance of	4194
Ps	7:13	for him the instruments of **d.**; he	4194
Ps	9:13	liftest me up from the gates of **d.**:	4194
Ps	13:3	lest I sleep the sleep of **d.**;	4194
Ps	18:4	The sorrows of **d.** compassed me,	4194
Ps	18:5	the snares of **d.** prevented me	4194
Ps	22:15	brought me into the dust of **d.**	4194
Ps	23:4	the valley of the shadow of **d.**,	6757
Ps	33:19	To deliver their soul from **d.**, and	4194
Ps	44:19	covered us with the shadow of **d.**	6757
Ps	48:14	he will be our guide even unto **d.**	4192
Ps	49:14	**d.** shall feed on them; and the	4194
Ps	55:4	the terrors of **d.** are fallen upon me	4194
Ps	55:15	Let **d.** seize upon them, and	4194
Ps	56:13	hast delivered my soul from **d.**:	4194
Ps	68:20	the Lord belong the issues from **d.**	4194
Ps	73:4	there are no bands in their **d.**:	4194
Ps	78:50	spared not their soul from **d.**,	4194
Ps	89:48	he that liveth, and shall not see **d.**?	4194
Ps	102:20	those that are appointed to **d.**;	8546
Ps	107:10	darkness and in the shadow of **d.**,	6757
Ps	107:14	of darkness and the shadow of **d.**,	6757
Ps	107:18	they draw near unto the gates of **d.**	4194
Ps	116:3	The sorrows of **d.** compassed me,	4194
Ps	116:8	delivered my soul from **d.**, mine	4194
Ps	116:15	of the Lord is the **d.** of his saints	4194
Ps	118:18	he hath not given me over unto **d.**	4194
Pr	2:18	her house inclineth unto **d.**, and	4194
Pr	5:5	Her feet go down to **d.**; her steps	4194
Pr	7:27	going down to the chambers of **d.**	4194
Pr	8:36	all they that hate me love **d.**	4194
Pr	:10:2	righteousness delivereth from **d.**	4194
Pr	11:4	righteousness delivereth from **d.**	4194
Pr	11:19	evil pursueth it to his own **d.**	4194
Pr	12:28	the pathway thereof there is no **d.**	4194
Pr	13:14	to depart from the snares of **d.**	4194
Pr	14:12	the end thereof are the ways of **d.**	4194
Pr	14:27	to depart from the snares of **d.**	4194
Pr	14:32	the righteous hath hope in his **d.**	4194
Pr	16:14	of a king is as messengers of **d.**:	4194
Pr	16:25	the end thereof are the ways of **d.**	4194
Pr	18:21	**D.** and life are in the power of the	4194
Pr	21:6	to and fro of them that seek **d.**	4194
Pr	24:11	them that are drawn unto **d.**, and	4194
Pr	26:18	casteth firebrands, arrows, and **d.**,	4194
Ec	7:1	day of **d.** than the day of one's birth	4194
Ec	7:26	more bitter than **d.** the woman,	4194
Ec	8:8	power in the day of **d.**: and there is	4194
Ca	8:6	love is strong as **d.**; jealousy is	4194
Isa	9:2	the land of the shadow of **d.**, upon	6757
Isa	25:8	He will swallow up **d.** in victory;	4194
Isa	28:15	We have made a covenant with **d.**,	4194
Isa	28:18	your covenant with **d.** shall be	4194
Isa	38:1	days was Hezekiah sick unto **d.**	4191
Isa	38:18	**d.** can not celebrate thee: they	4194
Isa	53:9	wicked, and with the rich in his **d.**;	4194
Isa	53:12	hath poured out his soul unto **d.**:	4194
Jer	2:6	drought, and of the shadow of **d.**,	6757
Jer	8:3	**d.** shall be chosen rather than	4194
Jer	9:21	**d.** is come up into our windows,	4194
Jer	13:16	he turn it into the shadow of **d.**,	6757
Jer	15:2	Such as are for **d.**, to **d.**; and such	4194
Jer	18:21	let their men be put to **d.**; let	4194
Jer	21:8	the way of life, and the way of **d.**	4194
Jer	26:15	if ye put me to **d.**, ye shall surely	4191
Jer	26:19	and all Judah put him at all to **d.**?	4191
Jer	26:21	the king sought to put him to **d.**:	4191
Jer	26:24	hand of the people to put him to **d.**	4191
Jer	38:4	let this man be put to **d.**: for thus	4191
Jer	38:15	wilt thou not surely put me to **d.**?	4191
Jer	38:16	I will not put thee to **d.**, neither	4191
Jer	38:25	we will not put thee to **d.**; also	4191
Jer	43:3	that they might put us to **d.**, and	4191
Jer	43:11	such as are for **d.** to **d.**; and such	4194
Jer	52:11	in prison till the day of his **d.**	4194
Jer	52:27	smote them, and put them to **d.**	4191
Jer	52:34	a portion until the day of his **d.**,	4194
La	1:20	bereaveth, at home there is as **d.**	4194
Eze	18:32	pleasure in the **d.** of him that dieth,	4194
Eze	31:14	they are all delivered unto **d.**, to the	4194
Eze	33:11	no pleasure in the **d.** of the wicked;	4194
Ho	13:14	I will redeem them from **d.**: O **d.**,	4194
Am	5:8	turneth the shadow of **d.** into the	6757
Jon	4:9	well to be angry, even unto **d.**	4194
Hab	2:5	his desire as hell, and is as **d.**,	4194
Mt	2:15	was there until the **d.** of Herod:	*5054*
Mt	4:16	in the region and shadow of **d.**	*2288*
Mt	10:21	**deliver up the brother to d.,**	*2288*
Mt	10:21	**and cause them to be put to d**	*2289*
Mt	14:5	he would have put him to **d.**,	*615*
Mt	15:4	**or mother, let him die the d**	*2288*
Mt	16:28	**shall not taste of d., till they see**	*2288*
Mt	20:18	**and they shall condemn him to d.,**	*2288*
Mt	26:38	**exceeding sorrowful, even unto d.:**	*2288*
Mt	26:59	against Jesus, to put him to **d.**;	*2289*
Mt	26:66	and said, He is guilty of **d.**	*2288*
Mt	27:1	against Jesus, to put him to **d.**:	*2289*
Mk	5:23	daughter lieth at the point of **d.**:	*2079*
Mk	7:10	**let him die the d.: But ye say,**	*2288*
Mk	9:1	**shall not taste of d., till they have**	*2288*
Mk	10:33	**shall condemn him to d., and shall**	*2288*
Mk	13:12	**shall betray the brother to d.,**	*2288*
Mk	13:12	**shall cause them to be put to d**	*2289*
Mk	14:1	him by craft, and put him to **d.**	*615*
Mk	14:34	**is exceeding sorrowful unto d.:**	*2288*
Mk	14:55	against Jesus to put him to **d.**; and	*2289*
Mk	14:64	condemned him to be guilty of **d.**	*2288*
Lu	1:79	and in the shadow of **d.**, to guide	*2288*
Lu	2:26	that he should not see **d.**, before	*2288*
Lu	9:27	**which shall not taste of d., till**	*2288*
Lu	18:33	**scourge him, and put him to d.:**	*615*
Lu	21:16	**shall they cause to be put to d**	*2289*
Lu	22:33	thee; both into prison, and to **d.**	*2288*
Lu	23:15	nothing worthy of **d.** is done unto	*2288*
Lu	23:22	found no cause of **d.** in him: I will	*2288*
Lu	23:32	led with him to be put to **d.**	*337*
Lu	24:20	to be condemned to **d.**, and have	*2288*
Joh	4:47	for he was at the point of **d.**	*599*
Joh	5:24	**but is passed from d. unto life**	*2288*
Joh	8:51	**my saying, he shall never see d.**	*2288*
Joh	8:52	saying, he shall never taste of **d.**	*2288*
Joh	11:4	**This sickness is not unto d., but**	*2288*
Joh	11:13	Jesus spake of his **d.**; but they	*2288*
Joh	11:53	together for to put him to **d.**	*615*
Joh	12:10	they might put Lazarus also to **d.**;	*615*
Joh	12:33	signifying what **d.** he should die,	*2288*
Joh	18:31	lawful for us to put any man to **d.**;	*615*
Joh	18:32	signifying what **d.** he should die	*2288*
Joh	21:19	by what **d.** he should glorify God	*2288*
Ac	2:24	up, having loosed the pains of **d.**:	*2288*
Ac	8:1	Saul was consenting unto his **d.**	*336*
Ac	12:19	that they should be put to **d.**	*520*
Ac	13:28	they found no cause of **d.** in him,	*2288*
Ac	22:4	I persecuted this way unto the **d.**,	*2288*
Ac	22:20	by, and consenting unto his **d.**,	*336*
Ac	23:29	charge worthy of **d.** or of bonds	*336*
Ac	25:11	committed any thing worthy of **d.**,	*336*
Ac	25:25	committed nothing worthy of **d.**,	*336*
Ac	26:10	when they were put to **d.**, I gave	*337*
Ac	26:31	nothing worthy of **d.** or of bonds	*2288*
Ac	28:18	there was no cause of **d.** in me	*2288*
Ro	1:32	such things are worthy of **d.**,	*2288*
Ro	5:10	by the **d.** of his Son, much more,	*2288*
Ro	5:12	and **d.** by sin; and so **d.** passed	*2288*
Ro	5:14	**d.** reigned from Adam to Moses,	*2288*
Ro	5:17	man's offence **d.** reigned by one;	*2288*
Ro	5:21	That as sin hath reigned unto **d.**,	*2288*
Ro	6:3	Christ were baptized into his **d.**?	*2288*
Ro	6:4	with him by baptism into **d.**:	*2288*
Ro	6:5	in the likeness of his **d.**, we shall be	*2288*
Ro	6:9	**d.** hath no more dominion over him	*2288*
Ro	6:16	of sin unto **d.**, or of obedience	*2288*
Ro	6:21	the end of those things is **d.**	*2288*
Ro	6:23	For the wages of sin is **d.**; but the	*2288*
Ro	7:5	to bring forth fruit unto **d.**	*2288*
Ro	7:10	life, I found to be unto **d.**	*2288*
Ro	7:13	which is good made **d.** unto me?	*2288*
Ro	7:13	might appear sin, working **d.** in me	*2288*
Ro	7:24	me from the body of this **d.**?	*2288*
Ro	8:2	free from the law of sin and **d.**	*2288*
Ro	8:6	to be carnally minded is **d.**;	*2288*
Ro	8:38	neither **d.**, nor life, nor angels, nor	*2288*
1Co	3:22	or life, or **d.**, or things present,	*2288*
1Co	4:9	last, as it were appointed to **d.**:	*1935*
1Co	11:26	ye do shew the Lord's **d.** till he	*2288*
1Co	15:21	by man came **d.**, by man came	*2288*
1Co	15:26	that shall be destroyed is **d.**	*2288*
1Co	15:54	**D.** is swallowed up in victory	*2288*
1Co	15:55	O **d.**, where is thy sting? O grave	*2288*
1Co	15:56	sting of **d.** is sin; and the strength	*2288*
2Co	1:9	had the sentence of **d.** in ourselves,	*2288*
2Co	1:10	delivered us from so great a **d.**,	*2288*
2Co	2:16	one we are the savour of **d.** unto **d.**;	*2288*
2Co	3:7	the ministration of **d.**, written and	*2288*
2Co	4:11	delivered unto **d.** for Jesus' sake,	*2288*
2Co	4:12	then **d.** worketh in us, but life in	*2288*
2Co	7:10	the sorrow of the world worketh **d.**	*2288*
Php	1:20	whether it be by life, or by **d.**	*2288*
Php	2:8	and became obedient unto **d.**,	*2288*
Php	2:8	even the **d.** of the cross	*2288*
Php	2:27	he was sick nigh unto **d.**: but God	*2288*
Php	2:30	he was nigh unto **d.**, not regarding	*2288*
Php	3:10	made conformable unto his **d.**;	*2288*
Col	1:22	In the body of his flesh through **d.**,	*2288*
2Ti	1:10	who hath abolished **d.**, and	*2288*
Heb	2:9	for the suffering of **d.**, crowned	*2288*
Heb	2:9	God should taste **d.** for every man	*2288*
Heb	2:14	through **d.** he might destroy him	*2288*
Heb	2:14	that had the power of **d.**,	*2288*
Heb	2:15	fear of **d.** were all their lifetime	*2288*
Heb	5:7	to save him from **d.**, and was heard	*2288*
Heb	7:23	to continue by reason of **d.**:	*2288*
Heb	9:15	by means of **d.**, for the redemption	*2288*
Heb	9:16	must also of necessity be the **d.**	*2288*
Heb	11:5	that he should not see **d.**;	*2288*
Jas	1:15	it is finished, bringeth forth **d.**	*2288*
Jas	5:20	save a soul from **d.**, and shall hide	*2288*
1Pe	3:18	being put to **d.** in the flesh,	*2289*
1Jo	3:14	we have passed from **d.** unto life,	*2288*
1Jo	3:14	not his brother abideth in **d.**	*2288*
1Jo	5:16	a sin which is not unto **d.**, he shall	*2288*
1Jo	5:16	life for them that sin not unto **d.**	*2288*
1Jo	5:16	There is a sin unto **d.**: I do not	*2288*
1Jo	5:17	and there is a sin not unto **d.**	*2288*
Re	1:18	**the keys of hell and of d**	*2288*
Re	2:10	**be thou faithful unto d., and I will**	*2288*
Re	2:11	**shall not be hurt of the second d**	*2288*
Re	2:23	**I will kill her children with d.;**	*2288*
Re	6:8	his name that sat on him was **D.**,	*2288*

Re 6:8 and with hunger, and with **d.**, *2288*
Re 9:6 men seek **d.**, and shall not find it; *2288*
Re 9:6 and **d.** shall flee from them. *2288*
Re 12:11 loved not their lives unto the **d.**. *2288*
Re 13:3 as it were wounded to **d.**; and his *2288*
Re 18:8 day, **d.**, and mourning, and famine; *2288*
Re 20:6 the second **d.** hath no power, but *2288*
Re 20:13 **d.** and hell delivered up the dead *2288*
Re 20:14 **d.** and hell were cast into the *2288*
Re 20:14 lake of fire. This is the second **d.**, *2288*
Re 21:4 be no more **d.**, neither sorrow, *2288*
Re 21:8 brimstone: which is the second **d.**. *2288*

DEATHS
Jer 16:4 They shall die of grievous **d.**; 4463
Eze 28:8 the **d.** of them that are slain 4463
Eze 28:10 die the **d.** of the uncircumcised 4194
2Co 11:23 prisons more frequent in **d.** oft. *2288*

DEBAR See LO-DEBAR.

DEBASE
Isa 57:9 didst **d.** thyself even unto hell. 8213

DEBATE See also DEBATES.
Pr 25:9 **D.** thy cause with thy neighbour 7378
Isa 27:8 forth, thou wilt **d.** with it: 7378
Isa 58:4 fast for strife and **d.**, and to smite 4683
Ro 1:29 murder, **d.**, deceit, malignity; *2054*

DEBATES
2Co 12:20 there be **d.**, envyings, wraths, *2054*

DEBIR (de'-bur) See also KIRJATH-SANNAH; KIRJATH-SEPHER.
Jos 10:3 unto **D.** king of Eglon, saying, 1688
Jos 10:38 and all Israel with him, to **D.**; 1688
Jos 10:39 did to **D.**, and to the king thereof; 1688
Jos 11:21 from Hebron, from **D.**, from Anab, 1688
Jos 12:13 king of **D.**, one; the king of Geder, 1688
Jos 13:26 Mahanaim unto the border of **D.**; 1688
Jos 15:7 the border went up toward **D.** 1688
Jos 15:15 up thence to the inhabitants of **D.**: 1688
Jos 15:15 of **D.** before was Kirjath-sepher. 1688
Jos 15:49 and Kirjath-sannah, which is **D.**, 1688
Jos 21:15 Holon with her suburbs, and **D.** 1688
Jg 1:11 up against the inhabitants of **D.**: 1688
Jg 1:11 of **D.** before was Kirjath-sepher. 1688
1Ch 6:58 Hilen with her suburbs, **D.** with 1688

DEBORAH (deb'-o-rah)
Ge 35:8 But **D.** Rebekah's nurse died, 1683
Jg 4:4 **D.**, a prophetess, the wife of 1683
Jg 4:5 dwelt under the palm tree of **D.**, 1683
Jg 4:9 **D.** arose, and went with Barak 1683
Jg 4:10 and **D.** went up with him. 1683
Jg 4:14 **D.** said unto Barak, Up; for this 1683
Jg 5:1 Then sang **D.** and Barak the son of 1683
Jg 5:7 until that I **D.** arose, that I arose 1683
Jg 5:12 Awake, awake, **D.**: awake, awake, 1683
Jg 5:15 princes of Issachar were with **D.**; 1683

DEBT See also DEBTS; INDEBTED.
1Sa 22:2 every one that was in **d.**, and 5378
2Ki 4:7 sell the oil, and pay thy **d.**, 5386
Ne 10:31 and the exaction of every **d.** 3027
Mt 18:27 **him, and forgave him the d.** *1156*
Mt 18:30 **prison, till he should pay the d.** *3784*
Mt 18:32 **I forgave thee all that d., because** *3782*
Ro 4:4 not reckoned of grace, but of **d.** *3783*

DEBTOR See also DEBTORS.
Eze 18:7 hath restored to the **d.** his pledge, 2326
Mt 23:16 **the gold of the temple, he is a d.!** *3784*
Ro 1:14 I am **d.** both to the Greeks, and *3781*
Ga 5:3 he is a **d.** to do the whole law. *3781*

DEBTORS
Mt 6:12 **our debts, as we forgive our d.** *3781*
Lu 7:41 **certain creditor which had two d.**: *5533*
Lu 16:5 **called every one of his lord's d.** *5533*
Ro 8:12 we are **d.**, not to the flesh, *3781*
Ro 15:27 them verily; and their **d.** they are *3781*

DEBTS
Pr 22:26 of them that are sureties for **d.** 4859
Mt 6:12 **forgive us our d., as we forgive** *3783*

DECAPOLIS (de-cap'-o-lis)
Mt 4:25 and from **D.**, and from Jerusalem, *1179*
Mk 5:20 and began to publish in **D.** how *1179*
Mk 7:31 the midst of the coasts of **D.** *1179*

DECAY See also DECAYED; DECAYETH.
Le 25:35 and fallen in **d.** with thee; 4131

DECAYED
Ne 4:10 of the bearers of burdens is **d.**, 3782
Isa 44:26 and I will raise up the **d.** places 2723

DECAYETH
Job 14:11 the flood **d.** and drieth up: 2717
Ec 10:18 slothfulness the building **d.**; 4355
Heb 8:13 that which **d.** and waxeth old *3822*

DECEASE See also DECEASED.
Lu 9:31 spake of his **d.** which he should *1841*
2Pe 1:15 may be able after my **d.** to have *1841*

DECEASED
Isa 26:14 they are **d.**, they shall not rise: 7496
Mt 22:25 when he had married a wife, **d.**, *5053*

DECEIT See also DECEITFUL; DECEITS.
Job 15:35 and their belly prepareth **d.**. 4820
Job 27:4 nor my tongue utter **d.**. 7423
Job 31:5 if my foot hath hasted to **d.**; 4820
Ps 10:7 His mouth is full of cursing and **d.** 4820
Ps 36:3 of his mouth are iniquity and **d.**: 4820
Ps 50:19 to evil, and thy tongue frameth **d.**. 4820
Ps 55:11 **d.** and guile depart not from her 8496
Ps 72:14 shall redeem their soul from **d.** 8496
Ps 101:7 **d.** shall not dwell within my 7423
Ps 119:118 statutes: for their **d.** is falsehood. 8649
Pr 12:5 the counsels of the wicked are **d.** 4820
Pr 12:17 but a false witness **d.**. 4820
Pr 12:20 **D.** is in the heart of them that 4820
Pr 14:8 but the folly of fools is **d.**. 4820
Pr 20:17 Bread of **d.** is sweet to a man; 8267
Pr 26:24 and layeth up **d.** within him; 4820
Pr 26:26 Whose hatred is covered by **d.**, 4860
Isa 53:9 neither was any **d.** in his mouth. 4820
Jer 5:27 their houses full of **d.**: therefore 4820
Jer 8:5 hold fast **d.**, they refuse to return. 8649
Jer 9:6 habitation is in the midst of **d.**; 4820
Jer 9:6 through **d.** they refuse to know me, 4820
Jer 9:8 it speaketh **d.**: one speaketh 4820
Jer 14:14 nought, and the **d.** of their heart. 8649
Jer 23:26 of the **d.** of their own heart; 8649
Ho 11:12 and the house of Israel with **d.**: 4820
Ho 12:7 the balances of **d.** are in his hand: 4820
Am 8:5 and falsifying the balances by **d.**? 4820
Zep 1:9 houses with violence and **d.**. 4820
Mk 7:22 **wickedness, d., lasciviousness, an** *1388*
Ro 1:29 full of envy, murder, debate, **d.**, *1388*
Ro 3:13 their tongues they have used **d.**; *1387*
Col 2:8 through philosphy and vain **d.**, *539*
1Th 2:3 our exhortation was not of **d.**, *4106*

DECEITFUL
Ps 5:6 will abhor the bloody and **d.** man. 4820
Ps 35:20 devise **d.** matters against them 4820
Ps 43:1 me from the **d.** and unjust man. 4820
Ps 52:4 words, O thou **d.** tongue. 4820
Ps 55:23 bloody and **d.** men shall not live 4820
Ps 78:57 were turned aside like a **d.** bow. 7423
Ps 109:2 of the **d.** are opened against me: 4820
Ps 120:2 from lying lips, and from a **d.** 7423
Pr 11:18 The wicked worketh a **d.** work: 8267
Pr 14:25 but a **d.** witness speaketh lies. 4820
Pr 23:3 his dainties: for they are **d.** meat. 3577
Pr 27:6 but the kisses of an enemy are **d.**. 6280
Pr 29:13 and the **d.** man meet together: 8501
Pr 31:30 Favour is **d.**, and beauty is vain: 8267
Jer 17:9 The heart is **d.** above all things, 6121
Ho 7:16 High: they are like a **d.** bow: 7423
Mic 6:11 and with the bag of **d.** weights? 4820
Mic 6:12 their tongue is **d.** in heir mouth. 7423
Zep 3:13 **d.** tongue be found in their mouth: 8649
2Co 11:13 false apostles, **d.** workers, *1386*
Eph 4:22 corrupt according to the **d.** lusts; *539*

DECEITFULLY
Ge 34:13 Shechem and Hamor his father **d.**, 4820
Ex 8:29 let not Pharaoh deal **d.** any more 2048
Ex 21:8 seeing he hath dealt **d.** with her. 898
Le 6:4 thing which he hath **d.** gotten. 6231
Job 6:15 brethren have dealt **d.** as a brook, 898
Job 13:7 for God? and talk **d.** for him? 7423
Ps 24:4 his soul unto vanity, nor sworn **d.**. 4820
Ps 52:2 like a sharp razor, working **d.**. 7423
Jer 48:10 doeth the work of the Lord **d.**, 7423
Da 11:23 he shall work **d.**: for he shall 4820
2Co 4:2 nor handling the word of God **d.**, *1389*

DECEITFULNESS
Mt 13:22 **the d. of riches, choke the word,** *539*
Mk 4:19 **the d. of riches, and the lusts of** *539*
Heb 3:13 be hardened through the **d.** of sin. *539*

DECEITS
Ps 38:12 and imagine **d.** all the day long. 4820
Isa 30:10 us smooth things, prophesy **d.**: 4123

DECEIVABLENESS
2Th 2:10 with all **d.** of unrighteousness in *539*

DECEIVE See also DECEIVED; DECEIVETH; DECEIVING.
2Sa 3:25 that he came to **d.** thee, and to 6601
2Ki 4:28 did I not say, Do not **d.** me? 7952
2Ki 18:29 Let not Hezekiah **d.** you: for he 5377
2Ki 19:10 God in whom thou trustest **d.** thee, 5377
2Ch 32:15 let not Hezekiah **d.** you, nor 5377
Pr 24:28 cause; and **d.** not with thy lips. 6601
Isa 36:14 Let not Hezekiah **d.** you: for he 5377
Isa 37:10 God, in whom thou trustest, **d.** thee, 5377
Jer 9:5 will **d.** every one his neighbour, 2048
Jer 29:8 that be in the midst of you **d.** you, 5377
Jer 37:9 **D.** not yourselves, saying, The 5377
Zec 13:4 they wear a rough garment to **d.**: 3584
Mt 24:4 **Take heed that no man d. you.** *4105*
Mt 24:5 **I am Christ; and shall d. many.** *4105*
Mt 24:11 **shall rise and shall d. many.** *4105*
Mt 24:24 **they shall d. the very elect.** *4105*
Mk 13:5 **Take heed lest any man d. you:** *4105*
Mk 13:6 **I am Christ; and shall d. many.** *4105*
Ro 16:18 speeches **d.** the hearts of the *1818*
1Co 3:18 Let no man **d.** himself. If any *1818*
Eph 4:14 whereby they lie in wait to **d.**; *4106*
Eph 5:6 Let no man **d.** you with vain words: *538*
2Th 2:3 Let no man **d.** you by any means: *1818*
1Jo 1:8 we **d.** ourselves, and the truth *4105*
1Jo 3:7 let no man **d.** you: he that doeth *4105*
Re 20:3 that he should **d.** the nations no *4105*
Re 20:8 go out to **d.** the nations which are *4105*

DECEIVED
Ge 31:7 your father hath **d.** me, and 2048
Le 6:2 violence, or hath **d.** his neighbour; 6231
De 11:16 that your heart be not **d.**, 6601
1Sa 19:17 Why hast thou **d.** me so, and sent 7411
1Sa 28:12 Why hast thou **d.** me? for thou art 7411
2Sa 19:26 my servant **d.** me: for thy servant 7411
Job 12:16 the **d.** and the deceiver are his. 7683
Job 15:31 not him that is **d.** trust in vanity: 8582
Job 31:9 If mine heart have been **d.** by a 6601
Pr 20:1 whosoever is **d.** thereby is not 7686
Isa 19:13 the princes of Noph are **d.**: 5377
Isa 44:20 a **d.** heart had turned him aside, 2048
Jer 4:10 thou hast greatly **d.** this people 5377
Jer 20:7 thou hast **d.** me, and I was **d.**: 6601
Jer 49:16 Thy terribleness hath **d.** thee, 5377
La 1:19 I called for my lovers, but they **d.** 7411
Eze 14:9 if the prophet be **d.** when he hath 6601
Eze 14:9 I the Lord have **d.** that prophet, 6601
Ob 3 pride of thine heart hath **d.** thee, 5377
Ob 7 at peace with thee hath **d.** thee, 5377
Lu 21:8 **Take heed that ye be not d.** *4105*
Joh 7:47 the Pharisees, Are ye also **d.**? *4105*
Ro 7:11 **d.** me, and by it slew me. *1818*
1Co 6:9 Be not **d.**: neither fornicators, nor *4105*
1Co 15:33 Be not **d.**; evil communications *4105*
Ga 6:7 Be not **d.**; God is not mocked: *4105*
1Ti 2:14 Adam was not **d.**, but the woman *538*
1Ti 2:14 being **d.** was in the transgression. *538*
2Ti 3:13 worse, deceiving, and being **d.** *4105*
Tit 3:3 **d.**, serving divers lusts and *4105*
Re 18:23 thy sorceries were all nations **d.** *4105*
Re 19:20 with which he **d.** them that had *4105*
Re 20:10 the devil that **d.** them was cast *4105*

DECEIVER See also DECEIVERS.
Ge 27:12 I shall seem to him as a **d.**; 8591
Job 12:16 he deceived and the **d.** are his. 7686
Mal 1:14 cursed be the **d.**, which hath in 5230
Mt 27:63 we remember that that **d.** said, *4108*
2Jo 7 This is a **d.** and an antichrist. *4108*

DECEIVERS
2Co 6:8 good report: as **d.**, and yet true; *4108*
Tit 1:10 unruly and vain talkers and **d.**, *5423*
2Jo 7 For many **d.** are entered into the *4108*

DECEIVETH
Pr 26:19 the man that **d.** his neighbour, 7411
Joh 7:12 said, Nay; but he **d.** the people. *4105*
Ga 6:3 when he is nothing, he **d.** himself. *5422*
Jas 1:26 his tongue, but **d.** his own heart, *538*
Re 12:9 Satan, which **d.** the whole world: *4105*
Re 13:14 **d.** them that dwell on the earth *4105*

DECEIVING See also DECEIVINGS.
2Ti 3:13 worse and worse, **d.**, and being *4105*
Jas 1:22 hearers only, **d.** your own selves. *3884*

DECEIVINGS
2Pe 2:13 their own **d.** while they feast, *539*

DECENTLY
1Co 14:40 all things be done **d.** and in order. *2156*

DECIDED
1Ki 20:40 judgment be; thyself hast **d.** it. 2782

DECISION
Joe 3:14 multitudes in the valley of **d.**: for 2742
Joe 3:14 the Lord is near in the valley of **d.** 2742

DECK See also DECKED; DECKEST; DECKETH.
Job 40:10 **D.** thyself now with majesty 5710
Jer 10:4 **d.** it with silver and with gold; 3302

DECKED See also DECKEDST.
Pr 7:16 I have **d.** my bed with coverings 7234
Eze 16:11 I **d.** thee also with ornaments, 5710
Eze 16:13 wast thou **d.** with gold and silver; 5710
Ho 2:13 she **d.** herself with her earrings 5710
Re 17:4 **d.** with gold and precious stones *5558*
Re 18:16 **d.** with gold, and precious stones, *5558*

DECKEDST
Eze 16:16 and **d.** thy high places with divers 6213
Eze 23:40 and **d.** thyself with ornaments, 5710

DECKEST
Jer 4:30 thou **d.** thee with ornaments of 5710

DECKETH
Isa 61:10 as a bridegroom **d.** himself with 3547

DECLARATION
Es 10:2 **d.** of the greatness of Mordecai 6575
Job 13:17 and my **d.** with your ears. 262
Lu 1:1 to set forth in order a **d.** of those *1335*
2Co 8:19 and **d.** of your ready mind:

DECLARE See also DECLARED; DECLARETH; DECLARING.
Ge 41:24 was none that could **d.** it to me. 5046
De 1:5 began Moses to **d.** this law, saying, 874
Jos 20:4 and shall **d.** his cause in the ears 1696
Jg 14:12 **d.** it me within the seven days of 5046
Jg 14:13 if ye cannot **d.** it me, then shall ye 5046
Jg 14:15 that he may **d.** unto us the riddle, 5046
1Ki 22:13 prophets **d.** good unto the king
1Ch 16:24 **D.** his glory among the heathen; 5608
2Ch 18:12 the words of the prophets **d.** good
Es 4:8 and to **d.** unto her, and to charge 5046
Job 12:8 the fishes of the sea shall **d.** unto 5608
Job 15:17 that which I have seen I will **d.**; 5608
Job 21:31 Who shall **d.** his way to his face? 5046
Job 28:27 Then did he see it, and **d.** it; 5608
Job 31:37 I would **d.** unto him the number 5046
Job 38:4 **d.**, if thou hast understanding. 5046
Job 38:18 earth? **d.** if thou knowest it all. 5046
Job 40:7 of thee, and **d.** thou unto me. 3045
Job 42:4 of thee, and **d.** thou unto me. 3045
Ps 2:7 I will **d.** the decree: the Lord 5608
Ps 9:11 **d.** among the people his doings. 5046
Ps 19:1 The heavens **d.** the glory of God; 5608
Ps 22:22 **d.** thy name unto my brethren: 5608
Ps 22:31 **d.** his righteousness unto a people 5046
Ps 30:9 praise thee? shall it **d.** thy truth? 5046
Ps 38:18 For I will **d.** mine iniquity; 5046
Ps 40:5 if I would **d.** and speak of them, 5046
Ps 50:6 heavens shall **d.** his righteousness: 5046
Ps 50:16 hast thou to do to **d.** my statutes, 5608
Ps 64:9 and shall **d.** the work of God; 5046
Ps 66:16 and I will **d.** what he hath done 5608
Ps 73:28 that I may **d.** all thy works. 5608
Ps 75:1 is near thy wondrous works **d.** 5608
Ps 75:9 But I will **d.** for ever; I will 5046
Ps 78:6 and **d.** them to their children: 5608
Ps 96:3 **D.** his glory among the heathen, 5608
Ps 97:6 The heavens **d.** his righteousness, 5046
Ps 102:21 To **d.** the name of the Lord in 5608
Ps 107:22 and **d.** his works with rejoicing. 5608
Ps 118:17 but live, and **d.** the works of the 5608
Ps 145:4 and shall **d.** thy mighty acts. 5046
Ps 145:8 acts: and I will **d.** thy greatness. 5608
Ec 8:1 to **d.** all this, that the righteous, 952
Isa 3:9 they **d.** their sin as Sodom, they 5046
Isa 12:4 **d.** his doings among the people, 3045
Isa 21:6 let him **d.** what he seeth. 5046
Isa 41:22 or **d.** us things for to come. 8085
Isa 42:9 new things do I **d.**: before they 5046
Isa 42:12 unto Lord, and **d.** his praise 5046
Isa 43:9 who among them can **d.** this, 5046
Isa 43:26 **d.** thou, that thou mayest be 5608
Isa 44:7 as I shall call, and shall **d.** it, 5046
Isa 45:19 I **d.** things that are right. 5046
Isa 48:6 all this; and will not ye **d.** it? 5046
Isa 48:20 with a voice of singing **d.** ye, 5046
Isa 53:8 and who shall **d.** his generation? 7878
Isa 57:12 I will **d.** thy righteousness, and 5046
Isa 66:19 and they shall **d.** my glory among 5046
Jer 4:5 **D.** ye in Judah, and publish in 5046
Jer 5:20 **D.** this in the house of Jacob, 5046
Jer 9:12 **d.** it, for what the land perisheth 5046
Jer 31:10 and **d.** it in the isles afar off, 5046
Jer 38:15 If I **d.** it unto thee, wilt thou not 5046
Jer 38:25 **D.** unto us now what thou hast 5046
Jer 42:4 I will **d.** it unto you; I will keep 5046
Jer 42:20 **d.** unto us, and we will do it. 5046
Jer 46:14 **D.** ye in Egypt, and publish in 5046
Jer 50:2 **D.** ye among the nations, and 5046
Jer 50:28 to **d.** in Zion the vengeance of the 5046
Jer 51:10 and let us **d.** in Zion the work of 5608
Eze 12:16 they may **d.** all their abominations 5608
Eze 23:36 **d.** unto them their abominations; 5046
Eze 40:4 **d.** all that thou seest to the house 5046
Da 4:18 **d.** the interpretation thereof, 560
Mic 1:10 **D.** ye it not at Gath, weep ye not 5046
Mic 3:8 to **d.** unto Jacob his transgression, 5046
Zec 9:12 even to day do I **d.** that I will 5046
Mt 13:36 **D.** unto us the parable of the *5419*
Mt 15:15 unto him, **D.** unto us this parable. *5419*
Joh 17:26 **them thy name, and will d. it:** *1107*
Ac 8:33 and who shall **d.** his generation? *1334*
Ac 13:32 we **d.** unto you glad tidings, how *2097*
Ac 13:41 though a man **d.** it unto you. *1555*
Ac 17:23 worship, him **d.** I unto you. *2605*
Ac 20:27 to **d.** unto you the counsel of God. *312*
Ro 3:25 to **d.** his righteousness for the *1732*
Ro 3:26 To **d.**, I say, at this time his *1732*
1Co 3:13 for the day shall **d.** it, because *1213*
1Co 11:17 Now in this that I **d.** unto you *3853*
1Co 15:1 brethren I **d.** unto you the gospel *1107*
Col 4:7 state shall Tychicus **d.** unto you, *1107*
Heb 2:12 will **d.** thy name unto my brethren, *518*
Heb 11:14 **d.** plainly that they seek a *1718*
1Jo 1:3 seen and heard **d.** we unto you, *518*
1Jo 1:5 **d.** unto you, that God is light, *312*

DECLARED
Ex 9:16 my name may be **d.** throughout 5608
Le 23:44 And Moses **d.** unto the children 1696
Nu 1:18 and they **d.** their pedigrees after
Nu 15:34 was not **d.** what should be done 6567
De 4:13 And he **d.** unto you his covenant 5046
2Sa 19:6 thou hast **d.** this day, that thou 5046
Ne 8:12 the words that were **d.** unto them. 3045
Job 26:3 hast thou plentifully **d.** the thing 3045
Ps 40:10 I have **d.** thy faithfulness and thy 559
Ps 71:17 have I **d.** thy wondrous works. 5046
Ps 77:14 **d.** thy strength among the people. 3045
Ps 88:11 Shall thy lovingkindness be **d.** 5608
Ps 119:13 With my lips have I **d.** all the 5608
Ps 119:26 I have **d.** my ways, and thou 5608
Isa 21:2 A grievous vision is **d.** unto me; 5046
Isa 21:10 of Israel, have I **d.** unto you. 5046
Isa 41:26 Who hath **d.** from the beginning, 5046
Isa 43:12 I have **d.**, and have saved, and I 5046
Isa 44:8 from that time, and have **d.** it? 5046
Isa 45:21 who hath **d.** this from ancient 8085
Isa 48:3 I have **d.** the former things from 5046
Isa 48:5 from the beginning **d.** it to thee; 5046
Isa 48:14 among them hath **d.** these things? 5046
Jer 36:13 Then Michaiah **d.** unto them all 5046
Jer 42:21 And now I have this day **d.** it 5046
Lu 8:47 **d.** unto him before all the people *518*
Joh 1:18 the Father, he hath **d.** him: *1834*
Joh 17:26 **I have d. unto them thy name,** *1107*
Ac 9:27 **d.** unto them how he had seen the *1334*
Ac 10:8 when he had **d.** all these things *1834*
Ac 12:17 **d.** unto them how the Lord had *1334*
Ac 15:4 **d.** all things that God had done *312*
Ac 15:14 Simeon hath **d.** how God at the *1834*
Ac 21:19 **d.** particularly what things God *1834*
Ac 25:14 **d.** Paul's cause unto the king, *394*
Ro 1:4 **d.** to be the Son of God with power, *3724*
Ro 9:17 my name might be **d.** throughout *1229*
1Co 1:11 it hath been **d.** unto me of you, *1213*
2Co 3:3 manifestly **d.** to be the epistle of *5319*
Col 1:3 Who also **d.** unto us your love *1213*
Re 10:7 **d.** to his servants the prophets. *2097*

DECLARETH
Isa 41:26 there is none that **d.**, yea, there is 5046
Jer 4:15 For a voice **d.** from Dan, and 5046
Ho 4:12 and their staff **d.** unto them: for 5046
Am 4:13 **d.** unto man what is his thought. 5046

DECLARING
Isa 46:10 **D.** the end from the beginning, 5046
Ac 15:3 **d.** the conversion of the Gentiles: *1555*
Ac 15:12 **d.** what miracles and wonders *1834*
1Co 2:1 **d.** unto you the testimony of God. *2605*

DECLINE See also DECLINED; DECLINETH.
Ex 23:2 **d.** after many to wrest judgment: 5186
De 17:11 shalt not **d.** from the sentence 5493
Ps 119:157 do I not **d.** from thy testimonies. 5186
Pr 4:5 neither **d.** from the words of my 5186
Pr 7:25 Let not thine heart **d.** to her ways, 7847

DECLINED
2Ch 34:2 **d.** neither to the right hand, nor 5493
Job 23:11 his way have I kept and not **d.** 5186
Ps 44:18 have our steps **d.** from thy way; 5186
Ps 119:51 yet have I not **d.** from thy law. 5186

DECLINETH
Ps 102:11 days are like a shadow that **d.**; 5186
Ps 109:23 gone like the shadow when it **d.**: 5186

DECREASE See also DECREASED.
Ps 107:38 and suffereth not their cattle to **d.** 4591
Joh 3:30 He must increase, but I must **d.** *1642*

DECREASED
Ge 8:5 the waters **d.** continually until 2637

DECREE See also DECREED; DECREES.
2Ch 30:5 So they established a **d.** to make 1697
Ezr 5:13 Cyrus made a **d.** to build this 2942
Ezr 5:17 that a **d.** was made of Cyrus the 2942
Ezr 6:1 Darius the king made a **d.**, and 2942
Ezr 6:3 same Cyrus the king made a **d.** 2942
Ezr 6:8 I make a **d.** what ye shall do to 2942
Ezr 6:11 I have made a **d.**, that whosoever 2942
Ezr 6:12 I Darius have made a **d.**: let it 2942
Ezr 7:13 I make a **d.**, that all they of the 2942
Ezr 7:21 I Artaxerxes the king, do make a **d.** 2942
Es 1:20 the king's **d.** which he shall make 6599
Es 2:8 and his **d.** was heard, and when 1881
Es 3:15 and the **d.** was given in Shushan 1881
Es 4:3 commandment and his **d.** came, 1881
Es 4:8 the copy of the writing of the **d.** 1881
Es 8:14 And the **d.** was given at Shushan 1881
Es 8:17 commandment and his **d.** came, 1881
Es 9:1 and his **d.** drew near to be put in 1881
Es 9:13 according unto this day's **d.**, and let 1881
Es 9:14 the **d.** was given at Shushan; and 1881
Es 9:32 And the **d.** of Esther confirmed 3982
Job 22:28 Thou shalt also **d.** a thing, and it 1504
Job 28:26 When he made a **d.** for the rain, 2706
Ps 2:7 I will declare the **d.**: the Lord hath 2706
Ps 148:6 made a **d.** which shall not pass. 2706
Pr 8:15 reign, and princes **d.** justice. 2710
Pr 8:29 When he gave to the sea his **d.**, 2706
Isa 10:1 unto them that **d.** unrighteous 2710
Jer 5:22 of the sea by a perpetual **d.**, 2706
Da 2:9 there is but one **d.** for you: 1882
Da 2:13 And the **d.** went forth that wise men 1882
Da 2:15 is the **d.** so hasty from the king? 1882
Da 3:10 Thou, O king, hast made a **d.**, 2942
Da 3:29 I make a **d.**, That every people, 2942
Da 4:6 Therefore made I a **d.** to bring in 2942
Da 4:17 by the **d.** of the watchers, and the 1510
Da 4:24 and this is the **d.** of the most High, 1510
Da 6:7 to make a firm **d.**, that whosoever 633
Da 6:8 O king, establish the **d.**, and sign 633
Da 6:9 signed the writing and the **d.** 633
Da 6:12 king concerning the king's **d.**; 633

Da 6:12 Hast thou not signed a d., that... 633
Da 6:13 nor the d. that thou hast signed,... 633
Da 6:15 no d. nor statute which the king... 633
Da 6:26 I make a d., That in every... 2942
Jon 3:7 the d. of the king and his nobles,... 2940
Mic 7:11 day shall the d. be far removed.... 2706
Zep 2:2 Before the d. bring forth, before... 2706
Lu 2:1 there went out a d. from Caesar... *1378*

DECREED
Es 2:1 and what was d. against her.... 1504
Es 9:31 and as they had d. for themselves... 6965
Job 38:10 brake up for it my d. place... 2706
Isa 10:22 the consumption d. shall overflow... 2782
1Co 7:37 hath so d. in his heart that he... *2919*

DECREES
Isa 10:1 that decree unrighteous d., and... 2711
Ac 16:4 delivered them the d. for to keep,... *1378*
Ac 17:7 all do contrary to the d. of Caesar... *1378*

DEDAN (de'-dan) See also DEDANIM.
Ge 10:7 sons of Raamah; Sheba, and D.... 1719
Ge 25:3 Jokshan begat Sheba and D.... 1719
Ge 25:3 the sons of D. were Asshurim, and... 1719
1Ch 1:9 sons of Raamah; Sheba, and D.... 1719
1Ch 1:32 sons of Jokshan; Sheba, and D.... 1719
Jer 25:23 D., and Tema, and Buz, and all... 1719
Jer 49:8 dwell deep, O inhabitants of D.;... 1719
Eze 25:13 they of D. shall fall by the sword.... 1719
Eze 27:15 The men of D. were thy merchants;... 1719
Eze 27:20 D. was thy merchant in precious... 1719
Eze 38:13 Sheba, and D., and the merchants... 1719

DEDANIM (ded'-a-nim) See also DODANIM.
Isa 21:13 O ye travelling companies of D.... 1720

DEDICATE See also DEDICATED; DEDICATING.
De 20:5 battle, and another man d. it.... 2596
2Sa 8:11 Which also king David did d.... 6942
1Ch 26:27 did they d. to maintain the house... 6942
2Ch 2:4 to d. it to him, and to burn... 6942

DEDICATED
De 20:5 new house, and hath not d. it?... 2596
Jg 17:3 wholly d. the silver unto the Lord... 6942
2Sa 8:11 the silver and gold that he had d.... 6942
1Ki 7:51 which David his father had d.;... 6944
1Ki 8:63 and all the children of Israel d.... 2596
1Ki 15:15 things which his father had d.,... 6944
1Ki 15:15 the things which himself had d.,... 6944
2Ki 12:4 money of the d. things that is... 6944
2Ki 12:18 kings of Judah, had d., and his... 6942
1Ch 18:11 king David d. unto the Lord,... 6942
1Ch 26:20 over the treasures of the d. things... 6944
1Ch 26:26 all the treasures of the d. things,... 6944
1Ch 26:26 the captains of the host, had d.... 6942
1Ch 26:28 Joab the son of Jeruiah, had d.;... 6942
1Ch 26:28 and whosoever had d. any thing,... 6942
1Ch 28:12 of the treasuries of the d. things:... 6944
2Ch 5:1 things that David his father had d.;... 6944
2Ch 7:5 and all the people d. the house... 2596
2Ch 15:18 the things that his father had d.,... 6944
2Ch 15:18 and that he himself had d.,... 6944
2Ch 24:7 d. things of the house of the Lord... 6944
2Ch 31:12 and the d. things faithfully: over... 6944
Eze 44:29 every d. thing in Israel shall be... 2764
Heb 9:18 testament was d. without blood.... *1457*

DEDICATING
Nu 7:10 princes offered for d. of the altar... 2598
Nu 7:11 on his day, for the d. of the altar.... 2598

DEDICATION
Nu 7:84 the d. of the altar, in the day... 2598
Nu 7:88 This was the d. of the altar,... 2598
2Ch 7:9 they kept the d. of the altar... 2598
Ezr 6:16 kept the d. of this house of God... 2597
Ezr 6:17 And offered at the d. of this house... 2597
Ne 12:27 at the d. of the wall of Jerusalem... 2598
Ne 12:27 to keep the d. with gladness,... 2598
Ps 30:*title* at the d. of the house of David.... 2598
Da 3:2 come to the d. of the image... 2597
Da 3:3 together unto the d. of the image... 2597
Joh 10:22 at Jerusalem the feast of the d.,... *1456*

DEED See also DEEDS; INDEED.
Ge 44:15 What d. is this that ye have done?... 4639
Ex 9:16 And in very d. for this cause... 199
Jg 19:30 There was no such d. done nor...
1Sa 25:34 For in very d., as the Lord God of... 199
1Sa 26:4 that Saul was come in very d..... 3559
2Sa 12:14 by this d. thou hast given great... 1697
2Ch 6:18 But will God in very d. dwell with men...
Es 1:17 For this d. of the queen shall... 1697
Es 1:18 have heard of the d. of the queen.... 1697
Lu 23:51 to the counsel and d. of them;... *4234*
Lu 24:19 mighty in d. and word before God... *2041*
Ac 4:9 good d. done to the impotent man,... *2108*
Ro 15:18 Gentiles obedient, by word and d.,... *2041*
1Co 5:2 hath done this d. might be taken... *2041*
1Co 5:3 him that hath so done this d.,...
2Co 10:11 also in d. when we are present.... *2041*
Col 3:17 ye do in word or d., do all in the... *2041*
Jas 1:25 man shall be blessed in his d..... *4162*
1Jo 3:18 tongue; but in d. and in truth.... *2041*

DEEDS See also ALMSDEEDS.
Ge 20:9 thou hast done d. unto me that... 4639
1Ch 16:8 make known his d. among the... 5949
2Ch 35:27 And his d., first and last, behold,... 1697
Ezr 9:13 for our evil d., and for our... 4639
Ne 6:19 reported his good d. before him,...
Ne 13:14 wipe not out my good d. that I...
Ps 28:4 Give them according to their d.,... 6467
Ps 105:1 make known his d. among the... 5949
Isa 59:18 According to their d.,... 1578
Jer 5:28 overpass the d. of the wicked:... 1697
Jer 25:14 them according to their d., and... 6467
Lu 11:48 **ye allow the d. of your fathers:**... *2041*
Lu 23:41 the due reward of our d.... *3739,4238*
Joh 3:19 **because their d. were evil**... *2041*
Joh 3:20 **lest his d. should be reproved**... *2041*
Joh 3:21 **his d. may be made manifest**... *2041*
Joh 8:41 **Ye do the d. of your father**... *2041*
Ac 7:22 was mighty in words and in d..... *2041*
Ac 19:18 confessed, and shewed their d..... *4234*
Ac 24:2 and that very worthy d. are done... *2735*
Ro 2:6 to every man according to his d.:... *2041*
Ro 3:20 by the d. of the law there shall no... *2041*
Ro 3:28 faith without the d. of the law.... *2041*
Ro 8:13 do mortify the d. of the body,... *4234*
2Co 12:12 and wonders, and mighty d..... *1411*
Col 3:9 put off the old man with his d.;... *4234*
2Pe 2:8 to day with their unlawful d.;... *2041*
2Jo 11 speed is partaker of his evil d.... *2041*
3Jo 10 his d. which he doeth, prating... *2041*
Jude 15 of all their ungodly d. which... *2041*
Re 2:6 **hatest the d. of the Nicolaitanes**... *2041*
Re 2:22 **except they repent of their d**... *2041*
Re 16:11 and repented not of their d.... *2041*

DEEMED
Ac 27:27 shipmen d. that they drew near... *5282*

DEEP See also DEEPER; DEEPS.
Ge 1:2 was upon the face of the d.... 8415
Ge 2:21 God caused a d. sleep to fall upon... 8639
Ge 7:11 fountains of the great d. broken... 8415
Ge 8:2 The fountains also of the d. and... 8415
Ge 15:12 down, a d. sleep fell upon Abram;... 8639
Ge 49:25 blessings of the d. that lieth under,... 8415
De 33:13 for the d. that coucheth beneath,... 8415
1Sa 26:12 d. sleep from the Lord was fallen... 8639
Job 4:13 when d. sleep falleth on men,... 8639
Job 12:22 He discovereth d. things out of... 6013
Job 33:15 when d. sleep falleth upon men,... 8639
Job 38:30 and the face of the d. is frozen.... 8415
Job 41:31 maketh the d. to boil like a pot:... 4688
Job 41:32 would think the d. to be hoary.... 8415
Ps 36:6 thy judgments are a great d.:... 8415
Ps 42:7 D. calleth unto d. at the noise of... 8415
Ps 64:6 one of them, and the heart, is d..... 6013
Ps 69:2 I sink in d. mire, when there is no... 4688
Ps 69:2 I am come into d. waters, where... 4615
Ps 69:14 hate me, and out of the d. waters.... 4615
Ps 69:15 neither let the d. swallow me up,... 4688
Ps 80:9 and didst cause it to take d. root,... 8328
Ps 92:5 and thy thoughts are very d..... 6009
Ps 95:4 In his hand are the d. places of the... 4278
Ps 104:6 Thou coveredst it with the d. as... 8415
Ps 107:24 Lord, and his wonders in the d..... 4688
Ps 135:6 in the seas, and all d. places.... 8415
Ps 140:10 into the fire; into d. pits, that... 4113
Pr 8:28 the fountains of the d.:... 8415
Pr 18:4 of a man's mouth are as d. waters,... 6013
Pr 19:15 casteth into a d. sleep; and an... 8639
Pr 20:5 in the heart of man is like d. water;... 6013
Pr 22:14 mouth of strange women is a d. pit;... 6013
Pr 23:27 whore is a d. ditch; and a strange... 6013
Ec 7:24 far off, and exceeding d., who can... 6013
Isa 29:10 the spirit of d. sleep, and hath... 8639
Isa 29:15 Woe unto them that seek d. to... 6009
Isa 30:33 he hath made it d. and large:... 6009
Isa 44:27 That saith to the d., Be dry,... 6683
Isa 51:10 sea, the waters of the great d.;... 8415
Isa 63:13 That led them through the d., as... 8415
Jer 49:8 dwell d., O inhabitants of Dedan;... 6009
Jer 49:30 dwell d. O ye inhabitants of Hazor,... 6009
Eze 23:32 shalt drink of thy sister's cup d.... 6013
Eze 26:19 when I shall bring up the d. upon... 8415
Eze 31:4 the d. set him up on high with her... 8415
Eze 31:15 I covered the d. for him, and I... 8415
Eze 32:14 Then will I make their waters d.,... 8257
Eze 34:18 to have drunk of the d. waters,... 4950
Da 2:22 revealeth the d. and secret things:... 5994
Da 8:18 I was in a d. sleep on my face.... 7290
Da 10:9 then was I in a d. sleep on my face.... 7290
Am 7:4 it devoured the great d., and did... 8415
Jon 2:3 thou hadst cast me into the d.,... 4688
Hab 3:10 the d. uttered his voice, and lifted... 8415
Lu 5:4 **Launch out into the d., and let**... *899*
Lu 6:48 **built an house, and digged d.,** ..*2532,900*
Lu 8:31 them to go out into the d..... *12*
Joh 4:11 to draw with, and the well is d.:... *901*
Ac 20:9 being fallen into a d. sleep:... *901*
Ro 10:7 Who shall descend into the d.?... *12*
1Co 2:10 things, yea, the d. things of God.... *899*
2Co 8:2 their d. poverty abounded unto the... *899*
2Co 11:25 and a day I have been in the d.;... *1037*

DEEPER
Le 13:3 plague in sight be d. than the skin,... 6013
Le 13:4 and in sight be not d. than the skin,... 6013
Le 13:25 and it be in sight d. than the skin;... 6013
Le 13:30 it it be in sight d. than the skin;... 6013
Le 13:31 it be not in sight d. than the skin... 6013
Le 13:32 in sight d. than the skin;... 6013
Le 13:34 nor be in sight d. than the skin;... 6013
Job 11:8 d. than hell; what canst thou know?... 6013
Isa 33:19 a people of d. speech than thou... 6012

DEEPLY
Isa 31:6 children of Israel have d. revolted... 6009
Ho 9:9 They have d. corrupted themselves,... 6009
Mk 8:12 he sighed d. in his spirit, and saith,... *389*

DEEPNESS
Mt 13:5 **because they had no d. of earth:**... *899*

DEEPS
Ne 9:11 thou threwest into the d., as a... 4688
Ps 88:6 lowest pit, in darkness, in the d.... 4688
Ps 148:7 the earth, ye dragons, and all d.:... 8415
Zec 10:11 the d. of the river shall dry up:... 4688

DEER See also FALLOWDEER.
De 14:5 the roebuck, and the fallow d.,... 3180

DEFAMED
1Co 4:13 Being d., we intreat: we are made... *987*

DEFAMING
Jer 20:10 For I heard the d. of many, fear... 1681

DEFEAT
2Sa 15:34 me d. the counsel of Ahithophel.... 6565
2Sa 17:14 d. the good counsel of Ahithophel,... 6565

DEFENCE See also DEFENCED.
Nu 14:9 their d. is departed from them,... 6738
2Ch 11:5 Jerusalem, and built cities for d.... 4692
Job 22:25 the Almighty shall be thy d., and... 1220
Ps 7:10 My d. is of God, which saveth... 4043
Ps 31:2 for an house of d. to save me... 4686
Ps 59:9 wait upon thee: for God is my d..... 4869
Ps 59:16 thou hast been my d. and refuge... 4869
Ps 59:17 God is my d., and the God of my... 4869
Ps 62:2 and my salvation; he is my d.;... 4869
Ps 62:6 he is my d.; I shall not be moved.... 4869
Ps 89:18 For the Lord is our d.: and the... 4043
Ps 94:22 the Lord is my d.; and my God... 4869
Ec 7:12 wisdom is a d., and money is a d.:... 6738
Isa 4:5 upon all the glory shall be a d.... 2646
Isa 19:6 the brooks of d. shall be emptied... 4692
Isa 33:16 place of d. shall be the munition... 4869
Na 2:5 and the d. shall be prepared.... 5526
Ac 19:33 have made his d. unto the people.... *626*
Ac 22:1 hear ye my d., which I make... *627*

Php 1:7 **d.** and confirmation of the gospel, ... *627*
Php 1:17 I am set for the **d.** of the gospel......... *627*

DEFENCED
Isa 25:2 of a **d.** city a ruin: a palace of........... 1219
Isa 27:10 Yet the **d.** city shall be desolate......... 1219
Isa 36:1 against all the **d.** cities of Judah,......... 1219
Isa 37:26 to lay waste **d.** cities into ruinous....... 1219
Jer 1:18 have made thee this day a **d.** city,...... 4013
Jer 4:5 and let us go into the **d.** cities. 4013
Jer 8:14 and let us enter into the **d.** cities, ... 4013
Jer 34:7 for these **d.** cities remained of........... 4013
Eze 21:20 and to Judah in Jerusalem the **d.**. 1219

DEFEND See DEFENDED; DEFENDEST; DEFENDING.
Jg 10:1 arose to **d.** Israel Tola the son of....... 3467
2Ki 19:34 For I will **d.** this city, to save it,........ 1598
2Ki 20:6 will **d.** this city for mine own sake,..... 1598
Ps 20:1 name of the God of Jacob **d.** thee;...... 7682
Ps 59:1 **d.** me from them that rise up........... 7682
Ps 82:3 **D.** the poor and fatherless: do........... 8199
Isa 31:5 the Lord of hosts **d.** Jerusalem; 1598
Isa 37:35 For I will **d.** this city to save it.......... 1598
Isa 38:6 of Assyria: and I will **d.** this city. 1598
Zec 9:15 The Lord of hosts shall **d.** them;........ 1598
Zec 12:8 In that day shall the Lord **d.** the 1598

DEFENDED
2Sa 23:12 and **d.** it, and slew the Philistines:...... 5337
Ac 7:24 suffer wrong, he **d.** him; and smote...... *292*

DEFENDEST
Ps 5:11 because thou **d.** them: let them 5526

DEFENDING
Isa 31:5 **d.** also he will deliver it; and............ 1598

DEFER See also DEFERRED; DEFERRETH.
Ec 5:4 **d.** not to pay it; for he hath no........... 309
Isa 48:9 will I **d.** mine anger, and for my.......... 748
Da 9:19 **d.** not, for thine own sake, O my 309

DEFERRED
Ge 34:19 young man **d.** not to do the thing,........ 309
Pr 13:12 Hope **d.** maketh the heart sick:.......... 4900
Ac 24:22 of that way, he **d.** them, and said, ... *306*

DEFERRETH
Pr 19:11 discretion of a man **d.** his anger;.......... 748

DEFIED
Nu 23:8 defy, whom the Lord hath not **d.**? 2194
1Sa 17:36 seeing he hath **d.** the armies of.......... 2778
1Sa 17:45 armies of Israel, whom thou hast **d.**.... 2778
2Sa 21:21 And when he **d.** Israel, Jonathan 2778
2Sa 23:9 when they **d.** the Philistines that........ 2778
1Ch 20:7 But when he **d.** Israel, Jonathan......... 2778

DEFILE See also DEFILED; DEFILETH.
Le 11:44 neither shall ye **d.** yourselves.............. 2930
Le 15:31 when they **d.** my tabernacle that is..... 2930
Le 18:20 neighbour's wife, to **d.** thyself with..... 2930
Le 18:23 thou lie with any beast to **d.** thyself.... 2930
Le 18:24 **D.** not ye yourselves in any of these.... 2930
Le 18:28 spue not you out also, when ye **d.** it,.. 2930
Le 18:30 that ye **d.** not yourselves therein:....... 2930
Le 20:3 to **d.** my sanctuary, and to profane..... 2930
Le 21:4 shall not **d.** himself, being a chief 2930
Le 21:11 nor **d.** himself for his father, or for..... 2930
Le 22:8 not eat to **d.** himself therewith:........... 2930
Nu 5:3 that they **d.** not their camps, in the 2930
Nu 35:34 **D.** not therefore the land which ye..... 2930
2Ki 23:13 children of Ammon, did the king **d.**..... 2930
Ca 5:3 my feet; how shall I **d.** them?............ 2936
Isa 30:22 Ye shall **d.** also the covering of thy..... 2930
Jer 32:34 called by my name, to **d.** it. 2930
Eze 7:22 robbers shall enter into it, and **d.**....... 2490
Eze 9:7 he said unto them, **D.** the house,........ 2930
Eze 20:7 **d.** not yourselves with the idols of...... 2930
Eze 20:18 nor **d.** yourselves with their idols: 2930
Eze 22:3 maketh idols against herself to **d.** 2930
Eze 28:7 and they shall **d.** thy brightness. 2490
Eze 33:26 ye **d.** every one his neighbour's 2930
Eze 37:23 Neither shall they **d.** themselves 2930
Eze 43:7 shall the house of Israel no more **d.**,... 2930
Eze 44:25 no dead person to **d.** themselves:......... 2930
Eze 44:25 husband, they may **d.** themselves. 2930
Da 1:8 he would not **d.** himself with the 1351
Da 1:8 that he might not **d.** himself. 1351
Mt 15:18 the heart; and they d. the man...... *2840*
Mt 15:20 are the things which d. a man: *2840*
Mk 7:15 entering into him can d. him: but . *2840*
Mk 7:15 him, those are they that d. the...... *2840*
Mk 7:18 into the man, it cannot d. him;..... *2840*
Mk 7:23 come from within, and d. the man. *2840*
1Co 3:17 If any man **d.** the temple of God, ... *5351*
1Ti 1:10 that **d.** themselves with mankind,......... *733*
Jude 8 these filthy dreamers **d.** the flesh, ... *3392*

DEFILED See also DEFILEDST.
Ge 34:2 and lay with her, and **d.** her............. 6031
Ge 34:5 Jacob heard that he had **d.** Dinah........ 2930
Ge 34:13 he had **d.** Dinah their sister:............. 2930
Ge 34:27 because they had **d.** their sister. 2930
Le 5:3 that a man shall be **d.** withal, and....... 2930
Le 11:43 them, that ye should be **d.** thereby..... 2933
Le 13:46 shall be in him he shall be **d.**;............ 2930
Le 15:32 from him, and is **d.** therewith;........... 2930
Le 18:24 all these the nations are **d.** which....... 2930
Le 18:25 the land is **d.**: therefore I do visit....... 2930
Le 18:27 before you, and the land is **d.**;........... 2930
Le 19:31 wizards, to be **d.** by them: I am the ... 2930
Le 21:1 There shall none be **d.** for the........... 2930
Le 21:3 no husband; for her may he be **d.**. 2930
Nu 5:2 and whosoever is **d.** by the dead:....... 2931
Nu 5:13 kept close, and she be **d.**, and........... 2930
Nu 5:14 jealous of his wife, and she be **d.** 2930
Nu 5:14 of his wife, and she be not **d.**............ 2930
Nu 5:20 if thou be **d.** and some man have 2930
Nu 5:27 if she be **d.**, and have done trespass... 2930
Nu 5:28 if the woman be not **d.**, but be 2930
Nu 5:29 instead of her husband, and is **d.**;....... 2930
Nu 6:9 and he hath **d.** the head of his........... 2930
Nu 6:12 lost, because his separation was **d.**..... 2930
Nu 9:6 men, who were **d.** by the dead.......... 2931
Nu 9:7 We are **d.** by the dead body of a......... 2931
Nu 19:20 hath **d.** the sanctuary of the Lord:...... 2930
De 21:23 that thy land be not **d.**, which the 2930
De 22:9 the fruit of thy vineyard, be **d.**. 6942
De 24:4 after that she is **d.**; for that is........... 2930
2Ki 23:8 and **d.** the high places where the........ 2930
2Ki 23:10 And he **d.** Topheth, which is in.......... 2930
1Ch 5:1 forasmuch as he **d.** his father's 2490
Neh 13:29 they have **d.** the priesthood, ... 1351
Job 16:15 and **d.** my horn in the dust. 5953
Ps 74:7 they have **d.** by casting down the........ 2490
Ps 79:1 thy holy temple have they **d.**;............ 2930
Ps 106:39 Thus were they **d.** with their own...... 2930
Isa 24:5 The earth also is **d.** under the........... 2610
Isa 59:3 your hands are **d.** with blood, and 1351
Jer 2:7 when ye entered, ye **d.** my land, ... 2930
Jer 3:9 she **d.** the land, and committed.......... 2610
Jer 16:18 because they have **d.** my land,........... 2490
Jer 19:13 be **d.** as the place of Tophet, ... 2931
Eze 4:13 Israel eat their **d.** bread among.......... 2931
Eze 5:11 thou hast **d.** my sanctuary with.......... 2930
Eze 7:24 and their holy places shall be **d.**. 2490
Eze 18:6 hath **d.** his neighbour's wife,............. 2930
Eze 18:11 and **d.** his neighbour's wife,............... 2930
Eze 18:15 hath not **d.** his neighbour's wife, ... 2930
Eze 20:43 wherein ye have been **d.**; and ye 2930
Eze 22:4 and hast **d.** thyself in thine idols......... 2930
Eze 22:11 hath lewdly **d.** his daughter in law; 2930
Eze 23:7 with all their idols she **d.** herself. 2930
Eze 23:13 Then I saw that she was **d.**, that 2930
Eze 23:17 they **d.** her with their whoredom,........ 2930
Eze 23:38 they have **d.** my sanctuary in the 2930
Eze 28:18 Thou hast **d.** thy sanctuaries by......... 2490
Eze 36:17 dwelt in their own land, they **d.** it 2930
Eze 43:8 they have even **d.** my holy name........ 2930
Hos 5:3 whoredom, and Israel is **d.**................ 2930
Hos 6:10 whoredom of Ephraim, Israel is **d.**...... 2930
Mic 4:11 that say, Let her be **d.**, and let our...... 2610
Mk 7:2 eat bread with **d.**, that is to say,........ *2839*
Joh 18:28 lest they should be **d.**; but that.......... *3392*
1Co 8:7 their conscience being weak is **d.**. *3435*
Tit 1:15 but unto them that are **d.** and............ *3392*
Tit 1:15 their mind and conscience is **d.**. *3392*
Heb 12:15 you, and thereby many be **d.**;............ *3392*
Re 3:4 which have not d. their garments;.. *3435*
Re 14:4 which were not **d.** with women;......... *3435*

DEFILEDST
Ge 49:4 then **d.** thou it: he went up to........... 2490

DEFILETH
Ex 31:14 every one that **d.** it shall surely 2490
Nu 19:13 **d.** the tabernacle of the Lord:........... 2930
Nu 35:33 for blood it **d.** the land: and the 2610
Mt 15:11 into the mouth d. a man; but that.. *2840*
Mt 15:11 out of the mouth, this d. a man.... *2840*
Mt 15:20 with unwashen hands d. not a....... *2840*
Mk 7:20 of the man, that d. the man.......... *2840*
Jas 3:6 members, that it **d.** the whole body, ... *4695*
Re 21:27 enter into it any thing that **d.**, ... *2840*

DEFRAUD See also DEFRAUDED.
Le 19:13 Thou shalt not **d.** thy neighbour, ... 6231
Mr 10:19 D. not, Honour thy father and........ *650*
1Co 6:8 Nay, ye do wrong, and **d.**, and that....... *650*
1Co 7:5 **D.** ye not one the other, except it *650*
1Th 4:6 and **d.** his brother in any matter:........ *4122*

DEFRAUDED
1Sa 12:3 I taken? or whom have I **d.**? 6231
1Sa 12:4 Thou hast not **d.** us, nor oppressed.... 6231
1Co 6:7 rather suffer yourselves to be **d.**? *650*
2Co 7:2 no man, we have **d.** no man............. *4122*

DEFY See also DEFIED.
Nu 23:7 me Jacob, and come, **d.** Israel. 2194
Nu 23:8 hath not cursed? or how shall I **d.**, ... 2194
1Sa 17:10 I **d.** the armies of Israel this day;....... 2778
1Sa 17:25 surely to **d.** Israel is he come up:....... 2778
1Sa 17:26 that he should **d.** the armies of the..... 2778

DEGENERATE
Jer 2:21 art thou turned into the **d.** plant......... 5494

DEGREE See also DEGREES.
1Ch 15:18 of the second **d.**, Zechariah, Ben,............
1Ch 17:17 to the estate of a man of high **d.**,............
Ps 62:9 **d.** are vanity, and men of high **d.** ....
Lu 1:52 seats, and exalted them of low **d.**....... *5011*
1Ti 3:13 purchase to themselves a good **d.**, ... *898*
Jas 1:9 Let the brother of low **d.** rejoice........ *5011*

DEGREES
2Ki 20:9 the shadow go forward ten **d.**,........... 4609
2Ki 20:9 or go back ten **d.**?......................... 4609
2Ki 20:10 for the shadow to go down ten **d.** 4609
2Ki 20:10 shadow return backward ten **d.**.......... 4609
2Ki 20:11 the shadow ten **d.** backward, by......... 4609
Ps 120:*title* A Song of **d.**................................ 4609
Ps 121:*title* A Song of **d.**................................ 4609
Ps 122:*title* A Song of **d.** of David...................... 4609
Ps 123:*title* A Song of **d.**,.............................. 4609
Ps 124:*title* A Song of **d.**, of David..................... 4609
Ps 125:*title* A Song of **d.**................................ 4609
Ps 126:*title* A Song of **d.**................................ 4609
Ps 127:*title* A Song of **d.** for Solomon. 4609
Ps 128:*title* A Song of **d.**................................ 4609
Ps 129:*title* A Song of **d.**,.............................. 4609
Ps 130:*title* A Song of **d.**................................ 4609
Ps 131:*title* A Song of **d.** of David...................... 4609
Ps 132:*title* A Song of **d.**................................ 4609
Ps 133:*title* A Song of **d.** of David...................... 4609
Ps 134:*title* A Song of **d.**................................ 4609
Isa 38:8 bring again the shadow of the **d.**, ... 4609
Isa 38:8 Ahaz, ten **d.** backward. So the sun..... 4609
Isa 38:8 ten **d.**, by which **d.** it was gone 4609

DEHAVITES (de-ha'-vites)
Ezr 4:9 the **D.**, and the Elamites, ... 1723

DEKAR (de'-kar)
1Ki 4:9 The son of **D.**, in Makaz, and in 1857

DELAIAH (del-a-i'-ah) See also DALAIAH.
1Ch 24:18 The three and twentieth to **D.**,.......... 1806
Ezr 2:60 The children of **D.**, the children of...... 1806
Ne 6:10 houe of Shemaiah the son of **D.** 1806
Ne 7:62 The children of **D.**, the children of...... 1806
Jer 36:12 and **D.** the son of Shemaiah, ... 1806
Jer 36:25 Nevertheless Elnathan and **D.** and...... 1806

DELAY See also DELAYED; DELAYETH.
Ex 22:29 Thou shalt not **d.** to offer the.............. 309
Ac 9:38 that he would not **d.** to come *3635*
Ac 25:17 without any **d.** on the morrow *311*

DELAYED
Ex 32:1 Moses **d.** to come down out of the 954
Ps 119:60 I made haste, and **d.** not to keep 4102

DELAYETH
Mt 24:48 My lord d. his coming; and shall... *5549*
Lu 12:45 My lord d. his coming; and shall... *5549*

DELECTABLE
Isa 44:9 their **d.** things shall not profit; 2530

DELICACIES
Rev 18:3 through the abundance of her **d.** *4764*

DELICATE See also DELICATES.
De 28:54 is tender among you, and very **d.**, 6028
De 28:56 The tender and **d.** woman among 6028
Isa 47:1 no more be called tender and **d.** 6028
Jer 6:2 to a comely and **d.** woman. 6026
Mic 1:16 and poll thee for thy **d.** children; 8588

DELICATELY
1Sa 15:32 And Agag came unto him **d.**. 4574
Pr 29:21 He that **d.** bringeth up his servant 6445
La 4:5 They that did feed **d.** are desolate 4574
Lu 7:25 **and live d., are in king's courts** *5172*

DELICATENESS
De 28:56 of her foot upon the ground for **d.** 6026

DELICATES
Jer 51:34 he hath filled his belly with my **d.**, 5730

DELICIOUSLY
Re 18:7 glorified herself, and lived **d.**, *4763*
Re 18:9 and lived **d.** with her, shall *4763*

DELIGHT See also DELIGHTED; DELIGHTEST; DELIGHTETH; DELIGHTS; DELIGHTSOME.
Ge 34:19 he had **d.** in Jacob's daughter: 2654
Nu 14:8 If the Lord **d.** in us, then he will 2654
De 10:15 the Lord had a **d.** in thy fathers 2836
De 21:14 if thou have no **d.** in her, then 2654
1Sa 15:22 Hath the Lord as great **d.** in burnt 2656
1Sa 18:22 the king hath **d.** in thee, and all 2654
2Sa 15:26 I have no **d.** in thee; behold, here 2654
2Sa 24:3 doth my lord the king **d.** in this 2654
Es 6:6 To whom would the king **d.** to do 2654
Job 22:26 then shalt thou have thy **d.** in the 6026
Job 27:10 Will he **d.** himself in the Almighty? 6026
Job 34:9 that he should **d.** himself with God. 7521
Ps 1:2 But his **d.** is in the law of the Lord; 2656
Ps 16:3 excellent, in whom is all my **d.**, 2656
Ps 37:4 **D.** thyself also in the Lord; and 6026
Ps 37:11 **d.** themselves in the abundance 6026
Ps 40:8 I **d.** to do thy will, O my God: 2654
Ps 62:4 they **d.** in lies: they bless with 7521
Ps 68:30 thou the people that **d.** in war. 2654
Ps 94:19 me thy comforts **d.** my soul. 8173
Ps 119:16 I will **d.** myself in thy statutes: 8173
Ps 119:24 Thy testimonies also are my **d.** 8191
Ps 119:35 for therein do I **d.**. 2654
Ps 119:47 **d.** myself in thy commandments, 8173
Ps 119:70 fat as grease; but I **d.** in thy law. 8173
Ps 119:77 I may live: for thy law is my **d.**. 8191
Ps 119:174 O Lord; and thy law is my **d.**. 8191
Pr 1:22 the scorners **d.** in their scorning, 2531
Pr 2:14 and **d.**, in the frowardness of the 1523
Pr 8:30 I was daily his **d.**, rejoicing always 8191
Pr 11:1 but a just weight is his **d.**, 7522
Pr 11:20 but such as are upright are his **d.** 7522
Pr 12:22 but they that deal truly are his **d.** 7522
Pr 15:8 the prayer of the upright is his **d.** 7522
Pr 16:13 Righteous lips are the **d.** of kings; 7522
Pr 18:2 fool hath no **d.** in understanding. 2654
Pr 19:10 **D.** is not seemly for a fool; 8588
Pr 24:25 them that rebuke him shall be **d.**, 5276
Pr 29:17 he shall give **d.** unto thy soul. 4574
Ca 2:3 under his shadow with great **d.**, 2530
Isa 1:11 I **d.** not in the blood of bullocks, 2654
Isa 13:17 as for gold, they shall not **d.** in it. 2654
Isa 55:2 let your soul **d.** itself in fatness, 6026
Isa 58:2 me daily, and **d.** to know my ways, 2654
Isa 58:2 take **d.** in approaching to God. 2654
Isa 58:13 call the sabbath a **d.**, the holy of 6027
Isa 58:14 shalt thou **d.** thyself in the Lord; 6026
Jer 6:10 reproach; they have no **d.** in it. 2654
Jer 9:24 these things I **d.**, saith the Lord. 2654
Mal 3:1 of the covenant, whom ye **d.** in: 2655
Ro 7:22 For I **d.** in the law of God after *4913*

DELIGHTED
1Sa 19:2 Saul's son **d.** much in David: 2654
2Sa 22:20 delivered me, because he **d.** in me. 2654
1Ki 10:9 which **d.** in thee, to set thee on the 2654
2Ch 9:8 which **d.** in thee to set thee on his 2654
Ne 9:25 and **d.** themselves in thy great 5727
Es 2:14 no more, except the king **d.** in her, 2654
Ps 18:19 delivered me, because he **d.** in me. 2654
Ps 22:8 deliver him, seeing he **d.** in him. 2654
Ps 109:17 as he **d.** not in blessing, so let it be 2654
Isa 65:12 did choose that wherein I **d.** not. 2654
Isa 66:4 and chose that in which I **d.** not. 2654
Isa 66:11 and be **d.** with the abundance 6026

DELIGHTEST
Ps 51:16 thou **d.** not in burnt offering. 7521

DELIGHTETH
Es 6:6 man whom the king **d.** to honour? 2654
Es 6:7 man whom the king **d.** to honour, 2654
Es 6:9 withal whom the king **d.** to honour 2654
Es 6:9, 11 whom the king **d.** to honour. 2654
Ps 37:23 Lord: and he **d.** in his way. 2654
Ps 112:1 **d.** greatly in his commandments. 2654
Ps 147:10 **d.** not in the strength of the horse: 2654
Pr 3:12 a father the son in whom he **d.**. 7521
Isa 42:1 mine elect, in whom my soul **d.**; 7521
Isa 62:4 the Lord **d.** in thee, and thy land 2654
Isa 66:3 their soul **d.** in their abominations. 2654
Mic 7:18 for ever, because he **d.** in mercy. 2654
Mal 2:17 and he **d.** in them; or, Where is the 2654

DELIGHTS
2Sa 1:24 you in scarlet, with other **d.**, 5730
Ps 119:92 Unless thy law had been my **d.**, 8191
Ps 119:143 thy commandments are my **d.** 8191
Pr 8:31 my **d.** were with the sons of men. 8191
Ec 2:8 and the **d.** of the sons of men, 8588
Ca 7:6 pleasant art thou, O love, for **d.**! 8588

DELIGHTSOME
Mal 3:12 for ye shall be a **d.** land, 2656

DELILAH (de-li'-lah)
Jg 16:4 of Sorek, whose name was **D.**. 1807
Jg 16:6 **D.** said to Samson, Tell me, I pray 1807
Jg 16:10 **D.** said unto Samson, Behold, thou 1807
Jg 16:12 **D.** therefore took new ropes, and 1807
Jg 16:13 **D.** said unto Samson, Hitherto thou 1807
Jg 16:18 **D.** saw that he had told her all 1807

DELIVER See also DELIVERED; DELIVEREST; DELIVERETH; DELIVERING.
Ge 32:11 **D.** me, I pray thee, from the hand 5337
Ge 37:22 to **d.** him to his father again. 7725
Ge 40:13 **d.** Pharaoh's cup into his hand, 5414
Ge 42:34 will I **d.** you your brother, and ye 5414
Ge 42:37 **d.** him into my hand, and I will 5414
Ex 3:8 I am come down to **d.** them 5337
Ex 5:18 yet shall ye **d.** the tale of bricks. 5414
Ex 21:13 but God **d.** him into his hand; 579
Ex 22:7 a man shall **d.** unto his neighbour 5414
Ex 22:10 If a man **d.** unto his neighbour 5414
Ex 22:26 thou shalt **d.** it unto him by that 7725
Ex 23:31 **d.** the inhabitants of the land into 5414
Le 26:26 shall **d.** you your bread again 7725
Nu 21:2 If thou wilt indeed **d.** this people 5414
Nu 35:25 congregation shall **d.** the slayer 5337
De 1:27 to **d.** us into the hand of the 5414
De 2:30 that he might **d.** him into thy hand, 5414
De 3:2 **d.** him, and all his people, into 5414
De 7:2 Lord thy God shall **d.** them before 5414
De 7:16 the Lord thy God shall **d.** thee; 5414
De 7:23 the Lord thy God shall **d.** them unto 5414
De 7:24 shall **d.** their kings into thine hand, 5414
De 19:12 **d.** him into the hand of the avenger 5414
De 23:14 the midst of thy camp, to **d.** thee, 5337
De 23:15 not **d.** unto his master the servant 5462
De 24:13 shalt **d.** him the pledge again 7725
De 25:11 to **d.** her husband out of the hand 5337
De 32:39 any that can **d.** out of my hand. 5337
Jos 2:13 have, and **d.** our lives from death. 5337
Jos 7:7 to **d.** us into the hand of the 5414
Jos 8:7 the Lord your God will **d.** it into 5414
Jos 11:6 about this time will I **d.** them up 5414
Jos 20:5 **d.** the slayer up into his hand; 5462
Jg 4:7 and I will **d.** him into thine hand. 5414
Jg 7:7 I save you, and **d.** the Midianites 5414
Jg 10:11 not I **d.** you from the Egyptians
Jg 10:13 wherefore I will **d.** you no more. 3467
Jg 10:14 let them **d.** you in the time of 3467
Jg 10:15 **d.** us only, we pray thee, this day. 5337
Jg 11:9 and the Lord **d.** them before me, 5414
Jg 11:30 **d.** the children of Ammon into mine 5414
Jg 13:5 he shall begin to **d.** Israel out of 3467
Jg 15:12 that we may **d.** thee into the hand 5414
Jg 15:13 fast, and **d.** thee into their hand: 5414
Jg 20:13 Now therefore **d.** us the men, the 5414
Jg 20:28 I will **d.** them into thine hand. 5414
1Sa 4:8 who shall **d.** us out of the hand of 5337
1Sa 7:3 he will **d.** you out of the hand of the 5337
1Sa 7:14 the coasts theeof did Israel **d.** out 5337
1Sa 12:10 but now **d.** us out of the hand of our 5337
1Sa 12:21 things, which cannot profit nor **d.**; 5337
1Sa 14:37 **d.** them into the hand of Israel? 5414
1Sa 17:37 he will **d.** me out of the hand of 5337
1Sa 17:46 the Lord **d.** thee into mine hand; 5462
1Sa 23:4 **d.** the Philistines into thine hand. 5414
1Sa 23:11 Will the men of Keilah **d.** me up 5462
1Sa 23:12 Will the men of Keilah **d.** me and 5462
1Sa 23:12 Lord said, They will **d.** thee up. 5462
1Sa 23:20 to **d.** him into the king's hand. 5462
1Sa 24:4 I will **d.** thine enemy into thine 5414
1Sa 24:15 and **d.** me out of thine hand. 8199
1Sa 26:24 him **d.** me out of all tribulation. 5337
1Sa 28:19 Lord will also **d.** Israel with thee 5414
1Sa 28:19 the Lord also shall **d.** the host into 5414
1Sa 30:15 nor **d.** me into the hands of my 5462
2Sa 3:14 **D.** me my wife Michal, which I 5414
2Sa 5:19 wilt thou **d.** them into mine hand? 5414
2Sa 5:19 will doubtless **d.** the Philistines into 5414
2Sa 14:7 **D.** him that smote his brother that 5414
2Sa 14:16 **d.** his handmaid out of the hand 5337
2Sa 20:21 **d.** him only, and I will depart. 5414
1Ki 8:46 **d.** them to the enemy, so that they 5414
1Ki 18:9 thou wouldst **d.** thy servant into 5414
1Ki 20:5 Thou shalt **d.** me thy silver, and 5414
1Ki 20:13 I will **d.** it into thine hand 5414
1Ki 20:28 I **d.** all this great multitude into 5414
1Ki 22:6 shall **d.** it into the hand of the king. 5414
1Ki 22:12 Lord shall **d.** it into the king's hand. 5414
1Ki 22:15 shall **d.** into the hand of the king. 5414
2Ki 3:10, 13 **d.** them into the hand of Moab! 5414
2Ki 3:18 he will **d.** the Moabites also into 5414
2Ki 12:7 **d.** it for the breaches of the house. 5414
2Ki 17:39 he shall **d.** you out of the hand of 5337
2Ki 18:23 will **d.** thee two thousand horses, 5414
2Ki 18:29 he shall not be able to **d.** you 5337
2Ki 18:30 The Lord will surely **d.** us, and this 5337
2Ki 18:32 you, saying, The Lord will **d.** us, 5337
2Ki 18:35 the Lord should **d.** Jerusalem out 5337
2Ki 20:6 I will **d.** thee and this city out of the 5337
2Ki 21:14 and **d.** them into the hand of their 5414
2Ki 22:5 And let them **d.** it into the hand of 5414
1Ch 14:10 thou **d.** them into mine hand? 5414
1Ch 14:10 for I will **d.** them into thine hand. 5414
1Ch 16:35 and **d.** us from the heathen, that 5337
2Ch 6:36 angry with them, and **d.** them over 5414
2Ch 18:5 God will **d.** it into the king's hand. 5414
2Ch 18:11 shall **d.** it into the hand of the king. 5414
2Ch 25:15 could not **d.** their own people 5337
2Ch 25:20 that he might **d.** them into the 5414
2Ch 28:11 and **d.** the captives again, which 7725
2Ch 32:11 The Lord our God shall **d.** us out 5337
2Ch 32:13 **d.** their lands out of mine hand? 5337
2Ch 32:14 **d.** his people out of mine hand, 5337
2Ch 32:14 God should be able to **d.** you out 5337
2Ch 32:15 able to **d.** his people out of mine 5337
2Ch 32:15 your God **d.** you out of mine hand? 5337
2Ch 32:17 God of Hezekiah **d.** his people out 5337
Ezr 7:19 those **d.** thou before the God of 8000
Ne 9:28 many times didst thou **d.** them 5337
Job 5:4 neither is there any to **d.** them. 5337
Job 5:19 He shall **d.** thee in six troubles: 5337
Job 6:23 **D.** me from the enemy's hand? 4422
Job 10:7 there is none that can **d.** out of 5337
Job 22:30 **d.** the island of the innocent: 4422
Job 33:24 **D.** him from going down to the 6308
Job 33:28 He will **d.** his soul from going 6299
Job 36:18 a great ransom cannot **d.** thee, 5186
Ps 6:4 Return, O Lord, **d.** my soul: oh 2502
Ps 7:1 that persecute me, and **d.** me: 5337
Ps 7:2 in pieces, while there is none to **d.**. 5337
Ps 17:13 **d.** my soul from the wicked, 6403
Ps 22:4 trusted, and thou didst **d.** them. 6403
Ps 22:8 on the Lord that he would **d.** him: 6403
Ps 22:8 **d.** him, seeing he delighted in 5337
Ps 22:20 **D.** my soul from the sword; my 5337
Ps 25:20 O keep my soul, and **d.** me: 5337
Ps 27:12 **D.** me not over unto the will of 5414
Ps 31:1 **d.** me in thy righteousness. 6403
Ps 31:2 **d.** me speedily: be thou my strong 5337
Ps 31:15 **d.** me from the hand of mine 5337
Ps 33:17 he **d.** any by his great strength. 4422
Ps 33:19 To **d.** their soul from death, and 5337
Ps 37:40 **d.** them: he shall **d.** them from 6403

Ps 39:8 **D.** me from all my transgressions: 5337
Ps 40:13 Be pleased, O Lord, to **d.** me: 5337
Ps 41:1 Lord will **d.** him in time of trouble. 4422
Ps 41:2 thou wilt not **d.** him unto the will 5414
Ps 43:1 O **d.** me from the deceitful and 6403
Ps 50:15 the day of trouble: I will **d.** thee, 2502
Ps 50:22 in pieces, and there be none to **d.**. 5337
Ps 51:14 **D.** me from bloodguiltiness, O God, 5337
Ps 56:13 not thou **d.** my feet from falling, 5337
Ps 59:1 **D.** me from mine enemies, O my 5337
Ps 59:2 **D.** me from the workers of iniquity, 5337
Ps 69:14 **D.** me out of the mire, and let me 5337
Ps 69:18 **d.** me because of mine enemies. 6299
Ps 70:1 Make haste, O God, to **d.** me: 5337
Ps 71:2 **D.** me in thy righteousness, and 5337
Ps 71:4 **D.** me, O my God, out of the 6403
Ps 71:11 for there is none to **d.** him. 5337
Ps 72:12 shall **d.** the needy when he crieth; 5337
Ps 74:19 O **d.** not the soul of thy turtledove 5414
Ps 79:9 **d.** us, and purge away our sins, 5337
Ps 82:4 **D.** the poor and needy:rid them 6403
Ps 89:48 shall he **d.** his soul from the hand 4422
Ps 91:3 he shall **d.** thee from the snare 5337
Ps 91:14 will I **d.** him: I will set him on 6403
Ps 91:15 I will **d.** him, and honour him. 2502
Ps 106:43 Many times did he **d.** them; but 5337
Ps 109:21 thy mercy is good, **d.** thou me. 5337
Ps 116:4 Lord, I beseech thee, **d.** my soul. 4422
Ps 119:134 **D.** me from the oppression of 6299
Ps 119:153 mine affliction and **d.** me: for I 2502
Ps 119:154 Plead my cause, and **d.** me: 1350
Ps 119:170 **d.** me according to thy word. 5337
Ps 120:2 **D.** my soul, O Lord, from lying 5337
Ps 140:1 **D.** me, O Lord, from the evil man: 2502
Ps 142:6 **d.** me from my persecutors; for 5337
Ps 143:9 **D.** me, O Lord, from mine enemies: 5337
Ps 144:7 and **d.** me out of great waters, 5337
Ps 144:11 and **d.** me from the hand of strange 5337
Pr 2:12 To **d.** thee from the way of the evil 5337
Pr 2:16 To **d.** thee from the strange woman 5337
Pr 4:9 a crown of glory shall she **d.** to 4042
Pr 6:3 this now, my son, and **d.** thyself, 5337
Pr 6:5 **D.** thyself as a roe from the hand 5337
Pr 11:6 of the upright shall **d.** them: 5337
Pr 12:6 mouth of the upright shall **d.** them. 5337
Pr 19:19 if thou **d.** him, yet thou must 5337
Pr 23:14 and shall **d.** his soul from hell. 5337
Pr 24:11 If thou forbear to **d.** them that are 5337
Ec 8:8 neither shall wickedness **d.** those 4422
Isa 5:29 away safe, and none shall **d.** it. 5337
Isa 19:20 a great one, and he shall **d.** them. 5337
Isa 29:11 men **d.** to one that is learned, 5414
Isa 31:5 defending also he will **d.** it, 5337
Isa 36:14 he shall not be able to **d.** you. 5337
Isa 36:15 The Lord will surely **d.** us: this city 5337
Isa 36:18 you, saying, The Lord will **d.** us. 5337
Isa 36:20 that the Lord should **d.** Jerusalem. 5337
Isa 38:6 And I will **d.** thee and this city 5337
Isa 43:13 there is none that can **d.** out of my 5337
Isa 44:17 **D.** me; for thou art my god. 5337
Isa 44:20 he cannot **d.** his soul, nor say, 5337
Isa 46:2 they could not **d.** the burden, but 4422
Isa 46:4 I will carry, and will **d.** you. 4422
Isa 47:14 they shall not **d.** themselves from 5337
Isa 50:2 or have I no power to **d.**? 5337
Isa 57:13 let thy companies **d.** thee; but the 5337
Jer 1:8 I am with thee to **d.** thee, saith 5337
Jer 1:19 with thee, saith the Lord, to **d.** thee 5337
Jer 15:9 the residue of them will I **d.** to the 5414
Jer 15:20 to save thee and to **d.** thee, 5337
Jer 15:21 And I will **d.** thee out of the hand 5337
Jer 18:21 **d.** up their children to the famine, 5414
Jer 20:5 will **d.** all the strength of the city, 5414
Jer 21:7 I will **d.** Zedekiah king of Judah, 5414
Jer 21:12 and **d.** him that is spoiled out of 5337
Jer 22:3 and **d.** the spoiled out of the hand 5337
Jer 24:9 And I will **d.** them to be removed 5414
Jer 29:18 and will **d.** them to be removed 5414
Jer 29:21 I will **d.** them into the hand of 5414
Jer 38:19 lest they **d.** me into their hand, 5414
Jer 38:20 They shall not **d.** thee. Obey, I 5414
Jer 39:17 But I will **d.** thee in that day, 5337
Jer 39:18 I will surely **d.** thee, and thou 4422
Jer 42:11 and to **d.** you from his hand. 5337
Jer 43:3 to **d.** us into the hand of the 5414
Jer 43:11 and **d.** such as are for death to
Jer 46:26 and I will **d.** them into the hand 5414
Jer 51:6 and **d.** every man his soul: be 4422
Jer 51:45 and **d.** ye every man his soul. 4422
La 5:8 there is none that doth **d.** us out 6561
Eze 7:19 gold shall not be able to **d.** them 5337
Eze 11:9 and **d.** you into the hands of 5414
Eze 13:21 and **d.** my people out of your 5337
Eze 13:23 for I will **d.** my people out of your 5337
Eze 14:14 they should **d.** but their own souls 5337
Eze 14:16 **d.** neither sons nor daughters; they 5337
Eze 14:18 **d.** neither sons nor daughters, but 5337
Eze 14:20 shall **d.** neither son nor daughter; 5337
Eze 14:20 they shall but **d.** their own souls 5337
Eze 21:31 and **d.** thee into the hand of 5414
Eze 23:28 I will **d.** thee into the hand of them 5414
Eze 25:4 I will **d.** thee to the men of the 5414
Eze 25:7 and will **d.** thee for a spoil to the 5414
Eze 33:5 taketh warning shall **d.** his soul. 4422
Eze 33:12 of the righteous shall not **d.** him. 5337
Eze 34:10 I will **d.** my flock from their mouth, 5337
Eze 34:12 and will **d.** them out of all places 5337
Da 3:15 who is that God that shall **d.** you 7804
Da 3:17 is able to **d.** us from the burning 7804
Da 3:17 he will **d.** us out of thine hand, 7804
Da 3:29 God that can **d.** after this sort. 5338
Da 6:14 set his heart on Daniel to **d.** him: 7804
Da 6:14 going down of the sun to **d.** him. 5338
Da 6:16 servest continually, he will **d.** thee. 7804
Da 6:20 able to **d.** thee from the lions? 7804
Da 8:4 was there any that could **d.** out of 5337
Da 8:7 was none that could **d.** the ram. 5337
Ho 2:10 shall **d.** her out of mine hand. 5337
Ho 11:8 how shall I **d.** thee, Israel? 4042
Am 1:6 captivity, to **d.** them up to Edom: 5462
Am 2:14 shall the mighty **d.** himself: 4422
Am 2:15 swift of foot shall not **d.** himself: 4422
Am 2:15 he that rideth the horse **d.** himself. 4422
Am 6:8 therefore will I **d.** up the city 5462
Jon 4:6 head, to **d.** him from his grief. 5337
Mic 5:6 shall he **d.** us from the Assyrian, 5337
Mic 5:8 teareth in pieces, and none can **d.**. 5337
Mic 6:14 shalt take hold, but shalt not **d.**; 6043
Zep 1:18 shall be able to **d.** them in the day 5337
Zec 2:7 **D.** thyself, O Zion, that dwellest 4422
Zec 11:6 I will **d.** the men every one 4672
Zec 11:6 out of their hand I will not **d.** them. 5337
Mt 5:25 adversary **d.** thee to the judge, *3860*
Mt 5:25 and the judge **d.** thee to the *3860*
Mt 6:13 temptation, but **d.** us from evil: *4506*
Mt 10:17 will **d.** you up to the councils, *3860*
Mt 10:19 But when they **d.** you up, take *3860*
Mt 10:21 the brother shall **d.** up the brother *3860*
Mt 20:19 And shall **d.** him to the Gentiles *3860*
Mt 24:9 Then shall they **d.** you up to the *3860*
Mt 26:15 and I will **d.** him unto you? *3860*
Mt 27:43 let him **d.** him now, if he will have *4506*
Mk 10:33 and shall **d.** him to the Gentiles: *3860*
Mk 13:9 they shall **d.** you up to councils; *3860*
Mk 13:11 and **d.** you up, take no thought *3860*
Lu 11:4 temptation: but **d.** us from evil *4506*
Lu 12:58 the judge **d.** thee to the officer, *3860*
Lu 20:20 that so they might **d.** him unto the *3860*
Ac 7:25 God by his hand would **d.** them: *1325*
Ac 7:34 and am come down to **d.** them. *1807*
Ac 21:11 and shall **d.** him into the hands of *3860*
Ac 25:11 no man may **d.** me unto them. *5483*
Ac 25:16 to **d.** any man to die, before that *5483*
Ro 7:24 who shall **d.** me from the body of *4506*
1Co 5:5 To **d.** such an one unto Satan *3860*
2Co 1:10 a death, and doth **d.**: in whom *4506*
2Co 1:10 we trust that he will yet **d.** us; *4506*
Ga 1:4 that he might **d.** us from this *1807*
2Ti 4:18 the Lord shall **d.** me from every *4506*
Heb 2:15 and **d.** them who through fear of *525*
2Pe 2:9 The Lord knoweth how to **d.** the *4506*

DELIVERANCE See also DELIVERANCES.
Ge 45:7 save your lives by a great **d.** 6413
Jg 15:18 Thou hast given this great **d.** 8668
2Ki 5:1 Lord had given **d.** unto Syria: 8668
2Ki 13:17 The arrow of the Lord's **d.**, 8668
2Ki 13:17 the arrow of **d.** from Syria 8668
1Ch 11:14 Lord saved them by a great **d.**. 8668
2Ch 12:7 but I will grant them some **d.**; 6413
Ezr 9:13 hast given us such **d.** as this; 6413
Es 4:14 enlargement and **d.** arise to the 2020
Ps 18:50 Great **d.** giveth he to his king; 3444
Ps 32:7 me about with the songs of **d.**. 6405
Isa 26:18 we have not wrought any **d.** in 3444
Joe 2:32 and in Jerusalem shall be **d.** 6413
Ob 17 upon Mount Zion shall be **d.** 6413
Lu 4:18 to preach **d.** to the captives, and *859*
Heb 11:35 were tortured, not accepting **d.**; *629*

DELIVERANCES
Ps 44:4 O God: command **d.** for Jacob. 3444

DELIVERED See also DELIVEREDST.
Ge 9:2 sea; into your hand are they **d.** 5414
Ge 14:20 hath **d.** thine enemies into thy 4042
Ge 25:24 her days to be **d.** were fulfilled, 3205
Ge 32:16 And he **d.** them into the hand of 5414
Ge 37:21 and he **d.** him out of their hands; 5337
Ex 1:19 and are **d.** ere the midwives come 3205
Ex 2:19 An Egyptian **d.** us out of the hand 5337
Ex 5:23 neither hast thou **d.** thy people at 5337
Ex 12:27 the Egyptians, and **d.** our houses. 5337
Ex 18:4 **d.** me from the sword of Pharaoh: 5337
Ex 18:8 way, and how the Lord **d.** them. 5337
Ex 18:9 whom he had **d.** out of the hand 5337
Ex 18:10 who hath **d.** you out of the hand of 5337
Ex 18:10 of Pharaoh, who hath **d.** the people 5337
Le 6:2 which was **d.** him to keep, or in 6487
Le 6:4 which was **d.** him to keep, or the 6487
Le 26:25 and ye shall be **d.** into the 5414
Nu 21:3 and **d.** up the Canaanites; and they 5414
Nu 21:34 I have **d.** him into thy hand, 5414
Nu 31:5 they were **d.** out of the thousands 4560
De 2:33 And the Lord our God **d.** him 5414
De 2:36 the Lord our God **d.** all unto us: 5414
De 3:3 So the Lord our God **d.** into our 5414
De 5:22 of stone, and **d.** them unto me. 5414
De 9:10 And the Lord **d.** unto me two tables 5414
De 20:13 God hath **d.** it into thine hands, 5414
De 21:10 the Lord thy God hath **d.** them 5414
De 31:9 and **d.** it unto the priests the sons 5414
Jos 2:24 the Lord hath **d.** into our hands 5414
Jos 9:26 and **d.** them out of the hand of the 5337
Jos 10:8 I have **d.** them into thine hand; 5414
Jos 10:12 the Lord **d.** up the Amorites before 5414
Jos 10:19 the Lord your God hath **d.** them 5414
Jos 10:30 And the Lord **d.** it also, and the 5414
Jos 10:32 And the Lord **d.** Lachish into the 5414
Jos 11:8 **d.** them into the hand of Israel, 5414
Jos 21:44 the Lord **d.** all their enemies into 5414
Jos 22:31 ye have **d.** the children of Israel. 5337
Jos 24:10 so I **d.** you out of his hand. 5337
Jos 24:11 and I **d.** them into your hand. 5414
Jg 1:2 I have **d.** the land into his hand. 5414
Jg 1:4 and the Lord **d.** the Canaanites 5414
Jg 2:14 and he **d.** them into the hands of 5414
Jg 2:16 which **d.** them out of the hand of 3467
Jg 2:18 and **d.** them out of the hand of 3467
Jg 2:23 neither **d.** he them into the hand 5414
Jg 3:9 children of Israel who **d.** them, 3467
Jg 3:10 the Lord **d.** Chushan-rishathaim 5414
Jg 3:28 hath **d.** your enemies the Moabites 5414
Jg 3:31 ox-goad: and he also **d.** Israel. 3467
Jg 4:14 hath **d.** Sisera into thine hand: 5414
Jg 5:11 are **d.** from the noise of archers
Jg 6:1 **d.** them into the hand of Midian 5414
Jg 6:9 And I **d.** you out of the hand of 5337
Jg 6:13 and **d.** us into the hands of the 5414
Jg 7:9 I have **d.** it into thine hand. 5414
Jg 7:14 into his hand hath God **d.** Midian, 5414
Jg 7:15 the Lord hath **d.** into your hand 5414
Jg 8:3 God hath **d.** into your hands the 5414
Jg 8:7 when the Lord hath **d.** Zebah and 5414
Jg 8:22 **d.** us from the hand of Midian. 3467
Jg 8:34 Lord their God, who had **d.** them 5337
Jg 9:17 **d.** you out of the hand of Midian: 5337
Jg 10:12 and I **d.** you out of their hand. 3467
Jg 11:21 the Lord God of Israel **d.** Sihon 5414
Jg 11:32 the Lord **d.** them into his hands. 5414
Jg 12:2 ye **d.** me not out of their hands. 3467
Jg 12:3 And when I saw that ye **d.** me not, 3467
Jg 12:3 the Lord **d.** them into my hand: 5414
Jg 13:1 and the Lord **d.** them into the hand 5414
Jg 16:23 hath **d.** Samson our enemy into our 5414
Jg 16:24 hath **d.** into our hands our enemy, 5414
1Sa 4:19 was with child, near to be **d.**: 3205
1Sa 10:18 and **d.** you out of the hand of the 5337
1Sa 12:11 and **d.** you out of the hand of your 5337
1Sa 14:10 hath **d.** them into our hand: 5414
1Sa 14:12 **d.** them into the hand of Israel. 5414
1Sa 14:48 **d.** Israel out of the hands of them 5337

1Sa 17:35 and **d.** it out of his mouth: 5337
1Sa 17:37 **d.** me out of the paw of the lion, 5337
1Sa 23:7 God hath **d.** him into mine hand; 5234
1Sa 23:14 God **d.** him not into his hand. 5414
1Sa 24:10 the Lord had **d.** thee to day 5414
1Sa 24:18 Lord had **d.** me into thine hand, 5462
1Sa 26:8 **d.** thine enemy into thine hand 5462
1Sa 26:23 the Lord **d.** thee into my hand 5414
1Sa 30:23 and **d.** the company that came 5414
2Sa 3:8 not **d.** thee into the hand of David, 4672
2Sa 10:10 the rest of the people he **d.** 5414
2Sa 12:7 I **d.** thee out of the hand of Saul; 5337
2Sa 16:8 and the Lord hath **d.** the kingdom 5414
2Sa 18:28 hath **d.** up the men that lifted 5462
2Sa 19:9 and he **d.** us out of the hand of 4422
2Sa 21:6 Let seven men of his sons be **d.** 5414
2Sa 21:9 And he **d.** them into the hands of 5414
2Sa 22:1 the Lord had **d.** him out of the 5337
2Sa 22:18 He **d.** me from my strong enemy, 5337
2Sa 22:20 he **d.** me, because he delighted in 2502
2Sa 22:44 **d.** me from the strivings of my 6403
2Sa 22:49 hast **d.** me from the violent man. 5337
1Ki 3:17 **d.** of a child with her in the house 3205
1Ki 3:18 the third day after that I was **d.**, 3205
1Ki 3:18 that this woman was **d.** also: 3205
1Ki 13:26 Lord hath **d.** him unto the lion, 5414
1Ki 15:18 and **d.** them into the hand of his 5414
1Ki 17:23 and **d.** him unto his mother: and 5414
2Ki 12:15 they **d.** the money to be bestowed 5414
2Ki 13:3 **d.** them into the hand of Hazael 5414
2Ki 17:20 **d.** them into the hand of spoilers, 5414
2Ki 18:30 shall not be **d.** into the hand 5414
2Ki 18:33 any of the gods of the nations, **d.** 5337
2Ki 18:34 **d.** Samaria out of mine hand? 5337
2Ki 18:35 **d.** their country out of mine hand, 5337
2Ki 19:10 Jerusalem shall not be **d.** into 5414
2Ki 19:11 utterly: and shalt thou be **d.**? 5337
2Ki 19:12 the gods of the nation **d.** them. 5337
2Ki 22:7 the money that was **d.** into their 5414
2Ki 22:9 and have **d.** it into the hand of 5414
2Ki 22:10 Hilkiah the priest hath **d.** me a 5414
1Ch 5:20 Hagarites were **d.** into their hand, 5414
1Ch 11:14 **d.** it, and slew the Philistines; 5337
1Ch 16:7 David **d.** first this psalm to thank 5414
1Ch 19:11 the rest of the people he **d.** unto 5414
2Ch 13:16 and God **d.** them into their hand. 5414
2Ch 16:8 Lord, he **d.** them into thine hand. 5414
2Ch 18:14 and they shall be **d.** into your hand 5414
2Ch 23:9 Moreover Jehoiada the priest **d.** to 5414
2Ch 24:24 **d.** a very great host into their hand, 5414
2Ch 28:5 Lord his God **d.** him into the hand 5414
2Ch 28:5 he was also **d.** into the hand of 5414
2Ch 28:9 he hath **d.** them into your hand, 5414
2Ch 29:8 and he hath **d.** them to trouble, 5414
2Ch 32:17 not **d.** their people out of mine 5337
2Ch 34:9 the high priest, they **d.** the money 5414
2Ch 34:15 Hilkiah **d.** the book to Shaphan 5414
2Ch 34:17 **d.** it into the hand of the overseers, 5414
Ezr 5:14 and they were **d.** unto one, 3052
Ezr 8:31 **d.** us from the hand of the enemy, 5337
Ezr 8:36 they **d.** the king's commissions 5414
Ezr 9:7 our priests, been **d.** into the hand 5414
Es 6:9 let this apparel and horse be **d.** 5414
Job 16:11 God hath **d.** me to the ungodly, 5462
Job 22:30 **d.** by the pureness of thine hands. 4422
Job 23:7 I be **d.** for ever from my judge 6403
Job 29:12 I **d.** the poor that cried, and the 4422
Ps 7:4 have **d.** him that without cause 2502
Ps 18:*title* the Lord **d.** him from the hand 5337
Ps 18:17 He **d.** me from my strong enemy, 5337
Ps 18:19 he **d.** me, because he delighted in 2502
Ps 18:43 hast **d.** me from the striving 6403
Ps 18:48 **d.** me from the violent man. 5337
Ps 22:5 They cried unto thee and were **d.**: 4422
Ps 33:16 a mighty man is not **d.** by much 5337
Ps 34:4 and **d.** me from all my fears. 5337
Ps 54:7 he hath **d.** me out of all trouble: 5337
Ps 55:18 He hath **d.** my soul in peace 6299
Ps 56:13 thou hast **d.** my soul from death: 5337
Ps 60:5 That thy beloved may be **d.**; save 2502
Ps 69:14 me be **d.** from them that hate me, 5337
Ps 78:42 he **d.** them from the enemy. 6299
Ps 78:61 And **d.** his strength into captivity, 5414
Ps 81:6 his hands were **d.** from the pots. 5674
Ps 81:7 calledst in trouble, and I **d.** thee; 2502
Ps 86:13 and thou hast **d.** my soul from the 5337
Ps 107:6 he **d.** them out of their distresses. 5337
Ps 107:20 **d.** them from their destructions. 4422
Ps 108:6 That thy beloved may be **d.**: save 2502
Ps 116:8 thou hast **d.** my soul from death, 2502
Pr 11:8 The righteous is **d.** out of trouble, 2502
Pr 11:9 knowledge shall the just be **d.**. 2502
Pr 11:21 seed of the righteous shall be **d.**. 4422
Pr 28:26 walketh wisely, he shall be **d.**. 4422
Ec 9:15 and he by his wisdom **d.** the city; 4422
Isa 20:6 to be **d.** from the king of Assyria: 5337
Isa 29:12 And the book is **d.** to him that is 5414
Isa 34:2 he hath **d.** them to the slaughter. 5414
Isa 36:15 this city shall not be **d.** into the 5414
Isa 36:18 the gods of the nations **d.** his land 5337
Isa 36:19 have they **d.** Samaria out of my 5337
Isa 36:20 that have **d.** their land out of my 5337
Isa 37:11 them utterly; and shalt thou be **d.**? 5337
Isa 37:12 Have the gods of the nations **d.** them. 5337
Isa 38:17 hast in love to my soul **d.** it from the
Isa 49:24 mighty, or the lawful captive **d.**? 4422
Isa 49:25 the prey of the terrible shall be **d.**: 4422
Isa 66:7 came, she was **d.** of a man child. 4422
Jer 7:10 are **d.** to do all these abominations? 5337
Jer 20:13 he hath **d.** the soul of the poor 5337
Jer 32:4 surely be **d.** into the hand of the 5414
Jer 32:16 when I had **d.** the evidence of the 5414
Jer 32:36 It shall be **d.** into the hand of the 5414
Jer 34:3 shalt surely be taken, and **d.** into 5414
Jer 37:17 thou shalt be **d.** into the hand of the 5414
Jer 46:24 she shall be **d.** into the hand of the 5414
La 1:14 Lord hath **d.** me into their hands, 5414
Eze 3:19 iniquity; but thou hast **d.** thy soul. 5337
Eze 3:21 warned; also thou hast **d.** thy soul. 5337
Eze 14:16 they only shall be **d.**, but the land 5337
Eze 14:18 they only shall be **d.** themselves. 5337
Eze 16:21 and **d.** them to cause them to pass 5414
Eze 16:27 and **d.** thee unto the will of them 5414
Eze 17:15 he break the covenant, and be **d.**? 4422
Eze 23:9 I have **d.** her into the hand of her 5414
Eze 31:11 I have therefore **d.** him into the 5414
Eze 31:14 they are all **d.** unto death, to the 5414
Eze 32:20 she is **d.** to the sword: draw her 5414
Eze 33:9 iniquity; but thou hast **d.** thy soul. 5337
Eze 34:27 and **d.** them out of the hand of those 5337
Da 3:28 hath sent his angel, and **d.** his 7804
Da 6:27 who hath **d.** Daniel from the power 7804
Da 12:1 thy people shall be **d.**, every one 4422
Joe 2:32 the name of the Lord shall be **d.**: 4422
Am 1:9 they **d.** up the whole captivity to 5462
Am 9:1 escapeth of them I shall not be **d.** 4422
Ob 14 neither shouldest thou have **d.** up 5462
Mic 4:10 there shalt thou be **d.**; there the 5337
Hab 2:9 that he may be **d.** from the power 5337
Mal 3:15 they that tempt God are even **d.**. 4422
Mt 11:27 **All things are d. unto me of my** 3860
Mt 18:34 **and d. him to the tormentors, till** 3860
Mt 25:14 **and d. unto them his goods.** 3860
Mt 27:2 and **d.** him to Pontius Pilate the 3860
Mt 27:18 that for envy they had **d.** him. 3860
Mt 27:26 Jesus, he **d.** him to be crucified. 3860
Mt 27:58 commanded the body to be **d.**. 591
Mk 7:13 **your tradition, which ye have d.:** 3860
Mk 9:31 **is d. into the hands of men, and** 3860
Mk 10:33 **the Son of man shall be d. unto** 3860
Mk 15:1 him away, and **d.** him to Pilate. 3860
Mk 15:10 chief priests had **d.** him for envy. 3860
Mk 15:15 and **d.** Jesus, when he had scourged 3860
Lu 1:2 Even as they **d.** them unto us, 3860
Lu 1:57 time came that she should be **d.**; 5088
Lu 1:74 that we being **d.** out of the hand 4506
Lu 2:6 accomplished that she should be **d.**. 5088
Lu 4:6 of them; for that is **d.** unto me; 3860
Lu 4:17 was **d.** unto him the book of the 1929
Lu 7:15 And he **d.** him to his mother 1325
Lu 9:42 and **d.** him again to his father. 591
Lu 9:44 **Son of man shall be d. into the** 3860
Lu 10:22 **things are d. to me of my Father.** 3860
Lu 12:58 **that thou mayest be d. from him;** 525
Lu 18:32 **he shall be d. unto the Gentiles,** 3860
Lu 19:13 **d. them ten pounds. and said unto** 1325
Lu 23:25 but he **d.** Jesus to their will. 3860
Lu 24:7 must be **d.** into the hands of sinful 3860
Lu 24:20 and our rulers **d.** him to be 3860
Joh 16:21 **as soon as she is d. of the child,** 1080
Joh 18:30 we would not have **d.** him up unto 3860
Joh 18:35 chief priests have **d.** thee unto me: 3860
Joh 18:36 **that I should not be d. to the Jews:** 3860
Joh 19:11 **therefore he that d. me unto thee.** 3860
Joh 19:16 Then **d.** he him therefore unto 3860
Ac 2:23 Him being **d.** by the determinate 1560
Ac 3:13 whom ye **d.** up, and denied him 3860
Ac 6:14 the customs which Moses **d.** us. 3860
Ac 7:10 And **d.** him out of all his afflictions, 1807
Ac 12:4 and **d.** him to four quaternions of 3860
Ac 12:11 and hath **d.** me out of the hand of 1807
Ac 15:30 together, they **d.** the epistle: 1929
Ac 16:4 **d.** them the decrees for to keep 3860
Ac 23:33 **d.** the epistle to the governor, 325
Ac 27:1 they **d.** Paul and certain other 3860
Ac 28:16 the centurion **d.** the prisoners to 3860
Ac 28:17 yet was I **d.** prisoner from 3860
Ro 4:25 Who was **d.** for our offences, and 3860
Ro 6:17 form of doctrine which was **d.** you. 3860
Ro 7:6 now we are **d.** from the law, 2673
Ro 8:21 shall be **d.** from the bondage of 1659
Ro 8:32 own Son, but **d.** him up for us all, 3860
Ro 15:31 That I may be **d.** from them that 4506
1Co 11:2 ordinances, as I **d.** them to you. 3860
1Co 11:23 which also I **d.** unto you, that the 3860
1Co 15:3 For I **d.** unto you first of all that 3860
1Co 15:24 when he shall have **d.** up the 3860
2Co 1:10 Who **d.** us from so great a death, 4506
2Co 4:11 are alway **d.** unto death for Jesus' 3860
Col 1:13 **d.** us from the power of darkness, 4506
1Th 1:10 Jesus which **d.** us from the wrath 4506
2Th 3:2 we may be **d.** from unreasonable 4506
1Ti 1:20 whom I have **d.** unto Satan, that 3860
2Ti 3:11 out of them all the Lord **d.** me. 4506
2Ti 4:17 was **d.** out of the mouth of the lion. 4506
Heb 11:11 and was **d.** of a child when she 5088
2Pe 2:4 **d.** them into chains of darkness, 3860
2Pe 2:7 And **d.** just Lot, vexed with the 4506
2Pe 2:21 holy commandment **d.** unto them. 3860
Jude 3 faith which was once **d.** unto the 3860
Re 12:2 in birth, and pained to be **d.**. 5088
Re 12:4 woman which was ready to be **d.**, 5088
Re 20:13 death and hell **d.** up the dead 1325

DELIVEREDST
Ne 9:27 Therefore thou **d.** them into the 5414
Mt 25:20 **Lord, thou d. unto me five talents:** 3860
Mt 25:22 **Lord, thou d. unto me two talents:** 3860

DELIVERER
Jg 3:9 the Lord raised up a **d.** to the 3467
Jg 3:15 the Lord raised them up a **d.**, 3467
Jg 18:28 there was no **d.**, because it was 5337
2Sa 22:2 rock, and my fortress, and my **d.**; 6403
Ps 18:2 my fortress, and my **d.**; my God, 6403
Ps 40:17 thou art my help and my **d.**; make 6403
Ps 70:5 thou art my help and my **d.**; O Lord, 6403
Ps 144:2 my high tower, and my **d.**: my 6403
Ac 7:35 God send to be a ruler and a **d.** by 3086
Ro 11:26 shall come out of Sion the **D.**, 4506

DELIVEREST
Ps 35:10 which **d.** the poor from him that 5337
Mic 6:14 which thou **d.** will I give up to 6403

DELIVERETH
Job 36:15 He **d.** the poor in his affliction, 2502
Ps 18:48 He **d.** me from mine enemies: 6403
Ps 34:7 them that fear him, and **d.** them. 2502
Ps 34:17 **d.** them out of all their troubles. 5337
Ps 34:19 the Lord **d.** him out of them all. 5337
Ps 97:10 he **d.** them out of the hand of the 5337
Ps 144:10 who **d.** David his servant from 6475
Pr 10:2 but righteousness **d.** from death. 5337
Pr 11:4 but righteousness **d.** from death. 5337
Pr 14:25 A true witness **d.** souls: but a 5337
Pr 31:24 and **d.** girdles unto the merchant. 5414
Isa 42:22 for a prey, and none **d.**; for a spoil, 5337
Da 6:27 He **d.** and rescueth, and he 7804

DELIVERING
Lu 21:12 **d. you up to the synagogues, and** 3860
Ac 22:4 and **d.** into prisons both men and 3860
Ac 26:17 **D. thee from the people, and from** 1807

DELIVERY
Isa 26:17 draweth near the time of her **d.**, 3205

DELUSION
See also DELUSIONS.
2Th 2:11 God shall send them strong **d.** 4106

DELUSIONS
Isa 66:4 I also will choose their **d.**, 8586

DEMAND See also DEMANDED.
Job 38:3 for I will d. of thee, and answer 7592
Job 40:7 like a man: I will d. of thee, and 7592
Job 42:4 will speak: I will d. of thee, and 7592
Da 4:17 the d. by the word of the holy ones: 7595

DEMANDED
Ex 5:14 were beaten, and d., Wherefore 559
2Sa 11:7 David d. of him how Joab did, 7592
Da 2:27 The secret which the king hath d. 7593
Mt 2:4 he d. of them where Christ should *4441*
Lu 3:14 soldiers likewise d. of him, saying, *1905*
Lu 17:20 when he was d. of the Pharisees, *1905*
Ac 21:33 and d. who he was, and what *4441*

DEMAS (de'-mas)
Col 4:14 the beloved physician, and D., *1214*
2Ti 4:10 For D. hath forsaken me, having *1214*
Phm 24 Marcus, Aristarchus, D., Lucas, *1214*

DEMETRIUS (de-me'-tre-us)
Ac 19:24 For a certain man named D., a *1216*
Ac 19:38 Wherefore if D., and the craftsmen *1216*
3Jo 12 D. hath good report of all men, *1216*

DEMONSTRATION
1Co 2:4 in d. of the Spirit and of power: *585*

DEN See also DENS.
Ps 10:9 in wait secretly as a lion in his d.: 5520
Isa 11:8 his hand on the cockatrice' d. 3975
Jer 7:11 a d. of robbers in your eyes? 4631
Jer 9:11 heaps, and a d. of dragons; and I 4583
Jer 10:22 desolate, and a d. of dragons 4583
Da 6:7 shall be cast into the d. of lions. 1358
Da 6:12 d. of lions? The king answered 1358
Da 6:16 and cast him into the d. of lions. 1358
Da 6:17 and laid upon the mouth of the d.; 1358
Da 6:19 went in haste unto the d. of lions. 1358
Da 6:20 when he came to the d. he cried 1358
Da 6:23 should take Daniel up out of the d. 1358
Da 6:23 Daniel was taken up out of the d., 1358
Da 6:24 they cast them into the d. of lions, 1358
Da 6:24 they came at the bottom of the d. 1358
Am 3:4 will a young lion cry out of his d., 4585
Mt 21:13 **but ye have made it a d. of thieves** *4693*
Mk 11:17 **but ye have made it a d. of thieves** *4693*
Lu 19:46 **but ye have made it a d. of thieves** *4693*

DENIED
Ge 18:15 Sarah d., saying, I laughed not; 3584
1Ki 20:7 my gold, and I d. him not. 4513
Job 31:28 have d. the God that is above. 3584
Mt 26:70 he d. before them all, saying, *720*
Mt 26:72 again he d. with an oath, I do not *720*
Mk 14:68 But he d., saying, I know not, *720*
Mk 14:70 And he d. it again. And a little after, *720*
Lu 8:45 When all d., Peter and they that *720*
Lu 12:9 **be d. before the angels of God** *533*
Lu 22:57 he d. him, saying, Woman, I know *720*
Joh 1:20 he confessed, and d. not; but 720
Joh 13:38 **crow, till thou hast d. me thrice** *533*
Joh 18:25 He d. it, and said, I am not, *720*
Joh 18:27 Peter then d. again: and *720*
Ac 3:13 d. him in the presence of Pilate, *720*
Ac 3:14 ye d. the Holy One and the Just, *720*
1Ti 5:8 he hath d. the faith, and is worse *720*
Re 2:13 **hast not d. my faith, even in those** *720*
Re 3:8 **word, and hast not d. my name** 720

DENIETH
Lu 12:9 **he that d. me before men shall be** *720*
1Jo 2:22 he that d. that Jesus is the Christ? *720*
1Jo 2:22 that d. the Father and the Son. *720*
1Jo 2:23 Whosoever d. the Son, the same *720*

DENOUNCE
De 30:18 I d. unto you this day, that ye 5046

DENS
Jg 6:2 of Israel made them the d. which 4492
Job 37:8 Then the beasts go into d., and 695
Job 38:40 When they couch in their d., and 4585
Ps 104:22 and lay them down in their d. 4585
Ca 4:8 from the lions' d., from the 4585
Isa 32:14 forts and towers shall be for d. 4631
Na 2:12 with prey, and his d. with ravin. 4585
Heb 11:38 and in d. and caves of the earth *4693*
Re 6:15 hid themselves in the d. and in *4693*

DENY See also DENIED; DENIETH; DENYING.
Jos 24:27 unto you, lest ye d. your God. 3584
1Ki 2:16 one petition of thee, d. me not. 7725
Job 8:18 then it shall d. him, saying, I have 3584
Pr 30:7 d. me them not before I die: 4513
Pr 30:9 be full, and d. thee, and say, Who 3584
Mt 10:33 **whosoever shall d. me before men,** *720*
Mt 10:33 **him will I also d. before my Father** *720*
Mt 16:24 **come after me, let him d. himself,** *533*
Mt 26:34 **cock crow, thou shalt d. me thrice** *533*
Mt 26:35 die with thee, yet will I not d. thee *533*
Mt 26:75 cock crow, thou shalt d. me thrice. *533*
Mk 8:34 **let him d. himself, and take up** *533*
Mk 14:30 **crow twice, thou shalt d. me thrice** *533*
Mk 14:31 I will not d. thee in any wise. *533*
Mk 14:72 twice, thou shalt d. me thrice. *533*
Lu 9:23 **come after me, let him d. himself,** *533*
Lu 20:27 d. that there is any resurrection; *483*
Lu 22:34 **thrice d. that thou knowest me** *533*
Lu 22:61 cock crow, thou shalt d. me thrice. *533*
Ac 4:16 Jerusalem; and we cannot d. it. *720*
2Ti 2:12 if we d. him, he also will d. us: *720*
2Ti 2:13 faithful: he cannot d. himself. *720*
Tit 1:16 but in works they d. him, being *720*

DENYING
2Ti 3:5 of godliness, but d. the power *720*
Tit 2:12 d. ungodliness and worldly lusts, *720*
2Pe 2:1 d. the Lord that bought them, *720*
Jude 4 d. the only Lord God, and our Lord *720*

DEPART See also DEPARTED; DEPARTETH; DEPARTING.
Ge 13:9 or if thou d. to the right hand,
Ge 49:10 sceptre shall not d. from Judah, 5493
Ex 8:11 And the frogs shall d. from thee, 5493
Ex 8:29 that the swarms of flies may d. 5493
Ex 18:27 And Moses let his father in law d.; 7971
Ex 21:22 so that her fruit d. from her, 3318
Ex 33:1 D., and go up hence, thou and 3212
Le 25:41 And then shall he d. from thee, 3318
Nu 10:30 but I will d. to mine own land, 3212
Nu 16:26 D., I pray you, from the tents of 5493
De 4:9 lest they d. from thy heart all the 5493
De 9:7 from the day that thou didst d. 3318
Jos 1:8 This book of the law shall not d. 4185
Jos 24:28 So Joshua let the people d., 7971
Jg 6:18 D. not hence, I pray thee, 4185
Jg 7:3 let him return and d. early from 6852
Jg 19:5 he rose up to d.: and the damsel's 3212
Jg 19:7 the man rose up to d., his father 3212
Jg 19:8 the morning on the fifth day to d.: 3212
Jg 19:9 the man rose up to d., he, and his 3212
1Sa 15:6 d., get you down from among 5493
1Sa 22:5 d., and get thee into the land of 3212
1Sa 29:10 in the morning, and have light, d. 3212
1Sa 29:11 and his men rose up early to d. 3212
1Sa 30:22 they may lead them away, and d. 3212
2Sa 7:15 mercy shall not d. away from him, 5493
2Sa 11:12 and to morrow I will let thee d. 7971
2Sa 12:10 shall never d. from thine house; 5493
2Sa 15:14 make speed to d., lest he overtake 3212
2Sa 20:21 and I will d. from the city. 3212
2Sa 22:23 statutes, I did not d. from them. 5493
1Ki 11:21 Let me d., that I may go to mine 7971
1Ki 12:5 unto them, D. yet for three days, 3212
1Ki 12:24 returned to d., according to the 3212
1Ki 15:19 king of Israel, that he may d. from 5927
2Ch 16:3 king of Israel, that he may d. from 5927
2Ch 18:31 God moved them to d. from him.
2Ch 35:15 might not d. from their service: 5493
Job 7:19 long wilt thou not d. from me. 8159
Job 15:30 He shall not d. out of darkness; 5493
Job 20:28 The increase of his house shall d., 1540
Job 21:14 they say unto God, D. from us; 5493
Job 22:17 Which said unto God, D. from us: 5493
Job 28:28 to d. from evil is understanding. 5493
Ps 6:8 D. from me, all ye workers of 5493
Ps 34:14 D. from evil, and do good; seek 5493
Ps 37:27 D. from evil, and do good; and 5493
Ps 55:11 and guile d. not from her streets. 4185
Ps 101:4 froward heart shall d. from me: 5493
Ps 119:115 D. from me, ye evildoers: for I 5493
Ps 139:19 d. from me therefore, ye bloody 5493
Pr 3:7 fear the Lord, and d. from evil. 5493
Pr 3:21 let not them d. from thine eyes: 3868
Pr 4:21 Let them not d. from thine eyes; 3868
Pr 5:7 d. not from the words of my 5493
Pr 13:14 to d. from the snares of death. 5493
Pr 13:19 abomination to fools to d. from 5493
Pr 14:27 to d. from the snares of death. 5493
Pr 15:24 that he may d. from hell beneath. 5493
Pr 16:6 fear of the Lord men d. from evil. 5493
Pr 16:17 of the upright is to d. from evil: 5493
Pr 17:13 evil shall not d. from his house. 4185
Pr 22:6 he is old, he will not d. from it. 5493
Pr 27:22 not his foolishness d. from him. 5493
Isa 11:13 The envy also of Ephraim shall d., 5493
Isa 14:25 shall his yoke d. from off them, 5493
Isa 14:25 burden d. from off their shoulders. 5493
Isa 52:11 D. ye, d. ye, go ye out from thence, 5493
Isa 54:10 the mountains shall d., and the 4185
Isa 54:10 but my kindness shall not d. from 4185
Isa 59:21 have put in thy mouth, shall not d. 4185
Jer 6:8 lest my soul d. from thee; lest 3363
Jer 17:13 and they that d. from me shall be 3249
Jer 31:36 ordinances d. from before me, 4185
Jer 32:40 that they shall not d. from me. 5493
Jer 37:9 The Chaldeans shall surely d. 1980
Jer 37:9 from us: for they shall not d. 1980
Jer 50:3 they shall d., both man and beast. 1980
La 4:15 They cried unto them, D. ye; it 5493
La 4:15 it is unclean; d., d., touch not: 5493
Eze 16:42 my jealously shall d. from thee, 5493
Ho 9:12 woe also to them when I d. from 5493
Mic 2:10 Arise ye, and d.; for this is not 3212
Zec 10:11 sceptre of Egypt shall d. away. 5493
Mt 7:23 **d. from me, ye that work iniquity** *672*
Mt 8:18 gave the commandment to d. unto *565*
Mt 8:34 he would d. out of their coasts. *3327*
Mt 10:14 **ye d. out of that house or city,** *1831*
Mt 14:16 unto them, **They need not d;** *565*
Mt 25:41 **D. from me, ye cursed, into** *4198*
Mk 5:17 pray him to d. out of their coasts. *565*
Mk 6:10 **abide till ye d. from that place** *1831*
Mk 6:11 **ye d. thence, shake off the dust** *1607*
Lu 2:29 lettest thou thy servant d. in peace, *630*
Lu 4:42 that he should not d. from them. *4198*
Lu 5:8 saying, D. from me; for I am a *1831*
Lu 8:37 besought him to d. from them; *565*
Lu 9:4 **into, there abide, and thence d.,** *1831*
Lu 12:59 **thou shalt not d. thence, till thou** *1831*
Lu 13:27 **d. from me, all ye workers of** *868*
Lu 13:31 Get thee out, and d. hence: for *4198*
Lu 21:21 **which are in the midst of it d. out;** *1633*
Joh 7:3 D. hence, and go into Judaea, *3327*
Joh 13:1 that he should d. out of this world *3327*
Joh 16:7 **but if I d., I will send him unto** *4198*
Ac 1:4 they should not d. from Jerusalem *5562*
Ac 16:36 therefore d., and go in peace. *1831*
Ac 16:39 desired them to d. out of the city. *1831*
Ac 18:2 all Jews to d. from Rome: *5562*
Ac 20:7 them, ready to d. on the morrow; *1826*
Ac 22:21 **D.: for I will send thee far hence** *4198*
Ac 23:22 then let the young man d., and *630*
Ac 25:4 himself would d. shortly thither. *1607*
Ac 27:12 part advised to d. thence also, *321*
1Co 7:10 not the wife d. from her husband *5562*
1Co 7:11 she d., let her remain unmarried, *5562*
1Co 7:15 if the unbelieving d., let him d. *5562*
2Co 12:8 thrice, that it might d. from me. *868*
Php 1:23 having a desire to d., and to be *360*
1Ti 4:1 some shall d. from the faith, *868*
2Ti 2:19 name of Christ d. from iniquity. *868*
Jas 2:16 say unto them, D. in peace, be ye *5217*

DEPARTED
Ge 12:4 Abram d., as the Lord had spoken 3212
Ge 12:4 old when he d. out of Haran. 3318
Ge 14:12 and his goods, and d. 3212
Ge 21:14 and she d., and wandered in the 3212
Ge 24:10 the camels of his master, and d.; 3212
Ge 26:17 And Isaac d. thence, and pitched 3212
Ge 26:31 and they d. from him in peace. 3212
Ge 31:40 and my sleep d. from mine eyes. 5074
Ge 31:55 and Laban d., and returned unto 3212
Ge 37:17 They are d. hence; for I heard 5265
Ge 42:26 asses with the corn, and d. thence. 3212
Ge 45:24 his brethren away, and they d.: 3212
Ex 19:2 For they were d. from Rephidim, 5265
Ex 33:11 d. not out of the tabernacle. 4185
Ex 35:20 of the children of Israel d. 3318
Le 13:58 if the plague be d. from them, 5493
Nu 10:33 d. from the mount of the Lord 5265
Nu 12:9 kindled against them; and he d. 3212
Nu 12:10 cloud d. from off the tabernacle; 5493
Nu 14:9 their defence is d. from them, 5493
Nu 14:44 Moses, d. not out of the camp. 4185

Nu 22:7 the elders of Midian **d.** with the........ 3212
Nu 33:3 they **d.** from Rameses in the first....... 5265
Nu 33:6 And they **d.** from Succoth, and......... 5265
Nu 33:8 they **d.** from before Pi-hahiroth,......... 5265
Nu 33:13 And they **d.** from Dophkah, and......... 5265
Nu 33:15 And they **d.** from Rephidim, and 5265
Nu 33:17 they **d.** from Kibroth-hattaavah, ... 5265
Nu 33:18 And they **d.** from Hazeroth, and......... 5265
Nu 33:19 And they **d.** from Rithmah, and......... 5265
Nu 33:20 And they **d.** from Rimmon-parez, ... 5265
Nu 33:27 And they **d.** from Tahath, and 5265
Nu 33:30 And they **d.** from Hashmonah, ... 5265
Nu 33:31 And they **d.** from Moseroth, and........ 5265
Nu 33:35 And they **d.** from Ebronah, and......... 5265
Nu 33:41 And they **d.** from mount Hor, and 5265
Nu 33:42 And they **d.** from Zalmonah, and 5265
Nu 33:43 And they **d.** from Punon, and 5265
Nu 33:44 And they **d.** from Oboth, and 5265
Nu 33:45 And they **d.** from Iim, and pitched...... 5265
Nu 33:48 **d.** from the mountains of Abarim, ... 5265
De 1:19 when we **d.** from Horeb, we went...... 5265
De 24:2 when she is **d.** out of his house, ... 3318
Jos 2:21 she sent them away, and they **d.**: 3212
Jos 22:9 and **d.** from the children of Israel....... 3212
Jg 6:21 angel of the Lord **d.** out of his............ 1980
Jg 9:55 that Abimelech was dead they **d.**......... 3212
Jg 16:20 he wist not that the Lord was **d.**......... 5493
Jg 17:8 And the man **d.** out of the city........... 3212
Jg 18:7 Then the five men **d.**, and came to........ 3212
Jg 18:21 So they turned and **d.**, and put 3212
Jg 19:10 he rose up and **d.**, and came over......... 3212
Jg 21:24 And the children of Israel **d.**.............. 1980
1Sa 4:21 saying, The glory is **d.** from Israel:..... 1540
1Sa 4:22 is **d.** from Israel: for the ark of God ... 1540
1Sa 6:6 let the people go, and they **d.**? 3212
1Sa 10:2 When thou art **d.** from me to day,...... 3212
1Sa 15:6 So the Kenites **d.** from among the...... 5493
1Sa 16:14 the Spirit of the Lord **d.** from Saul, ... 5493
1Sa 16:23 and the evil spirit **d.** from him. 5493
1Sa 18:12 with him, and was **d.** from Saul.......... 5493
1Sa 20:42 he arose and **d.**: and Jonathan............ 3212
1Sa 22:1 David therefore **d.** thence, and 3212
1Sa 22:5 David **d.**, and came into the forest...... 3212
1Sa 23:13 six hundred, **d.** out of Keilah, ... 3318
1Sa 28:15 God is **d.** from me, and answereth 5493
1Sa 28:16 seeing the Lord is **d.** from thee, ... 5493
2Sa 6:19 So all the people **d.** every one.......... 3212
2Sa 11:8 Uriah **d.** out of the king's house,........ 3318
2Sa 12:15 And Nathan **d.** unto his house............ 3212
2Sa 17:21 after they were **d.**, that they came..... 3212
2Sa 19:24 the day the king **d.** until the day 3212
2Sa 22:22 have not wickedly **d.** from my God...........
1Ki 12:5 again to me. And the people **d.**........... 3212
1Ki 12:16 So Israel **d.** unto their tents............. 3212
1Ki 14:17 Jeroboam's wife arose, and **d.**, and..... 3212
1Ki 19:19 So he **d.** thence, and found Elisha 3212
1Ki 20:9 the messengers **d.**, and brought......... 3212
1Ki 20:36 as thou art **d.** from me a lion shall...... 1980
1Ki 20:36 as soon as he was **d.** from him, ... 3212
1Ki 20:38 So the prophet **d.**, and waited 3212
2Ki 1:4 shalt surely die. And Elijah **d.**........... 3212
2Ki 3:3 to sin; he **d.** not therefrom. 5493
2Ki 3:27 they **d.** from him, and returned.......... 5265
2Ki 5:5 **d.**, and took with him ten talents....... 3212
2Ki 5:19 So he **d.** from him a little way........... 3212
2Ki 5:24 he let the men go, and they **d.**. 3212
2Ki 8:14 So he **d.** from Elisha, and came to...... 3212
2Ki 10:12 he arose and **d.**, and came to.............. 935
2Ki 10:15 when he was **d.** thence, he lighted 3212
2Ki 10:29 Jehu **d.** not from after them, ... 5493
2Ki 10:31 **d.** not from the sins of Jeroboam,....... 5493
2Ki 13:2 Israel to sin; he **d.** not therefrom. 5493
2Ki 13:6 They **d.** not from the sins of the 5493
2Ki 13:11 **d.** not from all the sins of Jeroboam.... 5493
2Ki 14:24 **d.** not from all the sins of Jeroboam.... 5493
2Ki 15:9 he **d.** not from the sins of Jeroboam.... 5493
2Ki 15:18 he **d.** not all his days from the sins..... 5493
2Ki 15:24, 28 **d.** not from the sins of Jeroboam.... 5493
2Ki 17:22 he did; they **d.** not from them; 5493
2Ki 18:6 and **d.** not from following him, ... 5493
2Ki 19:8 that he was **d.** from Lachish................ 5265
2Ki 19:36 So Sennacherib king of Assyria **d.**,...... 5265
1Ch 16:43 And all the people **d.** every man 3212
1Ch 21:4 Joab **d.**, and went throughout all......... 3318
2Ch 8:15 **d.** not from the commandment........... 5493
2Ch 10:5 three days. And the people **d.**. 3212
2Ch 20:32 **d.** not from it, doing that which 5493
2Ch 21:20 and **d.** without being desired. 3212
2Ch 24:25 And when they were **d.** from him,...... 3212
2Ch 34:33 **d.** not from following the Lord, ... 5493
Ezr 8:31 we **d.** from the river of Ahava 5265
Ne 9:19 cloud **d.** not from them by day,........... 5493
Ps 18:21 have not wickedly **d.** from my God. ....
Ps 34:*title* who drove him away, and he **d.**. 3212
Ps 105:38 Egypt was glad when they **d.**: 3318
Ps 119:102 have not **d.** from thy judgments: 5493
Isa 7:17 from the day that Ephraim **d.** 5493
Isa 37:8 that he was **d.** from Lachish.............. 5265
Isa 37:37 So Sennacherib king of Assyria **d.**,..... 5265
Isa 38:12 Mine age is **d.**, and is removed.......... 5265
Jer 29:2 smiths were **d.** from Jerusalem: 3318
Jer 37:5 of them, they **d.** from Jerusalem. 5927
Jer 41:10 **d.** to go over to the Ammonites.......... 3212
Jer 41:17 they **d.**, and dwelt in the habitation..... 3212
La 1:6 of Zion all her beauty is **d.**:............... 3318
Eze 6:9 their whorish heart, which hath **d.** 5493
Eze 10:18 the glory of the Lord **d.** from off........ 3318
Da 4:31 The kingdom is **d.** from thee. 5709
Ho 10:5 thereof, because it is **d.** from it. 1540
Mal 2:8 ye are **d.** out of the way; 5493
Mt 2:9 they **d.**; and, lo, the star, which......... *4198*
Mt 2:12 **d.** into their own country another......... *402*
Mt 2:13 when they were **d.**, behold, the angel... *402*
Mt 2:14 mother by night, and **d.** into Egypt: *402*
Mt 4:12 into prison, he **d.** into Galilee;............ *402*
Mt 9:7 And he arose and **d.** to his house *565*
Mt 9:27 And when Jesus **d.** thence, two *3855*
Mt 9:31 when they were **d.**, spread abroad...... *1831*
Mt 11:1 he **d.** thence to teach and to preach.... *3327*
Mt 11:7 as they **d.**, Jesus began to say.......... *4198*
Mt 12:9 And when he was **d.** thence, he......... *3327*
Mt 13:53 these parables, he **d.** thence. *3332*
Mt 14:13 he **d.** thence by ship into a desert........ *402*
Mt 15:21 and **d.** into the coasts of Tyre and....... *402*
Mt 15:29 Jesus **d.** from thence, and came *3327*
Mt 16:4 **Jonas.** And he left them, and **d.**. *565*
Mt 17:18 he **d.** out of him: and the child.......... *1831*
Mt 19:1 he **d.** from Galilee, and came unto......... *3332*
Mt 19:15 his hands on them, and **d.** thence. *4198*
Mt 20:29 **d.** from Jericho, a great multitude...... *1607*
Mt 24:1 and **d.** from the temple: and his *4198*
Mt 27:5 in the temple, and **d.**, and went........... *402*
Mt 27:60 the door of the sepulchre, and **d.**.......... *565*
Mt 28:8 they **d.** quickly from the sepulchre...... *1831*
Mk 1:35 he went out, and **d.** into a solitary *565*
Mk 1:42 the leprosy **d.** from him, and he was *565*
Mk 5:20 he **d.**, and began to publish in *565*
Mk 6:32 they **d.** into a desert place by ship *565*
Mk 6:46 he **d.** into a mountain to pray.............. *565*
Mk 8:13 the ship again **d.** to the other side. *565*
Mk 9:30 And they **d.** thence, and passed......... *1831*
Lu 1:23 he **d.** to his own house..................... *565*
Lu 1:38 word. And the angel **d.** from her. *565*
Lu 2:37 which **d.** not from the temple,............. *868*
Lu 4:13 he **d.** from him for a season............... *868*
Lu 4:42 was day, he **d.** and went into *1831*
Lu 5:13 the leprosy **d.** from him.................... *565*
Lu 5:25 **d.** to his own house, glorifying God...... *565*
Lu 7:24 the messengers of John were **d.**, ... *565*
Lu 8:35, 38 out of whom the devils were **d.**..... *1831*
Lu 9:6 **d.**, and went through the towns, ... *1831*
Lu 9:33 as they **d.** from him, Peter said *1316*
Lu 10:30 **him, d., leaving him half dead**........ *565*
Lu 10:35 **morrow when he d., he took out** ... *1831*
Lu 24:12 clothes laid by themselves, and **d.**,....... *565*
Joh 4:3 Judaea, and **d.** again into Galilee. *565*
Joh 4:43 after two days he **d.** thence, and *565*
Joh 5:15 The man **d.**, and told the Jews............ *565*
Joh 6:15 **d.** again into a mountain himself........... *402*
Joh 12:36 These things spake Jesus, and **d.**,........ *565*
Ac 5:41 And they **d.** from the presence of....... *4198*
Ac 10:7 spake unto Cornelius was **d.**, he *565*
Ac 11:25 Then **d.** Barnabas to Tarsus, for......... *1831*
Ac 12:10 forthwith the angel **d.** from him. *868*
Ac 12:17 And he **d.**, and went into another....... *1831*
Ac 13:4 **d.** unto Seleucia; and from thence....... *2718*
Ac 13:14 when they **d.** from Perga, they *1330*
Ac 14:20 he **d.** with Barnabas to Derbe............ *1831*
Ac 15:38 **d.** from them from Pamphylia,............. *868*
Ac 15:39 they **d.** asunder one from the............. *673*
Ac 15:40 Paul chose Silas, and **d.**, being.......... *1831*
Ac 16:40 they comforted them, and **d.**,............ *1831*
Ac 17:15 come to him with all speed, they **d.**, ... *1826*
Ac 17:33 So Paul **d.** from among them............ *1831*
Ac 18:1 Paul **d.** from Athens, and came to *5562*
Ac 18:7 he **d.** thence, and entered into a *1831*
Ac 18:23 he **d.**, and went over all the country ... *1831*
Ac 19:9 he **d.** from them, and separated.......... *868*
Ac 19:12 and the diseases **d.** from them, ... *525*
Ac 20:1 and **d.** for to go into Macedonia. *1831*
Ac 20:11 even till break of day, so he **d.**, ... *1831*
Ac 21:5 we **d.** and went our way; and they *1831*
Ac 21:8 that were of Paul's company **d.**, and ... *1831*
Ac 22:29 Then straightway they **d.** from him *868*
Ac 28:10 when we **d.**, they laded us with *321*
Ac 28:11 we **d.** in a ship of Alexandria,.............. *321*
Ac 28:25 not among themselves, they **d.**,........... *630*
Ac 28:29 Jews **d.**, and had great reasoning......... *565*
Php 4:15 when I **d.** from Macedonia, no........... *1831*
Phm 15 For perhaps he therefore **d.** for a....... *5563*
2Ti 4:10 and is **d.** unto Thessalonica; *4198*
Re 6:14 the heaven **d.** as a scroll when it is...... *673*
Re 18:14 lusted after are **d.** from thee, and........ *565*
Re 18:14 and goodly are **d.** from thee, and......... *565*

DEPARTETH

Job 27:21 carrieth him away, and he **d.**:........... 3212
Pr 14:16 A wise man feareth, and **d.** from....... 5493
Ec 6:4 and **d.** in darkness, and his name 3212
Isa 59:15 and he that **d.** from evil maketh 5493
Jer 3:20 a wife treacherously **d.** from her ....
Jer 17:5 and whose heart **d.** from the Lord, ... 5493
Na 3:1 lies and robbery; the prey **d.** not;...... 4185
Lu 9:30 bruising him hardly **d.** from him, ... *672*

DEPARTING

Ge 35:18 her soul was in **d.** (for she died), ... 3318
Ex 16:1 after their **d.** out of the land of.......... 3318
Isa 59:13 **d.** away from our God, speaking 5253
Da 9:5 even by **d.** from thy precepts and....... 5493
Da 9:11 transgressed thy law, even by **d.**, ... 5493
Ho 1:2 great whoredom, **d.** from the Lord. ....
Mk 6:33 And the people saw them **d.**, and........ *5217*
Mk 7:31 again, **d.** from the coast of Tyre *1831*
Ac 13:13 John **d.** from them returned to *672*
Ac 20:29 I know this, that after my **d.** *867*
Heb 3:12 unbelief, in **d.** from the living God........ *868*
Heb 11:22 the **d.** of the children of Israel........... *1841*

DEPARTURE

Eze 26:18 the sea shall be troubled at thy **d.**. 3318
2Ti 4:6 and the time of my **d.** is at hand.......... *359*

DEPOSED

Da 5:20 he was **d.** from his kingly throne, ... 5182

DEPRIVED

Ge 27:45 why should I be **d.** also of you.......... 7921
Job 39:17 God hath **d.** her of wisdom, ... 5382
Isa 38:10 I am **d.** of the residue of my years. 6485

DEPTH See also DEPTHS.

Job 28:14 The **d.** saith, It is not in me:............ 8415
Job 38:16 walked in the search of the **d.**? 8415
Ps 33:7 layeth up the **d.** in storehouses.......... 8415
Pr 8:27 compass upon the face of the **d.**:........ 8415
Pr 25:3 for height, and the earth for **d.**, ... 6012
Isa 7:11 ask it either in the **d.** or in the 6009
Jon 2:5 the **d.** closed me round about, the....... 8415
Mt 18:6 **were drowned in the d. of the sea**... *3989*
Mk 4:5 **because it had no d. of earth:**......... *899*
Ro 8:39 Nor height, nor **d.**, nor any other *899*
Ro 11:33 O the **d.** of the riches both of the........ *899*
Eph 3:18 the breadth, and length, and **d.**, and..... *899*

DEPTHS

Ex 15:5 The **d.** have covered them; they 8415
Ex 15:8 **d.** were congealed in the heart 8415
De 8:7 of fountains and **d.** that spring out 8415
Ps 68:22 again from the **d.** of the sea:............. 4688
Ps 71:20 up again from the **d.** of the earth. 8415
Ps 77:16 afraid: the **d.** also were troubled. 8415
Ps 78:15 them drink as out of the great **d.**. 8415
Ps 106:9 so he led them through the **d.**, ... 8415
Ps 107:26 they go down again to the **d.**:........... 8415
Ps 130:1 Out of the **d.** have I cried unto thee, .. 4615
Pr 3:20 By his knowledge the **d.** are.............. 8415
Pr 8:24 When there were no **d.**, I was............ 8415
Pr 9:18 her guests are in the **d.** of hell. 6010
Isa 51:10 that hath made the **d.** of the sea 4615
Eze 27:34 by the seas in the **d.** of the waters..... 4615

Mic 7:19 their sin into the **d.** of the sea........... 4688
Re 2:24 **have not known the d. of Satan,**..... *899*

DEPUTED
2Sa 15:3 there is no man **d.** of the king to hear.......

DEPUTIES
Es 8:9 the **d.** and rulers of the provinces....... 6346
Es 9:3 the **d.** and officers of the king,........... 6346
Ac 19:38 the law is open, and there are **d.**:........ *446*

DEPUTY See also DEPUTIES.
1Ki 22:47 no king in Edom: a **d.** was king. 5324
Ac 13:7 was with the **d.** of the country, ... *446*
Ac 13:8 turn away the **d.** from the faith. *446*
Ac 13:12 Then the **d.**, when he saw what *446*
Ac 18:12 when Gallio was **d.** of Achaia, ... *446*

DERBE (der'-by)
Ac 14:6 and fled unto Lystra and **D.**, ... *1191*
Ac 14:20 he departed with Barnabas to **D.**........ *1191*
Ac 16:1 Then came he to **D.** and Lystra:........ *1191*
Ac 20:4 and Secundus; and Gaius of **D.**, and.... *1191*

DERIDE See also DERIDED.
Hab 1:10 they shall **d.** every strong hold; 7832

DERIDED
Lu 16:14 all these things: and they **d.** him. *1592*
Lu 23:35 the rulers also with them **d.** him. *1592*

DERISION
Job 30:1 are younger than I have me in **d.**, ... 7832
Ps 2:4 the Lord shall have them in **d.**............ 3932
Ps 44:13 a scorn and a **d.** to them that are....... 7047
Ps 59:8 shalt have all the heathen in **d.**.......... 3932
Ps 79:4 a scorn and **d.** to them that are 7047
Ps 119:51 proud have had me greatly in **d.**:........ 3887
Jer 20:7 am in **d.** daily, every one mocketh...... 7814
Jer 20:8 a reproach unto me, and a **d.**, ... 7047
Jer 48:26 and he also shall be in **d.**................ 7814
Jer 48:27 was not Israel a **d.** unto thee? 7814
Jer 48:39 so shall Moab be a **d.** and a 7814
La 3:14 I was a **d.** to all my people; 7814
Eze 23:32 laughed to scorn and had in **d.**; 3932
Eze 36:4 which became a prey and **d.** to the..... 3932
Ho 7:16 shall be their **d.** in the land of Egypt... 3932

DESCEND See also DESCENDED; DESCENDETH; DESCENDING.
Nu 34:11 and the border shall **d.**, and shall........ 3381
1Sa 26:10 he shall **d.** into battle, and perish. 3381
Ps 49:17 his glory shall not **d.** after him........... 3381
Isa 5:14 he that rejoiceth, shall **d.** into it. 3381
Eze 26:20 them that **d.** into the pit, with the...... 3381
Eze 31:16 them that **d.** into the pit: and all 3381
Mk 15:32 Let Christ the king of Israel **d.**.......... *2597*
Ac 11:5 A certain vessel **d.**, as it had been *2597*
Ro 10:7 Or, Who shall **d.** into the deep? *2597*
1Th 4:16 Lord himself shall **d.** from heaven....... *2597*

DESCENDED
Ex 19:18 the Lord **d.** upon it in fire: and.......... 3381
Ex 33:9 the cloudy pillar **d.**, and stood at......... 3381
Ex 34:5 And the Lord **d.** in the cloud,.............. 3381
De 9:21 the brook that **d.** out of the mount. 3381
Jos 2:23 returned, and **d.** from the mountain, ... 3381
Jos 17:9 And the coast **d.** unto the river.......... 3381
Jos 18:13 the border **d.** to Atarot-adar,.............. 3381
Jos 18:16 and **d.** to the valley of Hinnom,.......... 3381
Jos 18:16 south, and **d.** to En-rogel,................. 3381
Jos 18:17 and **d.** to the stone of Bohan the........ 3381
Ps 133:3 **d.** upon the mountains of Zion: 3381
Pr 30:4 ascended up into heaven, or **d.**?.......... 3381
Mt 7:25, 27 **And the rain d., and the floods** ..*2597*
Mt 28:2 for the angel of the Lord **d.** from *2597*
Lu 3:22 the Holy Ghost **d.** in a bodily shape *2597*
Ac 24:1 the high priest **d.** with the elders,....... *2597*
Eph 4:9 but that he also **d.** first into the *2597*
Eph 4:10 He that **d.** is the same also that......... *2597*

DESCENDETH
Jas 3:15 This wisdom **d.** not from above,......... *2718*

DESCENDING
Ge 28:12 angels of God ascending and **d.**........... 3381
Mt 3:16 Spirit of God **d.** like a dove,.............. *2597*
Mk 1:10 the Spirit like a dove **d.** upon him........ *2597*
Joh 1:32 I saw the Spirit **d.** from heaven *2597*
Joh 1:33 whom thou shalt see the Spirit **d.**,...... *2597*
Joh 1:51 **angels of God ascending and d.**......... *2597*
Ac 10:11 a certain vessel **d.** unto him, ... *2597*
Re 21:10 Jerusalem, **d.** out of heaven from *2597*

DESCENT
Lu 19:37 at the **d.** of the mount of Olives,........ *2600*
Heb 7:3 without mother, without **d.**,................ *35*
Heb 7:6 whose **d.** is not counted from............. *1075*

DESCRIBE See also DESCRIBED; DESCRIBETH.
Jos 18:4 and go through the land, and **d.** it 3789
Jos 18:6 ye shall therefore **d.** the land into....... 3789
Jos 18:8 them that went to **d.** the land,........... 3789
Jos 18:8 walk through the land, and **d.** it, ... 3789

DESCRIBED
Jos 18:9 and **d.** it by cities into seven parts...... 3789
Jg 3:14 and he **d.** unto him the princes of....... 3789

DESCRIBETH
Ro 4:6 as David also **d.** the blessedness *3004*
Ro 10:5 Moses **d.** the righteousness which...... *1125*

DESCRIPTION
Jos 18:6 and bring the **d.** hither to me ....

DESCRY
Jg 1:23 the house of Joseph sent to **d.**........... 8446

DESERT See also DESERTS.
Ex 3:1 to the backside of the **d.**, and........... 4057
Ex 5:3 three days' journey into the **d.**,.......... 4057
Ex 19:2 were come to the **d.** of Sinai, and 4057
Ex 23:31 and from the **d.** unto the river:.......... 4057
Nu 20:1 into the **d.** of Zin in the first............. 4057
Nu 27:14 in the **d.** of Zin, in the strife of.......... 4057
Nu 33:16 removed from the **d.** of Sinai, and 4057
De 32:10 He found him in a **d.** land, and.......... 4057
2Ch 26:10 he built towers in the **d.**, and 4057
Job 24:5 wild asses in the **d.**, go they forth....... 4057
Ps 28:4 hands; render to them their **d.**........... 1576
Ps 78:40 and grieve him in the **d.**!................. 3452
Ps 102:6 I am like an owl of the **d.**.................. 2723
Ps 106:14 and tempted God in the **d.**................ 3452
Isa 13:21 beasts of the **d.** shall lie there; 6728
Isa 21:1 burden of the **d.** of the sea. 4057
Isa 21:1 through; so it cometh from the **d.**, ... 4057
Isa 34:14 The wild beasts of the **d.** shall............ 6728
Isa 35:1 the **d.** shall rejoice, and blossom 6160
Isa 35:6 break out, and streams in the **d.**......... 6160
Isa 40:3 make straight in the **d.** a highway....... 6160
Isa 41:19 I will set in the **d.** the fir tree, ... 6160
Isa 43:19 wilderness, and rivers in the **d.**.......... 3452
Isa 43:20 rivers in the **d.**, to give drink to my ... 3452
Isa 51:3 her **d.** like the garden of the Lord; 6160
Jer 17:6 like the heath in the **d.**, and shall 6160
Jer 25:24 people that dwell in the **d.**, ... 4057
Jer 50:12 wilderness, a dry land, and a **d.**.......... 6160
Jer 50:39 Therefore the wild beasts of the **d.**....... 6728
Eze 47:8 go down into the **d.**, and go into 6160
Mt 14:13 by ship into a **d.** place apart: *2048*
Mt 14:15 This is a **d.** place, and the time is *2048*
Mt 24:26 **Behold, he is in the d.; go not** *2048*
Mk 1:45 was without in **d.** places: and they....... *2048*
Mk 6:31 **yourselves apart into a d. place,**.... *2048*
Mk 6:32 they departed into a **d.** place by.......... *2048*
Mk 6:35 This is a **d.** place, and now the........... *2048*
Lu 4:42 departed and went into a **d.** place:...... *2048*
Lu 9:10 into a **d.** place belonging to the.......... *2048*
Lu 9:12 for we are here in a **d.** place. *2048*
Joh 6:31 fathers did eat manna in the **d.**; *2048*
Ac 8:26 Jerusalem unto Gaza, which is **d.**......... *2048*

DESERTS
Isa 48:21 he led them through the **d.**: he.......... 2723
Jer 2:6 a land of **d.** and of pits,.................... 6160
Eze 7:27 and according to their **d.** will I........... 4941
Eze 13:4 are like the foxes in the **d.**................ 2723
Lu 1:80 and was in the **d.** till the day of *2048*
Heb 11:38 wandered in **d.**, and in mountains, ... *2047*

DESERVE See also DESERVETH; DESERVING.
Ezr 9:13 us less than our iniquities **d.**, and ....

DESERVETH
Job 11:6 of thee less than thine iniquity **d.**............

DESERVING
Jg 9:16 according to the **d.** of his hands; 1576

DESIRABLE
Eze 23:6 rulers, all of them **d.** young men, ... 2531
Eze 23:12 riding upon horses, all of them **d.**........ 2531
Eze 23:23 **d.** young men, captains and rulers, ... 2531

DESIRE See also DESIRABLE; DESIRED; DESIRES; DESIREST; DESIRETH; DESIRING.
Ge 3:16 thy **d.** shall be to thy husband. 8669
Ge 4:7 unto thee shall be his **d.**, and thou...... 8669
Ex 10:11 serve the Lord; for that ye did **d.** 1245
Ex 34:24 neither shall any man **d.** thy land........ 2530
De 5:21 shalt thou **d.** thy neighbour's wife....... 2530
De 7:25 shalt not **d.** the silver or gold........... 2530
De 18:6 come with all the **d.** of his mind.......... 183
De 21:11 and hast a **d.** unto her, that thou........ 2836
Jg 8:24 I would **d.** a request of you,.............. 7592
1Sa 9:20 on whom is all the **d.** of Israel?.......... 2532
1Sa 23:20 according to all the **d.** of thy soul........ 183
2Sa 23:5 all my salvation, and all my **d.**, ... 2656
1Ki 2:20 I **d.** one small petition of thee;........... 7592
1Ki 5:8 I will do all thy **d.** concerning 2656
1Ki 5:9 thou shalt accomplish my **d.**, in.......... 2656
1Ki 5:10 fir trees according to all his **d.**........... 2656
1Ki 9:1 all Solomon's **d.** which he was 2837
1Ki 9:11 according to all his **d.**,) that then........ 2656
1Ki 10:13 unto the queen of Sheba all her **d.**,..... 2656
2Ki 4:28 Did I **d.** a son of my lord? 7592
2Ch 9:12 to the queen of Sheba all her **d.**,........ 2656
2Ch 15:15 sought him with their whole **d.**; 7522
Ne 1:11 who **d.** to fear thy name: and............ 2655
Job 13:3 and I **d.** to reason with God............... 2654
Job 14:15 thou wilt have a **d.** to the work of...... 3700
Job 21:14 we **d.** not the knowledge of thy 2654
Job 31:16 withheld the poor from their **d.**.......... 2656
Job 31:35 my **d.** is, that the Almighty would 8420
Job 33:32 speak, for I **d.** to justify thee............. 2654
Job 34:36 My **d.** is that Job may be tried............. 15
Job 36:20 **D.** not the night, when people are....... 7602
Ps 10:3 wicked boasteth of his heart's **d.**, ... 8378
Ps 10:17 hast heard the **d.** of the humble: 8378
Ps 21:2 Thou hast given him his heart's **d.**,..... 8378
Ps 38:9 Lord, all my **d.** is before thee;........... 8378
Ps 40:6 and offering thou didst not **d.**; 2654
Ps 45:11 shall the king greatly **d.** thy beauty: 183
Ps 54:7 mine eye hath seen his **d.** upon mine ....
Ps 59:10 let me see my **d.** upon mine enemies. ....
Ps 70:2 put to confusion, that **d.** my hurt........ 2655
Ps 73:25 upon earth that I **d.** beside thee......... 2654
Ps 78:29 for he gave them their own **d.**; 8378
Ps 92:11 shall see my **d.** upon mine enemies,..........
Ps 92:11 ears shall hear my **d.** of the wicked ....
Ps 112:8 he see his **d.** upon his enemies. ....
Ps 112:10 the **d.** of the wicked shall perish. 8378
Ps 118:7 therefore shall I see my **d.** upon them.......
Ps 145:16 satisfiest the **d.** of every living........... 7522
Ps 145:19 He will fulfill the **d.** of them that 7522
Pr 3:15 all the things thou canst not **d.** are......... 2656
Pr 10:24 but the **d.** of the righteous shall......... 8378
Pr 11:23 The **d.** of the righteous is only good: .. 8378
Pr 13:12 when the **d.** cometh, it is a tree of....... 8378
Pr 13:19 The **d.** accomplished is sweet to 8378
Pr 18:1 Through **d.** a man, having separated ... 8378
Pr 19:22 The **d.** of a man is his kindness: 8378
Pr 21:25 The **d.** of the slothful killeth him; 8378
Pr 23:6 neither **d.** thou his dainty meats: 183
Pr 24:1 men, neither **d.** to be with them............ 183
Ec 6:9 than the wandering of the **d.**: 5315
Ec 12:5 be a burden, and **d.** shall fail: 35
Ca 7:10 beloved's, and his **d.** is toward me...... 8669
Isa 26:8 the **d.** of our soul is to thy name,........ 8378
Isa 53:2 no beauty that we should **d.** him. 2530
Jer 22:27 whereunto they **d.** to return....... 5375,5315
Jer 42:22 the place whither ye **d.** to go 2654
Jer 44:14 which they have a **d.** to return ... 5375,5315
Eze 24:16 away from thee the **d.** of thine 4261
Eze 24:21 strength, the **d.** of your eyes, ... 4261
Eze 24:25 of the glory, the **d.** of their eyes,........ 4261
Da 2:18 That they would **d.** mercies of the...... 1156
Da 11:37 nor the **d.** of women, nor regard........ 2532
Ho 10:10 It is in my **d.** that I should chastise...... 183
Am 5:18 Woe unto you that **d.** the day of.......... 183
Mic 7:3 he uttereth his mischievous **d.**: 5315
Hab 2:5 who enlargeth his **d.** as hell, and......... 5315
Hag 2:7 the **d.** of all nations shall come:.......... 2532
Mk 9:35 **If any man d. to be first,**............. *2309*
Mk 10:35 do for us whatsoever we shall **d.**.......... *154*
Mk 11:24 **What things soever ye d., when** *154*
Mk 15:8 began to **d.** him to do as he had.......... *154*
Lu 17:22 **ye shall d. to see one of the days** .. *1937*
Lu 20:46 **the scribes, which d. to walk in** *2309*
Lu 22:15 **With d. I have desired to eat this** .. *1939*
Ac 23:20 The Jews have agreed to **d.** thee *2065*
Ac 28:22 we **d.** to hear of thee what thou.......... *515*
Ro 10:1 Brethren, my heart's **d.** and prayer..... *2107*
Ro 15:23 having a great **d.** these many *1974*

1Co	14:1	and **d.** spiritual gifts, but rather	*2206*
2Co	7:7	he told us your earnest **d.**, your	*1972*
2Co	7:11	yea, what vehement **d.**, yea, what	*1972*
2Co	11:12	from them which **d.** occasion;	*2309*
2Co	12:6	For though I would **d.** to glory,	*2309*
Ga	4:9	ye **d.** again to be in bondage?	*2309*
Ga	4:20	I **d.** to be present with you now,	*2309*
Ga	4:21	Tell me, ye that **d.** to be under the	*2309*
Ga	6:12	As many as **d.** to make a fair shew	*2309*
Ga	6:13	but **d.** to have you circumcised,	*2309*
Eph	3:13	I **d.** that ye faint not at my	*154*
Php	1:23	having a **d.** to depart, and to be	*1939*
Php	4:17	Not because I **d.** a gift:	*1934*
Php	4:17	but I **d.** fruit that may abound	*1934*
Col	1:9	and to **d.** that ye might be filled	*154*
1Th	2:17	to see your face with great **d.**	*1939*
1Ti	3:1	If a man **d.** the office of a bishop,	*3713*
Heb	6:11	And we **d.** that every one of you	*1937*
Heb	11:16	But now they **d.** a better country,	*3713*
Jas	4:2	kill, and **d.** to have, and cannot	*2206*
1Pe	1:12	which things the angels **d.** to look	*1937*
1Pe	2:2	**d.** the sincere milk of the word,	*1971*
Re	9:6	and shall **d.** to die, and death shall	*1937*

DESIRED See also DESIREDST.

Ge	3:6	and a tree to be **d.** to make one	2530
1Sa	12:13	chosen, and whom ye have **d.**!	7592
1Ki	9:19	that which Solomon **d.** to build in	2836
2Ch	8:6	all that Solomon **d.** to build in	2836
2Ch	11:23	And he **d.** many wives.	7592
2Ch	21:20	and departed without being **d.**	2532
Es	2:13	whatsoever she **d.** was given her	559
Job	20:20	shall not save of that which he **d.**	2530
Ps	19:10	More to be **d.** are they than gold,	2530
Ps	27:4	One thing have I **d.** of the Lord,	7592
Ps	107:30	bringeth them unto their **d.** haven.	2656
Ps	132:13	he hath **d.** it for his habitation.	183
Ps	132:14	here will I dwell; for I have **d.** it	183
Pr	8:11	all the things that may be **d.** are	2656
Pr	21:20	There is treasure to be **d.** and oil	2530
Ec	2:10	whatsoever mine eyes **d.** I kept	7592
Isa	1:29	the oaks which ye have **d.**, and ye	2530
Isa	26:9	With my soul have I **d.** thee	183
Jer	17:16	neither have I **d.** the woeful day;	183
Da	2:16	Daniel went in, and **d.** of the king	1156
Da	2:23	known unto me now what we **d.**	1156
Ho	6:6	For I **d.** mercy, and not sacrifice	2654
Mic	7:1	my soul **d.** the first ripe fruit	183
Zep	2:1	gather together, O nation not **d.**;	3700
Mt	13:17	**righteous men have d. to see those**	*1939*
Mt	16:1	**d.** him that he would shew them	*1905*
Mk	15:6	one prisoner, whomsoever they **d.**	*154*
Lu	7:36	And one of the Pharisees **d.** him	*2065*
Lu	9:9	things? And he **d.** to see him	*2212*
Lu	10:24	**prophets and kings have d. to see**	*2309*
Lu	22:15	**With desire I have d. to eat this**	*1937*
Lu	22:31	**Satan hath d. to have you, that**	*1809*
Lu	23:25	into prison, whom they had **d.**;	*154*
Joh	12:21	**d.** him, saying, Sir, we would see	*2065*
Ac	3:14	the Just, and **d.** a murderer to	*154*
Ac	7:46	**d.** to find a tabernacle for the God	*154*
Ac	8:31	And he **d.** Philip that he would	*3870*
Ac	9:2	**d.** of him letters to Damascus to	*154*
Ac	12:20	their friend, **d.** peace; because	*154*
Ac	13:7	and **d.** to hear the word of God.	*1934*
Ac	13:21	afterward they **d.** a king: and	*154*
Ac	13:28	yet **d.** they Pilate that he should	*154*
Ac	16:39	them out, and **d.** them to depart	*2065*
Ac	18:20	When they **d.** him to tarry longer	*2065*
Ac	25:3	**d.** favour against him, that he	*154*
Ac	28:14	and were **d.** to tarry with them	*3870*
1Co	16:12	Apollos, I greatly **d.** him to come	*3870*
2Co	8:6	Insomuch that we **d.** Titus, that	*3870*
2Co	12:18	I **d.** Titus, and with him I sent	*3870*
1Jo	5:15	the petitions that we **d.** of him.	*154*

DESIREDST

De	18:16	According to all that thou **d.** of the	7592
Mt	18:32	**all that debt, because thou d. me:**	*3870*

DESIRES

Ps	37:4	give thee the **d.** of thine heart.	4862
Ps	140:8	Grant not, O Lord, the **d.** of the	3970
Eph	2:3	fulfilling the **d.** of the flesh and of	*2307*

DESIREST

Ps	51:6	thou **d.** truth in the inward parts:	2654
Ps	51:16	For thou **d.** not sacrifice; else	2654

DESIRETH

De	14:26	or for whatsoever thy soul **d.**	7592
1Sa	2:16	take as much as thy soul **d.**;	8378
1Sa	18:25	The king **d.** not any dowry,	2656
1Sa	20:4	Whatsoever thy soul **d.**,	559
2Sa	3:21	reign over all that thine heart **d.**	8378
1Ki	11:37	according to all that thy soul **d.**,	8378
Job	7:2	As a servant earnestly **d.** the	7602
Job	23:13	what his soul **d.** even that he	183
Ps	34:12	What man is he that **d.** life,	2655
Ps	68:16	the hill which God **d.** to dwell in;	2530
Pr	12:12	The wicked **d.** the net of evil men:	2530
Pr	13:4	The soul of the sluggard **d.**, and	183
Pr	21:10	The soul of the wicked **d.** evil:	183
Ec	6:2	for his soul of all that he **d.**,	183
Lu	5:39	**drunk old wine straightway d.**	*2309*
Lu	14:32	**and d. conditions of peace.**	*2065*
1Ti	3:1	of a bishop, he **d.** a good work.	*1937*

DESIRING

Mt	12:46	without, **d.** to speak with him.	*2212*
Mt	12:47	without, **d.** to speak with thee.	*2212*
Mt	20:20	and **d.** a certain thing of him.	*154*
Lu	8:20	stand without, **d.** to see thee.	*2309*
Lu	16:21	**d. to be fed with the crumbs**	*1937*
Ac	9:38	**d.** him that he would not delay	*3870*
Ac	19:31	**d.** him that he would not	*3870*
Ac	25:15	**d.** to have judgment against him.	*154*
2Co	5:2	earnestly **d.** to be clothed upon	*1971*
1Th	3:6	**d.** greatly to see us, as we also	*1971*
1Ti	1:7	**D.** to be teachers of the law;	*2309*
2Ti	1:4	Greatly **d.** to see thee, being	*1971*

DESIROUS

Pr	23:3	Be not **d.** of his dainties: for they	183
Lu	23:8	for he was **d.** to see him a long	*2309*
Joh	16:19	they were **d.** to ask him, and said	*2309*
2Co	11:32	garrison, **d.** to apprehend me:	*2309*
Ga	5:26	Let us not be **d.** of vain glory,	*2755*
1Th	2:8	So being affectionately **d.** of you,	*2442*

DESOLATE

Ge	47:19	not die, that the land be not **d.**	3456
Ex	23:29	lest the land become **d.** and the	8077
Le	26:22	and your high ways shall be **d.**	8074
Le	26:33	your land shall be **d.**, and your	8077
Le	26:34	as long as it lieth **d.**, and ye be in	8074
Le	26:35	As long as it lieth **d.**, it shall rest;	8074
Le	26:43	while she lieth **d.** without them:	8074
2Sa	13:20	Tamar remained **d.** in her brother	8076
2Ch	36:21	as long as she lay **d.**, she kept	8074
Job	3:14	built **d.** places for themselves;	2723
Job	15:28	he dwelleth in **d.** cities, and in	3582
Job	15:34	of hypocrites shall be **d.**, and fire	1565
Job	16:7	hast made **d.** all my company.	8074
Job	30:3	in former time **d.** and waste.	7722
Job	38:27	satisfy the **d.** and waste ground,	7722
Ps	25:16	upon me; for I am **d.** and afflicted.	3173
Ps	34:21	hate the righteous shall be **d.**	816
Ps	34:22	them that trust in him shall be **d.**	816
Ps	40:15	Let them be **d.** for a reward of	8074
Ps	69:25	Let their habitation be **d.**; and	8074
Ps	109:10	bread also out of their **d.** places.	2723
Ps	143:4	me; my heart within me is **d.**	8074
Isa	1:7	Your country is **d.**, your cities are	8077
Isa	1:7	in your presence, and it is **d.**,	8077
Isa	3:26	being **d.** shall sit upon the ground.	5352
Isa	5:9	many houses shall be **d.**, even	8047
Isa	6:11	and the land be utterly **d.**,	8077
Isa	7:19	all of them in the **d.** valleys,	1327
Isa	13:9	fierce anger, to lay the land **d.**	8047
Isa	13:22	shall cry in their **d.** house,	490
Isa	15:6	the waters of Nimrim shall be **d.**	4923
Isa	24:6	they that dwell therein are **d.**	816
Isa	27:10	the defenced city shall be **d.**,	910
Isa	49:8	cause to inherit the **d.** heritages;	8076
Isa	49:19	thy waste and thy **d.** places, and	8074
Isa	49:21	children, and am **d.**, a captive,	1565
Isa	54:1	the children of the **d.** than the	8074
Isa	54:3	make the **d.** cities to be inhabited	8077
Isa	59:10	we are in **d.** places as dead men	820
Isa	62:4	thy land any more be termed **D.**:	8077
Jer	2:12	be ye very **d.**, saith the Lord.	2717
Jer	4:7	his place to make thy land **d.**;	8047
Jer	4:27	The whole land shall be **d.**; yet	8077
Jer	6:8	lest I make thee **d.**, a land not	8077
Jer	7:34	bride: for the land shall be **d.**	2723
Jer	9:11	will make the cities of Judah **d.**,	8077
Jer	10:22	to make the cities of Judah **d.**,	8077
Jer	10:25	and have made his habitation **d.**	8074
Jer	12:10	pleasant portion a **d.** wilderness.	8077
Jer	12:11	They have made it **d.**, and	8074
Jer	12:11	being **d.** it mourneth unto me;	8077
Jer	12:11	the whole land is made **d.**, because	8074
Jer	18:16	To make their land **d.**, and a	8047
Jer	19:8	I will make this city **d.**, and an	8047
Jer	25:38	for their land is **d.** because of	8047
Jer	26:9	this city shall be **d.** without an	2717
Jer	32:43	It is **d.** without man or beast;	8077
Jer	33:10	which ye say shall be **d.** without	2717
Jer	33:10	streets of Jerusalem, that are **d.**,	8074
Jer	33:12	Again in this place, which is **d.**	2717
Jer	44:6	they are wasted and **d.**, as at	8077
Jer	46:19	for Noph shall be waste and **d.**	3341
Jer	48:9	for the cities thereof shall be **d.**,	8047
Jer	48:34	waters also of Nimrim shall be **d.**	4923
Jer	49:2	it shall be a **d.** heap, and her	8077
Jer	49:20	shall make their habitations **d.**	8074
Jer	50:3	shall make her land **d.**, and none	8047
Jer	50:13	but it shall be wholly **d.**	8077
Jer	50:45	he shall make their habitation **d.**	8074
Jer	51:26	but thou shalt be **d.** for ever,	8077
Jer	51:62	but that it shall be **d.** for ever.	8077
La	1:4	feasts: all her gates are **d.**: and	8076
La	1:13	made me **d.** and faint all the day.	8076
La	1:16	my children are **d.**, because the	8076
La	3:11	in pieces: he hath made me **d.**	8076
La	4:5	They that did feed delicately are **d.**	8074
La	5:18	the mountain of Zion, which is **d.**,	8074
Eze	6:4	And your altars shall be **d.**, and	8074
Eze	6:6	the high places shall be **d.**; that	3456
Eze	6:6	may be laid waste and made **d.**,	816
Eze	6:14	and make the land **d.**, yea,	8077
Eze	6:14	more **d.** than the wilderness	8047
Eze	12:19	that her land may be **d.** from all	3456
Eze	12:20	waste, and the land shall be **d.**;	8077
Eze	14:15	spoil it, so that it be **d.**,	8077
Eze	14:16	delivered, but the land shall be **d.**	8077
Eze	15:8	I will make the land **d.**, because	8077
Eze	19:7	he knew their **d.** places, and he	490
Eze	19:7	their cities; and the land was **d.**,	3456
Eze	20:26	that I might make them **d.**, to the	8074
Eze	25:3	land of Israel, when it was **d.**;	8074
Eze	25:13	I will make it **d.** from Teman;	2723
Eze	26:19	I shall make thee a **d.** city,	2717
Eze	26:20	of the earth, in places **d.** of old,	2723
Eze	29:9	the land of Egypt shall be **d.**	8077
Eze	29:10	of Egypt utterly waste and **d.**,	8077
Eze	29:12	I will make the land of Egypt **d.**	8077
Eze	29:12	midst of the countries that are **d.**,	8074
Eze	29:12	laid waste shall be **d.** forty years:	8077
Eze	30:7	they shall be **d.** in the midst of	8074
Eze	30:7	midst of the countries that are **d.**,	8074
Eze	30:14	And I will make Pathros **d.**, and	8074
Eze	32:15	I shall make the land of Egypt **d.**,	8077
Eze	33:28	For I will lay the land most **d.**,	8077
Eze	33:28	mountains of Israel shall be **d.**,	8074
Eze	33:29	when I have laid the land most **d.**	8077
Eze	35:3	I will make thee most **d.**	8077
Eze	35:4	cities waste, and thou shalt be **d.**,	8077
Eze	35:7	will I make mount Seir most **d.**,	8077
Eze	35:12	They are laid **d.**, they are given	8074
Eze	35:14	rejoiceth, I will make thee **d.**	8077
Eze	35:15	house of Israel, because it was **d.**,	8074
Eze	35:15	I do unto thee: thou shalt be **d.**,	8077
Eze	36:3	Because they have made you **d.**,	8074
Eze	36:4	to the valleys, to the **d.** wastes,	8076
Eze	36:34	And the **d.** land shall be tilled,	8074
Eze	36:34	whereas it lay **d.** in the sight	8077
Eze	36:35	This land that was **d.** is become	8074
Eze	36:35	waste and **d.** and ruined cities	8074
Eze	36:36	places, and plant that that was **d.**	8074
Eze	38:12	thine hand upon the **d.** places	2723
Da	9:17	upon thy sanctuary that is **d.**,	8074
Da	9:27	he shall make it **d.**, even until the	8074
Da	9:27	shall be poured upon the **d.**	8076
Da	11:31	the abomination that maketh **d.**	8074
Da	12:11	abomination that maketh **d.** set up,	8074
Ho	5:9	Ephraim shall be **d.** in the day	8047
Ho	13:16	Samaria shall become **d.**; for she	816
Joe	1:17	the garners are laid **d.**, the barns	8074
Joe	1:18	the flocks of sheep are made **d.**	816
Joe	2:3	behind them a **d.** wilderness;	8077

Joe 2:20 him into a land barren and **d.**, 8077
Joe 3:19 and Edom shall be a **d.** wilderness, 8077
Am 7:9 high places of Isaac shall be **d.**, 8074
Mic 1:7 the idols thereof will I lay **d.**: 8077
Mic 6:13 making thee **d.** because of thy sins. 8074
Mic 7:13 land shall be **d.** because of them 8077
Zep 3:6 their towers are **d.**; I made their 8074
Zec 7:14 the land was **d.** after them, that 8074
Zec 7:14 for they laid the pleasant land **d.**. 8047
Mal 1:4 return and build the **d.** places: 2723
Mt 23:38 **your house is left unto you d.**. *2048*
Lu 13:35 **your house is left unto you d.**: *2048*
Ac 1:20 Let his habitation be **d.**, and let *2048*
Ga 4:27 the **d.** hath many more children *2048*
1Ti 5:5 that is a widow indeed, and **d.**, *3443*
Re 17:16 shall make her **d.** and naked, *2049*
Re 18:19 for in one hour is she made **d.** *2049*

DESOLATION See also DESOLATIONS.
Le 26:31 bring your sanctuaries unto **d.**, 8074
Le 26:32 And I will bring the land into **d.**: 8074
Jos 8:28 for ever, even a **d.** unto this day. 8077
2Ki 22:19 should become a **d.** and a curse, 8047
2Ch 30:7 gave them up to **d.**, as ye see. 8047
Job 30:14 in the **d.** they rolled themselves 7722
Ps 73:19 How are they brought into **d.**, 8047
Pr 1:27 When your fear cometh as **d.**, 7584
Pr 3:25 neither of the **d.** of the wicked, 7722
Isa 10:3 and in the **d.** which shall come 7722
Isa 17:9 of Israel: and there shall be **d.** 8077
Isa 24:12 In the city is left **d.**, and the gate 8047
Isa 47:11 **d.** shall come upon thee suddenly, 7722
Isa 51:19 **d.**, and destruction, and the 7701
Isa 64:10 is a wilderness, Jerusalem a **d.**. 8077
Jer 22:5 that this house shall become a **d.**. 2723
Jer 25:11 this whole land shall be a **d.**, 2723
Jer 25:18 make them a **d.**, an astonishment, 2723
Jer 34:22 Judah a **d.** without an inhabitant. 8077
Jer 44:2 this day they are **d.**, and no man 2723
Jer 44:22 therefore is your land a **d.**, and an 2723
Jer 49:13 Bozrah shall become a **d.**, 8047
Jer 49:17 Edom shall be a **d.**: every one 8047
Jer 49:33 for dragons, and a **d.** for ever: 8077
Jer 50:23 Babylon become a **d.** among the 8047
Jer 51:29 Babylon a **d.** without an inhabitant. 8047
Jer 51:43 Her cities are a **d.**, a dry land, 8047
La 3:47 come upon us, **d.** and destruction. 7612
Eze 7:27 prince shall be clothed with **d.**, 8077
Eze 23:33 the cup of astonishment and **d.**, 8077
Da 8:13 transgression of **d.**, to give both 8074
Ho 12:1 he daily increaseth lies and **d.**; 7701
Joe 3:19 Egypt shall be a **d.**, and Edom 8077
Mic 6:16 that I should make thee a **d.**, 8047
Zep 1:13 a booty, and their houses a **d.**: 8047
Zep 1:15 a day of wasteness, and **d.**, a day 4875
Zep 2:4 be forsaken, and Ashkelon a **d.**: 8077
Zep 2:9 and salt pits, and a perpetual **d.**: 8077
Zep 2:13 will make Nineveh a **d.**, and dry 8077
Zep 2:14 **d.** shall be in the thresholds: 2721
Zep 2:15 how is she become a **d.**, a place 8047
Mt 12:25 **against itself is brought to d.**; *2049*
Mt 24:15 **the abomination of d., spoken of** *2050*
Mk 13:14 **ye shall see the abomination of d.**, *2050*
Lu 11:17 **against itself is brought to d.**; *2049*
Lu 21:20 **know that the d. thereof is nigh.** *2050*

DESOLATIONS
Ezr 9:9 to repair the **d.** thereof, and to 2723
Ps 46:8 what **d.** he hath made in the 8047
Ps 74:3 thy feet unto the perpetual **d.**; 4876
Isa 61:4 they shall raise up the former **d.**, 8074
Isa 61:4 cities, the **d.** of many generations. 8074
Jer 25:9 and an hissing, perpetual **d.** 2723
Jer 25:12 and will make it perpetual **d.**. 8077
Eze 35:9 I will make thee perpetual **d.**, and 8077
Da 9:2 years in the **d.** of Jerusalem. 2723
Da 9:18 thine eyes, and behold our **d.**, 8074
Da 9:26 end of the war **d.** are determined. 8074

DESPAIR See also DESPAIRED.
1Sa 27:1 and Saul shall **d.** of me, to seek 2976
Ec 2:20 my heart to **d.** of all the labour 2976
2Co 4:8 we are perplexed, but not in **d.**; *1820*

DESPAIRED
2Co 1:8 insomuch that we **d.** even of life: *1820*

DESPERATE
Job 6:26 and speeches of one that is **d.**, 2976
Isa 17:11 the day of grief and of **d.** sorrow. 605

DESPERATELY
Jer 17:9 above all things, and **d.** wicked: 605

DESPISE See also DESPISED; DESPISEST; DESPISETH; DESPISING.
Le 26:15 if ye shall **d.** my statues, or if 3988
1Sa 2:30 and they that **d.** me shall be lightly 959
2Sa 19:43 why then did ye **d.** us, that our 7043
Es 1:17 that they shall **d.** their husbands 959
Job 5:17 **d.** not thou the chastening of the 3988
Job 9:21 my soul: I would **d.** my life. 3988
Job 10:3 shouldst **d.** the work of thine hands, 3988
Job 31:13 did **d.** the cause of my manservant 3988
Ps 51:17 heart, O God, thou wilt not **d.**. 959
Ps 73:20 awakest, thou shalt **d.** their image. 959
Ps 102:17 destitute, and not **d.** their prayer. 959
Pr 1:7 fools **d.** wisdom and instruction. 936
Pr 3:11 **d.** not the chastening of the Lord; 3988
Pr 6:30 Men do not **d.** a thief, if he steal 936
Pr 23:9 he will **d.** the wisdom of thy words. 936
Pr 23:22 **d.** not thy mother when she is old. 936
Isa 30:12 Because ye **d.** this word, and trust 3988
Jer 4:30 thy lovers will **d.** thee, they 3988
Jer 23:17 They say still unto them that **d.** 5006
La 1:8 all that honoured her **d.** her, 2107
Eze 16:57 of the Philistines, which **d.** thee 7590
Eze 28:26 upon all those that **d.** them 7590
Am 5:21 I hate, I **d.** your feast days, and I 3988
Mal 1:6 you, O priests, that **d.** my name. 959
Mt 6:24 **hold to the one, and d. the other.** *2706*
Mt 18:10 **ye d. not one of these little ones;** *2706*
Lu 16:13 **hold to the one, and d. the other.** *2706*
Ro 14:3 Let not him that eateth **d.** him. *1848*
1Co 11:22 or **d.** ye the church of God, *2706*
1Co 16:11 Let no man therefore **d.** him: *1848*
1Th 5:20 **D.** not prophesyings. Prove all *1848*
1Ti 4:12 Let no man **d.** thy youth; but be *2706*
1Ti 6:2 masters, let them not **d.** them, *2706*
Tit 2:15 authority. Let no man **d.** thee. *4065*
Heb 12:5 **d.** not thou the chastening of *3643*
2Pe 2:10 uncleanness, and **d.** government. *2706*
Jude 8 **d.** dominion, and speak evil *114*

DESPISED
Ge 16:4 her mistress was **d.** in her eyes. 7043
Ge 16:5 conceived, I was **d.** in her eyes: 7043
Ge 25:34 way: thus Esau **d.** his birthright. 959
Le 26:43 because they **d.** my judgments, 3988
Nu 11:20 ye have **d.** the Lord which is 3988
Nu 14:31 know the land which ye have **d.**. 3988
Nu 15:31 he hath **d.** the word of the Lord, 959
Jg 9:38 this the people that thou hast **d.**? 3988
1Sa 10:27 And they **d.** him, and brought him 959
2Sa 6:16 and she **d.** him in her heart. 959
2Sa 12:9 **d.** the commandment of the Lord, 959
2Sa 12:10 because thou hast **d.** me, and hast 959
2Ki 19:21 the daughter of Zion hath **d.** thee, 959
1Ch 15:29 and she **d.** him in her heart. 959
2Ch 36:16 and **d.** his words, and misused his 959
Ne 2:19 and **d.** us, and said, What is this 959
Ne 4:4 Hear, O our God; for we are **d.**: 939
Job 12:5 a lamp **d.** in the thought of him 937
Job 19:18 young children **d.** me; I arose, 3988
Ps 22:6 of men, and **d.** of the people. 959
Ps 22:24 not **d.** nor abhorred the afflictions 959
Ps 53:5 because God hath **d.** them. 3988
Ps 106:24 Yea, they **d.** the pleasant land, 3988
Ps 119:141 I am small and **d.**: yet do not I 959
Pr 1:30 counsel: they **d.** all my reproof. 5006
Pr 5:12 and my heart **d.** reproof; 5006
Pr 12:8 is of a perverse heart shall be **d.**. 937
Pr 12:9 He that is **d.**, and hath a servant, 7034
Ec 9:16 the poor man's wisdom is **d.**, 959
Ca 8:1 kiss thee; yea, I should not be **d.**. 937
Isa 5:24 **d.** the word of the Holy One of 5006
Isa 33:8 he hath **d.** the cities, he regardeth 3988
Isa 37:22 **d.** thee, and laughed thee to scorn; 959
Isa 53:3 He is **d.** and rejected of men; a 959
Isa 53:3 he was **d.**, and we esteemed him not. 959
Isa 60:14 all they that **d.** thee shall bow 5006
Jer 22:28 Is this man Coniah a **d.** broken idol? 959
Jer 33:24 they have **d.** my people, that they 5006
Jer 49:15 the heathen, and **d.** among men. 959
La 2:6 **d.** in the indignation of his anger 5006
Eze 16:59 hast **d.** the oath in breaking the 959
Eze 17:16 oath he **d.**, and whose covenant 959
Eze 17:18 Seeing he **d.** the oath by breaking 959
Eze 17:19 surely mine oath that he hath **d.**, 959
Eze 20:13 they **d.** my judgments, which if 3988
Eze 20:16 they **d.** my judgments, and walked 3988
Eze 20:24 **d.** my statutes, and had polluted 3988
Eze 22:8 Thou hast **d.** mine holy things, 959
Eze 28:24 round about them, that **d.** them: 7590
Am 2:4 they have **d.** the law of the Lord, 3988
Ob 2 the heathen: thou art greatly **d.**. 959
Zec 4:10 hath **d.** the day of small things? 937
Mal 1:6 Wherein have we **d.** thy name? 959
Lu 18:9 were righteous, and **d.** other: *1848*
Ac 19:27 Diana should be **d.**, *1519, 3762, 3049*
1Co 1:28 things which are **d.** hath God *1848*
1Co 4:10 ye are honourable, but we are **d.** *820*
Ga 4:14 in my flesh ye **d.** not, nor rejected; *1848*
Heb 10:28 He that **d.** Moses' law died without *114*
Jas 2:6 But ye have **d.** the poor. Do not *818*

DESPISERS
Ac 13:41 Behold, ye **d.**, and wonder, and *2707*
2Ti 3:3 fierce, **d.** of those that are good, *865*

DESPISEST
Ro 2:4 **d.** thou the riches of his goodness *2706*

DESPISETH
Job 36:5 God is mighty, and **d.** not any: 3988
Ps 69:33 the poor, and **d.** not his prisoners. 959
Pr 11:12 void of wisdom **d.** his neighbour: 936
Pr 13:13 Whoso **d.** the word shall be 936
Pr 14:2 that is perverse in his ways **d.** him. 959
Pr 14:21 He that **d.** his neighbour sinneth: 936
Pr 15:5 A fool **d.** his father's instruction: 5006
Pr 15:20 but a foolish man **d.** his mother. 959
Pr 15:32 refuseth instruction **d.** his own 3988
Pr 19:16 but he that **d.** his ways shall die. 959
Pr 30:17 father, and **d.** to obey his mother, 936
Isa 33:15 he that **d.** the gain of oppressions, 3988
Isa 49:7 to him whom man **d.**, to him whom 960
Lu 10:16 **he that d. you d. me;** *114*
Lu 10:16 **and he that d. me d. him that sent** *114*
1Th 4:8 He therefore that **d.**, **d.** not man, *114*

DESPISING
Heb 12:2 the cross, **d.** the shame, and is *2706*

DESPITE See also DESPITEFUL; DESPITEFULLY.
Eze 25:6 rejoiced in heart with all thy **d.** 7589
Heb 10:29 and hath done **d.** unto the Spirit *1796*

DESPITEFUL
Eze 25:15 taken vengeance with a **d.** heart, 7589
Eze 36:5 with **d.** minds, to cast it out for 7589
Ro 1:30 Backbiters, haters of God, **d.**, *5197*

DESPITEFULLY
Mt 5:44 **pray for them which d. use you,** *1908*
Lu 6:28 **pray for them which d. use you.** *1908*
Ac 14:5 to use them **d.**, and to stone them, *5195*

DESTITUTE
Ge 24:27 not left **d.** my master of his mercy 5800
Ps 102:17 will regard the prayer of the **d.**, 6199
Ps 141:8 is my trust; leave not my soul **d.**. 6168
Pr 15:21 joy to him that is **d.** of wisdom: 2638
Eze 32:15 and the country shall be **d.** of that 8047
1Ti 6:5 corrupt minds and **d.** of the truth, *650*
Heb 11:37 being **d.**, afflicted, tormented; *5302*
Jas 2:15 be naked, and **d.** of daily food, *3007*

DESTROY See also DESTROYED; DESTROYEST; DESTROYETH; DESTROYING.
Ge 6:7 And the Lord said, I will **d.** man 4229
Ge 6:13 I will **d.** them with the earth. 7843
Ge 6:17 to **d.** all flesh, wherein is the breath 7843
Ge 7:4 that I have made will I **d.** from off 4229
Ge 9:11 more be a flood to **d.** the earth. 7843
Ge 9:15 more become a flood to **d.** all flesh. 7843
Ge 18:23 **d.** the righteous with the wicked? 5595
Ge 18:24 wilt thou also **d.** and not spare 5595
Ge 18:28 thou **d.** all the city for lack of five? 7843
Ge 18:28 there forty and five, I will not **d.** it. 7843
Ge 18:31 I will not **d.** it for twenty's sake. 7843
Ge 18:32 I will not **d.** it for ten's sake. 7843
Ge 19:13 we will **d.** this place, because the 7843
Ge 19:13 the Lord hath sent us to **d.** it. 7843
Ge 19:14 place; for the Lord will **d.** this city. 7843
Ex 8:9 to **d.** the frogs from thee and thy 3772

Ex 12:13 be upon you to **d.** you, when I 4889
Ex 15:9 my sword, my hand shall **d.** them....... 3423
Ex 23:27 **d.** all the people to whom thou 2000
Ex 34:13 But ye shall **d.** their altars, ... 5422
Le 23:30 same soul will I **d.** from among his.......... 6
Le 26:22 **d.** your cattle, and make you few 3772
Le 26:30 And I will **d.** your high places, ... 8045
Le 26:44 to **d.** them utterly, and to break.......... 3615
Nu 21:2 then I will utterly **d.** their cities. 2763
Nu 24:17 and **d.** all the children of Sheth. 6979
Nu 24:19 and shall **d.** him that remaineth............... 6
Nu 32:15 and ye shall **d.** all this people............ 7843
Nu 33:52 before you, and **d.** all their pictures,........ 6
Nu 33:52 and **d.** all their molten images, ... 6
De 1:27 hand of the Amorites, to **d.** us........... 8045
De 2:15 to **d.** them from among the host, ... 2000
De 4:31 **d.** thee, nor forget the covenant of..... 7843
De 6:15 and **d.** thee from off the face of 8045
De 7:2 smite them, and utterly **d.** them;........ 2763
De 7:4 against you, and **d.** thee suddenly....... 8045
De 7:5 ye shall **d.** their altars, and break 5422
De 7:10 hate him to their face, to **d.** them: 6
De 7:23 and shall **d.** them with a mighty 2000
De 7:24 thou shalt **d.** their name from.................. 6
De 9:3 a consuming fire he shall **d.** them, ... 8045
De 9:3 thou drive them out, and **d.** them 6
De 9:14 Let me alone, that I may **d.** them, ... 8045
De 9:19 was wroth against you to **d.** you. 8045
De 9:25 the Lord had said he would **d.** you. 8045
De 9:26 God, **d.** not thy people and thine........ 7843
De 10:10 and the Lord would not **d.** thee. 7843
De 12:2 Ye shall utterly **d.** all the places,............ 6
De 12:3 and **d.** the names of them out of............. 6
De 20:17 But thou shalt utterly **d.** them; 2763
De 20:19 shalt not **d.** the trees thereof by 7843
De 20:20 thou shalt **d.** and cut them down; 7843
De 28:63 Lord will rejoice over you to **d.** you, ... 6
De 31:3 **d.** these nations from before thee,...... 8045
De 32:25 shall **d.** both the young man and......... 7921
De 33:27 thee; and shall say, **D.** them. 8045
Jos 7:7 hand of the Amorites, to **d.** us?.............. 6
Jos 7:12 **d.** the accursed from among you. 8045
Jos 9:24 to **d.** all the inhabitants of the land...... 8045
Jos 11:20 that he might **d.** them utterly, ... 2763
Jos 11:20 favour, but that he might **d.** them,...... 8045
Jos 22:33 **d.** the land wherein the children......... 7843
Jg 6:5 they entered into the land to **d.** it. 7843
Jg 21:11 Ye shall utterly **d.** every male,........... 2763
1Sa 15:3 smite Amalek, and utterly **d.** all 2763
1Sa 15:6 the Amalekites, lest I **d.** you with........ 622
1Sa 15:9 and would not utterly **d.** them: 2763
1Sa 15:18 **d.** the sinners the Amalekites, ... 2763
1Sa 23:10 to **d.** the city for my sake.................. 7843
1Sa 24:21 that thou wilt not **d.** my name 8045
1Sa 26:9 **D.** him not: for who can stretch.......... 7843
1Sa 26:15 came one of the people in to **d.** the 7843
2Sa 1:14 hand to **d.** the Lord's anointed?.......... 7843
2Sa 14:7 and we will **d.** the heir also:............. 8045
2Sa 14:11 revengers of blood to **d.** any more,...... 7843
2Sa 14:11 lest they **d.** my son. And he said, ... 8045
2Sa 14:16 the man that would **d.** me and my...... 8045
2Sa 20:19 seekest to **d.** a city and a mother....... 4191
2Sa 20:20 that I should swallow up or **d.** 7843
2Sa 22:41 I might **d.** them that hate me. 6789
2Sa 24:16 his hand upon Jerusalem to **d.** it,........ 7843
1Ki 9:21 also were not able utterly to **d.**,........... 2763
1Ki 13:34 and to **d.** it from off the face of the 8045
1Ki 16:12 did Zimri **d.** all the house Baasha,....... 8045
2Ki 8:19 Yet the Lord would not **d.** Judah........ 7843
2Ki 10:19 he might **d.** the worshippers of Baal........ 6
2Ki 13:23 would not **d.** them, neither cast 7843
2Ki 18:25 Lord against this place to **d.** it?......... 7843
2Ki 18:25 Go up against this land, and **d.** it....... 7843
2Ki 24:2 sent them against Judah to **d.** it, ... 6
1Ch 21:15 an angel unto Jerusalem to **d.** it: 7843
2Ch 12:7 I will not **d.** them, but I will grant 7843
2Ch 12:12 he would not **d.** him altogether: 7843
2Ch 20:23 Seir, utterly to slay and **d.** them: 8045
2Ch 20:23 every one helped to **d.** another, ... 4889
2Ch 21:7 would not **d.** the house of David, ... 7843
2Ch 25:16 God hath determined to **d.** thee, ... 3289
2Ch 35:21 who is with me, that he **d.** thee not.... 7843
Ezr 6:12 **d.** all kings and people, that shall....... 4049
Ezr 6:12 to alter and to **d.** this house of God.... 2255
Es 3:6 Haman sought to **d.** all the Jews 8045
Es 3:13 to **d.**, to kill, and to cause to perish,... 8045
Es 4:7 treasuries for the Jews, to **d.** them. 6
Es 4:8 was given at Shushan to **d.** them,........ 8045
Es 8:5 which he wrote to **d.** the Jews which....... 6
Es 8:11 **d.**, to slay, and to cause to perish, ... 8045
Es 9:24 devised against the Jews to **d.** them, ... 6
Es 9:24 to consume them, and to **d.** them; 6
Job 2:3 him, to **d.** him without cause. 1104
Job 6:9 it would please God to **d.** me; 1792
Job 8:18 If he **d.** him from his place,............... 1104
Job 10:8 round about; yet thou dost **d.** me....... 1104
Job 19:26 my skin worms **d.** this body, ... 5362
Ps 5:6 shalt **d.** them that speak leasing:............. 6
Ps 5:10 **D.** thou them, O God; let them........... 816
Ps 18:40 I might **d.** them that hate me. 6789
Ps 21:10 fruit shalt thou **d.** from the earth, ... 6
Ps 28:5 **d.** them, and not build them up.......... 2040
Ps 40:14 that seek after my soul to **d.** it; 5595
Ps 52:5 God shall likewise **d.** thee for ever, ... 5422
Ps 55:9 **D.**, O Lord, and divide their............... 1104
Ps 63:9 those that seek my soul, to **d.** it, ... 7722
Ps 69:4 they that would **d.** me, being............. 6789
Ps 74:8 Let us **d.** them together: they 3238
Ps 101:8 early **d.** all the wicked of the land;...... 6789
Ps 106:23 he would **d.** them, had not Moses 8045
Ps 106:23 his wrath, lest he should **d.** them. 7843
Ps 106:34 They did not **d.** the nations,.............. 8045
Ps 118:10, 11, 12 of the Lord will I **d.** them. 4135
Ps 119:95 wicked have waited for me to **d.** me:....... 6
Ps 143:12 and **d.** all them that afflict my soul: 6
Ps 144:6 out thine arrows, and **d.** them. 1949
Ps 145:20 but all the wicked will he **d.**. 8045
Pr 1:32 the prosperity of fools shall **d.** them. 6
Pr 11:3 of transgressors shall **d.** them.............. 7703
Pr 15:25 will **d.** the house of the proud:............ 5255
Pr 21:7 of the wicked shall **d.** them; 1641
Ec 5:6 and **d.** the work of thine hands? 2254
Ec 7:16 why shouldest thou **d.** thyself?........... 8074
Isa 3:12 and **d.** the way of thy paths. 1104
Isa 10:7 **d.** and cut off nations not a few. 8045
Isa 11:9 shall not hurt nor **d.** in all my 7843
Isa 11:15 Lord shall utterly **d.** the tongue of...... 2763
Isa 13:5 indignation, to **d.** the whole land......... 2254
Isa 13:9 **d.** the sinners thereof out of it........... 8045
Isa 19:3 and I will **d.** the counsel thereof:........ 1104
Isa 23:11 city, to **d.** the strong holds thereof. 8045
Isa 25:7 And he will **d.** in this mountain 1104
Isa 32:7 wicked devices to **d.** the poor with..... 2254
Isa 36:10 Lord against this land to **d.** it? 7843
Isa 36:10 Go up against this land, and **d.** it........ 7843
Isa 42:14 I will **d.** and devour at once. 5395
Isa 51:13 as if he were ready to **d.**? 7843
Isa 54:16 I have created the waster to **d.**. 2254
Isa 65:8 **D.** it not; for a blessing is in it: 7843
Isa 65:8 sakes, that I may not **d.** them all. 7843
Isa 65:25 They shall not hurt nor **d.** in all my 7843
Jer 1:10 to pull down, and to **d.**, and to.............. 6
Jer 5:10 Go ye up upon her walls, and **d.**; 7843
Jer 6:5 by night, and let us **d.** her palaces...... 7843
Jer 11:19 Let us **d.** the tree with the fruit.......... 7843
Jer 12:17 pluck up and **d.** that nation, ... 6
Jer 13:14 nor have mercy, but **d.** them............. 7843
Jer 15:3 of the earth, to devour and **d.**. 7843
Jer 15:6 my hand against thee, and **d.** thee;..... 7843
Jer 15:7 I will **d.** my people, since they return...... 6
Jer 17:18 **d.** them with double destruction. 7665
Jer 18:7 to pull down, and to **d.** it; 6
Jer 23:1 Woe be unto the pastors that **d.** and 6
Jer 25:9 utterly **d.** them, and make them......... 2763
Jer 31:28 break down, and to **d.**, and to afflict: 6
Jer 36:29 certainly come and **d.** this land,.......... 7843
Jer 46:8 I will **d.** the city and the inhabitants......... 6
Jer 48:18 and he shall **d.** thy strong holds. 7843
Jer 49:9 they will **d.** till they have enough........ 7843
Jer 49:38 and will **d.** from thence the king 6
Jer 50:21 waste and utterly **d.** after them,......... 2763
Jer 50:26 her up as heaps, and **d.** her utterly:.... 2763
Jer 51:3 men, **d.** ye utterly all her host........... 2763
Jer 51:11 device is against Babylon, to **d.** it;...... 7843
Jer 51:20 and with thee will I **d.** kingdoms; 7843
La 2:8 Lord hath purposed to **d.** the wall 7843
La 3:66 Persecute and **d.** them in anger 8045
Eze 5:16 and which I will send to **d.** you: 7843
Eze 6:3 and I will **d.** your high places. 6
Eze 9:8 wilt thou **d.** all the residue of Israel 7843
Eze 14:9 and will **d.** him from the midst 8045
Eze 21:31 of brutish men, and skilful to **d.**. 4889
Eze 22:27 to shed blood, and to **d.** souls, ... 6
Eze 22:30 the land, that I should not **d.** it; 7843
Eze 25:7 I will **d.** thee; and thou shalt know 8045
Eze 25:15 heart, to **d.** it for the old hatred;........ 4889
Eze 25:16 and **d.** the remnant of the sea coast. 9
Eze 26:4 they shall **d.** the walls of Tyrus,......... 7843
Eze 26:12 walls, and **d.** thy pleasant houses: 5422
Eze 28:16 I will **d.** thee; O covering cherub, ... 6
Eze 30:11 shall be brought to **d.** the land: 7843
Eze 30:13 I will also **d.** the idols, and I will............ 6
Eze 32:13 I will **d.** also all the beasts thereof 6
Eze 34:16 I will **d.** the fat and the strong; 8045
Eze 43:3 saw when I came to **d.** the city: 7843
Da 2:12 to **d.** all the wise men of Babylon........... 7
Da 2:24 to **d.** the wise men of Babylon. 7
Da 2:24 **D.** not the wise men of Babylon: 7
Da 4:23 Hew the tree down, and **d.** it; 2255
Da 7:26 consume and to **d.** it unto the end. 7
Da 8:24 **d.** wonderfully, and shall prosper, ... 7843
Da 8:24 **d.** the mighty and the holy people. 7843
Da 8:25 heart, and by peace shall **d.** many: 7843
Da 9:26 shall **d.** the city and the sanctuary; 7843
Da 11:26 portion of his meat shall **d.** him,......... 7665
Da 11:44 shall go forth with great fury to **d.**,..... 8045
Ho 2:12 will **d.** her vines and her fig trees,...... 8074
Ho 4:5 the night, and I will **d.** thy mother...... 1820
Ho 11:9 I will not return to **d.** Ephraim:.......... 7843
Am 9:8 and I will **d.** it from off the face of...... 8045
Am 9:8 I will not utterly **d.** the house of 8045
Ob 8 even **d.** the wise men out of Edom, ... 6
Mic 2:10 it is polluted, it shall **d.** you,............. 2254
Mic 5:10 of thee, and I will **d.** thy chariots: 6
Mic 5:14 of thee: so will I **d.** thy cities. 8045
Zep 2:5 the Philistines, I will even **d.** thee, ... 6
Zep 2:13 against the north, and **d.** Assyria; 6
Hag 2:22 **d.** the strength of the kingdoms 8045
Zec 12:9 seek to **d.** all the nations that come 8045
Mal 3:11 he shall not **d.** the fruits of your 7843
Mt 2:13 seek the young child to **d.** him. *622*
Mt 5:17 **not that I am come to d. the law,** ..*2647*
Mt 5:17 **I am not come to d., but to fulfil**.. *2647*
Mt 10:28 **able to d. both soul and body in** *622*
Mt 12:14 against him, how they might **d.** him...... *622*
Mt 21:41 He will miserably **d.** those wicked........ *622*
Mt 26:61 said, I am able to **d.** the temple......... *2647*
Mt 27:20 should ask Barabbas, and **d.** Jesus......... *622*
Mk 1:24 art thou come to **d.** us? I know thee *622*
Mk 3:6 against him, how they might **d.** him...... *622*
Mk 9:22 and into the waters, to **d.** him:............ *622*
Mk 11:18 sought how they might **d.** him:........... *622*
Mk 12:9 **will come and d. the husbandmen,** .. *622*
Mk 14:58 I will **d.** this temple that is made......... *2647*
Lu 4:34 Nazareth? art thou come to **d.** us? *622*
Lu 6:9 **to do evil? to save life, or to d. it?** .. *622*
Lu 9:56 **is not come to d. men's lives, but**.... *622*
Lu 19:47 chief of the people sought to **d.** him, ... *622*
Lu 20:16 **come and d. these husbandmen** *622*
Joh 2:19 **D. this temple, and in three days** .. *3089*
Joh 10:10 **for to steal, and to kill, and to d.:** .. *622*
Ac 6:14 Jesus of Nazareth shall **d.** this *2647*
Ro 14:15 **D.** not him with thy meat, for whom *622*
Ro 14:20 For meat **d.** not the work of God....... *2647*
1Co 1:19 I will **d.** the wisdom of the wise, ... *622*
1Co 3:17 temple of God, him shall God **d.**; *5351*
1Co 6:13 God shall **d.** both it and them. *2673*
2Th 2:8 and shall **d.** with the brightness.......... *2673*
Heb 2:14 through death he might **d.** him.......... *2673*
Jas 4:12 who is able to save and to **d.**: *622*
1Jo 3:8 that he might **d.** the works of the....... *3089*
Re 11:18 **d.** them which **d.** the earth. *1311*

DESTROYED

Ge 7:23 And every living substance was **d.**...... 4229
Ge 7:23 and they were **d.** from the earth: 4229
Ge 13:10 before the Lord **d.** Sodom and........... 7843
Ge 19:29 when God **d.** the cities of the plain, ... 7843
Ge 34:30 and I shall be **d.**, I and my house....... 8045
Ex 10:7 knowest thou not yet that Egypt is **d.**? 6
Ex 22:20 Lord only, he shall be utterly **d.**......... 2763
Nu 21:3 and they utterly **d.** them and their...... 2763
De 1:44 and **d.** you in Seir, even unto 3807
De 2:12 them, when they had **d.** them from..... 8045
De 2:21 but the Lord **d.** them before them:..... 8045
De 2:22 in Seir, when he **d.** the Horims.......... 8045
De 2:23 out of Caphtor, **d.** them, and dwelt..... 8045
De 2:34 and utterly **d.** the men, and the ....

De 3:6 And we utterly **d.** them, as we did 2763
De 4:3 thy God hath **d.** them from among 8045
De 4:26 days upon it, but shall utterly be **d.** 8045
De 7:20 hide themselves from thee, be **d.** 6
De 7:23 destruction, until they be **d.** 8045
De 7:24 before thee, until they have **d.** them. 8045
De 9:8 was angry with you to have **d.** you. 8045
De 9:20 angry with Aaron to have **d.** him: 8045
De 11:4 how the Lord hath **d.** them unto this 6
De 12:30 after that they be **d.** from before 8045
De 28:20 until thou be **d.**, and until thou 8045
De 28:24 down upon thee, until thou be **d.** 8045
De 28:45 and overtake thee, till thou be **d.**; 8045
De 28:48 thy neck, until he have **d.** thee. 8045
De 28:51 fruit of thy land, until thou be **d.**. 8045
De 28:51 thy sheep, until he have **d.** thee. 6
De 28:61 bring upon thee, until thou be **d.**. 8045
De 31:4 the land of them, whom he **d.**. 8045
Jos 2:10 Sihon and Og, whom ye utterly **d.** 2763
Jos 6:21 And they utterly **d.** all that was in 2763
Jos 8:26 until he had utterly **d.** all the 2763
Jos 10:1 taken Ai, and utterly **d.** it. 2763
Jos 10:28 and the king thereof he utterly **d.**, 2763
Jos 10:35 were therein he utterly **d.** that day, 2763
Jos 10:37 but **d.** it utterly, and all the souls 2763
Jos 10:39 and utterly **d.** all the souls that 2763
Jos 10:40 but utterly **d.** all that breathed, 2763
Jos 11:12 he utterly **d.** them, as Moses the 2763
Jos 11:14 until they had **d.** them, neither left 8045
Jos 11:21 Joshua **d.** them utterly with their 2763
Jos 23:15 until he have **d.** you from off this 8045
Jos 24:8 and **d.** them from before you. 8045
Jg 1:17 Zephath, and utterly **d.** it. 2763
Jg 4:24 until they had **d.** Jabin king of 3772
Jg 6:4 and **d.** the increase of the earth, 7843
Jg 20:21 Gibeah, and **d.** down to the ground 7843
Jg 20:25 second day, and **d.** down to the 7843
Jg 20:35 and the children of Israel **d.** of the 7843
Jg 20:42 the cities they **d.** in the midst of 7843
Jg 21:16 remain, seeing the women are **d.** 8045
Jg 21:17 Benjamin, that a tribe be not **d.** 4229
1Sa 5:6 Ashdod, and he **d.** them, and smote 8074
1Sa 15:8 and utterly **d.** all the people with 2763
1Sa 15:9 and refuse, that they **d.** utterly. 2763
1Sa 15:15 and the rest we have utterly **d.** 2763
1Sa 15:20 and have utterly **d.** the Amalekites. 2763
1Sa 15:21 which should have been utterly **d.**, 2764
2Sa 11:1 they **d.** the children of Ammon, 7843
2Sa 21:5 we should be **d.** from remaining 8045
2Sa 22:38 pursued mine enemies, and **d.** them; 8045
2Sa 24:16 the angel that **d.** the people, 7843
1Ki 15:13 and Asa **d.** her idol, and burnt it 3772
1Ki 15:29 that breathed, until he had **d.** him, 8045
2Ki 10:17 in Samaria, till he had **d.** him, 8045
2Ki 10:28 Thus Jehu **d.** Baal out of Israel. 8045
2Ki 11:1 she arose and **d.** all the seed royal. 6
2Ki 13:7 the king of Syria had **d.** them, 6
2Ki 19:12 them which my fathers have **d.**; 843
2Ki 19:17 of Assyria have **d.** the nations 2717
2Ki 19:18 stone, therefore they have **d.** them. 6
2Ki 21:3 which Hezekiah his father had **d.**; 6
2Ki 21:9 nations whom the Lord **d.** before 8045
1Ch 4:41 and **d.** them utterly unto this day, 2763
1Ch 5:25 land, whom God **d.** before them. 8045
1Ch 20:1 Joab smote Rabbah, and **d.** it, 2040
1Ch 21:12 three months to be **d.** before thy 5595
1Ch 21:15 and said to the angel that **d.**, 7843
2Ch 14:13 for they were **d.** before the Lord, 7665
2Ch 15:6 And nation was **d.** of nation, 3807
2Ch 20:10 turned from them, and **d.** them not; 8045
2Ch 22:10 she arose and **d.** all the seed royal 1696
2Ch 24:23 and **d.** all the princes of the people 7843
2Ch 31:1 until they had utterly **d.** them all. 3615
2Ch 32:14 nations that my fathers utterly **d.**, 2763
2Ch 33:9 whom the Lord had **d.** before the 8045
2Ch 34:11 which the kings of Judah had **d.**. 7843
2Ch 36:19 **d.** all the goodly vessels thereof. 7843
Ezr 4:15 for which cause was this city **d.**. 2718
Ezr 5:12 who **d.** this house, and carried the 5642
Es 3:9 it be written that they may be **d.**: 6
Es 4:14 and thy father's house shall be **d.**: 6
Es 7:4 to be **d.**, to be slain, and to perish. 8045
Es 9:6 Jews slew and **d.** five hundred men. 6
Es 9:12 Jews have slain and **d.** five hundred 6
Job 4:20 They are **d.** from morning to 3807
Job 19:10 He hath **d.** me on every side, 5422
Job 34:25 in the night, so that they are **d.** 1792
Ps 9:5 thou hast **d.** the wicked, thou hast 6
Ps 9:6 hast **d.** cities; their memorial 5428
Ps 11:3 If the foundations be **d.**, what can 2040
Ps 37:38 transgressors shall be **d.** together: 8045
Ps 73:27 thou hast **d.** all them that go a 6789
Ps 78:38 their iniquity, and **d.** them not: 7843
Ps 78:45 them; and frogs, which **d.** them. 7843
Ps 78:47 he **d.** their vines with hail, and 2026
Ps 92:7 it is that they shall be **d.** for ever: 8045
Ps 137:8 of Babylon, who art to be **d.**; 7703
Pr 13:13 despiseth the word shall be **d.**: 2254
Pr 13:20 a companion of fools shall be **d.** 7321
Pr 13:23 there is that is **d.** for want of 5595
Pr 29:1 shall suddenly be **d.**, and that 7665
Isa 9:16 they that are led of them are **d.** 1104
Isa 10:27 and the yoke shall be **d.** because 2254
Isa 14:17 and **d.** the cities thereof; 2040
Isa 14:20 because thou hast **d.** thy land, 7843
Isa 26:14 therefore hast thou visited and **d.** 8045
Isa 34:2 he hath utterly **d.** them, he hath 2763
Isa 37:12 them which my fathers have **d.**, 7843
Isa 37:19 stone: therefore they have **d.** them. 6
Isa 48:19 not have been cut off nor **d.** from 8045
Jer 12:10 Many pastors have **d.** my vineyard, 7843
Jer 22:20 passages: for all thy lovers are **d.** 7665
Jer 48:4 Moab is **d.**; her little ones have 7665
Jer 48:8 and the plain shall be **d.**, as the 8045
Jer 48:42 And Moab shall be **d.** from being a 8045
Jer 51:8 Babylon is suddenly fallen and **d.**: 7665
Jer 51:55 Babylon, and **d.** out of her the great 6
La 2:5 he hath **d.** his strong holds, and 7843
La 2:6 hath **d.** his places of the assembly: 7843
La 2:9 he hath **d.** and broken her bars: 6
Eze 26:17 How art thou **d.**, that wast inhabited 6
Eze 27:32 the **d.** in the midst of the sea? 1822
Eze 30:8 when all her helpers shall be **d.** 7665
Eze 32:12 the multitude thereof shall be **d.** 8045
Da 2:44 kingdom, which shall never be **d.**: 2255
Da 6:26 kingdom that which shall not be **d.**, 2255
Da 7:11 the beast was slain, and his body **d.**, 7
Da 7:14 kingdom that which shall not be **d.** 2255
Da 11:20 but within few days he shall be **d.**, 7665
Ho 4:6 My people are **d.** for lack of 1820
Ho 10:8 Aven, the sin of Israel, shall be **d.**: 8045
Ho 13:9 O Israel, thou hast **d.** thyself, but 7843
Am 2:9 Yet **d.** I the Amorite before them, 8045
Am 2:9 yet I **d.** his fruit from above, 8045
Zep 3:6 passeth by: their cities are **d.**, 6658
Mt 22:7 **and d. those murderers, and burned** *622*
Lu 17:27 **the flood came, and d. them all.** *622*
Lu 17:29 **from heaven, and d. them all** *622*
Ac 3:23 shall be **d.** from among the people. *1842*
Ac 9:21 Is not this he that **d.** them which *4199*
Ac 13:19 And when he had **d.** seven nations *2507*
Ac 19:27 her magnificence should be **d.**, *2507*
Ro 6:6 that the body of sin might be **d.**, *2673*
1Co 10:9 tempted and were **d.** of serpents. *622*
1Co 10:10 and were **d.** of the destroyer. *622*
1Co 15:26 The last enemy that shall be **d.** *2673*
2Co 4:9 forsaken; cast down, but not **d.**; *622*
Ga 1:23 the faith which once he **d.** *4199*
Ga 2:18 build again the things which I **d.**, *2647*
Heb 11:28 lest he that **d.** the first born *3645*
2Pe 2:12 beasts, made to be taken and **d.**, *5356*
Jude 5 afterward **d.** them that believed not. *622*
Re 8:9 the third part of the ships were **d.** *1311*

DESTROYER See also DESTROYERS.
Ex 12:23 will not suffer the **d.** to come in 7843
Jg 16:24 the **d.** of our country, which slew 2717
Job 15:21 the **d.** shall come upon him. 7703
Ps 17:4 kept me from the paths of the **d.** 6530
Pr 28:24 the same is the companion of a **d.** 7843
Jer 4:7 and the **d.** of the Gentiles is on his 7843
1Co 10:10 and were destroyed of the **d.** *3644*

DESTROYERS
Job 33:22 the grave, and his life to the **d.** 4191
Isa 49:17 thy **d.** and they that made thee 2040
Jer 22:7 And I will prepare **d.** against thee, 7843
Jer 50:11 O ye **d.** of mine heritage, because 8154

DESTROYEST
Job 14:19 earth; and thou **d.** the hope of man. 6
Jer 51:25 the Lord, which **d.** all the earth: 7843
Mt 27:40 Thou that **d.** the temple, and *2647*
Mk 15:29 Ah, thou that **d.** the temple, and *2647*

DESTROYETH
De 8:20 As the nations which the Lord **d.** 6
Job 9:22 He **d.** the perfect and the wicked. 3615
Job 12:23 increaseth the nations, and **d.** them: 6
Pr 6:32 he that doeth it **d.** his own soul. 7843
Pr 11:9 with his mouth **d.** his neighbour: 7843
Pr 31:3 thy ways to that which **d.** kings. 4229
Ec 7:7 man mad; and a gift **d.** the heart. 6
Ec 9:18 war: but one sinner **d.** much good. 6

DESTROYING
De 3:6 of Heshbon, utterly **d.** the men, 2763
De 13:15 **d.** it utterly, and all that is therein, 2763
Jos 11:11 edge of the sword, utterly **d.** them: 2763
2Ki 19:11 to all lands, by **d.** them utterly: 2763
1Ch 21:12 angel of the Lord **d.** throughout 7843
1Ch 21:15 and as he was **d.**, the Lord beheld 7843
Isa 28:2 a tempest of hail and a **d.** storm, 6986
Isa 37:11 by **d.** them utterly; and shalt thou 2763
Jer 2:30 your prophets, like a **d.** lion 7843
Jer 51:1 that rise up against me, a **d.** wind; 7843
Jer 51:25 I am against thee, O **d.** mountain, 4889
La 2:8 not withdrawn his hand from **d.**: 1104
Eze 9:1 every man with his **d.** weapon in 4892
Eze 20:17 eye spared them from **d.** them, 7843

DESTRUCTION See also DESTRUCTIONS.
De 7:23 destroy them with a mighty **d.**, 4103
De 32:34 burning heat, and with bitter **d.**: 6986
1Sa 5:9 the city with a very great **d.**: 4103
1Sa 5:11 there was a deadly **d.** throughout 4103
1Ki 20:42 whom I appointed to utter **d.**, 2764
2Ch 22:4 the death of his father to his **d.** 4889
2Ch 22:7 the **d.** of Ahaziah was of God by 8395
2Ch 26:16 his heart was lifted up to his **d.**: 7843
Es 8:6 how can I endure to see the **d.** of my 13
Es 9:5 slaughter, and **d.**, and did what 12
Job 5:21 neither shalt thou be afraid of **d.** 7701
Job 5:22 At **d.** and famine thou shalt laugh: 7701
Job 18:12 and **d.** shall be ready at his side. 343
Job 21:17 oft cometh their **d.** upon them! 343
Job 21:20 His eyes shall see his **d.**, and he 3589
Job 21:30 is reserved to the day of **d.**? 343
Job 26:6 him, and **d.** hath no covering. 11
Job 28:22 **D.** and death say, We have heard 11
Job 30:12 against me the ways of their **d.** 343
Job 30:24 grave, though they cry in his **d.** 6365
Job 31:3 Is not **d.** to the wicked? 343
Job 31:12 it is a fire that consumeth to **d.**, 11
Job 31:23 **d.** from God was a terror to me, 343
Job 31:29 If I rejoiced at the **d.** of him that 6365
Ps 35:8 **d.** come upon him at unawares; 7722
Ps 35:8 into that very **d.** let him fall. 7722
Ps 55:23 bring them down into the pit of **d.**: 7845
Ps 73:18 thou castedst them down into **d.** 4876
Ps 88:11 grave? or thy faithfulness in **d.**? 11
Ps 90:3 turnest man to **d.**; and sayest, 1793
Ps 91:6 the **d.** that wasteth at noonday. 6986
Ps 103:4 Who redeemeth thy life from **d.**: 7845
Pr 1:27 your **d.** cometh as a whirlwind; 343
Pr 10:14 the mouth of the foolish is near **d.** 4288
Pr 10:15 the **d.** of the poor is their poverty. 4288
Pr 10:29 but **d.** shall be to the workers of 4288
Pr 13:3 openeth wide his lips shall have **d.** 4288
Pr 14:28 want of people is the **d.** of the prince. 4288
Pr 15:11 Hell and **d.** are before the Lord: 11
Pr 16:18 Pride goeth before **d.**, and an 7667
Pr 17:19 that exalteth his gate seeketh **d.** 7667
Pr 18:7 A fool's mouth is his **d.**, and his 4288
Pr 18:12 Before **d.** the heart of man is 7667
Pr 21:15 but **d.** shall be to the workers of 4288
Pr 24:2 their heart studieth **d.**, and their 7701
Pr 27:20 Hell and **d.** are never full; 10
Pr 31:8 all such as are appointed to **d.** 2475
Isa 1:28 And the **d.** of the transgressors 7667
Isa 10:25 cease, and mine anger in their **d.** 8399
Isa 13:6 come as a **d.** from the Almighty. 7701
Isa 14:23 will sweep it with the besom of **d.**, 8045
Isa 15:5 they shall raise up a cry of **d.** 7667
Isa 19:18 one shall be called, The city of **d.** 2041
Isa 24:12 and the gate is smitten with **d.** 7591
Isa 49:19 the land of thy **d.**, shall even now 2035
Isa 51:19 desolation, and **d.**, and the famine, 7667

Isa 59:7 wasting and **d.** are in their paths. 7667
Isa 60:18 wasting nor **d.** within thy borders; 7667
Jer 4:6 evil from the north and a great **d.** 7667
Jer 4:20 **D.** upon **d.** is cried; for the whole 7667
Jer 6:1 out of the north, and great **d.** 7667
Jer 17:18 and destroy them with double **d.** 7670
Jer 46:20 but **d.** cometh; it cometh out of 7171
Jer 48:3 Horonaim, spoiling and great **d.** 7667
Jer 48:5 the enemies have heard a cry of **d.** 7667
Jer 50:22 battle is in the land and of great **d.** 7667
Jer 51:54 and great **d.** from the land of the 7667
La 2:11 **d.** of the daughter of my people; 7667
La 3:47 come upon us, desolation and **d.** 7667
La 3:48 **d.** of the daughter of my people. 7667
La 4:10 **d.** of the daughter of my people. 7667
Eze 5:16 which shall be for their **d.**, 4889
Eze 7:25 **D.** cometh; and they shall seek 7089
Eze 32:9 bring thy **d.** among the nations, 7667
Ho 7:13 **d.** unto them! because they have 7701
Ho 9:6 lo, they are gone because of **d.**: 7701
Ho 13:14 O grave, I will be thy **d.**: 6987
Joe 1:15 and as a **d.** from the Almighty 7701
Ob 12 of Judah in the day of their **d.**; 6
Mic 2:10 destroy you, even with a sore **d.** 2256
Zec 14:11 there shall be no more utter **d.**; 2764
Mt 7:13 broad is the way that leadeth to **d.**, *684*
Ro 3:16 **D.** and misery are in their ways: *4938*
Ro 9:22 vessels of wrath fitted to **d.** *684*
1Co 5:5 unto Satan for the **d.** of the flesh, *3639*
2Co 10:8 edification, and not for your **d.**, *2506*
2Co 13:10 me to edification, and not to **d.** *2506*
Php 3:19 Whose end is **d.**, whose God is *684*
1Th 5:3 sudden **d.** cometh upon them, *3639*
2Th 1:9 be punished with everlasting **d.** *3639*
1Ti 6:9 drown men in **d.** and perdition. *3639*
2Pe 2:1 bring upon themselves swift **d.** *684*
2Pe 3:16 other scriptures, unto their own **d.** *684*

DESTRUCTIONS
Ps 9:6 **d.** are come to a perpetual end: 2723
Ps 35:17 rescue my soul from their **d.**, 7722
Ps 107:20 and delivered them from their **d.** 7825

DETAIN See also DETAINED.
Jg 13:15 I pray thee, let us **d.** thee. 6113
Jg 13:16 Though thou **d.** me, I will not eat. 6113

DETAINED
1Sa 21:7 there that day, **d.** before the Lord; 6113

DETERMINATE
Ac 2:23 delivered by the **d.** counsel and *3724*

DETERMINATION
Zep 3:8 for my **d.** is to gather the nations, 4941

DETERMINE See DETERMINED.
Ex 21:22 and he shall pay as the judges **d.**

DETERMINED
1Sa 20:7 be sure that evil is **d.** by him. 3615
1Sa 20:9 evil were **d.** by my father to come 3615
1Sa 20:33 Jonathan knew that it was **d.** of his 3615
1Sa 25:17 evil is **d.** against our master. 3615
2Sa 13:32 this hath been **d.** from the day 7760
2Ch 2:1 Solomon **d.** to build an house for 559
2Ch 25:16 know that God hath **d.** to destroy 3289
Es 7:7 there was evil **d.** against him by 3615
Job 14:5 Seeing his days are **d.**, the number 2782
Isa 10:23 consumption, even **d.**, in the midst 2782
Isa 19:17 hosts, which he hath **d.** against it. 3289
Isa 28:22 a consumption, even **d.** upon 2782
Da 9:24 Seventy weeks are **d.** upon thy 2852
Da 9:26 end of the war desolations are **d.** 2782
Da 9:27 that **d.** shall be poured upon the 2782
Da 11:36 for that that is **d.** shall be done. 2782
Lu 22:22 Son of man goeth, as it was **d.** *3724*
Ac 3:13 Pilate, when he was **d.** to let him *2919*
Ac 4:28 counsel **d.** before to be done. *4309*
Ac 11:29 **d.** to send relief unto the brethren *3724*
Ac 15:2 they **d.** that Paul and Barnabas, *5021*
Ac 15:37 Barnabas **d.** to take with them *1011*
Ac 17:26 hath **d.** the times before appointed, *3724*
Ac 19:39 shall be **d.** in a lawful assembly. *1956*
Ac 20:16 Paul had **d.** to sail by Ephesus, *2919*
Ac 25:25 Augustus, I have **d.** to send him. *2919*
Ac 27:1 when it was **d.** that we should sail *2919*
1Co 2:2 For I **d.** not to know any thing *2919*
2Co 2:1 But I **d.** this with myself, that I *2919*
Tit 3:12 for I have **d.** there to winter. *2919*

DETEST See also DETESTABLE.
De 7:26 thou shalt utterly **d.** it, and thou 8262

DETESTABLE
Jer 16:18 their **d.** and abominable things. 8251
Eze 5:11 sanctuary with all thy **d.** things, 8251
Eze 7:20 and of their **d.** things therein: 8251
Eze 11:18 all the **d.** things thereof from 8251
Eze 11:21 **d.** things and their abominations, 8251
Eze 37:23 idols, nor with their **d.** things, 8251

DEUEL (de-oo'-el) See also REUEL.
Nu 1:14 of Gad; Eliasaph the son of **D.** 1845
Nu 7:42 sixth day Eliasaph the son of **D.**, 1845
Nu 7:47 offering of Eliasaph the son of **D.** 1845
Nu 10:20 Gad was Eliasaph the son of **D.** 1845

DEUTERONOMY (doo''-tur-on'-o-mee)
De *general title* Book Of Moses, Called **D.** 428,1697

DEVICE See also DEVICES.
2Ch 2:14 to find out every **d.** which shall 4284
Es 8:3 his **d.** that he had devised against 4284
Es 9:25 by letters that his wicked **d.**, which 4284
Ps 21:11 they imagined a mischievous **d.**,
Ps 140:8 further not his wicked **d.**; lest
Ec 9:10 for there is no work, nor **d.**, nor 2808
Jer 18:11 and devise a **d.** against you: 4284
Jer 51:11 for his **d.** is against Babylon, 4209
La 3:62 their **d.** against me all the day. 1902
Ac 17:29 stone, graven by art and man's **d.** *1761*

DEVICES
Job 5:12 He disappointeth the **d.** of the 4284
Job 21:27 **d.** which ye wrongfully imagine 4209
Ps 10:2 let them be taken in the **d.** that 4209
Ps 33:10 he maketh the **d.** of the people 4284
Ps 37:7 who bringeth wicked **d.** to pass. 4209
Pr 1:31 and be filled with their own **d.** 4156
Pr 12:2 man of wicked **d.** will he condemn. 4209
Pr 14:17 a man of wicked **d.** is hated. 4209
Pr 19:21 are many **d.** in a man's heart; 4284
Isa 32:7 he deviseth wicked **d.** to destroy 2154
Jer 11:19 they had devised **d.** against me, 4284
Jer 18:12 we will walk after our own **d.**, 4284
Jer 18:18 let us devise **d.** against Jeremiah; 4284
Da 11:24 forecast his **d.** against the strong 4284
Da 11:25 they shall forecast **d.** against him. 4284
2Co 2:11 we are not ignorant of his **d.** *3540*

DEVIL See also DEVILS.
Mt 4:1 wilderness to be tempted of the **d.** *1228*
Mt 4:5 **d.** taketh him up into the holy city, *1228*
Mt 4:8 Again the **d.** taketh him up into *1228*
Mt 4:11 Then the **d.** leaveth him, and, *1228*
Mt 9:32 a dumb man possessed with a **d.** *1139*
Mt 9:33 when the **d.** was cast out, the *1140*
Mt 11:18 and they say, He hath a **d.** *1140*
Mt 12:22 one possessed with a **d.**, blind, *1139*
Mt 13:39 enemy that sowed them is the **d.**; *1228*
Mt 15:22 is grievously vexed with a **d.** *1139*
Mt 17:18 Jesus rebuked the **d.**; and he *1140*
Mt 25:41 prepared for the **d.** and his angels: *1228*
Mk 5:15, 16 was possessed with the **d.**, *1139*
Mk 5:18 that had been possessed with a **d.**, *1139*
Mk 7:26 that he would cast forth the **d.** *1140*
Mk 7:29 **d.** is gone out of thy daughter. *1140*
Mk 7:30 she found the **d.** gone out, and her *1140*
Lu 4:2 Being forty days tempted of the **d.** *1228*
Lu 4:3 the **d.** said unto him, If thou be *1228*
Lu 4:5 **d.**, taking him up into an high *1228*
Lu 4:6 the **d.** said unto him, All this will *1228*
Lu 4:13 **d.** had ended all the temptation, *1228*
Lu 4:33 had a spirit of an unclean **d.**, *1140*
Lu 4:35 when the **d.** had thrown him in *1140*
Lu 7:33 wine; and ye say, He hath a **d.** *1140*
Lu 8:12 cometh the **d.**, and taketh away *1228*
Lu 8:29 of the **d.** into the wilderness. *1142*
Lu 9:42 **d.** threw him down, and tare him. *1140*
Lu 11:14 casting out a **d.**, and it was dumb. *1140*
Lu 11:14 to pass when the **d.** was gone out, *1140*
Joh 6:70 twelve, and one of you is a **d.**? *1228*
Joh 7:20 and said, Thou hast a **d.**: *1140*
Joh 8:44 Ye are of your father the **d.**, *1228*
Joh 8:48 art a Samaritan, and hast a **d.**? *1140*
Joh 8:49 Jesus answered, I have not a **d.**; *1140*
Joh 8:52 Now we know that thou hast a **d.**; *1140*
Joh 10:20 many of them said, He hath a **d.**; *1140*
Joh 10:21 the words of him that hath a **d.** *1139*
Joh 10:21 a **d.** open the eyes of the blind? *1140*
Joh 13:2 **d.** having now put into the heart *1228*
Ac 10:38 all that were oppressed of the **d.**; *1228*
Ac 13:10 thou child of the **d.**, thou enemy *1228*
Eph 4:27 Neither give place to the **d.** *1228*
Eph 6:11 stand against the wiles of the **d.** *1228*
1Ti 3:6 into the condemnation of the **d.** *1228*
1Ti 3:7 reproach and the snare of the **d.** *1228*
2Ti 2:26 out of the snare of the **d.**, who *1228*
Heb 2:14 power of death, that is, the **d.**; *1228*
Jas 4:7 Resist the **d.**, and he will flee from *1228*
1Pe 5:8 because your adversary the **d.**, *1228*
1Jo 3:8 that committeth sin is of the **d.**; *1228*
1Jo 3:8 **d.** sinneth from the beginning. *1228*
1Jo 3:8 might destroy the works of the **d.** *1228*
1Jo 3:10 manifest, and the children of the **d.**: *1228*
Jude 9 when contending with the **d.** he *1228*
Re 2:10 the **d.** shall cast some of you into *1228*
Re 12:9 that old serpent, called the **D.**, and *1228*
Re 12:12 the **d.** is come down unto you, *1228*
Re 20:2 that old serpent, which is the **D.**, *1228*
Re 20:10 the **d.** that deceived them was cast *1228*

DEVILISH
Jas 3:15 above, but is earthly, sensual, **d.** *1141*

DEVILS
Le 17:7 offer their sacrifices unto **d.**, after 8163
De 32:17 sacrificed unto **d.**, not to God; 7700
2Ch 11:15 and for the **d.**, and for the calves 8163
Ps 106:37 sons and their daughters unto **d.**, 7700
Mt 4:24 which were possessed with **d.**, *1139*
Mt 7:22 in thy name have cast out **d.**? *1140*
Mt 8:16 that were possessed with **d.**: *1139*
Mt 8:28 met him two possessed with **d.**, *1139*
Mt 8:31 So the **d.** besought him, saying, If *1142*
Mt 8:33 befallen to the possessed of the **d.**, *1139*
Mt 9:34 Pharisees said, He casteth out **d.** *1140*
Mt 9:34 through the prince of the **d.** *1140*
Mt 10:8 lepers, raise the dead, cast out **d.**: *1140*
Mt 12:24 This fellow doth not cast out **d.**, *1140*
Mt 12:24 by Beelzebub the prince of the **d.** *1140*
Mt 12:27 if I by Beelzebub cast out **d.**, *1140*
Mt 12:28 if I cast out **d.** by the Spirit of *1140*
Mk 1:32 them that were possessed with **d.** *1139*
Mk 1:34 diseases, and cast out many **d.**; *1140*
Mk 1:34 and suffered not the **d.** to speak, *1140*
Mk 1:39 all Galilee, and cast out **d.** *1140*
Mk 3:15 sicknesses, and to cast out **d.**: *1140*
Mk 3:22 and by the prince of the **d.** *1140*
Mk 3:22 casteth he out **d.** *1140*
Mk 5:12 all the **d.** besought him, saying, *1142*
Mk 6:13 they cast out many **d.**, and *1140*
Mk 9:38 one casting out **d.** in thy name, *1140*
Mk 16:9 out of whom he had cast seven **d.** *1140*
Mk 16:17 my name shall they cast out **d.**; *1140*
Lu 4:41 **d.** also came out of many, crying *1140*
Lu 8:2 out of whom went seven **d.**, *1140*
Lu 8:27 a certain man, which had **d.** long *1140*
Lu 8:30 because many **d.** were entered *1140*
Lu 8:33 Then went the **d.** out of the man, *1140*
Lu 8:35 of whom the **d.** were departed, *1140*
Lu 8:36 possessed of the **d.** was healed. *1139*
Lu 8:38 the man out of whom the **d.** were *1140*
Lu 9:1 power and authority over all **d.**, *1140*
Lu 9:49 Master, we saw one casting out **d.** *1140*
Lu 10:17 even the **d.** are subject unto us *1140*
Lu 11:15 casteth out **d.** through Beelzebub *1140*
Lu 11:15 the chief of the **d.** *1140*
Lu 11:18 I cast out **d.** through Beelzebub. *1140*
Lu 11:19 if I by Beelzebub cast out **d.**, *1140*
Lu 11:20 with the finger of God cast out **d.** *1140*
Lu 13:32 I cast out **d.**, and I do cures *1140*
1Co 10:20 sacrifice to **d.**, and not to God: *1140*
1Co 10:20 ye should have fellowship with **d.** *1140*
1Co 10:21 cup of the Lord, and the cup of **d.**: *1140*
1Co 10:21 Lord's table, and of the table of **d.** *1140*
1Ti 4:1 spirits, and doctrines of **d.**; *1140*
Jas 2:19 the **d.** also believe, and tremble. *1140*
Re 9:20 that they should not worship **d.** *1140*
Re 16:14 For they are the spirits of **d.**, *1142*
Re 18:2 is become the habitation of **d.**, *1142*

DEVISE See also DEVISED; DEVISETH.
Ex 31:4 To **d.** cunning works, to work in 2803
Ex 35:32 And to **d.** curious works, to work in 2803
Ex 35:35 and of those that **d.** cunning work. 2803
2Sa 14:14 yet doth he **d.** means, that his 2803
Ps 35:4 to confusion that **d.** my hurt. 2803
Ps 35:20 **d.** deceitful matters against them. 2803
Ps 41:7 against me do they **d.** my hurt. 2803
Pr 3:29 **D.** not evil against thy neighbour, 2790
Pr 14:22 Do they not err that **d.** evil? but 2790
Pr 14:22 shall be to them that **d.** good. 2790

Pr 16:30 shutteth his eyes of **d.** froward......... 2803
Jer 18:11 and **d.** a device against you: return..... 2803
Jer 18:18 let us **d.** devices against Jeremiah;...... 2803
Eze 11:2 the men that **d.** mischief, and give...... 2803
Mic 2:1 Woe to them that **d.** iniquity, and........ 2803
Mic 2:3 against this family do I **d.** an evil,....... 2803

DEVISED
2Sa 21:5 that **d.** against us that we should........ 1819
1Ki 12:33 in the month which he had **d.**.............. 908
Es 8:3 that he had **d.** against the Jews.......... 2803
Es 8:5 reverse the letters **d.** by Haman........ 4284
Es 9:24 had **d.** against the Jews to destroy...... 2803
Es 9:25 which he **d.** against the Jews,........... 2803
Ps 31:13 they **d.** to take away my life............. 2161
Jer 11:19 they had **d.** devices against me,......... 2803
Jer 48:2 in Heshbon they had **d.** evil.............. 2803
Jer 51:12 the Lord hath both **d.** and done......... 2161
La 2:17 hath done that which he had **d.**;......... 2161
2Pe 1:16 not followed cunningly **d.** fables,......... *4679*

DEVISETH
Ps 36:4 He **d.** mischief upon his bed; he......... 2803
Ps 52:2 tongue **d.** mischiefs; like a sharp........ 2803
Pr 6:14 heart, he **d.** mischief continually;........ 2790
Pr 6:18 heart that **d.** wicked imaginations,........ 2790
Pr 16:9 A man's heart **d.** his ways; but the..... 2803
Pr 24:8 He that **d.** to do evil shall be............ 2803
Isa 32:7 he **d.** wicked devices to destroy......... 3289
Isa 32:8 But the liberal **d.** liberal things;......... 3289

DEVOTE See also DEVOTED.
Le 27:28 that a man shall **d.** unto the Lord....... 2763

DEVOTED
Le 27:21 unto the Lord, as a field **d.**;............. 2764
Le 27:28 no **d.** thing, that a man shall devote.... 2764
Le 27:28 every **d.** thing is most holy unto........ 2764
Le 27:29 None **d.**, which shall be.................. 2764
Le 27:29 which shall be **d.** of men,................. 2763
Nu 18:14 Every thing **d.** in Israel shall be......... 2764
Ps 119:38 servant, who is **d.** to thy fear.................

DEVOTIONS
Ac 17:23 I passed by, and beheld your **d.**,........ *4574*

DEVOUR See also DEVOURED; DEVOUREST; DEVOURETH; DEVOURING.
Ge 49:27 the morning he shall **d.** the prey,......... 398
De 32:42 blood, and my sword shall **d.** flesh;...... 398
Jg 9:15 and **d.** the cedars of Lebanon............ 398
Jg 9:20 and **d.** the men of Shechem, and the.... 398
Jg 9:20 house of Millo, and **d.** Abimelech......... 398
2Sa 2:26 Shall the sword **d.** for ever?............... 398
2Ch 7:13 command the locusts to **d.** the land,.... 398
Job 18:13 It shall **d.** the strength of his skin:....... 398
Job 18:13 born of death shall **d.** his strength........ 398
Ps 21:9 wrath, and the fire shall **d.** them.......... 398
Ps 50:3 silence: a fire shall **d.** before him,........ 398
Ps 80:13 wild beasts of the field doth **d.** it....... 7462
Pr 30:14 to **d.** the poor from off the earth,........ 398
Isa 1:7 strangers **d.** it in your presence,.......... 398
Isa 9:12 shall **d.** Israel with open mouth............ 398
Isa 9:18 it shall **d.** the briers and thorns,.......... 398
Isa 10:17 and it shall burn and **d.** his thorns......... 398
Isa 26:11 of thine enemies shall **d.** them............ 398
Isa 31:8 not of a mean man, shall **d.** him:......... 398
Isa 33:11 your breath, as fire, shall **d.** you.......... 398
Isa 42:14 I will destroy and **d.** at once............. 7602
Isa 56:9 beasts of the field, come to **d.**,.......... 398
Jer 2:3 all that **d.** him shall offend:............... 398
Jer 5:14 people wood, and it shall **d.** them......... 398
Jer 12:9 the beasts of the field, come to **d.**........ 402
Jer 12:12 the sword of the Lord shall **d.**............ 398
Jer 15:3 of the earth, to **d.** and destroy............ 398
Jer 17:27 shall **d.** the palaces of Jerusalem,......... 398
Jer 21:14 and it shall **d.** all things round............ 398
Jer 30:16 Therefore all they that **d.** shall be........ 398
Jer 46:10 and the sword shall **d.**, and it shall....... 398
Jer 46:14 sword shall **d.** round about thee........... 398
Jer 48:45 and shall **d.** the corner of Moab,.......... 398
Jer 50:32 and it shall **d.** all round about him........ 398
Eze 7:15 famine and pestilence shall **d.** him........ 398
Eze 15:7 fire, and another fire shall **d.** them;...... 398
Eze 20:47 it shall **d.** every green tree in thee,...... 398
Eze 23:37 them through the fire to **d.** them......... 402
Eze 28:18 it shall **d.** thee, and I will bring........... 398
Eze 34:28 the beast of the land **d.** them;............ 398
Eze 36:14 thou shalt **d.** men no more, neither...... 398
Da 7:5 thus unto it, Arise, **d.** much flesh......... 399
Da 7:23 and shall **d.** the whole earth,.............. 399
Ho 5:7 now shall a month **d.** them with.......... 398
Ho 8:14 and it shall **d.** the palaces thereof......... 398
Ho 11:6 and **d.** them, because of their own....... 398
Ho 13:8 and there will I **d.** them like a lion:...... 398
Am 1:4 shall **d.** the palaces of Ben-hadad......... 398
Am 1:7 which shall **d.** the palaces thereof:........ 398
Am 1:10 of Tyrus, which shall **d.** the palaces...... 398
Am 1:12 shall **d.** the palaces of Bozrah............ 398
Am 1:14 and it shall **d.** the palaces thereof,........ 398
Am 2:2 Moab, and it shall **d.** the palaces.......... 398
Am 2:5 shall **d.** the palaces of Jerusalem.......... 398
Am 5:6 in the house of Joseph, and **d.** it,......... 398
Ob 18 shall kindle in them, and **d.** them;......... 398
Na 2:13 the sword shall **d.** thy young lions:....... 398
Na 3:13 enemies: the fire shall **d.** thy bars........ 398
Na 3:15 There shall the fire **d.** thee: the.......... 398
Hab 3:14 was as to **d.** the poor secretly............ 398
Zec 9:15 and they shall **d.**, and subdue with....... 398
Zec 11:1 that the fire may **d.** thy cedars............ 398
Zec 12:6 and they shall **d.** all the people............ 398
Mt 23:14 **ye d. widows' houses, and for**........ *2719*
Mk 12:40 **which d. widows' houses, and for** .. *2719*
Lu 20:47 **Which d. widows' houses, and for** ..*2719*
2Co 11:20 if a man **d.** you, if a man take........... *2719*
Ga 5:15 if ye bite and **d.** one another,............ *2719*
Heb 10:27 which shall **d.** the adversaries.......... *2068*
1Pe 5:8 about, seeking whom he may **d.**:......... *2666*
Re 12:4 for to **d.** her child as soon as............ *2719*

DEVOURED
Ge 31:15 and hath quite **d.** also our money......... 398
Ge 37:20 Some evil beast hath **d.** him: and......... 398
Ge 37:33 an evil beast hath **d.** him: Joseph......... 398
Ge 41:7 And the seven thin ears **d.** the.......... 1104
Ge 41:24 And the thin ears **d.** the seven.......... 1104
Le 10:2 and **d.** them, and they died before....... 398
Nu 26:10 the fire **d.** two hundred and fifty.......... 398
De 31:17 and they shall be **d.**, and many evils..... 398
De 32:24 and **d.** with burning heat, and........... 3898
2Sa 18:8 the wood **d.** more people.................. 398
2Sa 18:8 that day than the sword **d.**................ 398
2Sa 22:9 and fire out of his mouth **d.**:.............. 398
Ps 18:8 and fire out of his mouth **d.**:.............. 398
Ps 78:45 flies among them, which **d.** them;........ 398
Ps 79:7 For they have **d.** Jacob, and laid.......... 398
Ps 105:35 and **d.** the fruit of their ground............ 398
Isa 1:20 ye shall be **d.** with the sword:............. 398
Isa 24:6 hath the curse **d.** the earth................ 398
Jer 2:30 own sword hath **d.** your prophets,......... 398
Jer 3:24 shame hath **d.** the labour of our............ 398
Jer 8:16 they are come, and have **d.** the land,.... 398
Jer 10:25 have eaten up Jacob, and **d.** him,......... 398
Jer 30:16 they that devour thee shall be **d.**;......... 398
Jer 50:7 All that found them have **d.** them:......... 398
Jer 50:17 the king of Assyria hath **d.** him;........... 398
Jer 51:34 the king of Babylon hath **d.** me,........... 398
La 4:11 it hath **d.** the foundations thereof......... 398
Eze 15:5 when the fire hath **d.** it, and it is......... 398
Eze 16:20 thou sacrificed unto them to be **d.**......... 398
Eze 19:3 learned to catch the prey; it **d.** men...... 398
Eze 19:6 to catch the prey, and **d.** men............. 398
Eze 19:14 branches, which hath **d.** her fruit,......... 398
Eze 22:25 they have **d.** souls; they have taken...... 398
Eze 23:25 thy residue shall be **d.** by the fire......... 398
Eze 33:27 will I give to the beasts to be **d.**,.......... 398
Eze 39:4 to the beasts of the field to be **d.**........ 402
Da 7:7 teeth: it **d.** and brake in pieces,............ 399
Da 7:19 which **d.**, brake in pieces, and............. 399
Ho 7:7 an oven, and have **d.** their judges;........ 398
Ho 7:9 Strangers have **d.** his strength, and....... 398
Joe 1:19 to thee will I cry for the fire hath **d.**..... 398
Joe 1:20 the fire hath **d.** the pastures of the....... 398
Am 4:9 increased, the palmerworm **d.** them:...... 398
Am 7:4 and it **d.** the great deep, and did eat..... 398
Na 1:10 they shall be **d.** as stubble fully........... 398
Zep 1:18 shall be **d.** by the fire of his jealousy:... 398
Zep 3:8 be **d.** with the fire of my jealousy......... 398
Zec 9:4 and she shall be **d.** with fire............... 398
Mt 13:4 **the fowls came and d. them up:**.... *2719*
Mk 4:4 **fowls of the air came and d. it up.** .*2719*
Lu 8:5 **and the fowls of the air d. it**........ *2719*
Lu 15:30 **hath d. thy living with harlots,**..... *2719*
Re 20:9 out of heaven, and **d.** them............... *2719*

DEVOURER
Mal 3:11 I will rebuke the **d.** for your sakes,....... 398

DEVOUREST
Eze 36:13 Thou land **d.** up men, and hast............ 398

DEVOURETH
2Sa 11:25 sword **d.** one as well as another:.......... 398
Pr 19:28 mouth of the wicked **d.** iniquity.......... 1104
Pr 20:25 man who **d.** that which is holy,........... 3216
Isa 5:24 Therefore as the fire **d.** the stubble,..... 398
La 2:3 a flaming fire, which **d.** round about...... 398
Eze 15:4 the fire **d.** both the ends of it,............ 398
Joe 2:3 A fire **d.** before them; and behind......... 398
Joe 2:5 a flame of fire that **d.** the stubble,........ 398
Hab 1:13 when the wicked **d.** the man that....... 1104
Re 11:5 their mouth, and **d.** their enemies:...... *2719*

DEVOURING
Ex 24:17 like **d.** fire on the top of the mount...... 398
Ps 52:4 Thou lovest all **d.** words, O thou........ 1105
Isa 29:6 tempest, and the flame of **d.** fire......... 398
Isa 30:27 and his tongue as a **d.** fire:................. 398
Isa 30:30 and with the flame of a **d.** fire,............ 398
Isa 33:14 us shall dwell with the **d.** fire?............ 398

DEVOUT
Lu 2:25 the same man was just and **d.**,.......... *2126*
Ac 2:5 Jews, **d.** men, out of every nation...... *2126*
Ac 8:2 And **d.** men carried Stephen to his..... *2126*
Ac 10:2 A **d.** man, and one that feared God..... *2152*
Ac 10:7 a **d.** soldier of them that waited on..... *2152*
Ac 13:50 stirred up the **d.** and honourable........ *4576*
Ac 17:4 of the **d.** Greeks a great multitude,..... *4576*
Ac 17:17 the Jews, and with the **d.** persons,..... *4576*
Ac 22:12 a **d.** man according to the law,........... *2152*

DEW
Ge 27:28 God give thee of the **d.** of heaven,..... 2919
Ge 27:39 and of the **d.** of heaven from above;... 2919
Ex 16:13 the **d.** lay round about the host.......... 2919
Ex 16:14 when the **d.** that lay was gone........... 2919
Nu 11:9 when the **d.** fell upon the camp.......... 2919
De 32:2 my speech shall distil as the **d.**,......... 2919
De 33:13 for the **d.**, and for the deep............... 2919
De 33:28 also his heavens shall drop down **d.**.... 2919
Jg 6:37 if the **d.** be on the fleece only,........... 2919
Jg 6:38 wringed the **d.** out of the fleece,........ 2919
Jg 6:39 upon all the ground let there be **d.**.... 2919
Jg 6:40 there was **d.** on all the ground........... 2919
2Sa 1:21 Gilboa, let there be no **d.**, neither...... 2919
2Sa 17:12 light upon him as the **d.** falleth............ 2919
1Ki 17:1 there shall not be **d.** nor rain............. 2919
Job 29:19 the **d.** lay all night upon my branch..... 2919
Job 38:28 who hath begotten the drops of **d.**?.... 2919
Ps 110:3 thou hast the **d.** of thy youth.............. 2919
Ps 133:3 the **d.** [2919] of Hermon, and as the **d.**.....
Pr 3:20 and the clouds drop down the **d.**......... 2919
Pr 19:12 his favour is as **d.** upon the grass....... 2919
Ca 5:2 for my head is filled with **d.**,............... 2919
Isa 18:4 like a cloud of **d.** in the heart of.......... 2919
Isa 26:19 for thy **d.** is as the **d.** of herbs,........... 2919
Da 4:15 let it be wet with the **d.** of heaven,..... 2920
Da 4:23 **d.** of heaven, and let his portion be..... 2920
Da 4:25 they shall wet thee with the **d.** of....... 2920
Da 4:33 and his body was wet with the **d.** of.... 2920
Da 5:21 body was wet with the **d.** of heaven;.. 2920
Ho 6:4 and as the early **d.** it goeth away........ 2919
Ho 13:3 and as the early **d.** that passeth.......... 2919
Ho 14:5 I will be as the **d.** unto Israel:........... 2919
Mic 5:7 many people as a **d.** from the Lord,..... 2919
Hag 1:10 heaven over you is stayed from **d.**,...... 2919
Zec 8:12 the heavens shall give their **d.**;........... 2919

DIADEM
Job 29:14 judgment was as a robe and a **d.**......... 6797
Isa 28:5 and for a **d.** of beauty, unto the.......... 6843
Isa 62:3 a royal **d.** in the hand of thy God....... 6797
Eze 21:26 Remove the **d.**, and take off the.......... 4701

DIAL
2Ki 20:11 which it had gone down in the **d.**........ 4609
Isa 38:8 which is gone down in the sun **d.**........ 4609

DIAMOND
Ex 28:18 an emerald, a sapphire, and a **d.**........ 3095
Ex 39:11 an emerald, a sapphire, and a **d.**........ 3095
Jer 17:1 and with the point of a **d.**:................ 8068
Eze 28:13 the sardius, topaz, and the **d.**,........... 3095

DIANA (di-an'-ah)
Ac 19:24 which made silver shrines for **D.**.......... *735*
Ac 19:27 the temple of the great goddess **D.**....... *735*
Ac 19:28 Great is **D.** of the Ephesians............... *735*
Ac 19:34 out, Great is **D.** of the Ephesians......... *735*
Ac 19:35 worshipper of the great goddess **D.**,...... *735*

DIBLAIM (dib'-la-im)
Ho 1:3 took Gomer the daughter of **D.**; 1691

DIBLATH (dib'-lath)
Eze 6:14 than the wilderness toward **D.**, 1689

DIBLATHAIM See ALMON-DIBLATHAIM; BETH-DIBLATHAIM.

DIBON (di'-bon) See also DIBON-GAD; DIMON.
Nu 21:30 Heshbon is perished even unto **D.**, 1769
Nu 32:3 Ataroth, and **D.**, and Jazer, and 1769
Nu 32:34 And the children of Gad built **D.**, 1769
Jos 13:9 all the plain of Medeba unto **D.**; 1769
Jos 13:17 **D.**, and Bamoth-baal, and 1769
Ne 11:25 at **D.**, and in the villages thereof, 1769
Isa 15:2 He is gone up to Bajith, and to **D.**, 1769
Jer 48:18 daughter that dost inhabit **D.**, 1769
Jer 48:22 And upon **D.**, and upon Nebo, and 1769

DIBON-GAD (di'-bon-gad')
Nu 33:45 from Iim, and pitched in **D.** 1769
Nu 33:46 removed from **D.**, and encamped 1769

DIBRI (dib'-ri)
Le 24:11 Shelomith, the daughter of **D.**, 1704

DID See also DIDDEST; DIDST.
Ge 3:6 and **d.** eat, and gave also unto her
Ge 3:6 husband with her; and he **d.** eat.
Ge 3:12 she gave me of the tree, and I **d.** eat.
Ge 3:13 serpent beguiled me, and I **d.** eat.
Ge 3:21 unto his wife **d.** the Lord God make
Ge 6:22 Thus **d.** Noah; according to all 6213
Ge 6:22 God commanded him, so **d.** he. 6213
Ge 7:5 Noah **d.** according unto all that the 6213
Ge 7:20 cubits upward **d.** the waters prevail;
Ge 11:9 because the Lord **d.** there confound
Ge 11:9 thence **d.** the Lord scatter them.
Ge 18:8 under the tree, and they **d.** eat.
Ge 18:13 Wherefore **d.** Sarah laugh,
Ge 19:3 and **d.** bake unleavened bread,
Ge 21:1 **d.** unto Sarah as he had spoken. 6213
Ge 22:1 that God **d.** tempt Abraham and
Ge 22:23 these eight Milcah **d.** bear to Nahor,
Ge 24:54 and they **d.** eat and drink,
Ge 25:28 because he **d.** eat of his venison:
Ge 25:34 and he **d.** eat and drink, and rose up
Ge 26:20 the herdmen of Gerar **d.** strive
Ge 26:30 and they **d.** eat and drink,
Ge 27:25 brought it near to him, and he **d.** eat:
Ge 29:25 **d.** not I serve with thee for
Ge 29:28 Jacob **d.** so, and fulfilled her week: 6213
Ge 30:40 And Jacob **d.** separate the lambs,
Ge 30:41 the stronger cattle **d.** conceive,
Ge 31:46 and they **d.** eat thereupon the heap.
Ge 31:54 and they **d.** eat bread,
Ge 35:5 and they **d.** not pursue after the
Ge 38:10 which he **d.** displeased the Lord: 6213
Ge 38:11 he die also, as his brethren **d.**.
Ge 39:3 Lord made all that he **d.** to prosper 6213
Ge 39:6 save the bread which he **d.** eat.
Ge 39:19 this manner **d.** thy servant to me; 6213
Ge 39:22 they **d.** there, he was the doer of it. 6213
Ge 39:23 that which he **d.**, the Lord made 6213
Ge 40:17 birds **d.** eat them out of the basket
Ge 40:23 Yet **d.** not the chief butler remember
Ge 41:4 and the lean fleshed kine **d.** eat up
Ge 41:12 to his dream he **d.** interpret.
Ge 41:20 ill favored kine **d.** eat up the first
Ge 42:20 ye shall not die. And they **d.** so. 6213
Ge 42:25 way: and thus **d.** he unto them. 6213
Ge 43:3 man **d.** solemnly protest unto us,
Ge 43:17 And the man **d.** as Joseph bade; 6213
Ge 43:30 bowels **d.** yearn upon his brother:
Ge 43:32 which **d.** eat with him,
Ge 44:2 And he **d.** according to the word 6213
Ge 45:5 for God **d.** send me before you to
Ge 45:21 And the children of Israel **d.** so: 6213
Ge 47:22 **d.** eat their portion which Pharaoh
Ge 48:15 fathers Abraham and Isaac **d.** walk,
Ge 50:12 his sons **d.** unto him according as 6213
Ge 50:15 all the evil which we **d.** unto him 1580
Ge 50:16 father **d.** command before he died,
Ge 50:17 they **d.** unto thee evil: and now, 1580
Ex 1:11 **d.** set over them taskmasters
Ex 1:17 and **d.** not as the king of Egypt 6213
Ex 2:13 he said to him that **d.** the wrong,
Ex 4:30 and **d.** the signs in the sight of the 6213
Ex 5:8 which they **d.** make heretofore,
Ex 5:19 the children of Israel **d.** see that
Ex 6:8 the which I **d.** swear to give it to
Ex 7:6 Aaron **d.** as the Lord commanded 6213
Ex 7:6 Lord commanded them, so **d.** they. 6213
Ex 7:10 **d.** so as the Lord had commanded: 6213
Ex 7:11 magicians of Egypt, they also **d.** in 6213
Ex 7:20 And Moses and Aaron **d.** so, as the 6213
Ex 7:22 magicians of Egypt **d.** so with their 6213
Ex 7:22 neither **d.** he hearken unto them;
Ex 7:23 **d.** he set his heart to this also.
Ex 8:7 **d.** so with their enchantments, 6213
Ex 8:13 **d.** according to the word of Moses; 6213
Ex 8:17 they **d.** so; for Aaron stretched 6213
Ex 8:18 **d.** so with their enchantments 6213
Ex 8:24 the Lord **d.** so; and there came 6213
Ex 8:31 the Lord **d.** according to the word 6213
Ex 9:6 Lord **d.** that thing on the morrow, 6213
Ex 9:7 and he **d.** not let the people go.
Ex 10:11 for that ye **d.** desire.
Ex 10:15 they **d.** eat every herb of the land,
Ex 11:10 And Moses and Aaron **d.** all these 6213
Ex 12:28 children of Israel went away, and **d.** 6213
Ex 12:28 Moses and Aaron, so **d.** they. 6213
Ex 12:35 the children of Israel **d.** according 6213
Ex 12:50 Thus **d.** all the children of Israel; 6213
Ex 12:50 Moses and Aaron, so **d.** they. 6213
Ex 12:51 Lord **d.** bring the children of Israel
Ex 13:8 that which the Lord **d.** unto me 6213
Ex 14:4 I am the Lord. And they **d.** so. 6213
Ex 14:12 the word that we **d.** tell thee in
Ex 14:31 the Lord **d.** upon the Egyptians: 6313
Ex 16:3 and when we **d.** eat bread to the full;
Ex 16:17 And the children of Israel **d.** so, 6213
Ex 16:18 and when they **d.** mete it with an
Ex 16:24 and it **d.** not stink, neither was
Ex 16:35 the children of Israel **d.** eat manna
Ex 16:35 they **d.** eat manna, until they
Ex 17:2 the people **d.** chide with Moses
Ex 17:6 And Moses **d.** so in the sight of 6213
Ex 17:10 Joshua **d.** as Moses had said to him, 6213
Ex 18:7 his father in law, and **d.** obeisance,
Ex 18:14 father in law saw all that he **d.** to 6213
Ex 18:24 in law, and **d.** all that he had said. 6213
Ex 19:4 seen what I **d.** unto the Egyptians, 6213
Ex 24:11 nobles of the children of....and **d.** eat
Ex 32:12 For mischief **d.** he bring them out,
Ex 32:21 What **d.** this people unto thee, 6213
Ex 32:28 the children of Levi **d.** according 6213
Ex 33:4 and no man **d.** put on him his
Ex 34:28 **d.** neither eat bread, nor drink water.
Ex 35:24 that **d.** offer an offering of silver
Ex 35:25 that were wise hearted **d.** spin
Ex 36:22 thus **d.** he make for all the boards
Ex 36:29 **d.** both of them in both the corners. 6213
Ex 39:3 And they **d.** beat the gold into
Ex 39:21 **d.** bind the breastplate by his rings
Ex 39:32 children of Israel **d.** according to 6213
Ex 39:32 Lord commanded Moses, so **d.** they, 6213
Ex 39:43 And Moses **d.** look upon all the
Ex 40:16 Thus **d.** Moses: according to all 6213
Ex 40:16 command him, so **d.** he. And it 6213
Le 4:20 bullock as he **d.** with the bullock 6213
Le 8:4 Moses **d.** as the Lord commanded 6213
Le 8:9 **d.** he put the golden plate
Le 8:36 Aaron and his sons **d.** all the 6213
Le 9:14 **d.** wash the inwards and the legs,
Le 10:7 **d.** according to the word of Moses. 6213
Le 16:15 he **d.** with the blood of the bullock, 6213
Le 16:34 **d.** as the Lord commanded Moses. 6213
Le 24:23 Israel **d.** as the Lord commanded 6213
Le 26:35 it **d.** not rest in your sabbaths,
Le 27:24 possession of the land **d.** belong.
Nu 1:54 commanded Moses, so **d.** they. 6213
Nu 1:54 the children of Israel **d.** according 6213
Nu 2:34 the children of Israel **d.** according 6213
Nu 4:37 Moses and Aaron **d.** number
Nu 4:41 Moses and Aaron **d.** number
Nu 5:4 so **d.** the children of Israel. 6213
Nu 5:4 And the children of Israel **d.** so, 6213
Nu 7:18 prince of Issachar, **d.** offer:
Nu 7:24 children of Zebulun, **d.** offer:
Nu 7:30 the children of Reuben, **d.** offer:
Nu 7:36 the children of Simeon, **d.** offer:
Nu 8:3 Aaron **d.** so; he lighted the lamps 6213
Nu 8:20 **d.** the children on Israel unto them. 6213
Nu 8:20 **d.** to the Levites according unto all 6213
Nu 8:22 the Levites, so **d.** they unto them. 6213
Nu 9:5 Moses, so **d.** the children of Israel. 6213
Nu 10:21 the other **d.** set up the tabernacle
Nu 11:5 which we **d.** eat in Egypt freely;
Nu 11:25 they prophesied, and **d.** not cease.
Nu 14:22 my miracles, which I **d.** in Egypt, 6213
Nu 14:37 those men that **d.** bring up the evil
Nu 17:11 **d.** so: as the Lord commanded 6213
Nu 17:11 commanded him, so **d.** he. 6213
Nu 20:27 Moses **d.** as the Lord commanded: 6213
Nu 21:14 What he **d.** in the Read sea, and 2052
Nu 22:37 **D.** I not earnestly send unto thee
Nu 23:2 Balak **d.** as Balaam had spoken; 6213
Nu 23:30 And Balak **d.** as Balaam had said, 6213
Nu 25:2 and the people **d.** eat,
Nu 27:22 Moses **d.** as the Lord commanded 6213
Nu 31:31 **d.** as the Lord commanded Moses. 6213
Nu 32:8 **d.** your fathers, when I sent them 6213
Nu 36:10 so **d.** the daughters of Zelophehad: 6213
De 1:30 to all that he **d.** for you in Egypt 6213
De 1:32 ye **d.** not believe the Lord your God,
De 2:12 as Israel **d.** unto the land of his 6213
De 2:22 As he **d.** to the children of Esau, 6213
De 2:29 Moabites which dwell in Ar, **d.** unto 6213
De 3:6 we **d.** unto Sihon king of Heshbon, 6213
De 4:3 eyes have seen what the Lord **d.** 6213
De 4:4 **d.** cleave unto the Lord your God
De 4:33 **D.** ever people hear the voice of God
De 4:34 to all that the Lord your God **d.** 6213
De 5:23 for the mountain **d.** burn with fire,
De 7:7 the Lord **d.** not set his love upon you,
De 7:18 Lord thy God **d.** unto Pharaoh, 6213
De 8:3 neither **d.** thy fathers know;
De 8:4 neither **d.** thy foot swell,
De 9:9 I neither **d.** eat nor drink water:
De 9:18 I **d.** neither eat bread nor drink
De 11:3 which he **d.** in the midst of Egypt 6213
De 11:4 what he **d.** unto the army of Egypt, 6213
De 11:5 he **d.** unto you in the wilderness, 6213
De 11:6 he **d.** unto Dathan and Abiram, 6213
De 11:7 great acts of the Lord which he **d.** 6213
De 12:30 How **d.** these nations serve their
De 24:9 what the Lord thy God **d.** unto 6213
De 25:17 Remember what Amalek **d.** unto 6213
De 29:2 Ye have seen all that the Lord **d.** 6213
De 31:4 do unto them as he **d.** to Sihon and 6213
De 32:12 the Lord alone **d.** lead him,
De 32:38 which **d.** eat the fat of their sacrifices
De 33:9 neither **d.** he acknowledge his
De 34:9 and **d.** as the Lord commanded 6213
Jos 2:10 what ye **d.** unto the two kings of 6213
Jos 2:11 hearts **d.** melt, neither **d.** there remain
Jos 4:8 children of Israel **d.** so as Joshua 6213
Jos 4:18 over all his banks, as they **d.** before.
Jos 4:20 **d.** Joshua pitch in Gilgal.
Jos 4:23 as the Lord your God **d.** to the Red 6213
Jos 5:4 cause why Joshua **d.** circumcise
Jos 5:11 and they **d.** eat of the old corn
Jos 5:12 but they **d.** eat of the fruit of the
Jos 5:14 and **d.** worship, and said unto him,
Jos 5:15 is holy. And Joshua **d.** so. 6213
Jos 6:14 into the camp: so they **d.** six days. 6213
Jos 9:4 They **d.** work wilily, and went 6213
Jos 9:9 fame of him, and all that he **d.** in 6213
Jos 9:10 **d.** to the two kings of the Amorites, 6213
Jos 9:26 And so **d.** he unto them, and 6213
Jos 10:23 And they **d.** so, and brought forth 6213
Jos 10:28 **d.** to the king of Makkedah as he **d.** 6213
Jos 10:30 **d.** unto the king thereof as he **d.** 6213
Jos 10:39 he had done to Hebron, so he **d.** to 6213
Jos 10:42 kings and their land **d.** Joshua take
Jos 11:9 Joshua **d.** unto them as the Lord 6213
Jos 11:12 all the kings of them, **d.** Joshua take
Jos 11:13 Hazor only; that **d.** Joshua burn
Jos 11:15 Moses command Joshua, and so **d.** 6213
Jos 12:6 Them **d.** Moses the...smite:
Jos 13:12 for these **d.** Moses smite,
Jos 13:22 **d.** the children of Israel slay with the
Jos 13:32 which Moses **d.** distribute for
Jos 14:5 Moses, so the children of Israel **d.**, 6213
Jos 17:13 but **d.** not utterly drive them out
Jos 22:20 **D.** not Achan the son of Zerah commit
Jos 22:33 and **d.** not intend to go up against
Jos 24:5 according to that which I **d.** among 6213
Jos 24:13 a land for which ye **d.** not labour,
Jos 24:17 and which **d.** those great signs in 6213
Jg 1:21 children of Benjamin **d.** not drive out
Jg 1:27 Neither **d.** Manasseh drive out the
Jg 1:28 and **d.** not utterly drive them out.
Jg 1:29 Neither **d.** Ephraim drive out the

Jg 1:30 Neither **d.** Zebulun drive out the...
Jg 1:31 Neither **d.** Asher drive out the...
Jg 1:32 for they **d.** not drive them out...
Jg 1:33 Neither **d.** Naphtali drive out the...
Jg 2:7 works of the Lord, that he **d.** for... 6213
Jg 2:11 And the children of Israel **d.** evil in... 6213
Jg 2:17 of the Lord; but they **d.** not so... 6213
Jg 2:22 As their fathers **d.** keep it, or not...
Jg 3:7 And the children of Israel **d.** evil... 6213
Jg 3:12 the children of Israel **d.** evil again... 6213
Jg 3:16 he **d.** gird it under his raiment...
Jg 4:1 the children of Israel again **d.** evil... 6213
Jg 5:17 and why **d.** Dan remain in ships?...
Jg 6:1 the children of Israel **d.** evil in the... 6213
Jg 6:13 **D.** not the Lord bring us up from...
Jg 6:20 pour out the broth. And he **d.** so... 6213
Jg 6:27 and **d.** as the Lord had said unto... 6213
Jg 6:27 do it by day, that he **d.** it by night... 6213
Jg 6:40 And God **d.** so that night: for it was... 6213
Jg 8:1 And they **d.** chide with him sharply...
Jg 8:15 with whom ye **d.** upbraid me,...
Jg 8:25 and **d.** cast therein every man the...
Jg 9:27 and **d.** eat and drink,...
Jg 9:56 of Abimelech, which he **d.** unto... 6213
Jg 9:57 the men of Shechem **d.** God render...
Jg 10:6 And the children of Israel **d.** evil... 6213
Jg 10:11 **D.** not I deliver you from the...
Jg 10:12 and the Maonites, **d.** oppress you;...
Jg 11:7 **D.** not ye hate me, and expel me,...
Jg 11:25 or **d.** he ever fight against them,...
Jg 11:25 **d.** he ever strive against Israel,...
Jg 11:26 Why therefore **d.** ye not recover them...
Jg 11:39 father, who **d.** with her, according... 6213
Jg 13:1 Israel **d.** evil again in the sight of... 6213
Jg 13:19 and the angel **d.** wondrously;... 6213
Jg 13:21 angel of the Lord **d.** no more appear...
Jg 14:9 and they **d.** eat: but he told not...
Jg 15:11 As they **d.** unto me, so have I done... 6213
Jg 16:21 and he **d.** grind in the prison house...
Jg 17:6 every man **d.** that which was right... 6213
Jg 19:4 so they **d.** eat and drink,...
Jg 19:6 and **d.** eat and drink both of them...
Jg 19:8 and they **d.** eat both of them...
Jg 19:21 and **d.** eat and drink...
Jg 21:22 for ye **d.** not give unto them at this...
Jg 21:23 the children of Benjamin **d.** so,... 6213
Jg 21:25 every man **d.** that which was right... 6213
Ru 2:14 and she **d.** eat, and was sufficed,...
Ru 2:19 blessed be he that **d.** take knowledge...
Ru 3:6 unto the floor, and **d.** according... 6213
Ru 4:11 which two **d.** build the house of Israel:...
1Sa 1:7 And as he **d.** so year by year, when... 6213
1Sa 1:7 her; therefore she wept and **d.** not eat...
1Sa 1:18 went her way, and **d.** eat,...
1Sa 2:11 And the child **d.** minister unto the... 1961
1Sa 2:14 So they **d.** in Shiloh unto all the... 6213
1Sa 2:22 heard all that his sons **d.** unto all... 6213
1Sa 2:27 **D.** I plainly appear unto the house...
1Sa 2:28 and **d.** I choose him out of all the...
1Sa 2:28 and **d.** I give unto the house of thy...
1Sa 3:7 Now Samuel **d.** not yet know the Lord,...
1Sa 3:19 and **d.** let none of his words fall to the...
1Sa 4:20 neither **d.** she regard it...
1Sa 6:6 **d.** they not let the people go,...
1Sa 6:10 And the men **d.** so; and took two... 6213
1Sa 7:4 children of Israel **d.** put away Baalim...
1Sa 7:14 and the coasts thereof **d.** Israel deliver...
1Sa 9:24 So Saul **d.** eat with Samuel that day...
1Sa 12:7 Lord, which he **d.** to you and to... 6213
1Sa 13:6 then the people **d.** hide themselves in...
1Sa 14:32 and the people **d.** eat them with the...
1Sa 14:43 I **d.** but taste a little honey with the...
1Sa 15:2 remember that which Amalek **d.** to... 6213
1Sa 16:4 Samuel **d.** that which the Lord... 6213
1Sa 19:5 for he **d.** put his life in his hand,...
1Sa 20:34 and **d.** eat no meat the second day...
1Sa 21:11 **d.** they not sing one to another of...
1Sa 22:15 **D.** I then begin to enquire of God...
1Sa 22:17 and **d.** not shew it to me...
1Sa 22:18 and five persons that **d.** wear...
1Sa 25:4 David heard...that Nabal **d.** shear...
1Sa 27:11 saying, So **d.** David, and so will be... 6213
1Sa 28:24 and **d.** bake unleavened bread thereof:...
1Sa 28:25 and they **d.** eat. Then they rose up,...
1Sa 30:11 and he **d.** eat; and they made...
2Sa 1:2 he fell to the earth, and **d.** obeisance...
2Sa 2:3 were with him **d.** David bring up,...
2Sa 3:36 whatsoever the king **d.** pleased... 6219
2Sa 5:25 And David **d.** so, as the Lord had... 6219
2Sa 7:17 so **d.** Nathan speak unto David...
2Sa 8:11 king David **d.** dedicate unto the...
2Sa 9:6 fell on his face, and **d.** reverence...
2Sa 9:13 he **d.** eat continually at the king's...
2Sa 11:7 Joab **d.**, and how the people **d.**,... 7965
2Sa 11:13 he **d.** eat and drink before him;...
2Sa 11:20 ye so nigh...when ye **d.** fight?...
2Sa 11:21 **d.** not a woman cast a piece of...
2Sa 12:3 it **d.** eat of his own meat,...
2Sa 12:6 because he **d.** this thing, and... 6218
2Sa 12:17 neither **d.** he eat bread with them...
2Sa 12:20 bread before him, and he **d.** eat...
2Sa 12:31 and thus **d.** he unto all the cities... 6213
2Sa 13:8 and **d.** bake the cakes...
2Sa 13:29 the servants of Absalom **d.** unto... 6213
2Sa 14:4 face to the ground, and **d.** obeisance,...
2Sa 15:6 this manner **d.** Absalom to all... 6213
2Sa 17:15 Thus and thus **d.** Ahithophel counsel...
2Sa 19:19 that which thy servant **d.** perversely...
2Sa 19:28 among them that **d.** eat at thine own...
2Sa 19:43 why then **d.** ye despise us,...
2Sa 20:6 more harm than **d.** Absalom: take...
2Sa 21:6 whom the Lord **d.** choose...
2Sa 22:7 and he **d.** hear my voice out of his...
2Sa 22:7 my cry **d.** enter into his ears...
2Sa 22:11 he rode upon a cherub, and **d.** fly:...
2Sa 22:23 I **d.** not depart from them...
2Sa 22:37 so that my feet **d.** not slip...
2Sa 22:43 then **d.** I beat them as small as the...
2Sa 22:43 I **d.** stamp them as the mire of the...
2Sa 22:43 and **d.** spread them abroad...
2Sa 23:17 These things **d.** these three... 6213
2Sa 23:22 These things **d.** Benaiah the son of... 6213
2Sa 24:23 things **d.** Araunah, as a king,...
1Ki 1:16 Bath-sheba bowed, and **d.** obeisance...
1Ki 1:31 and **d.** reverence to the king,...
1Ki 2:5 the son of Zeruiah **d.** to me, and... 6213
1Ki 2:5 what he **d.** to the two captains... 6213
1Ki 2:35 and Zadok the priest **d.** the king put...
1Ki 2:42 **D.** I not make thee to swear by the...
1Ki 3:4 burnt offerings **d.** Solomon offer upon...
1Ki 3:14 as thy father David **d.** walk,...
1Ki 3:21 it was not my son, which I **d.** bear...
1Ki 5:18 builders and Hiram's **d.** hew them...
1Ki 7:15 a line of twelve cubits **d.** compass...
1Ki 7:18 and so **d.** he for the other chapiter... 6213
1Ki 7:23 a line of thirty cubits **d.** compass it...
1Ki 7:46 the plain of Jordan **d.** the king cast...
1Ki 7:51 the gold, and the vessels, **d.** he put...
1Ki 8:4 even those **d.** the priests...bring up...
1Ki 8:64 the same day **d.** the king hallow...
1Ki 9:21 upon those **d.** Solomon levy a tribute...
1Ki 9:22 the children of Israel **d.** Solomon...
1Ki 9:24 then **d.** he build Millo...
1Ki 9:25 And three times in a year **d.** Solomon...
1Ki 10:29 kings of Syria, **d.** they bring them out...
1Ki 11:6 And Solomon **d.** evil in the sight... 6213
1Ki 11:6 after the Lord, as **d.** David his...
1Ki 11:7 Then **d.** Solomon build an high place...
1Ki 11:8 likewise **d.** he for all his strange... 6213
1Ki 11:16 For six months **d.** Joab remain...
1Ki 11:25 beside the mischief that Hadad **d.**:...
1Ki 11:33 and my judgments as **d.** David his...
1Ki 11:38 as David my servant **d.**;... 6213
1Ki 11:41 and all that he **d.**, and his wisdom,... 6213
1Ki 12:9 which thy father **d.** put upon us...
1Ki 12:11 now whereas my father **d.** lade...
1Ki 12:32 So **d.** he in Beth-el, sacrificing... 6213
1Ki 13:19 and **d.** eat bread in his house,...
1Ki 13:22 which the Lord **d.** say to thee,...
1Ki 14:4 And Jeroboam's wife **d.** so, and... 6213
1Ki 14:16 who **d.** sin, and who made Israel...
1Ki 14:21 the city which the Lord **d.** choose...
1Ki 14:22 And Judah **d.** evil in the sight of... 6213
1Ki 14:24 and they **d.** according to all the... 6213
1Ki 14:29 and all that he **d.**, are they not... 6213
1Ki 15:4 for David's sake **d.** the Lord...give him...
1Ki 15:5 Because David **d.** that which was... 6213
1Ki 15:7 and all that he **d.**, are they not... 6213
1Ki 15:11 And Asa **d.** that which was right in... 6213
1Ki 15:11 of the Lord, as **d.** David his father...
1Ki 15:23 and all that he **d.**, and the cities... 6213
1Ki 15:26 he **d.** evil in the sight of the Lord,... 6213
1Ki 15:28 king of Judah **d.** Baasha slay him...
1Ki 15:31 and all that he **d.**, are they not... 6213
1Ki 15:34 he **d.** evil in the sight of the Lord,... 6213
1Ki 16:5 and what he **d.**, and his might, are... 6213
1Ki 16:7 the evil that he **d.** in the sight of... 6213
1Ki 16:12 Thus **d.** Zimri destroy all the house...
1Ki 16:14 Elah, and all that he **d.**, are they... 6213
1Ki 16:15 of Asa king of Judah **d.** Zimri reign...
1Ki 16:19 in his sin which he **d.**, to make... 6213
1Ki 16:25 and **d.** worse than all that were...
1Ki 16:27 the acts of Omri which he **d.**, and... 6213
1Ki 16:30 And Ahab the son of Omri **d.** evil... 6213
1Ki 16:33 Ahab **d.** more to provoke the Lord... 6213
1Ki 16:34 In his days **d.** Hiel the Bethelite build...
1Ki 17:5 So he went and **d.** according unto... 6213
1Ki 17:15 And she went and **d.** according to... 6213
1Ki 17:15 her house **d.** eat many days...
1Ki 17:16 neither **d.** the cruse of oil fail,...
1Ki 18:13 told my lord what I **d.** when... 6213
1Ki 18:34 And they **d.** it the second time...
1Ki 18:34 And they **d.** it the third time...
1Ki 19:6 And he **d.** eat and drink,...
1Ki 19:8 And he arose, and **d.** eat and drink,...
1Ki 19:21 gave unto the people, and they **d.** eat...
1Ki 20:25 unto their voice, and **d.** so... 6213
1Ki 20:33 Now the men **d.** diligently observe...
1Ki 20:33 and **d.** hastily catch it:...
1Ki 21:11 in his city, **d.** as Jezebel had... 6213
1Ki 21:13 Naboth **d.** blaspheme God and the...
1Ki 21:25 which **d.** sell himself to work wicked...
1Ki 21:26 he **d.** very abominably in following...
1Ki 21:26 to all things as **d.** the Amorites,... 6213
1Ki 22:18 **D.** I not tell thee that he would...
1Ki 22:39 acts of Ahab, and all that he **d.**,... 6213
1Ki 22:52 he **d.** evil in the sight of the Lord,... 6213
2Ki 1:18 the acts of Ahaziah which he **d.**... 6213
2Ki 2:18 **D.** I not say unto you, Go not?...
2Ki 4:1 thy servant **d.** fear the Lord:...
2Ki 4:28 **D.** I desire a son of my Lord?...
2Ki 4:28 **D.** I not say, do not deceive me?...
2Ki 4:44 he set it before them, and they **d.** eat...
2Ki 6:6 and the iron **d.** swim...
2Ki 6:29 we boiled my son, and **d.** eat him:...
2Ki 7:8 into one tent, and **d.** eat and drink,...
2Ki 8:2 **d.** after the saying of the man... 6213
2Ki 8:18 as **d.** the house of Ahab: for the... 6213
2Ki 8:18 was his wife: and he **d.** evil in the... 6213
2Ki 8:23 of Joram, and all that **d.**, are... 6213
2Ki 8:25 Ahab king of Israel **d.** Ahaziah...begin...
2Ki 8:27 **d.** evil in the sight of the Lord,... 6213
2Ki 8:27 as **d.** the house of Ahab: for he...
2Ki 9:27 they **d.** so at the going up to Gur...
2Ki 9:34 was come in, he **d.** eat and drink...
2Ki 10:19 But Jehu **d.** it in subtilty, to the... 6213
2Ki 10:34 and all that he **d.**, and all his might,... 6213
2Ki 11:3 Athaliah **d.** reign over the land...
2Ki 11:9 captains over the hundreds **d.**... 6213
2Ki 11:10 over hundreds **d.** the priest give...
2Ki 12:2 And Jehoash **d.** that which was... 6213
2Ki 12:11 the hands of them that **d.** the work,... 6213
2Ki 12:19 and all that he **d.**, are they not... 6213
2Ki 13:2 And he **d.** that which was evil in the... 6213
2Ki 13:7 neither **d.** he leave of the people...
2Ki 13:8 and all that he **d.**, and his might... 6213
2Ki 13:11 and he **d.** that which was evil in... 6213
2Ki 13:12 acts of Joash, and all that he **d.**... 6213
2Ki 13:25 three times **d.** Joash beat him,...
2Ki 14:3 And he **d.** that which was right... 6213
2Ki 14:3 he **d.** according to all things... 6213
2Ki 14:3 as Joash his father **d.**... 6213
2Ki 14:4 as yet the people **d.** sacrifice and...
2Ki 14:15 acts of Jehoash which he **d.**, and... 6213
2Ki 14:24 and he **d.** that which was evil in... 6213
2Ki 14:28 of Jeroboam, and all that he **d.**,... 6213
2Ki 15:3 And he **d.** that which was right... 6213
2Ki 15:6 and all that he **d.**, are they not... 6213
2Ki 15:8 king of Judah **d.** Zachariah...reign...
2Ki 15:9 And he **d.** that which was evil in... 6213
2Ki 15:18 **d.** that which was evil in the sight... 6213
2Ki 15:21 and all that he **d.**, are they not... 6213
2Ki 15:24 And he **d.** that which was evil in... 6213
2Ki 15:26 and all that he **d.**, behold, they are... 6213
2Ki 15:28 And he **d.** that which was evil in... 6213
2Ki 15:31 the acts of Pekah, and all that he **d.**,... 6213
2Ki 15:34 And he **d.** that which was right in... 6213
2Ki 15:34 he **d.** according to all that his... 6213
2Ki 15:36 acts of Jotham, and all that he **d.**,... 6213
2Ki 16:2 and **d.** not that which was right... 6213
2Ki 16:16 **d.** Urijah the priest, according to all... 6213

Book	Ref	Context	No.
2Ki	16:19	the acts of Ahaz which he **d.**, are	6213
2Ki	17:2	And he **d.** that which was evil in	6213
2Ki	17:9	children of Israel **d.** secretly those	
2Ki	17:11	the high places, as **d.** the heathen	
2Ki	17:14	that **d.** not believe in the Lord	
2Ki	17:22	the sins of Jeroboam which he **d.**;	6213
2Ki	17:40	Howbeit they **d.** not hearken,	
2Ki	17:40	**d.** after their former manner.	6213
2Ki	17:41	as **d.** their fathers, so do they unto	6213
2Ki	18:3	And he **d.** that which was right in	6213
2Ki	18:3	to all that David his father **d.**	6213
2Ki	18:4	children of Israel **d.** burn incense	
2Ki	18:11	of Assyria **d.** carry away Israel	
2Ki	18:13	king Hezekiah **d.** Sennacherib...come	
2Ki	18:16	time **d.** Hezekiah cut off the gold	
2Ki	21:2	And he **d.** that which was evil in	6213
2Ki	21:3	grove, as **d.** Ahab king of Israel	6213
2Ki	21:9	do more evil than **d.** the nations	
2Ki	21:11	above all that the Amorites **d.**,	6213
2Ki	21:17	and all that he **d.**, and his sin that	6213
2Ki	21:20	And he **d.** that which was evil in	6213
2Ki	21:20	Lord, as his father Manasseh **d.**	6213
2Ki	21:25	the acts of Amon which he **d.**,	6213
2Ki	22:2	And he **d.** that which was right in	6213
2Ki	23:9	**d.** eat of the unleavened bread	
2Ki	23:12	of the Lord, **d.** the king beat down,	
2Ki	23:13	of Ammon, **d.** the king defile.	
2Ki	23:19	and **d.** to them according to all	6213
2Ki	23:24	**d.** Josiah put away, that he might	
2Ki	23:28	and all that he **d.**, are they not	6213
2Ki	23:32	And he **d.** that which was evil in	6213
2Ki	23:37	he **d.** that which was evil in the	6213
2Ki	24:3	according to all that he **d.**;	6213
2Ki	24:5	all that he **d.**, are they not written	6213
2Ki	24:9	And he **d.** that which was evil in	6213
2Ki	24:11	and his servants **d.** besiege it.	
2Ki	24:19	And he **d.** that which was evil in	6213
2Ki	25:11	**d.** Nebuzar-adan...carry away.	
2Ki	25:13	**d.** the Chaldees break pieces,	
2Ki	25:27	**d.** lift up the head of Jehoiachin	
2Ki	25:29	and he **d.** eat bread continually.	
1Ch	4:27	**d.** all their family multiply,	
1Ch	9:22	David and Samuel the seer **d.** ordain	
1Ch	11:19	things **d.** these three mightiest.	6213
1Ch	11:24	**d.** Benaiah the son of Jehoiada	6213
1Ch	14:16	therefore **d.** as God commanded	6213
1Ch	15:13	because ye **d.** it not at the first,	
1Ch	15:24	**d.** blow with the trumpets before	
1Ch	17:15	so **d.** Nathan speak unto David	
1Ch	23:24	that **d.** the work for the service	6213
1Ch	26:27	**d.** they dedicate to maintain	
1Ch	27:26	And over them that **d.** the work	6213
1Ch	29:22	And **d.** eat and drink before the Lord	
2Ch	1:7	In that night **d.** God appear unto	
2Ch	2:7	whom David my father **d.** provide.	
2Ch	4:2	line of thirty cubits **d.** compass	
2Ch	4:3	which **d.** compass it round about:	
2Ch	4:16	**d.** Huram his father make to	
2Ch	4:17	of the Jordan **d.** the king cost them.	
2Ch	5:5	**d.** the priests and the Levites bring	
2Ch	5:11	and **d.** not then wait by course:	
2Ch	8:8	**d.** Solomon make to pay tribute	
2Ch	8:9	of Israel **d.** Solomon make no	
2Ch	10:9	that thy father **d.** put upon us?	
2Ch	12:14	**d.** evil, because he prepared not	6213
2Ch	13:20	Neither **d.** Jeroboam recover	
2Ch	14:2	And Asa **d.** that which was good	6213
2Ch	15:4	when they in their trouble **d.** turn.	
2Ch	15:6	**d.** vex them with all adversity.	
2Ch	18:16	I **d.** see all Israel scattered upon	
2Ch	18:17	**D.** I not tell thee that he would	
2Ch	19:8	in Jerusalem **d.** Jehoshaphat set	
2Ch	20:35	after this **d.** Jehoshaphat join	
2Ch	20:35	of Israel, who **d.** very wickedly:	6213
2Ch	21:6	like as **d.** the house of Ahab: for	6213
2Ch	21:10	same time also **d.** Libnah revolt	
2Ch	22:4	Wherefore he **d.** evil in the sight	6213
2Ch	23:8	Levites and all Judah **d.** according	6213
2Ch	24:2	Joash **d.** that which was right	6213
2Ch	24:7	**d.** they bestow on Baalim.	
2Ch	24:11	Thus they **d.** day by day, and	6213
2Ch	24:12	gave it to such as **d.** the work of	6213
2Ch	25:2	And he **d.** that which was right in	6213
2Ch	25:4	but **d.** as it is written in the law	
2Ch	25:12	alive **d.** the children of Judah carry	
2Ch	25:27	the time that Amaziah **d.** turn	
2Ch	26:4	And he **d.** that which was right in	6213
2Ch	26:4	to all that his father Amaziah **d.**	6213
2Ch	26:22	**d.** Isaiah the prophet,...write.	
2Ch	27:2	And he **d.** that which was right	6213
2Ch	27:2	to all that his father Uzziah **d.**:	6213
2Ch	27:2	And the people **d.** yet corruptly.	
2Ch	27:5	So much **d.** the children of Ammon pay	
2Ch	28:1	he **d.** not that which was right	6213
2Ch	28:16	**d.** king Ahaz send unto the kings	
2Ch	28:22	of his distress **d.** he trespass yet	
2Ch	29:2	And he **d.** that which was right	6213
2Ch	29:19	Ahaz in his reign **d.** cast away	
2Ch	29:34	the Levites **d.** help them,	
2Ch	30:18	yet **d.** they eat the passover	
2Ch	30:22	they **d.** eat throughout the feast	
2Ch	30:24	Hezekiah king of Judah **d.** give	
2Ch	31:20	**d.** Hezekiah throughout all Judah	6213
2Ch	31:21	he **d.** it with all his heart, and	6213
2Ch	32:3	and they **d.** help him.	
2Ch	32:9	After this **d.** Sennacherib...send	
2Ch	32:33	Jerusalem **d.** him honour at his	6213
2Ch	33:2	**d.** that which was evil in the sight	6213
2Ch	33:17	**d.** sacrifice still in the high places,	
2Ch	33:22	But he **d.** that which was evil	6213
2Ch	33:22	Lord, as **d.** Manasseh his father:	6213
2Ch	34:2	And he **d.** that which was right in	6213
2Ch	34:6	**d.** he in the cities of Manasseh,	
2Ch	34:12	the men **d.** the work faithfully:	6213
2Ch	34:32	the inhabitants of Jerusalem **d.**	6213
2Ch	35:3	David king of Israel **d.** build	
2Ch	35:12	And so **d.** they with the oxen.	
2Ch	35:18	neither **d.** all the kings of Israel keep	
2Ch	36:5	and he **d.** that which was evil in	6213
2Ch	36:8	and his abominations which he **d.**,	6213
2Ch	36:9	and he **d.** that which was evil in	6213
2Ch	36:12	he **d.** that which was evil in the	6213
Ezr	1:8	**d.** Cyrus king of Persia bring forth	
Ezr	1:11	All these **d.** Sheshbazzar bring up with	
Ezr	5:14	those **d.** Cyrus the king take out	
Ezr	6:13	the king had sent, so they **d.** speedily.	
Ezr	6:21	had separated themselves...**d.** eat,	
Ezr	10:6	he **d.** eat no bread, nor drink	
Ezr	10:16	the children of the captivity **d.** so.	6213
Ne	2:16	not whither I went, or what I **d.**;	6213
Ne	2:16	nor to the rest that **d.** the work	6213
Ne	3:3	gate **d.** the sons of Hassenaah build,	
Ne	5:13	**d.** according to this promise.	6213
Ne	5:15	but so **d.** not I, because of the fear	6213
Ne	9:25	so they **d.** eat, and were filled,	
Ne	9:28	they **d.** evil again before thee:	6213
Ne	11:12	their brethren that **d.** the work	6213
Ne	13:7	evil that Eliashib **d.** for Tobiah,	6213
Ne	13:10	and the singers, that **d.** the work	6213
Ne	13:18	**D.** [6213] not your fathers thus, and **d.**	
Ne	13:26	**D.** not Solomon king of Israel sin	
Ne	13:26	**d.** outlandish women cause to sin.	
Es	1:8	none **d.** compel: for so the king	
Es	1:21	king **d.** according to the word of	6213
Es	2:4	pleased the king; and he **d.** so.	6213
Es	2:11	to know how Esther **d.**, and what	7965
Es	2:20	for Esther **d.** the commandment	6213
Es	3:1	things **d.** king Ahasuerus promote	
Es	3:2, 5	bowed not, nor **d.** him reverence,	
Es	4:17	**d.** according to all that Esther	6213
Es	5:12	Esther the Queen **d.** let no man	
Es	8:1	that day **d.** the king Ahasuerus give	
Es	9:5	and **d.** what they would unto those	6213
Job	1:5	Thus **d.** Job continually.	6213
Job	2:10	In all this **d.** not Job sin with his lips.	
Job	3:11	why **d.** I not give up the ghost	
Job	3:12	Why **d.** the knees prevent me?	
Job	6:22	**D.** I say, Bring unto me?	
Job	28:27	Then **d.** he see it, and declare it;	
Job	30:25	**D.** not I weep for him that was in	
Job	31:13	If I **d.** despise the cause of my	
Job	31:15	**D.** not he that made me in the	
Job	31:15	**d.** not one fashion us in the womb?	
Job	31:32	The stranger **d.** not lodge in the	
Job	31:34	**D.** I fear a great multitude,	
Job	31:34	or **d.** the contempt of families	
Job	42:9	and **d.** according as the Lord	6213
Job	42:11	and **d.** eat bread with him in his	
Ps	14:2	if there any that **d.** understand,	
Ps	18:10	upon a cherub, and **d.** fly: yea,	
Ps	18:10	he **d.** fly upon the wings of the	
Ps	18:22	I **d.** not put away his statutes	
Ps	18:36	that my feet **d.** not slip.	
Ps	18:37	neither **d.** I turn again till they	
Ps	18:42	Then **d.** I beat them small as the dust	
Ps	18:42	I **d.** cast them out as the dirt in the	
Ps	31:11	they that **d.** see me without fled	
Ps	35:11	False witnesses **d.** rise up;	
Ps	35:15	they **d.** tear me, and ceased not:	
Ps	41:9	which **d.** eat of my bread,	
Ps	44:3	neither **d.** their own arm save them:	
Ps	45:9	upon the right hand **d.** stand the	
Ps	51:5	and in sin **d.** my mother conceive me.	
Ps	53:2	there were any that **d.** understand,	
Ps	53:2	that **d.** seek God.	
Ps	55:12	that **d.** magnify himself against me;	
Ps	66:6	there **d.** we rejoice in him.	
Ps	68:12	Kings of armies **d.** flee apace:	
Ps	78:12	Marvellous things **d.** he in the	6213
Ps	78:25	Man **d.** eat angel's food:	
Ps	78:29	so they **d.** eat, and were well filled:	
Ps	78:33	their days **d.** he consume in vanity.	
Ps	78:36	Nevertheless they **d.** flatter him	
Ps	78:38	and **d.** not stir up all his wrath.	
Ps	78:40	How oft **d.** they provoke him	
Ps	102:19	from heaven **d.** the Lord behold the	
Ps	105:35	And **d.** eat up all the herbs in	
Ps	106:34	They **d.** not destroy the nations,	
Ps	106:43	Many times **d.** he deliver them;	
Ps	119:23	also **d.** sit and speak against	
Ps	119:23	but thy servant **d.** meditate in thy	
Ps	135:6	pleased, that **d.** he in heaven, and	6213
Ps	139:16	Thine eyes **d.** see my substance, yet	
Ps	142:1	unto the Lord **d.** I make my	
Pr	1:29	and **d.** not choose the fear of the	
Isa	5:25	and the hills **d.** tremble,	
Isa	6:2	and with twain he **d.** fly.	
Isa	9:1	afterward **d.** more grievously	
Isa	10:10	and whose graven images **d.** excel	
Isa	13:1	which Isaiah the son of Amoz **d.** see.	
Isa	14:16	that **d.** shake kingdoms;	
Isa	20:2	And he **d.** so, walking naked and	6213
Isa	22:12	that day **d.** the Lord God of hosts call	
Isa	38:14	or a swallow, so **d.** I chatter:	
Isa	38:14	I **d.** mourn as a dove:	
Isa	42:24	**d.** not the Lord, he against whom	
Isa	48:3	I **d.** them suddenly, and they came	6213
Isa	53:4	yet we **d.** esteem him stricken	
Isa	58:2	as a nation that **d.** righteousness,	6213
Isa	65:12	when I called, ye **d.** not answer;	
Isa	65:12	when I spake, ye **d.** not hear:	
Isa	65:12	**d.** evil before mine eyes, and **d.**	6213
Isa	66:4	when I called, none **d.** answer;	
Isa	66:4	when I spake, they **d.** not hear:	
Isa	66:4	but they **d.** evil before mine eyes,	6213
Jer	7:12	and see what I **d.** to it for the	6213
Jer	7:26	they **d.** worse than their fathers.	
Jer	11:8	but they **d.** them not.	6213
Jer	14:6	the wild asses **d.** stand in the high	
Jer	14:6	their eyes **d.** fail,	
Jer	15:4	for that which he **d.** in Jerusalem.	6213
Jer	15:16	and I **d.** eat them;	
Jer	22:15	**d.** not thy father eat and drink,	
Jer	26:19	**D.** Hezekiah king of Judah...put him	
Jer	26:19	**d.** he not fear the Lord,	
Jer	31:19	I **d.** bear the reproach of my youth.	
Jer	36:8	the son of Neriah **d.** according to	6213
Jer	37:2	**d.** hearken unto the words of the	
Jer	38:12	the cords. And Jeremiah **d.** so,	6213
Jer	41:1	and there they **d.** eat bread together in	
Jer	44:19	**d.** we make her cakes to worship	
Jer	44:21	**d.** not the Lord remember them,	
Jer	46:15	because the Lord **d.** drive them.	
Jer	46:17	They **d.** cry there, Pharaoh king	
Jer	46:21	they **d.** not stand, because the day	
Jer	52:2	And he **d.** that which was evil in	6213
Jer	52:21	fillet of twelve cubits **d.** compass it;	
Jer	52:33	and he **d.** continually eat bread	
La	1:7	and none **d.** help her:	
La	1:7	and **d.** mock at her sabbaths.	
La	4:5	They that **d.** feed delicately are	
Eze	3:3	Then **d.** I eat it; and it was in	
Eze	6:13	the place where they **d.** offer sweet	
Eze	11:22	Then **d.** the cherubims lift up their	
Eze	12:7	And I **d.** so as I was commanded:	6213
Eze	16:49	neither **d.** she strengthen the hand	
Eze	17:7	this vine **d.** bend her roots toward	
Eze	18:18	and **d.** that which is not good	6213
Eze	20:8	they **d.** not every man cast away	
Eze	20:8	neither **d.** they forsake the idols of	
Eze	20:17	neither **d.** I make an end of them	

Eze 24:18 I **d.** in the morning as I was 6213
Eze 27:25 ships of Tarshish **d.** sing of thee,
Eze 31:6 branches **d.** all the beasts...bring
Eze 34:6 and none **d.** search or seek after
Eze 34:8 neither **d.** my shepherds search for
Eze 43:22 as they **d.** cleanse it with the
Eze 46:12 as he **d.** on the sabbath day: 6213
Da 1:15 children which **d.** eat the portion of
Da 3:24 **D.** not we cast three men bound
Da 4:7 but they **d.** not make known unto
Da 4:33 and **d.** eat grass as oxen,
Da 6:10 as he **d.** aforetime. 5648
Da 7:9 and the Ancient of days **d.** sit,
Da 8:4 but he **d.** according to his will, 6213
Da 8:27 I rose up, and **d.** the king's 6213
Da 10:3 neither **d.** I anoint myself at all,
Ho 2:8 For she **d.** not know that I gave her
Ho 9:17 because they **d.** not hearken unto
Ho 10:9 of iniquity **d.** not overtake them.
Ho 13:5 I **d.** know thee in the wilderness,
Am 1:11 because he **d.** pursue his brother
Am 1:11 and **d.** cast off all pity,
Am 1:11 and his anger **d.** tear perpetually,
Am 5:19 As if a man **d.** flee from a lion.
Am 7:4 and **d.** eat up a part
Ob 14 to cut off those of his that **d.** escape;
Ob 14 those of his that **d.** remain in the
Jon 3:10 do unto them: and he **d.** it not 6213
Jon 4:8 when the sun **d.** arise,
Na 2:12 The lion **d.** tear in pieces enough
Hab 1:1 which Habakkuk the prophet **d.** see.
Hab 3:6 the perpetual hills **d.** bow:
Hab 3:7 of the land of Midian **d.** tremble.
Hag 1:9 I **d.** blow upon it.
Hag 1:12 the people **d.** fear before the Lord.
Hag 1:14 they came and **d.** work in the 6213
Zec 1:4 but they **d.** not hear,
Zec 1:6 **d.** they not take hold of your
Zec 1:21 so that no man **d.** lift up his head:
Zec 7:5 seventy years **d.** ye at all fast
Zec 7:6 when ye **d.** eat, and when ye **d.** drink,
Zec 7:6 **d.** not ye eat for yourselves,
Zec 9:3 Tyrus **d.** build herself a stronghold,
Mal 2:6 and **d.** turn many away from
Mal 2:15 And **d.** not he make one?
Mt 1:24 being raised from sleep **d.** as *4160*
Mt 2:22 that Archelaus **d.** reign in Judaea
Mt 9:19 and so **d.** his disciples.
Mt 12:3 **Have ye not read what David d.** *4160*
Mt 12:4 **and d. eat the shewbread,**
Mt 13:58 And he **d.** not many mighty works *4160*
Mt 14:20 And they **d.** all eat, and were filled:
Mt 15:7 **well d. Esaias prophesy of you,**
Mt 15:37 And they **d.** all eat, and were filled:
Mt 15:38 they that **d.** eat were four thousand
Mt 17:2 and his face **d.** shine as the sun,
Mt 19:7 Why **d.** Moses then command to give
Mt 20:5 **and ninth hour, and d. likewise.** *4160*
Mt 21:6 went and **d.** as Jesus commanded *4160*
Mt 21:15 the wonderful things that he **d.**, *4160*
Mt 21:25 Why **d.** ye not then believe him?
Mt 21:31 **twain d. the will of his father?** *4160*
Mt 21:36 **and they d. unto them likewise** *4160*
Mt 21:42 **D. ye never read in the scriptures,**
Mt 25:44 **and d. not minister unto thee?**
Mt 25:45 **as ye d. it not to one of the least** *4160*
Mt 25:45 **of these, ye d. it not to me** *4160*
Mt 26:12 **on my body, she d. it for my** *4160*
Mt 26:19 disciples **d.** as Jesus had appointed *4160*
Mt 26:21 And as they **d.** eat, he said,
Mt 26:67 Then **d.** they spit in his face,
Mt 27:9 of the children of Israel **d.** value;
Mt 27:35 upon my vesture **d.** they cast lots,
Mt 27:51 and the earth **d.** quake,
Mt 28:4 for fear of him the keepers **d.** shake,
Mt 28:8 **d.** run to bring his disciples word.
Mt 28:15 money and **d.** as they were taught 4160
Mk 1:4 John **d.** baptize in the wilderness,
Mk 1:6 he **d.** eat locusts and wild honey;
Mk 1:32 And at even, when the sun **d.** set,
Mk 2:25 **read what David d., when he had** *4160*
Mk 2:26 **and d. eat the shrewbread,**
Mk 3:8 great things he **d.**, came unto him. *4160*
Mk 4:8 **and d. yield fruit that sprang up**
Mk 5:20 and all men **d.** marvel.
Mk 6:20 he **d.** many things, and heard *4160*
Mk 6:42 And they **d.** all eat, and were filled.
Mk 6:44 they that **d.** eat of the loaves were
Mk 8:6 **d.** set them before the people.
Mk 8:8 So they **d.** eat, and were filled:
Mk 10:3 **What d. Moses command you?**
Mk 11:31 Why then **d.** ye not believe him?
Mk 12:44 **they d. cast in of their abundance;**
Mk 12:44 **of her want d. cast in all that she had,**
Mk 14:18 and as they sat and **d.** eat;
Mk 14:22 as they **d.** eat, Jesus took bread,
Mk 14:59 neither so **d.** their witness agree
Mk 14:65 the servants **d.** strike him with
Mk 15:19 and **d.** spit upon him,
Lu 4:2 and in those days he **d.** eat nothing:
Lu 6:1 and **d.** eat, rubbing them in their
Lu 6:3 **what David d., when himself was** 4160
Lu 6:4 **and d. take and eat the shewbread,**
Lu 6:10 and he **d.** so: and his hand was *4160*
Lu 6:23 **the like manner d. their fathers** *4160*
Lu 6:26 **for so d. their fathers to the false** *4160*
Lu 6:49 **the stream d. beat vehemently,**
Lu 7:38 and **d.** wipe them with the hairs of
Lu 9:15 And they **d.** so, and made them all *4160*
Lu 9:17 And they **d.** eat, and were all filled:
Lu 9:43 at all things which Jesus **d.**, he *4160*
Lu 9:53 And they **d.** not receive him,
Lu 9:54 consume them, even as Elias did? *4160*
Lu 11:40 **d. not he that made that which is**
Lu 12:47 **neither d. according to his will,** *4160*
Lu 12:48 **d. commit things worthy of stripes,**
Lu 15:16 **with the husks that the swine d. eat:**
Lu 17:9 **because he d. things that were** *4160*
Lu 17:27, **28 They d. eat, they drank,**
Lu 19:22 **and reaping that I d. not sow:**
Lu 24:32 **D.** not our heart burn within us,
Lu 24:43 and **d.** eat before them.
Joh 1:45 the law, and the prophets, **d.** write,
Joh 2:11 of miracles **d.** Jesus, in Cana of *4160*
Joh 2:23 they saw the miracles which he **d.** *4160*
Joh 2:24 But Jesus **d.** not commit himself
Joh 4:29 all things that ever I **d.**: is not *4160*
Joh 4:39 He told me all that ever I **d.** *4160*
Joh 4:45 the things that he **d.** at Jerusalem *4160*
Joh 4:54 miracle that Jesus **d.**, when he was *4160*
Joh 5:16 therefore **d.** the Jews persecute Jesus,
Joh 6:2 which he **d.** on them that were *4160*
Joh 6:14 miracle that Jesus **d.**, said, This *4160*
Joh 6:23 where they **d.** eat bread.
Joh 6:26 **but because ye d. eat of the loaves,**
Joh 6:31 fathers **d.** eat manna in the desert;
Joh 6:49 **your fathers d. eat manna in the**
Joh 6:58 **not as your fathers d. eat manna,**
Joh 7:5 For neither **d.** his brethren believe
Joh 7:19 **D. not Moses give you the law,**
Joh 8:40 **of God: this d. not Abraham,** *4160*
Joh 9:2 Master, who **d.** sin, this man, or his
Joh 9:18 But the Jews **d.** not believe
Joh 9:22 man **d.** confess that he was Christ,
Joh 9:26 What **d.** he to thee? how opened *4160*
Joh 9:27 and ye **d.** not hear:
Joh 10:8 **but the sheep d. not hear them**
Joh 10:41 John **d.** no miracle: but all things *4160*
Joh 11:45 seen the things which Jesus **d.**, *4160*
Joh 12:36 and **d.** hide himself from them.
Joh 12:42 the Pharisees they **d.** not confess him,
Joh 15:24 **which none other man d., they** *4160*
Joh 18:15 followed Jesus, and so **d.** another
Joh 18:26 **D.** not I see thee in the garden with
Joh 18:34 **or d. others tell it thee of me?**
Joh 19:24 for my vesture they **d.** cast lots.
Joh 19:24 things therefore the soldiers **d.** *4160*
Joh 20:4 other disciples **d.** outrun Peter
Joh 20:30 other signs truly **d.** Jesus in *4160*
Joh 21:7 and **d.** cast himself into the sea.
Joh 21:25 many other things which Jesus **d.**, *4160*
Ac 2:22 which God **d.** by him in the midst *4160*
Ac 2:26 Therefore **d.** my heart rejoice,
Ac 2:31 neither his flesh **d.** see corruption.
Ac 2:40 many other words **d.** he testify
Ac 2:46 **d.** eat their meat with gladness and
Ac 3:17 through ignorance ye **d.** it, *4238*
Ac 3:17 as **d.** also your rulers.
Ac 4:25 Why **d.** the heathen rage, and the
Ac 5:28 **D.** not we straitly command you
Ac 6:8 faith and power, **d.** great wonders *4160*
Ac 7:27 that **d.** his neighbour wrong thrust *91*
Ac 7:35 the same **d.** God send to be a ruler
Ac 7:51 as your fathers **d.**, so do ye.
Ac 8:6 seeing the miracles which he **d.** *4160*
Ac 9:9 and neither **d.** eat nor drink.
Ac 9:36 works and almsdeeds which she **d.** *4160*
Ac 10:39 of all things which he **d.** both in *4160*
Ac 10:41 who **d.** eat and drink with him after
Ac 11:17 God gave them the like gift as he **d.**
Ac 11:30 Which also they **d.**, and sent it to *4160*
Ac 12:8 bind on thy sandels, so he **d.** *4160*
Ac 14:17 in that he **d.** good, and gave us rain *15*
Ac 15:8 Holy Ghost, even as he **d.** unto us;
Ac 15:14 God at the first **d.** visit the Gentiles
Ac 16:18 And this **d.** she many days. But *4160*
Ac 19:14 and chief of the priests which **d.** so. *4160*
Ac 21:9 virgins, which **d.** prophesy.
Ac 26:10 the saints **d.** I shut up in prison,
Ac 26:10 thing I also **d.** in Jerusalem: *4160*
Ac 26:22 and Moses **d.** say should come:
Ro 1:26 even their women **d.** change the
Ro 1:28 even as they **d.** not like to retain
Ro 3:3 For what if some **d.** not believe?
Ro 5:20 grace **d.** much more abound:
Ro 7:5 **d.** work in our members to bring
Ro 8:29 For whom he **d.** foreknow,
Ro 8:29 **d.** predestinate to be conformed
Ro 8:30 whom he **d.** predestinate,
Ro 10:19 **D.** not Israel know?
1Co 4:8 and I would to God ye **d.** reign,
1Co 10:3 **d.** all eat the same spiritual meat;
1Co 10:4 **d.** all drink the same spiritual drink:
1Co 15:27 which **d.** put all things under him.
2Co 1:17 **d.** I use lightness?
2Co 2:9 For to this end also **d.** I write,
2Co 5:20 as thou God **d.** beseech you
2Co 7:8 though I **d.** repent:
2Co 7:12 I **d.** it not for his cause that had
2Co 8:5 this they **d.**, not as we hoped,
2Co 12:16 But be it so, I **d.** not burden you:
2Co 12:17 **D.** I make a gain of you by any of
2Co 12:18 **D.** Titus make a gain of you?
Ga 2:12 he **d.** eat with the Gentiles:
Ga 4:8 ye **d.** service unto them which
Ga 5:7 Ye **d.** run well: who
Ga 5:7 who **d.** hinder you that ye should not
Php 4:14 **d.** communicate with my affliction.
2Th 3:8 Neither **d.** we eat any man's bread
1Ti 1:13 because I **d.** it ignorantly in
2Ti 4:14 Alexander the coppersmith **d.** me *1731*
Heb 3:16 when they had heard, **d.** provoke:
Heb 4:2 word preached **d.** not profit them:
Heb 4:4 God **d.** rest the seventh day from
Heb 4:10 his own works, as God **d.** from his.
Heb 7:19 bringing in of a better hope **d.**
Heb 7:27 for this he **d.** once, when he offered *4160*
Heb 9:9 him that **d.** the service perfect, *3000*
1Pe 1:11 Christ which was in them **d.** signify.
1Pe 1:12 unto us they **d.** minister the things,
1Pe 2:22 Who **d.** no sin, neither was guile *4160*
Re 12:4 and **d.** cast them to the earth:
Re 13:14 the wound by a sword, and **d.** live.
Re 19:2 which **d.** corrupt the earth with her
Re 21:33 for the glory of God **d.** lighten it,

DIDDEST See also DIDST.
Ac 7:28 thou **d.** the Egyptian yesterday? *337*

DIDST See also DIDDEST.
Ge 12:18 Why **d.** thou not tell me that
Ge 18:15 Nay; but thou **d.** laugh.
Ge 20:6 I know that thou **d.** this in the 6213
Ge 21:26 neither **d.** thou tell me,
Ge 31:27 Wherefore **d.** thou flee away
Ge 31:27 and **d.** not tell me,
Ge 31:39 of my hand **d.** thou require it,
Ex 15:10 Thou **d.** bow with thy wind,
Ex 40:15 as thou **d.** anoint their father,
Nu 21:34 do to him as thou **d.** unto Sihon 6213
De 3:2 as thou **d.** unto Sihon king of 6213
De 9:7 from the day that thou **d.** depart
De 32:14 and thou **d.** drink the pure
De 33:8 whom thou **d.** prove at Massah,
De 33:8 and with whom thou **d.** strive
Jos 2:18 window which thou **d.** let us down by:
Jos 8:2 thou **d.** unto Jericho and her king: 6213
Jg 12:1 and **d.** not call us to go with thee? we
Jg 13:8 man of God which thou **d.** send come
1Sa 3:6, 8 Here am I; for thou **d.** call me.
1Sa 15:19 Wherefore **d.** thou not obey the
1Sa 15:19 but **d.** fly upon the spoil,

1Sa 15:19 and **d.** evil in the sight of the ... 6213
1Sa 19:5 thou sawest it, and **d.** rejoice: ...
1Sa 20:19 the place where thou **d.** hide thyself ...
1Sa 25:25 of my lord, whom thou **d.** send ...
2Sa 11:10 Why then **d.** thou not go down ...
2Sa 12:12 For thou **d.** it secretly: but I will ... 6213
2Sa 12:21 thou **d.** fast and weep for the child, ...
2Sa 12:21 thou **d.** rise and eat bread ...
2Sa 13:16 the other that thou **d.** unto me. ... 6213
2Sa 18:11 and why **d.** thou not smite him ...
2Sa 19:28 yet **d.** thou set thy servant among ...
1Ki 1:13 **D.** not thou, my lord, O king, swear ...
1Ki 2:44 that thou **d.** to David my father: ... 6213
1Ki 8:18 thou **d.** well that it was in thine ...
1Ki 8:53 For thou **d.** separate them from among ...
1Ki 20:9 All that thou **d.** send for to thy ...
1Ki 21:10 Thou **d.** blaspheme God and the king. ...
1Ch 17:22 For thy people Israel **d.** thou make ...
2Ch 2:3 As thou **d.** deal with David my father. ...
2Ch 2:3 and **d.** send him cedars to build him ...
2Ch 6:8 **d.** well in that it was in thine heart: ...
2Ch 16:8 because thou **d.** rely on the Lord, ...
2Ch 20:7 who **d.** drive out the inhabitants ...
2Ch 34:27 thou **d.** humble thyself before God ...
2Ch 34:27 and **d.** rend thy clothes, and weep ...
Ne 9:7 the God, who **d.** choose Abram, ...
Ne 9:9 and **d.** see the affliction of our ...
Ne 9:10 So **d.** thou get thee a name, as it is ...
Ne 9:11 And thou **d.** divide the sea before them ...
Ne 9:17 wonder that thou **d.** among them; ... 6213
Ne 9:21 forty years **d.** thou sustain them in the ...
Ne 9:22 and **d.** divide them into corners: ...
Ne 9:28 and many times **d.** thou deliver them ...
Ne 9:30 Yet many years **d.** thou forbear them ...
Ne 9:31 thou **d.** not utterly consume them, ...
Ne 9:34 wherewith thou **d.** testify against ...
Ps 22:4 they trusted, and thou **d.** deliver them. ...
Ps 22:9 thou **d.** make me hope when I was upon ...
Ps 30:7 thou **d.** hide thy face, and I was ...
Ps 39:9 not my mouth; because thou **d.** it ... 6213
Ps 40:6 and offering thou **d.** not desire; ...
Ps 44:1 what work thou **d.** in their days, ... 6466
Ps 44:2 how thou **d.** drive out the heathen ...
Ps 44:2 how thou **d.** afflict the people, ...
Ps 60:10 **d.** not go out with our armies? ...
Ps 68:7 thou **d.** march through the wilderness: ...
Ps 68:9 Thou, O God, **d.** send a plentiful rain, ...
Ps 68:9 thou **d.** confine thine inheritance, ...
Ps 73:18 **d.** set them in slippery places: ...
Ps 74:13 Thou **d.** divide the sea by thy strength; ...
Ps 74:15 Thou **d.** cleave the fountain and the ...
Ps 76:8 Thou **d.** cause judgment to be heard ...
Ps 80:9 and **d.** cause it to take deep root, ...
Isa 14:12 which **d.** weaken the nations! ...
Isa 22:8 and thou **d.** look in that day to the ...
Isa 47:6 thou **d.** shew them no mercy; ...
Isa 47:7 so that thou **d.** not lay these things to ...
Isa 47:7 **d.** remember the latter end of it ...
Isa 48:6 and thou **d.** not know them. ...
Isa 54:1 barren, thou that **d.** not bear; ...
Isa 54:1 thou that **d.** not travail with child: ...
Isa 57:9 and **d.** increase thy perfumes, ...
Isa 57:9 and **d.** send thy messengers far off, ...
Isa 57:9 and **d.** debase thyself even unto hell. ...
Isa 63:14 so **d.** thou lead thy people, ...
Isa 64:3 When thou **d.** terrible things ... 6213
Jer 32:22 which thou **d.** swear to their fathers ...
Jer 36:17 How **d.** thou write all these words ...
Jer 45:3 Thou **d.** say, Woe is me now! ...
La 1:10 thou **d.** command that they should ...
Eze 16:13 thou **d.** eat fine flour, and honey, ...
Eze 16:13 and thou **d.** prosper into a kingdom ...
Eze 16:15 But thou **d.** trust in thine own beauty, ...
Eze 16:16 And of thy garments thou **d.** take, and ...
Eze 16:17 and **d.** commit whoredom with them, ...
Eze 16:36 which thou **d.** give unto them; ...
Eze 23:40 for whom thou **d.** wash thyself, ...
Eze 27:33 **d.** enrich the kings of the earth with ...
Eze 29:7 thou **d.** break, and rend all their ...
Eze 35:15 As thou **d.** rejoice at the inheritance ...
Da 10:12 **d.** set thine heart to understand, ...
Ho 10:13 because thou **d.** trust in thy way, ...
Hab 3:8 that thou **d.** ride upon thine horses ...
Hab 3:9 Thou **d.** cleave the earth with rivers. ...
Hab 3:12 Thou **d.** march through the land in ...
Hab 3:12 thou **d.** thresh the heathen in anger ...
Hab 3:14 Thou **d.** strike through with his slaves ...
Hab 3:15 Thou **d.** walk through the sea with ...
Mt 13:27 **d. not thou sow good seed in thy** ...
Mt 14:31 **wherefore d. thou doubt?**
Mt 20:13 **d. not thou agree with me for a penny?**
Lu 7:46 **My head with oil thou d. not anoint.** ...
Lu 19:21 **and reapest that thou d. not sow.** ...
Joh 17:8 **believed that thou d. send me.** ...
Ac 11:3 uncircumcised, and **d.** eat with them. ...
1Co 4:7 hast thou that thou **d.** not receive? ...
1Co 4:7 now if thou **d.** receive it, why dost thou ...
Heb 2:7 and **d.** set him over the works of thy ...
Re 17:7 Wherefore **d.** thou marvel? ...

DIDYMUS (did'-i-mus) See also THOMAS.
Joh 11:16 said Thomas, which is called **D.**, ... *1324*
Joh 20:24 one of the twelve, called **D.**, ... *1324*
Joh 21:2 Simon Peter, and Thomas called **D.**, ... *1324*

DIE See also DEAD; DIED; DIETH; DYING.
Ge 2:17 eatest thereof thou shalt surely **d.** ... 4191
Ge 3:3 neither shall ye touch it, lest ye **d.** ... 4191
Ge 3:4 the woman, Ye shall not surely **d.**: ... 4191
Ge 6:17 thing that is in the earth shall **d.** ... 1478
Ge 19:19 lest some evil take me, and I **d.**: ... 4191
Ge 20:7 thou shalt surely **d.**, thou, and all ... 4191
Ge 25:32 Behold, I am at the point to **d.**: ... 4191
Ge 26:9 Because I said, Lest I **d.** for her. ... 4191
Ge 27:4 my soul bless thee before I **d.** ... 4191
Ge 30:1 Give me children, or else I **d.** ... 4191
Ge 33:13 them one day, all the flock will **d.** ... 4191
Ge 38:11 Lest peradventure he **d.** also, as ... 4191
Ge 42:2 thence; that we may live, and not **d.** ... 4191
Ge 42:20 be verified, and ye shall not **d.** ... 4191
Ge 43:8 go; that we may live, and not **d.**, ... 4191
Ge 44:9 it be found, both let him **d.**, and we ... 4191
Ge 44:22 leave his father, his father would **d.** ... 4191
Ge 44:31 lad is not with us, that he will **d.**: ... 4191
Ge 45:28 I will go and see him before I **d.** ... 4191
Ge 46:30 Now let me **d.**, since I have seen ... 4191
Ge 47:15 why should we **d.** in thy presence? ... 4191
Ge 47:19 Wherefore shall we **d.** before thine ... 4191
Ge 47:19 seed, that we may live, and not **d.**, ... 4191
Ge 47:29 time drew nigh that Israel must **d.**: ... 4191
Ge 48:21 said unto Joseph, Behold, I **d.**: ... 4191
Ge 50:5 made me swear, saying, Lo, I **d.**: ... 4191
Ge 50:24 Joseph said unto his brethren, I **d.**: ... 4191
Ex 7:18 the fish that is in the river shall **d.**, ... 4191
Ex 9:4 there shall nothing **d.** of all that is ... 4191
Ex 9:19 down upon them, and they shall **d.** ... 4191
Ex 10:28 thou seest my face thou shalt **d.** ... 4191
Ex 11:5 in the land of Egypt shall **d.**, ... 4191
Ex 14:11 us away to **d.** in the wilderness? ... 4191
Ex 14:12 that we should **d.** in the wilderness. ... 4191
Ex 20:19 not God speak with us, lest we **d.** ... 4191
Ex 21:12 that smiteth a man, so that he **d.**, ... 4191
Ex 21:14 from mine altar, that he may **d.** ... 4191
Ex 21:18 or with his fist, and he **d.** not, ... 4191
Ex 21:20 a rod, and he **d.** under his hand; ... 4191
Ex 21:28 a man or a woman, that they **d.**: ... 4191
Ex 21:35 man's ox hurt another's, that he **d.**; ... 4191
Ex 22:2 up, and be smitten that he **d.**, ... 4191
Ex 22:10 it **d.**, or be hurt, or driven away, ... 4191
Ex 22:14 and it be hurt, or **d.**, the owner ... 4191
Ex 28:35 he cometh out, that he **d.** not. ... 4191
Ex 28:43 that they bear not iniquity, and **d.**: ... 4191
Ex 30:20 wash with water that they **d.** not; ... 4191
Ex 30:21 and their feet, that they **d.** not: ... 4191
Le 8:35 charge of the Lord, that ye **d.** not; ... 4191
Le 10:6 rend your clothes, lest ye **d.**, ... 4191
Le 10:7 of the congregation, lest ye **d.**: ... 4191
Le 10:9 of the congregation, lest ye **d.**: ... 4191
Le 11:39 any beast of which ye may eat, **d.**; ... 4191
Le 15:31 they **d.** not in their uncleanness, ... 4191
Le 16:2 is upon the ark; that he **d.** not: ... 4191
Le 16:13 the testimony, that he **d.** not: ... 4191
Le 20:20 their sin: they shall **d.** childless. ... 4191
Le 22:9 lest they bear sin for it, and **d.** ... 4191
Nu 4:15 touch any holy thing, lest they **d.**, ... 4191
Nu 4:19 that they may live, and not **d.**, ... 4191
Nu 4:20 holy things are covered, lest they **d.** ... 4191
Nu 6:7 or for his sister, when they **d.**: ... 4194
Nu 6:9 any man **d.** very suddenly by him, ... 4191
Nu 14:35 consumed, and there they shall **d.** ... 4191
Nu 16:29 If these men **d.** the common death ... 4191
Nu 17:10 from me, that they **d.** not. ... 4191
Nu 17:12 saying, Behold we **d.**, we perish, ... 1478
Nu 17:13 tabernacle of the Lord shall **d.**: ... 4191
Nu 18:3 that neither they, nor ye also, **d.** ... 4191
Nu 18:22 lest they bear sin, and **d.** ... 4191
Nu 18:32 the children of Israel, lest ye **d.** ... 4191
Nu 20:4 that we and our cattle should **d.** ... 4191
Nu 20:26 unto his people, and shall **d.** there, ... 4191
Nu 21:5 of Egypt to **d.** in the wilderness? ... 4191
Nu 23:10 me **d.** the death of the righteous, ... 4191
Nu 26:65 They shall surely **d.** in the ... 4191
Nu 27:8 If a man **d.**, and have no son, ... 4191
Nu 35:12 that the manslayer **d.** not, until he ... 4191
Nu 35:16 instrument of iron, so that he **d.**, ... 4191
Nu 35:17, 18 wherewith he may **d.**, and he **d.**, ... 4191
Nu 35:20 him by laying of wait, that he **d.**; ... 4191
Nu 35:21 him with his hand, that he **d.**: ... 4191
Nu 35:23 wherewith a man may **d.**, seeing ... 4191
Nu 35:23 cast it upon him, that he **d.**, ... 4191
Nu 35:30 any person to cause him to **d.** ... 4191
De 4:22 I must **d.** in this land, I must not ... 4191
De 5:25 Now therefore why should we **d.**? ... 4191
De 5:25 our God any more, then we shall **d.** ... 4191
De 13:10 stone him with stones, that he **d.**; ... 4191
De 17:5 stone them with stones, till they **d.** ... 4191
De 17:12 the judge, even that man shall **d.**: ... 4191
De 18:16 great fire any more that I **d.** not. ... 4191
De 18:20 gods, even that prophet shall **d.** ... 4191
De 19:5 upon his neighbour, that he **d.**; ... 4191
De 19:11 smite him mortally that he **d.**, ... 4191
De 19:12 avenger of blood, that he may **d.** ... 4191
De 20:5, 6, 7 lest he **d.** in the battle, and ... 4191
De 21:21 stone him with stones, that he **d.**: ... 4191
De 22:21 stone her with stones that she **d.**: ... 4191
De 22:22 then they shall both of them **d.**, ... 4191
De 22:24 stone them with stones that they **d.**; ... 4191
De 22:25 man only that lay with her shall **d.**: ... 4191
De 24:3 if the latter husband **d.**, which took ... 4191
De 24:7 that thief shall **d.**; and thou shalt ... 4191
De 25:5 dwell together, and one of them **d.**, ... 4191
De 31:14 days approach that thou must **d.**: ... 4191
De 32:50 And **d.** in the mount whither thou ... 4191
De 33:6 Let Reuben live, and not **d.**; and let ... 4191
Jos 20:9 not **d.** by the hand of the avenger ... 4191
Jg 6:23 thee; fear not: thou shalt not **d.** ... 4191
Jg 6:30 Bring out thy son, that he may **d.**: ... 4191
Jg 13:22 We shall surely **d.**, because we have ... 4191
Jg 15:18 and now shall I **d.** for thirst, and ... 4191
Jg 16:30 Let me **d.** with the Philistines. ... 4191
Ru 1:17 Where thou diest, will I **d.**, and ... 4191
1Sa 2:33 the increase of thine house shall **d.** ... 4191
1Sa 2:34 in one day they shall **d.** both of ... 4191
1Sa 12:19 the Lord thy God, that we **d.** not: ... 4191
1Sa 14:39 my son, he shall surely **d.** ... 4191
1Sa 14:43 in mine hand, and, lo, I must **d.** ... 4191
1Sa 14:44 for thou shalt surely **d.**, Jonathan. ... 4191
1Sa 14:45 Shall Jonathan **d.**, who hath ... 4191
1Sa 20:2 God forbid; thou shalt not **d.**: ... 4191
1Sa 20:14 kindness of the Lord, that I **d.** not: ... 4191
1Sa 20:31 unto me, for he shall surely **d.** ... 4191
1Sa 22:16 Thou shalt surely **d.**, Ahimelech, ... 4191
1Sa 26:10 his day shall come to **d.**; or he ... 4191
1Sa 26:16 ye are worthy to **d.**, because ye ... 4194
1Sa 28:9 for my life, to cause me to **d.**? ... 4191
2Sa 11:15 that he may be smitten, and **d.** ... 4191
2Sa 12:5 done this thing shall surely **d.**: ... 4194
2Sa 12:13 away thy sin; thou shalt not **d.** ... 4191
2Sa 12:14 is born unto thee shall surely **d.** ... 4191
2Sa 14:14 For we must needs **d.**, and are as ... 4191
2Sa 18:3 neither if half of us **d.**, will they ... 4191
2Sa 19:23 said unto Shimei, Thou shalt not **d.** ... 4191
2Sa 19:37 that I may **d.** in mine own city, ... 4191
1Ki 1:52 shall be found in him, he shall **d.** ... 4191
1Ki 2:1 David drew nigh that he should **d.**; ... 4191
1Ki 2:30 he said, Nay: but I will **d.** here. ... 4191
1Ki 2:37 certain that thou shalt surely **d.**: ... 4191
1Ki 2:42 whither, that thou shalt surely **d.**? ... 4191
1Ki 14:12 into the city, the child shall **d.** ... 4191
1Ki 17:12 that we may eat it, and **d.** ... 4191
1Ki 19:4 for himself that he might **d.**; ... 4191
1Ki 21:10 out, and stone him, that he may **d.** ... 4191
2Ki 1:4, 6, 16 gone up, but shalt surely **d.** ... 4191
2Ki 7:3 Why sit we here until we **d.**? ... 4191
2Ki 7:4 is in the city and we shall **d.** there: ... 4191
2Ki 7:4 and if we sit still here, we **d.** also. ... 4191
2Ki 7:4 and if they kill us, we shall but **d.** ... 4191
2Ki 8:10 showed me that he shall surely **d.** ... 4191
2Ki 18:32 that ye may live, and not **d.**: ... 4191
2Ki 20:1 for thou shalt **d.**, and not live. ... 4191
2Ch 25:4 The fathers shall not **d.** for the ... 4191
2Ch 25:4 neither shall the children **d.** for the ... 4191

2Ch 25:4 but every man shall **d.** for his own 4191
2Ch 32:11 to **d.** by famine and by thirst, ... 4191
Job 2:9 thine integrity? curse God, and **d.**. 4191
Job 4:21 they **d.**, even without wisdom 4191
Job 12:2 and wisdom shall **d.** with you 4191
Job 14:8 the stock thereof **d.** in the ground; 4191
Job 14:14 If a man **d.**, shall he live again? 4191
Job 27:5 that I should justify you: till I **d.** 1478
Job 29:18 Then I said, I shall **d.** in my nest, ... 1478
Job 34:20 In a moment shall they **d.**, and the 4191
Job 36:12 they shall **d.** without knowledge. 1478
Job 36:14 They **d.** in youth, and their life is 4191
Ps 41:5 When shall he **d.**, and his name 4191
Ps 49:10 For he seeth that wise men **d.**, ... 4191
Ps 79:11 those that are appointed to **d.**; 8546
Ps 82:7 But ye shall **d.** like men, and fall 4191
Ps 88:15 I am afflicted and ready to **d.** from 1478
Ps 104:29 they **d.**, and return to their dust. 1478
Ps 118:17 I shall not **d.**, but live, and declare 4191
Pr 5:23 He shall **d.** without instruction; 4191
Pr 10:21 but fools **d.** for want of wisdom. 4191
Pr 15:10 he that hateth reproof shall **d.**. 4191
Pr 19:16 he that despiseth his ways shall **d.** 4191
Pr 23:13 him with the rod, he shall not **d.**. 4191
Pr 30:7 deny me them not before I **d.** 4191
Ec 3:2 A time to be born, and a time to **d.**; 4191
Ec 7:17 why shouldest thou **d.** before thy 4191
Ec 9:5 the living know that they shall **d.**: 4191
Isa 22:13 drink; for to-morrow we shall **d.**. 4191
Isa 22:14 not be purged from you till ye **d.**, ... 4191
Isa 22:18 there shalt thou **d.**, and there the 4191
Isa 38:1 for thou shalt **d.**, and not live. 4191
Isa 51:6 they that dwell therein shall **d.** in 4191
Isa 51:12 be afraid of a man that shall **d.**. 4191
Isa 51:14 that he should not **d.** in the pit, ... 4191
Isa 65:20 the child shall **d.** an hundred years 4191
Isa 66:24 their worm shall not **d.**, neither 4191
Jer 11:21 Lord, that thou **d.** not by our hand: 4191
Jer 11:22 young men shall **d.** by the sword; 4191
Jer 11:22 sons and their daughters shall **d.**. 4191
Jer 16:4 They shall **d.** of grievous deaths; 4191
Jer 16:6 the great and the small shall **d.** in 4191
Jer 20:6 Babylon, and there thou shalt **d.**, ... 4191
Jer 21:6 they shall **d.** of a great pestilence. 4191
Jer 21:9 He that abideth in this city shall **d.** 4191
Jer 22:12 he shall **d.** in the place whither they ... 4191
Jer 22:26 not born; and there shall ye **d.**. 4191
Jer 26:8 him, saying, Thou shalt surely **d.**. 4191
Jer 26:11 This man is worthy to **d.**; for he 4194
Jer 26:16 This man is not worthy to **d.**: 4194
Jer 27:13 will ye **d.**, thou and thy people, ... 4191
Jer 28:16 this year thou shalt **d.**, because 4191
Jer 31:30 But every one shall **d.** for his own 4191
Jer 34:4 Thou shalt not **d.** by the sword: 4191
Jer 34:5 Thou shalt **d.** in peace: and with 4191
Jer 37:20 Jonathan the scribe, lest I **d.** there. 4191
Jer 38:2 that remaineth in this city shall **d.** 4191
Jer 38:9 and he is like to **d.** for hunger 4191
Jer 38:10 out of the dungeon, before he **d.** 4191
Jer 38:24 these words, and thou shalt not **d.**. 4191
Jer 38:26 to Jonathan's house, to **d.** there. 4191
Jer 42:16 in Egypt; and there ye shall **d.** 4191
Jer 42:17 they shall **d.** by the sword, by the 4191
Jer 42:22 know certainly that ye shall **d.** by 4191
Jer 44:12 they shall **d.**, from the least even 4191
Eze 3:18 Thou shalt surely **d.**; and thou 4191
Eze 3:18 the same wicked man shall **d.** in 4191
Eze 3:19 way, he shall **d.** in his iniquity; 4191
Eze 3:20 he shall **d.**: because thou hast not 4191
Eze 3:20 him warning, he shall **d.** in his sin, ... 4191
Eze 5:12 of thee shall **d.** with the pestilence, ... 4191
Eze 6:12 He that is far off shall **d.** of the 4191
Eze 6:12 remaineth and is besieged shall **d.** 4191
Eze 7:15 he that is in the field shall **d.** with 4191
Eze 12:13 not see it, though he shall **d.** there 4191
Eze 13:19 to slay the souls that should not **d.**, ... 4191
Eze 17:16 in the midst of Babylon he shall **d.** 4191
Eze 18:4 the soul that sinneth, it shall **d.** 4191
Eze 18:13 he shall surely **d.**; his blood shall 4191
Eze 18:17 he shall not **d.** for the iniquity of 4191
Eze 18:18 even he shall **d.** in his iniquity. 4191
Eze 18:20 The soul that sinneth, it shall **d.** 4191
Eze 18:21 he shall surely live, he shall not **d.**. 4191
Eze 18:23 at all that the wicked should **d.**? 4194
Eze 18:24 hath sinned, in them shall he **d.**. 4191
Eze 18:26 that he hath done shall he **d.** 4191
Eze 18:28 he shall surely live, he shall not **d.**. 4191
Eze 18:31 why will ye **d.**, O house of Israel? 4191
Eze 28:8 and thou shalt **d.** the deaths of them ... 4191
Eze 28:10 Thou shalt **d.** the deaths of the 4191
Eze 33:8 thou shalt surely **d.**; if thou dost 4191
Eze 33:8 his way, that wicked man shall **d.** 4191
Eze 33:9 his way he shall **d.** in his iniquity; 4191
Eze 33:11 why will ye **d.**, O house of Israel? 4191
Eze 33:13 hath committed, he shall **d.** for it. 4191
Eze 33:14 Thou shalt surely **d.**; if he turn 4191
Eze 33:15 he shall surely live, he shall not **d.**. 4191
Eze 33:18 iniquity, he shall even **d.** thereby 4191
Eze 33:27 the caves shall **d.** of the pestilence. 4191
Am 2:2 and Moab shall **d.** with tumult, ... 4191
Am 6:9 in one house, that they shall **d.** 4191
Am 7:11 Jeroboam shall **d.** by the sword, ... 4191
Am 7:17 thou shalt **d.** in a polluted land: 4191
Am 9:10 the sinners of my people shall **d.** 4191
Jon 4:3 is better for me to **d.** than to live. 4194
Jon 4:8 wished in himself to **d.**, and said, ... 4191
Jon 4:8 It is better for me to **d.** than to live. .. 4191
Hab 1:12 mine Holy One? we shall not **d.**. 4191
Zec 11:9 feed you: that that dieth, let it **d.**; 4191
Zec 13:8 therein shall be cut off and **d.**; 1478
Mt 15:4 **or mother, let him d. the death** *5053*
Mt 22:24 Master, Moses said, If a man **d.**, ... *599*
Mt 26:35 Though I should **d.** with thee, yet *599*
Mk 7:10 **let him d. the death: But ye say,** ... *5053*
Mk 12:19 If a man's brother **d.**, and leave *599*
Mk 14:31 If I should **d.** with thee, I will not *4880*
Lu 7:2 him, was sick, and ready to **d.** *5053*
Lu 20:28 If any man's brother **d.**, having a *599*
Lu 20:28 wife, and he **d.** without children, ... *599*
Lu 20:36 **Neither can they d. any more: for** ... *599*
Joh 4:49 Sir, come down ere my child **d.** *599*
Joh 6:50 **a man may eat thereof, and not d** *599*
Joh 8:21 **seek me, and shall d. in your sins:** .. *599*
Joh 8:24 **that ye shall d. in your sins: for if** .. *599*
Joh 8:24 **unto you ye shall d. in your sins** *599*
Joh 11:16 also go, that we may **d.** with him *599*
Joh 11:26 **and believeth in me shall never d** *599*
Joh 11:50 one man should **d.** for the people, ... *599*
Joh 11:51 that Jesus should **d.** for that nation; *599*
Joh 12:24 **wheat fall into the ground and d.,** .. *599*
Joh 12:24 **it abideth alone: but if it d., it** *599*
Joh 12:33 signifying what death he should **d.** *599*
Joh 18:14 one man should **d.** for the people *622*
Joh 18:32 signifying what death he should **d.** *599*
Joh 19:7 and by our law he ought to **d.**, ... *599*
Joh 21:23 that disciple should not **d.**: yet *599*
Joh 21:23 said not unto him, He shall not **d.**; *599*
Ac 21:13 also to **d.** at Jerusalem for the *599*
Ac 25:11 worthy of death, I refuse not to **d.** *599*
Ac 25:16 Romans to deliver any man to **d.**, ... *684*
Ro 5:7 for a righteous man will one **d.** *599*
Ro 5:7 man some would even dare to **d.** *599*
Ro 8:13 ye live after the flesh, ye shall **d.** *599*
Ro 14:8 whether we **d.**, we **d.** unto the Lord: ... *599*
Ro 14:8 therefore, or **d.**, we are the Lord's. *599*
1Co 9:15 better for me to **d.**, than that any *599*
1Co 15:22 For as in Adam all **d.**, even so *599*
1Co 15:31 in Christ Jesus our Lord, I **d.** daily *599*
1Co 15:32 eat and drink; for to morrow we **d.** *599*
1Co 15:36 is not quickened, except it **d.**: *599*
2Co 7:3 our hearts to **d.** and live with you. *4880*
Php 1:21 to live is Christ, and to **d.** is gain. *599*
Heb 7:8 here men that **d.** receive tithes; *599*
Heb 9:27 it is appointed unto men once to **d.**, ... *599*
Re 3:2 **which remain, that are ready to d** ... *599*
Re 9:6 not find it; and shall desire to **d.**, ... *599*
Re 14:13 are the dead which **d.** in the Lord *599*

DIED

Ge 5:5 and thirty years: and he **d.** 4191
Ge 5:8 and twelve years: and he **d.** 4191
Ge 5:11 hundred and five years: and he **d.** 4191
Ge 5:14 hundred and ten years: and he **d.** 4191
Ge 5:17 ninety and five years: and he **d.** 4191
Ge 5:20 sixty and two years: and he **d.** 4191
Ge 5:27 sixty and nine years: and he **d.** 4191
Ge 5:31 seventy and seven years: and he **d.** 4191
Ge 7:21 And all flesh **d.** that moved upon 1478
Ge 7:22 all that was in the dry land, **d.** 4191
Ge 9:29 hundred and fifty years: and he **d.** 4191
Ge 11:28 Haran **d.** before his father Terah 4191
Ge 11:32 five years: and Terah **d.** in Haran, ... 4191
Ge 23:2 And Sarah **d.** in Kirjath-arba; the 4191
Ge 25:8 **d.** in a good old age, an old man, ... 4191
Ge 25:17 and he gave up the ghost and **d.**; 4191
Ge 25:18 he **d.** in the presence of all his 5307
Ge 35:8 But Deborah Rebekah's nurse **d.**, ... 4191
Ge 35:18 soul was in departing, (for she **d.**) 4191
Ge 35:19 And Rachel **d.**, and was buried in 4191
Ge 35:29 Isaac gave up the ghost, and **d.**, ... 4191
Ge 36:33 And Bela **d.**, and Jobab the son of 4191
Ge 36:34 And Jobab **d.**, and Husham of the 4191
Ge 36:35 And Husham **d.**, and Hadad the son 4191
Ge 36:36 And Haddad **d.**, and Samlah of 4191
Ge 36:37 Samlah **d.**, and Saul of Rehoboth 4191
Ge 36:38 Saul **d.**, and Baal-hanan the son of 4191
Ge 36:39 Baal-hanan the son of Achbor **d.**, ... 4191
Ge 38:12 daughter of Shuah Judah's wife **d.**; 4191
Ge 46:12 and Onan **d.** in the land of Canaan. 4191
Ge 48:7 Rachel **d.** by me in the land of 4191
Ge 50:16 father did command before he **d.**, ... 4194
Ge 50:26 Joseph **d.**, being an hundred and 4191
Ex 1:6 Joseph **d.**, and all his brethren, ... 4191
Ex 2:23 of time that the king of Egypt **d.** 4191
Ex 7:21 the fish that was in the river **d.**; 4191
Ex 8:13 and the frogs **d.** out of the houses, ... 4191
Ex 9:6 and all the cattle of Egypt **d.** 4191
Ex 9:6 of the children of Israel **d.** not one. 4191
Ex 16:3 Would to God we had **d.** by the 4191
Le 10:2 them, and they **d.** before the Lord. 4191
Le 16:1 offered before the Lord, and **d.**; 4191
Le 17:15 soul that eateth that which **d.** of 5038
Nu 3:4 and Abihu **d.** before the Lord, ... 4191
Nu 14:2 we had **d.** in the land of Egypt! 4191
Nu 14:2 God we had **d.** in this wilderness! 4191
Nu 14:37 up the evil report upon the land, **d.** 4191
Nu 15:36 stoned him with stones, and he **d.**; 4191
Nu 16:49 they that **d.** in the plague were 4191
Nu 16:49 that **d.** about the matter of Korah 4191
Nu 20:1 Miriam **d.** there, and was buried 4191
Nu 20:3 Would God that we had **d.** when 1478
Nu 20:3 our brethren **d.** before the Lord! 1478
Nu 20:28 Aaron **d.** there in the top of the 4191
Nu 21:6 and much people of Israel **d.** 4191
Nu 25:9 those that **d.** in the plague were 4191
Nu 26:10 when that company **d.**, what time 4194
Nu 26:11 the children of Korah **d.** not 4191
Nu 26:19 and Onan **d.** in the land of Canaan. 4191
Nu 26:61 And Nadab and Abihu **d.**, when 4191
Nu 27:3 Our father **d.** in the wilderness, and 4191
Nu 27:3 **d.** in his own sin, and had no sons 4191
Nu 33:38 of the Lord, and **d.** there, ... 4191
Nu 33:39 old when he **d.** in mount Hor 4194
De 10:6 Aaron **d.**, and there he was buried; 4191
De 32:50 Aaron thy brother **d.** in mount Hor, ... 4191
De 34:5 Moses the servant of the Lord **d.** 4191
De 34:7 and twenty years old when he **d.** 4194
Jos 5:4 **d.** in the wilderness by the way, ... 4191
Jos 10:11 them unto Azekah, and they **d.** 4191
Jos 10:11 more which **d.** with hailstones than 4191
Jos 24:29 of Nun, the servant of the Lord, **d.** ... 4191
Jos 24:33 Eleazar the son of Aaron **d.**; and 4191
Jg 1:7 him to Jerusalem, and there he **d.** 4191
Jg 2:8 of Nun, the servant of the Lord, **d.**, ... 4191
Jg 2:21 which Joshua left when he **d.** 4191
Jg 3:11 And Othniel the son of Kenaz **d.** 4191
Jg 4:21 fast asleep and weary. So he **d.** 4191
Jg 8:32 And Gideon the son of Joash **d.** 4191
Jg 9:49 the men of the tower of Shechem **d.** ... 4191
Jg 9:54 man thrust him through, and he **d.** 4191
Jg 10:2 twenty and three years, and **d.**, ... 4191
Jg 10:5 And Jair **d.**, and was buried in 4191
Jg 12:7 Then **d.** Jephthah the Gileadite, and 4191
Jg 12:10 Then **d.** Ibzan, and was buried at 4191
Jg 12:12 And Elon the Zebulonite **d.**, and was ... 4191
Jg 12:15 son of Hillel the Pirathonite **d.**, ... 4191
Ru 1:3 Elimelech Naomi's husband **d.**; 4191
Ru 1:5 and Chilion **d.** also both of them; 4191
1Sa 4:18 and his neck brake, and he **d.** 4191
1Sa 5:12 the men that **d.** not were smitten 4191
1Sa 14:45 rescued Jonathan, that he **d.** not. 4191
1Sa 25:1 Samuel **d.**; and all the Israelites 4191
1Sa 25:37 that his heart **d.** within him, and he 4191
1Sa 25:38 the Lord smote Nabal, that he **d.** 4191
1Sa 31:5 upon his sword, and **d.** with him. 4191
1Sa 31:6 So Saul **d.**, and his three sons, ... 4191
2Sa 1:15 And he smote him that he **d.** 4191
2Sa 2:23 and **d.** in the same place: and it 4191
2Sa 2:23 Asahel fell down and **d.** stood still. 4191
2Sa 2:31 hundred and threescore men **d.** 4191
2Sa 3:27 under the fifth rib, that he **d.**, ... 4191

2Sa 3:33 said, D. Abner as a fool dieth? 4191
2Sa 6:7 and there he d. by the ark of God. 4191
2Sa 10:1 king of the children of Ammon d., 4191
2Sa 10:18 captain of their host, who d. there. 4191
2Sa 11:17 and Uriah the Hittite d. also. 4191
2Sa 11:21 the wall, that he d. in Thebez? 4191
2Sa 12:18 the seventh day, that the child d.. 4191
2Sa 17:23 and hanged himself, and d., and 4191
2Sa 18:33 would God I had d. for thee, 4191
2Sa 19:6 all we had d. this day, then it had 4191
2Sa 20:10 struck him not again; and he d. 4191
2Sa 24:15 there d. of the people from Dan 4191
1Ki 2:25 and he fell upon him that he d.. 4191
1Ki 2:46 and fell upon him, that he d.. 4191
1Ki 3:19 woman's child d. in the night; 4191
1Ki 12:18 stoned him with stones, that he d.. 4191
1Ki 14:17 threshold of the door, the child d.: 4191
1Ki 16:18 house over him with fire, and d., 4191
1Ki 16:22 so Tibni d., and Omri reigned. 4191
1Ki 21:13 stoned him with stones, that he d.. 4191
1Ki 22:35 against the Syrians, and d. at even: 4191
1Ki 22:37 So the king d., and was brought to 4191
2Ki 1:17 So he d. according to the word of 4191
2Ki 4:20 on her knees till noon, and then d.. 4191
2Ki 7:17 upon him in the gate, and he d., as 4191
2Ki 7:20 upon him in the gate, and he d.. 4191
2Ki 8:15 spread it on his face, so that he d.: 4191
2Ki 9:27 he fled to Megiddo, and d. there. 4191
2Ki 12:21 his servants, smote him, and he d.; 4191
2Ki 13:14 sick of his sickness whereof he d.. 4191
2Ki 13:20 And Elisha d., and they buried him. 4191
2Ki 13:24 So Hazael king of Syria d.; and 4191
2Ki 23:34 he came to Egypt, and d. there. 4191
2Ki 25:25 and smote Gedaliah, that he d., 4191
1Ch 1:51 Hadad d. also. And the dukes of 4191
1Ch 2:30 but Seled d. without children. 4191
1Ch 2:32 and Jether d. without children. 4191
1Ch 10:5 fell likewise on the sword, and d.. 4191
1Ch 10:6 So Saul d., and his three sons, 4191
1Ch 10:6 and all his house d. together. 4191
1Ch 10:13 So Saul d. for his transgression. 4191
1Ch 13:10 and there he d. before God. 4191
1Ch 19:1 king of the children of Ammon d., 4191
1Ch 23:22 And Eleazar d., and had no sons, 4191
1Ch 24:2 Nadab and Abihu d. before their 4191
1Ch 29:28 And he d. in a good old age, 4191
2Ch 10:18 stoned him with stones, that he d.. 4191
2Ch 13:20 the Lord struck him, and he d.. 4191
2Ch 16:13 and d. in the one and fortieth year 4191
2Ch 18:34 time of the sun going down he d.. 4191
2Ch 21:19 sickness: so he d. of sore diseases. 4191
2Ch 24:15 and was full of days when he d.; 4191
2Ch 24:15 years old was he when he d.. 4194
2Ch 24:22 And when he d., he said, The Lord 4191
2Ch 24:25 slew him on his bed, and he d.: 4191
2Ch 35:24 him to Jerusalem, and he d., 4191
Job 3:11 Why d. I not from the womb? 4191
Job 42:17 Job d., being old and full of days. 4191
Isa 6:1 In the year that king Uzziah d. 4194
Isa 14:28 In the year that king Ahaz d. 4194
Jer 28:17 So Hananiah the prophet d. the 4191
Eze 11:13 Pelatiah the son of Benaiah d.. 4191
Eze 24:18 and at even my wife d.; and I did 4191
Ho 13:1 when he offended in Baal, he d.. 4191
Mt 22:27 And last of all the woman d. also. *599*
Mk 12:21 the second took her, and d., neither *599*
Mk 12:22 seed: last of all the woman d. also. *599*
Lu 16:22 **it came to pass, that the beggar d.,** *599*
Lu 16:22 **rich man also d., and was buried;** *599*
Lu 20:29 a wife, and d. without children. *599*
Lu 20:30 her to wife, and he d. childless. *599*
Lu 20:31 and they left no children, and d.. *599*
Lu 20:32 Last of all the woman d. also. *599*
Joh 11:21, 32 here, my brother had not d.. *599*
Joh 11:37 even this man should not have d.? *599*
Ac 7:15 Egypt, and d., he, and our fathers, *5053*
Ac 9:37 days, that she was sick, and d.: *599*
Ro 5:6 time Christ d. for the ungodly. *599*
Ro 5:8 were yet sinners, Christ d. for us. *599*
Ro 6:10 in that he d., he d. unto sin once: *599*
Ro 7:9 came, sin revived, and I d.. *599*
Ro 8:34 It is Christ that d., yea rather, *599*
Ro 14:9 To this end Christ both d., and rose, *599*
Ro 14:15 with thy meat, for whom Christ d.. *599*
1Co 8:11 brother perish, for whom Christ d.? *599*
1Co 15:3 how that Christ d. for our sins *599*
2Co 5:14 one d. for all, then were all dead: *599*
2Co 5:15 that he d. for all, that they which *599*
2Co 5:15 but unto him which d. for them, *599*
1Th 4:14 that Jesus d. and rose again, even *599*
1Th 5:10 Who d. for us, that, whether we *599*
Heb 10:28 Moses' law d. without mercy under *599*
Heb 11:13 These all d. in faith, not having *599*
Heb 11:22 By faith Joseph when he d., made *5053*
Re 8:9 were in the sea, and had life, d.; *599*
Re 8:11 many men d. of the waters, *599*
Re 16:3 every living soul d. in the sea. *599*

DIEST
Ru 1:17 Where thou d., will I die, and 4191

DIET
Jer 52:34 And for his d., there was a 737
Jer 52:34 there was a continual d. given 737

DIETH
Le 7:24 fat of the beast that d. of itself, 5038
Le 22:8 That which d. of itself, or is torn 5038
Nu 19:14 when a man d. in a tent: 4191
De 14:21 eat of any thing that d. of itself: 5038
2Sa 3:33 said, Died Abner as a fool d.? 4194
1Ki 14:11 Him that d. of Jeroboam in the 4191
1Ki 14:11 eat; and him that d. in the field 4191
1Ki 16:4 Him that d. of Baasha in the city 4191
1Ki 16:4 and him that d. of his in the fields 4191
1Ki 21:24 Him that d. of Ahab in the city 4191
1Ki 21:24 eat; and him that d. in the field 4191
Job 14:10 But man d., and wasteth away: 4191
Job 21:23 One d. in his full strength, being 4191
Job 21:25 d. in the bitterness of his soul, 4191
Ps 49:17 when he d. he shall carry nothing 4194
Pr 11:7 a wicked man d., his expectation 4194
Ec 2:16 And how d. the wise man? as the 4191
Ec 3:19 as the one d., so d. the other; 4194
Isa 50:2 is no water, and d. for thirst. 4191
Isa 59:5 he that eateth of their eggs d., 4191
Eze 4:14 eaten of that which d. of itself, 5038
Eze 18:26 iniquity, and d. in them; 4191
Eze 18:32 pleasure in the death of him that d., 4191
Zec 11:9 feed you: that that d., let it die; 4191
Mk 9:44, 46 **Where their worm d. not, and** *5053*
Mk 9:48 **Where their worm d. not, and** *5053*
Ro 6:9 raised from the dead, d. no more; *599*
Ro 14:7 himself, and no man d. to himself. *599*

DIFFER See also DIFFERETH; DIFFERING.
1Co 4:7 maketh thee to d. from another? *1252*

DIFFERENCE See also DIFFERENCES.
Ex 11:7 the Lord doth put a d. between 6395
Le 10:10 And that ye may put d. between holy 914
Le 11:47 d. between the unclean and the 914
Le 20:25 shall therefore put d. between 914
Eze 22:26 they have put no d. between the
Eze 22:26 have they showed d. between
Eze 44:23 the d. between the holy and
Ac 15:9 no d. between us and them. *1252*
Ro 3:22 that believe: for there is no d.: *1293*
Ro 10:12 no d. between the Jew and the *1293*
1Co 7:34 There is d. also between a wife *3307*
Jude 22 have compassion, making a d.: *1252*

DIFFERENCES
1Co 12:5 there are d. of administrations, *1243*

DIFFERETH
1Co 15:41 for one star d. from another star *1308*
Ga 4:1 a child, d. nothing from a servant, *1308*

DIFFERING
Ro 12:6 gifts d. according to the grace *1313*

DIG See also DIGGED; DIGGETH.
Ex 21:33 if a man shall d. a pit, and not 3738
De 8:9 whose hills thou mayest d. brass. 2672
De 23:13 thou shalt d. therewith, and shalt 2658
Job 3:21 d. for it more than for hid treasures: 2658
Job 6:27 and ye d. a pit for your friend. 3738
Job 11:18 yea, thou shalt d. about thee, 2658
Job 24:16 the dark they d. through houses, 2864
Eze 8:8 Son of man, d. now in the wall: 2864
Eze 12:5 D. thou through the wall in their 2864
Eze 12:12 d. through the wall to carry out, 2864
Am 9:2 Though they d. into hell, thence 2864
Lu 13:8 **I shall d. about it, and dung it:** *4626*
Lu 16:3 **I cannot d.; to beg I am ashamed.** *4626*

DIGGED See also DIGGEDST.
Ge 21:30 unto me, that I have d. this well. 2658
Ge 26:15 had d. in the days of Abraham 2658
Ge 26:18 Isaac d. again the wells of water; 2658
Ge 26:18 which they had d. in the days of 2658
Ge 26:19 Isaac's servants d. in the valley. 2658
Ge 26:21 And they d. another well, and 2658
Ge 26:22 from thence, and d. another well; 2658
Ge 26:25 there Isaac's servants d. a well. 3738
Ge 26:32 the well which they had d., and 2658
Ge 49:6 their selfwill they d. down a wall. 6131
Ge 50:5 in my grave which I have d. for 3738
Ex 7:24 the Egyptians d. round about the 2658
Nu 21:18 The princes d. the well, 2658
Nu 21:18 the nobles of the people d. it 3738
De 6:11 wells d., which thou diggedst not, 2672
2Ki 19:24 d. and drunk strange waters, 5365
2Ch 26:10 in the desert, and d. many wells: 2672
Ne 9:25 houses full of all goods, wells d., 2672
Ps 7:15 He made a pit, and d. it, and is 2658
Ps 35:7 cause they have d. for my soul. 2658
Ps 57:6 they have d. a pit before me, into 3738
Ps 94:13 until the pit be d. for the wicked. 3738
Ps 119:85 The proud have d. pits for me, 3738
Isa 5:6 it shall not be pruned, nor d.; 5737
Isa 7:25 on all hills that shall be d. with 5737
Isa 37:25 I have d., and drunk water; and 5365
Isa 51:1 hole of the pit whence ye are d.. 5365
Jer 13:7 Then I went to Euphrates, and d., 2658
Jer 18:20 they have d. a pit for my soul, 3738
Jer 18:22 they have d. a pit to take me, 3738
Eze 8:8 and when I had d. in the wall, 2864
Eze 12:7 in the even I d. through the wall 2864
Mt 21:33 **and d. a winepress in it, and built** *3736*
Mt 25:18 **and d. in the earth, and hid his** *3736*
Mk 12:1 **and d. a place for the winefat,** *3736*
Lu 6:48 **d. deep, and laid the foundation** *4626*
Ro 11:3 and d. down thine altars; *2679*

DIGGEDST
De 6:11 wells digged, which thou d. not, 2672

DIGGETH
Pr 16:27 An ungodly man d. up evil: and 3738
Pr 26:27 Whoso d. a pit shall fall therein: 3738
Ec 10:8 He that d. a pit shall fall into it; 2658

DIGNITIES
2Pe 2:10 are not afraid to speak evil of d.. *1391*
Jude 8 dominion, and speak evil of d.. *1391*

DIGNITY See also DIGNITIES.
Ge 49:3 the excellency of d., and the 7613
Es 6:3 What honour and d. has been done 1420
Ec 10:6 Folly is set in great d., and the 4791
Hab 1:7 d. shall proceed of themselves. 7613

DIKLAH (dik'-lah)
Ge 10:27 And Hadoram and Uzal, and D., 1853
1Ch 1:21 Hadoram also, and Uzal, and D., 1853

DILEAN (dil'-e-an)
Jos 15:38 and D., and Mizpeh, and Joktheel, 1810

DILIGENCE
Pr 4:23 Keep thy heart with all d.; for out 4929
Lu 12:58 **way, give d. that thou mayest be** *2039*
Ro 12:8 he that ruleth, with d.; he that *4710*
2Co 8:7 and knowledge, and in all d., and *4710*
2Ti 4:9 thy d. to come shortly unto me: *4704*
2Ti 4:21 Do thy d. to come before winter. *4704*
Heb 6:11 the same d. to the full assurance *4710*
2Pe 1:5 giving all d., add to your faith *4710*
2Pe 1:10 give d. to make your calling and *4710*
Jude 3 when I gave all d. to write unto *4710*

DILIGENT See also DILIGENCE; DILIGENTLY.
De 19:18 judges shall make d. inquisition: 3190
Jos 22:5 d. heed to do the commandment 3966
Ps 64:6 they accomplish a d. search:
Ps 77:6 heart: and my spirit made d. search.
Pr 10:4 the hand of the d. maketh rich 2742
Pr 12:24 The hand of the d. shall bear rule: 2742
Pr 12:27 substance of a d. man is precious. 2742
Pr 13:4 the soul of the d. shall be made fat 2742
Pr 21:5 The thoughts of the d. tend only to 2742
Pr 22:29 thou a man d. in his business? 4106
Pr 27:23 Be thou d. to know the state of
2Co 8:22 often proved d. in many things, *4705*
2Co 8:22 but now much more d., upon *4707*
Tit 3:12 d. to come unto me to Nicopolis: *4704*
2Pe 3:14 d. that ye may be found of him in *4704*

DILIGENTLY
Ex 15:26 If thou wilt d. hearken to the voice

Le 10:16 And Moses **d.** sought the goat of
De 4:9 keep thy soul **d.**, lest thou forget 3966
De 6:7 teach them **d.** unto thy children, 8150
De 6:17 Ye shall **d.** keep the commandments
De 11:13 hearken **d.** unto my commandments
De 11:22 For if ye shall **d.** keep all these
De 13:14 make search, and ask **d.**; and, 3190
De 17:4 hast heard of it, and enquired **d.**, 3190
De 24:8 of leprosy, that thou observe **d.**, 3966
De 28:1 if thou shalt hearken **d.** unto the
1Ki 20:33 did **d.** observe whether any thing 5172
Ezr 7:23 let it be **d.** done for the house of 149
Job 13:17 Hear **d.** my speech, and my
Job 21:2 Hear **d.** my speech, and let this be
Ps 37:10 thou shalt **d.** consider his place, 995
Ps 119:4 us to keep thy precepts **d.** 3966
Pr 7:15 **d.** to seek thy face, and I have 7836
Pr 11:27 He that **d.** seeketh good procureth 7836
Pr 23:1 ruler, consider **d.** what is before thee:
Isa 21:7 he hearkened **d.** with much heed 7182
Isa 55:2 hearken **d.** unto me, and eat ye that
Jer 2:10 and consider **d.**, and see if there 3966
Jer 12:16 if they will **d.** learn the ways
Jer 17:24 if ye **d.** hearken unto me, saith the
Zec 6:15 will **d.** obey the voice of the Lord
Mt 2:7 of them **d.** what time the star
Mt 2:8 search **d.** for the young child; *199*
Mt 2:16 had **d.** enquired of the wise men,
Lu 15:8 **house, and seek d. till she find it?** *1960*
Ac 18:25 he spake and taught **d.** the things *199*
1Ti 5:10 **d.** followed every good work.
2Ti 1:17 Rome, he sought me out very **d.**, *4706*
Tit 3:13 and Apollos on their journey **d.**, *4709*
Heb 11:6 reward of them that **d.** seek him. *1567*
Heb 12:15 Looking **d.** lest any man fail of
1Pe 1:10 have enquired and searched **d.**,

DIM
Ge 27:1 was old, and his eyes were **d.**, 3543
Ge 48:10 the eyes of Israel were **d.** for age, 3513
De 34:7 his eye was not **d.**, nor his 3543
1Sa 3:2 his eyes began to wax **d.**, that he 3544
1Sa 4:15 his eyes were **d.**, that he could 6965
Job 17:7 eye also is **d.** by reason of sorrow, 3543
Isa 32:3 of them that see shall not be **d.**, 8159
La 4:1 How is the gold become **d.**! how 6044
La 5:17 for these things our eyes are **d.** 2821

DIMINISH See also DIMINISHED; DIMINISHING; MINISH.
Ex 5:8 ye shall not **d.** ought thereof: for 1639
Ex 21:10 duty of marriage, shall he not **d.** 1639
Le 25:16 thou shalt **d.** the price of it: 4591
De 4:2 neither shall ye **d.** ought from it, 1639
De 12:32 not add thereto, nor **d.** from it. 1639
Jer 26:2 speak unto them; **d.** not a word: 1639
Eze 5:11 therefore will I also **d.** thee; 1639
Eze 29:15 for I will **d.** them, that they shall 4591

DIMINISHED See also MINISHED.
Ex 5:11 ought of your work shall be **d.** 1639
Pr 13:11 gotten by vanity shall be **d.**: 4591
Isa 21:17 children of Kedar, shall be **d.**: 4591
Jer 29:6 may be increased there, and not **d.** 4591
Eze 16:27 and have **d.** thine ordinary food, 1639

DIMINISHING
Ro 11:12 and the **d.** of them the riches of *2275*

DIMNAH (dim'-nah)
Jos 21:35 **D.** with her suburbs, Nahalal 1829

DIMNESS
Isa 8:22 and darkness, **d.** of anguish; 4588
Isa 9:1 the **d.** shall not be such as was 4155

DIMON (di'-mon) See also DIBON; DIMONAH.
Isa 15:9 waters of **D.** shall be full of blood: 1775
Isa 15:9 I will bring more upon **D.**, 1775

DIMONAH (di-mo'-nah) See also DIMON.
Jos 15:22 Kinah, and **D.**, and Adadah. 1776

DINAH See also DINAH'S.
Ge 30:21 daughter, and called her name **D.** 1783
Ge 34:1 **D.** the daughter of Leah, which 1783
Ge 34:3 soul clave unto **D.** the daughter of 1783
Ge 34:5 Jacob heard that he had defiled **D.** 1783
Ge 34:13 he had defiled **D.** their sister: 1783
Ge 34:26 took **D.** out of Shechem's house, 1783
Ge 46:15 Padan-aram, with his daughter **D.**: 1783

DINAH'S
Ge 34:25 Simeon, and Levi, **D.** brethren, 1783

DINAITES (di'-na-ites)
Ezr 4:9 the **D.**, the Apharsathchites, 1784

DINE See also DINED.
Ge 43:16 these men shall **d.** with me at noon. 398
Lu 11:37 besought him to **d.** with him: *709*
Joh 21:12 saith unto them, **Come and d.** *709*

DINED
Joh 21:15 So when they had **d.**, Jesus saith *709*

DINHABAH (din'-ha-bah)
Ge 36:32 and the name of his city was **D.** 1838
1Ch 1:43 and the name of his city was **D.** 1838

DINNER
Pr 15:17 is a **d.** of herbs where love is, 737
Mt 22:4 **Behold, I have prepared my d.:** *712*
Lu 11:38 had not first washed before **d.** *712*
Lu 14:12 **When thou makest a d. or a supper,** *712*

DIONYSIUS (di-on-ish'-yus)
Ac 17:34 the which was **D.** the Areopagite, *1354*

DIOTREPHES (di-ot'-re-feez)
3Jo 9 I wrote unto the church: but **D.**, *1361*

DIP See also DIPPED; DIPPETH.
Ex 12:22 **d.** it in the blood that is in the 2881
Le 4:6 shall **d.** his finger in the blood, 2881
Le 4:17 **d.** his finger in some of the blood, 2881
Le 14:6 shall **d.** them and the living bird 2881
Le 14:16 the priest shall **d.** his right finger 2881
Le 14:51 **d.** them in the blood of the slain 2881
Nu 19:18 and **d.** it in the water, and sprinkle 2881
De 33:24 and let him **d.** his foot in oil. 2881
Ru 2:14 and **d.** thy morsel in the vinegar. 2881
Lu 16:24 **that he may d. the tip of his finger.** *911*

DIPPED
Ge 37:31 and **d.** the coat in the blood; 2881
Le 9:9 and he **d.** his finger in the blood, 2881
Jos 3:15 were **d.** in the brim of the water, 2881
1Sa 14:27 and **d.** it in an honeycomb, and put 2881
2Ki 5:14 **d.** himself seven times in Jordan, 2881
2Ki 8:15 and **d.** it in the water, and spread it 2881
Ps 68:23 thy foot may be **d.** in the blood 4272
Joh 13:26 **give a sop when I have d. it** *911*
Joh 13:26 had **d.** the sop, he gave it to Judas *1686*
Re 19:13 with a vesture **d.** in blood: *911*

DIPPETH
Mt 26:23 **He that d. his hand with me in** *1686*
Mk 14:20 **that d. with me in the dish.** *1686*

DIRECT See also DIRECTED; DIRECTETH.
Ge 46:28 to **d.** his face unto Goshen; 3384
Ps 5:3 will I **d.** my prayer unto thee, 6186
Pr 3:6 him, and he shall **d.** thy paths. 3474
Pr 11:5 of the perfect shall **d.** his way: 3474
Ex 10:10 but wisdom is profitable to **d.** 3787
Isa 45:13 and I will **d.** all his ways: 3474
Isa 61:8 and I will **d.** their work in truth, 5414
Jer 10:23 man that walketh to **d.** his steps. 3559
1Th 3:11 Christ, **d.** our way unto you. *2720*
2Th 3:5 **d.** your hearts into the love of God, *2720*

DIRECTED
Job 32:14 hath not **d.** his words against me: 6186
Ps 119:5 ways were **d.** to keep thy statutes! 3559
Isa 40:13 Who hath **d.** the spirit of the Lord, 8505

DIRECTETH
Job 37:3 He **d.** it under the whole heaven, 3474
Pr 16:9 way: but the Lord **d.** his steps. 3559
Pr 21:29 as for the upright, he **d.** his way. 3559

DIRECTION
Nu 21:18 it, but the **d.** of the lawgiver,

DIRECTLY
Nu 19:4 blood **d.** before the tabernacle 413,5227
Eze 42:12 even the way **d.** before the wall 1903

DIRT
Jg 3:22 his belly; and the **d.** came out. 6574
Ps 18:42 them out as the **d.** in the streets. 2916
Isa 57:20 whose waters cast up mire and **d.** 2916

DISALLOW See also DISALLOWED.
Nu 30:5 if her father **d.** her in the day that 5106

DISALLOWED
Nu 30:5 her, because her father **d.** her 5106
Nu 30:8 her husband **d.** her on the day that 5106
Nu 30:11 his peace at her, and **d.** her not: 5106
1Pe 2:4 **d.** indeed of men, but chosen of *593*
1Pe 2:7 the stone which the builders **d.**, *593*

DISANNUL See also DISANNULLED; DISANNULLETH; DISANNULLING.
Job 40:8 Wilt thou also **d.** my judgment. 6565
Isa 14:27 purposed, and who shall **d.** it? 6565
Ga 3:17 years after, cannot **d.**, that it *208*

DISANNULLED
Isa 28:18 covenant with death shall be **d.**, 3722

DISANNULLETH
Ga 3:15 no man **d.**, or addeth thereto. *114*

DISANNULLING
Heb 7:18 verily a **d.** of the commandment *115*

DISAPPOINT See also DISAPPOINTED; DISAPPOINTETH.
Ps 17:13 Arise, O Lord, **d.** him, cast him 6923

DISAPPOINTED
Pr 15:22 Without counsel purposes are **d.**: 6565

DISAPPOINTETH
Job 5:12 He **d.** the devices of the crafty, 6565

DISCERN See also DISCERNED; DISCERNETH; DISCERNING.
Ge 31:32 **d.** thou what is thine with me, 5234
Ge 38:25 **D.**, I pray thee, whose are these, 5234
2Sa 14:17 lord the king to **d.** good and bad: 8085
2Sa 19:35 can I **d.** between good and evil? 3045
1Ki 3:9 I may **d.** between good and bad: 995
1Ki 3:11 understanding to **d.** judgment; 8085
Ezr 3:13 the people could not **d.** the noise 5234
Job 4:16 I could not **d.** the form thereof: 5234
Job 6:30 cannot my taste **d.** perverse things? 995
Eze 44:23 them to **d.** between the unclean 3045
Jon 4:11 that cannot **d.** between their right 3045
Mal 3:18 and **d.** between the righteous and 7200
Mt 16:3 **ye can d. the face of the sky;** *1252*
Mt 16:3 **but can ye not d. the signs of the**
Lu 12:56 **ye can d. the face of the sky and** *1381*
Lu 12:56 **is it that ye do not d. this time?**
Heb 5:14 exercised to **d.** both good and evil. *1253*

DISCERNED
Ge 27:23 he **d.** him not, because his hands 5234
1Ki 20:41 and the king of Israel **d.** him that 5234
Pr 7:7 I **d.** among the youths, a young 995
1Co 2:14 because they are spiritually **d.** *350*

DISCERNER
Heb 4:12 and is a **d.** of the thoughts and *2924*

DISCERNETH
Ec 8:5 and a wise man's heart **d.** both 3045

DISCERNING
1Co 11:29 himself, not **d.** the Lord's body. *1252*
1Co 12:10 to another **d.** of spirits; to another *1253*

DISCHARGE See also DISCHARGED.
Ec 8:8 and there is no **d.** in that war; 4917

DISCHARGED
1Ki 5:9 and will cause them to be **d.** there, 5310

DISCIPLE See also DISCIPLES.
Mt 10:24 **The d. is not above his master,** *3101*
Mt 10:25 **It is enough for the d. that he be** *3101*
Mt 10:42 **water only in the name of a d.,** *3101*
Mt 27:57 who also himself was Jesus' **d.**: *3100*
Lu 6:40 **The d. is not above his master:** *3101*
Lu 14:26 **own life also, he cannot be my d.** *3101*
Lu 14:27 **come after me, cannot be my d.** *3101*
Lu 14:33 **that he hath, he cannot be my d.,** *3101*
Joh 9:28 Thou art his **d.**; but we are Moses' *3101*
Joh 18:15 another **d.**: that **d.** was known *3101*
Joh 18:16 Then went out that other **d.**, which *3101*
Joh 19:26 and the **d.** standing by, whom he *3101*
Joh 19:27 Then saith he to the **d.**, **Behold thy** *3101*
Joh 19:27 from that hour that **d.** took her *3101*
Joh 19:38 of Arimathaea, being a **d.** of Jesus, *3101*
Joh 20:2 to the other **d.**, whom Jesus loved, *3101*
Joh 20:3 went forth, and that other **d.**, *3101*
Joh 20:4 and the other **d.** did outrun Peter, *3101*
Joh 20:8 Then went in also that other **d.**, *3101*
Joh 21:7 Therefore that **d.** whom Jesus loved *3101*
Joh 21:20 seeth the **d.** whom Jesus loved *3101*
Joh 21:23 that that **d.** should not die; *3101*
Joh 21:24 This is the **d.** which testifieth of *3101*
Ac 9:10 **d.** at Damascus, named Ananias; *3101*
Ac 9:26 believed not that he was a **d.** *3101*
Ac 9:36 Joppa a certain **d.** named Tabitha, *3102*
Ac 16:1 **d.** was there, named Timotheus, *3101*
Ac 21:16 **d.** with whom we should lodge. *3101*

DISCIPLES See also DISCIPLES'; FELLOWDISCIPLES.
Isa 8:16 seal the law among my **d.**. 3928
Mt 5:1 he was set, his **d.** came unto him: *3101*
Mt 8:21 another of his **d.** said unto him, *3101*
Mt 8:23 into a ship, his **d.** followed him. *3101*
Mt 8:25 his **d.** came to him, and awoke *3101*
Mt 9:10 and sat down with him and his **d.**. *3101*
Mt 9:11 they said unto his **d.**, Why eateth *3101*
Mt 9:14 came to him the **d.** of John, saying, *3101*
Mt 9:14 fast oft, but thy **d.** fast not? *3101*
Mt 9:19 and followed him, and so did his **d.**. *3101*
Mt 9:37 saith he unto his **d.**, **The harvest** *3101*
Mt 10:1 had called unto him his twelve **d.**, *3101*
Mt 11:1 end of commanding his twelve **d.**, *3101*
Mt 11:2 of Christ, he sent two of his **d.**, *3101*
Mt 12:1 **d.** were an hungred, and began to *3101*
Mt 12:2 thy **d.** do that which is not lawful *3101*
Mt 12:49 forth his hand toward his **d.**, *3101*
Mt 13:10 And the **d.** came, and said unto him, *3101*
Mt 13:36 into the house: and his **d.** came *3101*
Mt 14:12 his **d.** came, and took up the body, *3101*
Mt 14:15 his **d.** came to him, saying, This is *3101*
Mt 14:19 loaves to his **d.**, and the **d.** to the *3101*
Mt 14:22 constrained his **d.** to get into a ship, *3101*
Mt 14:26 the **d.** saw him walking on the sea, *3101*
Mt 15:2 Why do thy **d.** transgress the *3101*
Mt 15:12 Then came his **d.**, and said unto him, *3101*
Mt 15:23 And his **d.** came and besought him, *3101*
Mt 15:32 Jesus called his **d.** unto him, and *3101*
Mt 15:33 his **d.** say unto him, Whence *3101*
Mt 15:36 and brake them, and gave to his **d.**, *3101*
Mt 15:36 and the **d.** to the multitude. *3101*
Mt 16:5 his **d.** were come to the other side, *3101*
Mt 16:13 he asked his **d.**, saying, **Whom do** *3101*
Mt 16:20 Then charged he his **d.** that they *3101*
Mt 16:21 to shew unto his **d.**, how that he *3101*
Mt 16:24 said Jesus unto his **d.**, **If any man** *3101*
Mt 17:6 when the **d.** heard it, they fell *3101*
Mt 17:10 his **d.** asked him, saying, Why then *3101*
Mt 17:13 Then the **d.** understood that he *3101*
Mt 17:16 I brought him to thy **d.**, and they *3101*
Mt 17:19 Then came the **d.** to Jesus apart, *3101*
Mt 18:1 came the **d.** unto Jesus, saying, *3101*
Mt 19:10 His **d.** say unto him, If the case *3101*
Mt 19:13 and pray: and the **d.** rebuked them. *3101*
Mt 19:23 Then said Jesus unto his **d.**, **Verily** *3101*
Mt 19:25 When his **d.** heard it, they were *3101*
Mt 20:17 took the twelve **d.** apart in the way, *3101*
Mt 21:1 of Olives, then sent Jesus two **d.**, *3101*
Mt 21:6 And the **d.** went, and did as Jesus *3101*
Mt 21:20 when the **d.** saw it, they marvelled, *3101*
Mt 22:16 sent out unto him their **d.** with the *3101*
Mt 23:1 to the multitude, and to his **d.**, *3101*
Mt 24:1 his **d.** came to him for to shew him *3101*
Mt 24:3 the **d.** came unto him privately, *3101*
Mt 26:1 he said unto his **d.**, **Ye know that** *3101*
Mt 26:8 his **d.** saw it, they had indignation, *3101*
Mt 26:17 the **d.** came to Jesus, saying unto *3101*
Mt 26:18 **passover at thy house with my d.**. *3101*
Mt 26:19 the **d.** did as Jesus had appointed *3101*
Mt 26:26 gave it to the **d.**, and said, **Take,** *3101*
Mt 26:35 thee. Likewise also said all the **d.** *3101*
Mt 26:36 and saith unto the **d.**, **Sit ye here** *3101*
Mt 26:40 he cometh unto the **d.**, and findeth *3101*
Mt 26:45 Then cometh he to his **d.**, and saith *3101*
Mt 26:56 Then all the **d.** forsook him, and *3101*
Mt 27:64 lest his **d.** come by night, and steal *3101*
Mt 28:7 **d.** that is risen from the dead; *3101*
Mt 28:8 and did run to bring his **d.** word. *3101*
Mt 28:9 And as they went to tell his **d.**, *3101*
Mt 28:13 Say ye, His **d.** came by night, *3101*
Mt 28:16 eleven **d.** went away into Galilee, *3101*
Mk 2:15 together with Jesus and his **d.**: *3101*
Mk 2:16 they said unto his **d.**, How is it *3101*
Mk 2:18 And the **d.** of John and of the *3101*
Mk 2:18 Why do the **d.** of John and of the *3101*
Mk 2:18 Pharisees fast, but thy **d.** fast not? *3101*
Mk 2:23 his **d.** began, as they went, to pluck *3101*
Mk 3:7 himself with his **d.** to the sea: *3101*
Mk 3:9 spake to his **d.**, that a small ship *3101*
Mk 4:34 he expounded all things to his **d.**. *3101*
Mk 5:31 his **d.** said unto him, Thou seest *3101*
Mk 6:1 own country; and his **d.** follow him. *3101*
Mk 6:29 when his **d.** heard of it, they came *3101*
Mk 6:35 his **d.** came unto him, and said, *3101*
Mk 6:41 them to his **d.** to set before them: *3101*
Mk 6:45 constrained his **d.** to get into the *3101*
Mk 7:2 they saw some of his **d.** eat bread *3101*
Mk 7:5 Why walk not thy **d.** according to *3101*
Mk 7:17 his **d.** asked him concerning the *3101*
Mk 8:1 Jesus called his **d.** unto him, and *3101*
Mk 8:4 his **d.** answered him, From whence *3101*
Mk 8:6 gave to his **d.** to set before them; *3101*
Mk 8:10 entered into a ship with his **d.**, *3101*
Mk 8:14 Now the **d.** had forgotten to take
Mk 8:27 went out, and his **d.**, into the towns *3101*
Mk 8:27 and by the way he asked his **d.**, *3101*
Mk 8:33 looked on his **d.**, he rebuked Peter, *3101*
Mk 8:34 people unto him with his **d.** also, *3101*
Mk 9:14 when he came to his **d.**, he saw a *3101*
Mk 9:18 I spake to thy **d.** that they should *3101*
Mk 9:28 his **d.** asked him privately, Why *3101*
Mk 9:31 taught his **d.**, and said unto them, *3101*
Mk 10:10 in the house his **d.** asked him *3101*
Mk 10:13 his **d.** rebuked those that brought *3101*
Mk 10:23 and saith unto his **d.**, **How hardly** *3101*
Mk 10:24 the **d.** were astonished at his words. *3101*
Mk 10:46 went out of Jericho with his **d.** *3101*
Mk 11:1 he sendeth forth two of his **d.**, *3101*
Mk 11:14 **for ever.** And his **d.** heard it. *3101*
Mk 12:43 he called unto him his **d.**, and saith *3101*
Mk 13:1 one of his **d.** saith unto him, *3101*
Mk 14:12 **d.** said unto him, Where wilt thou *3101*
Mk 14:13 he sendeth forth two of his **d.**, *3101*
Mk 14:14 **shall eat the passover with my d.?** *3101*
Mk 14:16 his **d.** went forth, and came into *3101*
Mk 14:32 and he saith to his **d.**, **Sit ye here** *3101*
Mk 16:7 tell his **d.** and Peter that he goeth *3101*
Lu 5:30 murmured against his **d.**, saying, *3101*
Lu 5:33 Why do the **d.** of John fast often, *3101*
Lu 5:33 likewise the **d.** of the Pharisees
Lu 6:1 his **d.** plucked the ears of corn, *3101*
Lu 6:13 was day, he called unto him his **d.**: *3101*
Lu 6:17 company of his **d.**, and a great *3101*
Lu 6:20 And he lifted up his eyes on his **d.**, *3101*
Lu 7:11 and many of his **d.** went with him, *3101*
Lu 7:18 the **d.** of John shewed him of all *3101*
Lu 7:19 John calling unto him two of his **d.** *3101*
Lu 8:9 his **d.** asked him, saying, What *3101*
Lu 8:22 he went into a ship with his **d.**: *3101*
Lu 9:1 he called his twelve **d.** together, *3101*
Lu 9:14 he said to his **d.**, **Make them sit** *3101*
Lu 9:16 and gave to the **d.** to set before *3101*
Lu 9:18 praying, his **d.** were with him: *3101*
Lu 9:40 I besought thy **d.** to cast him out; *3101*
Lu 9:43 said unto his **d.**, **Let these sayings** *3101*
Lu 9:54 And when his **d.** James and John *3101*
Lu 10:23 he turned him unto his **d.**, and said. *3101*
Lu 11:1 one of his **d.** said unto him, Lord, *3101*
Lu 11:1 as John also taught his **d.** *3101*
Lu 12:1 he began to say unto his **d.** first of *3101*
Lu 12:22 he said unto his **d.**, **Therefore I say** *3101*
Lu 16:1 he said also unto his **d.**, **There was** *3101*
Lu 17:1 Then said he unto the **d.**, **It is** *3101*
Lu 17:22 said unto the **d.**, **The days will come,** *3101*
Lu 18:15 his **d.** saw it, they rebuked them. *3101*
Lu 19:29 of Olives, he sent two of his **d.**, *3101*
Lu 19:37 **d.** began to rejoice and praise God *3101*
Lu 19:39 unto him, Master, rebuke thy **d.**. *3101*
Lu 20:45 unto his **d.**, **Beware of the scribes,** *3101*
Lu 22:11 **eat the passover with my d.?** *3101*
Lu 22:39 Olives; and his **d.** also followed him. *3101*
Lu 22:45 was come to his **d.**, he found them *3101*
Joh 1:35 John stood, and two of his **d.**; *3101*
Joh 1:37 And the two **d.** heard him speak, *3101*
Joh 2:2 called, and his **d.**, to the marriage. *3101*
Joh 2:11 glory; and his **d.** believed on him. *3101*
Joh 2:12 and his brethren, and his **d.**: *3101*
Joh 2:17 his **d.** remembered that it was *3101*
Joh 2:22 his **d.** remembered that he had said *3101*
Joh 3:22 came Jesus and his **d.** into the land *3101*
Joh 3:25 between some of John's **d.** and the *3101*
Joh 4:1 and baptized more **d.** than John, *3101*
Joh 4:2 himself baptized not, but his **d.**,) *3101*
Joh 4:8 (For his **d.** were gone away unto *3101*
Joh 4:27 upon this came his **d.**, and marvelled *3101*
Joh 4:31 the meanwhile his **d.** prayed him, *3101*
Joh 4:33 Therefore said the **d.** one to *3101*
Joh 6:3 and there he sat with his **d.**. *3101*
Joh 6:8 One of his **d.**, Andrew, Simon *3101*
Joh 6:11 distributed to the **d.**, and the **d.** to *3101*
Joh 6:12 he said unto his **d.**, **Gather up the** *3101*
Joh 6:16 his **d.** went down unto the sea, *3101*
Joh 6:22 whereinto his **d.** were entered, *3101*
Joh 6:22 Jesus went not with his **d.** into the *3101*
Joh 6:22 that his **d.** were gone away alone; *3101*
Joh 6:24 was not there, neither his **d.**, they *3101*
Joh 6:60 Many therefore of his **d.**, when they *3101*
Joh 6:61 himself that his **d.** murmured at it, *3101*
Joh 6:66 many of his **d.** went back, and *3101*
Joh 7:3 that thy **d.** also may see the works *3101*
Joh 8:31 **word, then are ye my d. indeed;** *3101*
Joh 9:2 his **d.** asked him, saying, Master, *3101*
Joh 9:27 it again? will ye also be his **d.**? *3101*
Joh 9:28 his disciple; but we are Moses' **d.**. *3101*
Joh 11:7 saith he to his **d.**, **Let us go into** *3101*
Joh 11:8 His **d.** say unto him, Master, the *3101*
Joh 11:12 Then said his **d.**, Lord, if he sleep, *3101*
Joh 11:54 and there continued with his **d.**. *3101*
Joh 12:4 Then saith one of his **d.**, Judas *3101*
Joh 12:16 understood not his **d.** at the first: *3101*
Joh 13:22 Then the **d.** looked one on another, *3101*
Joh 13:23 one of his **d.**, whom Jesus loved. *3101*
Joh 13:35 **know that ye are my d., if ye have** *3101*
Joh 15:8 **much fruit; so shall ye be my d.** *3101*
Joh 16:17 Then said some of his **d.** among *3101*
Joh 16:29 His **d.** said unto him, Lo, now *3101*
Joh 18:1 he went forth with his **d.** over the *3101*
Joh 18:1 the which he entered, and his **d.** *3101*
Joh 18:2 resorted thither with his **d.**. *3101*
Joh 18:17 not thou also one of this man's **d.**? *3101*
Joh 18:19 priest then asked Jesus of his **d.**, *3101*
Joh 18:25 Art not thou also one of his **d.**? *3101*
Joh 20:10 Then the **d.** went away unto their *3101*
Joh 20:18 Magdalene came and told the **d.** *3101*
Joh 20:19 shut where the **d.** were assembled *3101*
Joh 20:20 Then were the **d.** glad, when they *3101*
Joh 20:25 The other **d.** therefore said unto *3101*
Joh 20:26 his **d.** were within, and Thomas *3101*
Joh 20:30 did Jesus in the presence of his **d.**, *3101*
Joh 21:1 himself again to the **d.** at the sea *3101*
Joh 21:2 of Zebedee, and two other of his **d.**. *3101*
Joh 21:4 the **d.** knew not that it was Jesus. *3101*
Joh 21:8 And the other **d.** came in a little *3101*
Joh 21:12 And none of the **d.** durst ask him, *3101*
Joh 21:14 Jesus shewed himself to his **d.**, *3101*
Ac 1:15 stood up in the midst of the **d.**, *3101*
Ac 6:1 number of the **d.** was multiplied, *3101*
Ac 6:2 called the multitude of the **d.** unto *3101*
Ac 6:7 the number of the **d.** multiplied in *3101*
Ac 9:1 against the **d.** of the Lord, went *3101*
Ac 9:19 certain days with the **d.** which *3101*
Ac 9:25 Then the **d.** took him by night, *3101*
Ac 9:26 assayed to join himself to the **d.**: *3101*
Ac 9:38 and the **d.** had heard that Peter *3101*
Ac 11:26 And the **d.** were called Christians *3101*
Ac 11:29 Then the **d.**, every man according *3101*
Ac 13:52 And the **d.** were filled with joy, *3101*
Ac 14:20 Howbeit, as the **d.** stood round *3101*
Ac 14:22 Confirming the souls of the **d.**, and *3101*
Ac 14:28 they abode long time with the **d.**. *3101*
Ac 15:10 a yoke upon the neck of the **d.**, *3101*
Ac 18:23 in order, strengthening all the **d.** *3101*
Ac 18:27 exhorting the **d.** to receive him: *3101*
Ac 19:1 Ephesus; and finding certain **d.**, *3101*
Ac 19:9 and separated the **d.**, disputing *3101*
Ac 19:30 people, the **d.** suffered him not. *3101*
Ac 20:1 Paul called unto him the **d.**, and *3101*
Ac 20:7 the **d.** came together to break *3101*
Ac 20:30 things, to draw away **d.** after them. *3101*
Ac 21:4 And finding **d.**, we tarried there *3101*
Ac 21:16 also certain of the **d.** of Caesarea, *3101*

DISCIPLES'
Joh 13:5 to wash the **d.** feet, and to wipe *3101*

DISCIPLINE
Job 36:10 He openeth also their ear to **d.**, 4148

DISCLOSE
Isa 26:21 the earth also shall **d.** her blood, 1540

DISCOMFITED
Ex 17:13 And Joshua **d.** Amalek and his 2522
Nu 14:45 smote them, and **d.** them, even 3807
Jos 10:10 And the Lord **d.** them before 1949
Jg 4:15 And the Lord **d.** Sisera, and all his 2000
Jg 8:12 and Zalmunna, and **d.** all the host. 2729
1Sa 7:10 the Philistines, and **d.** them; and 1949
2Sa 22:15 them; lightning, and **d.** them. 2000
Ps 18:14 shot out lightnings, and **d.** them. 1949
Isa 31:8 and his young men shall be **d.**. 4522

DISCOMFITURE
1Sa 14:20 and there was a very great **d.**. 4103

DISCONTENTED
1Sa 22:2 every one that was **d.**, 4751,5315

DISCONTINUE
Jer 17:4 And thou, even thyself, shalt **d.** 8058

DISCORD
Pr 6:14 continually; he soweth **d.**. 4066
Pr 6:19 that soweth **d.** among brethren. 4090

DISCOURAGE See also DISCOURAGED.
Nu 32:7 **d.** ye the heart of the children of 5106

DISCOURAGED
Nu 21:4 the soul of the people was much **d.** 7114
Nu 32:9 they **d.** the heart of the children 5106
De 1:21 thee: fear not, neither be **d.**. 2865
De 1:28 our brethren have **d.** our heart, 4549
Isa 42:4 He shall not fail nor be **d.**, till 7533
Col 3:21 children to anger, lest they be **d.**. *120*

DISCOVER See also DISCOVERED; DISCOVERETH; DISCOVERING.
De 22:30 wife, nor **d.** his father's skirt. 1540
1Sa 14:8 and we will **d.** ourselves unto them. 1540
Job 41:13 can **d.** the face of his garment? 1540
Pr 18:2 but that his heart may **d.** itself. 1540
Pr 25:9 and **d.** not a secret to another: 1540
Isa 3:17 Lord will **d.** their secret parts. 6168
Jer 13:26 Therefore will I **d.** thy skirts 2834
La 4:22 of Edom; he will **d.** thy sins. 1540
Eze 16:37 will **d.** thy nakedness unto them, 1540
Ho 2:10 now will I **d.** her lewdness in the 1540
Mic 1:6 I will **d.** the foundations thereof. 1540
Na 3:5 will **d.** thy skirts upon thy face, 1540

DISCOVERED
Ex 20:26 that thy nakedness be not **d.** 1540
Le 20:18 he hath **d.** her fountain, and she 6168
1Sa 14:11 And both of them **d.** themselves 1540
1Sa 22:6 Saul heard that David was **d.**, 3045
2Sa 22:16 foundations of the world were **d.**, 1540
Ps 18:15 foundations of the world were **d.** 1540
Isa 22:8 And he **d.** the covering of Judah, 1540
Isa 57:8 thou hast **d.** thyself to another 1540
Jer 13:22 thine iniquity are thy skirts **d.**, 1540
La 2:14 they have not **d.** thine iniquity, 1540
Eze 13:14 foundation thereof shall be **d.**, 1540
Eze 16:36 thy nakedness **d.** through thy 1540
Eze 16:57 thy wickedness was **d.**, as at the 1540
Eze 21:24 that your transgressions are **d.**, 1540
Eze 22:10 In thee have they **d.** their fathers' 1540
Eze 23:10 These **d.** her nakedness: they 1540
Eze 23:18 she **d.** her whoredoms, and **d.** her 1540
Eze 23:29 thy whoredoms shall be **d.**, both 1540
Ho 7:1 the iniquity of Ephraim was **d.**, 1540
Ac 21:3 when we had **d.** Cyprus, we left *398*
Ac 27:39 they **d.** a certain creek with a *2657*

DISCOVERETH
Job 12:22 He **d.** deep things out of darkness, 1540
Ps 29:9 and **d.** the forests: and in his 2834

DISCOVERING
Hab 3:13 **d.** the foundation unto the neck. 6168

DISCREET
Ge 41:33 look out a man **d.** and wise, 995
Ge 41:39 none so **d.** and wise as thou art: 995
Tit 2:5 To be **d.**, chaste, keepers at home, *4998*

DISCREETLY
Mk 12:34 saw that he answered **d.**, he said *3562*

DISCRETION
Ps 112:5 he will guide his affairs with **d.**. 4941
Pr 1:4 the young man knowledge and **d.**. 4209
Pr 2:11 **D.** shall preserve thee, 4209
Pr 3:21 eyes: keep sound wisdom and **d.**: 4209
Pr 5:2 That thou mayest regard **d.**, and 4209
Pr 11:22 a fair woman which is without **d.**. 2940
Pr 19:11 **d.** of a man deferreth his anger; 7922
Isa 28:26 his God doth instruct him to **d.**, 4941
Jer 10:12 out the heavens by his **d.**. 8394

DISDAINED
1Sa 17:42 and saw David, he **d.** him: for he 959
Job 30:1 whose fathers I would have **d.** to 3988

DISEASE See also DISEASED; DISEASES.
2Ki 1:2 whether I shall recover of this **d.**. 2483
2Ki 8:8, 9 Shall I recover of this **d.**? 2483
2Ch 16:12 until his **d.** was exceeding great: 2483
2Ch 16:12 yet in his **d.** he sought not to the 2483
2Ch 21:15 sickness by **d.** of thy bowels, until 4245
2Ch 21:18 his bowels with an incurable **d.**. 2483
Job 30:18 By the great force of my **d.** is my
Ps 38:7 are filled with a loathsome **d.**:
Ps 41:8 An evil **d.**, say they, cleaveth fast 1697
Ec 6:2 this is vanity, and it is an evil **d.**. 2483
Mt 4:23 all manner of **d.** among the people. *3119*
Mt 9:35 and every **d.** among the people. *3119*
Mt 10:1 of sickness and all manner of **d.**. *3119*
Joh 5:4 whole of whatsoever **d.** he had. *3553*

DISEASED
1Ki 15:23 his old age he was **d.** in his feet. 2470
2Ch 16:12 year of his reign was **d.** in his feet, 2470
Eze 34:4 The **d.** have ye not strengthened, 2456
Eze 34:21 pushed all the **d.** with your horns, 2456
Mt 9:20 was **d.** with an issue of blood
Mt 14:35 unto him all that were **d.**; *2560,2192*
Mk 1:32 unto him all that were **d.**, *2560,2192*
Joh 6:2 which he did on them that were **d.** *770*

DISEASES
Ex 15:26 put none of these **d.** upon thee, 4245
De 7:15 put none of the evil **d.** of Egypt, 4064
De 28:60 bring upon thee all the **d.** of Egypt, 4064
2Ch 21:19 his sickness: so he died of sore **d.** 8463
2Ch 24:25 (for they left him in great **d.**,) his 4251
Ps 103:3 iniquities: who healeth all thy **d.**; 8463
Mt 4:24 that were taken with divers **d.** *3554*
Mk 1:34 many that were sick of divers **d.**, *3554*
Lu 4:40 any sick with divers **d.** brought *3554*
Lu 6:17 him; and to be healed of their **d.**; *3554*
Lu 9:1 over all devils, and to cure **d.**. *3554*
Ac 19:12 and the **d.** departed from them, *3554*
Ac 28:9 which had **d.** in the island, came, *769*

DISFIGURE
Mt 6:16 **for they d. their faces, that they** *853*

DISGRACE
Jer 14:21 do not **d.** the throne of thy glory: 5034

DISGUISE See also DISGUISED; DISGUISETH.
1Ki 14:2 Arise, I pray thee, and **d.** thyself, 8138
1Ki 22:30 I will **d.** myself and enter into the 2664
2Ch 18:29 I will **d.** myself and will go to the 2664

DISGUISED
1Sa 28:8 And Saul **d.** himself, and put on 2664
1Ki 20:38 and **d.** himself with ashes upon 2664
1Ki 22:30 And the king of Israel **d.** himself, 2664
2Ch 18:29 So the king of Israel **d.** himself; 2664
2Ch 35:22 but **d.** himself, that he might fight 2664

DISGUISETH
Job 24:15 shall see me: and **d.** his face. 5643

DISH See DISHES; SNUFFDISH.
Jg 5:25 brought forth butter in a lordly **d.** 5602
2Ki 21:13 as a man wipeth a **d.**, wiping it, 6747
Mt 26:23 **dippeth his hand with me in the d.**,*5165*
Mk 14:20 **that dippeth with me in the d.**, *5165*

DISHAN (di'-shan) See also DISHON.
Ge 36:21 And Dishon, and Ezer, and **D.**: 1789
Ge 36:28 The children of **D.** are these: Uz 1789
Ge 36:30 Duke Dishon, duke Ezer, duke **D.**: 1789
1Ch 1:38 and Dishon, and Ezar, and **D.**. 1789
1Ch 1:42 The sons of **D.**; Uz, and Aran. 1789

DISHES
Ex 25:29 thou shalt make the **d.** thereof, 7086
Ex 37:16 the table, his **d.**, and his spoons, 7086
Nu 4:7 put thereon the **d.**, and the spoons, 7086

DISHON (di'-shon) See also DISHAN.
Ge 36:21 And **D.**, and Ezer, and Dishan: 1788
Ge 36:25 **D.**, and Aholibamah the daughter 1788
Ge 36:26 are the children of **D.**; Hemdan, 1788
Ge 36:30 Duke **D.**, duke Ezer, duke Dishan: 1788
1Ch 1:38 and **D.**, and Ezar, and Dishan. 1788
1Ch 1:41 The sons of Anah; **D.**. And the 1788
1Ch 1:41 sons of **D.**; Amram, and Eshban, 1788

DISHONEST
Eze 22:13 smitten mine hand at thy **d.** gain 1215
Eze 22:27 to destroy souls, to get **d.** gain. 1215

DISHONESTY
2Co 4:2 renounced the hidden things of **d.**, *152*

DISHONOUR See also DISHONOUREST; DISHONOURETH.
Ezr 4:14 meet for us to see the king's **d.**, 6173
Ps 35:26 be clothed with shame and **d.** that 3639
Ps 69:19 and my shame, and my **d.**: mine 3639
Ps 71:13 be covered with reproach and **d.** 3639
Pr 6:33 A wound and **d.** shall he get; 7036
Joh 8:49 **honour my Father, and ye do d. me.***818*
Ro 1:24 to **d.** their own bodies between *818*
Ro 9:21 unto honour, and another unto **d.**? *819*
1Co 15:43 It is sown in **d.**; it is raised in *819*
2Co 6:8 By honour and **d.**, by evil report *819*
2Ti 2:20 some to honour, and some to **d.**. *819*

DISHONOUREST
Ro 2:23 breaking the law **d.** thou God? *818*

DISHONOURETH
Mic 7:6 son **d.** the father, the daughter 5034
1Co 11:4 his head covered, **d.** his head. *2617*
1Co 11:5 her head uncovered **d.** her head: *2617*

DISINHERIT
Nu 14:12 with the pestilence, and **d.** them, 3423

DISMAYED
De 31:8 thee: fear not, neither be **d.**. 2865
Jos 1:9 neither be thou **d.**: for the Lord 2865
Jos 8:1 neither be thou **d.**: take all the 2865
Jos 10:25 Fear not, nor be **d.**, be strong and 2865
1Sa 17:11 Philistine, they were **d.**, and greatly 2865
2Ki 19:26 they were **d.** and confounded; 2865
1Ch 22:13 courage; dread not, nor be **d.**. 2865
1Ch 28:20 fear not, nor be **d.**: for the Lord 2865
2Ch 20:15 Be not afraid nor **d.** by reason of 2865
2Ch 20:17 fear not, nor be **d.**; to morrow go 2865
2Ch 32:7 be not afraid nor **d.** for the king of 2865
Isa 21:3 of it; I was **d.** at the seeing of it. 926
Isa 37:27 they were **d.** and confounded; 2865
Isa 41:10 be not **d.**; for I am thy God: 8159
Isa 41:23 that we may be **d.**, and behold it 8159
Jer 1:17 be not **d.** at their faces, lest I 2865
Jer 8:9 ashamed, they are **d.** and taken: 2865
Jer 10:2 be not **d.** at the signs of heaven; 2865
Jer 10:2 for the heathen are **d.** at them. 2865
Jer 17:18 be confounded: let them be **d.**, 2865
Jer 17:18 but let not me be **d.**: bring upon 2865
Jer 23:4 they shall fear no more, nor be **d.**, 2865
Jer 30:10 neither be **d.**, O Israel: for, lo, 2865
Jer 46:5 Wherefore have I seen them **d.** 2844
Jer 46:27 be not **d.**, O Israel: for, behold, 2865
Jer 48:1 Misgab is confounded and **d.**. 2865
Jer 49:37 For I will cause Elam to be **d.** 2865
Jer 50:36 mighty men; and they shall be **d.**. 2865
Eze 2:6 of their words, nor be **d.** at their 2865
Eze 3:9 neither be **d.** at their looks, though 2865
Ob 9 mighty men, O Teman, shall be **d.**, 2865

DISMAYING
Jer 48:39 a derision and a **d.** to all them 4288

DISMISSED
2Ch 23:8 Jehoiada the priest **d.** not the 6362
Ac 15:30 So when they were **d.**, they came *630*
Ac 19:41 thus spoken, he **d.** the assembly. *630*

DISOBEDIENCE
Ro 5:19 by one man's **d.** many were made *3876*
2Co 10:6 to revenge all **d.**, when your *3876*
Eph 2:2 now worketh in the children of **d.**: *543*
Eph 5:6 of God upon the children of **d.**: *543*
Col 3:6 of God cometh on the children of **d.**: *543*
Heb 2:2 transgression and **d.** received a *3876*

DISOBEDIENT
1Ki 13:26 the man of God, who was **d.** unto 4784
Ne 9:26 Nevertheless they were **d.**, and 4784
Lu 1:17 the **d.** to the wisdom of the just; *545*
Ac 26:19 was not **d.** unto the heavenly vision: *545*
Ro 1:30 of evil things, **d.** to parents, *545*
Ro 10:21 unto a **d.** and gainsaying people. *544*
1Ti 1:9 but for the lawless and **d.**, for the *506*
2Ti 3:2 blasphemers, **d.** to parents, *545*
Tit 1:16 being abominable, and **d.**, and unto *545*
Tit 3:3 sometimes foolish, **d.**, deceived, *545*
1Pe 2:7 but unto them which be **d.**, *544*
1Pe 2:8 stumble at the word, being **d.**: *544*
1Pe 3:20 Which sometime were **d.**, when *544*

DISOBEYED
1Ki 13:21 hast **d.** the mouth of the Lord, 4784

DISORDERLY
2Th 3:6 every brother that walketh **d.**, *814*
2Th 3:7 behaved not ourselves **d.** among *812*
2Th 3:11 some which walk among you **d.**, *814*

DISPATCH
Eze 23:47 and **d.** them with their swords; 1254

DISPENSATION
1Co 9:17 a **d.** of the gospel is committed........ *3622*
Eph 1:10 That in the **d.** of the fulness of......... *3622*
Eph 3:2 heard of the **d.** of the grace of God.... *3622*
Col 1:25 according to the **d.** of God which........ *3622*

DISPERSE See also DISPERSED.
1Sa 14:34 **D.** yourselves among the people, ... 6327
Pr 15:7 The lips of the wise **d.** knowledge: 2219
Eze 12:15 and **d.** them in the countries. 2219
Eze 20:23 and **d.** them through the countries;..... 2219
Eze 22:15 and **d.** thee in the countries, and........ 2219
Eze 29:12 and **d.** them through the countries. 2219
Eze 30:23 will **d.** them through the countries. 2219
Eze 30:26 and **d.** them among the countries; 2219

DISPERSED
2Ch 11:23 **d.** of all his children throughout.......... 6555
Es 3:8 and **d.** among the people in all.......... 6504
Ps 112:9 He hath **d.**, he hath given to the......... 6340
Pr 5:16 Let thy fountains be **d.** abroad,.......... 6327
Isa 11:12 gather together the **d.** of Judah.......... 5310
Eze 36:19 were **d.** through the countries: 2219
Zep 3:10 the daughter of my **d.**, shall bring......... 6327
Joh 7:35 unto the **d.** among the Gentiles? *1290*
Ac 5:37 as many as obeyed him, were **d.**.......... *1287*
2Co 9:9 He hath **d.** abroad; he hath given *4650*

DISPERSIONS
Jer 25:34 of your slaughter and of your **d.**........... 8600

DISPLAYED
Ps 60:4 may be **d.** because of the truth. 5127

DISPLEASE See also DISPLEASED.
Ge 31:35 Let it not **d.** my lord that I cannot...... 2734
Nu 22:34 **d.** thee, I will get me back 7489,5869
1Sa 29:7 thou **d.** not the lords of...... 6213,7451,5869
2Sa 11:25 Let not this thing **d.** thee, for..... 7489,5869
Pr 24:18 the Lord see it, and it **d.** him,..... 7489,5869

DISPLEASED
Ge 38:10 which he did **d.** the Lord:......... 7489,5869
Ge 48:17 And when Joseph...it **d.** him:...... 7489,5869
Nu 11:1 complained, it **d.** the Lord:.......... 7451,241
Nu 11:10 greatly; Moses also was **d.**........ 5869,7541
1Sa 8:6 But the thing **d.** Samuel, ... 7489,5869
1Sa 18:8 and the saying **d.** him; and he..... 7489,5869
2Sa 6:8 And David was **d.**, because the.......... 2734
2Sa 11:27 thing that David had done **d.**....... 7489,5869
1Ki 1:6 his father had not **d.** him at any......... 6087
1Ki 20:43 went to his house heavy and **d.**, ... 2198
1Ki 21:4 came into his house heavy and **d.**........ 2198
1Ch 13:11 And David was **d.**, because the........... 2734
1Ch 21:7 God was **d.** with this thing;........ 3415,5869
Ps 60:1 thou hast been **d.**; O turn thyself........... 599
Isa 59:15 it **d.** him that there was no........ 7489,5869
Da 6:14 was sore **d.** with himself, and set 888
Jon 4:1 But it **d.** Jonah exceedingly, ... 7489,5869
Hab 3:8 the Lord **d.** against the rivers? 2734
Zec 1:2 The Lord hath been sore **d.** with 7107
Zec 1:15 I am very sore **d.** with the heathen 7107
Zec 1:15 at ease: for I was but a little **d.**, ... 7107
Mt 21:15 son of David; they were sore **d.**, ... *23*
Mk 10:14 Jesus saw it, he was much **d.**, ... *23*
Mk 10:41 began to be much **d.** with James *23*
Ac 12:20 Herod was highly **d.** with them of........ *2371*

DISPLEASURE
De 9:19 was afraid of the anger and hot **d.**, ... 2534
Jg 15:3 though I do them a **d.**...................... 7451
Ps 2:5 and vex them in his sore **d.**. 2740
Ps 6:1 neither chasten me in thy hot **d.**. 2534
Ps 38:1 neither chasten me in thy hot **d.**. 2534

DISPOSED
Job 34:13 who hath **d.** the whole world?.......... 7760
Job 37:15 thou know when God **d.** them, ... 7760
Ac 18:27 he was **d.** to pass into Achaia, ... *1014*
1Co 10:27 you to a feast, and ye be **d.** to go;..... *2309*

DISPOSING
Pr 16:33 the whole **d.** thereof is of the Lord..... 4941

DISPOSITION
Ac 7:53 the law by the **d.** of angels, ... *1296*

DISPOSSESS See also DISPOSSESSED.
Nu 33:53 And ye shall **d.** the inhabitants 3423
De 7:17 more than I; how can I **d.** them?......... 3423

DISPOSSESSED
Nu 32:39 and **d.** the Amorite which was 3423
Jg 11:23 God of Israel hath **d.** the Amorites..... 3423

DISPUTATION See also DISPUTATIONS.
Ac 15:2 no small dissension and **d.** with.......... *4803*

DISPUTATIONS
Ro 14:1 receive ye, but not to doubtful **d.**....... *1253*

DISPUTE See also DISPUTED; DISPUTING.
Job 23:7 the righteous might **d.** with him, ... 3198

DISPUTED
Mk 9:33 **that ye d. among yourselves by** *1260*
Mk 9:34 they had **d.** among themselves,.......... *1256*
Ac 9:29 and **d.** against the Grecians:............. *4802*
Ac 17:17 **d.** he in the synagogue with the......... *1256*
Jude 9 he **d.** about the body of Moses, ... *1256*

DISPUTER
1Co 1:20 where is the **d.** of this world?........... *4804*

DISPUTING See also DISPUTINGS.
Ac 6:9 and of Asia, **d.** with Stephen. *4802*
Ac 15:7 when there had been much **d.**, ... *4803*
Ac 19:8 three months, **d.** and persuading *1256*
Ac 19:9 **d.** daily in the school of one *1256*
Ac 24:12 me in the temple **d.** with any man, ... *1256*

DISPUTINGS
Php 2:14 without murmurings and **d.**: *1261*
1Ti 6:5 Perverse **d.** of men of corrupt........... *3859*

DISQUIET See also DISQUIETED.
Jer 50:34 and **d.** the inhabitants of Babylon....... 7264

DISQUIETED
1Sa 28:15 Why hast thou **d.** me, to bring me...... 7264
Ps 39:6 shew: surely they are **d.** in vain:........ 1993
Ps 42:5 and why art thou **d.** in me? hope........ 1993
Ps 42:11 why art thou **d.** within me? hope........ 1993
Ps 43:5 why art thou **d.** within me? hope........ 1993
Pr 30:21 For three things the earth is **d.**, ... 7264

DISQUIETNESS
Ps 38:8 I have roared by reason of the **d.**........ 5100

DISSEMBLED See also DISSEMBLETH.
Jos 7:11 and have also stolen, and **d.** also,....... 3584
Jer 42:20 For ye **d.** in your hearts, when ye....... 8582
Ga 2:13 other Jews **d.** likewise with him; *4942*

DISSEMBLERS
Ps 26:4 neither will I go in with **d.**. 5956

DISSEMBLETH
Pr 26:24 he that hateth **d.** with his lips, ... 5234

DISSENSION
Ac 15:2 had no small **d.** and disputation *4714*
Ac 23:7 a **d.** between the Pharisees and the.... *4714*
Ac 23:10 And when there arose a great **d.**,........ *4714*

DISSIMULATION
Ro 12:9 Let love be without **d.** Abhor............. *505*
Ga 2:13 was carried away with their **d.**............ *5272*

DISSOLVE See also DISSOLVED; DISSOLVEST; DISSOLVING.
Da 5:16 interpretations, and **d.** doubts: 8271

DISSOLVED
Ps 75:3 the inhabitants therefore are **d.**: 4127
Isa 14:31 thou, whole Palestina, art **d.**: 4127
Isa 24:19 the earth is clean **d.**, the earth 6565
Isa 34:4 all the host of heaven shall be **d.**,......... 4743
Na 2:6 and the palace shall be **d.**. 4127
2Co 5:1 house of this tabernacle were **d.**, ... *2647*
2Pe 3:11 that all things shall be **d.**, ... *3089*
2Pe 3:12 heavens being on fire shall be **d.**, ... *3089*

DISSOLVEST
Job 30:22 upon it, and **d.** my substance............. 4127

DISSOLVING
Da 5:12 hard sentences, and **d.** of doubts,......... 8271

DISTAFF
Pr 31:19 and her hands hold the **d.**.................. 6418

DISTANT
Ex 36:22 equally **d.** one from another: 7947

DISTIL
De 32:2 my speech shall **d.** as the dew,........... 5140
Job 36:28 clouds do drop and **d.** upon man......... 7491

DISTINCTION
1Co 14:7 they give a **d.** in the sounds, ... *1293*

DISTINCTLY
Ne 8:8 in the book in the law of God **d.**, ... 6567

DISTRACTED
Ps 88:15 while I suffer thy terrors I am **d.**........ 6323

DISTRACTION
1Co 7:35 attend upon the Lord without **d.**.......... *563*

DISTRESS See also DISTRESSED; DISTRESSES.
Ge 35:3 answered me in the day of my **d.**,...... 6869
Ge 42:21 therefore is this **d.** come upon us....... 6869
De 2:9 **D.** not the Moabites, neither............ 6696
De 2:19 Ammon, **d.** them not, nor meddle........ 6696
De 28:53 thine enemies shall **d.** thee:............... 6693
De 28:55 thine enemies shall **d.** thee in all........ 6693
De 28:57 enemy shall **d.** thee in thy gates. 6693
Jg 11:7 unto me now when ye are in **d.**?........ 6887
1Sa 22:2 And every one that was in **d.**, ... 4689
2Sa 22:7 In my **d.** I called upon the Lord, ... 6862
1Ki 1:29 redeemed my soul out of all **d.**, ... 6869
2Ch 28:22 And in the time of his **d.** did he 6887
Ne 2:17 Ye see the **d.** that we are in,............. 7451
Ne 9:37 pleasure, and we are in great **d.**.......... 6869
Ps 4:1 enlarged me when I was in **d.**; 6862
Ps 18:6 In my **d.** I called upon the Lord, ... 6862
Ps 118:5 I called upon the Lord in **d.**:.............. 4712
Ps 120:1 In my **d.** I cried unto the Lord, ... 6869
Pr 1:27 **d.** and anguish cometh upon you. 6869
Isa 25:4 a strength to the needy in his **d.**, ... 6862
Isa 29:2 Yet I will **d.** Ariel, and there shall 6693
Isa 29:7 and her munition, and that **d.** her, ... 6693
Jer 10:18 and will **d.** them, that they may 6887
La 1:20 O Lord; for I am in **d.**: my bowels 6887
Ob 12 spoken proudly in the day of **d.**,.......... 6869
Ob 14 that did remain in the day of **d.**.......... 6869
Zep 1:15 a day of trouble and **d.**, a day of......... 4691
Zep 1:17 And I will bring **d.** upon men,............ 6887
Lu 21:23 **there shall be great d. in the land,** .. *318*
Lu 21:25 **and upon the earth d. of nations,** .. *4928*
Ro 8:35 tribulation, or **d.**, or persecution,........ *4730*
1Co 7:26 this is good for the present **d.**,............ *318*
1Th 3:7 our affliction and **d.** by your faith: *318*

DISTRESSED
Ge 32:7 Jacob was greatly afraid and **d.**: 3334
Nu 22:3 and Moab was **d.** because of the 6973
Jg 2:15 them: and they were greatly **d.**........... 3334
Jg 10:9 so that Israel was sore **d.**................ 3334
1Sa 13:6 (for the people were **d.**,) then the....... 5065
1Sa 14:24 the men of Israel were **d.** that day: 5065
1Sa 28:15 And Saul answered, I am sore **d.**; 6887
1Sa 30:6 And David was greatly **d.**; for the 3334
2Sa 1:26 I am **d.** for thee, my brother............. 6887
2Ch 28:20 **d.** him, but strengthened him not 6696
2Co 4:8 troubled on every side, yet not **d.**; *4729*

DISTRESSES
Ps 25:17 O bring thou me out of my **d.**............. 4691
Ps 107:6 he delivered them out of their **d.**......... 4691
Ps 107:13 he saved them out of their **d.**............ 4691
Ps 107:19 he saved them out of their **d.**............ 4691
Ps 107:28 he bringeth them out of their **d.**......... 4691
Eze 30:16 and Noph shall have **d.** daily............. 6862
2Co 6:4 in afflictions, in necessities, in **d.**,....... *4730*
2Co 12:10 persecutions, in **d.** for Christ's sake:... *4730*

DISTRIBUTE See also DISTRIBUTED; DISTRIBUTETH; DISTRIBUTING.
Jos 13:32 Moses did **d.** for inheritance in 5157
2Ch 31:14 to **d.** the oblations of the Lord,.......... 5414
Ne 13:13 was to **d.** unto their brethren. 2505
Lu 18:22 **d. unto the poor, and thou shalt** ... *1239*
1Ti 6:18 works, ready to **d.**, willing to *2130*

DISTRIBUTED
Jos 14:1 Israel, **d.** for inheritance to them........ 5157
1Ch 24:3 David **d.** them, both Zadok of............ 2505
2Ch 23:18 whom David had **d.** in the house of..... 2505
Joh 6:11 he **d.** to the disciples, and the *1239*
1Co 7:17 as God hath **d.** to every man,........... *3307*
2Co 10:13 rule which God hath **d.** to us,............ *3307*

DISTRIBUTETH
Job 21:17 God **d.** sorrows in his anger.............. 2505

DISTRIBUTING
Ro 12:13 **D.** to the necessity of saints; *2841*

DISTRIBUTION
Ac 4:35 feet: and **d.** was made unto every...... *1239*
2Co 9:13 and for your liberal **d.** unto them,...... *2842*

DITCH See also DITCHES.
Job 9:31 Yet shalt thou plunge me in the **d.**,..... 7845
Ps 7:15 is fallen into the **d.** which he 7845
Pr 23:27 For a whore is a deep **d.**; and a......... 7745
Isa 22:11 Ye made also a **d.** between the.......... 4724

Mt 15:14 **blind, both shall fall into the d** *999*
Lu 6:39 **they not both fall into the d.?** *999*

DITCHES
2Ki 3:16 Make this valley full of **d.** 1356

DIVERS See also DIVERSE.
De 22:9 sow thy vineyard with **d.** seeds:......... 3610
De 22:11 a garment of **d.** sorts, as of 8162
De 25:13 shalt not have in thy bag **d.** weights,.........
De 25:14 not have in thine house **d.** measures, ...
Jg 5:30 to Sisera a prey of **d.** colours, ... 6648
Jg 5:30 a prey of **d.** colours of needlework, ... 6648
Jg 5:30 of **d.** colours of needlework.............. 6648
2Sa 13:18 she had a garment of **d.** colours 6446
2Sa 13:19 rent her garment of **d.** colours........... 6446
1Ch 29:2 glistering stones, and of **d.** colours. 7553
2Ch 16:14 filled with sweet odours and **d.** kinds.........
2Ch 21:4 and **d.** also of the princes of Israel...........
2Ch 30:11 **d.** of Asher and Manesseh and 582
Ps 78:45 sent **d.** sorts of flies among them, ...
Ps 105:31 came **d.** sorts of flies, and lice ....
Pr 20:10 **D.** weights, and **d.** measures,..................
Pr 20:23 **D.** weights are an abomination.................
Ec 5:7 words there are also **d.** vanities: ....
Eze 16:16 thy high places with **d.** colours,.......... 2921
Eze 17:3 of feathers, which had **d.** colours,....... 7553
Mt 4:24 with **d.** diseases and torments, ... *4164*
Mt 24:7 **and earthquakes, in d. places** ....
Mk 1:34 many that were sick of **d.** diseases, ... *4164*
Mk 8:3 **for d. of them came from far** *5100*
Mk 13:8 **shall be earthquakes in d. places,** ....
Lu 4:40 sick with **d.** diseases brought............ *4164*
Lu 21:11 **great earthquakes shall be in d.** ....
Ac 19:9 But when **d.** were hardened, and *5100*
1Co 12:10 to another **d.** king of tongues;..................
2Ti 3:6 with sins, led away with **d.** lusts, ... *4164*
Tit 3:3 serving **d.** lusts and pleasures,.......... *4164*
Heb 1:1 times and in **d.** manners spake in *4187*
Heb 2:4 and with **d.** miracles, and gifts of....... *4164*
Heb 9:10 meats and drinks, and **d.** washings...... *1313*
Heb 13:9 with **d.** and strange doctrines. *4164*
Jas 1:2 when ye fall into **d.** temptations; *4164*

DIVERSE See also DIVERS.
Le 19:19 cattle gender with a **d.** kind:............. 3610
Es 1:7 vessels being **d.** one from another,).... 8138
Es 3:8 their laws are **d.** from all people;........ 8138
Da 7:3 the sea, **d.** one from another............. 8133
Da 7:7 and it was **d.** from all the beasts 8133
Da 7:19 which was **d.** from all the others, ... 8133
Da 7:23 which shall be **d.** from all kingdoms,.... 8133
Da 7:24 and he shall be **d.** from the first,........ 8133

DIVERSITIES
1Co 12:4 Now there are **d.** of gifts, but the *1243*
1Co 12:6 there are **d.** of operations, but it........ *1243*
1Co 12:28 helps, governments, **d.** of tongues *1085*

DIVIDE See also DIVIDED; DIVIDETH; DIVIDING.
Ge 1:6 let it **d.** the waters from the waters. 914
Ge 1:14 to **d.** the day from the night; 914
Ge 1:18 to **d.** the light from the darkness: 914
Ge 49:7 will **d.** them in Jacob, and scatter 2505
Ge 49:27 at night he shall **d.** the spoil. 2505
Ex 14:16 thine hand over the sea, and **d.** it:....... 1234
Ex 15:9 I will overtake, I will **d.** the spoil; 2505
Ex 21:35 the live ox, and **d.** the money of it; 2673
Ex 21:35 the dead ox also they shall **d.**.............. 2673
Ex 26:33 the vail shall **d.** unto you between........ 914
Le 1:17 thereof, but shall not **d.** it asunder: 914
Le 5:8 neck, but shall not **d.** it asunder: 914
Le 11:4 cud, or of them that **d.** the hoof:........ 6536
Le 11:7 the swine, though he **d.** the hoof,........ 6536
Nu 31:27 And **d.** the prey into two parts; 2673
Nu 33:54 And ye shall **d.** the land by lot for...... 5157
Nu 34:17 which shall **d.** the land unto you: 5157
Nu 34:18 tribe, to **d.** the land by inheritance...... 5157
Nu 34:29 Lord commanded to **d.** the inheritance.......
De 14:7 or of them that **d.** the cloven hoof;..... 6536
De 14:7 chew the cud, but **d.** not the hoof, ... 6536
De 19:3 **d.** the coasts ... into three parts, ...
Jos 1:6 shalt thou **d.** for an inheritance................
Jos 13:6 **d.** thou it by lot unto the Israelites 5307
Jos 13:7 **d.** this land for an inheritance 2505
Jos 18:5 And they shall **d.** it into seven........... 2505
Jos 22:8 **d.** the spoil of your enemies with 2505
2Sa 19:29 said, Thou and Ziba **d.** the land.......... 2505
1Ki 3:25 **D.** the living child in two, and........... 1504
1Ki 3:26 be neither mine nor thine, but **d.** it..... 1504
Ne 9:11 thou didst **d.** the sea before them,...... 1234
Ne 9:22 and didst **d.** them into corners: 2505
Job 27:17 and the innocent shall **d.** the silver. 2505
Ps 55:9 Destroy, O Lord, and **d.** their 6385
Ps 60:6 I will **d.** Shechem, and mete out 2505
Ps 74:13 Thou didst **d.** the sea by thy............ 6565
Ps 108:7 will rejoice, I will **d.** Shechem, and 2505
Pr 16:19 than to **d.** the spoil with the proud. 2505
Isa 9:3 rejoice when they **d.** the spoil........... 2505
Isa 53:12 Therefore will I **d.** him a portion 5312
Isa 53:12 he shall **d.** the spoil with the strong;... 5312
Eze 5:1 balances to weigh, and **d.** the hair. 2505
Eze 45:1 Moreover, when ye shall **d.** by lot...... 5307
Eze 47:21 So shall ye **d.** this land unto you 2505
Eze 47:22 shall **d.** it by lot for an inheritance 5307
Eze 48:29 ye shall **d.** by lot unto the tribes 5307
Da 11:39 and shall **d.** the land for gain. 2505
Lu 12:13 that he **d.** the inheritance with me. *3307*
Lu 22:17 **Take this, and d. it among** *1266*

DIVIDED
Ge 1:4 God **d.** the light from the darkness....... 914
Ge 1:7 and **d.** the waters which were under..... 914
Ge 10:5 were the isles of the Gentiles **d.** 6504
Ge 10:25 in his days was the earth **d.**; 6385
Ge 10:32 by these were the nations **d.** in the 5504
Ge 14:15 And he **d.** himself against them, ... 2505
Ge 15:10 and **d.** them in the midst, and laid 1334
Ge 15:10 another: but the birds **d.** he not.......... 1334
Ge 32:7 and he **d.** the people that was with..... 2673
Ge 33:1 And he **d.** the children unto Leah, ... 2673
Ex 14:21 dry land, and the waters were **d.**. 1234
Nu 26:53 Unto these the land shall be **d.**.......... 2505
Nu 26:55 the land shall be **d.** by lot: 2505
Nu 26:56 shall the possession thereof be **d.**......... 2505
Nu 31:42 which Moses **d.** from the men that 2673
De 4:19 which the Lord thy God hath **d.**.......... 2505
De 32:8 **d.** to the nations their inheritance, ...
Jos 14:5 Israel did, and they **d.** the land. 2505
Jos 18:10 there Joshua **d.** the land unto the 2505
Jos 19:51 **d.** for an inheritance by lot in ....
Jos 23:4 I have **d.** unto you by lot.................. 5307
Jg 5:30 have they not **d.** the prey; to 2505
Jg 7:16 And he **d.** the three hundred men 2673
Jg 9:43 and **d.** them into three companies,...... 2673
Jg 19:29 and **d.** her, together with her 5408
2Sa 1:23 in their death they were not **d.**: 6504
1Ki 16:21 Then were the people of Israel **d.** 2505
1Ki 18:6 So they **d.** the land between them...... 2505
2Ki 2:8 they were **d.** hither and thither, ... 2673
1Ch 1:19 in his days the earth was **d.**: 6385
1Ch 23:6 And David **d.** them into courses 2505
1Ch 24:4 of Ithamar; and thus were they **d.**. 2505
1Ch 24:5 Thus were they **d.** by lot, one sort..... 2505
2Ch 35:13 and **d.** them speedily among all 7323
Job 38:25 Who hath **d.** a watercourse for the 6385
Ps 68:12 that tarried at home **d.** the spoil......... 2505
Ps 78:13 He **d.** the sea, and caused them......... 1234
Ps 78:55 and **d.** them an inheritance by............ 5307
Ps 136:13 To him which **d.** the Red sea into 1504
Isa 33:23 is the prey of a great spoil **d.**;........... 2505
Isa 34:17 his hand hath **d.** it unto them by 2505
Isa 51:15 the Lord thy God, that **d.** the sea, ... 7280
La 4:16 anger of the Lord hath **d.** them;.......... 2505
Eze 37:22 neither shall they be **d.** into two 2673
Da 2:41 of iron, the kingdom shall be **d.**; 6386
Da 5:28 Thy kingdom is **d.**, and given 6537
Da 11:4 and shall be **d.** toward the four 2673
Ho 10:2 Their heart is **d.**; now shall they 2505
Am 7:17 and thy land shall be **d.** by line; 2505
Mic 2:4 away he hath **d.** our fields................. 2505
Zec 14:1 and thy spoil shall be **d.** in the............ 2505
Mt 12:25 **Every kingdom d. against itself is** . *3307*
Mt 12:25 **city or house d. against itself**........ *3307*
Mt 12:26 **Satan, he is d. against himself;** *3307*
Mk 3:24 **if a kingdom be d. against itself,** ... *3307*
Mk 3:25 **if a house be d. against itself,** *3307*
Mk 3:26 **and be d., he cannot stand, but** *3307*
Mk 6:41 the two fishes **d.** he among them all. .. *3307*
Lu 11:17 **Every kingdom d. against itself is** . *1266*
Lu 11:17 **house d. against a house falleth** ....
Lu 11:18 **If Satan also be d. against himself,** *1266*
Lu 12:52 **there shall be five in one house d.,** . *1266*
Lu 12:53 **father shall be d. against the son,** .. *1266*
Lu 15:12 **And he d. unto them his living**...... *1244*
Ac 13:19 he **d.** their land to them by lot.......... *2624*
Ac 14:4 the multitude of the city was **d.**: *4977*
Ac 23:7 and the multitude was **d.**. *4977*
1Co 1:13 Is Christ **d.**? was Paul crucified.......... *3307*
Re 16:19 the great city was **d.** into three *1096*

DIVIDER
Lu 12:14 **made me a judge or a d. over you?** .*3312*

DIVIDETH
Le 11:4, 5 the cud; but **d.** not the hoof; 6536
Le 11:6 the cud, but **d.** not the hoof;............. 6536
Le 11:26 every beast which **d.** the hoof, ... 6536
De 14:8 the swine, because it **d.** the hoof, ... 6536
Job 26:12 he **d.** the sea with his power,........... 7280
Ps 29:7 the Lord **d.** the flames of fire........... 2672
Jer 31:35 which **d.** the sea when the waves....... 7280
Mt 25:32 **as a shepherd d. his sheep from** *873*
Lu 11:22 **he trusted, and d. his spoils**.......... *1239*

DIVIDING
Jos 19:49 end of **d.** the land for inheritance.............
Jos 19:51 made an end of **d.** the country........... 2505
Isa 63:12 **d.** the water before them, to.............. 1234
Da 7:25 a time and times and the **d.** of........... 6387
1Co 12:11 **d.** to every man severally as he.......... *1244*
2Ti 2:15 rightly **d.** the word of truth.............. *3718*
Heb 4:12 even to the **d.** asunder of soul and *3311*

DIVINATION See also DIVINATIONS.
Nu 22:7 with the rewards of **d.** in their........... 7081
Nu 23:23 is there any **d.** against Israel: 7081
De 18:10 or that useth **d.**, or an observer......... 7081
2Ki 17:17 used **d.** and enchantments, and.......... 7081
Jer 14:14 a false vision and **d.**, and a thing........ 7081
Eze 12:24 vain vision nor flattering **d.** within...... 4738
Eze 13:6 vanity and lying **d.**, saying, The 7081
Eze 13:7 have ye not spoken a lying **d.**,........... 4738
Eze 21:21 head of the two ways, to use **d.**: 7081
Eze 21:22 hand was the **d.** for Jerusalem, ... 7081
Eze 21:23 be unto them as a false **d.** in their...... 7080
Ac 16:16 possessed with a spirit of **d.** met us,... *4436*

DIVINATIONS
Eze 13:23 see no more vanity, nor divine **d.**:...... 7081

DIVINE See also DIVINETH; DIVINING.
Ge 44:15 such a man as I can certainly **d.**? 5172
1Sa 28:8 **d.** unto me by the familiar spirit, ... 7080
Pr 16:10 A **d.** sentence is in the lips of the 7081
Eze 13:9 that see vanity, and that **d.** lies:......... 7080
Eze 13:23 no more vanity, nor **d.** divinations 7081
Eze 21:29 whiles they **d.** a lie unto thee, ... 7080
Mic 3:6 unto you, that ye shall not **d.**;........... 7080
Mic 3:11 the prophets thereof **d.** for money:...... 7080
Heb 9:1 had also ordinances of **d.** service,....... *2999*
2Pe 1:3 According as his **d.** power hath.......... *2304*
2Pe 1:4 might be partakers of the **d.** nature, ... *2304*
Re *general* *title* Revelation Of ... John The **D.**...... *2312*

DIVINERS
De 18:14 observers of times, and unto **d.**: 7080
1Sa 6:2 called for the priests, and the **d.**, ... 7080
Isa 44:25 of the liars, and maketh **d.** mad; 7080
Jer 27:9 to your **d.**, nor to your dreamers, ... 7080
Jer 29:8 Let not your prophets and your **d.**,...... 7080
Mic 3:7 ashamed, and the **d.** confounded:........ 7080
Zec 10:2 and the **d.** have seen a lie,................ 7080

DIVINETH
Ge 44:5 and whereby indeed he **d.**? 5172

DIVINING
Eze 22:28 seeing vanity, and **d.** lies unto 7080

DIVISION See also DIVISIONS.
Ex 8:23 I will put a **d.** between my people 6304
2Ch 35:5 and after the **d.** of the families........... 2515
Lu 12:51 **I tell you, Nay; but rather d.** *1267*
Joh 7:43 there was a **d.** among the people *4978*
Joh 9:16 there was a **d.** among them.............. *4978*
Joh 10:19 There was a **d.** therefore again.......... *4978*

DIVISIONS
Jos 11:23 to their **d.** by their tribes.................. 4256
Jos 12:7 a possession according to their **d.**;...... 4256
Jos 18:10 of Israel according to their **d.** 4256
Jg 5:15 For the **d.** of Reuben...thoughts.......... 6391
Jg 5:16 the **d.** of Reuben...searchings 6391
1Ch 24:1 are the **d.** of the sons of Aaron.......... 4256
1Ch 26:1 Concerning the **d.** of the porters: 4256
1Ch 26:12 these were the **d.** of the porters, ... 4256
1Ch 26:19 These are the **d.** of the porters 4256
2Ch 35:5 according to the **d.** of the families....... 6391
2Ch 35:12 according to the **d.** of the families....... 4653
Ezr 6:18 they set the priests in their **d.**,.......... 6392

Ne 11:36 of the Levites were **d.** in Judah,......... 4256
Ro 16:17 them which cause **d.** and offences....... *1370*
1Co 1:10 that there be no **d.** among you; *4978*
1Co 3:3 you envying, and strife, and **d.**, ... *1370*
1Co 11:18 hear that there be **d.** among you; *4978*

DIVORCE See also DIVORCED; DIVORCEMENT.
Jer 3:8 away, and given her a bill of **d.**;......... 3748

DIVORCED
Le 21:14 widow, or a **d.** woman, or profane,..... 1644
Le 22:13 priest's daughter be a widow, or **d.**, ... 1644
Nu 30:9 of a widow, and of her that is **d.**, ... 1644
Mt 5:32 **her that is d. committeth adultery**. ..*630*

DIVORCEMENT
De 24:1 then let him write her a bill of **d.**, ... 3748
De 24:3 hate her, and write her a bill of **d.**,..... 3748
Isa 50:1 Where is the bill of your mother's **d.**,.. 3748
Mt 5:31 **let him give her a writing of d**........ *647*
Mt 19:7 command to give a writing of **d.**, ... *647*
Mk 10:4 Moses suffered to write a bill of **d.**, ... *647*

DIZAHAB (diz'-a-hab)
De 1:1 and Laban, and Hazeroth, and **D.**....... 1774

DO See also ADO; DID; DOEST; DOETH; DOING; DONE; UNDO.
Ge 6:17 I, even I, **d.** bring a flood of waters..........
Ge 9:13 I **d.** set my bow in the cloud, and it..........
Ge 11:6 and this they begin to **d.**: and now 6213
Ge 11:6 which they have imagined to **d.**.......... 6213
Ge 16:6 hand; **d.** to her as it pleaseth thee...... 6213
Ge 18:5 they said, So **d.**, as thou hast said...... 6213
Ge 18:17 Abraham that thing which I **d.**; 6213
Ge 18:19 Lord, to **d.** justice and judgment; 6213
Ge 18:25 from thee to **d.** after this manner, ... 6213
Ge 18:25 the Judge of all the earth **d.** right?...... 6213
Ge 18:29 said, I will not **d.** it for forty's sake. ... 6213
Ge 18:30 I will not **d.** it, if I find thirty there..... 6213
Ge 19:7 you, brethren, **d.** not so wickedly............
Ge 19:8 you, and **d.** ye to them as is good...... 6213
Ge 19:8 only unto these men **d.** nothing;.......... 6213
Ge 19:22 for I cannot **d.** any thing till thou........ 6213
Ge 21:23 thou shalt **d.** unto me, and to the....... 6213
Ge 22:12 the lad, neither **d.** thou any thing 6213
Ge 24:42 thou **d.** prosper my way which I go: ....
Ge 25:32 profit shall this birthright **d.** to me?..........
Ge 26:29 That thou wilt **d.** us no hurt, a 6213
Ge 27:37 and what shall I **d.** now unto thee, ... 6213
Ge 27:46 what good shall my life **d.** me?.................
Ge 30:31 if thou wilt **d.** this thing for me, I....... 6213
Ge 31:16 God hath said unto thee, **d.**................ 6213
Ge 31:29 power of my hand to **d.** you hurt: 6213
Ge 31:43 and what can I **d.** this day unto.......... 6213
Ge 32:12 saidst, I will surely **d.** thee good, ...
Ge 34:14 We cannot **d.** this thing, to give......... 6213
Ge 34:19 man deferred not to **d.** the thing, ... 6213
Ge 37:13 **D.** not thy brethren feed the flock in.........
Ge 39:9 can I **d.** this great wickedness, ... 6213
Ge 39:11 unto the house to **d.** his business;...... 6213
Ge 40:8 **D.** not interpretations belong to God?........
Ge 41:9 I **d.** remember my faults this day: ....
Ge 41:25 Pharaoh what he is about to **d.**.......... 6213
Ge 41:28 to **d.** he sheweth unto Pharaoh. 6213
Ge 41:34 Let Pharaoh **d.** this, and let him......... 6213
Ge 41:55 Joseph; what he saith to you, **d.**. 6213
Ge 42:1 Why **d.** ye look one upon another?............
Ge 42:18 This **d.**, and live; for I fear God:........ 6213
Ge 42:22 **D.** not sin against the child; ....
Ge 43:11 so now, **d.** this; take of the best........ 6213
Ge 44:7 thy servants should **d.** according 6213
Ge 44:17 said, God forbid that I should **d.** so:..... 6213
Ge 45:17 Say unto your brethren, This **d.** ye;.... 6213
Ge 45:19 thou art commanded, this **d.** ye; 6213
Ge 47:30 he said, I will **d.** as thou hast said. 6213
Ex 1:16 When ye **d.** the office of a midwife to........
Ex 3:20 I will **d.** in the midst thereof:............ 6213
Ex 4:15 will teach you what ye shall **d.**........... 6213
Ex 4:17 wherewith thou shalt **d.** signs. 6213
Ex 4:21 **d.** all those wonders before Pharaoh, .. 6213
Ex 5:4 Wherefore **d.** ye, Moses and Aaron, ...
Ex 5:17 Let us go and **d.** sacrifice to the ....
Ex 6:1 see what I will **d.** to Pharaoh:........... 6213
Ex 8:8 may **d.** sacrifice unto the Lord. ....
Ex 8:26 Moses said, It is not meet so to **d.**; ... 6213
Ex 9:5 To morrow the Lord shall **d.** this 6213
Ex 15:26 **d.** that which is right in his sight,....... 6213
Ex 17:2 wherefore **d.** ye tempt the Lord? ....
Ex 17:4 What shall I **d.** unto this people? 6213
Ex 18:16 **d.** make them know the statutes ....
Ex 18:20 and the work that they must **d.**. 6213
Ex 18:23 If thou shalt **d.** this thing, and God 6213
Ex 19:8 the Lord hath spoken we will **d.**.......... 6213
Ex 20:9 thou labour, and **d.** all thy work: 6213
Ex 20:10 in it thou shalt not **d.** any work,......... 6213
Ex 21:7 not go out as the menservants **d.**........ 3318
Ex 21:11 if he **d.** not these three unto her,....... 6213
Ex 22:30 shalt thou **d.** with thine oxen, and 6213
Ex 23:2 shalt not follow a multitude to **d.** evil; ....
Ex 23:12 Six days thou shalt **d.** thy work, ... 6213
Ex 23:22 his voice, and **d.** all that I speak; 6213
Ex 23:24 them, nor **d.** after their works: 6213
Ex 24:3 which the Lord hath said will we **d.**. ... 6213
Ex 24:7 that the Lord hath said will we **d.**,...... 6213
Ex 24:14 any man have any matters to **d.**,........ 1167
Ex 29:1 is the thing that thou shalt **d.** unto........ 6213
Ex 29:35 And thus shalt thou **d.** unto Aaron,..... 6213
Ex 29:41 shalt **d.** according to the meat 6213
Ex 31:11 commanded thee shall they **d.**............ 6213
Ex 32:14 he thought to **d.** unto his people. 6213
Ex 32:18 the noise of them that sing **d.** I hear.........
Ex 33:5 may know what to **d.** unto thee. 6213
Ex 33:17 I will **d.** this thing also that thou 6213
Ex 34:10 all thy people I will **d.** marvels,.......... 6213
Ex 34:10 thing that I will **d.** with thee............. 6213
Ex 34:15 gods, and **d.** sacrifice unto their gods, ...
Ex 35:1 commanded, that ye should **d.** 6213
Ex 35:19 to **d.** service in the holy place..................
Ex 35:35 weaver, even of them that **d.** any....... 6213
Ex 36:2 up to come unto the work to **d.** it: 6213
Ex 39:1, 41 to **d.** service in the holy place, ...
Le 4:2 and shall **d.** against any of them: 6213
Le 4:3 that is anointed **d.** sin according ....
Le 4:20 And he shall **d.** with the bullock 6213
Le 4:20 offering, so shall he **d.** with this:........ 6213
Le 5:1 if he **d.** not utter it, then he shall............
Le 5:4 his lips to **d.** evil, or to **d.** good, ...
Le 8:34 the Lord hath commanded to **d.**, ... 6213
Le 9:6 commanded that ye should **d.**: 6213
Le 10:9 **D.** not drink wine nor strong...................
Le 16:15 and **d.** with that blood as he did.......... 6213
Le 16:16 so shall he **d.** for the tabernacle......... 6213
Le 16:29 souls, and **d.** no work at all,.............. 6213
Le 18:3 wherein ye dwelt, shall ye not **d.**: 6213
Le 18:3 whither I bring you, shall ye not **d.**:.... 6213
Le 18:4 Ye shall **d.** my judgments, and........... 6213
Le 18:5 if a man **d.**, he shall live in them:....... 6213
Le 18:25 therefore I **d.** visit the iniquity.................
Le 19:15 ye shall **d.** no unrighteousness in........ 6213
Le 19:29 **D.** not prostitute thy daughter, ...
Le 19:35 Ye shall **d.** no unrighteousness in 6213
Le 19:37 judgments, and **d.** them; I am the 6213
Le 20:4 **d.** any ways hide their eyes from ....
Le 20:8 keep my statutes, and **d.** them: 6213
Le 20:22 all my judgments, and **d.** them:.......... 6213
Le 21:6 the bread of their God, they **d.** offer:........
Le 21:15 for I the Lord **d.** sanctify him. ....
Le 21:23 for I the Lord **d.** sanctify them. ....
Le 22:9 it: I the Lord **d.** sanctify them. ....
Le 22:16 for I the Lord **d.** sanctify them. ....
Le 22:31 my commandments, and **d.** them;........ 6213
Le 23:3 ye shall **d.** no work therein: 6213
Le 23:7 ye shall **d.** no servile work therein...... 6213
Le 23:8 ye shall **d.** no servile work................. 6213
Le 23:21 ye shall **d.** no servile work therein:...... 6213
Le 23:25 Ye shall **d.** no servile work therein: 6213
Le 23:28 shall **d.** no work in that same day:...... 6213
Le 23:31 Ye shall **d.** no manner of work: it......... 6213
Le 23:35 ye shall **d.** no servile work therein...... 6213
Le 23:36 and ye shall **d.** no servile work 6213
Le 25:18 Wherefore ye shall **d.** my statutes, ... 6213
Le 25:18 keep my judgments, and **d.** them; 6213
Le 25:45 strangers that **d.** sojourn among you, ...
Le 26:3 my commandments, and **d.** them;....... 6213
Le 26:14 not **d.** all these commandments;.......... 6213
Le 26:15 will not **d.** all my commandments,....... 6213
Le 26:16 I also will **d.** this unto you; I will........ 6213
Le 27:11 of which they **d.** not offer a sacrifice ....
Nu 2:5 those that **d.** pitch next unto him............
Nu 3:7 congregation, to **d.** the service of......... 5647
Nu 3:8 of Israel, to **d.** the service of the 5647
Nu 4:3 to **d.** the work in the tabernacle of..... 6213
Nu 4:19 **d.** unto them, that they may live,....... 6213
Nu 4:23 the service, to **d.** the work in the 5647
Nu 4:30 the service, to **d.** the work of the 5647
Nu 4:37, 41 **d.** service in the tabernacle........... 5647
Nu 4:47 to **d.** the service of the ministry,........ 5647
Nu 5:6 to **d.** a trespass against the Lord,....... 6213
Nu 6:21 **d.** after the law of his separation. 6213
Nu 7:5 to **d.** the service of the tabernacle...... 5647
Nu 8:7 And thus shalt thou **d.** unto them, ... 6213
Nu 8:15 the Levites go in to **d.** the service 5647
Nu 8:19 to **d.** the service of the children of 5647
Nu 8:22 Levites in to **d.** their service 5647
Nu 8:26 the charge, and shall **d.** no service. 5647
Nu 8:26 Thus shalt thou **d.** unto the............... 6213
Nu 9:14 the manner thereof, so shall ye **d.**: 6213
Nu 10:29 with us, and we will **d.** thee good:............
Nu 10:32 goodness the Lord shall **d.** unto us, ... 3190
Nu 10:32 the same will we **d.** unto thee. 3190
Nu 11:27 and Medad **d.** prophesy in the camp..........
Nu 14:28 in mine ears, so will I **d.** to you:........ 6213
Nu 14:35 will surely **d.** it unto all this evil 6213
Nu 14:41 Wherefore **d.** ye now transgress ....
Nu 15:12 shall ye **d.** to every one according...... 6213
Nu 15:13 of the country shall **d.** these things..... 6213
Nu 15:14 as ye **d.**, so he shall **d.**. 6213
Nu 15:20 ye **d.** the heave offering of the.................
Nu 15:39 of the Lord, and **d.** them;................. 6213
Nu 15:40 and **d.** all my commandments,............ 6213
Nu 16:6 This **d.**; Take you censers, Korah, ... 6213
Nu 16:9 near to himself to **d.** the service 5647
Nu 16:28 sent me to **d.** all these works;........... 6213
Nu 18:6 gift for the Lord, to **d.** the service 5647
Nu 18:23 But the Levites shall **d.** the service 5647
Nu 21:34 **d.** to him as thou didst unto Sihon...... 6213
Nu 22:17 **d.** whatsoever thou sayest unto me: ... 6213
Nu 22:18 Lord my God, to **d.** less or more. 6213
Nu 22:20 say unto thee, that shalt thou **d.**. 6213
Nu 22:30 was I ever wont to **d.** so unto thee?... 6213
Nu 23:19 he said, and shall he not **d.** it?........... 6213
Nu 23:26 the Lord speaketh, that I must **d.**?....... 6213
Nu 24:13 **d.** either good or bad of mine own...... 6213
Nu 24:14 thee what this people shall **d.**........... 6213
Nu 24:18 and Israel shall **d.** valiantly................ 6213
Nu 28:18 shall **d.** no manner of servile work...... 6213
Nu 28:25 ye shall **d.** no servile work................ 6213
Nu 28:26 ye shall **d.** no servile work:............... 6213
Nu 29:1 ye shall **d.** no servile work: it is a...... 6213
Nu 29:7 ye shall not **d.** any work therein:......... 6213
Nu 29:12 ye shall **d.** no servile work, and ye...... 6213
Nu 29:35 ye shall **d.** no servile work therein:..... 6213
Nu 29:39 things ye shall **d.** unto the Lord 6213
Nu 30:2 he shall **d.** according to all that 6213
Nu 31:19 and **d.** ye abide without the camp............
Nu 32:20 If ye will **d.** this thing, if ye will........ 6213
Nu 32:23 But if ye will not **d.** so, behold, ye 6213
Nu 32:24 and **d.** that which hath proceeded....... 6213
Nu 32:25 Thy servants will **d.** as my lord 6213
Nu 32:31 unto thy servants, so will we **d.**......... 6213
Nu 33:56 shall **d.** unto you, as I thought to **d.** ... 6213
De 1:14 hast spoken is good for us to **d.**.......... 6213
De 1:18 all the things which ye should **d.**. 6213
De 1:44 you, and chased you, as bees **d.**, ... 6213
De 3:2 thou shalt **d.** unto him as thou........... 6213
De 3:21 so shall the Lord **d.** unto all the......... 6213
De 3:24 or in earth, that can **d.** according 6213
De 4:1 which I teach you, for to **d.** them,...... 6213
De 4:5 that ye should **d.** so in the land.......... 6213
De 4:6 Keep therefore and **d.** them; for 6213
De 4:14 that ye might **d.** them in the land....... 6213
De 4:25 shall **d.** evil in the sight of the Lord...... 6213
De 5:1 learn them, and keep, and **d.** them. 6213
De 5:13 Six days thou shall labour, and **d.**....... 6213
De 5:14 in it thou shalt not **d.** any work,.......... 6213
De 5:27 and we will hear it, and **d.** it. 6213
De 5:31 teach them, that they may **d.** them..... 6213
De 5:32 ye shall observe to **d.** therefore as 6213
De 6:1 to teach you, that ye might **d.** them.... 6213
De 6:3 O Israel, and observe to **d.** it;........... 6213
De 6:18 And thou shalt **d.** that which is 6213
De 6:24 Lord commanded us to **d.** all these...... 6213
De 6:25 if we observe to **d.** all these............. 6213
De 7:11 I command thee this day, to **d.** them. ..6213
De 7:12 and keep, and **d.** them, that the........ 6213
De 7:19 shall the Lord thy God **d.** unto all...... 6213
De 8:1 shall ye observe to **d.**, that ye may 6213
De 8:16 prove thee, to **d.** thee good at thy...........
De 8:19 if thou **d.** at all forget the Lord................
De 11:22 to **d.** them, to love the Lord your...... 6213
De 11:32 And ye shall observe to **d.** all the....... 6213
De 12:1 which ye shall observe to **d.** in the..... 6213
De 12:4 Ye shall not **d.** so unto the Lord 6213
De 12:8 not **d.** after all the things that we **d.**.... 6213

De 12:14 and there thou shalt **d.** all that I 6213
De 12:25 **d.** that which is right in the sight 6213
De 12:30 serve their gods? even so will I **d.** 6213
De 12:31 Thou shalt not **d.** so unto the Lord 6213
De 12:32 I command you, observe to **d.** it: 6213
De 13:11 and shall **d.** no more any such 6213
De 13:18 **d.** that which is right in the sight 6213
De 15:5 to observe to **d.** all these 6213
De 15:17 maidservant thou shalt **d.** likewise. 6213
De 15:19 shalt **d.** no work with the firstling
De 16:8 Lord thy God: thou shalt **d.** no 6213
De 16:12 and thou shalt observe and **d.** 6213
De 17:10 And thou shalt **d.** according to the 6213
De 17:10 to **d.** according to all that they 6213
De 17:11 they shall tell thee, thou shalt **d.** 6213
De 17:12 man that will **d.** presumptuously, 6213
De 17:13 and **d.** no more presumptuously.
De 17:19 and these statutes, to **d.** them: 6213
De 18:7 as all his brethren the Levites **d.**,
De 18:9 shalt not learn to **d.** after the 6213
De 18:12 all that **d.** these things are an 6213
De 18:14 God hath not suffered thee so to **d.**.
De 19:9 to **d.** them, which I command 6213
De 19:19 Then shall ye **d.** unto him, as he 6213
De 20:3 fear not, and **d.** not tremble,
De 20:15 Thus shalt thou **d.** unto all the 6213
De 20:18 That they teach you not to **d.** after 6213
De 21:9 when thou shalt **d.** that which is 6213
De 22:3 **d.** with his ass; and so shalt thou **d.** 6213
De 22:3 hast found, shalt thou **d.** likewise: 6213
De 22:5 all that **d.** so are an abomination 6213
De 22:26 unto the damsel thou shalt **d.** nothing;
De 24:8 and **d.** according to all that the 6213
De 24:8 them, so ye shall observe to **d.**. 6213
De 24:18, 22 therefore I command thee to **d.** 6213
De 25:16 For all that **d.** such things, and all 6213
De 25:16 all that **d.** unrighteously, are an 6213
De 26:16 hath commanded thee to **d.** these 6213
De 26:16 thou shalt therefore keep and **d.** 6213
De 27:10 and **d.** his commandments and his 6213
De 27:26 not all the words of this law to **d.** 6213
De 28:1 thy God, to observe and to **d.** all his 6213
De 28:13 thee this day, to observe and to **d.** 6213
De 28:15 thy God, to observe to **d.** all his 6213
De 28:20 settest thine hand unto for to **d.**, 6213
De 28:58 If thou wilt not observe to **d.** all the 6213
De 28:63 rejoiced over you to **d.** you good,
De 29:9 this covenant, and **d.** them, that 6213
De 29:9 ye may prosper in all that ye **d.**. 6213
De 29:14 Neither with you only **d.** I make this
De 29:29 that we may **d.** all the words of 6213
De 30:5 and he will **d.** thee good, and
De 30:8 and **d.** all his commandments 6213
De 30:12, 13 that we may hear it, and **d.** it? 6213
De 30:14 thy heart, that thou mayest **d.** it. 6213
De 31:4 And the Lord shall **d.** unto them as 6213
De 31:5 that ye may **d.** unto them according 6213
De 31:12 and observe to **d.** all the words of 6213
De 31:29 ye will **d.** evil in the sight of the 6213
De 32:6 **D.** ye thus requite the Lord,
De 32:46 your children to observe to **d.**, 6213
De 34:11 the Lord sent him to **d.** in the land 6213
Jos 1:2 the land which I **d.** give to them,
Jos 1:7 to **d.** according to all the law, 6213
Jos 1:8 to **d.** according to all that is written 6213
Jos 1:16 thou commandest us we will **d.**, 6213
Jos 2:24 the country **d.** faint because of us.
Jos 3:5 morrow the Lord will **d.** wonders 6213
Jos 6:3 Thus shalt thou **d.** six days. 6213
Jos 7:9 what wilt thou **d.** unto thy great 6213
Jos 8:2 And thou shalt **d.** to Ai and her king 6213
Jos 8:8 of the Lord shall ye **d.**. 6213
Jos 9:20 This we will **d.** to them: we will 6213
Jos 9:25 right unto thee to **d.** unto us, **d.**. 6213
Jos 10:25 thus shall the Lord **d.** to all your 6213
Jos 22:5 take diligent heed to **d.** the 6213
Jos 22:24 What have ye to **d.** with the Lord
Jos 22:27 that we might **d.** the service of the 5647
Jos 23:6 courageous to keep and to **d.** all 6213
Jos 23:12 Else if ye **d.** in any wise go back,
Jos 24:13 which ye planted not **d.** ye eat.
Jos 24:20 will turn and **d.** you hurt, and consume
Jg 6:27 of the city, that he could not **d.** 6213
Jg 7:17 unto them, Look on me, and **d.** 6213
Jg 7:17 it shall be that, as I **d.**, so shall ye **d.**. 6213
Jg 8:3 was I able to **d.** in comparison of 6213
Jg 9:33 thou **d.** to them as thou shalt find 6213
Jg 9:48 What ye have seen me **d.**, make 6213
Jg 9:48 make haste, and **d.** as I have done. 6213
Jg 10:15 **d.** thou unto us whatsoever seemeth 6213
Jg 11:10 if we **d.** not so according to thy 6213
Jg 11:12 What hast thou to **d.** with me, that
Jg 11:36 unto the Lord, **d.** to me according 6213
Jg 13:8 teach us what we shall **d.** unto the 6213
Jg 13:12 child, and how shall we **d.** unto 4640
Jg 13:17 come to pass we may **d.** thee honour?
Jg 14:10 for so used the young men to **d.**. 6213
Jg 15:3 Philistines, though I **d.** them a 6213
Jg 15:10 come up, to **d.** to him as he hath 6213
Jg 17:13 know I that the Lord will **d.** me good.
Jg 18:14 **D.** ye know that there is in these
Jg 18:14 consider what ye have to **d.** 6213
Jg 18:18 the priest unto them, What **d.** ye? 6213
Jg 19:23 nay, I pray you, **d.** not so wickedly:
Jg 19:23 into mine house, **d.** not this folly. 6213
Jg 19:24 **d.** with them what seemeth good 6213
Jg 19:24 but unto this man **d.** not so vile a 6213
Jg 20:9 the thing which we will **d.** to 6213
Jg 20:10 that they may **d.**, when they come 6213
Jg 21:7 How shall we **d.** for wives for them 6213
Jg 21:11 this is the thing that ye shall **d.**, 6213
Jg 21:16 How shall we **d.** for wives for them 6213
Ru 1:17 the Lord **d.** so to me, and more also, 6213
Ru 2:9 eyes be on the field that they **d.** reap,
Ru 3:4 he will tell thee what thou shalt **d.** 6213
Ru 3:5 All thou sayest unto me I will **d.**. 6213
Ru 3:11 I will **d.** for thee all that thou 6213
Ru 3:13 well; let him **d.** the kinsman's part:
Ru 3:13 but if he will not **d.** the part of a
Ru 3:13 will I **d.** the part of a kinsman to
Ru 4:11 and **d.** thou worthily in Ephratah, 6213
1Sa 1:23 said unto her, **D.** what seemeth 6213
1Sa 2:23 he said unto them, Why **d.** ye such 6213
1Sa 2:35 priest, that shall **d.** according to 6213
1Sa 3:11 Behold, I will **d.** a thing in Israel, 6213
1Sa 3:17 God **d.** so to thee, and more also, if 6213
1Sa 3:18 let him **d.** what seemeth him good. 6213
1Sa 5:8 What shall we **d.** with the ark of the 6213
1Sa 6:2 What shall we **d.** to the ark of the 6213
1Sa 6:6 Wherefore then **d.** ye harden your
1Sa 7:3 If ye **d.** return unto the Lord with
1Sa 8:8 served other gods, so **d.** they also 6213
1Sa 10:2 you, saying, What shall I **d.** for my 6213
1Sa 10:7 that thou **d.** as occasion serve thee; 6213
1Sa 10:8 and shew thee what thou shalt **d.**. 6213
1Sa 11:10 ye shall **d.** with us all that seemeth 6213
1Sa 12:16 which the Lord will **d.** before your 6213
1Sa 12:25 But if ye shall still **d.** wickedly, ye
1Sa 14:7 said unto him, **D.** all that is in 6213
1Sa 14:36 **D.** whatsoever seemeth good unto 6213
1Sa 14:40 unto Saul, **D.** what seemeth good 6213
1Sa 14:44 And Saul answered, God **d.** so and 6213
1Sa 16:3 will shew thee what thou shalt **d.**: 6213
1Sa 20:2 my father will **d.** nothing either 6213
1Sa 20:4 thy soul desireth, I will even **d.** it 6213
1Sa 20:13 The Lord **d.** so and much more to 6213
1Sa 20:13 if it please my father to **d.** thee evil,
1Sa 20:30 **d.** not I know that thou hast
1Sa 22:3 till I know what God will **d.** for me. 6213
1Sa 24:4 that thou mayest **d.** to him as it 6213
1Sa 24:6 Lord forbid that I should **d.** this 6213
1Sa 25:17 and consider what thou wilt **d.**; 6213
1Sa 25:22 So and more also **d.** God unto the 6213
1Sa 26:21 I will no more **d.** thee harm, because
1Sa 26:25 David: thou shalt both **d.** great 6213
1Sa 28:2 shalt know what thy servant can **d.** 6213
1Sa 28:15 known unto me what I shall **d.** 6213
1Sa 29:3 the Philistines, What **d.** these Hebrews
1Sa 30:23 Ye shall not **d.** so, my brethren, 6213
2Sa 3:8 which against Judah **d.** shew 6213
2Sa 3:9 So **d.** God to Abner, and more 6213
2Sa 3:9 sworn to David, even so I **d.** to him; 6213
2Sa 3:18 Now then **d.** it: for the Lord hath 6213
2Sa 3:35 So **d.** God to me, and more also, if 6213
2Sa 7:3 Nathan said to the king, Go, **d.** all 6213
2Sa 7:23 to make him a name, and to **d.** for 6213
2Sa 7:25 establish it for ever, and **d.** as thou 6213
2Sa 9:11 his servant, so shall thy servant **d.**. 6213
2Sa 10:12 Lord **d.** that which seemeth him 6213
2Sa 11:11 soul liveth, I will not **d.** this thing. 6213
2Sa 12:9 commandment of the Lord, to **d.** 6213
2Sa 12:12 but I will **d.** this thing before all 6213
2Sa 13:2 thought it hard for him to **d.** any 6213
2Sa 13:12 in Israel: d. not thou this folly. 6213
2Sa 13:12 Nay, my brother, **d.** not force me
2Sa 15:4 unto me, and I would **d.** him justice!
2Sa 15:5 nigh to him to **d.** him obeisance,
2Sa 15:15 thy servants are ready to **d.**
2Sa 15:26 let him **d.** to me as seemeth good 6213
2Sa 16:10 What have I to **d.** with you, ye sons of
2Sa 16:11 more now may this Benjamite **d.** it?
2Sa 16:20 among you what we shall **d.**. 6213
2Sa 17:6 shall we **d.** after his saying? if not, 6213
2Sa 18:4 What seemeth you best I will **d.**. 6213
2Sa 18:32 rise against thee to **d.** thee hurt, be as
2Sa 19:13 God **d.** so to me, and more also, if 6213
2Sa 19:18 and to **d.** what he thought good. 6213
2Sa 19:19 neither **d.** thou remember that which
2Sa 19:22 What have I to **d.** with you, ye sons of
2Sa 19:22 for **d.** not I know that I am this day
2Sa 19:27 **d.** therefore what is good in thine 6213
2Sa 19:37 and **d.** to him what shall seem 6213
2Sa 19:38 will **d.** to him that which shall seem 6213
2Sa 19:38 shalt require of me, that will I **d.** 6213
2Sa 20:6 the son of Bichri **d.** us more harm
2Sa 20:17 And he answered, I **d.** hear.
2Sa 21:3 What shall I **d.** for you? and 6213
2Sa 21:4 ye shall say, that will I **d.** for you. 6213
2Sa 23:17 that I should **d.** this: is not this the 6213
2Sa 24:12 of them, that I may **d.** it unto thee. 6213
1Ki 1:30 even so will I certainly **d.** this day. 6213
1Ki 2:6 **D.** therefore according to thy 6213
1Ki 2:9 knowest what thou oughtest to **d.** 6213
1Ki 2:23 God **d.** so to me, and more also, if 6213
1Ki 2:31 the king said unto him, **D.** as he 6213
1Ki 2:38 hath said, so will thy servant **d.**. 6213
1Ki 3:28 wisdom of God was in him, to **d.** 6213
1Ki 5:8 and I will **d.** all thy desire 6213
1Ki 8:32 Then hear thou in heaven, and **d.**, 6213
1Ki 8:39 and forgive, and **d.**, and give to 6213
1Ki 8:43 and **d.** according to all that the 6213
1Ki 8:43 fear thee, as **d.** thy people Israel;
1Ki 9:1 which he was pleased to **d.**, That 6213
1Ki 9:4 to **d.** according to all that I have 6213
1Ki 10:9 made he thee king, to **d.** judgment 6213
1Ki 11:12 I will not **d.** it for David thy 6213
1Ki 11:33 have not walked in my ways, to **d.** 6213
1Ki 11:38 and **d.** that is right in my sight, to 6213
1Ki 12:6 **d.** ye advise that I may answer
1Ki 12:27 If this people go up to **d.** sacrifice 6213
1Ki 14:8 to **d.** that only which was right in 6213
1Ki 17:13 go and **d.** as thou hast said: but 6213
1Ki 17:18 What have I to **d.** with thee, O thou
1Ki 18:34 And he said, **D.** it the second time.
1Ki 18:34 And he said, **D.** it the third time.
1Ki 19:2 So let the gods **d.** to me, and more 6213
1Ki 20:9 I will **d.**: but this thing I may not **d.**. 6213
1Ki 20:10 Thy gods **d.** so unto me, and more 6213
1Ki 20:24 And **d.** this thing, Take the kings 6213
1Ki 22:22 prevail also: go forth, and **d.** so. 6213
2Ki 2:9 Ask what I shall **d.** for thee, before 6213
2Ki 3:13 What have I to **d.** with thee? get
2Ki 4:2 What shall I **d.** for thee? tell me, 6213
2Ki 4:16 thou man of God, **d.** not lie unto thine
2Ki 4:28 did I not say, **D.** not deceive me?
2Ki 5:13 the prophet had bid thee **d.** some
2Ki 6:15 Alas, my master! how shall we **d.**? 6213
2Ki 6:27 And he said, If the Lord **d.** not help
2Ki 6:31 God **d.** so and more also to me, if 6213
2Ki 7:9 We **d.** not well: this day is a day of 6213
2Ki 8:12 the evil that thou wilt **d.** unto the 6213
2Ki 8:13 servant a dog, that he should **d.** 6213
2Ki 9:18, 19 What hast thou to **d.** with peace?
2Ki 10:5 and will **d.** all that thou shalt bid 6213
2Ki 10:5 **d.** thou that which is good in thine 6213
2Ki 10:19 I have a great sacrifice to **d.** to Baal:
2Ki 11:5 This is the thing that ye shall **d.**; 6213
2Ki 17:12 said unto them, Ye shall not **d.** this 6213
2Ki 17:15 that they should not **d.** like them 6213
2Ki 17:17 sold themselves to **d.** evil in the 6213
2Ki 17:34 Unto this day they **d.** after the 6213
2Ki 17:34 they fear not the Lord, neither **d.** 6213
2Ki 17:36 and to him shall ye **d.** sacrifice,
2Ki 17:37 shall observe to **d.** for evermore; 6213
2Ki 17:41 so **d.** they unto this day 6213
2Ki 18:12 would not hear them, nor **d.** them. 6213
2Ki 19:31 of the Lord of hosts shall **d.** this. 6213
2Ki 20:9 that the lord will **d.** the thing that 6213
2Ki 21:8 observe to **d.** according to all that 6213
2Ki 21:9 seduced them to **d.** more evil than 6213
2Ki 22:9 hand of them that **d.** the work, 6213

2Ki 22:13 this book, to **d.** according unto all....... 6213
1Ch 11:19 that I should **d.** this thing: shall I........ 6213
1Ch 12:32 to know what Israel ought to **d.**;......... 6213
1Ch 13:4 said that they would **d.** so: for............ 6213
1Ch 16:21 He suffered no man to **d.** them wrong:.......
1Ch 16:22 anointed, and **d.** my prophets no harm.......
1Ch 16:40 **d.** according to all that is written...............
1Ch 17:2 **D.** all that is in thine heart; for.......... 6213
1Ch 17:23 for ever, and **d.** as thou hast said.......... 6213
1Ch 19:13 the Lord **d.** that which is good in........ 6213
1Ch 21:8 thee, **d.** away the iniquity of thy......... 5674
1Ch 21:10 them, that I may **d.** it unto thee......... 6213
1Ch 21:23 let my lord the king **d.** that which....... 6213
1Ch 28:7 constant to **d.** my commandments....... 6213
1Ch 28:10 sanctuary: be strong, and **d.** it........... 6213
1Ch 28:20 and of good courage, and **d.** it:............ 6213
1Ch 29:19 and to **d.** all these things, and to......... 6213
2Ch 6:23 hear thou from heaven and **d.**,............ 6213
2Ch 6:33 and **d.** according to all that the........... 6213
2Ch 7:17 **d.** according to all that I have............ 6213
2Ch 9:8 king over them, to **d.** judgment.......... 6213
2Ch 14:4 **d.** the law and the commandment........ 6213
2Ch 18:21 also prevail: go out, and **d.** even so..... 6213
2Ch 19:6 Take heed what ye **d.**: for ye judge..... 6213
2Ch 19:7 be upon you; take heed and **d.** it:......... 6213
2Ch 19:9 shall ye **d.** in the fear of the Lord,...... 6213
2Ch 19:10 this **d.**, and ye shall not trespass......... 6213
2Ch 20:12 neither know we what to **d.**:.............. 6213
2Ch 22:3 was his counseller to **d.** wickedly............
2Ch 23:4 This is the thing that ye shall **d.**;......... 6213
2Ch 25:8 But if thou wilt go, **d.** it, be strong...... 6213
2Ch 25:9 shall we **d.** for the hundred talents...... 6213
2Ch 30:12 one heart to **d.** the commandment....... 6213
2Ch 32:10 Whereon **d.** ye trust, that ye abide............
2Ch 33:8 will take heed to **d.** all that I have....... 6213
2Ch 33:9 and to **d.** worse than the heathen,....... 6213
2Ch 34:16 to thy servants, they **d.** it................ 6213
2Ch 34:21 **d.** after all that is written in this......... 6213
2Ch 35:6 they may **d.** according to the word....... 6213
2Ch 35:21 What have I to **d.** with thee, thou king.......
Ezr 4:2 for we seek your God, as ye **d.**;...............
Ezr 4:2 we **d.** sacrifice unto him since the............
Ezr 4:3 Ye have nothing to **d.** with us..................
Ezr 4:22 now that ye fail not to **d.** this:............ 5648
Ezr 6:8 what ye shall **d.** to the elders of......... 5648
Ezr 7:10 and to **d.** it, and to teach in Israel....... 6213
Ezr 7:18 to **d.** with the rest of the silver.......... 5648
Ezr 7:18 that **d.** after the will of your God........ 5648
Ezr 7:21 I Artaxerxes the king, **d.** make.................
Ezr 7:26 whosoever will not **d.** the law of......... 5648
Ezr 10:4 be of good courage, and **d.** it.......... 6213
Ezr 10:5 should **d.** according to this word......... 6213
Ezr 10:11 your fathers, and **d.** his pleasure:........ 6213
Ezr 10:12 As thou hast said, so must we **d.**......... 6213
Ne 1:9 my commandments, and **d.** them;......... 6213
Ne 2:12 in my heart to **d.** at Jerusalem:........... 6213
Ne 2:19 What is this thing that ye **d.**?............. 6213
Ne 4:2 What **d.** thee feeble Jews?................. 6213
Ne 5:9 I said, It is not good that ye **d.**:........... 6213
Ne 5:12 them; so will we **d.** as thou sayest...... 6213
Ne 5:12 should **d.** according to this promise...... 6213
Ne 6:2 they thought to **d.** me mischief........... 6213
Ne 6:13 should be afraid, and **d.** so, and sin,..... 6213
Ne 9:24 might **d.** with them as they would....... 6213
Ne 9:29 which if a man **d.**, he shall live in........ 6213
Ne 10:29 and **d.** all the commandments of.......... 6213
Ne 13:17 What evil thing is this that ye **d.**,........ 6213
Ne 13:21 **d.** so again, I will lay hands on you............
Ne 13:27 hearken unto you to **d.** all this........... 6213
Es 1:8 should **d.** according to every man's...... 6213
Es 1:15 shall we **d.** unto the queen Vashti....... 6213
Es 3:11 to **d.** with them as it seemeth good..... 6213
Es 4:11 of the king's provinces, **d.** know, that........
Es 5:5 he may **d.** as Esther hath said........... 6213
Es 5:8 **d.** to morrow as the king hath said..... 6213
Es 6:6 the king delight to **d.** honour more...... 6213
Es 6:10 said, and **d.** even so to Mordecai........ 6213
Es 7:5 presume in his heart to **d.** so?........... 6213
Es 9:13 in Shushan to **d.** to morrow also......... 6213
Es 9:23 undertook to **d.** as they had begun,..... 6213
Job 6:4 terrors of God **d.** set themselves in...........
Job 6:26 **D.** ye imagine to reprove words,.............
Job 7:20 what shall I **d.** unto thee, O thou........ 6466
Job 9:13 proud helpers **d.** stoop under him.............
Job 10:2 **D.** not condemn me; shew me.................
Job 11:8 as heaven; what can thou **d.**?............ 6466
Job 13:2 ye know, the same **d.** I know also:...........
Job 13:9 another, **d.** ye so mock him?....................
Job 13:10 if ye **d.** secretly accept persons...............
Job 13:14 Wherefore **d.** I take my flesh in................
Job 13:20 Only **d.** not two things unto me:......... 6213
Job 15:3 wherewith he can **d.** no good?............ 5953
Job 15:12 and what **d.** thy eyes wink at,..................
Job 16:4 I also could speak as ye **d.**:........................
Job 17:10 all, **d.** ye return, and come now:...............
Job 19:22 Why **d.** ye persecute me as God,.............
Job 20:2 Therefore **d.** my thoughts cause me.........
Job 21:7 Wherefore **d.** the wicked live, become........
Job 21:29 and **d.** ye not know their tokens,..............
Job 22:17 can the Almighty **d.** for them?............ 6466
Job 24:1 **d.** they that know him not see.................
Job 31:14 shall I **d.** when God riseth up?.................
Job 32:9 **d.** the aged understand judgment...............
Job 34:10 God, that he should **d.** wickedness;...........
Job 34:12 God will not **d.** wickedly, neither..............
Job 34:32 done iniquity, I will **d.** no more.......... 6466
Job 36:28 Which the clouds **d.** drop and....................
Job 37:12 **d.** whatsoever he commandeth............ 6467
Job 37:24 men **d.** therefore fear him:.......................
Job 39:1 thou mark when the hinds **d.** calve?...........
Job 41:8 him, remember the battle, **d.** no more.......
Job 42:2 know that thou canst **d.** every thing,..........
Ps 2:1 Why **d.** the heathen rage, and the............
Ps 7:1 my God, in thee **d.** I put my trust:............
Ps 11:3 what can the righteous **d.**?................. 6466
Ps 12:2 with a double heart **d.** they speak............
Ps 16:1 for in thee **d.** I put my trust....................
Ps 25:1 thee, O Lord, **d.** I lift up my soul............
Ps 25:5 on thee **d.** I wait all the day....................
Ps 31:1 In thee, O Lord, **d.** I put my trust; let.......
Ps 34:10 young lions **d.** lack, and suffer hunger:.......
Ps 34:14 Depart from evil, and **d.** good;........... 6213
Ps 34:16 Lord is against them that **d.** evil,......... 6213
Ps 36:3 off to be wise, and to **d.** good..................
Ps 37:3 Trust in the Lord and **d.** good;........... 6213
Ps 37:8 not thyself in any wise to **d.** evil...............
Ps 37:27 Depart from evil, and **d.** good;........... 6213
Ps 38:15 For in thee, O Lord, **d.** I hope:................
Ps 40:8 I delight to **d.** thy will, O my God:....... 6213
Ps 41:7 against me **d.** they devise my hurt............
Ps 50:16 hast thou to **d.** to declare my statutes,........
Ps 51:18 **D.** good in thy good pleasure....................
Ps 56:4 fear what flesh can **d.** unto me........... 6213
Ps 56:11 afraid what man can **d.** unto me.......... 6213
Ps 58:1 **D.** ye indeed speak righteousness,............
Ps 58:1 **d.** ye judge uprightly, O ye sons of............
Ps 60:12 God we shall **d.** valiantly: for he.......... 6213
Ps 64:4 suddenly **d.** they shoot at him, and fear......
Ps 71:1 In thee, O Lord, **d.** I put my trust:...........
Ps 75:1 unto thee, O God, **d.** we give thanks,........
Ps 80:12 which pass by the way **d.** pluck her?..........
Ps 82:3 **d.** justice to the afflicted and needy...........
Ps 83:9 **D.** unto them as unto the.................. 6213
Ps 86:4 unto thee, O Lord, **d.** I lift up my soul.......
Ps 89:50 how **d.** I bear in my bosom the..................
Ps 92:7 all the workers of iniquity **d.** flourish;.........
Ps 95:10 a people that **d.** err in their heart,.............
Ps 103:18 his commandments to **d.** them........... 6213
Ps 103:20 that **d.** his commandments,................ 6213
Ps 103:21 of his, that **d.** his pleasure................ 6213
Ps 104:20 beasts of the forest **d.** creep forth............
Ps 105:14 suffered no man to **d.** them wrong:...........
Ps 105:15 anointed, and **d.** my prophets no harm.......
Ps 107:23 that **d.** business in great waters;......... 6213
Ps 108:13 Through God we shall **d.** valiantly:...... 6213
Ps 109:21 But **d.** thou for me, O God the.......... 6213
Ps 111:10 they that **d.** his commandments:.......... 6213
Ps 118:6 fear: what can man **d.** unto me?.......... 6213
Ps 119:3 They also **d.** no iniquity: they............ 6466
Ps 119:21 which **d.** err from thy commandments........
Ps 119:35 commandments; for therein **d.** I................
Ps 119:83 yet **d.** I not forget thy statutes.................
Ps 119:109 yet **d.** I not forget thy law.......................
Ps 119:113 vain thoughts: but thy law **d.** I love...........
Ps 119:132 as thou usest to **d.** unto those that............
Ps 119:141 yet **d.** not I forget thy precepts................
Ps 119:153 for I **d.** not forget thy law......................
Ps 119:157 yet **d.** I not decline from thy...................
Ps 119:163 lying: but thy law **d.** I love.....................
Ps 119:164 seven times a day **d.** I praise thee............
Ps 119:176 I **d.** not forget thy commandments.............
Ps 125:4 **D.** good, O Lord, unto those that............
Ps 129:8 Neither **d.** they which go by say,..............
Ps 130:5 and in his word **d.** I hope........................
Ps 131:1 neither **d.** I exercise myself in..................
Ps 137:6 If I **d.** not remember thee, let my............
Ps 139:21 **D.** not I hate them, O Lord, that hate........
Ps 143:8 morning: for in thee **d.** I trust:.................
Ps 143:10 Teach me to **d.** thy will; for thou.......... 6213
Pr 2:14 Who rejoice to **d.** evil, and delight....... 6213
Pr 3:27 in the power of thine hand to **d.** it....... 6213
Pr 6:3 **D.** this now, my son, and deliver........ 6213
Pr 6:30 Men **d.** not despise a thief, if he..............
Pr 8:13 and the froward mouth, **d.** I hate...............
Pr 10:23 as sport to a fool to **d.** mischief:.......... 6213
Pr 14:22 **D.** they not err that devise evil?..............
Pr 17:7 much less **d.** lying lips a prince.................
Pr 19:7 brethren of the poor **d.** hate him:..............
Pr 19:7 how much more **d.** his friends go..............
Pr 19:19 deliver him, yet thou must **d.** it again.........
Pr 20:30 so **d.** stripes the inward parts of...............
Pr 21:3 To **d.** justice and judgment is............. 6213
Pr 21:7 because they refuse to **d.** judgment..... 6213
Pr 21:15 It is joy to the just to **d.** judgment:...... 6213
Pr 24:8 He that deviseth to **d.** evil shall be.........
Pr 24:29 I will **d.** so to him as he hath done...... 6213
Pr 25:8 lest thou know not what to **d.** in......... 6213
Pr 28:12 When righteous men **d.** rejoice,................
Pr 31:12 She will **d.** him good and not evil........ 1580
Ec 2:3 which they should **d.** under the........... 6213
Ec 2:11 labour that I had laboured to **d.**:......... 6213
Ec 2:12 what can the man **d.** that cometh..............
Ec 3:12 rejoice, and to **d.** good in his life......... 6213
Ec 4:8 For whom **d.** I labour, and bereave............
Ec 5:1 they consider not that they **d.** evil......... 6213
Ec 6:6 no good: **d.** not all go to one place?...........
Ec 8:11 men is fully set in them to **d.** evil........ 6213
Ec 8:12 Though a sinner **d.** evil an hundred...... 6213
Ec 9:10 hand findeth to **d.**, **d.** it with thy.......... 6213
Ec 10:10 iron be blunt, and he **d.** not whet the.........
Ec 11:5 how the bones **d.** grow in the womb..........
Ca 1:3 therefore **d.** the virgins love thee.............
Ca 8:8 what shall we **d.** for our sister in........ 6213
Isa 1:16 before mine eyes; cease to **d.** evil;..............
Isa 1:17 Learn to **d.** well; seek judgment,..............
Isa 5:5 you what I will **d.** to my vineyard,........ 6213
Isa 9:13 neither **d.** they seek the Lord of..............
Isa 10:3 will ye **d.** in the day of visitation,........ 6213
Isa 10:11 so **d.** to Jerusalem and her idols?......... 6213
Isa 14:21 that they **d.** not rise, nor possess.............
Isa 19:15 or tail, branch or rush, may **d.**........... 6213
Isa 19:21 shall **d.** sacrifice and oblation;............ 5647
Isa 23:4 neither **d.** I nourish up young men,............
Isa 24:4 people of the earth **d.** languish.................
Isa 24:7 all the merryhearted **d.** sigh.....................
Isa 24:18 the foundations of the earth **d.** shake.........
Isa 27:3 I the Lord **d.** keep it; I will water.............
Isa 28:21 that he may **d.** his work, his............. 6213
Isa 29:13 and with their lips **d.** honour me,..............
Isa 29:14 I will proceed to **d.** a marvellous work........
Isa 37:32 of the Lord of hosts shall **d.** this......... 6213
Isa 38:7 that the Lord will **d.** this thing that...... 6213
Isa 38:19 he shall praise thee, as I **d.** this day:.........
Isa 41:23 yea, **d.** good, or **d.** evil, that we..............
Isa 42:9 and new things **d.** I declare:.....................
Isa 42:16 These things will I **d.** unto them,......... 6213
Isa 43:19 Behold, I will **d.** a new thing;............. 6213
Isa 45:7 I the Lord **d.** all these things............. 6213
Isa 46:10 and I will **d.** all my pleasure:............. 6213
Isa 46:11 I have purposed it, I will also **d.** it....... 6213
Isa 48:11 even for mine own sake, will I **d.** it:.... 6213
Isa 48:14 will **d.** his pleasure on Babylon,.......... 6213
Isa 55:2 Wherefore **d.** ye spend money for that.......
Isa 56:1 Keep ye judgment, and **d.** justice:....... 6213
Isa 57:4 Against whom **d.** ye sport yourselves?.......
Isa 58:4 ye shall not fast as ye **d.** this day,............
Isa 64:6 and we all **d.** fade as a leaf;.....................
Isa 65:8 so will I **d.** for my servants' sakes,....... 6213
Jer 2:8 walked after things that **d.** not profit.........
Jer 2:18 hast thou to **d.** in the way of Egypt,..........
Jer 2:18 hast thou to **d.** in the way of Assyria,........
Jer 4:22 they are wise to **d.** evil, but to.................
Jer 4:22 to **d.** good they have no knowledge...........
Jer 4:30 thou art spoiled, what wilt thou **d.**?..... 6213
Jer 5:28 right of the needy **d.** they not judge..........
Jer 5:31 what will ye **d.** in the end thereof?...... 6213
Jer 7:10 We are delivered to **d.** all these.......... 6213
Jer 7:14 Therefore will I **d.** unto this house,..... 6213
Jer 7:17 Seest thou not what they **d.** in the...... 6213
Jer 7:19 **D.** they provoke me to anger?.................
Jer 7:19 **d.** they not provoke themselves to...........

Book	Ref	Context	Strong's
Jer	8:8	How **d.** ye say, We are wise,	
Jer	8:14	Why **d.** we sit still? assemble	
Jer	9:7	for how shall I **d.** for the daughter	6213
Jer	10:5	for they cannot **d.** evil, neither	
Jer	10:5	also is it in them to **d.** good.	
Jer	11:4	Obey my voice, and **d.** them,	6213
Jer	11:6	words of this covenant, and **d.** them.	6213
Jer	11:8	which I commanded them to **d.**;	6213
Jer	11:15	hath my beloved to **d.** in mine house,	
Jer	12:5	then how wilt thou **d.** in the	6213
Jer	13:12	**D.** we not certainly know that every	
Jer	13:23	then may ye also **d.** good, that are	
Jer	13:23	that are accustomed to **d.** evil.	
Jer	14:7	**d.** thou it for thy name's sake:	6213
Jer	14:21	**D.** not abhor us, for thy name's sake,	
Jer	14:21	**d.** not disgrace the throne of thy glory:	
Jer	17:22	neither **d.** ye any work, but hallow	6213
Jer	17:24	sabbath day, to **d.** no work therein;	6213
Jer	18:6	cannot I **d.** with you as this potter?	6213
Jer	18:8	evil that I thought to **d.** unto them	6213
Jer	18:10	If it **d.** evil in my sight, that it obey	6213
Jer	18:12	we will every one **d.** the imagination	6213
Jer	19:12	Thus will I **d.** unto this place, saith	6213
Jer	22:3	and **d.** no wrong, **d.** no violence to	
Jer	22:4	For if ye **d.** this thing indeed,	6213
Jer	22:15	and **d.** judgment and justice, and	6213
Jer	22:17	oppression, and for violence, to **d.** it	6213
Jer	23:24	**D.** not I fill heaven and earth?	
Jer	23:32	and **d.** tell them, and cause my people	
Jer	25:6	hands; and I will **d.** you no hurt.	
Jer	26:3	which I purpose to **d.** unto them	6213
Jer	26:14	**d.** with me as seemeth good and	6213
Jer	28:6	the Lord **d.** so: the Lord perform	6213
Jer	29:32	good that I will **d.** for my people,	6213
Jer	30:6	wherefore **d.** I see every man with	
Jer	31:20	I **d.** earnestly remember him still:	
Jer	32:23	that thou commandest them to **d.**:	6213
Jer	32:35	they should **d.** this abomination,	6213
Jer	32:40	away from them, to **d.** them good;	
Jer	32:41	rejoice over them to **d.** them good,	
Jer	33:9	shall hear all the good that I **d.**	6213
Jer	33:18	meat offerings, and to **d.** sacrifice	6213
Jer	36:3	which I purpose to **d.** unto them;	6213
Jer	38:5	is not he that can **d.** any thing	
Jer	39:12	**d.** him no harm: but **d.** unto him	6213
Jer	40:16	Thou shalt not **d.** this thing: for	6213
Jer	42:2	as thine eyes **d.** behold us:)	
Jer	42:3	and the thing that we may **d.**	6213
Jer	42:5	if we **d.** not even according to all	6213
Jer	42:20	declare unto us, and we will **d.** it.	6213
Jer	44:4	Oh, **d.** not this abominable thing	6213
Jer	44:17	we will certainly **d.** whatsoever	6213
Jer	50:15	as she hath done, **d.** unto her	6213
Jer	50:21	saith the Lord, and **d.** according to	6213
Jer	50:29	that she hath done, **d.** unto her:	6213
Jer	51:47	that I will **d.** judgment upon the	
Jer	51:52	that I will **d.** judgment upon her	
Jer	51:55	when her waves **d.** roar like great	
La	1:4	The ways of Zion **d.** mourn,	
La	1:22	and **d.** unto them, as thou hast	5953
La	2:11	Mine eyes **d.** fail with tears,	
Eze	2:4	I **d.** send thee unto them;	
Eze	5:9	And I will **d.** in thee that which I	6213
Eze	5:9	and whereunto I will not **d.** any	6213
Eze	6:10	I would **d.** this evil unto them	6213
Eze	7:27	I will **d.** unto them after their way,	6213
Eze	8:6	seest thou what they **d.**? even the	6213
Eze	8:9	abominations that they **d.** here.	6213
Eze	8:12	of the house of Israel **d.** in the dark,	6213
Eze	8:13	greater abominations that they **d.**	6213
Eze	11:20	and **d.** them: and they shall be my	6213
Eze	15:3	be taken thereof to **d.** any work?	6213
Eze	16:5	pitied thee, to **d.** any of these unto	6213
Eze	18:5	but if a man be just and **d.** that	6213
Eze	18:21	**d.** that which is lawful and right,	6213
Eze	20:11	man **d.**, he shall even live in them.	6213
Eze	20:13	man **d.**, he shall even live in them;	6213
Eze	20:19	keep my judgments, and **d.** them;	6213
Eze	20:21	to **d.** them, which if a man **d.**, he	6213
Eze	21:24	all your doings your sins **d.** appear;	
Eze	22:14	Lord have spoken it, and will **d.** it.	6213
Eze	23:30	I will **d.** these things unto thee,	6213
Eze	23:48	taught not to **d.** after your lewdness.	6213
Eze	24:14	and I will **d.** it; I will not go back.	6213
Eze	24:22	And ye shall **d.** as I have done: ye	6213
Eze	24:24	to all that he hath done shall ye **d.**:	6213
Eze	25:8	Because that Moab and Seir **d.** say,	
Eze	25:14	they shall **d.** in Edom according	6213
Eze	33:9	if he **d.** not turn from his way,	
Eze	33:14,	19 and **d.** that which is lawful and	6213
Eze	33:31	but they will not **d.** them: for with	6213
Eze	33:32	thy words, but they **d.** them not.	6213
Eze	34:2	to the shepherds of Israel that **d.** feed	
Eze	35:11	even **d.** according to thine anger,	6213
Eze	35:15	so will I **d.** unto thee: thou shalt	6213
Eze	36:11	and will **d.** better unto you than at	
Eze	36:22	I **d.** not this for your sakes, O	6213
Eze	36:27	keep my judgments and **d.** them.	6213
Eze	36:32	Not for your sakes **d.** I this, saith	6213
Eze	36:36	Lord have spoken it, and I will **d.** it	6213
Eze	36:37	house of Israel, to **d.** it for them;	6213
Eze	37:24	observe my statutes, and **d.** them.	6213
Eze	37:28	I the Lord **d.** sanctify Israel,	
Eze	39:17	my sacrifice that I **d.** sacrifice for	
Eze	43:11	ordinances thereof, and **d.** them.	6213
Eze	44:13	near unto me, to **d.** the office of a	
Eze	45:20	And so shalt thou **d.** the seventh	6213
Eze	45:25	shall he **d.** the like in the feast of	6213
Da	3:14	**d.** not ye serve my gods, nor	
Da	4:26	have known that the heavens **d.** rule.	
Da	9:18	for we **d.** not present our supplications	
Da	9:19	O Lord, hearken and **d.**; defer not	6213
Da	11:3	dominion, and **d.** according to his	6213
Da	11:16	shall **d.** according to his own will,	6213
Da	11:17	thus shall he **d.**: and he shall give	6213
Da	11:24	he shall **d.** that which his fathers	6213
Da	11:27	shall be to **d.** mischief, and they	
Da	11:28	he shall **d.** exploits, and return to	6213
Da	11:30	so shall he **d.**; he shall even return	6213
Da	11:32	and such as **d.** wickedly against	
Da	11:32	the people that **d.** know their God	
Da	11:32	shall be strong, and **d.** exploits,	6213
Da	11:36	king shall **d.** according to his will;	6213
Da	11:39	he **d.** in the most strong holds	6213
Da	12:10	but the wicked shall **d.** wickedly:	
Ho	4:18	her rulers with shame **d.** love,	
Ho	6:4	Ephraim, what shall I **d.** unto thee?	6213
Ho	6:4	Judah, what shall I **d.** unto thee?	6213
Ho	7:10	**d.** not return to the Lord their God,	
Ho	7:15	yet **d.** they imagine mischief against	
Ho	9:5	What will ye **d.** in the solemn day,	6213
Ho	10:3	what then should a king **d.** to us?	6213
Ho	10:15	So shall Beth-el **d.** unto you	6213
Ho	12:1	and they **d.** make a covenant with	
Ho	14:8	What have I to **d.** any more with idols?	
Joe	1:18	How **d.** the beasts groan?	
Joe	2:21	for the Lord will **d.** great things,	6213
Joe	2:22	pastures of the wilderness **d.** spring	
Joe	2:26	and the vine **d.** yield their strength.	
Joe	3:4	what have ye to **d.** with me, O Tyre,	
Am	3:7	the Lord God will **d.** nothing, but	6213
Am	3:10	know not to **d.** right, saith the Lord,	6213
Am	4:12	thus will I **d.** unto thee, O Israel:	6213
Am	4:12	because I will **d.** this unto thee,	6213
Jon	1:11	What shall we **d.** unto thee, that	6213
Jon	3:10	that he would **d.** unto them: and	6213
Jon	4:9	he said, I **d.** well to be angry,	
Mic	2:3	against this family **d.** I devise an evil,	
Mic	2:7	**d.** not my words **d.** good to him	
Mic	2:11	in the spirit and falsehood **d.** lie,	
Mic	6:8	to **d.** justly, and to love mercy,	6213
Mic	7:3	that they may **d.** evil with both hands	
Na	1:9	What **d.** ye imagine against the Lord?	
Zep	1:12	will not **d.** good,	
Zep	1:12	neither will he **d.** evil.	
Zep	3:5	not **d.** iniquity: every morning	6213
Zep	3:13	Israel shall not **d.** iniquity, nor	6213
Hag	2:3	and how **d.** ye see it now?	
Hag	2:12	and with his skirt **d.** touch bread,	
Zec	1:5	and the prophets, **d.** they live for ever?	
Zec	1:6	Lord of hosts thought to **d.** unto us,	6213
Zec	1:21	What come these to **d.**? And he	6213
Zec	5:10	Whither **d.** these bear the ephah?	
Zec	8:15	days to **d.** well unto Jerusalem	
Zec	8:16	things that ye shall **d.**; Speak ye	6213
Zec	9:12	even to day **d.** I declare that I will	
Zec	12:7	of Jerusalem **d.** not magnify	
Mal	1:10	**d.** ye kindle fire on mine altar	
Mal	2:2	because ye **d.** not lay it to heart.	
Mal	2:10	why **d.** we deal treacherously every	
Mal	4:1	and all that **d.** wickedly shall be	6213
Mal	4:3	day that I **d.** this, saith the Lord	6213
Mt	5:6	**Blessed are they which d. hunger**	
Mt	5:15	**neither d. men light a candle, and**	
Mt	5:19	**whosoever shall d. and teach**	*4160*
Mt	5:44	**d. good to them that hate you,**	*4160*
Mt	5:46	**d. not even the publicans the**	*4160*
Mt	5:47	**what d. ye more than others?**	*4160*
Mt	5:47	**d. not even the publicans so?**	*4160*
Mt	6:1	**Take heed that ye d. not your**	*4160*
Mt	6:2	**d. not sound a trumpet before thee,**	
Mt	6:2	**as the hypocrites d. in the**	*4160*
Mt	6:7	**repetitions, as the heathen d.:**	
Mt	6:20	**where thieves d. not break through**	
Mt	6:26	**they sow not, neither d. they reap,**	
Mt	6:28	**they toil not, neither d. they spin:**	
Mt	6:32	**all these things d. the Gentiles seek:**	
Mt	7:12	**ye would that men should d. to**	*4160*
Mt	7:12	**d. ye even so to them: for this is**	*4160*
Mt	7:16	**D. men gather grapes of thorns,**	
Mt	8:9	**D. this, and he doeth it.**	*4160*
Mt	8:29	What have we to **d.** with thee, Jesus,	
Mt	9:14	Why **d.** we and the Pharisees fast oft,	
Mt	9:17	**Neither d. men put new wine into**	
Mt	9:28	**ye that I am able to d. this?**	*4160*
Mt	11:3	or **d.** we look for another?	
Mt	11:4	**again these things which ye d. hear**	
Mt	12:2	thy disciples **d.** that which is not	*4160*
Mt	12:2	not lawful to **d.** upon the sabbath	*4160*
Mt	12:12	**Wherefore it is lawful to d. well**	*4160*
Mt	12:27	**d. your children cast them out?**	
Mt	12:50	**For whosoever shall d. the will**	*4160*
Mt	13:13	**neither d. they understand.**	
Mt	13:41	**and them which d. iniquity;**	*4160*
Mt	14:2	mighty works **d.** shew forth	
Mt	15:2	Why **d.** thy disciples transgress the	
Mt	15:3	**Why d. ye also transgress the**	
Mt	15:9	**vain they d. worship me, teaching**	
Mt	15:17	**d. not ye yet understand,**	
Mt	16:9	**D. ye not yet understand,**	
Mt	16:11	**How is it that ye d. not understand**	
Mt	16:13	**Whom d. men say that I the Son of**	
Mt	17:25	**of whom d. the kings of the earth**	
Mt	18:10	**heaven their angels d. always behold**	
Mt	18:35	**heavenly Father d. also unto you,**	*4160*
Mt	19:16	what good thing shall I **d.**, that I	*4160*
Mt	19:18	**Thou shalt d. no murder. Thou**	
Mt	20:13	**I d. thee no wrong: didst not thou**	*91*
Mt	20:15	**for me to d. what I will with mine**	*4160*
Mt	20:32	**will ye that I shall d. unto you?**	*4160*
Mt	21:21	**ye shall not only d. this which is**	*4160*
Mt	21:24,	**27 by what authority I d. these**	*4160*
Mt	21:40	**will he d. unto those husbandmen?**	*4160*
Mt	22:29	**d. err, not knowing the Scriptures,**	
Mt	23:3	**you observe, that observe and d.;**	*4160*
Mt	23:3	**but d. not ye after their works:**	*4160*
Mt	23:3	**for they say and d. not.**	*4160*
Mt	23:5	**But all their works they d. for to**	*4160*
Mt	26:72	I **d.** not know the man.	
Mt	27:19	thou nothing to **d.** with that just man:	
Mt	27:22	What shall I **d.** then with Jesus	*4160*
Mk	1:24	have we to **d.** with thee, thou Jesus	
Mk	1:27	spirits, and they **d.** obey him.	
Mk	2:18	Why **d.** the disciples of John and of	
Mk	2:24	why **d.** they on the sabbath day	*4160*
Mk	3:4	**to d. good on the sabbath days,**	*15*
Mk	3:4	**to d. evil? to save life, or to kill?**	*2554*
Mk	3:35	**whosoever shall d. the will of God,**	
Mk	5:7	What have I to **d.** with thee, Jesus	
Mk	6:5	he could there **d.** no mighty work,	*4160*
Mk	6:14	**d.** shew forth themselves in him.	
Mk	7:7	**Howbeit in vain d. they worship me,**	
Mk	7:8	**many other such like things ye d.**	*4160*
Mk	7:12	**ye suffer him no more to d. ought**	*4160*
Mk	7:13	**and many such like things d. ye.**	*4160*
Mk	7:18	**D. ye not perceive, that whatsoever**	
Mk	8:18	**and d. ye not remember?**	
Mk	8:21	**How is it that ye d. not understand?**	
Mk	8:27	**Whom d. men say that I am?**	
Mk	9:22	canst **d.** any thing, have compassion	
Mk	9:39	**no man which shall d. a miracle**	*4160*
Mk	10:17	what shall I **d.** that I may inherit	*4160*
Mk	10:19	**D. not commit adultery, D. not kill,**	
Mk	10:19	**D. not steal, D. not bear false**	
Mk	10:35	that thou shouldest **d.** for us	*4160*
Mk	10:36	**What would ye that I should d.**	*4160*
Mk	10:51	**What wilt thou that I should d.**	*4160*
Mk	11:3	**Why d. ye this? say ye that the**	*4160*
Mk	11:5	them, What **d.** ye, loosing the colt?	*4160*
Mk	11:26	**But if ye d. not forgive, neither**	
Mk	11:28	this authority to **d.** these things?	*4160*

Mk 11:29, 33 by what authority I d. these 4160
Mk 11:33 d. I tell you by what authority
Mk 12:9 the lord of the vineyard d.? he 4160
Mk 12:24 D. ye not therefore err, because
Mk 12:27 living: ye therefore d. greatly err.
Mk 13:11 neither d. ye premeditate:
Mk 14:7 ye will ye may d. them good: but 4160
Mk 15:8 desire him to d. as he had ever done
Mk 15:12 I shall d. unto him whom ye call 4160
Lu 2:27 to d. for him after the custom of 4160
Lu 3:10 saying, What shall we d. then? 4160
Lu 3:11 that hath meat, let him d. likewise 4160
Lu 3:12 him, Master, what shall we d.? 4160
Lu 3:14 And what shall we d.? And he 4160
Lu 3:14 D. violence to no man, neither 1286
Lu 4:23 d. also here in thy country. 4160
Lu 4:34 have we to d. with thee, thou Jesus
Lu 5:30 Why d. ye eat and drink with publicans
Lu 5:33 Why d. the disciples of John fast
Lu 6:2 Why d. ye that which is not lawful 4160
Lu 6:2 to d. on the sabbath days? 4160
Lu 6:9 on the sabbath days to d. good, 15
Lu 6:9 or to d. evil? 2554
Lu 6:11 what they might d. to Jesus. 4160
Lu 6:27 Love your enemies, d. good to 4160
Lu 6:31 would that men should d. to you, 4160
Lu 6:31 d. ye also to them likewise. 4160
Lu 6:33 And if ye d. good to them which
Lu 6:33 d. good to you, what thank have ye? 15
Lu 6:33 for sinners also d. even the same 4160
Lu 6:35 love your enemies, and d. good. 15
Lu 6:44 For of thorns men d. not gather figs,
Lu 6:46 and d. not the things which I say? 4160
Lu 7:4 worthy for whom he should d. this: 3930
Lu 7:8 servant, D. this, and he doeth it. 4160
Lu 8:21 hear the word of God, and d. it 4160
Lu 8:28 What have I to d. with thee, Jesus,
Lu 10:11 dust...we d. wipe off against you:
Lu 10:25 shall I d. to inherit eternal life? 4160
Lu 10:28 answered right: this d., and thou 4160
Lu 10:37 unto him, Go, and d. thou likewise, 4160
Lu 11:19 by whom d. your sons cast them 4160
Lu 11:39 Now d. ye Pharisees make clean the
Lu 12:4 have no more that they can d. 4160
Lu 12:17 What shall I d., because I have no 4160
Lu 12:18 will I d.: I will pull down my 4160
Lu 12:26 not able to d. that thing which is least.
Lu 12:30 all these things d. the nations of the
Lu 12:56 that ye d. not discern this time?
Lu 13:32 I d. cures to day and to morrow, 2005
Lu 15:29 these many years d. I serve thee,
Lu 16:3 What shall I d.? for my lord 4160
Lu 16:4 I am resolved what to d., that 4160
Lu 17:10 that which was our duty to d. 4160
Lu 18:18 shall I d. to inherit eternal life? 4160
Lu 18:20 D. not commit adultery, D. not kill,
Lu 18:20 D. not steal, D. not bear false witness.
Lu 18:41 thou that I shall d. unto thee? 4160
Lu 19:31 Why d. ye loose him?
Lu 19:48 could not find what they might d.: 4160
Lu 20:8 by what authority I d. these 4160
Lu 20:13 What shall I d.? I will send my 4160
Lu 20:15 lord of the vineyard d. unto them? 4160
Lu 22:19 you: this d. in remembrance of me. 4160
Lu 22:23 it was that should d. this thing 4238
Lu 23:31 d. these things in a green tree 4160
Lu 23:34 for they know not what they d. 4160
Lu 24:38 why d. thoughts arise in your hearts?
Joh 2:4 what have I to d. with thee? mine
Joh 2:5 Whatsoever he saith unto you, d. 4160
Joh 3:2 for no man can d. these miracles 4160
Joh 3:11 We speak that we d. know,
Joh 4:34 My meat is to d. the will of him 4160
Joh 5:19 The Son can d. nothing of himself, 4160
Joh 5:19 what he seeth the Father d.: for 4160
Joh 5:30 I can of mine own self d. nothing; 4160
Joh 5:36 same works that I d., bear witness 4160
Joh 5:45 D. not think that I will accuse
Joh 6:6 himself knew what he would d. 4160
Joh 6:28 What shall we d., that we might 4160
Joh 6:38 not to d. mine own will, but the 4160
Joh 7:4 thou d. these things, shew thyself 4160
Joh 7:17 If any man will d. his will, he 4160
Joh 7:26 D. the rulers know indeed that
Joh 7:31 will he d. more miracles than 4160
Joh 8:11 neither d. I condemn thee: go and
Joh 8:28 and that I d. nothing of myself; 4160
Joh 8:29 for I d. always those things that 4160
Joh 8:38 and ye d. that which ye have seen. 4160
Joh 8:39 ye would d. the works of Abraham. 4160
Joh 8:41 Ye d. the deeds of your father 4160
Joh 8:43 d. ye not understand my speech?
Joh 8:44 the lusts of your father ye will d. 4160
Joh 8:46 the truth, why d. ye not believe me?
Joh 8:49 and ye d. dishonour me.
Joh 9:15 and I washed, and d. see.
Joh 9:16 that is a sinner d. such miracles? 4160
Joh 9:33 not of God, he could d. nothing. 4160
Joh 10:25 that I d. in my Father's name, 4160
Joh 10:32 for which of these works d. ye
Joh 10:37 If I d. not the work of my Father, 4160
Joh 10:38 if I d., though ye believe not me, 4160
Joh 11:12 Lord, if he sleep, he shall d. well. 4982
Joh 11:47 What d. we? for this man doeth 4160
Joh 13:7 What I d. thou knowest not now; 4160
Joh 13:15 ye should d. as I have done to you. 4160
Joh 13:17 things, happy are ye if ye d. them, 4160
Joh 13:27 That thou doest, d. quickly. 4160
Joh 14:12 the works that I d. shall he d. also; 4160
Joh 14:12 works than these shall he d.; 4160
Joh 14:13 that will I d., that the Father may 4160
Joh 14:14 any thing in my name, I will d. it. 4160
Joh 14:31 commandment, even so I d., Arise, 4160
Joh 15:5 for without me ye can d. nothing. 4160
Joh 15:14 ye d. whatsoever I command you, 4160
Joh 15:21 But all these things will they d. 4160
Joh 16:3 these things will they d. unto you, 4160
Joh 16:19 D. ye enquire among yourselves of
Joh 16:31 D. ye now believe?
Joh 17:4 work which thou gavest me to d. 4160
Joh 21:21 Lord, and what shall this man d.?
Ac 1:1 Jesus began both to d. and teach, 4160
Ac 2:11 we d. hear them speak in our tongues
Ac 2:37 and brethren, what shall we d.? 4160
Ac 4:16 What shall we d. to these men? 4160
Ac 4:28 For to d. whatsoever thy hand and 4160
Ac 5:35 to d. as touching these men. 4238
Ac 7:26 why d. ye wrong one to another? 91
Ac 7:51 as your fathers did, so d. ye.
Ac 7:51 ye d. always resist the Holy Ghost:
Ac 9:6 have me to d.? And the Lord 4160
Ac 9:6 be told thee what thou must d., 4160
Ac 10:6 thee what thou oughtest to d. 4160
Ac 14:15 Sirs, why d. ye these things? 4160
Ac 15:29 ye shall d. well. Fare ye well. 4238
Ac 15:36 of the Lord, and see how they d. 2192
Ac 16:20 Jews, d. exceedingly trouble our city,
Ac 16:28 D. thyself no harm: for we are 4238
Ac 16:30 Sirs, what must I d. to be saved? 4160
Ac 16:37 now d. they thrust us out privily?
Ac 17:7 all d. contrary to the decrees 4160
Ac 19:36 be quiet, and to d. nothing rashly, 4160
Ac 21:23 D. therefore this that we say to 4160
Ac 22:10 I said, What shall I d., Lord? 4160
Ac 22:10 which are appointed for thee to d. 4160
Ac 23:21 But d. not thou yield unto them:
Ac 24:10 I d. the more cheerfully answer for
Ac 24:16 and herein d. I exercise myself,
Ac 25:9 willing to d. the Jews a pleasure, 2698
Ac 26:9 ought to d. many things contrary 4238
Ac 26:20 d. works meet for repentance, 4238
Ro 1:28 to d. those things which are not 4160
Ro 1:32 not only d. the same, but have
Ro 1:32 pleasure in them that d. them. 4238
Ro 2:3 them which d. such things, and 4238
Ro 2:8 and d. not obey the truth,
Ro 2:14 have not the law, d. by nature 4160
Ro 3:8 Let us d. evil, that good may come? 4160
Ro 3:31 D. we then make void the law
Ro 7:15 For that which I d. I allow not: 2716
Ro 7:15 for what I would, that d. I not; 4238
Ro 7:15 but what I hate, that d. I. 4160
Ro 7:16 If then I d. that which I would not 4160
Ro 7:17 it is no more I that d. it, but sin 2716
Ro 7:19 the good that I would I d. not: but 4160
Ro 7:19 evil which I would not, that I d. 4238
Ro 7:20 Now if I d. that I would not, 4160
Ro 7:20 no more I that d. it, but sin that 2716
Ro 7:21 I would d. good, evil is present 4160
Ro 8:3 law could not d., in that it was weak
Ro 8:5 flesh d. mind the things of the flesh;
Ro 8:13 d. mortify the deeds of the body,
Ro 8:25 then d. we with patience wait for it.
Ro 12:8 giveth, let him d. it with simplicity;
Ro 12:15 Rejoice with them that d. rejoice,
Ro 13:3 d. that which is good, and thou 4160
Ro 13:4 But if thou d. that which is evil, 4160
Ro 15:31 that d. not believe in Judaea;
1Co 5:12 I to d. to judge them also that are
1Co 5:12 d. not ye judge them that are
1Co 6:2 D. ye not know that the saints shall
1Co 6:7 Why d. ye not rather take wrong?
1Co 6:7 d. ye not rather suffer yourselves
1Co 6:8 Nay, ye d. wrong, and defraud,
1Co 7:36 let him d. what he will, 4160
1Co 9:3 answer to them that d. examine me
1Co 9:13 D. ye not know that they which
1Co 9:17 For if I d. this thing willingly, I 4238
1Co 9:23 And this I d. for the gospel's sake, 4160
1Co 9:25 d. it to obtain a corruptible crown;
1Co 10:22 D. we provoke the Lord to jealousy?
1Co 10:31 ye d., d. all to the glory of God. 4160
1Co 11:24 this d. in remembrance of me. 4160
1Co 11:25 this d. ye, as oft as ye drink it in 4160
1Co 11:26 ye d. show the Lord's death till
1Co 12:30 d. all speak with tongues?
1Co 12:30 d. all interpret?
1Co 15:29 Else what shall they d. which are 4160
1Co 15:35 and with what body d. they come?
1Co 16:1 even so d. ye. Upon the first day 4160
1Co 16:5 for I d. pass through Macedonia
1Co 16:10 the work of the lord, as I also d.
2Co 1:17 d. I purpose according to the flesh,
2Co 3:1 D. we begin again to commend
2Co 5:4 that are in this tabernacle d. groan,
2Co 7:8 I d. not repent, though I did repent:
2Co 8:1 d. you to wit of the grace of God 1107
2Co 8:10 only to d., but also to be forward 4160
2Co 8:23 Whether any d. enquire of Titus,
2Co 10:3 we d. not war after the flesh:
2Co 10:7 D. ye look on things after the
2Co 11:8 wages of them to d. you service.
2Co 11:12 But what I d., that I will d., that 4160
2Co 12:19 but we d. all things dearly
2Co 13:7 d. no evil; d. that which is honest, 4160
2Co 13:8 we can d. nothing against the truth,
Ga 1:10 d. I now persuade me, or God?
Ga 1:10 or d. I seek to please men?
Ga 2:10 which I also was forward to d. 4160
Ga 2:14 and not as d. the Jews,
Ga 2:14 to live as d. the Jews? We who
Ga 2:21 d. not frustrate the grace of God:
Ga 3:10 in the book of the law to d. them. 4160
Ga 4:21 d. ye not hear the law?
Ga 5:3 he is a debtor to d. the whole law. 4160
Ga 5:11 why d. I yet suffer persecution?
Ga 5:17 d. the things that ye would. 4160
Ga 5:21 that they which d. such things 4238
Ga 6:10 let us d. good unto all men, 2038
Eph 3:20 is able to d. exceeding abundantly 4160
Eph 6:9 d. the same things unto them, 4160
Eph 6:21 know my affairs, and how I d., 4238
Php 1:18 and I therefore d. rejoice,
Php 2:13 and to d. of his good pleasure. 1754
Php 2:14 D. all things without murmurings 4160
Php 2:18 For the same cause also d. ye joy,
Php 3:8 loss of all things, and d. count them
Php 3:13 but this one thing I d., forgetting
Php 4:9 heard, and seen in me, d.: and 4238
Php 4:13 can d. all things through Christ 2480
Col 1:9 d. not cease to pray for you,
Col 3:13 as Christ forgave you, so also d. ye.
Col 3:17 ye d. in word or deed, d. all in 4160
Col 3:23 And whatsoever ye d., 4160
Col 3:23 d. it heartily, as to the Lord, 2038
1Th 3:12 even as we d. toward you:
1Th 4:10 And indeed ye d. it toward all the 4160
1Th 4:11 be quiet, and to d. your business 4238
1Th 5:6 let us not sleep, as d. others; but
1Th 5:11 one another, even as also ye d. 4160
1Th 5:24 calleth you, who also will d. it. 4160
2Th 3:4 that ye both d., and will d. the 4160
1Ti 1:4 edifying which is in faith: so d.
1Ti 6:2 rather d. them service, because 1398
1Ti 6:18 That they d. good, that they be rich 14
2Ti 2:23 knowing that they d. gender strifes
2Ti 3:8 so d. these also resist the truth: men
2Ti 4:5 d. the work of an evangelist, make 4160
2Ti 4:9 D. thy diligence to come shortly 4704
2Ti 4:21 D. thy diligence to come before 4704
Phm 14 thy mind would I d. nothing; 4160

Phm 19 albeit I d. not say to thee how thou..........
Phm 21 thou wilt also d. more than I say........ 4160
Heb 3:10 They d. always err in their heart;.............
Heb 4:3 For we which have believed d. enter ....
Heb 4:13 him with whom we have to d.. ... 3588,3056
Heb 6:3 And this will we d. if God permit. 4160
Heb 6:10 have ministered to the saints and d...........
Heb 6:11 every one of you d. shew the same.........
Heb 10:7 written of me,) to d. thy will, O God.. 4160
Heb 10:9 Lo, I come to d. thy will, O God. 4160
Heb 11:3 not made of things which d. appear...........
Heb 11:29 assaying to d. were drowned..............
Heb 13:6 not fear what man shall d. unto me...........
Heb 13:16 to d. good and to communicate 2140
Heb 13:17 that they may d. it with joy,........... 4160
Heb 13:19 beseech you the rather to d. this, ... 4160
Heb 13:21 in every good work to d. his will,....... 4160
Jas 1:16 D. not err, my beloved brethren...........
Jas 2:6 D. not rich men oppress you,..............
Jas 2:7 D. they not blaspheme that worthy...........
Jas 2:8 neighbour as thyself, ye d. well: 4160
Jas 2:11 that said, D. not commit adultery,............
Jas 2:11 said also, D. not kill. ....
Jas 2:12 So speak ye, and so d., as they......... 4160
Jas 4:5 D. ye think that the scripture saith..........
Jas 4:15 we shall live, and d. this, or that........ 4160
Jas 4:17 to him that knoweth to d. good,......... 4160
Jas 5:19 any of you d. err from the truth,.............
1Pe 1:21 Who by him d. believe in God, ...
1Pe 2:14 for the praise of them that d. well......... 17
1Pe 2:20 if, when ye d. well, and suffer for it, ... 15
1Pe 3:6 daughters ye are, as long as ye d......... 15
1Pe 3:11 him eschew evil, and d. good; 4160
1Pe 3:12 Lord is against them that d. evil. 4160
1Pe 4:11 let him d. it as of the ability...................
2Pe 1:10 for if ye d. these things, ye shall........ 4160
2Pe 1:19 ye d. well that ye take heed, as......... 4160
2Pe 3:16 they d. also the other Scriptures,...........
1Jo 1:6 we lie, and d. not the truth:............. 4160
1Jo 2:3 hereby we d. know that we know............
1Jo 3:22 d. those things that are pleasing......... 4160
1Jo 4:14 and d. testify that the Father..................
1Jo 5:16 I d. not say that he shall pray for it..........
3Jo 6 a godly sort, thou shalt d. well; 4160
Re 2:5 **and repent, and d. the first works;** .4160
Re 3:9 **are Jews, and are not, but d. lie;**.........
Re 3:18 **thy nakedness d. not appear;**...............
Re 9:19 and with them they d. hurt...................
Re 13:14 which he had the power to d. in 4160
Re 14:13 and their works d. follow them. ....
Re 19:10 See thou d. it not: I am thy fellow...........
Re 21:24 the kings of the earth d. bring their..........
Re 22:9 saith he unto me, See thou d. it not; ....
Re 22:14 they that d. his commandments,......... 4160

DOCTOR See also DOCTORS.
Ac 5:34 named Gamaliel, a d. of the law......... 3547

DOCTORS
Lu 2:46 sitting in the midst of the d.,............. 1320
Lu 5:17 and d. of the law sitting by, ... 3547

DOCTRINE See also DOCTRINES.
De 32:2 My d. shall drop as the rain,............ 3948
Job 11:4 My d. is pure, and I am clean in 3948
Pr 4:2 I give you good d., forsake ye not...... 3948
Isa 28:9 shall he make to understand d.? 8052
Isa 29:24 that murmured shall learn d.. 3948
Jer 10:8 the stock is a d. of vanities............. 4148
Mt 7:28 people were astonished at his d.: 1322
Mt 16:12 of the d. of the Pharisees and of........ 1322
Mt 22:33 they were astonished at his d.. 1322
Mk 1:22 they were astonished at his d.: 1322
Mk 1:27 what new d. is this? for with............. 1322
Mk 4:2 and said unto them in his d., ... 1322
Mk 11:18 people was astonished at his d........... 1322
Mk 12:38 he said unto them in his d., ... 1322
Lu 4:32 they were astonished at his d.: 1322
Joh 7:16 **My d. is not mine, but his that** 1322
Joh 7:17 **he shall know of the d., whether**... 1322
Joh 18:19 of his disciples, and of his d.. 1322
Ac 2:42 in the apostles' d. and fellowship, ... 1322
Ac 5:28 filled Jerusalem with your d.,............ 1322
Ac 13:12 astonished at the d. of the Lord.......... 1322
Ac 17:19 what this new d., whereof thou 1322
Ro 6:17 form of d. which was delivered 1322
Ro 16:17 offences contrary to the d. which 1322
1Co 14:6 or by prophesying, or by d.? 1322
1Co 14:26 of you hath a psalm, hath a d., ... 1322
Eph 4:14 about with every wind of d., ... 1319
1Ti 1:3 some that they teach no other d., ...
1Ti 1:10 that is contrary to sound d.; 1319
1Ti 4:6 up in words of faith and of good d., ... 1319
1Ti 4:13 to reading, to exhortation, to d., ... 1319
1Ti 4:16 unto thyself, and unto the d.; 1319
1Ti 5:17 who labour in the word and d., ... 1319
1Ti 6:1 God and his d. be not blasphemed...... 1319
1Ti 6:3 to the d. which is according to............ 1319
2Ti 3:10 thou hast fully known my d., ... 1319
2Ti 3:16 is profitable for d., for reproof, ... 1319
2Ti 4:2 with all longsuffering and d.............. 1322
2Ti 4:3 they will not endure sound d.; 1319
Tit 1:9 able by sound d. both to exhort 1319
Tit 2:1 things which become sound d.: 1319
Tit 2:7 in d. shewing uncorruptness, ... 1319
Tit 2:10 adorn the d. of God our Saviour......... 1319
Heb 6:1 leaving the principles of the d........... 3056
Heb 6:2 Of the d. of baptisms, and of............ 1322
2Jo 9 abideth not in the d. of Christ, ... 1322
2Jo 9 that abideth in the d. of Christ, ... 1322
2Jo 9 bring not this d., receive him not 1322
Re 2:14 **that hold the d. of Balaam, who** ... 1322
Re 2:15 **hold the d. of the Nicolaitanes,** 1322
Re 2:24 **as many as have not this d.,** 1322

DOCTRINES
Mt 15:9 **for d. the commandments of men**...1319
Mk 7:7 **for d. the commandments of men**...1319
Col 2:22 the commandments and d. of men?..... 1319
1Ti 4:1 seducing spirits, and d. of devils; 1319
Heb 13:9 about with divers and strange d.. 1322

DODAI (do'-dahee) See also DODO.
1Ch 27:4 second month was D. an Ahohite, ... 1739

DODANIM (do'da-nim) See also RODANIM.
Ge 10:4 and Tarshish, Kittim, and D.. 1721
1Ch 1:7 and Tarshish, Kittim, and D.. 1721

DODAVAH (do'da-vah)
2Ch 20:37 Then Eliezer the son of D. of........... 1735

DODO (do'-do) See also DODAI.
Jg 10:1 the son of D., a man of Issachar; 1734
2Sa 23:9 Eleazar the son of D. the Ahohite, ... 1734
2Sa 23:24 Elhanan the son of D. of Beth-lehem,.. 1734
1Ch 11:12 him was Eleazar the son of D.,.......... 1734
1Ch 11:26 Elhanan the son of D. of Beth-lehem,.. 1734

DOEG (do'-eg)
1Sa 21:7 his name was D., an Edomite,........... 1673
1Sa 22:9 Then answered D. the Edomite, ... 1673
1Sa 22:18 the king said to D., Turn thou,......... 1673
1Sa 22:18 D. the Edomite turned, and he fell..... 1673
1Sa 22:22 when D. the Edomite was there, ... 1673
Ps 52 *title* when D. the Edomite came and......... 1673

DOER See also DOERS.
Ge 39:22 did there, he was the d. of it. 6213
2Sa 3:39 Lord shall reward the d. of evil.......... 6213
Ps 31:23 plentifully rewardeth the proud d......... 6213
Pr 17:4 wicked d. giveth heed to false lips;..........
2Ti 2:9 as an evil d., even unto bonds; 2557
Jas 1:23 hearer of the word, and not a d., ... 4163
Jas 1:25 hearer, but a d. of the work,............. 4163
Jas 4:11 not a d. of the law, but a judge.......... 4163

DOERS
2Ki 22:5 the hand of the d. of the work,.......... 6213
2Ki 22:5 them give it to the d. of the work,...... 6213
Job 8:20 neither will he help the evil d.: ....
Ps 26:5 hated the congregation of evil d.; ....
Ps 101:8 that I may cut off all wicked d. 6466
Ro 2:13 d. of the law shall be justified............ 4163
Jas 1:22 be ye d. of the word, and not.............. 4163

DOEST See also DOST.
Ge 4:7 If thou d. well, shalt thou not be..........
Ge 4:7 and if thou d. not well, sin lieth at...........
Ge 21:22 is with thee in all that thou d.:........... 6213
Ex 18:14 What is this thing that thou d. to 6213
Ex 18:17 unto him, The thing that thou d. is..... 6213
De 12:28 when thou d. that which is good 6213
De 14:29 work of thine hand which thou d. 6213
De 15:18 shall bless thee in all that thou d....... 6213
Jg 11:27 thou d. me wrong to war against........ 6213
2Sa 3:25 in, and to know all that thou d........... 6213
1Ki 2:3 mayest prosper in all that thou d., ... 6213
1Ki 19:9 he said unto him, What d. thou here, ...
1Ki 19:13 and said, What d. thou here, Elijah?..........
1Ki 20:22 mark, and see what thou d.: for........ 6213
Job 9:12 will say unto him, What d. thou?........ 6213
Job 35:6 what d. thou against him? or if 6466
Job 35:6 be multiplied, what d. thou unto.......... 6213
Ps 49:18 men will praise thee, when thou d. well.....
Ps 77:14 Thou art the God that d. wonders:...... 6213
Ps 86:10 thou art great, and d. wondrous.......... 6213
Ps 119:68 Thou art good, and d. good; teach me.......
Ec 8:4 may say unto him, What d. thou? 6213
Jer 11:15 when thou d. evil, then thou rejoicest. ......
Jer 15:5 go aside to ask how thou d.? 7965
Eze 12:9 said unto thee, What d. thou?............ 6213
Eze 16:30 seeing thou d. all these things, the...... 6213
Eze 24:19 these things are to us, that thou d. 6213
Da 4:35 or say unto him, What d. thou? 5648
Jon 4:4 the Lord, D. thou well to be angry? ....
Jon 4:9 D. thou well to be angry for the gourd?.....
Mt 6:2 **when thou d. thine alms, do not**.... 4160
Mt 6:3 **But when thou d. alms, let not** 4160
Mt 21:23 By what authority d. thou these......... 4160
Mk 11:28 By what authority d. thou these......... 4160
Lu 20:2 by what authority d. thou these 4160
Joh 2:18 seeing that thou d. these things? 4160
Joh 3:2 that thou d., except God be with 4160
Joh 7:3 may see the works that thou d.. 4160
Joh 13:27 **That thou d., do quickly**............... 4160
Ac 22:26 Take heed what thou d.: for this......... 4160
Ro 2:1 thou that judgest d. the same........... 4238
Ro 2:3 and d. the same, that thou shalt......... 4160
Jas 2:19 that there is one God; thou d. well:.... 4160
3Jo 5 d. faithfully whatsoever thou d. to...... 4160

DOETH See also DOTH.
Ge 31:12 seen all that Laban d. unto thee....... 6213
Ex 31:14 whosoever d. any work therein,......... 6213
Ex 31:15 whosoever d. any work in the 6213
Ex 35:2 whosoever d. work therein shall be 6213
Le 4:27 while he d. somewhat against 6213
Le 6:3 of all these that a man d., sinning....... 6213
Le 23:30 whatsoever soul it be that d. any 6213
Nu 15:30 soul that d. ought presumptuously, ... 6213
Nu 24:23 who shall live when God d. this! 7760
Job 5:9 d. great things and unsearchable; 6213
Job 9:10 Which d. great things past finding....... 6213
Job 23:13 his soul desireth, even that he d.. 6213
Job 24:21 and d. not good to the widow.................
Job 37:5 great things d. he, which we............. 6213
Ps 1:3 and whatsoever he d. shall prosper...... 6213
Ps 14:1 works, there is none that d. good. 6213
Ps 14:3 there is none that d. good, no, not..... 6213
Ps 15:3 nor d. evil to his neighbour, nor......... 6213
Ps 15:5 He that d. these things shall never..... 6213
Ps 53:1 iniquity: there is none that d. good. 6213
Ps 53:3 there is none that d. good, no, not..... 6213
Ps 72:18 of Israel, who only d. wondrous........ 6213
Ps 106:3 and he that d. righteousness at all...... 6213
Ps 118:15, 16 hand of the Lord d. valiantly. 6213
Ps 136:4 him who alone d. great wonders: 6213
Pr 6:32 he that d. it destroyeth his own soul... 6213
Pr 11:17 The merciful man d. good to his 1580
Pr 15:7 but the heart of the foolish d. not so..........
Pr 17:21 He that begetteth a fool d. it to his ....
Pr 17:22 A merry heart d. good like a................
Pr 28:17 A man that d. violence to the ....
Ec 2:2 is mad: and of mirth, What d. it? 6213
Ec 3:14 I know that, whatsoever God d., it..... 6213
Ec 3:14 and God d. it, that men should fear 6213
Ec 7:20 just man upon earth, that d. good....... 6213
Ec 8:3 for he d. whatsoever pleaseth him...... 6213
Isa 49:18 bind them on thee, as a bride d.. ....
Isa 56:2 Blessed is the man that d. this, ... 6213
Jer 5:19 Wherefore d. the Lord our God all 6213
Jer 48:10 Cursed be he that d. the work of the.. 6213
Eze 17:15 shall he escape that d. such things? 6213
Eze 18:10 and that d. the like to any one of....... 6213
Eze 18:11 And that d. not any of those duties,.... 6213
Eze 18:14 and considereth, and d. not such........ 6213
Eze 18:24 iniquity, and d. according to all the 6213
Eze 18:24 that the wicked man d., shall he 6213
Eze 18:27 and d. that which is lawful and........... 6213
Da 4:35 and he d. according to his will........... 5648
Da 9:14 in all his work which he d.: 6213
Am 9:12 saith the Lord that d. this,................ 6213
Mal 2:12 the man that d. this, the master 6213
Mal 2:17 Every one that d. evil is good in......... 6213
Mt 6:3 **what thy right hand d.:** 4160
Mt 7:21 **he that d. the will of my Father**.... 4160
Mt 7:24 **and d. them, I will liken him unto** .4160

Mt 7:26 **and d. them not, shall be likened..** *4160*
Mt 8:9 my servant, Do this, and he **d.** it. *4160*
Lu 6:47 **my sayings, and d. them, I will** *4160*
Lu 6:49 **heareth, and d. not, is like a man** *4160*
Lu 7:8 my servant, Do this, and he **d.** it. *4238*
Joh 3:20 **For every one that d. evil hateth** *4160*
Joh 3:21 **But he that d. truth cometh to the** *4160*
Joh 5:19 **for what things soever he d.,** *4160*
Joh 5:19 **these also d. the Son likewise** *4160*
Joh 5:20 **him all things that himself d.; and** *4160*
Joh 7:4 there is no man that **d.** any thing *4160*
Joh 7:51 hear him, and know what he **d.**? *4160*
Joh 9:31 and **d.** his will, him he heareth. *4160*
Joh 11:47 What do we? for this man **d.** many *4160*
Joh 14:10 **dwelleth in me, he d. the works** *4160*
Joh 15:15 **knoweth not what his lord d.: but** *4160*
Joh 16:2 **will think that he d. God service,** *4374*
Ac 15:17 the Lord who **d.** all these things, *4160*
Ac 26:31 This man **d.** nothing worthy of *4238*
Ro 2:9 soul of man that **d.** evil, of the
Ro 3:12 there is none that **d.** good, no, not *4160*
Ro 10:5 the man which **d.** those things *4160*
Ro 13:4 wrath upon him that **d.** evil. *4238*
1Co 6:18 that a man **d.** is without the body; *4160*
1Co 7:37 he will keep his virgin, **d.** well. *4160*
1Co 7:38 giveth her in marriage, **d.** well; *4160*
1Co 7:38 her not in marriage **d.** better. *4160*
Ga 3:5 **d.** he it by the works of the law, or
Ga 3:12 The man that **d.** them shall live *4160*
Eph 6:8 whatsoever good thing any man **d.**, *4160*
Col 3:25 But he that **d.** wrong shall receive *91*
Jas 4:17 knoweth to do good, and **d.** it not, *4160*
1Jo 2:17 but he that **d.** the will of God *4160*
1Jo 2:29 that **d.** righteousness is born of him. *4160*
1Jo 3:7 that **d.** righteousness is righteous, *4160*
1Jo 3:10 Whosoever **d.** not righteousness is *4160*
3Jo 10 remember his deeds which he **d.**, *4160*
3Jo 11 He that **d.** good is of God: but he *15*
3Jo 11 he that **d.** evil hath not seen God. *2554*
Re 13:13 And he **d.** great wonders, so that *4160*

DOG See also DOG'S; DOGS.
Ex 11:7 shall not a **d.** move his tongue, 3611
De 23:18 the price of a **d.**, into the house 3611
Jg 7:5 with his tongue, as a **d.** lappeth, 3611
1Sa 17:43 Am I a **d.**, that thou comest to me 3611
1Sa 24:14 after a dead **d.**, after a flea. 3611
2Sa 9:8 look upon such a dead **d.** as I am? 3611
2Sa 16:9 Why should this dead **d.** curse my 3611
2Ki 8:13 is thy servant a **d.**, that he should 3611
Ps 22:20 darling from the power of the **d.**. 3611
Ps 59:6 they make a noise like a **d.**, and go 3611
Ps 59:14 let them make a noise like a **d.**, 3611
Pr 26:11 As a **d.** returneth to his vomit, 3611
Pr 26:17 one that taketh a **d.** by the ears. 3611
Ec 9:4 living **d.** is better than a dead lion. 3611
2Pe 2:22 The **d.** is turned to his own vomit *2965*

DOG'S
2Sa 3:8 Am I a **d.** head, which against 3611
Isa 66:3 a lamb, as if he cut off a **d.** neck; 3611

DOGS
Ex 22:31 the field; ye shall cast it to the **d.**. 3611
1Ki 14:11 in the city shall the **d.** eat; and him 3611
1Ki 16:4 Baasha in the city shall the **d.** eat; 3611
1Ki 21:19 place where **d.** licked the blood of 3611
1Ki 21:19 Naboth shall **d.** lick thy blood, 3611
1Ki 21:23 The **d.** shall eat Jezebel by the wall 3611
1Ki 21:24 Ahab in the city, the **d.** shall eat: 3611
1Ki 22:38 and the **d.** licked up his blood; 3611
2Ki 9:10 the **d.** shall eat Jezebel in the 3611
2Ki 9:36 shall **d.** eat the flesh of Jezebel: 3611
Job 30:1 to have set with the **d.** of my flock. 3611
Ps 22:16 For **d.** have compassed me: the 3611
Ps 68:23 and the tongue of thy **d.** in the 3611
Isa 56:10 all ignorant, they are all dumb **d.**, 3611
Isa 56:11 Yea, they are greedy **d.** which can 3611
Jer 15:3 and the **d.** to tear, and the fowls 3611
Mt 7:6 **not that which is holy unto the d.,** *2965*
Mt 15:26 **bread, and to cast it to d.** *2952*
Mt 15:27 yet the **d.** eat of the crumbs which *2952*
Mk 7:27 **bread, and to cast it unto the d.** *2952*
Mk 7:28 yet the **d.** under the table eat of the *2952*
Lu 16:21 **the d. came and licked his sores** *2965*
Php 3:2 Beware of **d.**, beware of evil *2965*
Re 22:15 For without are **d.**, and sorcerers, *2965*

DOING See also DOINGS.
Ge 31:28 hast now done foolishly in so **d.** 6213
Ge 44:5 ye have done evil in so **d.** 6213
Ex 15:11 fearful in praises, **d.** wonders? 6213
Nu 20:19 I will only, without **d.** any thing
De 9:18 in **d.** wickedly in the sight of the 6213
1Ki 7:40 Hiram made an end of **d.** all the 6213
1Ki 16:19 he sinned in **d.** evil in the sight of 6213
1Ki 22:43 **d.** that which was right in the eyes 6213
2Ki 21:16 in **d.** that which was evil in the 6213
1Ch 22:16 Arise therefore and be **d.**, and the 6213
2Ch 20:32 and departed not from it, **d.** that 6213
Ezr 9:1 **d.** according to their abominations,
Ne 6:3 I am doing a great work, so that 6213
Job 32:22 in so **d.** my Maker would soon
Ps 64:9 shall wisely consider of his **d.**. 4640
Ps 66:5 is terrible in his **d.** toward the 5949
Ps 118:23 This is the Lord's **d.**; it is 854
Isa 56:2 keepeth his hand from **d.** any evil. 6213
Isa 58:13 **d.** thy pleasure on my holy day; 6213
Isa 58:13 honour him, not **d.** thine own ways, 6213
Mt 21:42 **this is the Lord's d., and it is** *1096*
Mt 24:46 **when he cometh shall find so d** *4160*
Mk 12:11 **This was the Lord's d., and it is** *1096*
Lu 12:43 **when he cometh shall find so d** *4160*
Ac 10:38 who went about **d.** good, and *2109*
Ac 24:20 found any evil **d.** in me, while I *92*
Ro 2:7 by patient continuance in well **d.** *2041*
Ro 12:20 for in so **d.** thou shalt heap coals *4160*
2Co 8:11 Now therefore perform the **d.** ot it; *4160*
Ga 6:9 be weary in well **d.**: for in due *4160*
Eph 6:6 servants of Christ, **d.** the will of *4160*
Eph 6:7 With good will **d.** service, as to *1398*
2Th 3:13 brethren, be not weary in well **d.**. *2569*
1Ti 4:16 for in **d.** this thou shalt both save *4160*
1Ti 5:21 one before another, **d.** nothing by *4160*
1Pe 2:15 that with well **d.** ye may put to *15*
1Pe 3:17 be so, that ye suffer for well **d.** *15*
1Pe 3:17 than for evil **d.**. *2554*
1Pe 4:19 of their souls to him in well **d.**, as *16*

DOINGS
Le 18:3 after the **d.** of the land of Egypt 4640
Le 18:3 and after the **d.** of the land of 4640
De 28:20 of the wickedness of thy **d.**, 4611
Jg 2:19 they ceased not from their own **d.**, 4611
1Sa 25:3 was churlish and evil in his **d.**: 4611
2Ch 17:4 and not after the **d.** of Israel. 4640
Ps 9:11 declare among the people his **d.**. 5949
Ps 77:12 all thy work, and talk of thy **d.**, 5949
Pr 20:11 Even a child is known by his **d.**, 4611
Isa 1:16 put away the evil of your **d.** from 4611
Isa 3:8 and their **d.** are against the Lord, 4611
Isa 3:10 they shall eat the fruit of their **d.**. 4611
Isa 12:4 declare his **d.** among the people, 5949
Jer 4:4 it, because of the evil of your **d.**. 4611
Jer 4:18 Thy way and thy **d.** have procured 4611
Jer 7:3 Amend your ways and your **d.**, 4611
Jer 7:5 amend your ways and your **d.**; 4611
Jer 11:18 then thou shewedst me their **d.**. 4611
Jer 17:10 and according to the fruit of his **d.**. 4611
Jer 18:11 make your ways and your **d.** good. 4611
Jer 21:12 because of the evil of your **d.**. 4611
Jer 21:14 according to the fruit of your **d.**, 4611
Jer 23:2 visit upon you the evil of your **d.**, 4611
Jer 23:22 way, and from the evil of their **d.**. 4611
Jer 25:5 and from the evil of your **d.**, and 4611
Jer 26:3 because of the evil of their **d.**. 4611
Jer 26:13 amend your ways and your **d.**, 4611
Jer 32:19 according to the fruit of his **d.**: 4611
Jer 35:15 his evil way, and amend your **d.**, 4611
Jer 44:22 because of the evil of your **d.**, and 4611
Eze 14:22 shall see their way and their **d.**: 5949
Eze 14:23 ye see their ways and their **d.**: 5949
Eze 20:43 all your **d.** wherein ye have been 5949
Eze 20:44 nor according to your corrupt **d.**, 5949
Eze 21:24 in all your **d.**, your sins do appear; 5949
Eze 24:14 and according to thy **d.**, shall they 5949
Eze 36:17 by their own way and by their **d.**: 5949
Eze 36:19 according to their **d.** I judged them, 5949
Eze 36:31 own evil ways, and your **d.** that 4611
Ho 4:9 ways, and reward them their **d.**. 4611
Ho 5:4 They will not frame their **d.** to turn 4611
Ho 7:2 now their own **d.** have beset them 4611
Ho 9:15 for the wickedness of their **d.** I 4611
Ho 12:2 to his **d.** will he recompense him. 4611
Mic 2:7 are these his **d.**? do not my words 4611
Mic 3:4 behaved themselves ill in their **d.**. 4611
Mic 7:13 therein, for the fruit of their **d.**. 4611
Zep 3:7 early, and corrupted all their **d.**. 5949
Zep 3:11 thou not be ashamed for all thy **d.**, 5949
Zec 1:4 and from your evil **d.**: but they did 4611
Zec 1:6 according to our **d.**, so hath he 4611

DOLEFUL
Isa 13:21 houses shall be full of **d.** creatures; 255
Mic 2:4 and lament with a **d.** lamentation, 5093

DOMINION See also DOMINIONS.
Ge 1:26 and let them have **d.** over the fish 7287
Ge 1:28 and have **d.** over the fish of the sea, 7287
Ge 27:40 pass when thou shalt have the **d.**, 7300
Ge 37:8 shalt thou indeed have **d.** over us? 4910
Nu 24:19 shall come he that shall have **d.**, 7287
Jg 5:13 made him that remaineth have **d.** 7287
Jg 5:13 made me have **d.** over the mighty. 7287
Jg 14:4 the Philistines had **d.** over Israel. 4910
1Ki 4:24 he had **d.** over all the region on 7287
1Ki 9:19 and in all the land of his **d.**. 4475
2Ki 20:13 in his house, nor in all his **d.**, 4475
1Ch 4:22 Saraph, who had the **d.** in Moab, 1166
1Ch 18:3 his **d.** by the river Euphrates. 3027
2Ch 8:6 throughout all the land of his **d.**, 4475
2Ch 21:8 from under the **d.** of Judah, and 3027
Ne 9:28 so that they had the **d.** over them: 7287
Ne 9:37 also they have **d.** over our bodies, 4910
Job 25:2 **D.** and fear are with him, he 4910
Job 38:33 canst thou set the **d.** thereof in 4896
Ps 8:6 Thou madest him to have **d.** over 4910
Ps 19:13 let them not have **d.** over me: 4910
Ps 49:14 and the upright shall have **d.** over 7287
Ps 72:8 He shall have **d.** also from sea to 7287
Ps 103:22 his works in all places of his **d.**: 4475
Ps 114:2 was his sanctuary, and Israel his **d.**. 4475
Ps 119:133 let not iniquity have **d.** over me. 7980
Ps 145:13 and thy **d.** endureth throughout 4475
Isa 26:13 beside thee have had **d.** over us: 1166
Isa 39:2 nor in all his **d.**, that Hezekiah 4475
Jer 34:1 the kingdoms of the earth of his **d.**, 4475
Jer 51:28 thereof, and all the land of his **d.**. 4475
Da 4:3 and his **d.** is from generation to 7985
Da 4:22 and thy **d.** to the end of the earth. 7985
Da 4:34 whose **d.** is an everlasting **d.**, 7985
Da 6:26 That in every **d.** of my kingdom 7985
Da 6:26 his **d.** shall be even unto the end. 7985
Da 7:6 four heads; and **d.** was given to it. 7985
Da 7:12 they had their **d.** taken away: 7985
Da 7:14 there was given him **d.**, and glory, 7985
Da 7:14 his **d.** is an everlasting **d.**, 7985
Da 7:26 and they shall take away his **d.**, 7985
Da 7:27 And the kingdom and **d.**, and the 7985
Da 11:3 up, that shall rule with great **d.**, 4474
Da 11:4 according to his **d.** which he ruled: 4915
Da 11:5 be strong above him, and have **d.**; 4910
Da 11:5 his **d.** shall be a great 4474
Da 11:5 shall be a great **d.**. 4475
Mic 4:8 shall it come, even the first **d.**; 4475
Zec 9:10 and his **d.** shall be from sea to 4915
Mt 20:25 **princes of the Gentiles exercise d** *2634*
Ro 6:9 death hath no more **d.** over him. *2961*
Ro 6:14 sin shall not have **d.** over you: *2961*
Ro 7:1 the law hath **d.** over a man as long *2961*
2Co 1:24 that we have **d.** over your faith, *2961*
Eph 1:21 might, and **d.**, and every name that *2963*
1Pe 4:11 be praise and **d.** for ever and ever. *2904*
1Pe 5:11 To him be glory and **d.** for ever *2904*
Jude 8 despise **d.**, and speak evil of *2963*
Jude 25 **d.** and power, both now and ever *2904*
Re 1:6 to him be glory and **d.** for ever *2904*

DOMINIONS
Da 7:27 all **d.** shall serve and obey him. 7985
Col 1:16 or **d.**, or principalities, or powers: *2963*

DONE See also UNDONE.
Ge 3:13 What is this that thou hast **d.**? 6213
Ge 3:14 Because thou hast **d.** this, thou art 6213
Ge 4:10 What hast thou **d.**? the voice of 6213
Ge 8:21 every living thing, as I have **d.**. 6213
Ge 9:24 knew what his younger son had **d.**. 6213
Ge 12:18 is this that thou hast **d.** unto me? 6213
Ge 18:21 whether they have **d.** altogether 6213
Ge 20:5 of my hands have I **d.** this. 6213
Ge 20:9 What hast thou **d.** unto us? 6213
Ge 20:9 thou hast **d.** deeds unto me that 6213
Ge 20:9 unto me that ought not to be **d.**. 6213

Ge 20:10 thou, that thou hast **d.** this thing? 6213
Ge 21:23 kindness that I have **d.** unto thee, 6213
Ge 21:26 I wot not who hath **d.** this thing: 6213
Ge 22:16 because thou hast **d.** this thing, 6213
Ge 24:15 pass, before he had **d.** speaking, 3615
Ge 24:19 when she had **d.** giving him drink, 3615
Ge 24:19 also, until they have **d.** drinking. 3615
Ge 24:22 pass, as the camels had **d.** drinking, 3615
Ge 24:45 I had **d.** speaking in mine heart, 3615
Ge 24:66 Isaac all things that he had **d.**. 6213
Ge 26:10 What is this thou hast **d.** unto us? 6213
Ge 26:29 have **d.** unto thee nothing but good, 6213
Ge 27:19 **d.** according as thou badest me: 6213
Ge 27:45 that which thou hast **d.** to him: 6213
Ge 28:15 I have **d.** that which I have spoken 6213
Ge 29:25 What is this thou hast **d.** unto me? 6213
Ge 29:26 It must not be so **d.** in our country, 6213
Ge 30:26 my service which I have **d.** thee. 5647
Ge 31:26 What hast thou **d.**, that thou hast 6213
Ge 31:28 hast now **d.** foolishly in so doing.
Ge 34:7 which thing ought not to be **d.**. 6213
Ge 40:15 and here also have I **d.** nothing 6213
Ge 42:28 is this that God hath **d.** unto us? 6213
Ge 44:5 divineth? ye have **d.** evil in so doing.
Ge 44:15 What deed is this that ye have **d.**? 6213
Ex 1:18 Why have ye **d.** this thing, and 6213
Ex 2:4 to wit what would be **d.** to him. 6213
Ex 3:16 that which is **d.** to you in Egypt: 6213
Ex 5:23 he hath **d.** evil to this people;
Ex 10:2 which I have **d.** among them; 7760
Ex 12:16 no manner of work shall be **d.** in 6213
Ex 12:16 eat, that only may be **d.** of you. 6213
Ex 13:8 This is **d.** because of that which
Ex 14:5 Why have we **d.** this, that we have 6213
Ex 18:1 of all that God had **d.** for Moses, 6213
Ex 18:8 that the Lord had **d.** unto Pharoah 6213
Ex 18:9 which the Lord had **d.** to Israel, 6213
Ex 21:31 judgment shall it be **d.** unto him. 6213
Ex 31:15 Six days may work be **d.**; but in 6213
Ex 34:10 have not been **d.** in all the earth, 1254
Ex 34:33 Moses had **d.** speaking with them, 3615
Ex 35:2 Six days shall work be **d.**, but on 6213
Ex 39:43 **d.** it as the Lord had commanded, 6213
Ex 39:43 even so had they **d.** it: and Moses 6213
Le 4:2 things which ought not to be **d.**, 6213
Le 4:13 and they have **d.** somewhat against 6213
Le 4:13 should not be **d.**, and are guilty; 6213
Le 4:22 When a ruler hath sinned, and **d.** 6213
Le 4:22 things which should not be **d.**, 6213
Le 4:27 things ought not to be **d.**, 6213
Le 5:16 for the harm that he hath **d.** in
Le 5:17 to be **d.** by the commandments 6213
Le 6:7 he hath **d.** in trespassing therein. 6213
Le 8:5 the Lord commanded to be **d.**. 6213
Le 8:34 As he hath **d.** this day, so the Lord 6213
Le 11:32 vessel it be, wherein any work is **d.**, 6213
Le 18:27 have the men of the land **d.**, which 6213
Le 19:22 for his sin which he hath **d.**:
Le 19:22 he hath **d.** shall be forgiven him.
Le 23:3 six days shall work be **d.**: but 6213
Le 24:19 he hath **d.**, so shall it be **d.** to him; 6213
Le 24:20 so shall it be **d.** to him again. 5414
Nu 5:7 their sin which they have **d.**: 6213
Nu 5:27 **d.** trespass against her husband,
Nu 12:11 wherein we have **d.** foolishly, and
Nu 15:11 Thus shall it be **d.** for one bullock, 6213
Nu 15:34 declared what should be **d.** to him. 6213
Nu 16:28 have not **d.** them of mine own mind.
Nu 22:2 that Israel had **d.** to the Amorites. 6213
Nu 22:28 What have I **d.** unto thee, that 6213
Nu 23:11 What hast thou **d.** unto me? 6213
Nu 27:4 name of our father be **d.** away 1639
Nu 32:13 **d.** evil in the sight of the Lord, 6213
De 3:21 God hath **d.** unto these two kings: 6213
De 10:21 **d.** for thee these great and terrible 6213
De 12:31 Lord, which he hateth, have they **d.** 6213
De 19:19 to have **d.** unto his brother: 6213
De 20:18 which they have **d.** unto their gods;
De 25:9 So shall it be **d.** unto that man 6213
De 26:14 **d.** according to all that thou hast 6213
De 29:24 Wherefore hath the Lord **d.** thus 6213
De 32:27 and the Lord hath not **d.** all this. 6466
Jos 5:8 **d.** circumcising all the people, 8552
Jos 7:19 tell me now what thou hast **d.**; 6213
Jos 7:20 and thus and thus have I **d.**: 6213
Jos 9:3 what Joshua had **d.** unto Jericho 6213
Jos 9:24 of you, and have **d.** this thing. 6213
Jos 10:1 **d.** to Jericho and her king, 6213
Jos 10:1 so he had **d.** to Ai and her 6213
Jos 10:32 to all that he had **d.** to Libnah. 6213
Jos 10:35 to all that he had **d.** to Lachish. 6213
Jos 10:37 to all that he had **d.** to Eglon; 6213
Jos 10:39 as he had **d.** to Hebron, so he did 6213
Jos 10:39 as he had **d.** also to Libnah, and to 6213
Jos 22:24 rather **d.** it for fear of this thing, 6213
Jos 23:3 all that the Lord your God hath **d.** 6213
Jos 23:8 God, as ye have **d.** unto this day. 6213
Jos 24:7 seen what I have **d.** in Egypt: 6213
Jos 24:20 you, after that he hath **d.** you good.
Jos 24:31 Lord, that he had **d.** for Israel. 6213
Jg 1:7 have **d.**, so God hath requited me. 6213
Jg 2:2 my voice: why have ye **d.** this? 6213
Jg 2:10 yet the works which he had **d.** 6213
Jg 3:12 Israel, because they had **d.** evil 6213
Jg 6:29 another, Who hath **d.** this thing? 6213
Jg 6:29 the son of Joash hath **d.** this thing. 6213
Jg 8:2 What have I **d.** now, in comparison 6213
Jg 9:16 Now therefore, if ye have **d.** truly 6213
Jg 9:16 **d.** unto him according to the 6213
Jg 9:24 That the cruelty **d.** to the three
Jg 9:48 do, make haste, and do as I have **d.**.
Jg 11:37 Let this thing be **d.** for me: 6213
Jg 14:6 or his mother what he had **d.**. 6213
Jg 15:6 Philistines said, Who hath **d.** this? 6213
Jg 15:7 Though ye have **d.** this, yet will 6213
Jg 15:10 up, to do to him as he hath **d.** to us. 6213
Jg 15:11 is this that thou hast **d.** unto us? 6213
Jg 15:11 unto me, so have I **d.** unto them. 6213
Jg 19:30 There was no such deed **d.** nor 1961
Jg 20:12 wickedness is this that is **d.** 1961
Ru 2:11 hast **d.** unto thy mother in law 6213
Ru 3:3 shall have **d.** eating and drinking 3615
Ru 3:16 told her all that the man had **d.** 6213
1Sa 4:16 What is there **d.**, my son? 1697
1Sa 6:9 to Beth-shemesh, then he hath **d.** 6213
1Sa 8:8 works which they have **d.** since the 6213
1Sa 11:7 Samuel, so shall it be **d.** unto his 6213
1Sa 12:17 ye have **d.** in the sight of the Lord, 6213
1Sa 12:20 not: ye have **d.** all this wickedness: 6213
1Sa 12:24 consider how great things he hath **d.**
1Sa 13:11 Samuel said, What hast thou **d.**? 6213
1Sa 13:13 said to Saul, Thou hast **d.** foolishly:
1Sa 14:43 Tell me what thou hast **d.** 6213
1Sa 17:26 shall be **d.** to the man that killeth 6213
1Sa 17:27 it be **d.** to the man that killeth him. 6213
1Sa 17:29 David said, What have I now **d.**? 6213
1Sa 19:18 told him all that Saul had **d.** to him. 6213
1Sa 20:1 before Jonathan, What have I **d.**? 6213
1Sa 20:32 shall he be slain? what hath he **d.**? 6213
1Sa 20:34 because his father had **d.** him shame.
1Sa 24:19 that thou hast **d.** unto me this day. 6213
1Sa 25:30 the Lord shall have **d.** to my lord 6213
1Sa 26:16 thing is not good that thou hast **d.** 6213
1Sa 26:18 for what have I **d.**? or what evil is 6213
1Sa 28:9 thou knowest what Saul hath **d.**, 6213
1Sa 28:17 the Lord hath **d.** to him, as he 6213
1Sa 28:18 therefore hath the Lord **d.** this 6213
1Sa 29:8 unto Achish, But what have I **d.**? 6213
1Sa 31:11 the Philistines had **d.** to Saul; 6213
2Sa 2:6 because ye have **d.** this thing. 6213
2Sa 3:24 and said, What hast thou **d.**? 6213
2Sa 7:21 thou **d.** all these great things, 6213
2Sa 11:27 But the thing that David had **d.** 6213
2Sa 12:5 the man that hath **d.** this thing 6213
2Sa 12:21 thing is this that thou hast **d.**? 6213
2Sa 13:12 such thing ought to be **d.** in Israel: 6213
2Sa 14:20 hath thy servant Joab **d.** this thing: 6213
2Sa 14:21 Behold now, I have **d.** this thing: 6213
2Sa 15:24 all the people had **d.** passing out 8552
2Sa 16:10 Wherefore hast thou **d.** so? 6213
2Sa 21:11 Aiah, the concubine of Saul, had **d.** 6213
2Sa 23:20 who had **d.** many acts, he slew 6213
2Sa 24:10 sinned greatly in that I have **d.**: 6213
2Sa 24:10 for I have **d.** very foolishly. For
2Sa 24:17 sinned, and I have **d.** wickedly:
2Sa 24:17 but these sheep what have they **d.**? 6213
1Ki 1:6 Why hast thou **d.** so? 6213
1Ki 1:27 thing **d.** by my lord the king, 6213
1Ki 3:12 Behold, I have **d.** according to thy 6213
1Ki 8:47 have sinned, and have **d.** perversely,
1Ki 8:66 that the Lord had **d.** for David 6213
1Ki 9:8 Why hath the Lord **d.** thus unto 6213
1Ki 11:11 Forasmuch as this is **d.** of thee,
1Ki 13:11 the man of God had **d.** that day 6213
1Ki 14:9 But hast **d.** evil above all that were 6213
1Ki 14:22 above all that their fathers had **d.**. 6213
1Ki 15:3 which he had **d.** before him: and 6213
1Ki 18:36 **d.** all these things at thy word. 6213
1Ki 19:1 all that Elijah had **d.**, and withal 6213
1Ki 19:20 for what have I **d.** to thee? 6213
1Ki 22:53 to all that his father had **d.**: wouldest 6213
2Ki 4:13 what is to be **d.** for thee? wouldest 6213
2Ki 4:14 what is then to be **d.** for her? 6213
2Ki 5:13 wouldest thou not have **d.** it? 6213
2Ki 7:12 what the Syrians have **d.** to us. 6213
2Ki 8:4 great things that Elisha hath **d.**. 6213
2Ki 10:10 Lord hath **d.** that which he spake 6213
2Ki 10:30 thou hast **d.** well in executing that
2Ki 10:30 hast **d.** unto the house of Ahab 6213
2Ki 15:3 all that his father Amaziah had **d.**; 6213
2Ki 15:9 as his fathers had **d.**: he departed 6213
2Ki 15:34 to all that his father Uzziah had **d.**. 6213
2Ki 17:4 he had **d.** year by year: therefore
2Ki 19:11 what the kings of Assyria have **d.** 6213
2Ki 19:25 long ago how I have **d.** it, and of 6213
2Ki 20:3 have **d.** that which is good in thy 6213
2Ki 21:11 Judah hath **d.** these abominations, 6213
2Ki 21:11 and hath **d.** wickedly above all 6213
2Ki 21:15 they have **d.** that which was evil 6213
2Ki 23:17 that thou hast **d.** against the altar 6213
2Ki 23:19 the acts that he hath **d.** in Beth-el. 6213
2Ki 23:32, 37 to all that his fathers had **d.**. 6213
2Ki 24:9 to all that his father had **d.** 6213
2Ki 24:19 to all that Jehoiakim had **d.** 6213
1Ch 10:11 that the Philistines had **d.** to Saul, 6213
1Ch 11:22 who had **d.** many acts, he slew two
1Ch 16:12 marvellous works that he hath **d.**, 6213
1Ch 17:19 hast thou **d.** all this greatness, 6213
1Ch 21:8 because I have **d.** this thing; 6213
1Ch 21:8 for I have **d.** very foolishly.
1Ch 21:17 have sinned and **d.** evil indeed;
1Ch 21:17 for these sheep, what have they **d.**? 6213
2Ch 6:37 We have sinned, we have **d.** amiss,
2Ch 7:21 Why hath the Lord **d.** thus unto 6213
2Ch 11:4 for this thing is **d.** of me.
2Ch 16:9 Herein thou hast **d.** foolishly:
2Ch 24:16 because he had **d.** good in Israel, 6213
2Ch 24:22 Jehoiada his father had **d.** to 6213
2Ch 25:16 because thou hast **d.** this, and hast 6213
2Ch 29:2 to all that David his father had **d.**. 6213
2Ch 29:6 **d.** that which was evil in the sight 6213
2Ch 29:36 for the thing was **d.** suddenly.
2Ch 30:5 they had not **d.** it of a long time 6213
2Ch 32:13 what I and my fathers have **d.** 6213
2Ch 32:25 according to the benefit **d.** unto him;
2Ch 32:31 wonder that was **d.** in the land,
Ezr 6:12 made a decree; let it be **d.** with 5648
Ezr 7:21 require of you, it be **d.** speedily, 5648
Ezr 7:23 let it be diligently **d.** for the house 5648
Ezr 9:1 Now when these things were **d.**, 3615
Ezr 10:3 let it be **d.** according to the law. 6213
Ne 5:19 all that I have **d.** for this people. 6213
Ne 6:8 There are no such things **d.** as
Ne 6:9 from the work, that it be not **d.**. 6213
Ne 8:17 not the children of Israel **d.** so. 6213
Ne 9:33 for thou hast **d.** right, 6213
Ne 9:33 but we have **d.** wickedly:
Ne 13:14 deeds that I have **d.** for the house 6213
Es 1:16 hath not **d.** wrong unto the king
Es 2:1 and what she had **d.**, and what 6213
Es 4:1 Mordecai perceived all that was **d.**, 6213
Es 6:3 hath been **d.** to Mordecai for this? 6213
Es 6:3 him, There is nothing **d.** for him. 6213
Es 6:6 What shall be **d.** unto the man 6213
Es 6:9 Thus shall it be **d.** to the man 6213
Es 6:11 Thus shall it be **d.** unto the man 6213
Es 9:12 they **d.** in the rest of the king's 6213
Es 9:12 request further? and it shall be **d.** 6213
Es 9:14 the king commanded it so to be **d.**: 6213
Job 21:31 shall repay him what he hath **d.**? 6213
Job 34:29 whether it be **d.** against a nation,
Job 34:32 if I have **d.** iniquity, I will do no 6466
Ps 7:3 O Lord my God, if I have **d.** this; 6213
Ps 14:1 they have **d.** abominable works,
Ps 22:31 be born, that he hath **d.** this. 6213
Ps 33:4 and all his works are **d.** in truth.
Ps 33:9 For he spake, and it was **d.**; he
Ps 40:5 works which thou hast **d.**, and thy 6213
Ps 50:21 These things hast thou **d.**, and I 6213
Ps 51:4 sinned, and **d.** this evil in thy sight: 6213
Ps 52:9 because thou hast **d.** it: and I will 6213

Ps 53:1 and have **d.** abominable iniquity:
Ps 66:16 what he hath **d.** for my soul 6213
Ps 71:19 who hast **d.** great things: O God 6213
Ps 74:3 hath **d.** wickedly in the sanctuary
Ps 78:4 wonderful works that he hath **d.** 6213
Ps 98:1 for he hath **d.** marvellous things: 6213
Ps 105:5 marvellous works that he hath **d.**; 6213
Ps 106:6 iniquity, we have **d.** wickedly 6213
Ps 106:21 saviour, which had **d.** great things
Ps 109:27 hand; that thou, Lord, hast **d.** it 6213
Ps 111:8 are **d.** in truth and uprightness 6213
Ps 115:3 **d.** whatsoever he hath pleased 6213
Ps 119:121 I have **d.** judgment and justice: 6213
Ps 119:166 and **d.** thy commandments 6213
Ps 120:3 what shall be **d.** unto thee, thou 3254
Ps 126:2 hath **d.** great things for them 6213
Ps 126:3 Lord hath **d.** great things for us; 6213
Pr 3:30 if he have **d.** thee no harm 1580
Pr 4:16 sleep not, except they have **d.** mischief;
Pr 24:29 do so to him as he hath **d.** to me: 6213
Pr 30:20 saith, I have **d.** no wickedness 6466
Pr 30:32 hast **d.** foolishly in lifting up thyself,
Pr 31:29 daughters have **d.** virtuously, 6213
Ec 1:9 which is **d.** is that which shall be **d.**: 6213
Ec 1:13 things that are **d.** under heaven: 6213
Ec 1:14 works that are **d.** under the sun; 6213
Ec 2:12 that which hath been already **d.** 6213
Ec 4:1 that are **d.** under the sun: 6213
Ec 4:3 the evil work that is **d.** under the 6213
Ec 8:9 my heart unto every work that is **d.** 6213
Ec 8:10 in the city where they had so **d.**: 6213
Ec 8:14 a vanity which is **d.** upon the earth; 6213
Ec 8:16 business that is **d.** upon the earth: 6213
Ec 8:17 cannot find out the work that is **d.** 6213
Ec 9:3 things that are **d.** under the sun, 6213
Ec 9:6 any thing that is **d.** under the sun 6213
Isa 5:4 have been **d.** more to my vineyard, 6213
Isa 5:4 that I have not **d.** in it? 6213
Isa 10:11 **d.** unto Samaria and her idols, so 6213
Isa 10:13 strength of my hand I have **d.** it, 6213
Isa 12:5 for he hath **d.** excellent things: 6213
Isa 24:13 grapes when the vintage is **d.** 3615
Isa 25:1 thou hast **d.** wonderful things; 6213
Isa 33:13 that are far off, what I have **d.**; 6213
Isa 37:11 the kings of Assyria have **d.** to all 6213
Isa 37:26 heard long ago, how I have **d.** it; 6213
Isa 38:3 and have **d.** that which is good in 6213
Isa 38:15 unto me, and himself hath **d.** it: 6213
Isa 41:4 Who hath wrought and **d.** it, 6213
Isa 41:20 the hand of the Lord hath **d.** this, 6213
Isa 44:23 ye heavens; for the Lord hath **d.** it: 6213
Isa 46:10 the things that are not yet **d.**, 6213
Isa 48:5 say, Mine idol hath **d.** them, 6213
Isa 53:9 because he had **d.** no violence, 6213
Jer 2:23 the valley, know what thou hast **d.**: 6213
Jer 3:5 thou hast spoken and **d.** evil things 6213
Jer 3:6 which backsliding Israel hath **d.**? 6213
Jer 3:7 after she had **d.** all these things, 6213
Jer 3:16 neither shall that be **d.** any more 6213
Jer 5:13 thus shall it be **d.** unto them 6213
Jer 7:13 because ye have **d.** all these works, 6213
Jer 7:14 your fathers, as I have **d.** to Shiloh 6213
Jer 7:30 children of Judah have **d.** evil in 6213
Jer 8:6 saying, What have I **d.**? 6213
Jer 11:17 **d.** against themselves to provoke 6213
Jer 16:12 have **d.** worse than your fathers; 6213
Jer 18:13 the virgin of Israel hath **d.** a very 6213
Jer 22:8 hath the Lord **d.** thus unto this 6213
Jer 30:15 I have **d.** these things unto thee 6213
Jer 30:24 until he have **d.** it, and until he 6213
Jer 31:37 that they have **d.**, saith the Lord, 6213
Jer 32:23 they have **d.** nothing of all that 6213
Jer 32:30 children of Judah have only **d.** evil 6213
Jer 32:32 have **d.** to provoke me to anger, 6213
Jer 34:15 **d.** right in my sight, in proclaiming 6213
Jer 35:10 obeyed, and **d.** according to all 6213
Jer 35:18 **d.** according unto all that he hath 6213
Jer 38:9 these men have **d.** evil in all that
Jer 38:9 have **d.** to Jeremiah the prophet, 6213
Jer 40:3 brought it, and **d.** according as he 6213
Jer 41:11 the son of Nethaniah had **d.**, 6213
Jer 42:10 the evil that I have **d.** unto you 6213
Jer 44:17 as we have **d.**, we, and our fathers, 6213
Jer 48:19 that escapeth, and say, What is **d.**?
Jer 50:15 as she hath **d.**, do unto her 6213
Jer 50:29 according to all that she hath **d.**, 6213
Jer 51:12 both devised and **d.** that which 6213
Jer 51:24 they have **d.** in Zion in your sight 6213
Jer 51:35 The violence **d.** to me and to my flesh
Jer 52:2 all that Jehoiakim had **d.** 6213
La 1:12 which is **d.** unto me, wherewith 5953
La 1:21 they are glad that thou has **d.** it: 6213
La 1:22 unto them, as thou hast **d.** unto 5953
La 2:17 The Lord hath **d.** that which he 6213
La 2:20 to whom thou hast **d.** this 5953
Eze 3:20 his righteousness which he hath **d.** 6213
Eze 5:7 **d.** according to the judgments 6213
Eze 5:9 which I have not **d.**, and whereunto 6213
Eze 9:4 that be **d.** in the midst thereof 6213
Eze 9:11 **d.** as thou hast commanded me 6213
Eze 11:12 **d.** after the manners of the heathen 6213
Eze 12:11 have **d.**, so shall it be **d.** unto them 6213
Eze 12:28 shall be **d.**, saith the Lord God, 6213
Eze 14:23 I have not **d.** without cause all that 6213
Eze 14:23 I have **d.** in it, saith the Lord God 6213
Eze 16:47 nor **d.** after their abominations: 6213
Eze 16:48 hath not **d.**, she nor her daughters, 6213
Eze 16:48 hast **d.**, thou and thy daughters 6213
Eze 16:51 abominations which thou hast **d.** 6213
Eze 16:54 confounded in all that thou hast **d.**, 6213
Eze 16:59 deal with thee as thou hast **d.**, 6213
Eze 16:63 toward thee for all that thou hast **d.**, 6213
Eze 17:18 and hath **d.** all these things, he 6213
Eze 17:24 Lord have spoken and have **d.** it 6213
Eze 18:13 he hath **d.** all these abominations; 6213
Eze 18:14 his father's sins which he hath **d.**, 6213
Eze 18:19 **d.** that which is lawful and right, 6213
Eze 18:19 hath **d.** them, he shall surely live 6213
Eze 18:22 that he hath **d.** he shall live 6213
Eze 18:24 he hath **d.** shall not be mentioned: 6213
Eze 18:26 that he hath **d.** shall he die 6213
Eze 23:38 Moreover this they have **d.** unto me: 6213
Eze 23:39 they **d.** in the midst of mine house 6213
Eze 24:22 And ye shall do as I have **d.**: ye 6213
Eze 24:24 according to all that he hath **d.** 6213
Eze 33:16 **d.** that which is lawful and right; 6213
Eze 39:8 Behold, it is come, and it is **d.**,
Eze 39:24 have I **d.** unto them, and hid my 6213
Eze 43:11 of all that they have **d.**, shew them 6213
Eze 44:14 and for all that shall be **d.** therein 6213
Da 6:22 thee, O King, have I **d.** no hurt 5648
Da 9:5 have **d.** wickedly, and have rebelled,
Da 9:12 hath not been **d.** as hath been **d.** 6213
Da 9:15 we have sinned, we have **d.** wickedly
Da 11:24 which his fathers have not **d.**, nor 6213
Da 11:36 that that is determined shall be **d.** 6213
Hos 2:5 conceived them hath **d.** shamefully:
Joe 2:20 because he hath **d.** great things 6213
Am 3:6 and the Lord hath not **d.** it? 6213
Ob 15 as thou hast **d.**, it shall be **d.** unto 6213
Jon 1:10 Why hast thou **d.** this? For the 6213
Jon 1:14 O Lord, hast **d.** as it pleased thee 6213
Mic 6:3 what have I **d.** unto thee? and 6213
Zep 3:4 they have **d.** violence to the law,
Zec 7:3 as I have **d.** these so many years? 6213
Mal 2:13 And this have ye **d.** again, 6213
Mt 1:22 Now all this was **d.**, that it might 1096
Mt 6:10 **Thy will be d. in earth** 1096
Mt 7:22 **in thy name d. many wonderful** 4160
Mt 8:13 **so be it d. unto thee** 1096
Mt 11:20 most of his mighty works were **d.**, 1096
Mt 11:21 **which were d. in you,** 1096
Mt 11:21 **had been d. in Tyre and Sidon,** 1096
Mt 11:23 **which have been d. in thee,** 1096
Mt 11:23 **had been d. in Sodom, it would** 1096
Mt 13:28 **An enemy hath d. this** 4160
Mt 17:12 **but have d. unto him whatsoever** 4160
Mt 18:19 **it shall be d. for them of my** 1096
Mt 18:31 **saw what was d., they were very** 1096
Mt 18:31 **told unto their lord all that was d.** 1096
Mt 21:4 All this was **d.**, that it might be 1096
Mt 21:21 **this which is d. to the fig tree, but**
Mt 21:21 **cast into the sea; and it shall be d.** 1096
Mt 23:23 **these ought ye to have d., and not** 4160
Mt 25:21 **Well d., thou good and faithful**
Mt 25:23 **Well d., good and faithful servant;**
Mt 25:40 **as ye have d. it unto one of the** 4160
Mt 25:40 **brethren, ye have d. it unto me** 4160
Mt 26:13 **that this woman hath d., be told** 4160
Mt 26:42 **except I drink it, thy will be d.** 1096
Mt 26:56 **But all this was d. that the** 1096
Mt 27:23 Why, what evil hath he **d.**? But 4160
Mt 27:54 and those things that were **d.**, 1096
Mt 28:11 priests all the things that were **d.** 1096
Mk 4:11 **all these things are d. in parables:** 1096
Mk 5:14 to see what it was that was **d.** 1096
Mk 5:19 **the Lord hath d. for thee, and** 4160
Mk 5:20 great things Jesus had **d.** for him: 4160
Mk 5:32 to see her that had **d.** this thing 4160
Mk 5:33 knowing what was **d.** in her, came 1096
Mk 6:30 both what they had **d.**, and what 4160
Mk 7:37 He hath **d.** all things well; 4160
Mk 9:13 **they have d. unto him whatsoever** 4160
Mk 13:30 **pass, till all these things be d.** 1096
Mk 14:8 **She hath d. what she could: she** 4160
Mk 14:9 **this also that she hath d. shall be** 4160
Mk 15:8 do as he had ever **d.** unto them 4160
Mk 15:14 what evil hath he **d.**? And they 4160
Lu 1:49 he that is mighty hath **d.** to me 4160
Lu 3:19 all the evils which Herod had **d.** 4160
Lu 4:23 **whatsoever we have heard d. in** 1096
Lu 5:6 when they had this **d.**, they inclosed 4160
Lu 8:34 that fed them saw what was **d.**, 1096
Lu 8:35 they went out to see what was **d.**; 1096
Lu 8:39 **great things God hath d. unto** 4160
Lu 8:39 how great things Jesus had **d.** unto 4160
Lu 8:56 should tell no man what was **d.** 1096
Lu 9:7 heard all that was **d.** by him: and 1096
Lu 9:10 told him all that they had **d.** 4160
Lu 10:13 **works had been d. in Tyre and** 1096
Lu 10:13 **which have been d. in you, they** 1096
Lu 11:2 **Thy will be d., as in heaven, so in** 1096
Lu 11:42 **these ought ye to have d., and not** 4160
Lu 13:17 glorious things that were **d.** by 1096
Lu 14:22 **it is d. as thou hast commanded** 1096
Lu 16:8 **because he had d. wisely; for the** 4160
Lu 17:10 **when ye shall have d. all those** 4160
Lu 17:10 **unprofitable servants: we have d.** 4160
Lu 22:42 **not my will, but thine, be d.** 1096
Lu 23:8 have seen some miracle **d.** by him 1096
Lu 23:15 worthy of death is **d.** unto him 4238
Lu 23:22 time, Why, what evil hath he **d.**? 4160
Lu 23:31 **what shall be d. in the dry?** 1096
Lu 23:41 this man hath **d.** nothing amiss 4238
Lu 23:47 saw what was **d.**, he glorified God, 1096
Lu 23:48 the things which were **d.**, smote 1096
Lu 24:21 day since these things were **d.** 1096
Lu 24:35 what things were **d.** in the way,
Joh 1:28 These things were **d.** in Bethabara 1096
Joh 5:16 because he had **d.** these things on 4160
Joh 5:29 **they that have d. good, unto the** 4160
Joh 5:29 **of life; and they that have d. evil** 4238
Joh 7:21 **I have d. one work, and ye all** 4160
Joh 7:31 than these which this man hath **d.**? 4160
Joh 11:46 them what things Jesus had **d.** 4160
Joh 12:16 and that they had **d.** these things 4160
Joh 12:18 they heard that he had **d.** this 4160
Joh 12:37 But though he had **d.** so many 4160
Joh 13:12 **Know ye what I have d. to you?** 4160
Joh 13:15 **ye should do as I have d. to you** 4160
Joh 15:7 **what ye will, and it shall be d.** 1096
Joh 15:24 **If I had not d. among them the** 4160
Joh 18:35 thee unto me: what hast thou **d.**? 4160
Joh 19:36 For these things were **d.**, that the 1096
Ac 2:43 wonders and were **d.** by the 1096
Ac 4:7 by what name, have ye **d.** this? 4160
Ac 4:9 the good deed **d.** to the impotent
Ac 4:16 notable miracle hath been **d.** by 1096
Ac 4:21 glorified God for that which was **d.** 1096
Ac 4:28 determined before to be **d.** 1096
Ac 4:30 may be **d.** by the name of thy holy 1096
Ac 5:7 not knowing what was **d.**, came in, 1096
Ac 8:13 miracles and signs which were **d.**, 1096
Ac 9:13 much evil he hath **d.** to thy saints 4160
Ac 10:16 This was **d.** thrice: and the vessel 1096
Ac 10:33 and thou hast **d.** well that thou 4160
Ac 11:10 And this was **d.** three times: and 1096
Ac 12:9 true which was **d.** by the angel; 1096
Ac 13:12 when he saw what was **d.**, 1096
Ac 14:3 signs and wonders to be **d.** by their 1096
Ac 14:11 saw what Paul had **d.**, they lifted 4160
Ac 14:13 and would have **d.** sacrifice with the
Ac 14:18 that they had not **d.** sacrifice unto
Ac 14:27 all that God had **d.** with them, and 4160
Ac 15:4 all things that God had **d.** with 4160
Ac 21:14 The will of the Lord be **d.** 1096
Ac 21:33 who he was, and what he had **d.** 4160
Ac 24:2 worthy deeds are **d.** unto this 1096
Ac 25:10 have I **d.** no wrong, as thou very 91
Ac 26:26 this thing was not **d.** in a corner 4238

Ac 28:9 So when this was **d.**, others also,....... *1096*
Ro 9:11 neither having **d.** any good or evil, ... *4238*
1Co 5:2 that he that hath **d.** this deed *4160*
1Co 5:3 him that hath so **d.** this deed,............ *2716*
1Co 9:15 that it should be so **d.** unto me:......... *1096*
1Co 13:10 which is in part shall be **d.** away. *2673*
1Co 14:26 Let all things be **d.** unto edifying. *1096*
1Co 14:40 Let all things be **d.** decently and in..... *1096*
1Co 16:14 all your things be **d.** with charity........ *1096*
2Co 3:7 which glory was to be **d.** away: *2673*
2Co 3:11 For if that which is **d.** away was *2673*
2Co 3:14 which vail is **d.** away in Christ. *2673*
2Co 5:10 may receive the things **d.** in his body,.......
2Co 5:10 according to that he hath **d.**, ... *4238*
2Co 7:12 that had **d.** the wrong, nor for his *91*
Eph 5:12 those things which are **d.** of them *1096*
Eph 6:13 in the evil day, and having **d.** all,........ *2716*
Php 2:3 Let nothing be **d.** through strife or ....
Php 4:14 Notwithstanding ye have well **d.**,........ *4160*
Col 3:25 for the wrong which he hath **d.**:......... *91*
Col 4:9 unto you all things which are **d.** here. ....
Tit 3:5 righteousness which we have **d.**, ... *4160*
Heb 10:29 hath **d.** despite unto the Spirit of........ *1796*
Heb 10:36 after ye have **d.** the will of God, ... *4160*
Re 16:17 from the throne, saying, It is **d.**......... *1096*
Re 21:6 And he said unto me, It is **d.**. *1096*
Re 22:6 things which must shortly be **d.**. *1096*

DOOR See also DOORKEEPER; DOORS.
Ge 4:7 doest not well, sin lieth at the **d.**. 6607
Ge 6:16 and the **d.** of the ark shalt thou set 6607
Ge 18:1 he sat in the tent **d.** in the heat of 6607
Ge 18:2 ran to meet them from the tent **d.**, ... 6607
Ge 18:10 Sarah heard it in the tent **d.**,............ 6607
Ge 19:6 Lot went out at the **d.** unto them,...... 6607
Ge 19:6 and shut the **d.** after him,................ 1817
Ge 19:9 and came near to break the **d.**........... 1817
Ge 19:10 house to them, and shut to the **d.**. 1817
Ge 19:11 the men that were at the **d.**............... 6607
Ge 19:11 wearied themselves to find the **d.**....... 6607
Ge 43:19 with him at the **d.** of the house,......... 6607
Ex 12:7 on the **d.** post of the houses, ... 4947
Ex 12:22 go out at the **d.** of his house 6607
Ex 12:23 the Lord will pass over the **d.**, ... 6607
Ex 21:6 he shall also bring him to the **d.**,........ 1817
Ex 21:6 unto the **d.** post; and his master 4201
Ex 26:36 shalt make an hanging for the **d.** 6607
Ex 29:4 bring unto the **d.** of the tabernacle...... 6607
Ex 29:11 Lord, by the **d.** of the tabernacle 6607
Ex 29:32 in the basket, by the **d.** of the.......... 6607
Ex 29:42 at the **d.** of the tabernacle of the........ 6607
Ex 33:8 and stood every man at his tent **d.**, ... 6607
Ex 33:9 stood at the **d.** of the tabernacle, ... 6607
Ex 33:10 pillar stand at the tabernacle **d.**: 6607
Ex 33:10 worshipped, everyman in his tent **d.**. .. 6607
Ex 35:15 and the hanging for the **d.** at the........ 6607
Ex 35:17 hanging for the **d.** of the court, ... 8179
Ex 36:37 for the tabernacle **d.** of blue, ... 6607
Ex 38:8 which assembled at the **d.** of the........ 6607
Ex 38:30 the sockets to the **d.** of the 6607
Ex 39:38 the hanging for the tabernacle **d.**,........ 6607
Ex 40:5 and put the hanging of the **d.** to the.... 6607
Ex 40:6 before the **d.** of the tabernacle of....... 6607
Ex 40:12 and his sons unto the **d.** of the.......... 6607
Ex 40:28 he set up the hanging at the **d.**.......... 6607
Ex 40:29 by the **d.** of the tabernacle of the....... 6607
Le 1:3 voluntary will at the **d.** of the........... 6607
Le 1:5 the altar that is by the **d.** of the......... 6607
Le 3:2 kill it at the **d.** of the tabernacle......... 6607
Le 4:4 unto the **d.** of the tabernacle 6607
Le 4:7 which is at the **d.** of the tabernacle..... 6607
Le 4:18 burnt offering, which is at the **d.** of 6607
Le 8:3 congregation together unto the **d.**........ 6607
Le 8:4 was gathered together unto the **d.**...... 6607
Le 8:31 the flesh at the **d.** of the tabernacle.... 6607
Le 8:33 And ye shall not go out of the **d.** 6607
Le 8:35 Therefore shall ye abide at the **d.**........ 6607
Le 10:7 And ye shall not go out from the **d.**.... 6607
Le 12:6 sin offering, unto the **d.** of the.......... 6607
Le 14:11 Lord, at the **d.** of the tabernacle 6607
Le 14:23 the priest, unto the **d.** of the............ 6607
Le 14:38 the house to the **d.** of the house, ... 6607
Le 15:14 Lord unto the **d.** of the tabernacle...... 6607
Le 15:29 the priest, to the **d.** of the................. 6607
Le 16:7 at the **d.** of the tabernacle of the........ 6607
Le 17:4 And bringeth it not unto the **d.** of....... 6607
Le 17:5 unto the Lord, unto the **d.** of the 6607
Le 17:6 altar of the Lord at the **d.** of............. 6607
Le 17:9 bringeth it not unto the **d.** of the........ 6607
Le 19:21 offering unto the Lord, unto the **d.**..... 6607
Nu 3:25 for the **d.** of the tabernacle 6607
Nu 3:26 the curtain for the **d.** of the court,....... 6607
Nu 4:25 for the **d.** of the tabernacle 6607
Nu 4:26 the hanging for the **d.** at the gate....... 6607
Nu 6:10 priest, to the **d.** of the tabernacle....... 6607
Nu 6:13 unto the **d.** of the tabernacle 6607
Nu 6:18 his separation at the **d.** of the............ 6607
Nu 10:3 at the **d.** of the tabernacle 6607
Nu 11:10 every man in the **d.** of his tent: 6607
Nu 12:5 stood in the **d.** of the tabernacle, ... 6607
Nu 16:18 stood in the **d.** of the tabernacle 6607
Nu 16:19 them unto the **d.** of the tabernacle........ 6607
Nu 16:27 and stood in the **d.** of their tents,........ 6607
Nu 16:50 returned unto Moses unto the **d.** of.... 6607
Nu 20:6 unto the **d.** of the tabernacle of the 6607
Nu 25:6 before the **d.** of the tabernacle........... 6607
Nu 27:2 the congregation, by the **d.** of the 6607
De 11:20 upon the **d.** posts of thine house, ... 4201
De 15:17 it through his ear unto the **d.**, ... 1817
De 22:21 to the **d.** of her father's house, ... 6607
De 31:15 stood over the **d.** of the tabernacle..... 6607
Jos 19:51 Lord, at the **d.** of the tabernacle 6607
Jg 4:20 Stand in the **d.** of the tent, and it....... 6607
Jg 9:52 went hard unto the **d.** of the tower..... 6607
Jg 19:22 beat at the **d.**, and spake to the......... 1817
Jg 19:26 down at the **d.** of the man's house...... 6607
1Sa 2:22 that assembled at the **d.** of the 6607
2Sa 11:9 Uriah slept at the **d.** of the king's....... 6607
2Sa 13:17 from me, and bolt the **d.** after her...... 1817
2Sa 13:18 her out, and bolted the **d.** after her. ... 1817
1Ki 6:8 The **d.** for the middle chamber 6907
1Ki 6:33 made he for the **d.** of the temple 6907
1Ki 6:34 leaves of the one **d.** were folding, ... 1817
1Ki 6:34 and the two leaves of the other **d.**........ 1817
1Ki 14:6 her feet, as she came in at the **d.**, ... 6607
1Ki 14:17 threshold of the **d.**, the child died;...... 1004
1Ki 14:27 kept the **d.** of the king's house. 6607
2Ki 4:4 thou shalt shut the **d.** upon thee 1817
2Ki 4:5 shut the **d.** upon her and upon her 1817
2Ki 4:15 had called her, she stood in the **d.**....... 6607
2Ki 4:21 shut the **d.** upon him, and went out. ....
2Ki 4:33 and shut the **d.** upon them twain, ... 1817
2Ki 5:9 at the **d.** of the house of Elisha.......... 6607
2Ki 6:32 the **d.**, and hold him fast at the **d.**:..... 1817
2Ki 9:3 Then open the **d.**, and flee, and......... 1817
2Ki 9:10 And he opened the **d.**, and fled.......... 1817
2Ki 12:9 that kept the **d.** put therein.............. 5592
2Ki 22:4 keepers of the **d.** have gathered......... 5592
2Ki 23:4 keepers of the **d.**, to bring forth 5592
2Ki 25:18 and the three keepers of the **d.**: 5592
1Ch 9:21 porter of the **d.** of the tabernacle 6607
Ne 3:20 unto the **d.** of the house of Eliashib 6607
Ne 3:21 from the **d.** of the house of Eliashib.... 6607
Es 2:21 which kept the **d.**, were wroth, ... 5592
Es 6:2 the keepers of the **d.**, who sought...... 5592
Job 31:9 laid wait at my neighbour's **d.**;........... 6607
Job 31:34 silence, and went not out of the **d.**?.... 6607
Ps 141:3 my mouth; keep the **d.** of my lips. 1817
Pr 5:8 come not nigh the **d.** of her house:...... 6607
Pr 9:14 she sitteth at the **d.** of her house,...... 6607
Pr 26:14 As the **d.** turneth upon his hinges,...... 1817
Ca 5:4 the hole of the **d.**, and my bowels ....
Ca 8:9 if she be a **d.**, we will enclose 1817
Isa 6:4 posts of the **d.** moved at the voice 5592
Jer 35:4 of Shallum, the keeper of the **d.**:........ 5592
Jer 52:24 and the three keepers of the **d.**: 5592
Eze 8:3 to the **d.** of the inner gate that 6607
Eze 8:7 brought me to the **d.** of the court;...... 6607
Eze 8:8 had digged in the wall, behold a **d.**. 6607
Eze 8:14 he brought me to the **d.** of the gate.... 6607
Eze 8:16 at the **d.** of the temple of the Lord,..... 6607
Eze 10:19 one stood at the **d.** of the east gate.... 6607
Eze 11:1 and behold at the **d.** of the gate five ... 6607
Eze 40:13 and twenty cubits, **d.** against **d.**. 6607
Eze 41:2 breadth of the **d.** was ten cubits;........ 6607
Eze 41:2 the sides of the **d.** were five cubits....... 6607
Eze 41:3 and measured the post of the **d.**, ... 6607
Eze 41:3 two cubits; and the **d.**, six cubits. 6607
Eze 41:3 the breadth of the **d.**, seven cubits..... 6607
Eze 41:11 one **d.** toward the north, and............ 6607
Eze 41:11 another **d.** toward the south:............ 6607
Eze 41:16 The **d.** posts, and the narrow............ 5592
Eze 41:16 against the **d.**, cieled with wood......... 5592
Eze 41:17 To that above the **d.**, even unto 6607
Eze 41:20 From the ground unto above the **d.**..... 6607
Eze 41:24 leaves for the one **d.**, and...other **d.**.. 1817
Eze 42:2 hundred cubits was the north **d.**,........ 6607
Eze 42:12 was a **d.** in the head of the way,........ 6607
Eze 46:3 shall worship at the **d.** of this gate...... 6607
Eze 47:1 me again unto the **d.** of the house; 6607
Ho 2:15 the valley of Achor for a **d.** of hope: ... 6607
Am 9:1 he said, Smite the lintel of the **d.**, ...
Mt 6:6 **when thou hast shut thy d.,**.......... *2374*
Mt 25:10 **marriage; and the d. was shut**...... *2374*
Mt 27:60 stone to the **d.** of the sepulchre,........ *2374*
Mt 28:2 rolled back the stone from the **d.**, ... *2374*
Mk 1:33 was gathered together at the **d.**......... *2374*
Mk 2:2 no, not so much as about the **d.**: *2374*
Mk 11:4 colt tied by the **d.** without in a place... *2374*
Mk 15:46 stone unto the **d.** of the sepulchre........ *2374*
Mk 16:3 stone from the **d.** of the sepulchre? *2374*
Lu 11:7 **the d. is now shut, and my**.......... *2374*
Lu 13:25 **up, and hath shut to the d.,**.......... *2374*
Lu 13:25 **to knock at the d., saying, Lord,**.. *2374*
Joh 10:1 **by the d. into the sheepfold, but**... *2374*
Joh 10:2 **the d. is the shepherd of the sheep**. *2374*
Joh 10:7 **unto you, I am the d. of the sheep**. *2374*
Joh 10:9 **I am the d.: by me if any man**...... *2374*
Joh 18:16 Peter stood at the **d.** without. *2374*
Joh 18:16 spake unto her that kept the **d.**, ... *2377*
Joh 18:17 the damsel that kept the **d.**............... *2377*
Ac 5:9 at the **d.**, and shall carry thee out. *2374*
Ac 12:6 before the **d.** kept the prison............ *2374*
Ac 12:13 Peter knocked at the **d.** of the gate, ...
Ac 12:16 and when they had opened the **d.**,............
Ac 14:27 opened the **d.** of faith unto the *2374*
1Co 16:9 a great **d.** and effectual is opened....... *2374*
2Co 2:12 and a **d.** was opened unto me............ *2374*
Col 4:3 open unto us a **d.** of utterance,.......... *2374*
Jas 5:9 the judge standeth before the **d.**. *2374*
Re 3:8 **set before thee an open d.,**............ *2374*
Re 3:20 **I stand at the d., and knock: if**..... *2374*
Re 3:20 **hear my voice, and open the d.,**.... *2374*
Re 4:1 a **d.** was opened in heaven:.............. *2374*

DOORKEEPER See also DOORKEEPERS.
Ps 84:10 I had rather be a **d.** in the house 5605

DOORKEEPERS
1Ch 15:23 and Elkanah were **d.** for the ark......... 7778
1Ch 15:24 and Jehiah were **d.** for the ark. 7778

DOOR-POST See DOOR and POST.

DOORS
Jos 2:19 shall go out of the **d.** of thy house...... 1817
Jg 3:23 the **d.** of the parlour upon him,.......... 1817
Jg 3:24 the **d.** of the parlour were locked, ... 1817
Jg 3:25 he opened not the **d.** of the parlour; ... 1817
Jg 11:31 cometh forth of the **d.** of my house 1817
Jg 16:3 took the **d.** of the gate of the city, ... 1817
Jg 19:27 and opened the **d.** of the house, and... 1817
1Sa 3:15 the **d.** of the house of the Lord. 1817
1Sa 21:13 scrabbled on the **d.** of the gate, and.... 1817
1Ki 6:31 the oracle he made **d.** of olive tree:.... 1817
1Ki 6:32 The two **d.** also were of olive tree; 1817
1Ki 6:34 the two **d.** were of fir tree: the two ... 1817
1Ki 7:5 all the **d.** and posts were square, ... 6607
1Ki 7:50 of the **d.** of the inner house, the 1817
1Ki 7:50 place, and for the **d.** of the house,...... 1817
2Ki 18:16 the **d.** of the temple of the Lord, ... 1817
1Ch 22:3 the nails of the **d.** of the gates,.......... 1817
2Ch 3:7 and the **d.** thereof, with gold;............ 1817
2Ch 4:9 great court and **d.** for the court, ... 1817
2Ch 4:9 and overlaid the **d.** of them with 1817
2Ch 4:22 the inner **d.** thereof for the most......... 1817
2Ch 4:22 and the **d.** of the house of the 1817
2Ch 23:4 Levites, shall be porters of the **d.**; 5592
2Ch 28:24 up the **d.** of the house of the Lord, ... 1817
2Ch 29:3 the **d.** of the house of the Lord, ... 1817
2Ch 29:7 have shut up the **d.** of the porch, ... 1817
2Ch 34:9 the Levites that kept the **d.** had......... 5592
Ne 3:1 set up the **d.** of it; even unto the....... 1817
Ne 3:3, 6,13,14,15 and set up the **d.** thereof,.. 1817
Ne 6:1 that time I had not set up the **d.**........ 1817
Ne 6:10 let us shut the **d.** of the temple: 1817
Ne 7:1 I had set up the **d.**, and the porters,.... 1817
Ne 7:3 let them shut the **d.** and bar them: 1817
Job 3:10 up the **d.** of my mother's womb, ... 1817
Job 31:32 but I opened my **d.** to the traveller..... 1817
Job 38:8 Or who shut up the sea with **d.**, ... 1817
Job 38:10 decreed place, and set bars and **d.**, ... 1817
Job 38:17 thou seen the **d.** of the shadow.......... 8179

Job 41:14 Who can open the **d.** of his face? 1817
Ps 24:7 be ye lift up, ye everlasting **d.**; 6607
Ps 24:9 lift them up, ye everlasting **d.**; 6607
Ps 78:23 and opened the **d.** of heaven, 1817
Pr 8:3 city, at the coming in at the **d.**. 6607
Pr 8:34 waiting at the posts of my **d.** 6607
Ec 12:4 the **d.** shall be shut in the streets, 1817
Isa 26:20 shut thy **d.** about thee: hide 1817
Isa 57:8 Behind the **d.** also and the posts 1817
Eze 33:30 and in the **d.** of the houses, 6607
Eze 41:11 And the **d.** of the side chambers 6607
Eze 41:23 and the sanctuary had two **d.**. 1817
Eze 41:24 the **d.** had two leaves apiece, 1817
Eze 41:25 on the **d.** of the temple, cherubims 1817
Eze 42:4 and their **d.** toward the north. 6607
Eze 42:11 fashions, and according to their **d.**. 6607
Eze 42:12 according to the **d.** of the chambers 6607
Mic 7:5 keep the **d.** of my mouth from her 6607
Zec 11:1 open thy **d.**, O Lebanon, that the 1817
Mal 1:10 that would shut the **d.** for nought? 1817
Mt 24:33 **it is near, even at the d.**. *2374*
Mk 13:29 **it is nigh, even at the d.**. *2374*
Joh 20:19 when the **d.** were shut where the *2374*
Joh 20:26 the **d.** being shut, and stood in the *2374*
Ac 5:19 opened the prison **d.**, and brought *2374*
Ac 5:23 standing without before the **d.**: *2374*
Ac 16:26 immediately all the **d.** were opened, *2374*
Ac 16:27 seeing the prison **d.** open, he drew *2374*
Ac 21:30 and forthwith the **d.** were shut. *2374*

DOPHKAH (dof'-kah)
Nu 33:12 of Sin, and encamped in **D.**. 1850
Nu 33:13 And they departed from **D.**, and 1850

DOR (dor) See also EN-DOR.
Jos 11:2 the borders of **D.** on the west, 1756
Jos 12:23 The king of **D.** in the coast of **D.**, 1756
Jos 17:11 the inhabitants of **D.** and her towns, 1756
Jg 1:27 the inhabitants of **D.** and her towns, 1756
1Ki 4:11 of Anbinadab, in all the region of **D.**; 1756
1Ch 7:29 and her towns, **D.** and her towns. 1756

DORCAS (dor'-cas) See also TABITHA.
Ac 9:36 by interpretation is called **D.**: *1393*
Ac 9:39 **D.** made, while she was with them. *1393*

DOST See also DOEST.
Ge 32:29 is it that thou **d.** ask after my name?
Ge 44:4 Thou **d.** overtake them, say unto them,
De 9:5 **d.** thou go to possess their land:
De 24:10 thou **d.** lend thy brother any thing,
De 24:11 the man to whom thou **d.** lend shall
Jg 14:16 Thou **d.** but hate me, and lovest me
1Sa 24:14 after whom **d.** thou pursue? after
1Sa 28:16 Wherefore then **d.** thou ask of me,
1Ki 2:22 **d.** thou ask Abishag the Shunammite
1Ki 21:7 **D.** thou now govern the kingdom of
2Ki 18:20 Now on whom **d.** thou trust, that
2Ch 6:26 their sin, when thou **d.** afflict them;
Ne 2:4 For what **d.** thou make request?
Job 2:9 **D.** thou still retain thine integrity?
Job 7:21 **d.** thou not pardon my transgression
Job 10:8 round about; yet thou **d.** destroy
Job 14:3 And **d.** thou open thine eyes upon
Job 14:16 **d.** thou not watch over my sin?
Job 15:8 **d.** thou restrain wisdom for thyself?
Job 30:20 unto thee, and thou **d.** not hear me:
Job 33:13 Why **d.** thou strive against him?
Job 37:15 **D.** thou know when God disposed
Job 37:16 **D.** thou know the balancings of the
Ps 39:11 thou with rebukes **d.** correct man for
Ps 43:2 why **d.** thou cast me off? why go
Ps 44:12 and **d.** not increase thy wealth
Ps 99:4 thou **d.** establish equity, thou executest
Pr 4:8 to honour, when thou **d.** embrace her.
Ec 7:10 **d.** not enquire wisely concerning this
Ca 5:9 that thou **d.** so charge us?
Isa 26:7 most upright, **d.** weigh the path of the
Isa 36:5 now on whom **d.** thou trust, that thou
Jer 32:3 Wherefore **d.** thou prophesy, and say,
Jer 40:14 **D.** thou certainly know that Baalis
Jer 48:18 daughter that **d.** inhabit Dibon,
La 5:20 Wherefore **d.** thou forget us for ever,
Eze 2:6 and thou **d.** dwell among scorpions:
Eze 32:19 Whom **d.** thou pass in beauty?
Eze 33:8 if thou **d.** not speak to warn the
Mic 4:9 why **d.** thou cry out aloud? is there
Hab 1:3 Why **d.** thou shew me iniquity, and
Lu 10:40 Lord, **d.** thou not care that my sister
Lu 23:40 **D.** not thou fear God, seeing thou art
Joh 6:30 believe thee? what **d.** thou work?
Joh 9:34 and **d.** thou teach us? And they cast
Joh 9:35 **D. thou believe on the Son of God?**
Joh 10:24 How long **d.** thou make us to doubt?
Joh 13:6 Lord, **d.** thou wash my feet?
Ro 2:21 man should not steal, **d.** thou steal?
Ro 2:22 **d.** thou commit adultery? thou that
Ro 2:22 idols, **d.** thou commit sacrilege?
Ro 2:27 and circumcision **d.** transgress
Ro 14:10 But why **d.** thou judge thy brother?
Ro 14:10 or why **d.** thou set at nought thy
1Co 4:7 why **d.** thou glory, as if thou hadst
Re 6:10 Lord, holy and true, **d.** thou not judge

DOTE See also DOTED; DOTING.
Jer 50:36 and they shall **d.**: a sword is upon 2973

DOTED
Eze 23:5 and she **d.** on her lovers, on the 5689
Eze 23:7 with all on whom she **d.**; with all 5689
Eze 23:9 of the Assyrians, upon whom she **d.**. 5689
Eze 23:12 She **d.** upon the Assyrians her 5689
Eze 23:16 she saw them with her eyes, she **d.** 5689
Eze 23:20 For she **d.** upon their paramours, 5689

DOTH See also DOETH.
Ge 3:5 God **d.** know that in the day ye eat
Ge 27:42 Esau, as touching thee, **d.** comfort
Ge 45:3 **d.** my father yet live?
Ex 11:7 how that the Lord **d.** put a difference
Ex 31:13 am the Lord that **d.** sanctify you.
Ex 32:11 why **d.** thy wrath wax hot against thy
Le 11:31 **d.** touch them, when they be dead,
Le 11:32 when they are dead, **d.** fall, it shall be
Le 25:16 years of the fruits **d.** he sell unto thee,
Nu 5:21 the Lord **d.** make thy thigh to rot,
Nu 16:7 the man whom the Lord **d.** choose,
Nu 36:6 thing which the Lord **d.** command
De 1:20 Lord our God **d.** give unto us.
De 1:25 the Lord our God **d.** give us.
De 1:31 God bare thee, as a man **d.** bear his
De 5:24 this day that God **d.** talk with man,
De 8:3 that man **d.** not live by bread only,
De 8:3 of the mouth of the Lord **d.** man live.
De 9:4 the Lord **d.** drive them out from before
De 9:5 thy God **d.** drive them out from before
De 10:12 **d.** the Lord thy God require of thee,
De 10:18 he **d.** execute the judgment of the
De 16:19 a gift **d.** blind the eyes of the wise,
De 18:12 the Lord thy God **d.** drive them out
De 20:16 the Lord thy God **d.** give thee for
De 31:6 thy God, he it is that **d.** go with thee;
De 31:8 Lord, he it is that **d.** go before thee;
Jos 1:18 Whosoever he be that **d.** rebel
Jos 20:4 when he that **d.** flee unto one of
Jg 4:20 any man **d.** come and enquire of thee,
Ru 3:11 for all the city of my people **d.** know
1Sa 9:13 because he **d.** bless the sacrifice; and
1Sa 23:19 **d.** not David hide himself with us
1Sa 26:1 **D.** not David hide himself in the hill
1Sa 26:18 Wherefore **d.** my lord thus pursue
1Sa 26:20 flea, as when one **d.** hunt a partridge
2Sa 10:3 Thinkest thou that David **d.** honour
2Sa 14:13 for the king **d.** speak this thing
2Sa 14:13 in that the king **d.** not fetch home
2Sa 14:14 **d.** God respect any person: yet **d.**
2Sa 19:8 Behold, the king **d.** sit in the gate.
2Sa 19:20 servant **d.** know that I have sinned:
2Sa 24:3 but why **d.** my lord the king delight
2Sa 24:24 that which **d.** cost me nothing.
1Ki 1:11 Adonijah the son of Haggith **d.** reign,
1Ki 1:13 throne? why then **d.** Adonijah reign?
1Ki 22:8 **d.** not prophesy good concerning me,
2Ki 2:15 The spirit of Elijah **d.** rest on Elisha.
2Ki 5:7 this man **d.** send unto me to recover
1Ch 19:3 thou that David **d.** honour thy father,
1Ch 21:3 then **d.** my lord require this thing?
2Ch 6:33 and fear thee, as **d.** thy people Israel,
2Ch 32:11 **D.** not Hezekiah persuade you to give
Job 1:9 said, **D.** Job fear God for nought?
Job 4:21 **D.** not their excellency which is
Job 5:6 **d.** trouble spring out of the ground;
Job 6:5 **D.** the wild ass bray when he hath
Job 6:25 but what **d.** your arguing reprove?
Job 8:3 **D.** God pervert judgment? or **d.** the
Job 12:11 **D.** not the ear try words? and the
Job 15:12 Why **d.** thine heart carry thee away?
Job 16:13 my reins asunder, and **d.** not spare;
Job 17:2 **d.** not mine eye continue in their
Job 22:13 How **d.** God know? can he judge
Job 23:9 on the left hand, where he **d.** work,
Job 24:19 **d.** the grave those which have sinned.
Job 25:3 upon whom **d.** not his light arise?
Job 31:4 **D.** not he see my ways, and count all
Job 35:16 **d.** Job open his mouth in vain;
Job 36:7 he **d.** establish them for ever, and
Job 39:26 **D.** the hawk fly by thy wisdom, and
Job 39:27 **D.** the eagle mount up at thy
Job 41:18 By his neesings a light **d.** shine,
Ps 1:2 and in his law **d.** he meditate day and
Ps 10:2 his pride **d.** persecute the poor:
Ps 10:8 in the secret places **d.** he murder the
Ps 10:9 **d.** catch the poor, when he draweth
Ps 10:13 Wherefore **d.** the wicked contemn
Ps 11:7 his countenance **d.** behold the
Ps 29:9 in his temple **d.** every one speak
Ps 41:11 because mine enemy **d.** not triumph
Ps 54:*title* **D.** not David hide himself with us?
Ps 59:7 their lips: for who, say they, **d.** hear?
Ps 68:33 lo, he **d.** send out his voice, and
Ps 73:11 How **d.** God know? and is there
Ps 74:1 why **d.** thine anger smoke against
Ps 77:8 **d.** his promise fail for evermore?
Ps 80:13 boar out of the wood **d.** waste it,
Ps 80:13 wild beast of the field **d.** devour it.
Ps 92:6 neither **d.** a fool understand this.
Ps 119:129 therefore **d.** my soul keep them.
Ps 130:5 **d.** wait, and in his word do I hope.
Ps 147:2 The Lord **d.** build up Jerusalem:
Pr 6:16 These six things **d.** the Lord hate:
Pr 8:1 **D.** not wisdom cry? and understanding
Pr 14:10 stranger **d.** not intermeddle with his
Pr 22:5 **d.** keep his soul shall be far from
Pr 24:12 **d.** not he that pondereth the heart
Pr 24:12 keepeth thy soul, **d.** not he know it?
Pr 25:23 so **d.** an angry countenance a
Pr 26:14 upon his hinges, so **d.** the slothful
Pr 27:9 so **d.** the sweetness of a man's friend
Pr 27:24 and **d.** the crown endure to every
Pr 29:6 but the righteous **d.** sing and rejoice.
Pr 30:11 and **d.** not bless their mother.
Pr 31:11 husband **d.** safely trust in her,
Ec 10:1 so **d.** a little folly him that is in
Ca 2:6 and his right hand **d.** embrace me.
Isa 1:3 but Israel **d.** not know,
Isa 1:3 my people **d.** not consider.
Isa 1:23 **d.** the cause of the widow come unto
Isa 3:1 the Lord of hosts, **d.** take away from
Isa 3:9 shew of their countenance **d.** witness
Isa 10:7 neither **d.** his heart think so;
Isa 28:24 **D.** the plowman plow all day to sow?
Isa 28:24 **d.** he open and break the clods of his
Isa 28:25 **d.** he not cast abroad the fitches,
Isa 28:26 **d.** instruct him to discretion, and **d.**
Isa 30:33 a stream of brimstone **d.** kindle it.
Isa 42:11 the villages that Kedar **d.** inhabit:
Isa 44:14 an ash, and the rain **d.** nourish it.
Isa 52:6 that day that I am he that **d.** speak:
Isa 59:9 us, neither **d.** judgment overtake us:
Jer 2:11 glory for that which **d.** not profit.
Jer 10:7 for to thee **d.** it appertain:
Jer 12:1 **d.** the way of the wicked prosper?
Jer 14:10 therefore the Lord **d.** not accept them:
Jer 15:10 yet every one of them **d.** curse me.
Jer 23:14 none **d.** return from his wickedness:
Jer 30:6 whether a man **d.** travail with child?
Jer 31:10 keep him, as a shepherd **d.** his flock.
Jer 49:1 why then **d.** their king inherit Gad,
Jer 51:43 **d.** any son of man pass thereby.
La 1:1 How **d.** the city sit solitary, that was
La 3:33 For he **d.** not afflict willingly nor
La 3:39 Wherefore **d.** a living man complain.
La 5:8 **d.** deliver us out of their hand.
Eze 3:20 When a righteous man **d.** turn from
Eze 3:21 and he **d.** not sin, he shall surely live
Eze 18:19 Why? **d.** not the son bear the iniquity
Eze 20:49 me, **D.** he not speak in parables?
Ho 4:14 the people that **d.** not understand
Ho 5:5 pride of Israel **d.** testify to his face:
Mic 6:8 and what **d.** the Lord require of thee,
Hab 1:4 and judgment **d.** never go forth: for
Hab 1:4 **d.** compass about the righteous;
Zep 3:5 morning **d.** he bring his judgment

Mt 6:19 where moth and rust d. corrupt,
Mt 6:20 neither moth nor rust d. corrupt,
Mt 12:24 This fellow d. not cast out devils,
Mt 17:24 D. not your master pay tribute?
Mt 18:12 d. he not leave the ninety and nine,
Mt 19:9 is put away d. commit adultery
Mt 22:43 then d. David in spirit call him Lord,
Mt 24:42 not what hour your Lord d. come
Mt 26:46 he is at hand that d. betray me
Mk 2:7 d. this man thus speak blasphemies?
Mk 2:22 new wine d. burst the bottles,
Mk 8:12 d. this generation seek after a sign?
Lu 1:46 My soul d. magnify the Lord,
Lu 6:43 neither d. a corrupt tree bring
Lu 11:36 a candle d. give thee light
Lu 13:15 Thou hypocrite, d. not each one of
Lu 13:34 a hen d. gather her brood under
Lu 14:27 And whosoever d. not bear his cross,
Lu 15:4 if he lose one of them, d. not leave the
Lu 15:8 lose one piece, d. not light a candle,
Lu 17:9 D. he thank that servant because he
Lu 22:26 that is chief, as he that d. serve
Joh 2:10 beginning d. set forth good wine;
Joh 6:61 said unto them, D. this offend you?
Joh 7:51 D. our law judge any man, before
Joh 9:19 born blind? how then d. he now see?
Joh 10:17 Therefore d. my Father love me,
Ac 4:10 even by him d. this man stand here
Ac 8:36 what d. hinder me to be baptized?
Ac 22:5 the high priest d. bear me witness,
Ac 26:24 much learning d. make thee mad
Ro 8:24 seeth, why d. he yet hope for?
Ro 9:19 Why d. he yet find fault? For who
Ro 14:6 to the Lord he d. not regard it.
1Co 9:9 D. God take care for oxen?
1Co 11:14 D. not even nature itself teach you,
1Co 13:5 D. not behave itself unseemly,
1Co 15:50 d. corruption inherit incorruption.
2Co 1:10 so great a death, and d. deliver:
2Co 3:9 d. the ministration of righteousness
Eph 5:13 d. make manifest is light
Col 1:6 d. also in you, since the day ye heard
1Th 2:11 you, as a father d. his children
2Th 2:7 mystery of iniquity d. already work:
2Ti 2:17 their word will eat as d. a canker:
Heb 1:11 all shall wax old as d. a garment;
Heb 12:1 the sin which d. so easily beset us,
Jas 2:14 What d. it profit, my brethren, though
Jas 2:16 to the body; what d. it profit?
Jas 3:11 D. a fountain send forth at the same
Jas 5:6 killed the just; and he d. not resist
1Pe 3:21 even baptism d. also now save us,
1Pe 5:13 you; and so d. Marcus my son
1Jo 3:2 and it d. not yet appear what we
1Jo 3:9 is born of God d. not commit sin;
3Jo 10 d. he himself receive the brethren,
Re 19:11 righteousness he d. judge and make

DOTHAN (do'-than)
Ge 37:17 I heard them say, Let us go to D.. 1886
Ge 37:17 his brethren, and found them in D.. 1886
2Ki 6:13 him, saying, Behold, he is in D. 1886

DOTING
1Ti 6:4 but d. about questions and strifes 3552

DOUBLE See also DOUBLED; DOUBLETONGUED.
Ge 43:12 take d. money in your hand; 4932
Ge 43:15 they tood d. money in their hand, 4932
Ex 22:4 or sheep; and he shall restore d. 8147
Ex 22:7 the thief be found, let him pay d.: 8147
Ex 22:9 shall pay d. unto his neighbour 8147
Ex 26:9 and shalt d. the sixth curtain in 3717
Ex 39:9 they made the breastplate d.: a 3717
De 15:18 worth a d. hired servant to thee, 4932
De 21:17 by giving him a d. portion of all 8147
2Ki 2:9 d. portion of thy spirit be upon me. 8147
1Ch 12:33 they were not of d. heart.
Job 11:6 of wisdom, that they are d. 3718
Job 41:13 who can come to him with his d. 3718
Ps 12:2 and with a d. heart do they speak.
Isa 40:2 received of the Lord's hand d. for 3718
Isa 61:7 shall have d.; and for confusion 4932
Isa 61:7 they shall possess the d.: 4932
Jer 16:18 their iniquity and their sin d.; 4932
Jer 17:18 destroy them with d. destruction. 4932
Zec 9:12 that I will render d. unto thee; 4932
1Ti 5:17 be counted worthy of d. honour, 1362
Jas 1:8 A d. minded man is unstable in all 1374
Jas 4:8 purify your hearts, ye d. minded. 1374
Re 18:6 rewarded you, and d. unto her 1363
Re 18:6 d. according to her works: 3588,1362
Re 18:6 which she hath filled fill to her d.. 1362

DOUBLED
Ge 41:32 for that the dream was d. unto 8138
Ex 28:16 Foursquare it shall be being d.; 3717
Ex 39:9 the breadth thereof, being d.. 3717
Eze 21:14 and let the sword be d. the third 3717

DOUBLE-MINDED See DOUBLE and MINDED.

DOUBLETONGUED
1Ti 3:8 not d., not given to much wine, 1351

DOUBT See also DOUBTED; DOUBTETH; DOUBTFUL; DOUBTING; DOUBTLESS; DOUBTS.
Ge 37:33 Joseph is without d. rent in pieces.
De 28:66 life shall hand in d. before thee:
Job 12:2 No d. but ye are the people, 551
Mt 14:31 faith, wherefore didst thou d.? 1365
Mt 21:21 If ye have faith, and d. not, ye 1252
Mk 11:23 shall not d. in his heart, but shall 1252
Lu 11:20 no d. the kingdom of God is come 686
Joh 10:24 dost thou make us to d.? 142,5590
Ac 2:12 were all amazed, and were in d., 1280
Ac 28:4 No d. this man is a murderer, 3843
1Co 9:10 our sakes, no d., this is written: 1063
Ga 4:20 voice; for I stand in d. of you. 639
1Jo 2:19 they would no d. have continued 639

DOUBTED
Mt 28:17 worshipped him: but some d.. 1365
Ac 5:24 they d. of them whereunto this 1280
Ac 10:17 while Peter d. in himself what 1280
Ac 25:20 d. of such manner of questions, 639

DOUBTETH
Ro 14:23 he that d. is damned if he eat, 1252

DOUBTFUL
Lu 12:29 drink, neither be ye of d. mind. 3349
Ro 14:1 ye, but not to d. disputations. 1261

DOUBTING
Joh 13:22 on another, d. of whom we spake. 639
Ac 10:20 and go with them, d. nothing: 1252
Ac 11:12 bade me go with them, nothing d.. 1252
1Ti 2:8 holy hands, without wrath and d. 1261

DOUBTLESS
Nu 14:30 D. ye shall not come into the 518
2Sa 5:19 I will d. deliver the Philistines
Ps 126:6 d. come again with rejoicing,
Isa 63:16 D. thou art our Father, though 3588
1Co 9:2 unto others, ye d. I am to you: 1065
2Co 12:1 not expedient for me d. to glory. 1211
Php 3:8 Yea d., and I count all things 3304

DOUBTS
Da 5:12 and dissolving of d., were found 7001
Da 5:16 interpretations, and dissolve d.: 7001

DOUGH
Ex 12:34 the people took their d. before it. 1217
Ex 12:39 baked unleavened cakes of the d. 1217
Nu 15:20 a cake of the first of your d. for an 6182
Nu 15:21 the first of your d. ye shall give 6182
Ne 10:37 the first fruits of your d., and our 6182
Jer 7:18 the women knead their d., to 1217
Eze 44:30 the first of your d., that he may 6182
Ho 7:4 after he hath kneaded the d., 1217

DOVE See also DOVE'S; DOVES; TURTLEDOVE.
Ge 8:8 he sent forth a d. from him, to 3123
Ge 8:9 the d. found no rest for the sole of 3123
Ge 8:10 again he sent forth the d. out of 3123
Ge 8:11 d. came in to him in the evening; 3123
Ge 8:12 seven days; and sent forth the d.; 3123
Ps 55:6 O that I had wings like a d.! for 3123
Ps 68:13 ye be as the wings of a d. covered 3123
Ca 2:14 O my d., that art in the clefts of 3123
Ca 5:2 to me, my sister, my love, my d., 3123
Ca 6:9 My d., my undefiled is but one; 3123
Isa 38:14 I did mourn as a d.: mine eyes fail 3123
Jer 48:28 he like the d. that maketh her nest 3123
Ho 7:11 Ephraim also is like a silly d. 3123
Ho 11:11 as a d. out of the land of Assyria: 3123
Mt 3:16 Spirit of God descending like a d., 4058
Mk 1:10 and the Spirit like a d. descending 4058
Lu 3:22 in a bodily shape like a d. upon 4058
Joh 1:32 descending from heaven like a d. 4058

DOVE'S
2Ki 6:25 fourth part of a cab of d. dung 1686

DOVES See also DOVES'; TURTLEDOVES.
Ca 5:12 His eyes are as the eyes of d. 3123
Isa 59:11 like bears, and mourn sore like d.: 3123
Isa 60:8 and as the d. to their windows? 3123
Eze 7:16 shall be on the mountains like d. 3123
Na 2:7 lead her as with the voice of d., 3123
Mt 10:16 as serpents, and harmless as d.. 4058
Mt 21:12 the seats of them that sold d., 4058
Mk 11:15 the seats of them that sold d.; 4058
Joh 2:14 that sold oxen and sheep and d.
Joh 2:16 said unto them that sold d., Take 4058

DOVES'
Ca 1:15 thou art fair; thou hast d. eyes. 3123
Ca 4:1 thou hast d. eyes within thy locks: 3123

DOWN See also DOWNSITTING; DOWNWARD.
Ge 11:5 the Lord came d. to see the city 3381
Ge 11:7 Go to, let us go d., and there 3381
Ge 12:10 Abram went d. into Egypt to 3381
Ge 15:11 fowls came d. upon the carcasses, 3381
Ge 15:12 And when the sun was going d., 935
Ge 15:17 to pass, that, when the sun went d., 935
Ge 18:21 I will go d. now, and see whether 3381
Ge 19:4 But before they lay d., the men
Ge 19:33, 35 perceived not when she lay d.
Ge 21:16 and sat her d. over against him
Ge 23:12 And Abraham bowed d. himself 7812
Ge 24:11 he made his camels to kneel d. 1288
Ge 24:14 Let d. thy pitcher, I pray thee, 5186
Ge 24:16 and she went d. to the well, and 3381
Ge 24:18 let d. her pitcher upon her hand, 3381
Ge 24:26 And the man bowed d. his head, 6915
Ge 24:45 and she went d. unto the well, and 3381
Ge 24:46 she let d. her pitcher from her 3381
Ge 24:48 And I bowed d. my head, and 6915
Ge 26:2 Go not d. into Egypt; dwell in 3381
Ge 27:29 thee, and nations bow d. to thee; 7812
Ge 27:29 thy mother's sons bow d. to thee: 7812
Ge 28:11 and lay d. in that place to sleep.
Ge 37:10 come to bow d. ourselves to thee 7812
Ge 37:25 And they sat d. to eat bread: and
Ge 37:25 going to carry it d. to Egypt, 3381
Ge 37:35 I will go d. into the grave unto my 3381
Ge 38:1 Judah went d. from his brethren, 3381
Ge 39:1 Joseph was brought d. to Egypt; 3381
Ge 39:1 which had brought him d. thither. 3381
Ge 42:2 get you d. thither, and buy for us 3381
Ge 42:3 Joseph's ten brethren went d. to 3381
Ge 42:6 came, and bowed d. themselves 7812
Ge 42:38 my son shall not go d. with you;
Ge 42:38 shall ye bring d. my gray hairs 3381
Ge 43:4 we will go d. and buy thee food: 3381
Ge 43:5 not send him, we will not go d.: 3381
Ge 43:7 would say, Bring your brother d.? 3381
Ge 43:11 and carry d. the man a present, 3381
Ge 43:15 and rose up, and went d. to Egypt, 3381
Ge 43:20 came indeed d. at the first time 3381
Ge 43:22 other money have we brought d. 3381
Ge 43:28 And they bowed d. their heads, 6915
Ge 44:11 they speedily took d. every man 3381
Ge 44:21 Bring him d. unto me, that I may 3381
Ge 44:23 your youngest brother come d. with 3381
Ge 44:26 And we said, We cannot go d.: if 3381
Ge 44:26 be with us, then will we go d.: 3381
Ge 44:29 ye shall bring d. my gray hairs 3381
Ge 44:31 shall bring d. the gray hairs of thy 3381
Ge 45:9 come d. unto me, tarry not: 3381
Ge 45:13 and bring d. my father hither 3381
Ge 46:3 fear not to go d. into Egypt; for I 3381
Ge 46:4 I will go d. with thee into Egypt; 3381
Ge 49:6 selfwill they digged d. a wall. 6131
Ge 49:8 children shall bow d. before thee. 7812
Ge 49:9 stooped d., he couched as a lion,
Ge 49:14 a strong ass couching d. between
Ge 50:18 went and fell d. before his face;
Ex 2:5 daughter of Pharoah came d. to 3381
Ex 2:15 of Midian: and he sat d. by a well.
Ex 3:8 I am come d. to deliver them out 3381
Ex 7:10 cast d. his rod before Pharoah,
Ex 7:12 they cast d. every man his rod,
Ex 9:19 the hail shall come d. upon them, 3381

Ex 11:8 servants shall come **d.** unto me,......... 3381
Ex 11:8 and bow **d.** themselves unto me,.........7812
Ex 17:11 and when he let **d.** his hand,.............. 5117
Ex 17:12 steady until the going **d.** of the sun....... 935
Ex 19:11 third day the Lord will come **d.** in....... 3381
Ex 19:14 Moses went **d.** from the mount.......... 3381
Ex 19:20 Lord came **d.** upon mount Sinai,......... 3381
Ex 19:21 Go **d.**, charge the people, lest they..... 3381
Ex 19:24 Away, get thee **d.**, and thou shalt...... 3381
Ex 19:25 So Moses went **d.** unto the people,..... 3381
Ex 20:5 shalt not bow **d.** thyself to them,........ 7812
Ex 22:26 unto him by that the sun goeth **d.**:........935
Ex 23:24 shalt now bow **d.** to their gods,.......... 7812
Ex 23:24 and quite break **d.** their images...........7665
Ex 32:1 to come **d.** out of the mount,............. 3381
Ex 32:6 people sat **d.** to eat and to drink,..............
Ex 32:7 said unto Moses, Go, get thee **d.**;.......3381
Ex 32:15 and went **d.** from the mount,............ 3381
Ex 34:13 images, and cut **d.** their groves:...........
Ex 34:29 Moses came **d.** from mount Sinai........ 3381
Ex 34:29 when he came **d.** from the mount,........3381
Le 9:22 came **d.** from offering of the sin..........3381
Le 11:35 for pots, they shall be broken **d.**:........ 5422
Le 14:45 And he shall break **d.** the house,.........5422
Le 18:23 before a beast to lie **d.** thereto:.......... 7250
Le 19:16 Thou shalt not go up and **d.** as a..............
Le 20:16 unto any beast, and lie **d.** thereto,.......7250
Le 22:7 when the sun is **d.**, he shall be........... 935
Le 26:1 in your land, to bow **d.** unto it:...........7812
Le 26:6 in the land, and ye shall lie **d.**,...................
Le 26:30 places, and cut **d.** your images,................
Nu 1:51 the Levites shall take it **d.**:..................3381
Nu 4:5 shall take **d.** the covering vail,............3381
Nu 10:17 And the tabernacle was taken **d.**;......... 3381
Nu 11:17 I will come **d.** and talk with thee..........3381
Nu 11:25 And the Lord came **d.** in a cloud,........3381
Nu 12:5 came **d.** in the pillar of the cloud,........3381
Nu 13:23 and cut **d.** from thence a branch...............
Nu 13:24 which the children of Israel cut **d.**.............
Nu 14:45 Amalekites came **d.**, and the............. 3381
Nu 16:30 and they go **d.** quick into the pit;........ 3381
Nu 16:33 went **d.** alive into the pit, and the....... 3381
Nu 20:15 How our fathers went **d.** into Egypt,... 3381
Nu 20:28 And Moses and Eleazar came **d.**......... 3381
Nu 21:15 brooks that goeth **d.** to the...............5186
Nu 22:27 of the Lord, she fell **d.** under............. 7257
Nu 22:31 bowed **d.** his head, and fell flat.......... 6915
Nu 23:24 he shall not lie **d.** until he eat of.......... 7901
Nu 24:9 He couched, he lay **d.** as a lion, and.... 7901
Nu 25:2 people did eat, and bowed **d.** to.......... 7812
Nu 33:52 and quite pluck **d.** all their high........... 8045
Nu 34:11 And the coast shall go **d.** from............3381
Nu 34:12 the border shall go **d.** to Jordan,......... 3381
De 1:25 brought it **d.** unto us, and brought....... 3381
De 5:9 Thou shalt not bow **d.** thyself unto...... 7812
De 6:7 when thou liest **d.**, and when thou.......7901
De 7:5 and break **d.** their images and..................
De 7:5 cut **d.** their groves, and..........................
De 9:3 he shall bring them **d.** before thy........ 3665
De 9:12 Arise, get thee **d.** quickly from........... 3381
De 9:15 I turned and came **d.** from the............3381
De 9:18 I fell **d.** before the Lord, as at the............
De 9:25 Thus I fell **d.** before the Lord forty...........
De 9:25 and forty nights, as I fell **d.** at the............
De 10:5 and came **d.** from the mount, and........3381
De 10:22 Thy fathers went **d.** into Egypt...........3381
De 11:19 when thou liest **d.**, and when thou.............
De 11:30 way where the sun goeth **d.**,............ 3996
De 12:3 and ye shall hew **d.** the graven.......... 1438
De 16:6 at the going **d.** of the sun, at the..........935
De 19:5 a stroke with the ax to cut **d.** the............
De 20:19 and thou shalt not cut them **d.**..................
De 20:20 thou shalt destroy and cut them **d.**;...........
De 21:4 elders of that city shall bring **d.**......... 3381
De 22:4 brother's ass or his ox fall **d.** by..............
De 23:11 when the sun is **d.**, he shall come.........935
De 24:13 pledge again when the sun goeth **d.**,...... 935
De 24:15 neither shall the sun go **d.** upon it;....... 935
De 24:19 thou cuttest **d.** thine harvest...................
De 25:2 shall cause him to lie **d.**, and to be............
De 26:4 and set it **d.** before the altar of the............
De 26:5 and he went **d.** into Egypt, and.......... 3381
De 26:15 Look **d.** from thy holy habitation..............
De 28:24 from heaven shall it come **d.** upon....... 3381
De 28:43 and thou shalt come **d.** very low......... 3381
De 28:52 thy high and fenced walls come **d.**,....... 3381
De 33:3 and they sat **d.** at thy feet;................8497
De 33:28 his heavens shall drop **d.** dew............6201
Jos 1:4 great sea toward the going **d.** of......... 3996
Jos 2:8 And before they were laid **d.**,..............7901
Jos 2:15 Then she let them **d.** by a cord.......... 3381
Jos 2:18 window which thou didst let us **d.**....... 3381
Jos 3:13 from the waters that come **d.** from......3381
Jos 3:16 the waters which came **d.** from...........3381
Jos 3:16 and those that came **d.** toward the...... 3381
Jos 4:8 they lodged, and laid them **d.**....................
Jos 6:5 walls of the city shall fall **d.** flat,................
Jos 6:20 shout, that the wall fell **d.** flat,...............
Jos 7:5 and smote them in the going **d.**:.......... 4174
Jos 8:29 and as soon as the sun was **d.**,............ 935
Jos 8:29 should take his carcase **d.** from...........3381
Jos 10:11 in the going **d.** to Beth-horon,............ 4174
Jos 10:11 the Lord cast **d.** great stones from...........
Jos 10:13 hasted not to go **d.** about a whole day........
Jos 10:27 at the time of the going **d.** of the..............
Jos 10:27 and they took them **d.** off the trees,..... 3381
Jos 15:10 and went **d.** to Beth-shemesh, and...... 3381
Jos 16:3 goeth **d.** westward to the coast of....... 3381
Jos 16:7 And it went **d.** from Janohah to...........3381
Jos 17:15 and cut **d.** for thyself there in the.............
Jos 17:18 is a wood, and thou shalt cut it **d.**:............
Jos 18:16 border came **d.** to the end of the........ 3381
Jos 18:18 northward, and went **d.** unto.............. 3381
Jos 24:4 Jacob and his children went **d.**............ 3381
Jg 1:9 Judah went **d.** to fight against the........ 3381
Jg 1:34 not suffer them to come **d.** to the........ 3381
Jg 2:2 ye shall throw **d.** their altars:............. 5422
Jg 2:19 to serve them, and to bow **d.** unto...... 7812
Jg 3:25 their lord was fallen **d.** dead on the............
Jg 3:27 the children of Israel went **d.** with....... 3381
Jg 3:28 And they went **d.** after him, and.......... 3381
Jg 4:14 Barak went **d.** from mount Tabor,........ 3381
Jg 4:15 so that Sisera lighted **d.** off his........... 3381
Jg 5:11 people of the Lord go **d.** to the.......... 3381
Jg 5:14 out of Machi came **d.** governors,.........3381
Jg 5:21 thou hast trodden **d.** strength...................
Jg 5:27 feet he bowed, he fell, he lay **d.**;........ 7901
Jg 5:27 where he bowed, there he fell **d.**..............
Jg 6:25 and throw **d.** the altar of Baal that.......2040
Jg 6:25 hath, and cut **d.** the grove that is.............
Jg 6:26 the grove which thou shalt cut **d.**.............
Jg 6:28 the altar of Baal was cast **d.**,............. 5422
Jg 6:28 and the grove was cut **d.** that was............
Jg 6:30 because he hath cast **d.** the altar..............
Jg 6:30 and because he hath cut **d.** the..................
Jg 6:31 because one hath cast **d.** his altar........5422
Jg 6:32 because he hath thrown **d.** his altar..... 5422
Jg 7:4 bring them **d.** unto the water, and.......3381
Jg 7:5 So he brought **d.** the people unto the... 3381
Jg 7:5 that boweth **d.** upon his knees to.............
Jg 7:6 all the rest of the people bowed **d.**,...........
Jg 7:9 Arise, get thee **d.** unto the host;........ 3381
Jg 7:10 But if thou fear to go **d.**, go thou........3381
Jg 7:10 with Phurah thy servant **d.** to the....... 3381
Jg 7:11 hands be strengthened to go **d.**........... 3381
Jg 7:11 Then went he **d.** with Phurah his........ 3381
Jg 7:24 Come **d.** against the Midianites, and.... 3381
Jg 8:9 again in peace, I will break **d.** this....... 5242
Jg 8:17 And he beat **d.** the tower of Penuel,.... 5242
Jg 9:36 Behold, there come people **d.** from......3381
Jg 9:37 See there come people **d.** by the........ 3381
Jg 9:45 that was therein, and beat **d.** the........ 5422
Jg 9:48 and cut **d.** a bough from the trees,...........
Jg 9:49 all the people likewise cut **d.** every...........
Jg 11:37 go up and **d.** upon the mountains,....... 3381
Jg 14:1 And Samson went **d.** to Timnath,........ 3381
Jg 14:5 Then went Samson **d.**, and his........... 3381
Jg 14:7 And he went **d.**, and talked with the.... 3381
Jg 14:10 So his father went **d.** unto the............3381
Jg 14:18 seventh day before the sun went **d.**,.... 3381
Jg 14:19 and he went **d.** to Ashkelon, and.........3381
Jg 15:8 and he went **d.** and dwelt in the..........3381
Jg 15:12 We are come **d.** to bind thee, that.......3381
Jg 16:21 his eyes, and brought him **d.** to.......... 3381
Jg 16:31 the house of his fathers came **d.**,......... 3381
Jg 19:6 And they sat **d.**, and did eat and drink........
Jg 19:14 and the sun went **d.** upon them when.........
Jg 19:15 he sat him **d.** in a street of the city:..........
Jg 19:26 and fell **d.** at the door of the man's............
Jg 19:27 his concubine was fallen **d.** at the.............
Jg 20:21 of Gibeah, and destroyed **d.** to the............
Jg 20:25 destroyed **d.** to the ground of the............
Jg 20:32 They are smitten **d.** before us, as at..........
Jg 20:39 Surely they are smitten **d.** before us,.........
Jg 20:43 and trode them **d.** with ease over.............
Ru 3:3 upon thee, and get thee **d.** to the........3381
Ru 3:4 And it shall be, when he lieth **d.**,......... 7901
Ru 3:4 uncover his feet, and lay thee **d.**;........7901
Ru 3:6 And she went **d.** unto the floor,...........3381
Ru 3:7 he went to lie **d.** at the end of the...... 7901
Ru 3:7 uncovered his feet, and laid her **d.**...... 7901
Ru 3:13 liveth: lie **d.** until the morning............ 7901
Ru 4:1 up to the gate, and sat him **d.** there:.........
Ru 4:1 such a one! turn aside, sit **d.** here.............
Ru 4:1 And he turned aside, and sat **d.**.................
Ru 4:2 said, Sit ye **d.** here. And they sat **d.**...........
1Sa 2:6 he bringeth **d.** to the grave, and......... 3381
1Sa 3:2 when Eli was laid **d.** in his place,......... 7901
1Sa 3:3 and Samuel was laid **d.** to sleep;.......... 7901
1Sa 3:5 lie **d.** again. And he...lay **d.**................ 7901
1Sa 3:6 I called not, my son; lie **d.** again.......... 7901
1Sa 3:9 Eli said unto Samuel, Go, lie **d.**:........... 7901
1Sa 3:9 went and lay **d.** in his place............... 7901
1Sa 6:15 And the Levites took **d.** the ark of...... 3381
1Sa 6:18 Abel, whereon they set **d.** the ark............
1Sa 6:21 the ark of the Lord; come ye **d.**,......... 3381
1Sa 9:25 come **d.** from the high place into.......... 3381
1Sa 9:27 were going **d.** to the end of the city,... 3381
1Sa 10:5 coming **d.** from the high place............ 3381
1Sa 10:8 shalt go **d.** before me to Gilgal;.......... 3381
1Sa 10:8 behold, I will come **d.** unto thee,......... 3381
1Sa 13:12 The Philistines will come **d.** now.......... 3381
1Sa 13:20 Israelites went **d.** to the Philistines,..... 3381
1Sa 14:16 went on beating **d.** one another................
1Sa 14:36 Let us go **d.** after the Philistines.........3381
1Sa 14:37 Shall I go **d.** after the Philistines?........3381
1Sa 15:6 get you **d.** from among the................ 3381
1Sa 15:12 passed on, and gone **d.** to Gilgal......... 3381
1Sa 16:11 we will not sit **d.** till he come hither..........
1Sa 17:8 you, and let him come **d.** to me...........3381
1Sa 17:28 said, Why comest thou **d.** hither?......... 3381
1Sa 17:28 thou art come **d.** that thou mightest.....3381
1Sa 17:52 Philistines fell **d.** by the way to.................
1Sa 19:12 let David **d.** through a window:...........3381
1Sa 19:24 lay **d.** naked all that day and all.................
1Sa 20:19 then thou shalt go **d.** quickly,............. 3381
1Sa 20:24 the king sat him **d.** to eat meat.................
1Sa 21:13 his spittle fall **d.** upon his beard.......... 3381
1Sa 22:1 it, they went **d.** thither to him............3381
1Sa 23:4 and said, Arise, go **d.** to Keilah;.......... 3381
1Sa 23:6 came **d.** with an ephod in his hand.......3381
1Sa 23:8 to go **d.** to Keilah, to besiege David.... 3381
1Sa 23:11 And the Lord said, He will come **d.**...... 3381
1Sa 23:11 come **d.** as thy servant hath heard?..... 3381
1Sa 23:20 O king, come **d.** according to all......... 3381
1Sa 23:20 the desire of thy soul to come **d.**;......... 3381
1Sa 23:25 wherefore he came **d.** into a rock,........3381
1Sa 25:1 went **d.** to the wilderness of Paran...... 3381
1Sa 25:20 that she came **d.** by the covert of....... 3381
1Sa 25:20 and his men came **d.** against her;......... 3381
1Sa 26:2 Saul arose, and went **d.** to the........... 3381
1Sa 26:6 Who will go **d.** with me to Saul to....... 3381
1Sa 26:6 Abishai said, I will go **d.** with thee.......3381
1Sa 29:4 let him not go **d.** with us to battle,...... 3381
1Sa 30:15 Canst thou bring me **d.** to this............3381
1Sa 30:15 will bring thee **d.** to this company......... 3381
1Sa 30:16 And when he had brought him **d.**,........ 3381
1Sa 30:24 part is that goeth **d.** to the battle,........ 3381
1Sa 31:1 and fell **d.** slain in mount Gilboa................
2Sa 2:16 so they fell **d.** together: wherefore.............
2Sa 2:13 the pool of Gideon: and they sat **d.**.............
2Sa 2:23 and he fell **d.** there, and died in................
2Sa 2:23 where Asahel fell **d.** and died stood...........
2Sa 2:24 and the sun went **d.** when they were.........
2Sa 3:35 or ought else, till the sun be **d.**............935
2Sa 5:17 of it, and went **d.** to the hold............. 3381
2Sa 8:2 with a line, casting them **d.** to the....... 7901
2Sa 11:8 Go **d.** to thy house, and wash thy....... 3381
2Sa 11:9 lord, and went not **d.** to his house,...... 3381
2Sa 11:10 Uriah went not **d.** unto his house,....... 3381
2Sa 11:10 why then didst thou not go **d.** unto...... 3381
2Sa 11:13 servants of his lord, but went not **d.**..... 3381
2Sa 13:5 Lay thee **d.** on thy bed, and make....... 7901
2Sa 13:6 So Amnon lay **d.** and made himelf....... 7901
2Sa 13:8 Amnon's house; and he was laid **d.**........ 7901
2Sa 15:20 make thee go up and **d.** with us?........ 5128
2Sa 15:24 and they set **d.** the ark of God;.......... 3332
2Sa 17:18 court; whither they went **d.**................ 3381
2Sa 18:28 he fell **d.** to the earth upon his........... 7812
2Sa 19:16 hasted and came **d.** with the men........3381
2Sa 19:18 Shimei the son of Gera fell **d.** before..........

2Sa 19:20 of all the house of Joseph to go **d.** 3381
2Sa 19:24 Mephibosheth the son of Saul came **d.** 3381
2Sa 19:31 Gileadite came **d.** from Rogelim, 3381
2Sa 20:15 battered the wall, to throw it **d.** 5307
2Sa 21:15 and David went **d.**, and his 3381
2Sa 22:10 the heavens also, and came **d.**; 3381
2Sa 22:28 that thou mayest bring them **d.** 3381
2Sa 22:48 and that bringest **d.** the people 8213
2Sa 23:13 of the thirty chief went **d.**, 3381
2Sa 23:20 he went **d.** also and slew a lion in 3381
2Sa 23:21 but he went **d.** to him with a staff 3381
1Ki 1:25 he is gone **d.** this day, and hath slain 3381
1Ki 1:33 mule, and bring him **d.** to Gihon; 3381
1Ki 1:38 and the Pelethites, went **d.**, and 3381
1Ki 1:53 and they brought him **d.** from the 3381
1Ki 2:6 let not his hoar head go **d.** to the 3381
1Ki 2:8 he came **d.** to meet me at Jordan, 3381
1Ki 2:9 his hoar head bring thou **d.** to the 3381
1Ki 2:19 and sat **d.** on his throne, and caused a
1Ki 5:9 shall bring them **d.** from Lebanon 3381
1Ki 8:33 When thy people Israel be smitten **d.**
1Ki 17:23 and brought him **d.** out of the 3381
1Ki 18:30 altar of the lord that was broken **d.**
1Ki 18:40 Elijah brought them **d.** to the 3281
1Ki 18:42 he cast himself **d.** upon the earth, 1457
1Ki 18:44 and get thee **d.**, that the rain stop 3381
1Ki 19:4 and came and sat down under a
1Ki 19:6 and drink, and laid him **d.** again 7901
1Ki 19:10 covenant, thrown **d.** thine altars, 2040
1Ki 19:14 thrown **d.** thine altars, and slain 2040
1Ki 21:4 And he laid him **d.** upon his bed, 7901
1Ki 21:16 Ahab rose up to go **d.** to the 3381
1Ki 21:18 Arise, go **d.** to meet Ahab king of 3381
1Ki 21:18 whither he is gone **d.** to possess it 3381
1Ki 22:2 the king of Judah came **d.** to the 3381
1Ki 22:36 about the going **d.** of the sun,
2Ki 1:2 And Ahaziah fell **d.** through a
2Ki 1:4 Thou shalt not come **d.** from that 3381
2Ki 1:6 therefore thou shalt not come **d.** 3381
2Ki 1:9 God, the king hath said, Come **d.** 3381
2Ki 1:10 let fire come **d.** from heaven, and 3381
2Ki 1:10 thy fifty. And there came **d.** fire 3381
2Ki 1:11 the king said, Come **d.** quickly 3381
2Ki 1:12 let fire come **d.** from heaven, and 3381
2Ki 1:12 fifty. And the fire of God came **d.** 3381
2Ki 1:14 Behold, there came **d.** fire from 3381
2Ki 1:15 Go **d.** with him: be not afraid of 3381
2Ki 1:15 he arose, and went **d.** with him unto 3381
2Ki 1:16 thou shalt not come **d.** off that bed 3381
2Ki 2:2 thee. So they went **d.** to Beth-el 3381
2Ki 3:12 the king of Edom went **d.** to him. 3381
2Ki 3:25 And they beat **d.** the cities, and 2040
2Ki 5:14 went he **d.**, and dipped himself 3381
2Ki 5:18 I bow **d.** myself in the house of 7812
2Ki 5:21 he lighted **d.** from his chariot to
2Ki 6:4 to the Jordan they cut **d.** wood,
2Ki 6:6 And he cut **d.** a stick, and cast it
2Ki 6:9 thither the Syrians are come **d.** 5181
2Ki 6:18 And when they came **d.** to him, 3381
2Ki 6:33 the messenger came **d.** unto him: 3381
2Ki 7:17 when the king came **d.** to him. 3381
2Ki 8:29 king of Judah went **d.** to see Joram 3381
2Ki 9:16 Judah was come **d.** to see Joram. 3381
2Ki 9:24 and he sunk **d.** in his chariot.
2Ki 9:33 Throw her **d.** So...threw her **d.**: 8058
2Ki 10:13 we go **d.** to salute the children of 3381
2Ki 10:27 they brake **d.** the image of Baal. 5422
2Ki 10:27 and brake **d.** the house of Baal. 5422
2Ki 11:6 house, that it be not broken **d.** 4535
2Ki 11:18 the house of Baal, and break it **d.**; 5422
2Ki 11:19 they brought **d.** the king from the 3381
2Ki 12:20 of Millo, which goeth **d.** to Silla. 3381
2Ki 13:14 king of Israel came **d.** unto him, 3381
2Ki 13:21 and when the man was let **d.**, and 3212
2Ki 14:9 in Lebanon, and trode **d.** the thistle.
2Ki 14:13 brake **d.** the wall of Jerusalem
2Ki 16:17 and took **d.** the sea from off the 3381
2Ki 18:4 and cut **d.** the groves, and brake
2Ki 19:16 Lord, bow **d.** thine ear, and hear: 5186
2Ki 19:23 and will cut **d.** the tall cedars
2Ki 20:10 the shadow to go **d.** ten degrees: 5186
2Ki 20:11 by which it had gone **d.** in the 3381
2Ki 21:13 wiping it, and turning it upside **d.**
2Ki 23:5 he put **d.** the idolatrous priests, 7673
2Ki 23:7 And he brake **d.** the houses of the 5422
2Ki 23:8 and brake **d.** the high places of
2Ki 23:12 did the king beat **d.**, and
2Ki 23:12 and brake them **d.** from thence, 7323
2Ki 23:14 and cut **d.** the groves, and filled
2Ki 23:15 and the high places he brake **d.**, 5422
2Ki 25:10 brake **d.** the walls of Jerusalem 5422
1Ch 5:22 For there fell **d.** many slain, 5422
1Ch 7:21 because they came **d.** to take 3381
1Ch 10:1 and fell **d.** slain in mount Gilboa.
1Ch 11:15 went **d.** to the rock to David, into 3381
1Ch 11:22 he went **d.** and slew a lion in a pit 3381
1Ch 11:23 and he went **d.** to him with a staff, 3381
1Ch 29:20 and bowed **d.** their heads, and 6915
2Ch 6:13 kneeled **d.** upon his knees before
2Ch 7:1 the fire came **d.** from heaven, 3381
2Ch 7:3 of Israel saw how the fire came **d.**, 3381
2Ch 13:17 so there fell **d.** slain of Israel five
2Ch 14:3 and brake **d.** the images,
2Ch 14:3 and cut **d.** the groves:
2Ch 15:16 Asa cut **d.** her idol, and stamped
2Ch 18:2 certain years he went **d.** to Ahab 3381
2Ch 18:34 time of the sun going **d.** he died
2Ch 20:16 To morrow go ye **d.** against them; 3381
2Ch 22:6 Jehoram king of Judah went **d.** to 3381
2Ch 23:17 the house of Baal, and brake it **d.**, 5422
2Ch 23:20 and brought **d.** the king from the 3381
2Ch 25:8 power to help, and to cast **d.** 3782
2Ch 25:12 cast them **d.** from the top of the rock,
2Ch 25:14 and bowed **d.** himself before them, 7812
2Ch 25:18 Lebanon, and trode **d.** the thistle.
2Ch 25:23 brake **d.** the wall of Jerusalem
2Ch 26:6 and brake **d.** the wall of Gath, and
2Ch 31:1 in pieces, and **d.** the groves, and 1438
2Ch 31:1 and threw **d.** the high places and 5422
2Ch 32:30 brought it straight **d.** to the west 4295
2Ch 33:3 Hezekiah his father had broken **d.**, 5422
2Ch 34:4 brake **d.** the altars of Baalim in 5422
2Ch 34:4 on high above them, he cut **d.**; 1438
2Ch 34:7 when he had broken **d.** the altars 5422
2Ch 34:7 powder, and cut **d.** all the idols 1438
2Ch 36:3 the king of Egypt put him **d.** at 5493
2Ch 36:19 brake **d.** the wall of Jerusalem, 5422
Ezr 6:11 be pulled **d.** from his house,
Ezr 9:3 of my beard, and sat **d.** astonied.
Ezr 10:1 weeping and casting himself **d.** 5307
Ezr 10:16 sat **d.** in the first day of the tenth
Ne 1:3 of Jerusalem also is broken **d.**,
Ne 1:4 I sat **d.** and wept, and mourned
Ne 2:13 Jerusalem, which were broken **d.**,
Ne 3:15 the stairs that go **d.** from the city 3381
Ne 4:3 even break **d.** their stone wall.
Ne 6:3 I cannot come **d.**: why should the 3381
Ne 6:3 I leave it, and come **d.** to you? 3381
Ne 6:16 much cast **d.** in their own eyes: 5307
Ne 9:13 camest **d.** also upon mount Sinai, 3381
Es 3:15 the king and Haman sat **d.** to drink;
Es 8:3 fell **d.** at his feet, and besought
Job 1:7 and from walking up and **d.** in it.
Job 1:20 and fell **d.** upon the ground, and
Job 2:2 and from walking up and **d.** in it.
Job 2:8 and he sat **d.** among the ashes
Job 2:13 they sat **d.** with him upon the ground
Job 6:21 see my casting **d.** and are afraid
Job 7:4 When I lie **d.**, I say, When shall I 7901
Job 7:9 so he that goeth **d.** to the grave 3381
Job 7:19 me alone till I swallow **d.** my spittle?
Job 8:12 and not cut **d.**, it withereth before
Job 11:19 Also thou shalt lie **d.**, and none 7257
Job 12:14 breaketh **d.**, and it cannot be built 2040
Job 14:2 forth as a flower, and is cut **d.**:
Job 14:7 is hope of a tree, if it be cut **d.**,
Job 14:12 So man lieth **d.**, and riseth not: 7901
Job 17:3 Lay **d.** now, put me in a surety
Job 17:16 shall go **d.** to the bars of the pit, 3381
Job 18:7 and his counsel shall cast him **d.**
Job 20:11 shall lie **d.** with him in the dust. 7901
Job 20:15 He hath swallowed **d.** riches, and he
Job 20:18 shall not swallow it **d.**: according
Job 21:13 in a moment go **d.** to the grave. 5181
Job 21:26 They shall lie **d.** alike in the dust, 7901
Job 22:16 Which were cut **d.** out of time,
Job 22:20 our substance is not cut **d.**, but
Job 22:29 When men are cast **d.**, then thou 8213
Job 27:19 The rich man shall lie **d.**, but he 7901
Job 29:24 my countenance they cast not **d.** 5307
Job 31:10 and let others bow **d.** upon her 3766
Job 32:13 God thrusteth him **d.**, not man
Job 33:24 him from going **d.** to the pit: 3381
Job 36:27 they pour **d.** rain according to the
Job 40:12 and tread **d.** the wicked in their place
Job 41:1 with a cord which thou lettest **d.**? 8257
Job 41:9 one be cast **d.** even at the sight 2904
Ps 3:5 I laid me **d.** and slept; I awaked: 7901
Ps 4:8 both lay me **d.** in peace, and sleep; 7901
Ps 7:5 yea, let him tread **d.** my life upon the
Ps 7:16 dealing shall come **d.** upon his 3381
Ps 9:15 The heathen are sunk **d.** in the pit
Ps 14:2 Lord looked **d.** from heaven upon
Ps 17:11 have set their eyes bowing **d.** to 5186
Ps 17:13 disappoint him, cast him **d.** 3766
Ps 18:9 the heavens also, and came **d.**: 3381
Ps 18:27 but wilt bring **d.** high looks. 8213
Ps 20:8 They are brought **d.** and fallen: 3766
Ps 22:29 that go **d.** to the dust shall bow 3381
Ps 23:2 me to lie **d.** in green pastures, 7257
Ps 28:1 like them that go **d.** into the pit. 3381
Ps 30:3 that I should not go **d.** to the pit. 3381
Ps 30:9 in my blood, when I go **d.** to the pit? 3381
Ps 31:2 Bow **d.** thine ear to me; deliver 5186
Ps 35:14 I bowed **d.** heavily, as one that 7817
Ps 36:12 they are cast **d.**, and shall not be 1760
Ps 37:2 For they shall soon be cut **d.** like 5243
Ps 37:14 to cast **d.** the poor and needy, and 5307
Ps 37:24 he shall not be utterly cast **d.**: for 2904
Ps 38:6 I am bowed **d.** greatly; I go 7817
Ps 42:5 Why art thou cast **d.**, O my soul? 7817
Ps 42:6 God, my soul is cast **d.** within me: 7817
Ps 42:11 Why art thou cast **d.**, O my soul? 7817
Ps 43:5 Why art thou cast **d.**, O my soul? 7817
Ps 44:5 thee will we push **d.** our enemies:
Ps 44:25 our soul is bowed **d.** to the dust: 7743
Ps 50:1 the sun unto the going **d.** thereof.
Ps 53:2 God looked **d.** from heaven upon
Ps 55:15 let them go **d.** quick into hell: 3381
Ps 55:23 shalt bring them **d.** into the pit of 3381
Ps 56:7 thine anger cast **d.** the people, O God.
Ps 57:6 my soul is bowed **d.**; they have
Ps 59:11 bring them **d.**, O Lord our shield. 3381
Ps 59:15 Let them wander up and **d.** for meat,
Ps 60:12 it is that shall tread **d.** our enemies,
Ps 62:4 They only consult to cast him **d.**
Ps 72:6 He shall come **d.** like rain upon 3381
Ps 72:11 all kings shall fall **d.** before him: 7812
Ps 73:18 castedst them **d.** into destruction 5307
Ps 74:6 they break **d.** the carved work
Ps 74:7 by casting **d.** the dwellingplace
Ps 75:7 he putteth **d.** one, and setteth up 8213
Ps 78:16 caused waters to run **d.** like rivers.
Ps 78:24 And had rained **d.** manna upon them
Ps 78:31 smote **d.** the chosen men of Israel. 3766
Ps 80:12 thou then broken **d.** her hedges,
Ps 80:14 look **d.** from heaven, and behold,
Ps 80:16 It is burned with fire, it is cut **d.**:
Ps 85:11 shall look **d.** from heaven.
Ps 86:1 Bow **d.** thine ear, O Lord, hear 5186
Ps 88:4 am counted with them that go **d.** 3381
Ps 89:23 I will beat **d.** his foes before his
Ps 89:40 hast broken **d.** all his hedges;
Ps 89:44 cast his throne **d.** to the ground.
Ps 90:6 in the evening it is cut **d.**, and
Ps 95:6 come, let us worship and bow **d.**: 3766
Ps 102:10 hast lifted me up, and cast me **d.**
Ps 102:19 he hath looked **d.** from the height
Ps 104:8 they go **d.** by the valleys unto 3381
Ps 104:19 the sun knoweth his going **d.**
Ps 104:22 and lay them **d.** in their dens. 7257
Ps 107:12 brought **d.** their heart with labour; 3665
Ps 107:12 they fell **d.**, and there was none 3782
Ps 107:23 that go **d.** to the sea in ships, 3381
Ps 107:26 they go **d.** again to the depths: 3381
Ps 108:13 he that shall tread **d.** our enemies.
Ps 109:23 am tossed up and **d.** as the locust.
Ps 113:3 sun unto the going **d.** of the same
Ps 115:17 any that go **d.** into silence 3381
Ps 119:118 hast trodden **d.** all them that err
Ps 119:136 Rivers of waters run **d.** mine eyes,
Ps 133:2 head, that ran **d.** upon the beard, 3381
Ps 133:2 that went **d.** to the skirts of his 3381
Ps 137:1 rivers of Babylon, there we sat **d.**,
Ps 139:3 my path and my lying **d.** 7252
Ps 143:3 smitten my life **d.** to the ground;
Ps 143:7 unto them that go **d.** into the pit. 3381
Ps 144:5 thy heavens, O Lord, and come **d.**: 3381
Ps 145:14 up all those that be bowed **d.**
Ps 146:8 raiseth them that are bowed **d.**:

Ps 146:9 the wicked he turneth upside **d.**..............
Ps 147:6 casteth the wicked **d.** to the.............. 8213
Pr 1:12 as those that go **d.** into the pit: 3381
Pr 3:20 and the clouds drop **d.** the dew.......... 7491
Pr 3:24 When thou liest **d.**, thou shalt not 7901
Pr 3:24 thou shalt lie **d.**, and thy sleep.......... 7901
Pr 5:5 Her feet go **d.** to death;.................. 3381
Pr 7:26 she hath cast **d.** many wounded: ....
Pr 7:27 to hell, going **d.** to the chambers........ 3381
Pr 14:1 plucketh it **d.** with her hands............ 8045
Pr 18:8 go **d.** into the innermost parts of......... 3381
Pr 21:22 and casteth **d.** the strength of the 3381
Pr 22:17 Bow **d.** thine ear, and hear the.......... 5186
Pr 23:34 lieth **d.** in the midst of the sea,.......... 7901
Pr 24:31 stone wall thereof was broken **d.**......... 2040
Pr 25:26 A righteous man falling **d.** before..............
Pr 25:28 is like a city that is broken **d.**,..............
Pr 26:22 go **d.** into the innermost parts of......... 3381
Ec 1:5 also ariseth, and the sun goeth **d.**,............
Ec 3:3 a time to break **d.**, and a time to ....
Ca 2:3 I sat **d.** under his shadow with great........
Ca 6:2 beloved is gone **d.** into his garden, ... 3381
Ca 6:11 I went **d.** into the garden of nuts 3381
Ca 7:9 that goeth **d.** sweetly, causing the...........
Isa 2:9 And the mean man boweth **d.**,........... 7817
Isa 2:11 shall be bowed **d.**,............................ 7817
Isa 2:17 loftiness of man shall be bowed **d.**, ... 7817
Isa 5:5 and break **d.** the wall thereof,..................
Isa 5:5 and it shall be trodden **d.**:......................
Isa 5:15 mean man shall be brought **d.**,........... 7817
Isa 9:10 The bricks are fallen **d.**, but we..............
Isa 9:10 the sycamores are cut **d.**, but we....... 1438
Isa 10:4 Without me they shall bow **d.**............ 3766
Isa 10:6 and to tread them **d.** like the mire...........
Isa 10:13 I have put **d.** the inhabitants like........ 3381
Isa 10:33 ones of stature shall be hewn **d.**, ... 1438
Isa 10:34 And he shall cut **d.** the thickets..............
Isa 11:6 leopard shall lie **d.** with the kid;......... 7257
Isa 11:7 young ones shall lie **d.** together: 7257
Isa 14:8 Since thou art laid **d.**, no feller is 7901
Isa 14:11 pomp is brought **d.** to the grave,......... 3381
Isa 14:12 art thou cut **d.** to the ground,........... 1438
Isa 14:15 thou shalt be brought **d.** to hell,......... 3381
Isa 14:19 that go **d.** to the stones of the pit; 3381
Isa 14:30 the needy shall lie **d.** in safety: 7257
Isa 16:8 of the heathen have broken **d.**..................
Isa 17:2 be for flocks, which shall lie **d.**, ... 7257
Isa 18:2 a nation meted out and trodden **d.**,...........
Isa 18:5 away and cut **d.** the branches....................
Isa 21:3 was bowed **d.** at the hearing of it;...........
Isa 22:5 day of trouble, and of treading **d.**,...........
Isa 22:5 breaking **d.** the walls, and of ....
Isa 22:10 and the houses have ye broken **d.**....... 5422
Isa 22:19 from thy state shall he pull thee **d.**.........
Isa 22:25 and be cut **d.**, and fall;...................... 1438
Isa 24:1 it waste, and turneth it upside **d.**,...........
Isa 24:10 The city of confusion is broken **d.**:..........
Isa 24:19 The earth is utterly broken **d.**, ...
Isa 25:5 bring **d.** the noise of strangers,.......... 3665
Isa 25:10 Moab shall be trodden **d.** under................
Isa 25:10 straw is trodden **d.** for the dunghill..........
Isa 25:11 and he shall bring **d.** their pride 8213
Isa 25:12 fort of thy walls shall he bring **d.**,....... 7817
Isa 26:5 bringeth **d.** them that dwell on........... 7817
Isa 26:6 The foot shall tread it **d.**,.......................
Isa 27:10 and there shall he lie **d.**,.................... 7257
Isa 28:2 cast **d.** to the earth with the hand. ....
Isa 28:18 then ye shall be trodden **d.** by it. ....
Isa 29:4 And thou shalt be brought **d.**,............ 8213
Isa 29:16 your turning of things upside **d.**...............
Isa 30:2 That walk to go **d.** into Egypt, ... 3381
Isa 30:30 show the lighting **d.** of his arm, ... 5183
Isa 30:31 shall the Assyrian be beaten **d.**, ...
Isa 31:1 that go **d.** to Egypt for help; 3381
Isa 31:3 he that is holpen shall fall **d.**,...................
Isa 31:4 so shall the Lord of hosts come **d.** 3381
Isa 32:19 hail, coming **d.** on the forest; 3381
Isa 33:9 Lebanon is ashamed and hewn **d.**: ....
Isa 33:20 that shall not be taken **d.**;......................
Isa 34:4 and all their host shall fall **d.**,................
Isa 34:5 it shall come **d.** upon Idumea,............ 3381
Isa 34:7 unicorn shall come **d.** with them,........ 3381
Isa 37:24 will cut **d.** the tall cedars thereof,..........
Isa 38:8 is gone **d.** in the sun dial of Ahaz, ...
Isa 38:8 by which degrees it was gone **d.**. ....
Isa 38:18 they that go **d.** into the pit cannot...... 3381

Isa 42:10 ye that go **d.** to the sea, and all......... 3381
Isa 43:14 have brought **d.** all their nobles,......... 3381
Isa 43:17 they shall lie **d.** together, they shall.... 3381
Isa 44:14 He heweth him **d.** cedars,......................
Isa 44:15 it a graven image, and falleth **d.**.......... 5456
Isa 44:17 falleth **d.** unto it, and worshippeth 5456
Isa 44:19 fall **d.** to the stock of a tree?............ 5456
Isa 45:8 Drop **d.**, ye heavens, from above, ...
Isa 45:8 the skies pour **d.** righteousness:..............
Isa 45:14 and they shall fall **d.** unto thee,.......... 7812
Isa 46:1 Bel boweth **d.**, Nebo stoopeth, ... 3766
Isa 46:2 They stoop, they bow **d.** together; 3766
Isa 46:6 they fall **d.**, yea, they worship. 5456
Isa 47:1 Come **d.**, and sit in the dust,............. 3381
Isa 49:23 shall bow **d.** to thee with their........... 7812
Isa 50:11 ye shall lie **d.** in sorrow.................... 7901
Isa 51:23 Bow **d.**, that we may go over:........... 7812
Isa 52:2 arise, and sit **d.**, O Jerusalem: ....
Isa 52:4 went **d.** aforetime into Egypt............. 3381
Isa 55:10 For as the rain cometh **d.**, and the..... 3381
Isa 56:10 sleeping, lying **d.**, loving to.............. 7901
Isa 58:5 to bow **d.** his head as a bulrush, ...
Isa 60:14 **d.** at the soles of thy feet;................ 7812
Isa 60:20 Thy sun shall no more go **d.**;..................
Isa 63:6 And I will tread **d.** the people in..............
Isa 63:6 and I will bring **d.** their strength..............
Isa 63:14 a beast goeth **d.** into the valley,.......... 3381
Isa 63:15 Look **d.** from heaven, ...
Isa 63:18 our adversaries have trodden **d.** thy..........
Isa 64:1 that thou wouldest come **d.**,............... 3381
Isa 64:1 the mountains might flow **d.** at................
Isa 64:3 looked not for, thou camest **d.**,........... 3381
Isa 64:3 mountains flowed **d.** at thy....................
Isa 65:10 place for the herds to lie **d.** in, ... 7257
Isa 65:12 shall all bow **d.** to the slaughter; 3766
Jer 1:10 to root out, and to pull **d.**, and to...........
Jer 1:10 throw **d.**, to build, and to plant. 2040
Jer 3:25 We lie **d.** in our shame,.................... 7901
Jer 4:26 the cities thereof were broken **d.** 5422
Jer 6:6 Hew ye **d.** trees, and cast a mount...........
Jer 6:15 they shall be cast **d.**, saith the........... 3782
Jer 8:12 they shall be cast **d.**, saith the Lord.... 3782
Jer 9:18 our eyes may run **d.** with tears,..............
Jer 13:17 and run **d.** with tears, because.................
Jer 13:18 Humble yourselves, sit **d.**: for ....
Jer 13:18 your principalities shall come **d.**,.......... 3381
Jer 14:17 Let mine eyes run **d.** with tears...............
Jer 15:9 sun is gone **d.** while it was yet day:..........
Jer 18:2 and go **d.** to the potter's house,.......... 3381
Jer 18:3 Then I went **d.** to the potter's........... 3381
Jer 18:7 and to pull **d.**, and to destroy it; ....
Jer 21:13 Who shall come **d.** against us? 5181
Jer 22:1 Go **d.** to the house of the king........... 3381
Jer 22:7 shall cut **d.** thy choice cedars,...............
Jer 24:6 build them, and not pull them **d.**;.............
Jer 25:37 cut **d.** because of the fierce anger............
Jer 26:10 sat **d.** in the entry of the new gate..........
Jer 31:28 pluck up, and to break **d.**, and........... 5422
Jer 31:28 and to throw **d.**, and to destroy.......... 2040
Jer 31:40 nor thrown **d.** any more for ever........ 2040
Jer 33:4 are thrown **d.** by the mounts,............ 5422
Jer 33:12 causing their flock to lie **d.**................ 7901
Jer 36:12 went **d.** into the king's house, ... 3381
Jer 36:15 Sit **d.** now, and read it in our ears...........
Jer 38:6 they let **d.** Jeremiah with cords........... 7971
Jer 38:11 and let them **d.** by cords into the....... 7971
Jer 39:8 brake **d.** the walls of Jerusalem. 5422
Jer 42:10 and not pull you **d.**, and I will..................
Jer 45:4 which I have built will I break **d.**,....... 2040
Jer 46:5 their mighty ones are beaten **d.**, ...
Jer 46:23 They shall cut **d.** her forest,....................
Jer 48:2 thou shalt be cut **d.**, O Madmen;..............
Jer 48:5 for in the going **d.** of Horonaim.......... 4174
Jer 48:15 men are gone **d.** to the slaughter, ... 3381
Jer 48:18 come **d.** from thy glory, and sit in...... 3381
Jer 48:20 it is broken **d.**: howl and cry; ....
Jer 48:39 How is it broken **d.**! how hath.................
Jer 49:16 I will bring thee **d.** from thence, ... 3381
Jer 50:15 her walls are thrown **d.**: for it is 2040
Jer 50:27 bullocks; let them go **d.** to the........... 3381
Jer 51:25 and roll thee **d.** from the rocks, and..........
Jer 51:40 I will bring them **d.** like lambs to........ 3381
Jer 52:14 brake **d.** all the walls of Jerusalem...... 5422
La 1:9 she came **d.** wonderfully:.................... 3381
La 1:16 mine eye runneth **d.** with water, ...
La 2:1 and cast **d.** from heaven unto ....
La 2:2 he hath thrown **d.** in his wrath........... 2040

La 2:2 brought them **d.** to the ground:................
La 2:10 hang **d.** their heads to the ground....... 3381
La 2:17 thrown **d.**, and hath not pitied: 2040
La 2:18 tears run **d.** like a river day and night: ......
La 3:48 eye runneth **d.** with rivers of water ....
La 3:49 eye trickleth **d.**, and ceaseth not, ...
La 3:50 Till the Lord look **d.**, and behold..............
La 3:63 their sitting **d.**, and their rising up; ....
Eze 1:13 it went up and **d.** among the living...........
Eze 1:24 they stood, they let **d.** their wings...... 7503
Eze 1:25 stood, and had let **d.** their wings........ 7503
Eze 6:4 and I will cast **d.** your slain men 5307
Eze 6:6 and your images may be cut **d.**, ... 1438
Eze 11:13 Then fell I **d.** upon my face, and ....
Eze 13:14 I break **d.** the wall that ye have......... 2040
Eze 13:14 and bring it **d.** to the ground, ...
Eze 16:39 throw **d.** thine eminent place, ... 2040
Eze 16:39 shall break **d.** thy high places: 5422
Eze 17:24 have brought **d.** the high tree, ... 8213
Eze 19:2 thy mother? A lioness: she lay **d.**........ 7257
Eze 19:6 went up and **d.** among the lions, ...
Eze 19:12 she was cast **d.** to the ground, ...
Eze 24:16 neither shall thy tears run **d.**..................
Eze 26:4 and break **d.** her towers: I will 2040
Eze 26:9 axes he shall break **d.** thy towers........ 5422
Eze 26:11 shall he tread **d.** all thy streets: he...........
Eze 26:11 shall go **d.** to the ground.................. 3381
Eze 26:12 and they shall break **d.** thy walls, ... 2040
Eze 26:16 shall come **d.** from their thrones, ... 3381
Eze 26:20 I shall bring thee **d.** with them........... 3381
Eze 26:20 with them that go **d.** to the pit, ... 3381
Eze 27:29 shall come **d.** from their ships,............ 3381
Eze 28:8 They shall bring thee **d.** to the pit, ... 3381
Eze 28:14 thou hast walked up and **d.** in the............
Eze 30:4 her foundations shall be broken **d.**, ... 2040
Eze 30:6 pride of her power shall come **d.**:.......... 3381
Eze 30:25 the arms of Pharoah shall fall **d.**; ....
Eze 31:12 are gone **d.** from his shadow, and.............
Eze 31:14 with them that go **d.** to the pit........... 3381
Eze 31:15 day when he went **d.** to the grave...... 3381
Eze 31:16 when I cast him **d.** to hell with.......... 3381
Eze 31:17 They also went **d.** into hell with......... 3381
Eze 31:18 thou be brought **d.** wih the trees........ 3381
Eze 32:18 and cast them **d.**, even her, and the ... 3381
Eze 32:18 with them that go **d.** into the pit. 3381
Eze 32:19 go **d.**, and be thou laid with the 3381
Eze 32:21 gone **d.**, they lie uncircumcised, ... 3381
Eze 32:24 are gone **d.** uncircumcised into........... 3381
Eze 32:24 with them that go **d.** to the pit. 3381
Eze 32:25 that go **d.** to the pit: he is put in......... 3381
Eze 32:27 gone **d.** to hell with their weapons...... 3381
Eze 32:29 with them that go **d.** to the pit. 3381
Eze 32:30 which are gone **d.** with the slain;......... 3381
Eze 32:30 with them that go **d.** to the pit. 3381
Eze 34:15 them to lie **d.**, saith the Lord God...... 7901
Eze 34:18 ye must tread **d.** with your feet the..........
Eze 34:26 I will cause the shower to come **d.**........ 3381
Eze 37:1 and set me **d.** in the midst of a valley ....
Eze 38:20 the mountains shall be thrown **d.**,........ 2040
Eze 39:10 cut **d.** any out of the forests; for.............
Eze 47:1 came **d.** from under from the right 3381
Eze 47:8 and go **d.** into the desert, and go 3381
Da 3:5 ye fall **d.** and worship the golden.............
Da 3:6 falleth not **d.** and worshippeth..................
Da 3:7 fell **d.** and worshipped the golden ....
Da 3:10 shall fall **d.** and worship the golden ....
Da 3:11 falleth not **d.** and worshippeth,..................
Da 3:15 ye fall **d.** and worship the image................
Da 3:23 fell **d.** bound into the midst of the..............
Da 4:13 an holy one came **d.** from heaven; 5182
Da 4:14 Hew **d.** the tree, and cut off his...............
Da 4:23 one coming **d.** from heaven, and 5182
Da 4:23 Hew the tree **d.**, and destroy it; ....
Da 5:19 and whom he would he put **d.**. 8214
Da 6:14 till the going **d.** of the sun 4606
Da 7:9 till the thrones were cast **d.**, and.............
Da 7:23 and shall tread it **d.** and break it...............
Da 8:7 but he cast him **d.** to the ground,.............
Da 8:10 and it cast **d.** some of the host.......... 5307
Da 8:11 place of his sanctuary was cast **d.**.............
Da 8:12 and it cast **d.** the truth to the....................
Da 11:12 shall cast **d.** many ten thousands: 5307
Da 11:26 and many shall fall **d.** slain. ....
Ho 2:18 will make them to lie **d.** safely........... 7901

Ho 7:12 I will bring them d. as the fowls ... 3381
Ho 10:2 he shall break d. their altars, he...
Joe 1:17 the barns are broken d.; for the... 2040
Joe 2:23 cause to come d. for you the rain,... 3381
Joe 3:2 will bring them d. into the valley... 3381
Joe 3:11 mighty ones to come d., O Lord,... 5181
Joe 3:13 come, get you d.; for the press is... 3381
Joe 3:18 mountains shall drop d. new wine...
Am 2:8 lay themselves d. upon clothes...
Am 3:11 and he shall bring d. thy strength... 3381
Am 5:24 let judgment run d. as waters, and...
Am 6:2 go d. to Gath of the Philistines:... 3381
Am 8:9 the sun to go d. at noon, and I will...
Am 9:2 thence will I bring them d.:... 3381
Ob 3 shall bring me d. to the ground?... 3381
Ob 4 I bring thee d., saith the Lord... 3381
Ob 16 and they shall swallow d., and they...
Jon 1:3 went d. to Joppa; and he found... 3381
Jon 1:3 fare thereof, and went d. into it,... 3381
Jon 1:5 Jonah was gone d. into the sides... 3381
Jon 2:6 I went d. to the bottoms of the... 3381
Mic 1:3 and will come d., and tread upon... 3381
Mic 1:4 that are poured d. a steep place...
Mic 1:6 I will pour d. the stones thereof...
Mic 1:12 but evil came d. from the Lord... 3381
Mic 3:6 the sun shall go d. over the prophets,...
Mic 5:8 both treadeth d., and teareth in pieces,...
Mic 5:11 and throw d. all thy strong holds:... 2040
Mic 6:14 and thy casting d. shall be in the...
Mic 7:10 shall she be trodden d. as the mire...
Na 1:6 the rocks are thrown d. by him... 5422
Na 1:12 thus shall they be cut d., when he...
Zep 1:11 the merchant people are cut d.;...
Zep 2:7 Ashkelon shall they lie d. in the... 7257
Zep 2:14 And flocks shall lie d. in the midst... 7257
Zep 2:15 a place for beasts to lie d. in!... 4769
Zep 3:13 they shall feed and lie d., and none... 4769
Hag 2:22 riders shall come d., every one... 3381
Zec 10:5 which tread d. their enemies in the...
Zec 10:11 Assyria shall be brought d., and... 3381
Zec 10:12 shall walk up and d. in his name,...
Zec 11:2 forest of the vintage is come d... 3381
Mal 1:4 I will throw d.; and they shall... 2040
Mal 1:11 even unto the going d. of the same...
Mal 4:3 ye shall tread d. the wicked;...
Mt 2:11 and fell d., and worshipped him:... 4098
Mt 3:10 not forth good fruit is hewn d.,... 1581
Mt 4:6 the Son of God, cast thyself d.:... 2736
Mt 4:9 if thou wilt fall d. and worship me... 4098
Mt 7:19 is hewn d., and cast into the fire .1581
Mt 8:1 When he was come d. from the... 2597
Mt 8:11 shall sit d. with Abraham, and... 347
Mt 8:32 swine ran violently d. a steep place... 2596
Mt 9:10 and sinners came and sat d... 347
Mt 11:23 shall be brought d. to hell:... 2601
Mt 13:48 and sat d., and gathered the good.. 2523
Mt 14:19 the multitude to sit d. on the grass,... 347
Mt 14:29 when Peter was come d. out of the... 2597
Mt 15:29 into a mountain, and sat d. there... 2521
Mt 15:30 and cast them d. at Jesus' feet;... 4496
Mt 15:35 multitudes to sit d. on the ground... 377
Mt 17:9 And as they came d. from the... 2597
Mt 17:14 kneeling d. to him, and saying,...
Mt 18:26 The servant therefore fell d., and...
Mt 18:29 And his fellow servant fell d. at his...
Mt 21:8 others cut d. branches from the... 2875
Mt 24:2 that shall not be thrown d... 2647
Mt 24:17 housetop not come d. to take any.. 2597
Mt 26:20 even was come, he sat d. with the... 345
Mt 27:5 And he cast d. the pieces of silver... 4496
Mt 27:19 he was set d. on the judgment... 2521
Mt 27:36 And sitting d. they watched him... 2521
Mt 27:40 If thou be the Son of God, come d... 2597
Mt 27:42 let him now come d. from the cross... 2597
Mk 1:7 not worthy to stoop d. and unloose...
Mk 1:40 and kneeling d. to him, and saying...
Mk 2:4 they let d. the bed wherein the sick... 5465
Mk 3:11 fell d. before him, and cried,...
Mk 3:22 the scribes which came d. from... 2597
Mk 5:13 the herd ran violently d. a steep... 2596
Mk 5:33 came and fell d. before him, and...
Mk 6:39 to make all sit d. by companies... 347
Mk 6:40 they sat d. in ranks, by hundreds,... 377
Mk 8:6 the people to sit d. on the ground:... 377
Mk 9:9 And as they came d. from the... 2597
Mk 9:35 he sat d., and called the twelve,... 2523
Mk 11:8 and others cut d. branches off the... 2523
Mk 13:2 that shall not be thrown d... 2647
Mk 13:15 on the housetop not go d. into... 2597
Mk 15:30 and come d. from the cross... 2597
Mk 15:36 Elias will come to take him d... 2507
Mr 15:46 and took him d., and wrapped him... 2507
Lu 1:52 He hath put d. the mighty from... 2507
Lu 2:51 And he went d. with them, and... 2597
Lu 3:9 good fruit is hewn d., and cast... 1581
Lu 4:9 of God, cast thyself d. from hence;... 2736
Lu 4:20 again to the minister, and sat d... 2523
Lu 4:29 they might cast him d. headlong... 2630
Lu 4:31 And came d. to Capernaum, a city... 2718
Lu 5:3 he sat d., and taught the people... 2523
Lu 5:4 let d. your nets for a draught,... 5465
Lu 5:5 at thy word will I let d. the net... 5465
Lu 5:8 he fell d. at Jesus' knees, saying,...
Lu 5:19 and let him d. through the tiling... 2524
Lu 5:29 of others that sat d. with them... 2621
Lu 6:17 he came d. with them, and stood... 2597
Lu 6:38 measure, pressed d., and shaken...
Lu 7:36 the Pharisee's house, and sat d. to... 347
Lu 8:5 it was trodden d., and the fowls... 2662
Lu 8:23 and there came d. a storm of wind... 2597
Lu 8:28 he cried out, and fell d. before him,...
Lu 8:33 herd ran violently d. a steep place... 2596
Lu 8:41 fell d. at Jesus' feet, and besought...
Lu 8:47 and falling d. before him, she...
Lu 9:14 Make them sit d. by fifties in a... 2625
Lu 9:15 and made them all sit d... 347
Lu 9:37 when they were come d. from the... 2778
Lu 9:42 the devil threw him d., and tare him...
Lu 9:44 Let these sayings sink d. into...
Lu 9:54 fire to come d. from heaven, and... 2597
Lu 10:15 to heaven, shalt be thrust d. to... 2601
Lu 10:30 A certain man went d. from... 2597
Lu 10:31 chance there came d. a certain...
Lu 11:37 and he went in, and sat d. to meat... 377
Lu 12:18 I will pull d. my barns, and... 2507
Lu 12:37 them to sit d. to meat, and will... 347
Lu 13:7 cut it d.; why cumbereth it the... 1581
Lu 13:9 after that thou shalt cut it d... 1581
Lu 13:29 and shall sit d. in the kingdom... 347
Lu 14:8 sit not d. in the highest room;... 2625
Lu 14:10 go and sit d. in the lowest room,... 377
Lu 14:28 sitteth not d. first, and counteth... 2523
Lu 14:31 sitteth not d. first, and consulteth..2523
Lu 16:6 thy bill, and sit d. quickly, and... 2523
Lu 17:7 the field, Go and sit d. to meat?... 377
Lu 17:16 And fell d. on his face at his feet,...
Lu 17:31 him not come d. to take it away:.. 2597
Lu 18:14 this man went d. to his house... 2597
Lu 19:5 make haste, and come d.; for... 2597
Lu 19:6 And he made haste, and came d.,... 2597
Lu 19:21 takest up that thou layedst not d.,...
Lu 19:22 taking up that I laid not d., and...
Lu 21:6 that shall not be thrown d... 2647
Lu 21:24 Jerusalem shall be trodden d. of...
Lu 22:14 he sat d., and the twelve apostles... 377
Lu 22:41 a stone's cast, and kneeled d., and...
Lu 22:44 drops of blood falling d. to the... 2597
Lu 22:55 and were set d. together,... 4776
Lu 22:55 Peter sat d. among them... 2521
Lu 23:53 And he took it d., and wrapped it... 2507
Lu 24:5 bowed d. their faces to the earth,...
Lu 24:12 stooping d., he beheld the... 3879
Joh 2:12 this he went d. to Capernaum,... 2597
Joh 3:13 but he that came d. from heaven;.. 2597
Joh 4:47 he would come d., and heal his son:... 2597
Joh 4:49 Sir, come d. ere my child die,... 2597
Joh 4:51 as he was now going d., his servants.. 2597
Joh 5:4 angel went d. at a certain season... 2597
Joh 5:7 another steppeth d. before me,... 2597
Joh 6:10 Make the men sit d. Now there... 377
Joh 6:10 So the men sat d., in number... 377
Joh 6:11 disciples to them that were set d.;... 345
Joh 6:16 his disciples went d. unto the sea,... 2597
Joh 6:33 which cometh d. from heaven,... 2597
Joh 6:38 For I came d. from heaven, not... 2597
Joh 6:41 bread which came d. from heaven... 2597
Joh 6:42 he saith, I came d. from heaven?... 2597
Joh 6:50 which cometh d. from heaven,... 2597
Joh 6:51 living bread which came d. from... 2597
Joh 6:58 bread which came d. from heaven: .2597
Joh 8:2 and he sat d., and taught them... 2523
Joh 8:6 Jesus stooped d., and with his... 2736
Joh 8:8 And again he stooped d., and wrote... 2736
Joh 10:15 and I lay d. my life for the sheep...
Joh 10:17 because I lay d. my life, that I...
Joh 10:18 I lay it d. of myself. I have power...
Joh 10:18 to lay it d., and I have power to...
Joh 11:32 she fell d. at his feet, saying unto...
Joh 13:12 and was set d. again, he said unto... 377
Joh 13:37 I will lay d. my life for thy sake...
Joh 13:38 Wilt thou lay d. thy life for my...
Joh 15:13 that a man lay d. his life for his...
Joh 19:13 and sat d. in the judgment seat in... 2523
Joh 20:5 And he stooping d., and looking... 3879
Joh 20:11 she stooped d., and looked into... 3879
Ac 4:35 laid them d. at the apostles' feet:...
Ac 5:5 hearing these words fell d., and...
Ac 5:10 Then fell she d. straightway at his...
Ac 7:15 So Jacob went d. into Egypt, and... 2597
Ac 7:34 and am come d. to deliver them... 2597
Ac 7:58 laid d. their clothes at a young...
Ac 7:60 And he kneeled d., and cried with a...
Ac 8:5 Philip went d. to the city of... 2718
Ac 8:15 when they were come d., prayed... 2597
Ac 8:26 way that goeth d. from Jerusalem... 2597
Ac 8:38 and they went d. both into the water.. 2597
Ac 9:25 and let him d. by the wall in a... 2524
Ac 9:30 they brought him d. to Caesarea,... 2609
Ac 9:32 he came d. also to the saints... 2718
Ac 9:40 and kneeled d., and prayed; and...
Ac 10:11 corners, and let d. to the earth;... 2524
Ac 10:20 and get thee d., and go with them,... 2597
Ac 10:21 Then Peter went d. to the men... 2597
Ac 10:25 fell d. at his feet, and worshipped...
Ac 11:5 great sheet, let d. from heaven by... 2524
Ac 12:19 he went d. from Judaea to Caesarea,.. 2718
Ac 13:14 on the sabbath day, and sat d... 2523
Ac 13:29 they took him d. from the tree,... 2507
Ac 14:11 The gods are come d. to us in the... 2597
Ac 14:25 Perga, they went d. into Attalia:... 2597
Ac 15:1 men which came d. from Judaea... 2718
Ac 15:16 of David, which is fallen d.; and...
Ac 16:8 passing by Mysia came d. to... 2597
Ac 16:13 and we sat d., and spake unto the... 2523
Ac 16:29 and fell d. before Paul and Silas,...
Ac 17:6 turned the world upside d. are... 387
Ac 18:22 the church, he went d. to Antioch... 2597
Ac 19:35 image which fell d. from Jupiter?...
Ac 20:9 he sunk d. with sleep, and... 2736
Ac 20:9 and fell d. from the third loft...
Ac 20:10 And Paul went d., and fell on him,... 2597
Ac 20:36 he kneeled d., and prayed with them...
Ac 21:5 and we kneeled d. on the shore, and...
Ac 21:10 there came d. from Judaea a... 2718
Ac 21:32 and ran d. unto them: and when... 2701
Ac 22:30 and brought Paul d., and set him... 2609
Ac 23:10 commanded the soldiers to go d.,... 2597
Ac 23:15 that he bring him d. unto you... 2609
Ac 23:20 thou wouldest bring d. Paul... 2609
Ac 24:22 chief captain shall come d., I... 2597
Ac 25:5 you are able, go d. with me,... 4782
Ac 25:6 he went d. unto Caesarea: and... 2597
Ac 25:7 which came d. from Jerusalem... 2597
Ac 27:27 as we were driven up and d. in... 1308
Ac 27:30 when they had let d. the boat into... 5465
Ac 28:6 or fallen d. dead suddenly: but... 2667
Ro 10:6 to bring Christ d. from above:)... 2609
Ro 11:3 and digged d. thine altars; and... 2679
Ro 11:10 and bow d. their back alway... 4781
Ro 16:4 Who have for my life laid d. their... 5294
1Co 10:7 The people sat d. to eat and drink,... 2523
1Co 14:25 and so falling d. on his face he...
1Co 15:24 when he shall have put d. all rule... 2673
2Co 4:9 cast d., but not destroyed;... 2598
2Co 7:6 those that are cast d., comforted... 5011
2Co 10:4 to the pulling d. of strong holds:)... 2506
2Co 10:5 Casting d. imaginations, and... 2504
2Co 11:33 a basket was I let d. by the wall,... 5465
Eph 2:14 and hath broken d. the middle wall of...
Eph 4:26 let not the sun go d. upon your... 1931
Heb 1:3 himself purged our sins, sat d. on... 2523
Heb 10:12 sat d. on the right hand of God;... 2523
Heb 11:30 the walls of Jericho fell d.,...
Heb 12:2 sit d. at the right hand of the throne... 2523
Heb 12:12 which hang d., and the feeble... 3935
Jas 1:17 cometh d. from the Father of lights,... 2597
Jas 5:4 labourers who have reaped d...
1Pe 1:12 Holy Ghost sent d. from heaven;...
2Pe 2:4 but cast them d. to hell,...
1Jo 3:16 because he laid d. his life...

1Jo 3:16 we ought to lay d. our lives
Re 1:13 clothed with a garment d. to the foot.
Re 3:12 Jerusalem, which cometh d. out *2597*
Re 3:21 d. with my Father in his throne *2523*
Re 4:10 The four and twenty elders fall d.
Re 5:8 elders fell d. before the Lamb,
Re 5:14 the four and twenty elders fell d.
Re 10:1 angel come d. from heaven, *2597*
Re 12:10 accuser of our brethren is cast d., *2598*
Re 12:12 for the devil is come d. unto you, *2597*
Re 13:13 maketh fire come d. from heaven *2597*
Re 18:1 I saw another angel come d. from *2597*
Re 18:21 great city Babylon be thrown d.,
Re 19:4 and the four beasts fell d. and
Re 20:1 an angel come d. from heaven, *2597*
Re 20:9 and fire came d. from God out of *2597*
Re 21:2 Jerusalem, coming d. from God out *2597*
Re 22:8 I fell d. to worship before the feet

DOWNSITTING
Ps 139:2 Thou knowest my d. and mine 3427

DOWNWARD
2Ki 19:30 shall yet again take root d., and 4295
Ec 3:21 the spirit of the beast that goeth d. 4295
Isa 37:31 shall again take root d., and bear 4295
Eze 1:27 appearance of his loins even d., I saw. 4295
Eze 8:2 appearance of his loins even d., fire 4295

DOWRY
Ge 30:20 hath endued me with a good d.; 2065
Ge 34:12 Ask me never so much d. and gift, 4119
Ex 22:17 pay money according to the d. of 4119
1Sa 18:25 The king desireth not any d., but 4119

DRAG See also DRAGGING.
Hab 1:15 net, and gather them in their d.: 4365
Hab 1:16 burn incense unto their d.; because 4365

DRAGGING
Joh 21:8 cubits,) d. the net with fishes. *4951*

DRAGON See also DRAGONS.
Ne 2:13 even before the d. well, and 8577
Ps 91:13 the young lion and the d. shalt 8577
Isa 27:1 he shall slay the d. that is in the 8577
Isa 51:9 cut Rahab, and wounded the d.? 8577
Jer 51:34 hath swallowed me up like a d., 8577
Eze 29:3 the great d. that lieth in the midst 8577
Re 12:3 behold a great red d., having *1404*
Re 12:4 the d. stood before the woman *1404*
Re 12:7 his angels fought against the d.; *1404*
Re 12:7 and the d. fought and his angels, *1404*
Re 12:9 the great d. was cast out, that *1404*
Re 12:13 when the d. saw that he was cast *1404*
Re 12:16 the flood which the d. cast out *1404*
Re 12:17 the d. was wroth with the woman, *1404*
Re 13:2 and the d. gave him his power, *1404*
Re 13:4 they worshipped the d. which gave *1404*
Re 13:11 like a lamb, and he spake as a d. *1404*
Re 16:13 out of the mouth of the d., *1404*
Re 20:2 he laid hold on the d., that old *1404*

DRAGONS
De 32:33 Their wine is the poison of d., 8577
Job 30:29 I am a brother to d., and a 8577
Ps 44:19 sore broken us in the place of d., 8577
Ps 74:13 thou breakest the heads of the d. 8577
Ps 148:7 the earth, ye d., and all deeps: 8577
Isa 13:22 and d. in their pleasant palaces; 8577
Isa 34:13 it shall be an habitation of d., 8577
Isa 35:7 in the habitation of d., where 8577
Isa 43:20 honour me, the d. and the owls: 8577
Jer 9:11 Jerusalem heaps, and a den of d.; 8577
Jer 10:22 Judah desolate, and a den of d. 8577
Jer 14:6 they snuffed up the wind like d.; 8577
Jer 49:33 Hazor shall be a dwelling for d., 8577
Jer 51:37 a dwellingplace for d., an 8577
Mic 1:8 make a wailing like the d., and 8577
Mal 1:3 waste for the d. of the wilderness. 8563

DRAGON-WELL See DRAGON and WELL.

DRAMS
1Ch 29:7 talents and ten thousand d., 150
Ezr 2:69 and one thousand d. of gold, 1871
Ezr 8:27 of gold, of a thousand d; and 150
Ne 7:70 thousand d. of gold, fifty basons, 1871
Ne 7:71 twenty thousand d. of gold, and 1871
Ne 7:72 gave was twenty thousand d. 1871

DRANK
Ge 9:21 And he d. of the wine, and was 8354
Ge 24:46 I d., and she made the camels drink 8354
Ge 27:25 he brought him wine, and he d. 8354
Ge 43:34 they d., and were merry with him. 8354
Nu 20:11 and the congregation d., and their
De 32:38 d. the wine of their drink offerings? 8354
2Sa 12:3 and d. of his own cup, and lay in 8354
1Ki 13:19 bread in his house, and d. water. 8354
1Ki 17:6 evening; and he d. of the brook.
Da 1:5 and of the wine which he d.: 4960
Da 1:8 nor with the wine which he d.: 4960
Da 5:1 and d. wine before the thousand. 8355
Da 5:3 his wives, and his concubines, d. 8355
Da 5:4 They d. wine, and praised the gods 8355
Mk 14:23 it to them; and they all d. of it. *4095*
Lu 17:27 They did eat, they d., they married *4095*
Lu 17:28 they did eat, they d., they bought, *4095*
Joh 4:12 us the well, and d. thereof himself, *4095*
1Co 10:4 for they d. of that spiritual Rock *4095*

DRAUGHT
2Ki 10:27 made it d. house unto this day. 4280
Mt 15:17 and is cast out into the d.? *856*
Mk 7:19 goeth out into the d., purging *856*
Lu 5:4 and let down your nets for a d. *61*
Lu 5:9 at the d. of the fishes which they *61*

DRAUGHT-HOUSE See DRAUGHT and HOUSE.

DRAVE See also DROVE.
Ex 14:25 that they d. them heavily: so that 5090
Jos 16:10 they d. not out the Canaanites 3423
Jos 24:12 d. them out from before you, 1644
Jos 24:18 the Lord d. out from before us 1644
Jg 1:19 he d. out the inhabitants of the 3423
Jg 6:9 and d. them out from before you, 1644
1Sa 30:20 and the herds, which they d. 5090
2Sa 6:3 sons of Abinadab, d. the new cart. 5090
2Ki 16:6 and d. the Jews from Elath: 5394
2Ki 17:21 d. Israel from following the Lord, 5071
1Ch 13:7 and Uzza and Ahio d. the cart. 5090
Ac 7:45 whom God d. out before the face *1856*
Ac 18:16 d. them from the judgment seat. *556*

DRAW See also DRAWETH; DRAWING; DRAWN; DREW; WITHDRAW.
Ge 24:11 that women go out to d. water. 7579
Ge 24:13 of the city come out to d. water: 7579
Ge 24:19 I will d. water for thy camels also, 7579
Ge 24:20 ran unto the well to d. water, 7579
Ge 24:43 virgin cometh forth to d. water, 7579
Ge 24:44 I will also d. for thy camels: 7579
Ex 3:5 D. not nigh hither: put off thy
Ex 12:21 D. out and take you a lamb 4900
Ex 15:9 I will d. my sword, mine hand 7324
Le 26:33 and will d. out a sword after you; 7324
Jg 3:22 he could not d. the dagger out 8025
Jg 4:6 and d. toward mount Tabor, and 4900
Jg 4:7 And I will d. unto thee to the river 4900
Jg 9:54 D. thy sword, and slay me, that 8025
Jg 19:13 us d. near to one of these places
Jg 20:32 and d. them from the city unto 5423
1Sa 9:11 maidens going out to d. water, 7579
1Sa 14:36 Let us d. near hither unto God.
1Sa 14:38 D. ye near hither, all the chief of
1Sa 31:4 his armourbearer, D. thy sword, 8025
2Sa 17:13 and we will d. it into the river, 5498
1Ch 10:4 D. thy sword, and thrust me 8025
Job 21:33 and every man shall d. after him. 4900
Job 40:23 that he can d. up Jordan 1518
Job 41:1 Canst thou d. out leviathan with 4900
Ps 28:3 D. me not away with the wicked, 4900
Ps 35:3 D. out also the spear, and stop 7324
Ps 69:18 D. nigh unto my soul, and redeem
Ps 73:28 is good for me to d. near to God:
Ps 85:5 wilt thou d. out thine anger to all 4900
Ps 107:18 d. near unto the gates of death.
Ps 119:150 d. nigh that follow after mischief:
Pr 20:5 of understanding will d. it out. 1802
Ec 12:1 d. nigh, when thou shalt say,
Ca 1:4 D. me, we will run after thee: 4900
Isa 5:18 d. iniquity with cords of vanity, 4900
Isa 5:19 of the Holy One of Israel d. nigh
Isa 12:3 Therefore with joy shall ye d. 7579
Isa 29:13 people d. near me with their mouth,
Isa 45:20 d. near together, ye that are escaped
Isa 57:3 But d. near hither, ye sons of the
Isa 57:4 mouth, and d. out the tongue? 748
Isa 58:10 d. out thy soul to the hungry, 6329
Isa 66:19 d. the bow, to Tubal, and Javan, 4900
Jer 30:21 and I will cause him to d. near,
Jer 46:3 and shield, and d. near to battle.
Jer 49:20 shall d. them out; surely he shall 5498
Jer 50:45 of the flock shall d. them out: 5498
La 4:3 sea monsters d. out the breast, 2502
Eze 5:2 in the wind; and I will d. out a 7324
Eze 5:12 I will d. out a sword after them. 7324
Eze 9:1 charge over the city to d. near,
Eze 12:14 will d. out the sword after them. 7324
Eze 21:3 and will d. forth my sword out of 3318
Eze 22:4 thy days to d. near, and art
Eze 28:7 d. their swords against the beauty 7324
Eze 30:11 d. their swords against Egypt, 7324
Eze 32:20 d. her and all her multitudes. 4900
Joe 3:9 let all the men of war d. near;
Na 3:14 D. thee waters for the siege, 7579
Hag 2:16 press at for to d. out fifty vessels 2834
Joh 2:8 saith unto them, D. out now, and *501*
Joh 4:7 a woman of Samaria to d. water: *501*
Joh 4:11 Sir, thou hast nothing to d. with, *502*
Joh 4:15 not, neither come hither to d. *501*
Joh 6:44 Father which hath sent me d. him: *1670*
Joh 12:32 the earth, will d. all men unto me. *1670*
Joh 21:6 now they were not able to d. it for *1670*
Ac 20:30 to d. away disciples after them. *645*
Heb 7:19 by the which we d. nigh unto God.
Heb 10:22 Let us d. near with a true heart *4334*
Heb 10:38 but if any man d. back, my soul *5288*
Heb 10:39 we are not of them who d. back *5289*
Jas 2:6 rich men oppress you, and d. you *1670*
Jas 4:8 D. nigh to God, and he will d. nigh.

DRAWER See also DRAWERS.
De 29:11 the hewer of thy wood unto the d. 7579

DRAWERS
Jos 9:21 hewers of wood and d. of water 7579
Jos 9:23 d. of water for the house of my God 7579
Jos 9:27 d. of water for the congregation, 7579

DRAWEST See WITHDRAWEST.

DRAWETH See also WITHDRAWETH.
De 25:11 and the wife of the one d. near
Jg 19:9 the day d. toward evening, 7503
Job 24:22 he d. also the mighty with his 4900
Job 33:22 his soul d. near unto the grave,
Ps 10:9 when he d. him into his net. 4900
Ps 88:3 my life d. nigh unto the grave.
Isa 26:17 d. near the time of her delivery,
Eze 7:12 the day d. near: let not the
Mt 15:8 This people d. nigh unto me with
Lu 21:8 the time d. near: go ye not
Lu 21:28 for your redemption d. nigh.
Jas 5:8 the coming of the Lord d. nigh.

DRAWING
Jg 5:11 archers in the places of d. water, 4857
Joh 6:19 the sea, and d. nigh unto the ship; *1096*

DRAWN See also WITHDRAWN.
Nu 22:23, 31 and his sword d. in his hand: 8025
De 21:3 which hath not d. in the yoke; 4900
De 30:17 but shall be d. away, and worship 5080
Jos 5:13 against him with his sword d. 8025
Jos 8:6 till we have d. them from the city; 5423
Jos 8:16 and were d. away from the city. 5423
Jos 15:9 And the border was d. from the 8388
Jos 15:9 and the border was d. to Baalah, 8388
Jos 15:11 and the border was d. to Shicron, 8388
Jos 18:14 And the border was d. thence, 8388
Jos 18:17 And was d. from the north, and 8388
Jg 20:31 were d. away from the city; and 5423
Ru 2:9 that which the young men have d., 7579
1Ch 21:16 having a d. sword in his hand 8025
Job 20:25 It is d., and cometh out of the 8025
Ps 37:14 The wicked have d. out the sword, 6605
Ps 55:21 than oil, yet were they d. swords. 6609
Pr 24:11 them that are d. unto death, 3947
Isa 21:15 the swords, from the d. sword, 5203
Isa 28:9 the milk, and d. from the breasts. 6267
Jer 22:19 burial of an ass, d. and cast forth 5498
Jer 31:3 lovingkindness have I d. thee. 4900
La 2:3 he hath d. back his right hand 7725
Eze 21:5 I the Lord have d. forth my sword 3318
Eze 21:28 The sword, the sword is d.: for 6605
Ac 11:10 all were d. up again into heaven. *385*
Jas 1:14 when he is d. away of his own lust, *1828*

DREAD See also DREADFUL.
Ge 9:2 the fear of you and the **d.** of you 2844
Ex 15:16 Fear and **d.** shall fall upon them; 6343
De 1:29 **D.** not, neither be afraid of them. 6206
De 2:25 the **d.** of thee and the fear of thee 6343
De 11:25 and the **d.** of you upon all the land 4172
1Ch 22:13 courage; **d.** not, nor be dismayed. 3372
Job 13:11 afraid? and his **d.** fall upon you? 6343
Job 13:21 and let not thy **d.** make me afraid. 367
Isa 8:13 fear, and let him be your **d.**. 6206

DREADFUL
Ge 28:17 How **d.** is this place! this is none 3372
Job 15:21 A **d.** sound is in his ears: 6343
Eze 1:18 were so high that they were **d.**; 3374
Da 7:7 a fourth beast, **d.** and terrible, 1763
Da 7:19 from all the others, exceeding **d.**, 1763
Da 9:4 O Lord, the great and **d.** God, 3372
Hab 1:7 They are terrible and **d.**: their 3372
Mal 1:14 name is **d.** among the heathen. 3372
Mal 4:5 the great and **d.** day of the Lord: 3372

DREAM See also DREAMED; DREAMETH; DREAMS.
Ge 20:3 to Abimelech in a **d.** by night, 2472
Ge 20:6 And God said unto him in a **d.**, 2472
Ge 31:10 and saw in a **d.**, and, behold, the 2472
Ge 31:11 spake unto me in a **d.**, saying, 2472
Ge 31:24 came to Laban the Syrian in a **d.** 2472
Ge 37:5 Joseph dreamed a **d.**, and he told 2472
Ge 37:6 you, this **d.** which I have dreamed: 2472
Ge 37:9 he dreamed yet another **d.**, and 2472
Ge 37:9 Behold, I have dreamed a **d.** 2472
Ge 37:10 What is this **d.** that thou hast 2472
Ge 40:5 they dreamed a **d.** both of them, 2472
Ge 40:5 each man his **d.** in one night, 2472
Ge 40:5 to the interpretation of his **d.**, 2472
Ge 40:8 We have dreamed a **d.**, and there 2472
Ge 40:9 chief butler told his **d.** to Joseph, 2472
Ge 40:9 In my **d.**, behold, a vine was 2472
Ge 40:16 I also was in my **d.**, and, behold, I 2472
Ge 41:7 awoke, and behold, it was a **d.**. 2472
Ge 41:8 Pharaoh told them his **d.**; but there 2472
Ge 41:11 we dreamed a **d.** in one night, I and 2472
Ge 41:11 to the interpretation of his **d.**. 2472
Ge 41:12 to each man according to his **d.** 2472
Ge 41:15 I have dreamed a **d.**, and there is 2472
Ge 41:15 that thou canst understand a **d.** 2472
Ge 41:17 In my **d.**, behold, I stood upon the 2472
Ge 41:22 I saw in my **d.**, and, behold, seven 2472
Ge 41:25 The **d.** of Pharaoh is one: God 2472
Ge 41:26 ears are seven years: the **d.** is one. 2472
Ge 41:32 for that the **d.** was double unto 2472
Nu 12:6 and will speak unto him in a **d.**. 2472
Jg 7:13 a man that told a **d.** unto his fellow, 2472
Jg 7:13 and said, Behold, I dreamed a **d.**, 2472
Jg 7:15 Gideon heard the telling of the **d.**, 2472
1Ki 3:5 Lord appeared to Solomon in a **d.** 2472
1Ki 3:15 awoke; and, behold, it was a **d.**, 2472
Job 20:8 He shall fly away as a **d.**, and shall 2472
Job 33:15 In a **d.**, in a vision of the night, 2472
Ps 73:20 As a **d.** when one awaketh; 2472
Ps 126:1 Zion, we were like them that **d.**. 2472
Ec 5:3 a **d.** cometh through the multitude 2472
Isa 29:7 shall be as a **d.** of a night vision. 2472
Jer 23:28 The prophet that hath a **d.**, let him 2472
Jer 23:28 let him tell a **d.**: and he that hath 2472
Da 2:3 I have dreamed a **d.**, and my spirit 2472
Da 2:3 was troubled to know the **d.**. 2472
Da 2:4 tell thy servants the **d.**, and we 2493
Da 2:5 not make known unto me the **d.**, 2493
Da 2:6 But if ye shew the **d.**, and the 2493
Da 2:6 honour: therefore shew me the **d.**, 2493
Da 2:7 the king tell his servants the **d.**, 2493
Da 2:9 not make known unto me the **d.**, 2493
Da 2:9 therefore tell me the **d.**, and I shall 2493
Da 2:26 able to make known unto me the **d.** 2493
Da 2:28 Thy **d.**, and the visions of thy head 2493
Da 2:36 This is the **d.**; and we will tell the 2493
Da 2:45 and the **d.** is certain, and the 2493
Da 4:5 I saw a **d.** which made me afraid, 2493
Da 4:6 unto me the interpretation of the **d.** 2493
Da 4:7 and I told the **d.** before them; 2493
Da 4:8 and before him I told the **d.**, 2493
Da 4:9 tell me the visions of my **d.** that I 2493
Da 4:18 This **d.** I king Nebuchadnezzar 2493
Da 4:19 let not the **d.**, or the interpretation 2493
Da 4:19 the **d.** be to them that hate thee, 2493
Da 7:1 Daniel had a **d.** and visions of his 2493
Da 7:1 then he wrote the **d.**, and told the 2493
Joe 2:28 your old men shall **d.** dreams, your 2492
Mt 1:20 Lord appeared unto him in a **d.**, *3677*
Mt 2:12 being warned of God in a **d.** that *3677*
Mt 2:13 Lord appeareth to Joseph in a **d.**, *3677*
Mt 2:19 Lord appeareth in a **d.** to Joseph *3677*
Mt 2:22 being warned of God in a **d.**, he *3677*
Mt 27:19 this day in a **d.** because of him. *3677*
Ac 2:17 and your old men shall **d.** dreams: *1798*

DREAMED
Ge 28:12 And he **d.**, and behold a ladder set 2492
Ge 37:5 And Joseph **d.** a dream, and he told 2492
Ge 37:6 you, this dream which I have **d.**: 2492
Ge 37:9 And he **d.** yet another dream, and 2492
Ge 37:9 Behold, I have **d.** a dream more; 2492
Ge 37:10 is this dream that thou hast **d.**? 2492
Ge 40:5 And they **d.** a dream both of them, 2492
Ge 40:8 We have **d.** a dream, and there is no 2492
Ge 41:1 of two full years, that Pharaoh **d.**: 2492
Ge 41:5 he slept and **d.** the second time: 2492
Ge 41:11 And we **d.** a dream in one night, I 2492
Ge 41:11 we **d.** each man according to the 2492
Ge 41:15 unto Joseph, I have **d.** a dream, 2492
Ge 42:9 the dreams which he **d.** of them, 2492
Jg 7:13 said, Behold, I **d.** a dream, and, 2492
Jer 23:25 name, saying, I have **d.**, I have **d.** 2492
Jer 29:8 dreams, which ye cause to be **d.** 2492
Da 2:1 Nebuchadnezzar **d.** dreams, 2492
Da 2:3 I have **d.** a dream, and my spirit 2492

DREAMER See also DREAMERS.
Ge 37:19 Behold, this **d.** cometh. 1167,2472
De 13:1 you a prophet, or a **d.** of dreams, 2492
De 13:3 that prophet, or that **d.** of dreams: 2492
De 13:5 that prophet, or that **d.** of dreams, 2492

DREAMERS
Jer 27:9 nor to your **d.**, nor to your 2492
Jude 8 Likewise also these filthy **d.** defile *1797*

DREAMETH
Isa 29:8 as when an hungry man **d.**, and, 2492
Isa 29:8 as when a thirsty man **d.**, 2492

DREAMS
Ge 37:8 hated him yet the more for his **d.**, 2472
Ge 37:20 see what will become of his **d.** 2472
Ge 41:12 he interpreted to us our **d.**; to each 2472
Ge 42:9 Joseph remembered the **d.** which 2472
De 13:1 or a dreamer of **d.**, and giveth thee 2472
De 13:3 that prophet, or that dreamer of **d.**: 2472
De 13:5 that prophet, or that dreamer of **d.** 2472
1Sa 28:6 neither by **d.**, nor by Urim, nor by 2472
1Sa 28:15 neither by prophets, nor by **d.**: 2472
Job 7:14 Then thou scarest me with **d.**, and 2472
Ec 5:7 in the multitude of **d.** and many 2472
Jer 23:27 to forget my name by their **d.** 2472
Jer 23:32 against them that prophesy false **d.** 2472
Jer 29:8 neither hearken to your **d.** which 2472
Da 1:17 understanding in all visions and **d.** 2472
Da 2:1 Nebuchadnezzar dreamed **d.**, 2472
Da 2:2 for to shew the king his **d.** 2472
Da 5:12 interpreting of **d.**, and shewing of 2493
Joe 2:28 your old men shall dream **d.**, your 2472
Zec 10:2 seen a lie, and have told false **d.**; 2472
Ac 2:17 and your old men shall dream **d.**: *1797*

DREGS
Ps 75:8 but the **d.** thereof, all the wicked 8105
Isa 51:17 thou hast drunken the **d.** of the 6907
Isa 51:22 even the **d.** of the cup of my fury; 6907

DRESS See also DRESSED; DRESSETH.
Ge 2:15 of Eden to **d.** it and to keep it. 5647
Ge 18:7 young man; and he hasted to **d.** it. 6213
De 28:39 shalt plant vineyards, and **d.** them, 5647
2Sa 12:4 to **d.** for the wayfaring man that 6213
2Sa 13:5 meat, and **d.** the meat in my sight, 6213
2Sa 13:7 Amnon's house, and **d.** him meat. 6213
1Ki 17:12 that I may go in and **d.** it for me 6213
1Ki 18:23 I will **d.** the other bullock, and lay 6213
1Ki 18:25 one bullock for yourselves, and **d.** it 6213

DRESSED See also UNDRESSED.
Ge 18:8 milk, and the calf which he had **d.**, 6213
Le 7:9 all that is **d.** in the fryingpan, 6213
1Sa 25:18 and five sheep ready **d.**, and five 6213
2Sa 12:4 and **d.** it for the man that was come 6213
2Sa 19:24 had neither **d.** his feet, nor trimmed 6213
1Ki 18:26 which was given them, and they **d.** 6213
Heb 6:7 for them by whom it is **d.** *1090*

DRESSER See also DRESSERS.
Lu 13:7 **said he unto the d. of his vineyard,** *289*

DRESSERS See also VINEDRESSERS.
2Ch 26:10 and vine **d.** in the mountains, and 3755

DRESSETH
Ex 30:7 when he **d.** the lamps, he shall 3190

DREW See also DREWEST; WITHDREW.
Ge 18:23 And Abraham **d.** near, and said,
Ge 24:20 water, and **d.** for all his camels. 7579
Ge 24:45 down unto the well, and **d.** water. 7579
Ge 37:28 and they **d.** and lifted up Joseph 4900
Ge 38:29 to pass, as he **d.** back his hand, 7725
Ge 47:29 time **d.** nigh that Israel must die:
Ex 2:10 Because I **d.** him out of the water. 4871
Ex 2:16 they came and **d.** water, and filled 1802
Ex 2:19 and also **d.** water enough for us, 1802
Ex 14:10 when Pharaoh **d.** nigh, the
Ex 20:21 **d.** near unto the thick darkness
Le 9:5 and all the congregation **d.** near
Jos 8:11 went up, and **d.** nigh, and came
Jos 8:26 Joshua **d.** not his hand back, 7725
Jg 8:10 thousand men that **d.** sword. 8025
Jg 8:20 But the youth **d.** not his sword: 8025
Jg 20:2 thousand footmen that **d.** sword. 8025
Jg 20:15 six thousand men that **d.** sword, 8025
Jg 20:17 thousand men that **d.** sword:
Jg 20:25, 35 men; all these **d.** the sword.
Jg 20:37 liers in wait **d.** themselves along, 4900
Jg 20:46 thousand men that **d.** the sword; 8025
Ru 4:8 for thee. So he **d.** off his shoe. 8025
1Sa 7:6 together to Mizpeh, and **d.** water, 7579
1Sa 7:10 the Philistines **d.** near to battle
1Sa 9:18 Saul **d.** near to Samuel in the gate,
1Sa 17:16 the Philistine **d.** near morning
1Sa 17:40 and he **d.** near to the Philistine.
1Sa 17:41 Philistine came on and **d.** near
1Sa 17:48 arose, and came and **d.** nigh
1Sa 17:51 **d.** it out of the sheath thereof, 8025
2Sa 10:13 And Joab **d.** nigh, and the people
2Sa 18:25 And he came apace, and **d.** near.
2Sa 22:17 he **d.** me out of many waters; 4871
2Sa 23:16 and **d.** water out of the well of 7579
2Sa 24:9 valiant men that **d.** the sword; 8025
1Ki 2:1 Now the days of David **d.** nigh
1Ki 8:8 And they **d.** out the staves, 748
1Ki 22:34 certain man **d.** a bow at a venture, 4900
2Ki 3:26 hundred men that **d.** swords, 8025
2Ki 9:24 **d.** a bow with his full strength,
1Ch 11:18 of the Philistines, and **d.** water 7579
1Ch 19:14 people that were with him **d.** nigh
1Ch 19:16 and **d.** forth the Syrians that were 3318
1Ch 21:5 thousand men that **d.** swords: 8025
1Ch 21:5 ten thousand men that **d.** sword. 8025
2Ch 5:9 they **d.** out the staves of the ark, 748
2Ch 14:8 that bare shields and **d.** bows, 1869
2Ch 18:33 certain man **d.** a bow at a venture 4900
Es 5:2 So Esther **d.** near, and touched
Es 9:1 and his decree **d.** near to be put
Ps 18:16 he **d.** me out of many waters. 4871
Isa 41:5 the earth were afraid, **d.** near,
Jer 38:13 they **d.** up Jeremiah with cords, 4900
Ho 11:4 I **d.** them with cords of a man, 4900
Zep 3:2 Lord; she **d.** not near to her God.
Mt 13:48 **they d. to shore, and sat down,** *307*
Mt 21:1 they **d.** nigh unto Jerusalem,
Mt 21:34 **when the time of the fruit d. near,**
Mt 26:51 and **d.** his sword, and struck a *645*
Mk 6:53 Gennesaret, and **d.** to the shore. *4358*
Mk 14:47 them that stood by **d.** a sword, *4685*
Lu 15:1 Then **d.** near unto him all the
Lu 15:25 **he came and d. nigh to the house,**
Lu 22:1 feast of unleavened bread **d.** nigh,
Lu 22:47 **d.** near unto Jesus to kiss him.
Lu 23:54 preparation, and the sabbath **d.** on. *2020*
Lu 24:15 Jesus himself **d.** near, and went
Lu 24:28 And they **d.** nigh unto the village,
Joh 2:9 servants which **d.** the water knew;) *501*
Joh 18:10 Peter having a sword **d.** it, and *1670*
Joh 21:11 Peter went up, and **d.** the net to *1670*
Ac 5:37 **d.** away much people after him: *868*
Ac 7:17 the time of the promise **d.** nigh,
Ac 7:31 and as he **d.** near to behold it, *4334*

Ac 10:9 and **d.** nigh unto the city, Peter
Ac 14:19 Paul, **d.** him out of the city, *4951*
Ac 16:19 Paul and Silas, and **d.** them into *1670*
Ac 16:27 he **d.** out his sword, and would *4685*
Ac 17:6 **d.** Jason and certain brethren *4951*
Ac 19:33 **d.** Alexander out of the multitude, *4264*
Ac 21:30 and **d.** him out of the temple: *1670*
Ac 27:27 they **d.** near to some country; *4317*
Re 12:4 **d.** the third part of the stars *4951*

DREWEST
La 3:57 Thou **d.** near in the day that I

DRIED See also DRIEDST.
Ge 8:7 until the waters were **d.** up from 3001
Ge 8:13 were **d.** up from off the earth: 2717
Ge 8:14 of the month, was the earth **d.**. 3001
Le 2:14 green ears of corn **d.** by the fire, 7033
Nu 6:3 nor eat moist grapes, or **d.**. 3002
Nu 11:6 now our soul is **d.** away; there 3001
Jos 2:10 **d.** up the water of the Red sea 3001
Jos 4:23 God **d.** up the waters of Jordan 3001
Jos 4:23 which he **d.** up from before us, 3001
Jos 5:1 the Lord had **d.** up the waters of 3001
Jg 16:7 green withs that were never **d.**, 2717
Jg 16:8 green withs which had not been **d.**, 2717
1Ki 13:4 he put forth against him, **d.** up, 3001
1Ki 17:7 that the brook **d.** up, because 3001
2Ki 19:24 with the sole of my feet have I **d.** 2717
Job 18:16 His roots shall be **d.** up beneath, 3001
Job 28:4 they are **d.** up, they are gone 1809
Ps 22:15 strength is **d.** up like a potsherd; 3001
Ps 69:3 my throat is **d.**: mine eyes fail 2787
Ps 106:9 Red sea also, and it was **d.** up: 2717
Isa 5:13 their multitude **d.** up with thirst. 6704
Isa 19:5 river shall be wasted and **d.** up. 3001
Isa 19:6 shall be emptied and **d.** up: 2717
Isa 37:25 the sole of my feet have I **d.** 2717
Isa 51:10 thou not it which hath **d.** the sea, 2717
Jer 23:10 of the wilderness are **d.** up. 3001
Jer 50:38 waters; and they shall be **d.** up: 3001
Eze 17:24 have **d.** up the green tree, and have 3001
Eze 19:12 the east wind **d.** up her fruit: 3001
Eze 37:11 they say, Our bones are **d.**, and 3001
Ho 9:16 their root is **d.** up, they shall bear 3001
Ho 13:15 and his fountain shall be **d.** up: 2717
Joe 1:10 the new wine is **d.** up, the oil 3001
Joe 1:12 The vine is **d.** up, and the fig tree 3001
Joe 1:20 the rivers of waters are **d.** up, and 3001
Zec 11:17 his arm shall be clean **d.** up, and 3001
Mk 5:29 fountain of her blood was **d.** up; *3583*
Mk 11:20 the fig tree **d.** up from the roots. *3583*
Re 16:12 and the water thereof was **d.** up, *3583*

DRIEDST
Ps 74:15 flood: thou **d.** up mighty rivers. 3001

DRIETH
Job 14:11 the flood decayeth and **d.** up: 3001
Pr 17:22 but a broken spirit **d.** the bones. 3001
Na 1:4 it dry, and **d.** up all the rivers: 2717

DRINK See also DRANK; DRINKETH; DRINKING; DRINKS; DRUNK.
Ge 19:32 let us make our father **d.** wine, 8248
Ge 19:33 And they made their father **d.** wine 8248
Ge 19:34 make him **d.** wine this night also; 8248
Ge 19:35 And they made their father **d.** wine 8248
Ge 21:19 with water, and gave the lad **d.**. 8248
Ge 24:14 pitcher, I pray thee, that I may **d.**; 8354
Ge 24:14 and she shall say, **D.**, and I will 8354
Ge 24:14 I will give thy camels **d.** also: 8248
Ge 24:17 Let me, I pray thee, **d.** a little 1572
Ge 24:18 And she said, **D.**, my lord: and 8354
Ge 24:18 upon her hand, and gave him **d.**. 8248
Ge 24:19 when she had done giving him **d.**, 8248
Ge 24:43 a little water of thy pitcher to **d.**; 8248
Ge 24:44 And she say to me, Both **d.** thou, 8354
Ge 24:45 unto her, Let me **d.**, I pray thee 8248
Ge 24:46 from her shoulder, and said, **D.**, 8354
Ge 24:46 I will give thy camels **d.** also: 8248
Ge 24:46 and she made the camels **d.** also. 8354
Ge 24:54 they did eat and **d.**, he and the 8354
Ge 25:34 he did eat and **d.**, and rose up, and 8354
Ge 26:30 a feast, and they did eat and **d.**. 8354
Ge 30:38 when the flocks came to **d.**, that 8354
Ge 30:38 conceive when they came to **d.**. 8354
Ge 35:14 poured a **d.** offering thereon, 5262
Ex 7:18 Egyptians shall lothe to **d.** of the 8354
Ex 7:21 the Egyptians could not **d.** of the 8354
Ex 7:24 about the river for water to **d.**; 8354
Ex 7:24 for they could not **d.** of the water 8354
Ex 15:23 they could not **d.** of the waters of 8354
Ex 15:24 Moses, saying, What shall we **d.**? 8354
Ex 17:1 was no water for the people to **d.**. 8354
Ex 17:2 Give us water that we may **d.**. 8354
Ex 17:6 out of it, that the people may **d.**. 8354
Ex 24:11 they saw God, and did eat and **d.**. 8354
Ex 29:40 him of wine for a **d.** offering 5262
Ex 29:41 according to the **d.** offering thereof. 5262
Ex 30:9 shall ye pour **d.** offering thereon. 5262
Ex 32:6 people sat down to eat and to **d.**, 8354
Ex 32:20 and made the children of Israel **d.** 8248
Ex 34:28 neither eat bread, nor **d.** water. 8354
Le 10:9 Do not **d.** wine nor strong 8354
Le 10:9 wine nor strong **d.**, thou, nor thy 7941
Le 11:34 all **d.** that may be drunk in 4945
Le 23:13 and the **d.** offering thereof 5262
Le 23:18 and their **d.** offerings, even an 5262
Le 23:37 a sacrifice, and **d.** offerings, every 5262
Nu 5:24 cause the woman to **d.** the bitter 8248
Nu 5:26 cause the woman to **d.** the water. 8248
Nu 5:27 he hath made her to **d.** the water, 8248
Nu 6:3 himself from wine and strong **d.**, 7941
Nu 6:3 and shall **d.** no vinegar of wine, 8354
Nu 6:3 of wine, or vinegar of strong **d.**, 7941
Nu 6:3 shall he **d.** any liquor of grapes 8354
Nu 6:15 offering, and their **d.** offerings. 5262
Nu 6:17 meat offering, and his **d.** offering. 5262
Nu 6:20 that the Nazarite may **d.** wine. 8354
Nu 15:5 of an hin of wine for a **d.** offering 5262
Nu 15:7 for a **d.** offering thou shalt offer 5262
Nu 15:10 for a **d.** offering half an hin of wine, 5262
Nu 15:24 and his **d.** offering, according to 5262
Nu 20:5 neither is there any water to **d.**. 8354
Nu 20:8 congregation and their beasts **d.**. 8248
Nu 20:17 neither will we **d.** of the water 8354
Nu 20:19 if I and my cattle **d.** of thy water, 8354
Nu 21:22 we will not **d.** of the waters 8354
Nu 23:24 prey, and **d.** the blood of the slain. 8354
Nu 28:7 And the **d.** offering thereof shall 5262
Nu 28:7 unto the Lord for a **d.** offering. 5262
Nu 28:8 and as the **d.** offering thereof, thou 5262
Nu 28:9 oil, and the **d.** offering thereof: 5262
Nu 28:10 burnt offering, and his **d.** offering. 5262
Nu 28:14 their **d.** offerings shall be half an 5262
Nu 28:15, 24 offering, and his **d.** offering. 5262
Nu 28:31 blemish) and their **d.** offerings. 5262
Nu 29:6 **d.** offerings, according unto their 5262
Nu 29:11 offering of it, and their **d.** offerings. 5262
Nu 29:16 meat offering, and his **d.** offering 5262
Nu 29:18 their **d.** offerings for the bullocks, 5262
Nu 29:19 thereof, and their **d.** offerings. 5262
Nu 29:21 meat offering and their **d.** offerings 5262
Nu 29:22 meat offering, and his **d.** offering. 5262
Nu 29:24 their **d.** offerings for the bullocks, 5262
Nu 29:25 meat offering, and his **d.** offering. 5262
Nu 29:27 meat offering and their **d.** offerings 5262
Nu 29:28 meat offering, and his **d.** offering. 5262
Nu 29:30 offering and their **d.** offerings 5262
Nu 29:31 meat offering, and his **d.** offering. 5262
Nu 29:33 their **d.** offerings for the bullocks, 5262
Nu 29:34 meat offering, and his **d.** offering. 5262
Nu 29:37 meat offering and their **d.** offerings 5262
Nu 29:38 meat offering, and his **d.** offerings 5262
Nu 29:39 and for your **d.** offerings, and for 5262
Nu 33:14 was no water for the people to **d.**. 8354
De 2:6 them for money, that ye may **d.**. 8354
De 2:28 water for money, that I may **d.**: 8354
De 9:9 neither did eat bread, nor **d.** water, 8354
De 9:18 neither eat bread nor **d.** water, 8354
De 14:26 for wine, or for strong **d.**, or for 7941
De 28:39 but shalt neither **d.** of the wine, 8354
De 29:6 have ye drunk wine or strong **d.**: 7941
De 32:14 **d.** the pure blood of the grape. 8354
De 32:38 the wine of their **d.** offerings? 5257
Jg 4:19 I pray thee, a little water to **d.**; 8248
Jg 4:19 and gave him **d.**, and covered him. 8248
Jg 7:5 boweth down upon his knees to **d.**. 8354
Jg 7:6 bowed down upon their knees to **d.**. 8354
Jg 9:27 eat and **d.**, and cursed Abimelech. 8354
Jg 13:4 and **d.** not wine nor strong 8354
Jg 13:4 not wine nor strong **d.**, and eat 7941
Jg 13:7 no wine nor strong **d.**, neither 7941
Jg 13:7 and now **d.** no wine nor strong 8354
Jg 13:14 neither let her **d.** wine or strong 8354
Jg 13:14 wine or strong **d.**, nor eat any 7941
Jg 19:4 did eat and **d.**, and lodged there 8354
Jg 19:6 did eat and **d.** both of them 8354
Jg 19:21 washed their feet, and did eat and **d.**. 8354
Ru 2:9 and **d.** of that which the young men 8354
1Sa 1:15 drunk neither wine nor strong **d.**, 7941
1Sa 30:11 eat; and they made him **d.** water: 8248
2Sa 11:11 to eat and to **d.**, and to lie with my 8354
2Sa 11:13 he did eat and **d.** before him; 8354
2Sa 16:2 be faint in the wilderness may **d.** 8354
2Sa 19:35 taste what I eat or what I **d.**? 8354
2Sa 23:15 one would give me **d.** of the water 8248
2Sa 23:16 he would not **d.** thereof, but 8354
2Sa 23:17 lives? therefore he would not **d.** it. 8354
1Ki 1:25 they eat and **d.** before him, and say, 8354
1Ki 13:8 neither will I eat bread nor **d.** water 8354
1Ki 13:9 Eat no bread, nor **d.** water, nor turn 8354
1Ki 13:16 will I eat bread nor **d.** water with 8354
1Ki 13:17 shalt eat no bread nor **d.** water 8354
1Ki 13:18 he may eat bread and **d.** water. 8354
1Ki 13:22 Eat no bread, and **d.** no water 8354
1Ki 17:4 be, that thou shalt **d.** of the brook; 8354
1Ki 17:10 water into a vessel, that I may **d.**. 8354
1Ki 18:41 unto Ahab, Get thee up, eat and **d.**; 8354
1Ki 18:42 Ahab went up to eat and to **d.**. 8354
1Ki 19:6 he did eat and **d.**, and laid him 8354
1Ki 19:8 eat and **d.**, and went in the strength 8354
2Ki 3:17 water, that ye may **d.**, both ye, and 8354
2Ki 6:22 that they may eat and **d.**, and go to 8354
2Ki 7:8 into one tent, and did eat and **d.**, 8354
2Ki 9:34 was come in, he did eat and **d.**, 8354
2Ki 16:13 and poured his **d.** offering, and 5262
2Ki 16:15 offering, and their **d.** offerings; 5262
2Ki 18:27 and **d.** their own piss with you? 8354
2Ki 18:31 and **d.** ye every one the waters 8354
1Ch 11:17 would give me **d.** of the water 8248
1Ch 11:18 David would not **d.** of it, but poured 8354
1Ch 11:19 shall I **d.** the blood of these men 8354
1Ch 11:19 it. Therefore he would not **d.** it. 8354
1Ch 29:21 lambs, with their **d.** offerings, 5262
1Ch 29:22 did eat and **d.** before the Lord 8353
2Ch 28:15 and gave them to eat and to **d.**, 8248
2Ch 29:35 and the **d.** offerings for every 5262
Ezr 3:7 meat, and **d.**, and oil, unto them 4960
Ezr 7:17 their **d.** offerings, and offer them 5261
Ezr 10:6 he did eat no bread, nor **d.** water: 8354
Ne 8:10 eat the fat, and **d.** the sweet, 8354
Ne 8:12 went their way to eat, and to **d.**, 8354
Es 1:7 gave them **d.** in vessels of gold, 8248
Es 3:15 king and Haman sat down to **d.**; 8354
Es 4:16 neither eat nor **d.** three days, night 8354
Job 1:4 sisters to eat and to **d.** with them. 8354
Job 21:20 **d.** of the wrath of the Almighty 8354
Job 22:7 not given water to the weary to **d.**, 8248
Ps 16:4 **d.** offerings of blood will I not 5262
Ps 36:8 thou shalt make them **d.** of the 8248
Ps 50:13 of bulls, or **d.** the blood of goats? 8354
Ps 60:3 to **d.** the wine of astonishment. 8248
Ps 69:21 thirst they gave me vinegar to **d.**. 8248
Ps 75:8 wring them out, and **d.** them. 8354
Ps 78:15 gave them **d.** as out of the great 8248
Ps 78:44 floods, that they could not **d.**. 8354
Ps 80:5 tears to **d.** in great measure. 8248
Ps 102:9 and mingled my **d.** with weeping, 8249
Ps 104:11 give **d.** to every beast of the field: 8248
Ps 110:7 shall **d.** of the brook in the way: 8354
Pr 4:17 and **d.** the wine of violence. 8354
Pr 5:15 **D.** waters out of thine own cistern, 8354
Pr 9:5 eat of my bread, and **d.** of the wine 8354
Pr 20:1 is a mocker, strong **d.** is raging: 7941
Pr 23:7 Eat and **d.**, saith he to thee; 8354
Pr 25:21 be thirsty, give him water to **d.** 8248
Pr 31:4 it is not for kings to **d.** wine; 8354
Pr 31:4 wine, nor for princes strong **d.** 7941
Pr 31:5 Lest they **d.**, and forget the law, 8354
Pr 31:6 Give strong **d.** unto him that is 7941
Pr 31:7 Let him **d.**, and forget his 8354
Ec 2:24 that he should eat and **d.**, and 8354
Ec 3:13 every man should eat and **d.**, and 8354
Ec 5:18 comely for one to eat and to **d.** 8354
Ec 8:15 to eat, and to **d.**, and to be merry: 8354
Ec 9:7 **d.** thy wine with a merry heart; 8354
Ca 5:1 eat, O friends; **d.**, yea, 8354
Ca 5:1 yea, **d.** abundantly, O beloved, 7937
Ca 8:2 I would cause thee to **d.** of spiced 8248
Isa 5:11 that they may follow strong **d.**; 7941
Isa 5:22 them that are mighty to **d.** wine, 8354
Isa 5:22 of strength to mingle strong **d.** 7941

Book	Ref	Context	No.
Isa	21:5	watch in the watchtower, eat, **d.**	8354
Isa	22:13	drinking wine: let us eat and **d.**;	8354
Isa	24:9	They shall not **d.** wine with a song;	8354
Isa	24:9	strong **d.** shall be bitter to them	7941
Isa	24:9	shall be bitter to them that **d.** it	8354
Isa	28:7	strong **d.** are out of the way;	7941
Isa	28:7	have erred through strong **d.**,	7941
Isa	28:7	out of the way through strong **d.**;	7941
Isa	29:9	stagger, but not with strong **d.**	7941
Isa	32:6	he will cause the **d.** of the thirsty	4945
Isa	36:12	and **d.** their own piss with you?	8354
Isa	36:16	**d.** ye every one the waters of his	8354
Isa	43:20	desert, to give **d.** to my people,	8248
Isa	51:22	thou shalt no more **d.** it again:	8354
Isa	56:12	will fill ourselves with strong **d.**;	7941
Isa	57:6	hast thou poured a **d.** offering,	5262
Isa	62:8	the stranger shall not **d.** thy wine,	8354
Isa	62:9	**d.** it in the courts of my holiness	8354
Isa	65:11	**d.** offering unto that number	4469
Isa	65:13	shall **d.**, but ye shall be thirsty:	8354
Jer	2:18	to **d.** the waters of Sihor? or what	8354
Jer	2:18	to **d.** the waters of the river?	8354
Jer	7:18	**d.** offerings unto other gods, that	5262
Jer	8:14	and given us water of gall to **d.**,	8248
Jer	9:15	and give them water of gall to **d.**.	8248
Jer	16:7	them the cup of consolation to **d.**	8248
Jer	16:8	to sit with them to eat and to **d.**.	8354
Jer	19:13	have poured out **d.** offerings unto	5262
Jer	22:15	did not thy father eat and **d.**,	8354
Jer	23:15	make them **d.** the water of gall:	8248
Jer	25:15	to whom I send thee, to **d.** it	8248
Jer	25:16	And they shall **d.**, and be moved,	8354
Jer	25:17	and made all the nations to **d.**,	8248
Jer	25:26	of Sheshach shall **d.** after them	8354
Jer	25:27	**D.** ye, and be drunken, and spue,	8354
Jer	25:28	take the cup at thine hand to **d.**,	8354
Jer	25:28	Lord of hosts; Ye shall certainly **d.**	8354
Jer	32:29	out **d.** offerings unto other gods,	5262
Jer	35:2	and give them wine to **d.**	8248
Jer	35:5	I said unto them, **D.** ye wine	8354
Jer	35:6	We will **d.** no wine: for Jonadab	8354
Jer	35:6	Ye shall **d.** no wine, neither ye,	8354
Jer	35:8	to **d.** no wine all our days,	8354
Jer	35:14	commanded his sons not to **d.** wine,	8354
Jer	35:14	for unto this day they **d.** none,	8354
Jer	44:17,	18 pour out **d.** offerings unto her,	5262
Jer	44:19	poured out **d.** offerings unto her,	5262
Jer	44:19	and pour out **d.** offerings unto her,	5262
Jer	44:25	to pour out **d.** offerings unto her:	5262
Jer	49:12	whose judgment was not to **d.** of	8354
Jer	49:12	but thou shalt surely **d.** of it	8354
Eze	4:11	shall **d.** also water by measure,	8354
Eze	4:11	from time to time shalt thou **d.**.	8354
Eze	4:16	they shall **d.** water by measure,	8354
Eze	12:18	and **d.** thy water with trembling	8354
Eze	12:19	**d.** their water with astonishment,	8354
Eze	20:28	poured out there their **d.** offerings,	5262
Eze	23:32	Thou shalt **d.** of thy sister's cup	8354
Eze	23:34	shalt even **d.** it and suck it out,	8354
Eze	25:4	fruit, and they shall **d.** thy milk	8354
Eze	31:14	in their height, all that **d.** water:	8354
Eze	31:16	all that **d.** water, shall be comforted	8354
Eze	34:19	they **d.** that which ye have fouled	8354
Eze	39:17	that ye may eat flesh, and **d.** blood	8354
Eze	39:18	**d.** the bloof of the princes of the	8354
Eze	39:19	and **d.** blood till ye be drunken,	8354
Eze	44:21	Neither shall any priest **d.** wine,	8354
Eze	45:17	meat offerings, and **d.** offerings,	5262
Da	1:10	appointed your meat and your **d.**:	4960
Da	1:12	pulse to eat, and water to **d.**	8354
Da	1:16	and the wine that they should **d.**;	4960
Da	5:2	his concubines, might **d.** therein	8355
Ho	2:5	and my flax, mine oil and my **d.**,	8250
Ho	4:18	Their **d.** is sour: they have	5435
Joe	1:9	the **d.** offering is cut off from the	5262
Joe	1:13	and the **d.** offering is withholden	5262
Joe	2:14	a **d.** offering unto the Lord your	5262
Joe	3:3	girl for wine, that they might **d.**	8354
Am	2:8	they **d.** the wine of the condemned	8354
Am	2:12	ye gave the Nazarites wine to **d.**;	8248
Am	4:1	masters, Bring, and let us **d.**	8354
Am	4:8	unto one city, to **d.** water;	8354
Am	5:11	but ye shall not **d.** wine of them	8354
Am	6:6	That **d.** wine in bowls, and anoint	8354
Am	9:14	vineyards, and **d.** the wine thereof;	8354
Ob	16	all the heathen **d.** continually,	8354
Ob	16	yea, they shall **d.**, and they	8354
Jon	3:7	let them not feed, nor **d.** water:	8354
Mic	2:11	thee of wine and of strong **d.**;	7941
Mic	6:15	and sweet wine, but shalt not **d.**	8354
Hab	2:15	him that giveth his neighbour **d.**,	8248
Hab	2:16	**d.** thou also, and let thy foreskin	8354
Zep	1:13	but not **d.** the wine thereof	8354
Hag	1:6	ye **d.**, but ye are not filled	8354
Hag	1:6	but ye are not filled with **d.**;	7937
Zec	7:6	did eat, and when ye did **d.**,	8354
Zec	7:6	yourselves, and **d.** for yourselves?	8354
Zec	9:15	they shall **d.**, and make a noise	8354
Mt	6:25	**ye shall eat, or what ye shall d.;**	*4095*
Mt	6:31	**What shall we d.? or, Wherewithal**	*4095*
Mt	10:42	**whosoever shall give to d. unto**	*4222*
Mt	20:22	**to d. of the cup that I shall d. of,**	*4095*
Mt	20:23	**Ye shall d. indeed of my cup,**	*4095*
Mt	24:49	**to eat and d. with the drunken;**	*4095*
Mt	25:35	**I was thirsty, and ye gave me d.:**	*4222*
Mt	25:37	**or thirsty, and gave thee d.?**	*4222*
Mt	25:42	**I was thirsty and ye gave me no d.:**	*4222*
Mt	26:27	to them, saying, **D.** ye all of it;	*4095*
Mt	26:29	**I will not d. henceforth of this**	*4095*
Mt	26:29	**day when I d. it new with you**	*4095*
Mt	26:42	**except I d. it, thy will be done.**	*4095*
Mt	27:34	vinegar to **d.** mingled with gall:	*4095*
Mt	27:34	tasted thereof, he would not **d.**,	*4095*
Mt	27:48	on a reed, and gave him to **d.**.	
Mk	9:41	**shall give you a cup of water to d.**	*4222*
Mk	10:38	**can ye d. of the cup that I d. of?**	*4095*
Mk	10:39	**indeed d. of the cup that I d. of;**	*4095*
Mk	14:25	**I will d. no more of the fruit of**	*4095*
Mk	14:25	**vine, until that day that I d. it**	*4095*
Mk	15:23	And they gave him to **d.** wine	*4095*
Mk	15:36	gave him to **d.**, saying, Let alone;	*4222*
Mk	16:18	**and if they d. any deadly thing,**	*4095*
Lu	1:15	shall **d.** neither wine nor strong	*4095*
Lu	1:15	neither wine nor strong **d.**;	*4608*
Lu	5:30	do ye eat and **d.** with publicans	*4095*
Lu	5:33	Pharisees; but thine eat and **d.**?	*4095*
Lu	12:19	**thine ease, eat, d., and be merry.**	*4095*
Lu	12:29	**ye shall eat or what ye shall d.**	*4095*
Lu	12:45	**to eat and d., and to be drunken;**	*4095*
Lu	17:8	**afterward thou shalt eat and d.?**	*4095*
Lu	22:18	**will not d. of the fruit of the vine,**	*4095*
Lu	22:30	**ye may eat and d. at my table**	*4095*
Joh	4:7	Jesus saith unto her, **Give me to d.,**	*4095*
Joh	4:9	askest **d.** of me, which am a woman	*4095*
Joh	4:10	**Give me to d.; thou wouldest**	*4095*
Joh	6:53	**and d. his blood, ye have no life**	*4095*
Joh	6:55	**and my blood is d. indeed.**	*4215*
Joh	7:37	**let him come unto me, and d.**	*4095*
Joh	18:11	**hath given me, shall I not d. it?**	*4095*
Ac	9:9	sight, and neither did eat nor **d.**	*4095*
Ac	10:41	who did eat and **d.** with him	*4844*
Ac	23:12	they would neither eat nor **d.** till	*4095*
Ac	23:21	they will neither eat nor **d.** till	*4095*
Ro	12:20	if he thirst, give him **d.**: for in so	*4222*
Ro	14:17	of God is not meat and **d.**;	*4213*
Ro	14:21	nor to **d.** wine, nor any thing	*4095*
1Co	9:4	we not power to eat and to **d.**?	*4095*
1Co	10:4	And did all **d.** the same spiritual	*4095*
1Co	10:4	same spiritual **d.**: for they drank	*4188*
1Co	10:7	The people sat down to eat and **d.**,	*4095*
1Co	10:21	Ye cannot **d.** the cup of the Lord,	*4095*
1Co	10:31	Whether therefore ye eat, or **d.**, or	*4095*
1Co	11:22	ye not houses to eat and to **d.** in?	*4095*
1Co	11:25	**this do ye, as oft as ye d. it,**	*4095*
1Co	11:26	ye eat this bread, and **d.** this cup,	*4095*
1Co	11:27	**d.** this cup of the Lord, unworthily,	*4095*
1Co	11:28	of that bread, and **d.** of that cup.	*4095*
1Co	12:13	all made to **d.** into one Spirit	*4222*
1Co	15:32	let us eat and **d.**; for to morrow	*4095*
Col	2:16	judge you in meat, or in **d.**,	*4213*
1Ti	5:23	**D.** no longer water, but use a	*5202*
Re	14:8	because she made all nations **d.**	*4222*
Re	14:10	The same shall **d.** of the wine	*4095*
Re	16:6	thou hast given them blood to **d.**;	*4095*

DRINKERS

Book	Ref	Context	No.
Joe	1:5	howl, all ye **d.** of wine, because of	8354

DRINKETH

Book	Ref	Context	No.
Ge	44:5	Is not this it in which my lord **d.**,	8354
De	11:11	**d.** water of the rain of heaven:	8354
Job	6:4	poison whereof **d.** up my spirit:	8354
Job	15:16	man, which **d.** iniquity like water?	8354
Job	34:7	Job, who **d.** up scorning like water?	8354
Job	40:23	Behold, he **d.** up a river, and	6231
Pr	26:6	cutteth off the feet, and **d.** damage	8354
Isa	29:8	behold, he **d.**; but he awaketh,	8354
Isa	44:12	he **d.** no water, and is faint	8354
Mk	2:16	**d.** with publicans and sinners?	*4095*
Joh	4:13	**d. of this water shall thirst again:**	*4095*
Joh	4:14	**But whosoever d. of the water**	*4095*
Joh	6:54	**and d. my blood, hath eternal life;**	*4095*
Joh	6:56	**eateth my flesh, and d. my blood,**	*4095*
1Co	11:29	For he that eateth and **d.**	*4095*
1Co	11:29	unworthily, eateth and **d.** damnation	*4095*
Heb	6:7	the earth which **d.** in the rain	*4095*

DRINKING

Book	Ref	Context	No.
Ge	24:19	also, until they have done **d.**.	8354
Ge	24:22	to pass, as the camels had done **d.**,	8354
Ru	3:3	he shall have done eating and **d.**.	8354
1Sa	30:16	earth, eating and **d.**, and dancing,	8354
1Ki	4:20	eating and **d.**, and making merry	8354
1Ki	10:21	all king Solomon's **d.** vessels were	4945
1Ki	16:9	in Tirzah, **d.** himself drunk in the	8354
1Ki	20:12	message, as he was **d.**, he and the	8354
1Ki	20:16	Ben-hadad was **d.** himself drunk in	8354
1Ch	12:39	David three days, eating and **d.**:	8354
2Ch	9:20	all the **d.** vessels of king Solomon	4945
Es	1:8	And the **d.** was according to the	8360
Job	1:13	his daughters were eating and **d.**	8354
Job	1:18	thy daughters were eating and **d.**	8354
Isa	22:13	sheep, eating flesh, and **d.** wine:	8354
Mt	11:18	**John came neither eating nor d.,**	*4095*
Mt	11:19	**Son of man came eating and d.,**	*4095*
Mt	24:38	**they were eating and d., marrying**	*4095*
Lu	7:33	**neither eating bread nor d. wine;**	*4095*
Lu	7:34	**Son of man is come eating and d.;**	*4095*
Lu	10:7	**eating and d. such things as they**	*4095*

DRINK-OFFERING See DRINK and OFFERING.

DRINKS

Book	Ref	Context	No.
Heb	9:10	Which stood only in meats and **d.**,	*4188*

DRIVE See also DRAVE; DROVE; DRIVEN; DRIVETH; DRIVING; OVERDRIVE.

Book	Ref	Context	No.
Ex	6:1	with a strong hand shall he **d.** them	1644
Ex	23:28	which shall **d.** out the Hivite, the	1644
Ex	23:29	I will not **d.** them out from before	1644
Ex	23:30	By little and little I will **d.** them	1644
Ex	23:31	and thou shalt **d.** them out before	1644
Ex	33:2	and I will **d.** out the Canaanite, the	1644
Ex	34:11	I **d.** out before thee the Amorite,	1644
Nu	22:6	and that I may **d.** them out of the	1644
Nu	22:11	to overcome them, and **d.** them out	1644
Nu	33:52	ye shall **d.** out all the inhabitants	3423
Nu	33:55	if ye will not **d.** out the inhabitants	3423
De	4:38	To **d.** out nations from before thee	3423
De	9:3	so shalt thou **d.** them out, and	3423
De	9:4	the Lord doth **d.** them out from	3423
De	9:5	the Lord thy God doth **d.** them out	3423
De	11:23	Then will the Lord **d.** out all these	3423
De	18:12	the Lord thy God doth **d.** them out	3423
Jos	3:10	and that he will without fail **d.** out	3423
Jos	13:6	them will I **d.** out from before the	3423
Jos	14:12	then I shall be able to **d.** them out,	3423
Jos	15:63	children of Judah could not **d.** them	3423
Jos	17:12	children of Mannasseh could not **d.**	3423
Jos	17:13	but did not utterly **d.** them out.	3423
Jos	17:18	thou shalt **d.** out the Canaanites,	3423
Jos	23:5	and **d.** them from out of your sight;	3423
Jos	23:13	your God will no more **d.** out any	3423
Jg	1:19	could not **d.** out the inhabitants of	3423
Jg	1:21	the children of Benjamin did not **d.**	3423
Jg	1:27	Manasseh **d.** out the inhabitants of	3423
Jg	1:28	and did not utterly **d.** them out	3423
Jg	1:29	did Ephraim **d.** out the Canaanites	3423
Jg	1:30	did Zebulun **d.** out the inhabitants	3423
Jg	1:31	did Asher **d.** out the inhabitants	3423
Jg	1:32	land: for they did not **d.** them out.	3423
Jg	1:33	did Naphtali **d.** out the inhabitants	3423
Jg	2:3	I will not **d.** them out from before	1644
Jg	2:21	I also will not henceforth **d.** out	3423
Jg	11:24	the Lord our God shall **d.** out	3423
2Ki	4:24	**D.**, and go forward; slack not thy	5090
2Ch	20:7	didst **d.** out the inhabitants of this	3423
Job	18:11	side, and shall **d.** him to his feet.	6327
Job	24:3	**d.** away the ass of the fatherless,	5090
Ps	44:2	thou didst **d.** out the heathen with	3423
Ps	68:2	is driven away, so **d.** them away:	5086
Pr	22:15	the rod of correction shall **d.** it far	
Isa	22:19	I will **d.** thee from thy station,	1920

Jer 24:9 all places whither I shall **d.** them. 5080
Jer 27:10 that I should **d.** you out, and ye 5080
Jer 27:15 that I might **d.** you out, and that 5080
Jer 46:15 not, because the Lord did **d.** them 1920
Eze 4:13 Gentiles, whither I will **d.** them. 5080
Da 4:25 they shall **d.** thee from men, and 2957
Da 4:32 And they shall **d.** thee from men, 2957
Ho 9:15 I will **d.** them out of mine house, 1644
Joe 2:20 and will **d.** him into a land barren 5080
Zep 2:4 they shall **d.** out Ashdod at the 1644
Ac 27:15 up into the wind, we let her **d.**. 1929

DRIVEN

Ge 4:14 thou hast **d.** me out this day from 1644
Ex 10:11 they were **d.** out from Pharaoh's 1644
Ex 22:10 die, or be hurt, or **d.** away, no man 7617
Nu 32:21 until he hath **d.** out his enemies 3423
De 4:19 shouldest be **d.** to worship them, 5080
De 30:1 whither the Lord thy God hath **d.** 5080
De 30:4 If any of thine be **d.** out unto the 5080
Jos 23:9 the Lord hath **d.** out from before 3423
1Sa 26:19 for they have **d.** me out this day 1644
Job 6:13 and is wisdom **d.** quite from me? 5080
Job 13:25 thou break a leaf **d.** to and fro? 5086
Job 18:18 He shall be **d.** from light into 1920
Job 30:5 They were **d.** forth from among 1644
Ps 40:14 let them be **d.** backward and put 5472
Ps 68:2 As smoke is **d.** away, so drive 5086
Ps 114:3 it, and fled: Jordan was **d.** back 5437
Ps 114:5 thou Jordan, that thou wast **d.** 5437
Pr 14:32 The wicked is **d.** away in his 1760
Isa 8:22 they shall be **d.** to darkness. 5080
Isa 19:7 by the brooks, shall wither, be **d.** 5086
Isa 41:2 sword, and as **d.** stubble to his bow 5086
Jer 8:3 the places whither I have **d.** them, 5080
Jer 16:15 the lands whither he had **d.** them: 5080
Jer 23:2 scattered my flock, and **d.** them 5080
Jer 23:3 all countries whither I have **d.** them 5080
Jer 23:8 all countries whither I had **d.** them; 5080
Jer 23:12 they shall be **d.** on, and fall 1760
Jer 29:14 all the places whither I have **d.** 5080
Jer 29:18 the nations whither I have **d.** them: 5080
Jer 32:37 all countries, whither I have **d.** 5080
Jer 40:12 all places whither they were **d.**, 5080
Jer 43:5 nations, whither they had been **d.**, 5080
Jer 46:28 the nations whither I have **d.** thee: 5080
Jer 49:5 and ye shall be **d.** out every man 5080
Jer 50:17 the lions have **d.** him away: 5080
Eze 31:11 have **d.** him out for his wickedness. 1644
Eze 34:4 brought again that which was **d.** 5080
Eze 34:16 bring again that which was **d.** away, 5080
Da 4:33 he was **d.** from men, and did eat 2957
Da 5:21 he was **d.** from the sons of men; 2957
Da 9:7 countries whither thou hast **d.** 5080
Ho 13:3 chaff that is **d.** with the whirlwind 5590
Mic 4:6 I will gather her that is **d.** out, 5080
Zep 3:19 and gather her that was **d.** out; 5080
Lu 8:29 **d.** of the devil into the wilderness.) *1643*
Ac 27:17 strake sail, and so were **d.** *5342*
Ac 27:27 we were **d.** up and down in Adria, *1308*
Jas 1:6 the sea **d.** with the wind and tossed. *416*
Jas 3:4 are **d.** of fierce winds, yet are they *1643*

DRIVER

1Ki 22:34 he said unto the **d.** of his chariot, 7395
Job 39:7 regardeth he the crying of the **d.**. 5065

DRIVETH

2Ki 9:20 son of Nimshi; for he **d.** furiously. 5090
Ps 1:4 the chaff which the wind **d.** away. 5086
Pr 25:23 The north wind **d.** away rain: so 2342
Mk 1:12 spirit **d.** him into the wilderness. 1544

DRIVING

Jg 2:23 without **d.** them out hastily; 3423
2Ki 9:20 and the **d.** is like the **d.** of Jehu 4491
1Ch 17:21 by **d.** out nations from before thy 1644

DROMEDARIES

1Ki 4:28 and **d.** brought they unto the 7409
Es 8:10 mules, camels, and young **d.**: 7424
Isa 60:6 the **d.** of Midian and Ephah; 1070

DROMEDARY See also DROMEDARIES.

Jer 2:23 a swift **d.** traversing her ways; 1072

DROP See also DROPPED; DROPPETH; DROPPING; DROPS.

De 32:2 My doctrine shall **d.** as the rain, 6201
De 33:28 also his heaven shall **d.** down dew. 6201
Job 36:28 the clouds do **d.** and distil upon 5140
Ps 35:11 goodness; and thy paths **d.** fatness. 7491
Ps 35:12 They **d.** upon the pastures of the 7491
Pr 3:20 and the clouds **d.** down the dew 7491
Pr 5:3 woman **d.** as an honeycomb, 5197
Ca 4:11 my spouse, **d.** as the honeycomb: 5197
Isa 40:15 a **d.** of a bucket, and are counted 4752
Isa 45:8 **D.** down, ye heavens, from above, 7491
Eze 20:46 and **d.** thy word toward the south, 5197
Eze 21:2 and **d.** thy word toward the holy 5197
Joe 3:18 the mountains shall **d.** down new 5197
Am 7:16 **d.** not thy word against the house 5197
Am 9:13 and the mountains shall **d.** sweet 5197

DROPPED

Jg 5:4 the heavens **d.**, the clouds also **d.** 5197
1Sa 14:26 behold, the honey **d.**; but no man 1982
2Sa 21:10 until water **d.** upon them out of 5413
Job 29:22 and my speech **d.** upon them 5197
Ps 68:8 heavens also **d.** at the presence of 5197
Ca 5:5 my hands **d.** with myrrh, and my 5197

DROPPETH

Ec 10:18 the hands the house **d.** through 1811

DROPPING

Pr 19:13 of a wife are a continual **d.** 1812
Pr 27:15 A continual **d.** in a very rainy day 1812
Ca 5:13 lilies, **d.** sweet smelling myrrh. 5197

DROPS

Job 36:27 he maketh small the **d.** of water: 5197
Job 38:28 who hath begotten the **d.** of dew? 96
Ca 5:2 my locks with the **d.** of the night. 7447
Lu 22:44 as it were great **d.** of blood falling *2361*

DROPSY

Lu 14:2 man before him which had the **d.**. *5203*

DROSS

Ps 119:119 all the wicked of the earth like **d.**: 5509
Pr 25:4 Take away the **d.** from the silver, 5509
Pr 26:23 a potsherd covered with silver **d.**. 5509
Isa 1:22 Thy silver is become **d.**, thy wine 5509
Isa 1:25 purely purge away thy **d.**, and take 5509
Eze 22:18 house of Israel is to me become **d.**; 5509
Eze 22:18 they are even the **d.** of silver. 5509
Eze 22:19 all become **d.**, behold, therefore 5509

DROUGHT

Ge 31:40 in the day the **d.** consumed me, 2721
De 8:15 serpents, and scorpions, and **d.**, 6774
Job 24:19 **D.** and heat consume the snow 6723
Ps 32:4 is turned into the **d.** of summer. 2725
Isa 58:11 and satisfy thy soul in **d.**, and 6710
Jer 2:6 through a land of **d.**, and of the 6723
Jer 17:8 not be careful in the year of **d.**, 1226
Jer 50:38 A **d.** is upon her waters; and they 2721
Ho 13:5 wilderness, in the land of great **d.**. 8514
Hag 1:11 I called for a **d.** upon the land, 2721

DROVE See also DRAVE; DROVES.

Ge 3:24 So he **d.** out the man; and he 1644
Ge 15:11 carcases, Abram **d.** them away. 5380
Ge 32:16 every **d.** by themselves; and said 5739
Ge 32:16 put a space betwixt **d.** and **d.** 5739
Ge 33:8 What meanest thou by all this **d.** 4264
Ex 2:17 came and **d.** them away: but 1644
Nu 21:32 and **d.** out the Amorites that were 3423
Jos 15:14 Caleb **d.** thence the three sons of 3423
1Ch 8:13 who **d.** away the inhabitants of 1272
Ps 34:*title* who **d.** him away, and he 1644
Hab 3:6 and **d.** asunder the nations; and 5425
Joh 2:15 he **d.** them all out of the temple, *1544*

DROVES

Ge 32:19 all that followed the **d.**, saying, 5739

DROWN See also DROWNED.

Ca 8:7 neither can the floods **d.** it: if a 7857
1Ti 6:9 which **d.** men in destruction and *1036*

DROWNED

Ex 15:4 his chosen captains also are **d.** 2883
Am 8:8 and it shall be cast out and **d.**, as 8248
Am 9:5 and shall be **d.**, as by the flood of 8248
Mt 18:6 **he were d. in the depth of the sea.** *2670*
Heb 11:29 Egyptians assaying to do were **d.**. *2666*

DROWSINESS

Pr 23:21 **d.** shall clothe a man with rags. 5124

DRUNK See also DRUNKEN.

Le 11:34 all drink that may be **d.** in every 8354
De 29:6 neither have ye **d.** wine or strong 8354
De 32:42 make mine arrows **d.** with blood, 7937
Jg 15:19 and when he had **d.**, his spirit 8354
Ru 3:7 when Boaz had eaten and **d.**, and 8354
1Sa 1:9 in Shiloh, and after they had **d.**. 8354
1Sa 1:15 I have **d.** neither wine nor strong 8354
1Sa 30:12 eaten no bread, nor **d.** any water, 8354
2Sa 11:13 and he made him **d.**: and at even 7937
1Ki 13:22 and **d.** water in the place, of the 8354
1Ki 13:23 after he had **d.**, that he saddled 8354
1Ki 16:9 drinking himself **d.** in the house of 7910
1Ki 20:16 drinking himself **d.** in the pavailions, 7910
2Ki 6:23 when they had eaten and **d.**, he 8354
2Ki 19:24 digged and **d.** strange waters, and 8354
Ca 5:1 I have **d.** my wine with my milk: 8354
Isa 37:25 I have digged, and **d.** water; and 8354
Isa 51:17 which hast **d.** at the hand of the 8354
Isa 63:6 and make them **d.** in my fury, 7937
Jer 46:10 and made **d.** with their blood: 7301
Jer 51:57 And I will make **d.** her princes, 7937
Eze 34:18 to have **d.** of the deep waters, 8354
Da 5:23 have **d.** wine in them; and thou 8355
Ob 16 have **d.** upon my holy mountain, 8354
Lu 5:39 **No man also having d. old wine** *4095*
Lu 13:26 **have eaten and d. in thy presence,** *4095*
Joh 2:10 when men have well **d.**, then *3184*
Eph 5:18 And be not **d.** with wine, wherein *3182*
Re 17:2 have been made **d.** with the wine *3182*
Re 18:3 all nations have **d.** of the wine

DRUNKARD See also DRUNKARDS.

De 21:20 voice; he is a glutton, and a **d.**. 5435
Pr 23:21 the **d.** and the glutton shall come 5435
Pr 26:9 goeth up into the hand of a **d.**, 7910
Isa 24:20 shall reel to and fro like a **d.**, 7910
1Co 5:11 railer, or a **d.**, or an extortioner; *3183*

DRUNKARDS

Ps 69:12 and I was the song of the **d.** 8354,7941
Isa 28:1 of pride, to the **d.** of Ephraim, 7910
Isa 28:3 crown of pride, the **d.** of Ephraim, 7910
Joe 1:5 Awake, ye **d.**, and weep; and howl. 7910
Na 1:10 while they are drunken as **d.**, 5435
1Co 6:10 nor **d.**, nor revilers, nor *3183*

DRUNKEN

Ge 9:21 he drank of the wine, and was **d.**; 7943
1Sa 1:13 Eli thought she had been **d.**. 7910
1Sa 1:14 How long wilt thou be **d.**? put 7937
1Sa 25:36 within him, for he was very **d.** 7910
Job 12:25 them to stagger like a **d.** man 7910
Ps 107:27 and stagger like a **d.** man, 7910
Isa 19:14 a **d.** man staggereth in his vomit. 7910
Isa 29:9 they are **d.**, but not with wine; 7937
Isa 49:26 shall be **d.** with their own blood, 7937
Isa 51:17 thou hast **d.** the dregs of the cup 8354
Isa 51:21 and **d.**, but not with wine: 7937
Jer 23:9 I am like a **d.** man, and like a 7910
Jer 25:27 Drink ye, and be **d.**, and spue, 7937
Jer 48:26 Make ye him **d.**: for he magnified 7937
Jer 49:12 of the cup have assuredly **d.**; 7937
Jer 51:7 that made all the earth **d.** 7937
Jer 51:7 the nations have **d.** of her wine; 8354
Jer 51:39 feasts, and I will make them **d.**, 7937
La 3:15 hath made me **d.** with wormwood 7301
La 4:21 thou shalt be **d.**, and shalt make 7937
La 5:4 We have **d.** our water for money; 8354
Eze 39:19 and drink blood till ye be **d.**, 7943
Na 1:10 while they are **d.** as drunkards, 5435
Na 3:11 Thou also shalt be **d.**: thou shalt 7937
Hab 2:15 to him, and makest him **d.** also, 7937
Mt 24:49 **and to eat and drink with the d.;** *3184*
Lu 12:45 **eat and drink, and to be d.;** *3182*
Lu 17:8 **till I have eaten and d.; and** *4095*
Ac 2:15 these are not **d.**, as ye suppose, *3184*
1Co 11:21 one is hungry, and another is **d.** *3184*
1Th 5:7 they that be **d.** are **d.** in the night. *3184*
Re 17:6 **d.** with the blood of the saints, *3184*

DRUNKENNESS

De 29:19 mine heart, to add **d.** to thirst: 7302
Ec 10:17 for strength, and not for **d.**! 8358
Jer 13:13 inhabitants of Jerusalem, with **d.** 7943
Eze 23:33 shalt be filled with **d.** and sorrow, 7943
Lu 21:34 **and d., and cares of this life,** *3178*
Ro 13:13 rioting and **d.**, not in chambering *3178*
Ga 5:21 Envyings, murders, **d.**, revellings, *3178*

DRUSILLA (dru-sil'-lah)
Ac 24:24 when Felix came with his wife **D.**....... *1409*

DRY See also DRIED; DRIETH; DRYSHOD.
Ge 1:9 let the **d.** land appear: and it was....... 3004
Ge 1:10 And God called the **d.** land Earth; 3004
Ge 7:22 of all that was in the **d.** land, died. 2724
Ge 8:13 the face of the ground was **d.**.......... 2720
Ex 4:9 pour it upon the **d.** land: and the......... 3004
Ex 4:9 become blood upon the **d.** land; 3006
Ex 14:16 of Israel shall go on **d.** ground........... 3004
Ex 14:21 the sea **d.** land, and the waters.......... 2724
Ex 14:22 of the sea upon the **d.** ground: 3004
Ex 14:29 of Israel walked upon **d.** land.......... 3004
Ex 15:19 children of Israel went on **d.** land....... 3004
Le 7:10 offering mingled with oil, and **d.**, ... 2720
Le 13:30 it is a **d.** scall, even a leprosy upon 5424
Jos 3:17 stood firm on **d.** ground in the........... 2724
Jos 3:17 Israelites passed over on **d.** ground, ... 2724
Jos 4:18 were lifted up unto the **d.** land,.......... 2724
Jos 4:22 came over this Jordan on **d.** land........ 3004
Jos 9:5 their provision was **d.** and mouldy. 3001
Jos 9:12 behold, it is **d.**, and it is mouldy:........ 3001
Jg 6:37 be **d.** upon all the earth beside, ... 2721
Jg 6:39 it now be **d.** only upon the fleece, ... 2721
Jg 6:40 for it was **d.** upon the fleece only, ... 2721
2Ki 2:8 they two went over on **d.** ground....... 2724
Ne 9:11 midst of the sea on the **d.** land; 3004
Job 12:15 the waters, and they **d.** up: also 3001
Job 13:25 wilt thou pursue the **d.** stubble?......... 3002
Job 15:30 the flame shall **d.** up his branches,...... 3001
Ps 63:1 for thee in a **d.** and thirsty land, ... 6723
Ps 66:6 He turned the sea into **d.** land: 3004
Ps 68:6 the rebellious dwell in a **d.** land.......... 6707
Ps 95:5 and his hands formed the **d.** land......... 3006
Ps 105:41 ran in the **d.** places like a river.......... 6723
Ps 107:33 the watersprings into **d.** ground; 6774
Ps 107:35 and **d.** ground into watesprings............ 6723
Pr 17:1 is a **d.** morsel, and quietness.......... 2720
Isa 25:5 strangers, as the heat in a **d.** place,.... 6724
Isa 32:2 as rivers of water in a **d.** place, ... 6724
Isa 41:18 and the **d.** land springs of water......... 6723
Isa 42:15 and **d.** up all their herbs; and I 3001
Isa 42:15 islands, and I will **d.** up the pools. 3001
Isa 44:3 and floods upon the **d.** ground: 3004
Isa 44:27 saith to the deep, Be **d.**,.................. 2717
Isa 44:27 and I will **d.** up thy rivers................ 3001
Isa 50:2 at my rebuke I **d.** up the sea,............ 2717
Isa 53:2 as a root out of a **d.** ground: 6723
Isa 56:3 say, Behold, I am a **d.** tree.............. 3002
Jer 4:11 A **d.** wind of the high places.............. 6703
Jer 50:12 a **d.** land, and a desert.................... 6723
Jer 51:36 I will **d.** up her sea, and make........... 2717
Jer 51:36 and make her springs **d.**.................. 3001
Jer 51:43 a **d.** land, and a wilderness,.............. 6723
Eze 17:24 have made the **d.** tree to flourish: 3002
Eze 19:13 in a **d.** and thirsty ground. 6723
Eze 20:47 tree in thee, and every **d.** tree: 3002
Eze 30:12 I will make the rivers **d.**, and sell......... 2724
Eze 37:2 valley; and, lo, they were very **d.**. 3002
Eze 37:4 O ye **d.** bones, hear the word of........ 3002
Ho 2:3 set her like a **d.** land, and slay........... 6723
Ho 9:14 miscarrying womb and **d.** breasts. 6784
Ho 13:15 and his spring shall become **d.**,........... 954
Jon 1:9 hath made the sea and the **d.** land...... 3004
Jon 2:10 vomited out Jonah upon the **d.** land..... 3004
Na 1:4 rebuketh the sea, and maketh it **d.**, ... 3001
Na 1:10 be devoured as stubble fully **d.**........ 3002
Zep 2:13 desolation, and **d.** like a wilderness..... 6723
Hag 2:6 and the sea, and the **d.** land;............. 2724
Zec 10:11 the deeps of the river shall **d.** up: 3001
Mt 12:43 **he walketh through d. places,**......... *504*
Lu 11:24 **he walketh through d. places,**......... *504*
Lu 23:31 **what shall be done in the d.?** *3584*
Heb 11:29 through the Red sea as by **d.** land: *3584*

DRY-GROUND See DRY and GROUND.

DRY-LAND See DRY and LAND.

DRYSHOD
Isa 11:15 streams, and make men go over **d.**,..... 5275

DUE See also DUES.
Le 10:13 it is thy **d.**, and thy sons' **d.**,............. 2706
Le 10:14 they be thy **d.**, and thy sons **d.**, ... 2706
Le 26:4 I will give thee rain in **d.** season, ...
Nu 28:2 offer unto me in their **d.** season. ....
De 11:14 rain of your land in his **d.** season,............
De 18:3 be the priest's **d.** from the people, ... 4941
De 32:35 their foot shall slide in **d.** time: ....
1Ch 15:13 sought him not after the **d.** order. ....
1Ch 16:29 Give unto the Lord the glory **d.**..............
Ne 11:23 for the singers, **d.** for every day. 1697
Ps 29:2 Lord the glory **d.** unto his name;............
Ps 96:8 the Lord the glory **d.** unto his name: ....
Ps 104:27 give them their meat in **d.** season............
Ps 145:15 them their meat in **d.** season. ....
Pr 3:27 good from them to whom it is **d.**,........ 1167
Pr 15:23 a word spoken in **d.** season, how ....
Ec 10:17 princes eat in **d.** season, for strength, ...
Mt 18:34 **pay all that was d. unto him,**......... *3784*
Mt 24:45 **to give them meat in d. season?** ....
Lu 12:42 **their portion of meat in d. season?**......
Lu 23:41 receive the **d.** reward of our deeds; *514*
Ro 5:6 in **d.** time Christ died for the ungodly. .. *514*
Ro 13:7 dues: tribute to whom tribute is **d.**;...... *514*
1Co 7:3 unto the wife **d.** benevolence: *3784*
1Co 15:8 as of one born out of **d.** time...................
Ga 6:9 for in **d.** season we shall reap,........... *2398*
1Ti 2:6 for all, to be testified in **d.** time. *2398*
Tit 1:3 in **d.** time manifested his word........... *2398*
1Pe 5:6 that he may exalt you in **d.** time: *2398*

DUES
Ro 13:7 Render therefore to all their **d.**.............. *3782*

DUG See DIGGED.

DUKE See also DUKES.
Ge 36:15 **d.** Tenman, **d.** Omar, ... 441
Ge 36:15 **d.** Zepho, **d.** Kenaz,............................. 441
Ge 36:16 **D.** Korah, **d.** Gatam, and **d.** Amalek:.... 441
Ge 36:17 **d.** Nahath, **d.** Zerah, ... 441
Ge 36:17 **d.** Shammah, **d.** Mizzah: 441
Ge 36:18 **d.** Jeush, **d.** Jaalam, **d.** Korah: 441
Ge 36:29 **d.** Lotan, **d.** Shobal,............................. 441
Ge 36:29 **d.** Zibeon, **d.** Anah,............................. 441
Ge 36:30 **D.** Dishon, **d.** Ezer, **d.** Dishan: 441
Ge 36:40 **d.** Timnah, **d.** Alvah, **d.** Jetheth,........... 441
Ge 36:41 **D.** Aholibamah, **d.** Elah, **d.** Pinon, ... 441
Ge 36:42 **D.** Kenaz, **d.** Teman, **d.** Mibzar, ... 441
Ge 36:43 **D.** Magdiel, **d.** Iram:............................ 441
1Ch 1:51 **d.** Timnah, **d.** Aliah, **d.** Jetheth, ... 441
1Ch 1:52 **D.** Aholibamah, **d.** Elah, **d.** Pinon,......... 441
1Ch 1:53 **D.** Kenaz, **d.** Teman, **d.** Mibzar, ... 441
1Ch 1:54 **D.** Magdiel, **d.** Iram.............................. 441

DUKES
Ge 36:15 These were **d.** of the sons.................. 441
Ge 36:16 are the **d.** that came of Eliphaz............ 441
Ge 36:17 are the **d.** that came of Reuel 441
Ge 36:18 the **d.** that came of Aholibamah 441
Ge 36:19 is Edom, and these are their **d.**............ 441
Ge 36:21 these are the **d.** of the Horites,............ 441
Ge 36:29 the **d.** that came of the Horites; 441
Ge 36:30 are the **d.** that came of Hori, ... 441
Ge 36:30 among their **d.** in the land of Seir. 441
Ge 36:40 of the **d.** that came of Esau, ... 441
Ge 36:43 these be the **d.** of Edom,..................... 441
Ex 15:15 the **d.** of Edom shall be amazed;........... 441
Jos 13:21 were **d.** of Sihon, dwelling in the........ 5257
1Ch 1:51 And the **d.** of Edom were; 441
1Ch 1:54 These are the **d.** of Edom. ....

DULCIMER
Da 3:5, 10,15 **d.**, and all kinds of musick, ... 5481

DULL
Mt 13:15 **their ears are d. of hearing, and**..... *917*
Ac 28:27 their ears are **d.** of hearing, and.......... *917*
Heb 5:11 seeing ye are **d.** of hearing. *3576*

DUMAH (doo'-mah)
Ge 25:14 Mishma, and **D.**, and Massa,............. 1746
Jos 15:52 Arab, and **D.**, and Eshean,................. 1746
1Ch 1:30 and **D.**, Massa, Hadad, and Tema, ... 1746
Isa 21:11 The burden of **D.**. He calleth to.......... 1746

DUMB
Ex 4:11 or who maketh the **d.**, or deaf, ... 483
Ps 38:13 and I was as a **d.** man that openeth...... 483
Ps 39:2 I was **d.** with silence, I held my 481
Ps 39:9 I was **d.**, I opened not my mouth; 481
Pr 31:8 Open thy mouth for the **d.** in the......... 483
Isa 35:6 and the tongue of the **d.** sing:............. 483
Isa 53:7 a sheep before her shearers is **d.**, ... 481
Isa 56:10 they are all **d.** dogs, they cannot 483
Eze 3:26 thou shalt be **d.**, and shalt not be 481
Eze 24:27 shalt speak, and be no more **d.**: 481
Eze 33:22 was opened, and I was no more **d.**. 481
Da 10:15 toward the ground, and I became **d.**...... 481
Hab 2:18 trusteth therein, to make **d.** idols? 483
Hab 2:19 Awake; to the **d.** stone, Arise, ... 1748
Mt 9:32 brought to him a **d.** man possessed..... *2974*
Mt 9:33 devil was cast out, the **d.** spake:........ *2974*
Mt 12:22 with a devil, blind, and **d.**: and he *2974*
Mt 12:22 that the blind and **d.** both spake......... *2974*
Mt 15:30 blind, **d.**, maimed, and many others, ... *2974*
Mt 15:31 when they saw the **d.** to speak, ... *2974*
Mk 7:37 deaf to hear, and the **d.** to speak......... *216*
Mk 9:17 my son, which hath a **d.** spirit;............ *216*
Mk 9:25 **Thou d. and deaf spirit, I charge**.... *216*
Lu 1:20 shalt be **d.**, and not able to speak,...... *4623*
Lu 11:14 casting out a devil, and it was **d.**....... *2974*
Lu 11:14 devil was gone out, the **d.** spake........ *2974*
Ac 8:32 like a lamb **d.** before his shearer,.......... *880*
1Co 12:2 carried away unto these **d.** idols, ... *880*
2Pe 2:16 **d.** ass speaking with man's voice *880*

DUNG See also DUNGHILL.
Ex 29:14 bullock, and his skin, and his **d.**, ... 6569
Le 4:11 his legs, and his inwards, and his **d.**,.... 6569
Le 8:17 and his hide, his flesh, and his **d.**, ... 6569
Le 16:27 skins, their flesh, and their **d.**,........... 6569
Nu 19:5 flesh, and her blood, with her **d.**, ... 6569
1Ki 14:10 as a man taketh away **d.**, till it be 1557
2Ki 6:25 fourth part of a cab of dove's **d.**.......... 2755
2Ki 9:37 Jezebel shall be as **d.** upon the face 1828
2Ki 18:27 they may eat their own **d.**, ... 2716 (6675)
Ne 2:13 and to the **d.** port, and viewed the....... 830
Ne 3:13 cubits on the wall unto the **d.** gate. 830
Ne 3:14 But the **d.** gate repaired Malchiah 830
Ne 12:31 upon the wall toward the **d.** gate: 830
Job 20:7 shall perish for ever like his own **d.**: ... 1561
Ps 83:10 they became as **d.** for the earth. 1828
Isa 36:12 may eat their own **d.**,............ 2716 (6675)
Jer 8:2 they shall be for **d.** upon the face......... 1828
Jer 9:22 shall fall as **d.** upon the open field,...... 1828
Jer 16:4 they shall be as **d.** upon the face of..... 1828
Jer 25:33 they shall be **d.** upon the ground. 1828
Eze 4:12 and thou shalt bake it with **d.** that...... 1561
Eze 4:15 Lo I have given thee cow's **d.** 6832
Eze 4:15 for man's **d.**, and thou shalt............. 1561
Zep 1:17 as dust, and their flesh as the **d.**........ 1561
Mal 2:3 spread **d.** upon your faces, even 6569
Mal 2:3 even the **d.** of your solemn feasts; 6569
Lu 13:8 **I shall dig about it, and d. it:**.. *906,2874*
Php 3:8 and do count them but **d.**, that I......... *4657*

DUNGEON
Ge 40:15 that they should put me into the **d.**. 953
Ge 41:14 brought him hastily out of the **d.**:......... 953
Ex 12:29 the captive that was in the **d.**; 1004,953
Jer 37:16 was entered into the **d.**, ... 1004,953
Jer 38:6 cast him into the **d.** of Malchiah the 953
Jer 38:6 And in the **d.** there was no water, but.. 953
Jer 38:7 they had put Jeremiah into the **d.**;......... 953
Jer 38:9 whom they have cast into the **d.**; and... 953
Jer 38:10 Jeremiah the prophet out of the **d.**, ... 953
Jer 38:11 let them down by cords into the **d.** to.... 953
Jer 38:13 cords, and took him up out of the **d.** 953
La 3:53 They have cut off my life in the **d.**,....... 953
La 3:55 thy name, O Lord, out of the low **d.** 953

DUNG-GATE See DUNG and GATE.

DUNGHILL See also DUNGHILLS.
1Sa 2:8 lifted up the beggar from the **d.**,.......... 830
Ezr 6:11 his house be made a **d.** for this.......... 5122
Ps 113:7 and lifteth the needy out of the **d.**;........ 830
Isa 25:10 as straw is trodden down for the **d.**.... 4087
Da 2:5 your houses shall be made a **d.**.......... 5122
Da 3:29 their houses shall be made a **d.**:......... 5122
Lu 14:35 **for the land, nor yet for the d.;**....... *2874*

DUNGHILLS
La 4:5 brought up in scarlet embrace **d.**. 830

DURA (doo'-rah)
Da 3:1 he set it up in the plain of **D.**, in the .. 1757

DURABLE
Pr 8:18 yea, **d.** riches and righteousness. 6276
Isa 23:18 sufficiently, and for **d.** clothing. 6266

DURETH See also ENDURETH.
Mt 13:21 **root in himself, but d. for a while:** *2076*

DURST
Es 7:5 that **d.** presume in his heart to do so?.......

Job 32:6 and **d.** not shew you mine opinion. 3372
Mt 22:46 neither **d.** any man from that day *5111*
Mk 12:34 no man after that **d.** ask him any........ *5111*
Lu 20:40 they **d.** not ask him any question........ *5111*
Joh 21:12 none of the disciples **d.** ask him, ... *5111*
Ac 5:13 And of the rest **d.** no man join........... *5111*
Ac 7:32 Moses trembled, and **d.** not behold..... *5111*
Jude 9 **d.** not bring against him a railing *5111*

DUST

Ge 2:7 Lord God formed man of the **d.** of..... 6083
Ge 3:14 and **d.** shalt thou eat all the days of.... 6083
Ge 3:19 wast thou taken; for **d.** thou art, ... 6083
Ge 3:19 and unto **d.** shalt thou return............. 6083
Ge 13:16 as the **d.** of the earth: so that if a 6083
Ge 13:16 man can number the **d.** of the earth,... 6083
Ge 18:27 Lord, which am but **d.** and ashes: 6083
Ge 28:14 shall be as the **d.** of the earth,.......... 6083
Ex 8:16 smite the **d.** of the land, that it.......... 6083
Ex 8:17 and smote the **d.** of the earth,........... 6083
Ex 8:17 in beast; all the **d.** of the land............ 6083
Ex 9:9 And it shall become small **d.** in all 80
Le 14:41 they shall pour out the **d.** that 6083
Le 17:13 blood thereof, and cover it with **d.**....... 6083
Nu 5:17 and of the **d.** that is in the floor of 6083
Nu 23:10 Who can count the **d.** of Jacob,.......... 6083
De 9:21 until it was as small as **d.**: and.......... 6083
De 9:21 I cast the **d.** thereof into the brook..... 6083
De 28:24 the rain of thy land powder and **d.**:...... 6083
De 32:24 the poison of serpents of the **d.**. 6083
Jos 7:6 and put **d.** upon their heads............... 6083
1Sa 2:8 raiseth up the poor out of the **d.**, ... 6083
2Sa 16:13 threw stones at him, and cast **d.**. 6083
2Sa 22:43 I beat them as small as the **d.** of........ 6083
1Ki 16:2 I exalted thee out of the **d.**, ... 6083
1Ki 18:38 the wood, and the stones, and the **d.**, . 6083
1Ki 20:10 if the **d.** of Samaria shall suffice 6083
2Ki 13:7 and had made them like the **d.** by 6083
2Ki 23:12 cast the **d.** of them into the brook...... 6083
2Ch 1:19 people like the **d.** of the earth 6083
2Ch 34:4 and made **d.** of them, and strowed 1854
Job 2:12 sprinkled **d.** upon their heads............ 6083
Job 4:19 whose foundation is in the **d.**, ... 6083
Job 5:6 affliction cometh not forth of the **d.**,..... 6083
Job 7:5 with worms and with clods of **d.**; 6083
Job 7:21 now shall I sleet in the **d.**; and 6083
Job 10:9 wilt thou bring me into **d.** again? 6083
Job 14:19 grow out of the **d.** of the earth; 6083
Job 16:15 and defiled my horn in the **d.**............. 6083
Job 17:16 our rest together is in the **d.**............. 6083
Job 20:11 shall lie down with him in the **d.** 6083
Job 21:26 They shall lie down alike in the **d.**, ... 6083
Job 22:24 Then shalt thou lay up gold as **d.**, ... 6083
Job 27:16 Though he heap up silver as the **d.**,.... 6083
Job 28:6 sapphires: and it hath **d.** of gold......... 6083
Job 30:19 I am become like **d.** and ashes........... 6083
Job 34:15 man shall turn again unto **d.**. 6083
Job 38:38 When the **d.** groweth into hardness, ... 6083
Job 39:14 earth, and warmeth them in **d.**, ... 6083
Job 40:13 Hide them in the **d.** together;............ 6083
Job 42:6 and repent in **d.** and ashes................ 6083
Ps 7:5 and lay mine honour in the **d.**. 6083
Ps 18:42 I beat them small as the **d.** before...... 6083
Ps 22:15 brought me into the **d.** of death. 6083
Ps 22:29 they that go down to the **d.** shall 6083
Ps 30:9 Shall the **d.** praise thee? shall it 6083
Ps 44:25 our soul is bowed down to the **d.**........ 6083
Ps 72:9 and his enemies shall lick the **d.**......... 6083
Ps 78:27 rained flesh also upon them as **d.**, ... 6083
Ps 102:14 stones, and favour the **d.** thereof. 6083
Ps 103:14 he remembereth that we are **d.**. 6083
Ps 104:29 they die, and return to their **d.**. 6083
Ps 113:7 raiseth up the poor out of the **d.**, ... 6083
Ps 119:25 My soul cleaveth unto the **d.**:............ 6083
Pr 8:26 highest part of the **d.** of the world...... 6083
Ec 3:20 all are of the **d.**, and all turn to **d.**...... 6083
Ec 12:7 shall the **d.** return to the earth 6083
Isa 2:10 and hide thee in the **d.**, for fear of 6083
Isa 5:24 their blossom shall go up as **d.**............. 80
Isa 25:12 to the ground, even to the **d.**, ... 6083
Isa 26:5 he bringeth it even to the **d.**. 6083
Isa 26:19 and sing, ye that dwell in **d.**: 6083
Isa 29:4 speech shall be low out of the **d.**,........ 6083
Isa 29:4 speech shall whisper out of the **d.**. 6083
Isa 29:5 strangers shall be like small **d.**,............ 80
Isa 34:7 their **d.** made fat with fatness. 6083
Isa 34:9 and the **d.** thereof into brimstone, ... 6083
Isa 40:12 comprehended the **d.** of the earth....... 6083
Isa 40:15 as the small **d.** of the balance: 7834
Isa 41:2 gave them as the **d.** to his sword, ... 6083
Isa 47:1 Come down, and sit in the **d.**, ... 6083
Isa 49:23 and lick up the **d.** of thy feet; 6083
Isa 52:2 Shake thyself from the **d.**; arise, ... 6083
Isa 65:25 and **d.** shall be the serpent's meat. 6083
La 2:10 have cast up **d.** upon their heads; 6083
La 3:29 He putteth his mouth in the **d.**; 6083
Eze 24:7 the ground, to cover it with **d.**; 6083
Eze 26:4 I will also scrape her **d.** from her, ... 6083
Eze 26:10 his horses their **d.** shall cover thee: 80
Eze 26:12 timber and thy **d.** in the midst of......... 6083
Eze 27:30 shall cast up **d.** upon their heads, ... 6083
Da 12:2 many of them that sleep in the **d.**........ 6083
Am 2:7 that pant after the **d.** of the earth....... 6083
Mic 1:10 of Aphrah roll thyself in the **d.**. 6083
Mic 7:17 shall lick the **d.** like a serpent, ... 6083
Na 1:3 the clouds are the **d.** of his feet. 80
Na 3:18 thy nobles shall dwell in the **d.**:................
Hab 1:10 they shall heap **d.**, and take it. 6083
Zep 1:17 blood shall be poured out as **d.**, ... 6083
Zec 9:3 heaped up silver as the **d.**, and fine 6083
Mt 10:14 **city, shake off the d. of your feet**...*2868*
Mk 6:11 **shake off the d. under your feet** *5522*
Lu 9:5 **shake off the very d. from your** *2868*
Lu 10:11 **Even the very d. of your city,** *2868*
Ac 13:51 they shook off the **d.** of their feet *2868*
Ac 22:23 clothes, and threw **d.** into the air, ... *2868*
Re 18:19 And they cast **d.** on their heads, ... *5522*

DUTIES

Eze 18:11 And that doeth not any of those **d.** but......

DUTY

Ex 21:10 and her **d.** of marriage, shall he not..........
De 25:5 **d.** of an husband's brother unto her. ....
De 25:7 the **d.** of my husband's brother. ....
2Ch 8:14 as the **d.** of every day required:......... 1697
Ezr 3:4 as the **d.** of every day required;......... 1697
Ec 12:13 for this is the whole **d.** of man........... 1697
Lu 17:10 **done that which was our d. to do**.. *3784*
Ro 15:27 their **d.** is also to minister unto.......... *3784*

DWARF

Le 21:20 crookbackt, or a **d.**, or that hath........ 1851

DWELL See also DWELLED; DWELLEST; DWELLETH; DWELLING; DWELT.

Ge 4:20 the father of such as **d.** in tents, ... 3427
Ge 9:27 he shall **d.** in the tents of Shem; 7931
Ge 13:6 that they might **d.** together: for 3427
Ge 13:6 so that they could not **d.** together, ... 3427
Ge 16:12 he shall **d.** in the presence of all 7931
Ge 19:30 he feared to **d.** in Zoar: and he........... 3427
Ge 20:15 thee: **d.** where it pleaseth thee. 3427
Ge 24:3 the Canaanites, among whom I **d.**:....... 3427
Ge 24:37 the Canaanites, in whose land I **d.**: 3427
Ge 26:2 **d.** in the land which I shall tell........... 7931
Ge 30:20 now will my husband **d.** with me, ... 2082
Ge 34:10 And ye shall **d.** with us: and the 3427
Ge 34:10 **d.** and trade ye therein, and get you... 3427
Ge 34:16 and we will **d.** with you, and we 3427
Ge 34:21 therefore let them **d.** in the land, ... 3427
Ge 34:22 consent unto us for to **d.** with us, ... 3427
Ge 34:23 unto them, and they will **d.** with us. ... 3427
Ge 35:1 go up to Beth-el, and **d.** there: and 3427
Ge 36:7 than that they might **d.** together; 3427
Ge 45:10 thou shalt **d.** in the land of Goshen, ... 3427
Ge 46:34 ye may **d.** in the land of Goshen; 3427
Ge 47:4 servants **d.** in the land of Goshen. 3427
Ge 47:6 make thy father and brethren to **d.**;.... 3427
Ge 47:6 in the land of Goshen let them **d.**: 3427
Ge 49:13 Zebulun shall **d.** at the haven of 7931
Ex 2:21 Moses was content to **d.** with the 3427
Ex 8:22 Goshen, in which my people **d.**, ... 5975
Ex 15:17 thou hast made for thee to **d.**, in, ... 3427
Ex 23:33 They shall not **d.** in thy land, lest....... 3427
Ex 25:8 that I may **d.** among them. 7931
Ex 29:45 **d.** among the children of Israel, ... 7931
Ex 29:46 that I may **d.** among them: I am 7931
Le 13:46 he shall **d.** alone; without the camp..... 3427
Le 20:22 whither I bring you to **d.** therein, ... 3427
Le 23:42 Ye shall **d.** in booths seven days; 3427
Le 23:42 Israelites born shall **d.** in booths:........ 3427
Le 23:43 children of Israel to **d.** in booths, ... 3427
Le 25:18 ye shall **d.** in the land in safety. 3427
Le 25:19 your fill, and **d.** therein in safety. 3427
Le 26:5 the full, and **d.** in your land safely. 3427
Le 26:32 your enemies which **d.** therein.......... 3427
Nu 5:3 camps, in the midst whereof I **d.**,......... 7931
Nu 13:19 what the land is that they **d.** in, ... 3427
Nu 13:19 that they **d.** in, whether in tents, ... 3427
Nu 13:28 people be strong that **d.** in the land, ... 3427
Nu 13:29 The Amalekites **d.** in the land of 3427
Nu 13:29 the Amorites, **d.** in the mountains: 3427
Nu 13:29 and the Canaanites **d.** by the sea, ... 3427
Nu 14:30 make you **d.** therein, save Caleb 7931
Nu 23:9 the people shall **d.** alone, and shall...... 7931
Nu 32:17 ones shall **d.** in the fenced cities 3427
Nu 33:53 of the land, and **d.** therein: for I 3427
Nu 33:55 vex you in the land wherein ye **d.** 3427
Nu 35:2 of their possession cities to **d.** in;....... 3427
Nu 35:3 the cities shall they have to **d.** in; 3427
Nu 35:32 should come again to **d.** in the land,.... 3427
Nu 35:34 ye shall inhabit, wherein I **d.**: for 7931
Nu 35:34 **d.** among the children of Israel. 7931
De 2:4 children of Esau, which **d.** in Seir;....... 3427
De 2:29 children of Esau which **d.** in Seir, ... 3427
De 2:29 and the Moabites which **d.** in Ar, ... 3427
De 11:30 which **d.** in the champaign over.......... 3427
De 11:31 ye shall possess it, and **d.** therein. 3427
De 12:10 and **d.** in the land which the Lord....... 3427
De 12:10 round about, so that ye **d.** in safety; ... 3427
De 12:11 to cause his name to **d.** there;........... 7931
De 13:12 God hath given thee to **d.** there,........ 3427
De 17:14 possess it, and shalt **d.** therein, ... 3427
De 23:16 He shall **d.** with thee, even among 3427
De 25:5 If brethren **d.** together, and one of..... 3427
De 28:30 and thou shalt not **d.** therein: 3427
De 30:20 that thou mayet **d.** in the land........... 3427
De 33:12 Lord shall **d.** in safety by him; 7931
De 33:12 he shall **d.** between his shoulders. 7931
De 33:28 Israel then shall **d.** in safety 7931
Jos 9:7 Peradventure ye **d.** among us;........... 3427
Jos 9:22 from you; when ye **d.** among us? 3427
Jos 10:6 **d.** in the mountains are gathered........ 3427
Jos 13:13 the Maachathites **d.** among the 3427
Jos 14:4 cities to **d.** in, with their suburbs 3427
Jos 15:63 Jebusites **d.** with the children 3427
Jos 16:10 but the Canaanites **d.** among the 3427
Jos 17:12 Canaanites would **d.** in that land. 3427
Jos 17:16 that **d.** in the land of the valley.......... 3427
Jos 20:4 place, that he may **d.** among them...... 3427
Jos 20:6 And he shall **d.** in that city,............... 3427
Jos 21:2 of Moses to give us cities to **d.** in,..... 3427
Jos 24:13 ye built not, and ye **d.** in them; 3427
Jos 24:15 the Amorites, in whose land ye **d.**: 3427
Jg 1:21 Jebusites **d.** with the children 3427
Jg 1:27 Canaanites would **d.** in that land. 3427
Jg 1:35 Amorites would **d.** in mount Heres 3427
Jg 6:10 in whose land ye **d.**: but ye have 3427
Jg 9:41 they should not **d.** in Shechem............ 3427
Jg 17:10 Micah said unto him, **D.** with me, ... 3427
Jg 17:11 the Levite was content to **d.** with....... 3427
Jg 18:1 sought them an inheritance to **d.** in;.... 3427
1Sa 12:8 and made them **d.** in this place. 3427
1Sa 27:5 country, that I may **d.** there: for......... 3427
1Sa 27:5 why should thy servant **d.** in the......... 3427
2Sa 7:2 I **d.** in an house of cedar, but the ark.. 3427
2Sa 7:5 build me an house for me to **d.** in? 3427
2Sa 7:10 that they may **d.** in a place of their..... 7931
1Ki 2:36 house in Jerusalem, and **d.** there, ... 3427
1Ki 3:17 I and this woman **d.** in one house;....... 3427
1Ki 6:13 And I will **d.** among the children 7931
1Ki 8:12 The Lord said that he would **d.** in 7931
1Ki 8:13 built thee an house to **d.** in, a.............. 2073
1Ki 8:27 will God indeed **d.** on the earth? 3427
1Ki 17:9 belongeth to Zidon, and **d.** there: 3427
2Ki 4:13 I **d.** among mine own people. 3427
2Ki 6:1 the place where we **d.** with thee......... 3427
2Ki 6:2 a place there, where we may **d.**.......... 3427
2Ki 17:27 let them go and **d.** there, ... 3427
2Ki 25:24 **d.** in the land, and serve the king........ 3427
1Ch 17:1 I **d.** in an house of cedars, ... 3427
1Ch 17:4 not build me an house to **d.** in: 3427
1Ch 17:9 and they shall **d.** in their place, ... 7931
1Ch 23:25 may **d.** in Jerusalem for ever: 7931
2Ch 2:3 build him an house to **d.** therein, ... 3427
2Ch 6:1 he would **d.** in the thick darkness. 7931
2Ch 6:18 will God in very deed **d.** with men...... 3427
2Ch 8:2 the children of Israel to **d.** there. 3427
2Ch 8:11 shall not **d.** in the house of David....... 3427
2Ch 19:10 brethren that **d.** in their cities,.......... 3427
Ezr 4:17 companions that **d.** in Samaria,........... 3488

Ezr 6:12 hath caused his name to **d.** there 7932
Ne 8:14 the children of Israel should **d.** in 3427
Ne 11:1 to **d.** in Jerusalem the holy city, ... 3427
Ne 11:2 themselves to **d.** at Jerusalem........... 3427
Job 3:5 stain it; let a cloud **d.** upon it; 7931
Job 4:19 in them that **d.** in houses of clay, ... 7931
Job 11:14 wickedness **d.** in thy tabernacles. 7931
Job 18:15 It shall **d.** in his tabernacle,.............. 7931
Job 19:15 They that **d.** in mine house, and 1481
Job 30:6 To **d.** in the cliffs of the valleys, ... 7931
Ps 4:8 Lord, only makest me **d.** in safety...... 3427
Ps 5:4 neither shall evil **d.** with thee. 1481
Ps 15:1 who shall **d.** in thy holy hill?............ 7931
Ps 23:6 I will **d.** in the house of the Lord 3427
Ps 24:1 world, and they that **d.** therein. 3427
Ps 25:13 His soul shall **d.** at ease; and his 3885
Ps 27:4 I may **d.** in the house of the Lord 3427
Ps 37:3 So shalt thou **d.** in the land, and 7931
Ps 37:27 and do good; and **d.** for evermore. 7931
Ps 37:29 inherit the land, and **d.** therein for 7931
Ps 65:4 that he may **d.** in thy courts:............. 7931
Ps 65:8 They also that **d.** in the uttermost 3427
Ps 68:6 but the rebellious **d.** in a dry land....... 7931
Ps 68:16 hill which God desireth to **d.** in; 3427
Ps 68:16 yea, the Lord will **d.** in it for ever...... 7931
Ps 68:18 Lord God might **d.** among them 7931
Ps 69:25 and let none **d.** in their tents............. 3427
Ps 69:35 that they may **d.** there, and have 3427
Ps 69:36 they that love his name shall **d.** 7931
Ps 72:9 that **d.** in the wilderness shall bow............
Ps 78:55 made the tribes of Israel to **d.**........... 7931
Ps 84:4 Blessed are they that **d.** in thy 3427
Ps 84:10 to **d.** in the tents of wickedness. 1752
Ps 85:9 that glory may **d.** in our land............. 7931
Ps 98:7 world, and they that **d.** therein. 3427
Ps 101:6 the land, that they may **d.** with me:.... 3427
Ps 101:7 shall not **d.** within my house:............. 3427
Ps 107:4 way; they found no city to **d.** in. 4186
Ps 107:34 of them that **d.** therein...................... 3427
Ps 107:36 there he maketh the hungry to **d.**,....... 3427
Ps 120:5 I **d.** in the tents of Kedar! 7931
Ps 132:14 here will I **d.**; for I have desired it. 3427
Ps 133:1 brethren to **d.** together in unity! 3427
Ps 139:9 and **d.** in the uttermost parts of the.... 7931
Ps 140:13 upright shall **d.** in thy presence.......... 3427
Ps 143:3 he hath made me to **d.** in darkness,.... 3427
Pr 1:33 hearkeneth unto me shall **d.**............. 7931
Pr 2:21 the upright shall **d.** in the land, ... 7931
Pr 8:12 I wisdom **d.** with prudence, and......... 7931
Pr 21:9 to **d.** in the corner of the housetop,.... 3427
Pr 21:19 It is better to **d.** in the wilderness,..... 3427
Pr 25:24 to **d.** in the corner of the housetop,..... 3427
Isa 6:5 I **d.** in the midst of a people of.......... 3427
Isa 9:2 that **d.** in the land of the shadow........ 3427
Isa 11:6 wolf also shall **d.** with the lamb,......... 1481
Isa 13:21 owls shall **d.** there, and satyrs........... 7931
Isa 16:4 Let mine outcasts **d.** with thee, ... 1481
Isa 23:13 them that **d.** in the wilderness: ....
Isa 23:18 them that **d.** before the Lord, to.......... 3427
Isa 24:6 they that **d.** therein are desolate: 3427
Isa 26:5 down them that **d.** on high; the.......... 3427
Isa 26:19 and sing, ye that **d.** in dust: for 7931
Isa 30:19 For the people shall **d.** in Zion at 3427
Isa 32:16 shall **d.** in the wilderness, and 7931
Isa 32:18 **d.** in a peaceable habitation, ... 3427
Isa 33:14 shall **d.** with the devouring fire? 1481
Isa 33:14 shall **d.** with everlasting..................... 1481
Isa 33:16 He shall **d.** on high: his place of......... 7931
Isa 33:24 the people that **d.** therein shall 3427
Isa 34:11 the raven shall **d.** in it: and he........... 7931
Isa 34:17 generation shall they **d.** therein.......... 7931
Isa 40:22 them out as a tent to **d.** in:................ 3427
Isa 49:20 give place to me that I may **d.**........... 3427
Isa 51:6 **d.** therein shall die in like manner:...... 3427
Isa 57:15 I **d.** in the high and holy place, ... 7931
Isa 58:12 The restorer of paths to **d.** in............ 3427
Isa 65:9 and my servants shall **d.** there........... 7931
Jer 4:29 forsaken, and not a man **d.** therein. 3427
Jer 7:3 I will cause you to **d.** in this place. 7931
Jer 7:7 will I cause you to **d.** in this place, ... 7931
Jer 8:16 city, and those that **d.** therein. 3427
Jer 8:19 of them that **d.** in a far country:..............
Jer 9:26 corners, that **d.** in the wilderness: 3427
Jer 12:4 wickedness of them that **d.** therein?.... 3427
Jer 20:6 all that **d.** in thine house shall go........ 3427
Jer 23:6 Israel shall **d.** safely: and this 7931
Jer 23:8 they shall **d.** in their own land. 3427
Jer 24:8 them that **d.** in the land of Egypt: 3427
Jer 25:5 and **d.** in the land that the Lord 3427
Jer 25:24 people that **d.** in the desert,.............. 7931
Jer 27:11 they shall till it, and **d.** therein............ 3427
Jer 29:5 Build ye houses, and **d.** in them;........ 3427
Jer 29:28 build ye houses, and **d.** in them; 3427
Jer 29:32 a man to **d.** among his people;........... 3427
Jer 31:24 And there shall **d.** in Judah itself, ... 3427
Jer 32:37 and I will cause them to **d.** safely:...... 3427
Jer 33:16 and Jerusalem shall **d.** safely:............. 7931
Jer 35:7 all your days ye shall **d.** in tents; 3427
Jer 35:9 Nor to build houses for us to **d.** in: 3427
Jer 35:11 Syrians: so we **d.** at Jerusalem. 3427
Jer 35:15 and ye shall **d.** in the land which 3427
Jer 40:5 and **d.** with him among the people: 3427
Jer 40:9 **d.** in the land, and serve the king......... 3427
Jer 40:10 for me, behold, I will **d.** at Mizpah, ... 3427
Jer 40:10 and **d.** in your cities that ye have 3427
Jer 42:13 We will not **d.** in this land, neither...... 3427
Jer 42:14 of bread: and there will we **d.**: 3427
Jer 43:4 Lord, to **d.** in the land of Judah.......... 3427
Jer 43:5 driven, to **d.** in the land of Judah;....... 1481
Jer 44:1 which **d.** in the land of Egypt,............ 3427
Jer 44:1 which **d.** at Migdol, and at 3427
Jer 44:8 whither ye be gone to **d.**, that........... 1481
Jer 44:13 I will punish them that **d.** in the 3427
Jer 44:14 have a desire to return to **d.** there: 3427
Jer 44:26 Judah that **d.** in the land of Egypt;...... 3427
Jer 47:2 the city, and them that **d.** therein:...... 3427
Jer 48:9 desolate, without any to **d.** therein. 3427
Jer 48:28 O ye that **d.** in Moab, leave the......... 3427
Jer 48:28 cities, and **d.** in the rock, and be........ 7931
Jer 49:1 and his people **d.** in his cities? 3427
Jer 49:8 Flee ye, turn back, **d.** deep, O 3427
Jer 49:18 neither shall a son of man **d.** in it....... 1481
Jer 49:30 Flee, get you far off, **d.** deep, O ye..... 3427
Jer 49:31 gates nor bars which **d.** alone............ 7931
Jer 49:33 nor any son of man **d.** in it. 1481
Jer 50:3 none shall **d.** therein: they shall 3427
Jer 50:39 beasts of the island shall **d.** there, ... 3427
Jer 50:39 and the owls shall **d.** therein: and....... 3427
Jer 50:40 shall any son of man **d.** therein. 1481
Jer 51:1 against them that **d.** in the midst........ 3427
Eze 2:6 thou dost **d.** among scorpions: 3427
Eze 12:19 violence of all them that **d.** therein. 3427
Eze 16:46 daughters that **d.** at thy left hand: 3427
Eze 17:23 and under it shall **d.** all fowl.............. 7931
Eze 17:23 the branches thereof shall they **d.**....... 7931
Eze 28:25 then shall they **d.** in their land........... 3427
Eze 28:26 And they shall **d.** safely therein,.......... 3427
Eze 28:26 yea, they shall **d.** with confidence, ... 3427
Eze 32:15 shall smite all them that **d.** therein,..... 3427
Eze 34:25 and they shall **d.** safely in the........... 3427
Eze 34:28 but they shall **d.** safely, and none 3427
Eze 36:28 And ye shall **d.** in the land that.......... 3427
Eze 36:33 also cause you to **d.** in the cities, ... 3427
Eze 37:25 And they shall **d.** in the land that 3427
Eze 37:25 and they shall **d.** therein, even they,... 3427
Eze 38:8 and they shall **d.** safely all of them...... 3427
Eze 38:11 that are at rest, that **d.** safely, ... 3427
Eze 38:12 that **d.** in the midst of the land. 3427
Eze 39:6 among them that **d.** carelessly 3427
Eze 39:9 they that **d.** in the cities of Israel....... 3427
Eze 43:7 where I will **d.** in the midst of the...... 7931
Eze 43:9 and I will **d.** in the midst of them 7931
Da 2:38 wheresoever the children of men **d.**,... 1753
Da 4:1 that **d.** in all the earth; Peace be........ 1753
Da 6:25 that **d.** in all the earth; Peace be........ 1753
Ho 9:3 shall not **d.** in the Lord's land; 3427
Ho 12:9 make thee to **d.** in tabernacles,........... 3427
Ho 14:7 They that **d.** under his shadow 3427
Joe 3:20 Judah shall **d.** for ever, and.............. 3427
Am 3:12 be taken out that **d.** in Samaria.......... 3427
Am 5:11 but ye shall not **d.** in them;............... 3427
Am 9:5 all that **d.** therein shall mourn:............ 3427
Mic 4:10 and thou shalt **d.** in the field,............. 7931
Mic 7:13 because of them that **d.** therein, ... 3427
Mic 7:14 which **d.** solitarily in the wood, ... 7931
Na 1:5 the world, and all that **d.** therein. 3427
Na 3:18 thy nobles shall **d.** in the dust:........... 7931
Hab 2:8 the city, and of all that **d.** therein. 3427
Hab 2:17 city, and of all that **d.** therein. 3427
Zep 1:18 of all them that **d.** in the land. 3427
Hag 1:4 to **d.** in your cieled houses, and......... 3427
Zec 2:10 I come, and I will **d.** in the midst 7931
Zec 2:11 people: and I will **d.** in the midst........ 7931
Zec 8:3 will **d.** in the midst of Jerusalem:........ 7931
Zec 8:4 and old women **d.** in the streets.......... 3427
Zec 8:8 shall **d.** in the midst of Jerusalem: 7931
Zec 9:6 And a bastard shall **d.** in Ashdod, ... 3427
Zec 14:11 And men shall **d.** in it, and there........ 3427
Mt 12:45 **and they enter in and d. there:**...... *2730*
Lu 11:26 **and they enter in, and d. there:**..... *2730*
Lu 21:35 **all them that d. on the face of the** .*2521*
Ac 1:20 and let no man **d.** therein: *2730*
Ac 2:14 and all ye that **d.** at Jerusalem, ... *2730*
Ac 4:16 to all them that **d.** in Jerusalem;.......... *2730*
Ac 7:4 into this land, wherein ye now **d.**. *2730*
Ac 13:27 For they that **d.** at Jerusalem, and...... *2730*
Ac 17:26 to **d.** on all the face of the earth, ... *2730*
Ac 28:16 Paul was suffered to **d.** by himself...... *3306*
Ro 8:9 that the Spirit of God **d.** in you. *3611*
Ro 8:11 raised up Jesus from the dead **d.**......... *3611*
1Co 7:12 and she be pleased to **d.** with him, ... *3611*
1Co 7:13 if he be pleased to **d.** with her,........... *3611*
2Co 6:16 God hath said, I will **d.** in them, ... *1774*
Eph 3:17 That Christ may **d.** in your hearts *2730*
Col 1:19 that in him should all fulness **d.**;......... *2730*
Col 3:16 Let the word of Christ **d.** in you *1774*
1Pe 3:7 husbands **d.** with them according........ *4924*
1Jo 4:13 know we that we **d.** in him, ... *3306*
Re 3:10 **try them that d. upon the earth**. ... *2730*
Re 6:10 blood on them that **d.** on the earth?.... *2730*
Re 7:15 the throne shall **d.** among them.......... *4637*
Re 11:10 they that **d.** upon the earth shall *2730*
Re 11:10 tormented them that **d.** on the earth... *2730*
Re 12:12 heavens, and ye that **d.** in them.......... *4637*
Re 13:6 and them that **d.** in heaven. *4637*
Re 13:8 all that **d.** upon the earth shall *2730*
Re 13:12 which **d.** therein to worship the *2730*
Re 13:14 And deceiveth them that **d.** on the *2730*
Re 13:14 saying to them that **d.** on the earth, ... *2730*
Re 14:6 to preach unto them that **d.** on.......... *2730*
Re 17:8 and they that **d.** on the earth shall...... *2730*
Re 21:3 and he will **d.** with them, and they *4637*

DWELLED See also DWELT.
Ge 13:7 the Perizzite **d.** then in the land. 3427
Ge 13:12 Abram **d.** in the land of Canaan,......... 3427
Ge 13:12 and Lot **d.** in the cities of the plain, ... 3427
Ge 20:1 and **d.** between Kadesh and Shur, ... 3427
Ru 1:4 and they **d.** there about ten years. 3427
1Sa 12:11 on every side, and ye **d.** safe. 3427

DWELLERS
Isa 18:3 of the world, and **d.** on the earth, ... 7931
Ac 1:19 known unto all the **d.** at Jerusalem;..... *2730*
Ac 2:9 and the **d.** in Mesopotamia, and in...... *2730*

DWELLEST
De 12:29 them, and **d.** in their land; 3427
De 19:1 them, and **d.** in their cities,............... 3427
De 26:1 and possessest it, and **d.** therein;....... 3427
2Ki 19:15 which **d.** between the cherubims, ... 3427
Ps 80:1 that **d.** between the cherubims,.......... 3427
Ps 123:1 O thou that **d.** in the heavens............ 3427
Ca 8:13 Thou that **d.** in the gardens, the 3427
Isa 10:24 O my people that **d.** in Zion, ... 3427
Isa 37:16 that **d.** between the cherubims,........... 3427
Isa 47:8 to pleasures, that **d.** carelessly, ... 3427
Jer 49:16 O thou that **d.** in the clefts of the....... 7931
Jer 51:13 O thou that **d.** upon many waters, ... 7931
La 4:21 Edom, that **d.** in the land of Uz; 3427
Eze 7:7 O thou that **d.** in the land: 3427
Eze 12:2 thou **d.** in the midst of a rebellious 3427
Ob 3 that **d.** in the clefts of the rock, ... 7931
Zec 2:7 **d.** with the daughter of Babylon. 3427
Joh 1:38 Master,) where **d.** thou?................... *3306*
Re 2:13 **and where thou d., even where**..... *2730*

DWELLETH
Le 19:34 the stranger that **d.** with you............ 1481
Le 25:39 And if thy brother that **d.** by thee ....
Le 25:47 and thy brother that **d.** by him................
Nu 13:18 people that **d.** therein, whether.......... 3427
De 33:20 he **d.** as a lion, and teareth the arm.... 7931
Jos 6:25 and she **d.** in Israel even unto 3427
Jos 22:19 wherein the Lord's tabernacle **d.**, ... 7931
1Sa 4:4 which **d.** between the cherubims: 3427
1Sa 27:11 while he **d.** in the country of the........ 3427
2Sa 6:2 that **d.** between the cherubims.......... 3427
2Sa 7:2 the ark of God **d.** within curtains......... 3427
1Ch 13:6 that **d.** between the cherubims,.......... 3427
Job 15:28 And he **d.** in desolate cities, and 7931
Job 38:19 Where is the way where light **d.**?....... 7931

Job 39:28 She **d.** and abideth on the rock, 7931
Ps 9:11 to the Lord, which **d.** in Zion: 3427
Ps 26:8 the place where thine honour **d.** 4908
Ps 91:1 He that **d.** in the secret place of the 3427
Ps 113:5 the Lord our God, who **d.** on high 3427
Ps 135:21 of Zion, which **d.** at Jerusalem. 7931
Pr 3:29 seeing he **d.** securely by thee. 3427
Isa 8:18 of hosts, which **d.** in mount Zion. 7931
Isa 33:5 for he **d.** on high: he hath filled 7931
Jer 29:16 of all the people that **d.** in this 3427
Jer 44:2 desolation, and no man **d.** therein, 3427
Jer 49:31 nation that **d.** without care, 3427
Jer 51:43 a land wherein no man **d.**, neither 3427
La 1:3 she **d.** among the heathen, she 3427
Eze 16:46 that **d.** at thy right hand, is Sodom 3427
Eze 17:16 the place where the king **d.** that
Eze 38:14 when my people of Israel **d.** safely, 3427
Da 2:22 darkness, and the light **d.** with 8271
Ho 4:3 every one that **d.** therein shall 3427
Joe 3:21 cleansed: for the Lord **d.** in Zion. 7931
Am 8:8 every one mourn that **d.** therein? 3427
Mt 23:21 **by it, and by him that d. therein** *2730*
Joh 6:56 **my blood, d. in me, and I in him.** *3306*
Joh 14:10 **the Father that d. in me, he doeth** *3306*
Joh 14:17 **for he d. with you, and shall be** *3306*
Ac 7:48 the most High **d.** not in temples *2730*
Ac 17:24 of heaven and earth, **d.** not in temples *2730*
Ro 7:17 that do it, but sin that **d.** in me *3611*
Ro 7:18 is, in my flesh,) **d.** no good thing: *3611*
Ro 7:20 I that do it, but sin that **d.** in me. *3611*
Ro 8:11 bodies by his Spirit that **d.** in you. *1774*
1Co 3:16 and that the Spirit of God **d.** in you? *3611*
Col 2:9 in him **d.** all the fulness of the *2730*
2Ti 1:14 the Holy Ghost which **d.** in us. *1774*
Jas 4:5 The spirit that **d.** in us lusteth *2730*
2Pe 3:13 earth, wherein **d.** righteousness. *2730*
1Jo 3:17 how **d.** the love of God in him? *3306*
1Jo 3:24 his commandments **d.** in him, *3306*
1Jo 4:12 God **d.** in us, and his love is *3306*
1Jo 4:15 God **d.** in him, and he in God. *3306*
1Jo 4:16 he that **d.** in love **d.** in God, and *3306*
2Jo 2 the truth's sake, which **d.** in us, *3306*
Re 2:13 **slain among you, where Satan d.** *2730*

DWELLING See also DWELLINGPLACE; DWELLINGS.
Ge 10:30 their **d.** was from Mesha, as thou 4186
Ge 25:27 Jacob was a plain man, **d.** in tents. 3427
Ge 27:39 thy **d.** shall be the fatness of the 4186
Le 25:29 if a man sell a **d.** house in a walled 4186
Nu 21:15 that goeth down to the **d.** of Ar, 3427
Jos 13:21 dukes of Sihon, **d.** in the country. 3427
1Ki 8:30 and hear thou in heaven thy **d.** 3427
1Ki 8:39 Then hear thou in heaven thy **d.** 3427
1Ki 8:43 Hear thou in heaven thy **d.** place, 3427
1Ki 8:49 supplication in heaven thy **d.** place, 3427
1Ki 21:8 were in his city, **d.** with Naboth 3427
2Ki 17:25 the beginning of their **d.** there, that 3427
1Ch 6:32 they ministered before the **d.** 4908
1Ch 6:54 are their **d.** places throughout 4186
2Ch 6:2 a place for thy **d.** for ever. 3427
2Ch 6:21 hear thou from thy **d.** place, even 3427
2Ch 6:30 hear thou from heaven thy **d.** place, 3427
2Ch 6:33 even from thy **d.** place, and do 3427
2Ch 6:39 even from thy **d.** place, their prayer, 3427
2Ch 30:27 came up to his holy **d.** place, 4583
2Ch 36:15 his people, and on his **d.** place: 4583
Job 8:22 and the **d.** place of the wicked 168
Job 21:28 are the **d.** places of the wicked? 4908
Ps 49:11 their **d.** places to all generations; 4908
Ps 49:14 consume in the grave from their **d.** 2073
Ps 52:5 pluck thee out of thy **d.** place, 168
Ps 74:7 down the **d.** place of thy name 4908
Ps 76:2 and his **d.** place in Zion. 4585
Ps 79:7 Jacob, and laid waste his **d.** place. 5116
Ps 90:1 Lord, thou hast been our **d.** place 4583
Ps 91:10 shall any plague come nigh thy **d.** 168
Pr 21:20 and oil in the **d.** of the wise; 5116
Pr 24:15 against the **d.** of the righteous; 5116
Isa 4:5 every **d.** place of mount Zion, 4349
Isa 18:4 I will consider in my **d.** place 4349
Jer 46:19 O thou daughter **d.** in Egypt, 3427
Jer 49:33 Hazor shall be a **d.** for dragons, 4583
Eze 38:11 all of them **d.** without walls, and 3427
Eze 48:15 the city, for **d.**, and for suburbs: 4186
Da 2:11 gods, whose **d.** is not with flesh 4070
Da 4:25, 32 thy **d.** shall be with the beasts 4070
Da 5:21 and his **d.** was with the wild assess: 4070
Joe 3:17 the Lord your God **d.** in Zion, 7931
Na 2:11 Where is the **d.** of the lions, 4583
Zep 3:7 so their **d.** should not be cut off, 4583
Mk 5:3 Who had his **d.** among the tombs; *2731*
Ac 2:5 And there were **d.** at Jerusalem *2730*
Ac 19:17 Greeks also **d.** at Ephesus; and *2730*
1Ti 6:16 **d.** in the light which no man can *3611*
Heb 11:9 **d.** in tabernacles with Isaac and *2730*
2Pe 2:8 righteous man **d.** among them, *1460*

DWELLING-HOUSE See DWELLING and HOUSE.

DWELLINGPLACE See also DWELLING and PLACE; DWELLINGPLACES.
Nu 24:21 Strong is thy **d.**, and thou puttest 4186
Jer 51:37 Babylon shall become heaps, a **d.** 4583
1Co 4:11 are buffeted, have no certain **d.**; *790*

DWELLINGPLACES
Jer 30:18 tents, and have mercy on his **d.**; 4908
Jer 51:30 women: they have burned her **d.**; 4908
Eze 6:6 In all your **d.** the cities shall be 4186
Eze 37:23 I will save them out of all their **d.**, 4186
Hab 1:6 possess the **d.** that are not theirs. 4908

DWELLINGS
Ex 10:23 of Israel had light in their **d.** 4186
Le 3:17 throughout all your **d.**, that ye eat 4186
Le 7:26 fowl or of beast, in any of your **d.** 4186
Le 23:3 sabbath of the Lord in all your **d.** 4186
Le 23:14 your generations in all your **d.** 4186
Le 23:21 for ever in all your **d.** throughout 4186
Le 23:31 your generations in all your **d.** 4186
Nu 35:29 your generations in all your **d.** 4186
Job 18:19 nor any remaining in his **d.** 4033
Job 18:21 such are the **d.** of the wicked, 4908
Job 39:6 and the barren land his **d.** 4908
Ps 55:15 wickedness is in their **d.**, and 4033
Ps 87:2 Zion more than all the **d.** of Jacob 4908
Isa 32:18 and in sure **d.**, and in quiet resting 4908
Jer 9:19 because our **d.** have cast us out 4908
Eze 25:4 thee, and to make their **d.** in thee: 4908
Zep 2:6 And the sea coast shall be **d.** and 5116

DWELT See also DWELLED.
Ge 4:16 the Lord, and **d.** in the land of Nod, 3427
Ge 11:2 land of Shinar; and they **d.** there. 3427
Ge 11:31 came unto Haran, and **d.** there. 3427
Ge 13:18 and **d.** in the plain of Mamre, 3427
Ge 14:7 Amorites, that **d.** in Hazezon-tamar. 3427
Ge 14:12 who **d.** in Sodom, and his goods, 3427
Ge 14:13 for he **d.** in the plain of Mamre 7931
Ge 16:3 after Abram had **d.** ten years in 3427
Ge 19:29 the cities in the which Lot **d.** 3427
Ge 19:30 and **d.** in the mountain, and his two 3427
Ge 19:30 and he **d.** in a cave, he and his two 3427
Ge 21:20 grew, and **d.** in the wilderness, 3427
Ge 21:21 he **d.** in the wilderness of Paran: 3427
Ge 22:19 and Abraham **d.** at Beer-sheba. 3427
Ge 23:10 Ephron **d.** among the children of 3427
Ge 24:62 for he **d.** in the south country. 3427
Ge 25:11 Isaac **d.** by the well Lahai-roi. 3427
Ge 25:18 they **d.** from Havilah unto Shur, 7931
Ge 26:6 And Isaac **d.** in Gerar: 3427
Ge 26:17 the valley of Gerar, and **d.** there. 3427
Ge 35:22 when Israel **d.** in that land, that 7931
Ge 36:8 Thus **d.** Esau in mount Seir: 3427
Ge 37:1 And Jacob **d.** in the land wherein 3427
Ge 38:11 Tamar went and **d.** in her father's 3427
Ge 47:27 And Israel **d.** in the land of Egypt, 3427
Ge 50:22 And Joseph **d.** in Egypt, he, and his 3427
Ex 2:15 and **d.** in the land of Midian: 3427
Ex 12:40 of Israel, who **d.** in Egypt, 3427
Le 18:3 the land of Egypt, wherein ye **d.**, 3427
Le 26:35 sabbaths, when ye **d.** upon it. 3427
Nu 14:25 the Canaanites **d.** in the valley.) 3427
Nu 14:45 Canaanites which **d.** in that hill, 3427
Nu 20:15 we have **d.** in Egypt a long time; 3427
Nu 21:1 which **d.** in the south, heard tell 3427
Nu 21:25 and Israel **d.** in all the cities of the 3427
Nu 21:31 Israel **d.** in the land of the Amorites. 3427
Nu 21:34 Amorites, which **d.** at Heshbon. 3427
Nu 31:10 all their cities wherein they **d.**, 4186
Nu 32:40 Manasseh; and he **d.** therein. 3427
Nu 33:40 which **d.** in the south in the land of 3427
De 1:4 which **d.** in Heshbon, and Og the 3427
De 1:4 which **d.** at Astaroth in Edrei: 3427
De 1:6 have **d.** long enough in this mount: 3427
De 1:44 which **d.** in that mountain, came 3427
De 2:8 Esau, which **d.** in Seir, through 3427
De 2:10 Emims **d.** therein in times past, 3427
De 2:12 Horims also **d.** in Seir beforetime; 3427
De 2:12 before them, and **d.** in their stead; 3427
De 2:20 giants **d.** therein in old time; 3427
De 2:21 them, and **d.** in their stead: 3427
De 2:22 children of Esau, which **d.** in Seir, 3427
De 2:22 and **d.** in their stead even unto 3427
De 2:23 the Avims which **d.** in Hazerim, 3427
De 2:23 them, and **d.** in their stead.) 3427
De 3:2 the Amorites, which **d.** at Heshbon 3427
De 4:46 who **d.** at Heshbon, whom Moses 3427
De 8:12 built goodly houses, and **d.** therein; 3427
De 29:16 we have **d.** in the land of Egypt; 3427
De 33:16 will of him that **d.** in the bush: 7931
Jos 2:15 and she **d.** upon the wall. 3427
Jos 7:7 and **d.** on the other side Jordan! 3427
Jos 9:16 and that they **d.** among them. 3427
Jos 12:2 who **d.** in Heshbon, and ruled 3427
Jos 12:4 that **d.** at Ashtaroth and at Edrei, 3427
Jos 16:10 the Canaanites that **d.** in Gezer: 3427
Jos 19:47 possessed it, and **d.** therein, and 3427
Jos 19:50 he built the city, and **d.** therein. 3427
Jos 21:43 they possessed it, and **d.** therein. 3427
Jos 22:33 the children of Reuben and Gad **d.** 3427
Jos 24:2 **d.** on the other side of the flood 3427
Jos 24:7 **d.** in the wilderness a long season. 3427
Jos 24:8 **d.** on the other side Jordan; 3427
Jos 24:18 the Amorites which **d.** in the land: 3427
Jg 1:9 Canaanites, that **d.** in the mountain, 3427
Jg 1:10 Canaanites that **d.** in Hebron: 3427
Jg 1:16 they went and **d.** among the people. 3427
Jg 1:29 the Canaanites that **d.** in Gezer; 3427
Jg 1:29 but the Canaanites **d.** in Gezer 3427
Jg 1:30 but the Canaanites **d.** among them, 3427
Jg 1:32 Asherites **d.** among the Canaanites, 3427
Jg 1:33 but he **d.** among the Canaanites, 3427
Jg 3:3 Hivites that **d.** in mount Lebanon, 3427
Jg 3:5 of Israel **d.** among the Canaanites, 3427
Jg 4:2 **d.** in Harosheth of the Gentiles. 3427
Jg 4:5 **d.** under the palm tree of Deborah 3427
Jg 8:11 the way of them that **d.** in tents 7931
Jg 8:29 Joash went and **d.** in his own 3427
Jg 9:21 went to Beer, and **d.** there, for fear 3427
Jg 9:41 And Abimelech **d.** at Arumah: and 3427
Jg 10:1 he **d.** in Shamir in mount Ephraim. 3427
Jg 11:3 and **d.** in the land of Tob: 3427
Jg 11:26 Israel **d.** in Heshbon and her towns, 3427
Jg 15:8 and **d.** in the top of the rock Etam. 3427
Jg 18:7 they **d.** careless, after the manner 3427
Jg 18:28 they built a city, and **d.** therein. 3427
Jg 21:23 repaired the cities, and **d.** in them. 3427
Ru 2:23 and **d.** with her mother in law. 3427
1Sa 19:18 and Samuel went and **d.** in Naioth. 3427
1Sa 22:4 and they **d.** with him all the while 3427
1Sa 23:29 and **d.** in strong holds at En-gedi 3427
1Sa 27:3 And David **d.** with Achish at Gath, 3427
1Sa 27:7 **d.** in the country of the Philistines 3427
1Sa 31:7 Philistines came and **d.** in them. 3427
2Sa 2:3 and they **d.** in the cities of Hebron. 3427
2Sa 5:9 David **d.** in the fort, and called it 3427
2Sa 7:6 I have not **d.** in any house since 3427
2Sa 9:12 all that **d.** in the house of Ziba 4186
2Sa 9:13 Mephibosheth **d.** in Jerusalem: 3427
2Sa 14:28 So Absalom **d.** two full years in 3427
1Ki 2:38 Shimei **d.** in Jerusalem many days 3427
1Ki 4:25 And Judah and Israel **d.** safely, 3427
1Ki 7:8 his house where he **d.** had another 3427
1Ki 9:16 the Canaanites that **d.** in the city, 3427
1Ki 11:24 went to Damascus, and **d.** therein, 3427
1Ki 12:2 and Jeroboam **d.** in Egypt; 3427
1Ki 12:17 which **d.** in the cities of Judah, 3427
1Ki 12:25 in mount Ephraim, and **d.** therein; 3427
1Ki 13:11 there **d.** an old prophet in Beth-el; 3427
1Ki 13:25 the city where the old prophet **d.** 3427
1Ki 15:18 of Syria, that **d.** at Damascus. 3427
1Ki 15:21 of Ramah, and **D.** in Tirzah. 3427
1Ki 17:5 went and **d.** by the brook Cherith, 3427
2Ki 13:5 children of Israel **d.** in their tents, 3427
2Ki 15:5 his death, and **d.** in a several house 3427
2Ki 16:6 Elath, and **d.** there unto this day 3427
2Ki 17:24 Samaria, and **d.** in the cities thereof 3427
2Ki 17:28 came and **d.** in Beth-el, and taught 3427
2Ki 17:29 in their cities wherein they **d.** 3427
2Ki 19:36 and returned, and **d.** at Nineveh 3427
2Ki 22:14 she **d.** in Jerusalem in the college;) 3427
1Ch 2:55 of the scribes which **d.** at Jabez; 3427

1Ch 4:23 **d.** among plants and hedges: 3427
1Ch 4:23 there they **d.** with the king 3427
1Ch 4:28 **d.** at Beer-sheba, and Moladah, ... 3427
1Ch 4:40 they of Ham had **d.** there of old......... 3427
1Ch 4:41 this day, and **d.** in their rooms:.......... 3427
1Ch 4:43 escaped, and **d.** there unto this day. ... 3427
1Ch 5:8 who **d.** in Aroer, even unto Nebo.......... 3427
1Ch 5:10 they **d.** in their tents throughout 3427
1Ch 5:11 the children of Gad **d.** over against..... 3427
1Ch 5:16 And they **d.** in Gilead in Bashan, ... 3427
1Ch 5:22 **d.** in their steads until the captivity..... 3427
1Ch 5:23 tribe of Manasseh **d.** in the land:........ 3427
1Ch 7:29 In these **d.** the children of Joseph....... 3427
1Ch 8:28 chief men. These **d.** in Jerusalem........ 3427
1Ch 8:29 Gibeon **d.** the father of Gibeon; 3427
1Ch 8:32 **d.** with their brethren in Jerusalem, ... 3427
1Ch 9:2 Now the first inhabitants that **d.**.......... 3427
1Ch 9:3 in Jerusalem **d.** of the children of........ 3427
1Ch 9:16 that **d.** in the villages of the 3427
1Ch 9:34 generations; these **d.** at Jerusalem...... 3427
1Ch 9:35 in Gibeon **d.** the father of Gibeon; 3427
1Ch 9:38 **d.** with their brethren at Jerusalem, ... 3427
1Ch 10:7 Philistines came and **d.** in them.......... 3427
1Ch 11:7 And David **d.** in the castle; 3427
1Ch 17:5 I have not **d.** in an house since the..... 3427
2Ch 10:17 that **d.** in the cities of Judah, ... 3427
2Ch 11:5 And Rehoboam **d.** in Jerusalem, ... 3427
2Ch 16:2 king of Syria, that **d.** at Damascus, ... 3427
2Ch 19:4 And Jehoshaphat **d.** at Jerusalem: 3427
2Ch 20:8 And they **d.** therein, and have built...... 3427
2Ch 26:7 the Arabians that **d.** in Gur-baal, ... 3427
2Ch 26:21 **d.** in a several house, being a leper; ... 3427
2Ch 28:18 villages thereof: and they **d.** there. 3427
2Ch 30:25 of Israel, and that **d.** in Judah, ... 3427
2Ch 31:4 the people that **d.** in Jerusalem to....... 3427
2Ch 31:6 that **d.** in the cities of Judah, they 3427
2Ch 34:22 she **d.** in Jerusalem in the college:)..... 3427
Ezr 2:70 the Nethinims, **d.** in their cities,......... 3427
Ne 3:26 the Nethinims **d.** in Ophel, unto the.... 3427
Ne 4:12 the Jews which **d.** by them came,....... 3427
Ne 7:73 all Israel, **d.** in their cities; and 3427
Ne 11:1 of the people **d.** at Jerusalem:............ 3427
Ne 11:3 the province that **d.** in Jerusalem:....... 3427
Ne 11:3 but in the cities of Judah **d.** every 3427
Ne 11:4 at Jerusalem **d.** certain of the 3427
Ne 11:6 sons of Perez that **d.** at Jerusalem...... 3427
Ne 11:21 the Nethinims **d.** in Ophel; and 3427
Ne 11:25 of Judah **d.** at Kirjath-arba,................. 3427
Ne 11:30 they **d.** from Beer-sheba unto the....... 2583
Ne 11:31 also of Benjamin from Geba **d.** at ....
Ne 13:16 There **d.** men of Tyre also therein, ... 3427
Es 9:19 that **d.** in the unwalled towns, ... 3427
Job 22:8 and the honourable man **d.** in it.......... 3427
Job 29:25 and **d.** as a king in the army,............. 7931
Ps 68:10 congregation hath **d.** therein: 3427
Ps 74:2 mount Zion, wherein thou hast **d.**......... 7931
Ps 94:17 my soul had almost **d.** in silence........ 7931
Ps 120:6 My soul hath long **d.** with him 7931
Isa 13:20 neither shall it be **d.** in from............ 7931
Isa 29:1 to Ariel, the city where David **d.**!....... 2583
Isa 37:37 and returned, and **d.** at Nineveh........ 3427
Jer 2:6 through, and where no man **d.**? 3427
Jer 35:10 But we have **d.** in tents, and have...... 3427
Jer 39:14 home: so he **d.** among the people....... 3427
Jer 40:6 and **d.** with him among the people 3427
Jer 41:17 And they departed, and **d.** in the....... 3427
Jer 44:15 all the people that **d.** in the land of...... 3427
Jer 50:39 neither shall it be **d.** in from............. 7931
Eze 3:15 that **d.** by the river of Chebar, and..... 3427
Eze 31:6 and under his shadow **d.** all great....... 3427
Eze 31:17 that **d.** under his shadow in the......... 3427
Eze 36:17 the house of Israel **d.** in their own...... 3427
Eze 37:25 wherein your fathers have **d.**;............ 3427
Eze 39:26 when they **d.** safely in their land, ... 3427
Da 4:12 the fowls of the heaven **d.** in the........ 1753
Da 4:21 which the beasts of the field **d.**,......... 1753
Zep 2:15 rejoicing city that **d.** carelessly,.......... 3427
Mt 2:23 and **d.** in a city called Nazareth:......... *2730*
Mt 4:13 he came and **d.** in Capernaum,............ *2730*
Lu 1:65 on all that **d.** round about them:......... *4039*
Lu 13:4 **all men that d. in Jerusalem?**......... *2730*
Joh 1:14 and **d.** among us, (and we beheld........ *4637*
Joh 1:39 They came and saw where he **d.**,......... *3306*
Ac 7:2 Mesopotamia, before he **d.** in............ *2730*
Ac 7:4 Chaldeans, and **d.** in Charran:............ *2730*
Ac 9:22 the Jews which **d.** at Damascus,......... *2730*
Ac 9:32 to the saints which **d.** at Lydda......... *2730*
Ac 9:35 all that **d.** at Lydda and Saron saw...... *2730*
Ac 11:29 the brethren which **d.** in Judaea: *2730*
Ac 13:17 when they **d.** as strangers in the........ *3940*
Ac 19:10 all they which **d.** in Asia heard........... *2730*
Ac 22:12 of all the Jews which **d.** there,............ *2730*
Ac 28:30 Paul **d.** two whole years in his........... *3306*
2Ti 1:5 which **d.** first in thy grandmother *1774*
Re 11:10 them that **d.** on the earth. *2730*

DYED
Ex 25:5 rams' skins **d.** red, and badgers'..............
Ex 26:14 rams' skins **d.** red, and a covering...........
Ex 35:7 rams' skins **d.** red, and badgers'..............
Ex 36:19 rams' skins **d.** red, and a covering..........
Ex 39:34 rams' skins **d.** red, and the covering........
Isa 63:1 with **d.** garments from Bozrah?.......... 2556
Eze 23:15 exceeding in **d.** attire upon their......... 2871

DYING
Nu 17:13 shall we be consumed with **d.**? 1478
Mk 12:20 and the first took a wife, and **d.** *599*
Lu 8:42 years of age, and she lay a **d.** *599*
2Co 4:10 bearing about in the body the **d.** *3500*
2Co 6:9 known; as **d.**, and, behold, we live;...... *599*
Heb 11:21 Jacob, when he was a **d.**, blessed........ *599*

E.

EACH
Ge 15:10 laid **e.** piece one against another; 376
Ge 34:25 took **e.** man his sword, and came............
Ge 40:5 them, **e.** man his dream in one night, ...
Ge 40:5 one night, **e.** man according to the...........
Ge 41:11 dreamed **e.** man according to the ....
Ge 41:12 to **e.** man according to his dream he ....
Ge 45:22 he gave **e.** man changes of raiment;..........
Ex 18:7 asked **e.** other of their welfare;..............
Ex 30:34 of **e.** shall there be a like weight.......... 905
Le 24:7 put pure frankincense upon **e.** row,...........
Nu 1:44 **e.** one was for the house of his 376
Nu 7:3 of the princes, and for **e.** one an ox: ....
Nu 7:11 offer their offering, **e.** prince on his...... 259
Nu 7:85 **E.** charger of silver weighing an.......... 259
Nu 7:85 thirty shekels, **e.** bowl seventy:........... 259
Nu 14:34 even forty days, **e.** day for a year, ...
Nu 16:17 and Aaron, **e.** of you his censer........... 376
Nu 17:6 him a rod apiece, for **e.** prince one, ...
Nu 29:14 two tenth deals to **e.** ram of the.......... 259
Nu 29:15 a several tenth deal to **e.** lamb 259
Jos 18:4 from among you three men for **e.**.............
Jos 22:14 with him ten princes, of **e.** chief 259
Jos 22:14 **e.** one was an head of the house ....
Jg 8:18 **e.** one resembled the children of a............
Jg 21:22 not to **e.** man his wife in the war: ....
Ru 1:8 return **e.** to her mother's house:.......... 802
Ru 1:9 **e.** of you in the house of her husband... 802
1Ki 4:7 **e.** man his month in a year made......... 259
1Ki 6:23 two cherubims of olive tree, **e.** ten...........
1Ki 22:10 sat **e.** on his throne, having put on........ 376
2Ki 9:21 **e.** in his chariot, and they went out...... 376
2Ki 15:20 of **e.** man fifty shekels of silver, ... 259
1Ch 20:6 six on **e.** hand, and six on **e.** foot: ....
2Ch 3:15 the top of **e.** of them was five cubits.........
2Ch 4:13 two rows of pomegranates on **e.**........... 259
2Ch 9:18 stays on **e.** side of the sitting ....
Ne 13:24 according to the language of **e.** people. ......
Ps 85:10 and peace have kissed **e.** other. ....
Isa 2:20 they made **e.** one for himself to ....
Isa 6:2 seraphims: **e.** one had six wings; 259
Isa 35:7 of dragons, where **e.** lay, shall be............
Isa 57:2 **e.** one walking in his uprightness.............
Eze 4:6 have appointed thee **e.** day for a year,.......
Eze 40:16 and upon **e.** post were palm trees............
Eze 40:48 and measured **e.** post of the porch,...........
Lu 13:15 **doth not e. one of you on the**......... *1538*
Ac 2:3 fire, and it sat upon **e.** of them. *1538*
Php 2:3 let **e.** esteem other better than *240*
2Th 1:3 all toward **e.** other aboundeth;............. *240*
Re 4:8 And the four beasts had **e.** of them...... *303*

EAGLE See also EAGLE'S; EAGLES.
Le 11:13 the **e.**, and the ossifrage, and the....... 5404
Le 11:18 and the pelican and the gier **e.**,.......... 7360
De 14:12 not eat: the **e.**, and the ossifrage, ... 5404
De 14:17 the gier **e.**, and the cormorant, ... 7360
De 28:49 the earth, as swift as the **e.** flieth;...... 5404
De 32:11 As an **e.** stirreth up her nest,............ 5404
Job 9:26 as the **e.** that hasteth to the prey....... 5404
Job 39:27 Doth the **e.** mount up at thy.............. 5404
Pr 23:5 fly away as an **e.** toward heaven. 5404
Pr 30:19 The way of an **e.** in the air; 5404
Jer 48:40 Behold, he shall fly as an **e.**, ... 5404
Jer 49:16 make thy nest as high as the **e.**, ... 5404
Jer 49:22 and fly as the **e.**, and spread his 5404
Eze 1:10 they four also had the ace of an **e.**. 5404
Eze 10:14 and the fourth the face of an **e.**......... 5404
Eze 17:3 A great **e.** with great wings, long....... 5404
Eze 17:7 There was also another great **e.**......... 5404
Ho 8:1 He shall come as an **e.** against the...... 5404
Ob 4 Though thou exalt thyself as the **e.**,..... 5404
Mic 1:16 enlarge thy baldness as the **e.**; 5404
Hab 1:8 they shall fly as the **e.** that hasteth..... 5404
Re 4:7 the fourth beast was like a flying **e.**....... *105*
Re 12:14 were given two wings of a great **e.**, ... *105*

EAGLE'S
Ps 103:5 thy youth is renewed like the **e.**......... 5404
Da 7:4 was like a lion, and had **e.** wings; 5403

EAGLES See also EAGLES'.
2Sa 1:23 they were swifter than **e.**, they.......... 5404
Pr 30:17 and the young **e.** shall eat it.............. 5404
Isa 40:31 shall mount up with wings as **e.**; 5404
Jer 4:13 his horses are swifter than **e.**. 5404
La 4:19 swifter than the **e.** of the heaven:....... 5404
Mt 24:28 **is, there will the e. be gathered** *105*
Lu 17:37 **is, thither will the e. be gathered**.... *105*

EAGLES'
Ex 19:4 and how I bare you on **e.** wings,......... 5404
Da 4:33 his hairs were grown like **e.**.............. 5403

EAR See also EARED; EARING; EARRINGS; EARS; PLOW.
Ex 9:31 for the barley was in the **e.**,.................. 24
Ex 15:26 wilt give **e.** to his commandments,......... 238
Ex 21:6 his master shall bore his **e.** through...... 241
Ex 29:20 upon the tip of the right **e.** of Aaron,.... 241
Ex 29:20 upon the tip of the right **e.** of his........ 241
Le 8:23 upon the tip of Aaron's right **e.**, ... 241
Le 8:24 upon the tip of their right **e.**, and......... 241
Le 14:14, 17,25, 28 tip of the right **e.** of him......... 241
De 1:45 to your voice, nor give **e.** unto you. 238
De 15:17 it through his **e.** unto the door, ... 241
De 32:1 Give **e.**, O ye heavens, and I will 238
Jg 5:3 give **e.**, O ye princes; I, even I, will 238
1Sa 8:12 and will set them to **e.** his ground, ... 2790
1Sa 9:15 had told Samuel in his **e.** a day.......... 241
2Ki 19:16 Lord, bow down thine **e.**, and hear: 241
2Ch 24:19 them: but they would not give **e.**. 238
Ne 1:6 Let thine **e.** now be attentive, and....... 241
Ne 1:11 thine **e.** be attentive to the prayer 241
Ne 9:30 yet would they not give **e.**:................ 238
Job 4:12 mine **e.** received a little thereof. 241
Job 12:11 Doth not the **e.** try words? and the...... 241
Job 13:1 mine **e.** hath heard and understood....... 241
Job 29:11 the **e.** heard me, then it blessed me; 241
Job 29:21 Unto me men gave **e.**, and waited, ... 8085
Job 32:11 I gave **e.** to your reasons, whilst 238
Job 34:2 give **e.** unto me, ye that have 238
Job 34:3 the **e.** trieth words, as the mouth 241
Job 36:10 openeth also their **e.** to discipline,........ 241
Job 42:5 of thee by the hearing of the **e.**........... 241
Ps 5:1 Give **e.** to my words, O Lord, ... 238
Ps 10:17 thou wilt cause thine **e.** to hear: 241
Ps 17:1 my cry, give **e.** unto my prayer,.......... 238
Ps 17:6 incline thine **e.** unto me, and hear........ 241
Ps 31:2 Bow down thine **e.** to me; deliver........ 241
Ps 39:12 give **e.** unto my cry; hold not thy 238
Ps 45:10 and consider, and incline thine **e.**, ... 241
Ps 49:1 give **e.**, all ye inhabitants of the........... 238
Ps 49:4 I will incline mine **e.** to a parable: 241

Ps 54:2 give **e.** to the words of my mouth........ 238
Ps 55:1 Give **e.** to my prayer, O God;............ 238
Ps 58:4 deaf adder that stoppeth her **e.**; 241
Ps 71:2 incline thine **e.** unto me, and save........ 241
Ps 77:1 my voice; and he gave **e.** unto me. 238
Ps 78:1 Give **e.**, O my people, to my law:........ 238
Ps 80:1 Give **e.**, O Shepherd of Israel, ... 238
Ps 84:8 give **e.**, O God of Jacob. 238
Ps 86:1 down thine **e.**, O Lord, hear me: 241
Ps 86:6 Give **e.**, O Lord, unto my prayer;........ 238
Ps 88:2 incline thine **e.** unto my cry; 241
Ps 94:9 planted the **e.**, shall he not hear? 241
Ps 102:2 trouble; incline thine **e.** unto me: 241
Ps 116:2 he hath inclined his **e.** unto me, ... 241
Ps 141:1 give **e.** unto my voice, when I cry 238
Ps 143:1 O Lord, give **e.** to my supplications:..... 238
Pr 2:2 thou incline thine **e.** unto wisdom, ... 241
Pr 4:20 incline thine **e.** unto my sayings. 241
Pr 5:1 bow thine **e.** to my understanding: 241
Pr 5:13 mine **e.** to them that instructed me! 241
Pr 15:31 The **e.** that heareth the reproof of 241
Pr 17:4 liar giveth **e.** to a naughty tongue......... 238
Pr 18:15 **e.** of the wise seeketh knowledge. 241
Pr 20:12 The hearing **e.**, and the seeing eye, ... 241
Pr 22:17 Bow down thine **e.**, and hear the......... 241
Pr 25:12 a wise reprover upon an obedient **e.**....... 241
Pr 28:9 away his **e.** from hearing the law, ... 241
Ec 1:8 nor the **e.** filled with hearing. 241
Isa 1:2 O heavens, and give **e.**, O earth: 238
Isa 1:10 give **e.** unto the law of our God,.......... 238
Isa 8:9 and give **e.**, all ye of far countries: 238
Isa 28:23 Give ye **e.**, and hear my voice; 238
Isa 30:24 young asses that **e.** the ground 5647
Isa 32:9 daughters; give **e.** unto my speech. 238
Isa 37:17 Incline thine **e.**, O Lord, and hear; 241
Isa 42:23 among you will give **e.** to this? 238
Isa 48:8 time that thine **e.** was not opened: 241
Isa 50:4 wakeneth mine **e.** to hear as the........... 241
Isa 50:5 The Lord God hath opened mine **e.**,........ 241
Isa 51:4 give **e.** unto me, O my nation: 238
Isa 55:3 Incline your **e.**, and come unto me: 241
Isa 59:1 his **e.** heavy, that it cannot hear: 241
Isa 64:4 not heard, nor perceived by the **e.**, ... 238
Jer 6:10 behold, their **e.** is uncircumcised, ... 241
Jer 7:24 nor inclined their **e.**, but walked in....... 241
Jer 7:26 nor inclined their **e.**, but hardened........ 241
Jer 9:20 **e.** receive the word of his mouth, ... 241
Jer 11:8 nor inclined their **e.**, but walked 241
Jer 13:15 ye, and give **e.**; be not proud:............. 238
Jer 17:23 neither inclined their **e.**, but made......... 241
Jer 25:4 nor inclined your **e.** to hear. 241
Jer 34:14 unto me, neither inclined their **e.**. 241
Jer 35:15 but ye have not inclined your **e.**, ... 241
Jer 44:5 nor inclined their **e.** to turn from 241
La 3:56 hide not thine **e.** at my breathing, ... 241
Da 9:18 O my God, incline thine **e.**, and hear; ... 241
Ho 5:1 give ye **e.**, O house of the king; 238
Joe 1:2 Hear this, ye old men, and give **e.**, ... 238
Am 3:12 two legs, or a piece of an **e.**; 241
Mt 10:27 **what ye hear in the e., that preach** *3775*
Mt 26:51 high priest's, and smote off his **e.**........ *5621*
Mk 4:28 **first the blade, then the e., after**... *4719*
Mk 4:28 **after that the full corn in the e.**... *4719*
Mk 14:47 high priest, and cut off his **e.**............. *5621*
Lu 12:3 **which ye have spoken in the e.** *3775*
Lu 22:50 high priest, and cut off his right **e.**....... *3775*
Lu 22:51 he touched his **e.**, and healed him....... *5621*
Joh 18:10 servant, and cut off his right **e.**........... *5621*
Joh 18:26 his kinsman whose **e.** Peter cut off, ... *5621*
1Co 2:9 nor **e.** heard, neither have entered *3775*
1Co 12:16 And if the **e.** shall say, Because I....... *3775*
Re 2:7, 11,17,29 He that hath an **e.**, let him.... *3775*
Re 3:6, 13,22 He that hath an **e.**, let him *3775*
Re 13:9 If any man have an **e.**, let him hear. ... *3775*

EARED See also PLOWED.

De 21:4 which is neither **e.** nor sown, ... 5647

EARING See also PLOWING.

Ge 45:6 there neither be **e.** nor harvest. 2758
Ex 34:21 in **e.** time and in harvest thou.............. 2758

EARLY

Ge 19:2 rise up **e.**, and go on your ways......... 7925
Ge 19:27 Abraham gat up **e.** in the morning 7925
Ge 20:8 Abimelech rose **e.** in the morning, ... 7925
Ge 21:14 Abraham rose up **e.** in the morning,..... 7925
Ge 22:3 Abraham rose up **e.** in the morning,.... 7925
Ge 28:18 Jacob rose up **e.** in the morning, ... 7925
Ge 31:55 **e.** in the morning Laban rose up, ... 7925
Ex 8:20 Rise up **e.** in the morning, and........... 7925
Ex 9:13 Moses, Rise up **e.** in the morning,...... 7925
Ex 24:4 and rose up **e.** in the morning,........... 7925
Ex 32:6 And they rose up **e.** on the morrow,... 7925
Ex 34:4 Moses rose up **e.** in the morning,........ 7925
Nu 14:40 And they rose up **e.** in the morning. ... 7925
Jos 3:1 And Joshua rose **e.** in the morning;..... 7925
Jos 6:12 And Joshua rose **e.** in the morning,..... 7925
Jos 6:15 **e.** about the dawning of the day, ... 7925
Jos 7:16 Joshua rose up **e.** in the morning,....... 7925
Jos 8:10 Joshua rose up **e.** in the morning,....... 7925
Jos 8:14 they hasted and rose up **e.**, and the.... 7925
Jg 6:28 when the men of the city arose **e.**...... 7925
Jg 6:38 for he rose up **e.** on the morrow,......... 7925
Jg 7:1 Then Jerubbaal...rose up **e.**,............... 7925
Jg 7:3 and depart **e.** from mount Gilead. 6852
Jg 9:33 rise **e.**, and set upon the city:............ 7925
Jg 19:5 when they arose **e.** in the morning, ... 7925
Jg 19:8 And he arose **e.** in the morning.......... 7925
Jg 19:9 to morrow get you **e.** on your way,..... 7925
Jg 21:4 the morrow, that the people rose **e.**, .. 7925
1Sa 1:19 And they rose up in the morning **e.**, ... 7925
1Sa 5:3 they of Ashdod arose **e.** on the.......... 7925
1Sa 5:4 when they arose **e.** on the morrow..... 7925
1Sa 9:26 they arose **e.**: and it came to pass...... 7925
1Sa 15:12 when Samuel rose **e.** to meet Saul...... 7925
1Sa 17:20 David rose up **e.** in the morning,....... 7925
1Sa 29:10 now rise up **e.** in the morning............ 7925
1Sa 29:10 and as soon as ye be up **e.** in the....... 7925
1Sa 29:11 So David and his men rose up **e.** to.... 7925
2Sa 15:2 And Absalom rose up **e.**, and stood 7925
2Ki 3:22 And they rose up **e.** in the morning, ... 7925
2Ki 6:15 of the man of God was risen **e.**,.......... 7925
2Ki 19:35 when they arose **e.** in the morning, ... 7925
2Ch 20:20 And they rose **e.** in the morning, ... 7925
2Ch 29:20 Then Hezekiah the king rose **e.**,......... 7925
Job 1:5 and rose up **e.** in the morning,........... 7925
Ps 46:5 shall help her, and that right **e.**.......... 1242
Ps 57:8 I myself will awake **e.**. 7837
Ps 63:1 art my God; **e.** will I seek thee:.......... 7836
Ps 78:34 and enquired **e.** after God. 7836
Ps 90:14 satisfy us **e.** with thy mercy; 1242
Ps 101:8 I will **e.** destroy all the wicked of 1242
Ps 108:2 and harp: I myself will awake **e.**......... 7837
Ps 127:2 It is vain for you to rise up **e.**, ... 7925
Pr 1:28 they shall seek me **e.**, but they........... 7836
Pr 8:17 that seek me **e.** shall find me............ 7836
Pr 27:14 voice, rising **e.** in the morning, ... 7925
Ca 7:12 Let us get up **e.** to the vineyards;...... 7925
Isa 5:11 Woe unto them that rise up **e.**........... 7925
Isa 26:9 within me will I seek thee **e.**:............. 7836
Isa 37:36 they arose **e.** in the morning, ... 7925
Jer 7:13 you, rising up **e.** and speaking, ... 7925
Jer 7:25 rising up **e.** and sending them: 7925
Jer 11:7 rising **e.** and protesting, saying, ... 7925
Jer 25:3 unto you, rising **e.** and speaking; 7925
Jer 25:4 rising **e.** and sending them; 7925
Jer 26:5 rising up **e.**, and sending them, ... 7925
Jer 29:19 rising up **e.** and sending them; 7925
Jer 32:33 rising up **e.** and teaching them, ... 7925
Jer 35:14 rising **e.** and speaking; but ye 7925
Jer 35:15 rising up **e.** and sending them, ... 7925
Jer 44:4 rising **e.** and sending them. 7925
Da 6:19 king arose very **e.** in the morning,...... 8238
Ho 5:15 affliction they will seek me **e.**. 7836
Ho 6:4 as the **e.** dew it goeth away. 7925
Ho 13:3 as the **e.** dew that passeth away. 7925
Zep 3:7 but they rose **e.**, and corrupted all...... 7925
Mt 20:1 **went out e. in the morning to**. *260,4404*
Mk 16:2 And very **e.** in the morning the *260,4404*
Mk 16:9 risen **e.** the first day of the week,..*260,4404*
Lu 21:38 the people came **e.** in the morning...... *3719*
Lu 24:1 very **e.** in the morning, they came...... *3722*
Lu 24:22 which were **e.** at the sepulchre; *3721*
Joh 8:2 And **e.** in the morning he came.......... *3722*
Joh 18:28 it was **e.**; and they themselves *4405*
Joh 20:1 cometh Mary Magdalene **e.**, when...... *4404*
Ac 5:21 **e.** in the morning, and taught. *3722*
Jas 5:7 he receive the **e.** and latter rain. *4406*

EARNEST

Ro 8:19 the **e.** expectation of the creature *603*
2Co 1:22 the **e.** of the Spirit in our hearts. *728*
2Co 5:5 given unto us the **e.** of the Spirit. *728*
2Co 7:7 he told us your **e.** desire, your *1972*
2Co 8:16 put the same **e.** care into the heart..... *4710*
Eph 1:14 Which is the **e.** of our inheritance *728*
Php 1:20 to my **e.** expectation and my hope, ... *603*
Heb 2:1 we ought to give the more **e.** heed..... *4056*

EARNESTLY

Nu 22:37 Did I not **e.** send unto thee to call thee?....
1Sa 20:6 say, David **e.** asked leave of me that.........
1Sa 20:28 David **e.** asked leave of me to go to..........
Ne 3:20 the son of Zabbai **e.** repaired............. 2734
Job 7:2 As a servant **e.** desireth the shadow. ....
Jer 11:7 For I **e.** protested unto your fathers ....
Jer 31:20 him, I do **e.** remember him still:..............
Mic 7:3 may do evil with both hands **e.**, ... 3190
Lu 22:44 in an agony he prayed more **e.**: *1617*
Lu 22:56 and **e.** looked upon him, and said, ... *816*
Ac 3:12 why look ye so **e.** on us, ... *816*
Ac 23:1 Paul, **e.** beholding the council, ... *816*
1Co 12:31 But covet **e.** the best gifts: *2206*
2Co 5:2 **e.** desiring to be clothed upon............ *1971*
Jas 5:17 prayed **e.** that it might not rain: *4335*
Jude 3 ye should **e.** contend for the faith...... *1864*

EARNETH

Hag 1:6 he that **e.** wages, **e.** wages to put it ... 7936

EARRING See also EARRINGS.

Ge 24:22 golden **e.** of half a shekel weight, ... 5141
Ge 24:30 came to pass, when he saw the **e.**...... 5141
Ge 24:47 I put the **e.** upon her face,................ 5141
Job 42:11 and every one an **e.** of gold............. 5141
Pr 25:12 an **e.** of gold, and an ornament of....... 5141

EARRINGS

Ge 35:4 their **e.** which were in their ears;....... 5141
Ex 32:2 Break off the golden **e.**, which.......... 5141
Ex 32:3 people brake off the golden **e.** 5141
Ex 35:22 **e.**, and rings, and tablets, all jewels.... 5141
Nu 31:50 chains, and bracelets, rings, **e.**,.......... 5694
Jg 8:24 me every man the **e.** of his prey.......... 5141
Jg 8:24 (For they had golden **e.**, because they. 5141
Jg 8:25 every man the **e.** of his prey. 5141
Jg 8:26 And the weight of the golden **e.**......... 5141
Isa 3:20 and the tablets, and the **e.**, ... 3908
Eze 16:12 **e.** in thine ears, and a beautiful.......... 5694
Ho 2:13 herself with her **e.** and her jewels, ... 5141

EARS

Ge 20:8 and told all these things in their **e.**: 241
Ge 35:4 earrings which were in their **e.**;........... 241
Ge 41:5 seven **e.** of corn came up upon 7641
Ge 41:6 seven thin **e.** and blasted with the 7641
Ge 41:7 And the seven thin **e.** devoured the 7641
Ge 41:7 devoured the seven rank and full **e.**.... 7641
Ge 41:22 seven **e.** come up in one stalk, ... 7641
Ge 41:23 seven **e.**, withered, thin, and............. 7641
Ge 41:24 thin **e.** devoured the seven good **e.**:..... 7641
Ge 41:26 the seven good **e.** are seven years: 7641
Ge 41:27 the seven empty **e.** blasted with.......... 7641
Ge 44:18 spaeak a word in my lord's **e.**, ... 241
Ge 50:4 I pray you, in the **e.** of Pharaoh, ... 241
Ex 10:2 mayest tell in the **e.** of thy son,........... 241
Ex 11:2 Speak now in the **e.** of the people,....... 241
Ex 17:14 rehease it in the **e.** of Joshua: 241
Ex 32:2 which are in the **e.** of your wives,......... 241
Ex 32:3 earrings which were in their **e.**,............ 241
Le 2:14 of thy firstfruits green **e.** of corn........... 24
Le 2:14 even corn beaten out of full **e.**............ 3759
Le 23:14 nor parched corn, nor green **e.**, ... 3759
Nu 11:18 ye have wept in the **e.** of the Lord, ... 241
Nu 14:28 as ye have spoken in mine **e.**, so.......... 241
De 5:1 which I speak in your **e.** this day, ... 241
De 23:25 pluck the **e.** with thine hand; 4425
De 29:4 eyes to see, and **e.** to hear, unto this... 241
De 31:28 I may speak these words in their **e.**, ... 241
De 31:30 Moses spake in the **e.** of all the........... 241
De 32:44 this song in the **e.** of the people, ... 241
Jos 20:4 his cause in the **e.** of the elders........... 241
Jg 7:3 proclaim in the **e.** of the people, ... 241
Jg 9:2 Speak, I pray you, in the **e.** of all 241
Jg 9:3 in the **e.** of all the men of Shechem...... 241
Jg 17:2 and spakest of also in mine **e.**, ... 241
Ru 2:2 and glean **e.** of corn after him............ 7641
1Sa 3:11 the **e.** of every one that heareth.......... 241
1Sa 8:21 rehearse them in the **e.** of the Lord. 241
1Sa 11:4 the tidings in the **e.** of the people: 241
1Sa 15:14 bleating of the sheep in mine **e.**,.......... 241
1Sa 18:23 those words in the **e.** of David............ 241
2Sa 3:19 also spake in the **e.** of Benjamin: 241
2Sa 3:19 also to speak in the **e.** of David........... 241

2Sa 7:22 all that we have heard with our **e.** 241
2Sa 22:7 my cry did enter into his **e.** 241
2Ki 4:42 **e.** of corn in the husk thereof. 3759
2Ki 18:26 in the **e.** of the people that are on 241
2Ki 19:28 tumult is come up into mine **e.**, 241
2Ki 21:12 of it, both his **e.** shall tingle. 241
2Ki 23:2 read in their **e.** all the words of the 241
1Ch 17:20 all that we have heard with our **e.** 241
2Ch 6:40 and let thine **e.** be attent unto the 241
2Ch 7:15 and mine **e.** attent unto the prayer 241
2Ch 34:30 read in their **e.** all the words of the 241
Ne 8:3 and the **e.** of all the people were 241
Job 13:17 and my declaration with your **e.** 241
Job 15:21 A dreadful sound is in his **e.**: 241
Job 24:24 off as the tops of the **e.** of corn. 7641
Job 28:22 heard the fame thereof with our **e.** 241
Job 33:16 Then he openeth the **e.** of men, 241
Job 36:15 openeth their **e.** in oppression. 241
Ps 18:6 came before him, even into his **e.** 241
Ps 34:15 and his **e.** are open unto their cry. 241
Ps 40:6 mine **e.** hast thou opened: 241
Ps 44:1 We have heard with our **e.**, O God, 241
Ps 78:1 incline your **e.** to the words of my 241
Ps 92:11 mine **e.** shall hear my desire of 241
Ps 115:6 They have **e.**, but they hear not: 241
Ps 130:2 let thine **e.** be attentive to the voice 241
Ps 135:17 They have **e.**, but they hear not; 241
Pr 21:13 Whoso stoppeth his **e.** at the cry 241
Pr 23:9 Speak not in the **e.** of a fool: 241
Pr 23:12 thine **e.** to the words of knowledge. 241
Pr 26:17 one that taketh a dog by the **e.** 241
Isa 5:9 In mine **e.** said the Lord of hosts, 241
Isa 6:10 and make their **e.** heavy, and shut 241
Isa 6:10 their eyes, and hear with their **e.**, 241
Isa 11:3 reprove after the hearing of his **e.**: 241
Isa 17:5 and reapeth the **e.** with his arm; 7641
Isa 17:5 it shall be as he that gathereth **e.** 7641
Isa 22:14 revealed in mine **e.** by the Lord 241
Isa 30:21 And thine **e.** shall hear a word 241
Isa 32:3 **e.** of them that hear shall hearken. 241
Isa 33:15 stoppeth his **e.** from hearing of 241
Isa 35:5 **e.** of the deaf shall be unstopped. 241
Isa 36:11 in the **e.** of the people that are on 241
Isa 37:29 tumult, is come up into mine **e.**, 241
Isa 42:20 opening the **e.**, but he heareth not. 241
Isa 43:8 have eyes, and the deaf that have **e.** 241
Isa 49:20 other, shall say again in thine **e.**, 241
Jer 2:2 Go and cry in the **e.** of Jerusalem, 241
Jer 5:21 which have **e.**, and hear not: 241
Jer 19:3 whosoever heareth, his **e.** shall 241
Jer 26:11 as ye have heard with your **e.** 241
Jer 26:15 speak all these words in your **e.** 241
Jer 28:7 this word that I speak in thine **e.** 241
Jer 28:7 and in the **e.** of all the people; 241
Jer 29:29 this letter in the **e.** of Jeremiah. 241
Jer 36:6 in the **e.** of the people in the Lord's 241
Jer 36:6 in the **e.** of all Judah that come out 241
Jer 36:10 house, in the **e.** of all the people. 241
Jer 36:13 read the book in the **e.** of the people. 241
Jer 36:14 hast read in the **e.** of the people, 241
Jer 36:15 down now, and read it in our **e.** 241
Jer 36:15 So Baruch read it in their **e.** 241
Jer 36:20 all the words in the **e.** of the king. 241
Jer 36:21 Jehudi read it in the **e.** of the king, 241
Jer 36:21 and in the **e.** of all the princes 241
Eze 3:10 thine heart, and hear with thine **e.** 241
Eze 8:18 cry in mine **e.** with a loud voice, 241
Eze 9:1 cried also in mine **e.** with a loud 241
Eze 12:2 they have **e.** to hear, and hear not: 241
Eze 16:12 and earrings in thine **e.**, and a 241
Eze 23:25 take away thy nose and thine **e.**; 241
Eze 24:26 cause thee to hear it with thine **e.**? 241
Eze 40:4 thine eyes, and hear with thine **e.**, 241
Eze 44:5 and hear with thine **e.** all that I say 241
Mic 7:16 their mouth, their **e.** shall be deaf. 241
Zec 7:11 and stopped their **e.**, that they 241
Mt 11:15 **He that hath e. to hear, let him** *3775*
Mt 12:1 and began to pluck the **e.** of corn, *4719*
Mt 13:9 **Who hath e. to hear, let him hear.** *3775*
Mt 13:15 **and their e. are dull of hearing,** *3775*
Mt 13:15 **their eyes, and hear with their e.,** *3775*
Mt 13:16 **and your e., for they hear.** *3775*
Mt 13:43 **Who hath e. to hear, let him hear.** *3775*
Mt 28:14 if this come to the governor's **e.**, *191*
Mk 2:23 went, to pluck the **e.** of corn. *4719*
Mk 4:9 **He that hath e. to hear, let him** *3775*
Mk 4:23 **If any man have e. to hear,** *3775*
Mk 7:16 **If any man have e. to hear, let** *3775*
Mk 7:33 and put his fingers into his **e.**, *3775*
Mk 7:35 straightway his **e.** were opened, *189*
Mk 8:18 **and having e., hear ye not?** *3775*
Lu 1:44 thy salutation sounded in mine **e.**, *3775*
Lu 4:21 **this scripture fulfilled in your e.** *3775*
Lu 6:1 disciples plucked the **e.** of corn, *4719*
Lu 8:8 **He that hath e. to hear, let him** *3775*
Lu 9:44 **sayings sink down into your e.** *3775*
Lu 14:35 **He that hath e. to hear, let him** *3775*
Ac 7:51 and uncircumcised in heart and **e.** *3775*
Ac 7:57 and stopped their **e.** and ran upon *3775*
Ac 11:22 came unto the **e.** of the church *3775*
Ac 17:20 certain strange things to our **e.**: *189*
Ac 28:27 and their **e.** are dull of hearing, *3775*
Ac 28:27 their eyes, and hear with their **e.**, *3775*
Ro 11:8 and **e.** that they should not hear:) *3775*
2Ti 4:3 teachers, having itching **e.**; *189*
2Ti 4:4 turn away their **e.** from the truth, *189*
Jas 5:4 entered into the **e.** of the Lord *3775*
1Pe 3:12 his **e.** are open unto their prayers: *3775*

EARTH See also EARTHQUAKE.

Ge 1:1 God created the heaven and the **e.** 776
Ge 1:2 And the **e.** was without form, and 776
Ge 1:10 And God called the dry land **E.**; 776
Ge 1:11 said, Let the **e.** bring forth grass, 776
Ge 1:11 whose seed is in itself, upon the **e.**: 776
Ge 1:12 And the **e.** brought forth grass, 776
Ge 1:15 to give light upon the **e.**: and it was 776
Ge 1:17 to give light upon the **e.**, 776
Ge 1:20 and fowl that may fly above the **e.** in 776
Ge 1:22 and let fowl multiply in the **e.** 776
Ge 1:24 Let the **e.** bring forth the living 776
Ge 1:24 and beast of the **e.** after his kind: 776
Ge 1:25 God made the beast of the **e.** after 776
Ge 1:25 thing that creepeth upon the **e.** 127
Ge 1:26 and over all the **e.**, and over every 776
Ge 1:26 thing that creepeth upon the **e.** 776
Ge 1:28 multiply, and replenish the **e.**, and 776
Ge 1:28 living thing that moveth upon the **e.** 776
Ge 1:29 which is upon the face of all the **e.**, 776
Ge 1:30 to every beast of the **e.**, and to 776
Ge 1:30 thing that creepeth upon the **e.**, 776
Ge 2:1 the heavens and the **e.** were finished 776
Ge 2:4 of the heavens and of the **e.** when 776
Ge 2:4 day that the Lord God made the **e.** 776
Ge 2:5 of the field before it was in the **e.**, 776
Ge 2:5 had not caused it to rain upon thee **e.**, 776
Ge 2:6 there went up a mist from the **e.**, 776
Ge 4:11 now art thou cursed from the **e.**, 127
Ge 4:12 vagabond shalt thou be in the **e.** 776
Ge 4:14 this day from the face of the **e.**; 127
Ge 4:14 fugitive and a vagabond in the **e.**; 776
Ge 6:1 multiply upon the face of the **e.**, 127
Ge 6:4 were giants in the **e.** in those days; 776
Ge 6:5 of man was great in the **e.**, and that 776
Ge 6:6 that he had made man on the **e.**, 776
Ge 6:7 created from the face of the **e.**; 127
Ge 6:11 **e.** also was corrupt before God, 776
Ge 6:11 the **e.** was filled with violence. 776
Ge 6:12 God looked upon the **e.**, and, behold, 776
Ge 6:12 had corrupted his way upon the **e.**, 776
Ge 6:13 for the **e.** is filled with violence. 776
Ge 6:13 I will destroy them with the **e.** 776
Ge 6:17 bring a flood of waters upon the **e.**, 776
Ge 6:17 every thing that is in the **e.** shall die. 776
Ge 6:20 of every creeping thing of the **e.** 127
Ge 7:3 seed alive upon the face of all the **e.** 776
Ge 7:4 I will cause it to rain upon the **e.** 776
Ge 7:4 destroy from off the face of the **e.** 127
Ge 7:6 the flood of waters was upon the **e.** 776
Ge 7:8 thing that creepeth upon the **e.**, 127
Ge 7:10 waters of the flood were upon the **e.** 776
Ge 7:12 the rain was upon the **e.** forty days 776
Ge 7:14 creepeth upon the **e.** after his kind, 776
Ge 7:17 flood was forty days upon the **e.**; 776
Ge 7:17 and it was lift up above the **e.** 776
Ge 7:18 increased greatly upon the **e.**; 776
Ge 7:19 prevailed exceedingly upon the **e.**; 776
Ge 7:21 flesh died that moved upon the **e.**, 776
Ge 7:21 thing that creepeth upon the **e.**, 776
Ge 7:23 they were destroyed from the **e.** 776
Ge 7:24 the waters prevailed upon the **e.** 776
Ge 8:1 God made a wind to pass over the **e.**, 776
Ge 8:3 the waters returned from off the **e.** 776
Ge 8:7 were dried up from off the **e.**: 776
Ge 8:9 were on the face of the whole **e.**: 776
Ge 8:11 waters were abated from off the **e.** 776
Ge 8:13 were dried up from off the **e.**: 776
Ge 8:14 day of the month, was the **e.** dried. 776
Ge 8:17 thing that creepeth upon the **e.**; 776
Ge 8:17 may breed abundantly in the **e.**, 776
Ge 8:17 be fruitful, and multiply upon the **e.** 776
Ge 8:19 whatsoever creepeth upon the **e.**, 776
Ge 8:22 While the **e.** remaineth, seed time 776
Ge 9:1 and multiply, and replenish the **e.** 776
Ge 9:2 shall be upon every beast of the **e.**, 776
Ge 9:2 upon all that moveth upon the **e.**, 127
Ge 9:7 bring forth abundantly in the **e.**, 776
Ge 9:10 of every beast of the **e.** with you; 776
Ge 9:10 of the ark, to every beast of the **e.** 776
Ge 9:11 more be a flood to destroy the **e.** 776
Ge 9:13 a covenant between me and the **e.** 776
Ge 9:14 when I bring a cloud over the **e.**, 776
Ge 9:16 of all flesh that is upon the **e.** 776
Ge 9:17 and all flesh that is upon the **e.** 776
Ge 9:19 then was the whole **e.** overspread. 776
Ge 10:8 began to be a mighty one in the **e.** 776
Ge 10:25 in his days was the **e.** divided; 776
Ge 10:32 were the nations divided in the **e.** 776
Ge 11:1 the whole **e.** was of one language, 776
Ge 11:4 abroad upon the face of the whole **e.** 776
Ge 11:8 thence upon the face of all the **e.**: 776
Ge 11:9 confound the language of all the **e.**: 776
Ge 11:9 abroad upon the face of all the **e.** 776
Ge 12:3 shall all families of the **e.** be blessed. 127
Ge 13:16 make thy seed as the dust of the **e.**: 776
Ge 13:16 a man can number the dust of the **e.**, 776
Ge 14:19 God, possessor of heaven and **e.**: 776
Ge 14:22 God, the possessor of heaven and **e.**, 776
Ge 18:18 the nations of the **e.** shall be blessed 776
Ge 18:25 not the Judge of all the **e.** do right? 776
Ge 19:23 The sun was risen upon the **e.** when 776
Ge 19:31 there is not a man in the **e.** to come 776
Ge 19:31 us after the manner of all the **e.**: 776
Ge 22:18 all the nations of the **e.** be blessed; 776
Ge 24:3 of heaven, and the God of the **e.**, 776
Ge 24:52 the Lord, bowing himself to the **e.** 776
Ge 26:4 all the nations of the **e.** be blessed; 776
Ge 26:15 them, and filled them with **e.** 6083
Ge 27:28 the fatness of the **e.**, and plenty of 776
Ge 27:39 shall be the fatness of the **e.**, and of 776
Ge 28:12 behold a ladder set up on the **e.**, 776
Ge 28:14 shall be as the dust of the **e.**, 776
Ge 28:14 all the families of the **e.** be blessed. 127
Ge 37:10 down ourselves to thee to the **e.**? 776
Ge 41:47 the **e.** brought forth by handfuls. 776
Ge 41:56 was over all the face of the **e.** 776
Ge 42:6 before him with their faces to the **e.** 776
Ge 43:26 bowed themselves to him to the **e.** 776
Ge 45:7 to preserve you a posterity in the **e.** 776
Ge 48:12 himself with his face to the **e.**, 776
Ge 48:16 a multitude in the midst of the **e.** 776
Ex 8:17 and smote the dust of the **e.**, 776
Ex 8:22 I am the Lord in the midst of the **e.** 776
Ex 9:14 thee is none like me in all the **e.** 776
Ex 9:15 thou shalt be cut off from the **e.** 776
Ex 9:16 be declared throughout all the **e.** 776
Ex 9:29 know how that the **e.** is the Lord's. 776
Ex 9:33 the rain was not poured upon the **e.** 776
Ex 10:5 they shall cover the face of the **e.**, 776
Ex 10:5 that one cannot be able to see the **e.** 776
Ex 10:6 the day that they were upon the **e.** 127
Ex 10:15 they covered the face of the whole **e.**, 776
Ex 15:12 right hand, the **e.** swallowed them. 776
Ex 19:5 all people: for all the **e.** is mine: 776
Ex 20:4 or that is in the **e.** beneath, or 776
Ex 20:4 that is in the water under the **e.** 776
Ex 20:11 days the Lord made heaven and **e.**, 776
Ex 20:24 An altar of **e.** thou shalt make unto 127
Ex 31:17 days the Lord made heaven and **e.**, 776
Ex 32:12 them from the face of the **e.**? 127
Ex 33:16 that are upon the face of the **e.** 127
Ex 34:8 and bowed his head toward the **e.**, 776
Ex 34:10 as have not been done in all the **e.**, 776
Le 11:2 all the beasts that are on the **e.** 776
Le 11:21 feet, to leap withal upon the **e.**; 776
Le 11:29 things that creep upon the **e.**; 776
Le 11:41 thing that creepeth upon the **e.** 776
Le 11:42 things that creep upon the **e.**, 776
Le 11:44 thing that creepeth upon the **e.** 776
Le 11:46 creature that creepeth upon the **e.** 776

Le 15:12 the vessel of **e.**, that he toucheth........2789
Le 26:19 as iron, and your **e.** as brass:.............. 776
Nu 11:31 cubits high upon the face of the **e.**........ 776
Nu 12:3 which were upon the face of the **e.**.)..... 127
Nu 14:21 the **e.** shall be filled with the glory........ 776
Nu 16:30 and the **e.** open her mouth, and.......... 127
Nu 16:32 And the **e.** opened her mouth, and........ 776
Nu 16:33 and the **e.** closed upon them: and......... 776
Nu 16:34 Lest the **e.** swallow us up also............ 776
Nu 22:5 they cover the face of the **e.**, and they.. 776
Nu 22:11 which covereth the face of the **e.**:........ 776
Nu 26:10 And the **e.** opened her mouth, and........ 776
De 3:24 what God is there in heaven or in **e.**,.... 776
De 4:10 that they shall live upon the **e.**,............ 127
De 4:17 of any beast that is on the **e.**, the......... 776
De 4:18 that is in the waters beneath the **e.**:...... 776
De 4:26 I call heaven and **e.** to witness.......... 776
De 4:32 that God created man upon the **e.**,.......... 776
De 4:36 upon **e.** he shewed thee his great fire;... 776
De 4:39 above, and upon the **e.** beneath:........... 776
De 4:40 mayest prolong thy days upon the **e.**...... 127
De 5:8 or that is in the **e.** beneath, or that...... 776
De 5:8 is in the waters beneath the **e.**:.......... 776
De 6:15 thee from off the face of the **e.**............ 127
De 7:6 that are upon the face of the **e.**............ 127
De 10:14 the **e.** also, with all that therein is........ 776
De 11:6 now the **e.** opened her mouth, and........ 776
De 11:21 as the days of heaven upon the **e.**......... 776
De 12:1 all the days that ye live upon the **e.**...... 127
De 12:16 ye shall pour it upon the **e.** as water,.... 776
De 12:19 as long as thou livest upon the **e.**......... 127
De 12:24 thou shalt pour it upon the **e.** as.......... 776
De 13:7 from the one end of the **e.** even unto.... 776
De 13:7 even unto the other end of the **e.**;......... 776
De 14:2 all the nations that are upon the **e.**......... 127
De 26:2 the first of all the fruit of the **e.**,........... 127
De 28:1 on high above all nations of the **e.**:......... 776
De 28:10 all peole of the **e.** shall see that thou..... 776
De 28:23 and the **e.** that is under thee shall be..... 776
De 28:25 into all the kingdoms of the **e.**.............. 776
De 28:26 the air, and unto the beasts of the **e.**,..... 776
De 28:49 from afar, from the end of the **e.**,.......... 776
De 28:64 end of the **e.** even unto the other;........ 776
De 30:19 call heaven and **e.** to record this day..... 776
De 31:28 and **e.** to record against them,............. 776
De 32:1 hear, O **e.**, the words of my mouth....... 776
De 32:13 ride on the high places of the **e.**,........... 776
De 32:22 consume the **e.** with her increase,........ 776
De 33:16 And for the precious things of the **e.**...... 776
De 33:17 people together to the ends of the **e.**:... 776
Jos 2:11 in heaven above, and in **e.** beneath........ 776
Jos 3:11 the Lord of all the **e.** passeth over........ 776
Jos 3:13 Lord of all the **e.**, shall rest in the........ 776
Jos 4:24 That all the people of the **e.** might......... 776
Jos 5:14 Joshua fell on his face to the **e.**, and...... 776
Jos 7:6 and fell to the **e.** upon his face before.... 776
Jos 7:9 cut off our name from the **e.**:.............. 776
Jos 7:21 they are hid in the **e.** in the midst......... 776
Jos 23:14 I am going the way of all the **e.**:........... 776
Jg 3:25 lord was fallen down dead on the **e.**....... 776
Jg 5:4 the **e.** trembled, and the heavens.......... 776
Jg 6:4 destroyed the increase of the **e.**,........... 776
Jg 6:37 it be dry upon all the **e.** beside,........... 776
Jg 18:10 no want of anything that is in the **e.**....... 776
1Sa 2:8 the pillars of the **e.** are the Lord's,........ 776
1Sa 2:10 Lord shall judge the ends of the **e.**;........ 776
1Sa 4:5 a great shout, so that the **e.** rang......... 776
1Sa 4:12 rent, and with **e.** upon his head........... 127
1Sa 5:3 was fallen upon his face to the **e.**.......... 776
1Sa 14:15 also trembled, and the **e.** quaked:......... 776
1Sa 17:46 air, and to the wild beasts of the **e.**:...... 776
1Sa 17:46 that all the **e.** may know that there....... 776
1Sa 17:49 and he fell upon his face to the **e.**......... 776
1Sa 20:15 every one from the face of the **e.**.......... 127
1Sa 24:8 stooped with his face to the **e.**, and....... 776
1Sa 25:41 bowed herself on her face to the **e.**,....... 776
1Sa 26:8 the spear even to the **e.** at once,......... 776
1Sa 26:20 let not my blood fall to the **e.** before..... 776
1Sa 28:13 I saw gods ascending out of the **e.**......... 776
1Sa 28:20 fell straightway all along on the **e.**,........ 776
1Sa 28:23 So he rose from the **e.**, and sat upon.... 776
1Sa 30:16 were spread abroad upon all the **e.**........ 776
2Sa 1:2 clothes rent, and **e.** upon his head:....... 127
2Sa 1:2 he fell to the **e.**, and did obeisance........ 776
2Sa 4:11 and take you away from the **e.**?........... 776
2Sa 7:9 of the great men that are in the **e.**....... 776
2Sa 7:23 nation in the **e.** is like thy people,......... 776
2Sa 12:16 in, and lay all night upon the **e.**............ 776
2Sa 12:17 to him, to raise him up from the **e.**:...... 776
2Sa 12:20 Then David arose from the **e.**, and....... 776
2Sa 13:31 tare his garments, and lay on the **e.**;..... 776
2Sa 14:7 name nor remainder upon the **e.**........... 127
2Sa 14:11 not one hair of thy son fall to the **e.**...... 776
2Sa 14:20 know all things that are in the **e.**.......... 776
2Sa 15:32 his coat rent, and **e.** upon his head:....... 127
2Sa 18:9 up between the heaven and the **e.**;....... 776
2Sa 18:28 he fell down to the **e.** upon his face....... 776
2Sa 22:8 Then the **e.** shook and trembled;.......... 776
2Sa 22:43 them as small as the dust of the **e.**,....... 776
2Sa 23:4 tender grass springing out of the **e.**........ 776
1Ki 1:31 bowed with her face to the **e.**, and....... 776
1Ki 1:40 the **e.** rent with the sound of them........ 776
1Ki 1:52 not an hair of him fall to the **e.**:............ 776
1Ki 2:2 I go the way of all the **e.**: be thou........ 776
1Ki 4:34 from all kings of the **e.**, which had........ 776
1Ki 8:23 in heaven above, or on **e.** beneath,........ 776
1Ki 8:27 will God indeed dwell on the **e.**?........... 776
1Ki 8:43 that all people of the **e.** may know........ 776
1Ki 8:53 from among all the people of the **e.**,...... 776
1Ki 8:60 all the people of the **e.** may know......... 776
1Ki 10:23 exceeded all the kings of the **e.** for....... 776
1Ki 10:24 And all the **e.** sought to Solomon,........ 776
1Ki 13:34 destroy it from off the face of the **e.**...... 127
1Ki 17:14 the Lord sendeth rain upon the **e.**.......... 127
1Ki 18:1 and I will send rain upon the **e.**............ 127
1Ki 18:42 he cast himself down upon the **e.**,.......... 776
2Ki 5:15 that there is no God in all the **e.**,.......... 776
2Ki 5:17 servant two mules' burden of **e.**?........... 127
2Ki 10:10 there shall fall unto the **e.** nothing......... 776
2Ki 19:15 alone, of all the kingdoms of the **e.**;....... 776
2Ki 19:15 thou hast made heaven and **e.**.............. 776
2Ki 19:19 the kingdoms of the **e.** may know......... 776
1Ch 1:10 he began to be mighty upon the **e.**......... 776
1Ch 1:19 in his days the **e.** was divided:............ 776
1Ch 16:14 God; his judgments are in all the **e.**........ 776
1Ch 16:23 Sing unto the Lord, all the **e.**;.............. 776
1Ch 16:30 Fear before him, all the **e.**: the........... 776
1Ch 16:31 let the **e.** rejoice: and let men say......... 776
1Ch 16:33 because he cometh to judge the **e.**......... 776
1Ch 17:8 of the great men that are in the **e.**......... 776
1Ch 17:21 what one nation in the **e.** is like thy...... 776
1Ch 21:16 stand between the **e.** and the heaven,.... 776
1Ch 22:8 hast shed much blood upon the **e.**.......... 776
1Ch 29:11 in the heaven and in the **e.** is thine;...... 776
1Ch 29:15 our days on the **e.** are as a shadow,...... 776
2Ch 1:9 like the dust of the **e.** in multitude........ 776
2Ch 2:12 that made heaven and **e.**, who hath....... 776
2Ch 6:14 thee in the heaven, nor in the **e.**;......... 776
2Ch 6:18 very deed dwell with men on the **e.**?..... 776
2Ch 6:33 people of the **e.** may know thy name,.... 776
2Ch 9:22 passed all the kings of the **e.** in........... 776
2Ch 9:23 kings of the **e.** sought the presence....... 776
2Ch 16:9 and fro throughout the whole **e.**,.......... 776
2Ch 20:24 were dead bodies fallen to the **e.**,......... 776
2Ch 32:19 the gods of the people of the **e.**,........... 776
2Ch 36:23 All the kingdoms of the **e.** hath the........ 776
Ezr 1:2 given me all the kingdoms of the **e.**;....... 776
Ezr 5:11 of the God of heaven and **e.**, and.......... 772
Ne 9:1 with sackclothes, and **e.** upon them....... 127
Ne 9:6 **e.**, and all things that are therein,......... 776
Job 1:7 From going to and fro in the **e.**,........... 776
Job 1:8 that there is none like him in the **e.**,...... 776
Job 2:2 From going to and fro in the **e.**,........... 776
Job 2:3 that there is none like him in the **e.**,..... 776
Job 3:14 With kings and counsellors of the **e.**,..... 776
Job 5:10 Who giveth rain upon the **e.**, and.......... 776
Job 5:22 thou be afraid of the beasts of the **e.**..... 776
Job 5:25 offspring as the grass of the **e.**............. 776
Job 7:1 an appointed time to man upon **e.**?......... 776
Job 8:9 our days upon **e.** are a shadow:)........... 776
Job 8:19 and out of the **e.** shall others grow...... 6083
Job 9:6 shaketh the **e.** out of her place, and...... 776
Job 9:24 The **e.** is given into the hand of the...... 776
Job 11:9 thereof is longer than the **e.**, and.......... 776
Job 12:8 Or speak to the **e.**, and it shall............ 776
Job 12:15 them out, and they overturn the **e.**........ 776
Job 12:24 of the chief of the people of the **e.**,....... 776
Job 14:8 the root thereof wax old in the **e.**,......... 776
Job 14:19 which grow out of the dust of the **e.**;.... 776
Job 15:19 whom alone the **e.** was given,............... 776
Job 15:29 the perfection thereof upon the **e.**......... 776
Job 16:18 O **e.**, cover not thou my blood,............ 776
Job 18:4 shall the **e.** be forsaken for thee?........... 776
Job 18:17 shall perish from the **e.**, and he............ 776
Job 19:25 stand at the latter day upon the **e.**:...... 6083
Job 20:4 since man was placed upon **e.**,............. 776
Job 20:27 and the **e.** shall rise up against him........ 776
Job 22:8 for the mighty man, he had the **e.**;....... 776
Job 24:4 the poor of the **e.** hide themselves........ 776
Job 24:18 their portion is cursed in the **e.**:.......... 776
Job 26:7 and hangeth the **e.** upon nothing........... 776
Job 28:2 Iron is taken out of the **e.**,................ 6083
Job 28:5 for the **e.**, out of it cometh bread:........ 776
Job 28:24 For he looketh to the ends of the **e.**,...... 776
Job 30:6 caves of the **e.**, and in the rocks......... 6083
Job 30:8 men: they were viler than the **e.**........... 776
Job 34:13 given him a charge over the **e.**?........... 776
Job 35:11 us more than the beasts of the **e.**,......... 776
Job 37:3 his lightning unto the ends of the **e.**....... 776
Job 37:6 saith to the snow, Be thou on the **e.**;.... 776
Job 37:12 upon the face of the world in the **e.**....... 776
Job 37:17 quieteth the **e.** by the south wind?........ 776
Job 38:4 when I laid the foundations of the **e.**?.... 776
Job 38:13 might take hold of the ends of the **e.**,.... 776
Job 38:18 perceived the breadth of the **e.**?........... 776
Job 38:24 scattereth the east wind upon the **e.**?.... 776
Job 38:26 To cause it to rain on the **e.**,................ 776
Job 38:33 set the dominion thereof in the **e.**?........ 776
Job 39:14 Which leaveth her eggs in the **e.**,.......... 776
Job 41:33 Upon **e.** there is not his like,............. 6083
Ps 2:2 The kings of the **e.** set themselves,....... 776
Ps 2:8 parts of the **e.** for thy possession......... 776
Ps 2:10 be instructed ye judges of the **e.**........... 776
Ps 7:5 him tread down my life upon the **e.**,....... 776
Ps 8:1, 9 excellent is thy name in all the **e.**!...... 776
Ps 10:18 man of the **e.** may no more oppress...... 776
Ps 12:6 as silver tried in a furnace of **e.**,............ 776
Ps 16:3 But to the saints that are in the **e.**,........ 776
Ps 17:11 their eyes bowing down to the **e.**;........ 776
Ps 18:7 Then the **e.** shook and trembled;.......... 776
Ps 19:4 line is gone out through all the **e.**,......... 776
Ps 21:10 fruit shalt thou destroy from the **e.**,....... 776
Ps 22:29 All they that be fat upon **e.** shall eat...... 776
Ps 24:1 The **e.** is the Lord's, and the.............. 776
Ps 25:13 and his seed shall inherit the **e.**............ 776
Ps 33:5 **e.** is full of the goodness of the Lord..... 776
Ps 33:8 Let all the **e.** fear the Lord:................ 776
Ps 33:14 upon all the inhabitants of the **e.**........... 776
Ps 34:16 remembrance of them from the **e.**.......... 776
Ps 37:9 Lord, they shall inherit the **e.**............... 776
Ps 37:11 But the meek shall inherit the **e.**;......... 776
Ps 37:22 blessed of him shall inherit the **e.**;........ 776
Ps 41:2 he shall be blessed upon the **e.**:........... 776
Ps 44:25 our belly cleaveth unto the **e.**.............. 776
Ps 45:16 mayest make princes in all the **e.**........... 776
Ps 46:2 we fear, though the **e.** be removed,...... 776
Ps 46:6 he uttered his voice, the **e.** melted....... 776
Ps 46:8 desolations he hath made in the **e.**........ 776
Ps 46:9 was to cease unto the end of the **e.**;..... 776
Ps 46:10 am God: I will be exalted in the **e.**......... 776
Ps 47:2 he is a great King over all the **e.**........... 776
Ps 47:7 For God is the King of all the **e.**:......... 776
Ps 47:9 shields of the **e.** belong unto God:........ 776
Ps 48:2 joy of the whole **e.**, is mount Zion,...... 776
Ps 48:10 thy praise unto the ends of the **e.**:........ 776
Ps 50:1 the **e.** from the rising of the sun........... 776
Ps 50:4 heavens from above, and to the **e.**,....... 776
Ps 57:5, 11 let thy glory be above all the **e.**........ 776
Ps 58:2 violence of your hands in the **e.**............ 776
Ps 58:11 he is a God that judgeth in the **e.**......... 776
Ps 59:13 in Jacob unto the ends of the **e.**............ 776
Ps 60:2 hast made the **e.** to tremble;............... 776
Ps 61:2 From the end of the **e.** will I cry.......... 776
Ps 63:9 go into the lower parts of the **e.**........... 776
Ps 65:5 confidence of all the ends of the **e.**,........ 776
Ps 65:9 Thou visitest the **e.**, and waterest it:..... 776
Ps 66:4 All the **e.** shall worship thee, and.......... 776
Ps 67:2 That thy way may be known upon **e.**,..... 776
Ps 67:4 and govern the nations upon **e.**............ 776
Ps 67:6 Then shall the **e.** yield her increase;...... 776
Ps 67:7 all the ends of the **e.** shall fear him....... 776
Ps 68:8 The **e.** shook, the heavens also............ 776
Ps 68:32 unto God, ye kingdoms of the **e.**;......... 776
Ps 69:34 Let the heaven and **e.** praise him,......... 776
Ps 71:20 up again from the depths of the **e.**......... 776
Ps 72:6 grass: as showers that water the **e.**....... 776
Ps 72:8 the rivers unto the ends of the **e.**.......... 776
Ps 72:16 shall be an handful of corn in the **e.**........ 776
Ps 72:16 shall flourish like grass of the **e.**........... 776
Ps 72:19 the whole **e.** be filled with his glory;...... 776
Ps 73:9 their tongue walketh through the **e.**........ 776

Ps 73:25 there is none upon e. that I desire....... 776
Ps 74:12 salvation in the midst of the e.. 776
Ps 74:17 hast set all the borders of the e. 776
Ps 74:20 the dark places of the e. are full of 776
Ps 75:3 e. and all the inhabitants thereof......... 776
Ps 75:8 wicked of the e. shall wring them out, .. 776
Ps 76:8 heaven; the e. feared, and was still. 776
Ps 76:9 to save all the meek of the e.. 776
Ps 76:12 he is terrible to the kings of the e.. 776
Ps 77:18 the world: the e. trembled and shook. .. 776
Ps 78:69 e. which he hath established forever..... 776
Ps 79:2 thy saints unto the beasts of the e.. 776
Ps 82:5 all the foundations of the e. are out...... 776
Ps 82:8 Arise, O God, judge the e.: for thou 776
Ps 83:10 they became as dung for the e.. 127
Ps 83:18 art the most high over all the e.. 776
Ps 85:11 Truth shall spring out of the e.;.......... 776
Ps 89:11 The heavens are thine, the e. also is.... 776
Ps 89:27 higher than the kings of the e.. 776
Ps 90:2 or ever thou hadst formed the e. 776
Ps 94:2 Lift up thyself, thou judge of the e....... 776
Ps 95:4 hand are the deep places of the e. 776
Ps 96:1 sing unto the Lord, all the e.. 776
Ps 96:9 holiness: fear before him, all the e.. 776
Ps 96:11 rejoice, and let the e. be glad;........... 776
Ps 96:13 for he cometh to judge the e.............. 776
Ps 97:1 let the e. rejoice; let the multitude 776
Ps 97:4 world: the e. saw, and trembled. 776
Ps 97:5 presence of the Lord of the whole e.. ... 776
Ps 97:9 thou, Lord, art high above all the e. 776
Ps 98:3 all the ends of the e. have seen the 776
Ps 98:4 noise unto the Lord, all the e............. 776
Ps 98:9 for he cometh to judge the e.............. 776
Ps 99:1 the cherubims; let the e. be moved...... 776
Ps 102:15 and all the kings of the e. thy glory...... 776
Ps 102:19 heaven did the Lord behold the e.;....... 776
Ps 102:25 thou laid the foundation of the e. 776
Ps 103:11 the heaven is high above the e., ... 776
Ps 104:5 Who laid the foundations of the e., ... 776
Ps 104:9 they turn not again to cover the e........ 776
Ps 104:13 the e. is satisfied with the fruit of........ 776
Ps 104:14 may bring forth food out of the e.; 776
Ps 104:24 the e. is full of thy riches.................. 776
Ps 104:30 thou renewest the face of the e.. 127
Ps 104:32 looketh on the e., and it trembleth: 776
Ps 104:35 sinners be cousumed out of the e., ... 776
Ps 105:7 his judgments are in all the e.. 776
Ps 106:17 e. opened and swallowed up Dathan, ... 776
Ps 108:5 and thy glory above all the e.;........... 776
Ps 109:15 the memory of them from the e.. 776
Ps 112:2 His seed shall be mighty upon e. 776
Ps 113:6 that are in heaven, and in the e.! 776
Ps 114:7 Tremble, thou e., at the presence........ 776
Ps 115:15 the Lord, which made heaven and e.. ... 776
Ps 115:16 but the e. hath he given to the........... 776
Ps 119:19 I am a stranger in the e.................... 776
Ps 119:64 The e., O Lord, is full of thy mercy: 776
Ps 119:87 had almost consumed me upon e.;........ 776
Ps 119:90 thou hast established the e., and it....... 776
Ps 119:119 puttest away all the wicked of the e.. 776
Ps 121:2 the Lord, which made heaven and e.. ... 776
Ps 124:8 the Lord, who made heaven and e.. 776
Ps 134:3 The Lord that made heaven and e........ 776
Ps 135:6 that did he in heaven, and in e., ... 776
Ps 135:7 to ascend from the ends of the e.; 776
Ps 136:6 To him that stretched out the e.......... 776
Ps 138:4 All the kings of the e. shall praise........ 776
Ps 139:15 in the lowest parts of the e.. 776
Ps 140:11 speaker be established in the e........... 776
Ps 141:7 and cleaveth wood upon the e.. 776
Ps 146:4 goeth forth, he returneth to his e.; 127
Ps 146:6 Which made heaven, and e., the.......... 776
Ps 147:8 who prepareth rain for the e., who....... 776
Ps 147:15 forth his commandment upon e........... 776
Ps 148:7 Praise the Lord from the e.,.............. 776
Ps 148:11 Kings of the e., and all people;........... 776
Ps 148:11 princes, and all judges of the e........... 776
Ps 148:13 his glory is above the e. and heaven..... 776
Pr 2:22 wicked shall be cut off from the e., ... 776
Pr 3:19 by wisdom hath founded the e.;........... 776
Pr 8:16 even all the judges of the e.. 776
Pr 8:23 the beginning, or ever the e. was. 776
Pr 8:26 as yet he had not made the e.,............. 776
Pr 8:29 appointed the foundations of the e........ 776
Pr 8:31 in the habitable part of his e.; 776
Pr 10:30 the wicked shall not inhabit the e.. 776
Pr 11:31 shall be recompensed in the e. 776
Pr 17:24 of a fool are in the ends of the e.. 776
Pr 25:3 for height, and the e. for depth, ... 776
Pr 30:4 established all the ends of the e.? 776
Pr 30:14 to devour the poor from off the e., ... 776
Pr 30:16 the e. that is not filled with water; 776
Pr 30:21 For three things the e. is disquieted, ... 776
Pr 30:24 things which are little upon the e., ... 776
Ec 1:4 but the e. abideth for ever. 776
Ec 3:21 that goeth downward to the e.? 776
Ec 5:2 God is in heaven, and thou upon e....... 776
Ec 5:9 the profit of the e. is for all: 776
Ec 7:20 there is not a just man upon e., that 776
Ec 8:14 a vanity which is done upon the e.; 776
Ec 8:16 business that is done upon the e......... 776
Ec 10:7 walking as servants upon the e............ 776
Ec 11:2 what evil shall be upon the e............... 776
Ec 11:3 they empty themselves upon the e....... 776
Ec 12:7 Then shall the dust return to the e. 776
Ca 2:12 The flowers appear on the e.; 776
Isa 1:2 Hear, O heavens, and give ear, O e...... 776
Isa 2:19 rocks, and into the caves of the e.. 6083
Isa 2:19, 21 ariseth to shake terribly the e.. 776
Isa 4:2 fruit of the e. shall be excellent 776
Isa 5:8 placed alone in the midst of the e.! 776
Isa 5:26 unto them from the end of the e.:....... 776
Isa 6:3 the whole e. is full of his glory. 776
Isa 8:22 And they shall look unto the e.;........... 776
Isa 10:14 are left, have I gathered all the e.;....... 776
Isa 11:4 with equity for the meek of the e.: 776
Isa 11:4 and he shall smite the e. with the rod... 776
Isa 11:9 the e. shall be full of the knowledge 776
Isa 11:12 from the four corners of the e............ 776
Isa 12:5 things: this is known in all the e.. 776
Isa 13:13 and the e. shall remove out of her 776
Isa 14:7 The whole e. is at rest, and is quiet:.... 776
Isa 14:9 even all the chief ones of the e.; 776
Isa 14:16 the man that made the e. to tremble, ... 776
Isa 14:26 that is purposed upon the whole e.:...... 776
Isa 18:3 of the world, and dwellers on the e., ... 776
Isa 18:6 and to the beasts of the e.: and the 776
Isa 18:6 all the beasts of the e. shall winter...... 776
Isa 23:8 are the honourable of the e.? 776
Isa 23:9 contempt all the honourable of the e.. ... 776
Isa 23:17 the world upon the face of the e.. 127
Isa 24:1 the Lord maketh the e. empty, ... 776
Isa 24:4 The e. mourneth and fadeth away, ... 776
Isa 24:4 haughty people of the e. do languish..... 776
Isa 24:5 The e. also is defiled under the........... 776
Isa 24:6 hath the curse devoured the e., ... 776
Isa 24:6 the inhabitants of the e. are burned, ... 776
Isa 24:16 From the uttermost part of the e......... 776
Isa 24:17 upon thee, O inhabitant of the e.. 776
Isa 24:18 the foundations of the e. do shake........ 776
Isa 24:19 The e. is utterly broken down, the........ 776
Isa 24:19 e. is clean dissolved, the e. is moved 776
Isa 24:20 The e. shall reel to and fro like a......... 776
Isa 24:21 the kings of the e. upon the e.. 127
Isa 25:8 he take away from off all the e.: 776
Isa 26:9 when thy judgments are in the e., ... 776
Isa 26:15 it far unto all the ends of the e.. 776
Isa 26:18 wrought any deliverance in the e.; 776
Isa 26:19 and the e. shall cast out the dead. 776
Isa 26:21 to punish the inhabitants of the e. 776
Isa 26:21 the e. also shall disclose her blood, ... 776
Isa 28:2 shall cast down to the e. with the 776
Isa 28:22 even determined upon the whole e....... 776
Isa 30:23 bread of the increase of the e.. 127
Isa 33:9 The e. mourneth and languisheth: 776
Isa 34:1 let the e. hear, and all that is............. 776
Isa 37:16 alone, of all the kingdoms of the e.: 776
Isa 37:16 thou hast made heaven and e.. 776
Isa 37:20 all the kingdoms of the e. may know 776
Isa 40:12 and comprehended the dust of the e..... 776
Isa 40:21 from the foundations of the e.?........... 776
Isa 40:22 that sitteth upon the circle of the e., ... 776
Isa 40:23 he maketh the judges of the e. as 776
Isa 40:24 stock shall not take root in the e. 776
Isa 40:28 the Creator of the ends of the e., ... 776
Isa 41:5 the ends of the e. were afraid, ... 776
Isa 41:9 have taken from the ends of the e., ... 776
Isa 42:4 till he have set judgment in the e......... 776
Isa 42:5 he that spread forth the e., and that..... 776
Isa 42:10 his praise from the end of the e., ... 776
Isa 43:6 daughters from the ends of the e.; 776
Isa 44:23 shout, ye lower parts of the e............. 776
Isa 44:24 that spreadeth abroad the e. by........... 776
Isa 45:8 let the e. open, and let them bring....... 776
Isa 45:9 strive with the potsherds of the e.. 127
Isa 45:12 I have made the e., and created 776
Isa 45:18 God himself that formed the e. and 776
Isa 45:19 secret, in a dark place of the e............ 776
Isa 45:22 be ye saved, all the ends of the e........ 776
Isa 48:13 hath laid the foundation of the e.,....... 776
Isa 48:20 utter it even to the end of the e.;........ 776
Isa 49:6 my salvation unto the end of the e.. 776
Isa 49:8 to establish the e., to cause to........... 776
Isa 49:13 Sing, O heavens; and be joyful, O e.; ... 776
Isa 49:23 with their face toward the e., and........ 776
Isa 51:6 and look upon the e. beneath: for 776
Isa 51:6 the e. shall wax old like a garment, ... 776
Isa 51:13 and laid the foundations of the e.; 776
Isa 51:16 and lay the foundations of the e., ... 776
Isa 52:10 all the ends of the e. shall see the 776
Isa 54:5 The God of the whole e. shall he be..... 776
Isa 54:9 Noah should no more go over the e.; ... 776
Isa 55:9 the heavens are higher than the e., ... 776
Isa 55:10 but watereth the e., and maketh it....... 776
Isa 58:14 ride upon the high places of the e., ... 776
Isa 60:2 the darkness shall cover the e., ... 776
Isa 61:11 as the e. bringeth forth her bud,.......... 776
Isa 62:7 make Jerusalem a praise in the e.. 776
Isa 63:6 bring down their strength to the e.. 776
Isa 65:16 he who blesseth himself in the e......... 776
Isa 65:16 and he that sweareth in the e. shall...... 776
Isa 65:17 I create new heavens and a new e.: 776
Isa 66:1 throne, and the e. is my footstool: 776
Isa 66:8 Shall the e. be made to bring forth....... 776
Isa 66:22 as the new heavens and the new e....... 776
Jer 4:23 I beheld the e., and, lo, it was........... 776
Jer 4:28 For this shall the e. mourn, and the 776
Jer 6:19 Hear, O e.: behold, I will bring evil...... 776
Jer 6:22 be raised from the sides of the e., ... 776
Jer 7:33 heaven, and for the beasts of the e.; 776
Jer 8:2 be for dung upon the face of the e.. 127
Jer 9:3 valiant for the truth upon the e.:.......... 776
Jer 9:24 and righteousness, in the e.; 776
Jer 10:10 at his wrath the e. shall tremble, ... 776
Jer 10:11 not made the heavens and the e., ... 778
Jer 10:11 even they shall perish from the e., ... 772
Jer 10:12 He hath made the e. by his power, ... 776
Jer 10:13 to ascend from the ends of the e.; 776
Jer 14:4 for there was no rain in the e., ... 776
Jer 15:3 and the beasts of the e., to devour 776
Jer 15:4 removed into all kingdoms of the e.,...... 776
Jer 15:10 a man of contention to the whole e.! 776
Jer 16:4 as dung upon the face of the e. 127
Jer 16:4 heaven, and for the beasts of the e.. 776
Jer 16:19 unto thee from the ends of the e., ... 776
Jer 17:13 from me shall be written in the e., ... 776
Jer 19:7 heaven, and for the beasts of the e.. 776
Jer 22:29 O e., e., e., hear the word of the Lord. 776
Jer 23:5 judgment and justice in the e.. 776
Jer 23:24 Do not I fill heaven and e.? saith the 776
Jer 24:9 into all the kingdoms of the e. for 776
Jer 25:26 which are upon the face of the e......... 127
Jer 25:29 upon all the inhabitants of the e., ... 776
Jer 25:30 against all the inhabitants of the e.. 776
Jer 25:31 shall come even to the ends of the e.; .. 776
Jer 25:32 be raised from the coasts of the e........ 776
Jer 25:33 at that day from one end of the e. 776
Jer 25:33 even unto the other end of the e.: 776
Jer 26:6 a curse to all the nations of the e.. 776
Jer 27:5 I have made the e., the man and the.... 776
Jer 28:16 cast thee from off the face of the e. 127
Jer 29:18 to all the kingdoms of the e., to be a.... 776
Jer 31:8 them from the coasts of the e., ... 776
Jer 31:22 hath created a new thing in the e.,........ 776
Jer 31:37 foundations of the e. searched out........ 776
Jer 32:17 made the heaven and the e. by thy 776
Jer 33:9 before all the nations of the e., which... 776
Jer 33:25 the ordinances of heaven and e.;.......... 776
Jer 34:1 army, and all the kingdoms of the e...... 776
Jer 34:17 into all the kingdoms of the e............. 776
Jer 34:20 heaven, and to the beasts of the e.. 776
Jer 44:8 among all the nations of the e.? 776
Jer 46:8 will go up, and will cover the e.; 776
Jer 49:21 The e. is moved at the noise of their.... 776
Jer 50:23 whole e. cut asunder and broken! 776
Jer 50:41 raised up from the coasts of the e........ 776
Jer 50:46 taking of Babylon the e. is moved, ... 776
Jer 51:7 hand, that made all the e. drunken: 776
Jer 51:15 He hath made the e. by his power, ... 776
Jer 51:16 to ascend from the ends of the e. 776
Jer 51:25 Lord, which destroyest all the e. 776

Jer 51:41 the praise of the whole **e.** surprised! 776
Jer 51:48 Then the heaven and the **e.**, and all 776
Jer 51:49 shall fall the slain of all the **e.** 776
La 2:1 cast down from heaven unto the **e.** 776
La 2:11 my liver is poured upon the **e.**, 776
La 2:15 of beauty, The joy of the whole **e.**? 776
La 3:34 his feet all the prisoners of the **e.**, 776
La 4:12 The kings of the **e.**, and all the 776
Eze 1:15 behold one wheel upon the **e.** by the 776
Eze 1:19 creatures were lifted up from the **e.**, 776
Eze 1:21 those were lifted up from the **e.**, 776
Eze 7:21 to the wicked of the **e.** for a spoil; 776
Eze 8:3 up between the **e.** and the heaven, 776
Eze 8:12 not; the Lord hath forsaken the **e.** 776
Eze 9:9 The Lord hath forsaken the **e.**, and 776
Eze 10:16 their wings to mount up from the **e.**, 776
Eze 10:19 mounted up from the **e.** in my sight: 776
Eze 26:20 set thee in the low parts of the **e.**, 776
Eze 27:33 thou didst enrich the kings of the **e.** 776
Eze 28:18 will bring thee to ashes upon the **e.** 776
Eze 31:12 all the people of the **e.** are gone 776
Eze 31:14 death, to the nether parts of the **e.**, 776
Eze 31:16 in the nether parts of the **e.** 776
Eze 31:18 Eden unto the nether parts of the **e.**: 776
Eze 32:4 the beasts of the whole **e.** with thee. 776
Eze 32:18 unto the nether parts of the **e.**, with 776
Eze 32:24 into the nether parts of the **e.**, which 776
Eze 34:6 scattered upon all the face of the **e.**, 776
Eze 34:27 and the **e.** shall yield her increase, 776
Eze 35:14 When the whole **e.** rejoiceth, I will 776
Eze 38:20 things that creep upon the **e.**, 127
Eze 38:20 men that are upon the face of the **e.**, 127
Eze 39:14 remain upon the face of the **e.**, 776
Eze 39:18 the blood of the princes of the **e.** 776
Eze 43:2 and the **e.** shined with his glory. 776
Da 2:10 There is not a man upon the **e.** 3007
Da 2:35 mountain, and filled the whole **e.** 772
Da 2:39 which shall bear rule over all the **e.** 772
Da 4:1 languages, that dwell in all the **e.**; 772
Da 4:10 behold a tree in the midst of the **e.**, 772
Da 4:11 sight thereof to the end of all the **e.**: 772
Da 4:15 the stump of his roots in the **e.**, 772
Da 4:15 the beasts in the grass of the **e.**: 772
Da 4:20 and the sight thereof to all the **e.**; 772
Da 4:22 thy dominion to the end of the **e.** 772
Da 4:23 stump of the roots thereof in the **e.**, 772
Da 4:35 And all the inhabitants of the **e.** 772
Da 4:35 among the inhabitants of the **e.**: 772
Da 6:25 languages, that dwell in all the **e.**; 772
Da 6:27 and wonders in heaven and in **e.**, 772
Da 7:4 and it was lifted up from the **e.**, 772
Da 7:17 which shall arise out of the **e.** 772
Da 7:23 shall be the fourth kingdom upon **e.**, 772
Da 7:23 and shall devour the whole **e.**, and 772
Da 8:5 west on the face of the whole **e.**, 776
Da 12:2 them that sleep in the dust of the **e.** 127
Ho 2:18 sword and the battle out of the **e.**, 776
Ho 2:21 heavens, and they shall hear the **e.**; 776
Ho 2:22 And the **e.** shall hear the corn, 776
Ho 2:23 I will sow her unto me in the **e.**; 776
Ho 6:3 latter and former rain unto the **e.** 776
Joe 2:10 The **e.** shall quake before them; 776
Joe 2:30 in the heavens and in the **e.**, 776
Joe 3:16 the heavens and the **e.** shall shake: 776
Am 2:7 That pant after the dust of the **e.** 776
Am 3:2 known of all the families of the **e.**: 127
Am 3:5 a bird fall in a snare upon the **e.**, 776
Am 3:5 one take up a snare from the **e.**, 127
Am 4:13 upon the high places of the **e.**, 776
Am 5:7 leave off righteousness in the **e.**, 776
Am 5:8 them out upon the face of the **e.**: 776
Am 8:9 will darken the **e.** in the clear day: 776
Am 9:6 hath founded his troop in the **e.**; 776
Am 9:6 them out upon the face of the **e.**: 776
Am 9:8 destroy it from off the face of the **e.**; 127
Am 9:9 not the least grain fall upon the **e.** 776
Jon 2:6 the **e.** with her bars was about me 776
Mic 1:2 Hear, all ye people; hearken, O **e.**, 776
Mic 1:3 tread upon the high places of the **e.** 776
Mic 4:13 unto the Lord of the whole **e.** 776
Mic 5:4 he be great unto the ends of the **e.** 776
Mic 6:2 ye strong foundations of the **e.**: 776
Mic 7:2 good man is perished out of the **e.**: 776
Mic 7:17 of their holes like worms of the **e.**: 776
Na 1:5 and the **e.** is burned at his presence, 776
Na 2:13 I will cut off thy prey from the **e.**, 776
Hab 2:14 **e.** shall be filled with the knowledge 776
Hab 2:20 let all the **e.** keep silence before him, 776
Hab 3:3 and the **e.** was full of his praise. 776
Hab 3:6 He stood, and measured the **e.**: 776
Hab 3:9 Thou didst cleave the **e.** with rivers. 776
Zep 2:3 ye the Lord, all ye meek of the **e.**, 776
Zep 2:11 he will famish all the gods of the **e.**; 776
Zep 3:8 the **e.** shall be devoured with the fire 776
Zep 3:20 praise among all people of the **e.**, 776
Hag 1:10 and the **e.** is stayed from her fruit. 776
Hag 2:6 the heavens, and the **e.**, and the sea, 776
Hag 2:21 I will shake the heavens and the **e.**; 776
Zec 1:10 to walk to and fro through the **e.** 776
Zec 1:11 walked to and fro through the **e.**, 776
Zec 1:11 all the **e.** sitteth still, and is at rest. 776
Zec 4:10 run to and fro through the whole **e.** 776
Zec 4:14 stand by the Lord of the whole **e.** 776
Zec 5:3 forth over the face of the whole **e.**: 776
Zec 5:6 resemblance through all the **e.** 776
Zec 5:9 ephah between the **e.** and the heaven. 776
Zec 6:5 standing before the Lord of all the **e.** 776
Zec 6:7 and fro through the **e.**: and he said, 776
Zec 6:7 hence, walk to and fro through the **e.** 776
Zec 6:7 walked to and fro through the **e.** 776
Zec 9:10 the river even to the ends of the **e.** 776
Zec 12:1 and layeth the foundation of the **e.**, 776
Zec 12:3 though all the people of the **e.** be 776
Zec 14:9 Lord shall be king over all the **e.**: 776
Zec 14:17 families of the **e.** unto Jerusalem 776
Mal 4:6 come and smite the **e.** with a curse. 776
Mt 5:5 **meek: for they shall inherit the e.** *1093*
Mt 5:13 **Ye are the salt of the e.: but if the** *1093*
Mt 5:18 **Till heaven and e. pass, one jot or** *1093*
Mt 5:35 **Nor by the e.; for it is his** *1093*
Mt 6:10 **will be done in e., as it is in** *1093*
Mt 6:19 **for yourselves treasures upon e.,** *1093*
Mt 9:6 **hath power on e. to forgive sins,** *1093*
Mt 10:34 **I am come to send peace on e.:** *1093*
Mt 11:25 **O Father, Lord of heaven and e.,** *1093*
Mt 12:40 **three nights in the heart of the e.** *1093*
Mt 12:42 **uttemost parts of the e. to hear** *1093*
Mt 13:5 **where they had not much e.:** *1093*
Mt 13:5 **because they had no deepness of e.:** *1093*
Mt 16:19 **whatsoever thou shalt bind on e.** *1093*
Mt 16:19 **whatsoever thou shalt loose on e.** *1093*
Mt 17:25 **whom doth the kings of the e. take** *1093*
Mt 18:18 **Whatsoever ye shall bind on e.** *1093*
Mt 18:18 **and whatsoever ye shall loose on e.** *1093*
Mt 18:19 **if two of you shall agree on e. as** *1093*
Mt 23:9 **no man your father upon the e.:** *1093*
Mt 23:35 **righteous blood shed upon the e.,** *1093*
Mt 24:30 **shall the tribes of the e. mourn,** *1093*
Mt 24:35 **Heaven and e. shall pass away, but** *1093*
Mt 25:18 **one went and digged in the e.,** *1093*
Mt 25:25 **went and hid thy talent in the e.:** *1093*
Mt 27:51 **e.** did quake, and the rocks rent; *1093*
Mt 28:18 **given unto me in heaven and in e.** *1093*
Mk 2:10 **Son of man hath power on e. to** *1093*
Mk 4:5 **ground; where it had not much e.;** *1093*
Mk 4:5 **because it had no depth of e.:** *1093*
Mk 4:28 **e. bringeth forth fruit of herself;** *1093*
Mk 4:31 **it is sown in the e., is less than** *1093*
Mk 4:31 **all the seeds that be in the e.:** *1093*
Mk 9:3 as no fuller on **e.** can white them. *1093*
Mk 13:27 **from the uttemost part of the e.** *1093*
Mk 13:31 **Heaven and e. shall pass away:** *1093*
Lu 2:14 on **e.** peace, good will toward men. *1093*
Lu 5:24 **the Son of man hath power upon e.** *1093*
Lu 6:49 **built an house upon the e.;** *1093*
Lu 10:21 **O Father, Lord of heaven and e.,** *1093*
Lu 11:2 **be done, as in heaven, so in e.** *1093*
Lu 11:31 **from the utmost parts of the e. to** *1093*
Lu 12:49 **I am come to send fire on the e.;** *1093*
Lu 12:51 **I am come to give peace on e.?** *1093*
Lu 12:56 **the face of the sky and of the e.;** *1093*
Lu 16:17 **is easier for heaven and e. to pass,** *1093*
Lu 18:8 **shall he find faith on the e.?** *1093*
Lu 21:25 **and upon the e. distress of nations,** *1093*
Lu 21:26 **which are coming on the e.:** *3625*
Lu 21:33 **Heaven and e. shall pass away:** *1093*
Lu 21:35 **dwell on the face of the whole e.** *1093*
Lu 23:44 was a darkness over all the **e.** *1093*
Lu 24:5 bowed down their faces to the **e.**, *1093*
Joh 3:31 he that is of the **e.** is earthly, *1093*
Joh 3:31 and speaketh of the **e.**: *1093*
Joh 12:32 **if I be lifted up from the e.,** *1093*
Joh 17:4 **I have glorified thee on the e.:** *1093*
Ac 1:8 **unto the uttermost part of the e.** *1093*
Ac 2:19 and signs in the **e.** beneath; blood, *1093*
Ac 3:25 the kindreds of the **e.** be blessed. *1093*
Ac 4:24 which hast made heaven, and **e.**, *1093*
Ac 4:26 The kings of the **e.** stood up, *1093*
Ac 7:49 my throne, and **e.** is my footstool: *1093*
Ac 8:33 for his life is taken from the **e.** *1093*
Ac 9:4 he fell to the **e.**, and heard a voice *1093*
Ac 9:8 Saul arose from the **e.**; and when *1093*
Ac 10:11 corners, and let down to the **e.**: *1093*
Ac 10:12 of fourfooted beasts of the **e.**, and *1093*
Ac 11:6 and saw fourfooted beasts of the **e.**, *1093*
Ac 13:47 salvation unto the ends of the **e.** *1093*
Ac 14:15 God, which made heaven, and **e.**, *1093*
Ac 17:24 is Lord of heaven and **e.**, dwelleth *1093*
Ac 17:26 to dwell on all the face of the **e.**, *1093*
Ac 22:22 with such a fellow from the **e.**: *1093*
Ac 26:14 when we were all fallen to the **e.**, *1093*
Ro 9:17 be declared throughout all the **e.** *1093*
Ro 9:28 will the Lord make upon the **e.** *1093*
Ro 10:18 their sound went into all the **e.**, *1093*
1Co 8:5 gods, whether in heaven or in **e.**, *1093*
1Co 10:26 For the **e.** is the Lord's, and the *1093*
1Co 10:28 for the **e.** is the Lord's, and the *1093*
1Co 15:47 The first man is of the **e.**, earthy: *1093*
Eph 1:10 are in heaven, and which are on **e.**; *1093*
Eph 3:15 family in heaven and **e.** is named, *1093*
Eph 4:9 into the lower parts of the **e.**? *1093*
Eph 6:3 thou mayest live long on the **e.** *1093*
Php 2:10 things in heaven, and things in **e.**, *1919*
Php 2:10 and things under the **e.**; *2709*
Col 1:16 are in heaven, and that are in **e.**, *1093*
Col 1:20 whether they be things in **e.**, or *1093*
Col 3:2 above, not on things on the **e.** *1093*
Col 3:5 members which are upon the **e.**; *1093*
2Ti 2:20 but also of wood and of **e.**; and *3749*
Heb 1:10 hast laid the foundation of the **e.**; *1093*
Heb 6:7 the **e.** which drinketh in the rain *1093*
Heb 8:4 For if he were on **e.**, he should not *1093*
Heb 11:13 strangers and pilgrims on the **e.**: *1093*
Heb 11:38 and in dens and caves of the **e.** *1093*
Heb 12:25 who refused him that spake on **e.**, *1093*
Heb 12:26 Whose voice then shook the **e.**: *1093*
Heb 12:26 once more I shake not the **e.** only, *1093*
Jas 5:5 Ye have lived in pleasure on the **e.**, *1093*
Jas 5:7 for the precious fruit of the **e.**, *1093*
Jas 5:12 neither by heaven, neither by the **e.**, *1093*
Jas 5:17 it rained not on the **e.** by the space *1093*
Jas 5:18 and the **e.** brought forth her fruit. *1093*
2Pe 3:5 the **e.** standing out of the water *1093*
2Pe 3:7 heavens and the **e.**, which are now, *1093*
2Pe 3:10 the **e.** also and the works that are *1093*
2Pe 3:13 look for new heavens and a new **e.**, *1093*
1Jo 5:8 are three that bear witness in **e.**, *1093*
Re 1:5 the prince of the kings of the **e.** *1093*
Re 1:7 all kindreds of the **e.** shall wail *1093*
Re 3:10 **to try them that dwell upon the e.** *1093*
Re 5:3 nor in **e.**, neither under the **e.**, *1093*
Re 5:6 of God sent forth into all the **e.** *1093*
Re 5:10 and we shall reign on the **e.** *1093*
Re 5:13 and on the **e.**, and under the **e.**, *1093*
Re 6:4 thereon to take peace from the **e.**, *1093*
Re 6:8 them over the fourth part of the **e.**, *1093*
Re 6:8 death, and with the beasts of the **e.** *1093*
Re 6:10 blood on them that dwell on the **e.**? *1093*
Re 6:13 the stars of heaven fell unto the **e.**, *1093*
Re 6:15 kings of the **e.**, and the great men, *1093*
Re 7:1 on the four corners of the **e.**, *1093*
Re 7:1 holding the four winds of the **e.**, *1093*
Re 7:1 the wind should not blow on the **e.**, *1093*
Re 7:2 to whom it was given to hurt the **e.** *1093*
Re 7:3 Saying, Hurt not the **e.**, neither the *1093*
Re 8:5 altar, and cast it into the **e.**: *1093*
Re 8:7 and they were cast upon the **e.**: *1093*
Re 8:13 woe, to the inhabiters of the **e.** by *1093*
Re 9:1 a star fall from heaven unto the **e.**: *1093*
Re 9:3 of the smoke locusts upon the **e.**: *1093*
Re 9:3 the scorpions of the **e.** have power. *1093*
Re 9:4 should not hurt the grass of the **e.**, *1093*
Re 10:2 the sea, and his left foot on the **e.**, *1093*
Re 10:5 stand upon the sea and upon the **e.** *1093*
Re 10:6 **e.**, and the things that therein are, *1093*
Re 10:8 upon the sea and upon the **e.** *1093*
Re 11:4 standing before the God of the **e.** *1093*
Re 11:6 to smite the **e.** with all plagues, *1093*
Re 11:10 that dwell upon the **e.** shall rejoice *1093*
Re 11:10 tormented them that dwelt on the **e.** *1093*
Re 11:18 destroy them which destroy the **e.** *1093*

Re 12:4 and did cast them to the **e.**: *1093*
Re 12:9 he was cast out into the **e.**, *1093*
Re 12:12 Woe to the inhabiters of the **e.** and *1093*
Re 12:13 saw that he was cast unto the **e.**, *1093*
Re 12:16 And the **e.** helped the woman, *1093*
Re 12:16 and the **e.** opened her mouth, *1093*
Re 13:8 dwell upon the **e.** shall worship *1093*
Re 13:11 beast coming up out of the **e.**; *1093*
Re 13:12 causeth the **e.** and them which *1093*
Re 13:13 heaven on the **e.** in the sight of men *1093*
Re 13:14 deceiveth them that dwell on the **e.** *1093*
Re 13:14 saying to them that dwell on the **e.**, *1093*
Re 14:3 which were redeemed from the **e.** *1093*
Re 14:6 unto them that dwell on the **e.**, *1093*
Re 14:7 him that made heaven, and **e.**, *1093*
Re 14:15 for the harvest of the **e.** is ripe *1093*
Re 14:16 thrust in his sickle on the **e.**; *1093*
Re 14:16 and the **e.** was reaped *1093*
Re 14:18 the clusters of the vine of the **e.**; *1093*
Re 14:19 angel thrust his sickle into the **e.**, *1093*
Re 14:19 and gathered the vine of the **e.**, *1093*
Re 16:1 the wrath of God upon the **e.** *1093*
Re 16:2 poured out his vial upon the **e.**; *1093*
Re 16:14 of the **e.** and of the whole world, *1093*
Re 16:18 not since men were upon the **e.**, *1093*
Re 17:2 With whom the kings of the **e.** have *1093*
Re 17:2 of the **e.** have been made drunk *1093*
Re 17:5 harlots and abominations of the **e.** *1093*
Re 17:8 dwell upon the **e.** shall wonder, *1093*
Re 17:18 reigneth over the kings of the **e.** *1093*
Re 18:1 the **e.** was lightened with his glory. *1093*
Re 18:3 the **e.** have committed fornication *1093*
Re 18:3 merchants of the **e.** are waxed rich *1093*
Re 18:9 kings of the **e.**, who have committed *1093*
Re 18:11 the merchants of the **e.** shall weep *1093*
Re 18:23 were the great men of the **e.**; *1093*
Re 18:24 all that were slain upon the **e.** *1093*
Re 19:2 corrupt the **e.** with her fornication, *1093*
Re 19:19 the beast, and the kings of the **e.**, *1093*
Re 20:8 in the four quarters of the **e.**, *1093*
Re 20:9 went up on the breadth of the **e.**, *1093*
Re 20:11 the **e.** and the heaven fled away; *1093*
Re 21:1 I saw a new heaven and a new **e.**: *1093*
Re 21:1 and first **e.** were passed away; *1093*
Re 21:24 the kings of the **e.** do bring their *1093*

EARTHEN See also EARTHY.
Le 6:28 the **e.** vessel wherein it is sodden 2789
Le 11:33 every **e.** vessel, whereinto any of 2789
Le 14:5 birds be killed in an **e.** vessel 2789
Le 14:50 the one of the birds in an **e.** vessel 2789
Nu 5:17 take holy water in an **e.** vessel; 2789
2Sa 17:28 beds, and basons, and **e.** vessels, 3335
Jer 19:1 Go and get a potter's **e.** bottle, 2789
Jer 32:14 and put them in an **e.** vessel, 2789
La 4:2 are they esteemed as **e.** pitchers, 2789
2Co 4:7 have this treasure in **e.** vessels, *3749*

EARTHLY See also EARTHY.
Joh 3:12 **If I have told you e. things,** *1919*
Joh 3:31 that is of the earth is **e.**, *1537,3588,1093*
2Co 5:1 if our **e.** house of this tabernacle *1919*
Php 3:19 their shame, who mind **e.** things.) *1919*
Jas 3:15 above, but is **e.**, sensual, devilish. *1919*

EARTHQUAKE See also EARTHQUAKES.
1Ki 19:11 and after the wind an **e.**; 7494
1Ki 19:11 but the Lord was not in the **e.**: 7494
1Ki 19:12 after the **e.** a fire; but the Lord 7494
Isa 29:6 and with **e.**, and great noise, 7494
Am 1:1 two years before the **e.** 7494
Zec 14:5 the **e.** in the days of Uzziah 7494
Mt 27:54 saw the **e.**, and those things that *4578*
Mt 28:2 behold, there was a great **e.**: *4578*
Ac 16:26 And suddenly there was a great **e.**, *4578*
Re 6:12 lo, there was a great **e.**; *4578*
Re 8:5 and lightnings, and an **e.** *4578*
Re 11:13 same hour was there a great **e.**, *4578*
Re 11:13 and in the **e.** were slain of men *4578*
Re 11:19 and an **e.**, and great hail. *4578*
Re 16:18 and there was a great **e.**, *4578*
Re 16:18 so mighty an **e.**, and so great. *4578*

EARTHQUAKES
Mt 24:7 **and e., in divers places.** *4578*
Mk 13:8 **there shall be e. in divers places,** *4578*
Lu 21:11 **great e. shall be in divers places,** *4578*

EARTHY See also EARTHEN; EARTHLY.
1Co 15:47 The first man is of the earth, **e.**: *5517*
1Co 15:48 As is the **e.**, such are they also *5517*
1Co 15:48 such are they also that are **e.**: *5517*
1Co 15:49 we have born the image of the **e.**, *5517*

EASE See also EASED; DISEASE.
De 23:13 when thou wilt **e.** thyself abroad, 3427
De 28:65 these nations shalt thou find no **e.**, 7280
Jg 20:43 and trode them down with **e.** 4496
2Ch 10:4 **e.** thou somewhat the grievous 7043
2Ch 10:9 **E.** somewhat the yoke that thy 7043
Job 7:13 my couch shall **e.** my complaint; 5375
Job 12:5 the thought of him that is at **e.** 7600
Job 16:12 I was at **e.**, but he hath broken 7961
Job 21:23 being wholly at **e.** and quiet 7946
Ps 25:13 His soul shall dwell at **e.**; and 2896
Ps 123:4 scorning of those that are at **e.**, 7600
Isa 1:24 will **e.** me of mine adversaries, 5162
Isa 32:9 Rise up, ye women that are at **e.**; 7600
Isa 32:11 Tremble, ye women that are at **e.**; 7600
Jer 46:27 and be in rest and at **e.**, 7599
Jer 48:11 Moab hath been at **e.** from his 7599
Eze 23:42 a voice of a multitude being at **e.** 7961
Am 6:1 Woe to them that are at **e.** in Zion, 7600
Zec 1:15 with the heathen that are at **e.**: 7600
Lu 12:19 **take thine e., eat, drink, and be** *373*

EASED
Job 16:6 though I forbear, what am I **e.**? 1980
2Co 8:13 I mean not that other men be **e.**, *425*

EASIER
Ex 18:22 so shall it be **e.** for thyself, 7043
Mt 9:5 **whether is e., to say, Thy sins be** *2123*
Mt 19:24 **It is e. for a camel to go through** *2123*
Mk 2:9 **Whether it is e. to say to the sick** *2123*
Mk 10:25 **It is e. for a camel to go through** *2123*
Lu 5:23 **Whether is e., to say, Thy sins be** *2123*
Lu 16:17 **it is e. for heaven and earth to** *2123*
Lu 18:25 **For it is e. for a camel to go** *2123*

EASILY
1Co 13:5 not **e.** provoked, thinketh no evil;
Heb 12:1 the sin which doth so **e.** beset us,

EAST See also EASTWARD.
Ge 2:14 goeth toward the **e.** of Assyria 6926
Ge 3:24 at the **e.** of the garden of Eden 6924
Ge 4:16 the land of Nod, on the **e.** of Eden. 6926
Ge 10:30 was...Sephar a mount of the **e.** 6924
Ge 11:2 pass, as they journeyed from the **e.**, 6924
Ge 12:8 a mountain on the **e.** of Beth-el, 6924
Ge 12:8 his tent, having...Hai on the **e.**: 6924
Ge 13:11 and Lot journeyed **e.**: and they 6924
Ge 25:6 eastward, unto the **e.** country. 6924
Ge 28:14 abroad to the west, and to the **e.**, 6924
Ge 29:1 into the land of the people of the **e.** 6924
Ge 41:6 ears and blasted with the **e.** wind 6921
Ge 41:23 ears...blasted with the **e.** wind, 6921
Ge 41:27 empty ears blasted with the **e.** wind 6921
Ex 10:13 brought an **e.** wind upon the land 6921
Ex 10:13 the **e.** wind brought the locusts. 6921
Ex 14:21 to go back by a strong **e.** wind 6921
Ex 27:13 breadth of the court on the **e.** side 6924
Ex 38:13 for the **e.** side eastward fifty cubits. 6924
Le 1:16 it beside the altar on the **e.** part, 6924
Nu 2:3 on the **e.** side toward the rising of 6924
Nu 3:38 the tabernacle toward the **e.** 6924
Nu 10:5 the camps that lie on the **e.** parts 6924
Nu 23:7 out of the mountains of the **e.**, 6924
Nu 34:10 your **e.** border from Hazar-enan 6924
Nu 34:11 to Riblah, on the **e.** side of Ain; 6924
Nu 35:5 from without the city on the **e.** side 6924
Jos 4:19 Gilgal, in the **e.** border of Jericho. 4217
Jos 7:2 to Ai,...on the **e.** side of Beth-el, 6924
Jos 11:3 And to the Canaanite on the **e.** 4217
Jos 12:1 and all the plain on the **e.**: 4217
Jos 12:3 the sea of Chinneroth on the **e.**, 4217
Jos 12:3 even the salt sea on the **e.**, 4217
Jos 15:5 the **e.** border was the salt sea, 6924
Jos 16:1 the water of Jericho on the **e.**, 4217
Jos 16:5 of their inheritance on the **e.** side 4217
Jos 16:6 passed by it on the **e.** to Janohah; 4217
Jos 17:10 north, and in Issachar on the **e.** 4217
Jos 18:7 beyond Jordan on the **e.**, 4217
Jos 18:20 the border of it on the **e.** side. 6924
Jos 19:13 passeth on along on the **e.** 6924
Jg 6:3 the children of the **e.**,....came up 6924
Jg 6:33 children of the **e.** were gathered 6924
Jg 7:12 all the children of the **e.** lay along 6924
Jg 8:10 the hosts of the children of the **e.**: 6924
Jg 8:11 them that dwelt in tents on the **e.** 6924
Jg 11:18 came by the **e.** side of the land 4217,8121
Jg 21:19 on the **e.** side of the highway 4217,8121
1Ki 4:30 all the children of the **e.** country, 6924
1Ki 7:25 and three looking toward the **e.**: 4217
1Ch 4:39 unto the **e.** side of the valley, 4217
1Ch 5:10 tents throughout all the **e.** land 4217
1Ch 6:78 on the **e.** side of Jordan, were 4217
1Ch 9:24 the **e.**, west, north, and south. 4217
1Ch 12:15 toward the **e.**, and toward the west. 4217
2Ch 4:4 three looking toward the **e.**: and 4217
2Ch 4:10 on the right side of the **e.** end, 6924
2Ch 5:12 stood at the **e.** end of the altar, 4217
2Ch 29:4 them together into the **e.** street, 4217
2Ch 31:14 the porter toward the **e.**, was 4217
Ne 3:26 the water gate toward the **e.**, 4217
Ne 3:29 the keeper of the **e.** gate. 4217
Job 1:3 greatest of all the men of the **e.** 6924
Job 15:2 and fill his belly with the **e.** wind? 6921
Job 27:21 The **e.** wind carrieth him away, 6921
Job 38:24 which scattereth the **e.** wind upon 6921
Ps 48:7 ships of Tarshish with an **e.** wind. 6921
Ps 75:6 cometh neither from the **e.**, 4161
Ps 78:26 He caused an **e.** wind to blow in 6921
Ps 103:12 far as the **e.** is from the west, 4217
Ps 107:3 from the **e.**, and from the wet, 4217
Isa 2:6 they be replenished from the **e.**, 6924
Isa 11:14 shall spoil them of the **e.** together: 6924
Isa 27:8 wind in the day of the **e.** wind. 6921
Isa 41:2 up the righteous man from the **e.**, 4217
Isa 43:5 I will bring thy seed from the **e.**, 4217
Isa 46:11 Calling a ravenous bird from the **e.**, 4217
Jer 18:17 scatter them as with an **e.** wind 6921
Jer 19:2 is by the entry of the **e.** gate, 2777
Jer 31:40 of the horse gate toward the **e.**, 4217
Jer 49:28 and spoil the men of the **e.** 6924
Eze 8:16 their faces toward the **e.**; and they 6924
Eze 8:16 worshipped the sun toward the **e.** 6924
Eze 10:19 stood at the door of the **e.** gate 6931
Eze 11:1 brought me unto the **e.** gate 6931
Eze 11:23 mountain which is on the **e.** side 6924
Eze 17:10 when the **e.** wind toucheth it? 6921
Eze 19:12 the **e.** wind dried up her fruit: 6921
Eze 25:4 deliver thee to the men of the **e.** 6924
Eze 25:10 Unto the men of the **e.** with the 6924
Eze 27:26 the **e.** wind hath broken thee in 6921
Eze 39:11 passengers on the **e.** of the sea; 6926
Eze 40:6 gate which looketh toward the **e.**, 6921
Eze 40:22 the gate that looketh toward the **e.**; 6921
Eze 40:23 toward the north, and toward the **e.**; 6921
Eze 40:32 into the inner court toward the **e.**: 6921
Eze 40:44 at the side of the **e.** gate 6921
Eze 41:14 the separate place toward the **e.**, 6921
Eze 42:9 was the entry on the **e.** side, 6921
Eze 42:10 the wall of the court toward the **e.**, 6921
Eze 42:12 before the wall toward the **e.**, 6921
Eze 42:15 whose prospect is toward the **e.**, 6921
Eze 42:16 He measured the **e.** side with the 6921
Eze 43:1 the gate that looketh toward the **e.**: 6921
Eze 43:2 came from the way of the **e.**: 6921
Eze 43:4 whose prospect is toward the **e.** 6921
Eze 43:17 his stairs shall look toward the **e.** 6921
Eze 44:1 which looketh toward the **e.**: 6921
Eze 45:7 and from the **e.** side eastward: 6924
Eze 45:7 west border unto the **e.** border. 6921
Eze 46:1 court that looketh toward the **e.** 6921
Eze 46:12 gate that looketh toward the **e.**, 6921
Eze 47:1 of the house stood toward the **e.**, 6921
Eze 47:8 waters issue out toward the **e.** 6930
Eze 47:18 the **e.** side ye shall measure from 6921
Eze 47:18 from the border unto the **e.** sea. 6931
Eze 47:18 And this is the **e.** side. 6921
Eze 48:1 these are his sides **e.** and west; 6921
Eze 48:2 border of Dan, from the **e.** side 6921
Eze 48:3 border of Asher, from the **e.** side 6921
Eze 48:4 border of Naphtali, from the **e.** side 6921
Eze 48:5 border of Manasseh, from the **e.** 6921
Eze 48:6 border of Ephraim, from the **e.** side 6921
Eze 48:7 border of Reuben, from the **e.** side 6921
Eze 48:8 border of Judah, from the **e.** side 6921
Eze 48:8 the **e.** side unto the west side: 6921
Eze 48:10 and toward the **e.** ten thousand in 6921
Eze 48:16 the **e.** side four thousand and five 6921
Eze 48:17 the **e.** two hundred and fifty 6921
Eze 48:21 the oblation toward the **e.** border, 6921
Eze 48:23 from the **e.** side unto the west side, 6921
Eze 48:24 from the **e.** side unto the west 6921
Eze 48:25 border of Simeon, from the **e.** side 6921

Eze 48:26 border of Issachar, from the **e.** side.... 6921
Eze 48:27 border of Zebulun, from the **e.** side 6921
Eze 48:32 at the **e.** side four thousand and......... 6921
Da 8:9 the south, and toward the **e.**,.......... 4217
Da 11:44 But tidings out of the **e.** and out 4217
Ho 12:1 and followeth after the **e.** wind:.......... 6921
Ho 13:15 an **e.** wind shall come, the wind......... 6921
Joe 2:20 with his face toward the **e.** sea, ... 6931
Am 8:12 from the north even to the **e.**,........... 4217
Jon 4:5 and sat on the **e.** side of the city,....... 6924
Jon 4:8 God prepared a vehement **e.** wind; 6921
Hab 1:9 faces shall sup up as the **e.** wind, ... 6921
Zec 8:7 save my people from the **e.**............... 4217
Zec 14:4 is before Jerusalem on the **e.**,............ 6924
Zec 14:4 the midst thereof toward the **e.** 4217
Mt 2:1 men from the **e.** to Jerusalem, ... *395*
Mt 2:2 we have seen his star in the **e.**. *395*
Mt 2:9 the star, which they saw in the **e.**........ *395*
Mt 8:11 **shall come from the e. and west,**.... *395*
Mt 24:27 **the lightning cometh out of the e.,**..*395*
Lu 13:29 **they shall come from the e., and**.... *395*
Re 7:2 angel ascending from the **e.**, ... *395*
Re 16:12 the way of the kings of the **e.**............. *395*
Re 21:13 On the **e.** three gates; on the north *395*

EASTER
Ac 12:4 intending after **E.** to bring him........... *3957*

EAST-SIDE See EAST and SIDE.

EASTWARD
Ge 2:8 God planted a garden **e.** of Eden; 6924
Ge 13:14 southward, and **e.**, and westward: 6924
Ge 25:6 yet lived, **e.**, unto the east country..... 6924
Ex 27:13 east side **e.** shall be fifty cubits.......... 4217
Ex 38:13 the east side **e.** fifty cubits.................. 4217
Le 16:14 his finger upon the mercy seat **e.**; 6924
Nu 3:38 **e.**, shall be Moses, and Aaron 4217
Nu 32:19 fallen to us on this side Jordan **e.**. 4217
Nu 34:3 outmost coast of the salt sea **e.**; 6924
Nu 34:11 side of the sea of Chinnereth **e.**: 6924
Nu 34:15 Jericho **e.**, toward the sunrising.......... 6924
De 3:17 sea, under Ashdoth-pisgah **e.**............. 4217
De 3:27 northward, and southward, and **e.**,...... 4217
De 4:49 the plain on this side Jordan **e.**,.......... 4217
Jos 11:8 and unto the valley of Mizpeh **e.**; 4217
Jos 13:8 gave them, beyond Jordan **e.**,............ 4217
Jos 13:27 on the other side Jordan **e.**. 4217
Jos 13:32 other side Jordan, by Jericho, **e.**......... 4217
Jos 16:6 about **e.** unto Taanath-shiloh,............ 4217
Jos 19:12 from Sarid **e.** toward the sunrising...... 6924
Jos 20:8 other side Jordan by Jericho **e.**,......... 4217
1Sa 13:5 in Michmash, **e.** from Beth-aven......... 6926
1Ki 7:39 on the right side of the house **e.**, ... 6924
1Ki 17:3 Get thee hence, and turn thee **e.**, ... 6924
2Ki 10:33 Jordan **e.**, all...land of Gilead, ... 4217,8121
2Ki 13:17 And he said, Open the window **e.**....... 6924
1Ch 5:9 And **e.** he inhabited unto the 4217
1Ch 7:28 **e.** Naaran, and westward Gezer, ... 4217
1Ch 9:18 waited in the king's gate **e.**: 4217
1Ch 26:14 the lot **e.** fell to Shelemiah................ 4217
1Ch 26:17 **E.** were six Levites, northward four... 4217
Ne 12:37 even unto the water gate **e.**............... 4217
Eze 11:1 Lord's house, which looketh **e.**: 6921
Eze 40:10 little chambers of the gate **e.**....... 1870,6921
Eze 40:19 hundred cubits **e.** and northward. 6921
Eze 45:7 and from the east side **e.**:................ 6921
Eze 47:1 the threshold of the house **e.**:............ 6921
Eze 47:2 gate by the way that looketh **e.**; 6921
Eze 47:3 the line in his hand went forth **e.**,....... 6921
Eze 48:18 residue...shall be ten thousand **e.**, ... 6921

EAST WIND See EAST and WIND.

EASY See also EASIER.
Pr 14:6 knowledge is **e.** unto him that........... 7043
Mt 11:30 **For my yoke is e., and my burden**.*5543*
1Co 14:9 tongue words **e.** to be understood, ... *2154*
Jas 3:17 **e.** to be intreated, full of mercy *2138*

EAT See also ATE; EATEN; EATEST; EATETH; EATING.
Ge 2:16 garden thou mayest freely **e.**: 398
Ge 2:17 thou shalt not **e.** of it: for in the.......... 398
Ge 3:1 not **e.** of every tree of the garden? 398
Ge 3:2 We may **e.** of the fruit of the trees 398
Ge 3:3 God hath said, Ye shall not **e.** of it,...... 398
Ge 3:5 know that in the day ye **e.** thereof, ... 398
Ge 3:6 and did **e.**, and gave also unto her 398
Ge 3:6 husband with her; and he did **e.**........... 398
Ge 3:11 thee that thou shouldest not **e.**? 398
Ge 3:12 she gave me of the tree, and I did **e.**.. .. 398
Ge 3:13 serpent beguiled me, and I did **e.**......... 398
Ge 3:14 dust shalt thou **e.** all the days of thy..... 398
Ge 3:17 saying, Thou shalt not **e.** of it: 398
Ge 3:17 thou **e.** of it all the days of thy life; 398
Ge 3:18 thou shalt **e.** the herb of the field;........ 398
Ge 3:19 the sweat of thy face shalt thou **e.**....... 398
Ge 3:22 take also of the tree of life, and **e.**, ... 398
Ge 9:4 the blood thereof, shall ye not **e.**. 398
Ge 18:8 under the tree, and they did **e.**. 398
Ge 19:3 unleavened bread, and they did **e.**. 398
Ge 24:33 was set meat before him to **e.**:........... 398
Ge 24:33 but he said, I will not **e.**, ... 398
Ge 24:54 And they did **e.** and drink, he and........ 398
Ge 25:28 he did **e.** of his venison: 6310
Ge 25:34 he did **e.** and drink, and rose up, ... 398
Ge 26:30 made them a feast, and they did **e.** 398
Ge 27:4 bring it to me, that I may **e.**;............... 398
Ge 27:7 me savoury meat, that I may **e.**, ... 398
Ge 27:10 may **e.**, and that he may bless thee....... 398
Ge 27:19 sit and **e.** of my venison, that thy 398
Ge 27:25 and I will **e.** of my son's venison,......... 398
Ge 27:25 it near to him, and he did **e.**:.............. 398
Ge 27:31 arise, and **e.** of his son's venison, ... 398
Ge 28:20 I go, and will give me bread to **e.**,........ 398
Ge 31:46 and they did **e.** there upon the heap. 398
Ge 31:54 and called his brethren to **e.** bread, ... 398
Ge 31:54 did **e.** bread, and tarried all night......... 398
Ge 32:32 children of Israel **e.** not of the sinew 398
Ge 37:25 and they sat down to **e.** bread:............ 398
Ge 39:6 save the bread which he did **e.**........... 398
Ge 40:17 birds did **e.** them out of the basket 398
Ge 40:19 and the birds shall **e.** thy flesh............ 398
Ge 41:4 did **e.** up the seven well favoured 398
Ge 41:20 the...kine did **e.** up the first seven 398
Ge 43:25 that they should **e.** bread there. 398
Ge 43:32 Egyptians, which did **e.** with him, ... 398
Ge 43:32 not **e.** bread with the Hebrews;............ 398
Ge 45:18 and ye shall **e.** the fat of the land......... 398
Ge 47:22 and did **e.** their portion which.............. 398
Ex 2:20 call him, that he may **e.** bread............. 398
Ex 10:5 and they shall **e.** the residue of............ 398
Ex 10:5 shall **e.** every tree which groweth........ 398
Ex 10:12 and **e.** every herb of the land,............... 398
Ex 10:15 they did **e.** every herb of the land,........ 398
Ex 12:7 houses, wherein they shall **e.** it. 398
Ex 12:8 shall **e.** the flesh in that night............. 398
Ex 12:8 with bitter herbs they shall **e.** it. 398
Ex 12:9 **E.** not of it raw, nor sodden at all 398
Ex 12:11 And thus shall ye **e.** it; with your......... 398
Ex 12:11 and ye shall **e.** it in haste: 398
Ex 12:15 days shall ye **e.** unleavened bread; 398
Ex 12:16 save that which every man must **e.**, ... 398
Ex 12:18 ye shall **e.** unleavened bread, until........ 398
Ex 12:20 Ye shall **e.** nothing leavened; in all 398
Ex 12:20 shall ye **e.** unleavened bread. 398
Ex 12:43 There shall no stranger **e.** thereof:....... 398
Ex 12:44 him, then shall he **e.** thereof.............. 398
Ex 12:45 an hired servant shall not **e.** thereof. 398
Ex 12:48 no uncircumcised person shall **e.**......... 398
Ex 13:6 thou shalt **e.** unleavened bread, ... 398
Ex 16:3 when we did **e.** bread to the full; 398
Ex 16:8 give you in the evening flesh to **e.**, ... 398
Ex 16:12 At even ye shall **e.** flesh, and in the...... 398
Ex 16:15 which the Lord hath given you to **e.**..... 402
Ex 16:25 And Moses said, **E.** that to day;.......... 398
Ex 16:35 the children of Israel did **e.** manna 398
Ex 16:35 they did **e.** manna, until they came....... 398
Ex 18:12 **e.** bread with Moses' father in law 398
Ex 22:31 shall ye **e.** any flesh that is torn........... 398
Ex 23:11 that the poor of thy people may **e.**: 398
Ex 23:11 the beasts of the field shall **e.**. 398
Ex 23:15 **e.** unleavened bread seven days,.......... 398
Ex 24:11 they saw God, and did **e.** and drink. 398
Ex 29:32 And Aaron and his sons shall **e.**.......... 398
Ex 29:33 And they shall **e.** those things 398
Ex 29:33 but a stranger shall not **e.** thereof, ... 398
Ex 32:6 people sat down to **e.** and to drink, ... 398
Ex 34:15 and thou **e.** of his sacrifice;................. 398
Ex 34:18 thou shalt **e.** unleavened bread, ... 398
Ex 34:28 neither **e.** bread, nor drink water. 398
Le 3:17 that ye **e.** neither fat nor blood............. 398
Le 6:16 thereof shall Aaron and his sons **e.**:...... 398
Le 6:16 the congregation they shall **e.** it........... 398
Le 6:18 the children of Aaron shall **e.** of it. 398
Le 6:26 that offereth it for sin shall **e.** it:.......... 398
Le 6:29 among the priests shall **e.** thereof: 398
Le 7:6 among the priests shall **e.** thereof: 398
Le 7:19 all that be clean shall **e.** thereof. 398
Le 7:21 and **e.** of the flesh of the sacrifice 398
Le 7:23 Ye shall **e.** no manner of fat,................. 398
Le 7:24 but ye shall in no wise **e.** of it............. 398
Le 7:26 ye shall **e.** no manner of blood,............ 398
Le 8:31 and there **e.** it with the bread that is 398
Le 8:31 Aaron and his sons shall **e.** it. 398
Le 10:12 and **e.** it without leaven beside the....... 398
Le 10:13 And ye shall **e.** it in the holy place, ... 398
Le 10:14 and heave shoulder shall ye **e.**............. 398
Le 11:2 ye shall **e.** among all the beasts........... 398
Le 11:3 among the beasts, that shall ye **e.**. 398
Le 11:4 Nevertheless these shall ye not **e.** 398
Le 11:8 Of their flesh shall ye not **e.**, ... 398
Le 11:9 ye **e.** of all that are in the waters: 398
Le 11:9 and in the rivers, them shall ye **e.**. 398
Le 11:11 ye shall not **e.** of their flesh,............... 398
Le 11:21 Yet these may ye **e.** of every flying...... 398
Le 11:22 even these of them ye may **e.**;.............. 398
Le 11:39 any beast, of which ye may **e.**,............ 402
Le 11:42 them ye shall not **e.**; for they are 398
Le 17:12 No soul of you shall **e.** blood,.............. 398
Le 17:12 any stranger...among you **e.** blood. 398
Le 17:14 Ye shall **e.** the blood of no manner....... 398
Le 19:25 fifth year shall ye **e.** of the fruit.......... 398
Le 19:26 not **e.** anything with the blood, ... 398
Le 21:22 He shall **e.** the bread of his God, ... 398
Le 22:4 he shall not **e.** of the holy things,......... 398
Le 22:6 and shall not **e.** of the holy things, ... 398
Le 22:7 shall afterward **e.** the holy things; 398
Le 22:8 he shall not **e.** to defile himself............ 398
Le 22:10 no stranger **e.** of the holy thing: 398
Le 22:10 shall not **e.** of the holy thing................ 398
Le 22:11 he shall **e.** of it, and he that is born 398
Le 22:11 they shall **e.** of his meat..................... 398
Le 22:12 she may not **e.** of an offering 398
Le 22:13 she shall **e.** of her father's meat: 398
Le 22:13 there shall no stranger **e.** thereof......... 398
Le 22:14 if a man **e.** of the holy thing................ 398
Le 22:16 when they **e.** their holy things:............ 398
Le 23:6 days ye must **e.** unleavened bread........ 398
Le 23:14 And ye shall **e.** neither bread, nor........ 398
Le 24:9 they shall **e.** in in the holy place: 398
Le 25:12 ye shall **e.** the increase thereof out 398
Le 25:19 shall **e.** your fill, and dwell therein........ 398
Le 25:20 What shall we **e.** the seventh year?...... 398
Le 25:22 and **e.** yet of old fruit until the ninth..... 398
Le 25:22 ye shall **e.** of the old store. 398
Le 26:5 ye shall **e.** your bread to the full,......... 398
Le 26:10 ye shall **e.** old store, and bring forth..... 398
Le 26:16 for your enemies shall **e.** it................. 398
Le 26:26 ye shall **e.**, and not be satisfied. 398
Le 26:29 ye shall **e.** the flesh of your sons, ... 398
Le 26:29 flesh of your daughters shall ye **e.**........ 398
Le 26:38 land of your enemies shall **e.** you......... 398
Nu 6:3 nor **e.** moist grapes, or dried. 398
Nu 6:4 shall he **e.** nothing that is made 398
Nu 9:11 and **e.** it with unleavened bread 398
Nu 11:4 Who shall give us flesh to **e.**?.............. 398
Nu 11:5 remember the fish, which we did **e.** 398
Nu 11:13 Give us flesh, that we may **e.**. 398
Nu 11:18 and ye shall **e.** flesh: for ye have 398
Nu 11:18 Who shall give us flesh to **e.**?............. 398
Nu 11:18 will give you flesh, and ye shall **e.**........ 398
Nu 11:19 shall not **e.** one day, nor two days, ... 398
Nu 11:21 that they may **e.** a whole month. 398
Nu 15:19 when ye **e.** of the bread of the land,..... 398
Nu 18:10 most holy place shalt thou **e.** it;.......... 398
Nu 18:10 every male shall **e.** it:......................... 398
Nu 18:11 is clean in thy house shall **e.** of it......... 398
Nu 18:13 is clean in thine house shall **e.** of it. 398
Nu 18:31 And ye shall **e.** it in every place, ... 398
Nu 23:24 not lie down until he **e.** of the prey. 398
Nu 24:8 he shall **e.** up the nations 398
Nu 25:2 the people did **e.**, and bowed down 398
De 2:6 of them for money, that ye may **e.**;....... 398
De 2:28 me meat for money, that I may **e.**; 398
De 4:28 see, nor hear, nor **e.**, nor smell. 398
De 8:9 A land wherein thou shalt **e.** bread....... 398
De 9:9 did **e.** bread nor drink water: 398
De 9:18 neither **e.** bread, nor drink water, ... 398
De 11:15 that thou mayest **e.** and be full. 398
De 12:7 there ye shall **e.** before the Lord......... 398
De 12:15 kill and **e.** flesh in all thy gates, ... 398
De 12:15 and the clean may **e.** thereof,.............. 398
De 12:16 Only ye shall not **e.** the blood; 398
De 12:17 mayest not **e.** within thy gates 398

De 12:18 thou must **e.** them before the Lord 398
De 12:20 and thou shalt say, I will **e.** flesh, 398
De 12:20 because thy soul longeth to **e.** flesh; 398
De 12:20 thou mayest **e.** flesh, whatsoever 398
De 12:21 and thou shalt **e.** in thy gates 398
De 12:22 so thou shalt **e.** them: the unclean 398
De 12:22 and the clean shall **e.** of them alike 398
De 12:23 be sure that thou **e.** not the blood: 398
De 12:23 mayest not **e.** the life with the flesh. 398
De 12:24 Thou shalt not **e.** it; thou shalt pour 398
De 12:25 Thou shalt not **e.** it; that it may go 398
De 12:27 and thou shalt **e.** the flesh. 398
De 14:3 shalt not **e.** any abominable thing. 398
De 14:4 are the beasts which ye shall **e.**: 398
De 14:6 among the beasts, that ye shall **e.**. 398
De 14:7 Nevertheless these ye shall not **e.** 398
De 14:8 ye shall not **e.** of their flesh, 398
De 14:9 shall **e.** of all that are in the waters: 398
De 14:9 that have fins and scales shall ye **e.**: 398
De 14:10 not fins and scales ye may not **e.**; 398
De 14:11 Of all clean birds ye shall **e.**. 398
De 14:12 are they of which ye shall not **e.**: 398
De 14:20 But of all clean fowls ye may **e.** 398
De 14:21 Ye shall not **e.** of anything that 398
De 14:21 is in thy gates, that he may **e.** it; 398
De 14:23 And thou shalt **e.** before the Lord 398
De 14:26 thou shalt **e.** there before the Lord 398
De 14:29 come, and shall **e.** and be satisfied; 398
De 15:20 Thou shalt **e.** it before the Lord 398
De 15:22 and the clean person shall **e.** it alike,
De 15:22 Thou shalt **e.** it within thy gates: 398
De 15:23 thou shalt not **e.** the blood thereof; 398
De 16:3 shalt **e.** no leavened bread with it; 398
De 16:3 seven days shalt thou **e.** unleavened 398
De 16:7 And thou shalt roast and **e.** it 398
De 16:8 Six days shalt thou **e.** unleavened 398
De 18:1 shall **e.** the offerings of the Lord 398
De 18:8 They shall have like portions to **e.**, 398
De 20:6 battle, and another man **e.** of it 2490
De 20:14 shalt **e.** the spoil of thine enemies, 398
De 20:19 for thou mayest **e.** of them, and 398
De 23:24 then thou mayest **e.** grapes thy fill 398
De 26:12 that they may **e.** within thy gates, 398
De 27:7 **e.** there, and rejoice before the Lord 398
De 28:31 and thou shalt not **e.** thereof: 398
De 28:33 which thou knowest not **e.** up: 398
De 28:39 grapes; for the worms shall **e.** them. 398
De 28:51 he shall **e.** the fruit of thy cattle, 398
De 28:53 shalt **e.** the fruit of thine own body, 398
De 28:55 his children whom he shall **e.**: 398
De 28:57 shall **e.** them for want of all things 398
De 32:13 might **e.** the increase of the fields; 398
De 32:38 did **e.** the fat of their sacrifices, 398
Jos 5:11 And they did **e.** of the old corn 398
Jos 5:12 but they did **e.** of the fruit of the 398
Jos 24:13 which ye planted not do ye **e.**. 398
Jg 9:27 **e.** and drink, and cursed Abimelech. 398
Jg 13:4 and **e.** not any unclean thing: 398
Jg 13:7 drink, neither **e.** any unclean thing: 398
Jg 13:14 She may not **e.** of any thing that 398
Jg 13:14 nor **e.** any unclean thing: all that I 398
Jg 13:16 I will not **e.** of thy bread: 398
Jg 14:9 he gave them, and they did **e.** 398
Jg 19:4 did **e.** and drink, and lodged there 398
Jg 19:6 they sat down, and did **e.** and drink 398
Jg 19:8 and they did **e.** both of them 398
Jg 19:21 their feet, and did **e.** and drink 398
Ru 2:14 **e.** of the bread, and dip thy morsel 398
Ru 2:14 and she did **e.**, and was sufficed, 398
1Sa 1:7 therefore she wept, and did not **e.**. 398
1Sa 1:18 the woman went her way, and did **e.**, 398
1Sa 2:36 that I may **e.** a piece of bread. 398
1Sa 9:13 he go up to the high place to **e.** 398
1Sa 9:13 the people will not **e.** until he come, 398
1Sa 9:13 afterwards they **e.** that be bidden 398
1Sa 9:19 for ye shall **e.** with me to day, 398
1Sa 9:24 set it before thee, and **e.** for unto 398
1Sa 9:24 So Saul did **e.** with Samuel that day 398
1Sa 14:32 people did **e.** them with the blood. 398
1Sa 14:33 in that they **e.** with the blood. 398
1Sa 14:34 slay them here, and **e.**; and sin not 398
1Sa 20:24 the king sat him down to **e.** meat. 398
1Sa 20:34 and did **e.** no meat the second day 398
1Sa 28:22 **e.**, that thou mayest have strength, 398
1Sa 28:23 he refused, and said, I will not **e.**. 398
1Sa 28:25 before his servants; and they did **e.** 398
1Sa 30:11 and gave him bread, and he did **e.**; 398

2Sa 3:35 to cause David to **e.** meat while it 1262
2Sa 9:7 thou shalt not **e.** bread at my table 398
2Sa 9:10 master's son may have food to **e.**: 398
2Sa 9:10 thy master's son shall **e.** bread 398
2Sa 9:11 **e.** at my table, as one of the king's 398
2Sa 9:13 he did **e.** continually at the king's 398
2Sa 11:11 into mine house, to **e.** and to drink, 398
2Sa 11:13 And...he did **e.** and drink before him; 398
2Sa 12:3 it did **e.** of his own meat, 398
2Sa 12:17 neither did he **e.** bread with them 1262
2Sa 12:20 set bread before him, and he did **e.** 398
2Sa 12:21 thou didst rise and **e.** bread. 398
2Sa 13:5 that I may see it, and **e.** it at her hand. 398
2Sa 13:6 that I may **e.** at her hand 1262
2Sa 13:9 before him; but he refused to **e.** 398
2Sa 13:10 that I may **e.** of thine hand 1262
2Sa 13:11 had brought them unto him to **e.**, 398
2Sa 16:2 fruit for the young men to **e.**; 398
2Sa 17:29 the people that were with him, to **e.** 398
2Sa 19:28 them that did **e.** at thine own table 398
2Sa 19:35 taste what I **e.** or what I drink? 398
1Ki 1:25 they **e.** and drink before him, 398
1Ki 2:7 be of those that **e.** at thy table: 398
1Ki 13:8 neither will I **e.** bread nor drink 398
1Ki 13:9 **E.** no bread, nor drink water, nor 398
1Ki 13:15 Come home with me, and **e.** bread 398
1Ki 13:16 neither will I **e.** bread nor drink 398
1Ki 13:17 Thou shalt **e.** no bread nor drink 398
1Ki 13:18 he may **e.** bread and drink water. 398
1Ki 13:19 and did **e.** bread in his house, 398
1Ki 13:22 **E.** no bread, and drink no water; 398
1Ki 14:11 in the city shall the dogs **e.**; and 398
1Ki 14:11 the field shall the fowls of the air **e.** 398
1Ki 16:4 Baasha in the city shall the dogs **e.**; 398
1Ki 16:4 fields shall the fowls of the air **e.**, 398
1Ki 17:12 that we may **e.** it, and die. 398
1Ki 17:15 she, and he, and her house, did **e.** 398
1Ki 18:19 hundred, which **e.** at Jezebel's table 398
1Ki 18:41 Get thee up, **e.** and drink; for there 398
1Ki 18:42 Ahab went up to **e.** and to drink. 398
1Ki 19:5 and said unto him, Arise and **e.**. 398
1Ki 19:6 did **e.** and drink, and laid him down 398
1Ki 19:7 Arise and **e.**; because the journey is 398
1Ki 19:8 he arose, and did **e.** and drink, 398
1Ki 19:21 unto the people, and they did **e.**. 398
1Ki 21:4 his face, and would **e.** no bread. 398
1Ki 21:7 arise, and **e.** bread, and let thine 398
1Ki 21:23 dogs shall **e.** Jezebel by the wall 398
1Ki 21:24 Ahab in the city the dogs shall **e.**; 398
1Ki 21:24 field shall the fowls of the air **e.**. 398
2Ki 4:8 she constrained him to **e.** bread 398
2Ki 4:8 he turned in thither to **e.** bread. 398
2Ki 4:40 they poured out for the men to **e.** 398
2Ki 4:40 And they could not **e.** thereof. 398
2Ki 4:41 for the people, that they may **e.**. 398
2Ki 4:42 unto the people, that they may **e.**. 398
2Ki 4:43 Give the people, that they may **e.** 398
2Ki 4:43 shall **e.**, and shall leave thereof 398
2Ki 4:44 set it before them, and they did **e.**, 398
2Ki 6:22 **e.** and drink, and go to their master. 398
2Ki 6:28 thy son, that we may **e.** him to day, 398
2Ki 6:28 and we will **e.** my son to-morrow 398
2Ki 6:29 we boiled my son, and did **e.** him: 398
2Ki 6:29 Give thy son, that we may **e.** him: 398
2Ki 7:2 thine eyes, but shalt not **e.** thereof. 398
2Ki 7:8 into one tent, and did **e.** and drink, 398
2Ki 7:19 thine eyes, but shall not **e.** thereof 398
2Ki 9:10 dogs shall **e.** Jezebel in the portion 398
2Ki 9:34 he did **e.** and drink, annd said, Go, 398
2Ki 9:36 the portion of Jezreel shall dogs **e.** 398
2Ki 18:27 that they may **e.** their own dung, 398
2Ki 18:31 **e.** ye every man of his own vine, 398
2Ki 19:29 **e.** this year such things as grow 398
2Ki 19:29 vineyards, and **e.** the fruits thereof 398
2Ki 23:9 they did **e.** of the unleavened bread 398
2Ki 25:29 did **e.** bread continually before him 398
1Ch 29:22 did **e.** and drink before the Lord 398
2Ch 28:15 and gave them to **e.** and to drink, 398
2Ch 30:18 did they **e.** the passover otherwise 398
2Ch 30:22 and they did **e.** throughout the feast 398
2Ch 31:10 we have had enough to **e.**, and 398
Ezr 2:63 should not **e.** of the most holy things, 398
Ezr 6:21 seek the Lord God of Israel, did **e.**, 398
Ezr 9:12 and **e.** the good of the land, 398
Ezr 10:6 he did **e.** no bread, nor drink water: 398
Ne 5:2 for them, that we may **e.**, and live. 398
Ne 7:65 should not **e.** of the most holy things. 398

Ne 8:10 **e.** the fat, and drink the sweet, 398
Ne 8:12 the people went their way to **e.**, 398
Ne 9:25 so they did **e.**, and were filled, 398
Ne 9:36 our fathers to **e.** the fruit thereof 398
Es 4:16 neither **e.** nor drink three days, 398
Job 1:4 to **e.** and to drink with them. 398
Job 3:24 For my sighing cometh before I **e.**, 3899
Job 31:8 let me sow, and let another **e.**; 398
Job 42:11 did **e.** bread with him in his house: 398
Ps 14:4 **e.** up my people as they **e.** bread, 398
Ps 22:26 The meek shall **e.** and be satisfied: 398
Ps 22:29 fat upon earth shall **e.** and worship: 398
Ps 27:2 came upon me to **e.** up my flesh, 398
Ps 41:9 I trusted, which did **e.** of my bread, 398
Ps 50:13 Will I **e.** the flesh of bulls, or drink 398
Ps 53:4 **e.** up my people as they **e.** bread: 398
Ps 78:24 down manna upon them to **e.**, 398
Ps 78:25 Man did **e.** angels' food: he sent 398
Ps 78:29 So they did **e.**, and were well filled: 398
Ps 102:4 so that I forget to **e.** my bread. 398
Ps 105:35 did **e.** up all the herbs in their land, 398
Ps 127:2 up late, to **e.** the bread of sorrows: 398
Ps 128:2 shalt **e.** the labour of thine hands: 398
Ps 141:4 let me not **e.** of their dainties. 3898
Pr 1:31 **e.** of the fruit of their own way. 398
Pr 4:17 they **e.** the bread of wickedness. 3898
Pr 9:5 Come, **e.** of my bread, and drink of 3898
Pr 13:2 **e.** good by the fruit of his mouth: 398
Pr 13:2 of the transgressors shall **e.** violence.
Pr 18:21 they that love it shall **e.** the fruit 398
Pr 23:1 thou sittest to **e.** with a ruler, 3898
Pr 23:6 **E.** thou not the bread of him that 3898
Pr 23:7 **E.** and drink, said he to thee: 398
Pr 24:13 **e.** thou honey, because it is good; 398
Pr 25:16 **e.** so much as is sufficient for thee, 398
Pr 25:21 give him bread to **e.**; and if he be 398
Pr 25:27 It is not good to **e.** much honey: 398
Pr 27:18 fig tree shall **e.** the fruit thereof: 398
Pr 30:17 and the young eagles shall **e.** it. 398
Ec 2:24 than that he should **e.** and drink, 398
Ec 2:25 For who can **e.**, or who else can 398
Ec 3:13 that every man should **e.** and drink, 398
Ec 5:11 they are increased that **e.** them: 398
Ec 5:12 sweet, whether he **e.** little or much: 398
Ec 5:18 comely for one to **e.** and to drink, 398
Ec 5:19 hath given him power to **e.** thereof, 398
Ec 6:2 God giveth him not power to **e.** 398
Ec 8:15 than to **e.** and to drink 398
Ec 9:7 **e.** thy bread with joy, and drink 398
Ec 10:16 and thy princes **e.** in the morning! 398
Ec 10:17 and thy princes **e.** in due season, 398
Ca 4:16 garden, and **e.** his pleasant fruits. 398
Ca 5:1 **e.**, O friends; drink, yea, drink 398
Isa 1:19 ye shall **e.** the good of the land: 398
Isa 3:10 shall **e.** the fruit of their doings. 398
Isa 4:1 We will **e.** our own bread, and 398
Isa 5:17 of the fat ones shall strangers **e.** 398
Isa 7:15 Butter and honey shall he **e.**, that 398
Isa 7:22 he shall **e.** butter: for butter 398
Isa 7:22 and honey shall every one **e.** 398
Isa 9:20 and he shall **e.** on the left hand, 398
Isa 9:20 they shall **e.** every man the flesh of 398
Isa 11:7 the lion shall **e.** straw like the ox. 398
Isa 21:5 watch in the watchtower, **e.**, drink: 398
Isa 22:13 drinking wine: let us **e.** and drink; 398
Isa 23:18 to **e.** sufficiently, and for durable 398
Isa 30:24 shall **e.** clean provender, which 398
Isa 36:12 that they may **e.** their own dung, 398
Isa 36:16 and **e.** ye every one of his vine, 398
Isa 37:30 shall **e.** this year such as groweth 398
Isa 37:30 vineyards, and **e.** the fruit thereof. 398
Isa 50:9 the moth shall **e.** them up. 398
Isa 51:8 For the moth shall **e.** them up like 398
Isa 51:8 the worm shall **e.** them like wool: 398
Isa 55:1 come ye, buy, and **e.**; yea, come, 398
Isa 55:2 and **e.** ye that which is good, 398
Isa 61:6 shall **e.** the riches of the Gentiles, 398
Isa 62:9 that have gathered it shall **e.** it, 398
Isa 65:4 which **e.** swine's flesh, and broth 398
Isa 65:13 Behold, my servants shall **e.**, but 398
Isa 65:21 vineyards, and **e.** the fruit of them. 398
Isa 65:22 they shall not plant, and another **e.** 398
Isa 65:25 lion shall **e.** straw like the bullock 398
Jer 2:7 to **e.** the fruit thereof and the 398
Jer 5:17 And they shall **e.** up thine harvest 398
Jer 5:17 sons and thy daughters should **e.** 398
Jer 5:17 **e.** up thy flocks and thine herds 398

Jer 5:17 they shall e. up thy vines 398
Jer 7:21 unto your sacrifices, and e. flesh 398
Jer 15:16 were found, and I did e. them; 398
Jer 16:8 to sit with them to e. and to drink. 398
Jer 19:9 I will cause them to e. the flesh of 398
Jer 19:9 they shall e. every one the flesh of 398
Jer 22:15 did not thy father e. and drink, 398
Jer 22:22 wind shall e. up all thy pastors, 7462
Jer 29:5 gardens, and e. the fruit of them; 398
Jer 29:28 and plant gardens, and e. the fruit 398
Jer 31:5 shall e. them as common things
Jer 41:1 there they did e. bread together 398
Jer 52:33 and he did continually e. bread 398
La 2:20 Shall the women e. their fruit, and 398
Eze 2:8 open thy mouth, and e. that I give 398
Eze 3:1 Son of man, e. that thou findest; 398
Eze 3:1 e. this roll, and go speak 398
Eze 3:2 and he caused me to e. that roll. 398
Eze 3:3 Son of man, cause thy belly to e., 398
Eze 3:3 did I e. it; and it was in my mouth 398
Eze 4:9 days shalt thou e. thereof. 398
Eze 4:10 thy meat which thou shalt e. shall 398
Eze 4:10 from time to time shalt thou e. it 398
Eze 4:12 thou shalt e. it as barley cakes, 398
Eze 4:13 thus shall the children of Israel e. 398
Eze 4:16 and they shall e. bread by weight, 398
Eze 5:10 the fathers shall e. the sons 398
Eze 5:10 and the sons shall e. their fathers; 398
Eze 12:18 man, e. thy bread with quaking, 398
Eze 12:19 e. their bread with carefulness, 398
Eze 16:13 thou didst e. fine flour, and honey, 398
Eze 22:9 thee they e. upon the mountains: 398
Eze 24:17 and e. not the bread of men. 398
Eze 24:22 your lips, nor e. the bread of men. 398
Eze 25:4 they shall e. thy fruit, and they 398
Eze 33:25 Ye e. with the blood, and lift up 398
Eze 34:3 Ye e. the fat, and ye clothe you with 398
Eze 34:19 e. that which ye have trodden 7462
Eze 39:17 ye may e. flesh, and drink blood. 398
Eze 39:18 shall e. the flesh of the mighty. 398
Eze 39:19 And ye shall e. fat till ye be full, 398
Eze 42:13 Lord shall e. the most holy things: 398
Eze 44:3 he shall sit in it to e. bread 398
Eze 44:29 They shall e. the meat offering, and 398
Eze 44:31 The priests shall not e. of any thing 398
Da 1:12 let them give us pulse to e., 398
Da 1:13 e. of the portion of the king's meat: 398
Da 1:15 did e. the portion of the king's meat. 398
Da 4:25 they shall make thee to e. grass 2939
Da 4:32 make thee to e. grass as oxen, 2939
Da 4:33 and did e. grass as oxen, and his 399
Ho 2:12 the beasts of the field shall e. them 398
Ho 4:8 They e. up the sin of my people, 398
Ho 4:10 they shall e., and not have enough: 398
Ho 8:13 of mine offerings, and e. it; 398
Ho 9:3 shall e. unclean things in Assyria 398
Ho 9:4 that e. thereof shall be polluted: 398
Joe 2:26 And ye shall e. in plenty, and be 398
Am 6:4 and e. the lambs out of the flock, 398
Am 7:4 the great deep, and did e. up a part. 398
Am 7:12 there e. bread, and prophesy there: 398
Am 9:14 gardens, and e. the fruit of them. 398
Ob 7 they that e. thy bread have laid a
Mic 3:3 Who also e. the flesh of my people, 398
Mic 6:14 Thou shalt e., but not be satisfied; 398
Mic 7:1 vintage: there is no cluster to e.: 398
Na 3:15 e. thee up like the cankerworm: 398
Hab 1:8 as the eagle that hasteth to e. 398
Hag 1:6 ye e., but ye have not enough; 398
Zec 7:6 when ye did e., and when ye did 398
Zec 7:6 did not ye e. for yourselves, and 398
Zec 11:9 e. every one the flesh of another. 398
Zec 11:16 he shall e. the flesh of the fat, 398
Mt 6:25 **what ye shall e., or what ye shall** 5315
Mt 6:31 **What shall we e.? or, What** 5315
Mt 12:1 pluck the ears of corn, and to e. 2068
Mt 12:4 **and did e. the shewbread.** 5315
Mt 12:4 **was not lawful for him to e.,** 5315
Mt 14:16 **not depart; give ye them to e.** 5315
Mt 14:20 And they did all e., and were filled: 5315
Mt 15:2 wash not their hands when they e. 2068
Mt 15:20 **but to e. with unwashen hands** 5315
Mt 15:27 the dogs e. of the crumbs which 2068
Mt 15:32 **three days, and have nothing to e.:** 5315
Mt 15:37 they did all e., and were filled: 5315
Mt 15:38 did e. were four thousand men, 2068
Mt 24:49 **to e. and drink with the drunken;** 2068
Mt 26:17 prepare for thee to e. the passover? 5315
Mt 26:21 as they did e., he said, **Verily I say** 2068
Mt 26:26 said, **Take, e.; this is my body.** 5315
Mk 1:6 he did e. locusts and wild honey; 2068
Mk 2:16 e. with publicans and sinners, 2068
Mk 2:26 **and did e. the shewbread, which is** 5315
Mk 2:26 **not lawful to e. but for the priests,** 5315
Mk 3:20 could not so much as e. bread. 5315
Mk 5:43 should be given her to e. 5315
Mk 6:31 had no leisure so much as to e. 5315
Mk 6:36 bread: for they have nothing to e. 5315
Mk 6:37 said unto them, **Give ye them to e.** 5315
Mk 6:37 of bread, and give them to e.? 5315
Mk 6:42 And they did all e., and were filled. 5315
Mk 6:44 And they that did e. of the loaves 5315
Mk 7:2 saw some of his disciples e. bread 2068
Mk 7:3 e. not, holding the tradition of 2068
Mk 7:4 except they wash, they e. not. 2068
Mk 7:5 but e. bread with unwashen hands? 2068
Mk 7:28 yet the dogs under the table e. of 2068
Mk 8:1 having nothing to e., Jesus called 5315
Mk 8:2 **days, and have nothing to e.:** 5315
Mk 8:8 So they did e., and were filled: 5315
Mk 11:14 **No man e. fruit of thee hereafter** 5315
Mk 14:12 and prepare that thou mayest e. 5315
Mk 14:14 **where I shall e. the passover with** 5315
Mk 14:18 as they sat and did e., Jesus said, 2068
Mk 14:22 as they did e., Jesus took bread, 2068
Mk 14:22 said, **Take, e.; this is my body.** 5315
Lu 4:2 in those days he did e. nothing: 5315
Lu 5:30 ye e. and drink with publicans 2068
Lu 5:33 Pharisees; but thine e. and drink? 2068
Lu 6:1 and did e., rubbing them in their 2068
Lu 6:4 **did take and e. the shewbread,** 5315
Lu 6:4 **not lawful to e. but for the priests** 5315
Lu 7:36 him that he would e. with him. 5315
Lu 9:13 unto them, **Give ye them to e.** 5315
Lu 9:17 And they did e., and were all filled: 5315
Lu 10:8 **e. such things as are set before** 2068
Lu 12:19 **take thine ease, e., drink, and be** 5315
Lu 12:22 **for your life, what ye shall e.;** 5315
Lu 12:29 **seek not ye what ye shall e.,** 5315
Lu 12:45 **e. and drink, and to be drunken;** 2068
Lu 14:1 to e. bread on the sabbath day, 5315
Lu 14:15 Blessed is he that shall e. bread in 5315
Lu 15:16 **the husks that the swine did e.:** 2068
Lu 15:23 **and let us e., and be merry:** 5315
Lu 17:8 **afterward thou shalt e. and drink?** 5315
Lu 17:27 **They did e., they drank, they** 2068
Lu 17:28 **they did e., they drank, they** 2068
Lu 22:8 **us the passover, that we may e.** 5315
Lu 22:11 **where I shall e. the passover with** 5315
Lu 22:15 **I have desired to e. this passover** 5315
Lu 22:16 **I will not any more e. thereof,** 5315
Lu 22:30 **That ye may e. and drink at my** 2068
Lu 24:43 he took it, and did e. before them. 5315
Joh 4:31 prayed him, saying, Master, e. 5315
Joh 4:32 **I have meat to e. that ye know not** 5315
Joh 4:33 any man brought him ought to e.? 5315
Joh 6:5 **we buy bread, that these may e.?** 5315
Joh 6:23 the place where they did e. bread, 5315
Joh 6:26 **but because ye did e. of the loaves,** 5315
Joh 6:31 Our fathers did e. manna in the 5315
Joh 6:31 gave them bread from heaven to e. 5315
Joh 6:49 **Your fathers did e. manna in the** 5315
Joh 6:50 **a man may e. thereof, and not** 5315
Joh 6:51 **if any man e. of this bread,** 5315
Joh 6:52 can this man give us his flesh to e.? 5315
Joh 6:53 **Except ye e. the flesh of the Son of** 5315
Joh 6:58 **not as your fathers did e. manna,** 5315
Joh 18:28 but that they might e. the passover. 5315
Ac 2:46 did e. their meat with gladness 3335
Ac 9:9 sight, and neither did e. nor drink. 5315
Ac 10:13 Rise, Peter; kill, and e. 5315
Ac 10:41 who did e. and drink with him 4906
Ac 11:3 uncircumcised, and didst e. with 4906
Ac 11:7 Arise, Peter; slay and e. 5315
Ac 23:12 they would neither e. nor drink 5315
Ac 23:14 we will e. nothing until we have 1089
Ac 23:21 an oath, that they will neither e. 5315
Ac 27:35 he had broken it, he began to e. 2068
Ro 14:2 believeth that he may e. all things: 5315
Ro 14:21 It is good neither to e. flesh, nor to 5315
Ro 14:23 that doubteth is damned if he e., 5315
1Co 5:11 with such a one no not to e. 4906
1Co 8:7 e. it as a thing offered unto an 2068
1Co 8:8 neither, if we e., are we the better; 5315
1Co 8:8 if we e. not, are we the worse. 5315
1Co 8:10 e. those things which are offered 2068
1Co 8:13 I will e. no flesh while the world 5315
1Co 9:4 Have we not power to e. and to 5315
1Co 10:3 did all e. the same spiritual meat; 5315
1Co 10:7 people sat down to e. and drink, 5315
1Co 10:18 are they which e. of the sacrifices 2068
1Co 10:25 is sold in the shambles, that e., 2068
1Co 10:27 whatsoever is set before you, e., 2068
1Co 10:28 e. not for his sake that shewed it, 2068
1Co 10:31 Whether therefore ye e., or drink, 2068
1Co 11:20 this is not to e. the Lord's supper. 5315
1Co 11:22 have ye not houses to e. and to 2068
1Co 11:24 **Take, e.; this is my body, which** 5315
1Co 11:26 as often as ye e. this bread, 2068
1Co 11:27 whosoever shall e. this bread, and 2068
1Co 11:28 and so let him e. of that bread, 2068
1Co 11:33 when ye come together to e., tarry 5315
1Co 11:34 man hunger, let him e. at home; 2068
1Co 15:32 let us e. and drink; for to-morrow 5315
Ga 2:12 James, he did e. with the Gentiles: 4906
2Th 3:8 Neither did we e. any man's 5315
2Th 3:10 not work, neither should he e. 2068
2Th 3:12 with quietness they work, and e. 2068
2Ti 2:17 word will e. as doth a canker: 3542,2192
Heb 13:10 they have no right to e. which 5315
Jas 5:3 and shall e. your flesh as it were 5315
Re 2:7 **will I give to e. of the tree of life,** 5315
Re 2:14 **to e. things sacrificed unto idols,** 5315
Re 2:17 **will I give to e. of the hidden** 5315
Re 2:20 **to e. things sacrificed unto idols.** 5315
Re 10:9 Take it, and e. it up; and it shall 2719
Re 17:16 and shall e. her flesh, and burn her 5315
Re 19:18 That ye may e. the flesh of kings, 5315

EATEN

Ge 3:11 Hast thou e. of the tree, whereof I 398
Ge 3:17 hast e. of the tree, of which I 398
Ge 6:21 unto thee of all food that is e., 398
Ge 14:24 that which the young men have e., 398
Ge 27:33 I have e. of all before thou camest, 398
Ge 31:38 the rams of thy flock have I not e. 398
Ge 41:21 when they had e. them 935,413,7130
Ge 41:21 that they had e. them; 935,413,7130
Ge 43:2 when they had e. up the corn 398
Ex 12:46 In one house shall it be e.; 398
Ex 13:3 there shall no leavened bread be e. 398
Ex 13:7 unleavened bread shall be e. seven 398
Ex 21:28 and his flesh shall not be e.; 398
Ex 22:5 cause a field or vineyard to be e., 1197
Ex 29:34 it shall not be e., because it is holy. 398
Le 6:16 with unleavened bread shall it be e. 398
Le 6:23 be wholly burnt: it shall not be e. 398
Le 6:26 in the holy place shall it be e., 398
Le 6:30 no sin offering....shall be e.: 398
Le 7:6 it shall be e. in the holy place: 398
Le 7:15 shall be e. the same day that it is 398
Le 7:16 it shall be e. the same day that he 398
Le 7:16 the remainder of it shall be e.: 398
Le 7:18 his peace offerings be e. at all 398
Le 7:19 any unclean thing shall not be e.; 398
Le 10:17 Wherefore have ye not e. the sin 398
Le 10:18 ye should indeed have e. it in the 398
Le 10:19 and if I had e. the sin offering 398
Le 11:13 they shall not be e., they are an 398
Le 11:34 Of all meat which may be e., 398
Le 11:41 an abomination; it shall not be e. 398
Le 11:47 between the beast that may be e. 398
Le 11:47 and the beast that may not be e. 398
Le 17:13 any beast of fowl that may be e.; 398
Le 19:6 It shall be e. the same day ye offer 398
Le 19:7 if it be e. at all on the third day, 398
Le 19:23 it shall not be e. of. 398
Le 22:30 On the same day it shall be e. 398
Nu 28:17 days shall unleavened bread be e. 398
De 6:11 when thou shalt have e. and be 398
De 8:10 when thou hast e. and art full, 398
De 8:12 Lest when thou hast e. and art full, 398
De 12:22 the roebuck and the hart is e., 398
De 14:19 unto you: they shall not be e. 398
De 20:6 vineyard, and hath not yet e. of it? 2490
De 26:14 I have not e. thereof in my 398
De 29:6 Ye have not e. bread, neither have 398
De 31:20 and they shall have e. and filled 398
Jos 5:12 after they had e. of the old corn 398
Ru 3:7 when Boaz had e. and drunk, and 398
1Sa 1:9 Hannah rose up after they had e. in 398

1Sa 14:30 if haply the people had **e.** freely.......... 398
1Sa 28:20 he had **e.** no bread all the day,........... 398
1Sa 30:12 and when he had **e.**, his spirit came 398
1Sa 30:12 for he had **e.** no bread, nor drunk........ 398
2Sa 19:42 have we **e.** at all of the king's cost? 398
1Ki 13:22 and hast **e.** bread and drunk water....... 398
1Ki 13:23 it came to pass, after he had **e.**........... 398
1Ki 13:28 the lion had not **e.** the carcase, ... 398
2Ki 6:23 and when they had **e.** and drunk,.......... 398
Ne 5:14 my brethren have not **e.** the bread....... 398
Job 6:6 Can that which is unsavoury be **e.**........ 398
Job 13:28 as a garment that is moth **e.**................ 398
Job 31:17 Or have **e.** my morsel myself alone, ... 398
Job 31:17 the fatherless hath not **e.** thereof;........ 398
Job 31:39 If I have **e.** the fruits thereof............. 398
Ps 69:9 the zeal of thine house hath **e.** me 398
Ps 102:9 For I have **e.** ashes like bread,........... 398
Pr 9:17 and bread **e.** in secret is pleasant......... 398
Pr 23:8 The morsel which thou hast **e.**............ 398
Ca 5:1 I have **e.** my honeycomb with my 398
Isa 3:14 for ye have **e.** up the vineyard; 398
Isa 5:5 hedge thereof, and it shall be **e.** up; 398
Isa 6:13 it shall return, and shall be **e.**: 1197
Isa 44:19 I have roasted flesh, and **e.** it: 398
Jer 10:25 for they have **e.** up Jacob, and............ 398
Jer 24:2 naughty figs, which could not be **e.**, ... 398
Jer 24:3 evil, very evil, that cannot be **e.**,......... 398
Jer 24:8 as the evil figs, which cannot be **e.**, ... 398
Jer 29:17 like vile figs, that cannot be **e.**, ... 398
Jer 31:29 The fathers have **e.** a sour grape,........ 398
Eze 4:14 have I not **e.** of that which dieth.......... 398
Eze 18:2 The fathers have **e.** sour grapes,......... 398
Eze 18:6 and hath not **e.** upon the mountains,..... 398
Eze 18:11 even hath **e.** upon the mountains. 398
Eze 18:15 hath not **e.** upon the mountains, ... 398
Eze 34:18 to have **e.** up the good pasture, ... 7462
Eze 45:21 days; unleavened bread shall be **e.**. 398
Ho 10:13 ye have **e.** the fruit of lies:................ 398
Joe 1:4 worm hath left hath the locust **e.**; 398
Joe 1:4 hath left hath the cankerworm **e.** 398
Joe 1:4 hath left hath the caterpiller **e.**. 398
Joe 2:25 the years that the locust hath **e.**,......... 398
Mk 14:21 And they that had **e.** were about........ *2068*
Mk 8:9 And they that had **e.** were about........ *5315*
Lu 13:26 **We have e. and drunk in thy**......... *5315*
Lu 17:8 **till I have e. and drunken; and**...... *5315*
Joh 2:17 zeal of thine house hath **e.** me up....... *2719*
Joh 6:13 and above unto them that had **e.**.......... *977*
Ac 10:10 very hungry, and would have **e.**......... *1089*
Ac 10:14 for I have never **e.** anything that........ *5315*
Ac 12:23 and he was **e.** of worms, ... *4662*
Ac 20:11 had broken bread, and **e.**, and *1089*
Ac 27:38 when they had **e.** enough, they.......... *2880*
Re 10:10 as soon as I had **e.** it,...................... *5315*

EATER See also EATERS.
Jg 14:14 Out of the **e.** came forth meat,............ 398
Isa 55:10 to the sower, and bread to the **e.**........ 398
Na 3:12 even fall into the mouth of the **e.**........ 398

EATERS
Pro 23:20 among riotous **e.** of flesh: 2151

EATEST
Ge 2:17 the day that thou **e.** thereof thou......... 398
1Sa 1:8 weepest thou? and why **e.** thou not?..... 398
1Ki 21:5 spirit so sad, that thou **e.** no bread? 398

EATETH
Ex 12:15 whosoever **e.** leavened bread from....... 398
Ex 12:19 whosoever **e.** that which is leavened,.... 398
Le 7:18 the soul that **e.** of it shall bear his....... 398
Le 7:20 But the soul that **e.** of the flesh.......... 398
Le 7:25 For whosoever **e.** the fat of the........... 398
Le 7:25 even the soul that **e.** it shall be cut...... 398
Le 7:27 Whatsoever soul it be that **e.** any 398
Le 11:40 And he that **e.** of the carcase............. 398
Le 14:47 and he that **e.** in the house shall.......... 398
Le 17:10 that **e.** any manner of blood; I will 398
Le 17:10 against that soul that **e.** blood, ... 398
Le 17:14 whosoever **e.** it shall be cut off. 398
Le 17:15 every soul that **e.** that which died......... 398
Le 19:8 Therefore every one that **e.** it shall...... 398
Nu 13:32 **e.** up the inhabitants thereof; and......... 398
1Sa 14:24 the man that **e.** any food until 398
1Sa 14:28 Cursed be the man that **e.** any food 398
Job 5:5 the hungry **e.** up, and taketh it............ 398
Job 21:25 soul, and never **e.** with pleasure. 398
Job 40:15 he **e.** grass as an ox.......................... 398
Ps 106:20 the similitude of an ox that **e.** grass...... 398
Pr 13:25 The righteous **e.** to the satisfying of..... 398
Pr 30:20 she **e.**, and wipeth her mouth, ... 398
Pr 31:27 and **e.** not the bread of idleness........... 398
Ec 4:5 together, and **e.** his own flesh............ 398
Ec 5:17 All his days also he **e.** in darkness, ... 398
Ec 6:2 but a stranger **e.** it: this is vanity,........ 398
Isa 28:4 it is yet in his hand he **e.** it up............ 1104
Isa 29:8 man dreameth, and, behold, he **e.**; 398
Isa 44:16 with part thereof he **e.** flesh; 398
Isa 59:5 he that **e.** of their eggs dieth, ... 398
Jer 31:30 every man that **e.** the sour grape,......... 398
Mt 9:11 **e.** your Master with publicans........... *2068*
Mk 2:16 How is it that he **e.** and drinketh........ *2068*
Mk 14:18 **you, One of you which e. with me**.. *2068*
Lu 15:2 receiveth sinners, and **e.** with them. ... *4906*
Joh 6:54 **Whoso e. my flesh, and drinketh**... *5176*
Joh 6:56 **He hath e. my flesh, and drinketh.** *5176*
Joh 6:57 **so he that e. me, even he shall live.** *5176*
Joh 6:58 **he that e. of this bread shall live**... *5176*
Joh 13:18 **He that e. bread with me hath**...... *5176*
Ro 14:2 another, who is weak, **e.** herbs.......... *2068*
Ro 14:3 Let not him that **e.** despise him that ... *2068*
Ro 14:3 **e.** not; and let not him which **e.** not.... *2068*
Ro 14:3 not judge him that **e.**: *2068*
Ro 14:6 He that **e.**, **e.** to the Lord, for he *2068*
Ro 14:6 God thanks; and he that **e.** not, ... *2068*
Ro 14:6 not, to the Lord he **e.** not, ... *2068*
Ro 14:20 it is evil for that man who **e.** with *2068*
Ro 14:23 because he **e.** not of faith: *2068*
1Co 9:7 and **e.** not of the fruit thereof?........... *2068*
1Co 9:7 and **e.** not of the milk of the flock? *2068*
1Co 11:29 he that **e.** and drinketh unworthily, ... *2068*
1Co 11:29 **e.** and drinketh damnation to *2068*

EATING
Ex 12:4 every man according to his **e.** shall....... 400
Ex 16:16 of it every man according to his **e.**,...... 400
Ex 16:18 every man according to his **e.**. 400
Ex 16:21 every man acording to his **e.**: and....... 400
Jg 14:9 went on **e.**, and came to his father....... 398
Ru 3:3 until he shall have done **e.**, and 398
1Sa 14:34 sin not against the Lord in **e.**.............. 398
1Sa 30:16 **e.** and drinking, and dancing,............... 398
1Ki 1:41 as they had made an end of **e.**. 398
1Ki 4:20 **e.** and drinking, and making merry. 398
2Ki 4:40 as they were **e.** of the pottage,............ 398
1Ch 12:39 David three days, **e.** and drinking:......... 398
Job 1:13 his sons and his daughters were **e.**....... 398
Job 1:18 thy sons and thy daughters were **e.**...... 398
Job 20:23 rain it upon him while he is **e.**. 3894
Isa 22:13 killing sheep, **e.** flesh, and drinking...... 398
Isa 66:17 **e.** swine's flesh, and the abomination, ... 398
Am 7:2 when they had made an end of **e.** 398
Mt 11:18 **John came neither e. nor drinking,** *2068*
Mt 11:19 **Son of man came e. and drinking,**. *2068*
Mt 24:38 **were e. and drinking, marrying**..... *5176*
Mt 26:26 And as they were **e.**, Jesus took........ *2068*
Lu 7:33 **the Baptist came neither e. bread**.. *2068*
Lu 7:34 **The Son of man is come e. and**..... *2068*
Lu 10:7 **remain, e. and drinking such**........ *2068*
1Co 8:4 the **e.** of those things that are *1035*
1Co 11:21 For in **e.** every one taketh before....... *5315*

EBAL (e'-bal)
Ge 36:23 Alvan, and Manaheth, and **E.**, ... 5858
De 11:29 and the curse upon mount **E.**. 5858
De 27:4 command you this day, in mount **E.**,... 5858
De 27:13 shall stand upon mount **E.** to curse;.... 5858
Jos 8:30 Lord God of Israel in mount **E.**, ... 5858
Jos 8:33 half of them over against mount **E.**;.... 5858
1Ch 1:22 And **E.**, and Abimael, and Sheba, ... 5858
1Ch 1:40 Alian, and Manahath, and **E.**, ... 5858

EBED (e'-bed) See also EBED-MELECH.
Jg 9:26 Gaal the son of **E.** came with his 5651
Jg 9:28 Gaal the son of **E.** said, Who is 5651
Jg 9:30 the words of Gaal the son of **E.**, his... 5651
Jg 9:31 Behold, Gaal the son of **E.** and his..... 5651
Jg 9:35 Gaal the son of **E.** went out, and....... 5651
Ezr 8:6 **E.** the son of Jonathan, and with........ 5651

EBED-MELECH (e''-bed-me'-lek)
Jer 38:7 Now when **E.** the Ethiopian, ... 5663
Jer 38:8 **E.** went forth out of the king's 5663
Jer 38:10 Then the king commanded **E.** the....... 5663
Jer 38:11 So **E.** took the men with him, ... 5663
Jer 38:12 **E.** the Ethiopian said unto 5663
Jer 39:16 Go and speak to **E.** the Ethiopian,...... 5663

EBENEZER (eb-en-e'-zur)
1Sa 4:1 to battle, and pitched beside **E.**: 72
1Sa 5:1 and brought it from **E.** unto Ashdod....... 72
1Sa 7:12 and called the name of it **E.**. 72

EBER (e'-bur) See also HEBER.
Ge 10:21 the father of all the children of **E.**, ... 5677
Ge 10:24 begat Salah; and Salah begat **E.**. 5677
Ge 10:25 And unto **E.** were born two sons: 5677
Ge 11:14 lived thirty years, and begat **E.**: 5677
Ge 11:15 Salah lived after he begat **E.** 5677
Ge 11:16 And **E.** lived four and thirty years, ... 5677
Ge 11:17 And **E.** lived after he begat Peleg 5677
Nu 24:24 shall afflict **E.**, and he also shall......... 5677
1Ch 1:18 begat Shelah, and Shelah begat **E.**...... 5677
1Ch 1:19 And unto **E.** were born two sons; 5677
1Ch 1:25 **E.**, Peleg, Reu,................................ 5677
1Ch 8:12 **E.**, and Misham, and Shamed, who..... 5677
Ne 12:20 of Sallai, Kallai; of Amok, **E.**;............ 5677

EBIASAPH (e-bi'-a-saf) See also ABIASAPH.
1Ch 6:23 Elkanah his son, and **E.** his son, ... 43
1Ch 6:37 the son of Assir, the son of **E.**, ... 43
1Ch 9:19 the son of Kore, the son of **E.**, ... 43

EBONY
Eze 27:15 a present horns of ivory and **e.**. 1894

EBRONAH (eb-ro'-nah)
Nu 33:34 Jotbathah, and encamped at **E.**. 5684
Nu 33:35 And they departed from **E.**, and 5684

ECCLESIASTES (ek-kle''-ze-as'-teze)
Ec *general title* **E.**; Or, The Preacher 6953

ED (ed)
Jos 22:34 children of Gad called the altar **E.**: 5684

EDAR (e'-dar) See also EDER.
Ge 35:21 his tent beyond the tower of **E.**......... 5740

EDEN (e'-dun)
Ge 2:8 planted a garden eastward in **E.**;........ 5731
Ge 2:10 went out of **E.** to water the garden; ... 5731
Ge 2:15 him into the garden of **E.** to dress it... 5731
Ge 3:23 him forth from the garden of **E.**,........ 5731
Ge 3:24 east of the garden of **E.** Cherubims, ... 5731
Ge 4:16 the land of Nod, on the east of **E.**....... 5731
2Ki 19:12 of **E.** which were in Thelasar?........... 5731
2Ch 29:12 of Zimnah, and **E.** the son of Joah: 5731
2Ch 31:15 next him were **E.**, and Miniamin, ... 5731
Isa 37:12 of **E.** which were in Telassar? 5731
Isa 51:3 will make her wilderness like **E.**, ... 5731
Eze 27:23 Haran, and Canneh, and **E.**, the........ 5731
Eze 28:13 hast been in **E.** the garden of God; 5731
Eze 31:9 trees of **E.**, that were in the garden... 5731
Eze 31:16 the trees of **E.**, the choice and best ... 5731
Eze 31:18 greatness among the trees of **E.**?........ 5731
Eze 31:18 brought down with the trees of **E.** 5731
Eze 36:35 is become like the garden of **E.**; 5731
Joe 2:3 is as the garden of **E.** before them, ... 5731
Am 1:5 the sceptre from the house of **E.**: 5731

EDER (e'-dur) See also EDAR.
Jos 15:21 were Kabzeel, and **E.**, and Jagur,....... 5740
1Ch 23:23 Mahli, and **E.**, and Jeremoth, three. ... 5740
1Ch 24:30 Mahli, and **E.**, and Jerimoth. 5740

EDGE See also EDGES; SELVEDGE; TWOEDGED.
Ge 34:26 with the **e.** of the sword,................. 6310
Ex 13:20 Etham, in the **e.** of the wilderness...... 7097
Ex 17:13 people with the **e.** of the sword. 5310
Ex 26:4 upon the **e.** of the one curtain............ 8193
Ex 26:4 uttermost **e.** of another curtain, ... 8193
Ex 26:5 thou make in the **e.** of the curtain 7097
Ex 26:10 make fifty loops on the **e.** of the 8193
Ex 26:10 fifty loops in the **e.** of the curtain 8193
Ex 36:11 of blue on the **e.** of one curtain........... 8193
Ex 36:12 made he in the **e.** of the curtain......... 7097
Ex 36:17 the uttermost **e.** of the curtain........... 7097
Ex 36:17 made he upon the **e.** of the curtain..... 7097
Nu 21:24 smote him with the **e.** of the sword, ... 6310
Nu 33:6 Etham, which is in the **e.** of the......... 7097
Nu 33:37 Hor, in the **e.** of the land of Edom. 7097
De 13:15 that city with the **e.** of the sword, ... 6310
De 13:15 thereof, with the **e.** of the sword. 6310
De 20:13 thereof with the **e.** of the sword: 6310
Jos 6:21 and ass, with the **e.** of the sword. 6310
Jos 8:24 all fallen on the **e.** of the sword, ... 6310
Jos 8:24 smote it with the **e.** of the sword. 6310
Jos 10:28 smote it with the **e.** of the sword, ... 6310
Jos 10:30 he smote it with the **e.** of the sword,.. 6310
Jos 10:32, 35,37 and smote it with the **e.** of 6310
Jos 10:39 smote them with the **e.** of the sword, ..6310

Jos 11:11 therein with the **e.** of the sword, 6310
Jos 11:12 smote them with the **e.** of the sword, 6310
Jos 11:14 they smote with the **e.** of the sword, 6310
Jos 13:27 the **e.** of the sea of Chinnereth 7097
Jos 19:47 smote it with the **e.** of the sword, 6310
Jg 1:8 smitten it with the **e.** of the sword, 6310
Jg 1:25 the city with the **e.** of the sword; 6310
Jg 4:15 all his host, with the **e.** of the sword 6310
Jg 4:16 Sisera fell upon the **e.** of the sword; 6310
Jg 18:27 smote them with the **e.** of the sword, 6310
Jg 20:37 the city with the **e.** of the sword. 6310
Jg 20:48 smote them with the **e.** of the sword, 6310
Jg 21:10 with the **e.** of the sword, with the 6310
1Sa 15:8 the people with the **e.** of the sword. 6310
1Sa 22:19 smote he with the **e.** of the sword, 6310
1Sa 22:19 and sheep, with the **e.** of the sword. 6310
2Sa 15:14 the city with the **e.** of the sword. 6310
2Ki 10:25 them with the **e.** of the sword; 6310
Job 1:15 servants with the **e.** of the sword; 6310
Job 1:17 servants with the **e.** of the sword; 6310
Ps 89:43 also turned the **e.** of his sword, 6697
Ec 10:10 and he do not whet the **e.**, 6440
Jer 21:7 them with the **e.** of the sword; 6310
Jer 31:29 the children's teeth are set on **e.** 6949
Jer 31:30 his teeth shall be set on **e.** 6949
Eze 18:2 the children's teeth are set on **e.**? 6949
Eze 43:13 by the **e.** thereof round about shall 8193
Lu 21:24 **shall fall by the e. of the sword,** *4750*
Heb 11:34 escaped the **e.** of the sword, out of *4750*

EDGES
Ex 28:7 joined at the two **e.** thereof; 7098
Ex 39:4 two **e.** was it coupled together. 7099
Jg 3:13 a dagger which had two **e.**, 6366
Re 2:12 **hath the sharp sword with two e.;** *1366*

EDIFICATION
Ro 15:2 his neighbour for his good to **e.** *3619*
1Co 14:3 speaketh unto men to **e.**, *3619*
2Co 10:8 the Lord hath given us for **e.**, *3619*
2Co 13:10 the Lord hath given me to **e.**, *3619*

EDIFIED
Ac 9:31 the churches rest...and were **e.**; *3618*
1Co 14:17 thanks well, but the other is not **e.** *3618*

EDIFIETH
1Co 8:1 puffeth up, but charity **e.** *3618*
1Co 14:4 an unknown tongue **e.** himself; *3618*
1Co 14:4 he that propesieth **e.** the church. *3618*

EDIFY See also EDIFIED; EDIFIETH; EDIFYING.
Ro 14:19 wherewith one may **e.** another. *3619*
1Co 10:23 lawful for me, but all things **e.** not. *3618*
1Th 5:11 together, and **e.** one another, *3618*

EDIFYING
1Co 14:5 that the church may receive **e.** *3619*
1Co 14:12 may excel to the **e.** of the church. *3619*
1Co 14:26 Let all things be done unto **e.** *3619*
2Co 12:19 things, dearly beloved, for your **e.** *3619*
Eph 4:12 for the **e.** of the body of Christ: *3619*
Eph 4:16 unto the **e.** of itself in love. *3619*
Eph 4:29 which is good to the use of **e.**, *3619*
1Ti 1:4 than godly **e.** which is in faith: *3618*

EDOM (e'-dom) See also EDOMITES; ESAU; IDUMEA; OBED-EDOM.
Ge 25:30 therefore was his name called **E.** 123
Ge 32:3 the land of Seir, the country of **E.**, 123
Ge 36:1 the generations of Esau, who is **E.** 123
Ge 36:8 Esau in mount Seir; Esau is **E.** 123
Ge 36:16 came of Eliphaz in the land of **E.**; 123
Ge 36:17 came of Reuel in the land of **E.**; 123
Ge 36:19 are the sons of Esau, who is **E.** 123
Ge 36:21 children of Seir in the land of **E.** 123
Ge 36:31 kings that reigned in the land of **E.**, 123
Ge 36:32 Bela the son of Beor reigned in **E.**: 123
Ge 36:43 these be the dukes of **E.**, 123
Ex 15:15 the dukes of **E.** shall be amazed; 123
Nu 20:14 from Kadesh unto the king of **E.**, 123
Nu 20:18 **E.** said unto him, Thou shalt not 123
Nu 20:20 **E.** came out against him with much 123
Nu 20:21 **E.** refused to give Israel passage 123
Nu 20:23 by the coast of the land of **E.**, 123
Nu 21:4 to compass the land of **E.**: 123
Nu 24:18 And **E.** shall be a possession, 123
Nu 33:37 in the edge of the land of **E.** 123
Nu 34:3 of Zin along by the coast of **E.** 123
Jos 15:1 border of **E.** the wilderness of Zin 123
Jos 15:21 of Judah toward the coast of **E.** 123
Jg 5:4 marchedst out of the field of **E.**, 123
Jg 11:17 sent messengers unto the king of **E.**, 123
Jg 11:17 but the king of **E.** would not hearken 123
Jg 11:18 and compassed the land of **E.**, 123
1Sa 14:47 against **E.**, and against the kings of 123
2Sa 8:14 And he put garrisons in **E.**; 123
2Sa 8:14 throughout all **E.** put he garrisons. 123
2Sa 8:14 they of **E.** became David's servants. 123
1Ki 9:26 of the Red sea, in the land of **E.**, 123
1Ki 11:14 he was of the king's seed in **E.** 123
1Ki 11:15 came to pass, when David was in **E.**, 123
1Ki 11:15 he had smitten every male in **E.**; 123
1Ki 11:16 he had cut off every male in **E.**; 123
1Ki 22:47 There was then no king in **E.**: 123
2Ki 3:8 way through the wilderness of **E.** 123
2Ki 3:9 king of Judah, and the king of **E.**: 123
2Ki 3:12 the king of **E.** went down to him. 123
2Ki 3:20 there came water by the way of **E.**, 123
2Ki 3:26 through even unto the king of **E.**: 123
2Ki 8:20 **E.** revolted from under the hand of 123
2Ki 8:22 Yet **E.** revolted from under the hand 123
2Ki 14:7 He slew of **E.** in the valley of salt 123
2Ki 14:10 Thou hast indeed smitten **E.**, 123
1Ch 1:43 kings that reigned in the land of **E.** 123
1Ch 1:51 the dukes of **E.** were; duke Timnah; 123
1Ch 1:54 Iram. These are the dukes of **E.** 123
1Ch 18:11 from **E.**, and from Moab, and from 123
1Ch 18:13 And he put garrisons in **E.**; and all 123
2Ch 8:17 at the sea side in the land of **E.** 123
2Ch 25:20 they sought after the gods of **E.** 123
Ps 60:*title* smote in **E.** in the valley of salt 123
Ps 60:8 over **E.** will I cast out my shoe: 123
Ps 60:9 Who will lead me into **E.**? 123
Ps 83:6 of **E.**, and the Ishmaelites; 123
Ps 108:9 over **E.** will I cast out my shoe; 123
Ps 108:10 who will lead me into **E.**? 123
Ps 137:7 the children of **E.** in the day of 123
Isa 11:14 lay their hand upon **E.** and Moab; 123
Isa 63:1 Who is this that cometh from **E.**, 123
Jer 9:26 Egypt, and Judah, and **E.**, and the 123
Jer 25:21 **E.**, and Moab, and the children of 123
Jer 27:3 And send them to the king of **E.**, 123
Jer 40:11 among the Ammonites, and in **E.**, 123
Jer 49:7 concerning **E.**, thus saith the Lord 123
Jer 49:17 Also **E.** shall be a desolation: 123
Jer 49:20 that he hath taken against **E.**; 123
Jer 49:22 the heart of the mighty men of **E.** 123
La 4:21 and be glad, O daughter of **E.**, 123
La 4:22 thine iniquity, O daughter of **E.**; 123
Eze 25:12 **E.** hath dwelt against the house of 123
Eze 25:13 also stretch out mine hand upon **E.**, 123
Eze 25:14 I will lay my vengeannce upon **E.** 123
Eze 25:14 do in **E.** according to mine anger 123
Eze 32:29 There is **E.**, her kings, and all her 123
Da 11:41 out of his hand, even **E.**, and Moab, 123
Joe 3:19 **E.** shall be a desolate wilderness, 123
Am 1:6 captivity to deliver them up to **E.**: 123
Am 1:9 up the whole captivity to **E.**, and 123
Am 1:11 For three transgressions of **E.**, and 123
Am 2:1 burned the bones of the king of **E.** 123
Am 9:12 they may possess the remnant of **E.**, 123
Ob 1 saith the Lord God concerning **E.**; 123
Ob 8 even destroy the wise men out of **E.**, 123
Mal 1:4 **E.** saith, We are impoverished, 123

EDOMITE (e'-dum-ite) See also EDOMITES.
De 23:7 Thou shalt not abhor an **E.**: 130
1Sa 21:7 and his name was Doeg, an **E.**, 130
1Sa 22:9 Then answered Doeg the **E.**, 130
1Sa 22:18 And Doeg the **E.** turned, and he fell 130
1Sa 22:22 day, when Doeg the **E.** was there,
1Ki 11:14 unto Solomon, Hadad the **E.**: 130
Ps 52:*title* Doeg the **E.** came and told Saul, 130

EDOMITES (e'-dum-ites)
Ge 36:9 Esau the father of the **E.** in mount 130
Ge 36:43 he is Esau the father of the **E.** 130
1Ki 11:1 **E.**, Zidonians, and Hittites; 130
1Ki 11:17 Hadad fled, he and certain **E.**
2Ki 8:21 smote the **E.** which compassed him 130
1Ch 18:12 the son Zeruiah slew of the **E.** 130
1Ch 18:13 all the **E.** became David's servants. 130
2Ch 21:8 In his days the **E.** revolted from 130
2Ch 21:9 smote the **E.** which compassed him 130
2Ch 21:10 So the **E.** revolted from under the 130
2Ch 25:14 come from the slaughter of the **E.**, 130
2Ch 25:19 sayest, Lo, thou hast smitten the **E.**; 130
2Ch 28:17 **E.** had come and smitten Judah, 130

EDREI (ed'-re-i)
Nu 21:33 all his people, to the battle at **E.** 154
De 1:4 which dwelt at Astaroth in **E.**: 154
De 3:1 and all his people, to battle at **E.** 154
De 3:10 all Bashan, unto Salchah and **E.**, 154
Jos 12:4 that dwelt at Ashtaroth and at **E.**, 154
Jos 13:12 reigned in Ashtaroth and in **E.**, 154
Jos 13:31 half Gilead, and Ashtaroth, and **E.**, 154
Jos 19:37 And Kedesh, and **E.**, and En-hazor, 154

EFFECT See also EFFECTED.
Nu 30:8 shall make her vow...of none **e.**: 6565
2Ch 34:22 and they spake to her to that **e.**
Ps 33:10 devices of the people of none **e.** 5106
Isa 32:17 the **e.** of righteousness quietness 5656
Jer 48:30 his lies shall not so **e.** it. 6213
Eze 12:23 hand, and the **e.** of every vision. 1697
Mt 15:6 **commandment of God of none e.** *208*
Mk 7:13 **the word of God of none e.** *208*
Ro 3:3 make the faith of God without **e.**? *2673*
Ro 4:14 and the promise made of none **e.**: *2673*
Ro 9:6 word of God hath taken none **e.** *1601*
1Co 1:17 Christ should be made of none **e.** *2758*
Gal 3:17 make the promise of none **e.** *2673*
Gal 5:4 Christ is become of no **e.** unto *2673*

EFFECTED
2Ch 7:11 own house, he prosperously **e.** 6743

EFFECTUAL
1Co 16:9 a great door and **e.** is opened *1756*
2Co 1:6 which is **e.** in the enduring of the *1754*
Eph 3:7 by the **e.** working of his power. *1753*
Eph 4:16 the **e.** working in the measure of *1753*
Phm 6 become **e.** by the acknowledging *1756*
Jas 5:16 **e.** fervent prayer of a righteous *1754*

EFFECTUALLY
Gal 2:8 (For he that wrought **e.** in Peter *1754*
1Th 2:13 which **e.** worketh also in you *1754*

EFFEMINATE
1Co 6:9 adulterers, nor **e.**, nor abusers of *3120*

EGG See also EGGS.
Job 6:6 any taste in the white of an **e.**? 2495
Lu 11:12 **Or if he shall ask an e., will he** *5609*

EGGS
De 22:6 whether they be young ones, or **e.**, 1000
De 22:6 upon thy young, or upon the **e.**, 1000
Job 39:14 Which leaveth her **e.** in the earth, 1000
Isa 10:14 as one gathereth **e.** that are left, 1000
Isa 59:5 They hatch cockatrice' **e.**, and 1000
Isa 59:5 he that eateth of their **e.** dieth, 1000
Jer 17:11 As the partridge sitteth on **e.**, 1000

EGLAH (eg'-lah) See also MICHAL.
2Sa 3:5 Ithream, by **E.** David's wife. 5698
1Ch 3:3 the sixth, Ithream by **E.** his wife. 5698

EGLAIM (eg'-la-im) See also EN-EGLAIM.
Isa 15:8 the howling thereof unto **E.**, 97

EGLON (eg'-lon)
Jos 10:3 and unto Debir king of **E.**, saying, 5700
Jos 10:5 the king of Lachish, the king of **E.**, 5700
Jos 10:23 the king of Lachish, the king of **E.** 5700
Jos 10:34 Lachish Joshua passed unto **E.**, 5700
Jos 10:36 And Joshua went up from **E.**, 5700
Jos 10:37 to all that he had done to **E.**; 5700
Jos 12:12 The king of **E.**, one; the king of 5700
Jos 15:39 Lachish, Bozkath, and **E.**, 5700
Jg 3:12 Lord strengthened **E.** the king of 5700
Jg 3:14 children of Israel served **E.** the 5700
Jg 3:15 Israel sent a present unto **E.** the 5700
Jg 3:17 brought the present unto **E.** the 5700
Jg 3:17 And **E.** was a very fat man. 5700

EGYPT (e'-jipt) See also EGYPTIAN; MIZRAIM.
Ge 12:10 and Abram went down into **E.** 4714
Ge 12:11 was come near to enter into **E.**, 4714
Ge 12:14 when Abram was come into **E.**, 4714
Ge 13:1 Abram went up out of **E.**, he, 4714
Ge 13:10 of the Lord, like the land of **E.**, 4714
Ge 15:18 given this land, from the river of **E.** 4714
Ge 21:21 him a wife out of the land of **E.** 4714
Ge 25:18 **E.**, as thou goest toward Assyria: 4714
Ge 26:2 and said, Go not down into **E.**; 4714
Ge 37:25 going to carry it down to **E.** 4714
Ge 37:28 and they brought Joseph into **E.** 4714
Ge 37:36 sold him into **E.** unto Potiphar, 4714
Ge 39:1 Joseph was brought down to **E.**; 4714
Ge 40:1 that the butler of the king of **E.** 4714

Ge 40:1 offended their lord the king of **E.**. 4714
Ge 40:5 the baker of the king of **E.**, which 4714
Ge 41:8 the magicians of **E.**, and all the 4714
Ge 41:19 in all the land of **E.** for badness: 4714
Ge 41:29 throughout all the land of **E.**: 4714
Ge 41:30 be forgotten in the land of **E.**: 4714
Ge 41:33 and set him over the land of **E.**. 4714
Ge 41:34 up the fifth part of the land of **E.** 4714
Ge 41:36 which shall be in the land of **E.**; 4714
Ge 41:41 have set thee over all the land of **E.**. 4714
Ge 41:43 him ruler over all the land of **E.**. 4714
Ge 41:44 hand or foot in all the land of **E.**. 4714
Ge 41:45 went out over all the land of **E.**. 4714
Ge 41:46 he stood before Pharaoh king of **E.**. 4714
Ge 41:46 went throughout all the land of **E.**. 4714
Ge 41:48 which were in the land of **E.**, and 4714
Ge 41:53 that was in the land of **E.**, 4714
Ge 41:54 all the land of **E.** there was bread. 4714
Ge 41:55 all the land of **E.** was famished, 4714
Ge 41:56 famine waxed sore in the land of **E.**. 4714
Ge 41:57 And all the countries came into **E.**. 4714
Ge 42:1 saw that there was corn in **E.**, 4714
Ge 42:2 heard that there is corn in **E.**: 4714
Ge 42:3 went down to buy corn in **E.**. 4714
Ge 43:2 which they had brought out of **E.**, 4714
Ge 43:15 and went down to **E.**, and stood 4714
Ge 45:4 your brother, whom ye sold into **E.**. 4714
Ge 45:8 throughout all the land of **E.**. 4714
Ge 45:9 God hath made me lord of all **E.**: 4714
Ge 45:13 tell my father of all my glory in **E.**, 4714
Ge 45:18 give you the good of the land of **E.**, 4714
Ge 45:19 you wagons out of the land of **E.** 4714
Ge 45:20 good of all the land of **E.** is yours. 4714
Ge 45:23 laden with the good things of **E.**, 4714
Ge 45:25 they went up out of **E.**, and came 4714
Ge 45:26 governor over all the land of **E.**. 4714
Ge 46:3 fear not to go down into **E.**; for 4714
Ge 46:4 I will go down with thee into **E.**; 4714
Ge 46:6 and came into **E.**, Jacob, and all 4714
Ge 46:7 seed brought he with him into **E.**. 4714
Ge 46:8 of Israel, which came into **E.**, 4714
Ge 46:20 unto Joseph in the land of **E.** were 4714
Ge 46:26 that came with Jacob into **E.**, 4714
Ge 46:27 Joseph, which were born him in **E.**, 4714
Ge 46:27 which came into **E.**, were 4714
Ge 47:6 The land of **E.** is before thee; in 4714
Ge 47:11 them a possession in the land of **E.**, 4714
Ge 47:13 the land of **E.** and all the land of 4714
Ge 47:14 that was found in the land of **E.**, 4714
Ge 47:15 money failed in the land of **E.**, 4714
Ge 47:20 all the land of **E.** for Pharaoh; 4714
Ge 47:21 from one end of the borders of **E.** 4714
Ge 47:26 made it a law over the land of **E.** 4714
Ge 47:27 Israel dwelt in the land of **E.**, 4714
Ge 47:28 And Jacob lived in the land of **E.** 4714
Ge 47:29 bury me not, I pray thee, in **E.**: 4714
Ge 47:30 thou shalt carry me out of **E.**, 4714
Ge 48:5 born unto thee in the land of **E.** 4714
Ge 48:5 I came unto thee into **E.**, are mine; 4714
Ge 50:7 and all the elders of the land of **E.**, 4714
Ge 50:14 Joseph returned into **E.**, he, and 4714
Ge 50:22 Joseph dwelt in **E.**, he, and his 4714
Ge 50:26 and he was put in a coffin in **E.** 4714
Ex 1:1 of Israel, which came into **E.**; 4714
Ex 1:5 for Joseph was in **E.** already. 4714
Ex 1:8 there arose up a new king over **E.**, 4714
Ex 1:15 And the king of **E.** spake to the 4714
Ex 1:17 and did not as the king of **E.** 4714
Ex 1:18 And the king of **E.** called for the 4714
Ex 2:23 of time, that the king of **E.** died: 4714
Ex 3:7 of my people which are in **E.**, and 4714
Ex 3:10 the children of Israel out of **E.**, 4714
Ex 3:11 the children of Israel out of **E.**? 4714
Ex 3:12 brought forth the people out of **E.**, 4714
Ex 3:16 that which is done to you in **E.**: 4714
Ex 3:17 you up out of the affliction of **E.** 4714
Ex 3:18 unto the king of **E.**, and ye shall 4714
Ex 3:19 the king of **E.** will not let you go, 4714
Ex 3:20 stretch out my hand, and smite **E.** 4714
Ex 4:18 unto my brethren which are in **E.** 4714
Ex 4:19 in Midian, Go, return into **E.**: 4714
Ex 4:20 and he returned to the land of **E.**: 4714
Ex 4:21 return into **E.**, see that thou do all 4714
Ex 5:4 the king of **E.** said unto them, 4714
Ex 5:12 throughout all the land of **E.** to 4714
Ex 6:11 speak unto Pharaoh king of **E.**, 4714
Ex 6:13 and unto Pharoah king of **E.**, 4714
Ex 6:13 of Israel out of the land of **E.** 4714
Ex 6:26 from the land of **E.** according to 4714
Ex 6:27 spake to Pharaoh king of **E.**, 4714
Ex 6:27 out the children of Israel from **E.**: 4714
Ex 6:28 spake unto Moses in the land of **E.**. 4714
Ex 6:29 thou unto Pharaoh king of **E.** all 4714
Ex 7:3 and my wonders in the land of **E.**. 4714
Ex 7:4 lay my hand upon **E.**, and bring 4714
Ex 7:4 land of **E.** by great judgments. 4714
Ex 7:5 stretch forth mine hand upon **E.**, 4714
Ex 7:11 magicians of **E.**, they also did in 4714
Ex 7:19 thine hand upon the waters of **E.**, 4714
Ex 7:19 blood throughout all the land of **E.**, 4714
Ex 7:21 blood throughout all the land of **E.** 4714
Ex 7:22 the magicians of **E.** did so with 4714
Ex 8:5 to come up upon the land of **E.**. 4714
Ex 8:6 his hand over the waters of **E.**; 4714
Ex 8:6 came up, and covered the land of **E.**. 4714
Ex 8:7 up frogs upon the land of **E.** 4714
Ex 8:16 become lice throughout all...of **E.** 4714
Ex 8:17 became lice throughout all...of **E.**. 4714
Ex 8:24 houses, and into all the land of **E.**: 4714
Ex 9:4 of Israel and the cattle of **E.**: 4714
Ex 9:6 and all the cattle of **E.** died: 4714
Ex 9:9 small dust in all the land of **E.**, 4714
Ex 9:9 beast, throughout all the land of **E.** 4714
Ex 9:18 hail, such as hath not been in **E.** 4714
Ex 9:22 may be hail in all the land of **E.**, 4714
Ex 9:22 field, throughout the land of **E.**. 4714
Ex 9:23 rained hail upon the land of **E.** 4714
Ex 9:24 none like it in all the land of **E.** 4714
Ex 9:25 smote throughout all the land of **E.** 4714
Ex 10:2 what things I have wrought in **E.**, 4714
Ex 10:7 thou not yet that **E.** is destroyed? 4714
Ex 10:12 over the land of **E.** for the locusts, 4714
Ex 10:12 may come up upon the land of **E.**, 4714
Ex 10:13 forth his rod over the land of **E.**, 4714
Ex 10:14 went up over all the land of **E.**, 4714
Ex 10:14 and rested in all the coasts of **E.**: 4714
Ex 10:15 field, through all the land of **E.** 4714
Ex 10:19 one locust in all the coasts of **E.** 4714
Ex 10:21 be darkness over the land of **E.**, 4714
Ex 10:22 in all the land of **E.** three days: 4714
Ex 11:1 more upon Pharaoh, and upon **E.**; 4714
Ex 11:3 was very great in the land of **E.**, 4714
Ex 11:4 will I go out into the midst of **E.** 4714
Ex 11:5 firstborn in the land of **E.** shall die, 4714
Ex 11:6 cry throughout all the land of **E.**, 4714
Ex 11:9 be multiplied in the land of **E.**. 4714
Ex 12:1 Moses and Aaron in the land of **E.**, 4714
Ex 12:12 through the land of **E.** this night, 4714
Ex 12:12 all the firstborn in the land of **E.**, 4714
Ex 12:12 gods of **E.** I will execute judgment: 4714
Ex 12:13 you, when I smite the land of **E.** 4714
Ex 12:17 your armies out of the land of **E.**: 4714
Ex 12:27 of the children of Israel in **E.**, 4714
Ex 12:29 all the firstborn in the land of **E.**, 4714
Ex 12:30 and there was a great cry in **E.**; 4714
Ex 12:39 which they brought forth out of **E.**, 4714
Ex 12:39 because they were thrust out of **E.**, 4714
Ex 12:40 who dwelt in **E.**, was four hundred 4714
Ex 12:41 Lord went out from the land of **E.**. 4714
Ex 12:42 them out from the land of **E.**: 4714
Ex 12:51 of Israel out of the land of **E.** 4714
Ex 13:3 day, in which ye came out from **E.**, 4714
Ex 13:8 me when I came forth out of **E.**. 4714
Ex 13:9 the Lord brought thee out of **E.**. 4714
Ex 13:14 the Lord brought us out from **E.**, 4714
Ex 13:15 in the land of **E.**, both the firstborn 4714
Ex 13:16 the Lord brought us forth out of **E.**. 4714
Ex 13:17 see war, and they return to **E.**: 4714
Ex 13:18 harnessed out of the land of **E.** 4714
Ex 14:5 the king of **E.** that the people fled: 4714
Ex 14:7 the chariots of **E.**, and captains 4714
Ex 14:8 the heart of Pharaoh king of **E.**, 4714
Ex 14:11 Because there were no graves in **E.**, 4714
Ex 14:11 us, to carry us forth out of **E.**? 4714
Ex 14:12 that we did tell thee in **E.**, saying, 4714
Ex 16:1 departing out of the land of **E.** 4714
Ex 16:3 hand of the Lord in the land of **E.**, 4714
Ex 16:6 you out from the land of **E.**: 4714
Ex 16:32 you forth from the land of **E.**. 4714
Ex 17:3 thou hast brought us up out of **E.**, 4714
Ex 18:1 hath brought Israel out of **E.**; 4714
Ex 19:1 gone forth out of the land of **E.**, 4714
Ex 20:2 brought thee out of the land of **E.**, 4714
Ex 22:21 ye were strangers in the land of **E.**. 4714
Ex 23:9 ye were strangers in the land of **E.**. 4714
Ex 23:15 in it thou camest out from **E.**: 4714
Ex 29:46 out of the land of **E.**, that I may 4714
Ex 32:1 us up out of the land of **E.**, 4714
Ex 32:4 thee up out of the land of **E.** 4714
Ex 32:7 broughtest out of the land of **E.**, 4714
Ex 32:8 thee up out of the land of **E.** 4714
Ex 32:11 brought forth out of the land of **E.** 4714
Ex 32:23 brought us up out of the land of **E.**, 4714
Ex 33:1 brought up out of the land of **E.**, 4714
Ex 34:18 Abib thou camest out from **E.**. 4714
Le 11:45 of the land of **E.**, to be your God: 4714
Le 18:3 the land of **E.**, wherein ye dwelt, 4714
Le 19:34 strangers in the land of **E.**: I am 4714
Le 19:36 brought you out ot the land of **E.** 4714
Le 22:33 brought them out of the land of **E.**; 4714
Le 23:43 brought them out of the land of **E.**: 4714
Le 25:38 forth out of the land of **E.**, to give 4714
Le 25:42 forth out of the land of **E.**: they 4714
Le 25:55 forth out of the land of **E.**: I am 4714
Le 26:13 forth out of the land of **E.**, that ye 4714
Le 26:45 forth out of the land of **E.** in the 4714
Nu 1:1 come out of the land of **E.**, saying, 4714
Nu 3:13 all the firstborn in the land of **E.** 4714
Nu 8:17 of **E.** I sanctified them for myself. 4714
Nu 9:1 come out of the land **E.**, saying, 4714
Nu 11:5 fish, which we did eat in **E.** freely; 4714
Nu 11:18 eat? for it was well with us in **E.**: 4714
Nu 11:20 Why came we forth out of **E.**? 4714
Nu 13:22 built seven years before Zoan in **E.**.) 4714
Nu 14:2 we had died in the land of **E.**! 4714
Nu 14:3 not better for us to return into **E.**? 4714
Nu 14:4 captain, and let us return into **E.**, 4714
Nu 14:19 people, from **E.** even until now. 4714
Nu 14:22 I did in **E.** and in the wilderness, 4714
Nu 15:41 brought you out of the land of **E.**, 4714
Nu 20:5 up out of **E.**, to bring us in unto 4714
Nu 20:15 **E.**, and we have dwelt in **E.** a long 4714
Nu 20:16 hath brought us forth out of **E.**: 4714
Nu 21:5 out of **E.** to die in the wilderness? 4714
Nu 22:5 is a people come out from **E.**: 4714
Nu 22:11 out of **E.**, which covereth the face 4714
Nu 23:22 God brought them out of **E.**; he 4714
Nu 24:8 God brought him forth out of **E.**; 4714
Nu 26:4 went forth out of the land of **E.** 4714
Nu 26:59 her mother bare to Levi in **E.**: 4714
Nu 32:11 of the men that came up out of **E.**, 4714
Nu 33:1 went forth out of the land of **E.** 4714
Nu 33:38 the land of **E.**, in the first day of 4714
Nu 34:5 from Azmon unto the river of **E.**, 4714
De 1:27 the land of **E.**, to deliver us into 4714
De 1:30 did for you in **E.** before your eyes; 4714
De 4:20 of the iron furnace, even out of **E.**; 4714
De 4:34 Lord your God did for you in **E.** 4714
De 4:37 with his mighty power out of E; 4714
De 4:45 after they came forth out of **E.**, 4714
De 4:46 they were come forth out of **E.**: 4714
De 5:6 brought thee out of the land of **E.**, 4714
De 5:15 wast a servant in the land of **E.**, 4714
De 6:12 thee forth out of the land of **E.**, 4714
De 6:21 We were Pharaoh's bondmen in **E.**; 4714
De 6:21 the Lord brought us out of **E.** with 4714
De 6:22 wonders, great and sore, upon **E.** 4714
De 7:8 the hand of Pharaoh king of **E.** 4714
De 7:15 none of the evil diseases of **E.**, 4714
De 7:18 did unto Pharaoh, and unto all **E.**; 4714
De 8:14 thee forth out of the land of **E.**, 4714
De 9:7 didst depart out of the land of **E.**, 4714
De 9:12 thou hast brought forth out of **E.** 4714
De 9:26 out of **E.** with a mighty hand 4714
De 10:19 were strangers in the land of **E.**, 4714
De 10:22 Thy fathers went down into **E.** with 4714
De 11:3 acts, which he did in the midst of **E.** 4714
De 11:3 unto Pharaoh the king of **E.**, and 4714
De 11:4 what he did unto the army of **E.**, 4714
De 11:10 it, is not as the land of **E.**, from 4714
De 13:5 brought you out of the land of **E.**, 4714
De 13:10 brought thee out of the land of **E.**, 4714
De 15:15 wast a bondman in the land of **E.**, 4714
De 16:1 God brought thee forth out of **E.** by 4714
De 16:3 forth out of the land of **E.** in haste: 4714
De 16:3 out of the land of **E.** all the days of 4714
De 16:6 that thou camest forth out of **E.**. 4714
De 16:12 that thou wast a bondman in **E.**: 4714
De 17:16 cause the people to return to **E.**, 4714
De 20:1 brought thee up out of the land of **E.** 4714
De 23:4 way, when ye came forth out of **E.**; 4714

De 24:9 that ye were come forth out of **E.**....... 4714
De 24:18 that thou wast a bondman in **E.**, ... 4714
De 24:22 wast a bondman in the land of **E.**: 4714
De 25:17 when ye were come forth out of **E.**;.... 4714
De 26:5 and he went down into **E.**, and......... 4714
De 26:8 the Lord brought us forth out of **E.**..... 4714
De 28:27 will smite thee with the botch of **E.**,.... 4714
De 28:60 upon thee all the diseases of **E.**, ... 4714
De 28:68 Lord shall bring thee into **E.** again...... 4714
De 29:2 before your eyes in the land of **E.**....... 4714
De 29:16 we have dwelt in the land of **E.**;........ 4714
De 29:25 them forth out of the land of **E.**:........ 4714
De 34:11 sent him to do in the land of **E.**......... 4714
Jos 2:10 for you, when ye came out of **E.**; 4714
Jos 5:4 All the people that came out of **E.**,...... 4714
Jos 5:4 the way, after they came out of **E.**...... 4714
Jos 5:5 way as they came forth out of **E.**,....... 4714
Jos 5:6 men of war, which came out of **E.**, ... 4714
Jos 5:9 I rolled away the reproach of **E.** 4714
Jos 9:9 of him, and all that he did in **E.**, ... 4714
Jos 13:3 From Sihor, which is before **E.**,......... 4714
Jos 15:4 and went out unto the river of **E.**; 4714
Jos 15:47 her villages, unto the river of **E.**,........ 4714
Jos 24:4 his children went down into **E.**........... 4714
Jos 24:5 and I plagued **E.**, according to that..... 4714
Jos 24:6 I brought your fathers out of **E.**:........ 4714
Jos 24:7 have seen what I have done in **E.**: 4714
Jos 24:14 other side of the flood, and in **E.**; 4714
Jos 24:17 our fathers out of the land of **E.**, ... 4714
Jos 24:32 of Israel brought up out of **E.**,........... 4714
Jg 2:1 said, I made you to go up out of **E.**,.... 4714
Jg 2:12 brought them out of the land of **E.**, ... 4714
Jg 6:8 Israel, I brought you up from **E.**,........ 4714
Jg 6:13 not the Lord bring us up from **E.**? 4714
Jg 11:13 land, when they came up out of **E.**,.... 4714
Jg 11:16 When Israel came up from **E.**,........... 4714
Jg 19:30 came up out of the land of **E.** unto..... 4714
1Sa 2:27 thy father, when they were in **E.**........ 4714
1Sa 8:8 day that I brought them up out of **E.**... 4714
1Sa 10:18 I brought up Israel out of **E.**, and 4714
1Sa 12:6 fathers up out of the land of **E.**. 4714
1Sa 12:8 When Jacob was come into **E.**, and..... 4714
1Sa 12:8 brought forth your fathers out of **E.**,..... 4714
1Sa 15:2 the way, when he came up from **E.**.... 4714
1Sa 15:6 when they came up out of **E.**.......... 4714
1Sa 15:7 to Shur, that is over against **E.**. 4714
1Sa 27:8 to Shur, even unto the land of **E.**....... 4714
1Sa 30:13 I am a young man of **E.**, servant 4713
2Sa 7:6 up the children of Israel out of **E.**, ... 4714
2Sa 7:23 thou redeemedst to thee from **E.**, ... 4714
1Ki 3:1 affinity with Pharaoh king of **E.**,........ 4714
1Ki 4:21 and unto the border of **E.**: they......... 4714
1Ki 4:30 country, and all the wisdom of **E.**........ 4714
1Ki 6:1 were come out of the land of **E.**, ... 4714
1Ki 8:9 they came out of the land of **E.**.......... 4714
1Ki 8:16 my people Israel out of **E.**, I chose 4714
1Ki 8:21 brought them out of the land of **E.**...... 4714
1Ki 8:51 thou broughtest forth out of **E.**,......... 4714
1Ki 8:53 broughtest our fathers out of **E.**, ... 4714
1Ki 8:65 in of Hamath unto the river of **E.**,...... 4714
1Ki 9:9 their fathers out of the land of **E.**,...... 4714
1Ki 9:16 For Pharaoh king of **E.** had gone 4714
1Ki 10:28 had horses brought out of **E.**, and...... 4714
1Ki 10:29 and went out of **E.** for six hundred..... 4714
1Ki 11:17 servants with him, to go into **E.**; 4714
1Ki 11:18 came to **E.**, unto Pharaoh king of **E.**: ..4714
1Ki 11:21 And when Hadad heard in **E.** that 4714
1Ki 11:40 fled into **E.**, unto Shishak king of **E.**,.. 4714
1Ki 11:40 and was in **E.** until the death of......... 4714
1Ki 12:2 son of Nebat, who was yet in **E.**, ... 4714
1Ki 12:2 Solomon, and Jeroboam dwelt in **E.**; ... 4714
1Ki 12:28 brought thee up out of the land of **E.**...4714
1Ki 14:25 that Shishak king of **E.** came up......... 4714
2Ki 17:4 sent messengers to So king of **E.**, ... 4714
2Ki 17:7 them up out of the land of **E.**,........... 4714
2Ki 17:7 the hand of Pharaoh king of **E.**, ... 4714
2Ki 17:36 you up out of the land of **E.** with...... 4714
2Ki 18:21 of this bruised reed, even upon **E.**, ... 4714
2Ki 18:21 is Pharaoh king of **E.** unto all that...... 4714
2Ki 18:24 put thy trust on **E.** for chariots and.... 4714
2Ki 21:15 their fathers came forth out of **E.**,...... 4714
2Ki 23:29 Pharaoh-nechoh king of **E.** went up 4714
2Ki 23:34 and he came to **E.**, and died there. 4714
2Ki 24:7 And the king of **E.** came not again 4714
2Ki 24:7 had taken from the river of **E.** unto.... 4714
2Ki 24:7 all that pertained to the king of **E.**...... 4714
2Ki 25:26 arose, and came to **E.**: for they......... 4714
1Ch 13:5 Israel together, from Shihor of **E.** 4714
1Ch 17:21 whom thou hast redeemed out of **E.**?.. 4714
2Ch 1:16 had horses brought out of **E.**, and...... 4714
2Ch 1:17 and brought forth out of **E.** a 4714
2Ch 5:10 Israel, when they came out of **E.**....... 4714
2Ch 6:5 forth my people out of the land of **E.**... 4714
2Ch 7:8 in of Hamath unto the river of **E.**........ 4714
2Ch 7:22 them forth out of the land of **E.**,......... 4714
2Ch 9:26 Philistines, and to the border of **E.**..... 4714
2Ch 9:28 unto Solomon horses out of **E.**, ... 4714
2Ch 10:2 the son of Nebat, who was in **E.**, ... 4714
2Ch 10:2 that Jeroboam returned out of **E.**, ... 4714
2Ch 12:2 king Rehoboam, Shishak king of **E.**...... 4714
2Ch 12:3 that came with him out of **E.**;............ 4714
2Ch 12:9 Shishak king of **E.** came up against..... 4714
2Ch 20:10 they came out of the land of **E.**, ... 4714
2Ch 26:8 abroad even to the entering in of **E.**;.. 4714
2Ch 35:20 Necho king of **E.** came up to fight...... 4714
2Ch 36:3 And the king of **E.** put him down at.... 4714
2Ch 36:4 the king of **E.** made Eliakim his......... 4714
2Ch 36:4 his brother, and carried him to **E.**.. 4714
Ne 9:9 the affliction of our fathers in **E.**, ... 4714
Ne 9:18 that brought thee up out of **E.**,.......... 4714
Ps 68:31 Princes shall come out of E;............... 4714
Ps 78:12 of their fathers, in the land of **E.**, ... 4714
Ps 78:43 he had wrought his signs in **E.**, and.... 4714
Ps 78:51 And smote all the firstborn in **E.**;....... 4714
Ps 80:8 Thou hast brought a vine out of **E.**:..... 4714
Ps 81:5 he went out through the land of **E.**:.... 4714
Ps 81:10 brought thee out of the land of **E.**: 4714
Ps 105:23 Israel also came into **E.**; and Jacob..... 4714
Ps 105:38 **E.** was glad when they departed: 4714
Ps 106:7 understood not thy wonders in **E.**; 4714
Ps 106:21 which had done great things in **E.**; 4714
Ps 114:1 When Israel went out of **E.**, the 4714
Ps 135:8 Who smote the firstborn of **E.**, both... 4714
Ps 135:9 into the midst of thee, O **E.**,............. 4714
Ps 136:10 that smote **E.** in their firstborn: 4714
Pr 7:16 carved works, with fine linen of **E.**..... 4714
Isa 7:18 uttermost part of the rivers of **E.**,....... 4714
Isa 10:24 against thee, after the manner of **E.**. .. 4714
Isa 10:26 he lift it up after the manner of **E.**. 4714
Isa 11:11 and from **E.**, and from Pathros, and.... 4714
Isa 11:16 he came up out of the land of **E.**. 4714
Isa 19:1 The burden of **E.**, Behold, the Lord ... 4714
Isa 19:1 swift cloud, and shall come into **E.**: 4714
Isa 19:1 and the idols of **E.** shall be moved..... 4714
Isa 19:1 and the heart of **E.** shall melt in 4714
Isa 19:3 And the spirit of **E.** shall fail in the..... 4714
Isa 19:12 of hosts hath purposed upon **E.**. 4714
Isa 19:13 they have also seduced **E.**, even......... 4714
Isa 19:14 and they have caused **E.** to err in...... 4714
Isa 19:15 shall there be any work for **E.**,.......... 4714
Isa 19:16 day shall **E.** be like unto women: 4714
Isa 19:17 of Judah shall be a terror unto **E.**,...... 4714
Isa 19:18 five cities in the land of **E.** speak....... 4714
Isa 19:19 Lord in the midst of the land of **E.**,.... 4714
Isa 19:20 the Lord of hosts in the land of **E.**: 4714
Isa 19:21 the Lord shall be known to **E.**, and 4714
Isa 19:22 And the Lord shall smite **E.**: he......... 4714
Isa 19:23 shall there be a highway out of **E.** 4714
Isa 19:23 the Assyrian shall come into **E.**, and... 4714
Isa 19:24 shall Israel be the third with **E.** 4714
Isa 19:25 Blessed be **E.** my people, and........... 4714
Isa 20:3 for a sign and wonder upon **E.** and..... 4714
Isa 20:4 uncovered, to the shame of **E.**. 4714
Isa 20:5 expectation, and of **E.** their glory. 4714
Isa 23:5 As at the report concerning **E.**, so...... 4714
Isa 27:12 of the river unto the stream of **E.**,..... 4714
Isa 27:13 and the outcasts in the land of **E.**,...... 4714
Isa 30:2 That walk to go down into **E.**, and..... 4714
Isa 30:2 and to trust in the shadow of **E.**! 4714
Isa 30:3 the trust in the shadow of **E.** your 4714
Isa 31:1 that go down to **E.** for help; and........ 4714
Isa 36:6 the staff of this broken reed, on **E.**; ... 4714
Isa 36:6 so is Pharaoh king of **E.** to all that 4714
Isa 36:9 servants, and put thy trust on **E.**....... 4714
Isa 43:3 I gave **E.** for thy ransom, Ethiopia 4714
Isa 45:14 The labour of **E.**, and merchandise..... 4714
Isa 52:4 people went down aforetime into **E.**.... 4714
Jer 2:6 brought us up out of the land of **E.**, .. 4714
Jer 2:18 hast thou to do in the way of **E.**, ... 4714
Jer 2:36 thou also shalt be ashamed of **E.**,....... 4714
Jer 7:22 brought them out of the land of **E.**, ... 4714
Jer 7:25 came forth out of the land of **E.**......... 4714
Jer 9:26 **E.**, and Judah, and Edom, and the...... 4714
Jer 11:4 them forth out of the land of **E.**, ... 4714
Jer 11:7 them up out of the land of **E.**,........... 4714
Jer 16:14 of Israel out of the land of **E.**; 4714
Jer 23:7 of Israel out of the land of **E.**;........... 4714
Jer 24:8 them that dwell in the land of **E.**:........ 4714
Jer 25:19 Pharaoh king of **E.**, and his............... 4714
Jer 26:21 afraid, and fled, and went into **E.**; 4714
Jer 26:22 the king sent men into **E.**, namely,...... 4714
Jer 26:22 and certain men with him into **E.**. 4714
Jer 26:23 they fetched forth Urijah out of **E.**, ... 4714
Jer 31:32 bring them out of the land of **E.**; 4714
Jer 32:20 signs and wonders in the land of **E.**,... 4714
Jer 32:21 people Israel out of the land of **E.** 4714
Jer 34:13 them forth out of the land of **E.**, out... 4714
Jer 37:5 army was come forth out of **E.**:......... 4714
Jer 37:7 to help you, shall return to **E.** into..... 4714
Jer 41:17 Bethlehem, to go to enter into **E.**, ... 4714
Jer 42:14 but we will go into the land of **E.**,...... 4714
Jer 42:15 set your faces to enter into **E.**, ... 4714
Jer 42:16 overtake you there in the land of **E.**,.. 4714
Jer 42:16 follow close after you there in **E.**; 4714
Jer 42:17 that set their faces to go into **E.**......... 4714
Jer 42:18 you, when ye shall enter into **E.**:......... 4714
Jer 42:19 of Judah; Go ye not into **E.**:.............. 4714
Jer 43:2 sent thee to say, Go not into **E.** to 4714
Jer 43:7 they came into the land of **E.**: for 4714
Jer 43:11 he shall smite the land of **E.**, ... 4714
Jer 43:12 fire in the houses of the gods of **E.**; ... 4714
Jer 43:12 array himself with the land of **E.**, ... 4714
Jer 43:13 that is in the land of **E.**; and the........ 4714
Jer 44:1 Jews which dwell in the land of **E.**,..... 4714
Jer 44:8 unto other gods in the land of **E.**, ... 4714
Jer 44:12 their faces to go into the land of **E.**...... 4714
Jer 44:12 consumed, and fall in the land of **E.**;... 4714
Jer 44:13 them that dwell in the land of **E.**,........ 4714
Jer 44:14 which are gone into the land of **E.**...... 4714
Jer 44:15 people that dwelt in the land of **E.**, ... 4714
Jer 44:24 all Judah that are in the land of **E.**:..... 4714
Jer 44:26 Judah that dwell in the land of **E.**;..... 4714
Jer 44:26 man of Judah in all the land of **E.**, ... 4714
Jer 44:27 the land of **E.** shall be consumed by ... 4714
Jer 44:28 shall return out of the land of **E.**......... 4714
Jer 44:28 into the land of **E.** to sojourn there, ... 4714
Jer 44:30 give Pharaoh-hophra king of **E.**........... 4714
Jer 46:2 Against **E.**, against the army of 4714
Jer 46:2 Pharaoh-necho king of **E.**, which........ 4714
Jer 46:8 **E.** riseth up like a flood, and his........ 4714
Jer 46:11 balm, O virgin, the daughter of **E.**:..... 4714
Jer 46:13 come and smite the land of **E.**........... 4714
Jer 46:14 Declare ye in **E.**, and publish in......... 4714
Jer 46:17 Pharaoh king of **E.** is but a noise; 4714
Jer 46:19 O thou daughter dwelling in **E.**, ... 4714
Jer 46:20 **E.** is like a very fair heifer, but 4714
Jer 46:24 The daughter of **E.** shall be 4714
Jer 46:25 of No, and Pharaoh, and **E.**, with....... 4714
Eze 17:15 sending his ambassadors into **E.**,......... 4714
Eze 19:4 him with chains into the land of **E.**. 4714
Eze 20:5 known unto them in the land of **E.**, ... 4714
Eze 20:6 to bring them forth of the land of **E.**.... 4714
Eze 20:7 not yourselves with the idols of **E.**: 4714
Eze 20:8 did they forsake the idols of **E.**:......... 4714
Eze 20:8 them in the midst of the land of **E.**,.... 4714
Eze 20:9 them forth out of the land of **E.**......... 4714
Eze 20:10 to go forth out of the land of **E.**, ... 4714
Eze 20:36 in the wilderness of the land of **E.**,...... 4714
Eze 23:3 they committed whoredoms in **E.**;...... 4714
Eze 23:8 her whoredoms brought from **E.**: 4714
Eze 23:19 played the harlot in the land of **E.**.... 4714
Eze 23:27 brought from the land of **E.**: 4714
Eze 23:27 them, nor remember **E.** any more,..... 4714
Eze 27:7 linen with broidered work from **E.**....... 4714
Eze 29:2 face against Pharaoh king of **E.**,......... 4714
Eze 29:2 against him, and against all **E.**: 4714
Eze 29:3 Pharaoh king of **E.**, the great............ 4714
Eze 29:6 **E.** shall know that I am the Lord, ... 4714
Eze 29:9 the land of **E.** shall be desolate.......... 4714
Eze 29:10 make the land of **E.** utterly waste 4714
Eze 29:12 I will make the land of **E.** desolate 4714
Eze 29:14 will bring again the captivity of **E.**, ... 4714
Eze 29:19 I will give the land of **E.** unto........... 4714
Eze 29:20 given him the land of **E.** for his 4714
Eze 30:4 And the sword shall come upon **E.**, ... 4714
Eze 30:4 when the slain shall fall in **E.**,.......... 4714
Eze 30:6 They also that uphold **E.** shall fall;...... 4714
Eze 30:8 when I have set a fire in **E.**, and 4714
Eze 30:9 upon them, as in the day of **E.**: 4714
Eze 30:10 make the multitude of **E.** to cease...... 4714
Eze 30:11 shall draw their swords against **E.**,..... 4714

Eze 30:13 no more a prince of the land of **E.**: 4714
Eze 30:13 I will put a fear in the land of **E.**........ 4714
Eze 30:15 fury upon Sin, the strength of **E.**; 4714
Eze 30:16 And I will set fire in **E.**: Sin shall....... 4714
Eze 30:18 I shall break there the yokes of **E.**: 4714
Eze 30:19 will I execute judgments in **E.**: 4714
Eze 30:21 the arm of Pharaoh king of **E.**; 4714
Eze 30:22 I am against Pharaoh king of **E.**, ... 4714
Eze 30:25 stretch it out upon the land of **E.**....... 4714
Eze 31:2 speak unto Pharaoh king of **E.**,............ 4714
Eze 32:2 lamentation for Pharaoh king of **E.**,..... 4714
Eze 32:12 they shall spoil the pomp of **E.**,.......... 4714
Eze 32:15 shall make the land of **E.** desolate, ... 4714
Eze 32:16 shall lament for her, even for **E.**, ... 4714
Eze 32:18 man, wail for the multitude of **E.**, ... 4714
Da 9:15 people forth out of the land of **E.**....... 4714
Da 11:8 carry captives into **E.** their gods, ... 4714
Da 11:42 and the land of **E.** shall not escape. 4714
Da 11:43 over all the precious things of **E.**: 4714
Ho 2:15 she came up out of the land of **E.**: 4714
Ho 7:11 without heart: they call to **E.**, ... 4714
Ho 7:16 be their derision in the land of **E.**........ 4714
Ho 8:13 their sins: they shall return to **E.**........ 4714
Ho 9:3 Ephraim shall return to **E.**, and 4714
Ho 9:6 **E.** shall gather them up, Memphis...... 4714
Ho 11:1 him, and called my son out of **E.**. 4714
Ho 11:5 shall not return into the land of **E.**, ... 4714
Ho 11:11 shall tremble as a bird out of **E.**. 4714
Ho 12:1 and oil is carried into **E.**.................. 4714
Ho 12:9 thy God from the land of **E.** will yet ... 4714
Ho 12:13 the Lord brought Israel out of **E.**, ... 4714
Ho 13:4 Lord thy God from the land of **E.**, ... 4714
Joe 3:19 **E.** shall be a desolation, and Edom..... 4714
Am 2:10 up from the land of **E.**, and led you.... 4714
Am 3:1 up from the land of **E.**, saying, ... 4714
Am 3:9 and in the palaces in the land of **E.**,.... 4714
Am 4:10 pestilence after the manner of **E.**: 4714
Am 8:8 and drowned, as by the flood of **E.**..... 4714
Am 9:5 be drowned, as by the flood of **E.**....... 4714
Am 9:7 up Israel out of the land of **E.**?.......... 4714
Mic 6:4 thee up out of the land of **E.**,............ 4714
Mic 7:15 of thy coming out of the land of **E.**...... 4714
Na 3:9 Ethiopa and **E.** were her strength, ... 4714
Hag 2:5 with you when ye came out of **E.**, ... 4714
Zec 10:10 them again also out of the land of **E.**, ..4714
Zec 10:11 and the sceptre of **E.** shall depart 4714
Zec 14:18 if the family of **E.** go not up, and 4714
Zec 14:19 This shall be the punishment of **E.**, ... 4714
Mt 2:13 flee into **E.**, and be thou there........... *125*
Mt 2:14 by night, and departed into **E.**: *125*
Mt 2:15 Out of **E.** have I called my son. *125*
Mt 2:19 in a dream to Joseph in **E.**, ... *125*
Ac 2:10 in **E.**, and in the parts of Libya *125*
Ac 7:9 with envy, sold Joseph into **E.**: *125*
Ac 7:10 the sight of Pharaoh king of **E.**; *125*
Ac 7:10 he made him governor over **E.** *125*
Ac 7:11 came a dearth over all the land of **E.** ... *125*
Ac 7:12 Jacob heard that there was corn in **E.**,.. *125*
Ac 7:15 Jacob went down into **E.**, and died,...... *125*
Ac 7:17 people grew and multiplied in **E.**,......... *125*
Ac 7:34 of my people which is in **E.**,............... *125*
Ac 7:34 now come, I will send thee into **E.**. *125*
Ac 7:36 wonders and signs in the land of **E.**, ... *125*
Ac 7:39 hearts turned back again into **E.**,......... *125*
Ac 7:40 brought us out of the land of **E.**, ... *125*
Ac 13:17 as strangers in the land of **E.**,............ *125*
Heb 3:16 that came out of **E.** by Moses............. *125*
Heb 8:9 to lead them out of the land of **E.**;....... *125*
Heb 11:26 riches than the treasures in **E.**: *125*
Heb 11:27 By faith he forsook **E.**, not fearing....... *125*
Jude 5 the people out of the land of **E.**, ... *125*
Re 11:8 spiritually is called Sodom and **E.**,........ *125*

EGYPTIAN (e-jip'-shun) See also EGYPTIAN'S; EGYPTIANS.
Ge 16:1 an **E.**, whose name was Hagar. 4713
Ge 16:3 wife, took Hagar her maid the **E.**,....... 4713
Ge 21:9 Sarah saw the son of Hagar the **E.**,..... 4713
Ge 25:12 Hagar the **E.**, Sarah's handmaid, ... 4713
Ge 39:1 an **E.**, bought him of the hands of...... 4713
Ge 39:2 in the house of his master the **E.**........ 4713
Ex 1:19 women are not as the **E.** women; 4713
Ex 2:11 he spied an **E.** smiting an Hebrew,...... 4713
Ex 2:12 slew the **E.**, and hid him in the sand... 4713
Ex 2:14 to kill me, as thou killedst the **E.**?...... 4713
Ex 2:19 An **E.** delivered us out of the hand..... 4713
Le 24:10 woman, whose father was an **E.**, ... 4713
De 23:7 thou shalt not abhor an **E.**; because.... 4713
1Sa 30:11 And they found an **E.** in the field, ... 4713
2Sa 23:21 And he slew an **E.**, a goodly man:...... 4713
2Sa 23:21 the **E.** had a spear in his hand;.......... 4713
1Ch 2:34 And Sheshan had a servant, an **E.**,..... 4713
1Ch 11:23 slew an **E.**, a man of great stature, ... 4713
Isa 11:15 destroy the tongue of the **E.** sea; 4714
Isa 19:23 and the **E.** into Assyria, and............. 4714
Ac 7:24 was oppressed, and smote the **E.**:....... *124*
Ac 7:28 as thou didst the **E.** yesterday?.......... *124*
Ac 21:38 Art not thou that **E.**, which before....... *124*

EGYPTIAN'S (e-jip'-shuns)
Ge 39:5 the Lord blessed the **E.** house for...... 4713
2Sa 23:21 plucked the spear out of the **E.** 4713
1Ch 11:23 **E.** hand was a spear like a weaver's... 4713
1Ch 11:23 out of the **E.** hand, and slew him........ 4713

EGYPTIANS (e-jip'-shuns)
Ge 12:12 when the **E.** shall see thee, that........ 4713
Ge 12:14 Abram was come into Egypt, the **E.**.... 4713
Ge 41:55 Pharaoh said unto all the **E.**, Go........ 4714
Ge 41:56 storehouses, and sold unto the **E.**; 4714
Ge 43:32 by themselves, and for the **E.**,............ 4713
Ge 43:32 the **E.** might not eat bread with the.... 4713
Ge 43:32 is an abomination unto the **E.**. 4714
Ge 45:2 the **E.** and the house of Pharaoh........ 4714
Ge 46:34 is an abomination unto the **E.**............ 4714
Ge 47:15 the **E.** came unto Joseph, and said, ... 4714
Ge 47:20 for the **E.** sold every man his field, ... 4714
Ge 50:3 the **E.** mourned for him threescore..... 4714
Ge 50:11 is a grievous mourning to the **E.**:....... 4714
Ex 1:13 the **E.** made the children of Israel...... 4714
Ex 3:8 them out of the hand of the **E.**, ... 4714
Ex 3:9 wherewith the **E.** oppress them.......... 4714
Ex 3:21 people favour in the sight of the **E.**: ... 4714
Ex 3:22 and ye shall spoil the **E.**.................. 4714
Ex 6:5 whom the **E.** kept in bondage;........... 4714
Ex 6:6 from under the burdens of the **E.**,...... 4714
Ex 6:7 from under the burdens of the **E.**........ 4714
Ex 7:5 **E.** shall know that I am the Lord, ... 4714
Ex 7:18 the **E.** shall lothe to drink of the........ 4714
Ex 7:21 and the **E.** could not drink of............. 4714
Ex 7:24 **E.** digged round about the river.......... 4714
Ex 8:21 the houses of the **E.** shall be full........ 4714
Ex 8:26 abomination of the **E.** to the Lord...... 4714
Ex 8:26 abomination of the **E.** before their...... 4714
Ex 9:11 the magicians, and upon all the **E.**...... 4714
Ex 10:6 and the houses of all the **E.**;............ 4714
Ex 11:3 people favour in the sight of the **E.** ... 4714
Ex 11:7 a difference between the **E.** and 4714
Ex 12:23 will pass through to smite the **E.**; 4714
Ex 12:27 when he smote the **E.**, and.............. 4714
Ex 12:30 and all his servants, and all the **E.**;..... 4714
Ex 12:33 **E.** were urgent upon the people, ... 4714
Ex 12:35 borrowed of the **E.** jewels of silver,.... 4714
Ex 12:36 people favour in the sight of the **E.**. ... 4714
Ex 12:36 required. And they spoiled the **E.**. 4714
Ex 14:4 **E.** may know that I am the Lord. 4714
Ex 14:9 But the **E.** pursued after them, all...... 4714
Ex 14:10 the **E.** marched after them; and......... 4714
Ex 14:12 alone, that we may serve the **E.**? 4714
Ex 14:12 been better for us to serve the **E.**, ... 4714
Ex 14:13 the **E.** whom ye have seen to day,....... 4714
Ex 14:17 I will harden the hearts of the **E.**,...... 4714
Ex 14:18 **E.** shall know that I am the Lord, ... 4714
Ex 14:20 between the camp of the **E.** and........ 4714
Ex 14:23 **E.** pursued, and went in after them.... 4714
Ex 14:24 looked unto the host of the **E.**........... 4714
Ex 14:24 and troubled the host of the **E.**,......... 4714
Ex 14:25 the **E.** said, Let us flee from the 4714
Ex 14:25 fighteth for them against the **E.**. 4714
Ex 14:26 waters may come again upon the **E.**. .. 4714
Ex 14:27 the **E.** fled against it; and the Lord..... 4714
Ex 14:27 the **E.** in the midst of the sea. 4714
Ex 14:30 day out of the hand of the **E.**; 4714
Ex 14:30 saw the **E.** dead upon the sea shore... 4714
Ex 14:31 which the Lord did upon the **E.**: 4714
Ex 15:26 which I have brought upon the **E.**: 4714
Ex 18:8 and to the **E.** for Israel's sake, ... 4714
Ex 18:9 delivered out of the hand of the **E.**..... 4714
Ex 18:10 you out of the hand of the **E.**,............ 4714
Ex 18:10 from under the hand of the **E.**,.......... 4714
Ex 19:4 have seen what I did unto the **E.**,....... 4714
Ex 32:12 Wherefore should the **E.** speak,......... 4714
Nu 14:13 the Lord, Then the **E.** shall hear it,.... 4714
Nu 20:15 the **E.** vexed us, and our fathers: 4714
Nu 33:3 high hand in the sight of all the **E.**. 4714
Nu 33:4 the **E.** buried all their firstborn, ... 4714
De 26:6 **E.** evil entreated us, and afflicted....... 4713
Jos 24:6 **E.** pursued after your fathers 4714
Jos 24:7 and the **E.**, and brought the sea 4713
Jg 6:9 you out of the hand of the **e.**,........... 4714
Jg 10:11 Did not I deliver you from the **E.**,...... 4714
1Sa 4:8 are the Gods that smote the **E.**......... 4714
1Sa 6:6 do ye harden your hearts, as the **E.** ... 4714
1Sa 10:18 the **E.**, and out of the hand of all....... 4714
2Ki 7:6 the Hittites, and the kings of the **E.**, .. 4714
Ezr 9:1 Ammonites, the Moabites, the **E.**,....... 4713
Isa 19:2 I will set the **E.** against the **E.**:......... 4714
Isa 19:4 And the **E.** will I give over into the.... 4714
Isa 19:21 **E.** shall know the Lord in that day, ... 4714
Isa 19:23 **E.** shall serve with the Assyrians. 4714
Isa 20:4 Assyria lead away...**E.** prisoners,........ 4714
Isa 30:7 the **E.** shall help in vain, and to......... 4714
Isa 31:3 the **E.** are men, and not God; and...... 4714
Jer 43:13 the gods of the **E.** shall he burn 4714
La 5:6 to the **E.**, and to the Assyrians, ... 4714
Eze 16:26 committed fornication with the **E.**....... 4714
Eze 23:21 in bruising thy teats by the **E.** for...... 4714
Eze 29:12 scatter the **E.** among the nations, ... 4714
Eze 29:13 of forty years will I gather the **E.** 4714
Eze 30:23, 26 scatter the **E.** among the 4714
Ac 7:22 in all the wisdom of the **E.**,................ *124*
Heb 11:29 **E.** assaying to do were drowned. *124*

EHI (e'-hi) see also AHARAH.
Ge 46:21 Gera, and Naaman, **E.**, and Rosh, ... 278

EHUD (e'-hud)
Jg 3:15 raised them up a deliverer, **E.** 261
Jg 3:16 **E.** made him a dagger which had......... 261
Jg 3:20 And **E.** came unto him; and he was...... 261
Jg 3:20 **E.** said, I have a message from God 261
Jg 3:21 **E.** put forth his left hand, and took...... 261
Jg 3:23 **E.** went forth through the porch,......... 261
Jg 3:26 And **E.** escaped while they tarried, ... 261
Jg 4:1 of the Lord, when **E.** was dead........... 261
1Ch 7:10 Benjamin, and **E.**, and Chenaanah, ... 261
1Ch 8:6 And these are the sons of **E.**: these..... 261

EIGHT See also EIGHTEEN.
Ge 5:4 Seth were **e.** hundred years:.............. 8083
Ge 5:7 **e.** hundred and seven years, and......... 8083
Ge 5:10 **e.** hundred and fifteen years,............. 8083
Ge 5:13 **e.** hundred and forty years,................ 8083
Ge 5:16 Jared **e.** hundred and thirty years, ... 8083
Ge 5:17 **e.** hundred ninety and five years: 8083
Ge 5:19 begat Enoch **e.** hundred years, and....... 8083
Ge 17:12 is **e.** days old shall be circumcised...... 8083
Ge 21:4 his son Isaac being **e.** days old, as...... 8083
Ge 22:23 these **e.** Milcah did bear to Nahor, ... 8083
Ex 26:2 shall be **e.** and twenty cubits,.............. 8083
Ex 26:25 And they shall be **e.** boards, and......... 8083
Ex 36:9 curtain was twenty and **e.** cubits, ... 8083
Ex 36:30 And there were **e.** boards; and........... 8083
Nu 2:24 and **e.** thousand and an hundred, ... 8083
Nu 3:28 **e.** thousand and six hundred,............. 8083
Nu 4:48 were **e.** thousand and five hundred 8083
Nu 7:8 four wagons and **e.** oxen he gave 8083
Nu 29:29 on the sixth day **e.** bullocks,.............. 8083
Nu 35:7 Levites shall be forty and **e.** cities: 8083
De 2:14 Zered, was thirty and **e.** years;.......... 8083
Jos 21:41 forty and **e.** cities with their............... 8083
Jg 3:8 Chushan-rishathaim **e.** years. 8083
Jg 12:14 and he judged Israel **e.** years............. 8083
1Sa 4:15 Eli was ninety and **e.** years old; 8083
1Sa 17:12 was Jesse; and he had **e.** sons:.......... 8083
2Sa 23:8 against **e.** hundred, whom he slew...... 8083
2Sa 24:9 **e.** hundred thousand valiant men 8083
1Ki 7:10 of ten cubits, stones of **e.** cubits. 8083
2Ki 8:17 he reigned **e.** years in Jerusalem. 8083
2Ki 10:36 Samaria was twenty and **e.** years. 8083
2Ki 22:1 Josiah was **e.** years old when he 8083
1Ch 12:24 six thousand and **e.** hundred,............. 8083
1Ch 12:30 twenty thousand and **e.** hundred,........ 8083
1Ch 12:35 and **e.** thousand and six hundred. 8083
1Ch 16:38 their brethren, three score and **e.**; 8083
1Ch 23:3 man, was thirty and **e.** thousand......... 8083
1Ch 24:4 and **e.** among the sons of Ithamar....... 8083
1Ch 25:7 was two hundred fourscore and **e.**. 8083
2Ch 11:21 begat twenty and **e.** sons, and.......... 8083
2Ch 13:3 **e.** hundred thousand chosen men,........ 8083
2Ch 21:5 he reigned **e.** years in Jerusalem. 8083
2Ch 21:20 he reigned in Jerusalem **e.** years, ... 8083
2Ch 29:17 the house of the Lord in **e.** days; 8083
2Ch 34:1 Josiah was **e.** years old when he 8083

2Ch 36:9 Jehoiachin was **e.** years old when 8083
Ezr 2:6 thousand **e.** hundred and twelve. 8083
Ezr 2:16 Ater of Hezekiah, ninety and **e.**. 8083
Ezr 2:23 Anathoth, an hundred twenty and **e.**.... 8083
Ezr 2:41 Asaph, an hundred twenty and **e.**. 8083
Ezr 8:11 and with him twenty and **e.** males. 8083
Ne 7:11 and **e.** hundred and eighteen............ 8083
Ne 7:13 Zattu, **e.** hundred forty and five. 8083
Ne 7:15 Binnui, six hundred forty and **e.**. 8083
Ne 7:16 Bebai, six hundred twenty and **e.**. 8083
Ne 7:21 Ater of Hezekiah, ninety and **e.**. 8083
Ne 7:22 three hundred twenty and **e.**. 8083
Ne 7:26 an hundred fourscore and **e.**. 8083
Ne 7:27 an hundred twenty and **e.**. 8083
Ne 7:44 of Asaph, an hundred forty and **e.**. 8083
Ne 7:45 of Shobai, an hundred thirty and **e.**. 8083
Ne 11:6 threescore and **e.** valiant men. 8083
Ne 11:8 Sallai, nine hundred twenty and **e.**. 8083
Ne 11:12 were **e.** hundred twenty and two:....... 8083
Ne 11:14 of valour an hundred twenty and **e.**:..... 8083
Ec 11:2 a portion to seven, and also to **e.**;..... 8083
Jer 41:15 escaped from Johanan with **e.** men,..... 8083
Jer 52:29 from Jerusalem **e.** hundred thirty........ 8083
Eze 40:9 he the porch of the gate, **e.** cubits;..... 8083
Eze 40:31, 34,37 going up to it had **e.** steps........ 8083
Eze 40:41 **e.** tables, whereupon they slew......... 8083
Mic 5:5 shepherds, and **e.** principal men. 8083
Lu 2:21 when **e.** days were accomplished........ *3638*
Lu 9:28 an **e.** days after these sayings,.......... *3638*
Joh 5:5 an infirmity thirty and **e.** years.......... *3638*
Joh 20:26 after **e.** days again his disciples *3638*
Ac 9:33 which had kept his bed **e.** years, ... *3638*
1Pe 3:20 is, **e.** souls were saved by water........ *3638*

EIGHTEEN
Ge 14:14 house, three hundred and **e.**,....... 8083,6240
Jg 3:14 the king of Moab **e.** years........... 8083,6240
Jg 10:8 children of Israel: **e.** years, ... 8083,6240
Jg 20:25 Israel again **e.** thousand men; 8083,6240
Jg 20:44 Benjamin **e.** thousand men; 8083,6240
2Sa 8:13 salt, being **e.** thousand men......... 8083,6240
1Ki 7:15 brass, **e.** cubits high apiece: 8083,6240
2Ki 24:8 Jehoiachin was **e.** years old 8083,6240
2Ki 25:17 of one pillar was **e.** cubits, ... 8083,6240
1Ch 12:31 tribe of Manasseh **e.** thousand, ... 8083,6240
1Ch 18:12 the valley of salt **e.** thousand...... 8083,6240
1Ch 26:9 and brethren, strong men, **e.**........ 8083,6240
1Ch 29:7 of brass **e.** thousand talents,....... 7239,8083
2Ch 11:21 for he took **e.** wives, and 8083,6240
Ezr 8:9 him two hundred and **e.** males. ... 8083,6240
Ezr 8:18 his sons and his brethren, **e.**; 8083,6240
Ne 7:11 eight hundred and **e.**................ 8083,6240
Jer 52:21 of one pillar was **e.** cubits; 8083,6240
Eze 48:35 about **e.** thousand measures; 8083,6240
Lu 13:4 **Or those e., upon whom**..*1176,2532,3638*
Lu 13:11 spirit of infirmity **e.** years, .. *1176,2532,3638*
Lu 13:16 **lo, these e. years, be**...... *1176,2532,3638*

EIGHTEENTH
1Ki 15:1 the **e.** year of king Jeroboam...... 8083,6240
2Ki 3:1 Israel in Samaria the **e.** year............. 6240
2Ki 22:3 in the **e.** year of king Josiah, ... 6240
2Ki 23:23 in the **e.** year of king Josiah, ... 6240
1Ch 24:15 to Hezer, the **e.** to Aphses, ... 6240
1Ch 25:25 The **e.** to Hanani, he, his sons,.......... 6240
2Ch 13:1 the **e.** year of king Jeroboam............ 6240
2Ch 34:8 in the **e.** year of his reign, ... 6240
2Ch 35:19 **e.** year of the reign of Josiah............ 6240
Jer 32:1 the **e.** year of Nebuchadrezzar. 6240
Jer 52:29 the **e.** year of Nebuchadrezzar 6240

EIGHTEEN THOUSAND See EIGHTEEN and THOUSAND.

EIGHTH
Ex 22:30 the **e.** day thou shalt give it me. 8066
Le 9:1 it came to pass on the **e.** day, ... 8066
Le 12:3 the **e.** day the flesh of his foreskin...... 8066
Le 14:10 **e.** day he shall take two he lambs....... 8066
Le 14:23 he shall bring them on the **e.** day 8066
Le 15:14 **e.** day he shall take to him two.......... 8066
Le 15:29 **e.** day she shall take unto her two...... 8066
Le 22:27 from the **e.** day and thenceforth......... 8066
Le 23:36 **e.** day shall be a holy convocation....... 8066
Le 23:39 on the **e.** day shall be a sabbath......... 8066
Le 25:22 ye shall sow the **e.** year, and eat 8066
Nu 6:10 **e.** day he shall bring two turtles,........ 8066
Nu 7:54 the **e.** day offered Gamaliel the son..... 8066
Nu 29:35 On the **e.** day ye shall have a............ 8066
1Ki 6:38 month Bul, which is the **e.** month,...... 8066
1Ki 8:66 the **e.** day he sent the people away: ... 8066
1Ki 12:32 ordained a feast in the **e.** month,........ 8066
1Ki 12:33 the fifteenth day of the **e.** month,....... 8066
1Ki 16:29 in the thirty and **e.** year of Asa.......... 8083
2Ki 15:8 the thirty and **e.** year of Azariah 8083
2Ki 24:12 took him in the **e.** year of his reign..... 8083
1Ch 12:12 Johanan the **e.**, Elzabad the **e.**............ 8066
1Ch 24:10 to Hakkoz, the **e.** to Abijah,............... 8066
1Ch 25:15 The **e.** to Jeshaiah, he, his sons.......... 8066
1Ch 26:5 Peulthai the **e.**: for God blessed.......... 8066
1Ch 27:11 The **e.** captain for the **e.** month 8066
2Ch 7:9 **e.** day they made a solemn assembly:.. 8066
2Ch 29:17 and on the **e.** day of the month.......... 8066
2Ch 34:3 For in the **e.** year of his reign, ... 8083
Ne 8:18 the **e.** day was a solemn assembly...... 8066
Eze 43:27 upon the **e.** day, and so forward,......... 8066
Zec 1:1 In the **e.** month, in the second year.... 8066
Lu 1:59 **e.** day they came to circumcise *3590*
Ac 7:8 and circumcised him the **e.** day; *3590*
Php 3:5 Circumcised the **e.** day, of the........... *3637*
2Pe 2:5 but saved Noah the **e.** person,........... *3590*
Re 17:11 was, and is not, even he is the **e.**, ... *3590*
Re 21:20 the **e.**, beryl; the ninth, a topaz; *3590*

EIGHT HUNDRED See EIGHT and HUNDRED.

EIGHTIETH
1Ki 6:1 in the four hundred and **e.** year.......... 8084

EIGHT THOUSAND See EIGHT and THOUSAND.

EIGHTY
Ge 5:25 an hundred **e.** and seven years, ... 8084
Ge 5:26 seven hundred **e.** and two years,......... 8084
Ge 5:28 lived an hundred **e.** and two years, ... 8084

EITHER See also NEITHER.
Ge 31:24 speak not to Jacob **e.** good or bad. ....
Ge 31:29 thou speak not to Jacob **e.** good or bad......
Le 10:1 took **e.** of them his censer, and.......... 376
Le 13:49 or in the skin, **e.** in the warp, or 176
Le 13:51, 53 in the garment, **e.** in the warp, ... 176
Le 13:57 still in the garment, **e.** in the warp,...... 176
Le 13:58 And the garment, **e.** warp, or woof, ... 176
Le 13:59 or linen, **e.** in the warp, or woof,......... 176
Le 22:23 **E.** a bullock or a lamb that hath..............
Le 25:49 **E.** his uncle, or his uncle's son, ... 176
Nu 6:2 **e.** man or woman shall separate........... 376
Nu 22:26 no way to turn **e.** to the right hand..........
Nu 24:13 **e.** good or bad of mine own mind; ....
De 17:3 **e.** the sun, or moon, or any of................
De 28:51 also shall not leave thee **e.** corn, ...
Jg 9:2 **e.** that all the sons of Jerubbaal,...............
1Sa 20:2 will do nothing **e.** great or small, ...
1Sa 25:31 **e.** that thou hast shed blood causeless, ...
1Sa 30:2 slew not any, **e.** great or small, ...
1Ki 7:15 did compass **e.** of them about. 8145
1Ki 10:19 and there were stays on **e.** side ....
1Ki 18:27 **e.** he is talking, or he is pursuing, ... 3588
1Ch 21:12 **E.** three years' famine; or three.......... 518
2Ch 18:9 king of Judah sat **e.** of them on............ 376
Ec 9:1 man knoweth **e.** love or hatred 1571
Ec 11:6 not whether shall prosper, **e.** this............
Isa 7:11 ask it **e.** in the depth, or in the...............
Isa 17:8 **e.** the groves, or the images. ....
Eze 21:16 one way or other, **e.** on the right............
Mt 6:24 **for e. he will hate the one, and**..... *2228*
Mt 12:33 **E. make the tree good, and his**...... *2228*
Lu 6:42 **E. how canst thou say to thy**....... *2228*
Lu 15:8 **E. what woman having ten pieces**. *2228*
Lu 16:13 **two masters: for e. he will hate**.... *2228*
Joh 19:18 on **e.** side one, and Jesus in *1782,2532*
Ac 17:21 but **e.** to tell, or to hear some........... *2228*
1Co 14:6 shall speak to you **e.** by revelation,..... *2228*
Php 3:12 attained, **e.** were already perfect: *2228*
Jas 3:12 bear olive berries? **e.** a vine, figs? *2228*
Re 22:2 and on **e.** side of the river, ... *1782,2532*

EKER (e'-ker)
1Ch 2:27 were, Maaz, and Jamin, and **E.**.......... 6134

EKRON (ec'-ron) See also EKRONITES.
Jos 13:3 Egypt, even unto the borders of **E.**.... 6138
Jos 15:11 unto the side of **E.** northward: 6138
Jos 15:45 **E.**, with her towns and her villages: ... 6138
Jos 15:46 From **E.** even unto the sea, all.......... 6138
Jos 19:43 Elon, and Thimnathah, and **E.**, ... 6138
Jg 1:18 with the coast thereof, and **E.**........... 6138
1Sa 5:10 they sent the ark of God to **E.**. 6138
1Sa 5:10 pass, as the ark of God came to **E.**, ... 6138
1Sa 6:16 had seen it, they returned to **E.** 6138
1Sa 6:17 one, for Gath one, for **E.** one; 6138
1Sa 7:14 to Israel, from **E.** even unto Gath; 6138
1Sa 17:52 the valley, and to the gates of **E.**....... 6138
1Sa 17:52 even unto Gath, and unto **E.**............. 6138
2Ki 1:2 enquire of Baal-zebub the god of **E.**.... 6138
2Ki 1:3, 6 of Baal-zebub the god of **E.**? 6138
2Ki 1:16 enquire of Baal-zebub the god of **E.**,... 6138
Jer 25:20 and **E.**, and the remnant of Ashdod, ... 6138
Am 1:8 I will turn mine hand against **E.**: 6138
Zep 2:4 and **E.** shall be rooted up. 6138
Zec 9:5 and **E.**; for her expectation shall 6138
Zec 9:7 in Judah, and **E.** as a Jebusite............ 6138

EKRONITES (ek'-ron-ites)
Jos 13:3 the Gittites, and the **E.**; also the 6139
1Sa 5:10 that the **E.** cried out, saying, They..... 6139

EL See BETH-EL; EL-BETH-EL; EL-ELOHE-ISRAEL; EL-HARAN; JIPHTHAH-EL; MIGDAL-EL.

ELADAH (el'-a-dah)
1Ch 7:20 **E.** his son, and Tahath his son,........... 497

ELAH (e'-lah)
Ge 36:41 Duke Aholibamah, duke **E.**, duke......... 425
1Sa 17:2 and pitched by the valley of **E.**,........... 425
1Sa 17:19 were in the valley of **E.**, fighting 425
1Sa 21:9 thou slewest in the valley of **E.**,........... 425
1Ki 4:18 Shimei the son of **E.**, in Benjamin........ 425
1Ki 16:6 **E.** his son reigned in his stead. 425
1Ki 16:8 **E.** the son of Baasha to reign 425
1Ki 16:13 sins of Baasha, and the sins of **E.**........ 425
1Ki 16:14 the rest of the acts of **E.**, and all......... 425
2Ki 15:30 the son of **E.** made a conspiracy.......... 425
2Ki 17:1 began Hoshea the son of **E.** to reign.... 425
2Ki 18:1 the third year of Hoshea son of **E.**....... 425
2Ki 18:9 seventh year of Hoshea son of **E.**........ 425
1Ch 1:52 Duke Aholibamah, duke **E.**, duke.......... 425
1Ch 4:15 Jephunneh; Iru, **E.**, and Naam:............ 425
1Ch 4:15 and the sons of **E.**, even Kenaz. 425
1Ch 9:8 the son of Jeroham, and **E.** 425

ELAM (e'-lam) See also ELAMITES; PERSIA.
Ge 10:22 children of Shem; **E.**, and Ashur, ... 5867
Ge 14:1 Chedorlaomer king of **E.**, and............ 5867
Ge 14:9 With Chedorlaomer the king of **E.**, ... 5867
1Ch 1:17 The sons of Shem; **E.**, and Asshur,.... 5867
1Ch 8:24 Hananiah, and **E.**, and Antothijah,....... 5867
1Ch 26:3 **E.** the fifth, Jehohanan the sixth,....... 5867
Ezr 2:7 The children of **E.**, a thousand two..... 5867
Ezr 2:31 The children of the other **E.**, ... 5867
Ezr 8:7 And of the sons of **E.**; Jeshaiah 5867
Ezr 10:2 son of Jehiel, one of the sons of **E.**, ... 5867
Ezr 10:26 sons of **E.**; Mattaniah, Zechariah,........ 5867
Ne 7:12 children of **E.**, a thousand two........... 5867
Ne 7:34 The children of the other **E.**, ... 5867
Ne 10:14 people; Parosh, Pahath-moab, **E.**, ... 5867
Ne 12:42 and Malchijah, and **E.**, and Ezer. 5867
Isa 11:11 and from Cush, and from **E.**, and....... 5867
Isa 21:2 Go up, O **E.**: besiege, O Media;......... 5867
Isa 22:6 **E.** bare the quiver with chariots.......... 5867
Jer 25:25 and all the kings of **E.**, and all the...... 5867
Jer 49:34 Jeremiah the prophet against **E.**,........ 5867
Jer 49:35 Behold, I will break the bow of **E.**, ... 5867
Jer 49:36 upon **E.** will I bring the four winds 5867
Jer 49:36 the outcasts of **E.** shall not come. 5867
Jer 49:37 For I will cause **E.** to be dismayed..... 5867
Jer 49:38 And I will set my throne in **E.**, and.... 5867
Jer 49:39 bring again the captivity of **E.**,.......... 5867
Eze 32:24 is **E.** and all her multitude round........ 5867
Da 8:2 which is in the province of **E.**;........... 5867

ELAMITES (e'-lam-ites) See also PERSIANS.
Ezr 4:9 the Dehavites, and the **E.**,................ 5962
Ac 2:9 Parthians, and Medes, and **E.**, ... *1639*

ELASAH (el'-a-sah) See also ELEASA.
Ezr 10:22 Nethaneel, Jozabad, **E.**. 501
Jer 29:3 hand of **E.** the son of Shaphan, ... 501

ELATH (e'-lath) See also ELOTH.
De 2:8 the way of the plain from **E.**,............... 359
2Ki 14:22 built **E.**, and restored it to Judah, ... 359
2Ki 16:6 king of Syria recovered **E.** to Syria, ... 359
2Ki 16:6 and drave the Jews from **E.**:.............. 359
2Ki 16:6 Syrians came to **E.**, and dwelt there 359

EL-BETH-EL (el-beth'-el)
Ge 35:7 an altar, and called the place **E.**; 416

ELDAAH (el'-da-ah)
Ge 25:4 and Hanoch, and Abidah, and **E.**.......... 420
1Ch 1:33 and Henoch, and Abida, and **E.**, ... 420

ELDAD (el'-dad)
Nu 11:26 the name of the one was **E.**, ... 419

Nu 11:27 **E.** and Medad do prophesy in the 419

ELDER See also ELDERS.
Ge 10:21 the brother of Japheth the **e.**, 1419
Ge 25:23 and the **e.** shall serve the younger 7227
Ge 27:42 these words of Esau her **e.** son 1419
Ge 29:16 the name of the **e.** was Leah, 1419
1Sa 18:17 Behold my **e.** daughter Merab, 1419
1Ki 2:22 for he is mine **e.** brother; 1419
Job 15:10 men, much **e.** than thy father. 1419
Job 32:4 because they were **e.** than he 2205,3117
Eze 16:46 thine **e.** sister is Samaria, she and 1419
Eze 16:61 sisters, thine **e.** and thy younger: 1419
Eze 23:4 names of them were Aholah the **e.**, 1419
Lu 15:25 **Now his e. son was in the field:** *4245*
Ro 9:12 The **e.** shall serve the younger. *3187*
1Ti 5:1 Rebuke not an **e.**, but entreat him *4245*
1Ti 5:2 **e.** women as mothers; the younger *4245*
1Ti 5:19 an **e.** receive not an accusation, *4245*
1Pe 5:1 I exhort, who am also an **e.**, *4850*
1Pe 5:5 submit yourselves unto the **e.** *4245*
2Jo 1 The **e.** unto the elect lady and her *4245*
3Jo 1 The **e.** unto the well beloved Gaius, *4245*

ELDERS
Ge 50:7 of Pharaoh, the **e.** of his house, 2205
Ge 50:7 all the **e.** of the land of Egypt, 2205
Ex 3:16 Go, and gather the **e.** of Israel 2205
Ex 3:18 come, thou and the **e.** of Israel, 2205
Ex 4:29 gathered together all the **e.** of the 2205
Ex 12:21 Moses called for all the **e.** of Israel, 2205
Ex 17:5 take with thee of the **e.** of Israel; 2205
Ex 17:6 did so in the sight of the **e.** of 2205
Ex 18:12 Aaron came, all the **e.** of Israel, 2205
Ex 19:7 called for the **e.** of the people, 2205
Ex 24:1 seventy of the **e.** of Israel; and 2205
Ex 24:9 and seventy of the **e.** of Israel: 2205
Ex 24:14 he said unto the **e.**, Tarry ye here 2205
Le 4:15 the **e.** of the congregation shall 2205
Le 9:1 and his sons, and the **e.** of Israel; 2205
Nu 11:16 seventy men of the **e.** of Israel, 2205
Nu 11:16 knowest to be the **e.** of the people, 2205
Nu 11:24 seventy men of the **e.** of the people, 2205
Nu 11:25 and gave it unto the seventy **e.**: 2205
Nu 11:30 the camp, he and the **e.** of Israel. 2205
Nu 16:25 and the **e.** of Israel followed him. 2205
Nu 22:4 Moab said unto the **e.** of Midian, 2205
Nu 22:7 And the **e.** of Moab and the 2205
Nu 22:7 and the **e.** of Midian departed 2205
De 5:23 heads of your tribes, and your **e.**; 2205
De 19:12 Then the **e.** of his city shall send 2205
De 21:2 thy **e.** and thy judges shall come 2205
De 21:3 **e.** of that city shall take an heifer, 2205
De 21:4 And the **e.** of that city shall bring 2205
De 21:6 And all the **e.** of that city, 2205
De 21:19 him out unto the **e.** of his city, 2205
De 21:20 shall say unto the **e.** of his city, 2205
De 22:15 virginity unto the **e.** of the city 2205
De 22:16 damsel's father shall say unto the **e.**, 2205
De 22:17 the cloth before the **e.** of the city. 2205
De 22:18 And the **e.** of that city shall take 2205
De 25:7 go up to the gate unto the **e.**, 2205
De 25:8 the **e.** of his city shall call him, 2205
De 25:9 unto him in the presence of the **e.**, 2205
De 27:1 with the **e.** of Israel commanded 2205
De 29:10 your **e.**, and your officers, with all 2205
De 31:9 and unto all the **e.** of Israel. 2205
De 31:28 Gather unto me all the **e.** of your 2205
De 32:7 thy **e.**, and they will tell thee 2205
Jos 7:6 eventide, he and the **e.** of Israel, 2205
Jos 8:10 he and the **e.** of Israel, before the 2205
Jos 8:33 all Israel, and their **e.**, and officers, 2205
Jos 9:11 our **e.** and all the inhabitants 2205
Jos 20:4 his cause in the ears of the **e.** of 2205
Jos 23:2 for their **e.**, and for their heads, 2205
Jos 24:1 and called for the **e.** of Israel, 2205
Jos 24:31 days of the **e.** that overlived Joshua, 2205
Jg 2:7 days of the **e.** that outlived Joshua, 2205
Jg 8:14 and the **e.** thereof, even three score 2205
Jg 8:16 And he took the **e.** of the city, 2205
Jg 11:5 the **e.** of Gilead went to fetch 2205
Jg 11:7 Jephthah said unto the **e.** of Gilead, 2205
Jg 11:8 **e.** of Gilead said unto Jephthah, 2205
Jg 11:9 Jephthah said unto the **e.** of Gilead, 2205
Jg 11:10 the **e.** of Gilead said unto Jephthah, 2205
Jg 11:11 Jephthah went with the **e.** of Gilead, 2205
Jg 21:16 the **e.** of the congregation said, 2205
Ru 4:2 took ten men of the **e.** of the city. 2205
Ru 4:4 and before the **e.** of my people. 2205
Ru 4:9 And Boaz said unto the **e.**, 2205
Ru 4:11 and the **e.**, said, We are witnesses. 2205
1Sa 4:3 the **e.** of Israel said, Wherefore 2205
1Sa 8:4 Then all the **e.** of Israel gathered 2205
1Sa 11:3 the **e.** of Jabesh said unto him, 2205
1Sa 15:30 thee, before the **e.** of my people, 2205
1Sa 16:4 the **e.** of the town trembled at his 2205
1Sa 30:26 he sent of the spoil unto the **e.** of 2205
2Sa 3:17 communication with the **e.** of 2205
2Sa 5:3 the **e.** of Israel came to the king 2205
2Sa 12:17 the **e.** of his house arose, and went 2205
2Sa 17:4 Absalom well, and all the **e.** of 2205
2Sa 17:15 Absalom and the **e.** of Israel; 2205
2Sa 19:11 Speak unto the **e.** of Judah, saying, 2205
1Ki 8:1 Solomon assembled the **e.** of Israel, 2205
1Ki 8:3 And all the **e.** of Israel came, 2205
1Ki 20:7 king of Israel called all the **e.** of 2205
1Ki 20:8 And all the **e.** and all the people 2205
1Ki 21:8 and sent the letters unto the **e.** and 2205
1Ki 21:11 even the **e.** and the nobles who were 2205
2Ki 6:32 and the **e.** sat with him; 2205
2Ki 6:32 came to him, he said to the **e.**, 2205
2Ki 10:1 unto the rulers of Jezreel, to the **e.**, 2205
2Ki 10:5 the **e.** also, and the bringers up 2205
2Ki 19:2 and the **e.** of the priests, covered 2205
2Ki 23:1 gathered unto him all the **e.** of 2205
1Ch 11:3 Therefore came all the **e.** of Israel, 2205
1Ch 15:25 So David, and the **e.** of Israel, 2205
1Ch 21:16 Then David and the **e.** of Israel, 2205
2Ch 5:2 Then Solomon assembled the **e.** of 2205
2Ch 5:4 And all the **e.** of Israel came; 2205
2Ch 34:29 gathered together all the **e.** of 2205
Ezr 5:5 of their God was upon the **e.** of 7868
Ezr 5:9 Then asked we those **e.**, and said 7868
Ezr 6:7 and the **e.** of the Jews build this 7868
Ezr 6:8 what ye shall do to the **e.** of these 7868
Ezr 6:14 And the **e.** of the Jews builded, 7868
Ezr 10:8 counsel of the princes and the **e.**, 2205
Ezr 10:14 with them the **e.** of every city, 2205
Ps 107:32 praise him in the assembly of the **e.** 2205
Pr 31:23 when he sitteth among the **e.** of the 2205
Isa 37:2 and the **e.** of the priests covered 2205
Jer 26:17 Then rose up certain of the **e.** of 2205
Jer 29:1 Jerusalem unto the residue of the **e.** 2205
La 1:19 my priests and mine **e.** gave up the 2205
La 2:10 The **e.** of the daughter of Zion 2205
La 4:16 priests, they favoured not the **e.** 2205
La 5:12 the faces of **e.** were not honoured. 2205
La 5:14 The **e.** have ceased from the gate, 2205
Eze 8:1 and the **e.** of Judah sat before me, 2205
Eze 14:1 Then came certain of the **e.** of 2205
Eze 20:1 certain of the **e.** of Israel came to 2205
Eze 20:3 of man speak unto the **e.** of Israel, 2205
Joe 1:14 assembly, gather the **e.** and all the 2205
Joe 2:16 congregation, assemble the **e.**, 2205
Mt 15:2 transgress the tradition of the **e.**? *4245*
Mt 16:21 suffer many things of the **e.** and *4245*
Mt 21:23 and the **e.** of the people came unto *4245*
Mt 26:3 scribes, and the **e.** of the people, *4245*
Mt 26:47 chief priests and **e.** of the people *4245*
Mt 26:57 scribes and the **e.** were assembled. *4245*
Mt 26:59 the chief priests, and **e.**, and all *4245*
Mt 27:1 chief priests and **e.** of the people *4245*
Mt 27:3 silver to the chief priests and **e.**, *4245*
Mt 27:12 accused of the chief priests and **e.**, *4245*
Mt 27:20 the chief priests and **e.** persuaded *4245*
Mt 27:41 with the scribes and **e.**, said, *4245*
Mt 28:12 they were assembled with the **e.**, *4245*
Mk 7:3 holding the tradition of the **e.** *4245*
Mk 7:5 according to the tradition of the **e.**, *4245*
Mk 8:31 and be rejected of the **e.**, and of the *4245*
Mk 11:27 priests, and the scribes, and the **e.**, *4245*
Mk 14:43 priests and the scribes and the **e.** *4245*
Mk 14:53 priests and the **e.** and the scribes *4245*
Mk 15:1 with the **e.** and scribes and the *4245*
Lu 7:3 he sent unto him the **e.** of the Jews, *4245*
Lu 9:22 **and be rejected of the e. and chief** *4245*
Lu 20:1 scribes came upon him with the **e.**, *4245*
Lu 22:52 captains of the temple, and the **e.**, *4245*
Lu 22:66 the **e.** of the people and the chief *4244*
Ac 4:5 that their rulers, and **e.**, and *4245*
Ac 4:8 of the people, and **e.** of Israel, *4245*
Ac 4:23 chief priests and **e.** had said unto *4245*
Ac 6:12 the people, and the **e.**, and the *4245*
Ac 11:30 and sent it to the **e.** by the hands *4245*
Ac 14:23 ordained them **e.** in every church, *4245*
Ac 15:2 unto the apostles and **e.** about this *4245*
Ac 15:4 and of the apostles and **e.**, and they *4245*
Ac 15:6 And the apostles and **e.** came *4245*
Ac 15:22 Then pleased it the apostles and **e.**, *4245*
Ac 15:23 The apostles and **e.** and brethren *4245*
Ac 16:4 were ordained of the apostles and **e.** *4245*
Ac 20:17 and called the **e.** of the church. *4245*
Ac 21:18 and all the **e.** were present. *4245*
Ac 22:5 and all the estate of the **e.**: *4244*
Ac 23:14 came to the chief priests and **e.**, *4245*
Ac 24:1 high priest descended with the **e.**, *4245*
Ac 25:15 the chief priests and the **e.** of the *4245*
1Ti 5:17 Let the **e.** that rule well be counted *4245*
Tit 1:5 ordain **e.** in every city, as I had *4245*
Heb 11:2 For by it the **e.** obtained a good *4245*
Jas 5:14 let him call for the **e.** of the church; *4245*
1Pe 5:1 The **e.** which are among you I *4245*
Re 4:4 I saw four and twenty **e.** sitting, *4245*
Re 4:10 The four and twenty **e.** fall down *4245*
Re 5:5 And one of the **e.** saith unto me, *4245*
Re 5:6 and in the midst of the **e.**, *4245*
Re 5:8 and four and twenty **e.** fell down *4245*
Re 5:11 and the beasts and the **e.**: *4245*
Re 5:14 the four and twenty **e.** fell down *4245*
Re 7:11 and about the **e.** and the four beasts, *4245*
Re 7:13 And one of the **e.** answered, saying *4245*
Re 11:16 the four and twenty **e.**, which sat *4245*
Re 14:3 before the four beasts, and the **e.**: *4245*
Re 19:4 the four and twenty **e.** and the four *4245*

ELDEST
Ge 24:2 Abraham said unto his **e.** servant 2205
Ge 27:1 he called Esau his **e.** son, and 1419
Ge 27:15 took goodly raiment of her **e.** son 1419
Ge 44:12 began at the **e.**, and left at the 1419
Nu 1:20 children of Reuben, Israel's **e.** son. 1060
Nu 26:5 Reuben, the **e.** son of Israel: the 1060
1Sa 17:13 And the three **e.** sons of Jesse 1419
1Sa 17:14 and the three **e.** followed Saul. 1419
1Sa 17:28 Eliab his **e.** brother heard when he 1419
2Ki 3:27 Then he took his **e.** son that 1060
2Ch 22:1 of men...had slain all the **e.** 7223
Job 1:13, 18 wine in their **e.** brother's 1060
Joh 8:9 beginning at the **e.**, even unto the *4245*

ELEAD (e'-le-ad)
1Ch 7:21 and Ezer, and **E.**, whom the men 496

ELEALEH (el-e-a'-leh)
Nu 32:3 Heshbon, and **E.**, and Shebam, 500
Nu 32:37 of Reuben built Heshbon, and **E.**, 500
Isa 15:4 And Heshbon shall cry, and **E.**: 500
Isa 16:9 with my tears, O Heshbon, and **E.**: 500
Jer 48:34 the cry of Heshbon even unto **E.**, 500

ELEASAH (el-e'-a-sah) See also ELASAH.
1Ch 2:39 begat Helez, and Helez begat **E.**, 501
1Ch 2:40 **E.** begat Sisamai, and Sisamai 501
1Ch 8:37 Rapha was his son, **E.** his son, 501
1Ch 9:43 Rephaiah his son, **E.** his son 501

ELEAZAR (el-e-a'-zar)
Ex 6:23 bare him Nadab, and Abihu, **E.**, 499
Ex 6:25 **E.** Aaron's son took him one of the 499
Ex 28:1 even Aaron, Nadab and Abihu, **E.** 499
Le 10:6 Moses said unto Aaron, and unto **E.** 499
Le 10:12 spake unto Aaron, and unto **E.** 499
Le 10:16 and he was angry with **E.** and 499
Nu 3:2 Nadab the firstborn, and Abihu, **E.**, 499
Nu 3:4 **E.** and Ithamar ministered in the 499
Nu 3:32 **E.** the son of Aaron the priest shall 499
Nu 4:16 to the office of **E.** the son of Aaron 499
Nu 16:37 Speak unto **E.** the son of Aaron the 499
Nu 16:39 **E.** the priest took the brazen 499
Nu 19:3 ye shall give her unto **E.** the priest, 499
Nu 19:4 **E.** the priest shall take of her blood 499
Nu 20:25 Take Aaron and **E.** his son, and 499
Nu 20:26, 28 garments, and put them upon **E.** 499
Nu 20:28 Moses and **E.** came down from the 499
Nu 25:7 when Phinehas, the son of **E.**, the 499
Nu 25:11 Phinehas, the son of **E.**, the son of 499
Nu 26:1 Lord spake unto Moses and unto **E.** 499
Nu 26:3 **E.** the priest spake with them in 499
Nu 26:60 was born Nadab, and Abihu, **E.** 499
Nu 26:63 Moses and **E.** the priest, who 499
Nu 27:2 stood before Moses, and before **E.** 499
Nu 27:19 And set him before **E.** the priest, 499
Nu 27:21 he shall stand before **E.** the priest, 499
Nu 27:22 took Joshua, and set him before **E.** 499

Nu 31:6 them and Phinehas the son of E. ... 499
Nu 31:12 and the spoil, unto Moses, and E. ... 499
Nu 31:13 Moses, and E. the priest, and all ... 499
Nu 31:21 E. the priest said unto the men of ... 499
Nu 31:26 thou, and E. the priest, and the ... 499
Nu 31:29 it of their half, and give it unto E. ... 499
Nu 31:31 Moses and E. the priest did as the ... 499
Nu 31:41 the Lord's heave offering, unto E. ... 499
Nu 31:51, 54 Moses and E. the priest took the ... 499
Nu 32:2 E. the priest, and unto the princes ... 499
Nu 32:28 Moses commanded E. the priest, ... 499
Nu 34:17 E. the priest, and Joshua the son ... 499
De 10:6 E. his son ministered in the priest's ... 499
Jos 14:1 in the land of Canaan, which E. the ... 499
Jos 17:4 they came near before E. the priest, ... 499
Jos 19:51 are the inheritances, which E. the ... 499
Jos 21:1 the fathers of the Levites unto E. ... 499
Jos 22:13 of Gilead, Phinehas the son of E. ... 499
Jos 22:31 the son of E. the priest said unto ... 499
Jos 22:32 the son of E. the priest, and the ... 499
Jos 24:33 E. the son of Aaron died; and they ... 499
Jg 20:28 son of E., the son of Aaron, stood ... 499
1Sa 7:1 sanctified E. his son to keep the ark ... 499
2Sa 23:9 after him was E. the son of Dodo ... 499
1Ch 6:3 of Aaron; Nadab, and Abihu, E., ... 499
1Ch 6:4 E. begat Phinehas, Phinehas begat ... 499
1Ch 6:50 these are the sons of Aaron, E. his ... 499
1Ch 9:20 Phinehas the son of E. was the ... 499
1Ch 11:12 after him was E. the son of Dodo, ... 499
1Ch 23:21 The sons of Mahli; E., and Kish ... 499
1Ch 23:22 E. died, and had no sons, ... 499
1Ch 24:1 of Aaron; Nadab, and Abihu, E., ... 499
1Ch 24:2 therefore E. and Ithamar executed ... 499
1Ch 24:3 both Zadok of the sons of E., and ... 499
1Ch 24:4 chief men found of the sons of E. ... 499
1Ch 24:4 Among the sons of E. there were ... 499
1Ch 24:5 were of the sons of E., and of the ... 499
1Ch 24:6 household being taken for E., ... 499
1Ch 24:28 of Mahli came E., who had no sons. ... 499
Ezr 7:5 the son of E., the son of Aaron the ... 499
Ezr 8:33 and with him was E. the son of ... 499
Ezr 10:25 Miamin, and E., and Malchijah ... 499
Ne 12:42 Shemaiah, and E., and Uzzi, ... 499
Mt 1:15 And Eliud begat E.; and E. begat ... *1648*

ELECT See also ELECTED; ELECT'S.
Isa 42:1 e., in whom my soul delighteth; ... 972
Isa 45:4 sake, and Israel mine e. ... 972
Isa 65:9 mine e. shall inherit it, and my ... 972
Isa 65:22 mine e. shall long enjoy the work ... 972
Mt 24:24 **they shall deceive the very e.** ... *1588*
Mt 24:31 **and shall gather together his e.** ... *1588*
Mk 13:22 **if it were possible, even the e.** ... *1588*
Mk 13:27 **and shall gather together his e.** ... *1588*
Lu 18:7 **shall not God avenge his own e.,** ... *1588*
Ro 8:33 any thing to the charge of God's e.? ... *1588*
Col 3:12 Put on therefore, as the e. of God, ... *1588*
1Ti 5:21 Lord Jesus Christ, and the e. angels, .. *1588*
Tit 1:1 according to the faith of God's e., ... *1588*
1Pe 1:2 E. according to the foreknowledge ... *1588*
1Pe 2:6 a chief corner stone, e., precious: ... *1588*
2Jo 1 The elder unto the e. lady and her ... *1588*
2Jo 13 The children of thy e. sister greet ... *1588*

ELECTED
1Pe 5:13 e. together with you, saluteth you; ... *4899*

ELECTION
Ro 9:11 the purpose of God according to e. ... *1589*
Ro 11:5 according to the e. of grace ... *1589*
Ro 11:7 the e. hath obtained it, and the rest ... *1589*
Ro 11:28 as touching the e., they are beloved ... *1589*
1Th 1:4 brethren beloved, your e. of God. ... *1589*
2Pe 1:10 make your calling and e. sure: ... *1589*

ELECT'S
Mt 24:22 **for the e. sake those days shall be** ... *1588*
Mk 13:20 **for the e. sake, whom he hath** ... *1588*
2Ti 2:10 endure all things for the e. sakes, ... *1588*

EL-ELOHE-ISRAEL (el-el-o″-he-iz′-rah-el)
Ge 33:20 there an altar, and called it E. ... 415

ELEMENTS
Ga 4:3 in bondage under the e. of the ... *4747*
Ga 4:9 to the weak and beggarly e., ... *4747*
2Pe 3:10 the e. shall melt with fervent heat, ... *4747*
2Pe 3:12 the e. shall melt with fervent heat? ... *4747*

ELEPH (e′-lef)
Jos 18:28 And Zelah, E., and Jebusi which is ... 507

ELEVEN
Ge 32:22 took....his e. sons, and passed ... 259,6240
Ge 37:9 and the moon and the e. stars ... 259,6240
Ex 26:7 e. curtains shalt thou make. ... 6249,6240
Ex 26:8 e. curtains shall be all of one ... 6249,6240
Ex 36:14 e. curtains he made them. ... 6249,6240
Ex 36:15 the e. curtains were of one ... 6249,6240
Nu 29:20 on the third day e. bullocks, ... 6249,6240
De 1:2 e. days' journey from Horeb ... 259,6240
Jos 15:51 e. cities with their villages ... 259,6240
Jg 16:5 one of us e. hundred pieces of ... 505,3967
Jg 17:2 e. hundred shekels of silver ... 505,3967
Jg 17:3 restored the e. hundred shekels ... 505,3967
2Ki 23:36 reign; and he reigned e. years ... 259,6240
2Ki 24:18 reign, and he reigned e. years ... 259,6240
2Ch 36:5, 11 and he reigned e. years in ... 259,6240
Jer 52:1 reigned e. years in Jerusalem. ... 259,6240
Eze 40:49 and the breadth e. cubits; ... 6249,6240
Mt 28:16 Then the e. disciples went away ... *1733*
Mk 16:14 he appeared unto the e. as they ... *1733*
Lu 24:9 told all these things unto the e., ... *1733*
Lu 24:33 found the e. gathered together, ... *1733*
Ac 1:26 was numbered with the e. apostles. ... *1733*
Ac 2:14 Peter, standing up with the e., ... *1733*

ELEVEN HUNDRED See also ELEVEN and HUNDRED.

ELEVENTH
Nu 7:72 the e. day of Pagiel...offered: ... 6249,6240
De 1:3 in the fortieth year, in the e. ... 6249,6240
1Ki 6:38 in the e. year, in the month ... 259,6240
2Ki 9:29 in the e. year of Joram the ... 6240
2Ki 25:2 the e. year of king Zedekiah. ... 6249,6240
1Ch 12:13 the tenth, Machbanai the e. ... 6240
1Ch 24:12 The e. to Eliashib, the twelfth ... 6240
1Ch 25:18 The e. to Azareel, he, his sons, ... 6240
1Ch 27:14 The e. captain for the e. month ... 6240
Jer 1:3 of the e. year of Zedekiah the ... 6240
Jer 39:2 in the e. year of Zedekiah, in ... 6240
Jer 52:5 was besieged unto the e. year ... 6240
Eze 26:1 in the e. year, in the first day ... 6240
Eze 30:20 came to pass in the e. year, ... 259,6240
Eze 31:1 the e. year, in the third month, ... 259,6240
Zec 1:7 twentieth day of...e. month, ... 6249,6240
Mt 20:6 **about the e. hour he went out,** ... *1734*
Mt 20:9 **that were hired about the e. hour,** . *1734*
Re 21:20 the e., a jacinth; the twelfth, an ... *1734*

ELHANAN (el-ha′-nan)
2Sa 21:19 where E. the son of Jaare-oregim, ... 445
2Sa 23:24 E. the son of Dodo of Bethlehem, ... 445
1Ch 11:26 brother of Joab, E. the son of Dodo ... 445
1Ch 20:5 E. the son of Jair slew Lahmi ... 445

ELI (e′-li) See also ELI'S; ELOI.
1Sa 1:3 sons of E., Hophni and Phinehas, ... 5941
1Sa 1:9 now E. the priest sat upon a seat ... 5941
1Sa 1:12 Lord, that E. marked her mouth. ... 5941
1Sa 1:13 E. thought she had been drunken. ... 5941
1Sa 1:14 And E. said unto her, How long ... 5941
1Sa 1:17 Then E. answered and said, Go in ... 5941
1Sa 1:25 and brought the child to E. ... 5941
1Sa 2:11 minister unto the Lord before E. ... 5941
1Sa 2:12 sons of E. were sons of Belial; ... 5941
1Sa 2:20 And E. blessed Elkanah and his ... 5941
1Sa 2:22 Now E. was very old, and heard ... 5941
1Sa 2:27 a man of God unto E., and said ... 5941
1Sa 3:1 ministered unto the Lord before E. .. 5941
1Sa 3:2 when E. was laid down in his place, .. 5941
1Sa 3:5 And he ran unto E., and said, Here ... 5941
1Sa 3:6 And Samuel arose and went to E., ... 5941
1Sa 3:8 he arose and went to E., and said, ... 5941
1Sa 3:8 And E. perceived that the Lord had ... 5941
1Sa 3:9 E. said unto Samuel, Go, lie down: ... 5941
1Sa 3:12 I will perform against E. all things ... 5941
1Sa 3:14 I have sworn unto the house of E., ... 5941
1Sa 3:15 Samuel feared to show E. the vision .. 5941
1Sa 3:16 Then E. called Samuel, and said, ... 5941
1Sa 4:4 sons of E., Hophni and Phinehas, ... 5941
1Sa 4:11 E., Hophni and Phinehas, were slain .. 5941
1Sa 4:13 E. sat upon a seat by the wayside ... 5941
1Sa 4:14 E. heard the noise of the crying, ... 5941
1Sa 4:14 man came in hastily, and told E. ... 5941
1Sa 4:15 Now E. was ninety and eight ... 5941
1Sa 4:16 And the man said unto E., I am he ... 5941
1Sa 14:3 son of Phinehas, the son of E., ... 5941
1Ki 2:27 spake concerning the house of E. ... 5941
Mt 27:46 **E., E., lama sabachthani? that is** ... *2241*

ELIAB (e′-le-ab) See also ELIAB'S; ELIEL.
Nu 1:9 Of Zebulun; E. the son of Helon ... 446
Nu 2:7 E. the son of Helon shall be captain ... 446
Nu 7:24 the third day E. the son of Helon, ... 446
Nu 7:29 the offering of E. the son of Helon ... 446
Nu 10:16 of the children of Zebulun was E. ... 446
Nu 16:1 Dathan and Abiram, the sons of E., ... 446
Nu 16:12 Dathan and Abiram, the sons of E. ... 446
Nu 26:8 And the sons of Pallu; E. ... 446
Nu 26:9 the sons of E.; Nemuel, and Dathan, ... 446
De 11:6 the sons of E., the son of Reuben: ... 446
1Sa 16:6 he looked on E., and said, Surely ... 446
1Sa 17:13 were E. the firstborn, and next unto ... 446
1Sa 17:28 E. his eldest brother heard when ... 446
1Ch 2:13 And Jesse begat his firstborn E., ... 446
1Ch 6:27 E. his son, Jeroham his son, ... 446
1Ch 12:9 Obadiah the second, E. the third, ... 446
1Ch 15:18 Jehiel, and unni, E., and Benaiah, ... 446
1Ch 15:20 Unni, and E., and Maaseiah, ... 446
1Ch 16:5 Mattithiah, and E., and Benaiah, ... 446
2Ch 11:18 Abihail the daughter of E. the son ... 446

ELIAB'S (e′-le-abs)
1Sa 17:28 E. anger was kindled against ... 446

ELIADA (e′-li′-a-dah) See also ELIADAH.
2Sa 5:16 Elishama, and E., and Eliphalet. ... 450
1Ch 3:8 E., and Eliphelet, nine ... 450
2Ch 17:17 E. a mighty man of valour, ... 450

ELIADAH (e-li′-a-dah) See also ELIADA.
1Ki 11:23 Rezon the son of E., which fled ... 450

ELIAH (e-li′-ah) see also ELIJAH.
1Ch 8:27 Jaresiah, and E., and Zichri, ... 452
Ezr 10:26 and Abdi, and Jeremoth, and E. ... 452

ELIAHBA (e-li′-ah-bah)
2Sa 23:32 E. the Shaalbonite, of the sons of ... 455
1Ch 11:33 the Baharumite, E. the Shaalbonite, ... 455

ELIAKIM (e-li′-a-kim) See also JEHOIAKIM.
2Ki 18:18 there came out to them E. the son ... 471
2Ki 18:26 Then said E. the son of Hilkiah, ... 471
2Ki 18:37 Then came E. the son of Hilkiah, ... 471
2Ki 19:2 And he sent E., which was over the ... 471
2Ki 23:34 Pharaoh-nechoh made E. the son of ... 471
2Ch 36:4 of Egypt made E. his brother king ... 471
Ne 12:41 the priests; E., Maaseiah, Miniamin, ... 471
Isa 22:20 I will call my servant E. the son of ... 471
Isa 36:3 Then came forth unto him E., ... 471
Isa 36:11 Then said E., and Shebna and Joah ... 471
Isa 36:22 Then came E., the son of Hilkiah, ... 471
Isa 37:2 And he sent E., who was over the ... 471
Mt 1:13 Abiud begat E.; and E. begat Azor; ... *1662*
Lu 3:30 Jonan, which was the son of E., ... *1662*

ELIAM (e′-le-am)
2Sa 11:3 Bath-sheba, the daughter of E., ... 463
2Sa 23:34 E. the son of Ahithophel the ... 463

ELIAS (e-li′-as) see also ELIJAH.
Mt 11:14 **is Elias, which was for to come.** ... *2243*
Mt 16:14 some, E.; and others, Jeremias, ... *2243*
Mt 17:3 Moses and E. talking with him. ... *2243*
Mt 17:4 and one for Moses, and one for E. ... *2243*
Mt 17:10 scribes that E. must first come? ... *2243*
Mt 17:11 **E. truly shall first come, and** ... *2243*
Mt 17:12 **unto you, That E. is come already,** *2243*
Mt 27:47 This man calleth for E. ... *2243*
Mt 27:49 whether E. will come to save him. ... *2243*
Mk 6:15 Others said, That it is E. ... *2243*
Mk 8:28 but some say, E.; and others, ... *2243*
Mk 9:4 unto them E. with Moses: ... *2243*
Mk 9:5 and one for Moses, and one for E. ... *2243*
Mk 9:11 that E. must first come? ... *2243*
Mk 9:12 **E. verily cometh first, and** ... *2243*
Mk 9:13 **unto you, That E. is indeed come,** . *2243*
Mk 15:35 Behold, he calleth E. ... *2243*
Mk 15:36 whether E. will come to take him ... *2243*
Lu 1:17 in the spirit and power of E., ... *2243*
Lu 4:25 **were in Israel in the days of E.,** ... *2243*
Lu 4:26 **But unto none of them was E.** ... *2243*
Lu 9:8 of some, that E. had appeared; ... *2243*
Lu 9:19 but some say, E.; and others say, ... *2243*
Lu 9:30 men, which were Moses and E.: ... *2243*
Lu 9:33 and one for Moses, and one for E.: ... *2243*

Lu 9:54 consume them, even as **E.** did? *2243*
Joh 1:21 What then? Art thou **E.**? And he *2243*
Joh 1:25 nor **E.**. neither that prophet? *2243*
Ro 11:2 what the scripture saith of **E.**? *2243*
Jas 5:17 **E.** was a man subject to like *2243*

ELIASAPH (e-li'-a-saf)
Nu 1:14 Of Gad; **E.** the son of Deuel 460
Nu 2:14 of the sons of Gad shall be **E.** 460
Nu 3:24 Gershonites shall be **E.** the son of 460
Nu 7:42 the sixth day **E.** the son of Deuel, 460
Nu 7:47 the offering of **E.** the son of Deuel. 460
Nu 10:20 tribe of the children of Gad was **E.** 460

ELIASHIB (e-li'-a-shib)
1Ch 3:24 Hodaiah, and **E.**, and Pelaiah, 475
1Ch 24:12 eleventh to **E.**, the twelfth to Jakim, 475
Ezr 10:6 chamber of Johanan the son of **E.**: 475
Ezr 10:24 Of the singers also; **E.**: 475
Ezr 10:27 Elioenai, **E.**, Mattaniah, 475
Ezr 10:36 Vaniah, Meremoth, **E.**, 475
Ne 3:1 Then **E.** the high priest rose up 475
Ne 3:20 unto the door of the house of **E.** 475
Ne 3:21 from the door of the house of **E.** 475
Ne 3:21 even to the end of the house of **E.**. 475
Ne 12:10 Joiakim also begat **E.**, 475
Ne 12:10 and **E.** begat Joiada, 475
Ne 12:22 Levites in the days of **E.**, Joiada, 475
Ne 12:23 the days of Johanan the son of **E.**. 475
Ne 13:4 **E.** the priest, having the oversight 475
Ne 13:7 the evil that **E.** did for Tobiah, 475
Ne 13:28 the son of **E.** the high priest, was 475

ELIATHAH (e-li'-a-thah)
1Ch 25:4 Hanani, **E.**, Giddalti, 448
1Ch 25:27 The twentieth to **E.**, he, his sons, 448

ELIDAD (e-li'-dad)
Nu 34:21 of Benjamin, **E.** the son of Chislon 449

ELIEL (e'-le-el) See also ELIAH.
1Ch 5:24 Epher, and Ishi, and **E.**, and Azriel, 447
1Ch 6:34 the son of Jeroham, the son of **E.**, 447
1Ch 8:20 And Elienai, and Zilthai, and **E.**, 447
1Ch 8:22 And Ishpan, and Heber, and **E.**, 447
1Ch 11:46 **E.** the Mahjavite, and Jeribai 447
1Ch 11:47 **E.**, and Obed, and Jasiel the 447
1Ch 12:11 Attai the sixth, **E.** the seventh, 447
1Ch 15:9 **E.** the chief, and his brethren 447
1Ch 15:11 Shemaiah, and **E.**, and Amminadab, 447
2Ch 31:13 Jozabad, and **E.**, and Ismachiah, 447

ELIENAI (e-li-e'-nahee)
1Ch 8:20 **E.**, and Zilthai, and Eliel, 462

ELIEZER (e-li-e'-zur)
Ge 15:2 the steward of my house is this **E.** 461
Ex 18:4 the name of the other was **E.**; 461
1Ch 7:8 Zemira, and Joash, and **E.**, 461
1Ch 15:24 Benaiah, and **E.**, the priests, did 461
1Ch 23:15 of Moses were, Gershom, and **E.** 461
1Ch 23:17 sons of **E.** were, Rehabiah the chief. 461
1Ch 23:17 And **E.** had none other sons; 461
1Ch 26:25 brethren by **E.**; Rehabiah his son, 461
1Ch 27:16 the ruler of the Reubenites was **E.** 461
2Ch 20:37 Then **E.** the son of Dodavah of 461
Ezr 8:16 Then sent I for **E.**, for Ariel, 461
Ezr 10:18 Maaseiah, and **E.**, and Jarib, 461
Ezr 10:23 Pethahiah, Judah, and **E.** 461
Ezr 10:31 of the sons of Harim, **E.**, Ishijah, 461
Lu 3:29 which was the son of **E.**, *1663*

ELIHOENAI (e-li-ho-e'-nahee) See also ELIOENAI.
Ezr 8:4 **E.** the son of Zerahiah, and with 454

ELIHOREPH (e-li-ho'-ref)
1Ki 4:3 **E.** and Ahiah, the sons of Shisha, 456

ELIHU (e-li'-hew)
1Sa 1:1 the son of **E.**, the son of Tohu, 453
1Ch 12:20 Jozabad, and **E.**, and Zilthai, 453
1Ch 26:7 strong men, **E.**, and Semachiah, 453
1Ch 27:18 **E.**, one of the brethren of David: 453
Job 32:2 Then was kindled the wrath of **E.** 453
Job 32:4 **E.** had waited till Job had spoken, 453
Job 32:5 **E.** saw that there was no answer 453
Job 32:6 **E.** the son of Barachel the Buzite 453
Job 34:1 **E.** answered and said, 453
Job 35:1 **E.** spake moreover, and said, 453
Job 36:1 **E.** also proceeded, and said, 453

ELIJAH (e-li'-jah) See also ELIAH; ELIAS.
1Ki 17:1 **E.** the Tishbite, who was of the 452
1Ki 17:13 **E.** said unto her, Fear not; go and 452
1Ki 17:15 did according to the saying of **E.**: 452
1Ki 17:16 of the Lord, which he spake by **E.** 452
1Ki 17:18 she said unto **E.**, What have I to do 452
1Ki 17:22 the Lord heard the voice of **E.**; and 452
1Ki 17:23 **E.** took the child, and brought him 452
1Ki 17:23 and **E.** said, See, thy son liveth. 452
1Ki 17:24 the woman said to **E.**, Now by this 452
1Ki 18:1 Lord came to **E.** in the third year, 452
1Ki 18:2 **E.** went to shew himself unto Ahab 452
1Ki 18:7 was in the way, behold, **E.** met him: 452
1Ki 18:7 Art thou that my lord **E.**? 452
1Ki 18:8 go, tell thy lord, Behold, **E.** is here. 452
1Ki 18:11 Go, tell thy lord, Behold, **E.** is here. 452
1Ki 18:14 Go, tell thy lord, Behold, **E.** is here: 452
1Ki 18:15 **E.** said, As the Lord of hosts liveth, 452
1Ki 18:16 and Ahab went to meet **E.**. 452
1Ki 18:17 it came to pass, when Ahab saw **E.**, 452
1Ki 18:21 **E.** came unto all the people, and 452
1Ki 18:22 Then said **E.** unto the people, I, 452
1Ki 18:25 **E.** said unto the prophets of Baal, 452
1Ki 18:27 **E.** mocked them, and said, Cry 452
1Ki 18:30 **E.** said unto all the people, Come 452
1Ki 18:31 **E.** took twelve stones, according to 452
1Ki 18:36 **E.** the prophet came near, and said, 452
1Ki 18:40 And **E.** said unto them, Take the 452
1Ki 18:40 **E.** brought them down to the brook 452
1Ki 18:41 **E.** said unto Ahab, Get thee up, eat 452
1Ki 18:42 **E.** went up to the top of Carmel; 452
1Ki 18:46 the hand of the Lord was on **E.**; 452
1Ki 19:1 told Jezebel all that **E.** had done, 452
1Ki 19:2 Jezebel sent a messenger unto **E.**, 452
1Ki 19:9 unto him, What doest thou here, **E.**? 452
1Ki 19:13 it was so, when **E.** heard it, that he 452
1Ki 19:13 and said, What doest thou here, **E.**? 452
1Ki 19:19 and **E.** passed by him, and cast his 452
1Ki 19:20 he left the oxen, and ran after **E.**, 452
1Ki 19:21 Then he arose, and went after **E.**, 452
1Ki 21:17 the Lord came to **E.** the Tishbite, 452
1Ki 21:20 Ahab said to **E.**, Hast thou found 452
1Ki 21:28 word of the Lord came to **E.** the 452
2Ki 1:3 said to **E.** the Tishbite, Arise, go up 452
2Ki 1:4 shalt surely die. And **E.** departed. 452
2Ki 1:8 And he said, It is **E.** the Tishbite. 452
2Ki 1:10 **E.** answered and said to the captain 452
2Ki 1:12 **E.** answered and said unto them, 452
2Ki 1:13 came and fell on his knees before **E.**, 452
2Ki 1:15 the angel of the Lord said unto **E.**, 452
2Ki 1:17 of the Lord which **E.** had spoken. 452
2Ki 2:1 Lord would take up **E.** into heaven 452
2Ki 2:1 **E.** went with Elisha from Gilgal. 452
2Ki 2:2 **E.** said unto, Elisha, Tarry here, I 452
2Ki 2:4 **E.** said unto him, Elisha, tarry here, 452
2Ki 2:6 **E.** said unto him, Tarry, I pray thee, 452
2Ki 2:8 **E.** took his mantle, and wrapped it 452
2Ki 2:9 **E.** said unto Elisha, Ask what I 452
2Ki 2:11 **E.** went up by a whirlwind into 452
2Ki 2:13 He took up also the mantle of **E.** 452
2Ki 2:14 And he took the mantle of **E.** that 452
2Ki 2:14 Where is the Lord God of **E.**? 452
2Ki 2:15 The spirit of **E.** doth rest on Elisha 452
2Ki 3:11 poured water on the hand of **E.**. 452
2Ki 9:36 which he spake by his servant **E.** the 452
2Ki 10:10 which he spake by his servant **E.** 452
2Ki 10:17 of the Lord, which he spake to **E.** 452
2Ch 21:12 there came a writing to him from **E.** 452
Ezr 10:21 Maaseiah, and **E.**, and Shemaiah, 452
Mal 4:5 I will send you **E.** the prophet 452

ELIKA (e-li'-kah)
2Sa 23:25 the Harodite, **E.** the Harodite, 470

ELIM (e'-lim) See also BEER-ELIM.
Ex 15:27 they came to **E.**, where were twelve 362
Ex 16:1 they took their journey from **E.**, 362
Ex 16:1 Sin, which is between **E.**, and Sinai, 362
Nu 33:9 from Marah, and came unto **E.**: 362
Nu 33:9 in **E.** were twelve fountains of water, 362
Nu 33:10 And they removed from **E.**, and 362

ELIMELECH (e-lim'-e-lek) See also ELIMELECH'S.
Ru 1:2 And the name of the man was **E.**, 458
Ru 1:3 And **E.** Naomi's husband died; 458
Ru 2:1 man of wealth, of the family of **E.**; 458
Ru 2:3 Boaz, who was of the kindred of **E.**. 458

ELIMELECH'S (e-lim'-e-leks)
Ru 4:3 of land, which was our brother **E.**: 458
Ru 4:9 that I have bought all that was **E.**, 458

ELIOENAI (e-li-o-e'-nahee) See also ELIHOENAI.
1Ch 3:23 sons of Neariah: **E.**, and Hezekiah, 454
1Ch 3:24 the sons of **E.** were, Hodaiah, and 454
1Ch 4:36 **E.**, and Jaakobah, and Jeshohaiah, 454
1Ch 7:8 Eliezer, and **E.**, and Omri, 454
1Ch 26:3 Jehohanan the sixth, **E.** the 454
Ezr 10:22 the sons of Pashur; **E.**, Maaseiah, 454
Ezr 10:27 of the sons of Zattu; **E.**, Eliashib, 454
Ne 12:41 Michaiah, **E.**, Zechariah, and 454

ELIPHAL (el'-i-fal)
1Ch 11:35 Sacar the Haraite, **E.** the son of Ur, 465

ELIPHALET (e-lif'-a-let) See also ELIPHELET; ELPALET.
2Sa 5:16 Elishama, and Eliada, and **E.**. 467
1Ch 4:7 Elishama, and Beeliada, and **E.**. 467

ELIPHAZ (el'-if-az)
Ge 36:4 And Adah bare to Esau **E.**; 464
Ge 36:10 **E.** the son of Adah the wife of Esau, 464
Ge 36:11 the sons of **E.** were Teman, Omar, 464
Ge 36:12 Timna was concubine to **E.** Esau's 464
Ge 36:12 and she bare to **E.** Amalek: 464
Ge 36:15 sons of **E.** the firstborn son of Esau; 464
Ge 36:16 these are the dukes that came of **E.** 464
1Ch 1:35 The sons of Esau; **E.**, Reuel. 464
1Ch 1:36 The sons of **E.**; Teman, and Omar, 464
Job 2:11 **E.** the Temanite, and Bildad the 464
Job 4:1 **E.** the Temanite answered and said, 464
Job 15:1 Then answered **E.** the Temanite, 464
Job 22:1 **E.** the Temanite answered and said, 464
Job 42:7 the Lord said to **E.** the Temanite, 464
Job 42:9 So **E.** the Temanite and Bildad the 464

ELIPHELEH (e-lif'-e-leh)
1Ch 15:18 Mattithiah, and **E.**, and Mikneiah, 465
1Ch 15:21 **E.**, and Mikneiah, and Obed-edom, 465

ELIPHELET (e-lif'-e-let) See also ELIPHALET.
2Sa 23:34 **E.** the son of Ahasbai, the son of 467
1Ch 3:6 Ibhar also, and Elishama, and **E.**, 467
1Ch 3:8 Elishama, and Eliada, and **E.**, nine. 467
1Ch 8:39 Jehush the second, and **E.** the third. 467
Ezr 8:13 whose names are these, **E.**, Jeiel, 467
Ezr 10:33 Zabad, **E.**, Jeremai, Manasseh, 467

ELI'S (e'-lize)
1Sa 3:14 the iniquity of **E.** house shall not 5941

ELISABETH (e-liz'-a-beth) See also ELISABETH'S.
Lu 1:5 of Aaron, and her name was **E.**. *1665*
Lu 1:7 child, because that **E.** was barren, *1665*
Lu 1:13 thy wife **E.** shall bear thee a son, *1665*
Lu 1:24 those days his wife **E.** conceived, *1665*
Lu 1:36 behold, thy cousin **E.**, she hath also *1665*
Lu 1:40 house of Zacharias, and saluted **E.** *1665*
Lu 1:41 **E.** heard the salutation of Mary, *1665*
Lu 1:41 **E.** was filled with the Holy Ghost: *1665*

ELISABETH'S (e-liz'-a-beths)
Lu 1:57 Now **E.** full time came that she *1665*

ELISAEUS See ELISEUS.

ELISEUS (el-i-se'-us) See also ELISHA.
Lu 4:27 **in the time of E. the prophet;** *1666*

ELISHA (e-li'-shah) See also ELISEUS.
1Ki 19:16 **E.** the son Shaphat of Abel-meholah 477
1Ki 19:17 from the sword of Jehu shall **E.** slay. 477
1Ki 19:19 he departed thence, and found **E.** 477
2Ki 2:1 Elijah went with **E.** from Gilgal. 477
2Ki 2:2 Elijah said unto **E.**, Tarry here, 477
2Ki 2:2 **E.** said unto him, As the Lord 477
2Ki 2:3 were at Beth-el came forth to **E.**, 477
2Ki 2:4 Elijah said unto him, **E.**, tarry here, 477
2Ki 2:5 that were at Jericho came to **E.**, 477
2Ki 2:9 Elijah said unto **E.**, Ask what I 477
2Ki 2:9 **E.** said, I pray thee, let a double 477
2Ki 2:12 **E.** saw it, and he cried, My father, 477
2Ki 2:14 and thither: and **E.** went over. 477
2Ki 2:15 The spirit of Elijah doth rest on **E.** 477
2Ki 2:19 the men of the city said unto **E.**, 477
2Ki 2:22 to the saying of **E.** which he spake. 477
2Ki 3:11 Here is **E.** the son of Shaphat, 477
2Ki 3:13 **E.** said unto the king of Israel, What 477
2Ki 3:14 **E.** said, As the Lord of hosts liveth, 477
2Ki 4:1 of the sons of the prophets unto **E.**, 477

2Ki 4:2 **E.** said unto her, What shall I do........ 477
2Ki 4:8 on a day, that **E.** passed to Shunem,.... 477
2Ki 4:17 season that **E.** had said unto her, ... 477
2Ki 4:32 when **E.** was come into the house, ... 477
2Ki 4:38 **E.** came again to Gilgal: and there 477
2Ki 5:8 when **E.** the man of God had heard...... 477
2Ki 5:9 stood at the door of the house of **E.**.... 477
2Ki 5:10 **E.** sent a messenger unto him, ... 477
2Ki 5:20 Gehazi, the servant of **E.** the man....... 477
2Ki 5:25 **E.** said unto him, Whence comest......... 477
2Ki 6:1 sons of the prophets said unto **E.**, ... 477
2Ki 6:12 but **E.**, the prophet that is in Israel,..... 477
2Ki 6:17 **E.** prayed, and said, Lord, I pray 477
2Ki 6:17 and chariots of fire round about **E.**........ 477
2Ki 6:18 **E.** prayed unto the Lord, and said, ... 477
2Ki 6:18 according to the word of **E.**................ 477
2Ki 6:19 **E.** said unto them, This is not the 477
2Ki 6:20 **E.** said, Lord, open the eyes of these .. 477
2Ki 6:21 the king of Israel said unto **E.**,............ 477
2Ki 6:31 the head of **E.** the son of Shaphat........ 477
2Ki 6:32 **E.** sat in his house, and the elders......... 477
2Ki 7:1 **E.** said, Hear ye the word of the Lord; .477
2Ki 8:1 Then spake **E.** unto the woman,.......... 477
2Ki 8:4 the great things that **E.** hath done. 477
2Ki 8:5 is her son, whom **E.** restored to life. ... 477
2Ki 8:7 And **E.** came to Damascus; and.......... 477
2Ki 8:10 **E.** said unto him, Go, say unto him,...... 477
2Ki 8:13 **E.** answered, The Lord hath shewed.... 477
2Ki 8:14 So he departed from **E.**, and came......... 477
2Ki 8:14 said to him, What said **E.** to thee?....... 477
2Ki 9:1 **E.** the prophet called one of the.......... 477
2Ki 13:14 **E.** was fallen sick of his sickness......... 477
2Ki 13:15 **E.** said unto him, Take bow and.......... 477
2Ki 13:16 **E.** put his hands upon the king's.......... 477
2Ki 13:17 Then **E.** said, Shoot. And he shot........ 477
2Ki 13:20 And **E.** died, and they buried him. 477
2Ki 13:21 the man into the sepulchre of **E.**: 477
2Ki 13:21 down, and touched the bones of **E.**,..... 477

ELISHAH (e-li'-shah)
Ge 10:4 the sons of Javan; **E.**, and Tarshish,.... 473
1Ch 1:7 the sons of Javan; **E.**, and Tarshish,..... 473
Eze 27:7 blue and purple from the isles of **E.** 473

ELISHAMA (e-lish'-a-mah) See also ELISHUA.
Nu 1:10 Ephraim; **E.** the son of Ammihud:........ 476
Nu 2:18 of the sons of Ephraim shall be **E.**........ 476
Nu 7:48 seventh day **E.** the son of Ammihud,.... 476
Nu 7:53 this was the offering of **E.** the son of... 476
Nu 10:22 over his host was **E.** the son of......... 476
2Sa 5:16 **E.**, and Eliada, and Eliphalet.............. 476
2Ki 25:25 the son of **E.**, of the seed royal, ... 476
1Ch 2:41 Jekamiah, and Jekamiah begat **E.**.. 476
1Ch 3:6 Ibhar also, and **E.**, and Eliphalet,......... 476
1Ch 3:8 **E.**, and Eliada, and Eliphelet, nine. 476
1Ch 7:26 Ammihud his son, **E.** his son, ... 476
1Ch 14:7 **E.**, and Beeliada, and Eliphalet............ 476
2Ch 17:8 and with them **E.** and Jehoram, ... 476
Jer 36:12 even **E.** the scribe, and Delaiah........... 476
Jer 36:20 in the chamber of **E.** the scribe, ... 476
Jer 36:21 out of **E.** the scribe's chamber. 476
Jer 41:1 the son of Nethaniah the son of **E.**, ... 476

ELISHAPHAT (e-lish'-a-fat)
2Ch 23:1 and **E.** the son of Zichri, into............. 478

ELISHEBA (e-lish'-e-bah)
Ex 6:23 Aaron took him **E.**, daughter of........... 472

ELISHUA (e-lish'-oo-ah) See also ELISHAMA.
2Sa 5:15 Ibhar also, and **E.**, and Nepheg, ... 474
1Ch 14:5 And Ibhar, and **E.**, and Elpalet,........... 474

ELITE See BETH-ELITE.

ELIUD (e-li'-ud)
Mt 1:14 begat Achim; and Achim begat **E.**; *1664*
Mt 1:15 And **E.** begat Eleazar; and................ *1664*

ELIZABETH See ELISABETH.

ELIZAPHAN (e-liz'-a-fan) See also ELZAPHAN.
Nu 3:30 of the Kohathites shall be **E.** 469
Nu 34:25 of Zebulun, **E.** the son of Parnach........ 469
1Ch 15:8 the sons of **E.**; Shemaiah the chief,....... 469
2Ch 29:13 of the sons of **E.**; Shimri, and Jeiel: 469

ELIZUR (e-li'-zur)
Nu 1:5 of Reuben; **E.** the son of Shedeur........ 468
Nu 2:10 the children of Reuben shall be **E.** 468
Nu 7:30 fourth day **E.** the son of Shedeur,........ 468
Nu 7:35 this was the offering of **E.** the son....... 468
Nu 10:18 host was **E.** the son of Shedeur. 468

ELKANAH (el-ka'-nah)
Ex 6:24 the sons of Korah; Assir, and **E.**,........ 511
1Sa 1:1 and his name was **E.**, the son of......... 511
1Sa 1:4 when the time was that **E.** offered,...... 511
1Sa 1:8 Then said **E.** her husband to her, ... 511
1Sa 1:19 and **E.** knew Hannah his wife;............. 511
1Sa 1:21 the man **E.**, and all his house, went..... 511
1Sa 1:23 **E.** her husband said unto her, Do........ 511
1Sa 2:11 And **E.** went to Ramah to his house..... 511
1Sa 2:20 And Eli blessed **E.** and his wife,.......... 511
1Ch 6:23 **E.** his son, and Ebiasaph his son, ... 511
1Ch 6:25 sons of **E.**; Amasai, and Ahimoth......... 511
1Ch 6:26 As for **E.**: the sons of **E.**; Zophai........ 511
1Ch 6:27 Jeroham his son, **E.** his son............... 511
1Ch 6:34 The son of **E.**, the son of Jeroham,...... 511
1Ch 6:35 The son of Zuph, the son of **E.**,.......... 511
1Ch 6:36 The son of **E.**, the son of Joel, ... 511
1Ch 9:16 the son of **E.**, that dwelt in the.......... 511
1Ch 12:6 **E.**, and Jesiah, and Azareel, ... 511
1Ch 15:23 Berechiah and **E.** were doorkeepers..... 511
2Ch 28:7 and **E.** that was next to the king......... 511

ELKOHSHITE (el'-ko-shite)
Na 1:1 book of the vision of Nahum the **E.**...... 512

ELLASAR (el'-la-sar)
Ge 14:1 Arioch kin of **E.**, Chedorlaomer.......... 495
Ge 14:9 and Arioch king of **E.**; four kings......... 495

ELMODAM (el-mo'-dam)
Lu 3:28 which was the son of **E.**, which......... *1678*

ELMS
Ho 4:13 under oaks and poplars and **E.**, ... 424

ELNAAM (el-na'-am)
1Ch 11:46 and Joshaviah, the sons of **E.**............. ,493

ELNATHAN (el-na'-than)
2Ki 24:8 the daughter of **E.** of Jerusalem.......... 494
Ezr 8:16 for **E.**, and for Jarib, and for **E.**,......... 494
Ezr 8:16 and for **E.**, men of understanding......... 494
Jer 26:22 **E.** the son of Achbor, and certain........ 494
Jer 36:12 **E.** the son of Achbor, and Gemariah 494
Jer 36:25 Nevertheless **E.** and Delaiah and......... 494

ELOHE See EL-ELOHE-ISRAEL.

ELOI (e-lo'-ee) See also ELI.
Mk 15:34 **E.,E., lama sabacthani?**............... *1682*

ELON (e'-lon) See also ELON-BETH-HANAN; ELONITES.
Ge 26:34 Bashemath the daughter of **E.** the 356
Ge 36:2 Adah the daughter of **E.** the.............. 356
Ge 46:14 sons of Zebulun; Sered, and **E.**, ... 356
Nu 26:26 of **E.** the family of the Elonites: 356
Jos 19:43 **E.**, and Thimnathah, and Ekron,.......... 356
Jg 12:11 And after him **E.**, a Zebulonite,.......... 356
Jg 12:12 And **E.** the Zebulonite died, and was.... 356

ELON-BETH-HANAN (e''-lon-beth-ha'-nan)
1Ki 4:9 and Beth-Shemesh, and **E.**; 358

ELONITES (e'-lon-ites)
Nu 26:26 of Elon, the family of the **E.**: 440

ELOQUENT
Ex 4:10 O my Lord, I am not **e.**,............ 376,1697
Isa 3:3 artificer, and the **e.** orator. 995
Ac 18:24 an **e.** man, and mighty in the............ *3052*

ELOTH (e'-loth) See also ELATH.
1Ki 9:26 Ezion-geber, which is beside **E.**, ... 359
2Ch 8:17 **E.**, at the sea side in the land of.......... 359
2Ch 26:2 He built **E.**, and restored it to Judah, ... 359

ELPAAL (el-pa'-al)
1Ch 8:11 Hushim he begat Abitub, and **E.**.......... 508
1Ch 8:12 The sons of **E.**; Eber, and Misham, ... 508
1Ch 8:18 Jezliah, and Jobab, the sons of **E.**; 508

ELPALET (el-pa'-let) See also ELIPHALET.
1Ch 14:5 And Ibhar, and elishua, and **E.**............ 467

EL-PARAN (el-pa'-ran)
Ge 14:6 unto **E.**, which is by the wilderness. 364

ELSE
Ge 30:1 Give me children, or **e.** I die.............. 369
Ge 42:16 or **e.** by the life of Pharaoh 518,3808
Ex 8:21 **E.**, if thou wilt not let my people....... 3588
Ex 10:4 **E.**, if thou refuse to let my people 3588
Nu 20:19 without doing anything **e.**, go through........
De 4:35 he is God; there is none **e.** beside...... 5750
De 4:39 the earth beneath: there is none **e.**...... 5750
Jos 23:12 **E.** if ye do in any wise go back, ... 3588
Jg 7:14 This is nothing **e.** save the sword..........
2Sa 3:35 if I taste bread, or ought **e.**, till the ....
2Sa 15:14 for we shall not **e.** escape from................
1Ki 8:60 is God, and that there is none **e.**........ 5750
1Ki 20:39 or **e.** thou shalt pay a talent of silver.........
1Ki 21:6 or **e.** if it please thee, I will give thee ......
1Ch 21:12 or **e.** three days the sword of the 518
2Ch 23:7 and whosoever **e.** cometh into the ....
Ne 2:2 this is nothing **e.** but sorrow of...............
Ps 51:16 thou desirest not sacrifice; **e.** would I........
Ec 2:25 or who **e.** can hasten hereunto,................
Isa 45:5 am the Lord, and there is none **e.**,........ 5750
Isa 45:6 I am the Lord, and there is none **e.**.... 5750
Isa 45:14 and there is none **e.**, there is no God.. 5750
Isa 45:18 I am the Lord; and there is none **e.**.... 5750
Isa 45:21 and there is no God **e.** beside me; a.... 5750
Isa 45:22 for I am God, and there is none **e.**.... 5750
Isa 46:9 I am God, and there is none **e.**: I...... 5750
Isa 47:8 I am, and none **e.** beside me; I shall... 5750
Isa 47:10 I am, and none **e.** beside me............. 5750
Joe 2:27 am the Lord your God, and none **e.**:... 5750
Mt 6:24 **he will hate the one.... or e. he**............
Mt 9:17 **e. the bottles break, and the wine** . *1490*
Mt 12:29 **Or e. how can one enter into the**.........
Mt 12:33 **or e. make the tree corrupt, and** ....
Mk 2:21 **e. the new piece that filled it up** ... *1490*
Mk 2:22 **e. the new wine doth burst the**...... *1490*
Lu 5:37 **e. the new wine will burst the**....... *1490*
Lu 14:32 **Or e., while the other is yet a**....... *1490*
Lu 16:13 **or e. he will hold to the one,**...............
Joh 14:11 **e. believe me for the very works'**... *1490*
Ac 17:21 spent their time in nothing **e.**, but *2087*
Ac 24:20 Or **e.** let these same here say, ...
Ro 2:15 accusing or **e.** excusing one............... *2532*
1Co 7:14 **e.** were your children unclean; *1893,686*
1Co 14:16 **E.** when thou shalt bless with the *1893*
1Co 15:29 **E.** what shall they do which are......... *1893*
Php 1:27 come and see you, or **e.** be absent, ...
Re 2:5 **or e. I will come unto thee** *1490*
Re 2:16 **Repent; or e. I will come unto** *1490*

ELTEKEH (el'-te-keh)
Jos 19:44 And **E.**, and Gibbethon, and Baalath,.... 514
Jos 21:23 out of the tribe of Dan, **E.** with her..... 514

ELTEKON (el'-te-kon)
Jos 15:59 Maarath, and Beth-anoth, and **E.**;........ 515

ELTOLAD (el-to'-lad)
Jos 15:30 And **E.**, and Chesil, and Hormah, ... 513
Jos 19:4 And **E.**, and Bethul, and Hormah,........ 513

ELUL (e'-lul)
Ne 6:15 and fifth day of the month **E.**,............. 435

ELUZAI (e-loo'-zahee)
1Ch 12:5 **E.**, and Jerimoth, and Bealiah, ... 498

ELYMAS (el'-i-mas) See also BAR-JESUS.
Ac 13:8 But **E.** the sorcerer (for so is his....... *1681*

ELZABAD (el'-za-bad)
1Ch 12:12 Johanan the eighth, **E.** the ninth, ... 443
1Ch 26:7 **E.**, whose brethren were strong.......... 443

ELZAPHAN (el'-za-fan) See also ELIZAPHAN.
Ex 6:22 the sons of Uzziel; Mishael, and **E.**,..... 469
Le 10:4 Moses called Mishael and **E.**, ... 469

EMBALM See also EMBALMED.
Ge 50:2 the physicians to **e.** his father: 2590

EMBALMED
Ge 50:2 and the physicians **e.** Israel. 2590
Ge 50:3 the days of those which are **e.**:.......... 2590
Ge 50:26 and they **e.** him, and he was put in..... 2590

EMBASSY See AMBASSAGE.

EMBOLDENED
1Co 8:10 of him which is weak be **e.** to eat....... *3618*

EMBOLDENETH
Job 16:3 what **e.** thee that thou answerest?...... 4834

EMBRACE See also EMBRACED; EMBRACING.
2Ki 4:16 time of life, thou shalt **e.** a son. 2263
Job 24:8 **e.** the rock for want of a shelter. 2263
Pr 4:8 to honour when thou dost **e.** her. 2263

Pr 5:20 and **e.** the bosom of a stranger? 2263
Ec 3:5 a time to **e.**, and a time to refrain 2263
Ca 2:6 and his right hand doth **e.** me. 2263
Ca 8:3 and his right hand should **e.** me. 2263
La 4:5 that were brought up in scarlet **e.** 2263

EMBRACED
Ge 29:13 he ran to meet him, and **e.** him, 2263
Ge 33:4 Esau ran to meet him, and **e.** him, 2263
Ge 48:10 he kissed them, and **e.** them. 2263
Ac 20:1 unto him the disciples, and **e.** *782*
Heb 11:13 **e.** them, and confessed that they *782*

EMBRACING
Ec 3:5 a time to refrain from **e.**; 2263
Ac 20:10 and fell on him, and **e.** him said, *4843*

EMBROIDER
Ex 28:39 And thou shalt **e.** the coat of fine 7660

EMBROIDERER
Ex 35:35 manner of work,...and of the **e.**, 7551
Ex 38:23 and an **e.** in blue, and in purple, 7551

EMEK See BETH-EMEK.

EMERALD See also EMERALDS.
Ex 28:18 And the second row shall be an **e.**, 5306
Ex 39:11 an **e.**, a sapphire, and a diamond. 5306
Eze 28:13 sapphire, the **e.**, and the carbuncle, 5306
Re 4:3 in sight like unto an **e.**. *4664*
Re 21:19 a chalcedony; the fourth, an **e.**; *4665*

EMERALDS
Eze 27:16 they occupied in thy fairs with **e.**, 5306

EMERODS (em'-e-rods)
De 28:27 and with the **e.**, and with the scab, 6076
1Sa 5:6 smote them with **e.**, even Ashdod 6076
1Sa 5:9 they had **e.** in their secret parts. 6076
1Sa 5:12 died not were smitten with the **e.**: 6076
1Sa 6:4 Five golden **e.**, and five golden 6076
1Sa 6:5 ye shall make images of your **e.**, 6076
1Sa 6:11 and the images of their **e.** 2914
1Sa 6:17 these are the golden **e.** which the 2914

EMIMS (e'-mims)
Ge 14:5 and the **E.** in Shaveh Kiriathaim, 368
De 2:10 **E.** dwelt therein in times past, 368
De 2:11 but the Moabites call them **E.** 368

EMINENCE See PRE-EMINENCE.

EMINENT
Eze 16:24 also built unto thee an **e.** place, 1354
Eze 16:31 thou buildest thine **e.** place in the 1354
Eze 16:39 shall throw down thine **e.** place, 1354
Eze 17:22 upon an high mountain and **e.**: 8524

EMMANUEL (em-man'-uel) See also IMMANUEL.
Mt 1:23 they shall call his name **E.**, *1694*

EMMAUS (em'-ma-us)
Lu 24:13 to a village called **E.**, which as *1695*

EMMOR (em'-mor) See also HAMOR.
Ac 7:16 of the sons of **E.** the father of *1697*

EMPIRE
Es 1:20 published throughout all his **e.**, 4438

EMPLOY See also EMPLOYED; EMPLOYMENT.
De 20:19 to **e.** them in the siege: 935,6440

EMPLOYED
1Ch 9:33 for they were **e.** in that work day 5921
Ezr 10:15 Tikvah were **e.** about this matter: 5975

EMPLOYMENT
Eze 39:14 shall sever out men of continual **e.**,

EMPTIED
Ge 24:20 she hasted, and **e.** her pitcher 6168
Ge 42:35 to pass as they **e.** their sacks, 7324
2Ch 24:11 officer came and **e.** the chest, 6168
Ne 5:13 thus be he shaken out, and **e.**. 7386
Isa 19:6 defence shall be **e.** and dried up; 1809
Isa 24:3 The land shall be utterly **e.**, and 1238
Jer 48:11 hath not been **e.** from vessel to 7324
Na 2:2 for the emptiers have **e.** them out, 1238

EMPTIERS
Na 2:2 for the **e.** have emptied them out, 1238

EMPTINESS
Isa 34:11 of confusion, and the stones of **e.**. 922

EMPTY See also EMPTIED.
Ge 31:42 thou hadst sent me away now **e.**. 7387
Ge 37:24 the pit was **e.**; there was no water 7386
Ge 41:27 the seven **e.** ears blasted with the 7386
Ex 3:21 when ye go, ye shall not go **e.**: 7387
Ex 23:15 and none shall appear before me **e.**:) 7387
Ex 34:20 And none shall appear before me **e.**. 7387
Le 14:36 command that they **e.** the house, 6437
De 15:13 thou shalt not let him go away **e.**: 7387
De 16:16 shall not appear before the Lord **e.**: 7387
Jg 7:16 **e.** pitchers, and lamps within the 7385
Ru 1:21 hath brought me home again **e.**; 7387
Ru 3:17 Go not **e.** unto thy mother in law. 7387
1Sa 6:3 send it not **e.**; but in any wise 7387
1Sa 20:18 missd because thy seat will be **e.**. 6485
1Sa 20:25 side, and David's place was **e.**. 6485
1Sa 20:27 that David's place was **e.**: and Saul 6485
2Sa 1:22 the sword of Saul returned not **e.** 7387
2Ki 4:3 borrow thee vessels...**e.** vessels; 7385
Job 22:9 Thou hast sent widows away **e.**, 7387
Job 26:7 out the north over the **e.** place, 8414
Ec 11:3 they **e.** themselves upon the earth; 7324
Isa 24:1 the Lord maketh the earth **e.**. 1238
Isa 29:8 he awaketh, and his soul is **e.**: 7385
Isa 32:6 to make **e.** the soul of the hungry, 7324
Jer 14:3 returned with their vessels **e.**; 7387
Jer 48:12 shall **e.** his vessels, and break 7324
Jer 51:2 shall fan her, and shall **e.** her land: 1238
Jer 51:34 he hath made me an **e.** vessel, 7385
Eze 24:11 set it **e.** upon the coals thereof, 7385
Ho 10:1 Israel is an **e.** vine, he bringeth 1238
Na 2:10 She is **e.**, and void, and waste: 950
Hab 1:17 Shall they therefore **e.** their net, 7324
Zec 4:12 through the two golden pipes **e.** 7324
Mt 12:44 **he findeth it e., swept, and** *4980*
Mk 12:3 **beat him, and sent him away e.** *2756*
Lu 1:53 the rich he hath sent **e.** away. *2756*
Lu 20:10 **beat him, and sent him away e.** *2756*
Lu 20:11 **shamefully, and sent him away e.** *2756*

EMULATION See also EMULATIONS.
Ro 11:14 I may provoke to **e.** them which *3863*

EMULATIONS
Ga 5:20 hatred, variance, **e.**, wrath, strife, *2205*

EN See EN-DOR; EN-EGLAIM; EN-GANNIM; EN-GEDI; EN-HADDAH; EN-HAKKORE; EN-HAZOR; EN-MISPHAT; EN-RIMMON; EN-ROGEL; EN-SHEMESH; EN-TAPPUAH.

ENABLED
1Ti 1:12 Jesus our Lord, who hath **e.** me, *1743*

ENAM (e'-nam)
Jos 15:34 and En-gannim, Tappuah, and **E.**, 5879

ENAN (e'-nan) See also HAZAR-ENAN.
Nu 1:15 of Naphtali; Ahira the son of **E.**. 5881
Nu 2:29 shall be Ahirah the son of **E.** 5881
Nu 7:78 the twelfth day Ahira the son of **E.**, 5881
Nu 7:83 the offering of Ahira the son of **E.** 5881
Nu 10:27 Naphtali was Ahira the son of **E.** 5881

ENCAMP See also ENCAMPED; ENCAMPETH; ENCAMPING.
Ex 14:2 turn and **e.** before Pi-hahiroth, 2583
Ex 14:2 before it shall ye **e.** by the sea. 2583
Nu 1:50 shall minister unto it, and shall **e.** 2583
Nu 2:17 as they **e.**, so shall they set forward, 2583
Nu 2:27 and those that **e.** by him shall be 2583
Nu 3:38 But those that **e.** before the 2583
Nu 10:31 how we are to **e.** in the wilderness, 2583
2Sa 12:28 and **e.** against the city, and take it: 2583
Job 19:12 and **e.** round about my tabernacle. 2583
Ps 27:3 Though an host should **e.** against 2583
Zec 9:8 And I will **e.** about mine house 2583

ENCAMPED
Ex 13:20 and **e.** in Etham, in the edge of the 2583
Ex 15:27 and they **e.** there by the waters. 2583
Ex 18:5 where he **e.** at the mount of God: 2583
Nu 33:10 and **e.** by the Red sea. 2583
Nu 33:11 and **e.** in the wilderness of Sin. 2583
Nu 33:12 and **e.** in Dophkah. 2583
Nu 33:13 and **e.** in Alush. 2583
Nu 33:14 and **e.** at Rephidim, where was no 2583
Nu 33:17 and **e.** at Hazeroth. 2583
Nu 33:24 and **e.** in Haradah. 2583
Nu 33:26 and **e.** at Tahath. 2583
Nu 33:30 and **e.** at Moseroth. 2583
Nu 33:32 and **e.** at Hor-hagidgad. 2583
Nu 33:34 and **e.** at Ebronah. 2583
Nu 33:35 and **e.** at Ezion-gaber. 2583
Nu 33:46 and **e.** in Almon-diblathaim. 2583
Jos 4:19 and **e.** in Gilgal, in the east border 2583
Jos 5:10 And the children of Israel **e.** in 2583
Jos 10:5 and **e.** before Gibeon, and made war 2583
Jos 10:31 and **e.** against it, and fought 2583
Jos 10:34 and they **e.** against it, and fought 2583
Jg 6:4 And they **e.** against them, and 2583
Jg 9:50 and **e.** against Thebez, and took it. 2583
Jg 10:17 gathered together, and **e.** in Gilead. 2583
Jg 10:17 together, and **e.** in Mizpeh. 2583
Jg 20:19 morning, and **e.** against Gibeah. 2583
1Sa 11:1 and **e.** against Jabesh-gilead: 2583
1Sa 13:16 but the Philistines **e.** in Michmash. 2583
2Sa 11:11 my lord, are **e.** in the open fields; 2583
1Ki 16:15 And the people were **e.** against 2583
1Ki 16:16 the people that were **e.** heard say, 2583
1Ch 11:15 the Philistines **e.** in the valley of 2583
2Ch 32:1 and **e.** against the fenced cities, 2583

ENCAMPETH
Ps 34:7 The angel of the Lord **e.** round 2583
Ps 53:5 the bones of him that **e.** against 2583

ENCAMPING
Ex 14:9 and overtook them **e.** by the sea, 2583

ENCHANTER See also ENCHANTERS.
De 18:10 spirits, or an **e.**, or a witch, 5172

ENCHANTERS
Jer 27:9 your **e.**, nor to your sorcerers, 6049

ENCHANTMENT See also ENCHANTMENTS.
Le 19:26 neither shall ye use **e.**, 5172
Nu 23:23 there is no **e.** against Jacob, 5172
Ec 10:11 the serpent will bite without **e.**; 3908

ENCHANTMENTS
Ex 7:11 did in like manner with their **e.**. 3858
Ex 7:22 of Egypt did so with their **e.**: 3909
Ex 8:7 the magicians did so with their **e.**, 3909
Ex 8:18 did so with their **e.** to bring forth 3909
Nu 24:1 to seek for **e.**, but he set his face 5172
2Ki 17:17 and used divination and **e.**, and 5172
2Ki 21:6 and observed times, and used **e.**, 5172
2Ch 33:6 also he observed times, and used **e.**, 5172
Isa 47:9 the great abundance of thine **e.** 2267
Isa 47:12 Stand now with thine **e.**, and with 2267

ENCOUNTERED
Ac 17:18 and of the Stoicks, **e.** him. *4820*

ENCOURAGE See also ENCOURAGED.
De 1:38 he shall go in thither: **e.** him: 2388
De 3:28 charge Joshua, and **e.** him, and 2388
2Sa 11:25 and overthrow it: and **e.** thou him. 2388
Ps 64:5 They **e.** themselves in an evil 2388

ENCOURAGED
Jg 20:22 the men of Israel **e.** themselves, 2388
1Sa 30:6 but David **e.** himself in the Lord. 2388
2Ch 31:4 that they might be **e.** in the law of 2388
2Ch 35:2 and **e.** them to the service of the 2388
Isa 41:7 So the carpenter **e.** the goldsmith, 2388

END See ENDEST; ENDETH; ENDING; ENDLESS; ENDS.
Ge 6:13 The **e.** of all flesh is come before 7093
Ge 8:3 after the **e.** of the hundred and 7097
Ge 8:6 came to pass at the **e.** of forty days, 7093
Ge 23:9 which is in the **e.** of his field; 7097
Ge 27:30 as Isaac had made an **e.** of blessing 3615
Ge 41:1 it came to pass at the **e.** of two full 7093
Ge 47:21 from one **e.** of the borders of Egypt 7097
Ge 47:21 even to the other **e.** thereof. 7097
Ge 49:33 And when Jacob had made an **e.** of 3615
Ex 8:22 to the **e.** thou mayest know that I 4616
Ex 12:41 at the **e.** of the four hundred and 7093
Ex 23:16 in the **e.** of the year, when thou 3318
Ex 25:19 one cherub on the one **e.**, and the 7098
Ex 25:19 the other cherub on the other **e.**: 7098
Ex 26:28 the boards shall reach from **e.** to **e.** 7097
Ex 31:18 choses, when he had made an **e.** of 3615
Ex 34:22 of ingathering at the year's **e.**. 8622
Ex 36:33 the boards from the one **e.** to the 7097
Ex 37:8 One cherub on the **e.** on this side, 7098
Ex 37:8 and another cherub on the other **e.** 7098
Le 8:33 of your consecration be at an **e.**: 4390
Le 16:20 hath made an **e.** of reconciling 3615
Le 17:5 To the **e.** that the children of 4616
Nu 4:15 have made an **e.** of covering 3615
Nu 16:31 as he had made an **e.** of speaking 3615

Nu 23:10 and let my last e. be like his!
Nu 24:20 but his latter e. shall be that he perish
De 8:16 to do thee good at thy latter e.;
De 9:11 at the e. of forty days and forty 7093
De 11:12 even unto the e. of the year. 319
De 13:7 from the one e. of the earth even 7097
De 13:7 even unto the other e. of the earth; 7097
De 14:28 At the e. of three years thou shalt 7097
De 15:1 At the e. of every seven years thou 7093
De 17:16 to the e. that he should multiply 4616
De 17:20 to the e. that he may prolong his 4616
De 20:9 officers have made an e. speaking 3615
De 26:12 thou hast made an e. of tithing all 3615
De 28:49 from the e. of the earth, as swift 7097
De 28:64 from the one e. of the earth even 7097
De 31:10 At the e. of every seven years, 7093
De 31:24 Moses had made an e. of writing 3615
De 32:20 I will see what their e. shall be: 319
De 32:29 they would consider their latter e.!
De 32:45 And Moses made an e. of speaking 3615
Jos 8:24 Israel had made an e. of slaying 3615
Jos 9:16 to pass at the e. of three days 7097
Jos 10:20 Israel had made an e. of slaying 3615
Jos 15:5 sea, even unto the e. of Jordan. 7097
Jos 15:8 at the e. of the valley of the giants 7097
Jos 18:15 from the e. of Kirjath-jearim, 7097
Jos 18:16 down to the e. of the mountain 7097
Jos 18:19 salt sea at the south e. of Jordan: 7097
Jos 19:49 they had made an e. of dividing 3615
Jos 19:51 So they made an e. of dividing the 3615
Jg 3:18 when he had made an e. to offer 3615
Jg 6:21 Lord put forth the e. of the staff 7097
Jg 11:39 to pass at the e. of two months, 7093
Jg 15:17 he had made an e. of speaking, 3615
Jg 19:9 behold, the day groweth to an e., 2583
Ru 2:23 unto the e. of barley harvest and 3615
Ru 3:7 at the e. of the heap of corn: 7097
Ru 3:10 more kindness at the latter e. than
1Sa 3:12 I begin, I will also make an e. 3615
1Sa 9:27 going down to the e. of the city, 7097
1Sa 10:13 he had made an e. of prophesying, 3615
1Sa 13:10 as he had made an e. of offering 3615
1Sa 14:27 he put forth the e. of the rod 7097
1Sa 14:43 a little honey with the e. of the rod 7097
1Sa 18:1 he had made an e. of speaking 3615
1Sa 24:16 David had made an e. of speaking 3615
2Sa 2:23 Abner with the hinder e. of the spear
2Sa 2:26 it will be bitterness in the latter e.?
2Sa 6:18 David had made an e. of offering 3615
2Sa 11:19 thou hast made an e. of telling 3615
2Sa 13:36 as he had made an e. of speaking, 3615
2Sa 14:26 every year's e. that he polled it: 7093
2Sa 24:8 at the e. of nine months and twenty 7097
1Ki 1:41 as they had made an e. of eating 3615
1Ki 2:39 to pass at the e. of three years, 7093
1Ki 3:1 he had made an e. of building 3615
1Ki 7:40 So Hiram made an e. of doing all 3615
1Ki 8:54 Solomon had made an e. of praying 3615
1Ki 9:10 to pass at the e. of twenty years, 7097
2Ki 8:3 came to pass at the seven years' e., 7097
2Ki 10:21 of Baal was full from one e. to 6310
2Ki 10:25 as he had made an e. of offering 3615
2Ki 18:10 at the e. of three years they took it: 7097
2Ki 21:16 Jerusalem from one e. to another; 6310
1Ch 16:2 David had made an e. of offering 3615
2Ch 4:10 sea on the right side of the east e.,
2Ch 5:12 stood at the east e. of the altar,
2Ch 7:1 Solomon had made an e. of praying, 3615
2Ch 8:1 to pass at the e. of twenty years, 7093
2Ch 20:16 find them at the e. of the brook, 5490
2Ch 20:23 had made an e. of the inhabitants 3615
2Ch 21:19 of time, after the e. of two years, 7093
2Ch 24:10 chest, until they had made an e. 3615
2Ch 24:23 came to pass at the e. of the year, 8622
2Ch 29:17 sixteenth day...they made an e. 3615
2Ch 29:29 they had made an e. of offering, 3615
Ezr 9:11 filled it from one e. to another 6310
Ezr 10:17 they made an e. with all the men 3615
Ne 3:21 to the e. of the house of Eliashib, 8503
Ne 2:2 will they make an e. in a day? 3615
Job 6:11 and what is mine e., that I should 7093
Job 8:7 thy latter e. should greatly increase.
Job 16:3 Shall vain words have an e.? 7093
Job 18:2 ere ye make an e. of words? 7078
Job 26:10 the day and night come to an e. 8503
Job 28:3 He setteth an e. to darkness, 7093
Job 34:36 that Job may be tried unto the e. 5331

Job 42:12 the Lord blessed the latter e. of Job
Ps 7:9 of the wicked come to an e.; 1584
Ps 9:6 are come to a perpetual e.: 8552
Ps 19:4 their words to the e. of the world. 7097
Ps 19:6 forth is from the e. of the heaven, 7097
Ps 30:12 To the e. that my glory may sing 4616
Ps 37:37 for the e. of that man is peace. 319
Ps 37:38 e. of the wicked shall be cut off. 319
Ps 39:4 Lord, make me to know mine e., 7093
Ps 46:9 to cease unto the e. of the earth; 7097
Ps 61:2 From the e. of the earth will I cry 7097
Ps 73:17 God; then understood I their e. 319
Ps 102:27 and thy years shall have no e. 8552
Ps 107:27 man, and are at their wit's e. 1104
Ps 119:33 I shall keep it unto the e. 6118
Ps 119:96 have seen an e. of all perfection: 7093
Ps 119:112 statutes alway, even unto the e. 6118
Pr 5:4 But her e. is bitter as wormwood, 319
Pr 14:12 e. thereof are the ways of death. 319
Pr 14:13 the e. of that mirth is heaviness. 319
Pr 16:25 the e. thereof are the ways of death. 319
Pr 19:20 thou mayest be wise in thy latter e.
Pr 20:21 the e. thereof shall not be blessed. 319
Pr 23:18 For surely there is an e.; and 319
Pr 25:8 what to do in the e. thereof, 319
Ec 3:11 from the beginning to the e. 5490
Ec 4:8 yet is there no e. of all his labour; 7093
Ec 4:16 There is no e. of all the people, 7093
Ec 7:2 for that is the e. of all men; 5490
Ec 7:8 Better is the e. of a thing than the 319
Ec 7:14 e. that man should find nothing 1700
Ec 10:13 the e. of his talk is mischievous 319
Ec 12:12 making many books there is no e.; 7093
Isa 2:7 is there any e. of their treasures; 7097
Isa 2:7 is there any e. of their chariots: 7097
Isa 5:26 unto them from the e. of the earth: 7097
Isa 7:3 at the e. of the conduit of the upper 7097
Isa 9:7 and peace there shall be no e., 7093
Isa 13:5 far country, from the e. of heaven, 7093
Isa 16:4 for the extortioner is at an e., 657
Isa 23:15 the e. of seventy years shall Tyre 7093
Isa 23:17 pass after the e. of seventy years, 7093
Isa 33:1 make an e. to deal treacherously, 5239
Isa 38:12, 13 wilt thou make an e. of me. 7999
Isa 41:22 and know the latter e. of them;
Isa 42:10 his praise from the e. of the earth, 7097
Isa 45:17 world without e. 5704,5769,5703
Isa 46:10 the e. from the beginning, 319
Isa 47:7 didst remember the latter e. of it.
Isa 48:20 it even to the e. of the earth; 7097
Isa 49:6 salvation unto the e. of the earth. 7097
Isa 62:11 proclaimed unto the e. of the world, 7097
Jer 1:3 unto the e. of the eleventh year 8537
Jer 3:5 will he keep it to the e.? 5331
Jer 4:27 yet will I not make a full e. 3615
Jer 5:10 but make not a full e.: take away 3615
Jer 5:18 I will not make a full e. with you. 3615
Jer 5:31 what will ye do in the e. thereof? 319
Jer 12:4 He shall not see our last e.
Jer 12:12 from the one e. of the land 7097
Jer 12:12 even to the other e. of the land: 7097
Jer 17:11 and at his e. shall be a fool. 319
Jer 25:33 from one e. of the earth even 7097
Jer 25:33 unto the other e. of the earth: 7097
Jer 26:8 had made an e. of speaking all 3615
Jer 29:11 of evil, to give you an expected e. 319
Jer 30:11 I make a full e. of all nations 3615
Jer 30:11 yet will I not make a full e. of thee: 3615
Jer 31:17 And there is hope in thine e., 319
Jer 34:14 At the e. of seven years let ye go 7093
Jer 43:1 had made an e. of speaking unto 3615
Jer 44:27 until there be an e. of them. 3615
Jer 46:28 will make a full e. of all the nations 3615
Jer 46:28 I will not make a full e. of thee, 3615
Jer 51:13 thine e. is come, and the measure 7093
Jer 51:31 that his city is taken at one e., 7097
Jer 51:63 made an e. of reading this book, 3615
La 1:9 she remembereth not her last e.;
La 4:18 our e. is near, our days are fulfilled; 7093
La 4:18 for our e. is come. 7093
Eze 3:16 to pass at the e. of seven days, 7097
Eze 7:2 An e., the e. is come upon the four 7093
Eze 7:3 Now is the e. come upon thee, 7093
Eze 7:6 An e. is come, the e. is come: 7093
Eze 11:13 God! wilt thou make a full e. of 3615
Eze 20:17 neither did I make an e. of them 3615
Eze 20:26 to the e. that they might know 4616

Eze 21:25 when iniquity shall have an e., 7093
Eze 21:29 their iniquity shall have an e. 7093
Eze 29:13 At the e. of forty years will I gather 7093
Eze 31:14 To the e. that none of all the trees 4616
Eze 35:5 that their iniquity had an e.: 7093
Eze 39:14 after the e. of seven months shall 7097
Eze 41:12 at the e. toward the west was 6285
Eze 42:15 he had made an e. of measuring 3615
Eze 43:23 hast made an e. of cleansing it, 3615
Eze 48:1 From the north e. to the coast of 7097
Da 1:5 at the e. thereof they might stand 7117
Da 1:15 And at the e. of ten days their 7117
Da 1:18 at the e. of the days that the king 7117
Da 4:11 thereof to the e. of all the earth: 5491
Da 4:22 thy dominion to the e. of the earth. 5491
Da 4:29 the e. of twelve months he walked 7118
Da 4:34 the e. of the days I Nebuchadnezzar 7118
Da 6:26 dominion shall be even unto the e. 5491
Da 7:26 and to destroy it unto the e. 5491
Da 7:28 Hitherto is the e. of the matter. 5491
Da 8:17 time of the e. shall be the vision. 7093
Da 8:19 in the last e. of the indignation:
Da 8:19 the time appointed the e. shall be, 7093
Da 9:24 and to make an e. of sins. 2856
Da 9:26 the e. thereof shall be with a flood, 7093
Da 9:26 and unto the e. of the war 7093
Da 11:6 in the e. of years they shall join 7093
Da 11:27 the e. shall be at the time appointed. 7093
Da 11:35 even to the time of the e.; 7093
Da 11:40 at the time of the e. shall the king 7093
Da 11:45 yet he shall come to his e., 7093
Da 12:4 book, even to the time of the e.: 7093
Da 12:6 it be to the e. of these wonders? 7093
Da 12:8 shall be the e. of these things? 319
Da 12:9 and sealed till the time of the e. 7093
Da 12:13 go thou thy way till the e. be: 7093
Da 12:13 stand in thy lot at the e. of the days. 7093
Am 3:15 the great houses shall have an e., 5486
Am 5:18 to what e. is it for you?
Am 7:2 they had made an e. of eating 3615
Am 8:2 The e. is come upon my people 7093
Am 8:10 and the e. thereof as a bitter day. 319
Ob 9 to the e. that every one of the 4616
Na 1:8 will make an utter e. of the place 3615
Na 1:9 the Lord? he will make an utter e.: 3615
Na 2:9 for there is none e. of the store 7097
Na 3:3 there is none e. of their corpses; 7097
Hab 2:3 but at the e. it shall speak, 7093
Mt 10:22 endureth to the e. shall be saved. *5056*
Mt 11:1 when Jesus had made an e. of *5055*
Mt 13:39 the harvest is the e. of the world; *4930*
Mt 13:40 so shall it be in the e. of this *4930*
Mt 13:49 So shall it be at the e. of the *4930*
Mt 24:3 and of the e. of the world? *4930*
Mt 24:6 come to pass, but the e. is not yet. *5056*
Mt 24:13 he that shall endure unto the e., *5056*
Mt 24:14 and then shall the e. come. *5056*
Mt 24:31 from one e. of heaven to the other *206*
Mt 26:58 with the servants, to see the e. *5056*
Mt 28:1 the e. of the sabbath, as it began *3796*
Mt 28:20 even unto the e. of the world. *4930*
Mk 3:26 he cannot stand, but hath an e. *5056*
Mk 13:7 but the e. shall not be yet. *5056*
Mk 13:13 he that shall endure unto the e., *5056*
Lu 1:33 of his kingdom there shall be no e. *5056*
Lu 18:1 a parable unto them to this e., that men
Lu 21:9 but the e. is not by and by. *5056*
Lu 22:37 things concerning me have an e. *5056*
Joh 13:1 world, he loved them unto the e. *5056*
Joh 18:37 To this e. was I born, and for this
Ac 7:19 to the e. they might not live. *1519*
Ro 1:11 to the e. ye may be established; *1519*
Ro 4:16 the e. the promise might be sure *1519*
Ro 6:21 for the e. of those things is death. *5056*
Ro 6:22 and the e. everlasting life. *5056*
Ro 10:4 For Christ is the e. of the law *5056*
Ro 14:9 to this e. Christ both died, and rose
1Co 1:8 shall also confirm you unto the e., *5056*
1Co 15:24 Then cometh the e., when he shall *5056*
2Co 1:13 shall acknowledge even to the e.; *5056*
2Co 2:9 to this e. also did I write, that I might
2Co 3:13 the e. of that which is abolished: *5056*
2Co 11:15 e. shall be according to their works. *5056*
Eph 3:21 ages, world without e. *165,3588,165*
Php 3:19 Whose e. is destruction, whose God *5056*
1Th 3:13 To the e. he may stablish your *1519*

1Ti 1:5 Now the e. of the commandment........ 5056
Heb 3:6 of the hope firm unto the e.. 5056
Heb 3:14 our confidence stedfast unto the e.; 5056
Heb 6:8 cursing; whose e. is to be burned......... 5056
Heb 6:11 full assurance of hope unto the e.:....... 5056
Heb 6:16 is to them an e. of all strife............... 4009
Heb 7:3 beginning of days, nor e. of life;.......... 5056
Heb 9:26 e. of the world hath he appeared........ 4930
Heb 13:7 the e. of their conversation. 1545
Jas 5:11 and have seen the e. of the Lord; 5056
1Pe 1:9 Receiving the e. of your faith, ... 5056
1Pe 1:13 and hope to the e. for the grace 5049
1Pe 4:7 But the e. of all things is at hand: 5056
1Pe 4:17 what shall the e. be of them that......... 5056
2Pe 2:20 the latter e. is worse with them.......... 2078
Re 2:26 **and keepeth my works unto the e.,**.5056
Re 21:6 the beginning and the e., I will give 5056
Re 22:13 **Omega, the beginning and the e.,**.. 5056

ENDAMAGE
Ezr 4:13 so thou shalt e. the revenue of.......... 5142

ENDANGER See also ENDANGERED.
Da 1:10 then shall ye make me e. my head 2325

ENDANGERED
Ec 10:9 he that cleaveth wood shall be e. 5533

ENDEAVOUR See also ENDEAVOURED; ENDEAVOURING; ENDEAVOURS.
2Pe 1:15 I will e. that ye may be able after 4704

ENDEAVOURED
Ac 16:10 we e. to go into Macedonia,.............. 2212
1Th 2:17 e. the more abundantly to see 4704

ENDEAVOURING
Eph 4:3 E. to keep the unity of the Spirit....... 4704

ENDEAVOURS
Ps 28:4 to the wickedness of their e.:........... 4611

ENDED
Ge 2:2 And on the seventh day God e. 3615
Ge 41:53 years of plenteousness...were e.. 3615
Ge 47:18 When that year was e., they came 8552
De 31:30 of this son, until they were e.. 8552
De 34:8 and mourning for Moses were e......... 8552
Ru 2:21 until they have e. all my harvest. 3615
2Sa 20:18 so they e. the matter.......................... 8552
1Ki 7:51 So was e. all the work that king.......... 7999
2Ch 29:34 till the work was e., and until the........ 3615
Job 31:40 The words of Job are e.. 8552
Ps 72:20 of David the son of Jesse are e.......... 3615
Isa 60:20 days of thy mourning shall be e.......... 7999
Jer 8:20 the summer is e., and we are not 3615
Eze 4:8 till thou hast e. the days of thy.......... 3615
Mt 7:28 when Jesus had e. these sayings, ... 4931
Lu 4:2 and when they were e., he 4931
Lu 4:13 And when the devil had e. all the....... 4931
Lu 7:1 when he had e. all his sayings............ 4137
Joh 13:2 supper being e., the devil having........ 1096
Ac 19:21 After these things were e., Paul 4137
Ac 21:27 the seven days were almost e., ... 4931

ENDETH
Isa 24:8 the noise of them that rejoice e., ... 2308

ENDING
Re 1:8 **Omega, the beginning and the e.,**.. 5056

ENDLESS
1Ti 1:4 to fables and e. genealogies, which....... 562
Heb 7:16 but after the power of an e. life........... 179

EN-DOR (en'-dor)
Jos 17:11 and the inhabitants of E. and her 5874
1Sa 28:7 that hath a familiar spirit at E........... 5874
Ps 83:10 Which perished at E.: they became 5874

ENDOW See also ENDUED.
Ex 22:16 he shall surely e. her to be his 4117

ENDS
Ex 25:18 in the two e. of the mercy seat. 7098
Ex 25:19 the cherubims on the two e. thereof. .. 7098
Ex 28:14 two chains of pure gold at the e.;....... 4020
Ex 28:22 the e. of wreathen work of pure 1383
Ex 28:23 on the two e. of the breastplate......... 7098
Ex 28:24 are on the e. of the breastplate.......... 7098
Ex 28:25 And the other two e. of the two 7098
Ex 28:26 upon the two e. of the breastplate...... 7098
Ex 37:7 on the two e. of the mercy seat;........ 7098
Ex 37:8 cherubims on the two e. thereof. 7099
Ex 38:5 four rings for the four e. of the.......... 7099
Ex 39:15 the breastplate chains at the e., ... 1383
Ex 39:16 in the two e. of the breastplate.......... 7098
Ex 39:17 rings on the e. of the breastplate. 7098
Ex 39:18 two e. of the two wreathen chains...... 7098
Ex 39:19 on the two e. of the breastplate,......... 7098
De 33:17 together to the e. of the earth: 657
1Sa 2:10 Lord shall judge the e. of the earth; 657
1Ki 8:8 the e. of the staves were seen out 7218
2Ch 5:9 the e. of the staves were seen from ... 7218
Job 28:24 he looketh to the e. of the earth, ... 7098
Job 37:3 lightning unto the e. of the earth. 3671
Job 38:13 take hold of the e. of the earth, ... 3671
Ps 19:6 and his circuit unto the e. of it:.......... 7098
Ps 22:27 All the e. of the world shall 657
Ps 48:10 thy praise unto the e. of the earth:..... 7099
Ps 59:13 in Jacob unto the e. of the earth. 657
Ps 65:5 confidence of all the e. of the earth,.... 7099
Ps 67:7 all the e. of the earth shall fear 657
Ps 72:8 the river unto the e. of the earth........... 657
Ps 98:3 all the e. of the earth have seen the..... 657
Ps 135:7 to ascend from the e. of the earth;..... 7097
Pr 17:24 of a fool are in the e. of the earth. 7097
Pr 30:4 established all the e. of the earth?........ 657
Isa 26:15 far unto all the e. of the earth. 7097
Isa 40:28 the Creator of the e. of the earth,...... 7098
Isa 41:5 the e. of the earth were afraid,........... 7098
Isa 41:9 have taken from the e. of the earth, ... 7098
Isa 43:6 my daughters from the e. of the 7097
Isa 45:22 saved, all the e. of the earth:.............. 657
Isa 52:10 all the e. of the earth shall see the....... 657
Jer 10:13 vapours to ascend from the e. of........ 7097
Jer 16:19 shall come unto thee from the e. of...... 657
Jer 25:31 come even to the e. of the earth;........ 7097
Jer 51:16 vapours to ascend from the e. of the... 7097
Eze 15:4 the fire devoureth both the e. of it, ... 7098
Mic 5:4 be great unto the e. of the earth. 657
Zec 9:10 the river even to the e. of the earth..... 657
Ac 13:47 salvation unto the e. of the earth......... 2078
Ro 10:18 their words unto the e. of the world. .. 4009
1Co 10:11 upon whom the e. of the world are...... 5056

ENDUED See also ENDOW.
Ge 30:20 God hath e. me with a good............. 2064
2Ch 2:12 a wise son, e. with prudence and 3045
2Ch 2:13 man, e. with understanding, ... 3045
Lu 24:49 **until ye be e. with power from on**..1746
Jas 3:13 e. with knowledge among you? 1990

ENDURE See also ENDURED; ENDURETH; ENDURING.
Ge 33:14 me and the children be able to e., ... 7272
Ex 18:23 then thou shalt be able to e.,............. 5975
Es 8:6 how can I e. to see the evil that 3201
Es 8:6 how can I e. to see the destruction 3201
Job 8:15 hold it fast, but it shall not e.. 6965
Job 31:23 of his highness I could not e.. ....
Ps 9:7 But the Lord shall e. for ever:........... 3427
Ps 30:5 weeping may e. for a night, but 3885
Ps 72:5 as long as the sun and moon e.,.......... 6440
Ps 72:17 His name shall e. for ever:................ 1961
Ps 89:29 His seed also will I make to e. forever, ...
Ps 89:36 His seed shall e. for ever, and his 1961
Ps 102:12 thou, O Lord, shalt e. for ever; 3427
Ps 102:26 shall perish, but thou shalt e.: 5975
Ps 104:31 glory of the Lord shall e. for ever: 1961
Pr 27:24 ever: and doth the crown e. to every........
Eze 22:14 Can thine heart e., or can thine 5975
Mt 24:13 **But he that shall e. unto the end,**..5278
Mk 4:17 **and so e. but for a time:**.............. 2076
Mk 13:13 **but he that shall e. unto the end,**.. 5278
2Th 1:4 and tribulations that ye e.:................. 430
2Ti 2:3 therefore e. hardness, as a good 2553
2Ti 2:10 Therefore I e. all things for the 5278
2Ti 4:3 they will not e. sound doctrine; 430
2Ti 4:5 e. afflictions, do the work of an.......... 2553
Heb 12:7 If ye e. chastening, God dealeth.......... 5278
Heb 12:20 (For they could not e. that which 5342
Jas 5:11 we count them happy which e............ 5278
1Pe 2:19 conscience toward God e. grief, ... 5297

ENDURED
Ps 81:15 their time should have e. for ever. 1961
Ro 9:22 e. with much longsuffering the........... 5342
2Ti 3:11 what persecutions I e.: but out of........ 5297
Heb 6:15 And so, after he had patiently e., ... 3114
Heb 10:32 ye e. a great fight of afflictions; 5278
Heb 11:27 for he e., as seeing him who is.......... 2594
Heb 12:2 e. the cross, despising the shame,...... 5278
Heb 12:3 him that e. such contradiction 5278

ENDURETH See also DURETH.
1Ch 16:34 he is good; for his mercy e. for ever. ....
1Ch 16:41 Lord because his mercy e. for ever; ....
2Ch 5:13 he is good; for his mercy e. for ever: ....
2Ch 7:3 he is good; for his mercy e. for ever. ....
2Ch 7:6 Lord, because his mercy e. for ever, ...
2Ch 20:21 the Lord; for his mercy e. for ever...........
Ezr 3:11 his mercy e. for ever toward Israel..........
Ps 30:5 For his anger e. but a moment; ....
Ps 52:1 the goodness of God e. continually...........
Ps 72:7 peace so long as the moon e.. 1097
Ps 100:5 and his truth e. to all generations. ....
Ps 106:1 he is good: for his mercy e. for ever. ....
Ps 107:1 he is good: for his mercy e. for ever. ....
Ps 111:3 and his righteousness e. for ever........ 5975
Ps 111:10 commandments: his praise e. for........ 5975
Ps 112:3 and his righteousness e. for ever........ 5975
Ps 112:9 poor; his righteousness e. for ever; 5975
Ps 117:2 and the truth of the Lord e. for ever. ....
Ps 118:1 is good: because his mercy e. for ever. .....
Ps 118:2 Israel now say, that his mercy e. for.........
Ps 118:3 Aaron now say, that his mercy e. for ....
Ps 118:4 Lord say, that his mercy e. for ever. ....
Ps 118:29 he is good: for his mercy e. for ever. ....
Ps 119:160 thy righteous judgments e. for ever. ....
Ps 135:13 Thy name, O Lord, e. for ever;...............
Ps 136:1 he is good: for his mercy e. for ever. ....
Ps 136:2 of gods: for his mercy e. for ever.............
Ps 136:3 of lords: for his mercy e. for ever. ....
Ps 136:4 wonders: for his mercy e. for ever............
Ps 136:5 heavens: for his mercy e. for ever............
Ps 136:6 the waters: for his mercy e. for ever. ....
Ps 136:7 lights: for his mercy e. for ever: ....
Ps 136:8 by day: for his mercy e. for ever: ....
Ps 136:9 by night: for his mercy e. for ever..........
Ps 136:10 firstborn: for his mercy e. for ever, ...
Ps 136:11 among them: for his mercy e...................
Ps 136:12 out arm: for his mercy e. for ever............
Ps 136:13 into parts: for his mercy e. for ever..........
Ps 136:14 the midst of it: for his mercy e. for ever. ..
Ps 136:15 the Red sea: for his mercy e. for ever. .....
Ps 136:16 wilderness: for his mercy e. for ever. ....
Ps 136:17 great kings: for his mercy e. for ever........
Ps 136:18 famous kings: for his mercy e. for ever. ....
Ps 136:19 the Amorites: for his mercy e. for ever. ....
Ps 136:20 of Bashan: for his mercy e. for ever. ....
Ps 136:21 an heritage: for his mercy e. for ever.........
Ps 136:22 his servant: for his mercy e. for ever........
Ps 136:23 low estate: for his mercy e. for ever.:.......
Ps 136:24 our enemies: for his mercy e. for ever. .....
Ps 136:25 to all flesh: for his mercy e. for ever. ....
Ps 136:26 of heaven: for his mercy e. for ever. ....
Ps 138:8 thy mercy, O Lord, e. for ever: forsake ....
Ps 145:13 and thy dominion e. throughout all............
Jer 33:11 for his mercy e. for ever: and of them .....
Mt 10:22 **that e. to the end shall be saved**.... 5278
Joh 6:27 **which e. unto everlasting life,**........ 3306
1Co 13:7 hopeth all things, e. all things. 5278
Jas 1:12 is the man that e. temptation:............ 5278
1Pe 1:25 the word of the Lord e. for ever........ 3306

ENDURING
Ps 19:9 of the Lord is clean, e. for ever:........ 5975
2Co 1:6 is effectual in the e. of the same 5281
Heb 10:3 a better and an e. substance. 3306

ENEAS See AENEAS.

EN-EGLAIM (en-eg'-la-im)
Eze 47:10 from Engedi even unto E.; 5882

ENEMIES See also ENEMIES'.
Ge 14:20 delivered thine e. into thy hand.......... 6862
Ge 22:17 seed shall possess the gate of his e.;.... 341
Ge 49:8 hand shall be in the neck of thine e.; 341
Ex 1:10 they join also unto our e., and........... 8130
Ex 23:22 I will be an enemy unto thine e., ... 341
Ex 23:27 make all thine e. turn their backs.......... 341
Ex 32:25 unto their shame among their e.:......... 6965
Le 26:7 And ye shall chase your e., ... 341
Le 26:8 and your e. shall fall before you........... 341
Le 26:16 seed in vain, for your e. shall eat it...... 341
Le 26:17 ye shall be slain before your e.:........... 341
Le 26:32 your e. which dwell therein shall be...... 341
Le 26:36 their hearts in the lands of their e.;...... 341
Le 26:37 no power to stand before your e.......... 341

Le 26:38 the land of your **e.** shall eat you up...... 341
Le 26:41 them into the land of their **e.**;.......... 341
Le 26:44 when they be in the land of their **e.**, ... 341
Nu 10:9 ye shall be saved from your **e.**. 341
Nu 10:35 Lord, and let thine **e.** be scattered;...... 341
Nu 14:42 ye be not smitten before your **e.**. 341
Nu 23:11 I took thee to curse mine **e.**, ... 341
Nu 24:8 he shall eat up the nations his **e.**,....... 6862
Nu 24:10 I called thee to curse mine **e.**,............ 341
Nu 24:18 also shall be a possession for his **e.**;..... 341
Nu 32:21 driven out his **e.** from before him,........ 341
De 1:42 lest ye be smitten before your **e.**......... 341
De 6:19 out all thine **e.** from before thee, ... 341
De 12:10 he giveth you rest from all your **e.**........ 341
De 20:1 goest out to battle against thine **e.**, ... 341
De 20:3 this day unto battle against your **e.**:...... 341
De 20:4 to fight for you against your **e.**, ... 341
De 20:14 thou shalt eat the spoil of thine **e.**........ 341
De 21:10 goest forth to war against thine **e.**, ... 341
De 23:9 host goeth forth against thine **e.**, ... 341
De 23:14 to give up thine **e.** before thee;........... 341
De 25:19 given thee rest from all thine **e.** 341
De 28:7 Lord shall cause thine **e.** that rise....... 341
De 28:25 thee to be smitten before thine **e.**:......... 341
De 28:31 sheep shall be given unto thine **e.**, ... 341
De 28:48 Therefore shalt thou serve thine **e.**...... 341
De 28:53 wherewith thine **e.** shall distress.......... 341
De 28:55 thine **e.** shall distress thee in all......... 341
De 28:68 ye shall be sold unto your **e.** for.......... 341
De 30:7 put all these curses upon thine **e.**, ... 341
De 32:31 our **e.** themselves being judges........... 341
De 32:41 will render vengeance to mine **e.**,....... 6862
De 33:7 be thou an help to him from his **e.**....... 6862
De 33:29 thine **e.** shall be found liars unto.......... 341
Jos 7:8 turneth their backs before their **e.**!........ 341
Jos 7:12 Israel could not stand before their **e.** 341
Jos 7:12 turned their backs before their **e.**,........ 341
Jos 7:13 thou canst not stand before thine **e.** 341
Jos 10:13 avenged themselves upon their **e.**. 341
Jos 10:19 but pursue after your **e.**, and smite...... 341
Jos 10:25 thus shall the Lord do to all your **e.** 341
Jos 21:44 stood not a man of all their **e.** before.... 341
Jos 21:44 delivered all their **e.** into their hand..... 341
Jos 22:8 divide the spoil of your **e.** with your..... 341
Jos 23:1 rest unto Israel from all their **e.** 341
Jg 2:14 sold them into the hands of their **e.**....... 341
Jg 2:14 any longer stand before their **e.**.......... 341
Jg 2:18 out of the hand of their **e.** all the.......... 341
Jg 3:28 for the Lord hath delivered your **e.** 341
Jg 5:31 So let all thine **e.** perish,.................... 341
Jg 8:34 out of the hands of all their **e.** on........ 341
Jg 11:36 taken vengeance for thee of thine **e.**,...... 341
1Sa 2:1 my mouth is enlarged over mine **e.**; 341
1Sa 4:3 save us out of the hand of our **e.**.......... 341
1Sa 12:10 deliver us out of the hand of our **e.**, ... 341
1Sa 12:11 out of the hand of your **e.** on every...... 341
1Sa 14:24 that I may be avenged on mine **e.**........ 341
1Sa 14:30 spoil of their **e.** which they found?......... 341
1Sa 14:47 against all his **e.** on every side, ... 341
1Sa 18:25 to be avenged of the king's **e.**. 341
1Sa 20:15 Lord hath cut off the **e.** of David 341
1Sa 20:16 require it at the hand of David's **e.**........ 341
1Sa 25:22 also do God unto the **e.** of David, ... 341
1Sa 25:26 let thine **e.**, and they that seek evil....... 341
1Sa 25:29 souls of thine **e.**, them shall he sling...... 341
1Sa 29:8 go fight against the **e.** of my lord 341
1Sa 30:26 the spoil of the **e.** of the Lord;............ 341
2Sa 3:18 out of the hand of all their **e.**. 341
2Sa 5:20 hath broken forth upon mine **e.** 341
2Sa 7:1 rest round about from all his **e.**; 341
2Sa 7:9 cut off all thine **e.** out of thy sight,........ 341
2Sa 7:11 caused thee to rest from all thine **e.**...... 341
2Sa 12:14 great occasion to the **e.** of the Lord 341
2Sa 18:19 the Lord hath avenged him of his **e.**..... 341
2Sa 18:32 The **e.** of my lord the king, and all....... 341
2Sa 19:6 thine **e.**, and hatest thy friends. 8130
2Sa 19:9 saved us out of the hand of our **e.**, ... 341
2Sa 22:1 him out of the hand of all his **e.**, and 341
2Sa 22:4 so shall I be saved from mine **e.**.......... 341
2Sa 22:38 I have pursued mine **e.**, and 341
2Sa 22:41 also given me the necks of mine **e.**, ... 341
2Sa 22:49 bringeth me forth from mine **e.**: 341
2Sa 24:13 flee three months before thine **e.**, ... 6862
1Ki 3:11 nor hast asked the life of thine **e.**; 341
1Ki 8:48 their soul, in the land of their **e.**, ... 341
2Ki 17:39 you out of the hand of all your **e.**.......... 341
2Ki 21:14 them into the hand of their **e.**; 341
2Ki 21:14 a prey and a spoil to all their **e.**;.......... 341
1Ch 12:17 be come to betray me to mine **e.**, ... 6862
1Ch 14:11 God hath broken in upon mine **e.**......... 341
1Ch 17:8 and have cut off all thine **e.** from 341
1Ch 17:10 Moreover I will subdue all thine **e.**....... 341
1Ch 21:12 while that the sword of thine **e.**.......... 341
1Ch 22:9 I will give him rest from all his **e.**......... 341
2Ch 1:11 or honour, nor the life of thine **e.**, ... 8130
2Ch 6:28 their **e.** besiege them in the cities........ 341
2Ch 6:34 go out to war against their **e.** by the 341
2Ch 6:36 deliver them over before their **e.**, ... 341
2Ch 20:27 made them to rejoice over their **e.**....... 341
2Ch 20:29 fought against the **e.** of Israel,............ 341
2Ch 25:20 deliver them into the hands of their **e.**,......
Ne 4:15 our **e.** heard that it was known............ 341
Ne 5:9 the reproach of the heathen our **e.**?...... 341
Ne 6:1 the Arabian, and the rest of our **e.**,...... 341
Ne 6:16 that when all our **e.** heard thereof,....... 341
Ne 9:27 them into the hand of their **e.**,.......... 6862
Ne 9:27 saved out of the hand of their **e.**. 6862
Ne 9:28 thou them in the hand of their **e.**, ... 341
Es 8:13 to avenge themselves on their **e.**.......... 341
Es 9:1 the day that the **e.** of the Jews hoped... 341
Es 9:5 Thus the Jews smote all their **e.**........... 341
Es 9:16 and had rest from their **e.**, and slew..... 341
Es 9:22 the Jews rested from their **e.**,............. 341
Job 19:11 me unto him as one of his **e.**............ 6862
Ps 3:7 thou hast smitten all mine **e.**................ 341
Ps 5:8 because of mine **e.**; make thy way......... 8324
Ps 6:7 waxeth old because of all mine **e.**. 6887
Ps 6:10 Let all mine **e.** be ashamed and........... 341
Ps 7:6 because of the rage of mine **e.**:............ 6887
Ps 8:2 strength because of thine **e.**, that....... 6887
Ps 9:3 When mine **e.** are turned back, ... 341
Ps 10:5 for all his **e.**, he puffeth at them......... 6887
Ps 17:9 from my deadly **e.**, who compass me.... 341
Ps 18:*title* him from the hand of all his **e.**,............ 341
Ps 18:3 so shall I be saved from mine **e.**.......... 341
Ps 18:37 I have pursued mine **e.**, and 341
Ps 18:40 also given me the necks of mine **e.**; 341
Ps 18:48 He delivereth me from mine **e.**:............ 341
Ps 21:8 Thine hand shall find out all thine **e.**: 341
Ps 23:5 me in the presence of mine **e.**: 6887
Ps 25:2 let not mine **e.** triumph over me. 341
Ps 25:19 consider mine **e.**; for they are many; 341
Ps 27:2 even mine **e.** and my foes, came........ 6862
Ps 27:6 head be lifted up above mine **e.**........... 341
Ps 27:11 a plain path, because of mine **e.**; 8324
Ps 27:12 not over unto the will of mine **e.**: 6862
Ps 31:11 was a reproach among all mine **e.**,...... 6887
Ps 31:15 me from the hand of mine **e.**,............... 341
Ps 35:19 Let not them that are mine **e.**.............. 341
Ps 37:20 and the **e.** of the Lord shall be as 341
Ps 38:19 But mine **e.** are lively, and they 341
Ps 41:2 deliver him unto the will of his **e.**......... 341
Ps 41:5 Mine **e.** speak evil of me, When........... 341
Ps 42:10 mine **e.** reproach me; while they 6887
Ps 44:5 thee will we push down our **e.**: 6862
Ps 44:7 thou hast saved us from our **e.**. 6862
Ps 45:5 in the heart of the king's **e.**: 341
Ps 54:5 He shall reward evil unto mine **e.**:...... 8324
Ps 54:7 hath seen his desire upon mine **e.**. 341
Ps 56:2 Mine **e.** would daily swallow me 8324
Ps 56:9 then shall mine **e.** turn back:............... 341
Ps 59:1 Deliver me from mine **e.**, O my God: ... 341
Ps 59:10 me see my desire upon mine **e.**. 8324
Ps 60:12 it is that shall tread down our **e.**. 6862
Ps 66:3 shall thine **e.** submit themselves 341
Ps 68:1 God arise, let his **e.** be scattered:......... 341
Ps 68:21 God shall wound the head of his **e.**,....... 341
Ps 68:23 be dipped in the blood of thine **e.**,......... 341
Ps 69:4 being mine **e.** wrongfully, are mighty: ... 341
Ps 69:18 deliver me because of mine **e.**.............. 341
Ps 71:10 For mine **e.** speak against me; 341
Ps 72:9 and his **e.** shall lick the dust................ 341
Ps 74:4 Thine **e.** roar in the midst of thy........ 6887
Ps 74:23 Forget not the voice of thine **e.**: 6887
Ps 78:53 but the sea overwhelmed their **e.**.......... 341
Ps 78:66 smote his **e.** in the hinder parts: 6862
Ps 80:6 our **e.** laugh among themselves............ 341
Ps 81:14 I should soon have subdued their **e.**, ... 341
Ps 83:2 For, lo, thine **e.** make a tumult: 341
Ps 89:10 scattered thine **e.** with thy strong 341
Ps 89:42 thou hast made all his **e.** to rejoice....... 341
Ps 89:51 Wherewith thine **e.** have reproached,.... 341
Ps 92:9 For, lo, thine **e.**, O Lord,.................... 341
Ps 92:9 for, lo, thine **e.** shall perish;................ 341
Ps 92:11 shall see my desire on mine **e.**, ... 7790
Ps 97:3 burneth up his **e.** round about.............. 6862
Ps 102:8 Mine **e.** reproach me all the day; 341
Ps 105:24 made them stronger than their **e.**. 6862
Ps 106:11 And the waters covered their **e.**:........ 6862
Ps 106:42 Their **e.** also oppressed them, and....... 341
Ps 108:13 it is that shall tread down our **e.**. 6862
Ps 110:1 until I make thine **e.** thy footstool. 341
Ps 110:2 rule thou in the midst of thine **e.**. 341
Ps 112:8 he see his desire upon his **e.**............. 6862
Ps 119:98 hast made me wiser than mine **e.**: 341
Ps 119:139 mine **e.** have forgotten thy words....... 6862
Ps 119:157 are my persecutors and mine **e.**; 6862
Ps 127:5 but they shall speak with the **e.**............ 341
Ps 132:18 His **e.** will I clothe with shame: 341
Ps 136:24 hath redeemed us from our **e.**: 6862
Ps 138:7 hand against the wrath of mine **e.**, ... 341
Ps 139:20 thine **e.** take thy name in vain. 6145
Ps 139:22 hatred: I count them mine **e.**................. 341
Ps 143:9 Deliver me, O Lord, from mine **e.**: 341
Ps 143:12 And of thy mercy cut off mine **e.**, ... 341
Pr 16:7 maketh even his **e.** to be at peace 341
Isa 1:24 and avenge me of mine **e.**: 341
Isa 9:11 and join his **e.** together;...................... 341
Isa 26:11 of thine **e.** shall devour them. 6862
Isa 42:13 he shall prevail against his **e.**................ 341
Isa 59:18 adversaries, recompence to his **e.**; 341
Isa 62:8 thy corn to be meat for thine **e.**; 341
Isa 66:6 rendereth recompence to his **e.**............ 341
Isa 66:14 and his indignation toward his **e.**.......... 341
Jer 12:7 my soul into the hand of her **e.**. 341
Jer 15:9 deliver to the sword before their **e.**,...... 341
Jer 15:14 make thee to pass with thine **e.**........... 341
Jer 17:4 I will cause thee to serve thine **e.**....... 341
Jer 19:7 to fall by the sword before their **e.**,...... 341
Jer 19:9 and straitness, wherewith their **e.**,........ 341
Jer 20:4 shall fall by the sword of their **e.**. 341
Jer 20:5 I give into the hand of their **e.**, ... 341
Jer 21:7 and into the hand of their **e.**, ... 341
Jer 34:20 give them into the hand of their **e.**, ... 341
Jer 34:21 I give into the hand of their **e.**, ... 341
Jer 44:30 king of Egypt into the hand of his **e.**,..... 341
Jer 48:5 **e.** have heard a cry of destruction. 6862
Jer 49:37 Elam to be dismayed before their **e.**,.... 341
La 1:2 with her, they are become her **e.**. 341
La 1:5 are the chief, her **e.** prosper;............... 341
La 1:21 mine **e.** have heard of my trouble; 341
La 2:16 thine **e.** have opened their mouth......... 341
La 3:46 All our **e.** have opened their mouths..... 341
La 3:52 Mine **e.** chased me sore, like a bird, ... 341
Eze 39:23 them into the hand of their **e.**;............ 6862
Da 4:19 interpretation thereof to thine **e.**. 6146
Am 9:4 go into captivity before their **e.**, ... 341
Mic 4:10 thee from the hand of thine **e.**.............. 341
Mic 5:9 all thine **e.** shall be cut off. 341
Mic 7:6 a man's **e.** are the men of his own....... 341
Na 1:2 he reserveth wrath for his **e.**. 341
Na 1:8 and darkness shall pursue his **e.**. 341
Na 3:13 be set wide open unto thine **e.**: 341
Zec 10:5 which tread down their **e.** in the..............
Mt 5:44 **Love your e., bless them that curse** *2190*
Mt 22:44 **till I make thine e. thy footstool?..** *2190*
Mk 12:36 **till I make thine e. thy footstool..** *2190*
Lu 1:71 That we should be saved from our **e.**,. *2190*
Lu 1:74 delivered out of the hand of our **e.** *2190*
Lu 6:27 **Love your e., do good to them that** *2190*
Lu 6:35 **love ye your e., and do good,** *2190*
Lu 19:27 **But those mine e., which would** *2190*
Lu 19:43 **thine e. shall cast a trench about** .. *2190*
Lu 20:43 **Till I make thine e. thy footstool.** .. *2190*
Ro 5:10 when we were **e.**, we were reconciled .*2190*
Ro 11:28 they are **e.** for your sakes: *2190*
1Co 15:25 till he hath put all **e.** under his feet..... *2190*
Php 3:18 that they are the **e.** of the cross of..... *2190*
Col 1:21 **e.** in your mind by wicked works,....... *2190*
Heb 1:13 until I make thine **e.** thy footstool? *2190*
Heb 10:13 till his **e.** be made his footstool. *2190*
Re 11:5 their mouth and devoureth their **e.**: *2190*
Re 11:12 and their **e.** beheld them.................... *2190*

ENEMIES'

Le 26:34 and ye be in your **e.** land; 341
Le 26:39 their iniquity in your **e.** lands;.............. 341
Eze 39:27 gathered them out of their **e.** lands, ... 341

ENEMY See also ENEMIES; ENEMY'S.

Ex 15:6 Lord hath dashed in pieces the **e.**. 341

Ex 15:9 The **e.** said, I will pursue, I will.......... 341
Ex 23:22 I will be an **e.** unto thine enemies, ... 340
Le 26:25 delivered into the hand of the **e.**. 341
Nu 10:9 the **e.** that oppresseth you, then.......... 341
Nu 35:23 that he die, and was not his **e.**, ... 341
De 28:57 wherewith thine **e.** shall distress.......... 341
De 32:27 not that I feared the wrath of the **e.**,.... 341
De 32:42 beginning of revenges upon the **e.**.......... 341
De 33:27 he shall thrust out the **e.** from.......... 341
Jg 16:23 hath delivered Samson our **e.** into........ 341
Jg 16:24 hath delivered into our hands our **e.**, ... 341
1Sa 2:32 shalt see an **e.** in my habitation,......... 6862
1Sa 18:29 Saul became David's **e.** continually......... 341
1Sa 19:17 and sent away mine **e.**, that he is 341
1Sa 24:4 will deliver thine **e.** into thine hand,...... 341
1Sa 24:19 For if a man find his **e.**, will he let....... 341
1Sa 26:8 hath delivered thine **e.** into thine.......... 341
1Sa 28:16 thee, and is become thine **e.**? 6145
2Sa 4:8 the son of Saul thine **e.**, which........... 341
2Sa 22:18 He delivered me from my strong **e.**,...... 341
1Ki 8:33 Israel be smitten down before the **e.**, ... 341
1Ki 8:37 if their **e.** besiege them in the land....... 341
1Ki 8:44 go out to battle against their **e.**, ... 341
1Ki 8:46 them, and deliver them to the **e.**, ... 341
1Ki 8:46 captives unto the land of the **e.**, ... 341
1Ki 21:20 Hast thou found me, O mine **e.**?.......... 341
2Ch 6:24 be put to the worse before the **e.**, ... 341
2Ch 25:8 shall make thee fall before the **e.**: 341
2Ch 26:13 to help the king against the **e.**.......... 341
Ezr 8:22 help us against the **e.** in the way: 341
Ezr 8:31 delivered us from the hand of the **e.**...... 341
Es 3:10 the Agagite, the Jews' **e.**. 6887
Es 7:4 the **e.** could not countervail the.......... 6862
Es 7:6 and **e.** is this wicked Haman. 341
Es 8:1 Haman the Jews' **e.** unto Esther......... 6887
Es 9:10 Hammedatha, the **e.** of the Jews, ... 6887
Es 9:24 the Agagite, the **e.** of all the Jews, ... 6887
Job 13:24 and holdest me for thine **e.**? 341
Job 16:9 mine **e.** sharpeneth his eyes upon....... 6862
Job 27:7 Let mine **e.** be as the wicked,............. 341
Job 33:10 he counteth me for his **e.**, ... 341
Ps 7:4 that without cause is mine **e.**:)........... 6887
Ps 7:5 Let the **e.** persecute my soul, ... 341
Ps 8:2 that thou mightest still the **e.** and 341
Ps 9:6 O thou **e.**, destructions are come......... 341
Ps 13:2 how long shall mine **e.** be exalted 341
Ps 13:4 Lest mine **e.** say, I have prevailed 341
Ps 18:17 He delivered me from my strong **e.**,....... 341
Ps 31:8 shut me up into the hand of the **e.**: 341
Ps 41:11 mine **e.** doth not triumph over me........ 341
Ps 42:9 because of the oppression of the **e.**?..... 341
Ps 43:2 because of the oppression of the **e.**?..... 341
Ps 44:10 us to turn back from the **e.**: 6862
Ps 44:16 by reason of the **e.** and avenger. 341
Ps 55:3 Because of the voice of the **e.**,............ 341
Ps 55:12 For it was not an **e.** that reproached 341
Ps 61:3 and a strong tower from the **e.**. 341
Ps 64:1 preserve my life from fear of the **e.**. 341
Ps 74:3 all that the **e.** hath done wickedly......... 341
Ps 74:10 shall the **e.** blaspheme thy name 341
Ps 74:18 this, that the **e.** hath reproached,......... 341
Ps 78:42 he delivered them from the **e.**. 6862
Ps 89:22 The **e.** shall not exact upon him;.......... 341
Ps 106:10 them from the hand of the **e.**. 341
Ps 107:2 redeemed from the hand of the **e.**; 6862
Ps 143:3 the **e.** hath persecuted my soul; 341
Pr 24:17 Rejoice not when thine **e.** falleth,......... 341
Pr 25:21 If thine **e.** be hungry, give him 8130
Pr 27:6 the kisses of an **e.** are deceitful. 8130
Isa 59:19 the **e.** shall come in like a flood,......... 6862
Isa 63:10 he was turned to be their **e.**, ... 341
Jer 6:25 for the sword of the **e.** and fear is on... 341
Jer 15:11 I will cause the **e.** to entreat thee......... 341
Jer 18:17 as with an east wind before the **e.**; 341
Jer 30:14 thee with the wound of an **e.**, ... 341
Jer 31:16 come again from the land of the **e.**....... 341
Jer 44:30 king of Babylon, his **e.**, and that.......... 341
La 1:5 gone into captivity before the **e.**. 6862
La 1:7 people fell into the hand of the **e.**, ... 6862
La 1:9 for the **e.** hath magnified himself. 341
La 1:16 desolate, because the **e.** prevailed. 341
La 2:3 his right hand from before the **e.**, ... 341
La 2:4 He hath bent his bow like an **e.**: 341
La 2:5 The Lord was as an **e.**: he hath........... 341
La 2:7 hath given up into the hand of the **e.**.... 341
La 2:17 he hath caused thine **e.** to rejoice 341
La 2:22 brought up hath mine **e.** consumed....... 341
La 4:12 and the **e.** should have entered into...... 341
Eze 36:2 Because the **e.** hath said against you, ... 341
Ho 8:3 is good: the **e.** shall pursue him........... 341
Mic 2:8 my people is risen up as an **e.**:........... 341
Mic 7:8 Rejoice not against me, O mine **e.**: 341
Mic 7:10 Then she that is mine **e.** shall see it,.... 341
Na 3:11 seek strength because of the **e.**........... 341
Zep 3:15 he hath cast out thine **e.**: 341
Mt 5:43 **thy neighbour, and hate thine e.**... *2190*
Mt 13:25 **his e. came and sowed tares among** *2190*
Mt 13:28 **unto them, An e. hath done this**.... *2190*
Mt 13:39 **The e. that sowed them is the**....... *2190*
Lu 10:19 **and over all the power of the e.** *2190*
Ac 13:10 devil, thou **e.** of all righteousness, ... *2190*
Ro 12:20 Therefore if thine **e.** hunger, feed......... *2190*
1Co 15:26 The last **e.** that shall be destroyed...... *2190*
Gal 4:16 Am I therefore become your **e.**,.......... *2190*
2Th 3:15 Yet count him not as an **e.**,............... *2190*
Jas 4:4 friend of the world is the **e.** of God. ... *2190*

ENEMY'S
Ex 23:4 If thou meet thine **e.** ox or his ass....... 341
Job 6:23 Deliver me from the **e.** hand?............. 6862
Ps 78:61 and his glory into the **e.** hand. 6862

ENFLAMING ee also INFLAME.
Isa 57:5 **E.** yourselves with idols under........... 2552

ENGAGED
Jer 30:21 for who is this that **e.** his heart to...... 6148

EN-GANNIM (en-gan'-nim)
Jos 15:34 And Zanoah, and **E.**, Tappuah, ... 5873
Jos 19:21 Remeth, and **E.**, and En-haddah,......... 5873
Jos 21:29 Jarmuth with her suburbs, **E.** with...... 5873

EN-GEDI (en-ghe'-di) See also HAZAZON-TAMAR.
Jos 15:62 and the city of Salt, and **E.**;............. 5872
1Sa 23:29 and dwelt in strong holds at **E.**.......... 5872
1Sa 24:1 David is in the wilderness of **E.**.......... 5872
2Ch 20:2 be in Hazazon-tamar, which is **E.**........ 5872
Ca 1:14 camphire in the vineyards of **E.**. 5872
Eze 47:10 fishers shall stand upon it from **E.**...... 5872

ENGINES
2Ch 26:15 And he made in Jerusalem **e.**,............ 2810
Eze 26:9 he shall set **e.** of war against thy........ 4239

ENGRAFTED See also GRAFFED.
Jas 1:21 with meekness the **e.** word, which...... *1721*

ENGRAVE See also ENGRAVEN; ENGRAVINGS.
Ex 28:11 shalt thou **e.** the two stones with....... 6605
Zec 3:9 behold, I will **e.** the graving thereof, ... 6605

ENGRAVEN
2Co 3:7 written and **e.** in stones, was *1795*

ENGRAVER
Ex 28:11 With the work of an **e.** in stone, ... 2796
Ex 35:35 all manner of work, of the **e.**,............ 2796
Ex 38:23 an **e.**, and a cunning workman, ... 2796

ENGRAVINGS
Ex 28:11 in stone, like the **e.** of a signet, ... 6603
Ex 28:21 names, like the **e.** of a signet; 6603
Ex 28:36 upon it, like the **e.** of a signet,........... 6603
Ex 39:14 names, like the **e.** of a signet, ... 6603
Ex 39:30 writing, like to the **e.** of a signet, ... 6603

EN-HADDAH (en-had'-dah)
Jos 19:21 and **E.**, and Beth-pazzez;.................. 5876

EN-HAKKORE (en-hak'-ko-re)
Jg 15:19 he called the name thereof **E.**, ... 5875

EN-HAZOR (en-ha'-zor)
Jos 19:37 And Kedesh, and Edrei, and **E.**, ... 5877

ENJOIN See also ENJOINED.
Phm 8 much bold in Christ to **e.** thee *2004*

ENJOINED
Es 9:31 and Esther the queen had **e.** them,..... 6965
Job 36:23 Who hath **e.** him his way? who 6485
Heb 9:20 which God hath **e.** unto you. *1781*

ENJOY See also ENJOYED.
Le 26:34 shall the land **e.** her sabbaths, ... 7521
Le 26:34 the land rest and **e.** her sabbaths. 7521
Le 26:43 shall **e.** her sabbaths, while she.......... 7521
Nu 36:8 children of Israel may **e.** every 3423
De 28:41 daughters, but thou shalt not **e.** 1961
Jos 1:15 land of your possession, and **e.** it, ... 3423
Ec 2:1 with mirth, therefore **e.** pleasure:....... 7200
Ec 2:24 he should make his soul **e.** good in 7200
Ec 3:13 and **e.** the good of all his labour, ... 7200
Ec 5:18 eat and drink, and to **e.** the good 7200
Isa 65:22 long **e.** the work of their hands. 1086
Ac 24:2 Seeing that by thee we **e.** great......... *5177*
1Ti 6:17 giveth us richly all things to **e.**; *619*
Heb 11:25 than to **e.** the pleasures of sin...... *2192,619*

ENJOYED
2Ch 36:21 until the land had **e.** her sabbaths: 7521

ENLARGE See also ENLARGED; ENLARGETH; ENLARGING.
Ge 9:27 God shall **e.** Japheth, and he shall....... 6601
Ex 34:24 before thee, and **e.** thy borders: 7337
De 12:20 When the Lord thy God shall **e.** thy.... 7337
De 19:8 if the Lord thy God **e.** thy coast, ... 7337
1Ch 4:10 wouldest bless....and **e.** my coast, ... 7235
Ps 119:32 when thou shalt **e.** my heart.............. 7337
Isa 54:2 **E.** the place of thy tent, and let.......... 7337
Am 1:13 that they might **e.** their border: 7337
Mic 1:16 **e.** thy baldness as the eagle for; 7337
Mt 23:5 **e. the borders of their garments,** ... *3170*

ENLARGED
1Sa 2:1 my mouth is **e.** over mine enemies; 7337
2Sa 22:37 Thou hast **e.** my steps under me;..... 7337
Ps 4:1 thou hast **e.** me when I was in........... 7337
Ps 18:36 Thou hast **e.** my steps under me,........ 7337
Ps 25:17 The troubles of my heart are **e.**: 7337
Isa 5:14 Therefore hell hath **e.** herself, ... 7337
Isa 57:8 gone up; thou hast **e.** thy bed,........... 7337
Isa 60:5 thine heart shall fear, and be **e.**; 7337
2Co 6:11 is open unto you, our heart is **e.**........ *4115*
2Co 6:13 unto my children,) be ye also **e.**......... *4115*
2Co 10:15 that we shall be **e.** by you *3170*

ENLARGEMENT
Es 4:14 shall there **e.** and deliverance 7305

ENLARGETH
De 33:20 Blessed be he that **e.** Gad: 7337
Job 12:23 he **e.** the nations, and straiteneth 7849
Hab 2:5 who **e.** his desire as hell, and is.......... 7337

ENLARGING
Eze 41:7 there was an **e.**, and a winding 7337

ENLIGHTEN See also ENLIGHTENED; ENLIGHTENING.
Ps 18:28 Lord my God will **e.** my darkness........ 5050

ENLIGHTENED
1Sa 14:27 his mouth; and his eyes were **e.**........... 215
1Sa 14:29 mine eyes have been **e.**, because.......... 215
Job 33:30 to be **e.** with the light of the living....... 215
Ps 97:4 His lightnings **e.** the world:................ 215
Eph 1:18 of your understanding being **e.**;.......... *5461*
Heb 6:4 those who were once **e.**, and have *5461*

ENLIGHTENING
Ps 19:8 of the Lord is pure, **e.** the eyes. 215

EN-MISHPAT (en-mish'-pat) See also KADESH.
Ge 14:7 they returned, and came to **E.**, ... 5880

ENMITY
Ge 3:15 put **e.** between thee and the woman,.... 342
Nu 35:21 Or in **e.** smite him with his hand,......... 342
Nu 35:22 thrust him suddenly without **e.**,...............
Lu 23:12 were at **e.** between themselves........... *2189*
Ro 8:7 the carnal mind is **e.** against God:....... *2189*
Eph 2:15 abolished in his flesh the **e.**,............. *2189*
Eph 2:16 having slain the **e.** thereby................ *2189*
Jas 4:4 friendship of the world is **e.** with......... *2189*

ENOCH (e'-nok) See also HENOCH.
Ge 4:17 and she conceived, and bare **E.** 2585
Ge 4:17 after the name of his son, **E.**.............. 2585
Ge 4:18 unto **E.** was born Irad: and Irad......... 2585
Ge 5:18 and two years, and he begat **E.**:.......... 2585
Ge 5:19 Jared lived after he begat **E.** eight...... 2585
Ge 5:21 And **E.** lived sixty and five years, ... 2585
Ge 5:22 **E.** walked with God after he begat..... 2585
Ge 5:23 the days of **E.** were three hundred...... 2585
Ge 5:24 **E.** walked with God: and he was not; ..2585
Lu 3:37 which was the son of **E.**, which......... *1802*
Heb 11:5 By faith **E.** was translated that he...... *1802*
Jude 14 **E.** also, the seventh from Adam, ... *1802*

ENON See AENON.

ENOS (e'-nos) See also ENOSH.
Ge 4:26 called his name **E.**: then began............ 583
Ge 5:6 and five years, and begat **E.**:............... 583

Ge 5:7 And Seth lived after he begat **E.**......... 583
Ge 5:9 **E.** lived ninety years, and begat.......... 583
Ge 5:10 **E.** lived after he begat Cainan............ 583
Ge 5:11 the days of **E.** were nine hundred........ 583
Lu 3:38 Which was the son of **E.**, which *1800*

ENOSH (e'-nosh) See also ENOS.
1Ch 1:1 Adam, Sheth, **E.**,............................ 583

ENOUGH
Ge 24:25 have both straw and provender **e.**, ... 7227
Ge 33:9 Esau said, I have **e.**, my brother;....... 7227
Ge 33:11 with me, and because I have **e.**. 3605
Ge 34:21 behold, it is large **e.** for them;.......... 3027
Ge 45:28 Israel said, It is **e.**; Joseph my.......... 7227
Ex 2:19 and also drew water **e.** for us. ....
Ex 9:28 Intreat the Lord (for it is **e.**) that....... 7227
Ex 36:5 much more than **e.** for the service........ 1767
De 1:6 Ye have dwelt long **e.** in this mount;.........
De 2:3 compassed this mountain long **e.**...............
Jos 17:16 The hill is not **e.** for us:................... 4672
2Sa 24:16 It is **e.**: stay now thine hand. And...... 7227
1Ki 19:4 It is **e.**; now, O Lord, take away........ 7227
1Ch 21:15 It is **e.**, stay now thine hand. And...... 7227
2Ch 31:10 we have had **e.** to eat, and have........ 7644
Pr 27:27 have goats' milk **e.** for thy food,......... 1767
Pr 28:19 persons shall have poverty **e.**.............. 7644
Pr 30:15 yea, four things say not, It is **e.**.......... 1952
Pr 30:16 and the fire that saith not, It is **e.**. 1952
Isa 56:11 dogs which can never have **e.**,............ 7654
Jer 49:9 they will destroy till they have **e.**. 1767
Ho 4:10 they shall eat, and not have **e.**:............ 7644
Ob 5 not have stolen till they had **e.**? 1767
Na 2:12 did tear in pieces **e.** for his whelps, ... 1767
Hag 1:6 little; ye eat, but ye have not **e.**; 7654
Mal 3:10 that there shall not be room **e.** 1767
Mt 10:25 **It is e. for the disciple that he be**... *713*
Mt 25:9 **there be not e. for us and your:**...... *714*
Mk 14:41 **your rest: it is e., the hour is come;**.*566*
Lu 15:17 **have bread e. and to spare, and I**.. *4052*
Lu 22:38 he said unto them, It is **e.**. *2425*
Ac 27:38 they had eaten **e.**, they lightened *2880*

ENQUIRE See also ENQUIRED; ENQUIREST; ENQUIRY.
Ge 24:57 We will call the damsel,and **e.** at........ 7592
Ge 25:22 And she went to **e.** of the Lord. 1875
Ex 18:15 people come unto me to **e.** of God: 1875
De 12:30 that thou **e.** not after their gods,........ 1875
De 13:14 shalt thou **e.**, and make search, ... 1875
De 17:9 and **e.**; and they shall shew thee......... 1875
Jg 4:20 man doth come and **e.** of thee,............ 7592
1Sa 9:9 when a man went to **e.** of God, ... 1875
1Sa 17:56 **E.** thou whose son the stripling is...... 7592
1Sa 22:15 Did I then begin to **e.** of God for 7592
1Sa 28:7 that I may go to her, and **e.** of her..... 1875
1Ki 22:5 **E.**, I pray thee, at the word of the..... 1875
1Ki 22:7 besides, that we might **e.** of him?........ 1875
1Ki 22:8 by whom we may **e.** of the Lord:.......... 1875
2Ki 1:2 **e.** of Baal-zebub the god of Ekron........ 1875
2Ki 1:3 that ye go to **e.** of Baal-zebub........... 1875
2Ki 1:6 thou sendest to **e.** of Baal-zebub 1875
2Ki 1:16 **e.** of Baal-zebub the god of Ekron, ... 1875
2Ki 1:16 no God in Israel to **e.** of his word? 1875
2Ki 3:11 that we may **e.** of the Lord by him?.... 1875
2Ki 8:8 and **e.** of the Lord by him,................. 1875
2Ki 16:15 altar shall be for me to **e.** by............. 1239
2Ki 22:13 Go ye, **e.** of the Lord for me, ... 1875
2Ki 22:18 which sent you to **e.** of the Lord,........ 1875
1Ch 10:13 had a familiar spirit, to **e.** of it: 1875
1Ch 18:10 his son to king David, to **e.** of his 7592
1Ch 21:30 could not go before it to **e.** of God: 1875
2Ch 18:4 **E.**, I pray thee, at the word of the....... 1875
2Ch 18:6 besides, that we might **e.** of him?....... 1875
2Ch 18:7 by whom we may **e.** of the Lord: 1875
2Ch 32:31 sent unto him to **e.** of the wonder 1875
2Ch 34:21 Go, **e.** of the Lord for me, and for 1875
2Ch 34:26 who sent you to **e.** of the Lord,......... 1875
Ezr 7:14 to **e.** concerning Judah and.............. 1240
Job 8:8 **e.**, I pray thee, of the former age, ... 7592
Ps 27:4 the Lord, and to **e.** in his temple......... 1239
Ec 7:10 dost not **e.** wisely concerning this....... 7592
Isa 21:12 if ye will **e.**, **e.** ye: return, come, ... 1158
Jer 21:2 **E.**, I pray thee, of the Lord for us;..... 1875
Jer 37:7 that sent you unto me to **e.** of me;..... 1875
Eze 14:7 prophet to **e.** of him concerning 1875
Eze 20:1 of Israel came to **e.** of the Lord,........ 1875
Eze 20:3 Are ye come to **e.** of me?................. 1875
Mt 10:11 **e. who in it is worthy; and there**... *1833*
Lu 22:23 began to **e.** among themselves,.......... *4802*
Joh 16:19 **Do ye e. among yourselves of that** *2212*
Ac 9:11 **e. in the house of Judas for one**.... *2212*
Ac 19:39 But if ye **e.** any thing concerning........ *1934*
Ac 23:15 as though ye would **e.** something........ *1231*
Ac 23:20 as though they would **e.** somewhat *4441*
2Co 8:23 Whether any do **e.** of Titus, he is............

ENQUIRED
De 17:4 **e.** diligently, and, behold, it be........... 1875
Jg 6:29 And when they **e.** and asked, ... 1875
Jg 8:14 a young man..., and **e.** of him:........... 7592
Jg 20:27 children of Israel **e.** of the Lord, ... 7592
1Sa 10:22 they **e.** of the Lord further, if the....... 7592
1Sa 22:10 And he **e.** of the Lord for him, ... 7592
1Sa 22:13 and hast **e.** of God for him,............... 7592
1Sa 23:2 Therefore David **e.** of the Lord,.......... 7592
1Sa 23:4 David **e.** of the Lord yet again............ 7592
1Sa 28:6 And when Saul **e.** of the Lord,........... 7592
1Sa 30:8 And David **e.** at the Lord, saying, ... 7592
2Sa 2:1 that David **e.** of the Lord, saying,........ 7592
2Sa 5:19 And David **e.** of the Lord, saying, ... 7592
2Sa 5:23 when David **e.** of the Lord, he said,.... 7592
2Sa 11:3 David sent and **e.** after the woman. 1875
2Sa 16:23 as if a man had **e.** at the oracle.......... 7592
2Sa 21:1 year; and David **e.** of the Lord. 1245
1Ch 10:14 And **e.** not of the Lord: therefore........ 1875
1Ch 13:3 we **e.** not at it in the days of Saul. 1875
1Ch 14:10 And David **e.** of God, saying, ... 7592
1Ch 14:14 Therefore David **e.** again of God; 7592
Ps 78:34 returned and **e.** early after God.......... 7836
Eze 14:3 should I be **e.** of at all by them?........ 1875
Eze 20:3 Lord God, I will not be **e.** of by you. .. 1875
Eze 20:31 and shall I be **e.** of by you, O house... 1875
Eze 20:31 Lord God, I will not be **e.** of by you. ....
Eze 36:37 I will yet for this be **e.** of by the........ 1875
Da 1:20 king **e.** of them, he found them.......... 1245
Zep 1:6 sought the Lord, nor **e.** for him. 1875
Mt 2:7 **e.** of them diligently what time the....... *198*
Mt 2:16 had diligently **e.** of the wise men. *198*
Joh 4:52 Then **e.** he of them the hour............ *4441*
2Co 8:23 or our brethren be **e.** of, they ....
1Pe 1:10 have **e.** and searched diligently,.......... *1567*

ENQUIREST
Job 10:6 That thou **e.** after mine iniquity,......... 1245

ENQUIRY
Pr 20:25 and after vows to make **e.**................ 1239
Ac 10:17 had made **e.** for Simon's house, ... *1331*

ENRICH See also ENRICHED; ENRICHEST.
1Sa 17:25 king will **e.** him with great riches,........ 6238
Eze 27:33 thou didst **e.** the kings of the earth..... 6238

ENRICHED
1Co 1:5 in every thing ye are **e.** by him,.......... *4148*
2Co 9:11 **e.** in every thing to all bountifulness,... *4148*

ENRICHEST
Ps 65:9 greatly **e.** it with the river of God, ... 6238

EN-RIMMON (en-rim'-mon) See also AIN and RIMMON.
Ne 11:29 And at **E.**, and at Zareah, and at......... 5884

EN-ROGEL (en-ro'-ghel)
Jos 15:7 the goings out thereof were at **E.**: 5883
Jos 18:16 on the south, and descended to **E.**, ... 5883
2Sa 17:17 and Ahimaaz stayed by **E.**; 5883
1Ki 1:9 stone of Zoheleth, which is by **E.**,....... 5883

ENSAMPLE See also ENSAMPLES; EXAMPLE.
Php 3:17 walk as ye have us for an **e.**. *5179*
2Th 3:9 to make ourselves an **e.** unto you....... *5179*
2Pe 2:6 making them an **e.** unto those........... *5262*

ENSAMPLES
1Co 10:11 things happened unto them for **e.**: *5179*
1Th 1:7 that ye were **e.** to all that believe....... *5179*
1Pe 5:3 but being **e.** to the flock. *5179*

EN-SHEMESH (en-she'-mesh)
Jos 15:7 passed toward the waters of **E.**, ... 5885
Jos 18:17 and went forth to **E.**, and went 5885

ENSIGN See also ENSIGNS.
Nu 2:2 the **e.** of their father's house:............. 226
Isa 5:26 he will lift up an **e.** to the nations....... 5251
Isa 11:10 shall stand for an **e.** of the people;....... 5251
Isa 11:12 he shall set up an **e.** for the nations,... 5251
Isa 18:3 lifteth up an **e.** on the mountains; 5251
Isa 30:17 and as an **e.** on an hill...................... 5251
Isa 31:9 his princes shall be afraid of the **e.**, ... 5251
Zec 9:16 lifted up as an **e.** upon his land. 5264

ENSIGNS
Ps 74:4 they set up their **e.** for signs. 226

ENSNARED
Job 34:30 reign not, lest the people be **e.**.......... 4170

ENSUE See also PURSUE.
1Pe 3:11 let him seek peace, and **e.** it. *1377*

ENTANGLE See also ENTANGLED; ENTANGLETH.
Mt 22:15 how they might **e.** him in his talk. *3802*

ENTANGLED
Ex 14:3 of Israel, They are **e.** in the land, ... 943
Ga 5:1 **e.** again with the yoke of bondage, ... *1758*
2Pe 2:20 they are again **e.** therein, and........... *1707*

ENTANGLETH
2Ti 2:4 **e.** himself with the affairs of the......... *1707*

EN-TAPPUAH (en-tap'-poo-ah)
Jos 17:7 hand, unto the inhabitants of **E.**,......... 5887

ENTER See also ENTERED; ENTERETH; ENTERING.
Ge 12:11 he was come near to **e.** into Egypt, ... 935
Ex 40:35 Moses was not able to **e.** into the........ 935
Nu 4:3 that **e.** into the host, to do the work.... 935
Nu 4:23 all that **e.** in to perform service, ... 935
Nu 5:24, 27 causeth the curse shall **e.** into......... 935
Nu 20:24 for he shall not **e.** into the land........... 935
De 23:1 member cut off, shall not **e.** into the..... 935
De 23:2 A bastard shall not **e.** into the 935
De 23:2 generation shall he not **e.** into the........ 935
De 23:3 or Moabite shall not **e.** into the 935
De 23:3 generation shall they not **e.** into the 935
De 23:8 begotten of them shall not **e.** into the... 935
De 29:12 thou shouldest **e.** into covenant.......... 5674
Jos 10:19 them not to **e.** into their cities:............ 935
Jg 18:9 and to **e.** to possess the land............... 935
2Sa 22:7 and my cry did **e.** into his ears. ....
1Ki 14:12 when thy feet **e.** into the city,............. 935
1Ki 22:30 myself, and **e.** into the battle; 935
2Ki 7:4 If we say, We will **e.** into the city,........ 935
2Ki 11:5 that **e.** in on the sabbath shall.............. 935
2Ki 19:23 **e.** into the lodgings of his borders,....... 935
2Ch 7:2 priests could not **e.** into the house....... 935
2Ch 23:19 unclean in any thing should **e.** in. 935
2Ch 30:8 and **e.** into his sanctuary, which he....... 935
Ne 2:8 for the house that I shall **e.** into. 935
Es 4:2 none might **e.** into the king's gate 935
Job 22:4 he **e.** with thee into judgment? 935
Job 34:23 that he should **e.** into judgment.......... 1980
Ps 37:15 sword shall **e.** into their own heart,...... 935
Ps 45:15 they shall **e.** into the king's palace........ 935
Ps 95:11 that they should not **e.** into my rest. 935
Ps 100:4 **E.** into his gates with thanksgiving, ... 935
Ps 118:20 into which the righteous shall **e.**. 935
Ps 143:2 And **e.** not into judgment with thy........ 935
Pr 4:14 **E.** not into the path of the wicked, ... 935
Pr 18:6 A fool's lips **e.** into contention, ... 935
Pr 23:10 and **e.** not into the fields of the 935
Isa 2:10 **E.** into the rock, and hide thee in......... 935
Isa 3:14 The Lord will **e.** into judgment with...... 935
Isa 26:2 which keepeth the truth may **e.** in......... 935
Isa 26:20 people, **e.** thou into thy chambers, ... 935
Isa 37:24 will **e.** into the height of his border, ... 935
Isa 57:2 shall **e.** into peace: they shall rest 935
Isa 59:14 in the street, and equity cannot **e.**. 935
Jer 7:2 that **e.** in at these gates to worship...... 935
Jer 8:14 and let us **e.** into the defenced cities, ... 935
Jer 14:18 if I **e.** into the city, then behold 935
Jer 16:5 **E.** not into the house of mourning, ... 935
Jer 17:20 Jerusalem, that **e.** in by these gates: 935
Jer 17:25 Then shall there **e.** into the gates 935
Jer 21:13 who shall **e.** into our habitations? 935
Jer 22:2 thy people that **e.** in by these gates: 935
Jer 22:4 then shall there **e.** in by the gates........ 935
Jer 41:17 Bethlehem, to go to **e.** into Egypt,........ 935
Jer 42:15 set your faces to **e.** into Egypt,............ 935
Jer 42:18 when ye shall **e.** into Egypt: 935
La 1:10 should not **e.** into thy congregation....... 935
La 3:13 caused the arrows of his quiver to **e.**..... 935
Eze 7:22 for the robbers shall **e.** into it. 935
Eze 13:9 they **e.** into the land of Israel;............. 935
Eze 20:38 shall not **e.** into the land of Israel:........ 935
Eze 26:10 when he shall **e.** into thy gates,........... 935
Eze 26:10 as men **e.** into a city wherein is............ 935
Eze 37:5 I will cause breath to **e.** into you, ... 935

Eze 42:14 When the priests **e.** therein, then 935
Eze 44:2 and no man shall **e.** in by it; 935
Eze 44:3 he shall **e.** by the way of the porch...... 935
Eze 44:9 in flesh, shall **e.** into my sanctuary, ... 935
Eze 44:16 They shall **e.** into my sanctuary, ... 935
Eze 44:17 when they **e.** in at the gates of the 935
Eze 44:21 when they **e.** into the inner court.......... 935
Eze 46:2 And the prince shall **e.** by the way....... 935
Eze 46:8 And when the prince shall **e.**, he 935
Da 11:7 army, and shall **e.** into the fortress....... 935
Da 11:17 He shall also set his face to **e.** 935
Da 11:24 He shall **e.** peaceably even upon 935
Da 11:40 and he shall **e.** into the countries, ... 935
Da 11:41 shall **e.** also into the glorious land, ... 935
Ho 11:9 and I will not **e.** into the city.............. 935
Joe 2:9 they shall **e.** in at the windows........... 935
Am 5:5 seek not Bethel, nor **e.** into Gilgal, ... 935
Jon 3:4 and Jonah began to **e.** into the city 935
Zec 5:4 and it shall **e.** into the house of the 935
Mt 5:20 **e. into the kingdom of heaven,** *1525*
Mt 6:6 **thou prayest, e. into thy closet,** *1525*
Mt 7:13 **E. ye in at the strait gate:** *1525*
Mt 7:21 **Lord, shall e. into the kingdom of.** *1525*
Mt 10:5 **city of the Samaritans e. ye not:** ... *1525*
Mt 10:11 **city or town ye shall e.,** *1525*
Mt 12:29 **one e. into a strong man's house,** .. *1525*
Mt 12:45 **and they e. in and dwell there:** *1525*
Mt 18:3 **not e. into the kingdom of heaven.** . *1525*
Mt 18:8 **thee to e. into life halt or maimed,** . *1525*
Mt 18:9 **thee to e. into life with one eye,** ... *1525*
Mt 19:17 **if thou wilt e. into life, keep the** ... *1525*
Mt 19:23 **shall hardly e. into the kingdom of** *1525*
Mt 19:24 **to e. into the kingdom of God.** *1525*
Mt 25:21, 23 **e. thou into the joy of thy lord.** . *1525*
Mt 26:41 **that ye e. not into temptation:** *1525*
Mk 1:45 no more openly **e.** into the city, ... *1525*
Mk 3:27 **can e. into a strong man's house,** .. *1525*
Mk 5:12 swine, that we may **e.** into them. *1525*
Mk 6:10 **place soever ye e. into an house,** ... *1525*
Mk 9:25 **of him, and e. no more into him.** .. *1525*
Mk 9:43 **for thee to e. into life maimed,** *1525*
Mk 9:45 **better for thee to e. halt into life,** . *1525*
Mk 9:47 **thee to e. into the kingdom of God.** *1525*
Mk 10:15 **little child, he shall not e. therein.** . *1525*
Mk 10:23 **shall...e. into the kingdom of God!** . *1525*
Mk 10:24 **riches to e. into the kingdom of** *1525*
Mk 10:25 **man to e. into the kingdom of** *1525*
Mk 13:15 **neither e. therein, to take any** *1525*
Mk 14:38 **pray, lest ye e. into temptation.** *1525*
Lu 7:6 thou shouldest **e.** under my roof:........ *1525*
Lu 8:16 **they which e. in may see the light.** *1531*
Lu 8:32 would suffer them to **e.** into them. *1525*
Lu 9:4 **house ye e. into, there abide,** *1525*
Lu 10:5 **whatsoever house ye e., first say,** .. *1525*
Lu 10:8 **into whatsoever city ye e., and** *1525*
Lu 10:10 **But into whatsoever city ye e.,** *1525*
Lu 11:26 **and they e. in, and dwell there:** *1525*
Lu 13:24 **Strive to e. in at the strait gate:** *1525*
Lu 13:24 **seek to e. in, and shall not be able.** *1525*
Lu 18:17 **child shall in no wise e. therein.** ... *1525*
Lu 18:24 **riches e. into the kingdom of God!** . *1525*
Lu 18:25 **man to e. into the kingdom of** *1525*
Lu 21:21 **are in the countries e. thereinto.** ... *1525*
Lu 22:40 **that ye e. not into temptation.** *1525*
Lu 22:46 **pray, lest ye e. into temptation.** *1525*
Lu 24:26 **things, and to e. into his glory?** *1525*
Joh 3:4 can he **e.** the second time into his *1525*
Joh 3:5 **cannot e. into the kingdom of God.** *1525*
Joh 10:9 **if any man e. in, he shall be saved,** *1525*
Ac 14:22 **e.** into the kingdom of God. *1525*
Ac 20:29 grievous wolves **e.** in among you,....... *1525*
Heb 3:11 They shall not **e.** into my rest.) *1525*
Heb 3:18 that they should not **e.** into his rest, ... *1525*
Heb 3:19 that they could not **e.** in because........ *1525*
Heb 4:3 which have believed do **e.** into rest,.... *1525*
Heb 4:3 wrath, if they shall **e.** into my rest: *1525*
Heb 4:5 again, If they shall **e.** into my rest...... *1525*
Heb 4:6 that some must **e.** therein, and they *1525*
Heb 4:11 therefore to **e.** into that rest, lest....... *1525*
Heb 10:19 boldness to **e.** into the holiest by........ *1529*
Re 15:8 was able to **e.** into the temple, ... *1525*
Re 21:27 there shall in no wise **e.** into it *1525*
Re 22:14 **E.** in through the gates into the city. .. *1525*

ENTERED

Ge 7:13 In the selfsame day **e.** Noah, and......... 935
Ge 19:3 unto him, and **e.** into his house; 935
Ge 19:23 the earth when Lot **e.** into Zoar. 935
Ge 31:33 Leah's tent, and **e.** into Rachel's.......... 935
Ge 43:30 and he **e.** into his chamber, and........... 935
Ex 33:9 as Moses **e.** into the tabernacle, ... 935
Jos 2:3 which are **e.** into thine house: for 935
Jos 8:19 and they **e.** into the city, and took it, ... 935
Jos 10:20 of them **e.** into fenced cities............... 935
Jg 6:5 they **e.** into the land to destroy it. 935
Jg 9:46 they **e.** into an hold of the house 935
2Sa 10:14 Abishai, and **e.** into the city. 935
2Ki 7:8 again, and **e.** into another tent,............ 935
2Ki 9:31 as Jehu **e.** in at the gate, ... 935
1Ch 19:15 and **e.** into the city. Then Joab 935
2Ch 12:11 king **e.** into the house of the Lord,....... 935
2Ch 15:12 **e.** into a covenant to seek the Lord...... 935
2Ch 27:2 howbeit he **e.** not into the temple 935
2Ch 32:1 and **e.** into Judah, and encamped.......... 935
Ne 2:15 and **e.** by the gate of the valley. 935
Ne 10:29 **e.** into a curse, and into an oath, ... 935
Job 38:16 Hast thou **e.** into the springs of the...... 935
Job 38:22 Hast thou **e.** into the treasures of 935
Jer 2:7 but when ye **e.**, ye defiled my land, ... 935
Jer 9:21 and is **e.** into our palaces, to cut off 935
Jer 34:10 which had **e.** into the covenant, ... 935
Jer 37:16 was **e.** into the dungeon, and into 935
La 1:10 the heathen **e.** into her sanctuary,........ 935
La 4:12 should have **e.** into the gates 935
Eze 2:2 the spirit **e.** into me when he spake 935
Eze 3:24 Then the spirit **e.** into me, and set....... 935
Eze 16:8 and **e.** into a covenant with thee, ... 935
Eze 36:20 when they **e.** unto the heathen, ... 935
Eze 41:6 and they **e.** into the wall 935
Eze 44:2 the God of Israel, hath **e.** in by it, ... 935
Ob 11 and foreigners **e.** into his gates............ 935
Ob 13 shouldest not have **e.** into the gate........ 935
Hab 3:16 rottenness **e.** into my bones, and I........ 935
Mt 8:5 when Jesus was **e.** into Capernaum, ... *1525*
Mt 8:23 when he was **e.** into a ship, ... *1684*
Mt 9:1 he **e.** into a ship, and passed over, ... *1684*
Mt 12:4 **How he e. into the house of God,** .. *1525*
Mt 24:38 **the day that Noe e. into the ark,** ... *1525*
Mk 1:21 he **e.** into the synagogue, and........... *1525*
Mk 1:29 they **e.** into the house of Simon *2064*
Mk 2:1 again he **e.** into Capernaum after........ *1525*
Mk 3:1 he **e.** again into the synagogue;.......... *1525*
Mk 4:1 he **e.** into a ship, and sat in the sea; ... *1684*
Mk 5:13 went out, and **e.** into the swine: *1525*
Mk 6:56 whithersoever he **e.**, into villages, ... *1531*
Mk 7:17 when he was **e.** into the house *1525*
Mk 7:24 **e.** into an house, and would have *1525*
Mk 8:10 he **e.** into a ship with his disciples, ... *1684*
Mk 11:2 **as soon as ye be e. into it,** *1531*
Mk 11:11 Jesus **e.** into Jerusalem, and into *1525*
Lu 1:40 And **e.** into the house of Zacharias, ... *1525*
Lu 4:38 synagogue, and **e.** into Simon's *1525*
Lu 5:3 he **e.** into one of the ships, which........ *1684*
Lu 6:6 **e.** into the synagogue and taught: *1525*
Lu 7:1 people, he **e.** into Capernaum. *1525*
Lu 7:44 **I e. into thine house, thou gavest** .. *1525*
Lu 8:30 many devils were **e.** into him............ *1525*
Lu 8:33 **e.** into the swine: and the herd ran...... *1525*
Lu 9:34 feared as they **e.** into the cloud.......... *1525*
Lu 9:52 they went, and **e.** into a village.......... *1525*
Lu 10:38 that he **e.** into a certain village:.......... *1525*
Lu 11:52 **ye e. not in yourselves, and them** .. *1525*
Lu 17:12 as he **e.** into a certain village, ... *1525*
Lu 17:27 **day that Noe e. into the ark,** *1525*
Lu 19:1 Jesus **e.** and passed through............. *1525*
Lu 22:3 Then **e.** Satan into Judas surnamed..... *1525*
Lu 22:10 **when ye are e. into the city, there** . *1525*
Lu 24:3 they **e.** in, and found not the body...... *1525*
Joh 4:38 **and ye are e. into their labours.** ... *1525*
Joh 6:17 **e.** into a ship, and went over the *1684*
Joh 6:22 whereinto his disciples were **e.**, ... *1684*
Joh 13:27 after the sop Satan **e.** into him........... *1525*
Joh 18:1 was a garden, into the which he **e.**, ... *1525*
Joh 18:33 Then Pilate **e.** into the judgment *1525*
Joh 21:3 They went forth, and **e.** into a ship *305*
Ac 3:2 ask alms of them that **e.** into the........ *1531*
Ac 3:8 and **e.** with them into the temple,........ *1525*
Ac 5:21 they **e.** into the temple early in the..... *1525*
Ac 9:17 went his way, and **e.** into the house;... *1525*
Ac 10:24 And the morrow after they **e.** into...... *1525*
Ac 11:8 hath at any time **e.** into my mouth...... *1525*
Ac 11:12 and we **e.** into the man's house:.......... *1525*
Ac 16:40 and **e.** into the house of Lydia: *1525*
Ac 18:7 and **e.** into a certain man's house, ... *2064*
Ac 18:19 **e.** the synagogue, and reasoned *1525*
Ac 19:30 Paul would have **e.** in unto the........... *1525*
Ac 21:8 we **e.** into the house of Philip *1525*
Ac 21:26 with them **e.** into the temple, to *1524*
Ac 23:16 **e.** into the castle, and told Paul.......... *1525*
Ac 25:23 and was **e.** into the place of hearing, ... *1525*
Ac 28:8 to whom Paul **e.** in, and prayed, ... *1525*
Ro 5:12 sin **e.** into the world, and death by *1525*
Ro 5:20 Moreover the law **e.**, that the *3922*
1Co 2:9 neither have **e.** into the heart of.......... *305*
Heb 4:6 **e.** not in because of unbelief:............ *1525*
Heb 4:10 For he that is **e.** into his rest, he........ *1525*
Heb 6:20 Whither the forerunner is for us **e.**, ... *1525*
Heb 9:12 he **e.** in once into the holy place, ... *1525*
Heb 9:24 For Christ is not **e.** into the holy........ *1525*
Jas 5:4 are **e.** into the ears of the Lord *1525*
2Jo 7 deceivers are **e.** into the world, ... *1525*
Re 11:11 spirit of life from God **e.** into them, ... *1525*

ENTERETH

Nu 4:30 that **e.** into the sevice, to do the 935
Nu 4:35, 39,43 that **e.** into the service, for 935
2Ch 31:16 every one that **e.** into the house of 935
Pr 2:10 When wisdom **e.** into thine heart, ... 935
Pr 17:10 A reproof **e.** more into a wise man..... 5181
Eze 21:14 which **e.** into their privy chambers............
Eze 42:12 toward the east, as one **e.** into them. ... 935
Eze 46:9 he that **e.** in by the way of the north.... 935
Eze 46:9 he that **e.** by the way of the south....... 935
Mt 15:17 **whatsoever e. in at the mouth** *1531*
Mk 5:40 **e.** in where the damsel was lying. *1531*
Mk 7:18 **from without e. into the man,** *1531*
Mk 7:19 **Because it e. not into his heart,** *1531*
Lu 22:10 **him into the house where he e. in.** . *1531*
Joh 10:1 **He that e. not by the door into** *1535*
Joh 10:2 **But he that e. in by the door is** *1535*
Heb 6:19 which **e.** into that within the veil; *1535*
Heb 9:25 as the high priest **e.** into the holy....... *1535*

ENTERING See also ENTRANCE.

Ex 35:15 at the **e.** in of the tabernacle, ... 6607
Jos 8:29 at the **e.** of the gate of the city,........... 6607
Jos 13:5 unto the **e.** into Hamath..................... 935
Jos 20:4 at the **e.** of the gate of the city,.......... 6607
Jg 3:3 unto the **e.** in of Hamath.................... 935
Jg 9:35 in the **e.** of the gate of the city:......... 6607
Jg 9:40 even unto the **e.** of the gate............. 6607
Jg 9:44 in the **e.** of the gate of the city:......... 6607
Jg 18:16 Dan, stood by the **e.** of the gate. 6607
Jg 18:17 priest stood in the **e.** of the gate........ 6607
1Sa 23:7 by **e.** into a town that hath gates 935
2Sa 10:8 in array at the **e.** in of the gate:........ 6607
2Sa 11:23 them even unto the **e.** of the gate. 6607
1Ki 6:31 And for the **e.** of the oracle he made .. 6607
1Ki 8:65 from the **e.** in of Hamath unto the........ 935
1Ki 19:13 and stood in the **e.** in of the cave. 6607
2Ki 7:3 leprous men at the **e.** in of the gate:... 6607
2Ki 10:8 two heaps at the **e.** in of the gate 6607
2Ki 14:25 **e.** of Hamath unto the sea of the 935
2Ki 23:8 in the **e.** in of the gate of Joshua 6607
2Ki 23:11 at the **e.** in of the house of the........... 935
1Ch 5:9 unto the **e.** in of the wildernes 935
1Ch 13:5 Egypt even unto the **e.** of Hemath, ... 935
2Ch 7:8 from the **e.** in of Hamath unto the........ 935
2Ch 18:9 void place at the **e.** in of the gate....... 6607
2Ch 23:4 part of you **e.** on the sabbath.............. 935
2Ch 23:13 king stood at his pillar at the **e.** 3996
2Ch 23:15 when she was come to the **e.** of 3996
2Ch 26:8 abroad even to the **e.** in of Egypt; 935
2Ch 33:14 even to the **e.** in at the fish gate, ... 935
Isa 23:1 so that there is no house, no **e.** in: 935
Jer 1:15 at the **e.** of the gates of Jerusalem,..... 6607
Jer 17:27 **e.** in at the gates of Jerusalem............ 935
Eze 44:5 mark well the **e.** in of the house, ... 3996
Am 6:14 afflict you from the **e.** in of Hemath...... 935
Mt 23:13 **suffer ye them that are e. to go in.** *1525*
Mk 4:19 **the lusts of other things e. in,** *1531*
Mk 7:15 **that e. into him can defile him;** *1531*
Mk 8:13 **e.** into the ship again departed.......... *1684*
Mk 16:5 **e.** into the sepulchre, they saw a *1525*
Lu 11:52 **them that were e. in ye hindered.** .. *1525*
Lu 19:30 **in the which at your e. ye shall** *1531*
Ac 8:3 As for Saul...**e.** into every house,........ *1531*
Ac 27:2 **e.** into a manner of ship of Adramyttium, ... *1910*
1Th 1:9 what manner of **e.** in we had unto *1529*
Heb 4:1 being left us of **e.** into his rest,.......... *1525*

ENTERPRISE
Job 5:12 hands cannot perform their **e.**........... 8454

ENTERTAIN See also ENTERTAINED.
Heb 13:2 Be not forgetful to **e.** strangers:......... *5381*

ENTERTAINED
Heb 13:2 some have **e.** angels unawares.......... *3579*

ENTICE See also ENTICED; ENTICETH.
Ex 22:16 if a man **e.** a maid that is not............ 6601
De 13:6 **e.** thee secretly, saying, Let us go..... 5496
Jg 14:15 **E.** thy husband, that he may............ 6601
Jg 16:5 **E.** him, and see wherein his great...... 6601
2Ch 18:19 Who shall **e.** Ahab king of Israel,........ 6601
2Ch 18:20 before the Lord, and said, I will **e.**..... 6601
2Ch 18:21 Thou shalt **e.** him, and thou shalt....... 6601
Pr 1:10 My son, if sinners **e.** thee, consent..... 6601

ENTICED
Job 31:27 my heart hath been secretly **e.**,......... 6601
Jer 20:10 Peradventure he will be **e.**, and......... 6601
Jas 1:14 drawn away of his own lust, and **e.**..... *1185*

ENTICETH
Pr 16:29 A violent man **e.** his neighbour.......... 6601

ENTICING
1Co 2:4 with **e.** words of man's wisdom,......... *3981*
Col 2:4 should beguile you with **e.** words,........ *4086*

ENTIRE
Jas 1:4 that ye may be perfect and **e.**,........... *3648*

ENTRANCE See also ENTERING; ENTRANCES; ENTRY.
Nu 34:8 border unto the **e.** of Hamath;............. 935
Jg 1:24 Shew us...the **e.** into the city,........... 3996
Jg 1:25 when he shewed them the **e.** into....... 3996
1Ki 18:46 ran before Ahab to the **e.** of Jezreel..... 935
1Ki 22:10 in the **e.** of the gate of Samaria;......... 6607
1Ch 4:39 they went to the **e.** of Gedor,............ 3996
2Ch 12:10 that kept the **e.** of the king's............ 6607
Ps 119:130 The **e.** of thy words giveth light;........ 6608
Eze 40:15 the face of the gate of the **e.**............. 2978
1Th 2:1 know our **e.** in unto you, that it......... *1529*
2Pe 1:11 an **e.** shall be ministered unto you...... *1529*

ENTRANCES
Mic 5:6 land of Nimrod in the **e.** thereof:........ 6607

ENTREAT See also ENTREATED; ENTREATETH; INTREAT.
Jer 15:11 cause the enemy to **e.** thee well........ 6293
Ac 7:6 and **e.** them evil four hundred........... *2559*

ENTREATED See also INTREATED.
Ge 12:16 he **e.** Abram well for her sake: ....
Ex 5:22 hast thou so evil **e.** this people? ....
De 26:6 And the Egyptians evil **e.** us,..................
Mt 22:6 **e. them spitefully, and slew them**...*5195*
Lu 18:32 **shall be mocked, and spitefully e.**, *5195*
Lu 20:11 **e. him shamefully, and sent him**..... *818*
Ac 7:19 evil **e.** our fathers, so that they......... *2559*
Ac 27:3 Julius courteously **e.** Paul, and.......... *5530*
1Th 2:2 before, and were shamefully **e.**.......... *5195*

ENTREATETH
Job 24:21 He evil **e.** the barren that beareth............

ENTREATY See INTREATY.

ENTRIES
Eze 40:38 the chambers and the **e.** thereof......... 6607

ENTRY See also ENTERING; ENTRANCE; ENTRIES.
2Ki 16:18 king's **e.** without, turned he from....... 3996
1Ch 9:19 of the Lord, were keepers of the **e.**.... 3996
2Ch 4:22 **e.** of the house, the inner doors......... 6607
Pr 8:3 at the **e.** of the city, at the coming..... 6310
Jer 19:2 which is by the **e.** of the east gate, ... 6607
Jer 26:10 sat down in the **e.** of the new gate..... 6607
Jer 36:10 court, at the **e.** of the new gate......... 6607
Jer 38:14 prophet unto him into the third **e.**........ 3996
Jer 43:9 is at the **e.** of Pharaoh's house........... 6607
Eze 8:5 this image of jealousy in the **e.**............ 872
Eze 27:3 art situate at the **e.** of the sea,.......... 3996
Eze 40:11 the breadth of the **e.** of the gate,........ 6607
Eze 40:40 goeth up to the **e.** of the north gate,..... 6607
Eze 42:9 was the **e.** on the east side,............... 3996
Eze 46:19 he brought me through the **e.**............ 3996

ENVIED
Ge 26:14 and the Philistines **e.** him................. 7065
Ge 30:1 no children, Rachel **e.** her sister;........ 7065
Ge 37:11 his brethren **e.** him; but his father...... 7065
Ps 106:16 They **e.** Moses also in the camp, ... 7065
Ec 4:4 this a man is **e.** of his neighbour. 7068
Eze 31:9 that all the trees of Eden....**e.** him. 7065

ENVIES
1Pe 2:1 guile, and hypocrisies, and **e.**, and...... 5355

ENVIEST
Nu 11:29 unto him, **E.** thou for my sake? 7065

ENVIETH
1Co 13:4 charity **e.** not; charity vaunteth.......... *2206*

ENVIOUS
Ps 37:1 neither be thou **e.** against the........... 7065
Ps 73:3 For I was **e.** at the foolish, when....... 7065
Pr 24:1 Be not thou **e.** against evil men,........ 7065
Pr 24:19 neither be thou **e.** at the wicked; 7065

ENVIRON
Jos 7:9 shall **e.** us round, and cut off our........ 5437

ENVY See also ENVIABLE; ENVIED; ENVIES; ENVIEST; ENVYING.
Job 5:2 and **e.** slayeth the silly one................ 7068
Pr 3:31 **E.** thou not the oppressor, and.......... 7065
Pr 14:30 but **e.** the rottenness of the bones...... 7068
Pr 23:17 Let not thine heart **e.** sinners: but...... 7065
Pr 27:4 who is able to stand before **e.**? 7068
Ec 9:6 their hatred, and their **e.**, is now........ 7068
Isa 11:13 The **e.** also of Ephraim shall depart,.... 7068
Isa 11:13 Ephraim shall not **e.** Judah, and......... 7065
Isa 26:11 for their **e.** at the people; yea,........... 7068
Eze 35:11 according to thine **e.** which thou......... 7068
Mt 27:18 that for **e.** they had delivered him....... *5355*
Mk 15:10 priests had delivered him for **e.**......... *5355*
Ac 7:9 patriarchs, moved with **e.**, sold.......... *2206*
Ac 13:45 were filled with **e.**, and spake............ *2205*
Ac 17:5 which believed not, moved with **e.**....... *2206*
Ro 1:29 full of **e.**, murder, debate, deceit,....... *5355*
Php 1:15 preach Christ even of **e.** and strife;..... *5355*
1Ti 6:4 whereof cometh **e.**, strife, railings, ... *5355*
Tit 3:3 living in malice and **e.**, hateful,........... *5355*
Jas 4:5 that dwelleth in us lusteth to **e.**? *5355*

ENVYING See also ENVYINGS.
Ro 13:13 wantonness, not in strife and **e.**. *2205*
1Co 3:3 **e.**, and strife, and divisions, are.......... *2205*
Ga 5:26 one another, **e.** one another. *5354*
Jas 3:14 But if ye have bitter **e.** and strife........ *2205*
Jas 3:16 For where **e.** and strife is, there........ *2205*

ENVYINGS
2Co 12:20 **e.**, wraths, strifes, backbitings, ... *2205*
Ga 5:21 **E.**, murders, drunkenness, ... *5355*

EPAENETUS (ep-en'-e-tus)
Ro 16:5 Salute my well beloved **E.**, who......... *1866*

EPAPHRAS (ep'-a-fras)
Col 1:7 As ye also learned of **E.** our dear *1889*
Col 4:12 **E.**, who is one of you, a servant of.... *1889*
Phm 23 salute thee **E.**, my fellowprisoner....... *1889*

EPAPHRODITUS (e-paf-ro-di'-tus)
Php 2:25 it necessary to send to you **E.**, ... *1891*
Php 4:18 having received of **E.** the things......... *1891*
Php *subscr.* Philippians from Rome by **E.**,............ *1891*

EPENETUS See EPAENETUS.

EPHAH (e'-fah)
Ex 16:36 an omer is the tenth part of an **e.**........ 374
Le 5:11 the tenth part of an **e.** of fine flour....... 374
Le 6:20 the tenth part of an **e.** of fine flour....... 374
Le 19:36 just weights, a just **e.**, and a just......... 374
Nu 5:15 tenth part of an **e.** of barley meal;........ 374
Nu 28:5 And a tenth part of an **e.** of flour......... 374
Jg 6:19 unleavened cakes of an **e.** of flour: 374
Ru 2:17 and it was about an **e.** of barley........... 374
1Sa 1:24 one **e.** of flour, and a bottle of wine, ... 374
1Sa 17:17 brethren an **e.** of this parched corn, ... 374
Isa 5:10 seed of an homer shall yield an **e.**......... 374
Eze 45:10 and a just **e.**, and a just bath.............. 374
Eze 45:11 The **e.** and the bath shall be of one...... 374
Eze 45:11 the **e.** the tenth part of an homer 374
Eze 45:13 part of an **e.** of an homer of wheat....... 374
Eze 45:13 part of an **e.** of an homer of barley:...... 374
Eze 45:24 an **e.** for a bullock, and an **e.** for a........ 374
Eze 45:24 a ram, and an hin of oil for an **e.**. 374
Eze 46:5 offering shall be an **e.** for a ram,......... 374
Eze 46:5 to give, and an hin of oil to an **e.**......... 374
Eze 46:7 an **e.** for a bullock, and an **e.** for a....... 374
Eze 46:7 unto, and an hin of oil to an **e.**. 374
Eze 46:11 an **e.** to a bullock, and an **e.** to a ram,.. 374
Eze 46:11 to give, and an hin of oil to an **e.**......... 374
Eze 46:14 morning, the sixth part of an **e.**,.......... 374
Am 8:5 making the **e.** small, and the shekel...... 374
Zec 5:6 This is an **e.** that goeth forth. 374
Zec 5:7 sitteth in the midst of the **e.**............... 374
Zec 5:8 he cast it into the midst of the **e.**; 374
Zec 5:9 they lifted up the **e.** between the......... 374
Zec 5:10 Whither do these bear the **e.**?............. 374

EPHAH (e'-fah)
Ge 25:4 And the sons of Midian; **E.**, and........ 5891
1Ch 1:33 **E.**, and Epher, and Henoch, and........ 5891
1Ch 2:46 **E.**, Caleb's concubine, bare Haran,..... 5891
1Ch 2:47 And Pelet, and **E.**, and Shaaph. 5891
Isa 60:6 the dromedaries of Midian and **E.**;...... 5891

EPHAI (e'-fahee)
Jer 40:8 the sons of **E.** the Netophathite,........ 5778

EPHER (e'-fur)
Ge 25:4 sons of Midian; Ephah, and **E.**,.......... 6081
1Ch 1:33 Ephah, and **E.**, and Henoch, and........ 6081
1Ch 4:17 were, Jether, and Mered, and **E.**, ... 6081
1Ch 5:24 the house of their fathers, even **E.**,..... 6081

EPHES-DAMMIN (e''-fes-dam'-min) See also PASDAMMIN.
1Sa 17:1 Shochoh and Azekah, in **E.**................ 658

EPHESIAN (e-fe'-zheun) See also EPHESIANS.
Ac 21:29 him in the city Trophimus an **E.**, ... *2180*

EPHESIANS (e-fe'-zheuns)
Eph *general title* The Epistle ... To The **E.** *2180*
Ac 19:28 saying, Great is Diana of the **E.**......... *2180*
Ac 19:34 cried out, Great is Diana of the **E.**. *2180*
Ac 19:35 the city of the **E.** is a worshipper....... *2180*
Eph *subscr.* Written from Rome unto the **E.**......... *2180*
2Ti *subscr.* first bishop of the church of the **E.**,.... *2180*

EPHESUS (ef'-e-sus) See also EPHESIAN.
Ac 18:19 And he came to **E.**, and left them...... *2181*
Ac 18:21 God will. And he sailed from **E.**......... *2181*
Ac 18:24 mighty in the scriptures, came to **E.**... *2181*
Ac 19:1 through the upper coasts came to **E.**.. *2181*
Ac 19:17 and Greeks also dwelling at **E.**, ... *2181*
Ac 19:26 that not alone at **E.**, but almost.......... *2181*
Ac 19:35 Ye men of **E.**, what man is there....... *2181*
Ac 20:16 Paul had determined to sail by **E.**,...... *2181*
Ac 20:17 And from Miletus he sent to **E.**......... *2181*
1Co 15:32 I have fought with beasts at **E.**,......... *2181*
1Co 16:8 I will tarry at **E.** until Pentecost. *2181*
Eph 1:1 to the saints which are at **E.**,............ *2181*
1Ti 1:3 besought thee to abide still at **E.**, ... *2181*
2Ti 1:18 he ministered unto me at **E.**, ... *2181*
2Ti 4:12 And Tychicus have I sent to **E.**.......... *2181*
Re 1:11 **unto E., and unto Smyrna, and**.... *2181*
Re 2:1 **angel of the church of E. write;**.... *2181*

EPHLAL (ef-lal)
1Ch 2:37 Zabad begat **E.**, and **E.** begat............ 654

EPHOD (e'-fod)
Ex 25:7 and stones to be set in the **e.**,............ 646
Ex 28:4 a breastplate, and an **e.**, and a robe, ... 646
Ex 28:6 they shall make the **e.** of gold, ... 646
Ex 28:8 And the curious girdle of the **e.**,.......... 642
Ex 28:12 upon the shoulders of the **e.** for 646
Ex 28:15 after the work of the **e.** thou shalt 646
Ex 28:25 shoulderpieces of the **e.** before it.......... 646
Ex 28:26 is in the side of the **e.** inward. 646
Ex 28:27 the two sides of the **e.** underneath,....... 646
Ex 28:27 above the curious girdle of the **e.**.......... 646
Ex 28:28 rings thereof unto the rings of the **e.**..... 646
Ex 28:28 above the curious girdle of the **e.**,......... 646
Ex 28:28 breastplate be not loosed from the **e.**.... 646
Ex 28:31 make the robe of the **e.** all of blue. 646
Ex 29:5 and the robe of the **e.**, and the **e.**,....... 646
Ex 29:5 with the curious girdle of the **e.**:.......... 646
Ex 35:9, 27 and stones to be set for the **e.**,....... 646
Ex 39:2 he made the **e.** of gold, blue,............. 646
Ex 39:5 And the curious girdle of his **e.**, ... 642
Ex 39:7 them on the shoulders of the **e.**,.......... 646
Ex 39:8 like the work of the **e.**; of gold,........... 646
Ex 39:18 shoulderpieces of the **e.**, before it. 646
Ex 39:19 was on the side of the **e.** inward.......... 646
Ex 39:20 the two sides of the **e.** underneath,....... 646
Ex 39:20 above the curious girdle of the **e.**.......... 646
Ex 39:21 his rings unto the rings of the **e.** with... 646

Ex 39:21 above the curious girdle of the **e.**,........ 646
Ex 39:21 it might not be loosed from the **e.**;........ 646
Ex 39:22 And he made the robe of the **e.** of........ 646
Le 8:7 put the **e.** upon him, and he girded 646
Le 8:7 with the curious girdle of the **e.**,........ 646
Jg 8:27 And Gideon made an **e.** thereof, ... 646
Jg 17:5 made an **e.**, and teraphim, and 646
Jg 18:14 there is in these houses an **e.**, ... 646
Jg 18:17 took the graven image, and the **e.**,........ 646
Jg 18:18 fetched the carved image, the **e.**,........ 646
Jg 18:20 he took the **e.**, and the teraphim, ... 646
1Sa 2:18 being a child, girded with a linen **e.**...... 646
1Sa 2:28 to wear an **e.** before me? and did 646
1Sa 14:3 priest in Shiloh, wearing an **e.**............ 646
1Sa 21:9 wrapped in a cloth behind the **e.**:......... 646
1Sa 22:18 persons that did wear a linen **e.**.......... 646
1Sa 23:6 came down with an **e.** in his hand.......... 646
1Sa 23:9 the priest, Bring hither the **e.**............ 646
1Sa 30:7 I pray thee, bring me hither the **e.**....... 646
1Sa 30:7 And Abiathar brought hither the **e.**........ 646
2Sa 6:14 David was girded with a linen **e.**........... 646
1Ch 15:27 David also had upon him an **e.** of........... 646
Ho 3:4 without an **e.**, and without teraphim:..... 646

EPHOD (e'-fod)
Nu 34:23 Manasseh, Hanniel the son of **E.**......... 641

EPHPHATHA (ef'-fath-ah)
Mk 7:34 unto him, **E.**, that is, Be opened............ *2188*

EPHRAIM (e'-fra-im) See also EPHRAIMITE; EPHRAIM'S; EPHRAIN.
Ge 41:52 name of the second called he **E.**.......... 669
Ge 46:20 were born Manasseh and **E.**, which...... 669
Ge 48:1 him his two sons, Manasseh and **E.**..... 669
Ge 48:5 now thy two sons, **E.** and Manasseh, ... 669
Ge 48:13 **E.** in his right hand toward Israel's 669
Ge 48:17 his right hand upon the head of **E.**,...... 669
Ge 48:20 God make thee as **E.** and as.............. 669
Ge 48:20 and he set **E.** before Manasseh,........... 669
Nu 1:10 of **E.**; Elishama the son of Ammihud: ... 669
Nu 1:32 namely, of the children of **E.**, ... 669
Nu 1:33 even of the tribe of **E.**, were forty 669
Nu 2:18 be the standard of the camp of **E.** 669
Nu 2:18 the captain of the sons of **E.** shall........ 669
Nu 2:24 were numbered of the camp of **E.** 669
Nu 7:48 prince of the children of **E.**, offered: 669
Nu 10:22 of the camp of the children of **E.**.......... 669
Nu 13:8 Of the tribe of **E.**, Oshea the son........ 669
Nu 26:28 families were Manasseh and **E.**............ 669
Nu 26:35 the sons of **E.** after their families: 669
Nu 26:37 are the families of the sons of **E.**......... 669
Nu 34:24 of the tribe of the children of **E.**,........ 669
De 33:17 they are the ten thousands of **E.**,......... 669
De 34:2 all Naphtali, and the land of **E.**,........... 669
Jos 14:4 were two tribes, Manasseh and **E.**:........ 669
Jos 16:4 Manasseh and **E.**, took their.............. 669
Jos 16:5 the border of the children of **E.**.......... 669
Jos 16:8 of the tribe of the children of **E.**.......... 669
Jos 16:9 separate cities for the children of **E.**..... 669
Jos 17:8 belonged to the children of **E.**;........... 669
Jos 17:9 these cities of **E.** are among the cities.. 669
Jos 17:15 if mount **E.** be too narrow for thee....... 669
Jos 17:17 the house of Joseph, even to **E.**.......... 669
Jos 19:50 Even Timnath-serah in mount **E.**.......... 669
Jos 20:7 and Shechem in mount **E.**, ... 669
Jos 21:5 of the families of the tribe of **E.**,......... 669
Jos 21:20 of their lot out of the tribe of **E.**........ 669
Jos 21:21 with her suburbs in mount **E.**, ... 669
Jos 24:30 Timnath-serah,...is in mount **E.**,.......... 669
Jos 24:33 which was given him in mount **E.**.......... 669
Jg 1:29 did **E.** drive out the Canaanites........... 669
Jg 2:9 in the mount of **E.**, on the north side... 669
Jg 3:27 a trumpet in the mountain of **E.**, ... 669
Jg 4:5 Ramah and Bethel in mount **E.**:........... 669
Jg 5:14 Out of **E.** was there a root of them 669
Jg 7:24 throughout all mount **E.**, saying,.......... 669
Jg 7:24 the men of **E.** gathered themselves...... 669
Jg 8:1 the men of **E.** said unto him. Why....... 669
Jg 8:2 the gleaning of the grapes of **E.** 669
Jg 10:1 he dwelt in Shamir in mount **E.**........... 669
Jg 10:9 and against the house of **E.**; 669
Jg 12:1 men of **E.** gathered themselves........... 669
Jg 12:4 of Gilead, and fought with **E.**: 669
Jg 12:4 and the men of Gilead smote **E.**, ... 669
Jg 12:4 Ye Gileadites are fugitives of **E.**.......... 669
Jg 12:15 in Pirathon in the land of **E.**, ... 669
Jg 17:1 there was a man of mount **E.**, ... 669
Jg 17:8 to mount **E.** to the house of Micah, ... 669
Jg 18:2 who when they came to mount **E.**, ... 669
Jg 18:13 they passed thence unto mount **E.**,...... 669
Jg 19:1 sojourning on the side of mount **E.**, ... 669
Jg 19:16 which was also of mount **E.**; and........ 669
Jg 19:18 toward the side of mount **E.**;.............. 669
1Sa 1:1 Ramathaim-zophim, of mount **E.**,......... 669
1Sa 9:4 he passed through mount **E.**, and........ 669
1Sa 14:22 had hid themselves in mount **E.**,.......... 669
2Sa 2:9 and over **E.**, and over Benjamin, ... 669
2Sa 13:23 in Baal-hazor, which is beside **E.**: 669
2Sa 18:6 and the battle was in the wood of **E.**;... 669
2Sa 20:21 but a man of mount **E.**, Sheba the....... 669
1Ki 4:8 The son of Hur, in mount **E.**:............... 669
1Ki 12:25 built Schechem in mount **E.**, ... 669
2Ki 5:22 there be come to me from mount **E.**...... 669
2Ki 14:13 from the gate of **E.** unto the corner..... 669
1Ch 6:66 of their coasts out of the tribe of **E.**..... 669
1Ch 6:67 Schechem in mount **E.** with her 669
1Ch 7:20 sons of **E.**; Shuthelah, and Bered 669
1Ch 7:22 **E.** their father mourned many days 669
1Ch 9:3 of the children of **E.**, and Manasseh; 669
1Ch 12:30 the children of **E.** twenty thousand....... 669
1Ch 27:10 the Pelonite, of the children of **E.**:........ 669
1Ch 27:14 Pirathonite, of the children of **E.**: 669
1Ch 27:20 Of the children of **E.**, Hoshea the........ 669
2Ch 13:4 Zemaraim, which is in mount **E.**, ... 669
2Ch 15:8 which he had taken from mount **E.**, ... 669
2Ch 15:9 the strangers with them out of **E.**......... 669
2Ch 17:2 and in the cities of **E.**, which Asa 669
2Ch 19:4 people from Beer-sheba to mount **E.**,.... 669
2Ch 25:7 to wit, with all the children of **E.**.......... 669
2Ch 25:10 that was come to him out of **E.**,........... 669
2Ch 25:23 from the gate of **E.** to the corner 669
2Ch 28:7 Zichri, a mighty man of **E.**, slew 669
2Ch 28:12 of the heads of the children of **E.**, ... 669
2Ch 30:1 and wrote letters also to **E.** and.......... 669
2Ch 30:10 to city through the country of **E.**.......... 669
2Ch 30:18 of people, even many of **E.**, ... 669
2Ch 31:1 in **E.** also and Manasseh, until the 669
2Ch 34:6 and **E.**, and Simeon, even unto 669
2Ch 34:9 and **E.**, and of all the remnant of.......... 669
Ne 8:16 in the street of the gate of **E.**............. 669
Ne 12:39 And from above the gate of **E.**,............ 669
Ps 60:7 **E.** also is the strength of mine head;.... 669
Ps 78:9 The children of **E.**, being armed, ... 669
Ps 78:67 and chose not the tribe of **E.**:............. 669
Ps 80:2 **E.** and Benjamin and Manasseh........... 669
Ps 108:8 **E.** also is the strength of mine head;.... 669
Isa 7:2 saying, Syria is confederate with **E.**..... 669
Isa 7:5 Syria, **E.**, and the son of Remaliah,...... 669
Isa 7:8 and five years shall **E.** be broken......... 669
Isa 7:9 And the head of **E.** is Samaria,............ 669
Isa 7:17 day that **E.** departed from Judah;......... 669
Isa 9:9 all the people shall know, even **E.** 669
Isa 9:21 Manasseh, **E.**; and **E.**, Manasseh: 669
Isa 11:13 The envy also of **E.** shall depart,......... 669
Isa 11:13 **E.** shall not envy Judah,..................... 669
Isa 11:13 and Judah shall not vex **E.**................ 669
Isa 17:3 fortress also shall cease from **E.**,........ 669
Isa 28:1 to the drunkards of **E.**, whose 669
Isa 28:3 the drunkards of **E.**, shall be trodden ... 669
Jer 4:15 publisheth affliction from mount **E.**....... 669
Jer 7:15 brethren, even the whole seed of **E.**..... 669
Jer 31:6 the watchmen upon the mount **E.**......... 669
Jer 31:9 to Israel, and **E.** is my firstborn.......... 669
Jer 31:18 surely heard **E.** bemoaning himself....... 669
Jer 31:20 Is **E.** my dear son? is he a pleasant 669
Jer 50:19 shall be satisfied upon mount **E.**.......... 669
Eze 37:16 For Joseph, the stick of **E.**,............... 669
Eze 37:19 which is in the hand of **E.**, and the 669
Eze 48:5 unto the west side, a portion for **E.**..... 669
Eze 48:6 by the border of **E.**, from the east....... 669
Ho 4:17 **E.** is joined to idols: let him alone........ 669
Ho 5:3 I know **E.**, and Israel is not hid.......... 669
Ho 5:3 for now, O **E.**, thou committest 669
Ho 5:5 therefore shall Israel and **E.** fall.......... 669
Ho 5:9 **E.** shall be desolate in the day of.......... 669
Ho 5:11 **E.** is oppressed and broken in............ 669
Ho 5:12 will I be unto **E.** as a moth,............... 669
Ho 5:13 **E.** saw his sickness, and Judah............ 669
Ho 5:13 then went **E.** to the Assyrian, and....... 669
Ho 5:14 I will be unto **E.** as a lion, ... 669
Ho 6:4 O **E.**, what shall I do unto thee? 669
Ho 6:10 there is the whoredom of **E.**,.............. 669
Ho 7:1 the iniquity of **E.** was discovered,........ 669
Ho 7:8 **E.**, he hath mixed himself among......... 669
Ho 7:8 **E.** is a cake not turned......................... 669
Ho 7:11 **E.** also is like a silly dove without........ 669
Ho 8:9 **E.** hath hired lovers.......................... 669
Ho 8:11 **E.** hath made many altars to sin, ... 669
Ho 9:3 but **E.** shall return to Egypt, ... 669
Ho 9:8 watchman of **E.** was with my God: 669
Ho 9:11 As for **E.**, their glory shall fly away 669
Ho 9:13 **E.**, as I saw Tyrus, is planted in......... 669
Ho 9:13 **E.** shall bring forth his children 669
Ho 9:16 **E.** is smitten, their root is dried up,..... 669
Ho 10:6 **E.** shall receive shame, and Israel........ 669
Ho 10:11 **E.** is as an heifer that is taught,.......... 669
Ho 10:11 I will make **E.** to ride; Judah shall........ 669
Ho 11:3 I taught **E.** also to go, taking them 669
Ho 11:8 How shall I give thee up, **E.**? 669
Ho 11:9 I will not return to destroy **E.**:............ 669
Ho 11:12 **E.** compasseth me about with lies,....... 669
Ho 12:1 **E.** feedeth on wind, and followeth........ 669
Ho 12:8 **E.** said, Yet I am become rich, ... 669
Ho 12:14 **E.** provoked him to anger most........... 669
Ho 13:1 When **E.** spake trembling, he............. 669
Ho 13:12 The iniquity of **E.** is bound up;............ 669
Ho 14:8 **E.** shall say, What have I to do any 669
Ob 19 they shall possess the fields of **E.**,....... 669
Zec 9:10 I will cut off the chariot from **E.**,......... 669
Zec 9:13 filled the bow with **E.**, and raised........ 669
Zec 10:7 And they of **E.** shall be like a mighty.... 669
Joh 11:54 into a city called **E.**, and there *2187*

EPHRAIMITE (e'-fra-im-ite) See also EPHRAIMITES.
Jg 12:5 said unto him, Art thou an **E.**? 673

EPHRAIMITES (e'-fra-im-ites)
Jos 16:10 Canaanites dwell among the **E.**............ 669
Jg 12:4 fugitives of Ephraim among the **E.**,....... 669
Jg 12:5 passages of Jordan before the **E.**: 669
Jg 12:5 those **E.** which were escaped said, ... 669
Jg 12:6 there fell at that time of the **E.**........... 669

EPHRAIM'S (e'-fra-ims)
Ge 48:14 and laid it upon **E.** head, who was....... 669
Ge 48:17 to remove it from **E.** head unto.......... 669
Ge 50:23 Joseph saw **E.** children of the third...... 669
Jos 17:10 Southward it was **E.**, and northward..... 669

EPHRAIN (e'-fra-in) See also EPHRAIM; EPHRON.
2Ch 13:19 and **E.** with the towns thereof........... 6085

EPHRATAH (ef'-rat-ah) See also BETHLEHEM; CALEB-EPHRATAH; EPHRATH; EPHRATHITE.
Ru 4:11 and do thou worthily in **E.**,................ 672
1Ch 2:50 the son of Hur, the firstborn of **E.**;...... 672
1Ch 4:4 **E.**, the father of Beth-lehem............. 672
Ps 132:6 Lo, we heard of it at **E.**: we found...... 672
Mic 5:2 But thou Beth-lehem **E.**, though........... 672

EPHRATH (e'-frath) See also EPHRATAH.
Ge 35:16 was but a little way to come to **E.**........ 672
Ge 35:19 and was buried in the way to **E.**,......... 672
Ge 48:7 but a little way to come unto **E.**.......... 672
Ge 48:7 I buried her there in the way of **E.**;...... 672
1Ch 2:19 Caleb took unto him **E.**, which bare 672

EPHRATHITE (ef'-rath-ite) See also EPHRATHITES.
1Sa 1:1 of John, the son of Zuph, an **E.**;.......... 673
1Sa 17:12 Now David was the son of that **E.**........ 673
1Ki 11:26 Jeroboam the son of Nebat, an **E.**.......... 673

EPHRATHITES (ef'-rath-ites)
Ru 1:2 **E.** of Beth-lehem-judah........................ 673

EPHRON (e'-fron) See also EPHRAIM; EPHRAIN.
Ge 23:8 for me to **E.** the son of Zohar, ... 6085
Ge 23:10 And **E.** dwelt among the children 6085
Ge 23:10 **E.** the Hittite answered Abraham........ 6085
Ge 23:13 he spake unto **E.** in the audience 6085
Ge 23:14 And **E.** answered Abraham, saying..... 6085
Ge 23:16 And Abraham hearkened unto **E.**;........ 6085
Ge 23:16 Abraham weighed to **E.** the silver, ... 6085
Ge 23:17 of **E.**, which was in Machpelah, ... 6085
Ge 25:9 of **E.** the son of Zohar the Hittite,....... 6085
Ge 49:29 that is in the field of **E.** the Hittite, ... 6085
Ge 49:30 with the field of **E.** the Hittite for a.... 6085
Ge 50:13 of a burying place of **E.** the Hittite, ... 6085
Jos 15:9 went out to the cities of mount **E.**; 6085

EPICUREANS (ep-i-cu-re'-ans)
Ac 17:18 certain philosophers of the **E.**,........... *1946*

EPISTLE See also EPISTLES.
Ac 15:30 together, they delivered the **e.** *1992*
Ac 23:33 delivered the **e.** to the governor,......... *1992*

Ro *general* *title* The **E.** Of Paul...Romans *1992*
Ro 16:22 I Tertius who wrote this **e.**, *1992*
1Co *general* *title* First **E.**..Corinthians *1992*
1Co 5:9 I wrote unto you in an **e.** *1992*
1Co *subscr.* The first **e.** to the Corinthians was
2Co *general* *title* Second **E.**...Corinthians *1992*
2Co 3:2 are our **e.** written in our hearts, *1992*
2Co 3:3 the **e.** of Christ ministered by us, *1992*
2Co 7:8 I perceive that the same **e.** hath *1992*
2Co *subscr.* The second **e.** to the Corinthians
Ga *general* *title* **E.** Of Paul...Galatians *1992*
Eph *general* *title* **E.** Of Paul...Ephesians *1992*
Php *general* *title* **E.** Of Paul...Philippians *1992*
Col *general* *title* **E.** Of Paul...Colossians *1992*
Col 4:16 when this **e.** is read among you, *1992*
Col 4:16 that ye likewise read the **e.** from
1Th *general* *title* First **E.** Of Paul...Thessalonians *1992*
1Th 5:27 this **e.** be read unto all the holy *1992*
1Th *subscr.* The first **e.** unto the Thessalonians *1992*
2Th *general* *title* Second **E.**...Thessalonians *1992*
2Th 2:15 whether my word, or our **e.** *1992*
2Th 3:14 our word by this **e.**, note that man, *1992*
2Th 3:17 which is the token in every **e.**: *1992*
2Th *subscr.* The second **e.** to the Thessalonians *1992*
1Ti *general* *title* First **E.** Of Paul...Timothy *1992*
2Ti *general* *title* Second **E.**...Timothy *1992*
2Ti *subscr.* The second **e.** unto Timotheus,
Tit *general* *title* The **E.** Of Paul to Titus *1992*
Phm *general* *title* The **E.** Of Paul To Philemon *1992*
Heb *general* *title* The **E.** Of Paul...Hebrews *1992*
Jas *general* *title* The General **E.** Of James *1992*
1Pe *general* *title* First **E.** General Of Peter *1992*
2Pe *general* *title* Second **E.** General of Peter *1992*
2Pe 3:1 second **e.**, beloved, I now write *1992*
1Jo *general* *title* First **E.** General of John *1992*
2Jo *general* *title* The Second **E.** Of John *1992*
3Jo *general* *title* The Third **E.** Of John *1992*
Ju *general* *title* The General **E.** Of Jude *1992*

EPISTLES
2Co 3:1 **e.** of commendation to you, or *1992*
2Pe 3:16 As also in all his **e.**, speaking in *1992*

EQUAL See also EQUALS; UNEQUAL.
Job 28:17 gold and the crystal cannot **e.** it: 6186
Job 28:19 topaz of Ethiopia shall not **e.** it, 6186
Ps 17:2 behold the things that are **e.** 4339
Ps 55:13 it was thou, a man mine **e.**, 6187
Pr 26:7 The legs of the lame are not **e.**: 1809
Isa 40:25 will ye liken me, or shall I be **e.**? 7737
Isa 46:5 will ye liken me, and make me **e.**, 7737
La 2:13 what shall I **e.** to thee, that I may 7737
Eze 18:25 The way of the Lord is not **e.**. 8505
Eze 18:25 house of Israel; Is not my way **e.**? 8505
Eze 18:29 The way of the Lord is not **e.** O 8505
Eze 18:29 of Israel, are not my ways **e.**? 8505
Eze 33:17 The way of the Lord is not **e.**: but 8505
Eze 33:17 as for them, their way is not **e.**. 8505
Eze 33:20 The way of the Lord is not **e.**. 8505
Mt 20:12 **thou hast made them e. unto us,** *2470*
Lu 20:36 **for they are e. unto the angels;** *2465*
Joh 5:18 making himself **e.** with God. *2470*
Php 2:6 it not robbery to be **e.** with God: *2470*
Col 4:1 servants that which is just and **e.**; *2471*
Re 21:16 breadth and the height of it are **e.** *2470*

EQUALITY
2Co 8:14 But by an **e.**, that now at this time *2471*
2Co 8:14 your want: that there may be **e.**: *2471*

EQUALLY See also UNEQUALLY.
Ex 36:22 **e.** distant one from another: 7947

EQUALS
Ga 1:14 many my **e.** in mine own nation, *4915*

EQUITY See also INIQUITY.
Ps 98:9 the world, and the people with **e.** 4339
Ps 99:4 doest establish **e.**, thou executest 4339
Pr 1:3 justice, and judgment, and **e.**; 4339
Pr 2:9 and judgment, and **e.**; yea, every 4339
Pr 17:26 good, nor to strike princes for **e.**. 3476
Ec 2:21 and in knowledge, and in **e.**; 3788
Isa 11:4 with **e.** for the meek of the earth: 4334
Isa 59:14 in the street, and **e.** cannot enter. 5229
Mic 3:9 abhor judgment, pervert all **e.** 3477
Mal 2:6 walked with me in peace and **e.**, 4334

ER (ur)
Ge 38:3 a son; and he called his name **E.** 6147
Ge 38:6 And Judah took a wife for **E.** his 6147
Ge 38:7 **E.**, Judah's firstborn, was wicked 6147
Ge 46:12 the sons of Judah; **E.**, and Onan, 6147
Ge 46:12 but **E.** and Onan died in the land 6147
Nu 26:19 sons of Judah were **E.**, and Onan: 6147
Nu 26:19 and **E.** and Onan died in the land 6147
1Ch 2:3 The sons of Judah; **E.**, and Onan, 6147
1Ch 2:3 And **E.**, the firstborn of Judah, 6147
1Ch 4:21 son of Judah were, **E.** the father 6147
Lu 3:28 Elmodam, which was the son of **E.**, *2262*

ERAN (e'-ran) See also ERANITES.
Nu 26:36 of **E.**, the family of the Eranites. 6197

ERANITES (e'-ran-ites)
Nu 26:36 of Eran, the family of the **E.**. 6198

ERASTUS (e-ras'-tus)
Ac 19:22 Timotheus and **E.**; but he himself *2037*
Ro 16:23 **E.** the chamberlain of the city *2037*
2Ti 4:20 **E.** abode at Corinth: but Trophimus *2037*

ERE
Ex 1:19 delivered **e.** the midwives come 2962
Nu 11:33 their teeth, **e.** it was chewed, 2962
Nu 14:11 how long will it be **e.** they believe 3808
1Sa 3:3 And **e.** the lamp of God went out 2962
2Sa 2:26 it be then, **e.** thou bid the people 3808
2Ki 6:32 but **e.** the messenger came to him, 2962
Job 18:2 How long will it be **e.** ye make an
Jer 47:6 how long will it be **e.** thou be quiet? 3808
Ho 8:5 how long will it be **e.** they attain 3808
Joh 4:49 Sir, come down **e.** my child die. *4250*

ERECH (e'-rek) See also ARCHEVITES.
Ge 10:10 Babel, and **E.**, and Accad, and 751

ERECTED
Ge 33:20 And he **e.** there an altar, 5324

ERI (e'-ri) See also ERITES.
Ge 46:16 Ezbon, **E.**, and Arodi, and Areli. 6179
Nu 26:16 of **E.**, the family of the Erites: 6179

ERITES (e'-rites)
Nu 26:16 of Eri, the family of the **E.**: 6180

ERR See also ERRED; ERRETH.
2Ch 33:9 So Manasseh made Judah....to **e.**, 8582
Ps 95:10 is a people that do **e.** in their heart, 8582
Ps 119:21 rebuked the proud...which do **e.** 7686
Ps 119:118 hast trodden down all them that **e.** 7686
Pr 14:22 Do they not **e.** that devise evil? 8582
Pr 19:27 the instruction that causeth to **e.** 7686
Isa 3:12 which lead thee cause thee to **e.**, 8582
Isa 9:16 of this people cause them to **e.**; 8582
Isa 19:14 they have caused Egypt to **e.** in 8582
Isa 28:7 they **e.** in vision, they stumble in 7686
Isa 30:28 of the people, causing them to **e.**. 8582
Isa 35:8 men, though fools, shall not **e.** 8582
Isa 63:17 why hast thou made us to **e.** from 8582
Jer 23:13 and caused my people Israel to **e.**. 8582
Jer 23:32 cause my people to **e.** by their lies, 8582
Ho 4:12 whoredoms hath caused them to **e.**, 8582
Am 2:4 and their lies caused them to **e.**, 8582
Mic 3:5 prophets that make my people **e.**, 8582
Mt 22:29 **Ye do e., not knowing the** *4105*
Mk 12:24 **Do ye not therefore e., because ye** *4105*
Mk 12:27 **ye therefore do greatly e.** *4105*
Heb 3:10 They do alway **e.** in their heart; *4105*
Jas 1:16 Do not **e.**, my beloved brethren. *4105*
Jas 5:19 Brethren, if any of you do **e.** from *4105*

ERRAND
Ge 24:33 not eat, until I have told mine **e.**. 1697
Jg 3:19 I have a secret **e.** unto thee, 1697
2Ki 9:5 I have an **e.** to thee, O captain. 1697

ERRED
Le 5:18 his ignorance wherein he **e.** and 7683
Nu 15:22 if ye have **e.**, and not observed all 7683
1Sa 26:21 the fool, and have **e.** exceedingly. 7683
Job 6:24 me to understand wherein I have **e.** 7683
Job 19:4 And be it indeed that I have **e.**, 7683
Ps 119:110 I have **e.** not from thy precepts. 8582
Isa 28:7 they also have **e.** through wine, 7686
Isa 28:7 priest and the prophet have **e.** 7686
Isa 29:24 They also that **e.** in spirit shall 8582
1Ti 6:10 they have **e.** from the faith, and *635*
1Ti 6:21 have **e.** concerning the faith. *795*
2Ti 2:18 Who concerning the truth have **e.**, *795*

ERRETH
Pr 10:17 but he that refuseth reproof **e.** 8582
Eze 45:20 every one that **e.** and for him that 7686

ERROR See also ERRORS.
2Sa 6:7 God smote him there for his **e.**; 7944
Job 19:4 mine **e.** remaineth with myself. 4879
Ec 5:6 neither say thou...it was an **e.**: 7684
Ec 10:5 as an **e.** which proceedeth from the 7684
Isa 32:6 and to utter **e.** against the Lord, 8432
Da 6:4 neither was there any **e.** or fault 7960
Mt 27:64 so the last **e.** shall be worse than *4106*
Ro 1:27 that recompence of their **e.** which *4106*
Jas 5:20 the sinner from the **e.** of his way *4106*
2Pe 2:18 escape from them who live in **e.**. *4106*
2Pe 3:17 being led away with the **e.** of the *4106*
1Jo 4:6 spirit of truth, and the spirit of **e.** *4106*
Jude 11 ran greedily after the **e.** of Balaam *4106*

ERRORS
Ps 19:12 Who can understand his **e.**? 7691
Jer 10:15 are vanity, and the work of **e.** 8595
Jer 51:18 They are vanity, the work of **e.** 8595
Heb 9:7 himself, and for the **e.** of the people *51*

ESAIAS (e-sah'-yas) See also ISAIAH.
Mt 3:3 spoken of by the prophet **E.**, *2268*
Mt 4:14 was spoken by **E.** the prophet, *2268*
Mt 8:17 fulfilled which was spoken by **E.** *2268*
Mt 12:17 fulfilled which was spoken by **E.** *2268*
Mt 13:14 **fulfilled the prophecy of E.,** *2268*
Mt 15:7 **hypocrites, well did E. prophesy** *2268*
Mk 7:6 **Well hath E. prophesied of you** *2268*
Lu 3:4 in the book of the words of **E.** *2268*
Lu 4:17 him the book of the prophet **E.**. *2268*
Joh 1:23 the Lord, as said the prophet **E.** *2268*
Joh 12:38 That the saying of **E.** the prophet *2268*
Joh 12:39 could not believe, because that **E.** *2268*
Joh 12:41 These things said **E.**, when he *2268*
Ac 8:28 sitting in his chariot read **E.** the *2268*
Ac 8:30 heard him read the prophet **E.**, *2268*
Ac 28:25 Well spake the Holy Ghost by **E.** *2268*
Ro 9:27 **E.** also crieth concerning Israel, *2268*
Ro 9:29 and as **E.** said before, Except the *2268*
Ro 10:16 **E.** saith, Lord, who hath believed *2268*
Ro 10:20 But **E.** is very bold, and saith, I *2268*
Ro 15:12 And again, **E.** saith, There shall *2268*

ESAR-HADDON (e''-zar-had'-dun)
2Ki 19:37 **E.** his son reigned in his stead. 634
Ezr 4:2 since the days of **E.** king of Assur, 634
Isa 37:38 **E.** his son reigned in his stead. 634

ESAU (e'-saw) See also EDOM; ESAU'S.
Ge 25:25 they called his name **E.** 6215
Ge 25:27 **E.** was a cunning hunter, a man of 6215
Ge 25:28 Isaac loved **E.**, because he did eat 6215
Ge 25:29 **E.** came from the field, and he was 6215
Ge 25:30 **E.** said to Jacob, Feed me, I pray 6215
Ge 25:32 **E.** said, Behold, I am at the point 6215
Ge 25:34 Then Jacob gave **E.** bread and 6215
Ge 25:34 Thus **E.** despised his birthright. 6215
Ge 26:34 And **E.** was forty years old when he 6215
Ge 27:1 he called **E.** his eldest son, and said 6215
Ge 27:5 heard when Isaac spake to **E.** 6215
Ge 27:5 And **E.** went to the field to hunt for 6215
Ge 27:6 I heard thy father speak unto **E.** 6215
Ge 27:11 Behold, **E.** my brother is a hairy 6215
Ge 27:15 goodly raiment of her eldest son **E.**, 6215
Ge 27:19 Jacob said unto his father, I am **E.** 6215
Ge 27:21 whether thou be my very son **E.** or 6215
Ge 27:22 but the hands are the hands of **E.**. 6215
Ge 27:24 he said, Art thou my very son **E.**? 6215
Ge 27:30 that **E.** his brother came in from 6215
Ge 27:32 said, I am thy son, thy firstborn **E.**. 6215
Ge 27:34 when **E.** heard the words of his 6215
Ge 27:37 Isaac answered and said unto **E.**, 6215
Ge 27:38 **E.** said unto his father, Hast thou 6215
Ge 27:38 **E.** lifted up his voice, and wept. 6215
Ge 27:41 And **E.** hated Jacob because of the 6215
Ge 27:41 **E.** said in his heart, The days of 6215
Ge 27:42 these words of **E.** her elder son 6215
Ge 27:42 Behold, thy brother **E.**, as touching 6215
Ge 28:6 When **E.** saw that Isaac had blessed 6215
Ge 28:8 And **E.** seeing that the daughters of 6215
Ge 28:9 Then went **E.** unto Ishmael, and 6215
Ge 32:3 sent messengers before him to **E.** 6215
Ge 32:4 shall ye speak unto my lord **E.**; 6215
Ge 32:6 We came to thy brother **E.**, and 6215
Ge 32:8 if **E.** come to the one company, 6215
Ge 32:11 of my brother, from the hand of **E.** 6215
Ge 32:13 hand a present for **E.** his brother; 6215

Ge 32:17 When **E.** my brother meeteth thee,.... 6215
Ge 32:18 sent unto my lord **E.**: and, behold,..... 6215
Ge 32:19 this manner shall ye speak unto **E.**,..... 6215
Ge 33:1 and, behold, **E.** came, and with him.... 6215
Ge 33:4 And **E.** ran to meet him, and 6215
Ge 33:9 **E.** said, I have enough, my brother;... 6215
Ge 33:15 And **E.** said, Let me now leave 6215
Ge 33:16 So **E.** returned that day on his way.... 6215
Ge 35:1 from the face of **E.** thy brother. 6215
Ge 35:29 his sons **E.** and Jacob buried him. 6215
Ge 36:1 generations of **E.**, who is Edom......... 6215
Ge 36:2 **E.** took his wives of the daughters..... 6215
Ge 36:4 And Adah bare to **E.** Eliphaz;........... 6215
Ge 36:5 these are the sons of **E.**, which......... 6215
Ge 36:6 And **E.** took his wives, and his sons,.. 6215
Ge 36:8 dwelt **E.** in Mount Seir: **E.** is Edom... 6215
Ge 36:9 of **E.** the father of the Edomites in..... 6215
Ge 36:10 the son of Adah the wife of **E.**,......... 6215
Ge 36:10 son of Bashemath the wife of **E.**......... 6215
Ge 36:14 she bare to **E.** Jeush, and Jaalam, ... 6215
Ge 36:15 were dukes of the sons of **E.**: 6215
Ge 36:15 of Eliphaz, the firstborn son of **E.**; 6215
Ge 36:19 are the sons of **E.**, who is Edom, ... 6215
Ge 36:40 of the dukes that came of **E.**,............. 6215
Ge 36:43 he is **E.** the father of the Edomites. ... 6215
De 2:4 children of **E.**, which dwell in Seir;..... 6215
De 2:5 Seir unto **E.** for a possession. 6215
De 2:8 children of **E.**, which dwelt in Seir,...... 6215
De 2:12 the children of **E.** succeeded them,..... 6215
De 2:22 As he did to the children of **E.**, ... 6215
De 2:29 children of **E.** which dwelt in Seir,...... 6215
Jos 24:4 I gave unto Isaac Jacob and **E.**: 6215
Jos 24:4 and I gave unto **E.** mount Seir, ... 6215
1Ch 1:34 The sons of Isaac; **E.** and Israel. 6215
1Ch 1:35 The sons of **E.**; Eliphaz, Reuel,......... 6215
Jer 49:8 bring the calamity of **E.** upon him,...... 6215
Jer 49:10 But I have made **E.** bare, I have 6215
Ob 6 are the things of **E.** searched out!...... 6215
Ob 8 the wise men out of the mount of **E.**.?.6215
Ob 9 every one of the mount of **E.** may 6215
Ob 18 and the house of **E.** for stubble, ... 6215
Ob 18 any remaining of the house of **E.**; 6215
Ob 19 shall possess the mount of **E.**;............. 6215
Ob 21 Zion to judge the mount of **E.**; 6215
Mal 1:2 Was not **E.** Jacob's brother? saith....... 6215
Mal 1:3 I hated **E.**, and laid his mountains 6215
Ro 9:13 I loved, but **E.** have I hated.............. *2269*
Heb 11:20 By faith Isaac blessed Jacob and **E.** *2269*
Heb 12:16 fornicator, or profane person, as **E.**,.... *2269*

ESAU'S (e'-saws)
Ge 25:26 his hand took hold on **E.** heel;........... 6215
Ge 27:23 hairy, as his brother **E.** hands; 6215
Ge 28:5 Rebekah, Jacob's and **E.** mother. 6215
Ge 36:10 are the names of **E.** sons; Eliphaz...... 6215
Ge 36:12 was concubine to Eliphaz **E.** son;........ 6215
Ge 36:12 were the sons of Adah **E.** wife. 6215
Ge 36:13 the sons of Bashemath **E.** wife. 6215
Ge 36:14 of Zibeon, **E.** wife: and she bare........ 6215
Ge 36:17 these are the sons of Reuel **E.** son; ... 6215
Ge 36:17 are the sons of Bashemath **E.** wife...... 6215
Ge 36:18 the sons of Aholibamah **E.** wife;.......... 6215
Ge 36:18 the daughter of Anah, **E.** wife. 6215

ESCAPE See also ESCAPED; ESCAPETH; ESCAPING.
Ge 19:17 **E.** for thy life; look not behind 4422
Ge 19:17 **e.** to the mountain, lest thou be......... 4422
Ge 19:19 I cannot **e.** to the mountain, lest 4422
Ge 19:20 Oh, let me **e.** thither, (is it not.......... 4422
Ge 19:22 Haste thee, **e.** thither; for I can not.... 4422
Ge 32:8 company which is left shall **e.**. 6413
Jos 8:22 let none of them remain or **e.**............ 6412
1Sa 27:1 I should speedily **e.** into the land........ 4422
1Sa 27:1 so shall I **e.** out of his hand............... 4422
2Sa 15:14 we shall not else **e.** from Absalom: 6413
2Sa 20:6 lest he get him fenced cities, and **e.**.... 5337
1Ki 18:40 let not one of them **e.**. And they........ 4422
2Ki 9:15 then let none go forth nor **e.**............. 6412
2Ki 10:24 If any of the men...**e.**, ... 4422
2Ki 19:31 and they that **e.** out of mount Zion: 6413
Ezr 9:8 to leave us a remnant to **e.**,.............. 6413
Es 4:13 thou shalt **e.** in the king's house,........ 4422
Job 11:20 they shall not **e.**, and their hope 4498,6
Ps 55:8 my **e.** from the windy storm and........ 4655
Ps 56:7 Shall they **e.** by iniquity: in thine 6405
Ps 71:2 cause me to **e.**: incline thine ear 6403
Ps 141:10 own nets, whilst that I withal **e.**......... 5674
Pr 19:5 he that speaketh lies shall not **e.**....... 4422
Ec 7:26 pleaseth God shall **e.** from her;.......... 4422
Isa 20:6 of Assyria: and how shall we **e.**? 4422
Isa 37:32 and they that **e.** out of mount Zion: 6413
Isa 66:19 I will send those that **e.** of them 6412
Jer 11:11 they shall not be able to **e.**; 3318
Jer 25:35 nor the principal of the flock to **e.**. 6413
Jer 32:4 shall not **e.** out of the hand of the 4422
Jer 34:3 thou shalt not **e.** out of his hand,......... 4422
Jer 38:18, 23 shalt not **e.** out of their hand......... 4422
Jer 42:17 none of them shall remain or **e.** 6412
Jer 44:14 of Egypt to sojourn there, shall **e.**...... 6412
Jer 44:14 shall return but such as shall **e.**.......... 6412
Jer 44:28 a small number that **e.** the sword....... 6412
Jer 46:6 flee away, nor the mighty man **e.**; 4422
Jer 48:8 no city shall **e.**: the valley also........... 4422
Jer 50:28 The voice of them that flee and **e.**...... 6412
Jer 50:29 let none thereof **e.**: recompense......... 6413
Eze 6:8 ye may have some that shall **e.**.......... 6412
Eze 6:9 they that **e.** of you shall remember..... 6412
Eze 7:16 But they that **e.** of them shall........... 6403
Eze 7:16 But they that...of them shall **e.**,......... 6412
Eze 17:15 shall he **e.** that doeth such things?...... 4422
Eze 17:18 all these things, he shall not **e.**. 4422
Da 11:41 But these shall **e.** out of his hand, ... 4422
Da 11:42 and the land of Egypt shall not **e.** 6413
Joe 2:3 yea, and nothing shall **e.** them. 6413
Ob 14 to cut off those of his that did **e.**;....... 6412
Mt 23:33 **ye e. the damnation of hell?**.... *5343,575*
Lu 21:36 **worthy to e. all these things** *1628*
Ac 27:42 of them should swim out, and **e.**........ *1309*
Ro 2:3 thou shalt **e.** the judgment of God? *1628*
1Co 10:13 temptation also make a way to **e.**, ... *1545*
1Th 5:3 with child; and they shall not **e.**. *1628*
Heb 2:3 How shall we **e.**, if we neglect so....... *1628*
Heb 12:25 earth, much more shall not we **e.**, ... *5343*

ESCAPED
Ge 14:13 And there came one that had **e.**, ... 6412
Ex 10:5 the residue of that which is **e.**, ... 6413
Nu 21:29 he hath given his sons that **e.**, ... 6412
De 23:15 servant which is **e.** from his master 5337
Jg 3:26 Ehud **e.** while they tarried, and.......... 4422
Jg 3:26 quarries, and **e.** unto Seirath. 4422
Jg 3:29 of valour; and there **e.** not a man. 4422
Jg 12:5 those Ephraimites which were **e.**......... 6412
Jg 21:17 for them that be **e.** of Benjamin, ... 6413
1Sa 14:41 were taken: but the people **e.**............ 3318
1Sa 19:10 and David fled, and **e.** that night. 4422
1Sa 19:12 and he went, and fled, and **e.**. 4422
1Sa 19:17 away mine enemy, that he is **e.**? 4422
1Sa 19:18 David fled and **e.**, and came to 4422
1Sa 22:1 thence, and **e.** to the cave Adullam: 4422
1Sa 22:20 sons of Ahimelech...**e.**, and fled 4422
1Sa 23:13 that David was **e.** from Keilah; 4422
1Sa 30:17 and there **e.** not a man of them, ... 4422
2Sa 1:3 Out of the camp of Israel am I **e.**.......... 4422
2Sa 4:6 Rechab and Baanah his brother **e.**....... 4422
1Ki 20:20 Ben-hadad the king of Syria **e.**............ 4422
2Ki 19:30 that is **e.** of the house of Judah.......... 6413
2Ki 19:37 they **e.** into the land of Armenia......... 4422
1Ch 4:43 of the Amalekites that were **e.**........... 6413
2Ch 16:7 the host of the king of Syria **e.** 4422
2Ch 20:24 fallen to the earth, and none **e.**, ... 6413
2Ch 30:6 the remnant of you, that are **e.**........... 6413
2Ch 36:20 them that had **e.** from the sword........ 7611
Ezr 9:15 we remain yet **e.**, as it is this day: 6413
Ne 1:2 concerning the Jews that had **e.**, ... 6413
Job 1:15, 16, 17, 19 I only am **e.** alone to tell.... 4422
Job 19:20 I am **e.** with the skin of my teeth....... 4422
Ps 124:7 Our soul is **e.** as a bird out of the 4422
Ps 124:7 the snare is broken, and we are **e.**. 4422
Isa 4:2 for them that are **e.** of Israel............ 6413
Isa 10:20 such as are **e.** of the house of Jacob. .. 6413
Isa 37:31 that is **e.** of the house of Judah.......... 6413
Isa 37:38 and they **e.** into the land of............... 4422
Isa 45:20 ye that are **e.** of the nations:............. 6412
Jer 41:15 Ishmael the son of Nethaniah **e.** 4422
Jer 51:50 Ye that have **e.** the sword, ... 6412
La 2:22 the day of the Lord's anger none **e.**..... 6412
Eze 24:27 mouth be opened to him which is **e.**,.... 6412
Eze 33:21 one that had **e.** out of Jerusalem 6412
Eze 33:22 evening, afore he that was **e.** came;.... 6412
Joh 10:39 him: but he **e.** out of their hand, ... *1831*
Ac 27:44 pass, that they **e.** all safe to land,....... *1295*
Ac 28:1 when they were **e.**, then they knew.... *1295*
Ac 28:4 whom, though he hath **e.** the sea, ... *1295*
2Co 11:33 was I let down by the wall, and **e.**....... *1628*
Heb 11:34 of fire, **e.** the edge of the sword, ... *5343*
Heb 12:25 For if they **e.** not who refused him..... *5343*
2Pe 1:4 having **e.** the corruption that is in *668*
2Pe 2:18 those that were clean **e.** from them...... *668*
2Pe 2:20 For if after they have **e.** the *668*

ESCAPETH
1Ki 19:17 him that **e.** the sword of Hazael......... 4422
1Ki 19:17 him that **e.** from the sword of Jehu..... 4422
Isa 15:9 lions upon him that **e.** of Moab, ... 6413
Jer 48:19 him that fleeth, and her that **e.**, ... 4422
Eze 24:26 he that **e.** in that day shall come 6412
Am 9:1 he that **e.** of them shall not be........... 6412

ESCAPING
Ezr 9:14 should be no remnant nor **e.**? 6413

ESCHEW See also ESCHEWED; ESCHEWETH.
1Pe 3:11 Let him **e.** evil, and do good; *1578*

ESCHEWED
Job 1:1 one that feared God, and **e.** evil......... 5493

ESCHEWETH
Job 1:8 son that feareth God and **e.** evil?........ 5493
Job 2:3 one that feareth God, and **e.** evil? 5493

ESEK (e'-sek)
Ge 26:20 he called the name of the well **E.**;...... 6320

ESH-BAAL (esh'-ba-al) See also ISH-BOSHETH.
1Ch 8:33 Malchi-shua, and Abinadab, and **E.**....... 792
1Ch 9:39 Malchi-shua, and Abinadab, and **E.**....... 792

ESH-BAN (esh'-ban)
Ge 36:26 Hemdan, and **E.**, and Ithran, ... 790
1Ch 1:41 Amram, and **E.**, and Ithran,................ 790

ESHCOL (esh'-col)
Ge 14:13 brother of **E.**, and brother of Aner:....... 812
Ge 14:24 men which went with me, Aner, **E.**, ... 812
Nu 13:23 they came unto the brook of **E.**, ... 812
Nu 13:24 The place was called the brook **E.**, ... 812
Nu 32:9 they went up unto the valley of **E.**,...... 812
De 1:24 came unto the valley of **E.**, and........... 812

ESHEAN (esh'-e-an)
Jos 15:52 Arab, and Dumah, and **E.**, ... 824

ESHEK (e'-shek)
1Ch 8:39 And the sons of **E.** his brother 6232

ESHKALONITES (esh'-ka-lon-ites)
Jos 13:3 Ashdothites, the **E.**, the Gittites,......... 832

ESHTAOL (esh'-ta-ol) See also ESHTAULITES.
Jos 15:33 in the valley, **E.**, and Zoreah, ... 847
Jos 19:41 Zorah, and **E.**, and Ir-shemesh............ 847
Jg 13:25 camp of Dan between Zorah and **E.**. 847
Jg 16:31 buried him between Zorah and **E.**......... 847
Jg 18:2 of valour, from Zorah, and from **E.**, ... 847
Jg 18:8 unto their brethren to Zorah and **E.**: 847
Jg 18:11 out of Zorah and out of **E.**, ... 847

ESHTAULITES (esh'-ta-u-lites)
1Ch 2:53 the Zareathites, and the **E.**................. 848

ESHTEMOA (esh-te-mo'-ah) See also ESHTEMOH.
Jos 21:14 and **E.** with her suburbs, ... 851
1Sa 30:28 and to them which were in **E.**,.............. 851
1Ch 4:17 and Ishbah the father of **E.**................... 851
1Ch 4:19 Garmite, and **E.** the Maachathite. 851
1Ch 6:57 Jattir, and **E.**, with their suburbs, ... 851

ESHTEMOH (esh'-te-moh) See also ESHTEMOA.
Jos 15:50 Anab, and **E.**, and Anim, ... 851

ESHTON (esh'-ton)
1Ch 4:11 Mehir, which was the father of **E.**. 850
1Ch 4:12 **E.** begat Beth-rapha, and Paseah,........ 850

ESLI (es'-li)
Lu 3:25 which was the son of **E.**, which......... *2069*

ESPECIALLY
Ps 31:11 but **e.** among my neighbours, ... 3966
Ac 26:3 **E.** because I know thee to be *3122*
Ga 6:10 men, **e.** unto them who are of the...... *3122*
1Ti 5:17 **e.** they who labour in the word and *3122*
2Ti 4:13 the books, but **e.** the parchments. *3122*

ESPIED
Ge 42:27 of them opened his sack...he **e.** 7200
Eze 20:6 into a land that I had **e.** for them, ... 8446

ESPOUSALS
Ca 3:11 crowned him in the day of his **e.**, 2861
Jer 2:2 of thy youth, the love of thine **e.**, 3623

ESPOUSED
2Sa 3:14 my wife Michal, which I **e.** to me 781
Mt 1:18 When as his mother Mary was **e.** *3423*
Lu 1:27 To a virgin **e.** to a man whose *3423*
Lu 2:5 To be taxed with Mary his **e.** wife, *3423*
2Co 11:2 For I have **e.** you to one husband, *718*

ESPY See also ESPIED; SPY.
Jos 14:7 sent…from Kadesh-barnea to **e.** 7270
Jer 48:19 stand by the way, and **e.**; ask him 6822

ESROM (es'-rom) See also HEZRON.
Mt 1:3 Phares begat **E.**; and **E.** begat *2074*
Lu 3:33 which was the son of **E.**, which *2074*

ESSAY See ASSAY.

ESTABLISH See also ESTABLISHED; ESTABLISHETH; STABLISH.
Ge 6:18 with thee will I **e.** my covenant; 6965
Ge 9:9 behold, I **e.** my covenant with you, 6965
Ge 9:11 And I will **e.** my covenant with you; 6965
Ge 17:7 And I will **e.** my covenant between 6965
Ge 17:19 and I will **e.** my covenant with him 6965
Ge 17:21 my covenant will I **e.** with Isaac, 6965
Le 26:9 you, and **e.** my covenant with you. 6965
Nu 30:13 her husband may **e.** it or her 6965
De 8:18 that he may **e.** his covenant which 6965
De 28:9 The Lord shall **e.** thee an holy people 6965
De 29:13 That he may **e.** thee to day 6965
1Sa 1:23 only the Lord **e.** his word. So the 6965
2Sa 7:12 and I will **e.** his kingdom 3559
2Sa 7:25 concerning his house, **e.** it for 6965
1Ki 9:5 Then I will **e.** the throne of thy 6965
1Ki 15:4 after him, and to **e.** Jerusalem. 5975
1Ch 17:11 and I will **e.** his kingdom 3559
1Ch 22:10 and I will **e.** the throne of his 3559
1Ch 28:7 Moreover I will **e.** his kingdom 3559
2Ch 9:8 loved Israel, to **e.** them for ever, 5975
Job 36:7 yea, he doth **e.** them for ever, 3427
Ps 7:9 but **e.** the just: for the righteous 3559
Ps 48:8 God will **e.** it for ever. Selah. 3559
Ps 87:5 and the highest himself shall **e.** her. 3559
Ps 89:2 thy faithfulness shalt thou **e.** in the 3559
Ps 89:4 Thy seed will I **e.** for ever, 3559
Ps 90:17 and **e.** thou the work of our hands 3559
Ps 90:17 the work of our hands **e.** thou it. 3559
Ps 99:4 thou dost **e.** equity, thou executest 3559
Pr 15:25 he will **e.** the border of the widow. 5324
Isa 9:7 and to **e.** it with judgment and 5582
Isa 49:8 of the people, to **e.** the earth, to 6965
Isa 62:7 And give him no rest, till he **e.**, 3559
Jer 33:2 the Lord that formed it, to **e.** it; 3559
Eze 16:60 I will **e.** unto thee an everlasting 6965
Eze 16:62 And I will **e.** my covenant with thee; 6965
Da 6:7 together to **e.** a royal statute, 6966
Da 6:8 Now, O king, **e.** the decree. 6966
Da 11:14 exalt themselves to **e.** the vision. 5975
Am 5:15 and **e.** judgment in the gate: 3322
Ro 3:31 God forbid: yea, we **e.** the law. *2476*
Ro 10:3 about to **e.** their own righteousness, *2476*
1Th 3:2 to **e.** you, and to comfort you *4741*
Heb 10:9 the first, that he may **e.** the second. *2476*

ESTABLISHED See also STABLISHED.
Ge 9:17 the covenant, which I have **e.** 6965
Ge 41:32 because the thing is **e.** by God, 3559
Ex 6:4 I have also **e.** my covenant with 6965
Ex 15:17 O Lord, which thy hands have **e.**. 3559
Lev 25:30 then the house…shall be **e.** 6965
De 19:15 witnesses, shall the matter be **e.** 6965
De 32:6 hath he not made thee, and **e.** thee? 3559
1Sa 3:20 knew that Samuel was **e.** to be a 539
1Sa 13:13 the Lord have **e.** thy kingdom. 3559
1Sa 20:31 shalt not be **e.**, nor thy kingdom. 3559
1Sa 24:20 the kingdom of Israel shall be **e.** 6965
2Sa 5:12 Lord had **e.** him king over Israel, 3559
2Sa 7:16 thy kingdom shall be **e.** for ever. 539
2Sa 7:16 thy throne shall be **e.** for ever. 3559
2Sa 7:26 house of thy servant David be **e.** 3559
1Ki 2:12 and his kingdom was **e.** greatly. 3559
1Ki 2:24 the Lord liveth, which hath **e.** me, 3559
1Ki 2:45 throne of David shall be **e.** before 3559
1Ki 2:46 the kingdom was **e.** in the hand of 3559
1Ch 17:14 his throne shall be **e.** for evermore. 3559
1Ch 17:23 let the thing…be **e.** for ever, 539
1Ch 17:24 Let it even be **e.**, that thy name be 539
1Ch 17:24 let the house of David…be **e.** 3559
2Ch 1:9 unto David my father be **e.**: 539
2Ch 12:1 when Rehoboam had **e.** the 3559
2Ch 20:20 so shall ye be **e.**; believe his 539
2Ch 25:3 when the kingdom was **e.** to him, 2388
2Ch 30:5 So they **e.** a decree to make 5975
Job 21:8 Their seed is **e.** in their sight 3559
Job 22:28 and it shall be **e.** unto thee: 6965
Ps 24:2 and **e.** it upon the floods. 3559
Ps 40:2 feet upon a rock, and **e.** my goings. 3559
Ps 78:5 For he **e.** a testimony in Jacob, 6965
Ps 78:69 earth which he hath **e.** for ever. 3245
Ps 89:21 with whom my hand shall be **e.**: 3559
Ps 89:37 It shall be **e.** for ever as the moon, 3559
Ps 93:2 Thy throne is **e.** of old: thou art 3559
Ps 96:10 the world also shall be **e.** that it 3559
Ps 102:28 their seed shall be **e.** before thee. 3559
Ps 112:8 His heart is **e.**, he shall not be 5564
Ps 119:90 thou hast **e.** the earth, and it 3559
Ps 140:11 Let not an evil speaker be **e.** 3559
Pr 3:19 by understanding hath he **e.** the 3559
Pr 4:26 and let all thy ways be **e.**. 3559
Pr 8:28 when he **e.** the clouds above: 553
Pr 12:3 man shall not be **e.** by wickedness: 3559
Pr 12:19 The lip of truth shall be **e.** for ever: 3559
Pr 15:22 of counsellors they are **e.**. 6965
Pr 16:3 and thy thoughts shall be **e.**. 3559
Pr 16:12 the throne is **e.** by righteousness. 3559
Pr 20:18 Every purpose is **e.** by counsel: 3559
Pr 24:3 and by understanding it is **e.**: 3559
Pr 25:5 and his throne shall be **e.** in 3559
Pr 29:14 his throne shall be **e.** for ever. 3559
Pr 30:4 hath **e.** all the ends of the earth? 6965
Isa 2:2 of the Lord's house shall be **e.** 3559
Isa 7:9 believe, surely ye shall not be **e.**. 539
Isa 16:5 in mercy shall the throne be **e.**: 3559
Isa 45:18 he hath **e.** it, he created it 3559
Isa 54:14 In righteousness shalt thou be **e.**: 3559
Jer 10:12 hath **e.** the world by his wisdom, 3559
Jer 30:20 their congregation shall be **e.** 3559
Jer 51:15 by his power, he hath **e.** the world 3559
Da 4:36 I was **e.** in my kingdom, 8627
Mic 4:1 be **e.** in the top of the mountains, 3559
Hab 1:12 thou hast **e.** them for correction. 3245
Zec 5:11 and it shall be **e.**, and set there 3559
Mt 18:16 **witnesses every word may be e.** *2476*
Ac 16:5 were the churches **e.** in the faith, *4732*
Ro 1:11 to the end ye may be **e.**; *4741*
2Co 13:1 witnesses shall every word be **e.** *2476*
Heb 8:6 was **e.** upon better promises. *3549*
Heb 13:9 that the heart be **e.** with grace; *950*
2Pe 1:12 and be **e.** in the present truth. *4741*

ESTABLISHETH
Nu 30:14 then he **e.** all her vows, or all her 6965
Pr 29:4 The king by judgment **e.** the land: 5975
Da 6:15 nor statute which the king **e.** 6966

ESTABLISHMENT
2Ch 32:1 After these things, and the **e.** 571

ESTATE See also ESTATES; STATE.
1Ch 17:17 regarded me according to the **e.** 8448
Es 1:19 give give her royal **e.** unto another
Ps 136:23 Who remembered us in our low **e.**:
Ec 1:16 Lo, I am come to great **e.**,
Ec 3:18 concerning the **e.** of the sons of 1700
Eze 16:55, 55 shall return to their former **e.**,
Eze 16:55, shall return to your former **e.**.
Da 11:7 shall one stand up in his **e.**, 3653
Da 11:20 Then shall stand up in his **e.** 3653
Da 11:21 And in his **e.** shall stand up a vile 3653
Da 11:38 in his **e.** shall he honour the God 3653
Lu 1:48 the low **e.** of his handmaiden:
Ac 22:5 and all the **e.** of the elders:
Ro 12:16 condescend to men of low **e.**,
Col 4:8 he might know your **e.**, and *3588,4012*
Jude 6 which kept not their first **e.**,

ESTATES
Eze 36:11 I will settle you after your old **e.**,
Mk 6:21 captains, and chief **e.** of Galilee;

ESTEEM See also ESTEEMED; ESTEEMETH; ESTEEMING.
Job 36:19 Will he **e.** thy riches? no, not 6186
Ps 119:128 I **e.** all thy precepts…to be right;
Isa 53:4 yet we did **e.** him stricken, 2803
Php 2:3 **e.** other better than themselves. *2233*
1Th 5:13 And to **e.** them very highly in love *2233*

ESTEEMED
De 32:15 lightly **e.** the Rock of his salvation. 5034
1Sa 2:30 despise me shall be lightly **e.** 7043
1Sa 18:23 I am a poor man, and lightly **e.**? 7043
Job 23:12 I have **e.** the words of his mouth 6845
Pr 17:28 shutteth his lips is **e.** a man of
Isa 29:16 shall be **e.** as the potter's clay 2803
Isa 29:17 fruitful field shall be **e.** as a forest? 2803
Isa 53:3 was despised, and we **e.** him not. 2803
La 4:2 are they **e.** as earthen pitchers, 2803
Lu 16:15 **which is highly e. among men**
1Co 6:4 them to judge who are least **e.** *1848*

ESTEEMETH
Job 41:27 He **e.** iron as straw, and brass 2803
Ro 14:5 One man **e.** one day above another: *2919*
Ro 14:5 another **e.** every day alike. *2919*
Ro 14:14 but to him that **e.** any thing to be *3049*

ESTEEMING
Heb 11:26 **E.** the reproach of Christ greater *2233*

ESTHER (est'-thur) See also ESTHER'S; HADASSAH.
Es *general title* The Book of **E.** 635
Es 2:7 brought up Hadassah, that is, **E.**, 635
Es 2:8 **E.** was brought also unto the king's 635
Es 2:10 **E.** had not shewed her people nor 635
Es 2:11 to know how **E.** did, and what 635
Es 2:15 Now when the turn of **E.**, the 635
Es 2:15 **E.** obtained favour in the sight of 635
Es 2:16 **E.** was taken unto king Ahasuerus 635
Es 2:17 king loved **E.** above all the women, 635
Es 2:20 **E.** had not yet shewed her kindred 635
Es 2:20 **E.** did the commandment of 635
Es 2:22 who told it unto **E.** the queen; 635
Es 2:22 and **E.** certified the king thereof 635
Es 4:5 Then called **E.** for Hatach, one of 635
Es 4:8 to shew it unto **E.**, and to declare 635
Es 4:9 Hatach came and told **E.** the words 635
Es 4:10 Again **E.** spake unto Hatach, and 635
Es 4:13 Mordecai commanded to answer **E.**, 635
Es 4:15 **E.** bade them return Mordecai this 635
Es 4:17 to all the **E.** had commanded 635
Es 5:1 that **E.** put on her royal apparel, 635
Es 5:2 when the king saw **E.** the queen 635
Es 5:2 held out to **E.** the golden sceptre 635
Es 5:2 **E.** drew near, and touched the top 635
Es 5:3 What wilt thou queen **E.**? 635
Es 5:4 **E.** answered, If it seem good unto 635
Es 5:5 that he may do as **E.** had said. 635
Es 5:5 the banquet that **E.** had prepared. 635
Es 5:6 said unto **E.** at the banquet of wine, 635
Es 5:7 Then answered **E.**, and said, My 635
Es 5:12 **E.** the queen did let no man come 635
Es 6:14 the banquet that **E.** had prepared. 635
Es 7:1 came to banquet with **E.** the queen. 635
Es 7:2 the king said again unto **E.** on the 635
Es 7:2 What is thy petition, queen **E.**? 635
Es 7:3 **E.** the queen answered and said, 635
Es 7:5 answered and said unto **E.** the 635
Es 7:6 **E.** said, The adversary and enemy 635
Es 7:7 to make request for his life to **E.** 635
Es 7:8 upon the bed whereon **E.** was. 635
Es 8:1 the Jews' enemy unto **E.** the queen. 635
Es 8:1 **E.** had told what he was unto her. 635
Es 8:2 **E.** set Mordecai over the house of 635
Es 8:3 **E.** spake yet again before the king, 635
Es 8:4 out the golden sceptre toward **E.**. 635
Es 8:4 **E.** arose, and stood before the king. 635
Es 8:7 Ahasuerus said unto **E.** the queen 635
Es 8:7 have given **E.** the house of Haman, 635
Es 9:12 the king said unto **E.** the queen, 635
Es 9:13 Then said **E.**, If it please the king, 635
Es 9:25 when **E.** came before the king,
Es 9:29 Then **E.** the queen, the daughter of 635
Es 9:31 **E.** the queen had enjoined them, 635
Es 9:32 the decree of **E.** confirmed these 635

ESTHER'S (es'-thurs)
Es 2:18 and his servants, even **E.** feast; 635
Es 4:4 **E.** maids and her chamberlains 635
Es 4:12 they told to Mordecai **E.** words 635

ESTIMATE
Le 27:14 then the priest shall **e.** it, whether 6186
Le 27:14 as the priest shall **e.** it, so shall 6186

ESTIMATION See also ESTIMATIONS.
Le 5:15 with thy **e.** by shekels of silver, 6187
Le 5:18 with thy **e.**, for a trespass offering, 6187
Le 6:6 with thy **e.**, for a trespass offering, 6187
Le 27:2 shall be for the Lord by thy **e.** 6187
Le 27:3 And thy **e.** shall be of the male 6187
Le 27:3 thy **e.** shall be fifty shekels of silver, 6187
Le 27:4 thy **e.** shall be thirty shekels. 6187
Le 27:5 then thy **e.** shall be of the male 6187
Le 27:6 **e.** shall be of the male five shekels 6187
Le 27:6 for the female thy **e.** shall be three 6187
Le 27:7 thy **e.** shall be fifteen shekels, 6187
Le 27:8 But if he be poorer than thy **e.**, 6187
Le 27:13 add a fifth part thereof unto thy **e.** 6187
Le 27:15 part of the money of thy **e.** unto it, 6187
Le 27:16 **e.** shall be according to the seed 6187
Le 27:17 year of jubile, according to thy **e.** 6187
Le 27:18 and it shall be abated from thy **e.** 6187
Le 27:19 part of the money of thy **e.** unto it, 6187
Le 27:23 unto him the worth of thy **e.**, even 6187
Le 27:23 he shall give thine **e.** in that day, 6187
Le 27:27 redeem it according to thine **e.**, 6187
Le 27:27 it shall be sold according to thy **e.** 6187
Nu 18:16 according to thine **e.**, for the money 6187

ESTIMATIONS
Le 27:25 thy **e.** shall be according to the 6187

ESTRANGED
Job 19:13 mine acquaintance are verily **e.** 2114
Ps 58:3 The wicked are **e.** from the womb: 2114
Ps 78:30 They were not **e.** from their lust. 2114
Jer 19:4 and have **e.** this place, and have 5234
Eze 14:5 they are all **e.** from me through 2114

ETAM (e'-tam)
Jg 15:8 dwelt in the top of the rock **E.** 5862
Jg 15:11 went to the top of the rock **E.**, and 5862
1Ch 4:3 And these were of the father of **E.**; 5862
1Ch 4:32 their villages were, **E.** and Ain, 5862
2Ch 11:6 He built even Bethlehem, and **E.**, 5862

ETERNAL
De 33:27 The **e.** God is thy refuge, and 6924
Isa 60:15 I will make thee an **e.** excellency, 5769
Mt 19:16 shall I do, that I may have **e.** life? *166*
Mt 25:46 but the righteous into life **e.** *166*
Mk 3:29 in danger of **e.** damnation: *166*
Mk 10:17 I do that I may inherit **e.** life? *166*
Mk 10:30 and in the world to come **e.** life, *166*
Lu 10:25 what shall I do to inherit **e.** life? *166*
Lu 18:18 what shall I do to inherit **e.** life? *166*
Joh 3:15 should not perish, but have **e.** life *166*
Joh 4:36 and gathereth fruit unto life **e.**: *166*
Joh 5:39 for in them ye think ye have **e.** life: *166*
Joh 6:54 and drinketh my blood, hath **e.** life; *166*
Joh 6:68 thou hast the words of **e.** life. *166*
Joh 10:28 And I give unto them **e.** life; *166*
Joh 12:25 this world shall keep it unto life **e.** *166*
Joh 17:2 he should give **e.** life to as many as *166*
Joh 17:3 this is life **e.**, that they might know *166*
Ac 13:48 many as were ordained to **e.** life *166*
Ro 1:20 even his **e.** power and Godhead; *126*
Ro 2:7 honour and immortality, **e.** life: *166*
Ro 5:21 through righteousness unto **e.** life *166*
Ro 6:23 but the gift of God is **e.** life through *166*
2Co 4:17 exceeding and **e.** weight of glory; *166*
2Co 4:18 the things which are not seen are **e.** *166*
2Co 5:1 made with hands, **e.** in the heavens. *166*
Eph 3:11 According the **e.** purpose which *165*
1Ti 1:17 Now unto the King **e.**, immortal, *165*
1Ti 6:12 lay hold on **e.** life, whereunto thou *166*
1Ti 6:19 that they may lay hold on **e.** life. *166*
2Ti 2:10 is in Christ Jesus with **e.** glory. *166*
Tit 1:2 In hope of **e.** life, which God, that *166*
Tit 3:7 according to the hope of **e.** life. *166*
Heb 5:9 became the author of **e.** salvation *166*
Heb 6:2 of the dead, and of **e.** judgment. *166*
Heb 9:12 having obtained **e.** redemption *166*
Heb 9:14 who through the **e.** Spirit offered *166*
Heb 9:15 the promise of **e.** redemption *166*
1Pe 5:10 who hath called us unto his **e.** glory *166*
1Jo 1:2 shew unto you that **e.** life, which *166*
1Jo 2:25 he hath promised us, even **e.** life. *166*
1Jo 3:15 no murderer hath **e.** life abiding in *166*
1Jo 5:11 that God hath given to us **e.** life, *166*
1Jo 5:13 ye may know that ye have **e.** life, *166*
1Jo 5:20 This is the true God, and **e.** life. *166*
Jude 7 suffering the vengeance of **e.** fire. *166*
Jude 21 of our Lord Jesus Christ unto **e.** life. *166*

ETERNITY
Isa 57:15 and lofty One that inhabiteth **e.**, 5703

ETHAM (e'-tham)
Ex 13:20 and encamped in **E.**, in the edge of 864
Nu 33:6 and pitched in **E.**, which is in the 864
Nu 33:7 they removed from **E.**, and turned 864
Nu 33:8 journey in the wilderness of **E.**, 864

ETHAN (e'-than)
1Ki 4:31 than **E.** the Ezrahite, and Heman, 387
1Ch 2:6 And the sons of Zera; Zimri, and **E.**, 387
1Ch 2:8 And the sons of **E.**; Azariah. 387
1Ch 6:42 The son of **E.**, the son of Zimmah, 387
1Ch 6:44 **E.** the son of Kishi, the son of Abdi, 387
1Ch 15:17 of Merari their brethren, **E.** the son 387
1Ch 15:19 the singers, Heman, Asaph, and **E.**, 387
Ps 89:*title* Maschil of **E.** the Ezrahite. 387

ETHANIM (eth'-a-nim)
1Ki 8:2 at the feast in the month **E.**, 388

ETHBAAL (eth'-ba-al)
1Ki 16:31 to wife Jezebel the daughter of **E.** 856

ETHER (e'-ther)
Jos 15:42 Libnah, and **E.**, and Ashan, 6281
Jos 19:7 Ain, Remmon, and **E.**, and Ashan; 6281

ETHIOPIA (e-the-o'-pe-ah) See also CUSH; ETHIOPIAN.
Ge 2:13 compasseth the whole land of **E.** 3568
2Ki 19:9 heard say of Tirhakah king of **E.** 3568
Es 1:1 reigned from India unto **E.**, 3568
Es 8:9 which are from India unto **E.**, 3568
Job 28:19 The topaz of **E.** shall not equal it, 3568
Ps 68:31 **E.** shall soon stretch out her hands 3568
Ps 87:4 behold Philistia, and Tyre, with **E.**; 3568
Isa 18:1 which is beyond the rivers of **E.**: 3568
Isa 20:3 wonder upon Egypt and upon **E.**; 3568
Isa 20:5 afraid and ashamed of **E.** their 3568
Isa 37:9 concerning Tirhakah king of **E.**, 3568
Isa 43:3 thy ransom, **E.** and Seba for thee. 3568
Isa 45:14 of Egypt, and merchandise of **E.** 3568
Eze 29:10 even unto the borders of **E.** 3568
Eze 30:4 and great pain shall be in **E.**, 3568
Eze 30:5 **E.**, and Libya, and Lydia, and all 3568
Eze 38:5 Persia, **E.**, and Libya with them; 3568
Na 3:9 **E.** and Egypt were her strength, 3568
Zep 3:10 From beyond the rivers of **E.** my 3568
Ac 8:27 and, behold, a man of **E.**, *128*

ETHIOPIAN See also ETHIOPIANS.
Nu 12:1 against Moses because of the **E.** 3569
Nu 12:1 for he had married an **E.** woman. 3569
2Ch 14:9 out against them Zerah the **E.** 3569
Jer 13:23 Can the **E.** change his skin, or the 3569
Jer 38:7 Now when Ebed-melech the **E.** 3569
Jer 38:10 commanded Ebed-melech the **E.**, 3569
Jer 38:12 Ebed-melech the **E.** said unto 3569
Jer 39:16 and speak to Ebed-melech the **E.**, 3569

ETHIOPIANS
2Ch 12:3 Lubims, the Sukkiims, and the **E.** 3569
2Ch 14:12 the Lord smote the **E.** before Asa, 3569
2Ch 14:12 before Judah; and the **E.** fled. 3569
2Ch 14:13 and the **E.** were overthrown, 3569
2Ch 16:8 Were not the **E.** and the Lubims 3569
2Ch 21:16 Arabians, that were near the **E.**: 3569
Isa 20:4 Egyptians prisoners, and the **E.** 3569
Jer 46:9 **E.** and the Libyans, that handle 3569
Eze 30:9 to make the careless **E.** afraid, 3569
Da 11:43 and the **E.** shall be at his steps. 3569
Am 9:7 not as children of the **E.** unto me, 3569
Zep 2:12 Ye **E.** also, ye shall be slain 3569
Ac 8:27 under Candace queen of the **E.**, *128*

ETHNAN (eth'-nan)
1Ch 4:7 Zereth, and Jezoar, and **E.** 869

ETHNI (eth'-ni) See also JEATERAI.
1Ch 6:41 The son of **E.**, the son of Zerah, 867

EUBULUS (yu-bu'-lus)
2Ti 4:21 **E.** greeteth thee, and Pudens, and *2103*

EUNICE (yu-ni'-see)
2Ti 1:5 Lois, and thy mother **E.**; and I am *2131*

EUNUCH See also EUNUCHS.
Isa 56:3 neither let the **e.** say, Behold, I 5631
Jer 52:25 **e.**, which had the charge of the 5631
Ac 8:27 and **e.** of great authority under *2135*
Ac 8:34 the **e.** answered Philip, and said, *2135*
Ac 8:36 the **e.** said, See, here is water; *2135*
Ac 8:38 the water, both Philip and the **e.**; *2135*
Ac 8:39 that the **e.** saw him no more: *2135*

EUNUCHS
2Ki 9:32 looked out to him two or three **e.** 5631
2Ki 20:18 and they shall be **e.** in the palace of 5631
Isa 39:7 and they shall be **e.** in the palace of 5631
Isa 56:4 thus saith the Lord unto the **e.** 5631
Jer 29:2 and the queen, and the **e.**, the 5631
Jer 34:19 the princes of Jerusalem, the **e.**, 5631
Jer 38:7 Ethiopian, one of the **e.** which 5631
Jer 41:16 the children, and the **e.**, whom 5631
Da 1:3 Ashpenaz the master of his **e.**, 5631
Da 1:7 the prince of the **e.** gave names: 5631
Da 1:8 he requested of the prince of the **e.** 5631
Da 1:9 tender love with the prince of the **e.** 5631
Da 1:10 prince of the **e.** said unto Daniel, 5631
Da 1:11 prince of the **e.** had set over Daniel, 5631
Da 1:18 prince of the **e.** brought them in 5631
Mt 19:12 For there are some **e.**, which were *2135*
Mt 19:12 and there are some **e.**, which *2134*
Mt 19:12 which were made **e.** of men: *2134*
Mt 19:12 and there be **e.**, which have made *2135*
Mt 19:12 have made themselves **e.** for the *2134*

EUODIAS (yu-o'-de-as)
Php 4:2 beseech **E.**, and beseech Syntyche, *2136*

EUPHRATES (yu-fra'-teze)
Ge 2:14 Assyria. And the fourth river is **E.** 6578
Ge 15:18 unto the great river, the river **E.**: 6578
De 1:7 unto the great river, the river **E.** 6578
De 11:24 from the river, the river **E.**, even 6578
Jos 1:4 unto the great river, the river **E.**, 6578
2Sa 8:3 recover his border at the river **E.** 6578
2Ki 23:29 the king of Assyria to the river **E.** 6578
2Ki 24:7 river of Egypt unto the river **E.** 6578
1Ch 5:9 the wilderness from the river **E.** 6578
1Ch 18:3 his dominion by the river **E.** 6578
2Ch 35:20 to fight against Carchemish by **E.** 6578
Jer 13:4 upon thy loins, and arise, go to **E.**, 6578
Jer 13:5 went, and hid it by **E.**, as the Lord 6578
Jer 13:6 Arise, go to **E.**, and take the girdle 6578
Jer 13:7 Then I went to **E.**, and digged, and 6578
Jer 46:2 of Egypt, which was by the river **E.** 6578
Jer 46:6 towards the north by the river **E.** 6578
Jer 46:10 the north country by the river **E.** 6578
Jer 51:63 it, and cast it into the midst of **E.**: 6578
Re 9:14 are bound in the great river **E.** *2166*
Re 16:12 his vial upon the great river **E.**; *2166*

EUROCLYDON (yu-roc'-lid-on)
Ac 27:14 a tempestuous wind, called **E.** *2148*

EUTYCHUS (yu'-tik-us)
Ac 20:9 a certain young man named **E.**, *2161*

EVANGELIST See also EVANGELISTS.
Ac 21:8 entered the house of Philip the **e.**, *2099*
2Ti 4:5 afflictions, do the work of an **e.**, *2099*

EVANGELISTS
Eph 4:11 and some, **e.**; and some, pastors *2099*

EVE (eev)
Ge 3:20 Adam called his wife's name **E.**; 2332
Ge 4:1 And Adam knew **E.** his wife; and 2332
2Co 11:3 the serpent beguiled **E.** through *2096*
1Ti 2:13 Adam was first formed, then **E.** *2096*

EVEN See also EVENING; EVENTIDE.
Ge 6:17 behold, I **e.** I, do bring a flood
Ge 9:3 **e.** as the green herb have I given
Ge 10:9 **E.** as Nimrod the mighty hunter
Ge 10:19 and Zeboim, **e.** unto Lasha.
Ge 10:21 **e.** to him were children born. 1571
Ge 13:3 from the south **e.** to Bethel,
Ge 13:10 **e.** as the garden of the Lord,
Ge 14:23 from a thread **e.** to a shoelatchet, 5704
Ge 19:1 came two angels to Sodom at **e.**; 6153
Ge 19:4 men of the city, **e.** the men of Sodom,
Ge 19:9 pressed sore upon the man, **e.** Lot,
Ge 20:5 she, **e.** she herself said, He is my 1571
Ge 21:10 be heir with my son, **e.** with Isaac.
Ge 23:7 **e.** to the children of Heth.
Ge 23:10 **e.** of all that went in at the gate of the
Ge 24:11 **e.** the time that women go to draw.
Ge 26:28 **e.** betwixt us and thee, and let us

Book	Ref	Context	No.
Ge	27:34	Bless me, **e.** me also, O my father.	1571
Ge	27:38	bless me, **e.** me also, O my father.	1571
Ge	34:29	spoiled **e.** all that was in the house.	
Ge	35:14	with him, **e.** a pillar of stone:	
Ge	37:18	**e.** before he came unto them,	
Ge	42:28	and, Lo, it is **e.** in my sack:	
Ge	44:18	servant: for thou art **e.** as Pharaoh.	
Ge	46:18	she bare unto Jacob, **e.** sixteen souls.	
Ge	46:34	our youth **e.** until now, both we,	
Ge	47:2	some of his brethren, **e.** five men,	
Ge	47:21	of the borders of Egypt **e.** to the other	
Ge	49:22	Joseph is..., **e.** a fruitful bough	
Ge	49:25	**E.** by the god of thy father, who	
Ex	3:1	mountain of God, **e.** to Horeb.	
Ex	4:16	**e.** he shall be to thee instead of	
Ex	4:22	Israel is my son, **e.** my firstborn:	
Ex	4:23	will slay thy son, **e.** thy firstborn.	
Ex	9:18	foundation thereof **e.** until now.	
Ex	10:12	eat every herb of the land, **e.** all	853
Ex	10:21	**e.** darkness that may be felt.	
Ex	11:5	**e.** unto the first born of the	
Ex	12:15	**e.** the first day ye shall put away	389
Ex	12:18	fourteenth day of the month at **e.**,	6153
Ex	12:18	twentieth day of the month at **e.**.	
Ex	12:38	flocks, and herds, **e.** very much cattle.	
Ex	12:41	**e.** the selfsame day it came to pass,	
Ex	14:23	the sea, **e.** all Pharaoh's horses,	
Ex	16:6	At **e.**, then ye shall know that the	6153
Ex	16:12	At **e.** ye shall eat flesh, and in the	6153
Ex	16:13	that at **e.** the quails came up, and	6153
Ex	18:14	by thee from morning unto **e.**?	6153
Ex	23:31	**e.** unto the sea of the Philistines,	
Ex	25:9	instruments thereof, **e.** so shall ye	
Ex	25:19	**e.** of the mercy seat shall ye make	
Ex	27:5	be **e.** to the midst of the altar.	
Ex	28:1	**e.** Aaron, Nadab and Abihu, Eleazar	
Ex	28:8	**e.** of gold, of blue, and purple,	
Ex	28:17	of stones, **e.** four rows of stones:	
Ex	28:42	from the loins **e.** unto the thighs	
Ex	29:27	**e.** of that which is for Aaron, and or	
Ex	29:28	**e.** their heave offering unto the Lord.	
Ex	29:39	other lamb thou shalt offer at **e.**:	6153
Ex	29:41	other lamb thou shalt offer at **e.**,	6153
Ex	30:8	Aaron lighteth the lamps at **e.**,	6153
Ex	30:21	**e.** to him and to his seed throughout	
Ex	30:23	so much, **e.** two hundred shekels,	
Ex	30:33	upon a stranger, shall **e.** be cut off	
Ex	30:38	to smell thereto, shall **e.** be cut off	
Ex	32:29	**e.** every man upon his son, and	3588
Ex	35:35	**e.** of them that do any work, and of	
Ex	36:2	**e.** every one whose heart stirred	
Ex	37:3	**e.** two rings upon the one side of it,	
Ex	37:9	**e.** to the mercy seatward were	
Ex	38:21	of the tabernacle, **e.** of the tabernacle	
Ex	38:24	**e.** the gold of the offering, was twenty	
Ex	39:37	**e.** with the lamps to be set in order,	
Ex	39:43	Lord had commanded, **e.** so had they	
Le	1:2	offering of the cattle, **e.** of the herd,	
Le	2:14	corn dried by the fire, **e.** corn	
Le	3:14	his offering, **e.** an offering made by	
Le	4:12	**E.** the whole bullock shall he carry	
Le	4:17	before the Lord **e.** before the vail.	
Le	5:12	of it, **e.** a memorial thereof, and	853
Le	6:5	shall **e.** restore it in the principal,	
Le	6:15	**e.** the memorial of it, unto the	
Le	7:8	**e.** the priest shall have to himself	
Le	7:20	upon him, **e.** that soul shall be cut	
Le	7:21	the Lord, **e.** that soul shall be cut	
Le	7:25	**e.** the soul that eateth it shall be	
Le	7:27	of blood, **e.** that soul shall be cut	
Le	8:9	mitre, **e.** upon his forefront, did	
Le	11:11	They shall be **e.** an abomination	
Le	11:22	**E.** these of them ye may eat; the	
Le	11:24	shall be unclean until the **e.**	6153
Le	11:25	clothes, and be unclean until the **e.**	6153
Le	11:27	carcase shall be unclean until the **e.**	6153
Le	11:28	clothes, and be unclean until the **e.**:	6153
Le	11:31	dead, shall be unclean until the **e.**	6153
Le	11:32	and it shall be unclean until the **e.**;	6153
Le	11:39	thereof shall be unclean until the **e.**	6153
Le	11:40	clothes, and be unclean until the **e.**:	6153
Le	11:40	and be unclean until the **e.**	6153
Le	13:12	from his head **e.** to his foot,	
Le	13:18	**e.** in the skin thereof, was a boil,	
Le	13:30	it is a dry scall, **e.** a leprosy upon	
Le	13:38	bright spots, **e.** white bright spots;	
Le	14:9	**e.** all his hair he shall shave off: and	
Le	14:31	**E.** such as he is able to get, the one	
Le	14:46	up shall be unclean until the **e.**	6153
Le	15:5,	6, 7, 8 and be unclean until the **e.**	6153
Le	15:10	him shall be unclean until the **e.**:	6153
Le	15:10,	11, 16, 17, 18 unclean until the **e.**	6153
Le	15:19	her shall be unclean until the **e.**	6153
Le	15:21,	22 and be unclean until the **e.**	6153
Le	15:23	he shall be unclean until the **e.**	6153
Le	15:27	water, and be unclean until the **e.**	6153
Le	16:32	linen clothes, **e.** the holy garments:	
Le	17:5	**e.** that they may bring them unto	
Le	17:9	**e.** that man shall be cut off from	
Le	17:10	I will **e.** set my face against that	
Le	17:13	**e.** pour out the blood thereof,	
Le	17:15	and be unclean until the **e.**:	6153
Le	18:9,	10 **e.** their nakedness thou shalt not	
Le	18:29	**e.** the souls that commit them shall	
Le	19:21	**e.** a ram for a trespass offering	
Le	20:6	I will **e.** set my face against that soul.	
Le	20:10	**e.** he that committeth adultery with	
Le	22:6	such shall be unclean until **e.**,	6153
Le	23:2	convocations, **e.** these are my feasts.	
Le	23:4	of the Lord, **e.** holy convocations,	
Le	23:5	day of the first month at **e.**	6153
Le	23:16	**E.** unto the morrow after the	
Le	23:18	**e.** an offering made by fire, of sweet	
Le	23:32	the ninth day of the month at **e.**,	6153
Le	23:32	from **e.** unto **e.**, shall ye celebrate	6153
Le	24:7	**e.** an offering made by fire unto the	
Le	26:16	I will **e.** appoint over you terror,	
Le	26:28	I, **e.** I, will chastise you seven	637
Le	26:34	**e.** then shall the land rest, and enjoy	
Le	26:43	because, **e.** because they despised	
Le	27:3	twenty years old **e.** unto sixty	
Le	27:3	**e.** thy estimation shall be fifty	
Le	27:5	years old **e.** unto twenty years old,	
Le	27:6	a month old **e.** unto five years old,	
Le	27:18	the years that remain, **e.** unto	
Le	27:23	**e.** unto the year of the jubilee:	
Le	27:24	**e.** to him to whom the possession of	
Le	27:32	**e.** to whatsoever passeth under	
Nu	1:21	**e.** of the tribe of Reuben, were	
Nu	1:23	**e.** of the tribe of Simeon, were	
Nu	1:25	**e.** of the tribe of Gad, were forty	
Nu	1:27	**e.** of the tribe of Judah, were	
Nu	1:29	**e.** of the tribe of Issachar, were	
Nu	1:31	**e.** of the tribe of Zebulun, were	
Nu	1:33	**e.** of the tribe of Ephraim, were	
Nu	1:35	**e.** of the tribe of Manasseh, were	
Nu	1:37	**e.** of the tribe of Benjamin, were	
Nu	1:39	**e.** of the tribe of Dan, were	
Nu	1:41	**e.** of the tribe of Asher, were	
Nu	1:43	**e.** of the tribe of Naphtali, were	
Nu	1:46	**E.** all they that were numbered were	
Nu	3:22	**e.** those that were numbered of them	
Nu	3:38	**e.** before the tabernacle of the	
Nu	3:47	shalt **e.** take five shekels apiece	
Nu	4:3	**e.** until fifty years old, all that	
Nu	4:14	**e.** the censers, the fleshhooks,	
Nu	4:30	**e.** unto fifty years old shalt thou	
Nu	4:35	years old and upward **e.** unto fifty	
Nu	4:39	and upward **e.** unto fifty years old,	
Nu	4:40	**E.** those that were numbered of them,	
Nu	4:43	**e.** unto fifty years old, every one	
Nu	4:44	**E.** those that were numbered of them	
Nu	4:47	**e.** unto fifty years old, every one	
Nu	4:48	**E.** those that were numbered of them,	
Nu	5:8	unto the Lord, **e.** to the priest;	
Nu	5:26	**e.** the memorial thereof, and burn	
Nu	6:4	from the kernels **e.** to the husk	
Nu	7:10	**e.** the princes offered their offering	
Nu	8:8	**e.** fine flour mingled with oil,	
Nu	8:16	**e.** instead of the firstborn of all the	
Nu	9:3	fourteenth day of this month, at **e.**,	6153
Nu	9:5	day of the first month at **e.** in the	6153
Nu	9:11	day of the second month at **e.** they	6153
Nu	9:13	**e.** the same soul shall be cut off	
Nu	9:15	and at **e.** there was upon the	6153
Nu	9:21	abode from **e.** unto the morning,	6153
Nu	11:20	But **e.** a whole month, until	5704
Nu	12:8	mouth to mouth, **e.** apparently,	
Nu	14:19	from Egypt **e.** until now.	
Nu	14:34	**e.** forty days, each day for a years,	
Nu	14:34	**e.** forty years, and ye shall know	
Nu	14:37	**E.** those men that did bring up the	
Nu	14:45	discomfited them, **e.** unto Hormah.	
Nu	15:23	**E.** all that the Lord hath commanded	
Nu	16:5	**E.** to morrow the Lord will shew	
Nu	16:5	**e.** him whom he hath chosen will	
Nu	17:6	fathers' houses, **e.** twelve rods:	
Nu	18:21	**e.** the service of the tabernacle of	
Nu	18:26	**e.** a tenth part of the tithe.	
Nu	18:29	**e.** the hallowed part thereof out of it.	853
Nu	19:7	shall be unclean until the **e.**	6153
Nu	19:8	and shall be unclean until the **e.**	6153
Nu	19:10	and be unclean until the **e.**:	6153
Nu	19:19	in water, shall be clean at **e.**	6153
Nu	19:21	shall be unclean until **e.**	6153
Nu	19:22	it shall be unclean until **e.**	6153
Nu	20:1	**e.** the whole congregation, into the	6153
Nu	20:22	**e.** the whole congregation, journeyed	
Nu	20:29	**e.** all the house of Israel.	
Nu	21:24	**e.** unto the children of Ammon:	
Nu	21:26	out of his hand, **e.** unto Arnon.	
Nu	21:30	is perished **e.** unto Dibon, and	
Nu	21:30	laid them waste **e.** unto Nophah,	
Nu	25:13	**e.** the covenant of an everlasting	
Nu	25:14	**e.** that was slain with the	
Nu	27:21	with him, **e.** all the congregation.	
Nu	28:4	other lamb shalt thou offer at **e.**;	6153
Nu	28:8	other lamb shalt thou offer at **e.**:	6153
Nu	31:47	**E.** of the children of Israel's half,	
Nu	31:51	them, **e.** all wrought jewels.	
Nu	32:4	**E.** the country which the Lord	
Nu	32:33	them, **e.** to the children of Gad,	
Nu	32:33	**e.** the cities of the country round	
Nu	33:49	from Beth-jesimoth **e.** unto	
Nu	34:2	**e.** the land of Canaan with the	
Nu	34:6	**e.** have the great sea for a border:	
Nu	36:10	**e.** as the Lord commanded Moses,	
De	1:44	you in Seir, **e.** unto Hormah.	
De	2:22	in their stead **e.** unto this day:	
De	2:23	**e.** unto Azzad, the Caphtorims,	
De	2:36	**e.** unto Gilead, there was not one	
De	3:16	from Gilead **e.** unto the river Jabbok,	
De	3:16	the border **e.** unto the river Jabbok,	
De	3:17	from Chinnereth **e.** unto the sea	
De	3:17	the sea, **e.** the salt sea, under	
De	4:5	**e.** as the Lord my God commanded	
De	4:13	to perform, **e.** ten commandments;	
De	4:19	stars, **e.** all the host of heaven,	
De	4:20	**e.** out of Egypt, to be unto him a	
De	4:24	consuming fire, **e.** a jealous God.	
De	4:30	**e.** in the latter days, if thou turn	
De	4:48	**e.** unto mount Sion, which is Hermon,	
De	4:49	**e.** unto the sea of the plain,	
De	5:3	but with us, **e.** us, who are all of	
De	5:23	**e.** all the heads of your tribes,	
De	9:9	**e.** the tables of the covenant which	
De	9:11	**e.** the tables of the covenant.	
De	9:21	**e.** until it was as small as dust:	
De	10:15	**e.** you above all people, as it is this	
De	11:12	the year **e.** unto the end of the	
De	11:24	**e.** unto the uttermost sea shall	
De	12:5	**e.** unto his habitation shall you	
De	12:22	**E.** as the roebuck and the hart	389
De	12:30	**e.** so will I do likewise.	1571
De	12:31	for **e.** their sons and their	1571
De	13:7	the earth, **e.** unto the other end	
De	16:3	bread therewith, **e.** the bread of	
De	16:4	first day at **e.**, remain all night	6153
De	16:6	sacrifice the passover at **e.**,	6153
De	17:5	**e.** that man or that woman, and	
De	17:12	unto the judge, **e.** that man shall die:	
De	18:20	**e.** that prophet shall die.	
De	20:14	**e.** all the spoil thereof, shalt thou	
De	21:3	**e.** the elders of that city shall take	
De	22:26	**e.** so is this matter:	
De	23:2	**e.** to his tenth generation shall	1571
De	23:3	**e.** to their tenth generation shall	1571
De	23:16	**e.** among you, in that place	
De	23:18	for **e.** both these are abomination	1571
De	23:23	**e.** a freewill offering, according	
De	25:18	**e.** all that were feeble behind	
De	26:9	**e.** a land that floweth with	
De	28:59	**e.** great plagues, and of long	
De	28:64	of the earth **e.** unto the other;	
De	28:64	have known, **e.** wood and stone.	
De	28:67	Would God it were **e.** and at **e.**	6153
De	29:24	**E.** all nations shall say,	
De	31:21	**e.** now, before I have brought	
De	32:31	**e.** our enemies themselves being	
De	32:39	that I, **e.** I, am he, and there is	

De 33:4 **e.** the inheritance of the
Jos 1:2 **e.** to the children of Israel.
Jos 1:4 **e.** unto the great river. the river,
Jos 2:1 Go view the land, **e.** Jericho.
Jos 2:24 for **e.** all the inhabitants of the 1571
Jos 3:16 of the plain, **e.** the salt sea, failed,
Jos 5:4 **e.** all the men of war, died in the
Jos 5:10 fourteenth day of the month at **e.** 6153
Jos 6:17 **e.** it, and all that are therein, to the
Jos 6:25 in Israel **e.** unto this day;
Jos 7:5 before the gate **e.** unto Shebarim,
Jos 7:11 **e.** taken of the accursed thing, 1571
Jos 7:11 put it **e.** among their own stuff. 1571
Jos 8:4 the city, **e.** behind the city:
Jos 8:11 **e.** the people of war that were with
Jos 8:13 **e.** all the host that was on the north
Jos 8:25 **e.** all the men of Ai.
Jos 8:28 **e.** a desolation unto this day.
Jos 9:20 we will **e.** let them live, lest
Jos 9:27 **e.** unto this day, in the place
Jos 10:41 Kadesh-barnea **e.** unto Gaza,
Jos 10:41 country of Goshen, **e.** unto Gibeon.
Jos 11:4 **e.** as the sand that is upon the sea
Jos 11:17 **E.** from the mount Halak,
Jos 11:17 **e.** unto Baal-gad in the valley of
Jos 12:2 Gilead, **e.** unto the river Jabbok,
Jos 12:3 **e.** the salt sea on the east,
Jos 12:7 **e.** unto the mount Halak,
Jos 13:3 **e.** unto the borders of Ekron
Jos 13:8 **e.** as Moses the servant of the Lord
Jos 13:24 **e.** unto the children of Gad
Jos 13:27 **e.** unto the edge of the sea of
Jos 13:31 **e.** to the one half of the children
Jos 14:10 **e.** since the Lord spake this word
Jos 14:11 **e.** so is my strength now, for
Jos 15:1 **e.** to the border of Edom the
Jos 15:5 **e.** unto the end of Jordan.
Jos 15:13 **e.** the city of Arba the father of
Jos 15:46 From Ekron **e.** unto the sea,
Jos 16:5 **e.** the border of their inheritance
Jos 17:11 and her towns, **e.** three countries.
Jos 17:17 **e.** to Ephraim and to Manasseh,
Jos 19:1 **e.** for the tribe of the children of
Jos 19:28 and Kanah, **e.** unto great Zidon;
Jos 19:32 **e.** for the children of Naphtali
Jos 19:50 **e.** Timnath-serah in mount
Jos 21:20 **e.** they had the cities of their lot
Jos 23:4 **e.** unto the great sea westward
Jos 23:12 **e.** these that remain among you,
Jos 24:2 **e.** Terah, the father of Abraham,
Jos 24:12 **e.** the two kings of the Amorites;
Jos 24:18 **e.** the Amorites which dwelt in the
Jg 3:1 **e.** as many of Israel as had not
Jg 3:9 **e.** Othniel the son of Kenaz, 853
Jg 4:13 **e.** nine hundred chariots of iron,
Jg 5:3 I, **e.** I, will sing unto the Lord;
Jg 5:5 **e.** that Sinai from before the Lord
Jg 5:11 **e.** the righteous acts toward the
Jg 5:15 **e.** Issachar, and also Barak:
Jg 6:3 the east, **e.** they came up against
Jg 6:25 **e.** the second bullock of seven years
Jg 7:22 fellow, **e.** throughout all the host:
Jg 8:14 **e.** threescore and seventeen men.
Jg 8:19 **e.** the sons of my mother:
Jg 8:27 put it in his city, **e.** in Ophrah:
Jg 9:40 **e.** unto the entering of the gate.
Jg 11:13 of Egypt, from Arnon **e.** unto Jabbok,
Jg 11:22 Amorites, from Arnon **e.** unto Jabbok.
Jg 11:22 the wilderness **e.** unto Jordan.
Jg 11:33 **e.** till thou come to Minnith,
Jg 11:33 **e.** twenty cities, and unto the plain
Jg 11:36 **e.** of the children of Ammon.
Jg 18:15 **e.** unto the house of Micah, and
Jg 19:16 there came an old man…at **e.**, 6153
Jg 20:1 from Dan **e.** to Beer-sheba,
Jg 20:2 **e.** of all the tribes of Israel,
Jg 20:23 wept before the Lord until **e.**. 6153
Jg 20:26 and fasted that day until **e.**, 6153
Jg 20:33 **e.** out of the meadows of Gibeah.
Jg 21:2 abode there till **e.** before God, 6153
Ru 2:7 continued **e.** from the morning 227
Ru 2:15 her glean **e.** among the sheaves, 1571
Ru 2:17 she gleaned in the field until **e.**, 6153
1Sa 3:20 from Dan **e.** to Beer-sheba knew
1Sa 5:6 **e.** Ashdod and the coasts thereof. 853
1Sa 6:18 **e.** unto the great stone of Abel,
1Sa 6:19 **e.** he smote of the people fifty
1Sa 7:14 from Ekron **e.** unto Gath;
1Sa 8:8 **e.** unto this day, wherewith they
1Sa 8:14 **e.** the best of them, and give them
1Sa 14:21 **e.** they also turned to be with
1Sa 14:22 **e.** they also followed hard after
1Sa 17:40 in a shepherd's bag…**e.** in a scrip:
1Sa 17:52 **e.** unto Gath, and unto Ekron.
1Sa 18:4 **e.** to his sword, and to his bow,
1Sa 18:11 smite David **e.** to the wall with it.
1Sa 19:10 David **e.** to the wall with the javelin:
1Sa 20:4 I will **e.** do it for thee.
1Sa 20:5 the field unto the third day at **e.**. 6153
1Sa 20:16 Lord **e.** require it at hand of
1Sa 20:25 set…**e.** upon a seat by the wall:
1Sa 25:25 regard this man of Belial, **e.** Nabal:
1Sa 25:27 it **e.** be given unto the young men
1Sa 26:8 him…**e.** to the earth at once,
1Sa 27:3 **e.** David with his two wives,
1Sa 27:8 **e.** unto the land of Egypt.
1Sa 28:3 him in Ramah, **e.** in his own city.
1Sa 28:17 it to thy neighbour, **e.** to David:
1Sa 30:17 the twilight **e.** unto the evening
1Sa 30:26 the elders of Judah, **e.** to his friends,
2Sa 1:2 It came **e.** to pass on the third day,
2Sa 1:12 and fasted until **e.**, for Saul, and 6153
2Sa 2:5 unto your Lord, **e.** unto Saul,
2Sa 3:9 to David, **e.** so I do to him; 3588
2Sa 3:10 from Dan **e.** to Beer-sheba.
2Sa 3:15 **e.** from Phaltiel the son of Laish.
2Sa 6:5 **e.** on harps, and on psalteries,
2Sa 6:19 **e.** among the whole multitude of
2Sa 7:6 out of Egypt, **e.** to this day,
2Sa 7:23 like thy people, **e.** like Israel,
2Sa 8:2 **e.** with two lines measured he to
2Sa 10:4 their garments…**e.** to their buttock,
2Sa 11:13 at **e.** he went out to lie on his bed 6153
2Sa 11:23 were upon them **e.** unto the entering
2Sa 14:25 his foot **e.** to the crown of his head
2Sa 15:12 from his city, **e.** from Giloh,
2Sa 15:21 **e.** there also will thy servant be. 3588
2Sa 17:11 from Dan **e.** to Beer-sheba,
2Sa 18:5 with the young men, **e.** with Absalom.
2Sa 19:11 come to the king, **e.** to his house.
2Sa 19:14 **e.** as the heart of one man;
2Sa 19:32 very aged man, **e.** fourscore years.
2Sa 20:2 from Jordan **e.** to Jerusalem.
2Sa 20:21 against the king, **e.** against David:
2Sa 22:42 **e.** unto the Lord, but he answered
2Sa 23:4 **e.** a morning without clouds:
2Sa 24:2 from Dan **e.** to Beer-sheba,
2Sa 24:7 south of Judah **e.** to Beer-sheba.
2Sa 24:15 **e.** to the time appointed:
2Sa 24:15 Dan **e.** to Beer-sheba seventy
1Ki 1:26 But me, **e.** me thy servant,
1Ki 1:30 **E.** as I sware unto thee by the 3588
1Ki 1:30 **e.** so will I certainly do this day, 3588
1Ki 1:37 **e.** so be he with Solomon, and
1Ki 1:48 mine eyes **e.** seeing it.
1Ki 2:22 **e.** for him, and for Abiathar the priest,
1Ki 4:12 **e.** unto the place that is beyond
1Ki 4:24 from Tiphsah **e.** to Azzah,
1Ki 4:25 from Dan **e.** to Beer-sheba,
1Ki 4:29 **e.** as the sand that is on the sea shore.
1Ki 4:33 **e.** unto the hyssop that springeth
1Ki 6:16 he **e.** built them for it within,
1Ki 6:16 **e.** for the oracle, **e.** for the most holy
1Ki 7:7 **e.** the porch of judgment:
1Ki 7:9 **e.** from the foundation unto the coping.
1Ki 7:10 costly stones, **e.** great stones,
1Ki 7:42 **e.** two rows of pomegranates for
1Ki 7:51 **e.** the silver, and the gold, 853
1Ki 8:4 **e.** those did the priests and the Levites
1Ki 8:6 **e.** under the wings of the cherubims.
1Ki 8:29 **e.** toward the place of which thou
1Ki 8:39 for thou, **e.** thou only, knowest the
1Ki 8:65 and seven days, **e.** fourteen days.
1Ki 11:26 Jeroboam…**e.** he lifted up his
1Ki 11:35 will give it unto thee, **e.** ten tribes.
1Ki 12:27 **e.** unto Rehoboam king of Judah,
1Ki 12:30 went to worship…**e.** unto Dan.
1Ki 12:33 **e.** in the month which he had devised
1Ki 13:34 **e.** to cut it off, and to destroy it
1Ki 14:14 that day: but what? **e.** now. 1571
1Ki 14:26 he **e.** took away all: and he took away
1Ki 15:13 Maachah…**e.** her he removed
1Ki 15:28 **E.** in the third year of Asa king of
1Ki 16:7 **e.** for all the evil that he did in
1Ki 18:22 I, **e.** I only, remain a prophet of the
1Ki 18:26 from morning **e.** until noon,
1Ki 19:10, 14 and I, **e.** I only, am left: and they
1Ki 20:3 children, **e.** the goodliest, are mine.
1Ki 20:14 **E.** by the young men of the
1Ki 20:15 people, **e.** all the children of Israel,
1Ki 21:11 **e.** the elders and the nobles who were
1Ki 21:13 against him, **e.** against Naboth, in the
1Ki 21:19 shall dogs lick thy blood, **e.** thine. 1571
1Ki 22:35 was stayed up…and died at **e.**: 6153
2Ki 3:24 Moabites, **e.** in their own country.
2Ki 3:26 **e.** unto the king of Edom:
2Ki 4:3 of thy neighbours, **e.** empty vessels;
2Ki 5:22 Behold, **e.** now there be come…two
2Ki 7:6 of horses, **e.** the noise of a great host:
2Ki 7:7 **e.** the camp as it was, and fled for
2Ki 7:13 they are **e.** as all the multitude of
2Ki 8:6 she left the land, **e.** until now.
2Ki 8:9 a present…**e.** of every good thing
2Ki 9:4 **e.** the young man the prophet, went
2Ki 9:6 anointed thee king…**e.** over Israel.
2Ki 9:20 saying, He came **e.** unto them, and
2Ki 10:3 Look **e.** out the best and meetest
2Ki 10:14 **e.** two and forty men;
2Ki 10:33 **e.** Gilead and Bashan.
2Ki 11:2 they hid him, **e.** him and his nurse,
2Ki 11:5 shall **e.** be keepers of the watch
2Ki 11:7 **e.** they shall keep the watch of the
2Ki 12:4 **e.** the money of every one that
2Ki 14:10 **e.** thou, and Judah with thee?
2Ki 14:29 **e.** with the kings of Israel;
2Ki 15:20 **e.** of all the mighty men of wealth,
2Ki 17:16 molten images, **e.** two calves,
2Ki 18:8 **e.** unto Gaza, and the borders
2Ki 18:10 **e.** in the sixth year of Hezekiah,
2Ki 18:21 **e.** upon Egypt, on which if a man
2Ki 19:15 thou art the God, **e.** thou alone,
2Ki 19:19 thou art the Lord God, **e.** thou only.
2Ki 19:22 **e.** against the Holy One of Israel.
2Ki 20:14 from a far country, **e.** from Babylon.
2Ki 21:15 out of Egypt, **e.** unto this day.
2Ki 22:16 **e.** all the words of the book which
2Ki 24:14 **e.** ten thousand captives, and all the
2Ki 24:16 the men of might, **e.** seven thousand,
2Ki 24:16 **e.** them the king of Babylon brought
2Ki 25:22 **e.** over them he made Gedaliah
2Ki 25:23 **e.** Ishmael the son of Nethaniah, and
1Ch 2:23 the towns thereof, **e.** threescore cities.
1Ch 4:15 and the sons of Elah, **e.** Kenaz.
1Ch 4:39 **e.** unto the east side of the valley,
1Ch 4:42 **e.** of the sons of Simeon, five hundred
1Ch 5:8 **e.** unto Nebo and Baal-meon
1Ch 5:24 **e.** Epher, and Ishi, and Eliel, and
1Ch 5:26 **e.** the Reubenites, and the Gadites,
1Ch 6:39 **e.** Asaph the son of Berachiah,
1Ch 10:13 **e.** against the word of the Lord,
1Ch 11:2 time past, **e.** when Saul was king, 1571
1Ch 11:8 city round about, **e.** from Millo 5704
1Ch 12:2 **e.** of Saul's brethren of Benjamin.
1Ch 12:40 **e.** unto Issachar and Zebulun and
1Ch 13:5 from Shihor of Egypt **e.** unto the
1Ch 14:16 smote the host…from Gibeon **e.**
1Ch 16:16 **E.** of the covenant which he made
1Ch 16:19 When ye were but few, **e.** a few,
1Ch 17:7 from the sheepcote, **e.** from
1Ch 17:24 Let it **e.** be established,
1Ch 17:24 Lord of hosts is…**e.** a God to Israel:
1Ch 20:3 **E.** so dealt David with all the
1Ch 21:2 Israel from Beer-sheba **e.** unto Dan;
1Ch 21:12 **e.** the pestilence, in the land, and the
1Ch 21:17 **e.** I it is that have sinned and done evil
1Ch 23:24 **e.** the chief of the fathers, as they were
1Ch 23:30 morning…and likewise at **e.**; 6153
1Ch 24:31 **e.** the principal fathers over against
1Ch 25:7 **e.** all that were cunning, was two
1Ch 26:12 divisions of the porters, **e.** among
1Ch 26:21 **e.** of Laadan the Gershonite,
1Ch 26:31 **e.** among the Hebronites, according to
1Ch 28:15 **E.** the weight for the candlesticks
1Ch 28:19 **e.** all the works of this pattern.
1Ch 28:20 the Lord God, **e.** my God, will be with
1Ch 28:21 **e.** they shall be with thee for all
1Ch 29:4 **E.** three thousand talents of gold,
1Ch 29:21 **e.** a thousand bullocks, a thousand
2Ch 2:3 As thou didst deal with David…**e.** so
2Ch 2:9 **E.** to prepare me timber in abundance:
2Ch 5:7 **e.** under the wings of the cherubims:

2Ch 5:13 It came **e.** to pass, as the trumpeters
2Ch 5:13 was filled with a cloud, **e.** the house of
2Ch 6:21 dwelling place, **e.** from heaven; and
2Ch 6:33 **e.** from thy dwelling place, and do
2Ch 6:39 **e.** from thy dwelling place, their prayer
2Ch 8:10 chief of king Solomon's officers, **e.** two
2Ch 8:13 **E.** after a certain rate every day,
2Ch 8:13 **e.** in the feast of unleavened bread,
2Ch 9:26 from the river **e.** unto the land of
2Ch 11:6 He built **e.** Beth-lehem, and Etam, and
2Ch 13:3 **e.** four hundred thousand chosen men:
2Ch 13:5 **e.** to him and to his sons by a covenant
2Ch 17:7 to his princes, **e.** to Ben-hail, and to
2Ch 17:8 he sent Levites, **e.** Shemaiah, and
2Ch 18:13 **e.** what my God saith, that will 3588
2Ch 18:21 prevail: go out, and do **e.** so.
2Ch 18:34 against the Syrians until the **e.**: 6153
2Ch 19:10 ye shall **e.** warn them that they
2Ch 20:4 **e.** out of all the cities of Judah 1571
2Ch 24:14 **e.** vessels to minister, and to offer
2Ch 25:13 from Samaria **e.** unto Beth-horon,
2Ch 25:19 thou shouldest fall, **e.** thou, and Judah
2Ch 26:8 spread abroad **e.** to the entering in
2Ch 26:19 leprosy **e.** rose up in his forehead
2Ch 28:10 are there not with you, **e.** with you, 7535
2Ch 28:27 buried him in the city, **e.** in
2Ch 30:5 from Beer-sheba **e.** to Dan,
2Ch 30:10 and Manasseh **e.** unto Zebulun:
2Ch 30:18 **e.** many of Ephraim, and Manasseh
2Ch 30:27 to his holy dwelling place, **e.** unto
2Ch 31:16 **e.** unto every one that entereth into
2Ch 33:14 **e.** to the entering in at the fish gate,
2Ch 34:6 and Simeon, **e.** unto Naphtali,
2Ch 34:11 **E.** to the artificers and builders give
2Ch 34:24 **e.** all the curses that are written in the
2Ch 34:27 I have **e.** heard thee also, saith
2Ch 34:33 **e.** to serve the Lord their God.
Ezr 1:8 **E.** those did Cyrus king of Persia
Ezr 3:3 **e.** burnt offerings morning and evening.
Ezr 4:5 **e.** until the reign of Darius king
Ezr 4:11 sent unto him, **e.** unto Artaxerxes
Ezr 5:1 unto the Jews…**e.** unto them,
Ezr 5:16 since that time **e.** until now
Ezr 6:8 of the king's goods, **e.** of the tribute
Ezr 7:11 **e.** a scribe of the words of the
Ezr 7:21 And I, **e.** I Artaxerxes the king,
Ezr 8:25 **e.** the offering of the house of our God,
Ezr 8:26 I **e.** weighed unto their hand six
Ezr 9:1 **e.** of the Canaanites, the Hittites,
Ne 2:13 **e.** before the dragon well,
Ne 3:1 **e.** unto the tower of Meah they
Ne 3:10 **e.** over against his house.
Ne 3:21 **e.** to the end of the house of
Ne 3:24 of the wall, **e.** unto the corner,
Ne 3:27 **e.** unto the wall of Ophel.
Ne 4:3 **E.** that which they build, 1571
Ne 4:3 he shall **e.** break down their stone
Ne 4:13 **e.** set the people after their families
Ne 5:8 and will ye **e.** sell your brethren? 1571
Ne 5:11 Restore…**e.** this day, their lands, their
Ne 5:13 **e.** thus be he shaken out, and 3602
Ne 5:14 twentieth year **e.** unto the two and
Ne 5:15 yea, **e.** their servants bare rule
Ne 8:13 **e.** to understand the words of the law.
Ne 9:6 Thou, **e.** thou, art Lord alone;
Ne 12:23 **e.** until the days of Johanan the son
Ne 12:37 **e.** unto the water gate eastward.
Ne 12:38 tower of the furnaces **e.** unto the broad
Ne 12:39 **e.** unto the sheep gate:
Ne 12:43 Jerusalem was heard **e.** afar off.
Ne 13:26 **e.** him did outlandish women
Es 1:1 from India **e.** unto Ethiopia,
Es 1:4 **e.** an hundred and fourscore days.
Es 2:18 made a great feast…**e.** Esther's 853
Es 3:6 **e.** the people of Mordecai.
Es 3:13 **e.** upon the thirteenth day of the
Es 4:2 came **e.** before the king's gate: 5704
Es 5:3 it shall be **e.** given thee to the half
Es 5:6 **e.** to the half of the kingdom it
Es 6:10 and do **e.** so to Mordecai the Jew,
Es 7:2 **e.** to the half of the kingdom.
Job 4:8 **E.** as I have seen, they that plow
Job 4:21 they die, **e.** without wisdom.
Job 5:5 and taketh it **e.** out of the thorns,
Job 6:9 **E.** that it would please God to destroy
Job 10:21 **e.** to the land of darkness and the
Job 15:26 runneth upon him, **e.** on his neck,
Job 17:5 **e.** the eyes of his children shall fail.
Job 17:11 **e.** the thoughts of my heart.
Job 18:13 **e.** the firstborn of death shall
Job 21:6 **E.** when I remember I am afraid,
Job 23:2 **E.** to day is my complaint bitter: 1571
Job 23:3 that I might come **e.** to his seat!
Job 23:13 his soul desireth, **e.** that he doeth.
Job 24:17 them **e.** as the shadow of death:
Job 25:5 Behold **e.** to the moon, and it
Job 28:4 **e.** the waters forgotten of the
Job 31:6 me be weighed in an **e.** balance, 6664
Job 34:17 Shall **e.** he that hateth right govern? 637
Job 36:16 **E.** so would he have removed
Job 41:9 cast down **e.** at the sight of him? 1571
Job 42:16 his sons's sons, **e.** four generations.
Ps 18:6 before him, **e.** into his ears.
Ps 18:41 **e.** unto the Lord, but he answered
Ps 21:4 **e.** length of days for ever and ever.
Ps 24:9 **e.** lift them up, ye everlasting
Ps 26:12 My foot standeth in an **e.** place: 4334
Ps 27:2 wicked, **e.** mine enemies and my foes,
Ps 35:23 to my judgment, **e.** unto my cause,
Ps 39:*title* the chief Musician, **e.** to Jeduthun,
Ps 39:2 I held my peace, **e.** from good;
Ps 40:3 in my mouth, **e.** praise unto our God:
Ps 45:12 **e.** the rich among the people shall
Ps 47:9 **e.** the people of the God of
Ps 48:14 he will be our guide **e.** unto death.
Ps 50:1 The mighty God, **e.** the Lord,
Ps 50:7 I am God, **e.** thy God.
Ps 55:19 **e.** he that abideth of old.
Ps 57:4 I lie **e.** among them that are set
Ps 57:4 **e.** the sons of men, whose teeth are
Ps 59:12 let them **e.** be taken in their pride:
Ps 64:3 to shoot their arrows, **e.** bitter words:
Ps 65:4 thy house, **e.** thy holy temple.
Ps 67:6 God, **e.** our own God, shall bless us.
Ps 68:8 **e.** Sinai itself was moved at the
Ps 68:17 thousand, **e.** thousands of angels:
Ps 68:19 loadeth…with benefits, **e.** the God of
Ps 68:24 **e.** the goings of my God, my King,
Ps 68:26 **e.** the Lord, from the fountain of
Ps 71:16 thy righteousness, **e.** of thine only.
Ps 71:22 **e.** thy truth, O my God:
Ps 73:1 **e.** to such as are of a clean heart.
Ps 74:3 **e.** all that the enemy hath done
Ps 74:11 thy hand, **e.** thy right hand?
Ps 76:7 Thou, **e.** thou, art to be feared:
Ps 77:1 **e.** unto God with my voice;
Ps 78:6 know them, **e.** the children which
Ps 78:54 **e.** to this mountain, which his right
Ps 84:2 yea, **e.** fainteth for the courts of 1571
Ps 84:3 **e.** thine altars, O Lord of hosts, my 853
Ps 90:2 **e.** from everlasting to everlasting,
Ps 90:11 **e.** according to thy fear, so is thy
Ps 91:9 **e.** the most High, thy habitation:
Ps 105:17 **e.** Joseph, who was sold for a
Ps 105:20 **e.** the ruler of the people, and let
Ps 106:7 him at the sea, **e.** at the Red sea.
Ps 106:38 blood, **e.** the blood of their sons
Ps 107:43 **e.** they shall understand the
Ps 108:1 and give praise, **e.** with my glory. 637
Ps 109:16 might **e.** slay the broken in heart.
Ps 113:8 **e.** with the princes of his people.
Ps 115:16 **e.** the heavens, are the Lord's:
Ps 118:27 **e.** unto the horns of the altar.
Ps 119:41 **e.** thy salvation, according to thy
Ps 119:112 thy statutes alway, **e.** unto the end.
Ps 121:8 time forth, and **e.** for evermore.
Ps 125:2 from hence forth **e.** for ever.
Ps 131:2 my soul is **e.** as a weaned child.
Ps 133:2 down upon the beard, **e.** Aaron's beard:
Ps 133:3 the blessing, **e.** life for evermore.
Ps 136:22 **E.** an heritage unto Israel his servant:
Ps 137:7 it, **e.** to the foundation thereof.
Ps 139:10 **E.** there shall thy hand lead me, 1571
Ps 139:11 **e.** the night shall be light about
Ps 146:10 **e.** thy God, O Zion, unto all
Ps 148:14 **e.** of the children of Israel, a people
Pr 2:16 **e.** from the stranger which flattereth
Pr 3:12 **e.** as a father the son in whom he
Pr 8:16 **e.** all the judges of the earth.
Pr 14:13 **E.** in laughter the heart is 1571
Pr 14:20 is hated **e.** of his own neighbour: 1571
Pr 16:4 **e.** the wicked for the day of evil. 1571
Pr 16:7 he maketh **e.** his enemies to be at 1571
Pr 17:15 **e.** they both are abomination to 1571
Pr 17:28 **E.** a fool, when he holdeth his 1571
Pr 20:11 **E.** a child is known by his doings, 1571
Pr 20:12 Lord hath made **e.** both of them. 1571
Pr 22:19 known to thee this day, **e.** to thee. 637
Pr 23:15 my heart shall rejoice, **e.** mine. 1571
Pr 28:9 **e.** his prayer shall be abomination. 1571
Pr 30:1 of Jakeh, **e.** the prophecy:
Pr 30:1 spake unto Ithiel, **e.** unto Ithiel
Ec 2:12 **e.** that which hath been already 853
Ec 2:15 so it happeneth **e.** to me; 1571
Ec 3:19 **e.** one thing befalleth them:
Ec 4:16 **e.** of all that have been before them:
Ec 7:25 of folly, **e.** of foolishness and
Ec 9:1 in my heart **e.** to declare all this,
Ec 11:5 **e.** so thou knowest not the works 3602
Ec 12:10 was upright, **e.** words of truth.
Ca 4:2 flock of sheep that are **e.** shorn,
Isa 1:6 soul of the foot **e.** unto the head
Isa 1:13 iniquity, **e.** the solemn meeting.
Isa 4:3 be called holy, **e.** every one that is
Isa 5:9 shall be desolate, **e.** great and fair,
Isa 7:6 in the midst…**e.** the son of Tabeal:
Isa 7:17 **e.** the king of Assyria. 853
Isa 7:23 it shall **e.** be for briers and thorns.
Isa 8:7 and many, **e.** the king of Assyria, 853
Isa 8:8 he shall reach **e.** to the neck;
Isa 9:7 justice henceforth **e.** for ever.
Isa 9:9 all the people…**e.** Ephraim and the
Isa 10:21 shall return, **e.** the remnant of Jacob,
Isa 10:23 **e.** determined, in the midst of all
Isa 13:3 **e.** them that rejoice in my highness.
Isa 13:5 **e.** the Lord, and the weapons of his
Isa 13:12 precious than fine gold; **e.** a man
Isa 14:9 **e.** all the chief ones of the earth;
Isa 14:18 kings…**e.** all of them, lie in glory,
Isa 15:4 shall be heard **e.** unto Jahaz:
Isa 16:6 **e.** of his haughtiness, and his pride,
Isa 16:8 they are come **e.** unto Jazer they
Isa 18:2 **e.** in vessels of bulrushes upon the
Isa 19:13 **e.** they that are the stay of the
Isa 19:22 they shall return **e.** to the Lord,
Isa 19:24 **e.** a blessing in the midst of the
Isa 20:4 **e.** with their buttocks uncovered,
Isa 22:15 unto this treasurer, **e.** unto Shebna,
Isa 22:24 **e.** to all the vessels of flagons.
Isa 23:4 spoken, **e.** the strength of the sea,
Isa 24:15 **e.** the name of the Lord God of
Isa 24:16 songs, **e.** glory to the righteous.
Isa 25:5 **e.** the heat with the shadow of a
Isa 25:10 **e.** as straw is trodden down for the
Isa 25:12 to the ground, **e.** to the dust.
Isa 26:5 he layeth it low, **e.** to the ground;
Isa 26:5 he bringeth it **e.** to the dust.
Isa 26:6 tread it down, **e.** the feet of the poor,
Isa 27:1 **e.** leviathan that crooked
Isa 28:22 **e.** determined upon the whole
Isa 29:7 fight against Ariel, **e.** all that fight
Isa 29:8 It shall **e.** be as when an hungry
Isa 29:14 **e.** a marvellous work and a wonder:
Isa 32:7 **e.** when the needy speaketh right.
Isa 35:2 rejoice **e.** with joy and singing: 637
Isa 35:4 **e.** God with a recompence;
Isa 37:16 thou art the God, **e.** thou alone,
Isa 37:20 thou art the Lord, **e.** thou only.
Isa 37:23 **e.** against the Holy One of Israel.
Isa 38:11 I shall not see the Lord, **e.** the Lord,
Isa 38:12 sickness: from day **e.** to night wilt
Isa 38:13 my bones: from day **e.** to night wilt
Isa 39:3 country unto me, **e.** from Babylon.
Isa 40:30 **E.** the youths shall faint and be weary,
Isa 41:3 **e.** by the way that he had not gone
Isa 41:12 **e.** them that contended with thee:
Isa 41:28 **e.** among them, and there was no
Isa 43:7 **E.** every one that is called by my
Isa 43:11 I, **e.** I, am the Lord;
Isa 43:19 **e.** make a way in the wilderness, 637
Isa 43:25 I, **e.** I, am he that blotteth out
Isa 44:8 ye are **e.** my witnesses.
Isa 44:17 maketh a god, **e.** his graven image:
Isa 44:28 **e.** saying to Jerusalem, Thou shalt be
Isa 45:4 have **e.** called thee by thy name:
Isa 45:12 I, **e.** my hands, have stretched out

Book	Ref	Context	No.
Isa	45:24	**e.** to him shall men come;	
Isa	46:4	And **e.** to your old age I am he;	
Isa	46:4	**e.** to hoar hairs will I carry you:	
Isa	46:4	**e.** I will carry, and will deliver	
Isa	47:15	**e.** thy merchants, from thy youth:	
Isa	48:5	I have **e.** from the beginning	
Isa	48:6	have showed you new...**e.** hidden	
Isa	48:7	**e.** before the day when thou	
Isa	48:11	For mine own sake, **e.** for mine	
Isa	48:15	I, **e.** I, have spoken;	
Isa	48:20	utter it **e.** to the end of the earth;	
Isa	49:10	**e.** by the springs of water shall he	
Isa	49:19	of thy destruction shall **e.** now be	3588
Isa	49:25	**E.** the captives of the mighty	1571
Isa	51:12	I, **e.** I, am he that comforteth you:	
Isa	51:22	**e.** the dregs of the cup of my fury;	
Isa	55:3	**e.** the sure mercies of David.	
Isa	56:5	**E.** unto them will I give in mine	
Isa	56:7	**E.** them will I bring to my holy	
Isa	57:6	**e.** to them hast thou poured a	1571
Isa	57:7	**e.** thither wentest thou up to offer	1571
Isa	57:9	didst debase thyself **e.** unto hell.	
Isa	57:11	have not I held my peace **e.** of old,	
Isa	65:6	**e.** recompense into their bosom,	
Isa	66:2	**e.** to him that is poor and of a contrite	
Jer	3:25	from your youth **e.** unto this day,	
Jer	4:12	**E.** a full wind from those places	
Jer	6:11	**e.** the husband with the wife	1571
Jer	6:13	the least of them **e.** unto the greatest	
Jer	6:13	from the prophet **e.** unto the priest	
Jer	6:19	**e.** the fruit of their thoughts,	
Jer	7:11	Behold, **e.** I have seen it,	1571
Jer	7:15	**e.** the whole seed of Ephraim.	853
Jer	7:25	unto this day I have **e.** sent	
Jer	8:10	from the least **e.** unto the greatest	
Jer	8:10	from the prophet **e.** unto the priest	
Jer	9:15	will feed them, **e.** this people, with	
Jer	9:22	**E.** the carcases of men shall fall	
Jer	10:11	**e.** they shall perish from the	
Jer	11:7	**e.** unto this day, rising early and	
Jer	11:13	**e.** altars to burn incense unto Baal	
Jer	11:23	**e.** the year of their visitation.	
Jer	12:6	For **e.** thy brethren, and the house	1571
Jer	12:6	of thy father, **e.** they have dealt	1571
Jer	12:12	from the one end of the land **e.** to	
Jer	13:10	to worship them, shall **e.** be as this	
Jer	13:13	inhabitants of this land, **e.** the kings	
Jer	13:14	one against another, **e.** the fathers	
Jer	13:18	shall come down, **e.** the crown of your	
Jer	15:13	for all thy sins, **e.** in all thy borders.	
Jer	16:5	**e.** lovingkindness and mercies.	853
Jer	17:4	And thou, **e.** thyself, shalt discontinue	
Jer	17:10	I try the reins, **e.** to give every man	
Jer	17:27	not to bear a burden, **e.** entering	
Jer	19:11	**E.** so will I break this people,	3602
Jer	19:12	and **e.** make this city as Tophet:	
Jer	21:5	with a strong arm, **e.** in anger,	
Jer	22:25	whose face thou fearest, **e.** into the	
Jer	23:12	**e.** the year of their visitation,	
Jer	23:19	in fury, **e.** a grievous whirlwind:	
Jer	23:33	I will **e.** forsake you,	
Jer	23:34	I will **e.** punish that man	
Jer	23:39	behold, I, **e.** I, will utterly forget	
Jer	24:2	very good figs, **e.** like the figs	
Jer	25:3	Amon king of Judah, **e.** unto this day,	
Jer	25:13	**e.** all that is written in this book	
Jer	25:31	noise shall come **e.** to the ends of	
Jer	25:33	one end of the earth **e.** unto the other	
Jer	28:6	**E.** the prophet Jeremiah said,	
Jer	28:11	**E.** so will I break the yoke	3602
Jer	29:23	I have not commanded them; **e.** I	
Jer	30:7	none is like it: it is **e.** the time	
Jer	31:2	grace in the wilderness; **e.** Israel,	
Jer	31:19	I was ashamed, yea, **e.** confounded,	1571
Jer	31:21	heart toward the highway, **e.** the way	
Jer	32:9	weighed him the money, **e.** seventeen	
Jer	32:20	land of Egypt, **e.** unto this day,	
Jer	32:31	they built it **e.** unto this day,	
Jer	33:10	beast, **e.** in the cities of Judah,	
Jer	33:24	he hath **e.** cast them off?	
Jer	34:20	I will **e.** give them into the hand	
Jer	36:2	the days of Josiah, **e.** unto this day.	
Jer	36:12	all the princes sat there **e.** Elishama	
Jer	39:3	in the middle gate, **e.** Nergal-sharezer,	
Jer	39:12	do unto him **e.** as he shall say	3651
Jer	39:14	**E.** they sent and took Jeremiah,	
Jer	40:7	in the fields, **e.** they and their men,	
Jer	40:8	to Mizpah, **e.** Ishmael the son	
Jer	40:12	**E.** all the Jews returned out	
Jer	41:1	the princes of the king, **e.** ten men	
Jer	41:3	that were with him, **e.** with Gedaliah,	
Jer	41:5	and from Samaria, **e.** fourscore men,	
Jer	41:10	that were in Mizpah, **e.** the king's	853
Jer	41:16	son of Ahikam, **e.** mighty men	
Jer	42:1	from the least **e.** unto the greatest,	
Jer	42:2	Lord thy God, **e.** for all this remnant;	
Jer	42:5	if we do not **e.** according to all	3651
Jer	42:8	from the least **e.** to the greatest,	
Jer	43:1	him to them, **e.** all these words,	853
Jer	43:6	**E.** men, and women, and children,	853
Jer	43:7	thus came they **e.** to Taphanhes.	
Jer	44:10	are not humbled **e.** unto this day,	
Jer	44:12	they shall **e.** be consumed.	
Jer	44:12	from the least **e.** unto the greatest,	
Jer	44:15	an great multitude, **e.** all the people	
Jer	45:4	I will pluck up, **e.** this whole land.	
Jer	46:25	and their king; **e.** Pharaoh,	
Jer	48:32	they reach **e.** to the sea of Jazer:	
Jer	48:34	the cry of Heshbon **e.** unto Elealeh,	
Jer	48:34	Elealeh, and **e.** unto Jahaz,	
Jer	48:34	from Zoar **e.** unto Horonaim,	
Jer	48:44	I will bring upon it, **e.** upon Moab,	
Jer	49:37	evil upon them, **e.** my fierce anger,	853
Jer	50:7	the habitation of justice, **e.** the Lord,	
Jer	50:21	land of Merathaim, **e.** against it,	
Jer	51:9	and is lifted up **e.** to the skies.	
Jer	51:56	is come upon her, **e.** upon Babylon,	
Jer	51:60	come upon Babylon, **e.** all these	853
La	4:3	**E.** the sea monsters draw out	1571
Eze	1:27	of his loins **e.** upward,	
Eze	1:27	of his loins **e.** downward,	
Eze	2:3	against me, **e.** unto this very day.	
Eze	4:1	upon it the city, **e.** Jerusalem:	853
Eze	4:13	said, **E.** thus shall the children	3602
Eze	4:14	from my youth up **e.** till now	
Eze	5:8	Behold, I, **e.** I, am against thee,	1571
Eze	6:3	Behold, I, **e.** I, will bring a sword	
Eze	7:14	the trumpet, **e.** to make all ready;	
Eze	8:2	of his loins **e.** downward,	
Eze	8:2	from his loins **e.** upward,	
Eze	8:6	**e.** the great abominations that the	
Eze	9:1	to draw near, **e.** every man	
Eze	10:2	the wheels, **e.** under the cherub,	
Eze	10:5	was heard **e.** to the outer court,	
Eze	10:12	full of eyes round about, **e.** the wheels	
Eze	11:15	thy brethren, **e.** thy brethren,	
Eze	11:17	**e.** gather you from the people,	
Eze	12:4	thou shalt go forth at **e.** in their	6153
Eze	12:7	in the **e.** I digged through the wall	6153
Eze	13:10	Because, **e.** because they have seduced	
Eze	13:13	I will **e.** rend it with a stormy wind	
Eze	13:20	will let the souls go, **e.** the souls that	
Eze	14:10	prophet shall be **e.** as the punishment	
Eze	14:22	**e.** concerning all that I have brought	
Eze	16:19	thou hast **e.** set it before them	
Eze	16:37	**e.** gather them round about against	
Eze	16:59	I will **e.** deal with thee as thou hast	
Eze	17:9	**e.** without great power or many	
Eze	17:16	whose covenant he brake, **e.** with him	
Eze	17:19	hath broken, **e.** it will I recompense	
Eze	18:11	but **e.** hath eaten upon the	1571
Eze	18:18	lo, **e.** he shall die in his iniquity	
Eze	20:11,	13, 21 he shall **e.** live in them.	
Eze	20:31	all your idols, **e.** unto this day:	
Eze	21:13	if the sword contemn **e.** the rod?	1571
Eze	21:28	concerning their reproach; **e.** say	
Eze	22:4	art come **e.** unto thy years:	
Eze	22:18	they are **e.** the dross of silver.	
Eze	23:34	Thou shalt **e.** drink it and suck it out,	
Eze	24:2	the name of the day, **e.** this same	
Eze	24:4	pieces thereof into it, **e.** every good	
Eze	24:9	will **e.** make the pile for fire great.	
Eze	24:18	and at **e.** my wife died;	6153
Eze	29:10	tower of Syene **e.** unto the border	
Eze	30:3	the day is near, **e.** the day of the Lord	
Eze	32:6	thou swimmest, **e.** to the mountains;	
Eze	32:16	shall lament for her, **e.** for Egypt,	
Eze	32:18	cast them down, **e.** her,	
Eze	32:31	all his multitude, **e.** Pharaoh	
Eze	32:32	are slain with the sword, **e.** Pharaoh	
Eze	33:18	he shall **e.** die thereby	
Eze	34:11	Behold, I, **e.** I, will both search	
Eze	34:20	Behold, I, **e.** I, will judge between the	
Eze	34:23	shall feed them, **e.** my servant	853
Eze	34:30	and they, **e.** the house of Israel,	
Eze	35:6	**e.** blood shall pursue thee.	
Eze	35:11	I will **e.** do according to thine	
Eze	35:15	and all Idumea, **e.** all of it:	
Eze	36:2	Aha, **e.** the ancient high places	
Eze	36:10	the house of Israel, **e.** all of it:	
Eze	36:12	to walk upon you, **e.** my people	853
Eze	37:19	put them with him, **e.** with the stick	853
Eze	37:25	they shall dwell therein, **e.** they,	
Eze	38:4	of armour, **e.** a great company	
Eze	39:17	sacrifice for you, **e.** a great sacrifice	
Eze	40:14	**e.** unto the post of the court	
Eze	41:17	the door, **e.** unto the inner house,	
Eze	42:12	the head of the way, **e.** the way	
Eze	43:1	**e.** the gate that looketh toward the	
Eze	43:3	I saw, **e.** according to the vision	
Eze	43:8	have **e.** defiled my holy name	
Eze	43:13	**e.** the bottom shall be a cubit,	
Eze	43:14	upon the ground **e.** to the lower	
Eze	43:14	settle **e.** the greater settle	
Eze	44:6	rebellious, **e.** to the house of Israel,	
Eze	44:7	to pollute it, **e.** my house,	853
Eze	44:10	they shall **e.** bear their iniquity	
Eze	44:19	into the utter court, **e.** into the utter	
Eze	47:10	from En-gedi **e.** unto En-eglain;	
Eze	47:19	of Tamar **e.** to the waters of	
Eze	48:3,	6 from the east side **e.** unto the west	
Eze	48:10	for them, **e.** for the priests,	
Eze	48:28	the border shall be **e.** from Tamar	
Da	1:21	Daniel continued **e.** unto the first	
Da	2:43	**e.** as iron is not mixed with clay.	1887
Da	4:15	roots in the earth, **e.** with a band	
Da	4:23	**e.** with a band of iron and brass,	
Da	5:14	I have **e.** heard of thee,	
Da	6:26	dominion shall be **e.** unto the end	
Da	7:11	I beheld **e.** till the beast was slain,	5705
Da	7:18	the kingdom for ever, **e.** for ever	5705
Da	7:20	before whom three fell; **e.** of that horn	
Da	8:1	appeared unto me, **e.** unto me Daniel,	
Da	8:10	it waxed great, **e.** to the host of heaven;	
Da	8:11	magnified himself **e.** to the prince of	
Da	8:15	when I, **e.** I Daniel, had seen	
Da	9:5	have rebelled, **e.** by departing	
Da	9:11	transgressed thy law, **e.** by departing	
Da	9:21	I was speaking in prayer, **e.** the man	
Da	9:25	the wall, **e.** in troublous times	
Da	9:27	**e.** until the consummation,	
Da	11:1	Darius the Mede, **e.** I, stood to	
Da	11:4	shall be plucked up, **e.** for others	
Da	11:10	be stirred up, **e.** to his fortress,	
Da	11:11	fight with him, **e.** with the king	
Da	11:24	enter peaceably **e.** upon the fattest	
Da	11:24	the strong hold, **e.** for a time.	
Da	11:30	he shall **e.** return, and have	
Da	11:35	make them white, **e.** to the time	
Da	11:41	escape out of his hand, **e.** Edom,	
Da	12:1	was a nation **e.** to that same time:	
Da	12:4	the book **e.** to the time of the end:	
Ho	2:20	I will **e.** betroth thee unto me	
Ho	5:14	I, **e.** I, will tear and go away;	
Ho	9:16	will I slay **e.** the beloved fruit of	
Ho	12:5	**E.** the Lord God of hosts;	
Joe	1:2	in your days, or **e.** in the days	518
Joe	1:12	and the apple trees, **e.** all the trees	
Joe	2:2	after it, **e.** to the years of many	
Joe	2:12	ye **e.** to me with all your heart,	
Joe	2:14	**e.** a meat offering and a drink offering	
Am	2:11	Is it not **e.** thus, O ye children	637
Am	3:11	then shall be **e.** round about the land;	
Am	5:1	up against you, **e.** a lamentation,	
Am	5:20	not light? **e.** very dark, and no	
Am	8:4	**e.** to make the poor of the land to	
Am	8:12	from the north **e.** to the east,	
Am	8:14	**e.** they shall fall and never rise	
Ob	7	brought thee **e.** to the border:	
Ob	8	**e.** destroy the wise men out of	
Ob	11	cast lots upon Jerusalem, **e.** thou	1571
Ob	20	Canaanites; **e.** unto Zarephath;	
Jon	2:5	compassed me about, **e.** to the soul:	
Jon	3:5	greatest of them **e.** to the least.	
Jon	4:9	do well to be angry, **e.** unto death.	
Mic	1:9	gate of my people, **e.** to Jerusalem.	
Mic	2:2	oppress a man in his house, **e.** a man	
Mic	2:8	**E.** of late my people is risen	
Mic	2:10	you **e.** with a sore destruction.	
Mic	2:11	shall **e.** be the prophet of this people,	
Mic	3:4	he will **e.** hide his face from them	

Mic 3:5 they e. prepare war against him.
Mic 4:7 from hence forth, e. for ever.
Mic 4:8 it come, e. the first dominion;
Mic 4:10 thou shalt go e. to Babylon:
Mic 7:12 he shall come e. to the river,
Mic 7:12 from the fortress e. to the river
Na 2:11 where the lion, e. the old lion,
Na 3:12 they shall e. fall into the mouth
Hab 1:2 e. cry out unto thee of violence,
Hab 3:9 oaths of the tribes, e. thy word.
Hab 3:13 e. for the salvation with thine
Zep 1:14 e. the voice of the day of the Lord:
Zep 1:18 shall make e. a speedy riddance
Zep 2:5 I will e. destroy thee,
Zep 2:9 e. the breeding of nettles,
Zep 2:11 from his place, e. all the isles
Zep 3:8 mine indignation, e. all my fierce
Zep 3:10 my suppliants, e. the daughter
Zep 3:15 the king of Israel, e. the Lord,
Zep 3:20 bring you again, e. in the time
Hag 2:18 the ninth month, e. from the day
Zec 3:2 O Satan; e. the Lord that hath
Zec 6:10 of the captivity, e. of Heldai,
Zec 6:13 E. he shall build the temple
Zec 7:1 the ninth month, e. in Chisleu;
Zec 7:5 and seventh month, e. those seventy
Zec 7:5 did ye at all fast unto me, e. to me?
Zec 8:23 e. shall take hold of the skirt of him
Zec 9:7 he that remaineth, e. he, shall be 1571
Zec 9:10 dominion shall be from sea e. to
Zec 9:10 and from the river e. to the ends
Zec 9:12 e. to day do I declare that I will 1571
Zec 11:7 flock of slaughter, e. you, O poor 3651
Zec 11:10 I took my staff, e. Beauty, 853
Zec 11:14 asunder mine other staff, e. Bands, 853
Zec 12:6 in her own place, e. in Jerusalem.
Zec 14:16 shall e. go up from year to year
Zec 14:17 the Lord of hosts, e. upon them.
Mal 1:10 Who is there e. among you 1571
Mal 1:11 rising of the sun e. unto the going
Mal 1:12 the fruit thereof, e. his meat,
Mal 2:2 I will e. send a curse upon you,
Mal 2:3 your faces, e. the dung of your
Mal 3:1 to his temple, e. the messenger
Mal 3:7 E. from the days of your father
Mal 3:9 ye have robbed me, e. this whole
Mal 3:15 that tempt God are e. delivered.
Mt 5:46 **do not e. the publicans the same?** *2532*
Mt 5:47 **do not e. publicans so?** *2532*
Mt 5:48 **perfect, e. as your Father** *5618*
Mt 6:29 **That e. Solomon in his glory was** *3761*
Mt 7:12 **do ye e. so to them: for this is** *2532*
Mt 7:17 **E. so every good tree bringeth**
Mt 8:16 When the e. was come, they *3798*
Mt 8:27 that e. the winds and the sea *2532*
Mt 9:18 My daughter is e. now dead: but *737*
Mt 11:26 **E. so, Father: for so it seemed**
Mt 12:8 **Son of man is Lord e. of the** *2532*
Mt 12:45 **E. so shall it be also unto this**
Mt 13:12 **taken away e. that he hath** *2532*
Mt 15:28 **be it unto thee e. as thou wilt**
Mt 18:14 **E. so it is not the will of your**
Mt 18:33 **on thy fellowservant, e. as I had** *2532*
Mt 20:8 **So when e. was come, the lord of** *3798*
Mt 20:14 **unto this last, e. as unto thee.** *2532*
Mt 20:28 **E. as the Son of man came not** *5618*
Mt 23:8 **one is your Master, e. Christ;**
Mt 23:10 **one is your Master, e. Christ**
Mt 23:28 **E. so ye also outwardly appear**
Mt 23:37 **e. as a hen gathereth her** *3739, 5158*
Mt 24:27 **and shineth e. unto the west;**
Mt 24:33 **that is is near, e. at the doors.**
Mt 25:29 **taken away e. that which he hath,** *2532*
Mt 26:20 Now when the e. was come, he say *3798*
Mt 26:38 **is exceedingly sorrowful, e. unto**
Mt 27:57 e. was come, there came a rich *3798*
Mt 28:20 **e. unto the end of the world**
Mk 1:27 commandeth he e. the unclean *2532*
Mk 1:32 at e., when the sun did set, *3798, 1096*
Mk 4:25 **shall be take e. that which he** *2532*
Mk 4:35 when the e. was come, he saith *3798*
Mk 4:36 took him e. as he was in the ship.
Mk 4:41 of man is this, that e. the wind *2532*
Mk 6:2 e. such mighty works are wrought *2532*
Mk 6:47 And when e. was come, the ship *3798*
Mk 10:45 **For e. the son of man came not** *2532*
Mk 11:6 them e. as Jesus had commanded: *2531*
Mk 11:19 when e. was come, he went out *3796*
Mk 12:44 **all that she had, e. all her living**
Mk 13:22 **if it were possible, e. the elect.** *2532*
Mk 13:29 **know that it is night, e. at the doors**
Mk 13:35 **at e., or at midnight, or at the** *3796*
Mk 14:30 **thee, That this day, e. in this night,**
Mk 14:54 e. into the palace of the high priest: *2193*
Mk 15:42 And now when the e. was come, *3798*
Lu 1:2 E. as they delivered them unto us, *2531*
Lu 1:15 Ghost, e. from his mother's womb *2089*
Lu 2:15 Let us now go e. unto Bethlehem,
Lu 6:33 **for sinners also do e. the same.** *2532*
Lu 8:18 **be taken e. that which he seemeth** *2532*
Lu 8:25 he commandeth e. the winds and *2532*
Lu 9:54 consume them, e. as Elias did? *2532*
Lu 10:11 **E. the very dust of your city,** *2532*
Lu 10:17 saying, Lord, e. the devils are *2532*
Lu 10:21 **e. so, Father; for so it seemed** *3483*
Lu 12:7 **But e. the very hairs of your head** *2532*
Lu 12:41 this parable unto us, or e. to all? *2532*
Lu 12:57 **and why e. of yourselves judge** *2532*
Lu 17:30 **E. thus shall it be in the days**
Lu 18:11 **or e. as this publican.** *2532*
Lu 19:26 **him that hath not, e. that he hath** *2532*
Lu 19:32 e. as he had said unto them. *2531*
Lu 19:37 when he was come nigh, e. now *2536*
Lu 19:42 **If thou hadst known, e. thou,** *2532*
Lu 19:44 **shall lay thee e. with the ground,**
Lu 20:37 **are raised, e. Moses shewed at** *2532*
Lu 24:24 found it e. as the woman had said: *3779*
Joh 1:12 to become the sons of God, e. to
Joh 3:13 **came down from heaven, e. the Son**
Joh 3:14 **e. so must the Son of man be lifted**
Joh 5:21 **e. so the Son quickeneth whom he** *2532*
Joh 5:23 **honour the Son, e. as they honour** *2531*
Joh 5:45 **that accuseth you, e. Moses,**
Joh 6:16 And when e. was now come, *3798*
Joh 6:57 **he that eateth me, e. he shall live** *2548*
Joh 8:9 beginning at the eldest, e. unto the
Joh 8:25 **E. the same that I said unto you** *2532*
Joh 8:41 we have one Father, e. God.
Joh 8:43 **e. because ye can not hear my word.**
Joh 10:15 **e. so know I the Father: and I lay** *2504*
Joh 11:22 But I know, that e. now, *2532*
Joh 11:37 have caused that e. this man *2532*
Joh 12:50 **e. as the Father said unto me,** *2531*
Joh 14:17 **E. the Spirit of truth;**
Joh 14:31 **gave me commandment, e. so I do.**
Joh 15:10 **e. as I have kept my Father's** *2531*
Joh 15:26 **from the Father, e. the Spirit of truth,**
Joh 17:14 **e. as I am not of the world.** *2531*
Joh 17:16 **They are not of the world, e. as I** *2531*
Joh 17:18 **e. so have I also sent them** *2504*
Joh 17:22 **they may be one e. as we are one:** *2531*
Joh 20:21 **hath sent me, e. so send I you.** *2504*
Joh 21:25 e. the world itself could not *3761*
Ac 2:39 are afar off, e. as many as
Ac 4:10 e. by him doth this man stand
Ac 5:37 and all, e. as many as obeyed him,
Ac 5:39 be found e. to fight against God. *2532*
Ac 9:17 the Lord, e. Jesus, hath appeared
Ac 10:41 chosen before of God, e. to us,
Ac 11:5 by four corners; and it came e. to *891*
Ac 12:15 constantly affirmed that it was e. so.
Ac 15:8 Holy Ghost, e. as he did unto us. *2532*
Ac 15:11 we shall be saved, e. as they. *2548*
Ac 20:11 talked a long while, e. till break
Ac 22:17 e. while I prayed in the temple
Ac 26:11 I persecuted them e. unto strange *2532*
Ac 27:25 it shall be e. as it was told me. *3779*
Ro 1:13 fruit among you also, e. as among *2532*
Ro 1:20 e. his eternal power and Godhead;
Ro 1:26 for e. their women did change the *5037*
Ro 1:28 e. as they did not like to retain God *2531*
Ro 3:22 E. the righteousness of God *1161*
Ro 4:6 E. as David also describeth the *2509*
Ro 4:17 whom he believed, e. God,
Ro 5:7 peradventure some would e. dare to die.
Ro 5:14 from Adam to Moses, e. over them *2532*
Ro 5:18 e. so by the righteousness of one *2532*
Ro 5:21 e. so might grace reign through *2532*
Ro 6:4 e. so we also should walk in
Ro 6:19 e. so now yield your members *3779*
Ro 7:4 married to another, e. to him who
Ro 8:23 e. we ourselves groan within *2532*
Ro 8:34 who is e. at the right hand of God, *2532*
Ro 9:10 conceived by one, e. by our father
Ro 9:17 unto Pharaoh, E. for this same
Ro 9:24 E. us, whom he hath called, *2532*
Ro 9:30 e. the righteousness which is of *1161*
Ro 10:8 word is nigh thee, e. in thy mouth
Ro 11:5 E. so then at this present time *2532*
Ro 11:31 E. so have these also now not
Ro 15:3 For e. Christ pleased not himself; *2532*
Ro 15:6 glorify God, e. the Father of our *2532*
1Co 1:6 E. as the testimony of Christ was *2531*
1Co 2:7 in a mystery, e. the hidden wisdom,
1Co 2:11 e. so the things of God knoweth no *2532*
1Co 3:1 as unto carnal, e. as unto babes
1Co 3:5 e. as the Lord gave to every man? *2532*
1Co 4:11 E. unto this present hour we both
1Co 5:7 For e. Christ our passover is *2532*
1Co 7:7 I would that all men were e. as I *2532*
1Co 7:8 good for them if they abide e. as I. *2504*
1Co 9:14 E. so hath the Lord ordained *2532*
1Co 10:33 E. as I please all men in all things, *2504*
1Co 11:1 e. as I also am of Christ. *2531*
1Co 11:5 that is e. all one as she were *2532*
1Co 11:12 e. so is the man also by the woman;
1Co 11:14 Doth not e. nature itself teach you, *3761*
1Co 12:2 these dumb idols, e. as ye were *5613*
1Co 13:12 shall I know e. as also I am known *2531*
1Co 14:7 And e. things without life giveth *3676*
1Co 14:12 E. so ye, forasmuch as ye are *2532*
1Co 15:22 e. so in Christ shall all be made *2532*
1Co 15:24 the kingdom of God, e. the Father; *2532*
1Co 16:1 churches of Galatia e. so do ye. *2532*
2Co 1:3 Blessed be God, e. the Father of *2532*
2Co 1:8 that we despaired e. of life: *2532*
2Co 1:13 shall acknowledge e. to the end; *2532*
2Co 1:14 e. as ye also are ours in the day *2509*
2Co 1:19 preached among you by us, e. by my
2Co 3:10 For e. that which was made *2532*
2Co 3:15 But e. unto this day, when Moses *2193*
2Co 3:18 from glory to glory, e. as by the Spirit
2Co 7:14 e. so our boasting, which I made *2532*
2Co 10:7 is Christ's, e. so are we Christ's. *2532*
2Co 10:13 a measure to reach e. unto you. *2532*
2Co 11:12 they may be found e. as we. *2532*
2Co 13:9 this also we wish e. your perfection.
Ga 2:16 e. we have believed in Jesus *2532*
Ga 3:6 E. as Abraham believed God, and *2531*
Ga 4:3 E. so we, when we were children, *2532*
Ga 4:14 as an angel of God, e. as Christ Jesus.
Ga 4:29 after the Spirit, e. so it is now. *2532*
Ga 5:12 I would they were e. cut off *2532*
Ga 5:14 law is fulfilled in one word, e. in this:
Eph 1:10 and which are on the earth; e. in him:
Eph 2:3 children of wrath, e. as other. *2532*
Eph 2:5 E. when we were dead in sins, *2532*
Eph 2:15 in his flesh the enmity, e. the law of
Eph 4:4 one Spirit, e. as ye are called *2532*
Eph 4:15 which is the head, e. Christ:
Eph 4:32 forgiving one another, e. as God *2532*
Eph 5:12 it is a shame e. to speak of those *2532*
Eph 5:23 the wife, e. as Christ is the head *2532*
Eph 5:25 love your wives, e. as Christ also *2531*
Eph 5:29 cherisheth it, e. as the Lord the *2532*
Eph 5:33 so love his wife e. as himself. *5613*
Php 1:7 E. as it is meet for me to think this *2531*
Php 1:15 preach Christ e. of envy *2532*
Php 2:8 obedient unto death, e. the death *1161*
Php 3:15 God shall reveal e. this unto you. *2532*
Php 3:18 now tell you e. weeping, *2532*
Php 3:21 he is able e. to subdue all things *2532*
Php 4:16 For e. Thessalonica ye sent once *2532*
Col 1:14 e. the forgiveness of sins:
Col 1:26 E. the mystery which hath
Col 3:13 e. as Christ forgave you, so also do *2532*
1Th 1:10 whom he raised from the dead, e. Jesus,
1Th 2:2 But e. after that we had suffered *2532*
1Th 2:4 e. so we speak; not as pleasing
1Th 2:7 gentle among; e. as a nurse
1Th 2:14 e. as they have of Jews: *2532*
1Th 2:18 e. I Paul, once again; but *3303*
1Th 2:19 Are not e. ye in the presence *2532*
1Th 3:4 suffer tribulation; e. as it came to *2532*
1Th 3:12 toward all men, e. as we do toward *2532*
1Th 3:13 holiness before God, e. our Father, *2532*
1Th 4:3 will of God, e. your sanctification
1Th 4:5 concupiscence, e. as the Gentiles *2532*

1Th 4:13 that ye sorrow not, e. as others 2532
1Th 4:14 e. so them also which sleep in
1Th 5:11 e. as also ye do. 2531
2Th 2:9 E. him, whose coming is after
2Th 2:16 and God, e. our Father, 2532
2Th 3:1 be glorified, e. as it is with you: 2532
2Th 3:10 For e. when we were with you, 2532
1Ti 3:11 E. so must their wives be grave, 5615
1Ti 6:3 wholesome words, e. the words
2Ti 2:9 as an evil doer, e. unto bonds;
Tit 1:12 One of themselves, e. a prophet
Tit 1:15 e. their mind and conscience is 2532
Phm 19 thou owest unto me e. thine own 2532
Heb 1:9 God, e. thy God, hath anointed
Heb 4:12 e. to the dividing asunder of soul
Heb 5:14 of full age, e. those who by reason
Heb 6:20 for us entered, e. Jesus made
Heb 7:4 whom e. the patriarch Abraham 2532
Heb 11:12 sprang there e. of one, 2532
Heb 11:19 to raise him up, e. from the dead; 2532
Jas 2:17 E. so faith, if it hath not works, 2532
Jas 3:5 E. so the tongue is a little member 2532
Jas 3:9 bless we God, e. the Father;
Jas 4:1 come they not hence, e. of your lusts
Jas 4:14 It is e. a vapour, that appeareth 1063
1Pe 1:9 end of your faith, e. the salvation
1Pe 2:8 rock of offence, e. to them which
1Pe 2:21 e. hereunto were ye called:
1Pe 3:4 not corruptible, e. the ornament
1Pe 3:6 E. as Sara obeyed Abraham, 5613
1Pe 3:21 whereunto e. baptism doth also
1Pe 4:10 received the gift, e. so minister
2Pe 1:14 e. as our Lord Jesus Christ 2532
2Pe 2:1 among the people, e. as there shall 2532
2Pe 2:1 damnable heresies, e. denying the 2532
2Pe 3:15 e. as our beloved brother Paul also 2531
1Jo 2:6 so to walk, e. as he walked 2531
1Jo 2:9 is in darkness e. until now.
1Jo 2:18 antichrist shall come, e. now are 2532
1Jo 2:25 he hath promised us, e. eternal life.
1Jo 2:27 e. as it hath taught you, ye shall 2531
1Jo 3:3 purifieth himself, e. as he is pure. 2531
1Jo 3:7 is righteous, e. as he is righteous. 2531
1Jo 4:3 it should come; and e. now 2532
1Jo 5:4 overcometh the world, e. our faith.
1Jo 5:6 by water and blood, e. Jesus Christ;
1Jo 5:20 is true, e. in his son Jesus Christ.
3Jo 2 health, e. as thy soul prospereth. 2531
3Jo 3 e. as thou walkest in the truth. 2531
Jude 7 E. as Sodom and Gomorrha, and 5613
Jude 23 hating e. the garment spotted 2532
Re 1:7 because of him. E. so, Amen. 3483
Re 2:13 **thou dwellest, e. where Satan's**
Re 2:13 **denied my faith. e. in those days** 2532
Re 2:27 **e. as I received of my father.** 2504
Re 3:4 **hast a few names e. in Sardis** 2532
Re 3:21 **e. as I also overcame, and am set** 2504
Re 6:13 fell unto the earth, e. as a fig tree
Re 14:20 e. unto the horse bridles,
Re 16:7 E. so, Lord God Almighty, true 3483
Re 17:11 e. he is the eighth, 2532
Re 18:6 Reward her e. as she rewarded you, 2532
Re 21:11 e. like a jasper stone, clear as 5613
Re 22:20 E. so, come, Lord Jesus. 3483

EVENING See also EVEN; EVENING; EVENTIDE.

Ge 1:5 e. and the morning were the first 6153
Ge 1:8 e. and the morning were the second 6153
Ge 1:13 e. and the morning were the third 6153
Ge 1:19 e. and the morning were the fourth 6153
Ge 1:23 e. and the morning were the fifth 6153
Ge 1:31 e. and the morning were the sixth 6153
Ge 8:11 the dove came in to him in the e.; 6153
Ge 24:11 at the time of the e., even the time 6153
Ge 29:23 it came to pass in the e., 6153
Ge 30:16 Jacob came out of the field in the e., 6153
Ex 12:6 Israel shall kill it in the e. 6153
Ex 16:8 shall give you in the e. flesh to eat, 6153
Ex 18:13 Moses from the morning unto the e. 6153
Ex 27:21 shall order it from e. to morning 6153
Le 24:3 e. unto the morning before the Lord 6153
De 23:11 when e. cometh on, he shall wash 6153
Jos 10:26 hanging upon the trees until the e. 6153
Jg 19:9 now the day draweth toward e., 6150
1Sa 14:24 man that eateth any food until e., 6150
1Sa 17:16 drew near morning and e., 6150
1Sa 30:17 unto the e. of the next day: 6153
1Ki 17:6 and bread and flesh in the e.; 6153
1Ki 18:29, 36 the offering of the e. sacrifice,
2Ki 16:15 e. meat offering, and the king's 6153
1Ch 16:40 continually morning and e., 6153
2Ch 2:4 burnt offerings morning and e., 6153
2Ch 13:11 Lord every morning and every e. 6153
2Ch 13:11 the lamps thereof, to burn every e.: 6153
2Ch 31:3 the morning and e. burnt offerings, 6153
Ezr 3:3 burnt offerings morning and e. 6153
Ezr 9:4 I sat astonished until the e. sacrifice. 6153
Ezr 9:5 at the e. sacrifice I arose up from 6153
Es 2:14 e. she went, and on the morrow 6153
Job 4:20 are destroyed from morning to e.: 6153
Ps 55:17 E., and morning, and at noon, 6153
Ps 59:6 They return at e.: they make a 6153
Ps 59:14 at e. let them return; and let them 6153
Ps 65:8 the morning and e. to rejoice. 6153
Ps 90:6 the e. it is cut down, and withereth. 6153
Ps 104:23 forth unto his work...until the e. 6153
Ps 141:2 up of my hands as the e. sacrifice. 6153
Pr 7:9 in the e., in the black and dark 6153
Ec 11:6 in the e. withhold not thine hand: 6153
Jer 6:4 shadows of the e. are stretched out. 6153
Eze 33:22 of the Lord was upon me in the e., 6153
Eze 46:2 gate shall not be shut until the e. 6153
Da 8:26 vision of the e. and the morning 6153
Da 9:21 about the time of the e. oblation. 6153
Hab 1:8 are more fierce than the e. wolves: 6153
Zep 2:7 shall they lie down in the e.: 6153
Zep 3:3 judges are e. wolves; they gnaw 6153
Zec 14:7 at e. time it shall be light. 6153
Mt 14:15 when it was e., his disciples came 3798
Mt 14:23 e. was come, he was there alone. 3798
Mt 16:2 **When it is e., ye say, it will be fair** 3798
Mk 14:17 in the e. he cometh with the twelve, 3798
Lu 24:29 toward e., and the day is far spent, 2073
Joh 20:19 same day at e., being the first 3798
Ac 28:23 the prophets, from morning till e. 2073

EVENINGS

Jer 5:6 a wolf of the e. shall spoil them, 6160

EVENINGTIDE See also EVENTIDE.

2Sa 11:12 it came to pass in an e., 6256,6153
Isa 17:14 And behold at e. trouble; 6256,6153

EVENT

Ec 2:14 one e. happeneth to them all. 4745
Ec 9:2 one e. to the righteous, and to the 4745
Ec 9:3 that there is one e. unto all: 4745

EVENTIDE See also EVENINGTIDE.

Ge 24:63 Isaac went out...at the e.: 6256,6153
Jos 7:6 the ark of the Lord until the e. 6153
Jos 8:29 he hanged on a tree until e.: 6256,6153
Mk 11:11 and now the e. was come, 3798,5610
Ac 4:3 the next day: for it was now e. 2073

EVER See also EVERLASTING; EVERMORE; NEVER; SOEVER.

Ge 3:22 life, and eat, and live for e.: 5769
Ge 13:15 I give it, and to thy seed for e. 5769
Ge 43:9 let me bear the blame for e.: 3605,3117
Ge 44:32 the blame to my father for e. 3605,3117
Ex 3:15 this is my name for e., and 5769
Ex 12:14 a feast by an ordinance for e. 5769
Ex 12:17 by an ordinance for e. 5769
Ex 12:24 to thee and to thy sons for e. 5769
Ex 14:13 them again no more for e. 5769
Ex 15:18 Lord shall reign for e. [5769] and e. 5703
Ex 19:9 thee, and believe thee for e. 5769
Ex 21:6 and he shall serve him for e. 5769
Ex 27:21 it shall be a statute for e. unto 5769
Ex 28:43 it shall be a statute for e. unto him 5769
Ex 29:28 for e. from the children of Israel; 5769
Ex 30:21 it shall be a statute for e. to them, 5769
Ex 31:17 the children of Israel for e.: 5769
Ex 32:13 and they shall inherit it for e. 5769
Le 6:13 e. be burning upon the altar; 8548
Le 6:18 statute for e. in your generations 5769
Le 6:22 a statute for e. unto the Lord; 5769
Le 7:34 for e. from among the children 5769
Le 7:36 for e. throughout their generations 5769
Le 10:9 for e. throughout your generations: 5769
Le 10:15 a statute for e.; as the Lord hath 5769
Le 16:29 shall be a statute for e. unto you: 5769
Le 16:31 afflict your souls, by a statute for e. 5769
Le 17:7 shall be a statute for e. unto them 5769
Le 23:14 for e. throughout your generations 5769
Le 23:21 statute for e. in all your dwellings 5769
Le 23:31 for e. throughout your generations 5769
Le 23:41 statute for e. in your generations: 5769
Le 24:3 statute for e. in your generations. 5769
Le 25:23 The land shall not be sold for e.: 6783
Le 25:30 shall be established for e. to him 6783
Le 25:46 shall be your bondmen for e.: 5769
Nu 10:8 for e. throughout your generations 5769
Nu 15:15 for e. in your generations: 5769
Nu 18:8 to thy sons, by an ordinance for e. 5769
Nu 18:11, 19 with thee, by a statute for e.: 5769
Nu 18:19 of salt for e. before the Lord 5769
Nu 18:23 for e. throughout your generations, 5769
Nu 19:10 among them, for a statute for e. 5769
Nu 22:30 which thou hast ridden e. since 5750
Nu 22:30 was I e. wont to do so unto thee?
Nu 24:20 end shall be that he perish for e. 5703
Nu 24:24 and he also shall perish for e. 5703
De 4:33 Did e. people hear the voice of God
De 4:40 thy God giveth thee, for e. 3605,3117
De 5:29 and with their children for e.! 5769
De 12:28 with thy children after thee for e., 5769
De 13:16 it shall be a heap for e.; 5769
De 15:17 and he shall be thy servant for e. 5769
De 18:5 Lord, him and his sons for e. 3605,3117
De 19:9 and to walk e. in his ways; 3605,3117
De 23:3 congregation of the Lord for e.: 5769
De 23:6 prosperity all thy days for e. 5769
De 28:46 wonder, and upon thy seed for e. 5769
De 29:29 unto us and to our children for e., 5769
De 32:40 and say, I live for e. 5769
Jos 4:7 unto the children of Israel for e. 5769
Jos 4:24 fear the Lord your God for e. 3605,3117
Jos 8:28 Ai, and made it an heap for e. 5769
Jos 14:9 and thy children's for e., 5769
Jg 11:25 did he e. strive against Israel,
Jg 11:25 or did he e. fight against them,
1Sa 1:22 the Lord, and there abide for e. 5769
1Sa 2:30 should walk before me for e.: 5769
1Sa 2:32 old man in thine house for e. 3605,3117
1Sa 2:35 before mine anointed for e. 3605,3117
1Sa 3:13 I will judge his house for e. 5769
1Sa 3:14 with sacrifice nor offering for e. 5769
1Sa 13:13 thy kingdom upon Israel for e. 5769
1Sa 20:15 thy kindness from my house for e.: 5769
1Sa 20:23 Lord between thee and me for e. 5769
1Sa 20:42 my seed and thy seed for e. 5769
1Sa 27:12 he shall be my servant for e. 5769
1Sa 28:2 keeper of mine head for e. 3605,3117
2Sa 2:26 Shall the sword devour for e.? 5331
2Sa 3:28 guiltless before the Lord for e. 5769
2Sa 7:13 the throne of his kingdom for e. 5769
2Sa 7:16 established for e. before thee: 5769
2Sa 7:16 throne shall be established for e. 5769
2Sa 7:24 to be a people unto thee for e.: 5769
2Sa 7:25 his house, establish it for e., 5769
2Sa 7:26 let thy name be magnified for e., 5769
2Sa 7:29 continue for e. before thee: 5769
2Sa 7:29 thy servant be blessed for e. 5769
1Ki 1:31 lord king David live for e. 5769
1Ki 2:33 the head of his seed for e.: 5769
1Ki 2:33 be peace for e. from the Lord. 5769
1Ki 2:45 established before the Lord for e.
1Ki 5:1 Hiram was e. a lover of David. 3605,3117
1Ki 8:13 place for thee to abide in for e. 5769
1Ki 9:3 to put my name there for e.; 5769
1Ki 9:5 kingdom upon Israel for e., 5769
1Ki 10:9 the Lord loved Israel for e., 5769
1Ki 11:39 seed of David, but not for e. 3605,3117
1Ki 12:7 they will be thy servants for e. 3605,3117
2Ki 5:27 thee, and unto thy seed for e. 5769
2Ki 21:7 will I put my name for e.: 5769
1Ch 15:2 and to minister unto him for e. 5769
1Ch 16:34 for his mercy endureth for e. 5769
1Ch 16:36 the Lord God of Israel for e. 5769
1Ch 16:36 Lord God of Israel...and e., 5704,5769
1Ch 16:41 for his mercy endureth for e.; 5769
1Ch 17:12 I will stablish his throne for e. 5769
1Ch 17:14 house and in my kingdom for e.: 5769
1Ch 17:22 thou make thine own people for e.; 5769
1Ch 17:23 his house be established for e., 5769
1Ch 17:24 thy name may be magnified for e., 5769
1Ch 17:27 it may be before thee for e.: 5769
1Ch 17:27 and it shall be blessed for e. 5769
1Ch 22:10 of his kingdom over Israel for e. 5769
1Ch 23:13 he and his sons for e., to burn 5769
1Ch 23:13 to bless in his name for e. 5769
1Ch 23:25 dwell in Jerusalem for e.: 5769

Book	Ref	Context	No.
1Ch	28:4	to be king over Israel for **e.**	5769
1Ch	28:7	establish his kingdom for **e.**,	5769
1Ch	28:8	for your children after you for **e.**	5769
1Ch	28:9	he will cast thee off for **e.**	5703
1Ch	29:10	Lord God of Israel our father, for **e.**	5769
1Ch	29:10	of Israel our father,...and **e.**	5769
1Ch	29:18	for **e.** in the imagination of	5769
2Ch	2:4	an ordinance for **e.** to Israel.	5769
2Ch	5:13	for his mercy endureth for **e.**:	5769
2Ch	6:2	a place for thy dwelling for **e.**	5769
2Ch	7:3	for his mercy endureth for **e.**	5769
2Ch	7:6	because his mercy endureth for **e.**,	5769
2Ch	7:16	that my name may be there for **e.**	5769
2Ch	9:8	to establish them for **e.**,	5769
2Ch	10:7	will be thy servants for **e.**	3605,3117
2Ch	13:5	over Israel to David for **e.**,	5769
2Ch	20:7	of Abraham thy friend for **e.**?	5769
2Ch	20:21	for his mercy endureth for **e.**	5769
2Ch	21:7	to him and to his sons for **e.**	3605,3117
2Ch	30:8	he hath sanctified for **e.**	5769
2Ch	33:4	shall my name be for **e.**	5769
2Ch	33:7	will I put my name for **e.**	5865
Ezr	3:11	for his mercy endureth for **e.**	5769
Ezr	9:12	their peace or their wealth for **e.**:	5769
Ezr	9:12	inheritance to your children for **e.**	5769
Ne	2:3	king, Let the king live for **e.**	5769
Ne	9:5	the Lord your God for **e.** and **e.**	5769
Ne	13:1	the congregation of God for **e.**;	5769
Job	4:7	who **e.** perished being innocent? or	
Job	4:20	they perish for **e.** without any	5331
Job	14:20	Thou prevailest for **e.** against him,	5331
Job	19:24	pen and lead in the rock for **e.**!	5703
Job	20:7	he shall perish for **e.** like his own	5331
Job	23:7	so should I be delivered for **e.** from	5331
Job	36:7	yea, he doth establish them for **e.**,	5331
Job	41:4	take him for a servant for **e.**	5760
Ps	5:11	let them **e.** shout for joy, because	5760
Ps	9:5	thou hast put out their name for **e.**	5760
Ps	9:5	hast put out their name...and **e.**	5703
Ps	9:7	the Lord shall endure for **e.**:	5769
Ps	9:18	of the poor shall not perish for **e.**	5703
Ps	10:16	The Lord is King for **e.**	5769
Ps	10:16	The Lord is King...and **e.**	5703
Ps	12:7	from this generation for **e.**,	5769
Ps	13:1	thou forget me, O Lord? for **e.**?	5331
Ps	19:9	the Lord is clean, enduring for **e.**:	5703
Ps	21:4	even length of days for **e.**	5769
Ps	21:4	even length of days...and **e.**	5703
Ps	21:6	made him most blessed for **e.**:	5703
Ps	22:26	him: your heart shall live for **e.**	5703
Ps	23:6	the house of the Lord for **e.**	753,3117
Ps	25:6	for they have been **e.** of old.	
Ps	25:15	Mine eyes are **e.** toward the Lord;	8548
Ps	28:9	them also, and lift them up for **e.**	5769
Ps	29:10	the Lord sitteth King for **e.**	5769
Ps	30:12	given thanks unto thee for **e.**	5769
Ps	33:11	counsel of the Lord standeth for **e.**,	5769
Ps	37:18	and their inheritance shall be for **e.**	5769
Ps	37:26	is **e.** merciful, and lendeth;	3605,3117
Ps	37:28	they are preserved for **e.**:	5769
Ps	37:29	the land, and dwell therein for **e.**	5703
Ps	41:12	settest me before thy face for **e.**	5769
Ps	44:8	and praise thy name for **e.**	5769
Ps	44:23	Lord? arise, cast us not off for **e.**	5331
Ps	45:2	God hath blessed thee for **e.**	5769
Ps	45:6	Thy throne, O God, is for **e.**	5769
Ps	45:6	Thy throne, O God, is...and **e.**;	5703
Ps	45:17	shall the people praise thee for **e.**	5769
Ps	45:17	the people praise thee...and **e.**	5703
Ps	48:8	God will establish it for **e.**	5769
Ps	48:14	God is our God for **e.** [5769] and **e.**	5703
Ps	49:8	precious, and it ceaseth for **e.**:)	5769
Ps	49:9	That he should still live for **e.**	5331
Ps	49:11	their houses shall continue for **e.**,	5769
Ps	51:3	and my sin is **e.** before me.	8548
Ps	52:5	shall likewise destroy thee for **e.**,	5331
Ps	52:8	trust in the mercy of God for **e.**	5769
Ps	52:8	trust in the mercy of God...and **e.**	5703
Ps	52:9	will praise thee for **e.**, because	5769
Ps	61:4	will abide in thy tabernacle for **e.**	5769
Ps	61:7	He shall abide before God for **e.**	5769
Ps	61:8	I sing praise unto thy name for **e.**,	5703
Ps	66:7	He ruleth by his power for **e.**;	5769
Ps	68:16	the Lord will dwell in it for **e.**	5331
Ps	72:17	name shall endure for **e.**	5769
Ps	72:19	be his glorious name for **e.**	5769
Ps	73:26	heart, and my portion for **e.**	5769
Ps	74:1	why hast thou cast us off for **e.**?	5331
Ps	74:10	enemy blaspheme thy name for **e.**?	5331
Ps	74:19	the congregation of thy poor for **e.**	5331
Ps	75:9	I will declare for **e.**; I will	5769
Ps	77:7	Will the Lord cast off for **e.**?	5769
Ps	77:8	Is his mercy clean gone for **e.**?	5331
Ps	78:69	he hath established for **e.**	5769
Ps	79:5	Lord? wilt thou be angry for **e.**?	5331
Ps	79:13	will give thee thanks for **e.**:	5769
Ps	81:15	should have endured for **e.**	5769
Ps	83:17	be confounded and troubled for **e.**;	5703
Ps	85:5	thou be angry with us for **e.**?	5769
Ps	89:1	of the mercies of the Lord for **e.**:	5769
Ps	89:2	Mercy shall be built up for **e.**:	5769
Ps	89:4	Thy seed will I establish for **e.**,	5769
Ps	89:29	also will I make to endure for **e.**,	5703
Ps	89:36	His seed shall endure for **e.**,	5769
Ps	89:37	It shall be established for **e.** as	5769
Ps	89:46	Lord? wilt thou hide thyself for **e.**?	5331
Ps	90:2	or **e.** thou hadst formed the earth	
Ps	92:7	that they shall be destroyed for **e.**:	5703
Ps	93:5	thine house, O Lord, for **e.**	753,3117
Ps	102:12	thou O Lord, shalt endure for **e.**;	5769
Ps	103:9	neither will he keep his anger for **e.**	5769
Ps	104:5	should not be removed for **e.**	5769,5703
Ps	104:31	glory of the Lord...endure for **e.**	5769
Ps	105:8	remembered his covenant for **e.**,	5769
Ps	106:1	for his mercy endureth for **e.**	5769
Ps	107:1	for his mercy endureth for **e.**	5769
Ps	110:4	Thou art a priest for **e.** after the	5769
Ps	111:3	his righteousness endureth for **e.**	5703
Ps	111:5	will **e.** be mindful of his covenant	5769
Ps	111:8	They stand fast for **e.**	5703
Ps	111:8	They stand fast...and **e.**,	5769
Ps	111:9	remembered his covenant for **e.**	5769
Ps	111:10	his praise endureth for **e.**	5769
Ps	112:3	his righteousness endureth for **e.**	5703
Ps	112:6	he shall not be moved for **e.**	5769
Ps	112:9	his righteousness endureth for **e.**,	5703
Ps	117:2	truth of the Lord endureth for **e.**	5769
Ps	118:1	because his mercy endureth for **e.**	5769
Ps	118:2,	3,4 that his mercy endureth for **e.**	5769
Ps	118:29	for his mercy endureth for **e.**	5769
Ps	119:44	I keep thy law continually for **e.**	5769
Ps	119:44	I keep thy law continually...and **e.**	5703
Ps	119:89	For **e.**, O Lord, thy word is settled	5769
Ps	119:98	enemies: for they are **e.** with me.	5769
Ps	119:111	have I taken as a heritage for **e.**:	5769
Ps	119:152	thou hast founded them for **e.**	5769
Ps	119:160	judgments endureth for **e.**	5769
Ps	125:1	be removed, but abideth for **e.**	5769
Ps	125:2	people from henceforth even for **e.**	5769
Ps	131:3	Lord from henceforth and for **e.**	5769
Ps	132:14	This is my rest for **e.**: here will I	5703
Ps	135:13	Thy name, O Lord, endureth for **e.**;	5769
Ps	136:1,	2,3,4,5,6 his mercy endureth for **e.**	5769
Ps	136:7,	8,10,11 his mercy endureth for **e.**	5769
Ps	136:9,	12,15,16 his mercy endureth for **e.**	5769
Ps	136:13,	14,17,18,19,20,21,23 for his mercy endureth for **e.**	5769
Ps	136:22,	24,25,26, his mercy endureth for **e.**	5769
Ps	138:8	thy mercy, O Lord, endureth for **e.**	5769
Ps	145:1	and I will bless thy name for **e.**	5769
Ps	145:1	and I will bless thy name...and **e.**	5703
Ps	145:2	and I will praise thy name for **e.**	5769
Ps	145:2	and I will praise thy name...and **e.**	5703
Ps	145:21	all flesh bless his holy name for **e.**	5769
Ps	145:21	flesh bless his holy name...and **e.**	5703
Ps	146:6	which keepeth truth for **e.**:	5769
Ps	146:10	The Lord shall reign for **e.**,	5769
Ps	148:6	hath also stablished them for **e.**	5703
Ps	148:6	hath also stablished them...and **e.**	5769
Pr	8:23	the beginning, or **e.** the earth	6924
Pr	12:19	truth shall be established for **e.**	5703
Pr	27:24	for riches are not for **e.**	5769
Pr	29:14	throne shall be established for **e.**	5703
Ec	1:4	but the earth abideth for **e.**	5769
Ec	2:16	more than of the fool for **e.**;	5769
Ec	3:14	God doeth, it shall be for **e.**	5769
Ec	9:6	they any more a portion for **e.**	5769
Ec	12:6	Or **e.** the silver cord be loosed,	
Ca	6:12	Or **e.** I was aware, my soul made	3808
Isa	9:7	from henceforth even for **e.**	5769
Isa	26:4	Trust ye in the Lord for **e.**	5703
Isa	28:28	because he will not **e.** be threshing	5331
Isa	30:8	may be for the time to come for **e.**	5703
Isa	30:8	be for the time to come...and **e.**:	5769
Isa	32:14	and towers shall be for dens for **e.**,	5769
Isa	32:17	quietness and assurance for **e.**	5769
Isa	33:20	thereof shall **e.** be removed,	5331
Isa	34:10	smoke thereof shall go up for **e.**:	5769
Isa	34:10	none shall pass through it for **e.**	5331
Isa	34:17	they shall posses it for **e.**, from	5769
Isa	40:8	word of our God shall stand for **e.**	5769
Isa	47:7	saidst, I shall be a lady for **e.**:	5769
Isa	51:6	but my salvation shall be for **e.**,	5769
Isa	51:8	but my righteousness shall be for **e.**,	5769
Isa	57:16	For I will not contend for **e.**,	5769
Isa	59:21	Lord, from henceforth and for **e.**	5769
Isa	60:21	they shall inherit the land for **e.**,	5769
Isa	64:9	neither remember iniquity for **e.**:	5703
Isa	65:18	But be ye glad and rejoice for **e.**	5703
Jer	3:5	Will he reserve his anger for **e.**?	
Jer	3:12	and I will not keep anger for **e.**	5769
Jer	7:7	gave to your fathers, for **e.** and **e.**	5769
Jer	17:4	anger, which shall burn for **e.**	5769
Jer	17:25	and this city shall remain for **e.**	5769
Jer	25:5	and to your fathers for **e.** and **e.**:	5769
Jer	31:36	a nation before me for **e.**	3605,3117
Jer	31:40	nor thrown down any more for **e.**	5769
Jer	32:39	that they may fear me for **e.**,	3605,3117
Jer	33:11	for his mercy endureth for **e.**	5769
Jer	35:6	neither ye, nor your sons for **e.**	5769
Jer	35:19	man to stand before me for **e.**	3605,3117
Jer	49:33	dragons, and a desolation for **e.**	5769
Jer	50:39	shall be no more inhabited for **e.**;	5331
Jer	51:26	but thou shalt be desolate for **e.**,	5769
Jer	51:62	but that it shall be desolate for **e.**	5769
La	3:31	For the Lord will not cast off for **e.**	5769
La	5:19	Thou O Lord, remainest for **e.**;	5769
La	5:20	dost thou forget us for **e.**,	5331
Eze	37:25	and their children's children for **e.**	5769
Eze	37:25	David shall be their prince for **e.**	5769
Eze	43:7	midst of the children of Israel for **e.**,	5769
Eze	43:9	will dwell in the midst of them for **e.**	5769
Da	2:4	O king, live for **e.**: tell thy servants	5957
Da	2:20	Blessed be...of God for **e.** and **e.**:	5957
Da	2:44	kingdoms, and it shall stand for **e.**	5957
Da	3:9	Nebuchadnezzar, O king, live for **e.**	5957
Da	4:34	and honoured him that liveth for **e.**,	5957
Da	5:10	O king, live for **e.**: let not thy	5957
Da	6:6	unto him, King Darius, live for **e.**	5957
Da	6:21	unto the king, O king, live for **e.**	5957
Da	6:24	all their bones in pieces or **e.** they	3809
Da	6:26	the living God, and stedfast for **e.**,	5957
Da	7:18	kingdom for **e.**, even for **e.** and **e.**	5957
Da	12:3	righteousness as the stars for **e.**	5769
Da	12:3	righteousness as the stars...and **e.**	5703
Da	12:7	and sware by him that liveth for **e.**,	5769
Ho	2:19	I will betroth thee unto me for **e.**;	5769
Joe	2:2	there hath not been **e.** the like,	5769
Joe	3:20	But Judah shall dwell for **e.**,	5769
Am	1:11	and he kept his wrath for **e.**:	5331
Ob	10	thou shalt be cut off for **e.**	5769
Jon	2:6	with her bars was about me for **e.**:	5769
Mic	2:9	have ye taken away my glory for **e.**	5769
Mic	4:5	name of the Lord our God for **e.**	5769
Mic	4:5	name of the Lord our God...and **e.**	5703
Mic	4:7	Zion from henceforth, even for **e.**	5769
Mic	7:18	he retaineth not his anger for **e.**,	5703
Zec	1:5	prophets, do they live for **e.**?	5769
Mal	1:4	the Lord hath indignation for **e.**	5769
Mt	6:13	**power, and the glory, for e.**	*165*
Mt	21:19	**on thee henceforward for e.**	*165*
Mt	24:21	**world to this time, no, nor e. shall**	3364
Mk	11:14	**fruit of thee hereafter for e.**	*165*
Mk	15:8	as he had **e.** done unto them.	*104*
Lu	1:33	over the house of Jacob for **e.**;	*165*
Lu	1:55	Abraham, and to his seed for **e.**	*165*
Lu	15:31	**Son, thou art e. with me, and all**	*3842*
Joh	4:29	told me all things that **e.** I did:	*3745*
Joh	4:39	testified, He told me all that **e.** I did.	*3745*
Joh	6:51	**this bread, he shall live for e.:**	*165*
Joh	6:58	**of this bread shall live for e.**	*165*
Joh	8:35	**abideth not in the house for e.:**	*165*
Joh	8:35	**but the Son abideth for e.**	*165*
Joh	10:8	**All that e. came before me are**	*3745*
Joh	12:34	law that Christ abideth for **e.**:	*165*
Joh	14:16	**he may abide with you for e.;**	*165*
Joh	18:20	**I e. taught in the synagogue, and**	*3842*
Ac	23:15	and we, or **e.** he come near, are	*4253*
Ro	1:25	Creator, who is blessed for **e.**	*165*
Ro	9:5	is over all, God blessed for **e.**	*165*

Ro 11:36 To whom be glory for e.. Amen. 165
Ro 16:27 through Jesus Christ for e.. 165
2Co 9:9 his righteousness remaineth for e......... 165
Ga 1:5 To whom be glory for e. and e.. 165
Eph 5:29 For no man e. yet hated his own 4218
Php 4:20 Father be glory for e. and e.. 165
1Th 4:17 and so shall we e. be with the.......... 3842
1Th 5:15 but e. follow that which is good, ... 3842
1Ti 1:17 honour and glory for e. and e.............. 165
2Ti 3:7 E. learning, and never able to 3842
2Ti 4:18 to whom be glory for e. and e.............. 165
Phm 15 thou shouldest receive him for e.;........ 166
Heb 1:8 thy throne, O God, is for e. and e.: 165
Heb 5:6 Thou art a priest for e. after the 165
Heb 6:20 made an high priest for e. after the...... 165
Heb 7:17, 21 Thou art a priest for e. after the..... 165
Heb 7:24 this man, because he continueth e.,...... 165
Heb 7:25 he e. liveth to make intercession........ 3842
Heb 10:12 for e. sat down on the right............. 1336
Heb 10:14 he hath perfected for e. them........... 1336
Heb 13:8 yesterday, and to day, and for e.. 165
Heb 13:21 whom be glory for e. and e.. 165
1Pe 1:23 which liveth and abideth for e.. 165
1Pe 1:25 the word of the Lord endureth for e..... 165
1Pe 4:11 praise and dominion for e. and e.. 165
1Pe 5:11 glory and dominion for e. and e.. 165
2Pe 2:17 of darkness is reserved for e. 165
2Pe 3:18 be glory both now and for e.. 2250,165
1Jo 2:17 doeth the will of God abideth for e...... 165
2Jo 2 and shall be with us for e.. 165
Jude 13 the blackness of darkness for e.. 165
Jude 25 and power, both now and for e..... 3956,165
Re 1:6 be glory and dominion for e. and e.. 165
Re 4:9 throne, who liveth for e. and e., ... 165
Re 4:10 worship him that liveth for e. and e.,..... 165
Re 5:13 and unto the Lamb for e. and e.. 165
Re 5:14 him that liveth for e. and e.. 165
Re 7:12 be unto our God for e. and e.. 165
Re 10:6 by him that liveth for e. and e.,........... 165
Re 11:15 and he shall reign for e. and e.. 165
Re 14:11 torment ascendeth up for e. and e.: 165
Re 15:7 God, who liveth for e. and e.. 165
Re 19:3 her smoke rose up for e. and e.. 165
Re 20:10 tormented day and night for e. and e.... 165
Re 22:5 and they shall reign for e. and e.. 165

EVERLASTING

Ge 9:16 I may remember the e. covenant........ 5769
Ge 17:7 an e. covenant, to be a God unto....... 5769
Ge 17:8 for an e. possession; and I will be 5769
Ge 17:13 be in your flesh for an e. covenant. 5769
Ge 17:19 with him for an e. covenant,............. 5769
Ge 21:33 name of the Lord, the e. God............ 5769
Ge 48:4 after thee for an e. possession........... 5769
Ge 49:26 the utmost bound of the e. hills: 5769
Ex 40:15 an e. priesthood throughout their........ 5769
Le 16:34 this shall be an e. statute unto you, ... 5769
Le 24:8 of Israel by an e. covenant................ 5769
Nu 25:13 the covenant of an e. priesthood; 5769
De 33:27 and underneath are the e. arms: 5769
2Sa 23:5 hath made with me an e. covenant,...... 5769
1Ch 16:17 and to Israel for an e. covenant, ... 5769
Ps 24:7 be ye lift up, ye e. doors;................ 5769
Ps 24:9 even lift them up, ye e. doors; 5769
Ps 41:13 Lord God of Israel from e., and to e.....5769
Ps 90:2 even from e. to e., thou art God......... 5769
Ps 93:2 established of old; thou art from e.. 5769
Ps 100:5 the Lord is good; his mercy is e.; 5769
Ps 103:17 mercy of the Lord is from e. to e. 5769
Ps 105:10 and to Israel for an e. covenant: 5769
Ps 106:48 the Lord God of Israel from e. to e.: .. 5769
Ps 112:6 shall be in e. remembrance. 5769
Ps 119:142 Thy righteousness is an e.................. 5769
Ps 119:144 of thy testimonies is e.:.................... 5769
Ps 139:24 and lead me in the way e.................... 5769
Ps 145:13 Thy kingdom is an e. kingdom, ... 5769
Pr 8:23 I was set up from e., from the.......... 5769
Pr 10:25 the righteous is an e. foundation......... 5769
Isa 9:6 The e. Father, The Prince of Peace.... 5703
Isa 24:5 ordinance, broken the e. covenant. 5769
Isa 26:4 in the Lord Jehovah is e. strength: 5769
Isa 33:14 us shall dwell with e. burnings?.......... 5769
Isa 35:10 and e. joy upon their heads:............. 5769
Isa 40:28 not heard, that the e. God, the Lord,.. 5769
Isa 45:17 in the Lord with an e. salvation:......... 5769
Isa 51:11 e. joy shall be upon their head:.......... 5769
Isa 54:8 with e. kindness will I have mercy...... 5769
Isa 55:3 I will make an e. covenant with you,... 5769
Isa 55:13 an e. sign that shall not be cut off. 5769
Isa 56:5 I will give them an e. name,............. 5769
Isa 60:19 Lord shall be unto thee an e. light,..... 5769
Isa 60:20 the Lord shall be thine e. light,.......... 5769
Isa 61:7 e. joy shall be unto them.................. 5769
Isa 61:8 I will make an e. covenant with.......... 5769
Isa 63:12 to make himself an e. name? 5769
Isa 63:16 redeemer; thy name is from e.. 5769
Jer 10:10 the living God, and an e. king:........... 5769
Jer 20:11 their e. confusion shall never be......... 5769
Jer 23:40 I will bring an e. reproach upon 5769
Jer 31:3 I have loved thee with an e. love: 5769
Jer 32:40 I will make an e. covenant with......... 5769
Eze 16:60 establish unto thee an e. covenant. 5769
Eze 37:26 shall be an e. covenant with them:...... 5769
Da 4:3 his kingdom is an e. kingdom,.......... 5957
Da 4:34 whose dominion is an e. dominion,...... 5957
Da 7:14 his dominion is an e. dominion, ... 5957
Da 7:27 whose kingdom is an e. kingdom, ... 5957
Da 9:24 and to bring in e. righteousness, ... 5769
Da 12:2 some to e. life, and some to shame 5769
Da 12:2 to shame and e. contempt................ 5769
Mic 5:2 forth have been from of old, from e.... 5769
Hab 1:12 Art thou not from e., O Lord 6924
Hab 3:6 the e. mountains were scattered. 5703
Hab 3:6 hills did bow: his ways are e.. 5769
Mt 18:8 **or two feet to be cast into e. fire**.... 166
Mt 19:29 **and shall inherit e. life**. 166
Mt 25:41 **from me, ye cursed, into e. fire**,........ 166
Mt 25:46 **shall go away into e. punishment**:...... 166
Lu 16:9 **receive you into e. habitations**.......... 166
Lu 18:30 **and in the world to come life e.**....... 166
Joh 3:16 **should not perish, but have e. life**... 166
Joh 3:36 believeth on the Son hath e. life; 166
Joh 4:14 **of water springing up into e. life**.... 166
Joh 5:24 **on him that sent me, hath e. life**,..... 166
Joh 6:27 **meat which endureth unto e. life**,..... 166
Joh 6:40 **on him, may have e. life**:.................. 166
Joh 6:47 **believeth on me hath e. life**.............. 166
Joh 12:50 **that his commandment is life e.**:........ 166
Ac 13:46 yourselves unworthy of e. life, lo,........ 166
Ro 6:22 unto holiness, and the end e. life. 166
Ro 16:26 the commandment of the e. God,........... 166
Ga 6:8 shall of the spirit reap life e.. 166
2Th 1:9 be punished with e. destruction 166
2Th 2:16 and hath given us e. consolation 166
1Ti 1:16 believe on him to life e.. 166
1Ti 6:16 to whom be honour and power e.. 166
Heb 13:20 the blood of the e. covenant, ... 166
2Pe 1:11 to the e. kingdom of our Lord and 166
Jude 6 he hath reserved in e. chains............. 126
Re 14:6 having the e. gospel to preach............ 166

EVERMORE

De 28:29 oppressed and spoiled e., ... 3605,3117
2Sa 22:51 unto David, and to his seed for e.. 5769
2Ki 17:37 ye shall observe to do for e.; 3605,3117
1Ch 17:14 throne shall be established for e.. 5769
Ps 16:11 hand there are pleasures for e.. 5331
Ps 18:50 David, and to his seed for e.. 5769
Ps 37:27 and do good; and dwell for e.. 5769
Ps 77:8 doth his promise fail for e.?.............. 1755
Ps 86:12 I will glorify they name for e.. 5769
Ps 89:28 My mercy will I keep for him for e.,... 5769
Ps 89:52 Blessed be the Lord for e.. Amen, ... 5769
Ps 92:8 thou, Lord, art most high for e.. 5769
Ps 105:4 and his strength: seek his face e.. 8548
Ps 106:31 unto all generations for e.. 5769
Ps 113:2 from this time forth and for e.. 5769
Ps 115:18 from this time forth and for e.. 5769
Ps 121:8 from this time forth, and even for e.... 5769
Ps 132:12 shall also sit upon thy throne for e.. 5703
Ps 133:3 the blessing, even life for e................ 5769
Eze 37:26 in the midst of them for e................. 5769
Eze 37:28 shall be in the midst of them for e...... 5769
Joh 6:34 Lord, e. give us this bread................ 3842
2Co 11:31 Christ, which is blessed for e.,..... 3588,165
1Th 5:16 Rejoice e...3842
Heb 7:28 Son, who is consecrated for e.. 3588,165
Re 1:18 **I am alive for e.**,.................... 3588,165

EVERY

Ge 1:21 and e. living creature that................ 3605
Ge 1:21 and e. winged fowl after his kind: 3605
Ge 1:25 e. thing that creepeth upon the 3605
Ge 1:26 over e. creeping thing that creepeth.... 3605
Ge 1:28 e. living thing that moveth upon......... 3605
Ge 1:29 given you e. herb bearing seed,......... 3605
Ge 1:29 and e. tree, in the which is the.......... 3605
Ge 1:30 e. beast of the earth, and to e. fowl ... 3605
Ge 1:30 and to e. thing that creepeth............ 3605
Ge 1:30 I have given e. green herb for meat:... 3605
Ge 1:31 God saw e. thing that he had made,.... 3605
Ge 2:5 And e. plant of the field before 3605
Ge 2:5 and e. herb of the field before 3605
Ge 2:9 to grow e. tree that is pleasant.......... 3605
Ge 2:16 e. tree of the garden thou mayest 3605
Ge 2:19 Adam called e. living creature that was......
Ge 2:19 God formed e. beast of the field,........ 3605
Ge 2:19 and e. fowl of the air;........................ 3605
Ge 2:20 and to e. beast of the field;............... 3605
Ge 3:1 not eat of e. tree of the garden? 3605
Ge 3:14 cattle, and above e. beast of the field;. 3605
Ge 3:24 flaming sword which turned e. way, ...
Ge 4:14 e. one that findeth me shall slay......... 3605
Ge 4:22 instructor of e. artificer in brass......... 3605
Ge 6:5 e. imagination of the thoughts............ 3605
Ge 6:17 e. thing that is in the earth shall 3605
Ge 6:19 And of e. living thing of all flesh,........ 3605
Ge 6:19 two of e. sort shalt thou bring............. 3605
Ge 6:20 of e. creeping thing of the earth......... 3605
Ge 6:20 two of e. sort shall come unto thee, ... 3605
Ge 7:2 Of e. clean beast thou shalt take 3605
Ge 7:4 e. living substance that I have 3605
Ge 7:8 and of e. thing that creepeth 3605
Ge 7:14 They, and e. beast after his kind,........ 3605
Ge 7:14 and e. creeping thing that creepeth..... 3605
Ge 7:14 and e. fowl after his kind.................. 3605
Ge 7:14 e. bird of e. sort................................ 3605
Ge 7:21 and of e. creeping thing that............. 3605
Ge 7:21 upon the earth, and e. man. 3605
Ge 7:23 And e. living substance was............... 3605
Ge 8:1 Noah, and e. living thing, and all 3605
Ge 8:17 Bring forth with thee E. living thing.... 3605
Ge 8:17 and of e. creeping thing that.............. 3605
Ge 8:19 E. beast, e. creeping thing, and e. 3605
Ge 8:20 and took of e. clean beast,................ 3605
Ge 8:20 and of e. clean fowl, ... 3605
Ge 8:21 smite any more e. thing living,............ 3605
Ge 9:2 and upon e. fowl of the air, upon......... 3605
Ge 9:2 upon e. beast of the earth,................ 3605
Ge 9:3 E. moving thing that liveth.................. 3605
Ge 9:5 at the hand of e. man's brother.................
Ge 9:10 And with e. living creature that.......... 3605
Ge 9:10 and of e. beast of the earth.............. 3605
Ge 9:10 of the ark, to e. beast of the earth. 3605
Ge 9:12 e. living creature that is with you, ... 3605
Ge 9:15 e. living creature of all flesh; 3605
Ge 9:16 e. living creature of all flesh that 3605
Ge 10:5 e. one after his tongue, after their 376
Ge 13:10 it was well watered e. where, ... 3605
Ge 16:12 his hand will be against e. man, ... 3605
Ge 16:12 and e. man's hand against him; 3605
Ge 17:10 E. man child among you shall be......... 3605
Ge 17:12 e. man child in your generations,........ 3605
Ge 17:23 e. male among the men of 3605
Ge 19:4 all the people from e. quarter: ....
Ge 20:13 at e. place whither we shall come,...... 3605
Ge 27:29 cursed be e. one that curseth thee, ...
Ge 30:33 e. one that is not speckled and 3605
Ge 30:35 e. one that had some white in it,........ 3605
Ge 32:16 e. drove by themselves ....
Ge 34:15 e. male of you be circumcised,........... 3605
Ge 34:22 e. male among us be circumcised, ... 3605
Ge 34:23 and e. beast of theirs be ours? 3605
Ge 34:24 e. male was circumcised,.................. 3605
Ge 41:48 which was round about e. city,..................
Ge 42:25 e. man's money into his sack,...................
Ge 42:35 e. man's bundle of money was ....
Ge 43:21 behold, e. man's money was in ....
Ge 44:1 and put e. man's money in his ....
Ge 44:11 took down e. man his sack.......................
Ge 44:11 opened e. man his sack. ....
Ge 44:13 laded e. man his ass, ...
Ge 45:1 Cause e. man to go out from me........ 3605
Ge 46:34 for e. shepherd is an abomination 3605
Ge 47:20 Egyptians sold e. man his field,..................
Ge 49:28 e. one according to his blessing.................
Ex 1:1 e. man and his household came ....
Ex 1:22 E. son that is born ye shall cast 3605
Ex 1:22 e. daughter ye shall save alive. 3605
Ex 3:22 But e. woman shall borrow of her............
Ex 7:12 they cast down e. man his rod, ... 376
Ex 9:19 upon e. man and beast which............. 3605

Ex 9:22 and upon **e.** herb of the field,............ 3605
Ex 9:25 hail smote **e.** herb of the field,............ 3605
Ex 9:25 break **e.** tree of the field.................. 3605
Ex 10:5 shall eat **e.** tree which groweth.......... 3605
Ex 10:12 eat **e.** herb of the land,..................... 3605
Ex 10:15 did eat **e.** herb of the land,................ 3605
Ex 11:2 let **e.** man borrow of his neighbour,..........
Ex 11:2 **e.** woman of her neighbour,.....................
Ex 12:3 shall take them **e.** man a lamb,.................
Ex 12:4 **e.** man according to his eating..................
Ex 12:16 save that which **e.** man must eat,........ 3605
Ex 12:44 But **e.** man's servant that is bought..... 3605
Ex 13:12 **e.** firstling that cometh of a............... 3605
Ex 13:13 And **e.** firstling of an ass.................. 3605
Ex 14:7 captains over **e.** one of them............. 3605
Ex 16:4 gather a certain rate **e.** day,....................
Ex 16:16 Gather of it **e.** man according to..............
Ex 16:16 an omer for **e.** man, according to.............
Ex 16:16 take ye **e.** man for them which are............
Ex 16:18 gathered **e.** man according to his..............
Ex 16:21 And they gathered it **e.** morning,...............
Ex 16:21 morning, **e.** man according to his...............
Ex 16:29 **e.** man in his place, let no man go............
Ex 18:22 **e.** great matter they shall bring........... 3605
Ex 18:22 **e.** small matter they shall judge:......... 3605
Ex 18:26 **e.** small matter they judged.................. 3605
Ex 25:2 of **e.** man that giveth it willingly.......... 3605
Ex 26:2 **e.** one of the curtains shall have.......... 3605
Ex 27:18 and the breadth fifty **e.** where............ 3605
Ex 28:21 **e.** one with his name shall they be........ 376
Ex 29:36 And thou shalt offer **e.** day.....................
Ex 30:7 thereon sweet incense **e.** morning:............
Ex 30:12 give **e.** man a ransom for his soul.............
Ex 30:13 **e.** one that passeth among them......... 3605
Ex 30:14 **E.** one that passeth among them......... 3605
Ex 31:14 **e.** one that defileth it shall surely.............
Ex 32:27 Put **e.** man his sword by his side,.............
Ex 32:27 slay **e.** man his brother,.........................
Ex 32:27 and **e.** man his companion,.......................
Ex 32:27 and **e.** man his neighbour........................
Ex 32:29 **e.** man upon his son, and upon his............
Ex 33:7 **e.** one which sought the Lord............. 3605
Ex 33:8 **e.** man at his tent door, and looked....... 376
Ex 33:10 worshipped, **e.** man in his tent door..........
Ex 34:19 **e.** firstling among thy cattle,.............. 3605
Ex 35:10 And **e.** wise hearted among you.......... 3605
Ex 35:21 they came, **e.** one whose heart........... 3605
Ex 35:21 **e.** one whom his spirit made............... 3605
Ex 35:22 and **e.** man that offered offered........... 3605
Ex 35:23 And **e.** man, with whom was.............. 3605
Ex 35:24 **E.** one that did offer an offering.......... 3605
Ex 35:24 **e.** man, with whom was found............ 3605
Ex 35:29 unto the Lord, **e.** man and woman,...... 3605
Ex 36:1 and **e.** wise hearted man, in whom...... 3605
Ex 36:2 and **e.** wise hearted man, in whose...... 3605
Ex 36:2 **e.** one whose heart stirred him........... 3605
Ex 36:3 free offerings **e.** morning........................
Ex 36:4 came **e.** man from his work.......................
Ex 36:8 And **e.** wise hearted man among......... 3605
Ex 36:30 silver, under **e.** board two sockets........ 259
Ex 38:26 for **e.** man, that is, half a shekel,.............
Ex 38:26 **e.** one that went to be numbered......... 3605
Ex 39:14 **e.** one with his name, according to......... 376
Le 2:13 And **e.** oblation of thy meat................ 3605
Le 6:12 burn wood on it **e.** morning,.....................
Le 6:18 **e.** one that toucheth them shall............. 3605
Le 6:23 For **e.** meat offering for the priest........ 3605
Le 7:6 **E.** male among the priests shall............ 3605
Le 7:10 And **e.** meat offering, mingled............. 3605
Le 11:15 **E.** raven after his kind;.............. 853,3605
Le 11:21 ye eat of **e.** flying creeping thing........ 3605
Le 11:26 The carcases of **e.** beast which........... 3605
Le 11:26 **e.** one that toucheth them shall be........ 3605
Le 11:33 And **e.** earthen vessel, whereinto......... 3605
Le 11:34 may be drunk in **e.** such vessel........... 3605
Le 11:35 And **e.** thing whereupon any part......... 3605
Le 11:41 **e.** creeping thing that creepeth.......... 3605
Le 11:46 of **e.** living creature that moveth......... 3605
Le 11:46 and of **e.** creature that creepeth.......... 3605
Le 15:4 **E.** bed, whereon he lieth that hath...... 3605
Le 15:4 **e.** thing, whereon he sitteth, shall...... 3605
Le 15:12 **e.** vessel of wood shall be rinsed......... 3605
Le 15:17 And **e.** garment, and **e.** skin,............ 3605
Le 15:20 And **e.** thing that she lieth upon.......... 3605
Le 15:20 **e.** thing also that she sitteth upon....... 3605
Le 15:26 **E.** bed whereon she lieth................... 3605
Le 17:15 **e.** soul that eateth that which died....... 3605
Le 19:3 Ye shall fear **e.** man his mother,..............
Le 19:8 Therefore **e.** one that eateth it.................
Le 19:10 gather **e.** grape of thy vineyard;................
Le 20:9 **e.** one that curseth his father or........... 376
Le 23:37 **e.** thing upon his day:...........................
Le 24:8 **E.** sabbath he shall set it in order.............
Le 25:10 return **e.** man unto his possession,.............
Le 25:10 shall return **e.** man unto his family.............
Le 25:13 return **e.** man unto his possession..............
Le 27:28 **e.** devoted thing is most holy............ 3605
Nu 1:2 **e.** male by their polls;........................ 3605
Nu 1:4 a man of **e.** tribe.................................. 376
Nu 1:4 **e.** one head of the house of his............ 376
Nu 1:20, 22 **e.** male from twenty years old........ 3605
Nu 1:52 **e.** man by his own camp,........................
Nu 1:52 and **e.** man by his own standard,...............
Nu 2:2 **E.** man of the children of Israel...............
Nu 2:17 **e.** man in his place by their......................
Nu 2:34 **e.** one after their families, according...... 376
Nu 3:15 **e.** male from a month old.................. 3605
Nu 4:19 appoint them **e.** one to his service........ 376
Nu 4:30, 35, 39, 43 **e.** one that entereth into..... 3605
Nu 4:47 **e.** one that came to do the service...... 3605
Nu 4:49 **e.** one according to his service, and...... 376
Nu 5:2 **e.** leper, and **e.** one that hath an......... 3605
Nu 5:9 **e.** offering of all the holy things.......... 3605
Nu 5:10 And **e.** man's hallowed things..................
Nu 7:5 to **e.** man according to his service............
Nu 8:16 instead of such as open **e.** womb,........ 3605
Nu 8:17 I smote **e.** firstborn in the land.......... 3605
Nu 11:10 **e.** man in the door of his tent:.................
Nu 13:2 **e.** tribe of their fathers shall ye............ 376
Nu 13:2 a man, **e.** one a ruler among them....... 3605
Nu 15:12 so shall ye do to **e.** one according............
Nu 16:3 congregation are holy, **e.** one of.......... 3605
Nu 16:17 take **e.** man his censer, and put...............
Nu 16:17 before the Lord **e.** man his censer,............
Nu 16:18 And they took **e.** man his censer,.............
Nu 16:27 the tabernacle of Korah,...on **e.** side:...... 376
Nu 17:2 and take of **e.** one of them a rod..............
Nu 17:2 write thou **e.** man's name upon.................
Nu 17:6 **e.** one of their princes gave him........... 3605
Nu 17:9 looked, and took **e.** man his rod................
Nu 18:7 office for **e.** thing of the altar,........... 3605
Nu 18:9 **e.** oblation of theirs,........................ 3605
Nu 18:9 **e.** meat offering................................. 3605
Nu 18:9 **e.** sin offering of theirs, **e.** trespass..... 3605
Nu 18:10 **e.** male shall eat it:........................ 3605
Nu 18:11 **e.** one that is clean in thy house......... 3605
Nu 18:13 **e.** one that is clean in thine house........ 3605
Nu 18:14 **E.** thing devoted in Israel shall be....... 3605
Nu 18:15 **E.** thing that openeth the matrix......... 3605
Nu 18:29 ye shall offer **e.** heave offering........... 3605
Nu 18:31 ye shall eat it in **e.** place,................. 3605
Nu 19:15 And **e.** open vessel, which hath no...... 3605
Nu 21:8 **E.** one that is bitten,........................ 3605
Nu 23:2 Balaam offered on **e.** altar a bullock..........
Nu 23:4 I have offered upon **e.** altar a bullock.........
Nu 23:14, 30 a bullock and a ram on **e.** altar.............
Nu 25:5 Slay ye **e.** one his men that................. 376
Nu 26:54 to **e.** one shall his inheritance be.......... 376
Nu 28:10 is the burnt offering of **e.** sabbath,.............
Nu 28:14 burnt offering for **e.** month.......................
Nu 28:21 deal shalt thou offer for **e.** lamb,..............
Nu 29:14 three tenth deals unto **e.** bullock........... 259
Nu 30:4 and **e.** bond wherewith she hath.......... 3605
Nu 30:9 But **e.** vow of a widow, and of her..........
Nu 30:11 **e.** bond wherewith she bound............. 3605
Nu 30:13 **E.** vow, and **e.** binding oath.............. 3605
Nu 31:4 Of **e.** tribe a thousand, throughout............
Nu 31:5 of Israel, a thousand of **e.** tribe,...............
Nu 31:6 to the war, a thousand of **e.** tribe,..............
Nu 31:17 Now therefore kill **e.** male among......... 3605
Nu 31:17 and kill **e.** woman that hath known....... 3605
Nu 31:23 **E.** thing that may abide the fire,.......... 3605
Nu 31:50 what **e.** man hath gotten, of jewels...........
Nu 31:53 had taken spoil, **e.** man for himself.)..........
Nu 32:18 inherited **e.** man his inheritance.................
Nu 32:27 pass over, **e.** man armed for war,....... 3605
Nu 32:29 Jordan, **e.** man armed to battle,.......... 3605
Nu 33:54 **e.** man's inheritance shall be in.................
Nu 34:18 take one prince of **e.** tribe,.......................
Nu 35:8 **e.** one shall give of his cities............... 376
Nu 35:15 **e.** one that killeth any person............. 3605
Nu 36:7 **e.** one of the children of Israel............. 376
Nu 36:8 **e.** daughter, that possesseth an.......... 3605
Nu 36:8 may enjoy **e.** man the inheritance.............
Nu 36:9 but **e.** one of the tribes of the............... 376
De 1:16 between **e.** man and his brother,..............
De 1:22 came near unto me **e.** one of you,........ 3605
De 1:41 on **e.** man his weapons of war,............... 376
De 2:34 of **e.** city, we left none to remain:....... 3605
De 3:6 and children, of **e.** city...................... 3605
De 3:20 return **e.** man, unto his possession,..........
De 4:4 are alive **e.** one of you this day........... 3605
De 8:3 but by **e.** word that proceedeth........... 3605
De 11:24 **E.** place whereon the soles of your..... 3605
De 12:2 and under **e.** green tree:.................... 3605
De 12:8 **e.** man whatsoever is right in his.............
De 12:13 offerings in **e.** place that thou............ 3605
De 12:31 for **e.** abomination to the Lord,........... 3605
De 13:16 and all the spoil thereof **e.** whit,........... 3632
De 14:6 And **e.** beast that parteth the hoof,....... 3605
De 14:14 And **e.** raven after his kind,............... 3605
De 14:19 And **e.** creeping thing that flieth......... 3605
De 15:1 end of **e.** seven years thou shalt...............
De 15:2 **E.** creditor that lendeth ought............ 3605
De 16:17 **E.** man shall give as he is able,...............
De 19:3 that **e.** slayer may flee thither............ 3605
De 20:13 thou shalt smite **e.** male thereof.......... 3605
De 21:5 shall **e.** controversy and **e.** stroke....... 3605
De 23:9 keep thee from **e.** wicked thing........... 3605
De 24:16 **e.** man shall be put to death....................
De 26:11 shalt rejoice in **e.** good thing.............. 3605
De 28:61 Also **e.** sickness, and **e.** plague........... 3605
De 30:9 plenteous in **e.** work.......................... 3605
De 31:10 at the end of **e.** seven years,....................
De 33:3 **e.** one shall receive of thy words..............
Jos 1:3 **E.** place that the sole of your foot....... 3605
Jos 3:12 of Israel, out of **e.** tribe a man.................
Jos 4:2 the people, out of **e.** tribe a man,..............
Jos 4:4 of Israel, out of **e.** tribe a man:.................
Jos 4:5 take you up **e.** man of you a stone............
Jos 4:10 until **e.** thing was finished that............ 3605
Jos 6:5 shall ascend up **e.** man straight................
Jos 6:20 **e.** man straight before him, and................
Jos 11:14 **e.** man they smote with the edge........ 3605
Jos 21:42 were **e.** one with their suburbs round.........
Jos 24:28 **e.** man unto his inheritance......................
Jg 2:6 **e.** man unto his inheritance to...................
Jg 5:30 to **e.** man a damsel or two;................ 7218
Jg 7:5 **E.** one that lappeth of the water......... 3605
Jg 7:5 **e.** one that boweth down upon his....... 3605
Jg 7:7 people go **e.** man unto his place...............
Jg 7:8 of Israel **e.** man unto his tent,..................
Jg 7:16 a trumpet in **e.** man's hand,................ 3605
Jg 7:18 on **e.** side of all the camp,.................. 3605
Jg 7:21 and they stood **e.** man in his place............
Jg 7:22 **e.** man's sword against his fellow.............
Jg 8:24 me **e.** man the earring of his prey............
Jg 8:25 cast therein **e.** man the earrings of...........
Jg 8:34 of all their enemies on **e.** side:........... 5437
Jg 9:49 cut down **e.** man his bough,......................
Jg 9:55 they departed **e.** man unto his place..........
Jg 16:5 **e.** one of us eleven hundred pieces....... 376
Jg 17:6 **e.** man did that which was right................
Jg 20:16 **e.** one could sling stones at an............ 3605
Jg 20:48 as well the men of **e.** city,.......................
Jg 21:11 destroy **e.** male, and **e.** woman........... 3605
Jg 21:21 and catch you **e.** man his wife..................
Jg 21:24 **e.** man to his tribe and to his family,..........
Jg 21:24 thence **e.** man to his inheritance................
Jg 21:25 **e.** man did that which was right in............
1Sa 2:36 **e.** one that is left in thine house.......... 3605
1Sa 3:11 ears of **e.** one that heareth it shall....... 3605
1Sa 3:18 Samuel told him **e.** whit,.................... 3605
1Sa 4:10 fled **e.** man into his tent:.........................
1Sa 8:22 Go ye **e.** man unto his city.......................
1Sa 10:25 people away, **e.** man to his house.............
1Sa 12:11 your enemies on **e.** side, and ye......... 5437
1Sa 13:2 he sent **e.** man to his tent.......................
1Sa 13:20 to sharpen **e.** man his share, and.............
1Sa 14:20 **e.** man's sword was against his..................
1Sa 14:34 Bring me hither **e.** man his ox,.................
1Sa 14:34 and **e.** man his sheep,...............................
1Sa 14:34 **e.** man his ox with him that night,............
1Sa 14:47 against all his enemies on **e.** side,........ 5437
1Sa 15:9 but **e.** thing that was vile.................... 3605
1Sa 20:15 And **e.** one from the face of the earth.... 376
1Sa 22:2 and **e.** one that was in distress,........... 3605
1Sa 22:2 and **e.** one that was in debt,............... 3605
1Sa 22:2 and **e.** on that was discontented,.......... 3605

1Sa 22:7 son of Jesse give **e.** one of you 3605
1Sa 23:14 And Saul sought him **e.** day, 3605
1Sa 25:10 away **e.** man from his master
1Sa 25:13 Gird ye on **e.** man his sword
1Sa 25:13 they girded on **e.** man his sword;
1Sa 26:23 The Lord render to **e.** man his
1Sa 27:3 **e.** man with his household, even
1Sa 30:6 **e.** man for his sons and for his
1Sa 30:22 **e.** man his wife and his children,
2Sa 2:3 **e.** man with his household: and
2Sa 2:16 **e.** one his fellow by the head, 376
2Sa 2:27 **e.** one from following his brother. 376
2Sa 6:19 to **e.** one a cake of bread, and a 376
2Sa 6:19 people departed **e.** one to his house. 376
2Sa 13:9 And they went out **e.** man from him.
2Sa 13:29 **e.** man gat him up upon his mule,
2Sa 13:37 David mourned for his son **e.** day. 3605
2Sa 14:26 was at **e.** year's end that he polled it:
2Sa 15:4 **e.** man which hath any suit or 3605
2Sa 15:30 covered **e.** man his head, and they
2Sa 15:36 send unto me **e.** thing that ye can 3605
2Sa 18:17 all Israel fled **e.** one to his tent 376
2Sa 19:8 Israel had fled **e.** man to his tent
2Sa 20:1 **e.** man to his tents, O Israel 376
2Sa 20:2 **e.** man of Israel went up from 376
2Sa 20:12 saw that **e.** one that came by him 3605
2Sa 20:22 from the city, **e.** man to his tent.
2Sa 21:20 had on **e.** hand six fingers,
2Sa 21:20 on **e.** foot six toes,
1Ki 1:49 rose up, and went **e.** man his way.
1Ki 4:25 **e.** man under his vine and under
1Ki 4:27 **e.** man in his month: they lacked
1Ki 4:28 **e.** man according to his charge
1Ki 5:3 which were about him on **e.** side, 5437
1Ki 5:4 God hath given me rest on **e.** side, 5437
1Ki 7:30 **e.** base had four brasen wheels, 259
1Ki 7:30 at the side of **e.** addition. 376
1Ki 7:36 the proportion of **e.** one, and 376
1Ki 7:38 and **e.** laver was four cubits: 259
1Ki 7:38 and upon **e.** one of the ten bases
1Ki 8:38 which shall know **e.** man the plague
1Ki 8:39 to **e.** man according to his ways,
1Ki 9:8 to one that passeth by it shall be 3605
1Ki 10:25 they brought **e.** man his present,
1Ki 11:15 had smitten **e.** male in Edom; 3605
1Ki 11:16 until he cut off **e.** male in Edom: 3605
1Ki 12:24 return **e.** man to his house; for
1Ki 14:23 groves, on **e.** high hill, 3605
1Ki 14:23 and under **e.** green tree. 3605
1Ki 19:18 and **e.** mouth which hath not 3605
1Ki 20:20 And they slew **e.** one his man: 376
1Ki 20:24 **e.** man out of his place, and put 376
1Ki 22:17 let them return **e.** man to his house
1Ki 22:28 Hearken, O people, **e.** one of you. 3605
1Ki 22:36 **E.** man to his city, and
1Ki 22:36 **e.** man to his own country.
2Ki 3:19 smite **e.** fenced city, and **e.** choice 3605
2Ki 3:19 and shall fell **e.** good tree, 3605
2Ki 3:19 mar **e.** good piece of land 3605
2Ki 3:25 on **e.** good piece of land 3605
2Ki 3:25 cast **e.** man his stone,
2Ki 6:2 and take thence **e.** man a beam,
2Ki 8:9 of **e.** good thing of Damascus, 3605
2Ki 9:13 took **e.** man his garment, and put
2Ki 11:8 **e.** man with his weapons in his
2Ki 11:9 they took **e.** man his men that were
2Ki 11:11 guard stood, **e.** man with weapons
2Ki 12:4 the money of **e.** one that passeth 3605
2Ki 12:4 the money that **e.** man is set at,
2Ki 12:5 them, **e.** man of his acquaintance:
2Ki 14:6 but **e.** man shall be put to death
2Ki 14:12 and they fled **e.** man to their tents
2Ki 16:4 the hills, and under **e.** green tree. 3605
2Ki 17:10 in **e.** high hill, and under **e.** green 3605
2Ki 17:29 Howbeit **e.** nation made gods
2Ki 17:29 **e.** nation in their cities wherein
2Ki 18:31 eat ye **e.** man of his own vine, and
2Ki 18:31 **e.** one of his fig...and drink ye **e.** one 376
2Ki 23:35 **e.** one according to his taxation, 376
2Ki 25:9 **e.** great man's house burnt he 3605
2Ki 25:30 a daily rate for **e.** day, all they days
1Ch 9:27 the opening thereof **e.** morning
1Ch 9:32 shewbread, to prepare it **e.** sabbath.
1Ch 13:1 hundreds, and with **e.** leader. 3605
1Ch 13:2 send abroad our brethren **e.** where,
1Ch 16:3 dealt to **e.** one of Israel, both man 376
1Ch 16:3 man and woman, to **e.** one a loaf 376
1Ch 16:37 before the ark continually, as **e.** day's
1Ch 16:43 departed **e.** man to his house:
1Ch 22:15 men for **e.** manner of work. 3605
1Ch 22:18 he not given you rest on **e.** side? 5437
1Ch 23:30 And to stand **e.** morning to thank
1Ch 26:13 cast lots...for **e.** gate.
1Ch 26:32 for **e.** matter pertaining to God, 3605
1Ch 27:1 of **e.** course were twenty and four 259
1Ch 28:14 instruments of **e.** kind of service: 3605
1Ch 28:15 by weight for **e.** candlestick,
1Ch 28:15 according to the use of **e.** candlestick.
1Ch 28:16 tables of shewbread, for **e.** table;
1Ch 28:17 he gave gold by weight for **e.** bason;
1Ch 28:17 silver by weight for **e.** bason of silver:
1Ch 28:21 workmanship **e.** willing skilful 3605
2Ch 1:2 and to **e.** governor in all Israel, 3605
2Ch 2:14 to find out **e.** device which 3605
2Ch 6:29 **e.** one shall know his own sore 376
2Ch 6:30 **e.** man according unto all his ways,
2Ch 7:21 an astonishment to **e.** one that 3605
2Ch 8:13 Even after a certain rate **e.** day,
2Ch 8:14 porters also by their courses at **e.** gate:
2Ch 8:14 as the duty of **e.** day required:
2Ch 9:21 **e.** three years once came the ships
2Ch 9:24 they brought **e.** man his present,
2Ch 10:16 **e.** man to your tents, O Israel:
2Ch 11:4 return **e.** man to his house; for this
2Ch 11:12 And in **e.** special city he put 3605
2Ch 11:23 Benjamin, unto **e.** fenced city: 3605
2Ch 13:11 **e.** morning and **e.** evening burnt
2Ch 13:11 lamps thereof, to burn **e.** evening:
2Ch 14:7 he hath given us rest on **e.** side. 5437
2Ch 18:16 therefore **e.** man to his house
2Ch 20:23 **e.** one helped to destroy another. 376
2Ch 20:27 they returned, **e.** man of Judah 3605
2Ch 23:7 **e.** man with his weapons in his
2Ch 23:8 **e.** man his men that were to come
2Ch 23:10 **e.** man having his weapon in his
2Ch 25:4 but **e.** man shall die for his own sin
2Ch 25:22 and they fled **e.** man to his tent.
2Ch 28:4 the hills, and under **e.** green tree. 3605
2Ch 28:24 altars in **e.** corner of Jerusalem. 3605
2Ch 28:25 And in **e.** several city of Judah 3605
2Ch 29:35 drink offerings for **e.** burnt offering.
2Ch 30:17 for **e.** one that was not clean, 3605
2Ch 30:18 The good Lord pardon **e.** one 3605
2Ch 31:1 **e.** man to his possession, into their
2Ch 31:2 **e.** man according to his service,
2Ch 31:16 even unto **e.** one that entereth 3605
2Ch 31:19 in **e.** several city, the men that 3605
2Ch 31:21 And in **e.** work that he began 3605
2Ch 32:22 and guided them on **e.** side. 5437
2Ch 35:15 and the porters waited at **e.** gate;
Ezr 2:1 and Judah, **e.** one unto his city; 376
Ezr 3:4 as the duty of **e.** day required;
Ezr 3:5 of **e.** one that willingly offered 3605
Ezr 6:5 at Jerusalem, **e.** one to his place,
Ezr 8:34 and by weight of **e.** one: 3605
Ezr 9:4 assembled unto me **e.** one that 3605
Ezr 10:14 with them the elders of **e.** city,
Ne 3:28 **e.** one over against his house. 376
Ne 4:15 to the wall, **e.** one unto his work. 376
Ne 4:17 **e.** one with one of his hands 376
Ne 4:18 **e.** one had his sword girded by his 376
Ne 4:22 Let **e.** one with his servant lodge 376
Ne 4:23 **e.** one put them off for washing. 376
Ne 5:7 exact usury, **e.** one of his brother. 376
Ne 5:13 shake out **e.** man from his house,
Ne 7:3 **e.** one in his watch, and **e.** one to be 376
Ne 7:6 and to Judah, **e.** one unto his city; 376
Ne 8:16 **e.** one upon the roof of his house, 376
Ne 10:28 **e.** one having knowledge, and 3605
Ne 10:31 and the exaction of **e.** debt 3605
Ne 11:3 **e.** one in his possession in their 376
Ne 11:20 of Judah, **e.** one in his inheritance. 376
Ne 11:23 be for the singers, due for **e.** day.
Ne 12:47 the singers and the porters, **e.** day
Ne 13:10 were fled **e.** one to his field. 376
Ne 13:30 the Levites, **e.** one in his business; 376
Es 1:8 do according to **e.** man's pleasure.
Es 1:22 king's provinces, into **e.** province
Es 1:22 to **e.** people after their language, 376
Es 1:22 that **e.** man should bear rule in
Es 1:22 to the language of **e.** people.
Es 2:11 Mordecai walked **e.** day before the
Es 2:12 Now when **e.** maid's turn was come
Es 2:13 came **e.** maiden unto the king;
Es 3:12 governors that were over **e.** province,
Es 3:12 rulers of **e.** people of province
Es 3:12 to people after their language;
Es 3:14 to be given in **e.** province 3605
Es 4:3 And in **e.** province, whithersoever 3605
Es 6:13 **e.** thing that had befallen him 3605
Es 8:9 unto **e.** province according to
Es 8:9 and unto **e.** people after their
Es 8:11 Jews which were in **e.** city to 3605
Es 8:13 to be given in **e.** province was 3605
Es 8:17 And in **e.** province, and in **e.** city. 3605
Es 9:27 their appointed time **e.** year; 3605
Es 9:28 **e.** [3605] generation, **e.** family.
Es 9:28 **e.** province, and **e.** city;
Job 1:4 their houses, **e.** one his day; 376
Job 1:10 about all that he hath on **e.** side? 5437
Job 2:11 came **e.** one from his own place; 376
Job 2:12 and they rent **e.** one his mantle, 376
Job 7:18 visit him **e.** morning, and try him **e.**
Job 12:10 the soul of **e.** living thing, 3605
Job 18:11 shall make him afraid on **e.** side, 5437
Job 19:10 He hath destroyed me on **e.** side, 5437
Job 20:22 **e.** hand of the wicked shall come 3605
Job 21:33 and **e.** man shall draw after him, 3605
Job 24:6 They reap **e.** one his corn
Job 28:10 his ye seeth **e.** precious thing 3605
Job 34:11 and cause **e.** man to find according
Job 36:25 **E.** man may see it; 3605
Job 37:7 sealeth up the hand of **e.** man; 3605
Job 39:8 he searcheth after **e.** green thing 3605
Job 40:11 behold **e.** one that is proud, 3605
Job 40:12 Look on **e.** one that is proud, 3605
Job 42:2 thou canst do **e.** thing, 3605
Job 42:11 **e.** man also gave him a piece of
Job 42:11 and **e.** one an earring 376
Ps 7:11 angry with the wicked **e.** day. 3605
Ps 12:2 vanity **e.** one with his neighbour: 376
Ps 12:8 The wicked walk on **e.** side, 5437
Ps 29:9 doth **e.** one speak on his glory 3605
Ps 31:13 fear was on **e.** side: 5437
Ps 32:6 For this shall **e.** one that is godly 3605
Ps 39:5 **e.** man at his best state is altogether 3605
Ps 39:6 **e.** man walketh in a vain shew:
Ps 39:11 surely **e.** man is vanity. Selah. 3605
Ps 50:10 For **e.** beast of the forest is mine, 3605
Ps 53:3 **E.** one of them is gone back: 3605
Ps 56:5 **E.** day they wrest my words: 3605
Ps 58:8 let **e.** one of them pass away:
Ps 62:12 to **e.** man according to his work.
Ps 63:11 **e.** one that sweareth by him shall 3605
Ps 64:6 inward thought of **E.** one of them, 376
Ps 65:12 the little hills rejoice on **e.** side.
Ps 68:30 till **e.** one submit himself with
Ps 69:34 the seas, and **e.** thing that moveth 3605
Ps 71:18 thy power to **e.** one that is to come 3605
Ps 71:21 and comfort me on **e.** side. 5437
Ps 74:14 plagued, and chastened **e.** morning.
Ps 84:7 **e.** one of them in Zion appeareth
Ps 92:2 and thy faithfulness **e.** night,
Ps 104:11 drink to **e.** beast of the field: 3605
Ps 115:8 so is **e.** one that trusteth in them. 3605
Ps 119:101 my feet from **e.** evil way, 3605
Ps 119:104 therefore I hate **e.** false way. 3605
Ps 119:128 and I hate **e.** false way. 3605
Ps 119:160 **e.** one of thy righteous judgments 3605
Ps 128:1 Blessed is **e.** one that feareth 3605
Ps 135:18 so is **e.** one that trusteth in them. 3605
Ps 145:2 **E.** day I will bless thee; 3605
Ps 145:16 the desire of **e.** living thing. 3605
Ps 150:6 Let **e.** thing that hath breath 3605
Pr 1:19 the ways of **e.** one that is greedy 3605
Pr 2:9 yea, **e.** good path. 3605
Pr 3:18 happy is **e.** one that retaineth her.
Pr 7:12 and lieth in wait at **e.** corner.) 3605
Pr 13:16 **E.** prudent man dealeth with 3605
Pr 14:1 **E.** wise woman buildeth her house:
Pr 14:15 The simple believeth **e.** word: 3605
Pr 15:3 The eyes of the Lord are in **e.** place, 3605
Pr 16:5 **E.** one that is proud in heart 3605
Pr 19:6 **e.** man that is a friend to him 3605
Pr 20:3 but **e.** fool will be meddling. 3605
Pr 20:6 **e.** one his own goodness: but a 376
Pr 20:18 **E.** purpose is established by counsel:
Pr 21:2 **E.** way of a man is right in his 3605

Pr 21:5 of **e.** one that is hasty only to want. 3605
Pr 24:12 to **e.** man according to his works?
Pr 24:26 **E.** man shall kiss his lips
Pr 27:7 soul **e.** bitter thing is sweet. 3605
Pr 27:24 crown endure to **e.** generation?
Pr 29:26 **e.** man's judgment cometh from
Pr 30:5 **E.** word of God is pure: 3605
Ec 3:1 To **e.** thing there is a season, 3605
Ec 3:1 to **e.** purpose under the heaven: 3605
Ec 3:11 **e.** thing beautiful in his time: 3605
Ec 3:13 that **e.** man should eat and drink, 3605
Ec 3:17 for **e.** purpose and for **e.** work 3605
Ec 4:4 all travail, and **e.** right work, 3605
Ec 5:19 **E.** man also to whom God hath 3605
Ec 8:6 Because to **e.** purpose there is 3605
Ec 8:9 unto **e.** work that is done under 3605
Ec 10:3 he saith to **e.** one that he is a fool 3605
Ec 10:15 wearieth **e.** one of them,
Ec 12:14 God shall bring **e.** work into 3605
Ec 12:14 with **e.** secret thing, whether it be 3605
Ca 3:8 **e.** man hath his sword upon his
Ca 4:2 whereof **e.** one bear twins, 3605
Ca 6:6 whereof **e.** one beareth twins, 3605
Ca 8:11 **e.** one for the fruit thereof was to 376
Isa 1:23 **e.** one loveth gifts, and followeth 3605
Isa 2:12 be upon **e.** one that is proud 3605
Isa 2:12 and upon **e.** one that is lifted up; 3605
Isa 2:15 **e.** high tower, and upon **e.** fenced 3605
Isa 3:5 be oppressed, **e.** one by another, 376
Isa 3:5 and **e.** one by his neighbour: 376
Isa 4:3 even **e.** one that is written among 3605
Isa 4:5 create upon **e.** dwelling place 3605
Isa 7:22 honey shall **e.** one eat that is 3605
Isa 7:23 that **e.** place shall be, where 3605
Isa 9:5 For **e.** battle of the warrior is 3605
Isa 9:17 **e.** one is an hypocrite and an 3605
Isa 9:17 and **e.** mouth speaketh folly, 3605
Isa 9:20 eat **e.** man the flesh of his own
Isa 13:7 **e.** man's heart shall melt: 3605
Isa 13:14 **e.** man turn to his own people, and
Isa 13:14 flee **e.** one into his own land. 376
Isa 13:15 **E.** one that is found shall be 3605
Isa 13:15 and **e.** one that is joined unto 3605
Isa 14:18 in glory, **e.** one in his own house. 376
Isa 15:2 and **e.** beard cut off. 3605
Isa 15:3 in their streets, **e.** one shall howl, 3605
Isa 16:7 for Moab, **e.** one shall howl: 3605
Isa 19:2 **e.** one against his brother, 376
Isa 19:2 and **e.** one against his neighbour; 376
Isa 19:7 and **e.** thing sown by the brooks 3605
Isa 19:14 Egypt to err in **e.** work thereof, 3605
Isa 19:17 **e.** one that maketh mention 3605
Isa 24:10 **e.** house is shut up, 3605
Isa 27:3 I will water it **e.** moment:
Isa 30:25 and upon **e.** high mountain 3605
Isa 30:25 and upon **e.** high hill, 3605
Isa 30:32 And in **e.** place where the grounded 3605
Isa 31:7 **e.** man shall cast away his idols
Isa 33:2 be thou their arm **e.** morning,
Isa 34:15 be gathered, **e.** one with her mate. 802
Isa 36:16 eat ye **e.** one of his vine, and **e.** one 376
Isa 36:16 drink ye **e.** one the waters of his 376
Isa 40:4 **E.** valley shall be exalted 3605
Isa 40:4 **e.** mountain and hill shall be made 3605
Isa 41:6 helped **e.** one his neighbour; 376
Isa 41:6 and **e.** one said to his brother, 376
Isa 43:7 **e.** one that is called by my name: 3605
Isa 44:23 O forest, and **e.** tree therein: 3605
Isa 45:23 unto me **e.** knee shall bow, 3605
Isa 45:23 **e.** tongue shall swear. 3605
Isa 47:15 they shall wander **e.** one to his 376
Isa 51:13 feared continually **e.** day because 3605
Isa 52:5 continually **e.** day is blasphemed. 3605
Isa 53:6 we have turned **e.** one to his own 376
Isa 54:17 **e.** tongue that shall rise against 3605
Isa 55:1 Ho, **e.** one that thirsteth, 3605
Isa 56:6 **e.** one that keepeth the sabbath 3605
Isa 56:11 **e.** one for his gain, from his quarter. 376
Isa 57:5 with idols under **e.** green tree, 3605
Isa 58:6 that ye break **e.** yoke? 3605
Jer 1:15 shall set **e.** one his throne at the 376
Jer 2:20 when upon **e.** high hill and under 3605
Jer 2:20 under **e.** green tree thou wanderest, 3605
Jer 3:6 gone up upon **e.** high mountain and 3605
Jer 3:6 and under **e.** green tree, and there 3605
Jer 3:13 to the strangers under **e.** green tree, 3605
Jer 4:29 **e.** city shall be forsaken, 3605
Jer 5:6 **e.** one that goeth out thence shall 3605
Jer 5:8 **e.** one neighed after his neighbour's 376
Jer 6:3 they shall feed **e.** one in his place. 376
Jer 6:13 **e.** one is given to covetousness; 3605
Jer 6:13 unto the priest **e.** one dealeth 3605
Jer 6:25 the enemy and fear is on **e.** side. 5437
Jer 8:6 **e.** one turned to his course, 3605
Jer 8:10 for **e.** one from the least even unto 3605
Jer 8:10 the priest **e.** one dealeth falsely. 3605
Jer 9:4 ye heed **e.** one of his neighbour, 376
Jer 9:4 for **e.** brother will utterly supplant 3605
Jer 9:4 **e.** neighbour will walk with slanders. 3605
Jer 9:5 deceive **e.** one his neighbour, 376
Jer 9:20 **e.** one her neighbour lamentation. 802
Jer 10:14 **E.** man is brutish in his 3605
Jer 10:14 **e.** founder is confounded by the 3605
Jer 11:8 walked **e.** one in the imagination 376
Jer 12:4 and the herbs of **e.** field wither, 3605
Jer 12:15 **e.** man to his heritage, and **e.** man
Jer 13:12 **E.** bottle shall be filled with wine: 3605
Jer 13:12 know that **e.** bottle shall be filled 3605
Jer 15:10 **e.** one of them doth curse me. 3605
Jer 16:12 **e.** one after the imagination of his 376
Jer 16:16 from **e.** mountain, and from **e.** hill, 3605
Jer 17:10 give **e.** man according to his ways,
Jer 18:11 return ye now **e.** one from his evil 376
Jer 18:12 we will **e.** one do the imagination 376
Jer 18:16 **e.** one that passeth thereby shall 3605
Jer 19:8 **e.** one that passeth thereby shall be 3605
Jer 19:9 and they shall eat **e.** one the flesh 376
Jer 20:7 daily, **e.** one mocketh me. 3605
Jer 20:10 defaming of many, fear on **e.** side. 5437
Jer 22:7 thee, **e.** one with his weapons; 376
Jer 22:8 shall say **e.** man to his neighbour,
Jer 23:17 they say unto **e.** one that walketh 3605
Jer 23:27 they tell **e.** man to his neighbour,
Jer 23:30 my words **e.** one from his neighbour 376
Jer 23:35 ye say **e.** one to his neighbour, and 376
Jer 23:35 and **e.** one to his brother, 376
Jer 23:36 **e.** man's word shall be his burden;
Jer 25:5 Turn ye again now **e.** one from his 376
Jer 26:3 and turn **e.** man from his evil way,
Jer 29:26 for **e.** man that is mad, and maketh
Jer 30:6 I see **e.** man with his hands on his 3605
Jer 30:16 **e.** one of them, shall go into 3605
Jer 31:25 replenished **e.** sorrowful soul. 3605
Jer 31:30 **e.** man that eateth the sour grape,
Jer 31:30 **e.** one shall die for his own iniquity: 376
Jer 31:34 teach no more **e.** man his neighbour,
Jer 31:34 and **e.** man his brother,
Jer 32:19 to give **e.** one according to his ways 376
Jer 34:9 **e.** man should let his manservant,
Jer 34:9 and **e.** man his maidservant,
Jer 34:10 **e.** one should let his manservant, 376
Jer 34:10 and **e.** one his maidservant, go free, 376
Jer 34:14 let ye go **e.** man his brother
Jer 34:15 proclaiming liberty **e.** man to his
Jer 34:16 **e.** man his servant, and **e.** man his
Jer 34:17 **e.** one to his brother, and **e.** man to
Jer 35:15 Return ye now **e.** man from his evil
Jer 36:3 return **e.** man from his evil way;
Jer 36:7 return **e.** one from his evil way: 376
Jer 37:10 rise up **e.** man in his tent,
Jer 43:6 and **e.** person that Nebuzar-adan 3605
Jer 47:4 from Tyrus and Zidon **e.** helper 3605
Jer 48:8 spoiler shall come upon **e.** city, 3605
Jer 48:37 For **e.** head shall be bald, 3605
Jer 48:37 and **e.** beard clipped: 3605
Jer 49:5 ye shall be driven out **e.** man
Jer 49:17 **e.** one that goeth by it shall be 3605
Jer 49:29 cry unto them, Fear is on **e.** side. 5437
Jer 50:13 **e.** one that goeth by Babylon shall 3605
Jer 50:16 shall turn **e.** one to his people, and 376
Jer 50:16 and they shall flee **e.** one 376
Jer 50:42 **e.** one put in array, like a man to the
Jer 51:6 and deliver **e.** man his soul:
Jer 51:9 go **e.** one into his own country: 376
Jer 51:17 **E.** man is brutish by his 3605
Jer 51:17 **e.** founder is confounded by the 3605
Jer 51:29 for **e.** purpose of the Lord shall be
Jer 51:45 and deliver ye **e.** man his soul
Jer 51:56 men are taken, **e.** one of their
Jer 52:34 **e.** day a portion until the day of his
La 2:19 for hunger in the top of **e.** street. 3605
La 3:23 They are new **e.** morning: great is
La 4:1 poured out in the top of **e.** street. 3605
Eze 1:6 **e.** one had four faces, and **e.** one
Eze 1:9 went **e.** one straight forward. 376
Eze 1:11 two wings of **e.** one were joined 376
Eze 1:12 they went **e.** one straight forward: 376
Eze 1:23 **e.** one had two, which covered on 376
Eze 1:23 this side, and **e.** one had two, 376
Eze 6:13 upon **e.** high hill,...under **e.** green 3605
Eze 6:13 and under **e.** thick oak, the place 3605
Eze 7:16 all of them mourning, **e.** one for his 376
Eze 8:10 and behold **e.** form of creeping 3605
Eze 8:11 with **e.** man his censer in his hand;
Eze 8:12 **e.** man in the chambers of his
Eze 9:1 even **e.** man with his destroying
Eze 9:2 and **e.** man a slaughter weapon
Eze 10:14 And **e.** one had four faces:
Eze 10:19 and **e.** one stood at the door
Eze 10:21 **E.** one had four faces apiece, and
Eze 10:21 and **e.** one four wings;
Eze 10:22 they went **e.** one straight forward. 376
Eze 11:5 into your mind, **e.** one of them,
Eze 12:14 And I will scatter toward **e.** wind 3605
Eze 12:22 The days are prolonged, and **e.** 3605
Eze 12:23 at hand, and the effect of **e.** vision 3605
Eze 13:18 kerchiefs upon the head of **e.** stature 3605
Eze 14:4 **E.** man of the house of Israel
Eze 14:7 **e.** one of the house of Israel, 376
Eze 16:15 thy fornications on **e.** one that 3605
Eze 16:24 made thee an high place in **e.** street. 3605
Eze 16:25 built thy high place at **e.** head of 3605
Eze 16:25 opened thy feet to **e.** one that 3605
Eze 16:31 eminent place in the head of **e.** way, 3605
Eze 16:31 makest thine high place in **e.** street; 3605
Eze 16:33 may come unto thee on **e.** side 5437
Eze 16:44 Behold, **e.** one that useth proverbs 3605
Eze 17:23 under it shall dwell all fowl of **e.** 3605
Eze 18:30 **e.** one according to his ways, saith 376
Eze 19:8 the nations set against him on **e.** 5437
Eze 20:7 Cast ye away **e.** man the
Eze 20:8 they did not **e.** man cast away
Eze 20:28 then they saw **e.** high hill, and all 3605
Eze 20:39 Go ye, serve ye **e.** one his idols, 376
Eze 20:47 **e.** green tree in thee, and **e.** dry 3605
Eze 21:7 and **e.** heart shall melt, and all 3605
Eze 21:7 and **e.** spirit shall faint, 3605
Eze 21:10 the rod of my son, as **e.** tree. 3605
Eze 22:6 **e.** one were in thee to their power 376
Eze 23:22 bring them against thee on **e.** side; 5437
Eze 24:4 even **e.** good piece, the thigh, and 3605
Eze 26:16 and shall tremble at **e.** moment, and
Eze 28:13 **e.** precious stone was thy covering, 3605
Eze 28:23 by the sword upon her on **e.** side; 5437
Eze 29:18 **e.** head was made bald, and 3605
Eze 29:18 and **e.** shoulder was peeled; 3605
Eze 32:10 and they shall tremble at **e.** moment,
Eze 32:10 **e.** man for his own life, in the day
Eze 33:20 I will judge you **e.** one after his ways 376
Eze 33:26 and ye defile **e.** one his neighbour's 376
Eze 33:30 **e.** one to his brother, saying, 376
Eze 34:6 the mountains, and upon **e.** high 3605
Eze 34:8 my flock became meat to **e.** beast 3605
Eze 36:3 and swallowed you up on **e.** side, 5437
Eze 37:21 and will gather them on **e.** side, 5437
Eze 38:20 and **e.** wall shall fall to the ground 3605
Eze 38:21 **e.** man's sword shall be against
Eze 39:4 unto the ravenous birds of **e.** sort, 3605
Eze 39:17 Speak unto **e.** feathered fowl, and 3605
Eze 39:17 and to **e.** beast of the field, 3605
Eze 39:17 gather yourselves on **e.** side to 5437
Eze 40:7 **e.** little chamber was one reed long,
Eze 41:5 and the breadth of **e.** side chamber,
Eze 41:5 round about the house on **e.** side. 5437
Eze 41:10 round about the house on **e.** side. 5437
Eze 41:18 and **e.** cherub had two faces;
Eze 43:25 shalt thou prepare **e.** day a goat for a
Eze 44:5 **e.** going forth of the sanctuary. 3605
Eze 44:29 and **e.** dedicated thing in Israel 3605
Eze 44:30 fruits of all things, and **e.** oblation 3605
Eze 44:30 of **e.** sort of your oblations, 3605
Eze 45:20 for **e.** one that erreth, and for him 376
Eze 46:13 thou shalt prepare it **e.** morning.
Eze 46:14 a meat offering for it **e.** morning,
Eze 46:15 **e.** offering, and the oil, **e.** morning
Eze 46:18 **e.** man from his possession.
Eze 46:21 in **e.** corner of the court there was a
Eze 47:9 come to pass, that **e.** thing that 3605
Eze 47:9 and **e.** thing shall live whither the 3605
Da 3:10 that **e.** man that shall hear the 3606
Da 3:29 **e.** people, nation, and language, 3606

Da 6:12 that **e.** man that shall ask a petition..... 3606
Da 6:26 in **e.** dominion of my kingdom............ 3606
Da 11:36 and magnify himself above **e.** god,....... 3605
Da 12:1 **e.** one shall be found written in.......... 3605
Ho 4:3 **e.** one that dwelleth therein shall.......... 3605
Ho 9:1 thou hast loved a reward upon **e.**........ 3605
Joe 2:7 and they shall march **e.** one on his........ 376
Joe 2:8 they shall walk **e.** one in his path:....... 1397
Am 2:8 clothes laid to pledge by **e.** altar,........ 3605
Am 4:3 **e.** cow at that which is before her;....... 802
Am 4:4 bring your sacrifices **e.** morning,..............
Am 8:3 be many dead bodies in **e.** place;......... 3605
Am 8:8 **e.** one mourn that dwelleth therein?..... 3605
Am 8:10 all loins, and baldness upon **e.** head;.... 3605
Ob 9 **e.** one of the mount of Esau................ 376
Jon 1:5 and cried **e.** man unto his god,................
Jon 1:7 and they said **e.** one to his fellow,......... 376
Jon 3:8 them turn **e.** one from his evil way,...... 376
Mic 4:4 sit **e.** man under his vine and under..........
Mic 4:5 walk **e.** one in the name of his god,........ 376
Mic 7:2 hunt **e.** man his brother with a net...........
Hab 1:10 they shall divide **e.** stronghold; for....... 3605
Zep 2:11 **e.** one from his place, even all the........ 376
Zep 2:15 **e.** one that passeth by her shall......... 3605
Zep 3:5 **e.** morning doth he bring his judgment........
Zep 3:19 fame in **e.** land where they have......... 3605
Hag 1:9 ye run **e.** man unto his own house.............
Hag 2:14 and so is **e.** work of their hands;......... 3605
Hag 2:22 **e.** one by the sword of his brother........ 376
Zec 3:10 call **e.** man his neighbour under.................
Zec 5:3 **e.** one that stealeth shall be cut.......... 3605
Zec 5:3 **e.** one that sweareth shall be cut........ 3605
Zec 7:9 compassions **e.** man to his brother:............
Zec 8:4 **e.** man with his staff in his hand...............
Zec 8:10 men **e.** one against his neighbour.............
Zec 8:16 **e.** man the truth to his neighbour;.............
Zec 10:1 to **e.** one grass in the field.................. 376
Zec 10:4 out of him **e.** oppressor together.......... 3605
Zec 11:6 **e.** one into his neighbour's hand,.......... 376
Zec 11:9 rest eat **e.** one the flesh of another....... 802
Zec 12:4 smite **e.** horse with astonishment,......... 3605
Zec 12:4 **e.** horse of the people with blindness... 3605
Zec 12:12 the land shall mourn, **e.** family apart;.........
Zec 12:14 families that remain, **e.** family apart,..........
Zec 13:4 be ashamed **e.** one of his vision............ 376
Zec 14:13 **e.** one on the hand of his neighbour,...... 376
Zec 14:16 **e.** one that is left of all the nations...... 3605
Zec 14:21 **e.** pot in Jerusalem and in Judah.......... 3605
Mal 1:11 in **e.** place incense shall be offered...... 3605
Mal 2:10 do we deal treacherously **e.** man................
Mal 2:17 **E.** one that doeth evil is good in......... 3605
Mt 3:10 **e.** tree which bringeth not forth............ *3956*
Mt 4:4 **but by e. word that proceedeth out.** *3956*
Mt 7:8 **For e. one that asketh receiveth;**.... *3956*
Mt 7:17 **so e. good tree bringeth forth good.** *3956*
Mt 7:19 **E. tree that bringeth not forth**....... *3956*
Mt 7:21 **Not e. one that saith unto me,**........... *3956*
Mt 7:26 **e. one that heareth these sayings**... *3956*
Mt 8:33 **e.** thing, and what was befallen........... *3956*
Mt 9:35 healing **e.** sickness and **e.** disease........ *3956*
Mt 12:25 **E. kingdom divided against**............ *3956*
Mt 12:25 **e. city or house divided against**...... *3956*
Mt 12:36 **e. idle word that men shall speak.**. *3956*
Mt 13:47 **the sea, and gathered of e. kind:**.... *3956*
Mt 13:52 **e. scribe which is instructed**.......... *3956*
Mt 15:13 **E. plant, which my heavenly**......... *3956*
Mt 16:27 **e. man according to his works**....... *1538*
Mt 18:16 **e. word may be established**............ *3956*
Mt 18:35 **e. one his brother their trespasses**.. *1538*
Mt 19:3 put away his wife for **e.** cause?............ *3956*
Mt 19:29 **e. one that hath forsaken houses,**... *3956*
Mt 20:9 **they received e. man a penny**.......... *303*
Mt 20:10 **likewise received e. man a penny**..... *303*
Mt 25:15 **e. man according to his several**...... *1538*
Mt 25:29 **e. one that hath shall be given,**...... *3956*
Mt 26:22 **e.** one of them to say unto him,........... *1538*
Mk 1:45 they came to him from **e.** quarter........ *3836*
Mk 7:14 **Hearken unto me e. one of you**...... *3956*
Mk 8:25 restored, and saw **e.** man clearly.......... *537*
Mk 9:49 **e. one shall be salted with fire,**...... *3956*
Mk 9:49 **and e. sacrifice shall be salted**....... *3956*
Mk 13:34 **and to e. man his work, and**.......... *1538*
Mk 15:24 them, what **e.** man should take........... *5100*
Mk 16:15 **preach the gospel to e. creature**..... *3956*
Mk 16:20 went forth, and preached **e.** where...... *3837*
Lu 2:3 to be taxed, **e.** one into his own city.... *1538*
Lu 2:23 **E.** male that openeth the womb.......... *3956*
Lu 2:41 **e.** year at the feast of the passover..... *2596*
Lu 3:5 **E.** valley shall be filled,.................... *3956*
Lu 3:5 and **e.** mountain and hill shall be.......... *3956*
Lu 3:9 **e.** tree therefore which bringeth not.... *3956*
Lu 4:4 **but by e. word of God**..................... *3956*
Lu 4:37 fame of him went out into **e.** place....... *3956*
Lu 4:40 laid his hands on **e.** one of them,......... *1538*
Lu 5:17 come out of **e.** town of Galilee,............ *3956*
Lu 6:30 **Give to e. man that asketh of thee;** *3956*
Lu 6:40 **but e. one that is perfect shall be**... *3956*
Lu 6:44 **e. tree is known by his own fruit**... *1538*
Lu 8:1 that he went throughout **e.** city............ *2596*
Lu 8:4 were come to him out of **e.** city,......... *2596*
Lu 9:6 the gospel, and healing **e.** where.......... *3837*
Lu 9:43 they wondered **e.** one at all things....... *3956*
Lu 10:1 into **e.** city and place, whither he......... *3956*
Lu 11:4 **forgive e. one that is indebted to**.... *3956*
Lu 11:10 **For e. one that asketh receiveth;**..... *3956*
Lu 11:17 **E. kingdom divided against itself**... *3956*
Lu 16:5 **called e. one of his lord's debtors**... *1538*
Lu 16:16 **and e. man presseth into it**............ *3956*
Lu 16:19 **and fared sumptuously e. day:**....... *2596*
Lu 18:14 **e. one that exalteth himself shall**... *3956*
Lu 19:15 **how much e. man had gained**......... *5101*
Lu 19:26 **e. one which hath shall be given**.... *3956*
Lu 19:43 **and keep thee in on e. side,**........... *3840*
Joh 1:9 lighteth **e.** man that cometh into.......... *3956*
Joh 2:10 **E.** man at the beginning doth set......... *3956*
Joh 3:8 **e. one that is born of the Spirit**...... *3956*
Joh 3:20 **e. one that doeth evil hateth the**.... *3956*
Joh 6:7 **e.** one of them may take a little........... *1538*
Joh 6:40 **e. one which seeth the Son, and**..... *3956*
Joh 6:45 **E. man therefore that hath heard,**. *3956*
Joh 7:23 **I have made a man e. whit whole**... *3650*
Joh 7:53 **e.** man went unto his own house........... *1538*
Joh 13:10 **but is clean e. whit: and ye are**....... *3650*
Joh 15:2 **E. branch in me that beareth not**... *3956*
Joh 15:2 **and e. branch that beareth fruit,**.... *3956*
Joh 16:32 **be scattered, e. man to his own,**..... *1538*
Joh 18:37 **E. one that is of the truth heareth.** *3956*
Joh 19:23 four parts, to **e.** soldier a part;........... *1538*
Joh 21:25 if they should be written **e.** one,........... *2596*
Ac 2:5 out of **e.** nation under heaven............. *3956*
Ac 2:6 **e.** man heard them speak in his.......... *1538*
Ac 2:8 hear we **e.** man in our own tongue,...... *1538*
Ac 2:38 and be baptized **e.** one of you............ *1538*
Ac 2:43 fear came upon **e.** soul: and many......... *3956*
Ac 2:45 all men, as **e.** man had need.............. *5100*
Ac 3:23 shall come to pass, that **e.** soul,.......... *3956*
Ac 3:26 in turning away **e.** one of you.............. *1538*
Ac 4:35 **e.** man according as he had need......... *1538*
Ac 5:16 and they were healed **e.** one................ *537*
Ac 5:42 and in **e.** house, they ceased not......... *2596*
Ac 8:3 entering into **e.** house, and haling......... *2596*
Ac 8:4 **e.** where preaching the word............... *1330*
Ac 10:35 in **e.** nation he that feareth him,.......... *3956*
Ac 11:29 **e.** man according to his ability,........... *1538*
Ac 13:27 which are read **e.** sabbath day,........... *3956*
Ac 14:23 ordained them elders in **e.** church,........ *2596*
Ac 15:21 in **e.** city them that preach him,.......... *2596*
Ac 15:21 in the synagogues **e.** sabbath day........ *3956*
Ac 15:36 and visit our brethren in **e.** city.......... *3956*
Ac 16:26 and **e.** one's bands were loosed.......... *3956*
Ac 17:27 he be not far from **e.** one of us:.......... *1538*
Ac 17:30 commandeth all men **e.** where to.......... *3837*
Ac 18:4 in the synagogue **e.** sabbath,............... *3956*
Ac 20:23 Holy Ghost witnesseth in **e.** city,.......... *2596*
Ac 20:31 to warn **e.** one night and day.............. *1538*
Ac 21:26 be offered for **e.** one of them............. *1538*
Ac 21:28 that teacheth all men **e.** where............ *3837*
Ac 22:19 beat in **e.** synagogue them that........... *2596*
Ac 26:11 them oft in **e.** synagogue,................... *3956*
Ac 28:2 and received us **e.** one, because......... *3956*
Ac 28:22 **e.** where it is spoken against................ *3837*
Ro 1:16 salvation to **e.** one that believeth;......... *3956*
Ro 2:6 to **e.** man according to his deeds:......... *1538*
Ro 2:9 **e.** soul of man doeth evil,................... *3956*
Ro 2:10 to **e.** man that worketh good, to the..... *3956*
Ro 3:2 Much **e.** way: chiefly, because that...... *3956*
Ro 3:4 by **e.** man a liar; as it is written.......... *3956*
Ro 3:19 that **e.** mouth may be stopped, and....... *3956*
Ro 10:4 to **e.** one that believeth.................... *3956*
Ro 12:3 to **e.** man that is among you, not......... *3956*
Ro 12:3 as God hath dealt to **e.** man................ *1538*
Ro 12:5 and **e.** one members one of............... *2596*
Ro 13:1 **e.** soul be subject unto the higher....... *3956*
Ro 14:5 another esteemeth **e.** day alike.......... *3956*
Ro 14:5 Let **e.** man be fully persuaded............ *1538*
Ro 14:11 **e.** knee shall bow to me,.................... *3956*
Ro 14:11 and **e.** tongue shall confess to God...... *3956*
Ro 14:12 **e.** one of us shall give account............ *1538*
Ro 15:2 **e.** one of us please his neighbour........ *1538*
1Co 1:2 with all that in **e.** place call upon......... *3956*
1Co 1:5 That in **e.** thing ye are enriched.......... *3956*
1Co 1:12 **e.** one of you saith, I am of Paul:......... *1538*
1Co 3:5 as the Lord gave to **e.** man?............... *1538*
1Co 3:8 **e.** man shall receive his own............. *1538*
1Co 3:10 let **e.** man take heed how he.............. *1538*
1Co 3:13 **E.** man's work shall be made............. *1538*
1Co 3:13 the fire shall try **e.** man's work.......... *1538*
1Co 4:5 shall **e.** man have praise of God.......... *1538*
1Co 4:17 as I teach **e.** where in....................... *3837*
1Co 4:17 as I teach...in **e.** church..................... *3956*
1Co 6:18 **E.** sin that a man doeth is without....... *3956*
1Co 7:2 let **e.** man have his own wife,............. *1538*
1Co 7:2 and let **e.** woman have her own.......... *1538*
1Co 7:7 **e.** man hath his proper gift of.............. *1538*
1Co 7:17 distributed to **e.** man, as the Lord....... *1538*
1Co 7:17 as the Lord hath called **e.** one, so....... *1538*
1Co 7:20 **e.** man abide in the same calling.......... *1538*
1Co 7:24 let **e.** man, wherein he is called,......... *1538*
1Co 8:7 Howbeit there is not in **e.** man............ *3956*
1Co 9:25 And **e.** man that striveth for the......... *3956*
1Co 10:24 but **e.** man another's wealth,.............. *1538*
1Co 11:3 the head of **e.** man is Christ;............... *3956*
1Co 11:4 **E.** man praying or prophesying,........... *3956*
1Co 11:5 But **e.** woman that prayeth or............ *3956*
1Co 11:21 in eating **e.** one taketh before............. *1538*
1Co 12:7 given to **e.** man to profit withal........... *1538*
1Co 12:11 to **e.** man severally as he will............. *1538*
1Co 12:18 **e.** one of them in the body,................ *1538*
1Co 14:26 **e.** one of you hath a psalm,............... *1538*
1Co 15:23 But **e.** man in his own order:............. *1538*
1Co 15:30 stand we in jeopardy **e.** hour?............. *3956*
1Co 15:38 and to **e.** seed his own body.............. *1538*
1Co 16:2 **e.** one of you lay by him in store,........ *1538*
1Co 16:16 and to **e.** one that helpeth with us,...... *3956*
2Co 2:14 his knowledge by us in **e.** place........... *3956*
2Co 4:2 to **e.** man's conscience in the sight...... *3956*
2Co 4:8 We are troubled one **e.** side,....... *1722,3956*
2Co 5:10 **e.** one may receive the things............ *1538*
2Co 7:5 but we were troubled one **e.** side;....... *3956*
2Co 8:7 as ye abound in **e.** thing,..................... *376*
2Co 9:7 **E.** man according as he...................... *1538*
2Co 9:8 may abound to **e.** good work:............. *3956*
2Co 9:11 in **e.** thing to all bountifulness,........... *3956*
2Co 10:5 **e.** high thing that exalteth itself.......... *3956*
2Co 10:5 **e.** thought to the obedience of............ *3956*
2Co 13:1 shall **e.** word be established.............. *3956*
Ga 3:10 **e.** one that continueth not in all.......... *3956*
Ga 3:13 is **e.** one that hangeth on a tree:.......... *3956*
Ga 5:3 For I testify again to **e.** man that........ *3956*
Ga 6:4 let **e.** man prove his own work,............ *1538*
Ga 6:5 **e.** man shall bear his own burden......... *1538*
Eph 1:21 and **e.** name that is named, not........... *3956*
Eph 4:7 unto **e.** one of us is given grace.......... *1538*
Eph 4:14 about with **e.** wind of doctrine,........... *3956*
Eph 4:16 by that which **e.** joint supplieth,......... *3596*
Eph 4:16 in the measure of **e.** part,........... *1520,1538*
Eph 4:25 **e.** man truth with his neighbour:.. *1520,1538*
Eph 5:24 to their own husbands in **e.** thing........ *3956*
Eph 5:33 let **e.** one of you in particular...... *2596,1520*
Php 1:3 upon **e.** remembrance of you,............. *3956*
Php 1:4 in **e.** prayer of mine for you all........... *3956*
Php 1:18 notwithstanding, **e.** way, whether......... *3956*
Php 2:4 not **e.** man on his own things,............. *1538*
Php 2:4 but **e.** man also on the things of.......... *1538*
Php 2:9 a name which is above **e.** name:.......... *3596*
Php 2:10 name of Jesus **e.** knee should bow,....... *3596*
Php 2:11 And that **e.** tongue should confess....... *3596*
Php 4:6 **e.** thing by prayer and supplication....... *3596*
Php 4:12 **e.** where and in all things I am........... *3596*
Php 4:21 Salute **e.** saint in Christ Jesus............ *3596*
Col 1:10 being fruitful in **e.** good work,............ *3596*
Col 1:15 God, the firstborn of **e.** creature:......... *3596*
Col 1:23 to **e.** creature which is under............... *3596*
Col 1:28 warning **e.** man, and teaching **e.** man... *3596*
Col 1:28 that we may present **e.** man.............. *3596*
Col 4:6 ye ought to answer **e.** man......... *1519,1538*

1Th 1:8 in **e.** place your faith to God-ward ... *3956*
1Th 2:11 and charged **e.** one of you, ... *1538*
1Th 4:4 That **e.** one of you should know ... *1538*
1Th 5:18 In **e.** thing give thanks: for this ... *3956*
2Th 1:3 the charity of **e.** one you all ... *1538*
2Th 2:17 stablish you in **e.** good word and ... *3956*
2Th 3:6 **e.** brother that walketh disorderly, ... *3956*
2Th 3:17 which is the token in **e.** epistle: ... *3956*
1Ti 2:8 that men pray **e.** where, ... *1722,3956*
1Ti 4:4 For **e.** creature of God is good, ... *3956*
1Ti 5:10 diligently followed **e.** good work. ... *3956*
2Ti 2:19 Let **e.** one that nameth the name ... *3956*
2Ti 2:21 and prepared unto **e.** good work ... *3956*
2Ti 4:18 shall deliver me from **e.** evil work, ... *3956*
Tit 1:5 and ordain elders in **e.** city, as I ... *2596*
Tit 1:16 and unto **e.** good work reprobate ... *3956*
Tit 3:1 to be ready to **e.** good work, ... *3956*
Phm 6 the acknowledging of **e.** good thing ... *3956*
Heb 2:2 **e.** transgression and disobedience ... *3956*
Heb 2:9 God should taste death for **e.** man. ... *3956*
Heb 3:4 For **e.** house is builded by some ... *3956*
Heb 5:1 For **e.** high priest taken from among ... *3956*
Heb 5:13 For **e.** one that useth milk is ... *3956*
Heb 6:11 desire that **e.** one of you do shew ... *1538*
Heb 8:3 For **e.** high priest is ordained to ... *3956*
Heb 8:11 **e.** man his neighbour, and **e.** man ... *1538*
Heb 9:7 high priest alone once **e.** year, ...
Heb 9:19 spoken **e.** precept to all the people ... *3956*
Heb 9:25 the high priest entereth...**e.** year ... *2596*
Heb 10:3 again made of sins **e.** year. ... *2596*
Heb 10:11 And **e.** priest standeth daily ... *3956*
Heb 12:1 let us lay aside **e.** weight, and the ... *3956*
Heb 12:6 and scourgeth **e.** son whom he ... *3956*
Heb 13:21 in **e.** good work to do his will, ... *3956*
Jas 1:14 **e.** man is tempted, when he is ... *1538*
Jas 1:17 **E.** good gift and **e.** perfect gift ... *3956*
Jas 1:19 let **e.** man be swift to hear, slow to ... *3956*
Jas 3:7 For **e.** king of beasts, and of birds, ... *3956*
Jas 3:16 there is confusion and **e.** evil work. ... *3956*
1Pe 1:17 according to **e.** man's work, ... *1538*
1Pe 2:13 yourself to **e.** ordinance of man ... *3956*
1Pe 3:15 answer to **e.** man that asketh you ... *3956*
1Pe 4:10 As **e.** man hath received the gift, ... *1538*
1Jo 2:29 **e.** one that doeth righteousness is ... *3956*
1Jo 3:3 And **e.** man that hath this hope ... *3956*
1Jo 4:1 believe not **e.** spirit, but try the ... *3956*
1Jo 4:2 **E.** spirit that confesseth that Jesus ... *3956*
1Jo 4:3 And **e.** spirit that confesseth not ... *3956*
1Jo 4:7 **e.** one that loveth is born of God, ... *3956*
1Jo 5:1 **e.** one that loveth him that begat, ... *3956*
Re 1:7 **e.** eye shall see him, and they also ... *3956*
Re 2:23 I will give unto **e.** one of you ... *1538*
Re 5:8 having **e.** one of them harps, and ... *1538*
Re 5:9 out of **e.** kindred, and tongue, ... *3956*
Re 5:13 And **e.** creature which is in heaven, ... *3956*
Re 6:11 were given unto **e.** one of them; ... *1538*
Re 6:14 **e.** mountain and island were ... *3956*
Re 6:15 **e.** bondman, and **e.** free man, hid ... *3956*
Re 14:6 **e.** nation, and kindred, and tongue, ... *3956*
Re 16:3 and **e.** living soul died in the sea. ... *3956*
Re 16:20 And **e.** island fled away, and the ... *3956*
Re 16:21 **e.** stone about the weight of a ...
Re 18:2 the hold of **e.** foul spirit, and a cage ... *3956*
Re 18:2 of **e.** unclean and hateful bird ... *3956*
Re 18:17 **e.** shipmaster, and all the company ... *3956*
Re 20:13 were judged **e.** man according to ... *1538*
Re 21:21 **e.** several gate was of one pearl: ... *1538*
Re 22:2 yielded her fruit **e.** month: ..*2596, 1520,1538*
Re 22:12 to give **e.** man according as his ... *1538*
Re 22:18 I testify unto **e.** man that heareth ... *3956*

EVERYONE See EVERY and ONE.

EVERYTHING See EVERY and THING.

EVERYWHERE See EVERY and WHERE.

EVI (e'-vi)
Nu 31:8 namely, **E.**, and Rekem, and Zur, ... 189
Jos 13:21 with the princes of Midian, **E.**, and ... 189

EVIDENCE See also EVIDENCES.
Jer 32:10 I subscribed the **e.**, and sealed it, ... 5612
Jer 32:11 So I took the **e.** of the purchase, ... 5612
Jer 32:12 And I gave the **e.** of the purchase ... 5612
Jer 32:14 this **e.** of the purchase, ... 5612
Jer 32:14 and this **e.** which is open; ... 5612
Jer 32:16 delivered the **e.** of the purchase ... 5612
Heb 11:1 the **e.** of things not seen. ... *1650*

EVIDENCES
Jer 32:14 Take these **e.**, this evidence of the ... 5612
Jer 32:44 and subscribe **e.**, and seal them, ... 5612

EVIDENT
Job 6:28 for it is **e.** unto you if I lie. ... 5921,6440
Ga 3:11 in the sight of God, it is **e.**: for, ... *1212*
Php 1:28 is to them an **e.** token of perdition, ... *1732*
Heb 7:14 For it is **e.** that our Lord sprang ... *4271*
Heb 7:15 And it is yet far more **e.**: for that ... *2612*

EVIDENTLY
Ac 10:3 He saw in a vision **e.**, about the ... *5320*
Ga 3:1 Jesus Christ hath been **e.** set forth, ... *4270*

EVIL See also EVILDOER; EVILFAVOUREDNESS; EVILS.
Ge 2:9 tree of knowledge of good and **e.** ... 7451
Ge 2:17 of the knowledge of good and **e.**, ... 7451
Ge 3:5 be as gods, knowing good and **e.** ... 7451
Ge 3:22 as one of us, to know good and **e.**: ... 7451
Ge 6:5 of his heart was only **e.** continually. ... 7451
Ge 8:21 imagination of man's heart is **e.** ... 7451
Ge 19:19 lest some **e.** take me, and I die: ... 7451
Ge 37:2 unto his father their **e.** report. ... 7451
Ge 37:20 Some **e.** beast hath devoured him: ... 7451
Ge 37:33 an **e.** beast hath devoured him; ... 7451
Ge 44:4 have ye rewarded **e.** for good? ... 7451
Ge 44:5 ye have done **e.** in so doing. ... 7489
Ge 44:34 lest...I see the **e.** that shall come ... 7451
Ge 47:9 few and **e.** have the days of the ... 7451
Ge 48:16 which redeemed me from all **e.**, ... 7451
Ge 50:15 the **e.** which we did unto him. ... 7451
Ge 50:17 their sin; for they did unto thee **e.**: ... 7451
Ge 50:20 for you, ye thought **e.** against me; ... 7451
Ex 5:19 Israel did see they were in **e.** case, ... 7451
Ex 5:22 hast thou so **e.** entreated this ... 7489
Ex 5:23 he hath done **e.** to this people; ... 7489
Ex 10:10 look to it; for **e.** is before you. ... 7451
Ex 23:2 not follow a multitude to do **e.**; ... 7451
Ex 32:12 repent of this **e.** against thy people. ... 7451
Ex 32:14 **e.** which he thought to do unto his ... 7451
Ex 33:4 the people heard these **e.** tidings, ... 7451
Le 5:4 pronouncing with his lips to do **e.**, ... 7489
Le 26:6 I will rid **e.** beasts out of the land, ... 7451
Nu 13:32 they brought up an **e.** report of ... 1681
Nu 14:27 I bear with this **e.** congregation, ... 7451
Nu 14:35 do it unto all this **e.** congregation, ... 7451
Nu 14:37 that did bring up the **e.** report ... 7451
Nu 20:5 to bring us in unto this **e.** place? ... 7451
Nu 32:13 the generation, that had done **e.** in ... 7451
De 1:35 these men of this **e.** generation see ... 7451
De 1:39 knowledge between good and **e.**, ... 7451
De 4:25 do **e.** in the sight of the Lord ... 7451
De 7:15 none of the **e.** diseases of Egypt, ... 7451
De 13:5 So shalt thou put the **e.** away ... 7451
De 15:9 thine eye be **e.** against thy poor ... 7489
De 17:7 put the **e.** away from among you. ... 7451
De 17:12 shalt put away the **e.** from Israel. ... 7451
De 19:19 put the **e.** away from among you. ... 7451
De 19:20 commit no more any such **e.** among ... 7451
De 21:21 so shalt thou put **e.** away from ... 7451
De 22:14 and bring up an **e.** name upon her, ... 7451
De 22:19 brought up an **e.** name upon a ... 7451
De 22:21 thou put **e.** away from among you ... 7451
De 22:22 shalt thou put away **e.** from Israel. ... 7451
De 22:24 thou shalt put away **e.** from among ... 7451
De 24:7 shalt put **e.** away from among you. ... 7451
De 26:6 the Egyptians **e.** entreated us, ... 7489
De 28:54 eye shall be **e.** toward his brother, ... 7489
De 28:56 her eye shall be **e.** toward the ... 7489
De 29:21 Lord shall separate him unto **e.** ... 7451
De 30:15 life and good, and death and **e.**; ... 7451
De 31:29 **e.** will befall you in the latter days; ... 7451
De 31:29 will do **e.** in the sight of the Lord, ... 7451
Jos 23:15 Lord bring upon you all **e.** things, ... 7451
Jos 24:15 if it seem **e.** unto you to serve the ... 7489
Jg 2:11 children of Israel did **e.** in the ... 7451
Jg 2:15 the Lord was against them for **e.**, ... 7451
Jg 3:7 did **e.** in the sight of the Lord, ... 7451
Jg 3:12 did **e.** again in the sight of the Lord: ... 7451
Jg 3:12 they had done **e.** in the sight of the ... 7451
Jg 4:1 the children of Israel again did **e.** ... 7451
Jg 6:1 children of Israel did **e.** in the sight ... 7451
Jg 9:23 God sent an **e.** spirit between ... 7451
Jg 9:57 all the **e.** of the men of Shechem ... 7451
Jg 10:6 did **e.** again in the sight of the Lord, ... 7451
Jg 13:1 did **e.** again in the sight of the Lord; ... 7451
Jg 20:13 death, and put away **e.** from Israel. ... 7451
Jg 20:34 but they knew not that **e.** was near ... 7451
Jg 20:41 saw that **e.** was come upon them. ... 7451
1Sa 2:23 I hear of your **e.** dealings by all this ... 7451
1Sa 6:9 he hath done us this great **e.**: ... 7451
1Sa 12:19 have added unto all our sins this **e.**, ... 7451
1Sa 15:19 didst **e.** in the sight of the Lord? ... 7451
1Sa 16:14 an **e.** spirit from the Lord troubled ... 7451
1Sa 16:15 **e.** spirit from God troubleth thee. ... 7451
1Sa 16:16 the **e.** spirit from God is upon thee, ... 7451
1Sa 16:23 it came to pass, when the **e.** spirit ... 7451
1Sa 16:23 the **e.** spirit departed from him. ... 7451
1Sa 18:10 **e.** spirit from God came upon Saul, ... 7451
1Sa 19:9 **e.** spirit from the Lord was upon ... 7451
1Sa 20:7 sure that **e.** is determined by him. ... 7451
1Sa 20:9 certainly that **e.** were determined ... 7451
1Sa 20:13 if it please my father to do thee **e.**, ... 7451
1Sa 24:11 **e.** nor transgression in mine hand, ... 7451
1Sa 24:17 whereas I have rewarded thee **e.** ... 7451
1Sa 25:3 was churlish and **e.** in his doings; ... 7451
1Sa 25:17 **e.** is determined against our master, ... 7451
1Sa 25:21 he hath requited me **e.** for good ... 7451
1Sa 25:26 they that seek **e.** to my lord, ... 7451
1Sa 25:28 and **e.** hath not been found in thee ... 7451
1Sa 25:39 and hath kept his servant from **e.**: ... 7451
1Sa 26:18 or what **e.** is in mine hand? ... 7451
1Sa 29:6 I have not found **e.** in thee ... 7451
2Sa 3:39 reward the doer of **e.** according ... 7451
2Sa 12:9 the Lord to do **e.** in his sight? ... 7451
2Sa 12:11 I will raise up **e.** against thee ... 7451
2Sa 13:16 **e.** in sending me away is greater ... 7451
2Sa 15:14 us suddenly, and bring **e.** upon us, ... 7451
2Sa 17:14 Lord might bring **e.** upon Absalom. ... 7451
2Sa 19:7 than all the **e.** that befell thee ... 7451
2Sa 19:35 I discern between good and **e.**? ... 7451
2Sa 24:16 the Lord repented him of the **e.**, ... 7451
1Ki 5:4 neither adversary nor **e.** occurrent ... 7451
1Ki 9:9 Lord brought upon them all this **e.** ... 7451
1Ki 11:6 Solomon did **e.** in the sight of the ... 7451
1Ki 13:33 Jeroboam returned not from his **e.** ... 7451
1Ki 14:9 done **e.** above all that were before ... 7489
1Ki 14:10 **e.** upon the house of Jeroboam, ... 7451
1Ki 14:22 Judah did **e.** in the sight of the Lord, .. 7451
1Ki 15:26, 34 did **e.** in the sight of the Lord, ... 7451
1Ki 16:7 **e.** that he did in the sight of the Lord, . 7451
1Ki 16:19 in doing **e.** in the sight of the Lord, ... 7451
1Ki 16:25 Omri wrought **e.** in the eyes of the ... 7451
1Ki 16:30 Ahab the son of Omri did **e.** in the ... 7451
1Ki 17:20 also brought **e.** upon the widow ... 7489
1Ki 21:20 thou hast sold thyself to work **e.** ... 7451
1Ki 21:21 Behold, I will bring **e.** upon thee, ... 7451
1Ki 21:29 I will not bring the **e.** in his days: ... 7451
1Ki 21:29 in his son's days will I bring the **e.** ... 7451
1Ki 22:8 doth not prophesy good...but **e.** ... 7451
1Ki 22:18 he would prophesy no good...but **e.**? ... 7451
1Ki 22:23 Lord hath spoken **e.** concerning ... 7451
1Ki 22:52 he did **e.** in the sight of the Lord, ... 7451
2Ki 3:2 wrought **e.** in the sight of the Lord; ... 7451
2Ki 6:33 Behold, this **e.** is of the Lord; ... 7451
2Ki 8:12 I know the **e.** that thou wilt do ... 7451
2Ki 8:18 he did **e.** in the sight of the Lord. ... 7451
2Ki 8:27 and did **e.** in the sight of the Lord, ... 7451
2Ki 13:2 was **e.** in the sight of the Lord, ... 7451
2Ki 13:11 did that which was **e.** in the sight ... 7451
2Ki 14:24 And he did that which was **e.** in the ... 7451
2Ki 15:9, 18, 24, 28 was **e.** in the sight of the ... 7451
2Ki 17:2 was **e.** in the sight of the Lord, ... 7451
2Ki 17:13 Turn ye from your **e.** ways, and ... 7451
2Ki 17:17 to do **e.** in the sight of the Lord, ... 7451
2Ki 21:2 was **e.** in the sight of the Lord, ... 7451
2Ki 21:9 seduced them to do more **e.** than ... 7451
2Ki 21:12 bringing such **e.** upon Jerusalem ... 7451
2Ki 21:15 done that which was **e.** in my sight, ... 7451
2Ki 21:16 doing that which was **e.** in the sight ... 7451
2Ki 21:20 did that which was **e.** in the sight ... 7451
2Ki 22:16 I will bring **e.** upon this place, ... 7451
2Ki 22:20 all the **e.** which I will bring upon ... 7451
2Ki 23:32, 37 he did that which was **e.** in the ... 7451
2Ki 24:9, 19 that which was **e.** in the sight ... 7451
1Ch 2:3 Er, the firstborn of Judah, was **e.** ... 7451
1Ch 4:10 thou wouldest keep me from **e.**, ... 7451
1Ch 7:23 because it went **e.** with his house ... 7451
1Ch 21:15 and he repented him of the **e.**, ... 7451
1Ch 21:17 is that have sinned and done **e.** ... 7489
2Ch 7:22 he brought all this **e.** upon them ... 7451
2Ch 12:14 he did **e.**, because he prepared ... 7451
2Ch 18:7 good unto me, but always **e.**: ... 7451
2Ch 18:17 prophesy good unto me, but **e.**? ... 7451

Book	Ref	Context	Strong's
2Ch	18:22	Lord hath spoken **e.** against thee	7451
2Ch	20:9	**e.** cometh upon us, as the sword,	7451
2Ch	21:6	was **e.** in the eyes of the Lord,	7451
2Ch	22:4	he did **e.** in the sight of the Lord	7451
2Ch	29:6	done that which was **e.** in the eyes	7451
2Ch	33:2	was **e.** in the sight of the Lord,	7451
2Ch	33:6	much **e.** in the sight of the Lord,	7451
2Ch	33:22	did that which was **e.** in the sight	7451
2Ch	34:24	I will bring **e.** upon this place,	7451
2Ch	34:28	**e.** that I will bring upon this place,	7451
2Ch	36:5	**e.** in the sight of the Lord his God.	7451
2Ch	36:9	was **e.** in the sight of the Lord.	7451
2Ch	36:12	he did that which was **e.** in the	7451
Ezr	9:13	is come upon us for our **e.** deeds,	7451
Ne	6:13	might have matter for an **e.** report,	7451
Ne	9:28	they did **e.** again before thee:	7451
Ne	13:7	understood of the **e.** that Eliashib	7451
Ne	13:17	What **e.** thing is this that ye do,	7451
Ne	13:18	our God bring all this **e.** upon us,	7451
Ne	13:27	to do all this great **e.**, to transgress	7451
Es	7:7	there was **e.** determined against	7451
Es	8:6	**e.** that shall come unto my people?	7451
Job	1:1	that feared god, and eschewed **e.**.	7451
Job	1:8	that feareth God, and escheweth **e.**?	7451
Job	2:3	that feareth God, and escheweth **e.**?	7451
Job	2:10	God, and shall we not receive **e.**?	7451
Job	2:11	this **e.** that was come upon him	7451
Job	5:19	seven there shall no **e.** touch thee.	7451
Job	8:20	neither will he help the **e.** doers:	7489
Job	24:21	He **e.** entreateth the barren that	7462
Job	28:28	depart from **e.** is understanding.	7451
Job	30:26	for good, then **e.** came upon me:	7451
Job	31:29	lifted up myself when **e.** found him:	7451
Job	35:12	because of the pride of **e.** men.	7451
Job	42:11	the **e.** that the Lord had brought	7451
Ps	5:4	neither shall **e.** dwell with thee.	7451
Ps	7:4	If I have rewarded **e.** unto him	7451
Ps	10:15	arm of the wicked and the **e.** man:	7451
Ps	15:3	nor doeth **e.** to his neighbour, nor	7451
Ps	21:11	For they intended **e.** against thee:	7451
Ps	23:4	I will fear no **e.**: for thou art	7451
Ps	26:5	have hated the congregation of **e.** doers;	
Ps	34:13	Keep thy tongue from **e.**, and thy	7451
Ps	34:14	Depart from **e.**, and do good; seek	7451
Ps	34:16	the Lord is against them that do **e.**,	7451
Ps	34:21	**E.** shall slay the wicked: and they	7451
Ps	35:12	They rewarded me **e.** for good to	7451
Ps	36:4	is not good; he abhorreth not **e.**.	7451
Ps	37:8	nor thyself in any wise to do **e.**.	7489
Ps	37:19	not be ashamed in the **e.** time:	7451
Ps	37:27	Depart from **e.**, and do good; and	7451
Ps	38:20	They also that render **e.** for good	7451
Ps	40:14	backward...that wish me **e.**.	7451
Ps	41:5	Mine enemies speak **e.** of me,	7451
Ps	41:8	An **e.** disease, say they, cleaveth	1100
Ps	49:5	should I fear in the days of **e.**,	7451
Ps	50:19	Thou givest thy mouth to **e.**, and	7451
Ps	51:4	and done this **e.** in thy sight:	7451
Ps	52:3	Thou lovest **e.** more than good;	7451
Ps	54:5	shall reward **e.** unto mine enemies:	7451
Ps	56:5	their thoughts are against me for **e.**.	7451
Ps	64:5	encourage themselves in an **e.**	7451
Ps	78:49	by sending **e.** angels among them.	7451
Ps	90:15	the years wherein we have seen **e.**	7451
Ps	91:10	There shall no **e.** befall thee,	7451
Ps	97:10	Ye that love the Lord, hate **e.**:	7451
Ps	109:5	have rewarded me **e.** for good,	7451
Ps	109:20	that speak **e.** against my soul.	7451
Ps	112:7	He shall not be afraid of **e.** tidings:	7451
Ps	119:101	refrained my feet from every **e.**	7451
Ps	121:7	Lord shall preserve thee from all **e.**:	7451
Ps	140:1	Deliver me, O Lord, from the **e.**	7451
Ps	140:11	an **e.** speaker be established	
Ps	140:11	**e.** shall hunt the violent man to	7451
Ps	141:4	not my heart to any **e.** thing,	7451
Pr	1:16	their feet run to **e.**, and make haste	7451
Pr	1:33	and shall be quiet from fear of **e.**	7451
Pr	2:12	me from the way of the **e.** man,	7451
Pr	2:14	Who rejoice to do **e.**, and delight	7451
Pr	3:7	fear the Lord, and depart from **e.**	7451
Pr	3:29	not **e.** against thy neighbour,	7451
Pr	4:14	go not in the way of **e.** men.	7451
Pr	4:27	to the left remove thy foot from **e.**	7451
Pr	5:14	I was almost in all **e.** in the midst	7451
Pr	6:24	To keep thee from the **e.** woman,	7451
Pr	8:13	The fear of the Lord is to hate **e.**:	7451
Pr	8:13	pride, and arrogancy, and the **e.**	7451
Pr	11:19	**e.** pursueth it to his own death.	7451
Pr	12:12	wicked desireth the net of **e.** men:	7451
Pr	12:20	the heart of them that imagine **e.**:	7451
Pr	12:21	shall no **e.** happen to the just:	205
Pr	13:19	to fools to depart from **e.**.	7451
Pr	13:21	**E.** pursueth sinners: but to the	7451
Pr	14:16	man feareth, and departeth from **e.**:	7451
Pr	14:19	The **e.** bow before the good;	7451
Pr	14:22	Do they not err that devise **e.**?	7451
Pr	15:3	eyes of the Lord...beholding the **e.**	7451
Pr	15:15	All the days of the afflicted are **e.**:	7451
Pr	15:28	the wicked pureth out **e.** things	7451
Pr	16:4	even the wicked for the day of **e.**.	7451
Pr	16:6	of the Lord men depart from **e.**.	7451
Pr	16:17	of the upright is to depart from **e.**:	7451
Pr	16:27	An ungodly man diggeth up **e.**:	7451
Pr	16:30	his lips he bringeth **e.** to pass.	7451
Pr	17:11	An **e.** man seeketh only rebellion:	7451
Pr	17:13	Whoso rewardeth **e.** for good,	7451
Pr	17:13	**e.** shall not depart from his house	7451
Pr	19:23	he shall not be visited with **e.**.	7451
Pr	20:8	A king...scattereth away all **e.** with	7451
Pr	20:22	Say not thou I will recompense **e.**;	7451
Pr	20:30	of a wound cleanseth away **e.**:	7451
Pr	21:10	The soul of the wicked desireth **e.**;	7451
Pr	22:3	A prudent man foreseeth the **e.**,	7451
Pr	23:6	bread of him that hath an **e.** eye,	7451
Pr	24:1	Be not thou envious against **e.** men,	7451
Pr	24:8	He that deviseth to do **e.** shall be	7489
Pr	24:19	Fret not thyself because of **e.** men.	7489
Pr	24:20	shall be no reward to the **e.** man;	7451
Pr	27:12	A prudent man foreseeth the **e.**,	7451
Pr	28:9	**E.** men understand not judgment:	7451
Pr	28:10	righteous to go astray in an **e.** way,	7451
Pr	28:22	hasteth to be rich hath an **e.** eye,	7451
Pr	29:6	the transgression of an **e.** man	7451
Pr	30:32	or if thou hast thought **e.**, lay thine	
Pr	31:12	She will do him good and not **e.**	7451
Ec	2:21	This also is vanity and a great **e.**	7451
Ec	4:3	**e.** work that is done under the sun.	7451
Ec	5:1	they consider not that they do **e.**.	7451
Ec	5:13	a sore **e.** which I have seen	7451
Ec	5:14	riches perish by **e.** travail: and he	7451
Ec	5:16	this also is a sore **e.**, that in all	7451
Ec	6:1	**e.** which I have seen under the sun,	7451
Ec	6:2	and it is an **e.** disease.	7451
Ec	8:3	stand not in an **e.** thing; for he	7451
Ec	8:5	the commandment shall feel no **e.**	7451
Ec	8:11	sentence against an **e.** work is not	7451
Ec	8:11	men is fully set in them to do **e.**.	7451
Ec	8:12	a sinner do **e.** an hundred times,	7451
Ec	9:3	**e.** among all things that are done	7451
Ec	9:3	heart of the sons of men is full of **e.**,	7451
Ec	9:12	fishes that are taken in an **e.** net,	7451
Ec	9:12	sons of men snared in an **e.** time,	7451
Ec	10:5	**e.** which I have seen under the sun,	7451
Ec	11:2	not what **e.** shall be upon the earth.	7451
Ec	11:10	and put away **e.** from thy flesh:	7451
Ec	12:1	while the **e.** days come not, nor the	7451
Ec	12:14	it be good, or whether it be **e.**.	7451
Isa	1:16	put away the **e.** of your doings	7455
Isa	1:16	before mine eyes, cease to do **e.**;	7489
Isa	3:9	rewarded **e.** unto themselves.	7451
Isa	5:20	them that call **e.** good, and good **e.**;	7451
Isa	7:5	taken **e.** counsel against thee,	7451
Isa	7:15	that he may know to refuse the **e.**,	7451
Isa	7:16	child show to refuse the **e.**,	7451
Isa	13:11	will punish the world for their **e.**,	7451
Isa	31:2	he also is wise, and will bring **e.**	7451
Isa	32:7	instruments also of the churl are **e.**:	7451
Isa	33:15	shutteth his eyes from seeing **e.**;	7451
Isa	41:23	do good,nor do **e.**, that we may be	7489
Isa	45:7	I make peace, and create **e.**: I	7451
Isa	47:11	Therefore shall **e.** come upon thee;	7451
Isa	56:2	his hand from doing any **e.**	7451
Isa	57:1	righteous is taken away from the **e.**	7451
Isa	59:7	Their feet run to **e.**,and they	7451
Isa	59:15	he that departeth from **e.** maketh	7451
Isa	65:12	hear; but did **e.** before mine eyes,	7451
Isa	66:4	but they did **e.** before mine eyes,	7451
Jer	1:14	an **e.** shall break forth upon all the	7451
Jer	2:3	**e.** shall come upon them, saith the	7451
Jer	2:19	it is an **e.** thing and bitter,	7451
Jer	3:5	hast spoken and done **e.** things	7451
Jer	3:17	the imagination of their **e.** heart.	7451
Jer	4:4	because of the **e.** of your doings.	7455
Jer	4:6	I will bring **e.** from the north,	7451
Jer	4:22	they are wise to do **e.**, but to	7489
Jer	5:12	neither shall **e.** come upon us;	7451
Jer	6:1	for **e.** appeareth out of the north,	7451
Jer	6:19	I will bring **e.** upon this people,	7451
Jer	7:24	in the imagination of their **e.** heart,	7451
Jer	7:30	Judah have done **e.** in my sight,	7451
Jer	8:3	them that remain of this **e.** family,	7451
Jer	9:3	they proceed from **e.** to **e.**, and	7451
Jer	10:5	they cannot do **e.**, neither also	7480
Jer	11:8	the imagination of their **e.** heart:	7451
Jer	11:11	Behold, I will bring **e.** upon them,	7451
Jer	11:15	thou doest **e.**, then thou rejoicest.	7451
Jer	11:17	hath pronounced **e.** against thee,	7451
Jer	11:17	for the **e.** of the house of Israel,	7451
Jer	11:23	**e.** upon the men of Anathoth,	7451
Jer	12:14	all mine **e.** neighbours that touch	7451
Jer	13:10	**e.** people, which refuse to hear	7451
Jer	13:23	ye...that are accustomed to do **e.**	7480
Jer	15:11	entreat thee well in the time of **e.**	7451
Jer	16:10	all this great **e.** against us?	7451
Jer	16:12	the imagination of his **e.** heart,	7451
Jer	17:17	thou art my hope in the day of **e.**.	7451
Jer	17:18	bring upon them the day of **e.**,	7451
Jer	18:8	If that nation,...turn from their **e.**,	7451
Jer	18:8	I will repent of the **e.** that I thought	7451
Jer	18:10	If it do **e.** in my sight, that it	7451
Jer	18:11	I frame **e.** against you, and devise	7451
Jer	18:11	ye now every one from his **e.** way,	7451
Jer	18:12	do the imagination of his **e.** heart.	7451
Jer	18:20	Shall **e.** be recompensed for good?	7451
Jer	19:3	I will bring **e.** upon this place,	7451
Jer	19:15	will bring upon this city...all the **e.**	7451
Jer	21:10	set my face against the city for **e.**,	7451
Jer	21:12	because of the **e.** of your doings.	7455
Jer	23:2	visit upon you the **e.** of your doings,	7455
Jer	23:10	their course is **e.**, and their force	7451
Jer	23:12	I will bring **e.** upon them, even	7451
Jer	23:17	No **e.** shall come upon you.	7451
Jer	23:22	turned them from their **e.** way,	7451
Jer	23:22	and from the **e.** of their doings.	7455
Jer	24:3	the **e.**, very **e.**, that cannot be eaten,	7451
Jer	24:3	cannot be eaten, they are so **e.**.	7455
Jer	24:8	the **e.** figs, which cannot be eaten,	7451
Jer	24:8	cannot be eaten, they are so **e.**;	7455
Jer	25:5	ye now every one from his **e.** way,	7451
Jer	25:5	and from the **e.** of your doings,	7455
Jer	25:29	I begin to bring **e.** on the city	7489
Jer	25:32	**e.** shall go forth form nation to	7451
Jer	26:3	turn every man from his **e.** way,	7451
Jer	26:3	that I may repent me of the **e.**,	7451
Jer	26:3	because of the **e.** of their doings.	7455
Jer	26:13	the Lord will repent him of the **e.**	7451
Jer	26:19	the Lord repented him of the **e.**	7451
Jer	26:19	procure great **e.** against our souls,	7451
Jer	28:8	war, and or **e.**, and of pestilence.	7451
Jer	29:11	thoughts of peace, and not of **e.**,	7451
Jer	29:17	cannot be eaten, they are so **e.**.	7455
Jer	32:23	all this **e.** to come upon them:	7451
Jer	32:30	have only done **e.** before me from	7451
Jer	32:32	the **e.** of the children of Israel	7451
Jer	32:42	all this great **e.** upon this people,	7451
Jer	35:15	now every man from his **e.** way,	7451
Jer	35:17	all the **e.** that I have pronounced	7451
Jer	36:3	all the **e.** which I purpose to do	7451
Jer	36:3	return every man from his **e.** way;	7451
Jer	36:7	return every one from his **e.** way:	7451
Jer	36:31	all the **e.** that I have pronounced	7451
Jer	38:9	these men have done **e.** in all	7480
Jer	39:16	my words upon this city for **e.**,	7451
Jer	40:2	pronounced this **e.** upon this place.	7451
Jer	41:11	the **e.** that Ishmael...had done,	7451
Jer	42:6	it be good, or whether it be **e.**,	7451
Jer	42:10	I repent me of the **e.** that I have	7451
Jer	42:17	escape from the **e.** that I will bring	7451
Jer	44:2	seen all the **e.** that I have brought	7451
Jer	44:7	Wherefore commit ye this great **e.**	7451
Jer	44:11	will set my face against you for **e.**,	7451
Jer	44:17	and were will, and saw no **e.**	7451
Jer	44:22	because of the **e.** of your doings,	7455
Jer	44:23	this **e.** is happened unto you,	7451
Jer	44:27	I will watch over them for **e.**,	7451
Jer	44:29	words shall surely stand...for **e.**:	7451
Jer	45:5	I will bring **e.** upon all flesh,	7451
Jer	48:2	they have devised **e.** against it:	7451
Jer	49:23	for they have heard **e.** tidings:	7451
Jer	49:37	and I will bring **e.** upon them,	7451
Jer	51:24	their **e.** that they have done in Zion	7451

Jer 51:60 e. that should come upon Babylon, ... 7451
Jer 51:64 the e. that I will bring upon her: 7451
Jer 52:2 which was e. in the eyes of the Lord, . 7451
La 3:38 High proceedeth not e. and good? 7451
Eze 5:16 upon them the e. arrows of famine. 7451
Eze 5:17 upon you famine and e. beasts, ... 7451
Eze 6:10 said in vain that I would do this e....... 7451
Eze 6:11 all the e. abominations of the house 7451
Eze 7:5 An e., and only e., behold, is come. ... 7451
Eze 14:22 the e. that I have brought upon 7451
Eze 33:11 turn ye from your e. ways; for 7451
Eze 34:25 will cause the e. beasts to cease 7451
Eze 36:31 ye remember your own e. ways, ... 7451
Eze 38:10 thou shalt think an e. thought: 7451
Da 9:12 by bringing upon us a great e.: 7451
Da 9:13 all this e. is come upon us: 7451
Da 9:14 hath the Lord watched upon the e., ... 7451
Joe 2:13 and repenteth him of the e................ 7451
Am 3:6 shall there be e. in a city, ... 7451
Am 5:13 that time; for it is an e. time. 7451
Am 5:14 Seek good, and not e., that ye may 7451
Am 5:15 Hate the e., and love the good, ... 7451
Am 6:3 Ye that put far away the e. day, ... 7451
Am 9:4 will set mine eyes upon them for e., ... 7451
Am 9:10 The e. shall not overtake...us........... 7451
Jon 1:7, 8 for whose cause that e. is upon us... 7451
Jon 3:8 turn every one from his e. way, ... 7451
Jon 3:10 that they turned from their e. way;..... 7451
Jon 3:10 God repented of the e., that he had.... 7451
Jon 4:2 and repentest thee of the e................ 7451
Mic 1:12 e. came down from the Lord unto 7451
Mic 2:1 and work e. upon their beds!............ 7451
Mic 2:3 against this family do I devise an e., ... 7451
Mic 2:3 go haughtily: for this time is e.. 7451
Mic 3:2 Who hate the good, and love the e.; ... 7451
Mic 3:11 none e. can come upon us. 7451
Mic 7:3 they may do e. with both hands 7451
Na 1:11 that imagineth e. against the Lord, ... 7451
Hab 1:13 art of purer eyes than to behold e.... 7451
Hab 2:9 that coveteth an e. covetousness....... 7451
Hab 2:9 delivered from the powers of e.! 7451
Zep 1:12 not do good, neither will he do e........ 7451
Zep 3:15 thou shalt not see e. any more. 7451
Zec 1:4 Turn ye now from your e. ways, ... 7451
Zec 1:4 and from your e. doings: 7451
Zec 7:10 none of you imagine e. against his 7451
Zec 8:17 let none of you imagine e. in your 7451
Mal 1:8 blind for the sacrifice, is it not e.? 7451
Mal 1:8 offer the lame and sick, is it not e.?.... 7451
Mal 2:17 Every one that doeth e. is good......... 7451
Mt 5:11 **shall say all manner of e. 4190,4487**
Mt 5:37 **is more than these cometh of e.... 4190**
Mt 5:39 **unto you, That ye resist not e. 4190**
Mt 5:45 **maketh his sun to rise on the e..... 4190**
Mt 6:13 **but deliver us from e.: 4190**
Mt 6:23 **in thine eye be e., thy whole body. 4190**
Mt 6:34 **Sufficient unto the day is the e..... 2549**
Mt 7:11 **If ye then, being e., know how to.. 4190**
Mt 7:17 **corrupt tree bringeth forth e. fruit. 4190**
Mt 7:18 **good tree cannot bring forth e. 4190**
Mt 9:4 **Wherefore think ye e. in your....... 4190**
Mt 12:34 **how can ye, being e., speak good .. 4190**
Mt 12:35 **an e. man out of the e. treasure.... 4190**
Mt 12:35 **bringeth forth e. things. 4190**
Mt 12:39 **An e. and adulterous generation.... 4190**
Mt 15:19 **of the heart proceed e. thoughts,... 4190**
Mt 20:15 **Is thine eye e., because I am good? 4190**
Mt 24:48 **and if that e. servant shall say...... 2556**
Mt 27:23 Why, what e. hath he done?............ 2556
Mk 3:4 **on the sabbath day, or to do e.?.... 2554**
Mk 7:21 **e. thoughts, adulteries, ... 2556**
Mk 7:22 **lasciviousness, an e. eye, ... 4190**
Mk 7:23 **these e. things come from within,. 4190**
Mk 9:39 **that can lightly speak e. of me...... 2551**
Mk 15:14 Why, what e. hath he done? 2556
Lu 6:9 **to do good, or to do e.? 2554**
Lu 6:22 **and cast out your name as e. 4190**
Lu 6:35 **unto the unthankful and to the e. .4190**
Lu 6:45 **and an e. man out of the e. 4190**
Lu 6:45 **bringeth forth that which is e. 4190**
Lu 7:21 and plagues, and of e. spirits; 4190
Lu 8:2 healed of e. spirits and infirmities, ... 4190
Lu 11:4 **but deliver us from e.. .... 4190**
Lu 11:13 **If ye then, being e., know how to.. 4190**
Lu 11:29 **This is an e. generation: they seek.4190**
Lu 11:34 **when thine eye is e., thy body also.4190**
Lu 16:25 **likewise Lazarus e. things: but...... 2556**
Lu 23:22 Why, what e. hath he done?.............. 2556
Joh 3:19 **light, because their deeds were e.... 4190**
Joh 3:20 **every one that doeth e. hateth the. 5337**
Joh 5:29 **they that have done e., unto the.... 5337**
Joh 7:7 **of that the works thereof are e., ... 4190**
Joh 17:15 **should keep them from the e......... 4190**
Joh 18:23 answered him, **If I have spoken e.,.. 2560**
Joh 18:23 **bear witness of the e.: but if well,. 2556**
Ac 7:6 entreat them e. four hundred............ 2559
Ac 7:19 e. entreated our fathers, so that 2559
Ac 9:13 of this man, how much e. he hath 2556
Ac 14:2 made their minds e. affected 2559
Ac 19:9 but spake e. of that way before the ....
Ac 19:12 the e. spirits went out of them. 4190
Ac 19:13 call over them which had e. spirits...... 4190
Ac 19:15 the e. spirit answered and said, ... 4190
Ac 19:16 the man in whom the e. spirit was...... 4190
Ac 23:5 Thou shalt not speak e. of the ruler.... 2560
Ac 23:9 We find no e. in this man: 2556
Ac 24:20 have found any e. doing in me, ... 92
Ro 1:30 inventors of e. things, disobedient 2556
Ro 2:9 every soul of man that doeth e., ... 2556
Ro 3:8 that we say,) Let us do e., that good.. 2556
Ro 7:19 but the e. which I would not, ... 2556
Ro 7:21 do good, e. is present with me. 2556
Ro 9:11 having done any good or e., ... 2556
Ro 12:9 Abhor that which is e.; cleave to........ 4190
Ro 12:17 Recompense to no man e. for e.. 2556
Ro 12:21 Be not overcome of e., but............... 2556
Ro 12:21 but overcome e. with good................ 2556
Ro 13:3 terror to good works, but to the e.. ... 2556
Ro 13:4 But if thou do that which is e., ... 2556
Ro 13:4 wrath upon him that doeth e. 2556
Ro 14:16 Let not then your good be e. spoken of:....
Ro 14:20 but it is e. for that man who eateth 2556
Ro 16:19 is good, and simple concerning e.. 2556
1Co 10:6 we should not lust after e. things, ... 2556
1Co 10:30 why am I e. spoken of for that for 987
1Co 13:5 easily provoked, thinketh no e.; 2556
1Co 15:33 e. communications corrupt good 2556
2Co 6:8 by e. report and good report: 1426
2Co 13:7 I pray to God that ye do no e.;.......... 2556
Ga 1:4 deliver us from this present e. 4190
Eph 4:31 clamour, and e. speaking, be put 988
Eph 5:16 the time, because the days are e........ 4190
Eph 6:13 be able to withstand in the e. day, ... 4190
Php 3:2 of dogs, beware of e. workers, ... 2556
Co 3:5 e. concupiscence, and covetousness, ... 2556
1Th 5:15 See that none render e. for e............ 2556
1Th 5:22 Abstain from all appearance of e.. 4190
2Th 3:3 stablish you, and keep you from e.. ... 4190
1Ti 6:4 envy, strife, railings, e. surmisings, ... 4190
1Ti 6:10 love of money is the root of all e.: 2556
2Ti 2:9 as an e. doer, even unto bonds: 2557
2Ti 3:13 But e. men and seducers shall wax........ 4190
2Ti 4:14 the coppersmith did me much e.: 2556
2Ti 4:18 deliver me from every e. work, ... 4190
Tit 1:12 e. beasts, slow bellies...................... 2556
Tit 2:8 having no e. thing to say of you. 5337
Tit 3:2 speak e. of no man, to be no 987
Heb 3:12 any of you an e. heart of unbelief, ... 4190
Heb 5:14 to discern both good and e................ 2556
Heb 10:22 sprinkled from an e. conscience, ... 4190
Jas 1:13 God cannot be tempted with e., ... 2556
Jas 2:4 are become judges of e. thoughts?...... 4190
Jas 3:8 an unruly e., full of deadly poison. 2556
Jas 3:16 is confusion and every e. work. 5337
Jas 4:11 Speak not e. one of another, ... 2635
Jas 4:11 that speaketh e. of his brother, ... 2635
Jas 4:11 speaketh e. of the law, and 2635
Jas 4:16 boastings: all such rejoicing is e.. 4190
1Pe 2:1 and envies, and all e. speakings, ... 2636
1Pe 3:9 Not rendering e. for e., or railing 2556
1Pe 3:10 refrain his tongue from e., ... 2556
1Pe 3:11 let him eschew e., and do good; 2556
1Pe 3:12 Lord is against them that do e.. 2556
1Pe 3:16 speak e. of you, as of evildoers, ... 2635
1Pe 3:17 for well doing, than for e. doing. 2554
1Pe 4:4 excess of riot, speaking e. of you: 987
1Pe 4:14 on their part he is e. spoken of, ... 987
2Pe 2:2 of truth shall be e. spoken of. 987
2Pe 2:10 not afraid to speak e. of dignities 987
2Pe 2:12 speak e. of the things that they........... 987
1Jo 3:12 Because his own works were e., ... 4190
2Jo 11 is partaker of his e. deeds. 4190
3Jo 11 follow not that which is e., but 2556
3Jo 11 that doeth e. hath not seen God. 2554
Jude 8 despise dominion, and speak e. of........ 987
Jude 10 these speak e. of those things............ 987
Re 2:2 **canst not bear them which are e.: ..2556**

EVIL-AFFECTED See EVIL and AFFECTED.

EVILDOER See also EVIL and DOER; EVILDOERS.
Isa 9:17 every one is a hypocrite and an e.. 7489
1Pe 4:15 or as an e., or as a busybody 2555

EVILDOERS
Ps 37:1 Fret not thyself because of e., ... 7489
Ps 37:9 e. shall be cut off: but those that 7489
Ps 94:16 will rise up for me against the e.? 7489
Ps 119:115 Depart from me, ye e.: for I will.......... 7489
Isa 1:4 a seed of e., children that are........... 7489
Isa 14:20 seed of e. shall never be renowned.... 7489
Isa 31:2 arise against the house of the e., ... 7489
Jer 20:13 soul of the poor from the hand of e.. .. 7489
Jer 23:14 strengthen also the hands of e., ... 7489
1Pe 2:12 they speak against you as e., ... 2555
1Pe 2:14 by him for the punishment of e., ... 2555
1Pe 3:16 speak evil of you, as of e., ... 2555

EVIL DOING See EVIL and DOING.

EVILFAVOUREDNESS
De 17:1 wherein is blemish, or any e. 1697,7451

EVIL-MERODACH (e″-vil-mer′-o-dak)
2Ki 25:27 that E. king of Babylon in the year 192
Jer 52:31 E. king of Babylon in the first year 192

EVILS
De 31:17 e. and troubles shall befall them 7451
De 31:17 Are not these e. come upon us, ... 7451
De 31:18 e. which they shall have wrought, ... 7451
De 31:21 e. and troubles are befallen them, ... 7451
Ps 40:12 innumerable e. have compassed me..... 7451
Jer 2:13 my people have committed two e.; 7451
Eze 6:9 the e. which they have committed 7451
Eze 20:43 all your e. that ye have committed...... 7451
Lu 3:19 all the e. which Herod had done, ... 4190

EVIL-SPEAKING See EVIL and SPEAKING

EWE See also EWES.
Ge 21:28 Abraham set seven e. lambs of.......... 3535
Ge 21:29 What mean these seven e. lambs 3535
Ge 21:30 seven e. lambs shalt thou take........... 3535
Le 14:10 and one e. lamb of the first year 3535
Le 22:28 cow or e., ye shall not kill it and........ 7716
Nu 6:14 and one e. lamb of the first year 3535
2Sa 12:3 one little e. lamb, which had had 3535

EWE-LAMB See EWE and LAMB.

EWES
Ge 31:38 thy e. and thy she goats have not 7353
Ge 32:14 two hundred e., and twenty rams, ... 7353
Ps 78:71 following the e. great with young........ 5763

EXACT See also EXACTED; EXACTETH.
De 15:2 shall not e. it of his neighbour, ... 5065
De 15:3 foreigner thou mayest e. it again: 5065
Ne 5:7 Ye e. usury, every one of his............ 5378
Ne 5:10 and my brethren,...might e. 5383
Ne 5:11 the corn,...that ye e. of them. 5383
Ps 89:22 The enemy shall not e. upon him; 5378
Isa 58:3 pleasure, and e. all your labours......... 5065
Lu 3:13 E. no more than that which is........... 4238

EXACTED
2Ki 15:20 Menahem e. the money of Israel, ... 3318
2Ki 23:35 he e. the silver and the gold of.......... 5065

EXACTETH
Job 11:6 God e. of thee less than thine........... 5382

EXACTION See also EXACTIONS.
Ne 10:31 year, and the e. of every debt. 4855

EXACTIONS
Eze 45:9 take away your e. from my people,..... 1646

EXACTORS
Isa 60:17 peace, and thine e. righteousness. 5065

EXALT See also EXALTED; EXALTEST; EXALTETH.
Ex 15:2 my father's God, and I will e. him. 7311
1Sa 2:10 and e. the horn of his anointed. 7311
Job 17:4 therefore shalt thou not e. them......... 7311
Ps 34:3 and let us e. his name together.......... 7311
Ps 37:34 shall e. thee to inherit the land: 7311
Ps 66:7 let not the rebellious e. themselves..... 7311

Ps 92:10 But my horn shalt thou **e.** like the 7311
Ps 99:5 **E.** ye the Lord our God, and 7311
Ps 99:9 **E.** the Lord our God, and worship 7311
Ps 107:32 **e.** him also in the congregation 7311
Ps 118:28 thou art my God, I will **e.** thee. 7311
Ps 140:8 device; lest they **e.** themselves. 7311
Pr 4:8 **E.** her, and she shall promote thee: 5549
Isa 13:2 **e.** the voice unto them, shake 7311
Isa 14:13 I will **e.** my throne above the stars 7311
Isa 25:1 thou art my god; I will **e.** thee, 7311
Eze 21:26 **e.** him that is low, and abase him 1361
Eze 29:15 neither shall it **e.** itself any more 5375
Eze 31:14 **e.** themselves for their height, 1361
Da 11:14 the robbers of thy people shall **e.** 5375
Da 11:36 shall **e.** himself, and magnify 7311
Ho 11:7 most High, none at all would **e.** him. 7311
Ob 4 Though thou **e.** thyself as the 1361
Mt 23:12 **And whosoever shall e. himself** *5312*
2Co 11:20 a man **e.** himself, if a man smite *1869*
1Pe 5:6 that he may **e.** you in due time: *5312*

EXALTED

Nu 24:7 and his kingdom shall be **e.**. 5375
1Sa 2:1 mine horn is **e.** in the Lord: 7311
2Sa 5:12 had **e.** his kingdom for his people 5375
2Sa 22:47 and **e.** be the God of the rock of 7311
1Ki 1:5 the son of Haggith **e.** himself, 5375
1Ki 14:7 I **e.** thee from among the people, 7311
1Ki 16:2 Forasmuch as I **e.** thee out of the 7311
2Ki 19:22 against whom hast thou **e.** thy 7311
1Ch 29:11 thou art **e.** as head above all. 5375
Ne 9:5 name, which is **e.** above all 7311
Job 5:11 which mourn may be **e.** to safety. 7682
Job 24:24 They are **e.** for a little while, 7426
Job 36:7 them forever, and they are **e.** 1361
Ps 12:8 when the vilest men are **e.**. 7311
Ps 13:2 how long shall mine enemy be **e.** 7311
Ps 18:46 let the God of my salvation be **e.**. 7311
Ps 21:13 Be thou **e.**, Lord, in thine own 7311
Ps 46:10 I will be **e.** among the heathen. 7311
Ps 46:10 I will be **e.** in the earth. 7311
Ps 47:9 belong unto god: he is greatly **e.**. 5927
Ps 57:5 thou **e.**, O God, above the heavens; 7311
Ps 57:11 thou **e.**, O God, above the heavens: 7311
Ps 75:10 horns of the righteous shall be **e.**. 7311
Ps 89:16 thy righteousness shall they be **e.**. 7311
Ps 89:17 in thy favour our horn shall be **e.**. 7311
Ps 89:19 **e.** one chosen out of the people. 7311
Ps 89:24 in my name shall his horn be **e.**. 7311
Ps 97:9 thou art **e.** far above all gods. 5927
Ps 108:5 thou **e.**, O God, above the heavens: 7311
Ps 112:9 his horn shall be **e.** with honour. 7311
Ps 118:16 The right hand of the Lord is **e.**: 7426
Pr 11:11 of the upright the city is **e.**: 7311
Isa 2:2 and shall be **e.** above the hills; 5375
Isa 2:11, 17 Lord alone shall be in that 7682
Isa 5:16 But the Lord of hosts shall be **e.** 1361
Isa 12:4 make mention that his name is **e.**. 7682
Isa 30:18 and therefore he will be **e.**, 7311
Isa 33:5 The Lord is **e.**, for he dwelleth on 7682
Isa 33:10 now will I be **e.**; now will I lift up 7311
Isa 37:23 against whom hast thou **e.** thy voice, 7311
Isa 40:4 Every valley shall be **e.**, and every 5375
Isa 49:11 and my highways shall be **e.**, 7311
Isa 52:13 he shall be **e.** and extolled, and be 7311
Eze 17:24 have **e.** the low tree, have dried 1361
Eze 19:11 was **e.** among the thick branches, 1361
Eze 31:5 Therefore his height was **e.** above 1361
Ho 13:1 Ephraim **e.** himself in Israel; 5375
Ho 13:6 filled, and their heart was **e.**; 7311
Mic 4:1 and it shall be **e.** above the hills: 5375
Mt 11:23 **which art e. unto heaven, shalt be** *5312*
Mt 23:12 **shall humble himself, shalt be e.** *5312*
Lu 1:52 seats, and **e.** them of low degree. *5312*
Lu 10:15 **which art e. to heaven, shalt be** *5312*
Lu 14:11 **that humbleth himself shall be e.** *5312*
Lu 18:14 **that humbleth himself shall be e.** *5312*
Ac 2:33 being by the right hand of God **e.**, *5312*
Ac 5:31 Him hath God **e.** with his right *5312*
Ac 13:17 **e.** the people when they dwelt as *5312*
2Co 11:7 abasing myself that ye might be **e.** *5312*
2Co 12:7 lest I should be **e.** above measure *5229*
2Co 12:7 lest I should be **e.** above measure. *5229*
Php 2:9 God also hath highly **e.** him, *5251*
Jas 1:9 low degree rejoice in that he is **e.** *5311*

EXALTEST

Ex 9:17 **e.** thou thyself against my people, 5549

EXALTETH

Job 36:22 Behold, God **e.** by his power: 7682
Ps 148:14 also **e.** the horn of his people, 7311
Pr 14:29 he that is hasty of spirit **e.** folly. 7311
Pr 14:34 Righteousness **e.** nation: but sin 7311
Pr 17:19 **e.** his gate seeketh destruction. 1361
Lu 14:11 **e. himself shall be abased;** *5312*
Lu 18:14 **that e. himself shall be abased;** *5312*
2Co 10:5 every high thing that **e.** itself *1869*
2Th 2:4 Who opposeth and **e.** himself *5229*

EXAMINATION

Ac 25:26 that, after **e.** had, I might have *351*

EXAMINE See also EXAMINED; EXAMINING.

Ezr 10:16 the tenth month to **e.** the matter. 1875
Ps 26:2 **E.** me, O Lord, and prove me; 974
1Co 9:3 to them that do **e.** me in this, *350*
1Co 11:28 let a man **e.** himself, and so let *1381*
2Co 13:5 **E.** yourselves, whether ye be in *3985*

EXAMINED

Lu 23:14 I, having **e.** him before you, *350*
Ac 4:9 If we this day be **e.** of the good deed *350*
Ac 12:19 found him not, he **e.** the keepers, *350*
Ac 22:24 he should be **e.** by scourging; *426*
Ac 22:29 him which should have **e.** him: *426*
Ac 28:18 Who, when they had **e.** me, *350*

EXAMINING

Ac 24:8 **e.** of whom thyself mayest take *350*

EXAMPLE See also ENSAMPLE; EXAMPLES.

Mt 1:19 make her a public **e.**, was minded *3856*
Joh 13:15 **For I have given you an e., that** *5262*
1Ti 4:12 be thou an **e.** of the believers, *5179*
Heb 4:11 after the same **e.** of unbelief. *5262*
Heb 8:5 serve unto the **e.** and shadow *5262*
Jas 5:10 for an **e.** of suffering affliction, *5262*
1Pe 2:21 leaving us an **e.**, that ye should *5261*
Jude 7 for an **e.**, suffering the vengeance *1164*

EXAMPLES

1Co 10:6 Now these things were our **e.**, *5179*

EXCEED See also EXCEEDED; EXCEEDEST; EXCEEDETH; EXCEEDING.

De 25:3 he may give him, and not **e.**: 3254
De 25:3 lest, if he should **e.**, and beat him 3254
Mt 5:20 **your righteousness shall e. the** *4052*
2Co 3:9 of righteousness **e.** in glory. *4052*

EXCEEDED

1Sa 20:41 one with another, until David **e.** 1431
1Ki 10:23 So king Solomon **e.** all the kings 1431
Job 36:9 transgressions that they have **e.** 1396

EXCEEDEST

2Ch 9:6 thou **e.** the fame that I heard 3254

EXCEEDETH

1Ki 10:7 thy wisdom and prosperity **e.** the 3254

EXCEEDING See also EXCEEDINGLY.

Ge 15:1 shield, and thy **e.** great reward. 3966
Ge 17:6 And I will make thee **e.** fruitful, 3966
Ge 27:34 with a great and **e.** bitter cry, 3966
Ex 1:7 multiplied, and waxed **e.** mighty; 3966
Ex 19:16 the voice of the trumpet **e.** loud; 3966
Nu 14:7 to search it, is an **e.** good land. 3966
1Sa 2:3 Talk no more so **e.** proudly;
2Sa 8:8 king David took **e.** much brass. 3966
2Sa 12:2 The rich man had **e.** many flocks 3966
1Ki 4:29 wisdom and understanding **e.** much, 3966
1Ki 7:47 because they were **e.** many: 3966
1Ch 20:2 also **e.** much spoil out of the city 3966
1Ch 22:5 the Lord must be **e.** magnifical, 4605
2Ch 11:12 and made them **e.** strong, 7235,3966
2Ch 14:14 for there was **e.** much spoil in 7235
2Ch 16:12 until his disease was **e.** great: 4605
2Ch 32:27 Hezekiah had **e.** much riches and 3966
Ps 21:6 him **e.** glad with thy countenance. 2302
Ps 43:4 altar of God, unto God my **e.** joy: 8057
Ps 119:96 thy commandment is **e.** broad. 3966
Pr 30:24 the earth, but they are **e.** wise:
Ec 7:24 That which is far off, and **e.** deep,
Jer 48:29 pride of Moab, (he is **e.** proud) 3966
Eze 9:9 Israel and Judah is **e.** great, 3966
Eze 16:13 and thou wast **e.** beautiful, and 3966
Eze 23:15 **e.** in dyed attire upon their heads, 5628
Eze 37:10 upon their feet, an **e.** great army. 3966
Eze 47:10 fish of the great sea, **e.** many. 3966
Da 3:22 and the furnace **e.** hot, the flame 3493
Da 6:23 was the king **e.** glad for him, 7689
Da 7:19 **e.** dreadful, whose teeth were of 3493
Da 8:9 waxed **e.** great, toward the south, 3499
Jon 3:3 Nineveh was an **e.** great city 430
Jon 4:6 Jonah was **e.** glad of the gourd 1419
Mt 2:10 they rejoiced with **e.** great joy. *4970*
Mt 2:16 of the wise men, was **e.** wroth, *3029*
Mt 4:8 him up into an **e.** high mountain, *3029*
Mt 5:12 **Rejoice, and be e. glad: for great**
Mt 8:28 coming out of the tombs, **e.** fierce, *3029*
Mt 17:23 And they were **e.** sorry. *4970*
Mt 26:22 And they were **e.** sorrowful, and *4970*
Mt 26:38 **soul is e. sorrowful, even unto** *4036*
Mk 6:26 And the king was **e.** sorry; yet for *4036*
Mk 9:3 became shining, **e.** white as snow; *3029*
Mk 14:34 **soul is e. sorrowful unto death:** *4036*
Lu 23:8 Herod saw Jesus he was **e.** glad: *3029*
Ac 7:20 and was **e.** fair, and nourished *3588,2316*
Ro 7:13 sin...might become **e.** sinful. *2596,5236*
2Co 4:17 a far more **e.** and eternal *1519,5236*
2Co 7:4 am **e.** joyful in all our tribulation. *5248*
2Co 9:14 for the **e.** grace of God in you. *5235*
Eph 1:19 And what is the **e.** greatness of *5235*
Eph 2:7 shew the **e.** riches of his grace *5235*
Eph 3:20 **e.** abundantly above all that we *5228*
1Ti 1:14 Lord was **e.** abundant with faith *5250*
1Pe 4:13 ye may be glad also with **e.** joy.
2Pe 1:4 us **e.** great and precious promises:
Jude 24 the presence of his glory with **e.** joy,
Re 16:21 the plague thereof was **e.** great. *4970*

EXCEEDINGLY See also EXCEEDING.

Ge 7:19 prevailed **e.** upon the earth; 3966
Ge 13:13 and sinners before the Lord **e.** 3966
Ge 16:10 I will multiply thy seed **e.**, 7235
Ge 17:2 and thee, and will multiply thee **e.** 3966
Ge 17:20 multiply him **e.**; twelve princes 3966
Ge 27:33 And Isaac trembled very **e.**. 1419
Ge 30:43 And the man increased **e.**, and 3966
Ge 47:27 and grew, and multiplied **e.**. 3966
1Sa 26:21 the fool, and have erred **e.** 7235,3966
2Sa 13:15 Then Amnon hated her **e.**; 1419,3966
2Ki 10:4 But they were **e.** afraid, and said, 3966
1Ch 29:25 the Lord magnified Solomon **e.** 4605
2Ch 1:1 was with him, and magnified him **e.**. 4605
2Ch 17:12 great **e.**; and he built in Judah 4605
2Ch 26:8 for he strengthened himself **e.** 4605
Ne 2:10 it grieved them **e.** that there was 1419
Es 4:4 Then was the queen **e.** grieved; 3966
Job 3:22 Which rejoice **e.**, and are glad, 413,1524
Ps 68:3 yea, let them **e.** rejoice. 8057
Ps 106:14 But lusted **e.** in the wilderness,
Ps 119:167 testimonies, and I love them **e.** 3966
Ps 123:3 for we are **e.** filled with contempt 7227
Ps 123:4 soul is **e.** filled with the scorning 7227
Isa 24:19 dissolved, the earth is moved **e.**
Da 7:7 strong **e.**; and it had great iron 3493
Jon 1:10 Then were the men **e.** afraid, and 1419
Jon 1:16 Then the men feared the Lord **e.**, 1419
Jon 4:1 it displeased Jonah **e.**, and he was 1419
Mt 19:25 they were **e.** amazed, saying, Who *4970*
Mk 4:41 they feared **e.**, and said one *5401,3173*
Mk 15:14 they cried out the more **e.**, Crucify *4056*
Ac 16:20 being Jews, do **e.** trouble our city, *1613*
Ac 26:11 and being **e.** mad against them, *4057*
Ac 27:18 we being **e.** tossed with a tempest, *4971*
2Co 7:13 **e.** the more joyed we for the joy of *4056*
Ga 1:14 more **e.** zealous of the traditions *4056*
1Th 3:10 Night and day praying **e.** *5228,1537,4053*
2Th 1:3 your faith growth **e.**, and the charity
Heb 12:21 Moses said, I **e.** fear and quake:) *1630*

EXCEL See also EXCELLED; EXCELLEST; EXCELLETH.

Ge 49:4 as water, thou shalt not **e.**; 3498
1Ch 15:21 with harps on the Sheminith to **e.** 5329
Ps 103:20 that **e.** in strength, that do his 1368
Isa 10:10 whose grave images did **e.** them of
1Co 14:12 that ye may **e.** to the edifying of *4052*

EXCELLED

1Ki 4:30 Solomon's wisdom **e.** the wisdom 7227

EXCELLENCY

Ge 49:3 **e.** of dignity, and the **e.** of power: 3499
Ex 15:7 the greatness of thine **e.** thou hast 1347
De 33:26 and in his **e.** on the sky. 1346
De 33:29 and who is the sword of thy **e.**! 1346
Job 4:21 Doth not their **e.** which is in them 3499

Job 13:11 Shall not his e. make you afraid? 7613
Job 20:6 Though his e. mount up to the 7863
Job 37:4 with the voice of his e.; and he will 1347
Job 40:10 thyself now with majesty and e.; 1363
Ps 47:4 the e. of Jacob whom he loved. 1347
Ps 62:4 to cast him down from his e.: 7613
Ps 68:34 his e. is over Israel, and his 1346
Ec 7:12 but the e. of knowledge is, that 3504
Isa 13:19 the beauty of the Chaldees' e., 1347
Isa 35:2 the e. of Carmel and Sharon, 1926
Isa 35:2 of the Lord, and the e. of our God. 1926
Isa 60:15 I will make thee an eternal e., 1347
Eze 24:21 the e. of your strength, the desire 1347
Am 6:8 I abhor the e. of Jacob, and hate 1347
Am 8:7 hath sworn by the e. of Jacob, 1347
Na 2:2 turned away the e. of Jacob, 1347
Na 2:2 as the e. of Israel; 1347
1Co 2:1 you, came not with e. of speech 5247
2Co 4:7 the e. of the power may be of God, 5236
Php 3:8 the e. of the knowledge of Christ 5242

EXCELLENT
Es 1:4 and the honour of his e. majesty 1420
Job 37:23 he is e. in power, and in judgment, 7689
Ps 8:1, 9 e. is thy name in all the earth! 117
Ps 16:3 to the e., in whom is all my delight. 117
Ps 36:7 e. is thy loving kindness, O God! 3368
Ps 76:4 Thou art more glorious and e. than 117
Ps 141:5 it shall be an e. oil, which shall 7218
Ps 148:13 his name alone is e.; his glory is 7682
Ps 150:2 him according to his e. greatness. 7230
Pr 8:6 for I will speak of e. things; 5057
Pr 12:26 The righteous is more e. than his 8446
Pr 17:7 E. speech becometh not a fool; 3499
Pr 17:27 of understanding is of an e. spirit. 7119
Pr 22:20 not I written to thee e. things in 7991
Ca 5:15 Lebanon, e. as the cedars. 977
Isa 4:2 the fruit of the earth shall be e. 1347
Isa 12:5 for he hath done e. things: 1348
Isa 28:29 in counsel, and e. in working. 1431
Eze 16:7 thou art come to e. ornaments: 5716
Da 2:31 image, whose brightness was e., 3493
Da 4:36 and e. majesty was added unto me, 3493
Da 5:12 Forasmuch as an e. spirit, and 3493
Da 5:14 and e. wisdom is found in thee. 3493
Da 6:3 because an e. spirit was in him; 3493
Lu 1:3 in order, most e. Theophilus, 2903
Ac 23:26 unto the most e. governor Felix. 2903
Ro 2:18 the things that are more e., being 1308
1Co 12:31 shew I unto you a more e. way. 2596,5236
Php 1:10 ye may approve things that are e.; 1308
Heb 1:4 obtained a more e. name than they. 1313
Heb 8:6 hath he obtained a more e. ministry, 1313
Heb 11:4 a more e. sacrifice than Cain, 4119
2Pe 1:17 a voice to him from the e. glory, 3169

EXCELLEST
Pr 31:29 virtuously, but thou e. them all. 5927

EXCELLETH
Ec 2:13 Then I saw that wisdom e. folly, 3504
Ec 2:13 as far as light e. darkness. 3504
2Co 3:10 by reason of the glory that e. 5235

EXCEPT See also EXCEPTED.
Ge 31:42 E. the God of my father, the God 3884
Ge 32:26 let thee go, e. thou bless me. 3588, 518
Ge 42:15 e. your youngest brother come 518
Ge 43:3 e. your brother be with you. 1115
Ge 43:5 not see my face, e. your brother 1115
Ge 43:10 e. we had lingered, surely now we 3884
Ge 44:23 E. your youngest brother 518,3808
Ge 44:26 e. our youngest brother be with 369
Ge 47:26 e. the land of the priests only, 7535
Nu 16:13 e. thou make thyself altogether 3588
De 32:30 e. their Rock had sold 518,3808,3588
Jos 7:12 e. ye destroy the accursed 518,3808
1Sa 25:34 e. thou hadst hasted and 3588,3884
2Sa 3:9 God to Abner, and more also, e., 3588
2Sa 3:13 not see my face, e. thou first 3588,518
2Sa 5:6 E. thou take away the blind 3588,518
2Ki 4:24 not thy riding for me, e. I bid 3588,518
Es 2:14 e. the king delighted in her, 3588,518
Es 4:11 e. such to whom the king shall 905
Ps 127:1 E. the Lord build the house, 518,3808
Ps 127:1 e. the Lord keep the city, the 3808
Pr 4:16 sleep not, e. they have done 3808
Isa 1:9 E. the Lord of hosts had left unto 3884
Da 2:11 e. the gods, whose dwelling is not 3861
Da 3:28 nor any god, e. their own God. 3861
Da 6:5 Daniel, e. we find it against him 3861
Am 3:3 walk together, e. they be agreed? 1115
Mt 5:20 e. your righteousness shall exceed. 3362
Mt 12:29 e. he first bind the strong man? 3362
Mt 18:3 E. ye be converted, and become 3362
Mt 19:9 e. it be for fornication, and shall 1508
Mt 24:22 e. those days should be shortened, 1508
Mt 26:42 e. I drink it, thy will be done. 3362
Mk 3:27 e. he will first bind the strong 3362
Mk 7:3 e. they wash their hands oft, 3362
Mk 7:4 e. they wash, they eat not. 3362
Mk 13:20 e. that the Lord had shortened 1508
Lu 9:13 e. we should go and buy meat for 1509
Lu 13:3, 5 e. ye repent, ye shall all 3362
Joh 3:2 that thou doest, e. God be with him. 3362
Joh 3:3 E. a man be born again, he cannot 3362
Joh 3:5 E. a man be born of water and of. 3362
Joh 3:27 e. it be given him from heaven. 3362
Joh 4:48 E. ye see signs and wonders, ye 3362
Joh 6:44 e. the Father which hath sent me 3362
Joh 6:53 E. ye eat the flesh of the Son of 3362
Joh 6:65 e. it were given unto him of my 3362
Joh 12:24 E. a corn of wheat fall into the 3362
Joh 15:4 e. it abide in the vine; no more 3362
Joh 15:4 no more can ye, e. ye abide in me. 3362
Joh 19:11 e. it were given thee from above: 1508
Joh 20:25 E. I shall see in his hands the print 3362
Ac 8:1 were all scattered...e. the apostles. 4133
Ac 8:31 How can I, e. some man should 3362
Ac 15:1 E. ye be circumcised after the 3362
Ac 24:21 E. it be for this one voice, that I 2228
Ac 26:29 such as I am, e. these bonds. 3923
Ac 27:31 E. these abide in the ship, ye 3362
Ro 7:7 e. the law had said, Thou shalt not 1508
Ro 9:29 E. the Lord of Sabaoth had left us 1508
Ro 10:15 e. they be sent, as it is written, 3362
1Co 7:5 e. it be with consent for a time, 1509
1Co 14:5 tongues, e. he interpret, that 1622,1508
1Co 14:6 e. I shall speak to you either by 3362
1Co 14:7 e. they give a distinction in the 3362
1Co 14:9 e. ye utter by the tongue words 3362
1Co 15:36 sowest is not quickened, e. it die: 3362
2Co 12:13 e. it be that I myself was not 1508
2Co 13:5 is in you, e. ye be reprobates? 1509
2Th 2:3 e. there come a falling away first, 3362
2Ti 2:5 not crowned, e. he strive lawfully. 3362
Re 2:5 out of his place, e. thou repent. 3362
Re 2:22 e. they repent of their deeds 3362

EXCEPTED
1Co 15:27 that he is e., which did put 1622

EXCESS
Mt 23:25 they are full of extortion and e. 192
Eph 5:18 drunk with wine, wherein is e.; 810
1Pe 4:3 e. of wine, revellings, 3632
1Pe 4:4 e. of riot, speaking evil of you: 401

EXCHANGE
Ge 47:17 them bread in e. for horses, and
Le 27:10 nd the e. thereof shall be holy. 8545
Job 28:17 and the e. of it shall not be 8545
Eze 48:14 e., nor alienate the first fruits 4171
Mt 16:26 shall a man give in e. for his soul? 465
Mk 8:37 shall a man give in e. for his soul? 465

EXCHANGERS
Mt 25:27 to have put my money to the e., 5133

EXCLUDE See also EXCLUDED.
Ga 4:17 yea, they would e. you, that ye 1576

EXCLUDED
Ro 3:27 Where is boasting then? It is e. 1576

EXCUSABLE See INEXCUSABLE.

EXCUSE See also EXCUSED, EXCUSING.
Lu 14:18 with one consent began to make e. 3868
Ro 1:20 so that they are without e.: 379
2Co 12:19 that we e. ourselves unto you? 626

EXCUSED
Lu 14:18 and see it: I pray thee have me e. 3868
Lu 14:19 prove them: I pray thee have me e.

EXCUSING
Ro 2:15 accusing or else e. one another;) 626

EXECRATION
Jer 42:18 be an e., and an astonishment, 423
Jer 44:12 shall be an e., and an astonishment, 423

EXECUTE See also EXECUTED; EXECUTEST; EXECUTETH; EXECUTING.
Ex 12:12 will e. judgment: I am the Lord. 6213
Nu 5:30 priest shall e. upon her all this law. 6213
Nu 8:11 may e. the service of the Lord. 5647
De 10:18 e. the judgment of the fatherless 6213
1Ki 6:12 and e. my judgments, and keep all 6213
Ps 119:84 when wilt thou e. judgment on 6213
Ps 149:7 To e. vengeance upon the heathen, 6213
Ps 149:9 To e. upon them the judgment 6213
Isa 16:3 Take counsel, e. judgment; make 6213
Jer 7:5 thoroughly e. judgment between 6213
Jer 21:12 E. judgment in the morning, and 1777
Jer 22:3 saith the Lord; E. ye judgment 6213
Jer 23:5 and prosper, and shall e. judgment 6213
Jer 33:15 and he shall e. judgment and 6213
Eze 5:8 and will e. judgments in the midst 6213
Eze 5:10 and I will e. judgments in thee, 6213
Eze 5:15 when I shall e. judgment in thee 6213
Eze 11:9 and will e. judgments among you. 6213
Eze 16:41 and e. judgments upon thee in the 6213
Eze 25:11 I will e. judgments upon Moab; 6213
Eze 25:17 will e. great vengeance upon them 6213
Eze 30:14 and will e. judgments in No. 6213
Eze 30:19 Thus will I e. judgments in Egypt: 6213
Eze 45:9 e. judgment and justice, take away 6213
Ho 11:9 not e. the fierceness of mine anger, 6213
Mic 5:15 And I will e. vengeance in anger 6213
Mic 7:9 my cause, and e. judgment for me: 6213
Zec 7:9 E. true judgment, and shew 8199
Zec 8:16 e. the judgment of truth and peace 8199
Joh 5:27 authority to e. judgment also, 4160
Ro 13:4 a revenger to e. wrath upon him
Jude 15 To e. judgment upon all, and to 4160

EXECUTED See also EXECUTEDST.
Nu 33:4 gods also the Lord e. judgments 6213
De 33:21 he e. the justice of the Lord, 6213
2Sa 8:15 David e. judgment and justice 6213
1Ch 6:10 (he it is that e. the priest's office in the
1Ch 18:14 e. judgment and justice among 6213
1Ch 24:2 and Ithamar e. the priest's office,
2Ch 24:24 they e. judgment against Joash. 6213
Ezr 7:26 judgment be e. speedily upon him, 5648
Ps 106:30 stood up Phinehas, and e. judgment:
Ec 8:11 an evil work is not e. speedily, 6213
Jer 23:20 until he have e., and till he have 6213
Eze 11:12 neither e. my judgments, but have 6213
Eze 18:8 hath e. true judgment between 6213
Eze 18:17 hath e. my judgment, hath walked 6213
Eze 20:24 they had not e. my judgments, 6213
Eze 23:10 for they had e. judgment upon her. 6213
Eze 28:22 I shall have e. judgments in her, 6213
Eze 28:26 when I have e. judgments upon all 6213
Eze 39:21 see my judgment that I have e., 6213
Lu 1:8 that while he e. the priest's office 2407

EXECUTEDST
1Sa 28:18 e. his fierce wrath upon Amalek, 6213

EXECUTEST
Ps 99:4 e. judgment and righteousness in 6213

EXECUTETH
Ps 9:16 by the judgment which he e.: 6213
Ps 103:6 The Lord e. righteousness and 6213
Ps 146:7 e. judgment for the oppressed: 6213
Isa 46:11 the man that e. my counsel from
Jer 5:1 if there be any that e. judgment, 6213
Joe 2:11 for he is strong that e. his word: 6213

EXECUTING
2Ki 10:30 thou hast done well in e. that 6213
2Ch 11:14 them off from e. the priest's office
2Ch 22:8 when Jehu was e. judgment upon

EXECUTION
Es 9:1 decree drew near to be put in e., 6213

EXECUTIONER
Mk 6:27 king sent an e., and commanded 4688

EXEMPTED
1Ki 15:22 none was e.: and they took away 5355

EXERCISE See also EXERCISED; EXERCISETH.
Ps 131:1 do I e. myself in great matters, 1980
Jer 9:24 the Lord which e. lovingkindness, 6213

Mt 20:25 **Gentiles e. dominion over them,** 2634
Mt 20:25 **are great e. authority upon them.** 2715
Mk 10:42 **the Gentiles e. lordship over them;** 2634
Mk 10:42 **great ones e. authority upon them.** 2715
Lu 22:25 **kings of the earth e. lordship** 2961
Lu 22:25 **they that e. authority upon them** 1850
Ac 24:16 herein do I e. myself, to have alway 778
1Ti 4:7 e. thyself rather unto godliness. 1128
1Ti 4:8 For bodily e. profiteth little: but 1129

EXERCISED
Ec 1:13 sons of man to be e. therewith. 6031
Ec 3:10 to the sons of men to be e. in it. 6031
Eze 22:29 and e. robbery, and have vexed
Heb 5:14 e. to discern both good and evil. 1128
Heb 12:11 unto them which are e. thereby. 1128
2Pe 2:14 have e. with covetous practices; 1128

EXERCISETH
Re 13:12 e. all the power of the first beast 4160

EXHORT See also EXHORTED; EXHORTETH; EXHORTING.
Ac 2:40 did he testify and e., saying, Save 3870
Ac 27:22 now I e. you to be of good cheer: 3867
2Co 9:5 it necessary to e. the brethren, 3870
1Th 4:1 and e. you by the Lord Jesus, 3870
1Th 5:14 we e. you, brethren, warn them 3870
2Th 3:12 and e. by our Lord Jesus Christ, 3870
1Ti 2:1 I e. therefore, that, first of all, 3870
1Ti 6:2 These things teach and e. 3870
2Ti 4:2 rebuke, e. with all long suffering 3870
Tit 1:9 to e. and to convince the gainsayers. 3870
Tit 2:6 likewise e. to be sober minded. 3870
Tit 2:9 E. servants to be obedient unto their
Tit 2:15 speak, and e., and rebuke with all 3870
Heb 3:13 But e. one another daily, while it 3870
1Pe 5:1 I e., who am also an elder, 3870
Jude 3 me to write unto you, and e. you 3870

EXHORTATION
Lu 3:18 e. preached he unto the people. 3870
Ac 13:15 any word of e. for the people, 3874
Ac 20:2 and had given them much e., 3870
Ro 12:8 Or he that exhorteth, on e.: 3874
1Co 14:3 edification, and e., and comfort. 3874
2Co 8:17 For indeed he accepted the e.; 3874
1Th 2:3 For our e. was not of deceit, 3874
1Ti 4:13 to reading, to e., to doctrine. 3874
Heb 12:5 forgotten the e. which speaketh 3874
Heb 13:22 brethren, suffer the word of e.: 3874

EXHORTED
Ac 11:23 and e. them all, that with purpose 3870
Ac 15:32 e. the brethren with many words, 3870
1Th 2:11 As ye know how we e. and

EXHORTETH
Ro 12:8 Or he that e., on exhortation: 3870

EXHORTING
Ac 14:22 e. them to continue in the faith, 3870
Ac 18:27 e. the disciples to receive him: 4389
Heb 10:25 but e. one another: and so much 3870
1Pe 5:12 written briefly, e., and testifying 3870

EXILE
2Sa 15:19 art a stranger, and also an e. 1540
Isa 51:14 The captive e. hasteneth that he 6808

EXODUS (ex´-o-dus)
Ex *general title* of Moses, Called **E.** 428,8031

EXORCISTS
Ac 19:13 vagabond Jews, e., took upon them 1845

EXPECTATION
Ps 9:18 the e. of the poor shall not perish 8615
Ps 62:5 my e. is from him. 8615
Pr 10:28 the e. of the wicked shall perish. 8615
Pr 11:7 man dieth, his e. shall perish: 8615
Pr 11:23 the e. of the wicked is wrath. 8615
Pr 23:18 and thine e. shall not be cut off. 8615
Pr 24:14 and thy e. shall not be cut off. 8615
Isa 20:5 Ethiopia their e., and of Egypt. 4007
Isa 20:6 such is our e. whither we flee 4007
Zec 9:5 Ekron; for her e. shall be ashamed; 4007
Lu 3:15 as the people were in e., 4328
Ac 12:11 all the e. of the people of the Jews. 4329
Ro 8:19 the earnest e. of the creature 603
Php 1:20 to my earnest e. and my hope, 603

EXPECTED
Jer 29:11 not of evil, to give you an e. end. 8615

EXPECTING
Ac 3:5 e. to receive something of them. 4328
Heb 10:13 e. till his enemies be made his 1551

EXPEDIENT
Joh 11:50 Nor consider that it is e. for us, 4851
Joh 16:7 **It is e. for you that I go away:** 4851
Joh 18:14 it was e. that one man should die 4851
1Co 6:12 unto me, but all things are not e.: 4851
1Co 10:23 but all things are not e.: 4851
2Co 8:10 this is e. of you, who have begun 4851
2Co 12:1 not e. for me doubtless to glory. 4851

EXPEL See also EXPELLED.
Jos 23:5 shall e. them from before you, 1920
Jg 11:7 Did not ye hate me, and e. me 1644

EXPELLED
Jos 13:13 of Israel e. not the Geshurites, 3423
Jg 1:20 e. thence the three sons of Anak. 3423
2Sa 14:14 his banished be not e. from him. 5080
Ac 13:50 and e. them out of their coasts. 1544

EXPENCES
Ezr 6:4 and let the e. be given out of the 5313
Ezr 6:8 forthwith e. be given unto these 5313

EXPENSE See EXPENCES.

EXPERIENCE
Ge 30:27 by e. that the Lord hath blessed 5172
Ec 1:16 my heart had great e. of wisdom 7200
Ro 5:4 And patience, e.; and e., hope: 1382

EXPERIMENT
2Co 9:13 by the e. of this ministration 1382

EXPERT
1Ch 12:33 e. in war, with all instruments of 6186
1Ch 12:35 of the Danites e. in war twenty 6186
1Ch 12:36 battle, e. in war, forty thousand. 6186
Ca 3:8 being e. in war: every man hath 3925
Jer 50:9 shall be as of a mighty e. man; 7919
Ac 26:3 be e. in all customs and questions 1109

EXPIRED
1Sa 18:26 and the days were not e. 4390
2Sa 11:1 after the year was e., at the time 8666
1Ch 17:11 when thy days be e. that thou 4390
1Ch 20:1 after the year was e., at the time 8666
2Ch 36:10 was e., king Nebuchadnezzar 8666
Es 1:5 And when these days were e., 4390
Eze 43:27 these days are e., it shall be, 3615
Ac 7:30 And when forty years were e., 4137
Re 20:7 when the thousand years are e., 5055

EXPLOITS
Da 11:28 and he shall do e., and return to
Da 11:32 God shall be strong, and do e.

EXPOUND See also EXPOUNDED.
Jg 14:14 they could not in three days e. 5046

EXPOUNDED
Jg 14:19 unto them which e. the riddle. 5046
Mk 4:34 he e. all things to his disciples. 1956
Lu 24:27 he e. unto them in all the 1329
Ac 11:4 e. it by order unto them, saying, 1620
Ac 18:26 and e. unto him the way of God 1620
Ac 28:23 to whom he e. and testified the 1620

EXPRESS See also EXPRESSED.
Heb 1:3 and the e. image of his person, 5481

EXPRESSED
Nu 1:17 men which are e. by their names: 5344
1Ch 12:31 which were e. by name, to come 5344
1Ch 16:41 were e. by name, to give thanks 5344
2Ch 28:15 which were e. by name rose up, 5344
2Ch 31:19 the men that were e. by name, to 5344
Ezr 8:20 all of them were e. by name.

EXPRESSLY
1Sa 20:21 If I e. say unto the lad, Behold, 559
Eze 1:3 word of the Lord came e. unto Ezekiel.
1Ti 4:1 Now the Spirit speaketh e., 4490

EXTEND See also EXTENDED; EXTENDETH.
Ps 109:12 Let there be none to e. mercy 4900
Isa 66:12 I will e. peace to her like a river, 5186

EXTENDED
Ezr 7:28 e. mercy unto me before the king, 5186
Ezr 9:9 hath e. mercy unto us in the sight 5186

EXTENDETH
Ps 16:2 my goodness e. not to thee;

EXTINCT
Job 17:1 breath is corrupt, my days are e., 2193
Isa 43:17 they are e., they are quenched as 1846

EXTOL See also EXTOLLED.
Ps 30:1 I will e. thee, O Lord; for thou 7311
Ps 68:4 e. him that rideth upon the 5549
Ps 145:1 I will e. thee, my God, O king; 7311
Da 4:37 I Nebuchadnezzar praise and e. 7313

EXTOLLED
Ps 66:17 and he was e. with my tongue. 7318
Isa 52:13 he shall be exalted and e., and be 5375

EXTORTION
Eze 22:12 gained of thy neighbours by e., 6233
Mt 23:25 **they are full of e. and excess.** 724

EXTORTIONER See also EXTORTIONERS.
Ps 109:11 Let the e. catch all that he hath; 5383
Isa 16:4 the e. is at an end, the spoiler 4160
1Co 5:11 a railer, or a drunkard, or an e.; 727

EXTORTIONERS
Lu 18:11 **not as other men are, e., unjust,** 727
1Co 5:10 covetous, or e., or with idolaters; 727
1Co 6:10 revilers, nor e., shall inherit the 727

EXTREME
De 28:22 an e. burning, and with the sword, 2746

EXTREMITY
Job 35:15 he knoweth it not in great e. 6580

EYE See also EYEBROWS; EYED; EYELIDS; EYE'S; EYES; EYESALVE; EYESERVICE; EYESIGHT; EYEWITNESSES.
Ex 21:24 E. for e., tooth for tooth, hand for 5869
Ex 21:26 if a man smite the e. of his servant, 5869
Ex 21:26 or the e. of his maid, that it perish 5869
Le 21:20 or that hath a blemish in his e., 5869
Le 24:20 e. for e., tooth for tooth: as he 5869
De 7:16 e. shall have no pity upon them: 5869
De 13:8 neither shall thine e. pity him, 5869
De 15:9 thine e. be evil against thy poor 5869
De 19:13 Thine e. shall not pity him, but 5869
De 19:21 And thine e. shall not pity; 5869
De 19:21 but life shall go for life, e. for e., 5869
De 25:12 hand, thine e. shall not pity her. 5869
De 28:54 e. shall be evil toward his brother, 5869
De 28:56 e. shall be evil toward the husband 5869
De 32:10 he kept him as the apple of his e. 5869
De 34:7 his e. was not dim, nor his natural 5869
1Sa 24:10 but mine e. spared thee; and I
2Sa 22:25 to my cleanness in his e. sight. 5869
Ezr 5:5 e. of their God was upon the elders 5870
Job 7:7 mine e. shall no more see good. 5869
Job 7:8 The e. of him that hath seen me 5869
Job 10:18 the ghost, and no e. had seen me! 5869
Job 13:1 Lo, mine e. hath seen all this, 5869
Job 16:20 mine e. poureth out tears unto God. 5869
Job 17:2 e. continue in their provocation? 5869
Job 17:7 e. also is dim by reason of sorrow, 5869
Job 20:9 The e. also which saw him shall see 5869
Job 24:15 The e. also of the adulterer 5869
Job 24:15 twilight, saying No e. shall see me: 5869
Job 28:7 the vulture's e. hath not seen: 5869
Job 28:10 his e. seeth every precious thing. 5869
Job 29:11 and when the e. saw me, it gave 5869
Job 42:5 but now mine e. seeth thee. 5869
Ps 6:7 e. is consumed because of grief; 5869
Ps 17:8 Keep me as the apple of the e., 5869
Ps 31:9 mine e. is consumed with grief, 5869
Ps 32:8 I will guide thee with mine e. 5869
Ps 33:18 the e. of the Lord is upon them 5869
Ps 35:19 neither let them wink with the e. 5869
Ps 35:21 Aha, aha, our e. hath seen it. 5869
Ps 54:7 and mine e. hath seen his desire 5869
Ps 88:9 e. mourneth by reason of affliction: 5869
Ps 92:11 Mine e. also shall see my desire 5869
Ps 94:9 he that formed the e., shall he not 5869
Pr 7:2 my law as the apple of thine e. 5869
Pr 10:10 that winketh with the e. causeth 5869
Pr 20:12 The hearing ear, and the seeing e., 5869
Pr 22:9 He that hath a bountiful e. shall 5869
Pr 23:6 bread of him that hath an evil e., 5869
Pr 28:22 hasteth to be rich hath an evil e. 5869
Pr 30:17 The e. that mocketh at his father, 5869
Ec 1:8 the e. is not satisfied with seeing, 5869

Ec 4:8 is his **e.** satisfied with riches; 5869
Isa 13:18 their **e.** shall not spare children. 5869
Isa 52:8 they shall see **e.** to **e.**, when the 5869
Isa 64:4 neither hath the **e.** seen, O God, 5869
Jer 13:17 mine **e.** shall weep sore, and run 5869
La 1:16 mine **e.**, mine **e.** runneth down with 5869
La 2:4 slew all that were pleasant to the **e.** 5869
La 2:18 let not the apple of thine **e.** cease. 5869
La 3:48 Mine **e.** runneth down with rivers of 5869
La 3:49 Mine **e.** trickleth down, and ceaseth 5869
La 3:51 Mine **e.** affecteth mine heart 5869
Eze 5:11 neither shall mine **e.** spare, neither 5869
Eze 7:4 And mine **e.** shall not spare thee, 5869
Eze 7:9 And mine **e.** shall not spare, neither 5869
Eze 8:18 mine **e.** shall not spare, neither 5869
Eze 9:5 let not your **e.** spare, neither have 5869
Eze 9:10 for me also, mine **e.** shall not spare, 5869
Eze 16:5 None **e.** pitied thee, to do any of 5869
Eze 20:17 **e.** spared them from destroying 5869
Mic 4:11 and let our **e.** look upon Zion. 5869
Zec 2:8 you toucheth the apple of his **e.** 5869
Zec 11:17 his arm, and upon his right **e.**: 5869
Zec 11:17 right **e.** shall be utterly darkened. 5869
Mt 5:29 **if thy right e. offend thee, pluck** *3788*
Mt 5:38 **e. for an e., and a tooth for a** *3788*
Mt 6:22 **The light of the body is the e.:** *3788*
Mt 6:22 **if therefore thine e. be single,** *3788*
Mt 6:23 **But if thine e. be evil, thy whole** *3788*
Mt 7:3 **mote that is in thy brother's e.,** *3788*
Mt 7:3 **the beam that is in thine own e.?** *3788*
Mt 7:4 **pull out the mote out of thine e.;** *3788*
Mt 7:4 **behold, a beam is in thine own e.?** *3788*
Mt 7:5 **out the beam out of thine own e.:** *3788*
Mt 7:5 **the mote out of thy brother's e** *3788*
Mt 18:9 **if thine e. offend thee, pluck it** *3788*
Mt 18:9 **thee to enter into life with one e.,** *3442*
Mt 19:24 **to go through the e. of a needle,** *5169*
Mt 20:15 **thine e. evil, because I am good?** *3788*
Mk 7:22 **an evil e., blasphemy, pride,** *3788*
Mk 9:47 **if thine e. offend thee, pluck it** *3788*
Mk 9:47 **the kingdom of God with one e.,** *3442*
Mk 10:25 **to go through the e. of a needle,** *5168*
Lu 6:41 **mote that is in thy brother's e.,** *3788*
Lu 6:41 **the beam that is in thine own e.?** *3788*
Lu 6:42 **out the mote that is in thine e.,** *3788*
Lu 6:42 **the beam that is in thine own e.?** *3788*
Lu 6:42 **first the beam out of thine own e.,** *3788*
Lu 6:42 **the mote that is in thy brother's e.** *3788*
Lu 11:34 **The light of the body is the e.:** *3788*
Lu 11:34 **therefore when thine e. is single,** *3788*
Lu 11:34 **but when thine e. is evil, thy** *3788*
Lu 18:25 **camel to go through a needle's e.,** *5168*
1Co 2:9 **E.** hath not seen, nor ear heard, *3788*
1Co 12:16 Because I am not the **e.**, I am not *3788*
1Co 12:17 If the whole body were an **e.**, where *3788*
1Co 12:21 the **e.** cannot say unto the hand, *3788*
1Co 15:52 in the twinkling of an **e.**, at the *3788*
Re 1:7 every **e.** shall see him, and they *3788*

EYEBROWS

Le 14:9 and his **e.**, even all his hair 1354,5869

EYED

Ge 29:17 Leah was tender **e.**; but Rachel 5869
1Sa 18:9 Saul **e.** David from that day 5770

EYELIDS

Job 16:16 on my **e.** is the shadow of death; 6079
Job 41:18 eyes are like the **e.** of the morning. 6079
Ps 11:4 his **e.** try, the children of men. 6079
Ps 132:4 mine eyes, or slumber to mine **e.**, 6079
Pr 4:25 thine **e.** look straight before thee. 6079
Pr 6:4 thine eyes, nor slumber to thine **e.** 6079
Pr 6:25 neither let her take thee with her **e.** 6079
Pr 30:13 and their **e.** are lifted up. 6079
Jer 9:18 and our **e.** gush out with waters. 6079

EYE'S

Ex 21:26 let him go free for his **e.** sake. 5869

EYES

Ge 3:5 then your **e.** shall be opened, and 5869
Ge 3:6 and that it was pleasant to the **e.**, 5869
Ge 3:7 the **e.** of them both were opened, 5869
Ge 6:8 found grace in the **e.** of the Lord. 5869
Ge 13:10 Lot lifted up his **e.**, and beheld 5869
Ge 13:14 Lift up now thine **e.**, and look 5869
Ge 16:4 her mistress was despised in her **e.** 5869
Ge 16:5 I was despised in her **e.**; the Lord 5869
Ge 18:2 And he lifted up his **e.** and looked, 5869
Ge 19:8 do ye to them as is good in your **e.**: 5869
Ge 20:16 he is to thee a covering of the **e.**, 5869
Ge 21:19 God opened her **e.**, and she saw a 5869
Ge 22:4 Abraham lifted up his **e.**, and saw 5869
Ge 22:13 Abraham lifted up his **e.**, and looked 5869
Ge 24:63 and he lifted up his **e.**, and saw, 5869
Ge 24:64 Rebekah lifted up her **e.**, and when 5869
Ge 27:1 Isaac was old, and his **e.** were dim, 5869
Ge 30:27 if I have found favour in thine **e.**, 5869
Ge 30:41 the rods before the **e.** of the cattle 5869
Ge 31:10 I lifted up mine **e.**, and saw in a 5869
Ge 31:12 Lift up now thine **e.**, and see, 5869
Ge 31:40 my sleep departed from mine **e.** 5869
Ge 33:1 Jacob lifted up his **e.**, and looked, 5869
Ge 33:5 lifted up his **e.**, and saw the women 5869
Ge 34:11 Let me find grace in your **e.**, 5869
Ge 37:25 they lifted up their **e.** and looked, 5869
Ge 39:7 his master's wife cast her **e.** upon 5869
Ge 41:37 was good in the **e.** of Pharaoh, 5869
Ge 41:37 and in the **e.** of all his servants. 5869
Ge 42:24 and bound him before their **e.** 5869
Ge 43:29 lifted up his **e.**, and saw his brother 5869
Ge 44:21 that I may set mine **e.** upon him. 5869
Ge 45:12 your **e.** see, and the **e.** of my brother. 5869
Ge 46:4 shall put his hand upon thine **e.** 5869
Ge 47:19 shall we die before thine **e.**, both 5869
Ge 48:10 the **e.** of Israel were dim for age, 5869
Ge 49:12 His **e.** shall be red with wine, 5869
Ge 50:4 now I have found grace in your **e.**, 5869
Ex 5:21 be abhorred in the **e.** of Pharaoh, 5869
Ex 5:21 and in the **e.** of his servants, 5869
Ex 8:26 of the Egyptians before their **e.**, 5869
Ex 13:9 for a memorial between thine **e.**, 5869
Ex 13:16 and for frontlets between thine **e.**: 5869
Ex 14:10 children of Israel lifted up their **e.**, 5869
Ex 24:17 in the **e.** of the children of Israel. 5869
Le 4:13 be hid from the **e.** of the assembly, 5869
Le 20:4 the land do any ways hide their **e.** 5869
Le 26:16 ague, that shall consume the **e.**, 5869
Nu 5:13 be hid from the **e.** of her husband, 5869
Nu 10:31 thou mayest be to us instead of **e.** 5869
Nu 11:6 beside this manna, before our **e.** 5869
Nu 15:39 your own heart and your own **e.**, 5869
Nu 16:14 thou put out the **e.** of these men? 5869
Nu 20:8 ye unto the rock before their **e.**; 5869
Nu 20:12 sanctify me in the **e.** of the children 5869
Nu 22:31 the Lord opened the **e.** of Balaam, 5869
Nu 24:2 Balaam lifted up his **e.**, and he saw 5869
Nu 24:3 man whose **e.** are open hath said: 5869
Nu 24:4 a trance, but having his **e.** open: 5869
Nu 24:15 man whose **e.** are open hath said: 5869
Nu 24:16 a trance, but having his **e.** open: 5869
Nu 27:14 me at the water before their **e.**: 5869
Nu 33:55 of them shall be pricks in your **e.**, 5869
De 1:30 did for you in Egypt before your **e.**; 5869
De 3:21 Thine **e.** have seen all that the Lord 5869
De 3:27 and lift up thine **e.** westward, and 5869
De 3:27 and behold it with thine **e.**: 5869
De 4:3 Your **e.** have seen what the Lord 5869
De 4:9 things which thine **e.** have seen, 5869
De 4:19 And lest thou lift up thine **e.** unto 5869
De 4:34 did for you in Egypt before your **e.**? 5869
De 6:8 be as frontlets between thine **e.** 5869
De 6:22 all his household, before our **e.**: 5869
De 7:19 temptations which thine **e.** saw, 5869
De 9:17 and brake them before your **e.** 5869
De 10:21 things, which thine **e.** have seen. 5869
De 11:7 your **e.** have seen all the great acts 5869
De 11:12 the **e.** of the Lord thy God are 5869
De 11:18 be as frontlets between your **e.** 5869
De 12:8 whatsoever is right in his own **e.** 5869
De 13:18 which is right in the **e.** of the Lord. 5869
De 14:1 make any baldness between your **e.** 5869
De 16:19 a gift doth blind the **e.** of the wise, 5869
De 21:7 neither have our **e.** seen it. 5869
De 24:1 that she find no favour in his **e.**, 5869
De 28:31 ox shall be slain before thine **e.**, 5869
De 28:32 and thine **e.** shall look, and fail with 5869
De 28:34 be mad for the sight of thine **e.** 5869
De 28:65 a trembling heart, and failing of **e.**, 5869
De 28:67 of thine **e.** which thou shalt see. 5869
De 29:2 all that the Lord did before your **e.** 5869
De 29:3 temptations which thine **e.** have 5869
De 29:4 a heart to perceive, and **e.** to see, 5869
De 34:4 caused thee to see it with thine **e.**, 5869
Jos 5:13 he lifted up his **e.** and looked, 5869
Jos 23:13 thorns in your **e.**, until ye perish 5869
Jos 24:7 your **e.** have seen what I have done 5869
Jg 16:21 took him, and put out his **e.**, 5869
Jg 16:28 of the Philistines for my two **e.** 5869
Jg 17:6 that which was right in his own **e.** 5869
Jg 19:17 when he had lifted up his **e.**, he saw 5869
Jg 21:25 that which was right in his own **e.** 5869
Ru 2:9 Let thine **e.** be on the field that 5869
Ru 2:10 have I found grace in thine **e.**, 5869
1Sa 2:33 shall be to consume thine **e.**, and 5869
1Sa 3:2 and his **e.** began to wax dim, 5869
1Sa 4:15 his **e.** were dim, that he could not 5869
1Sa 6:13 lifted up their **e.**, and saw the ark, 5869
1Sa 11:2 I may thrust out all your right **e.**, 5869
1Sa 12:3 bribe to blind mine **e.** therewith? 5869
1Sa 12:16 the Lord will do before your **e.** 5869
1Sa 14:27 and his **e.** were enlightened. 5869
1Sa 14:29 how mine **e.** have been enlightened, 5869
1Sa 20:3 I have found grace in thine **e.**; 5869
1Sa 20:29 if I have found favour in thine **e.**, 5869
1Sa 24:10 thine **e.** have seen how that the Lord 5869
1Sa 25:8 young men find favour in thine **e.**: 5869
1Sa 26:21 my soul was precious in thine **e.** 5869
1Sa 26:24 much set by this day in mine **e.**, 5869
1Sa 26:24 much set by in the **e.** of the Lord, 5869
1Sa 27:5 I have now found grace in thine **e.**, 5869
2Sa 6:20 to day in the **e.** of the handmaids 5869
2Sa 12:11 I will take thy wives before thine **e.**, 5869
2Sa 13:34 that kept the watch lifted up his **e.**, 5869
2Sa 15:25 find favour in the **e.** of the Lord, 5869
2Sa 18:24 and lifted up his **e.**, and looked, 5869
2Sa 19:27 therefore what is good in thine **e.** 5869
2Sa 22:28 thine **e.** are upon the haughty, 5869
2Sa 24:3 the **e.** of my lord the king may see 5869
1Ki 1:20 O king, the **e.** of all Israel are upon 5869
1Ki 1:48 this day, mine **e.** even seeing it. 5869
1Ki 8:29 **e.** may be open toward this house 5869
1Ki 8:52 That thine **e.** may be open unto the 5869
1Ki 9:3 **e.** and mine heart shall be there 5869
1Ki 10:7 mine **e.** had seen it: and, behold, 5869
1Ki 11:33 do that which is right in mine **e.**, 5869
1Ki 14:4 Ahijah could not see; for his **e.** 5869
1Ki 14:8 only which was right in mine **e.**; 5869
1Ki 15:5 was right in the **e.** of the Lord, 5869
1Ki 15:11 that which was right in the **e.** of 5869
1Ki 16:25 Omri wrought evil in the he **e.** of 5869
1Ki 20:6 whatsoever is pleasant in thine **e.**, 5869
1Ki 22:43 was right in the **e.** of the Lord: 5869
2Ki 4:34 and his **e.** upon his **e.**, and his hands 5869
2Ki 4:35 times, and the child opened his **e.** 5869
2Ki 6:17 Lord, I pray thee, open his **e.**, 5869
2Ki 6:17 opened the **e.** of the young man; 5869
2Ki 6:20 Lord, open the **e.** of these men, 5869
2Ki 6:20 And the Lord opened their **e.**, 5869
2Ki 7:2, 19 thou shalt see it with thine **e.**, 5869
2Ki 10:5 thou that which is good in thine **e.** 5869
2Ki 10:30 that which is right in mine **e.**, 5869
2Ki 19:16 open, Lord, thine **e.**, and see: 5869
2Ki 19:22 and lifted up thine **e.** on high? 5869
2Ki 22:20 thine **e.** shall not see all the evil. 5869
2Ki 25:7 the sons of Zedekiah before his **e.**, 5869
2Ki 25:7 and put out the **e.** of Zedekiah, 5869
1Ch 13:4 was right in the **e.** of all the people. 5869
1Ch 17:17 this was a small thing in thine **e.**, 5869
1Ch 21:16 And David lifted up his **e.**, and saw 5869
1Ch 21:23 do that which is good in his **e.**: 5869
2Ch 6:20 **e.** may be open upon this house 5869
2Ch 6:40 let, I beseech thee, thine **e.** be open, 5869
2Ch 7:15 Now mine **e.** shall be open, and 5869
2Ch 7:16 mine **e.** and mine heart shall be 5869
2Ch 9:6 mine **e.** had seen it: and, behold, 5869
2Ch 14:2 good and right in the **e.** of the Lord 5869
2Ch 16:9 the **e.** of the Lord run to and fro 5869
2Ch 20:12 but our **e.** are upon thee. 5869
2Ch 21:6 was evil in the **e.** of the Lord. 5869
2Ch 29:6 evil in the **e.** of the Lord our God, 5869
2Ch 29:8 to hissing, as ye see with your **e.** 5869
2Ch 34:28 neither shall thine **e.** see all the evil 5869
Ezr 3:12 house was laid before their **e.**, 5870
Ezr 9:8 that our God may lighten our **e.**, 5869
Ne 1:6 **e.** open, that thou mayest hear 5869
Ne 6:16 much cast down in their own **e.**: 5869
Es 1:17 despise their husbands in their **e.**, 5869
Es 8:5 the king, and I be pleasing in his **e.**, 5869

Job 2:12 they lifted up their **e.** afar off, 5869
Job 3:10 nor hid sorrow from mine **e.** 5869
Job 4:16 an image was before mine **e.**, 5869
Job 7:8 thine **e.** are upon me, and I am not 5869
Job 10:4 Hast thou **e.** of flesh? or seest the 5869
Job 11:4 and I am clean in thine **e.** 5869
Job 11:20 But the **e.** of the wicked shall fail, 5869
Job 14:3 open thine **e.** upon such an one, 5869
Job 15:12 and what do thy **e.** wink at, 5869
Job 16:9 enemy sharpeneth his **e.** upon me 5869
Job 17:5 even the **e.** of his children shall fail 5869
Job 19:27 and mine **e.** shall behold, and not 5869
Job 21:8 and their offspring before their **e.** 5869
Job 21:20 His **e.** shall see his destruction, 5869
Job 24:23 yet his **e.** are upon their ways 5869
Job 27:19 he openeth his **e.**, and he is not 5869
Job 28:21 it is hid from the **e.** of all living, 5869
Job 29:15 I was **e.** to the blind, and feet was I 5869
Job 31:1 I made a covenant with mine **e.**; 5869
Job 31:7 mine heart walked after mine **e.**, 5869
Job 31:16 caused the **e.** of the widow to fail; 5869
Job 32:1 he was righteous in his own **e.** 5869
Job 34:21 his **e.** are upon the ways of man, 5869
Job 36:7 not his **e.** from the righteous: 5869
Job 39:29 prey, and her **e.** behold afar off 5869
Job 40:24 He taketh it with his **e.**: his nose 5869
Job 41:18 and his **e.** are like the eyelids of the 5869
Ps 10:8 **e.** are privily set against the poor 5869
Ps 11:4 his **e.** behold, his eyelids try, 5869
Ps 13:3 lighten mine **e.**, lest I sleep 5869
Ps 15:4 whose **e.** a vile person is contemned; 5869
Ps 17:2 **e.** behold the things that are equal 5869
Ps 17:11 they have set their **e.** bowing down 5869
Ps 19:8 Lord is pure, enlightening the **e.** 5869
Ps 25:15 Mine **e.** are ever toward the Lord; 5869
Ps 26:3 lovingkindness is before mine **e.**: 5869
Ps 31:22 I am cut off from before thine **e.**: 5869
Ps 34:15 The **e.** of the Lord are upon the 5869
Ps 36:1 there is no fear of God before his **e.** 5869
Ps 36:2 he flattereth himself in his own **e.**, 5869
Ps 38:10 the light of mine **e.**, it also is gone 5869
Ps 50:21 set them in order before thine **e.** 5869
Ps 66:7 his **e.** behold the nations: let not 5869
Ps 69:3 mine **e.** fail while I wait for my God 5869
Ps 69:23 **e.** be darkened, that they see not; 5869
Ps 73:7 Their **e.** stand out with fatness: 5869
Ps 77:4 Thou holdest mine **e.** waking: I 5869
Ps 91:8 Only with thine **e.** shalt thou behold 5869
Ps 101:3 set no wicked thing before mine **e.**: 5869
Ps 101:6 Mine **e.** shall be upon the faithful 5869
Ps 115:5 **e.** have they, but they see not: 5869
Ps 116:8 soul from death, mine **e.** from tears, 5869
Ps 118:23 doing; it is marvellous in our **e.** 5869
Ps 119:18 Open thou mine **e.**, that I may 5869
Ps 119:37 mine **e.** from beholding vanity; 5869
Ps 119:82 Mine **e.** fail for thy word, saying, 5869
Ps 119:123 Mine **e.** fail for thy salvation, and 5869
Ps 119:136 Rivers of waters run down mine **e.**, 5869
Ps 119:148 Mine **e.** prevent the night watches, 5869
Ps 121:1 I will lift up mine **e.** unto the hills, 5869
Ps 123:1 Unto thee lift I up mine **e.**, O thou 5869
Ps 123:2 as the **e.** of servants look unto the 5869
Ps 123:2 as the **e.** of a maiden unto the hand 5869
Ps 123:2 our **e.** wait upon the Lord our God, 5869
Ps 131:1 is not haughty, nor mine **e.** lofty: 5869
Ps 132:4 I will not give sleep to mine **e.**, 5869
Ps 135:16 **e.** have they, but they see not; 5869
Ps 139:16 Thine **e.** did see my substance, yet 5869
Ps 141:8 But mine **e.** are unto thee, O God 5869
Ps 145:15 The **e.** of all wait upon thee: 5869
Ps 146:8 The Lord openeth the **e.** of the blind:
Pr 3:7 Be not wise in thine own **e.**: 5869
Pr 3:21 let not them depart from thine **e.**: 5869
Pr 4:21 Let them not depart from thine **e.**; 5869
Pr 4:25 Let thine **e.** look right on, and let 5869
Pr 5:21 man are before the **e.** of the Lord, 5869
Pr 6:4 Give not sleep to thine **e.**, nor 5869
Pr 6:13 winketh with his **e.**, he speaketh 5869
Pr 10:26 smoke to the **e.**, so is the sluggard 5869
Pr 12:15 way of a fool is right in his own **e.**: 5869
Pr 15:3 **e.** of the Lord are in every place, 5869
Pr 15:30 light of the **e.** rejoiceth the heart: 5869
Pr 16:2 of a man are clean in his own **e.**; 5869
Pr 16:30 shutteth his **e.** to devise froward 5869
Pr 17:8 as a precious stone in the **e.** of him 5869
Pr 17:24 but the **e.** of a fool are in the ends 5869
Pr 20:8 scattereth away all evil with his **e.** 5869
Pr 20:13 open thine **e.**, and thou shalt be 5869
Pr 21:2 way of a man is right in his own **e.**: 5869
Pr 21:10 findeth no favour in his **e.** 5869
Pr 22:12 The **e.** of the Lord preserve 5869
Pr 23:5 thine **e.** upon that which is not? 5869
Pr 23:26 and let thine **e.** observe my ways 5869
Pr 23:29 cause? who hath redness of **e.**? 5869
Pr 23:33 Thine **e.** shall behold strange 5869
Pr 25:7 prince whom thine **e.** have seen 5869
Pr 27:20 so the **e.** of man are never satisfied 5869
Pr 28:27 his **e.** shall have many a curse 5869
Pr 29:13 the Lord lighteneth both their **e.** 5869
Pr 30:12 that are pure in their own **e.**, 5869
Pr 30:13 O how lofty are their **e.**! 5869
Ec 2:10 **e.** desired I kept not from them, 5869
Ec 2:14 The wise man's **e.** are in his head; 5869
Ec 5:11 beholding of them with their **e.**? 5869
Ec 6:9 Better is the sight of the **e.** than 5869
Ec 8:16 nor night seeth sleep with his **e.**: 5869
Ec 11:7 thing it is for the **e.** to behold the 5869
Ec 11:9 heart, and in the sight of thine **e.**: 5869
Ca 1:15 thou art fair; thou hast doves' **e.** 5869
Ca 4:1 thou art fair; thou hast doves' **e.** 5869
Ca 4:9 my heart with one of thine **e.**, 5869
Ca 5:12 His **e.** are as the **e.** of doves 5869
Ca 6:5 Turn away thine **e.** from me, for 5869
Ca 7:4 **e.** like the fishpools in Heshbon: 5869
Ca 8:10 in his **e.** as one that found favour 5869
Isa 1:15 I will hide mine **e.** from you: yea, 5869
Isa 1:16 of your doings from before mine **e.**; 5869
Isa 3:8 Lord, to provoke the **e.** of his glory 5869
Isa 3:16 stretched forth necks and wanton **e.**, 5869
Isa 5:15 the **e.** of the lofty shall be humbled: 5869
Isa 5:21 them that are wise in their own **e.**, 5869
Isa 6:5 for mine **e.** have seen the King, 5869
Isa 6:10 their ears heavy, and shut their **e.**; 5869
Isa 6:10 lest they see with their **e.**, 5869
Isa 11:3 not judge after the sight of his **e.**, 5869
Isa 13:16 be dashed to pieces before their **e.**; 5869
Isa 17:7 and his **e.** shall have respect to the 5869
Isa 29:10 sleep, and hath closed your **e.**: 5869
Isa 29:18 the **e.** of the blind shall see out of 5869
Isa 30:20 but thine **e.** shall see thy teachers: 5869
Isa 32:3 **e.** of them that see shall not be dim, 5869
Isa 33:15 and shutteth his **e.** from seeing evil; 5869
Isa 33:17 **e.** shall see the King in his beauty: 5869
Isa 33:20 thine **e.** shall see Jerusalem a quiet 5869
Isa 35:5 the **e.** of the blind shall be opened, 5869
Isa 37:17 open then **e.**, O Lord, and see: 5869
Isa 37:23 and lifted up thine **e.** on high? 5869
Isa 38:14 mine **e.** fail with looking upward: 5869
Isa 40:26 Lift up your **e.** on high, and behold 5869
Isa 42:7 To open the blind **e.**, to bring out 5869
Isa 43:8 forth the blind people that have **e.**, 5869
Isa 44:18 he hath shut their **e.**, that they 5869
Isa 49:5 I be glorious in the **e.** of the Lord, 5869
Isa 49:18 Lift up thine **e.** round about, and 5869
Isa 51:6 Lift up your **e.** to the heavens, 5869
Isa 52:10 made bare his holy arm in the **e.** 5869
Isa 59:10 we grope as if we had no **e.**: 5869
Isa 60:4 Lift up thine **e.** round about, and 5869
Isa 65:12 but did evil before mine **e.**, and did 5869
Isa 65:16 because they are hid from mine **e.** 5869
Isa 66:4 but they did evil before mine **e.**, 5869
Jer 3:2 up thine **e.** unto the high places, 5869
Jer 5:3 are not thine **e.** upon the truth? 5869
Jer 5:21 which have **e.**, and see not; 5869
Jer 7:11 become a den of robbers in your **e.**? 5869
Jer 9:1 and mine **e.** a fountain of tears, 5869
Jer 9:18 that our **e.** may run down with tears 5869
Jer 13:20 Lift up your **e.**, and behold them 5869
Jer 14:6 their **e.** did fail, because there was 5869
Jer 14:17 Let mine **e.** run down with tears 5869
Jer 16:9 cease out of this place in your **e.**, 5869
Jer 16:17 mine **e.** are upon all their ways: 5869
Jer 16:17 is their iniquity hid from mine **e.** 5869
Jer 20:4 and thine **e.** shall behold it: and 5869
Jer 22:17 thine **e.** and thine heart are not 5869
Jer 24:6 set mine **e.** upon them for good, 5869
Jer 29:21 he shall slay them before your **e.**; 5869
Jer 31:16 weeping, and thine **e.** from tears: 5869
Jer 32:4 and his **e.** shall behold his **e.**; 5869
Jer 32:19 thine **e.** are open upon all the ways 5869
Jer 34:3 thine **e.** shall behold the **e.** of the 5869
Jer 39:6 Zedekiah in Riblah before his **e.**: 5869
Jer 39:7 Moreover he put out Zedekiah's **e.**, 5869
Jer 42:2 few of many, as thine **e.** do behold 5869
Jer 52:2 was evil in the **e.** of the Lord, 5869
Jer 52:10 the sons of Zedekiah before his **e.**: 5869
Jer 52:11 Then he put out the **e.** of Zedekiah; 5869
La 2:11 Mine **e.** do fail with tears, 5869
La 4:17 **e.** as yet failed for our vain help: 5869
La 5:17 for these things our **e.** are dim 5869
Eze 1:18 rings were full of **e.** round about 5869
Eze 6:9 their **e.**, which go a whoring after 5869
Eze 8:5 Son of man, lift up thine **e.** now 5869
Eze 8:5 So I lifted up mine **e.** the north, 5869
Eze 10:12 wheels, were full of **e.** round about, 5869
Eze 12:2 a rebellious house, which have **e.** 5869
Eze 12:12 he see not the ground with his **e.** 5869
Eze 18:6 neither hath lifted up his **e.** to the 5869
Eze 18:12 and hath lifted up his **e.** to the idols 5869
Eze 18:15 neither hath lifted up his **e.** to the 5869
Eze 20:7 man the abominations of his **e.**, 5869
Eze 20:8 away the abominations of their **e.**, 5869
Eze 20:24 **e.** were after their fathers' idols 5869
Eze 21:6 with bitterness sigh before their **e.** 5869
Eze 22:26 hid their **e.** from my sabbaths, 5869
Eze 23:16 soon as she saw them with her **e.**, 5869
Eze 23:27 thou shalt not lift up thine **e.** unto 5869
Eze 23:40 didst wash thyself, paintedst thy **e.**, 5869
Eze 24:16 from thee the desire of thine **e.** 5869
Eze 24:21 the desire of your **e.**, and that which 5869
Eze 24:25 their glory, the desire of their **e.**, 5869
Eze 33:25 lift up your **e.** toward your idols, 5869
Eze 36:23 be sanctified in you before their **e.** 5869
Eze 37:20 be in thine hand before their **e.** 5869
Eze 38:16 in thee, O Gog, before their **e.** 5869
Eze 38:23 known in the **e.** of many nations, 5869
Eze 40:4 Son of man, behold with thine **e.**, 5869
Eze 44:5 mark well, and behold with thine **e.**, 5869
Da 4:34 Nebuchadnezzar lifted up mine **e.** 5870
Da 7:8 this horn were **e.** like the **e.** of man, 5870
Da 7:20 even of that horn that had **e.**, 5870
Da 8:3 Then I lifted up mine **e.**, and saw, 5869
Da 8:5 had a notable horn between his **e.** 5869
Da 8:21 great horn that is between his **e.** 5869
Da 9:18 thine **e.**, and behold our desolations, 5869
Da 10:5 I lifted up mine **e.**, and looked, 5869
Da 10:6 his **e.** as lamps of fire, and his arms 5869
Ho 13:14 shall be hid from mine **e.** 5869
Joe 1:16 not the meat cut off before our **e.**, 5869
Am 9:4 will set mine **e.** upon them for evil, 5869
Am 9:8 the **e.** of the Lord God are upon 5869
Mic 7:10 mine **e.** shall behold her: now shall 5869
Hab 1:13 Thou art of purer **e.** than to behold 5869
Zep 3:20 back your captivity before your **e.**, 5869
Hag 2:3 not in your **e.** in comparison of it 5869
Zec 1:18 Then lifted I up mine **e.**, and saw, 5869
Zec 2:1 I lifted up mine **e.** again, and looked, 5869
Zec 3:9 upon one stone shall be seven **e.**: 5869
Zec 4:10 they are the **e.** of the Lord, which 5869
Zec 5:1 I turned, and lifted up mine **e.**, 5869
Zec 5:5 Lift up now thine **e.**, and see 5869
Zec 5:9 lifted I up mine **e.**, and looked, 5869
Zec 6:1 Then I turned, and lifted up mine **e.**, 5869
Zec 8:6 marvellous in the **e.** of the remnant 5869
Zec 8:6 it also be marvellous in mine **e.**? 5869
Zec 9:1 the **e.** of man, as of all the tribes 5869
Zec 9:8 for now have I seen with mine **e.** 5869
Zec 12:4 mine **e.** upon the house of Judah, 5869
Zec 14:12 their **e.** shall consume away in 5869
Mal 1:5 your **e.** shall see, and ye shall say, 5869
Mt 9:29 Then touched he their **e.**, saying, *3788*
Mt 9:30 their **e.** were opened; and Jesus *3788*
Mt 13:15 **and their e. they have closed;** *3788*
Mt 13:15 **time they should see with their e.**, *3788*
Mt 13:16 **blessed are your e., for they see:** *3788*
Mt 17:8 when they had lifted up their **e.**, *3788*
Mt 18:9 **rather than having two e. to be** *3788*
Mt 20:33 Lord, that our **e.** may be opened. *3788*
Mt 20:34 on them, and touched their **e.**: *3788*
Mt 20:34 their **e.** received sight, and they *3788*
Mt 21:42 **and it is marvellous in our e.?** *3788*
Mt 26:43 for their **e.** were heavy *3788*
Mk 8:18 **Having e., see ye not? having ears,** *3788*
Mk 8:23 and when he had spit on his **e.**, *3659*
Mk 8:25 put his hands again upon his **e.**, *3788*
Mk 9:47 **having two e. to be cast into hell** *3788*
Mk 12:11 **and it is marvellous in our e.?** *3788*
Mk 14:40 (for their **e.** were heavy,) neither *3788*
Lu 2:30 For mine **e.** have seen thy salvation, *3788*
Lu 4:20 And the **e.** of all them that were *3788*

Lu 6:20 he lifted up his **e.** on his disciples, 3788
Lu 10:23 **Blessed are the e. which see the** 3788
Lu 16:23 **And in hell he lifted up his e.,** 3788
Lu 18:13 **up so much as his e. unto heaven,** 3788
Lu 19:42 **but now they are hid from thine e.** 3788
Lu 24:16 **e.** were holden that they should 3788
Lu 24:31 And their **e.** were opened, and they 3788
Joh 4:35 **Lift up your e., and look on the** 3788
Joh 6:5 Jesus then lifted up his **e.**, and saw 3788
Joh 9:6 he anointed the **e.** of the blind man 3788
Joh 9:10 him, How were thine **e.** opened? 3788
Joh 9:11 and anointed mine **e.**, and said 3788
Joh 9:14 made the clay, and opened his **e.** 3788
Joh 9:15 He put clay upon mine **e.**, and I 3788
Joh 9:17 him, that he hath opened thine **e.**? 3788
Joh 9:21 who hath opened his **e.**, we know 3788
Joh 9:26 thee? how opened he thine **e.**? 3788
Joh 9:30 and yet he hath opened mine **e.** 3788
Joh 9:32 that any man opened the **e.** of one 3788
Joh 10:21 Can a devil open the **e.** of the blind? 3788
Joh 11:37 which opened the **e.** of the blind, 3788
Joh 11:41 Jesus lifted up his **e.**, and said, 3788
Joh 12:40 He hath blinded their **e.**, and 3788
Joh 12:40 they should not see with their **e.**, 3788
Joh 17:1 and lifted up his **e.** to heaven, and 3788
Ac 3:4 Peter, fastening his **e.** upon him with
Ac 9:8 his **e.** were opened, he saw no man: 3788
Ac 9:18 from his **e.** as it had been scales: 3788
Ac 9:40 And she opened her **e.**: and when 3788
Ac 11:6 when I had fastened mine **e.**, I
Ac 13:9 the Holy Ghost, set his **e.** on him,
Ac 26:18 **To open their e., and to turn them** 3788
Ac 28:27 and their **e.** have they closed; 3788
Ac 28:27 lest they should see with their **e.**, 3788
Ro 3:18 is not fear of God before their **e.** 3788
Ro 11:8 **e.** that they should not see, and 3788
Ro 11:10 Let their **e.** be darkened, that they 3788
Ga 3:1 before whose **e.** Jesus Christ hath 3788
Ga 4:15 have plucked out your own **e.**, 3788
Eph 1:18 The **e.** of your understanding being 3788
Heb 4:13 and opened unto the **e.** of him with 3788
1Pe 3:12 For the **e.** of the Lord are over the 3788
2Pe 2:14 Having **e.** full of adultery, and that 3788
1Jo 1:1 which we have seen with our **e.**, 3788
1Jo 2:11 that darkness hath blinded his **e.** 3788
1Jo 2:16 lust of the **e.**, and the pride of life, 3788
Re 1:14 and his **e.** were as a flame of fire; 3788
Re 2:18 **hath his e. like unto a flame of** 3788
Re 3:18 **and anoint thine e. with eyesalve,** 3788
Re 4:6 there four beasts full of **e.** before 3788
Re 4:8 and they were full of **e.** within: 3788
Re 5:6 seven **e.**, which are the seven spirits 3788
Re 7:17 wipe away all tears from their **e.** 3788
Re 19:12 His **e.** were as a flame of fire, 3788
Re 21:4 wipe away all tears from their **e.**; 3788

EYESALVE
Re 3:18 **and anoint thine eyes with e., that** 2854

EYESERVICE
Eph 6:6 Now with **e.**, as menpleasers; but as 3787
Col 3:22 not with **e.**, as menpleasers; but in 3787

EYESIGHT See also EYE and SIGHT.
Ps 18:24 cleanness of my hands in his **e.** 5869

EYEWITNESSES
Lu 1:2 which from the beginning were **e.**, 845
2Pe 1:16 but were **e.** of his majesty. 2030

EZAR (e'-zar) See also EZER.
1Ch 1:38 and Dishon, and **E.**, and Dishan. 687

EZBAI (ez'-bahee)
1Ch 11:37 Carmelite, Naarai the son of **E.**, 229

EZBON (ez'-bon)
Ge 46:16 Haggi, Shuni, and **E.**, Eri, 675
1Ch 7:7 the sons of Bela; and **E.**, and Uzzi 675

EZEKIAS (ez-e-ki'-as) See also HEZEKIAH.
Mt 1:9 Achaz; and Achaz begat **E.**; 1478
Mt 1:10 And **E.** begat Manasses; and 1478

EZEKIEL (e-zeke'-yel)
Eze *general* *title* Book Of The Prophet **E.** 3168
Eze 1:3 the Lord came expressly unto **E.** 3168
Eze 24:24 Thus **E.** is unto you a sign: 3168

EZEL (e'-zel) See also BETH-EZEL.
1Sa 20:19 and shalt remain by the stone **E.** 237

EZEM (e'-zem) See also AZEM.
1Ch 4:29 Bilhah, and at **E.**, and at Tolad, 6107

EZER (e'-zur) See also ABI-EZER; EBEN-EZER; EZAR; ROMAMTI-EZER.
Ge 36:21 And Dishon, and **E.**, and Dishan: 687
Ge 36:27 The children of **e.** are these; Bilhan, 687
Ge 36:30 Dishon, duke **E.**, duke Dishan: 687
1Ch 1:42 The sons of **E.**; Bilhan, and Zavan, 687
1Ch 4:4 and **E.** the father of Hushah. 5829
1Ch 7:21 and **E.**, and Elead, whom the men 5827
1Ch 12:9 **E.** the first, Obadiah the second, 5829
Ne 3:19 next to him repaired **E.** the son of 5829
Ne 12:42 and Malchijah, and Elam, and **E.** 5829

EZION-GABER (e''-ze-on-ga'-bur) See also EZIONGEBER.
Nu 33:35 Ebronah, and encamped at **E.** 6100
Nu 33:36 And they removed from **E.**, and 6100
De 2:8 from **E.**, we turned and passed 6100
2Ch 20:36 and they made the ships in **E.** 6100

EZION-GEBER (e''-ze-on-ghe'-bur) See also EZIONGABER.
1Ki 9:26 made a navy of ships in **E.**, 6100
1Ki 22:48 for the ships were broken at **E.** 6100
2Ch 8:17 went Solomon to **E.**, and to Eloth, 6100

EZNITE (ez'-nite)
2Sa 23:8 the same was Adino the **E.**: he 6112

EZRA (ez'-rah) See also AZARIAH; EZRAHITE.
1Ch 4:17 of **E.** were, Jether, and Mered, 5830
Ezr *general* *title* **E.** 5830
Ezr 7:1 **E.** the son of Seraiah, the son of 5830
Ezr 7:6 This **E.** went up from Babylon; 5830
Ezr 7:10 **E.** had prepared his heart to seek 5830
Ezr 7:11 Artaxerxes gave unto **E.** the priest, 5830
Ezr 7:12 kings of kings, Unto **E.** the priest, 5830
Ezr 7:21 whatsoever **E.** the priest, the scribe 5830
Ezr 7:25 **E.**, after the wisdom of thy God, 5830
Ezr 10:1 Now when **E.** had prayed, and 5830
Ezr 10:2 said unto **e.**, We have trespassed 5830
Ezr 10:5 Then arose **E.**, and made the chief 5830
Ezr 10:6 **E.** rose up from before the house 5830
Ezr 10:10 **E.** the priest stood up, and said 5830
Ezr 10:16 And **E.** the priest, with certain chief 5830
Ne 8:1 and they spake unto **E.** the scribe 5830
Ne 8:2 And **E.** the priest brought the law 5830
Ne 8:4 **E.** the scribe stood upon a pulpit 5830
Ne 8:5 **E.** opened the book in the sight of 5830
Ne 8:6 **E.** blessed the Lord, the great God 5830
Ne 8:9 and **E.** the priest the scribe, and the 5830
Ne 8:13 Levites, unto **E.** the scribe, even to 5830
Ne 12:1 Seraiah, Jeremiah, **E.**, 5830
Ne 12:13 Of **E.**, Meshullam; of Amariah, 5830
Ne 12:26 and of **E.** the priest, the scribe 5830
Ne 12:33 And Azariah, **E.**, Meshullam, 5830
Ne 12:36 of God, and **E.** the scribe before 5830

EZRAHITE (ez'-rah-hite)
1Ki 4:31 than Ethan the **E.**, and Heman, 250
Ps 88:*title* Maschil of Heman the **E.** 250
Ps 89:*title* Maschil of Ethan the **E.** 250

EZRI (ez'-ri)
1Ch 27:26 ground was **E.** the son of Chelub: 5836

EZRITE See ABI-EZRITE.

F.

FABLES
1Ti 1:4 Neither give heed to **f.** and endless 3454
1Ti 4:7 refuse profane and old wives' **f.**, 3454
2Ti 4:4 and shall be turned unto **f.** 3454
Tit 1:14 Not giving heed to Jewish **f.**, and 3454
2Pe 1:16 not followed cunningly devised **f.**, 3454

FACE See also FACES.
Ge 1:2 darkness was upon the **f.** of the 6440
Ge 1:2 Spirit of God moved upon the **f.** of 6440
Ge 1:29 which is upon the **f.** of all the earth, 6440
Ge 2:6 watered the whole **f.** of all the ground, 6440
Ge 3:19 In the sweat of thy **f.** shalt thou ear 639
Ge 4:14 driven me out this day from the **f.** 6440
Ge 4:14 of the earth; and from thy **f.** shall I 6440
Ge 6:1 to multiply on the **f.** of the earth, 6440
Ge 6:7 destroy...from the **f.** of the earth; 6440
Ge 7:3 seed alive upon the **f.** of all the earth 6440
Ge 7:4 destroy from off the **f.** of the earth 6440
Ge 7:18 ark went upon the **f.** of the waters 6440
Ge 7:23 was upon the **f.** of the ground, 6440
Ge 8:8 abated from off the **f.** of the ground; 6440
Ge 8:9 were on the **f.** of the whole earth: 6440
Ge 8:13 behold, the **f.** of the ground was dry 6440
Ge 11:4 upon the **f.** of the whole earth: 6440
Ge 11:8 thence upon the **f.** of all the earth: 6440
Ge 11:9 abroad upon the **f.** of all the earth. 6440
Ge 16:6 hardly with her, she fled from her **f.** 6440
Ge 16:8 I flee from the **f.** of my mistress 6440
Ge 17:3 And Abram fell on his **f.**: 6440
Ge 17:17 Then Abraham fell upon his **f.** 6440
Ge 19:1 with his **f.** toward the ground; 639
Ge 19:13 great before the **f.** of the Lord; 6440
Ge 24:47 and I put the earring upon her **f.**, 639
Ge 30:33 come for my hire before thy **f.**: 6440
Ge 31:21 set his **f.** toward the mount Gilead. 6440
Ge 32:20 and afterward I will see his **f.**; 6440
Ge 32:30 for I have seen God **f.** to **f.**, 6440
Ge 33:10 I have seen thy **f.**, and though I had 6440
Ge 33:10 though I had seen the **f.** of God, 6440
Ge 35:1 thou fleddest from the **f.** of Esau 6440
Ge 35:7 he fled from the **f.** of his brother. 6440
Ge 36:6 from the **f.** of his brother Jacob. 6440
Ge 38:15 because she had covered her **f.** 6440
Ge 41:56 was over all the **f.** of the earth: 6440
Ge 43:3 Ye shall not see my **f.**, except your 6440
Ge 43:5 unto us, Ye shall not see my **f.**, 6440
Ge 43:31 he washed his **f.**, and went out, 6440
Ge 44:23 with you, ye shall see my **f.** no more 6440
Ge 44:26 for we may not see the man's **f.**, 6440
Ge 46:28 him unto Joseph, to direct his **f.** 6440
Ge 46:30 let me die, since I have seen thy **f.**, 6440
Ge 48:11 I had not thought to see thy **f.**: 6440
Ge 48:12 bowed himself with his **f.** to the 639
Ge 50:1 Joseph fell upon his father's **f.**, 6440
Ge 50:18 went and fell down before his **f.**; 6440
Ex 2:15 Moses fled form the **f.** of Pharaoh, 6440
Ex 3:6 Moses hid his **f.**; for he was afraid 6440
Ex 10:5 they shall cover the **f.** of the earth, 5869
Ex 10:15 covered the **f.** of the whole earth, 5869
Ex 10:28 see my **f.** no more; for in that day 6440
Ex 10:28 thou seest my **f.** thou shalt die. 6440
Ex 10:29 I will see thy **f.** again no more. 6440
Ex 14:19 cloud went from before their **f.**,
Ex 14:25 Let us flee from the **f.** of Israel; 6440
Ex 16:14 upon the **f.** of the wilderness there 6440
Ex 32:12 to consume them from the **f.** of the 6440
Ex 33:11 the Lord spake unto Moses **f.** to **f.**, 6440
Ex 33:16 that are upon the **f.** of the earth. 6440
Ex 33:20 he said, Thou canst not see my **f.**: 6440
Ex 33:23 but my **f.** shall not be seen. 6440
Ex 34:29 wist not that the skin of his **f.** shone 6440
Ex 34:30 behold, the skin of his **f.** shone; 6440
Ex 34:33 he put a vail on his **f.** 6440
Ex 34:35 saw the **f.** of Moses, that the skin of 6440
Ex 34:35 the skin of Moses **f.** shone: 6440
Ex 34:35 and Moses put the vail upon his **f.** 6440
Le 13:41 the part of his head toward his **f.**, 6440
Le 17:10 I will even set my **f.** against that 6440
Le 19:32 and honour the **f.** of the old man, 6440
Le 20:3, 5 I will set my **f.** against that man, 6440
Le 20:6 I will even set my **f.** against that 6440
Le 26:17 And I will set my **f.** against you, 6440
Nu 6:25 Lord make his **f.** shine upon thee, 6440
Nu 11:31 cubits high upon the **f.** of the earth 6440
Nu 12:3 which were upon the **f.** of the earth.) 6440
Nu 12:14 If her father had but spit in her **f.** 6440
Nu 14:14 that thou Lord art seen **f.** to **f.**, 5869
Nu 16:4 Moses heard it, he fell upon his **f.**: 6440
Nu 19:3 and one shall slay her before his **f.**:
Nu 22:5 they cover the **f.** of the earth, 5869
Nu 22:11 which covereth the **f.** of the earth: 5869
Nu 22:31 and fell flat on his **f.** 639
Nu 24:1 set his **f.** toward the wilderness. 6440

De 1:17 shall not be afraid of the **f.** of man;......6440
De 5:4 Lord talked with you **f.** to **f.** in the......6440
De 6:15 thee from off the **f.** of the earth.........6440
De 7:6 that are upon the **f.** of the earth......... 6440
De 7:10 them that hate him to their **f.**,............6440
De 7:10 he will repay him to his **f.**................. 6440
De 8:20 Lord destroyeth before your **f.**,................
De 9:3 bring them down before thy **f.**:.................
De 25:2 and to be beaten before his **f.**,.................
De 25:9 and spit in his **f.**, and shall answer.......6440
De 28:7 to be smitten before thy **f.**,.....................
De 28:31 taken away from before thy **f.**:..................
De 31:5 shall give them up before your **f.**,.............
De 31:17 and I will hide my **f.** from them,......... 6440
De 31:18 I will surely hide my **f.** in that day.......6440
De 32:20 said, I will hide my **f.** from them,........6440
De 34:10 whom the Lord knew **f.** to **f.**,............ 6440
Jos 5:14 Joshua fell on his **f.** to the earth,.........6440
Jos 7:6 fell to the earth upon his **f.** before.......6440
Jos 7:10 liest thou thus upon thy **f.**?................6440
Jg 6:22 seen an angel of the Lord **f.** to **f.**........6440
Ru 2:10 Then she fell on her **f.**, and bowed.........6440
1Sa 5:3 was fallen upon his **f.** to the earth....... 6440
1Sa 5:4 was fallen upon his **f.** to the ground..... 6440
1Sa 17:49 he fell upon his **f.** to the earth............6440
1Sa 20:15 every one from the **f.** of the earth.......6440
1Sa 20:41 and fell on his **f.** to the ground,............639
1Sa 24:8 David stooped with his **f.** to the........... 639
1Sa 25:23 and fell before David on her **f.**,............6440
1Sa 25:41 bowed herself on her **f.** to the earth,......639
1Sa 26:20 earth before the **f.** of the Lord:.......... 6440
1Sa 28:14 stooped with his **f.** to the ground,..........639
2Sa 2:22 how then should I hold up my **f.**........... 6440
2Sa 3:13 Thou shalt not see my **f.**, except........ 6440
2Sa 3:13 when thou comest to see my **f.**........... 6440
2Sa 9:6 he fell on his **f.**, and did reverence...... 6440
2Sa 14:4 she fell on her **f.** to the ground,........... 639
2Sa 14:22 Joab fell to the ground on his **f.**,.......... 6440
2Sa 14:24 and let him not see my **f.**...................6440
2Sa 14:24 house, and saw not the king's **f.**.......... 6440
2Sa 14:28 and saw not the king's **f.**....................6440
2Sa 14:32 therefore let me see the king's **f.**;........6440
2Sa 14:33 himself on his **f.** to the ground............ 639
2Sa 18:8 over the **f.** of all the country:............6440
2Sa 18:28 his **f.** before the king, and said,............639
2Sa 19:4 But the king covered his **f.**,................6440
2Sa 24:20 king on his **f.** upon the ground............ 639
1Ki 1:23 the king with his **f.** to the ground......... 639
1Ki 1:31 bowed with her **f.** to the earth,............639
1Ki 8:14 And the king turned his **f.** about,........ 6440
1Ki 13:6 Intreat now the **f.** of the Lord............ 6440
1Ki 13:34 destroy it from off the **f.** of the earth...6440
1Ki 18:7 he knew him, and fell on his **f.**,.......... 6440
1Ki 18:42 and put his **f.** between his knees.........6440
1Ki 19:13 he wrapped his **f.** in his mantle,.......... 6440
1Ki 20:38 himself with ashes upon his **f.**............ 5869
1Ki 20:41 took the ashes away from his **f.**;.........5869
1Ki 21:4 turned away his **f.**, and would eat....... 6440
2Ki 4:29 lay my staff upon the **f.** of the child...... 6440
2Ki 4:31 the staff upon the **f.** of the child;.........6440
2Ki 8:15 spread it on his **f.**, so that he died:..... 6440
2Ki 9:30 she painted her **f.**, and tired her......... 5869
2Ki 9:32 he lifted up his **f.** to the window,........ 6440
2Ki 9:37 as dung upon the **f.** of the field...........6440
2Ki 12:17 set his **f.** to go up to Jerusalem.......... 6440
2Ki 13:14 and wept over his **f.**, and said,........... 6440
2Ki 14:8 let us look one another in the **f.**...........6440
2Ki 14:11 Judah looked one another in the **f.**.........6440
2Ki 18:24 thou turn away the **f.** of one captain.... 6440
2Ki 20:2 he turned his **f.** to the wall,............... 6440
1Ch 16:11 strength, seek his **f.** continually.......... 6440
1Ch 21:21 to David with his **f.** to the ground.........639
2Ch 6:3 And the king tuned his **f.**, and............ 6440
2Ch 6:42 not away the **f.** of thine anointed:........6440
2Ch 7:14 and pray, and seek my **f.**,................. 6440
2Ch 20:18 head with his **f.** to the ground:.............639
2Ch 25:17 let us see one another in the **f.**............6440
2Ch 25:21 they saw one another in the **f.**,............ 6440
2Ch 30:9 will not turn away his **f.** from you,...... 6440
2Ch 32:21 with shame of **f.** to his own land......... 6440
2Ch 35:22 Josiah would not turn his **f.** from.........6440
Ezr 9:6 and blush to lift up my **f.** to thee........ 6440
Ezr 9:7 to a spoil, and to confusion of **f.**,.......... 6440
Es 1:14 and Media, which saw the king's **f.**,.......6440
Es 7:8 mouth, they covered Haman's **f.**.......... 6440
Job 1:11 and he will curse thee to thy **f.**...........6440
Job 2:5 and he will curse thee to thy **f.**...........6440
Job 4:15 Then a spirit passed before my **f.**;...... 6440
Job 11:15 For then shalt thou lift up thy **f.**......... 6440
Job 13:24 Wherefore hidest thou thy **f.**, and....... 6440
Job 15:27 he covereth his **f.** with his fatness,.......6440
Job 16:8 in me beareth witness to my **f.**...........6440
Job 16:16 My **f.** is foul with weeping,.................6440
Job 21:31 Who shall declare his way to his **f.**?.....6440
Job 22:26 shalt lift up thy **f.** unto God.............. 6440
Job 23:17 covered the darkness from my **f.**......... 6440
Job 24:15 see me: and disguiseth his **f.**................6440
Job 26:9 holdeth back the **f.** of his throne,........ 6440
Job 30:10 and spare not to spit in my **f.**..............6440
Job 33:26 he shall see his **f.** with joy;..................6440
Job 34:29 and when he hideth his **f.**, who............6440
Job 37:12 the **f.** of the world in the earth........... 6440
Job 38:30 and the **f.** of the deep is frozen.......... 6440
Job 41:13 discover the **f.** of his garment?........... 6440
Job 41:14 Who can open the doors of his **f.**?.......6440
Ps 5:8 thy way straight before my **f.**...............6440
Ps 10:11 hideth his **f.**; he will never see it........ 6440
Ps 13:1 how long wilt thou hide thy **f.**............. 6440
Ps 17:15 will behold thy **f.** in righteousness:...... 6440
Ps 21:12 thy strings against the **f.** of them........ 6440
Ps 22:24 hath he hid his **f.** from him;................ 6440
Ps 24:6 that seek thy **f.**, O Jacob. Selah..........6440
Ps 27:8 Seek ye my **f.**; my hearts said unto..... 6440
Ps 27:8 Thy **f.**, Lord, will I seek..................... 6440
Ps 27:9 Hide not thy **f.** far from me;.............. 6440
Ps 30:7 hide thy **f.**, and I was troubled........... 6440
Ps 31:16 thy **f.** to shine upon thy servant:.........6440
Ps 34:16 The **f.** of the Lord is against them.......6440
Ps 41:12 settest me before thy **f.** for ever......... 6440
Ps 44:15 shame of my **f.** hath covered me,........6440
Ps 44:24 Wherefore hidest thou thy **f.**, and...... 6440
Ps 51:9 Hide thy **f.** from my sins,...................6440
Ps 67:1 and cause his **f.** to shine upon us;....... 6440
Ps 69:7 shame hath covered my **f.**.................. 6440
Ps 69:17 hide not thy **f.** from thy servant;..........6440
Ps 80:3 O God, and cause they **f.** to shine;......6440
Ps 80:7 of hosts, and cause thy **f.** to shine;......6440
Ps 80:19 of hosts, cause thy **f.** to shine:............6440
Ps 84:9 look upon the **f.** of thine anointed.......... 6440
Ps 88:14 why hidest thou thy **f.** from me?.........6440
Ps 89:14 and truth shall go before thy **f.**........... 6440
Ps 89:23 beat down his foes before his **f.**,..........6440
Ps 102:2 Hide not thy **f.** from me in the day......6440
Ps 104:15 and oil to make his **f.** to shine,............6440
Ps 104:29 hidest thy **f.**, they are troubled:............6440
Ps 104:30 thou renewest the **f.** of the earth........ 6440
Ps 105:4 strength: seek his **f.** evermore........... 6440
Ps 119:135 Make thy **f.** to shine upon thy............ 6440
Ps 132:10 not away the **f.** of thine anointed.........6440
Ps 143:7 faileth: hide not thy **f.** from me,..........6440
Pr 7:13 with an impudent **f.** said unto him,...... 6440
Pr 7:15 thee, diligently to seek thy **f.**,............ 6440
Pr 8:27 compass upon the **f.** of the depth:....... 6440
Pr 21:29 A wicked man hardeneth his **f.**:........... 6440
Pr 24:31 nettles had covered the **f.** thereof,...... 6440
Pr 27:19 As in water **f.** answereth to **f.**, so.......6440
Ec 8:1 wisdom maketh his **f.** to shine,........... 6440
Ec 8:1 boldness of his **f.** shall be changed.......6440
Isa 6:2 with twain he covered his **f.**,..............6440
Isa 8:17 his **f.** from the house of Jacob,........... 6440
Isa 14:21 fill the **f.** of the world with cities......... 6440
Isa 16:4 to them from the **f.** of the spoiler:........6440
Isa 23:17 the world upon the **f.** of the earth....... 6440
Isa 25:7 the **f.** of the covering cast over all.......6440
Isa 27:6 fill the **f.** of the world with fruit..........6440
Isa 28:25 he hath made plain the **f.** thereof,........ 6440
Isa 29:22 neither shall his **f.** now wax pale......... 6440
Isa 36:9 turn away the **f.** of one captain........... 6440
Isa 38:2 Hezekiah turned his **f.** toward the....... 6440
Isa 49:23 with their **f.** toward the earth,............ 639
Isa 50:6 my **f.** from shame and spitting............ 6440
Isa 50:7 have I set my **f.** like a flint,............... 6440
Isa 54:8 hid my **f.** from thee for a moment;....... 6440
Isa 59:2 your sins have hid his **f.** from you,...... 6440
Isa 64:7 thou hast hid thy **f.** from us,............... 6440
Isa 65:3 me to anger continually to my **f.**;......... 6440
Jer 1:13 the **f.** thereof is toward the north........6440
Jer 2:27 their back unto me, and not their **f.**:.....6440
Jer 4:30 thou rentest thy **f.** with painting,.........5869
Jer 8:2 for dung upon the **f.** of the earth:.........6440
Jer 13:26 I discover thy skirts upon thy **f.**,......... 6440
Jer 16:4 as dung upon the **f.** of the earth:......... 6440
Jer 16:17 ways: they are not hid from my **f.**,.......6440
Jer 18:17 shew them the back, and not the **f.**,..... 6440
Jer 21:10 I have set my **f.** against this city.........6440
Jer 22:25 of them whose **f.** thou fearest,........... 6440
Jer 25:26 which are upon the **f.** of the earth:......6440
Jer 28:16 thee from off the **f.** of the earth:.........6440
Jer 32:31 should remove it from before my **f.**,..... 6440
Jer 32:33 unto me the back, and not the **f.**:........6440
Jer 33:5 I have hid my **f.** from this city............6440
Jer 44:11 I will set my **f.** against you................. 6440
La 2:19 like water before the **f.** of the Lord:.... 6440
La 3:35 before the **f.** of the most High,............6440
Eze 1:10 the **f.** of a man, and the **f.** of a lion,.... 6440
Eze 1:10 had the **f.** of an ox on the left side;..... 6440
Eze 1:10 four also had the **f.** of an eagle.......... 6440
Eze 1:28 fell upon my **f.**, and I heard a voice..... 6440
Eze 3:8 thy **f.** strong against their faces,......... 6440
Eze 3:23 of Chebar: and I fell on my **f.**.............6440
Eze 4:3 and set thy **f.** against it, and it shall.....6440
Eze 4:7 shalt set thy **f.** toward the siege......... 6440
Eze 6:2 set thy **f.** toward the mountains.......... 6440
Eze 7:22 My **f.** will I turn also from them,........ 6440
Eze 9:8 I fell upon my **f.**, and cried,............... 6440
Eze 10:14 the first **f.** was the **f.** of a cherbub,..... 6440
Eze 10:14 the second **f.** was the **f.** of a man,...... 6440
Eze 10:14 and the third the **f.** of a lion,.............. 6440
Eze 10:14 and the fourth the **f.** of an eagle.......... 6440
Eze 11:13 Then fell I down upon my **f.**,.............. 6440
Eze 12:6 shalt cover thy **f.**, that thou see not.... 6440
Eze 12:12 shall cover his **f.**, that he see not........6440
Eze 13:17 set thy **f.** against the daughters of.......6440
Eze 14:3 of their iniquity before their **f.**:.......... 6440
Eze 14:4, 7 of his iniquity before his **f.**, and........6440
Eze 14:8 I will set my **f.** against that man,......... 6440
Eze 15:7 I will set my **f.** against them;............. 6440
Eze 15:7 when I set my **f.** against them............6440
Eze 20:35 there will I plead with you **f.** to **f.**.......6440
Eze 20:46 man, set thy **f.** toward the south,....... 6440
Eze 21:2 man, set thy **f.** toward Jerusalem,....... 6440
Eze 21:16 left, whithersoever thy **f.** is set.......... 6440
Eze 25:2 set thy **f.** against the Ammonites,....... 6440
Eze 28:21 of man, set thy **f.** against Zidon.......... 6440
Eze 29:2 of man, set thy **f.** against Pharaoh...... 6440
Eze 34:6 upon all the **f.** of the earth,............... 6440
Eze 35:2 man, set thy **f.** against mount Seir,...... 6440
Eze 38:2 Son of man, set thy **f.** against Gog,..... 6440
Eze 38:18 my fury shall come up in my **f.**............ 639
Eze 38:20 that are upon the **f.** of the earth,........ 6440
Eze 39:14 remain upon the **f.** of the earth,..........6440
Eze 39:23 therefore hid I my **f.** from them.........6440
Eze 39:24 and hid my **f.** from them.................. 6440
Eze 39:29 neither will I hide my **f.** any more....... 6440
Eze 40:15 And from the **f.** of the gate of the.......6440
Eze 40:15 entrance unto the **f.** of the porch....... 6440
Eze 41:14 the breadth of the **f.** of the house,...... 6440
Eze 41:19 **f.** of a man was toward the palm.........6440
Eze 41:19 **f.** of a young lion toward the palm.......6440
Eze 41:21 and the **f.** of the sanctuary;............... 6440
Eze 41:25 upon the **f.** of the porch without......... 6440
Eze 43:3 of Chebar; and I fell upon my **f.**...........6440
Eze 44:4 the Lord: and I fell upon my **f.**.......... 6440
Da 2:46 Nebuchadnezzar fell upon his **f.**,........... 600
Da 8:5 on the **f.** of the whole earth,..............6440
Da 8:17 I was afraid, and fell upon my **f.**:......... 6440
Da 8:18 I was in a deep sleep on my **f.**........... 6440
Da 9:3 I set my **f.** unto the Lord God,..............6440
Da 9:8 to us belongeth confusion of **f.**,............6440
Da 9:17 thy **f.** to shine upon thy sanctuary....... 6440
Da 10:6 **f.** as the appearance of lightning,.........6440
Da 10:9 then was I in a deep sleep on my **f.**,... 6440
Da 10:9 and my **f.** toward the ground............. 6440
Da 10:15 I set my **f.** toward the ground,........... 6440
Da 11:17 He shall also set his **f.** to enter.......... 6440
Da 11:18 shall he turn his **f.** unto the isles,........ 6440
Da 11:19 he shall turn his **f.** toward the fort.......6440
Ho 5:5 pride of Israel doth testify to his **f.**:..... 6440
Ho 5:15 their offence, and seek my **f.**:........... 6440
Ho 7:2 about: they are before my **f.**............... 6440
Ho 7:10 pride of Israel testifieth to his **f.**:........ 6440
Joe 2:6 Before their **f.** the people shall be....... 6440
Joe 2:20 with his **f.** toward the east sea,.......... 6440
Am 5:8 them out upon the **f.** of the earth:.......6440
Am 9:6 them out upon the **f.** of the earth:.......6440
Am 9:8 destroy it from off the **f.** of the earth;..6440
Mic 3:4 he will even hide his **f.** from them.......6440
Na 2:1 in pieces is come up before thy **f.**:...... 6440
Na 3:5 discover thy skirts upon thy **f.**,...........6440

Zec 5:3 over the f. of the whole earth: 6440
Mt 6:17 **anoint thine head, and wash thy f.;** *4383*
Mt 11:10 **I send my messenger before thy f.,** *4383*
Mt 16:3 **ye can discern the f. of the sky;** *4383*
Mt 17:2 and his f. did shine as the sun, *4383*
Mt 17:6 on their f., and were sore afraid. *4383*
Mt 18:10 **always behold the f. of my Father.** *4383*
Mt 26:39 and fell on his f., and prayed, *4383*
Mt 26:67 Then did they spit in his f., *4383*
Mk 1:2 I send my messenger before thy f., *4383*
Mk 14:65 to cover his f., and to buffet him, *4383*
Lu 1:76 shalt go before the f. of the Lord *4383*
Lu 2:31 prepared before the f. of all people; *4383*
Lu 5:12 who seeing Jesus fell on his f., *4383*
Lu 7:27 **I send my messenger before thy f.,** *4383*
Lu 9:51 set his f. to go to Jerusalem, *4383*
Lu 9:52 And sent messenger before thy f.: *4383*
Lu 9:53 because his f. was as though he *4383*
Lu 10:1 sent them two and two before his f. *4383*
Lu 12:56 **ye can discern the f. of the sky** *4383*
Lu 17:16 And fell down on his f. at his feet, *4383*
Lu 21:35 **dwell on the f. of the whole earth.** *4383*
Lu 22:64 struck him on the f., and asked *4383*
Joh 11:44 f. was bound about with a napkin. *3799*
Ac 2:25 the Lord always before my f., for *1799*
Ac 6:15 saw his f. as it had been the f. of *4383*
Ac 7:45 out before the f. of our fathers, *4383*
Ac 17:26 to dwell on all the f. of the earth, *4383*
Ac 20:25 shall see my f. no more. *4383*
Ac 20:38 that they should see his f. no more. *4383*
Ac 25:16 have the accusers f. to f., *4383*
1Co 13:12 a glass, darkly; but then f. to f.: *4383*
1Co 14:25 and so falling down on his f. *4383*
2Co 3:7 stedfastly behold the f. of Moses *4383*
2Co 3:13 which put a vail over his f., *4383*
2Co 3:18 with open f. beholding as in a glass *4383*
2Co 4:6 of God in the f. of Jesus Christ. *4383*
2Co 11:20 if a man smite you on the f. *4383*
Ga 1:22 unknown by f. unto the churches *4383*
Ga 2:11 I withstood him to the f., *4383*
Col 2:1 as have not seen my f. in the flesh; *4383*
1Th 2:17 to see your f. with great desire. *4383*
1Th 3:10 that we might see your f., *4383*
Jas 1:23 beholding his natural f. in a glass: *4383*
1Pe 3:12 the f. of the Lord is against them. *4383*
2Jo 12 and speak f. to f., that our joy may *4750*
3Jo 14 see thee, and we shall speak f. to f. *4750*
Re 4:7 the third beast had a f. as a man, *4383*
Re 6:16 hide us from the f. of him that *4383*
Re 10:1 and his f. was as it were the sun, *4383*
Re 12:14 a time, from the f. of the serpent. *4383*
Re 20:11 from whose f. the earth and the *4383*
Re 22:4 And they shall see his f.; *4383*

FACED See SHAMEFACEDNESS.

FACES
Ge 9:23 and their f. were backward, and 6440
Ge 18:22 their f. from thence, and went
Ge 30:40 and set the f. of the flocks 6440
Ge 42:6 with their f. to the earth. 639
Ex 19:7 before their f. all these words 6440
Ex 20:20 his fear may be before your f., 6440
Ex 25:20 their f. shall look one to another; 6440
Ex 25:20 shall the f. of the cherubims be. 6440
Ex 37:9 with their f. one to another; even 6440
Ex 37:9 were the f. of the cherubims. 6440
Le 9:24 they shouted, and fell on their f. 6440
Nu 14:5 Moses and Aaron fell on their f. 6440
Nu 16:22 they fell upon their f., and said, 6440
Nu 16:45 And they fell upon their f. 6440
Nu 20:6 they fell upon their f.: and the 6440
Jg 13:20 and fell on their f. to the ground. 6440
Jg 18:23 turned their f., and said unto Micah, 6440
2Sa 19:5 this day the f. of all thy servants, 6440
1Ki 2:15 all Israel set their f. on me, 6440
1Ki 18:39 they fell on their f.: and they said, 6440
1Ch 12:8 whose f. were like the f. of lions, 6440
1Ch 21:16 in sackcloth, fell upon their f. 6440
2Ch 3:13 feet, and their f. were inward. 6440
2Ch 7:3 with their f. to the ground upon the 639
2Ch 29:6 have turned away their f. from 6440
Ne 8:6 Lord with their f. to the ground. 639
Job 9:24 he covereth the f. of the judges 6440
Job 40:13 and bind their f. ins secret. 6440
Ps 34:5 and their f. were not ashamed. 6440
Ps 83:16 Fill their f. with shame; that they 6440
Isa 3:15 and grind the f. of the poor? 6440
Isa 13:8 their f. shall be as flames. 6440
Isa 25:8 wipe away tears from off all f.; 6440
Isa 53:3 we hid as it were our f. from him; 6440
Jer 1:8 Be not afraid of their f.: for I am 6440
Jer 1:17 be not dismayed at their f., 6440
Jer 5:3 made their f. harder than a rock; 6440
Jer 7:19 to the confusion of their own f.? 6440
Jer 30:6 all f. are turned into palenesss? 6440
Jer 42:15 If ye wholly set your f. to enter 6440
Jer 42:17 all the men that set their f. to 6440
Jer 44:12 that have set their f. to go into 6440
Jer 50:5 to Zion with their f. thitherward, 6440
Jer 51:51 shame hath covered our f.: for 6440
La 5:12 f. of elders were not honoured. 6440
Eze 1:6 And every one had four f., 6440
Eze 1:8 four had their f. and their wings. 6440
Eze 1:10 As for the likeness of their f., 6440
Eze 1:11 Thus were their f.: and their wings 6440
Eze 1:15 living creatures, with his four f. 6440
Eze 3:8 thy face strong against their f., 6440
Eze 7:18 and shame shall be upon all f., 6440
Eze 8:16 and their f. toward the east; 6440
Eze 10:14 And every one had four f.: 6440
Eze 10:21 Every one had four f. apiece, 6440
Eze 10:22 And the likeness of their f. was 6440
Eze 10:22 was the same f. which I saw 6440
Eze 14:6 f. from all your abominations. 6440
Eze 20:47 all f. from the south to the north 6440
Eze 41:18 and every cherub had two f.; 6440
Da 1:10 why should he see your f. worse 6440
Da 9:7 us confusion of f., as at this day; 6440
Joe 2:6 all f. shall gather blackness. 6440
Na 2:10 f. of them shall gather blackness. 6440
Hab 1:9 f. shall sup up as the east wind, 6440
Mal 2:3 and spread dung upon your f., 6440
Mt 6:16 **for they disfigure their f., that** *4383*
Lu 24:5 bowed down their f. to the earth, *4383*
Re 7:11 fell before the throne on their f., *4383*
Re 9:7 and their f. were as the f. of men. *4383*
Re 11:16 upon their f., and worshipped God, *4383*

FADE See also FADETH; FADING.
2Sa 22:46 Strangers shall f. away, and they 5034
Ps 18:45 strangers shall f. away, and be 5034
Isa 64:6 and we all do f. as a leaf; 5034
Jer 8:13 the fig tree, and the leaf shall f.; 5034
Eze 47:12 whose leaf shall not f., neither 5034
Jas 1:11 so also shall the rich man f. away. *3138*

FADETH
Isa 1:30 shall be as an oak whose leaf f., 5034
Isa 24:4 The earth mourneth and f. away, 5034
Isa 24:4 the world languisheth and f. away, 5034
Isa 40:7 the flower f.: because the spirit 5034
Isa 40:8 the flower f.: but the word of 5034
1Pe 1:4 undefiled, and that f. not away, *268*
1Pe 5:4 a crown of glory that f. not away. *262*

FADING
Isa 28:1 glorious beauty is a f. flower, 5034
Isa 28:4 shall be a f. flower, and as the 5034

FAIL See also FAILED; FAILETH; FAILING.
Ge 47:16 you for your cattle, if money f. 656
De 28:32 thine eyes shall look, and f. with 3615
De 31:6 he will not f. thee, nor forsake 7503
De 31:8 he will not f. thee, neither forsake 7503
Jos 1:5 I will not f. thee, nor forsake thee. 7503
Jos 3:10 that he will without f. drive out from
Jg 11:30 without f. deliver the children
1Sa 2:16 Let them not f. to burn the fat
1Sa 17:32 no man's heart f. because of him; 5307
1Sa 20:5 f. to sit with the king at meat:
1Sa 30:8 overtake them, and without f. recover
2Sa 3:29 not f. from the house of Joab 3772
1Ki 2:4 there shall not f. thee (said he) 3772
1Ki 8:25 There shall not f. thee a man in 3772
1Ki 9:5 There shall not f. thee a man upon 3772
1Ki 17:14 neither shall the cruse of oil f., 2637
1Ki 17:16 neither did the cruse of oil f., 2638
1Ch 28:20 will not f. thee, nor forsake thee, 7503
2Ch 6:16 There shall not f. thee a man in 3772
2Ch 7:18 There shall not f. thee a man to be 3772
Ezr 4:22 now that ye f. not to do this: 7960
Ezr 6:9 given them day by day without f.: 7960
Es 6:10 let nothing f. of all that thou 5307
Es 9:27 so as it should not f., that they 5674
Es 9:28 should not f. from among the Jews, 5674
Job 11:20 the eyes of the wicked shall f., 3615
Job 14:11 As the waters f. from the sea, 235
Job 17:5 the eyes of his children shall f. 3615
Job 31:16 caused the eyes of the widow to f.; 3615
Ps 12:1 f. from among the children of men. 6461
Ps 69:3 eyes f. while I wait for my God. 3615
Ps 77:8 doth his promise f. for evermore? 1584
Ps 89:33 nor suffer my faithfulness to f. 8266
Ps 119:82 Mine eyes f. for thy word, 3615
Ps 119:123 Mine eyes f. for thy salvation, 3615
Pr 22:8 and the rod of his anger shall f. 3615
Ec 12:5 and desire shall f.: because man 6565
Isa 19:3 And the spirit of Egypt shall f. 1238
Isa 19:5 the waters shall f. from the sea, 5405
Isa 21:16 and all the glory of Kedar shall f.: 3615
Isa 31:3 and they shall f. together. 3615
Isa 32:6 cause the drink of the thirst to f. 2637
Isa 32:10 the vintage shall f., the gathering 3615
Isa 34:16 no one of these shall f., none 5737
Isa 38:14 mine eyes f. with looking upward: 1809
Isa 42:4 shall not f. nor be discouraged, 3543
Isa 51:14 nor that his bread should f. 2637
Isa 57:16 the spirit should f. before me, 5848
Isa 58:11 spring of water, whose waters f. 3576
Jer 14:6 their eyes did f., because there 3615
Jer 15:18 and as waters that f.? 3808,539
Jer 48:33 and I have caused wine to f. from 7673
La 2:11 Mine eyes do f. with tears, my 3615
La 3:22 because his compassions f. not. 3615
Ho 9:2 and the new wine shall f. in her. 3584
Am 8:4 to make the poor of the land to f., 7673
Hab 3:17 the labour of the olive shall f., 3584
Lu 16:9 **when ye f., they may receive you** *1587*
Lu 16:17 **than one tittle of the law to f.** *4098*
Lu 22:32 **for thee, that thy faith f. not:** *1587*
1Co 13:8 there be prophecies, they shall f.; *2673*
Heb 1:12 same, and thy years shall not f. *1587*
Heb 11:32 time would f. me to tell of Gedeon, *1952*
Heb 12:15 any man f. of the grace of God; *5302*

FAILED
Ge 42:28 and their heart f. them, and they 3318
Ge 47:15 And when money f. in the land 8552
Jos 3:16 the plain, even the salt sea, f., 8552
Jos 21:45 f. not ought of any good thing 5307
Jos 23:14 thing hath f. of all the good things 5307
Jos 23:14 and not one thing hath f. thereof. 5307
1Ki 8:56 there hath not f. one word of all his 5307
Job 19:14 My kinsfolk have f., and my 2308
Ps 142:4 refuge f. me; no man cared for my 6
Ca 5:6 my soul f. when he spake: 3318
Jer 51:30 their might hath f.; they became 5405
La 4:17 eyes as yet f. for our vain help: 3615

FAILETH
Ge 47:15 thy presence? for the money f. 656
Job 21:10 Their bull gendereth, and f. not; 1602
Ps 31:10 my strength f. because of mine 3782
Ps 38:10 heart panteth, my strength f. me: 5800
Ps 40:12 therefore my heart f. me. 5800
Ps 71:9 me not when my strength f. 3615
Ps 73:26 My flesh and my heart f.: 3615
Ps 109:24 and my flesh f. of fatness. 3584
Ps 143:7 O Lord; my spirit f.: hide not 3615
Ec 10:3 his wisdom f. him, and he saith 2638
Isa 15:6 grass f., there is no green thing. 3615
Isa 40:26 he is strong in power; not one f. 5737
Isa 41:17 and their tongue f. for thirst, I the 5405
Isa 44:12 he is hungry, and his strength f.: 369
Isa 59:15 truth f.; and he that departeth 5737
Eze 12:22 prolonged, and every vision f.? 6
Zep 3:5 his judgment to light, he f. not; 5737
Lu 12:33 **treasure in the heavens that f. not,** *413*
1Co 13:8 Charity never f.: but whether *1601*

FAILING
De 28:65 a trembling heart, and f. of eyes, 3631
Lu 21:26 **Men's hearts f. them for fear,** *674*

FAIN
Job 27:22 he would f. flee out of his hand. 1272
Lu 15:16 **he would f. have filled his belly** *1987*

FAINT See also FAINTED; FAINTEST; FAINTETH; FAINTHEARTED.
Ge 25:29 came from the field, and he was f.: 5889
Ge 25:30 that same red pottage; for I am f.: 5889
De 20:3 let not your hearts f., fear not, 7401
De 20:8 lest his brethren's heart f. as well 4549

De 25:18 when thou wast f. and weary; 5889
Jos 2:9 inhabitants of the land f. because 4127
Jos 2:24 inhabitants of the country do f. 4127
Jg 8:4 men that were with him f., yet 5889
Jg 8:5 that follow me; for they be f., 5889
1Sa 14:28 And the people were f. 5774
1Sa 14:31 and the people were very f. 5774
1Sa 30:10 were so f. that they could not go 6296
1Sa 30:21 two hundred men, which were so f. 6296
2Sa 16:2 such as be f. in the wilderness 3287
2Sa 21:15 Philistines: and David waxed f. 5774
Pr 24:10 If thou f. in the day of adversity, 7503
Isa 1:5 is sick, and the whole heart f. 1742
Isa 13:7 Therefore shall all hands be f., 7503
Isa 29:8 he awaketh, and, behold, he is f., 5889
Isa 40:29 He giveth power to the f.; 3287
Isa 40:30 Even the youths shall f. and be 3286
Isa 40:31 and they shall walk, and not f. 3286
Isa 44:12 he drinketh no water, and is f. 3286
Jer 8:18 sorrow, my heart is f. in me. 1742
Jer 51:46 lest your heart f., and ye fear 7401
La 1:13 me desolate and f. all the day 1738
La 1:22 sighs are many, and my heart is f. 1742
La 2:19 young children, that f. for hunger 5848
La 5:17 for this our heart is f.; for these 1739
Eze 21:7 and every spirit shall f., and all 3543
Eze 21:15 that their heart may f., and their 4127
Am 8:13 the fair virgins and young men f. 5968
Mt 15:32 **lest they f. in the way.** *1590*
Mk 8:3 **they will f. by the way:** *1590*
Lu 18:1 always to pray, and not to f.; *1573*
2Co 4:1 we have received mercy, we f. not; *1573*
2Co 4:16 For which cause we f. not; but *1573*
Gal 6:9 we shall reap, if we f. not. *1590*
Eph 3:13 Wherefore I desire that ye f. not *1573*
Heb 12:3 be wearied and f. in your minds. *1590*
Heb 12:5 f. when thou art rebuked of him: *1590*

FAINTED

Ge 45:26 Jacob's heart f., for he believed 6313
Ge 47:13 all the land of Canaan f. by reason 3856
Ps 27:13 I had f., unless I had believed
Ps 107:5 thirsty, their soul f. in them. 5848
Isa 51:20 Thy sons have f., they lie at the 5968
Jer 45:3 I f. in my sighing, and I find no 3021
Eze 31:15 the trees of the field f. for him. 5969
Da 8:27 And I Daniel f., and was sick 1961
Jon 2:7 When my soul f. within me I 5848
Jon 4:8 upon the head of Jonah, that he f., 5968
Mt 9:36 they f., and were scattered *1590*
Re 2:3 **hast laboured, and hast not f.** *2577*

FAINTEST

Job 4:5 it is come upon thee, and thou f.; 3811

FAINTETH

Ps 84:2 My soul longeth, yea, even f. for 3615
Ps 119:81 My soul f. for thy salvation: 3615
Isa 10:18 be as when a standardbearer f. 4549
Isa 40:28 of the ends of the earth, f. not, 3286

FAINTHEARTED

De 20:8 there that is fearful and f.? 7390,3824
Isa 7:4 quiet; fear not, neither be f. 3824,7401
Jer 49:23 they are f.; there is sorrow on the 4127

FAINTNESS

Le 26:36 I will send a f. into their hearts 4816

FAIR See also FAIRER; FAIREST; FAIRS.

Ge 6:2 daughters of men that they were f.; 2896
Ge 12:11 I know that thou art a f. woman 3303
Ge 12:14 the woman that she was very f. 3303
Ge 24:16 damsel was very f. to look upon, 2896
Ge 26:7 because she was f. to look upon. 2896
1Sa 17:42 ruddy, and of a f. countenance. 3303
2Sa 13:1 the son of David had a f. sister, 3303
2Sa 14:27 was a woman of a f. countenance. 3303
1Ki 1:3 So they sought for a f. damsel 3303
1Ki 1:4 damsel was very f., and cherished 3303
Es 1:11 for she was f. to look on. 2896
Es 2:2 f. young virgins sought for 2896,4758
Es 2:3 together all the f. young virgins 2896,4758
Es 2:7 maid was f. and beautiful; 3303,8389
Job 37:22 F. weather cometh out of the 2091
Job 42:15 so f. as the daughters of Job: 3303
Pr 7:21 With her much f. speech she 3948
Pr 11:22 so is a f. woman which is without 3303
Pr 26:25 When he speaketh f., believe him 2603
Ca 1:15 Behold, thou art f., my love; 3302
Ca 1:15 behold, thou art f.; thou hast dove's 3302
Ca 1:16 Behold, thou art f., my beloved, 3302
Ca 2:10 Rise up, my love, my f. one, 3302
Ca 2:13 my love, my f. one, and come 3302
Ca 4:1 Behold, thou art f., my love; 3302
Ca 4:1 behold, thou art f.; thou hast dove's 3302
Ca 4:7 Thou art all f., my love; 3302
Ca 4:10 How f. is thy love, my sister, 3302
Ca 6:10 f. as the moon, clear as the sun, 3303
Ca 7:6 How f. and how pleasant art thou, 3302
Isa 5:9 be desolate, even great and f., 2896
Isa 54:11 will lay thy stones with f. colours, 6320
Jer 4:30 in vain shalt thou make thyself f.; 3302
Jer 11:16 olive tree, f., and of goodly fruit: 3303
Jer 12:6 they speak f. words unto thee. 2896
Jer 46:20 Egypt is like a very f. heifer, 3304
Eze 16:17 Thou hast also take n thy f. jewels 8597
Eze 16:39 and shall take thy f. jewels. 8597
Eze 23:26 and take away thy f. jewels 8597
Eze 31:3 cedar in Lebanon with f. branches, 3303
Eze 31:7 Thus was he f. in his greatness, 3302
Eze 31:9 made him f. by the multitude 3303
Da 4:12 The leaves thereof were f., and 8209
Da 4:21 Whose leaves were f., and the fruit 8209
Ho 10:11 passed over upon her f. neck: 2898
Am 8:13 In that day shall the f. virgins 3303
Zec 3:5 them set a f. mitre upon his head. 2889
Zec 3:5 they set a f. mitre upon his head, 2889
Mt 16:2 **ye say, It will be f. weather:** *2105*
Ac 7:20 was born, and was exceeding f., *791*
Ac 27:8 which is called The f. havens; *2568*
Ro 16:18 by good words and f. speeches *2129*
Gal 6:12 to make a f. shew in the flesh, *2146*

FAIRER

Jg 15:2 her younger sister f. than she? 2896
Ps 45:2 art f. than the children of men: 3302
Da 1:15 appeared f. and fatter in flesh 2896

FAIREST

Ca 1:8 O thou f. among women, go thy 3303
Ca 5:9 thou f. among women? what is thy 3303
Ca 6:1 O thou f. among women? whither 3303

FAIR-HAVENS See FAIR and HAVENS.

FAIRS

Eze 27:12 and lead, they traded in thy f. 5801
Eze 27:14 of Togarmah traded in thy f. 5801
Eze 27:16 occupied in thy f. with emeralds, 5801
Eze 27:19 going to an fro occupied in thy f.: 5801
Eze 27:22 in thy f. with chief of all spices, 5801
Eze 27:27 and thy f., thy merchandise, 5801

FAITH See also FAITHFUL; FAITHLESS.

De 32:20 children in whom is not f. 529
Hab 2:4 but the just shall live by his f. 530
Mt 6:30 **more clothe you, O ye of little f.?** *3640*
Mt 8:10 **I have not found so great f., no,** *4102*
Mt 8:26 **are ye fearful, O ye off little f.?** *3640*
Mt 9:2 Jesus seeing their f. said unto the *4102*
Mt 9:22 **thy f. hath made thee whole.** *4102*
Mt 9:29 **According to your f. be it unto** *4102*
Mt 14:31 **O thou of little f., wherefore didst** *3640*
Mt 15:28 **O woman, great is thy f.:** *4102*
Mt 16:8 **O ye of little f., why reason ye** *3640*
Mt 17:20 **If ye have f. as a grain of mustard** *4102*
Mt 21:21 **If ye have f., and doubt not,** *4102*
Mt 23:23 **the law, judgment, mercy, and f.:** *4102*
Mk 2:5 When Jesus saw their f., he said *4102*
Mk 4:40 **how is it that ye have no f.?** *4102*
Mk 5:34 **Daughter, thy f. hath made thee** *4102*
Mk 10:52 **way; thy f. hath made thee whole.** *4102*
Mk 11:22 saith unto them, **Have f. in God** *4102*
Lu 5:20 when he saw their f., he said unto *4102*
Lu 7:9 **I have not found so great f., no,** *4102*
Lu 7:50 **Thy f. hath saved thee; go in** *4102*
Lu 8:25 **Where is your f.?** And they being *4102*
Lu 8:48 **thy f. hath made thee whole; go** *4102*
Lu 12:28 **he clothe you, O ye of little f.?** *3640*
Lu 17:5 unto the Lord, Increase your f. *4102*
Lu 17:6 **If ye had f. as a grain of mustard** *4102*
Lu 17:19 **way: thy f. hath made thee whole.** *4102*
Lu 18:8 **shall he find f. on the earth?** *4102*
Lu 18:42 **thy sight: thy f. hath saved thee.** *4102*
Lu 22:32 **prayed for thee, that thy f. fail** *4102*
Ac 3:16 his name through f. in his name *4102*
Ac 3:16 yea, the f. which is by him *4102*
Ac 6:5 a man full of f. and of the Holy *4102*
Ac 6:7 the priests were obedient to the f. *4102*
Ac 6:8 Stephen, full of f. and power, *4102*
Ac 11:24 full of the Holy Ghost and of f.: *4102*
Ac 13:8 to turn away the deputy from the f. *4102*
Ac 14:9 that he had f. to be healed, *4102*
Ac 14:22 exhorting them to continue in the f., *4102*
Ac 14:27 how he had opened the door of f. *4102*
Ac 15:9 purifying their hearts by f. *4102*
Ac 16:5 the churches established in the f., *4102*
Ac 20:21 and f. toward our Lord Jesus Christ. *4102*
Ac 24:24 him concerning the f. in Christ. *4102*
Ac 26:18 **are sanctified by f. that is in me.** *4102*
Ro 1:5 for obedience to the f. among all *4102*
Ro 1:8 that your f. is spoken of throughout *4102*
Ro 1:12 by the mutual f. both of you and me. *4102*
Ro 1:17 God revealed from f. to f.: as it is *4102*
Ro 1:17 written, The just shall live by f. *4102*
Ro 3:3 make the f. of God without effect? *4102*
Ro 3:22 which is by f. of Jesus Christ unto *4102*
Ro 3:25 propitiation through f. in his blood, *4102*
Ro 3:27 of works? Nay: but by the law of f. *4102*
Ro 3:28 a man is justified by f. without the *4102*
Ro 3:30 justify the circumcision by f., and *4102*
Ro 3:30 and uncircumcision through f. *4102*
Ro 3:31 make void the law through f.? *4102*
Ro 4:5 his f. is counted for righteousness. *4102*
Ro 4:9 for we say that f. was reckoned to *4102*
Ro 4:11 seal of the righteousness of the f. *4102*
Ro 4:12 walk in the steps of that f. of our *4102*
Ro 4:13 through the righteousness of f. *4102*
Ro 4:14 f. is made void, and the promise *4102*
Ro 4:16 Therefore it is of f., that it might *4102*
Ro 4:16 which is of the f. of Abraham; *4102*
Ro 4:19 being not weak in f., he considered *4102*
Ro 4:20 but was strong in f., giving glory *4102*
Ro 5:1 being justified by f., we have peace *4102*
Ro 5:2 we have access by f. into this grace *4102*
Ro 9:30 the righteousness which is of f. *4102*
Ro 9:32 Because they sought it not by f., *4102*
Ro 10:6 but the righteousness which is of f. *4102*
Ro 10:8 is, the word of f., which we preach; *4102*
Ro 10:17 So then f. cometh by hearing, *4102*
Ro 11:20 broken off, and thou standest by f. *4102*
Ro 12:3 to every man the measure of f. *4102*
Ro 12:6 according to the proportion of f.; *4102*
Ro 14:1 Him that is weak in the f. receive *4102*
Ro 14:22 Hast thou f.? have it to thyself *4102*
Ro 14:23 because he eateth not of f.: for *4102*
Ro 14:23 whatsoever is not of f. is sin. *4102*
Ro 16:26 all nations for the obedience of f.: *4102*
1Co 2:5 That your f. should not stand in *4102*
1Co 12:9 To another f. by the same Spirit; *4102*
1Co 13:2 though I have all f., so that I could *4102*
1Co 13:13 And now abideth f., hope, charity *4102*
1Co 15:14 and your f. is also vain. *4102*
1Co 15:17 your f. is vain; ye are yet in your *4102*
1Co 16:13 Watch ye, stand fast in the f., *4102*
2Co 1:24 that we have dominion over your f., *4102*
2Co 1:24 of your joy: for by f. ye stand. *4102*
2Co 4:13 We having the same spirit of f., *4102*
2Co 5:7 (For we walk by f., not by sight:) *4102*
2Co 8:7 in f., and utterance, and knowledge, *4102*
2Co 10:15 hope, when your f. in increased, *4102*
2Co 13:5 yourselves, whether ye be in the f.; *4102*
Ga 1:23 now preacheth the f. which once *4102*
Ga 2:16 but by the f. of Jesus Christ, *4102*
Ga 2:16 be justified by the f. of Christ, *4102*
Ga 2:20 I live by the f. of the Son of God, *4102*
Ga 3:2,5 the law, or by the hearing of f.? *4102*
Ga 3:7 they which are of f., the same are *4102*
Ga 3:8 justify the heathen through f., *4102*
Ga 3:9 they which be of f. are blessed *4102*
Ga 3:11 for, The just shall live by f. *4102*
Ga 3:12 And the law is not of f.: *4102*
Ga 3:14 promise of the Spirit through f. *4102*
Ga 3:22 the promise by f. of Jesus Christ *4102*
Ga 3:23 But before f. came, we were kept *4102*
Ga 3:23 shut up unto the f., which should *4102*
Ga 3:24 that we might be justified by f. *4102*
Ga 3:25 But after that f. is come, *4102*
Ga 3:26 children of God by f. in Christ *4102*
Ga 5:5 the hope of righteousness by f. *4102*
Ga 5:6 but f. which worketh by love *4102*
Ga 5:22 gentleness, goodness, f., *4102*
Ga 6:10 who are of the household of f. *4102*
Eph 1:15 after I head of your f. in the Lord *4102*
Eph 2:8 by grace are ye saved through f.; *4102*
Eph 3:12 with confidence by the f. of him. *4102*

Eph 3:17 may dwell in your hearts by f.; 4102
Eph 4:5 One Lord, one f., one baptism, 4102
Eph 4:13 we all come in the unity of the f., 4102
Eph 6:16 Above all, taking the shield of f., 4102
Eph 6:23 and love with f., from God the 4102
Php 1:25 for your furtherance and joy of f.; 4102
Php 1:27 together for the f. of the gospel; 4102
Php 2:17 the sacrifice and service of your f., 4102
Php 3:9 which is through the f. of Christ, 4102
Php 3:9 righteousness which is of God by f.: 4102
Col 1:4 Since we heard of your f. in Christ 4102
Col 1:23 If ye continue in the f. grounded 4102
Col 2:5 the stedfastness of your f. in Christ 4102
Col 2:7 stablished in the f., as ye have been 4102
Col 2:12 through the f. of the operation of 4102
1Th 1:3 your work of f., and labour of love, 4102
1Th 1:8 f. to God-ward is spread abroad; 4102
1Th 3:2 to comfort you concerning your f.: 4102
1Th 3:5 forbear, I sent to know your f., 4102
1Th 3:6 good tidings of your f. and charity, 4102
1Th 3:7 affliction and distress by your f.: 4102
1Th 3:10 that which is lacking in your f.? 4102
1Th 5:8 the breastplate of f. and love; 4102
2Th 1:3 your f. groweth exceedingly, and 4102
2Th 1:4 for your patience and f. in all your 4102
2Th 1:11 and the work of f. with power: 4102
2Th 3:2 for all men have not f. 4102
1Ti 1:2 Timothy, my own son in the f.: 4102
1Ti 1:4 than godly edifying which is in f.: 4102
1Ti 1:5 conscience, and of f. unfeigned: 4102
1Ti 1:14 with f. and love which is in Christ 4102
1Ti 1:19 Holding f., and a good conscience; 4102
1Ti 1:19 concerning f. have made shipwreck: 4102
1Ti 2:7 of the Gentiles in f. and verity 4102
1Ti 2:15 if they continue in f. and charity 4102
1Ti 3:9 Holding the mystery of the f. in a 4102
1Ti 3:13 great boldness in the f. which is in 4102
1Ti 4:1 some shall depart from the f., 4102
1Ti 4:6 words of f. and of good doctrine, 4102
1Ti 4:12 in charity, in spirit, in f., in purity. 4102
1Ti 5:8 he hath denied the f., and is worse 4102
1Ti 5:12 they have cast off their first f. 4102
1Ti 6:10 they have erred from the f., 4102
1Ti 6:11 godliness, f., love, patience, 4102
1Ti 6:12 Fight the good fight of f., lay hold 4102
1Ti 6:21 have erred concerning the f. 4102
2Ti 1:5 the unfeigned f. that is in thee, 4102
2Ti 1:13 in f. and love which is in Christ 4102
2Ti 2:18 and overthrow the f. of some. 4102
2Ti 2:22 follow righteousness, f., charity, 4102
2Ti 3:8 minds, reprobate concerning the f. 4102
2Ti 3:10 f., long suffering, charity, patience, 4102
2Ti 3:15 through f. which is in Christ Jesus. 4102
2Ti 4:7 my course, I have kept the f.: 4102
Tit 1:1 according to the f. of God elect, 4102
Tit 1:4 mine own son after the common f.; 4102
Tit 1:13 that they may be sound in the he f.; 4102
Tit 2:2 sound in f., in charity, in patience. 4102
Tit 3:15 Greet them that love us in the f. 4102
Phm 5 Hearing of thy love and f., 4102
Phm 6 the communication of thy f. may 4102
Heb 4:2 not being mixed with f. in them 4102
Heb 6:1 dead works, and of f. toward God, 4102
Heb 6:12 who through f. and patience inherit 4102
Heb 10:22 a true heart in full assurance of f., 4102
Heb 10:23 hold fast the profession of our f. 1680
Heb 10:38 Now the just shall live by f.: 4102
Heb 11:1 Now f. is the substance of things 4102
Heb 11:3 Through f. we understand that the 4102
Heb 11:4 By f. Abel offered unto God a more 4102
Heb 11:5 By f. Enoch was translated that he 4102
Heb 11:6 without f. it is impossible to please 4102
Heb 11:7 By f. Noah, being warned of God 4102
Heb 11:7 of the righteousness which is by f. 4102
Heb 11:8 By f. Abraham, when he was called 4102
Heb 11:9 By f. he sojourned in the land of 4102
Heb 11:11 Through f....Sara herself received 4102
Heb 11:13 These all died in f., not having 4102
Heb 11:17 By f. Abraham, when he was tried, 4102
Heb 11:20 By f. Isaac blessed Jacob and Esau 4102
Heb 11:21 By f. Jacob, when he was a dying, 4102
Heb 11:22 By f. Joseph, when he died, made 4102
Heb 11:23 By f. Moses, when he was born, 4102
Heb 11:24 By f. Moses, when he was come to 4102
Heb 11:27 By f. he forsook Egypt, not fearing 4102
Heb 11:28 Through f. he kept the passover, 4102
Heb 11:29 by f. he passed through the Red 4102
Heb 11:30 By f. the walls of Jericho fell down, 4102
Heb 11:31 By f. the harlot Rahab perished not 4102
Heb 11:33 Who through f. subdued kingdoms, 4102
Heb 11:39 obtained a good report through f., 4102
Heb 12:2 the author and finisher of our f.; 4102
Heb 13:7 whose f. follow, considering the 4102
Jas 1:3 trying of your f. worketh patience. 4102
Jas 1:6 let him ask in f., nothing wavering 4102
Jas 2:1 My brethren, have not the f. of our 4102
Jas 2:5 rich in f., and heirs of the kingdom 4102
Jas 2:14 though a man say he hath f., and 4102
Jas 2:14 have not works? can f. save him? 4102
Jas 2:17 Even so f., if it hath not works, is 4102
Jas 2:18 Thou hast f., and I have works: 4102
Jas 2:18 shew me thy f. without thy works, 4102
Jas 2:18 I will shew thee my f. by my works. 4102
Jas 2:20 that f. without works is dead? 4102
Jas 2:22 Seest thou how f. wrought with his 4102
Jas 2:22 and by works was f. made perfect? 4102
Jas 2:24 man is justified, and not by f. only 4102
Jas 2:26 so f. without works is dead also. 4102
Jas 5:15 the prayer of f. shall save the sick, 4102
1Pe 1:5 through f. unto salvation ready to 4102
1Pe 1:7 That the trial of your f., being much 4102
1Pe 1:9 Receiving the end of your f., 4102
1Pe 1:21 your f. and hope might be in God. 4102
1Pe 5:9 Whom resist stedfast in the f., 4102
2Pe 1:1 obtained like precious f. with us 4102
2Pe 1:5 add to your f. virtue: and to virtue 4102
1Jo 5:4 overcometh the world, even our f. 4102
Jude 3 for the f. which was once delivered 4102
Jude 20 up yourselves on your most holy f., 4102
Re 2:13 **and hast not denied my f.,** 4102
Re 2:19 **and charity, and service, and f.,** 4102
Re 13:10 the patience and the f. of the saints 4102
Re 14:12 of God, and the f. of Jesus. 4102

FAITHFUL See also UNFAITHFUL.

Nu 12:7 who is f. in all mine house. 539
De 7:9 thy God, he is God, the f. God, 539
1Sa 2:35 I will raise me up a f. priest, 539
1Sa 22:14 who is so f. among all thy servants 539
2Sa 20:19 that are peaceable and f. in Israel: 539
Ne 7:2 he was a f. man, and feared God 571
Ne 9:8 foundest his heart f. before thee, 539
Ne 13:13 for they were counted f., and their 539
Ps 12:1 the f. fail from among the children 539
Ps 31:23 for the Lord preserveth the f., 539
Ps 89:37 and as a f. witness in heaven. 539
Ps 101:6 sages shall be upon the f. of the land, 539
Ps 119:86 All thy commandments are f.: 530
Ps 119:138 are righteous and very f. 530
Pr 11:13 he that is of a f. spirit concealeth 539
Pr 13:17 but a f. ambassador is health. 529
Pr 14:5 A f. witness will not lie: but a false 529
Pr 20:6 but a f. man who can find? 529
Pr 25:13 is a f. messenger to them that send 539
Pr 27:6 F. are the wounds of a friend; 539
Pr 28:20 A f. man shall abound with 530
Isa 1:21 How is the f. city become an harlot! 539
Isa 1:26 city of righteousness, the f. city. 539
Isa 8:2 And I took unto me f. witnesses to 539
Isa 49:7 because of the Lord that is f., 539
Jer 42:5 a true and f. witness between us, 539
Da 6:4 forasmuch as he was f., neither 540
Ho 11:12 and is f. with the saints. 539
Mt 24:45 **Who then is a f. and wise servant,** 4103
Mt 25:21 **done, thou good and f. servant:** 4103
Mt 25:21 **thou hast been f. over a few** 4103
Mt 25:23 **Well done, good and f. servant:** 4103
Mt 25:23 **thou hast been f. over a few** 4103
Lu 12:42 **then is that f. and wise steward,** 4103
Lu 16:10 **He that is f. in that which is** 4103
Lu 16:10 **is least is f. also in much:** 4103
Lu 16:11 **f. in the unrighteous mammon,** 4103
Lu 16:12 **And if ye have not been f. in that** 4103
Lu 19:17 **thou hast been f. in a very little,** 4103
Ac 16:15 have judged me to be f. to the Lord, 4103
1Co 1:9 God is f., by whom ye were called 4103
1Co 4:2 stewards, that a man be found f. 4103
1Co 4:17 my beloved son, and f. in the Lord, 4103
1Co 7:25 mercy of the Lord to be f. 4103
1Co 10:13 but God is f., who will not suffer 4103
Ga 3:9 faith are blessed with f. Abraham. 4103
Eph 1:1 and to the f. in Christ Jesus: 4103
Eph 6:21 and f. minister in the Lord, 4103
Col 1:2 saints and f. brethren in Christ 4103
Col 1:7 is for you a f. minister in Christ; 4103
Col 4:7 a f. minister and fellowservant in 4103
Col 4:9 Onesimus, a f. and beloved brother, 4103
1Th 5:24 F. is he that calleth you, 4103
2Th 3:3 Lord is f., who shall stablish you, 4103
1Ti 1:12 for that he counted me f., 4103
1Ti 1:15 This is a f. saying, and worthy of all 4103
1Ti 3:11 slanderers, sober, f. in all things. 4103
1Ti 4:9 This is a f. saying and worthy of all 4103
1Ti 6:2 because they are f. and beloved, 4103
2Ti 2:2 the same commit thou to f. men, 4103
2Ti 2:11 It is a f. saying: For if we be dead 4103
2Ti 2:13 ye he abideth f.: he cannot deny 4103
Tit 1:6 having f. children not accused 4103
Tit 1:9 the f. word as he hath been taught, 4103
Tit 3:8 This is a f. saying, and these things 4103
Heb 2:17 be a merciful and f. high priest in 4103
Heb 3:2 was f. to him that appointed him 4103
Heb 3:2 also Moses was f. in all his house.
Heb 3:5 Moses verily was f. in all his 4103
Heb 10:23 (for he is f. that promised;) 4103
Heb 11:11 judged him f. who had promised 4103
1Pe 4:19 in well doing, as unto a f. Creator. 4103
1Pe 5:12 By Silvanus, a f. brother unto you, 4103
1Jo 1:9 he is f. and just to forgive us our 4103
Re 1:5 Jesus Christ who is the f. witness, 4103
Re 2:10 **be thou f. unto death, and I will** 4103
Re 2:13 **Antipas was my f. martyr, who** 4103
Re 3:14 **the Amen, the f. and true witness,** 4103
Re 17:14 him are called, and chose, and f. 4103
Re 19:11 upon him was called F. and True, 4103
Re 21:5 for these words are true and f. 4103
Re 22:6 These saying are f. and true: 4103

FAITHFULLY See also UNFAITHFULLY.

2Ki 12:15 on workmen: for they dealt f. 530
2Ki 22:7 their hand, because they dealt f. 530
2Ch 19:9 Lord, f., and with a perfect heart. 530
2Ch 31:12 tithes and the dedicated things f.: 530
2Ch 34:12 And the men did the work f.: 530
Pr 29:14 The king that f. judgeth the poor, 571
Jer 23:28 let him speak my word f. 571
3Jo 5 doest f. whatsoever thou doest 4103

FAITHFULNESS

1Sa 26:23 man his righteousness and his f.: 530
Ps 5:9 there is no f. in their mouth; 3559
Ps 36:5 thy f. reacheth unto the clouds. 530
Ps 40:10 declared thy f. and thy salvation: 530
Ps 88:11 the grave? or thy f. in destruction? 530
Ps 89:1 mouth will I make known thy f. to all 530
Ps 89:2 thy f. shalt thou establish in the very 530
Ps 89:5 thy f. also in the congregation of the 530
Ps 89:8 or to thy f. round about thee? 530
Ps 89:24 But my f. and my mercy shall be with 530
Ps 89:33 nor suffer my f. to fail. 530
Ps 92:2 and thy f. every night, 530
Ps 119:75 that thou in f. hast afflicted me, 530
Ps 119:90 Thy f. is unto all generations: 530
Ps 143:1 in thy f. answer me, and in thy 530
Isa 11:5 and f. the girdle of his reins. 530
Isa 25:1 counsels of old are f. and truth. 530
La 3:23 every morning: great is thy f. 530
Ho 2:20 will even betroth thee unto me in f.: 530

FAITHLESS

Mt 17:17 said, **O f. and perverse generation,** 571
Mk 9:19 saith, **O f. generation, how long** 571
Lu 9:41 said, **O f. and perverse generation,** 571
Joh 20:27 **and be not f., but believing.** 571

FALL See also BEFALL; FALLEN; FALLEST; FALLETH; FALLING; FELL.

Ge 2:21 a deep sleep to f. upon Adam, 5370
Ge 43:18 occasion against us, and f. upon us, 5370
Ge 45:24 See that ye f. not out by the way. 7264
Ge 49:17 that his rider shall f. backward. 5307
Ex 5:3 lest he f. upon us with pestilence, 6293
Ex 15:16 and dread shall f. upon them; 5307
Ex 21:33 and an ox or an ass f. therein; 5307
Le 11:32 them, when they are dead, doth f., 5307
Le 11:37 if any part of their carcase f. upon 5307
Le 11:38 any part of their carcase f. thereon, 5307
Le 19:29 lest the land f. to whoredom,
Le 26:7 and they shall f. before you by the 5307
Le 26:8 your enemies shall f. before you by 5307
Le 26:36 they shall f. when none pursueth. 5307
Le 26:37 they shall f. one upon another, 3782

Nu 11:31 and let them f. by the camp, 5203
Nu 14:3 unto this land, to f. by the sword, 5307
Nu 14:29 carcases shall f. in this wilderness; 5307
Nu 14:32 they shall f. in this wilderness. 5307
Nu 14:43 and ye shall f. by the sword: 5307
Nu 34:2 is the land that shall f. unto you for 5307
De 22:4 thy brother's ass or his ox f. down 5307
De 22:8 if any man f. from thence. 5307
Jos 6:5 the wall of the city shall f. down 5307
Jg 8:21 Rise thou, and f. upon us: 6293
Jg 15:12 unto me that ye will not f. upon me 6293
Jg 15:18 thirst, and f. into the hand of the 5307
Ru 2:16 let f. also some of the handfuls 7997
Ru 3:18 thou know how the matter will f.: 5307
1Sa 3:19 and did let none of his words f. to 5307
1Sa 14:45 shall not one hair of his head f. to 5307
1Sa 18:25 Saul thought to make David f. by 5307
1Sa 21:13 his spittle f. down upon his beard 3381
1Sa 22:17 their hand to f. upon the priests 6293
1Sa 22:18 Turn thou, and f. upon the priests 6293
1Sa 26:20 let not my blood f. to the earth 5307
2Sa 1:15 said, Go near, and f. upon him. 6293
2Sa 14:11 shall not one hair of thy son f. to 5307
2Sa 24:14 us f. now into the hand of the Lord; 5307
2Sa 24:14 let me not f. into the hand of man. 5307
1Ki 1:52 there shall not an hair of him f. to 5307
1Ki 2:29 Jehoiada, saying, Go, f. upon him, 6293
1Ki 2:31 as he hath said, and f. upon him, 6293
1Ki 22:20 go up and f. at Ramoth-gilead? 5307
2Ki 7:4 us f. unto the host of the Syrians: 5307
2Ki 10:10 shall f. unto the earth nothing 5307
2Ki 14:10 shouldest f., even thou, and Judah 5307
2Ki 19:7 will cause him to f. by the sword 5307
1Ch 12:19 He will f. to his master Saul 5307
1Ch 21:13 f. now into the hand of the Lord; 5307
1Ch 21:13 let me not f. into the hand of man. 5307
2Ch 18:19 that he may go up and f. at 5307
2Ch 21:15 until thy bowels f. out by reason 3318
2Ch 25:8 God shall make thee f. before 3782
2Ch 25:19 shouldest f., even thou, and Judah 5307
Es 6:13 before whom thou hast began to f., 5307
Es 6:13 but shalt surely f. b before him 5307
Job 13:11 afraid? and his dread f. upon you? 5307
Job 31:22 arm f. from my shoulder blade, 5307
Ps 5:10 let them f. by their own counsels; 5307
Ps 9:3 they shall f. and perish at thy 3782
Ps 10:10 the poor may f. by his strong ones 5307
Ps 35:8 into that very destruction let him f. 5307
Ps 37:24 Though he f., he shall not be 5307
Ps 45:5 whereby the people f. under thee 5307
Ps 63:10 They shall f. by the sword: they 5064
Ps 64:8 make their own tongue to f. upon 3782
Ps 72:11 kings shall f. down before him: 7812
Ps 78:28 let it f. in the midst of their camp, 5307
Ps 82:7 and f. like one of the princes 5307
Ps 91:7 A thousand shall f. at thy side, 5307
Ps 118:13 thrust sore at me that I might f.: 5307
Ps 140:10 Let burning coals f. upon them: 4131
Ps 141:10 the wicked f. into their own nets, 5307
Ps 145:14 The Lord upholdeth all that f., 5307
Pr 4:16 unless they cause some to f. 3782
Pr 10:8 but a prating fool shall f. 3832
Pr 10:10 sorrow: but a prating fool shall f. 3832
Pr 11:5 shall f. by his own wickedness 5307
Pr 11:14 Where no counsel is, the people f.: 5307
Pr 11:28 that trusteth in his riches shall f.: 5307
Pr 16:18 and an haughty spirit before a f. 3783
Pr 22:14 of the Lord shall f. therein 5307
Pr 24:16 the wicked shall f. into mischief. 3782
Pr 26:27 diggeth a pit shall f. therein: 5307
Pr 28:10 he shall f. himself into his own pit: 5307
Pr 28:14 that hardeneth his heart shall f. 5307
Pr 28:18 is perverse in his ways shall f. at 5307
Pr 29:16 the righteous shall see their f. 4658
Ec 4:10 For if they f., the one will lift up 5307
Ec 10:8 that diggeth a pit shall f. into it; 5307
Ec 11:3 if the tree f. toward the south, 5307
Isa 3:25 Thy men shall f. by the sword, 5307
Isa 8:15 among them shall stumble, and f., 5307
Isa 10:4 and they shall f. under the slain. 5307
Isa 10:34 Lebanon shall f. by a mighty one 5307
Isa 13:15 unto them shall f. by the sword. 5307
Isa 22:25 removed, and be cut down, and f.; 5307
Isa 24:18 noise of the fear shall f. into the pit; 5307
Isa 24:20 and it shall f., and not rise again. 5307
Isa 28:13 they might go, and f. backward, 3782
Isa 30:13 as a breach ready to f., swelling 5307
Isa 30:25 slaughter, when the towers f. 5307
Isa 31:3 both he that helpeth shall f., and 3782
Isa 31:3 he that is holpen shall f. down, 5307
Isa 31:8 the Assyrian f. with the sword, 5307
Isa 34:4 all their host shall f. down, as 5034
Isa 37:7 will cause him to f. by the sword 5307
Isa 40:30 the young men shall utterly f.: 3782
Isa 44:19 I f. down to the stock of a tree? 5456
Isa 45:14 they shall f. down unto thee, 7812
Isa 46:6 they f. down, yea, they worship. 5456
Isa 47:11 and mischief shall f. upon thee; 5307
Isa 54:15 together against thee shall f. for thy 5307
Jer 3:12 not cause mine anger to f. upon 5307
Jer 6:15 they shall f. among them that f.: 5307
Jer 6:21 the sons together shall f. upon 3782
Jer 8:4 Shall they f., and not arise? shall 5307
Jer 8:12 shall they f. among them that f.: 5307
Jer 9:22 Even the carcases of men shall f. as 5307
Jer 15:8 I have caused him to f. upon it 5307
Jer 19:7 and I will cause them to f. by the 5307
Jer 20:4 and they shall f. by the sword 5307
Jer 23:12 shall be driven on, and f. therein: 5307
Jer 23:19 shall f. grievously upon the head 2342
Jer 25:27 be drunken, and spue, and f., 5307
Jer 25:34 ye shall f. like a pleasant vessel, 5307
Jer 30:23 shall f. with pain upon the head 2342
Jer 37:14 I f. not away to the Chaldeans 5307
Jer 39:18 thou shalt not f. by the sword, 5307
Jer 44:12 and f. in the land of Egypt: 5307
Jer 46:6 and f. toward the north by the 5307
Jer 46:16 made many to f., yea, one fell 3782
Jer 48:44 fleeth from the fear shall f. into 5307
Jer 49:21 is moved at the noise of their f., 5307
Jer 49:26 young men shall f. in her streets, 5307
Jer 50:30 shall her young men f. in the 5307
Jer 50:32 most proud shall stumble and f., 5307
Jer 51:4 Thus the slain shall f. in the land 5307
Jer 51:44 yea, the wall of Babylon shall f. 5307
Jer 51:47 all her slain shall f. in the midst 5307
Jer 51:49 hath caused the slain of Israel to f., 5307
Jer 51:49 so at Babylon shall f. the slain of 5307
La 1:14 he hath made made my strength to f., 3782
Eze 5:12 a third part shall f. by the sword 5307
Eze 6:7 the slain shall f. in the midst of you, 5307
Eze 6:11 for they shall f. by the sword, 5307
Eze 6:12 that is near shall f. by the sword; 5307
Eze 11:10 Ye shall f. by the sword; I will 5307
Eze 13:11 morter, that it shall f.: 5307
Eze 13:11 ye, O great hailstones, shall f.; 5307
Eze 13:14 and it shall f., and ye shall be 5307
Eze 17:21 fugitives with all his bands shall f. 5307
Eze 23:25 remnant shall fall by the sword: 5307
Eze 24:6 piece by piece; let no lot f. upon it 5307
Eze 24:21 daughters whom ye have left shall f. 5307
Eze 25:13 they of Dedan shall f. by the sword 5307
Eze 26:15 isles shake at the sound of thy f., 4658
Eze 26:18 isles tremble in the day of thy f.; 4658
Eze 27:27 is in the midst of thee, shall f. into 5307
Eze 27:34 in the midst of thee shall f. 5307
Eze 29:5 thou shalt f. upon the open fields; 5307
Eze 30:4 when the slain shall f. in Egypt, 5307
Eze 30:5 land that is in league, shall f. with 5307
Eze 30:6 also that uphold Egypt shall f.; 5307
Eze 30:6 shall they f. in it by the sword, 5307
Eze 30:17 of Pi-beseth shall f. by the sword 5307
Eze 30:22 I will cause the sword to f. out of 5307
Eze 30:25 the arms of Pharaoh shall f. down; 5307
Eze 31:16 to shake at the sound of this f., 4658
Eze 32:10 his own life, in the day of thy f. 4658
Eze 32:12 will I cause thy multitude to f., 4658
Eze 32:20 They shall f. in the midst of them 4658
Eze 33:12 he shall not f. thereby in the day 3782
Eze 33:27 the wastes shall f. by the sword, 5307
Eze 35:8 rivers, shall they f. that are slain 5307
Eze 36:15 shalt thou cause thy nations to f. 3782
Eze 38:20 and the steep places shall f., 5307
Eze 38:20 every wall shall f. to the ground. 5307
Eze 39:3 will cause thine arrows to f. out of 5307
Eze 39:4 Thou shalt f. upon the mountains 5307
Eze 39:5 Thou shalt f. upon the open field: 5307
Eze 44:12 house of Israel to f. into iniquity; 4383
Eze 47:14 and this land shall f. unto 5307
Da 3:5 ye f. down and worship the golden 5308
Da 3:10 shall f. down and worship the golden 5308
Da 3:15 ye f. down and worship the golden 5308
Da 11:14 establish...vision; but they shall f. 3782
Da 11:19 stumble and f., and not be found 5307
Da 11:26 overflow: and many shall f. down 5307
Da 11:33 yet they shall f. by the sword, 3782
Da 11:34 Now when they shall f., they shall 3782
Da 11:35 of them of understanding shall f., 3782
Ho 4:5 Therefore shalt thou f. in the day, 3782
Ho 4:5 and the prophet also shall f. with 3782
Ho 4:14 that doth not understand shall f. 3832
Ho 5:5 shall Israel and Ephraim f. in 3782
Ho 5:5 Judah also shall f. with them. 3782
Ho 7:16 their princes shall f. by the sword 5307
Ho 10:8 and to the hills, F. on us 5307
Ho 13:16 they shall f. by the sword: their 5307
Ho 14:9 the transgressors shall f. therein. 3872
Joe 2:8 when they f. upon the sword, 5307
Am 3:5 Can a bird f. in a snare upon the 5307
Am 3:14 be cut off, and f. to the ground. 5307
Am 7:17 sons and thy daughters shall f. by 5307
Am 8:14 they shall f., and never rise up 5307
Am 9:9 yet shall not the least grain f. upon 5307
Mic 7:8 enemy: when I f., I shall arise; 5307
Na 3:12 they shall even f. into the mouth of 5307
Mt 4:9 wilt f. down and worship me. *4098*
Mt 7:27 **and great was the f. of it** *4431*
Mt 10:29 **them shall not f. on the ground** *4098*
Mt 12:11 **if it f. into the pit on the sabbath** *1706*
Mt 15:14 **blind, both shall f. into the ditch** *409*
Mt 15:27 which f. from their masters' table. *409*
Mt 21:44 **whosoever shall f. on this stone** *409*
Mt 21:44 **on whomsoever it shall f., it will** *4[illegible]*
Mt 24:29 **and the stars shall f. from heaven,** *409*
Mk 13:25 **And the stars of heaven shall f.,** *1601*
Lu 2:34 child is set for the f. and rising *4431*
Lu 6:39 **shall they not both f. into the** *4098*
Lu 8:13 **and in time of temptation f. away** *868*
Lu 10:18 **as lightning f. from heaven** *4098*
Lu 20:18 **Whosoever shall f. upon that** *4098*
Lu 20:18 **but on whomsoever it shall f.,** *4098*
Lu 21:24 **shall f. by the edge of the sword,** *4098*
Lu 23:30 **F. on us; and to the hills, Cover** *4098*
Joh 12:24 **wheat f. into the ground and die,** *4098*
Ac 27:17 should f. into the quicksands, *1601*
Ac 27:32 ropes of the boat, and let her f. off. *1601*
Ac 27:34 shall not an hair f. from the head *4098*
Ro 11:11 they stumbled that they should f.? *4098*
Ro 11:11 through their f. salvation is come *3900*
Ro 11:12 Now if the f. of them be the riches *3900*
Ro 14:13 occasion to f. in his brother's way. *4625*
1Co 10:12 he standeth take heed lest he f. *4098*
1Ti 3:6 pride he f. into the condemnation *1706*
1Ti 3:7 he f. into reproach and the snare
1Ti 6:9 rich f. into temptation and a snare,
Heb 4:11 lest any man f. after the same *4098*
Heb 6:6 If they shall f. away, to renew *3895*
Heb 10:31 to f. into the hands of the living *1706*
Jas 1:2 when ye f. into divers temptations; *4045*
Jas 5:12 nay; lest ye f. into condemnation. *4098*
2Pe 1:10 do these things, ye shall never f.: *4417*
2Pe 3:17 f. from your own stedfastness, *1601*
Re 4:10 four and twenty elders f. down *4098*
Re 6:16 mountains and rocks, F. on us, *4098*
Re 9:1 and I saw a star f. from heaven *4098*

FALLEN See also BEFALLEN.

Ge 4:6 and why is thy countenance f.? 5307
Le 13:40 the man whose hair is f. off 4803
Le 13:41 he that hath his hair f. off 4803
Le 25:35 and f. in decay with thee; 4131,3027
Nu 32:19 because our inheritance is f. to us 935
Jos 2:9 and that your terror is f. upon us, 5307
Jos 8:24 were all f. on the edge of the sword, 5307
Jg 3:25 their lord was f. down dead on the 5307
Jg 18:1 inheritance had not f. unto them 5307
Jg 19:27 concubine was f. down at the door 5307
1Sa 5:3 was f. upon his face to the earth 5307
1Sa 5:4 was f. upon his face to the ground 5307
1Sa 26:12 from the Lord was f. upon them. 5307
1Sa 31:8 found Saul and his three sons f. in 5307
2Sa 1:4 many of the people also are f. and 5307
2Sa 1:10 could not live after that he was f.: 5307
2Sa 1:12 because they were f. by the sword 5307
2Sa 1:19 high places: how are the mighty f.! 5307
2Sa 1:25 How are the mighty f. in the midst 5307
2Sa 1:27 How are the mighty f., and the 5307
2Sa 3:28 there is a prince and a great man f. 5307
2Sa 22:39 yea, they are f. under my feet. 5307
2Ki 13:14 Now Elisha was f. sick of his sickness
1Ch 10:8 they found Saul and his sons f. in 5307

2Ch 20:24 were dead bodies f. to the earth, 5307
2Ch 29:9 our fathers have f. by the sword, 5307
Es 7:8 Haman was f. upon the bed where 5307
Job 1:16 The fire of God is f. from heaven, 5307
Ps 7:15 is f. into the ditch which he made. 5307
Ps 16:6 are f. unto me in pleasant places; 5307
Ps 18:38 they are f. under my feet. 5307
Ps 20:8 They are brought down and f.: 5307
Ps 36:12 There are the workers of iniquity f.: 5307
Ps 55:4 the terrors of death are f. upon me. 5307
Ps 57:6 whereof they are f. themselves. 5307
Ps 69:9 reproached thee are f. upon me. 5307
Isa 3:8 is ruined, and Judah is f.: 5307
Isa 9:10 The bricks are f. down, but we will 5307
Isa 14:12 How art thou f. from heaven, 5307
Isa 16:9 fruits and for thy harvest is f.. 5307
Isa 21:9 and said, Babylon is f., is f.; 5307
Isa 26:18 have the inhabitants of the world f. 5307
Isa 59:14 truth is f. in the street, and equity 3782
Jer 38:19 Jews that are f. to the Chaldeans, 5307
Jer 46:12 mighty, they are f. both together. 5307
Jer 48:32 the spoiler is f. upon thy summer 5307
Jer 50:15 her foundations are f., her walls 5307
Jer 51:8 Babylon is suddenly f. and 5307
La 2:21 my young men are f. by the sword; 5307
La 5:16 The crown is f. from our head: 5307
Eze 13:12 the wall is f., shall it not be said 5307
Eze 31:12 all the valleys his branches are f., 5307
Eze 32:22 all of them slain, f. by the sword: 5307
Eze 32:23, 24 all of them slain, f. by the sword, 5307
Eze 32:27 that are f. of the uncircumcised, 5307
Ho 7:7 all their kings are f.: there is none 5307
Ho 14:1 for thou hast f. by thine iniquity. 3782
Am 5:2 The virgin of Israel is f.; she 5307
Am 9:11 the tabernacle of David that is f., 5307
Zec 11:2 Howl, fir tree, for the cedar is f.; 5307
Lu 14:5 **have an ass or an ox f. into a pit,** *1706*
Ac 8:16 ye he was f. upon none of them: *1968*
Ac 15:16 of David, which is f. down, *4098*
Ac 20:9 being f. into a deep sleep: *2702*
Ac 26:14 when we were all f. to the earth, *2667*
Ac 27:29 lest we should have f. upon rocks, *1601*
Ac 28:6 should have swollen, or f. down *2667*
1Co 15:6 but some are f. asleep. *2837*
1Co 15:18 also which are f. asleep in Christ *2837*
Ga 5:4 by the law; ye are f. from grace. *1601*
Php 1:12 happened unto me have f. out *2064*
Re 2:5 **from whence thou art f.,** *1601*
Re 14:8 Babylon is f., is f., that great city, *4098*
Re 17:10 five are f., and one is, and the *4098*
Re 18:2 Babylon the great is f., is f., *4098*

FALLEST
Jer 37:13 Thou f. away to the Chaldeans, 5307

FALLETH See also BEFALLETH.
Ex 1:10 when there f. out any war, 7122
Le 11:33 vessel, whereinto any of them f., 5307
Le 11:35 any part of their carcase f. shall be 5307
Nu 33:54 in the place where his lot f.; 3318
2Sa 3:29 or that f. on the sword, or that 5307
2Sa 3:34 as a man f. before wicked men, 5307
2Sa 17:12 as the dew f. on the ground: 5307
Job 4:13 when deep sleep f. on men, 5307
Job 33:15 when deep sleep f. upon men, 5307
Pr 13:17 wicked messenger f. into mischief: 5307
Pr 17:20 that hath a perverse tongue f. into 5307
Pr 24:16 For a just man f. seven times, 5307
Pr 24:17 Rejoice not when thine enemy f., 5307
Ec 4:10 to him that is alone when he f.; 5307
Ec 9:12 when it f. suddenly upon them. 5307
Ec 11:3 in the place where the tree f., 5307
Isa 34:4 as the leaf f. off from the vine, 5034
Isa 44:15 image, and f. down thereto. 5456
Isa 44:17 he f. down unto it, and worshippeth. 5456
Jer 21:9 f. to the Chaldeans that besiege 5307
Da 3:6 f. not down and worshippeth shall 5308
Da 3:11 whoso f. not down and worshippeth, 5308
Mt 17:15 for ofttimes he f. into the fire, *4098*
Lu 11:17 **a house divided against a house f.** *4098*
Lu 15:12 **the portion of goods that f. to me.** *1911*
Ro 14:4 his own master he standeth or f.. *4098*
Jas 1:11 the grass, and the flower thereof f., *1601*
1Pe 1:24 and the flower thereof f. away: *1601*

FALLIBLE See INFALLIBLE.

FALLING
Nu 24:4, 16 f. into a trance, but having his 5307
Job 4:4 have upholden him that was f., 3782
Job 14:18 mountain f. cometh to nought, 5307
Ps 56:13 not thou deliver my feet from f., 1762
Ps 116:8 from tears, and my feet from f.. 1762
Pr 25:26 A righteous man f. down before 4131
Isa 34:4 as a f. fig from the fig tree. 5034
Lu 8:47 trembling, and f. down before him, *4363*
Lu 22:44 of blood f. down to the ground. *2597*
Ac 1:18 f. headlong, he burst asunder *4248,1096*
Ac 27:41 And f. into a place where two *4045*
1Co 14:25 and so f. down on his face he will *4098*
2Th 2:3 except there come a f. away first, *646*
Jude 24 that is able keep you from f., *679*

FALLOW See also FALLOWDEER.
De 14:5 and the roebuck and the f. deer, 3180
Jer 4:3 Break up your f. ground, and sow 5215
Ho 10:12 break up your f. ground: for it is 5215

FALLOWDEER See also FALLOW and DEER.
1Ki 4:23 harts, and roebucks, and f., 3180

FALLOW-GROUND See FALLOW and GROUND.

FALSE See also FALSEHOOD; FALSIFYING.
Ex 20:16 Thou shalt not bear f. witness 8267
Ex 23:1 Thou shalt not raise a f. report: 7723
Ex 23:7 Keep thee far from a f. matter; 8267
De 5:20 Neither shalt thou bear f. witness 7723
De 19:16 If a f. witness rise up against any 2555
De 19:18 if the witness be a f. witness, 8267
2Ki 9:12 they said, It is f.: tell us now. 8267
Job 36:4 truly my words shall not be f.: 8267
Ps 27:12 f. witnesses are risen up against 8267
Ps 35:11 F. witnesses did rise up' they 2555
Ps 119:104 therefore I hate every f. way. 8267
Ps 119:128 and I hate every f. way. 8267
Ps 120:3 done unto thee, thou f. tongue? 7423
Pr 6:19 A f. witness that speaketh lies, 8267
Pr 11:1 A f. balance is abomination to 4820
Pr 12:17 but a f. witness deceit. 8267
Pr 14:5 but a f. witness will utter lies. 8267
Pr 17:4 doer giveth heed to f. lips; 205
Pr 19:5,9 A f. witness shall not be 8267
Pr 20:23 and a f. balance is not good. 4820
Pr 21:28 A f. witness shall perish: but the 3577
Pr 25:14 boasteth himself of a f. gift is 8267
Pr 25:18 A man that beareth f. witness 8267
Jer 14:14 you a f. vision and divination, 8267
Jer 23:32 them that prophesy f. dreams, 8267
Jer 37:14 Then said Jeremiah, It is f.; 8267
La 2:14 have seen for thee f. burdens and 7723
Eze 21:23 as a f. divination in their sight, 7723
Zec 8:17 and love no f. oath: for all these 8267
Zec 10:2 a lie, and have told f. dreams; 7723
Mal 3:5 and against f. swearers, and *8267*
Mt 7:15 **Beware of f. prophets, which come.** *5578*
Mt 15:19 **thefts, f. witness, blasphemies:** *5577*
Mt 19:18 **Thou shalt not bear f. witness,** *5576*
Mt 24:11 **And many f. prophets shall rise,** *5578*
Mt 24:24 **For there shall arise f. Christs,**
Mt 24:24 **and f. prophets, and shall shew** *5578*
Mt 26:59 sought f. witness against Jesus, *5580*
Mt 26:60 though many f. witnesses came, *5575*
Mt 26:60 At the last came two f. witnesses, *5575*
Mk 10:19 **Do not bear f. witness, Defraud** *5576*
Mk 13:22 **f. Christs...shall rise, and shall** *5580*
Mk 13:22 **f. prophets shall rise, and shall** *5578*
Mk 14:56 For many bare f. witness against *5576*
Mk 14:57 and bare f. witness against him. *5576*
Lu 6:26 **their fathers to the f. prophets.** *5578*
Lu 18:20 **Do not bear f. witness, Honour** *5576*
Lu 19:8 from any man by f. accusation, *4811*
Ac 6:13 set up f. witnesses, which said, *5571*
Ac 13:6 sorcerer, a f. prophet, a Jew, *5578*
Ro 13:9 Thou shalt not bear f. witness, *5576*
1Co 15:15 we are found f. witnesses of God; *5575*
2Co 11:13 For such are f. apostles, deceitful *5570*
2Co 11:26 sea, in perils among f. brethren; *5569*
Ga 2:4 because of f. brethren unawares *5569*
2Ti 3:3 trucebreakers, f. accusers, *1228*
Tit 2:3 not f. accusers, not given to much *1228*
2Pe 2:1 there were f. prophets also among *5578*
2Pe 2:1 there shall be f. teachers among *5572*
1Jo 4:1 because many f. prophets are gone *5578*
Re 16:13 out of the mouth of the f. prophet *5578*
Re 19:20 f. prophet that wrought miracles *5578*
Re 20:10 the beast and the f. prophet are, *5578*

FALSE-ACCUSATION See FALSE and ACCUSATION.

FALSE-APOSTLES See FALSE and APOSTLES.

FALSE-BRETHREN See FALSE and BRETHREN.

FALSE-CHRISTS See FALSE and CHRISTS.

FALSEHOOD
2Sa 18:13 wrought f. against mine own life: 8267
Job 21:34 your answers there remaineth f.? 4604
Ps 7:14 mischief, and brought forth f.. 8267
Ps 119:118 thy statutes: for their deceit is f.. 8267
Ps 114:8 their right hand is a right hand of f.. 8267
Ps 114:11 their right hand is a right hand of f.: 8267
Isa 28:15 under f. have we hid ourselves: 8267
Isa 57:4 of transgression, a seed of f., 8267
Isa 59:13 uttering from the heart words of f.. 8267
Jer 10:14 for his molten image is f., and 8267
Jer 13:25 hast forgotten me, and trusted in f.. 8267
Jer 51:17 for his molten image is f., and 8267
Ho 7:1 for they commit f.; and the thief 8267
Mic 2:11 walking in the spirit and f. do lie, 8267

FALSELY
Ge 21:23 that thou wilt not deal f. with me, 8266
Le 6:3 it, and sweareth f.; 5921,8267
Le 6:5 that about which he hath sworn f.; 8267
Le 19:11 Ye shall not steal, neither deal f., 3584
Le 19:12 ye shall not swear by my name f., 8267
De 19:18 hath testified f. against his brother; 8267
Ps 44:17 neither have we dealt f. in thy 8266
Jer 5:2 Lord liveth; surely they swear f. 8267
Jer 5:31 prophets prophesy f., and the 8267
Jer 6:13 unto the priest every one dealeth f.. 8267
Jer 7:9 and commit adultery, and swear f., 8267
Jer 8:10 unto the priest every one dealeth f.. 8267
Jer 29:9 prophesy f. unto you in my name: 8267
Jer 40:16 for thou speakest f. of Ishmael. 8267
Jer 43:2 unto Jeremiah, Thou speakest f.: 8267
Hos 10:4 swearing f. in making a covenant: 7723
Zec 5:4 the house of him that sweareth f. 8267
Mt 5:11 **all manner of evil against you f.,** *5574*
Lu 3:14 neither accuse any f.; and be
1Ti 6:20 oppositions of science f. so called: *5581*
1Pe 3:16 ashamed that f. accuse your

FALSE-PROPHET See FALSE and PROPHET.

FALSE-TEACHER See FALSE and TEACHER.

FALSE-WITNESS See FALSE and WITNESS.

FALSIFYING
Am 8:5 and f. the balances by deceit? 5791

FAME See also DEFAME.
Ge 45:16 f. thereof was heard in Pharaoh's 6963
Nu 14:15 which have heard the f. of thee 8088
Jos 6:27 his f. was noised throughout all 8089
Jos 9:9 for we have heard the f. of him, 8089
1Ki 4:31 his f. was in all nations round 8034
1Ki 10:1 of Sheba heard of the f. of Solomon 8088
1Ki 10:7 exceedeth the f. which I heard. 8052
1Ch 14:17 the f. of David went out into all 8034
1Ch 22:5 magnifical, of f. and of glory 8034
2Ch 9:1 Sheba heard of the f. of Solomon, 8088
2Ch 9:6 thou exceedest the f. that I heard. 8052
Es 9:4 his f. went out throughout all the 8089
Job 28:22 We have heard the f. thereof with 8088
Is 66:19 afar off, that have not heard my f., 8088
Jer 6:24 We have heard the f. thereof: our 8089
Zep 3:19 I will get them praise and f. in 8034
Mt 4:24 his f. went throughout all Syria: *189*
Mt 9:26 the f. hereof went abroad into all *5345*
Mt 9:31 spread abroad his f. in all that *1310*
Mt 14:1 tetrarch heard of the f. of Jesus. *189*
Mk 1:28 immediately his f. spread abroad *189*
Lu 4:14 and there went out a f. of him *5345*
Lu 4:37 the f. of him went out into every *2279*
Lu 5:15 went there a f. abroad of him: *3056*

FAMILIAR See also FAMILIARS.
Le 19:31 not them that have f. spirits,
Le 20:6 turneth after such as have f. spirits,
Le 20:27 also or woman that hath a f. spirit,
De 18:11 or a consulter with f. spirits, or a
1Sa 28:3 put away those that had f. spirits,
1Sa 28:7 me a woman that hath a f. spirit,
1Sa 28:7 woman that hath a F. spirit at En-dor.
1Sa 28:8 divine unto me by the f. spirit, and
1Sa 28:9 hath cut off those that have f. spirits,

2Ki 21:6 and dealt with **f.** spirits and wizards:
2Ki 23:24 the workers with **f.** spirits, and the
1Ch 10:13 counsel of one that had a **f.** spirit,
2Ch 33:6 and dealt with a **f.** spirit, and with
Job 19:14 my **f.** friends have forgotten me. 3045
Ps 41:9 Yea, mine own **f.** friend, in whom 7965
Isa 8:19 unto them that have **f.** spirits, and
Isa 19:3 and to them that have **f.** spirits, and
Isa 29:4 as of one that hath a **f.** spirit,

FAMILIARS

Jer 20:10 all my **f.** watched for my halting. 7965

FAMILIAR-SPIRIT See FAMILIAR and SPIRIT.

FAMILIES

Ge 10:5 after their **f.**, in their nations. 4940
Ge 10:18 were the **f.** of the Canaanites 4940
Ge 10:20 are the sons of Ham, after their **f.**, 4940
Ge 10:31 are the sons of Shem, after their **f.**, 4940
Ge 10:32 These are the **f.** of the sons of Noah, 4940
Ge 12:3 shall all **f.** of the earth be blessed. 4940
Ge 28:14 all the **f.** of the earth be blessed. 4940
Ge 36:40 of Esau according to their **f.**, 4940
Ge 47:12 with bread, according to their **f.**. 2945
Ex 6:14 Carmi: these be the **f.** of Reuben. 4940
Ex 6:15 women: these are the **f.** of Simeon. 4940
Ex 6:17 and Shimi, according to their **f.**. 4940
Ex 6:19 these are the **f.** of Levi according 4940
Ex 6:24 these are the **f.** of the Korhites. 4940
Ex 6:25 of the Levites according to their **f.**. 4940
Ex 12:21 you a lamb according to your **f.**, 4940
Le 25:45 and of their **f.** that are with you, 4940
Nu 1:2 the children of Israel, after their **f.**, 4940
Nu 1:18 their pedigrees after their **f.**, 4940
Nu 1:20, 22,24,26,28,30,32,34,36,38,40 by their generations, after their **f.**, 4940
Nu 1:42 their generations, after their **f.**, by 4940
Nu 2:34 forward, every one after their **f.**, 4940
Nu 3:15 children of Levi,...after their **f.**; 4940
Nu 3:18 the sons of Gershon by their **f.**; 4940
Nu 3:19 the sons of Kohath by their **f.**; 4940
Nu 3:20 the sons of Merari by their **f.**; 4940
Nu 3:20 These are the **f.** of the Levites. 4940
Nu 3:21 these are the **f.** of the Gershonites. 4940
Nu 3:23 The **f.** of the Gershonites shall 4940
Nu 3:27 these are the **f.** of the Kohathites. 4940
Nu 3:29 The **f.** of the sons of Kohath 4940
Nu 3:30 father of the **f.** of the Kohathites. 4940
Nu 3:33 these are the **f.** of Merari. 4940
Nu 3:35 of the **f.** of Merari was Zuriel 4940
Nu 3:39 throughout their **f.**, all the males 4940
Nu 4:2 the sons of Levi, after their **f.**, 4940
Nu 4:18 tribe of the **f.** of the Kohathites 4940
Nu 4:22 houses of their fathers, by their **f.**; 4940
Nu 4:24 service of the **f.** of the Gershonites, 4940
Nu 4:28 of the **f.** of the sons of Gershon in 4940
Nu 4:29 shalt number them after their **f.**. 4940
Nu 4:33 of the **f.** of the sons of Merari, 4940
Nu 4:34 sons of the Kohathites after their **f.**, 4940
Nu 4:36 were numbered of them by their **f.** 4940
Nu 4:37 of the **f.** of the Kohathites, all that 4940
Nu 4:38 of Gershon, throughout their **f.**, 4940
Nu 4:40 throughout their **f.**, by the house of 4940
Nu 4:41 of the **f.** of the sons of Gershon. 4940
Nu 4:42 of the **f.** of the sons of Merari, 4940
Nu 4:42 throughout their **f.**, by the house of 4940
Nu 4:44 numbered of them after their **f.**. 4940
Nu 4:45 of the **f.** of the sons of Merari, 4940
Nu 4:46 of Israel, numbered after their **f.**, 4940
Nu 11:10 people weep throughout their **f.**, 4940
Nu 26:7 These are the **f.** of the Reubenites: 4940
Nu 26:12 The sons of Simeon after their **f.**: 4940
Nu 26:14 These are the **f.** of the Simeonites, 4940
Nu 26:15 The children of Gad after their **f.**: 4940
Nu 26:18 These are the **f.** of the children of 4940
Nu 26:20 sons of Judah after their **f.** were; 4940
Nu 26:22 These are the **f.** of Judah 4940
Nu 26:23 the sons of Issachar after their **f.**: 4940
Nu 26:25 These are the **f.** of Issachar 4940
Nu 26:26 the sons of Zebulun after their **f.**: 4940
Nu 26:27 These are the **f.** of the Zebulunites. 4940
Nu 26:28 The sons of Joseph after their **f.** 4940
Nu 26:34 These are the **f.** of Manasseh, after 4940
Nu 26:35 the sons of Ephraim after their **f.**: 4940
Nu 26:37 are the **f.** of the sons of Ephraim 4940
Nu 26:37 are the sons of Joseph after their **f.** 4940
Nu 26:38 The sons of Benjamin after their **f.**: 4940
Nu 26:41 the sons of Benjamin after their **f.**: 4940
Nu 26:42 are the sons of Dan after their **f.**; 4940
Nu 26:42 These are the **f.** of Dan after their **f.** 4940
Nu 26:43 All the **f.** of the Shuhamites, 4940
Nu 26:44 the children of Asher after their **f.**: 4940
Nu 26:47 These are the **f.** of the sons of Asher. 4940
Nu 26:48 Of the sons of Naphtali after their **f.**: 4940
Nu 26:50 **f.** of Naphtali according to their **f.**: 4940
Nu 26:57 of the Levites after their **f.**: 4940
Nu 26:58 These are the **f.** of the Levites: 4940
Nu 27:1 of the **f.** of Manasseh the son of 4940
Nu 33:54 for an inheritance among your **f.**: 4940
Nu 36:1 the **f.** of the children of Gilead, 4940
Nu 36:1 of the **f.** of the sons of Joseph, 4940
Nu 36:12 married into the **f.** of the sons of 4940
Jos 7:14 according to the **f.** thereof; and 4940
Jos 13:15 inheritance according to their **f.** 4940
Jos 13:23 children of Reuben after their **f.**, 4940
Jos 13:24 of Gad according to their **f.** 4940
Jos 13:28 the children of Gad after their **f.**, 4940
Jos 13:29 children of Manasseh by their **f.** 4940
Jos 13:31 the children of Machir by their **f.**. 4940
Jos 15:1 the children of Judah by their **f.**; 4940
Jos 15:12 round about according to their **f.**. 4940
Jos 15:20 of Judah according to their **f.**. 4940
Jos 16:5 of Ephraim according to their **f.** 4940
Jos 16:8 the children of Ephraim by their **f.** 4940
Jos 17:2 children of Manasseh by their **f.**; 4940
Jos 17:2 the son of Joseph by their **f.** 4940
Jos 18:11 came up according to their **f.**: 4940
Jos 18:20 round about, according to their **f.**. 4940
Jos 18:21 of Benjamin according to their **f.** 4940
Jos 18:28 of Benjamin according to their **f.**. 4940
Jos 19:1 of Simeon according to their **f.**: 4940
Jos 19:8 of Simeon according to their **f.** 4940
Jos 19:10 of Zebulun according to their **f.**: 4940
Jos 19:16 of Zebulun according to their **f.**, 4940
Jos 19:17 of Issachar according to their **f.**, 4940
Jos 19:23 of Issachar according to their **f.**, 4940
Jos 19:24 of Asher according to their **f.**. 4940
Jos 19:31 of Asher according to their **f.**, 4940
Jos 19:32 of Naphtali according to their **f.** 4940
Jos 19:39 of Naphtali according to their **f.**, 4940
Jos 19:40 of Dan according to their **f.**, 4940
Jos 19:48 of Dan according to their **f.**, 4940
Jos 21:4 for the **f.** of the Kohathites: 4940
Jos 21:5 of the **f.** of the tribe of Ephraim, 4940
Jos 21:6 of the **f.** of the tribe of Issachar, 4940
Jos 21:7 The children of Merari by their **f.** 4940
Jos 21:10 being of the **f.** of the Kohathites, 4940
Jos 21:20 And the **f.** of the children of Kohath, 4940
Jos 21:26 for the **f.** of the children of Kohath 4940
Jos 21:27 of Gershon, of the **f.** of the Levites, 4940
Jos 21:33 according to their **f.** were thirteen 4940
Jos 21:34 unto the **f.** of the children of Merari, 4940
Jos 21:40 the children of Merari by their **f.**, 4940
Jos 21:40 remaining of the **f.** of the Levites, 4940
1Sa 9:21 and my family the least of all the **f.** 4940
1Sa 10:21 Benjamin to come near by their **f.**, 4940
1Ch 2:53 And the **f.** of Kirjath-jearim; the 4940
1Ch 2:55 the **f.** of the scribes which dwelt 4940
1Ch 4:2 These are the **f.** of the Zorathites. 4940
1Ch 4:8 the **f.** of Aharhel the son of Harum. 4940
1Ch 4:21 and the **f.** of the house of them 4940
1Ch 4:38 names were princes in their **f.**: 4940
1Ch 5:7 And his brethren by their **f.**, 4940
1Ch 6:19 And these are the **f.** of the Levites 4940
1Ch 6:54 Aaron, of the **f.** of the Kohathites: 4940
1Ch 6:60 All their cities throughout their **f.** 4940
1Ch 6:62 of Gershom throughout their **f.** 4940
1Ch 6:63 given by lot, throughout their **f.**, 4940
1Ch 6:66 of the **f.** of the sons of Kohath had 4940
1Ch 7:5 among all the **f.** of Issachar were 4940
2Ch 35:5 divisions of the **f.** of the fathers 1004
2Ch 35:5 division of the **f.** of the Levites. 1004,1
2Ch 35:12 divisions of the **f.** of the people, 1004,1
Ne 4:13 after their **f.** with their swords, 4940
Job 31:34 did the contempt of **f.** terrify me, 4940
Ps 68:6 God setteth the solitary in **f.**: 1004
Ps 107:41 and maketh him **f.** like a flock. 4940
Jer 1:15 will call all the **f.** of the kingdoms 4940
Jer 2:4 all the **f.** of the house of Israel: 4940
Jer 10:25 the **f.** that call not on thy name: 4940
Jer 25:9 and take all the **f.** of the north, 4940
Jer 31:1 the God of all the **f.** of Israel, 4940
Jer 33:24 two **f.** which the Lord hath chosen, 4940
Eze 20:32 as the **f.** of the countries, to serve 4940
Am 3:2 I known of all the **f.** of the earth: 4940
Na 3:4 and **f.** through her witchcrafts. 4940
Zec 12:14 **f.** that remain, every family apart, 4940
Zec 14:17 come up of all the **f.** of the earth 4940

FAMILY See also FAMILIES.

Le 20:5 that man, and against his **f.**, 4940
Le 25:10 shall return every man unto his **f.**. 4940
Le 25:41 and shall return unto his own **f.**, 4940
Le 25:47 or to the stock of the stranger's **f.**: 4940
Le 25:49 is nigh of kin unto him of his **f.** 4940
Nu 3:21 Gershon was the **f.** of the Libnites, 4940
Nu 3:21 and the **f.** of the Shimites: 4940
Nu 3:27 Kohath was the **f.** of the Amramites, 4940
Nu 3:27 and the **f.** of the Izeharites, 4940
Nu 3:27 and the **f.** of the Hebronites, 4940
Nu 3:27 and the **f.** of the Uzzielites: 4940
Nu 3:33 Merari was the **f.** of the Mahlites, 4940
Nu 3:33 and the **f.** of the Mushites: 4940
Nu 26:5 cometh the **f.** of the Hanochites: 4940
Nu 26:5 of Pallu, the **f.** of the Palluites: 4940
Nu 26:6 Of Hezron, the **f.** of the Hezronites: 4940
Nu 26:6 of Carmi, the **f.** of the Carmites. 4940
Nu 26:12 Nemuel, the **f.** of the Nemuelites: 4940
Nu 26:12 of Jamin, the **f.** of the Jaminites: 4940
Nu 26:12 of Jachin, the **f.** of the Jachinites: 4940
Nu 26:13 Of Zerah, the **f.** of the Zarhites: 4940
Nu 26:13 of Shaul, the **f.** of the Shaulites. 4940
Nu 26:15 of Zephon, the **f.** of the Zephonites: 4940
Nu 26:15 of Haggi, the **f.** of the Haggites: 4940
Nu 26:15 of Shuni, the **f.** of the Shunites: 4940
Nu 26:16 Of Ozni, the **f.** of the Oznites: 4940
Nu 26:16 of Eri, the **f.** of the Erites: 4940
Nu 26:17 Of Arod, the **f.** of the Arodites: 4940
Nu 26:17 of Areli, the **f.** of the Arelites. 4940
Nu 26:20 of Shelah, the **f.** of the Shelanites: 4940
Nu 26:20 of Pharez, the **f.** of the Pharzites: 4940
Nu 26:20 of Zerah, the **f.** of the Zarhites. 4940
Nu 26:21 of Hezron, the **f.** of the Hezronites: 4940
Nu 26:21 of Hamul, the **f.** of the Hamulites. 4940
Nu 26:23 of Tola, the **f.** of the Tolaites: 4940
Nu 26:23 of Pua, the **f.** of the Punites: 4940
Nu 26:24 Of Jashub, **f.** of the Jashubites: 4940
Nu 26:24 Shimron, the **f.** of the Shimronites. 4940
Nu 26:26 of Sered, the **f.** of the Sardites: 4940
Nu 26:26 of Elon, the **f.** of the Elonites: 4940
Nu 26:26 of Jahleel, the **f.** of the Jahleelites. 4940
Nu 26:29 of Machir, the **f.** of the Machirites: 4940
Nu 26:29 Gilead come the **f.** of the Gileadites. 4940
Nu 26:30 of Jeezer, the **f.** of the Jeezerites: 4940
Nu 26:30 of Helek, the **f.** of the Helekites: 4940
Nu 26:31 of Asriel, the **f.** of the Asrielites: 4940
Nu 26:31 Shechem, the **f.** of the Shechemites: 4940
Nu 26:32 Shemida, the **f.** of the Shemidaites: 4940
Nu 26:32 Hepher, the **f.** of the Hepherites. 4940
Nu 26:35 Shuthelah, the **f.** of the Shuthalhites: 4940
Nu 26:35 of Becher, the **f.** of the Bachrites: 4940
Nu 26:35 of Tahan, the **f.** of the Tahahamites, 4940
Nu 26:36 of Eran, the **f.** of the Eranites. 4940
Nu 26:38 of Bela, the **f.** of the Belaites: 4940
Nu 26:38 of Ashbel, the **f.** of the Ashbelites: 4940
Nu 26:38 of Ahiram, the **f.** of the Ahiramites: 4940
Nu 26:39 Shupham, the **f.** of the Shuphamites: 4940
Nu 26:39 Hupham, the **f.** of the Huphamites. 4940
Nu 26:40 of Ard, the **f.** of the Ardites: 4940
Nu 26:40 of Naaman, the **f.** of the Naamites. 4940
Nu 26:42 Shuham, the **f.** of the Shuhamites. 4940
Nu 26:44 of Jimna, the **f.** of the Jimnites: 4940
Nu 26:44 of Jesui, the **f.** of the Jesuites: 4940
Nu 26:44 of Beriah, the **f.** of the Beriites. 4940
Nu 26:45 of Heber, the **f.** of the Heberites: 4940
Nu 26:45 Malchiel, the **f.** of the Malchielites. 4940
Nu 26:48 Jahzeel, the **f.** of the Jahzeelites: 4940
Nu 26:48 of Guni, the **f.** of the Gunites: 4940
Nu 26:49 of Jezer, the **f.** of the Jezerites: 4940
Nu 26:49 of Shillem, the **f.** of the Shillemites. 4940
Nu 26:57 Gershon, the **f.** of the Gershonites: 4940
Nu 26:57 Kohath, the **f.** of the Kohathites: 4940
Nu 26:57 of Merari, the **f.** of the Merarites. 4940
Nu 26:58 of the Levites: the **f.** of the Libnites, 4940
Nu 26:58 the **f.** of the Hebronites, 4940
Nu 26:58 the **f.** of the Mahlites, 4940
Nu 26:58 the **f.** of the Mushites, 4940
Nu 26:58 the **f.** of the Korathites. 4940
Nu 27:4 be done away from among his **f.**, 4940
Nu 27:11 that is next to him of his **f.**, 4940
Nu 36:6 only to the **f.** of the tribe of their 4940

Nu 36:8 wife unto one of the **f.** of the tribe..... 4940
Nu 36:12 or the tribe of the **f.** of their father. ... 4940
De 29:18 in **f.**, or tribe, whose heart turneth..... 4940
Jos 7:14 the **f.** which the Lord shall take......... 4940
Jos 7:17 And he brought the **f.** of Judah;......... 4940
Jos 7:17 and he took the **f.** of the Zarhites:....... 4940
Jos 7:17 he brought the **f.** of the Zarhites........ 4940
Jg 1:25 they let go the man and all his **f.**. 4940
Jg 6:15 behold, my **f.** is poor in Manasseh, ... 504
Jg 9:1 and with all the **f.** of the house of 4940
Jg 13:2 of Zorah, of the **f.** of the Danites, ... 4940
Jg 17:7 the **f.** of Judah, who was a Levite, ... 4940
Jg 18:2 of Dan sent of their **f.** five men 4940
Jg 18:11 from thence of the **f.** of the Danites,... 4940
Jg 18:19 unto a tribe and a **f.** in Israel?.......... 4940
Jg 21:24 every man to his tribe and to his **f.**, ... 4940
Ru 2:1 of wealth, of the **f.** of Elimelech;........ 4940
1Sa 9:21 my **f.** the least of all the families........ 4940
1Sa 10:21 the **f.** of Matri was taken,.................. 4940
1Sa 18:18 my life, or my father's **f.** in Israel, ... 4940
1Sa 20:6 yearly sacrifice there for all the **f.**. 4940
1Sa 20:29 for our **f.** hath a sacrifice in the city.... 4940
2Sa 14:7 **f.** is risen against thine handmaid,....... 4940
2Sa 16:5 a man of the **f.** of the house of Saul,... 4940
1Ch 4:27 neither did all their **f.** multiply, like..... 4940
1Ch 6:61 were left of the **f.** of that tribe, ... 4940
1Ch 6:70 the **f.** of the remnant of the sons 4940
1Ch 6:71 given out of the **f.** of the half tribe 4940
1Ch 13:14 ark of God remained with the **f.** of....... 1004
Es 9:28 every **f.**, every province, and every.... 4940
Jer 3:14 one of a city, and two of a **f.**,............ 4940
Jer 8:3 of them that remain of this evil **f.**,....... 4940
Am 3:1 the whole **f.** which I brought up......... 4940
Mic 2:3 against this **f.** do I devise an evil,....... 4940
Zec 12:12 shall mourn, every **f.** apart;.............. 4940
Zec 12:12 the **f.** of the house of David apart, ... 4940
Zec 12:12 the **f.** of the house of Nathan apart,.... 4940
Zec 12:13 The **f.** of the house of Levi apart, ... 4940
Zec 12:13 the **f.** of Shimei apart, and their......... 4940
Zec 12:14 families that remain, every **f.** apart, ... 4940
Zec 14:18 if the **f.** of Egypt go not up,.............. 4940
Eph 3:15 **f.** in heaven and earth is named. *3965*

FAMINE See also FAMINES.
Ge 12:10 And there was a **f.** in the land:........ 7458
Ge 12:10 for the **f.** was grievous in the land........ 7458
Ge 26:1 And there was a **f.** that was in the..... 7458
Ge 26:1 beside the first **f.** that was in the....... 7458
Ge 41:27 east wind shall be seven years of **f.**..... 7458
Ge 41:30 arise after them seven years of **f.**; 7458
Ge 41:30 and the **f.** shall consume the land; 7458
Ge 41:31 in the land by reason of that **f.** 7458
Ge 41:36 against the seven years of **f.**, which.... 7458
Ge 41:36 the land perish not through the **f.**....... 7458
Ge 41:50 before the years of **f.** came,............... 7458
Ge 41:56 And the **f.** was over all the face of..... 7458
Ge 41:56 and the **f.** waxed sore in the land of ... 7458
Ge 41:57 that the **f.** was so sore in all lands...... 7458
Ge 42:5 the **f.** was in the land of Canaan......... 7458
Ge 42:19 corn for the **f.** of your houses: 7459
Ge 42:33 food for the **f.** of your households, ... 7459
Ge 43:1 And the **f.** was sore in the land. 7458
Ge 45:6 years hath **f.** been in the land:........... 7458
Ge 45:11 yet there are five years of **f.**;............ 7458
Ge 47:4 the **f.** is sore in the land of Canaan:..... 7458
Ge 47:13 for the **f.** was very sore, so that the.... 7458
Ge 47:13 Canaan fainted by reason of the **f.**.... 7458
Ge 47:20 because the **f.** prevailed over them:.... 7458
Ru 1:1 that there was a **f.** in the land. 7458
2Sa 21:1 there was a **f.** in the days of David..... 7458
2Sa 24:13 Shall seven years of **f.** come unto....... 7458
1Ki 8:37 If there be in the land **f.**,................ 7458
1Ki 18:2 And there was a sore **f.** in Samaria..... 7458
2Ki 6:25 there was a great **f.** in Samaria:......... 7458
2Ki 7:4 then the **f.** is in the city, ... 7458
2Ki 8:1 the Lord hath called for a **f.**;............ 7458
2Ki 25:3 month the **f.** prevailed in the city, ... 7458
1Ch 21:12 Either three years' **f.**; or three.......... 7458
2Ch 20:9 judgment, or pestilence, or **f.**, ... 7458
2Ch 32:11 to die by **f.** and by thirst,................. 7458
Job 5:20 In **f.** he shall redeem thee from.......... 7458
Job 5:22 At destruction and **f.** thou shalt.......... 3720
Job 30:3 For want and **f.** they were solitary; 3720
Ps 33:19 and to keep them alive in **f.**.............. 7458
Ps 37:19 days of **f.** they shall be satisfied......... 7459
Ps 105:16 he called for a **f.** upon the land: 7458
Isa 14:30 I will kill thy root with **f.**,................ 7458
Isa 51:19 and the **f.**, and the sword:................ 7458
Jer 5:12 neither shall we see sword nor **f.**:....... 7458
Jer 11:22 and their daughters shall die by **f.**: 7458
Jer 14:12 them by the sword, and by the **f.**,...... 7458
Jer 14:13 the sword, neither shall ye have **f.**; 7458
Jer 14:15 and **f.** shall not be in this land;........... 7458
Jer 14:15 **f.** shall those prophets be consumed. .. 7458
Jer 14:16 because of the **f.** and the sword:......... 7458
Jer 14:18 behold them that are sick with **f.**!........ 7458
Jer 15:2 such as are for the **f.**, to the **f.**; 7458
Jer 16:4 consumed by the sword, and by **f.**;..... 7458
Jer 18:21 deliver up their children to the **f.**,...... 7458
Jer 21:7 from the sword, and from the **f.**, ... 7458
Jer 21:9 die by the sword, and by the **f.**, ... 7458
Jer 24:10 I will send the sword, the **f.**,............ 7458
Jer 27:8 with the sword, and with the **f.**, ... 7458
Jer 27:13 thy people, by the sword, by the **f.**,.... 7458
Jer 29:17 send upon them the sword, the **f.**, ... 7458
Jer 29:18 them with the sword, with the **f.**, ... 7458
Jer 32:24 because of the sword, and of the **f.**, ... 7458
Jer 32:36 Babylon by the sword, and by the **f.**,.. 7458
Jer 34:17 to the pestilence, and to the **f.**; 7458
Jer 38:2 shall die by the sword, by the **f.**, ... 7458
Jer 42:16 and the **f.**, whereof ye were afraid, ... 7458
Jer 42:17 shall die by the sword, by the **f.**, ... 7458
Jer 42:22 ye shall die by the sword, by the **f.**,... 7458
Jer 44:12, 12 by the sword and by the **f.**:......... 7458
Jer 44:13 Jerusalem, by the sword, by the **f.**, ... 7458
Jer 44:18 by the sword and by the **f.**. 7458
Jer 44:27 by the sword and by the **f.**, until........ 7458
Jer 52:6 month the **f.** was sore in the city, ... 7458
La 5:10 an oven because of the terrible **f.**....... 7458
Eze 5:12 and with **f.** shall they be consumed..... 7458
Eze 5:16 upon them the evil arrows of **f.**, ... 7458
Eze 5:16 and I will increase the **f.** upon you,..... 7458
Eze 5:17 So will I send upon you **f.** and evil 7458
Eze 6:11 they shall fall by the sword, by the **f.**. 7458
Eze 6:12 and is besieged shall die by the **f.**: 7458
Eze 7:15 the pestilence and the **f.** within:......... 7458
Eze 7:15 **f.** and pestilence shall devour him....... 7458
Eze 12:16 them from the sword, from the **f.**, ... 7458
Eze 14:13 and will send **f.** upon it, ... 7458
Eze 14:21 and the **f.**, and the noisome beast, ... 7458
Eze 36:29 and lay no **f.** upon you. 7458
Eze 36:30 shall receive no more reproach of **f.**.. 7458
Am 8:11 that I will send a **f.** in the land,.......... 7458
Am 8:11 not a **f.** of bread, nor a thirst of.......... 7458
Lu 4:25 **when great f. was throughout all** .. *3042*
Lu 15:14 **there arose a mighty f. in that**....... *3042*
Ro 8:35 or **f.**, or nakedness, or peril, or......... *3042*
Re 18:8 day, death, and mourning, and **f.**;....... *3042*

FAMINES
Mt 24:7 **there shall be f., and pestilences,** .. *3042*
Mk 13:8 **and there shall be f. and troubles:**. *3042*
Lu 21:11 **and f., and pestilences: and fearful**.*3042*

FAMISH See also FAMISHED.
Pr 10:3 the soul of the righteous to **f.**:........... 7456
Zep 2:11 will **f.** all the gods of the earth; 7329

FAMISHED
Ge 41:55 when all the land of Egypt was **f.**,....... 7456
Isa 5:13 and their honourable men are **f.**,......... 7458

FAMOUS See also INFAMOUS.
Nu 16:2 assembly, **f.** in the congregation,........ 7148
Nu 26:9 which were **f.** in the congregation,....... 7121
Ru 4:11 Ephratah...**f.** in Beth-lehem:........ 7121,8034
Ru 4:14 that his name may be **f.** in Israel........ 7121
1Ch 5:24 mighty men of valour, **f.** men, ... 8034
1Ch 12:30 **f.** throughout the house of their.......... 8034
Ps 74:5 A man was **f.** according as he had....... 3045
Ps 136:18 And slew **f.** kings: for his.................... 117
Eze 23:10 she became **f.** among women, ... 8034
Eze 32:18 the daughters of the **f.** nations, ... 117

FAN
Isa 30:24 with the shovel and with the **f.**.......... 4214
Isa 41:6 Thou shalt **f.** them, and the wind....... 2219
Jer 4:11 not to **f.**, nor to cleanse, ... 2219
Jer 15:7 And I will **f.** them...in the gates.......... 2219
Jer 15:7 And I will...with a **f.** in the gates 4214
Jer 51:2 Babylon fanners, that shall **f.** her,....... 2219
Mt 3:12 Whose **f.** is in his hand, and he.......... *4425*
Lu 3:17 Whose **f.** is in his hand, and he will *4425*

FANNERS
Jer 51:2 Babylon **f.**, that shall fan her, ... 2114

FAR See also ARAR; FARTHER.
Ge 18:25 That be **f.** from thee to do after 2486
Ge 18:25 as the wicked, that be **f.** from thee: ... 2486
Ge 44:4 and not yet **f.** off, Joseph said........... 7368
Ex 8:28 ye shall not go very **f.** away:............. 7368
Ex 23:7 Keep thee **f.** from a false matter;........ 7368
Nu 2:2 **f.** off about the tabernacle of the........ 5048
De 12:21 name there be too **f.** from thee, ... 7368
De 13:7 nigh unto thee, or **f.** off from thee,..... 7350
De 14:24 if the place be too **f.** from thee,......... 7368
De 20:15 the cities which are very **f.** off........... 7350
De 28:49 bring a nation against thee from **f.**,..... 7350
De 29:22 that shall come from a **f.** land,........... 7350
De 30:11 from thee, neither is it **f.** off. 7350
Jos 3:16 heap very **f.** from the city Adam, ... 7368
Jos 8:4 go not very **f.** from the city, ... 7368
Jos 9:6 We be come from a **f.** country:............ 7350
Jos 9:9 **f.** country thy servants are come 7350
Jos 9:22 We are very **f.** from you; when ye 7350
Jg 9:17 and adventured his life **f.**, and 5048
Jg 18:7 they were **f.** from the Zidonians,........ 7350
Jg 18:28 it was **f.** from Zidon, and they had....... 7350
Jg 19:11 by Jebus, the day was **f.** spent; 3966
1Sa 2:30 the Lord saith, Be it **f.** from me; 2486
1Sa 20:9 Jonathan said, **F.** be it from thee:....... 2486
1Sa 22:15 be it **f.** from me: let not the king 2486
2Sa 15:17 in a place that was **f.** off................... 4801
2Sa 20:20 said, **F.** be it, **f.** be it from me, ... 2486
2Sa 23:17 he said, Be it **f.** from me,.................. 2486
1Ki 8:41 cometh out of a **f.** country for thy...... 7350
1Ki 8:46 the land of the enemy, **f.** or near; 7350
2Ki 20:14 They are come from a **f.** country, ... 7350
2Ch 6:32 but is come from a **f.** country............ 7350
2Ch 6:36 unto a land **f.** off or near; 7350
2Ch 26:15 And his name spread **f.** abroad; 7350
Ezr 6:6 the river, be ye **f.** from thence: 7352
Ne 4:19 the wall, one **f.** from another............. 7350
Es 9:20 king Ahasuerus, both nigh and **f.**,........ 7350
Job 5:4 His children are **f.** from safety,.......... 7350
Job 11:14 be in thine hand, put it **f.** away,......... 7350
Job 13:21 Withdraw thine hand **f.** from me:........ 7350
Job 19:13 hath put my brethren **f.** from me, ... 7350
Job 21:16 counsel of the wicked is **f.** from me,... 7350
Job 22:18 but the counsel of the wicked is **f.**...... 7350
Job 22:23 shalt put away iniquity **f.** from thy...... 7350
Job 30:10 abhor me, they flee **f.** from me,.......... 7350
Job 34:10 **f.** be it from God, that he should 2486
Ps 10:5 are **f.** above out of his sight:............. 5048
Ps 22:1 art thou so **f.** from helping me,.......... 7350
Ps 22:11 Be not **f.** from me; for trouble is 7368
Ps 22:19 be not thou **f.** from me, O Lord:........ 7368
Ps 27:9 Hide not thy face **f.** from me;.................
Ps 35:22 O Lord, be not **f.** from me. 7368
Ps 38:21 O my God, be not **f.** from me. 7368
Ps 55:7 Lo, then would I wander **f.** off,.......... 7368
Ps 71:12 O God, be not **f.** from me: 7368
Ps 73:27 that are **f.** form thee shall perish:....... 7369
Ps 88:8 put away mine acquaintance **f.** 7368
Ps 88:18 and friend hast thou put **f.** from me, ... 7368
Ps 97:9 thou art exalted **f.** above all gods. 3966
Ps 103:12 As **f.** as the east is from the west,..... 7350
Ps 103:12 so **f.** hath he removed our............... 7350
Ps 109:17 so let it be **f.** from him. 7368
Ps 119:150 they are **f.** from thy law................. 7368
Ps 119:155 Salvation is **f.** from the wicked:......... 7350
Pr 4:24 and perverse lips put **f.** from thee...... 7368
Pr 5:8 Remove thy way **f.** from her, ... 7368
Pr 15:29 The Lord is **f.** from the wicked:......... 7350
Pr 19:7 do his friends go **f.** from him?........... 7368
Pr 22:5 keep his soul shall be **f.** from them..... 7368
Pr 22:15 rod of correction shall drive it **f.** 7368
Pr 25:25 is good news from a **f.** country. 4801
Pr 27:10 that is near than a brother **f.** off. 7350
Pr 30:8 Remove **f.** from me vanity and 7369
Pr 31:10 for her price is **f.** above rubies. 7350
Ec 2:13 folly, as **f.** as light excelleth darkness........
Ec 7:23 be wise; but it was **f.** from me. 7350
Ec 7:24 That which is **f.** off, and exceeding..... 7350
Isa 5:26 an ensign to the nations from **f.**, ... 7350
Isa 6:12 Lord have removed men **f.** away,......... 7368
Isa 8:9 give ear, all ye of **f.** countries: 4801
Isa 10:3 which shall come from **f.**? 4801
Isa 13:5 They come from a **f.** country, from 4801
Isa 17:13 they shall flee **f.** off, and shall........... 4801
Isa 19:6 they shall turn the rivers **f.** away; ....
Isa 22:3 together, which have fled from **f.**. 7350
Isa 26:15 removed it **f.** unto all the ends of....... 7368

Isa 29:13 removed their heart **f.** from me ... 7368
Isa 30:27 name of the Lord cometh from **f.**, ... 4801
Isa 33:13 hear, ye that are **f.** off, what I... 7350
Isa 33:17 behold the land that is very **f.** off... 4801
Isa 39:3 They are come from a **f.** country ... 7350
Isa 43:6 not back; bring my sons from **f.**, ... 7350
Isa 46:11 my counsel from a **f.** country: ... 4801
Isa 46:12 that are **f.** from righteousness: ... 7350
Isa 46:13 righteousness; it shall not be **f.** off, ... 7368
Isa 49:1 and hearken, ye people, from **f.**; ... 7350
Isa 49:12 Behold, these shall come from **f.**: ... 7350
Isa 49:19 swallowed thee up shall be **f.** away... 7368
Isa 54:14 thou shalt be **f.** from oppression; ... 7368
Isa 57:9 didst send thy messengers **f.** off, ... 7350
Isa 57:19 Peace, peace to him that is **f.** off, ... 7350
Isa 59:9 Therefore is judgment **f.** from us, ... 7368
Isa 59:11 salvation, but it is **f.** off from us... 7368
Isa 60:4 thy sons shall come from **f.**, and ... 7350
Isa 60:9 to bring thy sons from **f.**, their ... 7350
Jer 2:5 that they are gone **f.** from me, ... 7368
Jer 4:16 watchers come from a **f.** country, ... 4801
Jer 5:15 bing a nation upon you from **f.**, ... 4801
Jer 6:20 the sweet cane from a **f.** country? ... 4801
Jer 8:19 of them that dwell in a **f.** country; ... 4801
Jer 12:2 mouth, and **f.** from their reins. ... 7350
Jer 25:26 the kings of the north, **f.** and near... 7350
Jer 27:10 to remove you **f.** from your land; ... 7368
Jer 48:24 of the land of Moab, **f.** or near. ... 7350
Jer 48:47 Thus **f.** is the judgment of Moab. ... 2008
Jer 49:30 Flee, get you **f.** off, dwell deep, ... 3966
Jer 51:64 Thus **f.** are the words of Jeremiah... 2008
La 1:16 relieve my souls is **f.** from me: ... 7368
La 3:17 thou hast removed my soul **f.** off ... 2186
Eze 6:12 He that is **f.** off shall die ... 7350
Eze 7:20 therefore have I set it **f.** from ... 5079
Eze 8:6 go **f.** off from my sanctuary? ... 7368
Eze 11:15 Get you **f.** from the Lord: ... 7368
Eze 11:16 I have cast them **f.** off among the ... 7368
Eze 12:27 of the times that are **f.** off. ... 7350
Eze 22:5 and those that be **f.** from thee, ... 7350
Eze 23:40 sent for men to come from **f.**, ... 4801
Eze 43:9 carcases of their kings, **f.** from me, ... 7350
Eze 44:10 Levites that are gone away **f.** from... 7350
Da 9:7 that are near, and that are **f.** off, ... 7350
Da 11:2 fourth shall be **f.** richer than they ... 1419
Joe 2:20 I will remove **f.** off form you the... 7368
Joe 3:6 remove them **f.** from their border. ... 7368
Joe 3:8 the Sabeans, to a people **f.** off: ... 7350
Am 6:3 ye that put **f.** away the evil day, ...
Mic 4:7 her that was cast **f.** off a strong nation: ...
Mic 7:11 shall the decree be **f.** removed. ... 7368
Hab 1:8 their horsemen shall come from **f.**; ... 7350
Zec 6:15 they that are **f.** off shall come... 7350
Zec 10:9 shall remember me in **f.** countries; ... 4801
Mt 15:8 **but their heart is f. from me** ... *4206*
Mt 16:22 Be it **f.** from thee, Lord: ... *2436*
Mt 21:33 **and went into a f. country:** ...
Mt 25:14 **man travelling into a f. country,** ...
Mk 6:35 when the day was now **f.** spent, ... *4183*
Mk 6:35 and now the time is **f.** passed: ... *4183*
Mk 7:6 **but their heart is f. from me** ... *4206*
Mk 8:3 **for divers of them came from f.** ... *3113*
Mk 12:1 **and went into a f. country** ...
Mk 12:34 **not f. from the kingdom of God** ... *3112*
Mk 13:34 **as a man taking a f. journey** ...
Lu 7:6 was now not **f.** from the house, ... *3112*
Lu 15:13 **his journey into a f. country,** ... *3117*
Lu 19:12 **went into a f. country to receive** ... *3117*
Lu 20:9 **went into a f. country for a long time** ..
Lu 22:51 and said, **Suffer ye thus f.** ... *2193*
Lu 24:29 and the day is **f.** spent. ...
Lu 24:50 them out as **f.** as to Bethany, ... *2193*
Joh 21:8 for they were not **f.** from land, ... *3112*
Ac 11:19 Stephen travelled as **f.** as Phenice, ... *2193*
Ac 11:22 that he should go as **f.** as Antioch. ... *2193*
Ac 17:27 he be not **f.** from every one ... *3112*
Ac 22:21 **I will send thee f. hence unto the** .. *3112*
Ac 28:15 to meet us as **f.** as Appii forum, ... *891*
Ro 13:12 night is **f.** spent, the day is at hand: ...
2Co 4:17 for us a **f.** more exceeding ... *1519,5236*
2Co 10:14 we are come as **f.** as to you also in ... *891*
Eph 1:21 **F.** above all principality, and ... *5231*
Eph 2:13 ye who sometimes were **f.** off are ... *3112*
Eph 4:10 ascended up **f.** above all heavens, ... *5231*
Php 1:23 Christ; which is **f.** better: ... *4183,3123*
Heb 7:15 And it is yet **f.** more evident: ... *4054*

FARE See also FARED; FAREWELL; SEAFARING; WARFARE; WAYFARING; WELFARE.
1Sa 17:18 and look how thy brethren **f.**, ... 7965
Jon 1:3 he paid the **f.** thereof, and went... 7939
Ac 15:29 ye shall do well. **F.** ye well... *4517*

FARED
Lu 16:19 **and f. sumptuously every day:** ... *2165*

FAREWELL See also FARE and WELL.
Lu 9:61 but let me first go bid them **f.**, ... *657*
Ac 18:21 But bade them **f.**, saying, I must ... *657*
Ac 23:30 what they had against him. **F.** ... *4517*
2Co 13:11 Finally, brethren, **f.** Be perfect, ... *5463*

FARING See SEAFARING; WAYFARING.

FARM
Mt 22:5 and went their ways, one to his **f.** ... 68

FAR-OFF See FAR and OFF.

FARTHER See also FURTHER.
Ec 8:17 yea **f.**; though a wise man think ...
Mt 26:39 And he went a little **f.**, and fell ... *4281*
Mk 1:19 And when he had gone a little **f.** ... *4260*
Mk 10:1 by the **f.** side of Jordan: ... *4008*

FARTHING See also FARTHINGS.
Mt 5:26 **thou hast paid the uttermost f.** ... *2835*
Mt 10:29 **not two sparrows sold for a f.?** ... *787*
Mk 12:42 in two mites, which make a **f.** ... *2835*

FARTHINGS
Lu 12:6 **not five sparrows sold for two f.,** ... *787*

FASHION See also FASHIONED; FASHIONETH; FASHIONING; FASHIONS.
Ge 6:15 **f.** which thou shalt make it of: ...
Ex 26:30 according to the **f.** thereof which... 4941
Ex 37:19 made after the **f.** of almonds ...
1Ki 6:38 according to all the **f.** of it. ... 4941
2Ki 16:10 the **f.** of the altar, and the pattern... 1823
Job 31:15 did not one **f.** us in the womb? ... 3559
Eze 43:11 the house, and the **f.** thereof, ... 8498
Mk 2:12 We never saw it on this **f.** ... *3778*
Lu 9:29 the **f.** of his countenance was ... *1491*
Ac 7:44 to the **f.** that he had seen ... *5179*
1Co 7:31 for the **f.** of this world passeth ... *4976*
Php 2:8 And being found in **f.** as a man, ... *4976*
Jas 1:11 the grace of the **f.** of it perisheth: ... *4383*

FASHIONED
Ex 32:4 and **f.** it with a graving tool, ... 3335
Job 10:8 hands have made me and **f.** me ... 6213
Ps 119:73 hands have made me and **f.** me: ... 3559
Ps 139:16 which in continuance were **f.**, ... 3335
Isa 22:11 had respect unto him that **f.** it ... 3335
Eze 16:7 thy breasts are **f.**, and thine hair ... 3559
Php 3:21 be **f.** like unto his glorious body, ... *4832*

FASHIONETH
Ps 33:15 He **f.** their hearts alike; he ... 3335
Isa 44:12 the coals, and **f.** it with hammers, ... 3335
Isa 45:9 Shall the clay say to him that **f.** it, ... 3335

FASHIONING
1Pe 1:14 not **f.** yourselves according to the ... 4964

FASHIONS
Eze 42:11 out were both according to their **f.**, ... 4941

FAST See also FASTED; FASTING; STEDFAST.
Ge 20:18 Lord had **f.** closed up all the wombs ...
Jg 4:21 for he was **f.** asleep and weary. ...
Jg 15:13 No, but we will bind thee **f.**, ...
Jg 16:11 they bind me **f.** with new ropes ...
Ru 2:8 but abide here **f.** by my maidens: ...
Ru 2:21 Thou shalt keep **f.** by my young men, ...
Ru 2:23 So she kept **f.** by the maidens of Boaz ...
2Sa 12:21 didst **f.** and weep for the child, ... 6684
2Sa 12:23 he is dead, wherefore should I **f.**? ... 6684
1Ki 21:9 Proclaim a **f.**, and set Naboth ... 6685
1Ki 21:12 proclaimed a **f.**, and set Naboth ... 6685
2Ki 6:32 and hold him **f.** at the door: ...
2Ch 20:3 proclaimed a **f.** throughout all ... 6685
Ezr 5:8 and this work goeth **f.** on, ... 629
Ezr 8:21 Then I proclaimed a **f.** there, ... 6685
Es 4:16 and **f.** ye for me, and neither eat ... 6684
Es 4:16 and my maidens will **f.** likewise; ... 6684
Job 2:3 and still he holdeth **f.** his integrity, ...
Job 8:15 he shall hold it **f.**, but it shall not ...
Job 27:6 My righteousness I hold **f.**, and will ...
Job 38:38 and the clods cleave **f.** together? ...
Ps 33:9 he commanded, and it stood **f.** ...
Ps 38:2 For thine arrows stick **f.** in me, ...
Ps 41:8 disease, say they, cleaveth **f.** unto him: ...
Ps 65:6 his strength setteth **f.** the mountains: ...
Ps 89:28 my covenant shall stand **f.** with him. ...
Ps 111:8 They stand **f.** for ever and ever. ...
Pr 4:13 Take **f.** hold of instruction; let her not ...
Isa 58:3 Behold, in the day of your **f.** ye ... 6685
Isa 58:4 ye **f.** for strife and debate, ... 6684
Isa 58:4 ye shall not **f.** as ye do this day, ... 6684
Isa 58:5 Is it such a **f.** that I have chosen? ... 6685
Isa 58:5 wilt thou call this a **f.**, and an ... 6685
Isa 58:6 not this the **f.** that I have chosen? ... 6685
Jer 8:5 they hold **f.** deceit, they refuse to ...
Jer 14:12 When they **f.**, I will not hear their ... 6684
Jer 36:9 proclaimed a **f.** before the Lord ... 6685
Jer 46:14 Stand **f.**, and prepare thee; for ...
Jer 48:16 and his affliction hasteth **f.** ... 3966
Jer 50:33 took them captives held them **f.**; ...
Joe 1:14 Sanctify ye a **f.**, call a solemn ... 6685
Joe 2:15 sanctify a **f.**, call a solemn assembly: ... 6685
Jon 1:5 and he lay, and was **f.** asleep. ...
Jon 3:5 and proclaimed a **f.**, and put on ... 6685
Zec 7:5 did ye all **f.** unto me, even to me? ... 6684
Zec 8:19 The **f.** of the fourth month, ... 6685
Zec 8:19 and the **f.** of the fifth, ... 6685
Zec 8:19 and the **f.** of the seventh, ... 6685
Zec 8:19 and the **f.** of the tenth, ... 6685
Mt 6:16 **Moreover when ye f., be not, as** ... *3522*
Mt 6:16 **they may appear unto men to f.** ... *3522*
Mt 6:18 **thou appear not unto men to f.,** ... *3522*
Mt 9:14 Why do we and the Pharisees **f.** oft, ... *3522*
Mt 9:14 but thy disciples **f.** not? ... *3522*
Mt 9:15 **from them, and then shall they f.** .. *3522*
Mt 26:48 that same is he: hold him **f.**, ...
Mk 2:18 of the Pharisees used to **f.**: ... *3522*
Mk 2:18 of John and of the Pharisees **f.**, ... *3522*
Mk 2:18 but thy disciples **f.** not? ... *3522*
Mk 2:19 **children of the bridechamber f.** ... *3522*
Mk 2:19 **bridegroom with..., they cannot f.** .. *3522*
Mk 2:20 **then shall they f. in those days** ... *3522*
Lu 5:33 do the disciples of John **f.** often, ... *3522*
Lu 5:34 **children of the bridechamber f.,** ... *3522*
Lu 5:35 **then shall they f. in those days** ... *3522*
Lu 18:12 **I f. twice in the week,** ... *3522*
Ac 16:24 made their feet **f.** in the stocks. ... *805*
Ac 27:9 because the **f.** was now already ... *3521*
Ac 27:41 forepart stuck **f.**, and remained ...
1Co 16:13 Watch ye, stand **f.** in the faith, quit ...
Ga 5:1 Stand **f.** therefore in the liberty ...
Php 1:27 that ye stand **f.** in one spirit, with one ...
Php 4:1 so stand **f.** in the Lord, my dearly ...
1Th 3:8 now we live, if ye stand **f.** in the Lord. ...
1Th 5:21 hold **f.** that which is good. ... *2722*
2Th 2:15 brethren, stand **f.**, and hold the ...
2Ti 1:13 Hold **f.** the form of sound words, ...
Tit 1:9 Holding **f.** the faithful word as he ... *472*
Heb 3:6 if we hold **f.** the confidence and ... *2722*
Heb 4:14 let us hold **f.** our profession. ...
Heb 10:23 Let us hold **f.** the profession of our ... *2722*
Re 2:13 **and thou holdest f. my name,** ...
Re 2:25 **ye have already, hold f. till I come** ...
Re 3:3 **and hold f., and repent.** ...
Re 3:11 **hold that f. which thou hast, that no** ...

FASTED
Jg 20:26 **f.** that day until even, and offered ... 6684
1Sa 7:6 and **f.** on that day, and said there, ... 6684
1Sa 31:13 tree at jabesh, and **f.** seven days. ... 6684
2Sa 1:12 and **f.** until even, for Saul, ... 6684
2Sa 12:16 and David **f.**, and went in, ... 6684
2Sa 12:22 child was yet alive, I **f.** and wept: ... 6684
1Ki 21:27 and **f.**, and lay in sackcloth, ... 6684
1Ch 10:12 oak in Jabesh, and **f.** seven days. ... 6684
Ezr 8:23 So we **f.** and besought our God ... 6684
Ne 1:4 and **f.**, and prayed before the God of .. 6684
Isa 58:3 Wherefore have we **f.**, say they, ... 6684
Zec 7:5 When ye **f.** and mourned in the ... 6684
Mt 4:2 when he had **f.** forty days ... *3522*
Ac 13:2 they ministered to the Lord, and **f.**, ... *3522*
Ac 13:3 when they had **f.** and prayed, ... *3522*

FASTEN See also FASTENED; FASTENING.
Ex 28:14 and **f.** the wreathen chains to the ... 5414
Ex 28:25 thou shalt **f.** in the two ouches, ... 5414
Ex 39:31 to **f.** it on high upon the mitre; ... 5414
Isa 22:23 And I will **f.** him as a nail ... 8628
Jer 10:4 they **f.** it with nails and with ... 2388

FASTENED
Ex 39:18 chains they **f.** in the two ouches, ... 5414
Ex 40:18 and **f.** his sockets, and set up the 5414
Jg 4:21 and **f.** it into the ground: 6795
Jg 16:14 And she **f.** it with the pin, ... 8628
1Sa 31:10 and they **f.** his body to the wall of...... 8628
2Sa 20:8 with a sword **f.** upon his loins in 6775
1Ki 6:6 beams should not be **f.** in the.............. 270
1Ch 10:10 and **f.** his head in the temple of 8628
2Ch 9:18 which were **f.** to the throne,............... 270
Es 1:6 **f.** with cords of fine linen and purple 270
Job 38:6 are the foundations thereof **f.**? 2883
Ec 12:11 **f.** by the masters of assemblies, ... 5193
Isa 22:25 shall the nail that is **f.** in the sure....... 8628
Isa 41:7 **f.** it with nails, that it should not......... 2388
Eze 40:43 a hand broad, **f.** round about: 3559
Lu 4:20 in the synagogue were **f.** on him. *816*
Ac 11:6 which when I had **f.** mine eyes, I *816*
Ac 28:3 out of the heat, and **f.** on his hand. *2510*

FASTENING
Ac 3:4 Peter, **f.** his eyes upon him with *816*

FASTEST
Mt 6:17 **when thou f., anoint thine head,**... *3522*

FASTING See also FASTINGS.
Ne 9:1 of Israel were assembled with **f.**, ... 6685
Es 4:3 and **f.**, and weeping, and wailing; 6685
Ps 35:13 I humbled my soul with **f.**;................ 6685
Ps 69:10 and chastened my soul with **f.**, ... 6685
Ps 109:24 My knees are weak through **f.**;........... 6685
Jer 36:6 the Lord's house upon the **f.** day: 6685
Da 6:18 palace, and passed the night **f.**:......... 2908
Da 9:3 with **f.**, and sackcloth, and ashes:....... 6685
Joe 2:12 and with **f.**, and with weeping, and..... 6685
Mt 15:32 **I will not send them away f., lest..** *3523*
Mt 17:21 **not out but by prayer and f.** *3521*
Mk 8:3 **if I send them away f. to their.......** *3523*
Mk 9:29 **by nothing, but by prayer and f..** .. *3521*
Ac 10:30 Four days ago I was **f.** until this *3522*
Ac 14:23 prayed with **f.**, they commended.......... *521*
Ac 27:33 ye have tarried and continued **f.**, ... *777*
1Co 7:5 give yourselves to **f.** and prayer;........ *3521*

FASTINGS
Es 9:31 the matters of the **f.** and their cry...... 6685
Lu 2:37 with **f.** and prayers night and day. *3521*
2Co 6:5 in labours, in watchings, in **f.**; *3521*
2Co 11:27 in **f.** often, in cold and nakedness. *3521*

FASTNESS See STEDFASTNESS.

FAT See also FATFLESHED; FATLING; FATS; FATTED; FATTER; FATTEST; PRESSFAT; WINEFAT.
Ge 4:4 his flock and of the **f.** thereof. 2459
Ge 41:4 seven well favoured and **f.** kine.......... 1277
Ge 41:20 did eat up the first seven **f.** kine: 1277
Ge 45:18 ye shall eat the **f.** of the land. 2459
Ge 49:20 Out of Asher his bread shall be **f.**, ... 8082
Ex 23:18 shall the **f.** of my sacrifice remain....... 2459
Ex 29:13 shalt take all the **f.** that covereth 2459
Ex 29:13 kidneys, and the **f.** that is upon 2459
Ex 29:22 thou shalt take the ram the **f.**............ 2459
Ex 29:22 the **f.** that covereth the inwards,........ 2459
Ex 29:22 and the **f.** that is upon them,............. 2459
Le 1:8 the head, and the **f.**, in order upon..... 6309
Le 1:12 his pieces, with his head and his **f.**: 6309
Le 3:3 the **f.** that covereth the inwards,......... 2459
Le 3:3 all the **f.** that is upon the inwards,....... 2459
Le 3:4 and the **f.** that is on them,................ 2459
Le 3:9 the **f.** thereof, and the whole rump, ... 2459
Le 3:9 the **f.** that covereth the inwards,......... 2459
Le 3:9 all the **f.** that is upon the inwards,....... 2459
Le 3:10 the **f.** that is upon them, which is....... 2459
Le 3:14 the **f.** that covereth the inwards,......... 2459
Le 3:14 all the **f.** that is upon the inwards,...... 2459
Le 3:15 and the **f.** that is upon them,............. 2459
Le 3:16 savour: all the **f.** is the Lord's. 2459
Le 3:17 that ye eat neither **f.** nor blood.......... 2459
Le 4:8 shall take off from it all the **f.** of the... 2459
Le 4:8 the **f.** that covereth the inwards,......... 2459
Le 4:8 and the **f.** that is upon the inwards, ... 2459
Le 4:9 and the **f.** that is upon them,............. 2459
Le 4:19 he shall take all his **f.** from him,......... 2459
Le 4:26 he shall burn all his **f.** upon the.......... 2459
Le 4:26 as the **f.** of the sacrifice of............... 2459
Le 4:31 shall take away all the **f.** thereof, ... 2459
Le 4:31 as the **f.** is taken away from off......... 2459
Le 4:35 shall take away all the **f.** thereof, ... 2459
Le 4:35 as the **f.** of the lamb is taken away..... 2459
Le 6:12 he shall burn thereon the **f.** of the...... 2459
Le 7:3 offer of it all the **f.** thereof;.............. 2459
Le 7:3 the **f.** that covereth the inwards,.......... 2459
Le 7:4 and the **f.** that is on them,................ 2459
Le 7:23 Ye shall eat no manner of **f.**,............. 2459
Le 7:24 And the **f.** of the beast that dieth....... 2459
Le 7:24 and the **f.** of that which is torn 2459
Le 7:25 whosoever eateth the **f.** of the beast,.. 2459
Le 7:30 **f.** with the breast, it shall he bring, ... 2459
Le 7:31 And the priest shall burn the **f.**.......... 2459
Le 7:33 the peace offerings, and the **f.**, ... 2459
Le 8:16 the **f.** that was upon the inwards,....... 2459
Le 8:16 the two kidneys, and their **f.**, and 2459
Le 8:20 head, and the pieces, and the **f.**.......... 6309
Le 8:25 he took the **f.**, and the rump, and 2459
Le 8:25 the **f.** that was upon the inwards,....... 2459
Le 8:25 the two kidneys, and their **f.**, and 2459
Le 8:26 and put them on the **f.**, and upon....... 2459
Le 9:10 But the **f.**, and the kidneys, and 2459
Le 9:19 And the **f.** of the bullock and of the 2459
Le 9:20 they put the **f.** upon the breasts, ... 2459
Le 9:20 and he burnt the **f.** upon the altar: 2459
Le 9:24 altar the burnt offering and the **f.**: 2459
Le 10:15 the offerings made by fire of the **f.**, ... 2459
Le 16:25 And the **f.** of the sin offering shall...... 2459
Le 17:6 and burn the **f.** for a sweet savour 2459
Nu 13:20 land is, whether it be **f.** or lean, ... 8082
Nu 18:17 shalt burn their **f.** for an offering........ 2459
De 31:20 filled themselves, and waxen **f.**; 1878
De 32:14 with **f.** of lambs, and rams of the 2459
De 32:14 with the **f.** of kidneys of wheat; 2459
De 32:15 Jeshurun waxed **f.**, and kicked: 8080
De 32:15 art waxen **f.**, thou art grown thick,..... 8080
De 32:38 did eat the **f.** of their sacrifices, ... 2459
Jg 3:17 and Eglon was a very **f.** man............ 1277
Jg 3:22 and the **f.** closed upon the blade, ... 2459
1Sa 2:15 Also before they burnt the **f.**,............ 2459
1Sa 2:16 Let them not fail to burn the **f.**.......... 2459
1Sa 2:29 yourselves **f.** with the chiefest of 1254
1Sa 15:22 and to hearken than the **f.** of rams. 2459
1Sa 28:24 And the woman had a **f.** calf.............. 4770
2Sa 1:22 from the **f.** of the mighty, the bow 2459
1Ki 1:9 slew sheep and oxen and **f.** cattle....... 4806
1Ki 1:19 he hath slain oxen and **f.** cattle 4806
1Ki 1:25 slain oxen and **f.** cattle and sheep....... 4806
1Ki 4:23 Ten **f.** oxen, and twenty oxen out 1277
1Ki 8:64 and the **f.** of the peace offerings: 2459
1Ki 8:64 and the **f.** of the peace offerings. 2459
1Ch 4:40 they found **f.** pasture and good, ... 8082
2Ch 7:7 and the **f.** of the peace offerings, ... 2459
2Ch 7:7 the meat offerings, and the **f.**............ 2459
2Ch 29:35 with the **f.** of the peace offerings, ... 2459
2Ch 35:14 offerings and the **f.** until night;........... 2459
Ne 8:10 eat the **f.**, and drink the sweet, ... 4924
Ne 9:25 took strong cities, and a **f.** land, ... 8082
Ne 9:25 and were filled, and became **f.**, and 8082
Ne 9:35 and in the large and **f.** land which....... 8082
Job 15:27 maketh collops of **f.** on his flanks. 6371
Ps 17:10 They are inclosed in their own **f.**: 2459
Ps 22:29 All they that be **f.** upon earth shall 1879
Ps 37:20 Lord shall be as the **f.** of lambs: 3368
Ps 92:14 they shall be **f.** and flourishing; 1879
Ps 119:70 Their heart is as **f.** as grease;............ 2954
Pr 11:25 The liberal soul shall be made **f.**: 1878
Pr 13:4 soul of the diligent shall be made **f.**. ... 1878
Pr 15:30 a good report maketh the bones **f.**. 1878
Pr 28:25 trust in the Lord shall be made **f.**....... 1878
Isa 1:11 rams, and the **f.** of fed beasts; 2459
Isa 5:17 the waste places of the **f.** ones 4220
Isa 6:10 Make the heart of this people **f.**,........ 8082
Isa 10:16 send among his **f.** ones leanness; 4924
Isa 25:6 unto all people a feast of **f.** things, ... 8081
Isa 25:6 of **f.** things full of marrow,................ 8081
Isa 28:1 are on the head of the **f.** valleys of..... 8081
Isa 28:4 which is on the head of the **f.** valley, .. 8081
Isa 30:23 and it shall be **f.** and plenteous: 1879
Isa 34:6 it is made **f.** with fatness,................ 1878
Isa 34:6 with the **f.** of the kidneys of rams: 2459
Isa 34:7 their dust made **f.** with fatness. 1878
Isa 43:24 hast thou filled me with the **f.** of......... 2459
Isa 58:11 drought, and make **f.** thy bones: 2502
Jer 5:28 They are waxen **f.**, they shine:.......... 8080
Jer 50:11 ye are grown **f.** as the heifer............ 6335
Eze 34:3 Ye eat the **f.**, and ye clothe you 2459
Eze 34:14 in a **f.** pasture shall they feed........... 8082
Eze 34:16 will destroy the **f.** and the strong; 8082
Eze 34:20 I will judge between the **f.** cattle........ 1277
Eze 39:19 And ye shall eat **f.** till ye be full, ... 2459
Eze 44:7 my bread, the **f.** and the blood, ... 2459
Eze 44:15 offer unto me the **f.** and the blood,..... 2459
Eze 45:15 out of the **f.** pastures of Israel:.......... 4945
Am 5:22 peace offerings of your **f.** beasts. 4806
Hab 1:16 by them their portion is **f.**, ... 8082
Zec 11:16 but he shall eat the flesh of the **f.**, ... 1277

FATFLESHED
Ge 41:2 seven well favoured kine and **f.**;......... 1277
Ge 41:18 seven kine, **f.** and well favoured;........ 1277

FATHER See also FATHERLESS; FATHER'S; FATHERS.
Ge 2:24 a man leave his **f.** and his mother, ... 1
Ge 4:20 was the **f.** of such as dwell in tents,......... 1
Ge 4:21 the **f.** of all such as handle the harp......... 1
Ge 9:18 and Ham is the **f.** of Canaan. 1
Ge 9:22 And Ham, the **f.** of Canaan, saw the 1
Ge 9:22 saw the nakedness of his **f.**, ... 1
Ge 9:23 and covered the nakedness of their **f.**; 1
Ge 10:21 Shem also, the **f.** of all the children......... 1
Ge 11:28 And Haran died before his **f.** Terah......... 1
Ge 11:29 the **f.** of Milcah, and the **f.** of Iscah. 1
Ge 17:4 thou shalt be a **f.** of many nations. 1
Ge 17:5 **f.** of many nations have I made thee........ 1
Ge 19:31 Our **f.** is old, and there is not a man 1
Ge 19:32 Come, let us make our **f.** drink wine, ... 1
Ge 19:32 that we may preserve seed of our **f.**. 1
Ge 19:33 made their **f.** drink wine that night: 1
Ge 19:33 firstborn went in, and lay with her **f.**: 1
Ge 19:34 Behold, I lay yesternight with my **f.**: 1
Ge 19:34 that we may preserve seed of our **f.**. 1
Ge 19:35 And they made their **f.** drink wine 1
Ge 19:36 of Lot with child by their **f.**. 1
Ge 19:37 the same is the **f.** of the Moabites 1
Ge 19:38 is the **f.** of the children of Ammon 1
Ge 20:12 she is the daughter of my **f.**, but not....... 1
Ge 22:7 Abraham his **f.**, and said, My **f.**:............ 1
Ge 22:21 and Kemuel the **f.** of Aram,................... 1
Ge 26:3 which I swear unto Abraham thy **f.**; 1
Ge 26:15 digged in the days of Abraham his **f.**, ... 1
Ge 26:18 digged in the days of Abraham his **f.**; 1
Ge 26:18 by which his **f.** had called them. 1
Ge 26:24 I am the God of Abraham thy **f.**; 1
Ge 27:6 I heard thy **f.** speak unto Esau thy.......... 1
Ge 27:9 make them savoury meat for thy **f.**, ... 1
Ge 27:10 And thou shalt bring it to thy **f.**,............. 1
Ge 27:12 My **f.** peradventure will feel me, ... 1
Ge 27:14 savoury meat, such as his **f.** loved. 1
Ge 27:18 came unto his **f.**, and said, My **f.**:........... 1
Ge 27:19 And Jacob said unto his **f.**, I am Esau 1
Ge 27:22 Jacob went near unto Isaac his **f.**; 1
Ge 27:26 And his **f.** Isaac said unto him, Come 1
Ge 27:30 out from the presence of Isaac his **f.**, ... 1
Ge 27:31 and brought it unto his **f.**, and said.......... 1
Ge 27:31 and said unto his **f.**, Let my **f.** arise,....... 1
Ge 27:32 And Isaac his **f.** said unto him, Who 1
Ge 27:34 when Esau heard the words of his **f.**, ... 1
Ge 27:34 and said unto his **f.**, Bless me, even........ 1
Ge 27:34 Bless me, even me also, O my **f.**. 1
Ge 27:38 Esau said unto his **f.**, Hast thou but 1
Ge 27:38 but one blessing, my **f.**? bless me, ... 1
Ge 27:38 bless me, even me also, O my **f.**............ 1
Ge 27:39 And Isaac his **f.** answered and said........... 1
Ge 27:41 the blessing wherewith his **f.** blessed....... 1
Ge 27:41 the days of mourning for my **f.** are at...... 1
Ge 28:2 the house of Bethuel thy mother's **f.**; 1
Ge 28:7 Jacob obeyed his **f.** and his mother, ... 1
Ge 28:8 of Canaan pleased not Isaac his **f.**; 1
Ge 28:13 am the Lord God of Abraham thy **f.**, ... 1
Ge 29:12 and she ran and told her **f.**. 1
Ge 31:5 the God of my **f.** hath been with me. 1
Ge 31:6 all my power I have served your **f.**. 1
Ge 31:7 And your **f.** hath deceived me, and 1
Ge 31:9 hath taken away the cattle of your **f.**, ... 1
Ge 31:16 which God hath taken from our **f.**, ... 1
Ge 31:18 for to go to Isaac his **f.** in the land.......... 1
Ge 31:29 but the God of your **f.** spake unto me...... 1
Ge 31:35 And she said to her **f.**, Let it not............ 1
Ge 31:42 Except the God of my **f.**, the God of....... 1
Ge 31:53 the God of their **f.**, judge betwixt us. 1
Ge 31:53 sware by the fear of his **f.** Isaac. 1
Ge 32:9 Jacob said, O God of my **f.** Abraham, ... 1
Ge 32:9 and God of my **f.** Isaac, the Lord............ 1
Ge 33:19 children of Hamor, Shechem's **f.**, ... 1
Ge 34:4 Shechem spake unto his **f.** Hamor,........... 1
Ge 34:6 Hamor the **f.** of Shechem went out 1

Ge 34:11 Shechem said unto her **f.** and unto..........1
Ge 34:13 answered Shechem and Hamor his **f.**........1
Ge 34:19 than all the house of his **f.**..................... 1
Ge 35:18 but his **f.** called him Benjamin................. 1
Ge 35:27 Jacob came unto Isaac his **f.** unto........... 1
Ge 36:9 of Esau the **f.** of the Edomites in............1
Ge 36:24 as he fed the asses of Zibeon his **f.**..........1
Ge 36:43 he is Esau the **f.** of the Edomites........... 1
Ge 37:1 wherein his **f.** was a stranger,................ 1
Ge 37:2 brought unto his **f.** their evil report.........1
Ge 37:4 saw that their **f.** loved him more than.......1
Ge 37:10 And he told it to his **f.**, and to his........... 1
Ge 37:10 and his **f.** rebuked him, and said..............1
Ge 37:11 but his **f.** observed the saying.................1
Ge 37:22 to deliver him to his **f.** again.....................1
Ge 37:32 they brought it to their **f.**; and said,.........1
Ge 37:35 Thus his **f.** wept for him..............................1
Ge 38:13 thy **f.** in law goeth up to Timnath........2524
Ge 38:25 she sent to her **f.** in law, saying,........ 2524
Ge 42:13 the youngest is this day with our **f.**...........1
Ge 42:29 And they came unto Jacob their **f.**........... 1
Ge 42:32 be twelve brethren, sons of our **f.**;.......... 1
Ge 42:32 the youngest is this day with our **f.**..........1
Ge 42:35 they and their **f.** saw the bundles........... 1
Ge 42:36 And Jacob their **f.** said unto them,........... 1
Ge 42:37 Reuben spake unto his **f.**, saying,........... 1
Ge 43:2 their **f.** said unto them, Go again,............ 1
Ge 43:7 Is your **f.** yet alive? have ye another........ 1
Ge 43:8 And Judah said unto Israel his **f.**,.............1
Ge 43:11 And their **f.** Israel said unto them............1
Ge 43:23 the God of your **f.**, hath given you..........1
Ge 43:27 and said, Is your **f.** well, the old man....... 1
Ge 43:28 Thy servant our **f.** is in good health,........1
Ge 44:17 get you up in peace unto your **f.**................1
Ge 44:19 saying, Have ye a **f.**, or a brother?........... 1
Ge 44:20 my lord, We have a **f.**, an old man,..........1
Ge 44:20 his mother, and his **f.** loveth him.............1
Ge 44:22 The lad cannot leave his **f.**:..................... 1
Ge 44:22 for if he should leave his **f.**,.................... 1
Ge 44:22 his **f.** would die...
Ge 44:24 we came up unto thy servant my **f.**,..........1
Ge 44:25 And our **f.** said, Go again, and buy............1
Ge 44:27 thy servant my **f.** said unto us,............... 1
Ge 44:30 when I come to thy servant my **f.**,.......... 1
Ge 44:31 the gray hairs of thy servant our **f.**...........1
Ge 44:32 became surety for the lad unto my **f.**,........1
Ge 44:32 then I shall bear the blame to my **f.**......... 1
Ge 44:34 For how shall I go up to my **f.**,................1
Ge 44:34 see the evil that shall come on my **f.**.........1
Ge 45:3 I am Joseph; doth my **f.** yet live?............ 1
Ge 45:8 he hath made me a **f.** to Pharaoh,............1
Ge 45:9 Haste ye, and go up to my **f.**,................. 1
Ge 45:13 tell my **f.** of all my glory in Egypt,...........1
Ge 45:13 haste and bring down my **f.** hither..............
Ge 45:18 take your **f.** and your households,........... 1
Ge 45:19 and bring your **f.**, and come.................... 1
Ge 45:23 to his **f.** he sent after his manner;............ 1
Ge 45:23 and meat for his **f.** by the way...................1
Ge 45:25 land of Canaan unto Jacob their **f.**,............1
Ge 45:27 the spirit of Jacob their **f.** revived:...........1
Ge 46:1 sacrifices unto the God of his **f.** Isaac........1
Ge 46:3 I am God, the God of thy **f.**:..................... 1
Ge 46:5 carried Jacob their **f.**, and their................1
Ge 46:29 and went up to meet Israel his **f.**,..............1
Ge 47:1 and said, My **f.** and my brethren, and.......1
Ge 47:5 Thy **f.** and thy brethren are come............1
Ge 47:6 make thy **f.** and brethren to dwell;...........1
Ge 47:7 And Joseph brought in Jacob his **f.**,.......... 1
Ge 47:11 placed his **f.** and his brethren, and.......... 1
Ge 47:12 nourished his **f.**, and his brethren,........... 1
Ge 48:1 told Joseph, Behold, thy **f.** is sick:...........1
Ge 48:9 Joseph said unto his **f.**, They are............1
Ge 48:17 Joseph saw that his **f.** laid his right......... 1
Ge 48:18 said unto his **f.**, Not so, my **f.**: for........... 1
Ge 48:19 his **f.** refused, and said, I know it,.......... 1
Ge 49:2 and hearken unto Israel your **f.**.................. 1
Ge 49:25 Even by the God of thy **f.**, who shall........1
Ge 49:26 The blessings of thy **f.** have prevailed.......1
Ge 49:28 is it that their **f.** spake unto them,........... 1
Ge 50:2 the physicians to embalm his **f.**:............ 1
Ge 50:5 My **f.** made me swear, saying, Lo,........... 1
Ge 50:5 go up, I pray thee, and bury my **f.**,......... 1
Ge 50:6 Pharaoh said, Go up, and bury thy **f.**,........1
Ge 50:7 And Joseph went up to bury his **f.**:............ 1
Ge 50:10 a mourning for his **f.** seven days............ 1
Ge 50:14 went up with him to bury his **f.**..................1
Ge 50:14 after he had buried his **f.**.........................1
Ge 50:15 brethren saw that their **f.** was dead,........ 1
Ge 50:16 Thy **f.** did command before he died,.........1
Ge 50:17 the servants of the God of thy **f.**............. 1
Ex 2:18 when they came to Reuel their **f.**,............ 1
Ex 3:1 the flock of Jethro his **f.** in law,.......... 2859
Ex 3:6 I am the God of thy **f.**,..............................1
Ex 4:18 returned to Jethro his **f.** in law,.......... 2859
Ex 18:1 priest of Midian, Moses' **f.** in law,........ 2859
Ex 18:2 Then Jethro, Moses' **f.** in law, took..... 2859
Ex 18:4 God of my **f.**, said he, was mine help,....... 1
Ex 18:5 Jethro, Moses' **f.** in law, came with..... 2859
Ex 18:6 I thy **f.** in law Jethro am come unto..... 2859
Ex 18:7 went out to meet his **f.** in law,............ 2859
Ex 18:8 And Moses told his **f.** in law all that.... 2859
Ex 18:12 And Jethro, Moses' **f.** in law, took a.... 2859
Ex 18:12 to eat bread with Moses' **f.** in law....... 2859
Ex 18:14 when Moses' **f.** in law saw that he...... 2859
Ex 18:15 And Moses said unto his **f.** in law,...... 2859
Ex 18:17 And Moses' **f.** in law said unto him,.....2859
Ex 18:24 hearkened to the voice of his **f.** in....... 2859
Ex 18:27 And Moses let his **f.** in law depart;......2859
Ex 20:12 Honour they **f.** and thy mother:............... 1
Ex 21:15 he that smiteth his **f.**, or his mother.........1
Ex 21:17 he that curseth his **f.**, or his mother.........1
Ex 22:17 If her **f.** utterly refuse to give her.......... 1
Ex 40:15 as thou didst anoint their **f.**,.................. 1
Le 18:7 The nakedness of thy **f.**, or the.............. 1
Le 18:9 thy sister, the daughter of thy **f.**,............ 1
Le 18:11 begotten of thy **f.**, she is thy sister,..........1
Le 19:3 every man his mother, and his **f.**,............1
Le 20:9 For every man that curseth his **f.**............. 1
Le 20:9 he hath cursed his **f.** or his mother;.......... 1
Le 21:2 for his mother, and for his **f.**,.................. 1
Le 21:9 she profaneth her **f.**: she shall be............ 1
Le 21:11 nor defile himself for his **f.**,..................... 1
Le 24:10 whose **f.** was an Egyptian,........... 1121,376
Nu 3:4 office in the sight of Aaron their **f.**............1
Nu 3:24 chief of the house of the **f.** of the........... 1
Nu 3:30 **f.** of the families of the Kohathites............1
Nu 3:35 the **f.** of the families of Merari.................1
Nu 6:7 not make himself unclean for his **f.**,...........1
Nu 10:29 the Midianite, Moses' **f.** in law,........... 2859
Nu 11:12 nursing **f.** beareth the sucking child,..........
Nu 12:14 If her **f.** had but spit in her face,............. 1
Nu 18:2 the tribe of Levi, the tribe of thy **f.**,........ 1
Nu 27:3 Our **f.** died in the wilderness,.................. 1
Nu 27:4 the name of our **f.** be done away............. 1
Nu 27:4 among the brethren of our **f.**.................... 1
Nu 27:7 inheritance of their **f.** to pass unto........... 1
Nu 27:11 And if his **f.** have no brethren,................ 1
Nu 30:4 her **f.** hear her vow, and her bond........... 1
Nu 30:4 her **f.** shall hold his peace at her:............ 1
Nu 30:5 if her **f.** disallow her in the day............... 1
Nu 30:5 because her **f.** disallowed her................... 1
Nu 30:16 between the **f.** and his daughter,.............. 1
Nu 36:6 the tribe of their **f.** shall they marry.........1
Nu 36:8 the family of the tribe of her **f.**,................. 1
Nu 36:12 the tribe of the family of their **f.**...............1
De 5:16 Honour thy **f.** and thy mother,................... 1
De 21:13 and bewail her **f.** and her mother.............1
De 21:18 will not obey the voice of his **f.**,................1
De 21:19 shall his **f.** and his mother lay hold............1
De 22:15 Then shall the **f.** of the damsel,............... 1
De 22:16 And the damsel's **f.** shall say.....................1
De 22:19 give them unto the **f.** of the damsel,........ 1
De 22:29 shall give unto the damsel's **f.** fifty...........1
De 26:5 A Syrian ready to perish was my **f.**,..........1
De 27:16 be he that setteth light by his **f.**...............1
De 27:22 with his sister, the daughter of his **f.**,.......1
De 32:6 is not he thy **f.** that hath bought thee?......1
De 32:7 ask thy **f.**, and he will shew thee;.............1
De 33:9 Who said unto his **f.** and to his mother,.... 1
Jos 2:13 that ye will save alive my **f.**,.................... 1
Jos 2:18 shalt bring thy **f.**, and thy mother,............ 1
Jos 6:23 brought out Rahab, and her **f.**, and.......... 1
Jos 15:13 the city of Arba the **f.** of Anak,................1
Jos 15:18 she moved him to ask of her **f.** a field:..... 1
Jos 17:1 of Manasseh, the **f.** of Gilead:..................1
Jos 17:4 among the brethren of their **f.**....................1
Jos 19:47 after the name of Dan their **f.**....................1
Jos 21:11 the city of Arba the **f.** of Anak,................1
Jos 24:2 Terah, the **f.** of Abraham, and the **f.**........1
Jos 24:3 took your **f.** Abraham from the other.......... 1
Jos 24:32 the sons of Hamor the **f.** of Shechem....... 1
Jg 1:14 she moved him to ask of her **f.** a field:..... 1
Jg 1:16 Moses' **f.** in law, went up out of......... 2859
Jg 4:11 Hobab the **f.** in law of Moses,........... 2859
Jg 6:25 the altar of Baal that thy **f.** hath,............. 1
Jg 8:32 Joash his **f.**, in Ophrah of the..................1
Jg 9:1 of the house of his mother's **f.**,..................1
Jg 9:17 my **f.** fought for you, and adventured....... 1
Jg 9:28 the men of Hamor the **f.** of Shechem:........1
Jg 9:56 Abimelech, which he did unto his **f.**,.........1
Jg 11:36 And she said unto him, My **f.**, if thou....... 1
Jg 11:37 she said unto her **f.**, Let this thing...........1
Jg 11:39 she returned unto her **f.**, who did............ 1
Jg 14:2 up, and told his **f.** and his mother,........... 1
Jg 14:3 his **f.** and his mother said unto him,.......... 1
Jg 14:3 Samson said unto his **f.**, Get her for.........1
Jg 14:4 But his **f.** and his mother knew not.........1
Jg 14:5 went Samson down, and his **f.** and..........1
Jg 14:6 he told not his **f.** or his mother..............1
Jg 14:9 came to his **f.** and mother, and he........... 1
Jg 14:10 So his **f.** went down unto the woman:.........1
Jg 14:16 have not told it my **f.** nor my mother,...... 1
Jg 15:1 her **f.** would not suffer him to go in......... 1
Jg 15:2 And her **f.** said, I verily thought............ 1
Jg 15:6 and burnt her and her **f.** with fire........... 1
Jg 16:31 brethren and all the house of his **f.**........... 1
Jg 16:31 the burying-place of Manoah his **f.**............ 1
Jg 17:10 and be unto me a **f.** and a priest,............ 1
Jg 18:19 and be to us a **f.** and a priest:................. 1
Jg 18:29 after the name of Dan their **f.**,.................1
Jg 19:3 when the **f.** of the damsel saw him,......... 1
Jg 19:4 And his **f.** in law,...retained him;.........2859
Jg 19:4 law, the damsel's **f.**, retained him;.......... 1
Jg 19:5 damsel's **f.** said unto his son in law,........ 1
Jg 19:6 damsel's **f.** had said unto the man,.......... 1
Jg 19:7 his **f.** in law urged him: therefore........ 2859
Jg 19:8 damsel's **f.** said, Comfort thine heart,....... 1
Jg 19:9 his **f.** in law,...said unto him, Behold.... 2859
Jg 19:9 law, the damsel's **f.**, said unto him,.......... 1
Ru 2:11 thou hast left thy **f.** and thy mother,......... 1
Ru 4:17 he is the **f.** of Jesse, the **f.** of David........ 1
1Sa 2:25 not unto the voice of their **f.**,................. 1
1Sa 2:27 appear unto the house of thy **f.**,............... 1
1Sa 2:28 did I give unto the house of thy **f.**............ 1
1Sa 2:30 thy house, and the house of thy **f.**,.......... 1
1Sa 4:19 that her **f.** in law and her husband....... 2524
1Sa 4:21 of her **f.** in law and her husband......... 2524
1Sa 9:3 the asses of Kish Saul's **f.** were lost.........1
1Sa 9:5 lest my **f.** leave caring for the asses,........ 1
1Sa 10:2 thy **f.** hath left the care of the asses,....... 1
1Sa 10:12 and said, But who is their **f.**?................. 1
1Sa 14:1 But he told not his **f.**...............................1
1Sa 14:27 But Jonathan heard not when his **f.**.......... 1
1Sa 14:28 Thy **f.** straightly charged the people......... 1
1Sa 14:29 My **f.** hath troubled the land:....................1
1Sa 14:51 Kish was the **f.** of Saul; and Ner the........ 1
1Sa 14:51 the **f.** of Abner was the son of Abiel........ 1
1Sa 19:2 Saul my **f.** seeketh to kill thee:................ 1
1Sa 19:3 stand beside my **f.** in the field................. 1
1Sa 19:3 I will commune with my **f.** of thee;.......... 1
1Sa 19:4 spake good of David unto Saul his **f.**,.........1
1Sa 20:1 and what is my sin before thy **f.**,..............1
1Sa 20:2 behold, my **f.** will do nothing either........... 1
1Sa 20:2 and why should my **f.** hide this thing........ 1
1Sa 20:3 Thy **f.** certainly knoweth that I have......... 1
1Sa 20:6 If thy **f.** at all miss me, then say,............ 1
1Sa 20:8 shouldest thou bring me to thy **f.**?........... 1
1Sa 20:9 determined by my **f.** to come upon.......... 1
1Sa 20:10 what if thy **f.** answer thee roughly?.......... 1
1Sa 20:12 when I have sounded my **f.** about............ 1
1Sa 20:13 but if it please my **f.** to do thee evil,........ 1
1Sa 20:13 as he hath been with my **f.**...................... 1
1Sa 20:32 Jonathan answered Saul his **f.**, and..........1
1Sa 20:33 it was determined of his **f.** to slay............1
1Sa 20:34 because his **f.** had done him shame.......... 1
1Sa 22:3 Let my **f.** and my mother, I pray............1
1Sa 22:15 nor to all the house of my **f.**:...................1
1Sa 23:17 the hand of Saul my **f.** shall not find......... 1
1Sa 23:17 and that also Saul my **f.** knoweth.............1
1Sa 24:11 Moreover, my **f.**, see, yea, see the.........1
2Sa 2:32 buried him in the sepulchre of his **f.**,........1
2Sa 3:8 this day unto the house of Saul thy **f.**,....... 1
2Sa 6:21 Lord, which chose me before thy **f.**,.......... 1
2Sa 7:14 I will be his **f.**, and he shall be my.......... 1
2Sa 9:7 thee all the land of Saul thy **f.**;.................1
2Sa 10:2 as his **f.** shewed kindness unto me............1
2Sa 10:2 by the hand of his servants for his **f.**........ 1
2Sa 10:3 thou that David doth honour thy **f.**,............1
2Sa 13:5 and when thy **f.** cometh to see thee,........ 1
2Sa 16:3 restore me the kingdom of my **f.**..............1
2Sa 16:21 that thou art abhorred of thy **f.**:..............1

2Sa 17:8 thou knowest thy **f.** and his men,... 1
2Sa 17:8 and thy **f.** is a man of war, and will... 1
2Sa 17:10 knoweth that thy **f.** is a mighty man,... 1
2Sa 17:23 was buried in the sepulchre of his **f.**... 1
2Sa 19:37 and be buried by the grave of my **f.**... 1
2Sa 21:14 in the sepulchre of Kish his **f.**:... 1
1Ki 1:6 his **f.** had not displeased him at any... 1
1Ki 2:12 upon the throne of David his **f.**;... 1
1Ki 2:24 set me on the throne of David my **f.**,... 1
1Ki 2:26 ark of the Lord before David my **f.**,... 1
1Ki 2:26 in all wherein my **f.** was afflicted.... 1
1Ki 2:31 me, and from the house of my **f.**... 1
1Ki 2:32 my **f.** David not knowing thereof,... 1
1Ki 2:44 that thou didst to David my **f.**:... 1
1Ki 3:3 in the statues of David his **f.**:... 1
1Ki 3:6 shewed unto thy servant David my **f.**... 1
1Ki 3:7 servant king instead of David my **f.**:... 1
1Ki 3:14 as thy **f.** David did walk, then I will... 1
1Ki 5:1 him king in the room of his **f.**:... 1
1Ki 5:3 Thou knowest how that David my **f.**,... 1
1Ki 5:5 the Lord spake unto David my **f.**,... 1
1Ki 6:12 which I spake unto David thy **f.**:... 1
1Ki 7:14 and his **f.** was a man of Tyre,... 1
1Ki 7:51 which David his **f.** had dedicated;... 1
1Ki 8:15 with his mouth unto David my **f.**,... 1
1Ki 8:17 And it was in the heart of David my **f.**... 1
1Ki 8:18 and the Lord said unto David my **f.**,... 1
1Ki 8:20 risen up in the room of David my **f.**,... 1
1Ki 8:24 kept with thy servant David my **f.**... 1
1Ki 8:25 keep with thy servant David my **f.**... 1
1Ki 8:26 thou unto thy servant David my **f.**... 1
1Ki 9:4 before me, as David thy **f.** walked,... 1
1Ki 9:5 as I promised to David thy **f.**,... 1
1Ki 11:4 as was the heart of David his **f.**... 1
1Ki 11:6 after the Lord, as did David his **f.**... 1
1Ki 11:27 breaches of the city of David his **f.**... 1
1Ki 11:33 my judgments, as did David his **f.**... 1
1Ki 11:43 was buried in the city of David his **f.**:... 1
1Ki 12:4 Thy **f.** made our yoke grievous:... 1
1Ki 12:4 thou the grievous service of thy **f.**,... 1
1Ki 12:6 that stood before Solomon his **f.**... 1
1Ki 12:9 yoke which thy **f.** did put upon us.... 1
1Ki 12:10 saying, Thy **f.** made our yoke heavy,... 1
1Ki 12:11 whereas my **f.** did lade you with... 1
1Ki 12:11 my **f.** hath chastised you with whips,... 1
1Ki 12:14 My **f.** made your yoke heavy, and... 1
1Ki 12:14 my **f.** also chastised you with whips,... 1
1Ki 13:11 them they told also to their **f.**... 1
1Ki 13:12 their **f.** said unto them, What way... 1
1Ki 15:3 he walked in all the sins of his **f.**,... 1
1Ki 15:3 his God, as the heart of David his **f.**... 1
1Ki 15:11 eyes of the Lord, as did David his **f.**... 1
1Ki 15:15 things which his **f.** had dedicated,... 1
1Ki 15:19 thee, and between my **f.** and thy **f.**:... 1
1Ki 15:24 fathers in the city of David his **f.**;... 1
1Ki 15:26 and walked in the way of his **f.**,... 1
1Ki 19:20 thee, kiss my **f.** and my mother,... 1
1Ki 20:34 cities, which my **f.** took from thy **f.**,... 1
1Ki 20:34 Damascus, as my **f.** made in Samaria.... 1
1Ki 22:43 walked in the ways of Asa his **f.**;... 1
1Ki 22:46 which remained in the days of his **f.**... 1
1Ki 22:50 fathers in the city of David his **f.**;... 1
1Ki 22:52 and walked in the way of his **f.**,... 1
1Ki 22:53 according to all that is **f.** had done.... 1
2Ki 2:12 My **f.**, my **f.**, the chariot of Israel,... 1
2Ki 3:2 not like his **f.**, and like his mother:... 1
2Ki 3:2 image of Baal that his **f.** had made.... 1
2Ki 3:13 get thee to the prophets of thy **f.**,... 1
2Ki 4:18 he went out to his **f.** to the reapers.... 1
2Ki 4:19 he said unto his **f.**, My head, my head... 1
2Ki 5:13 My **f.**, if the prophet had bid thee do... 1
2Ki 6:21 My **f.**, shall I smite them? shall I... 1
2Ki 9:25 thou rode together after Ahab his **f.**,... 1
2Ki 13:14 and said, O my **f.**, my **f.**, the chariot... 1
2Ki 13:25 the hand of Jehoahaz his **f.** by war... 1
2Ki 14:3 yet not like David his **f.**:... 1
2Ki 14:3 to all things as Joash his **f.** did... 1
2Ki 14:5 which had slain the king his **f.**... 1
2Ki 14:21 him king instead of his **f.** Amaziah.... 1
2Ki 15:3 to all that his **f.** Amaziah had done;... 1
2Ki 15:34 to all that his **f.** Uzziah had done... 1
2Ki 15:38 fathers in the city of David his **f.**:... 1
2Ki 16:2 Lord his God, like David his **f.**... 1
2Ki 18:3 according to all that David his **f.** did... 1
2Ki 20:5 the Lord, the God of David thy **f.**,... 1
2Ki 21:3 which Hezekiah his **f.** had destroyed;... 1
2Ki 21:20 of the Lord, as his **f.** Manasseh did... 1
2Ki 21:21 all the way that his **f.** walked in,... 1
2Ki 21:21 served the idols that his **f.** served,... 1
2Ki 22:2 walked in all the way of David his **f.**,... 1
2Ki 23:34 king in the room of Josiah his **f.**,... 1
2Ki 24:9 according to all that his **f.** had done... 1
1Ch 2:17 and the **f.** of Amasa was Jether... 1
1Ch 2:21 daughter of Machir the **f.** of Gilead,... 1
1Ch 2:23 the sons of Machir the **f.** of Gilead.... 1
1Ch 2:24 bare him Ashur the **f.** of Tekoa... 1
1Ch 2:42 which was the **f.** of Ziph; and the... 1
1Ch 2:42 sons of Mareshah the **f.** of Hebron.... 1
1Ch 2:44 begat Raham, the **f.** of Jorkoam:... 1
1Ch 2:45 and Maon was the **f.** of Beth-zur.... 1
1Ch 2:49 Shaaph the **f.** of Madmannah,... 1
1Ch 2:49 Sheva the **f.** of Machbenah,... 1
1Ch 2:49 and the **f.** of Gibea:... 1
1Ch 2:50 Shobal the **f.** of Kirjath-jearlm,... 1
1Ch 2:51 Salma the **f.** of Beth-lehem,... 1
1Ch 2:51 Hareph the **f.** of Beth-gader... 1
1Ch 2:52 Shobal the **f.** of Kirjath-jearim had... 1
1Ch 2:55 the **f.** of the house of Rechab... 1
1Ch 4:3 And these were of the **f.** of Etam;... 1
1Ch 4:4 Penuel the **f.** of Gedor,... 1
1Ch 4:4 and Ezer the **f.** of Hushah.... 1
1Ch 4:4 of Ephrathah, the **f.** of Beth-lehem.... 1
1Ch 4:5 Ashur the **f.** of Tekoa had two wives,... 1
1Ch 4:11 Mehir, which was the **f.** of Eshton.... 1
1Ch 4:12 and Tehinnah the **f.** of Ir-nahash.... 1
1Ch 4:14 Joab the **f.** of the valley of Charashim,... 1
1Ch 4:17 and Ishbah the **f.** of Esthemoa.... 1
1Ch 4:18 bare Jered the **f.** of Gedor,... 1
1Ch 4:18 and Heber the **f.** of Socho,... 1
1Ch 4:18 and Jekuthiel the **f.** of Zanoah.... 1
1Ch 4:19 of Naham, the **f.** of Keilah the... 1
1Ch 4:21 were, Er the **f.** of Lecah,... 1
1Ch 4:21 and Laadah the **f.** of Mareshah,... 1
1Ch 7:14 bare Machir the **f.** of Gilead:... 1
1Ch 7:22 Ephraim their **f.** mourned many... 1
1Ch 7:31 Malchiel, who is the **f.** of Birzavith.... 1
1Ch 8:29 at Gibeon dwelt the **f.** of Gibeon... 25
1Ch 9:19 the house of his **f.**, the Korahites,... 1
1Ch 9:35 in Gibeon dwelt the **f.** of Gibeon,... 25
1Ch 17:13 will be his **f.**, and he shall be my son:... 25
1Ch 19:2 because his **f.** shewed kindness to me... 25
1Ch 19:2 to comfort him concerning his **f.**... 25
1Ch 19:3 thou that David doth honour thy **f.**,... 25
1Ch 22:10 be my son, and I will be his **f.**;... 25
1Ch 24:2 Nadab and Abihu died before their **f.**,... 25
1Ch 24:19 their manner, under Aaron their **f.**,... 25
1Ch 25:3 under the hands of their **f.** Jeduthun,... 25
1Ch 25:6 were under the hands of their **f.**... 25
1Ch 26:6 throughout the house of their **f.**:... 25
1Ch 26:10 yet his **f.** made him the chief;)... 25
1Ch 28:4 me before all the house of my **f.**... 25
1Ch 28:4 house of Judah, the house of my **f.**;... 25
1Ch 28:4 among the sons of my **f.** he liked me... 25
1Ch 28:6 him to be my son, and I will be his **f.**... 25
1Ch 28:9 my son, know thou the God of thy **f.**,... 25
1Ch 29:10 of Israel our **f.**, for ever and ever.... 25
1Ch 29:23 as king instead of David his **f.**,... 25
2Ch 1:8 great mercy unto David my **f.**,... 25
2Ch 1:9 unto David my **f.** be established:... 25
2Ch 2:3 As thou didst deal with David my **f.**,... 25
2Ch 2:7 whom David my **f.** did provide.... 25
2Ch 2:14 and his **f.** was a man of Tyre,... 25
2Ch 2:14 cunning men of my lord David thy **f.**... 25
2Ch 2:17 David his **f.** had numbered them;... 25
2Ch 3:1 the Lord appeared unto David his **f.**,... 25
2Ch 4:16 instruments did Huram his **f.** make... 25
2Ch 5:1 that David his **f.** had dedicated;... 25
2Ch 6:4 with his mouth to my **f.** David,... 25
2Ch 6:7 Now it was in the heart of David my **f.**... 25
2Ch 6:8 But the Lord said to David my **f.**,... 25
2Ch 6:10 risen up in the room of David my **f.**,... 25
2Ch 6:15 kept with thy servant David my **f.**... 25
2Ch 6:16 keep with thy servant David my **f.**... 25
2Ch 7:17 before me as David thy **f.** walked,... 25
2Ch 7:18 I have covenanted with David thy **f.**,... 25
2Ch 8:14 to the order of David his **f.**,... 25
2Ch 9:31 was buried in the city of David his **f.**:... 25
2Ch 10:4 Thy **f.** made our yoke grievous:... 25
2Ch 10:4 the grievous servitude of thy **f.**,... 25
2Ch 10:6 had stood before Solomon his **f.**... 25
2Ch 10:9 yoke that thy **f.** did put upon us?... 25
2Ch 10:10 Thy **f.** made our yoke heavy, but... 25
2Ch 10:11 my **f.** put a heavy yoke upon you,... 25
2Ch 10:11 my **f.** chastised you with whips, but I... 25
2Ch 10:14 My **f.** made your yoke heavy, but I... 25
2Ch 10:14 my **f.** chastised you with whips, but I... 25
2Ch 15:18 the things that his **f.** had dedicated,... 25
2Ch 16:3 there was between my **f.** and thy **f.**:... 25
2Ch 17:2 Ephraim, which Asa his **f.** had taken... 25
2Ch 17:3 in the first ways of his **f.** David,... 25
2Ch 17:4 sought to the Lord God of his **f.**,... 25
2Ch 20:32 he walked in the way of Asa his **f.**,... 25
2Ch 21:3 And their **f.** gave them great gifts of... 25
2Ch 21:4 risen up to the kingdom of his **f.**,... 25
2Ch 21:12 the Lord God of David thy **f.**,... 25
2Ch 21:12 in the ways of Jehoshaphat thy **f.**,... 25
2Ch 22:4 death of his **f.** to his destruction,... 25
2Ch 24:22 Jehoiada his **f.** had done to him,... 25
2Ch 25:3 that had killed the king his **f.**... 25
2Ch 26:1 king in the room of his **f.** Amaziah.... 25
2Ch 26:4 according to all that his **f.** Amaziah... 25
2Ch 27:2 according to all that his **f.** Uzziah... 25
2Ch 28:1 sight of the Lord, like David his **f.**:... 25
2Ch 29:2 to all that David his **f.** had done... 25
2Ch 33:3 Hezekiah his **f.** had broken down,...
2Ch 33:22 as did Manasseh his **f.**; for Amon... 1
2Ch 33:22 which Manasseh his **f.** had made,... 1
2Ch 33:23 as Manasseh his **f.** had humbled... 1
2Ch 34:2 walked in the ways of David his **f.**,... 1
2Ch 34:3 to seek after the God of David his **f.**:... 1
Es 2:7 for she had neither **f.** nor mother,... 1
Es 2:7 when her **f.** and mother were dead,... 1
Job 15:10 aged men, much elder than thy **f.**... 1
Job 17:14 said to corruption, Thou art my **f.**:... 1
Job 29:16 I was a **f.** to the poor: and the cause... 1
Job 31:18 was brought up with me, as with a **f.**,... 1
Job 38:28 Hath the rain a **f.**? or who hath... 1
Job 42:15 and their **f.** gave them inheritance... 1
Ps 27:10 my **f.** and my mother forsake me,... 1
Ps 68:5 A **f.** of the fatherless, and a judge of... 1
Ps 89:26 He shall cry unto me, Thou are my **f.**,... 1
Ps 103:13 Like as a **f.** pitieth his children, so... 1
Pr 1:8 My son, hear the instruction of thy **f.**,... 1
Pr 3:12 as a **f.** the son in whom he delighteth... 1
Pr 4:1 ye children, the instruction of a **f.**,... 1
Pr 10:1 A wise son maketh a glad **f.**: but a... 1
Pr 15:20 A wise son maketh a glad **f.**: but a... 1
Pr 17:21 and the **f.** of a fool hath no joy... 1
Pr 17:25 A foolish son is a grief to his **f.**, and... 1
Pr 19:13 foolish son is the calamity of his **f.**:... 1
Pr 19:26 that wasteth his **f.**, and chaseth... 1
Pr 20:20 Whoso curseth his **f.** or his mother,... 1
Pr 23:22 Hearken unto thy **f.** that begat thee,... 1
Pr 23:24 The **f.** of the righteous shall greatly... 1
Pr 23:25 Thy **f.** and thy mother shall be glad,... 1
Pr 28:7 of riotous men shameth his **f.**... 1
Pr 28:24 Whoso robbeth his **f.** or his mother,... 1
Pr 29:3 loveth wisdom rejoiceth his **f.**: but he... 1
Pr 30:11 is a generation that curseth their **f.**,... 1
Pr 30:17 The eye that mocketh at his **f.**, and... 1
Isa 3:6 of his brother of the house of his **f.**,... 1
Isa 8:4 to cry, My **f.**, and my mother,... 1
Isa 9:6 everlasting **F.**, The Prince of Peace.... 1
Isa 22:21 and he shall be a **f.** to the inhabitants... 1
Isa 38:5 the Lord, the God of David thy **f.**,... 1
Isa 38:19 **f.** to the children shall make known... 1
Isa 43:27 Thy first **f.** hath sinned, and thy... 1
Isa 45:10 Woe unto him that saith unto his **f.**,... 1
Isa 51:2 Look unto Abraham your **f.**, and... 1
Isa 58:14 with the heritage of Jacob thy **f.**:... 1
Isa 63:16 Doubtless thou art our **f.**, though... 1
Isa 63:16 thou, O Lord, art our **f.**, our... 1
Isa 64:8 But now, O Lord, thou art our **f.**;... 1
Jer 2:27 Saying to a stock, Thou art my **f.**;... 1
Jer 3:4 My **f.**, thou art the guide of my youth?... 1
Jer 3:19 I said, Thou shalt call me, My **f.**;... 1
Jer 12:6 thy brethren, and the house of thy **f.**,... 1
Jer 16:7 drink for their **f.** or for their mother.... 1
Jer 20:15 man who brought tidings to my **f.**,... 1
Jer 22:11 which reigned instead of Josiah his **f.**,... 1
Jer 22:15 did not thy **f.** eat and drink, and do... 1
Jer 31:9 for I am a **f.** to Israel, and Ephraim... 1
Jer 35:6 our **f.** commanded us, saying, Ye shall... 1
Jer 35:8 for Jonadab the son of Rechab our **f.**... 1
Jer 35:10 that Jonadab our **f.** commanded us... 1
Jer 35:16 the commandment of their **f.**,... 1
Jer 35:18 commandment of Jonadab your **f.**,... 1
Eze 16:3 thy **f.** was an Amorite, and thy mother... 1
Eze 16:45 an Hittite, and your **f.** an Amorite... 1
Eze 18:4 souls are mine; as the soul of the **f.**,... 1
Eze 18:17 shall not die for the iniquity of his **f.**,... 1

Eze 18:18 As for his f., because he cruelly............ 1
Eze 18:19 the son bear the iniquity of the f.?......... 1
Eze 18:20 shall not bear the iniquity of the f.,......... 1
Eze 18:20 neither shall the f. bear the iniquity.......... 1
Eze 22:7 have they set light by f. and mother:....... 1
Eze 44:25 but for f., or for mother, or for son,....... 1
Da 5:2 golden and silver vessels which his f. 2
Da 5:11 and in the days of thy f. light and........... 2
Da 5:11 the king Nebuchadnezzar thy f.,............... 2
Da 5:11 the king, I say, thy f., made master........ 2
Da 5:13 the king my f. brought out of Jewry?........ 2
Da 5:18 God gave Nebuchadnezzar thy f. a.......... 2
Am 2:7 a man and his f. will go in unto the......... 2
Mic 7:6 For the son dishonoureth the f., the........ 2
Zec 13:3 then his f. and his mother that begat...... 2
Zec 13:3 and his f. and his mother that begat........ 2
Mal 1:6 A son honoureth his f., and a servant...... 2
Mal 1:6 then I be a f., where is mine honour?...... 2
Mal 2:10 Have we not all one f.? hath not one........ 2
Mt 2:22 Judaea in the room of his f. Herod, ... 3962
Mt 3:9 We have Abraham to our f.: for I....... 3962
Mt 4:21 in a ship with Zebedee their f............ 3962
Mt 4:22 left the ship and their f., and............ 3962
Mt 5:16 glorify your F. which is in heaven. 3962
Mt 5:45 ye may be the children of your F.. 3962
Mt 5:48 even as your F. which is in heaven 3962
Mt 6:1 of your F. which is in heaven. 3962
Mt 6:4 and thy F. which seeth in secret... 3962
Mt 6:6 pray to thy F. which is in secret;.. 3962
Mt 6:6 and thy F. which seeth in secret... 3962
Mt 6:8 your F. knoweth what things ye.... 3962
Mt 6:9 F. which are in heaven, Hallowed. 3962
Mt 6:14 your heavenly F. will also forgive. 3962
Mt 6:15 neither will your F. forgive your... 3962
Mt 6:18 but unto thy F. which is in secret:.3962
Mt 6:18 and thy F., which seeth in secret,..3962
Mt 6:26 yet your heavenly F. feedeth them. 3962
Mt 6:32 for your heavenly F. knoweth that.3962
Mt 7:11 how much more shall your F....... 3962
Mt 7:21 he that doeth the will of my F....... 3962
Mt 8:21 suffer me first to go and bury my f.. .. 3962
Mt 10:20 Spirit of your F. which speaketh... 3962
Mt 10:21 the f. the child: and the children... 3962
Mt 10:29 fall on the ground without your F..3962
Mt 10:32 will I confess also before my F..... 3962
Mt 10:33 him will I also deny before my F. ..3962
Mt 10:35 man at variance against his f.,...... 3962
Mt 10:37 He that loveth f. or mother more.. 3962
Mt 11:25 I thank thee, O F., Lord of heaven 3962
Mt 11:26 Even so, F.: for so it seemed good.3962
Mt 11:27 delivered unto me of my F.: and... 3962
Mt 11:27 man knoweth the Son, but the F.; 3962
Mt 11:27 neither knoweth any man the F.,... 3962
Mt 12:50 shall do the will of my F............. 3962
Mt 13:43 the sun in the kingdom of their F..3962
Mt 15:4 thy f. and mother: and,............... 3962
Mt 15:4 He that curseth f. or mother, let... 3962
Mt 15:5 Whosoever shall say to his f. or.... 3962
Mt 15:6 And honour not his f. or his........... 3962
Mt 15:13 my heavenly F. hath not planted,.. 3962
Mt 16:17 but my F. which is in heaven........ 3962
Mt 16:27 shall come in the glory of his F.... 3962
Mt 18:10 do always behold the face of my F. 3962
Mt 18:14 so it is not the will of your F. 3962
Mt 18:19 if shall be done for them of my F. .3962
Mt 18:35 shall my heavenly F. do also unto. 3962
Mt 19:5 shall a man leave f. and mother,... 3962
Mt 19:19 Honour thy f. and thy mother:........ 3962
Mt 19:29 or brethren, or sisters, or f., or..... 3962
Mt 20:23 for whom it is prepared of my F.. ..3962
Mt 21:31 them twain did the will of his f.?.. 3962
Mt 23:9 call no man your f. upon the........ 3962
Mt 23:9 one is your F., which is in heaven..3962
Mt 24:36 angels in heaven, but my F. only. ..3962
Mt 25:34 Come, ye blessed of my F., inherit.3962
Mt 26:39 O my F., if it be possible, let this..3962
Mt 26:42 O my F., if this cup may not pass..3962
Mt 26:53 that I cannot now pray to my F.,.... 3962
Mt 28:19 them in the name of the F.,.......... 3962
Mk 1:20 they left their f. Zebedee in the ship.. 3962
Mk 5:40 he taketh the f. and the mother of..... 3962
Mk 7:10 Honour thy f. and thy mother;...... 3962
Mk 7:10 Whoso curseth f. or mother, let..... 3962
Mk 7:11 If a man shall say to his f. or....... 3962
Mk 7:12 him no more to do ought for his f..3962
Mk 8:38 cometh in the glory of his F. with.3962
Mk 9:21 he asked his f., How long is it ago.. 3962
Mk 9:24 And straightway the f. of the child...... 3962
Mk 10:7 this cause shall a man leave his f...3962
Mk 10:19 not, Honour thy f. and mother...... 3962
Mk 10:29 brethren, or sisters, of f., or........ 3962
Mk 11:10 be the kingdom of our f. David,......... 3962
Mk 11:25 that your F. also which is in........ 3962
Mk 11:26 neither will your F. which is in.... 3962
Mk 13:12 the f. the son; and the children..... 3962
Mk 13:32 neither the Son, but the F.......... 3962
Mk 14:36 he said, Abba, F., all things are...... 3962
Mk 15:21 f. of Alexander and Rufus, to bear...... 3962
Lu 1:32 unto him the throne of his f. David:.... 3962
Lu 1:59 Zacharias, after the name of his f.. 3962
Lu 1:62 And they made signs to his f., how..... 3962
Lu 1:67 his f. Zacharias was filled with the...... 3962
Lu 1:73 which he sware to our f. Abraham...... 3962
Lu 2:48 behold, thy f. and I have sought thee... 3962
Lu 3:8 We have Abraham to our f.: for I....... 3962
Lu 6:36 merciful, as your F. also is.......... 3962
Lu 8:51 f. and the mother of the maiden......... 3962
Lu 9:42 and delivered him again to his f.. 3962
Lu 9:59 suffer me first to go and bury my f.. .. 3962
Lu 10:21 I thank thee, O F., Lord of heaven 3962
Lu 10:21 even so, F.; for so it seemed good..3962
Lu 10:22 are delivered to me of my F.:........ 3962
Lu 10:22 but the F.; and who the F. is, but..3962
Lu 11:2 say, Our F. which art in heaven,... 3962
Lu 11:11 bread of any of you that is a f.,..... 3962
Lu 11:13 much more shall your heavenly F. .3962
Lu 12:30 your F. knoweth that ye have need 3962
Lu 12:53 The f. shall be divided against the. 3962
Lu 12:53 son, and the son against the f.;..... 3962
Lu 14:26 and hate not his f., and mother,.... 3962
Lu 15:12 of them said to his f., F., give me. 3962
Lu 15:18 I will arise and go to my f., and... 3962
Lu 15:18 say unto him, F., I have sinned.... 3962
Lu 15:20 And he arose, and came to his f.... 3962
Lu 15:20 f. saw him, and had compassion,... 3962
Lu 15:21 F., I have sinned against heaven,.. 3962
Lu 15:22 But the f. said to his servants....... 3962
Lu 15:27 and thy f. hath killed the fatted.... 3962
Lu 15:28 therefore came his f. out, and....... 3962
Lu 15:29 said to his f., Lo, these many....... 3962
Lu 16:24 he cried and said, F. Abraham,...... 3962
Lu 16:27 I pray thee therefore, f., that thou.3962
Lu 16:30 And he said, Nay, f. Abraham, but.3962
Lu 18:20 Honour thy f. and thy mother....... 3962
Lu 22:29 as my F. hath appointed unto me;. 3962
Lu 22:42 Saying, F., if thou be willing......... 3962
Lu 23:34 F., forgive them; for they know....3962
Lu 23:46 F., into thy hands I commend my..3962
Lu 24:49 I send the promise of my F. upon..3962
Joh 1:14 as of the only begotten of the F.,) 3962
Joh 1:18 in the bosom of the F., he hath......... 3962
Joh 3:35 The F. loveth the Son, and hath......... 3962
Joh 4:12 Art thou greater than our f. Jacob,..... 3962
Joh 4:21 yet at Jerusalem, worship the F.... 3962
Joh 4:23 shall worship the F. in spirit and.. 3962
Joh 4:23 in truth: for the F. seeketh such... 3962
Joh 4:53 So the f. knew that it was at the 3962
Joh 5:17 My F. worketh hitherto, and I...... 3962
Joh 5:18 but said also that God was his F.,...... 3962
Joh 5:19 but what he seeth the F. do: for.... 3962
Joh 5:20 For the F. loveth the Son, and...... 3962
Joh 5:21 For as the F. raiseth up the dead,. 3962
Joh 5:22 For the F. judgeth no man, but.... 3962
Joh 5:23 Son, even as they honour the F..... 3962
Joh 5:23 honoureth not the F. which hath... 3962
Joh 5:26 For as the F. hath life in himself;. 3962
Joh 5:30 but the will of the F. which hath.. 3962
Joh 5:36 the works which the F. hath given.3962
Joh 5:36 bear witness of me, that the F..... 3962
Joh 5:37 And the F. himself, which hath..... 3962
Joh 5:45 that I will accuse you to the F.:.... 3962
Joh 6:27 for him hath God the F. sealed..... 3962
Joh 6:32 but my F. giveth you the true....... 3962
Joh 6:37 All that the F. giveth me shall...... 3962
Joh 6:42 whose f. and mother we know? 3962
Joh 6:44 except the F. which hath sent me. 3962
Joh 6:45 hath learned of the F., cometh...... 3962
Joh 6:46 that any man hath seen the F.,..... 3962
Joh 6:46 is of God, he hath seen the F........ 3962
Joh 6:57 As the living F. hath sent me,...... 3962
Joh 6:57 and I live by the F.; so he that...... 3962
Joh 6:65 it were given unto him of my F.. .. 3962
Joh 8:16 but I and the F. that sent me. 3962
Joh 8:18 and the F. that sent me beareth.... 3962
Joh 8:19 they unto him, Where is thy F.?........ 3962
Joh 8:19 ye neither know me, nor my F.:..... 3962
Joh 8:19 ye should have known my F. also. .3962
Joh 8:27 not that he spake to them of the F..... 3962
Joh 8:28 as my F. hath taught me, I speak..3962
Joh 8:29 the F. hath not left me alone;....... 3962
Joh 8:38 which I have seen with my F.:...... 3962
Joh 8:38 which ye have seen with your f..... 3962
Joh 8:39 said unto him, Abraham is our f......... 3962
Joh 8:41 Ye do the deeds of your f............. 3962
Joh 8:41 we have one F., even God. 3962
Joh 8:42 God were your F., ye would love... 3962
Joh 8:44 Ye are of your f. the devil and the.3962
Joh 8:44 and the lusts of your f. ye will do: 3962
Joh 8:44 for he is a liar, and the f. of it. 3962
Joh 8:49 but I honour my F., and ye do...... 3962
Joh 8:53 Art thou greater than our f.............. 3962
Joh 8:54 it is my F. that honoureth me;..... 3962
Joh 8:56 Your f. Abraham rejoiced to see.... 3962
Joh 10:15 As the F. knoweth me, even so..... 3962
Joh 10:15 even so know I the F.:............... 3962
Joh 10:17 Therefore doth my F. love me,...... 3962
Joh 10:18 have I received of my F.............. 3962
Joh 10:29 My F. which gave them me, is...... 3962
Joh 10:30 I and my F. are one 3962
Joh 10:32 have I shewed you from my F.;..... 3962
Joh 10:36 him, whom the F. hath sanctified,.3962
Joh 10:37 not the works of my F., believe.... 3962
Joh 10:38 that the F. is in me, and I in him. 3962
Joh 11:41 F., I thank thee that thou hast...... 3962
Joh 12:26 serve me, him will my F. honour. . 3962
Joh 12:27 F., save me from this hour; but.... 3962
Joh 12:28 F., glorify thy name. Then came 3962
Joh 12:49 but the F. which sent me, he gave. 3962
Joh 12:50 even as the F. said unto me, so I.. 3962
Joh 13:1 depart out of this world unto the F.,.... 3962
Joh 13:3 that the F. had given all things into.... 3962
Joh 14:6 cometh unto the F., but by me...... 3962
Joh 14:7 ye should have known my F. also: 3962
Joh 14:8 Lord, shew us the F., and it.......... 3962
Joh 14:9 hath seen the F.; and how sayest.. 3962
Joh 14:9 thou then, Shew us the F.?........... 3962
Joh 14:10 I am in the F., and the F. in me?. 3962
Joh 14:10 but the F. that dwelleth in me, he. 3962
Joh 14:11 Believe me that I am in the F.,..... 3962
Joh 14:11 and the F. in me: or else believe.... 3962
Joh 14:12 he do; because I go unto my F...... 3962
Joh 14:13 that the F. may be glorified in the.3962
Joh 14:16 And I will pray the F., and he...... 3962
Joh 14:20 that I am in my F., and ye in me,. 3962
Joh 14:21 loveth me shall be loved of my F.,.3962
Joh 14:23 and my F. will love him, and we... 3962
Joh 14:26 whom the F. will send in my........ 3962
Joh 14:28 because I said, I go unto the F.:... 3962
Joh 14:28 for my F. is greater than I. 3962
Joh 14:31 may know that I love the F.; and.. 3962
Joh 14:31 as the F. gave me commandment,. 3962
Joh 15:1 and my F. is the husbandman...... 3962
Joh 15:8 Herein is my F. glorified, that ye.. 3962
Joh 15:9 As the F. hath loved me, so have I.3962
Joh 15:15 things that I have heard of my F. ..3962
Joh 15:16 ye shall ask of the F. in my name,.3962
Joh 15:23 that hateth me hateth my F. also.. 3962
Joh 15:24 they hated both me and my F........ 3962
Joh 15:26 I will send unto you from the F.,.. 3962
Joh 15:26 which proceedeth from the F.,...... 3962
Joh 16:3 they have not known the F., nor... 3962
Joh 16:10 because I go to my F., and ye see. 3962
Joh 16:15 things that the F. hath are mine:.. 3962
Joh 16:16 see me, because I go to the F. 3962
Joh 16:17 and, Because I go to the F.?............ 3962
Joh 16:23 ye shall ask the F. in my name,.... 3962
Joh 16:25 shall shew you plainly of the F..... 3962
Joh 16:26 that I will pray the F. for you:..... 3962
Joh 16:27 For the F. himself loveth you,...... 3962
Joh 16:28 I came forth from the F., and am..3962
Joh 16:28 leave the world, and go to the F. .. 3962
Joh 16:32 alone, because the F. is with me.. 3962
Joh 17:1 F., the hour is come; glorify thy... 3962
Joh 17:5 And now, O F., glorify thou me.... 3962
Joh 17:11 Holy F., keep through thine own.. 3962
Joh 17:21 as thou, F., art in me, and I in..... 3962
Joh 17:24 F., I will that they also, whom..... 3962
Joh 17:25 O righteous F., the world hath not 3962
Joh 18:11 cup which my F. hath given me,.... 3962
Joh 18:13 for he was f. in law to Caiphas, ... 3995
Joh 20:17 I am not yet ascended to my F.:... 3962

Joh 20:17 **I ascend unto my F., and your F.,** 3962
Joh 20:21 **as my F. hath sent me, even so** 3962
Ac 1:4 but **wait for the promise of the F.,** 3962
Ac 1:7 **the F. hath put in his own power** 3962
Ac 2:33 received of the **F.** the promise of 3962
Ac 7:2 appeared unto our **f.** Abraham, 3962
Ac 7:4 when his **f.** was dead, he removed 3962
Ac 7:14 and called his **f.** Jacob to him, 3962
Ac 7:16 sons of Emmor the **f.** of Sychem.
Ac 16:1 but his **f.** was a Greek: 3962
Ac 16:3 knew all that his **f.** was a Greek. 3962
Ac 28:8 that the **f.** of Publius lay sick of a 3962
Ro 1:7 and peace from God our **F.**, and the 3962
Ro 4:1 our **f.**, as pertaining to the flesh, 3962
Ro 4:11 be the **f.** of all them that believe, 3962
Ro 4:12 And the **f.** of circumcision to them 3962
Ro 4:12 of the faith of our **f.** Abraham, 3962
Ro 4:16 Abraham, who is the **f.** of us all, 3962
Ro 4:17 I have made thee a **f.** of many 3962
Ro 4:18 become the **f.** of many nations, 3962
Ro 6:4 the dead by the glory of the **F.**, 3962
Ro 8:15 adoption, whereby we cry, Abba, **F.** 3962
Ro 9:10 by one, even by our **f.** Isaac; 3962
Ro 15:6 God, even the **F.** of our Lord Jesus 3962
1Co 1:3 and peace, from God our **F.**, and 3962
1Co 8:6 one God, the **F.**, of whom are all 3962
1Co 15:24 the kingdom to God, even the **F.**; 3962
2Co 1:2 from God our **F.**, and from the 3962
2Co 1:3 even the **F.** of our Lord Jesus 3962
2Co 1:3 the **F.** of mercies, and the God of 3962
2Co 6:18 And will be a **F.** unto you, and ye 3962
2Co 11:31 The God and **F.** of our Lord Jesus 3962
Gal 1:1 and God the **F.**, who raised him 3962
Gal 1:3 peace from God the **F.**, and from 3962
Gal 1:4 to the will of God and our **F.**: 3962
Gal 4:2 until the time appointed of the **f.** 3962
Gal 4:6 unto your hearts, crying, Abba, **F.** 3962
Eph 1:2 from God and our **F.**, and from 3962
Eph 1:3 be the God and **F.** of our Lord 3962
Eph 1:17 the **F.** of glory, may give unto you 3962
Eph 2:18 access by one Spirit unto the **F.** 3962
Eph 3:14 my knees unto the **F.** of our Lord 3962
Eph 4:6 One God and **F.** of all, who is above 3962
Eph 5:20 unto God and the **F.** in the name 3962
Eph 5:31 a man leave his **f.** and mother, 3962
Eph 6:2 Honour thy **f.** and mother; which 3962
Eph 6:23 from God the **F.** and the Lord Jesus 3962
Php 1:2 from God our **F.**, and from the Lord 3962
Php 2:11 to the glory of God the **F.** 3962
Php 2:22 as a son with the **f.**, he hath served 3962
Php 4:20 Now unto God and our **F.** be glory 3962
Col 1:2 and peace, from God our **F.** and 3962
Col 1:3 God and the **F.** of our Lord Jesus 3962
Col 1:12 Giving thanks unto the **F.**, which 3962
Col 1:19 For it pleased the **F.** that in him
Col 2:2 and of the **F.**, and of Christ; 3962
Col 3:17 thanks to God and the **F.** by him. 3962
1Th 1:1 in God the **F.** and in the Lord 3962
1Th 1:1 and peace, from God our **F.**, and 3962
1Th 1:3 in the sight of God and our **F.**; 3962
1Th 2:11 of you, as a **f.** doth his children, 3962
1Th 3:11 Now God himself and our **F.**, and 3962
1Th 3:13 holiness before God, even our **F.**, 3962
2Th 1:1 in God our **F.** and the Lord Jesus 3962
2Th 1:2 and peace, from God our **F.** and the 3962
2Th 2:16 and God, even our **F.**, which hath 3962
1Ti 1:2 peace, from God our **F.** and Jesus 3962
1Ti 5:1 an elder, but intreat him as a **f.**; 3962
2Ti 1:2 peace, from God the **F.** and Christ 3962
Tit 1:4 and peace, from God the **F.** and the 3962
Phm 3 and peace, from God our **F.** and the 3962
Heb 1:5 And again, I will be to him a **F.**, 3962
Heb 7:3 Without **f.**, without mother, 540
Heb 7:10 he was yet in the loins of his **f.**, 3962
Heb 12:7 for what son is he whom the **f.** 3962
Heb 12:9 unto the **F.** of spirits, and live? 3962
Jas 1:17 cometh down from the **F.** of lights, 3962
Jas 1:27 undefiled before God and the **F.** is 3962
Jas 2:21 Was not Abraham our **f.** justified 3962
Jas 3:9 bless we God, even the **F.**; and 3962
1Pe 1:2 the foreknowledge of God the **F.**, 3962
1Pe 1:3 Blessed to the God and **F.** of our 3962
1Pe 1:17 And if ye call on the **F.**, who 3962
2Pe 1:17 For he received from God the **F.** 3962
1Jo 1:2 eternal life, which was with the **F.**, 3962
1Jo 1:3 our fellowship is with the **F.**, and 3962
1Jo 2:1 we have an advocate with the **F.**, 3962
1Jo 2:13 because ye have known the **F.** 3962
1Jo 2:15 the love of the **F.** is not in him. 3962
1Jo 2:16 is not the **F.**, but is of the world. 3962
1Jo 2:22 that denieth the **F.** and the Son. 3962
1Jo 2:23 the Son, the same hath not the **F.**: 3962
1Jo 2:23 acknowledgeth the Son hath the **F.**
1Jo 2:24 continue in the Son, and in the **F.** 3962
1Jo 3:1 of love the **F.** hath bestowed upon 3962
1Jo 4:14 **F.** sent the Son to the Saviour 3962
1Jo 5:7 **F.**, the Word, and the Holy Ghost: 3962
2Jo 3 and peace from God the **F.**, and from 3962
2Jo 3 the Son of the **F.**, in truth and love. 3962
2Jo 4 a commandment from the **F.** 3962
2Jo 9 he hath both the **F.** and the Son. 3962
Jude 1 that are sanctified by God the **F.**, 3962
Re 1:6 and priests unto God and his **F.**; 3962
Re 2:27 **even as I received of my F.** 3962
Re 3:5 **confess his name before my F.,** 3962
Re 3:21 **set down with my F. in his throne.** 3962

FATHER-IN-LAW See FATHER and LAW.

FATHERLESS
Ex 22:22 not afflict any widow, or **f.** child. 3490
Ex 22:24 be widows, and your children **f.** 3490
De 10:18 the judgment of the **f.** and widow, 3490
De 14:29 and the stranger, and the **f.**, and 3490
De 16:11 and the stranger, and the **f.**, and 3490
De 16:14 the stranger, and the **f.**, and the 3490
De 24:17 of the stranger, nor of the **f.**; 3490
De 24:19, 20,21 for the stranger, for the **f.**, 3490
De 26:12 Levite, the stranger, the **f.**, and the 3490
De 26:13 and unto the stranger, to the **f.**, and 3490
De 27:19 judgment of the stranger, **f.**, and 3490
Job 6:27 overwhelm the **f.**, and ye dig a pit 3490
Job 22:9 arms of the **f.** have been broken. 3490
Job 24:3 They drive away the ass of the **f.**, 3490
Job 24:9 They pluck the **f.** from the breast, 3490
Job 29:12 the poor that cried, and the **f.**, and 3490
Job 31:17 and the **f.** hath not eaten thereof; 3490
Job 31:21 lifted up my hand against the **f.**, 3490
Ps 10:14 thou art the helper of the **f.** 3490
Ps 10:18 to judge the **f.** and the oppressed, 3490
Ps 68:5 A father of the **f.**, and a judge of 3490
Ps 82:3 Defend the poor and **f.**: do justice 3490
Ps 94:6 the stranger, and murder the **f.** 3490
Ps 109:9 Let his children be **f.**, and his wife 3490
Ps 109:12 be any to favour his **f.** children. 3490
Ps 146:9 he relieveth the **f.** and widow: but 3490
Pr 23:10 enter not into the fields of the **f.**: 3490
Isa 1:17 judge the **f.**, plead for the widow. 3490
Isa 1:23 they judge not the **f.**, neither doth 3490
Isa 9:17 neither shall have mercy on their **f.** 3490
Isa 10:2 and that they may rob the **f.**! 3490
Jer 5:28 not the cause, the cause of the **f.**, 3490
Jer 7:6 oppress not the stranger, the **f.**, and 3490
Jer 22:3 no violence to the stranger, the **f.**, 3490
Jer 49:11 Leave thy **f.** children, I will preserve 3490
La 5:3 We are orphans and **f.**, our 369,1
Eze 22:7 in thee have they vexed the **f.** and 3490
Ho 14:3 for in thee the **f.** findeth mercy. 3490
Zec 7:10 oppress not the widow, nor the **f.**, 3490
Mal 3:5 in his wages, the widow, and the **f.**, 3490
Jas 1:27 To visit the **f.** and widows in their 3737

FATHER'S
Ge 9:23 and they saw not their **f.** nakedness. 1
Ge 12:1 thy kindred, and from thy **f.** house, 1
Ge 20:13 me to wander from my **f.** house, 1
Ge 24:7 which took me from my **f.** house, 1
Ge 24:23 is there room in thy **f.** house for us to 1
Ge 24:38 But thou shalt go unto my **f.** house, 1
Ge 24:40 of my kindred, and of my **f.** house: 1
Ge 26:15 which his **f.** servants had digged in 1
Ge 28:21 So that I come again to my **f.** house 1
Ge 29:9 Rachel came with her **f.** sheep: for 1
Ge 29:12 told Rachel that he was her **f.** brother, 1
Ge 31:1 taken away all that was our **f.**; and 1
Ge 31:1 that which was our **f.** hath he gotten 1
Ge 31:5 I see your **f.** countenance, that it is 1
Ge 31:14 inheritance for us in our **f.** house? 1
Ge 31:30 thou sore longedst after thy **f.** house, 1
Ge 35:22 and lay with Bilhah his **f.** concubine: 1
Ge 37:2 with the sons of Zilpah, his **f.** wives: 1
Ge 37:12 brethren went to feed their **f.** flock 1
Ge 38:11 Remain a widow at thy **f.** house. 1
Ge 38:11 Tamar went and dwelt in her **f.** house. 1
Ge 41:51 forget all my toil, and all my **f.** house. 1
Ge 46:31 his brethren, and unto his **f.** house, 1
Ge 46:31 My brethren, and my **f.** house, 1
Ge 47:12 brethren, and all his **f.** household, 1
Ge 48:17 and he held up his **f.** hand, 1
Ge 49:4 thou wentest up to thy **f.** bed; 1
Ge 49:8 thy **f.** children shall bow down before 1
Ge 50:1 And Joseph fell upon his **f.** face, 1
Ge 50:8 and his brethren, and his **f.** house: 1
Ge 50:22 dwelt in Egypt, he, and his **f.** house: 1
Ex 2:16 the troughs to water their **f.** flock. 1
Ex 6:20 him Jochebed his **f.** sister to wife; 1733
Ex 15:2 my **f.** God, and I will exalt him. 1
Le 16:32 in the priest's office in his **f.** stead, 1
Le 18:8 The nakedness of thy **f.** wife shalt 1
Le 18:8 not uncover: it is thy **f.** nakedness. 1
Le 18:11 nakedness of thy **f.** wife's daughter, 1
Le 18:12 uncover the nakedness of thy **f.** sister: 1
Le 18:12 she is thy **f.** near kinswoman. 1
Le 18:14 the nakedness of thy **f.** brother, 1
Le 20:11 the man that lieth with his **f.** wife 1
Le 20:11 hath uncovered his **f.** nakedness: 1
Le 20:17 shall take his sister, his **f.** daughter, 1
Le 20:19 mother's sister, nor of thy **f.** sister: 1
Le 22:13 and is returned unto her **f.** house, 1
Le 22:13 she shall eat of her **f.** meat: 1
Nu 2:2 with the ensign of their **f.** house: 1
Nu 18:1 and thy sons and thy **f.** house 1
Nu 27:7 inheritance among their **f.** brethren; 1
Nu 27:10 his inheritance unto his **f.** brethren. 1
Nu 30:3 being in her **f.** house in her youth; 1
Nu 30:16 yet in her youth in her **f.** house. 1
Nu 36:11 unto their **f.** brothers' sons: 1730
De 22:21 damsel to the door of her **f.** house, 1
De 22:21 to play the whore in her **f.** house: 1
De 22:30 A man shall not take his **f.** wife, 1
De 22:30 nor discover his **f.** skirt. 1
De 27:20 be he that lieth with his **f.** wife; 1
De 27:20 because he uncovereth his **f.** skirt. 1
Jos 2:12 shew kindness unto my **f.** house, 1
Jos 2:18 all thy **f.** household, home unto thee. 1
Jos 6:25 the harlot alive, and her **f.** household, 1
Jg 6:15 and I am the least in my **f.** house. 1
Jg 6:25 Take thy **f.** young bullock, even the 1
Jg 6:27 because he feared his **f.** household, 1
Jg 9:5 he went unto his **f.** house at Ophrah, 1
Jg 9:18 ye are risen up against my **f.** house 1
Jg 11:2 Thou shalt not inherit our **f.** house; 1
Jg 11:7 and expel me out of my **f.** house? 1
Jg 14:15 lest we burn thee and thy **f.** house 1
Jg 14:19 and he went up to his **f.** house. 1
Jg 19:2 away from him unto her **f.** house 1
Jg 19:3 she brought him into her **f.** house: 1
1Sa 2:31 thine arm, and the arm of thy **f.** house, 1
1Sa 9:20 not on thee, and on all thy **f.** house? 1
1Sa 17:15 to feed his **f.** sheep at Beth-lehem. 1
1Sa 17:25 and make his **f.** house free in Israel. 1
1Sa 17:34 Thy servant kept his **f.** sheep, 1
1Sa 18:2 him go no more home to his **f.** house. 1
1Sa 18:18 is my life, or my **f.** family in Israel, 1
1Sa 22:1 when his brethren and all his **f.** house 1
1Sa 22:11 son of Ahitub, and all his **f.** house, 1
1Sa 22:16 Ahimelech, thou, and all thy **f.** house. 1
1Sa 22:22 of all the persons of thy **f.** house. 1
1Sa 24:21 destroy my name out of my **f.** house. 1
2Sa 3:7 thou gone in unto my **f.** concubine? 1
2Sa 3:29 head of Joab, and on all his **f.** house; 1
2Sa 9:7 kindness for Jonathan thy **f.** sake, 1
2Sa 14:9 be on me, and on my **f.** house: 1
2Sa 15:34 as I have been thy **f.** servant hitherto, 1
2Sa 16:19 as I have served in thy **f.** presence, 1
2Sa 16:21 Go in unto thy **f.** concubines, which 1
2Sa 16:22 went in unto his **f.** concubines in the 1
2Sa 19:28 of my **f.** house were but dead men 1
2Sa 24:17 against me, and against my **f.** house. 1
1Ki 11:12 will not do it for David thy **f.** sake: 1
1Ki 11:17 certain Edomites of his **f.** servants 1
1Ki 12:10 shall be thicker than my **f.** loins. 1
1Ki 18:18 Israel; but thou and thy **f.** house, 1
2Ki 10:3 and set him on his **f.** throne, 1
2Ki 23:30 and made him king in his **f.** stead. 1
2Ki 24:17 made Mattaniah his **f.** brother 1730
1Ch 5:1 forasmuch as he defiled his **f.** bed, 1
1Ch 7:2 Shemuel, heads of their **f.** house, 1
1Ch 7:40 heads of their **f.** house, choice and 1
1Ch 12:28 his **f.** house twenty and two captains. 1
1Ch 21:17 be on me, and on my **f.** house; 1
1Ch 23:11 according to their **f.** house. 1

2Ch 2:13 understanding, of Huram my **f.**, 1
2Ch 10:10 shall be thicker than my **f.** loins. 1
2Ch 21:13 slain thy brethren of thy **f.** house, 1
2Ch 36:1 made him king his his **f.** stead in 1
Ezr 2:59 they could now slew their **f.** house, 1
Ne 1:6 both I and my **f.** house have sinned. 1
Ne 7:61 they could not shew their **f.** house,
Es 4:14 and thy **f.** house shall be destroyed: 1
Ps 45:10 thine own people, and thy **f.** house; 1
Pr 4:3 I was my **f.** son, tender and only 1
Pr 6:20 My son, keep thy **f.** commandment, 1
Pr 13:1 A wise son heareth his **f.** instruction: 1
Pr 15:5 A fool despiseth his **f.** instruction: 1
Pr 27:10 And thy **f.** friend forsake not: 1
Isa 7:17 thy people, and upon thy **f.** house, 1
Isa 22:23 for a glorious throne to his **f.** house. 1
Isa 22:24 upon him all the glory of his **f.** house, 1
Jer 35:14 but obey their **f.** commandment: 1
Eze 18:14 a son, that seeth all his **f.** sins which 1
Eze 22:11 humbled his sister, his **f.** daughter. 1
Mt 26:29 **new with you in my F. kingdom.** *3962*
Lu 2:49 **I must be about my F. business?** *3962*
Lu 9:26 **in his F., and of the holy angels.** *3962*
Lu 12:32 **it is your F. good pleasure to give.** *3962*
Lu 15:17 **hired servants of my f. have bread** *3962*
Lu 16:27 **wouldest send him to my f. house:** *3962*
Joh 2:16 **make not my F. house an house of** *3962*
Joh 5:43 **I am come in my F. name, and ye** *3962*
Joh 6:39 **And this is the F. will which hath** *3962*
Joh 10:25 **that I do in my F. name, they bear** *3962*
Joh 10:29 **to pluck them out of my F. hand.** *3962*
Joh 14:2 **In my F. house are many** *3962*
Joh 14:24 **not mine, but the F. which sent** *3962*
Joh 15:10 **I have kept my F. commandments,** *3962*
Ac 7:20 was nourished up in his **f.** house *3962*
1Co 5:1 that one should have his **f.** wife. *3962*
Re 14:1 having his **F.** name written in *3962*

FATHERS See also FATHERS'; FOREFATHERS.

Ge 15:15 And thou shalt go to thy **f.** in peace; 1
Ge 31:3 Return unto the land of thy **f.**, 1
Ge 46:34 until now, both we, and also our **f.**: 1
Ge 47:3 shepherds, both we, and also our **f.**. 1
Ge 47:9 of the years of the life of my **f.** in the 1
Ge 47:30 But I will lie with my **f.**, and thou 1
Ge 48:15 my **f.** Abraham and Isaac did walk, 1
Ge 48:16 name of my **f.** Abraham and Isaac; 1
Ge 48:21 you again unto the land of your **f.**. 1
Ge 49:29 bury me with my **f.** in the cave that is 1
Ex 3:13 The God of your **f.** hath sent me unto 1
Ex 3:15 of Israel, the Lord God of your **f.**, 1
Ex 3:16 unto them, The Lord God of your **f.**, 1
Ex 4:5 believe that the Lord God of their **f.**, 1
Ex 6:25 the heads of the **f.** of the Levites 1
Ex 10:6 thy **f.**, nor thy fathers' **f.** have seen. 1
Ex 12:3 according to the house of their **f.**, 1
Ex 13:5 he sware unto thy **f.** to give thee, 1
Ex 13:11 as he sware unto thee and to thy **f.**, 1
Ex 20:5 visiting the iniquity of the **f.** upon the 1
Ex 34:7 visiting the iniquity of the **f.** upon the 1
Le 25:41 possession of his **f.** shall he return. 1
Le 26:39 iniquities of their **f.** shall they pine 1
Le 26:40 and the iniquity of their **f.**, with their 1
Nu 1:2 families, by the house of their **f.**, 1
Nu 1:4 one head of the house of his **f.** 1
Nu 1:16 princes of the tribes of their **f.**, 1
Nu 1:18, 20 house of their **f.**, according 1
Nu 1:22 by the house of their **f.**, those that 1
Nu 1:24, 26,28,30,32,34,36,38,40 by the house of their **f.**, according to 1
Nu 1:42 by the house of their **f.** according 1
Nu 1:44 each one was for the house of his **f.** 1
Nu 1:45 the house of their **f.**, from twenty 1
Nu 1:47 Levites after the tribe of their **f.** were 1
Nu 2:32 of Israel by the house of their **f.**: 1
Nu 2:34 according to the house of their **f.** 1
Nu 3:15 of Levi after the house of their **f.**, 1
Nu 3:20 according to the house of their **f.** 1
Nu 4:2 families, by the house of their **f.**, 1
Nu 4:22 throughout the houses of their **f.**, 1
Nu 4:29 families by the house of their **f.**; 1
Nu 4:34 and after the house of their **f.**, 1
Nu 4:38 and by the house of their **f.**, 1
Nu 4:40 by the house of their **f.**, were two 1
Nu 4:42 families, by the house of their **f.**, 1
Nu 4:46 and after the house of their **f.**, 1
Nu 7:2 heads of the house of their **f.**, 1
Nu 11:12 which thou swarest unto their **f.**? 1
Nu 13:2 every tribe of their **f.** shall ye send 1
Nu 14:18 visiting the iniquity of the **f.** upon 1
Nu 14:23 the land which I sware unto their **f.**, 1
Nu 17:2 according to the house of their **f.**, 1
Nu 17:2 according to the house of their **f.** 1
Nu 17:3 the head of the house of their **f.**. 1
Nu 20:15 How our **f.** went down into Egypt, 1
Nu 20:15 the Egyptians vexed us, and our **f.**: 1
Nu 26:55 the names of the tribes of their **f.** 1
Nu 31:26 the chief **f.** of the congregation: 1
Nu 32:8 Thus did your **f.**, when I sent them 1
Nu 32:28 and the chief **f.** of the tribes of the 1
Nu 33:54 according to the tribes of your **f.** 1
Nu 34:14 Reuben according to...of their **f.**, 1
Nu 34:14 Gad according to the...of their **f.**, 1
Nu 36:1 And the chief **f.** of the families of 1
Nu 36:1 the chief **f.** of the children of Israel: 1
Nu 36:3 taken from the inheritance of our **f.**, 1
Nu 36:4 the inheritance of the tribe of our **f.**. 1
Nu 36:7 the inheritance of the tribe of his **f.**. 1
Nu 36:8 every man the inheritance of his **f.** 1
De 1:8 which the Lord sware unto your **f.**, 1
De 1:11 (The Lord God of your **f.** make you 1
De 1:21 the Lord God of thy **f.** hath said 1
De 1:35 which I sware to give unto your **f.**, 1
De 4:1 which the Lord God of your **f.** giveth 1
De 4:31 nor forget the covenant of thy **f.** which 1
De 4:37 because he loved thy **f.**, therefore he 1
De 5:3 made not this covenant with our **f.**, 1
De 5:9 visiting the iniquity of the **f.** upon the 1
De 6:3 the Lord God of thy **f.** hath promised 1
De 6:10 the land which he sware unto thy **f.**, 1
De 6:18 which the Lord sware unto thy **f.**, 1
De 6:23 the land which he sware unto our **f.**. 1
De 7:8 oath, which he had sworn unto your **f.**, 1
De 7:12 the mercy which he sware unto thy **f.**: 1
De 7:13 the land which he sware unto thy **f.** 1
De 8:1 which the Lord sware unto your **f.** 1
De 8:3 knewest not, neither did thy **f.** know; 1
De 8:16 with manna, which thy **f.** knew not, 1
De 8:18 covenant which he sware unto thy **f.**, 1
De 9:5 word which the Lord sware unto thy **f.**, 1
De 10:11 the land, which I sware unto their **f.** 1
De 10:15 the Lord had a delight in thy **f.** 1
De 10:22 Thy **f.** went down into Egypt with 1
De 11:9 which the Lord sware unto your **f.** 1
De 11:21 which the Lord sware unto your **f.** 1
De 12:1 the land, which the Lord God of thy **f.** 1
De 13:6 thou hast not known, thou, nor thy **f.**; 1
De 13:17 as he hath sworn unto thy **f.**; 1
De 19:8 coast, as he hath sworn unto thy **f.**, 1
De 19:8 which he promised to give unto thy **f.**; 1
De 24:16 The **f.** shall not be put to death for 1
De 24:16 children to put to death for the **f.**: 1
De 26:3 which the Lord sware unto our **f.** for 1
De 26:7 we cried unto the Lord God of our **f.**, 1
De 26:15 given us, as thou swarest unto our **f.**, 1
De 27:3 as the Lord God of thy **f.** hath 1
De 28:11 Lord sware unto thy **f.** to give thee. 1
De 28:36 neither thou nor thy **f.** have known; 1
De 28:64 neither thou nor thy **f.** have known, 1
De 29:13 as he hath sworn unto thy **f.**, 1
De 29:25 covenant of the Lord God of their **f.**, 1
De 30:5 into the land which thy **f.** possessed, 1
De 30:5 and multiply thee above thy **f.** 1
De 30:9 as he rejoiced over thy **f.**: 1
De 30:20 which the Lord sware unto thy **f.**, 1
De 31:7 the Lord hath sworn unto their **f.** 1
De 31:16 Behold, thou shalt sleep with thy **f.**; 1
De 31:20 the land which I sware unto their **f.**, 1
De 32:17 newly up, whom your **f.** feared not. 1
Jos 1:6 I sware unto their **f.** to give them. 1
Jos 4:6 children ask their **f.** in time to
Jos 4:21 children shall ask their **f.** in time to 1
Jos 5:6 which the Lord sware unto their **f.** 1
Jos 14:1 the heads of the **f.** of the tribes 1
Jos 18:3 land which the Lord God of your **f.** 1
Jos 19:51 the heads of the **f.** of the tribes. 1
Jos 21:1 the heads of the **f.** of the Levites 1
Jos 21:1 unto the heads of the **f.** of the tribes 1
Jos 21:43 which he sware to give unto their **f.**; 1
Jos 21:44 all that he sware unto their **f.**: 1
Jos 22:14 an head of the house of their **f.** 1
Jos 22:28 altar of the Lord, which our **f.** made, 1
Jos 24:2 Your **f.** dwelt on the other side of the 1
Jos 24:6 And I brought your **f.** out of Egypt: 1
Jos 24:6 the Egyptians pursued after your **f.** 1
Jos 24:14 the gods which your **f.** served on the 1
Jos 24:15 gods which your **f.** served that were 1
Jos 24:17 brought us up and our **f.** out of the 1
Jg 2:1 the land which I sware unto your **f.**; 1
Jg 2:10 were gathered unto their **f.**: and there 1
Jg 2:12 they forsook the Lord God of their **f.**, 1
Jg 2:17 the way which their **f.** walked in, 1
Jg 2:19 themselves more than their **f.**, 1
Jg 2:20 covenant which I commanded their **f.**, 1
Jg 2:22 as their **f.** did keep it, or not. 1
Jg 3:4 which he commanded their **f.** by the 1
Jg 6:13 his miracles which our **f.** told us of, 1
Jg 21:22 when their **f.** or their brethren come 1
1Sa 12:6 brought your **f.** up out of the land 1
1Sa 12:7 which he did to you and to your **f.**. 1
1Sa 12:8 and your **f.** cried unto the Lord, 1
1Sa 12:8 brought forth your **f.** out of Egypt, 1
1Sa 12:15 against you, as it was against your **f.** 1
2Sa 7:12 and thou shalt sleep with thy **f.**, 1
1Ki 1:21 lord the king shall sleep with his **f.**, 1
1Ki 2:10 David slept with his **f.**, and was buried 1
1Ki 8:1 the chief of the **f.** of the children 1
1Ki 8:21 the Lord, which he made with our **f.**, 1
1Ki 8:34 land which thou gavest unto their **f.** 1
1Ki 8:40 land which thou gavest unto our **f.**. 1
1Ki 8:48 land, which thou gavest unto their **f.**, 1
1Ki 8:53 thou broughtest our **f.** out of Egypt, 1
1Ki 8:57 be with us, as he was with our **f.**: 1
1Ki 8:58 which he commanded our **f.**. 1
1Ki 9:9 brought forth their **f.** out of the land 1
1Ki 11:21 in Egypt that David slept with his **f.**, 1
1Ki 11:43 Solomon slept with his **f.**, and was 1
1Ki 13:22 come unto the sepulchre of thy **f.**. 1
1Ki 14:15 good land, which he gave to their **f.**, 1
1Ki 14:20 he slept with his **f.**, and Nadab his 1
1Ki 14:22 above all that their **f.** had done 1
1Ki 14:31 And Rehoboam slept with his **f.**, 1
1Ki 14:31 and was buried with his **f.** in the city 1
1Ki 15:8 Abijam slept with his **f.**; and they 1
1Ki 15:12 all the idols that his **f.** had made. 1
1Ki 15:24 Asa slept with his **f.**, and was buried 1
1Ki 15:24 with his **f.** in the city of David his 1
1Ki 16:6 Baasha slept with his **f.**, and was 1
1Ki 16:28 Omri slept with his **f.**, and was buried 1
1Ki 19:4 for I am not better than my **f.** 1
1Ki 21:3 should give the inheritance of my **f.** 1
1Ki 21:4 not give thee the inheritance of my **f.**. 1
1Ki 22:40 Ahab slept with his **f.**; and Ahaziah 1
1Ki 22:50 And Jehoshaphat slept with his **f.**, 1
1Ki 22:50 and was buried with is **f.** in the city 1
2Ki 8:24 And Joram slept with his **f.**, 1
2Ki 8:24 and was buried with his **f.** in the city 1
2Ki 9:28 in his sepulchre with his **f.** in the city 1
2Ki 10:35 And Jehu slept with his **f.**: and they 1
2Ki 12:18 his **f.**, kings of Judah, had dedicated, 1
2Ki 12:21 and they buried him with his **f.** in the 1
2Ki 13:9 Jehoahaz slept with his **f.**; and they 1
2Ki 13:13 And Joash slept with his **f.**; and 1
2Ki 14:6 The **f.** shall not be put to death for 1
2Ki 14:6 children be put to death for the **f.**; 1
2Ki 14:16 Jehoash slept with his **f.**, and was 1
2Ki 14:20 was buried at Jerusalem with his **f.** 1
2Ki 14:22 after that the king slept with his **f.**. 1
2Ki 14:29 Jeroboam slept with his **f.**, even with 1
2Ki 15:7 So Azariah slept with his **f.**; and they 1
2Ki 15:7 buried him with his **f.** in the city of 1
2Ki 15:9 as his **f.** had done: he departed not 1
2Ki 15:22 And Menahem slept with his **f.**; and 1
2Ki 15:38 And Jotham slept with his **f.**, 1
2Ki 15:38 and was buried with his **f.** in the city 1
2Ki 16:20 And Ahaz slept with his **f.**, 1
2Ki 16:20 and was buried with his **f.** in the city 1
2Ki 17:13 the law which I commanded your **f.**, 1
2Ki 17:14 like to the neck of their **f.**, 1
2Ki 17:15 covenant that he made with their **f.**, 1
2Ki 17:41 as did their **f.**, so do they unto this 1
2Ki 19:12 them which my **f.** have destroyed; 1
2Ki 20:17 that which thy **f.** have laid up in 1
2Ki 20:21 And Hezekiah slept with his **f.**: and 1
2Ki 21:8 the land which I gave their **f.**; 1
2Ki 21:15 since the day their **f.** came forth 1
2Ki 21:18 Manasseh slept with his **f.**, and was 1
2Ki 21:22 he forsook the Lord God of his **f.**, 1
2Ki 22:13 our **f.** have not hearkened unto the 1

2Ki 22:20 I will gather thee unto thy f.,... 1
2Ki 23:32, 37 according to all that his f. had... 1
2Ki 24:6 So Jehoiakim slept with his f.:... 1
1Ch 4:38 house of their f. increased greatly... 1
1Ch 5:13 brethren of the house of their f... 1
1Ch 5:15 chief of the house of their f... 1
1Ch 5:24 the heads of the house of their f.,... 1
1Ch 5:24 and heads of the house of their f... 1
1Ch 5:25 trespassed against the God of their f.,... 1
1Ch 6:19 the Levites according to their f... 1
1Ch 7:4 after the house of their f., were... 1
1Ch 7:7, 9 heads of the house of their f.,... 1
1Ch 7:11 by the heads of their f., mighty... 1
1Ch 8:6 these are the heads of the f. of... 1
1Ch 8:10 were his sons, heads of the f... 1
1Ch 8:13 who were heads of the f. of the... 1
1Ch 8:28 These were heads of the f.,... 1
1Ch 9:9 of the f. in the house of their f... 1
1Ch 9:13 heads of the house of their f.,... 1
1Ch 9:19 and their f., being over the host... 1
1Ch 9:33 chief of the f. of the Levites,... 1
1Ch 9:34 These chief f. of the Levites were... 1
1Ch 12:17 the God of our f. look thereon, and... 1
1Ch 12:30 throughout the house of their f... 1
1Ch 15:12 chief of the f. of the Levites:... 1
1Ch 17:11 that thou must go to be with thy f.,... 1
1Ch 23:9 the chief of the f. of Laadan... 1
1Ch 23:24 Levi after the house of their f.;... 1
1Ch 23:24 the chief of the f., as they were... 1
1Ch 24:4 chief men of the house of their f.,... 1
1Ch 24:4 according to the house of their f... 1
1Ch 24:6 before the chief of the f. of the... 1
1Ch 24:30 Levites after the house of their f... 1
1Ch 24:31 the chief of the f. of the priests... 1
1Ch 24:31 and Levites, even the principal f... 1
1Ch 26:13 according to the house of their f.,... 1
1Ch 26:21 the Gershonite Laadan, chief f.,... 1
1Ch 26:26 David the king, and the chief f.,... 1
1Ch 26:31 to the generations of his f.,... 1
1Ch 26:32 and seven hundred chief f.,... 1
1Ch 27:1 chief f. and captains of thousands... 1
1Ch 29:6 the chief of the f. and princes... 1
1Ch 29:15 and sojourners, as were all our f.:... 1
1Ch 29:18 Abraham, Isaac, and of Israel, our f.,... 1
1Ch 29:20 blessed the Lord God of their f.,... 1
2Ch 1:2 in all Israel, the chief of the f... 1
2Ch 5:2 chief of the f. of the children of... 1
2Ch 6:25 thou gavest to them and to their f... 1
2Ch 6:31 land which thou gavest unto our f... 1
2Ch 6:38 land, which thou gavest unto their f.,... 1
2Ch 7:22 they forsook the Lord God of their f.,... 1
2Ch 9:31 Solomon slept with his f., and he... 1
2Ch 11:16 unto the Lord God of their f... 1
2Ch 12:16 Rehoboam slept with his f., and was... 1
2Ch 13:12 not against the Lord God of your f.;... 1
2Ch 13:18 relied upon the Lord God of their f... 1
2Ch 14:1 Abijah slept with his f., and they... 1
2Ch 14:4 to seek the Lord God of their f., and... 1
2Ch 15:12 to seek the Lord God of their f. with... 1
2Ch 16:13 And Asa slept with his f., and died... 1
2Ch 17:14 according to the house of their f.:... 1
2Ch 19:4 back unto the Lord God of their f... 1
2Ch 19:8 and of the chief of the f. of Israel,... 1
2Ch 20:6 And said, O Lord God of our f.,... 1
2Ch 20:33 their hearts unto the God of their f... 1
2Ch 21:1 Now Jehoshaphat slept with his f.,... 1
2Ch 21:1 and was buried with his f. in the city... 1
2Ch 21:10 had forsaken the Lord God of his f... 1
2Ch 21:19 for him, like the burning of his f... 1
2Ch 23:2 and the chief of the f. of Israel,... 1
2Ch 24:18 house of the Lord God of their f.,... 1
2Ch 24:24 forsaken the Lord God of their f... 1
2Ch 25:4 The f. shall not die for the children,... 1
2Ch 25:4 shall the children die for the f.,... 1
2Ch 25:5 according to the houses of their f.,... 1
2Ch 25:28 buried him with his f. in the city... 1
2Ch 26:2 after that the king slept with his f... 1
2Ch 26:12 whole number of the chief of the f... 1
2Ch 26:23 So Uzziah slept with his f., and they... 1
2Ch 26:23 buried him with is f. in the field... 1
2Ch 27:9 Jotham slept with his f., and they... 1
2Ch 28:6 forsaken the Lord God of their f... 1
2Ch 28:9 because the Lord God of your f. was... 1
2Ch 28:25 to anger the Lord God of his f... 1
2Ch 28:27 And Ahaz slept with his f., and they... 1
2Ch 29:5 the house of the Lord God of your f.,... 1
2Ch 29:6 for our f. have trespassed, and done... 1
2Ch 29:9 lo, our f. have fallen by the sword,... 1
2Ch 30:7 And be not ye like your f... 1
2Ch 30:7 against the Lord God of their f.,... 1
2Ch 30:8 be ye not stiffnecked, as your f. were,... 1
2Ch 30:19 to seek God, the Lord God his f.,... 1
2Ch 30:22 confession to the Lord God of their f... 1
2Ch 31:17 priests by the house of their f.,... 1
2Ch 32:13 what I and my f. have done unto all... 1
2Ch 32:14 nations that my f. utterly destroyed,... 1
2Ch 32:15 hand, and out of the hand of my f.:... 1
2Ch 32:33 Hezekiah slept with his f., and they... 1
2Ch 33:8 which I have appointed for your f.;... 1
2Ch 33:12 greatly before the God of his f.,... 1
2Ch 33:20 So Manasseh slept with his f.,... 1
2Ch 34:21 because our f. have not kept the word... 1
2Ch 34:28 Behold, I will gather thee to thy f.,... 1
2Ch 34:32 covenant of God, the God of their f... 1
2Ch 34:33 following the Lord, the God of their f... 1
2Ch 35:4 by the houses of your f., after... 1
2Ch 35:5 of the f. of your brethren... 1
2Ch 35:24 in one of the sepulchres of his f... 1
2Ch 36:15 the Lord God of their f. sent to them... 1
Ezr 1:5 Then rose up the chief of the f... 1
Ezr 2:68 And some of the chief of the f.,... 1
Ezr 3:12 Levites and chief of the f., who... 1
Ezr 4:2 and to the chief of the f., and said,... 1
Ezr 4:3 of the chiefs of the f. of Israel,... 1
Ezr 4:15 in the book of the records of thy f.:... 2
Ezr 5:12 f. had provoked the God of heaven... 2
Ezr 7:27 Blessed be the Lord God of our f.,... 1
Ezr 8:1 These are now the chief of their f.,... 1
Ezr 8:28 offering unto the Lord God of your f... 1
Ezr 8:29 and chief of the f. of Israel,... 1
Ezr 9:7 Since the days of our f. have we... 1
Ezr 10:11 unto the Lord God of your f., and do... 1
Ezr 10:16 the f., after the house of their f.,... 1
Ne 7:70 of the f. gave unto the work... 1
Ne 7:71 of the f. gave to the treasure... 1
Ne 8:13 together the chief of the f... 1
Ne 9:2 sins, and the iniquities of their f... 1
Ne 9:9 didst see the affliction of our f... 1
Ne 9:16 But they and our f. dealt proudly,... 1
Ne 9:23 which thou hadst promised to their f.,... 1
Ne 9:32 and on our f., and on all thy people,... 1
Ne 9:34 our priests, nor our f., kept thy law,... 1
Ne 9:36 the land that thou gavest unto our f... 1
Ne 10:34 after the houses of our f., at times... 1
Ne 11:13 And his brethren, chief of the f.,... 1
Ne 12:12 were priests, the chief of the f.:... 1
Ne 12:22 were recorded chief of the f.:... 1
Ne 12:23 the chief of the f., were written... 1
Ne 13:18 Did not your f. thus, and did not... 1
Job 8:8 thyself to the search of their f.:... 1
Job 15:18 wise men have told from their f.,... 1
Job 30:1 whose f. I would have disdained to... 1
Ps 22:4 Our f. trusted in thee; they trusted,... 1
Ps 39:12 and a sojourner, as all my f. were... 1
Ps 44:1 O God, our f. have told us, what... 1
Ps 45:16 Instead of thy f. shall be thy children,... 1
Ps 49:19 shall go to the generation of his f.;... 1
Ps 78:3 and known, and our f. have told us... 1
Ps 78:5 Israel, which he commanded our f.,... 1
Ps 78:8 And might not be as their f.,... 1
Ps 78:12 things did he in the sight of their f.,... 1
Ps 78:57 and dealt unfaithfully like their f.:... 1
Ps 95:9 When your f. tempted me, proved... 1
Ps 106:6 We have sinned with our f., we have... 1
Ps 106:7 Our f. understood not thy wonders... 1
Ps 109:14 the iniquity of his f. be remembered... 1
Pr 17:6 and the glory of children are their f... 1
Pr 19:14 and riches are the inheritance of f.:... 1
Pr 22:28 landmark, which thy f. have set... 1
Isa 14:21 children for the iniquity of their f.;... 1
Isa 37:12 which my f. have destroyed, as Gozan,... 1
Isa 39:6 that which thy f. have laid up in... 1
Isa 49:23 And kings shall be thy nursing f.,...
Isa 64:11 house, where our f. praised thee,... 1
Isa 65:7 the iniquities of your f. together,... 1
Jer 2:5 iniquity have your f. found in me,... 1
Jer 3:18 given for an inheritance unto your f... 1
Jer 3:24 hath devoured the labour of our f... 1
Jer 3:25 the Lord our God, we and our f.,... 1
Jer 6:21 the f. and the sons together shall fall... 1
Jer 7:7 the land that I gave to your f.,... 1
Jer 7:14 which I gave to you and to your f.,... 1
Jer 7:18 and the f. kindle the fire, and the... 1
Jer 7:22 For I spake unto your f.,... 1
Jer 7:25 Since the day that your f. came forth... 1
Jer 7:26 they did worse than their f... 1
Jer 9:14 Baalim, which their f. taught them:... 1
Jer 9:16 neither they nor their f. have known:... 1
Jer 11:4 Which I commanded your f. in the... 1
Jer 11:5 oath which I have sworn unto your f.,... 1
Jer 11:7 I earnestly protested unto your f... 1
Jer 11:10 covenant which I made with their f... 1
Jer 13:14 even the f. and the sons together,... 1
Jer 14:20 wickedness, and the iniquity of our f.:... 1
Jer 16:3 concerning their f. that begat them... 1
Jer 16:11 Because your f. have forsaken me,... 1
Jer 16:12 ye have done worse than your f.;... 1
Jer 16:13 ye know not, neither ye nor your f.;... 1
Jer 16:15 their land that I gave unto their f... 1
Jer 16:19 Surely our f. have inherited lies,... 1
Jer 17:22 sabbath day, as I commanded your f... 1
Jer 19:4 neither they nor their f. have known,... 1
Jer 23:27 as their f. have forgotten my name... 1
Jer 23:39 the city that I gave you and your f.,... 1
Jer 24:10 that I gave unto them and to their f... 1
Jer 25:5 hath given unto you and to your f... 1
Jer 30:3 to the land that I gave to their f.,... 1
Jer 31:29 The f. have eaten a sour grape,... 1
Jer 31:32 covenant that I made with their f... 1
Jer 32:18 recompensest the iniquity of the f... 1
Jer 32:22 land, which thou didst swear to their f... 1
Jer 34:5 and with the burnings of thy f., the... 1
Jer 34:13 I made a covenant with your f. in the... 1
Jer 34:14 but your f. hearkened not unto me,... 1
Jer 35:15 I have given to you and to your f.:... 1
Jer 44:3 not, neither they, ye, nor your f.,... 1
Jer 44:9 forgotten the wickedness of your f.,... 1
Jer 44:10 I set before you, and before your f... 1
Jer 44:17 as we have done, we, and our f.,... 1
Jer 44:21 ye, and your f., your kings, and your... 1
Jer 47:3 the f. shall not look back to their... 1
Jer 50:7 even the Lord, the hope of their f... 1
La 5:7 Our f. have sinned, and are not;... 1
Eze 2:3 their f. have transgressed against... 1
Eze 5:10 Therefore the f. shall eat the sons in... 1
Eze 5:10 and the sons shall eat their f.;... 1
Eze 18:2 saying, The f. have eaten sour grapes,... 1
Eze 20:4 to know the abominations of their f... 1
Eze 20:18 Walk ye not in the statutes of your f.,... 1
Eze 20:27 Yet in this your f. have blasphemed... 1
Eze 20:30 polluted after the manner of your f.?... 1
Eze 20:36 Like as I pleaded with your f. in the... 1
Eze 20:42 up mine hand to give it to your f... 1
Eze 36:28 the land that I gave to your f.;... 1
Eze 37:25 wherein your f. have dwelt; and they... 1
Eze 47:14 up mine hand to give it unto your f.:... 1
Da 2:23 praise thee, O thou God of my f.,... 2
Da 9:6 our princes, and our f., and to all... 1
Da 9:8 to our princes, and to our f., because... 1
Da 9:16 and for the iniquities of our f.,... 1
Da 11:24 f. have not done, nor his fathers' f.;... 1
Da 11:37 shall he regard the God of his f., nor... 1
Da 11:38 and a god whom his f. knew not shall... 1
Ho 9:10 I saw your f. as the firstripe in the fig... 1
Joe 1:2 or even in the days of your f.?... 1
Am 2:4 after the which their f. have walked:... 1
Mic 7:20 hast sworn unto our f. from the days... 1
Zec 1:2 been sore displeased with your f... 1
Zec 1:4 Be ye not as your f., unto whom the... 1
Zec 1:5 Your f. where are they? and the... 1
Zec 1:6 did they not take hold of your f.?... 1
Zec 8:14 when your f. provoked me to wrath... 1
Mal 2:10 by profaning the covenant of our f.?... 1
Mal 3:7 Even from the days of your f. ye are... 1
Mal 4:6 the heart of the f. to the children,... 1
Mal 4:6 the heart of the children to their f.,... 1
Mt 23:30 **we had been in the days of our f.,..** 3962
Mt 23:32 **ye up then the measure of your f.,** 3962
Lu 1:17 to turn the hearts of the f. to the... 3962
Lu 1:55 As he spake to our f., to Abraham,... 3962
Lu 1:72 the mercy promised to our f.,... 3962
Lu 6:23 **did their f. unto the prophets...** 3962
Lu 6:26 **did their f. to the false prophets...** 3962
Lu 11:47 **prophets, and your f. killed them...** 3962
Lu 11:48 **that ye allow the deeds of your f.:...** 3962
Joh 4:20 f. worshipped in this mountain;... 3962
Joh 6:31 Our f. did eat manna in the desert;... 3962
Joh 6:49 **f. did eat manna in the wilderness,** 3962
Joh 6:58 **not as your f. did eat manna,...** 3962

Joh 7:22 **it is of Moses, but of the f.;)**......... *3962*
Ac 3:13 God of our **f.**, hath glorified his Son.... *3962*
Ac 3:22 For Moses truly said unto the **f.**, ... *3962*
Ac 3:25 which God made with our **f.**,............ *3962*
Ac 5:30 The God of our **f.** raised up Jesus, ... *3962*
Ac 7:2 Men, brethren, and **f.**, hearken;......... *3962*
Ac 7:11 and our **f.** found no sustenance.......... *3962*
Ac 7:12 Egypt, he sent out our **f.** first........... *3962*
Ac 7:15 Egypt, and died, he, and our **f.**,........ *3962*
Ac 7:19 evil entreated our **f.**, so that they *3962*
Ac 7:32 Saying, I am the God of thy **f.**,.......... *3962*
Ac 7:38 the mount Sina, and with our **f.**: *3962*
Ac 7:39 To whom our **f.** would not obey,......... *3962*
Ac 7:44 **f.** had the tabernacle of witness *3962*
Ac 7:45 Which also our **f.** that came after *3962*
Ac 7:45 drave out before the face of our **f.**, ... *3962*
Ac 7:51 as your **f.** did, so do ye. *3962*
Ac 7:52 have not your **f.** persecuted?............. *3962*
Ac 13:17 chose our **f.**, and exalted the people ... *3962*
Ac 13:32 which was made unto the **f.**, ... *3962*
Ac 13:36 and was laid unto his **f.**, and saw *3962*
Ac 15:10 our **f.** nor we were able to bear? *3962*
Ac 22:1 Men, brethren, and **f.**, hear ye.......... *3962*
Ac 22:3 manner of the law of the **f.**,.............. *3971*
Ac 22:14 God of our **f.** hath chosen thee,......... *3962*
Ac 24:14 so worship I the God of my **f.**,........... *3971*
Ac 26:6 promise made of God unto our **f.**:;...... *3962*
Ac 28:17 the people, or customs of our **f.**, ... *3971*
Ac 28:25 Esaias the prophet unto our **f.**, ... *3962*
Ro 9:5 Whose are the **f.**, and of whom *3962*
Ro 15:8 the promises made unto the **f.**:........... *3962*
1Co 4:15 yet have ye not many **f.**:................... *3962*
1Co 10:1 all our **f.** were under the cloud, ... *3962*
Ga 1:14 zealous of the traditions of my **f.**......... *3967*
Eph 6:4 ye **f.**, provoke not your children to..... *3962*
Col 3:21 **F.**, provoke not your children to.......... *3962*
1Ti 1:9 for murderers of **f.** and murderers...... *3964*
Heb 1:1 spake in time past unto the **f.** by *3962*
Heb 3:9 When your **f.** tempted me, proved...... *3962*
Heb 8:9 that I made with their **f.** in the day..... *3962*
Heb 12:9 Furthermore we have had **f.** of our..... *3962*
1Pe 1:18 received by tradition from your **f.**;...... *3970*
2Pe 3:4 since the **f.** fell asleep, all things *3962*
1Jo 2:13 I write unto you, **f.**, because ye......... *3962*
1Jo 2:14 I have written unto you, **f.**, because ... *3962*

FATHERS'
Ex 6:14 These be the heads of their **f.** houses:..... 1
Ex 10:6 fathers, nor thy **f.** fathers have seen, ... 1
Nu 17:6 according to their **f.** houses, even.......... 1
Nu 26:2 upward, throughout their **f.** house,.......... 1
Nu 32:14 ye are risen up in your **f.** stead, an......... 1
Ne 2:3 the place of my **f.** sepulchres, lieth 1
Ne 2:5 the city of my **f.** sepulchres, that I.......... 1
Eze 20:24 their eyes were after their **f.** idols. 1
Eze 22:10 they discovered their **f.** nakedness: 1
Ro 11:28 they are beloved for the **f.** sakes. *3962*

FATHOMS
Ac 27:28 sounded, and found it twenty **f.**: *3712*
Ac 27:28 again, and found it fifteen **f.**. *3712*

FATLING See also FATLINGS.
Isa 11:6 young lion and the **f.** together; 4806

FATLINGS
1Sa 15:9 and of the **f.**, and the lambs,............. 4932
2Sa 6:13 he sacrificed oxen and **f.**.................... 4806
Ps 66:15 unto thee burnt sacrifices of **f.**,.......... 4220
Eze 39:18 bullocks, all of them **f.** of Bashan. 4806
Mt 22:4 **my oxen and my f. are killed,**....... *4619*

FATNESS
Ge 27:28 of heaven, and the **f.** of the earth,...... 4924
Ge 27:39 dwelling shall be the **f.** of the earth, ... 4924
De 32:15 thick, thou art covered with **f.**; ....
Jg 9:9 Should I leave my **f.**, wherewith 1880
Job 15:27 he covereth his face with his **f.**,.......... 2459
Job 36:16 thy table should be full of **f.**.............. 1880
Ps 36:8 satisfied with the **f.** of thy house;....... 1880
Ps 63:5 be satisfied as with marrow and **f.**;..... 1880
Ps 65:11 goodness; and thy paths drop **f.**........... 1880
Ps 73:7 Their eyes stand out with **f.**:.............. 2459
Ps 109:24 and my flesh faileth of **f.**................. 8081
Isa 17:4 the **f.** of his flesh shall wax lean.......... 4924
Isa 34:6 it is made fat with **f.**, and with the 2459
Isa 34:7 and their dust made fat with **f.**. 2459
Isa 55:2 let your soul delight itself in **f.**........... 1880

Jer 31:14 the soul of the priests with **f.**,........... 1880
Ro 11:17 the root and **f.** of the olive tree; *4096*

FATS
Joe 2:24 the **f.** shall overflow with wine and..... 3342
Joe 3:13 the press is full, the **f.** overflow;........ 3342

FATTED
1Ki 4:23 and fallowdeer, and **f.** fowl. 75
Jer 46:21 the midst of her like **f.** bullocks; 4770
Lu 15:23 **And bring hither the f. calf, and...** *4618*
Lu 15:27 **thy father hath killed the f. calf,...** *4618*
Lu 15:30 **thou hast killed for him the f. calf,** *4618*

FATTER
Da 1:15 appeared fairer and **f.** in flesh........... 1277

FATTEST
Ps 78:31 upon them, and slew the **f.** of them,... 4924
Da 11:24 upon the **f.** places of the province; 4924

FAULT See also FAULTS; FAULTNESS.
Ex 5:16 but the **f.** is in thine own people. 2398
De 25:2 before his face, according to his **f.**..... 7564
1Sa 29:3 I have found no **f.** in him since 3972
2Sa 3:8 with a **f.** concerning this woman? 5771
Ps 59:4 prepare themselves without my **f.**: 5771
Da 6:4 could find none occasion nor **f.**;.......... 7844
Da 6:4 there any error of **f.** found in him...... 7844
Mt 18:15 **and tell him his f. between thee....** *1651*
Mk 7:2 unwashen, hands, they found **f.**.......... *3201*
Lu 23:4 I find no **f.** in this man. *158*
Lu 23:14 have found no **f.** in this man *158*
Joh 18:38 I find in him no **f.** at all...................... *156*
Joh 19:4 know that I find no **f.** in him............... *156*
Joh 19:6 for I find no **f.** in him......................... *156*
Ro 9:19 Why doth he yet find **f.**? For who *3201*
1Co 6:7 there is utterly a **f.** among you, ... *2275*
Ga 6:1 if a man be overtaken in a **f.**, ... *3900*
Heb 8:8 For finding **f.** with them, he saith,...... *3201*
Re 14:5 are without **f.** before the throne *299*

FAULTLESS
Heb 8:7 if that first covenant had been **f.**,......... *273*
Jude 24 and to present you **f.** before the.......... *299*

FAULTS
Ge 41:9 I do remember my **f.** this day: 2399
Ps 19:12 cleanse thou me from secret **f.**. ....
Jas 5:16 Confess your **f.** one to another, ... *3900*
1Pe 2:20 if, when ye be buffeted for your **f.**, ... *264*

FAULTY
2Sa 14:13 this thing as one which is **f.**,................ 818
Ho 10:2 now shall they be found **f.**:................. 816

FAVOUR See also FAVOURABLE; FAVOURED; FAVOUREST; FAVOURETH.
Ge 18:3 now I have found **f.** in thy sight, ... 2580
Ge 30:27 if I have found **f.** in thine eyes,.......... 2580
Ge 39:21 him **f.** in the sight of the keeper 2580
Ex 3:21 will give this people **f.** in the sight....... 2580
Ex 11:3 And the Lord gave the people **f.** in..... 2580
Ex 12:36 Lord gave the people **f.** in the sight.... 2580
Nu 11:11 have I not found **f.** in thy sight, ... 2580
Nu 11:15 if I have found **f.** in thy sight;............ 2580
De 24:1 pass that she find no **f.** in his eyes, ... 2580
De 28:50 the old, nor shew **f.** to the young:....... 2603
De 33:23 O Naphtali, satisfied with **f.**, and........ 7522
Jos 11:20 and that they might have no **f.**,.......... 8467
Ru 2:13 Let me find **f.** in thy sight, ... 2580
1Sa 2:26 and was in **f.** both with the Lord,....... 2896
1Sa 16:22 for he hath found **f.** in my sight. 2580
1Sa 20:29 if I have found **f.** in thine eyes,.......... 2580
1Sa 25:8 young men find **f.** in thine eyes:.......... 2580
1Sa 29:6 the lords **f.** thee not......................... 2896
2Sa 15:25 if I shall find **f.** in the eyes of the....... 2580
1Ki 11:19 Hadad found great **f.** in the sight.......... 2580
Ne 2:5 if thy servant have found **f.** in thy 3190
Es 2:15 Esther obtained **f.** in the sight of........ 2580
Es 2:17 she obtained grace and **f.** in his 2617
Es 5:2 that she obtained **f.** in his sight:.......... 2580
Es 5:8 If I have found **f.** in the sight of the.... 2580
Es 7:3 I I have found **f.** in thy sight, O.......... 2580
Es 8:5 and if I have found **f.** in his sight,....... 2580
Job 10:12 Thou hast granted me like and **f.**, ... 2617
Ps 5:12 with **f.** wilt thou compass him as........ 7522
Ps 30:5 his **f.** is life: weeping may endure........ 7522
Ps 30:7 **f.** thou hast made my mountain.......... 7522
Ps 35:27 glad, that **f.** my righteous cause: 2655
Ps 44:3 because thou hadst a **f.** unto them...... 7520

Ps 45:12 the people shall intreat thy **f.**. 6440
Ps 89:17 thy **f.** our horn shall be exalted.......... 7522
Ps 102:13 for the time to **f.** her, yea, the set..... 2603
Ps 102:14 stones, and **f.** the dust thereof. 2603
Ps 106:4 with the **f.** that thou bearest unto....... 7522
Ps 109:12 neither let there be any to **f.** his........ 2603
Ps 112:5 man sheweth **f.**, and lendeth: 2603
Ps 119:58 I intreated thy **f.** with my whole 6440
Pr 3:4 So shalt thou find **f.** and good........... 2580
Pr 8:35 and shall obtain **f.** of the Lord. 7522
Pr 11:27 seeketh good procureth **f.**: but 7522
Pr 12:2 good man obtaineth **f.** of the Lord: 7522
Pr 13:15 Good understanding giveth **f.**:............ 2580
Pr 14:9 among the righteous there is **f.**.......... 7522
Pr 14:35 king's **f.** is toward a wise servant:...... 7522
Pr 16:15 **f.** is as a cloud of the latter rain.......... 7522
Pr 18:22 thing, and obtaineth **f.** of the Lord...... 7522
Pr 19:6 will intreat the **f.** of the prince:.......... 6440
Pr 19:12 his **f.** is as dew upon the grass. 7522
Pr 21:10 neighbour findeth no **f.** in his eyes...... 2603
Pr 22:1 **f.** rather than silver and gold............ 2580
Pr 28:23 find more **f.** than he that flattereth 2580
Pr 29:26 Many seek the ruler's **f.**;.................. 6440
Pr 31:30 **F.** is deceitful, and beauty if vain: 2580
Ec 9:11 nor yet **f.** to men of skill; 2580
Ca 8:10 I in his eyes as one that found **f.**. 7965
Isa 26:10 Let **f.** be shewed to the wicked, ... 2603
Isa 27:11 formed them will shew them no **f.**...... 2603
Isa 60:10 but in my **f.** have I had mercy on........ 7522
Jer 16:13 where I will not shew you **f.**. 2594
Da 1:9 God had brought Daniel into **f.**........... 2617
Lu 1:30 for thou hast found **f.** with God.......... *5485*
Lu 2:52 and in **f.** with God and man.............. *5485*
Ac 2:47 and having **f.** with all the people......... *5485*
Ac 7:10 him **f.** and wisdom in the sight of....... *5485*
Ac 7:46 Who found **f.** before God, and *5485*
Ac 25:3 And desired **f.** against him, that......... *5485*

FAVOURABLE
Jg 21:22 Be **f.** unto them for our sakes: 2603
Job 33:26 and he will be **f.** unto him:................ 7520
Ps 77:7 and will he be **f.** no more?................. 7520
Ps 85:1 thou hast been **f.** unto thy land: 7520

FAVOURED See also EVILFAVOUREDNESS.
Ge 29:17 Rachel was beautiful and well **f.**. 4758
Ge 39:6 was a goodly person, and well **f.**........ 4758
Ge 41:2 out of the river seven well **f.** kine 4758
Ge 41:3 seven other kine...ill **f.** and............. 4758
Ge 41:4 the ill **f.**...kine did eat up the seven.... 4758
Ge 41:4 kine did eat up the seven well **f.**........ 4758
Ge 41:18 kine, fatfleshed and well **f.**;............... 8389
Ge 41:19 poor and very ill **f.** and leanfleshed, ... 8389
Ge 41:20 the lean and the ill **f.** kine did eat............
Ge 41:21 were still ill **f.**, as at the beginning.............
Ge 41:27 And the seven thin and ill **f.** kine............
La 4:16 priests, and **f.** not the elders............. 2603
Da 1:4 was no blemish, but well **f.**,.............. 4758
Lu 1:28 Hail, thou that art highly **f.**, ... *5487*

FAVOUREST
Ps 41:11 By this I know that thou **f.** me, ... 2654

FAVOURETH
2Sa 20:11 He that **f.** Joab, and he that is for 2654

FEAR See also FEARED; FEAREST; FEARETH; FEARFUL; FEARING; FEARS.
Ge 9:2 the **f.** of you and the dread of you...... 4172
Ge 15:1 **F.** not, Abram: I am thy shield,......... 3372
Ge 20:11 the **f.** of God is not in this place; 3374
Ge 21:17 What aileth thee, Hagar? **f.** not:......... 3372
Ge 26:24 **f.** not, for I am with thee, and will 3372
Ge 31:42 and the **f.** of Isaac, had been with 6343
Ge 31:53 Jacob sware by the **f.** of his father....... 6343
Ge 32:11 I **f.** him, lest he will come and........... 3373
Ge 35:17 **F.** not; thou shalt have this son 3372
Ge 42:18 This do, and live; for I **f.** God:.......... 3373
Ge 43:23 he said, Peace be to you, **f.** not:......... 3372
Ge 46:3 **f.** not to go down into Egypt;............ 3372
Ge 50:19 Joseph said unto them, **F.** not: 3372
Ge 50:21 Now therefore **f.** ye not: I will 3372
Ex 9:30 I know that ye will not yet **f.** the 3372
Ex 14:13 **F.** ye not, stand still, and see the 3372
Ex 15:16 **F.** and dread shall fall upon them; 367
Ex 18:21 people able men, such as **f.** God, ... 3373
Ex 20:20 Moses said unto the people, **F.** not: ... 3372
Ex 20:20 that his **f.** may be before your........... 3374

Book	Ref	Context	No.
Ex	23:27	I will send my **f.** before thee,	367
Le	19:3	Ye shall **f.** every man his mother,	3372
Le	19:14	but shalt **f.** thy God: I am the	3372
Le	19:32	face of the old man, and **f.** thy God:	3372
Le	25:17	but thou shalt **f.** thy God: for I am	3372
Le	25:36	but **f.** thy God; that thy brother	3372
Le	25:43	with rigour; but shalt **f.** thy God	3372
Nu	14:9	neither **f.** ye the people of the land;	3372
Nu	14:9	the Lord is with us; **f.** them not	3372
Nu	21:34	Lord said unto Moses, **F.** him not:	3372
De	1:21	said unto thee; **f.** not, neither be	3372
De	2:25	the dread of thee and the **f.** of thee	3374
De	3:2	Lord said unto me, **F.** him not:	3372
De	3:22	Ye shall not **f.** them: for the Lord	3372
De	4:10	that they may learn to **f.** me	3372
De	5:29	that they would **f.** me, and keep all	3372
De	6:2	That thou mightest **f.** the Lord thy	3372
De	6:13	Thou shalt **f.** the Lord thy God,	3372
De	6:24	to **f.** the Lord our God, for our	3372
De	8:6	to walk in his ways, and to **f.** him	3372
De	10:12	but to **f.** the Lord thy God,	3372
De	10:20	Thou shalt **f.** the Lord thy God;	3372
De	11:25	the **f.** of you and the dread of you	6343
De	13:4	the Lord your God, and **f.** him,	3372
De	13:11	And all Israel shall hear, and **f.**,	3372
De	14:23	thou mayest learn to **f.** the Lord	3372
De	17:13	all the people shall hear, and **f.**,	3372
De	17:19	that he may learn to **f.** the Lord	3372
De	19:20	which remain shall hear, and **f.**,	3372
De	20:3	**f.** not, and do not tremble, neither	3372
De	21:21	and all Israel shall hear, and **f.**	3372
De	28:58	that thou mayest **f.** this glorious	3372
De	28:66	and thou shalt **f.** day and night,	6342
De	28:67	for the **f.** of thine heart wherewith	6343
De	28:67	heart wherewith thou shalt **f.**,	6342
De	31:6	**f.** not, nor be afraid of them:	3372
De	31:8	**f.** not, neither be dismayed	3372
De	31:12	they may learn, and **f.** the Lord	3372
De	31:13	and learn to **f.** the Lord your God,	3372
Jos	4:24	that ye might **f.** the Lord your God	3372
Jos	8:1	**F.** not, neither be thou dismayed:	3372
Jos	10:8	Lord said unto Joshua, **F.** them not:	3372
Jos	10:25	Joshua said unto them, **F.** not, nor	3372
Jos	22:24	rather done it for **f.** of this thing,	1674
Jos	24:14	Now therefore **f.** the Lord, and	3372
Jg	4:18	my lord, turn in to me; **f.** not	3372
Jg	6:10	**f.** not the gods of the Amorites,	3372
Jg	6:23	Peace be unto thee; **f.** not: thou	3372
Jg	7:10	if thou **f.** to go down, go thou	3373
Jg	9:21	dwelt there, for **f.** of Abimelech	6440
Ru	3:11	my daughter, **f.** not; I will do to	3372
1Sa	4:20	**F.** not; for thou hast born a son	3372
1Sa	11:7	And the **f.** of the Lord fell on the	6343
1Sa	12:14	If ye will **f.** the Lord, and serve	3372
1Sa	12:20	Samuel said unto the people, **F.** not:	3372
1Sa	12:24	Only **f.** the Lord, and serve him in	3372
1Sa	21:10	and fled that day for **f.** of Saul,	6440
1Sa	22:23	Abide thou with me, **f.** not:	3372
1Sa	23:17	And he said unto him, **F.** not:	3372
1Sa	23:26	haste to get away for **f.** of Saul;	6440
2Sa	9:7	And David said unto him **F.** not:	3372
2Sa	13:28	Amnon; then kill him, **f.** not:	3372
2Sa	23:3	be just, ruling in the **f.** of God	3374
1Ki	8:40	That they may **f.** thee all the days	3372
1Ki	8:43	to **f.** thee, as do thy people Israel;	3372
1Ki	17:13	Elijah said unto her, **F.** not;	3372
1Ki	18:12	I thy servant **f.** the Lord from my	3372
2Ki	4:1	that thy servant did **f.** the Lord:	3373
2Ki	6:16	he answered, **F.** not: for they	3372
2Ki	17:28	taught them how they should **f.** the	3372
2Ki	17:34	manners: they **f.** not the Lord,	3373
2Ki	17:35	saying, Ye shall not **f.** other gods,	3372
2Ki	17:36	him shall ye **f.**, and him shall ye	3372
2Ki	17:37	and ye shall not **f.** other gods	3372
2Ki	17:38	neither shall ye **f.** other gods	3372
2Ki	17:39	the Lord your God ye shall **f.**;	3372
2Ki	25:24	**F.** not to be the servants of the	3372
1Ch	14:17	the Lord brought the **f.** of him	6343
1Ch	16:30	**F.** before him, all the earth:	2342
1Ch	28:20	do it: **f.** not, nor be dismayed:	3372
2Ch	6:31	That they may **f.** thee, to walk in	3372
2Ch	6:33	and **f.** thee, as doth thy people	3372
2Ch	14:14	the **f.** of the Lord came upon them:	6343
2Ch	17:10	the **f.** of the Lord fell upon all the	6343
2Ch	19:7	let the **f.** of the Lord be upon you;	6343
2Ch	19:9	Thus shall ye do in the **f.** of the	3374
2Ch	20:17	**f.** not, nor be dismayed;	3372
2Ch	20:29	And the **f.** of God was on all the	6343
Ezr	3:3	**f.** was upon them because of the	367
Ne	1:11	thy servants, who desire to **f.** thy	3372
Ne	5:9	ought ye not to walk in the **f.** of	3374
Ne	5:15	so did not I, because of the **f.** of	3374
Ne	6:14	that would have put me in **f.**	3372
Ne	6:19	Tobiah sent letters to put me in **f.**	3372
Es	8:17	the **f.** of the Jews fell upon them	6343
Es	9:2	the **f.** of them fell upon all people	6343
Es	9:3	the **f.** of Mordecai fell upon them	6343
Job	1:9	said, Doth Job **f.** God for nought?	3372
Job	4:6	Is not this thy **f.**, thy confidence,	3374
Job	4:14	**F.** came upon me, and trembling,	6343
Job	6:14	but he forsaketh the **f.** of the	3374
Job	9:34	and let not his **f.** terrify me:	367
Job	9:35	Then would I speak, and not **f.** him;	3372
Job	11:15	shalt be stedfast, and shalt not **f.**:	3372
Job	15:4	thou castest off **f.**, and restrainest	3374
Job	21:9	Their houses are safe from **f.**,	6343
Job	22:4	Will he reprove thee for **f.** of thee?	3374
Job	22:10	and sudden **f.** troubleth thee;	6343
Job	25:2	Dominion and **f.** are with him	6343
Job	28:28	the **f.** of the Lord, that is wisdom;	3374
Job	31:34	Did I **f.** a great multitude, or	6206
Job	37:24	Men do therefore **f.** him: he	3372
Job	39:16	her labour is in vain without **f.**:	6343
Job	39:22	He mocketh at **f.**, and is not	6343
Job	41:33	his like, who is made without **f.**	2844
Ps	2:11	Serve the Lord with **f.**, and rejoice	3374
Ps	5:7	and in thy **f.** will I worship toward	3374
Ps	9:20	Put them in **f.**, O Lord: that the	4172
Ps	14:5	There were they in great **f.**: for	6342
Ps	15:4	honoureth them that **f.** the Lord,	3373
Ps	19:9	The **f.** of the Lord is clean,	3374
Ps	22:23	Ye that **f.** the Lord, praise him:	3373
Ps	22:23	and **f.** him, all ye the seed of	1481
Ps	22:25	my vows before them that **f.** him	3373
Ps	23:4	I will **f.** no evil: for thou art with	3372
Ps	25:14	the Lord is with them that **f.** him;	3373
Ps	27:1	whom shall I **f.**? the Lord is the	3372
Ps	27:3	my heart shall not **f.**: though war	3372
Ps	31:11	and a **f.** to mine acquaintance;	6343
Ps	31:13	**f.** was on every side: while they	4032
Ps	31:19	hast laid up for them that **f.** thee;	3373
Ps	33:8	Let all the earth **f.** the Lord:	3372
Ps	33:18	the Lord is upon them that **f.** him;	3373
Ps	34:7	round about them that **f.** him,	3373
Ps	34:9	O **f.** the Lord, ye his saints;	3372
Ps	34:9	is not want to them that **f.** him	3373
Ps	34:11	I will teach you the **f.** of the Lord	3374
Ps	36:1	is no **f.** of God before his eyes	6343
Ps	40:3	many shall see it, and **f.**, and shall	3372
Ps	46:2	Therefore will not we **f.**, though	3372
Ps	48:6	**F.** took hold upon them there,	7461
Ps	49:5	should I **f.** in the days of evil,	3372
Ps	52:6	The righteous also shall see, and **f.**,	3372
Ps	53:5	There were they in great **f.**,	6343
Ps	53:5	There were...where no **f.** was:	6343
Ps	55:19	therefore they **f.** not God	3372
Ps	56:4	I will not **f.** what flesh can do unto	3372
Ps	60:4	a banner of them that **f.** thee,	3373
Ps	61:5	heritage of those that **f.** thy name	3373
Ps	64:1	I preserve my life from **f.** of the	6343
Ps	64:4	do they shoot at him, and **f.** not	3372
Ps	64:9	all men shall **f.**, and shall declare	3372
Ps	66:16	Come and hear, all ye that **f.** God,	3373
Ps	67:7	the ends of the earth shall **f.** him	3372
Ps	72:5	They shall **f.** thee as long as the	3372
Ps	85:9	salvation is nigh them that **f.** him;	3373
Ps	86:11	unite my heart to **f.** thy name	3372
Ps	90:11	even according to thy **f.**, so is thy	3374
Ps	96:9	**f.** before him, all the earth	2342
Ps	102:15	shall **f.** the name of the Lord,	3372
Ps	103:11	mercy toward them that **f.** him	3373
Ps	103:13	the Lord pitieth them that **f.** him	3373
Ps	103:17	everlasting upon them that **f.** him,	3373
Ps	105:8	for the **f.** of them fell upon them	6343
Ps	111:5	given meat unto them that **f.** him:	3373
Ps	111:10	The **f.** of the Lord is the beginning	3374
Ps	115:11	Ye that **f.** the Lord, trust in the	3373
Ps	115:13	He will bless them that **f.** the Lord,	3373
Ps	118:4	Let them now that **f.** the Lord say,	3373
Ps	118:6	Lord is on my side; I will not **f.**:	3372
Ps	119:38	servant, who is devoted to thy **f.**	3374
Ps	119:39	away my reproach which I **f.**:	3025
Ps	119:63	companion of all them that **f.** thee,	3372
Ps	119:74	They that **f.** thee will be glad	3373
Ps	119:79	those that **f.** thee turn unto me,	3373
Ps	119:120	My flesh trembleth for **f.** of thee;	6343
Ps	135:20	ye that **f.** the Lord, bless the Lord	3373
Ps	145:19	the desire of them that **f.** him:	3373
Ps	147:11	taketh pleasure in them that **f.** him,	3373
Pr	1:7	The **f.** of the Lord is the beginning	3374
Pr	1:26	will mock when your **f.** cometh;	6343
Pr	1:27	When your **f.** cometh as desolation,	6343
Pr	1:29	did not choose the **f.** of the Lord:	3374
Pr	1:33	and shall be quiet from **f.** of evil	6343
Pr	2:5	thou understand the **f.** of the Lord,	3374
Pr	3:7	**f.** the Lord, and depart from evil	3372
Pr	3:25	Be not afraid of sudden **f.**,	6343
Pr	8:13	The **f.** of the Lord is to hate evil:	3374
Pr	9:10	The **f.** of the Lord is the beginning	3374
Pr	10:24	The **f.** of the wicked, it shall come	4034
Pr	10:27	**f.** of the Lord prolongeth days:	3374
Pr	14:26	In the **f.** of the Lord is strong	3374
Pr	14:27	**f.** of the Lord is a fountain of life,	3374
Pr	15:16	Better is little with the **f.** of the	3374
Pr	15:33	The **f.** of the Lord is the instruction	3374
Pr	16:6	by the **f.** of the Lord men depart	3374
Pr	19:23	The **f.** of the Lord tendeth to life:	3374
Pr	20:2	The **f.** of the king is as the roaring	367
Pr	22:4	humility and the **f.** of the Lord	3374
Pr	23:17	be thou in the **f.** of the Lord	3374
Pr	24:21	**f.** thou the Lord and the king:	3372
Pr	29:25	The **f.** of man bringeth a snare:	2731
Ec	3:14	God doeth it, that men should **f.**	3372
Ec	5:7	divers vanities: but **f.** thou God	3372
Ec	8:12	shall be well with them that **f.** God,	3373
Ec	8:12	with them...which **f.** before him:	3372
Ec	12:13	matter: **F.** God, and keep his	3372
Ca	3:8	because of **f.** in the night	6343
Isa	2:10	in the dust, for **f.** of the Lord,	6343
Isa	2:19	of the earth, for **f.** of the Lord,	6343
Isa	2:21	ragged rocks, for **f.** of the Lord,	6343
Isa	7:4	Take heed, and be quiet; **f.** not,	3372
Isa	7:25	thither the **f.** of briers and thorns:	3374
Isa	8:12	neither **f.** ye...nor be afraid	3372
Isa	8:12	neither...their **f.**, nor be afraid	4172
Isa	8:13	let him be your **f.**, and let him be	4172
Isa	11:2	knowledge and of the **f.** of the	3374
Isa	11:3	understanding in the **f.** of the	3374
Isa	14:3	from thy sorrow and from thy **f.**,	7267
Isa	19:16	and **f.** because of the shaking of	6342
Isa	21:4	pleasure hath he turned into **f.**	2731
Isa	24:17	**F.**, and the pit, and the snare,	6343
Isa	24:18	who fleeth from the noise of the **f.**	6343
Isa	25:3	the terrible nations shall **f.** thee	3372
Isa	29:13	their **f.** toward me is taught by	3374
Isa	29:23	and shall **f.** the God of Israel	6206
Isa	31:9	pass over to his strong hold for **f.**,	4032
Isa	33:6	the **f.** of the Lord is his treasure	3374
Isa	35:4	Be strong, **f.** not: behold, your	3372
Isa	41:10	**F.** thou not; for I am with thee:	3372
Isa	41:13	thee, **F.** not; I will help thee	3372
Isa	41:14	**F.** not, thou worm Jacob, and ye	3372
Isa	43:1	**F.** not: for I have redeemed thee,	3372
Isa	43:5	**F.** not: for I am with thee: I will	3372
Isa	44:2	**F.** not, O Jacob, my servant;	3372
Isa	44:8	**F.** ye not, neither be afraid: have	6342
Isa	44:11	yet they shall **f.**, and they shall be	6342
Isa	51:7	**f.** ye not the reproach of men,	3372
Isa	54:4	**F.** not; for thou shalt not be	3372
Isa	54:14	oppression; for thou shalt not **f.**:	3372
Isa	59:19	shall they **f.** the name of the Lord	3372
Isa	60:5	and thine heart shall **f.**, and be	6342
Isa	63:17	hardened our heart from thy **f.**?	3374
Jer	2:19	that my **f.** is not in thee,	6345
Jer	5:22	**F.** ye not me? saith the Lord:	3372
Jer	5:24	Let us now **f.** the Lord our God,	3372
Jer	6:25	enemy, and **f.** is on every side	4032
Jer	10:7	Who would not **f.** thee, O King	3372
Jer	20:10	of many, **f.** on every side	4032
Jer	23:4	and they shall **f.** no more, nor be	3372
Jer	26:19	did he not **f.** the Lord, and	3373
Jer	30:5	a voice of trembling, of **f.**, and	6343
Jer	30:10	**f.** thou not, O my servant Jacob,	3372
Jer	32:39	that they may **f.** me for ever,	3372
Jer	32:40	I will put my **f.** in their hearts,	3374
Jer	33:9	and they shall **f.** and tremble	6342
Jer	35:11	for **f.** of the army of the Chaldeans,	6440
Jer	35:11	for **f.** of the army of the Syrians:	6440
Jer	37:11	for **f.** of Pharaoh's army,	6440
Jer	40:9	**F.** not to serve the Chaldeans:	3372
Jer	41:9	for **f.** of Baasha king of Israel:	6440

Jer 46:5 f. was round about, saith the 4032
Jer 46:27 f. not thou, O my servant Jacob, 3372
Jer 46:28 F. thou not, O Jacob my servant 3372
Jer 48:43 F., and the pit, and the snare, 6343
Jer 48:44 He that fleeth from the f. shall fall 6343
Jer 49:5 I will bring a f. upon thee, saith 6343
Jer 49:24 to flee, and f. hath seized on her: 7374
Jer 49:29 unto them, F. is on every side. 4032
Jer 50:16 for f. of the oppressing sword they 6440
Jer 51:46 lest your heart faint, and ye f. for 3372
La 3:47 F. and a snare is come upon us, 6343
La 3:57 upon thee: thou saidst, F. not. 3372
Eze 3:9 f. them not, neither be dismayed 3372
Eze 30:13 will put a f. in the land of Egypt. 3374
Da 1:10 I f. my lord the king, who hath 3373
Da 6:26 and f. before the God of Daniel: 1763
Da 10:12 Then said he unto me, F. not, 3372
Da 10:19 O man greatly beloved, f. not: 3372
Ho 3:5 shall f. the Lord and his goodness 6342
Ho 10:5 inhabitants of Samaria shall f. 1481
Joe 2:21 F. not, O land; be glad and 3372
Am 3:8 lion hath roared, who will not f.? 3372
Jon 1:9 I f. the Lord, the God of heaven, 3373
Mic 7:17 God, and shall f. because of thee. 3372
Zep 3:7 I said, Surely thou wilt f. me, 3372
Zep 3:16 be said to Jerusalem, F. thou not: 3372
Hag 1:12 the people did f. before the Lord. 3372
Hag 2:5 remaineth among you: f. ye not. 3372
Zec 8:13 f. not, but let your hands be strong. 3372
Zec 8:15 the house of Judah: f. ye not. 3372
Zec 9:5 Ashkelon shall see it, and f.; Gaza 3372
Mal 1:6 if I be a master, where is my f.? 4172
Mal 2:5 the f. wherewith he feared me, 4172
Mal 3:5 and f. not me, saith the Lord 3372
Mal 4:2 But unto you that f. my name 3373
Mt 1:20 f. not to take unto thee Mary 5399
Mt 10:26 **F. them not therefore: for there is** 5399
Mt 10:28 **f. not them which kill the body,** 5399
Mt 10:28 **f. him which is able to destroy** 5399
Mt 10:31 **F. ye not therefore, ye are of** 5399
Mt 14:26 a spirit; and they cried out for 5401
Mt 21:26 we f. the people; for all hold John 5399
Mt 28:4 for f. of him the keepers did shake, 5401
Mt 28:5 F. not ye: for I know that ye seek 5399
Mt 28:8 sepulchre with f. and great joy; 5401
Lu 1:12 was troubled, and f. fell upon him. 5401
Lu 1:13 F. not, Zacharias: for thy prayer 5399
Lu 1:30 F. not, Mary: for thou hast found 5399
Lu 1:50 his mercy is on them that f. him 5399
Lu 1:65 f. came on all that dwelt round 5401
Lu 1:74 enemies might serve him without f., 870
Lu 2:10 F. not: for, behold, I bring you 5399
Lu 5:10 And Jesus said unto Simon, **F. not;** 5399
Lu 5:26 were filled with f., saying, We have 5401
Lu 7:16 came a f. on all: and they glorified 5401
Lu 8:37 for they were taken with great f.: 5401
Lu 8:50 **F. not: believe only, and she shall** 5399
Lu 12:5 **whom ye shall f.: F. him, which** 5399
Lu 12:5 **yea, I say unto you, F. him** 5399
Lu 12:7 **F. not therefore: ye are of more** 5399
Lu 12:32 **F. not, little flock; for it is your** 5399
Lu 18:4 **I f. not God, nor regard man;** 5399
Lu 21:26 **Men's hearts failing them for f.,** 5401
Lu 23:40 Dost not thou f. God, seeing thou 5399
Joh 7:13 openly of him for f. of the Jews. 5401
Joh 12:15 F. not, daughter of Sion: behold, 5399
Joh 19:38 but secretly for f. of the Jews, 5401
Joh 20:19 assembled for f. of the Jews, came 5401
Ac 2:43 f. came upon every soul: and many 5401
Ac 5:5 great f. came on all them that heard 5401
Ac 5:11 great f. came upon all the church, 5401
Ac 9:31 and walking in the f. of the Lord, 5401
Ac 13:16 and ye that f. God, give audience 5399
Ac 19:17 f. fell on them all, and the name 5401
Ac 27:24 F. not, Paul; thou must be brought 5399
Ro 3:18 There is no f. of God before their 5401
Ro 8:15 the spirit of bondage again to f.; 5401
Ro 11:20 faith. Be not highminded, but f.: 5399
Ro 13:7 f. to whom f.; honour to whom 5401
1Co 2:3 and in f., and in much trembling. 5401
1Co 16:10 he may be with you without f.: 870
2Co 7:1 perfecting holiness in the f. of God. 5401
2Co 7:11 what indignation, yea, what f., yea, 5401
2Co 7:15 with f. and trembling ye received 5401
2Co 11:3 But I f., lest by any means, as the 5399
2Co 12:20 For I f., lest, when I come, I shall 5399
Eph 5:21 one to another in the f. of God. 5401
Eph 6:5 with f. and trembling, in singleness 5401
Php 1:14 bold to speak the word without f.. 870
Php 2:12 salvation with f. and trembling. 5401
1Ti 5:20 all, that others also may f. 5401,2192
2Ti 1:7 hath not given us the spirit of f.; 1167
Heb 2:15 who through f. of death were all 5401
Heb 4:1 Let us therefore f., lest, a promise 5399
Heb 11:7 moved with f., prepared an ark 2125
Heb 12:21 I exceedingly f. and quake:) 1630,1510
Heb 12:28 with reverence and godly f.: 2124
Heb 13:6 I will not f. what man shall do unto 5399
1Pe 1:17 time of your sojourning here in f.: 5401
1Pe 2:17 F. God. Honour the king. 5399
1Pe 2:18 subject to your masters with all f.; 5401
1Pe 3:2 chaste conversation coupled with f. 5401
1Pe 3:15 is in you with meekness and f.: 5401
1Jo 4:18 There is no f. in love; but perfect 5401
1Jo 4:18 love casteth out f.: because f. hath 5401
Jude 12 feeding themselves without f.: 870
Jude 23 others save with f., pulling them 5401
Re 1:17 saying unto me, **F. not; I am the** 5399
Re 2:10 **F. none of those things which** 5399
Re 11:11 great f. fell upon them which saw 5401
Re 11:18 saints, and them that f. thy name, 5399
Re 14:7 F. God, and give glory to him; 5399
Re 15:4 Who shall not f. thee, O Lord, 5399
Re 18:10, 15 afar off for the f. of her torment, 5401
Re 19:5 that f. him, both small and great. 5399

FEARED

Ge 19:30 for he f. to dwell in Zoar: 3372
Ge 26:7 for he f. to say, She is my wife; 3372
Ex 1:17 the midwives f. God, and did not as 3372
Ex 1:21 the midwives f. God, that he made 3372
Ex 2:14 And Moses f., and said, Surely this 3372
Ex 9:20 He that f. the word of the Lord 3373
Ex 14:31 people f. the Lord, and believed 3372
De 25:18 and he f. not God. 3373
De 32:17 up, whom your fathers f. not. 8175
De 32:27 that I f. the wrath of the enemy, 1481
Jos 4:14 sight of all Israel; and they f. him, 3372
Jos 4:14 they f. Moses, all the days of his life. 3372
Jos 10:2 they f. greatly, because Gibeon was 3372
Jg 6:27 because he f. his father's household, 3372
Jg 8:20 he f., because he was yet a youth. 3372
1Sa 3:15 Samuel f. to shew Eli the vision. 3372
1Sa 12:18 all the people greatly f. the Lord 3372
1Sa 14:26 mouth: for the people f. the oath. 3372
1Sa 15:24 because I f. the people, and obeyed 3372
2Sa 3:11 a word again, because he f. him. 3372
2Sa 10:19 the Syrians f. to help the children 3372
2Sa 12:18 And the servants of David f. to tell 3372
1Ki 1:50 Adonijah f. because of Solomon, 3372
1Ki 3:28 they f. the king: for they saw that 3372
1Ki 18:3 Obadiah f. the Lord greatly: 3373
2Ki 17:7 and had f. other gods, 3372
2Ki 17:25 they f. not the Lord: therefore the 3372
2Ki 17:32 they f. the Lord, and made unto 3373
2Ki 17:33 f. the Lord, and served their own 3373
2Ki 17:41 nations f. the Lord, and served 3373
1Ch 16:25 he also is to be f. above all gods. 3372
2Ch 20:3 Jehoshaphat f., and set himself to 3372
Ne 7:2 man, and f. God above many. 3372
Job 1:1 and one that f. God, and eschewed 3373
Job 3:25 thing which I greatly f. is come 6342
Ps 76:7 Thou, even thou, art to be f.: 3372
Ps 76:8 the earth f., and was still, 3372
Ps 76:11 unto him that ought to be f.. 4172
Ps 78:53 them on safely so that they f. not: 6342
Ps 89:7 God is greatly to be f. in the 6206
Ps 96:4 he is to be f. above all gods. 3372
Ps 130:4 with thee, that thou mayest be f. 3372
Isa 41:5 The isles saw it, and f.; the ends of 3372
Isa 51:13 and hast f. continually every day 6342
Isa 57:11 whom hast thou been afraid or f., 3372
Jer 3:8 her treacherous sister Judah f. not, 3372
Jer 42:16 sword, which ye f., shall overtake 3373
Jer 44:10 they f., nor walked in my law, 3372
Eze 11:8 Ye have f. the sword; and I will 3372
Da 5:19 languages, trembled and f. before 1763
Ho 10:3 because we f. not the Lord; what 3372
Jon 1:16 the men f. the Lord exceedingly, 3372
Mal 2:5 fear wherewith he f. me, and was 3372
Mal 3:16 they that f. the Lord spake often 3372
Mal 3:16 before him for them that f. the Lord, 3372
Mt 14:5 he f. the multitude, because they 5399
Mt 21:46 they f. the multitude, because they 5399
Mt 27:54 f. greatly, saying, Truly this was 5399
Mk 4:41 they f. exceedingly, and said 5399, 5401
Mk 6:20 For Herod f. John, knowing that 5399
Mk 11:18 they f. him, because all the people 5399
Mk 11:32 Of men; they f. the people: 5399
Mk 12:12 lay hold on him, but f. the people: 5399
Lu 9:34 f. as they entered into the cloud. 5399
Lu 9:45 they f. to ask him of that saying. 5399
Lu 18:2 **judge, which f. not God, neither** 5399
Lu 19:21 **For I f. thee, because thou art an** 5399
Lu 20:19 and they f. the people: for they 5399
Lu 22:2 kill him; for they f. the people. 5399
Joh 9:22 because they f. the Jews: for the 5399
Ac 5:26 for they f. the people, lest they 5399
Ac 10:2 one that f. God with all his house, 5399
Ac 16:38 they f., when they heard that they 5399
Heb 5:7 and was heard in that he f.; 2124

FEAREST

Ge 22:12 now I know that thou f. God, 3373
Isa 57:11 even of old, and thou f. me not? 3372
Jer 22:25 hand of them whose face thou f., 1481

FEARETH

1Ki 1:51 Behold, Adonijah f. king Solomon: 3372
Job 1:8 an upright man, one that f. God, 3373
Job 2:3 an upright man, one that f. God, 3373
Ps 25:12 What man is he that f. the Lord? 3373
Ps 112:1 Blessed is the man that f. the 3372
Ps 128:2 is every one that f. the Lord; 3373
Ps 128:4 shall the man be blessed that f. the 3373
Pr 13:13 but he that f. the commandment 3373
Pr 14:2 in his uprightness f. the Lord: 3373
Pr 14:16 A wise man f., and departeth from 3373
Pr 28:14 Happy is the man that f. alway: 6342
Pr 31:30 but a woman that f. the Lord, 3373
Ec 7:18 he that f. God shall come forth 3373
Ec 8:13 because he f. not before God. 3373
Ec 9:2 as he that f. an oath. 3373
Isa 50:10 Who is among you that f. the Lord, 3373
Ac 10:22 a just man, and one that f. God, 5399
Ac 10:35 But in every nation he that f. him, 5399
Ac 13:26 whosoever among you f. God, 5399
1Jo 4:18 He that f. is not made perfect in 5399

FEARFUL

Ex 15:11 f. in praises, doing wonders? 3372
De 20:8 What man is there that is f. and 3373
De 28:58 fear this glorious and f. name, 3372
Jg 7:3 Whosoever is f. and afraid, let 3373
Isa 35:4 Say to them that are of a f. heart, 4116
Mt 8:26 **Why are ye f., O ye of little faith?** 1169
Mk 4:40 said unto them, **Why are ye so f.?** 1169
Lu 21:11 **f. sights and great signs shall** 5400
Heb 10:27 certain f. looking for of judgment 5398
Heb 10:31 It is a f. thing to fall into the hands 5398
Re 21:8 the f., and unbelieving, and the 1169

FEARFULLY

Ps 139:14 I am f. and wonderfully made: 3372

FEARFULNESS

Ps 55:5 F. and trembling are come upon 3374
Isa 21:4 heart panted, f. affrighted me: 6427
Isa 33:14 f. hath surprised the hypocrites. 7461

FEARING

Jos 22:25 children cease from f. the Lord. 3372
Mk 5:33 But the woman f. and trembling, 5399
Ac 23:10 the chief captain, f. lest Paul 2125
Ac 27:17 and, f. lest they should fall into 5399
Ac 27:29 f. lest we should have fallen upon 5399
Ga 2:12 himself, f. them which were of the 5399
Col 3:22 but in singleness of heart, f. God: 5399
Heb 11:27 not f. the wrath of the king: 5399

FEARS

Ps 34:4 and delivered me from all my f. 4035
Ec 12:5 and f. shall be in the way, 2849
Isa 66:4 and will bring their f. upon them; 4035
2Co 7:5 were fightings, within were f. 5401

FEAST See also FEASTED; FEASTING; FEASTS.

Ge 19:3 he made them a f., and did bake 4960
Ge 21:8 Abraham made a great f. the same 4960
Ge 26:30 he made them a f., and they did eat 4960
Ge 29:22 men of the place, and made a f. 4960
Ge 40:20 he made a f. unto all his servants: 4960
Ex 5:1 that they may hold a f. unto me. 2287

Ex 10:9 we must hold a f. unto the Lord........ 2282
Ex 12:14 ye shall keep it a f. to the Lord........ 2282
Ex 12:14 shall keep it a f. by an ordinance........ 2287
Ex 12:17 observe the f. of unleavened bread;..........
Ex 13:6 in the seventh day shall be a f. to...... 2282
Ex 23:14 Three times thou shalt keep a f......... 2287
Ex 23:15 keep the f. of unleavened bread:........ 2282
Ex 23:16 And the f. of harvest, the firstfruits.... 2282
Ex 23:16 and the f. of ingathering, which is...... 2282
Ex 32:5 To morrow is a f. to the Lord.......... 2282
Ex 34:18 The f. of unleavened bread shalt........ 2282
Ex 34:22 thou shalt observe the f. of weeks, ... 2282
Ex 34:22 f. of ingathering at the year's end....... 2282
Ex 34:25 sacrifice of the f. of the passover........ 2282
Le 23:6 the f. of unleavened bread unto the 2282
Le 23:34 the f. of tabernacles for seven days.... 2282
Le 23:39 ye shall keep a f. unto the Lord........ 2282
Le 23:41 ye shall keep it a f. unto the Lord........ 2282
Nu 28:17 fifteenth day of this month is the f.:.... 2282
Nu 29:12 ye shall keep a f. unto the Lord........ 2282
De 16:10 thou shalt keep the f. of weeks 2282
De 16:13 shalt observe the f. of tabernacles...... 2282
De 16:14 And thou shalt rejoice in thy f., ... 2282
De 16:15 days shalt thou keep a solemn f......... 2287
De 16:16 in the f. of unleavened bread, and 2282
De 16:16 in the f. of weeks, and in the f. of..... 2282
De 31:10 of release, in the f. of tabernacles, ... 2282
Jg 14:10 Samson made there a f.; for so 4960
Jg 14:12 within the seven days of the f., ... 4960
Jg 14:17 seven days, while their f. lasted:........ 4960
Jg 21:19 Behold, there is a f. of the Lord........ 2282
1Sa 25:36 behold he held a f. in his house, ... 4960
1Sa 25:36 like the f. of a king; and Nabal's 4960
2Sa 3:20 the men that were with him a f.. 4960
1Ki 3:15 and made a f. to all his servants. 4960
1Ki 8:2 at the f. in the month Ethanim, ... 2282
1Ki 8:65 at that time Solomon held a f., ... 2282
1Ki 12:32 Jeroboam ordained a f. in the 2282
1Ki 12:32 like unto the f. that is in Judah, ... 2282
1Ki 12:33 a f. unto the children of Israel; 2282
2Ch 5:3 themselves unto the king in the f....... 2282
2Ch 7:8 Solomon kept the f. seven days, ... 2282
2Ch 7:9 seven days, and the f. seven days...... 2282
2Ch 8:13 even in the f. of unleavened bread,...... 2282
2Ch 8:13 and in the f. of weeks,...................... 2282
2Ch 8:13 and in the f. of tabernacles. 2282
2Ch 30:13 to keep the f. of unleavened bread..... 2282
2Ch 30:21 kept the f. of unleavened bread 2282
2Ch 30:22 eat throughout the f. seven days,....... 4150
2Ch 35:17 kept...the f. of unleavened bread........ 2282
Ezr 3:4 They kept also the f. of tabernacles,... 2282
Ezr 6:22 kept the f. of unleavened bread 2282
Ne 8:14 should dwell in booths in the f. of 2282
Ne 8:18 And they kept the f. seven days; 2282
Es 1:3 he made a f. unto all his princes 4960
Es 1:5 king made a f. unto all the people 4960
Es 1:9 Vashti the queen made a f. for the..... 4960
Es 2:18 Then the king made a great f. unto 4960
Es 2:18 and his servants, even Esther's f.; 4960
Es 8:17 and gladness, a f. and a good day....... 4960
Ps 81:3 appointed, on our solemn f. fay.......... 2282
Pr 15:15 a merry heart hath a continual f......... 4960
Ec 10:19 A f. is made for laughter, and........... 3899
Isa 25:6 unto all people a f. of fat things, ... 4960
Isa 25:6 a f. of wines on the lees, ... 4960
La 2:7 as in the day of a solemn f.. 4150
Eze 45:21 the passover, a f. of seven days; 2282
Eze 45:23 seven days of the f. he shall prepare .. 2282
Eze 45:25 shall he do the like in the f. of the 2282
Da 5:1 the king made a great f. to a............ 3900
Ho 2:11 her f. days, her new moons, and 2282
Ho 9:5 in the day of the f. of the Lord? 2282
Ho 12:9 as in the days of the solemn f.. 4150
Am 5:21 I hate, I despise your f. days, ... 2282
Zec 14:16 and to keep the f. of tabernacles........ 2282
Zec 14:18, 19 that come not up to keep the f...... 2282
Mt 26:2 **two days is the f. of the passover,** ....
Mt 26:5 But they said, Not on the f. day, ... *1859*
Mt 26:17 day of the f. of unleavened bread............
Mt 27:15 at that f. the governor was wont........ *1859*
Mk 14:1 two days was the f. of the passover, ...
Mk 14:2 But they said, Not on the f. day, ... *1859*
Mk 15:6 Now at that f. he released unto........ *1859*
Lu 2:41 every year at the f. of the passover. .. *1859*
Lu 2:42 Jerusalem after the custom of the f..... *1859*
Lu 5:29 Levi made him a great f. in his.......... *1408*
Lu 14:13 **when thou makest a f., call the**..... *1408*
Lu 22:1 the f. of unleavened bread drew......... *1859*
Lu 23:17 release one unto them at the f.. .... *1859*
Joh 2:8 **bear unto the governor of the f.**...... *755*
Joh 2:9 When the ruler of the f. had tasted...... *755*
Joh 2:9 the governor of the f. called the.......... *755*
Joh 2:23 at the passover, in the f. day, ... *1859*
Joh 4:45 that he did at Jerusalem at the f.: *1859*
Joh 4:45 for they also went unto the f............. *1859*
Joh 5:1 After this there was a f. of the Jews;.. *1859*
Joh 6:4 a f. of the Jews, was night................ *1859*
Joh 7:2 the Jews' f. of tabernacles was at....... *1859*
Joh 7:8 **Go ye up unto this f.;** *1859*
Joh 7:8 **I go not up yet unto this f.;** *1859*
Joh 7:10 then went he also up unto the f., ... *1859*
Joh 7:11 Then the Jews sought him at the f., ... *1859*
Joh 7:14 Now about the midst of the f. Jesus ... *1859*
Joh 7:37 last day, that great day of the f., ... *1859*
Joh 10:22 Jerusalem the f. of the dedication, ... *1456*
Joh 11:56 that he will not come to the f.? *1859*
Joh 12:12 people that were come to the f.,......... *1859*
Joh 12:20 that came up to worship at the f.: *1859*
Joh 13:1 Now before the f. of the passover,..... *1859*
Joh 13:29 we have need of against the f.;.......... *1859*
Ac 18:21 I must by all means keep this f.......... *1859*
1Co 5:8 Therefore let us keep the f.,............ *1858*
1Co 10:27 them that believe not bid you to a f.,.........
2Pe 2:13 deceivings while they f. with you; *4910*
Jude 12 of charity, when they f. with you, ... *4910*

FEAST-DAY See FEAST and DAY.

FEASTED
Job 1:4 his sons went and f. in their 6213,4960

FEASTING
Es 9:17,18 and made it a day of f. and.............. 4960
Es 9:19 Adar a day of gladness and f., ... 4960
Es 9:22 they should make them days of f........ 4960
Job 1:5 when the days of their f. were 4960
Ec 7:2 than to go to the house of f.: 4960
Jer 16:8 not also go into the house of f., ... 4960

FEASTS
Le 23:2 Concerning the f. of the Lord,........... 4150
Le 23:2 convocations, even these are my f..... 4150
Le 23:4 These are the f. of the Lord, even..... 4150
Le 23:37 These are the f. of the Lord, which.... 4150
Le 23:44 of Israel the f. of the Lord............. 4150
Nu 15:3 in your solemn f., to make a sweet 4150
Nu 29:39 do unto the Lord in your set f., ... 4150
1Ch 23:31 and on the set f., by number,............ 4150
2Ch 2:4 and on the solemn f. of the Lord 4150
2Ch 8:13 new moons, and on the solemn f........ 4150
2Ch 31:3 the new moons, and for the set f., ... 4150
Ezr 3:5 and of all the set f. of the Lord 4150
Ne 10:33 the set f., and for the holy things,...... 4150
Ps 35:16 With hypocritical mockers in f.,.......... 4580
Isa 1:14 your appointed f. my soul hateth: ....
Isa 5:12 and pipe and wine, are in their f.: 4960
Jer 51:39 In their heat I will make their f.,......... 4960
La 1:4 none come to the solemn f.: 4150
La 2:6 caused the solemn f. and sabbaths...... 4150
Eze 36:38 of Jerusalem in her solemn f.; 4150
Eze 45:17 to give drink...offerings, in the f., ... 2282
Eze 46:9 before the Lord in the solemn f., ... 4150
Eze 46:11 And in the f. and in the solemnities 2282
Ho 2:11 sabbaths, and all her solemn f.. 4150
Am 8:10 I will turn your f. into mourning,........ 2282
Na 1:15 keep thy solemn f., perform thy 2282
Zec 8:19 joy and gladness, and cheerful f.; 4150
Mal 2:3 even the dung of your solemn f.; 2282
Mt 23:6 **love the uppermost rooms at f.,**..... *1173*
Mk 12:39 **and the uppermost rooms at f.:** *1173*
Lu 20:46 **and the chief rooms at f.;** *1173*
Jude 12 are spots in your f. of charity..................

FEATHERED
Ps 78:27 and f. fowls like as the sand.............. 3671
Eze 39:17 Speak unto every f. fowl, and to........ 3671

FEATHERS
Le 1:16 pluck away his crop with his f., ... 5133
Job 39:13 wings and f. unto the ostrich? 2624
Ps 68:13 and her f. with yellow gold. 84
Ps 91:4 He shall cover thee with his f.,............ 84
Eze 17:3 great wings, long winged, full of f., ... 5133
Eze 17:7 with great wings and many f.: 5133
Da 4:33 hairs were grown like eagles' f., ...

FED
Ge 30:36 Jacob f. the rest of Laban's flocks 7462
Ge 36:24 as he f. the asses of Zibeon his 7462
Ge 41:2 fatfleshed; and they f. in a meadow. ... 7462
Ge 41:18 favoured; and they f. in a meadow:..... 7462
Ge 47:17 and he f. them with bread for all........ 5095
Ge 48:15 the God which f. me all my life.......... 7462
Ex 16:32 I have f. you in the wilderness, ... 398
De 8:3 to hunger, and f. thee with manna, ... 398
De 8:16 Who f. thee in the wilderness with....... 398
2Sa 20:3 put them in ward, and f. them,.......... 3557
1Ki 18:4 and f. them with bread and water.)........ 3557
1Ki 18:13 and f. them with bread and water? 3557
1Ch 27:29 over the herds that f. in Sharon......... 7462
Ps 37:3 and verily thou shalt be f.................. 7462
Ps 78:72 f. them according to the integrity....... 7462
Ps 81:16 He should have f. them also with......... 398
Isa 1:11 of rams, and the fat of f. beasts;........ 4806
Jer 5:7 when I had f. them to the full,.................
Jer 5:8 They were as f. horses in the 2109
Eze 16:19 and honey, wherewith I f. thee, ... 398
Eze 34:3 ye kill them that are f.: but ye 1277
Eze 34:8 but the shepherds f. themselves, ... 7462
Eze 34:8 and f. not my flock;........................... 7462
Da 4:12 and all flesh was f. of it.................... 2110
Da 5:21 they f. him with grass like oxen,........ 2939
Zec 11:7 called Bands; and I f. the flock. 7462
Mt 25:37 **thee an hungered, and f. thee?** *5142*
Mk 5:14 they that f. the swine fled, and.......... *1006*
Lu 8:34 they that f. them saw what was......... *1006*
Lu 16:21 **desiring to be f. with the crumbs**... *5526*
1Co 3:2 I have f. you with milk, and not......... *4222*

FEEBLE See also FEEBLEMINDED; FEEBLER.
Ge 30:42 But when the cattle were f., he......... 5848
De 25:18 even all that were f. behind thee,....... 2826
1Sa 2:5 hath many children is waxed f.. 535
2Sa 4:1 his hands were f., and all the 7503
2Ch 28:15 and carried all the f. of them upon...... 3782
Ne 4:2 What do these f. Jews? will they 537
Job 4:4 hast strengthened the f. knees, ... 3766
Ps 38:8 I am f. and sore broken: 6313
Ps 105:37 and there was not one f. person 3782
Pr 30:26 The conies are but a f. folk, ... 3808,6099
Isa 16:14 the remnant shall be very.......... 3808,3524
Isa 35:3 hands, and confirm the f. knees. 3782
Jer 6:24 our hands wax f.: anguish hath 7503
Jer 49:24 Damascus is waxed f., and turneth..... 7503
Jer 50:43 and his hands waxed f.: anguish......... 7503
Eze 7:17 All hands shall be f., and all knees...... 7503
Eze 21:7 and all hands shall be f.,.................... 7503
Zec 12:8 and he that is f. among them at......... 3782
1Co 12:22 which seem to be more f., are............ *772*
Heb 12:12 hang down, and the f. knees. *3886*

FEEBLEMINDED
1Th 5:14 comfort the f., support the weak,........ *3642*

FEEBLENESS
Jer 47:3 to their children for f. of hands;......... 7510

FEEBLER
Ge 30:42 so the f. were Laban's, and the......... 5848

FEED See also FED; FEEDEST; FEEDETH; FEEDING.
Ge 25:30 F. me, I pray thee, with that same 3938
Ge 29:7 ye the sheep, and go and f. them........ 7462
Ge 30:31 I will again f. and keep thy flock: 7462
Ge 37:12 went to f. their father's flock in 7462
Ge 37:13 Do not thy brethren f. the flock in 7462
Ge 37:16 tell me, I pray thee, where they f...... 7462
Ge 46:32 their trade hath been to f. cattle; ....
Ex 22:5 shall f. in another man's field;............. 1197
Ex 34:3 neither let the flocks nor herds f......... 7462
1Sa 17:15 from Saul to f. his father's sheep 7462
2Sa 5:2 Thou shalt f. my people Israel, ... 7462
2Sa 7:7 to f. my people Israel, saying, ... 7462
2Sa 19:33 and I will f. thee with me in.............. 3557
1Ki 17:4 commanded the ravens to f. thee 3557
1Ki 22:27 and f. him with bread of affliction......... 398
1Ch 11:2 Thou shalt f. my people Israel,.......... 7462
1Ch 17:6 I commanded to f. my people,............ 7462
2Ch 18:26 and f. him with bread of affliction.......... 398
Job 24:2 take away flocks, and f. thereof. 7462
Job 24:20 the worm shall f. sweetly on him; ....
Ps 28:9 f. them also, and lift them up............ 7462
Ps 49:14 death shall f. on them; and the 7462
Ps 78:71 brought him to f. Jacob his people, ... 7462
Pr 10:21 The lips of the righteous f. many: 7462

Pr 30:8 **f.** me with food convenient for me:..... 2963
Ca 1:8 **f.** thy kids beside the shepherds'........ 7462
Ca 4:5 twins, which **f.** among the lilies.......... 7462
Ca 6:2 bed of spices, to **f.** in the gardens,..... 7462
Isa 5:17 the lambs **f.** after their manner,.......... 7462
Isa 11:7 And the cow and the bear shall **f.**;...... 7462
Isa 14:30 And the firstborn of the poor shall **f.**,.. 7462
Isa 27:10 there shall the calf **f.**, and there......... 7462
Isa 30:23 shall thy cattle **f.** in large pastures...... 7462
Isa 40:11 shall **f.** his flock like a shepherd:......... 7462
Isa 49:9 They shall **f.** in the ways, and their.... 7462
Isa 49:26 I will **f.** them that oppress thee........... 398
Isa 58:14 **f.** thee with the heritage of Jacob......... 398
Isa 61:5 strangers shall stand and **f.** your........ 7462
Isa 65:25 wolf and the lamb shall **f.** together,..... 7462
Jer 3:15 which shall **f.** you with knowledge...... 7462
Jer 6:3 they shall **f.** every one in his place...... 7462
Jer 9:15 I will **f.** them, even this people,.......... 398
Jer 23:2 the pastors that **f.** my people;........... 7462
Jer 23:4 over them which shall **f.** them:.......... 7462
Jer 23:15 I will **f.** them with wormwood, and....... 398
Jer 50:19 he shall **f.** on Carmel and Bashan,...... 7462
La 4:5 They that did **f.** delicately are............ 398
Eze 34:2 the shepherds of Israel that do **f.**....... 7462
Eze 34:2 not the shepherds **f.** the flocks?......... 7462
Eze 34:3 that are fed; but ye **f.** not the flock.... 7462
Eze 34:10 shall the shepherds **f.** themselves....... 7462
Eze 34:13 and **f.** them upon the mountains of..... 7462
Eze 34:14 I will **f.** them in a good pasture,......... 7462
Eze 34:14 in a fat pasture they shall **f.** upon....... 7462
Eze 34:15 I will **f.** my flock, and I will cause...... 7462
Eze 34:16 I will **f.** them with judgment.............. 7462
Eze 34:23 he shall **f.** them, even my servant...... 7462
Eze 34:23 he shall **f.** them, and he shall be........ 7462
Da 11:26 that **f.** the portion of his meat............ 398
Ho 4:16 the Lord will **f.** them as a lamb......... 7462
Ho 9:2 and the winepress shall not **f.** them,... 7462
Jon 3:7 let them not **f.**, nor drink water:........ 7462
Mic 5:4 and **f.** in the strength of the Lord,...... 7462
Mic 7:14 **F.** thy people with thy rod, the......... 7462
Mic 7:14 let them **f.** in Bashan and Gilead,....... 7462
Zep 2:7 they shall **f.** thereupon: in the.......... 7462
Zep 3:13 for they shall **f.** and lie down,............ 7462
Zec 11:4 **F.** the flock of the slaughter;............. 7462
Zec 11:7 And I will **f.** the flock of slaughter,..... 7462
Zec 11:9 Then said I, I will not **f.** you:........... 7462
Zec 11:16 nor **f.** that that standeth still:.......... 3557
Lu 15:15 **him into his fields to f. swine**...... *1006*
Joh 21:15 He saith unto him, **F. my lambs**...... *1006*
Joh 21:16 He saith unto him, **F. my sheep**...... *4165*
Joh 21:17 Jesus saith unto him, **F. my sheep**... *1006*
Ac 20:28 overseers, to **f.** the church of God,.... *4165*
Ro 12:20 if thine enemy hunger, **f.** him; if........ *5595*
1Co 13:3 bestow all my goods to **f.** the poor,.... *5595*
1Pe 5:2 **F.** the flock of God which is.............. *4165*
Re 7:17 midst of the throne shall **f.** them,....... *4165*
Re 12:6 that they should **f.** her there a........... *5142*

FEEDEST

Ps 80:5 **f.** them with the bread of tears;.......... 398
Ca 1:7 my soul loveth, where thou **f.**,.......... 7462

FEEDETH

Pr 15:14 mouth of fools **f.** on foolishness.......... 7462
Ca 2:16 I am his: he **f.** among the lilies.......... 7462
Ca 6:3 is mine: he **f.** among the lilies........... 7462
Isa 44:20 He **f.** on ashes: a deceived heart....... 7462
Ho 12:1 Ephraim **f.** on wind, and followeth...... 7462
Mt 6:26 **yet your heavenly Father f. them**...*5142*
Lu 12:24 **and God f. them: how much more**..*5142*
1Co 9:7 who **f.** a flock, and eateth not............ *4165*

FEEDING See also FEEDINGPLACE.

Ge 37:2 was **f.** the flock with his brethren;...... 7462
Job 1:14 oxen were plowing, and the asses **f.**.... 7462
Eze 34:10 them to cease from **f.** the flock;.......... 7462
Mt 8:30 them an herd of many swine **f.**,......... *1006*
Mk 5:11 mountains a great herd of swine **f.**..... *1006*
Lu 8:32 many swine **f.** on the mountain:......... *1006*
Lu 17:7 **a servant plowing or f. cattle,**....... *4165*
Jude 12 you, **f.** themselves without fear:......... *4165*

FEEDINGPLACE

Na 2:11 and the **f.** of the young lions,............ 4829

FEEL See also FEELING; FELT.

Ge 27:12 will **f.** me, and I shall seem to him..... 4959
Ge 27:21 I pray thee, that I may **f.** thee,......... 4184
Jg 16:26 Suffer me that I may **f.** the pillars...... 4184
Job 20:20 shall not **f.** quietness in his belly,....... 3045
Ps 58:9 Before your pots can **f.** the thorns,...... 995
Ec 8:5 the commandment shall **f.** no evil....... 3045
Ac 17:27 if haply they might **f.** after him,......... *5584*

FEELING

Eph 4:19 Who being past **f.** have given............. *524*
Heb 4:15 cannot be touched with the **f.** of our... *4834*

FEET

Ge 18:4 wash your **f.**, and rest yourselves...... 7272
Ge 19:2 tarry all night, and wash your **f.**,........ 7272
Ge 24:32 and water to wash his **f.**, and the....... 7272
Ge 24:32 and the men's **f.** that were with him... 7272
Ge 43:24 water, and they washed their **f.**;........ 7272
Ge 49:10 nor a lawgiver from between his **f.**,.... 7272
Ge 49:33 he gathered up his **f.** into the bed,..... 7272
Ex 3:5 put off thy shoes from off thy **f.**,........ 7272
Ex 4:25 of her son, and cast it at his **f.**,......... 7272
Ex 12:11 your shoes on your **f.**, and your......... 7272
Ex 24:10 under his **f.** as it were a paved work.. 7272
Ex 25:26 that are on the four **f.** thereof............ 7272
Ex 30:19 shall wash their hands and their **f.**:........ 7272
Ex 30:21 shall wash their hands and their **f.**,..... 7272
Ex 37:13 that were in the four **f.** thereof........... 7272
Ex 40:31 washed their hands and their **f.**........... 7272
Le 8:24 the great toes of their right **f.**:.......... 7272
Le 11:21 which have legs above their **f.**, to....... 7272
Le 11:23 creeping things, which have four **f.**,.... 7272
Le 11:42 more **f.** among all creeping things....... 7272
Nu 20:19 anything else, go through on my **f.**..... 7272
De 2:28 only I will pass through on my **f.**;....... 7272
De 11:24 the soles of your **f.** shall tread........... 7272
De 28:57 cometh out from between her **f.**,........ 7272
De 33:3 and they sat down at thy **f.**;............... 7272
Jos 3:13 of the **f.** of the priests that bear........ 7272
Jos 3:15 and the **f.** of the priests that bare...... 7272
Jos 4:3 where the priests' **f.** stood firm,......... 7272
Jos 4:9 where the **f.** of the priests which....... 7272
Jos 4:18 soles of the priests' **f.** were lifted....... 7272
Jos 9:5 old shoes and clouted upon their **f.**,.... 7272
Jos 10:24 put your **f.** upon the necks of these.... 7272
Jos 10:24 put their **f.** upon the necks of them.... 7272
Jos 14:9 land whereon thy **f.** have trodden....... 7272
Jg 3:24 he covereth his **f.** in his summer........ 7272
Jg 4:10 with then thousand men at his **f.**:....... 7272
Jg 4:15 chariot, and fled away on his **f.**......... 7272
Jg 4:17 fled away on his **f.** to the tent........... 7272
Jg 5:27 At her **f.** he bowed, he fell, he lay..... 7272
Jg 5:27 at her **f.** he bowed, he fell: where...... 7272
Jg 19:21 they washed their **f.**, and did eat........ 7272
Ru 3:4 uncover his **f.**, and lay thee down;...... 4772
Ru 3:7 came softly, and uncovered his **f.**,....... 4772
Ru 3:8 behold, a woman lay at his **f.**,............ 4772
Ru 3:14 she lay at his **f.** until the morning:...... 4772
1Sa 2:9 He will keep the **f.** of his saints,........ 7272
1Sa 14:13 upon his hands and upon his **f.**,.......... 7272
1Sa 24:3 and Saul went in to cover his **f.**:......... 7272
1Sa 25:24 And fell at his **f.**, and said,................ 7272
1Sa 25:41 to wash the **f.** of the servants of......... 7272
2Sa 3:34 nor thy **f.** put into fetters: as a........... 7272
2Sa 4:4 had a son that was lame of his **f.**....... 7272
2Sa 4:12 cut off their hands and their **f.**,.......... 7272
2Sa 9:3 yet a son, which is lame on his **f.**,....... 7272
2Sa 9:13 and was lame on both his **f.**.............. 7272
2Sa 11:8 to thy house, and wash thy **f.**............ 7272
2Sa 19:24 had neither dressed his **f.**, nor.......... 7272
2Sa 22:10 and darkness was under his **f.**........... 7272
2Sa 22:34 He maketh my **f.** like hind's **f.**:.......... 7272
2Sa 22:37 so that my **f.** did not slip................. 7166
2Sa 22:39 yea, they are fallen under my **f.**......... 7272
1Ki 2:5 in his shoes that were on his **f.**......... 7272
1Ki 5:3 put them under the soles of his **f.**...... 7272
1Ki 14:6 Ahijah heard the sound of her **f.**,........ 7272
1Ki 14:12 when thy **f.** enter into the city,........... 7272
1Ki 15:23 old age he was diseased in his **f.**......... 7272
2Ki 4:27 she caught him by the **f.**: but............ 7272
2Ki 4:37 she went in, and fell at his **f.**,............ 7272
2Ki 6:32 sound of his master's **f.** behind.......... 7272
2Ki 9:35 the skull, and the **f.**, and the palms.... 7272
2Ki 13:21 he revived, and stood up on his **f.**....... 7272
2Ki 19:24 the sole of my **f.** have I dried up....... 6471
2Ki 21:8 Neither will I make the **f.** of Israel..... 7272
1Ch 28:2 David the king stood up upon his **f.**,... 7272
2Ch 3:13 they stood on their **f.**, and their......... 7272
2Ch 16:12 was diseased in his **f.**, until his.......... 7272
Neh 9:21 not old, and their **f.** swelled not......... 7272
Es 8:3 fell down at is **f.**, and besought.......... 7272
Job 12:5 He that is ready to slip with his **f.**........ 7272
Job 13:27 puttest my **f.** also in the stocks,......... 7272
Job 13:27 a print upon the heels of my **f.**........... 7272
Job 18:8 is cast into a net by his own **f.**.......... 7272
Job 18:11 shall drive him to his **f.**.................. 7272
Job 29:15 and **f.** was I to the lame.................. 7272
Job 30:12 they push away my **f.**, and they......... 7272
Job 33:11 He putteth my **f.** in the stocks,........... 7272
Ps 8:6 hast put all things under his **f.**:........... 7272
Ps 18:9 and darkness was under his **f.**............ 7272
Ps 18:33 He maketh my **f.** like hinds' **f.**,.......... 7272
Ps 18:36 under me, that my **f.** did not slip........ 7166
Ps 18:38 they are fallen under my **f.**................ 7272
Ps 22:16 they pierced my hands and my **f.**......... 7272
Ps 25:15 he shall pluck my **f.** out of the net...... 7272
Ps 31:8 thou hast set my **f.** in a large room..... 7272
Ps 40:2 and set my **f.** upon a rock,................ 7272
Ps 47:3 and the nations under our **f.**.............. 7272
Ps 56:13 not thou deliver my **f.** from falling,..... 7272
Ps 58:10 he shall wash his **f.** in the blood......... 6471
Ps 66:9 suffereth not our **f.** to be moved........ 7272
Ps 73:2 for me, my **f.** were almost gone;....... 7272
Ps 74:3 **f.** unto the perpetual desolations;....... 6471
Ps 91:13 dragon shalt thou trample under **f.**....... 6471
Ps 105:18 Whose **f.** they hurt with fetters:........ 7272
Ps 115:7 **f.** have they, but they walk not:......... 7272
Ps 116:8 from tears, and my **f.** from falling....... 7272
Ps 119:59 turned my **f.** unto thy testimonies...... 7272
Ps 119:101 refrained my **f.** from every evil way.... 7272
Ps 119:105 Thy word is a lamp unto my **f.**,.......... 7272
Ps 122:2 Our **f.** shall stand within thy gates,..... 7272
Pr 1:16 their **f.** run to evil, and make haste.... 7272
Pr 4:26 Ponder the path of thy **f.**, and let....... 7272
Pr 5:5 Her **f.** go down to death; her steps.... 7272
Pr 6:13 speaketh with his **f.**, he teacheth........ 7272
Pr 6:18 **f.** that be swift in running to............ 7272
Pr 6:28 coals, and his **f.** not be burned?......... 7272
Pr 7:11 her **f.** abide not in her house:............ 7272
Pr 19:2 he that hasteth with his **f.** sinneth...... 7272
Pr 26:6 the hand of a fool cutteth off the **f.**,.... 7272
Pr 29:5 spreadeth a net for his **f.**.................. 6471
Ca 5:3 I have washed my **f.**; how shall......... 7272
Ca 7:1 How beautiful are thy **f.** with............. 6471
Isa 3:16 making a tinkling with their **f.**:........... 7272
Isa 3:18 tinkling ornaments about their **f.**................
Isa 6:2 with twain he covered his **f.**, and....... 7272
Isa 7:20 the head, and the hair of the **f.**:......... 7272
Isa 14:19 as a carcase trodden under **f.**..................
Isa 23:7 her own **f.** shall carry her afar off....... 7272
Isa 26:6 it down, even the **f.** of the poor,........ 7272
Isa 28:3 Ephraim, shall be trodden under **f.**:.... 7272
Isa 32:20 thither the **f.** of the ox and the ass..... 7272
Isa 37:25 the sole of my **f.** have I dried up....... 6471
Isa 41:3 that he had not gone with his **f.**......... 7272
Isa 49:23 and lick up the dust of thy **f.**;........... 7272
Isa 52:7 the **f.** of him that bringeth good......... 7272
Isa 59:7 Their **f.** run to evil, and they make..... 7272
Isa 60:13 make the place of my **f.** glorious........ 7272
Isa 60:14 down at the soles of thy **f.**;............... 7272
Jer 13:16 your **f.** stumble upon the dark........... 7272
Jer 14:10 they have not refrained their **f.**,......... 7272
Jer 18:22 and hid snares for my **f.**.................. 7272
Jer 38:22 thy **f.** are sunk in the mire, and they.. 7272
La 1:13 he hath spread a net for my **f.**,.......... 7272
La 3:34 under his **f.** all the prisoners............ 7272
Eze 1:7 And their **f.** were straight **f.**;........... 7272
Eze 1:7 and the sole of their **f.** was like......... 7272
Eze 2:1 Son of man, stand upon my **f.**,.......... 7272
Eze 2:2 unto me, and set me upon my **f.**,....... 7272
Eze 3:24 into me, and set me upon my **f.**,........ 7272
Eze 16:25 opened thy **f.** to every one that........ 7272
Eze 24:17 and put on thy shoes upon thy **f.**,....... 7272
Eze 24:23 and your shoes upon your **f.**: ye........ 7272
Eze 25:6 hands, and stamped with the **f.**,......... 7272
Eze 32:2 troubledst the waters with thy **f.**,....... 7272
Eze 34:18 down with your **f.** the residue of......... 7272
Eze 34:18 must foul the residue with your **f.**?...... 7272
Eze 34:19 which ye have trodden with your **f.**;... 7272
Eze 34:19 which ye have fouled with your **f.**........ 7272
Eze 37:10 lived, and stood up upon their **f.**,....... 7272
Eze 43:7 and the place of the soles of my **f.**,.... 7272
Da 2:33 his **f.** part of iron and part of clay...... 7271
Da 2:34 smote the image upon his **f.**.............. 7271
Da 2:41 **f.** and toes, part of potters' clay,........ 7271
Da 2:42 And as the toes of the **f.**.................. 7271
Da 7:4 made stand upon the **f.** as a man,....... 7271
Da 7:7 stamped the residue with the **f.** of...... 7271

Da 7:19 stamped the residue with his f.; 7271
Da 10:6 his arms and his f. like in colour 4772
Na 1:3 the clouds are the dust of his f. 7272
Na 1:15 the f. of him that bringeth good 7272
Hab 3:5 burning coals went forth at his f. 7272
Hab 3:19 he will make my f. like hinds' f., 7272
Zec 14:4 And his f. shall stand in that day 7272
Zec 14:12 while they stand upon their f., 7272
Mal 4:3 ashes under the soles of your f. 7272
Mt 7:6 **they trample them under their f.,** 4228
Mt 10:14 **city, shake off the dust of your f.** 4228
Mt 15:30 and cast them down at Jesus' f.; 4228
Mt 18:8 **than having two hands or two f.** 4228
Mt 18:29 **fellowservant fell down at his f.,** 4228
Mt 28:9 they came and held him by the f., 4228
Mk 5:22 when he saw him, he fell at his f., 4228
Mk 6:11 **dust under your f. for a testimony** 4228
Mk 7:25 and came and fell at his f.: 4228
Mk 9:45 **having two f. to be cast into hell,** 4228
Lu 1:79 guide our f. into the way of peace. 4228
Lu 7:38 stood at his f. behind him weeping, 4228
Lu 7:38 and began to wash his f. with tears, 4228
Lu 7:38 kissed his f., and anointed them 4228
Lu 7:44 **thou gavest me no water for my f.:** 4228
Lu 7:44 **she hath washed my f. with tears,** 4228
Lu 7:45 **hath not ceased to kiss my f.** 4228
Lu 7:46 **hath anointed my f. with ointment.** 4228
Lu 8:35 sitting at the f. of Jesus, clothed, 4228
Lu 8:41 fell down at Jesus' f., and besought 4228
Lu 9:5 **off the very dust from your f. for** 4228
Lu 10:39 which also sat at Jesus's f., and 4228
Lu 15:22 **on his hand, and shoes on his f.:** 4228
Lu 17:16 And fell down on his face at his f., 4228
Lu 24:39 **Behold my hands and my f.,** 4228
Lu 24:40 shewed them his hands and his f. 4228
Joh 11:2 and wiped his f. with her hair, 4228
Joh 11:32 she fell down at his f., saying unto 4228
Joh 12:3 and anointed the f. of Jesus, 4228
Joh 12:3 and wiped his f. with her hair: 4228
Joh 13:5 and began to wash the disciples' f., 4228
Joh 13:6 Lord, dost thou wash my f.? 4228
Joh 13:8 Thou shalt never wash my f. 4228
Joh 13:9 Lord, not my f. only, but also my 4228
Joh 13:10 **needeth not save to wash his f.,** 4228
Joh 13:12 So after he had washed their f., 4228
Joh 13:14 **and Master, have washed your f.;** 4228
Joh 13:14 **ought to wash one another's f.** 4228
Joh 20:12 at the head, and the other at the f., 4228
Ac 3:7 his f. and ancle bones received 939
Ac 4:35 laid them down at the apostles' f.: 4228
Ac 4:37 money, and laid it at the apostles' f. 4228
Ac 5:2 part, and laid it at the apostles' f. 4228
Ac 5:9 the f. of them which have buried 4228
Ac 5:10 fell she down straightway at his f., 4228
Ac 7:33 Put off thy shoes from thy f.: 4228
Ac 7:58 their clothes at a young man's f., 4228
Ac 10:25 met him, and fell down at his f., 4228
Ac 13:25 of his f. I am not worthy to loose. 4228
Ac 13:51 they shook off the dust of their f. 4228
Ac 14:8 impotent in his f., being a cripple 4228
Ac 14:10 loud voice, Stand upright on thy f. 4228
Ac 16:24 and made their f. fast in the stocks. 4228
Ac 21:11 and bound his own hands and f., 4228
Ac 22:3 in this city at the f. of Gamaliel, 4228
Ac 26:16 **But rise, and stand upon thy f.:** 4228
Ro 3:15 Their f. are swift to shed blood: 4228
Ro 10:15 How beautiful are the f. of them 4228
Ro 16:20 bruise Satan under your f. shortly. 4228
1Co 12:21 nor again the head to the f., 4228
1Co 15:25 hath put all enemies under his f. 4228
1Co 15:27 he hath put all things under his f. 4228
Eph 1:22 And hath put all things under his f., 4228
Eph 6:15 your f. shod with the preparation 4228
1Ti 5:10 if she have washed the saints' f., 4228
Heb 2:8 all things in subjection under his f. 4228
Heb 12:13 And make straight paths for your f., 4228
Re 1:15 And his f. like unto fine brass, 4228
Re 1:17 I saw him, I fell at his f. as dead. 4228
Re 2:18 **and his f. are like fine brass;** 4228
Re 3:9 **to come and worship before thy f.,** 4228
Re 10:1 and his f. as pillars of fire: 4228
Re 11:11 and they stood upon their f.; and 4228
Re 12:1 the sun, and the moon under her f., 4228
Re 13:2 and his f. were as the f. of a bear, 4228
Re 19:10 I fell at his f. to worship him. 4228
Re 22:8 before the f. of the angel which 4228

FEIGN See also FEIGNED; FEIGNEST.
2Sa 14:2 thee, f. thyself to be a mourner,
1Ki 14:5 f. herself to be another woman. 5234
Lu 20:20 sent forth spies which would f. 5271

FEIGNED See also UNFEIGNED.
1Sa 21:13 and f. himself mad in their hands,
Ps 17:1 that goeth not out of f. lips. 4820
2Pe 2:3 with f. words make merchandise 4112

FEIGNEDLY
Jer 3:10 me with her whole heart, but f., 8267

FEIGNEST
1Ki 14:6 why f. thou thyself to be another? 5234
Ne 6:8 thou f. them out of thine own heart. 908

FELIX (fe'-lix) See also FELIX'.
Ac 23:24 him safe unto F. the governor. 5344
Ac 23:26 unto the most excellent governor F. 5344
Ac 24:3 and in all places, most noble F., 5344
Ac 24:22 And when F. heard these things, 5344
Ac 24:24 F. came with his wife Drusilla, 5344
Ac 24:25 F. trembled, and answered, Go thy 5344
Ac 24:27 and F., willing to shew the Jews a 5344
Ac 25:14 a certain man left in bonds by F.: 5344

FELIX' (fe'-lix)
Ac 24:27 Porcius Festus came into F. room: 5344

FELL See also BEFELL; FELLED; FELLEST; FELLING.
Ge 4:5 very wroth, and his countenance f. 5307
Ge 14:10 and Gomorrah fled, and f. there; 5307
Ge 15:12 a deep sleep f. upon Abram; and, 5307
Ge 15:12 an horror of great darkness f. upon 5307
Ge 17:3 And Abram f. on his face: and God 5307
Ge 17:17 Then Abraham f. upon his face, 5307
Ge 33:4 and f. on his neck, and kissed him: 5307
Ge 44:14 they f. before him on the ground. 5307
Ge 45:14 he f. upon his brother Benjamin's 5307
Ge 46:29 and he f. on his neck, and wept 5307
Ge 50:1 Joseph f. upon his father's face, 5307
Ge 50:18 his brethren also went and f. down 5307
Ex 32:28 and there f. of the people that day 5307
Le 9:24 they shouted, and f. on their faces. 5307
Le 16:9 goat upon which the Lord's lot f., 5927
Le 16:10 the goat, on which the lot f. to be the 5927
Nu 11:4 that was among them f. a lusting:
Nu 11:9 when the dew f. upon the camp 3381
Nu 11:9 in the night, the manna f. upon it. 3381
Nu 14:5 Moses and Aaron f. on their faces 5307
Nu 16:4 Moses heard it, he f. upon his face: 5307
Nu 16:22 they f. upon their faces, and said, 5307
Nu 16:45 And they f. upon their faces. 5307
Nu 20:6 and they f. upon their faces: and 5307
Nu 22:27 angel of the Lord, she f. down 7257
Nu 22:31 bowed down his head, and f. flat 7812
De 9:18 And I f. down before the Lord, 5307
De 9:25 Thus I f. down before the Lord 5307
De 9:25 forty nights, as I f. down at the first; 5307
Jos 5:14 Joshua f. on his face to the earth, 5307
Jos 6:20 shout, that the wall f. down flat, 5307
Jos 7:6 and f. the earth upon his face 5307
Jos 8:25 so it was, that all that f. that day, 5307
Jos 11:7 suddenly; and they f. upon them. 5307
Jos 16:1 of Joseph, f. from Jordan by 3318
Jos 17:5 there f. ten portions to Manasseh, 5307
Jos 22:20 wrath f. on all the congregation 1961
Jg 4:16 and all the host of Sisera f. upon 5307
Jg 5:27 feet he bowed, he f., he lay down: 5307
Jg 5:27 her feet he bowed, he f.: where he 5307
Jg 5:27 bowed, there he f. down dead. 5307
Jg 7:13 unto a tent, and smote it that it f., 5307
Jg 8:10 f. an hundred and twenty thousand 5307
Jg 12:6 f. at that time of the Ephraimites 5307
Jg 13:20 and f. on their faces to the ground. 5307
Jg 16:30 and the house f. upon the lords, 5307
Jg 19:26 f. down at the door of the man's 5307
Jg 20:44 f. of Benjamin eighteen thousand 5307
Jg 20:46 So that all which f. that day of 5307
Ru 2:10 Then she f. on her face, and bowed 5307
1Sa 4:10 there f. of Israel thirty thousand 5307
1Sa 4:18 he f. from off the seat backward 5307
1Sa 11:7 fear of the Lord f. on the people, 5307
1Sa 14:13 and they f. before Jonathan; and 5307
1Sa 17:49 and he f. upon his face to the earth. 5307
1Sa 17:52 the wounded of the Philistines f. 5307
1Sa 20:41 and f. on his face to the ground, 5307
1Sa 22:18 he f. upon the priests, and slew 6293

1Sa 25:23 and f. before David on her face, 5307
1Sa 25:24 And f. at his feet, and said, 5307
1Sa 28:20 Then Saul f. straightway all along 5307
1Sa 29:3 found no fault in him since he f. 5307
1Sa 30:13 because three days agone I f. sick.
1Sa 31:1 f. down slain in mount Gilboa. 5307
1Sa 31:4 Saul took a sword, and f. upon it. 5307
1Sa 31:5 he f. likewise upon his sword, and 5307
2Sa 1:2 f. to the earth, and did obeisance. 5307
2Sa 2:16 they f. down together: wherefore 5307
2Sa 2:23 and he f. down there, and died 5307
2Sa 2:23 Asahel f. down and died stood still. 5307
2Sa 4:4 as she made haste to flee, that he f., 5307
2Sa 9:6 he f. on his face, and did reverence. 5307
2Sa 11:17 and there f. some of the people 5307
2Sa 13:2 that he f. sick for his sister Tamar;
2Sa 14:4 to the king, she f. on her face 5307
2Sa 14:22 Joab f. to the ground on his face, 5307
2Sa 18:28 And he f. down to the earth 7812
2Sa 19:18 Shimei the son of Gera f. down 5307
2Sa 20:8 and as he went forth it f. out. 5307
2Sa 21:9 and they f. all seven together, 5307
2Sa 21:22 and f. by the hand of David, 5307
1Ki 2:25 and he f. upon him that he died. 6293
1Ki 2:32 f. upon two men more righteous 6293
1Ki 2:34 and f. upon him, and slew him: 6293
1Ki 2:46 and f. upon him, that he died. 6293
1Ki 14:1 Abijah the son of Jeroboam f. sick.
1Ki 17:17 the mistress of the house, f. sick;
1Ki 18:7 he knew him, and f. on his face, 5307
1Ki 18:38 Then the fire of the Lord f., 5307
1Ki 18:39 people saw it, they f. on their faces: 5307
1Ki 20:30 f. upon twenty and seven thousand 5307
2Ki 1:2 Ahaziah f. down through a lattice 5307
2Ki 1:13 and f. on his knees before Elijah, 3766
2Ki 2:13 mantle of Elijah that f. from him, 5307
2Ki 2:14 mantle of Elijah that f. from him, 5307
2Ki 3:19 and shall f. every good tree, 5307
2Ki 4:8 And it f. on a day, that Elisha 1961
2Ki 4:11 it f. on a day, that he came thither 1961
2Ki 4:18 the child was grown, it f. on a day, 1961
2Ki 4:37 she went in, and f. at his feet, 5307
2Ki 6:5 the axe head f. into the water: 5307
2Ki 6:6 Where f. it? And he shewed him 5307
2Ki 7:20 And so it f. out unto him: for the 1961
2Ki 25:11 fugitives that f. away to the king 5307
1Ch 5:10 Hagarites, who f. by their hand: 5307
1Ch 5:22 there f. down many slain, because 5307
1Ch 10:1 and f. down slain in mount Gilboa. 5307
1Ch 10:4 Saul took a sword, and f. upon it. 5307
1Ch 10:5 f. likewise on the sword, and died. 5307
1Ch 12:19 there f. some of Manasseh to David, 5307
1Ch 12:20 there f. to him of Manasseh, Adnah, 5307
1Ch 20:8 and they f. by the hand of David, 5307
1Ch 21:14 there f. of Israel seventy thousand 5307
1Ch 21:16 in sackcloth, f. upon their faces, 5307
1Ch 26:14 the lot eastward f. to Shelemiah 5307
1Ch 27:24 f. wrath for it against Israel; 1961
2Ch 13:17 so there f. down slain of Israel 5307
2Ch 15:9 they f. to him out of Israel 5307
2Ch 17:10 And the fear of the Lord f. upon 1961
2Ch 20:18 inhabitants of Jerusalem f. before 5307
2Ch 21:19 f. out by reason of his sickness: 3318
2Ch 25:13 f. upon the cities of Judah, from 6584
Ezr 9:5 I f. upon my knees, and spread 3766
Es 8:3 f. down at his feet, and besought 5307
Es 8:17 the fear of the Jews f. upon them. 5307
Es 9:2 fear of them f. upon all people. 5307
Es 9:3 the fear of Mordecai f. upon them. 5307
Job 1:15 And the Sabeans f. upon them, 5307
Job 1:17 bands, and f. upon the camels, 6584
Job 1:19 and it f. upon the young men, 5307
Job 1:20 and f. down upon the ground, and 5307
Ps 27:2 up my flesh, they stumbled and f. 5307
Ps 78:64 Their priests f. by the sword; and 5307
Ps 105:38 the fear of them f. upon them. 5307
Ps 107:12 they f. down, and there was none 3782
Jer 39:9 those that f. away, that f. to him, 5307
Jer 46:16 one f. upon another: and they said, 5307
Jer 52:15 that f. away, that f. to the king 5307
La 1:7 people f. into the hand of the enemy, 5307
La 5:13 the children f. under the wood 3782
Eze 1:28 when I saw it, I f. upon my face. 5307
Eze 3:23 of Chebar: and I f. on my face. 5307
Eze 8:1 of the Lord God f. there upon me. 5307
Eze 9:8 that I f. upon my face, and cried, 5307

Eze 11:5 the Spirit of the Lord f. upon me, ... 5307
Eze 11:13 Then f. I down upon my face, ... 5307
Eze 39:23 so f. they all by the sword................ 5307
Eze 43:3 river Chebar; and I f. upon my face.... 5307
Eze 44:4 of the Lord: and I f. upon my face, ... 5307
Da 2:46 Nebuchadnezzar f. upon his face, ... 5308
Da 3:7 f. down and worshipped the golden..... 5308
Da 3:23 f. down bound into the midst of the.... 5308
Da 4:31 there f. a voice from heaven, saying, .. 5308
Da 7:20 came up, and before whom three f.; ... 5308
Da 8:17 I was afraid, and f. upon my face: 5307
Da 10:7 but a great quaking f. upon them, ... 5307
Jon 1:7 lots, and the lot f. upon Jonah. 5307
Mt 2:11 and f. down, and worshipped him: 4098
Mt 7:25 and it f. not: for it was founded 4098
Mt 7:27 and it f.: and great was the fall 4098
Mt 13:4 some seeds f. by the way side,...... 4098
Mt 13:5 Some f. upon stony places, where.. 4098
Mt 13:7 And some f. among thorns; and..... 4098
Mt 13:8 But other f. into good ground, ... 4098
Mt 17:6 they f. on their face, and were sore ... 4098
Mt 18:26 therefore f. down, and worshipped..4098
Mt 18:29 fellowservant f. down at his feet. . 4098
Mt 26:39 and f. on his face, and prayed, ... 4098
Mk 3:11 they saw him, f. down before him, ... 4363
Mk 4:4 some f. by the way side, and the ... 4098
Mk 4:5 And some f. on stony ground, ... 4098
Mk 4:7 And some f. among thorns, and....... 4098
Mk 4:8 And other f. on good ground, and.. 4098
Mk 5:22 when he saw him, he f. at his feet, ... 4098
Mk 5:33 came and f. down before him, and...... 4363
Mk 7:25 and came and f. at his feet: 4363
Mk 9:20 he f. on the ground, and wallowed...... 4098
Mk 14:35 and f. on the ground, and prayed 4098
Lu 1:12 troubled, and fear f. upon him. 1968
Lu 5:8 he f. down at Jesus' knees, saying,...... 4363
Lu 5:12 f. on his face, and besought him, ... 4098
Lu 6:49 immediately it f.; and the ruin....... 4098
Lu 8:5 he sowed, some f. by the way side; .4098
Lu 8:6 And some f. upon a rock; and as ... 4098
Lu 8:7 And some f. among thorns; and..... 4098
Lu 8:8 And other f. on good ground, and.. 4098
Lu 8:14 which f. among thorns are they, ... 4098
Lu 8:23 as they sailed he f. asleep: and there........
Lu 8:28 cried out, and f. down before him, ... 4363
Lu 8:41 he f. down at Jesus's feet, and 4098
Lu 10:30 f. among thieves, which stripped ... 4045
Lu 10:36 him that f. among the thieves?....... 1706
Lu 13:4 upon whom the tower in Siloam f., 4098
Lu 15:20 and ran, and f. on his neck,.......... 1968
Lu 16:21 f. from the rich man's table: 4098
Lu 17:16 f. down on his face at his feet, ... 4098
Joh 11:32 f. down at his feet, saying unto him,... 4098
Joh 18:6 backward, and f. to the ground. 4098
Ac 1:25 from which Judas by transgression f.,........
Ac 1:26 and the lot f. upon Matthias; 4098
Ac 5:5 f. down, and gave up the ghost: 4098
Ac 5:10 Then f. she down straightway at........ 4098
Ac 7:60 when he had said this, he f. asleep...........
Ac 9:4 f. to the earth, and heard a voice....... 4098
Ac 9:18 there f. from his eyes as it had been.... 634
Ac 10:10 made ready, he f. into a trance,......... 1968
Ac 10:25 and f. down at his feet, and............... 4098
Ac 10:44 the Holy Ghost f. on all them which 1968
Ac 11:15 the Holy Ghost f. on them, as on us... 1968
Ac 12:7 his chains f. off from his hands. 1601
Ac 13:11 f. on him a mist and a darkness; 1968
Ac 13:36 f. on sleep, and was laid unto his ....
Ac 16:29 and f. down before Paul and Silas,....... 4363
Ac 19:17 and fear f. on them all, and the 1968
Ac 19:35 which f. down from Jupiter? 1356
Ac 20:9 and f. down from the third loft, ... 4098
Ac 20:10 Paul went down, and f. on him, ... 1968
Ac 20:37 f. on Paul's neck, and kissed him, ... 1968
Ac 22:7 I f. unto the ground, and heard............ 4098
Ro 11:22 on them which f., severity; but.......... 4098
Ro 15:3 that reproached thee f. on me. 1968
1Co 10:8 and f. in one day three and twenty..... 4098
Heb 3:17 carcasses f. in the wilderness? 4098
Heb 11:30 faith the walls of Jericho f. down, ... 4098
2Pe 3:4 since the fathers f. asleep, all things ....
Re 1:17 I saw him, I f. at his feet as dead. 4098
Re 5:8 elders f. down before the Lamb, ... 4098
Re 5:14 f. down and worshipped him that........ 4098
Re 6:13 stars of heaven f. unto the earth,....... 4098
Re 7:11 f. before the throne on their faces,..... 4098
Re 8:10 there f. a great star from heaven, ... 4098
Re 8:10 f. upon the third part of the rivers, ... 4098
Re 11:11 fear f. upon them which saw them...... 4098
Re 11:13 and the tenth part of the city f., ... 4098
Re 11:16 f. upon their faces, and worshipped 4098
Re 16:2 f. a noisome and grievous sore 1096
Re 16:19 and the cities of the nations f.: 4098
Re 16:21 there f. upon men a great hail 2597
Re 19:4 and the four beasts f. down and......... 4098
Re 19:10 And I f. at his feet to worship 4098
Re 22:8 I f. down to worship before the feet... 4098

FELLED
2Ki 3:25 and f. all the good trees: only in........ 5307

FELLER
Isa 14:8 no f. is come up against us. 3772

FELLEST
2Sa 3:34 before wicked men, so f. thou. 5307

FELLING
2Ki 6:5 But as one was f. a beam, ... 5307

FELLOES
1Ki 7:33 and their f., and their spokes, ... 2839

FELLOW See also FELLOWCITIZENS; FELLOWDISCIPLES; FELLOWHEIRS; FELLOWHELPER; FELLOWLABOURER; FELLOWPRISONER; FELLOW'S; FELLOWS; FELLOWSERVANT; FELLOWSHIP; FELLOWSOLDIER; FELLOWWORKERS; WORKFELLOW; YOKEFELLOW.
Ge 19:9 This one f. came in to sojourn, ...
Ex 2:13 Wherefore smitest thou thy f.? 7453
Jg 7:13 man that told a dream unto his f.,...... 7453
Jg 7:14 his f. answered and said, This is......... 7453
Jg 7:22 every man's sword against his f., ... 7453
1Sa 14:20 man's sword was against his f., ... 7453
1Sa 21:15 have brought this f. to play the mad ....
1Sa 21:15 shall this f. come into my house? ....
1Sa 25:21 in vain I have kept all that this f. hath.......
1Sa 29:4 Make this f. return, that he may 376
2Sa 2:16 caught every one his f. by the head,... 7453
1Ki 22:27 Put this f. in the prison, and feed him.......
2Ki 9:11 wherefore came this mad f. to thee? ....
2Ch 18:26 Put this f. in the prison, and feed him.......
Ec 4:10 the one will lift up his f.: 2270
Isa 34:14 and the satyr shall cry to his f.; 7453
Jon 1:7 And they said every one to his f., ... 7453
Zec 13:7 and against the man that is my f., ... 5997
Mt 12:24 This f. doth not cast out devils, ...
Mt 26:61 This f. said, I am able to destroy ....
Mt 26:71 This f. was also with Jesus of.................
Lu 22:59 a truth this f. also was with him:..............
Lu 23:2 We found this f. perverting the...............
Joh 9:29 as for this f., we know not from ....
Ac 18:13 Saying, This f. persuadeth men................
Ac 22:22 Away with such a f. from the ....
Ac 24:5 found this man a pestilent f., and ....

FELLOWCITIZENS
Eph 2:19 but f. with the saints, and of the........ 4847

FELLOWDISCIPLES
Joh 11:16 Didymus, unto his f., Let us also 4827

FELLOWHEIRS
Eph 3:6 That the Gentiles should be f., ... 4789

FELLOWHELPER See also FELLOWHELPERS.
2Co 8:23 partner and f. concerning you: 4904

FELLOWHELPERS
3Jo 8 that we might be f. to the truth. 4904

FELLOWLABOURER See also FELLOWLABOURERS.
1Th 3:2 our f. in the gospel of Christ, ... 4904
Phm 1 our dearly beloved, and f., ... 4904

FELLOWLABOURERS
Php 4:3 also, and with other my f., ... 4904
Phm 24 Demas, Lucas, my f.. 4904

FELLOWPRISONER See also FELLOWPRISONERS.
Col 4:10 Aristarchus my f. saluteth you, ... 4869
Phm 23 Epaphras, my f. in Christ Jesus; 4869

FELLOWPRISONERS
Ro 16:7 and Junia, my kinsmen, and my f., ... 4869

FELLOW'S
2Sa 2:16 thrust his sword in his f. side; 7453

FELLOWS
Jg 11:37 bewail my virginity, I and my f.. 7464
Jg 18:25 lest angry f. run upon thee, and 582
2Sa 6:20 as one of the vain f. shamelessly ....
Ps 45:7 the oil of gladness above thy f.. 2270
Isa 44:11 Behold, all his f. shall be ashamed: 2270
Eze 37:19 and the tribes of Israel his f., ... 2270
Da 2:13 they sought Daniel and his f. 2269
Da 2:18 that Daniel and his f. should not.......... 2269
Da 7:20 look was more stout than his f.. 2273
Zec 3:8 the high priest, thou, and thy f. 7453
Mt 11:16 markets, and calling unto their f., .2083
Ac 17:5 certain lewd f. of the baser sort, ... 435
Heb 1:9 the oil of gladness above thy f.. 3353

FELLOWSERVANT See also FELLOWSERVANTS.
Mt 18:29 And his f. fell down at his feet, ... 4889
Mt 18:33 have had compassion on thy f., ... 4889
Col 1:7 Epaphras our dear f., who is for 4889
Col 4:7 minister and f. in the Lord: 4889
Re 19:10 do it not: I am thy f., and of thy........ 4889
Re 22:9 do it not: for I am thy f., and of thy... 4889

FELLOWSERVANTS
Mt 18:28 went out, and found one of his f., . 4889
Mt 18:31 So when his f. saw what was done, 4889
Mt 24:49 And shall begin to smite his f., ... 4889
Re 6:11 their f. also and their brethren,........ 4889

FELLOWSHIP
Le 6:2 or in f., or in a thing taken 8667,3027
Ps 94:20 of iniquity have f. with thee, ... 2266
Ac 2:42 and f., and in breaking of bread, ... 2842
1Co 1:9 were called unto the f. of his Son........ 2842
1Co 10:20 that ye should have f. with devils. 2844
2Co 6:14 what f. hath righteousness with 3352
2Co 8:4 upon us the f. of the ministering 2842
Ga 2:9 and Barnabas the right hands of f.; 2842
Eph 3:9 see what is the f. of the mystery, ... 2842
Eph 5:11 And have no f. with the unfruitful........ 4790
Php 1:5 your f. in the gospel from the first 2842
Php 2:1 of love, if any f. of the Spirit, ... 2842
Php 3:10 and the f. of his sufferings, ... 2842
1Jo 1:3 ye also may have f. with us: and........ 2842
1Jo 1:3 truly our f. is with the Father, ... 2842
1Jo 1:6 If we say that we have f. with him, ... 2842
1Jo 1:7 light, we have f. one with another, ... 2842

FELLOWSOLDIER
Php 2:25 and companion in labour, and f.,......... 4961
Phm 2 and Archippus our f., and to the 4961

FELLOWWORKERS
Col 4:11 only are my f. unto the kingdom 4904

FELT
Ge 27:22 and he f. him, and said, the voice 4959
Ex 10:21 even darkness which may be f. 4959
Pr 23:35 I f. it not: when shall I awake? 3045
Mk 5:29 f. in her body that she was healed......... 1097
Ac 28:5 beast into the fire, and f. no harm. 3958

FEMALE
Ge 1:27 him; male and f. created he them. 5347
Ge 5:2 Male and f. created he them; and....... 5347
Ge 6:19 with thee; they shall be male and f.. ... 5347
Ge 7:2 thee by sevens, the male and his f.: 802
Ge 7:2 clean by two, the male and his f.. 802
Ge 7:3 air by sevens, the male and the f.; 5347
Ge 7:9 into the ark, the male and the f., ... 5347
Ge 7:16 went in male and f. of all flesh,........... 5347
Le 3:1 whether it be a male or f., he shall 5347
Le 3:6 flock; male or f., he shall offer it......... 5347
Le 4:28 of the goats, a f. without blemish, ... 5347
Le 4:32 shall bring it a f. without blemish. 5347
Le 5:6 a f. from the flock, a lamb or a kid..... 5347
Le 12:7 her that hath born a male or a f. 5347
Le 27:4 if it be a f., then thy estimation 5347
Le 27:5 and for the f. ten shekels. 5347
Le 27:6 and for the f. thy estimation shall....... 5347
Le 27:7 and for the f. ten shekels. 5347
Nu 5:3 Both male and f. shall ye put out, ... 5347
De 4:16 the likeness of male or f., ... 5347
De 7:14 there shall not be male or f. barren ....
Mt 19:4 beginning made them male and f., .2338
Mk 10:6 God made them male and f.. 2338
Gal 3:28 there is neither male nor f.: for 2338

FENCE See also DEFENCE; FENCED; OFFENCE.
Ps 62:3 shall ye be, and as a tottering f.. 1447

FENCED See also DEFENCED.
Nu 32:17 ones shall dwell in the f. cities........... 4013

Nu 32:36 **f.** cities: and folds for sheep........ 4013
De 3:5 cities were **f.** with high walls,........ 1219
De 9:1 cities great and **f.** up to heaven,........ 1219
De 28:52 thy high and **f.** walls come down,........ 1219
Jos 10:20 of them entered into **f.** cities........ 4013
Jos 14:12 that the cities were great and **f.**:........ 1219
Jos 19:35 the **f.** cities are Ziddim, Zer, and........ 4013
1Sa 6:18 **f.** cities, and of country villages,........ 4013
2Sa 20:6 he get him **f.** cities, and escape........ 1211
2Sa 23:7 that shall touch them must be **f.**........ 4390
2Ki 3:19 And ye shall smite every **f.** city,........ 4013
2Ki 10:2 a **f.** city also, and armour;........ 4013
2Ki 17:9 of the watchmen to the **f.** city........ 4013
2Ki 18:8 of the watchmen to the **f.** city........ 4013
2Ki 18:13 come up against all the **f.** cities........ 1219
2Ki 19:25 shouldest be to lay waste **f.** cities........ 1219
2Ch 8:5 **f.** cities, with walls, gates, and........ 4692
2Ch 11:10 Judah and in Benjamin **f.** cities........ 4694
2Ch 11:23 unto every **f.** city: and he gave........ 4694
2Ch 12:4 **f.** cities which pertained to Judah,........ 4694
2Ch 14:6 And he built **f.** cities in Judah:........ 4694
2Ch 17:2 placed forces in all the **f.** cities........ 1219
2Ch 17:19 whom the king put in the **f.** cities........ 4013
2Ch 19:5 all the **f.** cities of Judah, city by........ 1219
2Ch 21:3 things, with **f.** cities in Judah:........ 4694
2Ch 32:1 encamped against the **f.** cities,........ 1219
2Ch 33:14 war in all the **f.** cities of Judah........ 1219
Job 10:11 **f.** me with bones and sinews........ 7753
Job 19:8 **f.** up my way that I cannot pass,........ 1443
Isa 2:15 tower, and upon every **f.** wall,........ 1219
Isa 5:2 And he **f.** it, and gathered out........ 5823
Jer 5:17 shall impoverish thy **f.** cities,........ 4013
Jer 15:20 unto this people a **f.** brasen wall:........ 1219
Eze 36:35 and ruined cities are become **f.**,........ 1219
Da 11:15 and take the most **f.** cities; and........ 4013
Ho 8:14 Judah had multiplied **f.** cities:........ 1219
Zep 1:16 and alarm against the **f.** cities,........ 1219

FENCED-CITY See FENCED and CITY.

FENCED-WALL See FENCED and WALL.

FENS
Job 40:21 in the covert of the reed, and **f.**........ 1207

FERRET
Le 11:30 And the **f.**, and the chameleon,........ 604

FERRY
2Sa 19:18 And there went over a **f.** boat to........ 5679

FERRY-BOAT See FERRY and BOAT.

FERVENT
Ac 18:25 being **f.** in the spirit, he spake........ *2204*
Ro 12:11 **f.** in spirit; serving the Lord;........ *2204*
2Co 7:7 your **f.** mind toward me; so that........ *2205*
Jas 5:16 **f.** prayer of a righteous man........
1Pe 4:8 have **f.** charity among yourselves:........ *1618*
2Pe 3:10 the elements shall melt with **f.** heat,........
2Pe 3:12 the elements shall melt with **f.** heat?........

FERVENTLY
Col 4:12 labouring **f.** for you in prayers,........
1Pe 1:22 one another with a pure heart **f.**:........ *1619*

FESTUS (fes'-tus) See also FESTUS'.
Ac 24:27 Porcius **F.** came into Felix' room:........ *5347*
Ac 25:1 **F.** was come into the province,........ *5347*
Ac 25:4 But **F.** answered, that Paul should........ *5347*
Ac 25:9 But **F.**, willing to do the Jews a........ *5347*
Ac 25:12 Then **F.**, when he had conferred........ *5347*
Ac 25:13 came unto Caesarea to salute **F.**........ *5347*
Ac 25:14 **F.** declared Paul's cause unto the........ *5347*
Ac 25:22 Then Agrippa said unto **F.**, I would........ *5347*
Ac 25:24 and **F.** said, King Agrippa, and all........ *5347*
Ac 26:24 **F.** said with a loud voice, Paul,........ *5347*
Ac 26:25 I am not mad, most noble **F.**;........ *5347*
Ac 26:32 Then said Agrippa unto **F.**, This........ *5347*

FESTUS' (fes'-tus)
Ac 25:23 at **F.** commandment Paul was........ *5347*

FETCH See also FETCHED; FETCHETH; FETCHT.
Ge 18:5 And I will **f.** a morsel of bread,........ 3947
Ge 27:9 **f.** me from thence two good kids........ 3947
Ge 27:13 obey my voice, and go **f.** me them........ 3947
Ge 27:45 will send, and **f.** thee from thence:........ 3947
Ge 42:16 and let him **f.** your brother, and ye........ 3947
Ex 2:5 she sent her maid to **f.** it........ 3947
Nu 20:10 we **f.** you water out of this rock?........ 3318
Nu 34:5 the border shall **f.** a compass........
De 19:12 of his city shall send and **f.** him........ 3947
De 24:10 into his house to **f.** his pledge........ 5670
De 24:19 thou shalt not go again to **f.** it:........ 3947
De 30:4 and from thence will he **f.** thee:........ 3947
Jg 11:5 elders of Gilead went to **f.** Jephthah........ 3947
Jg 20:10 to **f.** victual for the people, that........ 3947
1Sa 4:3 Let us **f.** the ark of the covenant........ 3947
1Sa 6:21 come ye down, and **f.** it up to you........ 5927
1Sa 16:11 Send and **f.** him: for we will not........ 3947
1Sa 20:31 now send and **f.** him unto me, for........ 3947
1Sa 26:22 the young men come over and **f.** it........ 3947
2Sa 5:23 but **f.** a compass behind them,........
2Sa 14:13 the king doth not **f.** home again........ 7725
2Sa 14:20 To **f.** about this form of speech........ 5437
1Ki 17:10 **F.** me, I pray thee, a little water........ 3947
1Ki 17:11 And as she was going to **f.** it,........ 3947
2Ki 6:13 that I may send and **f.** him........ 3947
2Ch 18:8 **F.** quickly Micaiah the son of Imla........
Ne 8:15 and **f.** olive branches, and pine........ 935
Job 36:3 I will **f.** my knowledge from afar,........ 5375
Isa 56:12 I will **f.** wine, and we will fill........ 3947
Jer 36:21 the king sent Jehudi to **f.** the roll:........ 3947
Ac 16:37 come themselves and **f.** us out........ *1806*

FETCHED See also FETCHT.
Ge 18:4 Let a little water, I pray you, be **f.**,........ 3947
Ge 27:14 he went, and **f.**, and brought them........ 3947
Jos 15:3 and **f.** a compass to Karkaa........
Jg 18:18 **f.** the carved image, the ephod,........ 3947
1Sa 7:1 and **f.** up the ark of the Lord,........ 5927
1Sa 10:23 And they ran and **f.** him thence:........ 3947
2Sa 4:6 though they would have **f.** wheat;........ 3947
2Sa 9:5 king David sent, and **f.** him out of........ 3947
2Sa 11:27 sent and **f.** her to his house,........ 622
2Sa 14:2 and **f.** thence a wise woman, and........ 3947
1Ki 7:13 king Solomon sent and **f.** Hiram........ 3947
1Ki 9:28 to Ophir, and **f.** from thence gold........ 3947
2Ki 3:9 they **f.** a compass of seven days'........
2Ki 11:4 Jehoiada sent and **f.** the rulers........ 3947
2Ch 1:17 And they **f.** up, and brought forth........ 5927
2Ch 12:11 the guard came and **f.** them, and........ 5375
Jer 26:23 they **f.** forth Urijah out of Egypt,........ 3318
Ac 28:13 from thence we **f.** a compass, and........

FETCHETH
De 19:5 his hand **f.** a stroke with the axe........ 5080

FETCHT See also FETCHED.
Ge 18:7 and **f.** a calf tender and good,........ 3947

FETTERS
Jg 16:21 and bound him with **f.** of brass;........ 5178
2Sa 3:34 not bound, nor thy feet put into **f.**:........ 5178
2Ki 25:7 and bound him with **f.** of brass,........ 5178
2Ch 33:11 and bound him with **f.**, and carried........ 5178
2Ch 36:6 and bound him in **f.**, to carry him........ 5178
Job 36:8 And if they be bound in **f.**,........ 2131
Ps 105:18 Whose feet they hurt with **f.**: he........ 3525
Ps 149:8 and their nobles with **f.** of iron;........ 3525
Mk 5:4 often bound with **f.** and chains,........ *3976*
Mk 5:4 and the **f.** broken in pieces:........ *3976*
Lu 8:29 kept bound with chains and in **f.**;........ *3976*

FEVER
De 28:22 with a consumption, and with a **f.**,........ 6920
Mt 8:14 wife's mother laid, and sick of a **f.**........ *4445*
Mt 8:15 and the **f.** left her: and she arose,........ *4446*
Mk 1:30 wife's mother lay sick of a **f.**,........ *4445*
Mk 1:31 and immediately the **f.** left her,........ *4446*
Lu 4:38 mother was taken with a great **f.**;........ *4446*
Lu 4:39 and rebuked the **f.**; and it left her:........ *4446*
Joh 4:52 at the seventh hour the **f.** left him........ *4446*
Ac 28:8 lay sick of a **f.** and of a bloody flux:........ *4446*

FEW See also FEWER; FEWEST.
Ge 24:55 the damsel abide with us a **f.** days........
Ge 27:44 And tarry with him a **f.** days,........ 259
Ge 29:20 they seemed unto him but a **f.** days,........ 259
Ge 34:30 I being **f.** in number, they shall........ 4962
Ge 47:9 **f.** and evil have the days of the........ 4592
Le 25:52 if there remain but **f.** years unto........ 4592
Le 26:22 and make you **f.** in number;........ 4591
Nu 9:20 when the cloud was a **f.** days upon........ 4557
Nu 13:18 be strong or weak, **f.** or many;........ 4592
Nu 26:54 and to **f.** thou shalt give the less........ 4592
Nu 26:56 be divided between many and **f.**........ 4592
Nu 35:8 but from them that have **f.**........ 4592
Nu 35:8 ye shall give **f.**: every one........ 4591
De 4:27 and ye shall be left **f.** in number........ 4962
De 26:5 and sojourned there with a **f.**, and........ 4592
De 28:62 And ye shall be left **f.** in number,........ 4592
De 33:6 and let not his men be **f.**........ 4557
Jos 7:3 labour thither; for they are but **f.**........ 4592
1Sa 14:6 to save by many or by **f.**........ 4592
1Sa 17:28 with whom hast thou left those **f.**........ 4592
2Ki 4:3 empty vessels; borrow not a **f.**........ 4591
1Ch 16:19 When ye were but **f.**, even........ 4962
1Ch 16:19 even a **f.**, and strangers in it,........ 4592
2Ch 29:34 But the priests were too **f.**, so........ 4592
Ne 2:12 I and some **f.** men with me;........ 4592
Ne 7:4 but the people were **f.** therein, and........ 4592
Job 10:20 Are not my days **f.**? cease then,........ 4592
Job 14:1 that is born of woman is of **f.** days,........ 7116
Job 16:22 When a **f.** years are come, then I........ 4557
Ps 105:12 When they were but a **f.** men in........ 4962
Ps 105:12 yea, very **f.**, and strangers in it........ 4592
Ps 109:8 Let his days be **f.**: and let another........ 4592
Ec 5:2 therefore let thy words be **f.**........ 4592
Ec 9:14 a little city and **f.** men within it;........ 4592
Ec 12:3 grinders cease because they are **f.**,........ 4592
Isa 10:7 and cut off nations not a **f.**........ 4592
Isa 10:19 the trees of his forest shall be **f.**,........ 4557
Isa 24:6 earth are burned, and **f.** met left........ 4213
Jer 30:19 them, and they shall not be **f.**;........ 4591
Jer 42:2 we are left but a **f.** of many,........ 4592
Eze 5:3 also take thereof a **f.** in number,........ 4592
Eze 12:16 I will leave a **f.** men of them........ 4557
Da 11:20 **f.** days he shall be destroyed,........ 259
Mt 7:14 **and f. there be that find it**........ *3641*
Mt 9:37 **but the labourers are f.;**........ *3641*
Mt 15:34 Seven, and a **f.** little fishes........ *3641*
Mt 20:16 **for many be called, but f. chosen**........ *3641*
Mt 22:14 **many are called, but f. are chosen**........ *3641*
Mt 25:21, 23 **thou hast been faithful over a f.**........ *3641*
Mk 6:5 he laid hands upon a **f.** sick folk,........ *3641*
Mk 8:7 And they had a **f.** small fishes:........ *3641*
Lu 10:2 **is great, but the labourers are f.:**........ *3641*
Lu 12:48 **shall be beaten with f. stripes**........ *3641*
Lu 13:23 Lord, are there **f.** that be saved?........ *3641*
Ac 17:4 and of the chief women not a **f.**........ *3641*
Ac 17:12 were Greeks, and of men, not a **f.**........ *3641*
Ac 24:4 us of thy clemency a **f.** words,........ *4935*
Eph 3:3 (as I wrote afore in **f.** words,........ *3641*
Heb 12:10 verily for a **f.** days chastened us........ *3641*
Heb 13:22 a letter unto you in **f.** words........ *1024*
1Pe 3:20 wherein **f.**, that is, eight souls........ *3641*
Re 2:14 **But I have a f. things against thee,** *3641*
Re 2:20 **I have a f. things against thee,**........ *3641*
Re 3:4 **Thou hast a f. names even in**........ *3641*

FEWER
Nu 33:54 and to the **f.** ye shall give the less........ 4592

FEWEST
De 7:7 ye were the **f.** of all people:........ 4592

FEWNESS
Le 25:16 according to the **f.** of years thou........ 4591

FIDELITY
Tit 2:10 but shewing all good **f.**; that they........ *4102*

FIELD See also FIELDS.
Ge 2:5 every plant of the **f.** before it was........ 7704
Ge 2:5 every herb of the **f.** before it grew:........ 7704
Ge 2:19 God formed every beast of the **f.**,........ 7704
Ge 2:20 and to every beast of the **f.**;........ 7704
Ge 3:1 than any beast of the **f.** which the........ 7704
Ge 3:14 and above every beast of the **f.**;........ 7704
Ge 3:18 and thou shalt eat the herb of the **f.**;........ 7704
Ge 4:8 to pass, when they were in the **f.**,........ 7704
Ge 23:9 which is in the end of his **f.**;........ 7704
Ge 23:11 the **f.** give I thee, and the cave........ 7704
Ge 23:13 I will give thee money for the **f.**;........ 7704
Ge 23:17 And the **f.** of Ephron, which was in........ 7704
Ge 23:17 the **f.**, and the cave which was........ 7704
Ge 23:17 and all the trees that were in the **f.**,........ 7704
Ge 23:19 the cave of the **f.** of Machpelah........ 7704
Ge 23:20 the **f.**, and the cave that is therein,........ 7704
Ge 24:63 went out to meditate in the **f.** at the........ 7704
Ge 24:65 man is this that walketh in the **f.** to........ 7704
Ge 25:9 the **f.** of Ephron the son of Zohar........ 7704
Ge 25:10 The **f.** which Abraham purchased........ 7704
Ge 25:27 a cunning hunter, a man of the **f.**;........ 7704
Ge 25:29 and Esau came from the **f.**, and he........ 7704
Ge 27:3 and go out to the **f.** and take me........ 7704
Ge 27:5 And Esau went to the **f.** to hunt........ 7704
Ge 27:27 my son is as the smell of a **f.** which........ 7704

Ge 29:2 and behold a well in the f., ... 7704
Ge 30:14 found mandrakes in the f., and ... 7704
Ge 30:16 Jacob came out of the f. in the ... 7704
Ge 31:4 called Rachel and Leah to the f. ... 7704
Ge 33:19 he bought a parcel of a f., ... 7704
Ge 34:5 sons were with his cattle in the f.: ... 7704
Ge 34:7 sons of Jacob came out of the f. ... 7704
Ge 34:28 and that which was in the f., ... 7704
Ge 36:35 smote Midian in the f. of Moab, ... 7704
Ge 37:7 we were binding sheaves in the f., ... 7704
Ge 37:15 behold, he was wandering in the f.: ... 7704
Ge 39:5 he had in the house, and in the f., ... 7704
Ge 41:48 the food of the f., which was round ... 7704
Ge 47:20 Egyptians sold every man his f., ... 7704
Ge 47:24 seed of the f., and for your food, ... 7704
Ge 49:29 in the f. of Ephron the Hittite, ... 7704
Ge 49:30 In the cave that is in the f. of ... 7704
Ge 49:30 with the f. of Ephron the Hittite ... 7704
Ge 49:32 purchase of the f. and of the cave ... 7704
Ge 50:13 the cave of the f. of Machpelah, ... 7704
Ge 50:13 which Abraham bought with the f. ... 7704
Ex 1:14 in all manner of service in the f.: ... 7704
Ex 9:3 thy cattle which is in the f., ... 7704
Ex 9:19 all that thou hast in the f.; ... 7704
Ex 9:19 which shall be found in the f., ... 7704
Ex 9:21 servants and his cattle in the f. ... 7704
Ex 9:22 and upon every herb of the f., ... 7704
Ex 9:25 all that was in the f., both man and ... 7704
Ex 9:25 the hail smote every herb of the f., ... 7704
Ex 9:25 and brake every tree of the f.. ... 7704
Ex 10:5 which groweth for you out of the f.: ... 7704
Ex 10:15 or in the herbs of the f., ... 7704
Ex 16:25 ye shall not find it in the f.. ... 7704
Ex 22:5 If a man shall cause a f. or ... 7704
Ex 22:5 shall feed in another man's f.; ... 7704
Ex 22:5 of the best of his own f., ... 7704
Ex 22:6 corn, or the f. be consumed ... 7704
Ex 22:31 flesh that is torn of beasts in the f.; ... 7704
Ex 23:11 the beasts of the f. shall eat ... 7704
Ex 23:16 which thou hast sown in the f.: ... 7704
Ex 23:16 in thy labours out of the f.. ... 7704
Ex 23:29 the beast of the f. multiply against ... 7704
Le 14:7 living bird loose into the open f., ... 7704
Le 17:5 which they offer in the open f., ... 7704
Le 19:9 wholly reap the corners of thy f., ... 7704
Le 19:19 not sow thy f. with mingled seed: ... 7704
Le 23:22 riddance of the corners of thy f. ... 7704
Le 25:3 Six years thou shalt sow thy f., ... 7704
Le 25:4 thou shalt neither sow thy f., nor ... 7704
Le 25:12 the increase thereof out of the f.. ... 7704
Le 25:34 the f. of the suburbs of their cities ... 7704
Le 26:4 and the trees of the f. shall yield ... 7704
Le 27:16 unto the Lord some part of a f. of ... 7704
Le 27:17 his f. from the year of jubile, ... 7704
Le 27:18 he sanctify his f. after the jubile ... 7704
Le 27:19 he that sanctified the f. will in any ... 7704
Le 27:20 And if he will not redeem the f., ... 7704
Le 27:20 or if he have sold the f. to another ... 7704
Le 27:21 But the f. when it goeth out in the ... 7704
Le 27:21 unto the Lord, as a f. devoted; ... 7704
Le 27:22 a man sanctify unto the Lord a f. ... 7704
Le 27:24 the f. shall return unto him of ... 7704
Le 27:28 and of the f. of his possession, ... 7704
Nu 22:4 ox licketh up the grass of the f.. ... 7704
Nu 22:23 of the way, and went into the f.: ... 7704
Nu 23:14 brought him into the f. of Zophim, ... 7704
De 5:21 house, his f., or his manservant, ... 7704
De 7:22 lest the beasts of the f. increase ... 7704
De 14:22 the f. bringeth forth year by year ... 7704
De 20:19 the tree of the f. is man's life) ... 7704
De 21:1 lying in the f., and it be not known ... 7704
De 22:25 find a betrothed damsel in the f., ... 7704
De 22:27 For he found her in the f., ... 7704
De 24:19 cuttest down thine harvest in thy f., ... 7704
De 24:19 and hast forgot a sheaf in the f., ... 7704
De 28:3 blessed shalt thou be in the f.. ... 7704
De 28:16 cursed shalt thou be in the f.. ... 7704
De 28:38 carry much seed out into the f., ... 7704
Jos 8:24 all the inhabitants of Ai in the f., ... 7704
Jos 15:18 moved him to ask of her father a f.: ... 7704
Jg 1:14 moved him to ask of her father a f.: ... 7704
Jg 5:4 marchedst out from the f. of Edom, ... 7704
Jg 5:18 in the high places of the f.. ... 7704
Jg 9:32 and lie in wait in the f.: ... 7704
Jg 9:42 the people went out into the f.; ... 7704
Jg 9:43 laid wait in the f., and looked, ... 7704
Jg 13:9 the woman as she sat in the f.: ... 7704
Jg 19:16 old man from his work out of the f. ... 7704
Jg 20:31 the other to Gibeah in the f., ... 7704
Ru 2:2 Let me now go to the f., and glean ... 7704
Ru 2:3 gleaned in the f. after the reapers: ... 7704
Ru 2:3 part of the f. belonging unto Boaz, ... 7704
Ru 2:8 Go not to glean in another f., ... 7704
Ru 2:9 be on the f. that they do reap, ... 7704
Ru 2:17 she gleaned in the f. until even, ... 7704
Ru 2:22 they meet thee not in any other f., ... 7704
Ru 4:5 buyest the f. of the hand of Naomi, ... 7704
1Sa 4:2 they slew of the army in the f. ... 7704
1Sa 6:14 the f. of Joshua, a Beth-shemite, ... 7704
1Sa 6:18 remaineth unto this day in the f. ... 7704
1Sa 11:5 came after the herd out of the f.; ... 7704
1Sa 14:15 trembling in the host, in the f., ... 7704
1Sa 17:44 the air, and to the beasts of the f.. ... 7704
1Sa 19:3 stand beside my father in the f. ... 7704
1Sa 20:5 that I may hide myself in the f. ... 7704
1Sa 20:11 Come, and let us go out into the f., ... 7704
1Sa 20:11 went out both of them into the f.. ... 7704
1Sa 20:24 So David hid himself in the f.: ... 7704
1Sa 20:35 that Jonathan went out into the f. ... 7704
1Sa 30:11 they found an Egyptian in the f., ... 7704
2Sa 10:8 were by themselves in the f. ... 7704
2Sa 11:23 and came out unto us into the f., ... 7704
2Sa 14:6 they two strove together in the f., ... 7704
2Sa 14:30 See, Joab's f. is near mine, and he ... 2513
2Sa 14:30 Absalom's servants set the f. on fire ... 2513
2Sa 14:31 have thy servants set my f. on fire? ... 2513
2Sa 17:8 bear robbed of her whelps in the f.: ... 7704
2Sa 18:6 So the people went out into the f. ... 7704
2Sa 20:12 out of the highway into the f., ... 7704
2Sa 21:10 nor the beasts of the f. by night. ... 7704
1Ki 11:29 and they two were alone in the f.: ... 7704
1Ki 14:11 and him that dieth in the f. shall the ... 7704
1Ki 21:24 and him that dieth in the f. shall the ... 7704
2Ki 4:39 went out into the f. to gather herbs, ... 7704
2Ki 7:12 to hide themselves in the f., saying, ... 7704
2Ki 8:6 and all the fruits of the f. since the ... 7704
2Ki 9:25 in the portion of the f. of Naboth ... 7704
2Ki 9:37 the f. in the portion of Jezreel; ... 7704
2Ki 18:17 in the highway of the fuller's f.. ... 7704
2Ki 19:26 they were as the grass of the f., ... 7704
1Ch 1:46 smote Midian in the f. of Moab, ... 7704
1Ch 19:9 come were by themselves in the f. ... 7704
1Ch 27:26 them that did the work of the f. ... 7704
2Ch 26:23 the f. of the burial which belonged ... 7704
2Ch 31:5 and of all the increase of the f.; ... 7704
Ne 13:10 were fled every one to his f. ... 7704
Job 5:23 in league with the stones of the f.: ... 7704
Job 5:23 beasts of the f. shall be at peace ... 7704
Job 24:6 reap every one his corn in the f.: ... 7704
Job 40:20 where all the beasts of the f. play. ... 7704
Ps 8:7 yea, and the beasts of the f.; ... 7704
Ps 50:11 the wild beasts of the f. are mine ... 7704
Ps 78:12 the land of Egypt, in the f. of Zoan. ... 7704
Ps 78:43 and his wonders in the f. of Zoan: ... 7704
Ps 80:13 the wild beast of the f. doth devour ... 7704
Ps 96:12 Let the f. be joyful, and all that is ... 7704
Ps 103:15 flower of the f., so he flourisheth. ... 7704
Ps 104:11 drink to every beast of the f.: ... 7704
Pr 24:27 and make it fit for thyself in the f.; ... 7704
Pr 24:30 I went by the f. of the slothful, ... 7704
Pr 27:26 and the goats are the price of the f.. ... 7704
Pr 31:16 She considereth a f., and buyeth it: ... 7704
Ec 5:9 the king himself is served by the f.. ... 7704
Ca 2:7 and by the hinds of the f., that ye ... 7704
Ca 3:5 and by the hinds of the f., that ye ... 7704
Ca 7:11 beloved, let us go forth into the f.; ... 7704
Isa 5:8 join house to house, that lay f. to f., ... 7704
Isa 7:3 in the highway of the fuller's f.; ... 7704
Isa 10:18 of his forest, and of his fruitful f., ...
Isa 16:10 and joy out of the plentiful f.; ...
Isa 29:17 shall be turned into a fruitful f., ...
Isa 29:17 and the fruitful f. shall be esteemed ...
Isa 32:15 and the wilderness be a fruitful f., ...
Isa 32:15 the fruitful f. be counted for a forest. ...
Isa 32:16 righteousness remain in the fruitful f.. ...
Isa 36:2 in the highway of the fuller's f.. ... 7704
Isa 37:27 they were as the grass of the f., ... 7704
Isa 40:6 thereof is as the flower of the f.: ... 7704
Isa 43:20 The beast of the f. shall honour me, ... 7704
Isa 55:12 and all the trees of the f. shall clap ... 7704
Isa 56:9 ye beasts of the f., come to devour, ... 7704
Jer 4:17 As keepers of a f., are they against ... 7704
Jer 6:25 Go not forth into the f., nor walk ... 7704
Jer 7:20 and upon the trees of the f., ... 7704
Jer 9:22 fall as dung upon the open f., ... 7704
Jer 12:4 and the herbs of every f. wither, ... 7704
Jer 12:9 assemble all the beasts of the f., ... 7704
Jer 14:5 the hind also calved in the f., ... 7704
Jer 14:18 If I go forth into the f., then behold ... 7704
Jer 17:3 O my mountain in the f., I will give ... 7704
Jer 18:14 cometh from the rock of the f.? ... 7704
Jer 26:18 Zion shall be plowed like a f., ... 7704
Jer 27:6 the beasts of the f. have I given ... 7704
Jer 28:14 have given him the beasts of the f. ... 7704
Jer 32:7 Buy thee my f. that is in Anathoth: ... 7704
Jer 32:8 Buy my f., I pray thee, that is in ... 7704
Jer 32:9 And I bought the f. of Hanameel ... 7704
Jer 32:25 Buy thee the f. for money, and ... 7704
Jer 35:9 have we vineyard, nor f., nor seed: ... 7704
Jer 41:8 for we have treasures in the f., of ... 7704
Jer 48:33 gladness is taken from the plentiful f. ...
La 4:9 for want of the fruits of the f., ... 7704
Eze 7:15 he that is in the f. shall die with the ... 7704
Eze 16:5 but thou wast cast out in the open f., ... 7704
Eze 16:7 to multiply as the bud of the f., ... 7704
Eze 17:5 and planted it in a fruitful f.: ... 7704
Eze 17:24 all the trees of the f. shall know ... 7704
Eze 20:46 against the forest of the south f., ... 7704
Eze 26:6 her daughters which are in the f. ... 7704
Eze 26:8 the sword thy daughters in the f.: ... 7704
Eze 29:5 beasts of the f. and to the fowls ... 776
Eze 31:4 rivers unto all the trees of the f. ... 7704
Eze 31:5 exalted above all the trees of the f., ... 7704
Eze 31:6 beasts of the f. bring forth their ... 7704
Eze 31:13 beasts of the f. shall be upon his ... 7704
Eze 31:15 all the trees of the f. fainted for him. ... 7704
Eze 32:4 cast thee forth upon the open f., ... 7704
Eze 33:27 him that is in the open f. will I ... 7704
Eze 34:5 meat to all the beasts of the f., when ... 7704
Eze 34:8 meat to every beast of the f., because ... 7704
Eze 34:27 tree of the f. shall yield her fruit, ... 7704
Eze 36:30 the increase of the f., that ye shall ... 7704
Eze 38:20 heaven, and the beasts of the f., ... 7704
Eze 39:4 beasts of the f. to be devoured, ... 7704
Eze 39:5 Thou shalt fall upon the open f.: ... 7704
Eze 39:10 shall take no wood out of the f., ... 7704
Eze 39:17 and to every beast of the f., ... 7704
Da 2:38 the beasts of the f. and the fowls ... 1251
Da 4:12 the beasts of the f. had shadow ... 1251
Da 4:15 in the tender grass of the f.: and let ... 1251
Da 4:21 which the beasts of the f. dwelt, ... 1251
Da 4:23 in the tender grass of the f., and let ... 1251
Da 4:23 portion be with the beasts of the f., ... 1251
Da 4:25 shall be with the beasts of the f., ... 1251
Da 4:32 shall be with the beasts of the f.: ... 1251
Ho 2:12 beasts of the f. shall eat them. ... 7704
Ho 2:18 with the beasts of the f., and with ... 7704
Ho 4:3 languish, with the beasts of the f., ... 7704
Ho 10:4 hemlock in the furrows of the f. ... 7704
Joe 1:10 f. is wasted, the land mourneth; ... 7704
Joe 1:11 the harvest of the f. is perished. ... 7704
Joe 1:12 all the trees of the f., are withered: ... 7704
Joe 1:19 hath burned all the trees of the f.. ... 7704
Joe 1:20 beasts of the f. cry also unto thee: ... 7704
Joe 2:22 Be not afraid, ye beasts of the f.: ... 7704
Mic 1:6 make Samaria as an heap of the f., ... 7704
Mic 3:12 Zion for your sake be plowed as a f., ... 7704
Mic 4:10 and thou shalt dwell in the f., ... 7704
Zec 10:1 of rain, to every one grass in the f.. ... 7704
Mal 3:11 her fruit before the time in the f., ... 7704
Mt 6:28 **Consider the lilies of the f., how** ... *68*
Mt 6:30 **so clothe the grass of the f., which** ... *68*
Mt 13:24 **which sowed good seed in his f.:** ... *68*
Mt 13:27 **not thou sow good seed in thy f.?** ... *68*
Mt 13:31 **a man took, and sowed in his f.:** ... *68*
Mt 13:36 us the parable of the tares of the f.. ... *68*
Mt 13:38 **The f. is the world; the good seed** ... *68*
Mt 13:44 **is like unto treasure hid in a f.;** ... *68*
Mt 13:44 **all that he hath, and buyeth that f.** ... *68*
Mt 24:18 **Neither let him which is in the f.** ... *68*
Mt 24:40 **Then shall two be in the f.;** ... *68*
Mt 27:7 bought with them the potter's f., ... *68*
Mt 27:8 that f. was called, The f. of blood, ... *68*
Mt 27:10 And gave them for the potter's f., ... *68*
Mk 13:16 **him that is in the f. not turn back** ... *68*
Lu 2:8 shepherds abiding in the f., keeping ... *68*
Lu 12:28 **is to day in the f., and to-morrow** ... *68*
Lu 15:25 **Now his elder son was in the f.** ... *68*

Lu 17:7 and by, when he is come from the f., *68*
Lu 17:31 he that is in the f., let him likewise *68*
Lu 17:36 Two men shall be in the f.; *68*
Ac 1:18 purchased a **f.** with the reward of *5564*
Ac 1:19 **f.** is called in their proper tongue, *5564*
Ac 1:19 that is to say, The **f.** of blood *5564*

FIELDS
Ex 8:13 of the villages, and out of the **f.** 7704
Le 14:53 out of the city into the open **f.**, 7704
Le 25:31 counted as the **f.** of the country: 7704
Le 27:22 is not of the **f.** of his possession; 7704
Nu 16:14 us inheritance of **f.** and vineyards: 7704
Nu 19:16 slain with a sword in the open **f.**, 7704
Nu 20:17 we will not pass through the **f.**, 7704
Nu 21:22 we will not turn into the **f.**, or into 7704
De 11:15 I will send grass in thy **f.** 7704
De 32:13 might eat the increase of the **f.**; 7704
De 32:32 Sodom, and of the **f.** of Gomorrah: 7709
Jos 21:12 the **f.** of the city, and the villages 7704
Jg 9:27 And they went out into the **f.**, 7704
Jg 9:44 the people that were in the **f.**, 7704
1Sa 8:14 take your **f.**, and your vineyards, 7704
1Sa 22:7 Jesse give every one of you good **f.** 7704
1Sa 25:15 with them, when we were in the **f.**: 7704
2Sa 1:21 rain, upon you, nor **f.** of offerings: 7704
2Sa 11:11 encamped in the open **f.**; shall I 7704
1Ki 2:26 to Anathoth, unto thine own **f.**; 7704
1Ki 16:4 and him that dieth of his in the **f.** 7704
2Ki 23:4 Jerusalem in the **f.** of Kidron, 7709
1Ch 6:56 the **f.** of the city, and the villages 7704
1Ch 16:32 let the **f.** rejoice, and all that is 7704
1Ch 27:25 storehouses in the **f.**, in the cities, 7704
2Ch 31:19 which were in the **f.** of the suburbs 7704
Ne 11:25 And for the villages, with their **f.**, 7704
Ne 11:30 Lachish, and the **f.** thereof, at 7704
Ne 12:29 of the **f.** of Geba and Azmaveth: 7704
Ne 12:44 into them out of the **f.** of the cities 7704
Job 5:10 and sendeth waters upon the **f.**: 2351
Ps 107:37 sow the **f.**, and plant vineyards, 7704
Ps 132:6 we found it in the **f.** of the wood, 7704
Pr 8:26 had not made the earth, nor the **f.**, 2351
Pr 23:10 not into the **f.** of the fatherless: 7704
Isa 16:8 For the **f.** of Heshbon languish, 7709
Isa 32:12 for the teats, for the pleasant **f.**, 7704
Jer 6:12 with their **f.** and wives together: 7704
Jer 8:10 their **f.** to them that shall inherit 7704
Jer 13:27 abominations on the hills in the **f.** 7704
Jer 31:40 the **f.** unto the brook of Kidron, 8309
Jer 32:15 Houses and **f.** and vineyards shall 7704
Jer 32:43 And **f.** shall be bought in this land, 7704
Jer 32:44 Men shall buy **f.** for money, and 7704
Jer 39:10 vineyards and **f.** at the same time. 3010
Jer 40:7 of the forces which were in the **f.**, 7704
Jer 40:13 of the forces that were in the **f.**, 7704
Eze 29:5 thou shalt fall upon the open **f.**; 7704
Ho 12:11 heaps in the furrows of the **f.** 7704
Ob 19 **f.** of Ephraim, and the **f.** of Samaria: 7704
Mic 2:2 covet **f.**, and take them by violence; 7704
Mic 2:4 turning away he hath divided our **f.** 7704
Hab 3:17 and the **f.** shall yield no meat; 7709
Mk 2:23 that he went through the corn **f.** on
Lu 6:1 that he went through the corn **f.**; and
Lu 15:15 sent him into his f. to feed swine. *68*
Joh 4:35 look on the f.; for they are white *5561*
Jas 5:4 who have reaped down your **f.**, *5561*

FIERCE See also FIERCER.
Ge 49:7 Cursed be their anger, for it was **f.**; 5794
Ex 32:12 Turn from thy **f.** wrath, and repent 2740
Nu 25:4 **f.** anger of the Lord may be turned 2740
Nu 32:14 augment yet the **f.** anger of the 2740
De 28:50 A nation of **f.** countenance, which 5794
1Sa 20:34 arose from the table in **f.** anger, 2750
1Sa 28:18 nor executedst his **f.** wrath upon 2740
2Ch 28:11 **f.** wrath of the Lord is upon you. 2740
2Ch 28:13 and there is **f.** wrath against Israel. 2740
2Ch 29:10 that his **f.** wrath may turn away 2740
Ezr 10:14 until the **f.** wrath of our God for this 2740
Job 4:10 voice of the **f.** lion, and the teeth 7826
Job 10:16 Thou huntest me as a **f.** lion: 7826
Job 28:8 nor the **f.** lion passed by it 7826
Job 41:10 None is so **f.** that dare stir him up: 393
Ps 88:16 Thy **f.** wrath goeth over me; thy
Isa 7:4 the **f.** anger of Rezin with Syria, 2750
Isa 13:9 with wrath and **f.** anger, to lay 2740
Isa 13:13 and in the day of his **f.** anger. 2740
Isa 19:4 and a **f.** king shall rule over them, 5794
Isa 33:19 Thou shalt not see a **f.** people, 3267
Jer 4:8 **f.** anger of the Lord is not turned 2740
Jer 4:26 of the Lord, and by his **f.** anger. 2740
Jer 12:13 revenues because of the **f.** anger of 2740
Jer 25:37 cut down because of the **f.** anger of 2740
Jer 25:38 and because of his **f.** anger. 2740
Jer 30:24 The **f.** anger of the Lord shall not 2740
Jer 49:37 evil upon them, even my **f.** anger, 2740
Jer 51:45 man his soul from the **f.** anger of 2740
La 1:12 me in the day of his **f.** anger. 2740
La 2:3 He hath cut off in his **f.** anger all 2750
La 4:11 he hath poured out his **f.** anger, 2740
Da 8:23 a king of **f.** countenance, and 5794
Jon 3:9 and turn away from his **f.** anger, 2740
Hab 1:8 more **f.** than the evening wolves: 2300
Zep 2:2 the **f.** anger of the Lord come upon 2740
Zep 3:8 indignation, even all my **f.** anger: 2740
Mt 8:28 exceeding **f.**, so that no man might *5467*
Lu 23:5 they were the more **f.**, saying, *2001*
2Ti 3:3 false accusers, incontinent, **f.**, *434*
Jas 3:4 driven of **f.** winds, yet are they *4642*

FIERCENESS
De 13:17 turn from the **f.** of his anger, 2740
Jos 7:26 turned from the **f.** of his anger. 2740
2Ki 23:26 not from the **f.** of his great wrath, 2740
2Ch 30:8 the **f.** of his wrath may turn away 2740
Job 39:24 He swalloweth the ground with **f.** 7494
Ps 78:49 cast upon them the **f.** of his anger, 2740
Ps 85:3 thyself from the **f.** of thine anger. 2740
Jer 28:38 because of the **f.** of the oppressor, 2740
Ho 11:9 not execute the **f.** of mine anger, 2740
Na 1:6 can abide in the **f.** of his anger? 2740
Re 16:19 of the wine of the **f.** of his wrath. *2372*
Re 19:15 the **f.** and wrath of Almighty God. *2372*

FIERCER
2Sa 19:43 words of the men of Judah were **f.** 7185

FIERY
Nu 21:6 the Lord sent **f.** serpents among 8314
Nu 21:8 a **f.** serpent, and set it upon a pole: 8314
De 8:15 were **f.** serpents, and scorpions, 8314
De 33:2 right hand went a **f.** law for them. 799
Ps 21:9 Thou shalt make them as a **f.** oven 784
Isa 14:29 fruit shall be a **f.** flying serpent. 8314
Isa 30:6 the viper and **f.** flying serpent, 8314
Da 3:6, 11 midst of a burning **f.** furnace. 5135
Da 3:15 the midst of a burning **f.** furnace; 5135
Da 3:17 us from the burning **f.** furnace, 5135
Da 3:20 to cast them into the burning **f.** 5135
Da 3:21, 23 into the midst of the burning **f.** 5135
Da 3:26 the mouth of the burning **f.** furnace, 5135
Da 7:9 his throne was like the **f.** flame, 5135
Da 7:10 A **f.** stream issued and came forth 5135
Eph 6:16 all the **f.** darts of the wicked. *4448*
Heb 10:27 and **f.** indignation, which shall *4442*
1Pe 4:12 the **f.** trial which is to try you, *4451*

FIFTEEN
Ge 5:10 eight hundred and **f.** years, 2568,6240
Ge 7:20 **F.** cubits upward did the 6240
Ge 25:7 an hundred threescore and **f.** 7657,2568
Ex 27:14 of the gate shall be **f.** cubits: 2568,6240
Ex 27:15 shall be hangings **f.** cubits: 2568,6240
Ex 38:14 side of the gate were **f.** cubits; 2568,6240
Ex 38:15 were hangings of **f.** cubits; 2568,6240
Ex 38:25 threescore and **f.** shekels, 7657,2568
Le 27:7 estimation shall be **f.** shekels, 2568,6240
Nu 31:37 and threescore and **f.**, 7657,2568
Jg 8:10 about **f.** thousand men, all 2568,6240
2Sa 9:10 Ziba had **f.** sons and twenty 2568,6240
2Sa 19:17 house of Saul, and his **f.** sons 2568,6240
1Ki 7:3 forty five pillars, **f.** in a row. 2568,6240
2Ki 14:17 Jehoahaz king of Israel **f.** years 2568,6240
2Ki 20:6 will add unto thy days **f.** years; 2568,6240
2Ch 25:25 Jehoahaz king of Israel **f.** years 2568,6240
Isa 38:5 will add unto thy days **f.** years. 2568,6240
Eze 45:12 **f.** shekels, shall be your 6235,2568
Ho 3:2 to me for **f.** pieces of silver. 2568,6240
Joh 11:18 unto Jerusalem, about **f.** furlongs *1178*
Ac 7:14 threescore and **f.** souls. *1440,4002*
Ac 27:28 again, and found it **f.** fathoms. *1178*
Ga 1:18 Peter, and abode with him **f.** days. *1178*

FIFTEENTH
Ex 16:1 **f.** day of the second month 2568,6240
Le 23:6 the **f.** day of the same month 2568,6240
Le 23:34 **f.** day of this seventh month 2568,6240
Le 23:39 the **f.** day of the seventh month, 2568,6240
Nu 28:17 in the **f.** day of this month is 2568,6240
Nu 29:12 **f.** day of the seventh month ye 2568,6240
Nu 33:3 the **f.** day of the first month; 2568,6240
1Ki 12:32 the eighth month, on the **f.** day 2568,6240
1Ki 12:33 the **f.** day of the eighth month, 2568,6240
2Ki 14:23 In the **f.** year of Amaziah the 2568,6240
1Ch 24:14 The **f.** to Bilgah, the sixteenth 2568,6240
1Ch 25:22 **f.** to Jeremoth, he, his sons, 2568,6240
2Ch 15:10 the **f.** year of the reign of Asa. 2568,6240
Es 9:18 **f.** day of the same they rested, 2568,6240
Es 9:21 and the **f.** day of the same, 2568,6240
Eze 32:17 in the **f.** day of the month, 2568,6240
Eze 45:25 seventh month, in the **f.** day 2568,6240
Lu 3:1 Now in the **f.** year of the reign *4003*

FIFTH
Ge 1:23 and the morning were the **f.** day. 2549
Ge 30:17 conceived, and bare Jacob the **f.** 2549
Ge 41:34 and take up the **f.** part of the land 2567
Ge 47:24 that ye shall give the **f.** part unto 2549
Ge 47:26 that Pharaoh should have the **f.** 2569
Le 5:16 and shall add the **f.** part thereto, 2549
Le 6:5 add the **f.** part more thereto, and 2549
Le 19:25 And in the **f.** year shall ye eat of the 2549
Le 22:14 then he shall put the **f.** part thereof 2549
Le 27:13 then he shall add a **f.** part thereof 2549
Le 27:15, 19 shall add the **f.** part of the money 2549
Le 27:27 and shall add a **f.** part of it thereto: 2549
Le 27:31 shall add thereto the **f.** part thereof. 2549
Nu 5:7 and add unto it the **f.** part thereof. 2549
Nu 7:36 On the **f.** day Shelumiel the son of 2549
Nu 29:26 And on the **f.** day nine bullocks, 2549
Nu 33:38 in the first day of the **f.** month. 2549
De *general* *title* **F.** Book of Moses, Called
Jos 19:24 the **f.** lot came out for the tribe 2549
Jg 19:8 morning on the **f.** day to depart: 2549
2Sa 2:23 spear smote him under the **f.** rib, 2570
2Sa 3:4 and the **f.**, Shephatiah the son of 2549
2Sa 3:27 smote him there under the **f.** rib, 2570
2Sa 4:6 they smote him under the **f.** rib: 2570
2Sa 20:10 smote him therewith in the **f.** rib, 2570
1Ki 6:31 lintel and side posts were a **f.** part 2549
1Ki 14:25 in the **f.** year of king Rehoboam, 2549
2Ki 8:16 in the **f.** year of Joram the son of 2568
2Ki 25:8 the **f.** month, on the seventh day 2549
1Ch 2:14 Nethaneel the fourth, Raddai the **f.**, 2549
1Ch 3:3 The **f.**, Shephatiah of Abital: the 2549
1Ch 8:2 Nohah the fourth, and Rapha the **f.** 2549
1Ch 12:10 the fourth, Jeremiah the **f.**, 2549
1Ch 24:9 The **f.** to Malchijah, the sixth to 2549
1Ch 25:12 The **f.** to Nethaniah, he, his sons, 2549
1Ch 26:3 Elam the **f.**, Jehohanan the sixth, 2549
1Ch 26:4 Sacar the fourth, Nethaneel the **f.**, 2549
1Ch 27:8 The **f.** captain for the **f.** month 2549
2Ch 12:2 in the **f.** year of king Rehoboam 2549
Ezr 7:8 came to Jerusalem in the **f.** month, 2549
Ezr 7:9 on the first day of the **f.** month 2549
Ne 6:5 the **f.** time with an open letter 2549
Ne 6:15 finished in the twenty and **f.** day 2568
Jer 1:3 Jerusalem captive in the **f.** month. 2549
Jer 28:1 fourth year, and in the **f.** month, 2549
Jer 36:9 to pass in the **f.** year of Jehoiakim 2549
Jer 52:12 in the **f.** month, in the tenth day 2549
Eze 1:1 in the **f.** day of the month, as I was 2568
Eze 1:2 In the **f.** day of the month, which 2568
Eze 1:2 the **f.** year of king Jehoiachin's 2549
Eze 8:1 in the **f.** day of the month, as I sat 2568
Eze 20:1 the seventh year, in the **f.** month, 2549
Eze 33:21 in the **f.** day of the month, that one 2568
Zec 7:3 Should I weep in the **f.** month, 2549
Zec 7:5 mourned in the **f.** and seventh 2549
Zec 8:19 of the **f.**, and the last of the seventh, 2549
Re 6:9 when he had opened the **f.** seal, *3991*
Re 9:1 And the **f.** angel sounded, and I saw *3991*
Re 16:10 And the **f.** angel poured out his vial *3991*
Re 21:20 The **f.**, sardonyx; the sixth, sardius; *3991*

FIFTIES
Ex 18:21 rulers of **f.**, and rulers of tens: 2572
Ex 18:25 rulers of hundreds, ruler of **f.**, 2572
De 1:15 captains over **f.**, and captains over 2572
1Sa 8:12 captains over **f.**; and will set them 2572
2Ki 1:14 captains of the former **f.** with their 2572
Mk 6:40 in ranks, by hundreds, and by **f.** *4004*
Lu 9:14 them sit down by f. in a company. *4004*

FIFTIETH

Le 25:10 And ye shall hallow the **f.** year, ... 2572
Le 25:11 A jubile shall that **f.** year be unto 2572
2Ki 15:23 In the **f.** year of Azariah king of......... 2572
2Ki 15:27 In the two and **f.** year of Azariah 2572

FIFTY See also FIFTIES.

Ge 6:15 the breadth of it **f.** cubits, and........... 2572
Ge 7:24 the earth an hundred and **f.** days.......... 2572
Ge 8:3 the end of the hundred and **f.** days..... 2572
Ge 9:28 flood three hundred and **f.** years. 2572
Ge 9:29 of Noah were nine hundred and **f.** 2572
Ge 18:24 Peradventure there be **f.** righteous..... 2572
Ge 18:24 spare the place for the **f.** righteous..... 2572
Ge 18:26 said, If I find in Sodom **f.** righteous 2572
Ge 18:28 there shall lack five of the **f.** 2572
Ex 26:5 **F.** loops shalt thou make in the 2572
Ex 26:5 one curtain, and **f.** loops shalt thou..... 2572
Ex 26:6 thou shalt make **f.** taches of gold,....... 2572
Ex 26:10 shalt make **f.** loops on the edge of...... 2572
Ex 26:10 and **f.** loops in the edge of the............ 2572
Ex 26:11 thou shalt make **f.** taches of brass, ... 2572
Ex 27:12 side shall be hangings of **f.** cubits: 2572
Ex 27:13 side eastward shall be **f.** cubits. 2572
Ex 27:18 and the breadth **f.** every where, ... 2572
Ex 30:23 even two hundred and **f.** shekels,....... 2572
Ex 30:23 two hundred and **f.** shekels, ... 2572
Ex 36:12 **F.** loops made he in one curtain,........ 2572
Ex 36:12 and **f.** loops made he in the edge 2572
Ex 36:13 And he made **f.** taches of gold,.......... 2572
Ex 36:17 **f.** loops upon the uttermost edge 2572
Ex 36:17 and **f.** loops made he upon the edge ... 2572
Ex 36:18 And he made **f.** taches of brass 2572
Ex 38:12 side were hangings of **f.** cubits, ... 2572
Ex 38:13 the east side eastward **f.** cubits. 2572
Ex 38:26 and five hundred and **f.** men............. 2572
Le 23:16 sabbath shall ye number **f.** days; 2572
Le 27:3 thy estimation shall be **f.** shekels........ 2572
Le 27:16 be valued at **f.** shekels of silver. 2572
Nu 1:23 **f.** and nine thousand and three........... 2572
Nu 1:25 five thousand six hundred and **f.**......... 2572
Nu 1:29 were **f.** and four thousand and four..... 2572
Nu 1:31 were **f.** and seven thousand and four... 2572
Nu 1:43 were **f.** and three thousand and four ... 2572
Nu 1:46 thousand and five hundred and **f.**......... 2572
Nu 2:6 were **f.** and four thousand and four....... 2572
Nu 2:8 were **f.** and seven thousand and four... 2572
Nu 2:13 were **f.** and nine thousand and three ... 2572
Nu 2:15 thousand and six hundred and **f.**.......... 2572
Nu 2:16 an hundred thousand and **f.** and 2572
Nu 2:16 thousand and four hundred and **f.**, ... 2572
Nu 2:30 were **f.** and three thousand and four ... 2572
Nu 2:31 an hundred thousand and **f.** and 2572
Nu 2:32 thousand and five hundred and **f.**......... 2572
Nu 4:3 even until **f.** years old, all that........... 2572
Nu 4:23 until **f.** years old shalt thou number 2572
Nu 4:30 even unto **f.** years old shalt thou........ 2572
Nu 4:35 upward even unto **f.** years old, ... 2572
Nu 4:36 two thousand seven hundred and **f.**....... 2572
Nu 4:39, 43,47 upward even unto **f.** years........ 2572
Nu 8:25 the age of **f.** years they shall cease 2572
Nu 16:2 two hundred and **f.** princes of the,....... 2572
Nu 16:17 censer, two hundred and **f.** censers; ... 2572
Nu 16:35 consumed the two hundred and **f.**........ 2572
Nu 26:10 devoured two hundred and **f.** men: 2572
Nu 26:34 them, **f.** and two thousand and seven... 2572
Nu 26:47 were **f.** and three thousand and four ... 2572
Nu 31:30 thou shalt take one portion of **f.**,........ 2572
Nu 31:47 Moses took one portion of **f.**, both..... 2572
Nu 31:52 thousand seven hundred and **f.** 2572
De 22:29 unto the damsel's father **f.** shekels 2572
Jos 7:21 and a wedge of gold of **f.** shekels....... 2572
1Sa 6:19 he smote of the people **f.** thousand..... 2572
2Sa 15:1 and **f.** men to run before him. 2572
2Sa 24:24 and the oxen for **f.** shekels of silver.... 2572
1Ki 1:5 and **f.** men to run before him. 2572
1Ki 7:2 and the breadth thereof **f.** cubits, ... 2572
1Ki 7:6 the length thereof was **f.** cubits, ... 2572
1Ki 9:23 five hundred and **f.**, which bare rule.... 2572
1Ki 10:29 and an horse for an hundred and **f.**: 2572
1Ki 18:4 and hid them by **f.** in a cave,............ 2572
1Ki 18:13 the Lord's prophets by **f.** in a cave, ... 2572
1Ki 18:19 prophets of Baal four hundred and **f.**... 2572
1Ki 18:22 prophets are four hundred and **f.**........ 2572
2Ki 1:9 unto him a captain of **f.** with his **f.**. 2572
2Ki 1:10 and said to the captain of **f.**,............ 2572
2Ki 1:10 and consume thee and thy **f.**. 2572
2Ki 1:10 and consumed him and his **f.**. 2572
2Ki 1:11 him another captain of **f.** with his **f.**.... 2572
2Ki 1:12 and consume thee and thy **f.**. 2572
2Ki 1:12 and consumed him and his **f.**. 2572
2Ki 1:13 a captain of the third **f.** with his **f.**...... 2572
2Ki 1:13 And the third captain of **f.** went 2572
2Ki 1:13 the life of these **f.** thy servants,......... 2572
2Ki 2:7 **f.** men of the sons of the prophets 2572
2Ki 2:16 be with thy servants **f.** strong men;.... 2572
2Ki 2:17 They sent therefore **f.** men: and........ 2572
2Ki 13:7 people to Jehoahaz but **f.** horsemen, ... 2572
2Ki 15:2 and he reigned two and **f.** years in 2572
2Ki 15:20 of each man **f.** shekels of silver, ... 2572
2Ki 15:25 with him **f.** men of the Gileadites: 2572
2Ki 21:1 and reigned **f.** and five years in.......... 2572
1Ch 5:21 of their camels **f.** thousand, and......... 2572
1Ch 5:21 two hundred and **f.** thousand, ... 2572
1Ch 8:40 and sons' sons, an hundred and **f.**. 2572
1Ch 9:9 nine hundred and **f.** and six. 2572
1Ch 12:33 instruments of war, **f.** thousand, ... 2572
2Ch 1:17 an horse for an hundred and **f.**: 2572
2Ch 2:17 an hundred and **f.** thousand and 2572
2Ch 3:9 of the nails was **f.** shekels of gold. 2572
2Ch 8:10 two hundred and **f.**, that bare rule....... 2572
2Ch 8:18 four hundred and **f.** talents of gold,..... 2572
2Ch 26:3 and he reigned **f.** and two years in 2572
2Ch 33:1 and he reigned **f.** and five years in 2572
Ezr 2:7 thousand two hundred **f.** and four....... 2572
Ezr 2:14 of Bigvai, two thousand **f.** and six. 2572
Ezr 2:15 of Adin, four hundred **f.** and four........ 2572
Ezr 2:22 The men of Netophah, **f.** and six......... 2572
Ezr 2:29 The children of Nebo, **f.** and two. 2572
Ezr 2:30 of Magbish, an hundred **f.** and six. 2572
Ezr 2:31 thousand two hundred **f.** and four....... 2572
Ezr 2:37 of Immer, a thousand **f.** and two. 2572
Ezr 2:60 of Nekoda, six hundred **f.** and two...... 2572
Ezr 8:3 of the males an hundred and **f.**. 2572
Ezr 8:6 Jonathan, and with him **f.** males. 2572
Ezr 8:26 six hundred and **f.** talents of silver,..... 2572
Ne 5:17 an hundred and **f.** of the Jews and........ 2572
Ne 6:15 the month Elul, in **f.** and two days. 2572
Ne 7:10 of Arah, six hundred **f.** and two. 2572
Ne 7:12 thousand two hundred **f.** and four. 2572
Ne 7:20 of Adin, six hundred **f.** and five.......... 2572
Ne 7:33 of the other Nebo, **f.** and two. 2572
Ne 7:34 thousand two hundred **f.** and four....... 2572
Ne 7:40 of Immer, a thousand **f.** and two. 2572
Ne 7:70 **f.** basons, five hundred and thirty........ 2572
Es 5:14 gallows be made of **f.** cubits high,....... 2572
Es 7:9 also, the gallows **f.** cubits high,........... 2572
Isa 3:3 captain of **f.**, and the honourable 2572
Eze 40:15 of the inner gate were **f. cubits. 2572**
Eze 40:21 the length thereof was f. cubits,..... 2572
Eze 40:25 the length was **f.** cubits, and the........ 2572
Eze 40:29, 33 it was **f.** cubits long, and five 2572
Eze 40:36 the length was **f.** cubits, and the........ 2572
Eze 42:2 and the breadth was **f.** cubits. 2572
Eze 42:7 the length thereof was **f.** cubits. 2572
Eze 42:8 in the utter court was **f.** cubits: 2572
Eze 45:2 and **f.** cubits round about for the........ 2572
Eze 48:17 the north two hundred and **f.**, ... 2572
Eze 48:17 the south two hundred and **f.**, ... 2572
Eze 48:17 toward the east two hundred and **f.**, ... 2572
Eze 48:17 the west two hundred and **f.**. 2572
Hag 2:16 draw out **f.** vessels out of the press, .. 2572
Lu 7:41 **hundred pence, and the other f., ...** *4004*
Lu 16:6 **and sit down quickly, and write f ...** *4004*
Joh 8:57 Thou art not yet **f.** years old,........... *4004*
Joh 21:11 an hundred and **f.** and three: *4004*
Ac 13:20 of four hundred and **f.** years,............ *4004*
Ac 19:19 found it **f.** thousand pieces of *4002, 3461*

FIG See also FIGS.

Ge 3:7 and they sewed **f.** leaves together,..... 8384
De 8:8 barley, and vines, and **f.** trees, ... 8384
Jg 9:10 the trees said to the **f.** tree, ... 8384
Jg 9:11 But the **f.** tree said unto them,.......... 8384
1Ki 4:25 his vine and under his **f.** tree, ... 8384
2Ki 18:31 and every one of his **f.** tree, ... 8384
Ps 105:33 their vines also and their **f.** trees; 8384
Pr 27:18 Whoso keepeth the **f.** tree shall eat.... 8384
Ca 2:13 **f.** tree putteth forth her green figs, ... 8384
Isa 34:4 as a falling **f.** from the **f.** tree........ 8384
Isa 36:16 vine, and every one of his **f.** tree,...... 8384
Jer 5:17 eat up thy vines and thy **f.** trees:....... 8384
Jer 8:13 nor figs on the **f.** tree, and the leaf 8384
Ho 2:12 destroy her vines and her **f.** trees,..... 8384
Ho 9:10 as the firstripe in the **f.** tree 8384
Joe 1:7 vine waste, and barked my **f.** tree,..... 8384
Joe 1:12 and the **f.** tree languisheth; the.......... 8384
Joe 2:22 the **f.** tree and the vine do yield 8384
Am 4:9 your vineyards and your **f.** trees 8384
Mic 4:4 under his **f.** tree; and none shall 8384
Na 3:12 strong holds shall be like **f.** trees 8384
Hab 3:17 the **f.** tree shall not blossom, ... 8384
Hag 2:19 as yet the vine, and the **f.** tree,.......... 8384
Zec 3:10 the vine and under the **f.** tree. 8384
Mt 21:19 when he saw a **f.** tree in the way,...... *4808*
Mt 21:19 presently the **f.** tree withered away.... *4808*
Mt 21:20 soon is the **f.** tree withered away!...... *4808*
Mt 21:21 **this which is done to the f. tree, ...** *4808*
Mt 24:32 **learn a parable of the f. tree; ....** *4808*
Mk 11:13 a **f.** tree afar off having leaves, ... *4808*
Mk 11:20 they saw the **f.** tree dried up *4808*
Mk 11:21 the **f.** tree which thou cursedst........... *4808*
Mk 13:28 **learn a parable of the f. tree; ....** *4808*
Lu 13:6 **certain man had a f. tree planted ..** *4808*
Lu 13:7 **come seeking fruit on this f. tree, ..** *4808*
Lu 21:29 **Behold the f. tree, and all the ....** *4808*
Joh 1:48 when thou wast under the **f.** tree,........ *4808*
Joh 1:50 I saw thee under the **f.** tree,.............. *4808*
Jas 3:12 Can the **f.** tree, my brethren, bear....... *4808*
Re 6:13 a **f.** tree casteth her untimely figs, ... *4808*

FIGHT See also FIGHTETH; FIGHTING; FOUGHT.

Ex 1:10 also unto our enemies, and **f.**............ 3898
Ex 14:14 The Lord shall **f.** for you, and ye 3898
Ex 17:9 go out, **f.** with Amalek; tomorrow 3898
De 1:30 he shall go **f.** for you according to all .. 3898
De 1:41 we will go up and **f.**, according to 3898
De 1:42 Go not up, neither **f.**; for I am 3898
De 2:32 out he and all his people, to **f.**........... 4421
De 3:22 your God he shall **f.** for you............. 3898
De 20:4 to **f.** for you against your enemies,..... 3898
De 20:10 thou comest nigh unto a city to **f.** 3898
Jos 9:2 to **f.** with Joshua and with Israel, ... 3898
Jos 10:25 your enemies against whom ye **f.**........ 3898
Jos 11:5 of Merom, to **f.** against Israel............ 3898
Jos 19:47 children of Dan went up to **f.** 3898
Jg 1:1 Canaanites first, to **f.** against them?.... 3898
Jg 1:3 we may **f.** against the Canaanites; 3898
Jg 1:9 down to **f.** against the Canaanites, ... 3898
Jg 8:1 us not, when thou wentest to **f.**......... 3898
Jg 9:38 out, I pray now, and **f.** with them. 3898
Jg 10:9 to **f.** also against Judah, and 3898
Jg 10:18 is he that will begin to **f.** against 3898
Jg 11:6 that we may **f.** with the children 3898
Jg 11:8 **f.** against the children of Ammon,....... 3898
Jg 11:9 to **f.** against the children of Ammon,... 3898
Jg 11:12 come against me to **f.** in my land?...... 3898
Jg 11:25 or did he ever **f.** against them, ... 3898
Jg 11:32 the children of Ammon to **f.** against.... 3898
Jg 12:1 Wherefore passedst thou over to **f.** 3898
Jg 12:3 unto me this day, to **f.** against me? 3898
Jg 20:20 put themselves in array to **f.**............. 4421
1Sa 4:9 quit yourselves like men, and **f.**. 3898
1Sa 8:20 go out before us, and **f.** our battles. ... 3898
1Sa 13:5 gathered themselves together to **f.**...... 3898
1Sa 15:18 and **f.** against them until they be........ 3898
1Sa 17:9 If he be able to **f.** with me,............... 3898
1Sa 17:10 man, that we may **f.** together............ 3898
1Sa 17:20 the host was going forth to the **f.**,...... 4634
1Sa 17:32 go and **f.** with this Philistine.............. 3898
1Sa 17:33 to go against this Philistine to **f.**......... 3898
1Sa 18:17 for me, and **f.** the Lord's battles. 3898
1Sa 23:1 the Philistines **f.** against Keilah, ... 3898
1Sa 28:1 for warfare to **f.** with Israel............... 3898
1Sa 29:8 may not go **f.** against the enemies........ 3898
2Sa 11:20 nigh unto the city when ye did **f.**? 3898
1Ki 12:21 to **f.** against the house of Israel, ... 3898
1Ki 12:24 nor **f.** against your brethren the......... 3898
1Ki 20:23 us **f.** against them in the plain, ... 3898
1Ki 20:25 will **f.** against them in the plain, ... 3898
1Ki 20:26 up to Aphek, to **f.** against Israel. 4421
1Ki 22:31 **F.** neither with small nor great, ... 3898
1Ki 22:32 turned aside to **f.** against him: 3898
2Ki 3:21 the kings were come up to **f.**.............. 3898
2Ki 10:3 and **f.** for your master's house............ 3898
2Ki 19:9 he is come out to **f.** against thee:....... 3898
2Ch 11:1 to **f.** against Israel, that he might 3898
2Ch 11:4 nor **f.** against your brethren: 3898
2Ch 13:12 **f.** ye not against the Lord God 3898
2Ch 18:30 **F.** ye not with small or great, ... 3898
2Ch 18:31 they compassed about him to **f.** 3898

2Ch 20:17 shall not need to f. in this battle: 3898
2Ch 32:2 purposed to f. against Jerusalem, 4421
2Ch 32:8 to help us, and to f. our battles. 3898
2Ch 35:20 Necho king of Egypt came up to f. 3898
2Ch 35:22 might f. with him, and hearkened 3898
2Ch 35:22 came to f. in the valley of Megiddo. 3898
Ne 4:8 to f. against Jerusalem, and to 3898
Ne 4:14 and f. for your brethren, your 3898
Ne 4:20 our God shall f. for us. 3898
Ps 35:1 f. against them that f. against me. 3898
Ps 56:2 they be many that f. against me, 3898
Ps 144:1 to war, and my fingers to f.: 4421
Isa 19:2 and they shall f. every one against 3898
Isa 29:7 the nations that f. against Ariel, 6633
Isa 29:7 even all that f. against her and her 6633
Isa 29:8 be, that f. against mount Zion. 6633
Isa 30:32 in battles of shaking will he f. 3898
Isa 31:4 to f. for mount Zion, and for the 6633
Jer 1:19 they shall f. against thee; but 3898
Jer 15:20 and they shall f. against thee; 3898
Jer 21:4 ye f. against the king of Babylon, 3898
Jer 21:5 And I myself will f. against you 3898
Jer 32:5 though ye f. with the Chaldeans, 3898
Jer 32:24 of the Chaldeans, that f. against it, 3898
Jer 32:29 Chaldeans, that f. against this city, 3898
Jer 33:5 They come to f. with the Chaldeans, 3898
Jer 34:22 and they shall f. against it, and 3898
Jer 37:8 again, and f. against this city, 3898
Jer 37:10 army of the Chaldeans that f. 3898
Jer 41:12 to f. with Ishmael the son of 3898
Jer 51:30 men of Babylon have forborn to f., 3898
Da 10:20 will I return to f. with the prince 3898
Da 11:11 shall come forth and f. with him, 3898
Zec 10:5 and they shall f., because the Lord 3898
Zec 14:3 forth, and f. against those nations, 3898
Zec 14:14 Judah also shall f. at Jerusalem; 3898
Joh 18:36 **then would my servants f.,** *75*
Ac 5:39 be found even to f. against God. *2314*
Ac 23:9 let us not f. against God. *2313*
1Co 9:26 so f. I, not as one that beateth *4438*
1Ti 6:12 F. the good…of faith, lay hold on *75*
1Ti 6:12 the good f. of faith, lay hold on *73*
2Ti 4:7 a good f., I have finished my course, *73*
Heb 10:32 endured a great f. of afflictions; *119*
Heb 11:34 waxed valiant in f., turned to *4171*
Jas 4:2 ye f. and war, yet ye have not, *3164*
Re 2:16 **f. against them with the sword** *4170*

FIGHTETH
Ex 14:25 the Lord f. for them against the 3898
Jos 23:10 he it is that f. for you, as he hath 3898
1Sa 25:28 my lord f. the battles of the Lord, 3898

FIGHTING See also FIGHTINGS.
1Sa 17:19 of Elah, f. with the Philistines. 3898
2Ch 26:11 host of f. men, that went 6213,4421
Ps 56:1 me up; he f. daily oppresseth me. 3898

FIGHTINGS
2Co 7:5 without were f., within were fears. *3163*
Jas 4:1 come wars and f. among you? *3163*

FIG-LEAVES See FIG and LEAVES.

FIGS
Nu 13:23 the pomegranates, and of the f. 8384
Nu 20:5 it is no place of seed, or of f., 8384
1Sa 25:18 two hundred cakes of f., and laid
1Sa 30:12 they gave him a piece of a cake of f.,
2Ki 20:7 Isaiah said, Take a lump of f. 8384
1Ch 12:40 oxen, and meat, meal, cakes of f.,
Ne 13:15 also wine, grapes, and f., 8384
Ca 2:13 fig tree putteth forth her green f., 6291
Isa 38:21 let them take a lump of f., 8384
Jer 8:13 nor f. on the fig tree, and the leaf 8384
Jer 24:1 two baskets of f. were set before 8384
Jer 24:2 One basket had very good f., 8384
Jer 24:2 even like the f. that are first ripe: 8384
Jer 24:2 other basket had very naughty f. 8384
Jer 24:3 I said, F.; the good f., very good; 8384
Jer 24:5 Like these good f., so will I 8384
Jer 24:8 the evil, f. which cannot be eaten, 8384
Jer 29:17 I will make them like vile f., 8384
Na 3:12 like fig trees with the firstripe f.:
Mt 7:16 **grapes of thorns, or f. of thistles?** *4810*
Mk 11:13 for the time of f. was not yet. *4810*
Lu 6:44 **of thorns men do not gather f.,** *4810*
Jas 3:12 either a vine, f.? so can no fountain *4810*
Re 6:13 a fig tree casteth her untimely f., *3653*

FIG-TREE See FIG and TREE.

FIGURE See also DISFIGURE; FIGURES; TRANSFIGURED.
De 4:16 image, the similitude of any f., 5566
Isa 44:13 maketh it after the f. of a man, 8403
Ro 5:14 is the f. of him that was to come. *5179*
1Co 4:6 I have in a f. transferred to myself *3345*
Heb 9:9 was a f. for the time then present, *3850*
Heb 11:19 also he received him in a f. *3850*
1Pe 3:21 like f. whereunto even baptism *499*

FIGURES
1Ki 6:29 carved f. of cherubims and palm 4734
Ac 7:43 f. which ye made to worship *5179*
Heb 9:24 which are the f. of the true; *499*

FILE
1Sa 13:21 had a f. for the mattocks, 6477,6310

FILL See also FILLED; FILLEST; FILLETH; FILLING; FULFIL.
Ge 1:22 and f. the waters in the seas, 4390
Ge 42:25 Joseph commanded to f. their sacks 4390
Ge 44:1 F. the men's sacks with food, as 4390
Ex 10:6 And they shall f. thy houses, 4390
Ex 16:32 F. an omer of it to be kept 4393
Le 25:19 eat your f., and dwell therein 7648
De 23:24 thou mayest eat grapes thy f. at 7648
1Sa 16:1 f. thine horn with oil, and go, 4390
1Ki 18:33 F. four barrels with water, and 4390
Job 8:21 Till he f. thy mouth with laughing, 4390
Job 15:2 and f. his belly with the east wind? 4390
Job 20:23 When he is about to f. his belly, 4390
Job 23:4 and f. my mouth with arguments. 4390
Job 38:39 f. the appetite of the young lions, 4390
Job 41:7 thou f. his skin with barbed irons? 4390
Ps 81:10 thy mouth wide, and I will f. it. 4390
Ps 83:16 F. their faces with shame; that 4390
Ps 110:6 he shall f. the places with the dead 4390
Pr 1:13 we shall f. our houses with spoil: 4390
Pr 7:18 Come, let us take our f. of love 7301
Pr 8:21 and I will f. their treasures. 4390
Isa 8:8 shall f. the breadth of thy land, 4393
Isa 14:21 f. the face of the world with cities. 4390
Isa 27:6 f. the face of the world with fruit. 4390
Isa 56:12 f. ourselves with strong drink; 5433
Jer 13:13 I will f. all the inhabitants of 4390
Jer 23:24 Do not I f. heaven and earth? 4390
Jer 33:5 is to f. them with the dead bodies 4390
Jer 51:14 Surely I will f. thee with men, 4390
Eze 3:3 and f. thy bowels with this roll 4390
Eze 7:19 their souls, neither f. their bowels: 4390
Eze 9:7 and f. the courts with the slain: 4390
Eze 10:2 f. thine hand with coals of fire 4390
Eze 24:4 f. it with the choice bones. 4390
Eze 30:11 and f. the land with the slain. 4390
Eze 32:4 f. the beasts of the whole earth 7646
Eze 32:5 and f. the valleys with thy height. 4390
Eze 35:8 and I will f. his mountains with 4390
Zep 1:9 which f. their masters' houses 4390
Hag 2:7 and I will f. this house with glory, 4390
Mt 9:16 **which is put in to f. it up taketh** *4138*
Mt 15:33 as to f. so great a multitude? *5526*
Mt 23:32 **F. ye up then the measure of** *4137*
Joh 2:7 **F. the water pots with water** *1072*
Ro 15:13 f. you with all joy and peace in *4137*
Eph 4:10 that he might f. all things.) *4137*
Col 1:24 f. up that which is behind of the *466*
1Th 2:16 to f. up their sins alway: for the *378*
Re 18:6 she hath filled f. to her double. *2767*

FILLED See also FILLEDST; FULFILLED.
Ge 6:11 the earth was f. with violence. 4390
Ge 6:13 for the earth is f. with violence 4390
Ge 21:19 went, and f. the bottle with water, 4390
Ge 24:16 and f. her pitcher, and came up. 4390
Ge 26:15 them, and f. them with earth. 4390
Ex 1:7 and the land was f. with them. 4390
Ex 2:16 and f. the troughs to water their 4390
Ex 16:12 morning ye shall be f. with bread; 7646
Ex 28:3 whom I have f. with the spirit 4390
Ex 31:3 And I have f. him with the spirit 4390
Ex 35:31 And he hath f. him with the spirit 4390
Ex 35:35 hath he f. with wisdom of heart 4390
Ex 40:34, 35 and the glory of the Lord f. the 4390
Nu 14:21 the earth shall be f. with the glory 4390
De 26:12 eat within thy gates, and be f.; 7646
De 31:20 shall have eaten and f. themselves, 7646
Jos 9:13 these bottles of wine, which we f., 4390
1Ki 7:14 and he was f. with wisdom, and 4390
1Ki 8:10 the cloud f. the house of the Lord, 4390
1Ki 8:11 glory of the Lord had f. the house 4390
1Ki 18:35 he f. the trench also with water. 4390
1Ki 20:27 but the Syrians f. the country. 4390
2Ki 3:17 that valley shall be f. with water, 4390
2Ki 3:20 and the country was f. with water. 4390
2Ki 3:25 cast every man his stone, and f. it; 4390
2Ki 21:16 till he had f. Jerusalem from one 4390
2Ki 23:14 and f. their places with the bones. 4390
2Ki 24:4 for he f. Jerusalem with innocent 4390
2Ch 5:13 the house was f. with a cloud, 4390
2Ch 5:14 glory of the Lord had f. the house 4390
2Ch 7:1 the glory of the Lord f. the house. 4390
2Ch 7:2 glory of the Lord had f. the Lord's 4390
2Ch 16:14 which was f. with sweet odours 4390
Ezr 9:11 have f. it from one end to another. 4390
Ne 9:25 so they did eat, and were f., 7646
Job 3:15 who f. their houses with silver: 4390
Job 16:8 thou hast f. me with wrinkles, 7059
Job 22:18 f. their houses with good things: 4390
Ps 38:7 are f. with a loathsome disease: 4390
Ps 71:8 Let my mouth be f. with thy praise 4390
Ps 72:19 the whole earth be f. with his glory; 4390
Ps 78:29 they did eat, and were well f.: 7646
Ps 80:9 take deep root, and it f. the land. 4390
Ps 104:28 thy hand, they are f. with good. 7646
Ps 123:3 are exceedingly f. with contempt. 7646
Ps 123:4 exceedingly f. with the scorning 7646
Ps 126:2 was our mouth f. with laughter, 4390
Pr 1:31 fruit of their own way, and be f. 7646
Pr 3:10 shall thy barns be f. with plenty. 4390
Pr 5:10 strangers be f. with thy wealth; 7646
Pr 12:21 wicked shall be f. with mischief. 4390
Pr 14:14 backslider in heart shall be f. 7646
Pr 18:20 increase of his lips shall he be f.. 7646
Pr 20:17 his mouth shall be f. with gravel. 4390
Pr 24:4 shall the chambers be f. with all 4390
Pr 25:16 thou be f. therewith, and vomit 7646
Pr 30:16 the earth that is not f. with water, 7646
Pr 30:22 a fool when he is f. with meat; 7646
Ec 1:8 nor the ear f. with hearing. 4390
Ec 6:3 his soul be not f. with good, 7646
Ec 6:7 and yet the appetite is not f.. 4390
Ca 5:2 head is f. with dew, and my locks 4390
Isa 6:1 up, and his train f. the temple. 4390
Isa 6:4 and the house was f. with smoke. 4390
Isa 21:3 Therefore are my loins f. with 4390
Isa 33:5 he hath f. Zion with judgment 4390
Isa 34:6 sword of the Lord is f. with blood, 4390
Isa 43:24 neither hast thou f. me with the 7301
Isa 65:20 old man that hath not f. his days: 4390
Jer 13:12 Every bottle shall be f. with wine: 4390
Jer 13:12 every bottle shall be f. with wine? 4390
Jer 15:17 thou hast f. me with indignation. 4390
Jer 16:18 they have f. mine inheritance with 4390
Jer 19:4 have f. this place with the blood 4390
Jer 41:9 Ishmael the son of Nethaniah f. it 4390
Jer 46:12 and the cry hath f. the land: 4390
Jer 51:5 though their land was f. with sin 4390
Jer 51:34 hath f. his belly with my delicates, 4390
La 3:15 He hath f. me with bitterness. 7646
La 3:30 he is f. full with reproach. 7646
Eze 8:17 have f. the land with violence, 4390
Eze 10:3 and the cloud f. the inner court. 4390
Eze 10:4 the house was f. with the cloud, 4390
Eze 11:6 and ye have f. the streets thereof 4390
Eze 23:33 Thou shalt be f. with drunkenness 4390
Eze 28:16 f. the midst of thee with violence, 4390
Eze 36:38 the waste cities be f. with flocks 4390
Eze 39:20 Thus ye shall be f. at my table 7646
Eze 43:5 the glory of the Lord f. the house. 4390
Eze 44:4 the Lord f. the house of the Lord: 4390
Da 2:35 mountain, and f. the whole earth. 4391
Ho 13:6 to their pasture, so were they f.; 7646
Ho 13:6 they were f., and their heart was 7646
Na 2:12 and f. his holes with prey, and his 4390
Hab 2:14 shall be f. with the knowledge 4390
Hab 2:16 Thou art f. with shame for glory: 7646
Hag 1:6 but ye are not f. with drink;
Zec 9:13 f. the bow with Ephraim, and 4390
Zec 9:15 and they shall be f. like bowls, 4390
Mt 5:6 **righteousness: for they shall be f.** *5526*
Mt 14:20 And they did all eat, and were f.: *5526*
Mt 15:37 And they did all eat, and were f.: *5526*
Mt 27:48 a spunge, and f. it with vinegar, *4130*
Mk 2:21 **the new piece that f. it up** *4138*

Mk 6:42 And they did all eat, and were **f.**........ *5526*
Mk 7:27 **Let the children first be f.:** *5526*
Mk 8:8 So they did eat, and were **f.**: *5526*
Mk 15:36 and **f.** a spunge full of vinegar, ... *1072*
Lu 1:15 he shall be **f.** with the Holy Ghost,..... *4130*
Lu 1:41 Elisabeth was **f.** with the Holy.......... *4130*
Lu 1:53 He hath **f.** the hungry with good........ *1705*
Lu 1:67 Zacharias was **f.** with the Holy........... *4130*
Lu 2:40 strong in spirit, **f.** with wisdom:......... *4137*
Lu 3:5 Every valley shall be **f.**, and every..... *4137*
Lu 4:28 these things, were **f.** with wrath, ... *4130*
Lu 5:7 they came and **f.** both the ships,........ *4130*
Lu 5:26 and were **f.** with fear, saying,........... *4130*
Lu 6:11 And they were **f.** with madness; *4130*
Lu 6:21 **hunger now: for ye shall be f..** *5526*
Lu 8:23 and they were **f.** with water,............. *4845*
Lu 9:17 And they did eat, and were all **f.**:....... *5526*
Lu 14:23 **come in, that my house may be f.:** .*1072*
Lu 15:16 **And he would fain have f. his** *1072*
Joh 2:7 And they **f.** them up to the brim......... *1072*
Joh 6:12 When they were **f.**, he said unto........ *1705*
Joh 6:13 and **f.** twelve baskets with the........... *1072*
Joh 6:26 **ye did eat the loaves, and were f...** *5526*
Joh 12:3 the house was **f.** with the odour *4137*
Joh 16:6 **sorrow hath f. your heart.** *4137*
Joh 19:29 and they **f.** a spunge with vinegar,...... *4130*
Ac 2:2 **f.** all the house where they were *4137*
Ac 2:4 were all **f.** with the Holy Ghost, ... *4130*
Ac 3:10 and they were **f.** with wonder and...... *4130*
Ac 4:8 Then Peter, **f.** with the Holy Ghost,... *4130*
Ac 4:31 were all **f.** with the Holy Ghost, ... *4130*
Ac 5:3 hath Satan **f.** thine heart to lie........... *4137*
Ac 5:17 and were **f.** with indignation, ... *4130*
Ac 5:28 and, behold, ye have **f.** Jerusalem....... *4137*
Ac 9:17 and be **f.** with the Holy Ghost, ... *4130*
Ac 13:9 Paul,) **f.** with the Holy Ghost, set *4130*
Ac 13:45 they were **f.** with envy, and spake *4130*
Ac 13:52 And the disciples were **f.** with joy, ... *4137*
Ac 19:29 whole city was **f.** with confusion:........ *4130*
Ro 1:29 Being **f.** with all unrighteousness,....... *4137*
Ro 15:14 **f.** with all knowledge, able also to *4137*
Ro 15:24 somewhat **f.** with your company......... *1705*
2Co 7:4 **f.** with comfort, I am exceeding......... *4137*
Eph 3:19 might be **f.** with all the fulness of....... *4137*
Eph 5:18 but be **f.** with the Spirit; *4137*
Php 1:11 **f.** with the fruits of righteousness,....... *4137*
Col 1:9 might be **f.** with the knowledge.......... *4137*
2Ti 1:4 that I may be **f.** with joy; *4137*
Jas 2:16 in peace, be ye warmed and **f.**; *5526*
Re 8:5 **f.** it with fire to the altar, and cast..... *1072*
Re 15:1 in them is **f.** up the wrath of God....... *5055*
Re 15:8 the temple was **f.** with smoke *1072*
Re 18:6 she hath **f.** fill to her double............ *2767*
Re 19:21 the fowls were **f.** with their flesh. *5526*

FILLEDST
De 6:11 all good things, which thou **f.** not, ... 4390
Eze 27:33 thou **f.** many people: thou didst 7646

FILLEST
Ps 17:14 whose belly thou **f.** with thy hid......... 4390

FILLET See also FILLETED; FILLETS.
Jer 52:21 **f.** of twelve cubits did compass it; 2339

FILLETED
Ex 27:17 round about the court shall be **f.**........ 2836
Ex 38:17 all the pillars of the court were **f.**....... 2836
Ex 38:28 overlaid their chapiters, and **f.**........... 2836

FILLETH
Job 9:18 but **f.** me with bitterness.................. 7646
Ps 84:6 the rain also **f.** the pools. 5844
Ps 107:9 **f.** the hungry soul with goodness........... 4390
Ps 129:7 Wherewith the mower **f.** not his 4390
Ps 147:14 **f.** thee with the finest of the wheat. ... 7646
Eph 1:23 the fulness of him that **f.** all in all....... *4137*

FILLETS
Ex 27:10 and their **f.** shall be of silver. 2838
Ex 27:11 the pillars and their **f.** of silver. 2838
Ex 36:38 chapiters and their **f.** with gold. 2838
Ex 38:10 and their **f.** were of silver................. 2838
Ex 38:11 and their **f.** were of silver................. 2838
Ex 38:12 of the pillars and their **f.** of silver....... 2838
Ex 38:17 of the pillars and their **f.** of silver;...... 2838
Ex 38:19 their chapiters and their **f.** of silver..... 2838

FILLING See also FULFILLING.
Ac 14:17 **f.** our hearts with food and *1705*

FILTH
Isa 4:4 the **f.** of the daughters of Zion,.......... 6675
Na 3:6 I will cast abominable **f.** upon thee,...........
1Co 4:13 are made as the **f.** of the world, ... *4027*
1Pe 3:21 putting away of the **f.** of the flesh. *4509*

FILTHINESS
2Ch 29:5 forth the **f.** out of the holy place. 5079
Ezr 6:21 them from the **f.** of the heathen of..... 2932
Ezr 9:11 an unclean land with the **f.** of the 5079
Pr 30:12 yet is not washed from their **f.**.. 6675
Isa 28:8 all tables are full of vomit and **f.**,......... 6675
La 1:9 Her **f.** is in her skirts; she................ 2932
Eze 16:36 Because thy **f.** was poured out, ... 5178
Eze 22:15 will consume thy **f.** out of thee. 2932
Eze 24:11 that the **f.** of it may be molten in it, ... 2932
Eze 24:13 In thy **f.** is lewdness: because I......... 2932
Eze 24:13 shalt not be purged fron thy **f.**........... 2932
Eze 36:25 ye shall be clean: from all your **f.**,...... 2932
2Cor 7:1 from all **f.** of the flesh and spirit,....... *3436*
Eph 5:4 Neither **f.**, nor foolish talking, nor....... *151*
Jas 1:21 lay apart all **f.** and superfluity *4507*
Re 17:4 full of abominations and **f.** of her.......... *168*

FILTHY
Job 15:16 more abominable and **f.** is man, ... 444
Ps 14:3 aside, they are altogether become **f.**:.... 444
Ps 53:3 back: they are altogether become **f.**; 444
Isa 64:6 righteousness are as **f.** rags; 5708
Zep 3:1 Woe to her that is **f.** and polluted,...... 4754
Zec 3:3 was clothed with **f.** garments,............ 6674
Zec 3:4 Take away the **f.** garments from......... 6674
Col 3:8 **f.** communication out of your.............. *148*
1Ti 3:3 no striker, not greedy of **f.** lucre;............
1Ti 3:8 much wine, not greedy of **f.** lucre;............
Tit 1:7 no striker, not given to **f.** lucre; *150*
Tit 1:11 they ought not, for **f.** lucre's sake......... *150*
1Pe 5:2 not for **f.** lucre, but of a ready mind; *147*
2Pe 2:7 vexed with the **f.** conversation of......... *766*
Jude 8 also these **f.** dreamers defile ....
Re 22:11 he which is **f.**, let him be **f.** still: *4510*

FINALLY
2Co 13:11 **F.**, brethren, farewell. Be perfect, ... *3063*
Eph 6:10 **F.**, my brethren, be strong in the *3063*
Php 3:1 **F.**, my brethren, rejoice in the Lord.... *3063*
Php 4:8 **F.**, brethren, whatsoever things are ... *3063*
2Th 3:1 **F.**, brethren, pray for us, that the...... *3063*
1Pe 3:8 **F.**, be ye all of one mind, having *5056*

FIND See also FINDEST; FINDETH; FINDING; FOUND.
Ge 18:26 If I **f.** in Sodom fifty righteous 4672
Ge 18:28 If I **f.** there forty and five,............... 4672
Ge 18:30 I will not do it, if I **f.** thirty there....... 4672
Ge 19:11 wearied themselves to **f.** the door...... 4672
Ge 32:5 that I may **f.** grace in thy sight.......... 4672
Ge 32:19 speak unto Esau, when ye **f.** him....... 4672
Ge 33:8 to **f.** grace in the sight of my lord........ 4672
Ge 33:15 me **f.** grace in the sight of my lord..... 4672
Ge 34:11 Let me **f.** grace in your eyes,............ 4672
Ge 38:22 I cannot **f.** her; and also the men....... 4672
Ge 41:38 Can we **f.** such a one as this is,......... 4672
Ge 47:25 us **f.** grace in the sight of my lord...... 4672
Ex 5:11 get you straw where ye can **f.** it:....... 4672
Ex 16:25 ye shall not **f.** it in the field.............. 4672
Ex 33:13 that I may **f.** grace in thy sight: 4672
Nu 32:23 be sure your sin will **f.** you out.......... 4672
Nu 35:27 And the revenger of blood **f.** him 4672
De 4:29 thou shalt **f.** him, if thou seek him...... 4672
De 22:23 and a man **f.** her in the city, ... 4672
De 22:25 if a man **f.** a betrothed damsel........... 4672
De 22:28 a man **f.** a damsel that is a virgin, ... 4672
De 24:1 that she **f.** no favour in his eyes, ... 4672
De 28:65 these nations shalt thou **f.** no ease, ...
Jg 9:33 to them as thou shalt **f.** occasion........ 4672
Jg 14:12 and **f.** it out, then I will give you 4672
Jg 17:8 sojourn where he could **f.** a place;...... 4672
Jg 17:9 to sojourn where I may **f.** a place....... 4672
Ru 1:9 that ye may **f.** rest, each of you 4672
Ru 2:2 in whose sight I shall **f.** grace........... 4672
Ru 2:13 Let me **f.** favour in thy sight............ 4672
1Sa 1:18 handmaid **f.** grace in thy sight........... 4672
1Sa 9:13 ye shall straightway **f.** him,............... 4672
1Sa 9:13 about this time we shall **f.** him........... 4672
1Sa 10:2 **f.** two men by Rachel's sepulchre........ 4672
1Sa 20:21 saying, Go **f.** out the arrows. 4672
1Sa 20:36 **f.** out now the arrows which I shoot... 4672
1Sa 23:17 of Saul my father shall not **f.** thee; 4672
1Sa 24:19 a man **f.** his enemy, will he let him..... 4672
1Sa 25:8 let the young men **f.** favour in thine.... 4672
2Sa 15:25 if I shall **f.** favour in the eyes 4672
2Sa 16:4 that I may **f.** grace in thy sight.......... 4672
2Sa 17:20 had sought and could not **f.** them, ... 4672
1Ki 18:5 peradventure we may **f.** grass to........ 4672
1Ki 18:12 he cannot **f.** thee, he shall slay me: 4672
2Ch 2:14 and to **f.** out every device which......... 2803
2Ch 20:16 and ye shall **f.** them at the end......... 4672
2Ch 30:9 your children shall **f.** compassion..............
2Ch 32:4 Assyria come, and **f.** much water?...... 4672
Ezr 4:15 thou **f.** in the book of the records, ... 7912
Ezr 7:16 thou canst **f.** in all the province......... 7912
Job 3:22 glad, when they can **f.** the grave? 4672
Job 11:7 Canst thou by searching **f.** out God?... 4672
Job 11:7 canst thou **f.** out the Almighty 4672
Job 17:10 cannot **f.** one wise man among you..... 4672
Job 23:3 that I knew where I might **f.** him! 4672
Job 34:11 man to **f.** according to his ways. 4672
Job 37:23 Almighty we cannot **f.** him out:.......... 4672
Ps 10:15 out his wickedness till thou **f.** none..... 4672
Ps 17:3 tried me, and shalt **f.** nothing; 4672
Ps 21:8 Thine hand shall **f.** out all thine......... 4672
Ps 21:8 thy right hand shall **f.** out those 4672
Ps 132:5 Until I **f.** out a place for the Lord....... 4672
Pr 1:13 We shall **f.** all precious substance, ... 4672
Pr 1:28 me early, but they shall not **f.** me: 4672
Pr 2:5 Lord, and **f.** the knowledge of God..... 4672
Pr 3:4 **f.** favour and good understanding........ 4672
Pr 4:22 are life unto those that **f.** them, ... 4672
Pr 8:9 right to them that **f.** knowledge, ... 4672
Pr 8:12 and **f.** out knowledge of witty............ 4672
Pr 8:17 that seek me early shall **f.** me. 4672
Pr 16:20 a matter wisely shall **f.** good: 4672
Pr 19:8 keepeth understanding shall **f.**........... 4672
Pr 20:6 but a faithful man who can **f.**?............ 4672
Pr 28:23 shall **f.** more favour than he that 4672
Pr 31:10 Who can **f.** a virtuous woman?........... 4672
Ec 3:11 no man can **f.** out the work that God.. 4672
Ec 7:14 man should **f.** nothing after him.......... 4672
Ec 7:24 exceeding deep, who can **f.** it out? 4672
Ec 7:26 I **f.** more bitter than death the........... 4672
Ec 7:27 one by one, to **f.** out the account: 4672
Ec 7:28 yet my soul seeketh, but I **f.** not: 4672
Ec 8:17 that a man cannot **f.** out the work...... 4672
Ec 8:17 yet he shall not **f.** it: yea, farther;...... 4672
Ec 8:17 yet shall he not be able to **f.** it. 4672
Ec 11:1 for thou shalt **f.** it after many days. 4672
Ec 12:10 sought to **f.** out acceptable words:...... 4672
Ca 5:6 but I could not **f.** him; I called him. 4672
Ca 5:8 if ye **f.** my beloved, that ye tell him,... 4672
Ca 8:1 should **f.** thee without, I would kiss.... 4672
Isa 34:14 and **f.** for herself a place of rest......... 4672
Isa 41:12 seek them, and shalt not **f.** them, ... 4672
Isa 58:3 day of your fast ye **f.** pleasure,.......... 4672
Jer 2:24 in her month they shall **f.** her,........... 4672
Jer 5:1 if ye can **f.** a man, if there be any...... 4672
Jer 6:16 and ye shall **f.** rest for your souls...... 4672
Jer 10:18 distress them, that they may **f.** it....... 4672
Jer 29:13 And ye shall seek me, and **f.** me,........ 4672
Jer 45:3 in my sighing, and I **f.** no rest, ... 4672
La 1:6 like harts that **f.** no pasture,............. 4672
La 2:9 also **f.** no vision from the Lord. 4672
Da 6:4 to **f.** occasion against Daniel.............. 7912
Da 6:4 but they could **f.** none occasion.......... 7912
Da 6:5 not **f.** occasion against this Daniel,...... 7912
Da 6:5 Daniel, except we **f.** it against him 7912
Ho 2:6 that she shall not **f.** her paths........... 4672
Ho 2:7 seek them, but shall not **f.** them: 4672
Ho 5:6 they shall not **f.** him; he hath 4672
Ho 12:8 they shall **f.** none iniquity in me 4672
Am 8:12 of the Lord, and shall not **f.** it. 4672
Mt 7:7 **seek, and ye shall f.; knock, and**... *2147*
Mt 7:14 **and few there be that f. it**............ *2147*
Mt 10:39 **his life for my sake shall f. it**........ *2147*
Mt 11:29 **ye shall f. rest unto your souls**........ *2147*
Mt 16:25 **lose his life for my sake shall f. it**..*2147*
Mt 17:27 **thou shalt f. a piece of money:**...... *2147*
Mt 18:13 **if so be that he f. it, verily I say**... *2147*
Mt 21:2 **ye shall f. an ass tied, and a colt** .. *2147*
Mt 22:9 **as many as ye shall f., bid to the** .. *2147*
Mt 24:46 **when he cometh shall f. so doing**...*2147*
Mk 11:2 **ye shall f. a colt tied, whereon**...... *2147*
Mk 11:13 he might **f.** any thing thereon: *2147*
Mk 13:36 **suddenly he f. you sleeping**........... *2147*
Lu 2:12 Ye shall **f.** the babe wrapped in.......... *2147*

Lu 5:19 they could not f. by what way *2147*
Lu 6:7 might f. an accusation against him. *2147*
Lu 11:9 **given you; seek, and ye shall f.** *2147*
Lu 12:37 **when he cometh shall f. watching:** .*2147*
Lu 12:38 **and f. them so, blessed are those** ... *2147*
Lu 12:43 **when he cometh shall f. so doing.** ..*2147*
Lu 13:7 **fruit on this fig tree, and f. none:** ..*2147*
Lu 15:4 **that which is lost, until he f. it?** ... *2147*
Lu 15:8 **and seek diligently till she f. it?** *2147*
Lu 18:8 **shall he f. faith on the earth?** *2147*
Lu 19:30 **entering ye shall f. a colt tied,** *2147*
Lu 19:48 could not f. what they might do: *2147*
Lu 23:4 I f. no fault in this man. *2147*
Joh 7:34 **shall seek me, and shall not f. me:** .*2147*
Joh 7:35 we shall not f. him? will he go *2147*
Joh 7:36 and shall not f. me: and where I *2147*
Joh 10:9 **shall go in and out, and f. pasture.** *2147*
Joh 18:38 I f. in him no fault at all, ... *2147*
Joh 19:4 may know that I f. no fault in him. *2147*
Joh 19:6 for I f. no fault in him. *2147*
Joh 21:6 **side of the ship, and ye shall f.** *2147*
Ac 7:46 to f. a tabernacle for the God of *2147*
Ac 17:27 might feel after him, and f. him, ... *2147*
Ac 23:9 We f. no evil in this man: *2147*
Ro 7:18 that which is good I f. not. *2147*
Ro 7:21 I f. then a law, that, when I would *2147*
Ro 9:19 Why doth he yet f. fault? For who...........
2Co 9:4 with me, and f. you unprepared, ... *2147*
2Co 12:20 I shall not f. you such as I would, ... *2147*
2Ti 1:18 that he may f. mercy of the Lord *2147*
Heb 4:16 we may obtain mercy, and f. grace *2147*
Re 9:6 seek death, and shall not f. it; *2147*
Re 18:14 thou shalt f. them no more at all. *2147*

FINDEST
Ge 31:32 with whomsoever thou f. thy gods, ... 4672
Eze 3:1 Son of man, eat that thou f.; 4672

FINDETH
Ge 4:14 every one that f. me shall slay me. 4672
Job 33:10 Behold, he f. occasions against me, ... 4672
Ps 119:162 thy word as one that f. great spoil. 4672
Pr 3:13 Happy is the man that f. wisdom, ... 4672
Pr 8:35 whoso f. me, f. life, and shall 4672
Pr 14:6 scorner seeketh wisdom, and f. it not: ......
Pr 17:20 hath a froward heart f. no good: 4672
Pr 18:22 Whoso f. a wife f. a good thing, ... 4672
Pr 21:10 neighbour f. no favour in his eyes............
Pr 21:21 righteousness and mercy f. life, ... 4672
Ec 9:10 Whatsoever thy hand f. to do, do it 4672
La 1:3 she f. no rest: all her persecutors 4672
Ho 14:3 in thee the fatherless f. mercy.................
Mt 7:8 **he that seeketh f.; and to him** *2147*
Mt 10:39 **He that f. his life shall lose it:** *2147*
Mt 12:43 **places, seeking rest, and f. none** *2147*
Mt 12:44 **is come he f. it empty, swept, and** . *2147*
Mt 26:40 f. them asleep, and saith unto *2147*
Mk 14:37 he cometh, and f. them sleeping, ... *2147*
Lu 11:10 **receiveth; and he that seeketh f.;** .. *2147*
Lu 11:25 **he f. it swept and garnished** *2147*
Joh 1:41 He first f. his own brother Simon *2147*
Joh 1:43 and f. Philip, and saith unto him, ... *2147*
Joh 1:45 Philip f. Nathanael, and saith unto *2147*
Joh 5:14 Jesus f. him in the temple, and *2147*

FINDING
Ge 4:15 lest any f. him should kill him. 4672
Job 9:10 doeth great things past f. out; 2714
Isa 58:13 nor f. thine own pleasure, nor 4672
Lu 11:24 **and f. none, he saith, I will return** .*2147*
Ac 4:21 f. nothing how they might punish *2147*
Ac 19:1 and f. certain disciples. *2147*
Ac 21:2 And f. a ship sailing over unto *2147*
Ac 21:4 f. disciples, we tarried there seven *429*
Ro 11:33 and his ways past f. out! *421*
Heb 8:8 For f. fault with them, he saith ....

FINE See also FINEST; FINING; REFINE.
Ge 18:6 quickly three measures of f. meal, ... 5560
Ge 41:42 and arrayed him in vestures of f. linen, ...
Ex 25:4 scarlet, and f. linen, and goats' hair, ...
Ex 26:1 with ten curtains of f. twined linen, ...
Ex 26:31 and f. twined linen of cunning work: ....
Ex 26:36 and f. twined linen, wrought with ....
Ex 27:9 for the court of f. twined linen of an ....
Ex 27:16 purple and scarlet, and f. twined linen, ...
Ex 27:18 the height five cubits of f. twined linen, ...
Ex 28:5 and purple, and scarlet, and f. linen. ....
Ex 28:6 purple, of scarlet, and f. twined linen, ...
Ex 28:8 purple, and scarlet, and f. twined linen. .....
Ex 28:15 of f. twined linen, shalt thou make it. ....
Ex 28:39 shalt embroider the coat of f. linen, ...
Ex 28:39 thou shalt make the mitre of f. linen, ...
Ex 35:6, 23 scarlet, and f. linen, and goats' hair, ...
Ex 35:25 purple, and of scarlet, and of f. linen. ....
Ex 35:35 in purple, in scarlet, and in f. linen, ...
Ex 36:8 made ten curtains of f. twined linen, ...
Ex 36:35 and purple, and scarlet, and f. twined ....
Ex 36:37 and f. twined linen, of needlework; ....
Ex 38:9 of the court were of f. twined linen, an .....
Ex 38:16 round about were of f. twined linen. ....
Ex 38:18 purple, and scarlet, and f. twined linen: .....
Ex 38:23 in purple, and in scarlet, and f. linen. ....
Ex 39:2 purple, and scarlet, and f. twined linen, ...
Ex 39:3 and in the scarlet, and in the f. linen, ...
Ex 39:5 purple, and scarlet, and f. twined linen; .....
Ex 39:8 purple, and scarlet, and f. twined linen. .....
Ex 39:27 made coats of f. linen of woven work ....
Ex 39:28 And a mitre of f. linen, and goodly ....
Ex 39:28 and goodly bonnets of f. linen, and ....
Ex 39:28 and linen breeches of f. twined linen, ...
Ex 39:29 And a girdle of f. twined linen, and ....
Le 2:1 his offering shall be of f. flour; and ....
Le 2:4 shall be unleavened cakes of f. flour ....
Le 2:5 it shall be of f. flour unleavened, ...
Le 2:7 it shall be made of f. flour with oil, ...
Le 5:11 the tenth part of an ephah of f. flour ....
Le 6:20 the tenth part of an ephah of f. flour ....
Le 7:12 and cakes mingled with oil, of f. flour, ...
Le 14:10 and three tenth deals of f. flour for ....
Le 14:21 and one tenth deal of f. flour mingled ....
Le 23:13 two tenth deals of f. flour mingled ....
Le 23:17 tenth deals: they shall be of f. flour; ....
Le 24:5 And thou shalt take f. flour, and bake ....
Nu 6:15 cakes of f. flour mingled with oil ....
Nu 7:13, 19,25,31,37,43,49,55,61,67,73 both of them were full of f. flour ....
Nu 7:79 both of them full of f. flour mingled...........
Nu 8:8 even f. flour mingled with oil ....
1Ki 4:22 was thirty measures of f. flour, ...
2Ki 7:1 measure of f. flour be sold for a shekel, ...
2Ki 7:16 So a measure of f. flour was sold ....
2Ki 7:18 a measure of f. flour for a shekel, ...
1Ch 4:21 house of them that wrought f. linen, ...
1Ch 9:29 the f. flour, and the wine, and the oil, ...
1Ch 15:27 was clothed with a robe of f. linen, ...
1Ch 23:29 and for the f. flour for meat offering, ...
2Ch 2:14 in blue, and in f. linen, and in crimson: ......
2Ch 3:5 which he overlaid with f. gold, ... 2896
2Ch 3:8 and he overlaid it with f. gold, ... 2896
2Ch 3:14 purple, and crimson, and f. linen, ...
Ezr 8:27 two vessels of f. copper, precious 6668
Es 1:6 fastened with cords of f. linen and ....
Es 8:15 and with a garment of f. linen and ....
Job 28:1 place for gold where they f. it. 2212
Job 28:17 of it shall not be for jewels of f. gold. ....
Job 31:24 or have said to the f. gold, Thou art my ....
Ps 19:10 yea, than much f. gold: sweeter also ....
Ps 119:127 above gold; yea, above f. gold. ....
Pr 3:14 and the gain thereof than f. gold. ....
Pr 7:16 works, with f. linen of Egypt. ....
Pr 8:19 is better than gold, yea, than f. gold; ....
Pr 25:12 and an ornament of f. gold, so is a wise ....
Pr 31:24 She maketh f. linen, and selleth ....
Ca 5:11 His head is as the most f. gold, ...
Ca 5:15 marble, set upon sockets of f. gold: ....
Isa 3:23 The glasses, and the f. linen, and the ....
Isa 13:12 a man more precious than f. gold; ....
Isa 19:9 Moreover they that work in f. flax, ... 8305
La 4:1 how is the most f. gold changed! ....
La 4:2 sons of Zion, comparable to f. gold, ...
Eze 16:10 and I girded thee about with f. linen, ...
Eze 16:13 and thy raiment was of f. linen, ...
Eze 16:13 thou didst eat f. flour, and honey, ...
Eze 16:19 thee, f. flour, and oil, and honey, and ....
Eze 27:7 F. linen with broidered work from ....
Eze 27:16 and f. linen, and coral, and agate ....
Eze 46:14 of oil, to temper with the f. flour; ....
Da 2:32 This image's head was of f. gold, ... 2869
Da 10:5 were girded with f. gold of Uphaz: ....
Zec 9:3 and f. gold as the mire of the streets ....
Mk 15:46 And he bought f. linen, and took ....
Lu 16:19 **was clothed in purple and f. linen,** .....
Re 1:15 And his feet like unto f. brass, ...
Re 2:18 **and his feet are like f. brass;** ....
Re 18:12 and of pearls, and f. linen, and purple, ...
Re 18:13 and f. flour, and wheat, and *4585*
Re 18:16 great city, that was clothed in f. linen, ...
Re 19:8 that she should be arrayed in f. linen, ...
Re 19:8 the f. linen is the righteousness of............
Re 19:14 clothed in f. linen, white and clean............

FINER
Pr 25:4 come forth a vessel for the f. 6884

FINEST
Ps 81:16 them also with the f. of the wheat: 2459
Ps 147:14 filleth thee with the f. of the wheat. ... 2459

FINGER See also FINGERS.
Ex 8:19 Pharaoh, This is the f. of God: 676
Ex 29:12 the horns of the altar with thy, ... 676
Ex 31:18 stone, written with the f. of God. 676
Le 4:6 priest shall dip his f. in the blood, ... 676
Le 4:17 the priest shall dip his f. in some 676
Le 4:25 blood of the sin offering with his f., ... 676
Le 4:30 take of the blood thereof wiih his f., ... 676
Le 4:34 blood of the sin offering with his f., ... 676
Le 8:15 of the altar round about with his f., ... 676
Le 9:9 he dipped his f. in the blood, ... 676
Le 14:16 the priest shall dip his right f. in 676
Le 14:16 sprinkle of the oil with his f. seven 676
Le 14:27 shall sprinkle with his right f. some 676
Le 16:14 and sprinkle it with his f. seven 676
Le 16:14 of the blood with his f. seven times. 676
Le 16:19 blood upon it with his f. seven times, ... 676
Nu 19:4 shall take of her blood with his f., ... 676
De 9:10 them was written with the f. of God; ... 676
1Ki 12:10 My little f. shall be thicker than ....
2Ch 10:10 My little f. shall be thicker than ....
Isa 58:9 the putting forth of the f., and 676
Lu 11:20 **with the f. of God cast out devils,** ..*1147*
Lu 16:24 **may dip the tip of his f. in water,** . *1147*
Joh 8:6 with his f. wrote on the ground, ... *1147*
Joh 20:25 put my f. into the print of the nails, ... *1147*
Joh 20:27 **Reach hither thy f., and behold** *1147*

FINGERS
2Sa 21:20 that had on every hand six f., ... 676
1Ch 20:6 f. and toes were four and twenty, ... 676
Ps 8:3 thy heavens, the work of thy f., ... 676
Ps 144:1 my hands to war, and my f. to fight: 676
Pr 6:13 his feet, he teacheth with his f.; 676
Pr 7:3 Bind them upon thy f., write them 676
Ca 5:5 my f. with sweet smelling myrrh, ... 676
Isa 2:8 that which their own f. have made: 676
Isa 17:8 that which his f. have made, ... 676
Isa 59:3 and your f. with iniquity; your lips 676
Jer 52:21 the thickness thereof was four f.: 676
Da 5:5 In the same hour came forth f. of a 677
Mt 23:4 **move them with one of their f.** *1147*
Mk 7:33 put his f. into his ears, and he spit, ... *1147*
Lu 11:46 **the burdens with one of your f.** *1147*

FINING
Pr 17:3 The f. pot is for silver, and the 4715
Pr 27:21 As the f. pot for silver, and the 4715

FINING-POT See FINING and POT.

FINISH See also FINISHED.
Ge 6:16 in a cubit shalt thou f. it above; 3615
Da 9:24 to f. the transgression, and to 3607
Zec 4:9 his hands shall also f. it; 1214
Lu 14:28 **whether he have sufficient to f. it?** ..*535*
Lu 14:29 **foundation, and is not able to f. it,** *1615*
Lu 14:30 **to build, and was not able to f.** *1615*
Joh 4:34 **that sent me, and to f. his work** *5048*
Joh 5:36 **the Father hath given me to f.,** *5048*
Ac 20:24 I might f. my course with joy, ... *5048*
Ro 9:28 will f. the work, and cut it short *4931*
2Co 8:6 he would also f. in you the same *2005*

FINISHED
Ge 2:1 the heavens and the earth were f. 3615
Ex 39:32 of the tent of the congregation f.: 3615
Ex 40:33 So Moses f. the work 3615
De 31:24 law in a book, until they were f., ... 8552
Jos 4:10 until every thing was f. that the 8552
Ru 3:18 until he have f. the thing this day 3615
1Ki 6:9 he built the house, and f. it 3615
1Ki 6:14 Solomon built the house, and f. it 3615
1Ki 6:22 until he had f. all the house: 8552
1Ki 6:38 eighth month, was the house f. 3615
1Ki 7:1 and he f. all his house 3615
1Ki 7:22 so was the work of the pillars f.. 8552

1Ki 9:1 when Solomon had **f.** the building....... 3615
1Ki 9:25 the Lord. So he **f.** the house............ 7999
1Ch 27:24 Zeruiah began to number, but he **f.** 3615
1Ch 28:20 until thou hast **f.** all the work for 3615
2Ch 4:11 Huram **f.** the work that he was.......... 3615
2Ch 5:1 for the house of the Lord was **f.**: 7999
2Ch 7:11 Solomon **f.** the house of the Lord,...... 3615
2Ch 8:16 of the Lord, and until it was **f.**. 3615
2Ch 24:14 when they had **f.** it, they brought....... 3615
2Ch 29:28 until the burnt offering was **f.**............ 3615
2Ch 31:1 Now when all this was **f.**, all Israel..... 3615
2Ch 31:7 and **f.** them in the seventh month...... 3615
Ezr 5:16 building, and yet it is not **f.**.............. 8000
Ezr 6:14 And they builded, and **f.** it, ... 3635
Ezr 6:15 this house was **f.** on the third day...... 3319
Ne 6:15 So the wall was **f.** in the twenty 7999
Da 5:26 numbered thy kingdom, and **f.** it. 8000
Da 12:7 all these things shall be **f.**.. 3615
Mt 13:53 when Jesus had **f.** these parables, ... *5055*
Mt 19:1 when Jesus had **f.** these sayings,........ *5055*
Mt 26:1 when Jesus had **f.** all these sayings,.... *5055*
Joh 17:4 **I have f. the work which thou**....... *5048*
Joh 19:30 he said, **It is f.**: and he bowed.......... *5055*
Ac 21:7 And when we had **f.** our course......... *1274*
2Ti 4:7 I have **f.** my course, I have kept........ *5055*
Heb 4:3 works were **f.** from the foundation...... *1096*
Jas 1:15 sin, when it is **f.**, bringeth forth *658*
Re 10:7 the mystery of God should be **f.**, ... *5055*
Re 11:7 they shall have **f.** their testimony, ... *5055*
Re 20:5 until the thousand years were **f.**.......... *5055*

FINISHER
Heb 12:2 Jesus the author and **f.** of our........... *5047*

FINITE See INFINITE.

FINS
Le 11:9 hath **f.** and scales in the waters, ... 5579
Le 11:10 have not **f.** and scales in the seas,....... 5579
Le 11:12 Whatsoever hath no **f.** nor scales 5579
De 14:9 have **f.** and scales shall ye eat: 5579
De 14:10 not **f.** and scales ye may not eat; 5579

FIR
2Sa 6:5 of instruments made of **f.** wood, ... 1265
1Ki 5:8 and concerning timber of **f.**.. 1265
1Ki 5:10 gave Solomon cedar trees and **f.**......... 1265
1Ki 6:15 of the house with planks of **f.**............ 1265
1Ki 6:34 the two doors were of **f.** tree:........... 1265
1Ki 9:11 with cedar trees and **f.** trees, and....... 1265
2Ki 19:23 and the choice of **f.** trees thereof: 1265
2Ch 2:8 Send me also cedar trees, **f.** trees, ... 1265
2Ch 3:5 greater house he cieled with **f.** tree,... 1265
Ps 104:17 stork, the **f.** trees are her house........ 1265
Ca 1:17 are cedar, and our rafters of **f.**.......... 1266
Isa 14:8 Yea, the **f.** trees rejoice at thee,........ 1265
Isa 37:24 and the choice **f.** trees thereof:.......... 1265
Isa 41:19 I will set in the desert the **f.** tree, ... 1265
Isa 55:13 the thorn shall come up the **f.** tree,.... 1265
Isa 60:13 **f.** tree, the pine tree, and the box...... 1265
Eze 27:5 thy ship boards of **f.** trees of Senir:.... 1265
Eze 31:8 **f.** trees were not like his boughs,........ 1265
Ho 14:8 I am like a green **f.** tree.................. 1265
Na 2:3 **f.** trees shall be terribly shaken. 1265
Zec 11:2 **f.** tree; for the cedar is fallen; 1265

FIRE See also FIREBRAND; FIREPANS; FIRES.
Ge 19:24 brimstone and **f.** from the Lord out...... 784
Ge 22:6 and he took the **f.** in his hand, and a.... 784
Ge 22:7 Behold, the **f.** and the wood: 784
Ex 3:2 appeared unto him in a flame of **f.**......... 784
Ex 3:2 behold, the bush burned with **f.**,........... 784
Ex 9:23 the **f.** ran along upon the ground; 784
Ex 9:24 and **f.** mingled with the hail, very 784
Ex 12:8 roast with **f.**, and unleavened bread;..... 784
Ex 12:9 but with **f.**; his head with his legs,....... 784
Ex 12:10 the morning ye shall burn with **f.**......... 784
Ex 13:21 and by night in a pillar of **f.**. 784
Ex 13:22 nor the pillar of **f.** by night, ... 784
Ex 14:24 the pillar of **f.** and of the cloud, ... 784
Ex 19:18 the Lord descended upon it in **f.**:......... 784
Ex 22:6 If **f.** break out, and catch in thorns,...... 784
Ex 22:6 that kindled the **f.** shall surely 1200
Ex 24:17 like devouring **f.** on the top of the 784
Ex 29:14 his dung, shalt thou burn with **f.**.......... 784
Ex 29:18, 25 offering made by **f.** unto the Lord. ....
Ex 29:34 shalt burn the remainder with **f.**: 784
Ex 29:41 an offering made by **f.** unto the Lord. ....
Ex 30:20 an offering made by **f.** unto the Lord: ....
Ex 32:20 burnt it in the **f.**, and ground it 784
Ex 32:24 then I cast it into the **f.**, ... 784
Ex 35:3 Ye shall kindle no **f.** throughout........... 784
Ex 40:38 and **f.** was on it by night,.................... 784
Le 1:7 the priest shall put **f.** upon the altar, ... 784
Le 1:7 and lay the wood in order upon the **f.**:.. 784
Le 1:8 upon the wood that is on the **f.**............ 784
Le 1:9 burnt sacrifice, an offering made by **f.**, ...
Le 1:12 upon the wood that is on the **f.**............ 784
Le 1:13 offering made by **f.**, of a sweet savour ......
Le 1:17 upon the wood that is upon the **f.**: 784
Le 1:17 offering made by **f.**, of a sweet savour ......
Le 2:2 offering made by **f.**, of sweet savour.........
Le 2:3 the offerings of the Lord made by **f.**. ....
Le 2:9 offering made by **f.**, of sweet savour.........
Le 2:10 the offerings of the Lord made by **f.**. ....
Le 2:11 any offering of the Lord made by **f.**. ....
Le 2:14 green ears of corn dried by the **f.**......... 784
Le 2:16 an offering made by **f.** unto the Lord. ....
Le 3:3 an offering made by **f.** unto the Lord; ....
Le 3:5 upon the wood that is on the **f.**: 784
Le 3:5 offering made by **f.**, of a sweet savour ......
Le 3:9 an offering made by **f.** unto the Lord; ....
Le 3:11 the offering made by **f.** unto the Lord. ......
Le 3:14 an offering made by **f.** unto the Lord. ....
Le 3:16 offering made by **f.** of a sweet savour ....
Le 4:12 burn him on the wood with **f.**:............ 784
Le 4:35 the offerings made by **f.** unto the Lord:.....
Le 5:12 offerings made by **f.** unto the Lord: ....
Le 6:9 the **f.** of the altar shall be burning........ 784
Le 6:10 ashes which the **f.** hath consumed......... 784
Le 6:12 **f.** upon the altar shall be burning in...... 784
Le 6:13 The **f.** shall ever be burning upon 784
Le 6:17 portion of my offerings made by **f.**;...........
Le 6:18 the offerings of the Lord made by **f.**: ....
Le 6:30 it shall be burnt in the **f.**................... 784
Le 7:5 an offering made by **f.** unto the Lord: ....
Le 7:17 third day shall be burnt with **f.**............ 784
Le 7:19 be with **f.**: and as for the flesh,........... 784
Le 7:25 an offering made by **f.** unto the Lord; ....
Le 7:30 the offerings of the Lord made by **f.**, ...
Le 7:35 the offerings of the Lord made by **f.**, ...
Le 8:17 be burnt with **f.** without the camp;....... 784
Le 8:21 an offering made by **f.** unto the Lord; ....
Le 8:28 an offering made by **f.** unto the Lord. ....
Le 8:32 the bread shall ye burn with **f.**.............. 784
Le 9:11 he burnt with **f.** without the camp.......... 784
Le 9:24 came a **f.** out from before the Lord,..... 784
Le 10:1 them his censer, and put **f.** therein, ... 784
Le 10:1 offered strange **f.** before the Lord,....... 784
Le 10:2 there went out **f.** from the Lord,......... 784
Le 10:12 the offerings of the Lord made by **f.**, ...
Le 10:13 the sacrifices of the Lord made by **f.**: ....
Le 10:15 the offerings made by **f.** of the fat, ...
Le 13:52 it shall be burnt in the **f.**.................... 784
Le 13:55 thou shalt burn it in the **f.**;................. 784
Le 13:57 that wherein the plague is with **f.**. 784
Le 16:12 a censer full of burning coals of **f.**. 784
Le 16:13 he shall put the incense upon the **f.**...... 784
Le 16:27 they shall burn in the **f.** their skins, ... 784
Le 18:21 seed pass through the **f.** to Molech, ...
Le 19:6 it shall be burnt in the **f.**..................... 784
Le 20:14 be burnt with **f.**, both he and they;...... 784
Le 21:6 the offerings of the Lord made by **f.**, ...
Le 21:9 she shall be burnt with **f.**.. 784
Le 21:21 the offerings of the Lord made by **f.**: ....
Le 22:22 nor make an offering by **f.** of them ....
Le 22:27 an offering made by **f.** unto the Lord. ....
Le 23:8 ye shall offer an offering made by **f.**..........
Le 23:13 an offering made by **f.** unto the Lord ....
Le 23:18 an offering made by **f.**, of sweet savour.....
Le 23:25 ye shall offer an offering made by **f.**..........
Le 23:27 and offer an offering made by **f.** ....
Le 23:36 ye shall offer an offering made by **f.**..........
Le 23:36 ye shall offer an offering made by **f.**..........
Le 23:37 to offer an offering made by **f.**.................
Le 24:7 an offering made by **f.** unto the Lord. ....
Le 24:9 the offerings of the Lord made by **f.** ....
Nu 3:4 offered strange **f.** before the Lord,....... 784
Nu 6:18 put it in the **f.** which is under the 784
Nu 9:15 as it were the appearance of **f.**,........... 784
Nu 9:16 and the appearance of **f.** by night......... 784
Nu 11:1 **f.** of the Lord burnt among them, ... 784
Nu 11:2 unto the Lord, the **f.** was quenched. 784
Nu 11:3 because the **f.** of the Lord burnt.......... 784
Nu 14:14 and in a pillar of **f.** by night.............. 784
Nu 15:3 And will make an offering by **f.**...............
Nu 15:10 of wine, for an offering made by **f.**. ....
Nu 15:13 in offering an offering made by **f.**,..........
Nu 15:14 offering made by **f.**, of a sweet savour ......
Nu 15:25 a sacrifice made by **f.** unto the Lord, ...
Nu 16:7 put **f.** therein, and put incense 784
Nu 16:18 and put **f.** in them, and laid incense...... 784
Nu 16:35 there came out a **f.** from the Lord, ... 784
Nu 16:37 scatter thou the **f.** yonder; for they...... 784
Nu 16:46 put **f.** therein from off the altar, ... 784
Nu 18:9 holy things, reserved from the **f.**: 784
Nu 18:17 offering made by **f.**, for a sweet savour.....
Nu 21:28 there is a **f.** gone out of Heshbon,....... 784
Nu 26:10 time the **f.** devoured two hundred........ 784
Nu 26:61 offered strange **f.** before the Lord........ 784
Nu 28:2 bread for my sacrifices made by **f.**,...........
Nu 28:3 This is the offering made by **f.**.................
Nu 28:6 a sacrifice made by **f.** unto the Lord. ....
Nu 28:8 a sacrifice made by **f.**, of a sweet............
Nu 28:13 a sacrifice made by **f.** unto the Lord. ....
Nu 28:19 ye shall offer a sacrifice made by **f.**...........
Nu 28:24 the meat of the sacrifice made by **f.**,.........
Nu 29:6 a sacrifice made by **f.** unto the Lord. ....
Nu 29:13, 36 a sacrifice made by **f.**, of a sweet.........
Nu 31:10 and all their goodly castles, with **f.**........ 784
Nu 31:23 Every thing that may abide the **f.**, ... 784
Nu 31:23 ye shall make it go through the **f.**,....... 784
Nu 31:23 abideth not the **f.** ye shall make go 784
De 1:33 in **f.** by night, to shew you by what 784
De 4:11 the mountain burned with **f.** unto......... 784
De 4:12 unto you out of the midst of the **f.**:...... 784
De 4:15 Horeb out of the midst of the **f.**; 784
De 4:24 the Lord thy God is a consuming **f.**,...... 784
De 4:33 speaking out of the midst of the **f.**,...... 784
De 4:36 earth he shewed thee his great **f.**; 784
De 4:36 his words out of the midst of the **f.**...... 784
De 5:4 mount out of the midst of the **f.**, ... 784
De 5:5 ye were afraid by reason of the **f.**,........ 784
De 5:22 the mount out of the midst of the **f.**,..... 784
De 5:23 (for the mountain did burn with **f.**,)....... 784
De 5:24 his voice out of the midst of the **f.**:...... 784
De 5:25 for this great **f.** will consume us: 784
De 5:26 speaking out of the midst of the **f.**, ... 784
De 7:5 burn their graven images with **f.**.......... 784
De 7:25 of their gods shall ye burn with **f.**: 784
De 9:3 as a consuming **f.** he shall destroy 784
De 9:10 the mount out of the midst of the **f.**...... 784
De 9:15 and the mount burned with **f.**:............. 784
De 9:21 burnt it with **f.**, and stamped it, ... 784
De 10:4 the mount out of the midst of the **f.**..... 784
De 12:3 and burn their groves with **f.**; 784
De 12:31 have burnt in the **f.** to their gods......... 784
De 13:16 and shalt burn with **f.** the city,............ 784
De 18:1 offerings of the Lord made by **f.**, ...
De 18:10 his daughter to pass through the **f.**, ... 784
De 18:16 neither let me see this great **f.**............ 784
De 32:22 For a **f.** is kindled in mine anger,......... 784
De 32:22 set on **f.** the foundations of the.......... 3857
Jos 6:24 And they burnt the city with **f.**,........... 784
Jos 7:15 accursed thing shall be burnt with **f.**,.... 784
Jos 7:25 and burned them with **f.**, after they...... 784
Jos 8:8 that ye shall set the city on **f.**: 784
Jos 8:19 and hasted and set the city on **f.**. 784
Jos 11:6 and burn their chariots with **f.**.............. 784
Jos 11:9 and burnt their chariots with **f.**............ 784
Jos 11:11 and he burnt Hazor with **f.**.. 784
Jos 13:14 sacrifices of the Lord...made by **f.**...........
Jg 1:8 of the sword, and set the city on **f.**...... 784
Jg 6:21 there rose up **f.** out of the rock, ... 784
Jg 9:15 let **f.** come out of the bramble,............ 784
Jg 9:20 let **f.** come out from Abimelech, ... 784
Jg 9:20 and let **f.** come out from the men of..... 784
Jg 9:49 and set the hold on **f.** upon them;........ 784
Jg 9:52 of the tower to burn it with **f.**............. 784
Jg 12:1 burn thine house upon thee with **f.**........ 784
Jg 14:15 thee and thy father's house with **f.**:...... 784
Jg 15:5 when he had set the brands of **f.**, ... 784
Jg 15:6 burnt her and her father with **f.**.......... 784
Jg 15:14 as flax that was burnt with **f.**,............ 784
Jg 16:9 tow is broken when it toucheth the **f.**... 784
Jg 18:27 and burn the city with **f.**.. 784
Jg 20:48 also they set on **f.** all the cities 784
1Sa 2:28 offerings made by **f.** of the children ....
1Sa 30:1 Ziklag, and burned it with **f.**;.............. 784
1Sa 30:3 behold, it was burned with **f.**; 784
1Sa 30:14 and we burned Ziklag with **f.**................ 784
2Sa 14:30 hath barley there; go and set it on **f.**.... 784
2Sa 14:30 servants set the field on **f.** 784

2Sa 14:31 have thy servants set my field on **f.**? 784
2Sa 22:9 and **f.** out of his mouth devoured: 784
2Sa 22:13 before him were coals of **f.** kindled. 784
2Sa 23:7 they shall be utterly burned with **f.** 784
1Ki 9:16 taken Gezer, and burned it with **f.**, 784
1Ki 16:18 the king's house over him with **f.**, 784
1Ki 18:23 lay it on wood, and put no **f.** under: 784
1Ki 18:23 lay it on wood, and put no **f.** under: 784
1Ki 18:24 and the God that answereth by **f.**, 784
1Ki 18:25 of your gods, but put no **f.** under. 784
1Ki 18:38 Then the **f.** of the Lord fell, 784
1Ki 19:12 a **f.**; but the Lord was not in the **f.**: 784
1Ki 19:12 and after the **f.** a still small voice. 784
2Ki 1:10 then let **f.** come down from heaven, 784
2Ki 1:10 there came down **f.** from heaven, 784
2Ki 1:12 let **f.** come down from heaven, 784
2Ki 1:12 **f.** of God came down from heaven, 784
2Ki 1:14 there came **f.** down from heaven. 784
2Ki 2:11 a chariot of **f.**, and horses of **f.**, and 784
2Ki 6:17 was full of horses and chariots of **f.** 784
2Ki 8:12 their strong holds wilt thou set on **f.**, 784
2Ki 16:3 made his son to pass through the **f.**, 784
2Ki 17:17 daughters to pass through the **f.**, 784
2Ki 17:31 burnt their children in **f.** to 784
2Ki 19:18 And have cast their gods into the **f.**: 784
2Ki 21:6 he made his son pass through the **f.** 784
2Ki 23:10 to pass through the **f.** to Molech. 784
2Ki 23:11 the chariots of the sun with **f.**. 784
2Ki 25:9 great man's house burnt he with **f.** 784
1Ch 14:12 and they were burned with **f.** 784
1Ch 21:26 he answered him from heaven by **f.** 784
2Ch 7:1 the **f.** came down from heaven, 784
2Ch 7:3 Israel saw how the **f.** came down, 784
2Ch 28:3 and burnt his children in the **f.**, 784
2Ch 33:6 his children to pass through the **f.** 784
2Ch 35:13 they roasted the passover with **f.** 784
2Ch 36:19 burnt all the palaces thereof with **f.** 784
Ne 1:3 the gates thereof are burned with **f.** 784
Ne 2:3 gates thereof are consumed with **f.**? 784
Ne 2:13 gates thereof were consumed with **f.** 784
Ne 2:17 the gates thereof are burned with **f.**: 784
Ne 9:12 and in the night by a pillar of **f.** 784
Ne 9:19 neither the pillar of **f.** by night, 784
Job 1:16 The **f.** of God is fallen from heaven, 784
Job 15:34 **f.** shall consume the tabernacles of 784
Job 18:5 the spark of his **f.** shall not shine. 784
Job 20:26 a **f.** not blown shall consume him: 784
Job 22:20 remnant of them the **f.** consumeth. 784
Job 28:5 it is turned up as it were **f.**. 784
Job 31:12 For it is a **f.** that consumeth to 784
Job 41:19 and sparks of **f.** leap out. 784
Ps 11:6 **f.** and brimstone, and an horrible 784
Ps 18:8 and **f.** out of his mouth devoured: 784
Ps 18:12 passed, hail stones and coals of **f.** 784
Ps 18:13 his voice; hail stones and coals of **f.**. 784
Ps 21:9 wrath, and the **f.** shall devour them. 784
Ps 29:7 the Lord divideth the flames of **f.** 784
Ps 39:3 while I was musing the **f.** burned: 784
Ps 46:9 he burneth the chariot in the **f.**. 784
Ps 50:3 a **f.** shall devour before him, 784
Ps 57:4 even among them that are set on **f.**, 3857
Ps 66:12 through **f.** and through water: 784
Ps 68:2 as wax melteth before the **f.**, so let 784
Ps 74:7 They have cast **f.** into thy sanctuary, 784
Ps 78:14 and all the night with a light of **f.** 784
Ps 78:21 so a **f.** was kindled against Jacob. 784
Ps 78:63 The **f.** consumed their young men; 784
Ps 79:5 shall thy jealousy burn like **f.**? 784
Ps 80:16 It is burned with **f.**, it is cut down: 784
Ps 83:14 As the **f.** burneth a wood, and as 784
Ps 83:14 flame setteth the mountains on **f.**; 3857
Ps 89:46 shall thy wrath burn like **f.**? 784
Ps 97:3 A **f.** goeth before him, and burneth 784
Ps 104:4 spirits; his ministers a flaming **f.**: 784
Ps 105:32 rain, and flaming **f.** in their land. 784
Ps 105:39 and **f.** to give light in the night. 784
Ps 106:18 a **f.** was kindled in their company; 784
Ps 118:12 are quenched as the **f.** of thorns: 784
Ps 140:10 let them be cast into the **f.**; 784
Ps 148:8 **F.**, and hail; snow, and vapours; 784
Pr 6:27 Can a man take **f.** in his bosom, 784
Pr 16:27 in his lips there is as a burning **f.**. 784
Pr 25:22 shalt heap coals of **f.** upon his head,
Pr 26:20 no wood is, there the **f.** goeth out: 784
Pr 26:21 to burning coals, and wood to **f.**; 784
Pr 30:16 and the **f.** that saith not, It is 784
Ca 8:6 the coals thereof are coals of **f.**, 784
Isa 1:7 your cities are burned with **f.**: 784
Isa 4:5 the shining of a flaming **f.** by night: 784
Isa 5:24 as the **f.** devoureth the stubble, 784
Isa 9:5 shall be with burning and fuel of **f.**. 784
Isa 9:18 For wickedness burneth as the **f.**: 784
Isa 9:19 people shall be as the fuel of the **f.**: 784
Isa 10:16 a burning like the burning of a **f.**. 784
Isa 10:17 the light of Israel shall be for a **f.**, 784
Isa 26:11 the **f.** of thine enemies shall devour. 784
Isa 27:11 women come, and set them on **f.** 215
Isa 29:6 and the flame of devouring **f.**. 784
Isa 30:14 a sherd to take **f.** from the hearth, 784
Isa 30:27 and his tongue as a devouring **f.**: 784
Isa 30:30 the flame of a devouring **f.**, with 784
Isa 30:33 pile thereof is **f.** and much wood; 784
Isa 31:9 saith the Lord, whose **f.** is in Zion, 217
Isa 33:11 your breath, as **f.**, shall devour you. 784
Isa 33:12 cut up shall they be burned in the **f.** 784
Isa 33:14 shall dwell with the devouring **f.**? 784
Isa 37:19 And have cast their gods into the **f.**: 784
Isa 42:25 it hath set him on **f.** round about, 3857
Isa 43:2 when thou walkest through the **f.**, 784
Isa 44:16 He burneth part thereof in the **f.**; 784
Isa 44:16 I am warm, I have seen the **f.**: 217
Isa 44:19 I have burned part of it in the **f.**; 784
Isa 47:14 as stubble; the **f.** shall burn them; 784
Isa 47:14 to warm at, nor **f.** to sit before it. 217
Isa 50:11 Behold, all ye that kindle a **f.**. 784
Isa 50:11 walk in the light of your **f.**, and in 784
Isa 54:16 that bloweth the coals in the **f.**, 784
Isa 64:2 As when the melting **f.** burneth, 784
Isa 64:2 the **f.** causeth the waters to boil, 784
Isa 64:11 praised thee, is burned up with **f.**: 784
Isa 65:5 a **f.** that burneth all the day. 784
Isa 66:15 behold, the Lord will come with **f.**, 784
Isa 66:15 and his rebuke the flames of **f.**. 784
Isa 66:16 For by **f.** and by his sword will the 784
Isa 66:24 neither shall their **f.** be quenched; 784
Jer 4:4 lest my fury come forth like **f.**. 784
Jer 5:14 make my words in thy mouth **f.**, 784
Jer 6:1 up a sign of **f.** in Beth-haccerem:
Jer 6:29 the lead is consumed of the **f.**; 784
Jer 7:18 and the fathers kindle the **f.**, 784
Jer 7:31 sons and their daughters in the **f.**; 784
Jer 11:16 he hath kindled **f.** upon it, and the 784
Jer 15:14 for a **f.** is kindled in mine anger, 784
Jer 17:4 ye have kindled a **f.** in mine anger, 784
Jer 17:27 then will I kindle a **f.** in the gates 784
Jer 19:5 to burn their sons with **f.** for burnt 784
Jer 20:9 as a burning **f.** shut up in my bones, 784
Jer 21:10 and he shall burn it with **f.**. 784
Jer 21:12 lest my fury go out like **f.**, 784
Jer 21:14 and I will kindle a **f.** in the forest 784
Jer 22:7 cedars, and cast them into the **f.**. 784
Jer 23:29 Is not my word like as a **f.**? 784
Jer 29:22 king of Babylon roasted in the **f.**; 784
Jer 32:29 shall come and set **f.** on this city. 784
Jer 32:35 their daughters to pass through the **f.**
Jer 34:2 and he shall burn it with **f.**: 784
Jer 34:22 and take it, and burn it with **f.**: 784
Jer 36:22 and there was a **f.** on the hearth
Jer 36:23 into the **f.** that was on the hearth, 784
Jer 36:23 all the roll was consumed in the **f.** 784
Jer 36:32 king of Judah had burned in the **f.** 784
Jer 37:8 and take it, and burn it with **f.**. 784
Jer 37:10 tent, and burn this city with **f.**. 784
Jer 38:17 this city shall not be burnt with **f.**; 784
Jer 38:18 and they shall burn it with **f.**, 784
Jer 38:23 cause this city to be burned with **f.**. 784
Jer 39:8 the houses of the people, with **f.**, 784
Jer 43:12 And I will kindle a **f.** in the houses 784
Jer 43:13 Egyptians shall he burn with **f.** 784
Jer 48:45 **f.** shall come forth out of Heshbon, 784
Jer 49:2 daughters shall be burned with **f.**: 784
Jer 49:27 And I will kindle a **f.** in the wall of 784
Jer 50:32 and I will kindle a **f.** in his cities, 784
Jer 51:32 the reeds they have burned with **f.**, 784
Jer 51:58 high gates shall be burned with **f.**; 784
Jer 51:58 and the folk in the **f.**, and they shall 784
Jer 52:13 of the great men, burned he with **f.**: 784
La 1:13 above hath he sent **f.** into my bones, 784
La 2:3 against Jacob like a flaming **f.**, 784
La 2:4 he poured out his fury like **f.**. 784
La 4:11 and hath kindled a **f.** in Zion, 784
Eze 1:4 **f.** infolding itself, and a brightness 784
Eze 1:4 amber, out of the midst of the **f.**. 784
Eze 1:13 was like burning coals of **f.**, 784
Eze 1:13 the **f.** was bright, and out of the **f.** 784
Eze 1:27 as the appearance of **f.** round about 784
Eze 1:27 as it were the appearance of **f.**, 784
Eze 5:2 Thou shalt burn with **f.** a third part 217
Eze 5:4 cast them into the midst of the **f.**, 784
Eze 5:4 and burn them in the **f.**; 784
Eze 5:4 for thereof shall a **f.** come forth into 784
Eze 8:2 a likeness as the appearance of **f.**: 784
Eze 8:2 downward, **f.**; and from his loins 784
Eze 10:2 fill thine hand with coals of **f.** from 784
Eze 10:6 Take **f.** from between the wheels, 784
Eze 10:7 **f.** that was between the cherubims, 784
Eze 15:4 into the **f.** for fuel; the **f.** devoureth 784
Eze 15:5 when the **f.** hath devoured it, 784
Eze 15:6 which I have given to the **f.** for fuel, 784
Eze 15:7 they shall go out from one **f.**, 784
Eze 15:7 and another **f.** shall devour them; 784
Eze 16:21 them to pass through the **f.** for them?
Eze 16:41 they shall burn thine houses with **f.**, 784
Eze 19:12 withered; the **f.** consumed them. 784
Eze 19:14 And **f.** is gone out of a rod of her 784
Eze 20:26 through the **f.** all that openeth the
Eze 20:31 your sons to pass through the **f.**, 784
Eze 20:47 Behold, I will kindle a **f.** in thee, 784
Eze 21:31 against thee in the **f.** of my wrath, 784
Eze 21:32 Thou shalt be for fuel to the **f.**; 784
Eze 22:20 to blow the **f.** upon it, to melt it; 784
Eze 22:21 blow upon you in the **f.** of my wrath, 784
Eze 22:31 them with the **f.** of my wrath: 784
Eze 23:25 residue shall be devoured by the **f.**. 784
Eze 23:37 to pass for them through the **f.**, to
Eze 23:47 and burn up their houses with **f.**. 784
Eze 24:9 even make the pile for **f.** great.
Eze 24:10 Heap on wood, kindle the **f.**. 784
Eze 24:12 her scum shall be in the **f.**. 784
Eze 28:14 down in the midst of the stones of **f.** 784
Eze 28:16 from the midst of the stones of **f.**. 784
Eze 28:18 therefore will I bring forth a **f.** from 784
Eze 30:8 when I have set a **f.** in Egypt, 784
Eze 30:14 will set **f.** in Zoan, and will execute 784
Eze 30:16 And I will set **f.** in Egypt: 784
Eze 36:5 Surely in the **f.** of my jealousy have 784
Eze 38:19 in the **f.** of my wrath have I spoken, 784
Eze 38:22 great hailstones, **f.**, and brimstone. 784
Eze 39:6 And I will send a **f.** on Magog, 784
Eze 39:9 and shall set on **f.** and burn the 784
Eze 39:9 burn them with **f.** seven years: 784
Eze 39:10 shall burn the weapons with **f.**: 784
Da 3:22 the flame of the **f.** slew those men 5135
Da 3:24 bound into the midst of the **f.**? 5135
Da 3:25 loose, walking in the midst of the **f.**, 5135
Da 3:26 came forth of the midst of the **f.** 5135
Da 3:27 whose bodies the **f.** had no power, 5135
Da 3:27 the smell of **f.** had passed on them. 5135
Da 7:9 and his wheels as burning **f.**. 5135
Da 10:6 and his eyes as lamps of **f.**, 784
Ho 7:6 morning it burneth as a flaming **f.**. 784
Ho 8:14 but I will send a **f.** upon his cities, 784
Joe 1:19 for the **f.** hath devoured the pastures 784
Joe 1:20 the **f.** hath devoured the pastures 784
Joe 2:3 A **f.** devoureth before them; and 784
Joe 2:5 like the noise of a flame of **f.** that 784
Joe 2:30 blood, and **f.**, and pillars of smoke. 784
Am 1:4 I will send a **f.** into the house of 784
Am 1:7 I will send a **f.** on the wall of Gaza, 784
Am 1:10 I will send a **f.** on the wall of Tyrus, 784
Am 1:12 I will send a **f.** upon Teman, 784
Am 1:14 will kindle a **f.** in the wall of Rabbah, 784
Am 2:2 I will send a **f.** upon Moab, 784
Am 2:5 I will send a **f.** upon Judah, 784
Am 5:6 lest he break out like **f.** in the house 784
Am 7:4 Lord God called to contend by **f.**, 784
Ob 18 And the house of Jacob shall be a **f.**, 784
Mic 1:4 wax before the **f.**, and as the waters 784
Mic 1:7 thereof shall be burned with the **f.**. 784
Na 1:6 his fury is poured out like **f.**, 784
Na 3:13 the **f.** shall devour thy bars. 784
Na 3:15 There shall the **f.** devour thee; 784
Hab 2:13 people shall labour in the very **f.**, 784
Zep 1:18 land shall be devoured by the **f.** of 784
Zep 3:8 earth shall be devoured with the **f.** 784
Zec 2:5 will be unto her a wall of **f.** round 784
Zec 3:2 this a brand plucked out of the **f.**? 784
Zec 9:4 and she shall be devoured with **f.**. 784
Zec 11:1 that the **f.** may devour thy cedars. 784
Zec 12:6 like an hearth of **f.** among the wood, 784
Zec 12:6 and like a torch of **f.** in a sheaf; 784

Zec 13:9 bring the third part through the **f.**, 784
Mal 1:10 neither do ye kindle **f.** on mine altar
Mal 3:2 for he is like a refiner's **f.**, 784
Mt 3:10 is hewn down, and cast into the **f.** *4442*
Mt 3:11 with the Holy Ghost, and with **f.**: *4442*
Mt 3:12 up the chaff with unquenchable **f.** *4442*
Mt 5:22 **fool, shall be in danger of hell f.** *4442*
Mt 7:19 **is hewn down, and cast into the f.** *4442*
Mt 13:40 **are gathered and burned in the f.;** *4442*
Mt 13:42 **cast them into a furnace of f.:** *4442*
Mt 13:50 **cast them into the furnace of f.:** *4442*
Mt 17:15 for ofttimes he falleth into the **f.**, *4442*
Mt 18:8 **feet to be cast into everlasting f.** *4442*
Mt 18:9 **two eyes to be cast into hell f.** *4442*
Mt 25:41 **into everlasting f., prepared for** *4442*
Mk 9:22 it hath cast him into the **f.**, *4442*
Mk 9:43 **f. that never shall be quenched:** *4442*
Mk 9:44 **not, and the f. is not quenched:** *4442*
Mk 9:45 **f. that never shall be quenched;** *4442*
Mk 9:46 **not, and the f. is not quenched** *4442*
Mk 9:47 **two eyes to be cast into hell f.:** *4442*
Mk 9:48 **not, and the f. is not quenched** *4442*
Mk 9:49 **every one shall be salted with f.,** *4442*
Mk 14:54 and warmed himself at the **f.** *5457*
Lu 3:9 is hewn down, and cast into the **f.**, *4442*
Lu 3:16 with the Holy Ghost and with **f.**: *4442*
Lu 3:17 he will burn with **f.** unquenchable. *4442*
Lu 9:54 that we command **f.** to come down *4442*
Lu 12:49 **I am come to send f. on the earth;** *4442*
Lu 17:29 **it rained f. and brimstone from** *4442*
Lu 22:55 And when they had kindled a **f.** *4442*
Lu 22:56 beheld him as he sat by the **f.** *5457*
Joh 15:6 **them, and cast them into the f.,** *4442*
Joh 18:18 had made a **f.** of coals; for it was cold:
Joh 21:9 they saw a **f.** of coals there, and fish
Ac 2:3 them cloven tongues like as of **f.**, *4442*
Ac 2:19 blood, and **f.**, and vapour of smoke: *4442*
Ac 7:30 the Lord in a flame of **f.** in a bush. *4442*
Ac 28:8 they kindled a **f.**, and received us *4443*
Ac 28:3 of sticks, and laid them on the **f.** *4443*
Ac 28:5 he shook off the beast into the **f.**, *4442*
Ro 12:20 shalt heap coals of **f.** on his head. *4442*
1Co 3:13 shall be revealed by **f.**; and the **f.** *4442*
1Co 3:15 shall be saved; yet so as by **f.** *4442*
2Th 1:8 In flaming **f.** taking vengeance on *4442*
Heb 1:7 and his ministers a flame of **f.** *4442*
Heb 11:34 Quenched the violence of **f.**, *4442*
Heb 12:18 and that burned with **f.**, nor unto *4442*
Heb 12:29 For our God is a consuming **f.** *4442*
Jas 3:5 great a matter a little **f.** kindleth! *4442*
Jas 3:6 tongue is a **f.**, a world of iniquity: *4442*
Jas 3:6 setteth on **f.** the course of nature; *5394*
Jas 3:6 and it is set on **f.** of hell *5394*
Jas 5:3 shall eat your flesh as it were **f.** *4442*
1Pe 1:7 though it be tried with **f.**, might *4442*
2Pe 3:7 reserved unto **f.** against the day of *4442*
2Pe 3:12 being of **f.** shall be dissolved, *4448*
Jude 7 the vengeance of eternal **f.** *4442*
Jude 23 fear, pulling them out of the **f.**; *4442*
Re 1:14 and his eyes were as a flame of **f.**; *4442*
Re 2:18 **his eyes like unto a flame of f.,** *4442*
Re 3:18 **to buy of me gold tried in the f.,** *4442*
Re 4:5 seven lamps of **f.** burning before *4442*
Re 8:5 and filled it with **f.** of the altar, *4442*
Re 8:7 hail and **f.** mingled with blood, *4442*
Re 8:8 a great mountain burning with **f.** *4442*
Re 9:17 having breastplates of **f.**, and of *4447*
Re 9:17 out of their mouths issued **f.** and *4442*
Re 9:18 killed, by the **f.**, and by the smoke, *4442*
Re 10:1 and his feet as pillars of **f.**: *4442*
Re 11:5 **f.** proceedeth out of their mouth, *4442*
Re 13:13 maketh **f.** come down from heaven *4442*
Re 14:10 tormented with **f.** and brimstone *4442*
Re 14:18 which had power over **f.**; and cried *4442*
Re 15:2 were a sea of glass mingled with **f.**: *4442*
Re 16:8 unto him to scorch men with **f.** *4442*
Re 17:16 eat her flesh, and burn her with **f.** *4442*
Re 18:8 she shall be utterly burned with **f.**: *4442*
Re 19:12 His eyes were as a flame of **f.**, *4442*
Re 19:20 lake of **f.** burning with brimstone. *4442*
Re 20:9 and **f.** came down from God out of *4442*
Re 20:10 into the lake of **f.** and brimstone, *4442*
Re 20:14 hell were cast into the lake of **f.** *4442*
Re 20:15 of life was cast into the lake of **f.** *4442*
Re 21:8 burneth with **f.** and brimstone: *4442*

FIREBRAND See also FIREBRANDS.

Jg 15:4 turned tail to tail, and put a **f.** 3940
Am 4:11 ye were as a **f.** plucked out of the 181

FIREBRANDS

Jg 15:4 and took **f.** and turned tail to tail, 3940
Pr 26:18 As a mad man who casteth **f.**, 2131
Isa 7:4 for the two tails of these smoking **f.**, 181

FIREPANS

Ex 27:3 and his fleshhooks, and his **f.**; 4289
Ex 38:3 and the fleshhooks, and the **f.**: 4289
2Ki 25:15 And the **f.**, and the bowls, and such 4289
Jer 52:19 the basons, and the **f.**, and the bowls, 4289

FIRES

Isa 24:15 glorify ye the Lord in the **f.**, even 217

FIRKINS

Joh 2:6 containing two or three **f.** apiece. *3355*

FIRM See also AFFIRM; CONFIRM.

Jos 3:17 the covenant of the Lord stood **f.** 3559
Jos 4:3 where the priests' feet stood **f.**, 3559
Job 41:23 they are **f.** in themselves; they 3332
Job 41:24 His heart is as **f.** as a stone; they 3332
Ps 73:4 but their strength is **f.** 1277
Dan 6:7 and to make a **f.** decree, 8631
Heb 3:6 rejoicing of the hope **f.** unto the end. *949*

FIRMAMENT

Ge 1:6 Let there be a **f.** in the midst of 7549
Ge 1:7 God made the **f.**, and divided the 7549
Ge 1:7 which were under the **f.** from the 7549
Ge 1:7 the waters which were above the **f.**: 7549
Ge 1:8 And God called the **f.** Heaven. 7549
Ge 1:14 Let there be lights in the **f.** of the 7549
Ge 1:15 for lights in the **f.** of heaven to give 7549
Ge 1:17 God set them in the **f.** of heaven to 7549
Ge 1:20 earth in the open **f.** of heaven. 7549
Ps 19:1 and the **f.** sheweth his handywork. 7549
Ps 150:1 praise him in the **f.** of his power. 7549
Eze 1:22 the likeness of the **f.** upon the heads 7549
Eze 1:23 And under the **f.** were their wings 7549
Eze 1:25 And there was a voice from the **f.** 7549
Eze 1:26 And above the **f.** that was over their 7549
Eze 10:1 in the **f.** that was above the head 7549
Da 12:3 shine as the brightness of the **f.**; 7549

FIRST See also FIRSTBORN; FIRSTBEGOTTEN; FIRSTFRUIT; FIRSTLING; FIRSTRIPE.

Ge *general* *title* The **F.** Book of Moses, Called
Gen 1:5 and the morning were the **f.** day. 259
Gen 2:11 The name of the **f.** is Pison: 259
Gen 8:5 on the **f.** day of the month, were 259
Gen 8:13 in the six hundreth and **f.** year, in 259
Gen 8:13 the **f.** [7223] month, the **f.** day of the 259
Gen 13:4 which he had made there at the **f.**: 7223
Gen 25:25 And the **f.** came out red, all over 7223
Gen 26:1 the **f.** famine that was in the days 7223
Gen 28:19 that city was called Luz at the **f.** 7223
Gen 38:28 saying, This came out **f.** 7223
Gen 41:20 did eat up the **f.** seven fat kine: 7223
Gen 43:18 in our sacks at the **f.** time are we 8462
Gen 43:20 we came indeed down at the **f.** time 8462
Ex 4:8 hearken to the voice of the **f.** sign, 7223
Ex 12:2 be the **f.** month of the year to you. 7223
Ex 12:5 blemish, a male of the **f.** year; 1121
Ex 12:15 the **f.** day ye shall put away leaven 7223
Ex 12:15 from the **f.** day until the seventh 7223
Ex 12:16 in the **f.** day there shall be an holy 7223
Ex 12:18 In the **f.** month, on the fourteenth 7223
Ex 22:29 to offer the **f.** of thy ripe fruits, 4395
Ex 23:19 The **f.** of the firstfruits of thy land 7225
Ex 28:17 the **f.** row shall be a sardius, a
Ex 28:17 carbuncle: this shall be the **f.** row. 259
Ex 29:38 two lambs of the **f.** year day by 1121
Ex 34:1 tables of stone like unto the **f.**: 7223
Ex 34:1 the words that were in the **f.** tables, 7223
Ex 34:4 two tables of stone like unto the **f.**: 7223
Ex 34:26 The **f.** of the firstfruits of thy land 7225
Ex 39:10 the **f.** row was a sardius, a topaz,
Ex 39:10 a carbuncle: this was the **f.** row. 259
Ex 40:2 On the **f.** day of the...month shalt 7223
Ex 40:2 On the...day of the **f.** month shalt 259
Ex 40:17 the **f.** month in the second year, 7223
Ex 40:17 on the **f.** day of the month, that the 259
Le 4:21 and burn him as he burned the **f.** 7223
Le 5:8 that which is for the sin offering **f.**, 7223
Le 9:3 and a lamb, both of the **f.** year. 1121
Le 9:15 and offered it for sin, as the **f.** 7223
Le 12:6 shall bring a lamb of the **f.** year 1121
Le 14:10 and one ewe lamb of the **f.** year 1323
Le 23:5 the fourteenth day of the **f.** month 7223
Le 23:7 In the **f.** day ye shall have an holy 7223
Le 23:12 lamb without blemish of the **f.** 1121
Le 23:18 lambs without blemish of the **f.** 1121
Le 23:19 two lambs of the **f.** year for a 1121
Le 23:24 In the seventh month, in the **f.** day 259
Le 23:35 On the **f.** day shall be an holy 7223
Le 23:39 on the **f.** day shall be a sabbath, 7223
Le 23:40 take you on the **f.** day the boughs 7223
Nu 1:1, 18 the **f.** day of the second month, 259
Nu 2:9 armies. These shall **f.** set forth. 7223
Nu 6:12 shall bring a lamb of the **f.** year 1121
Nu 6:14 Lord, one he lamb of the **f.** year 1121
Nu 6:14 and one ewe lamb of the **f.** year 1323
Nu 7:12 he that offered his offering the **f.** 7223
Nu 7:15 one ram, one lamb of the **f.** year, 1121
Nu 7:17 goats, five lambs of the **f.** year: 1121
Nu 7:21 one lamb of the **f.** year, for a 1121
Nu 7:23 five lambs of the **f.** year: this 1121
Nu 7:27 one lamb of the **f.** year, for a 1121
Nu 7:29 goats, five lambs of the **f.** year: 1121
Nu 7:33 one ram, one lamb of the **f.** year, 1121
Nu 7:35 five lambs of the **f.** year: this 1121
Nu 7:39 one lamb of the **f.** year, for a 1121
Nu 7:41 five lambs of the **f.** year: this 1121
Nu 7:45 one ram, one lamb of the **f.** year, 1121
Nu 7:47 goats, five lambs of the **f.** year: 1121
Nu 7:51 one ram, one lamb of the **f.** year, 1121
Nu 7:53 goats, five lambs of the **f.** year: 1121
Nu 7:57 one ram, one lamb of the **f.** year, 1121
Nu 7:59 goats, five lambs of the **f.** year: 1121
Nu 7:63 one ram, one lamb of the **f.** year, 1121
Nu 7:65 goats, five lambs of the **f.** year: 1121
Nu 7:69 one ram, one lamb of the **f.** year, 1121
Nu 7:71 goats, five lambs of the **f.** year: 1121
Nu 7:75 one ram, one lamb of the **f.** year, 1121
Nu 7:77 goats, five lambs of the **f.** year: 1121
Nu 7:81 one ram, one lamb of the **f.** year, 1121
Nu 7:83 goats, five lambs of the **f.** year: 1121
Nu 7:87 the lambs of the **f.** year twelve, 1121
Nu 7:88 the lambs of the **f.** year sixty. 1121
Nu 9:1 in the **f.** month of the second year 7223
Nu 9:5 **f.** month at even in the wilderness 7223
Nu 10:13 they **f.** took their journey according 7223
Nu 10:14 In the **f.** place went the standard 7223
Nu 15:20 up a cake of the **f.** of your dough 7225
Nu 15:21 Of the **f.** of your dough ye shall give 7225
Nu 15:27 bring a she goat of the **f.** year 1323
Nu 18:13 whatsoever is **f.** ripe in the land, 1061
Nu 20:1 the desert of Zin in the **f.** month: 7223
Nu 24:20 Amalek was the **f.** of the nations; 7225
Nu 28:3, 9 lambs of the **f.** year without 1121
Nu 28:11 seven lambs of the **f.** year without 1121
Nu 28:16 fourteenth day of the **f.** month 7223
Nu 28:18 **f.** day shall be an holy convocation; 7223
Nu 28:19 and seven lambs of the **f.** year: 1121
Nu 28:27 ram, seven lambs of the **f.** year; 1121
Nu 29:1 in the seventh month, on the **f.** day 259
Nu 29:2 seven lambs of the **f.** year without 1121
Nu 29:8 and seven lambs of the **f.** year 1121
Nu 29:13 and fourteen lambs of the **f.** year; 1121
Nu 29:17, 20 fourteen lambs of the **f.** year 1121
Nu 29:23, 26,29,32 two rams, and fourteen lambs of the **f.** year without 1121
Nu 29:36 ram, seven lambs of the **f.** year 1121
Nu 33:3 from Rameses in the **f.** month, 7223
Nu 33:3 on the fifteenth day of the **f.** month; 7223
Nu 33:38 in the **f.** day of the fifth month. 259
De 1:3 the **f.** day of the month, that Moses 259
De 9:18 down before the Lord, as at the **f.**, 7223
De 9:25 as I fell down at the **f.**; because
De 10:1 two tables of stone like unto the **f.**, 7223
De 10:2 the words that were in the **f.** tables 7223
De 10:3 two tables of stone like unto the **f.**, 7223
De 10:4 according to the **f.** writing, the ten 7223
De 10:10 mount, according to the **f.** time, 7223
De 11:14 the **f.** rain and the latter rain, 3138
De 13:9 thine hand shall be **f.** upon him 7223
De 16:4 thou sacrificedst the **f.** day at even, 7223
De 17:7 hands of the witnesses shall be **f.** 7223
De 18:4 **f.** fleece of the fleece of thy sheep, 7225
De 26:2 thou shalt take of the **f.** of all the 7225
De 33:21 he provided the **f.** part for himself, 7225
Jos 4:19 on the tenth day of the **f.** month, 7223

Jos 8:5 come out against us, as at the f.,... 7223
Jos 8:6 They flee before us, as at the f.:... 7223
Jos 21:10 Levi, had: for theirs was the f. lot.... 7223
Jg 1:1 for us against the Canaanites f.,... 8462
Jg 18:29 name of the city was Laish at the f.... 7223
Jg 20:18 Which of us shall go up f. to the... 8462
Jg 20:18 Lord said, Judah shall go up f.... 8462
Jg 20:22 themselves in array the f. day.... 7223
Jg 20:32 smitten down before us, as at the f.... 7223
Jg 20:39 down before us, as in the f. battle... 7223
1Sa *general* *title* The F. Book of Samuel, [א]...
1Sa *general* *title* The F. Book Of The Kings...
1Sa 14:14 that f. slaughter, which Jonathan... 7223
1Sa 14:35 same was the f. altar that he built... 2490
2Sa 3:13 f. bring Michal Saul's daughter,... 6440
2Sa 17:9 of them be overthrown at the f.,... 8462
2Sa 19:20 I am come the f. this day of all the... 7223
2Sa 19:43 that our advice should not be f.... 7223
2Sa 21:9 the days of harvest, in the f. days,... 7223
2Sa 23:19 he attained not unto the f. three....
2Sa 23:23 but he attained not unto the f. three....
1Ki *general* *title* The F. Book Of The Kings, [א]...
1Ki 16:23 In the thirty and f. year of Asa... 259
1Ki 17:13 make me thereof a little cake f.,... 7223
1Ki 18:25 for yourselves, and dress it f.;... 7223
1Ki 20:9 send for to thy servant at the f.... 7223
1Ki 20:17 princes of the provinces went out f.;... 7223
1Ch *general* *title* The F. Book Of The Chronicles. [א]...
1Ch 9:2 f. inhabitants that dwelt in their... 7223
1Ch 11:6 Whosoever smiteth the Jebusites f.... 7223
1Ch 11:6 Joab the son of Zeruiah went f. up,... 7223
1Ch 11:21 howbeit he attained not to the f. three....
1Ch 11:25 but attained not to the f. three:...
1Ch 12:9 Ezer the f., Obadiah the second,... 7218
1Ch 12:15 went over Jordan in the f. month.... 7223
1Ch 15:13 because ye did it not at the f.,... 7223
1Ch 16:7 David delivered f. this psalm to... 7218
1Ch 23:19 Jeriah the f., Amariah the second,... 7218
1Ch 23:20 Micah the f., and Jesiah the... 7218
1Ch 24:7 the f. lot came forth to Jehoiarib,... 7223
1Ch 24:21 of Rehabiah, the f. was Isshiah.... 7218
1Ch 24:23 Jeriah the f., Amariah the second,...
1Ch 25:9 the f. lot came forth for Asaph... 7223
1Ch 27:2 Over the f. course for the f. month.... 7223
1Ch 27:3 captains of the host for the f. month... 7223
1Ch 29:29 acts of David the king, f. and last,... 7223
2Ch 3:3 f. measure was threescore cubits,... 7223
2Ch 9:29 the acts of Solomon, f. and last,... 7223
2Ch 12:15 the acts of Rehoboam, f. and last,... 7223
2Ch 16:11 the acts of Asa, f. and last,... 7223
2Ch 17:3 in the f. ways of his father David,... 7223
2Ch 20:34 the acts of Jehoshaphat, f. and last,... 7223
2Ch 25:26 the acts of Amaziah, f. and last,... 7223
2Ch 26:22 the acts of Uzziah, f. and last,... 7223
2Ch 28:26 acts and of all his ways, f. and last,... 7223
2Ch 29:3 He in the f. year of his reign,... 7223
2Ch 29:3 in the f. month, opened the doors of... 7223
2Ch 29:17 on the f. [259] day of the f. month to..7223
2Ch 29:17 in the sixteenth day of the f. month.... 7223
2Ch 35:1 the fourteenth day of the f. month... 7223
2Ch 35:27 And his deeds, f. and last, behold.... 7223
2Ch 36:22 the f. year of Cyrus king of Persia,... 259
Ezr 1:1 the f. year of Cyrus king of Persia,... 259
Ezr 3:6 From the f. day of the seventh month.. 259
Ezr 3:12 men, that had seen the f. house,... 7223
Ezr 5:13 But in the f. year of Cyrus the king.... 2298
Ezr 6:3 In the f. year of Cyrus the king... 2298
Ezr 6:19 the fourteenth day of the f. month... 7223
Ezr 7:9 For upon the f. day of the...month... 259
Ezr 7:9 day of the f. month began he to go.... 7223
Ezr 7:9 and on the f. day of the fifth month... 259
Ezr 8:31 on the twelfth day of the f. month,... 7223
Ezr 10:16 in the f. day of the tenth month to... 259
Ezr 10:17 wives by the f. day of the...month... 259
Ezr 10:17 wives by the...day of the f. month.... 7223
Ne 7:5 of them which came up at the f.... 7223
Ne 8:2 the f. day of the seventh month.... 259
Ne 8:18 from the f. day unto the last day,... 7223
Es 1:14 which sat the f. in the kingdom;)... 7223
Es 3:7 In the f. month, that is, the month... 7223
Es 3:12 the thirteenth day of the f. month,... 7223
Job 15:7 Art thou the f. man that was born?... 7223
Job 42:14 And he called the name of the f.,... 7223
Pr 18:17 He that is f. in his own cause... 7223
Isa 1:26 will restore thy judges as at the f.,... 7223
Isa 9:1 when at the f. he lightly afflicted... 7223
Isa 41:4 the Lord, the f., and with the last;... 7223
Isa 41:27 The f. shall say to Zion, Behold,... 7223
Isa 43:27 Thy f. father hath sinned, and thy... 7223
Isa 44:6 I am the f., and I am the last; and... 7223
Isa 48:12 he; I am the f., I also am the last.... 7223
Isa 60:9 the ships of Tarshish f., to bring... 7223
Jer 4:31 that bringeth forth her f. child,... 1069
Jer 7:12 where I set my name at the f.,... 7223
Jer 16:18 f. I will recompense their iniquity... 7223
Jer 24:2 even like the figs that are f. ripe:... 1073
Jer 25:1 was the f. year of Nebuchadrezzar... 7224
Jer 33:7 and will build them, as at the f.... 7223
Jer 33:11 the captivity of the land, as at the f.,.. 7223
Jer 36:28 words that were in the f. roll,... 7223
Jer 50:17 away: f. the king of Assyria hath... 7223
Jer 52:31 f. year of his reign lifted up the head...
Eze 10:14 the f. face was the face of a cherub,... 259
Eze 26:1 in the f. day of the month, that the... 259
Eze 29:17 in the f. month, in the...day of the... 7223
Eze 29:17 in the f. day of the month, the word... 259
Eze 30:20 the f. month, in the seventh day... 7223
Eze 31:1 in the f. day of the month, that the... 259
Eze 32:1 in the f. day of the month, that the... 259
Eze 40:21 were the measure of the f. gate:... 7223
Eze 44:30 And the f. of all the firstfruits... 7225
Eze 44:30 unto the priest the f. of your dough,... 7225
Eze 45:18 In the f. month, in the...day of the... 7223
Eze 45:18 in the f. day of the month, thou shalt... 259
Eze 45:21 In the f. month, in the fourteenth... 7223
Eze 46:13 of a lamb of the f. year without... 1121
Da 1:21 even unto the f. year of king Cyrus.... 259
Da 6:2 presidents of whom Daniel was f.:... 2298
Da 7:1 In the f. year of Belshazzar king... 2298
Da 7:4 The f. was like a lion, and had... 6933
Da 7:8 three of the f. horns plucked up... 6933
Da 7:24 he shall be diverse from the f.,... 6933
Da 8:1 which appeared unto me at the f.... 8462
Da 8:21 between his eyes is the f. king... 7223
Da 9:1 In the f. year of Darius the son of... 259
Da 9:2 In the f. year of his reign I Daniel... 259
Da 10:4 and twentieth day of the f. month,... 7223
Da 10:12 from the f. day that thou didst set... 7223
Da 11:1 Also I in the f. year of Darius the... 259
Ho 2:7 go and return to my f. husband:... 7223
Ho 9:10 in the fig tree at her f. time: but... 7225
Joe 2:23 and the latter rain in the f. month.... 7223
Am 6:7 captive with the f. that go captive,... 7218
Mic 4:8 the f. dominion; the kingdom... 7223
Hag 1:1 in the f. day of the month, came the... 259
Hag 2:3 saw this house in her f. glory?... 7223
Zec 6:2 In the f. chariot were red horses:... 7223
Zec 12:7 also shall save the tents of Judah f.,... 7223
Zec 14:10 gate unto the place of the f. gate,... 7223
Mt 5:24 **f. be reconciled to thy brother,**... *4412*
Mt 6:33 **But seek ye f. the kingdom of God,***4412*
Mt 7:5 **f. cast out the beam out of thine**... *4412*
Mt 8:21 suffer me f. to go and bury my... *4412*
Mt 10:2 The f., Simon, who is called Peter,... *4413*
Mt 12:29 **except he f. bind the strong man?**... *4412*
Mt 12:45 **of that man is worse than the f.**... *4413*
Mt 13:30 **Gather ye together f. the tares,**... *4412*
Mt 17:10 scribes that Elias must f. come?... *4412*
Mt 17:11 **Elias truly shall f. come, and**... *4412*
Mt 17:27 **take up the fish that f. cometh up;***4413*
Mt 19:30 **But many that are f. shall be last;***4413*
Mt 19:30 **be last; and the last shall be f.**... *4413*
Mt 20:8 **from the last unto the f.**... *4413*
Mt 20:10 **when the f. came, they supposed**... *4413*
Mt 20:16 **the last shall be f., and the f. last:***4413*
Mt 21:28 **and he came to the f., and said,**... *4413*
Mt 21:31 They say unto him, The f.... *4413*
Mt 21:36 **other servants more than the f.:**... *4413*
Mt 22:25 and the f., when he had married a... *4413*
Mt 22:38 **is the f. and great commandment.***4413*
Mt 23:26 **cleanse f. that which is within the***4412*
Mt 26:17 Now the f. day of the feast of... *4413*
Mt 27:64 last error shall be worse than the f.... *4413*
Mt 28:1 toward the f. day of the week,... *3391*
Mk 3:27 **he will f. bind the strong man;**... *4412*
Mk 4:28 **f. the blade, then the ear,**... *4412*
Mk 7:27 **Let the children f. be filled: for it** *4412*
Mk 9:11 the scribes that Elias must f. come?... *4412*
Mk 9:12 **Elias verily cometh f., and**... *4412*
Mk 9:35 **man desire to be f., the same shall***4413*
Mk 10:31 **But many that are f. shall be last;***4413*
Mk 10:31 **shall be last; and the last f.**... *4413*
Mk 12:20 f. took a wife, and dying left no... *4413*
Mk 12:28 Which is the f. commandment of... *4413*
Mk 12:29 **The f. of all the commandments**... *4413*
Mk 12:30 **this is the f. commandment.**... *4413*
Mk 13:10 **the gospel must f. be published**... *4412*
Mk 14:12 the f. day of unleavened bread,... *4413*
Mk 16:2 morning the f. day of the week,... *3391*
Mk 16:9 early the f. day of the week,... *4415*
Mk 16:9 he appeared f. to Mary Magdalene,... *4412*
Lu 1:3 of all things from the very f.,... *509*
Lu 2:2 taxing was f. made when Cyrenius... *4413*
Lu 6:1 the second sabbath after the f.,... *1207*
Lu 6:42 **hypocrite, cast out f. the beam**... *4412*
Lu 9:59 suffer me f. to go and bury my... *4412*
Lu 9:61 but let me f. go bid them farewell,... *4412*
Lu 10:5 **f. say, Peace be to this house**... *4412*
Lu 11:26 **of that man is worse than the f.**... *4413*
Lu 11:38 had not f. washed before dinner... *4412*
Lu 12:1 to say unto his disciples f. of all,... *4412*
Lu 13:30 **shall be f., and there are f. which**..*4413*
Lu 14:18 **f. said unto him, I have bought**... *4413*
Lu 14:28 **sitteth not down f., and counteth**.. *4412*
Lu 14:31 **sitteth not down f., and consulteth***4412*
Lu 16:5 **and said unto the f., How much**... *4413*
Lu 17:25 **But f. must he suffer many things,***4412*
Lu 19:16 **Then came the f., saying, Lord,**... *4413*
Lu 20:29 and the f. took a wife, and died... *4413*
Lu 21:9 **these things must f. come to pass;** *4412*
Lu 24:1 Now upon the f. day of the week,... *3391*
Joh 1:41 f. findeth his own brother Simon,... *4413*
Joh 5:4 then f. after the troubling of the... *4413*
Joh 8:7 **let him f. cast a stone at her.**... *4413*
Joh 10:40 place where John at f. baptized;... *4412*
Joh 12:16 not his disciples at the f.: but when... *4412*
Joh 18:13 And led him away to Annas f.; for... *4412*
Joh 19:32 and brake the legs of the f., and of... *4413*
Joh 19:39 at the f. came to Jesus by night,... *4412*
Joh 20:1 f. day of the week cometh Mary... *3391*
Joh 20:4 Peter, and came f. to the sepulchre... *4413*
Joh 20:8 which came f. to the sepulchre, and... *4413*
Joh 20:19 being the f. day of the week,... *3391*
Ac 3:26 Unto you f. God, having raised up... *4412*
Ac 7:12 Egypt, he sent out our fathers f.... *4412*
Ac 11:26 were called Christians f. in Antioch... *4412*
Ac 12:10 past the f. and the second ward,... *4413*
Ac 13:24 When John had f. preached before his...
Ac 13:46 should f. have been spoken to you:... *4412*
Ac 15:14 how God at the f. did visit the... *4412*
Ac 20:7 And upon the f. day of the week,... *3391*
Ac 20:18 know, from the f. day that I came... *4413*
Ac 26:4 at the f. among mine own nation... *746*
Ac 26:20 shewed f. unto them of Damascus... *4412*
Ac 26:23 should be the f. that should rise... *4413*
Ac 27:43 cast themselves f. into the sea,... *4413*
Ro 1:8 F., I thank my God through Jesus... *4412*
Ro 1:16 to the Jew f., and also to the Greek.. *4412*
Ro 2:9 the Jew f., and also of the Gentile;... *4412*
Ro 2:10 the Jew f., and also to the Gentile:... *4412*
Ro 10:19 F. Moses saith, I will provoke you... *4413*
Ro 11:35 Or who hath f. given to him,... *4272*
Ro 15:24 if f. I be somewhat filled with your... *4412*
1Co *general* *title* The F. Epistle Of Paul The... *4413*
1Co 11:18 For f. of all, when ye come... *4412*
1Co 12:28 f. apostles, secondarily prophets,... *4412*
1Co 14:30 sitteth by, let the f. hold his peace.... *4413*
1Co 15:3 I delivered unto you f. of all... *1722, 4413*
1Co 15:45 f. man Adam was made a living... *4413*
1Co 15:46 that was not f. which is spiritual,... *4412*
1Co 15:47 The f. man is of the earth, earthy:... *4413*
1Co 16:2 Upon the f. day of the week let... *3391*
1Co *subscr.* The f. epistle to the Corinthians... *4413*
2Co 8:5 f. gave their own selves to the... *4412*
2Co 8:12 if there be f. a willing mind,... *4295*
Ga 4:13 the gospel unto you at the f.... *4386*
Eph 1:12 who f. trusted in Christ... *4276*
Eph 4:9 also descended f. into the lower... *4412*
Eph 6:2 f. commandment with promise;... *4413*
Php 1:5 gospel from the f. day until now;... *4413*
1Th *general* *title* The F. Epistle Of Paul The... *4413*
1Th 4:16 the dead in Christ shall rise f.... *4412*
1Th *subscr.* f. epistle unto the Thessalonians... *4413*
2Th 2:3 except there come a falling away f.,... *4412*
1Ti *general* *title* The F. Epistle Of Paul The... *4413*
1Ti 1:16 in me f. Jesus Christ might shew... *4413*
1Ti 2:1 f. of all, supplications, prayers,... *4412*
1Ti 2:13 Adam was f. formed, then Eve.... *4413*
1Ti 3:10 And let these also f. be proved;... *4412*
1Ti 5:4 let them learn f. to shew piety... *4412*
1Ti 5:12 they have cast off their f. faith.... *4413*

1Ti *subscr.* The **f.** to Timothy was written for...... *4413*
2Ti 1:5 which dwelt **f.** in thy grandmother...... *4412*
2Ti 2:6 must be **f.** partaker of the fruits......... *4413*
2Ti 4:16 At my **f.** answer no man stood with.... *4413*
2Ti *subscr.* Timotheus, ordained the **f.** bishop *4413*
Tit 3:10 after the **f.** and second admonition....... *3391*
Tit *subscr.* Titus, ordained the **f.** bishop of the..... *4413*
Heb 2:3 which at the **f.** began to be spoken *746*
Heb 4:6 they to whom it was **f.** preached........ *4386*
Heb 5:12 **f.** principles of the oracles of God; *746*
Heb 7:2 **f.** being by interpretation King of *4412*
Heb 7:27 **f.** for his own sins, and then for......... *4386*
Heb 8:7 that **f.** covenant had been faultless,...... *4413*
Heb 8:13 covenant, he hath made the **f.** old. *4413*
Heb 9:1 Then verily the **f.** covenant had *4413*
Heb 9:2 the **f.**, wherein was the candlestick,.... *4413*
Heb 9:6 went always into the **f.** tabernacle, ... *4413*
Heb 9:8 while as the **f.** tabernacle was yet *4413*
Heb 9:15 that were under the **f.** testament, ... *4413*
Heb 9:18 the **f.** testament was dedicated *4413*
Heb 10:9 He taketh away the **f.**, that he may.... *4413*
Jas 3:17 is **f.** pure, then peaceable, gentle, ... *4412*
1Pe *general title* The **F.** Epistle General Of *4413*
1Pe 4:17 and if it **f.** begin at us, what shall....... *4412*
2Pe 1:20 Knowing this **f.**, that no prophecy *4412*
2Pe 3:3 Knowing this **f.**, that there shall......... *4412*
1Jo *general title* The **F.** Epistle General Of.......... *4413*
1Jo 4:19 love him, because he **f.** loved us........ *4413*
Jude 6 which kept not their **f.** estate,............ *746*
Re 1:5 and the **f.** begotten of the dead,......... *4416*
Re 1:11 **Alpha and Omega, the f. and the...** *4413*
Re 1:17 **Fear not; I am the f. and the last:** *4413*
Re 2:4 **because thou hast left thy f. love** . *4413*
Re 2:5 **and do the f. works; or else I will.** *4413*
Re 2:8 **saith the f. and the last, which**..... *4413*
Re 2:19 **the last to be more than the f.**..... *4413*
Re 4:1 and the **f.** voice which I heard was..... *4413*
Re 4:7 And the **f.** beast was like a lion, ... *4413*
Re 8:7 The **f.** angel sounded, and there *4413*
Re 13:12 all the power of the **f.** beast before *4413*
Re 13:12 therein to worship the **f.** beast, ... *4413*
Re 16:2 the **f.** went, and poured out his vial.... *4413*
Re 20:5 This is the **f.** resurrection................ *4413*
Re 20:6 hath part in the **f.** resurrection: *4413*
Re 21:1 the **f.** heaven and the **f.** earth were.... *4413*
Re 21:19 the **f.** foundation was jasper; the........ *4413*
Re 22:13 **and the end, the f. and the last** *4413*

FIRSTBEGOTTEN See also FIRST and BEGOTTEN.
Heb 1:6 bringeth in the **f.** into the world, ... *4416*

FIRSTBORN
Ge 10:15 Canaan begat Sidon his **f.**, and.......... 1060
Ge 19:31 And the **f.** said unto the younger,....... 1067
Ge 19:33 **f.** went in, and lay with her father,..... 1067
Ge 19:34 **f.** said unto the younger, Behold, ... 1067
Ge 19:37 **f.** bare a son, and called his name 1067
Ge 22:21 Huz his **f.**, and Buz his brother,......... 1060
Ge 25:13 **f.** of Ishmael, Nebajoth; and Kedar, ... 1060
Ge 27:19 I am Esau thy **f.**; I have done 1060
Ge 27:32 he said, I am thy son, thy **f.** Esau...... 1060
Ge 29:26 to give the younger before the **f.**. 1067
Ge 35:23 Reuben, Jacob's **f.**, and Simeon,......... 1060
Ge 36:15 sons of Eliphaz the **f.** son of Esau; 1060
Ge 38:6 And Judah took a wife for Er his **f.**,.... 1060
Ge 38:7 Er, Judah's **f.**, was wicked in the 1060
Ge 41:51 called the name of the **f.** Manasseh:.... 1060
Ge 43:33 the **f.** according to his birthright,........ 1060
Ge 46:8 and his sons; Reuben, Jacob's **f.**.......... 1060
Ge 48:14 for Manasseh was the **f.**.................... 1060
Ge 48:18 Not so, my father: for this is the **f.**; ... 1060
Ge 49:3 Reuben, thou art my **f.**, my might,..... 1060
Ex 4:22 Israel is my son, even my **f.**: 1060
Ex 4:23 I will slay thy son, even thy **f.**........... 1060
Ex 6:14 the **f.** of Israel; Hanoch and Pallu, ... 1060
Ex 11:5 all the **f.** in the land of Egypt shall...... 1060
Ex 11:5 die, from the **f.** of Pharaoh that 1060
Ex 11:5 unto the **f.** of the maidservant that 1060
Ex 11:5 the mill; and all the **f.** of beasts. 1060
Ex 12:12 and will smite all the **f.** in the land...... 1060
Ex 12:29 Lord smote all the **f.** in the land of..... 1060
Ex 12:29 from the **f.** of Pharaoh that sat on...... 1060
Ex 12:29 unto the **f.** of the captive that was...... 1060
Ex 12:29 dungeon; and all the **f.** of cattle. 1060
Ex 13:2 Sanctify unto me all the **f.**,............... 1060
Ex 13:13 the **f.** of man among thy children........ 1060
Ex 13:15 the Lord slew all the **f.** in the land 1060
Ex 13:15 of Egypt, both the **f.** of man, and....... 1060
Ex 13:15 of man, and the **f.** of beast: 1060
Ex 13:15 all the **f.** of my children I redeem....... 1060
Ex 22:29 the **f.** of thy sons shalt thou give 1060
Ex 34:20 the **f.** of thy sons thou shalt redeem, .. 1060
Nu 3:2 Nadab the **f.**, and Abihu, Eleazar,....... 1060
Nu 3:12 all the **f.** that openeth the matrix........ 1060
Nu 3:13 Because all the **f.** are mine; for on 1060
Nu 3:13 on the day that I smote all the **f.** of.... 1060
Nu 3:13 I hallowed unto me all the **f.** in.......... 1060
Nu 3:40 Number all the **f.** of the males of the.. 1060
Nu 3:41 instead of all the **f.** among the 1060
Nu 3:42 all the **f.** among the children of.......... 1060
Nu 3:43 And all the **f.** males by the number...... 1060
Nu 3:45 Take the Levites instead of all the **f.** .. 1060
Nu 3:46 of the **f.** of the children of Israel, ... 1060
Nu 3:50 Of the **f.** of the children of Israel 1060
Nu 8:16 even instead the **f.** of all the children .. 1060
Nu 8:17 For all the **f.** of the children of Israel.. 1060
Nu 8:17 day that I smote every **f.** in the land... 1060
Nu 8:18 have taken the Levites for all the **f.**.... 1060
Nu 18:15 **f.** of man shalt thou surely redeem, ... 1060
Nu 33:4 the Egyptians buried all their **f.**,......... 1060
De 21:15 the **f.** son be hers that was hated:...... 1060
De 21:16 not make the son of the beloved **f.**..... 1069
De 21:16 of the hated, which is indeed the **f.**: ... 1060
De 21:17 the son of the hated for the **f.**, ... 1060
De 21:17 strength; the right of the **f.** is his....... 1062
De 25:6 **f.** which she beareth shall succeed...... 1060
Jos 6:26 lay the foundation thereof in his **f.**, ... 1060
Jos 17:1 for he was the **f.** of Joseph; 1060
Jos 17:1 for Machir the **f.** of Manasseh, ... 1060
Jg 8:20 And he said unto Jether his **f.**,........... 1060
1Sa 8:2 Now the name off his **f.** was Joel; 1060
1Sa 14:49 the name of the **f.** Merab, ... 1067
1Sa 17:13 Eliab the **f.**, and next unto him 1060
2Sa 3:2 and his **f.** was Amnon, of Ahinoam 1060
1Ki 16:34 foundation thereof in Abiram his **f.**...... 1060
1Ch 1:13 And Canaan begat Zidon his **f.**, and..... 1060
1Ch 1:29 The **f.** of Ishmael, Nebaioth; then....... 1060
1Ch 2:3 And Er, the **f.** of Judah, was evil 1060
1Ch 2:13 begat his **f.** Eliab, and Abinadab 1060
1Ch 2:25 the **f.** of Hezron were, Ram the **f.**, ... 1060
1Ch 2:27 the sons of Ram the **f.** of Jerahmeel ... 1060
1Ch 2:42 of Jerahmeel were, Mesha his **f.**, ... 1060
1Ch 2:50 Hur, the **f.** of Ephratah; Shobal the 1060
1Ch 3:1 the **f.** Amnon, of Ahinoam the 1060
1Ch 3:15 **f.** Johanan, the second Jehoiakim, ... 1060
1Ch 4:4 the sons of Hur, the **f.** of Ephratah, ... 1060
1Ch 5:1 the sons of Reuben the **f.** of Israel, ... 1060
1Ch 5:1 (for he was the **f.**; but, forasmuch...... 1060
1Ch 5:3 I say, of Reuben the **f.** of Israel were, . 1060
1Ch 6:28 the sons of Samuel; the **f.** Vashni, ... 1060
1Ch 8:1 Now Benjamin begat Bela his **f.**, ... 1060
1Ch 8:30 And his **f.** son Abdon, and Zur, and.... 1060
1Ch 8:39 Ulam his **f.**, Jehush the second, ... 1060
1Ch 9:5 Asaiah the **f.**, and his sons................ 1060
1Ch 9:31 who was the **f.** of Shallum the 1060
1Ch 9:36 And his **f.** son Abdon, then Zur, and... 1060
1Ch 26:2 Zechariah the **f.**, Jediael the second, ... 1060
1Ch 26:4 were, Shemiah the **f.**, Jehozabad the... 1060
1Ch 26:10 not the **f.**, yet his father made him...... 1060
2Ch 21:3 to Jehoram; because he was the **f.**. 1060
Ne 10:36 Also the **f.** of our sons, and of our 1060
Job 18:13 the **f.** of death shall devour his 1060
Ps 78:51 And smote all the **f.** in Egypt; 1060
Ps 89:27 Also I will make him my **f.**,............... 1060
Ps 105:36 smote also all the **f.** in their land,....... 1060
Ps 135:8 Who smote the **f.** of Egypt, ... 1060
Ps 136:10 him that smote Egypt in their **f.**:........ 1060
Isa 14:30 And the **f.** of the poor shall feed, ... 1060
Jer 31:9 to Israel, and Ephraim is my **f.**.......... 1060
Mic 6:7 I give my **f.** for my transgression, ... 1060
Zec 12:10 as one that is in bitterness for his **f.**... 1060
Mt 1:25 she had brought forth her **f.** son: *4416*
Lu 2:7 And she brought forth her **f.** son,....... *4416*
Ro 8:29 be the **f.** among many brethren.......... *4416*
Col 1:15 God, the **f.** of every creature: *4416*
Col 1:18 the beginning, the **f.** from the dead;.... *4416*
Heb 11:28 destroyed the **f.** shall touch them....... *4416*
Heb 12:23 assembly and church of the **f.**,........... *4416*

FIRSTFRUIT See also FIRSTFRUITS.
De 18:4 **f.** also of thy corn, of thy wine, ... 7225
Ro 11:16 if the **f.** be holy, the lump is also......... *536*

FIRSTFRUITS
Ex 23:16 the **f.** of thy labours, which thou........ 1061
Ex 23:19 The first of the **f.** of thy land thou...... 1061
Ex 34:22 **f.** of wheat harvest, and the feast....... 1061
Ex 34:26 first of the **f.** of thy land thou shalt..... 1061
Le 2:12 the oblation of the **f.**, ye shall offer..... 7225
Le 2:14 offer a meat offering of thy **f.**............ 1061
Le 2:14 offer for the meat offering of thy **f.**...... 1061
Le 23:10 ye shall bring a sheaf of the **f.** of 7225
Le 23:17 they are the **f.** unto the Lord............ 1061
Le 23:20 wave them with the bread of the **f.** 1061
Nu 18:12 **f.** of them which they shall offer 7725
Nu 28:26 Also in the day of the **f.**, when ye...... 1061
De 26:10 I have brought the **f.** of the land, ... 7725
2Ki 4:42 bread of the **f.**, twenty loaves of........ 1061
2Ch 31:5 the **f.** of corn, wine, and oil, and........ 7225
Ne 10:35 And to bring the **f.** of our ground,...... 1061
Ne 10:35 and the **f.** of all fruit trees, yearly 1061
Ne 10:37 should bring the **f.** of our dough,........ 7225
Ne 12:44 for the **f.**, and for the tithes, to......... 7225
Ne 13:31 at times appointed, and for the **f.**. 1061
Pr 3:9 with the **f.** of all thine increase: 7225
Jer 2:3 the Lord, and the **f.** of his increase: ... 7225
Eze 20:40 and the **f.** of your oblations, ... 7225
Eze 44:30 the first of all the **f.** of all things, ... 1061
Eze 48:14 nor alienate the **f.** of the land: 7225
Ro 8:23 which have the **f.** of the Spirit,............ *536*
Ro 16:5 who is the **f.** of Achaia unto Christ........ *536*
1Co 15:20 and become the **f.** of them that slept,... *536*
1Co 15:23 Christ the **f.**; afterward they that......... *536*
1Co 16:15 Stephanas, that it is the **f.** of Achaia,.... *536*
Jas 1:18 be a kind of **f.** of his creatures, ... *536*
Re 14:4 the **f.** unto God and to the Lamb. *536*

FIRSTLING See also FIRSTLINGS.
Ex 13:12 every **f.** that cometh of a beast.......... 6363
Ex 13:13 every **f.** of an ass thou shalt redeem.... 6363
Ex 34:19 and every **f.** among thy cattle,............ 6363
Ex 34:20 the **f.** of an ass thou shalt redeem...... 6363
Le 27:26 Only the **f.** of the beasts, which......... 1060
Le 27:26 which should be the Lord's **f.**, no........ 1069
Nu 18:15 the **f.** of unclean beasts shall thou 1060
Nu 18:17 But the **f.** of a cow, or the **f.** of a....... 1060
Nu 18:17 a sheep, or the **f.** of a goat, thou....... 1060
De 15:19 All the **f.** males that come of thy......... 1060
De 15:19 no work with the **f.** of thy bullock, ... 1060
De 15:19 nor shear the **f.** of thy sheep............ 1060
De 33:17 glory is like the **f.** of his bullock,........ 1060

FIRSTLINGS
Ge 4:4 also brought of the **f.** of his flock 1062
Nu 3:41 instead of all the **f.** among the 1060
De 12:6 and the **f.** of your herds 1062
De 12:17 the **f.** of thy herds or of thy flock,....... 1062
De 14:23 the **f.** of your herds and of your......... 1062
Ne 10:36 **f.** of our herds and of our flocks, ... 1062

FIRSTRIPE See also FIRST and RIPE.
Nu 13:20 was the time of the **f.** grapes. 1061
Ho 9:10 I saw your fathers as the **f.** in the...... 1063
Mic 7:1 eat: my soul desired the **f.** fruit. 1063
Na 3:12 be like fig trees with the **f.** figs: 1063

FIR-TREE See FIR and TREE.

FIR-WOOD See FIR and WOOD.

FISH See also FISHERMEN; FISHER'S; FISHERS; FISHES; FISHHOOKS; FISHING; FISHPOOLS; FISH'S.
Ge 1:26, 28 dominion over the **f.** of the sea...... 1710
Ex 7:18 And the **f.** that is in the river shall 1710
Ex 7:21 And the **f.** that was in the river died;.. 1710
Nu 11:5 remember the **f.**, which we did eat..... 1710
Nu 11:22 or shall all the **f.** of the sea be........... 1709
De 4:18 of any **f.** that is in the waters............ 1710
2Ch 33:14 the entering in at the **f.** gate, ... 1709
Ne 3:3 **f.** gate did the sons of Hassenaah....... 1709
Ne 12:39 above the **f.** gate, and the tower......... 1709
Ne 13:16 which brought **f.**, and all manner........ 1709
Job 41:7 irons or his head with **f.** spears? 1709
Ps 8:8 the **f.** of the sea, and whatsoever....... 1709
Ps 105:29 into blood, and slew their **f.**.............. 1710
Isa 19:10 make sluices and ponds for **f.**........... 5315
Isa 50:2 their **f.** stinketh, because there is....... 1710
Jer 16:16 and they shall **f.** them; and after 1770
Eze 29:4 I will cause the **f.** of thy rivers to 1710
Eze 29:4 all the **f.** of thy rivers shall stick 1710
Eze 29:5 thee and all the **f.** of thy rivers:.......... 1710
Eze 47:9 be a very great multitude of **f.**,........... 1710
Eze 47:10 **f.** shall be according to their kinds,..... 1710
Eze 47:10 as the **f.** of the great sea,................. 1710

Jon 1:17 the Lord had prepared a great **f.** ... 1709
Jon 1:17 Jonah was in the belly of the **f.** ... 1709
Jon 2:10 And the Lord spake unto the **f.**, ... 1709
Zep 1:10 the noise of a cry from the **f.** gate, ... 1709
Mt 7:10 **Or if he ask a f., will he give him** ... *2486*
Mt 17:27 **take up the f. that first cometh** ... *2486*
Lu 11:11 **or if he ask a f., will he for a f.** ... *2486*
Lu 24:42 gave him a piece of a broiled **f.**, ... *2486*
Joh 21:9 and **f.** laid thereon, and bread ... *3795*
Joh 21:10 **the f. which ye have now caught** ... *3795*
Joh 21:13 and giveth them, and **f.** likewise ... *3795*

FISHERMEN
Lu 5:2 but the **f.** were gone out of them, ... *231*

FISHER'S
Joh 21:7 he girt his **f.** coat unto him, (for ... *1908*

FISHERS
Isa 19:8 The **f.** also shall mourn, and all ... 1771
Jer 16:16 Behold, I will send for many **f.**, ... 1728
Eze 47:10 that the **f.** shall stand upon it ... 1728
Mt 4:18 a net into the sea: for they were **f.** ... *231*
Mt 4:19 **I will make you f. of men** ... *231*
Mk 1:16 a net into the sea; for they were **f.** ... *231*
Mk 1:17 **I will make you to become f. of** ... *231*

FISHES
Ge 9:2 shall be upon all the **f.** of the sea; ... 1709
1Ki 4:33 and of creeping things, and of **f.** ... 1709
Job 12:8 the **f.** of the sea shall declare unto ... 1709
Ec 9:12 the **f.** that are taken in an evil net, ... 1709
Eze 38:20 So that the **f.** of the sea, and the ... 1709
Ho 4:3 the **f.** of the sea also shall be taken ... 1709
Hab 1:14 makest men as the **f.** of the sea, ... 1709
Zep 1:3 and the **f.** of the sea, and the ... 1709
Mt 14:17 here but five loaves, and two **f.** ... *2486*
Mt 14:19 took the five loaves, and the two **f.**, ... *2486*
Mt 15:34 said, Seven and a few little **f.** ... *2485*
Mt 15:36 took the seven loaves and the **f.**, ... *2486*
Mk 6:38 they say, Five, and two **f.** ... *2486*
Mk 6:41 taken the five loaves and the two **f.**, ... *2486*
Mk 6:41 the two **f.** divided he among them ... *2486*
Mk 6:43 full of the fragments, and of the **f.** ... *2486*
Mk 8:7 And they had a few small **f.**: ... *2485*
Lu 5:6 inclosed a great multitude of **f.** ... *2486*
Lu 5:9 draught of the **f.** which they had ... *2486*
Lu 9:13 no more but five loaves and two **f.**; ... *2486*
Lu 9:16 took the five loaves and the two **f.**; ... *2486*
Joh 6:9 barley loaves, and two small **f.**: ... *3795*
Joh 6:11 and likewise of the **f.** as much as ... *3795*
Joh 21:6 to draw it for the multitude of **f.** ... *2486*
Joh 21:8 dragging the net with **f.** ... *2486*
Joh 21:11 drew the net to land full of great **f.**, ... *2486*
1Co 15:39 another of **f.**, and another of birds ... *2486*

FISH-GATE See FISH and GATE.

FISHHOOKS
Am 4:2 and your posterity with **f.**, ... 5518,1729

FISHING
Joh 21:3 Peter saith unto them, I go a **f.** ... *239*

FISHPOOLS
Ca 7:4 thine eyes like the **f.** in Heshbon ... 1295

FISH'S
Jon 2:1 Lord his God out of the **f.** belly, ... 1710

FIST See also FISTS.
Ex 21:18 or with his **f.**, and he die not, ... 106
Isa 58:4 to smite with the **f.** of wickedness: ... 106

FISTS
Pr 30:4 hath gathered the wind in his **f.**? ... 2651

FIT See also FITTED; FITTETH.
Le 16:21 by the hand of a **f.** man into the ... 6261
1Ch 7:11 soldiers, **f.** to go out for war ...
1Ch 12:8 and men of war **f.** for the battle, ...
Job 34:18 Is it **f.** to say to a king, Thou art ...
Pr 24:27 make it **f.** for thyself in the field: ... 6257
Lu 9:62 **is f. for the kingdom of God** ... *2111*
Lu 14:35 **It is neither f. for the land, nor** ... *2111*
Ac 22:22 it is not **f.** that he should live ... *2520*
Col 3:18 husbands, as it is **f.** in the Lord ... *433*

FITCHES
Isa 28:25 cast abroad the **f.**, and scatter the ... 7100
Isa 28:27 For the **f.** are not threshed with a ... 7100
Isa 28:27 the **f.** are beaten out with a staff, ... 7100
Eze 4:9 and lentiles, and millet, and **f.**, ... 3698

FITLY
Pr 25:11 word **f.** spoken is like apples, ... 5921,655
Ca 5:12 washed with milk, and **f.** set ... 5921,4402
Eph 2:21 all the building **f.** framed together ... *4883*
Eph 4:16 the whole body **f.** joined together ... *4883*

FITTED
1Ki 6:35 with gold **f.** upon the carved work ... 3474
Pr 22:18 they shall withal be **f.** in thy lips ... 3559
Ro 9:22 vessels of wrath **f.** to destruction: ... *2675*

FITTETH
Isa 44:13 he **f.** it with planes, and he ... 6213

FIVE
Ge 5:6 lived an hundred and **f.** years, ... 2568
Ge 5:11 nine hundred and **f.** years: and ... 2568
Ge 5:15 Mahalaleel lived sixty and **f.** years, ... 2568
Ge 5:17 eight hundred ninety and **f.** years: ... 2568
Ge 5:21 Enoch lived sixty and **f.** years, ... 2568
Ge 5:23 three hundred sixty and **f.** years: ... 2568
Ge 5:30 **f.** hundred ninety and **f.** years ... 2568
Ge 5:32 Noah was **f.** hundred years old: ... 2568
Ge 11:11 **f.** hundred years, and begat sons ... 2568
Ge 11:12 Arphaxad lived **f.** and thirty years, ... 2568
Ge 11:32 were two hundred and **f.** years: ... 2568
Ge 12:4 Abram was seventy and **f.** years old ... 2568
Ge 14:9 of Ellasar; four kings with **f.** ... 2568
Ge 18:28 Peradventure there shall lack **f.** of ... 2568
Ge 18:28 destroy all the city for lack of **f.**? ... 2568
Ge 18:28 If I find there forty and **f.**, I will ... 2568
Ge 43:34 Benjamin's mess was **f.** times so ... 2568
Ge 45:6 and yet there are **f.** years, in the ... 2568
Ge 45:11 yet there are **f.** years of famine; ... 2568
Ge 45:22 silver, and **f.** changes of raiment ... 2568
Ge 47:2 some of his brethren, even **f.** men, ... 2568
Ex 22:1 he shall restore **f.** oxen for an ox, ... 2568
Ex 26:3 The **f.** curtains shall be coupled ... 2568
Ex 26:3 other **f.** curtains shall be coupled ... 2568
Ex 26:9 couple **f.** curtains by themselves, ... 2568
Ex 26:26 **f.** for the boards of the one side ... 2568
Ex 26:27 **f.** bars for the boards of the other ... 2568
Ex 26:27 **f.** bars for the boards of the side of ... 2568
Ex 26:37 make for the hanging **f.** pillars ... 2568
Ex 26:37 thou shalt cast **f.** sockets of brass ... 2568
Ex 27:1 **f.** cubits long, and **f.** cubits broad: ... 2568
Ex 27:18 the height **f.** cubits of fine twined ... 2568
Ex 30:23 of pure myrrh **f.** hundred shekels, ... 2568
Ex 30:24 And of cassia **f.** hundred shekels, ... 2568
Ex 36:10 the **f.** curtains one unto another: ... 2568
Ex 36:10 the other **f.** curtains he coupled ... 2568
Ex 36:16 coupled **f.** curtains by themselves, ... 2568
Ex 36:31 **f.** for the boards of the one side of ... 2568
Ex 36:32 **f.** bars for the boards of the other ... 2568
Ex 36:32 and **f.** bars for the boards of the ... 2568
Ex 36:38 **f.** pillars of it with their hooks: ... 2568
Ex 36:38 but their **f.** sockets were of brass ... 2568
Ex 38:1 **f.** cubits was the length thereof, ... 2568
Ex 38:1 and **f.** cubits the breadth thereof; ... 2568
Ex 38:18 height in the breadth was **f.** cubits, ... 2568
Ex 38:26 three thousand and **f.** hundred ... 2568
Ex 38:28 hundred seventy and **f.** shekels ... 2568
Le 26:8 **f.** of you shall chase an hundred, ... 2568
Le 27:5 from **f.** years old even unto twenty ... 2568
Le 27:6 a month old even unto **f.** years old, ... 2568
Le 27:6 of the male **f.** shekels of silver, ... 2568
Nu 1:21 and six thousand and **f.** hundred ... 2568
Nu 1:25 forty and **f.** thousand six hundred ... 2568
Nu 1:33 forty thousand and **f.** hundred ... 2568
Nu 1:37 and **f.** thousand and four hundred ... 2568
Nu 1:41 and one thousand and **f.** hundred ... 2568
Nu 1:46 thousand and **f.** hundred and fifty ... 2568
Nu 2:11 and six thousand and **f.** hundred ... 2568
Nu 2:15 **f.** thousand and six hundred and ... 2568
Nu 2:19 forty thousand and **f.** hundred ... 2568
Nu 2:23 and **f.** thousand and four hundred ... 2568
Nu 2:28 and one thousand and **f.** hundred ... 2568
Nu 2:32 thousand and **f.** hundred and fifty ... 2568
Nu 3:22 seven thousand and **f.** hundred ... 2568
Nu 3:47 shalt even take **f.** shekels apiece ... 2568
Nu 3:50 and threescore and **f.** shekels, ... 2568
Nu 4:48 and **f.** hundred and fourscore ... 2568
Nu 7:17, 23,29,35,41,47,53,59,65,71,77,83
f. rams, **f.** he goats, **f.** lambs of the ... 2568
Nu 8:24 from twenty and **f.** years old and ... 2568
Nu 11:19 two days, nor **f.** days, neither ten ... 2568
Nu 18:16 for the money of **f.** shekels, after ... 2568
Nu 26:18 forth thousand and **f.** hundred ... 2568
Nu 26:22 sixteen thousand and **f.** hundred ... 2568
Nu 26:27 threescore thousand and **f.** hundred ... 2568
Nu 26:37 and two thousand and **f.** hundred ... 2568
Nu 26:41 and **f.** thousand and six hundred ... 2568
Nu 26:50 and **f.** thousand and four hundred ... 2568
Nu 31:8 **f.** kings of Midian: Balaam also ... 2568
Nu 31:28 one soul of **f.** hundred, both of the ... 2568
Nu 31:32 thousand and **f.** thousand sheep, ... 2568
Nu 31:36 thirty thousand and **f.** hundred ... 2568
Nu 31:39 thirty thousand and **f.** hundred; ... 2568
Nu 31:43 seven thousand and **f.** hundred ... 2568
Nu 31:45 thousand asses and **f.** hundred, ... 2568
Jos 8:12 he took about **f.** thousand men, ... 2568
Jos 10:5 the **f.** kings of the Amorites, ... 2568
Jos 10:16 But these **f.** kings fled, and hid ... 2568
Jos 10:17 **f.** kings are found hid in a cave ... 2568
Jos 10:22 bring out those **f.** kings unto me ... 2568
Jos 10:23 brought forth those **f.** kings unto ... 2568
Jos 10:26 and hanged them on **f.** trees: ... 2568
Jos 13:3 **f.** lords of the Philistines; the ... 2568
Jos 14:10 these forty and **f.** years, even since ... 2568
Jos 14:10 day fourscore and **f.** years old ... 2568
Jg 3:3 **f.** lords of the Philistines, ... 2568
Jg 18:2 Dan sent of their family **f.** men ... 2568
Jg 18:7 Then the **f.** men departed, and ... 2568
Jg 18:14 answered the **f.** men that went ... 2568
Jg 18:17 the **f.** men that went to spy ... 2568
Jg 20:35 twenty and **f.** thousand and an ... 2568
Jg 20:45 in the highways **f.** thousand men; ... 2568
Jg 20:46 twenty and **f.** thousand men that ... 2568
1Sa 6:4 **F.** golden emerods, and **f.** golden ... 2568
1Sa 6:16 when the **f.** lords of the Philistines ... 2568
1Sa 6:18 Philistines belonging to the **f.** ... 2568
1Sa 17:5 was **f.** thousand shekels of brass ... 2568
1Sa 17:40 **f.** smooth stones out of the brook, ... 2568
1Sa 21:3 give me **f.** loaves of bread ... 2568
1Sa 22:18 fourscore and **f.** persons that did ... 2568
1Sa 25:18 and **f.** sheep ready dressed, ... 2568
1Sa 25:18 and **f.** measures of parched corn, ... 2568
1Sa 25:42 with **f.** damsels of hers that went ... 2568
2Sa 4:4 He was **f.** years old when the ... 2568
2Sa 21:8 **f.** sons of Michal the daughter of ... 2568
2Sa 24:9 were **f.** hundred thousand men ... 2568
1Ki 4:32 his songs were a thousand and **f.** ... 2568
1Ki 6:6 chamber was **f.** cubits broad, ... 2568
1Ki 6:10 against all the house, **f.** cubits ... 2568
1Ki 6:24 And **f.** cubits was the one wing ... 2568
1Ki 6:24 and **f.** cubits the other wing ... 2568
1Ki 7:3 on forty **f.** pillars, **f.** in a row ... 2568
1Ki 7:16 one chapiter was **f.** cubits, and the ... 2568
1Ki 7:16 height of the other chapiter was **f.** ... 2568
1Ki 7:23 and his height was **f.** cubits: and ... 2568
1Ki 7:39 put **f.** bases on the right side of the ... 2568
1Ki 7:39 **f.** on the left side of the house: ... 2568
1Ki 7:49 **f.** on the right side, ... 2568
1Ki 7:49 and **f.** on the left, ... 2568
1Ki 9:23 Solomon's work, **f.** hundred and ... 2568
1Ki 22:42 Jehoshaphat was thirty and **f.** ... 2568
1Ki 22:42 and he reigned twenty and **f.** years ... 2568
2Ki 6:25 a cab of dove's dung for **f.** pieces ... 2568
2Ki 7:13 **f.** of the horses that remain, ... 2568
2Ki 13:19 have smitten **f.** or six times; ... 2568
2Ki 14:2 twenty and **f.** years old when he ... 2568
2Ki 15:33 **F.** and twenty years old was he ... 2568
2Ki 18:2 Twenty and **f.** years old was he ... 2568
2Ki 19:35 hundred fourscore and **f.** thousand: ... 2568
2Ki 21:1 reigned fifty and **f.** years in ... 2568
2Ki 23:36 twenty and **f.** years old when he ... 2568
2Ki 25:19 and **f.** men of them that were in ... 2568
1Ch 2:4 All the sons of Judah were **f.** ... 2568
1Ch 2:6 and Dara, **f.** of them in all ... 2568
1Ch 3:20 Hasadiah, Jushab-hesed, **f.** ... 2568
1Ch 4:32 and Tochen, and Ashan, **f.** cities: ... 2568
1Ch 4:42 sons of Simeon, **f.** hundred men, ... 2568
1Ch 7:3 and Ishiah, **f.**: all of them chief ... 2568
1Ch 7:7 and Jerimoth, and Iri, **f.**; heads of ... 2568
1Ch 11:23 of great stature, **f.** cubits high; ... 2568
1Ch 29:7 **f.** thousand talents and ten ... 2568
2Ch 3:11 one wing of the one cherub was **f.** ... 2568
2Ch 3:11 other wing was likewise **f.** cubits ... 2568
2Ch 3:12 of the other cherub was **f.** cubits, ... 2568
2Ch 3:12 the other wing was **f.** cubits also, ... 2568
2Ch 3:15 two pillars of thirty and **f.** cubits ... 2568
2Ch 3:15 top of each of them was **f.** cubits, ... 2568
2Ch 4:2 and **f.** cubits the height thereof; ... 2568
2Ch 4:6 lavers, and put **f.** on the right hand, ... 2568
2Ch 4:6 and **f.** on the left, to wash in them: ... 2568

2Ch 4:7 in the temple, **f.** on the right hand,..... 2568
2Ch 4:7 right hand, and **f.** on the left. 2568
2Ch 4:8 in the temple, **f.** on the right side, ... 2568
2Ch 4:8 right side, and **f.** on the left. 2568
2Ch 6:13 brasen scaffold, of **f.** cubits long,........ 2568
2Ch 6:13 and **f.** cubits broad, and three cubits... 2568
2Ch 13:17 slain of Israel **f.** hundred thousand...... 2568
2Ch 15:19 **f.** and thirtieth year of the reign......... 2568
2Ch 20:31 thirty and **f.** years old when he.......... 2568
2Ch 20:31 and he reigned twenty and **f.** years..... 2568
2Ch 25:1 Amaziah was twenty and **f.** years....... 2568
2Ch 26:13 and seven thousand and **f.** hundred,.... 2568
2Ch 27:1 Jotham was twenty and **f.** years old.... 2568
2Ch 27:8 He was **f.** and twenty years old......... 2568
2Ch 29:1 when he was **f.** and twenty years old,. 2568
2Ch 33:1 and he reigned fifty and **f.** years in..... 2568
2Ch 35:9 **f.** thousand small cattle, and............. 2568
2Ch 35:9 small cattle, and **f.** hundred oxen........ 2568
2Ch 36:5 Jehoiakim was twenty and **f.** years...... 2568
Ezr 1:11 were **f.** thousand and four hundred..... 2568
Ezr 2:5 Arah, seven hundred seventy and **f.**.... 2568
Ezr 2:8 of Zattu, nine hundred forty and **f.**...... 2568
Ezr 2:20 children of Gibbar, ninety and **f.**........ 2568
Ezr 2:33 Ono, seven hundred twenty and **f.**........ 2568
Ezr 2:34 Jericho, three hundred forty and **f.**. 2568
Ezr 2:66 mules, two hundred forty and **f.**;........ 2568
Ezr 2:67 camels, four hundred thirty and **f.**; 2568
Ezr 2:69 and **f.** thousand pound of silver, ... 2568
Ne 7:13 of Zattu, eight hundred forty and **f.**..... 2568
Ne 7:20 of Adin, six hundred fifty and **f.**. 2568
Ne 7:25 children of Gibeon, ninety and **f.**. 2568
Ne 7:36 Jericho, three hundred forty and **f.**. 2568
Ne 7:67 hundred forty and **f.** singing men........ 2568
Ne 7:68 mules, two hundred forty and **f.**:........ 2568
Ne 7:69 camels, four hundred thirty and **f.**: 2568
Ne 7:70 **f.** hundred and thirty priests'........... 2568
Es 9:6 slew and destroyed **f.** hundred men, ... 2568
Es 9:12 and destroyed **f.** hundred men in........ 2568
Es 9:16 their foes seventy and **f.** thousand,..... 2568
Job 1:3 camels, and **f.** hundred yoke of oxen,.. 2568
Job 1:3 of oxen, and **f.** hundred she asses, ... 2568
Isa 7:8 and within threescore and **f.** years...... 2568
Isa 17:6 four or **f.** in the outmost fruitful........ 2568
Isa 19:18 that day shall **f.** cities in the land........ 2568
Isa 30:17 at the rebuke of **f.** shall ye flee:......... 2568
Isa 37:36 and fourscore and **f.** thousand:........... 2568
Jer 52:22 of one chapiter was **f.** cubits, ... 2568
Jer 52:30 seven hundred forty and **f.** persons:...... 2568
Jer 52:31 in the **f.** and twentieth day of the....... 2568
Eze 8:16 were about **f.** and twenty men,.......... 2568
Eze 11:1 door of the gate **f.** and twenty men; ... 2568
Eze 40:1 In the **f.** and twentieth year of our 2568
Eze 40:7 the little chambers were **f.** cubits;...... 2568
Eze 40:13 breadth was **f.** and twenty cubits,....... 2568
Eze 40:21, 25 the breadth **f.** and twenty cubits. ... 2568
Eze 40:29 and **f.** and twenty cubits broad........... 2568
Eze 40:30 were **f.** and twenty cubits long, ... 2568
Eze 40:30 long, and **f.** cubits broad............... 2568
Eze 40:33 and **f.** and twenty cubits broad........... 2568
Eze 40:36 the breadth **f.** and twenty cubits. 2568
Eze 40:48 the porch, **f.** cubits on this side, ... 2568
Eze 40:48 this side, and **f.** cubits on that side:.... 2568
Eze 41:2 the sides of the door were **f.** cubits.... 2568
Eze 41:2 and **f.** cubits on that side:................ 2568
Eze 41:9 chamber without, was **f.** cubits: 2568
Eze 41:11 was left was **f.** cubits round about. 2568
Eze 41:12 was **f.** cubits thick round about, ... 2568
Eze 42:16 reed, **f.** hundred reeds, with the........ 2568
Eze 42:17 the north side, **f.** hundred reeds, ... 2568
Eze 42:18 the south side, **f.** hundred reeds, ... 2568
Eze 42:19 and measured **f.** hundred reeds.......... 2568
Eze 42:20 round about, **f.** hundred reeds long, ... 2568
Eze 42:20 and **f.** hundred broad, to make.......... 2568
Eze 45:1 length of **f.** and twenty thousand........ 2568
Eze 45:2 sanctuary **f.** hundred in length, ... 2568
Eze 45:2 with **f.** hundred in breadth, square...... 2568
Eze 45:3 length of **f.** and twenty thousand, ... 2568
Eze 45:5 **f.** and twenty thousand of length, ... 2568
Eze 45:6 of the city **f.** thousand broad, ... 2568
Eze 45:6 and **f.** and twenty thousand long,......... 2568
Eze 45:12 **f.** and twenty shekels, fifteen............. 2568
Eze 48:8 offer of **f.** and twenty thousand.......... 2568
Eze 48:9 shall be of **f.** and twenty thousand...... 2568
Eze 48:10 the north **f.** and twenty thousand 2568
Eze 48:10 the south **f.** and twenty thousand 2568
Eze 48:13 shall have **f.** and twenty thousand....... 2568
Eze 48:13 shall be **f.** and twenty thousand,......... 2568
Eze 48:15 And the **f.** thousand, that are left....... 2568
Eze 48:15 against the **f.** and twenty thousand, ... 2568
Eze 48:16 north side four...and **f.** hundred, ... 2568
Eze 48:16 south side four...and **f.** hundred, ... 2568
Eze 48:16 east side four...and **f.** hundred,.......... 2568
Eze 48:16 west side four...and **f.** hundred.......... 2568
Eze 48:20 **f.** and twenty thousand by **f.** and 2568
Eze 48:21 city, over against the **f.** and twenty 2568
Eze 48:21 westward over against the **f.** and 2568
Eze 48:30 the north side, four thousand and **f.**.... 2568
Eze 48:32 the east side four thousand and **f.** 2568
Eze 48:33 the south side four thousand and **f.**..... 2568
Eze 48:34 the west side four thousand and **f.**...... 2568
Da 12:12 hundred and **f.** and thirty days. 2568
Mt 14:17 here but **f.** loaves, and two fishes. *4002*
Mt 14:19 the **f.** loaves, and the two fishes, ... *4002*
Mt 14:21 were about **f.** thousand men,............ *4000*
Mt 16:9 **neither remember the f. loaves of..** *4002*
Mt 16:9 **of the f. thousand, and how many.** *4000*
Mt 25:2 **And f. of them were wise,............** *4000*
Mt 25:2 **were wise, and f. were foolish.......** *4000*
Mt 25:15 **And unto one he gave f. talents,....** *4000*
Mt 25:16 **he that had received the f. talents ..** *4000*
Mt 25:16 **and made them other f. talents. ....** *4000*
Mt 25:20 **so he that had received f. talents..** *4000*
Mt 25:20 **came and brought other f. talents, .** *4000*
Mt 25:20 **thou deliveredst unto me f. talents:** *4000*
Mt 25:20 **gained beside them f. talents more.** *4000*
Mk 6:38 they say, **F.**, and two fishes. *4000*
Mk 6:41 when he had taken the **f.** loaves *4000*
Mk 6:44 loaves were about **f.** thousand men..... *4000*
Mk 8:19 **When I brake the f. loaves among.** *4002*
Mk 8:19 **loaves among the f. thousand,.......** *4000*
Lu 1:24 hid herself **f.** months, saying, ... *4002*
Lu 7:41 **one owed f. hundred pence, and ....** *4001*
Lu 9:13 more but **f.** loaves and two fishes;...... *4002*
Lu 9:14 For they were about **f.** thousand........ *4000*
Lu 9:16 the **f.** loaves and the two fishes, ... *4002*
Lu 12:6 **f. sparrows sold for two farthings, .** *4002*
Lu 12:52 **there shall be f. in one house........** *4002*
Lu 14:19 **I have bought f. yoke of oxen, ...** *4002*
Lu 16:28 **For I have f. brethren; that he......** *4002*
Lu 19:18 **thy pound hath gained f. pounds...** *4002*
Lu 19:19 **Be thou also over f. cities............** *4002*
Joh 4:18 **For thou hast had f. husbands; .....** *4002*
Joh 5:2 tongue Bethesda, having **f.** porches. ... *4002*
Joh 6:9 which hath **f.** barley loaves, and two... *4002*
Joh 6:10 in number about **f.** thousand.............. *4000*
Joh 6:13 fragments of the **f.** barley loaves,....... *4002*
Joh 6:19 rowed about **f.** and twenty or thirty.... *4002*
Ac 4:4 of the men was about **f.** thousand....... *4002*
Ac 20:6 came unto them to Troas in **f.** days;... *4002*
Ac 24:1 And after **f.** days Ananias the........... *4002*
1Co 14:19 church I had rather speak **f.** words..... *4002*
1Co 15:6 seen of above **f.** hundred brethren...... *4001*
2Co 11:24 **f.** times received I forty stripes *3999*
Re 9:5 should be tormented **f.** months: *4002*
Re 9:10 power was to hurt men **f.** months. *4002*
Re 17:10 **f.** are fallen, and one is, and the *4002*

FIVE HUNDRED See FIVE and HUNDRED.

FIVE THOUSAND See FIVE and THOUSAND.

FIVE TIMES See FIVE and TIMES.

FIXED
Ps 57:7 My heart is **f.**, O God, my heart........ 3559
Ps 57:7 O God, my heart is **f.**: I will sing....... 3559
Ps 108:1 O God, my heart is **f.**; I will sing....... 3559
Ps 112:7 his heart is **f.**, trusting in the Lord. 3559
Lu 16:26 **us and you there is a great gulf f.:** *4741*

FLAG See also FLAGS.
Job 8:11 can the **f.** grow without water? 260

FLAGON See also FLAGONS.
2Sa 6:19 piece of flesh, and a **f.** of wine. 809
1Ch 16:3 piece of flesh, and a **f.** of wine. 809

FLAGONS
Ca 2:5 Stay me with **f.**, comfort me with........ 809
Isa 22:24 even to all the vessels of **f.**............... 5035
Ho 3:1 to other gods, and love **f.** of wine........ 809

FLAGS
Ex 2:3 laid it in the **f.** by the river's brink. 5488
Ex 2:5 when she saw the ark among the **f.**.... 5488
Isa 19:6 the reeds and **f.** shall wither. 5488

FLAKES
Job 41:23 **f.** of his flesh are joined together: 4651

FLAME See also FLAMES; FLAMING; INFLAME.
Ex 3:2 the Lord appeared unto him in a **f.**..... 3827
Nu 21:28 a **f.** from the city of Sihon: 3852
Jg 13:20 when the **f.** went up toward heaven.... 3851
Jg 13:20 of the Lord ascended in the **f.** of......... 3851
Jg 20:38 make a great **f.** with smoke rise 4864
Jg 20:40 But when the **f.** began to rise............ 4864
Jg 20:40 the **f.** of the city ascended up............ 3632
Job 15:30 the **f.** shall dry up his branches,......... 7957
Job 41:21 and a **f.** goeth out of his mouth.......... 3851
Ps 83:14 as the **f.** setteth the mountains.......... 3852
Ps 106:18 the **f.** burned up the wicked............. 3852
Ca 8:6 which hath a most vehement **f.**.......... 7957
Isa 5:24 and the **f.** consumeth the chaff, so...... 3852
Isa 10:17 and his Holy One for a **f.**:................. 3852
Isa 29:6 and the **f.** of devouring fire. 3851
Isa 30:30 and with the **f.** of a devouring fire, ... 3851
Isa 43:2 neither shall the **f.** kindle upon........... 3852
Isa 47:14 themselves from the power of the **f.**:.. 3852
Jer 48:45 a **f.** from the midst of Sihon, ... 3852
Eze 20:47 flaming **f.** shall not be quenched, ... 7957
Da 3:22 the **f.** of the fire slew those men.......... 7631
Da 7:9 his throne was like the fiery **f.**,.......... 7631
Da 7:11 and given to the burning **f.**. 785
Da 11:33 shall fall by the sword, and by **f.**, ... 3852
Joe 1:19 the **f.** hath burned all the trees.......... 3852
Joe 2:3 and behind them a **f.** burneth: 3852
Joe 2:5 like the noise of a **f.** of fire............... 3851
Ob 18 and the house of Joseph a **f.**,............. 3852
Lu 16:24 **for I am tormented in this f..........** *5395*
Ac 7:30 in a **f.** of fire in a bush..................... *5395*
Heb 1:7 and his ministers a **f.** of fire.............. *5395*
Re 1:14 and his eyes were as a **f.** of fire; *5395*
Re 2:18 **hath his eyes like unto a f. of fire,** *5395*
Re 19:12 His eyes were as a **f.** of fire, ... *5395*

FLAMES
Ps 29:7 voice of the Lord divideth the **f.** 3852
Isa 13:8 their faces shall be as **f.**. 3851
Isa 66:15 and his rebuke with **f.** of fire............. 3851

FLAMING See also ENFLAMING.
Ge 3:24 **f.** sword which turned every way,...... 3858
Ps 104:4 and his ministers a **f.** fire:................ 3857
Ps 105:32 and **f.** fire in their land.................. 3852
Isa 4:5 the shining of a **f.** fire by night: 3852
La 2:3 burned against Jacob like a **f.** fire, ... 3852
Eze 20:47 the **f.** flame shall not be quenched, ... 3852
Ho 7:6 the morning it burneth as a **f.** fire, ... 3852
Na 2:3 shall be with **f.** torches in the day........ 784
2Th 1:8 In **f.** fire taking vengeance on............ *5395*

FLANKS
Le 3:4 is on them, which is by the **f.**,........... 3689
Le 3:10, 15 upon them which is by the **f.**, ... 3689
Le 4:9 is upon them, which is by the **f.**, ... 3689
Le 7:4 is on them, which is by the **f.**,........... 3689
Job 15:27 maketh collops of fat on his **f.**.......... 3689

FLASH
Eze 1:14 the appearance of a **f.** of lightning. 965

FLAT
Le 21:18 or he that hath a **f.** nose, ... 2763
Nu 22:31 bowed down his head, and fell **f.**..............
Jos 6:5 wall of the city shall fall down **f.**,......... 8478
Jos 6:20 that the wall fell down **f.**, so that 8478

FLATTER See also FLATTERETH; FLATTERING.
Ps 5:9 they **f.** with their tongue. 2505
Ps 78:36 Nevertheless they did **f.** him with....... 6601

FLATTERETH
Ps 36:2 For he **f.** himself in his own eyes,...... 2505
Pr 2:16 stranger which **f.** with her words; 2505
Pr 7:5 stranger which **f.** with her words. 2505
Pr 20:19 meddle not with him that **f.**............... 6601
Pr 28:23 than he that **f.** with the tongue. 2505
Pr 29:5 A man that **f.** his neighbour.............. 2505

FLATTERIES
Da 11:21 and obtain the kingdom by **f.**............ 2519
Da 11:32 covenant shall he corrupt by **f.**: 2514
Da 11:34 many shall cleave to them with **f.**........ 2519

FLATTERING
Job 32:21 let me give **f.** titles unto man. 3655
Job 32:22 I know not to give **f.** titles;............... 3655

Ps 12:2 **f.** lips and with a double heart 2513
Ps 12:3 The Lord shall cut off all **f.** lips, 2513
Pr 7:21 the **f.** of her lips she forced him. 2506
Pr 26:28 and a **f.** mouth worketh ruin. 2509
Eze 12:24 any vain vision nor **f.** divination 2509
1Th 2:5 used we **f.** words, as ye know, *2850*

FLATTERY See also FLATTERIES.
Job 17:5 that speaketh **f.** to his friends, 2506
Pr 6:24 from the **f.** of the tongue of a 2513

FLAX
Ex 9:31 the **f.** and the barley was smitten: 6594
Ex 9:31 in the ear, and the **f.** was bolled 6594
Jos 2:6 and hid them with the stalks of **f.** 6593
Jg 15:14 were upon his arms became of **f.** 6593
Pr 31:13 seeketh wool, and **f.**, and worketh 6593
Isa 19:9 Moreover they that work in fine **f.**, 6593
Isa 42:3 smoking **f.** shall he not quench: 6594
Eze 40:3 with a line of **f.** in his hand, 6593
Ho 2:5 my wool and my **f.**, mine oil and 6593
Ho 2:9 wool and my **f.** given to cover her 6593
Mt 12:20 smoking **f.** shall he not quench, *3043*

FLAY See also FLAYED.
Le 1:6 And he shall **f.** the burnt offering, 6584
2Ch 29:34 could not **f.** all the burnt offerings: 6584
Mic 3:3 and **f.** their skin from off them; 6584

FLAYED
2Ch 35:11 hands, and the Levites **f.** them. 6584

FLEA
1Sa 24:14 after a dead dog, after a **f.** 6550
1Sa 26:20 of Israel is come out to seek a **f.**, 6550

FLED See also FLEDDEST.
Ge 14:10 kings of Sodom and Gomorrah **f.**, 5127
Ge 14:10 that remained **f.** to the mountain. 5127
Ge 16:6 Sarai dealt hardly with her, she **f.** 1272
Ge 31:20 in that he told him not that he **f.** 1272
Ge 31:21 So he **f.** with all that he had; 1272
Ge 31:22 on the third day that Jacob was **f.** 1272
Ge 35:7 he **f.** from the face of his brother. 1272
Ge 39:12 his garment in her hand, and **f.**, 5127
Ge 39:13 his garment in her hand, and was **f.** 5127
Ge 39:15 with me and **f.**, and got him out. 5127
Ge 39:18 left his garment with me, and **f.** 5127
Ex 2:15 Moses **f.** from the face of Pharaoh, 1272
Ex 4:3 and Moses **f.** from before it. 5127
Ex 14:5 king of Egypt that the people **f.**: 1272
Ex 14:27 appeared; and the Egyptians **f.** 5127
Nu 16:34 that were round about them **f.** 5127
Nu 35:25 of his refuge, whither he was **f.**: 5127
Nu 35:26 of his refuge, whither he was **f.**; 5127
Nu 35:32 for him that is **f.** to the city of his 5127
Jos 7:4 and they **f.** before the men of Ai. 5127
Jos 8:15 and **f.** by the way of the wilderness. 5127
Jos 8:20 the people that **f.** to the wilderness. 5127
Jos 10:11 pass, as they **f.** from before Israel, 5127
Jos 10:16 But these five kings **f.**, and hid 5127
Jos 20:6 unto the city from whence he **f.** 5127
Jg 1:6 Adoni-bezek **f.**; and they pursued 5127
Jg 4:15 his chariot, and **f.** away on his feet. 5127
Jg 4:17 Sisera **f.** away on his feet to the 5127
Jg 7:21 the host ran, and cried, and **f.** 5127
Jg 7:22 and the host **f.** to Beth-shittah 5127
Jg 8:12 And when Zebah and Zalmunna **f.**, 5127
Jg 9:21 Jotham ran away, and **f.**, and went 1272
Jg 9:40 and he **f.** before him, and many 5127
Jg 9:51 thither **f.** all the men and women, 5127
Jg 11:3 Jephthah **f.** from his brethren, 1272
Jg 20:45 and **f.** toward the wilderness 5127
Jg 20:47 But six hundred men turned and **f.** 5127
1Sa 4:10 and they **f.** every man into his tent: 5127
1Sa 4:16 and I **f.** to day out of the army. 5127
1Sa 4:17 Israel is **f.** before the Philistines, 5127
1Sa 14:22 they heard that the Philistines **f.**, 5127
1Sa 17:24 **f.** from him, and were sore afraid. 5127
1Sa 17:51 their champion was dead, they **f.** 5127
1Sa 19:8 slaughter; and they **f.** from him. 5127
1Sa 19:10 David **f.**, and escaped that night. 5127
1Sa 19:12 and he went, and **f.**, and escaped. 1272
1Sa 19:18 So David **f.**, and escaped, and came. 1272
1Sa 20:1 David **f.** from Naioth in Ramah, 1272
1Sa 21:10 and **f.** that day for fear of Saul, 1272
1Sa 22:17 and because they knew when he **f.**, 1272
1Sa 22:20 escaped, and **f.** after David. 1272
1Sa 23:6 Abiathar the son of Ahimelech **f.** 1272
1Sa 27:4 it was told Saul that David was **f.** 1272
1Sa 30:17 which rode upon camels, and **f.** 5127
1Sa 31:1 the men of Israel **f.** from before 5127
1Sa 31:7 saw that the men of Israel **f.**, and 5127
1Sa 31:7 they forsook the cities, and **f.**; 5127
2Sa 1:4 the people are **f.** from the battle, 5127
2Sa 4:3 And the Beerothites **f.** to Gittaim, 1272
2Sa 4:4 and his nurse took him up, and **f.**: 5127
2Sa 10:13 Syrians: and they **f.** before him. 5127
2Sa 10:14 saw that the Syrians were **f.**, 5127
2Sa 10:14 then **f.** they also before Abishai, 5127
2Sa 10:18 And the Syrians **f.** before Israel: 5127
2Sa 13:29 gat him up upon his mule, and **f.** 5127
2Sa 13:34 Absalom **f.**. And the young man 1272
2Sa 13:37 Absalom **f.**, and went to Talmai, 1272
2Sa 13:38 So Absalom **f.**, and went to Geshur, 1272
2Sa 18:17 all Israel **f.** every one to his tent. 5127
2Sa 19:8 Israel had **f.** every man to his tent. 5127
2Sa 19:9 and now he is **f.** out of the land 1272
2Sa 23:11 the people **f.** from the Philistines. 1272
1Ki 2:7 **f.** because of Absalom thy brother. 1272
1Ki 2:28 And Joab **f.** unto the tabernacle 5127
1Ki 2:29 told king Solomon that Joab was **f.** 5127
1Ki 11:17 That Hadad **f.**, he and certain 1272
1Ki 11:23 which **f.** from his lord Hadadezer 1272
1Ki 11:40 Jeroboam arose, and **f.** into Egypt, 1272
1Ki 12:2 he was **f.** from the presence of king 1272
1Ki 20:20 the Syrians **f.**; and Israel pursued 5127
1Ki 20:30 the rest **f.** to Aphek, into the city; 5127
1Ki 20:30 Ben-hadad **f.**, and came into the 5127
2Ki 3:24 so that they **f.** before them: 5127
2Ki 7:7 they arose and **f.** in the twilight, 5127
2Ki 7:7 camp as it was, and **f.** for their life. 5127
2Ki 8:21 and the people **f.** into their tents. 5127
2Ki 9:10 And he opened the door, and **f.** 5127
2Ki 9:23 Joram turned his hands, and **f.**, 5127
2Ki 9:27 **f.** by the way of the garden house. 5127
2Ki 9:27 he **f.** to Megiddo, and died there. 5127
2Ki 14:12 they **f.** every man to their tents. 5127
2Ki 14:19 and he **f.** to Lachish; but they sent 5127
2Ki 25:4 and all the men of war **f.** by night
1Ch 10:1 the men of Israel **f.** from before 5127
1Ch 10:7 were in the valley saw that they **f.**, 5127
1Ch 10:7 they forsook their cities, and **f.**: 5127
1Ch 11:13 **f.** from before the Philistines. 5127
1Ch 19:14 the battle; and they **f.** before him. 5127
1Ch 19:15 saw that the Syrians were **f.**, they 5127
1Ch 19:15 they likewise **f.** before Abishai his 5127
1Ch 19:18 But the Syrians **f.** before Israel; 5127
2Ch 10:2 **f.** from the presence of Solomon 1272
2Ch 13:16 children of Israel **f.** before Judah: 5127
2Ch 14:12 Judah; and the Ethiopians **f.** 5127
2Ch 25:22 and they **f.** every man to his tent. 5127
2Ch 25:27 and he **f.** to Lachish: but they sent 5127
Ne 13:10 singers, that did the work, were **f.** 1272
Ps 3 *title* he **f.** from Absalom his son. 1272
Ps 31:11 they that did see me without **f.** 5074
Ps 57 *title* he **f.** from Saul in the cave. 1272
Ps 104:7 At thy rebuke they **f.**; at the voice 5127
Ps 114:3 the sea saw it, and **f.**: Jordan was 5127
Isa 10:29 is afraid; Gibeah of Saul is **f.** 5127
Isa 21:14 with their bread him that **f.** 5074
Isa 21:15 For they **f.** from the swords, from 5074
Isa 22:3 All thy rulers are **f.** together, 5074
Isa 22:3 together, which have **f.** from far. 1272
Isa 33:3 noise of the tumult the people **f.**; 5074
Jer 4:25 all the birds of the heavens were **f.** 5074
Jer 9:10 the heavens and the beast are **f.**; 5074
Jer 26:21 afraid and **f.**, and went into Egypt; 1272
Jer 39:4 then they **f.**, and went forth out of 1272
Jer 46:5 are beaten down, and are **f.** apace, 5127
Jer 46:21 back, and are **f.** away together: 5127
Jer 48:45 They that **f.** stood under the shadow 5127
Jer 52:7 all the men of war **f.**, and went 1272
La 4:15 when they **f.** away and wandered, 5132
Da 10:7 so that they **f.** to hide themselves. 1272
Ho 7:13 them! for they have **f.** from me: 5074
Ho 12:12 Jacob **f.** into the country of Syria, 1272
Jon 1:10 knew that he **f.** from the presence 1272
Jon 4:2 I **f.** before unto Tarshish: 1272
Zec 14:5 ye **f.** from before the earthquake 5127
Mt 8:33 And they that kept them **f.**, and *5343*
Mt 26:56 the disciples forsook him, and **f.** *5343*
Mk 5:14 And they that fed the swine **f.**, and *5343*
Mk 14:50 And they all forsook him, and **f.** *5343*
Mk 14:52 cloth, and **f.** from them naked. *5343*
Mk 16:8 quickly, and **f.** from the sepulchre; *5343*
Lu 8:34 they **f.** and went and told it in the *5343*
Ac 7:29 Then **f.** Moses at this saying, and *5343*
Ac 14:6 and **f.** unto Lystra and Derbe, *2703*
Ac 16:27 that the prisoners had been **f.** *1628*
Ac 19:16 they **f.** out of that house naked *1628*
Heb 6:18 who have **f.** for refuge to lay hold *2703*
Re 12:6 the woman **f.** into the wilderness, *5343*
Re 16:20 And every island **f.** away, and the *5343*
Re 20:11 the earth and the heaven **f.** away; *5343*

FLEDDEST
Ge 35:1 when thou **f.** from the face of Esau 1272
Ps 114:5 ailed thee, O thou sea, that thou **f.**? 5127

FLEE See also FLED; FLEETH; FLEEING.
Ge 16:8 **f.** from the face of my mistress 1272
Ge 19:20 now this city is near to **f.** unto, 5127
Ge 27:43 arise, **f.** thou to Laban my brother 1272
Ge 31:27 Wherefore didst thou **f.** away 1272
Ex 9:20 made his servants and his cattle **f.** 5127
Ex 14:25 Let us **f.** from the face of Israel; 5127
Ex 21:13 thee a place whither he shall **f.** 5127
Le 26:17 and ye shall **f.** when none pursueth. 5127
Le 26:36 and they shall **f.**, as fleeing from a 5127
Nu 10:35 and let them that hate thee **f.** 5127
Nu 24:11 Therefore now **f.** thou to thy place: 1272
Nu 35:6 that he may **f.** thither: and to 5127
Nu 35:11 that the slayer may **f.** thither, 5127
Nu 35:15 killeth any person unawares may **f.** 5127
De 4:42 That the slayer might **f.** thither, 5127
De 19:3 that every slayer may **f.** thither 5127
De 19:4 the slayer, which shall **f.** thither, 5127
De 19:5 he shall **f.** unto one of those cities, 5127
De 28:7 and **f.** before thee seven ways. 5127
De 28:25 and **f.** seven ways before them: 5127
Jos 8:5 first, that we will **f.** before them, 5127
Jos 8:6 They **f.** before us, as at the first: 5127
Jos 8:6 therefore we will **f.** before them. 5127
Jos 8:20 they had no power to **f.** this way 5127
Jos 20:3 unawares and unwittingly may **f.** 5127
Jos 20:4 And when he that doth **f.** unto one 5127
Jos 20:9 any person at unawares might **f.** 5127
Jg 20:32 Let us **f.**, and draw them from the 5127
2Sa 4:4 as she made haste to **f.**, that he fell, 5127
2Sa 15:14 and let us **f.**: for we shall not else 1227
2Sa 17:2 people that are with him shall **f.**; 5127
2Sa 18:3 for if we **f.** away, they will not 5127
2Sa 19:3 steal away when they **f.** in battle. 5127
2Sa 24:13 or wilt thou **f.** three months before 5127
1Ki 12:18 up to his chariot, to **f.** to Jerusalem. 5127
2Ki 9:3 open the door, and **f.**, and tarry not. 5127
2Ch 10:18 to his chariot, to **f.** to Jerusalem. 5127
Ne 6:11 Should such a man as I **f.**? 1272
Job 9:25 they **f.** away, they see no good. 1272
Job 20:24 He shall **f.** from the iron weapon, 1272
Job 27:22 he would fain **f.** out of his hand. 1272
Job 30:10 abhor me, they **f.** far from me, 7368
Job 41:28 The arrow cannot make him **f.**: 1272
Ps 11:1 **F.** as a bird to your mountain? 5110
Ps 64:8 all that see them shall **f.** away. 5074
Ps 68:1 them also that hate him **f.** before 5127
Ps 68:12 Kings of armies did **f.** apace: 5074
Ps 139:7 shall I **f.** from thy presence? 1272
Ps 143:9 enemies: I **f.** unto thee to hide me. 3680
Pr 28:1 wicked **f.** when no man pursueth: 5127
Pr 28:17 of any person shall **f.** to the pit; 5127
Ca 2:17 and the shadows **f.** away, turn, my 5127
Ca 4:6 and the shadows **f.** away, I will 5127
Isa 10:3 whom will ye **f.** for help? and where 5127
Isa 10:31 of Gebim gather themselves to **f.**
Isa 13:14 **f.** every one into his own land. 5127
Isa 15:5 his fugitives shall **f.** unto Zoar, an
Isa 17:13 and they shall **f.** far off, and shall 5127
Isa 20:6 we **f.** for help to be delivered 5127
Isa 30:16 **f.** upon horses; therefore shall ye **f.**: 5127
Isa 30:17 thousand shall **f.** at the rebuke of one;
Isa 30:17 at the rebuke of five shall ye **f.**: 5127
Isa 31:8 but he shall **f.** from the sword, 5127
Isa 35:10 sorrow and sighing shall **f.** away. 5127
Isa 48:20 **f.** ye from the Chaldeans, with a 1272
Isa 51:11 sorrow and mourning shall **f.** 5127
Jer 4:29 whole city shall **f.** for the noise 1272
Jer 6:1 gather yourselves to **f.** out of the 5756
Jer 25:35 shepherded shall have no way to **f.**, 4498
Jer 46:6 the swift **f.** away, nor the mighty 5127
Jer 48:6 **F.**, save your lives, and be like the 5127
Jer 48:9 Moab, that it may **f.** and get away: 5323

Jer 49:8 **F.** ye, turn back, dwell deep, 5127
Jer 49:24 feeble, and turneth herself to **f.**, 5127
Jer 49:30 **F.**, get you far off, dwell deep, 5127
Jer 50:16 they shall **f.** every one to his own 5127
Jer 50:28 voice of them that **f.** and escape 5127
Jer 51:6 **F.** out of the midst of Babylon, 5127
Am 2:16 the mighty shall **f.** away naked 5127
Am 5:19 As if a man did **f.** from a lion, 5127
Am 7:12 go, **f.** thee away into the land of 1272
Am 9:1 fleeth of them shall not **f.** away, 5127
Jon 1:3 Jonah rose up to **f.** unto Tarshish 1272
Na 2:8 yet they shall **f.** away. Stand, 5127
Na 3:7 they that look upon thee shall **f.** 5074
Na 3:17 when the sun ariseth they **f.** away, 5074
Zec 2:6 and **f.** from the land of the north, 5127
Zec 14:5 And ye shall **f.** to the valley of the 5127
Zec 14:5 yea, ye shall **f.**, like as ye fled from 5127
Mt 2:13 **f.** into Egypt, and be thou there *5343*
Mt 3:7 you to **f.** from the wrath to come? *5343*
Mt 10:23 **f. ye into another: for verily I say.** *5343*
Mt 24:16 **them which be in Judaea f.** *5343*
Mk 13:14 **them that be in Judaea f. to** *5343*
Lu 3:7 you to **f.** from the wrath to come? *5343*
Lu 21:21 **them which are in Judaea f. to the.** *5343*
Joh 10:5 **will f. from him: for they know** *5343*
Ac 27:30 were about to **f.** out of the ship, *5343*
1Co 6:18 **F.** fornication. Every sin that a *5343*
1Co 10:14 my dearly beloved, **f.** from idolatry. *5343*
1Ti 6:11 O man of God, **f.** these things; *5343*
2Ti 2:22 **F.** also youthful lusts: but follow *5343*
Jas 4:7 the devil, and he will **f.** from you. *5343*
Re 9:6 and death shall **f.** from them. *5343*

FLEECE
De 18:4 the first of the **f.** of thy sheep, 1488
Jg 6:37 I will put a **f.** of wool in the floor; 1492
Jg 6:37 and if the dew be on the **f.** only, 1492
Jg 6:38 thrust the **f.** together, and wringed 1492
Jg 6:38 and wringed the dew out of the **f.**. 1492
Jg 6:39 I pray thee, but this once with the **f.**; 1492
Jg 6:39 let it now be dry only upon the **f.**, 1492
Jg 6:40 for it was dry upon the **f.** only 1492
Job 31:20 if he were not warmed with the **f.** 1488

FLEEING
Le 26:36 they shall flee, as **f.** from a sword; 4499
De 4:42 and that **f.** unto one of these cities 5127
Job 30:3 **f.** into the wilderness in former 6207

FLEETH
De 19:11 and **f.** into one of these cities: 5127
Job 14:2 he **f.** also as a shadow, and 1272
Isa 24:18 who **f.** from the noise of the fear 5127
Jer 48:19 ask him that **f.**, and her that 5127
Jer 48:44 he that **f.** from the fear shall fall 5211
Am 9:1 he that **f.** of them shall not flee 5127
Na 3:16 cankerworm spoileth, and **f.** away 5775
Joh 10:12 **leaveth the sheep, and f.: and the.** *5343*
Joh 10:13 **The hireling f., because he is an** *5343*

FLESH See also FATFLESHED; FLESHHOOK; LEAN FLESHED.
Ge 2:21 closed up the **f.** instead thereof; 1320
Ge 2:23 bone of my bones, and **f.** of my **f.**; 1320
Ge 2:24 and they shall be one **f.** 1320
Ge 6:3 with man, for that he also is **f.**: 1320
Ge 6:12 for all **f.** had corrupted his way 1320
Ge 6:13 The end of all **f.** is come before me; 1320
Ge 6:17 destroy all **f.**, wherein is the breath 1320
Ge 6:19 And of every living thing of all **f.**, 1320
Ge 7:15 two of all **f.**, wherein is the breath 1320
Ge 7:16 went in male and female of all **f.**, 1320
Ge 7:21 all **f.** died that moved upon the 1320
Ge 8:17 of all **f.**, both of fowl, and of cattle, 1320
Ge 9:4 But **f.** with the life thereof, which is 1320
Ge 9:11 neither shall all **f.** be cut off any 1320
Ge 9:15 and every living creature of all **f.**; 1320
Ge 9:15 become a flood to destroy all **f.**. 1320
Ge 9:16 every living creature of all **f.** that is 1320
Ge 9:17 established between me and all **f.** 1320
Ge 17:11 circumcise the **f.** of your foreskin; 1320
Ge 17:13 my covenant shall be in your **f.** for 1320
Ge 17:14 whose **f.** of his foreskin is not 1320
Ge 17:23 circumcised the **f.** of their foreskin 1320
Ge 17:24, 25 circumcised in the **f.** of his 1320
Ge 29:14 Surely thou art my bone and my **f.** 1320
Ge 37:27 for he is our brother and our **f.** 1320
Ge 40:19 and the birds shall eat thy **f.** from 1320
Ex 4:7 it was turned again as his other **f.** 1320
Ex 12:8 they shall eat the **f.** in that night, 1320
Ex 12:46 carry forth ought of the **f.** abroad 1320
Ex 16:3 when we sat by the **f.** pots, 1320
Ex 16:8 give you in the evening **f.** to eat, 1320
Ex 16:12 At even ye shall eat **f.**, and in the 1320
Ex 21:28 and his **f.** shall not be eaten; 1320
Ex 22:31 shall ye eat any **f.** that is torn of 1320
Ex 29:14 the **f.** of the bullock, and his skin, 1320
Ex 29:31 and seethe his **f.** in the holy place. 1320
Ex 29:32 his sons shall eat the **f.** of the ram, 1320
Ex 29:34 ought of the **f.** of the consecrations, 1320
Ex 30:32 Upon man's **f.** shall it not be poured, 1320
Le 4:11 all his **f.**, with his head, and with 1320
Le 6:10 breeches shall he put upon his **f.**, 1320
Le 6:27 Whatsoever shall touch the **f.** 1320
Le 7:15 And the **f.** of the sacrifice of his 1320
Le 7:17 remainder of the **f.** of the sacrifice 1320
Le 7:18 And if any of the **f.** of the sacrifice 1320
Le 7:19 **f.** that toucheth any unclean thing 1320
Le 7:19 as for the **f.**, all that be clean shall 1320
Le 7:20 But the soul that eateth of the **f.** 1320
Le 7:21 and eat of the **f.** of the sacrifice of 1320
Le 8:17 the bullock, and his hide, his **f.**, 1320
Le 8:31 Boil the **f.** at the door of the 1320
Le 8:32 And that which remaineth of the **f.** 1320
Le 9:11 And the **f.** and the hide he burnt 1320
Le 11:8 Of their **f.** shall ye not eat, and their 1320
Le 11:11 ye shall not eat of their **f.**, but ye 1320
Le 12:3 the eighth day the **f.** of his foreskin 1320
Le 13:2 man shall have in the skin of his **f.** 1320
Le 13:2 and it be in the skin of his **f.** like 1320
Le 13:3 on the plague in the skin of his **f.**: 1320
Le 13:3 be deeper than the skin of his **f.**, 1320
Le 13:4 spot be white in the skin of his **f.**, 1320
Le 13:10 there be quick raw **f.** in the rising; 1320
Le 13:11 an old leprosy in the skin of his **f.**, 1320
Le 13:13 the leprosy have covered all his **f.**, 1320
Le 13:14 But when raw **f.** appeareth in him, 1320
Le 13:15 And the priest shall see the raw **f.**, 1320
Le 13:15 the raw **f.** is unclean: it is a leprosy 1320
Le 13:16 Or if the raw **f.** turn again, 1320
Le 13:18 The **f.** also, in which, even in the 1320
Le 13:24 there be any **f.**, in the skin whereof 1320
Le 13:24 and the quick **f.** that burneth have a
Le 13:38 in the skin of their **f.** bright spots, 1320
Le 13:39 bright spots in the skin of their **f.** 1320
Le 13:43 appeareth in the skin of the **f.**; 1320
Le 14:9 also he shall wash his **f.** in water, 1320
Le 15:2 hath a running issue out of his **f.**, 1320
Le 15:3 whether his **f.** run with his issue, 1320
Le 15:3 or his **f.** be stopped from his issue, 1320
Le 15:7 And he that toucheth the **f.** of him 1320
Le 15:13 and bathe his **f.** in running water, 1320
Le 15:16 then he shall wash all his **f.** in 1320
Le 15:19 and her issue in her **f.** be blood, 1320
Le 16:4 have the linen breeches upon his **f.**, 1320
Le 16:4 shall he wash his **f.** in water, and so 1320
Le 16:24 And he shall wash his **f.** with water 1320
Le 16:26 bathe his **f.** in water, and afterward 1320
Le 16:27 their skins, and their **f.**, and their 1320
Le 16:28 clothes, and bathe his **f.** in water, 1320
Le 17:11 For the life of the **f.** is in the blood; 1320
Le 17:14 For it is the life of all **f.**; 1320
Le 17:14 eat the blood of no manner of **f.**: 1320
Le 17:14 for the life of all **f.** is the blood 1320
Le 17:16 nor bathe his **f.**; then he shall bear 1320
Le 19:28 not make any cuttings in your **f.** 1320
Le 21:5 nor make any cuttings in their **f.** 1320
Le 22:6 unless he wash his **f.** with water 1320
Le 26:29 And ye shall eat the **f.** of your sons, 1320
Le 26:29 and the **f.** of your daughters shall 1320
Nu 8:7 and let them shave all their **f.**, 1320
Nu 11:4 said, Who shall give us **f.** to eat? 1320
Nu 11:13 Whence should I have **f.** to give unto 1320
Nu 11:13 saying, Give us **f.**, that we may eat. 1320
Nu 11:18 to-morrow, and ye shall eat **f.**: for 1320
Nu 11:18 saying, Who shall give us **f.** to eat? 1320
Nu 11:18 therefore the Lord will give you **f.**, 1320
Nu 11:21 thou hast said, I will give them **f.**, 1320
Nu 11:33 And while the **f.** was yet between 1320
Nu 12:12 of whom the **f.** is half consumed 1320
Nu 16:22 the God of the spirits of all **f.**, 1320
Nu 18:15 that openeth the matrix in all **f.**, 1320
Nu 18:18 And the **f.** of them shall be thine, 1320
Nu 19:5 her skin, and her **f.**, and her blood, 1320
Nu 19:7 and he shall bathe his **f.** in water, 1320
Nu 19:8 and bathe his **f.** in water, and shall 1320
Nu 27:16 the God of the spirits of all **f.**, 1320
De 5:26 For who is there of all **f.**, that hath 1320
De 12:15 kill and eat **f.** in all thy gates, 1320
De 12:20 and thou shalt say, I will eat **f.**, 1320
De 12:20 because thy soul longeth to eat **f.**; 1320
De 12:20 thou mayest eat **f.**, whatsoever 1320
De 12:23 mayest not eat the life with the **f.**. 1320
De 12:27 the **f.** and the blood, upon the altar 1320
De 12:27 thy God, and thou shalt eat the **f.**. 1320
De 14:8 ye shall not eat of their **f.**, nor 1320
De 16:4 shall there any thing of the **f.**, 1320
De 28:53 **f.** of thy sons and of thy daughters, 1320
De 28:55 **f.** of his children whom he shall eat: 1320
De 32:42 and my sword shall devour **f.**; 1320
Jg 6:19 the **f.** he put in a basket, and he put 1320
Jg 6:20 Take the **f.** and the unleavened 1320
Jg 6:21 touched the **f.** and the unleavened 1320
Jg 6:21 consumed the **f.** and the unleavened 1320
Jg 8:7 I will tear your **f.** with the thorns 1320
Jg 9:2 that I am your bone and your **f.** 1320
1Sa 2:13 came, while the **f.** was in seething, 1320
1Sa 2:15 Give **f.** to roast for the priest; for 1320
1Sa 2:15 he will not have sodden **f.** of thee; 1320
1Sa 17:44 and I will give thy **f.** unto the fowls 1320
1Sa 25:11 and my **f.** that I have killed for my 2878
2Sa 5:1 Behold, we are thy bone and thy **f.** 1320
2Sa 6:19 and a good piece of **f.**, and a flagon 829
2Sa 19:12 ye are my bones and my **f.**: 1320
2Sa 19:13 thou not of my bone, and of my **f.**? 1320
1Ki 17:6 him bread and **f.** in the morning, 1320
1Ki 17:6 and bread and **f.** in the evening; 1320
1Ki 19:21 boiled their **f.** with the instruments 1320
1Ki 21:27 sackcloth upon his **f.**, and fasted, 1320
2Ki 4:34 and the **f.** of the child waxed warm 1320
2Ki 5:10 and thy **f.** shall come again to thee, 1320
2Ki 5:14 his **f.** came again like unto the **f.** of 1320
2Ki 6:30 had sackcloth within upon his **f.** 1320
2Ki 9:36 shall dogs eat the **f.** of Jezebel: 1320
1Ch 11:1 Behold, we are thy bone and thy **f.** 1320
1Ch 16:3 a good piece of **f.**, and a flagon of 829
2Ch 32:8 With him is an arm of **f.**; 1320
Ne 5:5 Yet now our **f.** is as the **f.** of our 1320
Job 2:5 now, and touch his bone and his **f.**, 1320
Job 4:15 my face; the hair of my **f.** stood up: 1320
Job 6:12 of stones? or is my **f.** of brass? 1320
Job 7:5 My **f.** is clothed with worms and 1320
Job 10:4 Hast thou eyes of **f.**? or seest thou 1320
Job 10:11 hast clothed me with skin and **f.**, 1320
Job 13:14 Wherefore do I take my **f.** in my 1320
Job 14:22 his **f.** upon him shall have pain, 1320
Job 19:20 cleaveth to my skin and to my **f.**, 1320
Job 19:22 and are not satisfied with my **f.**? 1320
Job 19:26 yet in my **f.** shall I see God: 1320
Job 21:6 and trembling taketh hold on my **f.** 1320
Job 31:31 said not, Oh that we had of his **f.**! 1320
Job 33:21 His **f.** is consumed away, that it 1320
Job 33:25 His **f.** shall be fresher than a 1320
Job 34:15 All **f.** shall perish together, and 1320
Job 41:23 The flakes of his **f.** are joined 1320
Ps 16:9 my **f.** also shall rest in hope 1320
Ps 27:2 came upon me to eat up my **f.**, 1320
Ps 38:3 There is no soundness in my **f.** 1320
Ps 38:7 and there is no soundness in my **f.** 1320
Ps 50:13 Will I eat the **f.** of bulls, or drink 1320
Ps 56:4 I will not fear what **f.** can do unto 1320
Ps 63:1 my **f.** longeth for thee in a dry and 1320
Ps 65:2 unto thee shall all **f.** come 1320
Ps 73:26 My **f.** and my heart faileth: but 7607
Ps 78:20 can he provide **f.** for his people? 7607
Ps 78:27 rained **f.** also upon them as dust, 7607
Ps 78:39 remembered that they were but **f.**; 1320
Ps 79:2 the **f.** of thy saints unto the beasts 1320
Ps 84:2 my heart and my **f.** crieth out for 1320
Ps 109:24 fasting, and my **f.** faileth of fatness. 1320
Ps 119:120 My **f.** trembleth for fear of thee; 1320
Ps 136:25 Who giveth food to all **f.**: for his 1320
Ps 145:21 and let all **f.** bless his holy name 1320
Pr 4:22 find them, and health to all their **f.** 1320
Pr 5:11 thy **f.** and thy body are consumed, 1320
Pr 11:17 that is cruel troubleth his own **f.** 7607
Pr 14:30 a sound heart is the life of the **f.**: 1320
Pr 23:20 among riotous eaters of **f.**: 1320
Ec 4:5 together, and eateth his own **f.** 1320
Ec 5:6 not thy mouth to cause thy **f.** to sin; 1320
Ec 11:10 and put away evil from thy **f.**: 1320
Ec 12:12 much study is a weariness of the **f.** 1320
Isa 9:20 every man the **f.** of his own arm: 1320

Isa 17:4 the fatness of his f. shall wax lean... 1320
Isa 22:13 eating f., and drinking wine:... 1320
Isa 31:3 and their horses f., and not spirit... 1320
Isa 40:5 and all f. shall see it together:... 1320
Isa 40:6 What shall I cry? All f. is grass,... 1320
Isa 44:16 with part thereof he eateth f.; he... 1320
Isa 44:19 I have roasted f., and eaten it:... 1320
Isa 49:26 that oppress thee with their own f.;... 1320
Isa 49:26 and all f. shall know that I the Lord... 1320
Isa 58:7 hide not thyself from thine own f.?... 1320
Isa 65:4 which eat swine's f., and broth of... 1320
Isa 66:16 will the Lord plead with all f.:... 1320
Isa 66:17 the midst, eating swine's f., and the... 1320
Isa 66:23 all f. come to worship before me,... 1320
Isa 66:24 shall be an abhorring unto all f... 1320
Jer 7:21 unto your sacrifices, and eat f... 1320
Jer 11:15 and the holy f. is passed from thee?... 1320
Jer 12:12 the land: no f. shall have peace... 1320
Jer 17:5 in man, and maketh f. his arm,... 1320
Jer 19:9 cause them to eat the f. of their sons. 1320
Jer 19:9 and the f. of their daughters,... 1320
Jer 19:9 eat every one the f. of his friend in... 1320
Jer 25:31 he will plead with all f.; he will... 1320
Jer 32:27 I am the Lord, the God of all f.:... 1320
Jer 45:5 behold, I will bring evil upon all f.,... 1320
Jer 51:35 violence done to me and to my f... 7607
La 3:4 My f. and my skin hath he made... 1320
Eze 4:14 there abominable f. into my mouth... 1320
Eze 11:3 is the caldron, and we be the f... 1320
Eze 11:7 they are the f., and this city is the... 1320
Eze 11:11 neither shall ye be the f. in the midst.. 1320
Eze 11:19 take the stony heart out of their f.,... 1320
Eze 11:19 and will give them an heart of f.:... 1320
Eze 16:26 thy neighbours, great of f.; and... 1320
Eze 20:48 And all f. shall see that I the Lord... 1320
Eze 21:4 forth out of his sheath against all f.,... 1320
Eze 21:5 That all f. may know that I the Lord... 1320
Eze 23:20 whose f. is as the f. of asses,... 1320
Eze 24:10 consume the f., and spice it well,... 1320
Eze 32:5 will lay thy f. upon the mountains,... 1320
Eze 36:26 away the stony heart out of your f.,... 1320
Eze 36:26 and I will give you an heart of f... 1320
Eze 37:6 and will bring up f. upon you,... 1320
Eze 37:8 lo, the sinews and the f. came up... 1320
Eze 39:17 that ye may eat f., and drink blood... 1320
Eze 39:18 Ye shall eat the f. of the mighty,... 1320
Eze 40:43 and upon the tables was the f. of the.. 1320
Eze 44:7 and uncircumcised in f., to be in my... 1320
Eze 44:9 nor uncircumcised in f., shall enter... 1320
Da 1:15 appeared fairer and fatter in f... 1320
Da 2:11 gods, whose dwelling is not with f... 1321
Da 4:12 and all f. was fed of it... 1321
Da 7:5 thus unto it, Arise, devour much f... 1321
Da 10:3 came f. nor wine in my mouth,... 1320
Ho 8:13 They sacrifice f. for the sacrifices... 1320
Joe 2:28 will pour out my spirit upon all f.:... 1320
Mic 3:2 and their f. from off their bones;... 7607
Mic 3:3 Who also eat the f. of my people... 7607
Mic 3:3 and as f. within the caldron... 1320
Zep 1:17 as dust, and their f. as the dung... 3894
Hag 2:12 If one bear holy f. in the skirt of... 1320
Zec 2:13 Be silent, O all f., before the Lord:... 1320
Zec 11:9 rest eat every one the f. of another... 1320
Zec 11:16 but he shall eat the f. of the fat,... 1320
Zec 14:12 Their f. shall consume away while... 1320
Mt 16:17 **f. and blood hath not revealed it...** 4561
Mt 19:5 **and they twain shall be one f.?...** 4561
Mt 19:6 **they are no more twain, but one f.** 4561
Mt 24:22 **there should no f. be saved: but...** 4561
Mt 26:41 **indeed is willing, but the f. is...** 4561
Mk 10:8 **And they twain shall be one f.;...** 4561
Mk 10:8 **they are no more twain, but one f.** 4561
Mk 13:20 **no f. should be saved: but for the.** 4561
Mk 14:38 **truly is ready, but the f. is weak..** 4561
Lu 3:6 And all f. shall see the salvation of... 4561
Lu 24:39 **for a spirit hath not f. and bones,..** 4561
Joh 1:13 nor of the will of the f., nor of the... 4561
Joh 1:14 And the Word was made f., and... 4561
Joh 3:6 **That which is born of the f. is f.;.** 4561
Joh 6:51 **the bread that I will give is my f.,** 4561
Joh 6:52 can this man give us his f. to eat?... 4561
Joh 6:53 **Except ye eat the f. of the Son of.** 4561
Joh 6:54 **Whoso eateth my f., and drinketh.** 4561
Joh 6:55 **For my f. is meat indeed, and my..** 4561
Joh 6:56 **He that eateth my f., and drinketh** 4561
Joh 6:63 **quickeneth; the f. profiteth...** 4561
Joh 8:15 **judge after the f.; I judge no man.** 4561
Joh 17:2 **hast given him power over all f.,..** 4561
Ac 2:17 pour out of my Spirit upon all f.:... 4561
Ac 2:26 also my f. shall rest in hope:... 4561
Ac 2:30 fruit of his loins, according to the f.,... 4561
Ac 2:31 neither his f. did see corruption... 4561
Ro 1:3 seed of David according to the f.;... 4561
Ro 2:28 which is outward in the f.:... 4561
Ro 3:20 shall no f. be justified in his sight:... 4561
Ro 4:1 as pertaining to the f., hath found?... 4561
Ro 6:19 because of the infirmity of your f.:... 4561
Ro 7:5 For when we were in the f.,... 4561
Ro 7:18 in me, (that is, in my f.,)... 4561
Ro 7:25 but with the f. the law of sin... 4561
Ro 8:1 after the f., but after the Spirit... 4561
Ro 8:3 in that it was weak through the f.,... 4561
Ro 8:3 Son in the likeness of sinful f., and... 4561
Ro 8:3 for sin, condemned sin in the f.:... 4561
Ro 8:4 in us, who walk not after the f.,... 4561
Ro 8:5 For they that are after the f. do... 4561
Ro 8:5 do mind the things of the f.;... 4561
Ro 8:8 that are in the f. cannot please God... 4561
Ro 8:9 But ye are not in the f., but in the... 4561
Ro 8:12 we are debtors, not to the f.,... 4561
Ro 8:12 to live after the f... 4561
Ro 8:13 For if ye live after the f., ye shall... 4561
Ro 9:3 my kinsmen according to the f.:... 4561
Ro 9:5 as concerning the f. Christ came,... 4561
Ro 9:8 which are the children of the f.,... 4561
Ro 11:14 emulation them which are my f.,... 4561
Ro 13:14 and make not provision for the f... 4561
Ro 14:21 It is good neither to eat f., nor to... 2907
1Co 1:26 not many wise men after the f.,... 4561
1Co 1:29 no f. should glory in his presence... 4561
1Co 5:5 Satan for the destruction of the f.,... 4561
1Co 6:16 for two, saith he, shall be one f... 4561
1Co 7:28 such shall have trouble in the f.:... 4561
1Co 8:13 eat no f. while the world standeth,... 2907
1Co 10:18 Behold Israel after the f.: are not... 4561
1Co 15:39 All f. is not the same f.: but there... 4561
1Co 15:39 but there is one kind of f. of men,... 4561
1Co 15:39 another f. of beasts, another of... 4561
1Co 15:50 that f. and blood cannot inherit the... 4561
2Co 1:17 do I purpose according to the f.,... 4561
2Co 4:11 be made manifest in our mortal f... 4561
2Co 5:16 know we no man after the f.: yea,... 4561
2Co 5:16 we have known Christ after the f.,... 4561
2Co 7:1 all filthiness of the f. and spirit,... 4561
2Co 7:5 f. had no rest, but we were troubled.. 4561
2Co 10:2 as if we walked according to the f... 4561
2Co 10:3 in the f., we do not war after the f.:.. 4561
2Co 11:18 Seeing that many glory after the f.,... 4561
2Co 12:7 a thorn in the f., the messenger of... 4561
Ga 1:16 I conferred not with f. and blood:... 4561
Ga 2:16 of the law shall no f. be justified... 4561
Ga 2:20 the life which I now live in the f... 4561
Ga 3:3 are ye now made perfect by the f.?... 4561
Ga 4:13 infirmity of the f. I preached... 4561
Ga 4:14 my temptation which was in my f... 4561
Ga 4:23 bondwoman was born after the f.;... 4561
Ga 4:29 as then he that was born after the f... 4561
Ga 5:13 not liberty for an occasion to the f.,... 4561
Ga 5:16 ye shall not fulfil the lust of the f... 4561
Ga 5:17 the f. lusteth against the Spirit,... 4561
Ga 5:17 and the Spirit against the f.:... 4561
Ga 5:19 the works of the f. are manifest,... 4561
Ga 5:24 crucified the f. with the affections... 4561
Ga 6:8 soweth to his f. shall of the f. reap... 4561
Ga 6:12 desire to make a fair show in the f.,... 4561
Ga 6:13 that they may glory in your f... 4561
Eph 2:3 in the lusts of our f., fulfilling the... 4561
Eph 2:3 desires of the f. and of the mind;... 4561
Eph 2:11 being in time past Gentiles in the f.,... 4561
Eph 2:11 is called the Circumcision in the f... 4561
Eph 2:15 Having abolished in his f. the... 4561
Eph 5:29 no man ever yet hated his own f.;... 4561
Eph 5:30 his body, of his f., and of his bones... 4561
Eph 5:31 and they two shall be one f... 4561
Eph 6:5 your masters according to the f.,... 4561
Eph 6:12 we wrestle not against f. and blood,... 4561
Php 1:22 if I live in the f., this is the fruit of... 4561
Php 1:24 Nevertheless to abide in the f. is... 4561
Php 3:3 and have no confidence in the f... 4561
Php 3:4 might also have confidence in the f... 4561
Php 3:4 whereof he might trust in the f.,... 4561
Col 1:22 In the body of his f. through death,... 4561
Col 1:24 in my f. for his body's sake, which... 4561
Col 2:1 as have not seen my face in the f.;... 4561
Col 2:5 For though I be absent in the f.,... 4561
Col 2:11 off the body of the sins of the f. by... 4561
Col 2:13 and the uncircumcision of your f... 4561
Col 2:23 honour to the satisfying of the f... 4561
Col 3:22 your masters according to the f.;... 4561
1Ti 3:16 God was manifest in the f., justified... 4561
Phm 16 both in the f. and in the Lord?... 4561
Heb 2:14 the children are partakers of f. and... 4561
Heb 5:7 Who in the days of his f., when he... 4561
Heb 9:13 sanctifieth to the purifying of the f.:... 4561
Heb 10:20 the veil, that is to say, his f.;... 4561
Heb 12:9 we have had fathers of our f. which... 4561
Jas 5:3 and shall eat your f. as it were fire... 4561
1Pe 1:24 For all f. is grass, and all the glory... 4561
1Pe 3:18 to death in the f., but quickened... 4561
1Pe 3:21 putting away of the filth of the f.,... 4561
1Pe 4:1 Christ hath suffered for us in the f.,... 4561
1Pe 4:1 he that hath suffered in the f. hath... 4561
1Pe 4:2 live the rest of his time in the f. to... 4561
1Pe 4:6 be judged according to men in the f.,... 4561
2Pe 2:10 that walk after the f. in the lust of... 4561
2Pe 2:18 allure through the lusts of the f... 4561
1Jo 2:16 the lust of the f., and the lust of the... 4561
1Jo 4:2 that Jesus Christ is come in the f... 4561
1Jo 4:3 not that...Christ is come in the f... 4561
2Jo 7 that Jesus Christ is come in the f... 4561
Jude 7 going after strange f., are set forth... 4561
Jude 8 these filthy dreamers defile the f.,... 4561
Jude 23 even the garment spotted by the f... 4561
Re 17:16 and shall eat her f., and burn her... 4561
Re 19:18 f. of kings, and the f. of captains,... 4561
Re 19:18 captains, and the f. of mighty men,... 4561
Re 19:18 men, and the f. of horses, and of... 4561
Re 19:18 and the f. of all men, both free and... 4561
Re 19:21 the fowls were filled with their f... 4561

FLESHHOOK See also FLESHHOOKS.
1Sa 2:13 with a f. of three teeth in his hand;... 4207
1Sa 2:14 all that the f. brought up the priest... 4207

FLESHHOOKS
Ex 27:3 and his f., and his firepans: all the... 4207
Ex 38:3 and the f., and the firepans: all the... 4207
Nu 4:14 the censers, the f., and the shovels,... 4207
1Ch 28:17 pure gold for the f., and the bowls,... 4207
2Ch 4:16 and the shovels, and the f., and all... 4207

FLESHLY
2Co 1:12 not with f. wisdom, but by the... 4559
2Co 3:3 but in f. tables of the heart... 4560
Col 2:18 vainly puffed up by his f. mind,...
1Pe 2:11 abstain from f. lusts, which war... 4559

FLESH-POTS See FLESH and POTS.

FLEW
1Sa 14:32 And the people f. upon the spoil,... 6213
Isa 6:6 Then f. one of the seraphims unto... 5774

FLIES
Ex 8:21 I will send swarms of f. upon thee, and...
Ex 8:21 shall be full of swarms of f., and also...
Ex 8:22 that no swarms of f. shall be there;...
Ex 8:24 there came a grievous swarm of f. into...
Ex 8:24 corrupted by reason of the swarm of f...
Ex 8:29 that the swarms of f. may depart from...
Ex 8:31 and he removed the swarms of f. from...
Ps 78:45 He sent divers sorts of f. among... 6157
Ps 105:31 there came divers sorts of f., and... 6157
Ec 10:1 Dead f. cause the ointment of the... 2070

FLIETH
De 4:17 likeness of any winged fowl that f... 5774
De 14:19 creeping thing that f. is unclean... 5775
De 28:49 the earth as swift as the eagle f.;... 1675
Ps 91:5 nor for the arrow that f. by day;... 5774

FLIGHT
Le 26:8 you shall put ten thousand to f... 7291
De 32:30 and two put ten thousand to f.,... 5127
1Ch 12:15 and they put to f. all them of the... 1272
Isa 52:12 not go out with haste, nor go by f.:... 4499
Am 2:14 The f. shall perish from the swift... 4498
Mt 24:20 **But pray ye that your f. be not in.** 5437
Mk 13:18 **And pray ye that your f. be not in** 5437
Heb 11:34 turned to f. the armies of the aliens... 5437

FLINT
De 8:15 forth water out of the rock of f.;... 2496
Ps 114:8 the f. into a fountain of waters... 2496
Isa 5:28 hoofs shall be counted like f.,... 6864

Isa 50:7 have I set my face like a **f.**, 2496
Eze 3:9 As an adamant harder than **f.** have 6864

FLINTY

De 32:13 and oil out of the **f.** rock; 2496

FLOATS See also FLOTES.

1Ki 5:9 and I will convey them by sea in **f.** 1702

FLOCK See also FLOCKS.

Ge 4:4 the firstlings of his **f.** and the fat 6629
Ge 21:28 ewe lambs of the **f.** by themselves. 6629
Ge 27:9 Go now to the **f.**, and fetch me two 6629
Ge 29:10 and watered the **f.** of Laban his 6629
Ge 30:31 I will again feed and keep thy **f.** 6629
Ge 30:32 I will pass through all thy **f.** to day, 6629
Ge 30:40 all the brown in the **f.** of Laban; 6629
Ge 31:4 and Leah to the field unto his **f.** 6629
Ge 31:38 rams of thy **f.** have I not eaten. 6629
Ge 33:13 them one day, all the **f.** will die. 6629
Ge 37:2 years old was feeding the **f.** with his 6629
Ge 37:12 went to feed their father's **f.** in 6629
Ge 37:13 Do not thy brethren feed the **f.** in
Ge 38:17 I will send thee a kid from the **f.** 6629
Ex 2:16 troughs to water their father's **f.** 6629
Ex 2:17 helped them, and watered their **f.** 6629
Ex 2:19 enough for us, and watered the **f.** 6629
Ex 3:1 kept the **f.** of Jethro his father in 6629
Ex 3:1 the **f.** to the backside of the desert, 6629
Le 1:2 even of the herd, and of the **f.** 6629
Le 3:6 be of the **f.**; male or female, he 6629
Le 5:6 female from the **f.**, a lamb or a kid 6629
Le 5:18 ram without blemish out of the **f.**, 6629
Le 6:6 ram without blemish out of the **f.** 6629
Le 27:32 the tithe of the herd, or of the **f.**, 6629
Nu 15:3 the Lord, of the herd, or of the **f.**: 6629
De 12:17 firstlings of thy herds or of thy **f.**, 6629
De 12:21 shalt kill of thy herd and of thy **f.** 6629
De 15:14 out of thy **f.**, and out of thy floor, 6629
De 15:19 that come of thy herd and of thy **f.** 6629
De 16:2 of the **f.** and the herd, in the place 6629
1Sa 17:34 and took a lamb out of the **f.**: 5739
2Sa 12:4 he spared to take of his own **f.** and 6629
2Ch 35:7 Josiah gave to the people, of the **f.**, 6629
Ezr 10:19 they offered a ram of the **f.** for their 6629
Job 21:11 send forth their little ones like a **f.**, 6629
Job 30:1 to have set with the dogs of my **f.** 6629
Ps 77:20 Thou leddest thy people like a **f.** by 6629
Ps 78:52 them in the wilderness like a **f.** 5739
Ps 80:1 thou that leadest Joseph like a **f.**; 6629
Ps 107:41 and maketh him families like a **f.** 6629
Ca 1:7 thou makest thy **f.** to rest at noon:
Ca 1:8 way forth by the footsteps of the **f.**, 6629
Ca 4:1 thy hair is as a **f.** of goats, that 5739
Ca 4:2 Thy teeth are like a **f.** of sheep 5739
Ca 6:5 thy hair is as a **f.** of goats that 5739
Ca 6:6 Thy teeth are as a **f.** of sheep which 5739
Isa 40:11 He shall feed his **f.** like a shepherd: 5739
Isa 63:11 sea with the shepherd of his **f.**? 6629
Jer 13:17 Lord's **f.** is carried away captive. 5739
Jer 13:20 where is the **f.** that was given thee, 5739
Jer 13:20 was given thee, thy beautiful **f.**? 6629
Jer 23:2 have scattered my **f.**, and driven 6629
Jer 23:3 I will gather the remnant of my **f.** 6629
Jer 25:34 in the ashes, ye principal of the **f.**: 6629
Jer 25:35 nor the principal of the **f.** to escape. 6629
Jer 25:36 howling of the principal of the **f.** 6629
Jer 31:10 him, as a shepherd doth his **f.** 5739
Jer 31:12 young of the **f.** and of the herd: 6629
Jer 49:20 the least of the **f.** shall draw them 6629
Jer 50:45 the least of the **f.** shall draw them 6629
Jer 51:23 with thee the shepherd and his **f.**; 5739
Eze 24:5 Take the choice of the **f.**, and 6629
Eze 34:3 are fed: but ye feed not the **f.** 6629
Eze 34:6 my **f.** was scattered upon all the 6629
Eze 34:8 because my **f.** became a prey, 6629
Eze 34:8 and my **f.** became meat to every 6629
Eze 34:8 did my shepherds search for my **f.** 6629
Eze 34:8 fed themselves, and fed not my **f.**; 6629
Eze 34:10 I will require my **f.** at their hand, 6629
Eze 34:10 them to cease from feeding the **f.**; 6629
Eze 34:10 I will deliver my **f.** from their 6629
Eze 34:12 As a shepherd seeketh out his **f.** 5739
Eze 34:15 I will feed my **f.**, and I will cause 6629
Eze 34:17 And as for you, O my **f.**, thus saith 6629
Eze 34:19 And as for my **f.**, they eat that 6629
Eze 34:22 Therefore will I save my **f.**, and 6629
Eze 34:31 And ye my **f.**, the **f.** of my pasture, 6629
Eze 36:37 increase them with men like a **f.** 6629
Eze 36:38 the holy **f.**, as the **f.** of Jerusalem 6629
Eze 43:23, 25 a ram out of the **f.** without 6629
Eze 45:15 And one lamb out of the **f.**, out of 6629
Am 6:4 and eat the lambs out of the **f.**, and 6629
Am 7:15 Lord took me as I followed the **f.**, 6629
Jon 3:7 beast, herd nor **f.**, taste anything: 6629
Mic 2:12 as the **f.** in the midst of their fold: 5739
Mic 4:8 And thou, O tower of the **f.**, the 5739
Mic 7:14 thy rod, the **f.** of thine heritage, 6629
Hab 3:17 the **f.** shall be cut off from the fold, 6629
Zec 9:16 in that day as the **f.** of his people: 6629
Zec 10:2 they went their way as a **f.**, they 6629
Zec 10:3 Lord of hosts hath visited his **f.** 5739
Zec 11:4 Feed the **f.** of the slaughter; 6629
Zec 11:7 And I will feed the **f.** of slaughter, 6629
Zec 11:7 even you, O poor of the **f.** 6629
Zec 11:7 I called Bands; and I fed the **f.** 6629
Zec 11:11 poor of the **f.** that waited upon me 6629
Zec 11:17 idol shepherd that leaveth the **f.**! 6629
Mal 1:14 which hath in his **f.** a male, and 5739
Mt 26:31 **sheep of the f. shall be scattered** *4167*
Lu 2:8 watch over their **f.** by night. *4167*
Lu 12:32 **Fear not, little f.; for it is your** *4168*
Ac 20:28 unto yourselves, and to all the **f.**, *4168*
Ac 20:29 in among you, not sparing the **f.** *4168*
1Co 9:7 who feedeth a **f.**, and eateth not of *4167*
1Co 9:7 eateth not of the milk of the **f.**? *4167*
1Pe 5:2 the **f.** of God which is among you, *4168*
1Pe 5:3 but being ensamples to the **f.** *4168*

FLOCKS

Ge 13:5 with Abram, had **f.**, and herds, 6629
Ge 24:35 he hath given him **f.**, and herds, 6629
Ge 26:14 possession of **f.**, and possession of 6629
Ge 29:2 were three **f.** of sheep lying by it; 5739
Ge 29:2 out of that well they watered the **f.**: 5739
Ge 29:3 And thither were all the **f.** gathered: 5739
Ge 29:8 until all the **f.** be gathered together, 5739
Ge 30:36 Jacob fed the rest of Laban's **f.** 6629
Ge 30:38 which he had pilled before the **f.** 6629
Ge 30:38 when the **f.** came to drink, 6629
Ge 30:39 the **f.** conceived before the rods, 6629
Ge 30:40 of the **f.** toward the ringstraked, 6629
Ge 30:40 he put his own **f.** by themselves, 5739
Ge 32:5 and asses, **f.**, and menservants, 6629
Ge 32:7 the **f.**, and herds, and the camels, 6629
Ge 33:13 and the **f.** and herds with young 6629
Ge 37:14 brethren, and well with the **f.**: 6629
Ge 37:16 thee, where they feed their **f.**
Ge 45:10 and thy **f.**, and thy herds, and all 6629
Ge 46:32 and they have brought their **f.**, 6629
Ge 47:1 my brethren, and their **f.**, and their 6629
Ge 47:4 have no pasture for their **f.**; for the 6629
Ge 47:17 exchange for horses, and for the **f.**, 6629
Ge 50:8 only their little ones, and their **f.**, 6629
Ex 10:9 with our **f.** and with our herds will 6629
Ex 10:24 your **f.** and your herds be stayed: 6629
Ex 12:32 Also take your **f.** and your herds, 6629
Ex 12:38 and **f.**, and herds, even very much 6629
Ex 34:3 neither let the **f.** nor herds feed 6629
Le 1:10 And if his offering be of the **f.**, 6629
Le 5:15 ram without blemish out of the **f.**, 6629
Nu 11:22 Shall the **f.** and the herds be slain 6629
Nu 31:9 and all their **f.**, and all their goods. 4735
Nu 31:30 of the asses, and of the **f.**, of all 6629
Nu 32:36 Our little ones, our wives, our **f.**, 4735
De 7:13 and the **f.** of thy sheep, in the 6251
De 8:13 thy herds and thy **f.** multiply, 6629
De 12:6 of your herds and of your **f.**: 6629
De 14:23 of thy herds and of thy **f.**; 6629
De 28:4, 18 kine and the **f.** of thy sheep. 6251
De 28:51 of thy kine, or **f.** of thy sheep, 6251
Jg 5:16 to hear the bleatings of the **f.**? 5739
1Sa 30:20 David took all the **f.** and the herds, 6629
2Sa 12:2 had exceeding many **f.** and herds: 6629
1Ki 20:27 them like two little **f.** of kids; 2835
1Ch 4:39 valley, to seek pasture for their **f.** 6629
1Ch 4:41 there was pasture there for their **f.** 6629
1Ch 27:31 over the **f.** was Jazis the Hagerite. 6629
2Ch 17:11 the Arabians brought him **f.**, seven 6629
2Ch 32:28 manner of beasts, and cotes for **f.** 5739
2Ch 32:29 and possessions of **f.** and herds 6629
Ne 10:36 firstlings of our herds and of our **f.**, 6629
Job 24:2 they violently take away **f.**, and 5739
Ps 65:13 The pastures are clothed with **f.**; 6629
Ps 78:48 and their **f.** to hot thunderbolts. 4735
Pr 27:23 to know the state of thy **f.**, and 6629
Ca 1:7 as one that turneth aside by the **f.** 5739
Isa 17:2 they shall be for **f.**, which shall 5739
Isa 32:14 a joy of wild asses, a pasture of **f.**; 5739
Isa 60:7 the **f.** of Kedar shall be gathered 6629
Isa 61:5 shall stand and feed your **f.**, and the 6629
Isa 65:10 And Sharon shall be a fold of **f.**, 6629
Jer 3:24 their **f.** and their herds, their sons 6629
Jer 5:17 shall eat up thy **f.** and thine herds: 6629
Jer 6:3 shepherds with their **f.** shall come 5739
Jer 10:21 and all their **f.** shall be scattered. 4830
Jer 31:24 and they that go forth with **f.** 5739
Jer 33:12 shepherds causing their **f.** to lie 6629
Jer 33:13 the cities of Judah, shall the **f.** pass 6629
Jer 49:29 tents and their **f.** shall they take 6629
Jer 50:8 as the he goats before the **f.** 6629
Eze 25:5 Ammonites a couchingplace for **f.**; 6629
Eze 34:2 not the shepherds feed the **f.**? 6629
Eze 36:38 waste cities be filled with **f.** of men; 6629
Ho 5:6 with their **f.** and with their herds 6629
Joe 1:18 the **f.** of sheep are made desolate. 5739
Mic 5:8 young lion among the **f.** of sheep: 5739
Zep 2:6 for shepherds, and folds for **f.** 6629
Zep 2:14 And **f.** shall lie down in the midst 5739

FLOOD See also FLOODS; WATERFLOOD.

Ge 6:17 I do bring a **f.** of waters upon the 3999
Ge 7:6 the **f.** of waters was upon the earth. 3999
Ge 7:7 because of the waters of the **f.** 3999
Ge 7:10 waters of the **f.** were upon the earth. 3999
Ge 7:17 **f.** was forty days upon the earth; 3999
Ge 9:11 off any more by the waters of a **f.**; 3999
Ge 9:11 neither shall there any more be a **f.** 3999
Ge 9:15 waters shall no more become a **f.** 3999
Ge 9:28 And Noah lived after the **f.** three 3999
Ge 10:1 them were sons born after the **f.** 3999
Ge 10:32 divided in the earth after the **f.** 3999
Ge 11:10 Arphaxad two years after the **f.**: 3999
Jos 24:2 dwelt on the other side of the **f.** 5104
Jos 24:3 from the other side of the **f.**, 5104
Jos 24:14 served on the other side of the **f.**, 5104
Jos 24:15 were on the other side of the **f.**, 5104
Job 14:11 and the **f.** decayeth and drieth up: 5104
Job 22:16 was overflown with a **f.**: 5104
Job 28:4 The **f.** breaketh out from the 5158
Ps 29:10 The Lord sitteth upon the **f.**; yea, 3999
Ps 66:6 they went through the **f.** on foot: 5104
Ps 74:15 cleave the fountain and the **f.**: 5158
Ps 90:5 carriest them away as with a **f.**; 2229
Isa 28:2 **f.** of mighty waters overflowing, 2230
Isa 59:19 the enemy shall come in like a **f.**, 5104
Jer 46:7 Who is this that cometh up as a **f.**, 2975
Jer 46:8 Egypt riseth up like a **f.**, and his 2975
Jer 47:2 and shall be an overflowing **f.**, 5158
Dan 9:26 The end thereof shall be with a **f.**, 7858
Dan 11:22 with the arms of a **f.** shall they be 7858
Am 8:8 and it shall rise up wholly as a **f.**; 2975
Am 8:8 drowned, as by the **f.** of Egypt. 2975
Am 9:5 it shall rise up wholly like a **f.**; 2975
Am 9:5 be drowned, as by the **f.** of Egypt. 2975
Na 1:8 But with an overrunning **f.** he will 7858
Mt 24:38 **f. they were eating and drinking,** *2627*
Mt 24:39 **until the f. came, and took them** *2627*
Lu 6:48 **when the f. arose, the stream beat** *4132*
Lu 17:27 **the f. came, and destroyed them** *2627*
2Pe 2:5 bringing in the **f.** upon the world *2627*
Re 12:15 cast out of his mouth water as a **f.** *4215*
Re 12:15 her to be carried away of the **f.** *4216*
Re 12:16 mouth, and swallowed up the **f.** *4215*

FLOODS

Ex 15:8 the **f.** stood upright as an heap, 5140
2Sa 22:5 **f.** of ungodly men made me afraid; 5158
Job 20:17 He shall not see the rivers, the **f.**, 5104
Job 28:11 bindeth the **f.** from overflowing; 5104
Ps 18:4 **f.** of ungodly men made me afraid. 5158
Ps 24:2 and established it upon the **f.** 5104
Ps 32:6 surely in the **f.** of great waters 7858
Ps 69:2 waters, where the **f.** overflow me. 7641
Ps 78:44 rivers into blood; and their **f.**, 5140
Ps 93:3 The **f.** have lifted up, O Lord, 5104
Ps 93:3 the **f.** have lifted up their voice; 5104
Ps 93:3 the **f.** lift up their waves. 5104
Ps 98:8 the **f.** clap their hands: let the hills 5104
Ca 8:7 neither can the **f.** drown it: if a 5104
Isa 44:3 and **f.** upon the dry ground: 5140
Eze 31:15 **f.** thereof, and the great waters 5104

Jon 2:3 and the **f.** compassed me about: 5104
Mt 7:25, 27 **and the f. came, and the winds.** *4215*

FLOOR See also BARNFLOOR; CORNFLOOR; FLOORS; THRESHING-FLOOR.
Ge 50:11 the mourning in the **f.** of Atad, 1637
Nu 5:17 of the dust that is in the **f.** of the 7172
De 15:14 out of thy flock, and out of thy **f.**, 1637
Jg 6:37 will put a fleece of wool in the **f.**; 1637
Ru 3:3 and get thee down to the **f.**: 1637
Ru 3:6 And she went down unto the **f.**, 1637
Ru 3:14 that a woman came unto the **f.**. 1637
1Ki 6:15 the **f.** of the house, and the walls 7172
1Ki 6:15 covered the **f.** of the house with 7172
1Ki 6:16 the **f.** and the walls with boards 7172
1Ki 6:30 And the **f.** of the house he overlaid 7172
1Ki 7:7 from one side of the **f.** to the other. 7172
2Ch 34:11 to **f.** the houses which the kings 7136
Isa 21:10 threshing, and the corn of my **f.**: 1637
Ho 9:2 The **f.** and the winepress shall 1637
Ho 13:3 with the whirlwind out of the **f.**, 1637
Mic 4:12 them as the sheaves into the **f.** 1637
Mt 3:12 and he will throughly purge his **f.**, *257*
Lu 3:17 and he will throughly purge his **f.**, *257*

FLOORS See also THRESHINGFLOORS.
Joe 2:24 And the **f.** shall be full of wheat, 1637

FLOTES See also FLOATS.
2Ch 2:16 and we will bring it to thee in **f.** by 7513

FLOUR
Ex 29:2 wheaten **f.** shalt thou make them. 5560
Ex 29:40 tenth deal of **f.** mingled with the 5560
Le 2:1 his offering shall be of fine **f.**; 5560
Le 2:2 his handful of the **f.** thereof, 5560
Le 2:4 shall be unleavened cakes of fine **f.** 5560
Le 2:5 it shall be of fine **f.** unleavened, 5560
Le 2:7 it shall be made of fine **f.** with oil. 5560
Le 5:11 the tenth part of an ephah of fine **f.** 5560
Le 6:15 take of it his handful, of the **f.** 5560
Le 6:20 the tenth part of an ephah of fine **f.** 5560
Le 7:12 cakes mingled with oil, of fine **f.**, 5560
Le 14:10 and three tenth deals of fine **f.** 5560
Le 14:21 and one tenth deal of fine **f.** 5560
Le 23:13 shall be two tenth deals of fine **f.** 5560
Le 23:17 tenth deals: they shall be of fine **f.**; 5560
Le 24:5 thou shalt take fine **f.**, and bake 5560
Nu 6:15 cakes of fine **f.** mingled with oil, 5560
Nu 7:13 both of them were full of fine **f.** 5560
Nu 7:19, 25,31,37,43,49,55,61,67,73,79 full of fine **f.** mingled with oil for a 5560
Nu 8:8 even fine **f.** mingled with oil, 5560
Nu 15:4 meat offering of a tenth deal of **f.** 5560
Nu 15:6 offering two tenth deals of **f.** 5560
Nu 15:9 offering of three tenth deals of **f.** 5560
Nu 28:5 an ephah of **f.** for a meat offering, 5560
Nu 28:9 two tenth deals of fine **f.** for a 5560
Nu 28:12 three tenth deals of **f.** for a meat 5560
Nu 28:12 two tenth deals of **f.** for a meat 5560
Nu 28:13 And a several tenth deal of **f.** 5560
Nu 28:20 shall be of **f.** mingled with oil: 5560
Nu 28:28 their meat offering of **f.** mingled 5560
Nu 29:3 shall be of **f.** mingled with oil, 5560
Nu 29:9 shall be of **f.** mingled with oil, 5560
Nu 29:14 shall be of **f.** mingled with oil, 5560
Jg 6:19 cakes of an ephah of **f.**: 7058
1Sa 1:24 bullocks, and one ephah of **f.**, 7058
1Sa 28:24 and took **f.**, and kneaded it, 7058
2Sa 13:8 And she took **f.**, and kneaded it, 1217
2Sa 17:28 wheat, and barley, and **f.**, and 7058
1Ki 4:22 was thirty measures of fine **f.**, 5560
2Ki 7:1 a measure of fine **f.** be sold for a 5560
2Ki 7:16 So a measure of fine **f.** was sold for 5560
2Ki 7:18 a measure of fine **f.** for a shekel, 5560
1Ch 9:29 the fine **f.**, and the wine, and the 5560
1Ch 23:29 for the fine **f.** for meat offering, 5560
Eze 16:13 thou didst eat fine **f.**, and honey, 5560
Eze 16:19 gave thee fine **f.**, and oil, and honey, 5560
Eze 46:14 to temper with the fine **f.**; 5560
Re 18:13 fine **f.**, and wheat, and beasts, *4585*

FLOURISH See also FLOURISHED; FLOURISHETH; FLOURISHING.
Ps 72:7 In his days shall the righteous **f.**; 6524
Ps 72:16 and they of the city shall **f.** like 6692
Ps 92:7 all the workers of iniquity do **f.**; 6692
Ps 92:12 The righteous shall **f.** like the 6524
Ps 92:13 shall **f.** in the courts of our God 6524
Ps 132:18 upon himself shall his crown **f.** 6692
Pr 11:28 the righteous shall **f.** as a branch, 6524
Pr 14:11 tabernacle of the upright shall **f.** 6524
Ec 12:5 and the almond tree shall **f.**, 5006
Ca 7:12 let us see if the vine **f.**, 6524
Isa 17:11 shalt thou make thy seed to **f.**: 6524
Isa 66:14 your bones shall **f.** like an herb: 6524
Eze 17:24 and have made the dry tree to **f.**: 6524

FLOURISHED
Ca 6:11 and to see whether the vine **f.**, 6524
Php 4:10 your care of me hath **f.** again; *330*

FLOURISHETH
Ps 90:6 In the morning it **f.**, and groweth 6692
Ps 103:15 as a flower of the field, so he **f.** 6692

FLOURISHING
Ps 92:14 they shall be fat and **f.**; 7488
Da 4:4 mine house, and **f.** in my palace: 7487

FLOW See also FLOWED; FLOWETH; FLOWING; OVERFLOW.
Job 20:28 his goods shall **f.** away in the day 5064
Ps 147:18 wind to blow, and the waters **f.** 5140
Ca 4:16 that the spices thereof may **f.** out. 5140
Isa 2:2 and all nations shall **f.** unto it. 5102
Isa 48:21 the waters to **f.** out of the rock 5140
Isa 60:5 thou shalt see, and **f.** together, 5102
Isa 64:1 might **f.** down at thy presence, 2151
Jer 31:12 shall **f.** together to the goodness 5102
Jer 51:44 the nations shall not **f.** together 5102
Joe 3:18 the hills shall **f.** with milk, and 3212
Joe 3:18 all the rivers of Judah shall **f.** with 3212
Mic 4:1 and people shall **f.** unto it. 5102
Joh 7:38 **belly shall f. rivers of living water.** *4482*

FLOWED See also OVERFLOWED.
Jos 4:18 and **f.** over all his banks, as they 3212
Isa 64:3 mountains **f.** down at thy presence. 2151
La 3:54 Waters **f.** over mine head; then 6687

FLOWER See also FLOWERS.
Ex 25:33 a knop and a **f.** in one branch; 6525
Ex 25:33 other branch, with a knop and a **f.**: 6525
Ex 37:19 in one branch, a knop and a **f.**; 6525
Ex 37:19 another branch, a knop and a **f.**: 6525
1Sa 2:33 shall die in the **f.** of their age. 582
Job 14:2 He cometh forth like a **f.**, and is cut 6731
Job 15:33 shall cast off his **f.** as the olive. 5328
Ps 103:15 a **f.** of the field, so he flourisheth. 6731
Isa 18:5 sour grape is ripening in the **f.**, 5328
Isa 28:1 glorious beauty is a fading **f.**, 6731
Isa 28:4 shall be a fading **f.**, and as the 6733
Isa 40:6 thereof is as the **f.** of the field: 6731
Isa 40:7 the **f.** fadeth: because the spirit 6731
Isa 40:8 **f.** fadeth: but the word of our God 6731
Na 1:4 the **f.** of Lebanon languisheth. 6525
1Co 7:36 if she pass the **f.** of her age, *5230*
Jas 1:10 because as the **f.** of the grass *438*
Jas 1:11 the grass, and the **f.** thereof falleth, *438*
1Pe 1:24 the glory of man as the **f.** of grass. *438*
1Pe 1:24 and the **f.** thereof falleth away: *438*

FLOWERS
Ex 25:31 his bowls, his knops, and his **f.**, 6525
Ex 25:34 with their knops and their **f.** 6525
Ex 37:17 and his **f.** were of the same: 6525
Ex 37:20 like almonds, his knops, and his **f.**: 6525
Le 15:24 her **f.** be upon him, he shall be 5079
Le 15:33 And of her that is sick of her **f.**, 5079
Nu 8:4 the **f.** thereof, was beaten work: 6525
1Ki 6:18 knops and open **f.**: all was cedar; 6731
1Ki 6:29 palm trees and open **f.**, within and 6731
1Ki 6:32 palm trees and open **f.**, and overlaid 6731
1Ki 6:35 palm trees and open **f.**: and covered 6731
1Ki 7:26 the brim of a cup, with **f.** of lilies: 6525
1Ki 7:49 with the **f.**, and the lamps, and the 6525
2Ch 4:5 brim of a cup, and **f.** of lilies; 6525
2Ch 4:21 And the **f.**, and the lamps, and the 6525
Ca 2:12 The **f.** appear on the earth; 5339
Ca 5:13 as a bed of spices, as sweet **f.**: 4026

FLOWETH See also OVERFLOWETH.
Le 20:24 land that **f.** with milk and honey: 2100
Nu 13:27 surely it **f.** with milk and honey; 2100
Nu 14:8 land which **f.** with milk and honey. 2100
Nu 16:13, 14 that **f.** with milk and honey. 2100
De 6:3 land that **f.** with milk and honey. 2100
De 11:9 land that **f.** with milk and honey. 2100
De 26:9, 15 that **f.** with milk and honey. 2100
De 27:3 land that **f.** with milk and honey; 2100
De 31:20 land that **f.** with milk and honey; 2100
Jos 5:6 land that **f.** with milk and honey. 2100

FLOWING See also OVERFLOWING.
Ex 3:8 a land **f.** with milk and honey; 2100
Ex 3:17 unto a land **f.** with milk and honey. 2100
Ex 13:5 thee, a land **f.** with milk and honey, 2100
Ex 33:3 Unto a land **f.** with milk and 2100
Pr 18:4 wellspring of wisdom as a **f.** brook. 5042
Isa 66:12 the glory of the Gentiles like a **f.** 7857
Jer 11:5 to give them a land **f.** with milk 2100
Jer 18:14 the cold **f.** waters that come from 5140
Jer 32:22 a land **f.** with milk and honey; 2100
Jer 49:4 **f.** valley, O backsliding daughter? 2100
Eze 20:6 **f.** with milk and honey, which is 2100
Eze 20:15 them, **f.** with milk and honey, 2100

FLOWN See OVERFLOWN.

FLUTE
Da 3:5 ye hear the sound of the cornet, **f.**, 4953
Da 3:7 heard the sound of the cornet, **f.**, 4953
Da 3:10 hear the sound of the cornet, **f.**, 4953
Da 3:15 ye hear the sound of the cornet, **f.**, 4953

FLUTTERETH
De 32:11 up her nest, **f.** over her young, 7363

FLUX
Ac 28:8 sick of a fever and of a bloody **f.**: *1420*

FLY See also FLEW; FLIES; FLIETH; FLYING.
Ge 1:20 fowl that may **f.** above the earth 5774
1Sa 15:19 but didst **f.** upon the spoil, and 5860
2Sa 22:11 he rode upon a cherub, and did **f.**: 5774
Job 5:7 trouble, as the sparks **f.** upward. 5774
Job 20:8 He shall **f.** away as a dream, 5774
Job 39:26 Doth the hawk **f.** by thy wisdom, 82
Ps 18:10 rode upon a cherub, and did **f.**: 5774
Ps 18:10 yea, he did **f.** upon the wings 1675
Ps 55:6 would I **f.** away, and be at rest. 5774
Ps 90:10 it is soon cut off, and we **f.** away. 5774
Pr 23:5 they **f.** away as an eagle toward 5774
Isa 6:2 his feet, and with twain he did **f.** 5774
Isa 7:18 shall hiss for the **f.** that is in the 2070
Isa 11:14 they shall **f.** upon the shoulders 5774
Isa 60:8 Who are these that **f.** as a cloud, 5774
Jer 48:40 Behold, he shall **f.** as an eagle, 1675
Jer 49:22 shall come up and **f.** as the eagle, 1675
Eze 13:20 hunt the souls to make them **f.**, 6524
Eze 13:20 souls that ye hunt to make them **f.** 6524
Da 9:21 being caused to **f.** swiftly, touched 3286
Ho 9:11 glory shall **f.** away like a bird 5774
Hab 1:8 shall **f.** as the eagle that hasteth 5774
Re 12:14 she might **f.** into the wilderness, *4072*
Re 14:6 saw another angel **f.** in the midst *4072*
Re 19:17 to all the fowls that **f.** in the midst *4072*

FLYING
Le 11:21 ye eat of every **f.** creeping thing 5775
Le 11:23 But all other **f.** creeping things, 5775
Ps 148:10 creeping things, and **f.** fowl: 3671
Pr 26:2 as the swallow by **f.**, so the curse 5774
Isa 14:29 his fruit shall be a fiery **f.** serpent. 5774
Isa 30:6 the viper and the fiery **f.** serpent, 5774
Isa 31:5 birds **f.**, so will the Lord of hosts 5774
Zec 5:1 and looked, and behold a **f.** roll. 5774
Zec 5:2 And I answered, I see a **f.** roll; 5774
Re 4:7 fourth beast was like a **f.** eagle. *4072*
Re 8:13 **f.** through the midst of heaven, *4072*

FOAL See also FOALS.
Ge 49:11 Binding his **f.** unto the vine, and 5895
Zec 9:9 and upon a colt the **f.** of an ass. 1121
Mt 21:5 and a colt the **f.** of an ass. *5207*

FOALS
Ge 32:15 bulls, twenty she asses, and ten **f.** 5895

FOAM See also FOAMETH; FOAMING.
Ho 10:7 cut off as the **f.** upon the water. 7110

FOAMETH
Mk 9:18 he **f.**, and gnashed with his teeth, *875*
Lu 9:39 and it teareth him that he **f.** again, *876*

FOAMING
Mk 9:20 on the ground, and wallowed **f.** *875*
Jude 13 of the sea, **f.** out their own shame; *1890*

FODDER
Job 6:5 or loweth the ox over his **f.**? 1098

FOES
1Ch 21:12 to be destroyed before thy **f.**, ... 6862
Es 9:16 their **f.** seventy and five thousand,....... 8130
Ps 27:2 even mine enemies and my **f.**, ... 341
Ps 30:1 and hast not made my **f.** to rejoice....... 341
Ps 89:23 beat down his **f.** before his face. 6862
Mt 10:36 **a man's f. shall be they of his**....... *2190*
Ac 2:35 Until I make thy **f.** thy footstool......... *2190*

FOLD See also BLINDFOLD; FOLDEN; FOLDETH; FOLDING; FOLDS; FOURFOLD; HUNDREDFOLD; INFOLDING; MANIFOLD; SEVENFOLD; SHEEPFOLD; SIXTYFOLD; TENFOLD; THIRTYFOLD; THREEFOLD; TWOFOLD.
Isa 13:20 shall the shepherds make their **f.** 7257
Isa 65:10 And Sharon shall be a **f.** of flocks,...... 5116
Eze 34:14 mountains of Israel shall their **f.**......... 5116
Eze 34:14 there shall they lie in a good **f.**, ... 5116
Mic 2:12 the flock in the midst of their **f.**: 1699
Hab 3:17 flock shall be cut off from the **f.**, ... 4356
Joh 10:16 **I have, which are not of this f.**:...... *833*
Joh 10:16 **shall be one f., and one shepherd**. ..*4167*
Heb 1:12 as a vesture shalt thou **f.** them up,..... *1667*

FOLDEN
Na 1:10 they be **f.** together as thorns, ... 5440

FOLDETH
Ec 4:5 The fool **f.** his hands together, ... 2263

FOLDING See also INFOLDING.
1Ki 6:34 two leaves of the one door were **f.**,.... 1550
1Ki 6:34 two leaves of the other door were **f.** ..1550
Pr 6:10 a little **f.** of the hands to sleep:.......... 2264
Pr 24:33 a little **f.** of the hands to sleep:.......... 2264

FOLDS See also SHEEPFOLDS.
Nu 32:24 and **f.** for your sheep; and do that...... 1448
Nu 32:36 fenced cities: and **f.** for sheep. 1448
Ps 50:9 nor he goats out of thy **f.**. 4356
Jer 23:3 will bring them again to their **f.**;......... 5116
Zep 2:6 for shepherds, and **f.** for flocks. 1448

FOLK See also FOLKS; KINSFOLK.
Ge 33:15 now leave with thee some of the **f.** 5971
Pr 30:26 The conies are but a feeble **f.**, ... 5971
Jer 51:58 and the **f.** in the fire, and they........... 3816
Mk 6:5 laid his hands upon a few sick **f.**..............
Joh 5:3 a great multitude of impotent **f.**,..............

FOLKS See also KINSFOLKS.
Ac 5:16 bringing sick **f.**, and them which..............

FOLLOW See also FOLLOWED; FOLLOWETH; FOLLOWING.
Ge 24:5 will not be willing to **f.** me unto.... 3212,310
Ge 24:8 will not be willing to **f.** thee, then. 3212,310
Ge 24:39 the woman will not **f.** me............. 3212,310
Ge 44:4 Up, **f.** after the men; and when 7291
Ex 11:8 and all the people that **f.** thee:.......... 7272
Ex 14:4 that he shall **f.** after them;................ 7291
Ex 14:17 and they shall **f.** them: and................ 310
Ex 21:22 and yet no mischief **f.**: he shall.......... 1961
Ex 21:23 And if any mischief **f.**, then thou.......... 1961
Ex 23:2 not **f.** a multitude to do evil;........ 1961,310
De 16:20 is altogether just shalt thou **f.**,........... 7291
De 18:22 if the thing **f.** not, nor come to.......... 1961
Jg 3:28 he said unto them, **F.** after me:.......... 7291
Jg 8:5 bread unto the people that **f.** me;......... 7272
Jg 9:3 hearts inclined to **f.** Abimelech;....... 935,310
1Sa 25:27 young men that **f.** my lord......... 1980,7272
1Sa 30:21 so faint that they could not **f.**......... 3212,310
2Sa 17:9 among the people that **f.** Absalom. 310
1Ki 18:21 God, **f.** him: but if Baal, then **f.** ... 3212,310
1Ki 19:20 mother, and then I will **f.** thee. 3212,310
1Ki 20:10 for all the people that **f.** me. 7272
2Ki 6:19 **f.** me, and I will bring you 3212,310
Ps 23:6 goodness and mercy shall **f.** me 7291
Ps 38:20 I **f.** the thing that good is. 7291
Ps 45:14 virgins her companions that **f.** her........ 310
Ps 94:15 all the upright in heart shall **f.** it. 310
Ps 119:150 draw nigh that **f.** after mischief: 7291
Isa 5:11 that they may **f.** strong drink; 7291
Isa 51:1 me, ye that **f.** after righteousness, ... 7291
Jer 17:16 from being a pastor to **f.** thee: 310
Jer 42:16 **f.** close after you there in Egypt; 1692
Eze 13:3 foolish prophets, that **f.** their 1980,310
Ho 2:7 And she shall **f.** after her lovers,........ 7291
Ho 6:3 if we **f.** on to know the Lord:.............. 7291
Mt 4:19 he saith unto them, **F. me**, ... *1205,3694*
Mt 8:19 I will **f.** thee whithersoever thou.......... *190*
Mt 8:22 And Jesus said unto him, **F. me**;......... *190*
Mt 9:9 and he saith unto him, **F. me**. *190*
Mt 16:24 **and take up his cross, and f. me**..... *190*
Mt 19:21 **in heaven: and come and f. me**......... *190*
Mk 2:14 and said unto him, **F. me**. And he....... *190*
Mk 5:37 And he suffered no man to **f.** him,...... *4870*
Mk 6:1 country; and his disciples **f.** him. *190*
Mk 8:34 **and take up his cross, and f. me**..... *190*
Mk 10:21 **come, take up the cross, and f. me**. . *190*
Mk 14:13 **bearing a pitcher of water: f. him**. . *190*
Mk 16:17 **And these signs shall f. them that**..*3877*
Lu 5:27 and he said unto him, **F. me**. *190*
Lu 9:23 **take up his cross daily, and f. me**. . *190*
Lu 9:57 I will **f.** thee whithersoever thou.......... *190*
Lu 9:59 And he said unto another, **F. me**......... *190*
Lu 9:61 also said, Lord, I will **f.** thee; *190*
Lu 17:23 **go not after them, nor f. them**...... *1377*
Lu 18:22 **in heaven: and come, f. me**. *190*
Lu 22:10 **f. him into the house where he**....... *190*
Lu 22:49 were about him saw what would **f.**, ... *2071*
Joh 1:43 Philip, and saith unto him, **F. me**. *190*
Joh 10:4 **before them, and the sheep f. him**:. *190*
Joh 10:5 **And a stranger will they not f.**,...... *190*
Joh 10:27 **and I know them, and they f. me**:.. *190*
Joh 12:26 **If any man serve me, let him f. me**;.*190*
Joh 13:36 **not f. me now; but thou shalt f. me**.*190*
Joh 13:37 why cannot I **f.** thee now?................ *190*
Joh 21:19 he saith unto him, **F. me**................ *190*
Joh 21:22 **what is that to thee? f. thou me**. ... *190*
Ac 3:24 Samuel and those that **f.** after, ... *2517*
Ac 12:8 thy garment about thee, and **f.** me......... *190*
Ro 14:19 therefore **f.** after the things which...... *1377*
1Co 14:1 **F.** after charity, and desire............ *1377*
Php 3:12 I **f.** after, if that I may apprehend....... *1377*
1Th 5:15 but ever **f.** that which is good, ... *1377*
2Th 3:7 know how ye ought to **f.** us: *3401*
2Th 3:9 an ensample unto you to **f.** us. *3401*
1Ti 5:24 and some men they **f.** after............... *1872*
1Ti 6:11 **f.** after righteousness, godliness,........ *1377*
2Ti 2:22 **f.** righteousness, faith, charity, ... *1377*
Heb 12:14 **F.** peace with all men, and.............. *1377*
Heb 13:7 whose faith **f.**, considering the........... *3401*
1Pe 1:11 and the glory that should **f.**......... *3326,5023*
1Pe 2:21 example, that ye should **f.** his steps:... *1872*
2Pe 2:2 And many shall **f.** their pernicious....... *1811*
3Jo 11 Beloved, **f.** not that which is evil,....... *3401*
Re 14:4 These are they which **f.** the Lamb....... *190*
Re 14:13 and their works do **f.** them................ *190*

FOLLOWED See also FOLLOWEDST.
Ge 24:61 **f.** the man: and the servant......... 3212,310
Ge 32:19 all that **f.** the droves, saying, ... 1980,310
Nu 14:24 hath **f.** me fully, him will I bring.......... 310
Nu 16:25 and the elders of Israel **f.** him......... 3212,310
Nu 32:11 because they have not wholly **f.** me: 310
Nu 32:12 for they have wholly **f.** the Lord......... 310
De 1:36 because he hath wholly **f.** the Lord. 310
De 4:3 all the men that **f.** Baal-peor, ... 1980,310
Jos 6:8 the covenant of the Lord **f.** them.. 1980,310
Jos 14:8 but I wholly **f.** the Lord my God. 310
Jos 14:9 because thou hast wholly **f.** the Lord.... 310
Jos 14:14 he wholly **f.** the Lord God of Israel, ... 310
Jg 2:12 and **f.** other gods, of the gods...... 3212,310
Jg 9:4 and light persons, which **f.** him..... 3212,310
Jg 9:49 his bough, and **f.** Abimelech,......... 3212,310
1Sa 13:7 and all the people **f.** him trembling. 310
1Sa 14:22 even they also **f.** hard after them....... 1692
1Sa 17:13 and **f.** Saul to the battle;............ 1980,310
1Sa 17:14 and the three eldest **f.** Saul. 1980,310
1Sa 31:2 the Philistines **f.** hard upon Saul......... 1692
2Sa 1:6 chariots and horsemen **f.** hard after 1692
2Sa 2:10 the house of Judah **f.** David......... 1961,310
2Sa 3:31 And king David himself **f.** the....... 1980,310
2Sa 11:8 and there **f.** him a mess of meat.... 3318,310
2Sa 17:23 saw that his counsel was not **f.**, he...... 6213
2Sa 20:2 up from after David, and **f.** Sheba........ 310
1Ki 12:20 none that **f.** the house of David, ... 310
1Ki 14:8 who **f.** me with all his heart.........1980,310
1Ki 16:21 half of the people **f.** Tibni........... 1961,310
1Ki 16:21 make him king; and half **f.** Omri. 310
1Ki 16:22 the people that **f.** Omri prevailed......... 310
1Ki 16:22 against the people that **f.** Tibni............ 310
1Ki 18:18 Lord, and thou hast **f.** Baalim. 3212,310
1Ki 20:19 and the army which **f.** them................ 310
2Ki 3:9 and for the cattle that **f.** them. 7272
2Ki 4:30 And he arose, and **f.** her. 3112,310
2Ki 5:21 So Gehazi **f.** after Naaman................ 7291
2Ki 9:27 And Jehu **f.** after him, and said, ... 7291
2Ki 13:2 and **f.** the sins of Jeroboam the 3212,310
2Ki 17:15 they **f.** vanity, and became vain.... 3212,310
1Ch 10:2 And the Philistines **f.** hard after 1692
Ne 4:23 nor the men of the guard which **f.** 310
Ps 68:25 the players on instruments **f.** after;..........
Eze 10:11 the head looked they **f.** it;........... 3212,310
Am 7:15 the Lord took me as I **f.** the flock, ... 310
Mt 4:20 straightway left their nets, and **f.**......... *190*
Mt 4:22 the ship and their father, and **f.** him. *190*
Mt 4:25 **f.** him great multitudes of people *190*
Mt 8:1 mountain, great multitudes **f.** him,........ *190*
Mt 8:10 and said to them that **f.**, **Verily I say**.. *190*
Mt 8:23 into a ship, his disciples **f.** him. *190*
Mt 9:9 **Follow me.** And he arose, and **f.** *190*
Mt 9:19 And Jesus arose, and **f.** him,............... *190*
Mt 9:27 two blind men **f.** him, crying, and *190*
Mt 12:15 great multitudes **f.** him, and he *190*
Mt 14:13 they **f.** him on foot out of the cities...... *190*
Mt 19:2 great multitudes **f.** him; and he *190*
Mt 19:27 we have forsaken all, and **f.** thee;.......... *190*
Mt 19:28 **That ye which have f. me, in the**.... *190*
Mt 20:29 Jericho, a great multitude **f.** him. *190*
Mt 20:34 received sight, and they **f.** him............. *190*
Mt 21:9 that went before, and that **f.**,............... *190*
Mt 26:58 Peter **f.** him afar off unto the high *190*
Mt 27:55 **f.** Jesus from Galilee, ministering *190*
Mt 27:62 day, that **f.** the day of the *2076,3326*
Mk 1:18 they forsook their nets, and **f.** him......... *190*
Mk 1:36 they that were with him **f.** after......... *2614*
Mk 2:14 **Follow me.** And he arose and **f.** him... *190*
Mk 2:15 there were many, and they **f.** him......... *190*
Mk 3:7 great multitude from Galilee **f.** him,........ *190*
Mk 5:24 with him; and much people **f.** him, ... *190*
Mk 10:28 have left all, and have **f.** thee.............. *190*
Mk 10:32 and as they **f.**, they were afraid. *190*
Mk 10:52 he received his sight, and **f.** Jesus *190*
Mk 11:9 that went before, and they that **f.**,......... *190*
Mk 14:51 there **f.** him a certain young man,........ *190*
Mk 14:54 Peter **f.** him afar off, even into the *190*
Mk 15:41 when he was in Galilee, **f.** him, and *190*
Lu 5:11 they forsook all, and **f.** him................. *190*
Lu 5:28 And he left all, rose up, and **f.** him. *190*
Lu 7:9 and said unto the people that **f.** him, ... *190*
Lu 9:11 people, when they knew it, **f.** him: *190*
Lu 18:28 we have left all, and **f.** thee................ *190*
Lu 18:43 he received his sight, and **f.** him,......... *190*
Lu 22:39 and his disciples also **f.** him. *190*
Lu 22:54 priest's house. And Peter **f.** afar off. *190*
Lu 23:27 And there **f.** him a great company of.... *190*
Lu 23:49 and the women that **f.** him from........... *4870*
Lu 23:55 **f.** after, and beheld the sepulchre,....... *2628*
Joh 1:37 heard him speak, and they **f.** Jesus. *190*
Joh 1:40 which heard John speak, and **f.** him,..... *190*
Joh 6:2 And a great multitude **f.** him,.............. *190*
Joh 11:31 rose up hastily and went out, **f.** her, ... *190*
Joh 18:15 And Simon Peter **f.** Jesus, and so did.... *190*
Ac 12:9 And he went out, and **f.** him;.............. *190*
Ac 13:43 proselytes **f.** Paul and Barnabas:........... *190*
Ac 16:17 same **f.** Paul and us, and cried,........... *2628*
Ac 21:36 the multitude of the people **f.** after,...... *190*
Ro 9:30 which **f.** not after righteousness, ... *1377*
Ro 9:31 Israel, which **f.** after the law of.......... *1377*
1Co 10:4 of that spiritual Rock that **f.** them: *190*
1Ti 5:10 have diligently **f.** every good work...... *1872*
2Pe 1:16 we have not **f.** cunningly devised........ *1811*
Re 6:8 was Death, and Hell **f.** with him. *190*
Re 8:7 there **f.** hail and fire mingled with....... *1096*
Re 14:8 and there **f.** another angel, saying,....... *190*
Re 14:9 And the third angel **f.** them, saying....... *190*
Re 19:14 armies which were in heaven **f.** him *190*

FOLLOWEDST
Ru 3:10 as thou **f.** not young men,........... 3212,310

FOLLOWERS
1Co 4:16 I beseech you, be ye **f.** of me........... *3402*
1Co 11:1 Be ye **f.** of me, even as I also am...... *3402*
Eph 5:1 Be ye therefore **f.** of God,............... *3402*
Php 3:17 be **f.** together of me, and mark.......... *4831*
1Th 1:6 became **f.** of us, and of the Lord,....... *3402*
1Th 2:14 became **f.** of the churches of God....... *3402*
Heb 6:12 but **f.** of them who through faith *3402*
1Pe 3:13 if ye be **f.** of that which is good?......... *3402*

FOLLOWETH
2Ki 11:15 that **f.** her kill with the sword......... 935,310
2Ch 23:14 whoso **f.** her, let him be slain........ 935,310
Ps 63:8 My soul **f.** hard after thee: 1692

Pr 12:11 but he that f. vain persons is void 7291
Pr 15:9 him that f. after righteousness 7291
Pr 21:21 He that f. after righteousness and 7291
Pr 28:19 but he that f. after vain persons 7291
Isa 1:23 loveth gifts, and f. after rewards: 7291
Eze 16:34 none f. thee to commit whoredoms: 310
Ho 12:1 and f. after the east wind: he 7291
Mt 10:38 **and f. after me, is not worthy of** *190*
Mk 9:38 in thy name, and he f. not us: *190*
Mk 9:38 we forbad him, because he f. not *190*
Lu 9:49 we forbad him, because he f. not *190*
Joh 8:12 **he that f. me shall not walk in** *190*

FOLLOWING
Ge 41:31 by reason of that famine f.; 310,3651
De 7:4 will turn away thy son from f. me, 310
De 12:30 thou be not snared by f. them, 310
Jos 22:16 to turn away this day from f. the 310
Jos 22:18 must turn away this day from f. the 310
Jos 22:23 an altar to turn from f. the Lord, 310
Jos 22:29 to turn this day from f. the Lord, 310
Jg 2:19 in f. other gods to serve them, 3212,310
Ru 1:16 or to return from f. after thee:
1Sa 12:14 continue f. the Lord your God: 310
1Sa 12:20 yet turn not aside from f. the Lord, 310
1Sa 14:46 went up from f. the Philistines: 310
1Sa 15:11 for he is turned back from f. me, 310
1Sa 24:1 returned from f. the Philistines, 310
2Sa 2:19 hand nor to the left from f. Abner. 310
2Sa 2:21 would not turn aside from f. of him. 310
2Sa 2:22 Asahel, Turn thee aside from f. me: 310
2Sa 2:26 return from f. their brethren? 310
2Sa 2:27 up every one from f. his brother. 310
2Sa 2:30 And Joab returned from f. Abner; 310
2Sa 7:8 from f. the sheep, to be ruler over 310
1Ki 1:7 and they f. Adonijah helped him 310
1Ki 9:6 if ye shall at all turn from f. me, 310
1Ki 21:26 very abominably in f. idols, 3212,310
2Ki 17:21 drave Israel from f. the Lord, 310
2Ki 18:6 departed not from f. him, but kept 310
1Ch 17:7 sheepcote, even from f. the sheep, 310
2Ch 25:27 did turn away from f. the Lord 310
2Ch 34:33 they departed not from f. the Lord, 310
Ps 48:13 ye may tell it to the generation f. 314
Ps 78:71 From f. the ewes great with young 310
Ps 109:13 in the generation f. let their name 312
Mk 16:20 confirming the word with signs f. *1872*
Lu 13:33 **and tomorrow, and the day f.:** *2192*
Joh 1:38 Jesus turned, and saw them f., *190*
Joh 1:43 The day f. Jesus would go forth *1887*
Joh 6:22 The day f., when the people *1887*
Joh 20:6 Then cometh Simon Peter f. him, *190*
Joh 21:20 the disciple whom Jesus loved f.; *190*
Ac 21:1 and the day f. unto Rhodes, and *1836*
Ac 21:18 the day f. Paul went in with us *1966*
Ac 23:11 And the night f. the Lord stood
2Pe 2:15 f. the way of Balaam the son of *1811*

FOLLY
Ge 34:7 he had wrought f. in Israel 5039
De 22:21 she hath wrought f. in Israel, 5039
Jos 7:15 and because he hath wrought f. 5039
Jg 19:23 come into mine house, do not this f. 5039
Jg 20:6 committed lewdness and f. in 5039
Jg 20:10 f. that they have wrought in Israel. 5039
1Sa 25:25 Nabal is his name, and f. is with 5039
2Sa 13:12 done in Israel: do not thou this f. 5039
Job 4:18 his angels he charged with f.: 8417
Job 24:12 yet God layeth not f. to them 8604
Job 42:8 lest I deal with you after your f., 5039
Ps 49:13 This their way is their f.: 3689
Ps 85:8 but let them not turn again to f. 3690
Pr 5:23 in the greatness of his f. he shall 200
Pr 13:16 but a fool layeth open his f. 200
Pr 14:8 but the f. of fools is deceit 200
Pr 14:18 The simple inherit f.: but the 200
Pr 14:24 but the foolishness of fools is f. 200
Pr 14:29 he that is hasty of spirit exalteth f. 200
Pr 15:21 F. is joy to him that is destitute of 200
Pr 16:22 but the instruction of fools is f. 200
Pr 17:12 rather than a fool in his f. 200
Pr 18:13 matter before he heareth it, it is f. 200
Pr 26:4 Answer not a fool according to his f., 200
Pr 26:5 Answer a fool according to his f., 200
Pr 26:11 so a fool returneth to his f. 200
Ec 1:17 and to know madness and f.: 5531
Ec 2:3 to lay hold on f., till I might see 5531
Ec 2:12 wisdom, and madness, and f.: 5531
Ec 2:13 I saw that wisdom excelleth f., 5531
Ec 7:25 and to know the wickedness of f., 3689
Ec 10:1 so doth a little f. him that is in 5531
Ec 10:6 F. is set in great dignity, and the 5529
Isa 9:17 and every mouth speaketh f. 5039
Jer 23:13 I have seen f. in the prophets 8604
2Co 11:1 bear with me a little in my f.: *877*
2Ti 3:9 their f. shall be manifest unto all *454*

FOOD
Ge 2:9 to the sight, and good for f.; 3978
Ge 3:6 saw that the tree was good for f., 3978
Ge 6:21 unto thee of all f. that is eaten, 3978
Ge 6:21 and it shall be for f. for thee, 402
Ge 41:35 And let them gather all the f. 400
Ge 41:35 and let them keep f. in the cities. 400
Ge 41:36 And that f. shall be for store to the 400
Ge 41:48 And he gathered up all the f. of the 400
Ge 41:48 laid up the f. in the cities: the f. of 400
Ge 42:7 From the land of Canaan to buy f. 400
Ge 42:10 but to buy f. are thy servants come. 400
Ge 42:33 and take f. for the famine of your
Ge 43:2 Go again, buy us a little f. 400
Ge 43:4 we will go down and buy thee f.: 400
Ge 43:20 down at the first time to buy f.: 400
Ge 43:22 down in our hands to buy f.: 400
Ge 44:1 Fill the men's sacks with f., 400
Ge 44:25 Go again, and buy us a little f. 400
Ge 47:24 seed of the field, and for your f. 400
Ge 47:24 and for f. for your little ones. 398
Ex 21:10 her f., her raiment, and her duty 7607
Le 3:11, 16 it is the f. of the offering made 3899
Le 19:23 planted all manner of trees for f., 3978
Le 22:7 holy things; because it is his f. 3899
De 10:18 in giving him f. and raiment 3899
1Sa 14:24 be the man that eateth any f. until 3899
1Sa 14:24 So none of the people tasted any f. 3899
1Sa 14:28 be the man that eateth any f. this 3899
2Sa 9:10 master's son may have f. to eat: 3899
1Ki 5:9 desire, in giving f. for my household. 3899
1Ki 5:11 thousand measures of wheat for f. 4361
Job 23:12 mouth more than my necessary f.
Job 24:5 wilderness yieldeth f. for them 3899
Job 38:41 provideth for the raven his f.? 6718
Job 40:20 the mountains bring him forth f. 944
Ps 78:25 man did eat angels' f. he sent 3899
Ps 104:14 bring forth f. out of the earth; 3899
Ps 136:25 Who giveth f. to all flesh: for his 3899
Ps 146:7 which giveth f. to the hungry. 3899
Ps 147:9 He giveth to the beast his f., 3899
Pr 6:8 gathereth her f. in the harvest 3978
Pr 13:23 Much f. is in the tillage of the poor: 400
Pr 27:27 have goats' milk enough for thy f., 3899
Pr 27:27 for the f. of thy household, and for 3899
Pr 28:3 sweeping rain which leaveth no f. 3899
Pr 30:8 feed me with f. convenient for me: 3899
Pr 31:14 she bringeth her f. from afar. 3899
Eze 16:27 and have diminished thine ordinary f.,
Eze 48:18 f. unto them that serve the city. 3899
Ac 14:17 our hearts with f. and gladness. *5160*
2Co 9:10 both minister bread for your f., *1035*
1Ti 6:8 having f. and raiment let us be *1304*
Jas 2:15 be naked, and destitute of daily f., *5160*

FOOL See also FOOL'S; FOOLS.
1Sa 26:21 behold, I have played the f., and 5528
2Sa 3:33 said, Died Abner as a f. dieth? 5036
Ps 14:1 The f. hath said in his heart, 5036
Ps 49:10 the f. and the brutish person 3684
Ps 53:1 The f. hath said in his heart, 5036
Ps 92:6 neither doth a f. understand this 3684
Pr 7:22 f. to the correction of the stocks; 191
Pr 10:8 commandments: but a prating f. 191
Pr 10:10 sorrow: but a prating f. shall fall. 191
Pr 10:18 he that uttereth a slander, is a f. 3684
Pr 10:23 It is as sport to a f. to do mischief: 3684
Pr 11:29 f. shall be servant to the wise 191
Pr 12:15 of a f. is right in his own eyes: 191
Pr 13:16 but a f. layeth open his folly 3684
Pr 14:16 but the f. rageth, and is confident. 3684
Pr 15:5 f. despiseth his father's instruction: 191
Pr 17:7 speech becometh not a f.: 5036
Pr 17:10 than an hundred stripes into a f. 3684
Pr 17:12 rather than a f. in his folly. 3684
Pr 17:16 in the hand of a f. to get wisdom, 3684
Pr 17:21 He that begetteth a f. doeth it to his 3684
Pr 17:21 and the father of a f. hath no joy. 5036
Pr 17:24 the eyes of a f. are in the ends of 3684
Pr 17:28 a f., when he holdeth his peace, 191
Pr 18:2 A f. hath no delight in 3684
Pr 19:1 is perverse in his lips, and is a f. 3684
Pr 19:10 Delight is not seemly for a f.; 3684
Pr 20:3 but every f. will be meddling. 191
Pr 23:9 Speak not in the ears of a f.: 3684
Pr 24:7 Wisdom is too high for a f.: 191
Pr 26:1 So honour is not seemly for a f. 3684
Pr 26:4 Answer not a f. according to his 3684
Pr 26:5 Answer a f. according to his folly, 3684
Pr 26:6 a message by the hand of a f. 3684
Pr 26:8 so is he that giveth honour to a f. 3684
Pr 26:10 rewardeth the f., and rewardeth 3684
Pr 26:11 so a f. returneth to his folly. 3684
Pr 26:12 is more hope of a f. than of him. 3684
Pr 27:22 Though thou shouldest bray a f. in 191
Pr 28:26 trusteth in his own heart is a f.: 3684
Pr 29:11 A f. uttereth all his mind: 3684
Pr 29:20 is more hope of a f. than of him. 3684
Pr 30:22 a f. when he is filled with meat; 5030
Ec 2:14 but the f. walketh in darkness: 3684
Ec 2:15 As it happeneth to the f., so it 3684
Ec 2:16 of the wise more than of the f. 3684
Ec 2:16 how dieth the wise man? as the f. 3684
Ec 2:19 he shall be a wise man or a f.? 5530
Ec 4:5 The f. foldeth his hands together, 3684
Ec 6:8 hath the wise more than the f.? 3684
Ec 7:6 so is the laughter of the f.: 3684
Ec 10:3 he that is a f. walketh by the way, 5530
Ec 10:3 he saith to every one that he is a f. 5530
Ec 10:12 but the lips of a f. will swallow up 3684
Ec 10:14 A f. also is full of words: 5536
Jer 17:11 and at his end shall be a f. 5030
Ho 9:7 the prophet is a f., the spiritual 191
Mt 5:22 **but whosoever shall say, Thou f.,** *3474*
Lu 12:20 **Thou f., this night thy soul shall** *876*
1Co 3:18 become a f., that he may be wise. *3474*
1Co 15:36 Thou f., that which thou sowest *876*
2Co 11:16 Let no man think me a f.; *876*
2Co 11:16 yet as a f. receive me, *876*
2Co 11:23 (I speak as a f.) I am more; *3912*
2Co 12:6 I shall not be a f.; for I will say *876*
2Co 12:11 I am become a f. in glorying; *876*

FOOLISH
De 32:6 O f. people and unwise? is not he 5036
De 32:21 them to anger with a f. nation. 5036
Job 2:10 speakest as one of the f. women 5039
Job 5:2 For wrath killeth the f. man, 191
Job 5:3 I have seen the f. taking root: 191
Ps 5:5 The f. shall not stand in thy 1984
Ps 39:8 me not the reproach of the f. 5036
Ps 73:3 For I was envious at the f., 1984
Ps 73:22 So f. was I, and ignorant: I was 1198
Ps 74:18 the f. people have blasphemed 5036
Ps 74:22 the f. man reproacheth thee daily. 5036
Pr 9:6 Forsake the f., and live; and go 6612
Pr 9:13 A f. woman is clamorous: she is 3687
Pr 10:1 a f. son is the heaviness of his 3684
Pr 10:14 mouth of the f. is near destruction. 191
Pr 14:1 but the f. plucketh it down with 200
Pr 14:3 In the mouth of the f. is a rod of 191
Pr 14:7 Go from the presence of a f. man, 3684
Pr 15:7 but the heart of the f. doeth not so. 3684
Pr 15:20 but a f. man despiseth his mother. 3684
Pr 17:25 A f. son is grief to his father, 3684
Pr 19:13 A f. son is the calamity of his 3684
Pr 21:20 but a f. man spendeth it up 3684
Pr 29:9 wise man contendeth with a f. man, 191
Ec 4:13 an old and f. king, who will no 3684
Ec 7:17 neither be thou f.: why shouldest 5530
Ec 10:15 The labour of the f. wearieth 3684
Isa 44:25 and maketh their knowledge f.; 5528
Jer 4:22 For my people is f., they have not 191
Jer 5:4 they are f.: for they know not 2973
Jer 5:21 Hear now this, O f. people, 5530
Jer 10:8 they are altogether brutish and f.: 3688
La 2:14 seen vain and f. things for thee; 8602
Eze 13:3 Woe unto the f. prophets, that 5036
Zec 11:15 the instruments of a f. shepherd 196
Mt 7:26 **shall be likened unto a f. man,** *3474*
Mt 25:2 **them were wise, and five were f.** *3474*
Mt 25:3 **They that were f. took their lamps,** *3474*
Mt 25:8 **And the f. said unto the wise,** *3474*
Ro 1:21 and their f. heart was darkened *801*

Ro 2:20 An instructor of the f., a teacher........ *878*
Ro 10:19 by a f. nation I will anger you............ *801*
1Co 1:20 hath not God made f. the wisdom *3471*
1Co 1:27 God hath chosen the f. things of........ *3474*
Gal 3:1 O f. Galatians, who hath bewitched...... *453*
Gal 3:3 Are ye so f.? having begun in the........ *453*
Eph 5:4 nor f. talking, nor jesting,................. *3473*
1Ti 6:9 into many f. and hurtful lusts, ... *453*
2Ti 2:23 f. and unlearned questions avoid,........ *3474*
Tit 3:3 ourselves also were sometimes f., ... *453*
Tit 3:9 f. questions, and genealogies, ... *3474*
1Pe 2:15 to silence the ignorance of f. men: *878*

FOOLISHLY

Ge 31:28 thou hast now done f. in so doing. 5528
Nu 12:11 wherein we have done f., and 2973
1Sa 13:13 Thou hast done f.: thou hast not........ 5528
2Sa 24:10 servant; for I have done very f........... 5528
1Ch 21:8 thy servant; for I have done very f..... 5528
2Ch 16:9 Herein thou hast done f.: 5528
Job 1:22 sinned not, nor charged God f.. 8604
Ps 75:4 Deal not f.: and to the wicked, ... 1984
Pr 14:17 He that is soon angry dealeth f.: 200
Pr 30:32 If thou hast done f. in lifting up 5034
2Co 11:17 but as it were f., in this *1722,877*
2Co 11:21 (I speak f.,) I am bold also......... *1722,877*

FOOLISHNESS

2Sa 15:31 the counsel of Ahithophel into f.. 5528
Ps 38:5 and are corrupt because of my f.. 200
Ps 69:5 O God, thou knowest my f.; 200
Pr 12:23 the heart of fools proclaimeth f........... 200
Pr 14:24 but the f. of fools is folly. 200
Pr 15:2 mouth of fools poureth out f.. 200
Pr 15:14 the mouth of fools feedeth on f.. 200
Pr 19:3 The f. of man perverteth his way: 200
Pr 22:15 F. is bound in the heart of a child;....... 200
Pr 24:9 The thought of f. is sin:..................... 200
Pr 27:22 yet will not his f. depart from him. 200
Ec 7:25 of folly, even of f. and madness: 5531
Ec 10:13 of the words of his mouth is f.: 5531
Mk 7:22 **an evil eye, blasphemy, pride, f.:** *877*
1Co 1:18 the cross is to them that perish, f.;.... *3472*
1Co 1:21 the f. of preaching to save them *3472*
1Co 1:23 and unto the Greeks f.;..................... *3472*
1Co 1:25 the f. of God is wiser than men; *3474*
1Co 2:14 for they are f. unto him; *3472*
1Co 3:19 wisdom of this world is f. with God. ... *3472*

FOOL'S

Pr 12:16 A f. wrath is presently known: but....... 191
Pr 18:6 A f. lips enter into contention,.......... 3684
Pr 18:7 A f. mouth is his destruction, ... 3684
Pr 26:3 the ass, and a rod for the f. back....... 3684
Pr 27:3 a f. wrath is heavier than them 191
Ec 5:3 a f. voice is known by multitude 3684
Ec 10:2 but a f. heart at his left................... 3684

FOOLS

2Sa 13:13 shalt be as one of the f. in Israel. 5036
Job 12:17 and maketh the judges f.. 1984
Job 30:8 They were children of f., yea, ... 5036
Ps 75:4 I said unto the f., Deal not 1984
Ps 94:8 and ye f., when will ye be wise? 3684
Ps 107:17 F., because of their transgression, ... 191
Pr 1:7 f. despise wisdom and instruction......... 191
Pr 1:22 and f. hate knowledge? 3684
Pr 1:32 prosperity of f. shall destroy them....... 3684
Pr 3:35 shame shall be the promotion of f........ 3684
Pr 8:5 ye f., be ye of an understanding 3684
Pr 10:21 but f. die for want of wisdom............. 191
Pr 12:23 but the heart of f. proclaimeth........... 3684
Pr 13:19 it is abomination to f. to depart........... 3684
Pr 13:20 companion of f. shall be destroyed...... 3684
Pr 14:8 but the folly of f. is deceit. 3684
Pr 14:9 F. make a mock at sin: but 191
Pr 14:24 but the foolishness of f. is folly. 3684
Pr 14:33 that which is in the midst of f............ 3684
Pr 15:2 mouth of f. poureth out foolishness..... 3684
Pr 15:14 mouth of f. feedeth on foolishness..... 3684
Pr 16:22 but the instruction of f. is folly. 191
Pr 19:29 and stripes for the back of f.............. 3684
Pr 26:7, 9 is a parable in the mouth of f.......... 3684
Ec 5:1 than to give the sacrifice of f.:........... 3684
Ec 5:4 for he hath no pleasure in f.:............ 3684
Ec 7:4 but the heart of f. is in the house of... 3684
Ec 7:5 for a man to hear the song of f.......... 3684
Ec 7:9 for anger resteth in the bosom of f..... 3684
Ec 9:17 the cry of him that ruleth among f...... 3684
Isa 19:11 Surely the princes of Zoan are f., ... 191
Isa 19:13 The princes of Zoan are become f., ... 2973
Isa 35:8 wayfaring men, though f., shall not 191
Mt 23:17 **Ye f. and blind: for whether is**...... *3474*
Mt 23:19 **Ye f. and blind: for whether is**...... *3474*
Lu 11:40 **Ye f., did not he that made that**..... *878*
Lu 24:25 **O f., and slow of heart to believe**.... *453*
Ro 1:22 to be wise, they became f., ... *3471*
1Co 4:10 We are f. for Christ's sake, but ye..... *3474*
2Co 11:19 For ye suffer f. gladly, seeing ye *3878*
Eph 5:15 circumspectly, not as f., but as *781*

FOOT See also AFOOT; BAREFOOT; BROKENFOOTED; CLOVENFOOTED; FEET; FOOTMEN; FOOTSTEPS; FOOTSTOOL; FOURFOOTED.

Ge 8:9 found no rest for the sole of her f., ... 7272
Ge 41:44 shall no man lift up his hand or f........ 7272
Ex 12:37 about six hundred thousand on f.......... 7273
Ex 21:24 for tooth, hand for hand, f. for f., ... 7272
Ex 29:20 upon the great toe of their right f., ... 7272
Ex 30:18 a laver of brass, and his f. also.......... 3653
Ex 30:28 vessels, and the laver and his f.......... 3653
Ex 31:9 furniture, and the laver and his f., ... 3653
Ex 35:16 his vessels, the laver and his f., ... 3653
Ex 38:8 the laver of brass, and the f. of it 3653
Ex 39:39 his vessels, the laver and his f., ... 3653
Ex 40:11 laver and his f., and sanctify it........... 3653
Le 8:11 laver and his f., to sanctify them........ 3653
Le 8:23 upon the great toe of his right f.. 7272
Le 13:12 from his head even to his f., ... 7272
Le 14:14 upon the great toe of his right f.......... 7272
Le 14:17 upon the great toe of his right f., ... 7272
Le 14:25 upon the great toe of his right f.......... 7272
Le 14:28 upon the great toe of his right f., ... 7272
Nu 22:25 crushed Balaam's f. against the.......... 7272
De 2:5 no, not so much a a f. breadth; 7272
De 8:4 did thy f. swell, these forty years. 7272
De 11:10 wateredst it with thy f., as a garden... 7272
De 19:21 for tooth, hand for hand, f. for f., ... 7272
De 25:9 and loose his shoe from off his f., ... 7272
De 28:35 from the sole of thy f. unto the top..... 7272
De 28:56 the sole of her f. upon the ground...... 7272
De 28:65 shall the sole of thy f. have rest: 7272
De 29:5 shoe is not waxen old upon thy f.. 7272
De 32:35 their f. shall slide in due time: 7272
De 33:24 and let him dip his f. in oil. 7272
Jos 1:3 the sole of your f. shall tread upon, ... 7272
Jos 5:15 Loose thy shoe from off thy f.;........... 7272
Jg 5:15 he was sent on f. into the valley. 7272
2Sa 2:18 was as light of f. as a wild roe............ 7272
2Sa 14:25 the sole of his f. even to the crown.... 7272
2Sa 21:20 and on every f. six toes, four and 7272
2Ki 9:33 the horses: and he trode her under f. ....
1Ch 20:6 on each hand, and six on each f. ....
2Ch 33:8 any more remove the f. of Israel 7272
Job 2:7 the sole of his f. unto his crown. 7272
Job 23:11 My f. hath held his steps, his way...... 7272
Job 28:4 the waters forgotten of the f............. 7272
Job 31:5 if my f. hath hasted to deceit; 7272
Job 39:15 forgetteth that the f. may crush.......... 7272
Ps 9:15 which they hid is their own f. taken.... 7272
Ps 26:12 My f. standeth in an even place: 7272
Ps 36:11 Let not the f. of pride come against.... 7272
Ps 38:16 when my f. slippeth, they magnify...... 7272
Ps 66:6 they went through the flood on f........ 7272
Ps 68:23 thy f. may be dipped in the blood of ... 7272
Ps 91:12 thou dash thy f. against a stone. 7272
Ps 94:18 I said, My f. slippeth; thy mercy, ... 7272
Ps 121:3 will not suffer thy f. to be moved:....... 7272
Pr 1:15 refrain thy f. from their path: 7272
Pr 3:23 and thy f. shall not stumble................ 7272
Pr 3:26 shall keep thy f. from being taken. 7272
Pr 4:27 to the left: remove thy f. from evil. 7272
Pr 25:17 thy f. from thy neighbour's house;...... 7272
Pr 25:19 broken tooth, and a f. out of joint. 7272
Ec 5:1 Keep thy f. when thou goest to the.... 7272
Isa 1:6 From the sole of the f. even unto 7272
Isa 14:25 my mountains tread him under f. 947
Isa 18:7 meted out and trodden under f., ... 4001
Isa 20:2 and put off thy shoe from thy f. 7272
Isa 26:6 The f. shall tread it down, even the.... 7272
Isa 41:2 from the east, called him to his f., ... 7272
Isa 58:13 turn away thy f. from the sabbath, ... 7272
Jer 2:25 Withhold thy f. from being unshod, ... 7272
Jer 12:10 have trodden my portion under f., ... 947
La 1:15 Lord hath trodden under f. all 5541
Eze 1:7 was like the sole of a calf's f.: 7272
Eze 6:11 and stamp with thy f., and say, ... 7272
Eze 29:11 No f. of man shall pass through it, ... 7272
Eze 29:11 nor f. of beast shall pass through it, ... 7272
Eze 32:13 shall the f. of man trouble them......... 7272
Da 8:13 the host to be trodden under f.? 4823
Am 2:15 that is swift of f. shall not deliver....... 7272
Mt 4:6 lest at any time thou dash thy f. *4228*
Mt 5:13 **and to be trodden under f. of men.** .*2662*
Mt 14:13 followed him on f. out of the cities. *3979*
Mt 18:8 **if thy hand or thy f. offend thee,** .. *4228*
Mt 22:13 **Bind him hand and f., and take**.... *4228*
Mk 9:45 **if thy f. offend thee, cut it off:** *4228*
Lu 4:11 thou dash thy f. against a stone. *4228*
Joh 11:44 hand and f. with graveclothes:........... *4228*
Ac 7:5 not so much as to set his f. on: *4228*
1Co 12:15 If the f. shall say, Because I am not ... *4228*
Heb 10:29 trodden under f. the Son of God, ... *2662*
Re 1:13 with a garment down to the f., ... *4158*
Re 10:2 and he set his right f. upon the *4228*
Re 10:2 seas, and his left f. on the earth, ...
Re 11:2 the holy city shall they tread under f.........

FOOT-BREADTH See FOOT and BREADTH.

FOOTMEN

Nu 11:21 are six hundred thousand f.; and........ 7273
Jg 20:2 thousand f. that drew sword........ 376,7273
1Sa 4:10 fell of Israel thirty thousand f.. 7273
1Sa 15:4 two hundred thousand f., and ten....... 7273
1Sa 22:17 king said unto the f. that stood........... 7323
2Sa 8:4 and twenty thousand f.: and 376,7273
2Sa 10:6 twenty thousand f., and of king........... 7273
1Ki 20:29 hundred thousand f. in one day........... 7273
2Ki 13:7 and ten thousand f.; for the king......... 7273
1Ch 18:4 and twenty thousand f.:.............. 376,7273
1Ch 19:18 forty thousand f., and killed......... 376,7273
Jer 12:5 If thou hast run with the f., ... 7273

FOOTSTEPS

Ps 17:5 in thy paths, that my f. slip not. 6471
Ps 77:19 and thy f. are not known.................. 6119
Ps 89:51 reproached the f. of thine anointed. 6119
Ca 1:8 thy way forth by the f. of the flock,.... 6119

FOOTSTOOL

1Ch 28:2 and for the f. of our God,.......... 1916,7272
2Ch 9:18 to the throne with a f. of gold, ... 3534
Ps 99:5 and worship at his f.; for he....... 1916,7272
Ps 110:1 I make thine enemies thy f.. 1916,7272
Ps 132:7 we will worship at his f............ 1916,7272
Isa 66:1 and the earth is my f.: where..... 1916,7272
La 2:1 remembered not his f. in the...... 1916,7272
Mt 5:35 **earth; for it is his f.:**...... *5286,3588,4228*
Mt 22:44 **thine enemies thy f.?**....... *5286,3588,4228*
Mk 12:36 **thine enemies thy f.** *5286,3588,4228*
Lu 20:43 **thine enemies thy f..** *5286,3588,4228*
Ac 2:35 make thy foes thy f........... *5286,3588,4228*
Ac 7:49 and earth is my f.:........... *5286,3588,4228*
Heb 1:13 thine enemies thy f.? *5286,3588,4228*
Heb 10:13 enemies be made his f. *5286,3588,4228*
Jas 2:3 or sit here under my f.: *5286*

FOR See in the APPENDIX; also FORASMUCH; FORBEAR; FORBID; FORGET; FORGIVE; FORSAKE; FORSOMUCH; FORSWEAR.

FORASMUCH See also FORSOMUCH.

Ge 41:39 F. as God hath shewed thee all........... 310
Nu 10:31 f. as thou knowest how...... 3588,5921,3651
De 12:12 f. as he hath no part nor.................. 3588
De 17:16 f. as the Lord hath said unto you, Ye........
Jos 17:14 f. as the Lord hath blessed me.......... 5704
Jg 11:36 f. as the Lord hath taken........... 310,834
1Sa 20:42 f. as we have sworn both of us in the.......
1Sa 24:18 f. as when the Lord had.............. 854,834
2Sa 19:30 f. as my lord the king is come....... 310,834
1Ki 11:11 unto Solomon, F. as this is done .. 3282,834
1Ki 13:21 F. as thou hast disobeyed the 3282,834
1Ki 14:7 F. as I exalted thee from among .. 3282,834
1Ki 16:2 F. as I exalted thee out of the..... 3282,834
2Ki 1:16 F. as thou hast sent messengers .. 3282,834
1Ch 5:1 f. as he defiled his father's bed, ...
2Ch 6:8 F. as it was in thine heart to...................
Ezr 7:14 F. as thou art sent of........ 3606,6903,1768
Isa 8:6 F. as this people refuseth the...... 3282,365
Isa 29:13 F. as this people draw near me.... 3282,365
Jer 10:6 F. as there is none like unto thee, ...
Jer 10:7 f. as among all the wise men of the ....
Da 2:40 f. as iron breaketh in......... 3606,6903,1768
Da 2:41 f. as thou sawest the iron... 3606,6903,1768

Da 2:45 **F.** as thou sawest that....... 3606,6903,1768
Da 4:18 **f.** as all the wise men of 3606,6903,1768
Da 5:12 **F.** as an excellent spirit, ... 3606,6903,1768
Da 6:4 **f.** as he was faithful,......... 3606,6903,1768
Da 6:22 **f.** as before him...was........ 3606,6903,1768
Am 5:11 **F.** therefore as your treading is......... 3282
Mt 18:25 **But f. as he had not to pay,**................
Lu 1:1 **F.** as many have taken in hand.......... *1895*
Ac 9:38 And **f.** as Lydda was nigh to *5607*
Ac 11:17 **F.** then as God gave them the.......... *1487*
Ac 15:24 **F.** as we have heard, that certain....... *1894*
Ac 17:29 **F.** then as we are the offspring of...........
Ac 24:10 **F.** as I know that thou hast been of.........
1Co 11:7 **f.** as he is the image and glory of God: .....
1Co 14:12 **f.** as ye are zealous of spiritual *1893*
1Co 15:58 **f.** as ye know that your labour is not in.....
2Co 3:3 **F.** as ye are manifestly declared..............
Heb 2:14 **F.** then as the children are *1893*
1Pe 1:18 **F.** as ye know that ye were not..............
1Pe 4:1 **F.** then as Christ hath suffered for us ....

FORBAD
De 2:37 the Lord our God **f.** us. 6680
Mt 3:14 John **f.** him, saying, I have need *1254*
Mk 9:38 we **f.** him, because he followeth......... *2967*
Lu 9:49 we **f.** him, becaue he followeth.......... *2967*
2Pe 2:16 **f.** the madness of the prophet. *2967*

FORBARE
1Sa 23:13 and he **f.** to go forth....................... 2308
2Ch 25:16 Then the prophet **f.**, and said, I......... 2308
Jer 41:8 So he **f.**, and slew them not among 2308

FORBEAR See also FORBARE; FORBEARETH; FORBEARING; FORBORN.
Ex 23:5 and wouldest **f.** to help him,............. 2308
De 23:22 But if thou shalt **f.** to vow, ... 2308
1Ki 22:6 battle, or shall I **f.**? And they said, ... 2308
1Ki 22:15 or shall we **f.**? And he answered........ 2308
2Ch 18:5 or shall I **f.**? And they said, ... 2308
2Ch 18:14 to battle, or shall I **f.**? And he said, ... 2308
2Ch 25:16 **f.**; why shouldest thou be smitten? 2308
2Ch 35:21 **f.** thee from meddling with God, ... 2308
Ne 9:30 many years didst thou **f.** them, ... 4900
Job 16:6 and though I **f.**, what am I eased? 2308
Pr 24:11 If thou **f.** to deliver them that are 2820
Jer 40:4 to come with me into Babylon, **f.**: 2308
Eze 2:5 will hear, or whether they will **f.**,....... 2308
Eze 2:7 will hear, or whether they will **f.**:........ 2308
Eze 3:11 will hear, or whether they will **f.**........ 2308
Eze 3:27 he that forbeareth, let him **f.**:............ 2308
Eze 24:17 **F.** to cry, make no mourning 1826
Zec 11:12 and if not, **f.**. So they weighed 2308
1Co 9:6 have not we power to **f.** working?...... *3361*
2Co 12:6 I **f.**, lest any man should think of *5339*
1Th 3:1 when we could no longer **f.**, we......... *4722*
1Th 3:5 when I could no longer **f.**, I went....... *4722*

FORBEARANCE
Ro 2:4 the riches of his goodness and **f.** *463*
Ro 3:25 that are past, through the **f.** of God; *463*

FORBEARETH
Nu 9:13 and **f.** to keep the passover, even...... 2308
Eze 3:27 and he that **f.**, let him forbear: 2310

FORBEARING
Pr 25:15 by long **f.** is a prince persuaded,.......... 639
Jer 20:9 I was weary with **f.**, and I could 3557
Eph 4:2 **f.** one another in love;........................ *430*
Eph 6:9 things unto them, **f.** threatening: *447*
Col 3:13 **F.** one another, and forgiving one........ *430*

FORBID See also FORBAD; FORBIDDEN; FORBIDDETH; FORBIDDING.
Ge 44:7 God **f.** that thy servants should.......... 2486
Ge 44:17 God **f.** that I should do so: 2486
Nu 11:28 said, My lord Moses, **f.** them............. 3607
Jos 22:29 God **f.** that we should rebel 2486
Jos 24:16 God **f.** that we should forsake the 2486
1Sa 12:23 God **f.** that I should sin against......... 2486
1Sa 14:45 God **f.**: as the Lord liveth,................ 2486
1Sa 20:2 And he said unto him, God **f.**; 2486
1Sa 24:6 he said unto his men, The Lord **f.**...... 2486
1Sa 26:11 The Lord **f.** that I should stretch 2486
1Ki 21:3 The Lord **f.** it me, that I should......... 2486
1Ch 11:19 And said, My God **f.** it me,................ 2486
Job 27:5 God **f.** that I should justify you: 2486
Mt 19:14 **and f. them not, to come unto me:** .*2967*
Mk 9:39 But Jesus said, **F. him not:** *2967*
Mk 10:14 **to come unto me, and f. them not:** .*2967*
Lu 6:29 **f. not to take thy coat also.** *2967*
Lu 9:50 **F. him not: for he that is not** *2967*
Lu 18:16 **and f. them not: for of such is the** .*2967*
Lu 20:16 heard it, they said, God **f.**. *3361,1096*
Ac 10:47 Can any man **f.** water, that these....... *2967*
Ac 24:23 and that he should **f.** none of his........ *2967*
Ro 3:4 God **f.**: let God be true, but *3361,1096*
Ro 3:6 God **f.**; for then how shall God... *3361,1096*
Ro 3:31 God **f.**: yea, we establish the *3361,1096*
Ro 6:2 God **f.**. How shall we, that are ... *3361,1096*
Ro 6:15 law, but under grace? God **f.**...... *3361,1096*
Ro 7:7 Is the law sin? God **f.**. Nay, I *3361,1096*
Ro 7:13 made death unto me? God **f.**. *3361,1096*
Ro 9:14 unrighteousness...God? God **f.**.... *3361,1096*
Ro 11:1 cast away his people? God **f.**..... *3361,1096*
Ro 11:11 that they should fall? God **f.**: *3361,1096*
1Co 6:15 members of an harlot? God **f.**..... *3361,1096*
1Co 14:39 and **f.** not to speak with tongues. *2967*
Ga 2:17 the ministers of sin? God **f.** *3361,1096*
Ga 3:21 the promises of God? God **f.**: *3361,1096*
Ga 6:14 God **f.** that I should glory, ... *3361,1096*

FORBIDDEN
Le 5:17 things which are **f.** to be done by....... 3808
De 4:23 the Lord thy God hath **f.** thee. 6680
Ac 16:6 **f.** of the Holy Ghost to preach........... *2967*

FORBIDDETH
3Jo 10 **f.** them that would, and casteth *2967*

FORBIDDING
Lu 23:2 **f.** to give tribute to Caesar, saying..... *2967*
Ac 28:31 all confidence, no man **f.** him. *209*
1Th 2:16 **F.** us to speak to the Gentiles........... *2967*
1Ti 4:3 **F.** to marry, and commanding to........ *2967*

FORBORE See FORBARE.

FORBORN
Jer 51:30 men of Babylon have **f.** to fight,......... 2308

FORBORNE See FORBORN.

FORCE See also FORCED; FORCES; FORCIBLE; FORCING.
Ge 31:31 wouldest take by **f.** thy daughters 1497
De 22:25 the man **f.** her, and lie with her: 2388
De 34:7 not dim, nor his natural **f.** abated. 3893
1Sa 2:16 and if not, I will take it by **f.**............ 2394
2Sa 13:12 Nay, my brother, do not **f.** me; 6031
Ezr 4:23 them to cease by **f.** and power............ 153
Es 7:8 he **f.** the queen also before me.......... 3533
Job 30:18 By the great **f.** of my disease............ 3581
Job 40:16 and his **f.** is in the navel of his............ 202
Jer 18:21 their blood by the **f.** of the sword 3027
Jer 23:10 is evil, and their **f.** is not right.......... 1369
Jer 48:45 of Heshbon because of the **f.**:........... 3581
Eze 34:4 but with **f.** and with cruelty have........ 2394
Eze 35:5 by the **f.** of the sword in the time 3027
Am 2:14 strong shall not strengthen his **f.**,....... 3581
Mt 11:12 **and the violent take it by f.**............ *726*
Joh 6:15 take him by **f.**, to make him a king *726*
Ac 23:10 to take him by **f.** from among them,..... *726*
Heb 9:17 a testament is of **f.** after men are *949*

FORCED
Jg 1:34 Amorites **f.** the children of Dan.......... 3905
Jg 20:5 have they **f.**, that she is dead........... 6031
1Sa 13:12 I **f.** myself therefore, and offered a 662
2Sa 13:14 than she, **f.** her, and lay with her....... 6031
2Sa 13:22 because he had **f.** his sister.............. 6031
2Sa 13:32 from the day that he **f.** his sister 6031
Pr 7:21 the flattering of her lips she **f.** him. 5080

FORCES
2Ch 17:2 he placed **f.** in all the fenced cities...... 2428
Job 36:19 nor all the **f.** of strength.................. 3981
Isa 60:5 the **f.** of the Gentiles shall come 2428
Isa 60:11 unto thee the **f.** of the Gentiles, ... 2428
Jer 40:7 when all the captains of the **f.** which... 2428
Jer 40:13 and all the captains of the **f.** that........ 2428
Jer 41:11, 13,16 the **f.** that were with him, ... 2428
Jer 42:1 Then all the captains of the **f.**, and..... 2428
Jer 42:8 the **f.** which were with him, and all..... 2428
Jer 43:4 captains of the **f.**, and all the people, .. 2428
Jer 43:5 all the captains of the **f.**, took all........ 2428
Da 11:10 assemble a multitude of great **f.**: 2428
Da 11:38 shall he honour the God of **f.**:............ 4581
Ob 11 carried away captive his **f.**, and.......... 2428

FORCIBLE
Job 6:25 How **f.** are right words! but what....... 4834

FORCING
De 20:19 destroy the trees thereof by **f.** an...... 5080
Pr 30:33 **f.** of wrath bringeth forth strife.......... 4330

FORD See also FORDS.
Ge 32:22 and passed over the **f.** Jabbok. 4569

FORDS
Jos 2:7 the way to Jordan unto the **f.**: 4569
Jg 3:28 the **f.** of Jordan toward Moab, ... 4569
Isa 16:2 Moab shall be at the **f.** of Arnon. 4569

FORE See AFORE; BEFORE; FORECAST; FOREFATHERS; FOREFRONT; FOREHEAD; FOREKNOW; FOREKNOWLEDGE; FOREMEN; FOREMOST; FOREPART; FOREORDAINED; FORERUNNER; FORSAW; FORESEETH; FORESEEING; FORESHIP; FORESKIN; FORETELL; FORWARD; FOREWARN; HERETOFORE; THERETOFORE; WHEREFORE.

FORECAST
Da 11:24 **f.** his devices against the strong......... 2803
Da 11:25 they shall **f.** devices against him......... 2803

FOREFATHERS
Jer 11:10 back to the iniquities of their **f.**, ... 1,7223
2Ti 1:3 whom I serve from my **f.** with pure.... *4269*

FOREFRONT
Ex 26:9 in the **f.** of the tabernacle..........4136,6440
Ex 28:37 upon the **f.** of the mitre it shall... 4136,6440
Le 8:9 upon his **f.**, did he put the......... 4136,6440
1Sa 14:5 The **f.** of the one was situate 8127
2Sa 11:15 in the **f.** of the hottest battle,...... 4136,6440
2Ki 16:14 the **f.** of the house, from between...... 6440
2Ch 20:27 Jehoshaphat in the **f.** of them, ... 7218
Eze 40:19 from the **f.** of the lower gate unto...... 6440
Eze 40:19 the **f.** of the inner court without......... 6440
Eze 47:1 **f.** of the house stood toward the........ 6440

FOREHEAD See also FOREHEADS.
Ex 28:38 And it shall be upon Aaron's **f.**, ... 4696
Ex 28:38 and it shall be always upon his **f.**,....... 4696
Le 13:41 he is **f.** bald: yet is he clean............. 1371
Le 13:42 or bald **f.**, a white reddish sore;......... 1372
Le 13:42 in his bald head, or his bald **f.**. 1372
Le 13:43 or in his bald **f.**, as the leprosy.......... 1372
1Sa 17:49 and smote the Philistine in his **f.**,....... 4696
1Sa 17:49 that the stone sunk into his **f.**; 4696
2Ch 26:19 the leprosy even rose up in his **f.**....... 4696
2Ch 26:20 behold, he was leprous in his **f.**, ... 4696
Jer 3:3 and thou hadst a whore's **f.**,.............. 4696
Eze 3:8 **f.** strong against their foreheads......... 4696
Eze 3:9 harder than flint have I made thy **f.** ... 4696
Eze 16:12 And I put jewel on thy **f.**, ... 639
Re 14:9 and receive his mark in his **f.**, ... *3359*
Re 17:5 upon her **f.** was a name written, ... *3359*

FOREHEADS
Eze 3:8 forehead strong against their **f.**. 4696
Eze 9:4 set a mark upon the **f.** of the men...... 4696
Re 7:3 servants of our God in their **f.**........... *3359*
Re 9:4 have not the seal of God in their **f.**...... *3359*
Re 13:16 in their right hand, or in their **f.**:........ *3359*
Re 14:1 Father's name written in their **f.**. *3359*
Re 20:4 received his mark upon their **f.**, ... *3359*
Re 22:4 and his name shall be in their **f.**. *3359*

FOREIGNER See also FOREIGNERS.
Ex 12:45 A **f.** and an hired servant shall........... 8453
De 15:3 Of a **f.** thou mayest exact it again: 5237

FOREIGNERS
Ob 11 and **f.** entered into his gates, and....... 5237
Eph 2:19 ye are no more strangers and **f.**, ... *3941*

FOREKNEW
Ro 11:2 cast away his people which he **f.**......... *4267*

FOREKNOW See also FOREKNEW.
Ro 8:29 For whom he did **f.**, he also did......... *4267*

FOREKNOWLEDGE
Ac 2:23 and **f.** of God, ye have taken, and...... *4268*
1Pe 1:2 Elect according to the **f.** of God......... *4268*

FOREMOST
Ge 32:17 And he commanded the **f.**, saying,...... 7223
Ge 33:2 handmaids and their children **f.**, ... 7223
2Sa 18:27 the running of the **f.** is like the.......... 7223

FOREORDAINED
1Pe 1:20 Who verily was **f.** before the............ *4267*

FOREPART
Ex 28:27 toward the **f.** thereof, over against..... 6440

Ex 39:20 ephod underneath, toward the **f.** 6440
1Ki 6:20 oracle in the **f.** was twenty cubits 6440
Eze 42:7 court on the **f.** of the chambers, 6440
Ac 27:41 the **f.** stuck fast, and remained 4408

FORERUNNER
Heb 6:20 Whither the **f.** is for us entered, *4274*

FORESAW
Ac 2:25 I **f.** the Lord always before my *4308*

FORESEEING
Ga 3:8 the scripture, **f.** that God would *4275*

FORESEETH
Pr 22:3 A prudent man **f.** the evil, and 7200
Pr 27:12 A prudent man **f.** the evil, and 7200

FORESHIP
Ac 27:30 have cast anchors out of the **f.**, *4408*

FORESKIN See also FORESKINS.
Ge 17:11 circumcise the flesh of your **f.**; 6190
Ge 17:14 flesh of his **f.** is not circumcised, 6190
Ge 17:23 circumcised the flesh of their **f.** 6190
Ge 17:24, 25 circumcised in the flesh of his **f.** 6190
Ex 4:25 stone, and cut off the **f.** of her son, 6190
Le 12:3 flesh of his **f.** shall be circumcised. 6190
De 10:16 Circumcise therefore the **f.** of your 6190
Hab 2:16 and let thy **f.** be uncovered: 6188

FORESKINS
Jos 5:3 of Israel at the hill of the **f.** 6190
1Sa 18:25 an hundred **f.** of the Philistines, 6190
1Sa 18:27 David brought their **f.**, and they 6190
2Sa 3:14 an hundred **f.** of the Philistines. 6190
Jer 4:4 and take away the **f.** of your heart, 6190

FOREST See also FORESTS.
1Sa 22:5 and came into the **f.** of Hareth. 3293
1Ki 7:2 also the house of the **f.** of Lebanon; 3293
1Ki 10:17 in the house of the **f.** of Lebanon. 3293
1Ki 10:21 of the house of the **f.** of Lebanon 3293
2Ki 19:23 and into the **f.** of his Carmel. 3293
2Ch 9:16 in the house of the **f.** of Lebanon 3293
2Ch 9:20 of the house of the **f.** of Lebanon 3293
Ne 2:8 Asaph the keeper of the king's **f.**, 6508
Ps 50:10 For every beast of the **f.** is mine, 3293
Ps 104:20 all the beasts of the **f.** do creep 3293
Isa 9:18 kindle in the thickets of the **f.**, 3293
Isa 10:18 shall consume the glory of his **f.**, 3293
Isa 10:19 And the trees of his **f.** shall be few, 3293
Isa 10:34 shall cut down the thickets of the **f.** 3293
Isa 21:13 In the **f.** in Arabia shall ye lodge, 3293
Isa 22:8 the armour of the house of the **f.** 3293
Isa 29:17 field shall be esteemed as a **f.**? 3293
Isa 32:15 fruitful field be counted for a **f.** 3293
Isa 32:19 shall hail, coming down on the **f.**; 3293
Isa 37:24 border, and the **f.** of his Carmel. 3293
Isa 44:14 himself among the trees of the **f.**; 3293
Isa 44:23 O **f.**, and every tree therein: 3293
Isa 56:9 yea, all ye beasts in the **f.** 3293
Jer 5:6 a lion out of the **f.** shall slay them, 3293
Jer 10:3 one cutteth a tree out of the **f.**, 3293
Jer 12:8 is unto me as a lion in the **f.**; 3293
Jer 21:14 I will kindle a fire in the **f.** thereof, 3293
Jer 26:18 the house as the high places of a **f.** 3293
Jer 46:23 They shall cut down her **f.**, saith 3293
Eze 15:2 which is among the trees of the **f.**? 3293
Eze 15:6 vine tree among the trees of the **f.**, 3293
Eze 20:46 prophesy against the **f.** of the south 3293
Eze 20:47 And say to the **f.** of the south, 3293
Ho 2:12 and I will make them a **f.**, 3293
Am 3:4 Will a lion roar in the **f.**, when he 3293
Mic 3:12 the house as the high places of the **f.** 3293
Mic 5:8 as a lion among the beasts of the **f.**, 3293
Zec 11:2 the **f.** of the vintage is come down. 3293

FORESTS
2Ch 27:4 and in the **f.** he built castles and 2793
Ps 29:9 to calve, and discovereth the **f.**: 3295
Eze 39:10 neither cut down any out of the **f.**; 3293

FORETELL See also FORETOLD.
2Co 13:2 and **f.** you, as if I were present, *4302*

FORETOLD
Mr 13:23 behold, I have **f.** you all things. *4280*
Ac 3:24 have likewise **f.** of these days. *4293*

FOREVER See EVER.

FOREWARN See also FORWARNED.
Lu 12:5 I will **f.** you whom ye shall fear: *5263*

FOREWARNED
1Th 4:6 all such as we also have **f.** you and *4277*

FORFEITED
Ezr 10:8 all his substance should be **f.**, and 2763

FORGAT See also FORGOT.
Ge 40:23 remember Joseph, but **f.** him. 7911
Jg 3:7 and **f.** the Lord their God, and 7911
1Sa 12:9 when they **f.** the Lord their God, 7911
Ps 78:11 And **f.** his works, and his wonders 7911
Ps 106:13 They soon **f.** his works; they 7911
Ps 106:21 They **f.** God their saviour, which 7911
La 3:17 far off from peace: I **f.** prosperity. 5382
Ho 2:13 went after her lovers, and **f.** me, 7911

FORGAVE See also FORGAVEST.
Ps 78:38 **f.** their iniquity, and destroyed 3722
Mt 18:27 loosed him, and **f.** him the debt. *863*
Mt 18:32 I **f.** thee all that debt, because thou *863*
Lu 7:42 to pay, he frankly **f.** them both. *5483*
Lu 7:43 that he, to whom he **f.** most. *5483*
2Co 2:10 if I **f.** any thing, to whom I **f.** it, *5483*
2Co 2:10 for your sakes **f.** I it in the person
Col 3:13 even as Christ **f.** you, so also do ye.

FORGAVEST
Ps 32:5 and thou **f.** the iniquity of my sin. 5375
Ps 99:8 thou wast a God that **f.** them, 5375

FORGED
Ps 119:69 the proud have **f.** a lie against me: 2950

FORGERS
Job 13:4 But ye are **f.** of lies, ye are all 2950

FORGET See also FORGAT; FORGETFUL; FORGETTEST; FORGETTETH; FORGETTING; FORGOT; FORGOTTEN.
Ge 27:45 and he **f.** that which thou hast 7911
Ge 41:51 hath made me **f.** all my toil, 5382
De 4:9 lest thou **f.** the things which thine 7911
De 4:23 lest ye **f.** the covenant of the Lord 7911
De 4:31 nor **f.** the covenant of thy fathers 7911
De 6:12 Then beware lest thou **f.** the Lord, 7911
De 8:11 Beware that thou **f.** not the Lord 7911
De 8:14 and thou **f.** the Lord thy God, 7911
De 8:19 if thou do at all **f.** the Lord thy God, 7911
De 9:7 Remember, and **f.** not, how thou 7911
De 25:19 under heaven; thou shalt not **f.** it. 7911
1Sa 1:11 and not **f.** thine handmaid, but 7911
2Ki 17:38 have made with you ye shall not **f.**; 7911
Job 8:13 So are the paths of all that **f.** God; 7911
Job 9:27 If I say, I will **f.** my complaint, 7911
Job 11:16 Because thou shalt **f.** thy misery, 7911
Job 24:20 The womb shall **f.** him; the worm 7911
Ps 9:17 and all the nations that **f.** God. 7913
Ps 10:12 thine hand; **f.** not the humble. 7911
Ps 13:1 How long wilt thou **f.** me, O Lord? 7911
Ps 45:10 **f.** also thine own people, and thy 7911
Ps 50:22 ye that **f.** God, lest I tear you in 7911
Ps 59:11 slay them not, lest my people **f.**: 7911
Ps 74:19 **f.** not the congregation of thy poor 7911
Ps 74:23 **F.** not the voice of thine enemies: 7911
Ps 78:7 and not **f.** the works of God, 7911
Ps 102:4 so that I **f.** to eat my bread. 7911
Ps 103:2 my soul, and **f.** not all his benefits: 7911
Ps 119:16 thy statutes: I will not **f.** thy word. 7911
Ps 119:83 yet do I not **f.** thy statutes. 7911
Ps 119:93 I will never **f.** thy precepts: for 7911
Ps 119:109 in my hand: yet do I not **f.** thy law. 7911
Ps 119:141 yet do not I **f.** thy precepts. 7911
Ps 119:153 deliver me: for I do not **f.** thy law. 7911
Ps 119:176 I do not **f.** thy commandments. 7911
Ps 137:5 If I **f.** thee, O Jerusalem, 7911
Ps 137:5 let my right hand **f.** her cunning. 7911
Pr 3:1 My son, **f.** not my law; but let thine 7911
Pr 4:5 get understanding: **f.** it not; 7911
Pr 31:5 Lest they drink, and **f.** the law, 7911
Pr 31:7 Let him drink, and **f.** his poverty, 7911
Isa 49:15 Can a woman **f.** her sucking child, 7911
Isa 49:15 son of her womb? yea, they may **f.**, 7911
Isa 49:15 yet will I not **f.** thee. 7911
Isa 54:4 shalt **f.** the shame of thy youth, 7911
Isa 65:11 forsake the Lord, that **f.** my holy 7913
Jer 2:32 Can a maid **f.** her ornaments, 7911
Jer 23:27 to cause my people to **f.** my name 7911
Jer 23:39 I, even I, will utterly **f.** you, 5382
La 5:20 Wherefore dost thou **f.** us for ever, 7911
Ho 4:6 thy God, I will also **f.** thy children. 7911
Am 8:7 I will never **f.** any of their works. 7911
Heb 6:10 to **f.** your work and labour of love, *1950*
Heb 13:16 do good and to communicate **f.** not: *1950*

FORGETFUL
He 13:2 Be not **f.** to entertain strangers; *1950*
Jas 1:25 being not a **f.** hearer, but a doer *1953*

FORGETFULNESS
Ps 88:12 righteousness in the land of **f.**? 5388

FORGETTEST
Ps 44:24 and **f.** our affliction and our 7911
Isa 51:13 And **f.** the Lord thy maker, that 7911

FORGETTETH
Job 39:15 And **f.** that the foot may crush 7911
Ps 9:12 he **f.** not the cry of the humble. 7911
Pr 2:17 and **f.** the covenant of her God. 7913
Jas 1:24 **f.** what manner of man he was. *1950*

FORGETTING
Php 3:13 **f.** those things which are behind *1950*

FORGIVE See also FORGAVE; FORGIVEN; FORGIVETH; FORGIVING.
Ge 50:17 **F.**, I pray thee now the trespass, 5375
Ge 50:17 **f.** the trespass of the servants of the 5375
Ex 10:17 Now therefore **f.**, I pray thee, my 5375
Ex 32:32 Yet now, if thou wilt **f.** their sin--; 5375
Nu 30:5 the Lord shall **f.** her, because her 5545
Nu 30:8 effect: and the Lord shall **f.** her. 5545
Nu 30:12 void; and the Lord shall **f.** her, 5545
Jos 24:19 he will not **f.** your transgressions 5375
1Sa 25:28 I pray thee, **f.** the trespass of thine 5375
1Ki 8:30 and when thou hearest, **f.** 5545
1Ki 8:34 and **f.** the sin of thy people Israel, 5545
1Ki 8:36 and **f.** the sin of thy servants, 5545
1Ki 8:39 heaven thy dwelling place, and **f.**, 5545
1Ki 8:50 And **f.** thy people that have sinned 5545
2Ch 6:21 heaven; and when thou hearest, **f.** 5545
2Ch 6:25 hear thou from the heavens, and **f.** 5545
2Ch 6:27 hear thou from heaven, and **f.** 5545
2Ch 6:30 heaven, thy dwelling place, and **f.**, 5545
2Ch 6:39 and **f.** thy people which have 5545
2Ch 7:14 and will **f.** their sin, and will heal 5545
Ps 25:18 my pain; and **f.** all my sins. 5375
Ps 86:5 Lord, art good and ready to **f.**; 5546
Isa 2:9 himself: therefore **f.** them not. 5375
Jer 18:23 **f.** not their iniquity, neither blot 3722
Jer 31:34 I will **f.** their iniquity, and I will 5545
Jer 36:3 that I may **f.** their iniquity and 5545
Da 9:19 O Lord, hear; O Lord, **f.**; 5545
Am 7:2 O Lord God, **f.**, I beseech thee: 5545
Mt 6:12 **f.** us our debts, as we **f.** our *863*
Mt 6:14 For if ye **f.** men their trespasses, *863*
Mt 6:14 your heavenly Father will also **f.** *863*
Mt 6:15 if ye **f.** not men their trespasses, *863*
Mt 6:15 will your Father **f.** your trespasses. *863*
Mt 9:6 hath power on earth to **f.** sins, *863*
Mt 18:21 my brother sin against me and I **f.** *863*
Mt 18:35 **f.** not every one his brother their *863*
Mr 2:7 who can **f.** sins but God only? *863*
Mr 2:10 man hath power on earth to **f.** sins, *863*
Mr 11:25 **f.**, if ye have ought against any: *863*
Mr 11:25 may **f.** you your trespasses. *863*
Mr 11:26 if ye do not **f.**, neither will your *863*
Mr 11:26 in heaven **f.** your trespasses. *863*
Lu 5:21 Who can **f.** sins, but God alone? *863*
Lu 5:24 hath power upon earth to **f.** sins, *863*
Lu 6:37 **f.** and ye shall be forgiven: *630*
Lu 11:4 **f.** us our sins; for we also **f.** every *863*
Lu 17:3 and if he repent, **f.** him. *863*
Lu 17:4 saying, I repent; thou shalt **f.** him. *863*
Lu 23:34 Then said Jesus, Father, **f.** them; *863*
2Co 2:7 ought rather to **f.** him, and comfort *5483*
2Co 2:10 To whom ye **f.** any thing, I **f.** also: *5483*
2Co 12:13 to you? **f.** me this wrong. *5483*
1Jo 1:9 faithful and just to **f.** us our sins, *863*

FORGIVEN
Le 4:20 for them, and it shall be **f.** them. 5545
Le 4:26 concerning his sin, and it shall be **f.** 5545
Le 4:31 for him, and it shall be **f.** him. 5545
Le 4:35 committed, and it shall be **f.** him. 5545
Le 5:10 hath sinned, and it shall be **f.** him. 5545
Le 5:13 of these, and it shall be **f.** him: 5545

Le 5:16 offering, and it shall be f. him 5545
Le 5:18 it not, and it shall be forgiven him. 5545
Le 6:7 shall be f. him for any thing of all 5545
Le 19:22 which he hath done shall be f. him. 5545
Nu 14:19 and as thou hast f. this people, 5375
Nu 15:25 and it shall be f. them; for it is 5545
Nu 15:26 it shall be f. all the congregation 5545
Nu 15:28 for him; and it shall be f. him. 5545
De 21:8 And the blood shall be f. them. 3722
Ps 32:1 is he whose transgression is f., 5375
Ps 85:2 Thou hast f. the iniquity of thy 5375
Isa 33:24 that dwell therein shall be f. their 5375
Mt 9:2 be of good cheer; thy sins be f. *863*
Mt 9:5 to say, Thy sins be f. thee; *863*
Mt 12:31 and blasphemy shall be f. unto *863*
Mt 12:31 the Holy Ghost shall not be f. unto. *863*
Mt 12:32 the Son of man, it shall be f. him:. *863*
Mt 12:32 Holy Ghost, it shall not be f. him,. *863*
Mk 2:5 the palsy, Son, thy sins be f. thee. *863*
Mk 2:9 Thy sins be f. thee; or to say, Arise, *863*
Mk 3:28 All sins shall be f. unto the sons of. *863*
Mk 4:12 and their sins should be f. them. *863*
Lu 5:20 unto him, Man, thy sins are f. thee. *863*
Lu 5:23 Thy sins be f. thee; or to say, Rise *863*
Lu 6:37 forgive, and ye shall be f.: *630*
Lu 7:47 Her sins, which are many, are f.; *863*
Lu 7:47 whom little is f., the same loveth *863*
Lu 7:48 he said unto her, Thy sins are f. *863*
Lu 12:10 the Son of man, it shall be f. him;. *863*
Lu 12:10 the Holy Ghost it shall not be f. *863*
Ac 8:22 thought of thine heart may be f. thee. *863*
Ro 4:7 are they whose iniquities are f., *863*
Eph 4:32 God for Christ's sake hath f. you. *5483*
Col 2:13 him, having f. you all trespasses; *5483*
Jas 5:15 sins, they shall be f. him. *863*
1Jo 2:12 because your sins are f. you for *863*

FORGIVENESS See also FORGIVENESSES.
Ps 130:4 But there is f. with thee, that thou 5547
Mk 3:29 the Holy Ghost hath never f., *859*
Ac 5:31 repentance to Israel, and f. of *859*
Ac 13:38 preached unto you the f. of sins: *859*
Ac 26:18 that they may receive f. of sins, *859*
Eph 1:7 the f. of sins, according to the *859*
Col 1:14 through his blood, even the f. of sins: *859*

FORGIVENESSES
Da 9:9 to...God belong mercies and f., 5547

FORGIVETH
Ps 103:8 Who f. all thine iniquities; who 5545
Lu 7:49 Who is this that f. sins also? *863*

FORGIVING
Ex 34:7 for thousands, f. iniquity and 5375
Nu 14:18 of great mercy, f. iniquity and 5375
Eph 4:32 f. one another, even as God for *5483*
Col 3:13 and f. one another, if any man *5483*

FORGOT See also FORGAT; FORGOTTEN.
De 24:19 and hast f. a sheaf in the field, 7911

FORGOTTEN
Ge 41:30 and all the plenty shall be f. in 7911
De 26:13 neither have I f. them; 7911
De 31:21 for it shall not be f. out of the 7911
De 32:18 and hast f. God that formed thee. 7911
Job 19:14 and my familiar friends have f. me. 7911
Job 28:4 even the waters f. of the foot: 7911
Ps 9:18 the needy shall not always be f.; 7911
Ps 10:11 hath said in his heart, God hath f.: 7911
Ps 31:12 I am f. as a dead man out of 7911
Ps 42:9 Why hast thou f. me? why go I 7911
Ps 44:17 yet have we not f. thee, neither 7911
Ps 44:20 If we have f. the name of our God, 7911
Ps 77:9 Hath God f. to be gracious? hath 7911
Ps 119:61 but I have not f. thy law. 7911
Ps 119:139 because mine enemies have f. thy 7911
Ec 2:16 in the days to come shall all be f. 7911
Ec 8:10 and they were f. in the city where 7911
Ec 9:5 for the memory of them is f. 7911
Isa 17:10 Because thou hast f. the God of thy 7911
Isa 23:15 that Tyre shall be f. seventy years, 7911
Isa 23:16 thou harlot that hast been f.; 7911
Isa 44:21 Israel, thou shalt not be f. of me. 5382
Isa 49:14 and my Lord hath f. me. 7913
Isa 65:16 because the former troubles are f., 7911
Jer 2:32 yet my people have f. me days 7911
Jer 3:21 they have f. the Lord their God. 7911
Jer 13:25 because thou hast f. me, and 7911
Jer 18:15 my people hath f. me, they have 7911
Jer 20:11 their...confusion shall never be f. 7911
Jer 23:27 their fathers have f. my name 7911
Jer 23:40 shame, which shall not be f. 7911
Jer 30:14 All thy lovers have f. thee; 7911
Jer 44:9 f. the wickedness of your fathers, 7911
Jer 50:5 covenant that shall not be f. 7911
Jer 50:6 they have f. their restingplace. 7911
La 2:6 solemn feasts and sabbaths to be f. 7911
Eze 22:12 and hast f. me, saith the Lord God. 7911
Eze 23:35 Because thou hast f. me, and cast 7911
Ho 4:6 thou hast f. the law of thy God, 7911
Ho 8:14 For Israel hath f. his Maker, 7911
Ho 13:6 therefore have they f. me. 7911
Mt 16:5 side, they had f. to take bread. *1950*
Mk 8:14 disciples had f. to take bread, *1950*
Lu 12:6 not one of them is f. before God?. *1950*
Heb 12:5 And ye have f. the exhortation *1585*
2Pe 1:9 hath f. that he was purged *3024,2983*

FORKS
1Sa 13:21 the coulters, and for the f., 7969,7053

FORM See also FORMED; FORMETH; FORMS; INFORM; PERFORM; REFORM; TRANSFORM.
Ge 1:2 And the earth was without f., 8414
1Sa 28:14 said unto her, What f. is he of? 8389
2Sa 14:20 To fetch about this f. of speech 6440
2Ch 4:7 of gold according to their f., and 4941
Job 4:16 I could not discern the f. thereof: 4758
Isa 45:7 I f. the light, and create darkness: 3335
Isa 52:14 his f. more than the sons of men: 8389
Isa 53:2 he hath no f. nor comeliness; 8389
Jer 4:23 earth, and, lo, it was without f., 8414
Eze 8:3 he put forth the f. of an hand, 8403
Eze 8:10 behold every f. of creeping things, 8403
Eze 10:8 the f. of a man's hand under their 8403
Eze 43:11 shew them the f. of the house, 6699
Eze 43:11 may keep the whole f. thereof, 6699
Da 2:31 and the f. thereof was terrible. 7299
Da 3:19 the f. of his visage was changed 6755
Da 3:25 f. of the fourth is like the Son of 7299
Mk 16:12 he appeared in another f. unto *3444*
Ro 2:20 which hast the f. of knowledge *3446*
Ro 6:17 that f. of doctrine which was *5179*
Php 2:6 Who, being in the f. of God, *3444*
Php 2:7 took upon him the f. of a servant, *3444*
2Ti 1:13 Hold fast the f. of sound words, *5296*
2Ti 3:5 Having a f. of godliness, but *3446*

FORMED See also CONFORMED; DEFORMED; REFORMED; TRANSFORMED.
Ge 2:7 And the Lord God f. man of the 3335
Ge 2:8 he put the man whom he had f. 3335
Ge 2:19 the ground the Lord f. every beast 3335
De 32:18 hast forgotten God that f. thee. 2342
2Ki 19:25 of ancient times that I have f. it? 3335
Job 26:5 Dead things are f. from under 2342
Job 26:13 hand hath f. the crooked serpent 2342
Job 33:6 I also am f. out of the clay. 7169
Ps 90:2 or ever thou hadst f. the earth 2342
Ps 94:9 that f. the eye, shall he not see? 3335
Ps 95:5 and his hands f. the dry land. 3335
Pr 26:10 The great God that f. all things 2342
Isa 27:11 he that f. them will shew them 3335
Isa 37:26 of ancient times, that I have f. it? 3335
Isa 43:1 and he that f. thee, O Israel, 3335
Isa 43:7 I have f. him; yea, I have made 3335
Isa 43:10 before me there was no God f., 3335
Isa 43:21 This people have I f. for myself; 3335
Isa 44:2 and f. thee from the womb, 3335
Isa 44:10 Who hath f. a god, or molten a 3335
Isa 44:21 have f. thee; thou art my servant: 3335
Isa 44:24 and he that f. thee from the womb, 3335
Isa 45:18 God himself that f. the earth and 3335
Isa 45:18 he f. it to be inhabited: I am the 3335
Isa 49:5 the Lord that f. me from the womb 3335
Isa 54:17 No weapon that is f. against thee 3335
Jer 1:5 Before I f. thee in the belly 3335
Jer 33:2 the Lord that f. it, to establish it; 3335
Am 7:1 f. grasshoppers in the beginning 3335
Ro 9:20 the thing f. say to him that f. it, *4110*
Gal 4:19 until Christ be f. in you, *3445*
1Ti 2:13 Adam was first f., then Eve. *4111*

FORMER
Ge 40:13 after the f. manner when thou 7223
Nu 21:26 fought against the f. king Moab, 7223
De 24:4 Her f. husband, which sent her 7223
Ru 4:7 this was the manner in f. time 6440
1Sa 17:30 answered him again after the f. 7223
2Ki 1:14 two captains of the f. fifties with 7223
2Ki 17:34 they do after the f. manners: 7223
2Ki 17:40 but they did after their f. manner. 7223
Ne 5:15 the f. governors that had been 7223
Job 8:8 enquire, I pray thee, of the f. age, 7223
Job 30:3 in f. time desolate and waste. 570
Ps 79:8 not against us f. iniquities: 7223
Ps 89:49 where are thy f. lovingkindnesses, 7223
Ec 1:11 is no remembrance of f. things; 7223
Ec 7:10 the f. days were better than these? 7223
Isa 41:22 let them shew the f. things, what 7223
Isa 42:9 the f. things are come to pass, 7223
Isa 43:9 declare this, and shew us f. things? 7223
Isa 43:18 Remember ye not the f. things, 7223
Isa 46:9 Remember the f. things of old: 7223
Isa 48:3 I have declared the f. things from 7223
Isa 61:4 shall raise up the f. desolations, 7223
Isa 65:7 will I measure their f. work into 7223
Isa 65:16 the f. troubles are forgotten, 7223
Isa 65:17 and the f. shall not be remembered, 7223
Jer 5:24 rain, both the f. and the latter, 3138
Jer 10:16 for he is the f. of all things: 3335
Jer 34:5 f. kings which were before thee, 7223
Jer 36:28 f. words that were in the first roll, 7223
Jer 51:19 for he is the f. of all things: 3335
Eze 16:55 shall return to their f. estate, and 6927
Eze 16:55 shall return to their f. estate, then 6927
Eze 16:55 shall return to your f. estate. 6927
Da 11:13 a multitude greater than the f., 7223
Da 11:29 but it shall not be as the f., 7223
Ho 6:3 latter and f. rain unto the earth. 3138
Joe 2:23 given you the f. rain moderately. 4175
Joe 2:23 the f. rain, and the latter rain 4175
Hag 2:9 shall be greater than of the f., 7223
Zec 1:4 unto whom the f. prophets have 7223
Zec 7:7 Lord hath cried by the f. prophets, 7223
Zec 7:12 sent in his spirit by the f. prophets: 7223
Zec 8:11 of this people as in the f. days, 7223
Zec 14:8 half of them toward the f. sea. 6931
Mal 3:4 the days of old, and as in f. years. 6931
Ac 1:1 The f. treatise have I made, O *4413*
Eph 4:22 concerning the f. conversation *4387*
Heb 10:32 call to remembrance the f. days, *4386*
1Pe 1:14 according to the f. lusts in your *4386*
Re 21:4 for the f. things are passed away, *4413*

FORMETH See also PERFORMETH.
Am 4:13 For, lo, he that f. the mountains, 3335
Zec 12:1 and f. the spirit of man within him. 3335

FORMING See PERFORMING; TRANSFORMING.

FORMS
Eze 43:11 f. thereof, and all the ordinances 6699
Eze 43:11 all the f. thereof, and all the laws 6699

FORNICATION See also FORNICATIONS.
2Ch 21:11 of Jerusalem to commit f., and 2181
Isa 23:17 and shall commit f. with all the 2181
Eze 16:26 Thou hast also committed f. with 2181
Eze 16:29 hast moreover multiplied thy f. 8457
Mt 5:32 his wife, saving for the cause of f., *4202*
Mt 19:9 away his wife, except it be for f.,. *4202*
Joh 8:41 We be not born of f., we have one. *4202*
Ac 15:20 from f., and from things strangled *4202*
Ac 15:29 from things strangled, and from f.: *4202*
Ac 21:25 and from strangled, and from f. *4202*
Ro 1:29 f. wickedness, covetousness, *4202*
1Co 5:1 that there is f. among you, and *4202*
1Co 5:1 such f. as is not so much as *4202*
1Co 6:13 Now the body is not for f., *4202*
1Co 6:18 Flee f. Every sin that a man doeth *4202*
1Co 6:18 but he that committeth f. sinneth *4203*
1Co 7:2 to avoid f., let every man have *4202*
1Co 10:8 Neither let us commit f., as some *4203*
2Co 12:21 and f. and lasciviousness which *4202*
Ga 5:19 Adultery, f., uncleanness, *4202*
Eph 5:3 But f., and all uncleanness, or *4202*
Col 3:5 f., uncleanness, inordinate *4202*
1Th 4:3 that ye should abstain from f., *4202*
Jude 7 giving themselves over to f., *1608*
Re 2:14 unto idols, and to commit f. *4203*
Re 2:20 to commit f., and to eat things *4203*
Re 2:21 gave her space to repent of her f.;. *4202*
Re 9:21 nor of their f., nor of their thefts. *4202*

Re 14:8 the wine of the wrath of her **f.**. *4202*
Re 17:2 of the earth have committed **f.** *4203*
Re 17:2 drunk with the wine of her **f.**. *4202*
Re 17:4 and filthiness of her **f.**..................... *4202*
Re 18:3 of the wine of the wrath of her **f.**,...... *4202*
Re 18:3 have committed **f.** with her, and *4203*
Re 18:9 who have committed **f.** and lived........ *4203*
Re 19:2 did corrupt the earth with her **f.**, ... *4202*

FORNICATIONS
Eze 16:15 pouredst out thy **f.** on every one 8457
Mt 15:19 thoughts, murders, adulteries, **f.**,.. *4202*
Mk 7:21 evil thoughts, adulteries, **f.**,........... *4202*

FORNICATOR See also FORNICATORS.
1Co 5:11 Man that is called a brother be a **f.**, ... *4205*
Heb 12:16 Lest there be any **f.**, or profane *4205*

FORNICATORS
1Co 5:9 an epistle not to company with **f.** *4205*
1Co 5:10 altogether with the **f.** of this world. *4205*
1Co 6:9 neither **f.**, nor idolaters, nor............. *4205*

FORSAKE See FORSAKEN; FORSAKETH; FORSAKING; FORSOOK.
De 4:31 he will not **f.** thee, neither destroy 7503
De 12:19 heed to thyself that thou **f.** not.......... 5800
De 14:27 thou shalt not **f.** him; for he hath 5800
De 31:6 he will not fail thee, nor **f.** thee. 5800
De 31:8 will not fail thee, neither **f.** thee:........ 5800
De 31:16 will **f.** me, and break my covenant...... 5800
De 31:17 and I will **f.** them, and I will hide 5800
Jos 1:5 I will not fail thee, nor **f.** thee. 5800
Jos 24:16 forbid that we should **f.** the Lord, ... 5800
Jos 24:20 If ye **f.** the Lord, and serve strange ... 5800
Jg 9:11 Should I **f.** my sweetness, and my...... 2308
1Sa 12:22 the Lord will not **f.** his people for....... 5203
1Ki 6:13 and will not **f.** my people Israel.......... 5800
1Ki 8:57 let him not leave us, nor **f.** us; 5203
2Ki 21:14 And I will **f.** the remnant of mine 5203
1Ch 28:9 if thou **f.** him, he will cast thee off 5800
1Ch 28:20 he will not fail thee, nor **f.** thee, ... 5800
2Ch 7:19 if ye turn away, and **f.** my statutes..... 5800
2Ch 15:2 but if ye **f.** him, he will **f.** you. 5800
Ezr 8:22 is against all them that **f.** him. 5800
Ne 9:31 utterly consume them, nor **f.** them; 5800
Ne 10:39 we will not **f.** the house of our 5800
Job 20:13 Though he spare it, and **f.** it not; 5800
Ps 27:9 leave me not, neither **f.** me, O God.... 5800
Ps 27:10 my father and my mother **f.** me, ... 5800
Ps 37:8 Cease from anger, and **f.** wrath: 5800
Ps 38:21 **F.** me not, O Lord: O my God,........... 5800
Ps 71:9 **f.** me not when my strength faileth..... 5800
Ps 71:18 O God, **f.** me not; until I have............ 5800
Ps 89:30 If his children **f.** my law, and walk....... 5800
Ps 94:14 neither will he **f.** his inheritance. 5800
Ps 119:8 will keep thy statutes: O **f.** me not....... 5800
Ps 119:53 of the wicked that **f.** thy law. 5800
Ps 138:8 **f.** not the works of thine own............. 7503
Pr 1:8 and **f.** not the law of thy mother: 5203
Pr 3:3 Let not mercy and truth **f.** thee: 5800
Pr 4:2 good doctrine, **f.** ye not my law. 5800
Pr 4:6 **F.** her not, and she shall preserve...... 5800
Pr 6:20 and **f.** not the law of thy mother: 5203
Pr 9:6 **F.** the foolish, and live; and go 5800
Pr 27:10 and thy father's friend, **f.** not; 5800
Pr 28:4 that **f.** the law praise the wicked: 5800
Isa 1:28 that **f.** the Lord shall be consumed. 5800
Isa 41:17 the God of Israel will not **f.** them. 5800
Isa 42:16 I do unto them, and not **f.** them. 5800
Isa 55:7 Let the wicked **f.** his way, and the 5800
Isa 65:11 But ye are they that **f.** the Lord, ... 5800
Jer 17:13 all that **f.** thee shall be ashamed,......... 5800
Jer 23:33 I will even **f.** you, saith the Lord. 5203
Jer 23:39 and I will **f.** you, and the city 5203
Jer 51:9 but she is not healed: **f.** her,............. 5800
La 5:20 thou forget us for ever, and **f.** us....... 5800
Eze 20:8 did they **f.** the idols of Egypt:............ 5800
Da 11:30 them that **f.** the holy covenant............ 5800
Jon 2:8 lying vanities **f.** their own mercy. 5800
Ac 21:21 among the Gentiles to **f.** Moses, ... *646,575*
Heb 13:5 I will never leave thee, nor **f.** thee. *1459*

FORSAKEN
De 28:20 doings, whereby thou hast **f.** me. 5800
De 29:25 they have **f.** the covenant of the 5800
Jg 6:13 but now the Lord hath **f.** us,............. 5203
Jg 10:10 have **f.** our God, and also served 5800
Jg 10:13 have **f.** me, and served other gods: 5800
1Sa 8:8 have **f.** me, and served other gods, ... 5800
1Sa 12:10 have **f.** the Lord, and have served...... 5800
1Ki 11:33 have **f.** me, and have worshipped....... 5800
1Ki 18:18 **f.** the commandments of the Lord, ... 5800
1Ki 19:10, 14 of Israel have **f.** thy covenant. 5800
2Ki 22:17 Because they have **f.** me, and have 5800
2Ch 12:5 thus saith the Lord, Ye have **f.** me,.... 5800
2Ch 13:10 our God, and we have not **f.** him; 5800
2Ch 13:11 Lord our God, but ye have **f.** him. 5800
2Ch 21:10 had **f.** the Lord God of his fathers. 5800
2Ch 24:20 have **f.** the Lord, he hath also **f.** you. . 5800
2Ch 24:24 hand, because they had **f.** the Lord 5800
2Ch 28:6 men; because they had **f.** the Lord..... 5800
2Ch 29:6 have **f.** him, and have turned away..... 5800
2Ch 34:25 **f.** me, and have burned incense 5800
Ezr 9:9 yet our God hath not **f.** us.................. 5800
Ezr 9:10 for we have **f.** thy commandments,...... 5800
Ne 13:11 Why is the house of God **f.**? 5800
Job 18:4 shall the earth be **f.** for thee?............ 5800
Job 20:19 oppressed and hath **f.** the poor; 5800
Ps 9:10 hast not **f.** them that seek thee. 5800
Ps 22:1 my God, why hast thou **f.** me? 5800
Ps 37:25 have I not seen the righteous **f.**,......... 5800
Ps 71:11 God hath **f.** him; persecute and.......... 5800
Isa 1:4 they have **f.** the Lord, they have 5800
Isa 2:6 thou hast **f.** thy people the house....... 5203
Isa 7:16 that thou abhorrest shall be **f.** of........ 5800
Isa 17:2 The cities of Aroer are **f.**: they 5800
Isa 17:9 his strong cities be as a **f.** bough, ... 5800
Isa 27:10 the habitation **f.**, and left like a.......... 7971
Isa 32:14 palaces shall be **f.**; the multitude......... 5203
Isa 49:14 Zion said, The Lord hath **f.** me,.......... 5800
Isa 54:6 hath called thee as a woman **f.** and..... 5800
Isa 54:7 For a small moment have I **f.** thee, ... 5800
Isa 60:15 thou hast been **f.** and hated,.............. 5800
Isa 62:4 Thou shalt no more be termed **F.**; 5800
Isa 62:12 called, Sought out, A city not **f.**.......... 5800
Jer 1:16 who have **f.** me, and have burned 5800
Jer 2:13 have **f.** me the fountain of living......... 5800
Jer 2:17 in that thou hast **f.** the Lord thy 5800
Jer 2:19 that thou hast **f.** the Lord thy God, ... 5800
Jer 4:29 every city shall be **f.**, and not a man... 5800
Jer 5:7 thy children have **f.** me, and sworn..... 5800
Jer 5:19 Like as ye have **f.** me, and served 5800
Jer 7:29 and **f.** the generation of his wrath,....... 5203
Jer 9:13 they have **f.** my law which I set........ 5800
Jer 9:19 we have **f.** the land, because our 5800
Jer 12:7 I have **f.** mine house, I have left......... 5800
Jer 15:6 thou hast **f.** me, saith the lord,........... 5203
Jer 16:11 fathers have **f.** me, saith the Lord,...... 5800
Jer 16:11 and have **f.** me, and have not kept 5800
Jer 17:13 they have **f.** the Lord, the fountain...... 5800
Jer 18:14 come from another place be **f.**?.......... 5428
Jer 19:4 have **f.** me, and have estranged.......... 5800
Jer 22:9 have **f.** the covenant of the Lord......... 5800
Jer 25:38 he hath **f.** his covert, as the lion; 5800
Jer 51:5 Israel hath not been **f.**, nor Judah 488
Eze 8:12 not: the Lord hath **f.** the earth. 5800
Eze 9:9 say, The Lord hath **f.** the earth. 5800
Eze 36:4 the cities that are **f.**, which became 5800
Am 5:2 she is **f.** upon her land; there is......... 5203
Zep 2:4 Gaza shall be **f.**, and Ashkelon........... 5800
Mt 19:27 we have **f.** all, and followed thee; *863*
Mt 19:29 every one that hath **f.** houses, ... *863*
Mt 27:46 my God, why hast thou **f.** me? *1459*
Mk 15:34 God, my God, why hast thou **f.** me?... *1459*
2Co 4:9 persecuted, but not **f.**; cast down,...... *1459*
2Ti 4:10 Demas hath **f.** me, having loved......... *1459*
2Pe 2:15 Which have **f.** the right way, and *2641*

FORSAKETH
Job 6:14 he **f.** the fear of the Almighty........... 5800
Ps 37:28 judgment, and **f.** not his saints;........... 5800
Pr 2:17 Which **f.** the guide of her youth, ... 5800
Pr 15:10 is grievous unto him that **f.** the way; .. 5800
Pr 28:13 confesseth and **f.** them shall have........ 5800
Lu 14:33 of you that **f.** not all that he hath, . *657*

FORSAKING
Isa 6:12 there be a great **f.** in the midst 5805
Heb 10:25 Not **f.** the assembling of ourselves...... *1459*

FORSOMUCH See also FORASMUCH; INASMUCH.
Lu 19:9 **f.** as he also is a son of Abraham, . *2530*

FORSOOK See also FORSOOKEST.
De 32:15 then he **f.** God which made him, ... 5203
Jg 2:12 **f.** the Lord God of their fathers, ... 5800
Jg 2:13 they **f.** the Lord, and served Baal 5800
Jg 10:6 **f.** the Lord, and served not him......... 5800
1Sa 31:7 they **f.** the cities, and fled; and the..... 5800
1Ki 9:9 Because they **f.** the Lord their God,... 5800
1Ki 12:8 he **f.** the counsel of the old men, ... 5800
1Ki 12:13 and **f.** the old men's counsel that........ 5800
2Ki 21:22 he **f.** the Lord God of his fathers, ... 5800
1Ch 10:7 then they **f.** their cities, and fled;....... 5800
2Ch 7:22 they **f.** the Lord God of their fathers, ..5800
2Ch 10:8 he **f.** the counsel which the old men ... 5800
2Ch 10:13 Rehoboam **f.** the counsel of the old..... 5800
2Ch 12:1 he **f.** the law of the Lord, and all 5800
Ps 78:60 he **f.** the tabernacle of Shiloh,............ 5203
Ps 119:87 earth; but I **f.** not thy precepts.......... 5800
Isa 58:2 **f.** not the ordinance of their God;........ 5800
Jer 14:5 also calved in the field, and **f.** it,........ 5800
Mt 26:56 all the disciples **f.** him, and fled. *863*
Mk 1:18 they **f.** their nets, and followed *863*
Mk 14:50 And they all **f.** him, and fled. *863*
Lu 5:11 land, they **f.** all, and followed him. *863*
2Ti 4:16 stood with me, but all men **f.** me; *1459*
Heb 11:27 By faith he **f.** Egypt, not fearing *2641*

FORSOOKEST
Ne 9:17 great kindness, and **f.** them not. 5800
Ne 9:19 thy manifold mercies **f.** them not........ 5800

FORSWEAR
Mt 5:33 Thou shalt not **f.** thyself, but shalt.*1964*

FORT See also FORTS.
2Sa 5:9 David dwelt in the **f.**, and called......... 4686
Isa 25:12 fortress of the high **f.** of thy walls...... 4869
Eze 4:2 and build a **f.** against it, and cast........ 1785
Eze 21:22 to cast a mount, and to build a **f.**. 1785
Eze 26:8 he shall make a **f.** against thee, ... 1785
Da 11:19 shall turn his face toward the **f.** 4581

FORTH See also FORTHWITH; HENCEFORTH.
Ge 1:11 said, Let the earth bring **f.** grass, ... 1876
Ge 1:12 And the earth brought **f.** grass, ... 3318
Ge 1:20 God said, Let the waters bring **f.**....... 8317
Ge 1:21 the waters brought **f.** abundantly,....... 8317
Ge 1:24 earth bring **f.** the living creature 3318
Ge 3:16 thou shalt bring **f.** children; and 3205
Ge 3:18 thistles shall it bring **f.** to thee;......... 6779
Ge 3:22 lest he put **f.** his hand, and take 7971
Ge 3:23 God sent him **f.** from the garden...............
Ge 8:7 and he sent **f.** a raven, which went...........
Ge 8:7 a raven, which went **f.** to and fro,...... 3318
Ge 8:8 also he sent **f.** a dove from him, to...........
Ge 8:9 put **f.** his hand, and took her,.............. 7971
Ge 8:10 he sent **f.** his dove out of the ark;............
Ge 8:12 sent **f.** the dove; which returned not.........
Ge 8:16 Go **f.** of the ark, thou, and thy wife,... 3318
Ge 8:17 Bring **f.** with thee every living........... 3318
Ge 8:18 And Noah went **f.**, and his sons,......... 3318
Ge 8:19 their kinds, went **f.** out of the ark. 3318
Ge 9:7 bring **f.** abundantly in the earth,......... 8317
Ge 9:18 of Noah, that went **f.** of the ark,......... 3318
Ge 10:11 Out of that land went **f.** Asshur, ... 3318
Ge 11:31 they went **f.** with them from Ur of..... 3318
Ge 12:5 and they went **f.** to go into the land.... 3318
Ge 14:18 king of Salem brought **f.** bread........... 3318
Ge 15:4 come **f.** out of thine bowels,.............. 3318
Ge 15:5 he brought him **f.** abroad, and said, ... 3318
Ge 19:10 But the men put **f.** their hand,........... 7971
Ge 19:16 they brought him **f.**, and set him........ 3318
Ge 19:17 when they had brought **f.** abroad,....... 3318
Ge 22:10 Abraham stretched **f.** his hand, and...........
Ge 24:43 virgin cometh **f.** to draw water, ... 3318
Ge 24:45 Rebekah came **f.** with her pitcher........ 3318
Ge 24:53 servant brought **f.** jewels of silver, ... 3318
Ge 30:39 brought **f.** cattle ringstraked,............. 3209
Ge 38:24 And Judah said, Bring her **f.**, and....... 3318
Ge 38:25 When she was brought **f.**, she sent 3318
Ge 38:29 said, How hast thou broken **f.**?.......... 6556
Ge 39:13 in her hand, and was fled **f.**, ... 2351
Ge 40:10 budded, and her blossoms shot **f.**;............
Ge 40:10 thereof brought **f.** ripe grapes;........... 1310
Ge 41:47 the earth brought **f.** by handfuls. 6213
Ge 42:15 Pharaoh ye shall not go **f.** hence, ... 3318
Ex 3:10 that thou mayest bring **f.** my people ... 3318
Ex 3:11 should bring **f.** the children of Israel.... 3318
Ex 3:12 thou hast brought **f.** the people.......... 3318
Ex 4:4 Put **f.** thine hand and take it by 7971
Ex 4:4 he put **f.** his hand and caught it 7971
Ex 4:14 behold, he cometh **f.** to meet thee; 3318
Ex 5:20 as they came **f.** from Pharaoh:........... 3318
Ex 7:4 and bring **f.** mine armies, and my....... 3318

Ex 7:5 stretch **f.** mine hand upon Egypt.
Ex 8:3 shall bring **f.** frogs abundantly, 8317
Ex 8:5 Stretch **f.** thine hand with thy rod over
Ex 8:18 their enchantment to bring **f.** lice, 3318
Ex 8:20 lo, he cometh **f.** to the water; 3318
Ex 9:9 be a boil breaking **f.** with blains
Ex 9:10 a boil breaking **f.** with blains
Ex 9:22 Stretch **f.** thine hand toward heaven,
Ex 9:23 And Moses stretched **f.** his rod toward
Ex 10:13 Moses stretched **f.** his rod over the land
Ex 10:22 Moses stretched **f.** his hand toward
Ex 12:31 get you **f.** from among my people, 3318
Ex 12:39 which they brought **f.** out of Egypt, 3318
Ex 12:46 shalt not carry **f.** ought of the flesh 3318
Ex 13:8 unto me when I came **f.** out of Egypt. 3318
Ex 13:16 the Lord brought us **f.** out of Egypt 3318
Ex 14:11 with us, to carry us **f.** out of Egypt? 3318
Ex 14:27 stretched **f.** his hand over the sea,
Ex 15:7 sentest **f.** thy wrath, which consumed
Ex 15:13 in thy mercy hast led **f.** the people
Ex 16:3 brought us **f.** into this wilderness, 3318
Ex 16:32 when I brought you **f.** from the land 3318
Ex 19:1 Israel were gone **f.** out of the land 3318
Ex 19:17 Moses brought **f.** the people out of 3318
Ex 19:22 lest the Lord break **f.** upon them.
Ex 19:24 unto the Lord lest he break **f.** upon
Ex 25:20 cherubims shall stretch **f.** their
Ex 29:46 that brought them **f.** out of the land 3318
Ex 31:11 which thou hast brought **f.** out of 3318
Le 4:12 shall he carry **f.** without the camp 3318
Le 4:21 carry **f.** the bullock without the 3318
Le 6:11 carry **f.** the ashes without the camp 3318
Le 14:3 priest shall go **f.** out of the camp; 3318
Le 14:45 shall carry them **f.** out of the city 3318
Le 16:24 come **f.**, and offer his burnt offering, 3318
Le 16:27 one carry **f.** without the camp; 3318
Le 22:27 or a sheep, or a goat, is brought **f.**, 3205
Le 24:14 Bring **f.** him that hath cursed 3318
Le 24:23 should bring **f.** him that cursed 3318
Le 25:21 shall bring **f.** fruit for three years. 6213
Le 25:38 brought you **f.** out of the land of 3318
Le 25:42 which I brought **f.** out of the land 3318
Le 25:55 whom I brought **f.** out of the land 3318
Le 26:10 bring **f.** the old because of the new. 3318
Le 26:13 which brought you **f.** out of the land 3318
Le 26:45 whom I brought **f.** out of the land 3318
Nu 1:3 are able to go **f.** to war in Israel: 3318
Nu 1:20, 22,24,26,28,30,32,34,36,38,40,42,
all that were able to go **f.** to war; 3318
Nu 1:45 were able to go **f.** to war in Israel; 3318
Nu 2:9 armies. These shall first set **f.** 5265
Nu 2:16 they shall set **f.** in the second rank 5265
Nu 11:20 Why came we **f.** out of Egypt? 3318
Nu 11:31 there went **f.** a wind from the Lord, 5265
Nu 12:5 and they both came **f.**
Nu 17:8 was budded, and brought **f.** buds, 3318
Nu 19:3 may bring her **f.** without the camp, 3318
Nu 20:8 rock, and it shall give **f.** his water,
Nu 20:8 thou shalt bring **f.** to them water 3318
Nu 20:16 hath brought us **f.** out of Egypt; 3318
Nu 24:6 As the valley are they spread **f.**,
Nu 24:8 God brought him **f.** out of Egypt; 4161
Nu 26:4 went **f.** out of the land of Egypt 3318
Nu 31:13 went **f.** to meet them without the 3318
Nu 33:1 went **f.** out of the land of Egypt 3318
Nu 34:4 the going **f.** thereof shall be from 8444
Nu 34:8 goings **f.** of the border shall be to 8444
De 1:27 hath brought us **f.** out of the land 3318
De 2:23 which came **f.** out of Caphtor, 3318
De 4:20 and brought you **f.** out of the iron 3318
De 4:45 after they came **f.** out of Egypt, 3318
De 4:46 they were come **f.** out of Egypt: 3318
De 6:12 brought thee **f.** out of the land of 3318
De 8:14 brought thee **f.** out of the land of 4161
De 8:15 brought thee **f.** out of the rock of 4161
De 9:12, 26 hast brought **f.** out of the land 3318
De 14:22 the field bringeth **f.** year by year, 3318
De 14:28 shalt bring **f.** all the tithe of thine 3318
De 16:1 brought thee **f.** out of the land of 3318
De 16:3 for thou comest **f.** out of the land 3318
De 16:3 when thou camest **f.** out of the land 3318
De 16:6 that thou camest **f.** out of Egypt. 3318
De 17:5 then shalt thou bring **f.** that man or 3318
De 21:2 elders and thy judges shall come **f.**, 3318
De 21:10 thou goest **f.** to war against thine 3318
De 22:15 bring **f.** the tokens of the damsel's 3318
De 23:4 way, when ye came **f.** out of Egypt; 3318
De 23:9 host goeth **f.** against thine enemies, 3318
De 23:12 whither thou shalt go **f.** abroad: 3318
De 24:9 that we were come **f.** out of Egypt 3318
De 25:11 putteth **f.** her hand, and taketh 7971
De 25:17 when ye were come **f.** out of Egypt; 3318
De 26:8 Lord brought us **f.** out of Egypt 3318
De 29:25 he brought them **f.** out of the land 3318
De 33:2 he shined **f.** from Mount Paran, and
De 33:14 fruits brought **f.** by the sun,
De 33:14 things put **f.** by the moon. 1645
Jos 2:3 Bring **f.** the men that are come to 3318
Jos 5:5 as they came **f.** out of Egypt, them 3318
Jos 8:9 Joshua therefore sent them **f.**; and
Jos 9:12 day we came **f.** to go unto you; 3318
Jos 10:23 so, and brought **f.** those five kings 3318
Jos 18:11 coast of their lot came **f.** between 3318
Jos 18:17 went **f.** to En-shemesh, and went **f.** 3318
Jos 19:1 the second lot came **f.** to Simeon, 3318
Jg 1:24 spies saw a man come **f.** out of the 3318
Jg 3:21 Ehud put **f.** his left hand, and took 7971
Jg 3:23 Ehud went **f.** through the porch, 3318
Jg 5:25 brought **f.** water in a lordly dish 7126
Jg 5:31 sun when he goeth **f.** in his might. 3318
Jg 6:8 brought you **f.** out of the house of 3318
Jg 6:18 unto thee, and bring **f.** my present, 3318
Jg 6:21 the Lord put **f.** the end of the staff 7971
Jg 9:8 went **f.** on a time to anoint a king
Jg 9:43 were come **f.** out of the city; 3318
Jg 11:31 whatsoever cometh **f.** of the doors 3318
Jg 14:12 I will now put **f.** a riddle unto you: 2330
Jg 14:13 put **f.** thy riddle, that we may hear 2330
Jg 14:14 Out of the eater came **f.** meat, 3318
Jg 14:14 out of the strong came **f.** sweetness. 3318
Jg 14:16 thou hast put **f.** a riddle unto the 2330
Jg 15:15 of an ass, and put **f.** his hand, 7971
Jg 19:22 Bring **f.** the man that came into 3318
Jg 19:25 and brought her **f.** unto them; 3318
Jg 20:21 children of Benjamin came **f.** out 3318
Jg 20:25 And Benjamin went **f.** against 3318
Jg 20:33 the liers in wait of Israel came **f.** 1518
Ru 1:7 Wherefore she went **f.** out of the 3318
Ru 2:18 she brought **f.**, and gave to her 3318
1Sa 11:7 Whosoever cometh not **f.** after 3318
1Sa 12:8 brought **f.** your fathers up out 3318
1Sa 14:11 Hebrews come **f.** out of the holes 3318
1Sa 14:27 wherefore he put **f.** the end of the 7971
1Sa 17:20 the host was going **f.** to the fight, 3318
1Sa 17:55 And when Saul saw David go **f.** 3318
1Sa 18:30 princes of the Philistines went **f.**: 3318
1Sa 18:30 came to pass, after they went **f.**, 3318
1Sa 22:3 I pray thee, come **f.**, and be with 3318
1Sa 22:17 would not put **f.** their hand to fall 7971
1Sa 23:13 Keilah; and he forbare to go **f.** 3318
1Sa 24:6 to stretch **f.** mine hand against him,
1Sa 24:10 will not put **f.** mine hand against 7971
1Sa 26:9 for who can stretch **f.** his hand against
1Sa 26:11 that I should stretch **f.** mine hand
1Sa 26:23 but I would not stretch **f.** mine hand
1Sa 30:21 and they went **f.** to meet David, 3318
2Sa 1:14 thou not afraid to stretch **f.** thine hand
2Sa 5:20 The Lord hath broken **f.** upon
2Sa 6:6 Uzzah put **f.** his hand to the ark 7971
2Sa 11:1 at the time when kings go **f.** to 3318
2Sa 12:30 And he brought **f.** the spoil of the 3318
2Sa 12:31 And he brought **f.** the people that 3318
2Sa 13:39 king David longed to go **f.** unto 3318
2Sa 15:5 he put **f.** his hand, and took him, 7971
2Sa 15:16 And the king went **f.**, and all his 3318
2Sa 15:17 And the king went **f.**, and all the 3318
2Sa 16:5 he came **f.**, and cursed still as he 3318
2Sa 16:11 son, which came **f.** of my bowels, 3318
2Sa 18:2 And David sent **f.** a third part of the
2Sa 18:2 I will surely go **f.** with you myself 3318
2Sa 18:3 Thou shalt not go **f.**: for if we flee 3318
2Sa 18:12 yet would I not put **f.** mine hand 7971
2Sa 19:7 Now, therefore arise, go **f.**, and 3318
2Sa 19:7 swear by the Lord, if thou go not **f.**, 3318
2Sa 20:8 and as he went **f.** it fell out 3318
2Sa 22:20 He brought me **f.** also into a large 3318
2Sa 22:49 and that bringeth me **f.** from mine 4161
1Ki 2:30 Thus saith the king, Come **f.** 3318
1Ki 2:36 and go not **f.** thence any whither 3318
1Ki 6:27 and they stretched **f.** the wings of
1Ki 8:7 For the cherubims spread **f.** their
1Ki 8:16 I brought **f.** my people Israel out 3318
1Ki 8:19 thy son that shall come **f.** out of 3318
1Ki 8:22 spread **f.** his hands toward heaven:
1Ki 8:38 spread **f.** his hands toward this house:
1Ki 8:51 thou broughtest **f.** out of Egypt, 3318
1Ki 9:9 who brought **f.** their fathers out of 3318
1Ki 13:4 that he put **f.** his hand from the 7971
1Ki 13:4 And his hand which he put **f.** 7971
1Ki 19:11 And he said, Go **f.**, and stand upon 3318
1Ki 20:33 Then Ben-hadad came **f.** to him; 3318
1Ki 21:13 They carried him **f.** out of the city, 3318
1Ki 22:21 there came **f.** a spirit and stood 3318
1Ki 22:22 I will go **f.** and I will be a lying 3318
1Ki 22:22 and prevail also; go **f.**, and do so. 3318
2Ki 2:3 were at Beth-el came **f.** to Elisha, 3318
2Ki 2:21 And he went **f.** unto the spring of 3318
2Ki 2:23 there came **f.** little children out of 3318
2Ki 2:24 And there came **f.** two she bears 3318
2Ki 6:15 was risen early, and gone **f.**, 3318
2Ki 8:3 and she went **f.** to cry unto the 3318
2Ki 9:11 Then Jehu came **f.** to the servants 3318
2Ki 9:15 let none go **f.** nor escape out of the 3318
2Ki 10:22 Bring **f.** vestments for all the 3318
2Ki 10:22 And he brought them **f.** vestments. 3318
2Ki 10:25 and slay them; let none come **f.** 3318
2Ki 10:26 And they brought **f.** the images out 3318
2Ki 11:7 of all you that go **f.** on the sabbath, 3318
2Ki 11:12 And he brought **f.** the king's son, 3318
2Ki 11:15 her **f.** without the ranges; 3318
2Ki 18:7 whithersoever he went **f.**: 3318
2Ki 19:3 there is no strength to bring **f.** 3205
2Ki 19:31 Jerusalem shall go **f.** a remnant, 3318
2Ki 21:15 their fathers came **f.** out of Egypt, 3318
2Ki 23:4 to bring **f.** out of the temple of the 3318
1Ch 12:33, 36 such as went **f.** to battle, 3318
1Ch 13:9 Uzzah put **f.** his hand to hold the 7971
1Ch 14:11 like the breaking **f.** of waters: 7971
1Ch 14:15 for God is gone **f.** before thee to 3318
1Ch 16:23 shew **f.** from day to day his 1319
1Ch 19:16 and drew **f.** the Syrians that were 3318
1Ch 20:1 Joab led **f.** the power of the army,
1Ch 24:7 the first lot came **f.** to Jehoiarib, 3318
1Ch 25:9 Now the first lot came **f.** for Asaph 3318
1Ch 26:16 and Hosah the lot came **f.**
2Ch 1:17 they fetched up, and brought **f.** 3318
2Ch 3:13 cherubims spread themselves **f.**
2Ch 5:8 For the cherubims spread **f.** their
2Ch 6:5 Since the day that I brought **f.** my 3318
2Ch 6:9 but thy son which shall come **f.** out 3318
2Ch 6:12 of Israel, and spread **f.** his hands:
2Ch 6:13 of Israel, and spread **f.** his hands
2Ch 6:29 shall spread **f.** his hands in this
2Ch 7:22 brought them **f.** out of the land 3318
2Ch 20:20 early in themorning, and went **f.** 3318
2Ch 20:20 and as they went **f.**, Jehoshaphat 3318
2Ch 21:9 Then Jehoram went **f.** with his 5674
2Ch 23:14 Have her **f.** of the ranges; 3318
2Ch 25:9 able to go **f.** to war, that could 3318
2Ch 25:11 and led **f.** his people, and went to
2Ch 26:6 And he went **f.** and warred against 3318
2Ch 29:5 and carry **f.** the filthiness out of 3318
2Ch 29:23 And they brought **f.** the he goats
2Ch 32:21 that came **f.** of his own bowels 3329
Ezr 1:7 Also Cyrus the king brought **f.** 3318
Ezr 1:7 Nebuchadnezzer had brought **f.** 3318
Ezr 1:8 did Cyrus king of Persia bring **f.** 3318
Ezr 6:5 took **f.** out of the temple which is 5312
Ne 4:16 came to pass from that time **f.**, that
Ne 8:15 Go **f.** unto the mount, and fetch 3318
Ne 8:16 So the people went **f.**, and brought 3318
Ne 9:7 and broughtest him **f.** out of Ur of 3318
Ne 9:15 broughtest **f.** water for them out 3318
Ne 13:8 I cast **f.** all the household stuff
Ne 13:21 From that time **f.** came they no more
Es 4:6 So Hatach went **f.** to Mordecai 3318
Es 5:9 went Haman **f.** that day joyful and 3318
Job 1:11 But put **f.** thine hand now, and 7971
Job 1:12 upon himself put not **f.** thine hand, 7971
Job 1:12 went **f.** from the presence of the 3318
Job 2:5 But put **f.** thine hand now, and 7971
Job 2:7 went Satan **f.** from the presence 3318
Job 5:6 affliction cometh not **f.** of the dust, 3318
Job 8:16 and his branch shooteth **f.** in his 3318
Job 10:18 hast thou brought me **f.** out of the 3318
Job 11:17 thou shalt shine **f.**, thou shalt be
Job 14:2 He cometh **f.** like a flower, and is 3318
Job 14:9 it will bud, and bring **f.** boughs 6213
Job 15:35 and bring **f.** vanity, and their belly 3205
Job 21:11 They send **f.** their little ones like a

Job 21:30 they shall be brought **f.** to the day...........
Job 23:10 he hath tried me, I shall come **f.**..........3318
Job 24:5 wild asses in the desert, go they **f.**..... 3318
Job 28:9 He putteth **f.** his hand upon the......... 7971
Job 28:11 that is hid bringeth he **f.** to light........ 3318
Job 30:5 They were driven **f.** from among..............
Job 38:8 when it brake **f.**, as if it had issued..... 1518
Job 38:27 of the tender herb to spring **f.**?.......... 6779
Job 38:32 Canst thou bring **f.** Mazzaroth in.......... 3318
Job 39:1 when the wild goats bring **f.**? or......... 3205
Job 39:2 thou the time when they bring **f.**?....... 3205
Job 39:3 they bring **f.** their young ones,........... 6398
Job 39:4 they go **f.**, and return not unto.......... 3318
Job 40:20 the mountains bring him **f.** food,..............
Ps 1:3 that bringeth **f.** his fruit in his........... 5414
Ps 7:14 mischief, and brought **f.** falsehood....... 3205
Ps 9:1 I will shew **f.** all thy marvellous...............
Ps 9:14 that I may shew **f.** all thy praise..............
Ps 17:2 Let thy sentence come **f.** from........... 3318
Ps 18:19 He brought me **f.** also into a large.......3318
Ps 19:6 His going **f.** is from the end of the...... 4161
Ps 37:6 shall bring **f.** thy righteousness........... 3318
Ps 44:9 and goest not **f.** with our armies......... 3318
Ps 51:15 and my mouth shall shew **f.** thy..............
Ps 55:20 He hath put **f.** his hands against..........7971
Ps 57:3 God shall send **f.** his mercy and his..........
Ps 66:2 Sing **f.** the honour of his name; make.........
Ps 68:7 when thou wentest **f.** before thy......... 3318
Ps 71:15 shall shew **f.** thy righteousness............ 3318
Ps 78:52 But made his own people to go **f.**........ 5265
Ps 79:13 we will shew **f.** thy praise to all.......... 5608
Ps 80:1 between the cherubims, shine **f.**...............
Ps 88:8 am shut up, and I cannot come **f.**..........3318
Ps 90:2 the mountains were brought **f.**,............3205
Ps 92:2 To shew **f.** thy lovingkindness..................
Ps 92:14 still bring **f.** fruit in old age;............... 5107
Ps 96:2 shew **f.** his salvation from day to.............
Ps 104:14 that he may bring **f.** food out of.......... 3318
Ps 104:20 all the beasts of the forest do creep **f.**,........
Ps 104:23 Man goeth **f.** unto his work and.......... 3318
Ps 104:30 Thou sendest **f.** thy spirit, they are..........
Ps 105:30 brought **f.** frogs in abundance,............ 8317
Ps 105:37 brought them **f.** also with silver.......... 3318
Ps 105:43 he brought **f.** his people with joy,......... 3318
Ps 106:2 who can shew **f.** all his praise?................
Ps 107:7 he led them **f.** by the right way,...............
Ps 108:11 thou, O God, go **f.** with our hosts?......3318
Ps 113:2 from this time **f.** and for evermore...........
Ps 115:18 from this time **f.** and for evermore...........
Ps 121:8 thy coming in from this time **f.**,...............
Ps 125:3 the righteous put **f.** their hands.......... 7971
Ps 125:5 the Lord shall lead them **f.** with...............
Ps 126:6 He that goeth **f.** and weepeth,...............
Ps 138:7 thou shalt stretch **f.** thine hand against.......
Ps 141:2 be set **f.** before thee as incense;.............
Ps 143:6 I stretch **f.** my hands unto thee:..............
Ps 144:6 Cast **f.** lightning, and scatter them:...........
Ps 144:13 our sheep may bring **f.** thousands..............
Ps 146:4 His breath goeth **f.**, he returneth........ 3318
Ps 147:15 He sendeth **f.** his commandment..............
Ps 147:17 He casteth **f.** his ice like morsels:............
Pr 7:15 Therefore came I **f.** to meet thee,...... 3318
Pr 8:1 understanding put **f.** her voice?...............
Pr 8:24 were no depths, I was brought **f.**;.......2342
Pr 8:25 before the hills was I brought **f.**:.........2342
Pr 9:3 She hath sent **f.** her maidens:...................
Pr 10:31 of the just bringeth **f.** wisdom;.......... 5107
Pr 12:17 truth sheweth **f.** righteousness:.................
Pr 25:4 shall come **f.** a vessel for the finer...... 3318
Pr 25:6 Put not **f.** thyself in the presence........1921
Pr 25:8 Go out **f.** hastily to strive, lest thou.....3318
Pr 27:1 not what a day may bring **f.**................3205
Pr 30:27 go they **f.** all of them by bands;.......... 3318
Pr 30:33 churning of milk bringeth **f.** butter,...... 3318
Pr 30:33 of the nose bringeth **f.** blood:............. 3318
Pr 30:33 forcing of wrath bringeth **f.** strife........ 3318
Pr 31:20 yea, she reacheth **f.** her hands to........6566
Ec 2:6 the wood that bringeth **f.** trees:..........6779
Ec 5:15 he came **f.** of his mother's womb,....... 3318
Ec 7:18 God shall come **f.** of them all............ 3318
Ec 10:1 apothecary to send **f.** a stinking................
Ca 1:3 thy name is as ointment poured **f.**,...........
Ca 1:8 go thy way **f.** by the footsteps.......... 3318
Ca 1:12 spikenard sendeth **f.** the smell...................
Ca 2:9 he looketh **f.** at the windows,....................
Ca 2:13 fig tree putteth **f.** her green figs,........ 2590
Ca 3:11 Go **f.**, O ye daughters of Zion,........... 3318
Ca 6:10 that looketh **f.** as the morning,...................
Ca 7:11 let us go **f.** into the field;................... 3318
Ca 7:12 and the pomegranates bud **f.**:............. 5132
Ca 8:5 there thy mother brought thee **f.**;............ 2254
Ca 8:5 she brought thee **f.** that bare thee,...... 2254
Isa 1:15 And when ye spread **f.** your hands,...........
Isa 2:3 for out of Zion shall go **f.** the law,....... 3318
Isa 3:16 and walk with stretched **f.** necks..............
Isa 5:2 that it should bring **f.** grapes,............. 6213
Isa 5:2 and it brought **f.** wild grapes............... 6213
Isa 5:4 that it should bring **f.** grapes,............. 6213
Isa 5:4 brought it **f.** wild grapes?................... 6213
Isa 5:25 and he hath stretched **f.** his hand..............
Isa 7:3 Go **f.** now to meet Ahaz, thou,........... 3318
Isa 7:25 shall be for the sending **f.** of oxen,............
Isa 11:1 And there shall come **f.** a rod............ 3318
Isa 13:10 shall be darkened in his going **f.**,......... 3318
Isa 14:7 they break **f.** into singing.........................
Isa 14:29 root shall come **f.** a cockatrice,............ 3318
Isa 23:4 travail not, nor bring **f.** children,......... 3205
Isa 25:11 And he shall spread **f.** his hands in...........
Isa 25:11 as he that swimmeth spreadeth **f.** his.........
Isa 26:18 have as it were brought **f.** wind;......... 3205
Isa 27:8 In measure, when it shooteth **f.**,.................
Isa 28:19 from the time that it goeth **f.**.............. 5674
Isa 28:29 cometh **f.** from the Lord of hosts,........ 3318
Isa 31:4 multitude of shepherds is called **f.**.............
Isa 32:20 that send **f.** thither the feet of the ox.........
Isa 33:11 chaff, ye shall bring **f.** stubble:........... 3205
Isa 34:1 and all things that come **f.** of it.......... 6631
Isa 36:3 Then came **f.** unto him Eliakim,........... 3318
Isa 37:3 there is not strength to bring **f.**........... 3205
Isa 37:9 come **f.** to make war with thee............ 3318
Isa 37:32 For out of Jerusalem shall go **f.**.......... 3318
Isa 37:36 Then the angel of the Lord went **f.**,..... 3318
Isa 41:21 bring **f.** your strong reasons,...............5066
Isa 41:22 Let them bring them **f.**, and shew....... 5066
Isa 42:1 he shall bring **f.** judgment to the.......... 3318
Isa 42:3 bring **f.** judgment unto truth................ 3318
Isa 42:5 he that spread **f.** the earth,......................
Isa 42:9 before they spring **f.** I tell you..................
Isa 42:13 Lord shall go **f.** as a mighty man,........ 3318
Isa 43:8 Bring **f.** the blind people that have...... 3318
Isa 43:9 let them bring **f.** their witnesses,.............
Isa 43:17 bringeth **f.** the chariot and horse,........ 4161
Isa 43:19 now it shall spring **f.**;........................ 6779
Isa 43:21 they shall shew **f.** my praise.....................
Isa 44:23 break **f.** into singing, ye...........................
Isa 44:24 that stretcheth **f.** the heavens alone;..........
Isa 45:8 and let them bring **f.** salvation,........... 6509
Isa 45:10 What hast thou brought **f.**?............... 2342
Isa 48:1 come **f.** out of the waters of Judah,..... 3318
Isa 48:3 and they went **f.** out of my mouth,...... 3318
Isa 48:20 Go ye **f.** of Babylon, flee ye from........ 3318
Isa 49:9 mayest say to the prisoners, Go **f.**;..... 3318
Isa 49:13 and break **f.** into singing,........................
Isa 49:17 made thee waste shall go **f.** of thee.... 3318
Isa 51:5 my salvation is gone **f.**, and mine........ 3318
Isa 51:13 that hath stretched **f.** the heavens,...........
Isa 51:18 sons whom she hath brought **f.**;.......... 3205
Isa 52:9 Break **f.** into joy, sing together,...............
Isa 54:1 break **f.** into singing, and cry....................
Isa 54:2 and let them stretch **f.** the curtains..........
Isa 54:3 shalt break **f.** on the right hand.................
Isa 54:16 that bringeth **f.** an instrument............. 4161
Isa 55:10 and maketh it bring **f.** and bud,........... 3205
Isa 55:11 So shall my word be that goeth **f.**........ 3318
Isa 55:12 and be led **f.** with peace:................... 2986
Isa 55:12 and the hills shall break **f.**.....................
Isa 58:8 Then shall the light break **f.** as................
Isa 58:8 health shall spring **f.** speedily:.................
Isa 58:9 the putting **f.** of the finger, and.......... 7971
Isa 59:4 mischief, and bring **f.** iniquity............ 3205
Isa 60:6 shew **f.** the praises of the Lord..............
Isa 61:11 as the earth bringeth **f.** her bud,......... 3318
Isa 61:11 that are sown in it to spring **f.**;................
Isa 61:11 and praise to spring **f.** before all..............
Isa 62:1 the righteousness thereof go **f.**........... 3318
Isa 65:9 I will bring **f.** a seed out of Jacob,....... 3318
Isa 65:23 nor bring **f.** for trouble:...................... 3205
Isa 66:7 she travailed, she brought **f.**;............. 3205
Isa 66:8 be made to bring **f.** in one day?.......... 2342
Isa 66:8 she brought **f.** her children................ 3205
Isa 66:9 and not cause to bring **f.**? saith........... 3205
Isa 66:9 shall I cause to bring **f.**, and shut........ 3205
Isa 66:24 And they shall go **f.**, and look............ 3318
Jer 1:5 and before thou camest **f.** out of......... 3318
Jer 1:9 Then the Lord put **f.** his hand,........... 7971
Jer 1:14 the north an evil shall break **f.**.................
Jer 2:27 stone, Thou hast brought me **f.**:......... 3205
Jer 2:37 Yea, thou shalt go **f.** from him,........... 3318
Jer 4:4 lest my fury come **f.** like fire,............ 3318
Jer 4:7 is gone **f.** from his place to make........ 3318
Jer 4:31 anguish as of her that bringeth **f.**..............
Jer 6:25 Go not **f.** into the field, nor walk......... 3318
Jer 7:25 day that your fathers came **f.** out........ 3318
Jer 10:13 and bringeth **f.** the wind out of his....... 3318
Jer 10:20 my children are gone **f.** of me,........... 3318
Jer 10:20 there is none to stretch **f.** my tent...........
Jer 11:4 I brought them **f.** out of the land......... 3318
Jer 12:2 they grow, yea, they bring **f.** fruit;...... 6213
Jer 14:18 If I go **f.** into the field, then................ 3318
Jer 15:1 out of my sight, and, let them go **f.**..... 3318
Jer 15:2 Whither shall ye go **f.**? then thou........ 3318
Jer 15:19 and if thou take **f.** the precious........... 3318
Jer 17:22 carry **f.** a burden out of your houses.... 3318
Jer 19:2 And go **f.** unto the valley of the son.... 3318
Jer 20:8 Pashur brought **f.** Jeremiah out of....... 3318
Jer 20:18 Wherefore came I **f.** out of the.......... 3318
Jer 22:11 which went **f.** out of this place;.......... 3318
Jer 22:19 cast **f.** beyond the gates of Jerusalem,........
Jer 23:15 profaneness gone **f.** into all the........... 3318
Jer 23:19 the Lord is gone **f.** in fury, even.......... 3318
Jer 25:32 shall go **f.** from nation to nation,......... 3318
Jer 26:23 they fetched **f.** Urijah out of Egypt,...... 3318
Jer 29:16 not gone **f.** with you into captivity;...... 3318
Jer 30:23 the Lord goeth **f.** with fury, a............ 3318
Jer 31:4 shalt go **f.** in the dances of them......... 3318
Jer 31:24 and they that go **f.** with flocks........... 5265
Jer 31:39 shall yet go **f.** over against it............ 3318
Jer 32:21 brought **f.** thy people Israel out of....... 3318
Jer 34:13 I brought them **f.** out of the land......... 3318
Jer 37:5 Pharaoh's army was come **f.** out of...... 3318
Jer 37:7 which is come **f.** to help you, shall...... 3318
Jer 37:12 Jeremiah went **f.** out of Jerusalem....... 3318
Jer 38:2 he that goeth **f.** to the Chaldeans........ 3318
Jer 38:8 Ebed-melech went **f.** out of the.......... 3318
Jer 38:17 wilt assuredly go **f.** unto the king........ 3318
Jer 38:18 if thou wilt not go **f.** to the king.......... 3318
Jer 38:21 But if thou refuse to go **f.**, this is....... 3318
Jer 38:22 Judah's house shall be brought **f.**......... 4163
Jer 39:4 and went **f.** out of the city by night,.... 3318
Jer 41:6 went **f.** from Mizpah to meet them,...... 3318
Jer 42:18 my fury hath been poured **f.** upon............
Jer 42:18 shall my fury be poured **f.** upon you,.........
Jer 43:12 shall go **f.** from thence in peace.......... 3318
Jer 44:6 fury and mine anger was poured **f.**,...........
Jer 44:17 every thing goeth **f.** out of our........... 3318
Jer 46:4 and stand **f.** with your helmets;................
Jer 46:9 and let the mighty men come **f.**;.......... 3318
Jer 48:7 Chemosh shall go **f.** into captivity......... 3318
Jer 48:45 fire shall come **f.** out of Heshbon,........ 3318
Jer 49:5 driven out every man right **f.**;............. 6440
Jer 50:8 and go **f.** out of the land of the........... 3318
Jer 50:25 and hath brought **f.** the weapons of...... 3318
Jer 51:10 The Lord hath brought **f.** our............. 3318
Jer 51:16 and bringeth **f.** the wind out of his....... 3318
Jer 51:44 and I will bring **f.** out of his mouth...... 3318
Jer 52:7 and went **f.** out of the city by night..... 3318
Jer 52:31 and brought him **f.** out of prison,......... 3318
La 1:17 Zion spreadeth **f.** her hands, and...............
Eze 1:13 out of the fire went **f.** lightning........... 3318
Eze 1:22 the terrible crystal, stretched **f.** over.........
Eze 3:22 Arise, go **f.** into the plain, and I.......... 3318
Eze 3:23 and went **f.** into the plain: and,........... 3318
Eze 5:4 come **f.** into all the house of Israel...... 3318
Eze 7:10 the morning is gone **f.**; the rod hath.... 3318
Eze 8:3 And he put **f.** the form of an hand,....... 7971
Eze 9:7 go ye **f.**. And they went **f.**, and.......... 3318
Eze 10:7 cherub stretched **f.** his hand from.............
Eze 11:7 bring you **f.** out of the midst of it......... 3318
Eze 12:4 Thou shalt bring **f.** thy stuff by........... 3318
Eze 12:4 shalt go **f.** at even in their sight,......... 3318
Eze 12:4 as they that go **f.** into captivity........... 4161
Eze 12:6 and carry it **f.** in the twilight:............. 3318
Eze 12:7 I brought **f.** my stuff by day, as............ 3318
Eze 12:7 I brought it **f.** in the twilight, and........ 3318
Eze 12:12 in the twilight, and shall go **f.**:........... 3318
Eze 14:22 shall be brought **f.**, both sons and....... 4163
Eze 14:22 they shall come **f.** unto you, and ye..... 3318
Eze 16:14 And thy renown went **f.** among the..... 3318
Eze 17:2 Son of man, put **f.** a riddle, and.......... 2330
Eze 17:6 a vine and brought **f.** branches,.......... 6213

Eze 17:6 branches, and shot f. sprigs.
Eze 17:7 and shot f. her branches toward him,
Eze 17:8 that it might bring f. branches, 6213
Eze 17:23 and it shall bring f. boughs, and 5375
Eze 18:8 He that hath not given f. upon usury,
Eze 18:13 Hath given f. upon usury, and hath
Eze 20:6 bring them f. of the land of Egypt 3318
Eze 20:9 in bringing them f. out of the land 3318
Eze 20:10 Wherefore I caused them to go f. 3318
Eze 20:22 in whose sight I brought them f. 3318
Eze 20:38 bring them f. out of the country 3318
Eze 21:3 and will draw f. my sword out of 3318
Eze 21:4 shall my sword go f. out of his 3318
Eze 21:5 have drawn f. my sword out of his 3318
Eze 21:19 twain shall come f. out of one land: 3318
Eze 24:12 great scum went not f. out of her: 3318
Eze 27:7 which thou spreadest f. to be thy
Eze 27:10 they set f. thy comeliness.
Eze 27:33 thy wares went f. out of the seas, 3318
Eze 28:18 therefore will I bring f. a fire from 3318
Eze 29:21 house of Israel but f., and I will
Eze 30:9 shall messengers go f. from me 3318
Eze 31:5 multitude of waters, when he shot f.
Eze 31:6 of the field bring f. their young, 3205
Eze 32:2 and thou camest f. with thy rivers, 1518
Eze 32:4 will cast thee f. upon the open field,
Eze 33:30 that cometh f. from the Lord. 3318
Eze 36:8 ye shall shoot f. your branches, and
Eze 36:20 and are gone f. out of his land. 3318
Eze 38:4 I will bring thee f., and all thine 3318
Eze 38:8 it is brought f. out of the nations, 3318
Eze 39:9 cities of Israel shall go f., and shall 3318
Eze 42:1 he brought me f. into the utter 3318
Eze 42:15 he brought me f. toward the gate 3318
Eze 44:5 every going f. of the sanctuary. 4161
Eze 44:19 they go f. into the utter court, 3318
Eze 46:2 then he shall go f.; but the gate 3318
Eze 46:8 he shall go f. by the way thereof. 3318
Eze 46:9 go f. by the way of the north gate: 3318
Eze 46:9 but shall go f. over against it. 3318
Eze 46:10 and when they go f., shall go f. 3318
Eze 46:12 then he shall go f.; and after his 3318
Eze 46:12 after his going f. one shall shut the 3318
Eze 46:21 Then he brought me f. into the 3318
Eze 47:3 line in his hand went f. eastward, 3318
Eze 47:8 which being brought f. into the sea, 3318
Eze 47:10 shall be a place to spread f. nets;
Eze 47:12 it shall bring f. new fruit according
Da 2:13 decree went f. that the wise men 5312
Da 2:14 which was gone f. to slay the wise 5312
Da 3:26 come f., and come hither 5312
Da 3:26 and Abed-nego, came f. of the 5312
Da 5:5 In the same hour came f. fingers 5312
Da 7:10 stream issued and came f. from 5312
Da 8:9 out of one of them came f. a little 3318
Da 9:15 brought thy people f. out of the 3318
Da 9:22 I am now come f. to give thee skill 3318
Da 9:23 the commandment came f., and I 3318
Da 9:25 going f. of the commandment 4161
Da 10:20 and when I am gone f., lo, the 3318
Da 11:11 shall come f. and fight with him, 3318
Da 11:11 shall set f. a great multitude; 5975
Da 11:13 and shall set f. a multitude greater
Da 11:42 He shall stretch f. his hand also upon
Da 11:44 therefore he shall go f. with great 3318
Ho 6:3 his going f. is prepared as the 4161
Ho 6:5 are as the light that goeth f. 3318
Ho 9:13 shall bring f. his children to the 3318
Ho 9:16 though they bring f., yet will I 3205
Ho 10:1 he bringeth f. fruit unto himself: 7737
Ho 13:13 of the breaking f. of children. 4866
Ho 14:5 and cast f. his roots as Lebanon. 5221
Joe 2:16 bridegroom go f. of his chamber 3318
Joe 3:18 fountain shall come f. of the house 3318
Am 5:3 which went f. by an hundred shall 3318
Am 7:17 go into captivity f. of his land.
Am 8:3 shall cast them f. with silence.
Am 8:5 that we may set f. wheat, making 6605
Jon 1:5 cast f. the wares that were in the 2904
Jon 1:12 and cast me f. into the sea: so 2904
Jon 1:15 cast him f. into the sea: and the sea 2904
Mic 1:3 Lord cometh f. out of his place, 3318
Mic 1:11 Zaanan came not f. in the morning 3318
Mic 4:2 for the law shall go f. of Zion, and 3318
Mic 4:10 labour to bring f., O daughter of 1518
Mic 4:10 go f. out of the city, and thou 3318

Mic 5:2 shall he come f. unto me that is to 3318
Mic 5:2 be ruler in Israel; whose goings f. 4163
Mic 5:3 which travaileth hath brought f.: 3205
Mic 7:9 he will bring me f. to the light, 3318
Hab 1:4 and judgment doth never go f.: for 3318
Hab 3:5 burning coals went f. at his feet. 3318
Hab 3:13 Thou wentest f. for the salvation 3318
Zep 2:2 Before the decree bring f., before 3205
Hag 1:11 that which the ground bringeth f., 3318
Hag 2:19 the olive tree, hath not brought f.: 5375
Zec 1:16 shall be stretched f. upon Jerusalem,
Zec 2:3 angel that talked with me went f., 3318
Zec 2:6 Ho, ho, come f., and flee from the
Zec 3:8 bring f. my servant the Branch. 935
Zec 4:7 and he shall bring f. the headstone 3318
Zec 5:3 curse that goeth f. over the face of 3318
Zec 5:4 I will bring it f., saith the Lord of 3318
Zec 5:5 angel that talked with me went f., 3318
Zec 5:5 and see what is this that goeth f. 3318
Zec 5:6 This is an ephah that goeth f. 3318
Zec 6:5 which go f. from standing before 3318
Zec 6:6 therein go f. into the north country; 3318
Zec 6:6 and thewhite go f. after them; 3318
Zec 6:6 the grisled go f. toward the south 3318
Zec 6:7 the bay went f., and sought to go 3318
Zec 9:11 I have sent f. thy prisoners out of
Zec 9:14 arrow shall go f. as the lightning: 3318
Zec 10:4 Out of him came f. the corner, 3318
Zec 12:1 which stretcheth f. the heavens,
Zec 14:2 the city shall go f. into captivity, 3318
Zec 14:3 Then shall the Lord go f., and fight 3318
Mal 4:2 and ye shall go f., and grow up 3318
Mt 1:21 And she shall bring f. a son, and 5088
Mt 1:23 and shall bring f. a son, and they 5088
Mt 1:25 till she had brought f. her firstborn 5088
Mt 2:16 sent f., and slew all the children 649
Mt 3:8 Bring f. therefore fruits, meet for 4160
Mt 3:10 which bringeth not f. good fruit 4160
Mt 7:17 **good tree bringeth f. good fruit;** 4160
Mt 7:17 **corrupt tree bringeth f. evil fruit.** 4160
Mt 7:18 **good tree cannot bring f. evil fruit,** 4160
Mt 7:18 **neither can a corrupt tree bring f.** 4160
Mt 7:19 **tree that bringeth not f. good fruit** 4160
Mt 8:3 And Jesus put f. his hand, 1614
Mt 9:9 as Jesus passed f. from thence 3855
Mt 9:25 But when the people were put f., 1544
Mt 9:38 **that he will send f. labourers** 1544
Mt 10:5 These twelve Jesus sent f., and 649
Mt 10:16 **Behold, I send you f. as sheep** 649
Mt 12:13 **Stretch f. thine hand.** 1614
Mt 12:13 And he stretched it f.; 1614
Mt 12:20 till he send f. judgment unto 1544
Mt 12:35 **of the heart bringeth f. good** 1544
Mt 12:35 **treasure bringeth f. evil things**
Mt 12:49 And he stretched f. his hand 1614
Mt 13:3 **Behold a sower went f. to sow;** 1831
Mt 13:8 **good ground, and brought f. fruit,**
Mt 13:23 **beareth fruit, and bringeth f.,** 4160
Mt 13:24 Another parable put he f. unto 3908
Mt 13:26 **sprung up, and brought f. fruit,** 4160
Mt 13:31 Another parable put he f. unto 3908
Mt 13:41 **The son of man shall send f. his** 649
Mt 13:43 **Then shall the righteous shine f.** 1584
Mt 13:49 **the angels shall come f.,** 3318
Mt 13:52 **bringeth f. out of his treasure** 1544
Mt 14:2 therefore mighty works do shew f. 1754
Mt 14:14 And Jesus went f., and saw 1831
Mt 14:31 immediately Jesus stretched f. 1614
Mt 15:18 **mouth came f. from the heart;** 3318
Mt 16:21 From that time f. began Jesus to
Mt 21:43 **to a nation bringing f. the fruits** 4160
Mt 22:3 **sent f. his servants to call them** 649
Mt 22:4 **he sent f. other servants, saying,** 649
Mt 22:7 **sent f. his armies, and destroyed**
Mt 22:46 from that day f. ask him any more
Mt 24:26 **go not f.: behold, he is in the** 1831
Mt 24:32 **and putteth f. leaves, ye know that** 1631
Mt 25:1 **went f. to meet the bridegroom,** 1831
Mk 1:38 **there also: for therefore came I f.** 1831
Mk 1:41 put f. his hand, and touched him, 1614
Mk 2:12 and went f. before them all: 1831
Mk 2:13 And he went f. again by the sea side 1831
Mk 3:3 he saith...**Stand f.** 1519,3588,3319
Mk 3:5 the man, **Stretch f. thine hand.** 1614
Mk 3:6 And the Pharisees went f., and 1831
Mk 3:14 he might send them f. to preach, 649

Mk 4:8 **brought f., some thirty, and some** 5348
Mk 4:20 **and bring f. fruit, some thirtyfold,** 2592
Mk 4:28 **earth bringeth f. fruit of herself;** 2592
Mk 4:29 **fruit is brought f., immediately** 3860
Mk 6:7 to send them f. by two and two; 1614
Mk 6:14 mighty works do shew f. 1754
Mk 6:17 Herod himself had sent f. and laid 1614
Mk 6:24 And she went f. and said unto her 1831
Mk 7:26 he would cast f. the devil out of 1544
Mk 8:11 the Pharisees came f., and began 1831
Mk 9:29 **This kind can come f. by nothing,** 1831
Mk 10:17 when he was gone f. into the way, 1607
Mk 11:1 sendeth f. two of his disciples, 1614
Mk 13:28 **and putteth f. leaves, ye know** 1631
Mk 14:13 he sendeth f. two of his disciples, 1614
Mk 14:16 his disciples went f., and came 1831
Mk 16:20 they went f., and preached every 1831
Lu 1:1 to set f. in order a declaration 392
Lu 1:31 bring f. a son, and shalt call his 5088
Lu 1:57 be delivered; and she brought f. 1080
Lu 2:7 she brought f. her firstborn son. 5088
Lu 3:7 that came f. to be baptized of 1607
Lu 3:8 Bring f. therefore fruits worthy of 4160
Lu 3:9 which bringeth not f. good fruit 4160
Lu 5:13 he put f. his hand, and touched 1614
Lu 5:27 after these things he went f., and 1831
Lu 6:8 **Rise up, and stand f. in the midst.**
Lu 6:8 And he arose and stood f.
Lu 6:10 unto the man, **Stretch f. thy hand.** 1614
Lu 6:43 **bringeth not f. corrupt fruit;** 4160
Lu 6:43 **a corrupt tree bring f. good fruit.** 4160
Lu 6:45 **bringeth f. that which is good;** 4393
Lu 6:45 **treasure of his heart bringeth f.** 4393
Lu 7:17 of him went f. throughout all 1831
Lu 8:14 **when they have heard, go f., and** 4198
Lu 8:15 **and bring f. fruit with patience.**
Lu 8:22 **of the lake.** And they launched f. 321
Lu 8:27 And when he went f. to land, 1831
Lu 10:2 **that he would send f. labourers** 1544
Lu 10:3 **I send you f. as lambs among** 649
Lu 12:16 **rich man brought f. plentifully;** 2164
Lu 12:37 **and will come f. and serve them,** 3928
Lu 14:7 put f. a parable to those which 3004
Lu 15:22 **Bring f. the best robe, and put it** 1627
Lu 20:9 **and let it f. to husbandmen, and** 1554
Lu 20:20 sent f. spies, which should feign 649
Lu 21:30 **When they now shoot f., ye see** 4261
Lu 22:53 **ye stretched f. no hands against** 1614
Joh 1:43 Jesus would go f. into Galilee, 1831
Joh 2:10 doth set f. good wine; and when 5087
Joh 2:11 and manifested f. his glory; 5319
Joh 5:29 **And shall come f.; they that have** 1607
Joh 8:42 **I proceeded f. and came from God;** 1831
Joh 10:4 **when he putteth f. his own sheep,** 1544
Joh 11:43 a loud voice, **Lazarus, come f.,** 1854
Joh 11:44 he that was dead came f., bound 1831
Joh 11:53 from that day f. they took counsel
Joh 12:13 went f. to meet him, and cried, 1831
Joh 12:24 **if it die, it bringeth f. much fruit.**
Joh 15:2 **that it may bring f. more fruit,**
Joh 15:5 **the same bringeth f. much fruit:**
Joh 15:6 **he is cast f. as a branch, and is** 1854
Joh 15:16 **should go and bring f. fruit, and**
Joh 16:28 **I came f. from the Father, and** 1831
Joh 16:30 that thou camest f. from God. 1831
Joh 18:1 f. with his disciples over the brook 1831
Joh 18:4 went f., and said unto them, **Whom** 1831
Joh 19:4 Pilate therefore went f. again, 1854
Joh 19:4 unto them, Behold, I bring him f. 1854
Joh 19:5 came Jesus f., wearing the crown 1854
Joh 19:13 he brought Jesus f., and sat down 1854
Joh 19:17 went f. into a place called the 1831
Joh 20:3 Peter therefore went f., and that 1831
Joh 21:3 went f., and entered into a ship 1831
Joh 21:18 **thou shalt stretch f. thy hands,** 1614
Ac 1:26 And they gave f. their lots; and 1614
Ac 2:33 he hath shed f. this, which ye now 1632
Ac 4:30 By stretching f. thine hand to heal; 1614
Ac 5:10 and, carrying her f., buried her by 1627
Ac 5:15 brought f. the sick into the streets, 1627
Ac 5:19 and brought them f., and said, 1806
Ac 5:34 put the apostles f. a little space; 1854
Ac 7:7 shall they come f., and serve me 1831
Ac 9:30 Caesarea, and sent him f. to Tarsus. 1821
Ac 9:40 Peter put them all f., and kneeled 1854
Ac 11:22 they sent f. Barnabas, that he 1821

Ac 12:1 the king stretched **f.** his hands to....... *1911*
Ac 12:4 Easter to bring him **f.** to the people..... *321*
Ac 12:6 Herod would have brought him **f.**, ... *4254*
Ac 13:4 being sent **f.** by the Holy Ghost, ... *1599*
Ac 16:3 would Paul have to go **f.** with him; *1831*
Ac 17:18 to be a setter **f.** of strange gods: *2604*
Ac 21:2 we went aboard, and set **f.**.................. *321*
Ac 23:28 brought him **f.** into their council: *2609*
Ac 24:2 he was called **f.**, Tertullas began........ *2564*
Ac 25:17 the man to be brought **f.**.......................
Ac 25:23 Paul was brought **f.**..............................
Ac 25:26 have brought him **f.** before you,......... *4254*
Ac 26:1 Then Paul stretched **f.** the hand,........ *1614*
Ac 26:25 but speak **f.** the words of truth and...... *669*
Ac 27:21 Paul stood **f.** in the midst of them, ...
Ro 3:25 Whom God hath set **f.** to be a........... *4388*
Ro 7:4 that we should bring **f.** fruit unto.............
Ro 7:5 our members to bring **f.** fruit unto...........
Ro 10:21 I have stretched **f.** my hands unto...... *1600*
1Co 4:9 God hath set **f.** us the apostles *584*
1Co 16:11 but conduct him **f.** in peace, that........ *4311*
Ga 3:1 Christ hath been evidently set **f.**, ... *4270*
Ga 4:4 God sent **f.** his son, made of a *1821*
Ga 4:6 God hath sent **f.** the Spirit of his........ *1821*
Ga 4:27 **f.** and cry, thou that travailest *4486*
Php 2:16 Holding **f.** the word of life; that I *1907*
Php 3:13 and reaching **f.** unto those things........ *1901*
Col 1:6 and bringeth **f.** fruit, as it doth *1901*
1Ti 1:16 Jesus Christ might shew **f.** all............ *1731*
Heb 1:14 sent **f.** to minister for them who.......... *649*
Heb 6:7 bringeth **f.** herbs meet for them......... *5088*
Heb 13:13 Let us go **f.** therefore unto him *1831*
Jas 1:15 lust hath conceived, it bringeth **f.**.......... *616*
Jas 1:15 it is finished, bringeth **f.** death........... *5088*
Jas 3:11 Doth a fountain send **f.** at the same.... *1032*
Jas 5:18 and the earth brought **f.** her fruit......... *985*
1Pe 2:9 that ye should shew **f.** the praises...... *1804*
3Jo 7 for his name's sake they went **f.**, ... *1831*
Jude 7 are set **f.** for an example, suffering........ *4295*
Re 5:6 seven spirits of God sent **f.** into........ *649*
Re 6:2 went **f.** conquering, and to conquer..... *1831*
Re 12:5 And she brought **f.** a man child, ... *5088*
Re 12:13 woman which brought **f.** the man *5088*
Re 16:14 go **f.** unto the kings of the earth........ *1607*

FORTHWITH
Ezr 6:8 **f.** expences be given unto these 629
Mt 13:5 **f. they sprung up, because they**..... *2112*
Mt 26:49 **f.** he came to Jesus, and said, ... *2112*
Mk 1:29 **f.**, when they were come out of......... *2112*
Mk 1:43 charged him, and **f.** sent him away; *2112*
Mk 5:13 And **f.** Jesus gave them leave........... *2112*
Joh 19:34 **f.** came thereout blood and water....... *2117*
Ac 9:18 he received sight **f.**, and arose, ... *3916*
Ac 12:10 **f.** the angel departed from him. *2112*
Ac 21:30 and **f.** the doors were shut. *2112*

FORTIETH
Nu 33:38 and died there, in the **f.** year after....... 705
De 1:3 and it came to pass in the **f.** year, ... 705
1Ch 26:31 In the **f.** year of the reign of David...... 705
2Ch 16:13 and died in the one and **f.** year of........ 705

FORTIFIED
2Ch 11:11 And he **f.** the strong holds, and 2388
2Ch 26:9 turning of the wall, and **f.** them. 2388
Ne 3:8 **f.** Jerusalem unto the broad wall......... 5800
Mic 7:12 Assyria, and from the **f.** cities, ... 4692

FORTIFY See also FORTIFIED.
Jg 9:31 they **f.** the city against thee. 6696
Ne 4:2 Jews? will they **f.** themselves? 5800
Isa 22:10 ye broken down to **f.** the wall. 1219
Jer 51:53 should **f.** the height of her strength, ... 1219
Na 2:1 loins strong, **f.** thy power mightily. 553
Na 3:14 **f.** thy strong holds: go into clay, ... 2388

FORTRESS See also FORTRESSES.
2Sa 22:2 The Lord is my rock, and my **f.**, ... 4686
Ps 18:2 rock, and my **f.**, and my deliverer; 4686
Ps 31:3 For thou art my rock and my **f.**; 4686
Ps 71:3 for thou art my rock and my **f.**. 4686
Ps 91:2 He is my refuge and my **f.**: 4686
Ps 144:2 My goodness, and my **f.**; my high...... 4686
Isa 17:3 **f.** also shall cease from Ephraim,......... 4013
Isa 25:12 And the **f.** of the high fort of thy 4013
Jer 6:27 a tower and a **f.** among my people, ... 4013
Jer 10:17 the land, O inhabitant of the **f.**........... 4693
Jer 16:19 O Lord, my strength, and my **f.**, ... 4581
Da 11:7 shall enter into the **f.** of the king........ 4581
Da 11:10 and be stirred up, even to his **f.** 4581
Am 5:9 spoiled shall come against the **f.**......... 4013
Mic 7:12 and from the **f.** even to the river, ... 4693

FORTRESSES
Isa 34:13 and brambles in the **f.** thereof: 4013
Ho 10:14 and all thy **f.** shall be spoiled, ... 4013

FORTS
2Ki 25:1 they built **f.** against it round about...... 1785
Isa 29:3 and I will raise **f.** against thee. 4694
Isa 32:14 **f.** and towers shall be for dens 6076
Jer 52:4 and built **f.** against it round about. 1785
Eze 17:17 casting up mounts, and building **f.**,....... 1785
Eze 33:27 that be in the **f.** and in the caves 4679

FORTUNATUS (for-chu-na'-tus)
1Co 16:17 the coming of Stephanas and **F.**.......... *5415*
1Co *subscr.* Philippi by Stephanas, and **F.**. *5415*

FORTY See also FORTY'S.
Ge 5:13 Mahalaleel eight hundred and **f.**........... 705
Ge 7:4 upon the earth **f.** days and **f.** nights; 705
Ge 7:12 upon the earth **f.** days and **f.** nights 705
Ge 7:17 flood was **f.** days upon the earth;......... 705
Ge 8:6 it came to pass at the end of **f.** days, ... 705
Ge 18:28 he said, If I find there **f.** and five,........ 705
Ge 18:29 there shall be **f.** found there............... 705
Ge 25:20 Isaac was **f.** years old when he took..... 705
Ge 26:34 Esau was **f.** years old when he took..... 705
Ge 32:15 **f.** kine, and ten bulls, twenty she 705
Ge 47:28 Jacob was an hundred **f.** and seven 705
Ge 50:3 And **f.** days were fulfilled for him:........ 705
Ex 16:35 of Israel did eat manna **f.** years, ... 705
Ex 24:18 in the mount **f.** days and **f.** nights........ 705
Ex 26:19 thou shalt make **f.** sockets of silver...... 705
Ex 26:21 And their **f.** sockets of silver; two 705
Ex 34:28 with the Lord **f.** days and **f.** nights; 705
Ex 36:24 And **f.** sockets of silver he made 705
Ex 36:26 And their **f.** sockets of silver; 705
Le 25:8 shall be unto thee **f.** and nine years...... 705
Nu 1:21 **f.** and six thousand and five hundred..... 705
Nu 1:25 **f.** and five thousand six hundred.......... 705
Nu 1:33 were **f.** thousand and five hundred. 705
Nu 1:41 **f.** and one thousand and five hundred.... 705
Nu 2:11 **f.** and six thousand and five hundred..... 705
Nu 2:15 **f.** and five thousand and six hundred..... 705
Nu 2:19 were **f.** thousand and five hundred. 705
Nu 2:28 **f.** and one thousand and five hundred.... 705
Nu 13:25 searching of the land after **f.** days........ 705
Nu 14:33 wander in the wilderness **f.** years, ... 705
Nu 14:34 searched the land, even **f.** days, ... 705
Nu 14:34 bear your iniquities, even **f.** years,....... 705
Nu 26:7 numbered of them were **f.** and three 705
Nu 26:18 them, **f.** thousand and five hundred. 705
Nu 26:41 **f.** and five thousand and six hundred..... 705
Nu 26:50 were **f.** and five thousand and four........ 705
Nu 32:13 wander in the wilderness **f.** years, ... 705
Nu 35:6 them ye shall add **f.** and two cities........ 705
Nu 35:7 Levites shall be **f.** and eight cities:........ 705
De 2:7 these **f.** years the Lord thy God.......... 705
De 8:2 these **f.** years in the wilderness,.......... 705
De 8:4 did thy foot swell, these **f.** years. 705
De 9:9 in the mount **f.** days and **f.** nights........ 705
De 9:11 at the end of **f.** days and **f.** nights, ... 705
De 9:18 at the first, **f.** days and **f.** nights: 705
De 9:25 before the Lord **f.** days and **f.** nights,... 705
De 10:10 the first time, **f.** days and **f.** nights; 705
De 25:3 **F.** stripes he may give him, and.......... 705
De 29:5 led you **f.** years in the wilderness: 705
Jos 4:13 About **f.** thousand prepared for war...... 705
Jos 5:6 walked **f.** years in the wilderness,......... 705
Jos 14:7 **F.** years old was I when Moses the 705
Jos 14:10 as he said these **f.** and five years, ... 705
Jos 21:41 were **f.** and eight cities with their 705
Jg 3:11 And the land had rest **f.** years............ 705
Jg 5:8 seen among **f.** thousand in Israel? 705
Jg 5:31 And the land had rest **f.** years............ 705
Jg 8:28 country was in quietness **f.** years......... 705
Jg 12:6 Ephraimites **f.** and two thousand.......... 705
Jg 12:14 he had **f.** sons and thirty nephews, ... 705
Jg 13:1 the hand of the Philistines **f.** years....... 705
1Sa 4:18 And he had judged Israel **f.** years......... 705
1Sa 17:16 and presented himself **f.** days............. 705
2Sa 2:10 Ish-bosheth Saul's son was **f.** years...... 705
2Sa 5:4 to reign, and he reigned **f.** years. 705
2Sa 10:18 and **f.** thousand horsemen, and........... 705
2Sa 15:7 And it came to pass after **f.** years,....... 705
1Ki 2:11 reigned over Israel **f.** years: 705
1Ki 4:26 Solomon had **f.** thousand stalls of........ 705
1Ki 6:17 temple before it was, was **f.** cubits long. 705
1Ki 7:3 that lay on **f.** five pillars, fifteen in 705
1Ki 7:38 one layer contained **f.** baths:............... 705
1Ki 11:42 over all Israel was **f.** years................ 705
1Ki 14:21 Rehoboam was **f.** and one years old 705
1Ki 15:10 And **f.** and one years reigned he in 705
1Ki 19:8 of that meat **f.** days and **f.** nights 705
2Ki 2:24 tare **f.** and two children of them. 705
2Ki 8:9 of Damascus, **f.** camels' burden, ... 705
2Ki 10:14 even two and **f.** men; neither left he 705
2Ki 12:1 **f.** years reigned he in Jerusalem. 705
2Ki 14:23 and reigned **f.** and one years.............. 705
1Ch 5:18 were four and **f.** thousand seven........... 705
1Ch 12:36 to battle, expert in war, **f.** thousand..... 705
1Ch 19:18 chariots, and **f.** thousand footmen, ... 705
1Ch 29:27 he reigned over Israel was **f.** years;..... 705
2Ch 9:30 in Jerusalem over all Israel **f.** years...... 705
2Ch 12:13 Rehoboam was one and **f.** years old 705
2Ch 22:2 **F.** and two years old was Ahaziah........ 705
2Ch 24:1 he reigned **f.** years in Jerusalem. 705
Ezr 2:8 of Zattu, nine hundred **f.** and five......... 705
Ezr 2:10 of Bani, six hundred **f.** and two. 705
Ezr 2:24 children of Azmaveth, **f.** and two. 705
Ezr 2:25 seven hundred and **f.** and three............ 705
Ezr 2:34 of Jericho, three hundred **f.** and five..... 705
Ezr 2:38 thousand two hundred **f.** and seven. 705
Ezr 2:64 together was **f.** and two 702,7239
Ezr 2:66 mules, two hundred **f.** and five;........... 705
Ne 5:15 wine, beside **f.** shekels of silver; 705
Ne 7:13 of Zattu, eight hundred **f.** and five......... 705
Ne 7:15 of Binnui, six hundred **f.** and eight. 705
Ne 7:28 men of Beth-azmaveth, **f.** and two. 705
Ne 7:29 and Beeroth, seven hundred **f.** and 705
Ne 7:36 Jericho, three hundred **f.** and five. 705
Ne 7:41 thousand two hundred **f.** and seven. 705
Ne 7:44 of Asaph, an hundred **f.** and eight. 705
Ne 7:62 of Nekoda, six hundred **f.** and two. 705
Ne 7:66 was **f.** and two thousand three..... 702,7239
Ne 7:67 two hundred **f.** and five singing 705
Ne 7:68 mules, two hundred **f.** and five:............ 705
Ne 9:21 Yea, **f.** years didst thou sustain them.... 705
Ne 11:13 the fathers, two hundred **f.** and two: 705
Job 42:16 lived Job an hundred and **f.** years,........ 705
Ps 95:10 **F.** years long was I grieved with......... 705
Jer 52:30 seven hundred **f.** and five persons:....... 705
Eze 4:6 of the house of Judah **f.** days: 705
Eze 29:11 neither shall it be inhabited **f.** years...... 705
Eze 29:12 waste shall be desolate **f.** years:.......... 705
Eze 29:13 At the end of **f.** years will I gather 705
Eze 41:2 the length thereof, **f.** cubits: and the 705
Eze 46:22 were courts joined of **f.** cubits long 705
Am 2:10 you **f.** years through the wilderness, ... 705
Am 5:25 offerings in the wilderness **f.** years,...... 705
Jon 3:4 yet **f.** days, and Nineveh shall be.......... 705
Mt 4:2 he had fasted **f.** days and **f.** nights, ... *5062*
Mk 1:13 was there in the wilderness **f.** days, ... *5062*
Lu 4:2 Being **f.** days tempted of the devil...... *5062*
Joh 2:20 **F.** and six years was this temple........ *5062*
Ac 1:3 proofs, being seen of them **f.** days, ... *5062*
Ac 4:22 For the man was above **f.** years old,... *5062*
Ac 7:23 And when he was full **f.** years old, ... *5063*
Ac 7:30 And when **f.** years were expired, ... *5062*
Ac 7:36 sea, and in the wilderness **f.** years. *5062*
Ac 7:42 space of **f.** years in the wilderness? *5062*
Ac 13:18 And about the time of **f.** years........... *5063*
Ac 13:21 Benjamin, by the space of **f.** years. *5062*
Ac 23:13 were more than **f.** which had made...... *5062*
Ac 23:21 for him of them more than **f.** men, ... *5062*
2Co 11:24 times received I **f.** stripes save one.... *5062*
Heb 3:9 me, and saw my works **f.** years......... *5062*
Heb 3:17 with whom was he grieved **f.** years?... *5062*
Re 7:4 sealed an hundred and **f.** and four....... *5062*
Re 11:2 tread under foot **f.** and two months. ... *5062*
Re 13:5 him to continue **f.** and two months. *5062*
Re 14:1 with him an hundred **f.** and four......... *5062*
Re 14:3 but the hundred and **f.** and four *5062*
Re 21:17 an hundred and **f.** and four cubits, ... *5062*

FORTY'S
Ge 18:29 he said, I will not do it for **f.** sake. 705

FORTY-THOUSAND See FORTY and THOUSAND.

FORUM
Ac 28:15 came to meet us as far as Appii **f.** *675*

FORWARD See also HENCEFORWARD.
Ge 26:13 the man waxed great, and went **f.**,...... 1980
Ex 14:15 children of Israel, that they go **f.**:...... 5265
Nu 1:51 And when the tabernacle setteth **f.**,...... 5265
Nu 2:17 of the congregation shall set **f.**...... 5265
Nu 2:17 so shall they set **f.**, every man in...... 5265
Nu 2:24 they shall go **f.** in the third rank...... 5265
Nu 2:34 and so they set **f.**, every one after...... 5265
Nu 4:5 And when the camp setteth **f.**,...... 5265
Nu 4:15 as the camp is to set **f.**; after that,...... 5265
Nu 10:5 lie on the east parts shall go **f.**...... 5265
Nu 10:17 and the sons of Merari set **f.**,...... 5265
Nu 10:18 of the camp of Reuben set **f.**...... 5265
Nu 10:21 And the Kohathites set **f.**, bearing...... 5265
Nu 10:22 of the children of Ephraim set **f.**,...... 5265
Nu 10:25 camp of the children of Dan set **f.**,...... 5265
Nu 10:28 to their armies, when they set **f.**...... 5265
Nu 10:35 when the ark set **f.**, that Moses...... 5265
Nu 21:10 And the children of Israel set **f.**,...... 5265
Nu 22:1 And the children of Israel set **f.**,...... 5265
Nu 32:19 them on yonder side Jordan, or **f.**;...... 1973
Jg 9:44 that was with him, rushed **f.**, and...... 6584
1Sa 10:3 Then shalt thou go on **f.** from...... 1973
1Sa 16:13 upon David from that day **f.**...... 4605
1Sa 18:9 eyed David from that day and **f.**...... 1973
1Sa 30:25 And it was so from that day **f.**,...... 4605
2Ki 3:24 but they went **f.** smiting the Moabites,......
2Ki 4:24 Drive, and go **f.**; slack not thy riding......
2Ki 20:9 shall the shadow go **f.** ten degrees,......
1Ch 23:4 to set **f.** the work of the house...... 5921
2Ch 34:12 to set it **f.**; and other of the Levites,......
Ezr 3:8 to set **f.** the work of the house...... 5921
Ezr 3:9 set **f.** the workmen in the house...... 5921
Job 23:8 I go **f.**, but he is not there;...... 6924
Job 30:13 they set **f.** my calamity, they have...... 3276
Jer 7:24 and went backward, and not **f.**...... 6440
Eze 1:9 they went every one straight **f.**...... 6440
Eze 1:12 they went every one straight **f.**:...... 6440
Eze 10:22 they went every one straight **f.**...... 6440
Eze 39:22 their God from that day and **f.**...... 1973
Eze 43:27 and so **f.**, the priests shall make...... 1973
Zec 1:15 and they helped **f.** the affliction......
Mk 14:35 And he went **f.** a little, and fell on...... *4281*
Ac 19:33 the Jews putting him **f.**...... *4261*
2Co 8:10 but also to be **f.** a year ago...... *2309*
2Co 8:17 but being more **f.**, of his own...... *4707*
Gal 2:10 the same which I also was **f.** to do...... *4704*
3Jo 6 if thou bring **f.** on their journey...... *4311*

FORWARDNESS
2Co 8:8 by occasion of the **f.** of others, ... *4710*
2Co 9:2 For I know the **f.** of your mind,...... *4288*

FOUGHT
Ex 17:8 came Amalek, and **f.** with Israel...... 3898
Ex 17:10 said to him, and **f.** with Amalek:...... 3898
Nu 21:1 then he **f.** against Israel, and took...... 3898
Nu 21:23 to Jahaz, and **f.** against Israel...... 3898
Nu 21:26 who had **f.** against the former king...... 3898
Jos 10:14 the Lord **f.** for Israel...... 3898
Jos 10:29 for **f.** against Libnah:...... 3898
Jos 10:31, 34 against it, and **f.** against it:...... 3898
Jos 10:36 unto Hebron; and they **f.** against it:...... 3898
Jos 10:38 to Debir; and **f.** against it:...... 3898
Jos 10:42 the Lord God of Israel **f.** for Israel...... 3898
Jos 23:3 your God is he that hath **f.** for you...... 3898
Jos 24:8 and they **f.** with you: and I gave...... 3898
Jos 24:11 the men of Jericho **f.** against you,...... 3898
Jg 1:5 they **f.** against him, and they slew...... 3898
Jg 1:8 Now the children of Judah had **f.**...... 3898
Jg 5:19 kings came and **f.**, then **f.** the kings...... 3898
Jg 5:20 They **f.** from heaven;...... 3898
Jg 5:20 the stars in their courses **f.** against...... 3898
Jg 9:17 (For my father **f.** for you, and...... 3898
Jg 9:39 Shechem, and **f.** with Abimelech...... 3898
Jg 9:45 Abimelech **f.** against the city all...... 3898
Jg 9:52 and **f.** against it, and went hard...... 3898
Jg 11:20 in Jahaz, and **f.** against Israel...... 3898
Jg 12:4 and **f.** with Ephraim: and the men...... 3898
1Sa 4:10 And the Philistines **f.**, and Israel...... 3898
1Sa 12:9 Moab, and they **f.** against them...... 3898
1Sa 14:47 and **f.** against all his enemies on...... 3898
1Sa 19:8 went out, and **f.** with the Philistines,...... 3898
1Sa 23:5 Keilah, and **f.** with the Philistines,...... 3898
1Sa 31:1 the Philistines **f.** against Israel:...... 3898
2Sa 2:28 no more neither **f.** they any more...... 3898
2Sa 8:10 he had **f.** against Hadadezer, and...... 3898
2Sa 10:17 in array against David, and **f.** with...... 3898
2Sa 11:17 the men of the city went out, and **f.**...... 3898
2Sa 12:26 And Joab **f.** against Rabbah of the...... 3898
2Sa 12:27 I have **f.** against Rabbah, and have...... 3898
2Sa 12:29 and **f.** against it, and took it,...... 3898
2Sa 21:15 and **f.** against the Philistines...... 3898
2Ki 8:29 he **f.** against Hazael king of Syria,...... 3898
2Ki 9:15 he **f.** with Hazael king of Syria.)...... 3898
2Ki 12:17 Syria went up, and **f.** against Gath,...... 3898
2Ki 13:12 **f.** against Amaziah king of Judah,...... 3898
2Ki 14:15 he **f.** with Amaziah king of Judah,...... 3898
1Ch 10:1 the Philistines **f.** against Israel;...... 3898
1Ch 18:10 he had **f.** against Hadarezer, and...... 3898
1Ch 19:17 the Syrians, they **f.** with him...... 3898
1Ch 19:18 seven thousand men which **f.** in......
2Ch 20:29 the Lord **f.** against the enemies...... 3898
2Ch 22:6 when he **f.** with Hazeal king of Syria...... 3898
2Ch 27:5 He **f.** also with the king of the...... 3898
Ps 109:3 and **f.** against me without a cause...... 3898
Isa 20:1 and **f.** against Ashdod, and took it;...... 3898
Isa 63:10 enemy, and he **f.** against them...... 3898
Jer 34:1 the people, **f.** against Jerusalem,...... 3898
Jer 34:7 king of Babylon's army **f.** against...... 3898
Zec 14:3 as when he **f.** in the day of battle...... 3898
Zec 14:12 that have **f.** against Jerusalem;...... 6633
1Co 15:32 I have **f.** with beasts at Ephesus,...... *2341*
2Ti 4:7 I have **f.** a good fight, I have...... *75*
Re 12:7 his angels **f.** against the dragon;...... *4170*
Re 12:7 and the dragon **f.** and his angels,...... *4170*

FOUL See also FOULED.
Job 16:16 My face is **f.** with weeping, and...... 2560
Eze 34:18 ye must **f.** the residue with your...... 7515
Mt 16:3 **It will be f. weather to day: for**...... *5494*
Mk 9:25 he rebuked the **f.** spirit, saying...... *169*
Re 18:2 hold of every **f.** spirit, and a cage...... *169*

FOULED See also FOULEDST.
Eze 34:19 they drink that which ye have **f.**...... *4830*

FOULEDST
Eze 32:2 with thy feet, and **f.** their rivers...... 7515

FOUND See also CONFOUND; FOUNDED; FOUNDEST.
Ge 2:20 there was not **f.** an help meet...... 4672
Ge 6:8 Noah **f.** grace in the eyes of the...... 4672
Ge 8:9 **f.** no rest for the sole of her foot,...... 4672
Ge 11:2 that they **f.** a plain in the land of...... 4672
Ge 16:7 And the angel of the Lord **f.** her...... 4672
Ge 18:3 now I have **f.** favour in thy sight,...... 4672
Ge 18:29 Peradventure there shall be forty **f.**...... 4672
Ge 18:30 Peradventure there shall thirty be **f.**...... 4672
Ge 18:31 there shall be twenty **f.** there...... 4672
Ge 18:32 Peradventure ten shall be **f.** there...... 4672
Ge 19:19 servant hath **f.** grace in thy sight,...... 4672
Ge 26:19 **f.** there a well of springing water...... 4672
Ge 26:32 said unto him, We have **f.** water...... 4672
Ge 27:20 How is it that thou hast **f.** it so...... 4672
Ge 30:14 and **f.** mandrakes in the field,...... 4672
Ge 30:27 if I have **f.** favour in thine eyes,...... 4672
Ge 31:33 tents, but he **f.** them not...... 4672
Ge 31:34 all the tent, but **f.** them not...... 4672
Ge 31:35 he searched, but **f.** not the images...... 4672
Ge 31:37 hast thou **f.** of all thy household...... 4672
Ge 33:10 if now I have **f.** grace in thy sight,...... 4672
Ge 36:24 had **f.** the mules in the wilderness,...... 4672
Ge 37:15 And a certain man **f.** him, and,...... 4672
Ge 37:17 brethren, and **f.** them in Dothan...... 4672
Ge 37:32 This have we **f.**: know now...... 4672
Ge 38:20 woman's hand: but he **f.** her not...... 4672
Ge 38:23 this kid, and thou hast not **f.** her...... 4672
Ge 39:4 And Joseph **f.** grace in his sight,...... 4672
Ge 44:8 which we **f.** in our sacks' mouths,...... 4672
Ge 44:9 of thy servants it be **f.**, both let him...... 4672
Ge 44:10 he with whom it is **f.** shall be my...... 4672
Ge 44:12 the cup was **f.** in Benjamin's sack...... 4672
Ge 44:16 God hath **f.** out the iniquity of thy...... 4672
Ge 44:16 he also with whom the cup is **f.**...... 4672
Ge 44:17 man in whose hand the cup is **f.**,...... 4672
Ge 47:14 the money that was **f.** in the land...... 4672
Ge 47:29 If now I have **f.** grace in thy sight,...... 4672
Ge 50:4 If now I have **f.** grace in your eyes,...... 4672
Ex 9:19 man and beast which shall be **f.** in...... 4672
Ex 12:19 days shall there be no leaven **f.** in...... 4672
Ex 15:22 in the wilderness, and **f.** no water...... 4672
Ex 16:27 for to gather, and they **f.** none...... 4672
Ex 21:16 or if he be **f.** in his hand, he shall...... 4672
Ex 22:2 If a thief be **f.** breaking up, and be...... 4672
Ex 22:4 If the theft be certainly **f.** in his...... 4672
Ex 22:7 if the thief be **f.**, let him pay...... 4672
Ex 22:8 If the thief be not **f.**, then the...... 4672
Ex 33:12 thou hast also **f.** grace in my sight...... 4672
Ex 33:13 if I have **f.** grace in thy sight,...... 4672
Ex 33:16 people have **f.** grace in thy sight?...... 4672
Ex 33:17 thou hast **f.** grace in my sight,...... 4672
Ex 34:9 now I have **f.** grace in thy sight,...... 4672
Ex 35:23 with whom was **f.** blue, and purple,...... 4672
Ex 35:24 was **f.** shittim wood for any work...... 4672
Le 6:3 Or have **f.** that which was lost,...... 4672
Le 6:4 or the lost thing which he **f.**,...... 4672
Nu 11:11 have I now **f.** favour in thy sight,...... 4672
Nu 11:15 if I have **f.** favour in thy sight;...... 4672
Nu 15:32 they **f.** a man that gathered sticks...... 4672
Nu 15:33 they have **f.** him gathering sticks...... 4672
Nu 32:5 if we have **f.** grace in thy sight,...... 4672
De 17:2 If there be **f.** among you, within...... 4672
De 18:10 There shall not be **f.** among you...... 4672
De 20:11 all the people that is **f.** therein...... 4672
De 21:1 If one be **f.** slain in the land which...... 4672
De 22:3 which he hath lost, and thou hast **f.**,...... 4672
De 22:14 I came to her, I **f.** her not a maid:...... 4672
De 22:17 I **f.** not thy daughter a maid;...... 4672
De 22:20 virginity be not **f.** for the damsel;...... 4672
De 22:22 If a man be **f.** lying with a woman...... 4672
De 22:27 For he **f.** her in the field, and the...... 4672
De 22:28 and lie with her, and they be **f.**;...... 4672
De 24:1 hath **f.** some uncleanness in her:...... 4672
De 24:7 If a man be **f.** stealing any of his...... 4672
De 32:10 He **f.** him in a desert land,...... 4672
De 33:29 thine enemies shall be **f.** liars......
Jos 2:22 all the way, but **f.** them not...... 4672
Jos 10:17 The five kings are **f.** hid in a cave...... 4672
Jg 1:5 And they **f.** Adoni-bezek in Bezek:...... 4672
Jg 6:17 If now I have **f.** grace in thy sight,...... 4672
Jg 14:18 ye had not **f.** out my riddle...... 4672
Jg 15:15 he **f.** a new jawbone of an ass,...... 4672
Jg 21:12 And they **f.** among the inhabitants...... 4672
Ru 2:10 Why have I **f.** grace in thine eyes,...... 4672
1Sa 9:4 Shalisha, but they **f.** them not:...... 4672
1Sa 9:4 Benjamites, but they **f.** them not...... 4672
1Sa 9:11 they **f.** young maidens going out...... 4672
1Sa 9:20 thy mind on them; for they are **f.**...... 4672
1Sa 10:2 which thou wentest to seek are **f.**:...... 4672
1Sa 10:16 us plainly that the asses were **f.**...... 4672
1Sa 10:21 they sought him, he could not be **f.**...... 4672
1Sa 12:5 ye have not **f.** ought in my hand...... 4672
1Sa 13:19 smith **f.** throughout all the land...... 4672
1Sa 13:22 was neither sword nor spear **f.** in...... 4672
1Sa 13:22 with Jonathan his son was there **f.**...... 4672
1Sa 14:30 of their enemies which they **f.**?...... 4672
1Sa 16:22 for he hath **f.** favour in my sight...... 4672
1Sa 20:3 that I have **f.** grace in thine eyes;...... 4672
1Sa 20:29 if I have **f.** favour in thine eyes,...... 4672
1Sa 25:28 and evil hath not been **f.** in thee all...... 4672
1Sa 27:5 If I have now **f.** grace in thine eyes,...... 4672
1Sa 29:3 and I have **f.** no fault in him since...... 4672
1Sa 29:6 for I have not **f.** evil in thee since...... 4672
1Sa 29:8 what hast thou **f.** in thy servant...... 4672
1Sa 30:11 they **f.** an Egyptian in the field,...... 4672
1Sa 31:8 that they **f.** Saul and his three sons...... 4672
2Sa 7:27 hath thy servant **f.** in his heart...... 4672
2Sa 14:22 that I have **f.** grace in thy sight,...... 4672
2Sa 17:12 some place where he shall be **f.**,...... 4672
2Sa 17:13 be not one small stone **f.** there......
1Ki 1:3 and **f.** Abishag a Shunammite, and...... 4672
1Ki 1:52 if wickedness shall be **f.** in him,...... 4672
1Ki 7:47 was the weight of the brass **f.** out...... 2713
1Ki 11:19 Hadad **f.** great favour in the sight...... 4672
1Ki 11:29 the Shilonite **f.** him in the way;...... 4672
1Ki 13:14 and **f.** him sitting under an oak:...... 467
1Ki 13:28 he went and **f.** his carcase cast in...... 467
1Ki 14:13 in him there is **f.** some good thing...... 467
1Ki 18:10 and nation, that they **f.** thee not...... 467
1Ki 19:19 and **f.** Elisha the son of Shaphat,...... 467
1Ki 20:36 him, a lion **f.** him, and slew him...... 467
1Ki 20:37 Then he **f.** another man, and said,...... 467
1Ki 21:20 Hast thou **f.** me, O mine enemy?...... 467
1Ki 21:20 I have **f.** thee: because thou hast...... 467
2Ki 2:17 sought three days, but **f.** him not...... 467
2Ki 4:39 and **f.** a wild vine, and gathered...... 467
2Ki 9:35 **f.** no more of her than the skull,...... 467
2Ki 12:5 wheresoever any breach shall be **f.**...... 467
2Ki 12:10 the money that was **f.** in the house...... 467
2Ki 12:18 gold that was **f.** in the treasures...... 467
2Ki 14:14 vessels that were **f.** in the house...... 467
2Ki 16:8 the silver and gold that was **f.** in the...... 467

2Ki 17:4 the king of Assyria f. conspiracy 467
2Ki 18:15 the silver that was f. in the house 467
2Ki 19:8 and f. the king of Assyria warring 467
2Ki 20:13 and all that was f. in his treasures: 467
2Ki 22:8 I have f. the book of the law in the 467
2Ki 22:9 the money that was f. in the house, 467
2Ki 22:13 the words of this book that is f.: 467
2Ki 23:2 book of the covenant which was f. 467
2Ki 23:24 the book that Hilkiah the priest f. 467
2Ki 25:19 which were f. in the city, and the 467
2Ki 25:19 of the land that were f. in the city: 467
1Ch 4:40 And they f. fat pasture and good, 467
1Ch 4:41 the habitations that were f. there, 467
1Ch 10:8 they f. Saul and his sons fallen 467
1Ch 17:25 thy servant hath f. in his heart to 467
1Ch 20:2 and f. it to weigh a talent of gold, 467
1Ch 24:4 And there were more chief men f. 467
1Ch 26:31 were f. among them mighty men 467
1Ch 28:9 thou seek him, he will be f. of thee; 467
1Ch 29:8 with whom precious stones were f. 467
2Ch 2:17 and they were f. an hundred and 467
2Ch 4:18 the brass could not be f. out. 2713
2Ch 15:2 ye seek him, he will be f. of you; 4672
2Ch 15:4 and sought him, he was f. of them. 4672
2Ch 15:15 desire; and he was f. of them: 4672
2Ch 19:3 there are good things f. in thee, 4672
2Ch 20:25 they f. among them in abundance 4672
2Ch 21:17 that was f. in the king's house, 4672
2Ch 22:8 and f. the princes of Judah, and 4672
2Ch 25:5 and f. them three hundred...men, 4672
2Ch 25:24 vessels that were f. in the house 4672
2Ch 29:16 they f. in the temple of the Lord 4672
2Ch 34:14 Hilkiah the priest f. a book of the 4672
2Ch 34:15 I have f. the book of the law in the 4672
2Ch 34:17 the money that was f. in the house 4672
2Ch 34:21 the words of the book that is f.: 4672
2Ch 34:30 book of the covenant that was f. in 4672
2Ch 36:8 and that which was f. in him, 4672
Ezr 2:62 genealogy, but they were not f.: 4672
Ezr 4:19 and it is f. that this city of old 7912
Ezr 6:2 And there was f. at Achmetha, in 7912
Ezr 8:15 f. there none of the sons of Levi. 4672
Ezr 10:18 priests there were f. that had taken 4672
Ne 2:5 and if thy servant have f. favour in
Ne 5:8 peace, and f. nothing to answer. 4672
Ne 7:5 And I f. a register of the genealogy 4672
Ne 7:5 at the first, and f. written therein, 4672
Ne 7:64 by genealogy, but it was not f.: 4672
Ne 8:14 And they f. written in the law 4672
Ne 13:1 and therein was f. written, that the 4672
Es 2:23 made of the matter, it was f. out; 4672
Es 5:8 If I have f. favour in the sight of 4672
Es 6:2 it was f. written, that Mordecai 4672
Es 7:3 If I have f. favour in thy sight, 4672
Es 8:5 if I have f. favour in his sight, 4672
Job 19:28 the root of the matter is f. in me? 4672
Job 20:8 as a dream, and shall not be f.: 4672
Job 28:12 But where shall widom be f.? and 4672
Job 28:13 neither is it f. in the land of the 4672
Job 31:29 lifted up myself when evil f. him: 4672
Job 32:3 because they had f. no answer, and 4672
Job 32:13 should say, We have f. our wisdom: 4672
Job 33:24 down to the pit: I have f. a ransom. 4672
Job 42:15 were no women f. so fair as the 4672
Ps 32:6 in a time when thou mayest be f.: 4672
Ps 36:2 his inquity be f. to be hateful. 4672
Ps 37:36 sought him, but he could not be f. 4672
Ps 69:20 and for comforters, but I f. none 4672
Ps 76:5 men of might have f. their hands 4672
Ps 84:3 yea, the sparrow hath f. an house, 4672
Ps 89:20 I have f. David my servant: with 4672
Ps 107:4 way; they f. no city to dwell in. 4672
Ps 116:3 upon me: I f. trouble and sorrow. 4672
Ps 132:6 we f. it in the fields of the wood. 4672
Pr 6:31 But if he be f., he shall restore 4672
Pr 7:15 to seek thy face, and I have f. thee 4672
Pr 10:13 hath understanding wisdom is f.: 4672
Pr 16:31 it be f. in the way of righteousness. 4672
Pr 24:14 when thou hast f. it, then there 4672
Pr 25:16 Hast thou f. honey? eat so much 4672
Pr 30:6 he reprove thee, and thou be f. a liar.
Pr 30:10 curse thee, and thou be f. guilty.
Ec 7:27 this have I f., saith the preacher, 4672
Ec 7:28 man among a thousand have I f.; 4672
Ec 7:28 among all those have I not f. 4672
Ec 7:29 this only have I f., that God hath 4672
Ec 9:15 Now there was f. in it a poor wise 4672

Ca 3:1,2 I sought him, but I f. him not 4672
Ca 3:3 watchmen that go about the city f. 4672
Ca 3:4 but I f. him whom my soul loveth: 4672
Ca 5:7 that went about the city f. me, 4672
Ca 8:10 I in his eyes as one that f. favour. 4672
Isa 10:10 As my hand hath f. the kingdoms 4672
Isa 10:14 And my hand hath f. as a nest the 4672
Isa 13:15 Every one that is f. shall be thrust 4672
Isa 22:3 all that are f. in thee are bound 4672
Isa 30:14 there shall not be f. in the bursting 4672
Isa 35:9 it shall not be f. there; but the 4672
Isa 37:8 and f. the king of Assyria warring 4672
Isa 39:2 and all that was f. in his treasures: 4672
Isa 51:3 joy and gladness shall be f. therein, 4672
Isa 55:6 ye the Lord while he may be f., 4672
Isa 57:10 thou hast f. the life of thine hand; 4672
Isa 65:1 I am f. of them that sought me not: 4672
Isa 65:8 As the new wine is f. in the cluster, 4672
Jer 2:5 What iniquity have your fathers f. 4672
Jer 2:26 the thief is ashamed when he is f., 4672
Jer 2:34 in thy skirts is f. the blood of the 4672
Jer 2:34 I have not f. it by secret search, 4672
Jer 5:26 among my people are f. wicked 4672
Jer 11:9 A conspiracy is f. among the men 4672
Jer 14:3 came to the pits, and f. no water; 4672
Jer 15:16 Thy words were f., and I did eat 4672
Jer 23:11 have I f. there wickedness, saith 4672
Jer 29:14 And I will be f. of you, saith the 4672
Jer 31:2 were left of the sword f. grace in 4672
Jer 41:3 the Chaldeans that were f. there, 4672
Jer 41:8 But ten men were f. among them 4672
Jer 41:12 and f. him by the great waters that 4672
Jer 48:27 was he f. among thieves? for since 4672
Jer 50:7 that f. them have devoured them: 4672
Jer 50:20 shall not be f.: for I will pardon 4672
Jer 50:24 art f., and also caught, because 4672
Jer 52:25 which were f. in the city, and the 4672
Jer 52:25 that were f. in the midst of the city. 4672
La 2:16 for; we have f., we have seen it. 4672
Eze 22:30 not destroy it: but I f. none. 4672
Eze 26:21 yet shalt thou never be f. again, 4672
Eze 28:15 created, till iniquity was f. in thee. 4672
Da 1:19 them all was f. none like Daniel, 4672
Da 1:20 he f. them ten times better than all 4672
Da 2:25 I have f. a man of the captives of 4672
Da 2:35 that no place was f. for them: 7912
Da 5:11 wisdom of the gods, was f. in him; 7912
Da 5:12 doubts, were f. in the same Daniel, 7912
Da 5:14 and excellent wisdom is f. in thee. 7912
Da 5:27 in the balances, and art f. wanting. 7912
Da 6:4 was there any error or fault f. in 7912
Da 6:11 and f. Daniel praying and making 7912
Da 6:22 before him innocency was f. in me; 7912
Da 6:23 no manner of hurt was f. upon him, 7912
Da 11:19 stumble and fall, and not be f. 4672
Da 12:1 every one that shall be f. written 4672
Ho 9:10 I f. Israel like grapes in the 4672
Ho 10:2 now shall they be f. faulty:
Ho 12:4 he f. him in Beth-el, and there he 4672
Ho 12:8 I have f. me out substance: in all 4672
Ho 14:8 From me is thy fruit f. 4672
Jon 1:3 and he f. a ship going to Tarshish: 4672
Mic 1:13 the transgressions of Israel were f. 4672
Zep 3:13 shall a deceitful tongue be f. in 4672
Zec 10:10 and place shall not be f. for them. 4672
Mal 2:6 and iniquity was not f. in his lips: 4672
Mt 1:18 she was f. with child of the Holy *2147*
Mt 2:8 child; and when ye have f. him, *2147*
Mt 8:10 **I have not f. so great faith, no,** *2147*
Mt 13:44 **when a man hath f., he hideth** *2147*
Mt 13:46 **he had f. one pearl of great price,** *2147*
Mt 18:28 **and f. one of his fellowservants,** *2147*
Mt 20:6 **and f. others standing idle, and** *2147*
Mt 21:19 f. nothing thereon, but leaves only, *2147*
Mt 22:10 **all as many as they f., both bad** *2147*
Mt 26:43 he came and f. them asleep again: *2147*
Mt 26:60 But f. none: yea, though many *2147*
Mt 26:60 witnesses came, yet f. they none.
Mt 27:32 they f. a man of Cyrene, Simon by *2147*
Mk 1:37 And when they had f. him, they *2147*
Mk 7:2 unwashen, hands, they f. fault,
Mk 7:30 she f. the devil gone out, and her *2147*
Mk 11:4 and f. the colt tied by the door *2147*
Mk 11:13 to it, he f. nothing but leaves; *2147*
Mk 14:16 and f. as he had said unto them: *2147*
Mk 14:40 returned, he f. them asleep again, *2147*
Mk 14:55 to put him to death; and f. none. *2147*

Lu 1:30 Mary: for thou hast f. favour *2147*
Lu 2:16 came with haste, and f. Mary, and *429*
Lu 2:45 And when they f. him not, they *2147*
Lu 2:46 they f. him in the temple, sitting *2147*
Lu 4:17 f. the place where is was written, *2147*
Lu 7:9 **I have not f. so great faith, no,** *2147*
Lu 7:10 f. the servant whole that had been *2147*
Lu 8:35 and f. the man, out of whom the *2147*
Lu 9:36 voice was past, Jesus was f. alone *2147*
Lu 13:6 **sought fruit thereon, and f. none** *2147*
Lu 15:5 **when he hath f. it, he layeth it on** *2147*
Lu 15:6 **I have f. my sheep which was lost** *2147*
Lu 15:9 **when she hath f. it, she calleth** *2147*
Lu 15:9 **for I have f. the piece which I had** *2147*
Lu 15:24 **alive again; he was lost, and is f.** *2147*
Lu 15:32 **alive again; and was lost, and is f.** *2147*
Lu 17:18 **There are not f. that returned to** *2147*
Lu 19:32 and f. even as he had said unto *2147*
Lu 22:13 and f. as he had said unto them: *2147*
Lu 22:45 he f. them sleeping for sorrow, *2147*
Lu 23:2 We f. this fellow perverting the *2147*
Lu 23:14 you, have f. no fault in this man *2147*
Lu 23:22 I have f. no cause of death in him: *2147*
Lu 24:2 And they f. the stone rolled away *2147*
Lu 24:3 and f. not the body of the Lord *2147*
Lu 24:23 And when they f. not his body, they *2147*
Lu 24:24 and f. it even so as the women had *2147*
Lu 24:33 and f. the eleven gathered together, *2147*
Joh 1:41 We have f. the Messias, which is, *2147*
Joh 1:45 saith unto him, We have f. him, *2147*
Joh 2:14 And f. in the temple those that sold *2147*
Joh 6:25 And when they had f. him on the *2147*
Joh 9:35 and when he had f. him, he said *2147*
Joh 11:17 he f. that he had lain in the grave *2147*
Joh 12:14 he had f. a young ass, sat thereon; *2147*
Ac 5:10 young men came in, and f. her dead, *2147*
Ac 5:22 officers came, and f. them not in *2147*
Ac 5:23 prison truly f. we shut in all safety, *2147*
Ac 5:23 had opened, we f. no man within. *2147*
Ac 5:39 ye be f. even to fight against God. *2147*
Ac 7:11 and our fathers f. no sustenance, *2147*
Ac 7:46 Who f. favour before God, and *2147*
Ac 8:40 But Philip was f. at Azotus: *2147*
Ac 9:2 that if he f. any of this way, *2147*
Ac 9:33 And there he f. a certain man *2147*
Ac 10:27 f. many that were come together. *2147*
Ac 11:26 when he had f. him, he brought *2147*
Ac 12:19 f. him not, he examined the keepers, *2147*
Ac 13:6 f. a certain sorcerer, a false prophet, *2147*
Ac 13:22 I have f. David the son of Jesse, *2147*
Ac 13:28 though they f. no cause of death *2147*
Ac 17:6 when they f. them not, they drew *2147*
Ac 17:23 I f. an altar with this inscription, *2147*
Ac 18:2 And f. a certain Jew named Aquila, *2147*
Ac 19:19 f. it fifty thousand pieces of silver. *2147*
Ac 24:5 we have f. this man a pestilent *2147*
Ac 24:12 they neither f. me in the temple *2147*
Ac 24:18 Jews from Asia f. me purified in *2147*
Ac 24:20 if they have f. any evil doing in *2147*
Ac 25:25 when I f. that he had committed *2638*
Ac 27:6 And there the centurion f. a ship *2147*
Ac 27:28 sounded, and f. it twenty fathoms: *2147*
Ac 27:28 again, and f. it fifteen fathoms. *2147*
Ac 28:14 Where we f. brethren, and were *2147*
Ro 4:1 as pertaining to the flesh, hath f.? *2147*
Ro 7:10 to life, I f. to be unto death. *2147*
Ro 10:20 was f. of them that sought me not; *2147*
1Co 4:2 stewards, that a man be f. faithful. *2147*
1Co 15:15 Yea, and we are f. false witnesses *2147*
2Co 2:13 because I f. not Titus my brother: *2147*
2Co 5:3 clothed we shall not be f. naked. *2147*
2Co 7:14 made before Titus, is f. a truth, *1096*
2Co 11:12 they may be f. even as we. *2147*
2Co 12:20 and that I shall be f. unto you such *2147*
Ga 2:17 we ourselves also are f. sinners, *2147*
Php 2:8 And being f. in fashion as a man, *2147*
Php 3:9 And be f. in him, not having mine *2147*
1Ti 3:10 of a deacon, being f. blameless.
2Ti 1:17 me out very diligently, and f. me. *2147*
Heb 11:5 and was not f., because God had *2147*
Heb 12:17 for he f. no place of repentance, *2147*
1Pe 1:7 might be f. unto praise and honour *2147*
1Pe 2:22 neither was guile f. in his mouth: *2147*
2Pe 3:14 that ye may be f. of him in peace, *2147*
2Joh 4 f. of thy children walking in truth, *2147*
Re 2:2 **are not, and hast f. them liars:** *2147*
Re 3:2 **for I have not f. thy works perfect** *2147*

Re 5:4 no man was f. worthy to open and ... *2147*
Re 12:8 neither was their place f. any more ... *2147*
Re 14:5 And in their mouth was f. no guile: ... *2147*
Re 16:20 and the mountains were not f. ... *2147*
Re 18:21 and shall be f. no more at all ... *2147*
Re 18:22 he be, shall be f. any more in thee; ... *2147*
Re 18:24 in her was f. the blood of prophets, ... *2147*
Re 20:11 and there was f. no place for them ... *2147*
Re 20:15 And whosoever was not f. written ... *2147*

FOUNDATION See also FOUNDATIONS.
Ex 9:18 the f. thereof even until now ... 3245
Jos 6:26 he shall lay the f. thereof in his ... 3245
1Ki 5:17 stones, to lay the f. of the house ... 3245
1Ki 6:37 In the fourth year was the f. of the ... 3245
1Ki 7:9 even from the f. unto the coping, ... 4527
1Ki 7:10 And the f. was of costly stones, ... 3245
1Ki 16:34 he laid the f. thereof in Abiram his ... 3245
2Ch 8:16 unto the day of the f. of the house ... 4143
2Ch 23:5 a third part at the gate of the f. ... 3247
2Ch 31:7 began to lay the f. of the heaps, ... 3245
Ezr 3:6 f. of the temple of the Lord was not ... 3245
Ezr 3:10 when the builders laid the f. of the ... 3245
Ezr 3:11 the f. of the house of the Lord was ... 3245
Ezr 3:12 when the f. of the house was laid ... 3245
Ezr 5:16 and laid the f. of the house of God ... 787
Job 4:19 whose f. is in the dust, which are ... 3247
Job 22:16 whose f. was overflown with a flood: ... 3247
Ps 87:1 His f. is in the holy mountains ... 3248
Ps 102:25 Of old hast thou laid the f. of the ... 3245
Ps 137:7 rase it, even to the f. thereof ... 3247
Pr 10:25 the righteous is an everlasting f. ... 3247
Isa 28:16 I lay in Zion for a f. a stone, ... 3248
Isa 28:16 a precious corner stone, a sure f. ... 4143
Isa 44:28 to the temple. Thy f. shall be laid ... 3245
Isa 48:13 Mine hand also hath laid the f. of ... 3245
Eze 13:14 the f. thereof shall be discovered, ... 3247
Hab 3:13 discovering the f. unto the neck ... 3247
Hag 2:18 f. of the Lord's temple was laid ... 3245
Zec 4:9 have laid the f. of this house; ... 3248
Zec 8:9 the day that the f. of the house ... 3248
Zec 12:1 and layeth the f. of the earth, ... 3248
Mt 13:35 secret from the f. of the world ... *2602*
Mt 25:34 **for you from the f. of the world:** ... *2602*
Lu 6:48 **deep, and laid the f. on a rock:** ... *2310*
Lu 6:49 **without a f. built an house upon** ... *2310*
Lu 11:50 **shed from the f. of the world,** ... *2602*
Lu 14:29 **after he hath laid the f., and is** ... *2310*
Joh 17:24 **lovest me before the f. of the** ... *2602*
Ro 15:20 build upon anothers man's f. ... *2310*
1Co 3:10 I have laid the f., and another ... *2310*
1Co 3:11 For other f. can no man lay than ... *2310*
1Co 3:12 upon this f. gold, silver, precious ... *2310*
Eph 1:4 in him before the f. of the world, ... *2602*
Eph 2:20 built upon the f. of the apostles ... *2310*
1Ti 6:19 for themsleves a good f. against ... *2310*
2Ti 2:19 the f. of God standeth sure, having ... *2310*
Heb 1:10 hast laid the f. of the earth; ... *2311*
Heb 4:3 finished from the f. of the world ... *2602*
Heb 6:1 laying again the f. of repentance ... *2310*
Heb 9:26 suffered since the f. of the world: ... *2602*
1Pe 1:20 before the f. of the world, but was ... *2602*
Re 13:8 Lamb slain from the f. of the world ... *2602*
Re 17:8 of life from the f. of the world, ... *2602*
Re 21:19 The first f. was jasper; the second, ... *2310*

FOUNDATIONS
De 32:22 on fire the f. of the mountains ... 4146
2Sa 22:8 the f. of heaven moved and shook, ... 4146
2Sa 22:16 the f. of the world were discovered, ... 4146
Ezr 4:12 the wall thereof, and joined the f., ... 787
Ezr 6:3 let the f. thereof be strongly laid; ... 787
Job 38:4 thou when I laid the f. of the earth? ... 3245
Job 38:6 are the f. thereof fastened? or who ... 134
Ps 11:3 If the f. be destroyed, what can the ... 8356
Ps 18:7 the f. also of the hills moved and ... 4146
Ps 18:15 the f. of the world were discovered ... 4146
Ps 82:5 all of the f. of the earth are out of ... 4146
Ps 104:5 Who laid the f. of the earth, ... 4349
Pr 8:29 he appointed the f. of the earth: ... 4146
Isa 16:7 f. of Kir-hareseth shall ye mourn; ... 808
Isa 24:18 and the f. of the earth do shake ... 4146
Isa 40:21 understood from the f. of the earth? ... 4146
Isa 51:13 and laid the f. of the earth; ... 3245
Isa 51:16 and lay the f. of the earth, ... 3245
Isa 54:11 and lay thy f. with sapphires ... 3245
Isa 58:12 up the f. of many generations; ... 4146
Jer 31:37 and the f. of the earth searched out ... 4146
Jer 50:15 her f. are fallen, her walls are ... 803
Jer 51:26 thee a corner, nor a stone for f.: ... 4146
La 4:11 and it hath devoured the f. thereof ... 3247
Eze 30:4 and her f. shall be broken down ... 3247
Eze 41:8 f. of the side chambers were a full ... 4328
Mic 1:6 and I will discover the f. thereof ... 3247
Mic 6:2 and ye strong f. of the earth: ... 4146
Ac 16:26 the f. of the prison were shaken: ... *2310*
Heb 11:10 he looked for a city which hath f., ... *2310*
Re 21:14 the wall fo the city had twelve f., ... *2310*
Re 21:19 And the f. of the wall of the city ... *2310*

FOUNDED See also CONFOUNDED.
Ps 24:2 For he hath f. it upon the seas, ... 3245
Ps 89:11 fulness thereof, thou hast f. them ... 3245
Ps 104:8 place which thou hast f. for them ... 3245
Ps 119:152 that thou hast f. them for ever ... 3245
Pr 3:19 Lord by wisdom hath f. the earth; ... 3245
Isa 14:32 the Lord hath f. Zion, and the poor ... 3245
Isa 23:13 Assyrian f. it for them that dwell ... 3245
Am 9:6 and hath f. his troop in the earth; ... 3245
Mt 7:25 **fell not: for it was f. upon a rock** ... *2311*
Lu 6:48 **shake it: for it was f. upon a rock** ... *2311*

FOUNDER
Jg 17:4 and gave them to the f., who made ... 6884
Jer 6:29 f. melteth in vain: for the wicked ... 6884
Jer 10:9 hands of the f.: blue and purple ... 6884
Jer 10:14 every f. is confounded by the ... 6884
Jer 51:17 every f. is confounded by the ... 6884

FOUNDEST
Ne 9:8 f. his heart faithful before thee, ... 4672

FOUNTAIN See also FOUNTAINS.
Ge 16:7 found her by a f. of water in the ... 5869
Ge 16:7 by the f. in the way to Shur ... 5869
Le 11:36 nevertheless a f. or pit, wherein ... 4599
Le 20:18 he hath discovered her f., and she ... 4726
Le 20:18 she hath uncovered the f. of her ... 4726
De 33:28 f. of Jacob shall be upon a land ... 5869
Jos 15:9 the f. of the water of Nephtoah, ... 4599
1Sa 29:1 Israelites pitched by a f. which ... 5869
Ne 2:14 I went on to the gate of the f., ... 5869
Ne 3:15 the gate of the f. repaired Shallun ... 5869
Ne 12:37 And at the f. gate, which was over ... 5869
Ps 36:9 For with thee is the f. of life: ... 4726
Ps 68:26 the Lord, from the f. of Israel ... 4726
Ps 74:15 Thou didst cleave the f. and the ... 4599
Ps 114:8 water, the flint into a f. of waters ... 4599
Pr 5:18 Let thy f. be blessed: and rejoice ... 4726
Pr 13:14 The law of the wise is a f. of life, ... 4726
Pr 14:27 The fear of the Lord is a f. of life, ... 4726
Pr 25:26 troubled f., and a corrupt spring ... 4599
Ec 12:6 or the pitcher be broken at the f., ... 4002
Ca 4:12 a spring shut up, a f. sealed ... 4599
Ca 4:15 a f. of gardens, a well of living ... 4599
Jer 2:13 forsaken me the f. of living waters, ... 4726
Jer 6:7 As a f. casteth out her waters, ... 953
Jer 9:1 waters, and mine eyes a f. of tears, ... 4726
Jer 17:13 forsaken the Lord, the f. of living ... 4726
Ho 13:15 and his f. shall be dried up: ... 4599
Joe 3:18 a f. shall come forth of the house ... 4599
Zec 13:1 that day there shall be a f. opened ... 4726
Mk 5:29 straightway the f. of her blood ... *4077*
Jas 3:11 Doth a f. send forth at the same ... *4077*
Jas 3:12 so can no f. both yield salt water ... *4077*
Re 21:6 that is athirst of the f. of the water ... *4077*

FOUNTAINS
Ge 7:11 were all the f. of the great deep ... 4599
Ge 8:2 f. also of the deep and the windows ... 4599
Nu 33:9 in Elim were twelve f. of water, ... 5869
De 8:7 of f. and depths that spring out of ... 5869
1Ki 18:5 unto all f. of water, and unto all ... 4599
2Ch 32:3 to stop the waters of the f. which ... 5869
2Ch 32:4 stopped all the f., and the brook ... 4599
Pr 5:16 Let thy f. be dispersed abroad, ... 4599
Pr 8:24 when there were no f. abounding ... 4599
Pr 8:28 he strengthened the f. of the deep: ... 5869
Isa 41:18 and f. in the midst of the valleys: ... 4599
Re 7:17 shall lead them unto living f. of ... *4077*
Re 8:10 rivers, and upon the f. of waters; ... *4077*
Re 14:7 the sea, and the f. of waters ... *4077*
Re 16:4 upon the rivers and f. of waters: ... *4077*

FOUR See also FOURFOLD; FOURSCORE; FOURSQUARE; FOURTEEN.
Ge 2:10 parted, and became into f. heads ... 702
Ge 11:13 after he begat Salah f. hundred and ... 702
Ge 11:15 after he begat Eber f. hundred and ... 702
Ge 11:16 And Eber lived f. and thirty years, ... 702
Ge 11:17 after he begat Peleg f. hundred ... 702
Ge 14:9 king of Ellasar; f. kings with five ... 702
Ge 15:13 shall afflict them f. hundred years; ... 702
Ge 23:15 worth f. hundred shekels of silver; ... 702
Ge 23:16 Heth, f. hundred shekels of silver, ... 702
Ge 32:6 and f. hundred men with him ... 702
Ge 33:1 and with him f. hundred men ... 702
Ge 47:24 and f. parts shall be your own, ... 702
Ex 12:40 was f. hundred and thirty years ... 702
Ex 12:41 the f. hundred and thirty years, ... 702
Ex 22:1 an ox, and f. sheep for a sheep ... 702
Ex 25:12 thou shalt cast f. rings of gold for it, ... 702
Ex 25:12 and put them in the f. corners ... 702
Ex 25:26 shalt make for it f. rings of gold, ... 702
Ex 25:26 and put the rings in the f. corners ... 702
Ex 25:26 that are on the f. feet thereof ... 702
Ex 25:34 f. bowls made like unto almonds, ... 702
Ex 26:2,8 breadth of one curtain f. cubits, ... 702
Ex 26:32 f. pillars of shittim wood overlaid ... 702
Ex 26:32 gold, upon the f. sockets of silver ... 702
Ex 27:2 horns of it upon the f. corners ... 702
Ex 27:4 net shalt thou make f. brasen rings ... 702
Ex 27:4 rings in the f. corners thereof ... 702
Ex 27:16 and their pillars shall be f., ... 702
Ex 27:16 and their sockets f. ... 702
Ex 28:17 even f. rows of stones: the first row ... 702
Ex 36:9 the breadth of one curtain f. cubits: ... 702
Ex 36:15 f. cubits was the breadth of one ... 702
Ex 36:36 f. pillars of shittim wood, and ... 702
Ex 36:36 he cast for them f. sockets of silver ... 702
Ex 37:3 And he cast for it f. rings of gold, ... 702
Ex 37:3 to be set by the f. corners of it; ... 702
Ex 37:13 And he cast for it f. rings of gold, ... 702
Ex 37:13 and put the rings upon the f. corners ... 702
Ex 37:13 that were in the f. feet thereof ... 702
Ex 37:20 were f. bowls made like almonds, ... 702
Ex 38:2 the horns thereof on the f. corners ... 702
Ex 38:5 And he cast f. rings for the f. ends ... 702
Ex 38:19 And their pillars were f., ... 702
Ex 38:19 and their sockets of brass f.; ... 702
Ex 38:29 thousand and f. hundred shekels ... 702
Ex 39:10 they set in it f. rows of stones: ... 702
Le 11:20 fowls that creep, going upon all f., ... 702
Le 11:21 creeping thing that goeth upon all f., ... 702
Le 11:23 creeping things, which have f. feet, ... 702
Le 11:27 manner of beasts that go on all f., ... 702
Le 11:42 and whatsoever goeth upon all f., ... 702
Nu 1:29 fifty and f. thousand and f. hundred ... 702
Nu 1:31 and seven thousand and f. hundred ... 702
Nu 1:37 and five thousand and f. hundred ... 702
Nu 1:43 and three thousand and f. hundred ... 702
Nu 2:6 fifty and f. thousand and f. hundred ... 702
Nu 2:8 and seven thousand and f. hundred ... 702
Nu 2:9 and six thousand and f. hundred, ... 702
Nu 2:16 thousand and f. hundred and fifty, ... 702
Nu 2:23 and five thousand and f. hundred ... 702
Nu 2:30 and three thousand and f. hundred ... 702
Nu 7:7 Two wagons and f. oxen he gave ... 702
Nu 7:8 f. wagons and eight oxen he gave ... 702
Nu 7:85 thousand and f. hundred shekels, ... 702
Nu 7:88 were twenty and f. bullocks, the ... 702
Nu 25:9 plague were twenty and f. thousand ... 702
Nu 26:25 threescore and f. thousand and ... 702
Nu 26:43 and f. thousand and f. hundred ... 702
Nu 26:47 and three thousand and f. hundred ... 702
Nu 26:50 and five thousand and f. hundred ... 702
De 3:11 and f. cubits the breadth of it, ... 702
De 22:12 upon the f. quarters of thy vesture, ... 702
Jos 19:7 Ashan; f. cities and their villages: ... 702
Jos 21:18 Almon with her suburbs; f. cities ... 702
Jos 21:22 Beth-horon with her suburbs; f. ... 702
Jos 21:24 Gath-rimmon with her suburbs; f. ... 702
Jos 21:29 En-gannim wih her suburbs; f. ... 702
Jos 21:31 Rehob with her suburbs; f. cities ... 702
Jos 21:35 Nahalal with her suburbs; f. cities ... 702
Jos 21:37 Mephaath with her suburbs; f. ... 702
Jos 21:39 with her suburbs; f. cities in all ... 702
Jg 9:34 against Shechem in f. companies ... 702
Jg 11:40 of Jephthah the Gileadite f. days ... 702
Jg 19:2 and was there f. whole months ... 702
Jg 20:2 f. hundred thousand footmen that ... 702
Jg 20:17 f. hundred thousand men that drew ... 702
Jg 20:47 in the rock Rimmon f. months ... 702

Jg 21:12 **f.** hundred young virgins, that had 702
1Sa 4:2 in the field about **f.** thousand men. 702
1Sa 22:2 with him about **f.** hundred men. 702
1Sa 25:13 after David about **f.** hundred men; 702
1Sa 27:7 was a full year and **f.** months. 702
1Sa 30:10 David pursued, he and **f.** hundred 702
1Sa 30:17 save **f.** hundred young men, which 702
2Sa 21:20 six toes, **f.** and twenty in number; 702
2Sa 21:22 These **f.** were born to the giant in 702
1Ki 6:1 in the **f.** hundred and eightieth year 702
1Ki 7:2 upon **f.** rows of cedar pillars, with 702
1Ki 7:19 lily work in the porch, **f.** cubits. 702
1Ki 7:27 **f.** cubits was the length of one base, 702
1Ki 7:27 and **f.** cubits the breadth thereof, 702
1Ki 7:30 every base had **f.** brasen wheels, 702
1Ki 7:30 **f.** corners thereof had undersetters; 702
1Ki 7:32 under the borders were **f.** wheels; 702
1Ki 7:34 **f.** undersetters to the **f.** corners of 702
1Ki 7:38 and every layer was **f.** cubits: and 702
1Ki 7:42 **f.** hundred pomegranates for the 702
1Ki 9:28 gold, **f.** hundred and twenty talents, 702
1Ki 10:26 thousand and **f.** hundred chariots, 702
1Ki 15:33 in Tirzah twenty and **f.** years. 702
1Ki 18:19 the prophets of Baal **f.** hundred and 702
1Ki 18:19 prophets of the groves **f.** hundred, 702
1Ki 18:22 Baal's prophets are **f.** hundred and 702
1Ki 18:33 Fill **f.** barrels with water, and pour 702
1Ki 22:6 together, about **h.** hundred men, and 702
2Ki 7:3 And there were **f.** leprous men at 702
2Ki 14:13 unto the corner gate, **f.** hundred 702
1Ch 3:5 and Nathan, and Solomon, **f.**, 702
1Ch 5:18 **f.** and forty thousand seven hundred 702
1Ch 7:1 and Pua, Jashub, and Shimrom, **f.**. 702
1Ch 7:7 and two thousand and thirty and **f.** 702
1Ch 9:24 In **f.** quarters were the porters, 702
1Ch 9:26 the **f.** chief porters, were in their set 702
1Ch 12:26 Levi **f.** thousand and six hundred. 702
1Ch 20:6 whose fingers and toes were **f.** and 702
1Ch 21:5 **f.** hundred threescore and ten 702
1Ch 21:20 his **f.** sons with him hid themselves. 702
1Ch 23:4 twenty and **f.** thousand were to set 702
1Ch 23:5 Moreover **f.** thousand were porters; 702
1Ch 23:5 and **f.** thousand praised the Lord 702
1Ch 23:10 These **f.** were the sons fo Shimei. 702
1Ch 23:12 Izhar, Hebron, and Uzziel, **f.**. 702
1Ch 24:18 the **f.** and twentieth to Maaziah. 702
1Ch 25:31 **f.** and twentieth to Romamti-ezer. 702
1Ch 26:17 northward **f.** a day, southward **f.** a 702
1Ch 26:18 **f.** at the causeway, and two at 702
1Ch 27:1 of every course were...**f.** thousand. 702
1Ch 27:2 in his course were...**f.** thousand. 702
1Ch 27:4 likewise were...and **f.** thousand. 702
1Ch 27:5, 7,8,9,10,11,12,13,14,15 and in his
course were twenty and **f.** thousand 702
2Ch 1:14 a thousand and **f.** hundred chariots, 702
2Ch 4:13 **f.** hundred pomegranates on the 702
2Ch 8:18 **f.** hundred and fifty talents of gold, 702
2Ch 9:25 Solomon had **f.** thousand stalls for 702
2Ch 13:3 even **f.** hundred thousand chosen 702
2Ch 18:5 of prophets **f.** hundred men, and 702
2Ch 25:23 the corner gate, **f.** hundred cubits. 702
Ezr 1:10 basons of a second sort **f.** hundred 702
Ezr 1:11 were five thousand and **f.** hundred 702
Ezr 2:7 a thousand two hundred fifty, and **f.**. 702
Ezr 2:15 of Adin, **f.** hundred fifty and **f.**. 702
Ezr 2:31 a thousand two hundred fifty and **f.**. 702
Ezr 2:40 children of Holdaviah, seventy and **f.**. 702
Ezr 2:67 Their camels, **f.** hundred thirty and 702
Ezr 6:17 hundred rams, **f.** hundred lambs; 703
Ne 6:4 Yet they sent unto me **f.** times 702
Ne 7:12 thousand two hundred fifty and **f.** 702
Ne 7:23 Bezai, three hundred twenty and **f.**. 702
Ne 7:34 thousand two hundred fifty and **f.** 702
Ne 7:43 children of Hodevah, seventy and **f.**. 702
Ne 7:69 Their camels, **f.** hundred thirty 702
Ne 11:6 **f.** hundred three score and eight 702
Ne 11:18 were two hundred fourscore and **f.**, 702
Job 1:19 smote the **f.** corners of the house, 702
Job 42:16 his sons' sons, even **f.** generations. 702
Pr 30:15 **f.** things say not, It is enough: 702
Pr 30:18 yea, **f.** which I know not: 702
Pr 30:21 and for **f.** which it cannot bear: 702
Pr 30:24 **f.** things which are little upon the 702
Pr 30:29 yea, **f.** are comely in going: 702
Isa 11:12 from the **f.** corners of the earth. 702
Isa 17:6 **f.** or five in the outmost fruitful 702
Jer 15:3 I will appoint over them **f.** kinds, 702
Jer 36:23 Jehudi had read three or **f.** leaves, 702
Jer 49:36 the **f.** winds from the **f.** quarters 702
Jer 52:21 thickness thereof was **f.** fingers: 702
Jer 52:30 persons were **f.** thousand and six 702
Eze 1:5 the likeness of **f.** living creatures. 702
Eze 1:6 And every one had **f.** faces, 702
Eze 1:6 and every one had **f.** wings. 702
Eze 1:8 **f.** sides; and they **f.** had their faces 702
Eze 1:10 they **f.** had the face of a man, 702
Eze 1:10 and they **f.** had the face of an ox on 702
Eze 1:10 they **f.** also had the face of an eagle. 702
Eze 1:15 living creatures, with his **f.** faces. 702
Eze 1:16 they **f.** had one likeness: and their 702
Eze 1:17 went, they went upon their **f.** sides: 702
Eze 1:18 full of eyes round about them **f.**. 702
Eze 7:2 upon the **f.** corners of the land. 702
Eze 10:9 the **f.** wheels by the cherubims, 702
Eze 10:10 they **f.** had one likeness, as if a 702
Eze 10:11 went, they went upon their **f.** sides; 702
Eze 10:12 even the wheels that they **f.** had. 702
Eze 10:14 And every one had **f.** faces: the 702
Eze 10:21 Every one had **f.** faces apiece, 702
Eze 10:21 and every one **f.** wings; 702
Eze 14:21 when I send my **f.** sore judgments 702
Eze 37:9 come from the **f.** winds, O breath, 702
Eze 40:41 **F.** tables were on this side, 702
Eze 40:41 and **f.** tables on that side, 702
Eze 40:42 And the **f.** tables were of hewn 702
Eze 41:5 of every side chamber, **f.** cubits 702
Eze 42:20 He measured it by the **f.** sides: 702
Eze 43:14 the greater settle shall be **f.** cubits, 702
Eze 43:15 So the altar shall be **f.** cubits; 702
Eze 43:15 altar and upward shall be **f.** horns. 702
Eze 43:16 square in the **f.** squares thereof. 702
Eze 43:17 fourteen broad in the **f.** squares 702
Eze 43:20 **f.** horns of it, and on the **f.** corners 702
Eze 45:19 upon the **f.** corners of the settle 702
Eze 46:21 pass by the **f.** corners of the court; 702
Eze 46:22 In the **f.** corners of the court were 702
Eze 46:22 **f.** corners were of one measure. 702
Eze 46:23 in them round about them **f.**, and 702
Eze 48:16 the north side **f.** thousand and five 702
Eze 48:16 the south side **f.** thousand and five 702
Eze 48:16 the east side **f.** thousand and five 702
Eze 48:16 the west side **f.** thousand and five 702
Eze 48:30 on the north side, **f.** thousand and 702
Eze 48:32 at the east side, **f.** thousand and 702
Eze 48:33 at the side **f.** thousand and 702
Eze 48:34 At the west side **f.** thousand and 702
Da 1:17 these **f.** children, God gave them 702
Da 3:25 Lo, I see **f.** men loose, walking 703
Da 7:2 the **f.** winds of the heaven strove 703
Da 7:3 And **f.** great beasts came up from 703
Da 7:6 upon the back of it **f.** wings of a 703
Da 7:6 the beast had also **f.** heads; 703
Da 7:17 beasts, which are **f.**, are **f.** kings, 703
Da 8:8 and for it came up **f.** notable ones 702
Da 8:8 toward the **f.** winds of heaven. 702
Da 8:22 **f.** stood up for it, **f.** kingdoms shall 702
Da 10:4 in the **f.** and twentieth day of the 702
Da 11:4 be divided toward the **f.** winds of 702
Am 1:3 of Damascus, and for **f.**, I will not 702
Am 1:6 of Gaza, and for **f.**, I will not turn 702
Am 1:9 transgressions of Tyrus, and for **f.**, 702
Am 1:11 of Edom, and for **f.**, I will not turn 702
Am 1:13 Ammon, and for **f.**, I will not turn. 702
Am 2:1 of Moab, and for **f.**, I will not turn 702
Am 2:4 of Judah, and for **f.**, I will not turn 702
Am 2:6 of Israel, and for **f.**, I will not turn 702
Hag 1:15 In the **f.** and twentieth day of the 702
Hag 2:10 In the **f.** and twentieth day of the 702
Hag 2:18 from the **f.** and twentieth day of 702
Hag 2:20 In the **f.** and twentieth day of the 702
Zec 1:7 Upon the **f.** and twentieth day of 702
Zec 1:18 and saw, and behold **f.** horns. 702
Zec 1:20 the Lord shewed me **f.** carpenters. 702
Zec 2:6 as the **f.** winds of the heaven, 702
Zec 6:1 there came **f.** chariots out from 702
Zec 6:5 are the **f.** spirits of the heavens, 702
Mt 15:38 **f.** thousand men, beside women *5070*
Mt 16:10 **seven loaves of the f. thousand,** *5070*
Mt 24:31 **together his elect from the f.** *5064*
Mk 2:3 of the palsy, which was borne of **f.** *5064*
Mk 8:9 eaten were about **f.** thousand: *5070*
Mk 8:20 **the seven among f. thousand,** *5070*
Mk 13:27 **his elect from the f. winds,** *5064*
Lu 2:37 of about fourscore and **f.** years, *5064*
Joh 4:35 **not ye, There are yet f. months,** *5072*
Joh 11:17 lain in the grave **f.** days already. *5064*
Joh 11:39 for he hath been dead **f.** days. *5066*
Joh 19:23 **f.** parts, to every soldier a part; *5064*
Ac 5:36 number of men about **f.** hundred. *6071*
Ac 7:6 entreat them evil **f.** hundred years. *6071*
Ac 10:11 great sheet knit at the **f.** corners. *5064*
Ac 10:30 **F.** days ago I was fasting until *5067*
Ac 11:5 down from heaven by **f.** corners; *5064*
Ac 12:4 and delivered him to **f.** quaternions *5064*
Ac 13:20 the space of **f.** hundred and fifty *5071*
Ac 21:9 the same man had **f.** daughters, *5064*
Ac 21:23 We have **f.** men which have a vow *5064*
Ac 21:38 wilderness **f.** thousand men that *5070*
Ac 27:29 they cast **f.** anchors out of the *5064*
Ga 3:17 **f.** hundred and thirty years after, *5071*
Re 4:4 throne were **f.** and twenty seats: *5064*
Re 4:4 I saw **f.** and twenty elders sitting, *5064*
Re 4:6 **f.** beasts full of eyes before and *5064*
Re 4:8 And the **f.** beasts had each of them *5064*
Re 4:10 The **f.** and twenty elders fall down *5064*
Re 5:6 of the throne and of the **f.** beasts, *5064*
Re 5:8 **f.** beasts and **f.** and twenty elders *5064*
Re 5:14 And the **f.** beasts said, Amen. *5064*
Re 5:14 **f.** and twenty elders fell down *5064*
Re 6:1 one of the **f.** beasts saying, Come *5064*
Re 6:6 in the midst of the **f.** beasts say, *5064*
Re 7:1 after these things I saw **f.** angels *5064*
Re 7:1 on the **f.** corners of the earth, *5064*
Re 7:1 holding the **f.** winds of the earth, *5064*
Re 7:2 with a loud voice to the **f.** angels, *5064*
Re 7:4 hundred and forty and **f.** thousand *5064*
Re 7:11 about the elders and the **f.** beasts, *5064*
Re 9:13 I heard a voice from the **f.** horns *5064*
Re 9:14 Loose the **f.** angels which are *5064*
Re 9:15 And the **f.** angels were loosed, *5064*
Re 11:16 the **f.** and twenty elders, which sat *5064*
Re 14:1 and hundred forty and **f.** thousand, *5064*
Re 14:3 and before the **f.** beasts, and the *5064*
Re 14:3 hundred and forty and **f.** thousand *5064*
Re 15:7 And one of the **f.** beasts gave *5064*
Re 19:4 the **f.** and twenty elders and the **f.** *5064*
Re 20:8 are in the **f.** quarters of the earth, *5064*
Re 21:17 an hundred and forty and **f.** cubits, *5064*

FOURFOLD

2Sa 12:6 And he shall restore the lamb **f.**, 706
Lu 19:8 false accusation, I restore him **f.** *5073*

FOURFOOTED

Ac 10:12 manner of **f.** beasts of the earth, *5074*
Ac 11:6 and saw **f.** beasts of the earth, *5074*
Ro 1:23 **f.** beasts, and creeping things. *5074*

FOUR HUNDRED See FOUR and HUNDRED.

FOURSCORE

Ge 16:16 Abram was **f.** and six years old. 8084
Ge 35:28 of Isaac were an hundred and **f.** 8084
Ex 7:7 And Moss was **f.** years old. 8084
Ex 7:7 and Aaron **f.** and three years old, 8084
Nu 2:9 hundred thousand and **f.** thousand 8084
Nu 4:48 thousand and five hundred and **f.** 8084
Jos 14:10 I as this day **f.** and five years old. 8084
Jg 3:30 And the land had rest **f.** years. 8084
1Sa 22:18 slew on that day **f.** and five persons 8084
2Sa 19:32 a very aged man, even **f.** years old: 8084
2Sa 19:35 I am this day **f.** years old: and can 8084
1Ki 5:15 and **f.** thousand hewers in the 8084
1Ki 12:21 and hundred and **f.** thousand chosen 8084
2Ki 6:25 an ass's head was sold for **f.** pieces 8084
2Ki 10:24 Jehu appointed **f.** men without, 8084
2Ki 19:35 an hundred **f.** and five thousand: 8084
1Ch 7:5 genealogies **f.** and seven thousand. 8084
1Ch 15:9 Eliel the chief, and his brethren **f.** 8084
1Ch 25:7 was two hundred **f.** and eight 8084
2Ch 2:2 and **f.** thousand to hew in the 8084
2Ch 2:18 and **f.** thousand to be hewers in the 8084
2Ch 11:1 an hundred and **f.** thousand chosen 8084
2Ch 14:8 two hundred and **f.** thousand: all 8084
2Ch 17:15 him two hundred and **f.** thousand. 8084
2Ch 17:18 an hundred and **f.** thousand ready 8084
2Ch 26:17 and with him **f.** priests of the Lord, 8084
Ezr 8:8 Michael, and with him **f.** males. 8084
Ne 7:26 Netopha, and hundred and eight 8084
Ne 11:18 city were two hundred **f.** and four. 8084
Es 1:4 days, even an hundred and **f.** days. 8084
Ps 90:10 if by reason of strength they be **f.** 8084
Ca 6:8 queens, and **f.** concubines, and 8084

Isa 37:36 a hundred and **f.** and five thousand: 8084
Jer 41:5 and from Samaria, even **f.** men, ... 8084
Lu 2:37 widow of about **f.** and four years......... *3589*
Lu 16:7 take thy bill, and write **f.** *3589*

FOURSCORE THOUSAND See FOURSCORE and THOUSAND.

FOURSQUARE
Ex 27:1 the altar shall be **f.**: and the height..... 7251
Ex 28:16 **F.** it shall be being doubled; a span 7251
Ex 30:2 **f.** shall it be: and two cubits shall....... 7251
Ex 37:25 it was **f.**; and two cubits was the 7251
Ex 38:1 it was **f.**; and three cubits the 7251
Ex 39:9 It was **f.**; they made the 7251
1Ki 7:31 with their borders, **f.**, not round, ... 7251
Eze 40:47 an hundred cubits broad, **f.**; 7251
Eze 48:20 ye shall offer the holy oblation **f.**, ... 7243
Re 26:16 And the city lieth **f.**, and the length.... *5068*

FOURTEEN
Ge 31:41 I served thee **f.** years for thy 702,6240
Ge 46:22 Jacob: all the souls were **f.**.......... 702,6240
Nu 1:27 **f.** thousand and six hundred.......... 702,7657
Nu 2:4 **f.** thousand and six hundred......... 702,7657
Nu 16:49 were **f.** thousand and seven......... 702,7657
Nu 29:13 and **f.** lambs of the first year; 702,6246
Nu 29:15 to each lamb of the **f.** lambs: 702,6246
Nu 29:17, 20 **f.** lambs of the first year......... 702,6246
Nu 29:23, 26,29,32 and **f.** lambs of the........ 702,6246
Jos 15:36 **f.** cities with their villages. 702,6246
Jos 18:28 **f.** cities with their villages. 702,6246
1Ki 8:65 and seven days, even **f.** days....... 702,6246
1Ch 25:5 and God gave to Heman **f.** sons ... 702,6246
2Ch 13:21 mighty, and married **f.** wives, ... 702,6246
Job 42:12 for he had **f.** thousand sheep, ... 702,6246
Eze 43:17 settle shall be **f.** cubits long......... 702,6246
Eze 43:17 **f.** broad in the four squares......... 702,6246
Mt 1:17 Abraham to David are **f.** generations... *1180*
Mt 1:17 in to Babylon are **f.** generations; *1180*
Mt 1:17 unto Christ are **f.** generations. *1180*
2Co 12:2 a man in Christ above **f.** years ago, ... *1180*
Ga 2:1 **f.** years after I went up again to *1180*

FOURTEENTH
Ge 14:5 **f.** year came Chedorlaomer, ... 702,6240
Ex 12:6 shall keep it up until the **f.** day..... 702,6240
Ex 12:18 on the **f.** day of the month at....... 702,6240
Le 23:5 In the **f.** day of the first month 702,6240
Nu 9:3 In the **f.** day of this month, at....... 702,6240
Nu 9:5 the passover on the **f.** day of....... 702,6240
Nu 9:11 **f.** day of the second month at 702,6240
Nu 28:16 in the **f.** day of the first month..... 702,6240
Jos 5:10 the passover on the **f.** day of....... 702,6240
2Ki 18:13 in the **f.** year of king Hezekiah..... 702,6240
1Ch 24:13 Huppah, the **f.** to Jeshebeab, ... 702,6240
1Ch 25:21 **f.** to Mattithiah, he, his sons, ... 702,6240
2Ch 30:15 the passover on the **f.** day of....... 702,6240
2Ch 35:1 on the **f.** day of the first month. ... 702,6240
Ezr 6:19 the passover upon the **f.** day 702,6240
Es 9:15 on the **f.** day also of the month 702,6240
Es 9:17 and on the **f.** day of the same 702,6240
Es 9:18 and on the **f.** thereof;................ 702,6240
Es 9:19 the **f.** day of the month Adar 702,6240
Es 9:21 they should keep the **f.** day of 702,6240
Isa 36:1 in the **f.** year of king Hezekiah, ... 702,6240
Eze 40:1 the **f.** year after that the city....... 702,6240
Eze 45:21 first month, in the **f.** day of the.... 702,6240
Ac 27:27 But when the **f.** night was come, ... *5065*
Ac 27:33 is the **f.** day that ye have tarried........ *5065*

FOURTEEN THOUSAND See FOURTEEN and THOUSAND.

FOURTH
Ge 1:19 and the morning were the **f.** day......... 7243
Ge 2:14 And the **f.** river is Euphrates. 7243
Ge 15:16 the **f.** generation they shall come 7243
Ex 20:5 unto the third and **f.** generation 7256
Ex 28:20 the **f.** row a beryl, and an onyx, ... 7243
Ex 29:40 the **f.** part of an hin of beaten oil; 7253
Ex 29:40 and the **f.** part of an hin of wine.......... 7243
Ex 34:7 the third and to the **f.** generation. 7256
Ex 39:13 the **f.** row, a beryl, and onyx, ... 7243
Le 19:24 in the **f.** year all the fruit thereof 7243
Le 23:13 of wine, the **f.** part of an hin. 7243
Nu *title* The **F.** Book of Moses, Called..................
Nu 7:30 On the **f.** day Elizur the son of.......... 7243
Nu 14:18 unto the third and **f.** generation. 7256
Nu 15:4 with the **f.** part of an hin of oil........... 7243
Nu 15:5 And the **f.** part of an hin of wine........ 7243
Nu 23:10 the number of the **f.** part of Israel? 7255
Nu 28:5 the **f.** part of an hin of beaten oil. 7243
Nu 28:7 the **f.** part of an hin for the one 7243
Nu 28:14 and a **f.** part of an hin unto a lamb: 7243
Nu 29:23 And on the **f.** day ten bullocks, ... 7243
De 5:9 unto the third and **f.** generation 7256
Jos 19:17 the **f.** lot came out to Issachar, ... 7243
Jg 19:5 And it came to pass on the **f.** day, ... 7243
1Sa 9:8 the **f.** part of a shekel of silver: 7253
2Sa 3:4 And the **f.**, Adonijah the son of.......... 7243
1Ki 6:1 in the **f.** year of Solomon's reign 7243
1Ki 6:33 olive tree, a **f.** part of the wall. 7243
1Ki 6:37 In the **f.** year was the foundation 7243
1Ki 22:41 the **f.** year of Ahab king of Israel. 702
2Ki *title* The **F.** Book Of The Kings......................
2Ki 6:25 the **f.** part of a cab of dove's dung...... 7255
2Ki 10:30 children of the **f.** generation shall 7243
2Ki 15:12 of Israel unto the **f.** generation. 7243
2Ki 18:9 in the **f.** year of king Hezekiah, ... 7243
2Ki 25:3 of the **f.** month the famine prevailed ....
1Ch 2:14 Nethaneel the **f.**, Raddai the fifth, ... 7243
1Ch 3:2 the **f.**, Adonijah the son of Haggith: 7243
1Ch 3:15 the third Zedekiah, the **f.** Shallum......... 7243
1Ch 8:2 Nohah the **f.**, and Rapha the fifth. 7243
1Ch 12:10 Mishmannah the **f.**, Jeremiah the........ 7243
1Ch 23:19 the third, Jekameam the **f.**................ 7243
1Ch 24:8 third to Harim, the **f.** to Seorim, ... 7243
1Ch 24:23 the third, Jekameam the **f.**................ 7243
1Ch 25:11 The **f.** to Izri, he, his sons, ... 7243
1Ch 26:2 the third, Jathniel the **f.**,................... 7243
1Ch 26:4 Joah the third, Sacar the **f.**, and.......... 7243
1Ch 26:11 the third, Zechariah the **f.**:................ 7243
1Ch 27:7 The **f.** captain for the **f.** month was.... 7243
2Ch 3:2 month, in the **f.** year of his reign. 702
2Ch 20:26 And on the **f.** day they assembled 7243
Ezr 8:33 Now on the **f.** day was the silver 7243
Ne 9:1 Now in the twenty and **f.** day 702
Ne 9:3 their God one **f.** part of the day; of 7243
Ne 9:3 and another **f.** part they confessed,..... 7243
Jer 25:1 Judah in the **f.** year of Jehoiakim 7243
Jer 28:1 the **f.** year, and in the fifth month, ... 7243
Jer 36:1 pass in the **f.** year of Jehoiakim.......... 7243
Jer 39:2 the **f.** month, the ninth day of the 7243
Jer 45:1 the **f.** year of Jehoiakim the son of 7243
Jer 46:2 smote in the **f.** year of Jehoiakim 7243
Jer 51:59 Babylon in the **f.** year of his reign. 7243
Jer 52:6 And in the **f.** month, in the ninth day .. 7243
Eze 1:1 in the **f.** month, in the fifth day of...... 7243
Eze 10:14 and the **f.** the face of an eagle. 7243
Da 2:40 And the **f.** kingdom shall be strong 7244
Da 3:25 the form of the **f.** is like the Son of 7244
Da 7:7 and behold a **f.** beast, dreadful and 7244
Da 7:19 know the truth of the **f.** beast, ... 7244
Da 7:23 The **f.** beast shall be the **f.** kingdom ... 7244
Da 11:2 **f.** shall be far richer than they all: 7243
Zec 6:3 the **f.** chariot grisled and bay horses. .. 7243
Zec 7:1 pass in the **f.** year of king Darius......... 702
Zec 7:1 in the **f.** day of the ninth month, ... 702
Zec 8:19 The fast of the **f.** month, and the 7243
Mt 14:25 And in the **f.** watch of the night *5067*
Mk 6:48 and about the **f.** watch of the night *5067*
Re 4:7 the **f.** beast was like a flying eagle...... *5067*
Re 6:7 And when he had opened the **f.** seal,.. *5067*
Re 6:7 I heard the voice of the **f.** beast *5067*
Re 6:8 them over the **f.** part of the earth, ... *5067*
Re 8:12 And the **f.** angel sounded, and the....... *5067*
Re 16:8 And the **f.** angel poured out his vial.... *5067*
Re 21:19 a chalcedony; the **f.**, and emerald; *5067*

FOUR THOUSAND See FOUR and THOUSAND.

FOWL See also FOWLS.
Ge 1:20 and **f.** that may fly above the earth..... 5775
Ge 1:21 and every winged **f.** after his kind: 5775
Ge 1:22 and let **f.** multiply in the earth. 5775
Ge 1:26 of the sea, and over the **f.** of the air,.. 5775
Ge 1:28 and over the **f.** of the air, and over 5775
Ge 1:30 of the earth, and to every **f.** of the air, 5775
Ge 2:19 and every **f.** of the air; and brought 5775
Ge 2:20 and to the **f.** of the air, and to every .. 5775
Ge 7:14 every **f.** after his kind, every bird 5775
Ge 7:21 both of **f.**, and of cattle, and of........... 5775
Ge 7:23 the **f.** of the heaven; and they were.... 5775
Ge 8:17 both of **f.**, and of cattle, and of.......... 5775
Ge 8:19 every creeping thing, and every **f.**,...... 5775
Ge 8:20 clean beast, and of every clean **f.**, ... 5775
Ge 9:2 and upon every **f.** of the air, ... 5775
Ge 9:10 creature that is with you, of the **f.**, ... 5775
Le 7:26 manner of blood, whether it be of **f.** ... 5775
Le 11:46 the law of the beasts, and of the **f.**,.... 5775
Le 17:13 hunteth and catcheth any beast or **f.** ... 5775
Le 20:25 souls abominable by beast, or by **f.**,..... 5775
De 4:17 the likeness of any winged **f.** that....... 6833
1Ki 4:23 and fallowdeer, and fatted **f.**............. 1257
1Ki 4:33 he spake also of beasts, and of **f.**, ... 5775
Job 28:7 is a path which no **f.** knoweth, ... 5861
Ps 8:8 The **f.** of the air, and the fish of the ... 6833
Ps 148:10 creeping things, and flying **f.**: 6833
Jer 9:10 both the **f.** of the heavens and the....... 5775
Eze 17:23 shall dwell all **f.** of every wing; 6833
Eze 39:17 feathered **f.**, and to every beast......... 6833
Eze 44:31 or torn, whether it be **f.** or beast....... 5775
Da 7:6 the back of it four wings of a **f.**; 5776

FOWLER See also FOWLERS.
Ps 91:3 thee from the snare of the **f.**, and...... 3353
Pr 6:5 as a bird from the hand of the **f.**......... 3353
Ho 9:8 but the prophet is a snare of a **f.** 3353

FOWLERS
Ps 124:7 as a bird out of the snare of the **f.** 3369

FOWLS
Ge 6:7 thing, and the **f.** of the air; for it........ 5775
Ge 6:20 **f.** after their kind, and of cattle.......... 5775
Ge 7:3 Of **f.** also of the air by sevens, ... 5775
Ge 7:8 **f.**, and of every thing that creepeth 5775
Ge 15:11 **f.** came down upon the carcases, ... 5861
Le 1:14 his offering to the Lord be of **f.**, ... 5775
Le 11:13 have in abomination among the **f.**; 5775
Le 11:20 All **f.** that creep, going upon all.......... 5775
Le 20:25 between unclean **f.** and clean: 5775
De 14:20 But of all clean **f.** ye may eat. 5775
De 28:26 carcase shall be meat unto all **f.** of 5775
1Sa 17:44 and I will give thy flesh unto the **f.**..... 5775
1Sa 17:46 the Philistines this day unto the **f.** 5775
1Ki 14:11 the field shall the **f.** of the air eat:...... 5775
1Ki 16:4 the fields shall the **f.** of the air eat. 5775
1Ki 21:24 the field shall the **f.** of the air eat. 5775
Ne 5:18 also **f.** were prepared for me, and...... 6833
Job 12:7 and the **f.** of the air, and they shall..... 5775
Job 28:21 kept close from the **f.** of the air.......... 5775
Job 35:11 us wiser than the **f.** of heaven? 5775
Ps 50:11 I know all the **f.** of the mountains:...... 5775
Ps 78:27 and feathered **f.** like as the sand 5775
Ps 79:2 meat unto the **f.** of the heaven, ... 5775
Ps 104:12 By them shall the **f.** of the heaven 5775
Isa 18:6 unto the **f.** of the mountains, ... 5861
Isa 18:6 the **f.** shall summer upon them, ... 5861
Jer 7:33 people shall be meat for the **f.** of 5775
Jer 15:3 the **f.** of the heaven, and the beasts ... 5775
Jer 16:4 shall be meat for the **f.** of heaven,...... 5775
Jer 19:7 to be meat for the **f.** of the heaven, ... 5775
Jer 34:20 shall be for meat unto the **f.** of the..... 5775
Eze 29:5 field and to the **f.** of the heaven......... 5775
Eze 31:6 the **f.** of heaven made their nests....... 5775
Eze 31:13 all the **f.** of the heaven remain, ... 5775
Eze 32:4 all the **f.** of the heaven to remain 5775
Eze 38:20 the sea and the **f.** of the heaven, ... 5775
Da 2:38 and the **f.** of the heaven hath he 5776
Da 4:12 and the **f.** of the heaven dwelt in 6853
Da 4:14 it, and the **f.** from his branches:.......... 6853
Da 4:21 the **f.** of the heaven had their............. 6853
Ho 2:18 with the **f.** of the heaven, and with..... 5775
Ho 4:3 and with the **f.** of heaven; yea, the..... 5775
Ho 7:12 them down as the **f.** of heaven; I 5775
Zep 1:3 I will consume the **f.** of the heaven,.... 5775
Mt 6:26 Behold, the **f.** of the air: for they *4071*
Mt 13:4 the **f.** came and devoured them *4071*
Mk 4:4 and the **f.** of the air came and *4071*
Mk 4:32 the **f.** of the air my lodge under *4071*
Lu 8:5 and the **f.** of the air devoured it, ... *4071*
Lu 12:24 more are ye better than the **f.**? *4071*
Lu 13:19 and the **f.** of the air lodged in the *4071*
Ac 10:12 creeping things, and **f.** of the air. *4071*
Ac 11:6 creeping things, and **f.** of the air. *4071*
Re 19:17 saying to all the **f.** that fly in the........ *3732*
Re 19:21 the **f.** were filled with their flesh. *3732*

FOX See also FOXES.
Ne 4:3 if a **f.** go up, he shall even break 7776
Lu 13:32 Go ye, and tell that **f.**, Behold, I.... *258*

FOXES
Jg 15:4 went and caught three hundred **f.**, ... 7776

Ps 63:10 they shall be a portion for **f.** 7776
Ca 2:15 Take us the **f.**, the little **f.**, that 7776
La 5:18 is desolate, the **f.** walk upon it. 7776
Eze 13:4 are like the **f.** in the deserts. 7776
Mt 8:20 **The f. have holes, and the birds of..** *258*
Lu 9:58 **F. have holes, and birds of the air..** *258*

FRAGMENTS
Mt 14:20 took up of the **f.** that remained *2801*
Mk 6:43 up twleve baskets full of the **f.**, *2801*
Mk 8:19, **20 baskets full of f. took ye up?** *2801*
Lu 9:17 taken up of **f.** that remained to *2801*
Joh 6:12 **Gather up the f. that remain,** *2801*
Joh 6:13 filled twelve baskets with the **f.** *2801*

FRAIL
Ps 39:4 that I may know how **f.** I am 2310

FRAME See also FRAMED; FRAMETH.
Jg 12:6 could not **f.** to pronounce it right 3559
Ps 103:14 For he knoweth our **f.**; he 3336
Jer 18:11 I **f.** evil against you, and devise 3335
Eze 40:2 by which was as the **f.** of a city on 4011
Ho 5:4 They will not **f.** their doings to 5414

FRAMED
Isa 29:16 or shall the thing **f.** say of him 3336
Isa 29:16 say of him that **f.** it, He had no 3335
Eph 2:21 In whom all the building fitly **f.** *4883*
Heb 11:3 the worlds were **f.** by the word of *2675*

FRAMETH
Ps 50:19 evil, and thy tongue **f.** deceit 6775
Ps 94:20 which **f.** mischief by a law? 3335

FRANKINCENSE
Ex 30:34 these sweet spices with pure **f.**: 3828
Le 2:1 oil upon it, and put **f.** there on: 3828
Le 2:2 with all the **f.** there of; and the 3828
Le 2:15 and lay **f.** thereon: it is a meat 3828
Le 2:16 with all the **f.** thereof: it is an 3828
Le 5:11 neither shall he put any **f.** thereon: 3828
Le 6:15 all the **f.** which is upon the meat 3828
Le 24:7 shalt put pure **f.** upon each row, 3828
Nu 5:15 put **f.** thereon; for it is an offering 3828
1Ch 9:29 the oil, and the **f.**, and the spices 3828
Ne 13:5 the **f.**, and the vessels, and the 3828
Ne 13:9 with the meat offering and the **f.** 3828
Ca 3:6 perfumed with myrrh and **f.**, with 3828
Ca 4:6 of myrrh, and to the hill of **f.** 3828
Ca 4:14 with all trees of **f.**; myrrh and 3828
Mt 2:11 gifts; gold, and **f.**, and myrrh. *3030*
Re 18:13 **f.**, and wine, and oil, and fine flour, *3030*

FRANKLY
Lu 7:42 **to pay, he f. forgave them both** *5435*

FRAUD See also DEFRAUD.
Ps 10:7 full of cursing and deceit and **f.** 8496
Jas 5:4 which is of you kept back by **f.**, *650*

FRAY
De 28:26 and no man shall **f.** them away. 2729
Jer 7:33 and none shall **f.** them away. 2729
Zec 1:21 but these are come to **f.** them, 2729

FRECKLED
Le 13:39 it is a **f.** spot that groweth in the 933

FREE See also FREED; FREEMAN; FREEWILL; FREEWOMAN.
Ex 21:2 in the seventh he shall go out **f.** 2670
Ex 21:5 my children; I will not go out **f.** 2670
Ex 21:11 shall she go out **f.** without money 2600
Ex 21:26 let him go **f.** for his eye's sake. 2670
Ex 21:27 let him go **f.** for his tooth's sake. 2670
Ex 36:3 brought yet unto him **f.** offerings 5071
Le 19:20 to death, because she was not **f.** 2666
Nu 5:19 be thou **f.** from this bitter water 5352
Nu 5:28 then she shall be **f.**, and shall 5352
De 15:12 thou shalt let him go **f.** from thee 2670
De 15:13 thou sendest him out **f.** from thee, 2670
De 15:18 sendest him away **f.** from thee; 2670
De 24:5 he shall be **f.** at home one year, 5355
1Sa 17:25 his father's house **f.** in Israel. 2670
1Ch 9:33 in the chambers were **f.**: for they 6362
2Ch 29:31 and as many as were of a **f.** heart 5081
Job 3:19 the servant is **f.** from his master 2670
Job 39:5 Who hath sent out the wild ass **f.**? 2670
Ps 51:12 and uphold me with thy **f.** spirit. 5082
Ps 88:5 **F.** among the dead, like the slain 2670
Ps 105:20 of the people, and let him go **f.** 6605
Isa 58:6 and to let the oppressed go **f.**, 2670
Jer 34:9 an Hebrew or an Hebrewess, go **f.**; 2670
Jer 34:10 every one his maidservant, go **f.**, 2670
Jer 34:11 whom they had let go **f.**, to return, 2670
Jer 34:14 thou shalt let him go **f.** from thee: 2670
Am 4:5 and publish the **f.** offerings: 5071
Mt 15:6 **or his mother, he shall be f.**
Mt 17:26 unto him, **Then are the children f..** *1658*
Mk 7:11 **be profited by me; he shall be f.**
Joh 8:32 **and the truth shall make you f..** *1659*
Joh 8:33 sayest thou, Ye shall be made **f.**? *1658*
Joh 8:36 **Son therefore shall make you f..** *1659*
Joh 8:36 **ye shall be f. indeed.** *1658*
Ac 22:28 And Paul said, But I was **f.** born.
Ro 5:15 the offence, so also is the **f.** gift. *5486*
Ro 5:16 but the **f.** gift is of many offences *5486*
Ro 5:18 the **f.** gift came upon all men unto
Ro 6:18 Being then made **f.** from sin, ye *1659*
Ro 6:20 ye were **f.** from righteousness. *1658*
Ro 6:22 But now being made **f.** from sin *1659*
Ro 7:3 she is **f.** from that law; so that *1658*
Ro 8:2 hath made me **f.** from the law of *1659*
1Co 7:21 if thou mayest be made **f.**, use it *1658*
1Co 7:22 that is called, being **f.**, is Christ's *1658*
1Co 9:1 Am I not an apostle? am I not **f.**? *1658*
1Co 9:19 For though I be **f.** from all men, *1658*
1Co 12:13 whether we be bond or **f.**; and have *1658*
Ga 3:28 Greek, there is neither bond nor **f.**, *1658*
Ga 4:26 But Jerusalem which is above is **f.**, *1658*
Ga 4:31 of the bondwoman, but of the **f.** *1658*
Ga 5:1 wherewith Christ hath made us **f.**, *1659*
Eph 6:8 whether he be bond or **f.** *1658*
Col 3:11 Barbarian, Scythian, bond nor **f.**: *1658*
2Th 3:1 of the Lord may have **f.** course,
1Pe 2:16 As **f.**, and not using your liberty *1658*
Re 6:15 every bondman, and every **f.** man, *1658*
Re 13:16 rich and poor, **f.** and bond, to *1658*
Re 19:18 all men, both **f.** and bond, both *1658*

FREE-BORN See FREE and BORN.

FREED
Jos 9:23 there shall none of you be **f.** from 3772
Ro 6:7 For he that is dead is **f.** from sin. *1344*

FREEDOM
Le 19:20 at all redeemed, nor **f.** given her; 2668
Ac 22:28 a great sum obtained I this **f.** *4174*

FREELY
Ge 2:16 tree of the garden thou mayest **f.** eat:
Nu 11:5 which we did eat in Egypt **f.**; 2600
1Sa 14:30 if haply the people had eaten **f.** to day
Ezr 2:68 offered **f.** for the house of God to
Ezr 7:15 and his counsellors have **f.** offered unto
Ps 54:6 I will **f.** sacrifice unto thee: I 5071
Ho 14:4 I will love them **f.**: for mine anger 5071
Mt 10:8 **f. ye have received, f. give.** *1432*
Ac 2:29 let me **f.** speak unto you of *3326,3924*
Ac 26:26 before whom also I speak **f.**: *3955*
Ro 3:24 Being justified **f.** by his grace *1432*
Ro 8:32 shall he not with him also **f.** give us
1Co 2:12 we might know the things that are **f.**
2Co 11:7 to you the gospel of God **f.**? *1432*
Re 21:6 the fountain of the water of life **f.** *1432*
Re 22:17 let him take the water of life **f.** *1432*

FREEMAN
1Co 7:22 being a servant, is the Lord's **f.** *558*

FREEWILL See also FREE and WILL.
Le 22:18 all his **f.** offerings, which they 5071
Le 22:21 a **f.** offering in beeves or sheep, 5071
Le 22:23 mayest thou offer for a **f.** offering; 5071
Le 23:38 all your **f.** offerings, which ye give 5071
Nu 15:3 a vow, or in a **f.** offering, or in your 5071
Nu 29:39 your vows, and your **f.** offerings, for 5071
De 12:6 your vows, and your **f.** offerings, and 5071
De 12:17 thy **f.** offerings, or heave offering of 5071
De 16:10 of a **f.** offering of thine hand, which 5071
De 23:23 a **f.** offering, according as thou hast 5071
2Ch 31:14 the **f.** offerings of God, to distribute 5071
Ezr 1:4 the **f.** offering for the house of God 5071
Ezr 3:5 offered a **f.** offering unto the Lord. 5071
Ezr 7:13 which are minded of their own **f.** 5069
Ezr 7:16 with the **f.** offering of the people, 5069
Ezr 8:28 a **f.** offering unto the Lord God of 5071
Ps 119:108 the **f.** offerings of my mouth, O 5071

FREEWOMAN
Ga 4:22 by a bondmaid, the other by a **f.** *1658*
Ga 4:23 but he of the **f.** was by promise. *1658*
Ga 4:30 not be heir with the son of the **f.** *1658*

FREEZE See FROZEN.

FREQUENT
2Co 11:23 in prisons more **f.**, in deaths oft. *4056*

FRESH See also AFRESH; FRESHER; REFRESH.
Nu 11:8 taste of it was as the taste of **f.** oil 3955
Job 29:20 My glory was **f.** in me, and my 2319
Ps 92:10 I shall be anointed with **f.** oil. 7488
Jas 3:12 both yield salt water and **f.** *1099*

FRESHER
Job 33:25 His flesh shall be **f.** than a child's 7375

FRET See also FRETTED; FRETTETH; FRETTING.
Le 13:55 burn it in the fire; it is **f.** inward, 6356
1Sa 1:6 sore, for to make her **f.**, because 7481
Ps 37:1 **F.** not thyself because of 2734
Ps 37:7 **f.** not thyself because of him who 2734
Ps 37:8 **f.** not thyself in any wise to do evil. 2734
Pr 24:19 **F.** not thyself because of evil men, 2734
Isa 8:21 hungry, they shall **f.** themselves, 7107

FRETTED
Eze 16:43 hast **f.** me in all these things; but 7264

FRETTETH
Pr 19:3 and his heart **f.** agianst the Lord. 2196

FRETTING
Le 13:51 the plague is a **f.** leprosy: it is 3992
Le 13:52 it is a **f.** leprosy; it shall be burnt 3992
Le 14:44 it is a **f.** leprosy in the house: it is 3992

FRIED
Le 7:12 mingled with oil, of fine flour, **f.** 7246
1Ch 23:29 and for that which is **f.**, and for 7246

FRIEND See also FRIENDS; FREINDSHIP.
Ge 38:12 and his **f.** Hirah the Adullamite. 7453
Ge 38:20 sent the kid by the hand of his **f.** 7453
Ex 33:11 face, as a man speaketh unto his **f.** 7453
De 13:6 or the wife of thy bosom, or thy **f.**, 7453
Jg 14:20 whom he had used as his **f.** 7462
2Sa 13:3 Amnon had a **f.**, whose name was 7453
2Sa 15:37 Hushai David's **f.** came into 7463
2Sa 16:16 Hushai the Archite, David's **f.** 7463
2Sa 16:17 Is this thy kindness to thy **f.**? 7453
2Sa 16:17 why wentest thou not with thy **f.**? 7453
1Ki 4:5 principal officer, and the king's **f.**: 7463
2Ch 20:7 seed of Abraham thy **f.** for ever? 157
Job 6:14 pity should be shewed from his **f.**; 7453
Job 6:27 and ye dig a pit for your **f.** 7451
Ps 35:14 as though he had been my **f.** or 7453
Ps 41:9 mine own familiar **f.**, in whom I trusted
Ps 88:18 Lover and **f.** hast thou put far 7453
Pr 6:1 son, if thou be surety for thy **f.**, 7453
Pr 6:3 art come into the hand of thy **f.**; 7453
Pr 6:3 thyself, and make sure thy **f.** 7453
Pr 17:17 A **f.** loveth at all times, and a 7453
Pr 17:18 surety in the presence of his **f.** 7453
Pr 18:24 and there is a **f.** that sticketh closer 157
Pr 19:6 man is a **f.** to him that giveth gifts. 7453
Pr 22:11 of his lips the king shall be his **f.** 7453
Pr 27:6 Faithful are the wounds of a **f.**; 157
Pr 27:9 doth the sweetness of a man's **f.** by 7453
Pr 27:10 Thine own **f.**, and thy father's **f.**, 7453
Pr 27:14 blesseth his **f.** with a loud voice. 7453
Pr 27:17 a man...the countenance of his **f.** 7453
Ca 5:16 my **f.**, O daughters of Jerusalem. 7453
Isa 41:8 chosen, the seed of Abraham my **f.** 157
Jer 6:21 neighbour and his **f.** shall perish. 7453
Jer 19:9 eat every one the flesh of his **f.** in 7453
Ho 3:1 yet, love a woman beloved of her **f.**, 7453
Mic 7:5 Trust ye not in a **f.**, put ye not 7453
Mt 11:19 **a f. of publicans and sinners** *5384*
Mt 20:13 **F., I do thee no wrong: didst not ..** *2083*
Mt 22:12 **F., how camest thou in hither not** *2083*
Mt 26:50 **F., wherefore art thou come?** *2083*
Lu 7:34 **a f. of publicans and sinners!** *5384*
Lu 11:5 **Which of you shall have a f., and..** *5384*
Lu 11:5 **him, F., lend me three loaves;** *5384*
Lu 11:6 **For a f. of mine in his journey is ..** *5384*
Lu 11:8 **and give him, because he is his f.,** *5384*
Lu 14:10 **F., go up higher: then shalt thou** *5384*
Joh 3:29 but the **f.** of the bridegroom, which *5384*
Joh 11:11 **Our f. Lazarus sleepeth; but I go,** *5384*
Joh 19:12 thou art not Caesar's **f.**: whosoever *5384*

Ac 12:20 and having made Blastus their F., ... *3982*
Jas 2:23 and he was called the F. of God. *5384*
Jas 4:4 f. of the world is the enemy of God..... *5384*

FRIENDLY
Jg 19:3 to speak f. unto her, and to bring 3820
Ru 2:13 spoken f. unto thine handmaid, ... 3820
Pr 18:24 friends must shew himself f.: 7489

FRIENDS
Ge 26:26 and Ahuzzath one of his f., and......... 4828
1Sa 30:26 to his f., saying, Behold a present...... 7453
2Sa 3:8 to his brethren, and to his f., and 4828
2Sa 19:6 thine enemies, and hatest thy f.. 157
1Ki 16:11 of his kinsfolks, nor of his f.. and...... 7453
Es 5:10 he sent and called for his f., ... 157
Es 5:14 said Zeresh his wife and all his f......... 157
Es 6:13 told Zeresh his wife and all his f......... 157
Job 2:11 when Job's three f. heard of all.......... 7453
Job 16:20 My f. scorn me: but mine eye........... 7453
Job 17:5 He that speaketh flattery to his f., ... 7453
Job 19:14 and my familiar f. have forgotten me.........
Job 19:19 All my inward f. abhorred me:........... 4962
Job 19:21 have pity upon me, O ye my f.;......... 7453
Job 32:3 against his three f. was his wrath....... 7453
Job 42:7 thee, and against thy two f.: for ye 7453
Job 42:10 when he prayed for his f.: also the..... 7453
Ps 38:11 My lovers and my f. stand aloof......... 7453
Pr 14:20 but the rich hath many f.. 157
Pr 16:28 and a whisperer separateth chief f......... 441
Pr 17:9 he that...a matter separateth very f.. ... 441
Pr 18:24 A man that hath f. must shew 7453
Pr 19:4 Wealth maketh many f.; but the......... 7453
Pr 19:7 more do his f. go far from him? 4828
Ca 5:1 eat, O f.; drink, yea, drink 7453
Jer 20:4 terror to thyself, and to all thy f.:........ 157
Jer 20:6 be buried there, thou, and all thy f., ... 157
Jer 38:22 say, Thy f. have set thee on, ... 605,7965
La 1:2 her f. have dealt treacherously 7453
Zec 13:6 was wounded in the house of my f........ 157
Mk 3:21 when his f. heard of it, they *3588,3844*
Mk 5:19 Go home to thy f., and tell them ... *4674*
Lu 7:6 centurion sent f. to him, saying, ... *5384*
Lu 12:4 And I say unto you my f., Be not.. *5384*
Lu 14:12 call not thy f., nor thy brethren....... *5384*
Lu 15:6 he calleth together his f. and *5384*
Lu 15:9 calleth her f. and her neighbours .. *5384*
Lu 15:29 I might make merry with my f.:.... *5384*
Lu 16:9 to yourselves f. of the mammon of .*5384*
Lu 21:16 brethren, and kinsfolk, and f.; *5384*
Lu 23:12 day Pilate and Herod were made f....... *5384*
Joh 15:13 a man lay down his life for his f....*5384*
Joh 15:14 Ye are my f., if ye do whatsoever.. *5384*
Joh 15:15 I have called you f.; for all things . *5384*
Ac 10:24 together his kinsmen and near f.. .... *5384*
Ac 19:31 the chief of Asia, which were his f., ... *5384*
Ac 27:3 to go unto his f. to refresh himself. *5384*
3Jo 14 Our f. salute thee. *5384*
3Jo 14 Greet the f. by name............................ *5384*

FRIENDSHIP
Pr 22:24 Make no f. with an angry man;.......... 7462
Jas 4:4 f. of the world is enmity with God? *5373*

FRIGHT See AFFRIGHT.

FRINGE See also FRINGES.
Nu 15:38 put upon the f. of the borders a......... 6734
Nu 15:39 And it shall be unto you for a f.,........ 6734

FRINGES
Nu 15:38 may make them f. in the borders....... 6734
De 22:12 thee f. upon the four quarters 1434

FRO See also FROWARD.
Ge 8:7 raven, which went forth to and f., ... 7725
2Ki 4:35 walked in the house to and f.;...... 259,2008
2Ch 16:9 the eyes of the Lord run to and f....... 7751
Job 1:7 From going to and f. in the earth, ... 7751
Job 2:2 From going to and f. in the earth, ... 7751
Job 7:4 I am full of tossing to and f......................
Job 13:25 break a leaf driven to and f.?.................
Ps 107:27 They reel to and f., and stagger ....
Pr 21:6 a vanity tossed to and f. of them................
Isa 24:20 shall reel to and f. like a drunkard.............
Isa 33:4 as the running to and f. of locusts ....
Isa 49:21 a captive, and removing to and f.? ....
Jer 5:1 ye to and f. through the streets......... 7751
Jer 49:3 and run to and f. by the hedges:......... 7751
Eze 27:19 Dan also and Javan going to and f. 235
Da 12:4 many shall run to and f., and............ 7751
Joe 2:9 shall run to and f. in the city;........... 8264
Am 8:12 they shall run to and f. to seed the 7751
Zec 1:10 to walk to and f. through the earth..........
Zec 1:11 We have walked to and f. through the.......
Zec 4:10 of the Lord, which run to and f. 7751
Zec 6:7 might walk to and f. through the earth: .....
Zec 6:7 Get you hence, walk to and f. through .....
Zec 6:7 So they walked to and f. through the........
Eph 4:14 tossed to and f., and carried about *2831*

FROGS
Ex 8:2 will smite all thy borders with f.: 6854
Ex 8:3 And the river shall bring forth f. 6854
Ex 8:4 the f. shall come up both on thee....... 6854
Ex 8:5 and cause f. to come upon the land 6854
Ex 8:6 the f. came up, and covered the land.. 6854
Ex 8:7 and brought up f. upon the land of..... 6854
Ex 8:8 that he may take away the f. from 6854
Ex 8:9 the f. from thee and thy houses,......... 6854
Ex 8:11 And the f. shall depart from thee, ... 6854
Ex 8:12 of the f. which he had brought........... 6854
Ex 8:13 and the f. died out of the houses, ... 6854
Ps 78:45 and f., which destroyed them. 6854
Ps 105:30 land brought forth f. in abundance, ... 6854
Re 16:13 I saw three unclean spirits like f.......... *944*

FROM See in the APPENDIX; also THEREFROM.

FRONT See also FOREFRONT.
2Sa 10:9 Joab saw that the f. of the battle........ 6440
2Ch 3:4 that was in the f. of the house, ... 6440

FRONTIERS
Eze 25:9 from his cities which are on his f., ... 7097

FRONTLETS
Ex 13:16 and for f. between thine eyes:........... 2903
De 6:8 shall be as f. between thine eyes. 2903
De 11:18 they may be as f. between your eyes. .2903

FROST See also HOARFROST.
Ge 31:40 consumed me, and the f. by night; 7140
Ex 16:14 small as the hoar f. on the ground...... 3713
Job 37:10 By the breath of God f. is given: 7140
Job 38:29 and the hoary f. of heaven, who 3713
Ps 78:47 and their sycamore trees with f.. 2602
Jer 36:30 the heat, and in the night to the f.. 7140

FROWARD
De 32:20 for they are a very f. generation, ... 8419
2Sa 22:27 with the f. thou wilt shew thyself....... 6141
Job 5:13 counsel of the f. is carried................ 6617
Ps 18:26 and with the f. thou wilt shew,.......... 6141
Ps 18:26 with...thou wilt show thyself f., ... 6617
Ps 101:4 A f. heart shall depart from me: 6141
Pr 2:12 the man that speaketh f. things;......... 8419
Pr 2:15 and they f. in their paths:.................. 3868
Pr 3:32 the f. is abomination to the Lord:....... 3868
Pr 4:24 Put away from thee a f. mouth, ... 6143
Pr 6:12 man, walketh with a f. mouth, ... 6143
Pr 8:8 nothing f. or perverse in them........... 6617
Pr 8:13 and the f. mouth. do I hate............... 8419
Pr 10:31 but the f. tongue shall be cut out. 8419
Pr 11:20 are of a f. heart are abomination......... 6141
Pr 16:28 A f. man soweth strife: and a............. 8419
Pr 16:30 his eyes to devise f. things:.............. 8419
Pr 17:20 hath a f. heart findeth no good: 6141
Pr 21:8 way of man is f. and strange:............ 2019
Pr 22:5 snares are in the way of the f.: 6141
1Pe 2:18 good and gentle, but also to the f....... *4646*

FROWARDLY
Isa 57:17 he went on f. in the way of his.......... 7726

FROWARDNESSS
Pr 2:14 delight in the f. of the wicked;........... 8419
Pr 6:14 F. is in his heart, he deviseth............ 8419
Pr 10:32 mouth of the wicked speaketh f.. 8419

FROZEN
Job 38:30 and the face of the deep is f.. 3920

FRUIT See also FIRSTFRUIT; FRUITFUL; FRUITS.
Ge 1:11 f. tree yielding f. after his kind,......... 6529
Ge 1:12 yielding f., whose seed was in itself,... 6529
Ge 1:29 is the f. of a tree yielding seed;......... 6529
Ge 3:2 the f. of the trees of the garden: 6529
Ge 3:3 f. of the tree which is in the midst..... 6529
Ge 3:6 took of the f. thereof, and did eat, ... 6529
Ge 4:3 Cain brought of the f. of the ground ... 6529
Ge 30:2 from thee the f. of the womb?........... 6529
Ex 10:15 f. of the trees which the hail had 6529
Ex 21:22 so that her f. depart from her, ... 3206
Le 19:23 the f. thereof as uncircumcised: 6529
Le 19:24 year all the f. thereof shall be holy..... 6529
Le 19:25 year shall ye eat of the f. thereof,...... 6529
Le 23:39 have gathered in the f. of the land,..... 8393
Le 25:3 and gather in the f. thereof;.............. 8393
Le 25:19 And the land shall yield her f.,........... 6529
Le 25:21 and it shall bring forth f. for three...... 8393
Le 25:22 yet of old f. until the ninth year: 8393
Le 26:4 threes of the field shall yield their f.. .. 6529
Le 27:30 the f. of the tree, is the Lord's: 6529
Nu 13:20 and bring of the f. of the land........... 6529
Nu 13:26 and shewed them the f. of the land. ... 6529
Nu 13:27 and honey; and this is the f. of it. 6529
De 1:25 and they took of the f. of the land...... 6529
De 7:13 f. of thy womb, and the f. of thy 6529
De 11:17 that the land yield not her f.; 2981
De 22:9 lest the f. of thy seed...................... 4395
De 22:9 the f. of thy vineyard, be defiled. 8393
De 26:2 the first of all the f. of the earth. 6529
De 28:4 the f. of thy body, and the f. of thy ... 6529
De 28:4 ground, and the f. of thy cattle, ... 6529
De 28:11 in the f. of thy body, and in the f. of.. 6529
De 28:11 cattle, and in the f. of thy ground,....... 6529
De 28:18 f. of thy body, and the f. of thy land. . 6529
De 28:33 f. of thy land, and all thy labours,....... 6529
De 28:40 oil; for thine olive shall cast his f.............
De 28:42 All thy trees and f. of thy land............ 6529
De 28:51 the f. of thy cattle, and the f. of thy... 6529
De 28:53 shall eat the f. of thine own body,...... 6529
De 30:9 in the f. of thy body, and in the f. of.. 6529
De 30:9 thy cattle, and in the f. of thy land, ... 6529
Jos 5:12 they did eat of the f. of the land 8393
Jg 9:11 my sweetness, and my good f., ... 8270
2Sa 16:2 bread and summer f. for the young...........
2Ki 19:30 downward, and bear f. upward........... 6529
Ne 9:25 and f. trees in abundance:................. 3978
Ne 9:36 to eat the f. thereof and the good 6529
Ne 10:35 the firstfruits of all f. of all trees, ... 6529
Ne 10:37 and the f. of all manner of trees, ... 6529
Ps 1:3 bringeth forth his f. in his season; 6529
Ps 21:10 Their f. shalt thou destroy from.......... 6529
Ps 72:16 f. thereof shall shake like Lebanon:..... 6529
Ps 92:14 shall still bring forth f. in old age;...... 5107
Ps 104:13 satisfied with the f. of thy works........ 6529
Ps 105:35 devoured the f. of their ground.......... 6529
Ps 127:3 the f. of the womb is his reward........ 6529
Ps 132:11 Of the f. of thy body will I set upon ... 6529
Pr 1:31 they eat of the f. of their own way,.... 6529
Pr 8:19 My f. is better than gold, yea, than.... 6529
Pr 10:16 the f. of the wicked to sin. 8393
Pr 11:30 The f. of the righteous is a tree 6529
Pr 12:12 the root of the righteous yieldeth f.. ....
Pr 12:14 with good by the f. of his mouth: 6529
Pr 13:2 shall eat good by the f. of his mouth:.. 6529
Pr 18:20 satisfied with the f. of his mouth; 6529
Pr 18:21 that love it shall eat the f. thereof. 6529
Pr 27:18 the fig tree shall eat the f. thereof: 6529
Pr 31:16 the f. of her hands she planteth.......... 6529
Pr 31:31 Give her of the f. of her hands; 6529
Ca 2:3 and his f. was sweet to may taste...... 6529
Ca 8:11 evey one for the f. thereof was to...... 6529
Ca 8:12 those that keep the f. of their two...... 6529
Isa 3:10 they shall eat the f. of their doings...... 6529
Isa 4:2 the f. of the earth shall be excellent ... 6529
Isa 10:12 the f. of the stout heart of the king.... 6529
Isa 13:18 have no pity on the f. of the womb; ... 6529
Isa 14:29 his f. shall be a fiery flying serpent..... 6529
Isa 27:6 fill the face of the world with f.. 8570
Isa 27:9 is all the f. to take away his sin; 6529
Isa 28:4 the hasty f. before the summer; 1061
Isa 37:30 plant vineyards, and eat the f............ 6529
Isa 37:31 downward, and bear f. upward:........... 6529
Isa 57:19 I create the f. of the lips;................. 5108
Isa 65:21 plant vineyards, and eat the f. of......... 6529
Jer 2:7 eat the f. thereof and the goodness 6529
Jer 6:19 f. of their thoughts, because they....... 6529
Jer 7:20 and upon the f. of the ground;........... 6529
Jer 11:16 olive tree, fair, and of goodly f. 6529
Jer 11:19 Let us destroy the tree with the f...... 3899
Jer 12:2 they grow, yea, they bring forth f. 6529
Jer 17:8 neither shall cease from yielding f....... 6529
Jer 17:10 according to the f. of his doings......... 6529
Jer 21:14 according to the f. of your doings,...... 6529
Jer 29:5, 28 plant gardens, and eat the f. of...... 6529

Jer 32:19 according to the f. of his doings: 6529
La 2:20 Shall the women eat their f., and 6529
Eze 17:8 that it might bear f., that it might 6529
Eze 17:9 cut off the f. thereof, that it wither? 6529
Eze 17:23 bring forth boughs, and bear f.; 6529
Eze 19:12 and the east wind dried up her f.: 6529
Eze 19:14 which hath devoured her f., 6529
Eze 25:4 they shall eat thy f., and they shall 6529
Eze 34:27 tree of the field to shall yield her f., 6529
Eze 36:8 and yield your f. to my people 6529
Eze 36:11 they shall increase and bring f.: 6509
Eze 36:30 I will multiply the f. of the tree, 6529
Eze 47:12 the f. thereof be consumed: 6529
Eze 47:12 it shall bring forth new f. 1061
Eze 47:12 and the f. thereof shall be for meat, 6529
Da 4:12 the f. thereof much, and it was meat 4
Da 4:14 off his leaves, and scatter his f.: 4
Da 4:21 f. thereof much, and in it was meat 4
Ho 9:16 they shall bear no f.: yea, though 6529
Ho 9:16 yet will I slay even the beloved f.
Ho 10:1 bringeth forth f. unto himself: 6529
Ho 10:1 according to the multitide of his f. 6529
Ho 10:13 ye have eaten the f. of lies: 6529
Ho 14:8 From me is thy f. found. 6529
Joe 2:22 the tree beareth her f., the fig tree 6529
Am 2:9 I destroyed his f. from above, 6529
Am 6:12 f. of righteousness unto hemlock:
Am 7:14 and a gatherer of sycomore f.
Am 8:1 and behold a basket of summer f.
Am 8:2 And I said, A basket of summer f.
Am 9:14 make gardens, and eat the f. of 6529
Mic 6:7 f. of my body for the sin of my soul? 6529
Mic 7:1 my soul desired the first ripe f.
Mic 7:13 therein, for the f. of their doings 6529
Hab 3:17 neither shall f. be in the vines; 2981
Hag 1:10 the earth is stayed from her f. 2981
Zec 8:12 vine shall give her f., and the 6529
Mal 1:12 and the f. thereof, even his meat, 5108
Mal 3:11 your vine cast her f. before the 7920
Mt 3:10 which bringeth not forth good f. 2590
Mt 7:17 tree bringeth forth good f.; 2590
Mt 7:17 corrupt tree bringeth forth evil f. 2590
Mt 7:18 tree cannot bring forth evil f., 2590
Mt 7:18 a corrupt tree bring forth good f. 2590
Mt 7:19 that bringeth not forth good f. 2590
Mt 12:33 the tree good, and his f. good; 2590
Mt 12:33 tree corrupt, and his f. corrupt: 2590
Mt 12:33 for the tree is known by his f. 2590
Mt 13:8 and brought forth f., some an 2590
Mt 13:23 also beareth f., and bringeth forth, 2592
Mt 13:26 sprung up, and brought forth f., 2590
Mt 21:19 no f. grow on thee henceforward 2590
Mt 21:34 when the time of the f. drew near, 2590
Mt 26:29 henceforth of this f. of the vine, 1081
Mk 4:7 and choked it, and it yielded no f. 2590
Mk 4:8 and did yield f. that sprang up 2590
Mk 4:20 and bring forth f., some thirtyfold, 2592
Mk 4:28 earth bringeth forth f. of herself; 2592
Mk 4:29 But when the f. is brought forth, 2590
Mk 11:14 No man eat f. of thee hereafter 2590
Mk 12:2 from the husbandmen of the f. of 2590
Mk 14:25 drink no more of the f. of the 1081
Lu 1:42 blessed is the f. of thy womb. 2590
Lu 3:9 bringeth forth not good f. is hewn 2590
Lu 6:43 tree bringeth not forth corrupt f.; 2590
Lu 6:43 a corrupt tree bring forth good f. 2590
Lu 6:44 every tree is known by his own f. 2590
Lu 8:8 up, and bare f. an hundredfold 2590
Lu 8:14 and bring no f. to perfection 5062
Lu 8:15 and bring forth f. with patience 2592
Lu 13:6 he came and sought f. thereon 2590
Lu 13:7 these three years I come seeking f. 2590
Lu 13:9 And if it bear f., well: and if not, 2590
Lu 20:10 that they should give him of the f. 2590
Lu 22:18 will not drink of the f. of the vine, 1081
Joh 4:36 and gathereth f. unto life eternal: 2590
Joh 12:24 if it die, it bringeth forth much f. 2590
Joh 15:2 beareth not f. he taketh away: 2590
Joh 15:2 that beareth f., he purgeth it, 2590
Joh 15:2 that it may bring forth more f. 2590
Joh 15:4 that branch cannot bear f. of 2590
Joh 15:5 the same bringeth forth much f. 2590
Joh 15:8 glorified, that ye bear much f.; 2590
Joh 15:16 ye should go and bring forth f., 2590
Joh 15:16 and that your f. should remain: 2590
Ac 2:30 that of the f. of his loins, he would 2590
Ro 1:13 I might have some f. among you 2590
Ro 6:21 What f. had ye then in those things 2590
Ro 6:22 ye have your f. unto holiness, 2590
Ro 7:4 we should bring forth f. unto God. 2592
Ro 7:5 to bring forth f. unto death. 2592
Ro 15:28 and have sealed to them this f., 2590
1Co 9:7 and eateth not of the f. thereof? 2590
Ga 5:22 But the f. of the Spirit is love, 2590
Eph 5:9 f. of the Spirit is in all goodness 2590
Php 1:22 this is the f. of my labour: 2590
Php 4:17 but I desire f. that may abound 2590
Col 1:6 bringeth forth f., as it doth also 2592
Heb 12:11 it yieldeth the peaceable f. of 2590
Heb 13:15 the f. of our lips giving thanks 2590
Jas 3:18 And the f. of righteouness is sown 2590
Jas 5:7 for the precious f. of the earth, 2590
Jas 5:18 and the earth brought forth her f. 2590
Jude 12 three whose f. withereth, 5352
Jude 12 without f., twice dead, 175
Re 22:2 and yielded her f. every month: 2590

FRUITFUL See also UNFRUITFUL.

Ge 1:22 Be f., and multpily, and fill the 6509
Ge 1:28 Be f. and multiply, and replenish 6509
Ge 8:17 be f., and multiply upon the earth. 6509
Ge 9:1 Be f., and multiply, and replenish 6509
Ge 9:7 be ye f., and multiply; bring forth 6509
Ge 17:6 And I will make thee exceeding f., 6509
Ge 17:20 will make him f., and will multiply 6509
Ge 26:22 and we shall be f. in the land. 6509
Ge 28:3 bless thee, and make thee f., 6509
Ge 35:11 be f. and multiply; a nation 6509
Ge 41:52 God hath caused me to be f. 6509
Ge 48:4 Behold, I will make thee f., and 6509
Ge 49:22 Joseph is a f. bough, even a f. 6509
Ex 1:7 the children of Israel were f., and 6509
Le 26:9 respect unto you, and make you f., 6509
Ps 107:34 A f. land into barrenness, for the 6529
Ps 128:3 Thy wife shall be as a f. vine 6509
Ps 148:9 all hills; f. trees, and all cedars; 6529
Isa 5:1 a vineyard in a very f. hill: 1121,8081
Isa 10:18 of his forest, and of his f. field, 3759
Isa 17:6 the outmost f. branches thereof, 6509
Isa 29:17 Lebanon shall be turned into a f. 3759
Isa 29:17 field, and the f. field shall be 3759
Isa 32:12 the pleasant fields, for the f. vine. 6509
Isa 32:15 wilderness be a f. field, and the 3759
Isa 32:15 f. field be counted for a forest. 3759
Isa 32:16 righteousness remain in the f. field. 3759
Jer 4:26 lo, the f. place was a wilderness, 3759
Jer 23:3 and they shall be f. and increase. 6509
Eze 17:5 and planted it in a f. field; 2233
Eze 19:10 she was f. and full of branches 6509
Ho 13:15 he be f. among his brethren, 6500
Ac 14:17 and f. seasons, filling our hearts 2593
Col 1:10 being f. in every good work, 2592

FRUITS

Ge 43:11 take of the best f. in the land 2173
Ex 22:29 the first of thy ripe f., and of thy 4395
Ex 23:10 shalt gather in the f. thereof: 8393
Le 25:15 the f. he shall sell unto thee: 8393
Le 25:16 the f. doth he sell unto thee 8393
Le 25:22 until her f. come in ye shall eat 8393
Le 26:20 trees of the land yield their f. 6529
De 33:14 for the precious f. brought forth 8393
2Sa 9:10 bring in the f., that thy master's son
2Sa 16:1 hundred of summer f., and a bottle
2Ki 8:6 all the f. of the field since the day 8393
2Ki 19:29 vineyards, and eat the f. thereof. 6529
Job 31:39 If I have eaten the f. thereof 3581
Ps 107:37 which may yield f. of increase. 6529
Ec 2:5 trees in them of all kind of f.: 6529
Ca 4:13 with pleasant f.; camphire, with 6529
Ca 4:16 his garden, and eat his pleasant f. 6529
Ca 6:11 to see the f. of the valley, 3
Ca 7:13 are all manner of pleasant f.,
Isa 16:9 for the shouting for thy summer f.
Isa 33:9 and Carmel shake off their f.
Jer 40:10 gather ye wine, and summer f., and
Jer 40:12 gathered wine and summer f. very
Jer 48:32 spoiler is fallen upon they summer f.
La 4:9 for want of the f. of the field 8570
Mic 7:1 they have gathered the summer f.,
Mal 3:11 not destroy the f. of your ground; 6529
Mt 3:8 therefore f. meet for repentance: 2590
Mt 7:16 Ye shall know them by their f. 2590
Mt 7:20 by their f. ye shall know them 2590
Mt 21:34 they might receive the f. of it. 2590
Mt 21:41 render him the f. in their seasons. 2590
Mt 21:43 bringeth forth the f. thereof 2590
Lu 3:8 therefore f. worthy of repentance; 2590
Lu 12:17 no room where to bestow my f.? 2590
Lu 12:18 I bestow all my f. and my goods, 1081
2Co 9:10 the f. of your righteousness; 1081
Php 1:11 with the f. of righteousness, 2590
2Ti 2:6 must be first partaker of the f. 2590
Jas 3:17 full of mercy and good f., 2590
Re 18:14 the f. that thy soul lusted after 3703
Re 22:2 which bare twelve manner of f., 2590

FRUIT-TREE See also FRUIT and TREE.

FRUSTRATE See also FRUSTRATETH.

Ezr 4:5 to f. their purpose, all the days 656
Ga 2:21 I do not f. the grace of God: 114

FRUSTRATETH

Isa 44:25 That f. the tokens of the liars, 6565

FRYINGPAN

Le 2:7 a meat offering baken in the f. 4802
Le 7:9 all that is dressed in the f. 4802

FUEL

Isa 9:5 be with burning and f. of fire 3980
Isa 9:19 shall be as the f. of the fire: 3980
Eze 15:4 it is cast into the fire for f.; 402
Eze 15:6 I have given to the fire for f., 402
Eze 21:32 Thou shalt be for f. to the fire; 402

FUGITIVE See also FUGITIVES.

Ge 4:12 a f. and a vagabond shalt thou be 5128
Ge 4:14 I shall be a f. and a vagabond 5128

FUGITIVES

Jg 12:4 Ye Gileadites are f. of Ephraim 6412
2Ki 25:11 the f. that fell away to the king 5307
Isa 15:5 his f. shall flee unto Zoar, an 1280
Eze 17:21 his f. with all his bands shall fall 4015

FULFIL See also FULFILLED; FULFILLNG.

Ge 29:27 F. her week, and we will give thee 4390
Ex 5:13 F. your words, your daily tasks, 3615
Ex 23:26 the number of thy days I will f. 4390
1Ki 2:27 he might f. the word of the Lord, 4390
1Ch 22:13 takest heed to f. the statutes 6213
2Ch 36:21 To f. the word of the Lord by the 4390
2Ch 36:21 to f. threescore and ten years. 4390
Job 39:2 number the months that they f.?
Ps 20:4 and f. all thy counsel. 4390
Ps 20:5 the Lord f. all thy petitions. 4390
Ps 145:19 He will f. the desire of them that 6213
Mt 3:15 us to f. all righteousness. 4137
Mt 5:17 not come to destroy, but to f. 4137
Ac 13:22 heart, which shall f. all my will. 4160
Ro 2:27 it it f. the law, judge thee, 5055
Ro 13:14 provision for the flesh, to f. the lusts
Ga 5:16 shall not f. the lust of the flesh. 5055
Ga 6:2 and so f. the law of Christ, 378
Php 2:2 F. ye my joy, that ye be 4137
Col 1:25 for you, to f. the word of God; 4137
Col 4:17 in the Lord, that thou f. it. 4137
2Th 1:11 and f. all the good pleasure of his 4137
Jas 2:8 If ye f. the royal law according to 5055
Re 17:17 to f. his will, and to agree, and 4160

FULFILLED

Ge 25:24 her days to be delivered were f., 4390
Ge 29:21 my days are f., that I may go 4390
Ge 29:28 Jacob did so, and f. her week: 4390
Ge 50:3 And forty days were f. for him; 4390
Ge 50:3 for so are f. the days of those 4390
Ex 5:14 Wherefore have ye not f. your 3615
Ex 7:25 And seven days were f., after that 4390
Le 12:4 until the days of her purifying be f. 4390
Le 12:6 the days of her purifying are f., 4390
Nu 6:5 until the days be f., in the which 4390
Nu 6:13 the days of his separation are f.: 4390
2Sa 7:12 when thy days be f., and thou shalt 4390
2Sa 14:22 hath f. the request of his servant. 6213
1Ki 8:15 hath with his had f. it, saying, 4390
1Ki 8:24 and hasts f. it with thine hand, 4390
2Ch 6:4 who hath with his hands f. 4390
2Ch 6:15 and hast f. it with thine hand, 4390
Ezr 1:1 mouth of Jeremiah might be f., 3615
Job 36:17 f. the judgment of the wicked: 4390
Jer 44:25 spoken wth your mouths, and f. 4390

La 2:17 he hath f. his word that he had 1214
La 4:18 our end is near, our days are f.; 4390
Eze 5:2 when the days of the siege are f.: 4390
Da 4:33 The same hour was the thing f. 5487
Da 10:3 till three whole weeks were f. 4390
Mt 1:22 this was done, that it might be f. *4137*
Mt 2:15 it might be f. which was spoken *4137*
Mt 2:17 Then was f. that which was spoken *4137*
Mt 2:23 that it might be f. which was *4137*
Mt 4:14 it might be f. which was spoken *4137*
Mt 5:18 **from the law, till all be f.** *1096*
Mt 8:17 it might be f. which was spoken *4137*
Mt 12:17 be f. which was spoken by Esaias *4137*
Mt 13:14 **And in them is f. the prophecy** *378*
Mt 13:35 That it might be f. which was *4137*
Mt 21:4 it might be f. which was spoken by *4137*
Mt 24:34 **pass, till all these things be f.** *1096*
Mt 26:54 **then shall the scriptures be f.** *4137*
Mt 26:56 **of the prophets might be f.** *4137*
Mt 27:9 was f. that which was spoken *4137*
Mt 27:35 it might be f. which was spoken *4137*
Mk 1:15 **The time is f., and the kingdom** *4137*
Mk 13:4 when all these things shall be f.? *4931*
Mk 14:49 **but the scriptures must be f.** *4137*
Mk 15:28 the scripture was f., which saith, *4137*
Lu 1:20 which shall be f. in their season. *4137*
Lu 2:43 And when they had f. the days, *5048*
Lu 4:21 **is this scripture f. in your ears** *4137*
Lu 21:22 **things which are written may be f.** *4137*
Lu 21:24 **times of the Gentiles be f.** *4137*
Lu 21:32 **shall not pass away, till all be f.,** *1096*
Lu 22:16 **until it be f. in the kingdom** *4137*
Lu 24:44 **must be f., which were written** *4137*
Joh 3:29 this my joy therefore is f. *4137*
Joh 12:38 might be f., which he spake, Lord, *4137*
Joh 13:18 **but that the scripture may be f.,** *4137*
Joh 15:25 **word might be f. that is written** *4137*
Joh 17:12 **that the scripture might be f.** *4137*
Joh 17:13 **that they might have my joy f.** *4137*
Joh 18:9 saying might be f., which he spake *4137*
Joh 18:32 the saying of Jesus might be f., *4137*
Joh 19:24 scripture might be f., which saith, *4137*
Joh 19:28 that the scripture might be f., *5048*
Joh 19:36 the scripture should be f., A bone *4137*
Ac 1:16 scripture must needs have been f., *4137*
Ac 3:18 should suffer, he hath so f. *4137*
Ac 9:23 And after that many days were f., *4137*
Ac 12:25 when they had f. their ministry, *4137*
Ac 13:25 as John f. his course, he said, *4137*
Ac 13:27 have f. them in condemning him *4137*
Ac 13:29 f. all that was written of him, *5055*
Ac 13:33 God hath f. the same unto us *1603*
Ac 14:26 for the work which they f. *4137*
Ro 8:4 of the law might be f. in us, *4137*
Ro 13:8 loveth another hath f. the law *4137*
2Co 10:6 when your obedience is f. *4137*
Ga 5:14 all the law is f. in one word, *4137*
Jas 2:23 the scripture was f. which saith, *4137*
Re 6:11 killed as they were, should be f. *4137*
Re 15:8 of the seven angels were f. *5055*
Re 17:17 until the words of God shall be f. *5055*
Re 20:3 the thousand years should be f.: *5055*

FULFILLING

Ps 148:8 vapours; stormy wind f. his word: 6213
Ro 13:10 therefore love is the f. of the law *4138*
Eph 2:3 f. the desires of the flesh and of *4160*

FULL See also BEAUTIFUL; BOUNTIFUL; CHEERFUL; DECEITFUL; DESPITEFUL; DOUBTFUL; DREADFUL; FAITHFUL; FEARFUL; FORGETFUL; FRUITFUL; FULFIL; HANDFUL; HARMFUL; HATEFUL; HURTFUL; JOYFUL; LAWFUL; MERCIFUL; MINDFUL; MOURNFULLY; NEEDFUL; PAINFUL; PITIFUL; PLENTIFUL; POWERFUL; REPROACHFULLY; SCORNFUL; SHAMEFUL; SINFUL; SKILFUL; SLOTHFUL; SORROWFUL; THANKFUL; WATCHFUL; WILFULLY; WOEFUL; WONDERFUL; WRATHFUL; YOUTHFUL.

Ge 14:10 the vale of Siddim was f. of slimepits;
Ge 15:16 the Amorites is not yet f. 8003
Ge 25:8 an old man, and f. of years; 7649
Ge 35:29 old and f. of days: and his sons 7649
Ge 41:1 at the end of two f. years, 3117
Ge 41:7 the seven rank and f. ears 4392
Ge 41:22 came up in one stalk, f. and good: 4392
Ge 43:21 money in f. weight: and we have
Ex 8:21 of the Egyptians shall be f. 4390
Ex 16:3 when we did eat bread to the f.; 7648
Ex 16:8 in the morning bread to the f.; 7646
Ex 16:33 put an omer f. of manna therein, 4393
Ex 22:3 he should make f. restitution; 7999
Le 2:14 even corn beaten out of f. ears 3759
Le 16:12 shall take a censer f. of burning 4393
Le 16:12 f. of sweet incense beaten small, 4393
Le 19:29 the land become f. of wickedness. 4390
Le 25:29 within a f. year may he redeem it. 3117
Le 25:30 within the space of a f. year, 8549
Le 26:5 ye shall eat your bread to the f., 7648
Nu 7:13 both of them were f. of fine flour. 4392
Nu 7:14 of ten shekels of gold, f. of incense 4392
Nu 7:19 f. of fine flour mingled with oil 4392
Nu 7:20 of gold of ten shekels, f. of incense: 4392
Nu 7:25 f. of fine flour mingled with oil 4392
Nu 7:26 spoon of ten shekels, f. of incense 4392
Nu 7:31 both of them f. of fine flour 4392
Nu 7:32 spoon of ten shekels, f. of incense: 4392
Nu 7:37 f. of fine flour mingled with oil 4392
Nu 7:38 spoon of ten shekels, f. of incense 4392
Nu 7:43 both of them f. of fine flour 4392
Nu 7:44 spoon of ten shekels, f. of incense 4392
Nu 7:49 both of them f. of fine flour 4392
Nu 7:50 spoon of ten shekels, f. of incense: 4392
Nu 7:55 f. of fine flour mingled with oil 4392
Nu 7:56 spoon of ten shekels, f. of incense: 4392
Nu 7:61 f. of fine flour mingled with oil 4392
Nu 7:62 spoon of ten shekels, f. of incense: 4392
Nu 7:67 f. of fine flour mingled with oil 4392
Nu 7:68 spoon of ten shekels, f. of incense: 4392
Nu 7:73 f. of fine flour mingled with oil 4392
Nu 7:74 spoon of ten shekels, f. of incense: 4392
Nu 7:79 f. of fine flour mingled with oil for 4392
Nu 7:80 spoon of ten shekels, f. of incense: 4392
Nu 7:86 spoons were twelve, f. of incense, 4392
Nu 22:18 give me his house f. of silver 4393
Nu 24:13 give me his house f. of silver 4393
De 6:11 houses f. of all good things, 4392
De 6:11 thou shalt have eaten and be f.; 7646
De 8:10 When thou hast eaten and art f., 7646
De 8:12 when thou hast eaten and art f., 7646
De 11:15 that thou mayest eat and be f. 7646
De 21:13 father and her mother a f. month: 3117
De 33:23 f. with the blessing of the Lord: 4392
De 34:9 Nun was f. of the spirit of wisdom; 4392
Jg 6:38 of the fleece, a bowl f. of water 4392
Jg 16:27 house was f. of men and women; 4390
Ru 1:21 went out f., and the Lord hath 4390
Ru 2:12 and a f. reward be given thee 8003
1Sa 2:5 They that were f. have hired out 7646
1Sa 18:27 gave them in f. tale to the king, 4390
1Sa 27:7 of the Philistines was a f. year 3117
2Sa 8:2 and with one f. line to keep alive. 4393
2Sa 13:23 it came to pass after two f. years, 3117
2Sa 14:28 Absalom dwelt two f. years in 3117
2Sa 23:11 a piece of ground f. of lentiles: 4392
2Ki 3:16 Lord, Make this valley f. of ditches.
2Ki 4:4 shalt set aside that which is f. 4392
2Ki 4:6 when the vessels were f., that she 4390
2Ki 4:39 thereof wild gourds his lap f., 4393
2Ki 4:42 and f. ears of corn in the husk
2Ki 6:17 the mountain was f. of horses 4390
2Ki 7:15 was f. of garments and vessels, 4392
2Ki 9:24 drew a bow with his f. strength, 4390
2Ki 10:21 of Baal was f. from one end 4390
2Ki 15:13 reigned a f. month in Samaria 3117
1Ch 11:13 a parcel of ground f. of barley; 4392
1Ch 21:22 grant it me for the f. price: 4392
1Ch 21:24 I will verily buy it for the f. price: 4392
1Ch 23:1 David was old and f. of days, 7646
1Ch 29:28 f. of days, riches, and honour: 7646
2Ch 24:15 and was f. of days when he died; 7646
Ne 9:25 possessed houses f. of all goods, 4392
Es 3:5 then was Haman f. of wrath 4390
Es 5:9 he was f. of indignation against 4390
Job 5:26 shalt come to thy grave in a f. age, 3624
Job 7:4 and I am f. of tossings to and fro 7646
Job 10:15 I am f. of confusion; therefore see 7646
Job 11:2 should a man f. of talk be justified?
Job 14:1 is of few days, and f. of trouble. 7646
Job 20:11 His bones are f. of the sin of his 4390
Job 21:23 One dieth in his f. strength, being 8537
Job 21:24 His breasts are f. of milk, and 4390
Job 32:18 I am f. of matter, the spirit within 4390
Job 36:16 thy table should be f. of fatness. 4390
Job 42:17 Job died, being old and f. of days. 7646
Ps 10:7 His mouth is f. of cursing and 4390
Ps 17:14 they are f. of children, and leave 7646
Ps 26:10 their right hand is f. of bribes 4390
Ps 29:4 voice of the Lord is f. of majesty.
Ps 33:5 the earth is f. of the goodness of 4390
Ps 48:10 right hand is f. of righteousness. 4390
Ps 65:9 river of God, which is f. of water: 4390
Ps 69:20 and I am f. of heaviness: and I looked
Ps 73:10 waters of a f. cup are wrung out 4392
Ps 74:20 the earth are f. of the habitations 4390
Ps 75:8 it is f. of mixture; and he poureth 4392
Ps 78:25 he sent them meat to the f. 7648
Ps 78:38 he, being f. of compassion, forgave
Ps 86:15 a God f. of compassion, and gracious,
Ps 88:3 For my soul is f. of troubles: 7654
Ps 104:16 trees of the Lord are f. of sap; 7654
Ps 104:24 the earth is f. of thy riches 4390
Ps 111:4 Lord is gracious and f. of compassion
Ps 112:4 he is gracious, and f. of compassion,
Ps 119:64 earth, O Lord, is f. of thy mercy: 4390
Ps 127:5 that hath his quiver f. of them: 4390
Ps 144:13 That our garners may be f., 4392
Ps 145:8 Lord is gracious, and f. of compassion;
Pr 17:1 than an house f. of sacrifices 4392
Pr 27:7 f. soul loatheth an honeycomb; 7646
Pr 27:20 Hell and destruction are never f.; 7646
Pr 30:9 Lest I be f., and deny thee, and 7646
Ec 1:7 yet the sea is not f.; unto the 4392
Ec 1:8 All things are f. of labour; man
Ec 4:6 both the hands f. with travail 4393
Ec 9:3 of the sons of men is f. of evil, 4390
Ec 10:14 A fool also is f. of words: 7235
Ec 11:3 If the clouds be f. of rain, they 4390
Isa 1:11 I am f. of the burnt offerings of 7646
Isa 1:15 hear: your hands are f. of blood 4390
Isa 1:21 it was f. of judgment; 4392
Isa 2:7 land also is f. of silver and gold. 4390
Isa 2:7 their land is also f. of horses, 4390
Isa 2:8 Their land also is f. of idols; 4390
Isa 6:3 the whole earth is f. of his glory. 4393
Isa 11:9 earth shall be f. of the knowledge 4390
Isa 13:21 shall be f. of doleful creatures; 4390
Isa 15:9 of Dimon shall be f. of blood: 4390
Isa 22:2 art f. of stirs, a tumultuous city, 4392
Isa 22:7 valleys shall be f. of chariots, 4390
Isa 25:6 fat things f. of marrow, of wines
Isa 28:8 are f. of vomit and filthiness, 4390
Isa 30:27 his lips are f. of indignation, and 4390
Isa 51:20 they are f. of the fury of the Lord, 4392
Jer 4:12 a f. wind from those places shall 4392
Jer 4:27 yet will I not make a f. end.
Jer 5:7 when I had fed them to the f., 7646
Jer 5:10 but make not a f. end: take away
Jer 5:18 I will not make a f. end with you.
Jer 5:27 As a cage is f. of birds, 4392
Jer 5:27 so are their houses f. of deceit: 4392
Jer 6:11 I am f. of the fury of the Lord; 4392
Jer 6:11 aged with him that is f. of days. 4390
Jer 23:10 For the land is f. of adulterers; 4390
Jer 28:3 two f. years will I bring again 3117
Jer 28:11 within the space of two f. years. 3117
Jer 30:11 though I make a f. end of all nations
Jer 30:11 yet will I not make a f. end of thee:
Jer 35:5 pots f. of wine, and cups, and I 4392
Jer 46:28 I will make a f. end of all the nations
Jer 46:28 I will not make a f. end of thee,
La 1:1 solitary, that was f. of people! 7227
La 3:30 he is filled f. with reproach. 7646
Eze 1:18 their rings were f. of eyes round 4392
Eze 7:23 the land is f. of bloody crimes, 4390
Eze 7:23 and the city is f. of violence. 4390
Eze 9:9 and the land is f. of blood, 4390
Eze 9:9 and the city f. of perverseness: 4390
Eze 10:4 the court was f. of the brightness 4390
Eze 10:12 were f. of eyes round about, 4392
Eze 11:13 Lord God! wilt thou make a f. end
Eze 17:3 longwinged, f. of feathers, which 4392
Eze 19:10 she was fruitful and f. of branches
Eze 28:12 f. of wisdom, and perfect in 4392
Eze 32:6 and the rivers shall be f. of thee. 4390
Eze 32:15 destitute of that whereof it was f., 4393
Eze 37:1 the valley which was f. of bones, 4392
Eze 39:19 ye shall eat fat till ye be f. 7654
Eze 41:8 the side chambers were a f. reed 4393
Da 3:19 Was Nebuchadnezzar f. of fury, 4391
Da 8:23 transgressors are come to the f., 8552
Da 10:2 was mourning three f. weeks 3117
Joe 2:24 And the floors shall be f. of wheat, 4390

Joe 3:13 the press is f., the fats overflow: 4390
Am 2:13 is pressed that is f. of sheaves 4392
Mic 3:8 I am f. of power by the spirit 4390
Mic 6:12 rich men thereof are f. of violence, 4390
Na 3:1 it is all f. of lies and robbery; 4392
Hab 3:3 the earth was f. of his praise, 4390
Zec 8:5 the city shall be f. of boys and girls 4390
Mt 6:22 **the whole body shall be f. of light** *5460*
Mt 6:23 **whole body shall be f. of darkness** *5460*
Mt 13:48 **Which, when it was f., they drew** *4137*
Mt 14:20 that remained twelve baskets f. *4134*
Mt 15:37 that was left seven baskets f. *4134*
Mt 23:25 **within they are f. of extortion** *1073*
Mt 23:27 **are within f. of dead men's bones,** *1073*
Mt 23:28 **are f. of hypocrisy and iniquity** *3324*
Mk 4:28 **after that the f. corn in the ear** *4134*
Mk 4:37 the ship, so that it was now f. *1072*
Mk 6:43 baskets f. of the fragments. *4134*
Mk 7:9 **F. well ye reject the commandment**
Mk 8:19 **many baskets f. of fragments** *4134*
Mk 8:20 **how many baskets f. of fragments** *4138*
Mk 15:36 And one ran and filled a spunge f.
Lu 1:57 Elisabeth's f. time came that she *4130*
Lu 4:1 Jesus being f. of the Holy Ghost *4134*
Lu 5:12 behold a man f. of leprosy: who *4134*
Lu 6:25 **Woe unto you that are f.! for ye** *1705*
Lu 11:34 **the whole body also is f. of light;** *5460*
Lu 11:34 **thy body also is f. of darkness**
Lu 11:36 **whole body therefore be f. of light,** *5460*
Lu 11:36 **the whole shall be f. of light, as** *5460*
Lu 11:39 **your inward part is f. of ravening** *1073*
Lu 16:20 **laid at his gate f. of sores,**
Jon 1:14 the Father,) f. of grace and truth. *4134*
Jon 7:8 **my time is not yet f. come** *4137*
Jon 15:11 **and that your joy might be f.** *4137*
Jon 16:24 **receive, that your joy may be f.** *4137*
Jon 19:29 was set a vessel f. of vinegar: *3324*
Jon 21:11 f. of great fishes, an hundred and *3324*
Ac 2:13 These men are f. of new wine *3325*
Ac 2:28 thou shalt make me f. of joy with *4137*
Ac 6:3 f. of the Holy Ghost and wisdom, *4134*
Ac 6:5 f. of faith and of the Holy Ghost, *4134*
Ac 6:8 Stephen, f. of faith and power, *4134*
Ac 7:23 when he was f. forty years old, *4137*
Ac 7:55 he, being f. of the Holy Ghost, *4134*
Ac 9:36 this woman was f. of good works *4134*
Ac 11:24 f. of the Holy Ghost and of faith: *4134*
Ac 13:10 O f. of all subtilty and all mischief, *4134*
Ac 19:28 they were f. of wrath, and cried *4134*
Ro 1:29 f. of envy, murder, debate, deceit, *3324*
Ro 3:14 is f. of cursing and bitterness: *1073*
Ro 15:14 that ye are also f. of goodness, *3324*
1Co 4:8 Now ye are f., now ye are rich, *2880*
Php 2:26 you all, and was f. of heaviness,
Php 4:12 both to be f. and to be hungry, *5526*
Php 4:18 I am f., having received of *4137*
Col 2:2 the f. assurance of understanding, *4136*
2Ti 4:5 of an evangelist, make f. proof of *4135*
Heb 5:14 belongeth to them that are of f. *5046*
Heb 6:11 f. assurance of hope unto the end: *4136*
Heb 10:22 in f. assurance of faith, having *4136*
Jas 3:8 an unruly evil, f. of deadly poison. *3324*
Jas 3:17 f. of mercy and good fruits, without *3324*
1Pe 1:8 with joy unspeakable and f. of glory:
2Pe 2:14 Having eyes f. of adultery, and that *3324*
1Jo 1:4 you, that your joy may be f. *4137*
2Jo 8 but that we receive a f. reward. *4134*
2Jo 12 to face, that our joy may be f. *4137*
Re 4:6 f. of eyes before and behind. *1073*
Re 4:8 they were f. of eyes within: and *1073*
Re 5:8 harps, and golden vials f. of odours. *1073*
Re 15:7 f. of the wrath of God, who liveth *1073*
Re 16:10 his kingdom was f. of darkness;
Re 17:3 f. of names of blasphemy, having *1073*
Re 17:4 cup in her hand f. of abominations *1073*
Re 21:9 vials f. of the seven last plagues, *1073*

FULLER See also FULLER'S; FULLERS'.
Mk 9:3 as no f. on earth can white them. *1102*

FULLER'S
2Ki 18:17 is in the highway of the f. field. 3526
Isa 7:3 pool in the highway of the f. field; 3526
Isa 36:2 pool in the highway of the f. field. 3526

FULLERS'
Mal 3:2 like a refiner's fire, and like f. sope. 3526

FULLY See also MOURNFULLY; REPROACHFULLY; SHAMEFULLY; SKILFULLY; WILFULLY; WONDERFULLY.
Nu 7:1 had f. set up the tabernacle, 3615
Nu 14:24 and hath followed f., him will 4392
Ru 2:11 It hath f. been shewed me, all 5046
1Ki 11:6 went not f. after the Lord, as did 4390
Ec 8:11 heart of the sons of men is f. set 4390
Na 1:10 be devoured as stubble f. dry. 4390
Ac 2:1 the day of Pentecost was f. come, *4845*
Ro 4:21 And being f. persuaded that, what *4135*
Ro 14:5 Let every man be f. persuaded *4135*
Ro 15:19 I have f. preached the gospel of *4137*
2Ti 3:10 thou hast f. known my doctrine, *3877*
2Ti 4:17 the preaching might be f. known, *4135*
Re 14:18 for her grapes are f. ripe.

FULNESS See also SKILFULNESS; SLOTHFULNESS; THANKFULNESS.
Nu 18:27 and as the f. of the winepress. 4395
De 33:16 things of the earth and f. thereof, 4393
1Ch 16:32 Let the sea roar, and the f. thereof: 4393
Job 20:22 In the f. of his sufficiency he shall 4390
Ps 16:11 in thy presence is f. of joy; 7648
Ps 24:1 is the Lord's, and the f. thereof; 4393
Ps 50:12 world is mine, and the f. thereof. 4393
Ps 89:11 the world and the f. thereof, thou 4393
Ps 96:11 let the sea roar, and the f. thereof. 4393
Ps 98:7 Let the sea roar, and the f. thereof; 4393
Eze 16:49 f. of bread, and abundance of 7653
Eze 19:7 was desolate, and the f. thereof, 4393
Joh 1:16 of his f. have all we received. *4138*
Ro 11:12 Gentiles; how much more their f.? *4138*
Ro 11:25 the f. of the Gentiles be come *4138*
Ro 15:29 come in the f. of the blessing *4138*
1Co 10:26 is the Lord's and the f. thereof. *4138*
1Co 10:28 is the Lord's and the f. thereof; *4138*
Ga 4:4 when the f. of the time was come *4138*
Eph 1:10 despensation of the f. of times *4138*
Eph 1:23 the f. of him that filleth all in all. *4138*
Eph 3:19 be filled with all the f. of God. *4138*
Eph 4:13 the stature of the f. of Christ: *4138*
Col 1:19 that in him should all f. dwell; *4138*
Col 2:9 all the f. of the Godhead bodily. *4138*

FURBISH See also FURBISHED.
Jer 46:4 f. the spears, and put on the 4838

FURBISHED
Eze 21:9 sword is sharpened, and also f. 4803
Eze 21:10 it is f. that it may glitter: 4803
Eze 21:11 he hath given it to be f., 4803
Eze 21:11 and it is f., to give it into the hand 4803
Eze 21:28 the slaughter it is f., to consume 4803

FURIOUS
Pr 22:24 with a f. man thou shalt not go: 2534
Pr 29:22 and a f. man aboundeth in 2534
Eze 5:15 and in fury, and in f. rebukes. 2534
Eze 25:17 upon them with f. rebukes; 2534
Da 2:12 the king was angry and very f., 7108
Na 1:2 Lord revengeth, and is f.; 1167,2534

FURIOUSLY
2Ki 9:20 son of Nimshi; for he driveth f. 7697
Eze 23:25 and they shall deal f. with thee: 2534

FURLONGS
Lu 24:13 Jerusalem about threescore f. *4712*
Joh 6:19 about five and twenty or thirty f., *4712*
Joh 11:18 unto Jerusalem, about fifteen f. off: *4712*
Re 14:20 a thousand and six hundred f. *4712*
Re 21:16 the reed, twelve thousand f. *4712*

FURNACE See also FURNACES.
Ge 15:17 behold a smoking f., and a 8574
Ge 19:28 went up as the smoke of a f. 3536
Ex 9:8 to you handfuls of ashes of the f., 3536
Ex 9:10 And they took ashes of the f., 3536
Ex 19:18 ascended as the smoke of a f., 3536
De 4:20 you forth out of the iron f., 3564
1Ki 8:51 from the midst of the f. of iron: 3564
Ps 12:6 as silver tried in a f. of earth, 5948
Pr 17:3 and the f. for gold: but the Lord 3564
Pr 27:21 and the f. for gold; so is a man 3564
Isa 31:9 and his f. in Jerusalem. 8574
Isa 48:10 I have chosen thee in the f. of 3564
Jer 11:4 from the iron f., saying, Obey 3564
Eze 22:18 and lead, in the midst of the f.; 3564
Eze 22:20 into the midst of the f., 3564
Eze 22:22 is melted in the midst of the f., 3564
Da 3:6,11 the midst of a burning fiery f. 861
Da 3:15 into the midst of a burning fiery f.; 861
Da 3:17 deliver us from the burning fiery f., 861
Da 3:19 heat the f. one seven times more 861
Da 3:20 cast them into the burning fiery f. 861
Da 3:21 the midst of the burning fiery f. 861
Da 3:22 and the f. exceeding hot, the flame 861
Da 3:23 the midst of the burning fiery f. 861
Da 3:26 to the mouth of the burning fiery f. 861
Mt 13:42 **shall cast them into a f. of fire:** *2575*
Mt 13:50 **shall cast them into the f. of fire:** *2575*
Re 1:15 as if they burned in a f.; *2575*
Re 9:2 as the smoke of a great f.; *2575*

FURNACES
Ne 3:11 other piece, and the tower of the f. 8574
Ne 12:38 of the f. even unto the broad wall; 8574

FURNISH See also FURNISHED.
De 15:14 f. him liberally out of thy flock, 6059
Ps 78:19 God f. a table in the wilderness? 6186
Isa 65:11 the drink offering unto that 4390
Jer 46:19 f. thyself to go into captivity: 6213,3627

FURNISHED
1Ki 9:11 Hiram the king of Tyre had f. 5375
Pr 9:2 she hath also f. her table. 6186
Mt 22:10 **the wedding was f. with guests** *4130*
Mk 14:15 **large upper room f. and prepared:** *4766*
Lu 22:12 **shew you a large upper room f.:** *4766*
2Ti 3:17 throughly f. unto all good works. *1822*

FURNITURE
Ge 31:34 the camel's f., and sat upon them. 3733
Ex 31:7 and all the f. of the tabernacle, 3627
Ex 31:8 the table and his f., and the 3627
Ex 31:8 pure candlestick with all his f., 3627
Ex 31:9 of burnt offering with all his f., 3627
Ex 35:14 also for the light, and his f., 3627
Ex 39:33 all his f., his taches, his boards, 3627
Na 2:9 glory out of all the pleasant f. 3627

FURROW See also FURROWS.
Job 39:10 unicorn with his band in the f.? 8525

FURROWS
Job 31:38 the f. likewise thereof complain; 8525
Ps 65:10 settlest the f. thereof: thou makest 1417
Ps 129:3 they made long their f. 4618
Eze 17:7 it by the f. of her plantation. 6170
Eze 17:10 wither in the f. where it grew. 6170
Ho 10:4 as hemlock in the f. of the field. 8525
Ho 10:10 bind themselves in their two f. 5869
Ho 12:11 are as heaps in the f. of the fields. 8525

FURTHER See also FARTHER; FURTHERED; FURTHERMORE.
Nu 22:26 the angel of the Lord went f., 3254
De 20:8 shall speak f. unto the people, 3254
1Sa 10:22 enquired of the Lord f., if the man 5750
Es 9:12 is thy request f.? and it shall be 5750
Job 38:11 shalt thou come, but no f.: 3254
Job 40:5 yea, twice; but I will proceed no f.
Ps 140:8 f. not his wicked device; lest they 6329
Ec 12:12 And f. by these, my son, be 3148
Mt 26:65 what f. need have we of witnesses? *2089*
Mk 5:35 troublest thou the Master any f.? *2089*
Mk 14:63 What need we any f. witnesses? *2089*
Lu 22:71 What need we any f. witness? *2089*
Lu 24:28 as though he would have gone f. *4206*
Ac 4:17 spread no f. among the poeple, *1909,4118*
Ac 4:21 when they had f. threatened them,
Ac 12:3 he proceeded f. to take Peter also.
Ac 21:28 f. brought Greeks also into the *2089*
Ac 24:4 I be not f. tedious unto thee, *1909,4118*
Ac 27:28 when they had gone a little f., *1339*
2Ti 3:9 proceed no f.: for their folly, *1909,4118*
Heb 7:11 need was there that another *2089*

FURTHERANCE
Php 1:12 rather unto the f. of the gospel; *4297*
Php 1:25 for your f. and joy of faith; *4297*

FURTHERED
Ezr 8:36 they f. the people, and the house 5375

FURTHERMORE
Ex 4:6 And the Lord said f. unto him, 5750
De 4:21 F. the Lord was angry with me
De 9:13 F. the Lord spake unto me,
1Sa 26:10 David said f., As the Lord liveth,
1Ch 17:10 F. I tell thee that the Lord will

1Ch 27:16 **F.** over the tribes of Israel: the...
1Ch 29:1 **F.** David the king said unto...
2Ch 4:9 **F.** he made the court of the...
Job 34:1 **F.** Elihu answered and said,...
Eze 8:6 He said **f.** unto me, Son of man,...
Eze 23:40 And **f.**, that ye have sent for men... 637
2Co 2:12 **F.**, when I came to Troas to... *1161*
1Th 4:1 **F.** then we beseech you, brethren,... *3063*
Heb 12:9 **F.** we have had fathers of our... *1534*

FURY
Ge 27:44 until thy brother's **f.** turn away;... 2534
Le 26:28 walk contrary unto you also in **f.**;... 2534
Job 20:23 God shall cast the **f.** of his wrath... 2740
Isa 27:4 **F.** is not in me: who would set... 2534
Isa 34:2 and his **f.** upon all their armies:... 2534
Isa 42:25 upon him the **f.** of his anger,... 2534
Isa 51:13 because of the **f.** of the oppressor,... 2534
Isa 51:13 where is the **f.** of the oppressor?... 2534
Isa 51:17 of the Lord the cup of his **f.**;... 2534
Isa 51:20 they are full of the **f.** of the Lord,... 2534
Isa 51:22 the dregs of the cup of my **f.**;... 2534
Isa 59:18 **f.** to his adversaries, recompence... 2534
Isa 63:3 anger, and trample them in my **f.**;... 2534
Isa 63:5 and my **f.** it upheld me... 2534
Isa 63:6 and make them drunk in my **f.**,... 2534
Isa 66:15 to render his anger with **f.**, and... 2534
Jer 4:4 lest my **f.** come forth like fire,... 2534
Jer 6:11 I am full of the **f.** of the Lord;... 2534
Jer 7:20 mine anger and my **f.** shall be... 2534
Jer 10:25 Pour out thy **f.** upon the heathen... 2534
Jer 21:5 and in **f.**, and in great wrath... 2534
Jer 21:12 my **f.** go out like fire, and burn... 2534
Jer 23:19 the Lord is gone forth in **f.**,... 2534
Jer 25:15 Take the wine cup of this **f.** at my... 2534
Jer 30:23 of the Lord goeth forth with **f.**,... 2534
Jer 32:31 of mine anger and of my **f.**... 2534
Jer 32:37 and in my **f.**, and in great wrath;... 2534
Jer 33:5 in mine anger and in my **f.**,... 2534
Jer 36:7 **f.** that the Lord hath pronounced... 2534
Jer 42:18 and my **f.** hath been poured forth... 2534
Jer 42:18 my **f.** be poured forth upon you,... 2534
Jer 44:6 **f.** and mine anger was poured... 2534
La 2:4 he poured out his **f.** like fire... 2534
La 4:11 Lord hath accomplished his **f.**;... 2534
Eze 5:13 cause my **f.** to rest upon them,... 2534
Eze 5:13 have accomplished my **f.** in them... 2534
Eze 5:15 in **f.** and in furious rebukes.... 2534
Eze 6:12 I accomplish my **f.** upon them... 2534
Eze 7:8 Now will I shortly pour out my **f.**... 2534
Eze 8:18 Therefore will I also deal in **f.**:... 2534
Eze 9:8 in thy pouring out of thy **f.**... 2534
Eze 13:13 with a stormy wind in my **f.**;... 2534
Eze 13:13 hailstones in my **f.** to consume it... 2534
Eze 14:19 pour out my **f.** upon it in blood,... 2534
Eze 16:38 I will give thee blood in **f.**... 2534
Eze 16:42 I make my **f.** toward thee to rest,... 2534
Eze 19:12 plucked up in **f.**, she was cast... 2534
Eze 20:8 I will pour out my **f.** upon them,... 2534
Eze 20:13 I would pour out my **f.** upon them... 2534
Eze 20:21 would pour out my **f.** upon them,... 2534
Eze 20:33 and with **f.** poured out, will I rule... 2534
Eze 20:34 stretched out arm, and with **f.**... 2534
Eze 21:17 and I will cause my **f.** to rest:... 2534
Eze 22:20 in mine anger and in my **f.**,... 2534
Eze 22:22 have poured out my **f.** upon you,... 2534
Eze 24:8 That it might cause **f.** to come up... 2534
Eze 24:13 caused my **f.** to rest upon thee... 2534
Eze 25:14 anger and according to my **f.**;... 2534
Eze 30:15 I will pour my **f.** upon Sin,... 2534
Eze 36:6 in my jealousy and in my **f.**,... 2534
Eze 36:18 my **f.** upon them for the blood... 2534
Eze 38:18 my **f.** shall come up in my face... 2534
Da 3:13 rage and **f.** commanded to bring... 2528
Da 3:19 Then was Nebuchadnezzar full of **f.**,... 2528
Da 8:6 unto him in the **f.** of his power,... 2534
Da 9:16 thine anger and thy **f.** be turned... 2534
Da 11:44 go forth with great **f.** to destroy,... 2534
Mic 5:15 in anger and **f.** upon the heathen,... 2534
Na 1:6 **f.** is poured out like fire, and the... 2534
Zec 8:2 I was jealous for her with great **f.**... 2534

G.

GAAL (ga'-al)
Jg 9:26 And **G.** the son of Ebed came with... 1603
Jg 9:28 **G.** the son of Ebed said, Who is... 1603
Jg 9:30 words of **G.** the son of Ebed, his... 1603
Jg 9:31 Behold, **G.** the son of Ebed and his... 1603
Jg 9:35 **G.** the son of Ebed went out, and... 1603
Jg 9:36 **G.** was the people, he said to Zebul,... 1603
Jg 9:37 **G.** spake again and said, See... 1603
Jg 9:39 **G.** went out before the men of... 1603
Jg 9:41 thrust out **G.** and his brethren,... 1603

GAASH (ga'-ash)
Jos 24:30 on the north side of the hill of **G.**... 1608
Jg 2:9 on the north side of the hill **G.**... 1608
2Sa 23:30 Hiddai of the brooks of **G.**,... 1608
1Ch 11:32 Hurai of the brooks of **G.**, Abiel the... 1608

GABA (ga'-bah) See also GEBA.
Jos 18:24 and Ophni, and **G.**; twelve cities... 1387
Ezr 2:26 The children of Ramah and **G.**,... 1387
Ne 7:30 The men of Ramah and **G.**,... 1387

GABBAI (gab'-bahee)
Ne 11:8 And after him **G.**, Sallai, nine... 1373

GABBATHA (gab'-ba-thah)
Joh 19:13 but in the Hebrew, **G.**,... *1042*

GABER See EZION-GABER.

GABRIEL (ga'-bre-el)
Da 8:16 **G.**, make this man to understand... 1403
Da 9:21 even the man **G.**, whom I had seen... 1403
Lu 1:19 I am **G.**, that stand in the... *1043*
Lu 1:26 sixth month the angel **G.** was sent... *1043*

GAD See GADDEST.

GAD (gad) See also BAAL-GAD; DIBON-GAD; GADITE; MIGDAL-GAD.
Ge 30:11 and she called his name **G.**... 1410
Ge 35:26 Leah's handmaid; **G.**, and Asher:... 1410
Ge 46:16 And the sons of **G.**; Ziphion, and... 1410
Ge 49:19 **G.**, a troop shall overcome him:... 1410
Ex 1:4 Dan, and Naphtali, **G.**, and Asher... 1410
Nu 1:14 of **G.**, Eliasaph the son of Deuel... 1410
Nu 1:24 Of the children of **G.**, by their... 1410
Nu 1:25 even of the tribe of **G.**, were forty... 1410
Nu 2:14 Then the tribe of **G.**; and the... 1410
Nu 2:14 captain of the sons of **G.** shall be... 1410
Nu 7:42 of the children of **G.**, offered:... 1410
Nu 10:20 of the children of **G.** was Eliasaph... 1410
Nu 13:15 Of the tribe of **G.**, Geuel the son of... 1410
Nu 26:15 The children of **G.** after their... 1410
Nu 26:18 families of the children of **G.**... 1410
Nu 32:1 and the children of **G.** had a very... 1410
Nu 32:2 The children of **G.** and the... 1410
Nu 32:6 Moses said unto the children of **G.**... 1410
Nu 32:25 And the children of **G.** and the... 1410
Nu 32:29 If the children of **G.** and the... 1410
Nu 32:31 and the children of **G.** and the... 1410
Nu 32:33 even to the children of **G.**, and to... 1410
Nu 32:34 And the children of **G.** built Dibon... 1410
Nu 34:14 tribe of the children of **G.** according... 1410
De 27:13 Reuben, **G.**, and Asher, and... 1410
De 33:20 And of he said Blessed be... 1410
De 33:20 Blessed be he that enlargeth **G.**:... 1410
Jos 4:12 and the children of **G.**, and half... 1410
Jos 13:24 of **G.**,even unto the children of **G.**... 1410
Jos 13:28 children of **G.** after their families,... 1410
Jos 18:7 and **G.**, and Reuben, and half the... 1410
Jos 20:8 out of the tribe of **G.**, and Golan... 1410
Jos 21:7 out of the tribe of **G.**, and out of... 1410
Jos 21:38 And out of the tribe of **G.**, Ramoth... 1410
Jos 22:9, 10,11,13,15,21 children of **G.** and the... 1410
Jos 22:25 of Reuben and children of **G.**;... 1410
Jos 22:30 children of **G.** and the children of... 1410
Jos 22:31 children of **G.**, and to the children of... 1410
Jos 22:32 children of **G.**, out of the land of... 1410
Jos 22:33 children of Reuben and **G.** dwelt... 1410
Jos 22:34 children of **G.** called the altar Ed:... 1410
1Sa 13:7 Jordan to the land **G.** and Gilead... 1410
1Sa 22:5 prophet **G.** said unto David, Abide... 1410
2Sa 24:5 the river of **G.**, and toward Jazer:... 1410
2Sa 24:11 unto the prophet **G.**, David's seer,... 1410
2Sa 24:13 So **G.** came to David, and told him,... 1410
2Sa 24:14 David said unto **G.**, I am in a great... 1410
2Sa 24:18 And **G.** came that day to David,... 1410
2Sa 24:19 according to the saying of **G.**, went... 1410
1Ch 2:2 Benjamin, Nahtali, **G.**, and Asher... 1410
1Ch 5:11 And the children of **G.** dwelt over... 1410
1Ch 6:63 out of the tribe of **G.**, and out of the... 1410
1Ch 6:80 And out of the tribe of **G.**; Ramoth... 1410
1Ch 12:14 sons of **G.**, captains of the host:... 1410
1Ch 21:9 And the Lord spake unto **G.**,... 1410
1Ch 21:11 So **G.** came to David, and said unto... 1410
1Ch 21:13 David said unto **G.**, I am in a great... 1410
1Ch 21:18 Lord commanded **G.** to say to... 1410
1Ch 21:19 David went up at the saying **G.**,... 1410
1Ch 29:29 and in the book the **G.** the seer,... 1410
2Ch 29:25 of David, and of **G.** the king's seer,... 1410
Jer 49:1 why then doth their king inherit **G.**,... 1410
Eze 48:27 unto the west side, **G.** a portion... 1410
Eze 48:28 And by the border of **G.**, at the... 1410
Eze 48:34 one gate of **G.**, one gate of Asher,... 1410
Re 7:5 Of the tribe of **G.** were sealed... *1045*

GADARENES (gad-a-renes')
Mk 5:1 sea, into the country of the **G.**... *1046*
Lu 8:26 arrived at the country of the **G.**,... *1046*
Lu 8:37 of the country of the **G.** round... *1046*

GADDAH See HAZAR-GADDAH.

GADDEST
Jer 2:36 Why **g.** thou about so much to... 235

GADDI (gad'-di)
Nu 13:11 tribe of Manasseh, **G.** the son of... 1426

GADDIEL (gad'-de-el)
Nu 13:10 of Zebulun, **G.** the son of Sodi... 1427

GADER See BETH-GADER.

GADI (ga'-di)
2Ki 15:14 Menahem the son of **G.** went up... 1424
2Ki 15:17 Menahem the son of **G.** to reign... 1424

GADITE (gad'-ite) See also GADITES.
2Sa 23:36 of Zobah, Bani the **G.**,... 1425

GADITES (gad'-ites)
De 3:12 the Reubenites and to the **G.**... 1425
De 3:16 unto the **G.** I gave from Gilead even... 1425
De 4:43 Gilead, of the **G.**; and Golan in... 1425
De 29:8 and to the **G.**, and to the half tribe... 1425
Jos 1:12 and to the **G.**, and to half the tribe... 1425
Jos 12:6 unto the Reubenites, and the **G.**,... 1425
Jos 13:8 the Reubenites and the **G.** have... 1425
Jos 22:1 and the **G.**, and the half tribe of... 1425
2Ki 10:33 land of Gilead, the **G.**, and the... 1425
1Ch 5:18 and the **G.**, and half the tribe of... 1425
1Ch 5:26 and the **G.**, ad the half tribe of... 1425
1Ch 12:8 And of the **G.** there separated... 1425
1Ch 12:37 and the **G.**, and of the half tribe of... 1425
1Ch 26:32 the **G.**, and the half tribe of... 1425

GAHAM (ga'-ham)
Ge 22:24 bare also Tebah, and **G.**, and... 1514

GAHAR (ga'-har)
Ez 2:47 of Giddel, the children of **G.**, the... 1515
Ne 7:49 of Giddel, the children of **G.**,... 1515

GAIN See also AGAIN; GAINED; GAINS; GAINSAY.
Jg 5:19 they took no **g.** of money... 1214
Job 22:3 or is it **g.** to him, that thou makest... 1214
Pr 1:19 every one that is greedy of **g.**;... 1214
Pr 3:14 and the **g.** thereof than fine gold... 8393
Pr 15:27 He that is greedy of **g.** troubleth... 1214
Pr 28:8 by usury and unjust **g.** increaseth... 8636
Isa 33:15 despiseth the **g.** of oppressions,... 1214
Isa 56:11 one for his **g.**, from his quarter... 1214
Eze 22:13 mind hand at thy dishonest **g.**... 1214
Eze 22:27 destroy souls, to get dishonest **g.**... 1214
Da 2:8 certainty that ye would **g.** the time,... 2084
Da 11:39 and shall divide the land for **g.**... 4242
Mic 4:13 consecrate their **g.** unto the Lord,... 1214
Mt 16:26 **if he shall g. the whole world,**... *2770*

Mk 8:36 **if he shall g. the whole world, and** 2770
Lu 9:25 **if he g. the whole world, and lose** 2770
Ac 16:16 brought her masters much **g.** by 2039
Ac 19:24 brought no small **g.** unto the 2039
1Co 9:19 unto all, that I might **g.** the more 2770
1Co 9:20 that I might **g.** the Jews; 2770
1Co 9:20 that I might **g.** them that are under 2770
1Co 9:21 might **g.** them that are without law 2770
1Co 9:22 that I might **g.** the weak: 2770
2Co 12:17 Did I make a **g.** of you by any 4122
2Co 12:18 Did Titus make a **g.** of you? 4122
Php 1:21 to live is Christ, and to die is **g.** 2771
Php 3:7 But what things were **g.** to me, 2771
1Ti 6:5 supposing that **g.** is godliness: 4200
1Ti 6:6 with contentment is great **g.** 4200
Jas 4:13 and buy and sell, and get **g.**: 2770

GAINED
Job 27:8 though he hath **g.**, when God 1214
Eze 22:12 and thou hast greedily **g.** of thy 1214
Mt 18:15 **thee, thou hast g. thy brother** 2770
Mt 25:17 **received two, he also g. other two** 2770
Mt 25:20 **I have g. beside them five talents** 2770
Mt 25:22 **g. two other talents beside them** 2770
Lu 19:15 **every man had g. by trading** 1281
Lu 19:16 **thy pound hath g. ten pounds** 4333
Lu 19:18 **thy pound hath g. five pounds** 4160
Ac 27:21 to have **g.** this harm and loss. 2770

GAINS
Ac 16:19 the hope of their **g.** was gone, 2089

GAINSAY See also GAINSAYING.
Lu 21:15 **shall not be able to g. nor resist** 471

GAINSAYERS
Tit 1:9 to exhort and to convince the **g.** 483

GAINSAYING
Ac 10:29 came I unto you without **g.**, 369
Ro 10:21 a disobedient and **g.** people 483
Jude 11 and perished in the **g.** of Core 485

GAIUS (gah'-yus)
Ac 19:29 caught **G.** and Aristarchus, 1050
Ac 20:4 and **G.** of Derbe, and Timotheus; 1050
Ro 16:23 **G.** mine host, and of the whole 1050
1Co 1:14 none of you, but Crispus and **G.**; 1050
3Jo 1 The elder unto the wellbeloved **G.**, 1050

GALAL (ga'-lal)
1Ch 9:15 Heresh, and **G.**, and Mataniah 1559
1Ch 9:16 the son of **G.**, the son of Jeduthun, 1559
Ne 11:17 Shammua, the son of **G.**, the son of 1559

GALATIA (ga-la'-she-ah) See also GALATIANS.
Ac 16:6 Phrygia and the region of **G.**, 1054
Ac 18:23 country of **G.** and Phrygia in order, 1054
1Co 16:1 given order to the churches of **G.**, 1053
Ga 1:2 with me unto the churches of **G.**: 1053
2Ti 4:10 Crescens to **G.**, Titus unto 1053
1Pe 1:1 Pontus, **G.**, Cappadocia, Asia, 1053

GALATIANS (ga-la'-she-uns)
Ga *title* Paul [The Apostle] To the **G.** 1052
Ga 3:1 O foolish **G.** who hath bewitched 1052
Ga *subscr.* Unto the **G.** written from Rome 1052

GALBANUM (gal'-ba-num)
Ex 30:34 onycha, and **g.**; these sweet spices 2464

GALEED (ga'-le-ed) See also JAGAR-SAHADUTHA.
Ge 31:47 but Jacob called it **G.** 1567
Ge 31:48 was the name of it called **G.**; 1567

GALILAEAN (gal-i-le'-un) See also GALILAEANS.
Mk 14:70 for thou art a **G.**, and thy speech 1057
Lu 22:59 also was with him: for he is a **G.** 1057
Lu 23:6 asked whether the man were a **G.** 1057

GALILAEANS (gal-i-le'-uns)
Lu 13:1 some that told him of the **G.**, 1057
Lu 13:2 **Suppose ye that these G. were** 1057
Lu 13:2 **sinners above all the G.,** 1057
Joh 4:45 the **G.** received him, having seen 1057
Ac 2:7 are not all these which speak **G.**? 1057

GALILEE (gal'-i-lee) See also GALILAEAN.
Jos 20:7 Kedesh in **G.** in mount Naphtali, 1551
Jos 21:32 Kedesh in **G.** with her suburbs, 1551
1Ki 9:11 twenty cities in the land of **G.** 1551
2Ki 15:29 Hazor, and Gilead, and **G.**, all the 1551
1Ch 6:76 Kedesh in **G.** with her suburbs, 1551
Isa 9:1 beyond Jordan, in **G.** of the nations 1551
Mt 2:22 he turned aside in the parts of **G.** 1056
Mt 3:13 cometh Jesus from **G.** to Jordan 1056
Mt 4:12 into prison, he departed into **G.**; 1056
Mt 4:15 beyond Jordan, **G.** of the Gentiles; 1056
Mt 4:18 Jesus, walking by the sea of **G.**, 1056
Mt 4:23 And Jesus went about all **G.**, 1056
Mt 4:25 great multitudes of people from **G.** 1056
Mt 15:29 came nigh unto the sea of **G.**; 1056
Mt 17:22 while they abode in **G.**, Jesus said 1056
Mt 19:1 he departed from **G.**, and came 1056
Mt 21:11 the prophet of Nazareth of **G.** 1056
Mt 26:32 **I will go before you into G.** 1056
Mt 26:69 Thou also wast with Jesus of **G.** 1056
Mt 27:55 which followed Jesus from **G.**, 1056
Mt 28:7 he goeth before you in to **G.**; 1056
Mt 28:10 **that they go into G., and there** 1056
Mt 28:16 eleven disciples went away into **G.**, 1056
Mk 1:9 Jesus came from Nazareth of **G.**, 1056
Mk 1:14 Jesus came into **G.**, preaching the 1056
Mk 1:16 Now as he walked by the sea of **G.**, 1056
Mk 1:28 all the region round about **G.** 1056
Mk 1:39 synagogues throughout all **G.**, 1056
Mk 3:7 multitude from **G.** followed him, 1056
Mk 6:21 captains, and chief estates of **G.**; 1056
Mk 7:31 he came unto the sea of **G.**, 1056
Mk 9:30 thence, and passed through **G.**; 1056
Mk 14:28 **I will go before you into G.** 1056
Mk 15:41 when he was in **G.**, followed him, 1056
Mk 16:7 that he goeth before you into **G.**: 1056
Lu 1:26 unto a city of **G.**, named Nazareth, 1056
Lu 2:4 And Joseph also went up from **G.**, 1056
Lu 2:39 they returned into **G.**, to their own 1056
Lu 3:1 and Herod being tetrarch of **G.** 1056
Lu 4:14 in the power of the Spirit into **G.** 1056
Lu 4:31 down to Capernaum, a city of **G.** 1056
Lu 4:44 preached in the synagogues of **G.** 1056
Lu 5:17 were come out of every town of **G.**, 1056
Lu 8:26 which is over against **G.** 1056
Lu 17:11 the midst of Samaria and **G.** 1056
Lu 23:5 beginning from **G.** to this place. 1056
Lu 23:6 When Pilate heard of **G.**, he asked 1056
Lu 23:49 women that followed him from **G.**, 1056
Lu 23:55 which came with him from **G.**, 1056
Lu 24:6 unto you when he was yet in **G.**, 1056
Joh 1:43 Jesus would go forth into **G.**, 1056
Joh 2:1 there was a marriage in Cana of **G.**; 1056
Joh 2:11 miracles did Jesus in Cana of **G.**, 1056
Joh 4:3 Judea, and departed again into **G.** 1056
Joh 4:43 departed thence, and went into **G.** 1056
Joh 4:45 Then when he was come into **G.**, 1056
Joh 4:46 Jesus came again into Cana of **G.**, 1056
Joh 4:47 was come out of Judaea into **G.**, he 1056
Joh 4:54 he was come out of Judaea into **G.** 1056
Joh 6:1 Jesus went over the sea of **G.**, 1056
Joh 7:1 these things Jesus walked in **G.**: 1056
Joh 7:9 unto them, he abode still in **G.** 1056
Joh 7:41 said, Shall Christ come out of **G.**? 1056
Joh 7:52 Art thou also of **G.**? Search, and 1056
Joh 7:52 for out of **G.** ariseth no prophet. 1056
Joh 12:21 which was of Bethsaida of **G.**, 1056
Joh 21:2 and Nathanael of Cana in **G.**, 1056
Ac 1:11 Ye men of **G.**, why stand ye gazing 1056
Ac 5:37 After this man rose up Judas of **G.** 1056
Ac 9:31 all Judaea and **G.** and Samaria, 1056
Ac 10:37 began from **G.**, after the baptism 1056
Ac 13:31 which came up with him from **G.** 1056

GALL
De 29:18 that beareth **g.** and wormwood; 7219
De 32:32 their grapes are grapes of **g.** 7219
Job 16:13 out my **g.** upon the ground. 4845
Job 20:14 it is the **g.** of asps within him. 4846
Job 20:25 sword cometh out of his **g.**: 4846
Ps 69:21 gave me also **g.** for my meat; 7219
Jer 8:14 given us water of **g.** to drink, 7219
Jer 9:15 give them water of **g.** to drink. 7219
Jer 23:15 make them drink the water of **g.** 7219
La 3:5 compassed me with **g.** and travel. 7219
La 3:19 misery, the wormwood and the **g.** 7219
Am 6:12 ye have turned judgment into **g.**, 7219
Mt 27:34 vinegar to drink mingled with **g.**: 5521
Ac 8:23 thou art in the **g.** of bitterness, 5521

GALLANT
Isa 33:21 neither shall **g.** ship pass thereby 117

GALLERIES
Ca 7:5 the king is held in the **g.** 7298
Eze 41:15 and the **g.** thereof on the one side 862
Eze 41:16 windows, and the **g.** round about 862
Eze 42:5 for the **g.** were higher than these, 862

GALLERY See also GALLERIES.
Eze 42:3 **g.** against **g.** in the three stories. 862

GALLEY
Isa 33:21 wherein shall go no **g.** with oars, 590

GALLIM (gal'-lim)
1Sa 25:44 son of Laish, which was of **G.** 1554
Isa 10:30 Lift up thy voice, O daughter of **G.** 1554

GALLIO (gal'-le-o)
Ac 18:12 **G.** was the deputy of Achaia, 1058
Ac 18:14 **G.** said unto the Jews, If it were a 1058
Ac 18:17 And **G.** cared for none of those 1058

GALLOWS
Es 5:14 a **g.** be made of fifty cubits high, 6086
Es 5:14 he caused the **g.** to be made. 6086
Es 6:4 to hang Mordecai on the **g.** that he 6086
Es 7:9 Behold also, the **g.** fifty cubits high, 6086
Es 7:10 So they hanged Haman on the **g.** 6086
Es 8:7 they have hanged upon the **g.**, 6086
Es 9:13 ten sons be hanged upon the **g.** 6086
Es 9:25 his sons should be hanged on the **g.** 6086

GAMALIEL (gam-a'-le-el)
Nu 1:10 Manasseh; **G.** the son of Pedahzur. 1583
Nu 2:20 of Manasseh shall be **G.** the son of 1583
Nu 7:54 offered **G.** the son of Pedahzur 1583
Nu 7:59 this was the offering of **G.** the son 1583
Nu 10:23 of the children of Manasseh was **G.** 1583
Ac 5:34 a Pharisee, named **G.**, a doctor of 1059
Ac 22:3 in this city at the feet of **G.**, 1059

GAMMADIMS (gam'-ma-dims)
Eze 27:11 and the **G.** were in thy towers: 1575

GAMUL (ga'-mul) See also BETH-GAMUL.
1Ch 24:17 the two and twentieth to **G.**, 1577

GANNIM See EN-GANNIM.

GAOLER See JAILER.

GAP See also GAPED; GAPS.
Eze 22:30 and stand in the **g.** before me 6556

GAPED
Job 16:10 **g.** upon me with their mouth; 6473
Ps 22:13 **g.** upon me with their mouths, 6475

GAPS
Eze 13:5 Ye have not gone up into the **g.**, 6556

GARDEN
Ge 2:8 And the Lord God planted a **g.** 1588
Ge 2:9 also in the midst of the **g.**, 1588
Ge 2:10 out of Eden to water the **g.**; 1588
Ge 2:15 put him into the **g.** of Eden 1588
Ge 2:16 of the **g.** thou mayest freely eat: 1588
Ge 3:1 shall not eat of every tree of the **g.**? 1588
Ge 3:2 the fruit of the trees of the **g.**: 1588
Ge 3:3 which is in the midst of the **g.**, 1588
Ge 3:8 the Lord God walking in the **g.** 1588
Ge 3:8 amongst the trees of the **g.** 1588
Ge 3:10 I heard thy voice in the **g.**, 1588
Ge 3:23 sent him forth from the **g.** of Eden, 1588
Ge 3:24 at the east of the **g.** of Eden 1588
Ge 13:10 even as the **g.** of the Lord, 1588
De 11:10 with thy foot, as a **g.** of herbs; 1588
1Ki 21:2 that I may have it for a **g.** of herbs, 1588
2Ki 9:27 he fled by the way of the **g.** house. 1588
2Ki 21:18 buried in the **g.** of his own house, 1588
2Ki 21:18 in the **g.** of Uzza: and Amon his 1588
2Ki 21:26 his sepulchre in the **g.** of Uzza: 1588
2Ki 25:4 which is by the king's **g.** 1588
Ne 3:15 the pool of Siloah by the king's **g.**, 1588
Es 1:5 court of the **g.** of the king's palace; 1594
Es 7:7 his wrath went into the palace **g.** 1594
Es 7:8 king returned out of the palace **g.** 1594
Job 8:16 his branch shooteth forth in his **g.** 1593
Ca 4:12 A **g.** inclosed is my sister, my 1588
Ca 4:16 thou south; blow upon my **g.**, 1588
Ca 4:16 Let my beloved come into his **g.**, 1588
Ca 5:1 I am come into my **g.**, my sister, 1588
Ca 6:2 beloved is gone down into his **g.**, 1588
Ca 6:11 I went down into the **g.** of nuts 1594
Isa 1:8 as a lodge in a **g.** of cucumbers,
Isa 1:30 and as a **g.** that hath no water. 1593
Isa 51:3 her desert like the **g.** of the Lord; 1588

Isa 58:11 thou shalt be like a watered **g.**. 1588
Isa 61:11 and as the **g.** causeth the things......... 1593
Jer 31:12 their soul shall be as a watered **g.**;..... 1588
Jer 39:4 by the way of the king's **g.**, ... 1588
Jer 52:7 walls which was by the king's **g.**; 1588
La 2:6 as if it were of a **g.**: 1588
Eze 28:13 been in Eden the **g.** of God;............. 1588
Eze 31:8 The cedars in the **g.** of God............... 1588
Eze 31:8 nor any tree in the **g.** of God 1588
Eze 31:9 that were in the **g.** of God, ... 1588
Eze 36:35 is become like the **g.** of Eden; 1588
Joe 2:3 the land is as the **g.** of Eden 1588
Lu 13:19 **a man took, and cast into his g.**;... *2779*
Joh 18:1 where was a **g.**, into the which.......... *2779*
Joh 18:26 Did not I see thee in the **g.** *2779*
Joh 19:41 a **g.**; and in the **g.** a new sepulchre, ... *2779*

GARDENER
Joh 20:15 She, supposing him to be the **g.**,........ *2780*

GARDEN-HOUSE See GARDEN and HOUSE.

GARDENS
Nu 24:6 forth, as **g.** by the river's side, ... 1593
Ec 2:5 I made me **g.** and orchards, ... 1593
Ca 4:15 of **g.**, a well of living waters,............. 1588
Ca 6:2 in the **g.**, and to gather lilies. 1588
Ca 8:13 Thou that dwellest in the **g.**, ... 1588
Isa 1:29 for the **g.** that ye have chosen. 1593
Isa 65:3 that sacrificeth in **g.**, and burneth 1593
Isa 66:17 the **g.** behind one tree in the midst,.... 1593
Jer 29:5 plant **g.**, and eat the fruit of them; 1593
Jer 29:28 plant **g.**, and eat the fruit of them. 1593
Am 4:9 when your **g.** and your vineyards 1593
Am 9:14 make **g.**, and eat the fruit of them...... 1593

GAREB (ga'-reb)
2Sa 23:38 Ira an Ithrite, **G.** an Ithrite, ... 1619
1Ch 11:40 Ira the Ithrite, **G.** the Ithrite, ... 1619
Jer 31:39 upon the hill **G.**, and shall compass..... 1619

GARLANDS
Ac 14:13 brought oxen and **g.** unto the gates, ... *4725*

GARLICK
Nu 11:5 leeks, and the onions, and the **g.** 7762

GARMENT See also GARMENTS.
Ge 9:23 And Shem and Japheth took a **g.**, ... 8071
Ge 25:25 red, all over like an hairy **g.**; 155
Ge 39:12 she caught him by his **g.**, saying,......... 899
Ge 39:12 he left his **g.** in her hand,.................. 899
Ge 39:13 she saw that he had left his **g.** 899
Ge 39:15 that he left his **g.** with me,................. 899
Ge 39:16 she laid up his **g.** by her, ... 899
Ge 39:18 he left his **g.** with me, and fled............ 899
Le 6:10 the priest shall put on his linen **g.**, ... 4055
Le 6:27 of the blood thereof upon any **g.**,......... 899
Le 13:47 **g.** also that the plague of leprosy 899
Le 13:47 it be a woollen **g.**, or a linen **g.**; 899
Le 13:49 be greenish or reddish in the **g.**, ... 899
Le 13:51 plague be spread in the **g.**,................. 899
Le 13:52 He shall therefore burn that **g.**, ... 899
Le 13:53 be not spread in the **g.**, ... 899
Le 13:56 he shall rend it out of the **g.**,.............. 899
Le 13:57 if it appear still in the **g.**, ... 899
Le 13:58 And the **g.**, either warp, or woof,......... 899
Le 13:59 in a **g.** of woollen or linen, ... 899
Le 14:55 And for the leprosy of a **g.**,................ 899
Le 15:17 And every **g.**, and every skin,............. 899
Le 19:19 neither shall a **g.** mingled of linen......... 899
De 22:5 shall a man put on a woman's **g.** 8071
De 22:11 **g.** of divers sorts, as of woollen........... 8162
Jos 7:21 Babylonish **g.**, and two hundred........... 155
Jos 7:24 silver, and the **g.**, and the wedge 155
Jg 8:25 they spread a **g.**, and did cast............ 8071
2Sa 13:18 she had a **g.** of divers colours............ 3801
2Sa 13:19 and rent her **g.** of divers colours 3801
2Sa 20:8 Joab's **g.** that he had put on 4055
1Ki 11:29 he had clad himself with a new **g.**;...... 8008
1Ki 11:30 caught the new **g.** that was on him, ... 8008
2Ki 9:13 hasted, and took every man his **g.**, ... 899
Ezr 9:3 I rent my **g.** and my mantle, ... 899
Ezr 9:5 having rent my **g.** and my mantle,......... 899
Es 8:15 and with a **g.** of fine linen................. 8509
Job 13:28 as a **g.** that is moth eaten, ... 899
Job 30:18 of my disease is my **g.** changed: 3830
Job 38:9 I made the cloud the **g.** thereof, ... 3830
Job 38:14 and they stand as a **g.**. 3830
Job 41:13 Who can discover the face of his **g.**?... 3830
Ps 69:11 I made sackcloth also my **g.**; 3830
Ps 73:6 violence covereth them as a **g.**. 7897
Ps 102:26 all of them shall wax old like a **g.**;........ 899
Ps 104:2 thyself with light as with a **g.** 8008
Ps 104:6 with the deep as with a **g.**: 3830
Ps 109:18 with cursing like as with his **g.**, ... 4055
Ps 109:19 Let it be unto him as the **g.** 899
Pr 20:16 his **g.** that is surety for a stranger: 899
Pr 25:20 As he that taketh away a **g.**................. 899
Pr 27:13 Take his **g.** that is surety.................... 899
Pr 30:4 who hath bound the waters in a **g.**? 8071
Isa 50:9 they all shall wax old as a **g.**;.............. 899
Isa 51:6 the earth shall wax old like a **g.**,........... 899
Isa 51:8 shall eat them up like a **g.**, ... 899
Isa 61:3 the **g.** of praise for the spirit of 4594
Jer 43:12 as a shepherd putteth on his **g.**; 899
Eze 18:7 hath covered the naked with a **g.**;........ 899
Eze 18:16 hath covered the naked with a **g.**,........ 899
Da 7:9 whose **g.** was white as snow, ... 3831
Mic 2:8 ye pull off the robe with the **g.** 8008
Hag 2:12 holy flesh in the skirt of his **g.**, ... 899
Zec 13:4 wear a rough **g.** to deceive:............... 155
Mal 2:16 one covereth violence with his **g.**, ... 3830
Mt 9:16 **piece of new cloth unto an old g.**,.. *2440*
Mt 9:16 **to fill it up taketh from the g.**,..... *2440*
Mt 9:20 and touched the hem of his **g.** *2440*
Mt 9:21 If I may but touch his **g.**, ... *2440*
Mt 14:36 only touch the hem of his **g.**............... *2440*
Mt 22:11 **which had not on a wedding g.** *1742*
Mt 22:12 **in hither not having a wedding g.?**. *1742*
Mk 2:21 **piece of new cloth on an old g.**: *2440*
Mk 5:27 press behind, and touched his **g.**. *2440*
Mk 6:56 it were but the border of his **g.** *2440*
Mk 10:50 And he, casting away his **g.**, rose,...... *2440*
Mk 13:16 **back again for to take up his g.**.... *2440*
Mk 16:5 clothed in a long white **g.**:and............ *4749*
Lu 5:36 **a piece of a new g. upon an old;** ... *2440*
Lu 8:44 and touched the border of his **g.**: *2440*
Lu 22:36 **let him sell his g., and buy one,**.... *2440*
Ac 12:8 Cast thy **g.** about thee, ... *2440*
Heb 1:11 all shall wax old as doth a **g.**; *2440*
Jude 23 hating even the **g.** spotted by the....... *5509*
Re 1:13 clothed with a **g.** down to the foot,..... *4158*

GARMENTS
Ge 35:2 change your **g.**: 8071
Ge 38:14 she put her widow's **g.** off from........... 899
Ge 38:19 put on the **g.** of her widowhood........... 899
Ge 49:11 he washed his **g.** in wine, and his........ 3830
Ex 28:2 thou shalt make holy **g.** for Aaron........ 899
Ex 28:3 that they may make Aaron's **g.**............ 899
Ex 28:4 these are the **g.** which they shall......... 899
Ex 28:4 they shall make holy **g.** for Aaron 899
Ex 29:5 thou shalt take the **g.**, and put upon..... 899
Ex 29:21 and upon his **g.** and upon his sons,....... 899
Ex 29:21 and upon the **g.** of his sons with him: ... 899
Ex 29:21 he shall be hallowed, and his **g.**, and 899
Ex 29:21 his sons, and his sons' **g.** with him....... 899
Ex 29:29 And the holy **g.** of Aaron shall be 899
Ex 31:10 the holy **g.** for Aaron the priest, ... 899
Ex 31:10 the **g.** of his sons, to minister in.......... 899
Ex 35:19 the holy **g.** for Aaron the priest, ... 899
Ex 35:19 the **g.** of his sons, to minister in.......... 899
Ex 35:21 service, and for the holy **g.**. 899
Ex 39:1 and made the holy **g.** for Aaron; 899
Ex 39:41 the holy **g.** for Aaron the priest, ... 899
Ex 39:41 and his sons, **g.**, to minister in the....... 899
Ex 40:13 put upon Aaron the holy **g.**,................ 899
Le 6:11 put off his **g.**, and put on other **g.**, ... 899
Le 8:2 the **g.**, and the anointing oil, ... 899
Le 8:30 upon Aaron, and upon his **g.**, and 899
Le 8:30 and upon his sons' **g.** with him; 899
Le 8:30 Aaron, and his **g.**, and his sons, ... 899
Le 8:30 and his sons' **g.** with him. 899
Le 16:4 these are holy **g.**; therefore shall......... 899
Le 16:23 and shall put off the linen **g.**, ... 899
Le 16:24 put on his **g.**, and come forth,............. 899
Le 16:32 the linen clothes, even the holy **g.** 899
Le 21:10 is consecrated to put on the **g.**,............ 899
Nu 15:38 fringes in the borders of their **g.**.......... 899
Nu 20:26 strip Aaron of his **g.**, and put them 899
Nu 20:28 And Moses stripped Aaron of his **g.**, ... 899
Jos 9:5 and old **g.** upon them; and all the 8008
Jos 9:13 these our **g.** and our shoes 8008
Jg 14:12 and thirty changes of **g.** 899
Jg 14:13 sheets and thirty change of **g.**: 899
Jg 14:19 gave change of **g.** unto them ....
1Sa 18:4 and his **g.**, even to his sword, ... 4055
2Sa 10:4 cut off their **g.** in the middle,............. 4063
2Sa 13:31 the king arose, and tare his **g.**, ... 899
1Ki 10:25 vessels of gold, and **g.**, and................ 8008
2Ki 5:22 of silver, and two changes of **g.**........... 899
2Ki 5:23 two bags, with two changes of **g.**. 899
2Ki 5:26 and to receive **g.**, and oliveyards, ... 899
2Ki 7:15 all the way was full of **g.**....................... 899
2Ki 25:29 And changed his prison **g.**: and he 899
1Ch 19:4 and cut off their **g.** in the midst 4063
Ezr 2:69 and one hundred priests' **g.**. 3801
Ne 7:70 five hundred and thirty priests' **g.**....... 3801
Ne 7:72 threescore and seven priests' **g.**......... 3801
Job 37:17 How thy **g.** are warm, when he........... 899
Ps 22:18 They part my **g.** among them, ... 899
Ps 45:8 All thy **g.** smell of myrrh, and aloes, ... 899
Ps 133:2 went down to the skirts of his **g.**; 4060
Ec 9:8 Let thy **g.** be always white;................. 899
Ca 4:11 the smell of thy **g.** is like the smell..... 8008
Isa 9:5 noise, and **g.** rolled in blood; 8071
Isa 52:1 on thy beautiful **g.**, O Jerusalem, ... 899
Isa 59:6 Their webs shall not become **g.**,........... 899
Isa 59:17 he put on the **g.** of vengeance 899
Isa 61:10 clothed me with the **g.** of salvation,...... 899
Isa 63:1 Edom, with dyed **g.** from Bozrah?........ 899
Isa 63:2 and thy **g.** like him that treadeth.......... 899
Isa 63:3 shall be sprinkled upon my **g.**,............. 899
Jer 36:24 were not afraid, nor rent their **g.**,........ 899
Jer 52:33 And changed his prison **g.**: and he 899
La 4:14 that men could not touch their **g.**. 3830
Eze 16:16 And of thy **g.** thou didst take, ... 899
Eze 16:18 And tookest thy broidered **g.**, ... 899
Eze 26:16 robes, and put off their broidered **g.**..... 899
Eze 42:14 but there they shall lay their **g.** 899
Eze 42:14 and shall put on other **g.**, ... 899
Eze 44:17 they shall be clothed with linen **g.**; 899
Eze 44:19 they shall put off their **g.** wherein 899
Eze 44:19 and they shall put on other **g.**; 899
Eze 44:19 sanctify the people with their **g.**. 899
Da 3:21 and their other **g.**, and were cast 3831
Joe 2:13 rend your heart, and not your **g.**, ... 899
Zec 3:3 Joshua was clothed with filthy **g.**,......... 899
Zec 3:4 Take away the filthy **g.** from him......... 899
Zec 3:5 his head, and clothed him with **g.**......... 899
Mt 21:8 spread their **g.** in the way;................ *2440*
Mt 23:5 **enlarge the borders of their g.**,..... *2440*
Mt 27:35 and parted his **g.**, casting lots:.......... *2440*
Mt 27:35 They parted my **g.** among them, ... *2440*
Mk 11:7 and cast their **g.** on him; and he *2440*
Mk 11:8 many spread their **g.** in the way;......... *2440*
Mk 15:24 they parted his **g.**, casting lots........... *2440*
Lu 19:35 they cast their **g.** upon the colt,......... *2440*
Lu 24:4 men stood by them in shining **g.** *2067*
Joh 13:4 from supper, and laid aside his **g.**;....... *2440*
Joh 13:12 and had taken his **g.**, and was set *2440*
Joh 19:23 took his **g.** and made four parts, ... *2440*
Ac 9:39 shewing the coats and **g.** which.......... *2440*
Jas 5:2 and your **g.** are motheaten................ *2440*
Re 3:4 **which have not defiled their g.**...... *2440*
Re 16:15 that watcheth, and keepeth his **g.**,...... *2440*

GARMITE (gar'-mite)
1Ch 4:19 Keilah the **G.**, and Eshtemoa the 1636

GARNER See also GARNERS.
Mt 3:12 and gather his wheat into the **g.**; *596*
Lu 3:17 will gather the wheat into his **g.**; *596*

GARNERS
Ps 144:13 That our **g.** may be full, affording....... 4200
Joe 1:17 the **g.** are laid desolate, the barns........ 214

GARNISH See also GARNISHED.
Mt 23:29 **and g. the sepulchres of the**.......... *2885*

GARNISHED
2Ch 3:6 And he **g.** the house with precious 6823
Job 26:13 his spirit he hath **g.** the heavens; 8235
Mt 12:44 **he findeth it empty, swept, and g.**.. *2885*
Lu 11:25 **he findeth it swept and g.**............ *2885*
Re 21:19 of the wall of the city were **g.** *2885*

GARRISON See also GARRISONS.
1Sa 10:5 where is the **g.** of the Philistines:....... 5333
1Sa 13:3 Jonathan smote the **g.** of the 5333
1Sa 13:4 had smitten a **g.** of the Philistines,...... 5333
1Sa 13:23 the **g.** of the Philistines went out 4673
1Sa 14:1 let us go over to the Philistines' **g.**, ... 4673
1Sa 14:4 to go over unto the Philistines' **g.**,...... 4673
1Sa 14:6 Come, and let us go over unto the **g.** ..4673

1Sa 14:11 unto the **g.** of the Philistines; and 4673
1Sa 14:12 men of the **g.** answered Jonathan 4675
1Sa 14:15 people, the **g.**, and the spoilers, 4673
2Sa 23:14 and the **g.** of the Philistines was 4673
1Ch 11:16 the Philistines' **g.** was then at 5333
2Co 11:32 king kept the city of...with a **g.**, *5432*

GARRISONS
2Sa 8:6 Then David put **g.** in Syria of 5333
2Sa 8:14 And he put **g.** in Edom; 5333
2Sa 8:14 throughout all Edom put he **g.**, 5333
1Ch 18:6 Then David put **g.** in Syria-damascus;
1Ch 18:13 And he put **g.** in Edom; and all 5333
2Ch 17:2 and set **g.** in the land of Judah, 5333
Eze 26:11 and thy strong **g.** shall go down 4676

GASHMU (gash'-mu) See also GESHEM.
Ne 6:6 and **G.** saith it, that thou and the 1654

GAT See also BEGAT; FORGAT; GOT.
Ge 19:27 And Abraham **g.** up early in the
Ex 24:18 and **g.** him up into the mount: 5927
Nu 11:30 And Moses **g.** him into the camp, 622
Nu 14:40 and **g.** them up into the top of the 5927
Nu 16:27 so they **g.** up from the tabernacle 5927
Jg 9:48 Abimelech **g.** him up to mount 5927
Jg 9:51 and **g.** them up to the top of the 5927
Jg 19:28 the man rose up, and **g.** him unto 3212
1Sa 13:15 And Samuel arose, and **g.** him up 5927
1Sa 24:22 David and his men **g.** them up unto 5927
1Sa 26:12 and they **g.** them away, and no 3212
2Sa 4:7 and **g.** them away through the 3212
2Sa 8:13 And David **g.** him a name when 6213
2Sa 13:29 every man **g.** him up upon his 7392
2Sa 17:23 and **g.** him home to his house, 3212
2Sa 19:3 And the people **g.** them by stealth 935
1Ki 1:1 him with clothes, but he **g.** no heat.
Ps 116:3 the pains of hell **g.** hold upon me:
Ec 2:8 I **g.** me men singers and women 6213
La 5:9 We **g.** our bread with the peril of 935

GATAM (ga'-tam)
Ge 36:11 Omar, Zepho, and **G.**, and Kenaz. 1609
Ge 36:16 Duke Korah, duke **G.**, and duke 1609
1Ch 1:36 Omar, Zephi, and **G.**, Kenaz, and 1609

GATE See also GATES.
Ge 19:1 Lot sat in the gate of Sodom: 8179
Ge 22:17 possess the **g.** of his enemies; 8179
Ge 23:10 all that went in at the **g.** of his city, 8179
Ge 23:18 that went in at the **g.** of his city. 8179
Ge 24:60 let thy seed possess the **g.** of those 8179
Ge 28:17 and this is the **g.** of heaven. 8179
Ge 34:20 came unto the **g.** of their city, 8179
Ge 34:24 went out of the **g.** of his city; 8179
Ge 34:24 that went out of the **g.** of his city. 8179
Ex 27:14 The hangings of one side of the **g.**
Ex 27:16 And for the **g.** of the court 8179
Ex 32:26 Moses stood in the **g.** of the camp, 8179
Ex 32:27 from **g.** to **g.** throughout the camp, 8179
Ex 38:14 The hangings of the one side of the **g.**
Ex 38:15 for the other side of the court **g.**, 8179
Ex 38:18 the hanging for the **g.** of the court 8179
Ex 38:31 and the sockets of the court **g.**, 8179
Ex 39:40 and the hanging for the court **g.**, 8179
Ex 40:8 hang up the hanging at the court **g.** 8179
Ex 40:33 set up the hanging of the court **g.** 8179
Nu 4:26 the hanging for the door of the **g.** 8179
De 21:19 and unto the **g.** of his place; 8179
De 22:15 unto the elders of the city in the **g.** 8179
De 22:24 bring them both out unto the **g.** 8179
De 25:7 go up to the **g.** unto the elders, 8179
Jos 2:5 about the time of shutting of the **g.**, 8179
Jos 2:7 were gone out, they shut the **g.** 8179
Jos 7:5 chased them from before the **g.** 8179
Jos 8:29 cast it at the entering of the **g.** 8179
Jos 20:4 stand at the entering of the **g.** 8179
Jg 9:35 stood in the entering of the **g.** 8179
Jg 9:40 even unto the entering of the **g.** 8179
Jg 9:44 stood in the entering of the **g.** 8179
Jg 16:2 laid wait for him all night in the **g.** 8179
Jg 16:3 took the doors of the **g.** of the city, 8179
Jg 18:16 stood by the entering of the **g.** 8179
Jg 18:17 stood in the entering of the **g.** 8179
Ru 4:1 Then went Boaz up to the **g.**, 8179
Ru 4:10 and from the **g.** of his place: 8179
Ru 4:11 all the people that were in the **g.**, 8179
1Sa 4:18 seat backward by the side of the **g.**, 8179
1Sa 9:18 Saul drew near to Samuel in the **g.**, 8179
1Sa 21:13 scrabbled on the doors of the **g.**, 8179
2Sa 3:27 Joab took him aside in the **g.** 8179
2Sa 10:8 at the entering in of the **g.**: 8179
2Sa 11:23 even unto the entering of the **g.** 8179
2Sa 15:2 stood beside the way of the **g.**: 8179
2Sa 18:4 the king stood by the **g.** side, 8179
2Sa 18:24 went up to the roof over the **g.** 8179
2Sa 18:33 up to the chamber over the **g.**, 8179
2Sa 19:8 the king arose, and sat in the **g.** 8179
2Sa 19:8 the king doth sit in the **g.** 8179
2Sa 23:15 of Beth-lehem, which is by the **g.**! 8179
2Sa 23:16 that was by the **g.**, and took it, 8179
1Ki 17:10 when he came to the **g.** of the city, 6607
1Ki 22:10 the entrance of the **g.** of Samaria; 8179
2Ki 7:1 a shekel, in the **g.** of Samaria. 8179
2Ki 7:3 at the entering of the **g.** 8179
2Ki 7:17 to have the charge of the **g.** 8179
2Ki 7:17 the people trode upon him in the **g.**, 8179
2Ki 7:18 about this time in the **g.** of Samaria: 8179
2Ki 7:20 the people trode upon him in the **g.**, 8179
2Ki 9:31 as Jehu entered in at the **g.**, 8179
2Ki 10:8 entering in of the **g.** until the 8179
2Ki 11:6 third part shall be at the **g.** of Sur; 8179
2Ki 11:6 part at the **g.** behind the guard: 8179
2Ki 11:19 the way of the **g.** of the guard 8179
2Ki 14:13 **g.** of Ephraim unto the corner **g.**, 8179
2Ki 15:35 built the higher **g.** of the house 8179
2Ki 23:8 the **g.** of Joshua the governor of 8179
2Ki 23:8 left hand at the **g.** of the city 8179
2Ki 25:4 way of the **g.** between two walls, 8179
1Ch 9:18 hitherto waited in the king's **g.** 8179
1Ch 11:17 well of Beth-lehem, that is at the **g.**! 8179
1Ch 11:18 that was by the **g.**, and took it, 8179
1Ch 19:9 array before the **g.** of the city: 6607
1Ch 26:13 house of their fathers, for every **g.** 8179
1Ch 26:16 with the **g.** Shallecheth, by the 8179
2Ch 8:14 also by their courses at every **g.** 8179
2Ch 18:9 the entering in of the **g.** of Samaria; 8179
2Ch 23:5 part at the **g.** of the foundation: 8179
2Ch 23:15 to the entering of the horse **g.** 8179
2Ch 23:20 and they came through the high **g.** 8179
2Ch 24:8 set it without at the **g.** of the house 8179
2Ch 25:23 the **g.** of Ephraim to the corner **g.**, 8179
2Ch 26:9 the corner **g.**, and at the valley **g.**, 8179
2Ch 27:3 He built the high **g.** of the house 8179
2Ch 32:6 the street of the **g.** of the city, 8179
2Ch 33:14 the entering in at the fish **g.**, 8179
2Ch 35:15 and the porters waited at every **g.** 8179
Ne 2:13 by night by the **g.** of the valley, 8179
Ne 2:14 I went on to the **g.** of the fountain, 8179
Ne 2:15 entered by the **g.** of the valley, 8179
Ne 3:1 they builded the sheep **g.**; they 8179
Ne 3:3 fish **g.** did the sons of Hassenaah 8179
Ne 3:6 the old **g.** repaired Jehoiada 8179
Ne 3:13 The valley **g.** repaired Hanun, 8179
Ne 3:13 on the wall unto the dung **g.** 8179
Ne 3:14 the dung **g.** repaired Malchiah 8179
Ne 3:15 **g.** of the fountain repaired Shallun 8179
Ne 3:26 place over against the water **g.** 8179
Ne 3:28 the horse **g.** repaired the priests, 8179
Ne 3:29 the keeper of the east **g.** 8179
Ne 3:31 over against the **g.** Miphkad, 8179
Ne 3:32 unto the sheep **g.** repaired the 8179
Ne 8:1 street that was before the water **g.** 8179
Ne 8:3 street that was before the water **g.** 8179
Ne 8:16 and in the street of the water **g.**, 8179
Ne 8:16 in the street of the **g.** of Ephraim. 8179
Ne 12:31 upon the wall toward the dung **g.** 8179
Ne 12:37 And at the fountain **g.**, which was 8179
Ne 12:37 even unto the water **g.** eastward. 8179
Ne 12:39 from above the **g.** of Ephraim, 8179
Ne 12:39 the old **g.**, and above the fish **g.**, 8179
Ne 12:39 even unto the sheep **g.**: 8179
Ne 12:39 they stood still in the prison **g.** 8179
Es 2:19 then Mordecai sat in the king's **g.** 8179
Es 2:21 while Mordecai sat in the king's **g.** 8179
Es 3:2 servants, that were in the king's **g.**, 8179
Es 3:3 which were in the king's **g.**, 8179
Es 4:2 And came even before the king's **g.** 8179
Es 4:2 more might enter into the king's **g.** 8179
Es 4:6 which was before the king's **g.** 8179
Es 5:1 over against the **g.** of the house. 6607
Es 5:9 saw Mordecai in the king's **g.**, 8179
Es 5:13 the Jew sitting at the king's **g.** 8179
Es 6:10 Jew, that sitteth at the king's **g.** 8179
Es 6:12 came again to the king's **g.** 8179
Job 5:4 and they are crushed in the **g.**, 8179
Job 29:7 When I went out to the **g.** 8179
Job 31:21 when I saw my help in the **g.** 8179
Ps 69:12 They that sit in the **g.** speak 8179
Ps 118:20 This **g.** of the Lord, into which the 8179
Ps 127:5 speak with the enemies in the **g.** 8179
Pr 17:19 he that exalteth his **g.** seeketh 6607
Pr 22:22 oppress the afflicted in the **g.**; 8179
Pr 24:7 he openeth not his mouth in the **g.** 8179
Ca 7:4 Heshbon, by the **g.** of Bath-rabbim: 8179
Isa 14:31 Howl, O **g.**:cry, O city; thou, 8179
Isa 22:7 set themselves in array at the **g.** 8179
Isa 24:12 the **g.** is smitten with destruction. 8179
Isa 28:6 them that turn the battle to the **g.** 8179
Isa 29:21 for him that reproveth in the **g.**, 8179
Jer 7:2 Stand in the **g.** of the Lord's house, 8179
Jer 17:19 and stand in the **g.** of the children 8179
Jer 19:2 which is by the entry of the east **g.**, 8179
Jer 20:2 were in the high **g.** of Benjamin, 8179
Jer 26:10 down in the entry of the new **g.** 8179
Jer 31:38 Hananeel unto the **g.** of the corner. 8179
Jer 31:40 unto the corner of the horse **g.** 8179
Jer 36:10 at the entry of the new **g.** of the 8179
Jer 37:13 he was in the **g.** of Benjamin, 8179
Jer 38:7 the king then sitting in the **g.** 8179
Jer 39:3 came in, and sat in the middle **g.**, 8179
Jer 39:4 by the **g.** betwixt the two walls: 8179
Jer 52:7 of the **g.** between the two walls, 8179
La 5:14 elders have ceased from the **g.**, 8179
Eze 8:3 to the door of the inner **g.** that 8179
Eze 8:5 at the **g.** of the altar this image 8179
Eze 8:14 brought me to the door of the **g.** of 8179
Eze 9:2 from the way of the higher **g.**, 8179
Eze 10:19 stood at the door of the east **g.** 8179
Eze 11:1 unto the east **g.** of the Lord's house, 8179
Eze 11:1 behold at the door of the **g.** 8179
Eze 40:3 seed; he stood in the **g.** 8179
Eze 40:6 Then came he unto the **g.** which 8179
Eze 40:6 measured the threshold of the **g.**, 8179
Eze 40:6 and the other threshold of the **g.**,
Eze 40:7 and the threshold of the **g.** by the 8179
Eze 40:7 by the porch of the **g.** within was 8179
Eze 40:8 measured also the porch of the **g.** 8179
Eze 40:9 measured he the porch of the **g.**, 8179
Eze 40:9 the porch of the **g.** was inward. 8179
Eze 40:10 little chambers of the **g.** eastward 8179
Eze 40:11 breadth of the entry of the **g.**, ten 8179
Eze 40:11 and the length of the **g.**, thirteen 8179
Eze 40:13 measured then the **g.** from the roof 8179
Eze 40:14 post of the court round about the **g.** 8179
Eze 40:15 the face of the **g.** of the entrance 8179
Eze 40:15 porch of the inner **g.** were fifty 8179
Eze 40:16 posts within the **g.** round about, 8179
Eze 40:19 from the forefront of the lower **g.** 8179
Eze 40:20 And the **g.** of the outward court 8179
Eze 40:21 after the measure of the first **g.** 8179
Eze 40:22 the measure of the **g.** that looketh 8179
Eze 40:23 And the **g.** of the inner court was 8179
Eze 40:23 against the **g.** toward the north, 8179
Eze 40:23 from **g.** to **g.** an hundred cubits, 8179
Eze 40:24 behold a **g.** toward the south: 8179
Eze 40:27 there was a **g.** in the inner court 8179
Eze 40:27 he measured from **g.** to **g.** toward 8179
Eze 40:28 to the inner court by the south **g.** 8179
Eze 40:28 and he measured the south **g.** 8179
Eze 40:32 he measured the **g.** according to 8179
Eze 40:35 And he brought me to the north **g.**, 8179
Eze 40:39 And in the porch of the **g.** were two 8179
Eze 40:40 up to the entry of the north **g.**, 8179
Eze 40:40 at the porch of the **g.**, were two 8179
Eze 40:41 by the side of the **g.**; eight tables, 8179
Eze 40:44 And without the inner **g.** were the 8179
Eze 40:44 was at the side of the north **g.**; 8179
Eze 40:44 one at the side of the east **g.** having 8179
Eze 40:48 and the breadth of the **g.** was three 8179
Eze 42:15 forth toward the **g.** whose prospect 8179
Eze 43:1 to the **g.**, even the **g.** that looketh 8179
Eze 43:4 the house by the way of the **g.** 8179
Eze 44:1 the way of the **g.** whose prospect 8179
Eze 44:2 This **g.** shall be shut, it shall not 8179
Eze 44:3 by the way of the porch of that **g.**, 8179
Eze 44:4 brought...the way of the north **g.** 8179
Eze 45:19 posts of the **g.** of the inner court, 8179
Eze 46:1 **g.** of the inner court that looketh 8179
Eze 46:2 way of the porch of that **g.** without, 8179
Eze 46:2 and shall stand by the post of the **g.**, 8179
Eze 46:2 worship at the threshold of the **g.** 8179

Eze 46:2 but the g. shall not be shut until........ 8179
Eze 46:3 shall worship at the door of this g...... 8179
Eze 46:8 by the way of the porch of that g.,...... 8179
Eze 46:9 the way of the north g. to worship...... 8179
Eze 46:9 go out by the way of the south g.;...... 8179
Eze 46:9 entereth by the way of the south g..... 8179
Eze 46:9 go forth by the way of the north g..... 8179
Eze 46:9 shall not return by the way of the g.... 8179
Eze 46:12 the g. that looketh toward the east,.... 8179
Eze 46:12 going forth one shall shut the g......... 8179
Eze 46:19 which was at the side of the g.,......... 8179
Eze 47:2 he me out of the way of the g........... 8179
Eze 47:2 the way without unto the utter g........ 8179
Eze 48:31 gate northward; one g. of Reuben,..... 8179
Eze 48:31 one g. of Judah, one g. of Levi......... 8179
Eze 48:32 and three gates; one g. of Joseph,...... 8179
Eze 48:32 one g. of Benjamin, one g. of Dan...... 8179
Eze 48:33 and three gates: one g. of Simeon,..... 8179
Eze 48:33 g. of Issachar, one g. of Zebulun........ 8179
Eze 48:34 their three gates: one g. of God,...... 8179
Eze 48:34 g. of Asher, one g. of Naphtali.......... 8179
Da 2:49 Daniel sat in the g. of the king.......... 8651
Am 5:10 hate him that rebuketh in the g.,........ 8179
Am 5:12 they turn aside the poor in the g........ 8179
Am 5:15 and establish judgment in the g.:........ 8179
Ob 13 not have entered into the g. of.......... 8179
Mic 1:9 he is come unto the g. of my people,.. 8179
Mic 1:12 the Lord unto the g. of Jerusalem...... 8179
Mic 2:13 have passed through the g., and are... 8179
Zep 1:10 the noise of a cry from the fish g.,..... 8179
Zec 14:10 from Benjamin's g. unto the place....... 8179
Zec 14:10 of the first g., unto the corner g.,....... 8179
Mt 7:13 **Enter ye in at the strait g**............ *4439*
Mt 7:13 **for wide is the g., and broad is**...... *4439*
Mt 7:14 **Because strait is the g., and**......... *4439*
Lu 7:12 he came nigh to the g. of the city,..... *4439*
Lu 13:24 **Strive to enter in at the strait g**.... *4439*
Lu 16:20 **which was laid at his g., full of**.... *4440*
Ac 3:2 the g. of the temple which is called.... *2374*
Ac 3:10 at the Beautiful g. of the temple:....... *4439*
Ac 10:17 house, and stood before the g.,......... *4440*
Ac 12:10 they came unto the iron g. that......... *4439*
Ac 12:13 knocked at the door of the g.,........... *4440*
Ac 12:14 she opened not the g. for gladness,.... *4440*
Ac 12:14 told how Peter stood before the g...... *4440*
Heb 13:12 own blood, suffered without the g...... *4439*
Re 21:21 every...g. was of one pearl:....... *3588,4440*

GATES

Ex 20:10 thy stranger that is within thy g......... 8179
De 3:5 with high walls, g., and bars;............ 1817
De 5:14 thy stranger that is within thy g.;........ 8179
De 6:9 posts of thy house, and on thy g........ 8179
De 11:20 of thine house, and upon thy g.:........ 8179
De 12:12 the Levites that is within your g.;...... 8179
De 12:15 kill and eat flesh in all thy g.,........... 8179
De 12:17 Thou mayest not eat within thy g........ 8179
De 12:18 and the Levite that is within thy g.:.... 8179
De 12:21 and thou shalt eat in thy g............... 8179
De 14:21 unto the stranger that is in thy g.,...... 8179
De 14:27 the Levite that is within thy g.;......... 8179
De 14:28 and shalt lay it up within thy g.......... 8179
De 14:29 which are within thy g., shall come,..... 8179
De 15:7 of thy brethren within any of thy g..... 8179
De 15:22 Thou shalt eat it within thy g........... 8179
De 16:5 the passover within any of thy g.,...... 8179
De 16:11 and the Levite that is within thy g.,.... 8179
De 16:14 widow, that are within thy g............ 8179
De 16:18 shalt thou make thee in all thy g.,...... 8179
De 17:2 among you, within any of thy g.......... 8179
De 17:5 that wicked thing, unto thy g.,........... 8179
De 17:8 of controversy within thy g.:............. 8179
De 18:6 if a Levite come from any of thy g..... 8179
De 23:16 he shall choose in one of thy g.,......... 8179
De 24:14 that are in thy land within thy g......... 8179
De 26:12 that they may eat within thy g.,.......... 8179
De 28:52 he shall besiege thee in all thy g.,...... 8179
De 28:55 shall distress thee in all thy g........... 8179
De 28:57 enemy shall distress thee in thy g...... 8179
De 31:12 thy stranger that is within thy g.,........ 8179
Jos 6:26 son shall he set up the g. of it........... 1817
Jg 5:8 then was war in the g.: was there....... 8179
Jg 5:11 people of the Lord go down to the g... 8179
1Sa 17:52 the valley, and to the g. of Ekron...... 8179
1Sa 23:7 into a town that hath g. and bars....... 1817
2Sa 18:24 David sat between the two g.: and..... 8179
1Ki 16:34 up the g. thereof in his youngest........ 1817
2Ki 23:8 down the high places of the g........... 8179
1Ch 9:19 keepers of the g. of the tabernacle:..... 5592
1Ch 9:22 were chosen to be porters in the g...... 5592
1Ch 9:23 oversight of the g. of the house......... 8179
1Ch 22:3 for the nails for the doors of the g.,... 8179
2Ch 8:5 cities, with walls, g., and bars;.......... 1817
2Ch 14:7 walls, and towers, g., and bars,......... 1817
2Ch 23:19 And he set the porters at the g......... 8179
2Ch 31:2 to praise in the g. of the tents.......... 8179
Ne 1:3 the g. thereof are burned with fire...... 8179
Ne 2:3 g. thereof are consumed with fire?...... 8179
Ne 2:8 beams for the g. of the palace........... 8179
Ne 2:13 g. thereof were consumed with fire,.... 8179
Ne 2:17 the g. thereof are burned with fire:..... 8179
Ne 6:1 not set up the doors upon the g.;)....... 8179
Ne 7:3 Let not the g. of Jerusalem be........... 8179
Ne 11:19 and their brethren that kept the g.,..... 8179
Ne 12:25 ward at the thresholds of the g.......... 8179
Ne 12:30 the people, and the g., and the wall.... 8179
Ne 13:19 when the g. of Jerusalem began to...... 8179
Ne 13:19 that the g. should be shut,................ 1817
Ne 13:19 some of my servants set I at the g.,.... 8179
Ne 13:22 they should come and keep the g.,...... 8179
Job 38:17 Have the g. of death been opened........ 8179
Ps 9:13 liftest me up from the g. of death:...... 8179
Ps 9:14 in the g. of the daughter of Zion:........ 8179
Ps 24:7 your heads, O ye g.; and be ye lift up. 8179
Ps 24:9 your heads, O ye g.; even lift them..... 8179
Ps 87:2 The Lord loveth the g. of Zion.......... 8179
Ps 100:4 Enter into his g. with thanksgiving,..... 8179
Ps 107:16 he hath broken the g. of brass,........... 1817
Ps 107:18 draw near unto the g. of death........... 8179
Ps 118:19 Open to me the g. of righteousness:... 8179
Ps 122:2 Our feet shall stand within thy g.,....... 8179
Ps 147:13 strengthened the bars of thy g.;.......... 8179
Pr 1:21 in the openings of the g.: in the......... 8179
Pr 8:3 She crieth at the g., at the entry of..... 8179
Pr 8:34 watching daily at my g., waiting.......... 1817
Pr 14:19 wicked at the g. of the righteous......... 8179
Pr 31:23 Her husband is known in the g.,......... 8179
Pr 31:31 her own works praise her in the g...... 8179
Ca 7:13 our g. are all manner of pleasant........ 6607
Isa 3:26 her g. shall lament and mourn;........... 6607
Isa 13:2 go into the g. of the nobles............... 6607
Isa 26:2 Open ye the g., that the righteous...... 8179
Isa 38:10 I shall go to the g. of the grave:......... 8179
Isa 45:1 before him the two-leaved g.;............ 1817
Isa 45:1 and the g. shall not be shut;............. 8179
Isa 45:2 break in pieces the g. of brass,.......... 1817
Isa 54:12 and thy g. of carbuncles, and all......... 8179
Isa 60:11 thy g. shall be open continually;......... 8179
Isa 60:18 walls Salvation, and thy g. Praise....... 8179
Isa 62:10 through the g.; prepare ye the way..... 8179
Jer 1:15 the entering of the g. of Jerusalem,..... 8179
Jer 7:2 that enter in at these g. to worship..... 8179
Jer 14:2 Judah mourneth, and the g. thereof...... 8179
Jer 15:7 I will fan them with a fan in the g...... 8179
Jer 17:19 and in all the g. of Jerusalem;........... 8179
Jer 17:20 that enter in by these g.................. 8179
Jer 17:21 bring it in by the g. of Jerusalem;....... 8179
Jer 17:24 bring in no burden through the g........ 8179
Jer 17:25 Then shall there enter into the g........ 8179
Jer 17:27 entering in at the g. of Jerusalem...... 8179
Jer 17:27 I kindle a fire in the g. thereof,......... 8179
Jer 22:2 thy people that enter in by these g..... 8179
Jer 22:4 enter in by the g. of this house......... 8179
Jer 22:19 forth beyond the g. of Jerusalem........ 8179
Jer 49:31 which have neither g. nor bar............ 1817
Jer 51:58 and her high g. shall be burned.......... 8179
La 1:4 g. are desolate: her priests sigh,......... 8179
La 2:9 Her g. are sunk into the ground;......... 8179
La 4:12 entered into the g. of Jerusalem......... 8179
Eze 21:15 the sword against all their g.,........... 8179
Eze 21:22 battering rams against the g.,........... 8179
Eze 26:2 that was the g. of the people:........... 1817
Eze 26:10 when he shall enter into thy g.,.......... 8179
Eze 38:11 and having neither bars nor g.,.......... 1817
Eze 40:18 pavement by the side of the g. over... 8179
Eze 40:18 over against the length of the g........ 8179
Eze 40:38 thereof were by the posts of the g.,... 8179
Eze 44:11 charge at the g. of the house,........... 8179
Eze 44:17 in at the g. of the inner court,........... 8179
Eze 44:17 they minister in the g. of the inner..... 8179
Eze 48:31 And the g. of the city shall be........... 8179
Eze 48:31 g. northward; one gate of Reuben,...... 8179
Eze 48:32 three g.; and one gate of Joseph,........ 8179
Eze 48:33 three g.; and one gate of Simeon,....... 8179
Eze 48:34 their three g.; and one gate of Gad,... 8179
Ob 11 foreigners entered into his g.,........... 8179
Na 2:6 g. of the rivers shall be opened,........ 8179
Na 3:13 g. of thy land shall be set wide open... 8179
Zec 8:16 truth and peace in your g................ 8179
Mt 16:18 **the g. of hell shall not prevail**...... *4439*
Ac 9:24 they watched the g. day and night...... *4439*
Ac 14:13 oxen and garlands unto the g.,.......... *4440*
Re 21:12 and had twelve g.,......................... *4440*
Re 21:12 and at the g. twelve angels,.............. *4440*
Re 21:13 On the east three g.;....................... *4440*
Re 21:13 on the north three g.;...................... *4440*
Re 21:13 on the south three g.;...................... *4440*
Re 21:13 and on the west three g.................... *4440*
Re 21:15 and the g. thereof, and the wall......... *4440*
Re 21:21 the twelve g. were twelve pearls;...... *4440*
Re 21:25 And the g. of it shall not be shut...... *4440*
Re 22:14 enter in through the g. into the city,... *4440*

GATH (gath) See also GATH-HEPHER; GATH-RIMMON; GITTITE; MORESHETH-GATH.

Jos 11:22 only in Gaza, in G., and Ashdod,........ 1661
1Sa 5:8 of Israel be carried about unto G........ 1661
1Sa 6:17 Ashkelon one, for G. one, for Ekron... 1661
1Sa 7:14 to Israel, from Ekron even unto G.;... 1661
1Sa 17:4 Goliath, of G., whose height was........ 1661
1Sa 17:23 Philistine of G., Goliath by name,....... 1661
1Sa 17:52 Shaaraim, even unto G., and unto...... 1661
1Sa 21:10 and went to Achish the king of G....... 1661
1Sa 21:12 afraid of Achish the king of G........... 1661
1Sa 27:2 Achish, the son of Maoch, king of G... 1661
1Sa 27:3 David dwelt with Achish at G., he...... 1661
1Sa 27:4 told Saul that David was fled to G...... 1661
1Sa 27:11 woman alive, to bring tidings to G.,..... 1661
2Sa 1:20 Tell it not in G., publish it not in....... 1661
2Sa 15:18 men which came after him from G.,...... 1661
2Sa 21:20 was yet a battle in G., where was a.... 1661
2Sa 21:22 four were born to the giant in G.,....... 1661
1Ki 2:39 Achish son of Maachah king of G........ 1661
1Ki 2:39 Behold, thy servants be in G............. 1661
1Ki 2:40 saddled his ass, and went to G. to...... 1661
1Ki 2:40 and brought his servants from G......... 1661
1Ki 2:41 had gone from Jerusalem to G., and.... 1661
2Ki 12:17 went up, and fought against G.,......... 1661
1Ch 7:21 and Elead, whom the men of G. that.. 1661
1Ch 8:13 drove away the inhabitants of G......... 1661
1Ch 18:1 subdued them, and took G. and.......... 1661
1Ch 20:6 war at G., where was a man of........... 1661
1Ch 20:8 were born unto the giant in G.;.......... 1661
2Ch 11:8 And G., and Mareshah, and Ziph,........ 1661
2Ch 26:6 and brake down the wall of G., and.... 1661
Ps 56 *title* the Philistines took him in G............ 1661
Am 6:2 go down to G. of the Philistines:........ 1661
Mic 1:10 Declare ye it not at G., weep ye not.. 1661

GATHER See also GATHERED; GATHEREST; GATHERETH; GATHERING; TOGETHER.

Ge 6:21 and thou shalt g. it to thee;............... 622
Ge 31:46 said unto his brethren, G. stones;...... 3950
Ge 34:30 g. themselves together against me,...... 622
Ge 41:35 And let them g. all the food............. 6908
Ge 49:1 G. yourselves together, that I may...... 622
Ge 49:2 G. yourselves together, and hear,...... 6908
Ex 3:16 Go, and g. the elders of Israel............ 622
Ex 5:7 and g. straw for themselves,............. 7197
Ex 5:12 to g. stubble instead of straw............ 7197
Ex 9:19 therefore now, and g. thy cattle,........ 5756
Ex 16:4 the people shall go out and g........... 3950
Ex 16:5 twice as much as they g. daily........... 3950
Ex 16:16 G. of it every man according to his..... 3950
Ex 16:26 Six days ye shall g. it; but on the....... 3950
Ex 16:27 on the seventh day for to g............... 3950
Ex 23:10 shall g. in the fruits thereof:.............. 622
Le 8:3 g. thou all the congregation.............. 6950
Le 19:9 shalt thou g. the gleanings................ 3950
Le 19:109 neither shalt thou g. every grape....... 3950
Le 23:22 neither shalt thou g. any gleaning...... 3950
Le 25:3 prune thy vineyard, and g. in the........ 622
Le 25:5 neither g. the grapes of thy vine........ 1219
Le 25:11 nor g. the grapes in it of thy vine....... 1219
Le 25:20 not sow, nor g. in our increase:.......... 622
Nu 8:9 shalt g. the whole assembly of the...... 6950
Nu 10:4 of Israel, shall g. themselves........... 3259
Nu 11:16 G. unto me seventy men of the........... 622
Nu 19:9 And a man that is clean shall g......... 622
Nu 20:8 g. thou the assembly together,........... 6950
Nu 21:16 G. the people together, and I will........ 622
De 4:10 G. me the people together, and I........ 6950

De 11:14 that thou mayest **g.** in thy corn, 622
De 13:16 thou shalt **g.** all the spoil of it 6908
De 28:30 shalt not **g.** the grapes thereof 2490
De 28:38 shalt **g.** but little in; for the locust 622
De 28:39 nor **g.** the grapes; for the worm 103
De 30:3 and **g.** thee from all the nations, 6908
De 30:4 will the Lord thy God **g.** thee, 6908
De 31:12 **G.** the people together, men, and 6950
De 31:28 **G.** unto me all the elders of your 6950
Ru 2:7 me glean and **g.** after the reapers 622
1Sa 7:5 said, **G.** all Israel to Mizpeh, 6908
2Sa 3:21 and will **g.** all Israel unto my lord 6908
2Sa 12:28 **g.** the rest of the people together, 622
1Ki 18:19 **g.** to me all Israel unto mount 6908
2Ki 4:39 went out into the field to **g.** herbs, 3950
2Ki 22:20 I will **g.** thee unto thy fathers, 622
1Ch 13:2 they may **g.** themselves unto us: 6908
1Ch 16:35 and **g.** us together, and deliver us 6908
1Ch 22:2 David commanded to **g.** together 3664
2Ch 24:5 **g.** of all Israel money to repair 6908
2Ch 34:28 I will **g.** thee to thy fathers, 622
Ezr 10:7 they should **g.** themselves together 6908
Ne 1:9 yet will I **g.** them from thence, 6908
Ne 7:5 to **g.** together the nobles, and the 6908
Ne 12:44 to **g.** into them out of the fields 3664
Es 2:3 may **g.** together all the fair young 6908
Es 4:16 **g.** together all the Jews that are 3664
Es 8:11 to **g.** themselves together, and to 6950
Job 11:10 and shut up, or **g.** together, 6950
Job 24:6 they **g.** the vintage of the wicked 3953
Job 34:14 if he **g.** unto himself his spirit 622
Job 39:12 thy seed, and **g.** it into thy barn? 622
Ps 26:9 **G.** not my soul with sinners, 622
Ps 39:6 and knoweth not who shall **g.** them 622
Ps 50:5 **G.** my saints together unto me; 622
Ps 56:6 They **g.** themselves together, 1481
Ps 94:21 **g.** themselves together against 1413
Ps 104:22 they **g.** themselves together, and 622
Ps 104:28 That thou givest them they **g.**: 3950
Ps 106:47 **g.** us from among the heathen, 6908
Pr 28:8 **g.** it for him that will pity the poor 6908
Ec 2:26 to **g.** and to heap up, that he may 622
Ec 3:5 and a time to **g.** stones together; 3664
Ca 6:2 in the gardens, and to **g.** lilies 3950
Isa 10:31 the inhabitants of Gebim **g.** 5756
Isa 11:12 **g.** together the dispersed of Judah 6908
Isa 34:15 hatch, and **g.** under her shadow: 1716
Isa 40:11 shall **g.** the lambs with his arm, 6908
Isa 43:5 and **g.** thee from the west; 6908
Isa 49:18 all these **g.** themselves together, 6908
Isa 54:7 with great mercies will I **g.** thee 6908
Isa 54:15 they shall surely **g.** together, 1481
Isa 54:15 whosoever shall **g.** together against 1481
Isa 56:8 Yet will I **g.** others to him, 6908
Isa 60:4 all they **g.** themselves together, 6908
Isa 62:10 **g.** out the stones; lift up a 5619
Isa 66:18 I will **g.** all nations and tongues; 6908
Jer 4:5 the trumpet in the land: cry, **g.** 4390
Jer 6:1 ye children of Benjamin, **g.** 5756
Jer 7:18 children **g.** wood, and the fathers 3950
Jer 9:22 and none shall **g.** them 622
Jer 10:17 **G.** up thy wares out of the land, 622
Jer 23:3 I will **g.** the remnant of my flock 6908
Jer 29:14 I will **g.** you from all the nations, 6908
Jer 31:8 **g.** them from the coasts of the earth, 6908
Jer 31:10 He that scattered Israel will **g.** him, 6908
Jer 32:37 I will **g.** them out of all countries, 6908
Jer 40:10 ye, **g.** ye wine, and summer fruits, 622
Jer 49:5 shall **g.** up him that wandereth 6908
Jer 49:14 **G.** ye together, and come against 6908
Jer 51:11 the arrows; **g.** the shields: 4390
Eze 11:17 I will even **g.** you from the people, 6908
Eze 16:37 therefore I will **g.** all thy lovers, 6908
Eze 16:37 will even **g.** them round about 6908
Eze 20:34 and will **g.** you out of the countries 6908
Eze 20:41 and **g.** you out of the countries 6908
Eze 22:19 **g.** you into the midst of Jerusalem 6908
Eze 22:20 they **g.** silver, and brass, and iron, 6910
Eze 22:20 so will I **g.** you in mine anger 6908
Eze 22:21 Yea, I will **g.** you, and blow upon 3664
Eze 24:4 **G.** the pieces thereof into it, 622
Eze 29:13 At the end of forty years will I **g.** 6908
Eze 34:13 and **g.** them from the countries, 6908
Eze 36:24 and **g.** you out of all countries, 6908
Eze 37:21 and will **g.** them on every side, 6908
Eze 39:17 **g.** yourselves on every side to my 622
Da 3:2 sent to **g.** together the princes, 3673
Ho 8:10 now will I **g.** them, and they shall 6908
Ho 9:6 Egypt shall **g.** them up, Memphis 6908
Joe 1:14 **g.** the elders and all the 622
Joe 2:6 all faces shall **g.** blackness 6908
Joe 2:16 **G.** the people, sanctify the 622
Joe 2:16 assemble the elders, **g.** the children, 622
Joe 3:2 I will also **g.** all nations, and will 6908
Joe 3:11 **g.** yourselves together round about: 6908
Mic 2:12 surely **g.** the remnant of Israel; 6908
Mic 4:6 I will **g.** her that is driven out, 6908
Mic 4:12 for he shall **g.** them as the sheaves 6908
Mic 5:1 **g.** thyself in troops, O daughter 1413
Na 2:10 the faces of them all **g.** blackness 6908
Hab 1:9 shall **g.** the captivity as the sand 622
Hab 1:15 and **g.** them in their drag: 622
Zep 2:1 **G.** yourselves together, yea, 7197
Zep 2:1 **g.** together, O nation not desired; 7197
Zep 3:8 to **g.** the nations, that I may 622
Zep 3:18 I will **g.** them that are sorrowful 622
Zep 3:19 and **g.** her that was driven out; 6908
Zep 3:20 even in the time that I **g.** you: 6908
Zec 10:8 and **g.** them; for I have redeemed 6908
Zec 10:10 and **g.** them out of Assyria; and I 6908
Zec 14:2 **g.** all nations against Jerusalem 622
Mt 3:12 and **g.** his wheat into the garner; *4863*
Mt 6:26 **do they reap, nor g. into barns;** *4863*
Mt 7:14 **Do men g. grapes of thorns,** *4816*
Mt 13:28 **that we go and g. them up?** *4816*
Mt 13:29 **Nay; lest while ye g. up the tares,** *4816*
Mt 13:30 **G. ye together first the tares,** *4816*
Mt 13:30 **but g. the wheat into my barn,** *4863*
Mt 13:41 **they shall g. out of his kingdom** *4816*
Mt 24:13 **they shall g. together his elect** *1996*
Mt 25:26 **and g. where I have not strawed:** *4863*
Mk 13:27 **and shall g. together his elect** *1996*
Lu 3:17 will **g.** the wheat into his garner; *4863*
Lu 6:44 **of thorns men do not g. figs,** *4816*
Lu 6:44 **of a bramble bush g. they grapes** *5166*
Lu 13:34 **as a hen doth g. her brood under**
Joh 6:12 **G. up the fragments that remain,** *4863*
Joh 11:52 also he should **g.** together in one *4863*
Joh 15:6 **and men g. them, and cast them** *4863*
Eph 1:10 he might **g.** together in one all *346*
Re 14:18 **g.** the clusters of the vine of the *5166*
Re 16:14 to **g.** them to battle of that great *4863*
Re 19:17 Come and **g.** yourselves together *4863*
Re 20:8 to **g.** them together to battle: *4863*

GATHERED

Ge 1:9 be **g.** together unto one place, 6960
Ge 12:5 their substance that they had **g.**, 7408
Ge 25:8 of years; and was **g.** to his people 622
Ge 25:17 died; and was **g.** unto his people 622
Ge 29:3 And thither were all the flocks **g.**: 622
Ge 29:7 the cattle should be **g.** together: 622
Ge 29:8 until all the flocks be **g.** together, 622
Ge 29:22 And Laban **g.** together all the men 622
Ge 35:29 died, and was **g.** unto his people, 622
Ge 41:48 he **g.** up all the food of the seven 6908
Ge 41:49 And Joseph **g.** corn as the sand 6651
Ge 47:14 And Joseph **g.** up all the money 3950
Ge 49:29 I am to be **g.** unto my people: 622
Ge 49:33 he **g.** up his feet into the bed, 622
Ge 49:33 and was **g.** unto his people 622
Ex 4:29 **g.** together all the elders of Israel: 622
Ex 8:14 **g.** them together upon heaps: 6651
Ex 15:8 the waters were **g.** together, the 6192
Ex 16:17 and **g.**, some more, some less 3950
Ex 16:18 he that **g.** much had nothing over,
Ex 16:18 and he that **g.** little had no lack;
Ex 16:18 they **g.** every man according to his 3950
Ex 16:21 they **g.** it every morning, every man 3950
Ex 16:22 the sixth day they **g.** twice as much 3950
Ex 23:16 when thou hast **g.** in thy labours 622
Ex 32:1 **g.** themselves together unto Aaron, 6950
Ex 32:26 **g.** themselves together unto him 622
Ex 35:1 Moses **g.** all the congregation 6950
Le 8:4 and the assembly was **g.** together 6950
Le 23:39 ye have **g.** in the fruit of the land, 622
Le 26:25 and when ye are **g.** together within 622
Nu 10:7 congregation is to be **g.** together, 6950
Nu 11:8 the people went about, and **g.** it, 3950
Nu 11:22 all the fish of the sea be **g.** together 622
Nu 11:24 and **g.** the seventy men of the elders 622
Nu 11:32 and they **g.** the quails: 622
Nu 11:32 he that **g.** least...ten homers:
Nu 11:32 he that...least **g.** ten homers: 622
Nu 14:35 that are **g.** together against me: 3259
Nu 15:32 they found a man that **g.** sticks 7197
Nu 16:3 And they **g.** themselves together 6950
Nu 16:11 are **g.** together against the Lord: 3259
Nu 16:19 And Korah **g.** all the congregation 6950
Nu 16:42 the congregation was **g.** against 6950
Nu 20:2 And they **g.** themselves together 6950
Nu 20:10 And Moses and Aaron **g.** the 6950
Nu 20:24 Aaron shall be **g.** unto his people: 622
Nu 20:26 Aaron shall be **g.** unto his people, 622
Nu 21:23 but Sihon **g.** all his people together, 622
Nu 27:3 them that **g.** themselves together 3259
Nu 27:13 also shalt be **g.** unto thy people, 622
Nu 27:13 as Aaron thy brother was **g.** 622
Nu 31:2 shalt thou be **g.** unto thy people 622
De 16:13 after that thou hast **g.** in thy corn 622
De 32:50 and be **g.** unto thy people; as Aaron 622
De 32:50 and was **g.** unto his people: 622
De 33:5 the tribes of Israel were **g.** together 622
Jos 9:2 That they **g.** themselves together, 6908
Jos 10:5 **g.** themselves together, and went 622
Jos 10:6 in the mountains are **g.** together 6908
Jos 22:12 **g.** themselves together at Shiloh, 6950
Jos 24:1 Joshua **g.** all the tribes of Israel 622
Jg 1:7 **g.** their meat under my table: 3950
Jg 2:10 were **g.** unto their fathers: 622
Jg 3:13 And he **g.** unto him the children 622
Jg 4:13 Sisera **g.** together all his chariots, 2199
Jg 6:33 were **g.** together, and went over, 622
Jg 6:34 and Abi-ezer was **g.** after him 2199
Jg 6:35 Manasseh; who also was **g.** after 2199
Jg 7:23 the men of Israel **g.** themselves 6817
Jg 7:24 of Ephraim **g.** themselves together, 6817
Jg 9:6 the men of Shechem **g.** together, 622
Jg 9:27 and **g.** their vineyards, and trode 1219
Jg 9:47 of Shechem were **g.** together 6908
Jg 10:17 the children of Ammon were **g.** 6817
Jg 11:3 were **g.** vain men to Jephthah, 3950
Jg 11:20 Sihon **g.** all his people together, 622
Jg 12:1 the men of Ephraim **g.** themselves 6817
Jg 12:4 Jephthah **g.** together all the men 6908
Jg 16:23 of the Philistines **g.** them together 6908
Jg 18:22 to Micah's house were **g.** together, 2199
Jg 20:1 the congregation was **g.** together 6950
Jg 20:11 So all the men of Israel were **g.** 622
Jg 20:14 children of Benjamin **g.** themselves 622
1Sa 5:8 sent therefore and **g.** all the lords 622
1Sa 5:11 sent and **g.** together all the lords 622
1Sa 7:6 And they **g.** together to Mizpeh, 6908
1Sa 7:7 children of Israel were **g.** together 6908
1Sa 8:4 of Israel **g.** themselves together, 6908
1Sa 13:5 Philistines **g.** themselves together 622
1Sa 13:11 Philistines **g.** themselves together 622
1Sa 14:48 And he **g.** an host, and smote the 6213
1Sa 15:4 And Saul **g.** the people together, 8085
1Sa 17:1 Philistines **g.** together their armies 622
1Sa 17:1 and were **g.** together at Shochoh, 622
1Sa 17:2 the men of Israel were **g.** together, 622
1Sa 20:38 Jonathan's lad **g.** up the arrows, 3950
1Sa 22:2 was discontented, **g.** themselves 6908
1Sa 25:1 all the Israelites were **g.** together, 6908
1Sa 28:1 that the Philistines **g.** their armies 6908
1Sa 28:4 Philistines **g.** themselves together, 6908
1Sa 28:4 and Saul **g.** all Israel together, and 6908
1Sa 29:1 Now the Philistines **g.** together all 6908
2Sa 2:25 And the children of Benjamin **g.** 6908
2Sa 2:30 he had **g.** all the people together, 6908
2Sa 6:1 David **g.** together all the chosen 3254
2Sa 10:15 were smitten before Israel, they **g.** 622
2Sa 10:17 told David, he **g.** all Israel together, 622
2Sa 12:29 And David **g.** all the people together, 622
2Sa 14:14 which cannot be **g.** up again; 622
2Sa 17:11 all Israel be generally **g.** unto thee, 622
2Sa 20:14 and they were **g.** together, and 7035
2Sa 21:13 and they **g.** the bones of them 622
2Sa 23:9 that were there **g.** together to battle, 622
2Sa 23:11 the Philistines were **g.** together into 622
1Ki 10:26 And Solomon **g.** together chariots 622
1Ki 11:24 he **g.** men unto him, and became 6908
1Ki 18:20 and **g.** the prophets together unto 6908
1Ki 20:1 of Syria **g.** all his host together: 6908
1Ki 22:6 of Israel **g.** the prophets together, 6908
2Ki 3:21 they **g.** all that were able to put on 6817
2Ki 4:39 and **g.** thereof wild gourds his lap 3950
2Ki 6:24 Ben-hadad king of Syria **g.** all his 6908
2Ki 10:18 And Jehu **g.** all the people together, 6908
2Ki 22:4 of the door have **g.** of the people: 622

2Ki 22:9 Thy servants have **g.** the money........ 5413
2Ki 22:20 and thou shalt be **g.** into thy grave........ 622
2Ki 23:1 and they **g.** unto him all the elders........ 622
1Ch 11:1 all Israel **g.** themselves to David........ 6908
1Ch 11:13 the Philistines were **g.** together to........ 622
1Ch 13:5 So David **g.** all Israel together,........ 6950
1Ch 15:3 And David **g.** all Israel together........ 6950
1Ch 19:7 of Ammon **g.** themselves together........ 622
1Ch 19:17 and he **g.** all Israel, and passed over.... 622
1Ch 23:2 And he **g.** together all the princes........ 622
2Ch 1:14 And Solomon **g.** chariots and........ 622
2Ch 11:1 he **g.** of the house of Judah and........ 6950
2Ch 12:5 that were **g.** together to Jerusalem........ 622
2Ch 13:7 there are **g.** unto him vain men,........ 6908
2Ch 15:9 And he **g.** all Judah and Benjamin,........ 6908
2Ch 15:10 So they **g.** themselves together at........ 6908
2Ch 18:5 Therefore the king of Israel **g.**........ 6908
2Ch 20:4 And Judah **g.** themselves together,........ 6908
2Ch 23:2 **g.** the Levites out of all the cities........ 6908
2Ch 24:5 And he **g.** together the priests........ 6908
2Ch 24:11 day, and **g.** money in abundance........ 622
2Ch 25:5 Amaziah **g.** Judah together, and........ 6908
2Ch 28:24 And Ahaz **g.** together the vessels........ 622
2Ch 29:4 **g.** them together into the east street,... 622
2Ch 29:15 And they **g.** their brethren, and........ 622
2Ch 29:20 and **g.** the rulers of the city,........ 622
2Ch 30:3 the people **g.** themselves together........ 622
2Ch 32:4 was **g.** much people together,........ 6908
2Ch 32:6 and **g.** them together to him in the..... 6908
2Ch 34:9 had **g.** of the hand of Manasseh........ 622
2Ch 34:17 they have **g.** together the money........ 5413
2Ch 34:28 and thou shalt be **g.** to thy grave........ 622
2Ch 34:29 the king sent and **g.** together all the..... 622
Ezr 3:1 the people **g.** themselves together........ 622
Ezr 7:28 and I **g.** together out of Israel........ 6908
Ezr 8:15 And I **g.** them together to the river.... 6908
Ezr 10:9 the men of Judah and Benjamin **g.**........ 6908
Ne 5:16 all my servants were **g.** thither........ 6908
Ne 8:1 the people **g.** themselves together........ 622
Ne 8:13 on the second day were **g.** together..... 622
Ne 12:28 the singers **g.** themselves together,........ 622
Ne 13:11 I **g.** them together, and set them........ 6908
Es 2:8 and when many maidens were **g.**........ 6908
Es 2:19 when the virgins were **g.** together........ 6908
Es 9:2 The Jews **g.** themselves together........ 6950
Es 9:15 the Jews that were in Shushan **g.**........ 6950
Es 9:16 **g.** themselves together, and stood........ 6950
Job 16:10 they have **g.** themselves together........ 4390
Job 27:19 lie down, but he shall not be **g.**........ 622
Job 30:7 the nettles they were **g.** together........ 5596
Ps 35:15 and **g.** themselves together: yea,........ 622
Ps 35:15 the abjects **g.** themselves together........ 622
Ps 47:9 The princes of the people are **g.**........ 622
Ps 59:3 the mighty are **g.** against me;........ 1481
Ps 102:22 When the people are **g.** together,........ 6908
Ps 107:3 And **g.** them out of the lands,........ 6908
Ps 140:2 are they **g.** together for war........ 1481
Pr 27:25 and herbs of the mountains are **g.**........ 622
Pr 30:4 who hath **g.** the winds in his fists?........ 622
Ec 2:8 I **g.** me also silver and gold,........ 3664
Ca 5:1 I have **g.** my myrrh with my spice;........ 717
Isa 5:2 it, and **g.** out the stones thereof,........
Isa 10:14 are left, have I **g.** all the earth;........ 622
Isa 13:4 kingdoms of nations **g.** together:........ 622
Isa 22:9 and ye **g.** together the waters........ 6908
Isa 24:22 And they shall be **g.** together,........ 622
Isa 24:22 as prisoners are **g.** in the pit,........ 626
Isa 27:12 ye shall be **g.** one by one,........ 3950
Isa 33:4 spoil shall be **g.** like the gathering........ 622
Isa 34:15 there shall the vultures also be **g.**,........ 6908
Isa 34:16 and his spirit it hath **g.** them........ 6908
Isa 43:9 Let all the nations be **g.** together,........ 6908
Isa 44:11 let them all be **g.** together, let them... 6908
Isa 49:5 Though Israel be not **g.**, yet shall........ 622
Isa 56:8 beside those that are **g.** unto him,........ 6908
Isa 60:7 All the flocks of Kedar shall be **g.**........ 6908
Isa 62:9 they that have **g.** it shall eat it,........ 622
Jer 3:17 all the nations shall be **g.** unto it,........ 6960
Jer 8:2 they shall not be **g.**, nor be buried;........ 622
Jer 25:33 shall not be lamented, neither **g.**,........ 622
Jer 26:9 people were **g.** against Jeremiah........ 6950
Jer 40:12 and **g.** wine and summer fruits........ 622
Jer 40:15 **g.** unto thee should be scattered,........ 6908
Eze 28:25 I shall have **g.** the house of Israel........ 6908
Eze 29:5 not be brought together, nor **g.**:........ 6908
Eze 38:8 and is **g.** out of many people,........ 6908
Eze 38:12 upon the people that are **g.** out........ 622
Eze 38:13 **g.** thy company to take a prey?........ 6950
Eze 39:27 and **g.** them out of their enemies'........ 6908
Eze 39:28 have **g.** them unto their own land,........ 3664
Da 3:3 **g.** together unto the dedication........ 3673
Da 3:27 being **g.** together, saw these men,........ 3673
Ho 1:11 and the children of Israel be **g.**........ 6908
Ho 10:10 people shall be **g.** against them,........ 622
Mic 1:7 she **g.** it of the hire of an harlot,........ 6908
Mic 4:11 many nations are **g.** against thee,........ 622
Mic 7:1 they have **g.** the summer fruits,........ 622
Zec 12:3 people of the earth be **g.** together........ 622
Zec 14:14 round about shall be **g.** together,........ 622
Mt 2:4 he had **g.** all the chief priests........ *4863*
Mt 13:2 great multitudes were **g.** together........ *4863*
Mt 13:40 **As therefore the tares are g. and**... *4816*
Mt 13:47 **into the sea, and g. of every kind:**. *4863*
Mt 13:48 **and g. the good into vessels,**........ *4816*
Mt 18:20 **three are g. together in my name,**.. *4863*
Mt 22:10 **and g. together all as many as**........ *4863*
Mt 22:34 to silence, they were **g.** together........ *4863*
Mt 22:41 the Pharisees were **g.** together,........ *4863*
Mt 23:37 **ofter would I have g. thy children**.. *1996*
Mt 24:28 **will the eagles be g. together**........ *4863*
Mt 25:32 **before him shall be g. all nations:**.. *4863*
Mt 27:17 they were **g.** together, Pilate said........ *4863*
Mt 27:27 and **g.** unto him the whole band........ *4863*
Mk 1:33 city was **g.** together at the door........ *1996*
Mk 2:2 many were **g.** together, insomuch........ *4863*
Mk 4:1 was **g.** unto him a great multitude,........ *4863*
Mk 5:21 much people **g.** unto him: and he........ *4863*
Mk 6:30 the apostles **g.** themselves together.... *4863*
Lu 8:4 much people were **g.** together,........ *4896*
Lu 11:29 people were **g.** thick together........ *1865*
Lu 12:1 when there were **g.** together an........ *1996*
Lu 13:34 **how ofter would I have g. thy**........ *1996*
Lu 15:13 **the younger son g. all together,**.... *4863*
Lu 17:37 **will the eagles be g. together**........ *4863*
Lu 24:33 and found the eleven **g.** together........ *4867*
Joh 6:13 Therefore they **g.** them together,........ *4863*
Joh 11:47 Then **g.** the chief priests and the........ *4863*
Ac 4:6 were **g.** together at Jerusalem........ *4863*
Ac 4:26 rulers were **g.** together against the..... *4863*
Ac 4:27 and the people of Israel, were **g.**........ *4863*
Ac 12:12 many were **g.** together praying........ *4863*
Ac 14:27 and had **g.** the church together,........ *4863*
Ac 15:30 had **g.** the multitude together,........ *4863*
Ac 17:5 **g.** a company, and set all the city........ *3792*
Ac 20:8 where there they were **g.** together..... *4863*
Ac 28:3 And when Paul had **g.** a bundle........ *4962*
1Co 5:4 when ye are **g.** together, and my........ *4863*
2Co 8:15 He that had **g.** much had nothing........
2Co 8:15 and he that had **g.** little had no lack........
Re 14:19 and **g.** the vine of the earth,........ *5166*
Re 16:16 And he **g.** them together into a........ *4863*
Re 19:19 and their armies, **g.** together to........ *4863*

GATHERER
Am 7:14 and a **g.** of sycomore fruit:........ 1103

GATHEREST
De 24:21 When thou **g.** the grapes of thy........ 1219

GATHERETH
Nu 19:10 he that **g.** the ashes of the heifer........ 622
Ps 33:7 he **g.** the waters of the sea........ 3664
Ps 41:6 his heart **g.** iniquity to itself;........ 6908
Ps 147:2 **g.** together the outcasts of Israel........ 3664
Pr 6:8 and **g.** her food in the harvest........ 103
Pr 10:5 He that **g.** in summer is a wise son:..... 103
Pr 13:11 but he that **g.** by labour shall........ 6908
Isa 10:14 and as one **g.** eggs that are left,........ 622
Isa 17:5 when the harvestman **g.** the corn,........ 622
Isa 17:5 as he that **g.** ears in the valley........ 3950
Isa 56:8 which **g.** the outcasts of Israel........ 6908
Na 3:18 mountains, and no man **g.** them........ 6908
Hab 2:5 but **g.** unto him all nations,........ 622
Mt 12:30 **he that g. not with me scattereth**.. *4863*
Mt 23:37 **even as a hen g. her chickens**........ *1996*
Lu 11:23 **he that g. not with me scattereth**.. *4863*
Joh 4:36 **and g. fruit unto life eternal:**........ *4863*

GATHERING See also GATHERINGS.
Ge 1:10 and the **g.** together of the waters........ 4723
Ge 49:10 him shall the **g.** of the people be........ 3349
Nu 15:33 they that found him **g.** sticks........ 7197
1Ki 17:10 widow woman was there **g.** of sticks:.. 7197
1Ki 17:12 and, behold, I am **g.** two sticks,........ 7197
2Ch 20:25 were three days in **g.** of the spoil,........ 962
Isa 32:10 shall fail, the **g.** shall not come........ 625
Isa 33:4 the gathering of the caterpiller:........ 625
Mt 25:24 **g. where thou hast not strawed:**.... *4863*
Ac 16:10 assuredly **g.** that the Lord had........ *4822*
2Th 2:1 by our **g.** together unto him,........ *1997*

GATHERINGS
1Co 16:2 that there be no **g.** when I come........ *3048*

GATH-HEPHER (gath-he'-fer) See also GITTAH-HEPHER.
2Ki 14:25 the prophet, which was of **G.**........ 1662

GATH-RIMMON (gath-rim'-mon)
Jos 19:45 Jehud, and Bene-berak, and **G.**,........ 1667
Jos 21:24 her suburbs, **G.** with her suburbs;........ 1667
Jos 21:25 suburbs, and **G.** with her suburbs;........ 1667
1Ch 6:69 suburbs, and **G.** with her suburbs:........ 1667

GAVE See also FORGAVE; GAVEST.
Ge 2:20 And Adam **g.** names to all cattle,........ 7121
Ge 3:6 and **g.** also unto her husband........ 5414
Ge 3:12 to be with me, she **g.** me of the tree,. 5414
Ge 14:20 And he **g.** him tithes of all........ 5414
Ge 16:3 **g.** her to her husband Abram to be..... 5414
Ge 18:7 and **g.** it unto a young man; and he.... 5414
Ge 20:14 and **g.** them unto Abraham, and........ 5414
Ge 21:14 and **g.** it unto Hagar, putting it on........ 5414
Ge 21:19 with water, and **g.** the lad drink........
Ge 21:27 and **g.** them unto Abimelech; and........ 5414
Ge 24:18 upon her hand, and **g.** him drink........
Ge 24:32 and **g.** straw and provender for........ 5414
Ge 24:53 and **g.** them to Rebekah: he **g.** also.... 5414
Ge 25:5 And Abraham **g.** all that he had........ 5414
Ge 25:6 Abraham **g.** gifts, and sent them........ 5414
Ge 25:8 Then Abraham **g.** up the ghost, and........
Ge 25:17 and he **g.** up the ghost and died;........
Ge 25:34 Jacob **g.** Esau bread and pottage........ 5414
Ge 27:17 And she **g.** the savoury meat and........ 5414
Ge 28:4 which God **g.** unto Abraham........ 5414
Ge 28:6 he **g.** him a charge, saying, Thou........
Ge 29:24 And Laban **g.** unto his daughter........ 5414
Ge 29:28 and he **g.** him Rachel his daughter........ 5414
Ge 29:29 Laban **g.** to Rachel his daughter........ 5414
Ge 30:4 she **g.** him Bilhah her handmaid........ 5414
Ge 30:9 and **g.** her Jacob to wife........ 5414
Ge 30:35 and **g.** them into the hand of his........ 5414
Ge 35:4 And they **g.** unto Jacob all the........ 5414
Ge 35:12 the land which I **g.** Abraham and........ 5414
Ge 35:29 And Isaac **g.** up the ghost, and died,........
Ge 38:18 And he **g.** it her, and came in unto..... 5414
Ge 38:26 I **g.** her not to Shelah my son........ 5414
Ge 39:21 and **g.** him favour in the sight of........ 5414
Ge 40:11 and I **g.** the cup into Pharaoh's........ 5414
Ge 40:21 and he **g.** the cup into Pharaoh's........ 5414
Ge 41:45 and he **g.** him to wife Asenath the........ 5414
Ge 43:24 **g.** them water, and they washed........ 5414
Ge 43:24 their feet; and he **g.** their asses........ 5414
Ge 45:21 Joseph **g.** them wagons, according........ 5414
Ge 45:21 and **g.** them provision for the way........ 5414
Ge 45:22 he **g.** each man changes of raiment;.... 5414
Ge 45:22 to Benjamin he **g.** three hundred........ 5414
Ge 46:18 Zilpah, whom Laban **g.** to Leah........ 5414
Ge 46:25 Bilhah, which Laban **g.** unto........ 5414
Ge 47:11 and **g.** them a possession in the........ 5414
Ge 47:17 Joseph **g.** them bread in exchange........ 5414
Ge 47:22 eat their portion which Pharaoh **g.**........ 5414
Ex 2:21 and he **g.** Moses Zipporah his........ 5414
Ex 6:13 and **g.** them a charge unto the........
Ex 11:3 And the Lord **g.** the people favour........ 5414
Ex 12:36 the Lord **g.** the people favour in........ 5414
Ex 14:20 but it **g.** light by night to these:........
Ex 31:18 And he **g.** unto Moses, when he........ 5414
Ex 32:24 So they **g.** it me: then I cast it........ 5414
Ex 34:32 and he **g.** them in commandment........
Ex 36:6 And Moses **g.** commandment, and........
Nu 3:51 And Moses **g.** the money of them........ 5414
Nu 7:6 and **g.** them unto the Levites........ 5414
Nu 7:7 four oxen he **g.** unto the sons of........ 5414
Nu 7:8 eight oxen he **g.** unto the sons of........ 5414
Nu 7:9 unto the sons of Kohath he **g.** none:... 5414
Nu 11:25 and **g.** it unto the seventy elders:........ 5414
Nu 17:6 every one of their princes **g.** him a..... 5414
Nu 27:23 and **g.** him a charge, as the Lord........
Nu 31:41 And Moses **g.** the tribute, which........ 5414
Nu 31:47 and **g.** them unto the Levites,........ 5414
Nu 32:33 And Moses **g.** unto them, even to........ 5414
Nu 32:38 and **g.** other names unto the cities........ 7121
Nu 32:40 And Moses **g.** Gilead unto Machir........ 5414
De 2:12 his possession, which the Lord **g.**........ 5414
De 3:12 the cities thereof, **g.** I unto the........ 5414

De 3:13 the kingdom of Og, **g.** I unto the 5414
De 3:15 And I **g.** Gilead unto Machir............. 5414
De 3:16 **g.** from Gilead even unto the river 5414
De 9:11 the Lord **g.** me the two tables........... 5414
De 10:4 and the Lord **g.** them unto me........... 5414
De 22:16 I **g.** my daughter unto this man......... 5414
De 29:8 and **g.** it for an inheritance unto......... 5414
De 31:23 And he **g.** Joshua the son of Nun charge,...
Jos 1:14 the land which Moses **g.** you on......... 5414
Jos 1:15 which Moses the Lord's servant **g.**..... 5414
Jos 11:23 and Joshua **g.** it for an inheritance 5414
Jos 12:6 Moses the servant of the Lord **g.**....... 5414
Jos 12:7 which Joshua **g.** unto the tribes........... 5414
Jos 13:8 their inheritance, which Moses **g.**........ 5414
Jos 13:8 Moses the servant of the Lord **g.**....... 5414
Jos 13:14 tribe of Levi he **g.** none inheritance; ... 5414
Jos 13:15 And Moses **g.** unto the tribe of the 5414
Jos 13:24 **g.** inheritance unto the tribe of Gad, ... 5414
Jos 13:29 **g.** inheritance unto the half tribe of..... 5414
Jos 13:33 the tribe of Levi Moses **g.** not any..... 5414
Jos 14:3 but unto the Levites he **g.** none......... 5414
Jos 14:4 they **g.** no part unto the Levites 5414
Jos 14:13 and **g.** unto Caleb the son of.............. 5414
Jos 15:13 Caleb, the son of Jephunneh he **g.**....... 5414
Jos 15:17 and he **g.** him Achsah his daughter..... 5414
Jos 15:19 And he **g.** her the upper springs, ... 5414
Jos 17:4 he **g.** them an inheritance among........ 5414
Jos 18:7 the servant of the Lord **g.** them.......... 5414
Jos 19:49 children of Israel **g.** an inheritance...... 5414
Jos 19:50 they **g.** him the city which he asked,... 5414
Jos 21:3 of Israel **g.** unto the Levites out of..... 5414
Jos 21:8 And the children of Israel **g.** by lot..... 5414
Jos 21:9 And they **g.** out of the tribe of the 5414
Jos 21:11 And they **g.** them the city of Arba...... 5414
Jos 21:12 villages thereof, **g.** they to Caleb......... 5414
Jos 21:13 they **g.** to the children of Aaron.......... 5414
Jos 21:21 For they **g.** them Shechem with her ... 5414
Jos 21:27 tribe of Manasseh they **g.** Golan in..........
Jos 21:43 And the Lord **g.** unto Israel all 5414
Jos 21:44 Lord **g.** them rest round about,................
Jos 22:4 the servant of the Lord **g.** you 5414
Jos 22:7 **g.** Joshua among their brethren on...... 5414
Jos 24:3 his seed, and **g.** him Isaac. 5414
Jos 24:4 I **g.** unto Isaac Jacob and Esau;.......... 5414
Jos 24:4 and I **g.** unto Esau mount Seir,.......... 5414
Jos 24:8 and I **g.** them into your hand,............. 5414
Jg 1:13 and he **g.** him Achsah his daughter 5414
Jg 1:15 And Caleb **g.** her the upper springs 5414
Jg 1:20 And they **g.** Hebron unto Caleb, as..... 5414
Jg 3:6 and **g.** their daughters to their sons, ... 5414
Jg 4:19 bottle of milk, and **g.** him drink,...............
Jg 5:25 water, and she **g.** him milk; 5414
Jg 6:9 and **g.** you their land; 5414
Jg 9:4 **g.** him threescore and ten pieces........ 5414
Jg 14:9 and he **g.** them, and they did eat: 5414
Jg 14:19 **g.** change of garments unto them 5414
Jg 15:2 I **g.** her to thy companion: 5414
Jg 17:4 and **g.** them to the founder, who........ 5414
Jg 19:21 and **g.** provender unto the asses: and........
Jg 20:36 for the men of Israel **g.** place to 5414
Jg 21:14 and they **g.** them wives which they..... 5414
Ru 2:18 and **g.** to her that she had reserved.... 5414
Ru 3:17 six measures of barley **g.** he me; 5414
Ru 4:7 his shoe, and **g.** it to his neighbour:.... 5414
Ru 4:13 her, the Lord **g.**, her conception, ... 5414
Ru 4:17 her neighbours **g.** it a name, ... 7121
1Sa 1:4 he **g.** to Peninnah his wife, and to..... 5414
1Sa 1:5 Hannah he **g.** a worthy portion; 5414
1Sa 1:23 and **g.** her son suck until she weaned........
1Sa 9:23 Bring the portion which I **g.** thee, ... 5414
1Sa 10:9 Samuel, God **g.** him another heart: ....
1Sa 18:4 that was upon him, and **g.** it............. 5414
1Sa 18:27 and they **g.** them in full tale to the king.....
1Sa 18:27 Saul **g.** him Michal his daughter 5414
1Sa 20:40 And Jonathan **g.** his artillery unto 5414
1Sa 21:6 the priest **g.** him hallowed bread: 5414
1Sa 22:10 **g.** him victuals, and **g.** him the 5414
1Sa 27:6 Achish **g.** him Ziklag that day: 5414
1Sa 30:11 and **g.** him bread, and he did eat;....... 5414
1Sa 30:12 they **g.** him a piece of a cake of figs, .. 5414
2Sa 12:8 And I **g.** thee thy master's house, ... 5414
2Sa 12:8 and **g.** thee the house of Israel......... 5414
2Sa 18:5 the king **g.** all the captains charge.............
2Sa 24:9 And Joab **g.** up the sum of the........... 5414
1Ki 4:29 And God **g.** Solomon wisdom and....... 5414
1Ki 5:10 Hiram **g.** Solomon cedar trees and...... 5414
1Ki 5:11 And Solomon **g.** Hiram twenty........... 5414
1Ki 5:11 **g.** Solomon to Hiram year by year...... 5414
1Ki 5:12 the Lord **g.** Solomon wisdom, as........ 5414
1Ki 9:11 Solomon **g.** Hiram twenty cities 5414
1Ki 10:10 And she **g.** the king an hundred......... 5414
1Ki 10:10 queen of Sheba **g.** to king Solomon..... 5414
1Ki 10:13 king Solomon **g.** unto the queen of 5414
1Ki 10:13 Solomon **g.** her of his royal bounty. 5414
1Ki 11:18 of Egypt; which **g.** him an house, ... 5414
1Ki 11:18 him victuals, and **g.** him land. 5414
1Ki 11:19 that he **g.** him to wife the sister 5414
1Ki 12:13 men's counsel that they **g.** him; 3289
1Ki 13:3 And he **g.** a sign the same day, ... 5414
1Ki 14:8 the house of David, and **g.** it thee: 5414
1Ki 14:15 land which he **g.** to their fathers, ... 5414
1Ki 19:21 and **g.** unto the people, and they....... 5414
2Ki 10:15 And he **g.** him his hand; and he 5414
2Ki 11:12 upon him, and **g.** him the testimony;.........
2Ki 12:11 And they **g.** the money, being told, ... 5414
2Ki 12:14 But they **g.** that to the workmen,....... 5414
2Ki 13:5 (And the Lord **g.** Israel a saviour, ... 5414
2Ki 15:19 and Menahem **g.** Pul a thousand......... 5414
2Ki 17:3 his servant, and **g.** him presents. 7725
2Ki 18:15 And Hezekiah **g.** him all the silver...... 5414
2Ki 18:16 and **g.** it to the king of Assyria. 5414
2Ki 21:8 land which I **g.** their fathers;............. 5414
2Ki 22:8 Hilkiah **g.** the book to Shaphan, ... 5414
2Ki 23:35 Jehoiakim **g.** the silver and the.......... 5414
2Ki 25:6 and they **g.** judgment upon him. 1696
1Ch 2:35 Sheshan **g.** his daughter to Jarha 5414
1Ch 6:55 they **g.** them Hebron in the land 5414
1Ch 6:56 they **g.** to Caleb the son of.............. 5414
1Ch 6:57 Aaron they **g.** the cities of Judah, ... 5414
1Ch 6:64 of Israel **g.** to the Levites................. 5414
1Ch 6:65 And they **g.** by lot out of the tribe 5414
1Ch 6:67 And they **g.** unto them, of the cities ... 5414
1Ch 6:67 **g.** also Gezer with her suburbs,...............
1Ch 14:12 David **g.** a commandment, and they ....
1Ch 21:5 Joab **g.** the sum of the number 5414
1Ch 21:25 So David **g.** to Ornan for the place..... 5414
1Ch 25:5 God **g.** to Heman fourteen sons 5414
1Ch 28:11 Then David **g.** to Solomon his son...... 5414
1Ch 28:14 He **g.** of gold by weight for things............
1Ch 28:16 he **g.** gold for the tables of ....
1Ch 28:17 for the gold basons he **g.** gold by ....
1Ch 29:7 **g.** for the service of the house 5414
1Ch 29:8 precious stones were found **g.** them.... 5414
2Ch 9:9 And she **g.** the king an hundred......... 5414
2Ch 9:9 queen of Sheba **g.** king Solomon......... 5414
2Ch 9:12 Solomon **g.** to the queen of Sheba 5414
2Ch 10:8 counsel which the old men **g.** him,...... 3289
2Ch 11:23 he **g.** them victual in abundance. 5414
2Ch 13:5 God of Israel **g.** the kingdom over...... 5414
2Ch 13:15 Then the men of Judah **g.** a shout: ....
2Ch 15:15 and the Lord **g.** them rest round about......
2Ch 20:30 for his God **g.** him rest round about..........
2Ch 21:3 their father **g.** them great gifts 5414
2Ch 21:3 but the kingdom **g.** he to Jehoram; 5414
2Ch 23:11 the crown, and **g.** him the testimony,........
2Ch 24:12 And the king and Jehoiada **g.** it 5414
2Ch 26:8 the Ammonites **g.** gifts to Uzziah: 5414
2Ch 27:5 And the children of Ammon **g.** him 5414
2Ch 28:15 and **g.** them to eat and to drink, ...
2Ch 28:21 and **g.** it unto the king of Assyria: 5414
2Ch 30:7 therefore **g.** them up to desolation, ... 5414
2Ch 30:24 the princes **g.** to the congregation 7311
2Ch 32:24 unto him, and he **g.** him a sign. 5414
2Ch 34:10 and they **g.** it to the workmen........... 5414
2Ch 34:11 artificers and builders **g.** they it, ... 5414
2Ch 35:7 And Josiah **g.** to the people, of the..... 7311
2Ch 35:8 **g.** willingly unto the people, ... 7311
2Ch 35:8 **g.** unto the priests for the passover.... 5414
2Ch 35:9 of the Levites, **g.** unto the Levites..... 7311
2Ch 36:17 he **g.** them all into his hand.............. 5414
Ezr 2:69 They **g.** after their ability unto........... 5414
Ezr 3:7 **g.** money also unto the masons,......... 5414
Ezr 5:12 he **g.** them into the hand of.............. 3052
Ezr 7:11 the king Artaxerxes **g.** unto Ezra 5414
Ezr 10:19 And they **g.** their hands that they....... 5414
Ne 2:1 I took up the wine, and **g.** it 5414
Ne 2:9 river, and **g.** them the king's letters.... 5414
Ne 7:2 That I **g.** my brother Hanani,...charge.......
Ne 7:70 of the fathers **g.** unto the work.......... 5414
Ne 7:70 The Tirshatha **g.** to the treasure 5414
Ne 7:71 the chief of the fathers **g.** to the 5414
Ne 7:72 which the rest of the people **g.**.......... 5414
Ne 8:8 God distinctly, and **g.** the sense, ... 7760
Ne 12:31 companies of them that **g.** thanks, ...
Ne 12:38 other company of them that **g.** thanks.......
Ne 12:40 companies of them that **g.** thanks............
Ne 12:47 **g.** the portions of the singers 5414
Es 1:7 And they **g.** them drink in vessels of.........
Es 2:9 and he speedily **g.** her things for........ 5414
Es 2:18 and **g.** gifts, according to the state 5414
Es 3:10 his hand, and **g.** it unto Haman 5414
Es 4:5 and **g.** him a commandment to.................
Es 4:8 he **g.** him the copy of the writing....... 5414
Es 4:10 and **g.** him commandment unto..................
Es 8:2 Haman, and **g.** it unto Mordecai......... 5414
Job 1:21 Lord **g.**, and the Lord hath taken....... 5414
Job 19:16 servant, and he **g.** me no answer; ....
Job 29:11 the eye saw me, it **g.** witness to me:........
Job 29:21 Unto me men **g.** ear, and waited,.............
Job 32:11 I **g.** ear to your reasons, whilst..............
Job 42:10 also the Lord **g.** Job twice as much..... 3254
Job 42:11 man also **g.** him a piece of money, ... 5414
Job 42:15 their father **g.** them inheritance.......... 5414
Ps 18:13 and the Highest **g.** his voice;............ 5414
Ps 68:11 The Lord **g.** the word: great was....... 5414
Ps 69:21 They **g.** me also gall for my meat;...... 5414
Ps 69:21 in my thirst they **g.** me vinegar to drink. ...
Ps 77:1 and he **g.** ear unto me. ....
Ps 78:15 and **g.** them drink as out of the great........
Ps 78:29 for he **g.** them their own desire;.......... 935
Ps 78:46 He **g.** also their increase unto the 5414
Ps 78:48 **g.** up their cattle also to the hail, ... 5462
Ps 78:50 **g.** their life over to the pestilence; 5462
Ps 78:62 **g.** his people over also unto the......... 5462
Ps 81:12 So I **g.** them up unto their own 7971
Ps 99:7 the ordinance that he **g.** them............ 5414
Ps 105:32 **g.** them hail for rain, and flaming........ 5414
Ps 105:44 **g.** them the lands of the heathen:........ 5414
Ps 106:15 And he **g.** them their request; 5414
Ps 106:41 he **g.** them into the hand of the 5414
Ps 135:12 And **g.** their land for an heritage, ... 5414
Ps 136:21 And **g.** their land for an heritage: 5414
Pr 8:29 When he **g.** to the sea his decree,...... 7760
Ec 1:13 **g.** my heart to seek and search 5414
Ec 1:17 I **g.** my heart to know wisdom,........... 5414
Ec 12:7 spirit shall return unto God who **g.**...... 5414
Ec 12:9 yea, he **g.** good heed, and sought............
Ca 5:6 him, but he **g.** me no answer. ....
Isa 41:2 **g.** the nations before him, and........... 5414
Isa 41:2 **g.** them as the dust to his sword, ... 5414
Isa 42:24 Who **g.** Jacob for a spoil, and............. 5414
Isa 43:3 I **g.** Egypt for thy ransom,................ 5414
Isa 50:6 I **g.** my back to the smiters, ... 5414
Jer 7:7 the land that I **g.** to your fathers,....... 5414
Jer 7:14 the place which I **g.** to you and to...... 5414
Jer 16:15 land that I **g.** unto their fathers.......... 5414
Jer 17:4 from thine heritage that I **g.** thee; 5414
Jer 23:39 that I **g.** you and your fathers,............ 5414
Jer 24:10 the land that I **g.** unto them and to..... 5414
Jer 30:3 the land that I **g.** to their fathers,........ 5414
Jer 32:12 I **g.** the evidence of the purchase 5414
Jer 36:32 and **g.** it to Baruch the scribe............. 5414
Jer 39:5 where he **g.** judgment upon him. 1696
Jer 39:10 and **g.** them vineyards and fields 5414
Jer 39:11 king of Babylon **g.** charge ....
Jer 40:5 the captain of the guard **g.** him........... 5414
Jer 44:30 as I **g.** Zedekiah king of Judah............ 5414
Jer 52:9 where he **g.** judgment upon him. 1696
La 1:19 and mine elders **g.** up the ghost...............
Eze 16:19 My meat also which I **g.** thee,............ 5414
Eze 20:11 And I **g.** them my statutes, and......... 5414
Eze 20:12 also I **g.** them my sabbaths, ... 5414
Eze 20:25 Wherefore I **g.** them also statutes 5414
Eze 36:28 the land that I **g.** to your fathers;....... 5414
Eze 39:23 and **g.** them into the hand of their...... 5414
Da 1:2 And the Lord **g.** Jehoiakim king of...... 5414
Da 1:7 prince of the eunuchs **g.** names:......... 7760
Da 1:7 for he **g.** unto Daniel the name 7760
Da 1:16 should drink; and **g.** them pulse. 5414
Da 1:17 God **g.** them knowledge and skill........ 5414
Da 2:48 and **g.** him many great gifts, and........ 3052
Da 5:18 most high God **g.** Nebuchadnezzar...... 3052
Da 5:19 for the majesty that he **g.** him, ... 3052
Da 6:10 and **g.** thanks before his God, as he did.....
Ho 2:8 I **g.** her corn, and wine, and oil, ... 5414
Ho 13:11 I **g.** thee a king in mine anger, ... 5414
Am 2:12 ye **g.** the Nazarites wine to drink; ....
Mal 2:5 and I **g.** them to him for the fear 5414
Mt 8:18 he **g.** commandment to depart *2753*
Mt 10:1 **g.** them power against unclean........... *1325*
Mt 14:19 and **g.** the loaves to his disciples,....... *1325*

Mt 15:36 and **g.** thanks, and brake them,... *1325*
Mt 15:36 and **g.** to his disciples,... *1325*
Mt 21:23 who **g.** thee this authority?... *1325*
Mt 25:15 **unto one he g. five talents, to**... *1325*
Mt 25:35 **an hungred, and ye g. me meat:**... *1325*
Mt 25:35 **was thirsty, and ye g. me drink:**... *4222*
Mt 25:37 **or thirsty, and g. thee drink?**... *4222*
Mt 25:42 **an hungred, and ye g. me no meat:** *1325*
Mt 25:42 **thirsty, and ye g. me no drink:**... *4222*
Mt 26:26 brake it, and **g.** it to the disciples,... *1325*
Mt 26:27 **g.** thanks, and **g.** it to them, saying,... *1325*
Mt 26:48 that betrayed him **g.** them a sign,... *1325*
Mt 27:10 and **g.** them for the potter's field,... *1325*
Mt 27:34 **g.** him vinegar to drink mingled... *1325*
Mt 27:48 on a reed, and **g.** him to drink... *4222*
Mt 28:12 **g.** large money unto the soldiers,... *1325*
Mk 2:26 **g. also to them which were with**... *1325*
Mk 5:13 forthwith Jesus **g.** them leave... *2010*
Mk 6:7 and **g.** them power over unclean... *1325*
Mk 6:28 a charger, and **g.** it to the damsel:... *1325*
Mk 6:28 and the damsel **g.** it to her mother... *1325*
Mk 6:41 **g.** them to his disciples to set... *1325*
Mk 8:6 loaves and **g.** thanks, and brake,... *1325*
Mk 8:6 and **g.** to his disciples to set before... *1325*
Mk 11:28 who **g.** thee this authority to do... *1325*
Mk 13:34 **and g. authority to his servants,**... *1325*
Mk 14:22 brake it, and **g.** to them, and said,... *1325*
Mk 14:23 had given thanks, he **g.** it to them:... *1325*
Mk 15:23 And they **g.** him to drink wine... *1325*
Mk 15:36 and **g.** him to drink, saying, Let... *4222*
Mk 15:37 with a loud voice, and **g.** up the ghost,...
Mk 15:39 so cried out, and **g.** up the ghost,...
Mk 15:45 he **g.** the body to Joseph... *1433*
Lu 2:38 **g.** thanks likewise unto the Lord,... *437*
Lu 4:20 he **g.** it again to the minister, and... *591*
Lu 6:4 **g. also to them that were with**... *1325*
Lu 7:21 many that were blind he **g.** sight... *5483*
Lu 9:1 **g.** them power and authority over... *1325*
Lu 9:16 **g.** to the disciples to set before the... *1325*
Lu 10:35 **two pence, and g. them to the host.** *1325*
Lu 15:16 **and no man g. unto him**... *1325*
Lu 18:43 they saw it, **g.** praise unto God... *1325*
Lu 20:2 who is he that **g.** thee this authority?... *1325*
Lu 22:17 **g.** thanks, and said, **Take this,**...
Lu 22:19 and **g.** thanks, and brake it,...
Lu 22:19 and **g.** unto them, saying, **This is**... *1325*
Lu 23:24 Pilate **g.** sentence that it should be...
Lu 23:29 **and the paps which never g. suck**...
Lu 23:46 having said thus, he **g.** up the ghost...
Lu 24:30 blessed it, and brake and **g.** to them,... *1929*
Lu 24:42 they **g.** him a piece of a broiled fish,... *1929*
Joh 1:12 **g.** he power to become the sons... *1325*
Joh 3:16 **that he g. his only begotten Son,**... *1325*
Joh 4:5 that Jacob **g.** to his son Joseph... *1325*
Joh 4:12 Father Jacob, which **g.** us the well,... *1325*
Joh 6:31 **g.** them bread from heaven to eat... *1325*
Joh 6:32 **Moses g. you not that bread from**... *1325*
Joh 7:22 **Moses... g. unto you circumcision;**... *1325*
Joh 10:29 **Father, which g. them me, is**... *1325*
Joh 12:49 **he g. me a commandment, what I**... *1325*
Joh 13:26 the sop, he **g.** it to Judas Iscariot,... *1325*
Joh 14:31 **Father g. me commandment, even**... *1781*
Joh 18:14 Caiaphas was he, which **g.** counsel... *4823*
Joh 19:9 thou? But Jesus **g.** him no answer... *1325*
Joh 19:30 his head, and **g.** up the ghost... *3860*
Joh 19:38 and Pilate **g.** him leave. He came... *2010*
Ac 1:26 they **g.** forth their lots; and the lot... *1325*
Ac 2:4 as the Spirit **g.** them utterance... *1325*
Ac 3:5 he **g.** heed unto them, expecting to... *1907*
Ac 4:33 **g.** the apostles witness of the... *591*
Ac 5:5 fell down, and **g.** up the ghost:...
Ac 7:5 he **g.** him none inheritance in it,... *1325*
Ac 7:8 **g.** him the covenant of circumcision:... *1325*
Ac 7:10 **g.** him favour and wisdom in the... *1325*
Ac 7:42 **g.** them up to worship the host of... *3860*
Ac 8:6 **g.** heed unto these things which... *4337*
Ac 8:10 To whom they all **g.** heed, from the... *4337*
Ac 9:41 he **g.** her his hand, and lifted her... *1325*
Ac 10:2 which **g.** much alms to the people,... *4160*
Ac 11:17 God **g.** them the like gift as he did... *1325*
Ac 12:22 And the people **g.** a shout, saying,...
Ac 12:23 because he **g.** not God the glory:... *1325*
Ac 12:23 eaten of worms, and **g.** up the ghost...
Ac 13:20 after that he **g.** unto them judges... *1325*
Ac 13:21 God **g.** unto them Saul the son of... *1325*
Ac 13:22 to whom also he **g.** testimony, and... *3140*
Ac 14:3 which **g.** testimony unto the word... *3140*
Ac 14:17 and **g.** us rain from heaven, and... *1325*
Ac 15:12 **g.** audience to Barnabas and...
Ac 15:24 we **g.** no such commandment:... *1291*
Ac 22:22 **g.** him audience unto this word,...
Ac 23:30 **g.** commandment to his accusers...
Ac 26:10 I **g.** my voice against them... *2702*
Ac 27:3 **g.** him liberty to go unto his... *2010*
Ac 27:35 **g.** thanks to God in presence of them...
Ro 1:24 Wherefore God also **g.** them up to... *3860*
Ro 1:26 **g.** them up unto vile affections:... *3860*
Ro 1:28 God **g.** them over to a reprobate... *3860*
1Co 3:5 even as the Lord **g.** to every man?... *1325*
1Co 3:6 but God **g.** the increase...
2Co 8:5 **g.** their own selves to the Lord,... *1325*
Ga 1:4 Who **g.** himself for our sins, that... *1325*
Ga 2:5 whom we **g.** place by subjection,... *1502*
Ga 2:9 **g.** to me and Barnabas the right... *1325*
Ga 2:20 loved me, and **g.** himself for me... *3860*
Ga 3:18 God **g.** it to Abraham by promise... *5483*
Eph 1:22 **g.** him to be the head over all... *1325*
Eph 4:8 captive, and **g.** gifts unto men... *1325*
Eph 4:11 he **g.** some, apostles; and some,... *1325*
Eph 5:25 the church, and **g.** himself for it;... *3860*
1Th 4:2 we **g.** you by the Lord Jesus... *1325*
1Ti 2:6 Who **g.** himself a ransom for all,... *1325*
Tit 2:14 Who **g.** himself for us, that he might... *1325*
Heb 7:2 Abraham **g.** a tenth part of all;...
Heb 7:4 Abraham **g.** the tenth of the spoils,... *1325*
Heb 7:13 no man **g.** attendance at the altar,... *4337*
Heb 11:22 **g.** commandment concerning his...
Heb 12:9 we **g.** them reverence: shall we not... *1788*
Jas 5:18 the heaven **g.** rain, and the earth... *1325*
1Pe 1:21 from the dead, and **g.** him glory;... *1325*
1Jo 3:23 another as he **g.** us commandment... *1325*
1Jo 5:10 the record that God **g.** of his Son... *3140*
Jude 3 when I **g.** all diligence to write... *4160*
Re 1:1 which God **g.** unto him, to shew... *1325*
Re 2:21 **I g. her space to repent of her**... *1325*
Re 11:13 and **g.** glory to the God of heaven... *1325*
Re 13:2 the dragon **g.** him his power,... *1325*
Re 13:4 which **g.** power unto the beast:... *1325*
Re 15:7 **g.** unto the seven angels seven... *1325*
Re 20:13 sea **g.** up the dead which were in it;... *1325*

GAVEST See also FORGAVEST.
Ge 3:12 woman whom thou **g.** to be with... 5414
1Ki 8:34 unto the land which thou **g.** unto... 5414
1Ki 8:40 in the land which thou **g.** unto our... 5414
1Ki 8:48 their land, which thou **g.** unto their... 5414
2Ch 6:25 the land which thou **g.** to them... 5414
2Ch 6:31 in the land which thou **g.** unto our... 5414
2Ch 6:38 toward their land, which thou **g.**... 5414
2Ch 20:7 and **g.** it to the seed of Abraham... 5414
Ne 9:7 and **g.** him the name of Abraham;... 7760
Ne 9:13 **g.** them right judgments, and true... 5414
Ne 9:15 **g.** them bread from heaven for... 5414
Ne 9:20 **g.** also thy good spirit to instruct... 5414
Ne 9:20 and **g.** them water for their thirst... 5414
Ne 9:22 thou **g.** them kingdoms and nations,... 5414
Ne 9:24 **g.** them into their hands, with their... 5414
Ne 9:27 **g.** them saviours, who saved them... 5414
Ne 9:30 therefore **g.** thou them into the hand... 5414
Ne 9:35 great goodness that thou **g.** them,... 5414
Ne 9:35 fat land which thou **g.** before them... 5414
Ne 9:36 land that thou **g.** unto our fathers... 5414
Job 39:13 **G.** thou the goodly wings unto...
Ps 21:4 life of thee, and thou **g.** it him,... 5414
Ps 74:14 **g.** him to be meat to the people... 5414
Lu 7:44 **g. me no water for my feet:**... *1325*
Lu 7:45 **Thou g. me no kiss: but this**... *1325*
Lu 15:29 **and yet thou never g. me a kid,**... *1325*
Lu 19:23 **Wherefore then g. thou not my**... *1325*
Joh 17:4 **the work which thou g. me to do**... *1325*
Joh 17:6 **which thou g. me out of the world:** *1325*
Joh 17:6 **they were, and thou g. them me:**... *1325*
Joh 17:8 **them the words which thou g. me;** *1325*
Joh 17:12 **those that thou g. me I have kept,** *1325*
Joh 17:22 **glory which thou g. me I have**... *1325*
Joh 18:9 which thou **g.** me have I lost none... *1325*

GAY
Jas 2:3 the **g.** clothing, and say unto him,... *2986*

GAZA (ga'-zah) See also AZZAH; GAZITES.
Ge 10:19 as thou comest to Gerar, unto **G.**;... 5804
Jos 10:41 from Kadesh-barnea even unto **G.**,... 5804
Jos 11:22 only in **G.**, in Gath, and in Ashdod,... 5804
Jos 15:47 **G.** with her towns and her villages,... 5804
Jg 1:18 Also Judah took **G.** with the coast... 5804
Jg 6:4 till thou come unto **G.**; and left no... 5804
Jg 16:1 Then went Samson to **G.**, and saw... 5804
Jg 16:21 and brought him down to **G.**, and... 5804
1Sa 6:17 for Ashdod one, for **G.** one, for... 5804
2Ki 18:8 the Philistines, even unto **G.**,... 5804
1Ch 7:28 unto **G.** and the towns thereof:... 5804
Jer 47:1 before that Pharaoh smote **G.**... 5804
Jer 47:5 is come upon **G.**; Ashkelon is cut... 5804
Am 1:6 transgressions of **G.**, and for four,... 5804
Am 1:7 will send a fire on the wall of **G.**,... 5804
Zep 2:4 For **G.** shall be forsaken, and... 5804
Zec 9:5 **G.** also shall see it, and be very... 5804
Zec 9:5 and the king shall perish from **G.**,... 5804
Ac 8:26 down from Jerusalem unto **G.**,... *1048*

GAZATHITES (ga'-zath-ites) See also GAZITES.
Jos 13:3 lords of the Philistines; the **G.**,... 5841

GAZE See also GAZING.
Ex 19:21 break through unto the Lord to **g.**,... 7200

GAZER (ga'-zur) See also GEZER.
2Sa 5:25 from Geba until thou come to **G.**... 1507
1Ch 14:16 Philistines from Gibeon even to **G.**... 1507

GAZERS See STARGAZERS.

GAZEZ (ga'-zez)
1Ch 2:46 Moza, and **G.**: and Haran begat **G.**... 1495

GAZING See also GAZINGSTOCK.
Ac 1:11 why stand ye **g.** up into heaven?... *1689*

GAZINGSTOCK
Na 3:6 and will set thee as a **g.**... 7210
Heb 10:33 whilst ye were made a **g.** both by... *2301*

GAZITES (ga'-zites) See also GAZATHITES.
Jg 16:2 it was told the **G.**, saying, Samson... 5841

GAZZAM (gaz'-zam)
Ezr 2:48 of Nekoda, the children of **G.**,... 1502
Ne 7:51 The children of **G.**, the children of... 1502

GEBA (ghe'-bah) See also GABA; GIBEAH; GIBEON.
Jos 21:17 her suburbs, **G.** with her suburbs,... 1387
1Sa 13:3 of the Philistines that was in **G.**,... 1387
2Sa 5:25 Philistines from **G.** until thou come... 1387
1Ki 15:22 built with them **G.** of Benjamin,... 1387
2Ki 23:8 incense, from **G.** to Beer-sheba, and... 1387
1Ch 6:60 Benjamin; **G.** with her suburbs,... 1387
1Ch 8:6 fathers of the inhabitants of **G.**,... 1387
2Ch 16:6 he built therewith **G.** and Mizpah... 1387
Ne 11:31 of Benjamin from **G.** dwelt at... 1387
Ne 12:29 Gilgal, and out of the fields of **G.**... 1387
Isa 10:29 have taken up their lodging at **G.**;... 1387
Zec 14:10 turned as a plain from **G.** to... 1387

GEBAL (ghe'-bal) See also GIBLITES.
Ps 83:7 **G.**, and Ammon, and Amalek; the... 1381
Eze 27:9 The ancients of **G.** and the wise... 1381

GEBER See also EZION-GEBER.
1Ki 4:13 The son of **G.**, in Ramoth-gilead;... 1398
1Ki 4:19 **G.** the son Uri was in the country... 1398

GEBIM (ghe'-bim)
Isa 10:31 the inhabitants of **G.** gather... 1374

GEDALIAH (ghed-a-li'-ah)
2Ki 25:22 **G.** the son of Ahikam, the son of... 1436
2Ki 25:23 **G.** governor, there came to **G.** to... 1436
2Ki 25:24 **G.** sware to them, and to their men,... 1436
2Ki 25:25 smote **G.**, that he died, and the... 1436
1Ch 25:3 sons of Jeduthun; **G.**, and Zeri,... 1436
1Ch 25:9 the second to **G.**, who with his... 1436
Ezr 10:18 and Eliezer, and Jarib, and **G.**... 1436
Jer 38:1 **G.** the son of Pashur, and Jucal the... 1436
Jer 39:14 committed him unto **G.** the son of... 1436
Jer 40:5 Go back to **G.** the son of Ahikam... 1436
Jer 40:6 **G.** the son of Ahikam to Mizpah;... 1436
Jer 40:7 had made **G.** the son of Ahikam... 1436
Jer 40:8 came to **G.** to Mizpah, even Ishmael... 1436
Jer 40:9 And **G.** the son of Ahikam the son... 1436
Jer 40:11 over them **G.** the son of Ahikam... 1436
Jer 40:12 Judah, to **G.**, unto Mizpah, and... 1436
Jer 40:13 that were in the fields, came to **G.**... 1436
Jer 40:14 But **G.** the son of Ahikam believed... 1436
Jer 40:15 spake to **G.** in Mizpah secretly,... 1436
Jer 40:16 **G.** the son of Ahikam said unto... 1436
Jer 41:1 ten men with him, came unto **G.** the... 1436
Jer 41:2 smote **G.** the son of Ahikam the... 1436

Jer 41:3 even with **G.**, at Mizpah, and the 1436
Jer 41:4 second day after he had slain **G.**, 1436
Jer 41:6 unto them, Come to **G.**, the son of 1436
Jer 41:9 had slain because of **G.**, was it 1436
Jer 41:10 committed to **G.** the son of Ahikam; 1436
Jer 41:16 slain **G.** the son of Ahikam, even 1436
Jer 41:18 of Nehemiah had slain **G.** the son of 1436
Jer 43:6 guard had left with **G.** the son of 1436
Zep 1:1 Cushi, the son of **G.**, the son of 1436

GEDEON (ghed'-e-on) See also GIDEON.
He 11:32 time would fail me to tell of **G.**, *1066*

GEDER (ghe'-dur) See also BETH-GADER; GEDERITE; GEDOR.
Jos 12:13 Debir, one; the king of **G.**, one; 1445

GEDERAH (ghed'-e-rah) See also GEDERATHITE.
Jos 15:36 and Adithaim, and **G.**, and 1449

GEDERATHITE (ghed'-e-rath-ite)
1Ch 12:4 Johanan, and Josabad the **G.**, 1452

GEDERITE (ghed'-e-rite)
1Ch 27:28 low plains was Baal-hanan the **G.**: 1451

GEDEROTH (ghed'-e-roth)
Jos 15:41 And **G.**, Beth-dagon, and Naamah, 1450
2Ch 28:18 Ajalon, and **G.**, and Shocho with the 1450

GEDEROTHAIM (ghed-e-ro-tha'-im)
Jos 15:36 Adithaim, and Gederah, and **G.**; 1453

GEDI See EN-GEDI.

GEDOR (ghe'-dor) See also GEDER.
Jos 15:58 Halhul, Beth-zur, and **G.**, 1446
1Ch 4:4 Penuel the father of **G.**, Ezer the 1446
1Ch 4:18 Jered the father of **G.**, and Heber 1446
1Ch 4:39 entrance of **G.**, even unto the east 1446
1Ch 8:31 And **G.**, and Ahio, and Zacher 1446
1Ch 9:37 **G.**, and Ahio, and Zechariah, and 1446
1Ch 12:7 the sons of Jeroham of **G.** 1446

GEHAZI (ghe-ha'-zi)
2Ki 4:12 said to **G.** his servant, Call this 1522
2Ki 4:14 **G.** answered, Verily she hath no 1522
2Ki 4:25 to **G.** his servant, Behold, yonder is 1522
2Ki 4:27 **G.** came near to thrust her away 1522
2Ki 4:29 said to **G.**, Gird up thy loins, and 1522
2Ki 4:31 And **G.** passed on before them, 1522
2Ki 4:36 And he called **G.**, and said, Call 1522
2Ki 5:20 But **G.**, the servant of Elisha the 1522
2Ki 5:21 So **G.** followed after Naaman 1522
2Ki 5:25 Whence comest thou, **G.**? And he 1522
2Ki 8:4 **G.** the servant of the man of God, 1522
2Ki 8:5 **G.** said, My lord, O king, this is the 1522

GELILOTH (ghel'-il-oth)
Jos 18:17 went forth toward **G.**, which is 1553

GEMALLI (ghe-mal'-li)
Nu 13:12 of Dan, Ammiel the son of **G.** 1582

GEMARIAH (ghem-a-ri'-ah)
Jer 29:3 and **G.** the son of Hilkiah, (whom 1587
Jer 36:10 in the chamber of **G.** the son of 1587
Jer 36:11 Michaiah the son of **G.**, the son of 1587
Jer 36:12 Elnathan the son of Achbor, and **G.** 1587
Jer 36:25 Elnathan and Delaiah and **G.** had 1587

GENDER See also GENDERED; GENDERETH.
Le 19:19 Thou shalt not let thy cattle **g.** 7250
2Ti 2:23 knowing that they do **g.** strifes *1080*

GENDERED
Job 38:29 frost of heaven, who hath **g.** it? 3205

GENDERETH
Job 21:10 Their bull **g.**, and faileth not; 5674
Ga 4:24 **g.** to bondage, which is Agar *1080*

GENEALOGIES
1Ch 5:17 All these were reckoned by **g.** in 3187
1Ch 7:5 reckoned in all by their **g.** 3187
1Ch 7:7 and were reckoned by their **g.** 3187
1Ch 9:1 all Israel were reckoned by **g.**; 3187
2Ch 12:15 and of Iddo the seer concerning **g.**? 3187
2Ch 31:19 to all that were reckoned by **g.** 3187
1Ti 1:4 give heed to fables and endless **g.**, *1076*
Tit 3:9 But avoid foolish questions, and **g.**, *1076*

GENEALOGY See also GENEALOGIES.
1Ch 4:33 their habitations, and their **g.** 3188
1Ch 5:1 and the **g.** is not to be reckoned 3188
1Ch 5:7 when the **g.** of their generations 3188
1Ch 7:9 after their **g.** by their generations, 3188
1Ch 7:40 throughout the **g.** of them that 3188
1Ch 9:22 These were reckoned by their **g.** in 3188
2Ch 31:16 Beside their **g.** of males, from three 3188
2Ch 31:17 the **g.** of the priests by the house 3188
2Ch 31:18 And to the **g.** of all their little ones, 3188
Ezr 2:62 those that were reckoned by **g.** 3188
Ezr 8:1 and this is the **g.** of them that went 3188
Ezr 8:3 were reckoned by **g.** of the males 3188
Ne 7:5 that they might be reckoned by **g.** 3188
Ne 7:5 And I found a register of the **g.** of 3188
Ne 7:64 those that were reckoned by **g.**, 3188

GENERAL
1Ch 27:34 and the **g.** of the king's army 8269
Heb 12:23 to the **g.** assembly and church of *3831*
Jas *title* The **G.** Epistle Of James *2526*
1Pe *title* The First Epistle **G.** Of Peter *2526*
2Pe *title* Second Epistle **G.** Of Peter *2526*
1Jo *title* The First Epistle **G.** Of John *2526*
Jude *title* The **G.** Epistle of Jude *2526*

GENERALLY
2Sa 17:11 that all Israel be **g.** gathered *3831*
Jer 48:38 There shall be lamentation **g.** 3605

GENERATION See also GENERATIONS.
Ge 7:1 righteous before me in this **g.** 1755
Ge 15:16 But in the fourth **g.** they shall come 1755
Ge 50:23 Ephraim's children of the third **g.**
Ex 1:6 and all his brethren, and all that **g.** 1755
Ex 17:16 war with Amalek from **g.** to **g.** 1755
Ex 20:5 unto the third and fourth **g.** of them
Ex 34:7 unto the third and to the fourth **g.**
Nu 14:18 children unto the third and fourth **g.**
Nu 32:13 until all the **g.**, that had done evil 1755
De 1:35 one of these men of this evil **g.** 1755
De 2:14 all the **g.** of the men of war 1755
De 5:9 unto the third and fourth **g.** of them
De 23:2 even to his tenth **g.** shall he not 1755
De 23:3 even to their tenth **g.** shall they not 1755
De 23:8 of the Lord in their third **g.** 1755
De 29:22 So that the **g.** to come of your 1755
De 32:5 they are a perverse and crooked **g.** 1755
De 32:20 for they are a very froward **g.**, 1755
Jg 2:10 also all that **g.** were gathered unto 1755
Jg 2:10 there arose another **g.** after them, 1755
2Ki 10:30 thy children of the fourth **g.** shall sit
2Ki 15:12 throne of Israel unto the fourth **g.**
Es 9:28 kept throughout every **g.**, every 1755
Ps 12:7 preserve them from this **g.** for ever 1755
Ps 14:5 God is in the **g.** of the righteous 1755
Ps 22:30 be accounted to the Lord for a **g.** 1755
Ps 24:6 is the **g.** of them that seek him, 1755
Ps 48:13 ye may tell it to the **g.** following 1755
Ps 49:19 He shall go to the **g.** of his fathers; 1755
Ps 71:18 shewed thy strength unto this **g.**, 1755
Ps 73:15 against the **g.** of thy children 1755
Ps 78:4 shewing to the **g.** to come the 1755
Ps 78:6 That the **g.** to come might know 1755
Ps 78:8 a stubborn and rebellious **g.**; 1755
Ps 78:8 a **g.** that set not their heart aright, 1755
Ps 95:10 long was I grieved with this **g.**, 1755
Ps 102:18 shall be written for the **g.** to come: 1755
Ps 109:13 in the **g.** following let their name 1755
Ps 112:2 **g.** of the upright shall be blessed 1755
Ps 145:4 One **g.** shall praise thy works to 1755
Pr 27:24 doth the crown endure to every **g.**? 1755
Pr 30:11 is a **g.** that curseth their father, 1755
Pr 30:12 a **g.** that are pure in their own eyes, 1755
Pr 30:13 is a **g.**, O how lofty are their eyes! 1755
Pr 30:14 is a **g.**, whose teeth are as swords, 1755
Ec 1:4 One **g.** passeth away, and another **g.** 1755
Isa 13:20 shall it be dwelt in from **g.** to **g.**: 1755
Isa 34:10 from **g.** to **g.** it shall lie waste; 1755
Isa 34:17 from **g.** to **g.** shall they dwell therein 1755
Isa 51:8 my salvation from **g.** to **g.** 1755
Isa 53:8 and who shall declare his **g.**? for he 1755
Jer 2:31 O **g.**, see ye the word of the Lord 1755
Jer 7:29 and forsaken the **g.** of his wrath 1755
Jer 50:39 shall it be dwelt in from **g.** to **g.** 1755
La 5:19 thy throne from **g.** to **g.** 1755
Da 4:3 his dominion is from **g.** to **g.** 1859
Da 4:34 his kingdom is from **g.** to **g.**: 1859
Joe 1:3 and their children another **g.** 1755
Joe 3:20 and Jerusalem from **g.** to **g.** 1755
Mt 1:1 the book of the **g.** of Jesus Christ, *1078*
Mt 3:7 O **g.** of vipers, who hath warned *1081*
Mt 11:16 whereunto shall I liken this **g.**? *1074*
Mt 12:34 O **g.** of vipers, how can ye, *1081*
Mt 12:39 An evil and adulterous **g.** seeketh *1074*
Mt 12:41 shall rise in judgment with this **g.**, *1074*
Mt 12:42 up in the judgment with this **g.**, *1074*
Mt 12:45 shall it be also unto this wicked **g.** *1074*
Mt 16:4 wicked and adulterous **g.** seeketh *1074*
Mt 17:17 O faithless and perverse **g.**, how *1074*
Mt 23:33 Ye serpents, ye **g.** of vipers, how *1081*
Mt 23:36 things shall come upon this **g.** *1074*
Mt 24:34 This **g.** shall not pass, till all these *1074*
Mk 8:12 Why doth this **g.** seek after a sign? *1074*
Mk 8:12 shall no sign be given unto this **g.** *1074*
Mk 8:38 in this adulterous and sinful **g.** *1074*
Mk 9:19 O faithless **g.**, how long shall I be *1074*
Mk 13:30 that this **g.** shall not pass, till all *1074*
Lu 1:50 on them that fear him from **g.** to **g.** *1074*
Lu 3:7 O **g.** of vipers, who hath warned *1081*
Lu 7:31 shall I liken the men of this **g.**? *1074*
Lu 9:41 O faithless and perverse **g.**, how *1074*
Lu 11:29 he began to say, This is an evil **g.** *1074*
Lu 11:30 also the Son of man be to this **g.** *1074*
Lu 11:31 the men of this **g.**, and condemn *1074*
Lu 11:32 with this **g.**, and shall condemn it: *1074*
Lu 11:50 may be required of this **g.**; *1074*
Lu 11:51 It shall be required of this **g.** *1074*
Lu 16:8 in their **g.** wiser than the children *1074*
Lu 17:25 and be rejected of this **g.** *1074*
Lu 21:32 This **g.** shall not pass away, till *1074*
Ac 2:40 yourselves from this untoward **g.** *1074*
Ac 8:33 who shall declare his **g.**? for his *1074*
Ac 13:36 he had served his own **g.** by the *1074*
Heb 3:10 I was grieved with that **g.**, *1074*
1Pe 2:9 a chosen **g.**, a royal priesthood, *1085*

GENERATIONS
Ge 2:4 These are the **g.** of the heavens 8435
Ge 5:1 This is the book of the **g.** of Adam 8435
Ge 6:9 These are the **g.** of Noah: Noah was 8435
Ge 6:9 a just man and perfect in his **g.**, 8435
Ge 9:12 is with you, for perpetual **g.**: 1755
Ge 10:1 These are the **g.** of the sons of 8435
Ge 10:32 after their **g.**, in their nations: 8435
Ge 11:10 These are the **g.** of Shem: Shem was 8435
Ge 11:27 Now these are the **g.** of Terah: 8435
Ge 17:7 thy seed after thee in their **g.** for 1755
Ge 17:9 and thy seed after thee in their **g.** 1755
Ge 17:12 every man child in your **g.**, he that 1755
Ge 25:12 Now these are the **g.** of Ishmael, 8435
Ge 25:13 their names, according to their **g.** 8435
Ge 25:19 And these are the **g.** of Isaac, 8435
Ge 36:1 Now these are the **g.** of Esau, who 8435
Ge 36:9 And these are the **g.** of Esau the 8435
Ge 37:2 These are the **g.** of Jacob 8435
Ex 3:15 this is my memorial unto all **g.** 1755
Ex 6:16 sons of Levi according to their **g.** 8435
Ex 6:19 families of Levi according to their **g.** 8435
Ex 12:14 throughout your **g.**:ye shall keep 1755
Ex 12:17 ye observe this day in your **g.** 1755
Ex 12:42 the children of Israel in their **g.** 1755
Ex 16:32 to be kept for your **g.**;that they 1755
Ex 16:33 the Lord, to be kept for your **g.** 1755
Ex 27:21 a statute for ever unto their **g.** 1755
Ex 29:42 burnt offering throughout your **g.** 1755
Ex 30:8 before the Lord throughout your **g.** 1755
Ex 30:10 upon it throughout your **g.**: 1755
Ex 30:21 to his seed throughout their **g.** 1755
Ex 30:31 oil unto me throughout your **g.** 1755
Ex 31:13 me and you throughout your **g.**; 1755
Ex 31:16 the sabbath throughout their **g.**, 1755
Ex 40:15 priesthood throughout their **g.** 1755
Le 3:17 perpetual statute for your **g.** 1755
Le 6:18 a statute for ever in your **g.** 1755
Le 7:36 for ever throughout their **g.** 1755
Le 10:9 for ever throughout your **g.** 1755
Le 17:7 unto them throughout their **g.** 1755
Le 21:17 he be of thy seed in their **g.** 1755
Le 22:3 all your seed among your **g.**, 1755
Le 23:14 for ever throughout your **g.** in all 1755
Le 23:21 your dwellings throughout your **g.** 1755
Le 23:31 for ever throughout your **g.** 1755
Le 23:41 a statute for ever in your **g.**: 1755
Le 23:43 That your **g.** may know that I 1755
Le 24:3 a statute for ever in your **g.** 1755
Le 25:30 that bought it throughout his **g.**: 1755
Nu 1:20 Israel's eldest son, by their **g.**, 8435
Nu 1:22 children of Simeon, by their **g.**, after 8435

Nu 1:24 children of Gad, by their **g.**, after 8435
Nu 1:26 children of Judah, by their **g.**, after 8435
Nu 1:28 children of Assachar, by their **g.** 8435
Nu 1:30 children of Zebulun, by their **g.** 8435
Nu 1:32 children of Joseph, by their **g.**, by 8435
Nu 1:34 children of Manasseh, by their **g.**, 8435
Nu 1:36 children of Benjamin, by their **g.**, 8435
Nu 1:38 children of Dan, by their **g.**, after 8435
Nu 1:40 children of Asher, by their **g.**, after 8435
Nu 1:42 Naphtali, throughout their **g.**, after 8435
Nu 3:1 These also are the **g.** of Aaron 8435
Nu 10:8 for ever throughout your **g.** 1755
Nu 15:14 be among you in your **g.**, 1755
Nu 15:15 an ordinance for ever in your **g.** 1755
Nu 15:21 Lord an heave offering in your **g.** 1755
Nu 15:23 and henceforward among your **g.**; 1755
Nu 15:38 garments throughout their **g.**, 1755
Nu 18:23 for ever throughout your **g.**, 1755
Nu 35:29 throughout your **g.** in all your 1755
De 7:9 commandments to a thousand **g.**; 1755
De 32:7 consider the years of many **g.**: 1755
Jos 22:27 us, and you, and our **g.** after us, 1755
Jos 22:28 to us or to our **g.** in time to come, 1755
Jg 3:2 Only that the **g.** of the children 1755
Ru 4:18 Now these are the **g.** of Pharez: 8435
1Ch 1:29 these are their **g.**: The firstborn 8435
1Ch 5:7 genealogy of their **g.** was reckoned, 8435
1Ch 7:2 valiant men of might in their **g.**; 8435
1Ch 7:4 And with them, by their **g.**, after 8435
1Ch 7:9 after their genealogy by their **g.**, 8435
1Ch 8:28 the fathers, by their **g.**, chief men. 8435
1Ch 9:9 brethren, according to their **g.** 8435
1Ch 9:34 were chief throughout their **g.**; 8435
1Ch 16:15 he commanded to a thousand **g.**; 1755
1Ch 26:31 according to the **g.** of his fathers. 8435
Job 42:16 and his sons' sons, even four **g.** 1755
Ps 33:11 the thoughts of his heart to all **g.** 1755
Ps 45:17 name to be remembered in all **g.** 1755
Ps 49:11 and their dwelling places to all **g.**; 1755
Ps 61:6 and his years as many **g.** 1755
Ps 72:5 moon endure, throughout all **g.** 1755
Ps 79:13 will shew forth thy praise to all **g.** 1755
Ps 85:5 draw out thine anger to all **g.**? 1755
Ps 89:1 known thy faithfulness to all **g.** 1755
Ps 89:4 and build up thy throne to all **g.** 1755
Ps 90:1 been our dwelling place in all **g.** 1755
Ps 100:5 and his truth endureth to all **g.** 1755
Ps 102:12 and thy remembrance unto all **g.** 1755
Ps 102:24 thy years are throughout all **g.** 1755
Ps 105:8 he commanded to a thousand **g.** 1755
Ps 106:31 him for righteousness unto all **g.** 1755
Ps 119:90 Thy faithfulness is unto all **g.**: 1755
Ps 135:13 memorial, O Lord, throughout all **g.** 1755
Ps 145:13 endureth throughout all **g.** 1755
Ps 146:10 thy God, O Zion, unto all **g.** 1755
Isa 41:4 calling the **g.** from the beginning? 1755
Isa 51:9 in the ancient days, in the **g.** of old. 1755
Isa 58:12 up the foundations of many **g.**; 1755
Isa 60:15 excellency, a joy of many **g.** 1755
Isa 61:4 cities, the desolations of many **g.** 1755
Joe 2:2 even to the years of many **g.** 1755
Mt 1:17 So all the **g.** from Abraham to *1074*
Mt 1:17 Abraham to David are fourteen **g.**; *1074*
Mt 1:17 away into Babylon are fourteen **g.**; *1074*
Mt 1:17 Babylon unto Christ are fourteen **g.** *1074*
Lu 1:48 all **g.** shall call me blessed *1074*
Col 1:26 hid from ages and from **g.**, *1074*

GENESIS (jen'-e-sis)
Ge *general title* Book Of Moses, Called **G.** 7225

GENNESARET (ghen-nes'-a-ret) See also CHINNERETH.
Mt 14:34 they came into the land of **G.** *1082*
Mk 6:53 into the land of **G.**, and drew to *1082*
Lu 5:1 he stood by the lake of **G.**, *1082*

GENTILE (jen'-tile) See also GENTILES.
Ro 2:9 the Jew first, and also of the **G.**; *1672*
Ro 2:10 the Jew first, and also to the **G.** *1672*

GENTILES (jen'-tiles)
Ge 10:5 By these were the isles of the **G.** 1471
Jg 4:2 dwelt in Harosheth of the **G.** 1471
Jg 4:13 from Harosheth of the **G.** unto the 1471
Jg 4:16 the host, unto Harosheth of the **G.** 1471
Isa 11:10 to it shall the **G.** seek: and his 1471
Isa 42:1 bring forth judgment to the **G.** 1471
Isa 42:6 of the people, for a light of the **G.**; 1471
Isa 49:6 give thee for a light to the **G.**, 1471
Isa 49:22 I will lift up mine hand to the **G.**, 1471
Isa 54:3 and thy seed shall inherit the **G.**, 1471
Isa 60:3 the **G.** shall come to thy light, 1471
Isa 60:5 the forces of the **G.** shall come 1471
Isa 60:11 unto thee the forces of the **G.**, 1471
Isa 60:16 shalt also suck the milk of the **G.**, 1471
Isa 61:6 ye shall eat the riches of the **G.**, 1471
Isa 61:9 shall be known among the **G.**, 1471
Isa 62:2 **G.** shall see thy righteousness, 1471
Isa 66:12 of the **G.** like a flowing stream: 1471
Isa 66:19 declare my glory among the **G.** 1471
Jer 4:7 destroyer of the **G.** is on his way; 1471
Jer 14:22 among the vanities of the **G.** 1471
Jer 16:19 the **G.** shall come unto thee 1471
Jer 46:1 the prophet against the **G.**; 1471
La 2:9 her princes are among the **G.**: 1471
Eze 4:13 their defiled bread among the **G.**, 1471
Ho 8:8 shall they be among the **G.** as a 1471
Joe 3:9 Proclaim ye this among the **G.**; 1471
Mic 5:8 of Jacob shall be among the **G.** 1471
Zec 1:21 to cast out the horns of the **G.**, 1471
Mal 1:11 name shall be great among the **G.**; 1471
Mt 4:15 beyond Jordan, Galilee of the **G.**; *1484*
Mt 6:32 **all these things do the G. seek:)** *1484*
Mt 10:5 **Go not into the way of the G.,** *1484*
Mt 10:18 **testimony against them and the G.** *1484*
Mt 12:18 he shall shew judgment to the **G.** *1484*
Mt 12:21 in his name shall the **G.** trust. *1484*
Mt 20:19 **they shall deliver him to the G.** *1484*
Mt 20:25 **the princes of the G. exercise** *1484*
Mk 10:33 **and shall deliver him to the G.:** *1484*
Mk 10:42 **are accounted to rule over the G.** *1484*
Lu 2:32 A light to lighten the **G.**, and the *1484*
Lu 18:32 **he shall be delivered unto the G.,** *1484*
Lu 21:24 **shall be trodden down of the G.,** *1484*
Lu 21:24 **the times of the G. be fulfilled** *1484*
Lu 22:25 **kings of the G. exercise lordship** *1484*
Joh 7:35 the dispersed among the **G.**, *1672*
Joh 7:35 and teach the **G.**? *1672*
Ac 4:27 the **G.**, and the people of Israel, *1484*
Ac 7:45 into the possession of the **G.**, *1484*
Ac 9:15 **to bear my name before the G.,** *1484*
Ac 10:45 on the **G.** also was poured out *1484*
Ac 11:1 the **G.** had also received the word *1484*
Ac 11:18 hath God also to the **G.** granted *1484*
Ac 13:42 the **G.** besought that these words *1484*
Ac 13:46 lo, we turn to the **G.** *1484*
Ac 13:47 set thee to be a light of the **G.**, *1484*
Ac 13:48 the **G.** heard this, they were glad, *1484*
Ac 14:2 Jews stirred up the **G.**, *1484*
Ac 14:5 of the **G.**, and also of the Jews *1484*
Ac 14:27 the door of faith unto the **G.** *1484*
Ac 15:3 declaring the conversion of the **G.**: *1484*
Ac 15:7 the **G.** by my mouth should hear *1484*
Ac 15:12 wrought among the **G.** by them. *1484*
Ac 15:14 did visit the **G.**, to take out of them *1484*
Ac 15:17 all the **G.**, upon whom my name *1484*
Ac 15:19 from among the **G.** are turned *1484*
Ac 15:23 the brethren which are of the **G.** *1484*
Ac 18:6 henceforth I will go unto the **G.** *1484*
Ac 21:11 him into the hands of the **G.** *1484*
Ac 21:19 God had wrought among the **G.** *1484*
Ac 21:21 the Jews which are among the **G.** *1484*
Ac 21:25 As touching the **G.** which believe, *1484*
Ac 22:21 **send thee far hence unto the G.** *1484*
Ac 26:17 **from the people, and from the G.,** *1484*
Ac 26:20 to the **G.**, that they should repent *1484*
Ac 26:23 light unto the people, and to the **G.** *1484*
Ac 28:28 salvation of God is sent unto the **G.**, *1484*
Ro 1:13 you also, even as among other **G.** *1484*
Ro 2:14 the **G.**, which have not the law, *1484*
Ro 2:24 God is blasphemed among the **G.** *1484*
Ro 3:9 before proved both Jews and **G.**, *1672*
Ro 3:29 of the **G.**? Yes, of the **G.** also: *1484*
Ro 9:24 the Jews only, but also of the **G.**? *1484*
Ro 9:30 That the **G.**, which followed not *1484*
Ro 11:11 salvation is come unto the **G.**, *1484*
Ro 11:12 of them the riches of the **G.**; *1484*
Ro 11:13 For I speak to you **G.**, inasmuch as *1484*
Ro 11:13 I am the apostle of the **G.**, *1484*
Ro 11:25 until the fulness of the **G.** be come *1484*
Ro 15:9 And that the **G.** might glorify God *1484*
Ro 15:9 I will confess to thee among the **G.**, *1484*
Ro 15:10 he saith, Rejoice, ye **G.**, with his *1484*
Ro 15:11 Praise the Lord, all ye **G.**; and *1484*
Ro 15:12 shall rise to reign over the **G.**; *1484*
Ro 15:12 in him shall the **G.** trust. *1484*
Ro 15:16 minister of Jesus Christ to the **G.**, *1484*
Ro 15:16 the offering up of the **G.** might be *1484*
Ro 15:18 to make the **G.** obedient, by word *1484*
Ro 15:27 if the **G.** have been made partakers *1484*
Ro 16:4 but also all the churches of the **G.** *1484*
1Co 5:1 so much as named among the **G.**, *1484*
1Co 10:20 the things which the **G.** sacrifice, *1484*
1Co 10:32 neither to the Jews, nor to the **G.**, *1672*
1Co 12:2 Ye know that ye were **G.**, carried *1484*
1Co 12:13 whether we be Jews or **G.**, *1672*
Ga 2:2 which I preach among the **G.**, *1484*
Ga 2:8 was mighty in me toward the **G.**:) *1484*
Ga 2:12 he did eat with the **G.**: but when *1484*
Ga 2:14 livest after the manner of **G.**, *1483*
Ga 2:14 the **G.** to live as do the Jews? *1484*
Ga 2:15 nature, and not sinners of the **G.**, *1484*
Ga 3:14 come on the **G.** through Jesus *1484*
Eph 2:11 being in time past **G.** in the flesh, *1484*
Eph 3:1 prisoner of Jesus Christ for you **G.**, *1484*
Eph 3:6 That the **G.** should be fellowheirs, *1484*
Eph 3:8 that I should preach among the **G.** *1484*
Eph 4:17 walk not as other **G.** walk, in the *1484*
Col 1:27 of this mystery among the **G.**; *1484*
1Th 2:16 Forbidding us to speak to the **G.** *1484*
1Th 4:5 as the **G.** which know not God: *1484*
1Ti 2:7 a teacher of the **G.** in faith and *1484*
1Ti 3:16 preached unto the **G.**, believed *1484*
2Ti 1:11 apostle, and a teacher of the **G.** *1484*
2Ti 4:17 and that all the **G.** might hear: *1484*
1Pe 2:12 conversation honest among the **G.** *1484*
1Pe 4:3 to have wrought the will of the **G.**, *1484*
3Jo 7 forth, taking nothing of the **G.** *1484*
Re 11:2 for it is given unto the **G.** *1484*

GENTLE
1Th 2:7 But we were **g.** among you, even *2261*
2Ti 2:24 not strive; but be **g.** unto all men, *2261*
Tit 3:2 to be no brawlers, but **g.**, shewing *1933*
Jas 3:17 **g.**, and easy to be intreated, *1933*
1Pe 2:18 not only to the good and **g.**, but also *1933*

GENTLENESS
2Sa 22:36 and thy **g.** hath made me great. 6031
Ps 18:35 and thy **g.** hath made me great. 6038
2Co 10:1 by the meekness and **g.** of Christ, *1932*
Ga 5:22 longsuffering, **g.**, goodness, faith, *5544*

GENTLY
2Sa 18:5 Deal **g.** for my sake with the 3814
Isa 40:11 **g.** lead those that are with young.

GENUBATH (ghen'-u-bath)
1Ki 11:20 Tahpenes bare him **G.** his son, 1592
1Ki 11:20 and **G.** was in Pharaoh's household 1592

GERA (ghe'-rah)
Ge 46:21 and Becher, and Ashbel, **G.**, and 1617
Jg 3:15 Ehud the son of **G.**, a Benjamite, 1617
2Sa 16:5 name was Shimei, the son of **G.**; 1617
2Sa 19:16 Shimei the son of **G.**, a Benjamite 1617
2Sa 19:18 Shimei the son of **G.** fell down 1617
2Ki 2:8 hast with thee Shimei the son of **G.**, 1617
1Ch 8:3 Addar, and **G.**, and Abihud, 1617
1Ch 8:5 **G.**, and Shephuphan, and Huram. 1617
1Ch 8:7 Ahiah, and **G.**, he removed them, 1617

GERAHS (ghe'-rahs)
Ex 30:13 shekel is twenty **g.**:) an half shekel 1626
Le 27:25 twenty **g.** shall be the shekel. 1626
Nu 3:47 take them: (the shekel is twenty **g.**:) 1626
Nu 18:16 the sanctuary, which is twenty **g.** 1626
Eze 45:12 the shekel shall be twenty **g.**: 1626

GERAR (ghe'-rar)
Ge 10:19 as thou comest to **G.**, unto Gaza; 1642
Ge 20:1 and Shur, and sojourned in **G.** 1642
Ge 20:2 and Abimelech king of **G.** sent, 1642
Ge 26:1 king of the Philistines unto **G.** 1642
Ge 26:6 And Isaac dwelt in **G.** 1642
Ge 26:17 pitched his tent in the valley of **G.**, 1642
Ge 26:20 herdmen of **G.** did strive with 1642
Ge 26:26 Abimelech went to him from **G.**, 1642
2Ch 14:13 with him pursued them unto **G.** 1642
2Ch 14:14 smote all the cities round about **G.**; 1642

GERGESENES (ghur''-ghes-enes')
Mt 8:28 side into the country of the **G.**, *1086*

GERIZIM (gher'-iz-im)
De 11:29 put the blessing upon mount **G.**, 1630
De 27:12 upon mount **G.** to bless the people, 1630

Jos 8:33 against mount **G.**, and half of them..... 1630
Jg 9:7 in the top of mount **G.**, and lifted....... 1630

GERSHOM (ghur'-shom) See also GERSHON.
Ex 2:22 son, and he called his name **G.**.......... 1648
Ex 18:3 which the name of the one was **G.**; 1648
Jg 18:30 and Jonathan, the son of **G.**, the 1648
1Ch 6:16 The sons of Levi; **G.**, Kohath, and..... 1648
1Ch 6:17 the sons of **G.**; Libni, and Shimei. 1648
1Ch 6:20 **G.**; Libni his son, Jahath his son, ... 1648
1Ch 6:43 The son of Jahath, the son of **G.**,....... 1648
1Ch 6:62 of **G.** throughout their families........... 1648
1Ch 6:71 the sons of **G.** were given out of 1648
1Ch 15:7 Of the sons of **G.**; Joel the chief, ... 1648
1Ch 23:15 sons of Moses were, **G.**, and Eliezer. ..1648
1Ch 23:16 sons of **G.**, Shebuel was the chief. 1648
1Ch 26:24 And Shebuel the son of **G.**, the son.... 1648
Ezr 8:2 Of the sons of Phinehas; **G.**: of the 1648

GERSHON (ghur'-shon) See also GERSHOM; GERSHONITE.
Ge 46:11 sons of Levi; **G.**, Kohath, and 1647
Ex 6:16 **G.**, and Kohath, and Merari: and........ 1647
Ex 6:17 sons of **G.**, Libni, and Shimi,............. 1647
Nu 3:17 by their names; **G.**, and Kohath, ... 1647
Nu 3:18 the sons of **G.** by their families;.......... 1647
Nu 3:21 Of **G.** was the family of the Libnites, .. 1647
Nu 3:25 charge of the sons of **G.** in the.......... 1647
Nu 4:22 sum of the sons of **G.**, throughout...... 1647
Nu 4:28 the sons of **G.** in the tabernacle......... 1647
Nu 4:38 were numbered of the sons of **G.**,....... 1647
Nu 4:41 of the families of the sons of **G.**,.............
Nu 7:7 oxen he gave unto the sons of **G.**, ... 1647
Nu 10:17 sons of **G.** and the sons of Merari...... 1647
Nu 26:57 **G.**, the family of the Gershonites: 1647
Jos 21:6 **G.** had by lot out of the families......... 1647
Jos 21:27 unto the children of **G.**, of the........... 1647
1Ch 6:1 The sons of Levi; **G.**, Kohath, and..... 1647
1Ch 23:6 sons of Levi, namely **G.**, Kohath,....... 1647

GERSHONITE (ghur'-shon-ite) See also GERSHONITES.
1Ch 26:21 the sons of the **G.** Laadan, chief 1649
1Ch 26:21 even of Laadan the **G.**, were............. 1649
1Ch 29:8 Lord, by the hand of Jehiel the **G.**....... 1649

GERSHONITES (ghur'-shon-ites)
Nu 3:21 these are the families of the **G.**. 1649
Nu 3:23 The families of the **G.** shall pitch........ 1649
Nu 3:24 father of the **G.** shall be Eliasaph 1649
Nu 4:24 service of the families of the **G.**,......... 1649
Nu 4:27 service of the sons of the **G.**, in all 1649
Nu 26:57 of Gershon, the family of the **G.**: 1649
Jos 21:33 the cities of the **G.** according to.......... 1649
1Ch 23:7 Of the **G.** were, Laadan, and............. 1649
2Ch 29:12 and of the **G.**; Joah the son of........... 1649

GESHAM (ghe'-sham)
1Ch 2:47 Regem, and Jotham, and **G.**, and......... 1529

GESHEM (ghe'-shem) See also GASHMU.
Ne 2:19 and **G.** the Arabian, heard it,............. 1654
Ne 6:1 Tobiah, and **G.** the Arabian, and 1654
Ne 6:2 Sanballat and **G.** sent unto me, ... 1654

GESHUR (ghe-shur) See also GESHURITES.
2Sa 3:3 the daughter of Talmai king of **G.**;...... 1650
2Sa 13:37 the son of Ammihud, king of **G.**. 1650
2Sa 13:38 Absalom fled, and went to **G.**, ... 1650
2Sa 14:23 Joab arose and went to **G.**, and 1650
2Sa 14:32 Wherefore am I come from **G.**? 1650
2Sa 15:8 vow while I abode at **G.** in Syria, ... 1650
1Ch 2:23 And he took **G.**, and Aram, with........ 1650
1Ch 3:2 daughter of Talmai king of **G.**: 1650

GESHURI (ghesh'-u-ri) See also GESHURITES.
De 3:14 the coasts of **G.** and Maachathi;......... 1651
Jos 13:2 of the Philistines, and all **G.**, ... 1651

GESHURITES (ghesh'-u-rites)
Jos 12:5 of the **G.** and the Maachathites,......... 1651
Jos 13:11 border of the **G.** and Maachathites,..... 1651
Jos 13:13 Israel expelled not the **G.**, nor the 1651
Jos 13:13 the **G.** and the Maachathites dwell...... 1651
1Sa 27:8 invaded the **G.**, and the Gezrites,....... 1651

GET See also BEGET; FORGET; GAT; GETTETH; GETTING; GOT.
Ge 12:1 **G.** thee out of thy county, and 3212
Ge 19:14 said, Up, **g.** you out of this place; 3318
Ge 22:2 **g.** thee into the land of Moriah; 3212
Ge 31:13 **g.** thee out from this land, and 3318
Ge 34:4 saying, **G.** me this damsel to wife. 3947
Ge 34:10 therein, and **g.** you possessions therein. ....
Ge 42:2 **g.** you down thither, and buy for........ 3381
Ge 44:17 **g.** you up in peace unto your............. 5927
Ge 45:17 **g.** you unto the land of Canaan;........... 935
Ex 1:10 and so **g.** them up out of the land. 5927
Ex 5:4 **g.** you unto your burdens. 3212
Ex 5:11 **g.** you straw where ye can find it:...... 3947
Ex 7:15 **G.** thee unto Pharaoh in the............... 3212
Ex 10:28 **G.** thee from me, take heed to........... 3212
Ex 11:8 **G.** thee out, and all the people 3318
Ex 12:31 **g.** you forth from among my people, ... 3318
Ex 14:17 I will **g.** me honour upon Pharaoh,...... 3513
Ex 19:24 Away, **g.** thee down, and thou............ 3381
Ex 32:7 Go, **g.** thee down; for thy people, ... 3381
Le 14:21 he be poor, and cannot **g.** so much;.... 5381
Le 14:22 such as he is able to **g.**;...................... 5381
Le 14:30 young pigeons, such as he can **g.**; 5381
Le 14:31 Even such as he is able to **g.**, ... 5381
Le 14:32 whose hand is not able to **g.** that 5381
Nu 6:21 that that his hand shall **g.**: 5381
Nu 13:17 **G.** you up this way southward, ... 5927
Nu 14:25 and **g.** you into the wilderness by........ 5265
Nu 16:24 **G.** you up from about the.................. 5927
Nu 16:45 **G.** you up from among this 7426
Nu 22:13 **G.** you into your land: for the............ 3212
Nu 22:34 I will **g.** me back again. ....
Nu 27:12 **G.** thee up into this mount............... 5927
De 2:13 and **g.** you over the brook Zered........ 5974
De 3:27 **G.** thee up into the top of Pisgah, ... 5927
De 5:30 **G.** you into your tents again.............. 7725
De 8:18 that giveth the power to **g.** wealth,..... 6213
De 9:12 **g.** thee down quickly from hence;........ 3381
De 17:8 and **g.** thee up into the place.............. 5927
De 28:43 is within thee shall **g.** up above.......... 5927
De 32:49 **G.** thee up into this mountain............ 5927
Jos 2:16 **G.** you to the mountain, lest the 3212
Jos 7:10 **G.** thee up; wherefore liest thou 6965
Jos 17:15 **g.** thee up to the wood country, ... 5927
Jos 22:4 and **g.** you unto your tents, and.......... 3212
Jg 7:9 Arise, **g.** thee down unto the host; 3381
Jg 14:2 therefore **g.** her for me to wife.......... 3947
Jg 14:3 **G.** her for me; for she pleaseth me 3947
Jg 19:9 to morrow **g.** you early on your way,........
Ru 3:3 and **g.** thee down to the floor: 3381
1Sa 9:13 Now therefore **g.** you up; for 5927
1Sa 15:6 **g.** you down from among the............. 3381
1Sa 20:29 let me **g.** away, I pray thee, and......... 4422
1Sa 22:5 and **g.** thee into the land of Judah. 935
1Sa 23:26 David made haste to **g.** away for........ 3212
1Sa 25:5 **G.** you up to Carmel, and go to........... 5927
2Sa 20:6 lest he **g.** him fenced cities, and......... 4672
1Ki 1:2 that my lord the king may **g.** heat. ....
1Ki 1:13 Go and **g.** thee in unto king David, ... 935
1Ki 2:26 **G.** thee to Anathoth, unto thine 3212
1Ki 12:18 Rehoboam made speed to **g.** him........ 5927
1Ki 14:2 **g.** thee to Shiloh: behold, there is 1980
1Ki 14:12 Arise thou therefore, **g.** thee to.......... 3212
1Ki 17:3 **G.** thee hence, and turn the............... 3212
1Ki 17:9 Arise, **g.** thee to Zarephath, which 3212
1Ki 18:41 **G.** thee up, eat and drink; for............ 5927
1Ki 18:44 Prepare thy chariot, and **g.** thee 3381
2Ki 3:13 **g.** thee to the prophets of thy 3212
2Ki 7:12 shall catch them alive, and **g.** into........ 935
2Ch 10:18 Rehoboam made speed to **g.** him......... 5927
Ne 9:10 So didst thou **g.** thee a name, as it..... 6213
Ps 119:104 thy precepts I **g.** understanding:...............
Pr 4:5 **G.** wisdom, **g.** understanding:............ 7069
Pr 4:7 therefore **g.** wisdom: and with all 7069
Pr 4:7 thy getting **g.** understanding............. 7069
Pr 6:33 wound and dishonour shall he **g.**;........ 4672
Pr 16:16 better is it to **g.** wisdom than gold!..... 7069
Pr 16:16 to **g.** understanding rather to be......... 7069
Pr 17:16 the hand of a fool to **g.** wisdom, ... 7069
Pr 22:25 learn his ways, and **g.** a snare to 3947
Ec 3:6 A time to **g.**, and a time to lose;........ 1245
Ca 4:6 I will **g.** me to the mountain of 3212
Ca 7:12 Let us **g.** up early to the vineyards;..........
Isa 22:15 Go, **g.** thee unto this treasurer, ... 935
Isa 30:11 **G.** you out of the way, turn aside............
Isa 30:22 shalt say unto it, **G.** thee hence......... 3318
Isa 40:9 **g.** thee up into the high mountain;...... 5927
Isa 47:5 **g.** thee into darkness, O daughter........ 935
Jer 5:5 I will **g.** me unto the great men, ... 3212
Jer 13:1 Go and **g.** thee a linen girdle,............ 7069
Jer 19:1 and **g.** a potter's earthen bottle,......... 7069
Jer 46:4 **g.** up, ye horsemen, and stand 5927
Jer 48:9 that it may flee and **g.** away: for......... 3318
Jer 49:30 Flee, **g.** you far off, dwell deep,......... 5110
Jer 49:31 Arise, **g.** you up unto the wealthy 5927
La 3:7 me about, that I cannot **g.** out: 3318
Eze 3:4 go, **g.** thee unto the house of Israel, ... 935
Eze 3:11 go, **g.** thee to them of the captivity,..... 935
Eze 11:15 **G.** you far from the Lord; unto us...........
Eze 22:27 to destroy souls, to **g.** dishonest 1214
Da 4:14 let the beasts **g.** away from under 5111
Joe 3:13 come, **g.** you down; for the press 3381
Zep 3:19 and I will **g.** them praise and.............. 776
Zec 6:7 **G.** you hence, walk to and fro........... 3212
Mt 4:10 **G. thee hence, Satan: for it is**....... *5217*
Mt 14:22 his disciples to **g.** into a ship, ... *1684*
Mt 16:23 unto Peter, **G. thee behind me,**....... *5217*
Mk 6:45 his disciples to **g.** into the ship, ... *1684*
Mk 8:33 **G. thee behind me, Satan: for** *5217*
Lu 4:8 **G. thee behind me, Satan: for it**.... *5217*
Lu 9:12 and lodge, and **g.** victuals: for we....... *2147*
Lu 13:31 **G.** thee out, and depart hence:.......... *1831*
Ac 7:3 **G.** thee out of thy country, and *1831*
Ac 10:20 **g.** thee down, and go with them, ... *2597*
Ac 22:18 **g. thee quickly out of Jerusalem:** .. *1831*
Ac 27:43 first into the sea, and **g.** to land:........ *1826*
2Co 2:11 Lest Satan should **g.** an advantage...... *4122*
Jas 4:13 and buy and sell, and **g.** gain: ....

GETHER (ghe'-ther)
Ge 10:23 of Aram; Uz, and Hul, and **G.**, ... 1666
1Ch 1:17 Aram, and Uz, and Hul, and **G.**, ... 1666

GETHSEMANE (gheth-sem'-a-ne)
Mt 26:36 with them unto a place called **G.**, ... *1068*
Mk 14:32 to a place which was named **G.**........... *1068*

GETTETH See also BEGETTETH; FORGETTETH.
2Sa 5:8 Whosoever **g.** up to the gutter, ... 5060
Pr 3:13 the man that **g.** understanding. 6329
Pr 9:7 a scorner **g.** to himself shame: 3947
Pr 9:7 rebuketh a wicked man **g.** himself a ....
Pr 15:32 heareth reproof **g.** understanding........ 7069
Pr 18:15 heart of the prudent **g.** knowledge;..... 7069
Pr 19:8 He that **g.** wisdom loveth his own 7069
Jer 17:11 he that **g.** riches, and not by right, ... 6213
Jer 48:44 and he that **g.** up out of the pit.......... 5927

GETTING See also FORGETTING.
Ge 31:18 the cattle of his **g.**, which he had 7075
Pr 4:7 with all thy **g.** get understanding. 7069
Pr 21:6 **g.** of treasures by a lying tongue........ 6467

GEUEL (ghe-u'-el)
Nu 13:15 Of the tribe of Gad, **G.** the son of...... 1345

GEZER (ghe'-zur) See also GAZER; GEZRITES.
Jos 10:33 Horam king of **G.** came up to........... 1507
Jos 12:12 Eglon, one; the king of **G.**, one; 1507
Jos 16:3 Beth-horon the nether, and to **G.**: 1507
Jos 16:10 Canaanites that dwelt in **G.**: but......... 1507
Jos 21:21 of refuge for the slayer; and **G.** 1507
Jg 1:29 **G.**; but the Canaanites dwelt in **G.**..... 1507
1Ki 9:15 and Hazor, and Megiddo, and **G.**.......... 1507
1Ki 9:16 gone up, and taken **G.**, and burnt....... 1507
1Ki 9:17 Solomon built **G.**, and Beth-horon....... 1507
1Ch 6:67 they gave also **G.** with her suburbs, ... 1507
1Ch 7:28 eastward Naaran, and westward **G.**, ... 1507
1Ch 20:4 a war at **G.** with the Philistines;.......... 1507

GEZRITES (ghez'-rites)
1Sa 27:8 Geshurites, and the **G.**, and the......... 1511

GHOST
Ge 25:8 Then Abraham gave up the **g.**, ... 1478
Ge 25:17 and he gave up the **g.** and died;......... 1478
Ge 35:29 And Isaac gave up the **g.**, and died,.... 1478
Ge 49:33 and yielded up the **g.**, and was 1478
Job 3:11 why did I not give up the **g.** when...... 1478
Job 10:18 Oh that I had given up the **g.**, ... 1478
Job 11:20 shall be as the giving up of the **g.**. 5315
Job 13:19 tongue, I shall give up the **g.**............ 1478
Job 14:10 yea, man giveth up the **g.**, and 1478
Jer 15:9 she hath given up the **g.**; her sun......... 5315
La 1:19 mine elders gave up the **g.** in the........ 1478
Mt 1:18 found with child of the Holy **G.**.......... *4151*
Mt 1:20 in her is of the Holy **G.**..................... *4151*
Mt 3:11 with the Holy **G.**, and with fire: *4151*
Mt 12:31 **blasphemy against the Holy G.**....... *4151*
Mt 12:32 **speaketh against the Holy G.**,......... *4151*
Mt 27:50 yielded up the **g.**............................. *4151*
Mt 28:19 of the Son, and of the Holy **G.**: *4151*
Mk 1:8 baptize you with the Holy **G.**.............. *4151*
Mk 3:29 **blaspheme against the Holy G.**....... *4151*

Mk 12:36 himself said by the Holy G., ... 4151
Mk 13:11 ye that speak, but the Holy G...... 4151
Mk 15:37 a loud voice, and gave up the g.. 1606
Mk 15:39 so cried out, and gave up the g., ... 1606
Lu 1:15 be filled with the Holy G., ... 4151
Lu 1:35 Holy G. shall come upon thee,........... 4151
Lu 1:41 was filled with the Holy G. 4151
Lu 1:67 was filled with the Holy G.. 4151
Lu 2:25 and the Holy G. was upon him, ... 4151
Lu 2:26 unto him by the Holy G., ... 4151
Lu 3:16 baptize you with the Holy G............. 4151
Lu 3:22 And the Holy G. descended in........... 4151
Lu 4:1 Jesus being full of the Holy G........... 4151
Lu 12:10 against the Holy G......................... 4151
Lu 12:12 For the Holy G. shall teach 4151
Lu 23:46 said thus, he gave up the g............. 1606
Joh 1:33 baptizeth with the Holy G................ 4151
Joh 7:39 for the Holy G. was not yet............. 4151
Joh 14:26 Holy G., whom the Father............. 4151
Joh 19:30 his head, and gave up the g.. 4151
Joh 20:22 them, Receive ye the Holy G.: 4151
Ac 1:2 he through the Holy G. had 4151
Ac 1:5 be baptized with the Holy G. 4151
Ac 1:8 after that the Holy G. is come 4151
Ac 1:16 which the Holy G. by the mouth........ 4151
Ac 2:4 were all filled with the Holy G., ... 4151
Ac 2:33 the promise of the Holy G., ... 4151
Ac 2:38 receive the gift of the Holy G........... 4151
Ac 4:8 Peter, filled with the Holy G., ... 4151
Ac 4:31 were all filled with the Holy G., ... 4151
Ac 5:3 to lie to the Holy G., and to keep 4151
Ac 5:5 fell down, and gave up the g.: 1634
Ac 5:10 at his feet and yielded up the g.:........ 1634
Ac 5:32 and so is also the Holy G., ... 4151
Ac 6:3 full of the Holy G. and wisdom, ... 4151
Ac 6:5 of faith and of the Holy G., ... 4151
Ac 7:51 do always resist the Holy G.:............ 4151
Ac 7:55 he, being full of the Holy G.,............. 4151
Ac 8:15 they might receive the Holy G.:........ 4151
Ac 8:17 they received the Holy G.. 4151
Ac 8:18 Holy G. was given, he offered........... 4151
Ac 8:19 he may receive the Holy G.............. 4151
Ac 9:17 and be filled with the Holy G............ 4151
Ac 9:31 in the comfort of the Holy G., ... 4151
Ac 10:38 the Holy G. and with power:............ 4151
Ac 10:44 the Holy G. fell on all them............... 4151
Ac 10:45 out the gift of the Holy G.. 4151
Ac 10:47 have received the Holy G. as 4151
Ac 11:15 the Holy G. fell on them, as on 4151
Ac 11:16 be baptized with the Holy G.. 4151
Ac 11:24 man, and full of the Holy G.............. 4151
Ac 12:23 of worms and gave up the g............. 1634
Ac 13:2 the Holy G. said, Separate me........... 4151
Ac 13:4 being sent forth by the Holy G., ... 4151
Ac 13:9 Paul,) filled with the Holy G.,............ 4151
Ac 13:52 with joy, and with the Holy G.. 4151
Ac 15:8 giving them the Holy G., even........... 4151
Ac 15:28 it seemed good to the Holy G., ... 4151
Ac 16:6 were forbidden of the Holy G............ 4151
Ac 19:2 Have ye received the Holy G............ 4151
Ac 19:2 whether there be any Holy G............ 4151
Ac 19:6 the Holy G. came on them; and.......... 4151
Ac 20:23 that the Holy G. witnesseth 4151
Ac 20:28 Holy G. hath made you overseers, ... 4151
Ac 21:11 Thus saith the Holy G., So................ 4151
Ac 28:25 spake the Holy G. by Esaias 4151
Ro 5:5 by the Holy G. which is given........... 4151
Ro 9:1 me witness in the Holy G.,................ 4151
Ro 14:17 peace, and joy in the Holy G............ 4151
Ro 15:13 the power of the Holy G.. 4151
Ro 15:16 being sanctified by the Holy G........... 4151
1Co 2:13 the Holy G. teacheth; 4151
1Co 6:19 the temple of the Holy G.................. 4151
1Co 12:3 the Lord, but by the Holy G.............. 4151
2Co 6:6 the Holy G., by love unfeigned, ... 4151
2Co 13:14 the communion of the Holy G.,.......... 4151
1Th 1:5 in power, and in the Holy G.,............ 4151
1Th 1:6 with joy of the Holy G.: 4151
2Ti 1:14 by the Holy G. which dwelleth........... 4151
Tit 3:5 and renewing of the Holy G.; 4151
Heb 2:4 gifts of the Holy G., according........... 4151
Heb 3:7 (as the Holy G. saith, To day if 4151
Heb 6:4 made partakers of the Holy G., ... 4151
Heb 9:8 The Holy G. this signifying, ... 4151
Heb 10:15 Holy G. also is a witness to us: 4151
1Pe 1:12 Holy G. sent down from heaven;........ 4151
2Pe 1:21 were moved by the Holy G............... 4151
1Jo 5:7 Holy G.: and these three are one....... 4151
Jude 20 praying in the Holy G., ... 4151

GIAH (ghi'-ah)
2Sa 2:24 G. by the way of the wilderness 1520

GIANT See also GIANTS.
2Sa 21:16 which was of the sons of the g., ... 7497
2Sa 21:18 which was of the sons of the g.. 7497
2Sa 21:20 and he also was born to the g.. 7497
2Sa 21:22 four were born to the g. in Gath,....... 7497
1Ch 20:4 that was of the children of the g.: 7497
1Ch 20:6 and he also was the son of the g......... 7497
1Ch 20:8 were born unto the g. in Gath;.......... 7497
Job 16:14 he runneth upon me like a g.,............ 1368

GIANTS
Ge 6:4 were g. in the earth in those days;..... 5303
Nu 13:33 And there we saw the g., the sons..... 5303
Nu 13:33 of Anak, which come of the g............ 1368
De 2:11 accounted g., as the Anakims;........... 7497
De 2:20 accounted a land of g.: g. dwelt......... 7497
De 3:11 remained of the remnant of g.; 7497
De 3:13 which was called the land of g.. 7497
Jos 12:4 was of the remnants of the g., ... 7497
Jos 13:12 remained of the remnant of the g....... 7497
Jos 15:8 at the end of the valley of the g......... 7497
Jos 17:15 of the Perizzites and of the g., ... 7497
Jos 18:16 which is in the valley of the g............ 7497

GIBBAR (ghib'-bar) See also GIBEON.
Ezr 2:20 children of G., ninety and five. 1402

GIBBETHON (ghib'-be-thon)
Jos 19:44 Eltekeh, and G., and Baalath,............ 1405
Jos 21:23 Eltekeh with her suburbs, G. with...... 1405
1Ki 15:27 and Baasha smote him at G., ... 1405
1Ki 15:27 and all Israel laid siege to G.............. 1405
1Ki 16:15 encamped against G., which.............. 1405
1Ki 16:17 Omri went up from G., and all............ 1405

GIBEA (ghib'-e-ah) See also GIBEAH.
1Ch 2:49 Machbenah, and the father of G.......... 1388

GIBEAH (ghib'-e-ah) See also GIBEA; GIBEATH; GIBEON.
Jos 15:57 Cain, G., and Timnah; ten cities 1390
Jg 19:12 of Israel; we will pass over to G.......... 1390
Jg 19:13 lodge all night, in G., or in Ramah...... 1390
Jg 19:14 G., which belongeth to Benjamin......... 1390
Jg 19:15 thither, to go in and to lodge in G.:..... 1390
Jg 19:16 he sojourned in G.: but the men 1390
Jg 20:4 answered and said, I came into G........ 1390
Jg 20:5 And the men of G. rose against me, ... 1390
Jg 20:9 the thing which we will do to G.; 1390
Jg 20:10 when they come to G. of Benjamin,..... 1390
Jg 20:13 of Belial, which are in G., that we...... 1390
Jg 20:14 out of the cities unto G., to go out...... 1390
Jg 20:15 beside the inhabitants of G.,............... 1390
Jg 20:19 morning, and encamped against G....... 1390
Jg 20:20 array to fight against them at G.. 1390
Jg 20:21 Benjamin came forth out of G.,........... 1390
Jg 20:25 at G. the second day, and destroyed... 1390
Jg 20:29 set liers in wait round about G.. 1390
Jg 20:30 put themselves in array against G.,..... 1390
Jg 20:31 God, and the other to G. in the field,.. 1390
Jg 20:33 even out of the meadows of G............ 1390
Jg 20:34 came against G. ten thousand............ 1390
Jg 20:36 wait which they had set beside G....... 1390
Jg 20:37 wait hasted, and rushed upon G.; 1390
Jg 20:43 down with ease over against G........... 1390
1Sa 10:26 Saul also went home to G.; and.......... 1390
1Sa 11:4 came the messengers to G. of Saul, ... 1390
1Sa 13:2 thousand were with Jonathan in G. 1390
1Sa 13:15 and gat him up from Gilgal unto G...... 1390
1Sa 13:16 them, abode in G. of Benjamin: 1390
1Sa 14:2 tarried in the uttermost part of G........ 1390
1Sa 14:5 other southward over against G.......... 1390
1Sa 14:16 of Saul in G. of Benjamin looked; 1390
1Sa 15:34 went up to his house to G. of Saul. 1390
1Sa 22:6 in G. under a tree in Ramah,............. 1390
1Sa 23:19 came up the Ziphites to Saul to G., ... 1390
1Sa 26:1 the Ziphites came unto Saul to G., ... 1390
2Sa 6:3 of Abinadab that was in G.:.............. 1390
2Sa 6:4 of Abinadab which was at G., ... 1390
2Sa 21:6 unto the Lord in G. of Saul, whom..... 1390
2Sa 23:29 of G. of the children of Benjamin,....... 1390
1Ch 11:31 Ithai the son of Ribai of G., that 1390
2Ch 13:2 the daughter of Uriel of G. 1390
Isa 10:29 Ramah is afraid; G. of Saul is fled. 1390
Ho 5:8 Blow ye the cornet in G., and the...... 1390
Ho 9:9 themselves, as in the days of G......... 1390
Ho 10:9 hast sinned from the days of G.......... 1390
Ho 10:9 battle in G. against the children of...... 1390

GIBEATH (ghib'-e-ath) See also GIBEAH; GIBEATHITE.
Jos 18:28 Jebusi, which is in Jerusalem, G., ... 1394

GIBEATHITE (ghib'-e-ath-ite)
1Ch 12:3 of Shemaah the G.; and Jeziel,........... 1395

GIBEON (ghib'-e-on) See also GEBA; GIBEAH; GIBEONITE.
Jos 9:3 G. heard what Joshua had done.......... 1391
Jos 9:17 cities were G.. and Chephirah, ... 1391
Jos 10:1 inhabitants of G. had made peace 1391
Jos 10:2 because G. was a great city, as......... 1391
Jos 10:4 help me, that we may smite G.: 1391
Jos 10:5 and encamped before G., and made 1391
Jos 10:6 men of G. sent unto Joshua to the...... 1391
Jos 10:10 great slaughter at G., and chased....... 1391
Jos 10:12 Sun, stand thou still upon G.; and 1391
Jos 10:41 country of Goshen, even unto G.. 1391
Jos 11:19 the Hivites the inhabitants of G.......... 1391
Jos 18:25 G., and Ramah, and Beeroth,............ 1391
Jos 21:17 of Benjamin, G. with her suburbs, ... 1391
2Sa 2:12 went out from Mahanaim to G............ 1391
2Sa 2:13 and met together by the pool of G. 1391
2Sa 2:16 Helkath-hazzurim, which is in G.. 1391
2Sa 2:24 by the way of the wilderness of G...... 1391
2Sa 3:30 brother Asahel at G. in the battle....... 1391
2Sa 20:8 at the great stone which is in G.,........ 1391
1Ki 3:4 king went to G. to sacrifice there;...... 1391
1Ki 3:5 In G. the Lord appeared to............... 1391
1Ki 9:2 as he had appeared unto him at G.. 1391
1Ch 8:29 And at G. dwelt the father...whose..... 1391
1Ch 8:29 And at...dwelt the father of G.; whose... 25
1Ch 9:35 And in G. dwelt...Jehiel, whose 1391
1Ch 9:35 And...dwelt the father of G., Jehiel,....... 25
1Ch 14:16 Philistines from G. even to Gazer....... 1391
1Ch 16:39 in the high place that was at G.,......... 1391
1Ch 21:29 that season in the high place at G.. 1391
2Ch 1:3 to the high place that was at G.; 1391
2Ch 1:13 from...the high place that was at G..... 1391
Ne 3:7 the men of G., and of Mizpah, unto.... 1391
Ne 7:25 The children of G., ninety and five. ... 1391
Isa 28:21 shall be wroth as in the valley of G., .. 1391
Jer 28:1 Azur the prophet, which was of G.. 1391
Jer 41:12 by the great waters that are in G....... 1391
Jer 41:16 he had brought again from G.: 1391

GIBEONITE (ghib'-e-on-ite) See also GIBEONITES.
1Ch 12:4 Ismaiah the G., a mighty man........... 1393
Ne 3:7 Melatiah the G., and Jadon the 1393

GIBEONITES (ghib'-e-on-ites)
2Sa 21:1 house, because he slew the G.. 1393
2Sa 21:2 G. and said unto them; (now the G. ... 1393
2Sa 21:3 David said unto the G., What shall 1393
2Sa 21:4 the G. said unto him, We will have..... 1393
2Sa 21:9 them into the hands of the G., ... 1393

GIBLITES (ghib'-lites)
Jos 13:5 And the land of the G.,.................... 1382

GIDDALTI (ghid-dal'-ti)
1Ch 25:4 Hanani, Eliathah, G., and................. 1437
1Ch 25:29 and twentieth to G., he, his sons,........ 1437

GIDDEL (ghid'-del)
Ezr 2:47 The children of G., the children 1435
Ezr 2:56 of Darkon, the children of G., ... 1435
Ne 7:49 of Hanan, the children of G.,the......... 1435
Ne 7:58 of Darkon, the children of G., ... 1435

GIDEON (ghid'-e-on) See also GEDEON; JERUBBAAL.
Jg 6:11 his son G. threshed wheat by the....... 1439
Jg 6:13 G. said unto him, O my Lord, if the ... 1439
Jg 6:19 G. went in, and made ready a kid, ... 1439
Jg 6:22 G. perceived that he was an angel...... 1439
Jg 6:22 G. said, Alas, O Lord God! for........... 1439
Jg 6:24 G. build an altar there unto the.......... 1439
Jg 6:27 G. took ten men of his servants,........ 1439
Jg 6:29 G. the son of Joash hath done this...... 1439
Jg 6:34 Spirit of the Lord came upon G., ... 1439
Jg 6:36 G. said unto God, If thou wilt save..... 1439
Jg 6:39 G. said unto God, Let not thine.......... 1439
Jg 7:1 who is G., and all the people that....... 1439
Jg 7:2 said unto G., The people that are....... 1439
Jg 7:4 said unto G., The people are yet 1439
Jg 7:5 said unto G., Every one that............ 1439
Jg 7:7 said unto G., By the three hundred 1439
Jg 7:13 when G. was come, behold, there...... 1439

Jg 7:14 save the sword of **G.** the son of........ 1439
Jg 7:15 **G.** heard the telling of the dream,...... 1439
Jg 7:18 The sword of the Lord, and of **G.**...... 1439
Jg 7:19 So **G.**, and the hundred men that....... 1439
Jg 7:20 The sword of the Lord, and of **G.**...... 1439
Jg 7:24 **G.** sent messengers throughout all...... 1439
Jg 7:25 to **G.** on the other side Jordan........... 1439
Jg 8:4 **G.** came to Jordan, and passed............ 1439
Jg 8:7 **G.** said, Therefore when the Lord...... 1439
Jg 8:11 And **G.** went up by the way of them... 1439
Jg 8:13 **G.** the son of Joash returned from...... 1439
Jg 8:21 **G.** arose, and slew Zebah and........... 1439
Jg 8:22 Israel said unto **G.**, Rule thou over..... 1439
Jg 8:23 **G.** said unto them, I will not rule...... 1439
Jg 8:24 **G.** said unto them, I would desire...... 1439
Jg 8:27 **G.** made an ephod thereof, and put..... 1439
Jg 8:27 thing became a snare unto **G.**, and..... 1439
Jg 8:28 forty years in the days of **G.**............ 1439
Jg 8:30 **G.** had threescore and ten sons of...... 1439
Jg 8:32 **G.** the son of Joash died in a good...... 1439
Jg 8:33 as **G.** was dead, that the children of... 1439
Jg 8:35 house of Jerubbaal, namely, **G.**,.......... 1439

GIDEONI (ghid-e-o'-ni)

Nu 1:11 Benjamin; Abidan, the son of **G.**........ 1441
Nu 2:22 shall be Abidan the son of **G.**............ 1441
Nu 7:60 Abidan the son of **G.**, prince of the..... 1441
Nu 7:65 offering of Abidan the son of **G.**......... 1441
Nu 10:24 Benjamin was Abidan the son of **G.**... 1441

GIDOM (ghi'-dom)

Jg 20:45 pursued hard after them unto **G.**,....... 1440

GIER (jeer)

Le 11:18 the pelican, and the **g.** eagle,............ 7360
De 14:17 the pelican, and the **g.** eagle, and....... 7360

GIER-EAGLE See GIER and EAGLE.

GIFT See also GIFTS.

Ge 34:12 me never so much dowry and **g.**,........ 4976
Ex 23:8 And thou shalt take no **g.**:................ 7810
Ex 23:8 for the **g.** blindeth the wise,.............. 7810
Nu 8:19 I have given the Levites as a **g.**..............
Nu 18:6 are given as a **g.** for the Lord,.......... 4979
Nu 18:7 office unto you as a service of **g.**:...... 4979
Nu 18:11 the heave offering of their **g.**,............ 4976
De 16:19 neither take a **g.**: for a **g.** doth........... 7810
2Sa 19:42 or hath he given us any **g.**?............... 5379
Ps 45:12 of Tyre shall be there with a **g.**;........ 4503
Pr 17:8 A **g.** is as a precious stone in the....... 7810
Pr 17:23 A wicked man taketh a **g.** out of........ 7810
Pr 18:16 A man's **g.** maketh room for him,....... 4976
Pr 21:14 A **g.** in secret pacifieth anger:........... 4976
Pr 25:14 boasteth himself of a false **g.**............. 4991
Ec 3:13 of all his labour. it is the **g.** of God..... 4991
Ec 5:19 in his labour; this is the **g.** of God...... 4991
Ec 7:7 a **g.** destroyeth the heart.................. 4979
Eze 46:16 prince give a **g.** unto any of his sons,.. 4979
Eze 46:17 if he give a **g.** of his inheritance......... 4979
Mt 5:23 **if thou bring thy g. to the altar**.... *1435*
Mt 5:24 **leave there thy g. before the altar**, .*1435*
Mt 5:24 **and then come and offer thy g.**..... *1435*
Mt 8:4 **the g. that Moses commanded**....... *1435*
Mt 15:5 **It is a g., by whatsoever thou**....... *1435*
Mt 23:18 **sweareth by the g. that is upon it**...*1435*
Mt 23:19 **for whether is greater the g., or**.... *1435*
Mt 23:19 **or the altar that sanctifieth the g.?** *1435*
Mk 7:11 **Corban, that is to say, a g., by**..... *1435*
Joh 4:10 **If thou knewest the g. of God,**...... *1431*
Ac 2:38 receive the **g.** of the Holy Ghost........ *1431*
Ac 8:20 hast thought that the **g.** of God......... *1431*
Ac 10:45 poured out the **g.** of the Holy Ghost... *1431*
Ac 11:17 God gave them the like **g.** as he did... *1431*
Ro 1:11 impart unto you some spiritual **g.**,...... *5486*
Ro 5:15 as the offence, so also is the free **g.**... *5486*
Ro 5:15 grace of God, and the **g.** by grace,..... *1431*
Ro 5:16 by one that sinned, so is the **g.**:......... *1434*
Ro 5:16 the free **g.** is of many offences.......... *5486*
Ro 5:17 the **g.** of righteousness shall reign..... *1431*
Ro 5:18 the free **g.** came upon all men unto...........
Ro 6:23 but the **g.** of God is eternal life.......... *5486*
1Co 1:7 So that ye come behind in no **g.**;........ *5486*
1Co 7:7 every man hath his proper **g.** of God,...*5486*
1Co 13:2 though I have the **g.** of prophecy.............
2Co 1:11 for the **g.** bestowed upon us by.......... *5486*
2Co 8:4 that we would receive the **g.**, and...... *5485*
2Co 9:15 unto God for his unspeakable **g.**.......... *1431*
Eph 2:8 of yourselves: it is the **g.** of God:...... *1435*
Eph 3:7 according to the **g.** of the grace of...... *1431*
Eph 4:7 the measure of the **g.** of Christ.......... *1431*
Ph 4:17 Not because I desire a **g.**: but I.......... *1390*
1Ti 4:14 Neglect not the **g.** that is in thee,...... *5486*
2Ti 1:6 stir up the **g.** of God, which is in....... *5486*
Heb 6:4 have tasted of the heavenly **g.**,.......... *1431*
Jas 1:17 Every good **g.** and every perfect **g.**..... *1394*
1Pe 4:10 As every man hath received the **g.**,.... *5486*

GIFTS

Ge 25:6 Abraham gave **g.**, and sent them........ 4979
Ex 28:38 Israel shall hallow all their holy **g.**;....... 4979
Le 23:38 beside your **g.**, and beside all your..... 4979
Nu 18:29 Out of all your **g.** ye shall offer.......... 4979
2Sa 8:2 David's servants, and brought **g.**........ 4503
2Sa 8:6 to David, and brought **g.**.................. 4503
1Ch 18:2,6 servants and brought **g.**................... 4503
2Ch 19:7 of persons, nor taking of **g.**................ 7810
2Ch 21:3 their father gave them great **g.**........... 4979
2Ch 26:8 Ammonites gave **g.** to Uzziah:............ 4503
2Ch 32:23 many brought **g.** unto the Lord........... 4503
Es 2:18 to the provinces, and gave **g.**,........... 4864
Es 9:22 portions one to another, and **g.**........... 4979
Ps 68:18 thou hast received **g.** for men;........... 4979
Ps 72:10 of Sheba and Seba shall offer **g.**........... 814
Pr 6:35 though thou givest many **g.**................ 7810
Pr 15:27 but he that hateth **g.** shall live........... 4979
Pr 19:6 is a friend to him that giveth **g.**........... 4976
Pr 29:4 that receiveth **g.** overthroweth it........ 8641
Isa 1:23 every one loveth **g.**, and followeth...... 7810
Eze 16:33 They give **g.** to all whores:............... 5078
Eze 16:33 but thou givest thy **g.** to all thy.......... 5083
Eze 20:26 I polluted them in their own **g.**,.......... 4979
Eze 20:31 when ye offer your **g.**, when ye.......... 4979
Eze 20:39 holy name no more with your **g.**,........ 4979
Eze 22:12 have they taken **g.** to shed blood;...... 7810
Da 2:6 shall receive of me **g.** and rewards..... 4978
Da 2:48 and gave him many great **g.**, and....... 4978
Da 5:17 Let thy **g.** be to thyself, and give....... 4978
Mt 2:11 they presented unto him **g.**; gold,....... *1435*
Mt 7:11 **give good g. unto your children**,.... *1435*
Lu 11:13 **give good g. unto your children**:.... *1390*
Lu 21:1 casting their **g.** into the treasury........ *1435*
Lu 21:5 with goodly stones and **g.**,................. *334*
Ro 11:29 For the **g.** and calling of God are........ *5486*
Ro 12:6 Having then **g.** differing according....... *5486*
1Co 12:1 concerning spiritual **g.**, brethren,.............
1Co 12:4 there are diversities of **g.**, but the...... *5486*
1Co 12:9 to another the **g.** of healing by the..... *5486*
1Co 12:28 **g.** of healings, helps, governments,..... *5486*
1Co 12:30 Have all the **g.** of healing? do all........ *5486*
1Co 12:31 covet earnestly the best **g.**: and......... *5486*
1Co 14:1 desire spiritual **g.**, but rather that..............
1Co 14:12 as ye are zealous of spiritual **g.**,.............
Eph 4:8 captive, and gave **g.** unto men........... *1390*
Heb 2:4 miracles, and **g.** of the Holy Ghost,.... *3311*
Heb 5:1 may offer both **g.** and sacrifices......... *1435*
Heb 8:3 ordained to offer **g.** and sacrifices:...... *1435*
Heb 8:4 that there are priests that offer **g.**....... *1435*
Heb 9:9 were offered both **g.** and sacrifices,.... *1435*
Heb 11:4 God testifying of his **g.**: and by it....... *1435*
Re 11:10 shall send **g.** one to another;............ *1435*

GIHON (ghi'-hon)

Ge 2:13 the name of the second river is **G.**:.... 1521
1Ki 1:33 mule, and bring him down to **G.**:........ 1521
1Ki 1:38 mule, and brought him to **G.**.............. 1521
1Ki 1:45 have anointed him king in **G.**:............ 1521
2Ch 32:30 the upper watercourse of **G.**,............ 1521
2Ch 33:14 of David, on the west side of **G.**,........ 1521

GILALAI (ghil'-a-lahee)

Ne 12:36 Milalai, **G.**, Maai, Nethaneel, and....... 1562

GILBOA (ghil-bo'-ah)

1Sa 28:4 together, and they pitched in **G.**........ 1533
1Sa 31:1 and fell down slain in mount **G.**......... 1533
1Sa 31:8 his three sons fallen in mount **G.**........ 1533
2Sa 1:6 happened by chance upon mount **G.**,... 1533
2Sa 1:21 Ye mountains of **G.**, let there be no.... 1533
2Sa 21:12 Philistines had slain Saul in **G.**:........ 1533
1Ch 10:1 and fell down slain in mount **G.**......... 1533
1Ch 10:8 and his sons fallen in mount **G.**.......... 1533

GILEAD (ghil'-e-ad) See also GILEADITE; GILEAD'S; JABESH-GILEAD; RAMOTH-GILEAD.

Ge 31:21 set his face toward the mount **G.**........ 1568
Ge 31:23 they overtook him in the mount **G.**...... 1568
Ge 31:25 brethren pitched in the mount of **G.**..... 1568
Ge 37:25 of Ishmaelites came from **G.**............. 1568
Nu 26:29 Machir begat **G.**: of **G.** come the....... 1568
Nu 26:30 These are the sons of **G.**: of Jeezer,... 1568
Nu 27:1 Hepher, the son of **G.**, the son of...... 1568
Nu 32:1 and the land of **G.**, that, behold,........ 1568
Nu 32:26 shall be there in the cities of **G.**:........ 1568
Nu 32:29 ye shall give them the land of **G.**........ 1568
Nu 32:39 son of Manasseh went to **G.**, and........ 1568
Nu 32:40 Moses gave **G.** unto Machir the son... 1568
Nu 36:1 families of the children of **G.**,............ 1568
De 2:36 by the river, even unto **G.**, there....... 1568
De 3:10 cities of the plain, and all **G.**, and....... 1568
De 3:12 and half mount **G.**, and the cities........ 1568
De 3:13 rest of **G.**, and all Bashan, being........ 1568
De 3:15 And I gave **G.** unto Machir.............. 1568
De 3:16 Gadites I gave from **G.** even unto...... 1568
De 4:43 and Ramoth in **G.**, of the Gadites;...... 1568
De 34:1 shewed him all the land of **G.**,........... 1568
Jos 12:2 and from half **G.**, even unto the......... 1568
Jos 12:5 and half **G.**, the border of Sihon......... 1568
Jos 13:11 and **G.**, and the border of the............ 1568
Jos 13:25 and all the cities of **G.**, and half......... 1568
Jos 13:31 half **G.**, and Ashtaroth, and Edrei,...... 1568
Jos 17:1 the father of **G.**: because he.............. 1568
Jos 17:1 therefore he had **G.** and Bashan......... 1568
Jos 17:3 the son of **G.**, the son of Machir,....... 1568
Jos 17:5 besides the land of **G.** and Bashan,..... 1568
Jos 17:6 Manasseh's sons had the land of **G.**.... 1568
Jos 20:8 Ramoth in **G.** out of the tribe of......... 1568
Jos 21:38 Ramoth in **G.** with her suburbs,.......... 1568
Jos 22:9 to go into the country of **G.**, to the.... 1568
Jos 22:13 the land of **G.**, Phinehas the son........ 1568
Jos 22:15 unto the land of **G.**, and they spake....... 1568
Jos 22:32 Gad, out of the land of **G.**, unto the... 1568
Jg 5:17 **G.** abode beyond Jordan: and why...... 1568
Jg 7:3 depart early from mount **G.**............. 1568
Jg 10:4 day, which are in the land of **G.**......... 1568
Jg 10:8 of the Amorites, which is in **G.**........... 1568
Jg 10:17 together, and encamped in **G.**............ 1568
Jg 10:18 princes of **G.** said to one another,...... 1568
Jg 10:18 head over all the inhabitants of **G.**..... 1568
Jg 11:1 and **G.** begat Jephthah.................. 1568
Jg 11:5 elders of **G.** went to fetch Jephthah.... 1568
Jg 11:7 Jephthah said unto the elders of **G.**,.... 1568
Jg 11:8 elders of **G.** said unto Jephthah,......... 1568
Jg 11:8 head over all the inhabitants of **G.**..... 1568
Jg 11:9 Jephthah said unto the elders of **G.**,.... 1568
Jg 11:10 the elders of **G.** said unto Jephthah,.... 1568
Jg 11:11 with the elders of **G.**, and the people.. 1568
Jg 11:29 he passed over **G.**, and Manasseh,..... 1568
Jg 11:29 and passed over Mizpeh of **G.**,.......... 1568
Jg 11:29 and from Mizpeh of **G.** he passed....... 1568
Jg 12:4 gathered together all the men of **G.**,.... 1568
Jg 12:4 and the men of **G.** smote Ephraim,..... 1568
Jg 12:5 that the men of **G.** said unto him,....... 1568
Jg 12:7 buried in one of the cities of **G.**.......... 1568
Jg 20:1 with the land of **G.**, unto the Lord...... 1568
1Sa 13:7 Jordan to the land of Gad and **G.**......... 1568
2Sa 2:9 made him king over **G.**, and over....... 1568
2Sa 17:26 Absalom pitched in the land of **G.**....... 1568
2Sa 24:6 they came to **G.**, and to the land of.... 1568
1Ki 4:13 son of Manasseh, which are in **G.**;..... 1568
1Ki 4:19 son of Uri was in the country of **G.**,... 1568
1Ki 17:1 who was of the inhabitants of **G.**,...... 1568
1Ki 22:3 Know ye that Ramoth in **G.** is........... 1568
2Ki 10:33 all the land of **G.**, the Gadites,.......... 1568
2Ki 10:33 river Arnon, even **G.** and Bashan....... 1568
2Ki 15:29 and Hazor, and **G.**, and Galilee.......... 1568
1Ch 2:21 the father of **G.**, whom he married..... 1568
1Ch 2:22 and twenty cities in the land of **G.**....... 1568
1Ch 2:23 sons of Machir the father of **G.**.......... 1568
1Ch 5:9 were multiplied in the land of **G.**........ 1568
1Ch 5:10 throughout all the east land of **G.**,...... 1568
1Ch 5:14 the son Jaroah, the son of **G.**, the...... 1568
1Ch 5:16 and they dwelt in **G.**, in Bashan,......... 1568
1Ch 6:8 Ramoth in **G.** with her suburbs,......... 1568
1Ch 7:14 bare Machir the father of **G.**............. 1568
1Ch 7:17 the sons of **G.**, the son of Machir,...... 1568
1Ch 26:31 men of valour at Jazer of **G.**.............. 1568
1Ch 27:21 tribe of Manasseh in **G.**, Iddo the....... 1568
Ps 60:7 **G.** is mine, and Manasseh is mine:...... 1568
Ps 108:8 **G.** is mine, Manasseh is mine;........... 1568
Ca 4:1 goats, that appear from mount **G.**........ 1568
Ca 6:5 of goats that appear from **G.**:............. 1568
Jer 8:22 Is there no balm in **G.**:is there no...... 1568
Jer 22:6 Thou art **G.** unto me, and the head.... 1568

Jer 46:11 Go up into **G.**, and take balm, ... 1568
Jer 50:19 upon mount Ephraim and **G.**. ... 1568
Eze 47:18 and from Damascus, and from **G.**, ... 1568
Ho 6:8 **G.** is a city of them that work ... 1568
Ho 12:11 Is there iniquity in **G.**? surely ... 1568
Am 1:3 because they have threshed **G.** ... 1568
Am 1:13 the women with child of **G.**, ... 1568
Ob 19 and Benjamin shall possess **G.**. ... 1568
Mic 7:14 in Bashan and **G.**, as in the days of ... 1568
Zec 10:10 into the land of **G.** and Lebanon: ... 1568

GILEADITE (ghil'-e-ad-ite) See also GILEADITES.
Jg 10:3 after him arose Jair, a **G.**, and ... 1569
Jg 11:1 Jephthah the **G.** was a mighty ... 1569
Jg 11:40 the daughter of Jephthah the **G.** ... 1569
Jg 12:7 Then died Jephthah the **G.**, and ... 1569
2Sa 17:27 and Barzillai the **G.** of Rogelim, ... 1569
2Sa 19:31 And Barzillai the **G.** came down ... 1569
1Ki 2:7 of Barzillai the **G.**, and let them be ... 1569
Ezr 2:61 daughters of Barzillai the **G.**, and ... 1569
Ne 7:63 daughters of Barzillai the **G.** to ... 1569

GILEADITES (ghil'-e-ad-ites)
Nu 26:29 Gilead come the family of the **G.**. ... 1569
Jg 12:4 Ye **G.** are fugitives of Ephraim ... 1569
Jg 12:5 the **G.** took the passages of Jordan ... 1569
2Ki 15:25 and with him fifty men of the **G.**: ... 1569

GILEAD'S (ghil'-e-ads)
Jg 11:2 And **G.** wife bare him sons: ... 1568

GILGAL (ghil'-gal)
De 11:30 the champaign over against **G.**, ... 1537
Jos 4:19 and encamped in **G.**, in the east ... 1537
Jos 4:20 of Jordan, did Joshua pitch in **G.** ... 1537
Jos 5:9 place is called **G.** unto this day. ... 1537
Jos 5:10 Israel encamped in **G.**, and kept ... 1537
Jos 9:6 to Joshua unto the camp at **G.**, ... 1537
Jos 10:6 to the camp to **G.**, saying, Slack ... 1537
Jos 10:7 Joshua ascended from **G.**, he, and ... 1537
Jos 10:9 and went up from **G.** all night ... 1537
Jos 10:15, 43 with him, unto the camp to **G.**. ... 1537
Jos 12:23 the king of the nations of **G.**, one; ... 1537
Jos 14:6 came unto Joshua in **G.**: and ... 1537
Jos 15:7 looking toward **G.**, that is before ... 1537
Jg 2:1 Lord came up from **G.** to Bochim, ... 1537
Jg 3:19 quarries that were by **G.**, and said, ... 1537
1Sa 7:16 year in circuit to Beth-el, and **G.**, ... 1537
1Sa 10:8 shalt go down before me to **G.**; ... 1537
1Sa 11:14 Come, and let us go to **G.**, and ... 1537
1Sa 11:15 And all the people went to **G.**; ... 1537
1Sa 11:15 Saul king before the Lord in **G.**; ... 1537
1Sa 13:4 called together after Saul to **G.**. ... 1537
1Sa 13:7 As for Saul, he was yet in **G.**, and ... 1537
1Sa 13:8 but Samuel came not to **G.**; and ... 1537
1Sa 13:12 come down now upon me to **G.**, ... 1537
1Sa 13:15 gat him up from **G.** unto Gibeah of ... 1537
1Sa 15:12 passed on, and gone down to **G.**. ... 1537
1Sa 15:21 unto the Lord thy God in **G.**. ... 1537
1Sa 15:33 in pieces before the Lord in **G.** ... 1537
2Sa 19:15 And Judah came to **G.**, to go to ... 1537
2Sa 19:40 king went on to **G.**, and Chimham ... 1537
2Ki 2:1 Elijah went with Elisha from **G.**. ... 1537
2Ki 4:38 And Elisha came again to **G.**: and ... 1537
Ne 12:29 Also from the house of **G.**, and out ... 1537
Ho 4:15 and come not ye unto **G.**, neither ... 1537
Ho 9:15 All their wickedness is in **G.**: for ... 1537
Ho 12:11 they sacrifice bullocks in **G.**; yea, ... 1537
Am 4:4 at **G.** multiply transgression; ... 1537
Am 5:5 nor enter into **G.**, and pass not to ... 1537
Am 5:5 **G.** shall surely go into captivity, ... 1537
Mic 6:5 him, from Shittim unto **G.**; ... 1537

GILOH (ghi'-loh) See also GILONITE.
Jos 15:51 Goshen, and Holon, and **G.**; ... 1542
2Sa 15:12 city, even from **G.**, while he offered ... 1542

GILONITE (ghi'-lo-nite)
2Sa 15:12 Ahithophel the **G.**, David's ... 1526
2Sa 23:34 Eliam the son of Ahithophel the **G.**, ... 1526

GIMEL (ghee'-mel)
Ps 119:17 *title* [ג] **G.** ...

GIMZO (ghim'-zo)
2Ch 28:18 **G.** also and the villages thereof: ... 1579

GIN See also GINS.
Job 18:9 The **g.** shall take him by the heel, ... 6341
Isa 8:14 for a **g.** and for a snare to the ... 6341
Am 3:5 where no **g.** is for him? shall ... 4170

GINATH (ghi'-nath)
1Ki 16:21 Tibni the son of **G.**, to make him ... 1527
1Ki 16:22 Tibni the son of **G.**: so Tibni died, ... 1527

GINNETHO (ghin'-ne-tho) See also GINNETHON.
Ne 12:4 Iddo, **G.**, Abijah, ... 1599

GINNETHON (ghin'-ne-thon) See also GINNETHO.
Ne 10:6 Daniel, **G.**, Baruch, ... 1599
Ne 12:16 Iddo, Zechariah; of **G.**, Meshullam; ... 1599

GINS
Ps 140:5 wayside; they have set **g.** for me. ... 4170
Ps 141:9 the **g.** of the workers of iniquity. ... 4170

GIRD See also GIRDED; GIRDETH; GIRDING; GIRT.
Ex 29:5 and **g.** him with the curious girdle ... 640
Ex 29:9 thou shalt **g.** them with girdles, ... 2296
Jg 3:16 he did **g.** it under his raiment ... 2296
1Sa 25:13 **G.** ye on every man his sword. ... 2296
2Sa 3:31 **g.** you with sackcloth, and mourn ... 2296
2Ki 4:29 **G.** up thy loins, and take my staff ... 2296
2Ki 9:1 **G.** up thy loins, and take this box ... 2296
Job 38:3 **G.** up now thy loins like a man; ... 247
Job 40:7 **G.** up thy loins now like a man: ... 247
Ps 45:3 **G.** thy sword upon thy thigh, O ... 2296
Isa 8:9 **g.** yourselves, and ye shall be ... 247
Isa 15:3 **g.** themselves with sackcloth: ... 2296
Isa 32:11 and **g.** sackcloth upon your loins ... 2290
Jer 1:17 Thou therefore **g.** up thy loins, ... 2296
Jer 4:8 For this **g.** you with sackcloth, ... 2296
Jer 6:26 **g.** thee with sackcloth, and wallow ... 2296
Jer 49:3 **g.** you with sackcloth; lament, and ... 2296
Eze 7:18 They shall also **g.** themselves ... 2296
Eze 27:31 and **g.** them with sackcloth, and ... 2296
Eze 44:18 they shall not **g.** themselves with ... 2296
Joe 1:13 **G.** yourselves, and lament, ye ... 2296
Lu 12:37 **that he shall g. himself, and make** ... *4024*
Lu 17:8 **and g. thyself, and serve me, till** ... *4024*
Joh 21:18 **another shall g. thee, and carry** ... *2224*
Ac 12:8 **G.** thyself, and bind on thy ... *2224*
1Pe 1:13 Wherefore **g.** up the loins of your ... *328*

GIRDED See also GIRDEDST; GIFT; UNGIRDED.
Ex 12:11 shall ye eat it; with your loins **g.**, ... 2296
Le 8:7 and **g.** him with the girdle, and ... 2296
Le 8:7 he **g.** him with the curious girdle ... 2296
Le 8:13 them, and **g.** them with girdles, ... 2296
Le 16:4 and shall be **g.** with a linen girdle, ... 2296
De 1:41 And when ye had **g.** on every man ... 2296
1Sa 2:4 stumbled are **g.** with strength. ... 247
1Sa 2:18 a child, **g.** with a linen ephod. ... 2296
1Sa 17:39 And David **g.** his sword upon his ... 2296
1Sa 25:13 they **g.** on every man his sword: ... 2296
1Sa 25:13 and David also **g.** on his sword: ... 2296
2Sa 6:14 David was **g.** with a linen ephod ... 2296
2Sa 20:8 garment that he had put on was **g.** ... 2296
2Sa 21:16 he being **g.** with a new sword, ... 2296
2Sa 22:40 For thou hast **g.** me with strength ... 247
1Ki 18:46 and he **g.** up his loins, and ran ... 8151
1Ki 20:32 So they **g.** sackcloth on their loins, ... 2296
Ne 4:18 one had his sword **g.** by his side, ... 631
Ps 18:39 For thou hast **g.** me with strength ... 247
Ps 30:11 sackcloth, and **g.** me with gladness; ... 247
Ps 65:6 mountains; being **g.** with power: ... 247
Ps 93:1 wherewith he hath **g.** himself: ... 247
Ps 109:19 wherewith he is **g.** continually ... 2296
Isa 45:5 I **g.** thee, though thou hast not ... 247
La 2:10 they have **g.** themselves with ... 2296
Eze 16:10 and I **g.** thee about with fine linen, ... 2280
Eze 23:15 **G.** with girdles upon their loins, ... 2289
Da 10:5 whose loins were **g.** with fine gold ... 2296
Joe 1:8 like a virgin **g.** with sackcloth ... 2296
Lu 12:35 **Let your loins be g. about,** ... *4024*
Joh 13:4 and took a towel, and **g.** himself. ... *1241*
Joh 13:5 the towel wherewith he was **g.**. ... *1241*
Re 15:6 breasts **g.** with golden girdles. ... *4024*

GIRDEDST
Joh 21:18 **thou wast young, thou g. thyself** ... *2224*

GIRDETH
1Ki 20:11 Let not him that **g.** on his harness ... 2296
Job 12:18 and **g.** their loins with a girdle ... 631
Ps 18:32 It is God that **g.** me with strength, ... 247
Pr 31:17 She **g.** her loins with strength, ... 2296

GIRDING See also UNDERGIRDING.
Isa 3:24 of a stomacher a **g.** of sackcloth; ... 4228
Isa 22:12 baldness, and to **g.** with sackcloth: ... 2296

GIRDLE See also GIRDLES.
Ex 28:4 broidered coat, a mitre, and a **g.** ... 73
Ex 28:8 And the curious **g.** of the ephod, ... 2805
Ex 28:27 above the curious **g.** of the ephod. ... 2805
Ex 28:28 above the curious **g.** of the ephod, ... 2805
Ex 28:39 shalt make the **g.** of needlework. ... 73
Ex 29:5 with the curious **g.** of the ephod: ... 2805
Ex 39:5 And the curious **g.** of his ephod, ... 2805
Ex 39:20 above the curious **g.** of the ephod. ... 2805
Ex 39:21 above the curious **g.** of the ephod, ... 2805
Ex 39:29 a **g.** of fine twined linen, and blue, ... 73
Le 8:7 and girded him with the **g.**, and ... 73
Le 8:7 with the curious **g.** of the ephod, ... 2805
Le 16:4 and shall be girded with a linen **g.**, ... 73
1Sa 18:4 sword, and to his bow, and to his **g.**. ... 2290
2Sa 18:11 ten shekels of silver, and a **g.**. ... 2290
2Sa 20:8 upon it a **g.** with a sword fastened ... 2290
1Ki 2:5 put the blood of war upon his **g.** ... 2290
2Ki 1:8 girt with a **g.** of leather about his ... 232
Job 12:18 and girdeth their loins with a **g.** ... 232
Ps 109:19 and for a **g.** wherewith he is girded ... 4206
Isa 3:24 and instead of a **g.** a rent; and ... 2290
Isa 5:27 shall the **g.** of their loins be loosed, ... 232
Isa 11:5 righteousness shall be the **g.** of his ... 232
Isa 11:5 loins, and faithfulness the **g.** of his ... 232
Isa 22:21 strengthen him with thy **g.**, and I ... 73
Jer 13:1 Go and get thee a linen **g.**, and put ... 232
Jer 13:2 So I got a **g.** according to the word ... 232
Jer 13:4 Take the **g.** that thou hast got, ... 232
Jer 13:6 take the **g.** from thence, which I ... 232
Jer 13:7 took the **g.** from the place where I ... 232
Jer 13:7 **g.** was marred, it was profitable for ... 232
Jer 13:10 even be as this **g.**, which is good for ... 232
Jer 13:11 For as the **g.** cleaveth to the loins ... 232
Mt 3:4 and a leathern **g.** about his loins; ... *2223*
Mk 1:6 with a **g.** of a skin about his loins; ... *2223*
Ac 21:11 he took Paul's **g.**, and bound his ... *2223*
Ac 21:11 bind the man that owneth this **g.**, ... *2223*
Re 1:13 about the paps with a golden **g.**. ... *2223*

GIRDLES
Ex 28:40 shalt make for them **g.**, and bonnets ... 73
Ex 29:9 And thou shalt gird them with **g.**, ... 73
Le 8:13 girded them with **g.**, and put ... 73
Pr 31:24 delivereth **g.** unto the merchant. ... 2289
Eze 23:15 with **g.** upon their loins, exceeding ... 232
Re 15:6 breasts girded with golden **g.**. ... *2223*

GIRGASHITE (ghur'-gash-ite) See also GIRGASHITES; GIRGASITE.
1Ch 1:14 also, and the Amorite, and the **G.**, ... 1622

GIRGASHITES (ghur'-gash-ites)
Ge 15:21 the Canaanites, and the **G.**, and ... 1622
De 7:1 the Hittites, and the **G.**, and the ... 1622
Jos 3:10 the Perizzites, and the **G.**, and ... 1622
Jos 24:11 and the **G.**, the Hivites, and the ... 1622
Ne 9:8 Jebusites, and the **G.**, to give it, I ... 1622

GIRGASITE (ghur'-ga-site) See also GIRGASHITE.
Ge 10:16 and the Amorite, and the **G.**, ... 1622

GIRL See also GIRLS.
Joe 3:3 and sold a **g.** for wine, that they ... 3207

GIRLS
Zec 8:5 boys and **g.** playing in the streets ... 3207

GIRT See also GIRDED.
2Ki 1:8 and **g.** with a girdle of leather about ... 247
Joh 21:7 he **g.** his fisher's coat unto him, ... *1241*
Eph 6:14 your loins **g.** about with truth, ... *4024*
Re 1:13 and **g.** about the paps with a golden ... *4024*

GISPA (ghis'-pah)
Ne 11:21 and Ziha and **G.** were over the ... 1658

GITTAH-HEPHER (ghit''-tah-he'-fer) See also GATH-HEPHER.
Jos 19:13 on the east to **G.**, to Ittah-kazin, ... 1662

GITTAIM (ghit-ta'-im)
2Sa 4:3 Beerothites fled to **G.**, and were ... 1664
Ne 11:33 Hazor, Ramah, **G.**, ... 1664

GITTITE (ghit'-tite) See also GITTITES; GITTITH.
2Sa 6:10 the house of Obed-edom the **G.**. ... 1663
2Sa 6:11 house of Obed-edom the **G.** three ... 1663
2Sa 15:19 the king to Ittai the **G.**, Wherefore ... 1663
2Sa 15:22 Ittai the **G.** passed over, and all his ... 1663
2Sa 18:2 under the hand of Ittai the **G.** ... 1663
2Sa 21:19 slew the brother of Goliath the **G.**, ... 1663

1Ch 13:13 the house of Obed-edom the **G.** 1663
1Ch 20:5 the brother of Goliath the **G.**, 1663

GITTITES (ghit'-tites)
Jos 13:3 the **G.**, and the Ekronites; also the 1663
2Sa 15:18 and all the **G.**, six hundred men 1663

GITTITH (ghit'-tith)
Ps 8:*title* To the chief Musician upon **G.**, 1665
Ps 81:*title* To the chief Musician upon **G.**, 1665
Ps 84:*title* To the chief Musician upon **G.**, 1665

GIVE See also FORGIVE; GAVE; GIVEN; GIVEST; GIVETH; GIVING.
Ge 1:15, 17 heaven to **g.** light upon the earth,
Ge 12:7 Unto thy seed will I **g.** this land; 5414
Ge 13:15 to thee will I **g.** it, and to thy seed 5414
Ge 13:17 for will I **g.** it unto thee. 5414
Ge 14:21 **G.** me the persons, and take the 5414
Ge 15:2 what wilt thou **g.** me, seeing I go 5414
Ge 15:7 to **g.** thee this land to inherit it 5414
Ge 17:8 will **g.** unto thee, and to thy seed 5414
Ge 17:16 I will bless her, and **g.** thee a son 5414
Ge 23:4 **g.** me a possession of a...with you, 5414
Ge 23:9 may **g.** me the cave of Machpelah, 5414
Ge 23:9 he shall **g.** it me for a possession 5414
Ge 23:11 the field **g.** I thee, and the cave 5414
Ge 23:11 that is therein, I **g.** it thee; in the 5414
Ge 23:11 sons of my people **g.** I it thee: 5414
Ge 23:13 But if thou wilt **g.** it, I pray thee, 5414
Ge 23:13 I will **g.** thee money for the field; 5414
Ge 24:7 Unto thy seed will I **g.** this land; 5414
Ge 24:14 I will **g.** thy camels drink also:
Ge 24:41 if they **g.** not thee one, thou shalt 5414
Ge 24:43 **G.** me, I pray thee, a little...to drink;
Ge 24:46 I will **g.** thy camels drink also:
Ge 26:3 seed, I will **g.** all these countries, 5414
Ge 26:4 **g.** unto thy seed all these countries; 5414
Ge 27:28 God **g.** thee of the dew of heaven, 5414
Ge 28:4 **g.** thee the blessing of Abraham, 5414
Ge 28:13 to thee will I **g.** it, and to thy seed; 5414
Ge 28:20 and will **g.** me bread to eat, and 5414
Ge 28:22 and of all that thou shalt **g.** me 5414
Ge 28:22 I will surely **g.** the tenth unto thee.
Ge 29:19 better that I **g.** her to thee, than 5414
Ge 29:19 I should **g.** her to another man: 5414
Ge 29:21 **G.** me my wife, for my days are 3051
Ge 29:26 **g.** the younger before the firstborn. 5414
Ge 29:27 and we will **g.** thee this also for 5414
Ge 30:1 **G.** me children, or else I die. 3051
Ge 30:14 **G.** me, I pray thee, of thy son's 5414
Ge 30:26 **G.** me my wives and my children, 5414
Ge 30:28 me thy wages, and I will **g.** it 5414
Ge 30:31 And he said, What shall I **g.** thee? 5414
Ge 30:31 Thou shalt not **g.** me any thing: 5414
Ge 34:8 I pray you **g.** her him to wife. 5414
Ge 34:9 **g.** your daughters unto us, and 5414
Ge 34:11 what ye shall say unto me I will **g.** 5414
Ge 34:12 I will **g.** according as ye shall say 5414
Ge 34:12 but **g.** me the damsel to wife 5414
Ge 34:14 to **g.** our sister to one that is 5414
Ge 34:16 will we **g.** our daughters unto you, 5414
Ge 34:21 and let us **g.** them our daughters. 5414
Ge 35:12 Isaac, to thee will I **g.** it, and to thy 5414
Ge 35:12 seed after thee will I **g.** the land. 5414
Ge 38:9 he should **g.** seed to his brother. 5414
Ge 38:16 What wilt thou **g.** me, that thou 5414
Ge 38:17 Wilt thou **g.** me a pledge, till thou 5414
Ge 38:18 What pledge shall I **g.** thee? And 5414
Ge 41:16 God shall **g.** Pharaoh an answer of
Ge 42:25 to **g.** them provision for the way: 5414
Ge 42:27 to **g.** his ass provender in the inn, 5414
Ge 43:14 God Almighty **g.** you mercy before 5414
Ge 45:18 I will **g.** you the good of the land 5414
Ge 47:15 Joseph, and said, **G.** us bread: 3051
Ge 47:16 And Joseph said, **G.** your cattle; 3051
Ge 47:16 I will **g.** you for your cattle, 5414
Ge 47:19 and **g.** us seed, that we may live, 5414
Ge 47:24 shall **g.** the fifth part unto Pharaoh, 5414
Ge 48:4 and will **g.** this land to thy seed 5414
Ex 2:9 and I will **g.** thee thy wages. 5414
Ex 3:21 **g.** this people favour in the sight 5414
Ex 5:7 shall no more **g.** the people straw 5414
Ex 5:10 Pharaoh, I will not **g.** you straw. 5414
Ex 6:4 to **g.** them the land of Canaan, 5414
Ex 6:8 to **g.** it to Abraham, to Isaac, and 5414
Ex 6:8 and I will **g.** it you for an heritage: 5414
Ex 10:25 Thou must **g.** us also sacrifices 5414
Ex 12:25 the land which the Lord will **g.** you, 5414
Ex 13:5 sware unto thy fathers to **g.** thee, 5414
Ex 13:11 to thy fathers, and shall **g.** it thee, 5414
Ex 13:21 a pillar of fire, to **g.** them light;
Ex 15:26 and will **g.** ear to his commandments,
Ex 16:8 Lord shall **g.** you in the evening 5414
Ex 17:2 **G.** us water that we may drink. 5414
Ex 18:19 I will **g.** thee counsel, and God shall
Ex 21:23 then thou shalt **g.** life for life, 5414
Ex 21:30 then he shall **g.** for the ransom 5414
Ex 21:32 **g.** unto their master thirty shekels 5414
Ex 21:34 shall make it good, and **g.** money 7725
Ex 22:17 utterly refuse to **g.** her unto him, 5414
Ex 22:29 thy sons shalt thou **g.** unto me. 5414
Ex 22:30 the eighth day thou shalt **g.** it me 5414
Ex 24:12 and I will **g.** thee tables of stone, 5414
Ex 25:16 the testimony which I shall **g.** thee. 5414
Ex 25:21 the testimony that I shall **g.** thee. 5414
Ex 25:22 I will **g.** thee in commandment unto
Ex 25:37 that they may **g.** light over against it
Ex 30:12 shall they **g.** every man a ransom 5414
Ex 30:13 This they shall **g.**, every one that 5414
Ex 30:14 shall **g.** an offering unto the Lord. 5414
Ex 30:15 The rich shall not **g.** more,
Ex 30:15 shall not **g.** less than half a shekel,
Ex 30:15 when they **g.** an offering unto the 5414
Ex 32:13 will I **g.** unto your seed, and they 5414
Ex 33:1 unto thy seed will I **g.** it: 5414
Ex 33:14 go with thee, and I will **g.** thee rest
Le 5:16 thereto, and **g.** it unto the priest; 5414
Le 6:5 **g.** it unto him to whom it 5414
Le 7:32 shoulder shall ye **g.** unto the priest 5414
Le 14:34 land of Canaan, which I **g.** to you 5414
Le 15:14 and **g.** them unto the priest: 5414
Le 20:24 I will **g.** it unto you to possess it, 5414
Le 22:14 and shall **g.** it unto the priest 5414
Le 23:10 the land which I **g.** unto you, 5414
Le 23:38 offerings, which ye **g.** unto the Lord. 5414
Le 25:2 come into the land which I **g.** you, 5414
Le 25:37 Thou shalt not **g.** him thy money 5414
Le 25:38 to **g.** you the land of Canaan, 5414
Le 25:51 shall **g.** again the price of his 7725
Le 25:52 years shall he **g.** him again the 7725
Le 26:4 I will **g.** you rain in due season, 5414
Le 26:6 And I will **g.** peace in the land, 5414
Le 27:23 and he shall **g.** thine estimation 5414
Nu 3:9 shalt **g.** the Levites unto Aaron 5414
Nu 3:48 And thou shalt **g.** the money, 5414
Nu 5:7 and **g.** it unto him against whom he 5414
Nu 6:26 upon thee, and **g.** thee peace. 7760
Nu 7:5 shalt **g.** them unto the Levites, 5414
Nu 8:2 the seven lamps shall **g.** light over
Nu 10:29 the Lord said, I will **g.** it you: 5414
Nu 11:4 Who shall **g.** us flesh to eat?
Nu 11:13 flesh to **g.** unto all this people? 5414
Nu 11:13 **G.** us flesh, that we may eat. 5414
Nu 11:18 Who shall **g.** us flesh to eat?
Nu 11:18 therefore the Lord will **g.** you flesh, 5414
Nu 11:21 will **g.** them flesh, that they may eat 5414
Nu 13:2 the land of Canaan, which I **g.** unto 5414
Nu 14:8 bring us into this land, and **g.** it us; 5414
Nu 15:2 habitations, which I **g.** unto you, 5414
Nu 15:21 the first of your dough ye shall **g.** 5414
Nu 18:28 and ye shall **g.** thereof the Lord's 5414
Nu 19:3 And ye shall **g.** her unto Eleazar 5414
Nu 20:8 and it shall **g.** forth his water, 5414
Nu 20:8 thou shalt **g.** the congregation...drink.
Nu 20:21 Thus Edom refused to **g.** Israel 5414
Nu 21:16 I will **g.** them water. 5414
Nu 22:13 the Lord refuseth to **g.** me leave 5414
Nu 22:18 If Balak would **g.** me his house full 5414
Nu 24:13 If Balak would **g.** me his house full 5414
Nu 25:12 I **g.** unto him my covenant of peace: 5414
Nu 26:54 thou shalt **g.** the more inheritance.
Nu 26:54 thou shalt **g.** the less inheritance:
Nu 27:4 **G.** unto us therefore a possession? 5414
Nu 27:7 shalt surely **g.** them a possession 5414
Nu 27:9, 10,11 ye shall **g.** his inheritance 5414
Nu 27:19 and **g.** him a charge in their sight.
Nu 31:29 and **g.** it unto Eleazar the priest, 5414
Nu 31:30 and **g.** them unto the Levites, 5414
Nu 32:29 ye shall **g.** them the land of Gilead 5414
Nu 33:54 more ye shall **g.** the more inheritance,
Nu 33:54 fewer ye shall **g.** the less inheritance:
Nu 34:13 to **g.** unto the nine tribes, and to 5414
Nu 35:2 that they **g.** unto the Levites of the 5414
Nu 35:2 ye shall **g.** also unto the Levites 5414
Nu 35:4, 6 which ye shall **g.** unto the Levites 5414
Nu 35:7 which ye shall **g.** to the Levites 5414
Nu 35:7 them shall ye **g.** with their suburbs.
Nu 35:8 shall **g.** shall be of the possession 5414
Nu 35:8 that have many ye shall **g.** many;
Nu 35:8 that have few ye shall **g.** few:
Nu 35:8 every one shall **g.** of his cities 5414
Nu 35:13 cities which ye shall **g.** six cities 5414
Nu 35:14 Ye shall **g.** three cities on this side 5414
Nu 35:14 three cities shall ye **g.** in the land 5414
Nu 36:2 to **g.** the land for an inheritance 5414
Nu 36:2 to **g.** the inheritance of Zelophehad 5414
De 1:8 to **g.** unto them and to their seed 5414
De 1:20 Lord our God doth **g.** unto us. 5414
De 1:25 the Lord our God doth **g.** us. 5414
De 1:35 I sware to **g.** unto your fathers, 5414
De 1:36 to him will I **g.** the land that he 5414
De 1:39 unto them will I **g.** it, and they shall 5414
De 1:45 to your voice, nor **g.** ear unto you.
De 2:5 I will not **g.** you of their land, 5414
De 2:9 I will not **g.** thee of their land 5414
De 2:19 I will not **g.** thee of the land of the 5414
De 2:28 **g.** me water for money, that I may 5414
De 2:31 Behold, I have begun to **g.** Sihon 5414
De 4:38 to **g.** thee their land for an 5414
De 5:31 the land which I **g.** them to possess 5414
De 6:10 to **g.** thee great and goodly cities, 5414
De 6:23 to **g.** us the land which he sware 5414
De 7:3 thy daughter thou shalt not **g.** unto 5414
De 7:13 he sware unto thy fathers to **g.** 5414
De 10:11 I sware unto their fathers to **g.** 5414
De 11:9 to **g.** unto them and to their seed, 5414
De 11:14 I will **g.** you the rain of your land 5414
De 11:21 Lord sware unto your fathers to **g.** 5414
De 14:21 thou shalt **g.** it unto the stranger 5414
De 15:10 Thou shalt surely **g.** him, and thine 5414
De 15:14 blessed thee thou shalt **g.** unto him. 5414
De 16:10 shalt **g.** unto the Lord thy God, 5414
De 16:17 Every man shall **g.** as he is able,
De 18:3 **g.** unto the priest the shoulder, 5414
De 18:4 fleece of thy sheep, shalt thou **g.** 5414
De 19:8 and **g.** thee all the land which 5414
De 19:8 the land which he promised to **g.** 5414
De 20:16 the Lord thy God doth **g.** thee 5414
De 22:14 **g.** occasions of speech against 7760
De 22:19 and **g.** them unto the father of the 5414
De 22:29 shall **g.** unto the damsel's father 5414
De 23:14 to **g.** up thine enemies before thee: 5414
De 24:1 her a bill of divorcement, and **g.** it 5414
De 24:15 his day thou shalt **g.** him his hire, 5414
De 25:3 Forty stripes he may **g.** him, and
De 26:3 sware unto our fathers for to **g.** 5414
De 28:11 Lord sware unto thy fathers to **g.** 5414
De 28:12 **g.** the rain unto thy land in his 5414
De 28:55 So that he will not **g.** to any of them 5414
De 28:65 but the Lord shall **g.** thee there a 5414
De 30:20 to Isaac, and to Jacob, to **g.** them. 5414
De 31:5 And the Lord shall **g.** them up 5414
De 31:7 hath sworn unto their fathers to **g.** 5414
De 31:14 that I may **g.** him a charge
De 32:1 **G.** ear, O ye heavens, and I will speak;
De 32:49 the land of Canaan, which I **g.** 5414
De 32:52 which I **g.** the children of Israel. 5414
De 34:4 I will **g.** it unto thy seed: I have 5414
Jos 1:2 the land which I do **g.** to them, 5414
Jos 1:6 I sware unto their fathers to **g.** 5414
Jos 2:12 and **g.** me a true token: 5414
Jos 5:6 unto their fathers that he would **g.** 5414
Jos 7:19 **g.**, I pray thee, glory to the Lord 7760
Jos 8:18 for I will **g.** it into thine hand 5414
Jos 9:24 Moses to **g.** you all the land, and 5414
Jos 14:12 **g.** me this mountain, whereof the 5414
Jos 15:16 I **g.** Achsah my daughter to wife. 5414
Jos 15:19 **G.** me a blessing; for thou hast 5414
Jos 15:19 **g.** me also springs of water. 5414
Jos 17:4 to **g.** us an inheritance among our 5414
Jos 18:4 **G.** out from among you three 3051
Jos 20:4 and **g.** him a place, that he may 5414
Jos 21:2 to **g.** us cities to dwell in, with the 5414
Jos 21:43 the land which he sware to **g.** 5414
Jg 1:12 him will I **g.** Achsah my daughter 5414
Jg 1:15 **G.** me a blessing: for thou hast 3051
Jg 1:15 land; **g.** me also springs of water. 5414
Jg 4:19 **G.** me, I pray thee, a little...to drink;
Jg 5:3 **g.** ear, O ye princes; I, even I,
Jg 7:2 for me to **g.** the Midianites into 5414
Jg 8:5 **G.**, I pray you, loaves of bread 5414
Jg 8:6 should **g.** bread unto thine army? 5414

Jg 8:15 we should **g.** bread unto thy men... 5414
Jg 8:24 that ye would **g.** me every man the... 5414
Jg 8:25 We will willingly **g.** them... 5414
Jg 14:12 then I will **g.** you thirty sheets and... 5414
Jg 14:13 then shall ye **g.** me thirty sheets... 5414
Jg 16:5 we will **g.** thee every one of us... 5414
Jg 17:10 I will **g.** thee ten shekels of silver... 5414
Jg 20:7 **g.** here your advice and counsel... 3051
Jg 21:1 shall not any of us **g.** his daughters... 5414
Jg 21:7 will not **g.** them of our daughters... 5414
Jg 21:18 **g.** them wives of our daughters:... 5414
Jg 21:22 ye did not **g.** unto them at this time,... 5414
Ru 4:12 seed which the Lord shall **g.** thee... 5414
1Sa 1:11 wilt **g.** unto thine handmaid a man... 5414
1Sa 1:11 then I will **g.** him unto the Lord... 5414
1Sa 2:10 he shall **g.** strength unto his king,... 5414
1Sa 2:15 **G.** flesh to roast for the priest;... 5414
1Sa 2:16 but thou shalt **g.** it me now:... 5414
1Sa 2:20 Lord **g.** thee seed of this woman... 7760
1Sa 2:28 I **g.** unto the huse of thy father... 5414
1Sa 2:32 wealth which God shall **g.** Israel:... 3190
1Sa 6:5 **g.** glory unto the God of Israel:... 5414
1Sa 8:6 said, **G.** us a king to judge us... 5414
1Sa 8:14 them, and **g.** them to his servants... 5414
1Sa 8:15 and **g.** to his officers, and to his... 5414
1Sa 9:8 that will I **g.** to the man of God,... 5414
1Sa 10:4 and **g.** thee two loaves of bread;... 5414
1Sa 11:3 **G.** us seven days' respite, that we...
1Sa 14:41 **G.** a perfect lot. And Saul and... 3051
1Sa 17:10 **g.** me a man, that we may fight... 5414
1Sa 17:25 will **g.** him a daughter, and make... 5414
1Sa 17:44 I will **g.** thy flesh unto the fowls... 5414
1Sa 17:46 I will **g.** the carcases of the host... 5414
1Sa 17:47 and he will **g.** you into our hands... 5414
1Sa 18:17 Merab, her will I **g.** thee to wife:... 5414
1Sa 18:21 **g.** him her, that she may be a snare... 5414
1Sa 21:3 **g.** me five loaves of bread in mine... 5414
1Sa 21:9 There is none like that; **g.** it me... 5414
1Sa 22:7 will the son of Jesse **g.** every one... 5414
1Sa 25:8 **g.**, I pray thee, whatsoever cometh... 5414
1Sa 25:11 and **g.** it unto men, whom I know... 5414
1Sa 27:5 them **g.** me a place in some town... 5414
1Sa 30:22 will not **g.** them ought of the spoil... 5414
2Sa 12:11 wives before thine eyes, and **g.** them... 5414
2Sa 13:5 come, and **g.** me meat, and dress... 1262
2Sa 14:8 and I will **g.** charge concerning thee...
2Sa 16:20 **G.** counsel among you what we... 3051
2Sa 21:6 And the king said, I will **g.** them... 5414
2Sa 22:50 Therefore I will **g.** thanks unto thee,...
2Sa 23:15 one would **g.** me drink of the water...
2Sa 24:23 things did Araunah, as a king, **g.**... 5414
1Ki 1:12 let me, I pray thee, **g.** thee counsel,...
1Ki 2:17 he **g.** me Abishag the Shunammite... 5414
1Ki 3:5 God said, Ask what I shall **g.** thee... 5414
1Ki 3:9 **G.** therefore thy servant an... 5414
1Ki 3:21 in the morning to **g.** my child suck,...
1Ki 3:25 and **g.** half to the one,and half to... 5414
1Ki 3:26 **G.** her the living child, and in no... 5414
1Ki 3:27 **G.** her the living child, and in no... 5414
1Ki 5:6 thee will I **g.** hire for thy servants... 5414
1Ki 8:32 to **g.** him according to his... 5414
1Ki 8:36 **g.** rain upon thy land, which thou... 5414
1Ki 8:39 **g.** to every man according to his... 5414
1Ki 8:50 **g.** them compassion before them... 5414
1Ki 11:11 and will **g.** it to thy servant... 5414
1Ki 11:13 **g.** one tribe to thy son for David... 5414
1Ki 11:31 and will **g.** ten tribes to thee:... 5414
1Ki 11:35 will **g.** it unto thee, even ten tribes... 5414
1Ki 11:36 unto his son will I **g.** one tribe,... 5414
1Ki 11:38 and will **g.** Israel unto thee... 5414
1Ki 12:9 counsel **g.** ye that we may answer...
1Ki 13:7 and I will **g.** thee a reward... 5414
1Ki 13:8 If thou wilt **g.** me half thine house,... 5414
1Ki 14:16 **g.** Israel up because of the sins... 5414
1Ki 15:4 did the Lord his God **g.** him a lamp... 5414
1Ki 17:19 he said unto her, **G.** me thy son... 5414
1Ki 18:23 them therefore **g.** us two bullocks;... 5414
1Ki 21:2 **G.** me thy vineyard, that I may... 5414
1Ki 21:2 will **g.** thee for it a better vineyard... 5414
1Ki 21:2 **g.** thee the worth of it in money... 5414
1Ki 21:3 **g.** the inheritance of my fathers... 5414
1Ki 21:4 I will not **g.** thee the inheritance... 5414
1Ki 21:6 **G.** me thy vineyard for money; or... 5414
1Ki 21:6 I will **g.** thee another vineyard... 5414
1Ki 21:6 I will not **g.** thee my vineyard... 5414
1Ki 21:7 will **g.** thee the vineyard of Naboth... 5414
1Ki 21:15 he refused to **g.** thee for money;... 5414

2Ki 4:42 **G.** unto the people, that they may... 5414
2Ki 4:43 **G.** the people, that they may eat:... 5414
2Ki 5:22 **g.** them, I pray thee, a talent of... 5414
2Ki 6:28 **G.** thy son, that we may eat him to... 5414
2Ki 6:29 **G.** thy son, that we may eat him:... 5414
2Ki 8:19 to **g.** him alway a light, and to his... 5414
2Ki 10:15 **g.** me thine hand. And he gave... 5414
2Ki 11:10 over hundreds did the priest **g.**... 5414
2Ki 14:9 **G.** thy daughter to my son to wife:... 5414
2Ki 15:20 silver, to **g.** to the king of Assyria... 5414
2Ki 18:23 **g.** pledges to my lord the king of...
2Ki 22:5 and let them **g.** it to the doers of... 5414
2Ki 23:35 to **g.** the money according to the... 5414
2Ki 23:35 to **g.** it unto Pharaoh-nechoh... 5414
1Ch 11:17 Oh that one would **g.** me drink of the...
1Ch 16:8 **G.** thanks unto the Lord, call upon...
1Ch 16:18 thee will I **g.** the land of Canaan,... 5414
1Ch 16:28 **G.** unto the Lord, ye kindreds of... 3051
1Ch 16:28 **g.** unto the Lord glory and strength... 3051
1Ch 16:29 **G.** unto the Lord the glory due... 3051
1Ch 16:34 O **g.** thanks unto the Lord; for he is...
1Ch 16:35 that we may **g.** thanks to thy holy...
1Ch 16:41 to **g.** thanks to the Lord, because his...
1Ch 21:23 I **g.** thee the oxen also for burnt... 5414
1Ch 21:23 for the meat offering; I **g.** it all... 5414
1Ch 22:9 **g.** him rest from all his enemies...
1Ch 22:9 and I will **g.** peace and quietness... 5414
1Ch 22:12 the Lord **g.** thee wisdom and... 5414
1Ch 22:12 **g.** thee charge concerning Israel,...
1Ch 25:3 **g.** thanks and to praise the Lord...
1Ch 29:12 make great, and to **g.** strength unto all...
1Ch 29:19 **g.** unto Solomon my son a perfect... 5414
2Ch 1:7 Ask what I shall **g.** thee... 5414
2Ch 1:10 **G.** me now wisdom and knowledge,... 5414
2Ch 1:12 I will **g.** thee riches, and wealth,... 5414
2Ch 2:10 I will **g.** to thy servants, the hewers... 5414
2Ch 10:6 What counsel **g.** ye me to return...
2Ch 10:9 What advice **g.** ye that we may return...
2Ch 21:7 to **g.** a light to him and to his sons... 5414
2Ch 24:19 them: but they would not **g.** ear...
2Ch 25:9 The Lord is able to **g.** thee much... 5414
2Ch 25:18 **G.** thy daughter to my son to wife:... 5414
2Ch 30:12 to **g.** them one heart to do the... 5414
2Ch 30:24 Hezekiah king of Judah did **g.** to... 7311
2Ch 31:2 to minister, and to **g.** thanks, and to...
2Ch 31:4 to **g.** the portion of the priests... 5414
2Ch 31:15 to **g.** to their brethren by courses,... 5414
2Ch 31:19 to **g.** portions to all the males... 5414
2Ch 32:11 **g.** over yourselves to die by famine... 5414
2Ch 35:12 that they might **g.** according to... 5414
Ezr 4:21 **G.** ye now a commandment... 7761
Ezr 9:8 to **g.** us a nail in his holy place,... 5414
Ezr 9:8 and **g.** us a little reviving in our... 5414
Ezr 9:9 to **g.** us a reviving, to set up the... 5414
Ezr 9:9 and to **g.** us a wall in Judah... 5414
Ezr 9:12 **g.** not your daughters unto their... 5414
Ne 2:8 may **g.** me timber to make beams... 5414
Ne 4:4 and **g.** them for a prey in the land... 5414
Ne 9:8 to **g.** the land of the Canaanites,... 5414
Ne 9:8 to **g.** it, I say, to his seed,... 5414
Ne 9:12 fire, to **g.** them light in the way...
Ne 9:15 thou hadst sworn to **g.** them... 5414
Ne 9:30 yet would they not **g.** ear:...
Ne 10:30 we would not **g.** our daughters... 5414
Ne 12:24 to praise and to **g.** thanks, according...
Ne 13:25 Ye shall not **g.** your daughters... 5414
Es 1:19 and let the king **g.** her royal estate... 5414
Es 1:20 the wives shall **g.** to their husbands... 5414
Es 8:1 that day did the king Ahasuerus **g.**... 5414
Job 2:4 all that a man hath will he **g.** for... 5414
Job 3:11 why did I not **g.** up the ghost... 1478
Job 6:22 **G.** a reward for me of your substance?...
Job 13:19 tongue, I shall **g.** up the ghost... 1478
Job 32:21 neither let me **g.** flattering titles...
Job 32:22 For I know not to **g.** flattering titles;...
Job 34:2 and **g.** ear unto me, ye that have...
Ps 2:8 and I shall **g.** thee the heathen for... 5415
Ps 5:1 **G.** ear to my words, O Lord,...
Ps 6:5 in the grave who shall **g.** thee thanks?...
Ps 17:1 **g.** ear unto my prayer, that goeth...
Ps 18:49 Therefore will I **g.** thanks unto thee,...
Ps 28:4 **G.** them according to their deeds,... 5414
Ps 28:4 **g.** them after the work of their... 5414
Ps 29:1 **G.** unto the Lord, O ye mighty,... 3051
Ps 29:1 **g.** unto the Lord glory and strength... 3051
Ps 29:2 **G.** unto the Lord the glory due... 3051

Ps 29:11 The Lord will **g.** strength unto his... 5414
Ps 30:4 and **g.** thanks at the remembrance...
Ps 30:12 I will **g.** thanks unto thee for ever...
Ps 35:18 I will **g.** thee thanks in the great...
Ps 37:4 and he shall **g.** thee the desires of... 5414
Ps 39:12 **g.** ear unto my cry; hold not thy...
Ps 49:1 **g.** ear, all ye inhabitants of the...
Ps 49:7 nor **g.** to God a ransom for him:... 5414
Ps 51:16 not sacrifice; else would I **g.** it:... 5414
Ps 54:2 **g.** ear to the words of my mouth,...
Ps 55:1 **G.** ear to my prayer, O God;...
Ps 57:7 I will sing and **g.** praise...
Ps 60:11 **G.** us help from trouble: for vain... 3051
Ps 72:1 **G.** the king of thy judgments, O God,... 5414
Ps 75:1 Unto thee, O God, do we **g.** thanks,...
Ps 75:1 unto thee do we **g.** thanks:...
Ps 78:1 **G.** ear, O my people, to my law;...
Ps 78:20 he **g.** bread also? can he provide... 5414
Ps 79:13 pasture will **g.** thee thanks for ever:...
Ps 80:1 **G.** ear, O Shepherd of Israel,...
Ps 84:8 **g.** ear, O God of Jacob. Selah...
Ps 84:11 the Lord will **g.** grace and glory:... 5414
Ps 85:12 Lord shall **g.** that which is good;... 5414
Ps 86:6 **G.** ear, O Lord, unto my prayer;...
Ps 86:16 **g.** thy strength unto thy servant,... 5414
Ps 91:11 he shall **g.** his angels charge over...
Ps 92:1 It is a good thing to **g.** thanks...
Ps 94:13 That thou mayest **g.** him rest...
Ps 96:7 **G.** unto the Lord, O ye kindreds... 3051
Ps 96:7 **g.** unto the Lord glory and strength... 3051
Ps 96:8 **G.** unto the Lord the glory due... 3051
Ps 97:12 and **g.** thanks at the remembrance of...
Ps 104:11 **g.** drink to every beast of the field:...
Ps 104:27 that thou mayest **g.** them their... 5414
Ps 105:1 **g.** thanks unto the Lord; call upon...
Ps 105:11 Unto thee will I **g.** the land of... 5414
Ps 105:39 and fire to **g.** light in the night...
Ps 106:1 O **g.** thanks unto the Lord; for he is...
Ps 106:47 to **g.** thanks unto thy holy name, and...
Ps 107:1 **g.** thanks unto the Lord; for he is...
Ps 108:1 I will sing and **g.** praise, even...
Ps 108:12 **G.** us help from trouble: for vain... 3051
Ps 109:4 but I **g.** myself unto prayer...
Ps 111:6 that he may **g.** them the heritage... 5441
Ps 115:1 but unto thy name **g.** glory, for thy...
Ps 118:1, 29 O **g.** thanks unto the Lord; for he...
Ps 119:34 **G.** me understanding, and I shall keep...
Ps 119:62 I will rise to **g.** thanks unto thee...
Ps 119:73 **g.** me understanding, that I may learn...
Ps 119:125 **g.** me understanding, that I may know...
Ps 119:144 **g.** me understanding, and I shall live...
Ps 119:169 **g.** me understanding according to thy...
Ps 122:4 **g.** thanks unto the name of the Lord...
Ps 132:4 I will not **g.** sleep to mine eyes,... 5414
Ps 136:1 O **g.** thanks unto the Lord; for he is...
Ps 136:2 O **g.** thanks unto the God of gods:...
Ps 136:3 O **g.** thanks to the Lord of lords:...
Ps 136:26 O **g.** thanks unto the God of heaven:...
Ps 140:13 Surely the righteous shall **g.** thanks...
Ps 141:1 **g.** ear unto my voice, when I cry...
Ps 143:1 **g.** ear to my supplications: in thy...
Pr 1:4 To **g.** subtilty to the simple, and... 5414
Pr 3:28 to morrow I will **g.**; when thou hast... 5414
Pr 4:2 I **g.** you good doctrine, forsake ye... 5414
Pr 4:9 shall **g.** to thine head an ornament... 5414
Pr 5:9 thou **g.** thine honour unto others,... 5414
Pr 6:4 **G.** not sleep to thine eyes, nor... 5414
Pr 6:31 he shall **g.** all the substance of his... 5414
Pr 9:9 **G.** instruction to a wise man and... 5414
Pr 23:26 My son, **g.** me thine heart, and let... 5414
Pr 25:21 enemy be hungry, **g.** him bread to...
Pr 25:21 if he be thirsty, **g.** him water to drink:...
Pr 29:15 The rod and reproof **g.** wisdom:... 5414
Pr 29:17 correct thy son, and he shall **g.** thee...
Pr 29:17 he shall **g.** delight unto thy soul... 5414
Pr 30:8 **g.** me neither poverty nor riches;... 5414
Pr 30:15 hath two daughters, crying, **G.**, **g.**... 3051
Pr 31:3 **G.** not thy strength unto women,... 5414
Pr 31:6 **G.** strong drink unto him that is... 5414
Pr 31:31 **G.** her of the fruit of her hands;... 5414
Ec 2:3 heart to **g.** myself unto wine... 4900
Ec 2:26 that he may **g.** to him that is good... 5414
Ec 5:1 to hear, than to **g.** the sacrifice of... 5414
Ec 11:2 **G.** a portion to seven, and also to... 5414
Ca 2:13 the tender grape **g.** a good smell... 5414
Ca 7:12 there will **g.** thee my loves... 5414
Ca 7:13 The mandrakes **g.** a smell, and at... 5414

Ca 8:7 if a man would **g.** all the substance..... 5414
Isa 1:2 Hear, O heavens, and **g.** ear, O earth;......
Isa 1:10 **g.** ear unto the law of our God, ...
Isa 3:4 And I will **g.** children to be their........ 5414
Isa 7:14 Lord himself shall **g.** you a sign, ... 5414
Isa 7:22 of milk that they shall **g.**,................ 6213
Isa 8:9 and **g.** ear, all ye of far countries: ....
Isa 10:6 of my wrath will I **g.** him a charge,..........
Isa 13:10 thereof shall not **g.** their light: ....
Isa 14:3 day that the Lord shall **g.** thee rest ....
Isa 19:4 And the Egyptians will I **g.** over 5534
Isa 28:23 **G.** ye ear, and hear my voice;................
Isa 30:20 the Lord **g.** you the bread of............ 5414
Isa 30:23 Then shall he **g.** the rain of thy 5414
Isa 32:9 daughters; **g.** ear unto my speech. ....
Isa 36:8 **g.** pledges, I pray thee, to my................
Isa 36:8 and I will **g.** thee two thousand.......... 5414
Isa 41:27 **g.** to Jerusalem one that bringeth 5414
Isa 42:6 and **g.** thee for a covenant of the 5414
Isa 42:8 my glory will I not **g.** to another, ... 5414
Isa 42:12 Let them **g.** glory unto the Lord, ... 7760
Isa 42:23 Who among you will **g.** ear to this?...........
Isa 43:4 therefore will I **g.** men for thee, ... 5414
Isa 43:6 I will say to the north, **G.** up; 5414
Isa 43:20 I **g.** waters in the wilderness, and 5414
Isa 43:20 desert, to **g.** drink to my people, ...
Isa 45:3 And I will **g.** thee the treasures of...... 5414
Isa 48:11 I will not **g.** my glory unto another. 5414
Isa 49:6 I will also **g.** thee for a light............. 5414
Isa 49:8 and **g.** thee for a covenant of the 5414
Isa 49:20 **g.** place to me that I may dwell. 5066
Isa 51:4 **g.** ear unto me, O my nation: for a...........
Isa 55:10 that it may **g.** seed to the sower,........ 5414
Isa 56:5 Even unto them will I **g.** in mine........ 5414
Isa 56:5 I will **g.** them an everlasting name, ... 5414
Isa 60:19 shall the moon **g.** light unto thee: ....
Isa 61:3 to **g.** unto them beauty for ashes, ... 5414
Isa 62:7 And **g.** him no rest, till he establish, ... 5414
Isa 62:8 I will no more **g.** thy corn to be......... 5414
Jer 3:15 And I will **g.** you pastors according..... 5414
Jer 3:19 and **g.** thee a pleasant land, a............ 5414
Jer 4:12 will I **g.** sentence against them. 1696
Jer 4:16 and **g.** out their voice against 5414
Jer 6:10 shall I speak, and **g.** warning, ...
Jer 8:10 Therefore will I **g.** their wives........... 5414
Jer 9:15 and **g.** them water of gall to drink. ....
Jer 11:5 to **g.** them a land flowing with 5414
Jer 13:15 Hear ye, and **g.** ear; be not proud:...........
Jer 13:16 **G.** glory to the Lord your God, ... 5414
Jer 14:13 I will **g.** you assured peace in this 5414
Jer 14:22 or can the heavens **g.** showers?.......... 5414
Jer 15:13 thy treasures will I **g.** to the spoil 5414
Jer 16:7 shall men **g.** them the cup...to drink ....
Jer 17:3 I will **g.** thy substance and all thy....... 5414
Jer 17:10 **g.** every man according to his ways, ... 5414
Jer 18:18 let us not **g.** heed to any of his words.......
Jer 18:19 **G.** heed to me, O Lord, and hearken........
Jer 19:7 their carcases will I **g.** to be meat...... 5414
Jer 20:4 I will **g.** all Judah into the hand 5414
Jer 20:5 the kings of Judah will I **g.** into.......... 5414
Jer 22:25 And I will **g.** thee into the hand of....... 5414
Jer 24:7 will **g.** them an heart to know me,...... 5414
Jer 24:8 I **g.** Zedekiah the king of Judah, ... 5414
Jer 25:30 he shall **g.** a shout, as they that tread ....
Jer 25:31 he will **g.** them that are wicked.......... 5414
Jer 26:24 should not **g.** him into the hand.......... 5414
Jer 29:6 **g.** your daughters to husbands,.......... 5414
Jer 29:11 of evil, to **g.** you an expected end. 5414
Jer 30:16 upon thee will I **g.** for a prey. 5414
Jer 32:3 Behold, I will **g.** this city into the........ 5414
Jer 32:19 to **g.** every one according to his.......... 5414
Jer 32:22 to **g.** them, a land flowing with milk.... 5414
Jer 32:28 the Lord; Behold, I will **g.** this city..... 5414
Jer 32:39 And I will **g.** them one heart, and........ 5414
Jer 34:2 I will **g.** this city into the hand of 5414
Jer 34:18 **g.** the men that have transgressed...... 5414
Jer 34:20 I will even **g.** them into the hand 5414
Jer 34:21 Judah and his princes will I **g.** into...... 5414
Jer 35:2 and **g.** them wine to drink......................
Jer 37:21 **g.** him daily a piece of bread out 5414
Jer 38:15 if I **g.** thee counsel, wilt thou not ....
Jer 38:16 neither will I **g.** the into the 5414
Jer 44:30 I will **g.** Pharaoh-hophra king of 5414
Jer 45:5 life will I **g.** unto thee for a prey........ 5414
Jer 48:9 **G.** wings unto Moab, that it may........ 5414
Jer 50:34 that he may **g.** rest to the land, ...

La 2:18 **g.** thyself no rest; let not the 5414
La 3:65 **G.** them sorrow of heart, thy............ 5414
La 4:3 they **g.** suck to their young ones: the........
Eze 2:8 thy mouth, and eat that I **g.** thee. 5414
Eze 3:3 bowels with this roll that I **g.** thee...... 5414
Eze 3:17 and **g.** them warning from me..................
Eze 7:21 And I will **g.** it into the hands of 5414
Eze 11:2 and **g.** wicked counsel in this city: ....
Eze 11:17 I will **g.** you the land of Israel............ 5414
Eze 11:19 And I will **g.** them one heart, ... 5414
Eze 11:19 and will **g.** them an heart of flesh: 5414
Eze 15:6 fuel, so will I **g.** the inhabitants of...... 5414
Eze 16:33 They **g.** gifts to all whores; but 5414
Eze 16:36 which thou didst **g.** unto them; 5414
Eze 16:38 and I will **g.** thee blood in fury........... 5414
Eze 16:39 I will also **g.** thee into their hand,....... 5414
Eze 16:41 also shalt **g.** no hire any more. 5414
Eze 16:61 **g.** them unto thee for daughters,........ 5414
Eze 17:15 that they might **g.** him horses and....... 5414
Eze 20:28 lifted up mine hand to **g.** it to them, ... 5414
Eze 20:42 mine hand to **g.** it to your fathers....... 5414
Eze 21:11 to **g.** it into the hand of the slayer...... 5414
Eze 21:27 right it is; and I will **g.** it him. 5414
Eze 23:31 will I **g.** her cup into thine hand. 5414
Eze 23:46 and will **g.** them to be removed 5414
Eze 25:10 and will **g.** them in possession, ... 5414
Eze 29:19 I will **g.** the land of Egypt unto.......... 5414
Eze 29:21 **g.** thee the opening of the mouth 5414
Eze 32:7 the moon shall not **g.** her light.................
Eze 33:15 **g.** again that he had robbed, walk....... 7999
Eze 33:27 open field will I **g.** to the beasts.......... 5414
Eze 36:26 A new heart also will I **g.** you, ... 5414
Eze 36:26 and I will **g.** you an heart of flesh....... 5414
Eze 39:4 will **g.** thee unto the ravenous birds.... 5414
Eze 39:11 I will **g.** unto Gog a place there 5414
Eze 43:19 shalt **g.** to the priests the Levites 5414
Eze 44:28 **g.** them no possession in Israel: 5414
Eze 44:30 ye shall also **g.** unto the priest the 5414
Eze 45:8 the rest of the land shall they **g.** 5414
Eze 45:13 ye shall **g.** the sixth part of an ephah ....
Eze 45:16 land shall **g.** this oblation............. 1961,413
Eze 45:17 prince's part to **g.** burnt offerings ....
Eze 46:5 the lambs as he shall be able to **g.**, ... 4991
Eze 46:11 and to the lambs as he is able to **g.**,.... 4991
Eze 46:16 If the prince **g.** a gift unto any of 5414
Eze 46:17 if he **g.** a gift of his inheritance 5414
Eze 46:18 he shall **g.** his sons inheritance out of..........
Eze 47:14 hand to **g.** it unto your fathers:.......... 5414
Eze 47:23 shall ye **g.** him his inheritance,........... 5414
Da 1:12 let them **g.** us pulse to eat, and......... 5414
Da 2:16 king that he would **g.** him time, ... 5415
Da 5:17 and **g.** thy rewards to another; 3052
Da 6:2 might **g.** accounts unto them, ... 3052
Da 8:13 to **g.** both the sanctuary and the 5414
Da 9:22 **g.** thee skill and understanding.................
Da 11:17 **g.** him the daughter of women, ... 5414
Da 11:21 they shall not **g.** the honour of the 5414
Ho 2:5 **g.** me my bread and my water,........... 5414
Ho 2:15 And I will **g.** her her vineyards 5414
Ho 4:18 rulers with shame do love, **G.** ye. 3051
Ho 5:1 **g.** ye ear, O house of the king;................
Ho 9:14 **G.** them, O Lord: 5414
Ho 9:14 what wilt thou **g.**? 5414
Ho 9:14 **g.** them a miscarrying womb 5414
Ho 11:8 How shall I **g.** thee up, Ephraim?....... 5414
Ho 13:10 saidst, **G.** me a king and princes?....... 5414
Joe 1:2 Hear this, ye old men, and **g.** ear,............
Joe 2:17 **g.** not thine heritage to reproach, ... 5414
Mic 1:14 **g.** presents to Moresheth-gath:........... 5414
Mic 5:3 Therefore will he **g.** them up,............ 5414
Mic 6:7 shall I **g.** my firstborn for my 5414
Mic 6:14 which thou deliverest will I **g.** up 5414
Hag 2:9 will I **g.** peace, saith the Lord........... 5414
Zec 3:7 and I will **g.** thee places to walk......... 5414
Zec 8:12 the vine shall **g.** her fruit, and the 5414
Zec 8:12 ground shall **g.** her increase, and........ 5414
Zec 8:12 the heavens shall **g.** their dew; 5414
Zec 10:1 and **g.** them showers of rain, to......... 5414
Zec 11:12 If ye think good, **g.** me my price;........ 3051
Mal 2:2 to **g.** glory unto my name, saith......... 5414
Mt 4:6 He shall **g.** his angels charge ....
Mt 4:9 All these things will I **g.** thee, ... *1325*
Mt 5:31 **g. her a writing of divorcement:**.... *1325*
Mt 5:42 **G. to him that asketh thee, and**.... *1325*
Mt 6:11 **G. us this day our daily bread**....... *1325*
Mt 7:6 **G. not that which is holy unto the**. *1325*
Mt 7:9 **ask bread, will he g. him a stone?**. *1929*

Mt 7:10 **a fish, will he g. him a serpent?**.... *1929*
Mt 7:11 **g. good gifts unto your children,**... *1325*
Mt 7:11 **Father which is in heaven g. good**. *1325*
Mt 9:24 He said unto them, **G. place; for the**.. *402*
Mt 10:8 **freely ye have received, freely g.**... *1325*
Mt 10:42 **whosoever shall g. to drink unto**... *4222*
Mt 11:28 **heavy laden, and I will g. you rest**......
Mt 12:36 **shall g. account thereof in the day**.. *591*
Mt 14:7 **g.** her whatsoever she would ask. *1325*
Mt 14:8 **G.** me here John Baptist's head in...... *1325*
Mt 14:16 **need not depart; g. ye them to eat**.. *1325*
Mt 16:19 **I will g. unto thee the keys of the**.. *1325*
Mt 16:26 **a man g. in exchange for his soul?**. *1325*
Mt 17:27 **and g. unto them for me and thee**.. *1325*
Mt 19:7 to **g.** a writing of divorcement, ... *1325*
Mt 19:21 **g. to the poor, and thou shalt**....... *1325*
Mt 20:4 **whatsoever is right I will g. you**..........
Mt 20:8 **labourers, and g. them their hire,**... *591*
Mt 20:14 **g. unto this last, even as unto thee**. *1325*
Mt 20:23 **and on my left, is not mine to g.**,.. *1325*
Mt 20:28 **to g. his life a ransom for many**.... *1325*
Mt 22:17 Is it lawful to **g.** tribute unto *1325*
Mt 24:19 **them that g. suck in those days!** ....
Mt 24:29 **the moon shall not g. her light,** *1325*
Mt 24:45 **to g. them meat in due season?**..... *1325*
Mt 25:8 **G. us of your oil; for our lamps** *1325*
Mt 25:28 **g. it unto him which hath ten**...... *1325*
Mt 26:15 said unto them, What will ye **g.** me, ... *1325*
Mt 26:53 **he shall presently g. me more** *3936*
Mk 6:22 whatsoever thou wilt, and I will **g.**...... *1325*
Mk 6:23 I will **g.** it thee, unto the half *1325*
Mk 6:25 I will that thou **g.** me by and by......... *1325*
Mk 6:37 **G. ye them to eat. And they say**...... *1325*
Mk 6:37 of bread, and **g.** them to eat?............ *1325*
Mk 8:37 **what shall a man g. in exchange**... *1325*
Mk 9:41 **g. you a cup of water to drink** *4222*
Mk 10:21 **g. to the poor, and thou shalt have**. *1325*
Mk 10:40 **on my left hand is not mine to g.**;. *1325*
Mk 10:45 **to g. his life a ransom for many**.... *1325*
Mk 12:9 **will g. the vineyard unto others**. ... *1325*
Mk 12:14 Is it lawful to **g.** tribute to Caesar, ... *1325*
Mk 12:15 Shall we **g.**, or shall we not **g.**? *1325*
Mk 13:17 **to them that g. suck in those days!** .....
Mk 13:24 **the moon shall not g. her light,** *1325*
Mk 14:11 and promised to **g.** him money.......... *1325*
Lu 1:32 the Lord God shall **g.** unto him the..... *1325*
Lu 1:77 To **g.** knowledge of salvation unto *1325*
Lu 1:79 To **g.** light to them that sit in........... *2014*
Lu 4:6 All this power will I **g.** thee, ... *1325*
Lu 4:6 and to whomsoever I will I **g.** it......... *1325*
Lu 4:10 shall **g.** his angels charge over thee, ...
Lu 6:30 **G. to every man that asketh of** *1325*
Lu 6:38 **G., and it shall be given unto you;** . *1325*
Lu 6:38 **shall men g. into your bosom**........ *1325*
Lu 8:55 he commanded to **g.** her meat. *1325*
Lu 9:13 said unto them, **G. ye them to eat**.... *1325*
Lu 10:7 **drinking such things as they g.**:.... *3844*
Lu 10:19 **I g. unto you power to tread on**.... *1325*
Lu 11:3 **G. us day by day our daily bread**... *1325*
Lu 11:7 **I cannot rise and g. thee**............. *1325*
Lu 11:8 **he will not rise and g. him,** *1325*
Lu 11:8 **he will rise and g. him as many**.... *1325*
Lu 11:11 **will he g. him a stone? or if he**..... *1929*
Lu 11:11 **will he for a fish g. him a serpent?**. *1929*
Lu 11:13 **g. good gifts unto your children:**... *1325*
Lu 11:13 **your heavenly Father g. the Holy**.. *1325*
Lu 11:36 **of a candle doth g. thee light**........ *5461*
Lu 11:41 **g. alms of such things as ye have;**. *1325*
Lu 12:32 **Father's good pleasure to g. you** ... *1325*
Lu 12:33 **Sell that ye have, and g. alms;**...... *1325*
Lu 12:42 **to g. them their portion of meat**.... *1325*
Lu 12:51 **I am come to g. peace on earth?** ... *1325*
Lu 12:58 **g. diligence that thou mayest be**.... *1325*
Lu 14:9 **say to thee, G. this man place;**...... *1325*
Lu 15:12 **Father, g. me the portion of goods**. *1325*
Lu 16:2 **g. an account of thy stewardship;**... *591*
Lu 16:12 **g. you that which is your own?**..... *1325*
Lu 17:18 **that returned to g. glory to God,**... *1325*
Lu 18:12 **I g. tithes of all that I possess**. ....
Lu 19:8 half of my goods I **g.** to the poor; *1325*
Lu 19:24 **g. it to him that hath ten pounds**.. *1325*
Lu 20:10 **they should g. him of the fruit**...... *1325*
Lu 20:16 **and shall g. the vineyard to others**. *1325*
Lu 20:22 Is it lawful for us to **g.** tribute *1325*
Lu 21:15 **I will g. you a mouth and wisdom,**. *1325*

Lu 21:23 to them that g. suck, in those days!.... 1325
Lu 22:5 covenanted to g. him money. ... 1325
Lu 23:2 forbidding to g. tribute to Caesar, ... 1325
Joh 1:22 g. an answer to them that sent us... 1325
Joh 4:7 saith unto her, G. me to drink... 1325
Joh 4:10 saith to thee, G. me to drink; ... 1325
Joh 4:14 the water that I shall g. him shall..1325
Joh 4:14 water that I shall g. him shall ... 1325
Joh 4:15 g. me this water, that I thirst not, ... 1325
Joh 6:27 the Son of man shall g. unto you:. 1325
Joh 6:34 Lord, evermore g. us this bread. ... 1325
Joh 6:51 bread that I will g. is my flesh,... 1325
Joh 6:51 I will g. for the life of the world.. 1325
Joh 6:52 How can this man g. us his flesh... 1325
Joh 7:19 Did not Moses g. you the law,... 1325
Joh 9:24 said unto him, G. God the praise: ... 1325
Joh 10:28 And I g. unto them eternal life;... 1325
Joh 11:22 ask of God, God will g. it thee. ... 1325
Joh 13:26 to whom I shall g. a sop, when I... 1929
Joh 13:29 should g. something to the poor... 1325
Joh 13:34 A new commandment I g. unto... 1325
Joh 14:16 shall g. you another Comforter,... 1325
Joh 14:27 my peace I g. unto you: not as the.1325
Joh 14:27 as the world giveth, g. I unto you. .1325
Joh 15:16 in my name, he may g. it you... 1325
Joh 16:23 in my name, he will g. it you... 1325
Joh 17:2 he should g. eternal life to as... 1325
Ac 3:6 but such as I have g. I thee: In the... 1325
Ac 5:31 for to g. repentance to Israel, and... 1325
Ac 6:4 g. ourselves continually to prayer, ... 4342
Ac 7:5 promised that he would g. it to... 1325
Ac 7:38 the lively oracles to g. unto us: ... 1325
Ac 8:19 Saying, G. me also this power, that... 1325
Ac 10:43 g. all the prophets witness, that...
Ac 13:16 and ye that fear God, g. audience...
Ac 13:34 g. you the sure mercies of David. ... 1325
Ac 19:40 g. an account of this concourse. ... 591
Ac 20:32 to g. you an inheritance among all ... 1325
Ac 20:35 more blessed to g. than to receive. .1325
Ro 8:32 him also freely g. us all things?... 5483
Ro 12:19 but rather g. place unto wrath: ... 1325
Ro 12:20 if he thirst, g. him drink: for in so... 4222
Ro 14:12 shall g. account of himself to God... 1325
Ro 16:4 I g. thanks, but also all the churches...
1Co 7:5 ye may g. yourselves to fasting ... 4980
1Co 7:25 yet I g. my judgment, as one that ... 1325
1Co 10:30 for that for which I g. thanks? ...
1Co 10:32 G. none offence, neither to the... 1096
1Co 12:3 I g. you to understand, that no man...
1Co 13:3 though I g. my body to be burned, ... 3860
1Co 14:7 they g. a distinction in the sounds, ... 1325
1Co 14:8 the trumpet g. an uncertain sound, ... 1325
2Co 4:6 shined in our hearts, to g. the light...
2Co 5:12 g. you occasion to glory on our... 1325
2Co 8:10 herein I g. my advice: for this is... 1325
2Co 9:7 in his heart, so let him g.: not...
Eph 1:16 Cease not to g. thanks for you, ...
Eph 1:17 g. unto you the spirit of wisdom ... 1325
Eph 4:27 Neither g. place to the devil... 1325
Eph 4:28 have to g. to him that needeth. ... 3330
Eph 5:14 and Christ shall g. thee light...
Col 1:3 We g. thanks to God and the Father...
Col 4:1 g. unto your servants that which... 3930
1Th 1:2 We g. thanks to God always for...
1Th 5:18 In everything g. thanks: for this is the ...
2Th 2:13 bound to g. thanks alway to God...
2Th 3:16 g. you peace always by all means... 1325
1Ti 1:4 Neither g. heed to fables and endless...
1Ti 4:13 I come, g. attendance to reading, to...
1Ti 4:15 things; g. thyself wholly to them; ... 2468
1Ti 5:7 these things g. in charge that...
1Ti 5:14 g. none occasion to the adversary ... 1325
1Ti 6:13 g. thee charge in the sight of God, ...
2Ti 1:16 the Lord g. mercy unto the house... 1325
2Ti 2:7 Lord g. thee understanding in all... 1325
2Ti 2:25 if God peradventure will g. them... 1325
2Ti 4:8 judge, shall g. me at that day:... 591
Heb 2:1 to g. the more earnest heed to the...
Heb 13:17 they that must g. account, that ... 591
Jas 2:16 notwithstanding ye g. them not... 1325
1Pe 3:15 be ready always to g. an answer...
1Pe 4:5 Who shall g. account to him that is ... 591
2Pe 1:10 g. diligence to make your calling...
1Jo 5:16 he shall g. him life for them that... 1325
Re 2:7 will I g. to eat of the tree of life,.. 1325
Re 2:10 and I will g. thee a crown of life.. 1325
Re 2:17 that overcometh will I g. to eat... 1325
Re 2:17 and will g. him a white stone,... 1325
Re 2:23 and I will g. unto every one of you 1325
Re 2:26 to him will I g. power over the ... 1325
Re 2:28 And I will g. him the morning ... 1325
Re 4:9 those beasts g. glory and honour... 1325
Re 10:9 said unto him, G. me the little book... 1325
Re 11:3 will g. power unto my two witnesses, ..1325
Re 11:17 We g. thee thanks, O Lord God...
Re 11:18 g. reward unto thy servants the... 1325
Re 13:15 g. life unto the image of the beast, ... 1325
Re 14:7 Fear God, and g. glory to him; ... 1325
Re 16:9 they repented not to g. him glory... 1325
Re 16:19 to g. unto her the cup of the wine... 1325
Re 17:13 g. their power and strength unto... 1239
Re 17:17 g. their kingdom unto the beast, ... 1325
Re 18:7 much torment and sorrow g. her:... 1325
Re 19:7 and rejoice, an g. honour to him: ... 1325
Re 21:6 I will g. unto him that is athirst ... 1325
Re 22:12 g. every man according as his work.591

GIVEN See also FORGIVEN.
Ge 1:29 g. you every herb bearing seed, ... 5414
Ge 1:30 I have g. every green herb for meat: ...
Ge 9:3 as the green herb have I g. you... 5414
Ge 15:3 Behold, to me thou hast g. no seed:... 5414
Ge 15:18 Unto thy seed have I g. this land, ... 5414
Ge 16:5 I have g. my maid into thy bosom; ... 5414
Ge 20:16 I have g. thy brother a thousand... 5414
Ge 21:7 should have g. children suck? ...
Ge 24:35 he hath g. him flocks, and herds, ... 5414
Ge 24:36 and unto him hath he g. all ... 5414
Ge 27:37 all his brethren have I g. to him... 5414
Ge 29:33 he hath therefore g. me this son... 5414
Ge 30:6 and hath g. me a son: therefore... 5414
Ge 30:18 God hath g. me my hire, ... 5414
Ge 30:18 because I have g. my maiden ... 5414
Ge 31:9 cattle of your father, and g. them... 5414
Ge 33:5 hath graciously g. thy servant... 2603
Ge 38:14 she was not g. unto him to wife... 5414
Ge 43:23 the God of your father, hath g. you... 5414
Ge 48:9 my sons, whom God hath g. me ... 5414
Ge 48:22 I have g. to thee one portion above... 5414
Ex 5:16 is no straw g. unto thy servants, ... 5414
Ex 5:18 for there shall no straw be g. you, ... 5414
Ex 16:15 bread which the Lord hath g. you... 5414
Ex 16:29 the Lord hath g. you the sabbath, ... 5414
Ex 21:4 If his master have g. him a wife,... 5414
Ex 31:6 I have g. with him Aholiab, ... 5414
Le 6:17 g. it unto them for their portion... 5414
Le 7:34 have g. them unto Aaron the priest... 5414
Le 7:36 the Lord commanded to be g. them... 5414
Le 10:14 are g. out of the sacrifices of peace... 5414
Le 10:17 God hath g. it you to bear the... 5414
Le 17:11 I have g. it to you upon the altar ... 5414
Le 19:20 not at all redeemed, nor freedom g.... 5414
Le 20:3 he hath g. of his seed unto Molech,... 5414
Nu 3:9 they are wholly g. unto him out of... 5414
Nu 8:16 they are wholly g. unto me from... 5414
Nu 8:19 And I have g. the Levites as a gift ... 5414
Nu 16:14 or g. us inheritance of fields and ... 5414
Nu 18:6 they are g. as a gift for the Lord, ... 5414
Nu 18:7 g. your priest's office unto you ... 5414
Nu 18:8 also have g. thee the charge of mine... 5414
Nu 18:8 unto thee have I g. them by reason... 5414
Nu 18:11 I have g. them unto thee, and to thy .. 5414
Nu 18:12 unto the Lord, them have I g. thee. ... 5414
Nu 18:19 have I g. thee, and thy sons and... 5414
Nu 18:21 I have g. the children of Levi all ... 5414
Nu 18:24 I have g. the Levites to inherit: ... 5414
Nu 18:26 the tithes which I have g. you from... 5414
Nu 20:12 the land which I have g. them. ... 5414
Nu 20:24 which I have g. unto the children ... 5414
Nu 21:29 he hath g. his sons that escaped, ... 5414
Nu 26:54 every one shall his inheritance be g. ... 5414
Nu 26:62 there was no inheritance g. them ... 5414
Nu 27:12 the land which I have g. unto the... 5414
Nu 32:5 this land be g. unto thy servants... 5414
Nu 32:7 land which the Lord hath g. them? ... 5414
Nu 32:9 land which the Lord hath g. them... 5414
Nu 33:53 I have g. you the land to possess it... 5414
De 1:3 Lord had g. him in commandment...
De 2:5 I have g. mount Seir unto Esau ... 5414
De 2:9 have g. Ar unto the children of Lot... 5414
De 2:19 I have g. it unto the children of Lot... 5414
De 2:24 I have g. into thine hand Sihon ... 5414
De 9:18 Lord your God hath g. you this ... 5414
De 3:19 your cities which I have g. you;... 5414
De 3:20 have g. rest unto your brethren, ...
De 3:20 the Lord your God hath g. them... 5414
De 3:20 possession, which I have g. you... 5414
De 8:10 good land which he hath g. thee... 5414
De 9:23 the land which I have g. you; ... 5414
De 12:15 blessing...which he hath g. thee: ... 5414
De 12:21 flock, which the Lord hath g. thee,... 5414
De 13:12 God hath g. thee to dwell there, ... 5414
De 16:17 blessing...which he hath g. thee. ... 5414
De 20:14 the spoil...thy God hath g. thee. ... 5414
De 22:17 g. occasions of speech against ... 7760
De 25:19 the Lord thy God hath g. thee rest...
De 26:9 hath g. us this land, even a land ... 5414
De 26:10 which thou, O Lord, hast g. me... 5414
De 26:11 the Lord thy God hath g. unto thee,... 5414
De 26:12 and hast g. it unto the Levite, ... 5414
De 26:13 also have g. them unto the Levite, ... 5414
De 26:14 nor g. ought thereof for the dead: ... 5414
De 26:15 the land which thou hast g. us, ... 5414
De 28:31 shall be g. unto thine enemies, ... 5414
De 28:32 daughters shall be g. unto another... 5414
De 28:52 land...Lord thy God hath g. thee... 5414
De 28:53 daughters...thy God hath g. thee,... 5414
De 29:4 the Lord hath not g. you an heart ... 5414
De 29:26 whom he had not g. unto them: ... 2505
Jos 1:3 that have I g. unto you, as I said ... 5414
Jos 1:13 Lord your God hath g. you rest, ...
Jos 1:13 and hath g. you this land. ... 5414
Jos 1:15 the Lord have g. your brethren...
Jos 1:15 rest, as he hath g. you, ...
Jos 2:9 the Lord hath g. you the land, ... 5414
Jos 2:14 when the Lord hath g. us the land,... 5414
Jos 6:2 I have g. into thine hand Jericho, ... 5414
Jos 6:16 the Lord hath g. you the city. ... 5414
Jos 8:1 g. into thy hand the king of Ai, ... 5414
Jos 14:3 Moses had g. the inheritance of two... 5414
Jos 15:19 thou hast g. me a south land; ... 5414
Jos 17:14 Why hast thou g. me but one lot... 5414
Jos 18:3 Lord God of your fathers hath g. ... 5414
Jos 22:4 the Lord your God hath g. rest...
Jos 22:7 had g. possession in Bashan: ... 5414
Jos 23:1 the Lord had g. rest unto Israel...
Jos 23:13, 15 the Lord your God hath g. you... 5414
Jos 23:16 land which he hath g. unto you. ... 5414
Jos 24:13 And I have g. you a land for ... 5414
Jos 24:33 was g. him in mount Ephraim... 5414
Jg 1:15 for thou hast g. me a south land; ... 5414
Jg 14:20 Samson's wife was g. to his companion,...
Jg 15:6 wife, and g. her to his companion... 5414
Jg 15:18 Thou hast g. this great deliverance... 5414
Jg 18:10 God hath g. it into your hands; ... 5414
Ru 2:12 full reward be g. thee of the Lord...
1Sa 1:27 the Lord hath g. me my petition ... 5414
1Sa 15:28 hath g. it to a neighbour of thine,... 5414
1Sa 18:19 Saul's daughter should have been g.... 5414
1Sa 18:19 David, that she was g. unto Adriel ... 5414
1Sa 22:13 in that thou hast g. him bread, ... 5414
1Sa 25:27 it even be g. unto the young men ... 5414
1Sa 25:44 Saul had g. Michal his daughter,... 5414
1Sa 28:17 and g. it to thy neighbour, even to... 5414
1Sa 30:23 that which the Lord hath g. us, ... 5414
2Sa 4:10 I would have g. him a reward... 5414
2Sa 7:1 Lord had g. him rest round about...
2Sa 9:9 I have g. unto thy master's son ... 5414
2Sa 12:8 would moreover have g. unto thee ... 3254
2Sa 12:14 hast g. great occasion to the enemies...
2Sa 17:7 Ahithophel hath g. is not good ... 3289
2Sa 18:11 I would have g. thee ten shekels... 5414
2Sa 19:42 or hath he g. us any gift? ... 5375
2Sa 22:36 thou hast also g. me the shield ... 5414
2Sa 22:41 g. me the necks of mine enemies, ... 5414
1Ki 1:48 hath g. one to sit on my throne ... 5414
1Ki 2:21 Let Abishag the Shunammite be g. ... 5414
1Ki 3:6 g. him a son to sit on his throne, ... 5414
1Ki 3:12 I have g. thee a wise and an... 5414
1Ki 3:13 also g. thee that which thou hast... 5414
1Ki 5:4 the Lord my God hath g. me rest ...
1Ki 5:7 day, which hath g. unto David ... 5414
1Ki 8:36 thy land, which thou hast g. to thy... 5414
1Ki 8:56 the Lord, that hath g. rest unto his... 5414
1Ki 9:7 out of the land which I have g. ... 5414
1Ki 9:12 cities which Solomon had g. him;... 5414
1Ki 9:13 cities are these which thou hast g. ... 5414
1Ki 9:16 and g. it for a present unto his ... 5414
1Ki 12:8 old men, which they had g. him, ... 3289
1Ki 13:5 sign which the man of God had g. ... 5414

1Ki 18:26 the bullock which was **g.** them, 5414
2Ki 5:1 had **g.** deliverance unto Syria: 5414
2Ki 5:17 I pray thee, be **g.** to thy servant 5414
2Ki 8:29 wounds which the Syrians had **g.** 5221
2Ki 9:15 wounds which the Syrians had **g.** 5221
2Ki 23:11 kings of Judah had **g.** to the sun, 5414
2Ki 25:30 allowance **g.** him of the king, 5414
1Ch 5:1 was **g.** unto the sons of Joseph 5414
1Ch 6:61 cities **g.** out of the half tribe,
1Ch 6:63 Unto the sons of Merari were **g.** by
1Ch 6:71 Unto the sons of Gershom were **g.**
1Ch 6:77 the children of Merari were **g.** out of
1Ch 6:78 **g.** them out of the tribe of Reuben,
1Ch 22:18 he not **g.** you rest on every side?
1Ch 22:18 for he hath **g.** the inhabitants 5414
1Ch 23:25 The Lord God of Israel hath **g.** rest
1Ch 28:5 the Lord hath **g.** me many sons,) 5414
1Ch 29:3 gold and silver, which I have **g.** 5414
1Ch 29:14 and of thine own have we **g.** thee. 5414
2Ch 2:12 **g.** to David the king a wise son, 5414
2Ch 6:27 upon thy land, which thou hast **g.** 5414
2Ch 7:20 out of my land which I have **g.** 5414
2Ch 14:6 because the Lord had **g.** him rest
2Ch 14:7 he hath **g.** us rest on every side,
2Ch 20:11 which thou hast **g.** us to inherit.
2Ch 22:6 the wounds which were **g.** him at 5221
2Ch 25:9 hundred talents which I have **g.** 5414
2Ch 32:29 God had **g.** him substance very 5414
2Ch 34:14 the law of the Lord **g.** by Moses.
2Ch 34:18 the priest hath **g.** me a book. 5414
2Ch 36:23 hath the Lord God of heaven **g.** me; 5414
Ezr 1:2 The Lord God of heaven hath **g.** me 5414
Ezr 4:21 commandment shall be **g.** from 7761
Ezr 6:4 expences be **g.** out of the king's 3052
Ezr 6:8 expences be **g.** unto these men, 3052
Ezr 6:9 be **g.** them day by day without fail: 3052
Ezr 7:6 the Lord God of Israel had **g.**: 5414
Ezr 7:19 The vessels also that are **g.** thee 3052
Ezr 9:13 **g.** us such deliverance as this; 5414
Ne 2:7 letters be **g.** me to the governors 5414
Ne 10:29 God's law, which was **g.** by Moses 5414
Ne 13:5 commanded to be **g.** to the Levites,
Ne 13:10 the Levites had not been **g.** them 5414
Es 2:3 their things for purification be **g.** 5414
Es 2:9 which were meet to be **g.** her, 5414
Es 2:13 whatsoever she desired was **g.** her 5414
Es 3:11 silver is **g.** to thee, the people also, 5414
Es 3:14 a commandment to be **g.** in every 5414
Es 3:15 was **g.** in Shushan the palace. 5414
Es 4:8 the decree that was **g.** at Shushan 5414
Es 5:3 it shall be even **g.** thee to the half 5414
Es 7:3 let my life be **g.** me at my petition, 5414
Es 8:7 have **g.** Esther the house of Haman, 5414
Es 8:13 a commandment to be **g.** in every 5414
Es 8:14 was **g.** at Shushan the palace. 5414
Es 9:14 and the decree was **g.** at Shushan; 5414
Job 3:20 is light **g.** to him that is in misery, 5414
Job 3:23 Why is light **g.** to a man whose way
Job 9:24 is **g.** into the hand of the wicked: 5414
Job 10:18 O that I had **g.** up the ghost, 1478
Job 15:19 unto whom alone the earth was **g.**, 5414
Job 22:7 not **g.** water to the weary to drink,
Job 24:23 Though it be **g.** him to be in safety, 5414
Job 33:4 of the Almighty hath **g.** me life.
Job 34:13 **g.** him a charge over the earth?
Job 37:10 By the breath of God frost is **g.** 5414
Job 38:36 **g.** understanding to the heart? 5414
Job 39:19 Hast thou **g.** the horse strength? 5414
Ps 16:7 the Lord, who hath **g.** me counsel:
Ps 18:35 Thou hast also **g.** me the shield 5414
Ps 18:40 **g.** me the necks of mine enemies; 5414
Ps 21:2 hast **g.** him his heart's desire, 5414
Ps 44:11 **g.** us like sheep appointed for 5414
Ps 60:4 hast **g.** a banner to them that fear 5414
Ps 61:5 thou hast **g.** me the heritage of 5414
Ps 71:3 hast **g.** commandment to save me;
Ps 72:15 and to him shall be **g.** of the gold 5414
Ps 78:24 had **g.** them of the corn of heaven. 5414
Ps 78:63 maidens were not **g.** to marriage.
Ps 79:2 bodies of thy servants have they **g.** 5414
Ps 111:5 **g.** meat unto them that fear him: 5414
Ps 112:9 **g.** to the poor; his righteousness 5414
Ps 115:16 earth hath he **g.** to the children 5414
Ps 118:18 he hath not **g.** me over unto death. 5414
Ps 120:3 What shall be **g.** unto thee? or what 5414
Ps 124:6 who hath not **g.** us as a prey 5414
Pr 19:17 that which he hath **g.** will he pay 1576
Pr 23:2 if thou be a man **g.** to appetite. 1167
Pr 24:21 not with them that are **g.** to change:
Ec 1:13 sore travail hath God **g.** to the sons 5414
Ec 3:10 travail, which God hath **g.** to the 5414
Ec 5:19 to whom God hath **g.** riches and 5414
Ec 5:19 and hath **g.** him power to eat
Ec 6:2 man to whom God hath **g.** riches, 5414
Ec 8:8 deliver those that are **g.** to it. 1167
Ec 9:9 thy vanity, which he hath **g.** thee 5414
Ec 12:11 which are **g.** from one shepherd. 5414
Isa 3:11 reward of his hands shall be **g.** him 6213
Isa 8:18 children whom the Lord hath **g.** 5414
Isa 9:6 a child is born, unto us a son is **g.**: 5414
Isa 23:11 the Lord hath **g.** a commandment
Isa 33:16 bread shall be **g.** him; his waters 5414
Isa 35:2 glory of Lebanon shall be **g.** unto 5414
Isa 37:10 Jerusalem shall not be **g.** into the 5414
Isa 43:28 and have **g.** Jacob to the curse, 5414
Isa 47:6 and **g.** them into thine hand: 5414
Isa 47:8 thou that art **g.** to pleasures, that
Isa 50:4 Lord God hath **g.** me the tongue 5414
Isa 55:4 Behold, I have **g.** him for a witness 5414
Jer 3:8 away, and **g.** her a bill of divorce; 5414
Jer 3:18 I have **g.** for an inheritance unto your
Jer 6:13 every one is **g.** to covetousness;
Jer 8:10 the greatest is **g.** to covetousness,
Jer 8:13 the things that I have **g.** them 5414
Jer 8:14 and **g.** us water of gall to drink,
Jer 11:18 the Lord hath **g.** me knowledge
Jer 12:7 **g.** the dearly beloved of my soul 5414
Jer 13:20 where is the flock that was **g.** thee, 5414
Jer 15:9 she hath **g.** up the ghost; her sun 5301
Jer 21:10 shall be **g.** into the hand of the king 5414
Jer 25:5 land that the Lord hath **g.** unto you 5414
Jer 27:5 **g.** it unto whom it seemed meet 5414
Jer 27:6 now have I **g.** all these lands 5414
Jer 27:6 beasts of the field have I **g.** him 5414
Jer 28:14 **g.** him the beasts of the field also 5414
Jer 32:22 **g.** them this land, which thou didst 5414
Jer 32:24 and the city is **g.** into the hand of 5414
Jer 32:25 for the city is **g.** into the hand of the 5414
Jer 32:43 it is **g.** into the hand of the 5414
Jer 35:15 the land which I have **g.** to you 5414
Jer 38:3 This city shall surely be **g.** into the 5414
Jer 38:18 shall this city be **g.** into the hand 5414
Jer 39:17 thou shalt not be **g.** into the hand 5414
Jer 44:20 people which had **g.** him that answer,
Jer 47:7 the Lord hath **g.** it a charge against
Jer 50:15 hath **g.** her hand: her foundations 5414
Jer 52:34 continual diet **g.** him of the king 5414
La 1:11 **g.** their pleasant things for meat 5414
La 2:7 **g.** up into the hand of the enemy 5462
La 5:6 have **g.** the hand to the Egyptians, 5414
Eze 3:20 because thou hast not **g.** him warning,
Eze 4:15 **g.** thee cow's dung for man's dung, 5414
Eze 11:15 unto us is this land **g.** in possession. 5414
Eze 15:6 which I have **g.** to the fire for fuel 5414
Eze 16:17 of my silver, which I had **g.** thee. 5414
Eze 16:34 and no reward is **g.** unto thee, 5414
Eze 17:18 he had **g.** his hand, and hath done 5414
Eze 18:7 hath **g.** his bread to the hungry, 5414
Eze 18:8 that hath not **g.** forth upon usury, 5414
Eze 18:13 Hath **g.** forth upon usury, and hath 5414
Eze 18:16 hath **g.** his bread to the hungry, 5414
Eze 20:15 into the land which I had **g.** them, 5414
Eze 21:11 And he hath **g.** it to be furbished, 5414
Eze 28:25 land that I have **g.** to my servant 5414
Eze 29:5 have **g.** thee for meat to the beasts 5414
Eze 29:20 I have **g.** him the land of Egypt 5414
Eze 33:24 the land is **g.** us for inheritance 5414
Eze 35:12 desolate, they are **g.** us to consume. 5414
Eze 37:25 the land that I have **g.** unto Jacob 5414
Eze 47:11 they shall be **g.** to salt. 5414
Da 2:23 who hast **g.** me wisdom and might, 3052
Da 2:37 for the God of heaven hath **g.** thee 3052
Da 2:38 heaven hath he **g.** into thine hand, 3052
Da 4:16 let a beast's heart be **g.** unto him; 3052
Da 5:28 and **g.** to the Medes and Persians. 3052
Da 7:4 and a man's heart was **g.** to it. 3052
Da 7:6 and dominion was **g.** to it. 3052
Da 7:11 and **g.** to the burning flame. 3052
Da 7:14 And there was **g.** him dominion, 3052
Da 7:22 and judgment was **g.** to the saints 3052
Da 7:25 and they shall be **g.** into his hand 3052
Da 7:27 be **g.** to the people of the saints of 3052
Da 8:12 host was **g.** him against the daily 5414
Da 11:6 she shall be **g.** up, and they that 5414
Da 11:11 multitude shall be **g.** into his hand. 5414
Ho 2:9 flax **g.** to cover her nakedness.
Ho 2:12 rewards that my lovers have **g.** me: 5414
Joe 2:23 he hath **g.** you the former rain 5414
Joe 3:3 and have **g.** a boy for an harlot, 5414
Am 4:6 have **g.** you cleanness of teeth 5414
Am 9:15 their land which I have **g.** them, 5414
Na 1:14 And the Lord hath **g.** a commandment
Mt 7:7 **Ask, and it shall be g. you: seek,** *1325*
Mt 9:8 glorified God, which had **g.** such *1325*
Mt 10:19 **it shall be g. you in that same** *1325*
Mt 12:39 **and there shall no sign be g. to it,** *1325*
Mt 13:11 **g. unto you to know the mysteries** *1325*
Mt 13:11 **but to them it is not g.** *1325*
Mt 13:12 **whosoever hath, to him shall be g.** *1325*
Mt 14:9 he commanded it to be **g.** her. *1325*
Mt 14:11 in a charger, and **g.** to the damsel; *1325*
Mt 16:4 **there shall no sign be g. unto it,** *1325*
Mt 19:11 **save they to whom it is g.** *1325*
Mt 20:23 **it shall be g. to them for whom it**
Mt 21:43 **taken from you, and g. to a nation** *1325*
Mt 22:30 **marry, nor are g. in marriage,** *1547*
Mt 25:29 **every one that hath shall be g.,** *1325*
Mt 26:9 sold for much, and **g.** to the poor. *1325*
Mt 28:18 **All power is g. unto me in heaven.** *1325*
Mk 4:11 **you it is g. to know the mystery** *1325*
Mk 4:24 **you that hear shall more be g.** *4369*
Mk 4:25 **he that hath, to him shall be g.:** *1325*
Mk 5:43 something should be **g.** her to eat. *1325*
Mk 6:2 this which is **g.** unto him, that even *1325*
Mk 8:12 **no sign be g. unto this generation.** *1325*
Mk 10:40 **but it shall be g. to them for whom**
Mk 12:25 **marry, nor are g. in marriage:**
Mk 13:11 **shall be g. you in that hour,** *1325*
Mk 14:5 and have been **g.** to the poor. *1325*
Mk 14:23 cup, and when he had **g.** thanks,
Mk 14:44 him had **g.** them a token, saying, *1325*
Lu 6:38 **Give, and it shall be g. unto you;** *1325*
Lu 8:10 **you it is g. to know the mysteries** *1325*
Lu 8:18 **whosoever hath, to him shall be g.;** *1325*
Lu 11:9 **Ask, and it shall be g. you; seek.** *1325*
Lu 11:29 **there shall no sign be g. it, but the** *1325*
Lu 12:48 **unto whomsoever much is g., of** *1325*
Lu 17:27 **they were g. in marriage, until the**
Lu 19:15 **whom he had g. the money, that** *1325*
Lu 19:26 **every one which hath shall be g.;** *1325*
Lu 20:34 **marry, and are g. in marriage; but**
Lu 20:35 **neither marry, nor are g. in**
Lu 22:19 **This is my body which is g. for** *1325*
Joh 1:17 law was **g.** by Moses, but grace *1325*
Joh 3:27 except it be **g.** him from heaven. *1325*
Joh 3:35 hath **g.** all things into his hand. *1325*
Joh 4:10 **he would have g. thee living water.** *1325*
Joh 5:26 **so hath he g. to the Son to have** *1325*
Joh 5:27 **hath g. him authority to execute** *1325*
Joh 5:36 **which the Father hath g. me** *1325*
Joh 6:11 when he had **g.** thanks, he distributed
Joh 6:23 after that the Lord had **g.** thanks:)
Joh 6:39 **that of all which he hath g. me.** *1325*
Joh 6:65 **it were g. unto him of my Father.** *1325*
Joh 7:39 for the Holy Ghost was not yet **g.**;
Joh 11:57 Pharisees had **g.** a commandment, *1325*
Joh 12:5 hundred pence, and **g.** to the poor? *1325*
Joh 13:3 the Father had **g.** all things into his *1325*
Joh 13:15 **For I have g. you an example,** *1325*
Joh 17:2 **thou hast g. him power over all** *1325*
Joh 17:2 **to as many as thou hast g. him.** *1325*
Joh 17:7 **whatsoever thou hast g. me are of.** *1325*
Joh 17:8 **have g. unto them the words which** *1325*
Joh 17:9 **for them which thou hast g. me;** *1325*
Joh 17:11 **those whom thou hast g. me, that** *1325*
Joh 17:14 **I have g. them thy word; and the** *1325*
Joh 17:22 **thou gavest me I have g. them;** *1325*
Joh 17:24 **they also, whom thou hast g. me,** *1325*
Joh 17:24 **my glory, which thou hast g. me:** *1325*
Joh 18:11 **cup which my Father hath g. me,** *1325*
Joh 19:11 **except it were g. thee from above:** *1325*
Ac 1:2 Holy Ghost had **g.** commandments
Ac 3:16 hath **g.** him this perfect soundness *1325*
Ac 4:12 name under heaven **g.** among men, *1325*
Ac 5:32 whom God hath **g.** to them that *1325*
Ac 8:18 the Holy Ghost was **g.**, he offered *1325*
Ac 17:16 saw the city wholly **g.** to idolatry
Ac 17:31 whereof he hath **g.** assurance unto *3930*

Ac 20:2 and had **g.** them much exhortation,...
Ac 21:40 And when he had **g.** him licence, Paul...
Ac 24:26 money should have been **g.** him of... *1325*
Ac 27:24 God hath **g.** thee all them that... *5483*
Ro 5:5 by the Holy Ghost which is **g.** unto... *1325*
Ro 11:8 hath **g.** them the spirit of slumber,... *1325*
Ro 11:35 Or who hath first **g.** to him, and it... *4272*
Ro 12:3 say through the grace **g.** unto me,... *1325*
Ro 12:6 the grace that is **g.** to us, whether... *1325*
Ro 12:13 necessity of saints; **g.** to hospitality... *1377*
Ro 15:15 the grace that is **g.** to me of God,... *1325*
1Co 1:4 the grace of God which is **g.** you by... *1325*
1Co 2:12 know the things that are freely **g.**... *5483*
1Co 3:10 the grace of God which is **g.** unto... *1325*
1Co 11:15 for her hair is **g.** her for a covering... *1325*
1Co 11:24 And when he had **g.** thanks, he...
1Co 12:7 manifestation of the Spirit is **g.**... *1325*
1Co 12:8 to one is **g.** by the Spirit the word... *1325*
1Co 12:24 having **g.** more abundant honour... *1325*
1Co 16:1 as I have **g.** order to the churches...
2Co 1:11 thanks may be **g.** by many on our...
2Co 1:22 and **g.** the earnest of the Spirit... *1325*
2Co 5:5 also hath **g.** unto us the earnest of... *1325*
2Co 5:18 and hath **g.** to us the ministry... *1325*
2Co 9:9 **g.** to the poor: his righteousness... *1325*
2Co 10:8 the Lord hath **g.** us for edification,... *1325*
2Co 12:7 there was **g.** to me a thorn in the... *1325*
2Co 13:10 power which the Lord hath **g.** me... *1325*
Ga 2:9 the grace that was **g.** unto me, they... *1325*
Ga 3:21 for if there had been a law **g.**... *1325*
Ga 3:21 which could have **g.** life,... *2227*
Ga 3:22 might be **g.** to them that believe... *1325*
Ga 4:15 own eyes, and have **g.** them to me... *1325*
Eph 3:2 which is **g.** me to you-ward:... *1325*
Eph 3:7 the grace of God **g.** unto me by the... *1325*
Eph 3:8 is this grace **g.**, that I should preach... *1325*
Eph 4:7 unto every one of us is **g.** grace... *1325*
Eph 4:19 past feeling have **g.** themselves... *3860*
Eph 5:2 hath loved us, and hath **g.** himself... *3860*
Eph 6:19 that utterance may be **g.** unto me,... *1325*
Php 1:29 you it is **g.** in the behalf of Christ,... *5483*
Php 2:9 and **g.** him a name which is above... *5483*
Col 1:25 of God which is **g.** to me for you,... *1325*
1Th 4:8 also **g.** unto us his holy Spirit... *1325*
2Th 2:16 hath **g.** us everlasting consolation... *1325*
1Ti 3:2 **g.** to hospitality, apt to teach;...
1Ti 3:3 **g.** to wine, no striker, not greedy... *3943*
1Ti 3:8 not **g.** to much wine, not greedy... *4337*
1Ti 4:14 which was **g.** thee by prophecy,... *1325*
2Ti 1:7 For God hath not **g.** us the spirit... *1325*
2Ti 1:9 grace, which was **g.** us in Christ... *1325*
2Ti 3:16 All scripture is **g.** by inspiration...
Tit 1:7 not soon angry, not **g.** to wine,... *3943*
Tit 1:7 not **g.** to filthy lucre;...
Tit 2:3 not **g.** to much wine, teachers of... *1402*
Phm 22 prayers I shall be **g.** unto you... *5483*
Heb 2:13 the children which God hath **g.**... *1325*
Heb 4:8 For if Jesus had **g.** them rest, then...
Jas 1:5 upbraideth not; and it shall be **g.**... *1325*
2Pe 1:3 power hath **g.** unto us all things... *1433*
2Pe 1:4 Whereby are **g.** unto us exceeding... *1433*
2Pe 3:15 according to the wisdom **g.** unto... *1325*
1Jo 3:24 by the Spirit which he hath **g.** us... *1325*
1Jo 4:13 because he hath **g.** us of his Spirit... *1325*
1Jo 5:11 that God hath **g.** to us eternal life,... *1325*
1Jo 5:20 and hath **g.** us an understanding,... *1325*
Re 6:2 and a crown was **g.** unto him:... *1325*
Re 6:4 power was **g.** to him that sat thereon... *1325*
Re 6:4 and there was **g.** unto him a great... *1325*
Re 6:8 power was **g.** unto them over the... *1325*
Re 6:11 white robes were **g.** unto every one... *1325*
Re 7:2 to whom it was **g.** to hurt the earth... *1325*
Re 8:2 to them were **g.** seven trumpets... *1325*
Re 8:3 there was **g.** unto him much incense,... *1325*
Re 9:1 was **g.** the key of the bottomless pit... *1325*
Re 9:3 unto them was **g.** power, as the... *1325*
Re 9:5 to them it was **g.** that they should... *1325*
Re 11:1 there was **g.** me a reed like unto a... *1325*
Re 11:2 for it is **g.** unto the Gentiles:... *1325*
Re 12:14 to the woman were **g.** two wings... *1325*
Re 13:5 there was **g.** unto him a mouth... *1325*
Re 13:5 power was **g.** unto him to continue... *1325*
Re 13:7 it was **g.** unto him to make war... *1325*
Re 13:7 power was **g.** him over all kindreds,... *1325*
Re 16:6 thou hast **g.** them blood to drink;... *1325*
Re 16:8 power was **g.** unto him to scorch... *1325*
Re 20:4 and judgment was **g.** unto them:... *1325*

GIVER See also LAWGIVER.
Isa 24:2 so with the **g.** of usury to him...
2Co 9:7 for God loveth a cheerful **g.**... *1395*

GIVEST
De 15:9 thou **g.** him nought; and he cry... 5414
De 15:10 grieved when thou **g.** unto him?... 5414
Job 35:7 what **g.** thou him? or what... 5414
Ps 50:19 thou **g.** thy mouth to evil, and... 7971
Ps 80:5 and **g.** them tears to drink in great...
Ps 104:28 That thou **g.** them they gather:... 5414
Ps 145:15 thou **g.** them their meat in due... 5414
Pr 6:35 content, though thou **g.** many gifts...
Eze 3:18 thou **g.** him nor warning, nor speakest...
Eze 16:33 thou **g.** thy gifts to all thy lovers,... 5414
Eze 16:34 in that thou **g.** a reward, and no... 5414
1Co 14:17 For thou verily **g.** thanks well,...

GIVETH See also FORGIVETH.
Ge 49:21 hind let loose: he **g.** goodly words... 5414
Ex 16:29 therefore he **g.** you on the sixth... 5414
Ex 20:12 the land which the Lord thy God **g.**... 5414
Ex 25:2 every man that **g.** it willingly...
Le 20:2 **g.** any of his seed unto Molech;... 5414
Le 20:4 when he **g.** of his seed unto Molech,... 5414
Le 27:9 all that any man **g.** such unto the... 5414
Nu 5:10 whatsoever any man **g.** the priest,... 5414
De 2:29 the land which the Lord our God **g.**... 5414
De 4:1 the Lord God of your fathers **g.**... 5414
De 4:21 the Lord thy God **g.** thee for an... 5414
De 4:40 the land which the Lord thy God **g.**... 5414
De 5:16 the land which the Lord thy God **g.**... 5414
De 8:18 it is he that **g.** thee power to get... 5414
De 9:6 Lord thy God **g.** thee not this land... 5414
De 11:17 the good land which the Lord **g.**... 5414
De 11:31 land which the Lord your God **g.**... 5414
De 12:1 God of thy fathers **g.** thee to... 5414
De 12:9 which the Lord your God **g.** you... 5414
De 12:10 Lord your God **g.** you to inherit,...
De 12:10 and when he **g.** you rest from all...
De 13:1 and **g.** thee a sign or a wonder,... 5414
De 15:4 which the Lord thy God **g.** thee... 5414
De 15:7 God **g.** thee, thou shalt not harden... 5414
De 16:5 which the Lord thy God **g.** thee:... 5414
De 16:18 thy God **g.** thee, throughout thy... 5414
De 16:20 the land which the Lord thy God **g.**... 5414
De 17:2 the Lord thy God **g.** thee, man or... 5414
De 17:14 which the Lord thy God **g.** thee,... 5414
De 18:9 which the Lord thy God **g.** thee,... 5414
De 19:1 whose land the Lord thy God **g.**... 5414
De 19:2 which the Lord thy God **g.** thee to... 5414
De 19:3 God **g.** thee to inherit, into three...
De 19:10 thy God **g.** thee for an inheritance,... 5414
De 19:14 Lord thy God **g.** thee to possess... 5414
De 21:1 which the Lord thy God **g.** thee to... 5414
De 21:23 the Lord thy God **g.** thee for an... 5414
De 24:3 a bill of divorcement, and **g.** it... 5414
De 24:4 which the Lord thy God **g.** thee for... 5414
De 25:15 which the Lord thy God **g.** thee... 5414
De 25:19 the land which the Lord thy God **g.**... 5414
De 26:1 thy God **g.** thee for an inheritance,... 5414
De 26:2 that the Lord thy God **g.** thee, and... 5414
De 27:2 the Lord thy God **g.** thee, that thou... 5414
De 27:3 thy God **g.** thee, a land that floweth... 5414
De 28:8 which the Lord thy God **g.** thee... 5414
Jos 1:11 which the Lord your God **g.** you... 5414
Jos 1:15 which the Lord your God **g.** them:... 5414
Jg 11:24 Chemosh thy god **g.** thee to possess?...
Jg 21:18 Cursed be he that **g.** a wife to... 5414
Job 5:10 Who **g.** rain upon the earth, and... 5414
Job 14:10 yea, man **g.** up the ghost, and... 1478
Job 32:8 the Almighty **g.** them understanding...
Job 33:13 **g.** not account of any of his matters...
Job 34:29 When he **g.** queitness, who then...
Job 35:10 who **g.** songs in the night;... 5414
Job 35:12 There they cry, but none **g.** answer,...
Job 36:6 but **g.** right to the poor... 5414
Job 36:31 he **g.** meat in abundance... 5414
Ps 18:50 Great deliverance **g.** he to his king;...
Ps 37:21 righteous sheweth mercy, and **g.**... 5414
Ps 68:35 he that **g.** strength and power... 5414
Ps 119:130 The entrance of thy words **g.** light;...
Ps 119:130 it **g.** understanding unto the simple...
Ps 127:2 for so he **g.** his beloved sleep... 5414
Ps 136:25 Who **g.** food to all flesh: for his... 5414
Ps 144:10 is he that **g.** salvation unto kings:... 5414
Ps 146:7 which **g.** food to the hungry... 5414
Ps 147:9 He **g.** to the beast his food,... 5414
Ps 147:16 He **g.** snow like wool: he... 5414
Pr 2:6 For the Lord **g.** wisdom: out of his... 5414
Pr 3:34 but he **g.** grace unto the lowly... 5414
Pr 13:15 Good understanding **g.** favour;... 5414
Pr 17:4 A wicked doer **g.** heed to false lips;...
Pr 17:4 and a liar **g.** ear to a naughty tongue...
Pr 19:6 is a friend to him that **g.** gifts...
Pr 21:26 the righteous **g.** and spareth not... 5414
Pr 22:9 he **g.** of his bread to the poor... 5414
Pr 22:16 he that **g.** to the rich, shall surely... 5414
Pr 23:31 when it **g.** his colour in the cup,... 5414
Pr 24:26 kiss his lips that **g.** a right answer...
Pr 26:8 so is he that **g.** honour to a fool... 5414
Pr 28:27 that **g.** unto the poor shall not lack:... 5414
Pr 31:15 and **g.** meat to her household, and... 5414
Ec 2:26 For God **g.** to a man that is good... 5414
Ec 2:26 but to the sinner he **g.** travail to... 5414
Ec 5:18 days of his life, which God **g.** him:... 5414
Ec 6:2 God **g.** him not power to eat thereof,...
Ec 7:12 wisdom **g.** life to them that have...
Ec 8:15 which God **g.** him under the sun... 5414
Isa 40:29 He **g.** power to the faint; and to... 5414
Isa 42:5 that **g.** breath unto the people... 5414
Jer 5:24 the Lord our God, that **g.** rain,... 5414
Jer 22:13 and **g.** him not for his work;... 5414
Jer 31:35 Lord, which **g.** the sun for a light... 5414
La 3:30 **g.** his cheek to him that smiteth... 5414
Da 2:21 he **g.** wisdom unto the wise, and... 3052
Da 4:17 and **g.** it to whomsoever he will,... 5415
Da 4:25, 32 and **g.** it to whomsoever he will... 5415
Hab 2:15 him that **g.** his neighbour drink,...
Mt 5:15 **and it g. light unto all that are in...**
Joh 3:34 God **g.** not the Spirit by measure... *1325*
Joh 6:32 **my Father g. you the true bread...** *1325*
Joh 6:33 **and g. life unto the world...** *1325*
Joh 6:37 **All that the Father g. me shall...** *1325*
Joh 10:11 **good shepherd g. his life for the...** *5087*
Joh 14:27 **not as the world g., give I unto...** *1325*
Joh 21:13 taketh bread, and **g.** them, and fish... *1325*
Ac 17:25 seeing he **g.** to all life, and breath,... *1325*
Ro 12:8 he that **g.**, let him do it with... *3330*
Ro 14:6 for he **g.** God thanks; and he that...
Ro 14:6 eateth not, and **g.** God thanks...
1Co 3:7 but God that **g.** the increase...
1Co 7:38 he that **g.** her in marriage doeth well;...
1Co 7:38 but he that **g.** her not in marriage...
1Co 15:38 God **g.** it a body as it hath pleased... *1325*
1Co 15:57 God which **g.** us the victory through... *1325*
2Co 3:6 killeth, but the Spirit **g.** life...
1Ti 6:17 **g.** us richly all things to enjoy;... *3930*
Jas 1:5 ask of God, that **g.** to all men... *1325*
Jas 4:6 But he **g.** more grace. Wherefore... *1325*
Jas 4:6 but **g.** grace unto the humble... *1325*
1Pe 4:11 it as of the ability which God **g.**:... *5524*
1Pe 5:5 proud, and **g.** grace to the humble... *1325*
Re 22:5 for the Lord God **g.** them light:...

GIVING See also FORGIVING; THANKSGIVING.
Ge 24:19 when she had done **g.** him drink...
De 10:18 in **g.** him food and raiment... 5414
De 21:17 by **g.** him a double portion of all... 5414
Ru 1:6 visited his people in **g.** them bread... 5414
1Ki 5:9 in **g.** food for my household... 5414
2Ch 6:23 by **g.** him according to his... 5414
Ezr 3:11 praising and **g.** thanks unto the Lord;...
Job 11:20 shall be as the **g.** up of the ghost... 4646
Mt 24:38 **marrying and g. in marriage,...**
Lu 17:16 at his feet, **g.** him thanks: and he was...
Ac 8:9 **g.** out that himself was some... *3004*
Ac 15:8 **g.** them the Holy Ghost, even as... *1325*
Ro 4:20 strong in faith, **g.** glory to God;...
Ro 9:4 covenants, and the **g.** of the law,... *3548*
1Co 14:7 even things without life **g.** sound,... *1325*
1Co 14:16 say Amen at thy **g.** of thanks,...
2Co 6:3 **G.** no offence in any thing, that... *1325*
Eph 5:4 but rather **g.** of thanks...
Eph 5:20 **G.** thanks always for all things...
Php 4:15 concerning **g.** and receiving, but... *1394*
Col 1:12 **G.** thanks unto the Father, which...
Col 3:17 **g.** thanks to God and the Father...
1Ti 2:1 intercessions, and **g.** of thanks,...
1Ti 4:1 **g.** heed to seducing spirits, and...
Tit 1:14 Not **g.** heed to Jewish fables, and...
Heb 13:15 of our lips **g.** thanks to his name...
1Pe 3:7 **g.** honour unto the wife, as unto... *632*

2Pe 1:5 g. all diligence, add to your faith........ *3923*
Jude 7 g. themselves over to fornication........ *3923*

GIZONITE (ghi'-zo-nite)
1Ch 11:34 sons of Hashem the G., Jonathan....... 1493

GLAD
Ex 4:14 thee, he will be g. in his heart.......... 8056
Jg 18:20 And the priest's heart was g., ... 3190
1Sa 11:9 men of Jabesh; and they were g......... 8056
1Ki 8:66 joyful and g. of heart for all the 2896
1Ch 16:31 Let the heavens be g., and let.......... 8056
2Ch 7:10 g. and merry in heart for the............ 8056
Es 5:9 day joyful and with a g. heart: 2896
Es 8:15 of Shushan rejoiced and was g.. 8056
Job 3:22 rejoice exceedingly, and are g.,.......... 7797
Job 22:19 The righteous see it, and are g.......... 8056
Ps 9:2 I will be g. and rejoice in thee: 8056
Ps 14:7 rejoice, and Israel shall be g............ 8056
Ps 16:9 heart is g., and my glory rejoiceth:..... 8056
Ps 21:6 thou hast made him exceeding g. 2302
Ps 31:7 be g. and rejoice in thy mercy: 1523
Ps 32:11 Be g. in the Lord, and rejoice, ... 8056
Ps 34:2 shall hear thereof, and be g.. 8056
Ps 35:27 Let them shout for joy, and be g., ... 8056
Ps 40:16 rejoice and be g. in thee.......................
Ps 40:16 seek thee rejoice and be g. in thee:.... 8055
Ps 45:8 whereby they have made thee g. 8056
Ps 46:4 shall make g. the city of God,........... 8056
Ps 48:11 let the daughters of Judah be g.,......... 1523
Ps 53:6 rejoice, and Israel shall be g............. 8056
Ps 64:10 righteous shall be g. in the Lord, ... 8056
Ps 67:4 O let the nations be g. and sing......... 8056
Ps 68:3 But let the righteous be g.; let........... 8056
Ps 69:32 humble shall see this, and be g.: 8056
Ps 70:4 seek thee rejoice and be g. in thee:.... 8056
Ps 90:14 that we may rejoice and be g. all 8056
Ps 90:15 make us g. according to the days........ 8056
Ps 92:4 hast made me g. through thy work:.... 8056
Ps 96:11 and let the earth be g.; let the sea..... 1523
Ps 97:1 let the multitude of isles be g............ 8056
Ps 97:8 Zion hear, and was g.; and the 8056
Ps 104:15 wine that maketh g. the heart of........ 8056
Ps 104:34 I will be g. in the Lord. 8056
Ps 105:38 Egypt was g. when they departed: 8056
Ps 107:30 Then are they g. because they be...... 8056
Ps 118:24 we will rejoice and be g. in it. 8056
Ps 119:74 They that fear thee will be g............ 8056
Ps 122:1 I was g. when they said unto me, ... 8056
Ps 126:3 things for us; whereof we are g......... 8056
Pr 10:1 A wise son maketh a g. father:.......... 8056
Pr 12:25 but a good word maketh it g.. 8056
Pr 15:20 A wise son maketh a g. father:.......... 8056
Pr 17:5 and he that is g. at calamities........... 8056
Pr 23:25 father and thy mother shall be g., ... 8056
Pr 24:17 let not thine heart be g. when he....... 1523
Pr 27:11 be wise, and make my heart g.,......... 8056
Ca 1:4 he will be g. and rejoice in thee,........ 1523
Isa 25:9 we will be g. and rejoice in his 1523
Isa 35:1 solitary place shall be g. for them;...... 7796
Isa 39:2 And Hezekiah was g. of them,........... 8056
Isa 65:18 be ye g. and rejoice for ever.............. 7796
Isa 66:10 and be g. with her, all ye that love..... 1523
Jer 20:15 unto thee: making him very g............ 8056
Jer 41:13 were with him, then they were g......... 8056
Jer 50:11 Because ye were g., because ye........ 8056
La 1:21 they are g. that thou hast done it:...... 7796
La 4:21 Rejoice and be g., O daughter of......... 8056
Da 6:23 was the king exceeding g. for him, ... 2868
Ho 7:3 They make the king g. with their....... 8056
Joe 2:21 Fear not, O land; be g. and rejoice;.... 1523
Joe 2:23 Be g. then, ye children of Zion, ... 1523
Jon 4:6 so Jonah was exceeding g. of the 8056
Hab 1:15 therefore they rejoice and are g......... 1523
Zep 3:14 be g. and rejoice with all the............. 8056
Zec 10:7 shall see it, and be g.; their heart...... 8056
Mt 5:12 Rejoice, and be exceedingly g........... *21*
Mk 14:11 when they heard it, they were g.,......... *5463*
Lu 1:19 to shew thee these g. tidings. *2097*
Lu 8:1 the g. tidings of the kingdom............. *2097*
Lu 15:32 we should make merry, and be g... *5463*
Lu 22:5 And they were g., and covenanted...... *5463*
Lu 23:8 saw Jesus, he was exceeding g.......... *5463*
Joh 8:56 and he saw it, and was g.. .... *5463*
Joh 11:15 And I am g. for your sakes that.... *5463*
Joh 20:20 Then were the disciples g., when........ *5463*
Ac 2:26 rejoice, and my tongue was g.;............ *21*
Ac 11:23 was g., and exhorted them all, ... *5463*
Ac 13:32 we declare unto you g. tidings,.......... *2097*
Ac 13:48 Gentiles heard this, they were g.,...... *5463*
Ro 10:15 of peace, and bring g. tidings *2097*
Ro 16:19 I am g. therefore on your behalf: *5463*
1Co 16:17 am g. of the coming of Stephanas....... *5463*
2Co 2:2 who is he then that maketh me g.,..... *2165*
2Co 13:9 For we are g., when we are weak, ... *5463*
1Pe 4:13 be g. also with exceeding joy. *5463*
Re 19:7 Let us be g. and rejoice, and we........ *5463*

GLADLY
Mk 6:20 many things, and heard him g........... *2234*
Mk 12:37 the common people heard him g......... *2234*
Lu 8:40 the people g. received him:............... *2234*
Ac 2:41 they that g. received his word *780*
Ac 21:17 the brethren received us g.. .... *780*
2Co 11:19 For ye suffer fools g., seeing ye........ *2234*
2Co 12:9 Most g. therefore will I rather........... *2236*
2Co 12:15 I will very g. spend and be spent....... *2236*

GLADNESS
Nu 10:10 Also in the day of your g.,................ 8057
De 28:47 joyfulness, and with g. of heart, ... 2898
2Sa 6:12 into the city of David with g.............. 8057
1Ch 16:27 strength and g. are in his place.......... 2304
1Ch 29:22 Lord on that day with great g............ 8057
2Ch 29:30 they sang praises with g., and........... 8057
2Ch 30:21 bread seven days with great g.: 8057
2Ch 30:23 kept over seven days with g.. 8057
Ne 8:17 And there was very great g.. 8057
Ne 12:27 to keep the dedication with g., ... 8057
Es 8:16 The Jews had light, and g., and joy, ... 8057
Es 8:17 Jews had joy and g., a feast............. 8342
Es 9:17, 18 made it a day of feasting and g...... 8057
Es 9:19 day of the month Adar a day of g...... 8057
Ps 4:7 Thou hast put g. in my heart,............ 8057
Ps 30:11 sackcloth, and girded me with g.;....... 8057
Ps 45:7 anointed thee with the oil of g. 8342
Ps 45:15 With g. and rejoicing shall they.......... 8057
Ps 51:8 Make me to hear joy and g.;.............. 8057
Ps 97:11 and g. for the upright in heart. 8057
Ps 100:2 Serve the Lord with g.: come 8057
Ps 105:43 joy, and his chosen with g.: 7440
Ps 106:5 rejoice in the g. of thy nation, ... 8057
Pr 10:28 hope of the righteous shall be g.: 8057
Ca 3:11 in the day of the g. of his heart. 8057
Isa 16:10 And g. is taken away, and joy out 8057
Isa 22:13 behold joy and g., slaying oxen, ... 8057
Isa 30:29 and g. of heart, as when one goeth..... 8057
Isa 35:10 they shall obtain joy and g., and........ 8057
Isa 51:3 joy and g. shall be found therein, ... 8057
Isa 51:11 they shall obtain g. and joy; and......... 8057
Jer 7:34 voice of mirth, and the voice of g.,...... 8057
Jer 16:9 voice of mirth, and the voice of g.,...... 8057
Jer 25:10 voice of mirth, and the voice of g.,...... 8057
Jer 31:7 Sing with g. for Jacob, and shout........ 8057
Jer 33:11 The voice of joy, and the voice of g.,... 8057
Jer 48:33 And joy and g. is taken from the........ 8057
Joe 1:16 and g. from the house of our God?..... 1524
Zec 8:19 to the house of Judah joy and g., ... 8057
Mk 4:16 immediately receive it with g.;....... *5479*
Lu 1:14 And thou shalt have joy and g.;............. *20*
Ac 2:46 with g. and singleness of heart, ... *20*
Ac 12:14 she opened not the gate for g., ... *5479*
Ac 14:17 filling our hearts with food and g.. .... *2167*
Php 2:29 therefore in the Lord with all g.;........ *5479*
Heb 1:9 hath anointed thee with the oil of g........ *20*

GLASS See also GLASSES.
Job 37:18 and as a molten looking g.?.............. 7209
1Co 13:12 now we see through a g. darkly;........ *2072*
2Co 3:18 beholding as in a g. the glory of.......... *2734*
Jas 1:23 beholding his natural face in a g.: *2072*
Re 4:6 was a sea of g. like unto crystal:........ *5193*
Re 15:2 a sea of g. mingled with fire:............. *5193*
Re 15:2 sea of g., having the harps of God...... *5193*
Re 21:18 was pure gold, like unto clear g.. .... *5194*
Re 21:21 gold, as it were transparent g........... *5194*

GLASSES See also LOOKINGGLASSES.
Isa 3:23 The g., and the fine linen, and.......... 1549

GLEAN See also GLEANED; GLEANING.
Le 19:10 thou shalt not g. thy vineyard,.......... 5953
De 24:21 thou shalt not g. it afterward:........... 5953
Ru 2:2 and g. ears of corn after him............ 3950
Ru 2:7 let me g. and gather after the........... 3950
Ru 2:8 Go not to g. in another field,............ 3950
Ru 2:15 when she was risen up to g., ... 3950
Ru 2:15 Let her g. even among the sheaves,... 3950
Ru 2:16 that she may g. them, and rebuke...... 3950
Ru 2:23 to g. unto the end of barley harvest.... 3950
Jer 6:9 shall thoroughly g. the remnant.......... 5953

GLEANED
Jg 20:45 they g. of them in the highways......... 5953
Ru 2:3 g. in the field after the reapers:......... 3950
Ru 2:17 So she g. in the field until even, ... 3950
Ru 2:17 and beat out that she had g.............. 3950
Ru 2:18 mother in law saw what she had g...... 3950
Ru 2:19 Where hast thou g. to day?............... 3950

GLEANING See also GLEANINGS.
Le 23:22 shalt thou gather any g. of thy........... 3951
Jg 8:2 the g. of the grapes of Ephraim......... 5955
Isa 17:6 Yet g. grapes shall be left in it, ... 5955
Isa 24:13 as the g. grapes when the vintage...... 5955
Jer 49:9 they not leave some g. grapes? 5955

GLEANING-GRAPES See GLEANING and GRAPES.

GLEANINGS
Le 19:9 shalt thou gather the g. of thy........... 3951

GLEDE
De 14:13 And the g., and the kite, and the....... 7201

GLISTERING See also GLITTERING.
1Ch 29:2 g. stones, and of divers colours, ... 6320
Lu 9:29 his raiment was white and g.............. *1823*

GLITTER See also GLITTERING.
Eze 21:10 it is furbished that it may g.............. 1300

GLITTERING See also GLISTERING.
De 32:41 If I whet my g. sword, and mine........ 1300
Job 20:25 yea, the g. sword cometh out of........ 1300
Job 39:23 the g. spear and the shield............... 3851
Eze 21:28 to consume because of the g.:........... 1300
Na 3:3 the bright sword and the g. spear: 1300
Hab 3:11 at the shining of thy g. spear............ 1300

GLOOMINESS
Joe 2:2 A day of darkness and of g., a day...... 653
Zep 1:15 a day of darkness and g., a day of...... 653

GLORIEST
Jer 49:4 Wherefore g. thou in the valleys, ... 1984

GLORIETH
Jer 9:24 But let him that g. glory in this, ... 1984
1Co 1:31 that g., let him glory in the Lord. *2744*
2Co 10:17 that g., let him glory in the Lord. *2744*

GLORIFIED
Le 10:3 before all the people I will be g.. 3513
Isa 26:15 increased the nation: thou art g.: 3513
Isa 44:23 Jacob, and g. himself in Israel............ 6286
Isa 49:3 O Israel, in whom I will be g............ 6286
Isa 55:5 One of Israel; for he hath g. thee....... 6286
Isa 60:9 of Israel, because he hath g. thee. 6286
Isa 60:21 of my hands, that I may be g.. 6286
Isa 61:3 of the Lord, that he might be g.. 6286
Isa 66:5 Let the Lord be g.: but he shall.......... 3513
Eze 28:22 I will be g. in the midst of thee: 3513
Eze 39:13 that I shall be g., saith the Lord........ 3513
Da 5:23 are all thy ways, hast thou not g.:....... 1922
Hag 1:8 and I will be g., saith the Lord. 3513
Mt 9:8 they marvelled, and g. God, which *1392*
Mt 15:31 and they g. the God of Israel. *1392*
Mk 2:12 then were all amazed, and g. God, ... *1392*
Lu 4:15 their synagogues, being g. of all......... *1392*
Lu 5:26 were all amazed, and they g. God, ... *1392*
Lu 7:16 they g. God, saying, That a great *1392*
Lu 13:13 she was made straight, and g. God..... *1392*
Lu 17:15 and with a loud voice g. God............ *1392*
Lu 23:47 saw what was done, he g. God,......... *1392*
Joh 7:39 because that Jesus was not yet g..) *1392*
Joh 11:4 Son of God might be g. thereby..... *1392*
Joh 12:16 but when Jesus was g., then............ *1392*
Joh 12:23 that the Son of man should be g... *1392*
Joh 12:28 I have both g. it, and will glorify........ *1392*
Joh 13:31 Now is the Son of man g.,............ *1392*
Joh 13:31 and God is g. in him. *1392*
Joh 13:32 If God be g. in him, God shall...... *1392*
Joh 14:13 the Father may be g. in the Son. .. *1392*
Joh 15:8 Herein is my Father g., that ye..... *1392*
Joh 17:4 I have g. thee on the earth: I........ *1392*
Joh 17:10 and am g. in them....................... *1392*
Ac 3:13 hath g. his Son Jesus;.................... *1392*
Ac 4:21 for all men g. God for that which....... *1392*

Ac 11:18 they held their peace, and **g.** God, ... *1392*
Ac 13:48 and **g.** the word of the Lord: and *1392*
Ac 21:20 they **g.** the Lord, and said unto him, ... *1392*
Ro 1:21 they **g.** him not as God, neither *1392*
Ro 8:17 that we may be also **g.** together. *4888*
Ro 8:30 whom he justified, them he also **g.**.. .... *1392*
Ga 1:24 And they **g.** God in me. *1392*
2Th 1:10 shall come to be **g.** in his saints, ... *1740*
2Th 1:12 of our Lord Jesus Christ may be **g.** *1740*
2Th 3:1 may have free course and be **g.**, ... *1392*
Heb 5:5 Christ **g.** not himself to be made *1392*
1Pe 4:11 may be **g.** through Jesus Christ, ... *1392*
1Pe 4:14 but on your part he is **g.**.. .... *1392*
Re 18:7 How much she hath **g.** herself. *1392*

GLORIFIETH
Ps 50:23 Whoso offereth praise **g.** me: and 3513

GLORIFY See also GLORIFIED; GLORIFIETH; GLORIFYING.
Ps 22:23 all ye the seed of Jacob, **g.** him; 3513
Ps 50:15 deliver thee, and thou shalt **g.** me. 3513
Ps 86:9 O Lord; and shall **g.** thy name. 3513
Ps 86:12 I will **g.** thy name for evermore. 3513
Isa 24:15 Wherefore **g.** ye the Lord in the 3513
Isa 25:3 shall the strong people **g.** thee, ... 3513
Isa 60:7 I will **g.** the house of my glory. 6286
Jer 30:19 I will also **g.** them, and they shall 3513
Mt 5:16 **see your good works, and g. your** .. *1392*
Joh 12:28 **Father, g. thy name. Then came** ... *1392*
Joh 12:28 have both glorified it, and will **g.** it *1392*
Joh 13:32 **God shall also g. him in himself**.... *1392*
Joh 13:32 **and shall straightway g. him**......... *1392*
Joh 16:14 **He shall g. me: for he shall receive** *1392*
Joh 17:1 **g. thy Son, that thy Son also** *1392*
Joh 17:1 **that thy Son also may g. thee:** *1392*
Joh 17:5 **O Father, g. thou me with thine** ... *1392*
Joh 21:19 by what death he should **g.** God. *1392*
Ro 15:4 fear thee, O Lord, and **g.** thy name?... *1392*
Ro 15:6 one mind and one mouth **g.** God. *1392*
Ro 15:9 the Gentiles might **g.** God for his *1392*
1Co 6:20 therefore **g.** God in your body, ... *1392*
2Co 9:13 they **g.** God for your professed *1392*
1Pe 2:12 **g.** God in the day of visitation. *1392*
1Pe 4:16 let him **g.** God on this behalf. *1392*

GLORIFYING
Lu 2:20 **g.** and praising God for all things *1392*
Lu 5:25 departed to his own house, **g.** God. *1392*
Lu 18:43 and followed him, **g.** God: *1392*

GLORIOUS
Ex 15:6 O Lord, is become **g.** in power: 142
Ex 15:11 who is like thee, **g.** in holiness, ... 142
De 28:58 fear this **g.** and fearful name, ... 3513
2Sa 6:20 How **g.** was the king of Israel to day, . 3513
1Ch 29:13 thank thee, and praise thy **g.** name..... 8597
Ne 9:5 blessed be thy **g.** name, which is 3519
Es 1:4 shewed the riches of his **g.** kingdom ... 3519
Ps 45:13 king's daughter is all **g.** within: 3520
Ps 66:2 of his name: make his praise **g.** 3519
Ps 72:19 And blessed be his **g.** name for ever:.. 3519
Ps 76:4 Thou art more **g.** and excellent 215
Ps 87:3 **G.** things are spoken of thee, O......... 3513
Ps 111:3 His work is honourable and **g.**: 1926
Ps 145:5 I will speak of the **g.** honour of thy..... 3519
Ps 145:12 and the **g.** majesty of his kingdom. 3519
Isa 4:2 of the Lord be beautiful and **g.**, ... 3519
Isa 11:10 and his rest shall be **g.**.. 3519
Isa 22:23 and he shall be for a **g.** throne........... 3519
Isa 28:1 whose **g.** beauty is a fading flower, ... 6643
Isa 28:4 the **g.** beauty, which is on the head 6643
Isa 30:30 the Lord shall cause his **g.** voice 1935
Isa 33:21 But there the **g.** Lord will be............. 117
Isa 49:5 I be **g.** in the eyes of the Lord, ... 3513
Isa 60:13 I will make the place of my feet **g.**.. 3513
Isa 63:1 **g.** in his apparel, travelling in the 1921
Isa 63:12 with his **g.** arm, dividing the water 8597
Isa 63:14 people, to make thyself a **g.** name. 8597
Jer 17:12 A **g.** high throne from the................ 3519
Eze 27:25 wast replenished, and made very **g.**.. .. 3519
Da 11:16 and he shall stand in the **g.** land, ... 6643
Da 11:41 He shall enter also into the **g.** land, ... 6643
Da 11:45 the seas in the **g.** holy mountain; 6643
Lu 13:17 **g.** things that were done by him. *1741*
Ro 8:21 **g.** liberty of the children of God. *1391*
2Co 3:7 engraven in stones, was **g.**, ... *1722,1391*
2Co 3:8 of the spirit be rather **g.**? *1722,1391*
2Co 3:10 which was made **g.** had no glory *1392*
2Co 3:11 which is done away was **g.**, ... *1223,1391*
2Co 3:11 that which remaineth is **g.**.. .... *1722,1391*
2Co 4:4 the light of the **g.** gospel of Christ, ... *1391*
Eph 5:27 present it to himself a **g.** church, ... *1741*
Php 3:21 fashioned like unto his **g.** body, ... *1391*
Col 1:11 according to his **g.** power, unto *1391*
1Ti 1:11 the **g.** gospel of the blessed God, ... *1391*
Tit 2:13 the **g.** appearing of the great God....... *1391*

GLORIOUSLY
Ex 15:1 the Lord, for he hath triumphed **g.** ....
Ex 15:21 to the Lord, for he hath triumphed **g.** ....
Isa 24:23 and before his ancients **g.**.. 3519

GLORY See also GLORIEST; GLORIETH; GLORYING; VAINGLORY.
Ge 31:1 hath he gotten all this **g.**.. 3519
Ge 45:13 ye shall tell my father of all my **g.** 3519
Ex 8:9 Moses said unto Pharaoh, **G.** over...... 6286
Ex 16:7 ye shall see the **g.** of the Lord; 3519
Ex 16:10 **g.** of the Lord appeared in a cloud...... 3519
Ex 24:16 **g.** of the Lord abode upon mount 3519
Ex 24:17 **g.** of the Lord was like devouring....... 3519
Ex 28:2 thy brother for **g.** and for beauty. 3519
Ex 28:40 for them, for **g.** and for beauty. 3519
Ex 29:43 shall be sanctified by my **g.**.. 3519
Ex 33:18 I beseech thee, shew me thy **g.**.. 3519
Ex 33:22 while my **g.** passeth by, I will put 3519
Ex 40:34, 35 **g.** of the...filled the tabernacle....... 3519
Le 9:6 **g.** of the Lord shall appear unto you. .. 3519
Le 9:23 the **g.** of the Lord appeared unto all.... 3519
Nu 14:10 the **g.** of the Lord appeared in the...... 3519
Nu 14:21 be filled with the **g.** of the Lord. 3519
Nu 14:22 those men which have seen my **g.**, ... 3519
Nu 16:19 the **g.** of the Lord appeared unto all.... 3519
Nu 16:42 and the **g.** of the Lord appeared. 3519
Nu 20:6 **g.** of the Lord appeared unto them. 3519
De 5:24 Lord our God hath shewed us his **g.** ... 3519
De 33:17 His **g.** is like the firstling of his.......... 1926
Jos 7:19 thee, **g.** to the Lord God of Israel, ... 3519
1Sa 2:8 make them inherit the throne of **g.**: 3519
1Sa 4:21, 22 The **g.** is departed from Israel: 3519
1Sa 6:5 shall give **g.** unto the God of Israel: ... 3519
1Ki 8:11 **g.** of the Lord had filled the house...... 3519
2Ki 14:10 **g.** of this, and tarry at home: 3513
1Ch 16:10 **G.** ye in his holy name: let the 1984
1Ch 16:24 Declare his **g.** among the heathen;...... 3519
1Ch 16:27 **G.** and honour are in his presence; 1935
1Ch 16:28 give unto the Lord **g.** and strength. 3519
1Ch 16:29 the Lord the **g.** due unto his name: 3519
1Ch 16:35 holy name, and **g.** in thy praise. 7623
1Ch 22:5 and of **g.** throughout all countries; 8597
1Ch 29:11 and the power, and the **g.**, ... 8597
2Ch 5:14 **g.** of the Lord had filled the house.....: 3519
2Ch 7:1 the **g.** of the Lord filled the house. 3519
2Ch 7:2 **g.** of the Lord had filled the Lord's..... 3519
2Ch 7:3 the **g.** of the Lord upon the house, ... 3519
Es 5:11 Haman told them of the **g.** of his 3519
Job 19:9 He hath stripped me of my **g.**, ... 3519
Job 29:20 My **g.** was fresh in me, and my 3519
Job 39:20 the **g.** of his nostrils is terrible. 1935
Job 40:10 array thyself with **g.** and beauty. 1935
Ps 3:3 my **g.**, and the lifter up of mine 3519
Ps 4:2 long will ye turn my **g.** into shame? 3519
Ps 8:1 hast set thy **g.** above the heavens. 1935
Ps 8:5 crowned him with **g.** and honour. 3519
Ps 16:9 and my **g.** rejoiceth: my flesh also...... 3519
Ps 19:1 The heavens declare the **g.** of God; 3519
Ps 21:5 His **g.** is great in thy salvation: 3519
Ps 24:7 and the King of **g.** shall come in.......... 3519
Ps 24:8 Who is this King of **g.**? The Lord....... 3519
Ps 24:9 and the King of **g.** shall come in.......... 3519
Ps 24:10 Who is this King of **g.**? The Lord....... 3519
Ps 24:10 of hosts, he is the King of **g.**.. 3519
Ps 29:1 give unto the Lord **g.** and strength. 3519
Ps 29:2 the Lord the **g.** due unto his name; 3519
Ps 29:3 the God of **g.** thundereth: the Lord 3519
Ps 29:9 doth every one speak of his **g.**.. 3519
Ps 30:12 that my **g.** may sing praise to thee, ... 3519
Ps 45:3 with thy **g.** and thy majesty. 1935
Ps 49:16 the **g.** of his house is increased; 3519
Ps 49:17 his **g.** shall not descend after him. 3519
Ps 57:5 let thy **g.** be above all the earth. 3519
Ps 57:8 Awake up, my **g.**; awake, psaltery...... 3519
Ps 57:11 let thy **g.** be above all the earth. 3519
Ps 62:7 In God is my salvation and my **g.** 3519
Ps 63:2 To see thy power and thy **g.**, ... 3519
Ps 63:11 one that sweareth by him shall **g.** 1984
Ps 64:10 all the upright in heart shall **g.** 1984
Ps 72:19 whole earth be filled with his **g.**; 3519
Ps 73:24 and afterward receive me to **g.**.. 3519
Ps 78:61 and his **g.** into the enemy's hand. 8597
Ps 79:9 Help us...for the **g.** of thy name: 3519
Ps 84:11 the Lord will give grace and **g.**: 3519
Ps 85:9 that **g.** may dwell in our land. 3519
Ps 89:17 thou art the **g.** of their strength: 8597
Ps 89:44 Thou hast made his **g.** to cease, ... 2892
Ps 90:16 and thy **g.** unto their children. 1926
Ps 96:3 Declare his **g.** among the heathen, ... 3519
Ps 96:7 give unto the Lord **g.** and strength. 3519
Ps 96:8 the Lord the **g.** due unto his name: 3519
Ps 97:6 and all the people see his **g.**.. 3519
Ps 102:15 and all the kings of the earth thy **g.**.... 3519
Ps 102:16 he shall appear in his **g.**.. 3519
Ps 104:31 **g.** of the Lord shall endure for ever: ... 3519
Ps 105:3 **G.** ye in his holy name: let the 1984
Ps 106:5 I may **g.** with thine inheritance. 1984
Ps 106:20 Thus they changed their **g.** into 3519
Ps 108:1 and give praise, even with my **g.**.. 3519
Ps 108:5 and thy **g.** above all the earth; 3519
Ps 113:4 and his **g.** above the heavens. 3519
Ps 115:1 but unto thy name give **g.**, for thy...... 3519
Ps 138:5 for great is the **g.** of the Lord. 3519
Ps 145:11 speak of the **g.** of thy kingdom, ... 3519
Ps 148:13 **g.** is above the earth and heaven........ 1935
Ps 149:5 Let the saints be joyful in **g.**: 3519
Pr 3:35 The wise shall inherit **g.**: but............ 3519
Pr 4:9 a crown of **g.** shall she deliver 8597
Pr 16:31 The hoary head is a crown of **g.**, ... 8597
Pr 17:6 the **g.** of children are their fathers...... 8597
Pr 19:11 his **g.** to pass over a transgression. 8597
Pr 20:29 **g.** of young men is their strength: 8597
Pr 25:2 the **g.** of God to conceal a thing: 3519
Pr 25:27 to search their own **g.** is not **g.**.. 3519
Pr 28:12 men do rejoice, there is great **g.**: 8597
Isa 2:10 and for the **g.** of his majesty. 1926
Isa 2:19, 21 and for the **g.** of his majesty, ... 1926
Isa 3:8 to provoke the eyes of his **g.**.. 3519
Isa 4:5 upon all the **g.** shall be a defence. 3519
Isa 5:14 and their **g.**, and their multitude, ... 1926
Isa 6:3 the whole earth is full of his **g.**.. 3519
Isa 8:7 the king of Assyria, and all his **g.**: 3519
Isa 10:3 and where will ye leave your **g.**? 3519
Isa 10:12 and the **g.** of his high looks. 8597
Isa 10:16 and under his **g.** he shall kindle.......... 3519
Isa 10:18 shall consume the **g.** of his forest, ... 3519
Isa 13:19 Babylon, the **g.** of kingdoms, the........ 6643
Isa 14:18 nations, even all of them, lie in **g.**, ... 3519
Isa 16:14 the **g.** of Moab shall be contemned, ... 3519
Isa 17:3 shall be as the **g.** of the children 3519
Isa 17:4 the **g.** of Jacob shall be made thin, ... 3519
Isa 20:5 expectation, and of Egypt their **g.**.. 8597
Isa 21:16 and all the **g.** of Kedar shall fail: 3519
Isa 22:18 the chariots of thy **g.** shall be the 3519
Isa 22:24 him all the **g.** of his father's house, ... 3519
Isa 23:9 to stain the pride of all **g.**, and to 6643
Isa 24:16 songs, even **g.** to the righteous. 6643
Isa 28:5 Lord of hosts be for a crown of **g.**, ... 6643
Isa 35:2 **g.** of Lebanon shall be given unto 3519
Isa 35:2 they shall see the **g.** of the Lord, ... 3519
Isa 40:5 the **g.** of the Lord shall be revealed, ... 3519
Isa 41:16 shalt **g.** in the Holy One of Israel. 1984
Isa 42:8 my **g.** will I not give to another, ... 3519
Isa 42:12 Let them give **g.** unto the Lord, ... 3519
Isa 43:7 for I have created him for my **g.**, ... 3519
Isa 45:25 of Israel be justified, and shall **g.** 1984
Isa 46:13 salvation in Zion for Israel my **g.**.. 8597
Isa 48:11 I will not give my **g.** unto another. 3519
Isa 58:8 **g.** of the...shall be thy rereward. 3519
Isa 59:19 his **g.** from the rising of the sun.......... 3519
Isa 60:1 and the **g.** of the Lord is risen upon ... 3519
Isa 60:2 and his **g.** shall be seen upon thee...... 3519
Isa 60:7 I will glorify the house of my **g.**.. 8597
Isa 60:13 The **g.** of Lebanon shall come............ 3519
Isa 60:19 light, and thy God thy **g.**.. 8597
Isa 61:6 and in their **g.** shall ye boast 3519
Isa 62:2 and all kings thy **g.**: and thou shalt 3519
Isa 62:3 Thou shalt also be a crown of **g.** 8597
Isa 63:15 of thy holiness and of thy **g.**: 8597
Isa 66:11 with the abundance of her **g.**.. 3519
Isa 66:12 the **g.** of the Gentiles like a flowing 3519
Isa 66:18 they shall come, and see my **g.**.. 3519
Isa 66:19 neither have seen my **g.**; and they 3519
Isa 66:19 declare my **g.** among the Gentiles. 3519
Jer 2:11 my people have changed their **g.** 3519
Jer 4:2 and in him shall they **g.**.. 1984
Jer 9:23 Let not the wise man **g.** in his........... 1984

Jer	9:23	let the mighty man g. in his might,	1984
Jer	9:23	let not the rich man g. in his riches:	1984
Jer	9:24	But let him that glorieth g. in this,	1984
Jer	13:11	and for a praise, and for a g.:	8597
Jer	13:16	Give g. to the Lord your God,	3519
Jer	13:18	down, even the crown of your g.:	8597
Jer	14:21	not disgrace the throne of thy g.:	3519
Jer	22:18	saying, Ah Lord! or, Ah his g.!	1935
Jer	48:18	come down from thy g., and sit in	3519
Eze	1:28	the likeness of the g. of the Lord	3519
Eze	3:12	Blessed be the g. of the Lord from	3519
Eze	3:23	the g. of the Lord stood there,	3519
Eze	3:23	as the g. which I saw by the river	3519
Eze	8:4	the g. of the God of Israel was there,	3519
Eze	9:3	the g. of the God of Israel was gone	3519
Eze	10:4	the g. of the Lord went up from the	3519
Eze	10:4	of the brightness of the Lord's g.	3519
Eze	10:18	the g. of the Lord departed from off	3519
Eze	10:19	the g. of the God of Israel was over	3519
Eze	11:22	the g. of the God of Israel was over	3519
Eze	11:23	the g. of the Lord went up from the	3519
Eze	20:6	honey, which is the g. of all lands:	6643
Eze	20:15	honey, which is the g. of all lands;	
Eze	24:25	the joy of their g., the desire of	8597
Eze	25:9	his frontiers, the g. of the country,	6643
Eze	26:20	I shall set g. in the land of the	6643
Eze	31:18	To whom art thou thus like in g.	3519
Eze	39:21	I will set my g. among the heathen,	3519
Eze	43:2	g. of the God of Israel came from	3519
Eze	43:2	and the earth shined with his g.	3519
Eze	43:4	And the g. of the Lord came into	3519
Eze	43:5	the g. of the Lord filled the house.	3519
Eze	44:4	the g. of the Lord filled the house	3519
Da	2:37	power, and strength, and g.	3367
Da	4:36	and for the g. of my kingdom,	3367
Da	5:18	a kingdom, and majesty, and g.	3367
Da	5:20	and they took his g. from him:	3367
Da	7:14	was given him dominion, and g.,	3367
Da	11:20	of taxes in the g. of the kingdom:	1925
Da	11:39	acknowledge and increase with g.:	3519
Ho	4:7	therefore will I change their g.	3519
Ho	9:11	their g. shall fly away like a bird,	3519
Ho	10:5	that rejoiced in it, for the g. thereof,	3519
Mic	1:15	come unto Adullam the g. of Israel.	3519
Mic	2:9	have ye taken away my g. for ever.	1926
Na	2:9	is none end of the store and g.	3519
Hab	2:14	with the knowledge of the g. of the	3519
Hab	2:16	thou art filled with shame for g.:	3519
Hab	2:16	shameful spewing shall be on thy g.	3519
Hab	3:3	His g. covered the heavens, and	1935
Hag	2:3	that saw this house in her first g.?	3519
Hag	2:7	I will fill this house with g., saith	3519
Hag	2:9	The g. of this latter house shall be	3519
Zec	2:5	will be the g. in the midst of her.	3519
Zec	2:8	After the g. hath he sent me unto	3519
Zec	6:13	he shall bear the g., and shall sit	1935
Zec	11:3	for their g. is spoiled: a voice of	155
Zec	12:7	that the g. of the house of David	8597
Zec	12:7	and the g. of the inhabitants of	8597
Mal	2:2	give g. unto my name, saith the	3519
Mt	4:8	of the world, and the g. of them;	*1391*
Mt	6:2	**that they may have g. of men.**	*1392*
Mt	6:13	**the power, and the g., for ever**	*1391*
Mt	6:29	**even Solomon in all his g. was not**	*1391*
Mt	16:27	**come in the g. of his Father with**	*1391*
Mt	19:28	**shall sit in the throne of his g.,**	*1391*
Mt	24:30	**with power and great g.**	*1391*
Mt	25:31	**Son of man shall come in his g.,**	*1391*
Mt	25:31	**he sit upon the throne of his g.:**	*1391*
Mk	8:38	**cometh in the g. of his Father with**	*1391*
Mk	10:37	other on thy left hand, in thy g.	*1391*
Mk	13:26	**the clouds with great power and g.**	*1391*
Lu	2:9	and the g. of the Lord shone round	*1391*
Lu	2:14	G. to God in the highest, and on	*1391*
Lu	2:32	and the g. of thy people Israel.	*1391*
Lu	4:6	will I give thee, and the g. of them:	*1391*
Lu	9:26	**when he shall come in his own g.,**	*1391*
Lu	9:31	Who appeared in g., and spake of	*1391*
Lu	9:32	they saw his g., and the two men	*1391*
Lu	12:27	**that Solomon in all his g. was not**	*1391*
Lu	17:18	**returned to give g. to God, save**	*1391*
Lu	19:38	peace in heaven, and g. in the	*1391*
Lu	21:27	**in a cloud with power and great g.**	*1391*
Lu	24:26	**things, and to enter into his g.?**	*1391*
Joh	1:14	we beheld his g., the g. as of the	*1391*
Joh	2:11	and manifested forth his g.;	*1391*
Joh	7:18	**of himself seeketh his own g.: but**	*1391*
Joh	7:18	**he that seeketh his g. that sent**	*1391*
Joh	8:50	**I seek not mine own g.: there is**	*1391*
Joh	11:4	**but for the g. of God, that the Son**	*1391*
Joh	11:40	**thou shouldest see the g. of God?**	*1391*
Joh	12:41	said Esaias, when he saw his g.,	*1391*
Joh	17:5	**with the g. which I had with thee**	*1391*
Joh	17:22	**And the g. which thou gavest me**	*1391*
Joh	17:24	**that they may behold my g.,**	*1391*
Ac	7:2	The God of g. appeared unto our	*1391*
Ac	7:55	and saw the g. of God, and Jesus	*1391*
Ac	12:23	because he gave not God the g.:	*1391*
Ac	22:11	could not see for the g. of that light,	*1391*
Ro	1:23	the g. of the uncorruptible God into	*1391*
Ro	2:7	well doing seek for g. and honour	*1391*
Ro	2:10	g., honour, and peace, to every man	*1391*
Ro	3:7	through my lie unto his g.;	*1391*
Ro	3:23	and come short of the g. of God;	*1391*
Ro	4:2	he hath whereof to g.: but not	*2745*
Ro	4:20	strong in faith, giving g. to God;	*1391*
Ro	5:2	and rejoice in hope of the g. of God.	*1391*
Ro	5:3	but we g. in tribulations also:	*2744*
Ro	6:4	the dead by the g. of the Father,	*1391*
Ro	8:18	the g. which shall be revealed in us.	*1391*
Ro	9:4	the adoption, and the g., and the	*1391*
Ro	9:23	make known the riches of his g. on	*1391*
Ro	9:23	he had afore prepared unto g.,	*1391*
Ro	11:36	to whom be g. for ever. Amen.	*1391*
Ro	15:7	also received us to the g. of God.	*1391*
Ro	15:17	I have therefore whereof I may g.	*2746*
Ro	16:27	To God only wise, be g. through	*1391*
1Co	1:29	no flesh should g. in his presence.	*2744*
1Co	1:31	that glorieth, let him g. in the Lord.	*2744*
1Co	2:7	before the world unto our g.:	*1391*
1Co	2:8	not have crucified the Lord of g.	*1391*
1Co	3:21	Therefore let no man g. in men.	*2744*
1Co	4:7	why dost thou g., as if thou hadst	*2744*
1Co	9:16	I have nothing to g. of: for	*2745*
1Co	10:31	ye do, do all to the g. of God.	*1391*
1Co	11:7	as he is the image and g. of God:	*1391*
1Co	11:7	but the woman is the g. of the man.	*1391*
1Co	11:15	have long hair, it is a g. to her:	*1391*
1Co	15:40	but the g. of the celestial is one,	*1391*
1Co	15:40	the g. of the terrestial is another.	*1391*
1Co	15:41	There is one g. of the sun, and	*1391*
1Co	15:41	and another g. of the moon, and	*1391*
1Co	15:41	and another g. of the stars: for	*1391*
1Co	15:41	differeth from another star in g.	*1391*
1Co	15:43	sown in dishonour; it is raised in g.:	*1391*
2Co	1:20	Amen, unto the g. of God by us.	*1391*
2Co	3:7	g. of his countenance; which g. was	*1391*
2Co	3:9	ministration of condemnation be g.,	*1391*
2Co	3:9	of righteousness exceed in g.	*1391*
2Co	3:10	which was made glorious had no g.	*1392*
2Co	3:10	by reason of the g. that excelleth.	*1391*
2Co	3:18	as in a glass the g. of the Lord,	*1391*
2Co	3:18	into the same image from g. to g.,	*1391*
2Co	4:6	the knowledge of the g. of God	*1391*
2Co	4:15	of many redound to the g. of God.	*1391*
2Co	4:17	exceeding and eternal weight of g.;	*1391*
2Co	5:12	you occasion to g. on our behalf,	*2745*
2Co	5:12	them which g. in appearance,	*2744*
2Co	8:19	by us to the g. of the same Lord,	*1391*
2Co	8:23	the churches, and the g. of Christ.	*1391*
2Co	10:17	glorieth, let him g. in the Lord.	*2744*
2Co	11:12	that wherein they g., they may be	*2744*
2Co	11:18	Seeing that many g. after the flesh,	*2744*
2Co	11:18	after the flesh, I will g. also.	*2744*
2Co	11:30	If I must needs g., I will g. of the	*2744*
2Co	12:1	expedient for me doubtless to g.	*2744*
2Co	12:5	Of such an one will I g.:	*2744*
2Co	12:5	yet of myself I will not g.,	*2744*
2Co	12:6	For though I would desire to g.,	*2744*
2Co	12:9	will I rather g. in my infirmities,	*2744*
Ga	1:5	To whom be g. for ever and ever.	*1391*
Ga	5:26	Let us not be desirous of vain g.,	*2755*
Ga	6:13	that they may g. in your flesh.	*2744*
Ga	6:14	But God forbid that I should g.,	*2744*
Eph	1:6	To the praise of the g. of his grace,	*1391*
Eph	1:12	should be to the praise of his g.,	*1391*
Eph	1:14	possession unto the praise of his g.	*1391*
Eph	1:17	the Father of g., may give unto you	*1391*
Eph	1:18	riches of the g. of his inheritance	*1391*
Eph	3:13	tribulations for you, which is your g.	*1391*
Eph	3:16	according to the riches of his g.,	*1391*
Eph	3:21	Unto him be g. in the church by	*1391*
Php	1:11	unto the g. and praise of God.	*1391*
Php	2:11	is Lord, to the g. of God the Father.	*1391*
Php	3:19	and whose g. is in their shame,	*1391*
Php	4:19	to his riches in g. by Christ Jesus.	*1391*
Php	4:20	our Father be g. for ever and ever.	*1391*
Col	1:27	the riches of the g. of this mystery	*1391*
Col	1:27	is Christ in you, the hope of g.	*1391*
Col	3:4	shall ye also appear with him in g.	*1391*
1Th	2:6	Nor of men sought we g., neither	*1391*
1Th	2:12	called you unto his kingdom and g.	*1391*
1Th	2:20	For ye are our g. and joy.	*1391*
2Th	1:4	So that we ourselves g. in you	*2744*
2Th	1:9	and from the g. of his power;	*1391*
2Th	2:14	of the g. of our Lord Jesus Christ.	*1391*
1Ti	1:17	be honour and g. for ever and ever.	*1391*
1Ti	3:16	in the world, received up into g.	*1391*
2Ti	2:10	is in Christ Jesus with eternal g.	*1391*
2Ti	4:18	to whom be g. for ever and ever.	*1391*
Heb	1:3	Who being the brightness of his g.,	*1391*
Heb	2:7	crownedst him with g. and honour,	*1391*
Heb	2:9	suffering of death, crowned with g.	*1391*
Heb	2:10	in bringing many sons unto g.,	*1391*
Heb	3:3	worthy of more g. than Moses,	*1391*
Heb	9:5	it the cherubims of g. shadowing	*1391*
Heb	13:21	to whom be g. for ever and ever.	*1391*
Jas	2:1	Lord Jesus Christ, the Lord of g.,	*1391*
Jas	3:14	g. not, and lie not against the	*2620*
1Pe	1:7	honour and g. at the appearing of	*1391*
1Pe	1:8	joy unspeakable and full of g.:	*1392*
1Pe	1:11	and the g. that should follow.	*1391*
1Pe	1:21	up from the dead, and gave him g.;	*1391*
1Pe	1:24	the g. of man as the flower of grass.	*1391*
1Pe	2:20	For what g. is it, if, when ye be	*2811*
1Pe	4:13	when his g. shall be revealed,	*1391*
1Pe	4:14	the spirit of g. and of God resteth	*1391*
1Pe	5:1	a partaker of the g. that shall be	*1391*
1Pe	5:4	ye shall receive a crown of g. that	*1391*
1Pe	5:10	hath called us unto his eternal g.	*1391*
1Pe	5:11	him be g. and dominion for ever	*1391*
2Pe	1:3	that hath called us to g. and virtue:	*1391*
2Pe	1:17	from God the Father honour and g.,	*1391*
2Pe	1:17	voice to him from the excellent g.,	*1391*
2Pe	3:18	To him be g. both now and for ever.	*1391*
Jude	24	before the presence of his g. with	*1391*
Jude	25	our Saviour, be g. and majesty,	*1391*
Re	1:6	to him be g. and dominion for ever	*1391*
Re	4:9	those beasts give g. and honour	*1391*
Re	4:11	receive g. and honour and power:	*1391*
Re	5:12	and honour, and g., and blessing,	*1391*
Re	5:13	Blessing, and honour, and g., and	*1391*
Re	7:12	Saying, Amen: Blessing, and g.,	*1391*
Re	11:13	and gave g. to the God of heaven.	*1391*
Re	14:7	Fear God, and give g. to him;	*1391*
Re	15:8	with smoke from the g. of God,	*1391*
Re	16:9	they repented not to give him g.	*1391*
Re	18:1	the earth was lightened with his g.	*1391*
Re	19:1	Salvation, and g., and honour, and	*1391*
Re	21:11	Having the g. of God: and her light	*1391*
Re	21:23	for the g. of God did lighten it, and	*1391*
Re	21:24	bring their g. and honour into it.	*1391*
Re	21:26	they shall bring the g. and honour	*1391*

GLORYING

1Co	5:6	Your g. is not good. Know ye not	*2745*
1Co	9:15	any man should make my g. void.	*2745*
2Co	7:4	great is my g. of you:	*2746*
2Co	12:11	I am become a fool in g.; ye have	*2744*

GLUTTON

De	21:20	he is a g., and a drunkard.	2151
Pr	23:21	the drunkard and the g. shall come	2151

GLUTTONOUS

Mt	11:19	**a man g., and a winebibber, a**	*5314*
Lu	7:34	**a g. man, and a winebibber,**	*5314*

GNASH See also GNASHED; GNASHETH; GNASHING.

Ps	112:10	he shall g. with his teeth, and	2786
La	2:16	they hiss and g. the teeth: they	2786

GNASHED

Ps	35:16	they g. upon me with their teeth.	2786
Ac	7:54	they g. on him with their teeth.	*1031*

GNASHETH

Job	16:9	he g. upon me with his teeth;	2786
Ps	37:12	and g. upon him with his teeth.	2786
Mk	9:18	foameth, and g. with his teeth,	*5149*

GNASHING

Mt	8:12	**shall be weeping and g. of teeth.**	*1030*

Mt 13:42, 50 **shall be wailing and g. of teeth**..*1030*
Mt 22:13 **shall be weeping and g. of teeth**.....*1030*
Mt 24:51 **shall be weeping and g. of teeth**.....*1030*
Mt 25:30 **shall be weeping and g. of teeth**.....*1030*
Lu 13:28 **shall be weeping and g. of teeth**,....*1030*

GNAT
Mt 23:24 **which strain at a g., and swallow**...*2971*

GNAW See also GNAWED.
Zep 3:3 they **g.** not the bones till the.............1633

GNAWED
Re 16:10 and they **g.** their tongues for pain,...... *3145*

GO See also AGO; GOEST; GOETH; GOING; GONE; WENT.
Ge 3:14 upon thy belly shalt thou **g.**, and......... 3212
Ge 8:16 **G.** forth of the ark, thou, and thy........3318
Ge 9:10 **g.** out of the ark, to every beast.........3318
Ge 11:3 **G.** to, let us make brick, and burn...... 3051
Ge 11:4 **G.** to, let us build us a city and a.......3051
Ge 11:7 **G.** to, let us...down, and there...........3051
Ge 11:7 let us **g.** down, and there confound......3381
Ge 11:31 to **g.** into the land of Canaan;..............3212
Ge 12:5 forth to **g.** into the land of Canaan;......3212
Ge 12:19 thy wife, take her, and **g.** thy way...... 3212
Ge 13:9 then I will **g.** to the right; or if thou..........
Ge 13:9 right hand, then I will **g.** to the left..........
Ge 15:2 seeing I **g.** childless, and the..............1980
Ge 15:15 shalt **g.** to thy fathers in peace;.............935
Ge 16:2 I pray thee, **g.** in unto my maid;...........935
Ge 16:8 whither wilt thou **g.**? And she........... 3212
Ge 18:21 I will **g.** down now, and see.................. 3381
Ge 19:2 rise up early, and **g.** on your ways...... 1980
Ge 19:34 and **g.** thou in, and lie with him,............935
Ge 22:5 I and the lad will **g.** yonder and.......... 3212
Ge 24:4 But thou shalt **g.** unto my country,.......3212
Ge 24:11 that women **g.** out to draw water.........3318
Ge 24:38 shalt **g.** unto my father's house,...........3212
Ge 24:42 do prosper my way which I **g.**:...........1980
Ge 24:51 is before thee, take her, and **g.**,.......... 3212
Ge 24:55 at least ten; after that she shall **g.**........3212
Ge 24:56 away that I may **g.** to my master......... 3212
Ge 24:58 Wilt thou **g.** with this man?................ 3212
Ge 24:58 And she said, I will **g.**...................... 3212
Ge 26:2 **G.** not down into Egypt; dwell in........ 3381
Ge 26:16 said unto Isaac, **G.** from us;...............3212
Ge 27:3 and **g.** out to the field, and take..........3318
Ge 27:9 **G.** now to the flock, and fetch me.........3212
Ge 27:13 my voice, and **g.** fetch me them........ 3212
Ge 28:2 Arise, **g.** to Padan-aram, to the.......... 3212
Ge 28:20 in this way that I **g.**, and will give........1980
Ge 29:7 ye the sheep, and **g.** and feed............3212
Ge 29:21 that I may **g.** in unto her................. 935
Ge 30:3 **g.** in unto her; and she shall bear......... 935
Ge 30:25 I may **g.** unto mine own place,............3212
Ge 30:26 I have served thee, and let me **g.**:........ 3212
Ge 31:18 for to **g.** to Isaac his father in the..........935
Ge 32:26 And he said, Let me **g.**, for the day.... 7971
Ge 32:26 let thee **g.**, except thou bless me........ 7971
Ge 33:12 take our journey, and let us **g.**,.......... 3212
Ge 33:12 and I will **g.** before thee......................3212
Ge 35:1 unto Jacob, Arise, **g.** up to Beth-el,..... 5927
Ge 35:3 let us arise, and **g.** up to Beth-el;....... 5927
Ge 37:14 he said to him, **G.**, I pray thee,..........3212
Ge 37:17 Let us **g.** to Dothan. And Joseph........ 3212
Ge 37:30 is not; and I, whither shall I **g.**?.......... 935
Ge 37:35 I will **g.** down into the grave unto........ 3381
Ge 38:8 **G.** in unto thy brother's wife, and...........935
Ge 38:16 **G.** to, I pray thee, let me come in...... 3051
Ge 41:55 said unto all the Egyptians, **G.**..............3212
Ge 42:15 ye shall not **g.** forth hence, except........ 3318
Ge 42:19 **g.** ye, carry corn for the famine..........3212
Ge 42:38 My son shall not **g.** down with you;..... 3381
Ge 42:38 the way in which ye **g.**,...................... 3212
Ge 43:2 father said unto them, **G.** again,..........7725
Ge 43:4 will **g.** down and buy thee food:.........3381
Ge 43:5 not send him, we will not **g.** down:.......3381
Ge 43:8 we will arise and **g.**; that we may.........3212
Ge 43:13 your brother, and arise, **g.** again.........7725
Ge 44:25 our father said, **G.** again, and buy....... 7725
Ge 44:26 And we said, We cannot **g.** down:....... 3381
Ge 44:26 be with us, then will we **g.** down:........ 3381
Ge 44:33 the lad **g.** up with his brethren............. 5927
Ge 44:34 For how shall I **g.** up to my father,..... 5927
Ge 45:1 Cause every man to **g.** out from......... 3318
Ge 45:9 Haste ye, and **g.** up to my father,....... 5927
Ge 45:17 and **g.**, get you unto the land of..........3212
Ge 45:28 I will **g.** and see him before I die,....... 3212
Ge 46:3 fear not to **g.** down into Egypt;............ 3381
Ge 46:4 I will **g.** down with thee into Egypt;.....3381
Ge 46:31 I will **g.** up, and shew Pharaoh,........... 5927
Ge 50:5 let me **g.** up, I pray thee, and bury..... 5927
Ge 50:6 said, **G.** up, and bury thy father,.........5927
Ex 2:7 Shall I **g.** and call to thee a nurse.........3212
Ex 2:8 Pharaoh's daughter said to her, **G.**....... 3212
Ex 3:11 am I, that I should **g.** unto Pharaoh,.... 3212
Ex 3:16 **G.**, and gather the elders of Israel...... 3212
Ex 3:18 now let us **g.**, we beseech thee,.......... 3212
Ex 3:19 king of Egypt will not let you **g.**,.........1980
Ex 3:20 and after that he will let you **g.**...........7971
Ex 3:21 come to pass, that when ye **g.**,.......... 3212
Ex 3:21 ye shall not **g.** empty:...................... 3212
Ex 4:12 Now therefore **g.**, and I will be with.... 3212
Ex 4:18 Let me **g.**, I pray thee, and return...... 3212
Ex 4:18 Jethro said to Moses, **G.** in peace....... 3212
Ex 4:19 **G.**, return into Egypt: for all the.........3212
Ex 4:21 that he shall not let the people **g.**.........7971
Ex 4:23 Let my son **g.**, that he may serve....... 7971
Ex 4:23 if thou refuse to let him **g.**, behold,..... 7971
Ex 4:26 So he let him **g.**: then she said,........... 7503
Ex 4:27 **G.** into the wilderness to meet........... 3212
Ex 5:1 Let my people **g.**, that they may.........7971
Ex 5:2 obey his voice to let Israel **g.**?........... 7971
Ex 5:2 neither will I let Israel **g.**.................. 7971
Ex 5:3 let us **g.**, we pray thee, three days'.....3212
Ex 5:7 **g.** and gather straw for themselves......3212
Ex 5:8 Let us **g.** and sacrifice to our God.......3212
Ex 5:11 **G.** ye, get you straw where ye can..... 3212
Ex 5:17 us **g.** and do sacrifice to the Lord........3212
Ex 5:18 **G.** therefore now, and work; for...........3212
Ex 6:1 a strong hand shall he let them **g.**,....... 7971
Ex 6:11 **G.** in, speak unto Pharaoh king of.........935
Ex 6:11 that he let the children of Israel **g.**....... 7971
Ex 7:14 he refuseth to let the people **g.**.......... 7971
Ex 7:16 unto thee, saying, Let my people **g.**,... 7971
Ex 8:1 **G.** unto Pharaoh, and say unto............935
Ex 8:1 Let my people **g.**, that they may.........7971
Ex 8:2 if thou refuse to let them **g.**,...............7971
Ex 8:3 **g.** up and come into thine house,......... 5927
Ex 8:8 and I will let the people **g.**, that..........7971
Ex 8:20 Let my people **g.**, that they may.........7971
Ex 8:21 if thou wilt not let my people **g.**,..........7971
Ex 8:25 **G.** ye, sacrifice to your God in the...... 3212
Ex 8:27 We will **g.** three days' journey into...... 3212
Ex 8:28 said, I will let you **g.**, that ye may.......7971
Ex 8:28 only ye shall not **g.** very far away;...... 3212
Ex 8:29 Behold, I **g.** out from thee, and I........ 3318
Ex 8:29 letting the people **g.** to sacrifice..........7971
Ex 8:32 neither would he let the people **g.**........ 7971
Ex 9:1 **G.** in unto Pharaoh, and tell him,..........935
Ex 9:1 Let my people **g.**, that they may.........7971
Ex 9:2 For if thou refuse to let them **g.**,......... 7971
Ex 9:7 and he did not let the people **g.**.......... 7971
Ex 9:13 Let my people **g.**, that they may......... 7971
Ex 9:17 that thou wilt not let them **g.**?............ 7971
Ex 9:28 and I will let you **g.**, and ye shall........ 7971
Ex 9:35 he let the children of Israel **g.**;........... 7971
Ex 10:1 **G.** in unto Pharaoh, for I have............. 935
Ex 10:3 let my people **g.**, that they may.......... 7971
Ex 10:4 if thou refuse to let my people **g.**,........ 7971
Ex 10:7 let the men **g.**, that they may serve.... 7971
Ex 10:8 **G.**, serve the Lord your God:............. 3212
Ex 10:8 but who are they that shall **g.**?........... 1980
Ex 10:9 We will **g.** with our young and............3212
Ex 10:9 and with our herds will we **g.**;.............3212
Ex 10:10 as I will let you **g.**, and your little....... 7971
Ex 10:11 **g.** now ye that are men, and serve......3212
Ex 10:20 not let the children of Israel **g.**........... 7971
Ex 10:24 **G.** ye, serve the Lord; and let............ 3212
Ex 10:24 let your little ones also **g.** with you......3212
Ex 10:26 Our cattle also shall **g.** with us;........... 3212
Ex 10:27 and he would not let them **g.**............... 7971
Ex 11:1 afterwards he will let you **g.** hence:..... 7971
Ex 11:1 when he shall let you **g.**, he shall......... 7971
Ex 11:4 About midnight will I **g.** out into......... 3318
Ex 11:8 after that I will **g.** out. And he.............3318
Ex 11:10 not let the children of Israel **g.**............. 7971
Ex 12:22 none of you shall **g.** out at the............3318
Ex 12:31 and **g.**, serve the Lord, as ye have......3212
Ex 13:15 Pharaoh would hardly let us **g.**,........... 7971
Ex 13:17 Pharaoh had let the people **g.**,.............7971
Ex 13:21 light; to **g.** by day and night:...............3212
Ex 14:5 that we have let Israel **g.** from........... 7971
Ex 14:15 of Israel, that they **g.** forward:............ 5265
Ex 14:16 children of Israel shall **g.** on dry.......... 935
Ex 14:21 Lord caused the sea to **g.** back............3212
Ex 16:4 the people shall **g.** out and gather....... 3318
Ex 16:29 let no man **g.** of his place on the.........3318
Ex 17:5 **G.** on before the people, and............. 5674
Ex 17:5 take in thine hand, and **g.**.....................1980
Ex 17:9 Choose us out men, and **g.** out,..........3318
Ex 18:23 all this people shall also **g.** to...............935
Ex 19:10 **G.** unto the people, and sanctify......... 3212
Ex 19:12 that ye **g.** not up into the mount,......... 5927
Ex 19:21 **G.** down, charge the people, lest........ 3381
Ex 20:26 Neither shalt thou **g.** up by steps........ 5927
Ex 21:2 he shall **g.** out free for nothing........... 3318
Ex 21:3 he shall **g.** out by himself: if he...........3318
Ex 21:3 then his wife shall **g.** out with him........3318
Ex 21:4 and he shall **g.** out by himself..............3318
Ex 21:5 my children; I will not **g.** out free:.......3318
Ex 21:7 not **g.** out as the menservants do..........3318
Ex 21:11 then shall she **g.** out free without.........3318
Ex 21:26 let him **g.** free for his eye's sake.........7971
Ex 21:27 he shall let him **g.** free for his............ 7971
Ex 23:23 mine Angel shall **g.** before thee,.......... 3212
Ex 24:2 shall the people **g.** up with him........... 5927
Ex 30:20 When they **g.** into the tabernacle.......... 935
Ex 32:1 us gods, which shall **g.** before us;....... 3212
Ex 32:7 said unto Moses, **G.**, get thee down:... 3212
Ex 32:23 us gods, which shall **g.** before us:........ 3212
Ex 32:27 his sword by his side, and **g.** in.......... 5674
Ex 32:30 now I will **g.** up unto the Lord;............5927
Ex 32:34 Therefore now **g.**, lead the people.........3212
Ex 32:34 mine Angel shall **g.** before thee:.......... 3212
Ex 33:1 unto Moses, Depart, and **g.** up............5927
Ex 33:3 I will not **g.** up in the midst of thee;.... 5927
Ex 33:14 My presence shall **g.** with thee,............3212
Ex 33:15 If thy presence **g.** not with me,........... 1980
Ex 34:9 Lord, I pray thee, **g.** among us;.......... 3212
Ex 34:15 **g.** a whoring after their gods,...................
Ex 34:16 their daughters **g.** a whoring.....................
Ex 34:16 and make thy sons **g.** a whoring..................
Ex 34:24 when thou shalt **g.** up to appear...........5927
Le 6:13 on the altar; it shall never **g.** out..........3518
Le 8:33 ye shall not **g.** out of the door.............3318
Le 9:7 **G.** unto the altar, and offer thy............7126
Le 10:7 ye shall not **g.** out from the door......... 3318
Le 10:9 when ye **g.** into the tabernacle of......... 935
Le 11:27 that **g.** on all four, those are.............. 1980
Le 14:3 And the priest shall **g.** forth out...........3318
Le 14:36 before the priest **g.** into it to see......... 935
Le 14:36 the priest shall **g.** in to see the house:... 935
Le 14:38 priest shall **g.** out of the house............ 3318
Le 14:53 But he shall let **g.** the living bird.........7971
Le 15:16 man's seed of copulation **g.** out............3318
Le 16:10 to let him **g.** for a scapegoat.............. 7971
Le 16:18 And he shall **g.** out unto the altar........3318
Le 16:22 and he shall let **g.** the goat in the........7971
Le 16:26 he that let **g.** the goat for the.............7971
Le 19:16 **g.** up and down as a talebearer............3212
Le 20:5 all that **g.** a whoring after him,..................
Le 20:6 wizards, to **g.** a whoring after......................
Le 21:11 shall he **g.** in to any dead body............ 935
Le 21:12 shall he **g.** out of the sanctuary,............3318
Le 21:23 he shall not **g.** in unto the vail,...............935
Le 25:28 and in the jubile it shall **g.** out,............ 3318
Le 25:30 it shall not **g.** out in the jubile..............3318
Le 25:31 and they shall **g.** out in the jubile..........3318
Le 25:33 shall **g.** out in the year of jubile:........... 3318
Le 25:54 he shall **g.** out in the year of jubile,..... 3318
Le 26:6 the sword **g.** through your land............5674
Le 26:13 yoke, and made you **g.** upright............ 3212
Nu 1:3 all that are able to **g.** forth to war........ 3318
Nu 1:20, 22,24,26,30,32,34,36,38,40,42 all that
were able to **g.** forth to war;............. 3318
Nu 1:28 all that were able to **g.** forth to war;....3318
Nu 1:45 all that were able to **g.** forth to war.....3318
Nu 2:24 shall **g.** forward in the third rank......... 5265
Nu 2:31 **g.** hindmost with their standards.......... 5265
Nu 4:19 Aaron and his sons shall **g.** in,............. 935
Nu 4:20 But they shall not **g.** in to see when......935
Nu 5:12 man's wife **g.** aside, and commit a....... 7847
Nu 5:22 causeth the curse shall **g.** into thy........ 935
Nu 8:15 the Levites **g.** in to do the service......... 935
Nu 8:24 shall **g.** in to wait upon the service....... 935
Nu 10:5 the east parts shall **g.** forward............ 5265
Nu 10:9 And if ye **g.** to war in your land........... 935
Nu 10:30 he said unto him, I will not **g.**; but....... 3212
Nu 10:32 if thou **g.** with us, yea, it shall be,........3212
Nu 13:17 and **g.** up into the mountain:................ 5927

Book	Ref	Context	No.
Nu	13:30	Let us **g.** up at once, and possess it:	5927
Nu	13:31	We be not able to **g.** up against the	5927
Nu	14:40	**g.** up unto the place which the Lord	5927
Nu	14:42	**G.** not up, for the Lord is not among	5927
Nu	14:44	presumed to **g.** up unto the hill top:	5927
Nu	15:39	which ye use to **g.** a whoring:	
Nu	16:30	they **g.** down quick into the pit;	3381
Nu	16:46	**g.** quickly unto the congregation,	3212
Nu	20:17	we will **g.** by the king's high way,	3212
Nu	20:19	him, We will **g.** by the high way;	5927
Nu	20:19	doing anyting else, **g.** through	5674
Nu	20:20	said, Thou shalt not **g.** through	5674
Nu	21:22	**g.** along by the king's high way,	3212
Nu	22:12	Thou shalt not **g.** with them; thou	3212
Nu	22:13	to give me leave to **g.** with you	1980
Nu	22:18	cannot **g.** beyond the word of the	5674
Nu	22:20	thee, rise up, and **g.** with them;	3212
Nu	22:35	**G.** with the men: but only the word	3212
Nu	23:3	by thy burnt offering, and I will **g.**:	3212
Nu	23:16	**G.** again unto Balak, and say thus	7725
Nu	24:13	**g.** beyond the commandment of	5674
Nu	24:14	now, behold, I **g.** unto my people:	1980
Nu	26:2	all that are able to **g.** to war in	3318
Nu	27:17	Which may **g.** out before them,	3318
Nu	27:17	which may **g.** in before them,	935
Nu	27:21	at his word shall they **g.** out, and	3318
Nu	31:3	let them **g.** against the Midianites,	1961
Nu	31:23	shall make it **g.** through the fire,	5674
Nu	31:23	ye shall make **g.** through the water	5674
Nu	32:6	Shall your brethren **g.** to war,	935
Nu	32:9	that they should not **g.** into the land	935
Nu	32:17	ourselves will **g.** ready armed before	
Nu	32:20	if ye will **g.** armed before the Lord	
Nu	32:21	**g.** all of you armed over Jordan	5674
Nu	34:4	and shall **g.** on to Hazar-addar,	3318
Nu	34:9	the border shall **g.** on to Ziphron,	3318
Nu	34:11	coast shall **g.** down from Shepham,	3381
Nu	34:12	the border shall **g.** down to Jordan,	3381
De	1:7	**g.** to the mount of the Amorites,	935
De	1:8	**g.** in and possess the land which	935
De	1:21	before thee: **g.** up and possess it,	5927
De	1:22	by what way we must **g.** up, and	5927
De	1:26	ye would not **g.** up, but rebelled	5927
De	1:28	Whither shall we **g.** up? our	5927
De	1:33	you by what way ye should **g.**,	3212
De	1:37	Thou also shalt not **g.** in thither	935
De	1:38	he shall **g.** in thither: encourage	935
De	1:39	they shall **g.** in thither, and unto	935
De	1:41	we will **g.** up and fight, according	5927
De	1:41	ye were ready to **g.** up into the hill	5927
De	1:42	**G.** not up, neither fight; for I am	5927
De	2:27	I will **g.** along by the high way,	3212
De	3:25	I pray thee, let me **g.** over, and	5674
De	3:27	thou shalt not **g.** over this Jordan	5674
De	3:28	he shall **g.** over before this people,	5674
De	4:1	and **g.** in and possess the land	935
De	4:5	the land whither ye **g.** to possess it	935
De	4:14	them in the land whither ye **g.** over	5674
De	4:21	that I should not **g.** over Jordan,	5674
De	4:21	and that I should not **g.** in unto that	935
De	4:22	land, I must not **g.** over Jordan	5674
De	4:22	but ye shall **g.** over, and possess	5674
De	4:26	ye **g.** over Jordan to possess it;	5674
De	4:34	hath God assayed to **g.** and take him	935
De	4:40	that it may **g.** well with thee, and with	
De	5:16	that it may **g.** well with thee, in the	
De	5:27	**G.** thou near, and hear all that	7126
De	5:30	**G.** say to them, Get you into your	3212
De	6:1	the land whither ye **g.** to possess	5674
De	6:14	Ye shall not **g.** after other gods,	3212
De	6:18	that thou mayest **g.** in and possess	935
De	8:1	and **g.** in and possess the land which	935
De	9:1	to **g.** in to possess nations greater	935
De	9:5	dost thou **g.** to possess their land;	935
De	9:23	**G.** up and possess the land which	5927
De	10:11	may **g.** in and possess the land,	935
De	11:8	and **g.** in and possess the land	935
De	11:8	land, whither ye **g.** to possess it;	5674
De	11:11	the land whither ye **g.** to possess it,	
De	11:28	to **g.** after other gods, which ye	3212
De	11:31	Jordan to **g.** in to possess the land	935
De	12:10	when ye **g.** over Jordan, and dwell	5674
De	12:25	that it may **g.** well with thee, and with	
De	12:26	**g.** unto the place which the Lord	935
De	12:28	that it may **g.** well with thee, and with	
De	13:2	Let us **g.** after other gods, which	3212
De	13:6	**g.** and serve other gods, which thou	3212
De	13:13	**g.** and serve other gods, which ye	3212
De	14:25	**g.** unto the place which the Lord	1980
De	15:12	shalt let him **g.** free from thee	7971
De	15:13	shalt not let him **g.** away empty:	7971
De	15:16	I will not **g.** away from thee;	3318
De	16:7	morning, and **g.** unto thy tents	1980
De	19:13	that it may **g.** well with thee	
De	19:21	life shall **g.** for life, eye for eye, tooth	
De	20:5	let him **g.** and return to his house,	3212
De	20:6	also **g.** and return unto his house,	3212
De	20:7, 8	him **g.** and return unto his house,	3212
De	21:13	after that thou shalt **g.** in unto her,	935
De	21:14	shalt let her **g.** whither she will;	7971
De	22:1	brother's ox or his sheep **g.** astray,	
De	22:7	shalt in any wise let the dam **g.**,	7971
De	22:13	and **g.** in unto her, and hate her,	935
De	23:10	shall he **g.** abroad out of the camp,	3318
De	23:12	whither thou shalt **g.** forth abroad:	3318
De	24:2	out of his house, she may **g.** and be	1980
De	24:5	he shall not **g.** out to war, neither	3318
De	24:10	thou shalt not **g.** into his house	935
De	24:15	shall the sun **g.** down upon it;	935
De	24:19	thou shalt not **g.** again to fetch it:	7725
De	24:20	shalt not **g.** over the boughs again:	
De	25:5	brother shall **g.** in unto her, and	935
De	25:7	then let his brother's wife **g.** up	5927
De	26:2	and shalt **g.** unto the place which	1980
De	26:3	And thou shalt **g.** unto the priest	935
De	27:3	that thou mayest **g.** in unto the land	935
De	28:14	thou shalt not **g.** aside from any	5493
De	28:14	**g.** after other gods to serve them	3212
De	28:25	shalt **g.** out one way against them,	3318
De	28:41	for they shall **g.** into captivity,	3212
De	29:18	to **g.** and serve the gods of these	3212
De	30:12	Who shall **g.** up for us to heaven,	5927
De	30:13	Who shall **g.** over the sea for us,	5674
De	30:18	over Jordan to **g.** to possess it	935
De	31:2	I can no more **g.** out and come in:	3318
De	31:2	Thou shalt not **g.** over this Jordan	5674
De	31:3	he will **g.** over before thee, and he	5674
De	31:3	Joshua, he shall **g.** over before thee,	5674
De	31:6	he it is that doth **g.** with thee;	1980
De	31:7	for thou must **g.** with this people	935
De	31:8	he it is that doth **g.** before thee;	1980
De	31:13	ye **g.** over Jordan to possess it	5674
De	31:16	and **g.** a whoring after the gods	
De	31:16	whither they **g.** to be among them,	935
De	31:21	imagination which they **g.** about,	6213
De	32:47	ye **g.** over Jordan to possess it	5674
De	32:52	but thou shalt not **g.** thither unto	935
De	34:4	but thou shalt not **g.** over thither	5674
Jos	1:2	therefore arise, **g.** over this Jordan,	5674
Jos	1:11	to **g.** in to possess the land, which	935
Jos	1:16	thou sendest us, we will **g.**	3212
Jos	2:1	**G.** view the land, even Jericho	3212
Jos	2:16	afterward may ye **g.** your way	3212
Jos	2:19	that whosoever shall **g.** out of the	3318
Jos	3:3	from your place, and **g.** after it	1980
Jos	3:4	the way by which ye must **g.**:	3212
Jos	6:3	and **g.** round about the city once	5362
Jos	6:22	**G.** into the harlot's house, and	935
Jos	7:2	**G.** up and view the country	5927
Jos	7:3	Let not all the people **g.** up; but let	5927
Jos	7:3	about two or three thousand **g.** up	5927
Jos	8:1	**g.** up to Ai: see, I have given into	5927
Jos	8:3	people of war, to **g.** up against Ai:	5927
Jos	8:4	**g.** not very far from the city,	7368
Jos	9:11	and **g.** to meet them, and say unto	3212
Jos	9:12	day we came forth to **g.** unto you;	3212
Jos	10:13	hasted not to **g.** down about a	935
Jos	14:11	both to **g.** out, and to come in	3318
Jos	18:3	ye slack to **g.** to possess the land,	935
Jos	18:4	rise, and **g.** through the land,	1980
Jos	18:8	**G.** and walk through the land,	3212
Jos	22:9	to **g.** unto the country of Gilead,	3212
Jos	22:12	to **g.** up to war against them	5927
Jos	22:33	not intend to **g.** up against them	5927
Jos	23:12	if ye do in any wise **g.** back, and	7725
Jos	23:12	**g.** in unto them, and they to you:	935
Jg	1:1	Who shall **g.** up for us against	5927
Jg	1:2	the Lord said, Judah shall **g.** up:	5927
Jg	1:3	will **g.** with thee into thy lot	1980
Jg	1:25	let **g.** the man and all his family	7971
Jg	2:1	I made you to **g.** up out of Egypt,	5927
Jg	2:6	Joshua had let the people **g.**,	7971
Jg	4:6	**G.** and draw toward mount Tabor,	3212
Jg	4:8	unto her, If thou wilt **g.** with me,	3212
Jg	4:8	then I will **g.**: but if thou	1980
Jg	4:8	but if thou wilt not **g.** with me,	3212
Jg	4:8	with me, then I will not **g.**	3212
Jg	4:9	she said, I will surely **g.** with thee:	3212
Jg	5:11	the people of the Lord **g.** down	3381
Jg	6:14	**G.** in this thy might, and thou	3212
Jg	7:3	**g.** to, proclaim in the ears of the	4994
Jg	7:4	unto thee, This shall **g.** with thee,	3212
Jg	7:4	the same shall **g.** with thee;	3212
Jg	7:4	thee, This shall not **g.** with thee,	3212
Jg	7:4	with thee, the same shall not **g.**	3212
Jg	7:7	all the other people **g.** every man	3212
Jg	7:10	But if thou fear to **g.** down,	3381
Jg	7:10	**g.** thou with Phurah...down to	3381
Jg	7:11	hands be strengthened to **g.** down	3381
Jg	9:9, 11,13	**g.** to be promoted over the	1980
Jg	9:38	**g.** out, I pray now, and fight with	3318
Jg	10:14	**G.** and cry unto the gods which	3212
Jg	11:8	that thou mayest **g.** with us, and	1980
Jg	11:35	and I cannot **g.** back	7725
Jg	11:37	two months, that I may **g.** up	3212
Jg	11:38	And he said, **G.**. And he sent her	3212
Jg	12:1	didst not call us to **g.** with thee?	3212
Jg	12:5	escaped said, Let me **g.** over;	5674
Jg	15:1	**g.** in to my wife into the chamber	935
Jg	15:1	father would not suffer him to **g.** in	935
Jg	15:5	the brands on fire, he let them **g.**	7971
Jg	16:17	then my strength will **g.** from me,	5493
Jg	16:20	**g.** out as at other times before,	3318
Jg	17:9	I **g.** to sojourn where I may find	1980
Jg	18:2	**G.**, search the land: who when	3212
Jg	18:5	which we **g.** shall be prosperous	1980
Jg	18:6	said unto them, **G.** in peace:	3212
Jg	18:6	Lord is your way wherein ye **g.**	3212
Jg	18:9	that we may **g.** up against them:	5927
Jg	18:9	be not slothful to **g.**, and to enter	3212
Jg	18:10	ye **g.**, ye shall come unto a people	935
Jg	18:19	**g.** with us, and be to us a father	3212
Jg	19:5	and afterward **g.** your way	3212
Jg	19:9	way, that thou mayest **g.** home	1980
Jg	19:15	to **g.** in and to lodge in Gibeah:	935
Jg	19:25	began to spring, they let her **g.**	7971
Jg	19:27	went out to **g.** his way: and,	3212
Jg	20:8	We will not any of us **g.** to his tent,	3212
Jg	20:9	will **g.** up by lot against it;	
Jg	20:14	to **g.** out to battle against the	3318
Jg	20:18	of us shall **g.** up first to the battle	5927
Jg	20:23	Shall I **g.** up again to battle	5066
Jg	20:23	And the Lord, **G.** up against him.)	5927
Jg	20:28	Shall I yet again **g.** out to battle	3318
Jg	20:28	And the Lord said, **G.** up; for to	5927
Jg	21:10	**G.** and smite the inhabitants of	3212
Jg	21:20	**G.** and lie in wait in the vineyards;	3212
Jg	21:21	and **g.** to the land of Benjamin	1980
Ru	1:8	**G.**, return each to her mother's	3212
Ru	1:11	why will ye **g.** with me? are there	3212
Ru	1:12	again, my daughters, **g.** your way;	3212
Ru	1:16	for whither thou goest, I will **g.**;	3212
Ru	1:18	stedfastly minded to **g.** with her,	3212
Ru	2:2	Let me now **g.** to the field,	3212
Ru	2:2	she said unto her, **G.**, my daughter	3212
Ru	2:8	**G.** not to glean in another field,	3212
Ru	2:8	neither **g.** from hence, but abide	5674
Ru	2:9	and **g.** thou after them: have I not	1980
Ru	2:9	art athirst, **g.** unto the vessels,	1980
Ru	2:22	that thou **g.** out with his maidens,	3318
Ru	3:4	shalt **g.** in, and uncover his feet,	935
Ru	3:17	**G.** not empty unto thy mother in	935
1Sa	1:17	Eli answered and said, **G.** in peace:	3212
1Sa	1:22	I will not **g.** up until the child be	
1Sa	3:9	Eli said unto Samuel, **G.**, lie down:	3212
1Sa	5:11	let it **g.** again to his own place,	7725
1Sa	6:6	did they not let the people **g.**,	7971
1Sa	6:8	and send it away, that it may **g.**	1980
1Sa	6:20	to whom shall he **g.** up from us?	5927
1Sa	8:20	**g.** out before us, and fight our	3318
1Sa	8:22	**G.** ye every man unto his city,	3212
1Sa	9:3	and arise, **g.** seek the asses	3212
1Sa	9:6	let us **g.** thither; peradventure he	3212
1Sa	9:6	shew us our way that we should **g.**	1980
1Sa	9:7	we **g.**, what shall we bring the man?	3212
1Sa	9:9	Come, and let us **g.** to the seer:	3212
1Sa	9:10	Well said; come, let us **g.**. So they	3212
1Sa	9:13	he **g.** up to the high place to eat:	5927
1Sa	9:14	for to **g.** up to the high place	5927
1Sa	9:19	**g.** up before me unto the high place;	5927

1Sa 9:19 and to morrow I will let thee **g.**,.........7971
1Sa 10:3 thou **g.** on forward from thence,.......... 2498
1Sa 10:8 shalt **g.** down before me to Gilgal;........3381
1Sa 10:9 turned his back to **g.** from Samuel,......3212
1Sa 11:14 Come, and let us **g.** to Gilgal,........... 3212
1Sa 12:21 for then should ye **g.** after vain things,.......
1Sa 14:1 let us **g.** over to the Philistines,.........5674
1Sa 14:4 Jonathan sought to **g.** over unto the.....5674
1Sa 14:6 and let us **g.** over unto the garrison.....5674
1Sa 14:9 still in our place, and will not **g.** up......5927
1Sa 14:10 up unto us; then we will **g.** up:...........5927
1Sa 14:36 Let us **g.** down after the Philistines..... 3381
1Sa 14:37 I **g.** down after the Philistines?........... 3381
1Sa 15:3 Now **g.** and smite Amalek, and............3212
1Sa 15:6 **G.**, depart, get you down from............3212
1Sa 15:18 **G.** and utterly destroy the sinners.......3212
1Sa 15:27 Samuel turned about to **g.** away,..........3212
1Sa 16:1 fill thine horn with oil, and **g.**,.............. 3212
1Sa 16:2 And Samuel said, How can I **g.**?........... 3212
1Sa 17:32 **g.** and fight with this Philistine...........3212
1Sa 17:33 not able to **g.** against this Philistine..... 3212
1Sa 17:37 Saul said unto David, **G.**, and the........3212
1Sa 17:39 he assayed to **g.**; for he had not........... 3212
1Sa 17:39 I cannot **g.** with these; for I have.........3212
1Sa 17:55 Saul saw David **g.** forth against...........3318
1Sa 18:2 **g.** no more home to his father's..........7725
1Sa 19:3 **g.** out and stand beside my father....... 3318
1Sa 19:17 He said unto me, Let me **g.**;............. 7971
1Sa 20:5 but let me **g.**, that I may hide............ 7971
1Sa 20:11 and let us **g.** out into the field............ 3318
1Sa 20:13 that thou mayest **g.** in peace: and....... 1980
1Sa 20:19 thou shalt **g.** down quickly,................ 3381
1Sa 20:21 saying, **G.**, find out the arrows............ 3212
1Sa 20:22 **g.** thy way: for the Lord hath sent...... 3212
1Sa 20:28 asked leave of me to **g.** to Bethlehem:.......
1Sa 20:29 he said, Let me **g.**, I pray thee;......... 7971
1Sa 20:40 him, **G.**, carry them to the city........... 3212
1Sa 20:42 Jonathan said to David, **G.** in peace,..... 3212
1Sa 23:2 I **g.** and smite these Philistines?..........3212
1Sa 23:2 **G.**, and smite the Philistines, and........3212
1Sa 23:4 Arise, **g.** down to Keilah; for I will...... 3381
1Sa 23:8 people together to war, to **g.** down..... 3381
1Sa 23:13 went whithersoever they could **g.**.........1980
1Sa 23:13 he forbare to **g.** forth...................... 3318
1Sa 23:22 **G.**, I pray you, prepare yet, and.........3212
1Sa 23:23 I will **g.** with you: and it shall.............1980
1Sa 24:19 will he let him **g.** well away?.............. 7971
1Sa 25:5 **g.** to Nabal, and greet him.................. 935
1Sa 25:19 her servants, **G.** on before me;.......... 5674
1Sa 25:35 **G.** up in peace to thine house;........... 5927
1Sa 26:6 will **g.** down with me to Saul to.......... 3381
1Sa 26:6 and Abishai said, I will **g.** down.......... 3381
1Sa 26:11 the cruse of water, and let us **g.**.........3212
1Sa 26:19 saying, **G.**, serve other gods..............3212
1Sa 28:1 shalt **g.** out with me to battle,............ 3318
1Sa 28:7 I may **g.** to her, and enquire of her..... 3212
1Sa 29:4 that he may **g.** again to his place.........7725
1Sa 29:4 him not **g.** down with us to battle,........3381
1Sa 29:7 now return, and **g.** in peace,.............. 3212
1Sa 29:8 not **g.** fight against the enemies............935
1Sa 29:9 not **g.** up with us to the battle............5927
1Sa 30:10 they could not **g.** over the brook.........5674
2Sa 1:15 **G.** near, and fall upon him.................. 5066
2Sa 2:1 Shall I **g.** up into any of the cities........5927
2Sa 2:1 And the Lord said unto him, **G.** up......5927
2Sa 2:1 David said, Whither shall I **g.** up?........5927
2Sa 3:16 said Abner unto him, **G.**, return..........3212
2Sa 3:21 I will arise and **g.**, and will gather....... 3212
2Sa 5:19 Shall I **g.** up to the Philistines?........... 5927
2Sa 5:19 Lord said unto David, **G.** up: for...........5927
2Sa 5:23 Thou shalt not **g.** up; but fetch a.........5927
2Sa 5:24 shall the Lord **g.** out before thee,........ 3318
2Sa 7:3 **G.**, do all that is in thine heart;.......... 3212
2Sa 7:5 **G.** and tell thy servant David,............ 3212
2Sa 11:1 time when kings **g.** forth to battle,...... 3318
2Sa 11:8 **G.** down to thy house, and wash.........3381
2Sa 11:10 not **g.** down unto thine house?............3381
2Sa 11:11 shall I then **g.** into mine house,.......... 935
2Sa 12:23 I shall **g.** to him, but he shall not........ 1980
2Sa 13:7 **G.** now to thy brother Amnon's.......... 3212
2Sa 13:13 shall I cause my shame to **g.**?............ 3212
2Sa 13:24 his servants **g.** with thy servant..........3212
2Sa 13:25 Nay, my son, let us not all now **g.**,...... 3212
2Sa 13:25 he would not **g.**, but blessed him........ 3212
2Sa 13:26 let my brother Amnon **g.** with us........ 3212
2Sa 13:26 Why should he **g.** with thee?..............3212
2Sa 13:27 Amnon and all the king's sons **g.**.........7971
2Sa 13:39 longed to **g.** forth unto Absalom:.........3318
2Sa 14:8 unto the woman, **G.** to thine house,.... 3212
2Sa 14:21 **g.** therefore, bring the young man....... 3212
2Sa 14:30 **g.** and set it on fire. And Absalom's.....3212
2Sa 15:7 let me **g.** and pay my vow,................3212
2Sa 15:9 the king said unto him, **G.** in peace..... 3212
2Sa 15:20 should I this day make thee **g.** up....... 3212
2Sa 15:20 seeing I **g.** whither I may,.................1980
2Sa 15:22 David said to Ittai, **G.** and pass.......... 3212
2Sa 16:9 let me **g.** over, I pray thee, and......... 5674
2Sa 16:21 **G.** in unto thy father's concubines,........ 935
2Sa 17:11 that thou **g.** to battle in thine own....... 1980
2Sa 18:2 surely **g.** forth with you myself........... 3318
2Sa 18:3 Thou shalt not **g.** forth: for if we.......... 3318
2Sa 18:21 **G.** tell the king what thou hast........... 3212
2Sa 19:7 Now therefore arise, **g.** forth, and.......3318
2Sa 19:7 by the Lord, if thou **g.** not forth,......... 3318
2Sa 19:15 to **g.** to meet the king, to conduct.......3212
2Sa 19:20 **g.** down to meet my lord the king...... 3381
2Sa 19:26 and **g.** to the king; because thy.......... 3212
2Sa 19:34 that I should **g.** up with the king......... 5927
2Sa 19:36 servant will **g.** a little way over.......... 5674
2Sa 19:37 servant Chimham; let him **g.** over....... 5674
2Sa 19:38 Chimham shall **g.** over with me,...........5674
2Sa 20:11 that is for David, let him **g.** after..............
2Sa 21:17 Thou shalt **g.** no more out with.......... 3318
2Sa 24:1 **G.**, number Israel and Judah............. 3212
2Sa 24:2 **G.** now through all the tribes of..........7751
2Sa 24:12 **G.** and say unto David, Thus saith...... 1980
2Sa 24:18 **G.** up, rear an altar unto the Lord.......5927
1Ki 1:13 **G.** and get thee in unto king.............. 3212
1Ki 1:53 Solomon said unto him, **G.** to thine......3212
1Ki 2:2 I **g.** the way of all the earth;.............. 1980
1Ki 2:6 let not his hoar head **g.** down to.......... 3381
1Ki 2:29 saying, **G.**, fall upon him..................... 3212
1Ki 2:36 **g.** not forth thence any whither........... 3318
1Ki 3:7 know not how to **g.** out or come in..... 3318
1Ki 8:44 If thy people **g.** out to battle.............. 3318
1Ki 9:6 but **g.** and serve other gods,..............1980
1Ki 11:2 Ye shall not **g.** in to them, neither........ 935
1Ki 11:10 that he should not **g.** after other.......... 3212
1Ki 11:17 servants with him, to **g.** into Egypt;...... 935
1Ki 11:21 that I may **g.** to mine own country...... 3212
1Ki 11:22 thou seekest to **g.** to thine own........... 3212
1Ki 11:22 Nothing: howbeit let me **g.** in any....... 7971
1Ki 12:24 saith the Lord, Ye shall not **g.** up,.......5927
1Ki 12:27 and **g.** again to Rehoboam king........... 7725
1Ki 12:27 this people **g.** up to do sacrifice........... 5927
1Ki 12:28 much for you to **g.** up to Jerusalem:.... 5927
1Ki 13:8 I will not **g.** in with thee, neither...........935
1Ki 13:16 nor **g.** in with thee: neither will I............935
1Ki 13:17 turn again to **g.** by the way that..........3212
1Ki 14:3 and **g.** to him: he shall tell thee............935
1Ki 14:7 **G.**, tell Jeroboam, Thus saith the........ 3212
1Ki 15:17 he might not suffer any to **g.** out......... 3318
1Ki 17:12 that I may **g.** in and dress it for.......... 935
1Ki 17:13 Fear not; **g.** and do as thou hast.......... 935
1Ki 18:1 **G.**, show thyself unto Ahab; and.......... 3212
1Ki 18:5 **G.** into the land, unto all fountains........ 3212
1Ki 18:8 I am: **g.**, tell thy lord, Behold, Elijah....3212
1Ki 18:11, 14 sayest, **G.**, tell thy lord, Behold,..... 3212
1Ki 18:43 **G.** up now, look toward the sea..........5927
1Ki 18:43 he said, **G.** again seven times.............7725
1Ki 18:44 **G.** up, say unto Ahab, Prepare........... 5927
1Ki 19:11 **G.** forth, and stand upon the..............3318
1Ki 19:15 **G.**, return on thy way to the.............. 3212
1Ki 19:20 he said unto him, **G.** back again:.......... 3212
1Ki 20:22 **G.**, strengthen thyself, and mark,.........3212
1Ki 20:31 and **g.** out to the king of Israel:............ 3318
1Ki 20:33 Then he said, **G.** ye, bring him............ 935
1Ki 20:42 Because thou hast let **g.** out of............. 7971
1Ki 20:42 therefore thy life shall **g.** for his..........1961
1Ki 21:16 Ahab rose up to **g.** down to the...........3381
1Ki 21:18 Arise, **g.** down to meet Ahab king.......3381
1Ki 22:4 Wilt thou **g.** with me to battle to.........3212
1Ki 22:6 Shall I **g.** against Ramoth-gilead........... 3212
1Ki 22:6 **G.** up; for the Lord shall deliver it.......5927
1Ki 22:12 **G.** up to Ramoth-gilead, and............. 5927
1Ki 22:15 shall we **g.** against Ramoth-gilead........ 3212
1Ki 22:15 **G.**, and prosper: for the Lord........... 5927
1Ki 22:20 persuade Ahab, that he may **g.** up........ 5927
1Ki 22:22 will **g.** forth, and I will be a lying........ 3318
1Ki 22:22 and prevail also: **g.** forth, and do.........3318
1Ki 22:25 when thou shalt **g.** into an inner........... 935
1Ki 22:48 ship of Tharshish to **g.** to Ophir..........3212
1Ki 22:49 my servants **g.** with thy servants........ 3212
2Ki 1:2 **G.**, enquire of Baal-zebub the god....... 3212
2Ki 1:3 **g.** up to meet the messengers of......... 5927
2Ki 1:3 ye **g.** to enquire to Baal-zebub............1980
2Ki 1:6 **G.**, turn again unto the king that.........3212
2Ki 1:15 **G.** down with him: be not afraid......... 3381
2Ki 2:16 let them **g.**, we pray thee, and seek.... 3212
2Ki 2:18 Did I not say unto you, **G.** not?.......... 3212
2Ki 2:23 **G.** up, thou bald head; **g.** up, thou...... 5927
2Ki 3:7 wilt thou **g.** with me against Moab.......3212
2Ki 3:7 And he said, I will **g.** up: I am as........5927
2Ki 3:8 Which way shall we **g.** up? And he...... 5927
2Ki 4:3 he said, **G.**, borrow thee vessels.......... 3212
2Ki 4:7 **G.**, sell the oil, and pay thy debt,.........3212
2Ki 4:23 Wherefore wilt thou **g.** to him............ 1980
2Ki 4:24 Drive, and **g.** forward; slack not......... 3212
2Ki 4:29 take my staff in thine hand, and **g.**....... 3212
2Ki 5:5 And the king of Syria said, **G.** to,.........3212
2Ki 5:5 **g.**, and I will send a letter.................... 935
2Ki 5:10 **G.** and wash in Jordan seven..............1980
2Ki 5:19 And he said unto him, **G.** in peace.......3212
2Ki 5:24 and he let the men **g.**, and they..........7971
2Ki 6:2 us **g.**, we pray thee, unto Jordan,......... 3212
2Ki 6:2 And he answered, **G.** ye.....................3212
2Ki 6:3 I pray thee, and **g.** with thy servants... 3212
2Ki 6:3 And he answered, I will **g.**................. 3212
2Ki 6:13 he said, **G.** and spy where he is,.......... 3212
2Ki 6:22 and drink, and **g.** to their master......... 3212
2Ki 7:5 **g.** unto the camp of the Syrians:.......... 935
2Ki 7:9 that we may **g.** and tell the king's.........935
2Ki 7:14 the Syrians, saying, **G.** and see.......... 3212
2Ki 8:1 and **g.** thou and thine household,...........3212
2Ki 8:8 and **g.**, meet the man of God, and.......3212
2Ki 8:10 **G.**, say unto him, Thou mayest............ 3212
2Ki 9:1 thine hand and **g.** to Ramoth-gilead:..... 3212
2Ki 9:2 and **g.** in, and make him arise up.......... 935
2Ki 9:15 let none **g.** forth nor escape out..........3318
2Ki 9:15 of the city, to **g.** to tell it in Jezreel.....3212
2Ki 9:34 **G.**, see now this cursed woman,..........6485
2Ki 10:13 and we **g.** down to salute the..............3381
2Ki 10:24 he that letteth him **g.**, his life shall be........
2Ki 10:25 **G.** in, and slay them; let none............. 935
2Ki 11:7 you that **g.** forth on the sabbath,..........3318
2Ki 11:9 that should **g.** out on the sabbath,........ 3318
2Ki 12:17 Hazael set his face to **g.** up to............5927
2Ki 17:27 and let them **g.** and dwell there,.......... 3212
2Ki 18:21 a man lean, it will **g.** into his hand,........ 935
2Ki 18:25 said to me, **G.** up against this land,...... 5927
2Ki 19:31 shall **g.** forth a remnant, and they....... 3318
2Ki 20:5 on the third day thou shalt **g.** up.........5927
2Ki 20:8 shall **g.** into the house of the Lord.......5927
2Ki 20:9 shall the shadow **g.** forward ten.......... 1980
2Ki 20:9 degrees, or **g.** back ten degrees?........ 7725
2Ki 20:10 shadow to **g.** down ten degrees:.......... 5186
2Ki 22:4 **G.** up to Hilkiah the high priest.......... 5927
2Ki 22:13 **G.** ye, enquire of the Lord for me,.......3212
1Ch 7:11 fit to **g.** out for war and battle............3318
1Ch 14:10 I **g.** up against the Philistines?............5927
1Ch 14:10 the Lord said unto him, **G.** up;........... 5927
1Ch 14:14 God said unto him, **G.** not up after...... 5927
1Ch 14:15 then thou shalt **g.** out to battle:.......... 3318
1Ch 17:4 **G.** and tell David my servant,............ 3212
1Ch 17:11 must **g.** to be with thy fathers,............3212
1Ch 20:1 time that kings **g.** out to battle,............ 3318
1Ch 21:2 **G.**, number Israel from Beer-sheba..... 3212
1Ch 21:10 **G.** and tell David, saying, Thus.......... 3212
1Ch 21:18 that David should **g.** up, and set......... 5927
1Ch 21:30 David could not **g.** before it to............3212
2Ch 1:10 that I may **g.** out and come in............ 3318
2Ch 6:34 If thy people **g.** out to war against.........3318
2Ch 7:19 and shall **g.** and serve other gods,.......1980
2Ch 11:4 Ye shall not **g.** up, nor fight against..... 5927
2Ch 14:11 we **g.** against this multitude..................935
2Ch 16:1 he might let none **g.** out or come in.....3318
2Ch 16:3 **g.**, break thy league with Baasha........ 3212
2Ch 18:2 persuaded him to **g.** up with him.......... 5927
2Ch 18:3 **g.** with me to Ramoth-gilead?............. 3212
2Ch 18:5 Shall we **g.** to Ramoth-gilead to.......... 3212
2Ch 18:5 **G.** up; for God will deliver it into......... 5927
2Ch 18:11 **G.** up to Ramoth-gilead, and.............. 5927
2Ch 18:14 Shall we **g.** to Ramoth-gilead to.......... 3212
2Ch 18:14 **G.** ye up, and prosper, and they......... 5927
2Ch 18:19 that he may **g.** up and fall at.............. 5927
2Ch 18:21 I will **g.** out, and be a lying spirit........ 3318
2Ch 18:21 also prevail; **g.** out, and do even so..... 3318
2Ch 18:24 that day when thou shalt **g.** into........... 935
2Ch 18:29 and will **g.** to the battle; but put...........935

2Ch 20:16 morrow **g.** ye down against them:.... 3381
2Ch 20:17 to morrow **g.** out against them:.... 3318
2Ch 20:27 to **g.** again to Jerusalem with joy;.... 7725
2Ch 20:36 to make ships to **g.** to Tarshish:.... 3212
2Ch 20:37 were not able to **g.** to Tarshish,.... 3212
2Ch 21:13 of Jerusalem to **g.** a whoring,....
2Ch 23:6 shall **g.** in, for they are holy:.... 935
2Ch 23:8 were to **g.** out on the sabbath:.... 3318
2Ch 24:5 **G.** out unto the cities of Judah,.... 3318
2Ch 25:5 able to **g.** forth to war, that could.... 3318
2Ch 25:7 the army of Israel **g.** with thee;.... 935
2Ch 25:8 But if thou wilt **g.**, do it, be strong.... 935
2Ch 25:10 out of Ephraim, to **g.** home again:.... 3212
2Ch 25:13 should not **g.** with him to battle,.... 3212
2Ch 26:18 **g.** out of the sanctuary; for thou.... 3318
2Ch 26:20 yea, himself hasted also to **g.** out,.... 3318
2Ch 34:21 **G.**, enquire of the Lord for me,.... 3212
2Ch 36:23 be with him, and let him **g.** up.... 5927
Ezr 1:3 be with him, and let him **g.** up to.... 5927
Ezr 1:5 to **g.** up to build the house of the.... 5927
Ezr 5:15 **g.**, carry them into the temple.... 236
Ezr 7:9 the first month began he to **g.** up.... 4609
Ezr 7:13 to **g.** to Jerusalem, **g.** with thee.... 1946
Ezr 7:28 chief men to **g.** up with me.... 5927
Ezr 8:31 to **g.** unto Jerusalem: and the.... 3212
Ezr 9:11 unto which ye **g.** to possess it,.... 935
Ne 3:15 stairs that **g.** down from the city.... 3381
Ne 4:3 if a fox **g.** up, he shall even break.... 5927
Ne 6:11 **g.** into the temple to save his life?.... 935
Ne 6:11 to save his life? I will not **g.** in.... 935
Ne 8:10 **G.** your way, eat the fat, and drink.... 3212
Ne 8:15 **G.** forth unto the mount, and.... 3318
Ne 9:12 the way wherein they should **g.**.... 3212
Ne 9:15 they should **g.** in to possess the land.... 935
Ne 9:19 the way wherein they should **g.**.... 3212
Ne 9:23 that they should **g.** in to possess it.... 935
Es 1:19 let there **g.** a royal commandment.... 3318
Es 2:12 maid's turn was come to **g.** into.... 935
Es 2:13 was given her to **g.** with her out.... 935
Es 2:15 was come to **g.** in unto the king.... 935
Es 4:8 that she should **g.** in unto the king,.... 935
Es 4:16 **G.**, gather together all the Jews.... 3212
Es 4:16 and so will I **g.** in unto the king,.... 935
Es 5:14 **g.** thou in merrily with the king.... 935
Job 4:21 which is in them **g.** away? they.... 5265
Job 6:18 they **g.** to nothing, and perish.... 5927
Job 10:21 I **g.** whence I shall not return,.... 3212
Job 15:13 such words **g.** out of thy mouth?.... 3318
Job 15:30 of his mouth shall he **g.** away.... 5493
Job 16:22 then I shall **g.** the way whence.... 1980
Job 17:16 They shall **g.** down to the bars of.... 3381
Job 20:26 it shall **g.** ill with him that is left.... 3381
Job 21:13 in a moment **g.** down to the grave.... 5181
Job 21:29 asked them that **g.** by the way?.... 5674
Job 23:8 Behold, I **g.** forward, but he is.... 1980
Job 24:5 asses in the desert, **g.** they forth.... 3318
Job 24:10 They cause him to **g.** naked.... 1980
Job 27:6 hold fast, and will not let it **g.**.... 7503
Job 31:37 prince would I **g.** near unto him.... 7126
Job 37:8 Then the beasts **g.** into dens, and.... 935
Job 38:35 send lightnings, that they may **g.**,.... 3212
Job 39:4 they **g.** forth, and return not.... 3318
Job 41:19 of his mouth **g.** burning lamps,.... 1980
Job 42:8 and **g.** to my servant Job, and.... 3212
Ps 22:29 all they that **g.** down to the dust.... 3381
Ps 26:4 will I **g.** in with dissemblers.... 935
Ps 28:1 them that **g.** down into the pit.... 3381
Ps 30:3 that I should not **g.** down to the pit.... 3381
Ps 30:9 when I **g.** down to the pit? shall.... 3381
Ps 32:8 the way which thou shalt **g.**?.... 3212
Ps 38:6 I **g.** mourning all the day long.... 1980
Ps 39:13 before I **g.** hence, and be no more.... 3212
Ps 42:9 why **g.** I mourning because of the.... 3212
Ps 43:2 why **g.** I mourning because of the.... 1980
Ps 43:4 will I **g.** unto the altar of God,.... 935
Ps 48:12 Zion, and **g.** round about her:.... 5362
Ps 49:19 He shall **g.** to the generation of.... 935
Ps 55:10 Day and night they **g.** about it.... 5437
Ps 55:15 let them **g.** down quick into hell:.... 3381
Ps 58:3 they **g.** astray as soon as they be.... 8582
Ps 59:6, 14 and **g.** round about the city.... 5437
Ps 60:10 didst not **g.** out with our armies?.... 3318
Ps 63:9 shall **g.** into the lower parts of the.... 935
Ps 66:13 I will **g.** into thy house with.... 935
Ps 71:16 I will **g.** in the strength of the.... 935
Ps 73:27 that **g.** a whoring from thee.... 935
Ps 78:52 made his own people to **g.** forth.... 5265
Ps 80:18 So will not we **g.** back from thee:.... 5472
Ps 84:7 They **g.** from strength to strength,.... 3212
Ps 85:13 Righteousness shall **g.** before him;.... 1980
Ps 88:4 them that **g.** down into the pit:.... 3381
Ps 89:14 and truth shall **g.** before thy face,.... 6923
Ps 104:8 They **g.** up by the mountains;.... 5927
Ps 104:8 they **g.** down by the valleys.... 3381
Ps 104:26 There **g.** the ships: there is that.... 1980
Ps 105:20 of the people, and let him **g.** free....
Ps 107:7 that they might **g.** to a city of.... 3212
Ps 107:23 They that **g.** down to the sea in.... 3381
Ps 107:26 they **g.** down again to the depths:.... 3381
Ps 108:11 wilt not thou, O God, **g.** forth with.... 3318
Ps 115:17 any that **g.** down into silence.... 3381
Ps 118:19 I will **g.** into them, and I will.... 935
Ps 119:35 Make me to **g.** in the path of thy.... 1869
Ps 122:1 Let us **g.** into the house of the.... 3212
Ps 122:4 Whither the tribes **g.** up, the.... 5927
Ps 129:8 Neither do they which **g.** by say,.... 5674
Ps 132:3 my house, nor **g.** up into my bed;.... 5927
Ps 132:7 We will **g.** into his tabernacles:.... 935
Ps 139:7 Whither shall I **g.** from thy spirit?.... 3212
Ps 143:7 them that **g.** down into the pit.... 3381
Pr 1:12 as those that **g.** down into the pit:.... 3381
Pr 2:19 None that **g.** unto her return again,.... 935
Pr 3:28 Say not unto thy neighbour, **G.**,.... 3212
Pr 4:13 hold of instruction; let her not **g.**?.... 7503
Pr 4:14 **g.** not in the way of evil men.... 833
Pr 5:5 Her feet **g.** down to death; her.... 3381
Pr 5:23 of his folly he shall **g.** astray.... 7686
Pr 6:3 **g.**, humble thyself, and make sure.... 3212
Pr 6:6 **G.** to the ant, thou sluggard;.... 3212
Pr 6:28 Can one **g.** upon hot coals, and.... 1980
Pr 7:25 **g.** not astray in her paths.... 8582
Pr 9:6 **g.** in the way of understanding.... 833
Pr 9:15 To call passengers who **g.** right on....
Pr 14:7 **G.** from the presence of a foolish.... 3212
Pr 15:12 neither will he **g.** unto the wise.... 3212
Pr 18:8 they **g.** down into the innermost.... 3381
Pr 19:7 do his friends **g.** far from him?.... 7368
Pr 22:6 a child in the way he should **g.**:.... 6310
Pr 22:10 and contention shall **g.** out; yea,.... 3318
Pr 22:24 a furious man thou shalt not **g.**:.... 935
Pr 23:30 they that **g.** to seek mixed wine.... 935
Pr 25:8 **G.** not forth hastily to strive,.... 3318
Pr 26:22 they **g.** down into the innermost.... 3381
Pr 27:10 neither **g.** into thy brother's house.... 935
Pr 28:10 causeth the righteous to **g.** astray.... 7686
Pr 30:27 yet **g.** they forth all of them by.... 3318
Pr 30:29 three things which **g.** well, yea,.... 6806
Ec 2:1 I said in mine heart, **G.** to now,.... 3212
Ec 3:20 All **g.** unto one place; all are of.... 1980
Ec 5:15 shall he return to **g.** as he came,.... 3212
Ec 5:16 so shall he **g.**: and what profit hath.... 3212
Ec 6:6 do not all **g.** to one place?.... 1980
Ec 7:2 to **g.** to the house of mourning,.... 3212
Ec 7:2 than to **g.** to the house of feasting:.... 3212
Ec 8:3 Be not hasty to **g.** out of his sight:.... 3212
Ec 9:3 and after that they **g.** to the dead....
Ec 9:7 **G.** thy way, eat thy bread with.... 3212
Ec 10:15 knoweth not how to **g.** to the city.... 3212
Ec 12:5 the mourners **g.** about the streets:.... 5437
Ca 1:8 **g.** thy way forth by the footsteps.... 3318
Ca 3:2 I will rise now, and **g.** about the.... 5437
Ca 3:3 watchmen that **g.** about the city.... 5437
Ca 3:4 him, and would not let him **g.**,.... 7503
Ca 3:11 **G.** forth, O ye daughters of Zion,.... 3318
Ca 6:6 as a flock of sheep which **g.** up.... 5927
Ca 7:8 said, I will **g.** up to the palm tree,.... 5927
Ca 7:11 let us **g.** forth into the field; let.... 3318
Isa 2:3 And many people shall **g.** and say,.... 1980
Isa 2:3 and let us **g.** up to the mountain.... 5927
Isa 2:3 out of Zion shall **g.** forth the law,.... 3318
Isa 2:19 And they shall **g.** into the holes.... 935
Isa 2:21 To **g.** into the clefts of he rocks,.... 935
Isa 3:16 walking and mincing as they **g.**,.... 3212
Isa 5:5 And now **g.** to; I will tell you what....
Isa 5:24 their blossom shall **g.** up as dust:.... 5927
Isa 6:8 who will **g.** for us? Then said I,.... 3212
Isa 6:9 he said, **G.**, and tell this people,.... 3212
Isa 7:3 **G.** forth now to meet Ahaz, thou,.... 3318
Isa 7:6 Let us **g.** up against Judah, and.... 5927
Isa 8:6 waters of Shiloah that **g.** softly.... 1980
Isa 8:7 channels, and **g.** over all his banks:.... 1980
Isa 8:8 he shall overflow and **g.** over,.... 5674
Isa 11:15 and make men **g.** over dryshod.... 1869
Isa 13:2 that they may **g.** into the gates.... 935
Isa 14:19 **g.** down to the stones of the pit;.... 3381
Isa 15:5 with weeping shall they **g.** it up;.... 5927
Isa 18:2 **G.**, ye swift messengers, to a.... 3212
Isa 20:2 **G.** and loose the sackcloth from off.... 3212
Isa 21:2 **G.** up, O Elam: besiege, O Media;.... 5927
Isa 21:6 **G.**, set a watchman, let him.... 3212
Isa 22:15 **G.**, get thee unto this treasurer,.... 3212
Isa 23:16 Take an harp, **g.** about the city,.... 5437
Isa 27:4 I would **g.** through them, I would.... 6585
Isa 28:13 they might **g.**, and fall backward,.... 3212
Isa 30:2 That walk to **g.** down into Egypt,.... 3381
Isa 30:8 **g.**, write it before them in a table,.... 935
Isa 31:1 to them that **g.** down to Egypt.... 3381
Isa 33:21 shall **g.** no galley with oars,.... 3212
Isa 34:10 smoke thereof shall **g.** up for ever:.... 5927
Isa 35:9 ravenous beast shall **g.** up thereon,.... 5927
Isa 36:6 man lean, it will **g.** into his hand,.... 935
Isa 36:10 **G.** up against this land, and.... 5927
Isa 37:32 out of Jerusalem shall **g.** forth a.... 3318
Isa 38:5 **G.**, and say to Hezekiah, Thus.... 1980
Isa 38:10 shall **g.** to the gates of the grave:.... 3212
Isa 38:15 I shall **g.** softly all my years in.... 1718
Isa 38:18 they that **g.** down into the pit.... 3381
Isa 38:22 What is the sign that I shall **g.** up.... 5927
Isa 42:10 ye that **g.** down to the sea, and all.... 3381
Isa 42:13 Lord shall **g.** forth as a mighty.... 3318
Isa 45:2 I will **g.** before thee, and make.... 3212
Isa 45:13 he shall let **g.** my captives, not.... 7971
Isa 45:16 shall **g.** to confusion together.... 1980
Isa 48:17 by the way that thou shouldest **g.**.... 3212
Isa 48:20 **G.** ye forth of Babylon, flee ye.... 3318
Isa 49:9 say to the prisoners, **G.** forth;.... 3318
Isa 49:17 that made thee waste shall **g.** forth.... 3318
Isa 51:23 Bow down, that we may **g.** over:.... 5674
Isa 52:11 **g.** ye out from thence, touch no.... 3318
Isa 52:11 **g.** ye out of the midst of her;.... 3318
Isa 52:12 ye shall not **g.** out with haste.... 3318
Isa 52:12 with haste, not **g.** by flight:.... 3212
Isa 52:12 for the Lord will **g.** before you:.... 1980
Isa 54:9 should no more **g.** over the earth;.... 5674
Isa 55:12 For ye shall **g.** out with joy, and.... 3318
Isa 58:6 and to let the oppressed **g.** free,.... 7971
Isa 58:8 righteousness shall **g.** before thee;.... 1980
Isa 60:20 Thy sun shall no more **g.** down;.... 935
Isa 62:1 thereof **g.** forth as brightness,.... 3318
Isa 62:10 **G.** through, **g.** through the gates;.... 5674
Isa 66:24 And they shall **g.** forth, and look.... 3318
Jer 1:7 shalt **g.** to all that I shall send.... 3212
Jer 2:2 **G.** and cry in the ears of.... 1980
Jer 2:25 strangers, and after them will I **g.**.... 3212
Jer 2:37 Yea, thou shalt **g.** forth from him.... 3318
Jer 3:1 and she **g.** from him, and become.... 1980
Jer 3:12 **G.** and proclaim these words.... 1980
Jer 4:5 let us **g.** into the defenced cities.... 935
Jer 4:29 shall **g.** into thickets, and climb up.... 935
Jer 5:10 **G.** ye up upon her walls, and.... 5927
Jer 6:4 arise, and let us **g.** up at noon.... 5927
Jer 6:5 Arise, and let us **g.** by night,.... 5927
Jer 6:25 **G.** not forth into the field, nor.... 3318
Jer 7:12 **g.** ye now unto my place which.... 3212
Jer 9:2 and **g.** from them! for they be all.... 3212
Jer 10:5 be borne, because they cannot **g.**.... 6805
Jer 11:12 and inhabitants of Jerusalem **g.**,.... 1980
Jer 13:1 **G.** and get thee a linen girdle,.... 1980
Jer 13:4 and arise, **g.** to Euphrates, and.... 3212
Jer 13:6 Arise, **g.** to Euphrates, and take.... 3212
Jer 14:18 If I **g.** forth into the field, then.... 3318
Jer 14:18 the prophet and the priest **g.** about.... 5503
Jer 15:1 my sight, and let them **g.** forth.... 3318
Jer 15:2 Whither shall we **g.** forth? then.... 3318
Jer 15:5 **g.** aside to ask how thou doest?.... 5493
Jer 16:5 **g.** to lament nor bemoan them:.... 3212
Jer 16:8 also **g.** into the house of feasting,.... 935
Jer 17:19 **G.** and stand in the gate of the.... 1980
Jer 17:19 by the which they **g.** out, and in.... 3318
Jer 18:2 Arise, and **g.** down to the potter's.... 3381
Jer 18:11 **g.** to, speak to the men of Judah,.... 4994
Jer 19:1 **G.** and get a potter's earthen.... 1980
Jer 19:2 **g.** forth unto the valley of the son.... 3318
Jer 19:10 sight of the men that **g.** with thee,.... 1980
Jer 20:6 that dwell in thine house shall **g.**.... 3212
Jer 21:2 that he may **g.** up from us.... 5927
Jer 21:12 lest my fury **g.** out like fire, and.... 3318
Jer 22:1 **G.** down to the house of the king.... 3381
Jer 22:20 **G.** up to Lebanon, and cry; and.... 5927
Jer 22:22 thy lovers shall **g.** into captivity:.... 3212
Jer 25:6 **g.** not after other gods to serve.... 3212

Book	Ref	Context	No.
Jer	25:32	evil shall **g.** forth from nation to	3318
Jer	27:18	at Jerusalem, **g.** not to Babylon.	935
Jer	28:13	**G.** and tell Hananiah, saying,	1980
Jer	29:12	and ye shall **g.** and pray unto me,	1980
Jer	30:16	of them, shall **g.** into captivity;	3212
Jer	31:4	and shalt **g.** forth in the dances of	3318
Jer	31:6	Arise ye, and let us **g.** up to Zion	5927
Jer	31:22	How long wilt thou **g.** about, O	2559
Jer	31:24	and they that **g.** forth with flocks.	5265
Jer	31:39	measuring line shall yet **g.** forth	3318
Jer	34:2	**G.** and speak to Zedekiah king of	1980
Jer	34:3	thou shalt **g.** to Babylon.	935
Jer	34:9	an Hebrewess, **g.** free; that none	7971
Jer	34:10	every one his maidservant, **g.** free;	7971
Jer	34:10	then they obeyed, and let them **g.**	7971
Jer	34:11	whom they had let **g.** free, to return,	7971
Jer	34:14	let ye **g.** every man his brother an	7971
Jer	34:14	thou shalt let him **g.** free from	7971
Jer	35:2	**G.** unto the house of the	1980
Jer	35:11	and let us **g.** to Jerusalem for fear	935
Jer	35:13	**G.** and tell the men of Judah and	1980
Jer	35:15	**g.** not after other gods to serve	3212
Jer	36:5	I cannot **g.** into the house of the	935
Jer	36:6	Therefore **g.** thou, and read in the	935
Jer	36:19	**G.**, hide thee, thou and Jeremiah;	3212
Jer	37:12	to **g.** into the land of Benjamin,	3212
Jer	38:17	thou wilt assuredly **g.** forth unto	3318
Jer	38:18	if thou wilt not **g.** forth to the king	3318
Jer	38:21	if thou refuse to **g.** forth, this is the	3318
Jer	39:16	**G.** and speak to Ebed-melech the	1980
Jer	40:1	guard had let him **g.** from Ramah,	7971
Jer	40:4	convenient for thee to **g.**, thither **g.**	3212
Jer	40:5	**G.** back also to Gedaliah the son	7725
Jer	40:5	or **g.** wheresoever it seemeth	3212
Jer	40:5	convenient unto thee to **g.**	3212
Jer	40:5	and a reward, and let him **g.**	7971
Jer	40:15	Let me **g.**, I pray thee, and I will	3212
Jer	41:10	and departed to **g.** over to the	5674
Jer	41:17	to **g.** to enter into Egypt,	3212
Jer	42:14	we will **g.** into the land of Egypt,	935
Jer	42:15	into Egypt, and **g.** to sojourn there;	935
Jer	42:17	that set their faces to **g.** into Egypt	935
Jer	42:19	**G.** ye not into Egypt: know	935
Jer	42:22	the place whither ye desire to **g.**	935
Jer	43:2	**G.** not into Egypt to sojourn there:	935
Jer	43:12	and he shall **g.** forth from thence	3318
Jer	44:12	have set their faces to **g.** into the	935
Jer	46:8	and he saith, I will **g.** up, and	5927
Jer	46:11	**G.** up into Gilead, and take balm,	5927
Jer	46:16	let us **g.** again to our own people,	7725
Jer	46:19	furnish thyself to **g.** into captivity:	
Jer	46:22	The voice thereof shall **g.** like a	3212
Jer	48:5	continual weeping shall **g.** up;	5927
Jer	48:7	and Chemosh shall **g.** forth into	3318
Jer	49:3	their king shall **g.** into captivity,	3212
Jer	49:12	that shall altogether **g.** unpunished?	
Jer	49:28	**g.** up to Kedar, and spoil the men	5927
Jer	50:4	they shall **g.**, and seek the Lord	3212
Jer	50:6	have caused them to **g.** astray,	8582
Jer	50:8	**g.** forth out of the land of the	3318
Jer	50:21	**G.** up against the land of	5927
Jer	50:27	them **g.** down to the slaughter:	3381
Jer	50:33	fast; they refused to let them **g.**	7971
Jer	51:9	and let us **g.** every one into his	3212
Jer	51:45	people, **g.** ye out of the midst of	3318
Jer	51:50	have escaped the sword, **g.** away,	1980
La	4:18	that we cannot **g.** in our streets:	3212
Eze	1:12	whither the spirit was to **g.**, they	3212
Eze	1:20	Whithersoever the spirit was to **g.**,	3212
Eze	1:20	thither was their spirit to **g.**;	3212
Eze	3:1	**g.** speak unto the house of Israel.	3212
Eze	3:4	of man, **g.**, get thee unto the house	3212
Eze	3:11	And **g.**, get thee to them of the	3212
Eze	3:22	Arise, **g.** forth into the plain,	3318
Eze	3:24	**G.**, shut thyself within thine house.	935
Eze	3:25	and thou shalt not **g.** out among	3318
Eze	6:9	**g.** a whoring after their idols:	3318
Eze	8:6	that I should **g.** far off from my	7368
Eze	8:9	**G.** in, and behold the wicked	935
Eze	9:4	**G.** through the midst of the city,	5674
Eze	9:5	**G.** ye after him through the city,	5674
Eze	9:7	**g.** ye forth, And they went forth,	3318
Eze	10:2	**G.** in between the wheels, even	935
Eze	12:4	thou shalt **g.** forth at even in their	3318
Eze	12:4	as they that **g.** forth into captivity.	4161
Eze	12:11	shall remove and **g.** into captivity.	3212
Eze	12:12	and shall **g.** forth: they shall dig	3318
Eze	13:20	and will let the souls **g.**, even the	7971
Eze	14:11	Israel may **g.** no more astray from	8582
Eze	14:17	Sword **g.** through the land; so	5674
Eze	15:7	they shall **g.** out from one fire,	3318
Eze	20:10	I caused them to **g.** forth out of the	3318
Eze	20:29	is the high place whereunto ye **g.**?	935
Eze	20:39	**G.** ye, serve ye every one his idols,	3212
Eze	21:4	therefore shall my sword **g.** forth	3318
Eze	21:16	**G.** thee one way or other, either on	258
Eze	23:44	as they **g.** in unto a woman that	935
Eze	24:14	I will not **g.** back, neither will I	6544
Eze	26:11	thy strong garrisons shall **g.** down	3381
Eze	26:20	with them that **g.** down to the pit,	3381
Eze	30:9	that day shall messengers **g.** forth	3318
Eze	30:17	these cities shall **g.** into captivity.	3212
Eze	30:18	daughters shall **g.** into captivity.	3212
Eze	31:14	with them that **g.** down to the pit.	3381
Eze	32:18	with them that **g.** down into the pit.	3381
Eze	32:19	**g.** down, and be thou laid with the	3381
Eze	32:24	with them that **g.** down to the pit.	3381
Eze	32:25	with them that **g.** down to the pit:	3381
Eze	32:29,	30 them that **g.** down to the pit.	3381
Eze	38:11	I will **g.** up to the land of unwalled	5927
Eze	38:11	I will **g.** to them that are at rest,	935
Eze	39:9	the cities of Israel shall **g.** forth,	3318
Eze	40:26	there were seven steps to **g.** up to	5930
Eze	42:14	shall they not **g.** out of the holy	3318
Eze	44:3	shall **g.** out by the way of the same.	3318
Eze	44:19	And when they **g.** forth into the	3318
Eze	46:2	then he shall **g.** forth; but the gate	3318
Eze	46:8	shall **g.** in by the way of the porch	935
Eze	46:8	shall **g.** forth by the way thereof.	3318
Eze	46:9	**g.** out by the way of the south gate;	3318
Eze	46:9	shall **g.** forth by the way of the	3318
Eze	46:9	but he shall **g.** forth over against it.	3318
Eze	46:10	when they **g.** in, shall **g.** in;	935
Eze	46:10	when they **g.** forth, shall **g.** forth.	3318
Eze	46:12	then he shall **g.** forth; and after	3318
Eze	47:8	and **g.** down into the desert,	3381
Eze	47:8	and **g.** into the sea: which being	935
Eze	47:15	of Hethlon, as men **g.** to Zedad;	935
Da	11:44	therefore he shall **g.** forth with	3318
Da	12:9	he said, **G.** thy way, Daniel: for	3212
Da	12:13	**g.** thou thy way till the end be:	3212
Ho	1:2	**G.** take unto thee a wife of	3212
Ho	2:5	I will **g.** after my lovers, that give	3212
Ho	2:7	**g.** and return to my first husband;	3212
Ho	3:1	**G.** yet, love a woman beloved of	3212
Ho	4:15	neither **g.** ye up to Beth-aven, nor	5927
Ho	5:6	They shall **g.** with their flocks	3212
Ho	5:14	I, even I, will tear and **g.** away;	3212
Ho	5:15	I will **g.** and return to my place,	3212
Ho	7:11	call to Egypt, they **g.** to Assyria.	1980
Ho	7:12	When they shall **g.**, I will spread	3212
Ho	11:3	taught Ephraim also to **g.**, taking	8637
Joe	2:16	let the bridegroom **g.** forth of his	3318
Am	1:5	people of Syria shall **g.** into captivity	
Am	1:15	their king shall **g.** into captivity,	1980
Am	2:7	his father will **g.** in unto the same	3212
Am	4:3	ye shall **g.** out at the breaches,	3318
Am	5:5	Gilgal shall surely **g.** into captivity,	
Am	5:27	will I cause you to **g.** into captivity	
Am	6:2	and from thence **g.** ye to Hamath	3212
Am	6:2	then **g.** down to Gath of the	3381
Am	6:7	Therefore now shall they **g.** captive	
Am	6:7	with the first that **g.** captive, and the	
Am	7:12	**g.**, flee thee away into the land of	3212
Am	7:15	**G.**, prophesy unto my people Israel.	3212
Am	7:17	Israel shall surely **g.** into captivity	3212
Am	8:9	cause the sun to **g.** down at noon	935
Am	9:4	though they **g.** into captivity	3212
Jon	1:2	Arise, **g.** to Nineveh, that great city,	3212
Jon	1:3	to **g.** with them unto Tarshish	935
Jon	3:2	Arise, **g.** unto Nineveh, that great	3312
Mic	1:8	I will **g.** stripped and naked: I will	3312
Mic	2:3	neither shall ye **g.** haughtily: for	3312
Mic	3:6	and the sun shall **g.** down over the	935
Mic	4:2	and let us **g.** up to the mountain	5927
Mic	4:2	the law shall **g.** forth of Zion,	3318
Mic	4:10	now shalt thou **g.** forth out of the	3318
Mic	4:10	and thou shalt **g.** even to Babylon;	935
Mic	5:8	if he **g.** through, both treadeth	5674
Na	3:14	**g.** into clay, and tread the morter,	935
Hab	1:4	judgment doth never **g.** forth: for	3318
Hag	1:8	**G.** up to the mountain, and bring	5927
Zec	6:5	which **g.** forth from standing	3318
Zec	6:6	**g.** forth into the north country;	3318
Zec	6:6	white **g.** forth after them; and	3318
Zec	6:6	grisled **g.** forth toward the south	3318
Zec	6:7	bay went forth, and sought to **g.**	3212
Zec	6:8	that **g.** toward the north country	3318
Zec	6:10	thou the same day, and **g.** into the	935
Zec	8:21	inhabitants of one city shall **g.**	1980
Zec	8:21	Let us **g.** speedily to pray before	3212
Zec	8:21	the Lord of hosts: I will **g.** also.	3212
Zec	8:23	We will **g.** with you: for we have	3212
Zec	9:14	and his arrow shall **g.** forth as the	3318
Zec	9:14	and shall **g.** with whirlwinds of	1980
Zec	14:2	and half of the city shall **g.** forth	3318
Zec	14:3	Then shall the Lord **g.** forth, and	3318
Zec	14:8	that living waters shall **g.** out from	3318
Zec	14:16	shall even **g.** up from year to year	5927
Zec	14:18	if the family of Egypt **g.** not up,	5927
Mal	4:2	and ye shall **g.** forth, and grow up	3318
Mt	2:8	**G.** and search diligently for the	*4198*
Mt	2:20	and **g.** into the land of Israel: for	*4198*
Mt	2:22	he was afraid to **g.** thither;	*565*
Mt	5:24	before the altar, and **g.** thy way;	*5217*
Mt	5:41	shall compel thee to **g.** a mile.	
Mt	5:41	a mile, **g.** with him twain.	*5217*
Mt	7:13	there be which **g.** in thereat:	*1525*
Mt	8:4	but **g.** thy way, shew thyself to	*5217*
Mt	8:9	I say to this man, **G.** and he goeth;	*4198*
Mt	8:13	**G.** thy way; and as thou hast	*5217*
Mt	8:21	suffer me first to **g.** and bury my	*565*
Mt	8:31	suffer us to **g.** away into the herd	*565*
Mt	8:32	And he said unto them, **G.**. And	*5217*
Mt	9:6	thy bed, and **g.** unto thine house.	*5217*
Mt	9:13	But **g.** ye and learn what that	*4198*
Mt	10:5	**G.** not into the way of the Gentiles,	*565*
Mt	10:6	But **g.** rather to the lost sheep	*4198*
Mt	10:7	And as ye **g.**, preach, saying,	*4198*
Mt	10:11	and there abide till ye **g.** thence.	*1831*
Mt	11:4	**G.** and shew John again those	*4198*
Mt	13:28	that we **g.** and gather them up?	*565*
Mt	14:15	that they may **g.** into the villages,	*565*
Mt	14:22	**g.** before him unto the other side,	*4254*
Mt	14:29	on the water, to **g.** to Jesus.	*2064*
Mt	16:21	that he must **g.** unto Jerusalem,	*565*
Mt	17:27	**g.** thou to the sea, and cast an	*4198*
Mt	18:15	**g.** and tell him his fault between	*5217*
Mt	19:21	**g.** and sell that thou hast, and give	*5217*
Mt	19:24	for a camel to **g.** through the eye	*1330*
Mt	20:4	**G.** ye also into the vineyard, and	*5217*
Mt	20:7	**G.** ye also into the vineyard; and	*5217*
Mt	20:14	Take that thine is, and **g.** thy way:	*5217*
Mt	20:18	Behold, we **g.** up to Jerusalem;	*305*
Mt	21:2	**G.** into the village over against	*4198*
Mt	21:28	**g.** work to day in my vineyard.	*5217*
Mt	21:30	And he answered and said I **g.**, sir:	*565*
Mt	21:31	**g.** into the kingdom of God before.	*4254*
Mt	22:9	**G.** ye therefore into the highways.	*4198*
Mt	23:13	ye neither **g.** in yourselves,	*1525*
Mt	23:13	ye them that are entering to **g.** in.	*1525*
Mt	24:26	he is in the desert; **g.** not forth:	*1831*
Mt	25:6	cometh; **g.** ye out to meet him.	*1831*
Mt	25:9	but **g.** ye rather to them that sell,	*4198*
Mt	25:46	these shall **g.** away into everlasting	*565*
Mt	26:18	**G.** into the city to such a man,	*5217*
Mt	26:32	I will **g.** before you into Galilee.	*4254*
Mt	26:36	here, while I **g.** and pray yonder.	*565*
Mt	27:65	**g.** your way, make it as sure as ye	*5217*
Mt	28:7	**g.** quickly, and tell his disciples	*4198*
Mt	28:10	Be not afraid: **g.** tell my brethren	*565*
Mt	28:10	brethren that they **g.** into Galilee,	*5217*
Mt	28:19	**G.** ye therefore, and teach all	*4198*
Mk	1:38	Let us **g.** into the next towns,	*71*
Mk	1:44	but **g.** thy way, shew thyself to	*5217*
Mk	2:11	and **g.** thy way into thine house.	*5217*
Mk	5:19	**G.** home to thy friends, and tell	*5217*
Mk	5:34	**g.** in peace, and be whole of thy	*5217*
Mk	6:36	that they may **g.** into the country	*565*
Mk	6:37	Shall we **g.** and buy two hundred	*565*
Mk	6:38	many loaves have ye? **g.** and see	*5217*
Mk	6:45	to **g.** to the other side before unto	*4254*
Mk	7:29	For this saying **g.** thy way; the	*5217*
Mk	8:26	Neither **g.** into the town, nor	*1525*
Mk	9:43	having two hands to **g.** into hell,	*565*
Mk	10:21	**g.** thy way, sell whatsoever thou	*5217*
Mk	10:25	to **g.** through the eye of a needle,	*1525*
Mk	10:33	Behold, we **g.** up to Jerusalem;	*305*
Mk	10:52	**G.** thy way; thy faith hath made	*5217*
Mk	11:2	**G.** your way into the village over	*5217*
Mk	11:6	commanded: and they let them **g.**	*863*

Mk 12:38 **which love to g. in long clothing,** 4043
Mk 13:15 **not g. down into the house,** 2597
Mk 14:12 wilt thou that we **g.** and prepare 565
Mk 14:13 **G. ye into the city, and there** 5217
Mk 14:14 **wheresoever he shall . in, say** 1525
Mk 14:28 **I will g. before you into Galilee** 4254
Mk 14:42 **Rise up, let us g.: lo, he that** 71
Mk 16:7 But **g.** your way, tell his disciples 5217
Mk 16:15 he said unto them, **G. ye into all** 4198
Lu 1:17 shall **g.** before him in the spirit 4281
Lu 1:76 **g.** before the face of the Lord 4313
Lu 2:15 us now **g.** even unto Bethlehem, 1330
Lu 5:14 **g., and shew thyself to the priest,** 565
Lu 5:24 **couch, and g. unto thine house** 4198
Lu 7:8 I say unto one, **G.**, and he goeth; 4198
Lu 7:22 **G. your way, and tell John what** 4198
Lu 7:50 **faith hath saved thee; g. in peace** 4198
Lu 8:14 **g. forth, and are choked with** 4198
Lu 8:22 **Let us g. over unto the other side** 1330
Lu 8:31 them to **g.** out into the deep 565
Lu 8:48 **made thee whole; g. in peace** 4198
Lu 8:51 he suffered no man to **g.** in, save 1525
Lu 9:5 **when ye g. out of that city,** 1831
Lu 9:12 that they may **g.** into the towns 565
Lu 9:13 except we should **g.** and buy meat 4198
Lu 9:51 set his face to **g.** to Jerusalem, 4198
Lu 9:53 though he would **g.** to Jerusalem. 4198
Lu 9:59 me first to **g.** and bury my father. 565
Lu 9:60 **g. thou and preach the kingdom** 565
Lu 9:61 let me first **g.** bid them farewell,
Lu 10:3 **G. your ways; Behold, I send you** 4198
Lu 10:7 **G. not from house to house.** 3327
Lu 10:10 **g. your ways out into the streets** 1831
Lu 10:37 unto him, **G.**, and do thou likewise 4198
Lu 11:5 **and shall g. unto him at midnight,** 4198
Lu 13:32 **G. ye, and tell that fox, Behold, I** 4198
Lu 14:4 and healed him, and let him **g.**; 630
Lu 14:10 **g. and sit down in the lowest** 4198
Lu 14:10 **Friend, g. up higher: then shalt** 4320
Lu 14:18 **and I must needs g. and see it:** 1831
Lu 14:19 **I g. to prove them: I pray thee** 4198
Lu 14:21 **G. out quickly into the streets** 1831
Lu 14:23 **G. out into the highways and** 1831
Lu 15:4 **and g. after that which is lost,** 4198
Lu 15:18 **I will arise and g. to my father,** 4198
Lu 15:28 **was angry, and would not g. in:** 1525
Lu 17:7 **G. and sit down to meat?** 3928
Lu 17:14 **G. shew yourselves unto the** 4198
Lu 17:19 **Arise, g. thy way: thy faith hath** 4198
Lu 17:23 **g. not after them, nor follow them** 565
Lu 18:25 **camel to g. through a needle's eye,** 1525
Lu 18:31 **we g. up to Jerusalem, and all** 305
Lu 19:30 **G. ye into the village over against** 5217
Lu 21:8 **g. ye not therefore after them** 4198
Lu 22:8 **G. and prepare us the passover,** 4198
Lu 22:33 am ready to **g.** with thee, both 4198
Lu 22:68 **not answer me, nor let me g.** 630
Lu 23:22 chastise him, and let him **g.** 630
Joh 1:43 Jesus would **g.** forth into Galilee, 1831
Joh 4:4 must needs **g.** through Samaria 1330
Joh 4:16 **G., call thy husband, and come** 5217
Joh 4:50 **G. thy way; thy son liveth. And** 4198
Joh 6:67 **Will ye also g. away?** 5217
Joh 6:68 Lord, to whom shall we **g.**? thou 565
Joh 7:3 Depart hence, and **g.** into Judaea, 5217
Joh 7:8 **G. ye up unto this feast: I g. not** 305
Joh 7:19 **Why g. ye about to kill me?** 2212
Joh 7:33 **then I g. unto him that sent me** 5217
Joh 7:35 Whither will he **g.**, that we shall 4198
Joh 7:35 will he **g.** unto the dispersed 4198
Joh 8:11 **do I condemn thee: g., and sin no** 4198
Joh 8:14 **whence I came, and whither I g.;** 5217
Joh 8:14 **whence I come, and whither I g** 5217
Joh 8:21 **I g. my way, and ye shall seek me,** 5217
Joh 8:21 **whither I g., ye cannot come** 5217
Joh 8:22 Whither I **g.**, ye cannot come 5217
Joh 9:7 **G., wash in the pool of Siloam,** 5217
Joh 9:11 **G.** to the pool of Siloam, and wash: 5217
Joh 10:9 **be saved, and shall g. in and** 1525
Joh 11:7 **Let us g. into Judaea again** 71
Joh 11:11 **but I g., that I may awake him** 4198
Joh 11:15 **nevertheless let us g. unto him** 71
Joh 11:16 Let us also **g.**, that we may die with 71
Joh 11:44 them, **Loose him, and let him g.** 5217
Joh 13:33 **Whither I g., ye cannot come; so** 5217
Joh 13:36 **Whither I g., thou canst not follow** 5217
Joh 14:2 **I g. to prepare a place for you** 4198
Joh 14:3 **if I g. and prepare a place for you,** 4198
Joh 14:4 **whither I g. ye know, and the way** 5217
Joh 14:12 **do; because I g. unto my Father** 4198
Joh 14:28 **I g. away, and come again unto** 5217
Joh 14:28 **I said, I g. unto the Father:** 4198
Joh 14:31 **even so I do. Arise, let us g. hence** 71
Joh 15:16 **ye should g. and bring forth fruit,** 5217
Joh 16:5 **I g. my way to him that sent me;** 5217
Joh 16:7 **expedient for you that I g. away:** 565
Joh 16:7 **for if I g. not away, the Comforter** 565
Joh 16:10 **because I g. to my Father, and ye** 5217
Joh 16:16 **see me, because I g. to my Father** 5217
Joh 16:17 and, Because I **g.** to the Father? 5217
Joh 16:28 **the world, and g. to the Father** 4198
Joh 18:8 **ye seek me, let these g. their way:** 5217
Joh 19:12 thou let this man **g.**, thou art not 630
Joh 20:17 **but g. to my brethren, and say** 4198
Joh 21:3 Peter saith unto them, I **g.** a fishing. 5217
Joh 21:3 unto him, We also **g.** with thee 2064
Ac 1:11 ye have seen him **g.** into heaven 4198
Ac 1:25 that he might **g.** to his own place. 4198
Ac 3:3 Peter and John about to **g.** into 1524
Ac 3:13 he was determined to let him **g.** 630
Ac 4:15 commanded them to **g.** aside out 565
Ac 4:21 they let them **g.**, finding nothing 630
Ac 4:23 And being let **g.**, they went to their 630
Ac 5:20 **G.**, stand and speak in the temple 4198
Ac 5:40 name of Jesus, and let them **g.** 630
Ac 7:40 Make us gods to **g.** before us: for 4313
Ac 8:26 Arise, and **g.** toward the south 4198
Ac 8:29 **G.** near, and join thyself to this 4334
Ac 9:6 **Arise, and g. into the city, and it** 1525
Ac 9:11 **Arise, and g. into the street which** 4198
Ac 9:15 **G. thy way: for he is a chosen** 4198
Ac 10:20 get thee down, and **g.** with them, 4198
Ac 11:12 the spirit bade me **g.** with them, 4905
Ac 11:22 he should **g.** as far as Antioch. 1330
Ac 12:17 he said, **G.** shew these things
Ac 15:2 should **g.** up to Jerusalem unto the 305
Ac 15:33 let **g.** in peace from the brethren 630
Ac 15:36 **g.** again and visit our brethren 1994
Ac 16:3 Paul have to **g.** forth with him; 1831
Ac 16:7 they assayed to **g.** into Bithynia: 4198
Ac 16:10 endeavoured to **g.** into Macedonia, 1831
Ac 16:35 serjeants, saying, Let those men **g.** 630
Ac 16:36 sent to let you **g.**: now therefore 630
Ac 16:36 therefore depart, and **g.** in peace. 4198
Ac 17:9 and of the other, they let them **g.** 630
Ac 17:14 Paul to **g.** as it were to the sea: 4198
Ac 18:6 I will **g.** unto the Gentiles 4198
Ac 19:21 to **g.** to Jerusalem, saying, After I 4198
Ac 20:1 departed for to **g.** into Macedonia 4198
Ac 20:13 appointed, minding himself to **g.** afoot
Ac 20:22 behold, I **g.** bound in the spirit 4198
Ac 21:4 he should not **g.** up to Jerusalem. 305
Ac 21:12 besought him not to **g.** up to 305
Ac 22:10 **Arise, and g. into Damascus; and** 4198
Ac 23:10 commanded the soldiers to **g.** 2597
Ac 23:23 hundred soldiers to **g.** to Caesarea, 4198
Ac 23:32 left the horsemen to **g.** with him, 4198
Ac 24:25 **G.** thy way for this time; when I 4198
Ac 25:5 **g.** down with me, and accuse this 4782
Ac 25:9 aid, Wilt thou **g.** up to Jerusalem, 305
Ac 25:12 Caesar? unto Caesar shalt thou **g.** 4198
Ac 25:20 whether he would **g.** to Jerusalem, 4198
Ac 27:3 him liberty to **g.** unto his friends 4198
Ac 28:18 would have let me **g.**, because 630
Ac 28:26 **G.** unto this people, and say, 4198
Ro 15:25 now I **g.** unto Jerusalem to minister 4198
1Co 5:10 must ye needs **g.** out of the world, 1831
1Co 6:1 another, **g.** to law before the unjust,
1Co 6:7 ye **g.** to law one with another
1Co 10:27 ye be disposed to **g.**; whatsoever 4198
1Co 16:4 it be meet that I **g.** also, they shall **g.** 4198
1Co 16:6 on my journey whithersoever I **g.** 4198
2Co 9:5 they would **g.** before unto you, 4281
Ga 2:9 that we should **g.** unto the heathen,
Eph 4:26 let not the sun **g.** down upon your 1931
Php 2:23 I shall see how it will **g.** with me.
1Th 4:6 no man **g.** beyond and defraud 5233
Heb 6:1 let us **g.** on unto perfection; not 5342
Heb 11:8 he was called to **g.** out into a place 1831
Heb 13:13 Let us **g.** forth therefore unto him 1831
Jas 4:13 **G.** to now, ye that say, To day or 33
Jas 4:13 we will **g.** into such a city, 4198
Jas 5:1 **G.** to now, ye rich men, weep and 33
Re 3:12 **and he shall g. no more out:** 1831
Re 10:8 **G.** and take the little book which 5217
Re 13:10 captivity shall **g.** into captivity: 5217
Re 16:1 **G.** your ways, and pour out the vials 5217
Re 16:14 **g.** forth unto the kings of the earth 1607
Re 17:8 pit, and **g.** into perdition: 5217
Re 20:8 shall **g.** out to deceive the nations 1831

GOAD See also GOADS.
Jg 3:31 six hundred men with an ox **g.** 4451

GOADS
1Sa 13:21 for the axes, and to sharpen the **g.**, 1861
Ec 12:11 The words of the wise are as **g.**, 1861

GOAT See also GOATS; GOATSKINS; SCAPEGOAT.
Ge 15:9 and a she **g.** of three years old, 5795
Le 3:12 if his offering be a **g.**, then he shall 5795
Le 4:24 his hand upon the head of the **g.**, 8163
Le 7:23 fat, of ox, or of sheep, or of **g.** 5795
Le 9:15 and took the **g.**, which was the sin 8163
Le 10:16 Moses diligently sought the **g.** of 8163
Le 16:9 Aaron shall bring the **g.** upon which 8163
Le 16:10 But the **g.**, on which the lot fell to be 8163
Le 16:15 Then shall he kill the **g.** of the sin 8163
Le 16:18 and of the blood of the **g.**, and put it 8163
Le 16:20 he shall bring the live **g.**: 8163
Le 16:21 hands upon the head of the live **g.** 8163
Le 16:21 putting them upon the head of the **g.** 8163
Le 16:22 the **g.** shall bear upon him all their 8163
Le 16:22 shall let go the **g.** in the wilderness. 8163
Le 16:26 that let go the **g.** for the scapegoat 8163
Le 16:27 and the **g.** for the sin offering 8163
Le 17:3 that killeth an ox, or lamb, or **g.** 5795
Le 22:27 When a bullock, or a sheep, or a **g.**, 5795
Nu 15:27 he shall bring a she **g.** of the first 5795
Nu 18:17 or the firstling of a **g.**, thou shalt 5795
Nu 28:22 And one **g.** for a sin offering, to 8163
Nu 29:22, 28,31,34,38 one **g.** for a sin 8163
De 14:4 eat: the ox, the sheep, and the **g.** 5795
De 14:5 and the wild **g.**, and the pygarg, 689
Pr 30:31 A greyhound; an he **g.** also; and 8495
Eze 43:25 every day a **g.** for a sin offering: 8163
Da 8:5 an he **g.** came from the west 5795
Da 8:5 and the **g.** had a notable horn 6842
Da 8:8 Therefore the he **g.** waxed very 6842
Da 8:21 the rough **g.** is the king of Grecia: 6842

GOATH (go'-ath)
Jer 31:39 and shall compass about to **G.** 1601

GOATS See also GOATS'.
Ge 27:9 thence two good kids of the **g.**; 5795
Ge 27:16 put the skins of the kids of the **g.** 5795
Ge 30:32 spotted and speckled among the **g.** 5795
Ge 30:33 speckled and spotted among the **g.**, 5795
Ge 30:35 he removed that day the he **g.** 8495
Ge 30:35 the she **g.** that were speckled and 5795
Ge 31:38 thy ewes and thy she **g.** have not 5795
Ge 32:14 Two hundred she **g.**, and twenty 5795
Ge 32:14 and twenty he **g.**, two hundred 8495
Ge 37:31 killed a kid of the **g.**, and dipped 5795
Ex 12:5 out from the sheep, or from the **g.** 5795
Le 1:10 of the sheep, or of the **g.** 5795
Le 4:23, 28 his offering, a kid of the **g.**, 5795
Le 5:6 a lamb or a kid of the **g.**, for a sin 5795
Le 9:3 Take ye a kid of the **g.** for a sin 5795
Le 16:5 two kids of the **g.** for a sin offering, 5795
Le 16:7 shall take the two **g.**, and present 8163
Le 16:8 shall cast lots upon the two **g.**; 8163
Le 22:19 beeves, of the sheep, or of the **g.** 5795
Le 23:19 kid of the **g.** for a sin offering, 5795
Nu 7:16 One kid of the **g.** for a sin offering: 5795
Nu 7:17 five rams, five he **g.**, five lambs of 6260
Nu 7:22 One kid of the **g.** for a sin offering: 5795
Nu 7:23 five he **g.**, five lambs of the first 6260
Nu 7:28 One kid of the **g.** for a sin offering: 5795
Nu 7:29 five he **g.**, five lambs of the first 6260
Nu 7:34 One kid of the **g.** for a sin offering: 5795
Nu 7:35 five he **g.**, five lambs of the first 6260
Nu 7:40 one kid of the **g.** for a sin offering: 5795
Nu 7:41 five he **g.**, five lambs of the first 6260
Nu 7:46 one kid of the **g.** for a sin offering. 5795
Nu 7:47 five he **g.**, five lambs of the first 6260
Nu 7:52 One kid of the **g.** for a sin offering: 5795
Nu 7:53 five he **g.**, five lambs of the first 6260
Nu 7:58 One kid of the **g.** for a sin offering: 5795
Nu 7:59 five he **g.**, five lambs of the first 6260
Nu 7:64 One kid of the **g.** for a sin offering: 5795
Nu 7:65 five he **g.**, five lambs of the first 6260

Nu 7:70 One kid of the **g.** for a sin offering: 5795
Nu 7:71 five he **g.**, five lambs of the first 6260
Nu 7:76 One kid of the **g.** for a sin offering: 5795
Nu 7:77 five he **g.**, five lambs of the first 6260
Nu 7:82 One kid of the **g.** for a sin offering: 5795
Nu 7:83 five he **g.**, five lambs of the first 6260
Nu 7:87 the kids of the **g.** for sin offering 5795
Nu 7:88 the rams sixty, the he **g.** sixty, 6260
Nu 15:24 one kid of the **g.** for a sin offering 5795
Nu 28:15 one kid of the **g.** for a sin offering 5795
Nu 28:30 And one kid of the **g.**, to make 5795
Nu 29:5 one kid of the **g.** for a sin offering 5795
Nu 29:11 One the **g.** for a sin offering; 5795
Nu 29:16, 19,25 And one kid of the **g.** for a 5795
De 32:14 of the breed of Bashan, and **g.**, 6260
1Sa 24:2 men upon the rocks of the wild **g.** 3277
1Sa 25:2 sheep, and a thousand **g.**: 5795
2Ch 17:11 thousand and seven hundred he **g.** 8495
2Ch 29:21 seven lambs, and seven he **g.** 5795
2Ch 29:23 they brought forth the he **g.** for 8163
Ezr 6:17 offering for all israel, twelve he **g.**, 5796
Ezr 8:35 twelve he **g.** for a sin offering: 6842
Job 39:1 wild **g.** of the rock bring forth? 3277
Ps 50:9 house, nor he **g.** out of thy folds 6260
Ps 50:13 of bulls, or drink the blood of **g.**? 6260
Ps 66:15 I will offer bullocks with **g.** 6260
Ps 104:18 hills are a refuge for the wild **g.**; 3277
Pr 27:26 and the **g.** are the price of the field. 6260
Ca 4:1 thy hair is as a flock of **g.**, that 5795
Ca 6:5 thy hair is as a flock of **g.** that 5795
Isa 1:11 the blood of bullocks...or of he **g.** 6260
Isa 34:6 and with the blood of lambs and **g.**, 6260
Jer 50:8 as the he **g.** before the flocks 6260
Jer 51:40 slaughter like rams with he **g.** 6260
Eze 27:21 thee in lambs, and rams, and **g.**: 6260
Eze 34:17 between the rams and the he **g.** 6260
Eze 39:18 of rams, of lambs, and of **g.**, of 6260
Eze 43:22 shalt offer a kid of the **g.** without 5795
Eze 45:23 a kid of the **g.** daily for a sin 5795
Zec 10:3 I punished the **g.**: for the Lord 6260
Mt 25:32 **divideth his sheep from the g.**: *2056*
Mt 25:33 **right hand, but the g. on the left.** *2055*
Heb 9:12 Neither by the blood of **g.** and *5131*
Heb 9:13 For if the blood of bulls and of **g.**, *5131*
Heb 9:19 took the blood of calves and of **g.** *5131*
Heb 10:4 that the blood of bulls and of **g.** *5131*

GOATS'
Ex 25:4 scarlet, and fine linen, and **g.** hair, 5795
Ex 26:7 thou shalt make curtains of **g.** hair 5795
Ex 35:6, 23 scarlet, and fine line, and **g.** hair, 5795
Ex 35:26 them up in wisdom spun **g.** hair. 5795
Ex 36:14 And he made curtains of **g.** hair 5795
Nu 31:20 all work of **g.** hair, and all things 5795
1Sa 19:13 put a pillow of **g.** hair for his bolster. 5795
1Sa 19:16 with a pillow of **g.** hair for his bolster, 5795
Pr 27:27 thou shalt have **g.** milk enough for 5795

GOATS'-HAIR See GOATS' and HAIR.

GOATSKINS
Heb 11:37 about in sheepskins and **g.**; *122,1192*

GOB (gob)
2Sa 21:18 a battle with the Philistines at **G.** 1359
2Sa 21:19 a battle in **G.** with the Philistines, 1359

GOBLET
Ca 7:2 Thy navel is like a round **g.** 101

GOD (or god) See also GODDESS; GODHEAD; GOD'S; GODS; GOD-WARD.
Ge 1:1 **G.** created the heaven and the 430
Ge 1:2 Spirit of **G.** moved upon the face 430
Ge 1:3 And **G.** said, Let there be light: 430
Ge 1:4 And **G.** saw the light, that it was 430
Ge 1:4 and **G.** divided the light from the 430
Ge 1:5 And **G.** called the light Day, and the 430
Ge 1:6 **G.** said, Let there be a firmament 430
Ge 1:7 **G.** made the firmament, and divided 430
Ge 1:8 **G.** called the firmament Heaven 430
Ge 1:9 **G.** said, Let the waters under the 430
Ge 1:10 And **G.** called the dry land Earth; 430
Ge 1:10 and **G.** saw that it was good 430
Ge 1:11 **G.** said, Let the earth bring forth 430
Ge 1:12 and **G.** saw that it was good 430
Ge 1:14 And **G.** said, Let there be lights 430
Ge 1:16 And **G.** made two great lights: the 430
Ge 1:17 And **G.** set them in the firmament 430
Ge 1:18 and **G.** saw that it was good 430
Ge 1:20 **G.** said, Let the waters bring forth 430
Ge 1:21 **G.** created great whales, and every 430
Ge 1:21 and **G.** saw that it was good 430
Ge 1:22 And **G.** blessed them, saying, Be 430
Ge 1:24 **G.** said, Let the earth bring forth 430
Ge 1:25 **G.** made the beast of the earth after 430
Ge 1:25 and **G.** saw that it was good 430
Ge 1:26 And **G.** said, Let us make man in 430
Ge 1:27 **G.** created man in his own image, 430
Ge 1:27 in the image of **G.** created he him; 430
Ge 1:28 **G.** blessed them, and **G.** said unto 430
Ge 1:29 And **G.** said, Behold, I have given 430
Ge 1:31 And **G.** saw everything that he had 430
Ge 2:2 the seventh day **G.** ended his work 430
Ge 2:3 And **G.** blessed the seventh day, and 430
Ge 2:3 his work which **G.** created and made. 430
Ge 2:4 day that the Lord **G.** made the earth 430
Ge 2:5 for the Lord **G.** had not caused it to 430
Ge 2:7 the Lord **G.** formed man of the dust 430
Ge 2:8 Lord **G.** planted a garden eastward 430
Ge 2:9 the Lord **G.** to grow every tree that 430
Ge 2:15 Lord **G.** took the man, and put him 430
Ge 2:16 the Lord **G.** commanded the man, 430
Ge 2:18 And the Lord **G.** said, It is not good 430
Ge 2:19 the Lord **G.** formed every beast of 430
Ge 2:21 the Lord **G.** caused a deep sleep to 430
Ge 2:22 the Lord **G.** had taken from man, 430
Ge 3:1 field which the Lord **G.** had made 430
Ge 3:1 hath **G.** said, Ye shall not eat of every 430
Ge 3:3 **G.** hath said, Ye shall not eat of it, 430
Ge 3:5 For **G.** doth know that in the day 430
Ge 3:8 they heard the voice of the Lord **G.** 430
Ge 3:8 from the presence of the Lord **G.** 430
Ge 3:9 And the Lord **G.** called unto Adam, 430
Ge 3:13 the Lord **G.** said unto the woman, 430
Ge 3:14 the Lord **G.** said unto the serpent, 430
Ge 3:21 did the Lord **G.** make coats of skins, 430
Ge 3:22 Lord **G.** said, Behold, the man is 430
Ge 3:23 Therefore the Lord **G.** sent him forth 430
Ge 4:25 For **G.**, said she, hath appointed me 430
Ge 5:1 In the day that **G.** created man, 430
Ge 5:1 in the likeness of **G.** made he him 430
Ge 5:22 And Enoch walked with **G.**, after he 430
Ge 5:24 And Enoch walked with **G.**: and he 430
Ge 5:24 And he was not; for **G.** took him 430
Ge 6:2 the sons of **G.** saw the daughters 430
Ge 6:4 when the sons of **G.** came in unto 430
Ge 6:5 And **G.** saw that the wickedness of 3068
Ge 6:9 and Noah walked with **G.** 430
Ge 6:11 earth also was corrupt before **G.**, 430
Ge 6:12 And **G.** looked upon the earth, and, 430
Ge 6:13 **G.** said unto Noah, The end of all 430
Ge 6:22 according to all that **G.** commanded 430
Ge 7:9 female, as **G.** had commanded Noah. 430
Ge 7:16 as **G.** had commanded him: and the 430
Ge 8:1 And **G.** remembered Noah, and every 430
Ge 8:1 and **G.** made a wind to pass over the 430
Ge 8:15 And **G.** spake unto Noah, saying, 430
Ge 9:1 and **G.** blessed Noah and his sons, 430
Ge 9:6 in the image of **G.** made he man 430
Ge 9:8 **G.** spake unto Noah, and to his sons 430
Ge 9:12 And **G.** said, This is the token of 430
Ge 9:16 between **G.** and every living creature 430
Ge 9:17 **G.** said unto Noah, This is the token 430
Ge 9:26 Blessed be the Lord **G.** of Shem; 430
Ge 9:27 **G.** shall enlarge Japheth, and he 430
Ge 14:18 was the priest of the most high **G.**, 410
Ge 14:19 Blessed be Abram of the most high **G.**, 410
Ge 14:20 blessed be the most high **G.**, which 410
Ge 14:22 unto the Lord, the most high **G.**, 410
Ge 15:2 Abram said, Lord **G.**, what wilt 3069
Ge 15:8 he said, Lord **G.**, whereby shall I 3069
Ge 16:13 Thou **G.** seest me: for she said, 410
Ge 17:1 I am the Almighty **G.**; walk before 410
Ge 17:3 and **G.** talked with him, saying, 430
Ge 17:7 to be a **G.** unto thee, and to thy seed 430
Ge 17:8 possession; and I will be their **G.** 430
Ge 17:9 **G.** said unto Abraham, Thou shalt 430
Ge 17:15 **G.** said unto Abraham, As for Sarai 430
Ge 17:18 And Abraham said unto **G.**, O that 430
Ge 17:19 **G.** said, Sarah thy wife shall bear 430
Ge 17:22 and **G.** went up from Abraham. 430
Ge 17:23 selfsame day, as **G.** had said unto 430
Ge 19:29 when **G.** destroyed the cities of the 430
Ge 19:29 that **G.** remembered Abraham, 430
Ge 20:3 **G.** came to Abimelech in a dream 430
Ge 20:6 And **G.** said unto him in a dream, 430
Ge 20:11 the fear of **G.** is not in this place; 430
Ge 20:13 **G.** caused me to wander from my 430
Ge 20:17 So Abraham prayed unto **G.**: and **G.** 430
Ge 21:2 time of which **G.** had spoken to him. 430
Ge 21:4 old, as **G.** had commanded him 430
Ge 21:6 **G.** hath made me to laugh, so that 430
Ge 21:12 **G.** said unto Abraham, Let it not be 430
Ge 21:17 And **G.** heard the voice of the lad; 430
Ge 21:17 and the angel of **G.** called to Hagar 430
Ge 21:17 **G.** hath heard the voice of the lad 430
Ge 21:19 **G.** opened her eyes, and she saw 430
Ge 21:20 **G.** was with the lad; and he grew, 430
Ge 21:22 **G.** is with thee in all that thou doest: 430
Ge 21:23 therefore swear unto me here by **G.** 430
Ge 21:33 of the Lord, the everlasting **G.** 410
Ge 22:1 **G.** did tempt Abraham, and said 430
Ge 22:3 the place of which **G.** had told him. 430
Ge 22:8 **G.** will provide himself a lamb for a 430
Ge 22:9 to the place which **G.** had told him of 430
Ge 22:12 now I know that thou fearest **G.**, 430
Ge 24:3 **G.** of heaven, and the **G.** of the earth, 430
Ge 24:7 Lord **G.** of heaven, which took me 430
Ge 24:12 O Lord **G.** of my master Abraham, 430
Ge 24:27 the Lord **G.** of my master Abraham, 430
Ge 24:42 O Lord **G.** of my master Abraham, 430
Ge 24:48 the Lord **G.** of my master Abraham, 430
Ge 25:11 **G.** blessed his son Isaac; and Isaac 430
Ge 26:24 I am the **G.** of Abraham thy father: 430
Ge 27:20 the Lord thy **G.** brought it to me 430
Ge 27:28 **G.** give thee of the dew of heaven, 430
Ge 28:3 **G.** Almighty bless thee, and make 410
Ge 28:4 which **G.** gave unto Abraham. 430
Ge 28:12 the angels of **G.** ascending and 430
Ge 28:13 said, I am the Lord **G.** of Abraham 430
Ge 28:13 thy father, and the **G.** of Isaac: 430
Ge 28:17 is none other but the house of **G.**, 430
Ge 28:20 If **G.** will be with me, and will keep 430
Ge 28:21 then shall the Lord be my **G.** 430
Ge 30:6 Rachel said, **G.** hath judged me, and 430
Ge 30:17 **G.** hearkened unto Leah, and she 430
Ge 30:18 **G.** hath given me my hire, because 430
Ge 30:20 **G.** hath endued me with a good 430
Ge 30:22 **G.** remembered Rachel, and **G.** 430
Ge 30:23 **G.** hath taken away my reproach: 430
Ge 31:5 but the **G.** of my father hath been 430
Ge 31:7 **G.** suffered him not to hurt me. 430
Ge 31:9 Thus **G.** hath taken away the cattle 430
Ge 31:11 the angel of **G.** spake unto me in a 430
Ge 31:13 I am the **G.** of Beth-el, where thou 410
Ge 31:16 all the riches which **G.** hath taken 430
Ge 31:16 whatsoever **G.** hath said unto thee, 430
Ge 31:24 **G.** came to Laban the Syrian in a 430
Ge 31:29 the **G.** of your father spake unto me 430
Ge 31:42 **G.** of my father, the **G.** of Abraham, 430
Ge 31:42 **G.** hath seen mine affliction and the 430
Ge 31:50 **G.** is witness betwixt me and thee. 430
Ge 31:53 The **G.** of Abraham, and the **G.** of 430
Ge 31:53 Nathor, the **G.** of their father, 430
Ge 32:1 and the angels of **G.** met him 430
Ge 32:9 O **G.** of my father Abraham, 430
Ge 32:9 and **G.** of my father Isaac, 430
Ge 32:28 as a prince hast thou power with **G.** 430
Ge 32:30 for I have seen **G.** face to face, 430
Ge 33:5 which **G.** hath graciously given 430
Ge 33:10 as though I had seen the face of **G.**, 430
Ge 33:11 **G.** hath dealt graciously with me, 430
Ge 35:1 **G.** said unto Jacob, Arise, go up to 430
Ge 35:1 and make there an altar unto **G.**, 410
Ge 35:3 I will make there an altar unto **G.**, 410
Ge 35:5 terror of **G.** was upon the cities 430
Ge 35:7 there **G.** appeared unto him, 430
Ge 35:9 And **G.** appeared unto Jacob again 430
Ge 35:10 And **G.** said unto him, Thy name is 430
Ge 35:11 **G.** said unto him, I am...Almighty: 430
Ge 35:11 said unto him, I am **G.** Almighty: 410
Ge 35:13 **G.** went up from him in the place 430
Ge 35:15 the place where **G.** spake with him, 430
Ge 39:9 wickedness, and sin against **G.**? 430
Ge 40:8 Do not interpretations belong to **G.**? 430
Ge 41:16 **G.** shall give Pharaoh an answer of 430
Ge 41:25 **G.** hath shewed Pharaoh what he is 430
Ge 41:28 What **G.** is about to do he sheweth 430
Ge 41:32 the thing is established by **G.**, 430
Ge 41:32 and **G.** will shortly bring it to pass. 430
Ge 41:38 a man in whom the Spirit of **G.** is? 430

Book	Ref	Context	No.
Ge	41:39	as **G.** hath shewed thee all this,	430
Ge	41:51	the firstborn Manasseh: For **G.**,	430
Ge	41:52	**G.** hath caused me to be fruitful	430
Ge	42:18	This do, and live; for I fear **G.**:	430
Ge	42:28	What is this that **G.** hath done	430
Ge	43:14	And **G.** Almighty give you mercy	410
Ge	43:23	your **G.**, and the **G.** of your father,	430
Ge	43:29	**G.** be gracious unto thee,my son.	430
Ge	44:7	**G.** forbid that thy servants should	
Ge	44:16	**G.** hath found out the iniquity of	430
Ge	44:17	**G.** forbid that I should so:	
Ge	45:5	for **G.** did send me before you to	430
Ge	45:7	**G.** sent me before you to preserve	430
Ge	45:8	not you that sent me hither, but **G.**:	430
Ge	45:9	**G.** hath made me lord of all Egypt:	430
Ge	46:1	unto the **G.** of his father Isaac	430
Ge	46:2	**G.** spake unto Israel in the visions	430
Ge	46:3	And he said, I am **G.**,	410
Ge	46:3	the **G.** of thy father: fear not to	430
Ge	48:3	**G.** Almighty appeared unto me at	410
Ge	48:9	**G.** hath given me in this place	430
Ge	48:11	**G.** hath shewed me also thy seed.	430
Ge	48:15	**G.**, before whom my fathers	430
Ge	48:15	**G.** which fed me all my life long	430
Ge	48:20	**G.** make thee as Ephraim and	430
Ge	48:21	but **G.** shall be with you, and bring	430
Ge	49:24	by the hands of the mighty **G.**	
Ge	49:25	Even by the **G.** of thy father,	410
Ge	50:17	the servants of the **G.** of thy father,	430
Ge	50:19	for am I in the place of **G.**?	430
Ge	50:20	**G.** meant it unto good, to bring to	430
Ge	50:24	and **G.** will surely visit you, and	430
Ge	50:25	saying, **G.** will surely visit you, and	430
Ex	1:17	But the midwives feared **G.**, and did	430
Ex	1:20	**G.** dealt well with the midwives:	430
Ex	1:21	because the midwives feared **G.**,	430
Ex	2:23	their cry came up unto **G.** by reason	430
Ex	2:24	And **G.** heard their groaning, and	430
Ex	2:24	and **G.** remembered his covenant	430
Ex	2:25	And **G.** looked upon the children of	430
Ex	2:25	and **G.** had respect unto them.	430
Ex	3:1	the mountain of **G.**, even to Horeb.	430
Ex	3:4	**G.** called unto him out of the midst	430
Ex	3:6	I am the **G.** of thy father,	430
Ex	3:6	the **G.** of Abraham, the **G.** of Isaac	430
Ex	3:6	and the **G.** of Jacob.	430
Ex	3:6	for he was afraid to look upon **G.**	430
Ex	3:11	And Moses said unto **G.**, Who am I;	430
Ex	3:12	shall serve **G.** upon this mountain.	430
Ex	3:13	Moses said unto **G.**, Behold, when	430
Ex	3:13	The **G.** of your fathers hath sent me	430
Ex	3:14	**G.** said unto Moses, I Am that I Am:	430
Ex	3:15	And **G.** said moreover unto Moses,	430
Ex	3:15	The Lord **G.** of your fathers.	430
Ex	3:15	the **G.** of Abraham, the **G.** of Isaac,	430
Ex	3:15	and the **G.** of Jacob,	430
Ex	3:16	The Lord **G.** of your fathers,	430
Ex	3:16	the **G.** of Abraham, of Isaac, and	430
Ex	3:18	The Lord **G.** of the Hebrews hath	430
Ex	3:18	we may sacrifice to the Lord our **G.**	430
Ex	4:5	the Lord **G.** of their fathers,	430
Ex	4:5	the **G.** of Abraham, the **G.** of Isaac.	430
Ex	4:5	and the **G.** of Jacob, hath appeared	430
Ex	4:16	thou shalt be to him instead of **G.**	430
Ex	4:20	Moses took the rod of **G.** in his hand.	430
Ex	4:27	in the mount of **G.**, and kissed him,	430
Ex	5:1	Thus saith the Lord **G.** of Israel,	430
Ex	5:3	**G.** of the Hebrews hath met with us:	430
Ex	5:3	and sacrifice unto the Lord our **G.**;	430
Ex	5:8	Let us go and sacrifice to our **G.**	430
Ex	6:2	**G.** spake unto Moses, and said	430
Ex	6:3	by the name of **G.** Almighty, but	410
Ex	6:7	and I will be to you a **G.**:	430
Ex	6:7	know that I am the Lord your **G.**,	430
Ex	7:1	I have made thee a **G.** to Pharaoh:	430
Ex	7:16	Lord **G.** of the Hebrews hath sent	430
Ex	8:10	none like unto the Lord our **G.**	430
Ex	8:19	This is the finger of **G.**: and	430
Ex	8:25	sacrifice to your **G.** in the land.	430
Ex	8:26	of the Egyptians to the Lord our **G.**	430
Ex	8:27	sacrifice to the Lord our **G.**, as he	430
Ex	8:28	sacrifice to the Lord your **G.** in the	430
Ex	9:1,	13 saith the Lord **G.** of the Hebrews,	430
Ex	9:30	ye will not yet fear the Lord **G.**	430
Ex	10:3	saith the Lord **G.** of the Hebrews,	430
Ex	10:7	they may serve the Lord their **G.**:	430
Ex	10:8	Go, serve the Lord your **G.**: but who	430
Ex	10:16	sinned against the Lord your **G.**,	430
Ex	10:17	intreat the Lord your **G.**, that he	430
Ex	10:25	may sacrifice uto the Lord our **G.**	430
Ex	10:26	we take to serve the Lord our **G.**;	430
Ex	13:17	**G.** led them not through the way	430
Ex	13:17	**G.** said, Lest peradventure the	430
Ex	13:18	But **G.** led the people about,	430
Ex	13:19	**G.** will surely visit you; and ye	430
Ex	14:19	the angel of **G.**, which went before	430
Ex	15:2	become my salvation: he is my **G.**,	410
Ex	15:2	father's **G.**, and I will exalt him.	430
Ex	15:26	to the voice of the Lord thy **G.**,	430
Ex	16:3	Would to **G.** we had died by the hand of	
Ex	16:12	know that I am the Lord your **G.**	430
Ex	17:9	with the rod of **G.** in mine hand.	430
Ex	18:1	of all that **G.** had done for Moses,	430
Ex	18:4	for the **G.** of my father, said he,	430
Ex	18:5	he encamped at the mount of **G.**	430
Ex	18:12	burnt offering and sacrifices for **G.**	430
Ex	18:12	with Moses' father in law before **G.**	430
Ex	18:15	come unto me to enquire of **G.**:	430
Ex	18:16	make them know the statutes of **G.**,	430
Ex	18:19	counsel, and **G.** shall be with thee:	430
Ex	18:19	mayest bring the causes unto **G.**:	430
Ex	18:21	able men, such as fear **G.**, men of	430
Ex	18:23	this thing, and **G.** command thee so,	430
Ex	19:3	Moses went up unto **G.**, and the	430
Ex	19:17	out of the camp to meet with **G.**;	430
Ex	19:19	and **G.** answered him by a voice.	430
Ex	20:1	**G.** spake all these words, saying,	430
Ex	20:2	I am the Lord thy **G.**, which have	430
Ex	20:5	serve them: for I the Lord thy **G.**	430
Ex	20:5	a jealous **G.**, visiting the iniquity	410
Ex	20:7	name of the Lord thy **G.** in vain;	430
Ex	20:10	is the sabbath of the Lord thy **G.**	430
Ex	20:12	which the Lord thy **G.** giveth thee.	430
Ex	20:19	let not **G.** speak with us, lest we die.	430
Ex	20:20	**G.** is come to prove you, and that	430
Ex	20:21	the thick darkness where **G.** was.	430
Ex	21:13	but **G.** deliver him into his hand;	430
Ex	22:20	He that sacrificeth unto any **g.**,	430
Ex	23:17	shall appear before the Lord **G.**	3068
Ex	23:19	into the house of the Lord thy **G.**	430
Ex	23:25	ye shall serve the Lord your **G.**,	430
Ex	24:10	they saw the **G.** of Israel: and there	430
Ex	24:11	they saw **G.**, and did eat and drink.	430
Ex	24:13	Moses went up into the mount of **G.**	430
Ex	29:45	of Israel, and will be their **G.**	430
Ex	29:46	know that I am the Lord their **G.**,	430
Ex	29:46	among them: I am the Lord their **G.**	430
Ex	31:3	have filled him with the spirit of **G.**,	430
Ex	31:18	stone, written with the finger of **G.**	430
Ex	32:11	Moses besought the Lord his **G.**,	430
Ex	32:16	And the tables were the work of **G.**,	430
Ex	32:16	the writing was the writing of **G.**,	430
Ex	32:27	Thus saith the Lord **G.** of Israel,	430
Ex	34:6	Lord **G.**, merciful and gracious,	410
Ex	34:14	For thou shalt worship no other **g.**	410
Ex	34:14	name is Jealous, is a jealous **G.**	410
Ex	34:23	appear before the Lord **G.**,	3068
Ex	34:23	appear before...the **G.** of Israel,	430
Ex	34:24	appear before the Lord thy **G.**	430
Ex	34:26	unto the house of the Lord thy **G.**	430
Ex	35:31	hath filled him with the spirit of **G.**	430
Le	2:13	the salt of the covenant of thy **G.**	430
Le	4:22	commandments of the Lord his **G.**	430
Le	10:17	**G.** hath given it you to bear	
Le	11:44	For I am the Lord your **G.**	430
Le	11:45	of the land of Egypt, to be your **G.**	430
Le	18:2	unto them I am the Lord your **G.**	430
Le	18:4	therein: I am the Lord your **G.**	430
Le	18:21	thou profane the name of thy **G.**	430
Le	18:30	therein: I am the Lord your **G.**	430
Le	19:2	for I the Lord your **G.** am holy.	430
Le	19:3	am the Lord your **G.**	430
Le	19:4	molten gods, I am the Lord your **G.**	430
Le	19:10	stranger: I am the Lord your **G.**	430
Le	19:12	thou profane the name of thy **G.**;	430
Le	19:14	shalt fear thy **G.**: I am the Lord.	430
Le	19:25	thereof: I am the Lord your **G.**	430
Le	19:31	by them: I am the Lord your **G.**	430
Le	19:32	and fear thy **G.**: I am the Lord.	430
Le	19:34	of Egypt: I am the Lord your **G.**	430
Le	19:36	the Lord your **G.**, which brought	430
Le	20:7	be ye holy, for I am the Lord your **G.**	430
Le	20:24	I am the Lord your **G.**, which have	430
Le	21:6	They shall be holy unto their **G.**,	430
Le	21:6	not profane the name of their **G.**	430
Le	21:6	the bread of their **G.**, they do offer:	430
Le	21:7	for he is holy unto his **G.**	430
Le	21:8	for he offereth the bread of thy **G.**	430
Le	21:12	profane the sanctuary of his **G.**; for	430
Le	21:12	of the anointing oil of his **G.** is upon	430
Le	21:17	approach to offer the bread of his **G.**	430
Le	21:21	nigh to offer the bread of his **G.**	430
Le	21:22	He shall eat the bread of his **G.**,	430
Le	22:25	shall ye offer the bread of your **G.**	430
Le	22:33	the land of Egypt, to be your **G.**	430
Le	23:14	brought an offering unto your **G.**	430
Le	23:22	the stranger: I am the Lord your **G.**	430
Le	23:28	for you before the Lord your **G.**	430
Le	23:40	rejoice before the Lord your **G.**	430
Le	23:43	land of Egypt: I am the Lord your **G.**	430
Le	24:15	Whosoever curseth his **G.** shall	430
Le	24:22	country: for I am the Lord your **G.**	430
Le	25:17	but thou shalt fear thy **G.**	430
Le	25:17	for I am the Lord your **G.**	430
Le	25:36	but fear thy **G.**; that thy brother	430
Le	25:38	I am the Lord your **G.**, which	430
Le	25:38	land of Canaan, and to be your **G.**	430
Le	25:43	with rigour; but shalt fear thy **G.**,	430
Le	25:55	land of Egypt; I am the Lord your **G.**	430
Le	26:1	down into it: I am the Lord your **G.**	430
Le	26:12	among you, and will be your **G.**,	430
Le	26:13	am the Lord your **G.**, which brought	430
Le	26:44	them: for I am the Lord their **G.**	430
Le	26:45	that I might be their **G.**: I am the	430
Nu	6:7	consecration of his **G.** is upon his	430
Nu	10:9	remembered before...Lord your **G.**,	430
Nu	10:10	you for a memorial before your **G.**	430
Nu	10:10	I am the Lord your **G.**,	430
Nu	11:29	would **G.** that all the Lord's people	
Nu	12:13	Heal her now, O **G.**, I beseech thee.	410
Nu	14:2	Would **G.** that we had died in	
Nu	14:2	would **G.** we had died in this	
Nu	15:40	and be holy unto you **G.**	430
Nu	15:41	am the Lord your **G.**, which brought	430
Nu	15:41	the land of Egypt, to be your **G.**:	430
Nu	15:41	I am the Lord your **G.**	430
Nu	16:9	the **G.** of Israel hath separated	430
Nu	16:22	upon their faces, and said, O **G.**,	410
Nu	16:22	the **G.** of the spirits of all flesh,	430
Nu	20:3	Would **G.** that we had died when	
Nu	21:5	the people spake against **G.**, and	430
Nu	22:9	**G.** came unto Balaam, and said,	430
Nu	22:10	Balaam said unto **G.**, Balak the	430
Nu	22:12	**G.** said unto Balaam, Thou shalt	430
Nu	22:18	beyond the word of the Lord my **G.**,	430
Nu	22:20	**G.** came unto Balaam at night,	430
Nu	22:38	word that **G.** putteth in my mouth,	430
Nu	23:4	And **G.** met Balaam: and he said	430
Nu	23:8	How shall I curse, whom **G.** hath	410
Nu	23:19	**G.** is not a man, that he should	410
Nu	23:21	the Lord his **G.** is with him, and	430
Nu	23:22	**G.** brought them out of Egypt; he	410
Nu	23:23	What hath **G.** wrought!	410
Nu	23:27	peradventure it will please **G.**	430
Nu	24:2	the spirit of **G.** came upon him.	430
Nu	24:4	which heard the words of **G.**, which	410
Nu	24:8	**G.** brought him forth out of Egypt;	410
Nu	24:16	which heard the words of **G.**, and	410
Nu	24:23	who shall live when **G.** doeth this!	410
Nu	25:13	because he was zealous for his **G.**,	430
Nu	27:16	the **G.** of the spirits of all flesh,	430
De	1:6	The Lord our **G.** spake unto us	430
De	1:10	Lord your **G.** hath multiplied you,	430
De	1:11	Lord **G.** of your fathers make you	430
De	1:19	as the Lord our **G.** commanded us;	430
De	1:20	the Lord our **G.** doth give unto us.	430
De	1:21	the Lord thy **G.** hath set the land	430
De	1:21	Lord **G.** of thy fathers hath said	430
De	1:25	which the Lord our **G.** doth give us.	430
De	1:26	commandment of the Lord your **G.**;	430
De	1:30	Lord your **G.** which goeth before	430
De	1:31	the Lord thy **G.** bare thee, as a man	430
De	1:32	ye did not believe the Lord your **G.**,	430
De	1:41	that the Lord our **G.** commanded us.	430
De	2:7	the Lord thy **G.** hath blessed thee	430
De	2:7	Lord thy **G.** hath been with thee;	430
De	2:29	which the Lord our **G.** giveth us.	430
De	2:30	the Lord thy **G.** hardened his spirit,	430
De	2:33	our **G.** delivered him before us;	430
De	2:36	Lord our **G.** delivered all unto us:	430
De	2:37	whatsoever the Lord our **G.** forbad	430

Book	Ref	Context	No.
De	3:3	So the Lord our **G.** delivered into	430
De	3:18	The Lord your **G.** hath given you	430
De	3:20	the Lord your **G.** hath given them	430
De	3:21	that the Lord your **G.** hath done	430
De	3:22	Lord your **G.** he shall fight for you,	430
De	3:24	O Lord **G.**, thou hast begun to	3069
De	3:24	**G.** is there in heaven or in earth,	410
De	4:1	which the Lord **G.** of your father	430
De	4:2	commandments of the Lord your **G.**	430
De	4:3	Lord thy **G.** hath destroyed them	430
De	4:4	did cleave unto the Lord your **G.**	430
De	4:5	as the Lord my **G.** commanded me,	430
De	4:7	who hath **G.** so nigh unto them,	430
De	4:7	as the Lord our **G.** is in all things	430
De	4:10	before the Lord thy **G.** in Horeb,	430
De	4:19	which the Lord thy **G.** hath divided	430
De	4:21	which the Lord thy **G.** giveth thee	430
De	4:23	the covenant of the Lord your **G.**,	430
De	4:23	the Lord thy **G.** hath forbidden thee.	430
De	4:24	the Lord thy **G.** is a consuming fire,	430
De	4:24	consuming fire, even a jealous **G.**.	410
De	4:25	evil in the sight of the Lord thy **G.**,	430
De	4:29	thou shalt seek the Lord thy **G.**,	430
De	4:30	days, if thou turn to the Lord thy **G.**,	430
De	4:31	(For the Lord thy **G.** is a merciful	430
De	4:31	(For the Lord...is a merciful **G.**;)	410
De	4:32	since the day that **G.** created man	430
De	4:33	Did ever people hear the voice of **G.**	430
De	4:34	hath **G.** assayed to go and take him	430
De	4:34	all that the Lord your **G.** did for you	430
De	4:35	know that the Lord he is **G.**; there	430
De	4:39	the Lord he is **G.** in heaven above,	430
De	4:40	which the Lord thy **G.** giveth thee,	430
De	5:2	The Lord our **G.** made a covenant	430
De	5:6	am the Lord thy **G.**, which brought	430
De	5:9	for I the Lord thy **G.** am a jealous	430
De	5:9	a jealous **G.**, visiting the iniquity	410
De	5:11	the name of the Lord thy **G.** in vain:	430
De	5:12	as the Lord thy **G.** hath commanded.	430
De	5:14	is the sabbath of the Lord thy **G.**:	430
De	5:15	the Lord thy **G.** brought thee out	430
De	5:15	the Lord thy **G.** commanded thee	430
De	5:16	Lord thy **G.** hath commanded thee,	430
De	5:16	which the Lord thy **G.** giveth thee.	430
De	5:24	the Lord our **G.** hath hewed us his	430
De	5:24	that **G.** doth talk with man, and he	430
De	5:25	we hear the voice of the Lord our **G.**	430
De	5:26	hath heard the voice of the living **G.**	430
De	5:27	all that the Lord our **G.** shall say;	430
De	5:27	all that the Lord our **G.** shall speak	430
De	5:32	Lord your **G.** hath commanded you:	430
De	5:33	Lord your **G.** hath commanded you,	430
De	6:1	Lord your **G.** commanded to teach	430
De	6:2	thou mightest fear the Lord thy **G.**,	430
De	6:3	**G.** of thy fathers hath promised thee,	430
De	6:4	The Lord our **G.** is one Lord:	430
De	6:5	And thou shalt love the Lord thy **G.**	430
De	6:10	when the Lord thy **G.** shall have into	430
De	6:13	Thou shalt fear the Lord thy **G.**,	430
De	6:15	(For the Lord thy **G.** is a jealous	430
De	6:15	Lord...is a jealous **G.** among you)	410
De	6:15	lest the anger of the Lord thy **G.**	430
De	6:16	Ye shall not tempt the Lord your **G.**,	430
De	6:17	commandments of the Lord your **G.**,	430
De	6:20	Lord our **G.** hath commanded you?	430
De	6:24	to fear the Lord our **G.**, for our good	430
De	6:25	before the Lord our **G.**, as he hath	430
De	7:1	When the Lord thy **G.** shall bring	430
De	7:2	the Lord thy **G.** shall deliever them	430
De	7:6	holy people unto the Lord thy **G.**:	430
De	7:6	the Lord thy **G.** hath chosen thee	430
De	7:9	that the Lord thy **G.**, he is **G.**	430
De	7:9	the faithful **G.**, which keepeth	410
De	7:12	Lord thy **G.** shall keep unto thee	430
De	7:16	the Lord thy **G.** shall deliver thee;	430
De	7:18	the Lord thy **G.** did unto Pharaoh,	430
De	7:19	the Lord thy **G.** brought thee out:	430
De	7:19	so shall the Lord thy **G.** do unto all	430
De	7:20	Lord thy **G.** will send the hornet	430
De	7:21	for the Lord thy **G.** is among you,	430
De	7:21	you, a mighty **G.** and terrible	410
De	7:22	the Lord thy **G.** will put out those	430
De	7:23	the Lord thy **G.** shall deliver them	430
De	7:25	an abomination to the Lord thy **G.**.	430
De	8:2	way which the Lord thy **G.** led thee	430
De	8:5	so the Lord thy **G.** chasteneth thee	430
De	8:6	commandments of the Lord thy **G.**,	430
De	8:7	Lord thy **G.** bringeth thee into a	430
De	8:10	thou shalt bless the Lord thy **G.** for	430
De	8:11	that thou forget not the Lord thy **G.**,	430
De	8:14	up, and thou forget the Lord thy **G.**,	430
De	8:18	shalt remember the Lord thy **G.**:	430
De	8:19	at all forget the Lord thy **G.**, and	430
De	8:20	unto the voice of the Lord your **G.**.	430
De	9:3	Lord thy **G.** is he which goeth over	430
De	9:4	that the Lord thy **G.** hath cast them	430
De	9:5	the Lord thy **G.** doth drive them out	430
De	9:6	the Lord thy **G.** giveth thee not this	430
De	9:7	thou provokedst the Lord thy **G.** to	430
De	9:10	stone written with the finger of **G.**;	430
De	9:16	had sinned against the Lord your **G.**,	430
De	9:23	commandment of the Lord your **G.**,	430
De	9:26	O Lord **G.**, destroy not thy people	3069
De	10:9	as the Lord thy **G.** promised him	430
De	10:12	what doth the Lord thy **G.** require	430
De	10:12	of thee, but to fear the Lord thy **G.**.	430
De	10:12	and to serve the Lord thy **G.** with all	430
De	10:14	of heavens is the Lord's thy **G.**, the	430
De	10:17	For the Lord your **G.**, is **G.** of gods,	430
De	10:17	a great **G.**, and mighty, and a	410
De	10:20	Thou shalt fear the Lord thy **G.**;	430
De	10:21	He is thy praise, and he is thy **G.**,	430
De	10:22	Lord thy **G.** hath made thee as the	430
De	11:1	thou shalt love the Lord thy **G.**, and	430
De	11:2	chastisement of the Lord your **G.**,	430
De	11:12	which the Lord thy **G.** careth for:	430
De	11:12	eyes of the Lord thy **G.** are always	430
De	11:13	to love the Lord your **G.**, and to	430
De	11:22	to love the Lord your **G.**, to walk	430
De	11:25	the Lord your **G.** shall lay the fear	430
De	11:27	if ye obey the...of the Lord your **G.**,	430
De	11:28	not obey the...of the Lord your **G.**,	430
De	11:29	when the Lord thy **G.** hath brought	430
De	11:31	land which the Lord your **G.** giveth	430
De	12:1	land which the Lord **G.** of thy fathers	430
De	12:4	shall not do so unto the Lord your **G.**	430
De	12:5	the place which the Lord your **G.**	430
De	12:7	ye shall eat before the Lord your **G.**,	430
De	12:7	the Lord thy **G.** hath blessed thee.	430
De	12:9	inheritance...Lord your **G.** giveth	430
De	12:10	land which the Lord your **G.** giveth	430
De	12:11	Lord your **G.** shall choose to cause	430
De	12:12	shall rejoice before the Lord your **G.**,	430
De	12:15	to the blessing of the Lord thy **G.**	430
De	12:18	must eat them before the Lord thy **G.**	430
De	12:18	in the place which the Lord thy **G.**	430
De	12:18	shall rejoice before the Lord thy **G.**	430
De	12:20	When the Lord thy **G.** shall enlarge	430
De	12:21	which the Lord thy **G.** hath chosen	430
De	12:27	upon the altar of the Lord thy **G.**:	430
De	12:27	upon the altar of the Lord thy **G.**,	430
De	12:28	right in the sight of the Lord thy **G.**	430
De	12:29	Lord thy **G.** shall cut off the nations	430
De	12:31	shall not do so unto the Lord thy **G.**:	430
De	13:3	for the Lord your **G.** proveth you,	430
De	13:3	whether ye love the Lord your **G.**	430
De	13:4	shall walk after the Lord your **G.**,	430
De	13:5	you away from the Lord your **G.**,	430
De	13:5	which the Lord thy **G.** commanded	430
De	13:10	thee away from the Lord thy **G.**,	430
De	13:12	which the Lord thy **G.** hath given	430
De	13:16	every whit, for the Lord thy **G.**:	430
De	13:18	to the voice of the Lord thy **G.**,	430
De	13:18	right in the eyes of the Lord thy **G.**.	430
De	14:1	are the children of the Lord your **G.**.	430
De	14:2	an holy people unto the Lord thy **G.**,	430
De	14:21	an holy people unto the Lord thy **G.**	430
De	14:23	shalt eat before the Lord thy **G.**,	430
De	14:23	mayest learn to fear the Lord thy **G.**	430
De	14:24	which the Lord thy **G.** shall choose	430
De	14:24	when the Lord thy **G.** hath blessed	430
De	14:25	which the Lord thy **G.** shall choose:	430
De	14:26	eat there before the Lord thy **G.**.	430
De	14:29	that the Lord thy **G.** may bless thee	430
De	15:4	which the Lord thy **G.** giveth thee	430
De	15:5	unto the voice of the Lord thy **G.**,	430
De	15:6	For the Lord thy **G.** blesseth thee,	430
De	15:7	land which the Lord thy **G.** giveth	430
De	15:10	the Lord thy **G.** shall bless thee in	430
De	15:14	the Lord thy **G.** hath blessed thee	430
De	15:15	and the Lord thy **G.** redeemed thee:	430
De	15:18	and the Lord thy **G.** shall bless thee.	430
De	15:19	shalt sanctify unto the Lord thy **G.**	430
De	15:20	shalt eat it before the Lord thy **G.**	430
De	15:21	not sacrifice it unto the Lord thy **G.**.	430
De	16:1	the passover unto the Lord thy **G.**:	430
De	16:1	the Lord thy **G.** brought thee forth	430
De	16:2	the passover unto the Lord thy **G.**,	430
De	16:5	which the Lord thy **G.** giveth thee:	430
De	16:6	which the Lord thy **G.** shall choose	430
De	16:7	which the Lord thy **G.** shall choose:	430
De	16:8	solemn assembly to the Lord thy **G.**:	430
De	16:10	feast of weeks unto the Lord thy **G.**	430
De	16:10	shalt give unto the Lord thy **G.**,	
De	16:10	according as the Lord thy **G.** hath	430
De	16:11	shalt rejoice before the Lord thy **G.**,	430
De	16:11	which the Lord thy **G.** hath chosen	430
De	16:15	a solemn feast unto the Lord thy **G.**	430
De	16:15	the Lord thy **G.** shall bless thee in	430
De	16:16	appear before the Lord thy **G.** in the	430
De	16:17	to the blessing of the Lord thy **G.**	430
De	16:18	gates, which the Lord thy **G.** giveth	430
De	16:20	land which the Lord thy **G.** giveth	430
De	16:21	unto the altar of the Lord thy **G.**,	430
De	16:22	which the Lord thy **G.** hateth	430
De	17:1	not sacrifice unto the Lord thy **G.**	430
De	17:1	abomination unto the Lord thy **G.**.	430
De	17:2	gates which the Lord thy **G.** giveth	430
De	17:2	in the sight of the Lord thy **G.**, in	430
De	17:8	which the Lord thy **G.** shall choose;	430
De	17:12	minister...before the Lord thy **G.**	430
De	17:14	land which the Lord thy **G.** giveth	430
De	17:15	whom the Lord thy **G.** shall choose:	430
De	17:19	may learn to fear the Lord his **G.**,	430
De	18:5	the Lord thy **G.** hath chosen him	430
De	18:7	in the name of the Lord his **G.**,	430
De	18:9	land which the Lord thy **G.** giveth	430
De	18:12	the Lord thy **G.** doth drive them out	430
De	18:13	shalt be perfect with the Lord thy **G.**.	430
De	18:14	the Lord thy **G.** hath not suffered	430
De	18:15	The Lord thy **G.** will raise up unto	430
De	18:16	thou desiredst of the Lord thy **G.** in	430
De	18:16	again the voice of the Lord my **G.**,	430
De	19:1	When the Lord thy **G.** hath cut off	430
De	19:1	whose land the Lord thy **G.** giveth	430
De	19:2	Lord thy **G.** giveth thee to possess	430
De	19:3	Lord thy **G.** giveth thee to inherit	430
De	19:8	if the Lord thy **G.** enlarge thy	430
De	19:9	to love the Lord thy **G.**, and to	430
De	19:10	land, which the Lord thy **G.** giveth	430
De	19:14	land that the Lord thy **G.** giveth	430
De	20:1	for the Lord thy **G.** is with thee,	430
De	20:4	the Lord your **G.** is he that goeth	430
De	20:13	the Lord thy **G.** hath delivered it	430
De	20:14	which the Lord thy **G.** hath given	430
De	20:16	land which the Lord thy **G.** doth give	430
De	20:17	the Lord thy **G.** hath commanded	430
De	20:18	ye sin against the Lord your **G.**	430
De	21:1	land which the Lord thy **G.** giveth	430
De	21:5	them the Lord thy **G.** hath chosen	430
De	21:10	Lord thy **G.** hath delivered them	430
De	21:23	he that is hanged is accursed of **G.**;)	430
De	21:23	which the Lord thy **G.** giveth thee	430
De	22:5	abomination unto the Lord thy **G.**.	430
De	23:5	Nevertheless the Lord thy **G.** would	430
De	23:5	but the Lord thy **G.** turned the curse	430
De	23:5	because the Lord thy **G.** loved thee.	430
De	23:14	For the Lord thy **G.** walketh in the	430
De	23:18	into the house of the Lord thy **G.** for	430
De	23:18	abomination unto the Lord thy **G.**.	430
De	23:20	that the Lord thy **G.** may bless thee	430
De	23:21	vow a vow unto the Lord thy **G.**.	430
De	23:21	the Lord thy **G.** will surely require	430
De	23:23	hast vowed unto the Lord thy **G.**,	430
De	24:4	which the Lord thy **G.** giveth thee	430
De	24:9	Remember what the Lord thy **G.** did	430
De	24:13	unto thee before the Lord thy **G.**.	430
De	24:18	and the Lord thy **G.** redeemed thee	430
De	24:19	that the Lord thy **G.** may bless thee	430
De	25:15	land which the Lord thy **G.** giveth	430
De	25:16	abomination unto the Lord thy **G.**.	430
De	25:18	and he feared not **G.**	430
De	25:19	Lord thy **G.** hath given thee rest	430
De	25:19	land which the Lord thy **G.** giveth	430
De	26:1	land which the Lord thy **G.** giveth	430
De	26:2	land that the Lord thy **G.** giveth	430
De	26:2	the Lord thy **G.** shall choose to place	430
De	26:3	this day unto the Lord thy **G.**, that	430

De 26:4 before the altar of the Lord thy **G.**. 430
De 26:5 say before the Lord thy **G.**, A Syrian ... 430
De 26:7 unto the Lord **G.** of our fathers, ... 430
De 26:10 shalt set it before the Lord thy **G.**, ... 430
De 26:10 and worship before the Lord thy **G.**: 430
De 26:11 thing which the Lord thy **G.** hath 430
De 26:13 say before the Lord thy **G.**, I have 430
De 26:14 to the voice of the Lord my **G.**, and 430
De 26:16 Lord thy **G.** hath commanded thee 430
De 26:17 the Lord this day to be thy **G.**, ... 430
De 26:19 an holy people unto the Lord thy **G.**, ... 430
De 27:2 Lord thy **G.** giveth thee, that thou 430
De 27:3 Lord thy **G.** giveth thee, a land that 430
De 27:3 Lord **G.** of thy fathers hath promised 430
De 27:5 build an altar unto the Lord thy **G.**, ... 430
De 27:6 build the altar of the Lord thy **G.** of 430
De 27:6 thereon unto the Lord thy **G.**: 430
De 27:7 and rejoice before the Lord thy **G.**. 430
De 27:9 the people of the Lord thy **G.**. 430
De 27:10 obey the voice of the Lord thy **G.**, ... 430
De 28:1 unto the voice of the Lord thy **G.**, ... 430
De 28:1 Lord thy **G.** will set thee on high 430
De 28:2 unto the voice of the Lord thy **G.**. 430
De 28:8 land which the Lord thy **G.** giveth 430
De 28:9 shalt keep the...of the Lord thy **G.**, ... 430
De 28:13 hearken unto the...of the Lord thy **G.**, .. 430
De 28:15 unto the voice of the Lord thy **G.**, to ... 430
De 28:45 unto the voice of the Lord thy **G.**, ... 430
De 28:47 thou servedst not the Lord thy **G.** 430
De 28:52 which the Lord thy **G.** hath given 430
De 28:53 daughters...the Lord thy **G.** hath 430
De 28:58 fearful name, The Lord thy **G.**; 430
De 28:62 obey the voice of the Lord thy **G.**. 430
De 28:67 shalt say, Would **G.** it were even! .....
De 28:67 shalt say, Would **G.** it were morning! .....
De 29:6 know that I am the Lord your **G.**. 430
De 29:10 all of you before the Lord your **G.**; 430
De 29:12 convenant with the Lord thy **G.**, ... 430
De 29:12 the Lord thy **G.** maketh with thee 430
De 29:13 and that he may be unto thee a **G.**, ... 430
De 29:15 us this day before the Lord our **G.**, ... 430
De 29:18 away this day from the Lord our **G.**, ... 430
De 29:25 of the Lord **G.** of their fathers, ... 430
De 29:29 things belong unto the Lord our **G.**: 430
De 30:1 the Lord thy **G.** hath driven thee, ... 430
De 30:2 shalt return unto the Lord thy **G.**, ... 430
De 30:3 Lord thy **G.** will turn thy captivity 430
De 30:3 the Lord thy **G.** hath scattered thee 430
De 30:4 will the Lord thy **G.** gather thee, ... 430
De 30:5 the Lord thy **G.** will bring thee into 430
De 30:6 Lord thy **G.** will circumcise thine 430
De 30:6 love the Lord thy **G.** with all thine 430
De 30:7 the Lord thy **G.** will put all these 430
De 30:9 the Lord thy **G.** will make thee 430
De 30:10 unto the voice of the Lord thy **G.**, ... 430
De 30:10 if thou turn unto the Lord thy **G.** 430
De 30:16 to love the Lord thy **G.**, to walk in 430
De 30:16 and the Lord thy **G.** shall bless thee 430
De 30:20 thou mayest love the Lord thy **G.**, ... 430
De 31:3 The Lord thy **G.**, he will go before 430
De 31:6 Lord thy **G.**, he it is that doth go 430
De 31:11 to appear before the Lord thy **G.** 430
De 31:12 learn, and fear the Lord your **G.**, ... 430
De 31:13 and learn to fear the Lord your **G.**, ... 430
De 31:17 because our **G.** is not among us? 430
De 31:26 the covenant of the Lord your **G.**, ... 430
De 32:3 ascribe ye greatness unto our **G.**, ... 430
De 32:4 a **G.** of truth and without iniquity, ... 410
De 32:12 there was no strange **G.** with him 410
De 32:15 he forsook **G.** which made him, ... 433
De 32:17 sacrificed unto devils, not to **G.**; 433
De 32:18 hast forgotten **G.** that formed thee 410
De 32:21 jealousy with that which is not **G.**; 410
De 32:39 and there is no **g.** with me: 430
De 33:1 Moses the man of **G.** blessed the 430
De 33:26 none like unto the **G.** of Jeshurun, ... 410
De 33:27 The eternal **G.** is thy refuge, and 430
Jos 1:9 for the Lord thy **G.** is with thee 430
Jos 1:11 land, which the Lord your **G.** giveth 430
Jos 1:13 Lord your **G.** hath given you rest, ... 430
Jos 1:15 land which the Lord your **G.** giveth 430
Jos 1:17 the Lord thy **G.** be with thee, ... 430
Jos 2:11 the Lord your **G.**, he is **G.** in heaven ... 430
Jos 3:3 the covenant of the Lord your **G.**, ... 430
Jos 3:9 hear the words of the Lord your **G.**. 430
Jos 3:10 know that the living **G.** is among 410
Jos 4:5 before the ark of the Lord your **G.** 430
Jos 4:23 Lord your **G.** dried up the waters 430
Jos 4:23 Lord your **G.** did to the Red sea, ... 430
Jos 4:24 fear the Lord your **G.** for ever 430
Jos 7:7 Joshua said, Alas, O Lord **G.**, ... 3069
Jos 7:7 would to **G.** we had been content .....
Jos 7:13 thus saith the Lord **G.** of Israel, ... 430
Jos 7:19 glory to the Lord **G.** of Israel, ... 430
Jos 7:20 sinned against the Lord **G.** of Israel, ... 430
Jos 8:7 the Lord your **G.** will deliver it into 430
Jos 8:30 Lord **G.** of Israel in mount Ebal, ... 430
Jos 9:9 of the name of the Lord thy **G.**: for 430
Jos 9:18 had sworn unto them by the Lord **G.** ... 430
Jos 9:19 sworn unto them by the Lord **G.** of 430
Jos 9:23 of water for the house of my **G.** 430
Jos 9:24 that the Lord thy **G.** commanded 430
Jos 10:19 Lord your **G.** hath delivered them 430
Jos 10:40 the Lord **G.** of Israel commanded. 430
Jos 10:42 Lord **G.** of Israel fought for Israel 430
Jos 13:14 sacrifices of the Lord **G.** of Israel 430
Jos 13:33 the Lord **G.** of Israel was their 430
Jos 14:6 Lord said unto Moses the man of **G.** 430
Jos 14:8 I wholly followed the Lord my **G.**. 430
Jos 14:9 wholly followed the Lord my **G.**. 430
Jos 14:14 he wholly followed the Lord **G.** of 430
Jos 18:3 land, which the Lord **G.** of your 430
Jos 18:6 for you here before the Lord our **G.**. ... 430
Jos 22:3 commandment of the Lord your **G.**. 430
Jos 22:4 now the Lord your **G.** hath given 430
Jos 22:5 love the Lord your **G.**, and to walk 430
Jos 22:16 committed against the **G.** of Israel, ... 430
Jos 22:19 beside the altar of the Lord our **G.**. 430
Jos 22:22 Lord **G.** of gods, the Lord **G.** of 410
Jos 22:24 to do with the Lord **G.** of Israel? 430
Jos 22:29 **G.** forbid that we should rebel .....
Jos 22:29 beside the altar of the Lord our **G.** 430
Jos 22:33 the children of Israel blessed **G.**, ... 430
Jos 22:34 between us that the Lord is **G.**. 430
Jos 23:3 that the Lord your **G.** hath done 430
Jos 23:3 for the Lord your **G.** is he that hath 430
Jos 23:5 And the Lord your **G.**, he shall expel ... 430
Jos 23:5 as the Lord your **G.** hath promised 430
Jos 23:8 But cleave unto the Lord your **G.**, ... 430
Jos 23:10 for the Lord your **G.**, he it is that 430
Jos 23:11 that ye love the Lord your **G.**. 430
Jos 23:13 Lord your **G.** will no more drive 430
Jos 23:13 the Lord your **G.** hath given you. 430
Jos 23:14 things which the Lord your **G.** spake 430
Jos 23:15 the Lord your **G.** promised you; 430
Jos 23:15 the Lord your **G.** hath given you. 430
Jos 23:16 the covenant of the Lord your **G.**, ... 430
Jos 24:1 presented themselves before **G.** 430
Jos 24:2 Thus saith the Lord **G.** of Israel, ... 430
Jos 24:16 **G.** forbid that we should forsake .....
Jos 24:17 For the Lord our **G.**, he it is that 430
Jos 24:18 also serve the Lord; for he is our **G.** 430
Jos 24:19 the Lord: for he is an holy **G.**; 430
Jos 24:19 he is a jealous **G.**; he will forgive 410
Jos 24:23 heart unto the Lord **G.** of Israel. 430
Jos 24:24 The Lord our **G.** will we serve, ... 430
Jos 24:26 words in the book of the law of **G.**, ... 430
Jos 24:27 unto you, lest ye deny your **G.**. 430
Jg 1:7 have done, so **G.** had requited me. 430
Jg 2:12 forsook the Lord **G.** of their fathers, ... 430
Jg 3:7 forgat the Lord their **G.**, and served 430
Jg 3:20 have a message from **G.** unto thee 430
Jg 4:6 the Lord **G.** of Israel commanded 430
Jg 4:23 So **G.** subdued on that day Jabin 430
Jg 5:3 sing praise to the Lord **G.** of Israel. 430
Jg 5:5 from before the Lord **G.** of Israel. 430
Jg 6:8 Thus saith the Lord **G.** of Israel, ... 430
Jg 6:10 I am the Lord your **G.**; fear not 430
Jg 6:20 And the angel of **G.** said unto him, ... 430
Jg 6:22 Gideon said, Alas, O Lord **G.**! for 3069
Jg 6:26 build an altar unto the Lord thy **G.** 430
Jg 6:31 if he be a **g.**, let him plead for 430
Jg 6:36 Gideon said unto **G.**, If thou wilt 430
Jg 6:39 Gideon said unto **G.**, Let not thine 430
Jg 6:40 **G.** did so that night: for it was dry 430
Jg 7:14 his hand hath **G.** delivered Midian, ... 430
Jg 8:3 **G.** hath delivered into your hands 430
Jg 8:33 and made Baal-berith their **g.** 430
Jg 8:34 remembered not the Lord their **G.**, ... 430
Jg 9:7 that **G.** may hearken unto you 430
Jg 9:9 by me they honour **G.** and man, ... 430
Jg 9:13 which cheereth **G.** and man, and go 430
Jg 9:23 Then **G.** sent an evil spirit between 430
Jg 9:27 and went into the house of their **g.**, ... 430
Jg 9:29 would to **G.** this people were under my .....
Jg 9:46 hold of the house of the **g.** Berith 410
Jg 9:56 **G.** rendered the wickedness of 430
Jg 9:57 did **G.** render upon their heads: 430
Jg 10:10 because we have forsaken our **G.**, ... 430
Jg 11:21 Lord **G.** of Israel delivered Sihon 430
Jg 11:23 Son now the Lord **G.** of Israel hath 430
Jg 11:24 which Chemosh thy **g.** giveth thee to 430
Jg 11:24 the Lord our **G.** shall drive out from 430
Jg 13:5 a Nazarite unto **G.** from the womb: 430
Jg 13:6 A man of **G.** came unto me, ... 430
Jg 13:6 the countenance of an angel of **G.**, ... 430
Jg 13:7 be a Nazarite to **G.** from the womb 430
Jg 13:8 the man of **G.** which thou didst send 430
Jg 13:9 **G.** hearkened to the voice of Manoah; .. 430
Jg 13:9 and the angel of **G.** came again unto 430
Jg 13:22 surely die, because we have seen **G.** 430
Jg 15:19 **G.** clave and hollow place that was 430
Jg 16:17 Nazarite unto **G.** from my mother's 430
Jg 16:23 great sacrifice unto Dagon their **g.**, ... 430
Jg 16:23 Our **g.** hath delivered Samson our 430
Jg 16:24 praised their **g.**: for they said, Our **g.** ... 430
Jg 16:28 O Lord **G.**, remember me, I pray 3069
Jg 16:28 only this once, O **G.** that I may, ... 430
Jg 18:5 Ask counsel, we pray thee, of **G.**, ... 430
Jg 18:10 **G.** hath given it into your hands; 430
Jg 18:31 all the time that the house of **G.** was 430
Jg 20:2 in the assembly of the people of **G.**, ... 430
Jg 20:18 and went up to the house of **G.**, ... 1008
Jg 20:18 and asked counsel of **G.**, and said 430
Jg 20:26 came into the house of **G.**, and 1008
Jg 20:27 the ark of the covenant of **G.** 430
Jg 20:31 one goeth up to the house of **G.**, ... 1008
Jg 21:2 people came to the house of **G.**, ... 1008
Jg 21:2 and abode there till even before **G.**, ... 430
Jg 21:3 And said, O Lord **G.** of Israel, ... 430
Ru 1:16 my people, and thy **G.** my **G.**: 430
Ru 2:12 given thee of the Lord **G.** of Israel, ... 430
1Sa 1:17 **G.** of Israel grant thee thy petition 430
1Sa 2:2 neither is there any rock like our **G.**. ... 430
1Sa 2:3 the Lord is a **G.** of knowledge, ... 410
1Sa 2:27 there came a man of **G.** unto Eli, ... 430
1Sa 2:30 Wherefore the Lord **G.** of Israel 430
1Sa 2:32 the wealth which **G.** shall give Israel: .....
1Sa 3:3 And ere the lamp of **G.** went out in 430
1Sa 3:3 Lord, where the ark of **G.** was, and 430
1Sa 3:17 **G.** do so to thee, and more also, ... 430
1Sa 4:4 with the ark of the covenant of **G.**. 430
1Sa 4:7 they said, **G.** is come into the camp. 430
1Sa 4:11 And the ark of **G.** was taken; and 430
1Sa 4:13 his heart trembled for the ark of **G.**. 430
1Sa 4:17 are dead, and the ark of **G.** is taken 430
1Sa 4:18 he made mention of the ark of **G.**, ... 430
1Sa 4:19 that the ark of **G.** was taken, and 430
1Sa 4:21 because the ark of **G.** was taken, ... 430
1Sa 4:22 for the ark of **G.** is taken. 430
1Sa 5:1,2 the Philistines took the ark of **G.**, ... 430
1Sa 5:7 The ark of the **G.** of Israel shall not 430
1Sa 5:7 upon us, and upon Dagon our **g.** 430
1Sa 5:8 with the ark of the **G.** of Israel? 430
1Sa 5:8 Let the ark of the **G.** of Israel be 430
1Sa 5:8 carried the ark of the **G.** of Israel 430
1Sa 5:10 they sent the ark of **G.** to Ekron. 430
1Sa 5:10 as the ark of **G.** came to Ekron, ... 430
1Sa 5:10 brought about the ark of the **G.** of 430
1Sa 5:11 Send away the ark of the **G.** of Israel, .. 430
1Sa 5:11 hand of **G.** was very heavy there 430
1Sa 6:3 send away the ark of the **G.** of Israel, .. 430
1Sa 6:5 give glory unto the **G.** of Israel: 430
1Sa 6:20 to stand before this holy Lord **G.**? 430
1Sa 7:8 to cry unto the Lord our **G.** for us, ... 430
1Sa 9:6 now, there is in this city a man of **G.**, .. 430
1Sa 9:7 present to bring to the man of **G.**: 430
1Sa 9:8 that will I give to the man of **G.**, ... 430
1Sa 9:9 when a man went to inquire of **G.**, ... 430
1Sa 9:10 the city where the man of **G.** was 430
1Sa 9:27 I may shew thee the word of **G.**. 430
1Sa 10:3 meet thee three men going up to **G.** 430
1Sa 10:5 thou shalt come to the hill of **G.**, ... 430
1Sa 10:7 serve thee, for **G.** is with thee 430
1Sa 10:9 **G.** gave him another heart: and all 430
1Sa 10:10 and the Spirit of **G.** came upon him, ... 430
1Sa 10:18 Thus saith the Lord **G.** of Israel, ... 430
1Sa 10:19 ye have this day rejected your **G.**, ... 430
1Sa 10:24 and said, **G.** save the king. .....
1Sa 10:26 men, whose hearts **G.** had touched. 430
1Sa 11:6 And the Spirit of **G.** came upon Saul 430

Book	Ref.	Context	No.
1Sa	12:9	when they forgat the Lord their **G.**,	430
1Sa	12:12	the Lord your **G.** was your king.	430
1Sa	12:14	continue following the Lord your **G.**:	430
1Sa	12:19	thy servants unto the Lord thy **G.**,	430
1Sa	12:23	**G.** forbid that I should sin against	
1Sa	13:13	commandment of the Lord thy **G.**,	430
1Sa	14:18	Bring hither the ark of **G.**.	430
1Sa	14:18	For the ark of **G.** was at that time	430
1Sa	14:36	Let us draw near hither unto **G.**.	430
1Sa	14:37	And Saul asked counsel of **G.**,	430
1Sa	14:41	Saul said unto the Lord **G.** of Israel,	430
1Sa	14:44	**G.** do so and more also: for thou	430
1Sa	14:45	**G.** forbid: as the Lord liveth,	
1Sa	14:45	he hath wrought with **G.** this day	430
1Sa	15:15	sacrifice unto the Lord thy **G.**;	430
1Sa	15:21	sacrifice unto the Lord thy **G.** in	430
1Sa	15:30	that I may worship the Lord thy **G.**.	430
1Sa	16:15	evil spirit from **G.** troubleth thee.	430
1Sa	16:16	when the evil spirit from **G.** is upon	430
1Sa	16:23	evil spirit from **G.** was upon Saul,	430
1Sa	17:26	defy the armies of the living **G.**?	430
1Sa	17:36	defied the armies of the living **G.**.	430
1Sa	17:45	the **G.** of the armies of Israel, whom	430
1Sa	17:46	know that there is a **G.** in Israel	430
1Sa	18:10	evil spirit from **G.** came upon Saul,	430
1Sa	19:20	Spirit of **G.** was upon the messengers	430
1Sa	19:23	the Spirit of **G.** was upon him also,	430
1Sa	20:2	he said unto him, **G.** forbid; thou	
1Sa	20:12	O Lord **G.** of Israel, when I have	430
1Sa	22:3	till I know what **G.** will do for me.	430
1Sa	22:13	and hast enquired of **G.** for him,	430
1Sa	22:15	then begin to enquire of **G.** for him?	430
1Sa	23:7	**G.** hath delivered him into mine	430
1Sa	23:10	Then said David, O Lord **G.** of Israel,	430
1Sa	23:11	O Lord **G.** of Israel, I beseech thee,	430
1Sa	23:14	**G.** delivered him not into his hand.	430
1Sa	23:16	and strengthened his hand in **G.**.	430
1Sa	25:22	do **G.** unto the enemies of David,	430
1Sa	25:29	bundle of life with the Lord thy **G.**;	430
1Sa	25:32	Blessed be the Lord **G.** of Israel,	430
1Sa	25:34	Lord **G.** of Israel liveth, which hath	430
1Sa	26:8	**G.** hath delivered thine enemy into	430
1Sa	28:15	and **G.** is departed from me, and	430
1Sa	29:9	good in my sight, as an angel of **G.**:	430
1Sa	30:6	himself in the Lord his **G.**.	430
1Sa	30:15	Swear unto me by **G.**, that thou wilt	430
2Sa	2:27	Joab said, As **G.** liveth, unless thou	430
2Sa	3:9	So do **G.** to Abner, and more also,	430
2Sa	3:35	So do **G.** to me, and more also,	430
2Sa	5:10	the Lord **G.** of hosts was with him	430
2Sa	6:2	bring up from thence the ark of **G.**,	430
2Sa	6:3	set the ark of **G.** upon a new cart	430
2Sa	6:4	accompanying the ark of **G.**: and	430
2Sa	6:6	put forth his hand to the ark of **G.**,	430
2Sa	6:7	**G.** smote him there for his error;	430
2Sa	6:7	and there he died by the ark of **G.**,	430
2Sa	6:12	unto him, because of the ark of **G.**	430
2Sa	6:12	went and brought up the ark of **G.**	430
2Sa	7:2	ark of **G.** dwelleth within curtains.	430
2Sa	7:18	he said, Who am I, O Lord **G.**?	3069
2Sa	7:19	thing in thy sight, O Lord **G.**;	3069
2Sa	7:19	the manner of man, O Lord **G.**?	3069
2Sa	7:20	Lord **G.**, knowest thy servant.	3069
2Sa	7:22	thou art great, O Lord **G.**: for there	430
2Sa	7:22	neither is there any **G.** beside thee,	430
2Sa	7:23	**G.** went to redeem for a people to	430
2Sa	7:24	and thou, Lord, art become their **G.**	430
2Sa	7:25	Lord **G.**, the word that thou hast	430
2Sa	7:26	Lord of hosts is the **G.** over Israel:	430
2Sa	7:27	thou, O Lord of hosts, **G.** of Israel,	430
2Sa	7:28	And now O Lord **G.**, thou art	3069
2Sa	7:28	thou art that **G.**, and thou hast	430
2Sa	7:29	thou, O Lord **G.**, hast spoken it:	3069
2Sa	9:3	shew the kindness of **G.** unto him?	430
2Sa	10:12	people, and for the cities of our **G.**	430
2Sa	12:7	Thus saith the Lord **G.** of Israel,	430
2Sa	12:16	David therefore besought **G.** for the	430
2Sa	12:22	whether **G.** will be gracious to	3068
2Sa	14:11	king remember the Lord thy **G.**,	430
2Sa	14:13	a thing against the people of **G.**?	430
2Sa	14:14	neither doth **G.** respect any person:	430
2Sa	14:16	out of the inheritance of **G.**.	430
2Sa	14:17	for as an angel of **G.**, so is my lord	430
2Sa	14:17	therefore the Lord thy **G.** will be	430
2Sa	14:20	to the wisdom of an angel of **G.**,	430
2Sa	15:24	the ark of the covenant of **G.**;	430
2Sa	15:24	and they set down the ark of **G.**;	430
2Sa	15:25	back the ark of **G.** into the city:	430
2Sa	15:29	carried the ark of **G.** again to	430
2Sa	15:32	the mount, where he worshipped **G.**,	430
2Sa	16:16	**G.** save the king, **G.** save the	
2Sa	16:23	had enquired at the oracle of **G.**:	430
2Sa	18:28	Blessed be the Lord thy **G.**,	430
2Sa	18:33	would **G.** I...died for thee, O Absalom,	
2Sa	19:13	**G.** do so to me, and more also, if	430
2Sa	19:27	my lord the king is as an angel of **G.**:	430
2Sa	21:14	that **G.** was intreated for the land.	430
2Sa	22:3	**G.** of my rock; in him will I trust:	430
2Sa	22:7	and cried to my **G.**: and he did hear	430
2Sa	22:22	not wickedly departed from my **G.**.	430
2Sa	22:30	by my **G.** have I leaped over a wall	430
2Sa	22:31	As for **G.**, his way is perfect;	410
2Sa	22:32	For who is **G.**, save the Lord?	410
2Sa	22:32	and who is a rock, save our **G.**?	430
2Sa	22:33	**G.** is my strength and power:	410
2Sa	22:47	the **G.** of the rock of my salvation.	430
2Sa	22:48	It is **G.** that avengeth me, and	410
2Sa	23:1	the anointed of the **G.** of Jacob,	430
2Sa	23:3	The **G.** of Israel said, the Rock of	430
2Sa	23:3	must be just, ruling in the fear of **G.**.	430
2Sa	23:5	my house be not so with **G.**; yet	410
2Sa	24:3	Now the Lord thy **G.** add unto the	430
2Sa	24:23	The Lord thy **G.** accept thee.	430
2Sa	24:24	burnt offerings unto the Lord my **G.**	430
1Ki	1:17	thou swarest by the Lord thy **G.**	430
1Ki	1:25	and say, **G.** save king Adonijah.	
1Ki	1:30	unto thee by the Lord **G.** of Israel,	430
1Ki	1:34	and say, **G.** save king Solomon.	
1Ki	1:36	the Lord **G.** of my lord the king	430
1Ki	1:39	said, **G.** save king Solomon.	
1Ki	1:47	**G.** make the name of Solomon	430
1Ki	1:48	Blessed be the Lord **G.** of Israel,	430
1Ki	2:3	keep the charge of the Lord thy **G.**,	430
1Ki	2:23	**G.** do so to me, and more also, if	430
1Ki	2:26	thou barest the ark of the Lord **G.**	3069
1Ki	3:5	**G.** said, Ask what I shall give thee.	430
1Ki	3:7	O Lord my **G.**, thou hast made thy	430
1Ki	3:11	And **G.** said unto him, Because thou	430
1Ki	3:28	that the wisdom of **G.** was in him,	430
1Ki	4:29	And **G.** gave Solomon wisdom and	430
1Ki	5:3	unto the name of the Lord his **G.**	430
1Ki	5:4	But now the Lord my **G.** hath given	430
1Ki	5:5	unto the name of the Lord my **G.**,	430
1Ki	8:15	Blessed be the Lord **G.** of Israel,	430
1Ki	8:17	the name of the Lord **G.** of Israel.	430
1Ki	8:20	the name of the Lord **G.** of Israel	430
1Ki	8:23	And he said, Lord **G.** of Israel.	430
1Ki	8:23	there is no **G.** like thee, in heaven	430
1Ki	8:25	now, Lord **G.** of Israel, keep with thy	430
1Ki	8:26	And now, O **G.** of Israel, let thy word,	430
1Ki	8:27	will **G.** indeed dwell on the earth?	430
1Ki	8:28	to his supplication, O Lord my **G.**,	430
1Ki	8:53	fathers out of Egypt, O Lord **G.**.	3069
1Ki	8:57	The Lord our **G.** be with us,	430
1Ki	8:59	be nigh unto the Lord our **G.** by day	430
1Ki	8:60	earth may know that the Lord is **G.**.	430
1Ki	8:61	be perfect with the Lord our **G.**, to	430
1Ki	8:65	before the Lord our **G.**, seven days	430
1Ki	9:9	they forsook the Lord their **G.**, who	430
1Ki	10:9	Blessed be the Lord thy **G.**, which	430
1Ki	10:24	which **G.** had put in his heart.	430
1Ki	11:4	was not perfect with the Lord his **G.**,	430
1Ki	11:9	turned from the Lord **G.** of Israel,	430
1Ki	11:23	**G.** stirred him up another adversary,	430
1Ki	11:31	thus saith the Lord, the **G.** of Israel,	430
1Ki	11:33	Chemosh the **g.** of the Moabites,	430
1Ki	11:33	and Milcom the **g.** of the children	430
1Ki	12:22	But the word of **G.** came unto	430
1Ki	12:22	unto Shemaiah the man of **G.**,	430
1Ki	13:1	there came a man of **G.** out of Judah	430
1Ki	13:4	heard the saying of the man of **G.**,	430
1Ki	13:5	which the man of **G.** had given by	430
1Ki	13:6	and said unto the man of **G.**, Intreat	430
1Ki	13:6	now the face of the Lord thy **G.**,	430
1Ki	13:6	the man of **G.** besought the Lord,	430
1Ki	13:7	the king said unto the man of **G.**,	430
1Ki	13:8	the man of **G.** said unto the king,	430
1Ki	13:11	works that the man of **G.** had done	430
1Ki	13:12	seen what way the man of **G.** went,	430
1Ki	13:14	And went after the man of **G.**,	430
1Ki	13:14	man of **G.** that camest from Judah?	430
1Ki	13:21	And he cried unto the man of **G.**	430
1Ki	13:21	which the Lord thy **G.** commanded	430
1Ki	13:26	he said, It is the man of **G.**, who	430
1Ki	13:29	up the carcase of the man of **G.**,	430
1Ki	13:31	wherein the man of **G.** is buried;	430
1Ki	14:7	Thus saith the Lord **G.** of Israel,	430
1Ki	14:13	the Lord **G.** of Israel in the house	430
1Ki	15:3	not perfect with the Lord his **G.**,	430
1Ki	15:4	for David's sake did the Lord his **G.**	430
1Ki	15:30	he provoked the Lord **G.** of Israel	430
1Ki	16:13	in provoking the Lord **G.** of Israel	430
1Ki	16:26,	33 to provoke the Lord **G.** of Israel	430
1Ki	17:1	As the Lord **G.** of Israel liveth,	430
1Ki	17:12	she said, As the Lord thy **G.** liveth,	430
1Ki	17:14	thus saith the Lord **G.** of Israel,	430
1Ki	17:18	to do with thee, O thou man of **G.**?	430
1Ki	17:20	the Lord, and said, O Lord my **G.**,	430
1Ki	17:21	said, O Lord my **G.**, I pray thee,	430
1Ki	17:24	I know that thou art a man of **G.**,	430
1Ki	18:10	the Lord thy **G.** liveth, there is no	430
1Ki	18:21	If the Lord be **G.**, follow him: but	430
1Ki	18:24	and the **G.** that answereth by fire,	430
1Ki	18:24	answereth by fire, let him be **G.**	430
1Ki	18:27	and said, Cry aloud: for he is a **g.**;	430
1Ki	18:36	Lord **G.** of Abraham, Isaac, and of	430
1Ki	18:36	be known this day that thou art **G.**	430
1Ki	18:37	know that thou art the Lord **G.**,	430
1Ki	18:39	they said, The Lord, he is the **G.**;	430
1Ki	18:39	the Lord, he is the **G.**.	430
1Ki	19:8	nights unto Horeb the mount of **G.**.	430
1Ki	19:10,	14 jealous for the Lord **G.** of hosts:	430
1Ki	20:28	there came a man of **G.**, and spake	430
1Ki	20:28	said, The Lord is **G.** of the hills,	430
1Ki	20:28	but he is not **G.** of the valleys,	430
1Ki	21:10	didst blaspheme **G.** and the king.	430
1Ki	21:13	did blaspheme **G.** and the king,	430
1Ki	22:53	provoked to anger the Lord **G.** of	430
2Ki	1:2	of Baal-zebub the **g.** of Ekron	430
2Ki	1:3	is not a **G.** in Israel, that ye go to	430
2Ki	1:3	of Baal-zebub the **g.** of Ekron?	430
2Ki	1:6	not a **G.** in Israel, that thou sendest	430
2Ki	1:6	to enquire of Baal-zebub the **g.** of	430
2Ki	1:9	he spake unto him, Thou man of **G.**,	430
2Ki	1:10	If I be a man of **G.**, then let the fire	430
2Ki	1:11	and said unto him, O man of **G.**,	430
2Ki	1:12	If I be a man of **G.**, let fire come	430
2Ki	1:12	fire of **G.** came down from heaven,	430
2Ki	1:13	and said unto him, O man of **G.**,	430
2Ki	1:16	of Baal-zebub the **g.** of Ekron, is it	430
2Ki	1:16	not because there is no **G.** in Israel	430
2Ki	2:14	Where is the Lord **G.** of Elijah?	430
2Ki	4:7	she came and told the man of **G.**.	430
2Ki	4:9	that this is an holy man of **G.**, which	430
2Ki	4:16	Nay, my lord, thou man of **G.**, do not	430
2Ki	4:21	laid him on the bed of the man of **G.**	430
2Ki	4:22	that I may run to the man of **G.**,	430
2Ki	4:25	unto the man of **G.** to mount Carmel.	430
2Ki	4:25	when the man of **G.** saw her afar off,	430
2Ki	4:27	when she came to the man of **G.**	430
2Ki	4:27	the man of **G.** said, Let her alone;	430
2Ki	4:40	O thou man of **G.**, there is death	430
2Ki	4:42	and brought the man of **G.** bread	430
2Ki	5:3	Would **G.** my lord were with the	
2Ki	5:7	Am I **G.**, to kill and to make alive,	430
2Ki	5:8	Elisha the man of **G.** had heard	430
2Ki	5:11	call on the name of the Lord his **G.**	430
2Ki	5:14	to the saying of the man of **G.**:	430
2Ki	5:15	And he returned to the man of **G.**,	430
2Ki	5:15	now I know that there is no **G.** in	430
2Ki	5:20	the servant of Elisha the man of **G.**,	430
2Ki	6:6	the man of **G.** said, Where fell it?	430
2Ki	6:9	the man of **G.** sent unto the king	430
2Ki	6:10	place which the man of **G.** told him	430
2Ki	6:15	servant of the man of **G.** was risen	430
2Ki	6:31	**G.** do so and more also to me, if	430
2Ki	7:2	answered the man of **G.**, and said,	430
2Ki	7:17	he died, as the man of **G.** had said,	430
2Ki	7:18	as the man of **G.** had spoken to	430
2Ki	7:19	answered the man of **G.**, and said.	430
2Ki	8:2	after the saying of the man of **G.**	430
2Ki	8:4	servant of the man of **G.**, saying	430
2Ki	8:7	The man of **G.** is come hither.	430
2Ki	8:8	meet the man of **G.**, and enquire	430
2Ki	8:11	and the man of **G.** wept.	430
2Ki	9:6	Thus saith the Lord **G.** of Israel,	430
2Ki	10:31	in the law of the Lord **G.** of Israel	430
2Ki	11:12	hands, and said, **G.** save the king.	
2Ki	13:19	the man of **G.** was wroth with him,	430
2Ki	14:25	to the word of the Lord **G.** of Israel,	430
2Ki	16:2	right in the sight of the Lord his **G.**,	430

2Ki 17:7 sinned against the Lord their **G.**,... 430
2Ki 17:9 not right against the Lord their **G.**,... 430
2Ki 17:14 did not believe in the Lord their **G.**... 430
2Ki 17:16 left all the...of the Lord their **G.**,... 430
2Ki 17:19 kept not the...of the Lord their **G.**,... 430
2Ki 17:26 not the manner of the **G.** of the land:... 430
2Ki 17:26 not the manner of the **G.** of the land... 430
2Ki 17:27 the manner of the **G.** of the land... 430
2Ki 17:39 But the Lord your **G.** ye shall fear;... 430
2Ki 18:5 He trusted in the Lord **G.** of Israel;... 430
2Ki 18:12 not the voice of the Lord their **G.**,... 430
2Ki 18:22 We trust in the Lord our **G.**:... 430
2Ki 19:4 It may be the Lord thy **G.** will hear... 430
2Ki 19:4 hath sent to reproach the living **G.**;... 430
2Ki 19:4 words which the Lord thy **G.** hath... 430
2Ki 19:10 not thy **G.** in whom thou trustest... 430
2Ki 19:15 O Lord **G.** of Israel, which dwellest... 430
2Ki 19:15 thou art the **G.**, even thou alone,... 430
2Ki 19:16 sent him to reproach the living **G.**... 430
2Ki 19:19 Now therefore, O Lord our **G.**,... 430
2Ki 19:19 thou art the Lord **G.**, even thou only... 430
2Ki 19:20 Thus saith the Lord **G.** of Israel,... 430
2Ki 19:37 in the house or Nisroch his **g.**,... 430
2Ki 20:5 Lord, the **G.** of David thy father,... 430
2Ki 21:12 thus saith the Lord **G.** of Israel,... 430
2Ki 21:22 forsook the Lord **G.** of his fathers,... 430
2Ki 22:15 unto them, Thus saith the Lord **G.**... 430
2Ki 22:18 say to him, Thus saith the Lord **G.**... 430
2Ki 23:16 which the man of **G.** proclaimed,... 430
2Ki 23:17 It is the sepulchre of the man of **G.**,... 430
2Ki 23:21 the passover unto the Lord your **G.**,... 430
1Ch 4:10 Jabez called on the **G.** of Israel,... 430
1Ch 4:10 And **G.** granted him that which he... 430
1Ch 5:20 for they cried to **G.** in the battle,... 430
1Ch 5:22 slain, because the war was of **G.**... 430
1Ch 5:25 against the **G.** of their fathers, and... 430
1Ch 5:25 whom **G.** destroyed before them... 430
1Ch 5:26 the **G.** of Israel stirred up the spirit... 430
1Ch 6:48 the tabernacle of the house of **G.**... 430
1Ch 6:49 the servant of **G.** had commanded... 430
1Ch 9:11 the ruler of the house of **G.**;... 430
1Ch 9:13 of the service of the house of **G.**... 430
1Ch 9:26 and treasuries of the house of **G.**... 430
1Ch 9:27 lodged round about the house of **G.**,... 430
1Ch 11:2 and the Lord thy **G.** said unto thee,... 430
1Ch 11:19 My **G.** forbid it me, that I should... 430
1Ch 12:17 the **G.** of our fathers look thereon,... 430
1Ch 12:18 helpers; for thy **G.** helpeth thee... 430
1Ch 12:22 was a great host, like the host of **G.**... 430
1Ch 13:2 and that it be of the Lord our **G.**,... 430
1Ch 13:3 let us bring again the ark of our **G.**... 430
1Ch 13:5 the ark of **G.** from Kirjath-jearim... 430
1Ch 13:6 up thence the ark of **G.** the Lord,... 430
1Ch 13:7 they carried the ark of **G.** in a new... 430
1Ch 13:8 all Israel played before **G.** with... 430
1Ch 13:10 and there he died before **G.**... 430
1Ch 13:12 David was afraid of **G.** that day,... 430
1Ch 13:12 How shall I bring the ark of **G.**... 430
1Ch 13:14 ark of **G.** remained with the family... 430
1Ch 14:10 And David enquired of **G.**, saying,... 430
1Ch 14:11 said, **G.** hath broken in upon mine... 430
1Ch 14:14 David enquired again of **G.**; and **G.**... 430
1Ch 14:15 for **G.** is gone forth before thee to... 430
1Ch 14:16 therefore did as **G.** commanded... 430
1Ch 15:1 prepared a place for the ark of **G.**,... 430
1Ch 15:2 None ought to carry the ark of **G.**... 430
1Ch 15:2 Lord chosen to carry the ark of **G.**,... 430
1Ch 15:12 up the ark of the Lord **G.** of Israel... 430
1Ch 15:13 Lord our **G.** made a breach upon us,... 430
1Ch 15:14 up the ark of the Lord **G.** of Israel... 430
1Ch 15:15 the Levites bare the ark of **G.** upon... 430
1Ch 15:24 the trumpets before the ark of **G.**:... 430
1Ch 15:26 when **G.** helped the Levites that... 430
1Ch 16:1 So they brought the ark of **G.**,... 430
1Ch 16:1 and peace offerings before **G.**... 430
1Ch 16:4 and praise the Lord **G.** of Israel:... 430
1Ch 16:6 before the ark of the covenant of **G.**... 430
1Ch 16:14 is the Lord our **G.**; his judgments... 430
1Ch 16:35 Save us, O **G.** of our salvation,... 430
1Ch 16:36 Blessed be the Lord **G.** of Israel... 430
1Ch 16:42 and with musical instruments of **G.**... 430
1Ch 17:2 thine heart; for **G.** is with thee... 430
1Ch 17:3 that the word of **G.** came to Nathan,... 430
1Ch 17:16 Who am I, O Lord **G.**, and what is... 430
1Ch 17:17 a small thing in thine eyes, O **G.**;... 430
1Ch 17:17 a man of high degree, O Lord **G.**... 430
1Ch 17:20 neither is there any **G.** beside thee,... 430
1Ch 17:21 whom **G.** went to redeem to be his... 430
1Ch 17:22 and thou, Lord, becamest their **G.**... 430
1Ch 17:24 The Lord of hosts is the **G.** of Israel,... 430
1Ch 17:24 even a **G.** to Israel: and let the... 430
1Ch 17:25 For thou, O my **G.**, hast told thy... 430
1Ch 17:26 And now, Lord, thou art **G.**,... 430
1Ch 19:13 people, and for the cities of our **G.**:... 430
1Ch 21:7 **G.** was displeased with this thing;... 430
1Ch 21:8 David said unto **G.**, I have sinned... 430
1Ch 21:15 **G.** sent an angel unto Jerusalem to... 430
1Ch 21:17 And David said unto **G.**, Is it not I... 430
1Ch 21:17 O Lord my **G.**, be on me, and on my... 430
1Ch 21:30 not go before it to enquire of **G.**:... 430
1Ch 22:1 This is the house of the Lord **G.**,... 430
1Ch 22:2 stones to build the house of **G.**... 430
1Ch 22:6 an house for the Lord **G.** of Israel... 430
1Ch 22:7 unto the name of the Lord my **G.**:... 430
1Ch 22:11 build the house of the Lord thy **G.**,... 430
1Ch 22:12 keep the law of the Lord thy **G.**... 430
1Ch 22:18 Is not the Lord your **G.** with you?... 430
1Ch 22:19 your soul to seek the Lord your **G.**;... 430
1Ch 22:19 ye the sanctuary of the Lord **G.**,... 430
1Ch 22:19 holy vessels of **G.**, into the house... 430
1Ch 23:14 concerning Moses the man of **G.**,... 430
1Ch 23:25 The Lord **G.** of Israel hath given... 430
1Ch 23:28 of the service of the house of **G.**;... 430
1Ch 24:5 and governors of the house of **G.**,... 430
1Ch 24:19 Lord **G.** of Israel had commanded... 430
1Ch 25:5 the king's seer in the words of **G.**,... 430
1Ch 25:5 **G.** gave to Heman fourteen sons... 430
1Ch 25:6 for the service of the house of **G.**,... 430
1Ch 26:5 the eighth; for **G.** blessed him... 430
1Ch 26:20 over the treasures of the house of **G.**,... 430
1Ch 26:32 for every matter pertaining to **G.**... 430
1Ch 28:2 and for the footstool of our **G.**,... 430
1Ch 28:3 But **G.** said unto me, Thou shalt... 430
1Ch 28:4 Howbeit the Lord **G.** of Israel chose... 430
1Ch 28:8 and in the audience of our **G.**, keep... 430
1Ch 28:8 commandments of the Lord your **G.**:... 430
1Ch 28:9 know thou the **G.** of thy father,... 430
1Ch 28:12 of the treasuries of the house of **G.**,... 430
1Ch 28:20 nor be dismayed: for the Lord **G.**,... 430
1Ch 28:20 even my **G.**, will be with thee;... 430
1Ch 28:21 for all the service of the house of **G.**:... 430
1Ch 29:1 my son, whom alone **G.** hath chosen,... 430
1Ch 29:1 not for man, but for the Lord **G.**... 430
1Ch 29:2 all my might for the house of my **G.**... 430
1Ch 29:3 my affection to the house of my **G.**,... 430
1Ch 29:3 I have given to the house of my **G.**,... 430
1Ch 29:7 for the service of the house of **G.**... 430
1Ch 29:10 Blessed be thou, Lord **G.** of Israel... 430
1Ch 29:13 Now therefore, our **G.**, we thank... 430
1Ch 29:16 O Lord our **G.**, all this store that... 430
1Ch 29:17 I know also, my **G.**, that thou triest... 430
1Ch 29:18 O Lord **G.** of Abraham, Isaac, and... 430
1Ch 29:20 Now bless the Lord your **G.**. And... 430
1Ch 29:20 blessed the Lord **G.** of their fathers,... 430
2Ch 1:1 and the Lord his **G.** was with him,... 430
2Ch 1:3 tabernacle of the congregation of **G.**,... 430
2Ch 1:4 the ark of **G.** had David brought... 430
2Ch 1:7 In that night did **G.** appear unto... 430
2Ch 1:8 Solomon said unto **G.**, Thou hast... 430
2Ch 1:9 Lord **G.**, let thy promise unto David... 430
2Ch 1:11 **G.** said to Solomon, Because this... 430
2Ch 2:4 to the name of the Lord my **G.**,... 430
2Ch 2:4 solemn feasts of the Lord our **G.**... 430
2Ch 2:5 for great is our **G.** above all gods... 430
2Ch 2:12 Blessed be the Lord **G.** of Israel,... 430
2Ch 3:3 for the building of the house of **G.**... 430
2Ch 4:11 king Solomon for the house of **G.**;... 430
2Ch 4:19 vessels that were for the house of **G.**,... 430
2Ch 5:1 the treasures of the house of **G.**... 430
2Ch 5:14 the Lord had filled the house of **G.**... 430
2Ch 6:4 Blessed be the Lord **G.** of Israel,... 430
2Ch 6:7, 10 name of the Lord **G.** of Israel... 430
2Ch 6:14 **G.** of Israel, there is no **G.** like thee... 430
2Ch 6:16 Now therefore, O Lord **G.** of Israel,... 430
2Ch 6:17 Now then, O Lord **G.** of Israel,... 430
2Ch 6:18 But will **G.** in very deed dwell with... 430
2Ch 6:19 to his supplication, O Lord my **G.**,... 430
2Ch 6:40 Now, my **G.**, let, I beseech thee,... 430
2Ch 6:41 Now therefore arise, O Lord **G.**,... 430
2Ch 6:41 thy priests, O Lord **G.**, be clothed... 430
2Ch 6:42 O Lord **G.**, turn not away the face... 430
2Ch 7:5 people dedicated the house of **G.**... 430
2Ch 7:22 Because they forsook the Lord **G.**... 430
2Ch 8:14 David the man of **G.** commanded... 430
2Ch 9:8 Blessed be the Lord thy **G.**, which... 430
2Ch 9:8 Lord thy **G.**: because thy **G.** loved... 430
2Ch 9:23 wisdom, that **G.** had put in his heart... 430
2Ch 10:15 for the cause was of **G.**, that the... 430
2Ch 11:2 to Shemaiah the man of **G.**, saying... 430
2Ch 11:16 hearts to seek the Lord **G.** of Israel... 430
2Ch 11:16 unto the Lord **G.** of their fathers... 430
2Ch 13:5 to know that the Lord **G.** of Israel... 430
2Ch 13:10 But as for us, the Lord is our **G.**,... 430
2Ch 13:11 keep the charge of the Lord our **G.**;... 430
2Ch 13:12 **G.** himself is with us for our captain,... 430
2Ch 13:12 fight ye not against the Lord **G.** of... 430
2Ch 13:15 to pass, that **G.** smote Jeroboam... 430
2Ch 13:16 **G.** delivered them into their hand... 430
2Ch 13:18 they relied upon the Lord **G.** of... 430
2Ch 14:2 right in the eyes of the Lord his **G.**... 430
2Ch 14:4 to seek the Lord **G.** of their fathers,... 430
2Ch 14:7 we have sought the Lord our **G.**... 430
2Ch 14:11 And Asa cried unto the Lord his **G.**,... 430
2Ch 14:11 help us, O Lord our **G.**; for we rest... 430
2Ch 14:11 O Lord, thou art our **G.**; let not... 430
2Ch 15:1 the Spirit of **G.** came upon Azariah... 430
2Ch 15:3 Israel hath been without the true **G.**,... 430
2Ch 15:4 did turn unto the Lord **G.** of Israel,... 430
2Ch 15:6 **G.** did vex them with all adversity... 430
2Ch 15:9 that the Lord his **G.** was with him... 430
2Ch 15:12 a covenant to seek the Lord **G.** of... 430
2Ch 15:13 would not seek the Lord **G.** of Israel... 430
2Ch 15:18 And he brought into the house of **G.**... 430
2Ch 16:7 and not relied on the Lord thy **G.**... 430
2Ch 17:4 sought to the Lord **G.** of his father,... 430
2Ch 18:5 for **G.** will deliver it into the king's... 430
2Ch 18:13 even what my **G.** saith, that will I... 430
2Ch 18:31 **G.** moved them to depart from him... 430
2Ch 19:3 hast prepared thine heart to seek **G.**... 430
2Ch 19:4 unto the Lord **G.** of their fathers... 430
2Ch 19:7 is no iniquity with the Lord our **G.**,... 430
2Ch 20:6 And said, O Lord **G.** of our fathers,... 430
2Ch 20:6 art not thou **G.** in heaven?... 430
2Ch 20:7 Art not thou our **G.**, who didst drive... 430
2Ch 20:12 O our **G.**, wilt thou not judge them?... 430
2Ch 20:19 to praise the Lord **G.** of Israel with... 430
2Ch 20:20 Believe in the Lord your **G.**, so shall... 430
2Ch 20:29 fear of **G.** was on all the kingdoms... 430
2Ch 20:30 his **G.** gave him rest round about... 430
2Ch 20:33 hearts unto the **G.** of their fathers... 430
2Ch 21:10 forsaken the Lord **G.** of his fathers... 430
2Ch 21:12 Thus saith the Lord **G.** of David thy... 430
2Ch 22:7 destruction of Ahaziah was of **G.** by... 430
2Ch 22:12 was hid in the house of **G.** six years:... 430
2Ch 23:3 with the king in the house of **G.**... 430
2Ch 23:9 which were in the house of **G.**... 430
2Ch 23:11 him, and said, **G.** save the king...
2Ch 24:5 repair the house of your **G.** from... 430
2Ch 24:7 had broken up the house of **G.**;... 430
2Ch 24:9 Moses the servant of **G.** laid upon... 430
2Ch 24:13 they set the house of **G.** in his state,... 430
2Ch 24:16 toward **G.**, and toward his house... 430
2Ch 24:18 house of the Lord **G.** of their fathers,... 430
2Ch 24:20 Spirit of **G.** came upon Zechariah... 430
2Ch 24:20 Thus saith **G.**, Why transgress ye... 430
2Ch 24:24 had forsaken the Lord **G.** of their... 430
2Ch 24:27 and the repairing of the house of **G.**,... 430
2Ch 25:7 But there came a man of **G.** to him... 430
2Ch 25:8 **G.** shall make thee fall before the... 430
2Ch 25:8 for **G.** hath power to help, and to... 430
2Ch 25:9 And Amaziah said to the man of **G.**,... 430
2Ch 25:9 the man of **G.** answered, The Lord... 430
2Ch 25:16 I know that **G.** hath determined to... 430
2Ch 25:20 would not hear; for it came of **G.**,... 430
2Ch 25:24 the house of **G.** with Obed-edom,... 430
2Ch 26:5 sought **G.** in the days of Zechariah,... 430
2Ch 26:5 understanding in the visions of **G.**... 430
2Ch 26:5 the Lord, **G.** made him to prosper... 430
2Ch 26:7 And **G.** helped him against the... 430
2Ch 26:16 against the Lord his **G.**, and went... 430
2Ch 26:18 for thine honour from the Lord **G.**... 430
2Ch 27:6 his ways before the Lord his **G.**... 430
2Ch 28:5 the Lord his **G.** delivered him into... 430
2Ch 28:6 had forsaken the Lord **G.** of their... 430
2Ch 28:9 because the Lord **G.** of your fathers... 430
2Ch 28:10 you, sins against the Lord your **G.**?... 430
2Ch 28:24 the vessels of the house of **G.**, and... 430
2Ch 28:24 pieces the vessels of the house of **G.**,... 430
2Ch 28:25 provoked to anger the Lord **G.** of... 430
2Ch 29:5 house of the Lord **G.** of your fathers,... 430
2Ch 29:6 evil in the eyes of the Lord our **G.**,... 430

2Ch 29:7 holy place unto the **G.** of Israel. 430
2Ch 29:10 covenant with the Lord **G.** of Israel, 430
2Ch 29:36 that **G.** had prepared the people: 430
2Ch 30:1 passover unto the Lord **G.** of Israel. 430
2Ch 30:5 passover unto the Lord **G.** of Israel 430
2Ch 30:6 again unto the Lord **G.** of Abraham, 430
2Ch 30:7 against the Lord **G.** of their fathers, 430
2Ch 30:8 serve the Lord your **G.**, that the 430
2Ch 30:9 for the Lord your **G.** is gracious and 430
2Ch 30:12 the hand of **G.** was to give them one 430
2Ch 30:16 to the law of Moses the man of **G.**: 430
2Ch 30:19 That prepareth his heart to seek **G.**, 430
2Ch 30:19 the Lord **G.** of his fathers, though he 430
2Ch 30:22 to the Lord **G.** of their fathers. 430
2Ch 31:6 consecrated unto the Lord their **G.**, 430
2Ch 31:13 Azariah the ruler of the house of **G.**. 430
2Ch 31:14 was over the freewill offerings of **G.**, 430
2Ch 31:20 and truth before the Lord his **G.**. 430
2Ch 31:21 in the sevice of the house of **G.**, 430
2Ch 31:21 the commandments, to seek his **G.**, 430
2Ch 32:8 but with us is the Lord our **G.** to 430
2Ch 32:11 The Lord our **G.** shall deliver us 430
2Ch 32:14 your **G.** should be able to deliver 430
2Ch 32:15 for no **g.** of any nation or kingdom 433
2Ch 32:15 much less shall your **G.** deliver 430
2Ch 32:16 spake yet more against the Lord **G.**, 430
2Ch 32:17 to rail on the Lord **G.** of Israel. 430
2Ch 32:17 so shall not the **G.** of Hezekiah 430
2Ch 32:19 spake against the **G.** of Jerusalem, 430
2Ch 32:21 he was come to the house of his **g.**, 430
2Ch 32:29 for **G.** had given him substance 430
2Ch 32:31 **G.** left him, to try him, that he 430
2Ch 33:7 in the house of **G.**, of which **G.** had 430
2Ch 33:12 he besought the Lord his **G.**, and 430
2Ch 33:12 greatly before the **G.** of his fathers, 430
2Ch 33:13 knew that the Lord he was **G.**. 430
2Ch 33:16 Judah to serve the Lord **G.** of Israel. 430
2Ch 33:17 yet unto the Lord their **G.** only. 430
2Ch 33:18 and his prayer unto his **G.**, and the 430
2Ch 33:18 the name of the Lord **G.** of Israel, 430
2Ch 33:19 and how **G.** was intreated of him,
2Ch 34:3 began to seek after the **G.** of David 430
2Ch 34:8 repair the house of the Lord his **G.** 430
2Ch 34:9 was brought into the house of **G.**, 430
2Ch 34:23 Thus saith the Lord **G.** of Israel, 430
2Ch 34:26 Thus saith the Lord **G.** of Israel 430
2Ch 34:27 thou didst humble thyself before **G.**, 430
2Ch 34:32 according to the covenant of **G.**, 430
2Ch 34:32 the **G.** of their fathers. 430
2Ch 34:33 even to serve the Lord their **G.**. 430
2Ch 34:33 following the Lord, the **G.** of their 430
2Ch 35:3 serve now the Lord your **G.**, and 430
2Ch 35:8 rulers of the house of **G.**, gave unto 430
2Ch 35:21 **G.** commanded me to make haste: 430
2Ch 35:21 forbear thee from meddling with **G.**, 430
2Ch 35:22 words of Necho from the mouth of **G.**, 430
2Ch 36:5 evil in the sight of the Lord his **G.**. 430
2Ch 36:12 evil in the sight of the Lord his **G.**, 430
2Ch 36:13 who had made him swear by **G.**: 430
2Ch 36:13 turning unto the Lord **G.** of Israel. 430
2Ch 36:15 the Lord **G.** of their fathers sent 430
2Ch 36:16 they mocked the messengers of **G.**, 430
2Ch 36:18 all the vessels of the house of **G.**, 430
2Ch 36:19 And they burnt the house of **G.**, 430
2Ch 36:23 hath the Lord **G.** of heaven given me; 430
2Ch 36:23 The Lord his **G.** be with him, 430
Ezr 1:2 The Lord **G.** of heaven hath given 430
Ezr 1:3 his **G.** be with him, and let him go 430
Ezr 1:3 the house of the Lord **G.** of Israel, 430
Ezr 1:3 (he is the **G.**,) which is in 430
Ezr 3:4 freewill offering for the house of **G.** 430
Ezr 3:5 them whose spirit **G.** hath raised, 430
Ezr 2:68 offered freely for the house of **G.** to 430
Ezr 3:2 builded the altar of the **G.** of Israel, 430
Ezr 3:2 in the law of Moses the man of **G.** 430
Ezr 3:8 their coming unto the house of **G.** 430
Ezr 3:9 the workmen in the house of **G.**: 430
Ezr 4:1 temple unto the Lord **G.** of Israel; 430
Ezr 4:2 for we seek your **G.**, as ye do; 430
Ezr 4:3 to build an house unto our **G.**; 430
Ezr 4:3 will build unto the Lord **G.** of Israel, 430
Ezr 4:24 ceased the work of the house of **G.** 426
Ezr 5:1 in the name of the **G.** of Israel, 426
Ezr 5:2 and began to build the house of **G.** 426
Ezr 5:2 with them were the prophets of **G.** 426
Ezr 5:5 But the eye of their **G.** was upon 426
Ezr 5:8 to the house of the great **G.**, which 426
Ezr 5:11 are the servants of the **G.** of heaven 426
Ezr 5:12 had provoked the **G.** of heaven unto 426
Ezr 5:13 a decree to build this house of **G.**. 426
Ezr 5:14 gold and silver of the house of **G.**, 426
Ezr 5:15 and let the house of **G.** be builded 426
Ezr 5:16 the foundation of the house of **G.** 426
Ezr 5:17 build this house of **G.** at Jerusalem, 426
Ezr 6:3 the house of **G.** at Jerusalem, Let 426
Ezr 6:5 and silver vessels of the house of **G.**, 426
Ezr 6:5 and place them in the house of **G.**. 426
Ezr 6:7 the work of this house of **G.** alone; 426
Ezr 6:7 build this house of **G.** in his place, 426
Ezr 6:8 for the building of this house of **G.**: 426
Ezr 6:9 burnt offerings of the **G.** of heaven, 426
Ezr 6:10 savours unto the **G.** of heaven, 426
Ezr 6:12 the **G.** that hath caused his name 426
Ezr 6:12 to destroy this house of **G.** which is 426
Ezr 6:14 commandment of the **G.** of Israel, 426
Ezr 6:16 dedication of this house of **G.** with 426
Ezr 6:17 at the dedication of this house of **G.** 426
Ezr 6:18 for the service of **G.**, which is at 426
Ezr 6:21 to seek the Lord **G.** of Israel, did 430
Ezr 6:22 of the house of **G.**, the **G.** of Israel. 430
Ezr 7:6 the Lord **G.** of Israel had given: 430
Ezr 7:6 to the hand of the Lord his **G.** upon 430
Ezr 7:9 according to the good hand of his **G.** 430
Ezr 7:12 of the law of the **G.** of heaven, 426
Ezr 7:14 according to the law of thy **G.** which 426
Ezr 7:15 freely offered unto the **G.** of Israel, 426
Ezr 7:16 willingly for the house of their **G.** 426
Ezr 7:17 the altar of the house of your **G.** 426
Ezr 7:18 that do after the will of your **G.** 426
Ezr 7:19 the service of the house of thy **G.**, 426
Ezr 7:19 those deliver thou before the **G.** of 426
Ezr 7:20 be needful for the house of thy **G.**. 426
Ezr 7:21 scribe of the law of the **G.** of heaven, 426
Ezr 7:23 commanded by the **G.** of heaven, 426
Ezr 7:23 for the house of the **G.** of heaven: 426
Ezr 7:24 or ministers of this house of **G.**, 426
Ezr 7:25 Ezra, after the wisdom of thy **G.**, 426
Ezr 7:25 such as know the laws of thy **G.**; 426
Ezr 7:26 will not do the law of thy **G.**, and 426
Ezr 7:27 Blessed be the Lord **G.** of our 430
Ezr 7:28 as the hand of the Lord my **G.** was 430
Ezr 8:17 ministers for the house of our **G.** 430
Ezr 8:18 And by the good hand of our **G.** upon 430
Ezr 8:21 might afflict ourselves before our **G.**, 430
Ezr 8:22 The hand of our **G.** is upon all them 430
Ezr 8:23 fasted and besought our **G.** for this: 430
Ezr 8:25 the offering of the house of our **G.** 430
Ezr 8:28 unto the Lord **G.** of your fathers. 430
Ezr 8:30 unto the house of our **G.**. 430
Ezr 8:31 and the hand of our **G.** was upon us, 430
Ezr 8:33 weighed in the house of our **G.** by 430
Ezr 8:35 burnt offerings unto the **G.** of 430
Ezr 8:36 the people, and the house of **G.**. 430
Ezr 9:4 at the words of the **G.** of Israel, 430
Ezr 9:5 my hands unto the Lord my **G.**, 430
Ezr 9:6 O my **G.**, I am ashamed and blush 430
Ezr 9:6 to lift up my face to thee, my **G.**: 430
Ezr 9:8 been shewed from the Lord our **G.** 430
Ezr 9:8 that our **G.** may lighten our eyes, 430
Ezr 9:9 yet our **G.** hath not forsaken us 430
Ezr 9:9 to set up the house of our **G.**, and 430
Ezr 9:10 our **G.**, what shall we say after this? 430
Ezr 9:13 seeing that thou our **G.** hast 430
Ezr 9:15 O Lord **G.** of Israel, thou art 430
Ezr 10:1 down before the house of **G.**, there 430
Ezr 10:2 We have trespassed against our **G.**, 430
Ezr 10:3 make a covenant with our **G.** to put 430
Ezr 10:3 at the commandment of our **G.**; 430
Ezr 10:6 before the house of **G.**, and went 430
Ezr 10:9 sat in the street of the house of **G.**, 430
Ezr 10:11 make confession unto the Lord **G.** 430
Ezr 10:14 until the fierce wrath of our **G.** for 430
Ne 1:4 and prayed before the **G.** of heaven, 430
Ne 1:5 I beseech thee, O Lord **G.** of heaven, 430
Ne 1:5 the great and terrible **G.**, that 410
Ne 2:4 So I prayed to the **G.** of heaven. 430
Ne 2:8 to the good hand of my **G.** upon me. 430
Ne 2:12 what my **G.** had put in my heart 430
Ne 2:18 I told them of the hand of my **G.** to 430
Ne 2:20 The **G.** of heaven, he will prosper us; 430
Ne 4:4 Hear, O our **G.**; for we are despised: 430
Ne 4:9 we made our prayer unto our **G.**, 430
Ne 4:15 and **G.** had brought their counsel to 430
Ne 4:20 unto us: our **G.** shall fight for us. 430
Ne 5:9 walk in the fear of our **G.** because 430
Ne 5:13 So **G.** shake out every man from 430
Ne 5:15 did not I, because of the fear of **G.**. 430
Ne 5:19 Think upon me, my **G.**, for good, 430
Ne 6:9 therefore, O **G.**, strengthen my hands.
Ne 6:10 meet together in the house of **G.** 430
Ne 6:12 perceived that **G.** had not sent him; 430
Ne 6:14 My **G.**, think thou upon Tobiah and 430
Ne 6:16 this work was wrought of our **G.**. 430
Ne 7:2 a faithful man, and feared **G.** above 430
Ne 7:5 **G.** put into mine heart to gather 430
Ne 8:6 Ezra blessed the Lord, the great **G.** 430
Ne 8:8 they read in the book in the law of **G.** 430
Ne 8:9 day is holy unto the Lord your **G.**; 430
Ne 8:16 and in the courts of the house of **G.**, 430
Ne 8:18 he read in the book of the law of **G.** 430
Ne 9:3 book of the law of the Lord their **G.** 430
Ne 9:3 and worshipped the Lord their **G.**. 430
Ne 9:4 a loud voice unto the Lord their **G.**. 430
Ne 9:5 and bless the Lord your **G.** for ever 430
Ne 9:7 Thou art the Lord the **G.**, who didst 430
Ne 9:17 but thou art a **G.** ready to pardon, 433
Ne 9:18 This is thy **G.** that brought thee up 430
Ne 9:31 thou art a gracious and merciful **G.**. 410
Ne 9:32 our **G.**, the great, the mighty, and 430
Ne 9:32 terrible **G.**, who keepest covenant 410
Ne 10:28 of the lands unto the law of **G.**, 430
Ne 10:29 given by Moses the servant of **G.**, 430
Ne 10:32 the service of the house of our **G.**; 430
Ne 10:33 all the work of the house of our **G.**. 430
Ne 10:34 bring it into the house of our **G.**, 430
Ne 10:34 upon the altar of the Lord our **G.**, 430
Ne 10:36 to bring to the house of our **G.**, 430
Ne 10:36 that minister in the house of our **G.**: 430
Ne 10:37 chambers of the house of our **G.**; 430
Ne 10:38 the tithes unto the house of our **G.**, 430
Ne 10:39 will not forsake the house of our **G.**. 430
Ne 11:11 was the ruler of the house of **G.**. 430
Ne 11:16 outward business of the house of **G.** 430
Ne 11:22 over the business of the house of **G.** 430
Ne 12:24 of David the man of **G.**, ward 430
Ne 12:36 instruments of David the man of **G.**, 430
Ne 12:40 that gave thanks in the house of **G.**, 430
Ne 12:43 for **G.** had made them rejoice with 430
Ne 12:45 porters kept the ward of their **G.**, 430
Ne 12:46 praise and thanksgiving unto **G.**. 430
Ne 13:1 the congregation of **G.** for ever; 430
Ne 13:2 howbeit our **G.** turned the curse 430
Ne 13:4 the chamber of the house of our **G.**, 430
Ne 13:7 in the courts of the house of **G.**. 430
Ne 13:9 again the vessels of the house of **G.**, 430
Ne 13:11 Why is the house of **G.** forsaken? 430
Ne 13:14 Remember me, O my **G.**, concerning 430
Ne 13:14 I have done for the house of my **G.**. 430
Ne 13:18 did not our **G.** bring all this evil 430
Ne 13:22 Remember me, O my **G.**, concerning 430
Ne 13:25 made them swear by **G.**, saying, 430
Ne 13:26 like him, who was beloved of his **G.**, 430
Ne 13:26 and **G.** made him king over all. 430
Ne 13:27 to transgress against our **G.** in 430
Ne 13:29 Remember them, O my **G.**, because 430
Ne 13:31 Remember me, O my **G.**, for good. 430
Job 1:1 that feared **G.**, and eschewed evil. 430
Job 1:5 and cursed **G.** in their hearts. 430
Job 1:6 when the sons of **G.** came to present 430
Job 1:8 that feareth **G.**, and escheweth evil? 430
Job 1:9 said, Doth Job fear **G.** for nought? 430
Job 1:16 The fire of **G.** is fallen from heaven, 430
Job 1:22 sinned not, nor charged **G.** foolishly. 430
Job 2:1 a day when the sons of **G.** came 430
Job 2:3 upright man, one that feareth **G.**, 430
Job 2:9 retain thine integrity? curse **G.**, 430
Job 2:10 we receive good at the hand of **G.**, 430
Job 3:4 let not **G.** regard it from above, 433
Job 3:23 and whom **G.** hath hedged in? 433
Job 4:9 By the blast of **G.** they perish, 433
Job 4:17 mortal man be more just than **G.**? 433
Job 5:8 I would seek unto **G.**, and unto 410
Job 5:8 and unto **G.** would I commit my 430
Job 5:17 is the man whom **G.** correcteth: 433
Job 6:4 the terrors of **G.** do set themselves 433
Job 6:8 that **G.** would grant me the thing 433
Job 6:9 that it would please **G.** to destroy 433
Job 8:3 Doth **G.** pervert judgment? or doth 410
Job 8:5 thou wouldest seek unto **G.** betimes, 410

Book	Ref.	Context	No.
Job	8:13	are the paths of all that forget **G.**;	410
Job	8:20	**G.** will not cast away a perfect man,	410
Job	9:2	how should man be just with **G.**?	410
Job	9:13	**G.** will not withdraw his anger,	433
Job	10:2	I will say unto **G.**, Do not condemn	433
Job	11:5	But oh that **G.** would speak, and	433
Job	11:6	know therefore that **G.** exacteth of	433
Job	11:7	Canst thou by searching find out **G.**?	433
Job	12:4	who calleth upon **G.**, and he	433
Job	12:6	they that provoke **G.** are secure;	410
Job	12:6	into whose hand **G.** bringeth	433
Job	13:3	and I desire to reason with **G.**	410
Job	13:7	Will ye speak wickedly for **G.**?	410
Job	13:8	will ye contend for **G.**?	410
Job	15:4	and restrainest prayer before **G.**	410
Job	15:8	Hast thou heard the secret of **G.**?	433
Job	15:11	consolations of **G.** small with thee?	410
Job	15:13	thou turnest thy spirit against **G.**,	410
Job	15:25	stretcheth out his hand against **G.**,	410
Job	16:11	**G.** hath delivered me to the ungodly,	410
Job	16:20	eye poureth out tears unto **G.**	433
Job	16:21	one might plead for a man with **G.**,	433
Job	18:21	place of him that knoweth not **G.**	410
Job	19:6	now that **G.** hath overthrown me,	433
Job	19:21	the hand of **G.** hath touched me	433
Job	19:22	Why do ye persecute me as **G.**,	410
Job	19:26	yet in my flesh shall I see **G.**:	433
Job	20:15	**G.** shall cast them out of his belly	410
Job	20:23	**G.** shall cast the fury of his wrath upon	
Job	20:29	portion of a wicked man from **G.**,	430
Job	20:29	heritage appointed unto him by **G.**	410
Job	21:9	neither is the rod of **G.** upon them	433
Job	21:14	Therefore they say unto **G.**,	410
Job	21:17	**G.** distributeth sorrows in his anger	
Job	21:19	**G.** layeth up his iniquity for his	433
Job	21:22	Shall any teach **G.** knowledge?	410
Job	22:2	Can a man be profitable unto **G.**,	410
Job	22:12	Is not **G.** in the height of heaven?	433
Job	22:13	thou sayest, How doth **G.** know?	410
Job	22:17	said unto **G.**, Depart from us:	410
Job	22:26	and shalt lift up thy face unto **G.**	433
Job	23:16	For **G.** maketh my heart soft, and	410
Job	24:12	yet **G.** layeth not folly to them	433
Job	25:4	then can man be justified with **G.**?	410
Job	27:2	As **G.** liveth, who hath taken away	410
Job	27:3	the spirit of **G.** is in my nostrils;	433
Job	27:5	**G.** forbid that I should justify	
Job	27:8	when **G.** taketh away his soul?	433
Job	27:9	Will **G.** hear his cry when trouble	410
Job	27:10	will he always call upon **G.**?	433
Job	27:11	I will teach you by the hand of **G.**:	410
Job	27:13	the portion of a wicked man with **G.**,	410
Job	27:22	For **G.** shall cast upon him, and not	410
Job	28:23	**G.** understandeth the way thereof,	430
Job	29:2	in the days when **G.** preserved me;	433
Job	29:4	when the secret of **G.** was upon my	433
Job	31:2	portion of **G.** is there from above?	433
Job	31:6	that **G.** may know mine integrity	433
Job	31:14	then shall I do when **G.** riseth up?	410
Job	31:23	destruction from **G.** was a terror	410
Job	31:28	have denied the **G.** that is above	410
Job	32:2	he justified himself rather than **G.**	430
Job	32:13	**G.** thrusteth him down, not man,	410
Job	33:4	The Spirit of **G.** hath made me,	410
Job	33:12	thee, that **G.** is greater than man,	433
Job	33:14	For **G.** speaketh once, yea twice,	410
Job	33:26	He shall pray unto **G.**, and he will	433
Job	33:29	worketh **G.** oftentimes with man,	410
Job	34:5	**G.** hath taken away my judgment	410
Job	34:9	he should delight himself with **G.**	430
Job	34:10	far be it from **G.** that he should do	410
Job	34:12	Yea, surely **G.** will not do wickedly,	410
Job	34:23	should enter into judgment with **G.**	410
Job	34:31	Surely it is meet to be said unto **G.**,	410
Job	34:37	multiplieth his words against **G.**	410
Job	35:10	Where is **G.** my maker, who giveth	433
Job	35:13	Surely **G.** will not hear vanity,	410
Job	36:5	**G.** is mighty, and despiseth not any:	410
Job	36:22	Behold, **G.** exalteth by his power:	410
Job	36:26	**G.** is great, and we know him not,	410
Job	37:5	**G.** thundereth marvellously with	410
Job	37:10	By the breath of **G.** frost is given:	410
Job	37:14	consider the wondrous works of **G.**	410
Job	37:15	thou know when **G.** disposed them,	433
Job	37:22	with **G.** is terrible majesty	433
Job	38:7	all the sons of **G.** shouted for joy?	430
Job	38:41	when his young ones cry unto **G.**,	410
Job	39:17	**G.** hath deprived her of wisdom	433
Job	40:2	that reproveth **G.**, let him answer	433
Job	40:9	Hast thou an arm like **G.**? or canst	410
Job	40:19	He is the chief of the ways of **G.**:	410
Ps	3:2	There is not help for him in **G.**	430
Ps	3:7	Arise, O Lord; save me, O my **G.**:	430
Ps	4:1	O **G.** of my righteousness: thou	430
Ps	5:2	my King, and my **G.**: for unto thee	430
Ps	5:4	art not a **G.** that hath pleasure in	410
Ps	5:10	Destroy thou them, O **G.**; let them	430
Ps	7:1	my **G.**, in thee do I put my trust;	430
Ps	7:3	O Lord my **G.**, if I have done this;	430
Ps	7:9	the righteous **G.** trieth the hearts	430
Ps	7:10	My defence is of **G.**, which saveth	430
Ps	7:11	**G.** judgeth the righteous,	430
Ps	7:11	and **G.** is angry with the wicked	410
Ps	9:17	and all the nations that forget **G.**	430
Ps	10:4	countenance, will not seek after **G.**:	
Ps	10:4	**G.** is not in all his thoughts	430
Ps	10:11	in his heart, **G.** hath forgotten:	410
Ps	10:12	O **G.**, lift up thine hand: forget not	410
Ps	10:13	doth the wicked contemn **G.**? he	430
Ps	13:3	and hear me, O Lord my **G.**	430
Ps	14:1	said in his heart, There is no **G.**	430
Ps	14:2	that did understand, and seek **G.**	430
Ps	14:5	for **G.** is in the generation of the	430
Ps	16:1	Preserve me, O **G.**: for in thee do	410
Ps	16:4	that hasten after another **g.**: their	
Ps	17:6	for thou wilt hear me, O **G.**:	410
Ps	18:2	my **G.**, my strength, in whom I will	410
Ps	18:6	and cried unto my **G.**: he heard my	430
Ps	18:21	not wickedly departed from my **G.**	430
Ps	18:28	my **G.** will enlighten my darkness	430
Ps	18:29	and by my **G.** have I leaped over a	430
Ps	18:30	As for **G.**, his way is perfect:	410
Ps	18:31	For who is **G.** save the Lord?	433
Ps	18:31	or who is a rock save our **G.**?	430
Ps	18:32	**G.** that girdeth me with strength,	410
Ps	18:46	the **G.** of my salvation be exalted	430
Ps	18:47	It is **G.** that avengeth me, and	410
Ps	19:1	heavens declare the glory of **G.**;	410
Ps	20:1	of the **G.** of Jacob defend thee;	430
Ps	20:5	in the name of our **G.** we will set	430
Ps	20:7	the name of the Lord our **G.**	430
Ps	22:1	My **G.**, my **G.**, why hast thou	410
Ps	22:2	O my **G.**, I cry in the daytime,	430
Ps	22:10	art my **G.** from my mother's belly	410
Ps	24:5	from the **G.** of his salvation	430
Ps	25:2	O my **G.**, I trust in thee: let me not	430
Ps	25:5	for thou art the **G.** of my salvation;	430
Ps	25:22	Israel, O **G.**, out of all his troubles	430
Ps	27:9	forsake me, O **G.** of my salvation	430
Ps	29:3	**G.** of glory thundereth: the Lord	410
Ps	30:2	O Lord my **G.**, I cried unto thee,	430
Ps	30:12	O Lord my **G.**, I will give thanks	430
Ps	31:5	redeemed me, O Lord **G.** of truth,	410
Ps	31:14	I said, Thou art my **G.**	430
Ps	33:12	is the nation whose **G.** is the Lord;	430
Ps	35:23	unto my cause, my **G.** and my Lord	430
Ps	35:24	Judge me, O Lord my **G.**, according	430
Ps	36:1	is no fear of **G.** before his eyes	430
Ps	36:7	is thy lovingkindness, O **G.**!	430
Ps	37:31	The law of his **G.** is in his heart;	430
Ps	38:15	thou wilt hear, O Lord my **G.**	430
Ps	38:21	O my **G.**, be not far from me	430
Ps	40:3	even praise unto our **G.**: many shall	430
Ps	40:5	O Lord my **G.**, are thy wonderful	430
Ps	40:8	I delight to do thy will, O my **G.**:	430
Ps	40:17	make no tarrying, O my **G.**	430
Ps	41:13	Blessed be the Lord **G.** of Israel	430
Ps	42:1	so panteth my soul after thee, O **G.**	430
Ps	42:2	My soul thirsteth for **G.**,	430
Ps	42:2	for the living **G.**: when shall	410
Ps	42:2	I come and appear before **G.**?	430
Ps	42:3	say unto me, Where is thy **G.**?	430
Ps	42:4	I went with them to the house of **G.**,	430
Ps	42:5	hope thou in **G.**: for I shall yet	430
Ps	42:6	O my **G.**, my soul is cast down	430
Ps	42:8	my prayer unto the **G.** of my life	410
Ps	42:9	I will say unto **G.** my rock, Why	410
Ps	42:10	daily unto me, Where is thy **G.**?	430
Ps	42:11	hope thou in **G.**: for I shall yet	430
Ps	42:11	of my countenance, and my **G.**	430
Ps	43:1	Judge me, O **G.**, and plead my	430
Ps	43:2	For thou art the **G.** of my strength:	430
Ps	43:4	Then will I go unto the altar of **G.**,	430
Ps	43:4	unto **G.** my exceeding joy:	410
Ps	43:4	will I praise thee, O **G.** my **G.**	430
Ps	43:5	hope in **G.**: for I shall yet praise	430
Ps	43:5	of my countenance, and my **G.**	430
Ps	44:1	We have heard with our ears, O **G.**,	430
Ps	44:4	Thou art my King, O **G.**: command	430
Ps	44:8	In **G.** we boast all the day long,	430
Ps	44:20	have forgotten the name of our **G.**	430
Ps	44:20	out our hands to a strange **g.**	410
Ps	44:21	Shall not **G.** search this out?	430
Ps	45:2	therefore **G.** hath blessed thee for	430
Ps	45:6	thy throne, O **G.**, is for ever and	430
Ps	45:7	therefore **G.**, thy **G.**, hath anointed	430
Ps	46:1	**G.** is our refuge and strength, a	430
Ps	46:4	shall make glad the city of **G.**,	430
Ps	46:5	**G.** is in the midst of her; she shall	430
Ps	46:5	not be moved: **G.** shall help her,	430
Ps	46:7	the **G.** of Jacob is our refuge	430
Ps	46:10	and know that I am **G.**: I will be	430
Ps	46:11	the **G.** of Jacob is our refuge	430
Ps	47:1	unto **G.** with the voice of triumph	430
Ps	47:5	**G.** is gone up with a shout, the	430
Ps	47:6	Sing praises to **G.**, sing praises:	430
Ps	47:7	**G.** is the King of all the earth:	430
Ps	47:8	**G.** reigneth over the heathen:	430
Ps	47:8	**G.** sitteth upon the throne of his	430
Ps	47:9	the people of the **G.** of Abraham;	430
Ps	47:9	shields of the earth belong unto **G.**:	430
Ps	48:1	the city of our **G.**, in the mountain	430
Ps	48:3	**G.** is known in her palaces for a	430
Ps	48:8	Lord of hosts, in the city of our **G.**:	430
Ps	48:8	**G.** will establish it for ever	430
Ps	48:9	lovingkindness, O **G.**, in the midst	430
Ps	48:10	According to thy name, O **G.**, so is	430
Ps	48:14	this **G.** is our **G.** for ever and ever:	430
Ps	49:7	nor give to **G.** a ransom for him:	430
Ps	49:15	But **G.** will redeem my soul from	430
Ps	50:1	The mighty **G.**, even the Lord,	430
Ps	50:2	perfection of beauty, **G.** hath shined	430
Ps	50:3	Our **G.** shall come, and shall not	430
Ps	50:6	for **G.** is judge himself. Selah	430
Ps	50:7	I am **G.**, even thy **G.**	430
Ps	50:14	Offer unto **G.** thanksgiving; and	430
Ps	50:16	But unto the wicked **G.** saith, What	430
Ps	50:22	ye that forget **G.**, lest I tear you	433
Ps	50:23	will I shew the salvation of **G.**	430
Ps	51:1	Have mercy upon me, O **G.**;	430
Ps	51:10	Create in me a clean heart, O **G.**;	430
Ps	51:14	me from bloodguiltiness, O **G.**,	430
Ps	51:14	thou **G.** of my salvation:	430
Ps	51:17	sacrifices of **G.** are a broken spirit:	430
Ps	51:17	a broken and a contrite heart, O **G.**,	430
Ps	52:1	of **G.** endureth continually	410
Ps	52:5	**G.** shall likewise destroy thee for	410
Ps	52:7	man that made not **G.** his strength;	430
Ps	52:8	green olive tree in the house of **G.**:	430
Ps	52:8	I trust in the mercy of **G.** for ever	430
Ps	53:1	said in his heart, There is no **G.**	430
Ps	53:2	**G.** looked down from heaven upon	430
Ps	53:2	did understand, that did seek **G.**	430
Ps	53:4	they have not called upon **G.**	430
Ps	53:5	**G.** hath scattered the bones of him	430
Ps	53:5	because **G.** hath despised them	430
Ps	53:6	**G.** bringeth back the captivity of	430
Ps	54:1	Save me, O **G.**, by thy name,	430
Ps	54:2	Hear my prayer, O **G.**; give ear	430
Ps	54:3	they have not set **G.** before them	430
Ps	54:4	Behold, **G.** is mine helper: the Lord	430
Ps	55:1	Give ear to my prayer, O **G.**;	430
Ps	55:14	unto the house of **G.** in company	430
Ps	55:16	As for me, I will call upon **G.**;	430
Ps	55:19	**G.** shall hear, and afflict them,	410
Ps	55:19	therefore they fear not **G.**	430
Ps	55:23	But thou, O **G.**, shalt bring them	430
Ps	56:1	Be merciful unto me, O **G.**: for man	430
Ps	56:4	In **G.** I will praise his word,	430
Ps	56:4	in **G.** I have put my trust;	430
Ps	56:7	anger cast down the people, O **G.**	430
Ps	56:9	this I know; for **G.** is for me	430
Ps	56:10	In **G.** will I praise his word:	430
Ps	56:11	In **G.** have I put my trust:	430
Ps	56:12	Thy vows are upon me, O **G.**:	430
Ps	56:13	I may walk before **G.** in the light	430
Ps	57:1	Be merciful unto me, O **G.**, be	430
Ps	57:2	I will cry unto **G.** most high:	430
Ps	57:2	unto **G.** that performeth all	410
Ps	57:3	**G.** shall send forth his mercy and	430
Ps	57:5	exalted, O **G.**, above the heavens;	430

Ps	57:7	My heart is fixed, O **G.**, my heart is....	430
Ps	57:11	Be thou exalted, O **G.** above	430
Ps	58:6	Break their teeth, O **G.**, in their	430
Ps	58:11	he is a **G.** that judgeth in the earth.	430
Ps	59:1	me from mine enemies, O my **G.**, ...	430
Ps	59:5	Thou therefore, O Lord **G.** of hosts,....	430
Ps	59:5	the **G.** of Israel, awake to visit...........	430
Ps	59:9	upon thee: for **G.** is my defence...........	430
Ps	59:10	The **G.** of my mercy shall prevent	430
Ps	59:10	**G.** shall let me see my desire	430
Ps	59:13	them know that **G.** ruleth in Jacob	430
Ps	59:17	will I sing: for **G.** is my defence, ...	430
Ps	59:17	my defence, and the **G.** of my mercy. ..	430
Ps	60:1	O **G.**, thou hast cast us off..................	430
Ps	60:6	**G.** hath spoken in his holiness;............	430
Ps	60:10	Wilt not thou, O **G.**, which hadst.........	430
Ps	60:10	and thou, O **G.**. which didst not go......	430
Ps	60:12	Through **G.** we shall do valiantly:.........	430
Ps	61:1	Hear my cry, O **G.**; attend unto my.....	430
Ps	61:5	For thou, O **G.**, hast heard my vows:...	430
Ps	61:7	He shall abide before **G.** for ever:........	430
Ps	62:1	Truly my soul waiteth upon **G.**:...........	430
Ps	62:5	My soul, wait thou only upon **G.**;	430
Ps	62:7	In **G.** is my salvation and my glory:.......	430
Ps	62:7	strength, and my refuge, is in **G.**.........	430
Ps	62:8	before him: **G.** is a refuge for us.	430
Ps	62:11	**G.** hath spoken once; twice have I.......	430
Ps	62:11	that power belongeth unto **G.**.	430
Ps	63:1	O **G.**, thou art my...; early will I..........	430
Ps	63:1	thou art my **G.**; early will I	410
Ps	63:11	But the king shall rejoice in **G.**;...........	430
Ps	64:1	Hear my voice, O **G.**, in my prayer:	430
Ps	64:7	But **G.** shall shoot at them with an.......	430
Ps	64:9	and shall declare the work of **G.**;	430
Ps	65:1	waiteth for thee, O **G.**, in Sion:...........	430
Ps	65:5	answer us, O **G.** of our salvation;	430
Ps	65:9	enrichest it with the river of **G.**,..........	430
Ps	66:1	Make a joyful noise unto **G.**, all ye.......	430
Ps	66:3	Say unto **G.**, How terrible art thou	430
Ps	66:5	Come and see the works of **G.**:	430
Ps	66:8	O bless our **G.**, ye people, and make ...	430
Ps	66:10	For thou, O **G.**, hast proved us:.........	430
Ps	66:16	Come and hear, all ye that fear **G.**,......	430
Ps	66:19	But verily **G.** hath heard me;..............	430
Ps	66:20	Blessed be **G.**, which hath not	430
Ps	67:1	**G.** be merciful unto us, and bless	430
Ps	67:3,	5 Let the people praise thee, O **G.**;	430
Ps	67:6	**G.**, even our own **G.**, shall bless us.....	430
Ps	67:7	**G.** shall bless us; and all the ends........	430
Ps	68:1	Let **G.** arise, let his enemies be..........	430
Ps	68:2	wicked perish at the presence of **G.**.	430
Ps	68:3	let them rejoice before **G.**: yea, ...	430
Ps	68:4	Sing unto **G.**, sing praises to his..........	430
Ps	68:5	widows, is **G.** in his holy habitation.	430
Ps	68:6	**G.** setteth the solitary in families:	430
Ps	68:7	O **G.**, when thou wentest forth	430
Ps	68:8	dropped at the presence of **G.**:	430
Ps	68:8	the presence of **G.**, the **G.** of Israel,....	430
Ps	68:9	O **G.**, didst send a plentiful rain,..........	430
Ps	68:10	thou, O **G.**, hast prepared of thy.........	430
Ps	68:15	hill of **G.** is as the hill of Bashan;........	430
Ps	68:16	the hill which **G.** desireth to dwell........	430
Ps	68:17	The chariots of **G.** are twenty............	430
Ps	68:18	Lord **G.** might dwell among them.........	430
Ps	68:19	even the **G.** of our salvation.	410
Ps	68:20	that is our **G.** is the **G.** of salvation:.....	410
Ps	68:20	**G.** the Lord belong the issues	3069
Ps	68:21	**G.** shall wound the head of his	430
Ps	68:24	They have seen thy goings, O **G.**;	430
Ps	68:24	even the goings of my **G.**, my............	410
Ps	68:26	Bless ye **G.** in the congregations.	430
Ps	68:28	**G.** hath commanded thy strength:	430
Ps	68:28	strengthen, O **G.**, that which thou	430
Ps	68:31	soon stretch out her hands unto **G.**......	430
Ps	68:32	Sing unto **G.**, ye kingdoms of the	430
Ps	68:34	Ascribe ye strength unto **G.**:	430
Ps	68:35	O **G.**, thou art terrible out of thy.........	430
Ps	68:35	the **G.** of Israel is he that giveth	410
Ps	68:35	unto his people. Blessed be **G.**............	430
Ps	69:1	Save me, O **G.**; for the waters are	430
Ps	69:3	eyes fail while I wait for my **G.**.	430
Ps	69:5	O **G.**, thou knowest my foolishness;.....	430
Ps	69:6	wait on thee, O Lord **G.** of hosts, ...	3069
Ps	69:6	for my sake, O **G.** of Israel.	430
Ps	69:13	O **G.**, in the multitude of thy mercy.....	430
Ps	69:29	thy salvation, O **G.**, set me up on........	430
Ps	69:30	I will praise the name of **G.**...............	430
Ps	69:32	your heart shall live that seek **G.**.........	430
Ps	69:35	For **G.** will save Zion, and will build.....	430
Ps	70:1	Make haste, O **G.**, to deliver me;........	430
Ps	70:4	continually, Let **G.** be magnified.	430
Ps	70:5	make haste unto me, O **G.**: thou.........	430
Ps	71:4	Deliver me, O my **G.**, out of the.........	430
Ps	71:5	thou art my hope, O Lord **G.**:	3069
Ps	71:11	Saying, **G.** hath forsaken him:	430
Ps	71:12	O **G.**, be not far from me: O my **G.**, ...	430
Ps	71:16	go in the strength of the Lord **G.**;......	3069
Ps	71:17	O **G.**, thou hast taught me from..........	430
Ps	71:18	O **G.**, forsake me not; until I have.......	430
Ps	71:19	Thy righteousness also, O **G.**, is	430
Ps	71:19	O **G.**, who is like unto thee!..............	430
Ps	71:22	even thy truth, O my **G.**: unto thee.....	430
Ps	72:1	Give the king thy judgments, O **G.**, ...	430
Ps	72:18	be the Lord **G.**, the **G.** of Israel,.........	430
Ps	73:1	Truly **G.** is good to Israel, ...	430
Ps	73:11	they say, How doth **G.** know?..............	410
Ps	73:17	I went into the sanctuary of **G.**;	410
Ps	73:26	but **G.** is the strength of my heart, ...	430
Ps	73:28	is good for me to draw near to **G.**:	430
Ps	73:28	have put my trust in the Lord **G.**, ...	3069
Ps	74:1	O **G.**, why hast thou cast us off	430
Ps	74:8	burned up all the synagogues of **G.**	410
Ps	74:10	O **G.**, how long shall the adversary......	430
Ps	74:12	For **G.** is my King of old, working.........	430
Ps	74:22	Arise, O **G.**, plead thine own cause:.....	430
Ps	75:1	Unto thee, O **G.**, do we give thanks, ...	430
Ps	75:7	But **G.** is the judge: he putteth	430
Ps	75:9	will sing praises to the **G.** of Jacob.......	430
Ps	76:1	In Judah is **G.** known: his name is........	430
Ps	76:6	At the rebuke. O **G.** of Jacob,............	430
Ps	76:9	When **G.** arose to judgment, to save	430
Ps	76:11	and pay unto the Lord your **G.**:...........	430
Ps	77:1	**G.** with my voice, even unto **G.** with ...	430
Ps	77:3	I remembered **G.**, and was troubled:	430
Ps	77:9	Hath **G.** forgotten to be gracious?	410
Ps	77:13	Thy way, O **G.**, is in the sanctuary:	430
Ps	77:13	sanctuary: who is so great a **G.** as.......	410
Ps	77:13	who is so great...as our **G.**?	430
Ps	77:14	Thou art the **G.** that doest wonders:	410
Ps	77:16	waters saw thee, O **G.**, the waters.......	430
Ps	78:7	they might set their hope in **G.**, ...	430
Ps	78:7	and not forget the works of **G.**,............	410
Ps	78:8	whose spirit was not stedfast with **G.**...	410
Ps	78:10	They kept not the covenant of **G.**,.......	430
Ps	78:18	they tempted **G.** in their heart by	410
Ps	78:19	Yea, they spake against **G.**;................	430
Ps	78:19	they said, Can **G.** furnish a table	410
Ps	78:22	Because they believed not in **G.**, ...	430
Ps	78:31	The wrath of **G.** came upon them, ...	430
Ps	78:34	and enquired early after **G.**.................	410
Ps	78:35	they remembered that **G.** was their......	430
Ps	78:35	and the high **G.** their redeemer.	410
Ps	78:41	they turned back and tempted **G.**,.........	410
Ps	78:56	and provoked the most high **G.**,...........	430
Ps	78:59	When **G.** heard this, he was wroth,......	430
Ps	79:1	O **G.**, the heathen are come into	430
Ps	79:9	Help us, O **G.** of our salvation, ...	430
Ps	79:10	the heathen say, Where is their **G.**?	430
Ps	80:3	Turn us again, O **G.**, and cause thy	430
Ps	80:4	O Lord **G.** of hosts, how long wilt	430
Ps	80:7	Turn us again, O **G.** of hosts, ...	430
Ps	80:14	Return, we beseech thee, O **G.** of.......	430
Ps	80:19	Turn us again, O Lord **G.** of hosts,......	430
Ps	81:1	Sing aloud unto **G.** our strength:.........	430
Ps	81:1	make a joyful noise unto the **G.** of	430
Ps	81:4	and a law of the **G.** of Jacob.	430
Ps	81:9	There shall no strange **g.** be in thee:....	410
Ps	81:9	shalt thou worship any strange **g.**.	410
Ps	81:10	am the Lord thy **G.**, which brought......	430
Ps	82:1	**G.** standeth in the congregation of	430
Ps	82:8	Arise, O **G.**, judge the earth: for.........	430
Ps	83:1	Keep not thou silence, O **G.**:...............	430
Ps	83:1	not thy peace, and be not still, O **G.**....	410
Ps	83:12	the houses of **G.** in possession............	430
Ps	83:13	O my **G.**, make them like a wheel;	430
Ps	84:2	flesh crieth out for the living **G.**.	410
Ps	84:3	Lord of hosts, my King, and my **G.**.	430
Ps	84:7	them in Zion appeareth before **G.**.	430
Ps	84:8	O Lord **G.** of hosts, hear my prayer:.....	430
Ps	84:8	give ear, O **G.** of Jacob.	430
Ps	84:9	Behold, O **G.** our shield, and look........	430
Ps	84:10	doorkeeper in the house of my **G.**, ...	430
Ps	84:11	For the Lord **G.** is a sun and shield:	430
Ps	85:4	Turn us, O **G.** of our salvation,...........	430
Ps	85:8	I will hear what **G.** the Lord will	410
Ps	86:2	O thou my **G.**, save thy servant..........	430
Ps	86:10	wondrous things: thou art **G.** alone.	430
Ps	86:12	I will praise thee, O Lord my **G.**, ...	430
Ps	86:14	O **G.**, the proud are risen against	430
Ps	86:15	O Lord, art a **G.** full of compassion,.....	410
Ps	87:3	are spoken of thee, O city of **G.**..........	430
Ps	88:1	O Lord **G.** of my salvation, I have	430
Ps	89:7	**G.** is greatly to be feared in the	410
Ps	89:8	O Lord **G.** of hosts, who is a strong	430
Ps	89:26	Thou art my father, my **G.**, and..........	410
Ps	90:*title*	Prayer of Moses the man of **G.**...........	430
Ps	90:2	to everlasting, thou art **G.**...................	410
Ps	90:17	let the beauty of the Lord our **G.**	430
Ps	91:2	fortress: my **G.**; in him will I trust.......	430
Ps	92:13	shall flourish in the courts of our **G.**, ...	430
Ps	94:1	O Lord **G.**, to whom vengeance	410
Ps	94:1	O **G.**, to whom vengeance belongeth, ...	410
Ps	94:7	neither shall the **G.** of Jacob regard......	430
Ps	94:22	and my **G.** is the rock of my refuge.	430
Ps	94:23	the Lord our **G.** shall cut them off.	430
Ps	95:3	For the Lord is a great **G.**, and a........	410
Ps	95:7	For he is our **G.**; and we are the.........	430
Ps	98:3	have seen the salvation of our **G.**.	430
Ps	99:5	exalt ye the Lord our **G.**, and.............	430
Ps	99:8	answeredst them, O Lord our **G.**:........	430
Ps	99:8	thou wast a **G.** that forgavest them,.....	410
Ps	99:9	the Lord our **G.**, and worship at..........	430
Ps	99:9	hill; for the Lord our **G.** is holy.	430
Ps	100:3	Know ye that the Lord he is **G.**:	430
Ps	102:24	O my **G.**, take me not away in the	410
Ps	104:1	O Lord my **G.**,thou art very great;	430
Ps	104:21	and seek their meat from **G.**................	410
Ps	104:33	I will sing praise to my **G.** while I........	430
Ps	105:7	He is the Lord our **G.**: his	430
Ps	106:14	and tempted **G.** in the desert...............	410
Ps	106:21	They forgat **G.** their saviour, which......	410
Ps	106:47	Save us, O Lord our **G.**, and gather......	430
Ps	106:48	Blessed be the Lord **G.** of Israel	430
Ps	107:11	rebelled against the words of **G.**,.........	410
Ps	108:1	O **G.**, my heart is fixed; I will sing	430
Ps	108:5	Be thou exalted, O **G.**, above the........	430
Ps	108:7	**G.** hath spoken in his holiness;............	430
Ps	108:11	O **G.**, who hast cast us off? and..........	430
Ps	108:11	wilt not thou, O **G.**, go forth with........	430
Ps	108:13	Through **G.** we shall do valiantly:.........	430
Ps	109:1	Hold not thy peace, O **G.** of my...........	430
Ps	109:21	But do thou for me, O **G.** the Lord, ...	3069
Ps	109:26	Help me, O Lord my **G.**: O save.........	430
Ps	113:5	Who is like unto the Lord our **G.**,.........	430
Ps	114:7	at the presence of the **G.** of Jacob;	433
Ps	115:2	heathen say, Where is now their **G.**?....	430
Ps	115:3	But our **G.** is in the hevaens: he	430
Ps	116:5	yea, our **G.** is merciful.	430
Ps	118:27	**G.** is the Lord, which hath shewed	410
Ps	118:28	art my **G.** and I will praise thee:	410
Ps	118:28	thou art my **G.**, I will exalt thee..........	430
Ps	119:115	keep the commandments of my **G.**........	430
Ps	122:9	of the house of the Lord our **G.** I........	430
Ps	123:2	our eyes wait upon the Lord our **G.**,....	430
Ps	132:2	unto the mighty **G.** of Jacob;	
Ps	132:5	for the mighty **G.** of Jacob.	
Ps	135:2	the courts of the house of our **G.**, ...	430
Ps	136:2	unto the **G.** of Gods; for his mercy	430
Ps	136:26	give thanks unto the **G.** of heaven:	410
Ps	139:17	are thy thoughts unto me, O **G.**!	410
Ps	139:19	thou wilt slay the wicked, O **G.**:	433
Ps	139:23	Search me, O **G.**, and know my	410
Ps	140:6	unto the Lord, Thou art my **G.**;	410
Ps	140:7	O **G.** the Lord, the strength of my.....	3069
Ps	141:8	eyes are unto thee, O **G.** the Lord:....	3069
Ps	143:10	for thou art my **G.**: thy spirit............	430
Ps	144:9	sing a new song unto thee, O **G.**:........	430
Ps	144:15	that people whose **G.** is the Lord.	430
Ps	145:1	I will extol thee, my **G.**, O king;	430
Ps	146:2	I will sing praises unto my **G.** while	430
Ps	146:5	Happy is he that hath the **G.** of...........	410
Ps	146:5	whose hope is in the Lord his **G.**:........	430
Ps	146:10	thy **G.**, O Zion, unto all generations.	430
Ps	147:1	good to sing praises unto our **G.**;	430
Ps	147:7	praise upon the harp unto our **G.**:........	430
Ps	147:12	Jerusalem; praise thy **G.**, O Zion.	430
Ps	149:6	the high praises of **G.** be in their	410
Ps	150:1	Praise **G.** in his sanctuary: praise.........	410
Pr	2:5	and find the knowledge of **G.**.	430
Pr	2:17	forgetteth the covenant of her **G.**.	430
Pr	3:4	understanding in the sight of **G.** and.....	430

Book	Ref	Context	No.
Pr	21:12	but **G.** overthroweth the wicked	
Pr	25:2	the glory of **G.** to conceal a thing:	430
Pr	26:10	great **G.** that formed all things	
Pr	30:5	Every word of **G.** is pure: he is a	433
Pr	30:9	take the name of my **G.** in vain.	430
Ec	1:13	this sore travail hath **G.** given to	430
Ec	2:24	that it was from the hand of **G.**.	430
Ec	2:26	For **G.** giveth to a man that is good in	
Ec	2:26	to him that is good before **G.**.	430
Ec	3:10	**G.** hath given to the sons of men	430
Ec	3:11	find out the work that **G.** maketh	430
Ec	3:13	all his labour, it is the gift of **G.**.	430
Ec	3:14	whatsoever **G.** doeth, it shall be for	430
Ec	3:14	**G.** doeth it, that men should fear	430
Ec	3:15	and **G.** requireth that which is past.	430
Ec	3:17	**G.** shall judge the righteous and the	430
Ec	3:18	that **G.** might manifest them, and	430
Ec	5:1	when thou goest to the house of **G.**,	430
Ec	5:2	utter anything before **G.**: for **G.** is	430
Ec	5:4	When thou vowest a vow unto **G.**,	430
Ec	5:6	wherefore should **G.** be angry at	430
Ec	5:7	vanities: but fear thou **G.**.	430
Ec	5:18	of his life, which **G.** giveth him:	430
Ec	5:19	to whom **G.** hath given riches and	430
Ec	5:19	his labour; this is the gift of **G.**.	430
Ec	5:20	**G.** answereth him in the joy of his	430
Ec	6:2	man to whom **G.** hath given riches,	430
Ec	6:2	yet **G.** giveth him not power to eat	430
Ec	7:13	Consider the work of **G.**: for who	430
Ec	7:14	**G.** also hath set the one over	430
Ec	7:18	he that feareth **G.** shall come forth	430
Ec	7:26	pleaseth **G.** shall escape from her;	430
Ec	7:29	that **G.** hath made man upright;	430
Ec	8:2	and that in regard of the oath of **G.**	430
Ec	8:12	shall be well with them that fear **G.**,	430
Ec	8:13	because he feareth not before **G.**.	430
Ec	8:15	which **G.** giveth him under the sun	430
Ec	8:17	Then I beheld all the work of **G.**,	430
Ec	9:1	their works, are in the hand of **G.**	430
Ec	9:7	for **G.** now accepteth thy works.	430
Ec	11:5	thou knowest not the works of **G.**	430
Ec	11:9	**G.** will bring thee into judgment.	430
Ec	12:7	shall return unto **G.** who gave it.	430
Ec	12:13	matter: Fear **G.**, and keep his	430
Ec	12:14	For **G.** shall bring every work into	430
Isa	1:10	give ear unto the law of our **G.**,	430
Isa	2:3	to the house of the **G.** of Jacob;	430
Isa	3:15	of the poor? saith the Lord **G.**	3069
Isa	5:16	**G.** that is holy shall be sanctified	410
Isa	7:7	Thus saith the Lord **G.**, It shall	3069
Isa	7:11	Ask thee a sign of the Lord thy **G.**;	430
Isa	7:13	but will ye weary my **G.** also?	430
Isa	8:10	it shall not stand: for **G.** is with us	410
Isa	8:19	not a people seek unto their **G.**?	430
Isa	8:21	and curse their king and their **G.**,	430
Isa	9:6	The mighty **G.**, The everlasting	410
Isa	10:21	of Jacob, unto the mighty **G.**	410
Isa	10:23	the Lord **G.** of hosts shall make	3069
Isa	10:24	saith the Lord **G.** of hosts, O my	3069
Isa	12:2	Behold, **G.** is my salvation: I will	410
Isa	13:19	be as when **G.** overthrew Sodom	430
Isa	14:13	my throne above the stars of **G.**	410
Isa	17:6	thereof, saith the Lord **G.** of Israel.	430
Isa	17:10	forgotten the **G.** of thy salvation,	430
Isa	17:13	but **G.** shall rebuke them, and	
Isa	21:10	the Lord of hosts, the **G.** of Israel,	430
Isa	21:17	the Lord **G.** of Israel hath spoken	430
Isa	22:5	by the Lord **G.** of hosts in the	3069
Isa	22:12	day did the Lord **G.** of hosts call	3069
Isa	22:14	you till ye die, saith the Lord **G.**	3069
Isa	22:15	saith the Lord **G.** of hosts, Go,	3069
Isa	24:15	the name of the Lord **G.** of Israel	430
Isa	25:1	O Lord, thou art my **G.**; I will exalt	430
Isa	25:8	the Lord **G.** will wipe away tears	3069
Isa	25:9	in that day, Lo, this is our **G.**;	430
Isa	26:1	salvation will **G.** appoint for	
Isa	26:13	O Lord our **G.**, other lords beside	430
Isa	28:16	the Lord **G.**, Behold, I lay in Zion	3069
Isa	28:22	heard from the Lord **G.** of hosts	3069
Isa	28:26	**G.** doth instruct him to discretion,	430
Isa	29:23	and shall fear the **G.** of Israel.	430
Isa	30:15	saith the Lord **G.**, the Holy One	3069
Isa	30:18	for the Lord is a **G.** of judgment:	430
Isa	31:3	Egyptians are men, and not **G.**;	410
Isa	35:2	and the excellency of our **G.**.	430
Isa	35:4	your **G.** will come with vengeance,	430
Isa	35:4	even **G.** with a recompence;	430
Isa	36:7	We trust in the Lord our **G.**: is it	430
Isa	37:4	It may be the Lord thy **G.** will hear	430
Isa	37:4	hath sent to reproach the living **G.**	430
Isa	37:4	which the Lord thy **G.** hath heard:	430
Isa	37:10	Let not thy **G.**, in whom thou	430
Isa	37:16	O Lord of hosts, **G.** of Israel,	430
Isa	37:16	thou art the **G.**, even thou alone,	430
Isa	37:17	hath sent to reproach the living **G.**	430
Isa	37:20	Now therefore, O Lord our **G.**, save	430
Isa	37:21	Thus saith the Lord **G.** of Israel,	430
Isa	37:38	in the house of Nisroch his **g.**,	430
Isa	38:5	the **G.** of David thy father, I have	430
Isa	40:1	comfort ye my people, saith your **G.**.	430
Isa	40:3	in the desert a highway for our **G.**.	430
Isa	40:8	but the word of our **G.** shall stand	430
Isa	40:9	the cities of Judah, Behold your **G.**!	430
Isa	40:10	Lord **G.** will come with strong	3069
Isa	40:18	To whom then will ye liken **G.**?	410
Isa	40:27	is passed over from my **G.**?	430
Isa	40:28	**G.**, the Lord, the Creator	430
Isa	41:10	be not dismayed; for I am thy **G.**	430
Isa	41:13	I the Lord thy **G.** will hold thy	430
Isa	41:17	the **G.** of Israel will not forsake	430
Isa	42:5	Thus saith **G.** the Lord, he that	410
Isa	43:3	For I am the Lord thy **G.**, the Holy	430
Isa	43:10	before me there was no **G.** formed,	410
Isa	43:12	there was no strange **g.** among you:	
Isa	43:12	saith the Lord, that I am **G.**.	410
Isa	44:6	and beside me there is no **G.**.	430
Isa	44:8	Is there a **G.** beside me? yea,	433
Isa	44:8	there is no **G.**; I know not any.	6697
Isa	44:10	Who hath formed a **g.**, or molten	410
Isa	44:15	he maketh a **g.**, and worshippeth it;	410
Isa	44:17	the residue thereof he maketh a **g.**,	410
Isa	44:17	Deliver me; for thou art my **g.**.	410
Isa	45:3	by thy name, am the **G.** of Israel.	430
Isa	45:5	there is no **G.** beside me: I girded	430
Isa	45:14	Surely **G.** is in thee; and there is	410
Isa	45:14	there is none else, there is no **G.**.	430
Isa	45:15	Verily thou art a **G.** that hidest	410
Isa	45:15	thyself, O **G.** of Israel, the Saviour.	430
Isa	45:18	**G.** himself that formed the earth	430
Isa	45:20	pray unto a **g.** that cannot save.	410
Isa	45:21	there is no **G.** else beside me;	430
Isa	45:21	a just **G.** and a Saviour;	410
Isa	45:22	for I am **G.**, and there is none else.	410
Isa	46:6	he maketh it a **g.**: they fall down	410
Isa	46:9	for I am **G.**, and there is none else;	410
Isa	46:9	I am **G.**, and there is none like me,	430
Isa	48:1	make mention of the **G.** of Israel,	430
Isa	48:2	themselves upon the **G.** of Israel;	430
Isa	48:16	now the Lord **G.**, and his Spirit,	3069
Isa	48:17	I am the Lord thy **G.** which	430
Isa	49:4	and my work with my **G.**.	430
Isa	49:5	and my **G.** shall be my strength.	430
Isa	49:22	saith the Lord **G.**, Behold, I will	3069
Isa	50:4	The Lord **G.** hath given me the	3069
Isa	50:5	Lord **G.** hath opened mine ear,	3069
Isa	50:7	the Lord **G.** will help me;	3069
Isa	50:9	the Lord **G.** will help me; who is	3069
Isa	50:10	and stay upon his **G.**.	430
Isa	51:15	But I am the Lord thy **G.**,	430
Isa	51:20	of the Lord, the rebuke of thy **G.**.	430
Isa	51:22	and thy **G.** that pleadeth the cause	430
Isa	52:4	saith the Lord **G.**, My people	3069
Isa	52:7	saith unto Zion, Thy **G.** reigneth!	430
Isa	52:10	shall see the salvation of our **G.**.	430
Isa	52:12	and the **G.** of Israel will be your	430
Isa	53:4	stricken, smitten of **G.**, and afflicted.	430
Isa	54:5	The **G.** of the whole earth shall he	430
Isa	54:6	thou wast refused, saith thy **G.**.	430
Isa	55:5	because of the Lord thy **G.**, and for	430
Isa	55:7	and to our **G.**, for he will abundantly	430
Isa	56:8	The Lord **G.** which gathereth	3069
Isa	57:21	peace, saith my **G.**, to the wicked.	430
Isa	58:2	not the ordinance of their **G.**	430
Isa	58:2	take delight in approaching to **G.**.	430
Isa	59:2	separated between you and your **G.**,	430
Isa	59:13	and departing away from our **G.**,	430
Isa	60:9	unto the name of the Lord thy **G.**,	430
Isa	60:19	and thy **G.** thy glory.	430
Isa	61:1	Spirit of the Lord **G.** is upon me;	3069
Isa	61:2	the day of vengeance of our **G.**;	430
Isa	61:6	call you the Ministers of our **G.**:	430
Isa	61:10	my soul shall be joyful in my **G.**;	430
Isa	61:11	Lord **G.** will cause righteousness	3069
Isa	62:3	royal diadem in the hand of thy **G.**.	430
Isa	62:5	so shall thy **G.** rejoice over thee.	430
Isa	64:4	neither hath the eye seen, O **G.**,	430
Isa	65:13	saith the Lord **G.**, Behold, my	3069
Isa	65:15	the Lord **G.** shall slay thee, and	3069
Isa	65:16	bless himself in the **G.** of truth;	430
Isa	65:16	shall swear by the **G.** of truth;	430
Isa	66:9	and shut the womb? saith thy **G.**.	430
Jer	1:6	Lord **G.**! behold, I cannot speak:	3069
Jer	2:17	forsaken the Lord thy **G.**, when	430
Jer	2:19	hast forsaken the Lord thy **G.**.	430
Jer	2:19	is not in thee, saith the Lord **G.**,	3069
Jer	2:22	before me, saith the Lord **G.**.	3069
Jer	3:13	against the Lord thy **G.**,	430
Jer	3:21	have forgotten the Lord their **G.**.	430
Jer	3:22	for thou art the Lord our **G.**.	430
Jer	3:23	our **G.** is the salvation of Israel.	430
Jer	3:25	sinned against the Lord our **G.**,	430
Jer	3:25	the voice of the Lord our **G.**.	430
Jer	4:10	Then said I, Ah, Lord **G.**!	3069
Jer	5:4	nor the judgment of their **G.**.	430
Jer	5:5	and the judgment of their **G.**: but	430
Jer	5:14	thus saith the Lord **G.** of hosts,	430
Jer	5:19	Wherefore doeth the Lord our **G.**	430
Jer	5:24	Let us now fear the Lord our **G.**,	430
Jer	7:3	the Lord of hosts, the **G.** of Israel,	430
Jer	7:20	saith the Lord **G.**; Behold, mine	3069
Jer	7:21	the Lord of hosts, the **G.** of Israel;	430
Jer	7:23	my voice, and I will be your **G.**.	430
Jer	7:28	not the voice of the Lord their **G.**,	430
Jer	8:14	for the Lord our **G.** hath put us	430
Jer	9:15	the Lord of hosts, the **G.** of Israel;	430
Jer	10:10	But the Lord is the true **G.**,	430
Jer	10:10	he is the living **G.**, and an	430
Jer	11:3	saith the Lord **G.** of Israel; Cursed	430
Jer	11:4	my people, and I will be your **G.**.	430
Jer	13:12	saith the Lord **G.** of Israel, Every	430
Jer	13:16	Give glory to the Lord your **G.**,	430
Jer	14:13	Ah, Lord **G.**! behold, the prophets	3069
Jer	14:22	art not thou he, O Lord our **G.**?	430
Jer	15:16	by thy name, O Lord **G.** of hosts.	430
Jer	16:9	the Lord of hosts, the **G.** of Israel;	430
Jer	16:10	committed against the Lord our **G.**?	430
Jer	19:3, 15	Lord of hosts, the **G.** of Israel;	430
Jer	21:4	saith the Lord **G.** of Israel; Behold,	430
Jer	22:9	the covenant of the Lord their **G.**,	430
Jer	23:2	saith the Lord **G.** of Israel against	430
Jer	23:23	Am I a **G.** at hand, saith the Lord,	430
Jer	23:23	and not a **G.** afar off?	430
Jer	23:36	perverted the words of the living **G.**,	430
Jer	23:36	of the Lord of hosts our **G.**.	430
Jer	24:5	saith the Lord, the **G.** of Israel; Like	430
Jer	24:7	and I will be their **G.**: for they shall	430
Jer	25:15	saith the Lord, **G.** of Israel unto me;	430
Jer	25:27	the Lord of hosts, the **G.** of Israel;	430
Jer	26:13	obey the voice of the Lord your **G.**;	430
Jer	26:16	in the name of the Lord our **G.**.	430
Jer	27:4	the Lord of hosts, the **G.** of Israel;	430
Jer	27:21	the Lord of hosts, the **G.** of Israel,	430
Jer	28:2	speaketh the Lord of hosts, the **G.**	430
Jer	28:14	the Lord of hosts, the **G.** of Israel;	430
Jer	29:4	the Lord of hosts, the **G.** of Israel,	430
Jer	29:8	the Lord of hosts, the **G.** of Israel;	430
Jer	29:21	the Lord of hosts, the **G.** of Israel,	430
Jer	29:25	speaketh the Lord of hosts, the **G.**	430
Jer	30:2	speaketh the Lord **G.** of Israel,	430
Jer	30:9	they shall serve the Lord their **G.**,	430
Jer	30:22	my people, and I will be your **G.**.	430
Jer	31:1	will I be the **G.** of all the families	430
Jer	31:6	up to Zion unto the Lord our **G.**.	430
Jer	31:18	for thou art the Lord my **G.**.	430
Jer	31:23	the Lord of hosts, the **G.** of Israel;	430
Jer	31:33	and will be their **G.**, and they shall	430
Jer	32:14	the Lord of hosts, the **G.** of Israel;	430
Jer	32:15	the Lord of hosts, the **G.** of Israel;	430
Jer	32:17	Ah, Lord **G.**! behold, thou hast	3069
Jer	32:18	the Great, the Mighty **G.**, the Lord	410
Jer	32:25	hast said unto me, O Lord **G.**,	3069
Jer	32:27	I am the Lord, the **G.** of all flesh:	430
Jer	32:36	thus saith the Lord, the **G.** of Israel,	430
Jer	32:38	my people, and I will be their **G.**:	430
Jer	33:4	thus saith the Lord, the **G.** of Israel,	430
Jer	34:2	saith the Lord, the **G.** of Israel; Go	430
Jer	34:13	saith the Lord, the **G.** of Israel; I	430
Jer	35:4	the son of Igdaliah, a man of **G.**.	430

Jer 35:13 the Lord of hosts, the **G.** of Israel;.......430
Jer 35:17 thus saith the Lord **G.** of hosts,........... 430
Jer 35:17 the **G.** of Israel; Behold, I will............. 430
Jer 35:18, 19 Lord of hosts, the **G.** of Israel;......... 430
Jer 37:3 Pray now unto the Lord our **G.** for....... 430
Jer 37:7 the Lord, the **G.** of Israel; Thus........... 430
Jer 38:17 thus saith the Lord, the **G.** of hosts,..... 430
Jer 38:17 the **G.** of Israel; If thou wilt................ 430
Jer 39:16 the Lord of hosts, the **G.** of Israel;....... 430
Jer 40:2 The Lord thy **G.** hath pronounced......... 430
Jer 42:2 pray for us unto the Lord thy **G.**,.......... 430
Jer 42:3 That the Lord thy **G.** may shew us....... 430
Jer 42:4 I will pray unto the Lord your **G.**......... 430
Jer 42:5 the Lord thy **G.** shall send thee........... 430
Jer 42:6 obey the voice of the Lord our **G.**,......... 430
Jer 42:6 obey the voice of the Lord our **G.**......... 430
Jer 42:9 saith the Lord, the **G.** of Israel, unto..... 430
Jer 42:13 obey the voice of the Lord your **G.**,....... 430
Jer 42:15, 18 Lord of hosts, the **G.** of Israel;......... 430
Jer 42:20 ye sent me unto the Lord your **G.**,........ 430
Jer 42:20 Pray for us unto the Lord our **G.**;......... 430
Jer 42:20 unto all that the Lord our **G.** shall......... 430
Jer 42:21 the voice of the Lord your **G.**,............. 430
Jer 43:1 all the words of the Lord their **G.**,......... 430
Jer 43:1 the Lord their **G.** had sent him to......... 430
Jer 43:2 the Lord our **G.** hath not sent thee....... 430
Jer 43:10 the Lord of hosts, the **G.** of Israel;....... 430
Jer 44:2 the Lord of hosts, the **G.** of Israel;....... 430
Jer 44:7 thus saith the Lord, the **G.** of hosts,..... 430
Jer 44:7 the **G.** of Israel; Wherefore................... 430
Jer 44:11 the Lord of hosts, the **G.** of Israel;....... 430
Jer 44:25 the Lord of hosts, the **G.** of Israel,....... 430
Jer 44:26 Egypt, saying, The Lord **G.** liveth....... 3069
Jer 45:2 Lord, the **G.** of Israel, unto thee,.......... 430
Jer 46:10 the day of the Lord **G.** of hosts,......... 3069
Jer 46:10 for the Lord **G.** of hosts hath a........... 3069
Jer 46:25 The Lord of hosts, the **G.** of Israel,...... 430
Jer 48:1 the Lord of hosts, the **G.** of Israel;....... 430
Jer 49:5 upon thee, saith the Lord **G.** of.......... 3069
Jer 50:4 go, and seek the Lord their **G.**............. 430
Jer 50:18 the Lord of hosts, the **G.** of Israel;....... 430
Jer 50:25 work of the Lord **G.** of hosts,............ 3069
Jer 50:28 vengeance of the Lord our **G.**,............. 430
Jer 50:31 most proud, saith the Lord **G.** of........ 3069
Jer 50:40 As **G.** overthrew Sodom and............... 430
Jer 51:5 nor Judah of his **G.**, of the Lord of........ 430
Jer 51:10 Zion the work of the Lord our **G.**........... 430
Jer 51:33 the Lord of hosts, the **G.** of Israel;....... 430
Jer 51:56 for the Lord **G.** of recompences........... 410
La 3:41 our heart with our hands unto **G.**.......... 410
Eze 1:1 opened, and I saw visions of **G.**........... 430
Eze 2:4 them, Thus saith the Lord **G.**............... 3069
Eze 3:11 saith the Lord **G.**; whether they......... 3069
Eze 3:27 saith the Lord **G.**; He that................. 3069
Eze 4:14 Ah Lord **G.**! behold, my soul............ 3069
Eze 5:5 saith the Lord **G.**: This is................. 3069
Eze 5:7 saith the Lord **G.**; Because ye............ 3069
Eze 5:8 saith the Lord **G.**; Behold, I,............. 3069
Eze 5:11 as I live, saith the Lord **G.**;............... 3069
Eze 6:3 hear the word of the Lord **G.**;.............. 3069
Eze 6:3 Thus saith the Lord **G.** to the........... 3069
Eze 6:11 saith the Lord **G.**; Smith with............ 3069
Eze 7:2 of man, thus saith the Lord **G.**............ 3069
Eze 7:5 saith the Lord **G.**; An evil, an............ 3069
Eze 8:1 the hand of the Lord **G.** fell there....... 3069
Eze 8:3 in the visions of **G.** to Jerusalem,......... 430
Eze 8:4 glory of the **G.** of Israel was there,....... 430
Eze 9:3 glory of the **G.** of Israel was gone......... 430
Eze 9:8 Ah Lord **G.**! wilt thou destroy............ 3069
Eze 10:5 as the voice of the Almighty **G.**............ 410
Eze 10:19 glory of the **G.** of Israel was over......... 430
Eze 10:20 I saw under the **G.** of Israel by the....... 430
Eze 11:7 saith the Lord **G.**; Your slain............. 3069
Eze 11:8 sword upon you, saith the Lord **G.**....... 3069
Eze 11:13 loud voice, and said, Ah Lord **G.**!........ 3069
Eze 11:16 saith the Lord **G.**; Although I............ 3069
Eze 11:17 saith the Lord **G.**; I will even............ 3069
Eze 11:20 my people, and I will be their **G.**.......... 430
Eze 11:21 own heads, saith the Lord **G.**.............. 3069
Eze 11:22 the glory of the **G.** of Israel................ 430
Eze 11:24 in a vision by the Spirit of **G.**............... 430
Eze 12:10 saith the Lord **G.**; This burden............ 3069
Eze 12:19 the Lord **G.** of the inhabitants of......... 3069
Eze 12:23 saith the Lord **G.**; I will make............ 3069
Eze 12:25 will perform it, saith the Lord **G.**......... 3069
Eze 12:28 saith the Lord **G.**; There shall............ 3069
Eze 12:28 shall be done, saith the Lord **G.**......... 3069
Eze 13:3 said the Lord **G.**; Woe unto the.......... 3069
Eze 13:8 saith the Lord **G.**; Because ye............ 3069
Eze 13:8 against you, saith the Lord **G.**........... 3069
Eze 13:9 shall know that I am the Lord **G.**......... 3069
Eze 13:13 saith the Lord **G.**; I will even............. 3069
Eze 13:16 is no peace, saith the Lord **G.**............ 3069
Eze 13:18 saith the Lord **G.**; Woe to the............ 3069
Eze 13:20 saith the Lord **G.**; Behold, I am......... 3069
Eze 14:4 saith the Lord **G.**; Every man of......... 3069
Eze 14:6 saith the Lord **G.**; Repent, and........... 3069
Eze 14:11 I may be their **G.**, saith the Lord......... 430
Eze 14:11 may be their...,saith the Lord **G.**......... 3069
Eze 14:14 righteousness, saith the Lord **G.**......... 3069
Eze 14:16 saith the Lord **G.**, they shall............. 3069
Eze 14:18 as I live, saith the Lord **G.**, they........ 3069
Eze 14:20 in it, as I live, saith the Lord **G.**,........ 3069
Eze 14:21 saith the Lord **G.**; How much............. 3069
Eze 14:23 have done in it, saith the Lord **G.**....... 3069
Eze 15:6 saith the Lord **G.**; As the vine........... 3069
Eze 15:8 a trespass, saith the Lord **G.**............. 3069
Eze 16:3 saith the Lord **G.** unto Jerusalem;....... 3069
Eze 16:8 saith the Lord **G.**, and thou............... 3069
Eze 16:14 put upon thee, saith the Lord **G.**......... 3069
Eze 16:19 thus it was, saith the Lord **G.**............ 3069
Eze 16:23 woe unto thee! saith the Lord **G.**;)...... 3069
Eze 16:30 is thine heart, saith the Lord **G.**,........ 3069
Eze 16:36 saith the Lord **G.**; Because thy........... 3069
Eze 16:43 thine head, saith the Lord **G.**:............ 3069
Eze 16:48 saith the Lord **G.**, Sodom thy............. 3069
Eze 16:59 saith the Lord **G.**; I will even deal....... 3069
Eze 16:63 thou hast done, saith the Lord **G.**........ 3069
Eze 17:3 saith the Lord **G.**; A great eagle.......... 3069
Eze 17:9 saith the Lord **G.**; Shall it prosper?..... 3069
Eze 17:16 saith the Lord **G.**, surely in the.......... 3069
Eze 17:19 saith the Lord **G.**; As I live,............... 3069
Eze 17:22 saith the Lord **G.**; I will also.............. 3069
Eze 18:3 saith the Lord **G.**, ye shall not........... 3069
Eze 18:9 surely live, saith the Lord **G.**............. 3069
Eze 18:23 should die? saith the Lord **G.**:............ 3069
Eze 18:30 to his ways, saith the Lord **G.**............. 3069
Eze 18:32 that dieth, saith the Lord **G.**:............... 3069
Eze 20:3 saith the Lord **G.**; Are ye come.......... 3069
Eze 20:3 saith the Lord **G.**, I will not be............ 3069
Eze 20:5 saith the Lord **G.**; In the day............. 3069
Eze 20:5 saying, I am the Lord your **G.**;............ 430
Eze 20:7 of Egypt: I am the Lord your **G.**........... 430
Eze 20:19 I am the Lord your **G.**; walk in my....... 430
Eze 20:20 know that I am the Lord your **G.**......... 430
Eze 20:27 saith the Lord **G.**; Yet in this............. 3069
Eze 20:30 saith the Lord **G.**; Are ye polluted...... 3069
Eze 20:31 As I live, saith the Lord **G.**, I will....... 3069
Eze 20:33 saith the Lord **G.**, surely with a.......... 3069
Eze 20:36 plead with you, saith the Lord **G.**......... 3069
Eze 20:39 saith the Lord **G.**; Go ye, serve.......... 3069
Eze 20:40 height of Israel, saith the Lord **G.**,....... 3069
Eze 20:44 house of Israel, saith the Lord **G.**........ 3069
Eze 20:47 saith the Lord **G.**; Behold, I will......... 3069
Eze 20:49 Ah Lord **G.**! they say of me, Doth...... 3069
Eze 21:7 to pass; saith the Lord **G.**................. 3069
Eze 21:13 be no more, saith the Lord **G.**............ 3069
Eze 21:24 saith the Lord **G.**; Because ye............ 3069
Eze 21:26 saith the Lord **G.**; Remove the............ 3069
Eze 21:28 saith the Lord **G.** concerning the......... 3069
Eze 22:3 saith the Lord **G.**, The city................ 3069
Eze 22:12 forgotten me, saith the Lord **G.**.......... 3069
Eze 22:19 saith the Lord **G.**: Because ye are...... 3069
Eze 22:28 saith the Lord **G.**, when the Lord....... 3069
Eze 22:31 their heads, saith the Lord **G.**............ 3069
Eze 23:22, 28 saith the Lord **G.**; Behold, I.......... 3069
Eze 23:32 saith the Lord **G.**; Thou shalt............. 3069
Eze 23:34 have spoken it, saith the Lord **G.**......... 3069
Eze 23:35 saith the Lord **G.**; Because thou......... 3069
Eze 23:46 saith the Lord **G.**; I will bring up........ 3069
Eze 23:49 shall know that I am the Lord **G.**......... 3069
Eze 24:3 saith the Lord **G.**; Set on a pot,......... 3069
Eze 24:6, 9 saith the Lord **G.**; Woe to the......... 3069
Eze 24:14 judge thee, saith the Lord **G.**............ 3069
Eze 24:21 saith the Lord **G.**; Behold, I will......... 3069
Eze 24:24 shall know that I am the Lord **G.**......... 3069
Eze 25:3 Hear the word of the Lord **G.**;............ 3069
Eze 25:3 the Lord **G.**; Because thou saidst,........ 3069
Eze 25:6 the Lord **G.**; Because thou hast........... 3069
Eze 25:8 the Lord **G.**; Because that Moab......... 3069
Eze 25:12 the Lord **G.**; Because that Edom........ 3069
Eze 25:13 saith the Lord **G.**; I will also............. 3069
Eze 25:14 my vengeance, saith the Lord **G.**......... 3069
Eze 25:15 saith the Lord **G.**; Because the........... 3069
Eze 25:16 saith the Lord **G.**; Behold, I will......... 3069
Eze 26:3 saith the Lord **G.**; Behold, I am.......... 3069
Eze 26:5 have spoken it, saith the Lord **G.**;........ 3069
Eze 26:7 saith the Lord **G.**; Behold, I will......... 3069
Eze 26:14 have spoken it, saith the Lord **G.**......... 3069
Eze 26:15 saith the Lord **G.** to Tyrus; Shall........ 3069
Eze 26:19 saith the Lord **G.**; When I shall......... 3069
Eze 26:21 found again, saith the Lord **G.**........... 3069
Eze 27:3 saith the Lord **G.**; O Tyrus, thou........ 3069
Eze 28:2 saith the Lord **G.**; Because thine........ 3069
Eze 28:2 and thou hast said, I am a **G.**,............. 410
Eze 28:2 I sit in the seat of **G.**, in the midst....... 430
Eze 28:2 thou art a man, and not **G.**, though....... 410
Eze 28:2 set thine heart as the heart of **G.**......... 430
Eze 28:6 saith the Lord **G.**; Because thou.......... 3069
Eze 28:6 set thine heart as the heart of **G.**;........ 430
Eze 28:9 him that slayeth thee, I am **G.**?........... 410
Eze 28:9 but thou shalt be a man, and no **G.**,....... 410
Eze 28:10 have spoken it, saith the Lord **G.**........ 3069
Eze 28:12 said the Lord **G.**: Thou sealest........... 3069
Eze 28:13 been in Eden the garden of **G.**;............ 430
Eze 28:14 was upon the holy mountain of **G.**;........ 430
Eze 28:16 profane out of the mountain of **G.**......... 430
Eze 28:22 saith the Lord **G.**; Behold, I am.......... 3069
Eze 28:24 shall know that I am the Lord **G.**......... 3069
Eze 28:25 saith the Lord **G.**; When I shall........... 3069
Eze 28:26 know that I am the Lord their **G.**.......... 430
Eze 29:3 saith the Lord **G.**; Behold, I am.......... 3069
Eze 29:8 saith the Lord **G.**; Behold, I will......... 3069
Eze 29:13 saith the Lord **G.**; At the end of......... 3069
Eze 29:16 shall know that I am the Lord **G.**......... 3069
Eze 29:19 saith the Lord **G.**; Behold, I will......... 3069
Eze 29:20 wrought for me, saith the Lord **G.**........ 3069
Eze 30:2 saith the Lord **G.**; Howl ye, Woe........ 3069
Eze 30:6 by the sword, saith the Lord **G.**.......... 3069
Eze 30:10 the Lord **G.**; I will also make............ 3069
Eze 30:13 the Lord **G.**; I will also destroy.......... 3069
Eze 30:22 saith the Lord **G.**; Behold, I am.......... 3069
Eze 31:8 The cedars in the garden of **G.**............ 430
Eze 31:8 nor any tree in the garden of **G.**........... 430
Eze 31:9 that were in the garden of **G.**,............. 430
Eze 31:10 said the Lord **G.**; Because thou.......... 3069
Eze 31:15 saith the Lord **G.**; In the day............. 3069
Eze 31:18 his multitude, saith the Lord **G.**......... 3069
Eze 32:3 Thus saith the Lord **G.**; I will............ 3069
Eze 32:8 upon thy land, saith the Lord **G.**......... 3069
Eze 32:11 saith the Lord **G.**; The sword of.......... 3069
Eze 32:14 to run like oil, saith the Lord **G.**......... 3069
Eze 32:16 her multitude, saith the Lord **G.**......... 3069
Eze 32:31 by the sword, saith the Lord **G.**.......... 3069
Eze 32:32 his multitude, saith the Lord **G.**......... 3069
Eze 33:11 As I live, saith the Lord **G.**, I............ 3069
Eze 33:25 thus saith the Lord **G.**; Ye eat........... 3069
Eze 33:27 saith the Lord **G.**; As I live,.............. 3069
Eze 34:2 the Lord **G.** unto the shepherds;.......... 3069
Eze 34:8 As I live, saith the Lord **G.**, surely...... 3069
Eze 34:10 Lord **G.**; Behold, I am against............ 3069
Eze 34:11 the Lord **G.**; Behold, I, even I,........... 3069
Eze 34:15 to lie down, saith the Lord **G.**............ 3069
Eze 34:17 saith the Lord **G.**; Behold, I judge....... 3069
Eze 34:20 saith the Lord **G.** unto them;.............. 3069
Eze 34:24 And I the Lord will be their **G.**,.......... 430
Eze 34:30 they know that I the Lord their **G.**........ 430
Eze 34:30 are my people, saith the Lord **G.**,........ 3069
Eze 34:31 are men, and I am your **G.**,................. 430
Eze 34:31 and I am...saith the Lord **G.**............... 3069
Eze 35:3 saith the Lord **G.**; Behold, O............. 3069
Eze 35:6 saith the Lord **G.**, I will prepare.......... 3069
Eze 35:11 saith the Lord **G.**, I will even do......... 3069
Eze 35:14 saith the Lord **G.**; When the.............. 3069
Eze 36:2 saith the Lord **G.**; Because the........... 3069
Eze 36:3 saith the Lord **G.**; Because they.......... 3069
Eze 36:4 hear the word of the Lord **G.**;............ 3069
Eze 36:4 the Lord **G.** to the mountains............. 3069
Eze 36:5 saith the Lord **G.**; Surely in the.......... 3069
Eze 36:6 saith the Lord **G.**; Behold, I have....... 3069
Eze 36:7 saith the Lord **G.**; I have lifted.......... 3069
Eze 36:13 saith the Lord **G.**; Because they......... 3069
Eze 36:14 nations...more, saith the Lord **G.**........ 3069
Eze 36:15 fall any more, saith the Lord **G.**.......... 3069
Eze 36:22 saith the Lord **G.**; I do not this.......... 3069
Eze 36:23 am the Lord, saith the Lord **G.**,.......... 3069
Eze 36:28 my people, and I will be your **G.**.......... 430
Eze 36:32 sakes do I this, saith the Lord **G.**,....... 3069
Eze 36:33 saith the Lord **G.**; In the day............. 3069
Eze 36:37 saith the Lord **G.**; I will yet............... 3069
Eze 37:3 And I answered, O Lord **G.**,.............. 3069

Eze 37:5 the Lord **G.** unto these bones; 3069
Eze 37:9 saith the Lord **G.**; Come from........... 3069
Eze 37:12 saith the Lord **G.**; Behold, O 3069
Eze 37:19 saith the Lord **G.**; Behold, I will........ 3069
Eze 37:21 saith the Lord **G.**; Behold, I will........ 3069
Eze 37:23 my people, and I will be their **G.**......... 430
Eze 37:27 I will be their **G.**, and they shall be...... 430
Eze 38:3 saith the Lord **G.**; Behold, I am......... 3069
Eze 38:10 saith the Lord **G.**; It shall also........... 3069
Eze 38:14 saith the Lord **G.**; In that day............ 3069
Eze 38:17 saith the Lord **G.**: Art thou he 3069
Eze 38:18 land of Israel, saith the Lord **G.**,......... 3069
Eze 38:21 my mountains, saith the Lord **G.**:....... 3069
Eze 39:1 saith the Lord **G.**; Behold I am............ 3069
Eze 39:5 have spoken it, saith the Lord **G.**........ 3069
Eze 39:8 and it is done, saith the Lord **G.**; 3069
Eze 39:10 robbed them, saith the Lord **G.**. 3069
Eze 39:13 be glorified, saith the Lord **G.**. 3069
Eze 39:17 saith the Lord **G.**; Speak unto 3069
Eze 39:20 all men of war, saith the Lord **G.**. 3069
Eze 39:22 I am the Lord their **G.** from that......... 430
Eze 39:25 saith the Lord **G.**; Now will I............ 3069
Eze 39:28 I am the Lord their **G.**, which............. 430
Eze 39:29 house of Israel, saith the Lord **G.**. 3069
Eze 40:2 In the visions of **G.** brought he me 430
Eze 43:2 glory of the **G.** of Israel came from...... 430
Eze 43:18 saith the Lord **G.**; These are the 3069
Eze 43:19 minister unto me, saith the Lord **G.**.... 3069
Eze 43:27 accept you, saith the Lord **G.**. 3069
Eze 44:2 because the Lord, the **G.** of Israel, ... 430
Eze 44:6 saith the Lord **G.**; O ye house of....... 3069
Eze 44:9 saith the Lord **G.**; No stranger, ... 3069
Eze 44:12 against them, saith the Lord **G.**, ... 3069
Eze 44:15 and the blood, saith the Lord **G.**; 3069
Eze 44:27 sin offering, saith the Lord **G.**. 3069
Eze 45:9 saith the Lord **G.**; Let it suffice........... 3069
Eze 45:9 my people, saith the Lord **G.**. 3069
Eze 45:15 for them, saith the Lord **G.**................ 3069
Eze 45:18 saith the Lord **G.**; In the first........... 3069
Eze 46:1 saith the Lord **G.**; The gate of 3069
Eze 46:16 saith the Lord **G.**; If the prince.......... 3069
Eze 47:13 saith the Lord **G.**; This shall be.......... 3069
Eze 47:23 inheritance, saith the Lord **G.**............ 3069
Eze 48:29 their portions, saith the Lord **G.**. 3069
Da 1:2 the vessels of the house of **G.** 430
Da 1:2 of Shinar to the house of his **g.**; 430
Da 1:2 into the treasure house of his **g.**.......... 430
Da 1:9 **G.** had brought Daniel into favour 430
Da 1:17 **G.** gave them knowledge and skill........ 430
Da 2:18 desire mercies of the **G.** of heaven 426
Da 2:19 Daniel blessed the **G.** of heaven. 426
Da 2:20 Blessed be the name of **G.** for ever 426
Da 2:23 O thou **G.** of my fathers, who hast 426
Da 2:28 is a **G.** in heaven that revealeth........... 426
Da 2:37 the **G.** of heaven hath given thee......... 426
Da 2:44 the **G.** of heaven set up a kingdom, ... 426
Da 2:45 **G.** hath made known to the king.......... 426
Da 2:47 that your **G.** is a **G.** of gods, ... 426
Da 3:15 who is that **G.** that shall deliver you..... 426
Da 3:17 **G.** whom we serve is able to deliver.... 426
Da 3:25 the fourth is like the Son of **G.**............ 426
Da 3:26 ye servants of the most high **G.**, ... 426
Da 3:28 Blessed be the **G.** of Shadrach, ... 426
Da 3:28 worship any **g.**, except their own **G.**. ... 426
Da 3:29 against the **G.** of Shadrach,................ 426
Da 3:29 is no other **G.** that can deliver 426
Da 4:2 and wonders that the high **G.** hath........ 426
Da 4:8 according to the name of my **g.**, and 426
Da 5:3 of the temple of the house of **G.** 426
Da 5:18 most high **G.** gave Nebuchadnezzar...... 426
Da 5:21 knew that the most high **G.** ruled 426
Da 5:23 the **G.** in whose hand thy breath is, ... 426
Da 5:26 **G.** hath numbered thy kingdom, ... 426
Da 6:5 concerning the law of his **G.**. 426
Da 6:7 shall ask a petition of any **G.** or........... 426
Da 6:10 gave thanks before his **G.**, as he did 426
Da 6:11 making supplication before his **G.**......... 426
Da 6:12 that shall ask a petition of any **G.** 426
Da 6:16 **G.** whom thou servest continually. 426
Da 6:20 servant of the living **G.**, is thy **G.**,....... 426
Da 6:22 My **G.** hath sent his angel, and 426
Da 6:23 him, because he believed in his **G.**....... 426
Da 6:26 and fear before the **G.** of Daniel: 426
Da 6:26 for he is the living **G.**, and stedfast...... 426
Da 9:3 And I set my face unto the Lord **G.**, ... 430
Da 9:4 I prayed unto the Lord my **G.**,............ 430
Da 9:4 O Lord, the great and dreadful **G.**, ... 410
Da 9:9 To the Lord our **G.** belong mercies...... 430
Da 9:10 obeyed the voice of the Lord our **G.**, ... 430
Da 9:11 law of Moses the servant of **G.**, ... 430
Da 9:13 prayer before the Lord our **G.**, ... 430
Da 9:14 for the Lord our **G.** is righteous 430
Da 9:15 now, O Lord our **G.**, thou hast 430
Da 9:17 Now therefore, O our **G.**, hear 430
Da 9:18 O my **G.**, incline thine ear, and hear; ... 430
Da 9:19 for thine own sake, O my **G.**: 430
Da 9:20 supplication before the Lord my **G.** 430
Da 9:20 for the holy mountain of my **G.**; 430
Da 10:12 to chasten thyself before thy **G.**, ... 430
Da 11:32 do know their **G.** shall be strong, ... 430
Da 11:36 magnify himself above every **g.** 410
Da 11:36 things against the **G.** of gods, ... 410
Da 11:37 he regard the **G.** of his fathers,........... 430
Da 11:37 nor regard any **g.**: for he shall............. 433
Da 11:38 the **G.** of forces: and a **g.** whom his...... 433
Da 11:39 most strong holds with a strange **g.**, ... 433
Ho 1:6 And **G.** said unto him, Call her ....
Ho 1:7 save them by the Lord their **G.**,.......... 430
Ho 1:9 said **G.**, Call his name Lo-ammi:..............
Ho 1:9 my people, and I will not be your **G.**. ....
Ho 1:10 Ye are the sons of the living **G.**. 410
Ho 2:23 they shall say, Thou art my **G.**. 430
Ho 3:5 seek the Lord their **G.**, and David 430
Ho 4:1 nor knowledge of **G.** in the land. 430
Ho 4:6 hast forgotten the law of thy **G.**, ... 430
Ho 4:12 a whoring from under their **G.**. 430
Ho 5:4 doings to turn unto their **G.**:............... 430
Ho 6:6 the knowledge of **G.** more than........... 430
Ho 7:10 return to the Lord their **G.**,................ 430
Ho 8:2 Israel shall cry unto me, My **G.**, ... 430
Ho 8:6 therefore it is not **G.**: but the calf......... 430
Ho 9:1 hast gone a whoring from thy **G.**, ... 430
Ho 9:8 of Ephraim was with my **G.**: but............ 430
Ho 9:8 and hatred in the house of his **G.**......... 430
Ho 9:17 My **G.** will cast them away, because 430
Ho 11:9 for I am **G.**, and not man;................... 410
Ho 11:12 but Judah yet ruleth with **G.**, and......... 430
Ho 12:3 his strength he had power with **G.**:...... 430
Ho 12:5 Even the Lord **G.** of hosts; the Lord.... 430
Ho 12:6 therefore turn thou to thy **G.**: keep...... 430
Ho 12:6 and wait on thy **G.** continually............ 430
Ho 12:9 And I that am the Lord thy **G.** from..... 430
Ho 13:4 Yet I am the Lord thy **G.** from the 430
Ho 13:4 and thou shalt know no **g.** but me:....... 430
Ho 13:16 she hath rebelled against her **G.**:......... 430
Ho 14:1 return unto the Lord thy **G.**; for.......... 430
Joe 1:13 ye ministers of my **G.**: for the meat..... 430
Joe 1:13 withholden from the house of your **G.**.... 430
Joe 1:14 into the house of the Lord your **G.**, ... 430
Joe 1:16 gladness from the house of our **G.**?...... 430
Joe 2:13 and turn unto the Lord your **G.**:.......... 430
Joe 2:14 offering unto the Lord your **G.**?........... 430
Joe 2:17 the people, Where is their **G.**?............ 430
Joe 2:23 and rejoice in the Lord your **G.**:.......... 430
Joe 2:26 praise the name of the Lord your **G.**, ... 430
Joe 2:27 am the Lord your **G.**, and none else:.... 430
Joe 3:17 I am the Lord your **G.** dwelling........... 430
Am 1:8 shall perish, saith the Lord **G.**. 3069
Am 2:8 condemned in the house of their **G.**...... 430
Am 3:7 the Lord **G.** will do nothing, but........... 3069
Am 3:8 the Lord **G.** hath spoken, who........... 3069
Am 3:11 saith the Lord **G.**; An adversary 3069
Am 3:13 of Jacob, saith the Lord **G.**, ... 3069
Am 3:13 saith the...the **G.** of hosts,................. 430
Am 4:2 The Lord **G.** hath sworn by his 3069
Am 4:5 of Israel, saith the Lord **G.**. 3069
Am 4:11 as **G.** overthrew Sodom and 430
Am 4:12 prepare to meet thy **G.**, O Israel......... 430
Am 4:13 The **G.** of hosts, is his name. 430
Am 5:3 saith the Lord **G.**; The city that......... 3069
Am 5:14 the **G.** of hosts, shall be with you, ... 430
Am 5:15 Lord **G.** of hosts will be gracious......... 430
Am 5:16 Therefore the Lord, the **G.** of hosts,.... 430
Am 5:26 the star of your **g.**, which ye made 430
Am 5:27 whose name is The **G.** of hosts............ 430
Am 6:8 Lord **G.** hath sworn by himself, ... 3069
Am 6:8 saith the Lord the **G.** of hosts,............ 430
Am 6:14 saith the Lord the **G.** of hosts;............ 430
Am 7:1 the Lord **G.** shewed unto me; 3069
Am 7:2 then I said, O Lord **G.**, forgive,.......... 3069
Am 7:4 the Lord **G.** shewed unto me: 3069
Am 7:4 the Lord **G.** called to contend by........ 3069
Am 7:5 Then said I, O Lord **G.**, cease, ... 3069
Am 7:6 shall not be, saith the Lord **G.**........... 3069
Am 8:1 the Lord **G.** shewed unto me: 3069
Am 8:3 that day, saith the Lord **G.**: there 3069
Am 8:9 that day, saith the Lord **G.**, that 3069
Am 8:11 days come, saith the Lord **G.**, ... 3069
Am 8:14 and say, Thy **g.**, O Dan, liveth;............ 430
Am 9:5 the Lord **G.** of hosts is he that.......... 3069
Am 9:8 the eyes of the Lord **G.** are upon....... 3069
Am 9:15 given them, saith the Lord thy **G.**........ 430
Ob 1 the Lord **G.** concerning Edom; 3069
Jon 1:5 cried every man unto his **g.**,............... 430
Jon 1:6 call upon thy **G.**, if so be that **G.**......... 430
Jon 1:9 I fear the Lord, the **G.** of heaven, ... 430
Jon 2:1 Jonah prayed unto the Lord his **G.**....... 430
Jon 2:6 from corruption, O Lord my **G.**............ 430
Jon 3:5 the people of Nineveh believed **G.**, ... 430
Jon 3:8 cry mightily unto **G.**: yea, ... 430
Jon 3:9 Who can tell if **G.** will turn and............ 430
Jon 3:10 **G.** saw their works, that they............. 430
Jon 3:10 **G.** repented of the evil, that he.......... 430
Jon 4:2 I knew that thou art a gracious **G.**, ... 410
Jon 4:6 the Lord **G.** prepared a gourd,............ 430
Jon 4:7 But **G.** prepared a worm when the....... 430
Jon 4:8 **G.** prepared a vehement east wind;...... 430
Jon 4:9 **G.** said to Jonah, Doest thou well 430
Mic 1:2 Lord **G.** be witness against you, ... 3069
Mic 3:7 for there is no answer of **G.**. 430
Mic 4:2 to the house of the **G.** of Jacob; 430
Mic 4:5 of the name of his **G.**, and we will....... 430
Mic 4:5 in the name of the Lord our **G.**.......... 430
Mic 5:4 of the name of the Lord his **G.**;.......... 430
Mic 6:6 and bow myself before the high **G.**? 430
Mic 6:8 and to walk humbly with thy **G.**? 430
Mic 7:7 will wait for the **G.** of my salvation: 430
Mic 7:7 salvation: my **G.** will hear me. 430
Mic 7:10 Where is the Lord thy **G.**? mine.......... 430
Mic 7:17 shall be afraid of the Lord our **G.**, ... 430
Mic 7:18 Who is a **G.** like unto thee, that.......... 410
Na 1:2 **G.** is jealous and the Lord................. 410
Hab 1:11 imputing this his power unto his **g.**...... 430
Hab 1:12 from everlasting, O Lord my **G.**, ... 430
Hab 1:12 mighty **G.**, thou hast established 6697
Hab 3:3 **G.** came from Teman, and the 433
Hab 3:18 joy in the **G.** of my salvation.............. 430
Hab 3:19 The Lord **G.** is my strength, and.......... 136
Zep 1:7 at the presence of the Lord **G.**: 3069
Zep 2:7 the Lord their **G.** shall visit them......... 430
Zep 2:9 the Lord of hosts, the **G.** of Israel, ... 430
Zep 3:2 she drew not near to her **G.**............. 430
Zep 3:17 The Lord thy **G.** in the midst of thee ... 430
Hag 1:12 the voice of the Lord their **G.**,............ 430
Hag 1:12 as the Lord their **G.** had sent him,....... 430
Hag 1:14 house of the Lord of hosts, their **G.**,.... 430
Zec 6:15 obey the voice of the Lord your **G.**...... 430
Zec 7:2 unto the house of **G.** Sherezer.......... 1008
Zec 8:8 I will be their **G.**, in truth.................. 430
Zec 8:23 we have heard that **G.** is with you. 430
Zec 9:7 even he, shall be for our **G.**, ... 430
Zec 9:14 Lord **G.** shall blow the trumpet,......... 3069
Zec 9:16 the Lord their **G.** shall save them........ 430
Zec 10:6 for I am the Lord their **G.**, and will...... 430
Zec 11:4 Thus saith the Lord my **G.**; Feed........ 430
Zec 12:5 strength in the Lord of hosts their **G.**... 430
Zec 12:8 the house of David shall be as **G.**. 430
Zec 13:9 they shall say, The Lord is my **G.**. 430
Zec 14:5 and the Lord my **G.** shall come, ... 430
Mal 1:9 beseech **G.** that he will be gracious...... 410
Mal 2:10 hath not one **G.** created us? why......... 410
Mal 2:11 married the daughter of a strange **g.** 410
Mal 2:16 For the Lord, the **G.** of Israel, saith..... 430
Mal 2:17 Where is the **G.** of judgment? 430
Mal 3:8 Will a man rob **G.**? Yet ye have........... 430
Mal 3:14 It is vain to serve **G.**: and what.......... 430
Mal 3:15 that tempt **G.** are even delivered......... 430
Mal 3:18 between him that serveth **G.** and......... 430
Mt 1:23 being interpreted is, **G.** with us. *2316*
Mt 2:12 being warned of **G.** in a dream that..........
Mt 2:22 warned of **G.** in a dream, he turned.........
Mt 3:9 **G.** is able of these stones to raise....... *2316*
Mt 3:16 he saw the Spirit of **G.** descending *2316*
Mt 4:3 If thou be the Son of **G.**, command..... *2316*
Mt 4:4 **proceedeth out of the mouth of G.**. *2316*
Mt 4:6 if thou be the Son of **G.**, cast........... *2316*
Mt 4:7 **shalt not tempt the Lord thy G.**...... *2316*
Mt 4:10 **shalt worship the Lord thy G.**,....... *2316*
Mt 5:8 **in heart; for they shall see G.**. *2316*
Mt 5:9 **shall be called the children of G.**.... *2316*
Mt 6:24 **Ye cannot serve G. and mammon**...*2316*

Mt 6:30 G. so clothe the grass of the field... 2316
Mt 6:33 seek ye first the kingdom of G.,.... 2316
Mt 8:29 Jesus, thou Son of G.? art thou ... 2316
Mt 9:8 and glorified G., which had given... 2316
Mt 12:4 he entered into the house of G.,.... 2316
Mt 12:28 cast out devils by the Spirit of G.... 2316
Mt 12:28 the kingdom of G. is come unto 2316
Mt 14:33 Of a truth thou art the Son of G.. ... 2316
Mt 15:3 the commandment of G. by your ... 2316
Mt 15:4 For G. commanded, saying, ... 2316
Mt 15:6 the commandment of G. of none ... 2316
Mt 15:31 and they glorified the G. of Israel... 2316
Mt 16:16 Christ, the Son of the living ... 2316
Mt 16:23 not the things that be of G.. ... 2316
Mt 19:6 therefore G. hath joined together.. 2316
Mt 19:17 none good but one, that is, G.:... 2316
Mt 19:24 to enter into the kingdom of G.. ... 2316
Mt 19:26 but with G. all things are possible.. 2316
Mt 21:12 into the temple of G., and cast out.... 2316
Mt 21:31 into the kingdom of G. before you. 2316
Mt 21:43 The kingdom of G. shall be taken . 2316
Mt 22:16 and teachest the way of G. in truth,... 2316
Mt 22:21 and unto G. the things that are.... 2316
Mt 22:29 the scriptures, nor the power of G.. 2316
Mt 22:30 but are as the angels of G. in ... 2316
Mt 22:31 which was spoken unto you by G., . 2316
Mt 22:32 I am the G. of Abraham... 2316
Mt 22:32 the G. of Isaac, and the G. of... 2316
Mt 22:32 G. is not the G. of the dead... 2316
Mt 22:37 Thou shalt love the Lord thy G.... 2316
Mt 23:22 sweareth by the throne of G., and .. 2316
Mt 26:61 to destroy the temple of G., and to.... 2316
Mt 26:63 I adjure thee by the living G., ... 2316
Mt 26:63 thou be the Christ, the Son of G... 2316
Mt 27:40 thou be the Son of G., come down..... 2316
Mt 27:43 He trusted in G.; let him deliver... 2316
Mt 27:43 for he said, I am the Son of G... 2316
Mt 27:46 My G., my G., why hast thou... 2316
Mt 27:54 Truly this was the Son of G... 2316
Mk 1:1 of Jesus Christ, the Son of G.; ... 2316
Mk 1:14 the gospel of the kingdom of G.,... 2316
Mk 1:15 the kingdom of G. is at hand:... 2316
Mk 1:24 who thou art, the Holy One of G.. ... 2316
Mk 2:7 who can forgive sins but G. only?... 2316
Mk 2:12 and glorified G., saying, We never... 2316
Mk 2:26 he went into the house of G... 2316
Mk 3:11 saying, Thou art the Son of G.. ... 2316
Mk 3:35 shall do the will of G., the same ... 2316
Mk 4:11 the mystery of the kingdom of G.: . 2316
Mk 4:26 So is the kingdom of G., as if... 2316
Mk 4:30 shall we liken the kingdom of G.? .. 2316
Mk 5:7 thou Son of the most high G.? ... 2316
Mk 5:7 adjure thee by G., that thou torment .. 2316
Mk 7:8 aside the commandment of G.,... 2316
Mk 7:9 ye reject the commandment of G... 2316
Mk 7:13 Making the word of G. of none.... 2316
Mk 8:33 not the things that be of G., but... 2316
Mk 9:1 they have seen the kingdom of G. . 2316
Mk 9:47 to enter into the kingdom of G. 2316
Mk 10:6 G. made them male and female.... 2316
Mk 10:9 therefore G. hath joined together, . 2316
Mk 10:14 for of such is the kingdom of G.... 2316
Mk 10:15 shall not receive the kingdom of G. 2316
Mk 10:18 is none good but one, that is, G.... 2316
Mk 10:23 enter into the kingdom of G.! ... 2316
Mk 10:24 to enter into the kingdom of G.! ... 2316
Mk 10:25 to enter into the kingdom of G.. ... 2316
Mk 10:27 impossible, but not with G.:... 2316
Mk 10:27 for with G. all things are possible. . 2316
Mk 11:22 saith unto them, Have faith in G.. ... 2316
Mk 12:14 teachest the way of G. in truth:... 2316
Mk 12:17 to G. the things that are God's... 2316
Mk 12:24 scriptures, neither the power of G.? 2316
Mk 12:26 how in the bush, G. spake unto.... 2316
Mk 12:26 saying, I am the G. of Abraham,... 2316
Mk 12:26 the G. of Isaac, and the G. of... 2316
Mk 12:27 He is not the G. of the dead, ... 2316
Mk 12:27 but the G. of the living:... 2316
Mk 12:29 The Lord our G. is one Lord:... 2316
Mk 12:30 thou shalt love the Lord thy G.... 2316
Mk 12:32 for there is one G.; and there is... 2316
Mk 12:34 not far from the kingdom of G... 2316
Mk 13:19 which G. created unto this time,... 2316
Mk 14:25 drink it new in the kingdom of G... 2316
Mk 15:34 My G., my G., why hast thou... 2316
Mk 15:39 Truly this man was the Son of G.. ... 2316
Mk 15:43 also waited for the kingdom of G.,... 2316
Mk 16:19 and sat on the right hand of G... 2316
Lu 1:6 they were both righteous before G.,... 2316
Lu 1:8 before G. in the order of his course,... 2316
Lu 1:16 shall he turn to the Lord their G... 2316
Lu 1:19 that stand in the presence of G.;... 2316
Lu 1:26 Gabriel was sent from G. unto a... 2316
Lu 1:30 for thou hast found favour with G... 2316
Lu 1:32 the Lord G. shall give unto him... 2316
Lu 1:35 of thee shall be called the Son of G.. .. 2316
Lu 1:37 G. nothing shall be impossible... 2316
Lu 1:47 hath rejoiced in G. my Saviour... 2316
Lu 1:64 and he spake, and praised G.. ... 2316
Lu 1:68 Blessed be the Lord G. of Israel;... 2316
Lu 1:78 the tender mercy of our G.;... 2316
Lu 2:13 of the heavenly host praising G.,... 2316
Lu 2:14 Glory to G. in the highest, and on... 2316
Lu 2:20 and praising G. for all the things... 2316
Lu 2:28 arms, and blessed G., and said, ... 2316
Lu 2:37 G. with fastings and prayers...
Lu 2:40 and the grace of G. was upon him..... 2316
Lu 2:52 and in favour with G. and man... 2316
Lu 3:2 the word of G. came unto John... 2316
Lu 3:6 flesh shall see the salvation of G.. ... 2316
Lu 3:8 G. is able of these stones to raise... 2316
Lu 3:38 of Adam, which was the son of G... 2316
Lu 4:3 If thou be the Son of G., command.... 2316
Lu 4:4 alone, but by every word of G... 2316
Lu 4:8 shalt worship the Lord thy G.,... 2316
Lu 4:9 thou be the Son of G., cast thyself.... 2316
Lu 4:12 shalt not tempt the Lord thy G.... 2316
Lu 4:34 who thou art, the Holy One of G.. ... 2316
Lu 4:41 Thou are Christ the Son of G... 2316
Lu 4:43 kingdom of G. to other cities also: . 2316
Lu 5:1 upon him to hear the word of G.,... 2316
Lu 5:21 Who can forgive sins, but G. alone?.... 2316
Lu 5:25 to his own house, glorifying G.. ... 2316
Lu 5:26 and they glorified G., and were filled... 2316
Lu 6:4 How he went into the house of G.,. 2316
Lu 6:12 continued all night in prayer to G.. ... 2316
Lu 6:20 for yours is the kingdom of G... 2316
Lu 7:16 and they glorified G., saying, That... 2316
Lu 7:16 G. hath visited his people... 2316
Lu 7:28 in the kingdom of G. is greater.... 2316
Lu 7:29 justified G., being baptized with... 2316
Lu 7:30 council of G. against themselves,... 2316
Lu 8:1 glad tidings of the kingdom of G.:... 2316
Lu 8:10 mysteries of the kingdom of G.:... 2316
Lu 8:11 The seed is the word of G... 2316
Lu 8:21 which hear the word of G., and do. 2316
Lu 8:28 Son of G. most high? I beseech... 2316
Lu 8:39 how great things G. hath done... 2316
Lu 9:2 to preach the kingdom of G., and... 2316
Lu 9:11 unto them of the kingdom of G.,... 2316
Lu 9:20 answering said, The Christ of G... 2316
Lu 9:27 till they see the kingdom of G... 2316
Lu 9:43 amazed at the mighty power of G... 2316
Lu 9:60 and preach the kingdom of G... 2316
Lu 9:62 back, is fit for the kingdom of G.... 2316
Lu 10:9 The kingdom of G. is come nigh ... 2316
Lu 10:11 the kingdom of G. is come nigh 2316
Lu 10:27 Thou shalt love the Lord thy G. ... 2316
Lu 11:20 But if I with the finger of G. cast.. 2316
Lu 11:20 no doubt the kingdom of G. is ... 2316
Lu 11:28 are they that hear the word of G.,. 2316
Lu 11:42 judgment and the love of G.:... 2316
Lu 11:49 said the wisdom of G., I will send. 2316
Lu 12:6 one of them is forgotten before G.? 2316
Lu 12:8 confess before the angels of G.:... 2316
Lu 12:9 be denied before the angels of G.. . 2316
Lu 12:20 But G. said unto him, Thou fool,.. 2316
Lu 12:21 and is not rich toward G.. ... 2316
Lu 12:24 G. feedeth them: how much more.. 2316
Lu 12:28 G. so clothed the grass, which is... 2316
Lu 12:31 rather seek ye the kingdom of G.;. 2316
Lu 13:13 was made straight, and glorified G... 2316
Lu 13:18 what is the kingdom of G. like?.... 2316
Lu 13:20 shall I liken the kingdom of G.?... 2316
Lu 13:28 the prophets, in the kingdom of G., 2316
Lu 13:29 sit down in the kingdom of G.. ... 2316
Lu 14:15 eat bread in the kingdom of G.. ... 2316
Lu 15:10 in the presence of the angels of G. 2316
Lu 16:13 Ye cannot serve G. and mammon... 2316
Lu 16:15 but G. knoweth your hearts; for.... 2316
Lu 16:15 is abomination in the sight of G.... 2316
Lu 16:16 the kingdom of G. is preached, and 2316
Lu 17:15 and with a loud voice glorified G., ... 2316
Lu 17:18 give glory to G., save this stranger. 2316
Lu 17:20 when the kingdom of G. should... 2316
Lu 17:20 kingdom of G. cometh not with..... 2316
Lu 17:21 the kingdom of G. is within you..... 2316
Lu 18:2 feared not G., neither regarded 2316
Lu 18:4 Though I fear not G., nor regard .. 2316
Lu 18:7 And shall not G. avenge his own... 2316
Lu 18:11 G., I thank thee, that I am not as.. 2316
Lu 18:13 G. be merciful to me a sinner... 2316
Lu 18:16 for of such is the kingdom of G..... 2316
Lu 18:17 shall not receive the kingdom of G. 2316
Lu 18:19 None is good, save one, that is, G.. 2316
Lu 18:24 enter into the kingdom of G.! ... 2316
Lu 18:25 enter into the kingdom of G.. ... 2316
Lu 18:27 with men are possible with G... 2316
Lu 18:43 followed him, glorifying G.; and all... 2316
Lu 18:43 they saw it, gave praise unto G.. ... 2316
Lu 19:11 kingdom of G. should immediately ... 2316
Lu 19:37 and praise G. with a loud voice for... 2316
Lu 20:16 heard it, they said, G. forbid..... 3361,1096
Lu 20:21 but teachest the way of G. truly: ... 2316
Lu 20:25 and unto G. the things which be ... 2316
Lu 20:36 and are the children of G., being... 2316
Lu 20:37 the Lord the G. of Abraham, ... 2316
Lu 20:37 G. of Isaac, and the G. of Jacob.... 2316
Lu 20:38 For he is not a G. of the dead,... 2316
Lu 21:4 cast in unto the offerings of G..... 2316
Lu 21:31 the kingdom of G. is nigh at hand.. 2316
Lu 22:16 be fulfilled in the kingdom of G.... 2316
Lu 22:18 the kingdom of G. shall come ... 2316
Lu 22:69 the right hand of the power of G.... 2316
Lu 22:70 Art thou then the Son of G.?... 2316
Lu 23:35 if he be Christ, the chosen of G... 2316
Lu 23:40 Dost not thou fear G., seeing thou..... 2316
Lu 23:47 he glorified G., saying, Certainly... 2316
Lu 23:51 waited for the kingdom of G... 2316
Lu 24:19 word before G. and all the people: 2316
Lu 24:53 temple, praising and blessing G..... 2316
Joh 1:1 was with G., and the Word was G.. ... 2316
Joh 1:2 same was in the beginning with G.. 2316
Joh 1:6 There was a man sent from G.,... 2316
Joh 1:12 power to become the sons of G.,... 2316
Joh 1:13 nor of the will of man, but of G.. ... 2316
Joh 1:18 No man hath seen G. at any time;... 2316
Joh 1:29 and saith, Behold the Lamb of G.,... 2316
Joh 1:34 record that this is the Son of G.. ... 2316
Joh 1:36 he saith, Behold the Lamb of G.! ... 2316
Joh 1:49 Rabbi, thou art the Son of G.; ... 2316
Joh 1:51 and the angels of G. ascending... 2316
Joh 3:2 thou art a teacher, come from G... 2316
Joh 3:2 thou doest, except G. be with him. 2316
Joh 3:3 he cannot see the kingdom of G.... 2316
Joh 3:5 enter into the kingdom of G... 2316
Joh 3:16 G. so loved the world, that he... 2316
Joh 3:17 G. sent not his Son into the world.. 2316
Joh 3:18 of the only begotten Son of G.. ... 2316
Joh 3:21 that they are wrought in G... 2316
Joh 3:33 hath set to his seal that G. is true... 2316
Joh 3:34 For he whom G. hath sent speaketh... 2316
Joh 3:34 words of G.: for G. giveth not the 2316
Joh 3:36 the wrath of G. abideth on him... 2316
Joh 4:10 If thou knewest the gift of G.,... 2316
Joh 4:24 G. is a Spirit: and they that... 2316
Joh 5:18 said also that G. was his Father,... 2316
Joh 5:18 making himself equal with G... 2316
Joh 5:25 hear the voice of the Son of G.:.... 2316
Joh 5:42 ye have not the love of G. in you.. 2316
Joh 5:44 honour that cometh from G. only? . 2316
Joh 6:27 for him hath G. the Father sealed.. 2316
Joh 6:28 we might work the works of G.?... 2316
Joh 6:29 This is the work of G., that ye... 2316
Joh 6:33 For the bread of G. is he which... 2316
Joh 6:45 And they shall be all taught of G.. 2316
Joh 6:46 he which is of G., he hath seen..... 2316
Joh 6:69 that Christ, the Son of the living G..... 2316
Joh 7:17 whether it be of G., or whether I.. 2316
Joh 8:40 truth which I have heard of G.:.... 2316
Joh 8:41 we have one Father, even G... 2316
Joh 8:42 If G. were your Father, ye would.. 2316
Joh 8:42 forth, and came from G.;... 2316
Joh 8:47 that is of G. heareth God's words:. 2316
Joh 8:47 them not, because ye are not of G.. 2316
Joh 8:54 whom ye say, that he is your G.: .. 2316
Joh 9:3 that the works of G. should be..... 2316
Joh 9:16 This man is not of G., because he... 2316
Joh 9:24 Give G. the praise: we know that 2316
Joh 9:29 know that G. spake unto Moses:... 2316
Joh 9:31 know that G. heareth not sinners: 2316

Joh 9:31 if any man be a worshipper of G., ... 2318
Joh 9:33 If this man were not of G., he.......... 2316
Joh 9:35 **thou believe on the Son of G.?** 2316
Joh 10:33 being a man, makest thyself G.......... 2316
Joh 10:35 **unto whom the word of G. came,** .. 2316
Joh 10:36 **because I said, I am the Son of G.?** 2316
Joh 11:4 **unto death, but for the glory of G.,** 2316
Joh 11:4 **the Son of G. might be glorified**.... 2316
Joh 11:22 whatsoever thou wilt ask of G., ... 2316
Joh 11:22 G. will give it thee........................ 2316
Joh 11:27 thou art the Christ, the Son of G., ... 2316
Joh 11:40 **thou shouldest see the glory of G.?** .2316
Joh 11:52 children of G. that were scattered...... 2316
Joh 12:43 of men more than the praise of G.. 2316
Joh 13:3 was come from G., and went to G.; ... 2316
Joh 13:31 **glorified, and G. is glorified in**...... 2316
Joh 13:32 **If G. be glorified in him,** 2316
Joh 13:32 **G. shall also glorify him in**.......... 2316
Joh 14:1 **ye believe in G., believe also in me.** 2316
Joh 16:2 **think that he doeth G. service**....... 2316
Joh 16:27 **believed that I came out from G**.... 2316
Joh 16:30 that thou camest forth from G.. 2316
Joh 17:3 **might know thee the only true G..** .2316
Joh 19:7 he made himself the Son of G.. 2316
Joh 20:17 **and to my G., and your G**............ 2316
Joh 20:28 said unto him, My Lord and my G.,.... 2316
Joh 20:31 Jesus is the Christ, the Son of G.; 2316
Joh 21:19 by what death he should glorify G.. 2316
Ac 1:3 pertaining to the kingdom of G.: 2316
Ac 2:11 tongue the wonderful works of G.. 2316
Ac 2:17 saith G., I will pour out of my........... 2316
Ac 2:22 a man approved of G. among you....... 2316
Ac 2:22 G. did by him in the midst of you,...... 2316
Ac 2:23 counsel and foreknowledge of G.,....... 2316
Ac 2:24 Whom G. hath raised up, having 2316
Ac 2:30 G. had sworn with an oath to him, ... 2316
Ac 2:32 This Jesus hath G. raised up, ... 2316
Ac 2:33 by the right hand of G. exalted........... 2316
Ac 2:36 that G. hath made that same Jesus, ... 2316
Ac 2:39 many as the Lord our G. shall call...... 2316
Ac 2:47 Praising G., and having favour........... 2316
Ac 3:8 and leaping, and praising G.. 2316
Ac 3:9 saw him walking and praising G.. 2316
Ac 3:13 The G. of Abraham, and of Isaac, ... 2316
Ac 3:13 and of Jacob, the G. of our fathers. 2316
Ac 3:15 whom G. hath raised from the dead;... 2316
Ac 3:18 things, which G. before had shewed.... 2316
Ac 3:21 which G. hath spoken by the mouth.... 2316
Ac 3:22 the Lord your G. raise up unto you.... 2316
Ac 3:25 convenant which G. made with our..... 2316
Ac 3:26 G., having raised up his Son Jesus,..... 2316
Ac 4:10 whom G. raised from the dead, ... 2316
Ac 4:19 right in the sight of G. to hearken 2316
Ac 4:19 unto you more than unto G.,............. 2316
Ac 4:21 all men glorified G. for that which 2316
Ac 4:24 they lifted up their voice to G. 2316
Ac 4:24 art G., which hast made heaven,........ 2316
Ac 4:31 they spake the word of G. with 2316
Ac 5:4 not lied unto men, but unto G.. 2316
Ac 5:29 ought to obey G. rather than men. 2316
Ac 5:30 The G. of our fathers raised up 2316
Ac 5:31 Him hath G. exalted with his............. 2316
Ac 5:32 G. hath given to them that obey 2316
Ac 5:39 But if it be of G., ye cannot............. 2316
Ac 5:39 be found even to fight against G.. 2314
Ac 6:2 we should leave the word of G., ... 2316
Ac 6:7 And the word of G. increased; and..... 2316
Ac 6:11 against Moses, and against G.. 2316
Ac 7:2 The G. of glory appeared unto our..... 2316
Ac 7:6 And G. spake on this wise, That........ 2316
Ac 7:7 in bondage will I judge, said G.:......... 2316
Ac 7:9 into Egypt; but G. was with him, ... 2316
Ac 7:17 which G. had sworn to Abraham, ... 2316
Ac 7:25 how that G. by his hand would 2316
Ac 7:32 Saying, I am the G. of thy fathers, ... 2316
Ac 7:32 thy fathers, the G. of Abraham, ... 2316
Ac 7:32 G. of Isaac, and the G. of Jacob. 2316
Ac 7:35 the same did G. send to be a ruler...... 2316
Ac 7:37 the Lord your G. raise up unto you.... 2316
Ac 7:42 Then G. turned, and gave them up..... 2316
Ac 7:43 and the star of your g. Remphan,....... 2316
Ac 7:45 whom G. drave out before the face 2316
Ac 7:46 favour before G., and desired to 2316
Ac 7:46 a tabernacle for the G. of Jacob. 2316
Ac 7:55 and saw the glory of G., and Jesus..... 2316
Ac 7:55 standing on the right hand of G.,........ 2316
Ac 7:56 standing on the right hand of G.......... 2316
Ac 7:59 stoned Stephen calling upon G., ...
Ac 8:10 This man is the great power of G.. 2316
Ac 8:12 concerning the kingdom of G., ... 2316
Ac 8:14 had received the word of G., ... 2316
Ac 8:20 hast thought that the gift of G. may.... 2316
Ac 8:21 heart is not right in the sight of G...... 2316
Ac 8:22 pray G., if perhaps the thought.......... 2316
Ac 8:37 that Jesus Christ is the Son of G......... 2316
Ac 9:20 synagogues, that he is the Son of G.. ..2316
Ac 10:2 that feared G. with all his house, ... 2316
Ac 10:2 people, and prayed to G. alway.......... 2316
Ac 10:3 an angel of G. coming in to him, ... 2316
Ac 10:4 come up for a memorial before G........ 2316
Ac 10:15 What G. hath cleansed, that call not.... 2316
Ac 10:22 and one that feareth G., and of good... 2316
Ac 10:22 was warned from G., by an holy angel ......
Ac 10:28 G. hath shewed me that I should 2316
Ac 10:31 in remembrance in the sight of G....... 2316
Ac 10:33 are we all here present before G., ... 2316
Ac 10:33 that are commanded thee of G........... 2316
Ac 10:34 that G. is no respecter of persons:..... 2316
Ac 10:36 The word which G. sent unto the............
Ac 10:38 G. anointed Jesus of Nazareth 2316
Ac 10:38 of the devil; for G. was with him. 2316
Ac 10:40 Him G. raised up the third day, ... 2316
Ac 10:41 witnesses chosen before of G., even... 2316
Ac 10:42 was ordained of G. to be the Judge 2316
Ac 10:46 speak with tongues, and magnify G..... 2316
Ac 11:1 had also received the word of G.. 2316
Ac 11:9 What G. hath cleansed, that call......... 2316
Ac 11:17 G. gave them the like gift as he did.... 2316
Ac 11:17 was I, that I could withstand G.? 2316
Ac 11:18 and glorified G., saying, then hath...... 2316
Ac 11:18 G. also to the Gentiles granted.......... 2316
Ac 11:23 had seen the grace of G., was glad,..... 2316
Ac 12:5 of the church unto G. for him............ 2316
Ac 12:22 the voice of a g., and not of a man..... 2316
Ac 12:23 because he gave not G. the glory:...... 2316
Ac 12:24 word of G. grew and multiplied.......... 2316
Ac 13:5 they preached the word of G. in the... 2316
Ac 13:7 and desirecd to hear the word of G.. .. 2316
Ac 13:16 ye that fear G., give audience. 2316
Ac 13:17 The G. of the people of Israel 2316
Ac 13:21 G. gave unto them Saul the son of..... 2316
Ac 13:23 this man's seed hath G. according 2316
Ac 13:26 whosoever among you feareth G., ... 2316
Ac 13:30 But G. raised him from the dead:....... 2316
Ac 13:33 G. hath fulfilled the same unto us....... 2316
Ac 13:36 by the will of G., fell on sleep, and...... 2316
Ac 13:37 But he, whom G. raised again, saw.... 2316
Ac 13:43 to continue in the grace of G............ 2316
Ac 13:44 together to hear the word of G........... 2316
Ac 13:46 the word of G. should first have 2316
Ac 14:15 unto the living G., which made 2316
Ac 14:22 enter into the kingdom of G.. 2316
Ac 14:26 to the grace of G. for the work 2316
Ac 14:27 all that G. had done with them, ... 2316
Ac 15:4 things that G. had done with them...... 2316
Ac 15:7 G. made choice among us, that the..... 2316
Ac 15:8 And G., which knoweth the hearts, ... 2316
Ac 15:10 now therefore why tempt ye G.,......... 2316
Ac 15:12 miracles and wonders G. had............ 2316
Ac 15:14 how G. at the first did visit the 2316
Ac 15:18 Known unto G. are all his works........ 2316
Ac 15:19 the Gentiles are turned to G.: 2316
Ac 15:40 brethren unto the grace of G............. 2316
Ac 16:14 which worshipped G., heard us: 2316
Ac 16:17 the servants of the most high G.,....... 2316
Ac 16:25 and sang praises unto G.: and 2316
Ac 16:34 believing in G. with all his house........ 2316
Ac 17:13 word of G. was preached of Paul 2316
Ac 17:23 To The Unknown G.. Whom............. 2316
Ac 17:24 G. that made the world and all 2316
Ac 17:29 then as we are the offspring of G.,..... 2316
Ac 17:30 ignorance G. winked at; but now........ 2316
Ac 18:7 one that worshipped G., whose........... 2316
Ac 18:11 the word of G. among them.............. 2316
Ac 18:13 to worship G. contrary to the law. 2316
Ac 18:21 return again unto you, if G. will. 2316
Ac 18:26 him the way of G. more perfectly....... 2316
Ac 19:8 concerning the kingdom of G............ 2316
Ac 19:11 G. wrought special miracles by the..... 2316
Ac 19:20 mightily grew the word of G. and........ 2962
Ac 20:21 repentance toward G., and faith......... 2316
Ac 20:24 the gospel of the grace of G.............. 2316
Ac 20:25 preaching the kingdom of G., ... 2316
Ac 20:27 unto you all the counsel of G............. 2316
Ac 20:28 to feed the church of G., which......... 2316
Ac 20:32 I commend you to G., and to 2316
Ac 21:19 things G. had wrought among the....... 2316
Ac 22:3 and was zealous toward G., as ye 2316
Ac 22:14 G. of our fathers hath chosen thee, ... 2316
Ac 23:1 in all good conscience before G.......... 2316
Ac 23:3 G. shall smite thee, thou whited 2316
Ac 23:9 let us not fight against G.. 2313
Ac 24:14 worship I the G. of my fathers, ... 2316
Ac 24:15 And have hope toward G., which 2316
Ac 24:16 void of offence toward G., ... 2316
Ac 26:6 made of G. unto our fathers:............. 2316
Ac 26:7 instantly serving G. day and night,............
Ac 26:8 that G. should raise the dead?........... 2316
Ac 26:18 **from the power of Satan unto G.,**.. 2316
Ac 26:20 repent and turn to G., and do............ 2316
Ac 26:22 therefore obtained help of G., I 2316
Ac 26:29 I would to G., that not only thou, ... 2316
Ac 27:23 the angel of G., whose I am, and....... 2316
Ac 27:24 G. hath given thee all them that........ 2316
Ac 27:25 for I believe G., that it shall be 2316
Ac 27:35 and gave thanks to G. in presence...... 2316
Ac 28:6 minds, and said that he was a g........ 2316
Ac 28:15 he thanked G., and took courage........ 2316
Ac 28:23 and testified the kingdom of G........... 2316
Ac 28:28 the salvation of G. is sent unto.......... 2316
Ac 28:31 Preaching the kingdom of G., and....... 2316
Ro 1:1 separated unto the gospel of G., ... 2316
Ro 1:4 And declared to be the Son of G.......... 2316
Ro 1:7 be in Rome, beloved of G., called 2316
Ro 1:7 from G. our Father, and the Lord 2316
Ro 1:8 thank my G. through Jesus Christ 2316
Ro 1:9 For G. is my witness, whom I serve .. 2316
Ro 1:10 by the will of G. to come unto you. 2316
Ro 1:16 for it is the power of G. unto............ 2316
Ro 1:17 therein is the righteousness of G........ 2316
Ro 1:18 For the wrath of G. is revealed 2316
Ro 1:19 may be known of G. is manifest......... 2316
Ro 1:19 for G. hath shewed it unto them.......... 2316
Ro 1:21 Because that, when they knew G.,...... 2316
Ro 1:21 they glorified him not as G.,.............. 2316
Ro 1:23 the glory of the uncorruptible G......... 2316
Ro 1:24 Wherefore G. also gave them up to..... 2316
Ro 1:25 changed the truth of G. into a lie, ... 2316
Ro 1:26 cause G. gave them up unto vile........ 2316
Ro 1:28 to retain G. in their knowledge, ... 2316
Ro 1:28 G. gave them over to a reprobate 2316
Ro 1:30 haters of G., despiteful, proud,.......... 2319
Ro 1:32 Who knowing the judgment of G., ... 2316
Ro 2:2 the judgment of G. is according 2316
Ro 2:3 shalt escape the judgment of G.?........ 2316
Ro 2:4 the goodness of G. leadeth thee to..... 2316
Ro 2:5 of the righteous judgment of G.; 2316
Ro 2:11 is no respect of persons with G.. 2316
Ro 2:13 are just before G., but the doers 2316
Ro 2:16 G. shall judge the secrets of men....... 2316
Ro 2:17 and makest thy boast of G., ... 2316
Ro 2:23 the law dishonourest thou G.? 2316
Ro 2:24 For the name of G. is blasphemed...... 2316
Ro 2:29 praise is not of men, but of G.. 2316
Ro 3:2 were committed the oracles of G.. 2316
Ro 3:3 the faith of G. without effect?............ 2316
Ro 3:4 G. forbid: yea, let.................... 3361,1096
Ro 3:4 let G. be true, but every man a.......... 2316
Ro 3:5 commend the righteousness of G.,....... 2316
Ro 3:5 Is G. unrighteous who taketh............. 2316
Ro 3:6 G. forbid: for then 3361,1096
Ro 3:6 how shall G. judge the world? 2316
Ro 3:7 truth of G. hath more abounded......... 2316
Ro 3:11 there is none that seeketh after G...... 2316
Ro 3:18 is no fear of G. before their eyes....... 2316
Ro 3:19 may become guilty before G............. 2316
Ro 3:21 righteousness of G. without the law.... 2316
Ro 3:22 Even the righteousness of G. which.... 2316
Ro 3:23 and come short of the glory of G.; 2316
Ro 3:25 Whom G. hath set forth to be a......... 2316
Ro 3:25 through the forbearance of G.;........... 2316
Ro 3:29 Is he the G. of the Jews only?........... 2316
Ro 3:30 Seeing it is one G., which shall.......... 2316
Ro 3:31 G. forbid: yea, we establish 3336,1096
Ro 4:2 to glory; but not before G.. 2316
Ro 4:3 Abraham believed G., and it was........ 2316
Ro 4:6 whom G. imputeth righteousness......... 2316
Ro 4:17 even G., who quickeneth the dead,..... 2316
Ro 4:20 promise of G. through unbelief;.......... 2316
Ro 4:20 strong in faith, giving glory to G.; 2316
Ro 5:1 we have peace with G. through our.... 2316

Book	Ref.	Text	No.
Ro	5:2	rejoice in hope of the glory of **G.**.	*2316*
Ro	5:5	the love of **G.** is shed abroad in our	*2316*
Ro	5:8	**G.** commendeth his love toward us,	*2316*
Ro	5:10	were reconciled to **G.** by the death	*2316*
Ro	5:11	we also joy in **G.** through our Lord	*2316*
Ro	5:15	much more the grace of **G.**, and the	*2316*
Ro	6:2	**G.** forbid. How shall we,	*3361,1096*
Ro	6:10	that he liveth, he liveth unto **G.**.	*2316*
Ro	6:11	alive unto **G.** through Jesus Christ	*2316*
Ro	6:13	yield yourselves unto **G.**, as those	*2316*
Ro	6:13	of righteousness unto **G.**.	*2316*
Ro	6:15	but under grace? **G.** forbid.	*3361,1096*
Ro	6:17	But **G.** be thanked, that ye were	*2316*
Ro	6:22	and become servants to **G.**, ye have	*2316*
Ro	6:23	but the gift of **G.** is eternal life	*2316*
Ro	7:4	should bring forth fruit unto **G.**.	*2316*
Ro	7:7	**G.** forbid. Nay, I had not	*3361,1096*
Ro	7:13	**G.** forbid. But sin, that it	*3361,1096*
Ro	7:22	For I delight in the law of **G.**	*2316*
Ro	7:25	I thank **G.** through Jesus Christ	*2316*
Ro	7:25	then I myself serve the law of **G.**;	*2316*
Ro	8:3	**G.** sending his own Son in the	*2316*
Ro	8:7	carnal mind is enmity against **G.**:	*2316*
Ro	8:7	for it is not subject to the law of **G.**,	*2316*
Ro	8:8	are in the flesh cannot please **G.**.	*2316*
Ro	8:9	if so be that the Spirit of **G.** dwell	*2316*
Ro	8:14	many as are led by the Spirit of **G.**:	*2316*
Ro	8:14	they are the sons of **G.**.	*2316*
Ro	8:16	that we are the children of **G.**:	*2316*
Ro	8:17	heirs of **G.**, and joint-heirs with	*2316*
Ro	8:19	the manifestation of the sons of **G.**.	*2316*
Ro	8:21	liberty of the children of **G.**	*2316*
Ro	8:27	saints according to the will of **G.**.	*2316*
Ro	8:28	for good to them that love **G.**, to	*2316*
Ro	8:31	If **G.** be for us, who can be against	*2316*
Ro	8:33	God's elect? It is **G.** that justifieth.	*2316*
Ro	8:34	who is even at the right hand of **G.**,	*2316*
Ro	8:39	to separate us from the love of **G.**,	*2316*
Ro	9:4	the service of **G.**, and the promises;	
Ro	9:5	who is over all, **G.** blessed forever.	*2316*
Ro	9:6	word of **G.** hath taken none effect,	*2316*
Ro	9:8	these are not the children of **G.**:	*2316*
Ro	9:11	purpose of **G.** according to election	*2316*
Ro	9:14	Is there unrighteousness with **G.**?	*2316*
Ro	9:14	unrighteousness...? **G.** forbid.	*3361,1096*
Ro	9:16	but of **G.** that sheweth mercy.	*2316*
Ro	9:20	art thou that repliest against **G.**?	*2316*
Ro	9:22	if **G.**, willing to shew his wrath,	*2316*
Ro	9:26	called the children of the living **G.**.	*2316*
Ro	10:1	and prayer to **G.** for Israel is, that	*2316*
Ro	10:2	have a zeal of **G.**, but not according	*2316*
Ro	10:3	unto the righteousness of **G.**.	*2316*
Ro	10:9	**G.** hath raised him from the dead,	*2316*
Ro	10:17	and hearing by the word of **G.**.	*2316*
Ro	11:1	Hath **G.** cast away his people?	*2316*
Ro	11:1	away his people? **G.** forbid.	*3361,1096*
Ro	11:2	**G.** hath not cast away his people	*2316*
Ro	11:2	how he maketh intercession to **G.**	*2316*
Ro	11:4	what saith the answer of **G.** unto him?	
Ro	11:8	**G.** hath given them the spirit of	*2316*
Ro	11:11	they should fall? **G.** forbid.	*3361,1096*
Ro	11:21	For if **G.** spared not the natural	*2316*
Ro	11:22	the goodness and severity of **G.**:	*2316*
Ro	11:23	for **G.** is able to graff them in	*2316*
Ro	11:29	For the gifts and calling of **G.**	*2316*
Ro	11:30	times past have not believed **G.**,	*2316*
Ro	11:32	For **G.** hath concluded them all in	*2316*
Ro	11:33	the wisdom and knowledge of **G.**!	*2316*
Ro	12:1	the mercies of **G.**, that ye present	*2316*
Ro	12:1	acceptable unto **G.**, which is your	*2316*
Ro	12:2	acceptable, and perfect, will of **G.**.	*2316*
Ro	12:3	according as **G.** hath dealt to every	*2316*
Ro	13:1	For there is no power but of **G.**:	*2316*
Ro	13:1	powers that be are ordained of **G.**.	*2316*
Ro	13:2	resisteth the ordinance of **G.**: and	*2316*
Ro	13:4	For he is the minister of **G.** to thee	*2316*
Ro	13:4	for he is the minister of **G.**,	*2316*
Ro	14:3	for **G.** hath received him.	*2316*
Ro	14:4	for **G.** is able to make him stand.	*2316*
Ro	14:6	the Lord, for he giveth **G.** thanks:	*2316*
Ro	14:6	eateth not, and giveth **G.** thanks.	*2316*
Ro	14:11	every tongue shall confess to **G.**.	*2316*
Ro	14:12	shall give account of himself to **G.**.	*2316*
Ro	14:17	For the kingdom of **G.** is not meat	*2316*
Ro	14:18	serveth Christ is acceptable to **G.**,	*2316*
Ro	14:20	meat destroy not the work of **G.**.	*2316*
Ro	14:22	faith? have it to thyself before **G.**.	*2316*
Ro	15:5	the **G.** of patience and consolation	*2316*
Ro	15:6	mind and one mouth glorify **G.**,	*2316*
Ro	15:7	also received us to the glory of **G.**.	*2316*
Ro	15:8	for the truth of **G.**, to confirm the	*2316*
Ro	15:9	Gentiles might glorify **G.** for his	*2316*
Ro	15:13	Now the **G.** of hope fill you with	*2316*
Ro	15:15	the grace that is given to me of **G.**,	*2316*
Ro	15:16	ministering the gospel of **G.**, that	*2316*
Ro	15:17	in those things which pertain to **G.**.	*2316*
Ro	15:19	by the power of the Spirit of **G.**;	*2316*
Ro	15:30	in your prayers to **G.** for me;	*2316*
Ro	15:32	unto you with joy by the will of **G.**,	*2316*
Ro	15:33	now the **G.** of peace be with you	*2316*
Ro	16:20	And the **G.** of peace shall bruise	*2316*
Ro	16:26	of the everlasting **G.**, made known	*2316*
Ro	16:27	To **G.** only wise, be glory through	*2316*
1Co	1:1	apostle...through the will of **G.**,	*2316*
1Co	1:2	Unto the church of **G.** which is at	*2316*
1Co	1:3	and peace, from **G.** our Father, and	*2316*
1Co	1:4	I thank my **G.** always on your	*2316*
1Co	1:4	behalf, for the grace of **G.** which	*2316*
1Co	1:9	**G.** is faithful, by whom ye were	*2316*
1Co	1:14	I thank **G.** that I baptized none of	*2316*
1Co	1:18	are saved it is the power of **G.**.	*2316*
1Co	1:20	not **G.** made foolish the wisdom	*2316*
1Co	1:21	For after that in the wisdom of **G.**	*2316*
1Co	1:21	the world by wisdom knew not **G.**,	*2316*
1Co	1:21	it pleased **G.** by the foolishness	*2316*
1Co	1:24	power of **G.**, and the wisdom of **G.**.	*2316*
1Co	1:25	the foolishness of **G.** is wiser than	*2316*
1Co	1:25	men; and the weakness of **G.** is	*2316*
1Co	1:27	**G.** hath chosen the foolish things	*2316*
1Co	1:27	**G.** hath chosen the weak things	*2316*
1Co	1:28	are despised, hath **G.** chosen,	*2316*
1Co	1:30	who of **G.** is made unto us wisdom,	*2316*
1Co	2:1	unto you the testimony of **G.**.	*2316*
1Co	2:5	of men, but in the power of **G.**.	*2316*
1Co	2:7	the wisdom of **G.** in a mystery,	*2316*
1Co	2:7	**G.** ordained before the world unto	*2316*
1Co	2:9	which **G.** hath prepared for them	*2316*
1Co	2:10	But **G.** hath revealed them unto us	*2316*
1Co	2:10	things, yea, the deep things of **G.**,	*2316*
1Co	2:11	even so the things of **G.** knoweth	*2316*
1Co	2:11	no man, but the Spirit of **G.**.	*2316*
1Co	2:12	but the spirit which is of **G.**; that	*2316*
1Co	2:12	that are freely given to us of **G.**.	*2316*
1Co	2:14	not the things of the Spirit of **G.**.	*2316*
1Co	3:6	watered; but **G.** gave the increase.	*2316*
1Co	3:7	but **G.** that giveth the increase.	*2316*
1Co	3:9	are labourers together with **G.**	*2316*
1Co	3:10	According to the grace of **G.** which	*2316*
1Co	3:16	that ye are the temple of **G.**, and	*2316*
1Co	3:16	that the Spirit of **G.** dwelleth in	*2316*
1Co	3:17	If any man defile the temple of **G.**,	*2316*
1Co	3:17	him shall **G.** destroy;	*2316*
1Co	3:17	for the temple of **G.** is holy, which	*2316*
1Co	3:19	this world is foolishness with **G.**,	*2316*
1Co	4:1	stewards of the mysteries of **G.**.	*2316*
1Co	4:5	shall every man have praise of **G.**.	*2316*
1Co	4:8	and I would to **G.** ye did reign,	
1Co	4:9	**G.** hath set forth us the apostles	*2316*
1Co	4:20	the kingdom of **G.** is not in word,	*2316*
1Co	5:13	them that are without **G.** judgeth.	*2316*
1Co	6:9	not inherit the kingdom of **G.**?	*2316*
1Co	6:10	shall inherit the kingdom of **G.**	*2316*
1Co	6:11	Jesus, and by the Spirit of our **G.**.	*2316*
1Co	6:13	**G.** shall destroy both it and them.	*2316*
1Co	6:14	**G.** hath both raised up the Lord,	*2316*
1Co	6:15	of an harlot? **G.** forbid.	*3361,1096*
1Co	6:19	which ye have of **G.**, and ye are	*2316*
1Co	6:20	therefore glorify **G.** in your body,	*2316*
1Co	7:7	man hath his proper gift of **G.**,	*2316*
1Co	7:15	but **G.** hath called us to peace.	*2316*
1Co	7:17	**G.** hath distributed to every man,	*2316*
1Co	7:19	of the commandments of **G.**	*2316*
1Co	7:24	he is called, therein abide with **G.**.	*2316*
1Co	7:40	also that I have the Spirit of **G.**.	*2316*
1Co	8:3	But if any man love **G.**, the same	*2316*
1Co	8:4	there is none other **G.** but one.	*2316*
1Co	8:6	there is but one **G.**, the Father,	*2316*
1Co	8:8	meat commendeth us not to **G.**:	*2316*
1Co	9:9	Doth **G.** take care of oxen?	*2316*
1Co	9:21	(being not without law to **G.**, but	*2316*
1Co	10:5	of them **G.** was not well pleased:	*2316*
1Co	10:13	**G.** is faithful, who will not suffer	*2316*
1Co	10:20	sacrifice to devils, and not to **G.**	*2316*
1Co	10:31	ye do, do all to the glory of **G.**	*2316*
1Co	10:32	Gentiles, nor to the church of **G.**	*2316*
1Co	11:3	and the head of Christ is **G.**	*2316*
1Co	11:7	as he is the image and glory of **G.**	*2316*
1Co	11:12	by the woman; but all things of **G.**	*2316*
1Co	11:13	woman pray unto **G.** uncovered?	*2316*
1Co	11:16	custom, neither the churches of **G.**	*2316*
1Co	11:22	or despise ye the church of **G.**, and	*2316*
1Co	12:3	speaking by the Spirit of **G.** calleth	*2316*
1Co	12:6	it is the same **G.** which worketh	*2316*
1Co	12:18	But now hath **G.** set the members	*2316*
1Co	12:24	but **G.** hath tempered the body	*2316*
1Co	12:28	**G.** hath set some in the church,	*2316*
1Co	14:2	not unto men, but unto **G.**	*2316*
1Co	14:18	thank my **G.**, I speak with tongues	*2316*
1Co	14:25	he will worship **G.**, and report	*2316*
1Co	14:25	report that **G.** is in you of a truth.	*2316*
1Co	14:28	let him speak to himself, and to **G.**	*2316*
1Co	14:33	**G.** is not the author of confusion,	*2316*
1Co	14:36	came the word of **G.** out from you?	*2316*
1Co	15:9	I persecuted the church of **G.**	*2316*
1Co	15:10	But by the grace of **G.** I am what	*2316*
1Co	15:10	but the grace of **G.** which was	*2316*
1Co	15:15	are found false witnesses of **G.**;	*2316*
1Co	15:15	have testified of **G.** that he raised	*2316*
1Co	15:24	delivered up the kingdom to **G.**,	*2316*
1Co	15:28	that **G.** may be all in all.	*2316*
1Co	15:34	some have not the knowledge of **G.**	*2316*
1Co	15:38	But **G.** giveth it a body as it hath	*2316*
1Co	15:50	cannot inherit the kingdom of **G.**;	*2316*
1Co	15:57	But thanks be to **G.**, which giveth	*2316*
1Co	16:2	in store, as **G.** has prospered him,	
2Co	1:1	an apostle...by the will of **G.**, and	*2316*
2Co	1:1	unto the church of **G.** which is at	*2316*
2Co	1:2	and peace from **G.** our Father, and	*2316*
2Co	1:3	Blessed be **G.**, even the Father	*2316*
2Co	1:3	and the **G.** of all comfort;	*2316*
2Co	1:4	we ourselves are comforted of **G.**.	*2316*
2Co	1:9	but in **G.** which raiseth the dead:	*2316*
2Co	1:12	but by the grace of **G.**, we have	*2316*
2Co	1:18	But as **G.** is true, our word toward	*2316*
2Co	1:19	For the Son of **G.**, Jesus Christ,	*2316*
2Co	1:20	For all the promises of **G.** in him	*2316*
2Co	1:20	unto the glory of **G.** by us.	*2316*
2Co	1:21	and hath anointed us, is **G.**;	*2316*
2Co	1:23	call **G.** for a record upon my soul,	*2316*
2Co	2:14	Now thanks be unto **G.**, which	*2316*
2Co	2:15	we are unto **G.** a sweet savour of	*2316*
2Co	2:17	many, which corrupt the word of **G.**:	*2316*
2Co	2:17	but as of **G.**, in the sight of **G.**	*2316*
2Co	3:3	with the Spirit of the living **G.**;	*2316*
2Co	3:5	but our sufficiency is of **G.**;	*2316*
2Co	4:2	handling the word of **G.** deceitfully;	*2316*
2Co	4:2	man's conscience in the sight of **G.**	*2316*
2Co	4:4	the **g.** of this world hath blinded	*2316*
2Co	4:4	who is the image of **G.**, should	*2316*
2Co	4:6	For **G.**, who commanded the light	*2316*
2Co	4:6	of the knowledge of the glory of **G.**	*2316*
2Co	4:7	of the power may be of **G.**, and not	*2316*
2Co	4:15	many redound to the glory of **G.**.	*2316*
2Co	5:1	we have a building of **G.**, an house	*2316*
2Co	5:5	us for the selfsame thing is **G.**,	*2316*
2Co	5:11	but we are made manifest unto **G.**;	*2316*
2Co	5:13	we be beside ourselves, it is to **G.**:	*2316*
2Co	5:18	And all things are of **G.**, who hath	*2316*
2Co	5:19	To wit, that **G.** was in Christ,	*2316*
2Co	5:20	though **G.** did beseech you by us:	*2316*
2Co	5:20	Christ's stead, be ye reconciled to **G.**.	*2316*
2Co	5:21	the righteousness of **G.** in him.	*2316*
2Co	6:1	receive not the grace of **G.** in vain,	*2316*
2Co	6:4	ourselves as the ministers of **G.**,	*2316*
2Co	6:7	by the power of **G.**, by the armour	*2316*
2Co	6:16	hath the temple of **G.** with idols?	*2316*
2Co	6:16	ye are the temple of the living **G.**;	*2316*
2Co	6:16	as **G.** hath said, I will be their **G.**,	*2316*
2Co	7:1	perfecting holiness in the fear of **G.**.	*2316*
2Co	7:6	**G.**, that comforteth those that are	*2316*
2Co	7:12	care for you in the sight of **G.**	*2316*
2Co	8:1	of the grace of **G.** bestowed on the	*2316*
2Co	8:5	and unto us by the will of **G.**	*2316*
2Co	8:16	But thanks be to **G.**, which put the	*2316*
2Co	9:7	for **G.** loveth a cheerful giver.	*2316*
2Co	9:8	And **G.** is able to make all grace	*2316*
2Co	9:11	through us thanksgiving to **G.**	*2316*
2Co	9:12	by many thanksgivings unto **G.**;	*2316*
2Co	9:13	they glorify **G.** for your professed	*2316*
2Co	9:14	the exceeding grace of **G.** in you.	*2316*
2Co	9:15	Thanks be unto **G.** for his...gift.	*2316*

2Co 10:4 mighty through **G.** to the pulling 2316
2Co 10:5 itself against the knowledge of **G.**, 2316
2Co 10:13 **G.** hath distributed to us, a 2316
2Co 11:1 Would to **G.** ye could bear with
2Co 11:7 preached to you the gospel of **G.** 2316
2Co 11:11 I love you not? **G.** knoweth 2316
2Co 11:31 **G.** and Father of our Lord Jesus 2316
2Co 12:2 I cannot tell: **G.** knoweth;) such 2316
2Co 12:3 I cannot tell: **G.** knoweth;) 2316
2Co 12:19 we speak before **G.** in Christ: but 2316
2Co 12:21 my **G.** will humble me among you, 2316
2Co 13:4 yet he liveth by the power of **G.** 2316
2Co 13:4 him by the power of **G.** toward you 2316
2Co 13:7 Now I pray to **G.** that ye do no evil; 2316
2Co 13:11 and the **G.** of love and peace shall 2316
2Co 13:14 the love of **G.**, and the communion 2316
Ga 1:1 and **G.** the Father, who raised him 2316
Ga 1:3 and peace from **G.** the Father, and 2316
Ga 1:4 according to the will of **G.** and our 2316
Ga 1:10 For do I now persuade men, or **G.**? 2316
Ga 1:13 I persecuted the church of **G.**, 2316
Ga 1:15 when it pleased **G.**, who separated 2316
Ga 1:20 behold, before **G.**, I lie not. 2316
Ga 1:24 And they glorified **G.** in me 2316
Ga 2:6 **G.** accepteth no man's person:) 2316
Ga 2:17 minister of sin? **G.** forbid 3361,1096
Ga 2:19 the law, that I might live unto **G.** 2316
Ga 2:20 live by the faith of the Son of **G.**, 2316
Ga 2:21 I do not frustrate the grace of **G.**: 2316
Ga 3:6 Even as Abraham believed **G.**, and 2316
Ga 3:8 that **G.** would justify the heathen 2316
Ga 3:11 by the law in the sight of **G.**, it is 2316
Ga 3:17 that was confirmed before of **G.** in 2316
Ga 3:18 **G.** gave it to Abraham by promise 2316
Ga 3:20 not a mediator of one, but **G.** is one 2316
Ga 3:21 law then against the promises of **G.**? 2316
Ga 3:21 **G.** forbid: for if there had 3361,1096
Ga 3:26 For ye are all the children of **G.** 2316
Ga 4:4 **G.** sent forth his Son, made of a 2316
Ga 4:6 **G.** hath sent forth the Spirit of his 2316
Ga 4:7 then an heir of **G.** through Christ. 2316
Ga 4:8 Howbeit then, when ye knew not **G.**, 2316
Ga 4:9 now, after that ye have known **G.**, 2316
Ga 4:9 or rather are known of **G.**, 2316
Ga 4:14 but received me as an angel of **G.**, 2316
Ga 5:21 shall not inherit the kingdom of **G.** 2316
Ga 6:7 **G.** is not mocked: for whatsoever 2316
Ga 6:14 But **G.** forbid that I should 3361,1096
Ga 6:16 and upon the Israel of **G.**, 2316
Eph 1:1 an apostle...by the will of **G.**, to 2316
Eph 1:2 and peace from **G.** our Father, and 2316
Eph 1:3 Blessed be the **G.** and Father of 2316
Eph 1:17 the **G.** of our Lord Jesus Christ, 2316
Eph 2:4 But **G.**, who is rich in mercy, for his 2316
Eph 2:8 of yourselves: it is the gift of **G.**: 2316
Eph 2:10 which **G.** hath before ordained that 2316
Eph 2:12 hope, and without **G.** in the world: 112
Eph 2:16 unto **G.** in one body by the cross, 2316
Eph 2:19 saints, and of the household of **G.**; 2316
Eph 2:22 for an habitation of **G.** through the 2316
Eph 3:2 of the grace of **G.** which is given me 2316
Eph 3:7 gift of the grace of **G.** given unto me 2316
Eph 3:9 of the world hath been hid in **G.**, 2316
Eph 3:10 church the manifold wisdom of **G.**, 2316
Eph 3:19 be filled with all the fulness of **G.** 2316
Eph 4:6 One **G.** and Father of all, who is 2316
Eph 4:13 of the knowledge of the Son of **G.**, 2316
Eph 4:18 alienated from the life of **G.** through 2316
Eph 4:24 after **G.** is created in righteousness 2316
Eph 4:30 And grieve not the holy Spirit of **G.**, 2316
Eph 4:32 even as **G.** for Christ's sake hath 2316
Eph 5:1 followers of **G.**, as dear children; 2316
Eph 5:2 sacrifice to **G.** for a sweetsmelling 2316
Eph 5:5 in the kingdom of Christ and of **G.** 2316
Eph 5:6 cometh the wrath of **G.** upon the 2316
Eph 5:20 thanks...unto **G.** and the Father 2316
Eph 5:21 one to another in the fear of **G.** 2316
Eph 6:6 the will of **G.** from the heart; 2316
Eph 6:11 Put on the whole armour of **G.**, 2316
Eph 6:13 unto you the whole armour of **G.**, 2316
Eph 6:17 the Spirit which is the word of **G.**: 2316
Eph 6:23 from **G.** the Father and the Lord 2316
Php 1:2 and peace, from **G.** our Father, and 2316
Php 1:3 I thank my **G.** upon every 2316
Php 1:8 For **G.** is my record, how greatly I 2316
Php 1:11 unto the glory and praise of **G.** 2316
Php 1:28 you of salvation, and that of **G.** 2316
Php 2:6 Who, being in the form of **G.**, 2316
Php 2:6 it not robbery to be equal with **G.**: 2316
Php 2:9 **G.** also hath highly exalted him, 2316
Php 2:11 to the glory of **G.** the Father 2316
Php 2:13 For it is **G.** which worketh in you 2316
Php 2:15 the sons of **G.**, without rebuke, 2316
Php 2:27 but **G.** had mercy on him; and not 2316
Php 3:3 which worship **G.** in the spirit, and 2316
Php 3:9 the righteousness which is of **G.** by 2316
Php 3:14 the prize of the high calling of **G.** 2316
Php 3:15 **G.** shall reveal even this unto you. 2316
Php 3:19 whose **G.** is their belly, and whose 2316
Php 4:6 requests be made known unto **G.** 2316
Php 4:7 And the peace of **G.**, which passeth 2316
Php 4:9 and the **G.** of peace shall be with 2316
Php 4:18 acceptable, well pleasing to **G.** 2316
Php 4:19 my **G.** shall supply all your need 2316
Php 4:20 unto **G.** and our Father be glory 2316
Col 1:1 an apostle...by the will of **G.**, and 2316
Col 1:2 and peace, from **G.** our Father and 2316
Col 1:3 give thanks to **G.** and the Father 2316
Col 1:6 and knew the grace of **G.** in truth: 2316
Col 1:10 increasing in the knowledge of **G.**; 2316
Col 1:15 is the image of the invisible **G.**, 2316
Col 1:25 dispensation of **G.** which is given 2316
Col 1:25 for you, to fulfil the word of **G.**; 2316
Col 1:27 **G.** would make known what is the 2316
Col 2:2 mystery of **G.**, and of the Father, 2316
Col 2:12 of **G.**, who hath raised him from the 2316
Col 2:19 increaseth with the increase of **G.** 2316
Col 3:1 sitteth on the right hand of **G.** 2316
Col 3:3 your life is hid with Christ in **G.** 2316
Col 3:6 wrath of **G.** cometh on the children 2316
Col 3:12 as the elect of **G.**, holy and beloved, 2316
Col 3:15 And let the peace of **G.** rule in 2316
Col 3:17 giving thanks to **G.** and the Father 2316
Col 3:22 in singleness of heart, fearing **G.**: 2316
Col 4:3 that **G.** would open unto us a door 2316
Col 4:11 unto the kingdom of **G.**, which 2316
Col 4:12 and complete in all the will of **G.** 2316
1Th 1:1 which is in **G.** the Father and in the 2316
1Th 1:1 and peace, from **G.** our Father, 2316
1Th 1:2 We give thanks to **G.** always for 2316
1Th 1:3 in the sight of **G.** and our Father; 2316
1Th 1:4 knowing...your election of **G.** 2316
1Th 1:9 and how ye turned to **G.** from idols 2316
1Th 1:9 to serve the living and true **G.**; 2316
1Th 2:2 were bold in our **G.** to speak unto 2316
1Th 2:2 to speak unto you the gospel of **G.** 2316
1Th 2:4 we were allowed of **G.** to be put 2316
1Th 2:4 not as pleasing men, but **G.**, which 2316
1Th 2:5 of covetousness; **G.** is witness: 2316
1Th 2:8 gospel of **G.** only, but also our own 2316
1Th 2:9 preached unto you the gospel of **G.** 2316
1Th 2:10 Ye are witnesses, and **G.** also, 2316
1Th 2:12 That ye would walk worthy of **G.**, 2316
1Th 2:13 also thank we **G.** without ceasing, 2316
1Th 2:13 the word of **G.** which ye heard of 2316
1Th 2:13 but as it is in truth, the word of **G.**, 2316
1Th 2:14 the churches of **G.** which in Judaea 2316
1Th 2:15 please not **G.**, and are contrary 2316
1Th 3:2 and minister of **G.**, and our 2316
1Th 3:9 can we render to **G.** again for you, 2316
1Th 3:9 joy for your sakes before our **G.**; 2316
1Th 3:11 Now **G.** himself and our Father, 2316
1Th 3:13 in holiness before **G.**, even our 2316
1Th 4:1 ought to walk and to please **G.**, 2316
1Th 4:3 For this is the will of **G.**, even 2316
1Th 4:5 as the Gentiles which know not **G.**: 2316
1Th 4:7 For **G.** hath not called us unto 2316
1Th 4:8 despiseth not man, but **G.**, who 2316
1Th 4:9 are taught of **G.** to love one 2312
1Th 4:14 which sleep in Jesus will **G.** bring 2316
1Th 4:16 and with the trump of **G.**: and the 2316
1Th 5:9 **G.** hath not appointed us to wrath, 2316
1Th 5:18 for this is the will of **G.** in Christ 2316
1Th 5:23 the very **G.** of peace sanctify you 2316
1Th 5:23 and I pray **G.** your whole spirit
2Th 1:1 church...in **G.** our Father and the 2316
2Th 1:2 peace, from **G.** our Father and the 2316
2Th 1:3 We are bound to thank **G.** always 2316
2Th 1:4 churches of **G.** for your patience 2316
2Th 1:5 of the righteous judgment of **G.**, 2316
2Th 1:5 worthy of the kingdom of **G.**, for 2316
2Th 1:6 it is a righteous thing with **G.** to 2316
2Th 1:8 on them that know not **G.**, 2316
2Th 1:11 our **G.** would count you worthy of 2316
2Th 1:12 according to the grace of our **G.** 2316
2Th 2:4 is called **G.**, or that is worshipped; 2316
2Th 2:4 he as **G.** sitteth in the temple of **G.**, 2316
2Th 2:4 shewing himself that he is **G.** 2316
2Th 2:11 **G.** shall send them strong delusion, 2316
2Th 2:13 to give thanks alway to **G.** for you, 2316
2Th 2:13 **G.** hath from the beginning chosen 2316
2Th 2:16 **G.**, even our Father, which hath 2316
2Th 3:5 into the love of **G.**, and into the 2316
1Ti 1:1 commandment of **G.** our Saviour, 2316
1Ti 1:2 peace, from **G.** our Father and Jesus 2316
1Ti 1:11 glorious gospel of the blessed **G.**, 2316
1Ti 1:17 the only wise **G.**, be honour and 2316
1Ti 2:3 in the sight of **G.** our Saviour; 2316
1Ti 2:5 For there is one **G.**, and one 2316
1Ti 2:5 one mediator between **G.** and men, 2316
1Ti 3:5 he take care of the church of **G.**?) 2316
1Ti 3:15 behave thyself in the house of **G.**, 2316
1Ti 3:15 which is the church of the living **G.**, 2316
1Ti 3:16 **G.** was manifest in the flesh, 2316
1Ti 4:3 **G.** hath created to be received with 2316
1Ti 4:4 For every creature of **G.** is good, 2316
1Ti 4:5 sanctified by the word of **G.** and 2316
1Ti 4:10 because we trust in the living **G.**, 2316
1Ti 5:4 is good and acceptable before **G.** 2316
1Ti 5:5 trusteth in **G.**, and continueth in 2316
1Ti 5:21 I charge thee before **G.**, and the 2316
1Ti 6:1 the name of **G.** and his doctrine 2316
1Ti 6:11 But thou, O man of **G.**, flee these 2316
1Ti 6:13 give thee charge in the sight of **G.**, 2316
1Ti 6:17 but in the living **G.**, who giveth us 2316
2Ti 1:1 an apostle...by the will of **G.**, 2316
2Ti 1:2 peace, from **G.** the Father and Christ 2316
2Ti 1:3 I thank **G.**, whom I serve from my 2316
2Ti 1:6 that thou stir up the gift of **G.**, 2316
2Ti 1:7 For **G.** hath not given us the spirit 2316
2Ti 1:8 according to the power of **G.**; 2316
2Ti 2:9 but the word of **G.** is not bound 2316
2Ti 2:15 to shew thyself approved unto **G.**, 2316
2Ti 2:19 the foundation of **G.** standeth sure, 2316
2Ti 2:25 if **G.** peradventure will give them 2316
2Ti 3:4 of pleasure more than lovers of **G.**; 5377
2Ti 3:16 is given by inspiration of **G.**, 2315
2Ti 3:17 That the man of **G.** may be perfect, 2316
2Ti 4:1 **G.**, and the Lord Jesus Christ, 2316
2Ti 4:16 I pray **G.** that it may not be laid
Tit 1:1 Paul, a servant of **G.**, and an 2316
Tit 1:2 which **G.**, that cannot lie, promised 2316
Tit 1:3 commandment of **G.** our Saviour; 2316
Tit 1:4 peace, from **G.** the Father and the 2316
Tit 1:7 blameless, as the steward of **G.**; 2316
Tit 1:16 They profess that they know **G.**; 2316
Tit 2:5 the word of **G.** be not blasphemed 2316
Tit 2:10 the doctrine of **G.** our Saviour 2316
Tit 2:11 For the grace of **G.** that bringeth 2316
Tit 2:13 appearing of the great **G.** and our 2316
Tit 3:4 kindness and love of **G.** our Saviour 2316
Tit 3:8 they which have believed in **G.** 2316
Phm 3 peace, from **G.** our Father and the 2316
Phm 4 I thank my **G.**, making mention of 2316
Heb 1:1 **G.**, who at sundry times and in 2316
Heb 1:6 all the angels of **G.** worship him 2316
Heb 1:8 Thy throne, O **G.**, is for ever and 2316
Heb 1:9 **G.**, even thy **G.**, hath anointed thee 2316
Heb 2:4 **G.** also bearing them witness, both 2316
Heb 2:9 that he by the grace of **G.** should 2316
Heb 2:13 children which **G.** hath given me. 2316
Heb 2:17 in things pertaining to **G.**, to make 2316
Heb 3:4 but he that built all things is **G.** 2316
Heb 3:12 in departing from the living **G.** 2316
Heb 4:4 **G.** did rest the seventh day from 2316
Heb 4:9 therefore a rest to the people of **G.** 2316
Heb 4:10 his own works, as **G.** did from his 2316
Heb 4:12 For the word of **G.** is quick, and 2316
Heb 4:14 high priest...Jesus the Son of **G.**, 2316
Heb 5:1 in things pertaining to **G.**, that he 2316
Heb 5:4 that is called of **G.**, as was Aaron 2316
Heb 5:10 called of **G.** an high priest after 2316
Heb 5:12 be principles of the oracles of **G.**; 2316
Heb 6:1 dead works, and of faith toward **G.**, 2316
Heb 6:3 And this will we do, if **G.** permit 2316
Heb 6:5 have tasted the good word of **G.**, 2316
Heb 6:6 to themselves the Son of **G.** afresh, 2316
Heb 6:7 receiveth blessing from **G.**: 2316
Heb 6:10 For **G.** is not unrighteous to forget 2316
Heb 6:13 when **G.** made promise to Abraham, 2316

Book	Ref	Context	Number
Heb	6:17	Wherein G., willing more	2316
Heb	6:18	it was impossible for G. to lie,	2316
Heb	7:1	priest of the most high G., who	2316
Heb	7:3	but made like unto the Son of G.;	2316
Heb	7:19	the which we draw nigh unto G..	2316
Heb	7:25	that come unto G. by him, seeing	2316
Heb	8:5	as Moses was admonished of G.	5537
Heb	8:10	I will be to them a G., and they	2316
Heb	9:6	accomplishing the service of G..	
Heb	9:14	without spot to G., purge your	2316
Heb	9:14	dead works to serve the living G.?	2316
Heb	9:20	G. hath injoined unto you	2316
Heb	9:24	appear in the presence of G. for us:	2316
Heb	10:7	written of one,) to do thy will, O G.	2316
Heb	10:9	Lo, I come to do thy will, O G.	2316
Heb	10:12	sat down on the right hand of G.;	2316
Heb	10:21	high priest over the house of G.;	2316
Heb	10:29	trodden under foot the Son of G.,	2316
Heb	10:31	fall into the hands of the living G.	2316
Heb	10:36	after ye have done the will of G.,	2316
Heb	11:3	were framed by the word of G.,	2316
Heb	11:4	faith Abel offered unto G. a more	2316
Heb	11:4	righteous, G. testifying of his gifts:	2316
Heb	11:5	G. had translated him: for before	2316
Heb	11:5	this testimony, that he pleased G..	2316
Heb	11:6	he that cometh to G. must believe	2316
Heb	11:7	Noah, being warned of G. of things	
Heb	11:10	whose builder and maker is G..	2316
Heb	11:16	wherefore G. is not ashamed to be	2316
Heb	11:16	ashamed to be called their G.:	2316
Heb	11:19	G. was able to raise him up, even	2316
Heb	11:25	affliction with the people of G.,	2316
Heb	11:40	G. having provided some better	2316
Heb	12:2	the right hand of the throne of G..	2316
Heb	12:7	G. dealeth with you as with sons;	2316
Heb	12:15	any man fail of the grace of G.;	2316
Heb	12:22	and unto the city of the living G.,	2316
Heb	12:23	and to G. the Judge of all, and to	2316
Heb	12:28	serve G. acceptably with reverence	2316
Heb	12:29	for our G. is a consuming fire	2316
Heb	13:4	and adulterers G. will judge.	2316
Heb	13:7	spoken unto you the word of G.:	2316
Heb	13:15	sacrifice of praise to G. continually,	2316
Heb	13:16	such sacrifices G. is well pleased	2316
Heb	13:20	Now the G. of peace, that brought	2316
Jas	1:1	James, a servant of G. and of the	2316
Jas	1:5	let him ask of G., that giveth to all	2316
Jas	1:13	he is tempted, I am tempted of G.:	2316
Jas	1:13	for G. cannot be tempted with evil,	2316
Jas	1:20	worketh not the righteousness of G.,	2316
Jas	1:27	religion and undefiled before G.	2316
Jas	2:5	Hath not G. chosen the poor of this	2316
Jas	2:19	Thou believest that there is one G.;	2316
Jas	2:23	Abraham believed G., and it was	2316
Jas	2:23	and he was called the Friend of G.,	2316
Jas	3:9	Therewith bless we G., even the	2316
Jas	3:9	are made after the similitude of G.,	2316
Jas	4:4	of the world is enmity with G.?	2316
Jas	4:4	of the world is the enemy of G..	2316
Jas	4:6	G. resisteth the proud, but given	2316
Jas	4:7	Submit yourselves therefore to G..	2316
Jas	4:8	Draw nigh to G., and he will draw	2316
1Pe	1:2	foreknowledge of G. the Father,	2316
1Pe	1:3	Blessed be the G. and Father of	2316
1Pe	1:5	Who are kept by the power of G.	2316
1Pe	1:21	do believe in G., that raised him	2316
1Pe	1:21	your faith and hope might be in G..	2316
1Pe	1:23	by the word of G., which liveth and	2316
1Pe	2:4	but chosen of G., and precious,	2316
1Pe	2:5	acceptable to G. by Jesus Christ.	2316
1Pe	2:10	but are now the people of G.:	2316
1Pe	2:12	glorify G. in the day of visitation.	2316
1Pe	2:15	For so is the will of G., that with	2316
1Pe	2:16	but as the servants of G.	2316
1Pe	2:17	Fear G.. Honour the king.	2316
1Pe	2:19	if a man for conscience toward G.	2316
1Pe	2:20	patiently, this is acceptable with G.	2316
1Pe	3:4	is in the sight of G. of great price.	2316
1Pe	3:5	holy women also, who trusted in G.,	2316
1Pe	3:15	the Lord G. in your hearts: and	2316
1Pe	3:17	it is better, if the will of G. be so,	2316
1Pe	3:18	that he might bring us to G., being	2316
1Pe	3:20	the longsuffering of G. waited in	2316
1Pe	3:21	of a good conscience toward G.,)	2316
1Pe	3:22	and is on the right hand of G.;	2316
1Pe	4:2	lusts of men, but to the will of G.,	2316
1Pe	4:6	live according to G. in the spirit.	2316
1Pe	4:10	of the manifold grace of G..	2316
1Pe	4:11	let him speak as the oracles of G.;	2316
1Pe	4:11	as of the ability which G. giveth:	2316
1Pe	4:11	G. in all things may be glorified	2316
1Pe	4:14	the spirit of glory and of G. resteth	2316
1Pe	4:16	let him glorify G. on this behalf.	2316
1Pe	4:17	must begin at the house of G.:	2316
1Pe	4:17	that obey not the gospel of G.?	2316
1Pe	4:19	according to the will of G. commit	2316
1Pe	5:2	Feed the flock of G. which is among	2316
1Pe	5:5	G. resisteth the proud, and giveth	2316
1Pe	5:6	under the mighty hand of G.,	2316
1Pe	5:10	But the G. of all grace, who hath	2316
1Pe	5:12	the true grace of G. wherein ye	2316
2Pe	1:1	through the righteousness of G.	2316
2Pe	1:2	through the knowledge of G., and of	2316
2Pe	1:17	For he received from G. the Father	2316
2Pe	1:21	holy men of G. spake as they were	2316
2Pe	2:4	For if G. spared not the angels that	2316
2Pe	3:5	that by the word of G. the heavens	2316
2Pe	3:12	unto the coming of the day of G.,	2316
1Jo	1:5	that G. is light, and in him is no	2316
1Jo	2:5	verily is the love of G. perfected:	2316
1Jo	2:14	and the word of G. abideth in you,	2316
1Jo	2:17	doeth the will of G. abideth for ever.	2316
1Jo	3:1	should be called the sons of G.:	2316
1Jo	3:2	now are we the sons of G., and	2316
1Jo	3:8	Son of G. was manifested, that he	2316
1Jo	3:9	is born of G. doth not commit sin;	2316
1Jo	3:9	sin, because he is born of G.	2316
1Jo	3:10	the children of G. are manifest,	2316
1Jo	3:10	doeth not righteousness is not of G.,	2316
1Jo	3:16	Hereby perceive we the love of G.,	
1Jo	3:17	how dwelleth the love of G. in him?	2316
1Jo	3:20	G. is greater than our heart, and	2316
1Jo	3:21	then have we confidence toward G..	2316
1Jo	4:1	the Spirits whether they are of G.:	2316
1Jo	4:2	Hereby know ye the Spirit of G.:	2316
1Jo	4:2	Christ is come in the flesh is of G.:	2316
1Jo	4:3	is come in the flesh is not of G.:	2316
1Jo	4:4	Ye are of G., little children, and	2316
1Jo	4:6	We are of G.: he that knoweth G.	2316
1Jo	4:6	he that is not of G. heareth not us.	2316
1Jo	4:7	for love is of G.; and every one that	2316
1Jo	4:7	loveth is born of G., and knoweth G.	2316
1Jo	4:8	knoweth not G.; for G. is love.	2316
1Jo	4:9	manifested the love of G. toward us,	2316
1Jo	4:9	G. sent his only begotten Son into	2316
1Jo	4:10	not that we loved G., but that he	2316
1Jo	4:11	if G. so loved us, we ought also to	2316
1Jo	4:12	No man hath seen G. at any time.	2316
1Jo	4:12	G. dwelleth in us, and his love is	2316
1Jo	4:15	that Jesus Christ is the Son of G.,	2316
1Jo	4:15	G. dwelleth in him, and he in G..	2316
1Jo	4:16	love that G. hath to us. G. is love;	2316
1Jo	4:16	dwelleth in G., and G. in him.	2316
1Jo	4:20	If a man say, I love G., and hateth	2316
1Jo	4:20	G. whom he hath not seen?	2316
1Jo	4:21	he who loveth G. love his brother	2316
1Jo	5:1	Jesus is the Christ is born of G.:	2316
1Jo	5:2	the children of G., when we love G.,	2316
1Jo	5:3	For this is the love of G., that	2316
1Jo	5:4	is born of G. overcometh the world:	2316
1Jo	5:5	that Jesus is the Son of G.?	2316
1Jo	5:9	men, the witness of G. is greater:	2316
1Jo	5:9	for this is the witness of G. which	2316
1Jo	5:10	He that believeth on the Son of G.	2316
1Jo	5:10	he that believeth not G. hath made	2316
1Jo	5:10	the record that G. gave of his Son.	2316
1Jo	5:11	G. hath given to us eternal life,	2316
1Jo	5:12	hath not the Son of G. hath not life.	2316
1Jo	5:13	on the name of the Son of G.;	2316
1Jo	5:13	believe on the name of the Son of G.	2316
1Jo	5:18	whosoever is born of G. sinneth	2316
1Jo	5:18	but he that is begotten of G.	2316
1Jo	5:19	And we know that we are of G., and	2316
1Jo	5:20	we know that the Son of G. is come,	2316
1Jo	5:20	This is the true G., and eternal life.	2316
2Jo	3	peace, from G. the Father, and from	2316
2Jo	9	the doctrine of Christ, hath not G..	2316
2Jo	10	house, neither bid him G. speed:	
2Jo	11	he that biddeth him G. speed is	
3Jo	11	He that doeth good is of G.: but	2316
3Jo	11	he that doeth evil hath not seen G..	2316
Jude	1	that are sanctified by G. the Father,	2316
Jude	4	grace of our G. into lasciviousness,	2316
Jude	4	and denying the only Lord G.,	2316
Jude	21	Keep yourselves in the love of G.,	2316
Jude	25	To the only wise G. our Saviour,	2316
Re	1:1	which G. gave unto him, to shew	2316
Re	1:2	Who bare record the word of G., and	2316
Re	1:6	made us kings and priests unto G.	2316
Re	1:9	for the word of G., and for the	2316
Re	2:7	**in the midst of the paradise of G.,**	2316
Re	2:18	**These things saith the Son of G.,**	2316
Re	3:1	**that hath the seven Spirits of G.,**	2316
Re	3:2	**found thy works perfect before G..**	2316
Re	3:12	**a pillar in the temple of my G.,**	2316
Re	3:12	**upon him the name of my G.,**	2316
Re	3:12	**and the name of the city of my G.,**	2316
Re	3:12	**down out of heaven from my G.:**	2316
Re	3:14	**beginning of the creation of G.;**	2316
Re	4:5	which are the seven Spirits of G..	2316
Re	4:8	Lord G. Almighty, which was, and	2316
Re	5:6	the seven Spirits of G. sent forth	2316
Re	5:9	and hast redeemed us to G. by thy	2316
Re	5:10	hast made us unto our G. kings	2316
Re	6:9	that were slain for the word of G.,	2316
Re	7:2	having the seal of the living G.:	2316
Re	7:3	sealed the sevants of our G. in	2316
Re	7:10	Salvation to our G. which sitteth	2316
Re	7:11	on their faces, and worshipped G.,	2316
Re	7:12	and might, be unto our G. for ever.	2316
Re	7:15	are they before the throne of G.,	2316
Re	7:17	G. shall wipe away all tears from	2316
Re	8:2	seven angels which stood before G.;	2316
Re	8:4	before G. out of the angel's hand.	2316
Re	9:4	not the seal of G. in their foreheads.	2316
Re	9:13	the golden altar which is before G.,	2316
Re	10:7	mystery of G. should be finished.	2316
Re	11:1	and measure the temple of G., and	2316
Re	11:4	standing before the G. of the	2316
Re	11:11	the Spirit of life from G. entered	2316
Re	11:13	and gave glory to the G. of heaven.	2316
Re	11:16	which sat before G. on their seats	2316
Re	11:16	their faces, and worshipped G.,	2316
Re	11:17	O Lord G. Almighty, which art, and	2316
Re	11:19	temple of G. was opened in heaven,	2316
Re	12:5	was caught up unto G., and to his	2316
Re	12:6	she hath a place prepared of G.,	2316
Re	12:10	kingdom of our G., and the power	2316
Re	12:10	accused them before our G. day	2316
Re	12:17	keep the commandments of G.,	2316
Re	13:6	mouth in blasphemy against G.,	2316
Re	14:4	firstfruits unto G. and to the Lamb.	2316
Re	14:5	fault before the throne of G..	2316
Re	14:7	Fear G., and give glory to him;	2316
Re	14:10	drink of the wine of the wrath of G.,	2316
Re	14:12	that keep the commandments of G.,	2316
Re	14:19	great winepress of the wrath of G..	2316
Re	15:1	in them is filled up the wrath of G..	2316
Re	15:2	sea of glass, having the harps of G..	2316
Re	15:3	the song of Moses the servant of G.,	2316
Re	15:3	are thy works, Lord G. Almighty;	2316
Re	15:7	vials full of the wrath of G., who	2316
Re	15:8	smoke from the glory of G., and	2316
Re	16:1	out the vials of the wrath of G.	2316
Re	16:7	say, Even so, Lord G. Almighty,	2316
Re	16:9	and blasphemed the name of G.,	2316
Re	16:11	And blasphemed the G. of heaven	2316
Re	16:14	of that great day of G. Almighty.	2316
Re	16:19	came in remembrance before G.,	2316
Re	16:21	men blasphemed G. because of the	2316
Re	17:17	For G. hath put in their hearts	2316
Re	17:17	the words of G. shall be fulfilled.	2316
Re	18:5	G. hath remembered her iniquities.	2316
Re	18:8	is the Lord G. who judgeth her.	2316
Re	18:20	for G. hath avenged you on her.	2316
Re	19:1	and power, unto the Lord our G.:	2316
Re	19:4	and worshipped G. that sat on the	2316
Re	19:5	Praise our G., all ye his servants,	2316
Re	19:6	the Lord G. omnipotent reigneth.	2316
Re	19:9	These are the true sayings of G..	2316
Re	19:10	worship G.: for the testimony of	2316
Re	19:13	his name is called The Word of G..	2316
Re	19:15	fierceness and wrath of Almighty G..	2316
Re	19:17	unto the supper of the great G.;	2316
Re	20:4	and for the word of G., and which	2316
Re	20:6	shall be priests of G. and of Christ,	2316
Re	20:9	came down from G. out of heaven,	2316
Re	20:12	small and great, stand before G.;	2316
Re	21:2	coming down from G. out of heaven,	2316
Re	21:3	the tabernacle of G. is with men,	2316
Re	21:3	and G. himself shall be with them,	2316

Re 21:3 be with them, and be their **G.**.......... *2316*
Re 21:4 And **G.** shall wipe away all tears........ *2316*
Re 21:7 and I will be his **G.**, and he shall be.... *2316*
Re 21:10 descending out of heaven from **G.**,..... *2316*
Re 21:11 Having the glory of **G.**: and her......... *2316*
Re 21:22 Lord **G.** Almighty and the Lamb......... *2316*
Re 21:23 for the glory of **G.** did lighten it,........ *2316*
Re 22:1 the throne of **G.** and of the Lamb........ *2316*
Re 22:3 the throne of **G.** and of the Lamb........ *2316*
Re 22:5 for the Lord **G.** giveth them light:...... *2316*
Re 22:6 the Lord **G.** of the holy prophets....... *2316*
Re 22:9 sayings of this book: worship **G.**......... *2316*
Re 22:18 **G.** shall add unto him the plagues....... *2316*
Re 22:19 **G.** shall take away his part out of....... *2316*

GODDESS
1Ki 11:5 went after Ashtoreth the **g.**................ 430
1Ki 11:33 Ashtoreth the **g.** of the Zidonians,........ 430
Ac 19:27 the temple of the great **g.** Diana........ *2299*
Ac 19:35 worshipper of the great **g.** Diana,....... *2299*
Ac 19:37 nor yet blasphemers of your **g.**.......... *2299*

GODHEAD
Ac 17:29 think that the **G.** is like unto gold,...... *2304*
Ro 1:20 even his eternal power and **G.**;.......... *2305*
Col 2:9 all the fulness of the **G.** bodily........... *2320*

GODLINESS See also UNGODLINESS.
1Ti 2:2 life in all **g.** and honesty.................. *2150*
1Ti 2:10 becometh women professing **g.**)......... *2317*
1Ti 3:16 great is the mystery of **g.**: God......... *2150*
1Ti 4:7 and exercise thyself rather unto **g.**..... *2150*
1Ti 4:8 but **g.** is profitable unto all things,...... *2150*
1Ti 6:3 doctrine which is according to **g.**;...... *2150*
1Ti 6:5 supposing that gain is **g.**: from such..... *2150*
1Ti 6:6 **g.** with contentment is great gain........ *2150*
1Ti 6:11 follow after righteousness, **g.**, faith,.... *2150*
2Ti 3:5 Having a form of **g.**, but denying......... *2150*
Tit 1:1 of the truth which is after **g.**;............ *2150*
2Pe 1:3 pertain unto life and **g.**, through......... *2150*
2Pe 1:6 patience; and to patience **g.**;............. *2150*
2Pe 1:7 And to **g.** brotherly kindness;............ *2150*
2Pe 3:11 in all holy conversation and **g.**,........... *2150*

GODLY See also UNGODLY.
Ps 4:3 apart him that is **g.** for himself:.......... 2623
Ps 12:1 Help, Lord; for the **g.** man ceaseth;..... 2623
Ps 32:6 this shall every one that is **g.** pray...... 2623
Mal 2:15 That he might seek a **g.** seed.............. 430
2Co 1:12 simplicity and **g.** sincerity, not........... *2316*
2Co 7:9 made sorry after a **g.** manner,..... *2596,2316*
2Co 7:10 **g.** sorrow worketh repentance..... *2596,2316*
2Co 7:11 that ye sorrowed after a **g.** sort,..*2596,2316*
2Co 11:2 jealous over you with **g.** jealousy:..*2596,2316*
1Ti 1:4 questions, rather than **g.** edifying........ *2316*
2Ti 3:12 all that will live **g.** in Christ Jesus........ *2153*
Tit 2:12 live soberly, righteously, and **g.**,......... *2153*
Heb 12:28 with reverence and **g.** fear:......................
2Pe 2:9 knoweth how to deliver the **g.** out....... *2152*
3Jo 6 their journey after a **g.** sort,......... *516,2316*

GOD'S
Ge 28:22 set for a pillar, shall be **G.** house:........ 430
Ge 30:2 I in **G.** stead, who hath witheld........... 430
Ge 32:2 he said, This is **G.** host: and he.......... 430
Nu 22:22 And **G.** anger was kindled because....... 430
De 1:17 the judgment is **G.**: and the cause........ 430
2Ch 20:15 for the battle is not your's, but **G.**....... 430
Ne 10:29 to walk in **G.** law, which was given....... 430
Job 33:6 according to thy wish in **G.** stead:........ 410
Job 35:2 My righteousness is more than **G.**?....... 410
Job 36:2 I have yet to speak on **G.** behalf.......... 433
Mt 5:34 **by heaven; for it is G. throne:**........ *2316*
Mt 22:21 **unto God the things that are G.**..... *2316*
Mk 12:17 **and to God the things that are G.**.. *2316*
Lu 18:29 **for the kingdom of G. sake,**........... *2316*
Lu 20:25 **unto God the things which be G.**,.. *2316*
Joh 8:47 **that is of God heareth G. words:**... *2316*
Ac 23:4 said, Revilest thou **G.** high priest?...... *2316*
Ro 8:33 thing to the charge of **G.** elect?.......... *2316*
Ro 10:3 being ignorant of **G.** righteousness,...... *2316*
Ro 13:6 they are **G.** ministers, attending......... *2316*
1Co 3:9 Ye are **G.** husbandry,....................... *2316*
1Co 3:9 ye are **G.** building............................ *2316*
1Co 3:23 ye are Christ's; and Christ is **G.**......... *2316*
1Co 6:20 and in your spirit, which are **G.**......... *2316*
Tit 1:1 according to the faith of **G.** elect......... *2316*
1Pe 5:3 as being lords over **G.** heritage,......... *2316*

GODS
Ge 3:5 ye shall be as **g.**, knowing good............ 430
Ge 31:30 wherefore hast thou stolen my **g.**?....... 430
Ge 31:32 whomsoever thou findest thy **g.**,.......... 430
Ge 35:2 the strange **g.** that are among you,...... 430
Ge 35:4 gave unto Jacob all the strange **g.**........ 430
Ex 12:12 all the **g.** of Egypt I will execute......... 430
Ex 15:11 unto thee, O Lord, among the **g.**?....... 410
Ex 18:11 the Lord is greater than all **g.**:............ 430
Ex 20:3 shalt have no other **g.** before me........... 430
Ex 20:23 not make with me **g.** of silver,............. 430
Ex 20:23 shall ye make unto you **g.** of gold......... 430
Ex 22:28 Thou shalt not revile the **g.** nor........... 430
Ex 23:13 mention of the name of other **g.**,.......... 430
Ex 23:24 Thou shalt not bow down to their **g.**,.... 430
Ex 23:32 with them, nor with their **g.**............... 430
Ex 23:33 if thou serve their **g.**, it will surely....... 430
Ex 32:1 make us **g.**, which shall go before us;... 430
Ex 32:4 be thy **g.**, O Israel, which brought....... 430
Ex 32:8 be thy **g.**, O Israel, which have........... 430
Ex 32:23 Make us **g.**, which shall go before........ 430
Ex 32:31 and have made them **g.** of gold........... 430
Ex 34:15 and they go a whoring after their **g.**,..... 430
Ex 34:15 and do sacrifice unto their **g.**,............. 430
Ex 34:16 and they go a whoring after their **g.**,..... 430
Ex 34:16 thy sons go a whoring after their **g.**...... 430
Ex 34:17 Thou shalt make thee no molten **g.**...... 430
Le 19:4 nor make to yourselves molten **g.**:....... 430
Nu 25:2 unto the sacrifices of their **g.**:............ 430
Nu 25:2 did eat, and bowed down to their **g.**...... 430
Nu 33:4 upon their **g.** also the Lord executed...... 430
De 4:28 there ye shall serve **g.**, the work of...... 430
De 5:7 Thou shalt have none other **g.** before... 430
De 6:14 Ye shall not go after other **g.**, of the.... 430
De 6:14 the **g.** of the people which are round.... 430
De 7:4 that they may serve other **g.**:............. 430
De 7:16 neither shalt thou serve their **g.**;......... 430
De 7:25 The graven images of their **g.** shall...... 430
De 8:19 walk after other **g.**, and serve them,.... 430
De 10:17 is God of **g.**, and Lord of lords,........... 430
De 11:16 and serve other **g.**, and worship.......... 430
De 11:28 to go after other **g.**, which ye have....... 430
De 12:2 ye shall possess served their **g.**,.......... 430
De 12:3 down the graven images of their **g.**,..... 430
De 12:30 enquire not after their **g.**, saying,......... 430
De 12:30 did these nations serve their **g.**?.......... 430
De 12:31 hateth, have they done unto their **g.**;.... 430
De 12:31 have burnt in the fire to their **g.**........... 430
De 13:2 Let us go after other **g.**, which thou..... 430
De 13:6 Let us go and serve other **g.**, which..... 430
De 13:7 the **g.** of the people which are round.... 430
De 13:13 Let us go and serve other **g.**, which..... 430
De 17:3 And hath gone and served other **g.**,..... 430
De 18:20 shall speak in the name of other **g.**,..... 430
De 20:18 which they have done unto their **g.**;..... 430
De 28:14 to go after other **g.** to serve them........ 430
De 28:36 there shalt thou serve other **g.**, wood... 430
De 28:64 there thou shalt serve other **g.**, which.. 430
De 29:18 go and serve the **g.** of these nations;.... 430
De 29:26 For they went and served other **g.**,..... 430
De 29:26 them, **g.** whom they knew not, and....... 430
De 30:17 drawn away, and worship other **g.**,....... 430
De 31:16 whoring after the **g.** of the strangers.... 430
De 31:18 they are turned unto other **g.**.............. 430
De 31:20 then will they turn unto other **g.**,......... 430
De 32:16 him to jealousy with strange **g.**,................
De 32:17 to **g.** whom they knew not,................ 430
De 32:17 to new **g.** that came newly up,................
De 32:37 he shall say, Where are their **g.**,......... 430
Jos 22:22 Lord God of **g.**, the Lord God of **g.**,.... 430
Jos 23:7 make mention of the name of their **g.**,.. 430
Jos 23:16 and have gone and served other **g.**,..... 430
Jos 24:2 and they served other **g.**..................... 430
Jos 24:14 put away the **g.** which your fathers....... 430
Jos 24:15 whether the **g.** which your fathers....... 430
Jos 24:15 or the **g.** of the Amorites, in whose..... 430
Jos 24:16 forsake the Lord, to serve other **g.**;..... 430
Jos 24:20 and serve strange **g.**, then he will........ 430
Jos 24:23 strange **g.** which are among you,......... 430
Jg 2:3 their **g.** shall be a snare unto you.......... 430
Jg 2:12 and followed other **g.**, of the **g.** of the.. 430
Jg 2:17 they went a whoring after other **g.**....... 430
Jg 2:19 in following other **g.** to serve them,..... 430
Jg 3:6 their sons, and served their **g.**............ 430
Jg 5:8 They chose new **g.**; then was war....... 430
Jg 6:10 fear not the **g.** of the Amorites,.......... 430
Jg 10:6 the **g.** of Syria, and the **g.** of Zidon,..... 430
Jg 10:6 and the **g.** of Moab, and the **g.** of the... 430
Jg 10:6 Ammon, and the **g.** of the Philistines,... 430
Jg 10:13 forsaken me, and served other **g.**:....... 430
Jg 10:14 unto the **g.** which ye have chosen;....... 430
Jg 10:16 And they put away the strange **g.**........ 430
Jg 17:5 the man Micah had an house of **g.**,...... 430
Jg 18:24 taken away my **g.** which I made,.......... 430
Ru 1:15 unto her people, and unto her **g.**:......... 430
1Sa 4:8 out of the hand of these mighty **G.**?..... 430
1Sa 4:8 these are the **G.** that smote the.......... 430
1Sa 6:5 from off you, and from off your **g.**,...... 430
1Sa 7:3 away the strange **g.** and Ashtaroth....... 430
1Sa 8:8 forsaken me, and served other **g.**,....... 430
1Sa 17:43 Philistine cursed David by his **g.**......... 430
1Sa 26:19 saying, Go, serve other **g.**................. 430
1Sa 28:13 saw **g.** ascending out of the earth........ 430
2Sa 7:23 from the nations and their **g.**?............ 430
1Ki 9:6 go and serve other **g.**, and worship....... 430
1Ki 9:9 and have taken hold upon other **g.**,...... 430
1Ki 11:2 turn away your heart after their **g.**:...... 430
1Ki 11:4 turned away his heart after other **g.**:.... 430
1Ki 11:8 incense and sacrificed unto their **g.**...... 430
1Ki 11:10 that he should not go after other **g.**:..... 430
1Ki 12:28 behold thy **g.**, O Israel, which............. 430
1Ki 14:9 hast gone and made thee other **g.**,....... 430
1Ki 18:24 call ye on the name of your **g.**,........... 430
1Ki 18:25 and call on the name of your **g.**,.......... 430
1Ki 19:2 So let the **g.** do to me, and more......... 430
1Ki 20:10 The **g.** do so unto me, and more.......... 430
1Ki 20:23 Their **g.** are **g.** of the hills;.............. 430
2Ki 5:17 nor sacrifice unto other **g.**, but unto..... 430
2Ki 17:7 and had feared other **g.**,..................... 430
2Ki 17:29 every nation made **g.** of their own,...... 430
2Ki 17:31 Anammelech, the **g.** of Sepharvaim....... 430
2Ki 17:33 served their own **g.**, after the manner.. 430
2Ki 17:35 Ye shall not fear other **g.**, nor bow...... 430
2Ki 17:37 and ye shall not fear other **g.**............. 430
2Ki 17:38 neither shall ye fear other **g.**.............. 430
2Ki 18:33 Hath any of the **g.** of the nations......... 430
2Ki 18:34 Where are the **g.** of Hamath, and of..... 430
2Ki 18:34 where are the **g.** of Sepharvaim,.......... 430
2Ki 18:35 among all the **g.** of the countries,........ 430
2Ki 19:12 Have the **g.** of the nations delivered..... 430
2Ki 19:18 And have cast their **g.** into the fire:..... 430
2Ki 19:18 for they were no **g.**, but the work....... 430
2Ki 22:17 have burned incense unto other **g.**,...... 430
1Ch 5:25 a whoring after the **g.** of the people..... 430
1Ch 10:10 his armour in the house of their **g.**,...... 430
1Ch 14:12 And when they had left their **g.** there,.. 430
1Ch 16:25 he also is to be feared above all **g.**........ 430
1Ch 16:26 For all the **g.** of the people are idols:... 430
2Ch 2:5 for great is our God above all **g.**........... 430
2Ch 7:19 go and serve other **g.**, and worship...... 430
2Ch 7:22 and laid hold on other **g.**, and............. 430
2Ch 13:8 which Jeroboam made you for **g.**.......... 430
2Ch 13:9 be a priest of them that are no **g.**......... 430
2Ch 14:3 away the altars of the strange **g.**,..............
2Ch 25:14 he brought the **g.** of the children of...... 430
2Ch 25:14 Seir, and set them up to be his **g.**,...... 430
2Ch 25:15 thou sought after the **g.** of the people,.. 430
2Ch 25:20 they sought after the **g.** of Edom......... 430
2Ch 28:23 sacrificed unto the **g.** of Damascus,...... 430
2Ch 28:23 **g.** of the kings of Syria help them......... 430
2Ch 28:25 to burn incense unto other **g.**, and....... 430
2Ch 32:13 were the **g.** of the nations of those...... 430
2Ch 32:14 Who was there among all the **g.** of........ 430
2Ch 32:17 the **g.** of the nations of other lands...... 430
2Ch 32:19 as against the **g.** of the people of the.... 430
2Ch 33:15 And he took away the strange **g.**,......... 430
2Ch 34:25 have burned incense unto other **g.**,...... 430
Ezr 1:7 had put them in the house of his **g.**;..... 430
Ps 82:1 mighty; he judgeth among the **g.**......... 430
Ps 82:6 I have said, Ye are **g.**; and all of you.... 430
Ps 86:8 Among the **g.** there is none like unto.... 430
Ps 95:3 and a great King above all **g.**.............. 430
Ps 96:4 he is to be feared above all **g.**............. 430
Ps 96:5 all the **g.** of the nations are idols:........ 430
Ps 97:7 worship him, all ye **g.**........................ 430
Ps 97:9 thou art exalted far above all **g.**........... 430
Ps 135:5 and that our Lord is above all **g.**:.......... 430
Ps 136:2 O give thanks unto the God of **g.**:....... 430
Ps 138:1 before the **g.** will I sing praise unto...... 430
Isa 21:9 images of her **g.** he hath broken unto... 430
Isa 36:18 Hath any of the **g.** of the nations......... 430
Isa 36:19 Where are the **g.** of Hamath and.......... 430
Isa 36:19 where are the **g.** of Sepharvaim?.......... 430

Isa 36:20 they among all the g. of these lands, 430
Isa 37:12 Have the g. of the nations delivered 430
Isa 37:19 And have cast their g. into the fire: 430
Isa 37:19 for they were no g., 430
Isa 41:23 that we may know that ye are g. 430
Isa 42:17 the molten images, Ye are our g.. 430
Jer 1:16 have burned incense unto other g., 430
Jer 2:11 changed their g., which are yet no g.? 430
Jer 2:28 But where are thy g. that thou hast 430
Jer 2:28 the number of thy cities are thy g., 430
Jer 5:7 and sworn by them that are no g.: 430
Jer 5:19 and served strange g. in your land. 430
Jer 7:6 walk after other g. to your hurt: 430
Jer 7:9 after other g. whom ye know not; 430
Jer 7:18 pour out...offerings unto other g., 430
Jer 10:11 g. that have not made the heavens 426
Jer 11:10 went after other g. to serve them: 430
Jer 11:12 go, and cry unto the g. unto whom 430
Jer 11:13 the number of thy cities were thy g.. 430
Jer 13:10 and walk after other g., to serve 430
Jer 16:11 and have walked after other g., and 430
Jer 16:13 there shall ye serve other g. day and 430
Jer 16:20 Shall a man make g. unto himself, 430
Jer 16:20 unto himself, and they are no g.? 430
Jer 19:4 burned incense in it unto other g. 430
Jer 19:13 out drink offerings unto other g.. 430
Jer 22:9 and worshipped other g., and served 430
Jer 25:6 And go not after other g. to serve 430
Jer 32:29 out drink offerings unto other g., 430
Jer 35:15 and go not after other g. to serve 430
Jer 43:12 in the houses of the g. of Egypt; 430
Jer 43:13 the houses of the g. of the Egyptians 430
Jer 44:3 and to serve other g., whom they 430
Jer 44:5 to burn no incense unto other g.. 430
Jer 44:8 burning incense unto other g. in the 430
Jer 44:15 had burned incense unto other g., 430
Jer 46:25 Pharaoh, and Egypt, with their g., 430
Jer 48:35 him that burneth incense to his g. 430
Da 2:11 except the g., whose dwelling is not 426
Da 2:47 your God is a God of g., and a Lord 426
Da 3:12 they serve not thy g., nor worship 426
Da 3:14 do not ye serve my g., nor worship 426
Da 3:18 we will not serve thy g., nor worship 426
Da 4:8 in whom is the spirit of the holy g.: 426
Da 4:9 the spirit of the holy g. is in thee, 426
Da 4:18 the spirit of the holy g. is in thee. 426
Da 5:4 praised the g. of gold, and of silver, 426
Da 5:11 in whom is the spirit of the holy g.; 426
Da 5:11 like the wisdom of the g., was found 426
Da 5:14 that the spirit of the g. is in thee, 426
Da 5:23 thou hast praised the g. of silver, 426
Da 11:8 carry captives into Egypt their g., 430
Da 11:36 things against the God of g., and 410
Ho 3:1 look to other g., and love flagons 430
Ho 14:3 work of our hands, Ye are our g. 430
Na 1:14 out of the house of thy g. will I 430
Zep 2:11 will famish all the g. of the earth; 430
Joh 10:34 **in your law, I said, Ye are g.?** *2316*
Joh 10:35 **If he called them g., unto whom** *2316*
Ac 7:40 Make us g. to go before us: for as *2316*
Ac 14:11 The g. are come down to us in the *2316*
Ac 17:18 to be a setter forth of strange g. *1140*
Ac 19:26 that they be no g., which are made *2316*
1Co 8:5 though there be that are called g., *2316*
1Co 8:5 (as there be g. many, and lords *2316*
Ga 4:8 them which by nature are no g.. *2316*

GOD-WARD

Ex 18:19 Be thou for the people to G., 4136,430
2Co 3:4 have we through Christ to G. *4314,2316*
1Th 1:8 your faith to G. is spread *4314,2316*

GOEST

Ge 10:19 Gaza; as thou g., unto Sodom, 935
Ge 10:30 as thou g., unto Sephar a mount 935
Ge 25:18 as thou g. toward Assyria: and he 935
Ge 28:15 thee in all places whither thou g., 3212
Ge 32:17 Whose art thou? and whither g. 3212
Ex 4:21 When thou g. to return into Egypt, 3212
Ex 33:16 is it not in that thou g. with us? 3212
Ex 34:12 the land whither thou g., lest it be 935
Nu 14:14 and that thou g. before them, 1980
De 7:1 land whither thou g. to possess it, 935
De 11:10 land, whither thou g. in to possess 935
De 11:29 land whither thou g. to possess it, 935
De 12:29 before thee, whither thou g. to 935
De 20:1 When thou g. out to battle against 3318
De 21:10 When thou g. forth to war against 3318
De 23:20 land whither thou g. to possess it. 935
De 28:6 shalt thou be when thou g. out. 3318
De 28:19 shalt thou be when thou g. out. 3318
De 28:21 land, whither thou g. to possess it. 935
De 28:63 land whither thou g. to possess it. 935
De 30:16 land whither thou g. to possess it. 935
De 32:50 in the mount whither thou g. up, 5927
Jos 1:7 prosper whithersoever thou g.. 3212
Jos 1:9 with thee whithersoever thou g. 3212
Jg 14:3 that thou g. to take a wife of the 1980
Jg 19:17 old man said, Whither g. thou? 3212
Ru 1:16 for whither thou g., I will go; 3212
1Sa 27:8 as thou g. to Shur, even unto the 935
1Sa 28:22 strength, when thou g. on thy way. 3212
2Sa 15:19 Wherefore g. thou also with us? 3212
1Ki 2:37 the day thou g. out, and passest 3318
1Ki 2:42 the day thou g. out, and walkest 3318
Ps 44:9 and g. not forth with our armies. 3318
Pr 4:12 When thou g., thy steps shall not 3212
Pr 6:22 When thou g., it shall lead thee; 1980
Ec 5:1 when thou g. to the house of God, 3212
Ec 9:10 in the grave, whither thou g. 1980
Jer 45:5 prey in all places whither thou g.. 3212
Zec 2:2 Whither g. thou? And he said 1980
Mt 8:19 follow thee whithersoever thou g. *565*
Lu 9:57 follow thee whithersoever thou g.. *565*
Lu 12:58 **When thou g. with thine adversary** *5217*
Joh 11:8 and g. thou thither again? *5217*
Joh 13:36 Lord, whither g. thou? Jesus *5217*
Joh 14:5 Lord, we know not whither thou g. *5217*
Joh 16:5 **you asketh me, Whither g. thou?** *5217*

GOETH

Ge 2:14 is it which g. toward the east of 1980
Ge 32:20 with the present that g. before me, 1980
Ge 33:14 as the cattle that g. before me
Ge 38:13 father in law g. up to Timnath 5927
Ex 7:15 he g. out unto the water; and thou 3318
Ex 22:26 him by that the sun g. down: 935
Ex 28:29 when he g. in unto the holy place, 935
Ex 28:30 when he g. in before the Lord: 935
Ex 28:35 when he g. in unto the holy place 935
Le 11:21 that g. upon all four, which 1980
Le 11:27 And whatsoever g. upon his paws, 1980
Le 11:42 Whatsoever g. upon the belly, and 1980
Le 11:42 and whatsoever g. upon all four, 1980
Le 14:46 that g. into the house all the while 935
Le 15:32 of him whose seed g. from him, 3318
Le 16:17 he g. in to make an atonement 935
Le 22:3 that g. unto the holy things, 7126
Le 22:4 a man whose seed g. from him; 3318
Le 27:21 when it g. out in the jubile, 3318
Nu 5:29 when a wife g. aside to another 7847
Nu 21:15 stream of the brooks that g. down 5186
De 1:30 your God which g. before you, 1980
De 9:3 is he which g. over before thee; 5674
De 11:30 where the sun g. down, in the 3996
De 19:5 As when a man g. into the wood 935
De 20:4 God is he that g. with you, to 1980
De 23:9 When the host g. forth against 3318
De 24:13 when the sun g. down, that he may 935
Jos 10:10 way that g. up to Beth-horon, 4609
Jos 11:17 mount Halak, that g. up to Seir, 5927
Jos 12:7 mount Halak, that g. up to Seir; 5927
Jos 16:1 wilderness...g. up from Jericho 5927
Jos 16:2 And g. out from Beth-el to Luz, 3318
Jos 16:3 g. down westward to the coast 3381
Jos 19:12 and then g. out to Daberath, 3318
Jos 19:12 g. up to Japhia, 5927
Jos 19:13 and g. out to Remmon-methoar 3318
Jos 19:27 and g. out to Cabul on the left 3318
Jos 19:34 g. out from thence to Hukkok, 3318
Jg 5:31 sun when he g. forth in his might 3318
Jg 20:31 one g. up to the house of God, 5927
Jg 21:19 highway that g. up from Beth-el 5927
1Sa 6:9 it g. up by the way of his own coast 5927
1Sa 22:14 in law, and g. at thy bidding, 5493
1Sa 30:24 part is that g. down to the battle, 3381
2Ki 5:18 when my master g. into the house 935
2Ki 11:8 be ye with the king as he g. out 3318
2Ki 12:20 of Millo, which g. down to Silla. 3381
2Ch 23:7 he cometh in, and when he g. out. 3318
Ezr 5:8 and this work g. fast on, and 5648
Job 7:9 so he that g. down to the grave 3381
Job 9:11 Lo, he g. by me, and I see him 5674
Job 34:8 g. in company with the workers of 732
Job 37:2 the sound that g. out of his mouth 3318
Job 39:21 he g. on to meet the armed men. 3318
Job 41:20 Out of his nostrils g. smoke, as out 3318
Job 41:21 and a flame g. out of his mouth. 3318
Ps 17:1 prayer, that g. not out of feigned
Ps 41:6 when he g. abroad, he telleth it. 3318
Ps 68:21 such an one as g. on still in his 1980
Ps 88:16 Thy fierce wrath g. over me; 5674
Ps 97:3 A fire g. before him, and burneth 3212
Ps 104:23 Man g. forth unto his work and to 3318
Ps 126:6 He that g. forth and weepeth, 3212
Ps 146:4 His breath g. forth, he returneth 3318
Pr 6:29 that g. in to his neighbour's wife; 935
Pr 7:22 He g. after her straightway, 1980
Pr 7:22 as an ox g. to the slaughter, 925
Pr 11:10 When it g. well with the righteous,
Pr 16:18 Pride g. before destruction, and an
Pr 20:19 He that g. about as a talebearer 1980
Pr 26:9 g. up into the hand of a drunkard, 5927
Pr 26:20 no wood is, there the fire g. out: 3518
Pr 31:18 her candle g. not out by night. 3518
Ec 1:5 and the sun g. down, and hasteth 935
Ec 1:6 The wind g. toward the south, and 1980
Ec 3:21 the spirit of man that g. upward, 5927
Ec 3:21 of the beast that g. downward 3381
Ec 12:5 because man g. to his long home, 1980
Ca 7:9 that g. down sweetly, causing the 1980
Isa 28:19 From the time that it g. forth 5674
Isa 30:29 as when one g. with a pipe to 1980
Isa 55:11 So shall my word be that g. forth 3318
Isa 59:8 whosoever g. therein shall not 1869
Isa 63:14 a beast g. down into the valley, 3318
Jer 5:6 every one that g. out thence shall 3318
Jer 6:4 the day g. away, for the shadows 6437
Jer 21:9 but he that g. out, and falleth to 3318
Jer 22:10 weep sore for him that g. away: 1980
Jer 30:23 whirlwind of the Lord g. forth 3318
Jer 38:2 he that g. forth to the Chaldeans 3318
Jer 44:17 whatsoever thing g. forth out of 3318
Jer 49:17 every one that g. by it shall be 5674
Jer 50:13 every one that g. by Babylon shall 5674
Eze 7:14 but none g. to the battle: for my 1980
Eze 33:31 heart g. after their covetousness 1980
Eze 40:40 one g. up to the entry of the north 5927
Eze 42:9 as one g. into them from the utter 935
Eze 44:27 in the day that he g. into the 935
Eze 48:1 one g. to Hamath, Hazar-enan, 935
Ho 6:4 as the early dew it g. away 1980
Ho 6:5 are as the light that g. forth. 3318
Zec 5:3 This is the curse that g. forth 3318
Zec 5:5 see what is this that g. forth. 3318
Zec 5:6 This is an ephah that g. forth. 3318
Mt 8:9 say to this man; Go, and he g. *4198*
Mt 12:45 **Then g. he, and taketh with** *4198*
Mt 13:44 **and for joy thereof g. and selleth** *5217*
Mt 15:11 **that which g. into the mouth** *1525*
Mt 15:17 **g. into the belly, and is cast out** *5562*
Mt 17:21 **this kind g. not out but by prayer** *1607*
Mt 18:12 **and g. into the mountains, and** *4198*
Mt 26:24 **The Son of man g. as it is written** *5217*
Mt 28:7 he g. before you into Galilee; *4254*
Mk 3:13 And he g. up into a mountain, and *305*
Mk 7:19 **g. out into the draught, purging** *1607*
Mk 14:21 **The Son of man indeed g., as it is** *5217*
Mk 14:45 he g. straightway to him, and *4334*
Mk 16:7 that he g. before you into Galilee: *4254*
Lu 7:8 I say unto one, Go, and he g.; *4198*
Lu 11:26 **Then g. he, and taketh to him** *4198*
Lu 22:22 **the Son of man g., as it was** *4198*
Joh 3:8 **it cometh, and whither it g.:** *5217*
Joh 7:20 devil: who g. about to kill thee? *2212*
Joh 10:4 **he g. before them, and the sheep** *4198*
Joh 11:31 She g. unto the grave to weep *5217*
Joh 12:35 **knoweth not whither he g.** *5217*
Ac 8:26 unto the way that g. down from *3597*
1Co 6:6 But brother g. to law with brother,
1Co 9:7 Who g. a warfare at any time at
Jas 1:24 beholdeth himself, and g. his way, *565*
1Jo 2:11 and knoweth not whither he g., *5217*
Re 14:4 the Lamb whithersoever he g.. *5217*
Re 17:11 and g. into perdition. *5217*
Re 19:15 his mouth g. a sharp sword, *1607*

GOG See also HAMON-GOG; MAGOG.

1Ch 5:4 Shemaiah his son, G. his son, 1463
Eze 38:2 Son of man, set thy face against G., 1463
Eze 38:3 I am against thee, O G., the chief 1463
Eze 38:14 prophesy and say unto G., Thus 1463

Eze 38:16 I shall be sanctified in thee, O **G.**, 1463
Eze 38:18 **G.** shall come against the land 1463
Eze 39:1 prophesy against **G.**, and say, 1463
Eze 39:1 I am against thee, O **G.**, the chief 1463
Eze 39:11 that I will give unto **G.** a place 1463
Eze 39:11 and there shall they bury **G.**, and 1463
Re 20:8 **G.** and Magog, to gather them *1136*

GOING See also GOINGS.
Ge 12:9 Abram journeyed, **g.** on...toward 1980
Ge 15:12 And when the sun was **g.** down, 935
Ge 37:25 **g.** to carry it down to Egypt. 1980
Ex 17:12 until the **g.** down of the sun 935
Ex 23:4 enemy's ox or his ass **g.** astray, 8582
Ex 37:18 six branches **g.** out of the sides 3318
Ex 37:19 branches **g.** out of the candlestick 3318
Ex 37:21 to the six branches **g.** out of it. 3318
Le 11:20 that creep, **g.** upon all four, 1980
Nu 32:7 children of Israel from **g.** over 5674
Nu 34:4 the **g.** forth thereof shall be from 8444
De 16:6 at the **g.** down of the sun, at the 935
De 33:18 Rejoice, Zebulun, in thy **g.** out; 3318
Jos 1:4 toward the **g.** down of the sun, 3996
Jos 6:9 after the ark, the priests **g.** on, 1980
Jos 6:11 **g.** about it once: and they came 5362
Jos 6:13 the priests **g.** on, and blowing 1980
Jos 7:5 and smote them in the **g.** down: 4174
Jos 10:11 were in the **g.** down to Beth-horon, 4174
Jos 10:27 the time of the **g.** down of the sun, 935
Jos 15:7 is before the **g.** up to Adummim, 4608
Jos 18:17 against the **g.** up of Adummim, 4608
Jos 23:14 I am **g.** the way of all the earth: 1980
Jg 1:36 from the **g.** up to Akrabbim, 4608
Jg 19:18 now **g.** to the house of the Lord; 1980
Jg 19:28 said unto her, Up, and let us be **g.** 3212
1Sa 9:11 they found young maidens **g.** out 3318
1Sa 9:27 were **g.** down to the end of the city, 3381
1Sa 10:3 meet thee three men **g.** up to God 5927
1Sa 17:20 the host was **g.** forth to the fight, 3318
1Sa 29:6 thy **g.** out and thy coming in with 3318
2Sa 2:19 in **g.** he turned not to the right 3212
2Sa 3:25 know thy **g.** out and thy coming in, 4161
2Sa 5:24 thou hearest the sound of a **g.** 6807
1Ki 17:11 as she was **g.** to fetch it, he called 3212
1Ki 22:36 about the **g.** down of the sun, 935
2Ki 2:23 as he was **g.** up by the way, 5927
2Ki 9:27 at the **g.** up to Gur, which is by 4608
2Ki 19:27 I know thy abode, and thy **g.** out, 3318
1Ch 14:15 thou shalt hear a sound of **g.** 6807
1Ch 26:16 by the causeway of the **g.** up, 5927
2Ch 11:4 from **g.** against Jeroboam. 3212
2Ch 18:34 the time of the sun **g.** down he 935
Ne 3:19 against the **g.** up to the armoury 5927
Ne 3:31 to the **g.** up of the corner. 5944
Ne 3:32 **g.** up of the corner unto the sheep 5944
Ne 12:37 at the **g.** up of the wall, above the 4608
Job 1:7 From **g.** to and fro in the earth, 7751
Job 2:2 From **g.** to and fro in the earth, and 7751
Job 33:24 Deliver him from **g.** down to the 3381
Job 33:28 his soul from **g.** into the pit, 5674
Ps 19:6 His **g.** forth is from the end of 4161
Ps 50:1 the sun unto the **g.** down thereof. 3996
Ps 104:19 the sun knoweth his **g.** down. 3996
Ps 113:3 unto the **g.** down of the same 3996
Ps 121:8 The Lord shall preserve thy **g.** out 3318
Ps 144:14 there be no breaking in, nor **g.** out; 3318
Pr 7:27 **g.** down to the chambers of death. 3381
Pr 14:15 man looketh well to his **g.** 838
Pr 30:29 four are comely in **g.**: 3212
Isa 13:10 shall be darkened in his **g.** forth, 3318
Isa 37:28 I know thy abode, and thy **g.** out, 3318
Jer 48:5 in the **g.** up of Luhith continual 4608
Jer 48:5 in the **g.** down of Horonaim the 4174
Jer 50:4 **g.** and weeping: they shall go, 1980
Eze 27:19 and Javan **g.** to and fro occupied 235
Eze 40:31, 34,37 **g.** up to it had eight steps, 4608
Eze 44:5 every **g.** forth of the sanctuary. 4161
Eze 46:12 after his **g.** forth one shall shut 3318
Da 6:14 laboured till the **g.** down of the sun 4606
Da 9:25 the **g.** forth of the commandment 4161
Ho 6:3 his **g.** forth is prepared as the 4161
Jon 1:3 he found a ship **g.** to Tarshish: 935
Mal 1:11 unto the **g.** down of the same 3996
Mt 4:21 And **g.** on from thence, he saw *4260*
Mt 20:17 Jesus **g.** up to Jerusalem took the *305*
Mt 26:46 **Rise, let us be g.: behold, he** *71*
Mt 28:11 Now when they were **g.**, behold *4108*
Mk 6:31 there were many coming and **g.**, *5217*
Mk 10:32 in the way **g.** up to Jerusalem; *305*
Lu 14:31 **g. to make war against another** *4198*
Joh 4:51 And as he was now **g.** down, *2597*
Joh 8:59 **g.** through the midst of them, *1330*
Ac 9:28 coming in and **g.** out at Jerusalem, *1607*
Ac 20:5 These **g.** before tarried for us at *4281*
Ro 10:3 and **g.** about to establish their *2212*
1Ti 5:24 **g.** before to judgment; and some *4254*
Heb 7:18 of the commandment **g.** before *4254*
1Pe 2:25 ye were as sheep **g.** astray; *4105*
Jude 7 **g.** after strange flesh, are set *565*

GOINGS See also OUTGOINGS.
Nu 33:2 And Moses wrote their **g.** out 4161
Nu 33:2 journeys according to their **g.** out, 4161
Nu 34:5 **g.** out of it shall be at the sea. 8444
Nu 34:8 the **g.** forth of the border shall be 8444
Nu 34:9 **g.** out of it shall be at Hazar-enan: 8444
Nu 34:12 **g.** out of shall be at the salt sea: 8444
Jos 15:4 the **g.** out of that coast were at the 8444
Jos 15:7 **g.** out thereof were at En-rogel: 8444
Jos 15:11 the **g.** out of the border were at the 8444
Jos 16:3 the **g.** out thereof are at the sea. 8444
Jos 16:8 the **g.** out thereof were at the sea. 8444
Jos 18:12 **g.** out...at the wilderness 8444
Jos 18:14 **g.** out...at Kirjath-baal, 8444
Job 34:21 man; and he seeth all his **g.** 6806
Ps 17:5 Hold up my **g.** in thy paths, 838
Ps 40:2 a rock, and established my **g.** 838
Ps 68:24 They have seen thy **g.**, O God; 1979
Ps 68:24 even the **g.** of my God, my King, 1979
Ps 140:4 purposed to overthrow my **g.** 6471
Pr 5:21 and he pondereth all his **g.** 4570
Pr 20:24 Man's **g.** are of the Lord; how 4703
Isa 59:8 there is no judgment in their **g.** 4570
Eze 42:11 their **g.** out were both according 4161
Eze 43:11 thereof, and the **g.** out thereof, 4161
Eze 48:30 these are the **g.** out of the city 8444
Mic 5:2 whose **g.** forth have been from of 4163

GOLAN (go'-lan)
De 4:43 **G.** in Bashan of the Manassites 1474
Jos 20:8 **G.** in Bashan out of the tribe of 1474
Jos 21:27 of Manasseh they gave **G.** in 1474
1Ch 6:71 Manasseh, **G.** in Bashan with her 1474

GOLD See also GOLDSMITH.
Ge 2:11 land of Havilah, where there is **g.**; 2091
Ge 2:12 And the **g.** of that land is good: 2091
Ge 13:2 in cattle, in silver, and in **g.** 2091
Ge 24:22 hands of ten shekels weight of **g.**; 2091
Ge 24:35 flocks, and herds, and silver, and **g.**, 2091
Ge 24:53 jewels of silver, and jewels of **g.**, 2091
Ge 41:42 put a **g.** chain about his neck; 2091
Ge 44:8 out of thy lord's house silver or **g.**? 2091
Ex 3:22 jewels of silver, and jewels of **g.**, 2091
Ex 11:2 jewels of silver, and jewels of **g.**, 2091
Ex 12:35 jewels of silver, and jewels of **g.**, 2091
Ex 20:23 Shall ye make unto you gods of **g.** 2091
Ex 25:3 take of them; **g.**, and silver, and 2091
Ex 25:11 overlay it with pure **g.**, within and 2091
Ex 25:11 make upon it a crown of **g.** round. 2091
Ex 25:12 thou shalt cast four rings of **g.** 2091
Ex 25:13 wood, and overlay them with **g.** 2091
Ex 25:17 make a mercy seat of pure **g.**: 2091
Ex 25:18 cherubims of **g.**, of beaten work 2091
Ex 25:24 thou shalt overlay it with pure **g.**, 2091
Ex 25:24 and make thereto a crown of **g.** 2091
Ex 25:26 shalt make for it four rings of **g.**, 2091
Ex 25:28 overlay them with **g.**, that the table 2091
Ex 25:29 of pure **g.** shalt thou make them. 2091
Ex 25:31 shalt make a candlestick of pure **g.**: 2091
Ex 25:36 shall be one beaten work of pure **g.** 2091
Ex 25:38 thereof, shall be of pure **g.** 2091
Ex 25:39 talent of pure **g.** shall he make it, 2091
Ex 26:6 thou shalt make fifty taches of **g.**, 2091
Ex 26:29 shalt overlay the boards with **g.**, 2091
Ex 26:29 and make their rings of **g.** 2091
Ex 26:29 thou shalt overlay the bars with **g.** 2091
Ex 26:32 of shittim wood overlaid with **g.**: 2091
Ex 26:32 their hooks shall be of **g.**, upon the 2091
Ex 26:37 and overlay them with **g.**, 2091
Ex 26:37 and their hooks shall be of **g.**: 2091
Ex 28:5 shall take **g.**, and blue, and purple, 2091
Ex 28:6 they shall make the ephod of **g.**, 2091
Ex 28:8 **g.**, of blue, and purple, and scarlet, 2091
Ex 28:11 them to be set in ouches of **g.** 2091
Ex 28:13 thou shalt make ouches of **g.**; 2091
Ex 28:14 two chains of pure **g.** at the ends; 2091
Ex 28:15 even of **g.**, of blue, and of purple, 2091
Ex 28:20 they shall be set in **g.** in their 2091
Ex 28:22 ends of wreathen work of pure **g.** 2091
Ex 28:23 upon the breastplate two rings of **g.**, 2091
Ex 28:24 put the two wreathen chains of **g.** 2091
Ex 28:26 And thou shalt make two rings of **g.**, 2091
Ex 28:27 And two other rings of **g.** thou shalt 2091
Ex 28:33 and bells of **g.** between them round 2091
Ex 28:36 thou shalt make a plate of pure **g.**, 2091
Ex 30:3 thou shalt overlay it with pure **g.**, 2091
Ex 30:3 make unto it a crown of **g.** round 2091
Ex 30:5 and overlay them with **g.** 2091
Ex 31:4 to work in **g.**, and in silver, and in 2091
Ex 32:24 Whosoever hath any **g.**, let them 2091
Ex 32:31 and have made them gods of **g.** 2091
Ex 35:5 offering of the Lord; **g.**, and silver, 2091
Ex 35:22 rings, and tablets, all jewels of **g.** 2091
Ex 35:22 an offering of **g.** unto the Lord. 2091
Ex 35:32 to work in **g.**, and in silver, and in 2091
Ex 36:13 And he made fifty taches of **g.**, 2091
Ex 36:34 And he overlaid the boards with **g.**, 2091
Ex 36:34 and made their rings of **g.** 2091
Ex 36:34 and overlaid the bars with **g.** 2091
Ex 36:36 and overlaid them with **g.**: 2091
Ex 36:36 their hooks were of **g.**; and he cast 2091
Ex 36:38 chapiters and their fillets with **g.**: 2091
Ex 37:2 he overlaid it with pure **g.** within 2091
Ex 37:2 and made a crown of **g.** to it round 2091
Ex 37:3 And he cast for it four rings of **g.**, 2091
Ex 37:4 and overlaid them with **g.** 2091
Ex 37:6 he made the mercy seat of pure **g.** 2091
Ex 37:7 And he made two cherubims of **g.**, 2091
Ex 37:11 And he overlaid it with pure **g.**, 2091
Ex 37:11 and made thereunto a crown of **g.** 2091
Ex 37:12 made a crown of **g.** for the border 2091
Ex 37:13 And he cast for it four rings of **g.**, 2091
Ex 37:15 and overlaid them with **g.**, to bear 2091
Ex 37:16 covers to cover withal, of pure **g.** 2091
Ex 37:17 he made the candlestick of pure **g.**: 2091
Ex 37:22 it was one beaten work of pure **g.** 2091
Ex 37:23 and his snuffdishes of pure **g.** 2091
Ex 37:24 Of a talent of pure **g.** made he it, 2091
Ex 37:26 And he overlaid it with pure **g.**, 2091
Ex 37:26 also he made unto it a crown of **g.** 2091
Ex 37:27 And he made two rings of **g.** for it 2091
Ex 37:28 and overlaid them with **g.** 2091
Ex 38:24 **g.** that was occupied for the work 2091
Ex 38:24 the **g.** of the offering, was twenty 2091
Ex 39:2 And he made the ephod of **g.**, blue, 2091
Ex 39:3 they did beat the **g.** into thin plates, 2091
Ex 39:5 of **g.**, blue, and purple, and scarlet, 2091
Ex 39:6 inclosed in ouches of **g.**, graven, as 2091
Ex 39:8 the ephod; of c, blue, and purple, 2091
Ex 39:13 inclosed in ouches of **g.**, in their 2091
Ex 39:15 ends, of wreathen work of pure **g.** 2091
Ex 39:16 two ouches of **g.**, and two **g.** rings, 2091
Ex 39:17 put the two wreathen chains of **g.** 2091
Ex 39:19 they made two rings of **g.**, and put 2091
Ex 39:25 and they made bells of pure **g.**, and 2091
Ex 39:30 of the holy crown of pure **g.**, 2091
Ex 40:5 thou shalt set the altar of **g.** for 2091
Nu 7:14 One spoon of ten shekels of **g.**, 2091
Nu 7:20 One spoon of **g.** of ten shekels, 2091
Nu 7:84 silver bowls, twelve spoons of **g.**: 2091
Nu 7:86 **g.** of the spoons was an hundred 2091
Nu 8:4 the candlestick was of beaten **g.**, 2091
Nu 22:18 me his house full of silver and **g.**, 2091
Nu 24:13 me his house full of silver and **g.**, 2091
Nu 31:22 Only the **g.**, and the silver, the 2091
Nu 31:50 gotten of jewels of **g.**, chains, and 2091
Nu 31:51 Eleazar the priest took the **g.** of 2091
Nu 31:52 all the **g.** of the offering that they 2091
Nu 31:54 priest took the **g.** of the captains 2091
De 7:25 shalt not desire the silver or **g.** that 2091
De 8:13 thy silver and thy **g.** is multiplied, 2091
De 17:17 multiply to himself silver and **g.** 2091
De 29:17 idols, wood and stone, silver and **g.**, 2091
Jos 6:19 all the silver, and **g.**, and vessels 2091
Jos 6:24 only the silver, and the **g.**, and the 2091
Jos 7:21 and a wedge of **g.** of fifty shekels 2091
Jos 7:24 the garment, and the wedge of **g.**, 2091
Jos 22:8 silver, and with **g.**, and with brass, 2091
Jg 8:26 and seven hundred shekels of **g.**; 2091
1Sa 6:8 the jewels of **g.**, which ye return 2091
1Sa 6:11 and the coffer with the mice of **g.** 2091

1Sa 6:15 wherein the jewels of **g.** were, and 2091
2Sa 1:24 ornaments of **g.** upon your apparel 2091
2Sa 8:7 And David took the shields of **g.** 2091
2Sa 8:10 vessels of **g.**, and vessels of brass: 2091
2Sa 8:11 Silver and **g.** that he had dedicated 2091
2Sa 12:30 weight whereof was a talent of **g.** 2091
2Sa 21:4 We will have no silver nor **g.** of 2091
1Ki 6:20 and he overlaid it with pure **g.**; 2091
1Ki 6:21 the house within with pure **g.**: 2091
1Ki 6:21 the chains of **g.** before the oracle; 2091
1Ki 6:21 and he overlaid it with **g.** 2091
1Ki 6:22 he overlaid with **g.**, until he had 2091
1Ki 6:22 oracle he overlaid with **g.** 2091
1Ki 6:28 he overlaid the cherubims with **g.** 2091
1Ki 6:30 of the house he overlaid with **g.**, 2091
1Ki 6:32 and overlaid them with **g.**, and 2091
1Ki 6:32 and spread **g.** upon the cherubims, 2091
1Ki 6:35 and covered them with **g.** fitted 2091
1Ki 7:48 the altar of **g.**, and the table of **g.**, 2091
1Ki 7:49 the candlesticks of pure **g.**, five on 2091
1Ki 7:49 the lamps, and the tongs of **g.**, 2091
1Ki 7:50 spoons, and the censers of pure **g.**; 2091
1Ki 7:50 and the hinges of **g.**, both for the 2091
1Ki 7:51 silver, and the **g.**, and the vessels, 2091
1Ki 9:11 trees and fir trees, and with **g.** 2091
1Ki 9:14 to the king sixscore talents of **g.** 2091
1Ki 9:28 from thence **g.**, four hundred and 2091
1Ki 10:2 that bare spices, and very much **g.**, 2091
1Ki 10:10 hundred and twenty talents of **g.**, 2091
1Ki 10:11 that brought **g.** from Ophir, brought 2091
1Ki 10:14 weight of **g.** that came to Solomon 2091
1Ki 10:14 threescore and six talents of **g.**, 2091
1Ki 10:16 two hundred targets of beaten **g.**: 2091
1Ki 10:16 six hundred shekels of **g.** went to 2091
1Ki 10:17 three hundred shields of beaten **g.**; 2091
1Ki 10:17 three pound of **g.** went to one shield: 2091
1Ki 10:18 and overlaid it with the best **g.** 2091
1Ki 10:21 drinking vessels were of **g.**, and all 2091
1Ki 10:21 forest of Lebanon were of pure **g.**; 2091
1Ki 10:22 the navy of Tharshish, bringing **g.**, 2091
1Ki 10:25 vessels of silver, and vessels of **g.**, 2091
1Ki 12:28 made two calves of **g.**, and said 2091
1Ki 14:26 he took away all the shields of **g.** 2091
1Ki 15:15 Lord, silver, and **g.**, and vessels. 2091
1Ki 15:18 Asa took all the silver and the **g.** 2091
1Ki 15:19 thee a present of silver and **g.**; 2091
1Ki 20:3 Thy silver and thy **g.** is mine; thy 2091
1Ki 20:5 silver, and thy **g.**, and thy wives, 2091
1Ki 20:7 and for my silver, and for my **g.**; 2091
1Ki 22:48 of Tharshish to go to Ophir for **g.** 2091
2Ki 5:5 six thousand pieces of **g.**, and ten 2091
2Ki 7:8 thence silver, and **g.**, and raiment, 2091
2Ki 12:13 vessels of **g.**, or vessels of silver. 2091
2Ki 12:18 **g.** that was found in the treasures 2091
2Ki 14:14 And he took all the **g.** and silver, 2091
2Ki 16:8 Ahaz took the silver and **g.** that 2091
2Ki 18:14 of silver and thirty talents of **g.** 2091
2Ki 18:16 Hezekiah cut off the **g.** from the
2Ki 20:13 silver, and the **g.**, and the spices, 2091
2Ki 23:33 talents of silver, and a talent of **g.** 2091
2Ki 23:35 the silver, and the **g.** to Pharaoh; 2091
2Ki 23:35 he exacted the silver and the **g.** 2091
2Ki 24:13 cut in pieces all the vessels of **g.** 2091
2Ki 25:15 such things as were of **g.**, in **g.**, 2091
1Ch 18:7 And David took the shields of **g.** 2091
1Ch 18:10 manner of vessels of **g.** and silver 2091
1Ch 18:11 and the **g.** that he brought from all 2091
1Ch 20:2 and found it to weigh a talent of **g.**, 2091
1Ch 21:25 hundred shekels of **g.** by weight. 2091
1Ch 22:14 an hundred thousand talents of **g.**, 2091
1Ch 22:16 Of the **g.**, the silver, and the brass, 2091
1Ch 28:14 He gave of **g.** by weight for things 2091
1Ch 28:14 by weight for things of **g.**, for all 2091
1Ch 28:15 weight for the candlesticks of **g.**, 2091
1Ch 28:15 and for their lamps of **g.**, 2091
1Ch 28:16 by weight he gave **g.** for the tables 2091
1Ch 28:17 Also pure **g.** for the fleshhooks, 2091
1Ch 28:17 for the golden basons he gave **g.**
1Ch 28:18 the altar of incense refined **g.** 2091
1Ch 28:18 **g.** for the pattern of the chariot 2091
1Ch 29:2 the **g.** for things to be made of **g.**, 2091
1Ch 29:3 own proper good, of **g.** and silver, 2091
1Ch 29:4 Even three thousand talents of **g.**, 2091
1Ch 29:4 of the **g.** of Ophir, and seven 2091
1Ch 29:5 The **g.** for things of **g.**, and the silver. 2091
1Ch 29:7 of **g.** five thousand talents and ten 2091
2Ch 1:15 made silver and **g.** at Jerusalem 2091
2Ch 2:7 a man cunning to work in **g.**, and in 2091
2Ch 2:14 skilful to work in **g.**, and in silver, 2091
2Ch 3:4 he overlaid it within with pure **g.** 2091
2Ch 3:5 which he overlaid with fine **g.**, and 2091
2Ch 3:6 and the **g.** was **g.** of Parvaim. 2091
2Ch 3:7 and the doors thereof, with **g.**; and 2091
2Ch 3:8 and overlaid it with fine **g.**, 2091
2Ch 3:9 of the nails was fifty shekels of **g.** 2091
2Ch 3:9 the upper chambers with **g.** 2091
2Ch 3:10 and overlaid them with **g.** 2091
2Ch 4:7 And he made ten candlesticks of **g.** 2091
2Ch 4:8 he made an hundred basons of **g.** 2091
2Ch 4:20 before the oracle, of pure **g.**; 2091
2Ch 4:21 made he of **g.**, and that perfect **g.** 2091
2Ch 4:22 spoons, and the censers, of pure **g.** 2091
2Ch 4:22 the house of the temple, were of **g.** 2091
2Ch 5:1 the silver, and the **g.**, and all the 2091
2Ch 8:18 four hundred and fifty talents of **g.**, 2091
2Ch 9:1 bare spices, and **g.** in abundance, 2091
2Ch 9:9 hundred and twenty talents of **g.**, 2091
2Ch 9:10 which brought **g.** from Ophir, 2091
2Ch 9:13 Now the weight of **g.** that came 2091
2Ch 9:13 threescore and six talents of **g.**; 2091
2Ch 9:14 brought **g.** and silver to Solomon. 2091
2Ch 9:15 two hundred targets of beaten **g.** 2091
2Ch 9:15 six hundred shekels of beaten **g.** 2091
2Ch 9:16 shields made he of beaten **g.** 2091
2Ch 9:16 three hundred shekels of **g.** went 2091
2Ch 9:17 ivory, and overlaid it with pure **g.** 2091
2Ch 9:18 with a footstool of **g.**, which were 2091
2Ch 9:20 vessels of king Solomon were of **g.**, 2091
2Ch 9:20 forest of Lebanon were of pure **g.**: 2091
2Ch 9:21 bringing **g.**, and silver, ivory, 2091
2Ch 9:24 vessels of silver, and vessels of **g.**, 2091
2Ch 12:9 carried away also the shields of **g.** 2091
2Ch 13:11 candlestick of **g.** with the lamps 2091
2Ch 15:18 himself had dedicated, silver, and **g.**, 2091
2Ch 16:2 Then Asa brought out silver and **g.** 2091
2Ch 16:3 I have sent thee silver and **g.**; go 2091
2Ch 21:3 them great gifts of silver, and of **g.**, 2091
2Ch 24:14 spoons, and vessels of **g.** and silver. 2091
2Ch 25:24 he took all the **g.** and the silver, 2091
2Ch 32:27 treasuries for silver, and for **g.**, 2091
2Ch 36:3 talents of silver and a talent of **g.**, 2091
Ezr 1:4 help him with silver, and with **g.**, 2091
Ezr 1:6 hands with vessels of silver, with **g.**, 2091
Ezr 1:9 thirty chargers of **g.**, a thousand 2091
Ezr 1:10 Thirty basons of **g.**, silver basons 2091
Ezr 1:11 All the vessels of **g.** and of silver 2091
Ezr 2:69 and one thousand drams of **g.**, 2091
Ezr 5:14 the vessels also of **g.** and silver 1722
Ezr 7:15 And to carry the silver and **g.**, 1722
Ezr 7:16 silver and **g.** that thou canst find 1722
Ezr 7:18 the rest of the silver and the **g.**, 1722
Ezr 8:25 unto them the silver, and the **g.**, 2091
Ezr 8:26 and of **g.** an hundred talents; 2091
Ezr 8:27 Also twenty basons of **g.**, of a 2091
Ezr 8:27 vessels of fine copper, precious as **g.** 2091
Ezr 8:28 the silver and the **g.** are a freewill 2091
Ezr 8:30 silver, and the **g.**, and the vessels, 2091
Ezr 8:33 and the **g.** and the vessels weighed 2091
Ne 7:70 thousand drams of **g.**, fifty basons, 2091
Ne 7:71 twenty thousand drams of **g.**, and 2091
Ne 7:72 was twenty thousand drams of **g.**, 2091
Es 1:6 the beds were of **g.** and silver, 2091
Es 1:7 gave them drink in vessels of **g.**, 2091
Es 8:15 with a great crown of **g.**, and with 2091
Job 3:15 Or with princes that had **g.**, who 2091
Job 22:24 Then shalt thou lay up **g.** as dust, 1220
Job 22:24 and the **g.** of Ophir as the stones
Job 23:10 tried me, I shall come forth as **g.** 2091
Job 28:1 a place for **g.** where they fine it 2091
Job 28:6 sapphires: and it hath dust of **g.** 2091
Job 28:15 It cannot be gotten for **g.**, 5458
Job 28:16 be valued with the **g.** of Ophir, 3800
Job 28:17 **g.** and the crystal cannot equal it: 2091
Job 28:17 shall not be for jewels of fine **g.** 6337
Job 28:19 shall it be valued with pure **g.** 3800
Job 31:24 If I have made **g.** my hope, 2091
Job 31:24 or have said to the fine **g.**, Thou 3800
Job 36:19 no, not **g.**, nor all the forces of 1222
Job 42:11 and every one an earring of **g.** 2091
Ps 19:10 More to be desired are they than **g.**, 2091
Ps 19:10 yea, than much fine **g.**: 6337
Ps 21:3 thou settest a crown of pure **g.** on 6337
Ps 45:9 did stand the queen in **g.** of Ophir. 3800
Ps 45:13 her clothing is of wrought **g.** 2091
Ps 68:13 and her feathers with yellow **g.** 2742
Ps 72:15 shall be given of the **g.** of Sheba: 2091
Ps 105:37 them forth also with silver and **g.**: 2091
Ps 115:4 Their idols are silver and **g.**, the 2091
Ps 119:72 better unto me than thousands of **g.** 2091
Ps 119:127 love thy commandments above **g.**; 2091
Ps 119:127 yea, above fine **g.** 6337
Ps 135:15 of the heathen are silver and **g.**, 2091
Pr 3:14 and the gain thereof than fine **g.**, 2742
Pr 8:10 knowledge rather than choice **g.** 2742
Pr 8:19 My fruit is better than **g.**; 2742
Pr 8:19 yea, than fine **g.**; and my 6337
Pr 11:22 a jewel of **g.** in a swine's snout, 2091
Pr 16:16 better is it to get wisdom than **g.**! 2742
Pr 17:3 the furnace for **g.**: but the Lord 2091
Pr 20:15 There is **g.**, and a multitude of 2091
Pr 22:1 favour rather than silver and **g.** 2091
Pr 25:11 apples of **g.** in pictures of silver 2091
Pr 25:12 As an earring of **g.**, and 2091
Pr 25:12 an ornament of fine **g.**, so is a 3800
Pr 27:21 the furnace for **g.**; so is a man 2091
Ec 2:8 I gathered me also silver and **g.**, 2091
Ca 1:10 jewels, thy neck with chains of **g.**
Ca 1:11 We will make thee borders of **g.** 2091
Ca 3:10 bottom thereof of **g.**, the covering 2091
Ca 5:11 His head is as the most fine **g.**, 6337
Ca 5:14 are as **g.** rings set with the beryl: 2091
Ca 5:15 marble, set upon sockets of fine **g.**: 6337
Isa 2:7 land also is full of silver and **g.**, 2091
Isa 2:20 his idols of **g.**, which they made 2091
Isa 13:12 a man more precious than fine **g.**; 6337
Isa 13:17 as for **g.**, they shall not delight 2091
Isa 30:22 of thy molten images of **g.**: 2091
Isa 31:7 idols of silver, and his idols of **g.**, 2091
Isa 39:2 silver, and the **g.**, and the spices, 2091
Isa 40:19 spreadeth it over with **g.**, and 2091
Isa 46:6 They lavish **g.** out of the bag, 2091
Isa 60:6 they shall bring **g.** and incense; 2091
Isa 60:9 their silver and their **g.** with them, 2091
Isa 60:17 For brass I will bring **g.**, and for 2091
Jer 4:30 deckest thee with ornaments of **g.**, 2091
Jer 10:4 They deck it with silver and with **g.**; 2091
Jer 10:9 and **g.** from Uphaz, the work of the 2091
Jer 52:19 cups; that which was of **g.** in **g.**, 2091
La 4:1 How is the **g.** become dim! 2091
La 4:1 how is the most fine **g.** changed! 3800
La 4:2 sons of Zion, comparable to fine **g.**, 6337
Eze 7:19 and their **g.** shall be removed: 2091
Eze 7:19 their silver and their **g.** shall not 2091
Eze 16:13 mast thou decked with **g.** and silver; 2091
Eze 16:17 fair jewels of my **g.** and of my silver, 2091
Eze 27:22 with all precious stones, and **g.** 2091
Eze 28:4 **g.** and silver into thy treasures: 2091
Eze 28:13 emerald, and the carbuncle, and **g.** 2091
Eze 38:13 to carry away silver and **g.**, to take 2091
Da 2:32 This image's head was of fine **g.**, 1722
Da 2:35 the brass, the silver, and the **g.**, 1722
Da 2:38 Thou art this head of **g.** 1722
Da 2:45 brass, the clay, the silver, and the **g.**; 1722
Da 3:1 the king made an image of **g.**, whose 1722
Da 5:4 and praised the gods of **g.**, and of 1722
Da 5:7 have a chain of **g.** about his neck, 1722
Da 5:16 have a chain of **g.** about thy neck, 1722
Da 5:23 praised the gods of silver, and **g.**, 1722
Da 5:29 and put a chain of **g.** about his neck, 1722
Da 10:5 were girded with fine **g.** of Uphaz: 3800
Da 11:8 precious vessels of silver and of **g.**; 2091
Da 11:38 shall he honour with **g.**, and silver, 2091
Da 11:43 have power over the treasures of **g.** 2091
Ho 2:8 multiplied her silver and **g.**, which 2091
Ho 8:4 their silver and their **g.** have they 2091
Joe 3:5 ye have taken my silver and my **g.**, 2091
Na 2:9 take the spoil of **g.**: for there is 2091
Hab 2:19 it is laid over with **g.** and silver, 2091
Zep 1:18 Neither their silver nor their **g.** 2091
Hag 2:8 The silver is mine, and the **g.** 2091
Zec 4:2 a candlestick all of **g.**, with a bowl 2091
Zec 6:11 Then take silver and **g.**, and make 2091
Zec 9:3 fine **g.** as the mire of the streets. 2742
Zec 13:9 and will try them as **g.** is tried: 2091
Zec 14:14 shall be gathered together, **g.**, and 2091
Mal 3:3 and purge them as **g.** and silver, 2091
Mt 2:11 him gifts; **g.**, and frankincense, *5557*
Mt 10:9 **Provide neither g., nor silver, nor** *5557*
Mt 23:16 **swear by the g. of the temple,** *5557*
Mt 23:17 **whether is greater, the g., or the** *5557*
Mt 23:17 **temple that sanctifieth the g.?** *5557*

Ac 3:6 said, Silver and **g.** have I none; *5553*
Ac 17:29 that the Godhead is like unto **g.**, ... *5557*
Ac 20:33 have coveted no man's silver, or **g.**, ... *5553*
1Co 3:12 upon this foundation **g.**, silver, ... *5557*
1Ti 2:9 not with broidered hair, or **g.**, or *5557*
2Ti 2:20 not only vessels of **g.** and of silver, ... *5552*
Heb 9:4 overlaid round about with **g.**, ... *5553*
Jas 2:2 with a **g.** ring, in goodly apparel, ... *5554*
Jas 5:3 Your **g.** and silver is cankered; *5557*
1Pe 1:7 much more precious than of **g.** *5553*
1Pe 1:18 corruptible things, as silver and **g.**, ... *5553*
1Pe 3:3 the hair, and of wearing of **g.**, ... *5553*
Re 3:18 **to buy of me g. tried in the fire,** ... *5553*
Re 4:4 had on their heads crowns of **g.**.......... *5552*
Re 9:7 were as it were crowns like **g.**, ... *5557*
Re 9:20 devils, and idols of **g.**, and *5552*
Re 17:4 decked with **g.** and precious *5557*
Re 18:12 The merchandise of **g.**, and silver,....... *5557*
Re 18:16 decked with **g.**, and precious stones,.... *5557*
Re 21:18 and the city was pure **g.**, like unto *5553*
Re 21:21 the street of the city was pure **g.**,....... *5553*

GOLDEN
Ge 24:22 the man took a **g.** earring of half a 2091
Ex 25:25 thou shalt make a **g.** crown to the...... 2091
Ex 28:34 **g.** bell and a pomegranate, a **g.** bell.... 2091
Ex 30:4 And two **g.** rings shalt thou make....... 2091
Ex 32:2 Break off the **g.** earrings, which are.... 2091
Ex 32:3 the people brake off the **g.** earrings 2091
Ex 39:20 And they made two other **g.** rings, ... 2091
Ex 39:38 the **g.** altar, and the anointing oil, ... 2091
Ex 40:26 he put the **g.** altar in the tent............ 2091
Lev 8:9 did he put the **g.** plate, the holy......... 2091
Nu 4:11 upon the **g.** altar they shall spread...... 2091
Nu 7:26, 32,38,44,50,56,62,68,74,80 One **g.** spoon of ten shekels, full of.............. 2091
Nu 7:86 The **g.** spoons were twelve, full of 2091
Jg 8:24 (For they had **g.** earrings, because 2091
Jg 8:26 the weight of the **g.** earrings that he... 2091
1Sa 6:4 Five **g.** emerods, and five **g.** mice, ... 2091
1Sa 6:17 these are the **g.** emerods which the.... 2091
1Sa 6:18 And the **g.** mice, according to the 2091
2Ki 10:29 the **g.** calves that were in Beth-el, ... 2091
1Ch 28:17 and for the **g.** basons he gave gold 2091
2Ch 4:19 the **g.** altar also, and the tables.......... 2091
2Ch 13:8 and there are with you **g.** calves, ... 2091
Ezr 6:5 also let the **g.** and silver vessels 1722
Es 4:11 king shall hold out the **g.** sceptre, ... 2091
Es 5:2 held out to Esther the **g.** sceptre 2091
Es 8:4 out the **g.** sceptre toward Esther. 2091
Ec 12:6 or the **g.** bowl be broken, or the......... 2091
Isa 13:12 a man that the **g.** wedge of Ophir....... 3800
Isa 14:4 the oppressed ceased! the **g.** city........ 4062
Jer 51:7 Babylon hath been a **g.** cup in the 2091
Da 3:5 down and worship the **g.** image.......... 1722
Da 3:7 down and worshipped the **g.** image 1722
Da 3:10 fall down and worship the **g.** image: 1722
Da 3:12 worship the **g.** image which thou........ 1722
Da 3:14 nor worship the **g.** image which I....... 1722
Da 3:18 worship the **g.** image which thou........ 1722
Da 5:2 commanded to bring the **g.** and.......... 1722
Da 5:3 they brought the **g.** vessels that......... 1722
Zec 4:12 which through the two **g.** pipes.......... 2091
Zec 4:12 empty the **g.** oil...of themselves? ....
Heb 9:4 Which had the **g.** censer, and the....... *5552*
Heb 9:4 wherein was the **g.** pot that had......... *5552*
Re 1:12 turned, I saw seven **g.** candlesticks; ... *5552*
Re 1:13 about the paps with a **g.** girdle. *5552*
Re 1:20 **and the seven g. candlesticks.** *5552*
Re 2:1 **midst of the seven g. candlesticks;** .*5552*
Re 5:8 harps, and **g.** vials full of odours, ... *5552*
Re 8:3 having a **g.** censer; and there was....... *5552*
Re 8:3 upon the **g.** altar which was before..... *5552*
Re 9:13 from the four horns of the **g.** altar....... *5552*
Re 14:14 having on his head a **g.** crown, ... *5552*
Re 15:6 their breasts girded with **g.** girdles. *5552*
Re 15:7 seven **g.** vials full of the wrath of....... *5552*
Re 17:4 having a **g.** cup in her hand full.......... *5552*
Re 21:15 had a **g.** reed to measure the city, ... *5552*

GOLDSMITH See also GOLDSMITH'S; GOLDSMITHS.
Isa 40:19 and the **g.** spreadeth it over with....... 6884
Isa 41:7 the carpenter encouraged the **g.**......... 6884
Isa 46:6 and hire a **g.**; and he maketh it.......... 6884

GOLDSMITH'S
Ne 3:31 repaired Malchiah the **g.** son unto....... 6885

GOLDSMITHS
Ne 3:8 the son of Harhaiah, of the **g.**........... 6884
Ne 3:32 repaired the **g.** and the merchants. 6884

GOLGOTHA (gol'-go-thah) See also CALVARY.
Mt 27:33 were come unto a place called **G.**, ... *1115*
Mk 15:22 they bring him unto the place **G.**, ... *1115*
Joh 19:17 which is called in the Hebrew **G.**........ *1115*

GOLIATH (go-li'-ath)
1Sa 17:4 named **G.**, of Gath, whose height....... 1555
1Sa 17:23 Gath, **G.** by name, out of the armies .. 1555
1Sa 21:9 sword of **G.** the Philistine, whom 1555
1Sa 22:10 and gave him the sword of **G.** the...... 1555
2Sa 21:19 slew the brother of **G.** the Gittite...... 1555
1Ch 20:5 slew...the brother of **G.** the Gittite,...... 1555

GOMER (go'-mer)
Ge 10:2 sons of Japheth; **G.**, and Magog, ... 1586
Ge 10:3 And the sons of **G.**; Ashkenaz, ... 1586
1Ch 1:5 sons of Japheth; **G.**, and Magog, ... 1586
1Ch 1:6 the sons of **G.**; Ashchenaz, and 1586
Ezr 38:6 **G.**, and all his bands; the house of 1586
Ho 1:3 went and took **G.** the daughter of....... 1586

GOMORRAH (go-mor'-rah) See also GOMORRHA.
Ge 10:19 thou goest, unto Sodom, and **G.**, ... 6017
Ge 13:10 the Lord destroyed Sodom and **G.**,..... 6017
Ge 14:2 and with Birsha king of **G.**, Shinab...... 6017
Ge 14:8 and the king of **G.**, and the king of..... 6017
Ge 14:10 and the kings of Sodom and **G.** fled, ... 6017
Ge 14:11 took all the goods of Sodom and **G.**, ... 6017
Ge 18:20 Because the cry of Sodom and **G.** is.... 6017
Ge 19:24 rained upon Sodom and upon **G.**,....... 6017
Ge 19:28 he looked toward Sodom and **G.**, ... 6017
De 29:23 like the overthrow of Sodom, and **G.**, . 6017
De 32:32 of Sodom, and of the fields of **G.**: 6017
Isa 1:9 we should have been like unto **G.**....... 6017
Isa 1:10 the law of our God, ye people of **G.**.. .. 6017
Isa 13:19 when God overthrew Sodom and **G.**.. 6017
Jer 23:14 and the inhabitants thereof as **G.**........ 6017
Jer 49:18 in the overthrow of Sodom and **G.**,..... 6017
Jer 50:40 As God overthrew Sodom and **G.**........ 6017
Am 4:11 as God overthrew Sodom and **G.**, ... 6017
Zep 2:9 and the children of Ammon as **G.**, ... 6017

GOMORRHA (go-mor'-rah) See also GOMORRAH.
Mt 10:15 **for the land of Sodom and G. in**.... *1116*
Mk 6:11 **more tolerable for Sodom and G.**... *1116*
Ro 9:29 and been made like unto **G.**. *1116*
2Pe 2:6 turning the cities of... and **G.**............ *1116*
Jude 7 Even as Sodom and **G.**, and the......... *1116*

GONE See also AGONE.
Ge 27:30 Jacob was yet scarce **g.** out from 3318
Ge 28:7 and was **g.** to Padan-aram;................ 3212
Ge 31:30 though thou wouldest needs be **g.**, ... 1980
Ge 34:17 our daughter, and we will be **g.**. 1980
Ge 42:33 of your households, and be **g.**:.......... 3212
Ge 44:4 when they were **g.** out of the city, ... 3318
Ge 49:9 the prey, my son, thou art **g.** up:......... 5927
Ex 9:29 As soon as I am **g.** out of the city, ... 3318
Ex 12:32 herds, as ye have said, and be **g.**;....... 3212
Ex 16:14 when the dew that lay was **g.** up, ... 5927
Ex 19:1 the children of Israel were **g.** forth...... 3318
Ex 33:8 until he was **g.** into the tabernacle. 935
Le 17:7 whom they have **g.** a whoring.................
Nu 5:19 hast not **g.** aside to uncleanness......... 7847
Nu 5:20 if thou hast **g.** aside to another 7847
Nu 7:89 And when Moses was **g.** into the......... 935
Nu 13:32 land, through which we have **g.** 5674
Nu 16:46 is wrath **g.** out from the Lord;............ 3318
Nu 21:28 there is a fire **g.** out of Heshbon, ... 3318
De 9:9 When I was **g.** up into the mount....... 5927
De 13:13 the children of Belial, are **g.** out......... 3318
De 17:3 hath **g.** and served other gods, ... 3212
De 23:23 That which is **g.** out of thy lips........... 4161
De 27:4 when ye be **g.** over Jordan, that 5674
De 32:36 he seeth that their power is **g.** 235
Jos 2:7 pursued after them were **g.** out. 3318
Jos 4:23 before us, until we were **g.** over:........ 5674
Jos 23:16 have **g.** and served other gods,........... 1980
Jg 3:24 When he was **g.** out, his servants 3318
Jg 4:12 the son of Abinoam was **g.** up 5927
Jg 4:14 is not the Lord **g.** out before thee?..... 3318
Jg 18:24 and ye are **g.** away: and what........... 3212
Jg 20:3 the children of Israel were **g.** up........ 5927
Ru 1:13 hand of the Lord is **g.** out against....... 3318
Ru 1:15 thy sister in law is **g.** back unto.......... 7725
1Sa 14:3 knew not that Jonathan was **g.**........... 1980
1Sa 14:17 now, and see who is **g.** from us......... 1980
1Sa 15:12 him up a place, and is **g.** about, ... 5437
1Sa 15:12 passed on, and **g.** down to Gilgal......... 3381
1Sa 15:20 **g.** the way which the Lord sent 3212
1Sa 20:41 And as soon as the lad was **g.**,............ 935
1Sa 25:37 when the wine was **g.** out of Nabal,.... 3318
2Sa 2:27 the people had **g.** up every one 5927
2Sa 3:7 Wherefore hast thou **g.** in unto.......... 935
2Sa 3:22 him away, and he was **g.** in peace. 3212
2Sa 3:23 him away, and he is **g.** in peace. 3212
2Sa 3:24 sent him away, and he is quite **g.**? 3212
2Sa 6:13 bare the ark of the Lord had **g.** six..... 6805
2Sa 13:15 Amnon said unto her, Arise, be **g.** 3212
2Sa 17:20 They be **g.** over the brook of water.... 5674
2Sa 17:22 one of them that was not **g.** over....... 5674
2Sa 23:9 the men of Israel were **g.** away: 5927
2Sa 24:8 So when they had **g.** through all......... 7751
1Ki 1:25 he is **g.** down this day, and hath 3381
1Ki 2:41 Shimei had **g.** from Jerusalem to 1980
1Ki 9:16 Pharaoh king of Egypt had **g.** up, ... 5927
1Ki 11:15 the captain of the host was **g.** up 5927
1Ki 13:24 when he was **g.**, a lion met him.......... 3212
1Ki 14:9 for thou hast **g.** and made thee 3212
1Ki 14:10 taketh away dung, till it be all **g.**. ....
1Ki 18:12 as soon as I am **g.** from thee, ... 3212
1Ki 20:40 was busy here and there, he was **g.**...... 369
1Ki 21:18 whither he is **g.** down to possess it, ... 3381
1Ki 22:13 the messenger that was **g.** to call........ 1980
2Ki 1:4, 6,16 bed on which thou art **g.** up, ... 5927
2Ki 2:9 when they were **g.** over, that Elijah.... 5674
2Ki 5:2 Syrians had **g.** out by companies, ... 3318
2Ki 6:15 God was risen early, and **g.** forth, ... 3318
2Ki 7:12 therefore are they **g.** out of the 3318
2Ki 20:4 afore Isaiah was **g.** out into the.......... 3318
2Ki 20:11 had **g.** down in the dial of Ahaz. 3381
1Ch 14:15 God is **g.** forth before thee to smite ... 3318
1Ch 17:5 but have **g.** from tent to tent,and 1961
Job 1:5 the days of their feasting were **g.**........ 5362
Job 7:4 shall I arise, and the night be **g.**? 4059
Job 19:10 and I am **g.**: and mine hope hath........ 3212
Job 23:12 Neither have I **g.** back from the......... 4185
Job 24:24 but are **g.** and brought low; 369
Job 28:4 they are **g.** away from men................ 5128
Ps 14:3 They are all **g.** aside, they are........... 5493
Ps 19:4 line is **g.** out through all the earth, ... 3318
Ps 38:4 mine iniquities are **g.** over mine 5674
Ps 38:10 mine eyes, it also is **g.** from me. 369
Ps 42:4 I had **g.** with the multitude,................ 5674
Ps 42:7 and thy billows are **g.** over me, ... 5674
Ps 47:5 God is **g.** up with a shout, the Lord.... 5927
Ps 51:*title* after he had **g.** in to Bath-sheba. 935
Ps 53:3 Every one of them is **g.** back: they 5472
Ps 73:2 as for me, my fleet were almost **g.**;.... 5186
Ps 77:8 Is his mercy clean **g.** for ever?............ 656
Ps 89:34 nor alter the thing that is **g.** out......... 4161
Ps 103:16 wind passeth over it, and it is **g.**; 369
Ps 109:23 I am **g.** like the shadow when it......... 1980
Ps 119:176 I have **g.** astray like a lost sheep; 8582
Ps 124:4 the stream had **g.** over our soul:........ 5674
Ps 124:5 proud waters had **g.** over our soul...... 5674
Pr 7:19 he is **g.** a long journey:.................... 1980
Pr 20:14 but when he is **g.** his way, then he...... 235
Ec 8:10 and **g.** from the place of the holy, ... 1980
Ca 2:11 is past, the rain is over and **g.**;.......... 1980
Ca 5:6 withdrawn himself, and was **g.**:.......... 5674
Ca 6:1 Whither is thy beloved **g.**, O thou 1980
Ca 6:2 beloved is **g.** down into his garden,..... 3381
Isa 1:4 they are **g.** away backward. 2114
Isa 5:13 my people are **g.** into captivity,...............
Isa 10:29 They are **g.** over the passage: they.... 5674
Isa 15:2 He is **g.** up to Bajith and to Dibon,..... 5927
Isa 15:8 cry is **g.** round about the borders....... 5362
Isa 16:8 they are **g.** over the sea.................... 5674
Isa 22:1 art wholly **g.** up to the housetops?...... 5927
Isa 24:11 the mirth of the land is **g.**................. 1540
Isa 38:8 is **g.** down in the sun dial of Ahaz, ... 3381
Isa 38:8 by which degrees it was **g.** down. 3381
Isa 41:3 that he had not **g.** with his feet. 935
Isa 45:23 the word is **g.** out of my mouth 3318
Isa 46:2 themselves are **g.** into captivity......... 1980
Isa 51:5 my salvation is **g.** forth, and mine...... 3318
Isa 53:6 All we like sheep have **g.** astray; 8582
Isa 57:8 to another than me, and art **g.** up; 5927
Jer 2:5 they are **g.** far from me, and have...........
Jer 2:23 I have not **g.** after Baalim? see.......... 1980

Jer 3:6 is **g.** up upon every high mountain... 1980
Jer 4:7 is **g.** forth from his place to make... 3318
Jer 5:23 they are revolted and **g.**... 3212
Jer 9:10 and the beast are fled; they are **g.**... 1980
Jer 10:20 my children are **g.** forth of me,... 3318
Jer 14:2 and the cry of Jerusalem is **g.** up... 5927
Jer 15:6 thou art **g.** backward: therefore... 3212
Jer 15:9 her sun is **g.** down while it was... 935
Jer 23:15 Jerusalem is profaneness **g.** forth... 3318
Jer 23:19 a whirlwind of the Lord is **g.** forth... 3318
Jer 29:16 your brethren that are not **g.** forth... 3318
Jer 34:21 army, which are **g.** up from you... 5927
Jer 40:5 while he was not yet **g.** back, he... 7725
Jer 44:8 land of Egypt, whither ye be **g.**... 935
Jer 44:14 which are **g.** into the land of Egypt... 935
Jer 44:28 that are **g.** into the land of Egypt... 935
Jer 48:11 neither hath he **g.** into captivity:... 1980
Jer 48:15 Moab is spoiled, and **g.** up out of... 5927
Jer 48:15 his chosen young men are **g.** down... 3381
Jer 48:32 thy plants are **g.** over the sea,... 5674
Jer 50:6 have **g.** from mountain to hill,... 1980
La 1:3 Judah is **g.** into captivity because...
La 1:5 her children are **g.** into captivity... 1980
La 1:6 and they are **g.** without strength... 3212
La 1:18 young men are **g.** into captivity... 1980
Eze 7:10 the morning is **g.** forth; the rod... 3318
Eze 9:3 glory of the God of Israel was **g.**... 5927
Eze 13:5 Ye have not **g.** up into the gaps,... 5927
Eze 19:14 And fire is **g.** out of a rod of her... 3318
Eze 23:30 because thou hast **g.** a whoring...
Eze 24:6 and whose scum is not **g.** out of it!... 3318
Eze 31:12 people of the earth are **g.** down... 3381
Eze 32:21 **g.** down, they lie uncircumcised,... 3381
Eze 32:24 which are **g.** down uncircumcised... 3381
Eze 32:27 **g.** down to hell with their weapons... 3381
Eze 32:30 which are **g.** down with the slain;... 3381
Eze 36:20 and are **g.** forth out of his land... 3318
Eze 37:21 whither they be **g.**, and will... 1980
Eze 44:10 the Levites that are **g.** away far...
Da 2:5 The thing is **g.** from me: if ye will... 230
Da 2:8 ye see the thing is **g.** from me... 230
Da 2:14 which was **g.** forth to slay the wise... 5312
Da 10:20 when I am **g.** forth, lo, the prince... 3318
Ho 4:12 and they have **g.** a whoring from...
Ho 8:9 For they are **g.** up to Assyria,... 5927
Ho 9:1 for thou hast **g.** a whoring from...
Ho 9:6 they are **g.** because of destruction:... 1980
Am 8:5 When will the new moon be **g.**,... 5674
Jon 1:5 Jonah was **g.** down into the sides... 3381
Mic 1:16 for they are **g.** into captivity from thee...
Mic 2:13 the gate, and are **g.** out by it:... 3318
Mal 3:7 **g.** away from mine ordinances,... 5493
Mt 10:23 **shall not have g. over the cities**... *5055*
Mt 12:43 **unclean spirit is g. out of a man,**... *1831*
Mt 14:34 when they were **g.** over, they... *1276*
Mt 18:12 **and one of them be g. astray,**... *4105*
Mt 18:12 **seeketh that which is g. astray?**...
Mt 25:8 **oil; for our lamps are g. out**... *4570*
Mt 26:71 when he was **g.** out into the porch,... *1831*
Mk 1:19 he had **g.** a little farther thence,... *4260*
Mk 5:30 that virtue had **g.** out of him,... *1831*
Mk 7:29 **the devil is g. out of thy daughter**.. *1831*
Mk 7:30 she found the devil **g.** out, and her... *1831*
Mk 10:17 when he was **g.** forth...the way,... *1607*
Lu 2:15 as the angels were **g.** away from... *565*
Lu 5:2 the fishermen were **g.** out of them,... *576*
Lu 8:46 **that virtue is g. out of me**... *1831*
Lu 11:14 when the devil was **g.** out, the... *1831*
Lu 11:24 **unclean spirit is g. out of a man**... *1831*
Lu 19:7 he was **g.** to be guest with a man... *1525*
Lu 24:28 though he would have **g.** further... *4198*
Joh 4:8 For his disciples were **g.** away unto... *565*
Joh 6:22 that his disciples were **g.** away... *565*
Joh 7:10 when his brethren were **g.** up, then... *305*
Joh 12:19 behold, the world is **g.** after him... *565*
Joh 13:31 Therefore, when he was **g.** out,... *1831*
Ac 13:6 when they had **g.** through the isle... *1330*
Ac 13:42 were **g.** out of the synagogue,... *1826*
Ac 16:6 when they had **g.** through Phrygia... *1330*
Ac 16:19 the hope of their gains was **g.**,... *1831*
Ac 18:22 landed at Caesarea, and **g.** up,... *305*
Ac 20:2 when he had **g.** over those parts,... *1330*
Ac 20:25 among whom I have **g.** preaching... *1330*
Ac 24:6 Who also hath **g.** about to profane... *3985*
Ac 26:31 when they were **g.** aside, they... *402*
Ac 27:28 when they had **g.** a little further,... *1339*
Ro 3:12 They are all **g.** out of the way,... *1578*
1Pe 3:22 Who is **g.** into heaven, and is on... *4198*
2Pe 2:15 and are **g.** astray, following the... *4105*
1Jo 4:1 false prophets are **g.** out into the... *1831*
Jude 11 they have **g.** in the way of Cain,... *4198*

GOOD See also BEST; BETTER; GOODMAN; GOODS.

Ge 1:4 God saw the light, that it was **g.**:... 2896
Ge 1:10, 12,18,21,25 God saw that it was **g.**... 2896
Ge 1:31 made, and, behold, it was very **g.**... 2896
Ge 2:9 pleasant to the sight and **g.** for food;... 2896
Ge 2:9 tree of knowledge of **g.** and evil... 2896
Ge 2:12 And the gold of that land is **g.**:... 2896
Ge 2:17 tree of the knowledge of **g.** and evil,... 2896
Ge 2:18 not **g.** that the man should be alone;... 2896
Ge 3:5 be as gods, knowing **g.** and evil... 2896
Ge 3:6 saw that the tree was **g.** for food,... 2896
Ge 3:22 to know **g.** and evil: and now, lest... 2896
Ge 15:15 shalt be buried in a **g.** old age... 2896
Ge 18:7 fetcht a calf tender and **g.**, and... 2896
Ge 19:8 do ye to them as is **g.** in your eyes;... 2896
Ge 21:16 down over against him a **g.** way... 7368
Ge 24:12 thee, send me **g.** speed this day,...
Ge 24:50 cannot speak unto thee bad or **g.**... 2896
Ge 25:8 died in a **g.** old age, an old man,... 2896
Ge 26:29 done unto thee nothing but **g.**,... 2896
Ge 27:9 fetch me from thence two **g.** kids... 2896
Ge 27:46 what **g.** shall my life do me?...
Ge 30:20 endued me with a **g.** dowry;... 2896
Ge 31:24, 29 not to Jacob either **g.** or bad... 2896
Ge 32:12 saidst, I will surely do thee **g.**,... 3190
Ge 40:16 that the interpretation was **g.**,... 2896
Ge 41:5 up upon one stalk, rank and **g.**... 2896
Ge 41:22 came up in one stalk, full and **g.**:... 2896
Ge 41:24 thin ears devoured the seven **g.**... 2896
Ge 41:26 The seven **g.** kine are seven years;... 2896
Ge 41:26 and the seven **g.** ears are seven... 2896
Ge 41:35 food of those **g.** years that come,... 2896
Ge 41:47 was **g.** in the eyes of Pharaoh,... 3190
Ge 43:28 servant our father is in **g.** health,... 7965
Ge 44:4 have ye rewarded evil for **g.**?... 2896
Ge 45:18 I will give you the **g.** of the land... 2898
Ge 45:20 for the **g.** of all the land of Egypt... 2898
Ge 45:23 laden with the **g.** things of Egypt,... 2898
Ge 46:29 and wept on his neck a **g.** while... 5750
Ge 49:15 he saw that rest was **g.**, and the... 2896
Ge 50:20 God meant it unto **g.**, to bring to... 2896
Ex 3:8 unto a **g.** land and a large, unto... 2896
Ex 18:17 The thing that thou doest is not **g.**... 2896
Ex 21:34 owner of the pit shall make it **g.**,... 7999
Ex 22:11 and he shall not make it **g.**... 7999
Ex 22:13 not make **g.** that which was torn... 7999
Ex 22:14 he shall surely make it **g.**... 7999
Ex 22:15 he shall not make it **g.**:... 7999
Le 5:4 to do evil, or to do **g.**, whatsoever... 3190
Le 24:18 killeth a beast shall make it **g.**;... 7999
Le 27:10 nor change it, a **g.** for a bad,... 2896
Le 27:10 or a bad for a **g.**:... 2896
Le 27:12 value it, whether it be **g.** or bad;... 2896
Le 27:14 estimate it, whether it be **g.** or bad:... 2896
Le 27:33 not search whether it be **g.** or bad,... 2896
Nu 10:29 with us, and we will do thee **g.**:... 2895
Nu 10:29 for the Lord hath spoken **g.**... 2896
Nu 13:19 whether it be **g.** or bad; and what... 2896
Nu 13:20 And be ye of **g.** courage, and bring...
Nu 14:7 search it, is an exceeding **g.** land... 2896
Nu 23:19 and shall he not make it **g.**?... 6965
Nu 24:13 to do either **g.** or bad of mine own... 2896
De 1:14 thing which thou hast spoken is **g.**... 2896
De 1:25 a **g.** land which the Lord our God... 2896
De 1:35 evil generation see that **g.** land,... 2896
De 1:39 no knowledge between **g.** and evil,... 2896
De 2:4 take ye **g.** heed unto yourselves... 3966
De 3:25 the **g.** land that is beyond Jordan,... 2896
De 4:15 herefore **g.** heed unto yourselves;... 3966
De 4:21 should not go in unto that **g.** land,... 2896
De 4:22 go over, and possess that **g.** land... 2896
De 6:11 And houses full of all **g.** things,... 2898
De 6:18 and **g.** in the sight of the Lord:... 2896
De 6:18 possess the **g.** land which the Lord... 2896
De 6:24 for our **g.** always, that he might... 2896
De 8:7 God bringeth thee into a **g.** land,... 2896
De 8:10 for the **g.** land which he hath given... 2896
De 8:16 to do thee **g.** at thy latter end;... 3190
De 9:6 God giveth thee not this **g.** land... 2896
De 10:13 command thee this day for thy **g.**?... 2896
De 11:17 perish quickly from off the **g.** land... 2896
De 12:28 doest that which is **g.** and right... 2896
De 26:11 And thou shalt rejoice in every **g.**... 2896
De 28:12 open unto thee his **g.** treasure,... 2896
De 28:63 rejoiced over you to do you **g.**,... 3190
De 30:5 he will do thee **g.**, and multiply... 3190
De 30:9 in the fruit of thy land, for **g.**:... 2896
De 30:9 again rejoice over thee for **g.**,... 2896
De 30:15 before thee this day life and **g.**,... 2896
De 31:6 Be strong and of a **g.** courage, fear not...
De 31:7, 23 Be strong and of a **g.** courage: for...
De 33:16 for the **g.** will of him that dwelt... 7522
Jos 1:6 Be strong and of a **g.** courage: for unto...
Jos 1:8 then thou shalt have **g.** success...
Jos 1:9 Be strong and of **g.** courage; be not...
Jos 1:18 only be strong, and of a **g.** courage;...
Jos 9:25 it seemeth **g.** and right unto thee... 2896
Jos 10:25 be strong and of **g.** courage: for thus...
Jos 21:45 failed not ought of any **g.** thing... 2896
Jos 23:11 Take **g.** heed therefore unto... 3966
Jos 23:13 perish from off this **g.** land which... 2896
Jos 23:14 hath failed of all the **g.** things... 2896
Jos 23:15 as all **g.** things are come upon you,... 2896
Jos 23:15 destroyed you from off this **g.** land... 2896
Jos 23:16 perish quickly from off the **g.** land... 2896
Jos 24:20 after that he hath done you **g.**... 3190
Jg 8:32 died in a **g.** old age, and was... 2896
Jg 9:11 my sweetness, and my **g.** fruit,... 2896
Jg 10:15 whatsoever seemeth **g.** unto thee:... 2896
Jg 17:13 I that the Lord will do me **g.**,... 3190
Jg 18:9 the land, and, behold, it is very **g.**:... 2896
Jg 18:22 a **g.** way from the house of Micah,... 7368
Jg 19:24 them what seemeth **g.** unto you:... 2896
Ru 2:22 It is **g.**, my daughter, that thou go... 2896
1Sa 1:23 Do what seemeth thee **g.**; tarry... 2896
1Sa 2:24 for it is no **g.** report that I hear:... 2896
1Sa 3:18 let him do what seemeth him **g.**... 2896
1Sa 11:10 all that seemeth **g.** unto you... 2896
1Sa 12:23 teach you the **g.** and the right way:... 2896
1Sa 14:36 whatsoever seemeth **g.** unto thee... 2896
1Sa 14:40 Do what seemeth **g.** unto thee... 2896
1Sa 15:9 all that was **g.**, and would not... 2896
1Sa 19:4 Jonathan spake **g.** of David unto... 2896
1Sa 19:4 have been to thee-ward very **g.**:... 2896
1Sa 20:12 behold, if there be **g.** toward David... 2896
1Sa 24:4 do to him as it shall seem **g.**... 3190
1Sa 24:17 for thou hast rewarded me **g.**,... 2896
1Sa 24:19 the Lord reward thee **g.** for that... 2896
1Sa 25:3 was a woman of **g.** understanding,... 2896
1Sa 25:8 for we come in a **g.** day: give, I... 2896
1Sa 25:15 But the men were very **g.** unto us,... 2896
1Sa 25:21 and he hath requited me evil for **g.**... 2896
1Sa 25:30 according to all the **g.** that he hath... 2896
1Sa 26:16 This thing is not **g.** that thou hast... 2896
1Sa 29:6 coming in with me in the host is **g.**... 2896
1Sa 29:9 know that thou art **g.** in my sight,... 2896
2Sa 3:19 all that seemed **g.** to Israel,... 2896
2Sa 3:19 that seemed **g.** to the whole house...
2Sa 4:10 to have brought **g.** tidings,... 1319
2Sa 6:19 a **g.** piece of flesh, and a flagon...
2Sa 10:12 Be of **g.** courage, and let us play...
2Sa 10:12 do that which seemeth him **g.**... 2896
2Sa 13:22 brother Amnon neither **g.** nor bad:... 2896
2Sa 14:17 the king to discern **g.** and bad:... 2896
2Sa 14:32 been **g.** for me to have been there... 2896
2Sa 15:3 See, thy matters are **g.** and right;... 2896
2Sa 15:26 let him do to me as seemeth **g.**... 2896
2Sa 16:12 will requite me **g.** for his cursing... 2896
2Sa 17:7 Ahithophel hath given is not **g.**... 2896
2Sa 17:14 appointed to defeat the **g.** counsel... 2896
2Sa 18:27 He is a **g.** man, and cometh with **g.**... 2896
2Sa 19:18 and to do what he thought **g.**... 2896
2Sa 19:27 do therefore what is **g.** in thine... 2896
2Sa 19:35 can I discern between **g.** and evil?... 2896
2Sa 19:37 what shall seem **g.** unto thee... 2896
2Sa 19:38 that which shall seem **g.** unto thee:... 2896
2Sa 24:22 offer up what seemeth **g.** unto him:... 2896
1Ki 1:42 man, and bringest **g.** tidings... 2896
1Ki 2:38 The saying is **g.**: as my lord the... 2896
1Ki 2:42 The word that I have heard is **g.**... 2896
1Ki 3:9 may discern between **g.** and bad:... 2896
1Ki 8:36 teach them the **g.** way wherein they... 2896
1Ki 8:56 one word of all his **g.** promise,... 2896
1Ki 12:7 and speak **g.** words to them, then... 2896
1Ki 14:13 him there is found some **g.** thing... 2896
1Ki 14:15 root up Israel out of this **g.** land,... 2896
1Ki 21:2 than it; or, if it seem **g.** to thee,... 2896
1Ki 22:8 not prophesy **g.** concerning me,... 2896
1Ki 22:13 prophets declare **g.** unto the king... 2896

Book	Ref	Context	No.
1Ki	22:13	and speak that which is **g.**	2896
1Ki	22:18	prophesy no **g.** concerning me,	2896
2Ki	3:19	and shall fell every **g.** tree, and stop	2896
2Ki	3:19	and mar every **g.** piece of land with	2896
2Ki	3:25	on every **g.** piece of land cast every	2896
2Ki	3:25	and felled all the **g.** trees: only in	2896
2Ki	7:9	this day is a day of **g.** tidings, and	
2Ki	8:9	of every **g.** thing of Damascus,	2898
2Ki	10:5	that which is **g.** in thine eyes	2896
2Ki	20:3	have done that which is **g.** in thy	2896
2Ki	20:19	**G.** is the word of the Lord which	2896
2Ki	20:19	And he said, Is it not **g.**, if peace	
1Ch	4:40	they found fat pasture and **g.**,	2896
1Ch	13:2	If it seem **g.** unto you, and that it	2895
1Ch	16:3	of bread, and a **g.** piece of flesh,	
1Ch	16:34	thanks unto the Lord; for he is **g.**;	2896
1Ch	19:13	Be of **g.** courage, and let us behave	
1Ch	19:13	do that which is **g.** in his sight	2896
1Ch	21:23	do that which is **g.** in his eyes:	
1Ch	22:13	be strong, and of **g.** courage; dread not	
1Ch	28:8	that ye may possess this **g.** land,	2896
1Ch	28:20	Be strong, and of **g.** courage; and do it:	
1Ch	29:3	I have of mine own proper **g.**,	
1Ch	29:28	died in a **g.** old age, full of days,	2896
2Ch	5:13	For he is **g.**; for his mercy endureth	2896
2Ch	6:27	thou hast taught them the **g.** way,	2896
2Ch	7:3	For he is **g.**; for his mercy endureth	2896
2Ch	10:7	speak **g.** words to them, they will	2896
2Ch	14:2	And Asa did that which was **g.** and	2896
2Ch	18:7	for he never prophesied **g.** unto me,	2896
2Ch	18:12	prophets declare **g.** to the king	2896
2Ch	18:12	one of theirs, and speak thou **g.**	2896
2Ch	18:17	he would not prophesy **g.** unto me,	2896
2Ch	19:3	there are **g.** things found in thee,	2896
2Ch	19:11	and the Lord shall be with the **g.**	2896
2Ch	24:16	because he had done **g.** in Israel,	2896
2Ch	30:18	The **g.** Lord pardon every one	2896
2Ch	30:22	that taught the **g.** knowledge of	2896
2Ch	31:20	wrought that which was **g.** and right	2896
Ezr	3:11	because he is **g.**, for his mercy	2896
Ezr	5:17	therefore, if it seem **g.** to the king,	2869
Ezr	7:9	according to the **g.** hand of his God	2896
Ezr	7:18	whatsoever shall seem **g.** to thee,	3191
Ezr	8:18	And by the **g.** hand of our God	2896
Ezr	8:22	all them for **g.** that seek him;	2896
Ezr	9:12	eat the **g.** of the land, and leave it	2898
Ezr	10:4	be of **g.** courage, and do it	
Ne	2:8	to the **g.** hand of my God upon me	2896
Ne	2:18	my God which was **g.** upon me;	2896
Ne	2:18	their hands for this **g.** work	2896
Ne	5:9	I said, It is not **g.** that ye do:	2896
Ne	5:19	Think upon me, my God, for **g.**,	2896
Ne	6:19	reported his **g.** deeds before me,	2896
Ne	9:13	**g.** statutes and commandments:	2896
Ne	9:20	Thou gavest also thy **g.** spirit to	2896
Ne	9:36	fruit thereof and the **g.** thereof,	2898
Ne	13:14	and wipe not out my **g.** deeds	2617
Ne	13:31	Remember me, O my God, for **g.**	2896
Es	3:11	do with them as it seemeth **g.**	2896
Es	5:4	If it seem **g.** unto the king,	2895
Es	7:9	who had spoken **g.** for the king,	2896
Es	8:17	gladness, a feast and a **g.** day	2896
Es	9:19	gladness and feasting, and a **g.** day,	2896
Es	9:22	and from mourning into a **g.** day:	2896
Job	2:10	we receive **g.** at the hand of God,	2896
Job	5:27	hear it, and know thou it for thy **g.**	2896
Job	7:7	mine eye shall no more see **g.**	2896
Job	9:25	they flee away, they see no **g.**	2896
Job	10:3	Is it **g.** unto thee that thou shouldest	2896
Job	13:9	**g.** that he should search you out?	2896
Job	15:3	wherewith he can do no **g.**?	3276
Job	21:16	their **g.** is not in their hand:	2898
Job	22:18	filled their house with **g.** things:	2896
Job	22:21	thereby **g.** shall come unto thee	2896
Job	24:21	and doeth not **g.** to the widow	3190
Job	30:26	I looked for **g.**, then evil came	2896
Job	34:4	know among ourselves what is **g.**	2896
Job	39:4	Their young ones are in **g.** liking,	2492
Ps	4:6	Who will shew us any **g.**? Lord,	2896
Ps	14:1	works, there is none that doeth **g.**	2896
Ps	14:3	filthy: there is none that doeth **g.**,	2896
Ps	25:8	**G.** and upright is the Lord:	2896
Ps	27:14	be of **g.** courage, and he shall	
Ps	31:24	Be of **g.** courage, and he shall	
Ps	34:8	taste and see that the Lord is **g.**:	2896
Ps	34:10	Lord shall not want any **g.** thing	2896
Ps	34:12	many days, that he may see **g.**?	2896
Ps	34:14	Depart from evil, and do **g.**; seek	2896
Ps	35:12	They rewarded me evil for **g.** to the	2896
Ps	36:3	hath left off to be wise, and to do **g.**	3190
Ps	36:4	himself in a way that is not **g.**;	2896
Ps	37:3	Trust in the Lord, and do **g.**:	2896
Ps	37:23	The steps of a **g.** man are ordered	
Ps	37:27	Depart from evil, and do **g.**; and	2896
Ps	38:20	They also that render evil for **g.**	2896
Ps	38:20	because I follow the thing that **g.** is	2896
Ps	39:2	I held my peace, even from **g.**;	2896
Ps	45:1	My heart is inditing a **g.** matter:	2896
Ps	51:18	Do **g.** in thy…pleasure unto Zion:	3190
Ps	51:18	Do…in thy **g.** pleasure unto Zion:	
Ps	52:3	Thou lovest evil more than **g.**;	2896
Ps	52:9	for it is **g.** before thy saints	2896
Ps	53:1	iniquity: there is none that doeth **g.**	2896
Ps	53:3	filthy: there is none that doeth **g.**	2896
Ps	54:6	thy name, O Lord; for it is **g.**	2896
Ps	69:16	Lord; for thy lovingkindness is **g.**:	2896
Ps	73:1	Truly God is **g.** to Israel,	2896
Ps	73:28	But it is **g.** for me to draw near	2896
Ps	84:11	no **g.** thing will he withhold from	2896
Ps	85:12	Lord shall give that which is **g.**;	2896
Ps	86:5	For thou, Lord, art **g.**, and ready to	2896
Ps	86:17	Shew me a token for **g.**; that they	2896
Ps	92:1	It is a **g.** thing to give thanks	2896
Ps	100:5	For the Lord is **g.**; his mercy is	2896
Ps	103:5	thy mouth with **g.** things: so that	2896
Ps	104:28	thine hand, they are filled with **g.**	2896
Ps	106:1	for he is **g.**: for his mercy endureth	2896
Ps	106:5	That I may see the **g.** of thy chosen,	2896
Ps	107:1	for he is **g.**: for his mercy endureth	2896
Ps	109:5	have rewarded me evil for **g.**,	2896
Ps	109:21	because thy mercy is **g.**, deliver thou	2896
Ps	111:10	a **g.** understanding have all they	2896
Ps	112:5	a **g.** man sheweth favour, and	2896
Ps	118:1	for he is **g.**: because his mercy	2896
Ps	118:29	for he is **g.**; for his mercy endureth	2896
Ps	119:39	I fear: for thy judgments are **g.**	2896
Ps	119:66	Teach me **g.** judgment and	2898
Ps	119:68	Thou art **g.**, and doest	2896
Ps	119:68	Thou art…,and doest **g.**;	2895
Ps	119:71	it is **g.** for me that I have been	2896
Ps	119:122	Be surety for thy servant for **g.**:	2896
Ps	122:9	the Lord our God I will seek thy **g.**	2896
Ps	125:4	Do **g.**, O Lord, unto those that be	2895
Ps	125:4	unto those that be **g.**, and to them	2896
Ps	128:5	thou shalt see the **g.** of Jerusalem	2898
Ps	133:1	how **g.** and how pleasant it is for	2896
Ps	135:3	for the Lord is **g.**: sing praises unto	2896
Ps	136:1	for he is **g.**: for his mercy endureth	2896
Ps	143:10	thy spirit is **g.**; lead me into the	2896
Ps	145:9	The Lord is **g.** to all: and his tender	2896
Ps	147:1	for it is **g.** to sing praises unto our	2896
Pr	2:9	and equity; yea, every **g.** path	2896
Pr	2:20	mayest walk in the way of **g.** men,	2896
Pr	3:4	find favour and **g.** understanding	2896
Pr	3:27	Withhold not **g.** from them to	2896
Pr	4:2	For I give you **g.** doctrine,	2896
Pr	11:17	The merciful man doeth **g.** to his	1580
Pr	11:23	desire of the righteous is only **g.**:	2896
Pr	11:27	diligently seeketh **g.** procureth	2896
Pr	12:2	A **g.** man obtaineth favour of the	2896
Pr	12:14	A man shall be satisfied with **g.**	2896
Pr	12:25	but a **g.** word maketh it glad	2896
Pr	13:2	A man shall eat **g.** by the fruit	2896
Pr	13:15	**G.** understanding giveth favour:	2896
Pr	13:21	to the righteous **g.** shall be repayed	2896
Pr	13:22	A **g.** man leaveth an inheritance	2896
Pr	14:14	and a **g.** man shall be satisfied	2896
Pr	14:19	The evil bow before the **g.**; and the	2896
Pr	14:22	shall be to them that devise **g.**	2896
Pr	15:3	beholding the evil and the **g.**	2896
Pr	15:23	word spoken in due season, how **g.**	2896
Pr	15:30	a **g.** report maketh the bones fat	2896
Pr	16:20	a matter wisely shall find **g.**:	2896
Pr	16:29	him into the way that is not **g.**	2896
Pr	17:13	Whoso rewarded evil for **g.**, evil	2896
Pr	17:20	hath a froward heart findeth no **g.**:	2896
Pr	17:22	A merry heart doeth **g.** like a	3190
Pr	17:26	Also to punish the just is not **g.**,	2896
Pr	18:5	It is not **g.** to accept the person of	2896
Pr	18:22	findeth a wife findeth a **g.** thing,	2896
Pr	19:2	without knowledge, it is not **g.**;	2896
Pr	19:8	keepeth understanding shall find **g.**	2896
Pr	20:18	and with **g.** advice make war	
Pr	20:23	and a false balance is not **g.**	2896
Pr	22:1	**g.** name is rather to be chosen than	
Pr	24:13	eat thou honey, because it is **g.**;	2896
Pr	24:23	It is not **g.** to have respect of	2896
Pr	24:25	a **g.** blessing shall come upon them	2896
Pr	25:25	so is **g.** news from a far country	2896
Pr	25:27	It is not **g.** to eat much honey:	2896
Pr	28:10	the upright shall have **g.** things	2896
Pr	28:21	To have respect of persons is not **g.**:	2896
Pr	31:12	She will do him **g.** and not evil	2896
Pr	31:18	that her merchandise is **g.**:	2896
Ec	2:3	was that **g.** for the sons of men,	2896
Ec	2:24	he should make his soul enjoy **g.**	2896
Ec	2:26	God giveth to a man that is **g.** in	2896
Ec	2:26	he may give to him that is **g.**	2896
Ec	3:12	I know that there is no **g.** in them,	2896
Ec	3:12	rejoice, and to do **g.** in his life	2896
Ec	3:13	and enjoy the **g.** of all his labour,	2896
Ec	4:8	and bereave my soul of **g.**?	2896
Ec	4:9	have a **g.** reward for their labour	2896
Ec	5:11	what **g.** is there to the owners	3788
Ec	5:18	it is **g.** and comely for one to eat	2896
Ec	5:18	to enjoy the **g.** of all his labour	2896
Ec	6:3	and his soul be not filled with **g.**,	2896
Ec	6:6	yet hath he seen no **g.**: do not all go	2896
Ec	6:12	who knoweth what is **g.** for man	2896
Ec	7:1	a **g.** name is better than precious	
Ec	7:11	Wisdom is **g.** with an inheritance:	2896
Ec	7:18	is **g.** that thou shouldest take hold	2896
Ec	7:20	just man upon earth, that doeth **g.**,	2896
Ec	9:2	to the **g.** and to the clean, and to the	2896
Ec	9:2	as is the **g.**, so is the sinner;	2896
Ec	9:18	but one sinner destroyeth much **g.**	2896
Ec	11:6	whether they both shall be alike **g.**	2896
Ec	12:9	yea, he gave **g.** heed, and sought	
Ec	12:14	whether it be **g.**, or whether it be	2896
Ca	1:3	of the savour of thy **g.** ointments	2896
Ca	2:13	tender grape give a **g.** smell	
Isa	1:19	ye shall eat the **g.** of the land:	2898
Isa	5:20	them that call evil **g.**, and **g.** evil;	2896
Isa	7:15	to refuse the evil, and choose the **g.**	2896
Isa	7:16	to refuse the evil, and choose the **g.**,	2896
Isa	38:3	and have done that which is **g.**	2896
Isa	39:8	**G.** is the word of the Lord which	2896
Isa	40:9	O Zion, that bringest **g.** tidings, get	1319
Isa	40:9	Jerusalem, that bringest **g.** tidings,	1319
Isa	41:6	said to his brother, Be of **g.** courage	1319
Isa	41:23	do **g.**, or do evil, that we may be	3190
Isa	41:27	one that bringeth **g.** tidings	1319
Isa	52:7	feet of him that bringeth **g.** tidings,	1319
Isa	52:7	him that bringeth…tidings of **g.**,	2896
Isa	55:2	and eat ye that which is **g.**,	2896
Isa	61:1	preach **g.** tidings unto the meek;	1319
Isa	65:2	walketh in a way that was not **g.**,	2896
Jer	4:22	to do **g.** they have no knowledge	3190
Jer	5:25	withholden **g.** things from you	2896
Jer	6:16	is the **g.** way, and walk therein,	2896
Jer	8:15	looked for peace, but no **g.** came;	2896
Jer	10:5	neither also is it in them to do **g.**	3190
Jer	13:10	this girdle, which is **g.** for nothing	6743
Jer	13:23	then may ye also do **g.**, that are	3190
Jer	14:11	not for this people for their **g.**	2896
Jer	14:19	and there is no **g.**; and for the time	2896
Jer	17:6	and shall not see when **g.** cometh;	2896
Jer	18:4	seemed **g.** to the potter to make it	3474
Jer	18:10	I will repent of the **g.**, wherewith	2896
Jer	18:11	your ways and your doings **g.**	3190
Jer	18:20	Shall evil be recompensed for **g.**?	2896
Jer	18:20	I stood before thee to speak **g.**	2896
Jer	21:10	this city for evil, and not for **g.**,	2896
Jer	24:2	One basket had very **g.** figs, even	2896
Jer	24:3	I said, Figs; the **g.** figs, very **g.**;	2896
Jer	24:5	these **g.** figs, so will I acknowledge	2896
Jer	24:5	land of the Chaldeans for their **g.**	2896
Jer	24:6	will set mine eyes upon them for **g.**,	2896
Jer	26:14	as seemeth **g.** and meet unto you	2896
Jer	29:10	perform my **g.** word toward you	2896
Jer	29:32	shall he behold the **g.** that I will do	2896
Jer	32:39	the **g.** of them, and of their children	2896
Jer	32:40	away from them, to do them **g.**;	3190
Jer	32:41	rejoice over them to do them **g.**,	2895
Jer	32:42	bring upon them all the **g.** that I	2896
Jer	33:9	hear all the **g.** that I do unto them:	2896
Jer	33:11	for the Lord is **g.**; for his mercy	2896
Jer	33:14	I will perform that **g.** thing which	2896
Jer	39:16	this city for evil, and not for **g.**;	2896
Jer	40:4	If it seem **g.** unto thee to come	2896
Jer	40:4	whither it seemeth **g.** and	2896

Jer 42:6 Whether it be g., or whether it be 2896
Jer 44:27 over them for evil, and not for g. 2896
La 3:25 The Lord is g. unto them that wait 2896
La 3:26 It is g. that a man should both hope 2896
La 3:27 It is g. for a man that he bear the 2896
La 3:38 High proceedeth not evil and g.? 2896
Eze 16:50 I took them away as I saw g.
Eze 17:8 was planted in a g. soil by great 2896
Eze 18:18 and did that which is not g. among 2896
Eze 20:25 them also statutes that were not g., 2896
Eze 24:4 even every g. piece, the thigh, and 2896
Eze 34:14 I will feed them in a g. pasture, 2896
Eze 34:14 there shall they lie in a g. fold, 2896
Eze 34:18 to have eaten up the g. pasture, 2896
Eze 36:31 your doings that were not g., 2896
Da 4:2 I thought it g. to shew the signs 8232
Ho 4:13 because the shadow thereof is g. 2896
Ho 8:3 cast off the thing that is g. 2896
Am 5:14 Seek g., and not evil, that ye may 2896
Am 5:15 Hate the evil, and love the g., 2896
Am 9:4 upon them for evil, and not for g. 2896
Mic 1:12 Maroth waited carefully for g.: 2896
Mic 2:7 do not my words do g. to him 3190
Mic 3:2 Who hate the g., and love the evil; 2896
Mic 6:8 shewed thee, O man, what is g.; 2896
Mic 7:2 The g. man is perished out of the 2623
Na 1:7 The Lord is g., a strong hold 2896
Na 1:15 of him that bringeth g. tidings, 1319
Zep 1:12 heart, The Lord will not do g., 3190
Zec 1:13 g. words and comfortable words 2896
Zec 11:12 If ye think g., give me my price; 2896
Mal 2:13 or receiveth it with g. will 7522
Mal 2:17 Every one that doeth evil is g. in 2896
Mt 3:10 which bringeth not forth g. fruit 2570
Mt 5:13 it is henceforth g. for nothing 2480
Mt 5:16 that they may see your g. works, 2570
Mt 5:44 do g. to them that hate you, and 2573
Mt 5:45 sun to rise on the evil and on the g., 18
Mt 7:11 to give g. gifts unto your children, 18
Mt 7:11 which is in heaven give g. things 18
Mt 7:17 Even so every g. tree bringeth forth 18
Mt 7:17 tree bringeth forth g. fruit; but a 2570
Mt 7:18 A g. tree cannot bring forth evil 18
Mt 7:18 a corrupt tree bring forth g. fruit 2570
Mt 7:19 that bringeth not forth g. fruit 2570
Mt 8:30 there was a g. way off from them 3112
Mt 9:2 be of g. cheer; thy sins be forgiven
Mt 9:22 Daughter, be of g. comfort; thy
Mt 11:26 for so it seemed g. in thy sight 2107
Mt 12:33 make the tree g., and his fruit g.; 2570
Mt 12:34 can ye, being evil, speak g. things? 18
Mt 12:35 A g. man out of the g. treasure of 18
Mt 12:35 the heart bringeth forth g. things: 18
Mt 13:8 fell into g. ground, and brought, 2570
Mt 13:23 received seed into the g. ground 2570
Mt 13:24 a man which sowed g. seed in his 2570
Mt 13:27 Sir, didst thou not sow g. seed in 2570
Mt 13:37 He that soweth the g. seed is the 2570
Mt 13:38 the g. seed are the children of the 2570
Mt 13:48 and gathered the g. into vessels, 2570
Mt 14:27 of g. cheer; it is I; be not afraid
Mt 17:4 Lord, it is g. for us to be here: 2570
Mt 19:10 with his wife, it is not g. to marry 4851
Mt 19:16 G. Master, what...thing shall I do, 18
Mt 19:16 what g. thing shall I do, that I may 18
Mt 19:17 callest thou me g.? there is none g. 18
Mt 20:15 Is thine eye evil, because I am g.? 18
Mt 22:10 many as they found, both bad and g.: 18
Mt 25:21 done, thou g. and faithful servant: 18
Mt 25:23 Well done, g. and faithful servant; 18
Mt 26:10 she hath wrought a g. work upon 18
Mt 26:24 it had been g. for that man if he 18
Mk 3:4 to do g. on the sabbath days, or to 15
Mk 4:8 And other fell on g. ground, and 2570
Mk 4:20 which are sown on g. ground; 2570
Mk 6:50 Be of g. cheer; it is I; be not afraid
Mk 9:5 Master, it is g. for us to be here: 2750
Mk 9:50 Salt is g.: but if the salt have lost 2750
Mk 10:17 G. Master, what shall I do that I 18
Mk 10:18 callest thou me g.? there is none g. 18
Mk 10:49 Be of g. comfort, rise; he calleth thee
Mk 14:6 hath wrought a g. work on me 2570
Mk 14:7 ye will ye may do them g.: but 2095
Mk 14:21 g. were it for that man if he had 2570
Lu 1:3 It seemed g. to me also, having had
Lu 1:53 He hath filled the hungry with g. 18
Lu 2:10 bring you g. tidings of great joy, 2097
Lu 2:14 earth peace, g. will toward men 2107
Lu 3:9 not forth g. fruit is hewn down, 2570
Lu 6:9 on the sabbath days to do g., or to 15
Lu 6:27 do g. to them which hate you, 2573
Lu 6:33 do g. to them which do g. to you, 15
Lu 6:35 do g., and lend, hoping for nothing 15
Lu 6:38 g. measure, pressed down, and 2570
Lu 6:43 For a g. tree bringeth not forth 2570
Lu 6:43 a corrupt tree bring forth g. fruit 2570
Lu 6:45 A g. man out of the g. treasure of 18
Lu 6:45 heart bringeth forth that which is g. 18
Lu 8:8 And other fell on g. ground, and 18
Lu 8:15 But that on the g. ground are they 2570
Lu 8:15 which in an honest and g. heart, 18
Lu 8:48 Daughter, be of g. comforth: thy
Lu 9:33 it is g. for us to be here: and let 2570
Lu 10:21 for so it seemed g. in thy sight
Lu 10:42 and Mary hath chosen that g. part, 18
Lu 11:13 know how to give g. gifts unto your 18
Lu 12:32 your Father's g. pleasure to give
Lu 14:34 Salt is g.: but if the salt have lost 2570
Lu 16:25 thy lifetime receivedst thy g. things, 18
Lu 18:18 G. Master, what shall I do to inherit 18
Lu 18:19 Why callest thou me g.? none is g., 18
Lu 19:17 Well, thou g. servant: because thou 18
Lu 23:50 and he was a g. man, and a just: 18
Joh 1:46 Can there any g. thing come out 18
Joh 2:10 doth set forth g. wine; and when 2570
Joh 2:10 but thou hast kept the g. wine 2570
Joh 5:29 they that have done g., unto the 18
Joh 7:12 some said, He is a g. man: others 18
Joh 10:11 the g. shepherd: the g. shepherd 2570
Joh 10:14 I am the g. shepherd, and know 2570
Joh 10:32 Many g. works have I shewed you 2570
Joh 10:33 For a g. work we stone thee not; 2570
Joh 16:33 but be of g. cheer; I have overcome
Ac 4:9 g. deed done to the impotent man, 2108
Ac 9:36 this woman was full of g. works 18
Ac 10:22 of g. report among all the nation 18
Ac 10:38 went about doing g., and healing 2109
Ac 11:24 For he was a g. man, and full of the 18
Ac 14:17 in that he did g., and gave us 15
Ac 15:7 that a g. while ago God made choice
Ac 15:25 It seemed g. unto us, being assembled
Ac 15:28 For it seemed g. to the Hold Ghost,
Ac 15:38 Paul thought not g. to take him 515
Ac 18:18 this tarried there yet a g. while, 2425
Ac 22:12 having a g. report of all the Jews
Ac 23:1 I have lived in all g. conscience until 18
Ac 23:11 Be of g. cheer, Paul: for as thou hast
Ac 27:22 And now I exhort you to be of g. cheer:
Ac 27:25 Wherefore, sirs, be of g. cheer: for I
Ac 27:36 Then were they all of g. cheer, and
Ro 2:10 peace to every man the worketh g., 18
Ro 3:8 Let us do evil, that g. may come? 18
Ro 3:12 there is none that doeth g., no, not 5544
Ro 5:7 for a g. man some would even dare 18
Ro 7:12 commandment holy, and just, and g. 18
Ro 7:13 Was then that which is g. made 18
Ro 7:13 death in me by that which is g.; 18
Ro 7:16 I consent unto the law that it is g. 2570
Ro 7:18 in my flesh,) dwelleth no g. thing: 18
Ro 7:18 how to perform that which is g. I 2570
Ro 7:19 For the g. that I would I do not: 18
Ro 7:21 a law, that when I would do g., 2570
Ro 8:28 all things work together for g. to 18
Ro 9:11 neither having done any g. or evil, 18
Ro 10:15 and bring glad tidings of g. things! 18
Ro 11:24 contrary to nature into a g. olive 2565
Ro 12:2 that ye may prove what is that g., 18
Ro 12:9 is evil; cleave to that which is g. 18
Ro 12:21 of evil, but overcome evil with g. 18
Ro 13:3 rulers are not a terror to g. works, 18
Ro 13:3 do that which is g., and thou shalt 18
Ro 13:4 the minister of God to thee for g., 18
Ro 14:16 Let not then your g. be evil spoken 18
Ro 14:21 It is g. neither to eat flesh, nor to 2570
Ro 15:2 please his neighbour for his g. to 18
Ro 16:18 by g. words and fair speeches 5542
Ro 16:19 have you wise unto that which is g., 18
1Co 5:6 Your glorying is not g.. Know ye 2570
1Co 7:1 It is g. for a man not to touch a 2570
1Co 7:8 It is g. for them if they abide even as 2570
1Co 7:26 that this is g. for the present 2570
1Co 7:26 that it is g. for a man so to be. 2570
1Co 15:33 evil communications corrupt g. 5543
2Co 5:10 hath done, whether it be g. or bad. 18
2Co 6:8 by evil report and g. report: as 2162
2Co 9:8 may abound to every g. work: 18
2Co 13:11 Be perfect, be of g. comfort, be
Ga 4:18 But it is g. to be zealously 2570
Ga 4:18 affected always in a g. thing, 2570
Ga 6:6 him that teacheth in all g. things. 18
Ga 6:10 let us do g. unto all men, especially 18
Eph 1:5 according to the g. pleasure of his
Eph 1:9 according to his g. pleasure which
Eph 2:10 created in Christ Jesus unto g. 18
Eph 4:28 his hands the thing which is g., 18
Eph 4:29 but that which is g. to the use of 18
Eph 6:7 With g. will doing service, as to 2133
Eph 6:8 whatsoever g. thing any man doeth, 18
Php 1:6 he which hath begun a g. work in 18
Php 1:15 and some also of g. will: 2107
Php 2:13 to will and to do of his g. pleasure
Php 2:19 that I also may be of g. comfort,
Php 4:8 whatsoever things are of g. report; 2163
Col 1:10 being fruitful in every g. work. 18
1Th 3:1 thought it g. to be left at Athens 2106
1Th 3:6 brought us g. tidings of your faith 2097
1Th 3:6 have g. remembrance of us always, 18
1Th 5:15 but ever follow that which is g., 18
1Th 5:21 things; hold fast that which is g. 2570
2Th 1:11 the g. pleasure of his goodness,
2Th 2:16 and g. hope through grace, 18
2Th 2:17 you in every g. word and work. 18
1Ti 1:5 a pure heart, and of a g. conscience, 18
1Ti 1:8 But we know that the law is g., 2570
1Ti 1:18 them mightest war a g. warfare; 2570
1Ti 1:19 Holding faith, and a g. conscience; 18
1Ti 2:3 For this is g. and acceptable in 2570
1Ti 2:10 professing godliness) with g. works 18
1Ti 3:1 of a bishop, he desireth a g. work. 2570
1Ti 3:2 vigilant, sober, of g. behaviour,
1Ti 3:7 he must have a g. report of them 2570
1Ti 3:13 purchase to themselves a g. degree, 2570
1Ti 4:4 For every creature of God is g., 2570
1Ti 4:6 thou shalt be a g. minister of Jesus 2570
1Ti 4:6 of faith and of g. doctrine, 2570
1Ti 5:4 for that is g. and acceptable 2570
1Ti 5:10 Well reported of for g. works; 2570
1Ti 5:10 diligently followed every g. work. 18
1Ti 5:25 the g. works of some are manifest 2570
1Ti 6:12 Fight the g. fight of faith, lay hold 2570
1Ti 6:12 and hast professed a g. profession 2570
1Ti 6:13 Pilate witnessed a g. confession; 2570
1Ti 6:18 That they do g., that they be 14
1Ti 6:18 that they be rich in g. works, 2570
1Ti 6:19 a g. foundation against the time 2570
2Ti 1:14 That g. thing which was committed 2570
2Ti 2:3 as a g. soldier of Jesus Christ 2570
2Ti 2:21 and prepared unto every g. work. 18
2Ti 3:3 despisers of those that are g., 865
2Ti 3:17 furnished unto all g. works. 18
2Ti 4:7 I have fought a g. fight, I have 2570
Tit 1:8 of hospitality, a lover of g. men, 5358
Tit 1:16 and unto every g. work reprobate. 18
Tit 2:3 much wine, teachers of g. things; 2567
Tit 2:5 keepers at home, g., obedient to 18
Tit 2:7 thyself a pattern of g. works: 2570
Tit 2:10 shewing all g. fidelity; that they 18
Tit 2:14 peculiar people, zealous of g. 2570
Tit 3:1 to be ready to every g. work, 18
Tit 3:8 be careful to maintain g. works. 2570
Tit 3:8 These things are g. and profitable 2570
Tit 3:14 also learn to maintain g. works for 2570
Phm 6 the acknowledging of every g. thing 18
Heb 5:14 to discern both g. and evil, 2570
Heb 6:5 And have tasted the g. word 2570
Heb 9:11 an high priest of g. things to come, 18
Heb 10:1 a shadow of g. things to come, 18
Heb 10:24 provoke unto love and to g. works: 2570
Heb 11:2 the elders obtained a g. report.
Heb 11:12 of one, and him as g. as dead,
Heb 11:39 a g. report through faith,
Heb 13:9 it is a g. thing that the heart be 2570
Heb 13:16 But to do g. and to communicate 2140
Heb 13:18 we trust we have a g. conscience, 2570
Heb 13:21 Make you perfect in every g. work 18
Jas 1:17 Every g. gift and every perfect gift 18
Jas 2:3 Sit thou here in a g. place; 2573
Jas 3:13 out of a g. conversation his works 2570
Jas 3:17 full of mercy and g. fruits, 18
Jas 4:17 to him that knoweth to do g., 2570
1Pe 2:12 they may by your g. works, which 2570

1Pe	2:18	not only to the g. and gentle, but	*18*
1Pe	3:10	he that will love life, and see g. days,	*18*
1Pe	3:11	Let him eschew evil, and do g.;	*18*
1Pe	3:13	be followers of that which is g.?	*18*
1Pe	3:16	Having a g. consceience; that,	*18*
1Pe	3:16	falsely accuse your g. conversation	*18*
1Pe	3:21	answer of a g. conscience toward	*18*
1Pe	4:10	as g. stewards of the manifold	*2570*
1Jo	3:17	whoso hath this world's g., and	*979*
3Jo	11	which is evil, but that which is g.	*18*
3Jo	11	He that doeth g. is of God:	*15*
3Jo	12	hath g. report of all men, and of	

GOODLIER

1Sa	9:2	of Israel a g. person than he: from	2896

GOODLIEST

1Sa	8:16	your g. young men, and your asses,	2896
1Ki	20:3	thy children, even the g., are mine	2896

GOODLINESS

Isa	40:6	all the g. thereof is as the flower	2617

GOODLY See also GOODLIER; GOODLIEST.

Ge	27:15	Rebekah took g. raiment of her	2530
Ge	39:6	Joseph was a g. person,	3303,8389
Ge	49:21	hind let loose; he giveth g. words.	8233
Ex	2:2	saw him that he was a g. child,	2896
Ex	39:28	and g. bonnets of fine linen, and	6287
Le	23:40	the boughs of g. trees, branches	1926
Nu	24:5	How g. are thy tents, O Jacob,	2896
Nu	31:10	and all their g. castles, with fire.	
De	3:25	that g. mountain, and Lebanon.	2896
De	6:10	to give thee great and g. cities,	2896
De	8:12	and hast built g. houses, and dwelt	2896
Jos	7:21	among the spoils a g. Babylonish	2896
1Sa	9:2	a choice young man, and a g.:	2896
1Sa	16:12	countenance, and g. to look to.	2896
2Sa	23:21	he slew an Egyptian, a g. man;	4758
1Ki	1:6	he also was a very g. man;	2896
2Ch	36:10	with the g. vessels of the house	2532
2Ch	36:19	destroyed all the g. vessels thereof,	4261
Job	39:13	the g. wings unto the peacocks?	7443
Ps	16:6	yea, I have a g. heritage.	8231
Ps	80:10	thereof were like the g. cedars.	410
Jer	3:19	a g. heritage of the hosts of	6643
Jer	11:16	fair, and of g. fruit: with	3303,8389
Eze	17:8	that it might be a g. vine.	155
Eze	17:23	and bear fruit, and be a g. cedar:	117
Ho	10:1	land they have made g. images.	2896
Joe	3:5	temples my g. pleasant things:	2896
Zec	10:3	as his g. horse in the battle.	1935
Zec	11:13	a g. price that I was prised at of	145
Mt	13:45	**merchant man, seeking g. pearls:**	*2573*
Lu	21:5	adorned with g. stones and gifts,	*2573*
Jas	2:2	in g. apparel, and there come	*2986*
Re	18:14	were dainty and g. are departed	*2986*

GOODMAN

Pr	7:19	For the g. is not at home,	376
Mt	20:11	**against the g. of the house.**	*3611*
Mt	24:43	**if the g. of the house had known**	*3611*
Mk	14:14	**say ye to the g. of the house,**	*3611*
Lu	12:39	**g. of the house had known what**	*3611*
Lu	22:11	**shall say unto the g. of the house,**	*3611*

GOODNESS See also GOODNESS'.

Ex	18:9	And Jethro rejoiced for all the g.	2896
Ex	33:19	make all my g. pass before thee,	2898
Ex	34:6	and abundant in g. and truth,	2617
Nu	10:32	g. the Lord shall do unto us,	2896
Jg	8:35	all the g. which he had shewed	2896
2Sa	7:28	promised this g. unto thy servant:	2896
1Ki	8:66	and glad of heart for all the g. that	2896
1Ch	17:26	promised this g. unto thy servant;	2896
2Ch	6:41	and let thy saints rejoice in g.	2896
2Ch	7:10	glad and merry in heart for the g.	2896
2Ch	32:32	the acts of Hezekiah, and his g.,	2617
2Ch	35:26	the acts of Josiah, and his g.,	2617
Ne	9:25	themselves in thy great g.	2898
Ne	9:35	and in thy great g. that thou gavest	2898
Ps	16:2	my g. extendeth not to thee;	2896
Ps	21:3	him with the blessings of g.: thou	2896
Ps	23:6	Surely g. and mercy shall follow me	2896
Ps	27:13	see the g. of the Lord in the land	2898
Ps	31:19	how great is thy g., which thou	2898
Ps	33:5	earth is full of the g. of the Lord.	2617
Ps	52:1	g. of God endureth continually.	2617
Ps	65:4	satisfied with the g. of thy house,	2898
Ps	65:11	crownest the year with thy g.;	2896
Ps	68:10	hast prepared of thy g. for the poor	2896
Ps	107:8	would praise the Lord for his g.,	2617
Ps	107:9	filleth the hungry soul with g.	2896
Ps	107:15,	21,31 praise the Lord for his g.,	2617
Ps	144:2	My g., and my fortress; my high	2617
Ps	145:7	utter the memory of thy great g.,	2898
Pr	20:6	proclaim every one his own g.:	2617
Isa	63:7	great g. toward the house of Israel,	2898
Jer	2:7	the fruit thereof and the g. thereof;	2898
Jer	31:12	flow together to the g. of the Lord,	2898
Jer	31:14	people shall be satisfied with my g.,	2898
Jer	33:9	fear and tremble for all the g.	2896
Ho	3:5	fear the Lord and his g. in the	2898
Ho	6:4	your g. is as a morning cloud,	2617
Ho	10:1	according to the g. of his land	2896
Zec	9:17	For how great is his g., and how	2898
Ro	2:4	despisest thou the riches of his g.	*5544*
Ro	2:4	not knowing that the g. of God	*5543*
Ro	11:22	the g. and severity of God:	*5544*
Ro	11:22	but toward thee, g., if thou	*5544*
Ro	11:22	if thou continue in his g.:	*5544*
Ro	15:14	ye also are full of g., filled with all	*19*
Ga	5:22	longsuffering, gentleness, g., faith,	*19*
Eph	5:9	the fruit of the Spirit is in all g.	*19*
2Th	1:11	all the good pleasure of his g.,	*19*

GOODNESS'

Ps	25:7	remember thou me for thy g. sake,	2898

GOODS

Ge	14:11	they took all the g. of Sodom	7399
Ge	14:12	Sodom, and his g., and departed.	7399
Ge	14:16	he brought back all the g., and also	7399
Ge	14:16	again his brother Lot, and his g.,	7399
Ge	14:21	persons, and take the g. to thyself.	7399
Ge	24:10	g. of his master were in his hand:	2898
Ge	31:18	all his g. which he had gotten,	7399
Ge	46:6	they took their cattle, and their g.	7399
Ex	22:8	his hand unto his neighbour's g.	4399
Ex	22:11	his hand unto his neighbour's g.;	4399
Nu	16:32	unto Korah, and all their g.	7399
Nu	31:9	all their flocks, and all their g.	2428
Nu	35:3	for their cattle, and for their g.,	7399
De	28:11	thee plenteous in g., in the fruit	2896
2Ch	21:14	and thy wives, and all thy g.:	7399
Ezr	1:4	silver, and with gold, and with g.,	7399
Ezr	1:6	vessels of silver, with gold, with g.,	7399
Ezr	6:8	the king's g., even of the tribute	5232
Ezr	7:26	or to confiscation of g., or to	5232
Ne	9:25	houses full of all g., wells digged,	2898
Job	20:10	his hands shall restore their g.	202
Job	20:21	shall no man look for his g.	2898
Job	20:28	and his g. shall flow away in the	
Ec	5:11	g. increase, they are increased	2896
Eze	38:12	which have gotten cattle and g.,	7075
Eze	38:13	to take away cattle and g., to take	7075
Zep	1:13	their g. shall become a booty,	2428
Mt	12:29	**and spoil his g., except he first**	*4632*
Mt	24:47	**make him ruler over all his g.**	*5224*
Mt	25:14	**and delivered unto them his g.**	*5224*
Mk	3:27	**spoil his g., except he will first**	*4632*
Lu	6:30	**away thy g. ask them not again.**	*4674*
Lu	11:21	**his palace, his g. are in peace:**	*5224*
Lu	12:18	**I bestow all my fruits and my g.**	*18*
Lu	12:19	**thou hast much g. laid up for many**	*18*
Lu	15:12	**me the portion of g. that falleth**	*3776*
Lu	16:1	**him that he had wasted his g.**	*5224*
Lu	19:8	Lord, the half of my g. I give to the	*5224*
Ac	2:45	And sold their possessions and g.,	*5223*
1Co	13:3	though I bestow all my g. to feed	*5224*
Heb	10:34	joyfully the spoiling of your g.,	*5224*
Re	3:17	**I am rich, and increased with g.,**	*4147*

GOPHER

Ge	6:14	Make thee an ark of g. wood;	1613

GOPHER-WOOD See GOPHER and WOOD.

GORE See also GORED.

Ex	21:28	If an ox g. a man or a woman,	5055

GORED

Ex	21:31	Whether he have g. a son,	5055
Ex	21:31	or have g. a daughter.	5055

GORGEOUS

Lu	23:11	arrayed him in a g. robe, and sent	*2986*

GORGEOUSLY

Eze	23:12	and rulers clothed most g.,	4358
Lu	7:25	**they which are g. apparelled**	*1741*

GOSHEN (go'-shen)

Ge	45:10	dwell in the land of G., and thou	1657
Ge	46:28	Joseph, to direct his face unto G.;	1657
Ge	46:28	and they came into the land of g.	1657
Ge	46:29	meet Israel his father, to G., and	1657
Ge	46:34	that ye may dwell in the land of G.;	1657
Ge	47:1	behold, they are in the land of G.	1657
Ge	47:4	servants dwell in the land of G.	1657
Ge	47:6	in the land of g. let them dwell:	1657
Ge	47:27	land of Egypt, in the country of G.;	1657
Ge	50:8	herds, they left in the land of G.	1657
Ex	8:22	sever in that day the land of G., in	1657
Ex	9:26	Only in the land of G., where the	1657
Jos	10:41	and all the country of G., even	1657
Jos	11:16	and all the land of G., and the	1657
Jos	15:51	And G., and Holon, and Giloh;	1657

GOSPEL See also GOSPEL'S.

Mt	*title*	G. According To...Matthew	*2098*
Mt	4:23	preaching the g. of the kingdom,	*2098*
Mt	9:35	preaching the g. of the kingdom,	*2098*
Mt	11:5	**have the g. preached to them.**	*2097*
Mt	24:14	**this g. of the kingdom shall be**	*2098*
Mt	26:13	**wheresoever this g. shall be**	*2098*
Mk	*title*	The G. According To...Mark	*2098*
Mk	1:1	beginning of the g. of Jesus Christ,	*2098*
Mk	1:14	preaching the g. of the kingdom of	*2098*
Mk	1:15	**repent ye, and believe the g.**	*2098*
Mk	13:10	**the g. must first be published**	*2098*
Mk	14:9	**this g. shall be preached through**	*2098*
Mk	16:15	**preach the g. to every creature**	*2098*
Lu	*title*	The G. According To...Luke	*2098*
Lu	4:18	**to preach the g. to the poor;**	*2097*
Lu	7:22	**to the poor the g. is preached.**	*2097*
Lu	9:6	preaching the g., and healing every	*2097*
Lu	20:1	in the temple, and preached the g.,	*2097*
Joh	*title*	The G. According To...John	*2098*
Ac	8:25	preached the g. in many villages	*2097*
Ac	14:7	And there they preached the g.,	*2097*
Ac	14:21	And when they had preached the g.	*2097*
Ac	15:7	should hear the word of the g.,	*2098*
Ac	16:10	to preach the g. unto them.	*2097*
Ac	20:24	testify the g. of the grace of God.	*2098*
Ro	1:1	separated unto the g. of God,	*2098*
Ro	1:9	my spirit in the g. of his Son,	*2098*
Ro	1:15	to preach the g. to you that are	*2097*
Ro	1:16	For I am not ashamed of the g.	*2098*
Ro	2:16	by Jesus Christ according to my g.	*2098*
Ro	10:15	them that preach the g. of peace,	*2097*
Ro	10:16	they have not all obeyed the	*2098*
Ro	11:28	As concerning the g., they are	*2098*
Ro	15:16	ministering the g. of God, that the	*2098*
Ro	15:19	have fully preached the g. of Christ.	*2098*
Ro	15:20	have I strived to preach the g.,	*2097*
Ro	15:29	of the blessing of the g. of Christ.	*2098*
Ro	16:25	stablish you according to my g.,	*2098*
1Co	1:17	but I preach the g.: not with	*2097*
1Co	4:15	have begotten you through the g.	*2098*
1Co	9:12	we should hinder the g. of Christ.	*2098*
1Co	9:14	that they which preach the g.	*2098*
1Co	9:14	should live of the g.	*2098*
1Co	9:16	For though I preach the g., I have	*2097*
1Co	9:16	is unto me, if I preach not the g.!	*2097*
1Co	9:17	a dispensation of the g. is	
1Co	9:18	that, when I preach the g., I may	*2097*
1Co	9:18	I may make the g. of Christ of no	*2098*
1Co	9:18	that I abuse not my power in the g.	*2098*
1Co	15:1	the g. which I preached unto you,	*2098*
2Co	2:12	to preach Christ's g., and a door	*2098*
2Co	4:3	But if our g. be hid, it is hid to them	*2098*
2Co	4:4	lest the light of the glorious g. of	*2098*
2Co	8:18	whose praise is in the g.	*2098*
2Co	9:13	subjection unto the g. of Christ,	*2098*
2Co	10:14	in preaching the g. of Christ:	*2098*
2Co	10:16	To preach the g. in the regions	*2097*
2Co	11:4	or another g., which ye have not	*2098*
2Co	11:7	have preached to you the g. of God	*2098*
Ga	1:6	grace of Christ unto another g.:	*2098*
Ga	1:7	and would pervert the g. of Christ.	*2098*
Ga	1:8	preach any other g. unto you than	*2097*
Ga	1:9	if any man preach any other g.	*2097*
Ga	1:11	that the g. which was preached	*2098*
Ga	2:2	communicated unto them that g.	*2098*

Ga 2:5 the truth of the **g.** might continue....... *2098*
Ga 2:7 the **g.** of the uncircumcision was........ *2098*
Ga 2:7 as the **g.** of the circumcision was.............
Ga 2:14 according to the truth of the **g.**,.......... *2098*
Ga 3:8 before the **g.** unto Abraham, ... *4283*
Ga 4:13 I preached the **g.** unto you................ *2097*
Eph 1:13 of truth the **g.** of your salvation: *2098*
Eph 3:6 promise in Christ by the **g.**:............... *2098*
Eph 6:15 the preparation of the **g.** of peace;....... *2098*
Eph 6:19 make known the mystery of the **g.**, ... *2098*
Php 1:5 For your fellowship in the **g.**.............. *2098*
Php 1:7 and confirmation of the **g.**, ye all........ *2098*
Php 1:12 unto the furtherance of the **g.**;........... *2098*
Php 1:17 I am set for the defence of the **g.**. *2098*
Php 1:27 be as it becometh the **g.** of Christ: *2098*
Php 1:27 together for the faith of the **g.**;.......... *2098*
Php 2:22 he hath served with me in the **g.**. *2098*
Php 4:3 which laboured with me in the **g.**, ... *2098*
Php 4:15 that in the beginning of the **g.**, ... *2098*
Col 1:5 in the word of the truth of the **g.**; *2098*
Col 1:23 away from the hope of the **g.**, ... *2098*
1Th 1:5 For our **g.** came not unto you............ *2098*
1Th 2:2 to speak unto you the **g.** of God *2098*
1Th 2:4 to be put in trust with the **g.**,............ *2098*
1Th 2:8 not the **g.** of God only, but also our..... *2098*
1Th 2:9 we preached unto you the **g.** of God... *2098*
1Th 3:2 fellowlabourer in the **g.** of Christ, ... *2098*
2Th 1:8 and that obey not the **g.** of our.......... *2098*
2Th 2:14 he called you by our **g.**, to the *2098*
1Ti 1:11 According to the glorious **g.** of the *2098*
2Ti 1:8 partaker of the afflictions of the **g.**....... *2098*
1Ti 1:10 immortality to light through the **g.**: *2098*
1Ti 2:8 from the dead according to my **g.**:...... *2098*
Phm 13 unto me in the bonds of the **g.**: *2098*
Heb 4:2 For unto us was the **g.** preached,....... *2097*
1Pe 1:12 by them that have preached the **g.**...... *2097*
1Pe 1:25 by the **g.** is preached unto you *2097*
1Pe 4:6 was the **g.** preached also to them......... *2097*
1Pe 4:17 them that obey not the **g.** of God? *2098*
Re 14:6 the evelasting **g.** to preach................ *2098*

GOSPEL'S
Mk 8:35 **his life for my sake and the g.,** *2098*
Mk 10:29 **or lands, for my sake, and the g.,** ..*2098*
1Co 9:23 And this I do for the **g.** sake,............ *2098*

GOT See also FORGOT; GAT; GOTTEN.
Ge 36:6 which he had **g.** in the land.............. 7408
Ge 39:12 her hand, and fled, and **g.** him out..... 3318
Ge 39:15 with me, and fled, and **g.** him out....... 3318
Ps 44:3 they **g.** not the land in possession 3423
Ec 2:7 I **g.** me servants and maidens,........... 7069
Jer 13:2 So I **g.** a girdle according to the......... 7069
Jer 13:4 Take the girdle that thou hast **g.**,........ 7069

GOTTEN See also BEGOTTEN; FORGOTTEN; GOT.
Ge 4:1 I have **g.** a man from the Lord. 7069
Ge 12:5 souls that they had **g.** in Haran; 6213
Ge 31:1 our father's hath he **g.** all this glory. ... 6213
Ge 31:18 all his goods which he had **g.**,............ 7408
Ge 31:18 of his getting, which he had **g.**........... 7408
Ge 46:6 their goods, which they had **g.**............ 7408
Ex 14:18 when I have **g.** me honour upon......... 7408
Le 6:4 thing which he hath deceitfully **g.**, ...
Nu 31:50 what every man hath **g.**, of................ 4672
De 8:17 mine hand hath **g.** me this 6213
2Sa 17:13 Moreover, if he be **g.** into a city, ... 622
Job 28:15 It cannot be **g.** for gold, neither......... 5414
Job 31:25 because mine hand hath **g.** much; 4672
Ps 98:1 arm, hath **g.** him the victory....................
Pr 13:11 Wealth **g.** by vanity shall be ....
Pr 20:21 inheritance may be **g.** hastily ....
Ec 1:16 and have **g.** more wisdom than 3254
Isa 15:7 the abundance they have **g.**,.............. 6213
Jer 48:36 riches that he hath **g.** are perished. 6213
Eze 28:4 thou hast **g.** thee riches, ... 6213
Eze 28:4 and hast **g.** gold and silver................ 6213
Eze 38:12 which have **g.** cattle and goods, ... 6213
Da 9:15 and hast **g.** thee renown, as at this..... 6213
Ac 21:1 after we were **g.** from them, ... *645*
Re 15:2 them that had **g.** the victory....................

GOURD See also GOURDS.
Jon 4:6 And the Lord God prepared a **g.**,....... 7021
Jon 4:6 Jonah was exceeding glad of the **g.**....... 7021
Jon 4:7 it smote the **g.** that it withered.......... 7021
Jon 4:9 thou well to be angry for the **g.**?........ 7021
Jon 4:10 Thou hast had pity on the **g.**, ... 7021

GOURDS
2Ki 4:39 gathered thereof wild **g.** his lap.......... 6498

GOVERN
1Ki 21:7 Dost thou now **g.** the kingdom........... 6213
Job 34:17 Shall even he that hateth right **g.**?...... 2280
Ps 67:4 and **g.** the nations upon earth. 5148

GOVERNMENT See also GOVERNMENTS.
Isa 9:6 the **g.** shall be upon his shoulder: 4951
Isa 9:7 Of the increase of his **g.** and peace..... 4951
Isa 22:21 and I will commit thy **g.** into his......... 4475
2Pe 2:10 of uncleanness, and despise **g.**. *2963*

GOVERNMENTS
1Co 12:28 helps, **g.**, diversities of tongues. *2941*

GOVERNOR See also GOVERNOR'S; GOVERNORS.
Ge 42:6 Joseph was the **g.** over the land,........ 7989
Ge 45:26 he is **g.** over all the land 4910
1Ki 18:3 Obadiah, which was **g.** of the 5921
1Ki 22:26 Amon the **g.** of the city, and to 8269
2Ki 23:8 gate of Joshua the **g.** of the city,........ 8269
2Ki 25:23 of Babylon had made Gedaliah **g.**........ 6485
1Ch 29:22 unto the Lord to be the chief **g.**,......... 5057
2Ch 1:2 every **g.** in all Israel, the chief.......... 5387
2Ch 18:25 back to Amon the **g.** of the city, ... 8269
2Ch 28:7 and Azrikam the **g.** of the house, ... 5057
2Ch 34:8 Maaseiah the **g.** of the city, ... 8269
Ezr 5:3 them Tatnai, **g.** on this side the......... 6347
Ezr 5:6 that Tatnai, **g.** on this side the 6347
Ezr 5:14 Sheshbazzar, whom he had made **g.**;... 6347
Ezr 6:6 Tatnai, **g.** beyond the river, ... 6347
Ezr 6:7 the **g.** of the Jews and the elders 6347
Ezr 6:13 Tatnai, **g.** on this side the river, ... 6347
Ne 3:7 the throne of the **g.** on this side 6346
Ne 5:14 I was appointed to be their **g.**............ 6346
Ne 5:14 have not eaten the bread of the **g.**. 6346
Ne 5:18 required not I the bread of the **g.**,...... 6346
Ne 12:26 in the days of Nehemiah the **g.**, ... 6346
Ps 22:28 he is the **g.** among the nations........... 4910
Jer 20:1 chief **g.** in the house of the Lord,....... 5057
Jer 30:21 and their **g.** shall proceed from 4910
Jer 40:5 made **g.** over the cities of Judah,........ 6485
Jer 40:7 has made Gedaliah...**g.** in the land, ... 6485
Jer 41:2 Babylon had made **g.** over the land..... 6485
Jer 41:18 of Babylon made **g.** in the land. 6485
Hag 1:1, 14 son of Shealtiel, **g.** of Judah, ... 6346
Hag 2:2, 21 the son of Shealtiel, **g.** of Judah, ... 6346
Zec 9:7 he shall be as a **g.** in Judah,................ 441
Mal 1:8 offer it now unto thy **g.**; will he 6346
Mt 2:6 shall come a **G.**, that shall rule *2233*
Mt 27:2 him to Pontius Pilate the **g.**................ *2232*
Mt 27:11 And Jesus stood before the **g.**:............ *2232*
Mt 27:11 and the **g.** asked him, saying, ... *2232*
Mt 27:14 that the **g.** marvelled greatly. *2232*
Mt 27:15 the **g.** was wont to release unto.......... *2232*
Mt 27:21 **g.** answered and said unto them,......... *2232*
Mt 27:23 And the **g.** said, Why, what evil......... *2232*
Mt 27:27 the soldiers of the **g.** took Jesus *2232*
Lu 2:2 when Cyrenius was **g.** of Syria.) *2230*
Lu 3:1 Pontius Pilate being **g.** of Judaea, ... *2230*
Lu 20:20 the power and authority of the **g.**. *2230*
Joh 2:8 **And bear unto the g. of the feast**.... *755*
Joh 2:9 the **g.** of the feast called the............ *755*
Ac 7:10 and he made him **g.** over Egypt.......... *2233*
Ac 23:24 bring him safe unto Felix the **g.**.......... *2232*
Ac 23:26 unto the most excellent **g.** Felix.......... *2232*
Ac 23:33 and delivered the epistle to the **g.**,...... *2232*
Ac 23:34 when the **g.** had read the letter, ... *2232*
Ac 24:1 who informed the **g.** against Paul........ *2232*
Ac 24:10 after that the **g.** had beckoned unto *2232*
Ac 26:30 the king rose up, and the **g.**,.............. *2232*
2Co 11:32 the **g.** under Aretas the king kept *1481*
Jas 3:4 whithersoever the **g.** listeth. *2116*

GOVERNOR'S
Mt 28:14 And if this come to the **g.** ears, ... *2232*

GOVERNORS
Jg 5:9 My heart is toward the **g.** of Israel,.... 2710
Jg 5:14 out of Machir came down **g.**,............. 2710
1Ki 10:15 and of the **g.** of the country. 6346
1Ch 24:5 the **g.** of the sanctuary, and **g.** of....... 8269
2Ch 9:14 **g.** of the country brought gold........... 6346
2Ch 23:20 and the **g.** of the peope, and all the 4910
Ezr 8:36 and to the **g.** on this side the river: 6346
Ne 2:7 given me to the **g.** beyond the river, .. 6346
Ne 2:9 Then I came to the **g.** beyond the...... 6346
Ne 5:15 But the former **g.** that had been 6346
Es 3:12 and to the **g.** that were over every..... 6346
Da 2:48 and chief of the **g.** over all the........... 5461
Da 3:2 gather together the princes, the **g.**, ... 5461
Da 3:3 Then the princes, the **g.**, and........... 5461
Da 3:27 And the princes, **g.**, and captains, ... 5461
Da 6:7 kingdom, the **g.** and the princes, the... 5461
Zec 12:5 And the **g.** of Judah shall say in.......... 441
Zec 12:6 day will I make the **g.** of Judah............ 441
Mt 10:18 **And ye shall be brought before g.**... *2232*
Gal 4:2 But is under tutors and **g.** until.......... *3623*
1Pe 2:14 Or unto **g.**, as unto them that are *2232*

GOZAN (go'-zan)
2Ki 17:6 and in Habor by the river of **G.**, ... 1470
2Ki 18:11 and in Habor by the river of **G.**, ... 1470
2Ki 19:12 my fathers have destroyed; as **G.**,...... 1470
1Ch 5:26 and Hara, and to the river **G.**,........... 1470
Isa 37:12 my fathers have destroyed, as **G.**,........ 1470

GRACE See also DISGRACE.
Ge 6:8 Noah found **g.** in the eyes of............ 2580
Ge 19:19 now, thy servant hath found **g.** in....... 2580
Ge 32:5 that I may find **g.** in thy sight............ 2580
Ge 33:8 to find **g.** in the sight of my lord. 2580
Ge 33:10 now I have found **g.** in thy sight, ... 2580
Ge 33:15 let me find **g.** in the sight of my......... 2580
Ge 34:11 Let me find **g.** in your eyes, ... 2580
Ge 39:4 And Joseph found **g.** in his sight,........ 2580
Ge 47:25 us find **g.** in the sight of my lord,........ 2580
Ge 47:29 now I have found **g.** in thy sight. 2580
Ge 50:4 now I have found **g.** in your eyes,....... 2580
Ex 33:12 hast also found **g.** in my sight............ 2580
Ex 33:13 if I have found **g.** in thy sight, ... 2580
Ex 33:13 that I may find **g.** in thy sight:........... 2580
Ex 33:16 people have found **g.** in thy sight? 2580
Ex 33:17 thou hast found **g.** in my sight, ... 2580
Ex 34:9 now I have found **g.** in thy sight, ... 2580
Nu 32:5 if we have found **g.** in thy sight, ... 2580
Jg 6:17 now I have found **g.** in thy sight, ... 2580
Ru 2:2 him in whose sight I shall find **g.**......... 2580
Ru 2:10 Why have I found **g.** in thine eyes, ... 2580
1Sa 1:18 handmaid find **g.** in thy sight. 2580
1Sa 20:3 knoweth that I have found **g.** in 2580
1Sa 27:5 I have now found **g.** in thine eyes, ... 2580
2Sa 14:22 knoweth that I have found **g.** in 2580
2Sa 16:4 that I may find **g.** in thy sight, my...... 2580
Ezr 9:8 a little space **g.** hath been shewed...... 8467
Es 2:17 she obtained **g.** and favour in his........ 2580
Ps 45:2 men; **g.** is poured into thy lips:.......... 2580
Ps 84:11 the Lord will give **g.** and glory:.......... 2580
Pr 1:9 an ornament of **g.** unto thy head, ... 2580
Pr 3:22 unto thy soul, and **g.** to thy neck. 2580
Pr 3:34 but he giveth **g.** unto the lowly. 2580
Pr 4:9 to thine head an ornament of **g.**: 2580
Pr 22:11 for the **g.** of his lips the king shall...... 2580
Jer 31:2 found **g.** in the wilderness;................ 2580
Zec 4:7 shoutings, crying, **G.**, **g.** unto it......... 2580
Zec 12:10 spirit of **g.** and of supplications:.......... 2580
Lu 2:40 and the **g.** of God was upon him. *5485*
Joh 1:14 of the Father,) full of **g.** and truth. *5485*
Joh 1:16 have all we received, and **g.** for **g.**..... *5485*
Joh 1:17 **g.** and truth came by Jesus Christ. *5485*
Ac 4:33 and great **g.** was upon them all. *5485*
Ac 11:23 had seen the **g.** of God, was glad,...... *5485*
Ac 13:43 them to continue in the **g.** of God. *5485*
Ac 14:3 testimony unto the word of his **g.**,....... *5485*
Ac 14:26 recommended to the **g.** of God for *5485*
Ac 15:11 through the **g.** of the Lord Jesus......... *5485*
Ac 15:40 by the brethren unto the **g.** of God..... *5485*
Ac 18:27 which had believed through **g.**: *5485*
Ac 20:24 testify the gospel of the **g.** of God...... *5485*
Ac 20:32 to God, and to the word of his **g.**,...... *5485*
Ro 1:5 By whom we have received **g.** and....... *5485*
Ro 1:7 **G.** to you and peace from God our..... *5485*
Ro 3:24 Being justified freely by his **g.**........... *5485*
Ro 4:4 not reckoned of **g.**, but of debt.......... *5485*
Ro 4:16 of faith, that it might be by **g.**; *5485*
Ro 5:2 faith into this **g.** wherein we stand,...... *5485*
Ro 5:15 the **g.** of God, and the gift by **g.**,....... *5485*
Ro 5:17 they which receive abundance of **g.**..... *5485*
Ro 5:20 **g.** did much more abound: *5485*
Ro 5:21 even so might **g.** reign through............ *5485*
Ro 6:1 continue in sin, that **g.** may abound? ... *5485*
Ro 6:14 are not under the law, but under **g.**.... *5485*
Ro 6:15 not under the law, but under **g.**?........ *5485*
Ro 11:5 according to the election of **g.**. *5485*
Ro 11:6 if by **g.**, then is it no more of works:.. *5485*

Ro 11:6 otherwise **g.** is no more **g.** *5485*
Ro 11:6 of works, then it is no more **g.**: *5485*
Ro 12:3 through the **g.** given unto me, to *5485*
Ro 12:6 according to the **g.** that is given to *5485*
Ro 15:15 because of the **g.** that is given to *5485*
Ro 16:20 The **g.** of our Lord Jesus Christ be *5485*
Ro 16:24 The **g.** of our Lord Jesus Christ *5485*
1Co 1:3 **G.** be unto you, and peace, from *5485*
1Co 1:4 for the **g.** of God which is given you *5485*
1Co 3:10 According to the **g.** of God which *5485*
1Co 10:30 For if I by **g.** be a partaker, why am *5485*
1Co 15:10 by the **g.** of God I am what I am: *5485*
1Co 15:10 and his **g.** which was bestowed upon *5485*
1Co 15:10 the **g.** of God which was with me *5485*
1Co 16:23 The **g.** of our Lord Jesus Christ be *5485*
2Co 1:2 **G.** be to you and peace from God *5485*
2Co 1:12 by the **g.** of God, we have had our *5485*
2Co 4:15 the abundant **g.** might through the *5485*
2Co 6:1 ye receive not the **g.** of God in vain. *5485*
2Co 8:1 you to wit of the **g.** of God bestowed *5485*
2Co 8:6 also finish in you the same **g.** also. *5485*
2Co 8:7 see that ye abound in this **g.** also. *5485*
2Co 8:9 ye know the **g.** of our Lord Jesus *5485*
2Co 8:19 to travel with us with this **g.**, which *5485*
2Co 9:8 God is able to make all **g.** abound *5485*
2Co 9:14 for the exceeding **g.** of God in you. *5485*
2Co 12:9 **My g. is sufficient for thee: for my** *5485*
2Co 13:14 The **g.** of the Lord Jesus Christ, *5485*
Ga 1:3 **G.** be to you and peace from God *5485*
Ga 1:6 that called you into the **g.** of Christ *5485*
Ga 1:15 womb, and called me by his **g.**, *5485*
Ga 2:9 perceived the **g.** that was given unto *5485*
Ga 2:21 I do not frustrate the **g.** of God: *5485*
Ga 5:4 by the law; ye are fallen from **g.** *5485*
Ga 6:18 the **g.** of our Lord Jesus Christ be *5485*
Ep 1:2 **G.** be to you, and peace, from God *5485*
Ep 1:6 To the praise of the glory of his **g.**, *5485*
Ep 1:7 according to the riches of his **g.**; *5485*
Ep 2:5 with Christ, (by **g.** ye are saved;) *5485*
Ep 2:7 the exceeding riches of his **g.** *5485*
Ep 2:8 by **g.** are ye saved through faith; *5485*
Ep 3:2 the dispensation of the **g.** of God *5485*
Ep 3:7 according to the gift of the **g.** of God *5485*
Ep 3:8 is this **g.** given, that I should preach *5485*
Ep 4:7 unto every one of us is given **g.** *5485*
Ep 4:29 it may minister **g.** unto the hearers *5485*
Ep 6:24 **G.** be with all them that love our *5485*
Php 1:2 **G.** be unto you, and peace, from *5485*
Php 1:7 ye all are partakers of my **g.** *5485*
Php 4:23 The **g.** of our Lord Jesus Christ be *5485*
Col 1:2 **G.** be unto you, and peace, from *5485*
Col 1:6 and knew the **g.** of God in truth: *5485*
Col 3:16 singing with **g.** in your hearts to *5485*
Col 4:6 your speech be always with **g.**, *5485*
Col 4:18 my bonds. **G.** be with you. Amen. *5485*
1Th 1:1 **G.** be unto you, and peace, from *5485*
1Th 5:28 The **g.** of our Lord Jesus Christ be *5485*
2Th 1:2 **G.** unto you, and peace, from God *5485*
2Th 1:12 according to the **g.** of our God and *5485*
2Th 2:16 and good hope through **g.**, *5485*
2Th 3:18 The **g.** of our Lord Jesus Christ be *5485*
1Ti 1:2 **G.**, mercy, and peace, from God *5485*
1Ti 1:14 the **g.** of our Lord was exceeding *5485*
1Ti 6:21 the faith. **G.** be with thee. Amen. *5485*
2Ti 1:2 , mercy, and peace, from God the *5485*
2Ti 1:9 to his own purpose and **g.**, *5485*
2Ti 2:1 be strong in the **g.** that is in Christ *5485*
2Ti 4:22 thy spirit. **G.** be with you. Amen. *5485*
Tit 1:4 **G.**, mercy, and peace, from God the *5485*
Tit 2:11 For the **g.** of God that bringeth *5485*
Tit 3:7 That being justified by his **g.**, we *5485*
Tit 3:15 faith. **G.** be with you all. Amen. *5485*
Phm 3 **G.** to you, and peace, from God our *5485*
Phm 25 The **g.** of our Lord Jesus Christ be *5485*
Heb 2:9 he by the **g.** of God should taste *5485*
Heb 4:16 come boldly unto the throne of **g.**, *5485*
Heb 4:16 and find **g.** to help in time of need. *5485*
Heb 10:29 done despite unto the Spirit of **g.**? *5485*
Heb 12:15 lest any man fail of the **g.** of God; *5485*
Heb 12:28 let us have **g.**, whereby we may *5485*
Heb 13:9 the heart be established with **g.**; *5485*
Heb 13:25 **G.** be with you all. Amen. *5485*
Jas 1:11 **g.** of the fashion of it perisheth: *2148*
Jas 4:6 But he giveth more **g.** Wherefore *5485*
Jas 4:6 but giveth **g.** unto the humble *5485*
1Pe 1:2 **G.** unto you, and peace, be *5485*
1Pe 1:10 the **g.** that should come unto you: *5485*
1Pe 1:13 for the **g.** that is to be brought *5485*
1Pe 3:7 heirs together of the **g.** of life; *5485*
1Pe 4:10 stewards of the manifold **g.** of God. *5485*
1Pe 5:5 proud, and giveth **g.** to the humble. *5485*
1Pe 5:10 But the God of all **g.**, who hath *5485*
1Pe 5:12 true **g.** of God wherein ye stand. *5485*
2Pe 1:2 **G.** and peace be multiplied unto *5485*
2Pe 3:18 grow in **g.**, and in the knowledge *5485*
2Jo 3 **G.** be with you, mercy, and peace, *5485*
Jude 4 turning the **g.** of our God into *5485*
Re 1:4 **G.** be unto you, and peace, from *5485*
Re 22:21 The **g.** of our Lord Jesus Christ be *5485*

GRACIOUS
Ge 43:29 God be **g.** unto thee, my son. 2603
Ex 22:27 that I will hear; for I am **g.** 2587
Ex 33:19 **g.** to whom I will be **g.**, and will 2603
Ex 34:6 The Lord God, merciful and **G.**, 2587
Nu 6:25 upon thee, and be **g.** unto thee: 2603
2Sa 12:22 God will be **g.** to me, that the child 2603
2Ki 13:23 And the Lord was **g.** unto them, 2603
2Ch 30:9 Lord your God is **g.** and merciful, 2587
Ne 9:17 ready to pardon, **g.** and merciful, 2587
Ne 9:31 thou art a **g.** and merciful God. 2587
Job 33:24 Then he is **g.** unto him, and saith, 2603
Ps 77:9 Hath God forgotten to be **g.**? 2589
Ps 86:15 a God full of compassion, and **g.**, 2587
Ps 103:8 the Lord is merciful and **g.**, slow to 2587
Ps 111:4 Lord is **g.** and full of compassion. 2587
Ps 112:4 he is **g.**, and full of compassion, 2587
Ps 116:5 **G.** is the Lord, and righteous; yea, 2587
Ps 145:8 Lord is **g.**, and full of compassion; 2587
Pr 11:16 A **g.** woman retaineth honour: 2580
Ec 10:12 of a wise man's mouth are **g.**: 2580
Isa 30:18 that he may be **g.** unto you, and 2603
Isa 30:19 he will be very **g.** unto thee at the 2603
Isa 33:2 O Lord, be **g.** unto us; we have 2603
Jer 22:23 **g.** shall thou be when pangs come 2603
Joe 2:13 is **g.** and merciful, slow to anger, 2587
Am 5:15 the Lord God of hosts will be **g.** 2587
Jon 4:2 I knew that thou art a **g.** God, 2587
Mal 1:9 God that he will be **g.** unto us: 2603
Lu 4:22 wondered at the **g.** words which *5485*
1Pe 2:3 ye have tasted that the Lord is **g.** *5543*

GRACIOUSLY
Ge 33:5 God hath **g.** given thy servant, 2603
Ge 33:11 God hath dealt **g.** with me, and 2603
Ps 119:29 lying: and grant me thy law **g.** 2603
Ho 14:2 receive us **g.**: so will we render 2896

GRAFF
Ro 11:23 God is able to **g.** them in again. *1461*

GRAFFED See also UNGRAFFED.
Ro 11:17 wert **g.** in among them, and with *1461*
Ro 11:19 broken off, that I might be **g.** in. *1461*
Ro 11:23 not still in unbelief, shall be **g.** in: *1461*
Ro 11:24 and wert **g.** contrary to nature *1461*
Ro 11:24 be **g.** into their own olive tree? *1461*

GRAFT See GRAFF.

GRAIN
Am 9:9 yet shall not the least **g.** fall 6872
Mt 13:31 **like to a g. of mustard seed,** *2848*
Mt 17:20 **faith as a g. of mustard seed, ye** *2848*
Mk 4:31 **It is like a g. of mustard seed,** *2848*
Lu 13:19 **It is like a g. of mustard seed,** *2848*
Lu 17:6 **faith as a g. of mustard seed, ye** *2848*
1Co 15:37 body that shall be, but bare **g.**, *2848*
1Co 15:37 of wheat, or of some other **g.**:

GRANDMOTHER
2Ti 1:5 which dwelt first in thy **g.** Lois, 3125

GRANT See also GRANTED.
Le 25:24 shall **g.** a redemption for the land. 5414
Ru 1:9 Lord **g.** you that ye may find rest, 5414
1Sa 1:17 God of Israel **g.** thee thy petition 5414
1Ch 21:22 **G.** me the place of this 5414
1Ch 21:22 shalt **g.** it me for the full price: 5414
2Ch 12:7 I will **g.** them some deliverance; 5414
Ezr 3:7 according to the **g.** that they had 7558
Ne 1:11 and **g.** him mercy in the sight of 5414
Es 5:8 it please the king to **g.** my petition, 5414
Job 6:8 and that God would **g.** me the thing 5414
Ps 20:4 **G.** thee according to thine own 5414
Ps 85:7 O Lord, and **g.** us thy salvation. 5414
Ps 119:29 and **g.** me thy law graciously. 5414
Ps 140:8 **G.** not, O Lord, the desires of the 5414
Mt 20:21 **G.** that these my two sons may *2036*
Mk 10:37 **G.** unto us that we may sit, one *1325*
Lu 1:74 That he would **g.** unto us, that we *1325*
Ac 4:29 **g.** unto thy servants, that with all *1325*
Ro 15:5 **g.** you to be likeminded one toward *1325*
Eph 3:16 That he would **g.** you, according to *1325*
2Ti 1:18 Lord **g.** unto him that he may find *1325*
Re 3:21 **that overcometh will I g. to sit** *1325*

GRANTED
1Ch 4:10 And God **g.** him that which he 935
2Ch 1:12 and knowledge is **g.** unto thee; 5414
Ezr 7:6 and the king **g.** him all his request, 5414
Ne 2:8 And the king **g.** me, according to 5414
Es 5:6 petition? and it shall be **g.** thee: 5414
Es 7:2 Esther? and it shall be **g.** thee: 5414
Es 8:11 the king **g.** the Jews which were in 5414
Es 9:12 petition? and it shall be **g.** thee: 5414
Es 9:13 let it be **g.** to the Jews which are in 5414
Job 10:12 Thou hast **g.** me life and favour, 6213
Pr 10:24 desire of the righteous shall be **g.** 5414
Ac 3:14 a murderer to be **g.** unto you; *5483*
Ac 11:18 Gentiles **g.** repentance unto life. *1325*
Ac 14:3 **g.** signs and wonders to be done *1325*
Re 19:8 to her was **g.** that she should *1325*

GRAPE See also GRAPEGATHERER; GRAPEGLEANINGS; GRAPES.
Le 19:10 neither shalt thou gather every **g.** 6528
De 32:14 drink the pure blood of the **g.** 6025
Job 15:33 He shall shake off his unripe **g.** 1154
Ca 2:13 the vines with the tender **g.** give 5563
Ca 7:12 whether the tennder **g.** appear, 5563
Isa 18:5 and the sour **g.** is ripening in 1155
Jer 31:29 The fathers have eaten a sour **g.**, 1155
Jer 31:30 every man that eateth the sour **g.**, 1155

GRAPEGATHERER See also GRAPEGATHERERS.
Jer 6:9 turn back thine hand as a **g.** into 1219

GRAPEGATHERERS
Jer 49:9 If **g.** come to thee, would they not 1219
Ob 5 if the **g.** came to thee, would they 1219

GRAPEGLEANINGS
Mic 7:1 as the **g.** of the vintage: 5955

GRAPES
Ge 40:10 thereof brought forth ripe **g.**: 6025
Ge 40:11 and I took the **g.**, and pressed them 6025
Ge 49:11 and his clothes in the blood of **g.**: 6025
Le 25:5 neither gather the **g.** of thy vine 6025
Le 25:11 nor gather the **g.** in it of thy vine
Nu 6:3 shall he drink any liquor of **g.** 6025
Nu 6:3 nor eat moist **g.**, or dried. 6025
Nu 13:20 was the time of the firstripe **g.** 6025
Nu 13:23 a branch with one cluster of **g.**, 6025
Nu 13:24 because of the cluster of **g.**
De 23:24 thou mayest eat **g.** thy fill at thine 6025
De 24:21 When thou gatherest the **g.** of thy
De 28:30 shalt not gather the **g.** thereof.
De 28:39 nor gather the **g.**: for the worms
De 32:32 their **g.** are **g.** of gall, their clusters 6025
Jg 8:2 the gleaning of the **g.** of Ephraim
Jg 9:27 and trode the **g.**, and made merry,
Ne 13:15 also wine, **g.**, and figs, and all 6025
Ca 2:15 for our vines have tender **g.** 5563
Ca 7:7 and thy breasts to clusters of **g.**
Isa 5:2 that it should bring forth **g.**, and 6025
Isa 5:2 it brought forth wild **g.**, 891
Isa 5:4 looked that it should bring forth **g.**, 6025
Isa 5:4 brought it forth wild **g.**? 891
Isa 17:6 gleaning **g.** shall be left in it, as
Isa 24:13 the gleaning **g.** when the vintage
Jer 8:13 there shall be no **g.** on the vine, 6025
Jer 25:30 as they that tread the **g.**, against
Jer 49:9 they not leave some gleaning **g.**?
Eze 18:2 The fathers have eaten sour **g.**, 1154
Ho 9:10 Israel like **g.** in the wilderness; 6025
Am 9:13 the treader of **g.** him that soweth 6025
Ob 5 would they not leave some **g.**? 6025
Mt 7:16 **Do men gather g. of thorns, or** *4718*
Lu 6:44 **of a bramble bush gather they g.** *4718*
Re 14:18 the earth; for her **g.** are fully ripe. *4718*

GRASS See also GRASSHOPPER.
Ge 1:11 Let the earth bring forth **g.**, the 1877
Ge 1:12 earth brought forth **g.**, and herb 1877
Nu 22:4 ox licketh up the **g.** of the field. 3418
De 11:15 I will send **g.** in thy fields 6212
De 29:23 nor any **g.** groweth therein, like 6212

De 32:2 and as the showers upon the **g.** 6212
2Sa 23:4 **g.** springing out of the earth by 1877
1Ki 18:5 peradventure we may find **g.** to 2682
2Ki 19:26 they were as the **g.** of the field, 6212
2Ki 19:26 herb, as the **g.** on the house tops, 2682
Job 5:25 offspring as the **g.** of the earth. 6212
Job 6:5 the wild ass bray when he hath **g.**? 1877
Job 40:15 with thee; he eateth **g.** as an ox. 2682
Ps 37:2 shall soon be cut down like the **g.**, 2682
Ps 72:6 upon the mown **g.**: as showers that
Ps 72:16 of the city shall flourish like **g.** of 6212
Ps 90:5 in the morning they are like **g.** 2682
Ps 92:7 When the wicked spring as the **g.**, 6212
Ps 102:4 is smitten, and withered like **g.**; 6212
Ps 102:11 and I am withered like **g.** 6212
Ps 103:15 As for man, his days are as **g.**: 2682
Ps 104:14 the **g.** to grow for the cattle, 2682
Ps 106:20 similitude of an ox that eateth **g.** 6212
Ps 129:6 as the **g.** upon the housetops, 2682
Ps 147:8 **g.** to grow upon the mountains. 2682
Pr 19:12 his favour is as dew upon the **g.** 6212
Pr 27:25 the tender **g.** sheweth itself, and 1877
Isa 15:6 the **g.** faileth, there is no green 1877
Isa 35:7 shall be **g.** with reeds and rushes. 2682
Isa 37:27 they were as the **g.** of the field, 6212
Isa 37:27 as the **g.** on the housetops, and as 2682
Isa 40:6 What shall I cry? All flesh is **g.**, 2682
Isa 40:7 The **g.** withereth, the flower fadeth: 2682
Isa 40:7 upon it: surely the people is **g.** 2682
Isa 40:8 The **g.** withereth, the flower fadeth: 2682
Isa 44:4 shall spring up as among the **g.**, 2682
Isa 51:12 man which shall be made as **g.**; 2682
Jer 14:5 forsook it, because there was no **g.** 1758
Jer 14:6 did fail, because there was no **g.** 6212
Jer 50:11 as the heifer at **g.**, and bellow 1877
Da 4:15 in the tender **g.** of the field; and 1883
Da 4:15 the beasts in the **g.** of the earth: 6211
Da 4:23 brass, in the tender **g.** of the field; 1883
Da 4:25 and they shall make thee to eat **g.** 6211
Da 4:32 they shall make thee to eat **g.** as 6211
Da 4:33 did eat **g.** as oxen, and his body 6211
Da 5:21 they fed him with **g.** like oxen, 6211
Am 7:2 make an end of eating the **g.** of 6212
Mic 5:7 as the showers upon the **g.**, that 6212
Zec 10:1 of rain, to every one **g.** in the field. 6212
Mt 6:30 **God so clothe the g. of the field,** *5528*
Mt 14:19 to sit down on the **g.**, and took *5528*
Mk 6:39 by companies upon the green **g.** *5528*
Lu 12:28 **If then God so clothe the g.,** *5528*
Joh 6:10 there was much **g.** in the place. *5528*
Jas 1:10 as the flower of the **g.** he shall pass *5528*
Jas 1:11 it withereth the **g.**, and the flower *5528*
1Pe 1:24 For all flesh is as **g.**, and all the *5528*
1Pe 1:24 glory of man as the flower of **g.** *5528*
1Pe 1:24 The **g.** withereth, and the flower *5528*
Re 8:7 and all green **g.** was burnt up. *5528*
Re 9:4 should not hurt the **g.** of the earth, *5528*

GRASSHOPPER See also GRASSHOPPERS.
Le 11:22 kind, and the **g.** after his kind. 2284
Job 39:20 thou make him afraid as a **g.**? 697
Ec 12:5 the **g.** shall be a burden, and desire 2284

GRASSHOPPERS
Nu 13:33 we were in our own sight as **g.** 2284
Jg 6:5 they came as **g.** for multitude; 697
Jg 7:12 lay along in the valley like **g.** 697
Isa 40:22 the inhabitants thereof are as **g.**; 2284
Jer 46:23 because they are more than the **g.**, 697
Am 7:1 he formed **g.** in the beginning of 1462
Na 3:17 as the great **g.**, which camp in the 1462

GRATE
Ex 27:4 shalt make for it a **g.** of network 4345
Ex 35:16 with his brasen **g.**, his staves, 4345
Ex 38:4 he made for the altar a brasen **g.** 4345
Ex 38:5 the four ends of the **g.** of brass, 4345
Ex 38:30 and the brasen **g.** for it, and all 4345
Ex 39:39 brasen altar, and his **g.** of brass, 4345

GRAVE See also ENGRAVE; GRAVECLOTHES; GRAVED; GRAVEN; GRAVE'S; GRAVES; GRAVETH; GRAVING.
Ge 35:20 Jacob set a pillar upon her **g.** 6900
Ge 35:20 that is the pillar of Rachel's **g.** 6900
Ge 37:35 go down into the **g.** unto my son 7585
Ge 42:38 gray hairs with sorrow to the **g.** 7585
Ge 44:29 gray hairs with sorrow to the **g.** 7585
Ge 44:31 our father with sorrow to the **g.** 7585
Ge 50:5 Lo, I die: in my **g.** which I have 6913
Ex 28:9 and **g.** on them the names of 6605
Ex 28:36 and **g.** upon it, like the engravings 6605
Nu 19:16 a **g.**, shall be unclean seven days. 6913
Nu 19:18 or one slain, or one dead, or a **g.**: 6913
1Sa 2:6 he bringeth down to the **g.**, and 7585
2Sa 3:32 and wept at the **g.** of Abner; 6913
2Sa 19:37 be buried by the **g.** of my father 6913
1Ki 2:6 head go down to the **g.** in peace. 7585
1Ki 2:9 head bring thou down to the **g.** 7585
1Ki 13:30 he laid his carcase in his own **g.**: 6913
1Ki 14:13 of Jeroboam shall come to the **g.**, 6913
2Ki 22:20 thou shalt be gathered into thy **g.** 6913
2Ch 2:7 to **g.** with the cunning men that 6603
2Ch 2:14 also to **g.** any manner of graving, 6605
2Ch 34:28 be gathered to thy **g.** in peace, 6913
Job 3:22 are glad, when they can find the **g.**? 6913
Job 5:26 Thou shalt come to thy **g.** in a full 6913
Job 7:9 goeth down to the **g.** shall come 7585
Job 10:19 carried from the womb to the **g.** 6913
Job 14:13 wouldest hide me in the **g.**, that 7585
Job 17:13 **g.** is mine house: I have made 7585
Job 21:13 in a moment go down to the **g.** 7585
Job 21:32 he be brought to the **g.**, and shall 6913
Job 24:19 so doth the **g.** those which have 7585
Job 30:24 stretch out his hand to the **g.**, 1164
Job 33:22 soul draweth near unto the **g.**, 7845
Ps 6:5 in the **g.** who shall give thee 7585
Ps 30:3 brought up my soul from the **g.** 7585
Ps 31:17 let them be silent in the **g.** 7585
Ps 49:14 sheep they are laid in the **g.**; 7585
Ps 49:14 beauty shall consume in the **g.** 7585
Ps 49:15 my soul from the power of the **g.** 7585
Ps 88:3 my life draweth nigh unto the **g.** 7585
Ps 88:5 like the slain that lie in the **g.**, 6913
Ps 88:11 be declared in the **g.**? or thy 6913
Ps 89:48 his soul from the hand of the **g.**? 7585
Pr 1:12 swallow them up alive as the **g.**; 7585
Pr 30:16 The **g.**; and the barren womb; 7585
Ec 9:10 knowledge, nor wisdom, in the **g.**, 7585
Ca 8:6 death; jealousy is cruel as the **g.** 7585
Isa 14:11 pomp is brought down to the **g.**, 7585
Isa 14:19 thou art cast out of thy **g.** like an 6913
Isa 38:10 I shall go to the gates of the **g.**: 7585
Isa 38:18 the **g.** cannot praise thee, death 7585
Isa 53:9 he made his **g.** with the wicked, 6913
Jer 20:17 my mother might have been my **g.**, 6913
Eze 31:15 when he went down to the **g.** I 7585
Eze 32:23 company is round about her **g.** 6900
Eze 32:24 her multitude round about her **g.**, 6900
Ho 13:14 them from the power of the **g.**; 7585
Ho 13:14 O **g.**, I will be thy destruction: 7585
Na 1:14 make thy **g.**; for thou art vile. 6913
Joh 11:17 he had lain in the **g.** four days *3419*
Joh 11:31 She goeth into the **g.** to weep *3419*
Joh 11:38 in himself cometh to the **g.** *3419*
Joh 12:17 he called Lazarus out of his **g.**, *3419*
1Co 15:55 sting? O **g.**, where is thy victory? *86*
1Ti 3:8 Likewise must the deacons be **g.**, *4586*
1Ti 3:11 Even so must their wives be **g.**, *4586*
Tit 2:2 aged men be sober, **g.**, temperate, *4586*

GRAVECLOTHES
Joh 11:44 bound hand and foot with **g.** *2750*

GRAVED See also GRAVEN.
1Ki 7:36 he **g.** cherubims, lions, and palm 6605
2Ch 3:7 and **g.** cherubims on the walls. 6605

GRAVEL
Pr 20:17 his mouth shall be filled with **g.** 2687
Isa 48:19 offspring of thy bowels like the **g.** 4579
La 3:16 broken my teeth with **g.** stones, 2687

GRAVEN See also GRAVED; ENGRAVEN.
Ex 20:4 not make unto thee any **g.** image, 6459
Ex 32:16 of God, **g.** upon the tables. 2801
Ex 39:6 **g.**, as signets are **g.**, with the 6605
Le 26:1 make you no idols nor **g.** image, 6459
De 4:16 and make you a **g.** image, 6459
De 4:23 you, and make you a **g.** image, or 6459
De 4:25 yourselves, and make a **g.** image, 6459
De 5:8 shalt not make thee any **g.** image, 6459
De 7:5 burn their **g.** images with fire. 6456
De 7:25 The **g.** images of their gods shall 6456
De 12:3 ye shall hew down the **g.** images 6456
De 27:15 maketh any **g.** or molten image, 6459
Jg 17:3 to make a **g.** image and a molten 6459
Jg 17:4 who made thereof a **g.** image and 6459
Jg 18:14 and teraphim, and a **g.** image, and 6459
Jg 18:17 took the **g.** image, and the ephod, 6459
Jg 18:20 the teraphim, and the **g.** image, 6459
Jg 18:30 children of Dan set up the **g.** image: 6459
Jg 18:31 they set them up Micah's **g.** image, 6459
2Ki 17:41 and served their **g.** images, both 6456
2Ki 21:7 he set a **g.** image of the grove 6459
2Ch 33:19 up groves and **g.** images, before 6456
2Ch 34:7 and had beaten the **g.** images into 6456
Job 19:24 they were **g.** with an iron pen 2672
Ps 78:58 to jealousy with their **g.** images. 6456
Ps 97:7 they that serve **g.** images, that 6459
Isa 10:10 and whose **g.** images did excel 6456
Isa 21:9 all the **g.** images of her gods 6456
Isa 30:22 the covering of thy **g.** images of 6456
Isa 40:19 workman melteth a **g.** image, 6459
Isa 40:20 to prepare a **g.** image, that shall 6459
Isa 42:8 neither my praise to **g.** images. 6456
Isa 42:17 that trust in **g.** images, that say 6459
Isa 44:9 They that make a **g.** image are all 6459
Isa 44:10 or molten a **g.** image that is 6459
Isa 44:15 maketh it a **g.** image, and falleth 6459
Isa 44:17 maketh a god, even his **g.** image: 6459
Isa 45:20 the wood of their **g.** image, and 6459
Isa 48:5 done them, and my **g.** image, and 6459
Isa 49:16 I have **g.** thee upon the palms 2710
Jer 8:19 me to anger with their **g.** images, 6456
Jer 10:14 is confounded by the **g.** image: 6459
Jer 17:1 **g.** upon the table of their heart, 2790
Jer 50:38 the land of **g.** images, and they 6456
Jer 51:17 is confounded by the **g.** image: 6459
Jer 51:47 the **g.** images of Babylon: and her 6456
Jer 51:52 do judgment upon her **g.** images: 6456
Ho 11:2 and burned incense to **g.** images. 6456
Mic 1:7 all the **g.** images thereof shall be 6456
Mic 5:13 Thy **g.** images also will I cut off, 6456
Na 1:14 will I cut off the **g.** image and the 6459
Hab 2:18 What profiteth the **g.** image that 6459
Hab 2:18 the maker thereof hath **g.** it; 6458
Ac 17:29 stone, **g.** by art and man's device. *5480*

GRAVE'S
Ps 141:7 are scattered at the **g.** mouth, 7585

GRAVES
Ex 14:11 Because there were no **g.** in Egypt, 6913
2Ki 23:6 the powder thereof upon the **g.** of 6913
2Ch 34:4 strowed it upon the **g.** of them 6913
Job 17:1 extinct, the **g.** are ready for me. 6913
Isa 65:4 Which remain among the **g.**, and 6913
Jer 8:1 of Jerusalem, out of their **g.** 6913
Jer 26:23 cast his dead body into the **g.** of 6913
Eze 32:22 company: his **g.** are about him: 6913
Eze 32:23 Whose **g.** are set in the sides of the 6913
Eze 32:25, 26 her **g.** are round about him: 6913
Eze 37:12 I will open your **g.**, and cause you 6913
Eze 37:12 you to come up out of your **g.**, 6913
Eze 37:13 when I have opened your **g.**, O my 6913
Eze 37:13 and brought you up out of your **g.**, 6913
Eze 39:11 give unto Gog a place there of **g.** 6913
Mt 27:52 the **g.** were opened; and many *3419*
Mt 27:53 And came out of the **g.** after his *3419*
Lu 11:44 **for ye are as g. which appear not,** *3419*
Joh 5:28 **that are in the g. shall hear his** *3419*
Re 11:9 their dead bodies to be put in **g.** *3418*

GRAVETH
Isa 22:16 and that **g.** an habitation for 2710

GRAVING See also GRAVINGS.
Ex 32:4 fashioned it with a **g.** tool, 2747
2Ch 2:14 also to grave any manner of **g.**, 6603
Zec 3:9 I will engrave the **g.** thereof, 6603

GRAVINGS
1Ki 7:31 also upon the mouth of it were **g.** 4734

GRAVING-TOOL See GRAVING and TOOL.

GRAVITY
1Ti 3:4 children in subjection with all **g.**; *4587*
Tit 2:7 uncorruptness, **g.**, sincerity, *4587*

GRAY See also GRAYHEADED; GREY.
Ge 42:38 down my **g.** hairs with sorrow 7872
Ge 44:29 bring down my **g.** hairs with sorrow 7872
Ge 44:31 **g.** hairs of thy servant our father 7872
De 32:25 also with the man of **g.** hairs. 7872
Pr 20:29 beauty of old men is the **g.** head 7872
Ho 7:9 **g.** hairs are here and there upon 7872

GRAYHEADED See also GREYHEADED.
1Sa 12:2 I am old and **g.**; and, behold, my........ 7867
Job 15:10 the **g.** and very aged men, much......... 7867
Ps 71:18 Now also when I am old and **g.**,.......... 7872
Ps 71:18 Now also when I am old and **g.**, O...... 7872

GREASE
Ps 119:70 Their heart is as fat as **g.**;.................2459

GREAT See also GREATER; GREATEST.
Ge 1:16 And God made two **g.** lights; the........ 1419
Ge 1:21 God created **g.** whales, and every....... 1419
Ge 6:5 that the wickedness of man was **g.**....... 7227
Ge 7:11 fountains of the **g.** deep broken up,..... 7227
Ge 10:12 and Calah: the same is a **g.** city.......... 1419
Ge 12:2 I will make of thee a **g.** nation, and..... 1419
Ge 12:2 bless thee, and make thy name **g.**;....... 1431
Ge 12:17 with **g.** plagues because of Sarai......... 1419
Ge 13:6 for their substance was **g.**, so that...... 7227
Ge 15:1 and thy exceeding **g.** reward............. 7235
Ge 15:12 horrow of **g.** darkness fell upon.......... 1419
Ge 15:14 they come out with **g.** substance.......... 1419
Ge 15:18 the **g.** river, the river Euphrates:......... 1419
Ge 17:20 and I will make him a **g.** nation.......... 1419
Ge 18:18 become a **g.** and mighty nation,........... 1419
Ge 18:20 cry of Sodom and Gomorrah is **g.**,........7227
Ge 19:11 with blindness, both small and **g.**:........1419
Ge 19:13 the cry of them is waxen **g.** before......1431
Ge 20:9 and on my kingdom a **g.** sin?.............1419
Ge 21:8 Abraham made a **g.** feast the same...... 1419
Ge 21:18 for I will make him a **g.** nation............1419
Ge 24:35 and he is become **g.**: and he hath........1431
Ge 26:13 And the man waxed **g.**, and............... 1431
Ge 26:13 and grew until he became very **g.**:........ 1431
Ge 26:14 of herds, and **g.** store of servants:...... 7227
Ge 27:34 a **g.** and exceeding bitter cry, and....... 1419
Ge 29:2 **g.** stone was upon the well's mouth..... 1419
Ge 30:8 **g.** wrestlings have I wrestled...............430
Ge 39:9 then can I do this **g.** wickedness,........ 1419
Ge 41:29 years of **g.** plenty throughout............. 1419
Ge 45:7 save your lives by a **g.** deliverance...... 1419
Ge 46:3 will there make of thee a **g.** nation:..... 1419
Ge 48:19 and he also shall be **g.**: but truly.........1431
Ge 50:9 and it was a very **g.** company.............3515
Ge 50:10 a **g.** and very sore lamentation:........... 1419
Ex 3:3 and see this **g.** sight, why the bush..... 1419
Ex 6:6 out arm, and with **g.** judgments:......... 1419
Ex 7:4 the land of Egypt by **g.** judgments.......1419
Ex 11:3 the man Moses was very **g.** in the...... 1419
Ex 11:6 there shall be a **g.** cry throughout....... 1419
Ex 11:8 out from Pharaoh in a **g.** anger.......... 2750
Ex 12:30 and there was a **g.** cry in Egypt;.........1419
Ex 14:31 Israel saw that **g.** work which the....... 1419
Ex 18:22 every **g.** matter they shall bring.........1419
Ex 29:20 and upon the **g.** toe of their right foot,.......
Ex 32:10 I will make of thee a **g.** nation............1419
Ex 32:11 of Egypt with **g.** power, and with........1419
Ex 32:21 brought so **g.** a sin upon them?.......... 1419
Ex 32:30 Ye have sinned a **g.** sin: and now.......1419
Ex 32:31 this people have sinned a **g.** sin.......... 1419
Le 8:23 upon the **g.** toe of his right foot..............
Le 8:24 upon the **g.** toes of their right feet:...........
Le 11:17 and the cormorant, and the **g.** owl,......3244
Le 14:14 upon the **g.** toe of his right foot:..............
Le 14:17 his right hand, and upon the **g.** toe...........
Le 14:25 upon the **g.** toe of his right foot:..............
Le 14:28 upon the **g.** toe of his right foot,...............
Nu 11:33 the people with a very **g.** plague......... 7227
Nu 13:28 walled, and very **g.**: and moreover...... 1419
Nu 13:32 we saw in it are men of a **g.** stature..........
Nu 14:17 let the power of my Lord be **g.**,.......... 1431
Nu 14:18 of **g.** mercy, forgiving iniquity.............7227
Nu 22:17 promote thee unto very **g.** honour,...........
Nu 23:24 people shall rise up as a **g.** lion,..........3833
Nu 24:9 down as a lion, and as a **g.** lion;...........3833
Nu 24:11 to promote thee unto **g.** honour;...............
Nu 32:1 of Gad had a very **g.** multitude........... 6099
Nu 34:6 have the **g.** sea for a border:............ 1419
Nu 34:7 from the **g.** sea ye shall point............ 1419
De 1:7 the **g.** river, the river Euphrates.........1419
De 1:17 hear the small as well as the **g.**;.......... 1419
De 1:19 all that **g.** and terrible wilderness,........ 1419
De 1:28 the cities are **g.** and walled up to......... 1419
De 2:7 walking through this **g.** wilderness:....... 1419
De 2:10 a people **g.**, and many, and tall,.......... 1419
De 2:21 A people **g.**, and many, and tall,.......... 1419
De 3:5 beside unwalled towns a **g.** many........ 3966
De 4:6 Surely this **g.** nation is a wise and....... 1419
De 4:7 For what nation is there so **g.**, who..... 1419
De 4:8 And what nation is there so **g.**, that..... 1419
De 4:32 any such thing as this **g.** thing is......... 1419
De 4:34 and by **g.** terrors, accordng to all......... 1419
De 4:36 earth he shewed thee his **g.** fire;.......... 1419
De 5:22 with a **g.** voice: and he added no.........1419
De 5:25 for this **g.** fire will consume us: if........1419
De 6:10 to give thee **g.** and goodly cities,......... 1419
De 6:22 wonders, **g.** and sore, upon Egypt,...... 1419
De 7:19 **g.** temptations which thine eyes.......... 1419
De 8:15 that **g.** and terrible wilderness,........... 1419
De 9:1 cities **g.** and fenced up to heaven,........ 1419
De 9:2 A people **g.** and tall, the children........ 1419
De 10:17 a **g.** God, a mighty, and a terrible,...... 1419
De 10:21 thee these **g.** and terrible things,......... 1419
De 11:7 eyes have seen all the **g.** acts of the.... 1419
De 14:16 and the **g.** owl, and the swan,........... 3244
De 18:16 let me see this **g.** fire any more..........1419
De 25:13 bag divers weights, a **g.** and a small.... 1419
De 25:14 divers measures, a **g.** and a small....... 1419
De 26:5 nation, **g.**, mighty, and populous:........ 1419
De 26:8 with **g.** terribleness, and with signs,..... 1419
De 27:2 thou shalt set thee up **g.** stones,.........1419
De 28:59 even **g.** plagues, and of long............. 1419
De 29:3 The **g.** temptations which thine...........1419
De 29:3 the signs, and those **g.** miracles:......... 1419
De 29:24 meaneth the heat of this **g.** anger?...... 1419
De 29:28 and in **g.** indignation, and cast............ 1419
De 34:12 in all the **g.** terror which Moses...........1419
Jos 1:4 even unto the **g.** river, the river......... 1419
Jos 1:4 unto the **g.** sea toward the going........ 1419
Jos 6:5 people shall shout with a **g.** shout;...... 1419
Jos 6:20 people shouted with a **g.** shout,.......... 1419
Jos 7:9 what wilt thou do unto thy **g.** name?.... 1419
Jos 7:26 raised over him a **g.** heap of stones..... 1419
Jos 8:29 raise thereon a **g.** heap of stones,....... 1419
Jos 9:1 the **g.** sea over agains Lebanon.......... 1419
Jos 10:2 Gibeon was a **g.** city, as one of.......... 1419
Jos 10:10 slew them with a **g.** slaughter at......... 1419
Jos 10:11 the Lord cast down **g.** stones from...... 1419
Jos 10:18 Roll **g.** stones upon the mouth of......... 1419
Jos 10:20 them with a very **g.** slaughter,........... 1419
Jos 10:27 laid **g.** stones in the cave's mouth,...... 1419
Jos 11:8 chased them unto **g.** Zidon, and......... 7227
Jos 14:12 that the cities were **g.** and fenced:...... 1419
Jos 14:15 a **g.** man among the Anakims............. 1419
Jos 15:12 border was to the **g.** sea, and the....... 1419
Jos 15:47 and the **g.** sea, and the border........... 1419
Jos 17:14 I am a **g.** people, forasmuch as...........7227
Jos 17:15 If thou be a **g.** people, then get thee... 7227
Jos 17:17 saying, Thou art a **g.** people,............. 7227
Jos 17:17 and hast **g.** power: thou shalt not........1419
Jos 19:28 and Kanah, even unto **g.** Zidon;........... 7227
Jos 22:10 by Jordan, a **g.** altar to see to............ 1419
Jos 23:4 even unto the **g.** sea westward.............1419
Jos 23:9 before you **g.** nations and strong:.........1419
Jos 24:17 which did those **g.** signs in our........... 1419
Jos 24:26 and took a **g.** stone, and set it up....... 1419
Jg 1:6 cut off his thumbs and his **g.** toes.............
Jg 1:7 their thumbs and their **g.** toes cut............
Jg 2:7 who had seen all the **g.** works of......... 1419
Jg 5:15 there were **g.** thoughts of heart.......... 1419
Jg 5:16 there were **g.** searchings of heart........1419
Jg 11:33 vineyards, with a very **g.** slaughter......1419
Jg 12:2 I and my people were at **g.** strife.........3966
Jg 15:8 hip and thigh with a **g.** slaughter:........ 1419
Jg 15:18 hast given this **g.** deliverance into....... 1419
Jg 16:5 see wherein his **g.** strength lieth,......... 1419
Jg 16:6 thee, wherein thy **g.** strength lieth,...... 1419
Jg 16:15 me wherein thy **g.** strength lieth.......... 1419
Jg 16:23 to offer a **g.** sacrifice unto Dagon......... 1419
Jg 20:38 that they should make a **g.** flame........ 7235
Jg 21:5 For they had made a **g.** oath..............1419
1Sa 2:17 men was very **g.** before the Lord:.......1419
1Sa 4:5 all Israel shouted with a **g.** shout,........ 1419
1Sa 4:6 the noise of this **g.** shout in the.......... 1419
1Sa 4:10 and there was a very **g.** slaugter;........1419
1Sa 4:17 there hath been also a **g.** slaughter...... 1419
1Sa 5:9 city with a very **g.** destruction:............1419
1Sa 5:9 of the city, both small and **g.**,............. 1419
1Sa 6:9 then he hath done us this **g.** evil:......... 1419
1Sa 6:14 where there was a **g.** stone: and..........1419
1Sa 6:15 and put them on the **g.** stone: and.......1419
1Sa 6:18 even unto the **g.** stone of Abel,........... 1419
1Sa 6:19 of the people with a **g.** slaughter......... 1419
1Sa 7:10 Lord thundered with a **g.** thunder........1419
1Sa 12:16 stand and see this **g.** thing, which....... 1419
1Sa 12:17 see that your wickedness is **g.**,........... 7227
1Sa 12:22 his people for his **g.** name's sake:....... 1419
1Sa 12:24 how **g.** things he hath done for you..... 1431
1Sa 14:15 so it was a very **g.** trembling..............430
1Sa 14:20 there was a very **g.** discomfiture......... 1419
1Sa 14:33 roll a **g.** stone unto me this day.......... 1419
1Sa 14:45 who hath wrought this **g.** salvation...... 1419
1Sa 15:22 Hath the Lord as **g.** delight in burnt..........
1Sa 17:25 king will enrich him with **g.** riches,...... 1419
1Sa 19:5 Lord wrought a **g.** salvation for all.......1419
1Sa 19:8 and slew them with a **g.** slaughter;...... 1419
1Sa 19:22 came to a **g.** well that is in Sechu:...... 1419
1Sa 20:2 will do nothing either **g.** or small,........ 1419
1Sa 23:5 and smote them with a **g.** slaughter..... 1419
1Sa 25:2 and the man was very **g.**, and he had...1419
1Sa 26:13 a **g.** space being between them:..........7227
1Sa 26:25 thou shalt both do **g.** things, and ....
1Sa 30:2 slew not any, either **g.** or small.......... 1419
1Sa 30:16 because of all the **g.** spoil that they..... 1419
1Sa 30:19 to them, neither small nor **g.**,............ 1419
2Sa 3:22 brought in a **g.** spoil with them:.......... 7227
2Sa 3:38 and a **g.** man fallen this day in............ 1419
2Sa 5:10 David went on, and grew **g.**, and......... 1419
2Sa 7:9 and have made thee a **g.** name, like.....1419
2Sa 7:9 like unto the name of the **g.** men........ 1419
2Sa 7:19 house for a **g.** while to come..............7350
2Sa 7:21 hast done all these **g.** things, to.......... 1420
2Sa 7:22 Wherefore thou art **g.**, O Lord............ 1431
2Sa 7:23 to do for you **g.** things and terrible,...... 1420
2Sa 12:14 thou hast given **g.** occasion to the....... 5006
2Sa 12:30 spoil of the city in **g.** abundance,..........3966
2Sa 18:7 and there was there a **g.** slaughter...... 1419
2Sa 18:9 under the thick boughs of a **g.** oak,..... 1419
2Sa 18:17 cast him into a **g.** pit in the wood,.......1419
2Sa 18:17 and laid a very **g.** heap of stones.........1419
2Sa 18:29 I saw a **g.** tumult, but I knew not......... 1419
2Sa 19:32 for he was a very **g.** man................... 1419
2Sa 20:8 they were at the **g.** stone which is...... 1419
2Sa 21:20 Gath, where was a man of **g.** stature,........
2Sa 22:36 thy gentleness hath made me **g.**.......... 7235
2Sa 23:10 wrought a **g.** victory that day;............ 1419
2Sa 23:12 and the Lord wrought a **g.** victory....... 1419
2Sa 24:14 I am in a **g.** strait: let us all..............3966
2Sa 24:14 for his mercies are **g.**: and let me....... 7227
1Ki 1:40 and rejoiced with **g.** joy, so that..........1419
1Ki 3:4 for that was the **g.** high place:............ 1419
1Ki 3:6 servant David my father **g.** mercy,....... 1419
1Ki 3:6 hast kept for him this **g.** kindness,....... 1419
1Ki 3:8 a **g.** people, that cannot be................ 7227
1Ki 3:9 to judge this thy so **g.** a people?......... 3515
1Ki 4:13 threescore **g.** cities with walls and....... 1419
1Ki 5:7 a wise son over this **g.** people............ 7227
1Ki 5:17 annd they brought **g.** stones, costly..... 1419
1Ki 7:9 on the outside toward the **g.** court...... 1419
1Ki 7:10 even **g.** stones, stones of ten cubits,... 1419
1Ki 7:12 the **g.** court round about was with....... 1419
1Ki 8:42 they shall hear of thy **g.** name,........... 1419
1Ki 8:65 with him, a **g.** congregation, from........1419
1Ki 10:2 to Jerusalem with a very **g.** train,.........3515
1Ki 10:10 and of spices very **g.** store, and..........7235
1Ki 10:11 in from Ophir a **g.** plenty of almug........ 3966
1Ki 10:18 king made a **g.** throne of ivory,........... 1419
1Ki 11:19 And Hadad found **g.** favour in the........ 3966
1Ki 18:32 **g.** as would contain two measures........ 1004
1Ki 18:45 and wind, and there was a **g.** rain....... 1419
1Ki 19:7 the journey is too **g.** for thee............. 7227
1Ki 19:11 and a **g.** and strong wind rent the....... 1419
1Ki 20:13 thou seen all this **g.** multitude?........... 1419
1Ki 20:21 slew the Syrians with a **g.** slaughter.... 1419
1Ki 20:28 deliver all this **g.** multitude into........... 1419
1Ki 22:31 Fight neither with small nor **g.**,............ 1419
2Ki 3:27 was **g.** indignation against Israel:......... 1419
2Ki 4:8 where was a **g.** woman; and she.......... 1419
2Ki 4:38 Set on the **g.** pot, and seethe..............1419
2Ki 5:1 was a **g.** man with his master, and...... 1419
2Ki 5:13 had bid thee do some **g.** thing,............ 1419
2Ki 6:14 and chariots, and a **g.** host: and........... 3515
2Ki 6:23 And he prepared **g.** provision for.........1419
2Ki 6:25 there was a **g.** famine in Samaria:........ 1419
2Ki 7:6 horses, even the noise of a **g.** host:.....1419
2Ki 8:4 the **g.** things that Elisha hath done....... 1419
2Ki 8:13 that he should do this **g.** thing?...........1419
2Ki 10:6 were with the **g.** men of the city,........1419
2Ki 10:11 all his **g.** men, and his kinsfolks,......... 1419

2Ki 10:19 I have a **g.** sacrifice to do to Baal;.......1419
2Ki 16:15 Upon the **g.** altar burn the morning..... 1419
2Ki 17:21 Lord, and made them sin a **g.** sin........1419
2Ki 17:36 of the land of Egypt with **g.** power...... 1419
2Ki 18:17 with a **g.** host against Jerusalem..........3515
2Ki 18:19 Thus saith the **g.** king, the king.......... 1419
2Ki 18:28 Hear the word of the **g.** king,............ 1419
2Ki 22:13 for **g.** is the wrath of the Lord........... 1419
2Ki 23:2 all the people, both small and **g.**:......... 1419
2Ki 23:26 from the fierceness of his **g.** wrath,...... 1419
2Ki 25:9 every **g.** man's house burnt he........... 1419
2Ki 25:26 all the people, both small and **g.**,........ 1419
1Ch 11:14 saved them by a **g.** deliverance...........1419
1Ch 11:23 slew an Egyptian, a man of **g.** stature,........
1Ch 12:22 until it was a **g.** host, like the............1419
1Ch 16:25 For **g.** is the Lord, and greatly to be... 1419
1Ch 17:8 like the name of the **g.** men that.........1419
1Ch 17:17 house for a **g.** while to come,.............7350
1Ch 17:19 making known all these **g.** things.........1420
1Ch 20:6 where was a man of **g.** stature,...............
1Ch 21:13 I am in a **g.** strait: let me fall............ 3966
1Ch 21:13 Lord; for very **g.** are his mercies:....... 7227
1Ch 22:8 hast made **g.** wars: thou shalt not....... 1419
1Ch 25:8 ward, as well the small as the **g.**,........1419
1Ch 26:13 lots, as well the small as the **g.**,.......... 1419
1Ch 29:1 and the work is **g.**: for the palace is.... 1419
1Ch 29:9 the king also rejoiced with **g.** joy.........1419
1Ch 29:12 and in thine hand it is to make **g.**,........ 1431
1Ch 29:22 Lord on that day with **g.** gladness....... 1419
2Ch 1:8 hast shewed **g.** mercy unto David....... 1419
2Ch 1:10 this thy people, that is so **g.**?............ 1419
2Ch 2:5 the house which I build is **g.**:............. 1419
2Ch 2:5 for **g.** is our God above all gods...........1419
2Ch 2:9 about to build shall be wonderful **g.**..... 1419
2Ch 4:9 and the **g.** court, and doors for the......1419
2Ch 4:18 all these vessels in **g.** abundance:........3966
2Ch 6:32 for thy **g.** name's sake, and thy.......... 1419
2Ch 7:8 a very **g.** congregation, from the.........1419
2Ch 9:1 with a very **g.** company, and............. 3515
2Ch 9:9 and of spices **g.** abundance, and.......... 3966
2Ch 9:17 the king made a **g.** throne of ivory,...... 1419
2Ch 13:8 and ye be a **g.** multitude, and there..... 7227
2Ch 13:17 slew them with a **g.** slaughter:.......... 7227
2Ch 15:5 but **g.** vexations were upon all the....... 7227
2Ch 15:13 put to death, whether small or **g.**,........1419
2Ch 16:12 until his disease was exceeding **g.**:............
2Ch 16:14 made a very **g.** burning for him.......... 1419
2Ch 17:12 And Jehoshaphat waxed **g.**.................. 1432
2Ch 18:30 Fight ye not with small or **g.**,.............1419
2Ch 20:2 There cometh a **g.** multitude.............. 7227
2Ch 20:12 this **g.** company that cometh.............. 7227
2Ch 20:15 by reason of this **g.** multitude; for....... 7227
2Ch 21:3 their father gave them **g.** gifts of....... 7227
2Ch 21:14 a **g.** plague will the Lord smite........... 1419
2Ch 21:15 shalt have **g.** sickness by disease........ 7227
2Ch 24:24 the Lord delivered a very **g.** host........7230
2Ch 24:25 (for they left him in **g.** diseases,)........ 7227
2Ch 25:10 they returned home in **g.** anger.......... 2750
2Ch 26:15 shoot arrows and **g.** stones withal....... 1419
2Ch 28:5 a **g.** multitude of them captives,......... 1419
2Ch 28:5 who smote him with a **g.** slaughter...... 1419
2Ch 28:13 for our trespass is **g.**, and there is...... 7227
2Ch 30:13 month, a very **g.** congregation............ 7230
2Ch 30:21 bread seven days with **g.** gladness:.......1419
2Ch 30:24 and a **g.** number of priests..................7230
2Ch 30:26 So there was **g.** joy in Jerusalem:.........1419
2Ch 31:10 and that which is left is this **g.** store..........
2Ch 31:15 as well to the **g.** as to the small:..........1419
2Ch 33:14 and raised it up a very **g.** height, and.........
2Ch 34:21 for **g.** is the wrath of the Lord........... 1419
2Ch 34:30 all the people, **g.** and small: and..........1419
2Ch 36:18 **g.** and small, and the treasures of....... 1419
Ezr 3:11 the people shouted with a **g.** shout,...... 1419
Ezr 4:10 the **g.** and noble Asnapper brought....... 7229
Ezr 5:8 to the house of the **g.** God, which....... 7229
Ezr 5:8 which is builded with **g.** stones,........... 1560
Ezr 5:11 which a **g.** king of Israel builded..........7229
Ezr 6:4 With three rows of **g.** stones, and....... 1560
Ezr 9:7 in a **g.** trespass unto this day;............ 1419
Ezr 9:13 and for our **g.** trespass, seeing that..... 1419
Ezr 10:1 a very **g.** congregation of men and...... 7227
Ezr 10:9 of this matter, and for the **g.** rain.............
Ne 1:3 are in **g.** affliction and reproach:..........1419
Ne 1:5 the **g.** and terrible God, that keepeth... 1419
Ne 1:10 thou hast redeemed by thy **g.** power,.. 1419
Ne 3:27 against the **g.** tower that lieth out,...... 1419
Ne 4:1 took **g.** indignation, and mocked.......... 7235
Ne 4:14 the Lord, which is **g.** and terrible,....... 1419
Ne 4:19 The work is **g.** and large, and we........7235
Ne 5:1 there was a **g.** cry of the people.......... 1419
Ne 5:7 I set a **g.** assembly against them......... 1419
Ne 6:3 I am doing a **g.** work, so that I...........1419
Ne 7:4 Now the city was large and **g.**:............ 1419
Ne 8:6 Ezra blessed the Lord, the **g.** God...... 1419
Ne 8:12 to make **g.** mirth, because they had..... 1419
Ne 8:17 And there was very **g.** gladness.......... 1419
Ne 9:17 slow to anger, and of **g.** kindness,....... 7227
Ne 9:18 and had wrought **g.** provocations;......... 1419
Ne 9:25 themselves in thy **g.** goodness............1419
Ne 9:26 and they wrought **g.** provocations.........1419
Ne 9:31 thy **g.** mercies' sake thou didst........... 7227
Ne 9:32 our God, the **g.**, the mighty, and........ 1419
Ne 9:35 and in thy **g.** goodness that thou.......... 7227
Ne 9:37 pleasure, and we are in **g.** distress...... 1419
Ne 11:14 the son of one of the **g.** men...............1419
Ne 12:31 appointed two **g.** companies of............1419
Ne 12:43 they offered **g.** sacrifices, and.............1419
Ne 12:43 God made them rejoice with **g.** joy:..... 1419
Ne 13:5 had prepared for him a **g.** chamber,...... 1419
Ne 13:27 to do all this **g.** evil, to transgress....... 1419
Es 1:5 the palace, both unto **g.** and small,...... 1419
Es 1:20 all his empire, (for it is **g.**,) all the.......7227
Es 1:20 honour, both to **g.** and small.............. 1419
Es 2:18 the king made a **g.** feast unto all.......... 1419
Es 4:3 was **g.** mourning among the Jews,....... 1419
Es 8:15 with the **g.** crown of gold, and with...... 1419
Es 9:4 **g.** in the king's house, and his fame..... 1419
Es 10:3 **g.** among the Jews, and accepted......... 1419
Job 1:3 a very **g.** household; so that this.......... 7227
Job 1:19 a **g.** wind from the wilderness,........... 1419
Job 2:13 saw that his grief was very **g.**............ 1431
Job 3:19 The small and **g.** are there; and...........1419
Job 5:9 doeth **g.** things and unsearchable;.........1419
Job 5:25 also that thy seed shall be **g.**, and....... 7227
Job 9:10 Which doeth **g.** things past............... 1419
Job 22:5 Is not thy wickedness **g.**? and............. 7227
Job 23:6 against me with his **g.** power?............ 7227
Job 30:18 By the **g.** force of my disease............ 7227
Job 31:25 because my wealth was **g.**,................. 7227
Job 31:34 Did I fear a **g.** multitude, or did..........7227
Job 32:9 **G.** men are not always wise:...............7227
Job 35:15 knoweth it not in **g.** extremity:............ 3966
Job 36:18 a **g.** ransom cannot deliver thee.......... 7227
Job 36:26 God is **g.**, and we know him not,......... 7689
Job 37:5 **g.** things doeth he, which we............. 1419
Job 37:6 small rain, and of the **g.** rain of...........4306
Job 38:21 the number of thy days is **g.**?..............7227
Job 39:11 him, because his strength is **g.**?........... 7227
Ps 14:5 There were they in **g.** fear: for God.... 6343
Ps 18:35 thy gentleness hath made me **g.**.......... 7235
Ps 18:50 **G.** deliverance giveth he to his........... 1431
Ps 19:11 keeping of them there is **g.** reward...... 7227
Ps 19:13 innocent from the **g.** transgression....... 7227
Ps 21:5 His glory is **g.** in thy salvation:........... 1419
Ps 22:25 be of thee in the **g.** congregation:........ 7227
Ps 25:11 pardon mine iniquity; for it is **g.**.......... 7227
Ps 31:19 how **g.** is thy goodness, which thou..... 7227
Ps 32:6 in the floods of **g.** waters they shall..... 7227
Ps 33:17 he deliver any by his **g.** strength.........7230
Ps 35:18 thee thanks in the **g.** congregation:...... 7227
Ps 36:6 is like the **g.** mountains;...................... 410
Ps 36:6 thy judgments are a **g.** deep:............. 7227
Ps 37:35 have seen the wicked in **g.** power,............
Ps 40:9 preached righteousness in the **g.**......... 7227
Ps 40:10 thy truth from the **g.** congregation........7227
Ps 47:2 he is a **g.** king over all the earth,........1419
Ps 48:1 **G.** is the Lord, and greatly to be......... 1419
Ps 48:2 the north, the city of the **g.** King......... 7227
Ps 53:5 were they in **g.** fear, where no fear was:....
Ps 57:10 thy mercy is **g.** unto the heavens,........ 1419
Ps 58:6 break out the **g.** teeth of the young..... 4459
Ps 68:11 **g.** was the company of those that........7227
Ps 71:19 who hast done **g.** things: O God,......... 1419
Ps 71:20 shewed me **g.** and sore troubles,.......... 7229
Ps 76:1 known: his name is **g.** in Israel............ 1419
Ps 77:13 who is so **g.** a God as our God?.......... 1419
Ps 77:19 the sea, thy path in the **g.** waters,...... 7227
Ps 78:15 drink as out of the **g.** depths..............7227
Ps 78:71 following the ewes **g.** with young.............
Ps 80:5 tears to drink in **g.** measure................7991
Ps 86:10 thou art **g.**, and doest wondrous.......... 1419
Ps 86:13 **g.** is thy mercy toward me: and.......... 1419
Ps 92:5 how **g.** are thy works! and thy........... 1431
Ps 95:3 the Lord is a **g.** God, and a **g.** King.... 1419
Ps 96:4 the Lord is **g.**, and greatly to be......... 1419
Ps 99:2 The Lord is **g.** in Zion; and he is........ 1419
Ps 99:3 praise thy **g.** and terrible name;........... 1419
Ps 103:11 **g.** is his mercy toward them that........ 1396
Ps 104:1 thou art very **g.**; thou art clothed......... 1431
Ps 104:25 So is this **g.** and wide sea, wherein..... 1419
Ps 104:25 innumerable, both small and **g.**........... 1419
Ps 106:21 which had done **g.** things in Egypt;...... 1419
Ps 107:23 that do business in **g.** waters;............ 7227
Ps 108:4 thy mercy is **g.** above the heavens:..... 1419
Ps 111:2 The works of the Lord are **g.**,............ 1419
Ps 115:13 fear the Lord, both small and **g.**.......... 1419
Ps 117:2 merciful kindness is **g.** toward us:....... 1396
Ps 119:156 **G.** are thy tender mercies, O............. 7227
Ps 119:162 word, as one that findth **g.** spoil......... 7227
Ps 119:165 **G.** peace have they which love thy...... 7227
Ps 126:2 Lord hath done **g.** things for them....... 1431
Ps 126:3 Lord hath done **g.** things for us;......... 1431
Ps 131:1 do I exercise myself in **g.** matters,...... 1419
Ps 135:5 I know that the Lord is **g.**, and...........1419
Ps 135:10 Who smote **g.** nations, and slew......... 7227
Ps 136:4 him who alone doeth **g.** wonders:......... 1419
Ps 136:7 To him that made **g.** lights: for his...... 1419
Ps 136:17 To him which smote **g.** kings: for........1419
Ps 138:5 for **g.** is the glory of the Lord............ 1419
Ps 139:17 O God! how **g.** is the sum of them!..... 6105
Ps 144:7 deliver me out of **g.** waters, from....... 7227
Ps 145:3 **G.** is the Lord, and greatly to be....... 1419
Ps 145:7 memory of thy **g.** goodness, and......... 7227
Ps 145:8 slow to anger, and of **g.** mercy...........1419
Ps 147:5 **G.** is our Lord, and of...power:.......... 1419
Ps 147:5 is our Lord, and of **g.** power: his........ 7227
Pr 13:7 himself poor, yet hath **g.** riches.......... 7227
Pr 14:29 to wrath is of **g.** understanding:........... 7227
Pr 15:16 Lord than **g.** treasure and trouble........7227
Pr 16:8 than **g.** revenues without right............ 7230
Pr 18:9 brother to him that is a **g.** waster....... 1167
Pr 18:16 and bringeth him before **g.** men.......... 1419
Pr 19:19 A man of **g.** wrath shall suffer..................
Pr 22:1 rather to be chosen than **g.** riches,...... 7227
Pr 25:6 stand not in the place of **g.** men:.........1419
Pr 26:10 The **g.** God that formed all things....... 7227
Pr 28:12 men do rejoice, there is **g.** glory:........ 7227
Pr 28:16 is also a **g.** oppressor: but he that....... 7227
Ec 1:16 I am come to **g.** estate, and have........1431
Ec 1:16 heart had **g.** experience of wisdom...... 7235
Ec 2:4 I made me **g.** works; I builded me........1431
Ec 2:7 house; also I had **g.** possessions of...... 7235
Ec 2:7 possessions of **g.** and small cattle........ 1241
Ec 2:9 I was **g.**, and increased more than.......1431
Ec 2:21 This also is vanity and a **g.** evil...........7227
Ec 8:6 the misery of man is **g.** upon him.........7227
Ec 9:13 the sun, and it seemed **g.** unto me:..... 1419
Ec 9:14 there came a **g.** king against it, and..... 1419
Ec 9:14 and built **g.** bulwarks against it:.......... 1419
Ec 10:4 for yielding pacifieth **g.** offences.......... 1419
Ec 10:6 Folly is set in **g.** dignity, and the..........7227
Ca 2:3 down under his shadow with **g.** delight,......
Isa 2:9 and the **g.** man humbleth himself:..............
Isa 5:9 **g.** and fair, without inhabitant:............ 1419
Isa 6:12 and there be a **g.** forsaking in the........7227
Isa 8:1 Take thee a **g.** roll, and write in it...... 1419
Isa 9:2 in darkness have seen a **g.** light:........ 1419
Isa 12:6 for **g.** is the Holy One of Israel...........1419
Isa 13:4 mountains, like as of a **g.** people;........ 7227
Isa 16:14 with all that **g.** multitude; and the........7227
Isa 19:20 send them a saviour, and a **g.** one,.......7227
Isa 23:3 And by **g.** waters the seed of Sihor,..... 7227
Isa 27:1 his sore and **g.** and strong sword........ 1419
Isa 27:13 that the **g.** trumpet shall be blown,...... 1419
Isa 29:6 and with earthquake, and **g.** noise,...... 1419
Isa 30:25 in the day of the **g.** slaughter,............ 7227
Isa 32:2 the shadow of a **g.** rock in a weary......3515
Isa 33:23 is the prey of a **g.** spoil divided;..........4766
Isa 34:6 **g.** slaughter in the land of Idumea,...... 1419
Isa 34:15 shall the **g.** owl make ner nest,........... 7091
Isa 36:2 King Hezekiah with a **g.** army............ 3515
Isa 36:4 the **g.** king, the king of Assyria,......... 1419
Isa 36:13 Hear ye the words of the **g.** king,........ 1419
Isa 38:17 for peace I had **g.** bitterness:....................
Isa 47:9 for the **g.** abundance of thine..............3966
Isa 51:10 the sea, the waters of the **g.** deep;..... 7227
Isa 53:12 divide him a portion with the **g.**,......... 7227
Isa 54:7 with **g.** mercies will I gather thee........1419
Isa 54:13 and **g.** shall be the peace of thy.......... 7227
Isa 63:7 the **g.** goodness toward the house....... 7227
Jer 4:6 the north, and a **g.** destruction........... 1419

Jer 5:5 me unto the g. men, and will speak.... 1419
Jer 5:27 therefore they are become g., and...... 1431
Jer 6:1 of the north, and g. destruction. 1419
Jer 6:22 and a g. nation shall be raised........... 1419
Jer 10:6 Lord; thou art g., and thy name is g... 1419
Jer 10:22 and a g. commotion out of the north... 1419
Jer 11:16 with the noise of a g. tumult he......... 1419
Jer 13:9 and the g. pride of Jerusalem. 7227
Jer 14:17 people is broken with a g. breach,...... 1419
Jer 16:6 the g. and the small shall die in 1419
Jer 16:10 pronounced all this g. evil against....... 1419
Jer 20:17 womb to be always g. with me. 2030
Jer 21:5 and in fury, and in g. wrath.............. 1419
Jer 21:6 they shall die of a g. pestilence......... 1419
Jer 22:8 Lord done thus unto this g. city? 1419
Jer 25:14 g. kings shall serve themselves of...... 1419
Jer 25:32 a g. whirlwind shall be raised up 1419
Jer 26:19 procure g. evil against our souls,........ 1419
Jer 27:5 g. power and by my outstretched....... 1419
Jer 27:7 many nations and g. kings shall.......... 1419
Jer 28:8 against g. kingdoms, of war, and of.... 1419
Jer 30:7 Alas! for that day is g., so that......... 1419
Jer 31:8 a g. company shall return thither........ 1419
Jer 32:17 heaven and the earth by thy g........... 1419
Jer 32:18 the G., the Mighty God, the Lord........ 1419
Jer 32:19 G. in counsel, and mighty in work: 1419
Jer 32:21 out arm, and with g. terror;............. 1419
Jer 32:37 and in my fury, and in g. wrath; 1419
Jer 32:42 all this g. evil upon this people, ... 1419
Jer 33:3 shew thee g. and mighty things, ... 1419
Jer 36:7 for g. is the anger and the fury.......... 1419
Jer 41:12 the g. waters that are in Gibeon. 7227
Jer 43:9 Take g. stones in thine hand, and....... 1419
Jer 44:7 ye this g. evil against your souls, ... 1419
Jer 44:15 a g. multitude, even all the people...... 1419
Jer 44:26 I have sworn by my g. name, saith..... 1419
Jer 45:5 seekest thou g. things for thyself?...... 1419
Jer 48:3 spoiling and g. destruction. 1419
Jer 50:9 an assembly of g. nations from the..... 1419
Jer 50:22 in the land, and of g. destruction........ 1419
Jer 50:41 and a g. nation, and many kings.......... 1419
Jer 51:54 g. destruction from the land of the 1419
Jer 51:55 destroyed out of her the g. voice;..... 1419
Jer 51:55 her waves do roar like g. waters,....... 7227
Jer 52:13 all the houses of the g. men,............. 1419
La 1:1 that was g. among the nations,.......... 7227
La 1:3 and because of g. servitude:.............. 7230
La 2:13 thy breach is g. like the sea: who 1419
La 3:23 morning: g. is thy faithfulness........... 7227
Eze 1:4 came out of the north, a g. cloud, ... 1419
Eze 1:24 like the noise of g. waters, as the...... 7227
Eze 3:12 behind me a voice of a g. rushing,...... 1419
Eze 3:13 them, and a noise of a g. rushing...... 1419
Eze 8:6 the g. abominations that the house 1419
Eze 9:9 Judah is exceeding g., and the land..... 1419
Eze 13:11 O g. hailstones, shall fail; and a.......... 417
Eze 13:13 g. hailstones in my fury to consume..... 417
Eze 16:7 thou hast increased and waxen g.,....... 1431
Eze 16:26 thy neighbours, g. of flesh; and.......... 1432
Eze 17:3 saith the Lord God; A g. eagle.......... 1419
Eze 17:3 eagle with g. wings, full of............... 1419
Eze 17:5 he placed it by g. waters, and set...... 7227
Eze 17:7 There was also another g. eagle 1419
Eze 17:7 with g. wings and many feathers,....... 1419
Eze 17:8 in a good soil by g. waters, that 7227
Eze 17:9 even withut g. power or many........... 1419
Eze 17:17 might army and g. company 7227
Eze 21:14 it is the sword of the g. men that 1419
Eze 23:23 g. lords and renowned, all of them 7991
Eze 24:9 will even make the pile for fire g........ 1431
Eze 24:12 her g. scum went not forth out of......... 7227
Eze 25:17 I will execute g. vengeance upon......... 1419
Eze 26:10 and g. waters shall cover thee;.......... 7227
Eze 27:26 have brought thee into g. waters:....... 7227
Eze 28:5 By thy g. wisdom and by thy 7230
Eze 29:3 g. dragon that lieth in the midst......... 1419
Eze 29:18 to serve a g. service against Tyrus:.... 1419
Eze 30:4 g. pain shall be in Ethiopia, when............
Eze 30:9 g. pain shall come upon them, as..............
Eze 30:16 Sin shall have g. pain, and No........... 2342
Eze 31:4 The waters made him g., the............ 1431
Eze 31:6 his shadow dwelt all g. nations.......... 7227
Eze 31:7 for his root was by g. waters. 7227
Eze 31:15 the g. waters were stayed: and I 7227
Eze 32:13 from beside the g. waters;................ 7227
Eze 36:23 I will sanctify my g. name, which 1419
Eze 37:10 their feet, an exceeding g. army. 1419
Eze 38:4 a g. company with bucklers and 7227
Eze 38:13 and goods, to take a g. spoil?............ 1419
Eze 38:15 a g. company, and a mighty army:...... 1419
Eze 38:19 there shall be a g. shaking in the 1419
Eze 38:22 g. hailstones, fire, and brimstone. 417
Eze 39:17 a g. sacrifice upon the mountains........ 1419
Eze 41:8 were a full reed of six g. cubits........... 679
Eze 47:9 shall be a very g. multitude of fish,..... 7227
Eze 47:10 as the fish of the g. sea, exceeding...... 1419
Eze 47:15 from the g. sea, the way of Hethlon, .. 1419
Eze 47:19 in Kadesh, the river to the g. sea. 1419
Eze 47:20 the g. sea from the border, till a........ 1419
Eze 48:28 and to the river toward the g. sea...... 1419
Da 2:6 and rewards and g. honour:.............. 7390
Da 2:31 and behold a g. image...................... 7390
Da 2:31 This g. image, whose brightness......... 7229
Da 2:35 became a g. mountain, and filled 7229
Da 2:45 the g. God hath made known to........... 7229
Da 2:48 the king made Daniel a g. man, ... 7236
Da 2:48 and gave him many g. gifts,............... 7260
Da 4:3 How g. are his signs! and how 7260
Da 4:10 and the height thereof was g............ 7690
Da 4:30 Is not this g. Babylon, that I............ 7227
Da 5:1 the king made a g. feast to a............. 7227
Da 7:2 the heavens strove upon the g. sea. ... 7227
Da 7:3 And four g. beasts came up from 7260
Da 7:7 and it had g. iron teeth: 7260
Da 7:8 and a mouth speaking g. things.......... 7260
Da 7:11 because of the voice of the g. words... 7260
Da 7:17 These g. beasts, which are four,......... 7260
Da 7:20 a mouth that spake very g. things, ... 7260
Da 7:25 And he shall speak g. words.....................
Da 8:4 to his will, and became g.................. 1431
Da 8:8 the he goat waxed very g.: and 1431
Da 8:8 the g. horn was broken;................... 1419
Da 8:9 exceeding g., toward the south, ... 1431
Da 8:10 And it waxed g., even to the host....... 1431
Da 8:21 the g. horn that is between his.......... 1419
Da 9:4 the g. and dreadful God, keeping........ 1419
Da 9:12 by bringing upon us a g. evil: 1419
Da 9:18 but for thy g. mercies...................... 7227
Da 10:4 I was by the side of the g. river, ... 1419
Da 10:7 a g. quaking fell upon them, so.......... 1419
Da 10:8 this g. vision, and there remained....... 1419
Da 11:3 that shall rule with g. dominion, ... 7227
Da 11:5 dominion shall be a g. dominion.......... 7227
Da 11:10 a multitude of g. forces: and one........ 7227
Da 11:11 he shall set forth a g. multitude; 7227
Da 11:13 with a g. army and with much 1419
Da 11:25 with a g. army; and the king of the 1419
Da 11:25 with a very g. and mighty army; 1419
Da 11:28 return into his land with g. riches;...... 1419
Da 11:44 go forth with g. fury to destroy, ... 1419
Da 12:1 the g. prince which standeth for.......... 1419
Ho 1:2 hath committed g. whoredom,..................
Ho 1:11 for g. shall be the day of Jezreel. 1419
Ho 8:12 written to him the g. things of........... 7239
Ho 9:7 thine iniquity, and the g. hatred. 7227
Ho 10:15 because of your g. wickedness:.......... 7451
Ho 13:5 in the land of g. drought.................. 8514
Joe 1:6 hath the cheek teeth of a g. lion. 3833
Joe 2:2 a g. people and a strong; there.......... 7227
Joe 2:11 for his camp is very g.: for he is........ 7227
Joe 2:11 of the Lord is g. and very terrible;..... 1419
Joe 2:13 to anger, and of g. kindness,............. 7227
Joe 2:20 because he hath done g. things.......... 1431
Joe 2:21 for the Lord will do g. things............. 1431
Joe 2:25 g. army which I sent among you. 1419
Joe 2:31 the g. and the terrible day of the 1419
Joe 3:13 for their wickedness is g.................. 7227
Am 3:9 g. tumults in the midst thereof, ... 7227
Am 3:15 the g. houses shall have an end, ... 7227
Am 6:2 go ye to Hamath the g.: then go......... 7227
Am 6:11 and he will smite the g. house........... 1419
Am 7:4 it devoured the g. deep, and did 7227
Am 8:5 and the shekel g., and falsifying 1431
Jon 1:2 go to Nineveh, that g. city, and cry.... 1419
Jon 1:4 the Lord sent out a g. wind into 1419
Jon 1:12 this g. tempest is upon you................ 1419
Jon 1:17 prepared a g. fish to swallow up 1419
Jon 3:2 go unto Nineveh, that g. city, and...... 1419
Jon 3:3 g. city of three days' journey............. 1419
Jon 4:2 to anger, and of g. kindness,.............. 7227
Jon 4:11 spare Nineveh, that g. city,............... 1419
Mic 2:12 they shall make g. noise by reason of........
Mic 5:4 now shall he be g. unto the ends 1431
Mic 7:3 and the g. man, he uttereth his 1419
Na 1:3 and g. in power, and will not............. 1431
Na 3:3 and a g. number of carcases; and........ 3514
Na 3:10 her g. men were bound in chains. 1419
Na 3:17 as the g. grasshoppers, which 1462
Hab 3:15 through the heap of g. waters. 7227
Zep 1:10 and a g. crashing from the hills.......... 1419
Zep 1:14 The g. day of the Lord is near, ... 1419
Zec 1:14 and for Zion with a g. jealousy............ 1419
Zec 4:7 Who art thou, O g. mountain? 1419
Zec 7:12 came a g. wrath from the Lord............ 1419
Zec 8:2 for Zion with g. jealousy, and I 1419
Zec 8:2 I was jealous for her with g. fury. 1419
Zec 9:17 how g. is his goodness, and how g. is.......
Zec 12:11 In that day shall there be a g. 1431
Zec 14:4 a very g. valley; and half of the 1419
Zec 14:13 a g. tumult from the Lord shall........... 7227
Zec 14:14 and apparel, in g. abundance. 3966
Mal 1:11 shall be g. among the Gentiles;........... 1419
Mal 1:11 shall be g. among the heathen, ... 1419
Mal 1:14 for I am a g. King, saith the Lord....... 1419
Mal 4:5 coming of the g. and dreadful day........ 1419
Mt 2:10 rejoiced with exceeding g. joy............ 3173
Mt 2:18 and g. mourning, Rachel weeping........ 4183
Mt 4:16 which sat in darkness saw g. light; 3173
Mt 4:25 him g. multitudes of people from......... 4183
Mt 5:12 for g. is your reward in heaven: 4183
Mt 5:19 shall be called g. in the kingdom... 3173
Mt 5:35 for it is the city of the g. King...... 3173
Mt 6:23 how g. is that darkness! 4214
Mt 7:27 and g. was the fall of it................. 3173
Mt 8:1 g. multitudes followed him. 4183
Mt 8:10 I have not found so g. faith, no, ... 5118
Mt 8:18 Jesus saw g. multitudes about............. 4183
Mt 8:24 arose a g. tempest in the sea,............ 3173
Mt 8:26 the sea; and there was a g. calm. 3173
Mt 12:15 and g. multitudes followed him,.......... 4183
Mt 13:2 And g. multitudes were gathered......... 4183
Mt 13:46 found one earl of g. price, went 4186
Mt 14:14 and saw a g. multitude, and was 4183
Mt 15:28 O woman, g. is thy faith: be it....... 3173
Mt 15:30 And g. multitudes came unto him, ... 4183
Mt 15:33 as to fill so g. a multitude?.............. 5118
Mt 19:2 And g. multitudes followed him;.......... 4183
Mt 19:22 sorrowful: for he had g. possessions. .. 4183
Mt 20:25 that are g. exercise authority........ 3171
Mt 20:26 whosoever will be g. among you,... 3173
Mt 20:29 a g. multitude followed him. 4183
Mt 21:8 And a very g. multitude spread.......... 4118
Mt 22:36 which is the g. commandment in......... 3173
Mt 22:38 is the first and g. commandment...... 3173
Mt 24:21 then shall be g. tribulation, such... 3173
Mt 24:24 shall shew g. signs and wonders;... 3173
Mt 24:30 of heaven with power and g. glory. 4183
Mt 24:31 with a g. sound of a trumpet, and . 3173
Mt 26:47 and with him a g. multitude with........ 4183
Mt 27:60 he rolled a g. stone to the door.......... 3173
Mt 28:2 there was a g. earthquake: for the 3173
Mt 28:8 with fear and g. joy; and did run......... 3173
Mk 1:35 rising up a g. while before day,.......... 3029
Mk 3:7 and a g. multitude from Galilee........... 4183
Mk 3:8 a g. multitude, when they had 4183
Mk 3:8 heard what g. things he did............... 3745
Mk 4:1 gathered unto him a g. multitude,........ 4183
Mk 4:32 and shooteth out g. branches; so... 3173
Mk 4:37 there arose a g. storm of wind, ... 3173
Mk 4:39 ceased; and there was a g. calm. 3173
Mk 5:11 a g. herd of swine feeding. 3173
Mk 5:19 tell them how g. things the Lord... 3745
Mk 5:20 how g. things Jesus had done for 3745
Mk 5:42 astonished with a g. astonishment....... 3173
Mk 7:36 so much the more a g. deal they......... 3123
Mk 8:1 the multitude being very g., and 3827
Mk 9:14 saw a g. multitude about them,........... 4183
Mk 10:22 grieved: for he had g. possessions...... 4183
Mk 10:42 their g. ones exercise authority....... 3173
Mk 10:43 whosoever will be g. among you,... 3173
Mk 10:46 his disciples and a g. number of.......... 2425
Mk 10:48 but he cried the more a g. deal, ... 4183
Mk 13:2 Seest thou these g. buildings? 3173
Mk 13:26 clouds with g. power and glory. 4183
Mk 14:43 and with him a g. multitude............... 4183
Mk 16:4 rolled away: for it was very g............ 3173
Lu 1:15 For he shall be g. in the sight of......... 3173
Lu 1:32 He shall be g., and shall be called 3173
Lu 1:49 hath done to me g. things; and........... 3167
Lu 1:58 had shewed g. mercy upon her;........... 3170
Lu 2:5 his espoused wife, being g. with child.......

Lu 2:10 I bring you good tidings of g. joy, 3173
Lu 2:36 she was of a g. age, and had lived 4183
Lu 4:25 when g. famine was throughout 3173
Lu 4:38 was taken with a g. fever; and 3173
Lu 5:6 inclosed a g. multitude of fishes: 4183
Lu 5:15 and g. multitudes came together 4183
Lu 5:29 Levi made him a g. feast in his 3173
Lu 5:29 and there was a g. company 4183
Lu 6:17 a g. multitude of people out of all 4183
Lu 6:23 your reward is g. in heaven: for 4183
Lu 6:35 and your reward shall be g., and 4183
Lu 6:49 and the ruin of that house was g. 3173
Lu 7:9 I have not found so g. faith, no, 5118
Lu 7:16 That a g. prophet is risen up 3173
Lu 8:37 they were taken with g. fear: and 3173
Lu 8:39 how g. things God hath done 3745
Lu 8:39 how g. things Jesus had done unto 3745
Lu 9:48 you all, the same shall be g. 3173
Lu 10:2 The harvest truly is g., but the 4183
Lu 10:13 they had a g. while ago repented, 3819
Lu 13:19 and waxed a g. tree; and the 3173
Lu 14:16 A certain man made a g. supper, 3173
Lu 14:25 there went g. multitudes with him: 4183
Lu 14:32 while the other is yet a g. way off, 4183
Lu 15:20 when he was yet a g. way off, 3112
Lu 16:26 there is a g. gulf fixed: so that 3173
Lu 21:11 g. earthquakes shall be in divers 3173
Lu 21:11 and g. signs shall there be 3173
Lu 21:23 shall be g. distress in the land, 3173
Lu 21:27 cloud with power and g. glory 4183
Lu 22:44 as it were g. drops of blood
Lu 23:27 a g. company of people, and of 4183
Lu 24:52 to Jerusalem with g. joy: 3173
Joh 5:3 a g. multitude of impotent folk, 4183
Joh 6:2 And a g. multitude followed him, 4183
Joh 6:5 saw a g. company come unto him, 4183
Joh 6:18 by reason of a g. wind that blew. 3173
Joh 7:37 that g. day of the feast, Jesus 3173
Joh 21:11 the net to land full of g. fishes, 3173
Ac 2:20 before that g. and notable day of 3173
Ac 4:33 with g. power gave the apostles 3173
Ac 4:33 and g. grace was upon them all 3173
Ac 5:5 and g. fear came on all them that 3173
Ac 5:11 And g. fear came upon all the 3173
Ac 6:7 and a g. company of the priests 4183
Ac 6:8 g. wonders and miracles among 3173
Ac 7:11 and Chanaan, and g. affliction: and 3173
Ac 8:1 there was a g. persectuion against 3173
Ac 8:2 and made g. lamentation over him. 3173
Ac 8:8 And there was g. joy in that city. 3173
Ac 8:9 that himself was some g. one: 3173
Ac 8:10 This man is the g. power of God. 3173
Ac 8:27 an eunuch of g. authority under
Ac 9:16 how g. things he must suffer for 3745
Ac 10:11 as it had been a g. sheet knit at 3173
Ac 11:5 as it had been a g. sheet, let down 3173
Ac 11:21 and a g. number believed, and 4183
Ac 11:28 that there should be g. dearth 3173
Ac 14:1 a g. multitude both of the Jews 4183
Ac 15:3 they caused g. joy unto all the 3173
Ac 16:26 there was a g. earthquake, so that 3173
Ac 17:4 devout Greeks a g. multitude, and 4183
Ac 19:27 of the g. goddess Diana should be 3173
Ac 19:28 G. is Diana of the Ephesians. 3173
Ac 19:34 out, G. is Diana of the Ephesians. 3173
Ac 19:35 of the g. goddess Diana, and of the 3173
Ac 21:40 there was made a g. silence, he 4183
Ac 22:6 shone from heaven a g. light round 2425
Ac 22:28 With a g. sum obtained I this 4183
Ac 23:9 And there arose a g. cry: and the 3173
Ac 23:10 there arose a g. dissension, the 4183
Ac 23:14 bound ourselves under a g. curse,
Ac 24:2 by thee we enjoy g. quietness, 4183
Ac 24:7 with g. violence took him away 4183
Ac 25:23 and Bernice, with g. pomp, and 4183
Ac 26:22 witnessing both to small and g., 3173
Ac 28:6 after they had looked a g. while, 4183
Ac 28:29 g. reasoning among themselves 4183
Ro 9:2 That I have g. heaviness and 3173
Ro 15:23 a g. desire these many years 1974
1Co 9:11 it is a g. thing if we shall reap 3173
1Co 16:9 a g. door and effectual is opened 3173
2Co 1:10 delivered us from so g. a death, 5082
2Co 3:12 we use g. plainness of speech: 4183
2Co 7:4 G. is my boldness of speech toward 4183
2Co 7:4 you, g. is my glorying of you: 4183
2Co 8:2 How that in a g. trial of affliction 4183
2Co 8:22 diligent, upon the g. confidence 4183
2Co 11:15 it is no g. thing if his ministers 3173
Eph 2:4 for his g. love wherewith he loved 4183
Eph 5:32 This is a g. mystery: but I speak 3173
Col 2:1 ye knew what g. conflict I have 2245
Col 4:13 that he hath a g. zeal for you, 4183
1Th 2:17 to see your face with g. desire. 4183
1Ti 3:13 and g. boldness in the faith which 4183
1Ti 3:16 g. is the mystery of godliness: 3173
1Ti 6:6 with contentment is g. gain. 3173
2Ti 2:20 But in a g. house there are not 3173
Tit 2:13 glorious appearing of the g. God 3173
Phm 7 have g. joy and consolation in 4183
Heb 2:3 if we neglect so g. salvation; 5082
Heb 4:14 that we have a g. high priest, 3173
Heb 7:4 consider how g. this man was, 4080
Heb 10:32 ye endured a g. fight of afflictions; 4183
Heb 10:35 hath g. recompence of reward. 3173
Heb 12:1 with so g. a cloud of witnesses, 5118
Heb 13:20 that g. shepherd of the sheep, 3173
Jas 3:4 which though they be so g., and 5082
Jas 3:5 member, and boasteth g. things. 3166
Jas 3:5 g. a matter a little fire kindleth! 2245
1Pe 3:4 in the sight of God of g. price. 4185
2Pe 1:4 g. and precious promises: 3176
2Pe 2:18 speak g. swelling words of vanity 5246
2Pe 3:10 shall pass away with a g. noise,
Jude 6 unto the judgment of the g. day. 3173
Jude 16 mouth speaketh g. swelling words, 5246
Re 1:10 and heard behind me a g. voice, 3173
Re 2:22 into g. tribulation, except they 3173
Re 6:4 was given unto him a g. sword. 3173
Re 6:12 and, lo, there was a g. earthquake; 3173
Re 6:15 kings of the earth, and the g. men. 3175
Re 6:17 the g. day of his wrath is come; 3173
Re 7:9 and, lo, a g. multitude, which no 4183
Re 7:14 which came out of g. tribulation, 3173
Re 8:8 as it were a g. mountain burning 3173
Re 8:10 there fell a g. star from heaven, 3173
Re 9:2 as the smoke of a g. furnace; and 3173
Re 9:14 are bound in the g. river Euphrates. 3173
Re 11:8 in the street of the g. city, which 3173
Re 11:11 g. fear fell upon them which saw 3173
Re 11:12 they heard a g. voice from heaven 3173
Re 11:13 hour was there a g. earthquake, 3173
Re 11:15 there were g. voices in heaven, 3173
Re 11:17 hast taken to thee thy g. power, 3173
Re 11:18 that fear thy name, small and g.; 3173
Re 11:19 and an earthquake, and g. hail. 3173
Re 12:1 a g. wonder in heaven; a woman 3173
Re 12:3 g. red dragon, having seven heads 3173
Re 12:9 And the g. dragon was cast out, 3173
Re 12:12 having g. wrath, because he 3173
Re 12:14 two wings of a g. eagle, that she 3173
Re 13:2 and his seat, and g. authority. 3173
Re 13:5 a mouth speaking g. things and 3173
Re 13:13 he doeth g. wonders, so that he 3173
Re 13:16 he causeth all, both small and g., 3173
Re 14:2 as the voice of a g. thunder: 3173
Re 14:8 that g. city, because she made 3173
Re 14:19 into the g. winepress of the wrath 3173
Re 15:1 g. and marvellous, seven angels 3173
Re 15:3 G. and marvelous are thy works, 3173
Re 16:1 I heard a g. voice out of the temple 3173
Re 16:9 men were scorched with g. heat, 3173
Re 16:12 vial upon the g. river Euphrates; 3173
Re 16:14 of that g. day of God Almighty. 3173
Re 16:17 came a g. voice out of the temple 3173
Re 16:18 there was a g. earthquake, such as 3173
Re 16:18 mighty an earthquake, and so g.. 3173
Re 16:19 the g. city was divided into three 3173
Re 16:19 g. Babylon came in remembrance 3173
Re 16:21 upon men a g. hail out of heaven, 3173
Re 16:21 plague thereof was exceeding g. 3173
Re 17:1 judgment of the g. whore that 3173
Re 17:5 Mystery, Babylon The G., The 3173
Re 17:6 I wondered with g. admiration. 3173
Re 17:18 is that g. city, which reigneth over 3173
Re 18:1 from heaven, having g. power; 3173
Re 18:2 Babylon the g. is fallen, is fallen, 3173
Re 18:10 Alas, alas that g. city Babylon, that 3173
Re 18:16 Alas, alas that g. city, that was 3173
Re 18:17 so g. riches is come to nought 5118
Re 18:18 What city is like unto this g. 3173
Re 18:19 Alas, alas that g. city, wherein 3173
Re 18:21 took up a stone like a g. millstone, 3173
Re 18:21 shall that g. city Babylon be thrown 3173
Re 18:23 thy merchants were the g. men 3175
Re 19:1 I heard a g. voice of much people 3173
Re 19:2 hath judged the g. whore, which 3173
Re 19:5 that fear him, both small and g.. 3173
Re 19:6 the voice of a g. multitude, and 4183
Re 19:17 unto the supper of the g. God; 3173
Re 19:18 free and bond, both small and g.. 3173
Re 20:1 and a g. chain in his hand. 3173
Re 20:11 I saw a g. white throne, and him 3173
Re 20:12 I saw the dead, small and g., 3173
Re 21:3 I heard a g. voice out of heaven 3173
Re 21:10 spirit to a g. and high mountain, 3173
Re 21:10 and shewed me that g. city, 3173
Re 21:12 had a wall g. and high, and had 3173

GREATER

Ge 1:16 the g. light to rule the day, and 1419
Ge 4:13 punishment is g. than I can bear. 1419
Ge 39:9 none g. in this house than I; 1419
Ge 41:40 throne will I be g. than thou 1431
Ge 48:19 shall be g. than he, and his seed 1431
Ex 18:11 the Lord is g. than all gods; 1419
Nu 14:12 make of thee a g. nation and 1419
De 1:28 The people is g. and taller than 1419
De 4:38 thee g. and mightier than thou art, 1419
De 7:1 seven nations g. and mightier 7227
De 9:1 nations g. and mightier than 1419
De 9:14 nation mightier and g. than they. 7227
De 11:23 ye shall possess g. nations and 1419
Jos 10:2 because it was g. than Ai, and all 1419
1Sa 14:30 not been now a much g. slaughter 7235
2Sa 13:15 g. than the love wherewith he had 1419
2Sa 13:16 g. than the other that thou didst 1419
1Ki 1:37 and make his throne g. than thee
1Ki 1:47 and make his throne g. than thy
1Ch 11:9 So David waxed g. and...: for the 1980
1Ch 11:9 and g.; for the Lord of hosts was 1419
2Ch 3:5 And the g. house he cieled with 1419
Es 9:4 this man Mordecai waxed g. and 1419
Es 9:4 this man Mordecai waxed...and g..
Job 33:12 thee, that God is g. than man 7235
La 4:6 people is g. than the punishment 1431
Eze 8:6 thou shalt see g. abominations. 1419
Eze 8:13 shalt see g. abominations that 1419
Eze 8:15 shalt see g. abominations than 1419
Eze 43:14 lesser settle even to the g. settle 1419
Da 11:13 a multitude g. than the former, 7227
Am 6:2 their border g. than your border? 7227
Hag 2:9 house shall be g. than the former, 1419
Mt 11:11 hath not risen a g. than John the 3187
Mt 11:11 kingdom of heaven is g. than he. 3187
Mt 12:6 place is one g. than the temple. 3187
Mt 12:41 behold, a g. than Jonas is here 1419
Mt 12:42 behold, a g. than Solomon is here. 1419
Mt 23:14 ye shall receive the g. damnation 4055
Mt 23:17 for whether is g., the gold, or the 3187
Mt 23:19 whether is g., the gift, or the 3187
Mk 4:32 becometh g. than all herbs, and 3187
Mk 12:31 none other commandment g. than 3187
Mk 12:40 these shall receive g. damnation 4055
Lu 7:28 there is not a g. prophet than 3187
Lu 7:28 is g. than he. 3187
Lu 11:31 behold, a g. than Solomon is here. 4119
Lu 11:32 behold, a g. than Jonas is here 4119
Lu 12:18 pull down my barns, and build g.; 3187
Lu 20:47 same shall receive g. damnation. 4055
Lu 22:27 For whether is g., he that sitteth 3187
Joh 1:50 thou shalt see g. things than these. 3187
Joh 4:12 Art thou g. than our father Jacob, 3187
Joh 5:20 g. works than these, that ye may 3187
Joh 5:36 But I have g. witness than that 3187
Joh 8:53 thou g. than our father Abraham. 3187
Joh 10:29 them me, is g. than all; and no 3187
Joh 13:16 The servant is not g. than his lord; 3187
Joh 13:16 neither he that is sent g. than he 3187
Joh 14:12 g. works than these shall he do; 3187
Joh 14:28 for my Father is g. than I. 3187
Joh 15:13 G. love hath no man than this, 3187
Joh 15:20 The servant is not g. than his 3187
Joh 19:11 me unto thee hath the g. sin 3187
Ac 15:28 to lay upon you no g. burden than 4119
1Co 14:5 for g. is he that prophesieth than 3187
1Co 15:6 g. part remain unto this present, 4119
Heb 6:13 could swear by no g., he sware by 3187
Heb 6:16 for men verily swear by the g.: 3187
Heb 9:11 a g. and more perfect tabernacle, 3187
Heb 11:26 reproach of Christ g. riches than 3187

Jas 3:1 shall receive the **g.** condemnation........*3187*
2Pe 2:11 which are **g.** in power and might,........*3187*
1Jo 3:20 God is **g.** than our heart, and............*3187*
1Jo 4:4 because **g.** is he that is in you, than....*3187*
1Jo 5:9 of men, the witness of God is **g.**:..........*3187*
3Jo 4 I have no **g.** joy than to hear that........*3186*

GREATEST
1Ch 12:14 an hundred, and the **g.** over a........... 1419
1Ch 12:29 the **g.** part of them had kept the.........4768
Job 1:3 was the **g.** of all the men of the...........1419
Jer 6:13 the least even unto the **g.** of them...... 1419
Jer 8:10 the least even unto the **g.** is given...... 1419
Jer 31:34 least of them unto the **g.** of them,.......1419
Jer 42:1 the least even unto the **g.**, came.........1419
Jer 42:8 people from the least even to the **g.**,....1419
Jer 44:12 the least even unto the **g.**, by the.......1419
Jon 3:5 the **g.** of them even to the least of......1419
Mt 13:32 **g. among herbs, and becometh**.......*3187*
Mt 18:1 Who is the **g.** in the kingdom of...........*3187*
Mt 18:4 **the same is g. in the kingdom of**...*3187*
Mt 23:11 **But he that is g. among you shall**..*3187*
Mr 9:34 themselves, who should be the **g.**........*3187*
Lu 9:46 which of them should be **g.**,.................*3187*
Lu 22:24 of them should be accounted the **g.** *3187*
Lu 22:26 **but he that is g. among you, let**......*3187*
Ac 8:10 heed, from the least to the **g.**,............*3173*
1Co 13:13 but the **g.** of these is charity..............*3187*
Heb 8:11 know me, from the least to the **g.**........*3173*

GREATLY
Ge 3:16 I will **g.** multiply thy sorrow and................
Ge 7:18 were increased **g.** upon the earth;....... 3966
Ge 19:3 pressed upon them **g.**; and they.............3966
Ge 24:35 Lord hath blessed my master **g.**;......... 3966
Ge 32:7 Jacob was **g.** afraid and distressed:...... 3966
Ex 19:18 and the whole mount quaked **g.**.......... 3966
Nu 11:10 anger of the Lord was kindled **g.**;....... 3966
Nu 14:39 Israel: and the people mourned **g.**......... 3966
De 15:4 for the Lord shall **g.** bless thee.................
De 17:17 neither shall he **g.** multiply to............3966
Jos 10:2 they feared **g.**, because Gibeon............3966
Jg 2:15 and they were **g.** distressed...............3966
Jg 6:6 And Israel was **g.** impoverished......... 3966
1Sa 11:6 and his anger was kindled **g.**.............. 3966
1Sa 11:15 all the men of Israel rejoiced **g.**........... 3966
1Sa 12:18 all the people **g.** feared the Lord........3966
1Sa 16:21 he loved him **g.**; and he became.......... 3966
1Sa 17:11 they were dismayed, and **g.** afraid....... 3966
1Sa 28:5 afraid, and his heart **g.** trembled......... 3966
1Sa 30:6 And David was **g.** distressed; for........ 3966
2Sa 10:5 because the men were **g.** ashamed:..... 3966
2Sa 12:5 anger was **g.** kindled against the......... 3966
2Sa 24:10 have sinned **g.** in that I have done:......3966
1Ki 2:12 his kingdom was established **g.**........... 3966
1Ki 5:7 of Solomon, that he rejoiced **g.**,.......... 3966
1Ki 18:3 (Now Obadiah feared the Lord **g.**:......... 3966
1Ch 4:38 house of their fathers increased **g.**........7230
1Ch 16:25 and **g.** to be praised: he also is...........3966
1Ch 19:5 for the men were **g.** ashamed.............3966
1Ch 21:8 said unto God, I have sinned **g.**,.......... 3966
2Ch 25:10 was **g.** kindled against Judah, and........ 3966
2Ch 33:12 and humbled himself **g.** before the....... 3966
Job 3:25 thing which I **g.** feared is come.................
Job 8:7 thy latter end should **g.** increase......... 3966
Ps 21:1 salvatin how **g.** shall he rejoice!............ 3966
Ps 28:7 therefore my heart **g.** rejoiceth; and.........
Ps 38:6 I am bowed down **g.**; I go.................. 3966
Ps 45:11 So shall the king **g.** desire thy..................
Ps 47:9 belong unto God: he is **g.** exalted........3966
Ps 48:1 and **g.** to be praised in the city...........3966
Ps 62:2 defence; I shall not be **g.** moved........ 7227
Ps 65:9 thou **g.** enrichest it with the..............7227
Ps 71:23 My lips shall **g.** rejoice when I.................
Ps 78:59 wroth, and **g.** abhorred Israel:............ 3966
Ps 89:7 God is **g.** to be feared in the...............7227
Ps 96:4 and **g.** to be praised: he is to............ 3966
Ps 105:24 And he increased his people **g.**;........... 3966
Ps 107:38 so that they are multiplied **g.**;............ 3966
Ps 109:30 I will **g.** praise the Lord with my.........3966
Ps 112:1 delighteth **g.** in his commandments...... 3966
Ps 116:10 have I spoken: I was **g.** afflicted:........ 3966
Ps 119:51 have had me **g.** in derision: yet........... 3966
Ps 145:3 the Lord, and **g.** to be praised;...........3966
Pr 23:24 father of the righteous shall **g.** rejoice:.......
Isa 42:17 they shall be **g.** ashamed, that..................
Isa 61:10 I will **g.** rejoice in the Lord, my soul.........
Jer 3:1 shall not that land be **g.** polluted?.............
Jer 4:10 surely thou hast **g.** deceived this...............
Jer 9:19 we are **g.** confounded, because we...... 3966
Jer 20:11 they shall be **g.** ashamed; for........... 3966
Eze 20:13 and my sabbaths they **g.** polluted:........ 3966
Eze 25:12 vengeance, and hath **g.** offended,..............
Da 5:9 was king Belshazzar **g.** troubled,......... 7690
Da 9:23 for thou art **g.** beloved: therefore.............
Da 10:11 man **g.** beloved, understand the word.........
Da 10:19 O man **g.** beloved, fear not:.....................
Ob 2 the heathen: thou art **g.** despised......... 3966
Zep 1:14 it is near, and hasteth **g.**, even........... 3966
Zec 9:9 Rejoice **g.**, O daughter of Zion;...........3966
Mt 27:14 that the governor marvelled **g.**............ *3029*
Mt 27:54 they feared **g.**, saying, Truly this........ *4970*
Mk 5:23 And besought him **g.**, saying, My........*4183*
Mk 5:38 and them that wept and wailed **g.**........*4183*
Mk 9:15 were **g.** amazed, and running to..........*1568*
Mk 12:27 **the living: ye therefore do g. err**.... *4183*
Joh 3:29 rejoiceth **g.** because of the...................*5479*
Ac 3:11 is called Solomon's, **g.** wondering,........ *1569*
Ac 6:7 multiplied in Jerusalem **g.**;.................. *4970*
1Co 16:12 **g.** desired him to come unto you.........*4183*
Php 1:8 how **g.** I long after you all in the.........*1971*
Php 4:10 I rejoiced in the Lord **g.**, that now...... *3171*
1Th 3:6 desiring **g.** to see us, as we also.........*1971*
2Ti 1:4 **G.** desiring to see thee, being............ *1971*
2Ti 4:15 he hath **g.** withstood our words.......... *3029*
1Pe 1:6 Wherein ye **g.** rejoice, though now for.......
2Jo 4 I rejoiced **g.** that I found of thy...........*3029*
3Jo 3 I rejoiced **g.**, when the brethren.......... *3029*

GREATNESS
Ex 15:7 And in the **g.** of thine excellency.........7230
Ex 15:16 by the **g.** of thine arm they................1419
Nu 14:19 unto the **g.** of thy mercy,.................. 1433
De 3:24 shew thy servant thy **g.**, and thy........ 1433
De 5:24 his glory and his **g.**, and we............... 1433
De 9:26 redeemed through thy **g.**, which......... 1433
De 11:2 his **g.**, his mighty hand, and his.......... 1433
De 32:3 Lord: ascribe ye **g.** unto our God....... 1433
1Ch 17:19 hast thou done all this **g.**, in............. 1420
1Ch 17:21 a name of **g.** and terribleness,............ 1420
1Ch 29:11 Thine, O Lord, is the **g.**, and............. 1420
2Ch 9:6 the **g.** of thy wisdom was not............. 4768
2Ch 24:27 and the **g.** of the burdens laid.............7230
Ne 13:22 according to the **g.** of thy mercy......... 7230
Es 10:2 the **g.** of Mordecai, whereunto the...... 1420
Ps 66:3 through the **g.** of thy power shall........ 7230
Ps 71:21 Thou shalt increase my **g.**, and........... 1420
Ps 79:11 according to the **g.** of thy power......... 1433
Ps 145:3 and his **g.** is unsearchable.................. 1420
Ps 145:6 acts: and I will declare thy **g.**............ 1420
Ps 150:2 according to his excellent **g.**.............. 1433
Pr 5:23 and in the **g.** of his folly he shall......... 7230
Isa 40:26 by the **g.** of his might, for that.......... 7230
Isa 57:10 wearied in the **g.** of thy way;............. 7230
Isa 63:1 travelling in the **g.** of his strength?...... 7230
Jer 13:22 For the **g.** of thine iniquity are.......... 7230
Eze 31:2 Whom art thou like in thy **g.**?............. 1433
Eze 31:7 Thus was he fair in his **g.**, in the......... 1433
Eze 31:18 in glory and in **g.** among the trees....... 1433
Da 4:22 for thy **g.** is grown, and reacheth........ 7238
Da 7:27 and the **g.** of the kingdom under......... 7238
Eph 1:19 **g.** of his power to us-ward who.......... *3174*

GREAT-OWL See GREAT and OWL.

GREAVES
1Sa 17:6 he had **g.** of brass upon his legs,......... 4697

GRECIA See also GRECIANS; GREECE.
Da 8:21 the rough goat is the king of **G.**:..........3120
Da 10:20 forth, lo, the prince of **G.** shall.......... 3120
Da 11:2 stir up all against the realm of **G.**......... 3120

GRECIANS See also GREEKS.
Joe 3:6 have ye sold unto the **G.**, that............3125
Ac 6:1 arose a murmuring of the **G.**.................*1675*
Ac 9:29 disputed against the **G.**: but............... *1675*
Ac 11:20 spake unto the **G.**, preaching............. *1675*

GREECE See also GRECIA.
Zec 9:13 O Zion, against thy sons, O **G.**,.............3120
Ac 20:2 exhortation, he came into **G.**,............... *1671*

GREEDILY
Pr 21:26 He coveteth **g.** all the day long:..........8378
Eze 22:12 and thou hast **g.** gained of thy...............
Jude 11 ran **g.** after the error of Balaam..........*1632*

GREEDINESS
Eph 4:19 to work all uncleanness with **g.**...........*4124*

GREEDY
Ps 17:12 as a lion that is **g.** of his prey,............3700
Pr 1:19 every one that is **g.** of gain;...............1214
Pr 15:27 He that is **g.** of gain troubleth his........1214
Isa 56:11 they are **g.** dogs which can......... 5794,5315
1Ti 3:3 no striker, not **g.** of filthy lucre;........... *866*
1Ti 3:8 much wine, not **g.** of filthy lucre;.......... *146*

GREEK See also GREEKS.
Mk 7:26 woman was a **G.**, a Syrophenician....... *1674*
Lu 23:38 of **G.**, and Latin, and Hebrew,.............*1673*
Joh 19:20 in Hebrew, and **G.**, and Latin...............*1676*
Ac 16:1 believed; but his father was a **G.**:....... *1672*
Ac 16:3 knew all that his father was a **G.**.........*1672*
Ac 21:37 Who said, Canst thou speak **G.**?......... *1676*
Ro 1:16 the Jew first, and also to the **G.**........... *1672*
Ro 10:12 between the Jew and the **G.**: for.........*1672*
Ga 2:3 who was with me, being a **G.**,..............*1672*
Ga 3:28 There is neither Jew nor **G.**, there...... *1672*
Col 3:11 there is neither **G.** nor Jew,.................*1672*
Re 9:11 in the **G.** tongue hath his name........... *1673*

GREEKS See also GRECIANS.
Joh 12:20 there were certain **G.** among............. *1672*
Ac 14:1 Jews and also of the **G.** believed........ *1672*
Ac 17:4 the devout **G.** a great multitude,........ *1672*
Ac 17:12 women which were **G.**, and of............ *1674*
Ac 18:4 persuaded the Jews and the **G.**............*1672*
Ac 18:17 the **G.** took Soshtenes, the chief...........*1672*
Ac 19:10 the Lord Jesus, both Jews and **G.**........ *1672*
Ac 19:17 known to all the Jews and **G.** also........ *1672*
Ac 20:21 to the Jews, and also to the **G.**,............*1672*
Ac 21:28 brought **G.** also into the temple,........... *1672*
Ro 1:14 I am debtor both to the **G.**, and to...... *1672*
1Co 1:22 and the **G.** seek after wisdom:............ *1672*
1Co 1:23 and unto the **G.** foolishness;................*1672*
1Co 1:24 which are called, both Jews and **G.**,...... *1672*

GREEN See also GREENISH.
Ge 1:30 have given every **g.** herb for meat:..... 3418
Ge 9:3 even as the **g.** herb have I given..........3418
Ge 30:37 Jacob took him rods of **g.** poplar,......... 3892
Ex 10:15 there remained not any **g.** thing.......... 3418
Le 2:14 of thy firstfruits **g.** ears of corn................
Le 23:14 parched corn, nor **g.** ears, until...............
De 12:2 the hills, and under every **g.** tree:........ 7488
Jg 16:7 seven **g.** withs that were never.......... 3892
Jg 16:8 seven **g.** withs which had not been....... 3892
1Ki 14:23 high hill, and under every **g.** tree........ 7488
2Ki 16:4 the hills, and under every **g.** tree......... 7488
2Ki 17:10 high hill, and under every **g.** tree:........ 7488
2Ki 19:26 and as the **g.** herb, as the grass on..... 3410
2Ch 28:4 the hills, and under every **g.** tree.......... 7488
Es 1:6 white, **g.**, and blue, hangings,.............3768
Job 8:16 He is **g.** before the sun, and his.......... 7373
Job 15:32 and his branch shall not be **g.**.............. 7488
Job 39:8 he searcheth after every **g.** thing........ 3387
Ps 23:2 me to lie down in **g.** pastures:............ 1877
Ps 37:2 grass, and wither as the **g.** herb.......... 3418
Ps 37:35 himself like a **g.** bay tree...................7488
Ps 52:8 am like a **g.** olive tree in the house..... 7488
Ca 1:16 yea, pleasant: also our bed is **g.**........... 7488
Ca 2:13 fig tree putteth forth her **g.** figs,..........6291
Isa 15:6 grass faileth, there is no **g.** thing........ 3418
Isa 37:27 and as the **g.** herb, as the grass.......... 3419
Isa 57:5 under every **g.** tree, slaying the.......... 7488
Jer 2:20 under every **g.** tree thou wanderest,..... 7488
Jer 3:6 under every **g.** tree, and there hath..... 7488
Jer 3:13 under every **g.** tree, and ye have........ 7488
Jer 11:16 A **g.** olive tree, fair, and of goodly....... 7488
Jer 17:2 the **g.** trees upon the high hills........... 7488
Jer 17:8 cometh, but her leaf shall be **g.**;.......... 7488
Eze 6:13 under every **g.** tree, and under............ 7488
Eze 17:24 have dried up the **g.** tree, and.............3892
Eze 20:47 shall devour every **g.** tree in thee,...... 3892
Ho 14:8 him: I am like a **g.** fir tree..................7488
Mr 6:39 by companies upon the **g.** grass............*5515*
Lu 23:31 **they do these things in a g. tree,**.....*5200*
Re 8:7 and all **g.** grass was burnt up.............*5515*
Re 9:4 neither any **g.** thing, neither any.......... *5515*

GREENISH
Le 13:49 if the plague be **g.** or reddish in.........3422

Le 14:37 hollow strakes, **g.** or reddish, which.... 3422

GREENNESS
Job 8:12 Whilst it is yet in his **g.**, and not cut 3

GREET See also GREETETH; GREETING.
1Sa 25:5 go to Nabal, and **g.** him in......... 7592,7965
Ro 16:3 **G.** Priscilla and Aquila my *782*
Ro 16:5 Likewise **g.** the church that is in ....
Ro 16:6 **G.** Mary; who bestowed much *782*
Ro 16:8 Amplias my beloved in the................ *782*
Ro 16:11 **G.** them that be of the household *782*
1Co 16:20 All the brethren **g.** you. **G.** ye *782*
2Co 13:12 **G.** one another with an holy kiss, ... *782*
Php 4:21 which are with me **g.** you.................. *782*
Col 4:14 physician, and Demas, **g.** you............ *782*
1Th 5:26 **G.** all the brethren with an holy.......... *782*
Tit 3:15 **G.** them that love us in the faith.......... *782*
1Pe 5:14 **G.** ye one another with a kiss of *782*
2Jo 13 of thy elect sister **g.** thee.................. *782*
3Jo 14 thee. **G.** the friends by name............. *782*

GREETETH
2Ti 4:21 Eubulus **g.** thee, and Pudens, ... *782*

GREETING See also GREETINGS.
Ac 15:23 send **g.** unto the brethren which *5463*
Ac 23:26 excellent governor Felix sendeth **g.**. ... *5463*
Jas 1:1 which are scattered abroad, **g.**........... *5463*

GREETINGS
Mt 23:7 **And g. in the markets, and to be**.... *783*
Lu 11:43 **synagogues and g. in the markets**... *783*
Lu 20:46 **love g. in the markets, and the**...... *783*

GREW
Ge 2:5 herb of the field before it **g.**:............ 6779
Ge 19:25 that which **g.** upon the ground............ 6780
Ge 21:8 the child **g.**, and was weaned: 1431
Ge 21:20 God was with the lad; and he **g.**, ... 1431
Ge 25:27 And the boys **g.**: and Esau was 1431
Ge 26:13 **g.** until he became very great:........... 1432
Ge 47:27 had possession therein, and **g.**,........... 6509
Ex 1:12 the more they multiplied and **g.**. 6555
Ex 2:10 And the child **g.**, and she brought....... 1431
Jg 11:2 and his wife's sons **g.** up, and they..... 1431
Jg 13:24 and the child **g.**, and the Lord 1431
1Sa 2:21 child Samuel **g.** before the Lord. 1431
1Sa 2:26 the child Samuel **g.** on, and was......... 1432
1Sa 3:19 And Samuel **g.**, and the Lord was 1431
2Sa 5:10 And David went on and **g.** great,..............
2Sa 12:3 it **g.** up together with him, and 1431
Eze 17:6 **g.**, and became a spreading vine 6779
Eze 17:10 wither in the furrows where it **g.**. 6780
Da 4:11 The tree **g.**, and was strong,and 7236
Da 4:20 tree that thou sawest, which **g.**. 7236
Mk 4:7 **thorns g. up, and choked it, and it**.. *305*
Mk 5:26 bettered, but rather **g.** worse, ... *2064*
Lu 1:80 And the child **g.**, and waxed strong...... *837*
Lu 2:40 And the child **g.**, and waxed strong...... *837*
Lu 13:19 **it g., and waxed a great tree**; *837*
Ac 7:17 people **g.** and multiplied in Egypt, ... *837*
Ac 12:24 the word of God **g.** and multiplied........ *837*
Ac 19:20 So mightily **g.** the word of God *837*

GREY (so most editions here) See also GRAY; GREYHEADED; GREYHOUND.
Pr 20:29 beauty of old men is the **g.** head. 7872

GREYHEADED (so most editions here)
Ps 71:18 Now also when I am old and **g.**, ... 7872

GREYHOUND
Pr 30:31 A **g.**; an he goat also, and a....... 2223,4975

GRIEF See also GRIEFS.
Ge 26:35 Which were a **g.** of mind unto Isaac.... 4786
1Sa 1:16 complaint and **g.** have I spoken.......... 3708
1Sa 25:31 this shall be no **g.** unto thee, nor 6330
2Ch 6:29 his own sore and his own **g.**,............ 4341
Job 2:13 saw that his **g.** was very great. 3511
Job 6:2 my **g.** were thoroughly weighed, ... 3708
Job 16:5 of my lips should asswage your **g.** ....
Job 16:6 I speak, my **g.** is not asswaged:.......... 3511
Ps 6:7 eye is consumed ecause of **g.**; 3708
Ps 31:9 mine eye is consumed with **g.**, yea, ... 3708
Ps 31:10 For my life is spent with **g.**,............... 3015
Ps 69:26 they talk to the **g.** of those whom 4341
Pr 17:25 A foolish son is a **g.** to his father, ... 3708
Ec 1:18 For in much wisdom is much **g.**: 3708
Ec 2:23 days are sorrows, and his travail **g.**; ... 3708
Isa 17:11 shall be a heap in the day of **g.**.......... 2470
Isa 53:3 sorrows, and acquainted with **g.**:.......... 2483
Isa 53:10 he hath put him to **g.**: when thou....... 2470
Jer 6:7 before me continually is **g.** and 2483
Jer 10:19 Truly this is a **g.**, and I must bear...... 2483
Jer 45:3 Lord hath added **g.** to my sorrow;...... 3015
La 3:32 though he cause **g.**, yet will he.......... 3013
Jon 4:6 head, to deliver him from his **g.**.......... 7451
2Co 2:5 if any have caused **g.**, he hath........... *3076*
Heb 13:17 do it with joy, and not with **g.**: *4727*
1Pe 2:19 conscience toward God endure **g.**,...... *3077*

GRIEFS
Isa 53:4 hath borne our **g.**, and carried our...... 2483

GRIEVANCE
Hab 1:3 and cause me to behold **g.**?.............. 5999

GRIEVE See also GRIEVED; GRIEVETH; GRIEVING.
1Sa 2:33 thine eyes, and to **g.** thine heart:......... 109
1Ch 4:10 from evil, that it may not **g.** me!........ 6087
Ps 78:40 wilderness, and **g.** him in the desert! .. 6087
La 3:33 willingly nor **g.** the children of 3013
Eph 4:30 And **g.** not the holy spirit of God, ... *3076*

GRIEVED
Ge 6:6 and it **g.** him at his heart,................. 6087
Ge 34:7 and the men were **g.**, and they were .. 6087
Ge 45:5 be not **g.**, nor angry with yourselves,... 6087
Ge 49:23 The archers have sorely **g.** him, ... 4843
Ex 1:12 And they were **g.** because of the 6973
De 15:10 thine heart shall not be **g.** when......... 7489
Jg 10:16 soul was **g.** for the misery of Israel. ... 7114
1Sa 1:8 thou not? and why is thy heart **g.**? 7489
1Sa 15:11 it **g.** Samuel; and he cried unto.......... 2734
1Sa 20:3 Jonathan know this, lest he be **g.**: 6087
1Sa 20:34 was **g.** for David, because his father... 6087
1Sa 30:6 the soul of all the people was **g.**, ... 4784
2Sa 19:2 the king was **g.** for his son. 6087
Ne 2:10 it **g.** them exceedingly that there........ 7489
Ne 8:11 the day is holy; neither be ye **g.**. 6087
Ne 13:8 And it **g.** me sore: therefore I cast..... 7489
Es 4:4 was the queen exceedingly **g.**; 2342
Job 4:2 with thee, wilt thou be **g.**?................. 3811
Job 30:25 was not my soul **g.** for the poor? 5701
Ps 73:21 Thus my heart was **g.**, and I was....... 2556
Ps 95:10 Forty years long was I **g.** with 6962
Ps 112:10 Tho wicked shall see it, and be **g.**; 3707
Ps 119:158 the transgressors, and was **g.**;............. 6962
Ps 139:21 am not I **g.** with those that rise up..... 6962
Isa 54:6 thee as a woman forsaken and **g.** 6087
Isa 57:10 hand; therefore thou wast not **g.**......... 2470
Jer 5:3 have not **g.**; thou hast consumed........ 2342
Da 7:15 I Daniel was **g.** in my spirit............... 3735
Da 11:30 he shall be **g.**, and return, ... 3512
Am 6:6 they are not **g.** for the affliction 2470
Mk 3:5 **g.** for the hardness of their hearts,...... *4818*
Mk 10:22 at that saying, and went away **g.**:....... 3076
Joh 21:17 Peter was **g.** because he said unto *3076*
Ac 4:2 **g.** that they taught the people, ... *1278*
Ac 16:18 Paul, being **g.**, turned and said to....... *1278*
Ro 14:15 if thy brother be **g.** with thy meat, ... *3076*
2Co 2:4 not that ye should be **g.**, but that....... *3076*
2Co 2:5 he hath not **g.** me, but in part: *3076*
Heb 3:10 I was **g.** with that generation,........... *4360*
Heb 3:17 with whom was he **g.** forty years?...... *4360*

GRIEVETH
Ru 1:13 for it **g.** me much for your sakes......... 4843
Pr 26:15 it **g.** him to bring it again to his 3811

GRIEVING
Eze 28:24 nor any **g.** thorn of all that are.......... 3510

GRIEVOUS
Ge 12:10 the famine was **g.** in the land............ 3515
Ge 18:20 and because their sin is very **g.**; 3513
Ge 21:11 the thing was very **g.** in Abraham's...... 7489
Ge 21:12 Let it not be **g.** in thy sight because ... 7489
Ge 41:31 following; for it shall be very **g.** 3515
Ge 50:11 is a **g.** mourning to the Egyptians:....... 3515
Ex 8:24 there came a **g.** swarm of flies 3515
Ex 9:3 there shall be a very **g.** murrain.......... 3515
Ex 9:18 will cause it to rain a very **g.** hail, ... 3515
Ex 9:24 fire mingled with the hail, very **g.**,........ 3515
Ex 10:14 coasts of Egypt; very **g.** were they; ... 3515
1Ki 2:8 cursed me with a **g.** curse in the........ 4834
1Ki 12:4 Thy father made our yoke **g.**............ 7185
1Ki 12:4 thou the **g.** service of thy father, ... 7186
2Ch 10:4 Thy father made our yoke **g.**: now 7185
2Ch 10:4 the **g.** servitude of thy father, ... 7186
Ps 10:5 His ways are always **g.**; thy.............. 2342
Ps 31:18 be put to silence; which speak **g.** 6277
Pr 15:1 wrath: but **g.** words stir up anger....... 6089
Pr 15:10 Correction is **g.** unto him that............ 7451
Ec 2:17 under the sun is **g.** unto me: for 7451
Isa 15:4 out; his life shall be **g.** unto him......... 3415
Isa 21:2 A **g.** vision is declared unto me;.......... 7186
Jer 6:28 They are all **g.** revolters,................. 5493
Jer 10:19 for my hurt! my wound is **g.**: 2470
Jer 14:17 a great breach, with a very **g.** blow. ... 2470
Jer 16:4 They shall die of **g.** deaths; they........ 8463
Jer 23:19 in fury, even a **g.** whirlwind: 2342
Jer 30:12 incurable, and thy wound is **g.**. 2470
Na 3:19 thy wound is **g.**: all that hear............ 2470
Mt 23:4 **heavy burdens and g. to be borne,**.. *1418*
Lu 11:46 **burdens g. to be borne, and ye**...... *1418*
Ac 20:29 shall **g.** wolves enter in among you, ... *926*
Ac 25:7 and **g.** complaints against Paul,............ *926*
Php 3:1 to me indeed is not **g.**, but for........... *3636*
Heb 12:11 seemeth to be joyous, but **g.**:............ *3077*
1Jo 5:3 and his commandments are not **g.**........ *926*
Re 16:2 noisome and **g.** sore upon the men..... *4190*

GRIEVOUSLY
Isa 9:1 afterward did more **g.** afflict her......... 3513
Jer 23:19 whirlwind: it shall fall **g.** upon 2342
La 1:8 Jerusalem hath **g.** sinned;.................... 2399
La 1:20 for I have **g.** rebelled: abroad the....... 4784
Eze 14:13 against me by trespassing **g.**, ... 4604
Mt 8:6 sick of the palsy, **g.** tormented. *1171*
Mt 15:22 daughter is **g.** vexed with a devil........ *2560*

GRIEVOUSNESS
Isa 10:1 that write **g.** which they have............ 5999
Isa 21:15 bent bow, and from the **g.** of war....... 3514

GRIND See also GRINDING; GROUND.
Jg 16:21 and he did **g.** in the prison house. 2912
Job 31:10 Then let my wife **g.** unto another, ... 2912
Isa 3:15 pieces, and **g.** the faces of the poor?... 2912
Isa 47:2 Take the millstones, and **g.** meal:......... 2912
La 5:13 They took the young men to **g.**. 2911
Mt 21:44 **shall fall, it will g. him to powder.**.*3039*
Lu 20:18 **shall fall, it will g. him to powder.**.*3039*

GRINDERS
Ec 12:3 the **g.** cease because they are few,..... 2912

GRINDING
Ec 12:4 when the sound of the **g.** is low,........ 2913
Mt 24:41 **Two women shall be g. at the mill;**..*229*
Lu 17:35 **Two women shall be g. together;** *229*

GRISLED
Ge 31:10 ringstraked, speckled, and **g.**,............ 1261
Ge 31:12 are ringstraked, speckled, and **g.**;......... 1261
Zec 6:3 forth chariot **g.** and bay horses. 1261
Zec 6:6 the **g.** go forth toward the south......... 1261

GROAN See also GROANED; GROANETH; GROANING.
Job 24:12 Men **g.** from out of the city, ... 5008
Jer 51:52 all her land the wounded shall **g.**.......... 602
Eze 30:24 he shall **g.** before him with the 5008
Joe 1:18 How do the beasts **g.**! the herds 584
Ro 8:23 we ourselves **g.** within ourselves,........ *4727*
2Co 5:2 in this we **g.**, earnestly desiring to *4727*
2Co 5:4 we that are in this tabernacle do **g.**, ... *4727*

GROANED
Joh 11:33 **g.** in the spirit, and was trouble, ... 1690

GROANETH
Ro 8:22 **g.** and travaileth in pain together........ *4959*

GROANING See also GROANINGS.
Ex 2:24 And God heard their **g.**, and God....... 5009
Ex 6:5 And I have also heard the **g.** of the 5009
Job 23:2 my stroke is heavier than my **g.**.......... 585
Ps 6:6 I am weary with my **g.**; all the............. 585
Ps 38:9 and my **g.** is not hid from thee............ 585
Ps 102:5 By reason of the voice of my **g.** my...... 585
Ps 102:20 To hear the **g.** of the prisoner;............ 603
Joh 11:38 therefore again **g.** in himself............... *1690*
Ac 7:34 and I have heard their **g.**, and *4726*

GROANINGS
Jg 2:18 because of their g. by reason of 5009
Eze 30:24 the g. of a deadly wounded man 5009
Ro 8:26 with g. which cannot be uttered. *4726*

GROPE See also GROPETH.
De 28:29 thou shalt g. at noonday, as the 4959
Job 5:14 g. in the noonday as in the night. 4959
Job 12:25 They g. in the dark without light, 4959
Isa 59:10 We g. for the wall like the blind, 1659
Isa 59:10 and we g. as if we had no eyes: 1659

GROPETH
De 28:29 as the blind g. in darkness, and 4959

GROSS
Isa 60:2 earth, and g. darkness the people: 6205
Jer 13:16 of death, and make it g. darkness 6205
Mt 13:15 **For this people's heart is waxed g.,** *3975*
Ac 28:27 the heart of this people is waxed g., *3975*

GROUND See also AGROUND; GROUNDED.
Ge 2:5 there was not a man to till the g. 127
Ge 2:6 and watered the whole face of the g. 127
Ge 2:7 formed man of the dust of the g., 127
Ge 2:9 out of the g. made the Lord God to 127
Ge 2:19 out of the g. the Lord God formed 127
Ge 3:17 cursed is the g. for thy sake; 127
Ge 3:19 bread, till thou return unto the g.; 127
Ge 3:23 to till the g. from whence he was 127
Ge 4:2 but Cain was a tiller of the g. 127
Ge 4:3 Cain brought of the fruit of the g. 127
Ge 4:10 blood crieth unto me from the g. 127
Ge 4:12 When thou tillest the g., it shall 127
Ge 5:29 the g. which the Lord hath cursed. 127
Ge 7:23 which was upon the face of the g., 127
Ge 8:8 abated from off the face of the g.; 127
Ge 8:13 behold, the face of the g. was dry. 127
Ge 8:21 I will not again curse the g. any 127
Ge 18:2 and bowed himself toward the g., 776
Ge 19:1 with his face toward the g.; 776
Ge 19:25 and that which grew upon the g., 127
Ge 33:3 himself to the g. seven times, 776
Ge 38:9 he spilled it on the g., lest that he 776
Ge 44:11 down every man his sack to the g., 776
Ge 44:14 and they fell before him on the g. 776
Ex 3:5 whereon thou standest is holy g. 127
Ex 4:3 And he said, Cast it on the g., 776
Ex 4:3 And he cast it on the g., 776
Ex 8:21 and also the g. whereon they are 127
Ex 9:23 the fire ran along upon the g.; 776
Ex 14:16 shall go on dry g. through the
Ex 14:22 midst of the sea upon the dry g.
Ex 16:14 as small as the hoar frost on the g. 776
Ex 32:20 the fire, and g. it to powder, 2912
Le 20:25 that creepeth on the g., which I 127
Nu 11:8 gathered it, and g. it in mills, 2912
Nu 16:31 g. clave asunder that was under 127
De 4:18 anything that creepeth on the g., 127
De 9:21 g. it very small, even until it was 2912
De 15:23 shalt pour it upon the g. as water. 776
De 22:6 in any tree, or on the g., whether 776
De 28:4 the fruit of thy g., and the fruit 127
De 28:11 the fruit of thy g., in the land 127
De 28:56 the sole of her foot upon the g. 776
Jos 3:17 stood firm on dry g. in the midst
Jos 3:17 Israelites passed over on dry g.,
Jos 24:32 a parcel of g. which Jacob bought 7704
Jg 4:21 fastened it into the g.: for he was 776
Jg 6:39 and upon all the g. let there be dew. 776
Jg 6:40 and there was dew on all the g. 776
Jg 13:20 and fell on their faces to the g. 776
Jg 20:21 Gibeah, and destroyed down to the g. 776
Jg 20:25 day, and destroyed down to the g. 776
Ru 2:10 bowed herself to the g., and said 776
1Sa 3:19 let none of his words fall to the g. 776
1Sa 5:4 was fallen upon his face to the g. 776
1Sa 8:12 and will set them to ear his g., 2758
1Sa 14:25 and there was honey upon the g. 7704
1Sa 14:32 calves, and slew them on the g.: 776
1Sa 14:45 one hair of his head fall to the g.; 776
1Sa 20:31 the son of Jesse liveth upon the g., 127
1Sa 20:41 fell on his face to the g., and bowed 776
1Sa 25:23 face, and bowed herself to the g., 776
1Sa 26:7 and his spear stuck in the g. at his 776
1Sa 28:14 and stooped with his face to the g., 776
2Sa 2:22 should I smite thee to the g.? 776
2Sa 8:2 casting them down to the g.; even 776
2Sa 14:4 she fell on her face to the g., and did 776
2Sa 14:14 water spilt on the g., which cannot 776
2Sa 14:22 Joab fell to the g. on his face, 776
2Sa 14:33 bowed himself on his face to the g. 776
2Sa 17:12 as the dew falleth on the g.; 127
2Sa 17:19 and spread g. corn thereon; 7383
2Sa 18:11 thou not smite him there to the g.? 776
2Sa 20:10 and shed out his bowels to the g., 776
2Sa 23:11 a piece of g. full of lentiles: and 7704
2Sa 23:12 stood in the midst of the g., and 2513
2Sa 24:20 the king on his face upon the g. 776
1Ki 1:23 the king with his face to the g. 776
1Ki 7:46 cast them, in the clay g. between 127
2Ki 2:8 so that they two went over on dry g.,
2Ki 2:15 themselves to the g. before him. 776
2Ki 2:19 is naught. and the g. barren 776
2Ki 4:37 bowed herself to the g., and took 776
2Ki 9:26 and cast him into the plat of g.,
2Ki 13:18 Smite upon the g.. And he smote 776
1Ch 11:13 was a parcel of g. full of barley; 7704
1Ch 21:21 to David with his face to the g. 776
1Ch 27:26 the field for tillage of the g. was 127
2Ch 4:17 king cast them, in the clay g. 127
2Ch 7:3 with their faces to the g. upon the 776
2Ch 20:18 his head with his face to the g.: 776
Ne 8:6 the Lord with their faces to the g. 776
Ne 10:35 to bring the firstfruits of our g., 127
Ne 10:37 the tithes of our g. unto the Levites, 127
Job 1:20 down upon the g., and worshipped, 776
Job 2:13 they sat down with him upon the g. 776
Job 5:6 doth trouble spring out of the g.; 127
Job 14:8 the stock thereof die in the g.; 6083
Job 16:13 poureth out my gall upon the g. 776
Job 18:10 The snare is laid for him in the g., 776
Job 38:27 To satisfy the desolate and waste g.;
Job 39:24 swalloweth the g. with fierceness 776
Ps 74:7 dwelling place of thy name to the g. 776
Ps 89:39 his crown by casting it to the g. 776
Ps 89:44 cast his throne down to the g. 776
Ps 105:35 and devoured the fruit of their g. 127
Ps 107:33 and the watersprings into dry g.;
Ps 107:35 and dry g. into watersprings. 127
Ps 143:3 hath smitten my life down to the g.; 776
Ps 147:6 casteth the wicked down to the g. 776
Isa 3:26 being desolate shall sit upon the g. 776
Isa 14:12 how art thou cut down to the g., 776
Isa 21:9 her gods he hath broken unto the g. 776
Isa 25:12 bring to the g., even to the dust, 776
Isa 26:5 he layeth it low, even to the g.; 776
Isa 28:24 and break the clods of his g.? 127
Isa 29:4 shalt speak out of the g., and thy 776
Isa 29:4 familiar spirit, out of the g., and 776
Isa 30:23 thou shalt sow the g. withal; 127
Isa 30:24 young asses that ear the g. shall eat 127
Isa 35:7 parched g. shall become a pool,
Isa 44:3 and floods upon the dry g.:
Isa 47:1 sit on the g.: there is no throne, 776
Isa 51:23 thou hast laid thy body as the g., 776
Isa 53:2 plant, and as a root out of a dry g.: 776
Jer 4:3 Break up your fallow g., and sow
Jer 7:20 and upon the fruit of the g.; 127
Jer 14:2 they are black unto the g.; 776
Jer 14:4 Because the g. is chat, for there 127
Jer 25:33 they shall be dung upon the g. 127
Jer 27:5 the beast that are upon the g. 776
La 2:2 hath brought them down to the g.: 776
La 2:9 Her gates are sunk into the g.; 776
La 2:10 sit upon the g., and keep silence: 776
La 2:10 hang down their heads to the g. 776
La 2:21 the old lie on the g. in the streets: 776
Eze 12:6 thy face, that thou see not the g.: 776
Eze 12:12 that he see not the g. with his eyes. 776
Eze 13:14 bring it down to the g., so that 776
Eze 19:12 she was cast down to the g., and the 776
Eze 19:13 wilderness, in a dry and thirsty g. 776
Eze 24:7 she poured it not upon the g., 776
Eze 26:11 garrisons shall go down to the g. 776
Eze 26:16 they shall sit upon the g., and 776
Eze 28:17 I will cast thee to the g., 776
Eze 38:20 every wall shall fall to the g. 776
Eze 41:16 and from the g. up to the windows, 776
Eze 41:20 From the g. unto above the door 776
Eze 42:6 and the middlemost from the g. 776
Eze 43:14 from the bottom upon the g. even 776
Da 8:5 earth, and touched not the g.: 776
Da 8:7 he cast him down to the g., and 776
Da 8:10 the host and of the stars to the g., 776
Da 8:12 it cast down the truth to the g.; 776
Da 8:18 sleep on my face toward the g.: 776
Da 10:9 my face, and my face toward the g. 776
Da 10:15 I set my face toward the g., 776
Ho 2:18 with the creeping things of the g.: 127
Ho 10:12 mercy; break up your fallow g.:
Am 3:14 be cut off, and fall to the g. 776
Ob 3 shall bring me down to the g.? 776
Hag 1:11 upon that which the g. bringeth 127
Zec 8:12 and the g. shall give her increase, 776
Mal 3:11 not destroy the fruits of your g.; 127
Mt 10:29 **shall not fall on the g. without** *1093*
Mt 13:8 **But other fell into good g., and** *1093*
Mt 13:23 **received seed into the good g. is** *1093*
Mt 15:35 multitude to sit down on the g. *1093*
Mk 4:5 **some fell on stony g., where it**
Mk 4:8 **other fell on good g., and did** *1093*
Mk 4:16 **which are sown on stony g., who,**
Mk 4:20 **they which are sown on good g.;** *1093*
Mk 4:26 **man should cast seed into the g.;** *1093*
Mk 8:6 people to sit down on the g.: *1093*
Mk 9:20 he fell on the g., and wallowed *1093*
Mk 14:35 fell on the g., and prayed that, if it *1093*
Lu 8:8 **other fell on good g., and sprang** *1093*
Lu 8:15 **But that on the good g. are they,** *1093*
Lu 12:16 **g. of a certain rich man brought** *5561*
Lu 13:7 **down; why cumbereth it the g.?** *1093*
Lu 14:18 **I have bought a piece of g., and I,** *68*
Lu 19:44 **shall lay thee even with the g.,** *1474*
Lu 22:44 of blood falling down to the g. *1093*
Joh 4:5 near to the parcel of g. that Jacob *5564*
Joh 8:6 with his finger wrote on the g., *1093*
Joh 8:8 stooped down, and wrote on the g. *1093*
Joh 9:6 he spat on the g., and made clay *5476*
Joh 12:24 **a corn of wheat fall into the g.** *1093*
Joh 18:6 went backward, and fell to the g. *5476*
Ac 7:33 where thou standest is holy g. *1093*
Ac 22:7 I fell unto the g., and heard *1475*
1Ti 3:15 the pillar and g. of the truth. *1477*

GROUNDED
Isa 30:32 every place where the g. staff 4145
Eph 3:17 ye, being rooted and g. in love, *2311*
Col 1:23 continue in the faith g. and settled, *2311*

GROVE See also GROVES.
Ge 21:33 And Abraham planted a g. in 815
De 16:21 Thou shalt not plant thee a g. 842
Jg 6:25 cut down the g. that is by it: 842
Jg 6:26 the wood of the g. which thou 842
Jg 6:28 the g. was cut down that was 842
Jg 6:30 he hath cut down the g. that was 842
1Ki 15:13 she had made an idol in a g.; 842
1Ki 16:33 Ahab made a g.; and Ahab did 842
2Ki 13:6 remained the g. also in Samaria.) 842
2Ki 17:16 even two calves, and made a g., 842
2Ki 21:3 and made a g., as did Ahab king 842
2Ki 21:7 set a graven image of the g. that 842
2Ki 23:4 for Baal, and for the g., and for 842
2Ki 23:6 he brought out the g. from the 842
2Ki 23:7 women wove hangings for the g. 842
2Ki 23:15 to powder, and burned the g. 842
2Ch 15:16 she had made an idol in a g.: 842

GROVES
Ex 34:13 images, and cut down their g. 842
De 7:5 images, and cut down their g., 842
De 12:3 and burn their g. with fire; 842
Jg 3:7 and served Baalim and the g. 842
1Ki 14:15 because they have made their g., 842
1Ki 14:23 and g., on every high hill, and 842
1Ki 18:19 prophets of the g. four hundred 842
2Ki 17:10 and g. in every high hill, and 842
2Ki 18:4 the images, and cut down the g., 842
2Ki 23:14 the images, and cut down the g., 842
2Ch 14:3 the images, and cut down the g., 842
2Ch 17:6 took away the high places, and g. 842
2Ch 19:3 thou hast taken away the g. 842
2Ch 24:18 fathers, and served g. and idols: 842
2Ch 31:1 in pieces, and cut down the g., 842
2Ch 33:3 and made g., and worshipped all 842
2Ch 33:19 and set up g. and graven images, 842
2Ch 34:3, 4 the g., and the carved images, 842
2Ch 34:7 altars and the g., and had beaten 842
Isa 17:8 either the g., or the images. 842

Isa 27:9 the **g.** and images shall not stand......... 842
Jer 17:2 their altars and their **g.** by the........... 842
Mic 5:14 I will pluck up thy **g.** out of the........... 842

GROW See also GREW; GROWETH; GROWN.
Ge 2:9 the Lord God to **g.** every tree........... 6779
Ge 48:16 and let them **g.** into a multitude......... 1711
Nu 6:5 locks of the hair of his head **g.**.......... 1431
Jg 16:22 the hair of his head began to **g.**......... 6779
2Sa 23:5 although he make it not to **g.**........... 6779
2Ki 19:29 such things as **g.** of themselves,......... 5599
Ezr 4:22 why should damage **g.** to the hurt...... 7680
Job 8:11 Can the rush **g.** up without mire?....... 1342
Job 8:11 can the flag **g.** without water?........... 1342
Job 8:19 out of the earth shall others **g.**.......... 6779
Job 14:19 washest away the things which **g.**....... 5599
Job 31:40 Let thistles **g.** instead of wheat,........ 3318
Job 39:4 good liking, they **g.** up with corn;....... 7235
Ps 92:12 shall **g.** like a cedar in Lebanon.......... 7685
Ps 104:14 causeth the grass to **g.** for the.......... 6779
Ps 147:8 who maketh grass to **g.** upon the......... 6779
Ec 11:5 how the bones do **g.** in the womb of.........
Isa 11:1 Branch shall **g.** out of his roots:.......... 6509
Isa 17:11 shalt thou make thy plant to **g.**,......... 7735
Isa 53:2 For he shall **g.** up before him............ 5927
Jer 12:2 they have taken root: they **g.**, yea,.... 3212
Jer 33:15 Branch of righteousness to **g.** up........ 6779
Eze 44:20 nor suffer their locks to **g.** long;........ 7971
Eze 47:12 this side and on that side, shall **g.**....... 5927
Ho 14:5 he shall **g.** as the lily, and cast........... 6524
Ho 14:7 as the corn, and **g.** as the vine:......... 6524
Jon 4:10 neither madest it **g.**; which came........ 1431
Zec 6:12 he shall **g.** up out of his place,........... 6779
Mal 4:2 and **g.** up as calves of the stall........... 6335
Mt 6:28 **the lilies of the field, how they g.;**... *837*
Mt 13:30 **both g. together until the harvest;**..*4886*
Mt 21:19 **no fruit g. on thee henceforward**... *1096*
Mk 4:27 **the seed should spring and g. up,**... *3373*
Lu 12:27 **Consider the lilies how they g.:**...... *837*
Ac 5:24 of them whereunto this would **g.**......... *1096*
Eph 4:15 may **g.** up into him in all things,.......... *837*
1Pe 2:2 the word, that ye may **g.** thereby:....... *837*
2Pe 3:18 **g.** in grace, and in the knowledge........ *837*

GROWETH
Ex 10:5 every tree which **g.** for you out of...... 6779
Le 13:39 freckled spot that **g.** in the skin;........ 6524
Le 25:5 That which **g.** of it own accord........... 5599
Le 25:11 reap that which **g.** of itself in it,......... 5599
De 29:23 beareth, nor any grass **g.** therein,...... 5927
Jg 19:9 the day **g.** to an end, lodge here,....... 2583
Job 38:38 When the dust **g.** into hardness,........ 3332
Ps 90:5 they are like grass which **g.** up........... 2498
Ps 90:6 morning it flourisheth, and **g.** up;....... 2498
Ps 129:6 which withereth afore it **g.** up:.......... 8025
Isa 37:30 eat this year such as **g.** of itself;........ 5599
Mk 4:32 **when it is sown, it g. up, and**......... *305*
Eph 2:21 **g.** unto an holy temple in the Lord;...... *837*
2Th 1:3 that your faith **g.** exceedingly,........... *5232*

GROWN
Ge 38:11 house, till Shelah my son be **g.**........... 1431
Ge 38:14 she saw that Shelah was **g.**, and........ 1431
Ex 2:11 when Moses was **g.**, that he went...... 1431
Ex 9:32 smitten: for they were not **g.** up.......... 648
Le 13:37 there is black hair **g.** up therein;........ 6779
De 32:15 thou art waxen fat, thou art **g.** thick,........
Ru 1:13 tarry for them till they were **g.**?........ 1431
2Sa 10:5 until your beards be **g.**, and then....... 6779
1Ki 12:8 that were **g.** up with him, and........... 1431
1Ki 12:10 that were **g.** up with him spake......... 1431
2Ki 4:18 And when the child was **g.**, it fell....... 1431
2Ki 19:26 as corn blasted before it be **g.** up....... 6965
1Ch 19:5 at Jericho until your beards be **g.**,...... 6779
Ezr 9:6 our trespass is **g.** up unto the........... 1431
Ps 144:12 as plants **g.** up in their youth;........... 1431
Pr 24:31 it was all **g.** over with thorns,............ 5927
Isa 37:27 as corn blasted before it be **g.** up......... 6965
Jer 50:11 are **g.** fat as the heifer at grass,........ 6335
Eze 16:7 are fashioned, and thine hair is **g.**,....... 6779
Da 4:22 that are **g.** and become strong:.......... 7236
Da 4:22 for thy greatness is **g.**,...................... 7236
Da 4:33 till his hairs were **g.** like eagles'......... 7236
Mt 13:32 **when it is g., it is the greatest**........ *837*

GROWTH
Am 7:1 the shooting up of the latter **g.**;......... 3954
Am 7:1 and, lo, it was the latter **g.** after........ 3954

GRUDGE See also GRUDGING.
Le 19:18 bear any **g.** against the children......... 5201
Ps 59:15 and **g.** if they be not satisfied............ 3885
Jas 5:9 **G.** not one against another,............... *4727*

GRUDGING
1Pe 4:9 one to another without **g.**................. *1112*

GRUDGINGLY
2Co 9:7 not **g.**, or of necessity:............. *1537,3077*

GUARD See also GUARDS; SAFEGUARD.
Ge 37:36 Pharaoh's, and captain of the **g.**......... 2876
Ge 39:1 of Pharaoh, captain of the **g.**, an........ 2876
Ge 40:3 the house of the captain of the **g.**,...... 2876
Ge 40:4 the **g.** charged Joseph with them,....... 2876
Ge 41:12 servant to the captain of the **g.**;......... 2876
2Sa 23:23 And David set him over his **g.**........... 4928
1Ki 14:27 the hands of the chief of the **g.**,.......... 7323
1Ki 14:28 that the **g.** bare them, and brought..... 7323
1Ki 14:28 them back into the **g.** chamber........... 7323
2Ki 10:25 that Jehu said to the **g.** and to the...... 7323
2Ki 10:25 the **g.** and the captains cast them....... 7323
2Ki 11:4 with the captains and the **g.**, and........ 7323
2Ki 11:6 third part at the gate behind the **g.**:.... 7323
2Ki 11:11 And the **g.** stood, every man with...... 7323
2Ki 11:13 Athaliah heard the noise of the **g.**........ 7323
2Ki 11:19 the captains, and the **g.**, and all......... 7323
2Ki 11:19 gate of the **g.** to the king's house....... 7323
2Ki 25:8 Nebuzar-adan, captain of the **g.**,......... 2876
2Ki 25:10 that were with the captain of the **g.**,... 2876
2Ki 25:11 the captain of the **g.** carry away......... 2876
2Ki 25:12 the captain of the **g.** left of the poor... 2876
2Ki 25:15 the captain of the **g.** took away......... 2876
2Ki 25:18 the captain of the **g.** took Seraiah....... 2876
2Ki 25:20 captain of the **g.** took these, and........ 2876
1Ch 11:25 and David set him over his **g.**,............ 4928
2Ch 12:10 the chief of the **g.**, that kept the........ 7323
2Ch 12:11 the **g.** came and fetched them,.......... 7323
2Ch 12:11 them again into the **g.** chamber.......... 7323
Ne 4:22 in the night they may be a **g.** to us,... 4929
Ne 4:23 men of the **g.** which followed me,....... 4929
Jer 39:9 the captain of the **g.** carried away....... 2876
Jer 39:10 the captain of the **g.** left of the poor... 2876
Jer 39:11 Nebuzar-adan the captain of the **g.**,..... 2876
Jer 39:13 the captain of the **g.** sent, and........... 2876
Jer 40:1 the captain of the **g.** had let him go.... 2876
Jer 40:2 the captain of the **g.** took Jeremiah,.... 2876
Jer 40:5 captain of the **g.** gave him victuals..... 2876
Jer 41:10 captain of the **g.** had committed......... 2876
Jer 43:6 the captain of the **g.** had left with....... 2876
Jer 52:12 the captain of the **g.**, which served....... 2876
Jer 52:14 the captain of the **g.**, brake down....... 2876
Jer 52:15 the captain of the **g.** carried away....... 2876
Jer 52:16 the captain of the **g.** left certain of...... 2876
Jer 52:19 took the captain of the **g.** away.......... 2876
Jer 52:24 the captain of the **g.** took Seraiah....... 2876
Jer 52:26 the captain of the **g.** took them,......... 2876
Jer 52:30 the captain of the **g.** carried away....... 2876
Eze 38:7 thee, and be thou a **g.** unto them....... 4929
Da 2:14 Arioch the captain of the king's **g.**,..... *2877*
Ac 28:16 prisoners to the captain of the **g.**:...... *4759*

GUARD'S
Ge 41:10 in the captain of the **g.** house,........... 2876

GUDGODAH (gud-go'-dah) See also HOR-HAGID-GAD.
De 10:7 unto **G.**; and from **G.** to Jotbath,........ 1412

GUEST See also GUESTCHAMBER; GUESTS.
Lu 19:7 gone to be **g.** with a man that is........ *2647*

GUESTCHAMBER
Mk 14:14 **The Master saith, Where is the g.,**.*2646*
Lu 22:11 **saith unto thee, Where is the g.,**... *2646*

GUESTS
1Ki 1:41 Adonijah and all the **g.** that were........ 7121
1Ki 1:49 the **g.** that were with Adonijah........... 7121
Pr 9:18 her **g.** are in the depths of hell.......... 7121
Zep 1:7 a sacrifice, he hath bid his **g.**............. 7121
Mt 22:10 **the wedding was furnished with g.**.. *345*
Mt 22:11 **when the king came to see the g.,**.. *345*

GUIDE See also GUIDED; GUIDES; GUIDING.
Job 38:32 canst thou **g.** Arcturus with his.......... 5148
Ps 25:9 The meek will he **g.** in judgment:....... 1869
Ps 31:3 name's sake lead me, and **g.** me........ 5095
Ps 32:8 I will **g.** thee with mine eye.............. 3289
Ps 48:14 he will be our **g.** even unto death....... 5090
Ps 55:13 my **g.**, and mine acquaintance............. 441
Ps 73:24 Thou shalt **g.** me with thy counsel,...... 5148
Ps 112:5 will **g.** his affairs with discretion......... 3557
Pr 2:17 forsaketh the **g.** of her youth,............. 441
Pr 6:7 having no **g.**, overseer, or ruler,......... 7101
Pr 11:3 of the upright shall **g.** them:............... 5148
Pr 23:19 and **g.** thine heart in the way............... 833
Isa 49:10 springs of water shall he **g.** them....... 5095
Isa 51:18 There is none to **g.** her among all...... 5095
Isa 58:11 And the Lord shall **g.** thee................ 5148
Jer 3:4 thou art the **g.** of my youth?............... 441
Mic 7:5 put ye not confidence in a **g.**:.............. 441
Lu 1:79 **g.** our feet into the way of peace....... *2720*
Joh 16:13 **he will g. you into all truth:**......... *3594*
Ac 1:16 was **g.** to them that took Jesus.......... *3595*
Ac 8:31 except some man should **g.** me?......... *3594*
Ro 2:19 art a **g.** of the blind, a light of........... *3595*
1Ti 5:14 **g.** the house, give none occasion........ *3616*

GUIDED
Ex 15:13 thou hast **g.** them in thy strength........ 5095
2Ch 32:22 other, and **g.** them on every side........ 5095
Job 31:18 a father, and I have **g.** her from......... 5148
Ps 78:52 and **g.** them in the wilderness............ 5090
Ps 78:72 **g.** them by the skilfulness of his......... 5148

GUIDES
Mt 23:16 **Woe unto you, ye blind g., which**.. *3595*
Mt 23:24 **Ye blind g., which strain at a gnat**.*3595*

GUIDING
Ge 48:14 Manasseh's head, **g.** his hands................

GUILE See also BEGUILE.
Ex 21:14 to slay him with **g.**; thou shalt........... 6195
Ps 32:2 in whose spirit there is no **g.**............. 7423
Ps 34:13 and thy lips from speaking **g.**............. 4820
Ps 55:11 deceit and **g.** depart not from her........ 4820
Joh 1:47 **Israelite indeed, in whom is no g.!** .*1388*
2Co 12:16 being crafty, I caught you with **g.**....... *1388*
1Th 2:3 nor of uncleanness, nor in **g.**:............ *1388*
1Pe 2:1 laying aside all malice, and all **g.**,........ *1388*
1Pe 2:22 neither was **g.** found in his mouth:....... *1388*
1Pe 3:10 his lips that they speak no **g.**:............ *1388*
Re 14:5 in their mouth was found no **g.**:.......... *1388*

GUILT See also GUILTLESS.
De 19:13 shalt put away the **g.** of innocent.............
De 21:9 put away the **g.** of innocent blood............

GUILTINESS See also BLOODGUILTINESS.
Ge 26:10 shouldest have brought **g.** upon us....... 817

GUILTLESS
Ex 20:7 the Lord will not hold him **g.**............. 5352
Nu 5:31 the man be **g.** from iniquity,............... 5352
Nu 32:22 be **g.** before the Lord, and before...... 5355
De 5:11 the Lord will not hold him **g.**............. 5352
Jos 2:19 upon his head, and we will be **g.**:....... 5355
1Sa 26:9 the Lord's anointed, and be **g.**?.......... 5352
2Sa 3:28 I and my kingdom are **g.**.................. 5355
2Sa 14:9 the king and his throne be **g.**............. 5355
1Ki 2:9 hold him not **g.**: for thou art............. 5352
Mt 12:7 **would not have condemned the g.**... *338*

GUILTY
Ge 42:21 verily **g.** concerning our brother,......... 816
Ex 34:7 and that will by no means clear the **g.**........
Le 4:13 should not be done, and are **g.**;........... 816
Le 4:22 should not be done, and is **g.**;............. 816
Le 4:27 ought not to be done, and be **g.**;......... 816
Le 5:2 he also shall be unclean, and **g.**........... 816
Le 5:3 knoweth of it, then he shall be **g.**......... 816
Le 5:4 then he shall be **g.** in one of these........ 816
Le 5:5 he shall be **g.** in one of these things,.... 816
Le 5:17 he wist it not, yet is he **g.**,................ 816
Le 6:4 he hath sinned, and is **g.**, that he........ 816
Nu 5:6 the Lord, and that person be **g.**;......... 816
Nu 14:18 and by no means clearing the **g.**,..............
Nu 35:27 he shall not be **g.** of blood:......................
Nu 35:31 a murderer, which is **g.** of death:....... 7563
Jg 21:22 at this time, that ye should be **g.**.......... 816
Ezr 10:19 wives; and being **g.**, they offered.......... 816
Pr 30:10 curse thee, and thou be found **g.**......... 816
Eze 22:4 Thou art become **g.** in thy blood.......... 816
Zec 11:5 hold themselves not **g.**: and they......... 816
Mt 23:18 **gift that is upon it, he is g.**......... *3784*
Mt 26:66 and said, He is **g.** of death................ *1777*
Mk 14:64 condemned him to be **g.** of death........ *1777*
Ro 3:19 world may become **g.** before God........ *5267*
1Co 11:27 shall be **g.** of the body and blood........ *1777*
Jas 2:10 offend in one point, he is **g.** of all....... *1777*

GULF
Lu 16:26 and you there is a great **g.** fixed: .. *5490*

GUNI (gu'-ni) See also GUNITES.
Ge 46:24 Jahzeel, and **G.** and Jezer, and ... 1476
Nu 26:48 of **G.**, the family of the Gunites: ... 1476
1Ch 5:15 the son of **G.**, chief of the house of ... 1476
1Ch 7:13 Jahziel, and **G.**, and Jezer, and ... 1476

GUNITES (gu'-nites)
Nu 26:48 of Guni, the family of the **G.**: ... 1477

GUR (gur) See also GUR-BAAL.
2Ki 9:27 they did so at the going up to **G.**, ... 1483

GUR-BAAL (gur-ba'-al)
2Ch 26:7 the Arabians that dwelt in , ... 1485

GUSH See also GUSHED.
Jer 9:18 our eyelids **g.** out with waters. ... 5140

GUSHED
1Ki 18:28 till the blood **g.** out upon them ... 8210
Ps 78:20 that the waters **g.** out, and the ... 2100
Ps 105:41 and the waters **g.** out; they ran in ... 2100
Isa 48:21 rock also, and the waters **g.** out. ... 2100
Ac 1:18 midst, and all his bowels **g.** out ... *1632*

GUTTER See also GUTTERS.
2Sa 5:8 Whosoever getteth up to the **g.** ... 6794

GUTTERS
Ge 30:38 pilled before the flocks in the **g.** ... 7298
Ge 30:41 the eyes of the cattle in the **g.** ... 7298

H.

HA See also AHA.
Job 39:25 **H.**, **h.**; and he smelleth the ... 1889

HAAHASHTARI (ha-a-hash'-te-ri)
1Ch 4:6 Hepher, and Temeni, and **H.** ... 326

HAAMMONAI See CHEPHAR-HAAMMONAI.

HABAIAH hab-ah'-yah)
Ezr 2:61 the children of **H.**, the children of ... 2252
Ne 7:63 the children of **H.**, the children of ... 2252

HABAKKUK (hab'-ak-kuk)
Hab *title* **H.** ... 2265
Hab 1:1 The burden which **H.** the prophet ... 2265
Hab 3:1 A prayer of **H.** the prophet upon ... 2265

HABAZINIAH (hab-az-in-i'-ah)
Jer 35:3 Jeremiah, the son of **H.**, and his ... 2262

HABERGEON See also HABERGEONS.
Ex 28:32 as it were the hole of an **h.**, ... 8473
Ex 39:23 robe, as the hole of an **h.**, ... 8473
Job 41:26 the spear, the dart, nor the **h.** ... 8302

HABERGEONS
2Ch 26:14 helmets, and **h.**, and bows, and ... 8302
Ne 4:16 shields, and the bows, and the **h.**; ... 8302

HABITABLE
Pr 8:31 in the **h.** part of his earth; ... 8398

HABITATION See also HABITATIONS.
Ex 15:2 and I will prepare him an **h.**; ... 5115
Ex 15:13 in thy strength unto the holy **h.** ... 5116
Le 13:46 without the camp shall his **h.** be ... 4186
De 12:5 even unto his **h.** shall ye seek, ... 7933
De 26:15 Look down from thy holy **h.**, ... 4583
1Sa 2:29 I have commanded n my **h.**; ... 4583
1Sa 2:32 shalt see an enemy in my **h.**, ... 4583
2Sa 15:25 shew me both it, and his **h.**: ... 5116
2Ch 6:2 have built an house of **h.** for thee, ... 2073
2Ch 29:6 their faces from the **h.** of the Lord, ... 4908
Ez 7:15 Israel, whose **h.** is in Jerusalem, ... 4907
Job 5:3 root: but suddenly I cursed his **h.**, ... 5116
Job 5:24 thou shalt visit thy **h.**, and shalt ... 5116
Job 8:6 **h.** of thy righteousness prosperous. ... 5116
Job 18:15 shall be scattered upon his **h.** ... 5116
Ps 26:8 I have loved the **h.** of thy house, ... 4583
Ps 33:14 From the place of his **h.** he looketh ... 3427
Ps 68:5 the widows, is God in his holy **h.** ... 4583
Ps 69:25 Let their **h.** be desolate; and let ... 2918
Ps 71:3 Be thou my strong **h.**, whereunto ... 4583
Ps 89:14 judgment...the **h.** of thy throne: ... 4349
Ps 91:9 refuge, even the most High, thy **h.**; ... 4583
Ps 97:2 judgment are the **h.** of his throne. ... 4349
Ps 104:12 fowls of the heaven have their **h.**, ... 7931
Ps 107:7 that they might go to a city of **h.**, ... 4186
Ps 107:36 that they may prepare a city for **h.**; ... 4186
Ps 132:5 **h.** for the mighty God of Jacob. ... 4908
Ps 132:13 he hath desired it for his **h.** ... 4186
Pr 3:33 but he blesseth the **h.** of the just. ... 5116
Isa 22:16 graveth an **h.** for himself in a rock? ... 4908
Isa 27:10 and the **h.** forsaken, and left like ... 5116
Isa 32:18 people shall dwell in a peaceable **h.**, ... 5116
Isa 33:20 eyes shall see Jerusalem a quiet **h.**, ... 5116
Isa 34:13 and it shall be an **h.** of dragons, ... 5116
Isa 35:7 in the **h.** of dragons, where each ... 5116
Isa 63:15 behold from the **h.** of thy holiness ... 2073
Jer 9:6 Thine **h.** is in the midst of deceit; ... 3427
Jer 10:25 and have made his **h.** desolate. ... 5116
Jer 25:30 utter his voice from his holy **h.**; ... 4583
Jer 25:30 shall mighty roar upon his **h.**; ... 5116
Jer 31:23 O **h.** of justice, and mountain of ... 5116
Jer 33:12 an **h.** of shepherds causing their ... 5116
Jer 41:17 dwelt in the **h.** of Chimham, ... 1628
Jer 49:19 against the **h.** of the strong: ... 5116
Jer 50:7 the **h.** of justice, even the Lord, ... 5116
Jer 50:19 I will bring Israel again to his **h.**, ... 5116
Jer 50:44 Jordan unto the **h.** of the strong; ... 5116
Jer 50:45 he shall make their **h.** desolate ... 5116
Eze 29:14 Pathros, into the land of their **h.**; ... 4351
Da 4:21 fowls of the heaven had their **h.** ... 7932
Ob 3 whose **h.** is high; that saith in his ... 3427
Hab 3:11 and moon stood still in their **h.** ... 2073
Zec 2:13 is raised up out of his holy **h.** ... 4583
Ac 1:20 Let his **h.** be desolate, and let no ... *1886*
Ac 17:26 and the bounds of their **h.**; ... *2733*
Eph 2:22 for an **h.** of God through the ... *2732*
Jude 6 but left their own **h.**, he hath ... *3613*
Re 18:2 and is become the **h.** of devils, ... *2732*

HABITATIONS
Ge 36:43 according to their **h.** in the land of ... 4186
Ge 49:5 of cruelty are in their **h.** ... 4380
Ex 12:20 in all your **h.** shall ye eat ... 4186
Ex 35:3 kindle no fire throughout your **h.** ... 4186
Le 23:17 Ye shall bring out of your **h.** two ... 4186
Nu 15:2 the land of your **h.**, which I give ... 4186
1Ch 4:33 These were their **h.**, and their ... 4186
1Ch 4:41 the **h.** that were found there, ... 4583
1Ch 7:28 possessions and **h.** were, Beth-el ... 4186
Ps 74:20 are full of the **h.** of cruelty. ... 4999
Ps 78:28 their camp, round about their **h.**, ... 4908
Isa 54:2 forth the curtains of thine **h.**: ... 4908
Jer 9:10 and for the **h.** of the wilderness ... 4999
Jer 21:13 or who shall enter into our **h.**? ... 4585
Jer 25:37 the peaceable **h.** are cut down ... 4999
Jer 49:20 he shall make their **h.** desolate ... 5116
La 2:2 swallowed up all the **h.** of Jacob, ... 4999
Eze 6:14 toward Diblath, in all their **h.**: ... 4186
Am 1:2 **h.** of the shepherds shall mourn, ... 4999
Lu 16:9 receive you into everlasting **h** ... *4633*

HABOR (ha'-bor)
2Ki 17:6 placed him in Halah and in **H.** ... 2249
2Ki 18:11 put them in Halah and in **H.** by ... 2249
1Ch 5:26 brought them unto Halah, and **H.**, ... 2249

HACCEREM See BETH-HACCEREM.

HACHALIAH (hak-a-li'-ah)
Ne 1:1 words of Nehemiah the son of **H.** ... 2446
Ne 10:1 the Tirshatha, the son of **H.**, ... 2446

HACHILAH (hak'-i-lah)
1Sa 23:19 in the hill of **H.**, which is on the ... 2444
1Sa 26:1 David hide himself in the hill of **H.**, ... 2444
1Sa 26:3 Saul pitched in the hill of **H.**, ... 2444

HACHMONI (hak'-mo-ni) See also HACHMONITE.
1Ch 27:32 of **H.** was with the king's sons; ... 2453

HACHMONITE (hak'-mo-nite) See also TACHMONITE.
1Ch 11:11 Jashobeam, an **H.**, the chief of ... 2453

HAD See also HADST.
Ge 1:31 every thing that he **h.** made, and ...
Ge 2:2 ended his work which he **h.** made: ...
Ge 2:2 from all his work which he **h.** made. ...
Ge 2:3 in it he **h.** rested from all his work ...
Ge 2:5 the Lord God **h.** not caused it to rain ...
Ge 2:8 put the man whom he **h.** formed ...
Ge 2:22 which the Lord God **h.** taken from ...
Ge 3:1 which the Lord God **h.** made. ...
Ge 4:4 And the Lord **h.** respect unto Abel ...
Ge 4:5 Cain and his offering he **h.** not respect. ...
Ge 5:4 after he **h.** begotten Seth were ...
Ge 6:6 that he **h.** made man on the earth, ...
Ge 6:12 for all flesh **h.** corrupted his way upon ...
Ge 7:9 and the female, as God **h.** commanded ...
Ge 7:16 of all flesh, as God had commanded ...
Ge 8:6 window of the ark which he **h.** made: ...
Ge 9:24 what his younger son h. done unto ...
Ge 11:3 **h.** brick for stone, and slime **h.** ... 1961
Ge 11:30 But Sarai was barren; she **h.** no child ...
Ge 12:1 Now the Lord **h.** said unto Abram, ...
Ge 12:4 departed, as the Lord **h.** spoken unto ...
Ge 12:5 their substance that they **h.** gathered ...
Ge 12:5 and all the souls that they **h.** gotten ...
Ge 12:16 and he **h.** sheep, and oxen, and ... 1961
Ge 12:20 away, and his wife, and all that he **h.** ...
Ge 13:1 and all that he **h.**, and Lot with him, ...
Ge 13:3 his tent **h.** been at the beginning, ...
Ge 13:4 the altar, which he **h.** made there at ...
Ge 13:5 And Lot also,... **h.** flocks, and herds, .. 1961
Ge 14:13 there came one that **h.** escaped, ...
Ge 16:1 and she **h.** an handmaid, an Egyptian, ...
Ge 16:3 after Abram **h.** dwelt ten years in the ...
Ge 16:4, 5 when she saw that she **h.** conceived, ...
Ge 17:23 selfsame day, as God **h.** said unto him. ...
Ge 18:8 and the calf which he **h.** dressed, and ...
Ge 18:33 as soon as he **h.** left communing with ...
Ge 19:17 when they **h.** brought them forth ...
Ge 20:4 But Abimelech **h.** not come near ...
Ge 20:18 For the Lord God **h.** fast closed up all ...
Ge 21:1 Lord visited Sarah as he **h.** said, and ...
Ge 21:1 Lord did unto Sarah as he **h.** spoken ...
Ge 21:2 the set time of which God **h.** spoken ...
Ge 21:4 days old, as God **h.** commanded him. ...
Ge 21:9 which she **h.** born unto Abraham, ...
Ge 21:25 which Abimelech's servants **h.** violently ...
Ge 22:3 the place of which God **h.** told him. ...
Ge 22:9 to the place which God **h.** told him of; ...
Ge 23:16 the silver which he **h.** named in the ...
Ge 24:1 and the Lord **h.** blessed Abraham in ...
Ge 24:2 house, that ruled over all that he **h.**, ...
Ge 24:15 before he **h.** done speaking, that, ...
Ge 24:16 virgin, neither **h.** any man known her; ...
Ge 24:19 And when she **h.** done giving him ...
Ge 24:21 whether the Lord **h.** made his journey ...
Ge 24:22 as the camels **h.** done drinking, that ...
Ge 24:29 And Rebekah **h.** a brother, and his ...
Ge 24:45 And before I **h.** done speaking in ...
Ge 24:48 which **h.** led me in the right way to ...
Ge 24:65 For she **h.** said unto the servant, ...
Ge 24:65 the servant **h.** said, It is my master ...
Ge 24:66 told Isaac all things that he **h.** done. ...
Ge 25:5 Abraham gave all that he **h.** unto Isaac. ...
Ge 25:6 of the concubines, which Abraham **h.**, ...
Ge 26:8 when he **h.** been there a long time, ...
Ge 26:14 For he **h.** possession of flocks, and ...
Ge 26:15 his father's servants **h.** digged in the ...
Ge 26:15 Philistines **h.** stopped them, and filled ...
Ge 26:18 which they **h.** digged in the days of ...
Ge 26:18 names by which his father **h.** called ...
Ge 26:32 concerning the well which they **h.** ...
Ge 27:17 and the bread, which she **h.** prepared, ...
Ge 27:30 as soon as Isaac **h.** made an end of ...
Ge 27:31 And he also **h.** made savoury meat, ...
Ge 28:6 Esau saw that Isaac **h.** blessed Jacob, ...
Ge 28:9 unto the wives which he **h.**, Mahalath ...
Ge 28:18 took the stone that he **h.** put for his ...
Ge 29:16 Laban **h.** two daughters: the name of ...
Ge 29:20 a few days, for the love he **h.** to her. ...
Ge 30:9 Leah saw that she **h.** left bearing, ...
Ge 30:25 Rachel **h.** borne Joseph, that Jacob said ...
Ge 30:35 and every one that **h.** some white in it, ...

Ge 30:38 which he **h.** pilled before the flocks
Ge 30:43 exceedingly, and **h.** much cattle, 1961
Ge 31:18 all his goods which he **h.** gotten,
Ge 31:18 which he **h.** gotten in Padan-aram,
Ge 31:19 Rachel **h.** stolen the images that
Ge 31:21 he fled with all that he **h.**; and he rose
Ge 31:25 Jacob **h.** pitched his tent in the mount:
Ge 31:32 knew not that Rachel **h.** stolen them.
Ge 31:34 Now Rachel had taken the images,
Ge 31:42 fear of Isaac, **h.** been with me, surely
Ge 32:23 the brook, and sent over that he **h.**.
Ge 33:10 though I **h.** seen the face of God.
Ge 33:19 a field, where he **h.** spread his tent,
Ge 34:5 Jacob heard that he **h.** defiled Dinah
Ge 34:7 because he **h.** wrought folly in Israel
Ge 34:13 and said, because he **h.** defiled Dinah
Ge 34:19 thing, because he **h.** delight in Jacob's
Ge 34:27 spoiled the city, because they **h.** defiled.
Ge 35:16 Rachel travailed, and she **h.** hard.
Ge 36:6 his substance, which he **h.** got in the
Ge 38:15 to be an harlot, because she **h.** covered
Ge 38:30 his brother, that **h.** the scarlet thread
Ge 39:1 the Ishmeelites, which **h.** brought him
Ge 39:4 all that he **h.** he put into his hand 3426
Ge 39:5 the time he **h.** made him overseer 3426
Ge 39:5 his house, and over all that he **h.**, 3426
Ge 39:5 the Lord was upon all that he **h.** in 3426
Ge 39:6 he left all that he **h.** in Joseph's hand;
Ge 39:6 he knew not ought he **h.**, save the
Ge 39:13 saw that he **h.** left his garment in her
Ge 40:1 and his baker **h.** offended their lord
Ge 40:16 I **h.** three white baskets on my
Ge 40:22 as Joseph **h.** interpreted to them.
Ge 41:21 And when they **h.** eaten them up, it
Ge 41:21 not be known that they **h.** eaten them;
Ge 41:43 ride in the second chariot which he **h.**;
Ge 41:54 to come, according as Joseph **h.** said:
Ge 43:2 when they **h.** eaten up the corn which
Ge 43:2 **h.** brought out of Egypt, their father
Ge 43:6 the man whether ye **h.** yet a brother?
Ge 43:10 **h.** lingered, surely now we **h.** returned
Ge 43:23 in your sacks: I **h.** your money. 935
Ge 44:2 to the word that Joseph **h.** spoken.
Ge 45:27 the words of Joseph, which he **h.** said
Ge 45:27 wagons which Joseph **h.** sent to carry
Ge 46:1 took his journey with all that he **h.**,
Ge 46:5 wagons which Pharaoh **h.** sent to
Ge 46:6 their goods which they **h.** gotten in
Ge 47:11 Rameses, as Pharaoh **h.** commanded.
Ge 47:22 the priests **h.** a portion assigned them
Ge 47:27 **h.** possessions therein, and grew,
Ge 48:11 I **h.** not thought to see thy face:
Ge 49:33 when Jacob **h.** made an end of
Ge 50:14 returned...after he **h.** buried his
Ex 2:6 And when she **h.** opened it, she saw
Ex 2:6 And she **h.** compassion on him, and
Ex 2:16 priest of Midian **h.** seven daughters:
Ex 2:25 children of Israel, and God **h.** respect
Ex 4:28 words of the Lord who **h.** sent him,
Ex 4:28 signs which he **h.** commanded him.
Ex 4:30 all the words which the Lord **h.** spoken
Ex 4:31 they heard that the Lord **h.** visited the
Ex 4:31 that he **h.** looked upon their affliction,
Ex 5:14 Pharaoh's taskmasters **h.** set over
Ex 7:10 they did so as the Lord **h.** commanded:
Ex 7:13 hearkened not...as the Lord **h.** said.
Ex 7:22 hearken unto them; as the Lord **h.** said.
Ex 7:25 after that the Lord **h.** smitten the river.
Ex 8:12 of the frogs which he **h.** brought
Ex 8:15 hearkened not...as the Lord **h.** said.
Ex 8:19 hearkened not...as the Lord **h.** said,
Ex 9:12 hearkened not...as the Lord **h.** spoken
Ex 9:35 as the Lord **h.** spoken by Moses.
Ex 10:15 fruit of the trees which the hail **h.** left:
Ex 10:23 children of Israel **h.** light in their 1961
Ex 12:28 as the Lord **h.** commanded Moses
Ex 12:39 **h.** they prepared for themselves any
Ex 13:17 when Pharaoh **h.** let the people go,
Ex 13:19 for he **h.** straitly sworn the children
Ex 14:12 it **h.** been better for us to serve
Ex 15:25 when he **h.** cast into the waters,
Ex 16:3 would to God we **h.** died by the hand
Ex 16:18 that gathered much **h.** nothing over,
Ex 16:18 he that gathered little **h.** no lack; they
Ex 17:10 Joshua did as Moses **h.** said to him,
Ex 18:1 Jethro...heard of all that God **h.** done
Ex 18:1 that the Lord **h.** brought Israel out of
Ex 18:2 after he **h.** sent her back, and her
Ex 18:8 all that the Lord **h.** done unto Pharaoh
Ex 18:8 all the travail that **h.** come upon them
Ex 18:9 the goodness which the Lord **h.** done.
Ex 18:9 whom he **h.** delivered out of the hand
Ex 18:24 hearkened...and did all that he **h.** said.
Ex 19:2 desert of Sinai, and **h.** pitched in
Ex 31:18 Moses, when he **h.** made an end of
Ex 32:4 a graving tool, after he **h.** made
Ex 32:20 he took the calf which they **h.** made,
Ex 32:25 (for Aaron **h.** made them naked
Ex 32:29 For Moses **h.** said, Consecrate
Ex 33:5 the Lord **h.** said unto Moses, Say
Ex 34:4 Sinai, as the Lord **h.** commanded
Ex 34:32 all that the Lord **h.** spoken with him
Ex 34:33 And till Moses **h.** done speaking with
Ex 35:25 and brought that which they **h.** spun,
Ex 35:29 the Lord **h.** commanded to be made
Ex 36:1 to all that the Lord **h.** commanded.
Ex 36:2 heart the Lord **h.** put wisdom, even
Ex 36:3 the children of Israel **h.** brought for
Ex 36:7 stuff they **h.** was sufficient for all 1961
Ex 36:22 board **h.** two tenons, equally distant
Ex 39:43 **h.** done it as the Lord **h.** commanded,
Ex 39:43 so **h.** they done it: and Moses blessed
Ex 40:23 the Lord; as the Lord **h.** commanded
Le 10:5 out of the camp; as Moses **h.** said,
Le 10:19 if I **h.** eaten the sin offering to day,
Le 21:3 unto him, which **h.** no husband; 1961
Le 24:23 bring forth him that **h.** cursed out of
Nu 1:48 the Lord **h.** spoken unto Moses:
Nu 3:4 of Sinai, and they **h.** no children: 1961
Nu 7:1 on the day that Moses **h.** fully set up
Nu 7:1 and **h.** anointed them, and sanctified
Nu 8:4 the pattern which the Lord **h.** shewed
Nu 8:22 as the Lord **h.** commanded Moses
Nu 12:1 Ethiopian woman whom he **h.** married:
Nu 12:1 for he **h.** married an Ethiopian woman.
Nu 12:14 If her father **h.** but spit in her face,
Nu 13:32 of the land which they **h.** searched
Nu 14:2 Would God that we **h.** died in the
Nu 14:2 would God we **h.** died in this
Nu 14:24 he **h.** another spirit with him, 1961
Nu 16:31 as he **h.** made an end of speaking
Nu 16:39 they that were burnt **h.** offered;
Nu 20:3 Would God that we **h.** died when our
Nu 21:9 if a serpent **h.** bitten any man,
Nu 21:26 who **h.** fought against the former king
Nu 22:2 saw all that Israel **h.** done to the
Nu 22:33 unless she **h.** turned from me, surely
Nu 22:33 now also I **h.** slain thee, and saved
Nu 23:2 Balak did as Balaam **h.** spoken;
Nu 23:30 did as Balaam **h.** said, and offered
Nu 26:33 the son of Hepher **h.** no sons, 1961
Nu 26:65 For the Lord **h.** said of them, They
Nu 27:3 in his own sin, and **h.** no sons. 1961
Nu 30:6 And if she **h.** at all an husband, 1961
Nu 31:32 which the men of war **h.** caught,
Nu 31:35 that **h.** not known man by lying
Nu 31:53 (For the men of war **h.** taken spoil,
Nu 32:1 the children of Gad **h.** a very great 1961
Nu 32:9 land which the Lord **h.** given them.
Nu 32:13 all the generation, that **h.** done evil
Nu 33:4 firstborn, which the Lord **h.** smitten
De 1:3 all that the Lord **h.** given him in
De 1:4 After he **h.** slain Sihon the king
De 1:39 **h.** no knowledge between good
De 1:41 when ye **h.** girded on every man
De 2:12 when they **h.** destroyed them
De 7:8 the oath which he **h.** sworn unto
De 9:16 behold, ye **h.** sinned against the Lord
De 9:16 and **h.** made you a molten calf:
De 9:16 ye **h.** turned aside quickly out of the way
De 9:16 which the Lord **h.** commanded you
De 9:21 the calf which ye **h.** made,
De 9:25 the Lord **h.** said he would destroy you.
De 10:5 tables in the ark which I **h.** made;
De 10:15 the Lord **h.** a delight in thy fathers
De 19:19 as he **h.** thought to have done unto
De 29:26 whom he **h.** not given unto them:
De 31:24 Moses **h.** made an end of writing
De 32:30 except their Rock **h.** sold them,
De 32:30 and the Lord **h.** shut them up?
De 34:9 Moses **h.** laid his hands upon him:
Jos 2:6 she **h.** brought them up to the roof
Jos 2:6 she **h.** laid in order upon the roof.
Jos 2:11 as soon as we **h.** heard these things,
Jos 4:4 twelve men, whom he **h.** prepared of
Jos 5:1 Lord **h.** dried up the waters of Jordan
Jos 5:5 them they **h.** not circumcised.
Jos 5:7 because they **h.** not circumcised.
Jos 5:8 when they **h.** done circumcising all
Jos 5:12 after they **h.** eaten of the old corn
Jos 5:12 neither **h.** the children of Israel 1961
Jos 6:8 Joshua **h.** spoken unto the people,
Jos 6:10 And Joshua **h.** commanded the people,
Jos 6:22 Joshua **h.** said unto the two men
Jos 6:22 that **h.** spied out the country, Go into
Jos 6:23 and her brethren, and all that she **h.**;
Jos 6:25 father's household, and all that she **h.**:
Jos 7:7 we **h.** been content, and dwelt on the
Jos 7:24 and his tent, and all that he **h.**:
Jos 7:25 they **h.** stoned them with stones.
Jos 8:13 And when they **h.** set the people,
Jos 8:18 stretched out the spear that he **h.**
Jos 8:19 soon as he **h.** stretched out his hand:
Jos 8:20 and they **h.** no power to flee this way
Jos 8:21 that the ambush **h.** taken the city.
Jos 8:24 Israel **h.** made an end of slaying
Jos 8:26 until he **h.** utterly destroyed all the
Jos 8:33 as Moses...**h.** commanded before.
Jos 9:3 Joshua **h.** done unto Jericho and to Ai,
Jos 9:4 made as if they **h.** been ambassadors,
Jos 9:16 they **h.** made a league with them,
Jos 9:18 **h.** sworn unto them by the Lord God
Jos 9:21 as the princes **h.** promised them.
Jos 10:1 taken Ai, and **h.** utterly destroyed it;
Jos 10:1 as he **h.** done to Jericho and her king;
Jos 10:1 **h.** heard how Joshua **h.** taken Ai,
Jos 10:1 so he **h.** done to Ai and her king,
Jos 10:1 Gibeon **h.** made peace with Israel,
Jos 10:13 the people **h.** avenged themselves
Jos 10:20 children of Israel **h.** made an end of
Jos 10:27 the cave wherein they **h.** been hid,
Jos 10:32 all that he **h.** done to Libnah.
Jos 10:33 until he **h.** left none remaining.
Jos 10:35 to all which he **h.** done to Lachish.
Jos 10:37 to all that he **h.** done to Eglon;
Jos 10:39 as he **h.** done to Hebron, so he did to
Jos 10:39 as he **h.** done also to Libnah, and to
Jos 11:1 Jabin king of Hazar **h.** heard those
Jos 11:14 until they **h.** destroyed them, neither
Jos 14:3 For Moses **h.** given the inheritance of
Jos 14:15 And the land **h.** rest from war.
Jos 17:1 man of war, therefore he **h.** Gilead 1961
Jos 17:3 the son of Manasseh, **h.** no sons, 1961
Jos 17:6 daughters of Manasseh **h.**...inheritance
Jos 17:6 of Manasseh's sons **h.** the land 1961
Jos 17:8 Manasseh **h.** the...of Tappuah: 1961
Jos 17:11 Manasseh **h.** in Issachar and in 1961
Jos 18:2 seven tribes, which **h.** not yet received
Jos 19:2 **h.** in their inheritance Beer-sheba,
Jos 19:9 of Simeon **h.** their inheritance
Jos 19:49 they **h.** made an end of dividing
Jos 21:4 **h.** by lot out of the tribe of Judah, 1961
Jos 21:5 children of Kohath **h.** by lot out of
Jos 21:6 And the children of Gershon **h.** by lot
Jos 21:7 Merari by their families **h.** out of the
Jos 21:10 were of the children of Levi, **h.**: 1961
Jos 21:20 of Kohath, even they **h.** the cities 1961
Jos 21:45 the Lord **h.** spoken unto the house of
Jos 22:7 Moses **h.** given possession in Bashan:
Jos 23:1 the Lord **h.** given rest unto Israel
Jos 24:31 **h.** known all the works of the Lord.
Jos 24:31 Lord, that he **h.** done for Israel.
Jg 1:8 children of Judah **h.** fought
Jg 1:8 Jerusalem, and **h.** taken it, and
Jg 1:19 because they **h.** chariots of iron.
Jg 2:6 And when Joshua **h.** let the people go,
Jg 2:7 who **h.** seen all the great works of the
Jg 2:10 the works which he **h.** done for Israel.
Jg 2:15 Lord **h.** said, and as the Lord **h.** sworn
Jg 3:1 as **h.** not known all the wars of
Jg 3:11 And the land **h.** rest forty years.
Jg 3:12 because they **h.** done evil in the sight
Jg 3:16 him a dagger which **h.** two edges,
Jg 3:18 And when he **h.** made an end to
Jg 3:20 a summer parlour, which he **h.**
Jg 3:30 And the land **h.** rest fourscore years.
Jg 4:3 he **h.** nine hundred chariots of iron;
Jg 4:11 **h.** severed himself from the Kenites

Book	Ref	Context	No.
Jg	4:18	when he **h.** turned in unto her	
Jg	4:24	until they **h.** destroyed Jabin king of	
Jg	5:26	When she **h.** pierced and stricken	
Jg	5:31	And the land **h.** rest forty years	
Jg	6:3	Israel **h.** sown, that the Midianites	
Jg	6:27	and did as the Lord **h.** said unto him:	
Jg	7:19	and they **h.** but newly set the watch:	
Jg	8:3	abated toward him, when he **h.** said	
Jg	8:8	the me of Succoth **h.** answered him.	
Jg	8:19	if ye **h.** saved them alive, I would not	
Jg	8:24	(For they **h.** golden earrings, because	
Jg	8:30	Gideon **h.** threescore and ten sons of	
Jg	8:30	begotten: for he **h.** many wives.	1961
Jg	8:34	their God, who **h.** delivered them out	
Jg	8:35	which he **h.** shewed unto Israel.	
Jg	9:22	Abimelech **h.** reigned three years	
Jg	10:4	And he **h.** thirty sons that rode on	1961
Jg	10:4	and they **h.** thirty cities, which are	
Jg	11:34	her he **h.** neither son nor daughter.	
Jg	11:39	to his vow which he **h.** vowed:	
Jg	12:9	And he **h.** thirty sons, and thirty	1961
Jg	12:14	**h.** forty sons, and thirty nephews,	1961
Jg	14:4	Philistines **h.** dominion over Israel.	
Jg	14:6	a kid, and he **h.** nothing in his hand:	
Jg	14:6	father or his mother what he **h.** done.	
Jg	14:9	that he **h.** taken the honey out of the	
Jg	14:18	**h.** not plowed with my heifer,	
Jg	14:18	ye **h.** not found out my riddle.	
Jg	14:20	whom he **h.** used as his friend.	
Jg	15:5	And when he **h.** set the brands on fire.	
Jg	15:6	because he **h.** taken his wife, and	
Jg	15:17	when he **h.** made an end of speaking.	
Jg	15:19	and when he **h.** drunk, his spirit came	
Jg	16:8	which **h.** not been dried, and she	
Jg	16:18	saw that he **h.** told her all his heart.	
Jg	17:3	he **h.** restored the eleven hundred	
Jg	17:3	I **h.** wholly dedicated the silver	
Jg	17:5	the man Micah **h.** an house of gods,	
Jg	18:1	all their inheritance **h.** not fallen	
Jg	18:7	Zidonians, and **h.** no business with any	
Jg	18:27	took the things which Micah **h.** made,	
Jg	18:27	and the priest which he **h.**,	1961
Jg	18:28	they **h.** no business with any man;	
Jg	19:6	damsel's father **h.** said unto the man,	
Jg	19:17	And when he **h.** lifted up his eyes,	
Jg	20:36	liers in wait which they **h.** set beside	
Jg	21:1	men of Israel **h.** sworn in Mizpeh,	
Jg	21:5	they **h.** made a great oath concerning	
Jg	21:12	virgins that **h.** known no man by lying	
Jg	21:14	they **h.** saved alive of the women	
Jg	21:15	because that the Lord **h.** made a breach	
Ru	1:6	she **h.** heard in the country of Moab	
Ru	1:6	Lord **h.** visited his people in giving	
Ru	2:1	Naomi **h.** a kinsman of her husband's,	
Ru	2:17	beat out that she **h.** gleaned:	
Ru	2:18	in law saw what she **h.** gleaned:	
Ru	2:18	she **h.** reserved after she was sufficed.	
Ru	2:19	with whom she **h.** wrought, and said,	
Ru	3:7	And when Boaz **h.** eaten and drunk,	
Ru	3:16	all that the man **h.** done to her.	
1Sa	1:2	he **h.** two wives; the name of the one	
1Sa	1:2	Peninnah **h.** children, but Hannah	1961
1Sa	1:2	children, but Hannah **h.** no children.	
1Sa	1:5	but the Lord **h.** shut up her womb.	
1Sa	1:6	because the Lord **h.** shut up her womb.	
1Sa	1:9	rose up after they **h.** eaten in Shiloh,	
1Sa	1:9	and after they **h.** drunk.	
1Sa	1:13	Eli thought she **h.** been drunken.	
1Sa	1:20	after Hannah **h.** conceived, that she	
1Sa	1:24	And when she **h.** weaned him, she	
1Sa	3:8	that the Lord **h.** called the child.	
1Sa	4:18	And he **h.** judged Israel forty years.	
1Sa	5:9	after they **h.** carried it about, the	
1Sa	5:9	they **h.** emerods in their secret parts.	
1Sa	6:6	he **h.** wrought wonderfully among	
1Sa	6:16	lords of the Philistines **h.** seen it,	
1Sa	6:19	because they **h.** looked into the ark	
1Sa	6:19	because the Lord **h.** smitten many of	
1Sa	7:14	cities which the Philistines **h.** taken	
1Sa	9:2	he **h.** a son, whose name was Saul,	1961
1Sa	9:15	Now the Lord **h.** told Samuel in his	
1Sa	10:9	when he **h.** turned his back to go	
1Sa	10:13	And when he **h.** made an end of	
1Sa	10:20	Samuel **h.** caused all the tribes	
1Sa	10:21	he **h.** caused the tribe of Benjamin	
1Sa	10:26	of men, whose hearts God **h.** touched.	
1Sa	13:1	and when he **h.** reigned two years	
1Sa	13:4	that Saul **h.** smitten a garrison of	
1Sa	13:4	that Israel also was **h.** in abomination	
1Sa	13:8	set time that Samuel **h.** appointed:	
1Sa	13:10	soon as he **h.** made an end of offering	
1Sa	13:21	Yet they **h.** a file for the mattocks,	
1Sa	14:11	out of the holes where they **h.** hid,	
1Sa	14:17	And when they **h.** numbered, behold	
1Sa	14:22	which **h.** hid themselves in mount	
1Sa	14:24	Saul **h.** adjured the people, saying,	
1Sa	14:30	the people **h.** eaten freely to day	
1Sa	14:30	for **h.** there not been now a much	
1Sa	15:35	repented that he **h.** made Saul king	
1Sa	17:5	he **h.** an helmet of brass upon his head,	
1Sa	17:6	And he **h.** greaves of brass upon his	
1Sa	17:12	name was Jesse; and he **h.** eight sons:	
1Sa	17:20	and went, as Jesse **h.** commanded him;	
1Sa	17:21	the Philistines **h.** put the battle in	
1Sa	17:39	assayed to go; for he **h.** not proved it.	
1Sa	17:40	in a shepherd's bag which he **h.**, even	
1Sa	18:1	when he **h.** made an end of speaking	
1Sa	19:18	told him all that Saul **h.** done to him.	
1Sa	20:34	because his father **h.** done him shame.	
1Sa	20:37	of the arrow which Jonathan **h.** shot,	
1Sa	22:21	that Saul **h.** slain the Lord's priests,	
1Sa	24:5	because he **h.** cut off Saul's skirt	
1Sa	24:10	the Lord **h.** delivered thee to day into	
1Sa	24:16	when David **h.** made an end of speaking	
1Sa	24:18	when the Lord **h.** delivered me into	
1Sa	25:2	great, and he **h.** three thousand sheep,	
1Sa	25:21	Now David **h.** said, Surely in vain have	
1Sa	25:34	there **h.** not been left unto Nabal	
1Sa	25:35	received...that which she **h.** brought	
1Sa	25:37	and his wife **h.** told him these things,	
1Sa	25:44	But Saul **h.** given Michal his daughter,	
1Sa	26:5	to the place where Saul **h.** pitched:	
1Sa	28:3	was dead, and all Israel **h.** lamented	
1Sa	28:3	And Saul **h.** put away those that	
1Sa	28:3	those that **h.** familiar spirits,	
1Sa	28:20	for he **h.** eaten no bread all the day,	
1Sa	28:24	And the woman **h.** a fat calf in the	
1Sa	30:1	the Amalekites **h.** invaded the land	
1Sa	30:2	And **h.** taken the women captives, that	
1Sa	30:4	wept, until they **h.** no more power to	
1Sa	30:12	and when he **h.** eaten, his spirit came	
1Sa	30:12	for he **h.** eaten no bread, nor drunk	
1Sa	30:16	And when he **h.** brought him down,	
1Sa	30:16	spoil that they **h.** taken out of the land	
1Sa	30:18	that the Amalekites **h.** carried away:	
1Sa	30:19	any thing that they **h.** taken to them:	
1Sa	30:21	whom they **h.** made also to abide at the	
1Sa	31:11	which the Philistines **h.** done to Saul;	
2Sa	1:1	and David **h.** abode two days in Ziklag;	
2Sa	1:21	as though he **h.** not been anointed	
2Sa	2:27	the people **h.** gone up every one from	
2Sa	2:30	and when he **h.** gathered all the people	
2Sa	2:31	servants of David **h.** smitten of	
2Sa	3:7	And Saul **h.** a concubine, whose name	
2Sa	3:17	And Abner **h.** communication with the	
2Sa	3:22	for he **h.** sent him away, and he was	
2Sa	3:30	because he **h.** slain their brother	
2Sa	4:2	And Saul's son **h.** two men that	1961
2Sa	4:4	Saul's son, **h.** a son that was lame of	
2Sa	5:12	that the Lord **h.** established him king	
2Sa	5:12	and that he **h.** exalted his kingdom for	
2Sa	5:17	heard that they **h.** anointed David	
2Sa	5:25	so, as the Lord **h.** commanded him;	
2Sa	6:8	because the Lord **h.** made a breach	
2Sa	6:13	the ark of the Lord **h.** gone six paces,	
2Sa	6:17	the tabernacle that David **h.** pitched	
2Sa	6:18	as David **h.** made an end of offering	
2Sa	6:22	of them shall I be **h.** in honour.	
2Sa	6:23	the daughter of Saul **h.** no child unto	
2Sa	7:1	and the Lord **h.** given him rest round	
2Sa	8:9	that David **h.** smitten all the host of	
2Sa	8:10	because he **h.** fought against	
2Sa	8:10	for Hadadezer **h.** wars with Toi.	
2Sa	8:11	silver and gold that he **h.** dedicated	
2Sa	9:2	And when they **h.** called him unto	
2Sa	9:10	Now Ziba **h.** fifteen sons and twenty	
2Sa	9:12	And Mephibosheth **h.** a young son,	
2Sa	11:10	And when they **h.** told David, saying,	
2Sa	11:13	And when David **h.** called him, he did	
2Sa	11:22	David all that Joab **h.** sent him for.	
2Sa	11:27	that David **h.** done displeased the	
2Sa	12:2	The rich man **h.** exceeding many	1961
2Sa	12:3	But the poor man **h.** nothing, save one	
2Sa	12:3	ewe lamb, which he **h.** bought and	
2Sa	12:6	this thing, and because he **h.** no pity	
2Sa	12:8	if that **h.** been too little, I would	
2Sa	13:1	the son of David **h.** a fair sister	
2Sa	13:3	But Amnon **h.** a friend, whose name	
2Sa	13:10	took the cakes which she **h.** made,	
2Sa	13:11	And when she **h.** brought them unto	
2Sa	13:15	the love wherewith he **h.** loved her.	
2Sa	13:18	And she **h.** a garment of divers colours	
2Sa	13:22	because he **h.** forced his sister Tamar.	
2Sa	13:23	that Absalom **h.** sheepshearers in	
2Sa	13:28	Now Absalom **h.** commanded his	
2Sa	13:29	Amnon as Absalom **h.** commanded.	
2Sa	13:36	as he **h.** made an end of speaking,	
2Sa	14:2	woman that **h.** a long time mourned	
2Sa	14:6	and thy handmaid **h.** two sons, and	
2Sa	14:32	it **h.** been good for me to have been	
2Sa	14:33	and when he **h.** called for Absalom,	
2Sa	15:2	any man that **h.** a controversy	1961
2Sa	15:24	until all the people **h.** done passing	
2Sa	15:30	and **h.** his head covered, and he went	
2Sa	16:23	as if a man **h.** enquired at the oracle	
2Sa	17:14	For the Lord **h.** appointed to defeat	
2Sa	17:18	which **h.** a well in his court; whither	
2Sa	17:20	And when they **h.** sought and could	
2Sa	18:18	Absalom...**h.** taken and reared up	
2Sa	18:33	would God I **h.** died for thee, O	
2Sa	19:6	perceive, that if Absalom **h.** lived,	
2Sa	19:6	and all we **h.** died this day,	
2Sa	19:6	then it **h.** pleased thee well.	
2Sa	19:8	for Israel **h.** fled every man to his tent.	
2Sa	19:24	and **h.** neither dressed his feet, nor	
2Sa	19:32	and he **h.** provided the king of	
2Sa	19:43	our advice should not be first **h.** in	
2Sa	20:3	whom he **h.** left to keep the house,	
2Sa	20:5	the set time which he **h.** appointed	
2Sa	20:8	garment that he **h.** put on was girded	
2Sa	21:2	children of Israel **h.** sworn unto them;	
2Sa	21:11	Aiah, the concubine of Saul, **h.** done.	
2Sa	21:12	which **h.** stolen them from the street	
2Sa	21:12	where the Philistines **h.** hanged them,	
2Sa	21:12	when the Philistines **h.** slain Saul	
2Sa	21:15	the Philistines **h.** yet war again	1961
2Sa	21:20	that **h.** on every hand six fingers, and	
2Sa	22:1	the day that the Lord **h.** delivered him	
2Sa	22:38	turned not again until I **h.** consumed	
2Sa	23:8	the mighty men whom David **h.**: the	
2Sa	23:18	and slew them, and **h.** the name among	
2Sa	23:20	who **h.** done many acts, he slew two	
2Sa	23:21	the Egyptian **h.** a spear in his hand;	
2Sa	23:22	and **h.** the name among three mighty	
2Sa	24:8	So when they **h.** gone through all the	
2Sa	24:10	after that he **h.** numbered the people,	
1Ki	1:6	And his father **h.** not displeased him	
1Ki	1:41	heard it as they **h.** made an end of	
1Ki	2:28	for Joab **h.** turned after Adonijah,	
1Ki	2:41	that Shimei **h.** gone from Jerusalem to	
1Ki	3:1	until he **h.** made an end of building	
1Ki	3:10	Pleased...that Solomon **h.** asked this	
1Ki	3:21	but when I **h.** considered it in the	
1Ki	3:28	judgment which the king **h.** judged;	
1Ki	4:2	these were the princes which he **h.**:	
1Ki	4:7	And Solomon **h.** twelve officers over	
1Ki	4:11	which **h.** Taphath the daughter of	
1Ki	4:14	the son of Iddo **h.** Mahanaim:	
1Ki	4:24	For he **h.** dominion over all the region	
1Ki	4:24	and he **h.** peace on all sides	1961
1Ki	4:26	And Solomon **h.** forty thousand stalls	
1Ki	4:34	earth which **h.** heard of his wisdom.	
1Ki	5:1	for he **h.** heard that they **h.** anointed	
1Ki	5:15	And Solomon **h.** three score and	1961
1Ki	6:22	until he **h.** finished all the house:	
1Ki	7:8	daughter, whom he **h.** taken to wife,	
1Ki	7:8	house where he dwelt **h.** another	
1Ki	7:20	pillars **h.** pomegranates also above,	
1Ki	7:28	they **h.** borders, and the borders were	
1Ki	7:30	And every base **h.** four brazen wheels,	
1Ki	7:30	four corners thereof **h.** undersetters	
1Ki	7:37	all of them **h.** one casting, one	
1Ki	7:51	which David his father **h.** dedicated;	
1Ki	8:11	glory of the Lord **h.** filled the house	
1Ki	8:54	Solomon **h.** made an end of praying	
1Ki	8:66	that the Lord **h.** done for David his	
1Ki	9:1	when Solomon **h.** finished the building	
1Ki	9:2	as he **h.** appeared unto him at Gibeon.	
1Ki	9:10	when Solomon **h.** built two houses, the	
1Ki	9:11	Hiram...**h.** furnished Solomon with	
1Ki	9:12	see the cities which Solomon **h.** given	

1Ki 9:16 Pharaoh...**h.** gone up, and taken
1Ki 9:19 the cities of stone that Solomon **h.**, ... 1961
1Ki 9:24 her house which Solomon **h.** built for
1Ki 9:27 shipmen that **h.** knowledge of the sea,
1Ki 10:4 when the queen of Sheba **h.** seen all
1Ki 10:4 and the house that he **h.** built,
1Ki 10:7 until I came, and mine eyes **h.** seen it;
1Ki 10:15 Beside...he **h.** of the merchantmen,
1Ki 10:19 The throne **h.** six steps, and the
1Ki 10:22 For the king **h.** at sea a navy of
1Ki 10:24 wisdom, which God **h.** put in his heart
1Ki 10:26 and he **h.** a thousand and four
1Ki 10:28 And Solomon **h.** horses brought out of
1Ki 11:3 And he **h.** seven hundred wives, 1961
1Ki 11:9 God of Israel, which **h.** appeared unto
1Ki 11:10 And **h.** commanded him concerning
1Ki 11:15 after he **h.** smitten every male in
1Ki 11:16 until he **h.** cut off every male in
1Ki 11:29 **h.** clad himself with a new garment;
1Ki 12:8 counsel...which they **h.** given him
1Ki 12:12 as the king **h.** appointed, saying,
1Ki 12:32 unto the calves that he **h.** made:
1Ki 12:32 the high places which he **h.** made.
1Ki 12:33 upon the altar which he **h.** made in
1Ki 12:33 the month which he **h.** devised of his
1Ki 13:4 which **h.** cried against the altar in
1Ki 13:5 the sign which the man of God **h.** given
1Ki 13:11 the man of God **h.** done that day in
1Ki 13:11 the words which he **h.** spoken unto the
1Ki 13:12 For his sons **h.** seen what way the man
1Ki 13:23 came to pass, after he **h.** eaten bread,
1Ki 13:23 and after he **h.** drunk, that he saddled
1Ki 13:28 the lion **h.** not eaten the carcase, nor
1Ki 13:31 after he **h.** buried him, that he spake
1Ki 14:22 with their sins...they **h.** committed,
1Ki 14:22 above all that their fathers **h.** done.
1Ki 14:26 shields of gold...Solomon **h.** made.
1Ki 15:3 which he **h.** done before him: and his
1Ki 15:12 the idols that his fathers **h.** made.
1Ki 15:13 because she **h.** made an idol in a
1Ki 15:15 things which his father **h.** dedicated,
1Ki 15:15 which himself **h.** dedicated, into the
1Ki 15:20 the captains of the hosts which he **h.**
1Ki 15:22 timber...wherewith Baasha **h.** built:
1Ki 15:29 until he **h.** destroyed him, according
1Ki 16:31 as if it **h.** been a light thing for him
1Ki 16:32 house of Baal, which he **h.** built in
1Ki 17:7 because there **h.** been no rain in 1961
1Ki 19:1 told Jezebel all that Elijah **h.** done,
1Ki 19:1 how he **h.** slain all the prophets
1Ki 21:1 Naboth the Jezreelite **h.** a vineyard 1961
1Ki 21:4 which Naboth...**h.** spoken to him:
1Ki 21:4 for he **h.** said, I will not give thee the
1Ki 21:11 did as Jezebel **h.** sent unto them, and
1Ki 21:11 the letters which she **h.** sent unto them.
1Ki 22:31 that **h.** rule over his chariots, saying,
1Ki 22:53 according to all that his father **h.** done
2Ki 1:17 word of the Lord...Elijah **h.** spoken.
2Ki 1:17 of Judah; because he **h.** no son. 1961
2Ki 2:14 when he also **h.** smitten the waters,
2Ki 3:2 image of Baal that his father **h.** made.
2Ki 4:12, 15 when he **h.** called her, she stood
2Ki 4:17 season that Elijah **h.** said unto her.
2Ki 4:20 And when he **h.** taken him,
2Ki 5:1 the Lord **h.** given deliverance unto Syria:
2Ki 5:2 the Syrians **h.** gone out by companies,
2Ki 5:2 and **h.** brought away captive out of the
2Ki 5:7 king of Israel **h.** read the letter,
2Ki 5:8 Elisha the man of God **h.** heard
2Ki 5:8 that the king of Israel **h.** rent his
2Ki 5:13 if the prophet **h.** bid thee do some
2Ki 6:23 when they **h.** eaten and drunk,
2Ki 6:30 he **h.** sackcloth upon his flesh.
2Ki 7:6 For the Lord **h.** made the host
2Ki 7:15 which the Syrians **h.** cast away
2Ki 7:17 as the man of God **h.** said,
2Ki 7:18 as the man of God **h.** spoken
2Ki 8:1 woman, whose son he **h.** restored
2Ki 8:5 how he **h.** restored a dead body
2Ki 8:5 whose son he **h.** restored to life,
2Ki 8:29 wounds which the Syrians **h.** given him
2Ki 9:14 Now Joram **h.** kept Ramoth-gilead,
2Ki 9:15 wounds which the Syrians **h.** given him,
2Ki 9:31 she said, **H.** Zimri peace, who slew his
2Ki 10:1 And Ahab **h.** seventy sons in Samaria,
2Ki 10:17 till he **h.** destroyed him, according to
2Ki 10:25 soon as he **h.** made an end of offering
2Ki 11:15 For the priest **h.** said, Let her not
2Ki 12:6 the priests **h.** not repaired the
2Ki 12:11 that **h.** the oversight of the house of
2Ki 12:18 his fathers, kings of Judah, **h.** dedicated,
2Ki 13:7 king of Syria **h.** destroyed them,
2Ki 13:7 and **h.** made them like the dust
2Ki 13:23 and **h.** compassion on them, and
2Ki 13:23 **h.** respect unto them, because of his
2Ki 13:25 which he **h.** taken out of the hand
2Ki 14:5 servants which **h.** slain the king
2Ki 15:3 his father Amaziah **h.** done;
2Ki 15:9 as his fathers **h.** done:
2Ki 15:34 that his father Uzziah **h.** done.
2Ki 16:11 that king Ahaz **h.** sent from Damascus
2Ki 16:18 that they **h.** built in the house,
2Ki 17:4 for he **h.** sent messengers to So king
2Ki 17:4 as he **h.** done year by year:
2Ki 17:7 children of Israel **h.** sinned against
2Ki 17:7 which **h.** brought them up out of
2Ki 17:7 and **h.** feared other gods,
2Ki 17:8 which they **h.** made.
2Ki 17:12 whereof the Lord **h.** said unto them,
2Ki 17:15 concerning whom the Lord **h.** charged
2Ki 17:20 until he **h.** cast them out
2Ki 17:23 as he **h.** said by all his servants
2Ki 17:28 priests whom they **h.** carried away
2Ki 17:29 which the Samaritans **h.** made,
2Ki 17:35 the Lord **h.** made a covenant,
2Ki 18:4 serpent that Moses **h.** made:
2Ki 18:16 Hezekiah king of Judah **h.** overlaid,
2Ki 18:18 when they **h.** called to the king,
2Ki 19:8 for he **h.** heard that he was departed
2Ki 20:11 by which it **h.** gone down in the dial
2Ki 20:12 for he **h.** heard that Hezekiah
2Ki 20:12 heard that Hezekiah **h.** been sick.
2Ki 21:3 Hezekiah his father **h.** destroyed;
2Ki 21:7 of the grove that he **h.** made
2Ki 21:16 till he **h.** filled Jerusalem
2Ki 21:24 slew all them that **h.** conspired
2Ki 22:11 when the king **h.** heard the words of
2Ki 23:5 whom the kings of Judah **h.** ordained
2Ki 23:8 where the priests **h.** burned incense,
2Ki 23:11 kings of Judah **h.** given to the sun,
2Ki 23:12 which the kings of Judah **h.** made,
2Ki 23:12 altars which Manasseh **h.** made
2Ki 23:13 Solomon...king of Israel **h.** builded
2Ki 23:15 Nebat, who made Israel to sin, **h.** made,
2Ki 23:19 kings of Israel **h.** made to provoke
2Ki 23:19 acts that he **h.** done in Beth-el,
2Ki 23:26 Manasseh **h.** provoked him
2Ki 23:29 slew him...when he **h.** seen him
2Ki 23:32, 37 all that his fathers **h.** done.
2Ki 24:7 king of Babylon **h.** taken from the
2Ki 24:9 all that his father **h.** done.
2Ki 24:13 Solomon king of Israel **h.** made
2Ki 24:13 As the Lord **h.** said.
2Ki 24:19 all that Jehoiakim **h.** done,
2Ki 24:20 until he **h.** cast them out
2Ki 25:16 bases which Solomon **h.** made
2Ki 25:17 and like unto these **h.** the second pillar
2Ki 25:22 king of Babylon **h.** left,
2Ki 25:23 king of Babylon **h.** made Gedaliah
1Ch 2:22 begat Jair, who **h.** three and 1961
1Ch 2:26 Jerahmeel **h.** also another wife, whose
1Ch 2:34 Now Sheshan **h.** no sons, but 1961
1Ch 2:34 Sheshan **h.** a servant, an Egyptian,
1Ch 2:52 Kirjath-jearim **h.** sons; Haroeh, and
1Ch 4:5 Ashur the father of Tekoa **h.** two 1961
1Ch 4:22 and Saraph, who **h.** the dominion in
1Ch 4:27 And Shimei **h.** sixteen sons and six
1Ch 4:27 but his brethren **h.** not many children,
1Ch 4:40 they of Ham **h.** dwelt there of old.
1Ch 6:31 the Lord, after that the ark **h.** rest
1Ch 6:32 until Solomon **h.** built the house
1Ch 6:49 the servant of God **h.** commanded.
1Ch 6:66 the sons of Kohath **h.** cities of 1961
1Ch 7:4 for they **h.** many wives and sons
1Ch 7:15 and Zelophehad **h.** daughters. 1961
1Ch 8:8 after he **h.** sent them away;
1Ch 8:38 And Azel **h.** six sons, whose names are
1Ch 8:40 and **h.** many sons, and sons' sons, an
1Ch 9:23 they and their children **h.** the
1Ch 9:28 And certain of them **h.** the charge of
1Ch 9:31 the Korahite, **h.** the set office over the
1Ch 9:44 And Azel **h.** six sons, whose names are
1Ch 10:9 when they **h.** stripped him,
1Ch 10:11 Philistines **h.** done to Saul,
1Ch 10:13 counsel of one that **h.** a familiar
1Ch 11:10 mighty men whom David **h.**, who
1Ch 11:11 the mighty men whom David **h.**;
1Ch 11:20 he slew them, and **h.** a name 1961
1Ch 11:22 who **h.** done many acts;
1Ch 11:24 and **h.** the name among the three
1Ch 12:15 when it **h.** overflown all his banks;
1Ch 12:29 greatest part of them **h.** kept the ward
1Ch 12:32 were men that **h.** understanding of
1Ch 12:39 their brethren **h.** prepared for them.
1Ch 13:11 because the Lord **h.** made a breach
1Ch 13:14 house of Obed-edom, and all that he **h.**
1Ch 14:2 that the Lord **h.** confirmed him
1Ch 14:4 his children which he **h.** in 1961
1Ch 14:12 when they **h.** left their gods
1Ch 15:3 which he **h.** prepared for it.
1Ch 15:27 David also **h.** upon him an ephod of
1Ch 16:1 that David **h.** pitched for it:
1Ch 16:2 when David **h.** made an end
1Ch 18:9 how David **h.** smitten all
1Ch 18:10 because he **h.** fought against
1Ch 18:10 (for Hadarezer **h.** war with Tou;) 1961
1Ch 19:6 they **h.** made themselves odious
1Ch 19:17 when David **h.** put the battle
1Ch 21:28 Lord **h.** answered him
1Ch 23:11 but Jeush and Beriah **h.** not many
1Ch 23:17 And Eliezer **h.** none other sons; 1961
1Ch 23:22 And Eliezer died, and **h.** no sons, 1961
1Ch 24:2 died before their father, and **h.** no 1961
1Ch 24:19 God of Israel **h.** commanded him.
1Ch 24:28 Of Mahli came Eleazar, who **h.** no 1961
1Ch 26:9 And Meshelemiah **h.** sons and
1Ch 26:10 of the children of Merari, **h.** sons;
1Ch 26:26 captain of the host, **h.** dedicated
1Ch 26:28 Joab the son of Zeruiah, **h.** dedicated;
1Ch 26:28 and whosoever **h.** dedicated
1Ch 27:23 because the Lord **h.** said
1Ch 28:2 As for me, I **h.** in mine heart to
1Ch 28:2 and **h.** made ready for the building:
1Ch 28:12 of all that he **h.** by the spirit, of the
1Ch 29:25 majesty as **h.** not been on any 1961
2Ch 1:3 servant of the Lord **h.** made 1961
2Ch 1:4 ark of God **h.** David brought
2Ch 1:4 place which David **h.** prepared
2Ch 1:4 for he **h.** pitched a tent
2Ch 1:5 the son of Hur, **h.** made,
2Ch 1:12 such as none of the kings have **h.** 1961
2Ch 1:14 and he **h.** a thousand and four 1961
2Ch 1:16 Solomon **h.** horses brought
2Ch 2:17 David his father **h.** numbered
2Ch 3:1 that David **h.** prepared
2Ch 5:1 David his father **h.** dedicated:
2Ch 5:14 glory of the Lord **h.** filled
2Ch 6:13 Solomon **h.** made a brasen
2Ch 6:13 and **h.** set it in the midst
2Ch 7:1 when Solomon **h.** made an end of praying,
2Ch 7:2 glory of the Lord **h.** filled
2Ch 7:6 the king **h.** made to praise
2Ch 7:7 altar which Solomon **h.** made
2Ch 7:10 the Lord **h.** shewed unto David
2Ch 8:1 wherein Solomon **h.** built
2Ch 8:2 which Huram **h.** restored
2Ch 8:6 store cities that Solomon **h.**, 1961
2Ch 8:11 house that he **h.** built for her:
2Ch 8:12 which he **h.** built before the porch.
2Ch 8:14 for so **h.** David the man of God
2Ch 8:18 ships, and servants that **h.** knowledge
2Ch 9:3 queen of Sheba **h.** seen the wisdom
2Ch 9:3 and the house that he **h.** built,
2Ch 9:6 and mine eyes **h.** seen it:
2Ch 9:12 which she **h.** brought unto the king
2Ch 9:23 that God **h.** put into his heart.
2Ch 9:25 And Solomon **h.** four thousand 1961
2Ch 10:2 whither he **h.** fled from
2Ch 10:6 the old men that **h.** stood before 1961
2Ch 11:14 his sons **h.** cast them off
2Ch 11:15 calves which he **h.** made.
2Ch 12:1 when Rehoboam **h.** established
2Ch 12:1 the kingdom, and **h.** strengthened
2Ch 12:2 they **h.** transgressed against the Lord,
2Ch 12:9 which Solomon **h.** made.
2Ch 12:13 city which the Lord **h.** chosen
2Ch 14:6 for the land **h.** rest, and
2Ch 14:6 he **h.** no war in those years;
2Ch 14:6 because the Lord **h.** given him rest.
2Ch 14:8 And Asa **h.** an army of men that 1961
2Ch 15:8 which he **h.** taken from mount

2Ch 15:11 spoil which they **h.** brought,
2Ch 15:15 for they **h.** sworn with all their hearts
2Ch 15:16 she **h.** made an idol in a grove:
2Ch 15:18 things that his father **h.** dedicated,
2Ch 15:18 and that he himself **h.** dedicated,
2Ch 16:14 which he **h.** made for himself
2Ch 17:2 which Asa his father **h.** taken.
2Ch 17:5 and he **h.** riches and honour in 1961
2Ch 17:9 taught in Judah, and **h.** the book
2Ch 17:13 And he **h.** much business in the 1961
2Ch 18:1 Now Jehoshaphat **h.** riches, and
2Ch 18:2 and for the people that he **h.** with
2Ch 18:10 son of Chenaanah **h.** made him horns
2Ch 18:30 king of Syria **h.** commanded
2Ch 20:21 when he **h.** consulted with
2Ch 20:23 when they **h.** made an end
2Ch 20:27 the Lord **h.** made them to rejoice
2Ch 20:29 when they **h.** heard that the Lord
2Ch 20:33 the people **h.** not prepared
2Ch 21:2 And he **h.** brethren the sons of
2Ch 21:6 for he **h.** the daughter of Ahab to 1961
2Ch 21:7 that he **h.** made with David,
2Ch 21:10 because he **h.** forsaken the Lord
2Ch 22:1 to the camp **h.** slain all the eldest
2Ch 22:7 whom the Lord **h.** anointed to cut
2Ch 22:9 and when they **h.** slain him,
2Ch 22:9 So the house of Ahaziah **h.** no power
2Ch 23:8 Jehoiada the priest **h.** commanded,
2Ch 23:9 that **h.** been king David's,
2Ch 23:18 whom David **h.** distributed in the
2Ch 23:21 that they **h.** slain Athaliah
2Ch 24:7 wicked woman, **h.** broken up
2Ch 24:10 until they **h.** made an end.
2Ch 24:14 And when they **h.** finished it.
2Ch 24:16 because he **h.** done good in Israel,
2Ch 24:22 his father **h.** done to him,
2Ch 24:24 because they **h.** forsaken the Lord
2Ch 25:3 servants that **h.** killed the king
2Ch 26:5 Zechariah, who **h.** understanding
2Ch 26:10 for he **h.** much cattle, both in the 1961
2Ch 26:11 Moreover Uzziah **h.** an host of fighting
2Ch 26:19 and **h.** a censer in his hand to burn
2Ch 26:20 because the Lord **h.** smitten him.
2Ch 28:3 whom the Lord **h.** cast out
2Ch 28:6 they **h.** forsaken the Lord God
2Ch 28:17 the Edomites **h.** come and smitten
2Ch 28:18 Philistines also **h.** invaded
2Ch 28:18 and **h.** taken Beth-shemesh,
2Ch 29:2 that David his father **h.** done.
2Ch 29:22 when they **h.** killed the rams,
2Ch 29:29 when they **h.** made an end
2Ch 29:34 other priests **h.** sanctified themselves:
2Ch 29:36 that God **h.** prepared the people:
2Ch 30:2 for the king **h.** taken counsel,
2Ch 30:3 the priests **h.** not sanctified
2Ch 30:3 neither **h.** the people gathered
2Ch 30:5 for they **h.** not done it of a long
2Ch 30:17 therefore the Levites **h.** the charge of
2Ch 30:18 Zebulun, **h.** not cleansed themselves,
2Ch 31:1 until they **h.** utterly destroyed
2Ch 31:10 we have **h.** enough to eat, and have
2Ch 32:27 And Hezekiah **h.** exceeding much 1961
2Ch 32:29 for God **h.** given him substance
2Ch 33:2 whom the Lord **h.** cast out
2Ch 33:3 his father **h.** broken down,
2Ch 33:4 whereof the Lord **h.** said,
2Ch 33:7 the idol which he **h.** made,
2Ch 33:7 of which God **h.** said to David,
2Ch 33:9 whom the Lord **h.** destroyed
2Ch 33:15 altars that he **h.** built in the mount
2Ch 33:22 Manasseh his father **h.** made,
2Ch 33:23 Manasseh his father **h.** humbled
2Ch 33:25 all them that **h.** conspired against
2Ch 34:4 that **h.** sacrificed unto them
2Ch 34:7 when he **h.** broken down the altars
2Ch 34:7 and **h.** beaten the graven images
2Ch 34:8 when he **h.** purged the land,
2Ch 34:9 Levites that kept the doors **h.** gathered
2Ch 34:10 the workmen that **h.** the oversight of
2Ch 34:11 kings of Judah **h.** destroyed.
2Ch 34:19 when the king **h.** heard the words
2Ch 34:22 they that the king **h.** appointed,
2Ch 35:20 when Josiah **h.** prepared the temple,
2Ch 35:24 in the second chariot that he **h.**:
2Ch 36:13 who **h.** made him swear
2Ch 36:14 the Lord which he **h.** hallowed
2Ch 36:15 because he **h.** compassion on his people,
2Ch 36:17 and **h.** no compassion upon young man
2Ch 36:20 And them that **h.** escaped from
2Ch 36:21 until the land **h.** enjoyed
Ezr 1:5 whose spirit God **h.** raised,
Ezr 1:7 which Nebuchadnezzar **h.** brought
Ezr 1:7 and **h.** put them in the house
Ezr 2:1 those which **h.** been carried away,
Ezr 2:1 king of Babylon **h.** carried away
Ezr 3:7 the grant that they **h.** of Cyrus king of
Ezr 3:12 that **h.** seen the first house,
Ezr 5:12 our fathers **h.** provoked the God
Ezr 5:14 whom he **h.** made governor;
Ezr 6:13 which Darius the king **h.** sent,
Ezr 6:21 all such as **h.** separated themselves
Ezr 6:22 the Lord **h.** made them joyful,
Ezr 7:6 Lord God of Israel **h.** given:
Ezr 7:10 For Ezra **h.** prepared his heart
Ezr 7:20 the princes **h.** appointed for the
Ezr 7:22 because we **h.** spoken unto the
Ezr 8:25 all Israel there present, **h.** offered:
Ezr 8:35 of those that **h.** been carried away,
Ezr 9:4 of those that **h.** been carried away;
Ezr 10:1 Now when Ezra **h.** prayed.
Ezr 10:1 and when he **h.** confessed,
Ezr 10:6 of them that **h.** been carried away.
Ezr 10:8 of those that **h.** been carried away.
Ezr 10:17 the men that **h.** taken strange
Ezr 10:18 were found that **h.** taken strange
Ezr 10:44 All these **h.** taken strange wives:
Ezr 10:44 and some of them **h.** wives 3426
Ezr 10:44 by whom they **h.** children. 7760
Ne 1:2 the Jews that **h.** escaped,
Ne 2:1 Now I **h.** not been beforetime
Ne 2:9 Now the king **h.** sent captains
Ne 2:12 what my God **h.** put in my heart
Ne 2:16 neither **h.** I as yet told it
Ne 2:18 words that he **h.** spoken unto me.
Ne 4:6 for the people **h.** a mind to work. 1961
Ne 4:15 and God **h.** brought their counsel
Ne 4:18 every one **h.** his sword girded by
Ne 5:15 governors that **h.** been before me
Ne 5:15 and **h.** taken of them bread and
Ne 6:1 heard that I **h.** builded the wall,
Ne 6:1 at that time I **h.** not set up the doors
Ne 6:12 that God **h.** not sent him;
Ne 6:12 and Sanballat **h.** hired him.
Ne 6:18 Johanan **h.** taken the daughter
Ne 7:1 and I **h.** set up the doors,
Ne 7:6 of those that **h.** been carried away,
Ne 7:6 king of Babylon **h.** carried away,
Ne 7:67 and they **h.** two hundred forty and five
Ne 8:1 which the Lord **h.** commanded
Ne 8:4 which they **h.** made for the purpose;
Ne 8:12 because they **h.** understood
Ne 8:14 law which the Lord **h.** commanded
Ne 8:17 unto that day **h.** not the children
Ne 9:18 when they **h.** made them a molten
Ne 9:18 and **h.** wrought great provocations;
Ne 9:28 But after they **h.** rest, they did evil
Ne 9:28 so that they **h.** the dominion over them:
Ne 10:28 all they that **h.** separated themselves
Ne 11:16 the Levites, **h.** the oversight of the
Ne 12:29 the singers **h.** builded them
Ne 12:43 for God **h.** made them rejoice
Ne 13:3 when they **h.** heard the law,
Ne 13:5 And he **h.** prepared for him
Ne 13:10 of the Levites **h.** not been given
Ne 13:23 Jews that **h.** married wives
Es 1:8 for so the king **h.** appointed
Es 2:1 and what she **h.** done,
Es 2:6 Who **h.** been carried away from
Es 2:6 which **h.** been carried away
Es 2:6 king of Babylon **h.** carried away.
Es 2:7 for she **h.** neither father nor mother.
Es 2:10 Esther **h.** not shewed her people
Es 2:10 Mordecai **h.** charged her that she
Es 2:12 After that she **h.** been twelve months.
Es 2:15 who **h.** taken her for his daughter,
Es 2:20 Esther **h.** not yet showed her
Es 2:20 as Mordecai **h.** charged her:
Es 3:2 for the king **h.** so commanded
Es 3:4 for he **h.** told them that he was
Es 3:6 for they **h.** shewed him the people
Es 3:12 to all that Haman **h.** commanded
Es 4:5 whom he **h.** appointed to attend
Es 4:7 of all that **h.** happened unto him,
Es 4:7 that Haman **h.** promised to pay
Es 4:17 to all that Esther **h.** commanded
Es 5:5 that Esther **h.** prepared.
Es 5:11 wherein the king **h.** promoted him,
Es 5:11 and how be **h.** advanced him
Es 5:12 that she **h.** prepared but myself;
Es 6:2 that Mordecai **h.** told of Bigthana
Es 6:4 gallows that he **h.** prepared for him.
Es 6:13 every thing that **h.** befallen him.
Es 6:14 banquet that Esther **h.** prepared.
Es 7:4 But if we **h.** been sold for bondmen
Es 7:4 I **h.** held my tongue,
Es 7:9 which Haman **h.** made for
Es 7:9 Mordecai, who **h.** spoken good
Es 7:10 that he **h.** prepared for Mordecai.
Es 8:1 for Esther **h.** told what he was unto
Es 8:2 which he **h.** taken from Haman,
Es 8:3 that he **h.** devised against the Jews.
Es 8:16 The Jews **h.** light, and gladness, and
Es 8:17 the Jews **h.** joy and gladness, a feast
Es 9:1 that the Jews **h.** rule over them that
Es 9:16 stood for their lives, and **h.** rest from
Es 9:23 to do as they **h.** begun,
Es 9:23 as Mordecai **h.** written unto them;
Es 9:24 all the Jews, **h.** devised against
Es 9:24 and **h.** cast Pur, that is, the lot,
Es 9:26 which they **h.** seen concerning
Es 9:26 and which **h.** come unto them,
Es 9:31 Esther the queen **h.** enjoined them.
Es 9:31 and as they **h.** decreed for themselves
Job 2:11 for they **h.** made an appointment
Job 3:13 then **h.** I been at rest,
Job 3:15 Or with princes that **h.** gold, who
Job 3:16 untimely birth I **h.** not been:
Job 3:26 neither **h.** I rest, neither was I quiet;
Job 6:20 confounded because they **h.** hoped;
Job 9:16 If I **h.** called, and he **h.** answered me:
Job 9:16 that he **h.** hearkened unto my voice.
Job 10:18 Oh that I **h.** given up the ghost,
Job 10:18 and no eye **h.** seen me!
Job 10:19 as though I **h.** not been;
Job 22:8 as for the mighty man, he **h.** the earth
Job 24:16 which they **h.** marked for
Job 29:12 and him that **h.** none to help him.
Job 31:25 because mine hand **h.** gotten
Job 31:31 Oh that we **h.** of his flesh! we cannot
Job 31:35 mine adversary **h.** written a book.
Job 32:3 because they **h.** found no answer,
Job 32:3 and yet **h.** condemned Job.
Job 32:4 Now Elihu **h.** waited
Job 32:4 till Job **h.** spoken,
Job 32:16 When I **h.** waited,
Job 38:8 as if it **h.** issued out of the womb?
Job 42:7 after the Lord **h.** spoken these words
Job 42:10 gave Job twice as much as he **h.** before.
Job 42:11 they that **h.** been of his acquaintance
Job 42:11 that the Lord **h.** brought upon him:
Job 42:12 for he **h.** fourteen thousand sheep, 1961
Job 42:13 He **h.** also seven sons and three 1961
Ps 27:13 I **h.** fainted, unless I **h.** believed to see
Ps 35:14 as though he **h.** been my friend
Ps 42:4 for I **h.** gone with the multitude,
Ps 51:*title* after he **h.** gone in to Bath-sheba
Ps 55:6 Oh that I **h.** wings like a dove! for then
Ps 73:2 my steps **h.** well nigh slipped.
Ps 74:5 according as he **h.** lifted up
Ps 78:11 wonders that he **h.** shewed them.
Ps 78:23 Though he **h.** commanded the
Ps 78:24 And **h.** rained down manna
Ps 78:24 and **h.** given them of the corn
Ps 78:43 How he **h.** wrought his signs
Ps 78:44 And **h.** turned their rivers into
Ps 78:54 which his right hand **h.** purchased.
Ps 81:13 that my people **h.** hearkened unto me,
Ps 81:13 and Israel **h.** walked in my ways?
Ps 84:10 I **h.** rather be a doorkeeper in the
Ps 89:7 and to be **h.** in reverence of all them
Ps 94:17 Unless the Lord **h.** been my help,
Ps 94:17 my soul **h.** almost dwelt in silence,
Ps 105:26 and Aaron whom he **h.** chosen.
Ps 106:21 which **h.** done great things
Ps 106:23 destroy them **h.** not Moses his 3884
Ps 119:51 The proud have **h.** me greatly in
Ps 119:56 This I **h.**, because I kept thy 1961
Ps 119:87 They **h.** almost consumed me
Ps 119:92 Unless thy law **h.** been my delights,
Ps 124:1 If it **h.** not been the Lord
Ps 124:2 If it **h.** not been the Lord

Ps 124:3 Then they **h.** swallowed us up
Ps 124:4 Then the waters **h.** overwhelmed us,
Ps 124:4 the stream **h.** gone over our soul:
Ps 124:5 Then the proud waters **h.**
Pr 8:26 While as yet he **h.** not made
Pr 24:31 and nettles **h.** covered the face
Ec 1:16 yea, my heart **h.** great experience of
Ec 2:7 and **h.** servants born in my house; 1961
Ec 2:7 also I **h.** great possessions of 1961
Ec 2:11 that my hands **h.** wrought,
Ec 2:11 labour that I **h.** laboured to do:
Ec 2:18 which I **h.** taken under the sun:
Ec 4:1 and they **h.** no comforter;
Ec 4:1 but they **h.** no comforter.
Ec 8:10 who **h.** come and gone from
Ec 8:10 city where they **h.** so done:
Ca 3:4 until I **h.** brought him
Ca 5:6 but my beloved **h.** withdrawn
Ca 8:11 Solomon **h.** a vineyard at Baal-hamon;
Isa 1:9 Except the Lord of hosts **h.** left unto
Isa 6:2 each one **h.** six wings;
Isa 6:6 which he **h.** taken with the tongs
Isa 22:11 neither **h.** respect unto him that
Isa 26:13 lords beside thee have **h.** dominion
Isa 29:16 He **h.** no understanding?
Isa 37:8 for he **h.** heard that he was
Isa 38:9 when he **h.** been sick,
Isa 38:17 Behold, for peace I **h.** great bitterness:
Isa 38:21 For Isaiah **h.** said, Let them take
Isa 38:22 Hezekiah also **h.** said,
Isa 39:1 for he **h.** heard that he
Isa 39:1 **h.** been sick, and was recovered.
Isa 41:3 way that he **h.** not gone with
Isa 48:18 then **h.** thy peace been as a river,
Isa 48:19 Thy seed also **h.** been as the
Isa 49:21 these, where **h.** they been?
Isa 52:15 for that which **h.** not been told
Isa 52:15 and that which they **h.** not heard
Isa 53:9 because he **h.** done no violence,
Isa 59:10 and we grope as if we **h.** no eyes:
Isa 60:10 but in my favour have I **h.** mercy on
Jer 2:21 Yet I **h.** planted thee a noble
Jer 3:7 after she **h.** done all these things,
Jer 3:8 adultery I **h.** put her away,
Jer 4:23 and the heavens, and they **h.** no light
Jer 5:7 when I **h.** fed them to the full,
Jer 6:15 ashamed when they **h.** committed
Jer 8:12 ashamed when they **h.** committed
Jer 9:2 Oh that I **h.** in the wilderness a lodging
Jer 11:19 I knew not that they **h.** devised
Jer 13:7 the place where I **h.** hid it:
Jer 16:15 the lands whither he **h.** driven them:
Jer 19:14 whither the Lord **h.** sent him
Jer 23:8 whither I **h.** driven them;
Jer 23:22 But if they **h.** stood in my counsel
Jer 23:22 and **h.** caused my people to hear my
Jer 24:1 king of Babylon **h.** carried away
Jer 24:1 from Jerusalem, and **h.** brought them
Jer 24:2 One basket **h.** very good figs, even
Jer 24:2 the other basket **h.** very naughty figs,
Jer 25:17 unto whom the Lord **h.** sent me:
Jer 26:8 when Jeremiah **h.** made an end
Jer 26:8 all that the Lord **h.** commanded
Jer 26:19 evil which he **h.** pronounced
Jer 28:12 the prophet **h.** broken the yoke
Jer 29:1 Nebuchadnezzar **h.** carried away
Jer 32:3 king of Judah **h.** shut him up,
Jer 32:16 Now when I **h.** delivered the evidence
Jer 34:8 king Zedekiah **h.** made a covenant
Jer 34:10 which **h.** entered into the covenant,
Jer 34:11 whom they **h.** let go free,
Jer 34:15 turned, and **h.** done right in my
Jer 34:15 and ye **h.** made a covenant
Jer 34:16 whom he **h.** set at liberty
Jer 34:18 which they **h.** made before me,
Jer 36:4 which he **h.** spoken unto him,
Jer 36:11 the son of Shaphan, **h.** heard out
Jer 36:13 all the words that he **h.** heard,
Jer 36:16 when they **h.** heard all the words,
Jer 36:23 Jehudi **h.** read three or four leaves,
Jer 36:25 and Gemariah **h.** made intercession
Jer 36:27 after that the king **h.** burned the
Jer 36:32 king of Judah **h.** burned in the fire:
Jer 37:4 for they **h.** not put him into prison
Jer 37:10 thought ye **h.** smitten the whole
Jer 37:15 for they **h.** made that the prison.
Jer 37:16 Jeremiah **h.** remained there
Jer 38:1 that Jeremiah **h.** spoken unto all
Jer 38:7 that they **h.** put Jeremiah in the
Jer 38:27 that the king **h.** commanded.
Jer 39:5 when they **h.** taken him,
Jer 39:10 poor of the people, which **h.** nothing,
Jer 40:1 of the guard **h.** let him go from
Jer 40:1 Ramah, when he **h.** taken him
Jer 40:7 king of Babylon **h.** made Gedaliah
Jer 40:7 and **h.** committed unto him
Jer 40:11 king of Babylon **h.** left a remnant
Jer 40:11 and that he **h.** set over them
Jer 41:2 king of Babylon **h.** made governor
Jer 41:4 after he **h.** slain Gedaliah,
Jer 41:9 wherein Ishmael **h.** cast all the dead
Jer 41:9 whom he **h.** slain because
Jer 41:9 Asa the king **h.** made for fear of
Jer 41:10 captain of the guard **h.** committed
Jer 41:11 the son of Nethaniah **h.** done,
Jer 41:14 that Ishmael **h.** carried away captive
Jer 41:16 whom he **h.** recovered from
Jer 41:16 after that he **h.** slain Gedaliah
Jer 41:16 whom he **h.** brought again
Jer 41:18 son of Nethaniah **h.** slain Gedaliah
Jer 43:1 when Jeremiah **h.** made an end
Jer 43:1 Lord their God **h.** sent him to them,
Jer 43:5 whither they **h.** been driven,
Jer 43:6 of the guard **h.** left with Gedaliah
Jer 44:15 that their wives **h.** burned incense
Jer 44:17 for then **h.** we plenty of victuals, 1961
Jer 44:20 which **h.** given him that answer,
Jer 45:1 when he **h.** written these words
Jer 52:2 to all that Jehoiakim **h.** done
Jer 52:3 till he **h.** cast them out from
Jer 52:20 which king Solomon **h.** made
Jer 52:25 which **h.** the charge of the men of 1961
La 1:7 pleasant things that she **h.** in the 1961
La 1:9 wonderfully: she **h.** no comforter
La 2:17 that which he **h.** devised;
La 2:17 his word that he **h.** commanded
Eze 1:5 they **h.** the likeness of a man.
Eze 1:6 And every one **h.** four faces,
Eze 1:6 and every one **h.** four wings
Eze 1:8 And they **h.** the hands of a man under
Eze 1:8 and they four **h.** their faces and their
Eze 1:10 they four **h.** the face of a man, and the
Eze 1:10 they four **h.** the face of an ox on the
Eze 1:10 they four also **h.** the face of an eagle
Eze 1:16 and they four **h.** one likeness: and
Eze 1:23 every one **h.** two, which covered on this
Eze 1:23 every one **h.** two, which covered on that
Eze 1:25 when they stood, and **h.** let down
Eze 1:27 and it **h.** brightness round about
Eze 3:6 Surely, **h.** I sent thee to them,
Eze 8:8 and when I **h.** digged in the wall,
Eze 9:3 which **h.** the writer's inkhorn by his
Eze 9:11 which **h.** the inkhorn by his side,
Eze 10:6 when he **h.** commanded the man
Eze 10:10 they four **h.** one likeness, as if a 1961
Eze 10:10 as if a wheel **h.** been in the midst
Eze 10:12 even the wheels that the four **h.**
Eze 10:14 and every one **h.** four faces: the first
Eze 10:21 Every one **h.** four faces apiece, and
Eze 11:24 vision that I **h.** seen went up
Eze 11:25 things that the Lord **h.** shewed me
Eze 16:14 which I **h.** put upon thee,
Eze 16:17 which I **h.** given thee,
Eze 17:3 full of feathers, which **h.** divers colours,
Eze 17:18 lo, he **h.** given his hand,
Eze 19:5 she saw that she **h.** waited,
Eze 19:11 And she **h.** strong rods for the 1961
Eze 20:6 a land that I **h.** espied for them,
Eze 20:15 which I **h.** given them, flowing
Eze 20:24 they **h.** not executed my judgments,
Eze 20:24 but **h.** despised my statutes,
Eze 20:24 and **h.** polluted my sabbaths,
Eze 20:28 when I **h.** brought them into
Eze 23:10 for they **h.** executed judgment
Eze 23:19 wherein she **h.** played the harlot
Eze 23:32 laughed to scorn and **h.** in derision;
Eze 23:39 when they **h.** slain their children
Eze 29:18 yet **h.** he no wages, nor his army, 1961
Eze 29:18 service that he **h.** served against
Eze 33:15 give again that he **h.** robbed,
Eze 33:21 that one that **h.** escaped out of
Eze 33:22 and **h.** opened my mouth,
Eze 35:5 Because thou hast **h.** a perpetual 1961
Eze 35:5 their iniquity **h.** an end:
Eze 36:18 the blood that they **h.** shed
Eze 36:18 wherewith they **h.** polluted it:
Eze 36:21 But I **h.** pity for mine holy name,
Eze 36:21 house of Israel **h.** profaned
Eze 40:10 and the posts **h.** one measure on this
Eze 40:26 and it **h.** palm trees, one on this side,
Eze 40:31, 34,37 the going up to it **h.** eight steps.
Eze 41:6 but they **h.** not hold in the wall 1961
Eze 41:18 and every cherub **h.** two faces;
Eze 41:23 and the sanctuary **h.** two doors.
Eze 41:24 And the doors **h.** two leaves apiece,
Eze 42:6 but **h.** not pillars as the pillars of the
Eze 42:15 Now when he **h.** made an end of
Eze 42:20 it **h.** a wall round about, five hundred
Eze 44:22 a widow that **h.** a priest before 1961
Eze 44:25 for sister that hath **h.** no husband, 1961
Eze 47:3 the man that **h.** the line in his hand
Eze 47:7 Now when I **h.** returned, behold,
Da 1:4 and such as **h.** ability in them to
Da 1:9 Now God **h.** brought Daniel into
Da 1:11 prince of the eunuchs **h.** set over
Da 1:17 Daniel **h.** understanding in all visions
Da 1:18 the king **h.** said he should bring
Da 2:24 whom the king **h.** ordained to
Da 3:2 Nebuchadnezzar the king **h.** set up.
Da 3:3 Nebuchadnezzar the king **h.** set up;
Da 3:3 image that Nebuchadnezzar **h.** set up.
Da 3:7 Nebuchadnezzar the king **h.** set up:
Da 3:27 upon whose bodies the fire **h.** no power,
Da 3:27 smell of fire **h.** passed on them.
Da 4:12 the beasts of the field **h.** shadow under
Da 4:21 fowls of the heaven **h.** their habitation;
Da 5:2 Nebuchadnezzar **h.** taken out
Da 6:24 those men which **h.** accused Daniel,
Da 6:24 and the lions **h.** the mastery of them
Da 7:1 Daniel **h.** a dream and visions of 2370
Da 7:4 and **h.** eagle's wings: I beheld till
Da 7:5 and it **h.** three ribs in the mouth
Da 7:6 which **h.** upon the back of it four
Da 7:6 the beast **h.** also four heads;
Da 7:7 and it **h.** great iron teeth:
Da 7:7 and it **h.** ten horns.
Da 7:12 they **h.** their dominion taken away:
Da 7:20 even of that horn that **h.** eyes, and a
Da 8:3 a ram which **h.** two horns: and the
Da 8:5 and the goat **h.** a notable horn
Da 8:6 to the ram that **h.** two horns
Da 8:6 which I **h.** seen standing before
Da 8:15 even I Daniel, **h.** seen the vision,
Da 9:21 whom I **h.** seen in the vision
Da 10:1 and **h.** understanding of the vision.
Da 10:11 And when he **h.** spoken this word
Da 10:15 And when he **h.** spoken such words
Da 10:19 And when he **h.** spoken unto me,
Ho 1:8 when she **h.** weaned Lo-ruhamah,
Ho 2:23 upon her that **h.** not obtained
Ho 12:3 his strength he **h.** power with God:
Ho 12:4 Yea, he **h.** power over the angel,
Am 7:2 when they **h.** made an end
Ob 5 have stolen till they **h.** enough?
Ob 16 as though they **h.** not been.
Jon 1:10 because he **h.** told them.
Jon 1:17 the Lord **h.** prepared a great fish
Jon 3:10 that he **h.** said that he would
Jon 4:10 Thou hast **h.** pity on the gourd, for
Na 3:8 the rivers, that **h.** the waters round
Hab 3:4 he **h.** horns coming out of his 1961
Hag 1:12 their God **h.** sent him,
Zec 1:12 against which thou hast **h.** indignation
Zec 5:9 for they **h.** wings like the wings of a
Zec 7:2 When they **h.** sent unto the
Zec 10:6 as though I **h.** not cast them off:
Zec 11:10 which I **h.** made with all the people.
Mal 2:15 Yet **h.** he the residue of the spirit
Mt 1:6 Solomon of her that **h.** been the wife
Mt 1:24 angel of the Lord **h.** bidden him.
Mt 1:25 till she **h.** brought forth her firstborn
Mt 2:3 Herod the king **h.** heard these things,
Mt 2:4 when he **h.** gathered all the chief
Mt 2:7 when he **h.** privily called the wise
Mt 2:9 When they **h.** heard the king,
Mt 2:11 when they **h.** opened their treasures,
Mt 2:16 time which he **h.** diligently enquired
Mt 3:4 And the same John **h.** his raiment *2192*

Mt 4:2 when he **h.** fasted forty days
Mt 4:12 when Jesus **h.** heard that John
Mt 4:24 lunatick, and those that **h.** the palsy;
Mt 7:28 when Jesus **h.** ended these sayings,
Mt 9:8 which **h.** given such power
Mt 10:1 And when he **h.** called unto him
Mt 11:1 when Jesus **h.** made an end
Mt 11:2 Now when John **h.** heard in the prison
Mt 11:21 **done in you, h. been done in Tyre**
Mt 11:23 **done in thee, h. been done in Sodom,**
Mt 12:7 **But if ye h. known what this**
Mt 12:10 a man which **h.** his hand withered. *2192*
Mt 13:5 **where they h. not much earth:** *2192*
Mt 13:5 **they h. no deepness of earth:** *2192*
Mt 13:6 **they h. no root, they withered** *2192*
Mt 13:46 **when he h. found one pearl**
Mt 13:46 **sold all that he h., and bought** *2192*
Mt 13:53 when Jesus **h.** finished these
Mt 14:3 For Herod **h.** laid hold on John,
Mt 14:13 when the people **h.** heard thereof,
Mt 14:21 And they that **h.** eaten were about
Mt 14:23 And when he **h.** sent the multitudes
Mt 14:35 the men of that place **h.** knowledge
Mt 16:5 they **h.** forgotten to take bread.
Mt 17:8 when they **h.** lifted up their eyes,
Mt 18:24 **And when he h. begun to reckon,**
Mt 18:25 **forasmuch as he h. not to pay, his** *2192*
Mt 18:25 **and children, and all that he h.,** *2192*
Mt 18:32 **after that he h. called him,**
Mt 18:33 **not thou also have h. compassion**
Mt 18:33 **fellowservant, even as I h. pity**
Mt 19:1 when Jesus **h.** finished these sayings,
Mt 19:22 sorrowful: for he **h.** great *2258,2193*
Mt 20:2 **And when he h. agreed with the**
Mt 20:11 **when they h. received it,**
Mt 20:34 So Jesus **h.** compassion on them, and
Mt 21:28 **A certain man h. two sons; and he** *2192*
Mt 21:32 **when ye h. seen it,**
Mt 21:45 and Pharisees **h.** heard his parables,
Mt 22:11 **a man which h. not on a wedding** *1746*
Mt 22:22 When they **h.** heard these words,
Mt 22:25 when he **h.** married a wife,
Mt 22:28 be of the seven? for they all **h.** her. *2192*
Mt 22:34 But when the Pharisees **h.** heard
Mt 22:34 that he **h.** put the Sadducees to silence,
Mt 23:30 **If we h. been in the days of our**
Mt 24:43 **of the house h. known in what hour**
Mt 25:16 **Then he that h. received the five**
Mt 25:17 **likewise he that h. received two,**
Mt 25:18 **But he that h. received one went**
Mt 25:20 **so he that h. received five talents,**
Mt 25:22 **He also that h. received two**
Mt 25:24 **Then he that h. received the one**
Mt 26:1 when Jesus **h.** finished all these
Mt 26:8 they **h.** indignation, saying, To what
Mt 26:19 as Jesus **h.** appointed them;
Mt 26:24 **it h. been good for that man**
Mt 26:24 **if he h. not been born,**
Mt 26:30 And when they **h.** sung an hymn,
Mt 26:57 they that **h.** laid hold on Jesus led
Mt 27:2 And when they **h.** bound him,
Mt 27:3 Then Judas, which **h.** betrayed him,
Mt 27:16 they **h.** then a notable prisoner, *2192*
Mt 27:18 that for envy they h. delivered him.
Mt 27:26 when he **h.** scourged Jesus,
Mt 27:29 they **h.** platted a crown of thorns,
Mt 27:31 after that they **h.** mocked him,
Mt 27:34 and when he **h.** tasted thereof,
Mt 27:50 Jesus, when he **h.** cried again
Mt 27:59 when Joseph **h.** taken the body,
Mt 27:60 which he **h.** hewn out in the rock:
Mt 28:12 with the elders, and **h.** taken counsel,
Mt 28:16 a mountain where Jesus **h.** appointed
Mk 1:19 when he **h.** gone a little farther
Mk 1:22 as one that **h.** authority, and not *2192*
Mk 1:26 when the unclean spirit **h.** torn him,
Mk 1:37 And when they **h.** found him,
Mk 1:42 as soon as he **h.** spoken,
Mk 2:4 and when they **h.** broken it up,
Mk 2:25 **what David did, when he h. need,** *2192*
Mk 3:1 a man there which **h.** a withered *2192*
Mk 3:3 the man which **h.** the withered *2192*
Mk 3:5 And when he **h.** looked round
Mk 3:8 they **h.** heard what great things he did,
Mk 3:10 For he **h.** healed many;
Mk 3:10 touch him, as many as **h.** plagues *2192*
Mk 4:5 **where it h. not much earth; and** *2192*
Mk 4:5 **sprang up, because it h. no depth** *2192*
Mk 4:6 **because it h. no root, it withered** *2192*
Mk 4:36 when they **h.** sent away the
Mk 5:3 Who **h.** his dwelling among the *2192*
Mk 5:4 Because that he **h.** been often bound
Mk 5:4 and the chains **h.** been plucked
Mk 5:15 with the devil, and **h.** the legion, *2192*
Mk 5:18 he that **h.** been possessed with the
Mk 5:19 **and hath h. compassion on thee.**
Mk 5:20 how great things Jesus **h.** done for
Mk 5:25 **h.** an issue of blood twelve years, *1510*
Mk 5:26 And **h.** suffered many things
Mk 5:26 of many physicians, and **h.** spent
Mk 5:26 all that she **h.**, and was nothing *3844*
Mk 5:27 When she **h.** heard of Jesus,
Mk 5:30 that virtue **h.** gone out of him,
Mk 5:32 to see her that **h.** done this thing.
Mk 5:40 But when he **h.** put them all out,
Mk 6:17 Herod himself **h.** sent forth
Mk 6:17 for he **h.** married her.
Mk 6:18 For John **h.** said unto Herod,
Mk 6:19 Therefore Herodias **h.** a quarrel
Mk 6:30 both what they **h.** done,
Mk 6:30 and what they **h.** taught.
Mk 6:31 and they **h.** no leisure so much as to
Mk 6:41 when he **h.** taken the five loaves
Mk 6:46 And when he **h.** sent them away,
Mk 6:49 they supposed it **h.** been a spirit,
Mk 6:53 And when they **h.** passed over,
Mk 7:14 when he **h.** called all the people
Mk 7:25 whose young daughter **h.** an *2192*
Mk 7:32 that was deaf, and **h.** an impediment
Mk 8:7 And they **h.** a few small fishes: *2192*
Mk 8:9 they that **h.** eaten were about four
Mk 8:14 Now the disciples **h.** forgotten to
Mk 8:14 neither **h.** they in the ship with *2192*
Mk 8:23 and when he **h.** spit on his eyes,
Mk 8:33 But when he **h.** turned about
Mk 8:34 and when he **h.** called the people
Mk 9:8 when they **h.** looked round about,
Mk 9:9 tell no man what things they **h.** seen,
Mk 9:34 they **h.** disputed among themselves,
Mk 9:36 and when he **h.** taken him in his
Mk 10:22 away grieved: for he **h.** great *2258,2192*
Mk 11:6 even as Jesus **h.** commanded:
Mk 11:11 and when he **h.** looked round about
Mk 12:12 knew that he **h.** spoken the parable
Mk 12:22 And the seven **h.** her, and left no *2983*
Mk 12:23 for the seven **h.** her to wife. *2192*
Mk 12:28 perceiving that he **h.** answered
Mk 12:44 **all that she h., even all her living.** *2192*
Mk 13:20 **except that the Lord h. shortened**
Mk 14:4 there were some that **h.** indignation
Mk 14:16 and found as he **h.** said unto them:
Mk 14:21 **if he h. never been born.**
Mk 14:23 and when he **h.** given thanks,
Mk 14:26 And when they **h.** sung an hymn,
Mk 14:44 he that betrayed him **h.** given them
Mk 15:7 with them that **h.** made insurrection
Mk 15:7 who **h.** committed murder in
Mk 15:8 to do as he **h.** ever done unto them
Mk 15:10 chief priests **h.** delivered him
Mk 15:15 when he **h.** scourged him,
Mk 15:20 And when they **h.** mocked him,
Mk 15:24 And when they **h.** crucified him,
Mk 15:44 whether he **h.** been any while dead.
Mk 16:1 and Salome **h.** bought sweet spices,
Mk 16:9 out of whom he **h.** cast seven devils.
Mk 16:10 told them that **h.** been with him,
Mk 16:11 when they **h.** heard that he was alive,
Mk 16:11 and **h.** been seen of her,
Mk 16:14 believed not them which **h.** seen him
Mk 16:19 after the Lord **h.** spoken unto them,
Lu 1:3 having **h.** perfect understanding
Lu 1:7 And they **h.** no child, because that *1510*
Lu 1:22 that he **h.** seen a vision in the temple:
Lu 1:58 how the Lord **h.** shewed great mercy
Lu 2:17 And when they **h.** seen it,
Lu 2:20 things that they **h.** heard and seen,
Lu 2:26 before he **h.** seen the Lord's Christ.
Lu 2:36 great age, and **h.** lived with an
Lu 2:39 when they **h.** performed all things
Lu 2:43 when they **h.** fulfilled the days,
Lu 3:19 evils which Herod **h.** done,
Lu 4:13 when the devil **h.** ended all the
Lu 4:16 where he **h.** been brought up:
Lu 4:17 And when he **h.** opened the book.
Lu 4:33 a man, which **h.** a spirit of an *2192*
Lu 4:35 when the devil **h.** thrown him
Lu 4:40 all they that **h.** any sick with *2192*
Lu 5:4 Now when he **h.** left speaking,
Lu 5:6 And when they **h.** this done,
Lu 5:9 of the fishes which they **h.** taken:
Lu 5:11 And when they **h.** brought their ships
Lu 6:8 the man which **h.** the withered *2192*
Lu 7:1 Now when he **h.** ended all his
Lu 7:10 servant whole that **h.** been sick.
Lu 7:13 saw her, he **h.** compassion on her, and
Lu 7:39 which **h.** bidden him saw it,
Lu 7:41 **a certain creditor which h. two** *1510*
Lu 7:42 **And when they h. nothing to pay,** *2192*
Lu 8:2 certain women, which **h.** been healed
Lu 8:8 And when he **h.** said these things,
Lu 8:27 which **h.** devils long time, and *2192*
Lu 8:29 For he **h.** commanded the unclean
Lu 8:29 For oftentimes it **h.** caught him:
Lu 8:39 how great things Jesus **h.** done unto
Lu 8:42 For he **h.** one only daughter, *1510*
Lu 8:43 which **h.** spent all her living
Lu 8:47 for what cause she **h.** touched him,
Lu 9:8 some, that Elias **h.** appeared;
Lu 9:10 told him what they **h.** done.
Lu 9:11 and healed them that **h.** need of *2192*
Lu 9:36 any of those things which they **h.** seen.
Lu 10:13 **if the mighty works h. been done**
Lu 10:13 **they h. a great while ago repented,**
Lu 10:33 **he saw him, he h. compassion**
Lu 10:39 And she **h.** a sister called Mary, *1510*
Lu 11:38 marvelled that he **h.** not first washed
Lu 12:39 **the goodman of the house h. known**
Lu 13:1 whose blood Pilot **h.** mingled with
Lu 13:6 **A certain man h. a fig tree** *2192*
Lu 13:11 a woman which **h.** a spirit of *2192*
Lu 13:14 because that Jesus **h.** healed on the
Lu 13:17 And when he **h.** said these things,
Lu 14:2 before him which **h.** the dropsy
Lu 15:9 **found the piece which I h. lost**
Lu 15:11 And he said, **A certain man h. two** *2192*
Lu 15:14 **And when he h. spent all**
Lu 15:20 **father saw him, and h. compassion**
Lu 16:1 **rich man, which h. a steward;** *2192*
Lu 16:1 **that he h. wasted his goods**
Lu 16:8 **because he h. done wisely:**
Lu 17:6 **ye h. faith as a grain of mustard** *2192*
Lu 19:15 **to whom he h. given the money,**
Lu 19:15 **how much every man h. gained**
Lu 19:28 And when he **h.** thus spoken,
Lu 19:32 and found even as he **h.** said
Lu 19:37 the mighty works that they **h.** seen;
Lu 20:19 that he **h.** spoken this parable
Lu 20:33 of them is she? for seven **h.** her *2192*
Lu 21:4 **cash in all the living that she h.** *2192*
Lu 22:13 and found as he **h.** said unto them:
Lu 22:55 And when they **h.** kindled a fire
Lu 22:61 how he **h.** said unto him,
Lu 22:64 And when they **h.** blindfolded him,
Lu 23:8 because he **h.** heard many things
Lu 23:13 when he **h.** called together the
Lu 23:25 whom they **h.** desired;
Lu 23:46 And when Jesus **h.** cried with a loud
Lu 23:51 The same **h.** not consented to the
Lu 24:1 the spices which they **h.** prepared,
Lu 24:14 all these things which **h.** happened
Lu 24:21 we trusted that it **h.** been he
Lu 24:23 they **h.** also seen a vision of angels,
Lu 24:24 even so as the women **h.** said:
Lu 24:37 supposed that they **h.** seen a spirit.
Lu 24:40 And when he **h.** thus spoken,
Joh 2:9 ruler of the feast **h.** tasted the
Joh 2:15 And when he **h.** made a scourge
Joh 2:22 remembered that he **h.** said this
Joh 2:22 and the word which Jesus **h.** said.
Joh 4:1 how the Pharisees **h.** heard
Joh 4:18 **For thou hast h. five husbands;** *2192*
Joh 4:50 the word that Jesus **h.** spoken
Joh 5:4 whole of whatsoever disease he **h.**, *2722*
Joh 5:5 which **h.** an infirmity thirty and *2192*
Joh 5:6 and knew that he **h.** been now
Joh 5:13 for Jesus **h.** conveyed himself away,
Joh 5:15 was Jesus, which **h.** made him whole.
Joh 5:16 because he **h.** done these things
Joh 5:18 he not only **h.** broken the sabbath,
Joh 5:46 **For h. ye believed Moses, ye**
Joh 6:11 and when he **h.** given thanks,

Joh 6:13 unto them that **h.** eaten.
Joh 6:14 when they **h.** seen the miracle
Joh 6:19 So when they **h.** rowed about
Joh 6:23 after that the Lord **h.** given thanks:
Joh 6:25 And when they **h.** found him
Joh 6:60 when they **h.** heard this, said,
Joh 7:9 When he **h.** said these words
Joh 8:3 when they **h.** set her in the midst,
Joh 8:10 When Jesus **h.** lifted up himself,
Joh 8:19 **if ye h. known me, ye should**
Joh 9:6 When he **h.** thus spoken,
Joh 9:8 they which before **h.** seen him
Joh 9:15 asked him how he **h.** received his
Joh 9:18 that he **h.** been blind,
Joh 9:18 that **h.** received his sight
Joh 9:22 for the Jews **h.** agreed already,
Joh 9:35 that they **h.** cast him out;
Joh 9:35 and when he **h.** found him,
Joh 11:6 When he **h.** heard therefore
Joh 11:13 they thought that he **h.** spoken
Joh 11:17 that he **h.** lain in the grave
Joh 11:21 my brother **h.** not died
Joh 11:28 And when she **h.** so said,
Joh 11:32 my brother **h.** not died
Joh 11:43 And when he thus **h.** spoken,
Joh 11:45 came to Mary, and **h.** seen the
Joh 11:46 what things Jesus **h.** done
Joh 11:57 and the Pharisees **h.** given a
Joh 12:1 Lazarus was which **h.** been dead,
Joh 12:6 he was a thief, and **h.** the bag, *2192*
Joh 12:9 whom he **h.** raised from the dead
Joh 12:14 when he **h.** found a young ass,
Joh 12:16 that they **h.** done these things
Joh 12:18 that he **h.** done this miracle.
Joh 12:37 But though he **h.** done so many
Joh 13:3 the Father **h.** given all things into
Joh 13:12 So after he **h.** washed their feet,
Joh 13:12 and **h.** taken his garments,
Joh 13:21 When Jesus **h.** thus said,
Joh 13:26 And when he **h.** dipped the sop,
Joh 13:29 because Judas **h.** the bag, that *2192*
Joh 13:29 that Jesus **h.** said unto him.
Joh 14:7 **If ye h. known me, ye should**
Joh 15:22 **If I h. not come and spoken**
Joh 15:22 **they h. not...sin, but now they**
Joh 15:22 **they...not h. sin: but now they** *2192*
Joh 15:24 **If I h. not done among them**
Joh 15:24 **they h. not...sin, but now have**
Joh 15:24 **they...not h. sin: but now have** *2192*
Joh 17:5 **the glory which I h. with thee** *2192*
Joh 18:1 When Jesus **h.** spoken these words,
Joh 18:6 as he **h.** said unto them,
Joh 18:18 who **h.** made a fire of coals;
Joh 18:22 And when he **h.** thus spoken,
Joh 18:24 Now Annas **h.** sent him bound
Joh 18:38 And when he **h.** said this,
Joh 19:23 when they **h.** crucified Jesus,
Joh 19:30 When Jesus therefore **h.** received the
Joh 20:12 where the body of Jesus **h.** lain
Joh 20:14 And when she **h.** thus said,
Joh 20:18 that she **h.** seen the Lord,
Joh 20:18 and that he **h.** spoken these things
Joh 20:20 And when he **h.** so said,
Joh 20:22 And when he **h.** said this,
Joh 21:15 So when they **h.** dined, Jesus
Joh 21:19 And when he **h.** spoken this,
Ac 1:2 Holy Ghost **h.** given commandments
Ac 1:2 unto the apostles whom he **h.** chosen:
Ac 1:9 And when he **h.** spoken these things,
Ac 1:17 and **h.** obtained part of this ministry
Ac 2:30 and knowing that God **h.** sworn
Ac 2:44 were together, and **h.** all things *2192*
Ac 2:45 to all men, as every man **h.** need *2192*
Ac 3:10 at that which **h.** happened
Ac 3:12 or holiness we **h.** made this man
Ac 3:18 which God before **h.** shewed
Ac 4:7 And when they **h.** set them in the
Ac 4:13 that they **h.** been with Jesus.
Ac 4:15 But when they **h.** commanded
Ac 4:21 when they **h.** further threatened
Ac 4:23 and elders **h.** said unto them.
Ac 4:31 And when they **h.** prayed,
Ac 4:32 but they **h.** all things common. *1510*
Ac 4:35 every man according as he **h.** need *2192*
Ac 5:23 but when we **h.** opened, we found
Ac 5:27 And when they **h.** brought them,
Ac 5:34 a doctor of the law, **h.** in reputation
Ac 5:40 when they **h.** called the apostles,
Ac 6:6 and when they **h.** prayed,
Ac 6:15 As it **h.** been the face of an angel
Ac 7:5 when as yet he **h.** no child *5607*
Ac 7:17 which God **h.** sworn to Abraham,
Ac 7:36 after that he **h.** shewed wonders
Ac 7:44 Our fathers **h.** the tabernacle of *1510*
Ac 7:44 as he **h.** appointed, speaking
Ac 7:44 to the fashion that he **h.** seen
Ac 7:60 And when he **h.** said this,
Ac 8:11 And to him they **h.** regard,
Ac 8:11 that of long time he **h.** bewitched them
Ac 8:14 heard that Samaria **h.** received the
Ac 8:25 when they **h.** testified and preached
Ac 8:27 who **h.** the charge of all her treasure,
Ac 8:27 and **h.** come to Jerusalem...to worship,
Ac 9:18 fell from his eyes as it **h.** been scales:
Ac 9:19 And when he **h.** received meat,
Ac 9:27 how he **h.** seen the Lord in the way,
Ac 9:27 and that he **h.** spoken to him,
Ac 9:27 and how he **h.** preached boldly
Ac 9:31 Then **h.** the churches rest *2192*
Ac 9:33 which **h.** kept his bed eight years,
Ac 9:37 whom when they **h.** washed,
Ac 9:38 the disciples **h.** heard that Peter
Ac 9:41 and when he **h.** called the saints
Ac 10:8 when he **h.** declared all these things
Ac 10:11 as it **h.** been a great sheet
Ac 10:17 which he **h.** seen should mean
Ac 10:17 Cornelius **h.** made enquiry for Simon's
Ac 10:24 and **h.** called together his
Ac 10:31 and thine alms are **h.** in remembrance
Ac 11:1 the Gentiles **h.** also received
Ac 11:5 as it **h.** been a great sheet,
Ac 11:6 when I **h.** fastened mine eyes,
Ac 11:13 how he **h.** seen an angel
Ac 11:23 and **h.** seen the grace of God,
Ac 11:26 And when he **h.** found him,
Ac 12:4 And when he **h.** apprehended him,
Ac 12:12 And when he **h.** considered the thing,
Ac 12:16 and when they **h.** opened the door,
Ac 12:17 how the Lord **h.** brought him out
Ac 12:19 And when Herod **h.** sought for him,
Ac 12:25 when they **h.** fulfilled their ministry,
Ac 13:1 which **h.** been brought up with
Ac 13:3 And when they **h.** fasted and
Ac 13:5 and then **h.** also John to their *2192*
Ac 13:6 when he **h.** gone through
Ac 13:19 when he **h.** destroyed seven nations
Ac 13:22 And when he **h.** removed him,
Ac 13:24 When John **h.** first preached
Ac 13:29 And when they **h.** fulfilled all that
Ac 13:36 after he **h.** served his own
Ac 14:8 who never **h.** walked:
Ac 14:9 perceiving that he **h.** faith to be *2192*
Ac 14:11 people saw what Paul **h.** done,
Ac 14:18 that they **h.** not done sacrifice
Ac 14:19 supposing he **h.** been dead
Ac 14:21 when they **h.** preached the gospel
Ac 14:21 to that city, and **h.** taught many
Ac 14:23 when they **h.** ordained them elders
Ac 14:23 in every church, and **h.** prayed
Ac 14:24 And after they **h.** passed throughout
Ac 14:25 And when they **h.** preached
Ac 14:26 from whence they **h.** been
Ac 14:27 and **h.** gathered the church
Ac 14:27 all that God **h.** done with them,
Ac 14:27 and how he **h.** opened the door
Ac 15:2 Paul and Barnabas **h.** no small *1096*
Ac 15:4 that God **h.** done with them.
Ac 15:7 when there **h.** been much disputing,
Ac 15:12 God **h.** wrought among the Gentiles
Ac 15:13 And after they **h.** held their peace,
Ac 15:30 and when they **h.** gathered the
Ac 15:31 Which when they **h.** read,
Ac 15:33 And after they **h.** tarried there
Ac 16:6 Now when they **h.** gone throughout
Ac 16:10 And after he **h.** seen the vision,
Ac 16:10 that the Lord **h.** called us for to
Ac 16:23 when they **h.** laid many stripes
Ac 16:27 that the prisoners **h.** been fled
Ac 16:34 when he **h.** brought them into
Ac 16:40 and when they **h.** seen the brethren,
Ac 17:1 when they **h.** passed through
Ac 17:9 when they **h.** taken security of Jason,
Ac 17:13 Jews of Thessalonica **h.** knowledge
Ac 18:2 Claudius **h.** commanded all
Ac 18:18 in Cenchrea: for he **h.** a vow *2192*
Ac 18:22 when he **h.** landed at Caesarea,
Ac 18:23 after he **h.** spent some time there,
Ac 18:26 Aquila and Priscilla **h.** heard,
Ac 18:27 which **h.** believed through grace:
Ac 19:6 when Paul **h.** laid his hands
Ac 19:13 over them which **h.** evil spirits *2192*
Ac 19:21 when he **h.** passed through
Ac 19:35 townclerk **h.** appeased the people,
Ac 19:41 And when he **h.** thus spoken,
Ac 20:2 when he **h.** gone over those parts,
Ac 20:2 and **h.** given them much
Ac 20:11 come up again, and **h.** broken bread,
Ac 20:13 for so he **h.** appointed,
Ac 20:16 For Paul **h.** determined to sail
Ac 20:36 And when he **h.** thus spoken,
Ac 21:1 gotten from them, and **h.** launched,
Ac 21:3 when we **h.** discovered Cyprus,
Ac 21:5 when we **h.** accomplished those
Ac 21:6 when we **h.** taken our leave
Ac 21:7 when we **h.** finished our course
Ac 21:9 the same man **h.** four daughters, *1510*
Ac 21:19 And when he **h.** saluted them,
Ac 21:19 what things God **h.** wrought among
Ac 21:29 For they **h.** seen before with him
Ac 21:29 supposed that Paul **h.** brought into
Ac 21:33 who he was, and what he **h.** done.
Ac 21:40 And when he **h.** given him license,
Ac 22:29 and because he **h.** bound him.
Ac 23:7 And when he **h.** so said, there arose a
Ac 23:12 eat nor drink till they **h.** killed Paul
Ac 23:13 than forty which **h.** made this
Ac 23:30 say before thee what they **h.** against
Ac 23:34 And when the governor **h.** read the
Ac 24:10 after that the governor **h.** beckoned
Ac 24:19 and object, if they **h.** ought *2192*
Ac 25:6 And when he **h.** tarried among them
Ac 25:12 Festus, when he **h.** conferred with the
Ac 25:14 And when they **h.** been there many
Ac 25:19 But **h.** certain questions against *2192*
Ac 25:21 But when Paul **h.** appealed to be
Ac 25:25 when I found that he **h.** committed
Ac 25:26 after examination **h.**, I might *1096*
Ac 26:30 And when he **h.** thus spoken,
Ac 26:32 if he **h.** not appealed unto Caesar.
Ac 27:4 And when we **h.** launched from
Ac 27:5 And when we **h.** sailed over the sea
Ac 27:7 And when we **h.** sailed slowly many
Ac 27:13 supposing that they **h.** obtained their
Ac 27:16 we **h.** much work to come by the
Ac 27:17 Which when they **h.** taken up, they
Ac 27:28 and when they **h.** gone a little further,
Ac 27:30 when they **h.** let down the boat into
Ac 27:35 And when he **h.** thus spoken,
Ac 27:35 and when he **h.** broken it, he began
Ac 27:38 And when they **h.** eaten enough,
Ac 27:40 And when they **h.** taken up the
Ac 28:3 And when Paul **h.** gathered a bundle
Ac 28:6 but after they **h.** looked a great while,
Ac 28:9 others also, which **h.** diseases in *2192*
Ac 28:11 which **h.** wintered in the isle,
Ac 28:18 Who, when they **h.** examined me,
Ac 28:19 not that I **h.** ought to accuse my *2192*
Ac 28:23 And when they **h.** appointed him a
Ac 28:25 after that Paul **h.** spoken one word,
Ac 28:29 And when he **h.** said these words,
Ac 28:29 and **h.** great reasoning among *2192*
Ro 1:2 Which he **h.** promised afore by his
Ro 4:11 faith which he **h.** yet being
Ro 4:12 which he **h.** being yet uncircumcised.
Ro 4:21 persuaded that, what he **h.** promised,
Ro 5:14 even over them that **h.** not sinned
Ro 6:21 What fruit **h.** ye then in those *2192*
Ro 7:7 Nay, I **h.** not known sin, but by the
Ro 7:7 for I **h.** not known lust, except the
Ro 7:7 law **h.** said, Thou shalt not covet.
Ro 9:10 but when Rebecca also **h.** conceived
Ro 9:23 which he **h.** afore prepared unto glory,
Ro 9:29 Except the Lord of Sabaoth **h.** left us
Ro 9:29 we **h.** been as Sodoma,
1Co 1:15 say that I **h.** baptized in mine own
1Co 2:8 for **h.** they known it, they would not
1Co 7:29 be as though they **h.** none; and *2192*
1Co 11:24 And when he **h.** given thanks, he brake
1Co 11:25 took the cup, when he **h.** supped
1Co 14:19 Yet in the church I **h.** rather speak five
2Co 1:9 But we **h.** the sentence of death in *2192*

2Co 1:12 we have **h.** our conversation in the....
2Co 2:13 I **h.** no rest in my spirit, because.... *2192*
2Co 3:10 which was made glorious **h.** no glory....
2Co 7:5 our flesh **h.** no rest, but we were.... *2192*
2Co 7:12 for his cause that **h.** done the wrong,....
2Co 8:6 we desired Titus, that as he **h.** begun....
2Co 8:15 He that **h.** gathered....
2Co 8:15 much **h.** nothing over;....
2Co 8:15 and he that **h.** gathered....
2Co 8:15 gathered little **h.** no lack....
2Co 9:5 whereof ye **h.** notice before, that the....
2Co 11:21 reproach, as though we **h.** been weak,....
Ga 1:23 But they **h.** heard only, That he which....
Ga 2:2 by any means I should run, or **h.** run,....
Ga 3:21 for if there **h.** been a law given which....
Ga 4:15 that, if it **h.** been possible, ye would....
Ga 4:22 Abraham **h.** two sons, the one by.... *2192*
Eph 2:3 Among whom also we all **h.** our....
Php 2:26 because that ye **h.** heard....
Php 2:26 that he **h.** been sick....
Php 2:27 but God **h.** mercy on him; and not on....
Php 3:12 Not as though I **h.** already attained....
1Th 1:9 what manner of entering in we **h.**.... *2192*
1Th 2:2 even after that we **h.** suffered before,....
2Th 2:12 believed not the truth, but **h.** pleasure....
Tit 1:5 elders in every city, as I **h.** appointed....
Heb 1:3 when he **h.** by himself purged our sins,....
Heb 2:14 he might destroy him that **h.** the.... *2192*
Heb 3:16 For some, when they **h.** heard, did....
Heb 3:17 was it not with them that **h.** sinned,....
Heb 4:8 For if Jesus **h.** given them rest,....
Heb 5:7 when he **h.** offered up prayers and....
Heb 6:15 And so, after he **h.** patiently endured,....
Heb 7:6 blessed him that **h.** the promises.... *2192*
Heb 8:7 if that first covenant **h.** been faultless,....
Heb 9:1 verily the first covenant **h.** also.... *2192*
Heb 9:4 Which **h.** the golden censer, and.... *2192*
Heb 9:4 the golden pot that **h.** manna,.... *2192*
Heb 9:19 when Moses **h.** spoken every precept....
Heb 10:2 once purged should have **h.** no.... *2192*
Heb 10:6 sacrifices for sin thou hast **h.** no....
Heb 10:12 But this man, after he **h.** offered one....
Heb 10:15 for after that he **h.** said before,....
Heb 10:34 ye **h.** compassion of me in my bonds,....
Heb 11:5 because God **h.** translated him:....
Heb 11:5 before his translation he **h.** this....
Heb 11:11 judged him faithful who **h.** promised....
Heb 11:15 if they **h.** been mindful of that country....
Heb 11:15 they might have **h.** opportunity.... *2192*
Heb 11:17 and he that **h.** received the promises....
Heb 11:26 for he **h.** respect unto the recompence....
Heb 11:31 she **h.** received the spies with peace....
Heb 11:36 others **h.** trial of cruel mockings.... *2983*
Heb 12:9 we have **h.** fathers of our flesh.... *2192*
Jas 2:21 when he **h.** offered Isaac his son....
Jas 2:25 when she **h.** received the messengers,....
Jas 2:25 and **h.** sent them out another way?....
1Pe 2:10 people of God: which **h.** not obtained....
2Pe 2:21 For it **h.** been better for them not....
1Jo 2:7 an old commandment which ye **h.**.... *2192*
1Jo 2:19 for if they **h.** been of us, they would....
2Jo 5 but that which we **h.** from the.... *2192*
3Jo 13 I **h.** many things to write, but I.... *2192*
Re 1:16 And he **h.** in his right hand seven.... *2192*
Re 4:4 and they **h.** on their heads crowns.... *2192*
Re 4:7 and the third beast **h.** a face as a.... *2192*
Re 4:8 And the four beasts **h.** each of.... *2192*
Re 5:6 stood a Lamb as it **h.** been slain,....
Re 5:8 and when he **h.** taken the book,....
Re 6:2 and he that sat on him **h.** a bow;.... *2192*
Re 6:3 And when he **h.** opened the second....
Re 6:5 And when he **h.** opened the third....
Re 6:5 and he that sat on him **h.** a pair.... *2192*
Re 6:7 And when he **h.** opened the fourth....
Re 6:9 And when he **h.** opened the fifth seal,....
Re 6:12 And I beheld when he **h.** opened the....
Re 8:1 And when he **h.** opened the seventh....
Re 8:6 seven angels which **h.** the seven.... *2192*
Re 8:9 were in the sea, and **h.** life, died;.... *2192*
Re 9:8 And they **h.** hair as the hair of.... *2192*
Re 9:9 And they **h.** breastplates, as it.... *2192*
Re 9:10 they **h.** tails like unto scorpions,.... *2192*
Re 9:11 And they **h.** a king over them,.... *2192*
Re 9:14 the sixth angel which **h.** the.... *2192*
Re 9:19 like unto serpents, and **h.** heads,.... *2192*
Re 10:2 And he **h.** in his hand a little book.... *2192*
Re 10:3 when he **h.** cried, seven thunders....
Re 10:4 when the seven thunders **h.** uttered....
Re 10:10 as soon as I **h.** eaten it, my belly was....
Re 13:11 and he **h.** two horns like a lamb,.... *2192*
Re 13:14 miracles which he **h.** power to do....
Re 13:14 the beast, which **h.** the wound.... *2192*
Re 13:15 And he **h.** power to give life unto....
Re 13:17 save he that **h.** the mark, or the.... *2192*
Re 14:18 another angel...which **h.** power.... *2192*
Re 14:18 with a cry to him that **h.** the sharp.... *2192*
Re 15:2 them that **h.** gotten the victory over....
Re 16:2 the men which **h.** the mark of.... *2192*
Re 17:1 of the seven angels which **h.** the.... *2192*
Re 18:19 were made rich all that **h.** ships in.... *2192*
Re 19:12 and he **h.** a name written, that no.... *2192*
Re 19:20 he deceived them that **h.** received....
Re 20:4 and which **h.** not worshipped the....
Re 20:4 neither **h.** received his mark....
Re 21:9 seven angels which **h.** the seven.... *2192*
Re 21:12 And **h.** a wall great and high.... *2192*
Re 21:12 and **h.** twelve gates, and at the.... *2192*
Re 21:14 And the wall of the city **h.** twelve.... *2192*
Re 21:15 And he that talked with me **h.** a.... *2192*
Re 21:23 And the city **h.** no need of the sun.... *2192*
Re 22:8 And when I **h.** heard and seen,....

HADAD (ha'-dad) See also BEN-HADAD; HADAD-RIMMON; HADAR.
Ge 36:35 And Husham died, and **H.** the son.... 1908
Ge 36:36 And **H.** died, and Samlah of.... 1908
1Ki 11:14 and adversary unto Solomon, **H.**.... 1908
1Ki 11:17 That **H.** fled, he and certain.... 1908
1Ki 11:17 **H.** being yet a little child.... 1908
1Ki 11:19 **H.** found great favour in the sight.... 1908
1Ki 11:21 when **H.** heard in Egypt that.... 1908
1Ki 11:21 **H.** said to Pharaoh, Let me depart,.... 1908
1Ki 11:25 besides the mischief that **H.** did:.... 1908
1Ch 1:30 Mishman, and Dumah, Massa, **H.**,.... 1908
1Ch 1:46 **H.** the son of Bedad, which smote.... 1908
1Ch 1:47 when **H.** was dead, Samlah of.... 1908
1Ch 1:50 Baal-hanan was dead, **H.** reigned.... 1908
1Ch 1:51 **H.** died also. And the dukes of.... 1908

HADADEZER (had-a-de'-zer) See also HADAREZER.
2Sa 8:3 David smote also **H.**, the son of.... 1909
2Sa 8:5 came to succour **H.** king of Zobah,.... 1909
2Sa 8:7 that were on the servants of **H.**,.... 1909
2Sa 8:8 Betah, and...Berothai, cities of **H.**,.... 1909
2Sa 8:9 had smitten all the host of **H.**,.... 1909
2Sa 8:10 because he had fought against **H.**,.... 1909
2Sa 8:10 for **H.** had wars with Toi.... 1909
2Sa 8:12 and of the spoil of **H.**, son of.... 1909
1Ki 11:23 which fled from his lord **H.**.... 1909

HADADRIMMON (ha''-dad-rim'-mon)
Zec 12:11 as the mourning of **H.** in the.... 1910

HADAR (ha'-dar) See also HADAD.
Ge 25:15 **H.**, and Tema, Jetur, Naphish,.... 1924
Ge 36:39 and **H.** reigned in his stead:.... 1924

HADAREZER (had-a-re'-zer) See also HADADEZER.
2Sa 10:16 And **H.** sent, and brought out.... 1928
2Sa 10:16 the captain of the host of **H.**.... 1928
2Sa 10:19 the kings that were servants to **H.**.... 1928
1Ch 18:3 David smote **H.** king of Zobah.... 1928
1Ch 18:5 came to help **H.** king of Zobah,.... 1928
1Ch 18:7 that were on the servants of **H.**,.... 1928
1Ch 18:8 and from Chun, cities of **H.**,.... 1928
1Ch 18:9 had smitten all the host of **H.**.... 1928
1Ch 18:10 because he had fought against **H.**,.... 1928
1Ch 18:10 for **H.** had war with Tou;.... 1928
1Ch 19:16 the captain of the host of **H.**.... 1928
1Ch 19:19 when the servants of **H.** saw that.... 1928

HADASHAH (had'-a-shah)
Jos 15:37 Zenan, and **H.**, and Migdal-gad,.... 2322

HADASSAH (ha-das'-sah) See also ESTHER.
Es 2:7 he brought up **H.**, that is Esther,.... 1919

HADATTAH (ha-dat'-tah) See also HAZOR-HADAT-TAH.
Jos 15:25 Hazor, **H.**, and Kerioth,.... 2675

HADDAH See EN-HADDAH.

HADDON See ESAR-HADDON.

HADID (ha'-did)
Ezr 2:33 The children of Lod, **H.**, and Ono,.... 2307
Ne 7:37 of Lod, **H.**, and Ono, seven.... 2307
Ne 11:34 **H.**, Zeboim, Neballat,.... 2307

HADLAI (had'-la-i)
2Ch 28:12 and Amasa the son of **H.**, stood.... 2311

HADORAM (ha-do'-ram) See also ADORAM.
Ge 10:27 And **H.**, and Uzal, and Diklah,.... 1913
1Ch 1:21 **H.** also, and Uzal, and Diklah,.... 1913
1Ch 18:10 He sent **H.** his son to king David,.... 1913
2Ch 10:18 Then king Rehoboam sent **H.**.... 1913

HADRACH (ha'-drak)
Zec 9:1 word of the Lord in the land of **H.**,.... 2317

HADST
Ge 30:30 For it was little which thou **h.** before I....
Ge 31:42 with me, surely thou **h.** sent me away....
Jg 15:2 thought that thou **h.** utterly hated....
1Sa 25:34 except thou **h.** hasted and come to....
2Sa 2:27 As God liveth, unless thou **h.** spoken,....
2Ki 13:19 then **h.** thou smitten Syria till thou **h.**,....
Ezr 9:14 be angry with us till thou **h.** consumed....
Ne 9:15 land which thou **h.** sworn to give them....
Ne 9:23 concerning which thou **h.** promised....
Ps 44:3 because thou **h.** a favour unto them....
Ps 60:10 O God, which **h.** cast us off?....
Ps 90:2 or ever thou **h.** formed the earth....
Isa 26:15 thou **h.** removed it far unto all the....
Isa 48:18 O that thou **h.** hearkened to my....
Jer 3:3 and thou **h.** a whore's forehead,....
Jon 2:3 For thou **h.** cast me into the deep,....
Lu 19:42 Saying, **If thou h. known, even thou**....
Joh 11:21 unto Jesus, Lord, if thou **h.** been here....
Joh 11:32 unto him, Lord, if thou **h.** been here,....
1Co 4:7 glory, as if thou **h.** not received it?....
Heb 10:8 not, neither **h.** pleasure therein;....

HAFT See also HANDLE.
Jg 3:22 the **h.** also went in after the blade;.... 5325

HAGAB (ha'-gab) See also HAGABA.
Ezr 2:46 The children of **H.**, the children.... 2285

HAGABA (hag'-a-bah) See also HAGAB; HAGABAH.
Ne 7:48 the children of **H.**, the children of.... 2286

HAGABAH (hag'-a-bah) See also HAGABA.
Ezr 2:45 the children of **H.**, the children of.... 2286

HAGAR (ha'-gar) See also AGAR; HAGARITES.
Ge 16:1 an Egyptian, whose name was **H.**.... 1904
Ge 16:3 Sarai, Abram's wife, took **H.** her.... 1904
Ge 16:4 he went in unto **H.**, and she.... 1904
Ge 16:8 he said, **H.**, Sarai's maid, whence.... 1904
Ge 16:15 **H.** bare Abram a son: and Abram.... 1904
Ge 16:15 called his son's name, which **H.** bare,.. 1904
Ge 16:16 when **H.** bare Ishmael to Abram.... 1904
Ge 21:9 Sarah saw the son of **H.** the.... 1904
Ge 21:14 and gave it unto **H.**, putting it.... 1904
Ge 21:17 and the angel of God called to **H.**.... 1904
Ge 21:17 unto her, What aileth thee, **H.**?.... 1904
Ge 25:12 Ishmael, Abraham's son, whom **H.**.... 1904

HAGARENES (haga-renes') See also HAGARITES.
Ps 83:6 Ishmaelites; of Moab, and the **H.**;.... 1905

HAGARITES (hag'-a-rites) See also HAGARENES; HAGERITE.
1Ch 5:10 they made war with the **H.**, who.... 1905
1Ch 5:19 they made war with the **H.**, with.... 1905
1Ch 5:20 and the **H.** were delivered into.... 1905

HAGERITE (hag'-e-rite) See also HAGARITES; HAGGERI.
1Ch 27:31 over the flocks was Jaziz the **H.**,.... 1905

HAGGAI (hag'-ga-i)
Ezr 5:1 the prophets, **H.** the prophet, and.... 2292
Ezr 6:14 through the prophesying of **H.** the.... 2292
Hag*general* *title* **H.**.... 2292
Hag 1:1 the Lord by **H.** the prophet unto.... 2292
Hag 1:3 the Lord by **H.** the prophet, saying,.... 2292
Hag 1:12 and the words of **H.** the prophet, as.... 2292
Hag 1:13 Then spake **H.** the Lord's.... 2292
Hag 2:1, 10 of the Lord by the prophet **H.**,.... 2292
Hag 2:13 Then said **H.**, if one that is unclean.... 2292
Hag 2:14 Then answered **H.**, and said, So is.... 2292
Hag 2:20 came unto **H.** in the four and.... 2292

HAGGERI (hag'-gher-i) See also HAGERITE.
1Ch 11:38 Mibhar the son of **H.**,.... 1905

HAGGI (hag'-ghi) See also HAGGITES.
Ge 46:16 Ziphion, and **H.**, Shuni, and.... 2291
Nu 26:15 of **H.**, the family of the Haggites:.... 2291

HAGGIAH (hag-ghi'-ah)
1Ch 6:30 Shimea his son, **H.** his son, ... 2293

HAGGITES (hag'-ghites) See also HAGGI.
Nu 26:15 of Haggi, the family of the **H.**:.......... 2291

HAGGITH (hag'-ghith)
2Sa 3:4 fourth, Adonijah the son of **H.**;.......... 2294
1Ki 1:5 Adonijah the son of **H.** exalted.......... 2294
1Ki 1:11 the son of **H.** doth reign, and.......... 2294
1Ki 2:13 the son of **H.** came to Bath-sheba...... 2294
1Ch 3:2 the fourth, Adonijah the son of **H.**:..... 2294

HAHIROTH See PI-HAHIROTH.

HAI (ha'-i) See also AI.
Ge 12:8 Beth-el on the west, and **H.** on........ 5857
Ge 13:3 between Beth-el and **H.**;................ 5857

HAIL See also HAILSTONES.
Ex 9:18 to rain a very grievous **h.**, such as..... 1259
Ex 9:19 the **h.** shall come down upon them,.... 1259
Ex 9:22 that there may be **h.** in all the.......... 1259
Ex 9:23 the Lord sent thunder and **h.**, and...... 1259
Ex 9:23 rained **h.** upon the land of Egypt........ 1259
Ex 9:24 was **h.**, and fire mingled with the **h.**,.. 1259
Ex 9:25 the **h.** smote throughout all the.......... 1259
Ex 9:25 the **h.** smote every herb of the field,.. 1259
Ex 9:26 of Israel were, was there no **h.**......... 1259
Ex 9:28 more mighty thunderings and **h.**:......... 1259
Ex 9:29 neither shall there be any more **h.**;..... 1259
Ex 9:33 the thunders and **h.** ceased, and........ 1259
Ex 9:34 saw that the rain and the **h.** and........ 1259
Ex 10:5 remaineth unto to you from the **h.**,...... 1259
Ex 10:12 even all that the **h.** hath left............ 1259
Ex 10:15 of the trees which the **h.** had left:...... 1259
Job 38:22 thou seen the treasures of the **h.**,...... 1259
Ps 18:12 thick clouds passed, **h.** stones and...... 1259
Ps 18:13 his voice; **h.** stones and coals of........ 1259
Ps 78:47 He destroyed their vines with **h.**,....... 1259
Ps 78:48 He gave up their cattle...to the **h.**,...... 1259
Ps 105:32 He gave them **h.** for rain, and........... 1259
Ps 148:8 Fire, and **h.**; snow, and vapours;....... 1259
Isa 28:2 as a tempest of **h.** and a destroying.... 1259
Isa 28:17 the **h.** shall sweep away the refuge..... 1259
Isa 32:19 When it shall **h.**, coming down on....... 1258
Hag 2:17 with mildew and with **h.** in all the........ 1259
Mt 26:49 and said, **H.**, master; and kissed....... *5463*
Mt 27:29 mocked him, saying, **H.**, King of the... *5463*
Mt 28:9 Jesus met them, saying, **All h.**.......... *5463*
Mk 15:18 salute him, **H.**, King of the Jews!....... *5463*
Lu 1:28 **H.**, thou that art highly favoured,....... *5463*
Joh 19:3 And said, **H.**, King of the Jews!......... *5463*
Re 8:7 followed **h.** and fire mingled with........ *5464*
Re 11:19 and an earthquake, and great **h.**......... *5464*
Re 16:21 there fell upon men a great **h.** out...... *5464*
Re 16:21 because of the plague of the **h.**;......... *5464*

HAIL See BEN-HAIL.

HAILSTONES See also HAIL and STONES.
Jos 10:11 more which died with **h.** than........ 68,1259
Isa 30:30 scattering, and tempest, and **h.**....... 68,1259
Eze 13:11 ye, O great **h.**, shall fall; and a....... 68,417
Eze 13:13 and great **h.** in my fury to............. 68,417
Eze 38:22 and great **h.**, fire, and brimstone..... 68,417

HAIR See also HAIRS.
Ex 25:4 scarlet, and fine linen, and goats' **h.**,.........
Ex 26:7 shalt make curtains of goats' **h.** to...........
Ex 35:6 scarlet, and fine linen, and goats **h.**,.........
Ex 35:23 and goats' **h.**, and red skins of rams,........
Ex 35:26 them up in wisdom spun goats' **h.**...........
Ex 36:14 And he made curtains of goats' **h.**............
Le 13:3 and when the **h.** in the plague is........ 8181
Le 13:4 and the **h.** thereof be not turned........ 8181
Le 13:10 it have turned the **h.** white, and.......... 8181
Le 13:20 and the **h.** thereof be turned white;.... 8181
Le 13:25 the **h.** in the bright spot be turned..... 8181
Le 13:26 no white **h.** in the bright spot,.......... 8181
Le 13:30 there be in it a yellow thin **h.**;.......... 8181
Le 13:31 and that there is no black **h.**............ 8181
Le 13:32 there be in it no yellow **h.**,.............. 8181
Le 13:36 priest shall not seek for yellow **h.**;..... 8181
Le 13:37 and that there is black **h.** grown up.... 8181
Le 13:40 whose **h.** is fallen off his head, he...... 4803
Le 13:41 he that hath his **h.** fallen off from...... 4803
Le 14:8 shave off all his **h.**, and wash........... 8181
Le 14:9 he shall shave all his **h.** off his head.... 8181
Le 14:9 eyebrows, even all his **h.** he shall....... 8181
Nu 6:5 let the locks of the **h.** of his head....... 8181
Nu 6:18 shall take the **h.** of the head............. 8181
Nu 6:19 of the Nazarite, after the **h.** of his...........
Nu 31:20 of goats' **h.**, and all things made of..........
Jg 16:22 the **h.** of his head began to grow....... 8181
Jg 20:16 could sling stones at an **h.** breadth,.... 8185
1Sa 14:45 there shall not one **h.** of his head....... 8185
1Sa 19:13 put a pillow of goats' **h.** for his bolster......
1Sa 19:16 a pillow of goats' **h.** for his bolster..........
2Sa 14:11 there shall not one **h.** of thy son........ 8185
2Sa 14:26 because the **h.** was heavy on him,...........
2Sa 14:26 he weighed the **h.** of his head........... 8181
1Ki 1:52 there shall not an **h.** of him fall.......... 8185
Ezr 9:3 plucked off the **h.** of my head............ 8181
Ne 13:25 and plucked off their **h.**, and made...........
Job 4:15 the **h.** of my flesh stood up:............. 8185
Ca 4:1 thy **h.** is as a flock of goats,............. 8181
Ca 6:5 thy **h.** is as a flock of goats............. 8181
Ca 7:5 and the **h.** of thine head like............. 1803
Isa 3:24 instead of well set **h.** baldness;.......... 4748
Isa 7:20 head, and the **h.** of the feet:............. 8181
Isa 50:6 to them that plucked off the **h.**:...............
Jer 7:29 Cut off thine **h.**, O Jerusalem, and...... 5145
Eze 5:1 balances to weigh and divide the **h.**.........
Eze 16:7 and thine **h.** is grown, whereas.......... 8181
Da 3:27 nor was an **h.** of their head singed,.... 8177
Da 7:9 and the **h.** of his head like the pure.... 8177
Mt 3:4 John had his raiment of camel's **h.**,..... *2359*
Mt 5:36 **canst not make one h. white or**..... *2359*
Mk 1:6 John was clothed with camel's **h.**,....... *2359*
Lu 21:18 **But there shall not an h. of your**.. *2359*
Joh 11:2 and wiped his feet with her **h.**,........... *2359*
Joh 12:3 wiped his feet with her **h.**:............... *2359*
Ac 27:34 an **h.** fall from the head.................... *2359*
1Co 11:14 if a man have long **h.**, it is a............ *2863*
1Co 11:15 But if a woman have long **h.**, it is a.... *2863*
1Co 11:15 for her **h.** is given her for a............. *2864*
1Ti 2:9 not with broided **h., or gold, or**........ *4117*
1Pe 3:3 of plaiting the **h.**, and of wearing......... *2359*
Re 6:12 black as sackcloth of **h.**,.................. *5155*
Re 9:8 And they had **h.** as the **h.** of............ *2359*

HAIR-BREADTH See HAIR and BREADTH.

HAIRS
Ge 42:38 bring down my gray **h.** with sorrow..........
Ge 44:29 bring down my gray **h.** with sorrow..........
Ge 44:31 the gray **h.** of thy servant our father.........
Le 13:21 no white **h.** therein, and if it be.......... 8181
De 32:25 suckling also with the man of gray **h.**........
Ps 40:12 they are more than the **h.** of mine...... 8185
Ps 69:4 cause are more than the **h.** of mine.... 8185
Isa 46:4 even to hoar **h.** will I carry you:...............
Da 4:33 his **h.** were grown like eagles'........... 8177
Ho 7:9 gray **h.** are here and there upon him,.........
Mt 10:30 **the very h. of your head are all**..... *2359*
Lu 7:38 wipe them with the **h.** of her head,..... *2359*
Lu 7:44 **wiped them with the h. of her**....... *2359*
Lu 12:7 **But even the very h. of your head** . *2359*
Re 1:14 His head and his **h.** were white.......... *2359*

HAIRY
Ge 25:25 red, all over like an **h.** garment;......... 8181
Ge 27:11 Esau my brother is a **h.** man, and...... 8163
Ge 27:23 because his hands were **h.**, as his...... 8163
2Ki 1:8 answered him, He was an **h.**...... 1167,8181
Ps 68:21 the **h.** scalp of such an one as
goeth.................................... 1167,8181

HAKKATAN (hak'-ka-tan)
Ezr 8:12 Johannan the son of **H.**, and with....... 6997

HAKKORE See EN-HAKKORE.

HAKKOZ (hak'-koz) See also KOZ.
1Ch 24:10 The seventh to **H.**, the eighth to....... 6976

HAKUPHA (ha-ku'-fah)
Ezr 2:51 the children of **H.**, the children of...... 2709
Ne 7:53 the children of **H.**, the children of...... 2709

HALAH (ha'-lah)
2Ki 17:6 and placed them in **H.** and in............ 2477
2Ki 18:11 and put them in **H.** and in Habor........ 2477
1Ch 5:26 and brought them unto **H.**, and.......... 2477

HALAK (ha'-lak)
Jos 11:17 mount **H.**, that goeth up to Seir,......... 2510
Jos 12:7 mount **H.**, that goeth up to Seir;......... 2510

HALE See also HALING.
Lu 12:58 **lest he h. thee to the judge,**.......... *2694*

HALF
Ge 24:22 a golden earring of **h.** a shekel.......... 1235
Ex 24:6 Moses took **h.** of the blood, and.......... 2677
Ex 24:6 and **h.** of the blood he sprinkled......... 2677
Ex 25:10 two cubits and a **h.** shall be the......... 2677
Ex 25:10 and a cubit and a **h.** the breadth......... 2677
Ex 25:10 thereof, and a cubit and a **h.**............. 2677
Ex 25:10 cubit and a **h.** the height.................. 2677
Ex 25:17 two cubits and a **h.** shall be the......... 2677
Ex 25:17 thereof, and a cubit and a **h.**............. 2677
Ex 25:23 cubit and a **h.** the height thereof......... 2677
Ex 26:12 the **h.** curtain that remaineth, shall...... 2677
Ex 26:16 a cubit and a **h.** shall be the............. 2677
Ex 30:13 **h.** a shekel after the shekel of the....... 4276
Ex 30:13 an **h.** shekel shall be the offering........ 4276
Ex 30:15 give less than **h.** a shekel,................ 4276
Ex 30:23 sweet cinnamon **h.** so much, even....... 4276
Ex 36:21 a board one cubit and a **h.**,............... 2677
Ex 37:1 two cubits and a **h.** was the length...... 2677
Ex 37:1 and a cubit and a **h.** the breadth of...... 2677
Ex 37:1 and a cubit and a **h.** the height of....... 2677
Ex 37:6 two cubits and a **h.** was the length...... 2677
Ex 37:6 one cubit and a **h.** the breadth........... 2677
Ex 37:10 a cubit and a **h.** the height thereof:..... 2677
Ex 38:26 **h.** a shekel, after the shekel of........... 4276
Le 6:20 **h.** of it in the morning, and **h.**.......... 4276
Nu 12:12 of whom the flesh is **h.** consumed...... 2677
Nu 15:9 mingled with **h.** an hin of oil............. 2677
Nu 15:10 for a drink offering **h.** an hin............. 2677
Nu 28:14 their drink offerings shall be **h.** an...... 2677
Nu 31:29 Take it of their **h.**, and give it unto.... 4276
Nu 31:30 And of the children of Israel's **h.**,........ 4276
Nu 31:36 the **h.**, which was the portion.............. 4275
Nu 31:42 And of the children of Israel's **h.**,........ 4276
Nu 31:43 the **h.** that pertained unto the............ 4275
Nu 31:47 Even of the children of Israel's **h.**,...... 4276
Nu 32:33 and unto **h.** the tribe of Manasseh...... 2677
Nu 34:13 nine tribes, and to the **h.** tribe:.......... 2677
Nu 34:14 and **h.** the tribe of Manasseh have...... 2677
Nu 34:15 The two tribes and the **h.** tribe........... 2677
De 3:12 **h.** mount Gilead, and the cities........... 2677
De 3:13 gave I unto the **h.** tribe of................. 2677
De 3:16 unto the river Arnon **h.** the............... 8432
De 29:8 and to the **h.** tribe of Manasseh........... 2677
Jos 1:12 and to **h.** the tribe of Manasseh,......... 2677
Jos 4:12 and **h.** the tribe of Manasseh,............ 2677
Jos 8:33 **h.** of them over against mount............ 2677
Jos 8:33 Gerizim, and **h.** of them over............. 2677
Jos 12:2 and from **h.** Gilead, even unto the...... 2677
Jos 12:5 Maachathites, and **h.** Gilead, the......... 2677
Jos 12:6 Gadites, and the **h.** tribe of................ 2677
Jos 13:7 nine tribes, and the **h.** tribe of........... 2677
Jos 13:25 and **h.** the land of the children........... 2677
Jos 13:29 unto the **h.** tribe of Manasseh: and..... 2677
Jos 13:29 was the possession of the **h.** tribe...... 2677
Jos 13:31 And **h.** Gilead, and Ashtaroth, and....... 2677
Jos 13:31 to the one **h.** of the children of........... 2677
Jos 14:2 nine tribes, and for the **h.** tribe,........... 2677
Jos 14:3 two tribes and an **h.** tribe on the........ 2677
Jos 18:7 Reuben, and **h.** the tribe of............... 2677
Jos 21:5 and out of the **h.** tribe of Manasseh,..... 2677
Jos 21:6 and out of the **h.** tribe of Manasseh..... 2677
Jos 21:25 And out of the **h.** tribe of................ 4276
Jos 21:27 out of the other **h.** tribe of............... 2677
Jos 22:1 the Gadites, and the **h.** tribe of.......... 2677
Jos 22:7 Now to the one **h.** of the tribe of......... 2677
Jos 22:7 but unto the other **h.** thereof gave...... 2677
Jos 22:9 the children of Gad and the **h.** tribe.... 2677
Jos 22:10 Gad and the **h.** tribe of Manasseh....... 2677
Jos 22:11 the children of Gad and the **h.** tribe.... 2677
Jos 22:13, 15 and to the **h.** tribe of Manasseh,.... 2677
Jos 22:21 and the **h.** tribe of Manasseh............ 2677
1Sa 14:14 within as it were an **h.** acre of land,.... 2677
2Sa 10:4 shaved off the one **h.** of their beards,.. 2677
2Sa 18:3 neither if **h.** of us die, will they......... 2677
2Sa 19:40 and also **h.** the people of Israel.......... 2677
1Ki 3:25 give **h.** to the one, and **h.** to the........ 2677
1Ki 7:31 a cubit and an **h.**: and also upon......... 2677
1Ki 7:32 a wheel was a cubit and **h.** a cubit...... 2677
1Ki 7:35 a round compass of **h.** a cubit high:.... 2677
1Ki 10:7 the **h.** was not told me: thy wisdom.... 2677
1Ki 13:8 If thou wilt give me **h.** thine house,..... 2677
1Ki 16:9 Zimri, captain of **h.** his chariots,........ 4276
1Ki 16:21 **h.** of the people followed Tibni........... 2677
1Ki 16:21 and **h.** followed Omri...................... 2677
1Ch 2:52 Haroeh, and **h.** of the Manahethites.... 2677

1Ch 2:54 Joab, and **h.** of the Manahethites, 2677
1Ch 5:18 and **h.** the tribe of Manasseh, of 2677
1Ch 5:23 the children of the **h.** tribe of 2677
1Ch 5:26 and the **h.** tribe of Manasseh, and 2677
1Ch 6:61 out of the **h.** tribe, namely, out 2677
1Ch 6:61 of the **h.** tribe of Manasseh, 4276
1Ch 6:70 And out of the **h.** tribe of Manasseh; 4276
1Ch 6:71 the **h.** tribe of Manasseh, Golan in 2677
1Ch 12:31 And of the **h.** tribe of Manasseh 2677
1Ch 12:37 and of the **h.** tribe of Manasseh, 2677
1Ch 26:32 and the **h.** tribe of Manasseh, for 2677
1Ch 27:20 of the **h.** tribe of Manasseh, Joel 2677
1Ch 27:21 Of the **h.** tribe of Manasseh in 2677
2Ch 9:6 the one **h.** of the greatness of thy 2677
Ne 3:9 ruler of the **h.** part of Jerusalem. 2677
Ne 3:12 ruler of the **h.** part of Jerusalem, 2677
Ne 3:16 the ruler of the **h.** part of Beth-zur, 2677
Ne 3:17 the ruler of the **h.** part of Keilah, 2677
Ne 3:18 the ruler of the **h.** part of Keilah. 2677
Ne 4:6 joined together unto the **h.** thereof: 2677
Ne 4:16 the **h.** of my servants wrought in 2677
Ne 4:16 and the other **h.** of them held 2677
Ne 4:21 **h.** of them held the spears 2677
Ne 12:32 and **h.** of the princes of Judah 2677
Ne 12:38 and the **h.** of the people upon the 2677
Ne 12:40 I, and the **h.** of the rulers with me: 2677
Ne 13:24 their children spake **h.** in the 2677
Es 5:3 given thee to the **h.** of the kingdom 2677
Es 5:6 the **h.** of the kingdom it shall be 2677
Es 7:2 even to the **h.** of the kingdom. 2677
Ps 55:23 shall not live out **h.** their days; 2673
Eze 16:51 Neither hath Samaria committed **h.** 2677
Eze 40:42 a cubit and an **h.** long, and 2677
Eze 40:42 a cubit and an **h.** broad, 2677
Eze 43:17 border about it shall be **h.** a cubit; 2677
Da 12:7 for a time, times, and an **h.**; and 2677
Ho 3:2 of barley, and an **h.** homer of
Zec 14:2 **h.** of the city shall go forth into 2677
Zec 14:4 **h.** of the mountain shall remove 2677
Zec 14:4 and **h.** of it toward the south 2677
Zec 14:8 **h.** of them toward the former sea, 2677
Zec 14:8 **h.** of them toward the hinder sea: 2677
Mk 6:23 it thee, unto the **h.** of my kingdom. *2255*
Lu 10:30 **departed, leaving him h. dead.** *2253*
Lu 19:8 the **h.** of my goods I give to the *2255*
Re 8:1 about the space of **h.** an hour. *2256*
Re 11:9 three days and an **h.**, and shall not *2255*
Re 11:11 three days and an **h.** the Spirit of life *2255*
Re 12:14 a time, and times, and **h.** a time, *2255*

HALF-DEAD See HALF and DEAD.

HALF-HOMER See HALF and HOMER.

HALHUL (hal'-hul)
Jos 15:58 **H.**, Beth-zur, and Gedor, 2478

HALI (ha'-li)
Jos 19:25 their border was Helkath, and **H.**, 2482

HALING
Ac 8:3 **h.** men and women committed *4951*

HALL
Mt 27:27 took Jesus into the common **h.**, *4232*
Mk 15:16 led him away into the **h.**, *833*
Lu 22:55 a fire in the midst of the **h.**, and *833*
Joh 18:28 led...unto the **h.** of judgment: *4232*
Joh 18:28 went not into the judgment **h.**; *4232*
Joh 18:33 Pilate entered...the judgment **h.** *4232*
Joh 19:9 went again into the judgment **h.**, *4232*
Ac 23:35 to be kept in Herod's judgment **h.** *4232*

HALLELUJAH See ALLELUIA.

HALLOHESH (hal-lo'-hesh) See also HALOHESH.
Ne 10:24 **H.**, Pileha, Shobek, 3873

HALLOW See also HALLOWED.
Ex 28:38 the children of Israel shall **h.** in 6942
Ex 29:1 to **h.** them, to minister unto me 6942
Ex 40:9 and shalt **h.** it, and all the vessels 6942
Le 16:19 cleanse it, and **h.** it from the 6942
Le 22:2 those things which they **h.** unto me: 6942
Le 22:3 which the children of Israel **h.** unto 6942
Le 22:32 I am the Lord which **h.** you, 6942
Le 25:10 And ye shall **h.** the fiftieth year, 6942
Nu 6:11 and shall **h.** his head that same day. 6942
1Ki 8:64 same day did the king **h.** the middle 6942
Jer 17:22 but **h.** ye the sabbath day, as I 6942
Jer 17:24 but **h.** the sabbath day, to do no 6942
Jer 17:27 to **h.** the sabbath day, and not to 6942
Eze 20:20 **h.** my sabbaths; and they shall be 6942
Eze 44:24 and they shall **h.** my sabbaths 6942

HALLOWED
Ex 20:11 blessed the sabbath day, and **h.** it. 6942
Ex 29:21 and he shall be **h.**, and his garments, 6942
Le 12:4 she shall touch no **h.** thing, nor 6944
Le 19:8 profaned the **h.** thing of the Lord: 6944
Le 22:32 I will be **h.** among the children 6942
Nu 3:13 I **h.** unto me all the firstborn 6942
Nu 5:10 every man's **h.** things shall be his: 6944
Nu 16:37 the fire yonder; for they are **h.** 6942
Nu 16:38 therefore they are **h.**: and they 6942
Nu 18:8 all the **h.** things of the children of 6944
Nu 18:29 even the **h.** part thereof out of it. 4720
De 26:13 I have brought away the **h.** things 6944
1Sa 21:4 there is **h.** bread; if the young 6944
1Sa 21:6 the priest gave him **h.** bread; for 6944
1Ki 9:3 I have **h.** this house, which thou 6942
1Ki 9:7 which I have **h.** for my name, 6942
2Ki 12:18 all the **h.** things that Jehoshaphat, 6944
2Ki 12:18 and his own **h.** things, and all 6944
2Ch 7:7 Moreover Solomon **h.** the middle 6942
2Ch 36:14 of the Lord which he had **h.** in 6942
Mt 6:9 **in heaven, H. be thy name.** *37*
Lu 11:2 **in heaven, H. be thy name.** *37*

HALOHESH (ha-lo'-hesh) See also HALLOHESH.
Ne 3:12 repaired Shallum the son of **H.**, 3873

HALT See also HALTED; HALTETH; HALTING.
1Ki 18:21 How long **h.** ye between two 6452
Ps 38:17 I am ready to **h.**, and my sorrow 6761
Mt 18:8 **to enter into life h. or maimed.** *5560*
Mk 9:45 **better for thee to enter h. into life,** *5560*
Lu 14:21 **the maimed, and the h., and the** *5560*
Joh 5:3 of blind, **h.**, withered, waiting for *5560*

HALTED
Ge 32:31 him, and he **h.** upon his thigh. 6761
Mic 4:7 I will make her that **h.** a remnant, 6761

HALTETH
Mic 4:6 will I assemble her that **h.**, and 6761
Zep 3:19 I will save her that **h.**, and gather 6761

HALTING
Jer 20:10 my familiars watched for my **h.**, 6761

HAM (ham)
Ge 5:32 Noah begat Shem, **H.**, and 2526
Ge 6:10 Noah begat three sons, Shem, **H.**, 2526
Ge 7:13 Noah, and Shem, and **H.**, and 2526
Ge 9:18 were Shem, and **H.**, and Japheth: 2526
Ge 9:18 and **H.** is the father of Caanan. 2526
Ge 9:22 And **H.**, the father of Caanan, saw 2526
Ge 10:1 Shem, **H.**, and Japheth: and unto 2526
Ge 10:6 the sons of **H.**; Cush, and Mizraim, 2526
Ge 10:20 These are the sons of **H.**, after their 2526
Ge 14:5 and the Zuzims in **H.**, and the 1990
1Ch 1:4 Noah, Shem, **H.**, and Japheth. 2526
1Ch 1:8 The sons of **H.**: Cush, and 2526
1Ch 4:40 for they of **H.** had dwelt there of 2526
Ps 78:51 strength in the tabernacles of **H.**: 2526
Ps 105:23 Jacob sojourned in the land of **H.** 2526
Ps 105:27 and wonders in the land of **H.** 2526
Ps 106:22 Wondrous works in the land of **H.**, 2526

HAMAN (ha'-man) See also HAMAN'S.
Es 3:1 **H.** the son of Hammedatha 2001
Es 3:2 bowed, and reverenced **H.**: for the 2001
Es 3:4 they told **H.**, to see whether 2001
Es 3:5 when **H.** saw that Mordecai bowed 2001
Es 3:5 then was **H.** full of wrath 2001
Es 3:6 wherefore **H.** sought to destroy all 2001
Es 3:7 that is, the lot, before **H.** from day 2001
Es 3:8 **H.** said unto king Ahasuerus, 2001
Es 3:10 and gave it unto **H.** the son of 2001
Es 3:11 the king said unto **H.**, The silver 2001
Es 3:12 according to all that **H.** had 2001
Es 3:15 the king and **H.** sat down to drink; 2001
Es 4:7 of the money that **H.** had promised 2001
Es 5:4 let the king and **H.** come this day 2001
Es 5:5 Cause **H.** to make haste, that he 2001
Es 5:5 So the king and **H.** came to the 2001
Es 5:8 let the king and **H.** come to the 2001
Es 5:9 Then went **H.** forth that day joyful 2001
Es 5:9 but when **H.** saw Mordecai in the 2001
Es 5:10 Nevertheless **H.** refrained himself: 2001
Es 5:11 **H.** told them of the glory of his 2001
Es 5:12 **H.** said moreover, Yea, Esther the 2001
Es 5:14 And the thing pleased **H.**; and he 2001
Es 6:4 Now **H.** was come into the outward 2001
Es 6:5 Behold, **H.** standeth in the court. 2001
Es 6:6 So **H.** came in. And the king 2001
Es 6:6 Now **H.** thought in his heart, To 2001
Es 6:7 **H.** answered the king, For the 2001
Es 6:10 Then the king said to **H.**, Make 2001
Es 6:11 Then took **H.** the apparel and the 2001
Es 6:12 But **H.** hasted to his house 2001
Es 6:13 And **H.** told Zeresh his wife 2001
Es 6:14 And hasted to bring **H.** unto the 2001
Es 7:1 So the king and **H.** came to 2001
Es 7:6 and enemy is this wicked **H.** 2001
Es 7:6 Then **H.** was afraid 2001
Es 7:7 and **H.** stood up to make request 2001
Es 7:8 and **H.** was fallen upon the bed 2001
Es 7:9 which **H.** had made for Mordecai, 2001
Es 7:9 standeth in the house of **H.** Then 2001
Es 7:10 So they hanged **H.** on the gallows 2001
Es 8:1 give the house of **H.** the Jews' 2001
Es 8:2 which he had taken from **H.**, and 2001
Es 8:2 Mordecai over the house of **H.**, 2001
Es 8:3 to put away the mischief of **H.** the 2001
Es 8:5 to reverse the letters devised by **H.**, 2001
Es 8:7 I have given Esther...house of **H.**, 2001
Es 9:10 The ten sons of **H.** the son of 2001
Es 9:12 the palace, and the ten sons of **H.**; 2001
Es 9:24 Because **H.** the son of 2001

HAMAN'S (ha'-mans)
Es 7:8 they covered **H.** face, 2001
Es 9:13 and let **H.** ten sons be hanged 2001
Es 9:14 and they hanged **H.** ten sons. 2001

HAMATH (ha'-math) See also HAMATHITE; HAMATH-ZOBAH; HEMATH.
Nu 13:21 unto Rehob, as men come to **H.** 2574
Nu 34:8 your border unto...entrance of **H.**; 2574
Jos 13:5 Hermon unto the entering into **H.** 2574
Jg 3:3 Baal-hermon...entering in of **H.** 2574
2Sa 8:9 When Toi king of **H.** heard that 2574
1Ki 8:65 from the entering in of **H.** unto the 2574
2Ki 14:25 from the entering of **H.** unto the 2574
2Ki 14:28 and **H.**, which belonged to Judah, 2574
2Ki 17:24 and from **H.**, and from Sepharvaim, 2574
2Ki 17:30 and the men of **H.** made Ashima, 2574
2Ki 18:34 Where are the gods of **H.**, and of 2574
2Ki 19:13 Where is the king of **H.**, and the 2574
2Ki 23:33 at Riblah in the land of **H.**, that he 2574
2Ki 25:21 slew them at Riblah...land of **H.** 2574
1Ch 18:3 Hadarezer king of Zobak unto **H.**, 2574
1Ch 18:9 when Tou king of **H.** heard how 2574
2Ch 7:8 of **H.** unto the river of Egypt. 2574
2Ch 8:4 store cities, which he built in **H.** 2574
Isa 10:9 is not **H.** as Arpad? is not 2574
Isa 11:11 from **H.**, and from the islands 2574
Isa 36:19 Where are the gods of **H.** and 2574
Isa 37:13 Where is the king of **H.**, and the 2574
Jer 39:5 **H.**, where he gave judgment upon 2574
Jer 49:23 **H.** is confounded, and Arpad: 2574
Jer 52:9 to Riblah in the land of **H.**; 2574
Jer 52:27 to death in Riblah in the land of **H.** 2574
Eze 47:16 **H.**, Berothah, Sibraim, which is 2574
Eze 47:16 of Damascus and the border of **H.** 2574
Eze 47:17 northward, and the border of **H.** 2574
Eze 47:20 till a man come over against **H.** 2574
Eze 48:1 of Hethlon, as one goeth to **H.**, 2574
Eze 48:1 Damascus northward...coast of **H.**; 2574
Am 6:2 from thence go ye to **H.** the great 2579
Zec 9:2 **H.** also shall border thereby; 2574

HAMATHITE (ham'-a-thite)
Ge 10:18 the Zemarite, and the **H.**: and 2577
1Ch 1:16 the Zemarite, and the **H.** 2577

HAMATH-ZOBAH (ha''-math-zo'-bah)
2Ch 8:3 And Solomon went to **H.**, and 2578

HAMMAHLEKOTH See SELA-HAMMAHLEKOTH.

HAMMATH (ham'-math)
Jos 19:35 and **H.**, Rakkath, and 2575

HAMMEDATHA (ham-med'-a-thah)
Es 3:1 the son of **H.** the Agagite. 4099
Es 3:10 Haman the son of **H.** the Agagite, 4099
Es 8:5 by Haman the son of **H.** the 4099
Es 9:10 sons of Haman the son of **H.**, the 4099
Es 9:24 son of **H.**, the Agagite, the enemy 4099

HAMMELECH (ham'-me-lek)
Jer 36:26 Jerahmeel the son of **H.**, and ... 4429
Jer 38:6 Malchiah the son of **H.**, that was ... 4429

HAMMER See also HAMMERS.
Jg 4:21 took an **h.** in her hand, and went ... 4718
Jg 5:26 right hand to the workmen's **h.**; ... 1989
Jg 5:26 and with the **h.** she smote ...
1Ki 6:7 neither **h.** nor axe nor any tool of ... 4717
Isa 41:7 he that smootheth with the **h.** ... 6360
Jer 23:29 and like a **h.** that breaketh ... 6360
Jer 50:23 the **h.** of the whole earth ... 6360

HAMMERS
Ps 74:6 work...at once with axes and **h.**. ... 3597
Isa 44:12 and fashioneth it with **h.**, and ... 4717
Jer 10:4 fasten it with nails and with **h.**, ... 4717

HAMMOLEKETH (ham-mol'-e-keth)
1Ch 7:18 And his sister **H.** bare Ishod, ... 4447

HAMMON (ham'-mon)
Jos 19:28 Hebron, and Rehob, and **H.**, ... 2540
1Ch 6:76 and **H.** with her suburbs, and ... 2540

HAMMOTH-DOR (ham''-moth-dor')
Jos 21:32 and **H.** with her suburbs, ... 2576

HAMON See BAAL-HAMON; HAMON-GOG.

HAMONAH (ha-mo'-nah)
Eze 39:16 the name of the city shall be **H.**. ... 1997

HAMON-GOG (ha''-mon-gog')
Eze 39:11 shall call it The valley of **H.**. ... 1996
Eze 39:15 have buried it in the valley of **H.**. ... 1996

HAMOR (ha'-mor) See also EMMOR; HAMOR'S.
Ge 33:19 at the hand of the children of **H.**, ... 2544
Ge 34:2 when Shechem the son of **H.** the ... 2544
Ge 34:4 Shechem spake unto his father **H.**, ... 2544
Ge 34:6 **H.** the father of Shechem went ... 2544
Ge 34:8 And **H.** communed with them, ... 2544
Ge 34:13 answered Shechem and **H.** his ... 2544
Ge 34:18 And their words pleased **H.** ... 2544
Ge 34:20 **H.** and Shechem his son came ... 2544
Ge 34:24 And unto **H.** and unto Shechem ... 2544
Ge 34:26 they slew **H.** and Shechem his son ... 2544
Jos 24:32 Jacob bought of the sons of **H.** ... 2544
Jg 9:28 serve the men of **H.** the father of ... 2544

HAMOR'S (ha'-mors)
Ge 34:18 and Shechem **H.** son. ... 2544

HAMUEL (ha-mu'-el)
1Ch 4:26 **H.** his son, Zacchur his son, ... 2536

HAMUL (ha'-mul) See also HAMULITES.
Gen 46:12 sons of Pharez...Hezron and **H.**. ... 2538
Nu 26:21 of **H.**, the family of the Hamulites. ... 2538
1Ch 2:5 sons of Pharez; Hezron, and **H.** ... 2538

HAMULITES (ha'-mu-lites)
Nu 26:21 of Hamul, the family of the **H.**. ... 2539

HAMUTAL (ha-mu'-tal)
2Ki 23:31 his mother's name was **H.**, ... 2537
2Ki 24:18 **H.**, the daughter of Jeremiah ... 2537
Jer 52:1 his mother's name was **H.** ... 2537

HANAMEEL (ha-nam'-e-el)
Jer 32:7 Behold, **H.** the son of Shallum ... 2601
Jer 32:8 So **H.** mine uncle's son came ... 2601
Jer 32:9 And I bought the field of **H.** ... 2601
Jer 32:12 in the sight of **H.** mine uncle's ... 2601

HANAN (ha'-nan) See also BAAL-HANAN; BEN-HANAN; ELON-BETH-HANAN.
1Ch 8:23 And Abdon, and Zichri, and **H.**, ... 2605
1Ch 8:38 Sheariah, and Obadiah, and **H.** ... 2605
1Ch 9:44 Obadiah, and **H.**: these were the ... 2605
1Ch 11:43 **H.** the son of Maachah, and ... 2605
Ezr 2:46 of Shalmai, the children of **H.**, ... 2605
Ne 7:49 The children of **H.**, the children ... 2605
Ne 8:7 Azariah, Jozabad, **H.**, Pelaiah, ... 2605
Ne 10:10 Kelita, Pelaiah, **H.**, ... 2605
Ne 10:22 Pelatiah, **H.**, Anaiah, ... 2605
Ne 10:26 And Ahijah, **H.**, Anan, ... 2605
Ne 13:13 and next to them was **H.** the son ... 2605
Jer 35:4 into the chamber of the sons of **H.**, ... 2605

HANANEEL (ha-nan'-e-el)
Ne 3:1 sanctified it unto the tower of **H.**. ... 2606
Ne 12:39 the tower of **H.**, and the tower of ... 2606
Jer 31:38 the tower of **H.** unto the gate ... 2606
Zec 14:10 the tower of **H.** unto the king's ... 2606

HANANI (ha-na'-ni)
1Ki 16:1 came to Jehu the son of **H.** ... 2607
1Ki 16:7 of the prophet Jehu, the son of **H.** ... 2607
1Ch 25:4 Hananiah, **H.**, Eliathah, Giddalti, ... 2607
1Ch 25:25 The eighteenth to **H.**, he, his sons, ... 2607
2Ch 16:7 at that time **H.** the seer came to ... 2607
2Ch 19:2 Jehu the son of **H.** the seer went ... 2607
2Ch 20:34 in the book of Jehu the son of **H.**, ... 2607
Ezr 10:20 of the sons of Immer; **H.**, and ... 2607
Ne 1:2 That **H.**, one of my brethren, ... 2607
Ne 7:2 That I gave my brother **H.**, and ... 2607
Ne 12:36 and Judah, **H.**, with the musical ... 2607

HANANIAH (han-a-ni'-ah) See also SHADRACH.
1Ch 3:19 Meshullam, and **H.**, and ... 2608
1Ch 3:21 the sons of **H.**; Pelatiah, and ... 2608
1Ch 8:24 **H.**, and Elam, and Antothijah, ... 2608
1Ch 25:4 Jerimoth, **H.**, Hanani, ... 2608
1Ch 25:23 The sixteenth to **H.**, he, his sons, ... 2608
2Ch 26:11 **H.**, one of the king's captains. ... 2608
Ezr 10:28 Jehohanan, **H.**, Zabbai, ... 2608
Ne 3:8 repaired **H.** the son of one of the ... 2608
Ne 3:30 repaired **H.**, the son of Shelemiah, ... 2608
Ne 7:2 and **H.** the ruler of the palace, ... 2608
Ne 10:23 Hoshea, **H.**, Hashub, ... 2608
Ne 12:12 of Jeremiah, **H.**; ... 2608
Ne 12:41 Zechariah, and **H.**, with trumpets; ... 2608
Jer 28:1 **H.** the son of Azur the prophet. ... 2608
Jer 28:5 Jeremiah said unto the prophet **H.** ... 2608
Jer 28:10 Then **H.** the prophet took the ... 2608
Jer 28:11 **H.** spake in the presence of all the ... 2608
Jer 28:12 after that **H.** the prophet had ... 2608
Jer 28:13 Go and tell **H.**, saying, Thus saith ... 2608
Jer 28:15 Then said...Jeremiah unto **H.** ... 2608
Jer 28:15 the prophet, Hear now, **H.**; ... 2608
Jer 28:17 So **H.** the prophet died the same ... 2608
Jer 36:12 and Zedekiah the son of **H.**, and ... 2608
Jer 37:13 Shelemiah the son of **H.**; and he ... 2608
Da 1:6 Daniel, **H.**, Mishael, and Azariah: ... 2608
Da 1:7 and to **H.**, of Shadrach; and to ... 2608
Da 1:11 over Daniel, **H.**, Mishael, and ... 2608
Da 1:19 none like Daniel, **H.**, Mishael, ... 2608
Da 2:17 and made the thing known to **H.**, ... 2608

HAND See also AFOREHAND; BEFOREHAND; HANDBREADTH; HANDED; HANDFUL; HANDKERCHIEFS; HANDMAID; HANDS; HAND-STAVES; HANDWRITING; HANDYWORK.
Ge 3:22 now, lest he put forth his **h.**, and ... 3027
Ge 4:11 thy brother's blood from thy **h.**; ... 3027
Ge 8:9 then he put forth his **h.**, and took ... 3027
Ge 9:2 fishes of the sea; into your **h.** are ... 3027
Ge 9:5 at the **h.** of every beast will I ... 3027
Ge 9:5 require it, and at the **h.** of man; ... 3027
Ge 9:5 at the **h.** of every man's ... 3027
Ge 13:9 if thou wilt take the left **h.**, ... 8041
Ge 13:9 or if thou depart to the right **h.**, ... 3225
Ge 14:15 which is on the left **h.** of Damascus. ... 8040
Ge 14:20 thine enemies into thy **h.** ... 3027
Ge 14:22 I have lift up mine **h.** unto the ... 3027
Ge 16:6 Behold, thy maid is in thy **h.**; ... 3027
Ge 16:12 his **h.** will be against every man, ... 3027
Ge 16:12 and every man's **h.** against him; ... 3027
Ge 19:10 the men put forth their **h.**, and ... 3027
Ge 19:16 the men laid hold upon his **h.**, and ... 3027
Ge 19:16 upon the **h.** of his wife, and upon ... 3027
Ge 19:16 the **h.** of his two daughters; ... 3027
Ge 21:18 hold him in thine **h.**; for I will ... 3027
Ge 21:30 lambs shalt thou take of my **h.**, ... 3027
Ge 22:6 he took the fire in his **h.**, and a ... 3027
Ge 22:10 Abraham stretched forth his **h.**, ... 3027
Ge 22:12 Lay not thine **h.** upon the lad, ... 3027
Ge 24:2 Put, I pray thee, thy **h.** under my ... 3027
Ge 24:9 the servant put his **h.** under the ... 3027
Ge 24:10 goods of his master were in his **h.** ... 3027
Ge 24:18 let down her pitcher upon her **h.**, ... 3027
Ge 24:49 that I may turn to the right **h.** ... 3225
Ge 25:26 and his **h.** took hold on Esau's heel: ... 3027
Ge 27:17 into the **h.** of her son Jacob. ... 3027
Ge 27:41 mourning for my father are at **h.**; ... 7126
Ge 30:35 gave them into the **h.** of his sons. ... 3027
Ge 31:29 It is in the power of my **h.** to do ... 3027
Ge 31:39 of my **h.** didst thou require it, ... 3027
Ge 32:11 Deliver me, I pray thee, from the **h.** .. 3027
Ge 32:11 of my brother, from the **h.** of Esau: ... 3027
Ge 32:13 that which came to his **h.** a present ... 3027
Ge 32:16 delivered them into the **h.** of his ... 3027
Ge 33:10 then receive my present at my **h.**: ... 3027
Ge 33:19 at the **h.** of the children of Hamor, ... 3027
Ge 35:4 strange gods which were in their **h.**, ... 3027
Ge 37:22 and lay no **h.** upon him; that he ... 3027
Ge 37:27 and let not our **h.** be upon him; ... 3027
Ge 38:18 thy staff that is in thine **h.**. ... 3027
Ge 38:20 sent the kid by the **h.** of his friend ... 3027
Ge 38:20 his pledge from the woman's **h.** ... 3027
Ge 38:28 put out his **h.**: and the midwife ... 3027
Ge 38:28 took and bound upon his **h.** a ... 3027
Ge 38:29 as he drew back his **h.**, that, ... 3027
Ge 38:30 had the scarlet thread upon his **h.** ... 3027
Ge 39:3 that he did to prosper in his **h.**. ... 3027
Ge 39:4 all that he had he put into his **h.**. ... 3027
Ge 39:6 left all that he had in Joseph's **h.**; ... 3027
Ge 39:8 committed all that he hath to my **h.**; ... 3027
Ge 39:12 left his garment in her **h.**, and fled, ... 3027
Ge 39:13 he had left his garment in her **h.**, ... 3027
Ge 39:22 committed to Joseph's **h.** all the ... 3027
Ge 39:23 any thing that was under his **h.**; ... 3027
Ge 40:11 Pharaoh's cup was in my **h.**: and I ... 3027
Ge 40:11 I gave the cup into Pharaoh's **h.**. ... 3709
Ge 40:13 deliver Pharaoh's cup into his **h.**, ... 3027
Ge 40:21 he gave the cup into Pharaoh's **h.**: ... 3709
Ge 41:35 lay up corn under the **h.** of ... 3027
Ge 41:42 took off his ring from his **h.**, and ... 3027
Ge 41:42 put it upon Joseph's **h.**, and ... 3027
Ge 41:44 shall no man lift up his **h.** ... 3027
Ge 42:37 deliver him into my **h.**, and I will ... 3027
Ge 43:9 of my **h.** shalt thou require him: ... 3027
Ge 43:12 take double money in your **h.**; and ... 3027
Ge 43:12 sacks, carry it again in your **h.**; ... 3027
Ge 43:15 they took double money in their **h.**, ... 3027
Ge 43:21 have brought it again in our **h.** ... 3027
Ge 43:26 present which was in their **h.** into ... 3027
Ge 44:17 in whose **h.** the cup is found, he ... 3027
Ge 46:4 Joseph shall put his **h.** upon thine ... 3027
Ge 47:29 put, I pray thee, thy **h.** under my ... 3027
Ge 48:13 them both, Ephraim in his right **h.** ... 3225
Ge 48:13 toward Israel's left **h.**. ... 8040
Ge 48:13 and Manasseh in his left **h.** ... 8040
Ge 48:13 toward Israel's right **h.**, ... 3225
Ge 48:14 Israel stretched out his right **h.**, ... 3225
Ge 48:14 his left **h.** upon Manasseh's head, ... 8040
Ge 48:17 laid his right **h.** upon the head ... 3225
Ge 48:17 he held up his father's **h.**, to remove .. 3027
Ge 48:18 put thy right **h.** upon his head. ... 3225
Ge 48:22 which I took out of the **h.** of the ... 3027
Ge 49:8 thy **h.** shall be in the neck of thine ... 3027
Ex 2:19 delivered us out of the **h.** of the ... 3027
Ex 3:8 deliver them out of the **h.** of the ... 3027
Ex 3:19 let you go, no, not by a mighty **h.** ... 3027
Ex 3:20 I will stretch out my **h.**, and smite ... 3027
Ex 4:2 What is that in thine **h.**? And he ... 3027
Ex 4:4 Put forth thine **h.**, and take it by ... 3027
Ex 4:4 And he put forth his **h.**, and ... 3027
Ex 4:4 it became a rod in his **h.** ... 3709
Ex 4:6 Put now thine **h.** into thy bosom. ... 3027
Ex 4:6 And he put his **h.** into his bosom: ... 3027
Ex 4:6 behold, his **h.** was leprous as snow ... 3027
Ex 4:7 Put thine **h.** into thy bosom again. ... 3027
Ex 4:7 And he put his **h.** into his bosom ... 3027
Ex 4:13 send, I pray thee, by the **h.** of him ... 3027
Ex 4:17 shalt take this rod in thine **h.**, ... 3027
Ex 4:20 took the rod of God in his **h.** ... 3027
Ex 4:21 which I have put in thine **h.**: ... 3027
Ex 5:21 to put a sword in their **h.** to slay us. .. 3027
Ex 6:1 for with a strong **h.** shall he let ... 3027
Ex 6:1 and with a strong **h.** shall he drive ... 3027
Ex 7:4 that I may lay my **h.** upon Egypt, ... 3027
Ex 7:5 when I stretch forth mine **h.** upon ... 3027
Ex 7:15 serpent shalt thou take in thine **h.** ... 3027
Ex 7:17 with the rod that is in mine **h.** ... 3027
Ex 7:19 stretch out thine **h.** upon the ... 3027
Ex 8:5 Stretch forth thine **h.** with thy rod ... 3027
Ex 8:6 Aaron stretched out his **h.** over the ... 3027
Ex 8:17 Aaron stretched out his **h.** with his ... 3027
Ex 9:3 the **h.** of the Lord is upon thy ... 3027
Ex 9:15 now I will stretch out my **h.**, that I ... 3027
Ex 9:22 Stretch forth thine **h.** toward ... 3027
Ex 10:12 Stretch out thine **h.** over the land ... 3027
Ex 10:21 Stretch out thine **h.** toward heaven, ... 3027
Ex 10:22 Moses stretched forth his **h.** ... 3027
Ex 12:11 your staff in your **h.**; and ye ... 3027
Ex 13:3 for by strength of **h.** the Lord ... 3027
Ex 13:9 a sign unto thee upon thine **h.**, ... 3027

Book	Ref	Context	No.
Ex	13:9	for with a strong **h.** hath the Lord	3027
Ex	13:14	By strength of **h.** the Lord brought	3027
Ex	13:16	for a token upon thine **h.**, and for	3027
Ex	13:16	for by strength of **h.** the Lord	3027
Ex	14:8	of Israel went out with an high **h.**.	3027
Ex	14:16	stretch out thine **h.** over the sea,	3027
Ex	14:21	Moses stretched out his **h.** over the	3027
Ex	14:22	on their right **h.**, and on their left.	3225
Ex	14:26	Stretch out thine **h.** over the sea,	3027
Ex	14:27	Moses stretched forth his **h.** over	3027
Ex	14:29	a wall unto them on their right **h.**,	3225
Ex	14:30	saved Israel that day out of the **h.**	3027
Ex	15:6	Thy right **h.**, O Lord, is become	3225
Ex	15:6	thy right **h.**, O Lord, hath dashed	3225
Ex	15:9	my sword, my **h.** shall destroy	3027
Ex	15:12	Thou stretchedst out thy right **h.**,	3225
Ex	15:20	took a timbrel in her **h.**; and all	3027
Ex	16:3	we had died by the **h.** of the Lord	3027
Ex	17:5	the river, take in thine **h.**, and go.	3027
Ex	17:9	with the rod of God in mine **h.**.	3027
Ex	17:11	Moses held up his **h.**, that Israel	3027
Ex	17:11	and when he let down his **h.**,	3027
Ex	18:9	delivered out of the **h.** of the	3027
Ex	18:10	delivered you out of the **h.** of the	3027
Ex	18:10	and out of the **h.** of Pharaoh,	3027
Ex	18:10	from under the **h.** of the Egyptians.	3027
Ex	19:13	There shall not an **h.** touch it,	3027
Ex	21:13	God deliver him into his **h.**; then I	3027
Ex	21:16	him, or if he be found in his **h.**,	3027
Ex	21:20	and he die under his **h.**; he shall be	3027
Ex	21:24	tooth for tooth, **h.** for **h.**, foot	3027
Ex	22:4	the theft be certainly found in his **h.**	3027
Ex	22:8	put his **h.** unto his neighbour's	3027
Ex	22:11	he hath not put his **h.** unto his	3027
Ex	23:1	put not thine **h.** with the wicked	3027
Ex	23:31	inhabitants of the land into your **h.**;	3027
Ex	24:11	of Israel he laid not his **h.**:	3027
Ex	25:25	a border of an **h.** breadth	2948
Ex	29:20	upon the thumb of their right **h.**,	3027
Ex	32:4	he received them at their **h.**, and	3027
Ex	32:11	great power, and with a mighty **h.**?	3027
Ex	32:15	of the testimony were in his **h.**:	3027
Ex	33:22	and will cover thee with my **h.**	3709
Ex	33:23	And I will take away mine **h.**,	3709
Ex	34:4	took in his **h.** the two tables of	3027
Ex	34:29	tables of testimony in Moses' **h.**.	3027
Ex	35:29	commanded to be made by the **h.**	3027
Ex	38:15	court gate, on this **h.** and that **h.**,	
Ex	38:21	by the **h.** of Ithamar, son to Aaron	3027
Le	1:4	he shall put his **h.** upon the head	3027
Le	3:2,8,	13 shall lay his **h.** upon the head	3027
Le	4:4	shall lay his **h.** upon the bullock's	3027
Le	4:24	lay his **h.** upon the head of the goat	3027
Le	4:29,	33 lay his **h.** upon the...sin	3027
Le	8:23	upon the thumb of his right **h.**,	3027
Le	8:36	the Lord commanded by the **h.** of	3027
Le	9:22	Aaron lifted up his **h.** toward the	3027
Le	10:11	spoken unto them by the **h.** of	3027
Le	14:14	upon the thumb of his right **h.**,	3027
Le	14:15	it into the palm of his own left **h.**:	8042
Le	14:16	the oil that is in his left **h.**, and	3709
Le	14:17	the rest of the oil that is in his **h.**	3709
Le	14:17	upon the thumb of his right **h.**,	3027
Le	14:18	the oil that is in the priest's **h.**	3709
Le	14:25	upon the thumb of his right **h.**,	3027
Le	14:26	oil into the palm of his own left **h.**:	8042
Le	14:27	the oil that is in his left **h.** seven	3709
Le	14:28	the oil that is in his **h.** upon the	3709
Le	14:28	upon the thumb of his right **h.**,	3027
Le	14:29	the oil that is in the priest's **h.** he	3709
Le	14:32	leprosy, whose **h.** is not able to get	3027
Le	16:21	send him away by the **h.** of a fit	3027
Le	22:25	Neither from a stranger's **h.** shall	3027
Le	25:14	ought of thy neighbour's **h.**,	3027
Le	25:28	shall remain in the **h.** of him that	3027
Le	26:25	ye shall be delivered into the **h.** of	3027
Le	26:46	in mount Sinai by the **h.** of Moses.	3027
Nu	4:28	charge shall be under the **h.** of	3027
Nu	4:33	congregation, under the **h.** of	3027
Nu	4:37	commandment...by the **h.** of Moses.	3027
Nu	4:45	word of...by the **h.** of Moses.	3027
Nu	4:49	were numbered by the **h.** of Moses,	3027
Nu	5:18	and the priest shall have in his **h.**	3027
Nu	5:25	offering out of the woman's **h.**,	3027
Nu	6:21	beside that that his **h.** shall get:	3027
Nu	7:8	under the **h.** of Ithamar the son of	3027
Nu	9:23	of the Lord by the **h.** of Moses.	3027
Nu	10:13	of the Lord by the **h.** of Moses.	3027
Nu	11:15	kill me, I pray thee, out of **h.**,	2026
Nu	11:23	Is the Lord's **h.** waxed short?	3027
Nu	15:23	by the **h.** of Moses, from the day	3027
Nu	16:40	Lord said to him by the **h.** of Moses	3027
Nu	20:11	Moses lifted up his **h.**, and with	3027
Nu	20:17	we will not turn to the right **h.** nor	3225
Nu	20:20	much people, and with a strong **h.**	3027
Nu	21:2	deliver this people into my **h.**, then	3027
Nu	21:26	taken all his land out of his **h.**	3027
Nu	21:34	I have delivered him into thy **h.**,	3027
Nu	22:7	rewards of divination in their **h.**;	3027
Nu	22:23	his sword drawn in his **h.**: and	3027
Nu	22:26	to the right **h.** or to the left.	3325
Nu	22:29	there were a sword in mine **h.**,	3027
Nu	22:31	sword drawn in his **h.**: and he	3027
Nu	25:7	and took a javelin in his **h.**;	3027
Nu	27:18	spirit, and lay thine **h.** upon him;	3027
Nu	27:23	commanded by the **h.** of Moses.	3027
Nu	31:6	the trumpets to blow in his **h.**.	3027
Nu	33:1	under the **h.** of Moses and Aaron.	3027
Nu	33:3	of Israel went out with an high **h.**	3027
Nu	35:18	if he smite him with an **h.** weapon	3027
Nu	35:21	in enmity smite him with his **h.**,	3027
Nu	35:25	out of the **h.** of the revenger of	3027
Nu	36:13	by the **h.** of Moses unto the	3027
De	1:27	deliver us into the hand of the	3027
De	2:7	the works of thy **h.**: he knoweth	3027
De	2:15	the **h.** of the Lord was against	3027
De	2:24	I have given into thine **h.** Sihon	3027
De	2:27	I will neither turn unto the right **h.**	3225
De	2:30	deliver him into thy **h.**, as	3027
De	3:2	and his land, into thy **h.**; and thou	3027
De	3:8	out of the **h.** of the two kings of the	3027
De	3:24	thy mighty **h.**: for what God	3027
De	4:34	and by a mighty **h.**, and by a	3027
De	5:15	through a mighty **h.** and by a	3027
De	5:32	turn aside to the right **h.** or to the	3225
De	6:8	a sign upon thine **h.**, and they	3027
De	6:21	out of Egypt with a mighty **h.**:	3027
De	7:8	you out with a mighty **h.**, and	3027
De	7:8	from the **h.** of Pharaoh king of	3027
De	7:19	and the mighty **h.**, and the	3027
De	7:24	deliver their kings into thine **h.**,	3027
De	8:17	the might of mine **h.** hath gotten	3027
De	9:26	out of Egypt, with a mighty **h.**.	3027
De	10:3	having the two tables in mine **h.**.	3027
De	11:2	his mighty **h.**, and his stretched	3027
De	11:18	a sign upon your **h.**, that they may	3027
De	12:6	heave offerings of your **h.**, and	3027
De	12:7	all that ye put your **h.** unto, ye	3027
De	12:11	the heave offering of your **h.**,	3027
De	12:17	or heave offering of thine **h.**:	3027
De	13:9	thine **h.** shall be first upon him to	3027
De	13:9	and afterwards the **h.** of all the	3027
De	13:17	the cursed thing to thine **h.**: that	3027
De	14:25	bind up the money in thine **h.**,	3027
De	14:29	the work of thine **h.** which thou	3027
De	15:3	thy brother thine **h.** shall release;	3027
De	15:7	nor shut thine **h.** from thy poor	3027
De	15:8	thou shalt open thine **h.** wide unto	3027
De	15:9	the year of release, is at **h.**;	7126
De	15:10	all that thou puttest thine **h.** unto.	3027
De	15:11	Thou shalt open thine **h.** wide unto	3027
De	16:10	a freewill offering of thine **h.**,	3027
De	17:11	to the right **h.**, nor to the left.	3225
De	17:20	to the right **h.**, or to the left: to the	3225
De	19:5	his **h.** fetcheth a stroke with the	3027
De	19:12	into the **h.** of the avenger of blood,	3027
De	19:21	for tooth, **h.** for **h.**, foot for foot.	3027
De	23:20	all that thou settest thine **h.** to in	3027
De	23:25	pluck the ears with thine **h.**;	3027
De	24:1	give it in her **h.**, and send her	3027
De	24:3	giveth it in her **h.**, and sendeth	3027
De	25:11	out of the **h.** of him that smiteth	3027
De	25:11	and putteth forth her **h.**,	3027
De	25:12	Then thou shalt cut off her **h.**,	3709
De	26:4	take the basket out of thine **h.**,	3027
De	26:8	with a mighty **h.**, and with	3027
De	28:8	all that thou settest thine **h.** unto;	3027
De	28:12	bless all the work of thine **h.**:	3027
De	28:14	to the right **h.**, or to the left.	3225
De	28:20	all that thou settest thine **h.** unto	3027
De	28:32	shall be no might in thine **h.**.	3027
De	30:9	every work of thine **h.**, in the	3027
De	32:27	Our **h.** is high, and the Lord	3027
De	32:35	the day of their calamity is at **h.**,	7138
De	32:39	that can deliver out of my **h.**.	3027
De	32:40	I lift up my **h.** to heaven, and say,	3027
De	32:41	mine **h.** take hold on judgment;	3027
De	33:2	from his right **h.** went a fiery law	3225
De	33:3	all his saints are in thy **h.**: and	3027
De	34:12	in all that mighty **h.**, and in all	3027
Jos	1:7	to the right **h.** or to the left,	3225
Jos	2:19	our head, if any **h.** be upon him.	3027
Jos	4:24	the **h.** of the Lord, that it is	3027
Jos	5:13	his sword drawn in his **h.**: and	3027
Jos	6:2	I have given into thine **h.** Jericho,	3027
Jos	7:7	into the **h.** of the Amorites, to	3027
Jos	8:1	I have given into thy **h.** the king	3027
Jos	8:7	God will deliver it into your **h.**	3027
Jos	8:18	the spear that is in thy **h.** toward	3027
Jos	8:18	for I will give it into thine **h.**.	3027
Jos	8:18	the spear that he had in his **h.**	3027
Jos	8:19	he had stretched out his **h.**: and	3027
Jos	8:26	Joshua drew not his **h.** back,	3027
Jos	9:25	we are in thine **h.**: as it	3027
Jos	9:26	out of the **h.** of the children of	3027
Jos	10:6	Slack not thy **h.** from thy servants;	3027
Jos	10:8	delivered them into thine **h.**;	3027
Jos	10:19	hath delivered them into your **h.**.	3027
Jos	10:30	the king thereof, into the **h.** of	3027
Jos	10:32	Lachish into the **h.** of Israel, which	3027
Jos	11:8	Lord delivered them into the **h.**	3027
Jos	14:2	by the **h.** of Moses, for the nine	3027
Jos	17:7	border went along on the right **h.**	3225
Jos	19:27	goeth out to Cabul on the left **h.**,	8040
Jos	20:2	I spake unto you by the **h.** of Moses:	3027
Jos	20:5	deliver the slayer up into his **h.**;	3027
Jos	20:9	by the **h.** of the avenger of blood,	3027
Jos	21:2	by the **h.** of Moses to give us	3027
Jos	21:8	commanded by the **h.** of Moses.	3027
Jos	21:44	all their enemies into their **h.**.	3027
Jos	22:9	of the Lord by the **h.** of Moses.	3027
Jos	22:31	out of the **h.** of the Lord.	3027
Jos	23:6	turn not aside...to the right **h.**	3225
Jos	24:8	I gave them into your **h.**, that ye	3027
Jos	24:10	I delivered you out of his **h.**	3027
Jos	24:11	and I delivered them into your **h.**	3027
Jg	1:2	I have delivered the land into his **h.**	3027
Jg	1:4	the Perizzites into their **h.**: and	3027
Jg	1:35	the **h.** of the house of Joseph	3027
Jg	2:15	the **h.** of the Lord was against them	3027
Jg	2:16	out of the **h.** of those that spoiled	3027
Jg	2:18	out of the **h.** of their enemies all	3027
Jg	2:23	them into the **h.** of Joshua.	3027
Jg	3:4	their fathers by the **h.** of Moses.	3027
Jg	3:8	into the **h.** of Chushan-rishathaim	3027
Jg	3:10	into his **h.**; and his **h.** prevailed	3027
Jg	3:21	Ehud put forth his left **h.**, and took	3027
Jg	3:28	enemies the Moabites into your **h.**.	3027
Jg	3:30	that day under the **h.** of Israel.	3027
Jg	4:2	Lord sold them into the **h.** of Jabin	3027
Jg	4:7	I will deliver him into thine **h.**.	3027
Jg	4:9	Sisera into the **h.** of a woman.	3027
Jg	4:14	hath delivered Sisera into thine **h.**:	3027
Jg	4:21	took an hammer in her **h.**, and	3027
Jg	4:24	the **h.** of the children of Israel	3027
Jg	5:26	She put her **h.** to the nail,	3027
Jg	5:26	and her right **h.** to the workmen's	3225
Jg	6:1	Lord delivered them into the **h.** of	3027
Jg	6:2	the **h.** of Midian prevailed against	3027
Jg	6:9	out of the **h.** of the Egyptians,	3027
Jg	6:9	out of the **h.** of all that oppressed	3027
Jg	6:14	from the **h.** of the Midianites:	3709
Jg	6:21	the staff that was in his **h.**,	3027
Jg	6:36	If thou wilt save Israel by mine **h.**,	3027
Jg	6:37	thou wilt save Israel by mine **h.**	3027
Jg	7:2	Mine own **h.** hath saved me.	3027
Jg	7:6	putting their **h.** to their mouth,	3027
Jg	7:7	deliver the Midianites into thine **h.**:	3027
Jg	7:8	the people took victuals in their **h.**.	3027
Jg	7:9	I have delivered it into thine **h.**	3027
Jg	7:14	into his **h.** hath God delivered	3027
Jg	7:15	Lord hath delivered into your **h.**	3027
Jg	7:16	put a trumpet in every man's **h.**,	3027
Jg	8:6	and Zalmunna now in thine **h.**,	3027
Jg	8:7	and Zalmunna into mine **h.**, then	3027
Jg	8:15	and Zalmunna now in thine **h.**,	3027
Jg	8:22	thou hast delivered us from the **h.**	3027
Jg	9:17	delivered you out of the **h.** of	3027
Jg	9:29	this people were under my **h.**! then	3027
Jg	9:48	Abimelech took an axe in his **h.**,	3027

Jg 10:12 I delivered you out of their **h.** 3027
Jg 11:21 into the **h.** of Israel, and they 3027
Jg 12:3 the Lord delivered them into my **h.**: 3027
Jg 13:1 delivered them into the **h.** of 3027
Jg 13:5 out of the **h.** of the Philistines 3027
Jg 14:6 he had nothing in his **h.**: 3027
Jg 15:12 deliver thee into the **h.** of the 3027
Jg 15:13 deliver thee into their **h.**: but 3027
Jg 15:15 put forth his **h.**, and took it, 3027
Jg 15:17 cast away the jawbone out of his **h.**, 3027
Jg 15:18 into the **h.** of thy servant: and now 3027
Jg 15:18 into the **h.** of the uncircumcised? 3027
Jg 16:18 and brought money in their **h.** 3027
Jg 16:23 Samson our enemy into our **h.** 3027
Jg 16:26 the lad that held him by the **h.**, 3027
Jg 16:29 the one with his right **h.**, and of the 3225
Jg 17:3 from my **h.** for my son, to make 3027
Jg 18:19 lay thine **h.** upon thy mouth, and 3027
Jg 20:28 I will deliver them into thine **h.** 3027
Jg 20:48 all that me to **h.**: also they 4672
Ru 1:13 the **h.** of the Lord is gone out 3027
Ru 4:5 thou buyest the field of the **h.** of 3027
Ru 4:9 and Mahlon's, of the **h.** of Naomi 3027
1Sa 2:13 a fleshhook of three teeth in his **h.**; 3027
1Sa 4:3 out of the **h.** of our enemies 3709
1Sa 4:8 out of the **h.** of these mighty Gods? 3027
1Sa 5:6 the **h.** of the Lord was heavy upon 3027
1Sa 5:7 his **h.** is sore upon us, and upon 3027
1Sa 5:9 the **h.** of the Lord was against the 3027
1Sa 5:11 **h.** of God was very heavy there 3027
1Sa 6:3 why his **h.** is not removed from 3027
1Sa 6:5 peradventure he will lighten his **h.** 3027
1Sa 6:9 we shall know that it is not his **h.** 3027
1Sa 6:12 turned not aside to the right **h.** 3225
1Sa 7:3 he will deliver you out of the **h.** of 3027
1Sa 7:8 he will save us out of the **h.** of the 3027
1Sa 7:13 the **h.** of the Lord was against the 3027
1Sa 9:8 I have here at **h.** the fourth part 3027
1Sa 9:16 out of the **h.** of the Philistines: 3027
1Sa 10:18 the **h.** of the Egyptians, and...the **h.** 3027
1Sa 12:3 or of whose **h.** have I received any 3027
1Sa 12:4 taken ought of any man's **h.** 3027
1Sa 12:5 ye have not found ought in my **h.** 3027
1Sa 12:9 he sold them into the **h.** of Sisera, 3027
1Sa 12:9 and into the **h.** of the Philistines, 3027
1Sa 12:9 and into the **h.** of the king of Moab, 3027
1Sa 12:10 deliver us out of the **h.** of our 3027
1Sa 12:11 delivered you out of the **h.** of your 3027
1Sa 12:15 then shall the **h.** of the Lord be 3027
1Sa 13:22 in the **h.** of any of the people 3027
1Sa 14:10 hath delivered them into our **h.**: 3027
1Sa 14:12 hath delivered them into the **h.** of 3027
1Sa 14:19 unto the priest; Withdraw thine **h.** 3027
1Sa 14:26 no man put his **h.** to his mouth: 3027
1Sa 14:27 rod that was in his **h.**, and dipped 3027
1Sa 14:27 and put his **h.** to his mouth; 3027
1Sa 14:37 wilt thou deliver them into the **h.** 3027
1Sa 14:43 the rod that was in mine **h.**, 3027
1Sa 16:16 he shall play with his **h.**, and thou 3027
1Sa 16:23 took an harp, and played with his **h.**: 3027
1Sa 17:22 David left his carriage in the **h.** of 3027
1Sa 17:37 me out of the **h.** of this Philistine 3027
1Sa 17:40 took his staff in his **h.**, and 3027
1Sa 17:40 his sling was in his **h.**: 3027
1Sa 17:46 the Lord deliver thee into mine **h.**; 3027
1Sa 17:49 David put his **h.** in his bag, and 3027
1Sa 17:50 there was no sword in the **h.** of 3027
1Sa 17:57 the head of the Philistine in his **h.** 3027
1Sa 18:10 David played with his **h.**, as at 3027
1Sa 18:10 there was a javelin in Saul's **h.** 3027
1Sa 18:17 Let not mine **h.** be upon him, but 3027
1Sa 18:17 the **h.** of the Philistines be upon 3027
1Sa 18:21 that the **h.** of the Philistines may be 3027
1Sa 18:25 fall by the **h.** of the Philistines 3027
1Sa 19:5 he did put his life in his **h.**, and 3709
1Sa 19:9 with his javelin in his **h.**: 3027
1Sa 19:9 and David played with his **h.** 3027
1Sa 20:16 at the **h.** of David's enemies 3027
1Sa 20:19 when the business was in **h.**, and
1Sa 21:3 what is under thine **h.**? give me 3027
1Sa 21:3 five loaves of bread in mine **h.**, 3027
1Sa 21:4 no common bread under mine **h.**, 3027
1Sa 21:8 is there not here under thine **h.** 3027
1Sa 22:6 having his spear in his **h.**, and all 3027
1Sa 22:17 their **h.** also is with David, and 3027
1Sa 22:17 king would not put forth their **h.** 3027
1Sa 23:4 deliver the Philistines into thine **h.** 3027
1Sa 23:6 came down with an ephod in his **h.** 3027
1Sa 23:7 hath delivered him into mine **h.**: 3027
1Sa 23:11 Keilah deliver me up into his **h.**? 3027
1Sa 23:12 me and my men into the **h.** of Saul? 3027
1Sa 23:14 God delivered him not into his **h.** 3027
1Sa 23:16 and strengthened his **h.** in God 3027
1Sa 23:17 **h.** of Saul my father shall not find 3027
1Sa 23:20 to deliver him into the king's **h.** 3027
1Sa 24:4 deliver thine enemy into thine **h.**, 3027
1Sa 24:6 to stretch forth mine **h.** against 3027
1Sa 24:10 delivered thee to day into mine **h.** 3027
1Sa 24:10 I will not put forth mine **h.** 3027
1Sa 24:11 see the skirt of thy robe in my **h.**: 3027
1Sa 24:11 nor transgression in mine **h.**, 3027
1Sa 24:12, 13 mine **h.** shall not be upon thee 3027
1Sa 24:15 and deliver me out of thine **h.** 3027
1Sa 24:18 had delivered me into thine **h.**, 3027
1Sa 24:20 shall be established in thine **h.** 3027
1Sa 25:8 whatsoever cometh to thine **h.** 3027
1Sa 25:26 avenging thyself with thine own **h.**, 3027
1Sa 25:33 avenging myself with mine own **h.** 3027
1Sa 25:35 David received of her **h.** that which 3027
1Sa 25:39 cause of my reproach from the **h.** 3027
1Sa 26:8 thine enemy into thine **h.** this day: 3027
1Sa 26:9 can stretch forth his **h.** against 3027
1Sa 26:11 that I should stretch forth mine **h.** 3027
1Sa 26:18 or what evil is in mine **h.**? 3027
1Sa 26:23 delivered thee into my **h.** to day, 3027
1Sa 26:23 I would not stretch forth mine **h.** 3027
1Sa 27:1 perish one day by the **h.** of Saul: 3027
1Sa 27:1 so shall I escape out of his **h.** 3027
1Sa 28:17 rent the kingdom out of thine **h.**, 3027
1Sa 28:19 into the **h.** of the Philistines: 3027
1Sa 28:19 Israel into the **h.** of the Philistines 3027
1Sa 28:21 I have put my life in my **h.**, 3709
1Sa 30:23 that came against us into our **h.** 3027
2Sa 1:14 not afraid to stretch forth thine **h.** 3027
2Sa 2:19 he turned not to the right **h.** 3225
2Sa 2:21 Turn thee aside to thy right **h.** 3225
2Sa 3:8 not delivered thee into the **h.** of 3027
2Sa 3:12 behold, my **h.** shall be with thee, 3027
2Sa 3:18 By the **h.** of my servant David I 3027
2Sa 3:18 save my people Israel out of the **h.** 3027
2Sa 3:18 Philistines, and out of the **h.** of all 3027
2Sa 4:11 require his blood of your **h.**, and 3027
2Sa 5:19 thou deliver them into mine **h.**? 3027
2Sa 6:6 Uzzah put forth his **h.** to the ark
2Sa 6:19 deliver the Philistines into thine **h.** 3027
2Sa 8:1 out of the **h.** of the Philistines 3027
2Sa 10:2 to comfort him by the **h.** of his 3027
2Sa 10:10 he delivered into the **h.** of Abishai 3027
2Sa 11:14 sent it by the **h.** of Uriah 3027
2Sa 12:7 I delivered thee out of the **h.** of 3027
2Sa 12:25 he sent by the **h.** of Nathan the 3027
2Sa 13:5 I may see it, and eat it at her **h.** 3027
2Sa 13:6 my sight, that I may eat at her **h.** 3027
2Sa 13:10 chamber, that I may eat of thine **h.**, 3027
2Sa 13:19 laid her **h.** on her head, and went 3027
2Sa 14:16 out of the **h.** of the man that 3709
2Sa 14:19 Is not the **h.** of Joab with thee 3027
2Sa 14:19 none can turn to the right **h.** 3231
2Sa 15:5 he put forth his **h.**, and took him, 3027
2Sa 16:6 might men were on his right **h.** 3225
2Sa 16:8 into the **h.** of Absalom thy son: 3027
2Sa 18:2 under the **h.** of Joab, and a third 3027
2Sa 18:2 under the **h.** of Abishai the son of 3027
2Sa 18:2 third part under the **h.** of Ittai 3027
2Sa 18:12 shekels of silver in mine **h.**, 3027
2Sa 18:12 yet would I not put forth mine **h.** 3027
2Sa 18:14 And he took three darts in his **h.** 3709
2Sa 18:28 that lifted up their **h.** against my 3027
2Sa 19:9 out of the **h.** of our enemies, and 3709
2Sa 19:9 he delivered us out of the **h.** of the 3709
2Sa 20:9 by the beard with the right **h.** 3027
2Sa 20:10 the sword that was in Joab's **h.**: 3027
2Sa 20:21 hath lifted up his **h.** against the 3027
2Sa 21:20 that had on every **h.** six fingers, 3027
2Sa 21:22 the **h.** of David, and by the **h.** of his 3027
2Sa 22:1 out of the **h.** of all his enemies, 3709
2Sa 22:1 enemies, and out of the **h.** of Saul: 3709
2Sa 23:10 smote the Philistines until his **h.** 3027
2Sa 23:10 was weary, and his **h.** clave unto 3027
2Sa 23:21 the Egyptian had a spear in his **h.**; 3027
2Sa 23:21 the spear out of the Egyptian's **h.**, 3027
2Sa 24:14 fall now into the **h.** of the Lord; 3027
2Sa 24:14 let me not fall into the **h.** of man 3027
2Sa 24:16 the angel stretched out his **h.** 3027
2Sa 24:16 It is enough: stay now thine **h.** 3027
2Sa 24:17 let thine **h.**, I pray thee, be against 3027
1Ki 2:19 and she sat on his right **h.** 3225
1Ki 2:25 king Solomon went by the **h.** of 3027
1Ki 2:46 kingdom was established in the **h.** 3027
1Ki 7:26 it was an **h.** breadth thick, and 2947
1Ki 8:15 and hath with his **h.** fulfilled it, 3027
1Ki 8:24 and hast fulfilled it with thine **h.**, 3027
1Ki 8:42 thy strong **h.**, and of thy stretched 3027
1Ki 8:53 by the **h.** of Moses thy servant, 3027
1Ki 8:56 by the **h.** of Moses his servant 3027
1Ki 11:12 I will rend it out of the **h.** of thy 3027
1Ki 11:26 he lifted up his **h.** against the king 3027
1Ki 11:27 the cause that he lifted up his **h.** 3027
1Ki 11:31 rend the kingdom out of the **h.** of 3027
1Ki 11:34 the whole kingdom out of his **h.**: 3027
1Ki 11:35 the kingdom out of his son's **h.**, 3027
1Ki 13:4 he put forth his **h.** from the altar, 3027
1Ki 13:4 And his **h.**, which he put forth 3027
1Ki 13:6 that my **h.** may be restored me 3027
1Ki 13:6 the king's **h.** was restored him 3027
1Ki 14:18 by the **h.** of his servant Ahijah 3027
1Ki 15:18 delivered them into the **h.** of his 3027
1Ki 16:7 by the **h.** of the prophet Jehu 3027
1Ki 17:11 a morsel of bread in thine **h.** 3027
1Ki 18:9 deliver thy servant into the **h.** of 3027
1Ki 18:44 out of the sea, like a man's **h.** 3709
1Ki 18:46 the **h.** of the Lord was on Elijah; 3027
1Ki 20:6 they shall put it in their **h.**, 3027
1Ki 20:13 I will deliver it into thine **h.** 3027
1Ki 20:28 this great multitude into thine **h.**, 3027
1Ki 20:42 thou hast let go out of thy **h.** 3027
1Ki 22:3 take it not out of the **h.** of the king 3027
1Ki 22:6 deliver it into the **h.** of the king 3027
1Ki 22:12 shall deliver it into the king's **h.** 3027
1Ki 22:15 deliver it into the **h.** of the king 3027
1Ki 22:19 on his right **h.** and on his left 3225
1Ki 22:34 Turn thine **h.**, and carry me out 3027
2Ki 3:10 deliver them into the **h.** of Moab! 3027
2Ki 3:13 to deliver them into the **h.** of 3027
2Ki 3:15 the **h.** of the Lord came upon him 3027
2Ki 3:18 the Moabites also into your **h.** 3027
2Ki 4:29 take my staff in thine **h.**, and go 3027
2Ki 5:11 strike his **h.** over the place, and 3027
2Ki 5:18 he leaneth on my **h.**, and I bow 3027
2Ki 5:24 he took them from their **h.**, 3027
2Ki 6:7 he put out his **h.**, and took it 3027
2Ki 7:2 a lord on whose **h.** the king leaned 3027
2Ki 7:17 the lord on whose **h.** he leaned 3027
2Ki 8:8 Take a present in thine **h.**, and go, 3027
2Ki 8:20 under the **h.** of Judah, and made a 3027
2Ki 8:22 revolted from under the **h.** of Judah 3027
2Ki 9:1 take this box of oil in thine **h.**, 3027
2Ki 9:7 the Lord, at the **h.** of Jezebel 3027
2Ki 10:15 If it be, give me thine **h.** 3027
2Ki 10:15 And he gave him his **h.**; 3027
2Ki 11:8 his weapons in his **h.**: and he that 3027
2Ki 11:11 man with his weapons in his **h.** 3027
2Ki 12:15 into whose **h.** they delivered the 3027
2Ki 13:3 into the **h.** of Hazael king of Syria, 3027
2Ki 13:3 and into the **h.** of Ben-hadad 3027
2Ki 13:5 from under the **h.** of the Syrians: 3027
2Ki 13:16 Put thine **h.** upon the bow 3027
2Ki 13:16 And he put his **h.** upon it: and 3027
2Ki 13:25 took again out of the **h.** of 3027
2Ki 13:25 which he had taken out of the **h.** of 3027
2Ki 14:5 kingdom was confirmed in his **h.**, 3027
2Ki 14:25 by the **h.** of his servant Jonah, 3027
2Ki 14:27 by the **h.** of Jeroboam the son of 3027
2Ki 15:19 that his **h.** might be with him to 3027
2Ki 15:19 confirm the kingdom in his **h.** 3027
2Ki 16:7 out of the **h.** of the king of Syria, 3709
2Ki 16:7 out of the **h.** of the king of Israel, 3709
2Ki 17:7 from under the **h.** of Pharaoh, 3027
2Ki 17:20 delivered them into the **h.** of 3027
2Ki 17:39 out of the **h.** of all your enemies 3027
2Ki 18:21 if a man lean, it will go into his **h.**, 3709
2Ki 18:29 to deliver you out of his **h.**: 3027
2Ki 18:30 delivered into the **h.** of the king 3027
2Ki 18:33 out of the **h.** of the king of Assyria? 3027
2Ki 18:34 delivered Samaria out of mine **h.**? 3027
2Ki 18:35 their country out of mine **h.**, that 3027
2Ki 18:35 deliver Jerusalem out of mine **h.**? 3027
2Ki 19:10 delivered into the **h.** of the king 3027
2Ki 19:14 letter of the **h.** of the messengers, 3027
2Ki 19:19 save thou us out of his **h.**, 3027
2Ki 20:6 thee and this city out of the **h.** of 3709

2Ki 21:14 into the **h.** of their enemies; 3027
2Ki 22:2 turned not aside to the right **h.** 3225
2Ki 22:5 let them deliver it into the **h.** of 3207
2Ki 22:7 them into their **h.**, because they 3207
2Ki 22:9 the **h.** of them that do the work, 3207
2Ki 23:8 were on a man's left **h.** at the gate
2Ki 23:13 on the right **h.** of the mount 3225
1Ch 4:10 that thine **h.** might be with me, 3027
1Ch 5:10 who fell by their **h.**: and they 3027
1Ch 5:20 were delivered into their **h.**, 3027
1Ch 6:15 and Jerusalem by the **h.** of 3027
1Ch 6:39 who stood on his right **h.**, even 3225
1Ch 6:44 sons of Merari stood on the left **h.**: 8040
1Ch 11:23 in the Egyptian's **h.** was a spear 3027
1Ch 11:23 the spear out of the Egyptian's **h.**, 3027
1Ch 12:2 could use both the right **h.** and the 3231
1Ch 13:9 Uzza put forth his **h.** to hold the 3027
1Ch 13:10 because he put his **h.** to the ark: 3027
1Ch 14:10 wilt thou deliver them into mine **h.**? 3027
1Ch 14:10 I will deliver them into thine **h.** 3027
1Ch 14:11 by mine **h.** like the breaking forth 3027
1Ch 16:7 into the **h.** of Asaph and his 3027
1Ch 18:1 out of the **h.** of the Philistines. 3027
1Ch 19:11 delivered unto the **h.** of Abishai his 3027
1Ch 20:6 six on each **h.**, and six on each foot:
1Ch 20:8 they fell by the **h.** of David, and 3027
1Ch 20:8 and by the **h.** of his servants 3027
1Ch 21:13 me fall now into the **h.** of the Lord; 3027
1Ch 21:13 but let me not fall into the **h.** of man. 3027
1Ch 21:15 It is enough, stay now thine **h.** 3027
1Ch 21:16 having a drawn sword in his **h.** 3027
1Ch 21:17 let thine **h.**, I pray thee, O Lord my 3027
1Ch 22:18 inhabitants of the land into mine **h.**; 3027
1Ch 26:28 it was under the **h.** of Shelomith, 3027
1Ch 28:19 in writing by his **h.** upon me, 3027
1Ch 29:8 by the **h.** of Jehiel the Gershonite. 3027
1Ch 29:12 and in thine **h.** is power and might; 3027
1Ch 29:12 and in thine **h.** it is to make great, 3027
1Ch 29:16 cometh of thine **h.**, and is all thine 3027
2Ch 3:17 one on the right **h.**, and the other 3225
2Ch 3:17 the name of that on the right **h.** 3227
2Ch 4:5 thickness of it was an **h.** breadth, 2947
2Ch 4:6 put five on the right **h.**, and five 3225
2Ch 4:7 in the temple, five on the right **h.**, 3225
2Ch 6:15 and hast fulfilled it with thine **h.**, 3027
2Ch 6:32 and thy mighty **h.**, and thy 3027
2Ch 10:15 he spake by the **h.** of Ahijah 3027
2Ch 12:5 I also left you in the **h.** of Shishak 3027
2Ch 12:7 upon Jerusalem by the **h.** of 3027
2Ch 13:8 in the **h.** of the sons of David; 3027
2Ch 13:16 God delivered them into their **h.** 3027
2Ch 16:7 the king...escaped out of thine **h.** 3027
2Ch 16:8 he delivered them into thine **h.** 3027
2Ch 17:5 stablished the kingdom in his **h.**; 3027
2Ch 18:5 God will deliver it into the king's **h.** 3027
2Ch 18:11 the Lord shall deliver it into the **h.** 3027
2Ch 18:14 they shall be delivered into your **h.** 3027
2Ch 18:18 of heaven standing on his right **h.** 3225
2Ch 18:33 Turn thine **h.**, that thou mayest 3027
2Ch 20:6 and in thine **h.** is there not power 3027
2Ch 21:10 from under the **h.** of Judah unto 3027
2Ch 21:10 Libnah revolt from under his **h.**; 3027
2Ch 23:7 man with his weapons in his **h.**; 3027
2Ch 23:10 man having his weapon in his **h.**, 3027
2Ch 23:18 by the **h.** of the priests the Levites, 3027
2Ch 24:11 by the **h.** of the Levites, and when 3027
2Ch 24:24 a very great host into their **h.**, 3027
2Ch 25:15 their own people out of thine **h.**? 3027
2Ch 25:20 into the **h.** of their enemies, 3027
2Ch 26:11 by the **h.** of Jeiel the scribe 3027
2Ch 26:11 under the **h.** of Hananiah, one of 3027
2Ch 26:13 under their **h.** was an army, three 3027
2Ch 26:19 and had a censer in his **h.** 3027
2Ch 28:5 into the **h.** of the king of Syria; 3027
2Ch 28:5 into the **h.** of the king of Israel, 3027
2Ch 28:9 he hath delivered them into your **h.**, 3027
2Ch 30:6 of the **h.** of the kings of Assyria. 3709
2Ch 30:12 the **h.** of God was to give them 3027
2Ch 30:16 they received of the **h.** of the 3027
2Ch 31:13 under the **h.** of Cononiah and 3027
2Ch 32:11 out of the **h.** of the king of 3709
2Ch 32:13 deliver their lands out of mine **h.**? 3027
2Ch 32:14 deliver his people out of mine **h.** 3027
2Ch 32:14 able to deliver you out of mine **h.**? 3027
2Ch 32:15 deliver his people out of mine **h.**, 3027
2Ch 32:15 and out of the **h.** of my fathers: 3027
2Ch 32:15 God deliver you out of mine **h.**? 3027
2Ch 32:17 delivered their people out of mine **h.**, 3027
2Ch 32:17 deliver his people out of mine **h.** 3027
2Ch 32:22 from the **h.** of Sennacherib the 3027
2Ch 32:22 and from the **h.** of all other, 3027
2Ch 33:8 the ordinances by the **h.** of Moses. 3027
2Ch 34:2 to the right **h.**, nor to the left. 3225
2Ch 34:9 gathered of the **h.** of Manasseh 3027
2Ch 34:10 put it in the **h.** of the workmen 3027
2Ch 34:17 into the **h.** of the overseers, and 3027
2Ch 34:17 to the **h.** of the workmen. 3027
2Ch 35:6 word of the Lord by the **h.** of Moses. 3027
2Ch 36:17 he gave them all into his **h.** 3027
Ezr 1:8 by the **h.** of Mithredath the 3027
Ezr 5:12 he gave them into the **h.** of 3028
Ezr 6:12 that shall put to their **h.** to alter 3028
Ezr 7:6 according to the **h.** of the Lord 3027
Ezr 7:9 according to the good **h.** of his God 3027
Ezr 7:14 of thy God which is in thine **h.**; 3028
Ezr 7:25 of thy God, that is in thine **h.**, 3028
Ezr 7:28 as the **h.** of the Lord my God was 3027
Ezr 8:18 by the good **h.** of our God upon us 3027
Ezr 8:22 The **h.** of our God is upon all 3027
Ezr 8:26 I even weighed unto their **h.** six 3027
Ezr 8:31 and the **h.** of our God was upon us, 3027
Ezr 8:31 and he delivered us from the **h.** of 3709
Ezr 8:33 by the **h.** of Meremoth the son of 3027
Ezr 9:2 yea, the **h.** of the princes and 3027
Ezr 9:7 into the **h.** of the kings of the lands, 3027
Ne 1:10 great power, and by thy strong **h.** 3027
Ne 2:8 according to the good **h.** of my God 3027
Ne 2:18 Then I told them of the **h.** of my 3027
Ne 4:17 and with the other **h.** held a weapon.
Ne 6:5 with an open letter in his **h.**; 3027
Ne 8:4 Hilkiah, and Maaseiah...right **h.**; 3225
Ne 8:4 and on his left **h.**, Pedaiah, and 8040
Ne 9:14 by the **h.** of Moses thy servant: 3027
Ne 9:27 into the **h.** of their enemies, who 3027
Ne 9:27 out of the **h.** of their enemies 3027
Ne 9:28 in the **h.** of their enemies, so that 3027
Ne 9:30 into the **h.** of the people of the 3027
Ne 11:24 son of Judah, was at the king's **h.** 3027
Ne 12:31 one went on the right **h.** upon the 3225
Es 2:21 sought to lay **h.** on the king 3027
Es 3:10 the king took his ring from his **h.**, 3027
Es 5:2 golden sceptre that was in his **h.** 3027
Es 6:2 who sought to lay **h.** on the king 3027
Es 6:9 the **h.** of one of the king's most 3027
Es 8:7 he laid his **h.** upon the Jews 3027
Es 9:2 to lay **h.** on such as sought their 3027
Es 9:10 on the spoil laid they not their **h.** 3027
Es 9:15 on the prey they laid not their **h.** 3027
Job 1:11 put forth thine **h.** now, and touch 3027
Job 1:12 upon himself put not forth thine **h.** 3027
Job 2:5 put forth thine **h.** now, and touch 3027
Job 2:6 Behold, he is in thine **h.**; but save 3027
Job 2:10 we receive good at the **h.** of God, 854
Job 5:15 and from the **h.** of the mighty. 3027
Job 6:9 that he would let loose his **h.**, 3027
Job 6:23 Deliver me from the enemy's **h.**? or, 3027
Job 6:23 Redeem me from the **h.** of the 3027
Job 9:24 The earth is given into the **h.** of 3027
Job 9:33 that might lay his **h.** upon us both. 3027
Job 10:7 none that can deliver out of thine **h.** 3027
Job 11:14 If iniquity be in thine **h.**, put it far 3027
Job 12:6 into whose **h.** God bringeth 3027
Job 12:9 the **h.** of the Lord hath wrought 3027
Job 12:10 In whose **h.** is the soul of every 3027
Job 13:14 and put my life in mine **h.**? 3709
Job 13:21 Withdraw thine **h.** far from me: 3709
Job 15:23 day of darkness is ready at his **h.** 3027
Job 15:25 stretcheth out his **h.** against God, 3027
Job 19:21 the **h.** of God hath touched me. 3027
Job 20:22 every **h.** of the wicked shall come 3027
Job 21:5 lay your **h.** upon your mouth. 3027
Job 21:16 their good is not in their **h.** 3027
Job 23:9 the left **h.**, where he doth work, 8040
Job 23:9 he hideth himself on the right **h.**, 3225
Job 26:13 his **h.** hath formed the crooked 3027
Job 27:11 I will teach you by the **h.** of God: 3027
Job 27:22 he would fain flee out of his **h.** 3027
Job 28:9 He putteth forth his **h.** upon the 3027
Job 29:9 and laid their **h.** on their mouth. 3709
Job 29:20 and my bow was renewed in my **h.** 3027
Job 30:12 Upon my right **h.** rise the youth; 3225
Job 30:21 with thy strong **h.** thou opposest 3027
Job 30:24 not stretch out his **h.** to the grave, 3027
Job 31:21 have lifted up my **h.** against the 3027
Job 31:25 and because mine **h.** had gotten 3027
Job 31:27 or my mouth hath kissed my **h.**: 3027
Job 33:7 neither shall my **h.** be heavy upon 405
Job 34:20 shall be taken away without **h.** 3027
Job 35:7 or what receiveth he of thine **h.**? 3027
Job 37:7 He sealeth up the **h.** of every man; 3027
Job 40:4 I will lay mine **h.** upon my mouth. 3027
Job 40:14 thine own right **h.** can save thee. 3225
Job 41:8 Lay thine **h.** upon him, remember 3709
Ps 10:12 O God, lift up thine **h.**: forget not 3027
Ps 10:14 spite, to requite it with thy **h.**: 3027
Ps 16:8 he is at my right **h.**, I shall not be 3225
Ps 16:11 at thy right **h.** there are pleasures 3225
Ps 17:7 O thou that savest by thy right **h.** 3225
Ps 17:14 From men which are thy **h.**, O 3027
Ps 18:*title* delivered him from the **h.** of all 3709
Ps 18:*title* enemies, and from the **h.** of Saul: 3027
Ps 18:35 and thy right **h.** hath holden me 3225
Ps 20:6 the saving strength of his right **h.** 3225
Ps 21:8 Thine **h.** shall find out all thine 3027
Ps 21:8 thy right **h.** shall find out those 3225
Ps 26:10 and their right **h.** is full of bribes 3225
Ps 31:5 Into thine **h.** I commit my spirit: 3027
Ps 31:8 me up into the **h.** of the enemy: 3027
Ps 31:15 My times are in thy **h.**: deliver me 3027
Ps 31:15 from the **h.** of mine enemies, 3027
Ps 32:4 day and night thy **h.** was heavy 3027
Ps 36:11 and let not the **h.** of the wicked 3027
Ps 37:24 Lord upholdeth him with his **h.** 3027
Ps 37:33 The Lord will not leave him in his **h.**, 3027
Ps 38:2 in me, and thy **h.** presseth me sore. 3027
Ps 39:10 consumed by the blow of thine **h.** 3027
Ps 44:2 drive out the heathen with thy **h.**, 3027
Ps 44:3 but thy right **h.**, and thine arm, 3225
Ps 45:4 thy right **h.** shall teach thee terrible 3225
Ps 45:9 upon thy right **h.** did stand the 3225
Ps 48:10 thy right **h.** is full of righteousness. 3225
Ps 60:5 save with thy right **h.**, and hear me 3225
Ps 63:8 thee: thy right **h.** upholdeth me. 3225
Ps 71:4 God, out of the **h.** of the wicked, 3027
Ps 71:4 out of the **h.** of the unrighteous 3709
Ps 73:23 hast holden me by my right **h.** 3027
Ps 74:11 Why withdrawest thou thy **h.**, 3027
Ps 74:11 even thy right **h.**? pluck it out 3225
Ps 75:8 in the **h.** of the Lord there is a 3027
Ps 77:10 the right **h.** of the most High. 3225
Ps 77:20 by the **h.** of Moses and Aaron. 3027
Ps 78:42 They remembered not his **h.**, nor 3027
Ps 78:54 mountain, which his right **h.** had 3225
Ps 78:61 his glory into the enemy's **h.** 3027
Ps 80:15 which thy right **h.** hath planted, 3225
Ps 80:17 Let thy **h.** be upon the man of thy 3027
Ps 80:17 upon the man of thy right **h.**, 3225
Ps 81:14 turned my **h.** against their 3027
Ps 82:4 rid them out of the **h.** of the wicked. 3027
Ps 88:5 they are cut off from thy **h.** 3027
Ps 89:13 mighty arm: strong is thy **h.**, 3027
Ps 89:13 and high is thy right **h.** 3225
Ps 89:21 my **h.** shall be established: mine 3027
Ps 89:25 I will set his **h.** also in the sea, 3027
Ps 89:25 and his right **h.** in the rivers. 3225
Ps 89:42 Thou hast set up the right **h.** of his 3225
Ps 89:48 his soul from the **h.** of the grave? 3027
Ps 91:7 ten thousand at thy right **h.**; but 3225
Ps 95:4 In his **h.** are the deep places 3027
Ps 95:7 pasture, and the sheep of his **h.** 3027
Ps 97:10 them out of the **h.** of the wicked 3027
Ps 98:1 his right **h.**, and his holy arm, 3225
Ps 104:28 thou openest thine **h.**, they are 3027
Ps 106:10 from the **h.** of him that hated them, 3027
Ps 106:10 and redeemed them from the **h.** of 3027
Ps 106:26 he lifted up his **h.** against them, 3027
Ps 106:41 into the **h.** of the heathen; and 3027
Ps 106:42 into subjection under their **h.** 3027
Ps 107:2 redeemed from the **h.** of the enemy; 3027
Ps 108:6 save with thy right **h.**, and answer 3225
Ps 109:6 let Satan stand at his right **h.** 3225
Ps 109:27 know that this is thy **h.**; that thou, 3027
Ps 109:31 at the right **h.** of the poor, to save 3225
Ps 110:1 Sit thou at my right **h.**, until I make 3225
Ps 110:5 The Lord at thy right **h.** shall strike 3225
Ps 118:15 right **h.** of the Lord doeth valiantly. 3225
Ps 118:16 The right **h.** of the Lord is exalted: 3225
Ps 118:16 right **h.** of the Lord doeth valiantly. 3225
Ps 119:109 My soul is continually in my **h.**: 3709

Ps 119:173 Let thine **h.** help me; for I have......... 3027
Ps 121:5 Lord is thy shade upon thy right **h.**..... 3027
Ps 123:2 the **h.** of their masters, and as the...... 3027
Ps 123:2 eyes of a maiden unto the **h.** of her..... 3027
Ps 127:4 As arrows are in the **h.** of a mighty..... 3027
Ps 129:7 the mower filleth not his **h.**;.............. 3709
Ps 136:12 With a strong **h.**, and with a............. 3027
Ps 137:5 let my right **h.** forget her cunning....... 3225
Ps 138:7 stretch forth thine **h.** against the......... 3027
Ps 138:7 thy right **h.** shall save me................... 3225
Ps 139:5 and before, and laid thine **h.** upon......... 3709
Ps 139:10 there shall thy **h.** lead me, and........... 3027
Ps 139:10 thy right **h.** shall hold me.................. 3225
Ps 142:4 I looked on my right **h.**, and................ 3225
Ps 144:7 Send thine **h.** from above; rid me,........ 3027
Ps 144:7 from the **h.** of strange children;............ 3027
Ps 144:8 and their right **h.** is at right **h.** of........ 3225
Ps 144:11 from the **h.** of strange children;.......... 3027
Ps 144:11 and their right **h.** is a right **h.** of......... 3225
Ps 145:16 Thou openest thine **h.**, and................ 3027
Ps 149:6 a twoedged sword in their **h.**;.............. 3027
Pr 1:24 I have stretched out my **h.**, and no..... 3027
Pr 3:16 Length of days is in her right **h.**;........ 3225
Pr 3:16 in her left **h.** riches and honour.......... 8040
Pr 3:27 the power of thine **h.** to do it............. 3027
Pr 4:27 Turn not to the right **h.** nor to the...... 3227
Pr 6:1 thou hast stricken thine **h.** with.......... 3709
Pr 6:3 art come into the **h.** of thy friend;........ 3709
Pr 6:5 as a roe from the **h.** of the hunter,....... 3027
Pr 6:5 and as a bird from the **h.** of the.......... 3027
Pr 10:4 poor that dealeth with a slack **h.**:......... 3709
Pr 10:4 but the **h.** of the diligent maketh......... 3027
Pr 11:21 Though **h.** join in **h.**, the wicked......... 3027
Pr 12:24 The **h.** of the diligent shall bear.......... 3027
Pr 16:5 though **h.** join in **h.**, he shall not......... 3027
Pr 17:16 is there a price in the **h.** of a fool....... 3027
Pr 19:24 A slothful man hideth his **h.** in his....... 3027
Pr 21:1 The king's heart is in the **h.** of the...... 3027
Pr 26:6 a message by the **h.** of a fool............. 3027
Pr 26:9 into the **h.** of a drunkard, so is a......... 3027
Pr 26:15 The slothful hideth his **h.** in his.......... 3027
Pr 27:16 and the ointment of his right **h.**,.......... 3225
Pr 30:32 lay thine **h.** upon thy mouth................ 3027
Pr 31:20 She stretcheth out her **h.** to the......... 3709
Ec 2:24 that it was from the **h.** of God............ 3027
Ec 5:14 and there is nothing in his **h.**............. 3027
Ec 5:15 which he may carry away in his **h.**...... 3027
Ec 7:18 from this withdraw not thine **h.**:......... 3027
Ec 9:1 their works, are in the **h.** of God:....... 3027
Ec 9:10 Whatsoever thy **h.** findeth to do,......... 3027
Ec 10:2 wise man's heart is at his right **h.**;...... 3225
Ec 11:6 evening withhold not thine **h.**:............ 3027
Ca 2:6 His left **h.** is under my head,............. 8040
Ca 2:6 and his right **h.** doth embrace me........ 3225
Ca 5:4 My beloved put in his **h.** by the........... 3027
Ca 8:3 His left **h.** should be under my........... 8040
Ca 8:3 his right **h.** should embrace me........... 3225
Isa 1:12 who hath required this at your **h.**,........ 3027
Isa 1:25 I will turn my **h.** upon thee,................ 3027
Isa 3:6 let this ruin be under thy **h.**:............... 3027
Isa 5:25 he hath stretched forth his **h.**.............. 3027
Isa 5:25 but his **h.** is stretched out still............ 3027
Isa 6:6 having a live coal in his **h.**,................ 3027
Isa 8:11 with a strong **h.**, and instructed me..... 3027
Isa 9:12, 17 but his **h.** is stretched out still........ 3027
Isa 9:20 he shall snatch on the right h.,........... 3225
Isa 9:20 and he shall eat on the left **h.**,............ 8040
Isa 9:21 but his **h.** is stretched out still............ 3027
Isa 10:4 but his **h.** is stretched out still............ 3027
Isa 10:5 the staff in their **h.** is mine................ 3027
Isa 10:10 my **h.** hath found the kingdoms........... 3027
Isa 10:13 the strength of mine **h.** I have done..... 3027
Isa 10:14 my **h.** hath found as a nest................ 3027
Isa 10:32 he shall shake his **h.** against the......... 3027
Isa 11:8 put his **h.** on the cockatrice' den.......... 3027
Isa 11:11 the Lord shall set his **h.** again........... 3027
Isa 11:14 they shall lay their **h.** upon Edom........ 3027
Isa 11:15 shall he shake his **h.** over the river,.... 3027
Isa 13:2 shake the **h.**, that they may go............ 3027
Isa 13:6 the day of the Lord is at **h.**;............... 7138
Isa 14:26 this is the **h.** that is stretched out....... 3027
Isa 14:27 and his **h.** is stretched out, and who.... 3027
Isa 19:4 into the **h.** of a cruel lord;.................. 3027
Isa 19:16 the shaking of the **h.** of the Lord......... 3027
Isa 22:21 commit thy government into his **h.**:...... 3027
Isa 23:11 He stretched out his **h.** over the sea,.. 3027
Isa 25:10 mountain shall the **h.** of the Lord........ 3027
Isa 26:11 when thy **h.** is lifted up, they will........ 3027
Isa 28:2 cast down to the earth with the **h.**....... 3027
Isa 28:4 while it is yet in his **h.** he eateth it...... 3709
Isa 30:21 when we turn to the right **h.**, and............
Isa 31:3 the Lord shall stretch out his **h.**,.......... 3027
Isa 34:17 and his **h.** hath divided it unto........... 3027
Isa 36:6 it will go into his **h.**, and pierce.......... 3709
Isa 36:15 into the **h.** of the king of Assyria........ 3027
Isa 36:18 out of the **h.** of the king of Assyria?..... 3027
Isa 36:19 delivered Samaria land out of my **h.**?... 3027
Isa 36:20 delivered their land out of my **h.**,........ 3027
Isa 36:20 deliver Jerusalem out of my **h.**?.......... 3027
Isa 37:10 into the **h.** of the king of Assyria......... 3027
Isa 37:14 from the **h.** of the messengers,........... 3027
Isa 37:20 save us from his **h.**, that all the.......... 3027
Isa 38:6 thee and this city out of the **h.**........... 3709
Isa 40:2 received of the Lord's **h.** double.......... 3027
Isa 40:10 Lord God will come with strong **h.**,...........
Isa 40:12 the waters in the hollow of his **h.**,.............
Isa 41:10 right **h.** of my righteousness.............. 3225
Isa 41:13 thy God will hold thy right **h.**,............. 3225
Isa 41:20 the **h.** of the Lord hath done this,........ 3027
Isa 42:6 will hold thine **h.**, and will keep.......... 3027
Isa 43:13 none that can deliver out of my **h.**:...... 3027
Isa 44:5 another shall subscribe with his **h.**....... 3027
Isa 44:20 Is there not a lie in my right **h.**?......... 3225
Isa 45:1 whose right **h.** I have holden, to.......... 3225
Isa 47:6 and given them into thine **h.**:.............. 3027
Isa 48:13 Mine **h.** also hath laid the.................. 3027
Isa 48:13 and my right **h.** hath spanned the........ 3225
Isa 49:2 in the shadow of his **h.** hath he........... 3027
Isa 49:22 I will lift up mine **h.** to the................ 3027
Isa 50:2 Is my **h.** shortened at all, that it......... 3027
Isa 50:11 This shall ye have of my **h.**; ye........... 3027
Isa 51:16 the shadow of mine **h.**, that I may........ 3027
Isa 51:17 hast drunk at the **h.** of the Lord......... 3027
Isa 51:18 that taketh her by the **h.** of all the...... 3027
Isa 51:22 I have taken out of thine **h.** the cup..... 3027
Isa 51:23 into the **h.** of them that afflict........... 3027
Isa 53:10 of the Lord shall prosper in his **h.**........ 3027
Isa 54:3 shalt break forth on the right **h.**........... 3225
Isa 56:2 keepeth his **h.** from doing...evil,......... 3027
Isa 57:10 thou hast found...life of thine **h.**;......... 3027
Isa 59:1 the Lord's **h.** is not shortened,........... 3027
Isa 62:3 crown of glory in the **h.** of the Lord,... 3027
Isa 62:3 royal diadem in the **h.** of thy God........ 3709
Isa 62:8 Lord hath sworn by his right **h.**,......... 3225
Isa 63:12 That led them by the right **h.** of......... 3225
Isa 64:8 we all are the work of thy **h.**.............. 3027
Isa 66:2 all those things hath mine **h.**.............. 3027
Isa 66:14 the **h.** of the Lord shall be known....... 3027
Jer 1:9 the Lord put forth his **h.**, and............ 3027
Jer 6:9 turn back thine **h.** as a.................... 3027
Jer 6:12 I will stretch out my **h.** upon the........ 3027
Jer 11:21 that thou die not by our **h.**:.............. 3027
Jer 12:7 soul into the **h.** of her enemies........... 3709
Jer 15:6 therefore will I stretch out my **h.**........ 3027
Jer 15:17 I sat alone because of thy **h.**:............. 3027
Jer 15:21 thee out of the **h.** of the wicked,......... 3027
Jer 15:21 thee out of the **h.** of the terrible.......... 3709
Jer 16:21 I will cause them to know mine **h.**........ 3027
Jer 18:4 marred in the **h.** of the potter:........... 3027
Jer 18:6 as the clay is in the potter's **h.**,.......... 3027
Jer 18:6 so are ye in mine **h.**, O house............ 3027
Jer 20:4 into the **h.** of the king of Babylon,........ 3027
Jer 20:5 into the **h.** of their enemies, which...... 3027
Jer 20:13 the poor from the **h.** of evildoers........ 3027
Jer 21:5 with an outstretched **h.** and with a...... 3027
Jer 21:7 into the **h.** of Nebuchadrezzar.............. 3027
Jer 21:7 and into the **h.** of their enemies,.......... 3027
Jer 21:7 **h.** of those that seek their life:........... 3027
Jer 21:10 into the **h.** of the king of Babylon,........ 3027
Jer 21:12 out of the **h.** of the oppressor,........... 3027
Jer 22:3 out of the **h.** of the oppressor:............ 3027
Jer 22:24 the signet upon my right **h.**, yet.......... 3027
Jer 22:25 the **h.** of them that seek thy life,........ 3027
Jer 22:25 **h.** of them whose face thou fearest,.... 3027
Jer 22:25 even into the **h.** of Nebuchadrezzar..... 3027
Jer 22:25 and into the **h.** of the Chaldeans......... 3027
Jer 23:23 Am I a God at **h.**, saith the Lord,....... 7138
Jer 25:15 the wine cup of this fury at my **h.**,....... 3027
Jer 25:17 the cup at the Lord's **h.**, and made....... 3027
Jer 25:28 take the cup at thine **h.** to drink......... 3027
Jer 26:14 I am in your **h.**: do with me................ 3027
Jer 26:24 the **h.** of Ahikam the son of............... 3027
Jer 26:24 give him into the **h.** of the people....... 3027
Jer 27:3 by the **h.** of the messengers which...... 3027
Jer 27:6 into the **h.** of Nebuchadnezzar the....... 3027
Jer 27:8 I have consumed them by his **h.**......... 3027
Jer 29:3 By the **h.** of Elasah the son of............ 3027
Jer 29:21 into the **h.** of Nebuchadrezzar king...... 3027
Jer 31:11 the **h.** of him that was stronger.......... 3027
Jer 31:32 the day that I took them by the **h.**...... 3027
Jer 32:3 into the **h.** of the king of Babylon,........ 3027
Jer 32:4 out of the **h.** of the Chaldeans,........... 3027
Jer 32:4 into the **h.** of the king of Babylon,........ 3027
Jer 32:21 and with a strong **h.**, and with a......... 3027
Jer 32:24 and the city is given into the **h.** of....... 3027
Jer 32:25 for the city is given into the **h.** of....... 3027
Jer 32:28 **h.** of the Chaldeans, and into the **h.**.... 3027
Jer 32:36 It shall be delivered into the **h.** of...... 3027
Jer 32:43 it is given into the **h.** of the............... 3027
Jer 34:2 into the **h.** of the king of Babylon,........ 3027
Jer 34:3 thou shalt not escape out of his **h.**,....... 3027
Jer 34:3 and delivered into his **h.**:.................... 3027
Jer 34:20 into the **h.** of their enemies, and......... 3027
Jer 34:20 the **h.** of them that seek their life:...... 3027
Jer 34:21 give into the **h.** of their enemies,......... 3027
Jer 34:21 **h.** of them that seek their life,........... 3027
Jer 34:21 and into the **h.** of the king of............. 3027
Jer 36:14 Take in thine **h.** the roll wherein......... 3027
Jer 36:14 took the roll in his **h.**, and came.......... 3027
Jer 37:17 into the **h.** of the king of Babylon........ 3027
Jer 38:3 into the **h.** of the king of Babylon's...... 3027
Jer 38:5 he is in your **h.**: for the king is not...... 3027
Jer 38:16 into the **h.** of these men that seek...... 3027
Jer 38:18 into the **h.** of the Chaldeans, and........ 3027
Jer 38:18 shalt not escape out of their **h.**,........... 3027
Jer 38:19 lest they deliver me into their **h.**,....... 3027
Jer 38:23 not escape out of their **h.**,................. 3027
Jer 38:23 shalt be taken by the **h.** of the king..... 3027
Jer 39:17 into the **h.** of the men of whom.......... 3027
Jer 40:4 the chains...were upon thine **h.**........... 3027
Jer 41:5 offerings and incense in their **h.**,......... 3027
Jer 42:11 and to deliver you from his **h.**............ 3027
Jer 43:3 into the **h.** of the Chaldeans,.............. 3027
Jer 43:9 Take great stones in thine **h.**, and....... 3027
Jer 44:25 and fulfilled with your **h.**, saying,........ 3027
Jer 44:30 into the **h.** of his enemies,................. 3027
Jer 44:30 the **h.** of them that seek his life;......... 3027
Jer 44:30 into the **h.** of Nebuchadrezzar king...... 3027
Jer 46:24 into the **h.** of the people of the north... 3027
Jer 46:26 the **h.** of those that seek their lives,.... 3027
Jer 46:26 into the **h.** of Nebuchadrezzar king...... 3027
Jer 46:26 and into the **h.** of his servants:........... 3027
Jer 50:15 she hath given her **h.**: her.................. 3027
Jer 51:7 a golden cup in the Lord's **h.**,............. 3027
Jer 51:25 I will stretch out mine **h.** upon........... 3027
La 1:7 her people fell into the **h.** of the......... 3027
La 1:10 The adversary...spread out his **h.**........ 3027
La 1:14 transgressions is bound by his **h.**:....... 3027
La 2:3 hath drawn back his right **h.**............... 3225
La 2:4 stood with his right **h.** as an.............. 3225
La 2:7 into the **h.** of the enemy the walls....... 3027
La 2:8 he hath not withdrawn his **h.** from........ 3027
La 3:3 he turneth his **h.** against me all.......... 3027
La 5:6 We have given the **h.** to the.............. 3027
La 5:8 that doth deliver us out of their **h.**....... 3027
La 5:12 Princes are hanged up by their **h.**:...... 3027
Eze 1:3 the **h.** of the Lord was there upon....... 3027
Eze 2:9 an **h.** was sent unto me; and, lo,......... 3027
Eze 3:14 but the **h.** of the Lord was strong....... 3027
Eze 3:18, 20 blood will I require at thine **h.**........ 3027
Eze 3:22 the **h.** of the Lord was there upon...... 3027
Eze 6:11 Smite with thine **h.**, and stamp.......... 3709
Eze 6:14 So will I stretch out my **h.** upon......... 3027
Eze 8:1 the **h.** of the Lord God fell there........ 3027
Eze 8:3 he put forth the form of an **h.**,........... 3027
Eze 8:11 every man his censer in his **h.**;.......... 3027
Eze 9:1 his destroying weapon in his **h.**........... 3027
Eze 9:2 a slaughter weapon in his **h.**;............. 3027
Eze 10:2 fill thine **h.** with coals of fire.............. 2651
Eze 10:7 one cherub stretched forth his **h.**......... 3027
Eze 10:8 the form of a man's **h.** under their....... 3027
Eze 12:7 I digged...the wall with mine **h.**;.......... 3027
Eze 12:23 The days are at **h.**, and the effect....... 7126
Eze 13:9 mine **h.** shall be upon the prophets...... 3027
Eze 13:21 deliver my people out of your **h.**,......... 3027
Eze 13:21 and they...be no more in your **h.**......... 3027
Eze 13:23 deliver my people out of your **h.**:......... 3027
Eze 14:9 I will stretch out my **h.** upon him,....... 3027
Eze 14:13 will I stretch out mine **h.** upon it,......... 3027
Eze 16:27 I have stretched out my **h.** over......... 3027
Eze 16:39 I will also give thee into their **h.**,......... 3027

Book	Ref	Context	No.
Eze	16:46	daughters that dwell at thy left **h.**:	8040
Eze	16:46	sister that dwelleth at thy right **h.**,	3225
Eze	16:49	neither did she strengthen the **h.**	3027
Eze	17:18	he had given his **h.**, and hath	3027
Eze	18:8	hath withdrawn his **h.** from	3027
Eze	18:17	hath taken off his **h.** from the poor,	3027
Eze	20:5	and lifted up mine **h.** unto the seed	3027
Eze	20:5	when I lifted up mine **h.** unto them,	3027
Eze	20:6	that I lifted up mine **h.** unto them,	3027
Eze	20:15	also I lifted up my **h.** unto them in	3027
Eze	20:22	I withdrew mine **h.**, and wrought	3027
Eze	20:23	I lifted up mine **h.** unto them also in	3027
Eze	20:28	for the which I lifted up mine **h.** to	3027
Eze	20:33	a mighty **h.**, and with a stretched	3027
Eze	20:34	ye are scattered, with a mighty **h.**,	3027
Eze	20:42	for the which I lifted up mine **h.** to	3027
Eze	21:11	to give it into the **h.** of the slayer.	3027
Eze	21:16	either on the right **h.**, or on...left,	3221
Eze	21:22	At his right **h.** was the divination	3225
Eze	21:24	ye shall be taken with the **h.**.	3079
Eze	21:31	deliver thee into the **h.** of brutish	3027
Eze	22:13	I have smitten mine **h.** at thy	3079
Eze	23:9	I have delivered her into the **h.**	3027
Eze	23:9	of her lovers, into the **h.** of the	3027
Eze	23:28	the **h.** of them whom thou hatest,	3027
Eze	23:28	**h.** of them from whom thy mind	3027
Eze	23:31	will I give her cup into thine **h.**	3027
Eze	25:7	I will stretch out mine **h.** upon	3027
Eze	25:13	I will also stretch out mine **h.** upon	3027
Eze	25:14	by the **h.** of my people Israel:	3027
Eze	25:16	I will stretch out mine **h.** upon	3027
Eze	27:15	the merchandise of thine **h.**: they	3027
Eze	28:9	in the **h.** of him that slayeth thee.	3027
Eze	28:10	by the **h.** of strangers: for I have	3027
Eze	29:7	they took hold of thee by thy **h.**,	3709
Eze	30:10	by the **h.** of Nebuchadrezzar king	3027
Eze	30:12	the land into the **h.** of the wicked:	3027
Eze	30:12	is therein, by the **h.** of strangers:	3027
Eze	30:22	the sword to fall out of his **h.**	3027
Eze	30:24	and put my sword in his **h.**:	3027
Eze	30:25	into the **h.** of the king of Babylon,	3027
Eze	31:11	into the **h.** of the mighty one	3027
Eze	33:6	will I require at the watchman's **h.**.	3027
Eze	33:8	his blood will I require at thine **h.**.	3027
Eze	33:22	Now the **h.** of the Lord was upon	3027
Eze	34:10	I will require my flock at their **h.**,	3027
Eze	34:27	out of the **h.** of those that served	3027
Eze	35:3	I will stretch out mine **h.** against	3027
Eze	36:7	I have lifted up mine **h.**, Surely the	3027
Eze	36:8	Israel; for they are at **h.** to come.	7126
Eze	37:1	The **h.** of the Lord was upon me,	3027
Eze	37:17	they shall become one in thine **h.**.	3027
Eze	37:19	which is in the **h.** of Ephraim, and	3027
Eze	37:19	they shall be one in mine **h.**.	3027
Eze	37:20	writest shall be in thine **h.** before	3027
Eze	38:12	turn thine **h.** upon the desolate	3027
Eze	39:3	smite the bow out of thy left **h.**,	3027
Eze	39:3	thine arrows to fall out of...right **h.**.	3027
Eze	39:21	my **h.** that I have laid upon them.	3027
Eze	39:23	them into the **h.** of their enemies:	3027
Eze	40:1	the **h.** of the Lord was upon me,	3027
Eze	40:3	a line of flax in his **h.**, and a	3027
Eze	40:5	and in the man's **h.** a measuring	3027
Eze	40:5	by the cubit and an **h.** breath	2948
Eze	40:43	hooks, an **h.** broad, fastened	2948
Eze	43:13	cubit is a cubit and an **h.** breadth;	2948
Eze	44:12	I lifted up mine **h.** against them,	3027
Eze	46:7	according as his **h.** shall attain	3027
Eze	47:3	man that had the line in his **h.**	3027
Eze	47:14	I lifted up mine **h.** to give it unto	3027
Da	1:2	into his **h.**, with part of the vessels	3027
Da	2:38	hath he given into thine **h.**, and	3028
Da	3:17	he will deliver us out of thine **h.**,	3028
Da	4:35	none can stay his **h.**, or say	3028
Da	5:5	came forth fingers of a man's **h.**,	3028
Da	5:5	saw the part of the **h.** that wrote.	3028
Da	5:23	and the God in whose **h.** thy breath	3028
Da	5:24	Then was the part of the **h.** sent	3028
Da	7:25	and they shall be given into his **h.**	3028
Da	8:4	that could deliver out of his **h.**;	3027
Da	8:7	deliver the ram out of his **h.**	3027
Da	8:25	cause craft to prosper in his **h.**;	3027
Da	8:25	but he shall be broken without **h.**.	3027
Da	9:15	land of Egypt with a mighty **h.**,	3027
Da	10:10	an **h.** touched me, which set me	3027
Da	11:11	multitude shall be given into his **h.**.	3027
Da	11:16	which by his **h.** shall be consumed.	3027
Da	11:41	escape out of his **h.**, even Edom,	3027
Da	11:42	He shall stretch forth his **h.** also	3027
Da	12:7	he held up his right **h.**	3225
Da	12:7	and his left **h.** unto heaven,	8040
Ho	2:10	shall deliver her out of mine **h.**	3027
Ho	7:5	stretched out his **h.** with scorners.	3027
Ho	12:7	the balances of deceit are in his **h.**:	3027
Joe	1:15	the day of the Lord is at **h.**.	7138
Joe	2:1	the day of the Lord...is nigh at **h.**;	
Joe	3:8	into the **h.** of the children of	3027
Am	1:8	I will turn mine **h.** against Ekron:	3027
Am	5:19	leaned his **h.** on the wall, and a	3027
Am	7:7	with a plumbline in his **h.**	3027
Am	9:2	hell, thence shall mine **h.** take	3027
Jon	4:11	cannot discern between ...right **h.**	3235
Jon	4:11	between their right...and...left **h.**.	8040
Mic	2:1	it is in the power of their **h.**	3027
Mic	4:10	thee from the **h.** of thine enemies.	3709
Mic	5:9	Thine **h.** shall be lifted up upon	3027
Mic	5:12	cut off witchcrafts out of thine **h.**;	3027
Mic	7:16	lay their **h.** upon their mouth,	3027
Hab	2:16	the Lord's right **h.** shall be turned	3225
Hab	3:4	he had horns coming out of his **h.**:	3027
Zep	1:4	I will also stretch out mine **h.**	3027
Zep	1:7	the day of the Lord is at **h.**:	7138
Zep	2:13	he will stretch out his **h.** against	3027
Zep	2:15	by her shall hiss, and wag his **h.**.	3027
Zec	2:1	with a measuring line in his **h.**.	3027
Zec	2:9	I will shake mine **h.** upon them,	3027
Zec	3:1	Satan standing at his right **h.** to	3225
Zec	4:10	plummet in the **h.** of Zerubbabel	3027
Zec	8:4	his staff in his **h.** for very age.	3027
Zec	11:6	every one into his neighbour's **h.**,	3027
Zec	11:6	and into the **h.** of his king:	3027
Zec	11:6	out of their **h.** I will not deliver	3027
Zec	12:6	on the right **h.** and on the left:	3225
Zec	13:7	I will turn mine **h.** upon the little	3027
Zec	14:13	shall lay hold every one on the **h.**	3027
Zec	14:13	of his neighbour, and...**h.** shall rise	3027
Zec	14:13	up against the **h.** of his neighbour	3027
Mal	1:10	will I accept an offering at your **h.**	3027
Mal	1:13	should I accept this of your **h.**?	3027
Mal	2:13	receiveth it with good will at your **h.**.	3027
Mt	3:2	for the kingdom of heaven is at **h.**	1448
Mt	3:12	Whose fan is in his **h.**, and he will	5495
Mt	4:17	**for the kingdom of heaven is at h.**	1448
Mt	5:30	**if thy right h. offend thee, cut it**	5495
Mt	6:3	**doest alms, let not thy left h.**	
Mt	6:3	**know what thy right h. doeth.**	
Mt	8:3	Jesus put forth his **h.**, and touched	5495
Mt	8:15	he touched her **h.**, and the fever	5495
Mt	9:18	lay thy **h.** upon her, and she shall	5495
Mt	9:25	took her by the **h.**, and the maid	5495
Mt	10:7	**The kingdom of heaven is at h.**	1448
Mt	12:10	a man which had his **h.** withered.	5495
Mt	12:13	to the man, **Stretch forth thine h.**	5495
Mt	12:49	he stretched forth his **h.** toward his	5495
Mt	14:31	Jesus stretched forth his **h.**, and	5495
Mt	18:8	**if thy h. or thy foot offend thee,**	5495
Mt	20:21	may sit, the one on thy right **h.**, and	
Mt	20:23	**to sit on my right h., and on my**	
Mt	22:13	**Bind him h. and foot, and take**	5495
Mt	22:44	**Sit thou on my right h., till I make**	
Mt	25:33	**shall set the sheep on his right h.,**	
Mt	25:34	**unto them on his right h., Come**	
Mt	25:41	**unto them on the left h., Depart**	
Mt	26:18	**The Master saith, My time is at h.;**	1451
Mt	26:23	**He that dippeth his h. with me**	5495
Mt	26:45	**behold, the hour is at h., and the**	1448
Mt	26:46	**he is at h. that doth betray me.**	1448
Mt	26:51	stretched out his **h.**, and drew his	5495
Mt	26:64	**sitting on the right h. of power,**	
Mt	27:29	his head, and a reed in his right **h.**:	
Mt	27:38	one on the right **h.**, and another on	
Mk	1:15	**the kingdom of God is at h.:**	1448
Mk	1:31	and took her by the **h.**, and lifted	5495
Mk	1:41	put forth his **h.**, and touched	5495
Mk	3:1	man there which had a withered **h.**	5495
Mk	3:3	had the withered **h.**, **Stand forth.**	5495
Mk	3:5	**Stretch forth thine h.** And he	5495
Mk	3:5	and his **h.** was restored whole as the	5495
Mk	5:41	took the damsel by the **h.**, and said	5495
Mk	7:32	beseech him to put his **h.** upon	5495
Mk	8:23	he took the blind man by the **h.**,	5495
Mk	9:27	took him by the **h.**, and lifted him	5495
Mk	9:43	**if thy h. offend thee, cut it off:**	5495
Mk	10:37	we may sit, one on thy right **h.**, and	
Mk	10:37	the other on thy left **h.**, in thy glory.	
Mk	10:40	**sit on my right h. and on my left h.,**	
Mk	12:36	**Sit thou on my right h., till I make**	
Mk	14:42	**lo, he that betrayeth me is at h.**	1448
Mk	14:62	**sitting on the right h. of power**	
Mk	15:27	the one on his right **h.**, and the other	
Mk	16:19	and sat on the right **h.** of God.	
Lu	1:1	many have taken in **h.** to set	2021
Lu	1:66	And the **h.** of the Lord was with	5495
Lu	1:71	and from the **h.** of all that hate us;	5495
Lu	1:74	being delivered out of the **h.** of our	5495
Lu	3:17	Whose fan is in his **h.**, and he will	5495
Lu	5:13	he put forth his **h.**, and touched	5495
Lu	6:6	man whose right **h.** was withered.	5495
Lu	6:8	which had the withered **h.**, **Rise up,**	5495
Lu	6:10	**Stretch forth thy h.** And he did so.	5495
Lu	6:10	his **h.** was restored whole as...other	5495
Lu	8:54	and took her by the **h.**, and called,	5495
Lu	9:62	**No man, having put his h. to the**	5495
Lu	15:22	**put a ring on his h., and shoes**	5495
Lu	20:42	**my Lord, Sit thou on my right h.,**	
Lu	21:30	**that summer is now nigh at h.**	
Lu	21:31	**kingdom of God is nigh at h..**	
Lu	22:21	**the h. of him that betrayeth me**	5495
Lu	22:69	**sit on the right h. of the power of**	
Lu	23:33	one on the right **h.**, and the other on	
Joh	2:13	the Jews' passover was at **h.**, and	1451
Joh	3:35	hath given all things into his **h.**.	5495
Joh	7:2	feast of tabernacles was at **h.**.	1451
Joh	10:28	**any man pluck them out of my h..**	5495
Joh	10:29	**them out of my Father's h.**	5495
Joh	10:39	him: but he escaped out of their **h.**,	5495
Joh	11:44	**h.** and foot with graveclothes;	5495
Joh	11:55	Jews' passover was nigh at **h.**: and	
Joh	18:22	struck Jesus with the palm of his **h.**,	
Joh	19:42	for the sepulchre was nigh at **h.**	
Joh	20:25	and thrust my **h.** into his side, I	5495
Joh	20:27	**reach hither thy h., and thrust**	5495
Ac	2:25	for he is on my right **h.**, that	
Ac	2:33	being by the right **h.** of God exalted,	
Ac	2:34	my Lord, Sit thou on my right **h.**,	
Ac	3:7	took him by the right **h.**, and	5495
Ac	4:28	whatsoever thy **h.** and thy counsel	5495
Ac	4:30	stretching forth thine **h.** to heal;	5495
Ac	5:31	hath God exalted with his right **h.**	5495
Ac	7:25	God by his **h.** would deliver them:	5495
Ac	7:35	by the **h.** of the angel which	5495
Ac	7:50	Hath not my **h.** made all these	5495
Ac	7:55	Jesus standing on the right **h.** of God,	
Ac	7:56	man standing on the right **h.** of God.	
Ac	9:8	they led him by the **h.**, and	5496
Ac	9:12	coming in, and putting his **h.** on	5495
Ac	9:41	he gave her his **h.**, and lifted	5495
Ac	11:21	And the **h.** of the Lord was with	5495
Ac	12:11	delivered me out of the **h.** of Herod,	5495
Ac	12:17	beckoning unto them with the **h.** to	5495
Ac	13:11	behold, the **h.** of the Lord is upon	5495
Ac	13:11	seeking some to lead him by the **h.**.	5497
Ac	13:16	beckoning with his **h.** said, Men of	5495
Ac	19:33	Alexander beckoned with the **h.**,	5495
Ac	21:3	Cyprus, we left it on the left **h.**,	
Ac	21:40	beckoned with the **h.** unto the	5495
Ac	22:11	being led by the **h.** of them that	5496
Ac	23:19	captain took him by the **h.**, and	5495
Ac	26:1	Paul stretched forth the **h.**, and	5495
Ac	28:3	of the heat, and fastened on his **h.**.	5495
Ac	28:4	beast hang on his **h.**, they said	5495
Ro	8:34	even at the right **h.** of God, who also	
Ro	13:12	night is far spent, the day is at **h.**:	1448
1Co	12:15	Because I am not the **h.**, I am not	5495
1Co	12:21	And the eye cannot say unto the **h.**,	5495
1Co	16:21	of me Paul with mine own **h.**	5495
2Co	6:7	on the right **h.** and on the left,	
2Co	10:16	of things made ready to our **h.**.	
Ga	3:19	by angels in the **h.** of a mediator,	5495
Ga	6:11	written unto you with mine own **h.**.	5495
Eph	1:20	set him at his own right **h.** in the	
Php	4:5	unto all men. The Lord is at **h.**.	1451
Col	3:1	Christ sitteth on the right **h.** of God,	
Col	4:18	salutation by the **h.** of me Paul.	5495
2Th	2:2	as that the day of Christ is at **h.**	1764
2Th	3:17	of Paul with mine own **h.**,	5495
2Ti	4:6	the time of my departure is at **h.**.	2186
Phm	19	written it with mine own **h.**,	5495

Heb 1:3 the right **h.** of the Majesty on high;..........
Heb 1:13 Sit on my right **h.**, until I make ....
Heb 8:1 set on the right **h.** of the throne ....
Heb 8:9 when I took them by the **h.** to lead.... *5495*
Heb 10:12 sat down on the right **h.** of God;..............
Heb 12:2 is set down at the right **h.** of the ....
1Pe 3:22 is on the right **h.** of God; angels, and.........
1Pe 4:7 the end of all things is at **h.**:............ *1448*
1Pe 5:6 under the mighty **h.** of God, that *5495*
Re 1:3 therein: for the time is at **h.**. *1451*
Re 1:16 he had in his right **h.** seven stars:...... *5495*
Re 1:17 he laid his right **h.** upon me, ... *5495*
Re 1:20 **which thou sawest in my right h.**,........
Re 2:1 **the seven stars in his right h.**,............
Re 5:1 I saw in the right **h.** of him that sat..........
Re 5:7 took the book out of the right **h.**..............
Re 6:5 him had a pair of balances in his **h.**..... *5495*
Re 8:4 up before God out of the angel's **h.**.... *5495*
Re 10:2 he had in his **h.** a little book................. *5495*
Re 10:5 the earth lifted up his **h.** to heaven,.... *5495*
Re 10:8 which is open in the **h.** of the angel..... *5495*
Re 10:10 book out of the angel's **h.**, and ate *5495*
Re 13:16 to receive a mark in their right **h.**, ... *5495*
Re 14:9 mark in his forehead, or in his **h.**, ... *5495*
Re 14:14 and in his **h.** a sharp sickle. *5495*
Re 17:4 having a golden cup in her **h.** full of.... *5495*
Re 19:2 the blood of his servants at her **h.**...... *5495*
Re 20:1 pit and a great chain in his **h.**............ *5495*
Re 22:10 of this book: for the time is at **h.**. *1451*

HANDBREADTH See also HAND and BREADTH.
Ex 37:12 a border of an **h.** round about;........... 2948
2Ch 4:5 And the thickness of it was an **h.**,....... 2947
Ps 39:5 thou hast made my days as an **h.**;...... 2947

HANDED See also BROKENHANDED; LEFTHANDED.
2Sa 17:2 he is weary and weak **h.**, and will...... 3027

HANDFUL See also HANDFULS.
Le 2:2 shall take thereout his **h.** of.......... 4393,7062
Le 5:12 priest shall take his **h.** of it,....... 4393,7062
Le 6:15 shall take of it his **h.**, of the flour....... 7062
Le 9:17 took an **h.** thereof, and burnt..... 4390,3709
Nu 5:26 And the priest shall take an **h.**........... 7061
1Ki 17:12 an **h.** of meal in a barrel,........... 4393,3709
Ps 72:16 There shall be an **h.** of corn................ 6451
Ec 4:6 Better is an **h.** with quietness, ... 4393,3709
Jer 9:22 as the **h.** after the harvestman,.......... 5995

HANDFULS
Ge 41:47 the earth brought forth by **h.**. 7062
Ex 9:8 Take to you **h.** of ashes of........ 4393,2651
Ru 2:16 let fall also some of the **h.**.................. 6653
1Ki 20:10 Samaria shall suffice for **h.** for all 8168
Eze 13:19 my people for **h.** of barley and for...... 8168

HANDIWORK See HANDYWORK.

HANDKERCHIEFS
Ac 19:12 brought unto the sick **h.** or aprons, ... *4676*

HANDLE See also HAFT; HANDLED; HANDLES; HANDLETH; HANDLING.
Ge 4:21 father of all such as **h.** the harp......... 8610
Jg 5:14 they that **h.** the pen of the writer. 4900
1Ch 12:8 that could **h.** shield and buckler,........ 6186
2Ch 25:5 that could **h.** spear and shield. 270
Ps 115:7 They have hands, but they **h.** not: 4184
Jer 2:8 and they that **h.** the law knew........... 8610
Jer 46:9 the Libyans, that **h.** the shield; and 8610
Jer 46:9 the Lydians, that **h.** and bend the........ 8610
Eze 27:29 all that **h.** the oar, the mariners,........ 8610
Lu 24:39 **h. me, and see; for a spirit**.......... *5584*
Col 2:21 touch not; taste not; **h.** not;............. *2345*

HANDLED
Eze 21:11 furbished, that it may be **h.** 8610,3709
Mk 12:4 **and sent him away shamefully h.**.... *821*
1Jo 1:1 looked upon, and...hands have **h.**, ... *5584*

HANDLES
Ca 5:5 upon the **h.** of the lock. 3709

HANDLETH
Pr 16:20 He that **h.** a matter wisely shall......... 5921
Jer 50:16 and him that **h.** the sickle................. 8610
Am 2:15 shall he stand that **h.** the bow; 8610

HANDLING
Eze 38:4 shields, all of them **h.** swords:........... 8610
2Co 4:2 **h.** the word of God deceitfully;.......... *1389*

HANDMAID See also HANDMAIDEN; HANDMAIDS.
Ge 16:1 she had an **h.**, an Egyptian, ... 8198
Ge 25:12 the Egyptian, Sarah's **h.**, bare unto..... 8198
Ge 29:24 Leah Zilpah his maid for an **h.**. 8198
Ge 29:29 Bilhah his **h.** to be her maid............. 8198
Ge 30:4 she gave him Bilhah her **h.** to wife..... 8198
Ge 35:25 the sons of Bilhah, Rachel's **h.**;.......... 8198
Ge 35:26 And the sons of Zilpah, Leah's **h.**;...... 8198
Ex 23:12 the son of thy **h.**, and the stranger, ... 519
Jg 19:19 also for me, and for thy **h.**, ... 519
Ru 2:13 spoken friendly unto thine **h.**,............ 8198
Ru 3:9 I am Ruth thine **h.**: spread................. 519
Ru 3:9 therefore thy skirt over thine **h.**;......... 519
1Sa 1:11 the affliction of thine **h.**, and.............. 519
1Sa 1:11 me, and not forget thine **h.**, ... 519
1Sa 1:11 but wilt give unto thine **h.**.................. 519
1Sa 1:16 Count not thine **h.** for a daughter 519
1Sa 1:18 Let thine **h.** find grace in thy sight. 8198
1Sa 25:24 let thine **h.**, I pray thee, speak in........ 519
1Sa 25:24 and hear the words of thine **h.**.............. 519
1Sa 25:25 but I thine **h.** saw not the young 519
1Sa 25:27 which thine **h.** hath brought unto........ 8198
1Sa 25:28 forgive the trespass of thine **h.** 519
1Sa 25:31 my lord, then remember thine **h.**.......... 519
1Sa 25:41 let thine **h.** be a servant 519
1Sa 28:21 thine **h.** hath obeyed thy voice,........... 8198
1Sa 28:22 also unto the voice of thine **h.**, ... 8198
2Sa 14:6 And thy **h.** had two sons, and they..... 8198
2Sa 14:7 family is risen against thine **h.**, ... 8198
2Sa 14:12 woman said, Let thine **h.**, I pray........ 8198
2Sa 14:15 and thy **h.** said, I will now speak........ 8198
2Sa 14:15 perform the request of his **h.**.............. 519
2Sa 14:16 to deliver his **h.** out of the hand 519
2Sa 14:17 Then thine **h.** said, The word of 8198
2Sa 14:19 words in the mouth of thine **h.**: 8198
2Sa 20:17 Hear the words of thine **h.**. And.......... 519
1Ki 1:13 O king, swear unto thine **h.**,............... 519
1Ki 1:17 the Lord thy God unto thine **h.**, ... 519
1Ki 3:20 while thine **h.** slept, and laid it.......... 519
2Ki 4:2 Thine **h.** hath not anything in the 8198
2Ki 4:16 man of God, do not lie unto thine **h.**.... 8198
Ps 86:16 and save the son of thine **h.**. 519
Ps 116:16 servant, and the son of thine **h.**: 519
Pr 30:23 and an **h.** that is heir to her............. 8198
Jer 34:16 every man his **h.**, whom he had.......... 8198
Lu 1:38 Behold the **h.** of the Lord; be it.......... *1399*

HANDMAIDEN See also HANDMAIDENS.
Lu 1:48 regarded the low estate of his **h.** *1399*

HANDMAIDENS
Ge 33:6 Then the **h.** came near, they and....... 8198
Ru 2:13 like unto one of thine **h.**.................. 8198
Ac 2:18 on my servants and on my **h.**............. *1399*

HANDMAIDS
Ge 33:1 Rachel, and unto the two **h.**................ 8198
Ge 33:2 he put the **h.** and their children 8198
2Sa 6:20 eyes of the **h.** of his servants, ... 519
Isa 14:2 them...for servants and **h.**: and.......... 8198
Jer 34:11 the servants and the **h.**, whom.......... 8198
Jer 34:11 subjection for servants and for **h.**. 8198
Jer 34:16 you for servants and for **h.**. 8198
Joe 2:29 upon the **h.** in those days will I 8198

HANDS
Ge 5:29 our work and toil of our **h.**. 3027
Ge 16:9 and submit thyself under her **h.**. 3027
Ge 20:5 innocency of my **h.** have I done.......... 3709
Ge 24:22 two bracelets for her **h.** of ten 3027
Ge 24:30 bracelets upon his sister's **h.**, and 3027
Ge 24:47 and the bracelets upon her **h.**............. 3027
Ge 27:16 of the kids of the goats upon his **h.**, ... 3027
Ge 27:22 but the **h.** are the **h.** of Esau. 3027
Ge 27:23 him not, because his **h.** were hairy..... 3027
Ge 27:23 hairy, as his brother Esau's **h.**:.......... 3027
Ge 31:42 the labour of my **h.**, and rebuked....... 3709
Ge 37:21 delivered him out of their **h.**; 3027
Ge 37:22 rid him out of their **h.**, to deliver 3027
Ge 39:1 bought him out of the **h.** of the.......... 3027
Ge 43:22 have we brought down in our **h.** 3027
Ge 48:14 guiding his **h.** wittingly; for 3027
Ge 49:24 the arms of his **h.** were made............. 3027
Ge 49:24 strong by the **h.** of the mighty God 3027
Ex 9:29 I will spread abroad my **h.**................. 3709
Ex 9:33 spread abroad his **h.** unto the............ 3709
Ex 15:17 Sanctuary, O Lord, which thy **h.**......... 3027
Ex 17:12 But Moses' **h.** were heavy; and......... 3027
Ex 17:12 Hur stayed up his **h.**, the one on the .. 3027
Ex 17:12 his **h.** were steady until the going 3027
Ex 29:10 **h.** upon the head of the bullock.......... 3027
Ex 29:15, 19 **h.** upon the head of the ram. 3027
Ex 29:24 the **h.** of Aaron, and in the **h.** of........ 3709
Ex 29:25 shalt receive them of their **h.**, ... 3027
Ex 30:19 sons shall wash their **h.** and their....... 3027
Ex 30:21 they shall wash their **h.** and their 3027
Ex 32:19 he cast the tables out of his **h.**. 3027
Ex 35:25 did spin with their **h.**, and brought...... 3027
Ex 40:31 washed their **h.** and their feet 3027
Le 4:15 lay their **h.** upon the head of the........ 3027
Le 7:30 His own **h.** shall bring the offerings 3027
Le 8:14 their **h.** upon the head of the............. 3027
Le 8:18 laid their **h.** upon...of the bullock......... 3027
Le 8:22 laid their **h.** upon the...of the ram. 3027
Le 8:24 upon the thumbs of their right **h.**, ... 3027
Le 8:27 he put all upon Aaron's **h.**, and.......... 3709
Le 8:27 and upon his sons' **h.**, and 3709
Le 8:28 Moses took them from off their **h.**, ... 3709
Le 15:11 and hath not rinsed his **h.** in water, ... 3027
Le 16:12 his **h.** full of sweet incense beaten....... 2651
Le 16:21 Aaron shall lay both his **h.** upon......... 3027
Le 24:14 lay their **h.** upon his head, and let 3027
Nu 5:18 the offering of memorial in her **h.**,....... 3709
Nu 6:19 upon the **h.** of the Nazarite, after....... 3709
Nu 8:10 put their **h.** upon the Levites: 3027
Nu 8:12 the Levites shall lay their **h.** upon...... 3027
Nu 24:10 he smote his **h.** together: and 3709
Nu 27:23 he laid his **h.** upon him, and gave....... 3027
De 1:25 of the fruit of the land in their **h.**, ... 3027
De 3:3 God delivered into our **h.** Og also, ... 3027
De 4:28 the work of men's **h.**, wood and 3027
De 9:15 of the covenant were in my two **h.**...... 3027
De 9:17 cast them out of my two **h.**, ... 3027
De 12:18 in all that thou puttest thine **h.** 3027
De 16:15 all the works of thine **h.**, therefore..... 3027
De 17:7 The **h.** of the witnesses shall be 3027
De 17:7 afterward the **h.** of all the people. 3027
De 20:13 delivered it into thine **h.**, thou 3027
De 21:6 shall wash their **h.** over the 3027
De 21:7 Our **h.** have not shed this blood,......... 3027
De 21:10 delivered them into thine **h.**,.............. 3027
De 24:19 bless thee in all the work of thine **h.**... 3027
De 27:15 work of the **h.** of the craftsman, ... 3027
De 31:29 anger through the work of your **h.**. 3027
De 33:7 let his **h.** be sufficient for him;........... 3027
De 33:11 accept the work of his **h.**: smite 3027
De 34:9 Moses had laid his **h.** upon him:......... 3027
Jos 2:24 the Lord hath delivered into our **h.**..... 3027
Jg 2:14 he delivered them into the **h.** of......... 3027
Jg 2:14 sold them into the **h.** of their 3027
Jg 6:13 us into the **h.** of the Midianites........... 3709
Jg 7:2 give the Midianites into their **h.**, ... 3027
Jg 7:11 shall thine **h.** be strengthened to go.... 3027
Jg 7:19 the pitchers that were in their **h.**. 3027
Jg 7:20 held the lamps in their left **h.**, and...... 3027
Jg 7:20 the trumpets in their right **h.** 3027
Jg 8:3 God hath delivered into your **h.** 3027
Jg 8:6, 15 said, Are the **h.** of Zebah and........ 3709
Jg 8:34 out of the **h.** of all their enemies......... 3027
Jg 9:16 according to...deserving of his **h.**; 3027
Jg 10:7 into the **h.** of the Philistines, and 3027
Jg 10:7 into the **h.** of the children of 3027
Jg 11:30 children of Ammon into mine **h.**, ... 3027
Jg 11:32 Lord delivered them into his **h.**............ 3027
Jg 12:2 ye delivered me not out of their **h.**..... 3027
Jg 12:3 I put my life in my **h.**, and................ 3709
Jg 13:23 a meat offering at our **h.**, neither....... 3027
Jg 14:9 he took thereof in his **h.**, and............ 3709
Jg 15:14 his bands loosed from off his **h.**. 3027
Jg 16:24 hath delivered into our **h.** our............. 3027
Jg 18:10 hath given it into your **h.**; a 3027
Jg 19:27 her **h.** were upon the threshold. 3027
1Sa 5:4 both the palms of his **h.** were cut......... 3027
1Sa 7:14 out of the **h.** of the Philistines. 3027
1Sa 10:4 thou shalt receive of their **h.**.............. 3027
1Sa 11:7 by the **h.** of messengers, saying, ... 3027
1Sa 14:13 Jonathan climbed up upon his **h.**......... 3027
1Sa 14:48 out of the **h.** of them that spoiled........ 3027
1Sa 17:47 and he will give you into our **h.**. 3027
1Sa 21:13 feigned himself mad in their **h.**,.......... 3027
1Sa 30:15 deliver me into the **h.** of my master, .. 3027
2Sa 2:7 now let your **h.** be strengthened, ... 3027
2Sa 3:34 Thy **h.** were not bound, nor thy 3027
2Sa 4:1 his **h.** were feeble, and all the 3027
2Sa 4:12 cut off their **h.** and their feet,............ 3027

2Sa 16:21 the **h.** of all that are with thee 3027
2Sa 21:9 he delivered them into the **h.** of 3027
2Sa 22:21 the cleanness of my **h.** hath he 3027
2Sa 22:35 He teacheth my **h.** to war; so that 3027
2Sa 23:6 they cannot be taken with **h.**: 3027
1Ki 8:22 spread forth his **h.** toward heaven: 3027
1Ki 8:38 spread forth his **h.** toward this 3027
1Ki 8:54 with his **h.** spread up to heaven. 3027
1Ki 14:27 the **h.** of the chief of the guard, 3027
1Ki 16:7 the work of his **h.**, in being like 3027
2Ki 3:11 poured water on the **h.** of Elijah. 3027
2Ki 4:34 and his **h.** upon his **h.**: 3709
2Ki 5:20 in not receiving at his **h.** that 3027
2Ki 9:23 Joram turned his **h.**, and fled, and 3027
2Ki 9:35 the feet, and the palms of her **h.**. 3027
2Ki 10:24 whom I have brought into your **h.** 3027
2Ki 11:12 they clapped their **h.**, and said, 3709
2Ki 11:16 they laid **h.** on her; and she went 3027
2Ki 12:11 the **h.** of them that did the work, 3027
2Ki 13:16 put his **h.** upon the king's **h.**. 3027
2Ki 19:18 the work of men's **h.**, wood and 3027
2Ki 22:17 the works of their **h.**; therefore 3027
1Ch 12:17 there is no wrong in mine **h.**, the 3709
1Ch 25:2 under the **h.** of Asaph, which 3027
1Ch 25:3 under the **h.** of their father 3027
1Ch 25:6 the **h.** of their father for song in 3027
1Ch 29:5 to be made by the **h.** of artificers. 3027
2Ch 6:4 who hath with his **h.** fulfilled that 3027
2Ch 6:12 of Israel, and spread forth his **h.**: 3709
2Ch 6:13 and spread forth his **h.** toward 3709
2Ch 6:29 and shall spread forth his **h.** in 3709
2Ch 8:18 by the **h.** of his servants ships, 3027
2Ch 12:10 the **h.** of the chief of the guard, 3027
2Ch 15:7 let not your **h.** be weak: for your 3027
2Ch 23:15 they laid **h.** on her; and when 3027
2Ch 29:23 they laid their **h.** upon them: 3027
2Ch 32:19 which were the work of the **h.** of 3027
2Ch 34:25 the works of their **h.**; therefore 3027
2Ch 35:11 sprinkled the blood from their **h.**, 3027
Ezr 1:6 about them strengthened their **h.** 3027
Ezr 4:4 weakened the **h.** of the people of 3027
Ezr 5:8 and prospereth in their **h.**. 3028
Ezr 6:22 to strengthen their **h.** in the 3027
Ezr 9:5 and spread out my **h.** unto the 3709
Ezr 10:19 gave their **h.** that they would 3027
Ne 2:18 they strengthened their **h.** for 3027
Ne 4:17 one of his **h.** wrought in the work, 3027
Ne 6:9 Their **h.** shall be weakened from 3027
Ne 6:9 O God, strengthen my **h.**. 3027
Ne 8:6 with lifting up their **h.**: and they 3027
Ne 9:24 and gavest them into their **h.**, 3027
Ne 13:21 ye do so again, I will lay **h.** on you. 3027
Es 3:6 he thought scorn to lay **h.** on 3027
Es 3:9 the **h.** of those that have the charge 3027
Es 9:16 but they laid not their **h.** on the 3027
Job 1:10 hast blessed the work of his **h.**, 3027
Job 4:3 hast strengthened the weak **h.** 3027
Job 5:12 their **h.** cannot perform their 3027
Job 5:18 woundeth, and his **h.** make whole 3027
Job 9:30 and make my **h.** never so clean; 3709
Job 10:3 despise the work of thine **h.**, and 3709
Job 10:8 Thine **h.** have made me and 3027
Job 11:13 stretch out thine **h.** toward him; 3709
Job 14:15 desire to the work of thine **h.**. 3027
Job 16:11 me over into the **h.** of the wicked. 3027
Job 16:17 any injustice in mine **h.**: also 3709
Job 17:3 who is he that will strike **h.** 3027
Job 17:9 he that hath clean **h.** shall be 3027
Job 20:10 and his **h.** shall restore their 3027
Job 22:30 by the pureness of thine **h.** 3709
Job 27:23 Men shall clap their **h.** at him, 3709
Job 30:2 the strength of their **h.** profit me, 3027
Job 31:7 if any blot hath cleaved to mine **h.**; 3709
Job 34:19 they all are the work of his **h.**. 3027
Job 34:37 he clappeth his **h.** among us, and
Ps 7:3 if there be iniquity in my **h.**; 3709
Ps 8:6 over the works of thy **h.**; 3027
Ps 9:16 snared in the work of his own **h.**. 3709
Ps 18:20 the cleanness of my **h.** hath he 3027
Ps 18:24 the cleanness of my **h.** in his 3027
Ps 18:34 He teacheth my **h.** to war, so that 3027
Ps 22:16 they pierced my **h.** and my feet. 3027
Ps 24:4 He that hath clean **h.**, and a pure 3709
Ps 26:6 I will wash mine **h.** in innocency: 3709
Ps 26:10 In whose **h.** is mischief, and their 3027
Ps 28:2 when I lift up my **h.** toward thy 3027
Ps 28:4 them after the work of their **h.**; 3027
Ps 28:5 the operation of his **h.**, he shall 3027
Ps 44:20 stretched out our **h.** to a strange 3709
Ps 47:1 O clap your **h.**, all ye people; 3709
Ps 55:20 He hath put forth his **h.** against 3027
Ps 58:2 the violence of your **h.** in the earth. 3027
Ps 63:4 I will lift up my **h.** in thy name. 3709
Ps 68:31 Ethiopia shall...stretch out her **h.** 3027
Ps 73:13 and washed my **h.** in innocency. 3709
Ps 76:5 men of might have found their **h.**. 3027
Ps 78:72 them by the skilfulness of his **h.**. 3709
Ps 81:6 his **h.** were delivered from the 3709
Ps 88:9 I have stretched out my **h.** unto 3709
Ps 90:17 the work of our **h.** upon us; yea, 3027
Ps 90:17 the work of our **h.** establish thou 3027
Ps 91:12 shall bear thee up in their **h.**. 3709
Ps 92:4 triumph in the works of thy **h.** 3027
Ps 95:5 his **h.** formed the dry land. 3027
Ps 98:8 Let the floods clap their **h.**: let 3709
Ps 102:25 heavens are the work of thy **h.** 3027
Ps 111:7 The works of his **h.** are verity 3027
Ps 115:4 and gold, the work of men's **h.**. 3027
Ps 115:7 They have **h.**, but they handle not: 3027
Ps 119:48 My **h.** also will I lift up unto thy 3709
Ps 119:73 Thy **h.** have made me and 3027
Ps 125:3 the righteous put forth their **h.** 3027
Ps 128:2 shalt eat the labour of thine **h.**: 3709
Ps 134:2 Lift up your **h.** in the sanctuary, 3027
Ps 135:15 and gold, the work of men's **h.** 3027
Ps 138:8 not the works of thine own **h.**. 3027
Ps 140:4 Lord, from the **h.** of the wicked; 3027
Ps 141:2 the lifting up of my **h.** as the 3709
Ps 143:5 I muse on the work of thy **h.**. 3027
Ps 143:6 I stretch forth my **h.** unto thee: 3027
Ps 144:1 teacheth my **h.** to war, and my 3027
Pr 6:10 a little folding of the **h.** to sleep: 3027
Pr 6:17 and **h.** that shed innocent blood, 3027
Pr 12:14 the recompence of a man's **h.** shall 3027
Pr 14:1 plucketh it down with her **h.**. 3027
Pr 17:18 void of understanding striketh **h.**, 3709
Pr 21:25 him; for his **h.** refuse to labour. 3027
Pr 22:26 one of them that strike **h.**, or of 3709
Pr 24:33 a little folding of the **h.** to sleep: 3027
Pr 30:28 The spider taketh hold with her **h.**, 3027
Pr 31:13 worketh willingly with her **h.**. 3709
Pr 31:16 the fruit of her **h.** she planteth 3709
Pr 31:19 She layeth her **h.** to the spindle, 3027
Pr 31:19 and her **h.** hold the distaff. 3709
Pr 31:20 reacheth forth her **h.** to the needy. 3027
Pr 31:31 Give her of the fruit of her **h.**; 3027
Ec 2:11 the works that my **h.** had wrought, 3027
Ec 4:5 The foot foldeth his **h.** together, 3027
Ec 4:6 than both the **h.** full with travail 2651
Ec 5:6 destroy the work of thine **h.**? 3027
Ec 7:26 her **h.** as bands: whose pleaseth 3027
Ec 10:18 through idleness of the **h.** the 3027
Ca 5:5 and my **h.** dropped with myrrh, 3027
Ca 5:14 His **h.** are as gold rings set with 3027
Ca 7:1 the work of the **h.** of a cunning 3027
Isa 1:15 when ye spread forth your **h.**, I 3709
Isa 1:15 your **h.** are full of blood. 3027
Isa 2:8 worship the work of their own **h.**, 3027
Isa 3:11 the reward of his **h.** shall be given 3027
Isa 5:12 consider the operation of his **h.** 3027
Isa 13:7 Therefore shall all **h.** be faint, and 3027
Isa 17:8 the work of his **h.**, neither shall 3027
Isa 19:25 and Assyria the work of my **h.**, 3027
Isa 25:11 And he shall spread forth his **h.** 3027
Isa 25:11 swimmeth spreadeth forth his **h.**
Isa 25:11 together with the spoils of their **h.**. 3027
Isa 29:23 the work of mine **h.**, in the midst 3027
Isa 31:7 your own **h.** have made unto you 3027
Isa 33:15 shaketh his **h.** from holding of 3709
Isa 35:3 Strengthen ye the weak **h.**, and 3027
Isa 37:19 the work of men's **h.**, wood and 3027
Isa 45:9 or thy work, He hath no **h.**? 3027
Isa 45:11 the work of my **h.** command ye me. 3027
Isa 45:12 I, even my **h.**, have stretched out 3027
Isa 49:16 thee upon the palms of my **h.**; 3709
Isa 55:12 of the field shall clap their **h.**. 3709
Isa 59:3 your **h.** are defiled with blood, and 3709
Isa 59:6 the act of violence is in their **h.**. 3709
Isa 60:21 the work of my **h.**, that I may 3027
Isa 65:2 I have spread out my **h.** all the 3027
Isa 65:22 long enjoy the work of their **h.**. 3027
Jer 1:16 the works of their own **h.** 3027
Jer 2:37 and thine **h.** upon thine head: for 3027
Jer 4:31 that spreadeth her **h.**, saying, 3709
Jer 6:24 our **h.** wax feeble: anguish hath 3027
Jer 10:3 the work of the **h.** of the workman, 3027
Jer 10:9 and of the **h.** of the founder: 3027
Jer 19:7 and by the **h.** of them that seek 3027
Jer 21:4 weapons of war that are in your **h.**, 3027
Jer 23:14 they strengthen also the **h.** of 3027
Jer 25:6 anger with the works of your **h.**; 3027
Jer 25:7 works of your **h.** to your own hurt. 3027
Jer 25:14 the works of their own **h.** 3027
Jer 30:6 his **h.** on his loins, as a woman 3027
Jer 32:30 the work of their **h.**, saith the Lord. 3027
Jer 33:13 the **h.** of him that telleth them, 3027
Jer 38:4 he weakeneth the **h.** of the men 3027
Jer 38:4 and the **h.** of all the people, 3027
Jer 44:8 the works of your **h.** burning 3027
Jer 47:3 their children for feebleness of **h.**; 3027
Jer 48:37 upon all the **h.** shall be cuttings, 3027
Jer 50:43 his **h.** waxed feeble: anguish took 3027
La 1:14 hath delivered me into their **h.**, 3027
La 1:17 Zion spreadeth forth her **h.**, and 3027
La 2:15 All that pass by clap their **h.** 3709
La 2:19 lift up thy **h.** toward him for the 3709
La 3:41 lift up our heart with our **h.** 3709
La 3:64 according to the work of their **h.** 3027
La 4:2 the work of the **h.** of the potter! 3027
La 4:6 moment, and no **h.** stayed on her. 3027
La 4:10 The **h.** of the pitiful women have 3027
Eze 1:8 And they had the **h.** of a man 3027
Eze 7:17 All **h.** shall be feeble, and all knees 3027
Eze 7:21 into the **h.** of the strangers for a 3027
Eze 7:27 and the **h.** of the people of the 3027
Eze 10:7 and put it into the **h.** of him 2651
Eze 10:12 and their **h.**, and their wings, 3027
Eze 10:21 **h.** of a man was under their wings. 3027
Eze 11:9 into the **h.** of strangers, and will 3027
Eze 13:22 strengthened the **h.** of the wicked, 3027
Eze 16:11 I put bracelets upon thy **h.**, and 3027
Eze 21:7 all **h.** shall be feeble, and every 3027
Eze 21:14 smite thine **h.** together, and let 3709
Eze 21:17 I will also smite mine **h.** together 3709
Eze 22:14 can thine **h.** be strong, in the days 3027
Eze 23:37 blood is in their **h.**, and with 3027
Eze 23:42 which put bracelets upon their **h.**, 3027
Eze 23:45 adulteresses, and blood is in her **h.**. 3027
Eze 25:6 thou hast clapped thine **h.**, and 3027
Da 2:34 a stone was cut out without **h.**, 3028
Da 2:45 cut out of the mountain without **h.**, 3028
Da 3:15 that shall deliver you out of my **h.**? 3028
Da 10:10 and upon the palms of my **h.**. 3027
Ho 14:3 any more to the work of our **h.**, 3027
Ob 13 laid **h.** on their substance in the
Jon 3:8 the violence that is in their **h.**. 3709
Mic 5:13 worship the work of thine **h.**. 3027
Mic 7:3 they may do evil with both **h.** 3709
Na 3:19 thee shall clap the **h.** over thee: 3709
Hab 3:10 and lifted up his **h.** on high. 3027
Zep 3:16 Zion, Let not thine **h.** be slack. 3027
Hag 1:11 upon all the labour of the **h.**. 3709
Hag 2:14 so is every work of their **h.**; 3027
Hag 2:17 in all the labours of your **h.**; 3027
Zec 4:9 The **h.** of Zerubbabel have laid 3027
Zec 4:9 his **h.** shall also finish it; 3027
Zec 8:9 Let your **h.** be strong, ye that 3027
Zec 8:13 fear not, but let your **h.** be strong. 3027
Zec 13:6 are these wounds in thine **h.**? 3027
Mt 4:6 in their **h.** they shall bear thee up, *5495*
Mt 15:2 for they wash not their **h.** when *5495*
Mt 15:20 **but to eat with unwashen h.** *5495*
Mt 17:22 **shall be betrayed into the h. of** *5495*
Mt 18:8 **rather than having two h. or two** *5495*
Mt 18:28 **and he laid h. on him, and took** *2902*
Mt 19:13 should put his **h.** on them, and *5495*
Mt 19:15 he laid his **h.** on them, and *5495*
Mt 21:46 when they sought to lay **h.** on *2902*
Mt 26:45 **is betrayed into the h. of sinners** *5495*
Mt 26:50 laid **h.** on Jesus, and took him. *5495*
Mt 26:67 smote him with the palms of their **h.**,
Mt 27:24 washed his **h.** before the multitude, *5495*
Mk 5:23 come and lay thy **h.** on her, that *5495*
Mk 6:2 works are wrought by his **h.**? *5495*
Mk 6:5 laid his **h.** upon a few sick folk, *5495*
Mk 7:2 with unwashen, **h.**, they found *5495*
Mk 7:3 except they wash their **h.** oft, eat *5495*
Mk 7:5 but eat bread with unwashen **h.**? *5495*
Mk 8:23 his eyes, and put his **h.** upon him, *5495*
Mk 8:25 he put his **h.** again upon his eyes, *5495*

Mk 9:31 **is delivered into the h. of men,** *5495*
Mk 9:43 **than having two h. to go into hell,** . *5495*
Mk 10:16 in his arms, put his **h.** upon them, ... *5495*
Mk 14:41 **is betrayed into the h. of sinners** ... *5495*
Mk 14:46 laid their **h.** on him, and took him. *5495*
Mk 14:58 this temple that is made with **h.**, ... *5499*
Mk 14:58 will build another made without **h.** *886*
Mk 14:65 strike him with the palms of their **h.** ....
Mk 16:18 **they shall lay h. on the sick, and** .. *5495*
Lu 4:11 And in their **h.** they shall bear thee *5495*
Lu 4:40 laid his **h.** on every one of them, ... *5495*
Lu 6:1 did eat, rubbing them in their **h.** *5495*
Lu 9:44 **shall be delivered into the h. of** *5495*
Lu 13:13 And he laid his **h.** on her: *5495*
Lu 20:19 hour sought to lay **h.** on him; *5495*
Lu 21:12 **they shall lay their h. on you,** *5495*
Lu 22:53 **ye stretched forth no h. against** *5495*
Lu 23:46 **into thy h. I commend my spirit:** .. *5495*
Lu 24:7 delivered into the **h.** of sinful............ *5495*
Lu 24:39 **Behold my h. and my feet, that it** . *5495*
Lu 24:40 he shewed them his **h.** and his *5495*
Lu 24:50 he lifted up his **h.**, and blessed *5495*
Joh 7:30 but no man laid **h.** on him, because *5495*
Joh 7:44 him; but no man laid **h.** on him. *5495*
Joh 8:20 and no man laid **h.** on him; for.......... *4084*
Joh 13:3 given all things into his **h.**, and *5495*
Joh 13:9 but also my **h.** and my head. *5495*
Joh 19:3 and they smote him with their **h.** *4475*
Joh 20:20 shewed unto them his **h.** and his *5495*
Joh 20:25 I shall see in his **h.** the print of the *5495*
Joh 20:27 **thy finger, and behold my h.;** *5495*
Joh 21:18 **thou shalt stretch forth thy h.,** *5495*
Ac 2:23 by wicked **h.** have crucified and *5495*
Ac 4:3 they laid **h.** on them, and put *5495*
Ac 5:12 by the **h.** of the apostles were.......... *5495*
Ac 5:18 laid their **h.** on the apostles, and........ *5495*
Ac 6:6 prayed, they laid their **h.** on them. *5495*
Ac 7:41 in the works of their own **h.** *5495*
Ac 7:48 not in temples made with **h.**; *5499*
Ac 8:17 Then laid they their **h.** on them, ... *5495*
Ac 8:18 laying on of the apostles' **h.** *5495*
Ac 8:19 that on whomsoever I lay **h.**, he *5495*
Ac 9:17 and putting his **h.** on him said, ... *5495*
Ac 11:30 by the **h.** of Barnabas and Saul. *5495*
Ac 12:1 the king stretched forth his **h.** to *5495*
Ac 12:7 And his chains fell off from his **h.** *5495*
Ac 13:3 prayed, and laid their **h.** on them, ... *5495*
Ac 14:3 and wonders to be done by their **h.** *5495*
Ac 17:24 not in temples made with **h.**; *5499*
Ac 17:25 is worshipped with men's **h.**, ... *5495*
Ac 19:6 when Paul had laid his **h.** upon *5495*
Ac 19:11 special miracles by the **h.** of Paul: *5495*
Ac 19:26 no gods, which are made with **h.**: *5495*
Ac 20:34 these **h.** have ministered unto my *5495*
Ac 21:11 bound his own **h.** and feet, ... *5495*
Ac 21:11 shall deliver him into the **h.** of the...... *5495*
Ac 21:27 all the people, and laid **h.** on him, ... *5495*
Ac 24:7 took him away out of our **h.**, ... *5495*
Ac 27:19 out with our own **h.** the tackling.......... *849*
Ac 28:8 laid his **h.** on him, and healed him. *5495*
Ac 28:17 into the **h.** of the Romans................ *5495*
Ro 10:21 I have stretched forth my **h.** unto *5495*
1Co 4:12 labour, working with our own **h.**: *5495*
2Co 5:1 an house not made with **h.**, eternal *886*
2Co 11:33 by the wall, and escaped his **h.** *5495*
Ga 2:9 the right **h.** of fellowship: that *1188*
Eph 2:11 Circumcision in...flesh made by **h.**; *5499*
Eph 4:28 working with his **h.** the thing............. *5495*
Col 2:11 the circumcision made without **h.**, ... *886*
1Th 4:11 and to work with your own **h.**, ... *5495*
1Ti 2:8 lifting up holy **h.**, without wrath *5495*
1Ti 4:14 with the laying on of the **h.** of the *5495*
1Ti 5:22 Lay **h.** suddenly on no man, neither *5495*
2Ti 1:6 in thee by the putting on of my **h.** *5495*
Heb 1:10 heavens are the works of thine **h.**: *5495*
Heb 2:7 set him over the works of thy **h.**: *5495*
Heb 6:2 of baptisms, and of laying on of **h.**, ... *5495*
Heb 9:11 tabernacle, not made with **h.**, that *5499*
Heb 9:24 into the holy places made with **h.**, ... *5499*
Heb 10:31 to fall into the **h.** of the living God. *5495*
Heb 12:12 lift up the **h.** which hang down.......... *5495*
Jas 4:8 Cleanse your **h.**, ye sinners; and......... *5495*
1Jo 1:1 and our **h.** have handled, of the *5495*
Re 7:9 white robes, and palms in their **h.**; *5495*
Re 9:20 not of the works of their **h.**, that *5495*
Re 20:4 upon their foreheads, or in their **h.**; *5495*

HANDSTAVES
Eze 39:9 the arrows, and the **h.**, and 4731,3027

HAND-WEAPON See HAND and WEAPON.

HANDWRITING
Col 2:14 Blotting out the **h.** of ordinances *5498*

HANDYWORK
Ps 19:1 firmament sheweth his **h.** 4639,3027

HANES (ha'-nees) See also TAHPANES.
Isa 30:4 and his ambassadors came to **H.** 2609

HANG See also HANGED; HANGETH; HANGING.
Ge 40:19 and shall **h.** thee on a tree; 8518
Ex 26:12 shall **h.** over the backside of the 5628
Ex 26:13 it shall **h.** over the sides of the ... 1961,5628
Ex 26:32 And thou shalt **h.** it upon four........... 5414
Ex 26:33 And thou shalt **h.** up the vail under..... 5414
Ex 40:8 and **h.** up the hanging at the 5414
Nu 25:4 and **h.** them up before the Lord......... 3363
De 21:22 and thou **h.** him on a tree: 8518
De 28:66 thy life shall **h.** in doubt before 8511
2Sa 21:6 and we will **h.** them up unto the 3363
Es 6:4 to **h.** Mordecai on the gallows 8518
Es 7:9 Then the king said, **H.** him thereon. ... 8518
Ca 4:4 whereon there **h.** a thousand............. 8518
Isa 22:24 And they shall **h.** upon him all the 8518
La 2:10 the virgins of Jerusalem **h.** down........ 3381
Eze 15:3 will men take a pin of it to **h.** 8518
Mt 22:40 **h. all the law and the prophets.** *2910*
Ac 28:4 venomous beast **h.** on his hand, ... *2910*
Heb 12:12 lift up the hands which **h.** down, ... *3935*

HANGED See also HANGETH; HANGING; HUNG.
Ge 40:22 But he **h.** the chief baker: 8518
Ge 41:13 unto mine office, and him he **h.** 8518
De 21:23 he that is **h.** is accursed of God; 8518
Jos 8:29 the king of Ai he **h.** on a tree........... 8518
Jos 10:26 them: and **h.** them on five trees: 8518
2Sa 4:12 and **h.** them up over the pool............ 8518
2Sa 17:23 and **h.** himself, and died, and was....... 2614
2Sa 18:10 I saw Absalom **h.** in an oak............... 8518
2Sa 21:9 and they **h.** them in the hill.............. 3363
2Sa 21:12 where the Philistines had **h.** them, ... 8511
2Sa 21:13 the bones of them that were **h.** 3363
Ezr 6:11 let him be **h.** thereon; and let his 4223
Es 2:23 therefore they were both **h.** on a 8518
Es 5:14 king that Mordecai may be **h.** 8518
Es 7:10 So they **h.** Haman on the gallows....... 8518
Es 8:7 him they have **h.** upon the gallows, ... 8518
Es 9:13 let Haman's ten sons be **h.** upon........ 8518
Es 9:14 and they **h.** Haman's ten sons. 8518
Es 9:25 that he and his sons should be **h.** 8518
Ps 137:2 We **h.** our harps upon the willows 8518
La 5:12 Princes are **h.** up by their hand: 8518
Eze 27:10 they **h.** the shield and helmet in......... 8518
Eze 27:11 they **h.** their shields upon thy walls 8518
Mt 18:6 **that a millstone were h. about his** . *2910*
Mt 27:5 departed, and went and **h.** himself. *519*
Mk 9:42 **that a millstone were h. about his** . *4029*
Lu 17:2 **that a millstone were h. about his** . *4029*
Lu 23:39 of the malefactors which were **h.** *2910*
Ac 5:30 whom ye slew and **h.** on a tree. *2910*
Ac 10:39 whom they slew and **h.** on a tree: *2910*

HANGETH
Job 26:7 and **h.** the earth upon nothing........... 8518
Ga 3:13 Cursed is every one that **h.** on a *2910*

HANGING See also HANGINGS.
Ex 26:36 shalt make an **h.** for the door............ 4539
Ex 26:37 thou shalt make for the **h.** five 4539
Ex 27:16 gate of the court shall be an **h.** 4539
Ex 35:15 and the **h.** for the door at the............ 4539
Ex 35:17 the **h.** for the door of the court, ... 4539
Ex 36:37 he made an **h.** for the tabernacle........ 4539
Ex 38:18 And the **h.** for the gate of the court ... 4539
Ex 39:38 and the **h.** for the tabernacle door, ... 4539
Ex 39:40 the **h.** for the court gate, his cords, ... 4539
Ex 40:5 the **h.** of the door to the tabernacle. ... 4539
Ex 40:8 hang up the **h.** at the court gate. 4539
Ex 40:28 he set up the **h.** at the door of the..... 4539
Ex 40:33 and set up the **h.** of the court gate..... 4539
Nu 3:25 **h.** for the door of the tabernacle 4539
Nu 3:31 and the **h.**, and all the service 4539
Nu 4:25 **h.** for the door of the tabernacle 4539
Nu 4:26 and the **h.** for the door of the gate..... 4539
Jos 10:26 they were **h.** upon the trees until....... 8518

HANGINGS
Ex 27:9 side southward there shall be **h.** 7050
Ex 27:11 side in length there shall be **h.** 7050
Ex 27:12 west side shall be **h.** of fifty.............. 7050
Ex 27:14 The **h.** of one side of the gate........... 7050
Ex 27:15 on the other side shall be **h.** 7050
Ex 35:17 The **h.** of the court, his pillars,.......... 7050
Ex 38:9 the **h.** of the court were of fine 7050
Ex 38:11 side the **h.** were an hundred cubits, ...
Ex 38:12 for the west side were **h.** 7050
Ex 38:14 The **h.** of the one side of the gate...... 7050
Ex 38:15 that hand, were **h.** of fifteen cubits; 7050
Ex 38:16 All the **h.** of the court round about 7050
Ex 38:18 answerable to the **h.** of the court. 7050
Ex 39:40 The **h.** of the court, his pillars,.......... 7050
Nu 3:26 And the **h.** of the court, and the 7050
Nu 4:26 And the **h.** of the court, and the 7050
2Ki 23:7 where the women wove **h.** for the 1004
Es 1:6 were white, green, and blue, **h.**, ...

HANIEL (ha'-ne-el) See also HANNIEL.
1Ch 7:39 sons of Ulla; Arah, and **H.**, ... 2592

HANNAH (han'-nah)
1Sa 1:2 the name of the one was **H.**, ... 2584
1Sa 1:2 but **H.** had no children. 2584
1Sa 1:5 unto **H.** he gave a worthy portion; 2584
1Sa 1:5 for he loved **H.**; but the Lord........... 2584
1Sa 1:8 **H.**, why weepest thou? and why 2584
1Sa 1:9 So **H.** rose up after they had eaten 2584
1Sa 1:13 Now **H.**, she spake in her heart; 2584
1Sa 1:15 **H.** answered and said, No, my lord, ... 2584
1Sa 1:19 and Elkanah knew **H.** his wife; 2584
1Sa 1:20 about after **H.** had conceived, ... 2584
1Sa 1:22 But **H.** went not up; for she said 2584
1Sa 2:1 **H.** prayed, and said, My heart........... 2584
1Sa 2:21 the Lord visited **H.**, so that she......... 2584

HANNATHON (han'-na-thon)
Jos 19:14 it on the north side to **H.**: 2615

HANNIEL (han'-ne-el) See also HANIEL.
Nu 34:23 Manasseh, **H.** the son of Ephod......... 2592

HANOCH (ha'-nok) See also HANOCHITES; HENOCH.
Ge 25:4 Ephah, and Epher, and **H.**, and 2585
Ge 46:9 of Reuben: **H.**, and Phallu, and.......... 2585
Ex 6:14 **H.**, and Pallu, Hezron, and Carmi: 2585
Nu 26:5 **H.**, of whom cometh the family of...... 2585
1Ch 5:3 **H.**, and Pallu, Hezron, and Carmi....... 2585

HANOCHITES (ha'-nok-ites)
Nu 26:5 cometh the family of the **H.** 2599

HANUN (ha'-nun)
2Sa 10:1 **H.** his son reigned in his stead. 2586
2Sa 10:2 I will shew kindness unto **H.** the........ 2586
2Sa 10:3 of Ammon said unto **H.** their lord, ... 2586
2Sa 10:4 Wherefore **H.** took David's 2586
1Ch 19:2 said, I will shew kindness unto **H.** 2586
1Ch 19:2 of the children of Ammon to **H.**, ... 2586
1Ch 19:3 said to **H.**, Thinkest thou that 2586
1Ch 19:4 **H.** took David's servants, and 2586
1Ch 19:6 **H.** and the children of Ammon............ 2586
Ne 3:13 The valley gate repaired **H.**, and........ 2586
Ne 3:30 and **H.** the sixth son of Zalaph, ... 2586

HAP See also PERHAPS.
Ru 2:3 her **h.** was to light on a part of.......... 4745

HAPHRAIM (haf-ra'-im)
Jos 19:19 And **H.**, and Shihon, and 2663

HAPLY
1Sa 14:30 if **h.** the people had eaten freely 3863
Mk 11:13 if **h.** he might find any thing............... *686*
Lu 14:29 **Lest h., after he hath laid the** *3379*
Ac 5:39 lest **h.** ye be found even to fight........ *3379*
Ac 17:27 if **h.** they might feel after him, ... *686*
2Co 9:4 Lest **h.** if they of Macedonia come *3381*

HAPPEN See also HAPPENED; HAPPENETH.
1Sa 28:10 there shall no punishment **h.** to.......... 7136
Pr 12:21 There shall no evil **h.** to the just: 579
Isa 41:22 shew us what shall **h.**: let them 7136
Mk 10:32 what things should **h.** unto him, ... *4819*

HAPPENED
1Sa 6:9 it was a chance that **h.** to us............ 1961
2Sa 1:6 As I **h.** by chance upon mount........... 7136
2Sa 20:1 there **h.** to be there a man of............ 7122
Es 4:7 all that had **h.** unto him, and of.......... 7136

Jer 44:23 therefore this evil is **h.** unto you, 7122
Lu 24:14 of all these things which had **h.** *4819*
Ac 3:10 at that which had **h.** unto him. *4819*
Ro 11:25 blindness in part is **h.** to Israel, *1096*
1Co 10:11 all these things **h.** unto them for *4819*
Php 1:12 that the things which **h.** unto me
1Pe 4:12 as though some strange thing **h.** *4819*
2Pe 2:22 But it is **h.** unto them according to *4819*

HAPPENETH
Ec 2:14 that one event **h.** to them all. 7136
Ec 2:15 As it **h.** to the fool, 4745
Ec 2:15 it **h.** even to me: 7136
Ec 8:14 men, unto whom it **h.** according 5060
Ec 8:14 wicked men, to whom it **h.** 5060
Ec 9:11 time and chance **h.** to them all. 7136

HAPPIER
1Co 7:40 But she is **h.** if she so abide, *3107*

HAPPUCH See KEREN-HAPPUCH.

HAPPY See also HAPPIER.
Ge 30:13 Leah said, **H.** am I, for the 837
De 33:29 **H.** art thou, O Israel: who is like 835
1Ki 10:8 **H.** are thy men, **h.** are these thy 835
2Ch 9:7 **H.** are thy men, and **h.** are these 835
Job 5:17 **h.** is the man whom God correcteth: 835
Ps 127:5 **H.** is the man that hath his quiver 835
Ps 128:2 **h.** shalt thou be, and it shall be 835
Ps 137:8 **h.** shall he be, that rewardeth thee 835
Ps 137:9 **H.** shall he be, that taketh and 835
Ps 144:15 **H.** is that people, that is in such a 835
Ps 144:15 **h.** is that people, whose God is the 835
Ps 146:5 **H.** is he that hath the God 835
Pr 3:13 **H.** is the man that findeth wisdom, 835
Pr 3:18 **h.** is every one that retaineth her. 833
Pr 14:21 hath mercy on the poor, **h.** is he. 835
Pr 16:20 trusteth in the Lord, **h.** is he. 835
Pr 28:14 **H.** is the man that feareth alway: 835
Pr 29:18 he that keepeth the law, **h.** is he. 835
Jer 12:1 are all they **h.** that deal very 7951
Mal 3:15 And now we call the proud **h.**; 833
Joh 13:17 **h. are ye if you do them.** *3107*
Ac 26:2 I think myself **h.**, king Agrippa, *3107*
Ro 14:22 **H.** is he that condemneth not *3107*
Jas 5:11 we count them **h.** which endure. *3106*
1Pe 3:14 for righteousness's sake, **h.** are ye; *3107*
1Pe 4:14 for the name of Christ, **h.** are ye; *3107*

HARA (ha'-rah)
1Ch 5:26 Habor, and **H.**, and to the river 2024

HARADAH (har'-a-dah)
Nu 33:24 Shapher, and encamped in **H.** 2732
Nu 33:25 And they removed from **H.**, and 2732

HARAN (ha'-ran) See also BETH-HARAN; CHARRAN.
Ge 11:26 begat Abram, Nahor, and **H.** 2039
Ge 11:27 Nahor, and **H.**; and **H.** begat 2039
Ge 11:28 **H.** died before his father Terah 2039
Ge 11:29 Milcah, the daughter of **H.**, the 2039
Ge 11:31 Lot the son of **H.** his son's son, 2039
Ge 11:31 they came unto **H.**, and dwelt 2771
Ge 11:32 five years: and Terah died in **H.** 2771
Ge 12:4 when he departed out of **H.** 2771
Ge 12:5 souls that they had gotten in **H.**; 2771
Ge 27:43 thou to Laban my brother to **H.**; 2771
Ge 28:10 Beer-sheba, and went toward **H.** 2771
Ge 29:4 And they said, Of **H.** are we. 2771
2Ki 19:12 as Gozan, and **H.**, and Rezeph, 2771
1Ch 2:46 Caleb's concubine, bare **H.**, and 2771
1Ch 2:46 and Gazez: and **H.** begat Gazez. 2771
1Ch 23:9 Shelomith, and Haziel, and **H.**, 2039
Isa 37:12 **H.**, and Rezeph, and the children 2771
Eze 27:23 **H.**, and Canneh, and Eden, the 2771

HARARITE (har'-a-rite)
2Sa 23:11 Shammah the son of Agee the **H.** 2043
2Sa 23:33 Shammath the **H.**, Ahiam the son of 2043
2Sa 23:33 Ahiam the son of Sharar the **H.**, 2043
1Ch 11:34 Jonathan the son of Shage the **H.**, 2043
1Ch 11:35 Ahiam the son of Sacar the **H.**, 2043

HARBONA (har-bo'-nah) See also HARBONAH.
Es 1:10 Biztha, **H.**, Bigtha, and Abagtha, 2726

HARBONAH (har-bo'-nah) See also HARBONA.
Es 7:9 **H.**, one of the chamberlains, 2726

HARD See also HARDER; HARDHEARTED.
Ge 18:14 Is any thing too **h.** for the Lord? 6381
Ge 35:16 travailed, and she had **h.** labour. 7185
Ge 35:17 when she was in **h.** labour, that 7185
Ex 1:14 their lives bitter with **h.** bondage, 7186
Ex 18:26 the **h.** causes they brought unto 7186
Lev 3:9 he take off **h.** by the backbone; 5980
De 1:17 the cause that is too **h.** for you, 7185
De 15:18 It shall not seem **h.** unto thee, 7185
De 17:8 If there arise a matter too **h.** for 6381
De 26:6 us, and laid upon us **h.** bondage: 7186
Jg 9:52 and went **h.** unto the door of the 5066
Jg 20:45 and pursued **h.** after them unto
1Sa 14:22 even they also followed **h.** after 1692
1Sa 31:2 the Philistines followed **h.** upon 1692
2Sa 1:6 and horsemen followed **h.** after 1692
2Sa 3:39 the sons of Zeruiah be too **h.** for 7186
2Sa 13:2 and Amnon thought it **h.** for him 6381
1Ki 10:1 to prove him with **h.** questions. 2420
1Ki 21:1 **h.** by the palace of Ahab king of 681
2Ki 2:10 Thou hast asked a **h.** thing: 7185
1Ch 10:2 the Philistines followed **h.** after 5221
1Ch 19:4 in the midst **h.** by their buttocks,
2Ch 9:1 prove Solomon with **h.** questions 2420
Job 41:24 **h.** as a piece of the nether 3332
Ps 60:3 hast shewed thy people **h.** things: 7186
Ps 63:8 My soul followeth **h.** after thee: 1692
Ps 88:7 Thy wrath lieth **h.** upon me, and 5564
Ps 94:4 they utter and speak **h.** things? 6277
Pr 13:15 the way of transgressors is **h.** 386
Isa 14:3 the **h.** bondage wherein thou 7186
Jer 32:17 and there is nothing too **h.** for thee: 6381
Jer 32:27 is there any thing too **h.** for me? 6381
Eze 3:5 and of an **h.** language, but to the 3515
Eze 3:6 and of an **h.** language, whose words 3515
Da 5:12 and shewing of **h.** sentences, and 280
Jon 1:13 men rowed **h.** to bring it to the land;
Mt 25:24 **that thou art an h. man, reaping** *4642*
Mk 10:24 **how h. is it for them that trust** *1422*
Joh 6:60 This is an **h.** saying; who can *4642*
Ac 9:5 **h. for thee to kick against the** *4642*
Ac 18:7 house joined **h.** to the synagogue. *4927*
Ac 26:14 **it is h. for thee to kick against** *4642*
Heb 5:11 things to say, and **h.** to be uttered, *1421*
2Pe 3:16 some things **h.** to be understood, *1425*
Jude 15 and of all their **h.** speeches which *4642*

HARDEN See also HARDENED.
Ex 4:21 but I will **h.** his heart, that he 2388
Ex 7:3 I will **h.** Pharaoh's heart, and 7185
Ex 14:4 I will **h.** Pharaoh's heart, that he 2388
Ex 14:17 will **h.** the hearts of the Egyptians, 2388
De 15:7 thou shalt not **h.** thine heart, nor 553
Jos 11:20 was of the Lord to **h.** their hearts, 2388
1Sa 6:6 Wherefore then do ye **h.** your 5513
Job 6:10 yea, I would **h.** myself in sorrow: 5339
Ps 95:8 **H.** not your heart, as in the 7185
Heb 3:8 **H.** not your hearts, as in the *4645*
Heb 3:15 voice, **h.** not your hearts, as in the *4645*
Heb 4:7 his voice, **h.** not your hearts. *4645*

HARDENED
Ex 7:13 And he **h.** Pharaoh's heart, that 2388
Ex 7:14 Pharaoh's heart is **h.**, he refuseth 3515
Ex 7:22 Pharaoh's heart was **h.**, neither 2388
Ex 8:15 he **h.** his heart, and hearkened not 3513
Ex 8:19 and Pharaoh's heart was **h.**, and 2388
Ex 8:32 And Pharaoh **h.** his heart at this 3513
Ex 9:7 And the heart of Pharaoh was **h.**, 3515
Ex 9:12 the Lord **h.** the heart of Pharaoh, 2388
Ex 9:34 sinned yet more, and **h.** his heart, 3513
Ex 9:35 And the heart of Pharaoh was **h.**, 2388
Ex 10:1 I have **h.** his heart, and the heart 3513
Ex 10:20 the Lord **h.** Pharaoh's heart, so 2388
Ex 10:27 the Lord **h.** Pharaoh's heart, and 2388
Ex 11:10 the Lord **h.** Pharaoh's heart, so 2388
Ex 14:8 the Lord **h.** the heart of Pharaoh 2388
De 2:30 the Lord thy God **h.** his spirit, 7185
1Sa 6:6 and Pharaoh **h.** their hearts? 3513
2Ki 17:14 would not hear, but **h.** their necks, 7185
2Ch 36:13 and **h.** heart from turning 553
Ne 9:16 **h.** their necks, and hearkened not 7185
Ne 9:17 but **h.** their necks, and in their 7185
Ne 9:29 **h.** their neck, and would not hear. 7185
Job 9:4 who hath **h.** himself against him, 7185
Job 39:16 She is **h.** against her young 7188
Isa 63:17 from thy ways, and **h.** our heart 7188
Jer 7:26 but **h.** their neck: they did worse 7185
Jer 19:15 they have **h.** their necks, that 7185
Da 5:20 up, and his mind **h.** in pride, 8631
Mk 6:52 loaves: for their heart was **h.** *4456*
Mk 8:17 **have ye your heart yet h.?** *4456*
Joh 12:40 blinded their eyes, and **h.** their *4456*
Ac 19:9 But when divers were **h.**, and *4645*
Heb 3:13 **h.** through the deceitfulness of sin. *4645*

HARDENETH
Pr 21:29 A wicked man **h.** his face: but as 5810
Pr 28:14 but he that **h.** his heart shall fall 7185
Pr 29:1 being often reproved **h.** his neck, 7185
Ro 9:18 mercy, and whom he will he **h.** *4645*

HARDER
Pr 18:19 A brother offended is **h.** to be won
Jer 5:3 made their faces **h.** than a rock; 2388
Eze 3:9 As an adamant **h.** than flint 2389

HARDHEARTED
Eze 3:7 Israel are impudent and **h.** 7186,3820

HARDLY
Ge 16:6 And when Sarai dealt **h.** with her, 6031
Ex 13:15 Pharaoh would **h.** let us go, 7185
Isa 8:21 through it, **h.** bestead and hungry: 7185
Mt 19:23 **a rich man shall h. enter into** *1423*
Mk 10:23 **How h. shall they that have riches.** *1423*
Lu 9:39 bruising him **h.** departeth from *3425*
Lu 18:24 How **h.** shall they that have riches *1423*
Ac 27:8 And, **h.** passing it, came unto a *3433*

HARDNESS
Job 38:38 the dust groweth into **h.**, and 4165
Mt 19:8 **because of the h. of your hearts** *4641*
Mk 3:5 grieved for the **h.** of their hearts, *4457*
Mk 10:5 **For the h. of your heart he wrote** *4641*
Mk 16:14 their unbelief and **h.** of heart, *4641*
Ro 2:5 thy **h.** and impenitent heart *4643*
2Ti 2:3 therefore endure **h.**, as a good *2553*

HARE
Le 11:6 the **h.**, because he cheweth the cud, 768
De 14:7 the camel, and the **h.**, and the 768

HAREPH (ha'-ref)
1Ch 2:51 **H.** the father of Beth-gader. 2780

HARESHA See TEL-HARESHA.

HARETH (ha'-reth)
1Sa 22:5 and came into the forest of **H.** 2802

HARHAIAH (har-ha-i'-ah)
Ne 3:8 the son of **H.**, of the goldsmiths. 2736

HARHAS (has'-has) See also HASRAH.
2Ki 22:14 the son of **H.**, keeper of the 2745

HARHUR (har'-hur)
Ezr 2:51 of Hakupha, the children of **H.**, 2744
Ne 7:53 of Hakupha, the children of **H.**, 2744

HARIM (ha'-rim)
1Ch 24:8 The third to **H.**, the fourth to 2766
Ezr 2:32 The children of **H.**, three hundred 2766
Ezr 2:39 the children of **H.**, a thousand and 2766
Ezr 10:21 the sons of **H.**; Maaseiah, and 2766
Ezr 10:31 of the sons of **H.**; Eliezer, Ishijah, 2766
Ne 3:11 Malchijah the son of **H.**, and 2766
Ne 7:35 The children of **H.**, three hundred 2766
Ne 7:42 The children of **H.**, a thousand 2766
Ne 10:5 **H.**, Meremoth, Obadiah, 2766
Ne 10:27 Malluch, **H.**, Baanah. 2766
Ne 12:15 Of **H.**, Adna; of Meraioth, Helkai; 2766

HARIPH (ha'-rif) See also JORAH.
Ne 7:24 The children of **H.**, an hundred 2756
Ne 10:19 **H.**, Anathoth, Nebai, 2756

HARLOT See also HARLOT'S; HARLOTS.
Ge 34:31 with our sister as with an **h.**? 2181
Ge 38:15 he thought her to be an **h.**; 2181
Ge 38:21 Where is the **h.**, that was openly 6948
Ge 38:21 There was no **h.** in this place. 6948
Ge 38:22 there was no **h.** in this place. 6948
Ge 38:24 daughter in law hath played the **h.**; 2181
Le 21:14 or rofane, or an **h.**, these shall 2181
Jos 6:17 only Rahab the **h.** shall live, she 2181
Jos 6:25 Joshua saved Rahab the **h.** alive, 2181
Jg 11:1 he was the son of an **h.**: 2181
Jg 16:1 saw there an **h.**, and went 2181
Pr 7:10 a woman with the attire of an **h.**, 2181
Isa 1:21 the faithful city become an **h.**! 2181
Isa 23:15 years shall Tyre sin as an **h.** 2181

Isa 23:16 thou h. that hast been forgotten;........ 2181
Jer 2:20 tree thou wanderest, playing the h.. ... 2181
Jer 3:1 played the h. with many lovers;......... 2181
Jer 3:6 tree, and there hath played the h.. 2181
Jer 3:8 but when and played the h. also......... 2181
Eze 16:15 and playedst the h. because of thy 2181
Eze 16:16 and playedst the h. thereupon: 2181
Eze 16:28 yea, thou hast played the h. with....... 2181
Eze 16:31 hast not been as an h., in that thou.... 2181
Eze 16:35 O h., hear the word of the Lord:........ 2181
Eze 16:41 thee to cease from playing the h......... 2181
Eze 23:5 And Aholah played the h. when she..... 2181
Eze 23:19 wherein she had played the h. in........ 2181
Eze 23:44 unto a woman that playeth the h.:........ 2181
Ho 2:5 their mother hath played the h.: 2181
Ho 3:3 thou shalt not play the h., and........... 2181
Ho 4:15 Though thou, Israel, play the h.,......... 2181
Joe 3:3 have given a boy for an h.,.................. 2181
Am 7:17 Thy wife shall be an h. in the city,...... 2181
Mic 1:7 she gathered it of the hire of an h.,....... 2181
Mic 1:7 shall return to the hire of an h.......... 2181
Na 3:4 of the wellfavoured h., the mistress.... 2181
1Co 6:15 make them the members of an h.? *4204*
1Co 6:16 is joined to an h. is one body?........... *4204*
Heb 11:31 By faith the h. Rahab perished not...... *4204*
Jas 2:25 was not Rahab the h. justified by....... *4204*

HARLOT'S
Jos 2:1 came into an h. house, named.......... 2181
Jos 6:22 Go into the h. house, and bring.......... 2181

HARLOTS See also HARLOTS'.
1Ki 3:16 two women, that were h., unto the.... 2181
Pr 29:3 he that keepeth company with h. 2181
Ho 4:14 they sacrifice with h.: therefore......... 6948
Mt 21:31 **and the h. go into the kingdom**...... *4204*
Mt 21:32 **and the h. believed him: and ye,**..... *4204*
Lu 15:30 **devoured thy living with h., thou** .. *4204*
Re 17:5 mother of h. and abominations........... *4204*

HARLOTS'
Jer 5:7 by troops in the h. houses................ 2181

HARM See also HARMFUL.
Ge 31:52 and this pillar unto me, for h............ 7451
Le 5:16 for the h. that he hath done in........... 2398
Nu 35:23 his enemy, neither sought his h.:....... 7451
1Sa 26:21 I will no more do thee h., ... 7489
2Sa 20:6 the son of Bichri do us more h.......... 3415
2Ki 4:41 there was no h. in the pot......... 1697,7451
1Ch 16:22 and do my prophets no h................... 7489
Ps 105:15 and do my prophets no h................... 7489
Pr 3:30 if he have done thee no h.................. 7451
Jer 39:12 look well to him, and do him no h.;..... 7451
Ac 16:28 Do thyself no h.: for we are all *2556*
Ac 27:21 to have gained this h. and loss. *5196*
Ac 28:5 into the fire, and felt no h.. .... *2556*
Ac 28:6 saw no h. come to him, they.............. *824*
Ac 28:21 shewed or spake any h. of thee......... *4190*
1Pe 3:13 who is he that will h. you,................ *2559*

HARMLESS
Mt 10:16 **wise as serpents, and h. as doves**.... *185*
Php 2:15 That ye may be blameless and h., ... *185*
Heb 7:26 who is holy, h., undefiled,.................. *172*

HARNEPHER (har-ne'-fur)
1Ch 7:36 Suah, and H., and Shual,................... 2774

HARNESS See also HARNESSED.
1Ki 20:11 him that girdeth on his h. boast..............
1Ki 22:34 between the joints of the h.:............ 8302
2Ch 9:24 raiment, h., and spices, horses,......... 5402
2Ch 18:33 between the joints of the h.:............ 8302
Jer 46:4 H. the horses; and get up, ye............ 631

HARNESSED
Ex 13:18 the children of Israel went up h......... 2571

HAROD (ha'-rod) See also HARODITE.
Jg 7:1 and pitched beside the well of H.:....... 5878

HARODITE (ha'-ro-dite) See also HARORITE.
2Sa 23:25 Shammah the H., Elika the H., ... 2733

HAROEH (ha-ro'-eh) See also REAIAH.
1Ch 2:52 H., and half of the Manahethites........ 7204

HARORITE (ha'-ro-rite) See also HARODITE.
1Ch 11:27 Shammoth the H., Helez the............ 2033

HAROSHETH (har'-o-sheth)
Jg 4:2 which dwelt in H. of the Gentiles....... 2800
Jg 4:13 from H. of the Gentiles unto the........ 2800
Jg 4:16 the host, unto H. of the Gentiles: 2800

HARP See also HARPED; HARPING; HARPS.
Ge 4:21 such as handle the h. and organ......... 3658
Ge 31:27 songs, with tabret, and with h.?........ 3658
1Sa 10:5 a pipe, and a h., before them;........... 3658
1Sa 16:16 a cunning player on an h.: 3658
1Sa 16:23 David took an h., and played............. 3658
1Ch 25:3 who prophesied with a h., to give...... 3658
Job 21:12 They take the timbrel and h., and...... 3658
Job 30:31 My h. also is turned to mourning....... 3658
Ps 33:2 Praise the Lord with h.: sing unto...... 3658
Ps 43:4 upon the h. will I praise thee, ... 3658
Ps 49:4 open my dark saying upon the h.. 3658
Ps 57:8 awake, psaltery and h.: I myself........ 3658
Ps 71:22 unto thee will I sing with the h.,....... 3658
Ps 81:2 the pleasant h. with the psaltery. 3658
Ps 92:3 upon the h. with a solemn sound........ 3658
Ps 98:5 Sing unto the Lord with the h.; 3658
Ps 98:5 with the h., and the voice of a........... 3658
Ps 108:2 Awake, psaltery and h.: I myself........ 3658
Ps 147:7 sing praise upon the h. unto our 3658
Ps 149:3 unto him with the timbrel and h......... 3658
Ps 150:3 praise him with the psaltery and h...... 3658
Isa 5:12 the h., and the viol, the tabret, and.... 3658
Isa 16:11 my bowels shall sound like an h.......... 3658
Isa 23:16 Take an h., go about the city............ 3658
Isa 24:8 endeth, the joy of the h. ceaseth. 3658
Da 3:5, 7,10,15 flute, h., sackbut,................ 7030
1Co 14:7 giving sound. whether pipe or h.,....... *2788*

HARPED
1Co 14:7 be known what is piped or h.?........... *2789*

HARPERS
Re 14:2 I heard the voice of h. harping *2790*
Re 18:22 And the voice of h., and musicians, ... *2790*

HARPING
Re 14:2 voice of harpers h. with their *2789*

HARPS
2Sa 6:5 even on h., and on psalteries, and...... 3658
1Ki 10:12 h. also and psalteries for singers:...... 3658
1Ch 13:8 and with h., and with psalteries, ... 3658
1Ch 15:16 psalteries and h. and cymbals............ 3658
1Ch 15:21 with h. on the Sheminith.................. 3658
1Ch 15:28 a noise with psalteries and h.. 3658
1Ch 16:5 Jeiel with psalteries and with h.; 3658
1Ch 25:1 who should prophesy with h., with...... 3658
1Ch 25:6 with cymbals psalteries, and h., for 3658
2Ch 5:12 cymbals and psalteries and h., ... 3658
2Ch 9:11 and h. and psalteries for singers: 3658
2Ch 20:28 with psalteries and h. and................ 3658
2Ch 29:25 with psalteries, and with h.,.............. 3658
Ne 12:27 cymbals, psalteries, and with h.......... 3658
Ps 137:2 We hanged our h. upon the willows.... 3658
Isa 30:32 it shall be with tabrets and h.:........... 3658
Eze 26:13 sound of thy h. shall no more be........ 3658
Re 5:8 having every one of them h., ... *2788*
Re 14:2 of harpers harping with their h.: *2788*
Re 15:2 sea of glass, having the h. of God. *2788*

HARROW See also HARROWS.
Job 39:10 will he h. the valleys after thee? 7702

HARROWS
2Sa 12:31 saws, and under h. of iron, and......... 2757
1Ch 20:3 and with h. of iron, and with axes 2757

HARASA See TEL-HARSA.

HARSHA (har'-shah)
Ezr 2:52 of Mehida, the children of H., ... 2797
Ne 7:54 of Mehida, the children of H., ... 2797

HART See also HARTS.
De 12:15 the roebuck, and as of the h.,.......... 354
De 12:22 as the roebuck and the h. is eaten,...... 354
De 14:5 The h., and the roebuck, and the 354
De 15:22 as the roebuck, and as the h.. 354
Ps 42:1 As the h. panteth after the water 354
Ca 2:9 is like a roe or a young h.:................. 354
Ca 2:17 or a young h. upon the mountains........ 354
Ca 8:14 to a young h. upon the mountains........ 354
Isa 35:6 shall the lame man leap as an h.,......... 354

HARTS
1Ki 4:23 an hundred sheep, beside h.,.............. 354
La 1:6 her princes are become like h............. 354

HARUM (ha'-rum)
1Ch 4:8 families of Aharhel the son of H.......... 2037

HARUMAPH (ha-ru'-maf)
Ne 3:10 repaired Jedaiah the son of H., ... 2739

HARUPHITE (ha'-ru-fite)
1Ch 12:5 Shermariah, and Shephatiah the H., ... 2741

HARUZ (ha'-ruz)
2Ki 21:19 Meshullemeth, the daughter of H........ 2743

HARVEST See also HARVESTMAN.
Ge 8:22 seedtime and h., and cold and 7105
Ge 30:14 in the days of wheat h., and found 7105
Ge 45:6 there shall neither be earing nor h...... 7105
Ex 23:16 the feast of h., the firstfruits of.......... 7105
Ex 34:21 in earing time and in h. thou shalt...... 7105
Ex 34:22 the firstfruits of wheat h., and the...... 7105
Le 19:9 when ye reap the h. of your land, ... 7105
Le 19:9 thou gather the gleanings of thy h.. 7105
Le 23:10 shall reap the h. thereof, then ye....... 7105
Le 23:10 a sheaf of the firstfruits of your h....... 7105
Le 23:22 when ye reap the h. of your land, ... 7105
Le 23:22 thou gather any gleaning of thy h.:..... 7105
Le 25:5 growth of its own accord of thy h........ 7105
De 24:19 When thou cuttest down thine h. 7105
Jos 3:15 all his banks all the time of h.,........... 7105
Jg 15:1 in the time of wheat h., ... 7105
Ru 1:22 in the beginning of barley h................ 7105
Ru 2:21 until they have ended all my h............ 7105
Ru 2:23 end of barley h. and of wheat h.;........ 7105
1Sa 6:13 their wheat h. in the valley:.............. 7105
1Sa 8:12 to reap his h., and to make his........... 7105
1Sa 12:17 Is it not wheat h. to day?.................. 7105
2Sa 21:9 were put to death in the days of h., ... 7105
2Sa 21:9 in the beginning of barley h............... 7105
2Sa 21:10 from the beginning of h. until............ 7105
2Sa 23:13 came to David in the h. time............. 7105
Job 5:5 Whose h. the hungry eateth up,.......... 7105
Pr 6:8 and gathereth her food in the h. 7105
Pr 10:5 he that sleepeth in h. is a son........... 7105
Pr 20:4 therefore shall he beg in h., and 7105
Pr 25:13 the cold of snow in the time of h., ... 7105
Pr 26:1 as rain in h., so honour is not 7105
Isa 9:3 according to the joy in h., and as....... 7105
Isa 16:9 thy summer fruits and for thy h.......... 7105
Isa 17:11 the h. shall be a heap in the day of 7105
Isa 18:4 like a cloud of dew in the heat of h.. .. 7105
Isa 18:5 For afore the h., when the bud is 7105
Isa 23:3 the h. of the river, is her revenue;...... 7105
Jer 5:17 they shall eat up thine h., and thy....... 7105
Jer 5:24 us the appointed weeks of the h.. 7105
Jer 8:20 The h. is past, the summer is........... 7105
Jer 50:16 the sickle in the time of h.:................ 7105
Jer 51:33 the time of her h. shall come. 7105
Ho 6:11 he hath set an h. for thee,................. 7105
Joe 1:11 the h. of the field is perished. 7105
Joe 3:13 the sickle, for the h. is ripe: 7105
Am 4:7 were yet three months to the h......... 7105
Mt 9:37 **The h. truly is plenteous, but the** .. *2326*
Mt 9:38 **Lord of the h., that he will send** ... *2326*
Mt 9:38 **send forth labourers into his h.** *2326*
Mt 13:30 **both grow together until the h.** *2326*
Mt 13:30 **and in the time of h. I will say** *2326*
Mt 13:39 **the h. is the end of the world;** *2326*
Mk 4:29 **the sickle, because the h. is come.** .*2326*
Lu 10:2 **The h. truly is great, but the** *2326*
Lu 10:2 **ye therefore the Lord of the h.** *2326*
Lu 10:2 **send forth labourers into his h.** *2326*
Joh 4:35 **four months, and then cometh h.?** ... *2326*
Joh 4:35 **for they are white already to h.** *2326*
Re 14:15 the h. of the earth is ripe.................. *2326*

HARVESTMAN
Isa 17:5 when the h. gathereth the corn, ... 7105
Jer 9:22 as the handful after the h., ... 7114

HAS See HATH.

HASADIAH (has-a-di'-ah)
1Ch 3:20 and H., Jushab-hesed, five................. 2619

HASENUAH (has-e-nu'-ah) See also SENUAH.
1Ch 9:7 son of Hodaviah, the son of H., ... 5574

HASH See MAHER-SHALAL-HASH-BAZ.

HASHABIAH (hash-a-bi'-ah)
1Ch 6:45 The son of H., the son of Amaziah,.... 2811
1Ch 9:14 son of H., of the sons of Merari; 2811

1Ch 25:3 Jeshaiah, **H.**, and Mattithiah, 2811
1Ch 25:19 The twelfth, to **H.**, he, his sons, 2811
1Ch 26:30 Heronites, **H.** and his brethren, 2811
1Ch 27:17 Of the Levites, **H.** the son of 2811
2Ch 35:9 his brethren, and **H.** and Jeiel 2811
Ezr 8:19 **H.**, and with him Jeshaiah of 2811
Ezr 8:24 **H.** and ten of their brethren 2811
Ne 3:17 Next unto him repaired **H.**, 2811
Ne 10:11 Micha, Rehob, **H.**, 2811
Ne 11:15 the son of **H.**, the son of Bunni; 2811
Ne 11:22 the son of Bani, the son of **H.**, 2811
Ne 12:21 Of Hilkiah, **H.**; of Jedaiah, 2811
Ne 12:24 chief of the Levites: **H.**, Sherebiah, 2811

HASHABNAH (hash-ab'-nah)
Ne 10:25 Rehum, **H.**, Maaseiah, 2812

HASHABNIAH (hash-ab-ni'-ah)
Ne 3:10 repaired Hattush the son of **H.** 2813
Ne 9:5 Bani, **H.**, Sherebiah, Hadijah, 2813

HASHBADANA (hash-bad'-a-nah)
Ne 8:4 Hashum, and **H.**, Zechariah, 2806

HASHEM (ha'-shem)
1Ch 11:34 The sons of **H.** the Gizonite, 2044

HASHMONAH (hash-mo'-nah)
Nu 33:29 from Mithcah, and pitched in **H.** 2832
Nu 33:30 And they departed from **H.**, and 2832

HASHUB (ha'-shub) See also HASSHUB.
Ne 3:11 and **H.** the son of Pahath-moab, 2815
Ne 3:23 him repaired Benjamin and **H.** 2815
Ne 10:23 Hoshea, Hananiah, **H.**, 2815
Ne 11:15 Shemaiah the son of **H.**, the son 2815

HASHUBAH (hash-u'-bah)
1Ch 3:20 **H.**, and Ohel, and Berechiah, 2807

HASHUM (ha'-shum)
Ezr 2:19 The children of **H.**, two hundred 2828
Ezr 10:33 Of the sons of **H.**; Mattenai, 2828
Ne 7:22 The children of **H.**, three hundred 2828
Ne 8:4 and Malchiah, and **H.**, and 2828
Ne 10:18 Hodijah, **H.**, Bezai, 2828

HASHUPHA (hash-u'-fah) See also HASUPHA.
Ne 7:46 the children of **H.**, the children 2817

HASRAH (has'-rah) See also HARHAS.
2Ch 34:22 the son of **H.** keeper of the 2641

HASSENAAH (has-se-na'-ah) See also SENAAH.
Ne 3:3 fish gate did the sons of **H.** build, 5574

HASSHUB (hash'-ub) See also HASHUB.
1Ch 9:14 Shemaiah the son of **H.**, the son 2815

HAST
Ge 3:11 **H.** thou eaten of the tree,
Ge 3:13 What is this that thou **h.** done?
Ge 3:14 Because thou **h.** done this, thou art
Ge 3:17 Because thou **h.** hearkened unto the
Ge 3:17 and **h.** eaten of the tree, of which I
Ge 4:10 And he said, What **h.** thou done?
Ge 4:14 Behold, thou **h.** driven me out this
Ge 12:18 What is this that thou **h.** done unto
Ge 15:3 Behold, to me thou **h.** given no seed:
Ge 18:5 And they said, so do, as thou **h.** said.
Ge 19:12 unto Lot, **H.** thou here any besides?
Ge 19:12 whatsoever thou **h.** in the city, bring
Ge 19:19 and thou **h.** magnified thy mercy,
Ge 19:19 which thou **h.** shewed unto me in
Ge 19:21 this city, for the which thou **h.** spoken.
Ge 20:3 woman which thou **h.** taken; for she
Ge 20:9 and said unto him, What **h.** thou done
Ge 20:9 that thou **h.** brought on me and my
Ge 20:9 thou **h.** done deeds unto me that ought
Ge 20:10 What sawest thou, that thou **h.** done
Ge 21:23 the land wherein thou **h.** sojourned.
Ge 21:29 ewe lambs which thou **h.** set by
Ge 22:12 seeing thou **h.** not withheld thy son,
Ge 22:16 for because thou **h.** done this thing,
Ge 22:16 and **h.** not withheld thy son, thine
Ge 22:18 because thou **h.** obeyed my voice.
Ge 24:14 same be she that thou **h.** appointed
Ge 24:14 I know that thou **h.** shewed kindness
Ge 26:10 What is this thou **h.** done unto us?
Ge 27:20 How is it that thou **h.** found it so
Ge 27:36 **H.** thou not reserved a blessing for
Ge 27:38 **H.** thou but one blessing, my father?
Ge 27:45 forget that which thou **h.** done to
Ge 29:25 What is this that thou **h.** done unto
Ge 29:25 wherefore then **h.** thou beguiled me?
Ge 30:15 Is it a small matter that thou **h.** taken
Ge 31:26 said to Jacob, What **h.** thou done,
Ge 31:26 that thou **h.** stolen away unawares to
Ge 31:28 And **h.** not suffered me to kiss my
Ge 31:28 thou **h.** now done foolishly in so doing.
Ge 31:30 yet wherefore **h.** thou stolen my gods?
Ge 31:36 my sin, that thou **h.** so hotly pursued
Ge 31:37 Whereas thou **h.** searched all my stuff,
Ge 31:37 what **h.** thou found of all thy
Ge 31:41 and thou **h.** changed my wages ten
Ge 32:10 which thou **h.** shewed unto thy
Ge 32:28 for as a prince **h.** thou power with
Ge 32:28 God and with men, and **h.** prevailed.
Ge 33:9 my brother; keep that thou **h.** unto
Ge 37:10 is this dream that thou **h.** dreamed?
Ge 38:23 this kid, and thou **h.** not found her.
Ge 38:29 she said, How **h.** thou broken forth?
Ge 39:17 servant, which thou **h.** brought
Ge 45:10 and thy herds, and all that thou **h.**:
Ge 45:11 and thy household, and all that thou **h.**,
Ge 47:25 And they said, Thou **h.** saved our lives:
Ge 47:30 And he said, I will do as thou **h.** said.
Ex 3:12 When thou **h.** brought forth the people
Ex 4:10 nor since thou **h.** spoken unto thy
Ex 5:22 **h.** thou so evil entreated this
Ex 5:22 why is it that thou **h.** sent me?
Ex 5:23 neither **h.** thou delivered thy people
Ex 9:19 gather thy cattle, and all that thou **h.**
Ex 10:29 And Moses said, Thou **h.** spoken well,
Ex 12:44 when thou **h.** circumcised him, then
Ex 13:12 cometh of a beast which thou **h.**: 1961
Ex 14:11 **h.** thou taken us away to die in the
Ex 14:11 wherefore **h.** thou dealt thus
Ex 15:7 thou **h.** overthrown them that rose
Ex 15:13 Thou in thy mercy **h.** led forth the
Ex 15:13 the people which thou **h.** redeemed:
Ex 15:13 thou **h.** guided them in thy strength
Ex 15:16 pass over, which thou **h.** purchased.
Ex 15:17 O Lord, which thou **h.** made for
Ex 17:3 this that thou **h.** brought us up
Ex 20:25 thy tool upon it, thou **h.** polluted it.
Ex 23:16 thy labours, which thou **h.** sown
Ex 23:16 when thou **h.** gathered in thy
Ex 29:36 when thou **h.** made an atonement
Ex 32:11 which thou **h.** brought forth out of the
Ex 32:21 that thou **h.** brought so great a sin
Ex 32:32 of thy book which thou **h.** written.
Ex 33:1 people which thou **h.** brought up
Ex 33:12 and thou **h.** not let me know whom
Ex 33:12 Yet thou **h.** said, I know thee by
Ex 33:12 and thou **h.** also found grace in my
Ex 33:17 this thing also that thou **h.** spoken:
Ex 33:17 for thou **h.** found grace in my sight,
Nu 5:19 and if thou **h.** not gone aside to
Nu 5:20 but if thou **h.** gone aside to another
Nu 11:11 Wherefore **h.** thou afflicted thy
Nu 11:21 and thou **h.** said, I will give them
Nu 14:17 be great, according as thou **h.** spoken,
Nu 14:19 and as thou **h.** forgiven this people,
Nu 16:13 a small thing that thou **h.** brought us
Nu 16:14 Moreover thou **h.** not brought us into
Nu 22:28 that thou **h.** smitten me these three
Nu 22:29 Because thou **h.** mocked me: I would
Nu 22:30 thine ass, upon which thou **h.** ridden
Nu 22:32 Wherefore **h.** thou smitten thine ass
Nu 23:11 What **h.** thou done unto me? I took
Nu 23:11 and, behold, thou **h.** blessed them
Nu 24:10 thou **h.** altogether blessed them these
Nu 27:13 And when thou **h.** seen it, thou also
De 1:14 The thing...thou **h.** spoken is good
De 1:31 where thou **h.** seen how that the Lord
De 2:7 with thee; thou **h.** lacked nothing.
De 3:24 O Lord God, thou **h.** begun to shew thy
De 4:33 the midst of the fire, as thou **h.** heard,
De 8:10 When thou **h.** eaten and art full
De 8:12 Lest when thou **h.** eaten and art full,
De 8:12 and **h.** build goodly houses, and dwelt
De 8:13 and all that thou **h.** is multiplied;
De 9:2 thou **h.** heard say, Who can stand
De 9:12 for thy people which thou **h.** brought
De 9:26 inheritance, which thou **h.** redeemed:
De 9:26 which thou **h.** brought forth out of
De 12:26 Only thy holy things which thou **h.**, 1961
De 13:2 which thou **h.** not known, and let us
De 13:6 which thou **h.** not known, thou, nor
De 16:13 after that thou **h.** gathered in thy corn
De 17:4 and thou **h.** heard of it, and enquired
De 21:8 people Israel, whom thou **h.** redeemed,
De 21:10 and thou **h.** taken them captive,
De 21:11 a beautiful woman, and **h.** a desire
De 21:14 of her, because thou **h.** humbled her.
De 22:3 which he hath lost, and thou **h.** found,
De 22:9 fruit of thy seed which thou **h.** sown,
De 23:23 according as thou **h.** vowed unto the
De 23:23 which thou **h.** promised with thy
De 24:19 harvest in thy field, and **h.** forgot a
De 26:10 land, which thou, O Lord, **h.** given me.
De 26:12 When thou **h.** made an end of tithing
De 26:12 and **h.** given it unto the Levite, the
De 26:13 which thou **h.** commanded me:
De 26:14 to all that thou **h.** commanded me.
De 26:15 the land which thou **h.** given us, as
De 26:17 Thou **h.** avouched the Lord this day
De 28:20 doings, whereby thou **h.** forsaken me:
De 32:18 art unmindful, and **h.** forgotten God
Jos 2:17 this thine oath...**h.** made us swear.
Jos 2:20 of thine oath...**h.** made us to swear.
Jos 7:7 wherefore **h.** thou at all brought
Jos 7:19 and tell me now what thou **h.** done;
Jos 7:25 And Joshua said, Why **h.** thou troubled
Jos 14:9 because thou **h.** wholly followed the
Jos 15:19 for thou **h.** given me a south land;
Jos 17:14 Why **h.** thou given me but one lot and
Jos 17:17 Thou art a great people, and **h.** great
Jg 1:15 Give me a blessing: for thou **h.** given
Jg 5:21 O my soul, thou **h.** trodden down
Jg 6:36 Israel by mine hand, as thou **h.** said,
Jg 6:37 Israel by mine hand, as thou **h.** said.
Jg 8:1 said unto him, Why **h.** thou served us
Jg 8:22 for thou **h.** delivered us from the hand
Jg 9:38 the people that thou **h.** despised?
Jg 11:12 saying, What **h.** thou to do with me,
Jg 11:35 Alas, my daughter! thou **h.** brought
Jg 11:36 My father, if thou **h.** opened thy mouth
Jg 14:16 thou **h.** put forth a riddle unto the
Jg 14:16 children of my people, and **h.** not told
Jg 15:11 what is this that thou **h.** done unto
Jg 15:18 Thou **h.** given this great deliverance
Jg 16:10 Behold, thou **h.** mocked me, and told
Jg 16:13 Hitherto thou **h.** mocked me, and
Jg 16:15 thou **h.** mocked me these three times,
Jg 16:15 and **h.** not told me wherein thy great
Jg 18:3 in this place? and what **h.** thou here?
Ru 2:11 thou **h.** done unto thy mother in
Ru 2:11 and how thou **h.** left thy father and
Ru 2:13 for that thou **h.** comforted me, and
Ru 2:13 and for that thou **h.** spoken friendly
Ru 2:19 Where **h.** thou gleaned to-day?
Ru 3:10 for thou **h.** shewed more kindness
Ru 3:15 Bring the vail that thou **h.** upon thee,
1Sa 1:17 thy petition that thou **h.** asked him.
1Sa 4:20 fear not; for thou **h.** born a son.
1Sa 12:4 And they said, Thou **h.** not defrauded
1Sa 12:4 neither **h.** thou taken ought of any
1Sa 13:11 And Samuel said, What **h.** thou done?
1Sa 13:13 said to Saul, Thou **h.** done foolishly:
1Sa 13:13 thou **h.** not kept the commandment
1Sa 13:14 because thou **h.** not kept that...the Lord
1Sa 14:43 Tell me what thou **h.** done. And
1Sa 15:23 Because thou **h.** rejected the word of
1Sa 15:26 for thou **h.** rejected the word of the
1Sa 17:28 and with whom **h.** thou left those few
1Sa 17:45 armies of Israel, whom thou **h.** defied.
1Sa 19:17 Why **h.** thou deceived me so, and sent
1Sa 20:8 for thou **h.** brought thy servant into a
1Sa 20:19 And when thou **h.** stayed three days,
1Sa 20:30 do not I know that thou **h.** chosen the
1Sa 22:13 in that thou **h.** given him bread, and a
1Sa 22:13 and a sword, and **h.** enquired of God
1Sa 24:17 for thou **h.** rewarded me good,
1Sa 24:18 And thou **h.** shewed this day how
1Sa 24:18 how that thou **h.** dealt well with me:
1Sa 24:19 good for that thou **h.** done unto me
1Sa 25:6 and peace be upon all that thou **h.**
1Sa 25:7 I have heard that thou **h.** shearers:
1Sa 25:31 either that thou **h.** shed blood
1Sa 25:33 be thou which **h.** kept me this day
1Sa 26:15 wherefore then **h.** thou not kept thy
1Sa 26:16 thing is not good that thou **h.** done
1Sa 28:12 Why **h.** thou deceived me? for thou
1Sa 28:15 Why **h.** thou disquieted me, to bring
1Sa 29:4 place which thou **h.** appointed him,

1Sa 29:6 as the Lord liveth, thou **h.** been
1Sa 29:8 and what **h.** thou found in thy servant
2Sa 1:26 very pleasant **h.** thou been unto me:
2Sa 3:7 Wherefore **h.** thou gone in unto my
2Sa 3:24 the king, and said, What **h.** thou done?
2Sa 3:24 why is it that thou **h.** sent him away,
2Sa 6:22 maidservants which thou **h.** spoken of,
2Sa 7:18 my house, that thou **h.** brought me
2Sa 7:19 but thou **h.** spoken also of thy
2Sa 7:21 to thine own heart, **h.** thou done all
2Sa 7:24 For thou **h.** confirmed to thyself thy
2Sa 7:25 the word that thou **h.** spoken
2Sa 7:25 it forever, and do as thou **h.** said
2Sa 7:27 God of Israel, **h.** revealed to thy
2Sa 7:28 and thou **h.** promised this goodness
2Sa 7:29 for thou, O Lord God, **h.** spoken it:
2Sa 11:19 When thou **h.** made an end of telling
2Sa 12:9 Wherefore **h.** thou despised the
2Sa 12:9 thou **h.** killed Uriah the Hittite with
2Sa 12:9 and **h.** taken his wife to be thy wife,
2Sa 12:9 and **h.** slain him with the sword of
2Sa 12:10 because thou **h.** despised me,
2Sa 12:10 and **h.** slain with the sword of the
2Sa 12:14 by this deed thou **h.** given great
2Sa 12:21 What thing is this that thou **h.** done?
2Sa 14:13 Wherefore then **h.** thou thought such
2Sa 15:35 And **h.** thou not there with thee Zadok
2Sa 16:8 Saul, in whose stead thou **h.** reigned:
2Sa 16:10 say, Wherefore **h.** thou done so?
2Sa 18:21 Go tell the king what thou **h.** seen
2Sa 18:22 son, seeing that thou **h.** no tidings
2Sa 19:5 Thou **h.** shamed this day the faces of
2Sa 19:6 For thou **h.** declared this day, that
2Sa 22:36 Thou **h.** also given me the shield of
2Sa 22:37 Thou **h.** enlarged my steps under me;
2Sa 22:40 for thou **h.** girded me with strength to
2Sa 22:40 rose up against me **h.** thou subdued
2Sa 22:41 Thou **h.** also given me the necks of
2Sa 22:44 Thou also **h.** delivered me from the
2Sa 22:44 thou **h.** kept me to be the head of the
2Sa 22:49 thou also **h.** lifted me up on high
2Sa 22:49 thou **h.** delivered me from the violent
1Ki 1:6 Why **h.** thou done so? and he also was
1Ki 1:11 **H.** thou not heard that Adonijah the
1Ki 1:24 my Lord, O king, **h.** thou said,
1Ki 1:27 and thou **h.** not shewed it unto thy
1Ki 2:8 And behold, thou **h.** with thee
1Ki 2:26 and because thou **h.** been afflicted in
1Ki 2:43 Why then **h.** thou not kept the oath of
1Ki 3:6 Thou **h.** shewed unto thy servant
1Ki 3:6 and thou **h.** kept for him this great
1Ki 3:6 that thou **h.** given him a son to sit on
1Ki 3:7 O Lord my God, thou **h.** made thy
1Ki 3:8 thy people which thou **h.** chosen,
1Ki 3:11 Because thou **h.** asked this thing, and
1Ki 3:11 and **h.** not asked for thyself long life;
1Ki 3:11 neither **h.** asked riches for thyself,
1Ki 3:11 nor **h.** asked the life of thine enemies;
1Ki 3:11 but **h.** asked for thyself understanding
1Ki 3:13 which thou **h.** not asked, both riches,
1Ki 8:24 Who **h.** kept with thy servant David
1Ki 8:24 and **h.** fulfilled it with thine hand,
1Ki 8:25 walk before me as thou **h.** walked
1Ki 8:29 the place of which thou **h.** said, My
1Ki 8:36 which thou **h.** given to thy people for
1Ki 8:44 toward the city which thou **h.** chosen,
1Ki 8:48 the city which thou **h.** chosen, and the
1Ki 9:3 thy supplication, that thou **h.** made
1Ki 9:3 this house, which thou **h.** built, to put
1Ki 9:13 cities are these which thou **h.** given
1Ki 11:11 and thou **h.** not kept my covenant and
1Ki 11:22 But what **h.** thou lacked with me,
1Ki 13:21 forasmuch as thou **h.** disobeyed the
1Ki 13:21 and **h.** not kept the commandment
1Ki 13:22 But camest back, and **h.** eaten bread
1Ki 14:8 and yet thou **h.** not been as my
1Ki 14:9 But **h.** done evil above all that were
1Ki 14:9 for thou **h.** gone and made thee other
1Ki 14:9 to provoke me to anger, and **h.** cast
1Ki 16:2 and thou **h.** walked in the way of
1Ki 16:2 and **h.** made my people Israel to sin,
1Ki 17:13 Fear not; go and do as thou **h.** said:
1Ki 17:20 **h.** thou also brought evil upon the
1Ki 18:18 of the Lord and thou **h.** followed
1Ki 18:37 and that thou **h.** turned their heart
1Ki 20:13 **H.** thou seen all this great multitude?
1Ki 20:25 like the army that thou **h.** lost, horse
1Ki 20:36 Because thou **h.** not obeyed the voice
1Ki 20:40 judgment be; thyself **h.** decided it
1Ki 20:42 Because thou **h.** let go out of thy hand
1Ki 21:19 **H.** thou killed, and also taken
1Ki 21:20 said to Elijah, **H.** thou found me, O
1Ki 21:20 because thou **h.** sold thyself to work
1Ki 21:22 wherewith thou **h.** provoked me to
2Ki 1:16 Forasmuch as thou **h.** sent messengers
2Ki 2:10 Thou **h.** asked a hard thing:
2Ki 4:2 tell me, what **h.** thou in the house? 3426
2Ki 4:13 thou **h.** been careful for us with all
2Ki 5:8 Wherefore **h.** thou rent thy clothes?
2Ki 6:22 smite those whom thou **h.** taken
2Ki 9:18 said, What **h.** thou to do with peace?
2Ki 9:19 answered, What **h.** thou to do with
2Ki 10:30 Because thou **h.** done well in
2Ki 10:30 and **h.** done unto the house of Ahab
2Ki 14:10 Thou **h.** indeed smitten Edom, and
2Ki 17:26 The nations which thou **h.** removed,
2Ki 19:6 of the words which thou **h.** heard,
2Ki 19:11 Behold, thou **h.** heard what the kings
2Ki 19:15 thou **h.** made heaven and earth
2Ki 19:20 That which thou **h.** prayed to me
2Ki 19:22 Whom **h.** thou reproached and
2Ki 19:22 and against whom **h.** thou exalted thy
2Ki 19:23 By the messengers thou **h.** reproached
2Ki 19:23 and **h.** said, With the multitude of my
2Ki 19:25 **H.** thou not heard long ago how I
2Ki 20:19 word of the Lord which thou **h.**
2Ki 22:18 the words which thou **h.** heard;
2Ki 22:19 and thou **h.** humbled thyself
2Ki 22:19 and **h.** rent thy clothes, and wept
2Ki 23:17 that thou **h.** done against the altar of
1Ch 17:8 thee whithersoever thou **h.** walked,
1Ch 17:16 that thou h. brought me hitherto?
1Ch 17:17 for thou **h.** also spoken of thy servant's
1Ch 17:17 and **h.** regarded me according to the
1Ch 17:19 to thine own heart, **h.** thou done all
1Ch 17:21 thy people, whom thou **h.** redeemed
1Ch 17:23 let the thing that thou **h.** spoken
1Ch 17:23 forever, and do as thou **h.** said
1Ch 17:25 For thou, O my God, **h.** told thy
1Ch 17:26 Lord, thou art God, and **h.** promised
1Ch 22:8 saying, Thou **h.** shed blood
1Ch 22:8 and **h.** made great wars: thou shalt
1Ch 22:8 because thou **h.** shed much blood
1Ch 28:3 because thou **h.** been a man of war,
1Ch 28:3 a man of war, and **h.** shed blood
1Ch 28:20 until thou **h.** finished all the work
1Ch 29:17 triest the heart, and **h.** pleasure in
2Ch 1:8 Thou **h.** shewed great mercy unto
2Ch 1:8 and **h.** made me to reign in his stead
2Ch 1:9 for thou **h.** made me king over a
2Ch 1:11 and thou **h.** not asked riches, wealth,
2Ch 1:11 neither yet **h.** asked long life;
2Ch 1:11 but **h.** asked wisdom and knowledge
2Ch 6:15 Thou which **h.** kept with thy servant
2Ch 6:15 that which thou **h.** promised him;
2Ch 6:15 and **h.** fulfilled it with thine hand
2Ch 6:16 that which thou **h.** promised him
2Ch 6:16 walk in my law, as thou **h.** walked
2Ch 6:17 which thou **h.** spoken unto thy
2Ch 6:20 the place whereof thou **h.** said that
2Ch 6:27 when thou **h.** taught them the good
2Ch 6:27 which thou **h.** given unto thy people
2Ch 6:34 this city which thou **h.** chosen, and
2Ch 6:38 the city which thou **h.** chosen, and
2Ch 16:7 Because thou **h.** relied on the king of
2Ch 16:9 Herein thou **h.** done foolishly:
2Ch 19:3 in that thou **h.** taken away the groves
2Ch 19:3 and **h.** prepared thine heart to seek
2Ch 20:11 which thou **h.** given us to inherit
2Ch 20:37 Because thou **h.** joined thyself with
2Ch 21:12 Because thou **h.** not walked in the
2Ch 21:13 But **h.** walked in the way of the kings
2Ch 21:13 and **h.** made Judah...to go a whoring,
2Ch 21:13 and also **h.** slain thy brethren of thy
2Ch 24:6 Why **h.** thou not required of the
2Ch 25:15 Why **h.** thou sought after the gods of
2Ch 25:16 destroy thee, because thou **h.** done
2Ch 25:16 and **h.** not hearkened unto my counsel
2Ch 25:19 Thou savest, Lo, thou **h.** smitten the
2Ch 26:18 sanctuary; for thou **h.** trespassed;
2Ch 34:26 the words which thou **h.** heard;
Ezr 9:11 Which thou **h.** commanded by thy
Ezr 9:13 that thou our God **h.** punished us
Ezr 9:13 and **h.** given us such deliverance as
Ezr 10:12 As thou **h.** said, so must we do
Ne 1:10 whom thou **h.** redeemed by thy great
Ne 6:7 And thou **h.** also appointed prophets
Ne 9:6 thou **h.** made heaven, the heaven of
Ne 9:8 to his seed, and **h.** performed thy
Ne 9:33 for thou **h.** done right, but we have
Ne 9:37 whom thou **h.** set over us because of
Es 6:10 and the horse, as thou **h.** said,
Es 6:10 nothing fail of all that thou **h.** spoken,
Es 6:13 before whom thou **h.** begun to fall,
Job 1:8 **H.** thou considered my servant Job,
Job 1:10 **H.** not thou made an hedge about
Job 1:10 thou **h.** blessed the work of his hands,
Job 2:3 **H.** thou considered my servant Job,
Job 4:3 Behold, thou **h.** instructed many, and
Job 4:3 and thou **h.** strengthened the weak
Job 4:4 and thou **h.** strengthened the feeble
Job 7:20 why **h.** thou set me as a mark against
Job 10:4 **H.** thou eyes of flesh? or seest thou as
Job 10:9 that thou **h.** made me as the clay;
Job 10:10 **H.** thou not poured me out as milk,
Job 10:11 Thou **h.** clothed me with skin and
Job 10:11 and **h.** fenced me with bones and
Job 10:12 Thou **h.** granted me life and favour,
Job 10:13 And these things **h.** thou hid in
Job 10:18 Wherefore then **h.** thou brought me
Job 11:4 For thou **h.** said, My doctrine is
Job 14:5 thou **h.** appointed his bounds that he
Job 15:8 **H.** thou heard the secret of God?
Job 16:7 thou **h.** made desolate all my
Job 16:8 And thou **h.** filled me with wrinkles,
Job 17:4 For thou **h.** hid their heart from
Job 22:6 For thou **h.** taken a pledge from thy
Job 22:7 Thou **h.** not given water to the weary
Job 22:7 and thou **h.** withholden bread from
Job 22:9 Thou **h.** sent widows away empty,
Job 22:15 **H.** thou marked the old way which
Job 26:2 How **h.** thou helped him that is
Job 26:3 How **h.** thou counselled him that hath
Job 26:3 and how **h.** thou plentifully declared
Job 26:4 To whom **h.** thou uttered words? and
Job 33:8 Surely thou **h.** spoken in mine hearing,
Job 33:32 If thou **h.** anything to say, answer 3426
Job 34:16 If now thou **h.** understanding, hear
Job 36:17 But thou **h.** fulfilled the judgment of
Job 36:21 for this **h.** thou chosen rather than
Job 36:23 can say, Thou **h.** wrought iniquity?
Job 37:18 **H.** thou with him spread out the sky,
Job 38:4 declare if thou **h.** understanding
Job 38:12 **H.** thou commanded the morning
Job 38:16 **H.** thou entered into the springs of
Job 38:16 or **h.** thou walked in the search of the
Job 38:17 **h.** thou seen the doors of the shadow
Job 38:18 **H.** thou perceived the breadth of the
Job 38:22 **H.** thou entered into the treasures of
Job 38:22 **h.** thou seen the treasures of the hail,
Job 39:19 **H.** thou given the horse strength?
Job 39:19 **h.** thou clothed his neck with
Job 40:9 **H.** thou an arm like God? or canst
Ps 3:7 for thou **h.** smitten all mine enemies
Ps 3:7 thou **h.** broken the teeth of the ungodly
Ps 4:1 thou **h.** enlarged me when I was in
Ps 4:7 Thou **h.** put gladness in my heart,
Ps 7:6 judgment that thou **h.** commanded
Ps 8:1 who **h.** set thy glory above the heavens
Ps 8:2 babes and sucklings **h.** thou ordained
Ps 8:3 the stars, which thou **h.** ordained;
Ps 8:5 For thou **h.** made him a little lower
Ps 8:5 and **h.** crowned him with glory and
Ps 8:6 thou **h.** put all things under his feet:
Ps 9:4 For thou **h.** maintained my right and
Ps 9:5 Thou **h.** rebuked the heathen,
Ps 9:5 thou **h.** destroyed the wicked,
Ps 9:5 thou **h.** put out their name for ever
Ps 9:6 end: and thou **h.** destroyed cities;
Ps 9:10 for thou, Lord, **h.** not forsaken them
Ps 10:14 Thou **h.** seen it; for thou beholdest
Ps 10:17 Lord, thou **h.** heard the desire of the
Ps 16:2 O my soul, thou **h.** said unto the Lord,
Ps 17:3 Thou **h.** proved mine heart; thou
Ps 17:3 mine heart; thou **h.** visited me in the
Ps 17:3 thou **h.** tried me, and shalt find
Ps 18:35 Thou **h.** also given me the shield of
Ps 18:36 Thou **h.** enlarged my steps under me,
Ps 18:39 For thou **h.** girded me with strength
Ps 18:39 thou **h.** subdued under me those that
Ps 18:40 Thou **h.** also given me the necks of

Ps	18:43	Thou **h.** delivered me from the
Ps	18:43	and thou **h.** made me the head of the
Ps	18:48	thou **h.** delivered me from the
Ps	21:2	Thou **h.** given him his heart's desire,
Ps	21:2	and **h.** not withholden the request of
Ps	21:5	honour and majesty **h.** thou laid upon
Ps	21:6	For thou **h.** made him most blessed
Ps	21:6	thou **h.** made him exceeding glad with
Ps	22:1	My God, my God, why **h.** thou forsaken
Ps	22:15	and thou **h.** brought me into the dust
Ps	22:21	for thou **h.** heard me from the horns
Ps	27:9	thou **h.** been my help; leave me
Ps	30:1	O Lord, for thou **h.** lifted me up,
Ps	30:1	and **h.** not made my foes to rejoice
Ps	30:2	I cried unto thee, and thou **h.** healed
Ps	30:3	thou **h.** brought up my soul from the
Ps	30:3	thou **h.** kept me alive, that I should not
Ps	30:7	thou **h.** made my mountain to stand
Ps	30:11	Thou **h.** turned for me my mourning
Ps	30:11	thou **h.** put off my sackcloth, and
Ps	31:5	thou **h.** redeemed me, O Lord God of
Ps	31:7	in thy mercy: for thou **h.** considered
Ps	31:7	thou **h.** known my soul in adversities;
Ps	31:8	And **h.** not shut me up into the hands
Ps	31:8	thou **h.** set my feet in a large room
Ps	31:19	which thou **h.** laid up for them that
Ps	31:19	which thou **h.** wrought for them that
Ps	35:22	This thou **h.** seen, O Lord: keep not
Ps	39:5	Behold, thou **h.** made my days as an
Ps	40:5	wonderful works which thou **h.** done,
Ps	40:6	desire; mine ears **h.** thou opened:
Ps	40:6	and sin-offering **h.** thou not required
Ps	42:9	Why **h.** thou forgotten me? why go I
Ps	44:7	But thou **h.** saved us from our enemies,
Ps	44:7	and **h.** put them to shame that hated
Ps	44:9	But thou **h.** cast off, and put us to
Ps	44:11	Thou **h.** given us like sheep appointed
Ps	44:11	and **h.** scattered us among the
Ps	44:19	Though thou **h.** sore broken us in the
Ps	50:16	What **h.** thou to do to declare my
Ps	50:18	and **h.** been partaker with adulterers
Ps	50:21	These things **h.** thou done and I kept
Ps	51:8	that the bones which thou **h.** broken
Ps	52:9	because thou **h.** done it: and I will
Ps	53:5	thou **h.** put them to shame, because
Ps	56:13	For thou **h.** delivered my soul from
Ps	59:16	for thou **h.** been my defence and
Ps	60:1	O God, thou **h.** cast us off, thou
Ps	60:1	cast us off, thou **h.** scattered us, thou
Ps	60:1	thou **h.** been displeased; O turn
Ps	60:2	Thou **h.** made the earth to tremble;
Ps	60:2	thou **h.** broken it: heal the breaches
Ps	60:3	Thou **h.** shewed thy people hard
Ps	60:3	thou **h.** made us to drink the wine of
Ps	60:4	Thou **h.** given a banner to them that
Ps	61:3	For thou **h.** been a shelter for me,
Ps	61:5	For thou, O God, **h.** heard my vows:
Ps	61:5	thou **h.** given me the heritage of those
Ps	63:7	Because thou **h.** been my help,
Ps	65:9	them corn, when thou **h.** so provided
Ps	66:10	For thou, O God, **h.** proved us: thou
Ps	66:10	thou **h.** tried us as silver is tried
Ps	66:12	Thou **h.** caused men to ride over our
Ps	68:10	thou, O God, **h.** prepared of thy
Ps	68:18	Thou **h.** ascended on high, thou
Ps	68:18	on high, thou **h.** led captivity captive:
Ps	68:18	thou **h.** received gifts for men; yea,
Ps	68:28	that which thou **h.** wrought for us
Ps	69:19	Thou **h.** known my reproach, and my
Ps	69:26	persecute him whom thou **h.** smitten;
Ps	69:26	grief of those whom thou **h.** wounded
Ps	71:3	thou **h.** given commandment to save
Ps	71:17	O God, thou **h.** taught me from my
Ps	71:19	is very high, who **h.** done great things:
Ps	71:20	Thou, which **h.** shewed me great
Ps	71:23	and my soul, which thou **h.** redeemed
Ps	73:23	thou **h.** holden me by my right hand
Ps	73:27	thou **h.** destroyed all them that go a
Ps	74:1	O God, why **h.** thou cast us off for ever?
Ps	74:2	which thou **h.** purchased of old; the
Ps	74:2	inheritance, which thou **h.** redeemed;
Ps	74:2	mount Zion, wherein thou **h.** dwelt
Ps	74:16	thou **h.** prepared the light and the sun
Ps	74:17	Thou **h.** set all the borders of the
Ps	74:17	thou **h.** made summer and winter
Ps	77:14	thou **h.** declared thy strength among
Ps	77:15	Thou **h.** with thine arm redeemed thy
Ps	80:8	Thou **h.** brought a vine out of Egypt:
Ps	80:8	thou **h.** cast out the heathen and
Ps	80:12	Why **h.** thou then broken down her
Ps	85:1	Lord, thou **h.** been favourable unto thy
Ps	85:1	thou **h.** brought back the captivity of
Ps	85:2	Thou **h.** forgiven the iniquity of thy
Ps	85:2	people, thou **h.** covered all their sins
Ps	85:3	Thou **h.** taken away all thy wrath: thou
Ps	85:3	thou **h.** turned thyself from the
Ps	86:9	All nations whom thou **h.** made shall
Ps	86:13	and thou **h.** delivered my soul from
Ps	86:17	because thou, O Lord, **h.** holpen me,
Ps	88:6	Thou **h.** laid me in the lowest pit,
Ps	88:7	thou **h.** afflicted me with all thy waves
Ps	88:8	Thou **h.** put away mine acquaintance
Ps	88:8	thou **h.** made me an abomination
Ps	88:18	Lover and friend **h.** thou put far from
Ps	89:10	Thou **h.** broken Rahab in pieces, as
Ps	89:10	thou **h.** scattered thine enemies with
Ps	89:11	the fulness thereof, thou **h.** founded
Ps	89:12	north and the south thou **h.** created
Ps	89:13	Thou **h.** a mighty arm: strong is thy
Ps	89:38	But thou **h.** cast off and abhorred,
Ps	89:38	thou **h.** been wroth with thine
Ps	89:39	Thou **h.** made void the covenant of thy
Ps	89:39	thou **h.** profaned his crown by casting
Ps	89:40	Thou **h.** broken down all his hedges;
Ps	89:40	thou **h.** brought his strong holds to
Ps	89:42	Thou **h.** set up the right hand of his
Ps	89:42	thou **h.** made all his enemies to rejoice
Ps	89:43	Thou **h.** also turned the edge of his
Ps	89:43	and **h.** not made him to stand in the
Ps	89:44	Thou **h.** made his glory to cease, and
Ps	89:45	days of his youth **h.** thou shortened:
Ps	89:45	thou **h.** covered him with shame
Ps	89:47	wherefore **h.** thou made...men in vain?
Ps	90:1	thou **h.** been our dwelling place
Ps	90:8	Thou **h.** set our iniquities before thee,
Ps	90:15	wherein thou **h.** afflicted us, and the
Ps	91:9	Because thou **h.** made the Lord, which
Ps	92:4	For thou, Lord, **h.** made me glad
Ps	102:10	for thou **h.** lifted me up, and cast me
Ps	102:25	Of old **h.** thou laid the foundation of
Ps	104:8	the place which thou **h.** founded for
Ps	104:9	Thou **h.** set a bound that they may not
Ps	104:24	in wisdom **h.** thou made them all:
Ps	104:26	whom thou **h.** made to play therein
Ps	108:11	Wilt not thou, O God, who **h.** cast us
Ps	109:27	thy hand; that thou, Lord, **h.** done it
Ps	110:3	morning: thou **h.** the dew of thy youth
Ps	116:8	For thou **h.** delivered my soul from
Ps	116:16	handmaid: thou **h.** loosed my bonds,
Ps	118:13	Thou **h.** thrust sore at me that I might
Ps	118:21	for thou **h.** heard me, and art become
Ps	119:4	Thou **h.** commanded us to keep thy
Ps	119:21	Thou **h.** rebuked the proud that are
Ps	119:49	upon which thou **h.** caused me to hope
Ps	119:65	Thou **h.** dealt well with thy servant
Ps	119:75	thou in faithfulness **h.** afflicted me,
Ps	119:90	thou **h.** established the earth, and it
Ps	119:93	for with them thou **h.** quickened me
Ps	119:98	commandments **h.** made me wiser
Ps	119:102	judgments: for thou **h.** taught me
Ps	119:118	Thou **h.** trodden down all them that
Ps	119:138	testimonies that thou **h.** commanded
Ps	119:152	that thou **h.** founded them for ever
Ps	119:171	when thou **h.** taught me thy statutes
Ps	137:8	rewardeth thee as thou **h.** served us
Ps	138:2	for thou **h.** magnified thy word above
Ps	139:1	O Lord, thou **h.** searched me, and
Ps	139:5	Thou **h.** beset me behind and before,
Ps	139:13	For thou **h.** possessed my reins: thou
Ps	139:13	thou **h.** covered me in my mother's
Ps	140:7	thou **h.** covered my head in the day of
Pr	3:28	will give; when thou **h.** it by thee 3426
Pr	6:1	if thou **h.** stricken thy hand with a
Pr	22:27	If thou **h.** nothing to pay, why should
Pr	23:8	The morsel which thou **h.** eaten shalt
Pr	24:14	when thou **h.** found it, then there shall
Pr	25:16	**H.** thou found honey? eat so much as
Pr	30:32	If thou **h.** done foolishly in lifting up
Pr	30:32	or if thou **h.** thought evil, lay thine
Ec	5:4	pay that which thou **h.** vowed
Ec	7:22	that thou thyself likewise **h.** cursed
Ca	1:15	thou art fair; thou **h.** doves' eyes
Ca	4:1	thou **h.** doves' eyes within thy locks:
Ca	4:9	Thou **h.** ravished my heart, my sister,
Ca	4:9	thou **h.** ravished my heart with one of
Isa	2:6	Therefore thou **h.** forsaken thy people
Isa	3:6	Thou **h.** clothing, be thou our ruler,
Isa	9:3	Thou **h.** multiplied the nation, and
Isa	9:4	For thou **h.** broken the yoke of his
Isa	14:13	For thou **h.** said in thine heart, I will
Isa	14:20	because thou **h.** destroyed thy land,
Isa	17:10	Because thou **h.** forgotten the God of
Isa	17:10	and **h.** not been mindful of the rock
Isa	22:16	What **h.** thou here? and whom
Isa	22:16	here? and whom **h.** thou here, that
Isa	22:16	that thou **h.** hewed thee out a
Isa	23:16	thou harlot that **h.** been forgotten;
Isa	25:1	for thou **h.** done wonderful things; thy
Isa	25:2	For thou **h.** made of a city an heap; of
Isa	25:4	For thou **h.** been a strength to the
Isa	26:12	for thou also **h.** wrought all our works
Isa	26:14	therefore **h.** thou visited and destroyed
Isa	26:15	Thou **h.** increased the nation, O Lord,
Isa	26:15	O Lord, thou **h.** increased the nation:
Isa	37:6	words that thou **h.** heard, wherewith
Isa	37:11	Behold, thou **h.** heard what the kings
Isa	37:16	thou **h.** made heaven and earth
Isa	37:21	Israel, Whereas thou **h.** prayed to me
Isa	37:23	Whom **h.** thou reproached and
Isa	37:23	and against whom **h.** thou exalted thy
Isa	37:24	By thy servants **h.** thou reproached
Isa	37:24	and **h.** said, By the multitude of my
Isa	37:26	**H.** thou not heard long ago, how I
Isa	38:17	but thou **h.** in love to my soul
Isa	38:17	for thou **h.** cast all my sins behind
Isa	39:8	of the Lord which thou **h.** spoken
Isa	40:28	**H.** thou not known? **h.** thou not heard,
Isa	43:4	thou **h.** been honourable, and I have
Isa	43:22	But thou **h.** not called upon me, O
Isa	43:22	but thou **h.** been weary of me, O Israel
Isa	43:23	Thou **h.** not brought me the small
Isa	43:23	neither **h.** thou honoured me with thy
Isa	43:24	Thou **h.** bought me no sweet cane with
Isa	43:24	neither **h.** thou filled me with the fat
Isa	43:24	but thou **h.** made me to serve with
Isa	43:24	thou **h.** wearied me with thine
Isa	45:4	thee, though thou **h.** not known me
Isa	45:5	thee, though thou **h.** not known me:
Isa	45:10	woman, What **h.** thou brought forth?
Isa	47:6	upon the ancient **h.** thou very heavily
Isa	47:10	For thou **h.** trusted in thy wickedness:
Isa	47:10	thou **h.** said, None seeth me. Thy
Isa	47:10	and thou **h.** said in thine heart, I am,
Isa	47:12	wherein thou **h.** laboured from thy
Isa	47:15	with whom thou **h.** laboured, even thy
Isa	48:6	Thou **h.** heard, see all this; and will
Isa	49:20	after thou **h.** lost the other, shall say
Isa	51:13	and **h.** feared continually every day
Isa	51:17	which **h.** drunk at the hand of the Lord
Isa	51:17	thou **h.** drunken the dregs of the cup
Isa	51:23	and thou **h.** laid thy body as the
Isa	57:6	even to them **h.** thou poured a drink
Isa	57:6	offering, thou **h.** offered a meat offering
Isa	57:7	and high mountain **h.** thou set thy bed:
Isa	57:8	**h.** thou set up thy remembrance:
Isa	57:8	for thou **h.** discovered thyself to
Isa	57:8	thou **h.** enlarged thy bed, and made
Isa	57:10	thou **h.** found the life of thine hand;
Isa	57:11	and of whom **h.** thou been afraid or
Isa	57:11	afraid or feared, that thou **h.** lied,
Isa	57:11	and **h.** not remembered me, nor laid
Isa	60:15	Whereas thou **h.** been forsaken
Isa	62:8	for the which thou **h.** laboured:
Isa	63:17	O Lord, why **h.** thou made us to err
Isa	64:7	for thou **h.** hid thy face from us,
Isa	64:7	and **h.** consumed us, because of our
Jer	1:12	Thou **h.** well seen: for I will hasten
Jer	2:17	**H.** thou not procured this unto thyself
Jer	2:17	in that thou **h.** forsaken the Lord thy
Jer	2:18	**h.** thou to do in the way of Egypt,
Jer	2:18	**h.** thou to do in the way of Assyria,
Jer	2:19	that thou **h.** forsaken the Lord thy God,
Jer	2:23	know what thou **h.** done; thou art a
Jer	2:27	Thou **h.** brought me forth: for they
Jer	2:28	are thy gods that thou **h.** made thee?
Jer	2:33	therefore **h.** thou also taught the
Jer	3:1	but thou **h.** played the harlot with
Jer	3:2	and see where thou **h.** not been lien

Jer 3:2 In the ways **h.** thou sat for them,
Jer 3:2 and thou **h.** polluted the land with
Jer 3:5 Behold, thou **h.** spoken and done evil
Jer 3:6 **H.** thou seen that which backsliding
Jer 3:13 that thou **h.** transgressed against the
Jer 3:13 and **h.** scattered thy ways to the
Jer 4:10 surely thou **h.** greatly deceived this
Jer 4:19 because thou **h.** heard, O my soul, the
Jer 5:3 thou **h.** stricken them, but they have
Jer 5:3 thou **h.** consumed them, but they have
Jer 12:2 Thou **h.** planted them, yea, they have
Jer 12:3 thou **h.** seen me, and tried mine heart
Jer 12:5 If thou **h.** run with the footmen,
Jer 13:4 Take the girdle that thou **h.** got,
Jer 13:21 thou **h.** taught them to be captains,
Jer 13:25 because thou **h.** forgotten me, and
Jer 14:19 **H.** thou utterly rejected Judah? hath
Jer 14:19 why **h.** thou smitten us, and there is
Jer 14:22 for thou **h.** made all these things.
Jer 15:6 Thou **h.** forsaken me, saith the Lord,
Jer 15:10 thou **h.** borne me a man of strife
Jer 15:17 for thou **h.** filled me with indignation.
Jer 20:6 friends, to whom thou **h.** prophesied
Jer 20:7 O Lord, thou **h.** deceived me, and I
Jer 20:7 art stronger than I, and **h.** prevailed:
Jer 26:9 Why **h.** thou prophesied in the name
Jer 28:6 thy words which thou **h.** prophesied,
Jer 28:13 Thou **h.** broken the yokes of wood; but
Jer 28:16 because thou **h.** taught rebellion
Jer 29:25 Because thou **h.** sent letters in thy
Jer 29:27 therefore why **h.** thou not reproved
Jer 30:13 thou **h.** no healing medicines.
Jer 31:18 Thou **h.** chastised me, and I was
Jer 32:17 thou **h.** made the heaven and the earth
Jer 32:20 Which **h.** set signs and wonders in
Jer 32:20 and **h.** made thee a name, as at this
Jer 32:21 And **h.** brought forth thy people Israel
Jer 32:22 And **h.** given them this land, which
Jer 32:23 therefore thou **h.** caused all this evil
Jer 32:24 and what thou **h.** spoken is come to
Jer 32:25 And thou **h.** said unto me, O Lord
Jer 36:6 which thou **h.** written from my mouth,
Jer 36:14 wherein thou **h.** read in the ears of
Jer 36:29 Thus saith the Lord; Thou **h.** burned
Jer 36:29 Why **h.** thou written therein, saying,
Jer 38:25 now what thou **h.** said unto the king,
Jer 39:18 because thou **h.** put thy trust in me,
Jer 44:16 As for the word that thou **h.** spoken
Jer 48:7 For because thou **h.** trusted in thy
Jer 50:24 caught, because thou **h.** striven
Jer 51:62 O Lord, thou **h.** spoken against this
Jer 51:63 when thou **h.** made an end of reading
La 1:21 they are glad that thou **h.** done it:
La 1:21 the day that thou **h.** called, and
La 1:22 unto them, as thou **h.** done unto me
La 2:20 and consider to whom thou **h.** done
La 2:21 thou **h.** slain them in the day of thine
La 2:21 thine anger; thou **h.** killed, and not
La 2:22 Thou **h.** called as in the solemn day
La 3:17 And thou **h.** removed my soul far off
La 3:42 have rebelled: thou **h.** not pardoned.
La 3:43 Thou **h.** covered with anger, and
La 3:43 Thou **h.** slain, thou **h.** not pitied.
La 3:44 Thou **h.** covered thyself with a cloud,
La 3:45 Thou **h.** made us as the offscouring
La 3:56 Thou **h.** heard my voice: hide not
La 3:58 O Lord, thou **h.** pleaded the causes of
La 3:58 of my soul; thou **h.** redeemed my life
La 3:59 O Lord, thou **h.** seen my wrong:
La 3:60 Thou **h.** seen all their vengeance and
La 3:61 Thou **h.** heard their reproach, O Lord,
La 5:22 But thou **h.** utterly rejected us; thou
Eze 3:19 but thou **h.** delivered thy soul.
Eze 3:20 thou **h.** not given him warning,
Eze 3:21 also thou **h.** delivered thy soul.
Eze 4:6 And when thou **h.** accomplished them,
Eze 4:8 till thou **h.** ended the days of thy
Eze 5:11 because thou **h.** defiled my sanctuary
Eze 8:12 Son of man, **h.** thou seen what the
Eze 8:15, 17 **H.** thou seen this, O son of man?
Eze 9:11 I have done as thou **h.** commanded
Eze 16:7 and thou **h.** increased and waxen
Eze 16:17 Thou **h.** also taken thy fair jewels of
Eze 16:18 and thou **h.** set mine oil and mine
Eze 16:19 I fed thee, thou **h.** even set it before
Eze 16:20 Moreover thou **h.** taken thy sons and
Eze 16:20 whom thou **h.** borne unto me, and
Eze 16:20 and these **h.** thou sacrificed unto
Eze 16:21 That thou **h.** slain my children and
Eze 16:22 whoredoms thou **h.** not remembered
Eze 16:24 That thou **h.** also built unto thee an
Eze 16:24 and **h.** made thee a high place in every
Eze 16:25 Thou **h.** built thy high place at every
Eze 16:25 and **h.** made thy beauty to be
Eze 16:25 and **h.** opened thy feet to every one
Eze 16:26 Thou **h.** also committed fornication
Eze 16:26 and **h.** increased thy whoredoms, to
Eze 16:28 Thou **h.** played the whore also with
Eze 16:28 yea, thou **h.** played the harlot with
Eze 16:29 Thou **h.** moreover multiplied thy
Eze 16:31 and **h.** not been as an harlot, in
Eze 16:37 with whom thou **h.** taken pleasure,
Eze 16:37 and all them that thou **h.** loved, with
Eze 16:37 with all them that thou **h.** hated; I
Eze 16:43 Because thou **h.** not remembered the
Eze 16:43 but **h.** fretted me in all these things;
Eze 16:47 Yet **h.** thou not walked after their
Eze 16:48 as thou **h.** done, thou and thy
Eze 16:51 thou **h.** multiplied thine abominations
Eze 16:51 and **h.** justified thy sisters in all
Eze 16:51 abominations which thou **h.** done.
Eze 16:52 Thou also, which **h.** judged thy sisters,
Eze 16:52 that thou **h.** committed more
Eze 16:52 in that thou **h.** justified thy sisters.
Eze 16:54 all that thou **h.** done, in that thou art
Eze 16:58 Thou **h.** borne thy lewdness and
Eze 16:59 even deal with thee as thou **h.** done,
Eze 16:59 which **h.** despised the oath in
Eze 16:63 for all that thou **h.** done, saith the Lord
Eze 22:4 guilty in thy blood that thou **h.** shed;
Eze 22:4 and **h.** defiled thyself in thine idols
Eze 22:4 thine idols which thou **h.** made; and
Eze 22:4 and thou **h.** caused thy days to draw
Eze 22:8 Thou **h.** despised mine holy things,
Eze 22:8 and **h.** profaned my sabbaths.
Eze 22:12 to shed blood; thou **h.** taken usury
Eze 22:12 and thou **h.** greedily gained of thy
Eze 22:12 and **h.** forgotten me, saith the Lord
Eze 22:13 gain which thou **h.** made, and at thy
Eze 23:30 because thou **h.** gone a whoring after
Eze 23:31 Thou **h.** walked in the way of thy
Eze 23:35 Because thou **h.** forgotten me, and
Eze 23:41 whereupon thou **h.** set mine incense
Eze 25:6 Because thou **h.** clapped thine hands,
Eze 27:3 O Tyrus, thou **h.** said, I am of perfect
Eze 28:2 and thou **h.** said, I am a god, I sit in
Eze 28:4 understanding thou **h.** gotten thee
Eze 28:4 and **h.** gotten gold and silver into thy
Eze 28:5 and by the traffick **h.** thou increased
Eze 28:6 Because thou **h.** set thine heart as
Eze 28:13 Thou **h.** been in Eden the garden
Eze 28:14 thou **h.** walked up and down in the
Eze 28:16 and thou **h.** sinned: therefore I will
Eze 28:17 thou **h.** corrupted thy wisdom by
Eze 28:18 Thou **h.** defiled thy sanctuaries by the
Eze 31:10 Because thou **h.** lifted up thyself in
Eze 32:9 countries which thou **h.** not known.
Eze 33:9 but thou **h.** delivered thy soul.
Eze 35:5 Because thou **h.** had a perpetual
Eze 35:5 and **h.** shed the blood of the children
Eze 35:6 thou **h.** not hated blood, even blood
Eze 35:10 Because thou **h.** said, These two
Eze 35:11 which thou **h.** used out of thy hatred
Eze 35:12 which thou **h.** spoken against the
Eze 36:13 up men, and **h.** bereaved thy nations;
Eze 38:13 **h.** thou gathered thy company to take
Eze 43:23 When thou **h.** made an end of cleansing
Eze 47:6 Son of man, **h.** thou seen this? Then
Da 2:23 and **h.** made known unto me now
Da 2:23 for thou **h.** now made known unto
Da 2:23 my fathers, who **h.** given me wisdom
Da 3:10 Thou, O king, **h.** made a decree, that
Da 3:12 certain Jews whom thou **h.** set over
Da 3:12, 18 golden image which thou **h.** set up.
Da 5:22 **h.** not humbled thine heart, though
Da 5:23 But **h.** lifted up thyself against the
Da 5:23 and thou **h.** praised the gods of silver,
Da 5:23 are all thy ways, **h.** thou not glorified:
Da 6:12 **H.** thou not signed a decree, that
Da 6:13 the decree that thou **h.** signed, but
Da 9:7 whither thou **h.** driven them, because
Da 9:15 that **h.** brought thy people forth out
Da 9:15 and **h.** gotten thee renown, as at this
Da 10:19 speak; for thou **h.** strengthened me.
Ho 4:6 because thou **h.** rejected knowledge,
Ho 4:6 seeing thou **h.** forgotten the law of
Ho 9:1 for thou **h.** gone a whoring from thy
Ho 9:1 thou **h.** loved a reward upon every
Ho 10:9 O Israel, thou **h.** sinned from the
Ho 13:9 O Israel, thou **h.** destroyed thyself;
Ho 14:1 thy God; for thou **h.** fallen by thine
Ob 15 as thou **h.** done, it shall be done unto
Jon 1:10 Why **h.** thou done this? For the men
Jon 1:14 for thou, O Lord, **h.** done as it pleased
Jon 2:6 yet **h.** thou brought up my life from
Jon 4:10 Then said the Lord, Thou **h.** had pity
Jon 4:10 for the which thou **h.** not laboured,
Mic 7:20 which thou **h.** sworn unto our fathers
Na 3:16 Thou **h.** multiplied thy merchants
Hab 1:12 O Lord, thou **h.** ordained them for
Hab 1:12 thou **h.** established them for correction
Hab 2:8 Because thou **h.** spoiled many nations,
Hab 2:10 Thou **h.** consulted shame to thy house
Hab 2:10 people, and **h.** sinned against thy soul
Zep 3:11 thou **h.** transgressed against me: for
Zec 1:12 thou **h.** had indignation these
Mal 1:2 Wherein **h.** thou loved us? Was not
Mal 2:14 against whom thou **h.** dealt
Mt 5:26 thou **h.** paid the uttermost farthing.
Mt 6:6 when thou **h.** shut thy door, pray
Mt 8:13 as thou **h.** believed, so be it done
Mt 11:25 because thou **h.** hid these things
Mt 11:25 and **h.** revealed them unto babes,
Mt 17:27 and when thou **h.** opened his mouth
Mt 18:15 if he shall hear thee thou **h.** gained
Mt 19:21 go and sell that thou **h.**, and give.. *5224*
Mt 20:12 and thou **h.** made them equal unto us,
Mt 21:16 babes and sucklings thou **h.** perfected..
Mt 25:21, 23 thou **h.** been faithful over a few
Mt 25:24 reaping where thou **h.** not sown,
Mt 25:24 gathering where thou **h.** not strawed:
Mt 25:25 lo, there thou **h.** that is thine. *2192*
Mt 26:25 He said unto him, Thou **h.** said.
Mt 26:64 Jesus saith unto him, Thou **h.** said:
Mt 27:46 my God, why **h.** thou forsaken me?
Mk 10:21 sell whatsoever thou **h.**, and give... *2192*
Mk 12:32 Well, Master, thou **h.** said the truth:
Mk 15:34 my God, why **h.** thou forsaken me?
Lu 1:4 wherein thou **h.** been instructed.
Lu 1:30 Fear not, Mary: for thou **h.** found
Lu 2:31 Which thou **h.** prepared before the
Lu 2:48 Son, why **h.** thou thus dealt with us?
Lu 7:43 unto him, Thou **h.** rightly judged.
Lu 10:21 earth, that thou **h.** hid these things
Lu 10:21 and **h.** revealed them unto babes:
Lu 10:28 Thou **h.** answered right: this do,
Lu 11:27 and the paps which thou **h.** sucked.
Lu 12:19 Soul, thou **h.** much goods laid up.. *2192*
Lu 12:20 things be which thou **h.** provided?
Lu 12:59 thence, till thou **h.** paid the very
Lu 13:26 and thou **h.** taught in our streets.
Lu 14:22 it is done as thou **h.** commanded,
Lu 15:30 thou **h.** killed for him the fatted
Lu 18:22 sell all that thou **h.**, and distribute. *2192*
Lu 19:17 because thou **h.** been faithful in a
Lu 20:39 said, Master, thou **h.** well said.
Lu 24:18 and **h.** not known the things which
Joh 2:10 but thou **h.** kept the good wine until
Joh 4:11 Sir, thou **h.** nothing to draw with, *2192*
Joh 4:11 from whence then **h.** thou that *2192*
Joh 4:17 Thou **h.** well said, I have no
Joh 4:18 For thou **h.** had five husbands: *2192*
Joh 4:18 he whom thou now **h.** is not thy *2192*
Joh 6:68 thou **h.** the words of eternal life *2192*
Joh 7:20 Thou **h.** a devil: who goeth about *2192*
Joh 8:48 art a Samaritan, and **h.** a devil? *2192*
Joh 8:52 Now we know that thou **h.** a devil *2192*
Joh 8:57 years old, and **h.** thou seen Abraham?
Joh 9:37 Thou **h.** both seen him, and it is
Joh 11:41 I thank thee that thou **h.** heard
Joh 11:42 may believe that thou **h.** sent me.
Joh 13:8 If I wash thee not, thou **h.** no *2192*
Joh 13:38 crow, till thou **h.** denied me thrice.
Joh 14:9 and yet **h.** thou not known me,
Joh 17:2 As thou **h.** given him power over all
Joh 17:2 life to as many as thou **h.** given him.
Joh 17:3 and Jesus Christ, whom thou **h.** sent.
Joh 17:7 whatsoever thou **h.** given me are of
Joh 17:9 but for them which thou **h.** given me;
Joh 17:11 name those whom thou **h.** given me,

Joh 17:18 **As thou h. sent me into the world**......
Joh 17:21 **world may believe that thou h. sent**.....
Joh 17:23 **world may know that thou h. sent me**, .
Joh 17:23 **h. loved them, as thou h. loved me**......
Joh 17:24 **whom thou h. given me, be with me**....
Joh 17:24 **glory which thou h. given me: for**.......
Joh 17:25 **these have known that thou h. sent**.....
Joh 17:26 **thou h. loved me may be in them, and**..
Joh 18:35 thee unto me: what **h.** thou done?...........
Joh 20:15 tell me where thou **h.** laid him, and I........
Joh 20:29 **Thomas, because thou h. seen me**,.......
Joh 20:29 **thou h. believed: blessed are they that**..
Ac 1:24 whether of these two thou **h.** chosen,.......
Ac 2:28 Thou **h.** made known to me the ways.......
Ac 4:24 which **h.** made heaven, and earth,...........
Ac 4:25 by the mouth of David **h.** said, Why.........
Ac 4:27 child Jesus whom thou **h.** anointed,..........
Ac 5:4 why **h.** thou conceived this thing in...........
Ac 5:4 thou **h.** not lied unto men, but unto...........
Ac 8:20 because thou **h.** thought that the gift.........
Ac 8:21 Thou **h.** neither part nor lot in this..... *2076*
Ac 10:33 and thou **h.** well done that thou art..........
Ac 22:15 unto all men of what thou **h.** seen and.......
Ac 23:11 **for as thou h. testified of me in**..........
Ac 23:19 What is that thou **h.** to tell me?......... *2192*
Ac 23:22 thou **h.** shewed these things to me..........
Ac 24:10 I know that thou **h.** been of many...........
Ac 25:12 **H.** thou appealed unto Caesar? unto.........
Ac 26:16 **of these things which thou h. seen**,.....
Ro 2:20 which **h.** the form of knowledge......... *2192*
Ro 9:20 formed it, Why **h.** thou made me thus?.....
Ro 14:22 **H.** thou faith? have it to thyself......... *2192*
1Co 4:7 and what **h.** thou that thou didst.......... *2192*
1Co 7:28 and if thou marry, thou **h.** not sinned;.......
1Co 8:10 see thee which **h.** knowledge sit......... *2192*
Col 4:17 the ministry which thou **h.** received..........
1Ti 4:6 doctrine, whereunto thou **h.** attained..........
1Ti 6:12 and **h.** professed a good profession..........
2Ti 1:13 which thou **h.** heard of me, in faith and.....
2Ti 2:2 And the things that thou **h.** heard of..........
2Ti 3:10 But thou **h.** fully known my doctrine,........
2Ti 3:14 in the things which thou **h.** learned..........
2Ti 3:14 learned and **h.** been assured of,..............
2Ti 3:14 knowing of whom thou **h.** learned............
2Ti 3:15 And that from a child thou **h.** known.........
Phm 5 which thou **h.** toward the Lord.......... *2192*
Heb 1:9 Thou **h.** loved righteousness, and............
Heb 1:10 Thou, Lord, in the beginning **h.** laid..........
Heb 2:8 Thou **h.** put all things in subjection..........
Heb 10:5 not, but a body **h.** thou prepared me:.......
Heb 10:6 for sin thou **h.** had no pleasure...............
Jas 2:18 Thou **h.** faith, and I have works:......... *2192*
Re 1:19 **Write the things which thou h. seen**,...
Re 2:2 **thou h. tried them which say they are**.
Re 2:2 **and are not, and h. found them liars**:..
Re 2:3 **And h. borne, and...patience**..............
Re 2:3 **borne, and h. patience, and for**..... *2192*
Re 2:3 **and for my name's sake h**..................
Re 2:3 **laboured, and h. not fainted**...............
Re 2:4 **thee, because thou h. left thy first**......
Re 2:6 **But this thou h., that thou hatest**..*2192*
Re 2:13 **and h. not denied my faith, even in**.....
Re 2:14 **because thou h. there them that**.... *2192*
Re 2:15 **So h. thou also them that hold the**.*2192*
Re 3:1 **that thou h. a name that thou**...... *2192*
Re 3:3 **therefore how thou h. received**............
Re 3:4 **Thou h. a few names even in**........ *2192*
Re 3:8 **for thou h. a little strength**,.......... *2192*
Re 3:8 **strength, and h. kept my word**............
Re 3:8 **my word, and h. not denied my name**..
Re 3:10 **Because thou h. kept the word of my**..
Re 3:11 **hold that fast which thou h., that**..*2192*
Re 4:11 for thou **h.** created all things, and...........
Re 5:9 for thou wast slain, and **h.** redeemed........
Re 5:10 And **h.** made us unto our God kings.........
Re 11:17 because thou **h.** taken to thee thy...........
Re 11:17 thee thy great power, and **h.** reigned........
Re 16:5 shalt be, because thou **h.** judged thus........
Re 16:6 thou **h.** given them blood to drink;...........

HASTE See also HASTED; HASTETH; HASTING.

Ge 19:22 **H.** thee, escape thither: for I........... 4116
Ge 24:46 And she made **h.**, and let down her.... 4116
Ge 43:30 And Joseph made **h.**; for his.............. 4116
Ge 45:9 **H.** ye, and go up to my father,.......... 4116
Ge 45:13 and ye shall **h.** and bring down.......... 4116
Ex 10:16 called for Moses and Aaron in **h.**;....... 4116
Ex 12:11 ye shall eat it in **h.**: it is the............ 2649
Ex 12:33 send them out of the land in **h.**;......... 4416
Ex 34:8 And Moses made **h.**, and bowed........ 4416
De 16:3 out of the land of Egypt in **h.**:........... 2649
De 32:35 shall come upon them make **h.**......... 2363
Jg 9:48 make **h.**, and do as I have done......... 4116
Jg 13:10 And the woman made **h.**, and ran,...... 4116
1Sa 9:12 make **h.** now, for he came to day....... 4116
1Sa 20:38 Make speed, **h.**, stay not. And.......... 2363
1Sa 21:8 the king's business required **h.**......... 5169
1Sa 23:26 David made **h.** to get away for.......... 2648
1Sa 23:27 **H.** thee, and come; for the.............. 4116
1Sa 25:18 Then Abigail made **h.**, and took......... 4116
2Sa 4:4 as she made **h.** to flee, that he.......... 2648
2Ki 7:15 Syrians had cast away in their **h.**......... 2648
2Ch 35:21 God commanded me to make **h.**:......... 926
Ezr 4:23 they went up in **h.** to Jerusalem.......... 924
Es 5:5 Cause Haman to make **h.**, that.......... 4116
Es 6:10 Make **h.**, and take the apparel........... 4116
Job 20:2 answer, and for this I make **h.**.......... 2363
Ps 22:19 my strength, **h.** thee to help me........ 2363
Ps 31:22 For I said in my **h.**. I am cut........... 2648
Ps 38:22 Make **h.** to help me, O Lord............. 2363
Ps 40:13 O Lord, make **h.** to help me............. 2363
Ps 70:1 Make **h.**, O God, to deliver me;.............
Ps 70:1 make **h.** to help me, O Lord............. 2363
Ps 70:5 make **h.** unto me, O God: thou.......... 2363
Ps 71:12 my God, make **h.** for my help............ 2439
Ps 116:11 I said in my **h.**, All men are liars...... 2648
Ps 119:60 I made **h.**, and delayed not to keep.... 2363
Ps 141:1 I cry unto thee: make **h.** unto me;..... 2363
Pr 1:16 evil, and make **h.** to shed blood......... 4116
Pr 28:20 but he that maketh **h.** to be rich.......... 213
Ca 8:14 Make **h.**, my beloved, and be............ 1272
Isa 28:16 that believeth shall not make **h.**......... 2363
Isa 49:17 Thy children shall make **h.**; thy.......... 4116
Isa 52:12 ye shall not go out with **h.**,............... 2649
Isa 59:7 they make **h.** to shed innocent........... 4116
Jer 9:18 And let them make **h.**, and take.......... 4116
Da 2:25 in Daniel before the king in **h.**,........... 927
Da 3:24 was astonished, and rose up in **h.**,....... 927
Da 6:19 and went in **h.** unto the den of lions..... 927
Na 2:5 they shall make **h.** to the wall............ 4116
Mk 6:25 she came in straightway with **h.**.......... *4710*
Lu 1:39 went into the hill country with **h.**,...... *4710*
Lu 2:16 And they came with **h.**, and found...... *4692*
Lu 19:5 **Zacchaeus, make h., and come**........ *4692*
Lu 19:6 And he made **h.**, and came down,...... *4692*
Ac 22:18 **Make h., and get thee quickly out**. *4692*

HASTED See also HASTENED.

Ge 18:7 young man; and he **h.** to dress it....... 4116
Ge 24:18 and she **h.**, and let down her............ 4116
Ge 24:20 And she **h.**, and emptied her............ 4116
Ex 5:13 the taskmasters **h.** them, saying,......... 213
Jos 4:10 and the people **h.** and passed over..... 4116
Jos 8:14 that they **h.** and rose up early,.......... 4116
Jos 8:19 and **h.** and set the city on fire........... 4116
Jos 10:13 **h.** not to go down about a whole......... 213
Jg 20:37 the liers in wait **h.**, and rushed.......... 2363
1Sa 17:48 that David **h.**, and ran toward.......... 4116
1Sa 25:23 when Abigail saw David, she **h.**,........ 4116
1Sa 25:34 except thou hadst **h.** and come to...... 4116
1Sa 25:42 And Abigail **h.**, and arose, and.......... 4116
1Sa 28:24 and she **h.**, and killed it, and took...... 4116
2Sa 19:16 was of Bahurim, **h.** and came........... 4116
1Ki 20:41 And he **h.**, and took the ashes.......... 4116
2Ki 9:13 Then they **h.**, and took every man..... 4116
2Ch 26:20 himself **h.** also to go out, because...... 1765
Es 6:12 **h.** to his house mourning, and.......... 1765
Es 6:14 and **h.** to bring Haman unto the.......... 926
Job 31:5 of if my foot hath **h.** to deceit;........... 2363
Ps 48:5 they were troubled, and **h.** away........ 2648
Ps 104:7 voice of thy thunder they **h.** away...... 2648
Ac 20:16 for he **h.**, if it were possible for......... *4692*

HASTEN See also HASTENED; HASTENETH.

1Ki 22:9 **H.** hither Micaiah the son of............. 4116
2Ch 24:5 and see that ye **h.** the matter............ 4116
Ps 16:4 be multiplied that **h.** after............... 4116
Ps 55:8 I would **h.** my escape from the.......... 2363
Ec 2:25 or who else can **h.** hereunto, more..... 2363
Isa 5:19 Let him make speed, and **h.**.............. 2363
Isa 60:22 I the Lord will **h.** it in his time.......... 2363
Jer 1:12 I will **h.** my word to perform it,......... 8245

HASTENED See also HASTED.

Ge 18:6 And Abraham **h.** into the tent............ 4116
Ge 19:15 then the angels **h.** Lot, saying,............ 213
2Ch 24:5 Howbeit the Levites **h.** it not........... 4116
Es 3:15 The posts went out, being **h.**............ 1765
Es 8:14 being **h.** and pressed on by the........... 926
Jer 17:16 I have not **h.** from being a pastor........ 213

HASTENETH See also HASTETH.

Isa 51:14 The captive exile **h.** that he may........ 4116

HASTETH See also HASTENETH.

Job 9:26 as the eagle that **h.** to the prey......... 2907
Job 40:23 drinketh up a river, and **h.** not:......... 2648
Pr 7:23 as a bird **h.** to the snare,................. 4116
Pr 19:2 and he that **h.** with his feet sinneth..... 213
Pr 28:22 He that **h.** to be rich hath an evil......... 926
Ec 1:5 the sun goeth down, and **h.** to his...... 7602
Jer 48:16 to come, and his affliction **h.** fast......... 4116
Hab 1:8 fly as the eagle that **h.** to eat........... 2363
Zep 1:14 is near, it is near, and **h.** greatly,....... 4116

HASTILY

Ge 41:14 and they brought him **h.** out of.......... 7323
Jg 2:23 without driving them out **h.**;.............. 4118
Jg 9:54 he called **h.** unto the young man........ 4120
1Sa 4:14 And the man came in **h.**, and told...... 4116
1Ki 20:33 and did **h.** catch it: and they said,...... 4116
Pr 20:21 inheritance may be gotten **h.** at........... 926
Pr 25:8 Go not forth **h.** to strive, lest thou..... 4118
Joh 11:31 that she rose up **h.** and went out,...... *5030*

HASTING

Isa 16:5 judgment, and **h.** righteousness.......... 4106
2Pe 3:12 **h.** unto the coming of the day of........ *4692*

HASTY

Pr 14:29 but he that is **h.** of spirit exalteth....... 7116
Pr 21:5 every one that is **h.** only to want......... 213
Pr 29:20 Seest thou a man that is **h.** in his........ 213
Ec 5:2 let not thine heart be **h.** to utter........ 4116
Ec 7:9 Be not **h.** in thy spirit to be.............. 926
Ec 8:3 Be not **h.** to go out of his sight:.......... 926
Isa 28:4 the **h.** fruit before the summer;......... 1061
Da 2:15 Why is the decree so **h.** from the...... 2685
Hab 1:6 that bitter and **h.** nation, which.......... 4116

HASUPHA (has-u'-fah) See also HASHUPHA.

Ezr 2:43 the children of **H.**, the children.......... 2817

HATACH (ha'-tak)

Es 4:5 called Esther for **H.**, one of the......... 2047
Es 4:6 So **H.** went forth to Mordecai unto..... 2047
Es 4:9 And **H.** came and told Esther the....... 2047
Es 4:10 Esther spake unto **H.**, and gave......... 2047

HATCH See also HATCHETH.

Isa 34:15 make her nest, and lay, and **h.**,......... 1234
Isa 59:5 They **h.** cockatrice' eggs, and............ 1234

HATCHETH

Jer 17:11 partridge sitteth on eggs, and **h.**......... 3205

HATE See also HATED; HATEFUL; HATEST; HATETH; HATING.

Ge 24:60 the gate of those which **h.** them........ 8130
Ge 26:27 come ye to me, seeing ye **h.** me,........ 8130
Ge 50:15 Joseph will peradventure **h.** us,......... 7852
Ex 20:5 fourth generation of them that **h.**........ 8130
Le 19:17 Thou shalt not **h.** thy brother in......... 8130
Le 26:17 they that **h.** you shall reign over........ 8130
Nu 10:35 let them that **h.** thee flee before......... 8130
De 5:9 fourth generation of them that **h.**........ 8130
De 7:10 repayeth them that **h.** him to their..... 8130
De 7:15 them upon all them that **h.** thee......... 8130
De 19:11 But if any man **h.** his neighbour,........ 8130
De 22:13 go in unto her, and **h.** her............... 8130
De 24:3 And if the latter husband **h.** her,........ 8130
De 30:7 on them that **h.** thee, which.............. 8130
De 32:41 and will reward them that **h.** me......... 8130
De 33:11 and of them that **h.** him, that they...... 8130
Jg 11:7 Did not ye **h.** me, and expel me out... 8130
Jg 14:16 Thou dost but **h.** me, and lovest me... 8130
2Sa 22:41 that I might destroy them that **h.**........ 8130
1Ki 22:8 but I **h.** him; for he doth not............. 8130
2Ch 18:7 but I **h.** him; for he never................ 8130
2Ch 19:2 and love them that **h.** the Lord?......... 8130
Job 8:22 They that **h.** thee shall be clothed...... 8130
Ps 9:13 of them that **h.** me, thou that liftest.... 8130
Ps 18:40 that I might destroy them that **h.**........ 8130
Ps 21:8 shall find out those that **h.** thee......... 8130
Ps 25:19 they **h.** me with cruel hatred............ 8130
Ps 34:21 and they that **h.** the righteous........... 8130
Ps 35:19 eye that **h.** me without a cause.......... 8130
Ps 38:19 they that **h.** me wrongfully are.......... 8130
Ps 41:7 All that **h.** me whisper together......... 8130

Ps 44:10 and they which **h.** us spoil for 8130
Ps 55:3 me, and in wrath they **h.** me 7852
Ps 68:1 let them also that **h.** him flee 8130
Ps 69:4 They that **h.** me without a cause 8130
Ps 69:14 delivered from them that **h.** me, 8130
Ps 83:2 and they that **h.** thee have lifted up 8130
Ps 86:17 that they which **h.** me may see 8130
Ps 89:23 face, and plague them that **h.** him. 8130
Ps 97:10 Ye that love the Lord, **h.** evil: 8130
Ps 101:3 I **h.** the work of them that turn 8130
Ps 105:25 turned their heart to **h.** his people, 8130
Ps 118:7 see my desire upon them that **h.** 8130
Ps 119:104 therefore I **h.** every false way. 8130
Ps 119:113 I **h.** vain thoughts: but thy law 8130
Ps 119:128 right; and I **h.** every false way. 8130
Ps 119:163 I **h.** and abhor lying: but thy law 8130
Ps 129:5 and turned back that **h.** Zion. 8130
Ps 139:21 I **h.** them, O Lord, that **h.** thee? 8130
Ps 139:22 I **h.** them with perfect hatred: 8130
Pr 1:22 scorning, and fools **h.** knowledge? 8130
Pr 6:16 These six things doth the Lord **h.**: 8130
Pr 8:13 The fear of the Lord is to **h.** evil: 8130
Pr 8:13 and the froward mouth, do I **h.** 8130
Pr 8:36 all they that **h.** me love death. 8130
Pr 9:8 Reprove not a scorner, lest he **h.** 8130
Pr 19:7 the brethren of the poor do **h.** him: 8130
Pr 25:17 he be weary of thee, and so **h.** thee. 8130
Pr 29:10 The bloodthirsty **h.** the upright: 8130
Ec 3:8 A time to love, and a time to **h.**; 8130
Isa 61:8 I **h.** robbery for burnt offering; and 8130
Jer 44:4 this abominable thing that I **h.**. 8130
Eze 16:27 unto the will of them that **h.** thee, 8130
Da 4:19 the dream be to them that **h.** thee, 8131
Am 5:10 They **h.** him that rebuketh in the 8130
Am 5:15 **H.** the evil, and love the good, 8130
Am 5:21 I **h.**, I despise your feast days, 8130
Am 6:8 and **h.** his palaces: therefore will I 8130
Mic 3:2 Who **h.** the good, and love the evil; 8130
Zec 8:17 for all these are things that I **h.**, 8130
Mt 5:43 **shalt love thy neighbour, and h.** *3404*
Mt 5:44 **do good to them that h. you.** *3404*
Mt 6:24 **for either he will h. the one,** *3404*
Mt 24:10 **another, and shall h. one another.** *3404*
Lu 1:71 from the hand of all that **h.** us; *3404*
Lu 6:22 **when men shall h. you, and when** *3404*
Lu 6:27 **enemies, do good to them which h.** *3404*
Lu 14:26 **and h. not his father, and mother,** *3404*
Lu 16:13 **either he will h. the one, and love** *3404*
Joh 7:7 **cannot h. you; but me it hateth,** *3404*
Joh 15:18 **If the world h. you, ye know that** *3404*
Ro 7:15 do I not; but what I **h.**, that do I. *3404*
1Jo 3:13 my brethren, if the world **h.** you. *3404*
Re 2:6 **Nicolaitanes, which I also h.** *3404*
Re 2:15 **the Nicolaitanes, which thing I h.** *3404*
Re 17:16 these shall **h.** the whore, and shall *3404*

HATED
Ge 27:41 And Esau **h.** Jacob because of the 7852
Ge 29:31 the Lord saw that Leah was **h.**, 8130
Ge 29:33 the Lord hath heard that I was **h.**, 8130
Ge 37:4 than all his brethren, they **h.** him, 8130
Ge 37:5 and they **h.** him yet the more. 8130
Ge 37:8 they **h.** him yet the more for his 8130
Ge 49:23 and shot at him, and **h.** him: 7852
De 1:27 Because the Lord **h.** us, he hath 8135
De 4:42 **h.** him not in times past; 8130
De 9:28 and because he **h.** them, he hath 8135
De 19:4 whom he **h.** not in times past; 8130
De 19:6 as he **h.** him not in time past, 8130
De 21:15 one beloved, and another **h.**, and 8130
De 21:15 both the beloved and the **h.**; 8130
De 21:15 firstborn son be her's that was **h.**: 8146
De 21:16 firstborn before the son of the **h.**, 8130
De 21:17 acknowledge the son of the **h.** for 8130
Jos 20:5 neighbour unwittingly, and **h.** him 8130
Jg 15:2 thought that thou hadst utterly **h.** 8130
2Sa 5:8 that are **h.** of David's soul, he shall 8130
2Sa 13:15 Then Amnon **h.** her exceedingly; so 8130
2Sa 13:15 the hatred wherewith he **h.** her was 8130
2Sa 13:22 for Absalom **h.** Amnon, because he 8130
2Sa 22:18 enemy, and from them that **h.** me: 8130
Es 9:1 Jews had rule over them that **h.** 8130
Es 9:5 what they would unto those that **h.** 8130
Job 31:29 the destruction of him that **h.** me, 8130
Ps 18:17 enemy, and from them which **h.** me 8130
Ps 26:5 I have **h.** the congregation of evil 8130
Ps 31:6 I have **h.** them that regard lying 8130
Ps 44:7 hast put them to shame that **h.** us 8130
Ps 55:12 neither was it he that **h.** me that 8130
Ps 106:10 from the hand of him that **h.** them, 8130
Ps 106:41 and they that **h.** them ruled over 8130
Pr 1:29 For that they **h.** knowledge, and 8130
Pr 5:12 How have I **h.** instruction, and my 8130
Pr 14:17 a man of wicked devices is **h.** 8130
Pr 14:20 The poor is **h.** even of his own 8130
Ec 2:17 Therefore I **h.** life; because the 8130
Ec 2:18 Yea, I **h.** all my labour which I had 8130
Isa 60:15 thou hast been forsaken and **h.**, so 8130
Isa 66:5 Your brethren that **h.** you, that 8130
Jer 12:8 against me: therefore have I **h.** it, 8130
Eze 16:37 with all them that thou hast **h.**; 8130
Eze 35:6 sith thou hast not **h.** blood, even 8130
Ho 9:15 for there I **h.** them: for the 8130
Mal 1:3 I **h.** Esau, and laid his mountains 8130
Mal 24:9 and ye shall be **h.** of all nations for 8130
Mt 10:22 **ye shall be h. of all men for my** *3404*
Mt 24:9 **ye shall be h. of all nations**
Mk 13:13 **ye shall be h. of all men for my** *3404*
Lu 19:14 **But his citizens h. him, and sent** *3404*
Lu 21:17 **And ye shall be h. of all men my** *3404*
Joh 15:18 **ye know that it h. me before it** *3404*
Joh 15:18 **me before it h. you**
Joh 15:24 **they both seen and h. both me** *3404*
Joh 15:25 **They h. me without a cause.** *3404*
Joh 17:14 **the world hath h. them, because** *3404*
Ro 9:13 I loved, but Esau have I **h.** *3404*
Eph 5:29 no man ever yet **h.** his own flesh; *3404*
Heb 1:9 loved righteousness, and **h.** iniquity; *3404*

HATEFUL
Ps 36:2 his iniquity be found to be **h.** 8130
Tit 3:3 envy, **h.**, and hating one another. *4767*
Re 18:2 of every unclean and **h.** bird. *3404*

HATEFULLY
Eze 23:29 they shall deal with thee **h.**, 8135

HATERS
Ps 81:15 The **h.** of the Lord should have 8130
Ro 1:30 **h.** of God, despiteful, proud, *2319*

HATEST
2Sa 19:6 thine enemies, and **h.** thy friends 8130
Ps 5:5 thou **h.** all workers of iniquity. 8130
Ps 45:7 righteousness, and **h.** wickedness: 8130
Ps 50:17 Seeing thou **h.** instruction, and 8130
Eze 23:28 the hand of them whom thou **h.**, 8130
Re 2:6 **thou h. the deeds of...Nicolaitanes,** *3404*

HATETH
Ex 23:5 see the ass of him that **h.** thee 8130
De 7:10 will not be slack to him that **h.** him, 8130
De 12:31 which he **h.**, have they done unto 8130
De 16:22 image; which the Lord thy God **h.** 8130
De 22:16 unto this man to wife, and he **h.** her; 8130
Job 16:9 teareth me in his wrath, who **h.** me: 7852
Job 34:17 even he that **h.** right govern? 8130
Ps 11:5 him that loveth violence his soul **h.** 8130
Ps 120:6 long dwelt with him that **h.** peace. 8130
Pr 11:15 and he that **h.** suretiship is sure 8130
Pr 12:1 but he that **h.** reproof is brutish. 8130
Pr 13:5 A righteous man **h.** lying: but a 8130
Pr 13:24 He that spareth his rod **h.** his son: 8130
Pr 15:10 and he that **h.** reproof shall die. 8130
Pr 15:27 but he that **h.** gifts shall live. 8130
Pr 26:24 He that **h.** dissembleth with his lips, 8130
Pr 26:28 A lying tongue **h.** those that are 8130
Pr 28:16 he that **h.** covetousness shall 8130
Pr 29:24 partner with a thief **h.** his own soul: 8130
Isa 1:14 your appointed feasts my soul **h.**: 8130
Mal 2:16 saith that he **h.** putting away: 8130
Joh 3:20 **h. the light, neither cometh to** *3404*
Joh 7:7 **cannot hate you; but me it h.,** *3404*
Joh 12:25 **he that h. his life in this world** *3404*
Joh 15:19 **world, therefore the world h. you.** *3404*
Joh 15:23 **He that h. me h. my Father also.** *3404*
1Jo 2:9 is in the light, and **h.** his brother, *3404*
1Jo 2:11 But he that **h.** his brother is in *3404*
1Jo 3:15 Whosoever **h.** his brother, is a *3404*
1Jo 4:20 and **h.** his brother, he is a liar: *3404*

HATH
Ge 1:20 the moving creature that **h.** life,
Ge 3:1 Yea, **h.** God said, Ye shall not eat of
Ge 3:3 God **h.** said, Ye shall not eat of it,
Ge 4:11 earth, which **h.** opened her mouth to
Ge 4:25 For God, said she, **h.** appointed me
Ge 5:29 ground which the Lord **h.** cursed.
Ge 14:20 the most high God, which **h.** delivered
Ge 16:2 Behold now, the Lord **h.** restrained
Ge 16:11 because the Lord **h.** heard thy
Ge 17:14 people; he **h.** broken my covenant.
Ge 18:19 Abraham that which he **h.** spoken.
Ge 19:13 and the Lord **h.** sent us to destroy it.
Ge 19:19 thy servant **h.** found grace in thy
Ge 21:6 Sarah said, God **h.** made me to laugh,
Ge 21:12 in all that Sarah **h.** said unto thee,
Ge 21:17 for God **h.** heard the voice of the lad
Ge 21:26 I wot not who **h.** done this thing:
Ge 22:20 Behold, Milcah, she **h.** also born
Ge 23:9 me the cave of Machpelah, which he **h.**,
Ge 24:27 who **h.** not left destitute my master
Ge 24:35 And the Lord **h.** blessed my master
Ge 24:35 and he **h.** given him flocks,
Ge 24:36 unto him **h.** he given all that he **h.**.
Ge 24:44 woman whom the Lord **h.** appointed
Ge 24:51 son's wife, as the Lord **h.** spoken.
Ge 24:56 seeing the Lord **h.** prospered my way;
Ge 26:22 For now the Lord **h.** made room for
Ge 27:27 of a field which the Lord **h.** blessed:
Ge 27:33 where is he that **h.** taken venison,
Ge 27:35 came with subtility, and **h.** taken
Ge 27:36 for he **h.** supplanted me these two
Ge 27:36 behold, now he **h.** taken away my
Ge 29:32 Surely the Lord **h.** looked upon my
Ge 29:33 Because the Lord **h.** heard that I was
Ge 29:33 he **h.** therefore given me this son.
Ge 30:2 who **h.** withheld from thee the fruit
Ge 30:6 And Rachel said, God **h.** judged me,
Ge 30:6 and **h.** also heard my voice, and
Ge 30:6 voice, and **h.** given me a son:
Ge 30:18 Leah said, God **h.** given me my hire,
Ge 30:20 God **h.** endued me with a good dowry;
Ge 30:23 and said, God **h.** taken away my
Ge 30:27 the Lord **h.** blessed me for thy sake.
Ge 30:30 and the Lord **h.** blessed thee since
Ge 31:1 saying, Jacob **h.** taken away all that
Ge 31:1 which was our father's **h.** he gotten
Ge 31:5 the God of my father **h.** been with me.
Ge 31:7 And your father **h.** deceived me,
Ge 31:9 Thus God **h.** taken away the cattle of
Ge 31:15 of him strangers? for he **h.** sold us,
Ge 31:15 and **h.** quite devoured also our
Ge 31:16 riches which God **h.** taken from
Ge 31:16 whatsoever God **h.** said unto thee,
Ge 31:42 God **h.** seen mine affliction and the
Ge 33:5 which God **h.** graciously given thy
Ge 33:11 because God **h.** dealt graciously with
Ge 37:20 Some evil beast **h.** devoured him:
Ge 37:33 an evil beast **h.** devoured him;
Ge 38:24 Tamar thy daughter in law **h.** played
Ge 38:26 She **h.** been more righteous than I;
Ge 39:8 me in the house, and he **h.** committed
Ge 39:8 all that he **h.** to my hands; 3426
Ge 39:9 neither **h.** he kept back anything from
Ge 39:14 See, he **h.** brought in an Hebrew unto
Ge 41:25 God **h.** shewed Pharaoh what he is
Ge 41:39 Forasmuch as God **h.** shewed thee all
Ge 41:51 For God, said he, **h.** made me forget
Ge 41:52 For God **h.** caused me to be fruitful
Ge 42:28 What is this that God **h.** done unto us?
Ge 43:23 God of your father, **h.** given you
Ge 44:16 God **h.** found out the iniquity of thy
Ge 45:6 For these two years **h.** the famine been
Ge 45:8 but God: and he **h.** made me a father
Ge 45:9 God **h.** made me lord of all Egypt:
Ge 46:32 their trade **h.** been to feed cattle;
Ge 46:34 Thy servants' trade **h.** been about
Ge 47:18 my lord also **h.** our herds of cattle, 413
Ge 48:9 my sons, whom God **h.** given me
Ge 48:11 and, lo, God **h.** shewed me also thy
Ex 3:13 The God of your fathers **h.** sent me
Ex 3:14 I Am **h.** sent me unto you.
Ex 3:15 the God of Jacob, **h.** sent me unto you:
Ex 3:18 The Lord God of the Hebrews **h.** met
Ex 4:1 The Lord **h.** not appeared unto thee.
Ex 4:5 the God of Jacob, **h.** appeared unto
Ex 4:11 unto him, Who **h.** made man's mouth?
Ex 5:3 The God of the Hebrews **h.** met with
Ex 5:23 to speak in thy name, he **h.** done evil
Ex 7:16 Lord God of the Hebrews **h.** sent me
Ex 9:18 hail, such as **h.** not been in Egypt
Ex 10:12 even all that the hail **h.** left.
Ex 12:25 give you, according as he **h.** promised,

Ex 13:9 strong hand **h.** the Lord brought thee........
Ex 14:3 the wilderness **h.** shut them in................
Ex 15:1 unto the Lord, for he **h.** triumphed..........
Ex 15:1 the horse and his rider **h.** he thrown..........
Ex 15:4 and his host **h.** he cast into the sea:..........
Ex 15:6 thy right hand, O Lord, **h.** dashed in..........
Ex 15:21 ye to the Lord, for he **h.** triumphed..........
Ex 15:21 the horse and his rider **h.** he thrown..........
Ex 16:6 that the Lord **h.** brought you out.............
Ex 16:9 for he **h.** heard your murmurings..............
Ex 16:15 bread which the Lord **h.** given you to........
Ex 16:16 thing which the Lord **h.** commanded,..........
Ex 16:23 This is that which the Lord **h.** said,..........
Ex 16:29 See, for that the Lord **h.** given you the......
Ex 17:16 Because the Lord **h.** sworn that..............
Ex 18:10 who **h.** delivered you out of the hand of.....
Ex 18:10 who **h.** delivered the people from under.....
Ex 19:8 All that the Lord **h.** spoken we will do.......
Ex 21:8 her master, who **h.** betrothed her to..........
Ex 21:8 seeing he **h.** dealt deceitfully with............
Ex 21:29 and it **h.** been testified to his owner,.........
Ex 21:29 and he **h.** not kept him in, but................
Ex 21:29 that he **h.** killed a man or a woman;..........
Ex 21:36 that the ox **h.** used to push in time...........
Ex 21:36 and his owner **h.** not kept him in;............
Ex 22:11 that he **h.** not put his hand unto his...........
Ex 24:3 All the words which the Lord **h.** said.........
Ex 24:7 All that the Lord **h.** said will we do,..........
Ex 24:8 which the Lord **h.** made with you..............
Ex 32:24 Whosoever **h.** any gold, let them..............
Ex 32:33 Whosoever **h.** sinned against me,..............
Ex 35:1 words which the Lord **h.** commanded,........
Ex 35:10 make all that the Lord **h.** commanded;.......
Ex 35:30 See, the Lord **h.** called by name...............
Ex 35:31 And he **h.** filled him with the spirit...........
Ex 35:34 And he **h.** put in his heart that he............
Ex 35:35 Them **h.** he filled with wisdom of..............
Le 4:3 bring for his sin, which he **h.** sinned,.........
Le 4:22 When a ruler **h.** sinned, and done..............
Le 4:23 Or if his sin, wherein he **h.** sinned,...........
Le 4:28 Or if his sin, which he **h.** sinned...............
Le 4:28 blemish, for his sin which he **h.** sinned.......
Le 4:35 for his sin which he **h.** committed,.............
Le 5:1 whether he **h.** seen or known of it;...........
Le 5:5 shall confess that he **h.** sinned in..............
Le 5:6 Lord for his sin which he **h.** sinned,...........
Le 5:7 his trespass, which he **h.** committed,.........
Le 5:10 for him for his sin which he **h.** sinned,.......
Le 5:13 that he **h.** sinned in one of these,.............
Le 5:16 the harm that he **h.** done in thy holy..........
Le 5:19 he **h.** certainly trespassed against.............
Le 6:2 or **h.** oppressed his neighbour;..................
Le 6:4 Then it shall be, because he **h.** sinned,.......
Le 6:4 thing which he **h.** deceitfully gotten,..........
Le 6:5 all that about which he **h.** sworn...............
Le 6:7 for any thing of all that he **h.** done...........
Le 6:10 the ashes which the fire **h.** consumed........
Le 7:8 the burnt-offering which he **h.** offered........
Le 8:34 As he **h.** done this day, so the Lord..........
Le 8:34 **h.** commanded to do, to make an...............
Le 10:6 burning which the Lord **h.** kindled............
Le 10:11 statutes which the Lord **h.** spoken...........
Le 10:15 for ever; as the Lord **h.** commanded...........
Le 10:17 and God **h.** given it you to bear the..........
Le 11:9 whatsoever **h.** fins and scales in the..........
Le 11:12 Whatsoever **h.** no fins nor scales in...........
Le 11:42 whatsoever **h.** more feet among all.............
Le 12:7 the law for her that **h.** born a male...........
Le 13:4 shut up him that **h.** the plague seven.........
Le 13:7 after that he **h.** been seen of the.............
Le 13:12 skin of him that **h.** the plague from............
Le 13:13 him clean that **h.** the plague: it is.............
Le 13:17 him clean that **h.** the plague: he is............
Le 13:31 shall shut up him that **h.** the plague...........
Le 13:33 shall shut up him that **h.** the scall.............
Le 13:41 And he that **h.** his hair fallen off..............
Le 13:50 shut up it that **h.** the plague seven............
Le 14:43 after that he **h.** taken away the stones,.......
Le 14:43 and after he **h.** scraped the house,..........
Le 14:48 behold, the plague **h.** not spread in............
Le 15:2 When any man **h.** a running issue........1961
Le 15:4 bed, whereon he lieth that **h.** the issue,.....
Le 15:6 whereon he sat that **h.** the issue.............
Le 15:7 the flesh of him that **h.** the issue.............
Le 15:8 And if he that **h.** the issue spit upon.........
Le 15:9 he rideth upon that **h.** the issue...............
Le 15:11 he toucheth that **h.** the issue,..................
Le 15:11 and **h.** not rinsed his hands in water,.........
Le 15:12 that he toucheth which **h.** the issue,..........
Le 15:13 And when he that **h.** an issue is...............
Le 15:32 This is the law of him that **h.** an issue,......
Le 15:33 and of him that **h.** an issue, of the............
Le 16:20 when he **h.** made an end of reconciling.......
Le 17:2 thing which the Lord **h.** commanded,.........
Le 17:4 unto that man; he **h.** shed blood;..............
Le 19:8 because he **h.** profaned the hallowed..........
Le 19:22 for his sin which he **h.** done:....................
Le 19:22 and the sin which he **h.** done shall be.........
Le 20:3 because he **h.** given of his seed unto.........
Le 20:9 he **h.** cursed his father or his mother;........
Le 20:11 with his father's wife **h.** uncovered............
Le 20:17 he **h.** uncovered his sister's nakedness;......
Le 20:18 he **h.** discovered her fountain,..................
Le 20:18 and she **h.** uncovered the fountain..............
Le 20:20 he **h.** uncovered his uncle's nakedness:......
Le 20:21 he **h.** uncovered his brother's..................
Le 20:27 also or woman that **h.** a familiar..........1961
Le 21:3 him, which **h.** had no husband;..................
Le 21:17 generations that **h.** any blemish,.......... 1961
Le 21:18 man he be that **h.** a blemish,....................
Le 21:18 or a lame, or that he **h.** a flat nose,...........
Le 21:20 or a dwarf, or that **h.** a blemish in his........
Le 21:20 or scabbed, or **h.** his stones broken;..........
Le 21:21 No man that **h.** a blemish of the seed........
Le 21:21 he **h.** a blemish; he shall not come............
Le 21:23 unto the altar, because he **h.** a blemish;.....
Le 22:4 is a leper, or **h.** a running issue;.............
Le 22:5 whatsoever uncleanness he **h.**;...............
Le 22:6 The soul which **h.** touched any such..........
Le 22:20 But whatsoever **h.** a blemish, that.............
Le 22:23 bullock or a lamb that **h.** any thing...........
Le 24:14 Bring forth him that **h.** cursed...................
Le 24:19 as he **h.** done, so shall it be done.............
Le 24:20 as he **h.** caused a blemish in a man...........
Le 25:25 brother be waxen poor, and **h.** sold...........
Le 25:28 hand of him that **h.** bought it until............
Le 27:22 the Lord a field which he **h.** bought,..........
Le 27:28 devote unto the Lord of all that he **h.**,........
Nu 5:2 leper, and every one that **h.** an issue,.........
Nu 5:7 him against whom he **h.** trespassed..........
Nu 5:27 And when he **h.** made her to drink...........
Nu 6:9 and he **h.** defiled the head of his..............
Nu 6:21 law of the Nazarite who **h.** vowed,.............
Nu 10:29 the Lord **h.** spoken good concerning..........
Nu 12:2 **H.** the Lord indeed spoken only by..........
Nu 12:2 **h.** he not spoken also by us?...................
Nu 14:3 And wherefore **h.** the Lord brought............
Nu 14:16 therefore he **h.** slain them in the..............
Nu 14:24 and **h.** followed me fully, him will.............
Nu 14:40 the place which the Lord **h.** promised:.......
Nu 15:22 which the Lord **h.** spoken unto.................
Nu 15:23 Even all that the Lord **h.** commanded........
Nu 15:31 Because he **h.** despised the word of the.....
Nu 15:31 and **h.** broken his commandment,..............
Nu 16:5 whom he **h.** chosen will he cause to..........
Nu 16:9 that the God of Israel **h.** separated..........
Nu 16:10 And he **h.** brought thee near to him,..........
Nu 16:28 shall know that the Lord **h.** sent me..........
Nu 16:29 then the Lord **h.** not sent me...................
Nu 19:2 law which the Lord **h.** commanded,...........
Nu 19:15 open vessel, which **h.** no covering.............
Nu 19:20 because he **h.** defiled the sanctuary...........
Nu 19:20 of separation **h.** not been sprinkled............
Nu 20:14 all the travel that **h.** befallen us;..............
Nu 20:16 and **h.** brought us forth out of Egypt:.........
Nu 21:28 it **h.** consumed Ar of Moab, and...............
Nu 21:29 he **h.** given his sons that escaped,.............
Nu 22:10 king of Moab, **h.** sent unto me, saying,......
Nu 23:7 Balak the king of Moab **h.** brought me.......
Nu 23:8 I curse, whom God **h.** not cursed?............
Nu 23:8 whom the Lord **h.** not defied?...............
Nu 23:12 that which the Lord **h.** put in my..............
Nu 23:17 him, What **h.** the Lord spoken?..................
Nu 23:19 **h.** he said, and shall he not do it?............
Nu 23:19 or **h.** he spoken, and shall he not..............
Nu 23:20 and he **h.** blessed; and I cannot.............
Nu 23:21 He **h.** not beheld iniquity in Jacob,...........
Nu 23:21 neither **h.** he seen perverseness in...........
Nu 23:22 he **h.** as it were the strength of an............
Nu 23:23 and of Israel, What **h.** God wrought!..........
Nu 24:3 said, Balaam the son of Beor **h.** said,.........
Nu 24:3 man whose eyes are open **h.** said:...........
Nu 24:4 He **h.** said, which heard the words of.........
Nu 24:6 aloes which the Lord **h.** planted,..............
Nu 24:8 he **h.** as it were the strength of an...........
Nu 24:11 the Lord **h.** kept thee back from...............
Nu 24:15 Balaam the son of Beor **h.** said,................
Nu 24:15 man whose eyes are open **h.** said:...........
Nu 24:16 He **h.** said, which heard the words of.........
Nu 25:11 son of Aaron the priest, **h.** turned my.........
Nu 27:4 his family, because he **h.** no son?.............
Nu 30:1 thing which the Lord **h.** commanded..........
Nu 30:4 her bond wherewith she **h.** bound...............
Nu 30:4 every bond wherewith she **h.** bound..........
Nu 30:5 her bonds wherewith she **h.** bound............
Nu 30:12 if her husband **h.** utterly made them..........
Nu 30:12 her husband **h.** made them void;...............
Nu 30:15 them void after that he **h.** heard them;.......
Nu 31:17 kill every woman that **h.** known man..........
Nu 31:19 whosoever **h.** killed any person,...............
Nu 31:19 and whosoever **h.** touched any slain,..........
Nu 31:50 what every man **h.** gotten, of jewels..........
Nu 32:7 the land which the Lord **h.** given...............
Nu 32:21 until he **h.** driven out his enemies............
Nu 32:24 that which **h.** proceeded out of your............
Nu 32:31 As the Lord **h.** said unto thy servants,.......
Nu 36:5 of the sons of Joseph **h.** said well.............
De 1:10 The Lord your God **h.** multiplied you,.........
De 1:11 and bless you, as he **h.** promised you!.......
De 1:21 the Lord thy God **h.** set the land..............
De 1:21 as the Lord God of thy fathers **h.** said.......
De 1:27 hates us, he **h.** brought us forth...............
De 1:36 I give the land that he **h.** trodden.............
De 1:36 because he **h.** wholly followed the.............
De 2:7 For the Lord thy God **h.** blessed thee.........
De 2:7 the Lord thy God **h.** been with thee:..........
De 3:18 The Lord your God **h.** given you this.........
De 3:20 The Lord your God **h.** given them.............
De 3:21 all that the Lord your God **h.** done...........
De 4:3 the Lord thy God **h.** destroyed them...........
De 4:7 great, who **h.** God so nigh unto them,........
De 4:8 that **h.** statutes and judgments..................
De 4:19 which the Lord thy God **h.** divided.............
De 4:20 But the Lord **h.** taken you, and................
De 4:23 which the Lord thy God **h.** forbidden..........
De 4:32 whether there **h.** been any such thing.........
De 4:32 as this great thing is, or **h.** been heard.......
De 4:34 Or **h.** God assayed to go and take him.......
De 5:12 as the Lord...God **h.** commanded thee.......
De 5:16 as the Lord...God **h.** commanded thee;.......
De 5:24 Lord our God **h.** shewed us his glory..........
De 5:26 of all flesh, that **h.** heard the voice..........
De 5:32 as the Lord...God **h.** commanded you;.........
De 5:33 which the Lord...God **h.** commanded.........
De 6:3 Lord God of thy fathers **h.** promised...........
De 6:17 his statutes, which he **h.** commanded.........
De 6:19 before thee, as the Lord **h.** spoken.............
De 6:20 the Lord our God **h.** commanded..............
De 6:25 as he **h.** commanded us..........................
De 7:1 and **h.** cast out many nations before..........
De 7:6 the Lord thy God **h.** chosen thee to be......
De 7:8 unto your fathers, **h.** the Lord brought.......
De 8:10 for the good land which he **h.** given...........
De 8:17 the might of mine hand **h.** gotten me.........
De 9:3 them quickly, as the Lord **h.** said.............
De 9:4 after that the Lord thy God **h.** cast...........
De 9:4 the Lord **h.** brought me in to possess.........
De 9:28 he **h.** brought them out to slay them..........
De 10:9 Levi **h.** no part nor inheritance........... 1961
De 10:21 he is thy God, that **h.** done for thee..........
De 10:22 now the Lord thy God **h.** made thee as......
De 11:4 and how the Lord **h.** destroyed them...........
De 11:25 ye shall tread upon, as he **h.** said unto.......
De 11:29 when the Lord thy God **h.** brought............
De 12:7 wherein the Lord thy God **h.** blessed.........
De 12:12 forasmuch as he **h.** no part nor.................
De 12:15 of the Lord thy God which he **h.** given.......
De 12:20 enlarge thy border, as he **h.** promised.......
De 12:21 the Lord thy God **h.** chosen to put............
De 12:21 thy flock which the Lord **h.** given thee,.......
De 13:5 because he **h.** spoken to turn you.............
De 13:10 because he **h.** sought to thrust thee..........
De 13:12 which the Lord thy God **h.** given thee........
De 13:17 as he **h.** sworn unto thy fathers;..............
De 14:2 and the Lord **h.** chosen thee to be a...........
De 14:10 And whatsoever **h.** not fins and scales........
De 14:24 when the Lord thy God **h.** blessed..............
De 14:27 he **h.** no part nor inheritance with............
De 14:29 And the Levite, (because he **h.** no part.......
De 15:14 wherewith the Lord thy God **h.** blessed......
De 15:18 for he **h.** been worth a double hired...........

2Sa 18:28 the Lord thy God, which **h.** delivered
2Sa 18:31 for the Lord **h.** avenged thee this day
2Sa 19:27 And he **h.** slandered thy servant unto
2Sa 19:42 or **h.** he given us any gift?
2Sa 20:21 Bichri by name, **h.** lifted up his hand
2Sa 22:21 of my hands **h.** recompensed me.
2Sa 22:25 Therefore the Lord **h.** recompensed
2Sa 22:36 and thy gentleness **h.** made me great.
2Sa 23:5 yet he **h.** made with me an everlasting
1Ki 1:19 And he **h.** slain oxen and fat cattle
1Ki 1:19 and **h.** called all the sons of the king,
1Ki 1:19 Solomon thy servant **h.** he not called.
1Ki 1:25 gone down this day, and **h.** slain oxen
1Ki 1:25 and **h.** called all the king's sons,
1Ki 1:26 thy servant Solomon, **h.** he not called.
1Ki 1:29 As the Lord liveth, that **h.** redeemed
1Ki 1:37 As the Lord **h.** been with my lord
1Ki 1:43 lord king David **h.** made Solomon king.
1Ki 1:44 And the king **h.** sent with him Zadok
1Ki 1:48 which **h.** given one to sit on my throne
1Ki 1:51 lo, he **h.** caught hold on the horns of
1Ki 2:24 the Lord liveth, which **h.** established
1Ki 2:24 and who **h.** made me an house,
1Ki 2:31 Do as he **h.** said, and fall upon him,
1Ki 2:38 as my lord the king **h.** said, so will
1Ki 5:4 the Lord my God **h.** given me rest
1Ki 5:7 the Lord this day, which **h.** given unto
1Ki 8:15 and **h.** with his hand fulfilled it,
1Ki 8:20 And the Lord **h.** performed his word
1Ki 8:56 Blessed be the Lord, that **h.** given rest
1Ki 8:56 there **h.** not failed one word of all his
1Ki 9:8 Why **h.** the Lord done thus unto this
1Ki 9:9 therefore **h.** the Lord brought upon
1Ki 12:11 father **h.** chastised you with whips,
1Ki 13:3 is the sign which the Lord **h.** spoken;
1Ki 13:26 therefore the Lord **h.** delivered him
1Ki 13:26 unto the lion, which **h.** torn him,
1Ki 14:11 the air eat: for the Lord **h.** spoken it.
1Ki 16:16 Zimri **h.** conspired, and **h.** also slain
1Ki 18:10 whither my Lord **h.** not sent to seek
1Ki 19:18 and every mouth which **h.** not kissed
1Ki 22:23 behold, the Lord **h.** put a lying spirit
1Ki 22:23 and the Lord **h.** spoken evil concerning
1Ki 22:28 the Lord **h.** not spoken by me.
2Ki 1:9 Thou man of God, the king **h.** said,
2Ki 1:11 O man of God, thus **h.** the king said,
2Ki 2:2 for the Lord **h.** sent me to Beth-el
2Ki 2:4 for the Lord **h.** sent me to Jericho
2Ki 2:6 for the Lord **h.** sent me to Jordan.
2Ki 2:16 the Spirit of the Lord **h.** taken him up,
2Ki 3:7 The king of Moab **h.** rebelled against
2Ki 3:10 that the Lord **h.** called these three
2Ki 3:13 for the Lord **h.** called these three
2Ki 4:2 Thine handmaid **h.** not any thing in
2Ki 4:14 Verily she **h.** no child, and her
2Ki 4:27 and the Lord **h.** hid it from me,
2Ki 4:27 hid it from me, and **h.** not told me.
2Ki 5:20 Behold, my master **h.** spared Naaman
2Ki 5:22 My master **h.** sent me, saying,
2Ki 6:29 eat him: and she **h.** hid her son.
2Ki 6:32 this son of a murderer **h.** sent to take
2Ki 7:6 Lo, the king of Israel **h.** hired against
2Ki 8:1 for the Lord **h.** called for a famine;
2Ki 8:4 the great things that Elisha **h.** done.
2Ki 8:9 king of Syria **h.** sent me to thee,
2Ki 8:10 the Lord **h.** shewed me that he shall
2Ki 8:13 The Lord **h.** shewed me that thou shalt
2Ki 10:10 for the Lord **h.** done that which he
2Ki 14:10 and thine heart **h.** lifted thee up:
2Ki 17:26 therefore he **h.** sent lions among
2Ki 18:22 and whose altars Hezekiah **h.** taken
2Ki 18:22 and **h.** said to Judah and Jerusalem,
2Ki 18:27 **H.** my master sent me to thy master,
2Ki 18:27 **h.** he not sent me to the men which
2Ki 18:33 **H.** any of the gods of the nations
2Ki 19:4 king of Assyria his master **h.** sent to
2Ki 19:4 which the Lord thy God **h.** heard:
2Ki 19:16 which **h.** sent him to reproach the
2Ki 19:21 the word that the Lord **h.** spoken
2Ki 19:21 the daughter of Zion **h.** despised thee,
2Ki 19:21 the daughter of Jerusalem **h.** shaken
2Ki 20:9 will do the thing that he **h.** spoken:
2Ki 21:11 Manasseh king of Judah **h.** done these
2Ki 21:11 abominations, and **h.** done wickedly
2Ki 21:11 and **h.** made Judah also to sin
2Ki 22:10 Hilkiah the priest **h.** delivered
2Ki 22:16 book which the king of Judah **h.** read:
1Ch 14:11 God **h.** broken in upon mine enemies
1Ch 15:2 for them **h.** the Lord chosen to carry
1Ch 16:12 his marvellous works that he **h.** done,
1Ch 16:17 And **h.** confirmed the same to Jacob
1Ch 17:25 therefore thy servant **h.** found in his
1Ch 19:3 that he **h.** sent comforters unto thee?
1Ch 22:11 house of the Lord thy God, as he **h.** said
1Ch 22:18 and **h.** he not given you rest on every
1Ch 22:18 for he **h.** given the inhabitants of the
1Ch 23:25 The Lord God of Israel **h.** given rest
1Ch 28:4 for he **h.** chosen Judah to be the ruler;
1Ch 28:5 for the Lord **h.** given me many sons,
1Ch 28:5 he **h.** chosen Solomon my son to sit
1Ch 28:10 for the Lord **h.** chosen thee to build an
1Ch 29:1 whom alone God **h.** chosen, is yet
2Ch 2:11 Because the Lord **h.** loved his people,
2Ch 2:11 he **h.** made thee king over them.
2Ch 2:12 who **h.** given to David the king a wise
2Ch 2:15 which my lord **h.** spoken of, let him
2Ch 6:1 The Lord **h.** said that he would dwell
2Ch 6:4 who **h.** with his hands fulfilled that
2Ch 6:10 The Lord therefore **h.** performed his
2Ch 6:10 that he **h.** spoken: for I am risen
2Ch 7:21 Why **h.** the Lord done thus unto this
2Ch 7:22 therefore **h.** he brought all this evil
2Ch 8:11 the ark of the Lord **h.** come
2Ch 13:6 is risen up, and **h.** rebelled against
2Ch 14:7 we have sought him, and he **h.** given
2Ch 15:3 long season Israel **h.** been without
2Ch 18:22 the Lord **h.** put a lying spirit in the
2Ch 18:22 and the Lord **h.** spoken evil against
2Ch 18:27 in peace, then **h.** not the Lord spoken
2Ch 20:37 the Lord **h.** broken thy works.
2Ch 23:3 as the Lord **h.** said of the sons of
2Ch 24:20 forsaken the Lord, he **h.** also forsaken
2Ch 25:8 for God **h.** power to help, and to 3426
2Ch 25:16 I know that God **h.** determined to
2Ch 28:9 he **h.** delivered them into your hand,
2Ch 29:8 and he **h.** delivered them to trouble,
2Ch 29:11 for the Lord **h.** chosen you to stand
2Ch 30:8 his sanctuary, which he **h.** sanctified
2Ch 31:10 for the Lord **h.** blessed his people;
2Ch 32:12 **H.** not the same Hezekiah taken
2Ch 34:18 Hilkiah the priest **h.** given me a book
2Ch 36:23 kingdoms of the earth **h.** the Lord
2Ch 36:23 heaven given me; and he **h.** charged
Ezr 1:2 The Lord God of heaven **h.** given me
Ezr 1:2 and he **h.** charged me to build him
Ezr 4:3 the king of Persia **h.** commanded us.
Ezr 4:18 ye sent unto us **h.** been plainly read
Ezr 4:19 commanded, and search **h.** been made,
Ezr 4:19 this city of old time **h.** made
Ezr 5:3 Who **h.** commanded you to build this
Ezr 5:16 even until now **h.** it been in building
Ezr 6:12 the God that **h.** caused his name to
Ezr 7:27 which **h.** put such a thing as this in
Ezr 7:28 And **h.** extended mercy unto me
Ezr 9:2 princes and rulers **h.** been chief
Ezr 9:8 little space grace **h.** been shewed
Ezr 9:9 yet our God **h.** not forsaken us in our
Ezr 9:9 but **h.** extended mercy unto us in the
Ne 9:32 that **h.** come upon us, on our kings, on
Es 1:15 because she **h.** not performed the
Es 1:16 Vashti the queen **h.** not done wrong
Es 5:5 that he may do as Esther **h.** said.
Es 5:8 will do to morrow as the king **h.** said.
Es 6:3 What honour and dignity **h.** been done
Job 1:10 about all that he **h.** on every side?
Job 1:11 touch all that he **h.**, and he will curse
Job 1:12 all that he **h.** is in thy power; only
Job 1:16 and **h.** burned up the sheep, and the
Job 1:21 the Lord gave, and the Lord **h.** taken
Job 2:4 all that a man **h.** will he give for his
Job 3:23 and whom God **h.** hedged in?
Job 5:16 So the poor **h.** hope, and iniquity 1961
Job 6:5 the wild ass bray when he **h.** grass?
Job 7:8 The eye of him that **h.** seen me shall
Job 9:4 who **h.** hardened himself against him,
Job 9:4 against him and **h.** prospered?
Job 10:12 and thy visitation **h.** preserved my
Job 12:9 the hand of the Lord **h.** wrought this?
Job 12:13 and strength, he **h.** counsel and
Job 13:1 Lo, mine eye **h.** seen all this,
Job 13:1 mine ear **h.** heard and understood it.
Job 16:7 But now he **h.** made me weary:
Job 16:11 God **h.** delivered me to the ungodly,
Job 16:12 I was at ease, but he **h.** broken me
Job 16:12 he **h.** also taken me by my neck,
Job 17:6 He **h.** made me also a byword of the
Job 17:9 and he that **h.** clean hands shall
Job 19:6 Know now that God **h.** overthrown
Job 19:6 and **h.** compassed me with his net.
Job 19:8 He **h.** fenced up my way that I cannot
Job 19:8 pass, and he **h.** set darkness in my
Job 19:9 He **h.** stripped me of my glory,
Job 19:10 He **h.** destroyed me on every side,
Job 19:10 and mine hope **h.** he removed like a
Job 19:11 He **h.** also kindled his wrath against
Job 19:13 He **h.** put my brethren far from me,
Job 19:21 for the hand of the Lord **h.** touched
Job 20:15 He **h.** swallowed down riches, and
Job 20:19 Because he **h.** oppressed and
Job 20:19 oppressed and **h.** forsaken the poor;
Job 20:19 he **h.** violently taken away an house
Job 21:21 For what pleasure **h.** he in his house
Job 21:31 shall repay him what he **h.** done?
Job 23:10 when he **h.** tried me, I shall come
Job 23:11 My foot **h.** held his steps, his way
Job 23:17 neither **h.** he covered the darkness
Job 26:2 the arm that **h.** no strength?
Job 26:3 counselled him that **h.** no wisdom?
Job 26:6 and destruction **h.** no covering.
Job 26:10 He **h.** compassed the waters with
Job 26:13 By his spirit he **h.** garnished the
Job 26:13 his hand **h.** formed the crooked
Job 27:2 As God liveth, who **h.** taken away my
Job 27:2 the Almighty, who **h.** vexed my soul;
Job 27:8 the hypocrite, though he **h.** gained,
Job 28:6 of sapphires: and it **h.** dust of gold.
Job 28:7 which the vulture's eye **h.** not seen:
Job 30:11 Because he **h.** loosed my cord, and
Job 30:19 He **h.** cast me into the mire, and I
Job 31:5 or my foot **h.** hasted to deceit;
Job 31:7 If my step **h.** turned out of the way,
Job 31:7 and if any blot **h.** cleaved to mine
Job 31:17 the fatherless **h.** not eaten thereof;
Job 31:27 my heart **h.** been secretly enticed,
Job 31:27 or my mouth **h.** kissed my hand:
Job 32:14 Now he **h.** not directed his words
Job 32:19 my belly is as wine which **h.** no vent;
Job 33:2 my tongue **h.** spoken in my mouth.
Job 33:4 The Spirit of God **h.** made me,
Job 33:4 breath of the Almighty **h.** given me
Job 34:5 For Job **h.** said, I am righteous:
Job 34:5 and God **h.** taken away my judgment.
Job 34:9 For he **h.** said, It profiteth a man
Job 34:13 Who **h.** given him a charge over the
Job 34:13 or who **h.** disposed the whole world?
Job 34:35 Job **h.** spoken without knowledge,
Job 35:15 it is not so, he **h.** visited in his anger;
Job 36:23 Who **h.** enjoined him his way?
Job 38:5 Who **h.** laid the measures thereof,
Job 38:5 or who **h.** stretched the line upon it
Job 38:25 Who **h.** divided a watercourse for the
Job 38:28 **H.** the rain a father? or who 3426
Job 38:28 **h.** begotten the drops of dew?
Job 38:29 hoary frost of heaven, who **h.** gendered
Job 38:36 Who **h.** put wisdom in the inward
Job 38:36 or who **h.** given understanding to the
Job 39:5 Who **h.** sent out the wild ass free?
Job 39:5 or who **h.** loosed the bands of the
Job 39:17 Because God **h.** deprived her of
Job 39:17 neither **h.** he imparted to her
Job 41:11 Who **h.** prevented me, that I should
Job 42:7 that is right as my servant Job **h.**
Ps 2:7 the Lord **h.** said unto me, Thou art
Ps 4:3 know that the Lord **h.** set apart him
Ps 5:4 thou art not a God that **h.** pleasure in
Ps 6:8 for the Lord **h.** heard the voice of my
Ps 6:9 The Lord **h.** heard my supplication;
Ps 7:12 he **h.** bent his bow, and made it ready.
Ps 7:13 He **h.** also prepared for him the
Ps 7:14 iniquity, and **h.** conceived mischief,
Ps 9:7 he **h.** prepared his throne for
Ps 10:6 He **h.** said in his heart, I shall not
Ps 10:11 He **h.** said in his heart, God
Ps 10:11 said in his heart, God **h.** forgotten:
Ps 10:13 he **h.** said in his heart, Thou wilt
Ps 13:6 because he **h.** dealt bountifully with
Ps 14:1 The fool **h.** said in his heart, There is
Ps 16:7 bless the Lord, who **h.** given me

Ps 18:20 of my hands **h.** he recompensed me
Ps 18:24 Therefore **h.** the Lord recompensed
Ps 18:35 and thy right hand **h.** holden me
Ps 18:35 and thy gentleness **h.** made me great
Ps 19:4 In them **h.** he set a tabernacle for the
Ps 22:24 For he **h.** not despised nor abhorred
Ps 22:24 neither **h.** he hid his face from him;
Ps 22:31 shall be born, that he **h.** done this.
Ps 24:2 For he **h.** founded it upon the seas.
Ps 24:4 He that **h.** clean hands, and a pure
Ps 24:4 who **h.** not lifted up his soul unto
Ps 28:6 because he **h.** heard the voice
Ps 31:21 for he **h.** shewed me his marvellous
Ps 33:12 and the people whom he **h.** chosen
Ps 35:8 let his net that he **h.** hid catch
Ps 35:21 Aha, aha, our eye **h.** seen it.
Ps 35:27 which **h.** pleasure in the prosperity
Ps 36:3 he **h.** left off to be wise, and to do
Ps 37:16 little that a righteous man **h.** is better
Ps 40:3 And he **h.** put a new song in my
Ps 41:9 which did eat of my bread, **h.** lifted up
Ps 44:15 and the shame of my face **h.** covered
Ps 45:2 therefore God **h.** blessed thee for ever
Ps 45:7 thy God, **h.** anointed thee with the oil
Ps 46:8 what desolations he **h.** made in the
Ps 50:1 even the Lord, **h.** spoken, and called
Ps 50:2 perfection of beauty, God **h.** shined.
Ps 53:1 The fool **h.** said in his heart, There is
Ps 53:5 for God **h.** scattered the bones of
Ps 53:5 because God **h.** despised them
Ps 54:7 For he **h.** delivered me out of all my
Ps 54:7 and mine eye **h.** seen his desire upon
Ps 55:5 and horror **h.** overwhelmed me
Ps 55:18 He **h.** delivered my soul in peace
Ps 55:20 He **h.** put forth his hands against
Ps 55:20 with him: he **h.** broken his covenant.
Ps 60:6 God **h.** spoken in his holiness;
Ps 62:11 God **h.** spoken once; twice have I
Ps 66:14 have uttered, and my mouth **h.** spoken,
Ps 66:16 I will declare what he **h.** done for my
Ps 66:19 But verily God **h.** heard me;
Ps 66:19 he **h.** attended to the voice of my
Ps 66:20 Blessed be God, which **h.** not turned
Ps 68:10 Thy congregation **h.** dwelt therein:
Ps 68:28 Thy God **h.** commanded thy strength:
Ps 69:7 borne reproach; shame **h.** covered my
Ps 69:9 zeal of thine house **h.** eaten me up;
Ps 69:20 Reproach **h.** broken my heart; and I
Ps 69:31 an ox or bullock that **h.** horns and
Ps 71:11 saying, God **h.** forsaken him:
Ps 72:12 poor also, and him that **h.** no helper.
Ps 74:3 all that the enemy **h.** done wickedly
Ps 74:18 that the enemy **h.** reproached, O Lord,
Ps 77:9 **H.** God forgotten to be gracious?
Ps 77:9 **h.** he in anger shut up his tender
Ps 78:4 his wonderful works that he **h.** done.
Ps 78:69 like the earth which he **h.** established
Ps 80:15 which thy right hand **h.** planted,
Ps 84:3 Yea, the sparrow **h.** found an house,
Ps 88:4 I am as a man that **h.** no strength:
Ps 91:14 Because he **h.** set his love upon me,
Ps 91:14 because he **h.** known my name
Ps 93:1 wherewith he **h.** girded himself: the
Ps 98:1 for he **h.** done marvellous things: his
Ps 98:1 his holy arm, **h.** gotten him the victory
Ps 98:2 The Lord **h.** made known his
Ps 98:2 his righteousness **h.** he openly shewed
Ps 98:3 He **h.** remembered his mercy and his
Ps 100:3 it is he that **h.** made us, and not we
Ps 101:5 him that **h.** an high look and a proud
Ps 102:19 For he **h.** looked down from the
Ps 103:10 He **h.** not dealt with us after our sins;
Ps 103:12 far **h.** he removed our transgressions
Ps 103:19 The Lord **h.** prepared his throne in
Ps 104:16 of Lebanon, which he **h.** planted;
Ps 105:5 his marvellous works that he **h.** done;
Ps 105:8 He **h.** remembered his covenant
Ps 107:2 whom he **h.** redeemed from the hand
Ps 107:16 For he **h.** broken the gates of brass,
Ps 108:7 God **h.** spoken in his holiness;
Ps 109:11 Let the extortioner catch all that he **h.**;
Ps 110:4 The Lord **h.** sworn, and will not
Ps 111:4 He **h.** made his wonderful works to be
Ps 111:5 He **h.** given meat unto them that fear
Ps 111:6 He **h.** shewed his people the power
Ps 111:9 he **h.** commanded his covenant
Ps 112:9 He **h.** dispersed, he **h.** given to the
Ps 115:3 God is in the heavens: he **h.** done
Ps 115:3 done whatsoever he **h.** pleased.
Ps 115:12 The Lord **h.** been mindful of us:
Ps 115:16 but the earth **h.** he given to the
Ps 116:1 I love the Lord, because he **h.** heard
Ps 116:2 Because he **h.** inclined his ear unto
Ps 116:7 for the Lord **h.** dealt bountifully with
Ps 118:18 The Lord **h.** chastened me sore:
Ps 118:18 but he **h.** not given me over unto
Ps 118:24 is the day which the Lord **h.** made;
Ps 118:27 God is the Lord, which **h.** shewed us
Ps 119:20 the longing that it **h.** unto thy
Ps 119:50 for thy word **h.** quickened me
Ps 119:53 Horror **h.** taken hold upon me because
Ps 119:139 My zeal **h.** consumed me, because
Ps 119:167 My soul **h.** kept thy testimonies;
Ps 120:6 My soul **h.** long dwelt with him that
Ps 124:6 who **h.** not given us as a prey to their
Ps 126:2 Lord **h.** done great things for them.
Ps 126:3 The Lord **h.** done great things for us;
Ps 127:5 Happy is the man that **h.** his quiver
Ps 129:4 he **h.** cut asunder the cords of the
Ps 132:11 The Lord **h.** sworn in truth unto
Ps 132:13 **h.** chosen Zion: he **h.** desired it for his
Ps 135:4 For the Lord **h.** chosen Jacob unto
Ps 136:24 And **h.** redeemed us from our
Ps 138:6 Lord be high, yet **h.** he respect unto
Ps 143:3 For the enemy **h.** persecuted my soul;
Ps 143:3 he **h.** smitten my life down to the
Ps 143:3 he **h.** made me to dwell in darkness,
Ps 146:5 Happy is he that **h.** the God of Jacob
Ps 147:13 For he **h.** strengthened the bars of thy
Ps 147:13 he **h.** blessed thy children within thee.
Ps 147:20 He **h.** not dealt so with any nation:
Ps 148:6 He **h.** also stablished them for ever
Ps 148:6 he **h.** made a decree which shall not
Ps 150:6 Let every thing that **h.** breath praise
Pr 3:19 The Lord by wisdom **h.** founded the
Pr 3:19 by understanding **h.** he established
Pr 7:20 He **h.** taken a bag of money with him,
Pr 7:26 For she **h.** cast down many wounded:
Pr 9:1 Wisdom **h.** builded her house,
Pr 9:1 she **h.** hewn out her seven pillars:
Pr 9:2 She **h.** killed her beasts;
Pr 9:2 she **h.** mingled her wine;
Pr 9:2 she **h.** also furnished her table.
Pr 9:3 She **h.** sent forth her maidens:
Pr 10:13 the lips of him that **h.** understanding
Pr 10:23 a man of understanding **h.** wisdom.
Pr 12:9 He that is despised, and **h.** a servant,
Pr 13:4 the sluggard desireth, and **h.** nothing:
Pr 13:7 maketh himself rich, yet **h.** nothing:
Pr 13:7 himself poor, yet **h.** great riches.
Pr 14:20 but the rich **h.** many friends.
Pr 14:21 but he that **h.** mercy on the poor,
Pr 14:31 but he that honoureth him **h.** mercy on
Pr 14:32 but the righteous **h.** hope in his death.
Pr 14:33 heart of him that **h.** understanding:
Pr 15:14 the heart of him that **h.** understanding
Pr 15:15 a merry heart **h.** a continual feast.
Pr 15:23 A man **h.** joy by the answer of his
Pr 16:4 The Lord **h.** made all things for
Pr 16:22 of life unto him that **h.** it. 1167
Pr 17:8 stone in the eyes of him that **h.** it: 1167
Pr 17:16 seeing he **h.** no heart to it?
Pr 17:20 He that **h.** a froward heart findeth no
Pr 17:20 and he that **h.** a perverse tongue
Pr 17:21 and the father of a fool **h.** no joy.
Pr 17:24 is before him that **h.** understanding;
Pr 17:27 He that **h.** knowledge spareth his
Pr 18:2 A fool **h.** no delight in understanding,
Pr 18:24 A man that **h.** friends must shew
Pr 19:17 He that **h.** pity upon the poor lendeth
Pr 19:17 that which he **h.** given will he pay
Pr 19:23 and he that **h.** it shall abide satisfied;
Pr 19:25 reprove one that **h.** understanding,
Pr 20:12 the Lord **h.** made even both of them.
Pr 22:9 He that **h.** a bountiful eye shall be
Pr 23:6 the bread of him that **h.** an evil eye,
Pr 23:29 Who **h.** woe? who **h.** sorrow?
Pr 23:29 who **h.** contentions? who **h.** babbling?
Pr 23:29 who **h.** wounds without cause?
Pr 23:29 who **h.** redness of eyes?
Pr 24:29 I will do so to him as he **h.** done to me:
Pr 25:8 thy neighbour **h.** put thee to shame.
Pr 25:28 He that **h.** no rule over his own
Pr 28:11 but the poor that **h.** understanding
Pr 28:22 He that hasteth to be rich **h.** an evil
Pr 30:4 Who **h.** ascended up into heaven, or
Pr 30:4 who **h.** gathered the winds in his fists?
Pr 30:4 who **h.** bound the waters in a garment?
Pr 30:4 who **h.** established all the ends of the
Pr 30:15 The horseleach **h.** two daughters,
Ec 1:3 What profit **h.** a man of all his labour
Ec 1:9 The thing that **h.** been, it is that which
Ec 1:10 it **h.** been already of old time.
Ec 1:13 this sore travail **h.** God given to the
Ec 2:12 even that which **h.** been already done.
Ec 2:21 yet to a man that **h.** not laboured
Ec 2:22 For what **h.** man of all his labour, 1933
Ec 2:22 he **h.** laboured under the sun?
Ec 3:9 What profit **h.** he that worketh in that
Ec 3:10 the travail, which God **h.** given to the
Ec 3:11 He **h.** made every thing beautiful in
Ec 3:11 also he **h.** set the world in their heart,
Ec 3:15 That which **h.** been is now; and
Ec 3:15 that which is to be **h.** already been;
Ec 3:19 so that a man **h.** no preeminence
Ec 4:3 both they, which **h.** not yet been,
Ec 4:3 who **h.** not seen the evil work that
Ec 4:8 yea, he **h.** neither child nor brother:
Ec 4:10 for he **h.** not another to help him up.
Ec 5:4 to pay it; for he **h.** no pleasure in fools:
Ec 5:16 so shall he go: and what profit **h.** he
Ec 5:16 he that **h.** laboured for the wind?
Ec 5:17 and he **h.** much sorrow and wrath
Ec 5:19 to whom God **h.** given riches and
Ec 5:19 and **h.** given him power to eat thereof,
Ec 6:2 A man to whom God **h.** given riches,
Ec 6:5 Moreover he **h.** not seen the sun,
Ec 6:5 this **h.** more rest than the other.
Ec 6:6 years twice told, yet **h.** he seen no
Ec 6:8 For what **h.** the wise more than the
Ec 6:8 what **h.** the poor, that knoweth to
Ec 6:10 That which **h.** been is named
Ec 7:13 straight, which he **h.** made crooked?
Ec 7:14 God also **h.** set the one over against
Ec 7:29 found, that God **h.** made man upright;
Ec 8:8 There is no man that **h.** power over the
Ec 8:8 neither **h.** he power in the day of
Ec 8:15 because a man **h.** no better thing
Ec 9:9 which he **h.** given thee under the sun,
Ec 10:20 and that which **h.** wings shall tell 1167
Ca 1:4 the king **h.** brought me into his
Ca 1:6 because the sun **h.** looked upon me:
Ca 3:8 every man **h.** his sword upon his
Ca 8:6 which **h.** a most vehement flame.
Ca 8:8 little sister, and she **h.** no breasts:
Isa 1:2 O earth: for the Lord **h.** spoken, I
Isa 1:12 who **h.** required this at your hand,
Isa 1:20 for the mouth of the Lord **h.** spoken it,
Isa 1:30 and as a garden that **h.** no water.
Isa 5:1 My wellbeloved **h.** a vineyard in a
Isa 5:14 Therefore hell **h.** enlarged herself,
Isa 5:25 and he **h.** stretched forth his hand
Isa 5:25 them, and **h.** smitten them:
Isa 6:7 and said, Lo, this **h.** touched thy lips;
Isa 8:18 children whom the Lord **h.** given me
Isa 9:2 death, upon them **h.** the light shined.
Isa 9:8 word into Jacob, and it **h.** lighted upon
Isa 10:10 As my hand **h.** found the kingdoms of
Isa 10:12 when the Lord **h.** performed his whole
Isa 10:14 And my hand **h.** found as a nest the
Isa 10:28 at Michmash he **h.** laid up his
Isa 12:5 the Lord; for he **h.** done excellent
Isa 14:4 and say, How **h.** the oppressor ceased!
Isa 14:5 The Lord **h.** broken the staff of the
Isa 14:9 it **h.** raised up from their thrones all
Isa 14:24 The Lord of hosts **h.** sworn, saying,
Isa 14:27 For the Lord of hosts **h.** purposed, and
Isa 14:32 That the Lord **h.** founded Zion,
Isa 16:13 the word that the Lord **h.** spoken
Isa 16:14 But now the Lord **h.** spoken, saying,
Isa 19:12 what the Lord of hosts **h.** purposed
Isa 19:14 The Lord **h.** mingled a perverse spirit
Isa 19:17 which he **h.** determined against it.
Isa 20:3 Like as my servant Isaiah **h.** walked
Isa 21:4 the night of my pleasure **h.** he turned
Isa 21:6 For thus **h.** the Lord said unto me, Go,
Isa 21:9 images of her gods he **h.** broken unto
Isa 21:16 For thus **h.** the Lord said unto me,
Isa 21:17 for the Lord God of Israel **h.** spoken it.
Isa 22:25 shall be cut off: for the Lord **h.** spoken
Isa 23:4 O Zidon: for the sea **h.** spoken,

Isa 23:8 Who **h.** taken this counsel against
Isa 23:9 The Lord of hosts **h.** purposed it, to
Isa 23:11 the Lord **h.** given a commandment
Isa 24:3 for the Lord **h.** spoken this word.
Isa 24:6 Therefore **h.** the curse devoured the
Isa 25:8 all the earth: for the Lord **h.** spoken it.
Isa 27:7 **H.** he smitten him, as he smote those
Isa 28:2 the Lord **h.** a mighty and strong one,
Isa 28:25 When he **h.** made plain the face
Isa 29:4 as of one that **h.** a familiar spirit,
Isa 29:8 he is faint, and his soul **h.** appetite:
Isa 29:10 For the Lord **h.** poured out upon you
Isa 29:10 of deep sleep, and **h.** closed your eyes:
Isa 29:10 your rulers, the seers **h.** he covered.
Isa 30:24 which **h.** been winnowed with the
Isa 30:33 it is prepared; he **h.** made it deep and
Isa 31:4 For thus **h.** the Lord spoken unto me,
Isa 33:5 he **h.** filled Zion with judgment and
Isa 33:8 he **h.** broken the covenant,
Isa 33:8 he **h.** despised the cities, he regardeth
Isa 33:14 fearfulness **h.** surprised the
Isa 34:2 he **h.** utterly destroyed them,
Isa 34:2 he **h.** delivered them to the slaughter
Isa 34:6 for the Lord **h.** a sacrifice in Bozrah.
Isa 34:16 for my mouth it **h.** commanded, and
Isa 34:16 his spirit it **h.** gathered them.
Isa 34:17 And he **h.** cast the lot for them, and
Isa 34:17 his hand **h.** divided it unto them by
Isa 36:7 whose altars Hezekiah **h.** taken away,
Isa 36:12 said, **H.** my master sent me to thy
Isa 36:12 **h.** he not sent me to the men that sit
Isa 36:18 **H.** any of the gods of the nations
Isa 37:4 his master **h.** sent to reproach the
Isa 37:4 which the Lord thy God **h.** heard:
Isa 37:17 which **h.** sent to reproach the living
Isa 37:22 the word which the Lord **h.** spoken
Isa 37:22 the daughter of Zion, **h.** despised thee,
Isa 37:22 the daughter of Jerusalem **h.** shaken
Isa 38:7 will do this thing that he **h.** spoken;
Isa 38:15 he **h.** both spoken unto me,
Isa 38:15 and himself **h.** done it: I shall go
Isa 40:2 for she **h.** received of the Lord's hand
Isa 40:5 for the mouth of the Lord **h.** spoken
Isa 40:12 Who **h.** measured the waters in the
Isa 40:13 Who **h.** directed the Spirit of the Lord,
Isa 40:13 or being his counsellor **h.** taught him?
Isa 40:20 impoverished that he **h.** no oblation
Isa 40:21 **h.** it not been told you from the
Isa 40:26 and behold who **h.** created these
Isa 41:4 Who **h.** wrought and done it, calling
Isa 41:20 the hand of the Lord **h.** done this, and
Isa 41:20 the Holy One of Israel **h.** created it.
Isa 41:26 Who **h.** declared from the beginning,
Isa 42:25 Therefore he **h.** poured upon him the
Isa 42:25 and it **h.** set him on fire round about,
Isa 43:27 Thy first father **h.** sinned, and thy
Isa 44:10 who **h.** formed a god, or molten a
Isa 44:18 for he **h.** shut their eyes, that they
Isa 44:20 a deceived heart **h.** turned him aside,
Isa 44:23 O ye heavens; for the Lord **h.** done it:
Isa 44:23 for the Lord **h.** redeemed Jacob, and
Isa 45:9 or thy work, He **h.** no hands?
Isa 45:18 he **h.** established it, he created it not
Isa 45:21 counsel together: who **h.** declared this
Isa 45:21 from ancient time. who **h.** told it
Isa 47:10 thy knowledge, it **h.** perverted thee;
Isa 48:5 Mine idol **h.** done them, and my
Isa 48:5 molten image, **h.** commanded
Isa 48:13 Mine hand also **h.** laid the foundation
Isa 48:13 and my right hand **h.** spanned the
Isa 48:14 which among them **h.** declared these
Isa 48:14 The Lord **h.** loved him: he will do
Isa 48:16 the Lord God, and his Spirit, **h.** sent
Isa 48:20 The Lord **h.** redeemed his servant
Isa 49:1 The Lord **h.** called me from the womb;
Isa 49:1 of my mother **h.** he made mention of
Isa 49:2 And he **h.** made my mouth like a sharp
Isa 49:2 in the shadow of his hand **h.** he hid
Isa 49:2 in his quiver **h.** he hid me;
Isa 49:10 for he that **h.** mercy on them shall
Isa 49:13 for the Lord **h.** comforted his people,
Isa 49:14 But Zion said, The Lord **h.** forsaken
Isa 49:14 and my Lord **h.** forgotten me.
Isa 49:21 Who **h.** begotten me these, seeing I
Isa 49:21 and who **h.** brought up these?
Isa 50:4 The Lord God **h.** given me the tongue
Isa 50:5 The Lord God **h.** opened mine ear,
Isa 50:10 walketh in darkness, and **h.** no light?
Isa 51:9 Art thou not it that **h.** cut Rahab,
Isa 51:10 Art thou not it which **h.** dried the sea,
Isa 51:10 that **h.** made the depths of the sea
Isa 51:13 that **h.** stretched forth the heavens,
Isa 51:18 all the sons whom she **h.** brought forth;
Isa 51:18 of all the sons that she **h.** brought up.
Isa 52:9 for the Lord **h.** comforted his people,
Isa 52:9 he **h.** redeemed Jerusalem.
Isa 52:10 The Lord **h.** made bare his holy arm
Isa 53:1 Who **h.** believed our report?
Isa 53:2 **h.** no form nor comeliness;
Isa 53:4 Surely he **h.** borne our griefs, and
Isa 53:6 and the Lord **h.** laid on him the
Isa 53:10 bruise him; he **h.** put him to grief:
Isa 53:12 because he **h.** poured out his soul
Isa 54:6 For the Lord **h.** called thee as a
Isa 54:10 saith the Lord that **h.** mercy on thee.
Isa 55:1 the waters, and he that **h.** no money;
Isa 55:5 Holy One of Israel; for he **h.** glorified
Isa 56:3 stranger, that **h.** joined himself to
Isa 56:3 The Lord **h.** utterly separated me
Isa 58:14 for the mouth of the Lord **h.** spoken it.
Isa 59:3 your tongue **h.** muttered perverseness.
Isa 60:9 because he **h.** glorified thee.
Isa 61:1 because the Lord **h.** anointed me to
Isa 61:1 he **h.** sent me to bind up the
Isa 61:9 the seed which the Lord **h.** blessed.
Isa 61:10 for he **h.** clothed me with the garments
Isa 61:10 he **h.** covered me with the robe of
Isa 62:8 The Lord **h.** sworn by his right hand,
Isa 62:11 Behold, the Lord **h.** proclaimed unto
Isa 63:7 to all that the Lord **h.** bestowed on us,
Isa 63:7 which he **h.** bestowed on them
Isa 64:4 by the ear, neither **h.** the eye seen,
Isa 64:4 beside thee, what he **h.** prepared for
Isa 65:20 nor an old man that **h.** not filled his
Isa 66:2 all those things **h.** mine hand made,
Isa 66:8 Who **h.** heard such a thing?
Isa 66:8 who **h.** seen such things?
Jer 2:11 **H.** a nation changed their gods,
Jer 2:30 your own sword **h.** devoured your
Jer 2:37 the Lord **h.** rejected thy confidences,
Jer 3:3 and there **h.** been no latter rain;
Jer 3:6 which backsliding Israel **h.** done?
Jer 3:6 and there **h.** played the harlot.
Jer 3:10 Judah **h.** not turned unto me with
Jer 3:11 backsliding Israel **h.** justified herself
Jer 3:24 For shame **h.** devoured the labour of
Jer 4:17 because she **h.** been rebellious against
Jer 4:27 For thus **h.** the Lord said, The whole
Jer 5:23 But this people **h.** a revolting and a
Jer 6:6 For thus **h.** the Lord of hosts said,
Jer 6:24 anguish **h.** taken hold of us, and pain,
Jer 6:30 because the Lord **h.** rejected them.
Jer 7:29 for the Lord **h.** rejected and forsaken
Jer 8:14 the Lord our God **h.** put us to silence,
Jer 8:21 astonishment **h.** taken hold on me.
Jer 9:12 whom the mouth of the Lord **h.** spoken,
Jer 10:12 He **h.** made the earth by his power,
Jer 10:12 he **h.** established the world by his
Jer 10:12 and **h.** stretched out the heavens by
Jer 11:15 What **h.** my beloved to do in mine
Jer 11:15 seeing she **h.** wrought lewdness
Jer 11:16 of a great tumult he **h.** kindled fire
Jer 11:17 that planted thee, **h.** pronounced evil
Jer 11:18 And the Lord **h.** given me knowledge
Jer 13:15 not proud: for the Lord **h.** spoken.
Jer 14:19 Judah? **h.** thy soul lothed Zion?
Jer 15:9 She that **h.** borne seven languisheth:
Jer 15:9 she **h.** given up the ghost;
Jer 15:9 she **h.** been ashamed and confounded:
Jer 16:10 Wherefore **h.** the Lord pronounced all
Jer 18:13 heathen, who **h.** heard such things:
Jer 18:13 of Israel **h.** done a very horrible thing.
Jer 18:15 Because my people **h.** forgotten me,
Jer 20:3 The Lord **h.** not called thy name
Jer 20:13 for he **h.** delivered the soul of the poor
Jer 22:8 Wherefore **h.** the Lord done thus unto
Jer 22:21 This **h.** been thy manner from thy
Jer 23:9 like a man whom wine **h.** overcome,
Jer 23:17 The Lord **h.** said, Ye shall have peace;
Jer 23:18 For who **h.** stood in the counsel of the
Jer 23:18 and **h.** perceived and heard his word?
Jer 23:18 who **h.** marked his word, and heard it?
Jer 23:28 The prophet that **h.** a dream, let him
Jer 23:28 a dream; and he that **h.** my word, let
Jer 23:35 What **h.** the Lord answered?
Jer 23:35 and, What **h.** the Lord spoken?
Jer 23:37 What **h.** the Lord answered thee?
Jer 23:37 and, What **h.** the Lord spoken?
Jer 25:3 the word of the Lord **h.** come unto me,
Jer 25:4 And the Lord **h.** sent unto you all
Jer 25:5 in the land that the Lord **h.** given
Jer 25:13 Jeremiah **h.** prophesied against all
Jer 25:31 for the Lord **h.** a controversy with the
Jer 25:36 for the Lord **h.** spoiled their pasture.
Jer 25:38 He **h.** forsaken his covert, as the lion:
Jer 26:11 for he **h.** prophesied against this city,
Jer 26:13 him of the evil that he **h.** pronounced
Jer 26:15 for of a truth the Lord **h.** sent me
Jer 26:16 for he **h.** spoken to us in the name of
Jer 27:13 as the Lord **h.** spoken against the
Jer 28:9 that the Lord **h.** truly sent him.
Jer 28:15 The Lord **h.** not sent thee; but thou
Jer 29:15 The Lord **h.** raised us up prophets in
Jer 29:26 The Lord **h.** made thee priest in the
Jer 29:31 Because that Shemaiah **h.** prophesied
Jer 29:32 because he **h.** taught rebellion
Jer 31:3 The Lord **h.** appeared of old unto me,
Jer 31:11 For the Lord **h.** redeemed Jacob,
Jer 31:22 for the Lord **h.** created a new thing in
Jer 32:31 For this city **h.** been to me as a
Jer 33:24 families which the Lord **h.** chosen,
Jer 33:24 he **h.** even cast them off?
Jer 34:14 an Hebrew, which **h.** been sold unto
Jer 34:14 and when he **h.** served thee six years,
Jer 35:8 our father in all that he **h.** charged us,
Jer 35:16 but this people **h.** not hearkened unto
Jer 35:18 unto all that he **h.** commanded you:
Jer 36:7 the Lord **h.** pronounced against this
Jer 36:28 Jehoiakim the king of Judah **h.** burned.
Jer 38:21 the word that the Lord **h.** shewed me:
Jer 40:2 The Lord thy God **h.** pronounced this
Jer 40:3 Now the Lord **h.** brought it, and done
Jer 40:3 done according as he **h.** said:
Jer 40:5 the king of Babylon **h.** made governor
Jer 40:14 king of the Ammonites **h.** sent Ishmael
Jer 42:18 anger and my fury **h.** been poured
Jer 42:19 The Lord **h.** said concerning you,
Jer 42:21 for the which he **h.** sent me unto you.
Jer 43:2 the Lord our God **h.** not sent thee to
Jer 45:3 for the Lord **h.** added grief to my
Jer 46:10 God of hosts **h.** a sacrifice in the north
Jer 46:12 and thy cry **h.** filled the land:
Jer 46:12 for the mighty man **h.** stumbled
Jer 46:17 he **h.** passed the time appointed.
Jer 47:7 seeing the Lord **h.** given it a charge
Jer 47:7 the sea shore? there **h.** he appointed
Jer 48:8 be destroyed, as the Lord **h.** spoken.
Jer 48:11 and he **h.** settled on his lees,
Jer 48:11 and **h.** not been emptied from vessel to
Jer 48:11 neither **h.** he gone into captivity:
Jer 48:11 Moab **h.** been at ease from his youth,
Jer 48:36 because the riches that he **h.** gotten
Jer 48:39 how **h.** Moab turned the back with
Jer 48:42 because he **h.** magnified himself
Jer 49:1 **H.** Israel no sons? **h.** he no heir?
Jer 49:16 Thy terribleness **h.** deceived thee,
Jer 49:20 that he **h.** taken against Edom;
Jer 49:20 and his purposes, that he **h.** purposed
Jer 49:24 to flee, and fear **h.** seized on her:
Jer 49:30 king of Babylon **h.** taken counsel
Jer 49:30 you, and **h.** conceived a purpose
Jer 50:6 My people **h.** been lost sheep:
Jer 50:14 for she **h.** sinned against the Lord.
Jer 50:15 she **h.** given her hand: her foundations
Jer 50:15 as she **h.** done, do unto her.
Jer 50:17 king of Assyria **h.** devoured him;
Jer 50:17 king of Babylon **h.** broken his bones.
Jer 50:25 The Lord **h.** opened his armoury,
Jer 50:25 and **h.** brought forth the weapons
Jer 50:29 according to all that she **h.** done, do
Jer 50:29 she **h.** been proud against the Lord,
Jer 50:43 The king of Babylon **h.** heard the
Jer 50:45 the Lord, that he **h.** taken against
Jer 50:45 and his purposes, that he **h.** purposed
Jer 51:5 For Israel **h.** not been forsaken,
Jer 51:7 Babylon **h.** been a golden cup in the
Jer 51:10 The Lord **h.** brought forth our
Jer 51:11 the Lord **h.** raised up the spirit of the
Jer 51:12 for the Lord **h.** both devised and done

Jer	51:14	The Lord of hosts **h.** sworn by himself,
Jer	51:15	He **h.** made the earth by his power,
Jer	51:15	he **h.** established the world by his
Jer	51:15	and **h.** stretched out the heaven by his
Jer	51:30	their might **h.** failed; they became as
Jer	51:34	the king of Babylon **h.** devoured me,
Jer	51:34	he **h.** crushed me,
Jer	51:34	he **h.** made me an empty vessel,
Jer	51:34	he **h.** swallowed me up like a dragon,
Jer	51:34	he **h.** filled his belly with my delicates.
Jer	51:34	he **h.** cast me out.
Jer	51:44	that which he **h.** swallowed up:
Jer	51:49	As Babylon **h.** caused the slain of
Jer	51:51	shame **h.** covered our faces:
Jer	51:55	Because the Lord **h.** spoiled Babylon,
La	1:2	among all her lovers she **h.** none to
La	1:5	for the Lord **h.** afflicted her for the
La	1:8	Jerusalem **h.** grievously sinned;
La	1:9	for the enemy **h.** magnified himself.
La	1:10	The adversary **h.** spread out his hand
La	1:10	she **h.** seen that the heathen entered
La	1:12	the Lord **h.** afflicted me in the day
La	1:13	From above **h.** he sent fire into my
La	1:13	he **h.** spread a net for my feet,
La	1:13	he **h.** turned me back:
La	1:13	he **h.** made me desolate and faint all
La	1:14	he **h.** made my strength to fall,
La	1:14	the Lord **h.** delivered me into their
La	1:15	The Lord **h.** trodden under foot all my
La	1:15	he **h.** called an assembly against me
La	1:15	the Lord **h.** trodden the virgin, the
La	1:17	Lord **h.** commanded concerning Jacob,
La	2:1	How **h.** the Lord covered the daughter
La	2:2	The Lord **h.** swallowed up all the
La	2:2	of Jacob, and **h.** not pitied:
La	2:2	he **h.** thrown down in his wrath the
La	2:2	he **h.** brought them down to the ground:
La	2:2	he **h.** polluted the kingdom and
La	2:3	He **h.** cut off in his fierce anger all the
La	2:3	he **h.** drawn back his right hand
La	2:4	He **h.** bent his bow like an enemy:
La	2:5	an enemy: he **h.** swallowed up Israel,
La	2:5	he **h.** swallowed up all her palaces:
La	2:5	he **h.** destroyed his strong holds,
La	2:5	and **h.** increased in the daughter of
La	2:6	and he **h.** violently taken away his
La	2:6	he **h.** destroyed his places of the
La	2:6	the Lord **h.** caused the solemn feasts
La	2:6	and **h.** despised in the indignation of
La	2:7	The Lord **h.** cast off his altar,
La	2:7	he **h.** abhorred his sanctuary,
La	2:7	he **h.** given up into the hand of the
La	2:8	The Lord **h.** purposed to destroy the
La	2:8	he **h.** stretched out a line,
La	2:8	he **h.** not withdrawn his hand from
La	2:9	he **h.** destroyed and broken her bars:
La	2:17	The Lord **h.** done that which he had
La	2:17	he **h.** fulfilled his word that he had
La	2:17	he **h.** thrown down, and **h.** not pitied:
La	2:17	and he **h.** caused thine enemy to
La	2:17	he **h.** set up the horn of thine
La	2:22	up **h.** mine enemy consumed.
La	3:1	I am the man that **h.** seen affliction by
La	3:2	He **h.** led me, and brought me into
La	3:4	My flesh and my skin **h.** he made old:
La	3:4	he **h.** broken my bones.
La	3:5	He **h.** builded against me, and
La	3:6	He **h.** set me in dark places,
La	3:7	He **h.** hedged me about, that I cannot
La	3:7	he **h.** made my chain heavy.
La	3:9	He **h.** inclosed my ways with hewn
La	3:9	he **h.** made my paths crooked.
La	3:11	He **h.** turned aside my ways,
La	3:11	he **h.** made me desolate.
La	3:12	He **h.** bent his bow, and set me as
La	3:13	He **h.** caused the arrows of his quiver
La	3:15	He **h.** filled me with bitterness,
La	3:15	he **h.** made me drunken with
La	3:16	He **h.** also broken my teeth with gravel
La	3:16	he **h.** covered me with ashes.
La	3:20	My soul **h.** them still in remembrance,
La	3:28	because he **h.** borne it upon him.
La	4:11	The Lord **h.** accomplished his fury;
La	4:11	he **h.** poured out his fierce anger,
La	4:11	and **h.** kindled a fire in Zion,
La	4:11	and it **h.** devoured the foundations
La	4:16	The anger of the Lord **h.** divided them;
Eze	2:3	to a rebellious nation that **h.** rebelled
Eze	2:5	that there **h.** been a prophet
Eze	3:20	his righteousness which he **h.** done
Eze	4:14	behold, my soul **h.** not been polluted:
Eze	5:6	And she **h.** changed my judgments
Eze	6:9	whorish heart, which **h.** departed
Eze	7:10	the rod **h.** blossomed, pride **h.** budded.
Eze	8:12	not; the Lord **h.** forsaken the earth.
Eze	9:9	The Lord **h.** forsaken the earth, and
Eze	12:9	**h.** not the house of Israel...said
Eze	13:6	and the Lord **h.** not sent them:
Eze	14:9	be deceived when he **h.** spoken a
Eze	15:5	when the fire **h.** devoured it, and it is
Eze	16:48	Sodom thy sister **h.** not done, she nor
Eze	16:51	Neither **h.** Samaria committed half
Eze	17:12	come to Jerusalem, and **h.** taken the
Eze	17:13	And **h.** taken of the king's seed,
Eze	17:13	and **h.** taken an oath of him:
Eze	17:13	he **h.** also taken the mighty of the
Eze	17:18	given his hand, and **h.** done all these
Eze	17:19	surely mine oath that he **h.** despised,
Eze	17:19	and my covenant that he **h.** broken,
Eze	17:20	his trespass that he **h.** trespassed
Eze	18:6	And **h.** not eaten upon the mountains,
Eze	18:6	neither **h.** lifted up his eyes to the idols
Eze	18:6	neither **h.** defiled his neighbour's wife
Eze	18:6	neither **h.** come near to a menstruous
Eze	18:7	And **h.** not oppressed any,
Eze	18:7	but **h.** restored to the debtor his
Eze	18:7	**h.** spoiled none by violence,
Eze	18:7	**h.** given his bread to the hungry,
Eze	18:7	and **h.** covered the naked with a
Eze	18:8	He that **h.** not given forth upon usury,
Eze	18:8	neither **h.** taken any increase,
Eze	18:8	that **h.** withdrawn his hand from
Eze	18:8	**h.** executed true judgment between
Eze	18:9	**H.** walked in my statutes,
Eze	18:9	and **h.** kept my judgments, to deal
Eze	18:11	but even **h.** eaten upon the mountains,
Eze	18:12	**H.** oppressed the poor and needy,
Eze	18:12	**h.** spoiled by violence,
Eze	18:12	**h.** not restored the pledge, and
Eze	18:12	**h.** not lifted up his eyes to the idols
Eze	18:12	**h.** committed abomination,
Eze	18:13	**H.** given forth upon usury,
Eze	18:13	and **h.** taken increase:
Eze	18:13	he **h.** done all these abominations;
Eze	18:14	all his father's sins which he **h.** done,
Eze	18:15	That **h.** not eaten upon the mountains,
Eze	18:15	neither **h.** lifted up his eyes to the idols
Eze	18:15	**h.** not defiled his neighbour's wife,
Eze	18:16	Neither **h.** oppressed any,
Eze	18:16	**h.** not withholden the pledge,
Eze	18:16	neither **h.** spoiled by violence,
Eze	18:16	but **h.** given his bread to the hungry,
Eze	18:16	**h.** covered the naked with a garment,
Eze	18:17	That **h.** taken off his hand from the
Eze	18:17	that **h.** not received usury nor increase,
Eze	18:17	**h.** executed my judgments,
Eze	18:17	**h.** walked in my statutes;
Eze	18:19	When the son **h.** done that which is
Eze	18:19	and right, and **h.** kept all my statutes,
Eze	18:19	and **h.** done them, he shall surely live.
Eze	18:21	from all his sins that he **h.** committed,
Eze	18:22	transgressions that he **h.** committed,
Eze	18:22	in his righteousness that he **h.** done
Eze	18:24	righteousness that he **h.** done shall not
Eze	18:24	in his trespass that he **h.** trespassed,
Eze	18:24	and in his sin that he **h.** sinned,
Eze	18:26	for his iniquity that he **h.** done shall
Eze	18:27	his wickedness that he **h.** committed,
Eze	18:28	transgressions that he **h.** committed,
Eze	19:14	her branches, which **h.** devoured her
Eze	19:14	so that she **h.** no strong rod to be a
Eze	21:11	And he **h.** given it to be furbished,
Eze	22:11	And one **h.** committed abomination
Eze	22:11	and another **h.** lewdly defiled his
Eze	22:11	and another in thee **h.** humbled his
Eze	22:13	thy blood which **h.** been in the midst
Eze	22:28	God, when the Lord **h.** not spoken.
Eze	24:12	She **h.** wearied herself with lies,
Eze	24:24	according to all that he **h.** done shall
Eze	25:12	Because that Edom **h.** dealt against
Eze	25:12	and **h.** greatly offended, and revenged
Eze	26:2	because that Tyrus **h.** said against
Eze	27:26	east wind **h.** broken thee in the midst
Eze	29:3	which **h.** said, My river is mine own,
Eze	29:9	because he **h.** said, The river is mine,
Eze	31:10	and he **h.** shot up his top among the
Eze	33:13	for his iniquity that he **h.** committed,
Eze	33:16	sins that he **h.** committed shall be
Eze	33:16	he **h.** done that which is lawful and
Eze	33:32	song of one that **h.** a pleasant voice,
Eze	33:33	a prophet **h.** been among them
Eze	36:2	Because the enemy **h.** said against
Eze	44:2	the God of Israel, **h.** entered in by it,
Eze	44:25	or for sister that **h.** had no husband,
Da	1:10	who **h.** appointed your meat and your
Da	2:27	secret which the king **h.** demanded
Da	2:37	for the God of heaven **h.** given thee a
Da	2:38	fowls of the heaven **h.** he given into
Da	2:38	hand, and **h.** made thee ruler over
Da	2:45	the great God **h.** made known to the
Da	3:5	Nebuchadnezzar the king **h.** set up;
Da	3:28	who **h.** sent his angel, and delivered
Da	4:2	that the high God **h.** wrought toward
Da	5:26	God **h.** numbered thy kingdom, and
Da	6:22	My God **h.** sent his angel, and
Da	6:22	**h.** shut the lions' mouths,
Da	6:27	who **h.** delivered Daniel from the
Da	9:12	And he **h.** confirmed his words, which
Da	9:12	the whole heaven **h.** not been done
Da	9:12	as **h.** been done upon Jerusalem.
Da	9:14	Therefore **h.** the Lord watched upon
Da	11:12	And when he **h.** taken away the
Ho	1:2	for the land **h.** committed great
Ho	2:5	For their mother **h.** played the harlot:
Ho	2:5	conceived them **h.** done shamefully:
Ho	2:12	whereof she **h.** said, These are my
Ho	4:1	for the Lord **h.** a controversy with the
Ho	4:12	for the spirit of whoredoms **h.** caused
Ho	4:19	The wind **h.** bound her up in her
Ho	5:6	he **h.** withdrawn himself from them.
Ho	6:1	for he **h.** torn, and he will heal us;
Ho	6:1	he **h.** smitten, and he will bind us up.
Ho	6:11	Also, O Judah, he **h.** sent an harvest
Ho	7:4	after he **h.** kneaded the dough, until
Ho	7:8	Ephraim, he **h.** mixed himself among
Ho	7:12	them, as their congregation **h.** heard.
Ho	8:3	Israel **h.** cast off the thing that is good:
Ho	8:5	Thy calf, O Samaria, **h.** cast thee off;
Ho	8:7	it **h.** no stalk: the bud shall yield no
Ho	8:9	alone by himself: Ephraim **h.** hired
Ho	8:11	Because Ephraim **h.** made many altars
Ho	8:14	For Israel **h.** forgotten his Maker,
Ho	8:14	and Judah **h.** multiplied fenced cities:
Ho	10:1	multitude of his fruit he **h.** increased
Ho	12:2	The Lord **h.** also a controversy with
Ho	13:16	for she **h.** rebelled against her God:
Joe	1:2	**H.** this been in your days, or
Joe	1:4	That which the palmerworm **h.** left
Joe	1:4	**h.** the locust eaten; and that
Joe	1:4	and that which the locust **h.** left
Joe	1:4	left **h.** the cankerworm eaten;
Joe	1:4	and that which the cankerworm **h.** left
Joe	1:4	left **h.** the caterpiller eaten.
Joe	1:6	and he **h.** the cheek teeth of a great
Joe	1:7	He **h.** laid my vine waste, and barked
Joe	1:7	he **h.** made it clean bare, and cast it
Joe	1:19	for the fire **h.** devoured the pastures
Joe	1:19	and the flame **h.** burned all the trees
Joe	1:20	and the fire **h.** devoured the pastures
Joe	2:2	there **h.** not been ever the like,
Joe	2:20	because he **h.** done great things.
Joe	2:23	for he **h.** given you the former rain
Joe	2:25	you the years that the locust **h.** eaten,
Joe	2:26	that **h.** dealt wondrously with you:
Joe	2:32	as the Lord **h.** said, and in the
Joe	3:8	people far off: for the Lord **h.** spoken
Am	3:1	word that the Lord **h.** spoken against
Am	3:4	when he **h.** no prey? will a young lion
Am	3:6	evil in a city, and the Lord **h.** not done
Am	3:8	The lion **h.** roared, who will not fear?
Am	3:8	the Lord God **h.** spoken, who can but
Am	4:2	The Lord God **h.** sworn by his holiness,
Am	6:8	The Lord God **h.** sworn by himself,
Am	7:1,4	Thus **h.** the Lord God shewed unto
Am	7:10	Amon **h.** conspired against thee in
Am	8:1	Thus **h.** the Lord God shewed unto
Am	8:7	The Lord **h.** sworn by the excellency
Am	9:6	and **h.** founded his troop in the
Ob	3	The pride of thine heart **h.** deceived

Ob	18	house of Esau; for the Lord h. spoken	
Jon	1:9	which h. made the sea and the dry	
Mic	2:4	he h. changed the portion of my	
Mic	2:4	how h. he removed it from me!	
Mic	2:4	turning away he h. divided our fields	
Mic	4:4	mouth of the Lord of hosts h. spoken	
Mic	5:1	daughter of troops: he h. laid siege	
Mic	5:3	which travaileth h. brought forth:	
Mic	6:2	for the Lord h. a controversy with his	
Mic	6:8	He h. shewed thee, O man, what is	
Mic	6:9	ye the rod, and who h. appointed it.	
Na	1:3	the Lord h. his way in the whirlwind	
Na	1:14	the Lord h. given a commandment	
Na	2:2	For the Lord h. turned away the	
Na	3:19	whom h. not thy wickedness passed	
Hab	2:18	that the maker thereof h. graven it;	
Zep	1:7	for the Lord h. prepared a sacrifice,	
Zep	1:7	he h. bid his guests.	
Zep	3:15	Lord h. taken away thy judgments,	
Zep	3:15	he h. cast out thine enemy:	
Hag	2:19	the olive tree, h. not brought forth:	
Zec	1:2	The Lord h. been sore displeased	
Zec	1:6	according to our doings, so h. he dealt	
Zec	1:10	they whom the Lord h. sent to walk to	
Zec	2:8	After the glory h. he sent me unto the	
Zec	2:9	that the Lord of hosts h. sent me.	
Zec	2:11	the Lord of hosts h. sent me unto thee.	
Zec	3:2	the Lord that h. chosen Jerusalem	
Zec	4:9	the Lord of hosts h. sent me unto you.	
Zec	4:10	For who h. despised the day of small	
Zec	6:15	the Lord of hosts h. sent me unto you.	
Zec	7:7	words which the Lord h. cried by the	
Zec	7:12	which the Lord of hosts h. sent in his	
Zec	10:3	the Lord of hosts h. visited his flock	
Zec	10:3	and h. made them as his goodly horse	
Zec	13:4	of his vision, when he h. prophesied;	
Mal	1:4	against whom the Lord h. indignation	
Mal	1:9	this h. been by your means: will	
Mal	1:14	the deceiver, which h. in his flock a	
Mal	2:10	all one father? h. not one God created	
Mal	2:11	Judah h. dealt treacherously, and an	
Mal	2:11	Judah h. profaned the holiness of the	
Mal	2:11	and h. married the daughter of a	
Mal	2:14	Because the Lord h. been witness	
Mt	3:7	who h. warned you to flee from the	
Mt	5:23	**that thy brother h. ought against**	2192
Mt	5:28	**to lust after her h. committed**	
Mt	5:31	**It h. been said, Whosoever shall**	
Mt	5:33	**ye have heard that it h. been said**	
Mt	5:38,	**43 Ye have heard that it h. been**	
Mt	8:20	**Son of man h. not where to lay**	2192
Mt	9:6	**the Son of man h. power on earth.**	2192
Mt	9:22	**thy faith h. made thee whole.**	
Mt	11:11	**born of women there h. not risen**	
Mt	11:15	**He that h. ears to hear, let him**	2192
Mt	11:18	**and they say, He h. a devil.**	2192
Mt	13:9	**Who h. ears to hear, let him hear.**	2192
Mt	13:12	**For whosoever h., to him shall be**	2192
Mt	13:12	**but whosoever h. not, from him**	2192
Mt	13:12	**taken away even that he h.**	2192
Mt	13:21	**Yet h. he not root in himself, but**	2192
Mt	13:27	**from whence then h. it tares?**	2192
Mt	13:28	**unto them, An enemy h. done this**	
Mt	13:43	**Who h. ears to hear, let him hear.**	2192
Mt	13:44	**the which when a man h. found,**	
Mt	13:44	**goeth and selleth all that he h.,**	2192
Mt	13:54	Whence h. this man this wisdom,	
Mt	13:56	Whence then h. this man all these	
Mt	15:13	**my heavenly Father h. not planted,**	
Mt	16:17	**flesh and blood h. not revealed it**	
Mt	19:6	**What therefore God h. joined,**	
Mt	19:29	**every one that h. forsaken houses,**	
Mt	20:7	**Because no man h. hired us.**	
Mt	21:3	**ye shall say, The Lord h. need of**	2192
Mt	24:45	**his lord h. made ruler over his**	
Mt	25:28	**unto him which h. ten talents.**	2192
Mt	25:29	**every one that h. shall be given,**	2192
Mt	25:29	**from him that h. not shall be**	2192
Mt	25:29	**taken away even that which he h.**	2192
Mt	26:10	**she h. wrought a good work upon**	
Mt	26:12	**For in that she h. poured this**	
Mt	26:13	**that this woman h. done, be told**	
Mt	26:65	saying, He h. spoken blasphemy;	
Mt	27:23	Why, what evil h. he done?	
Mk	2:10	**the Son of man h. power on earth.**	2192
Mk	3:22	He h. Beelzebub, and by the prince	2192
Mk	3:26	he cannot stand, but h. an end	2192
Mk	3:29	**Holy Ghost h. never forgiveness**	2192
Mk	3:30	they said, He h. an unclean spirit.	2192
Mk	4:9	**He that h. ears to hear, let him**	2192
Mk	4:25	**he that h., to him shall be given:**	2192
Mk	4:25	**and he that h. not, from him shall**	2192
Mk	4:25	**be taken even that which he h.**	2192
Mk	5:19	**things the Lord h. done for thee.**	
Mk	5:19	**and h. had compassion on thee**	
Mk	5:34	**thy faith h. made thee whole;**	
Mk	6:2	From whence h. this man these	
Mk	7:6	**Well h. Esaias prophesied of you**	
Mk	7:37	He h. done all things well: he maketh	
Mk	9:17	my son, which h. a dumb spirit;	2192
Mk	9:22	And ofttimes it h. cast him into the	
Mk	10:9	**What therefore God h. joined**	
Mk	10:29	**There is no man that h. left house,**	
Mk	10:52	**thy faith h. made thee whole.**	
Mk	11:3	**ye that the Lord h. need of him;**	2192
Mk	12:43	**this poor widow h. cast more in,**	
Mk	13:20	**the elect's sake, whom he h. chosen,**	
Mk	13:20	**he h. shortened the days.**	
Mk	14:6	**she h. wrought a good work on me**	
Mk	14:8	**She h. done what she could: she is**	
Mk	14:9	**this also that she h. done shall be**	
Mk	15:14	Why, what evil h. he done?	
Lu	1:25	Thus h. the Lord dealt with me	
Lu	1:36	she h. also conceived a son in her old	
Lu	1:47	And my spirit h. rejoiced in God my	
Lu	1:48	For he h. rearded the low estate of	
Lu	1:49	he that is mighty h. done to me great	
Lu	1:51	He h. shewed strength with his arm;	
Lu	1:51	he h. scattered the proud in the	
Lu	1:52	He h. put down the mighty from	
Lu	1:53	He h. filled the hungry with good	
Lu	1:53	and the rich he h. sent empty away.	
Lu	1:54	He h. holpen his servant Israel,	
Lu	1:68	for he h. visited and redeemed his	
Lu	1:69	And h. raised up an horn of salvation	
Lu	1:78	the dayspring from on high h. visited	
Lu	2:15	the Lord h. made known unto us.	
Lu	3:7	who h. warned you to flee from the	
Lu	3:11	He that h. two coats, let him	2192
Lu	3:11	impart to him that h. none;	2192
Lu	3:11	and he that h. meat, let him do	2192
Lu	4:18	**he h. anointed me to preach**	
Lu	4:18	**h. sent me to heal ... brokenhearted,**	
Lu	5:24	**Son of man h. power upon earth**	2192
Lu	7:5	and he h. built us a synagogue.	
Lu	7:16	That God h. visited his people.	
Lu	7:20	they said, John Baptist h. sent us unto	
Lu	7:33	**wine; and ye say, He h. a devil.**	2192
Lu	7:44	**she h. washed my feet with tears,**	
Lu	7:45	**time I came in h. not ceased to**	
Lu	7:46	**this woman h. anointed my feet**	
Lu	7:50	**Thy faith h. saved thee; go in peace**	
Lu	8:8	**He that h. ears to hear, let him**	2192
Lu	8:16	**No man, when he h. lighted a**	
Lu	8:18	**whosoever h., to him shall be**	2192
Lu	8:18	**and whosoever h. not from him**	2192
Lu	8:39	**great things God h. done unto thee.**	
Lu	8:46	said, Somebody h. touched me:	
Lu	8:48	**thy faith h. made thee whole;**	
Lu	9:58	**the Son of man h. not where to**	2192
Lu	10:40	that my sister h. left me to serve	
Lu	10:42	**and Mary h. chosen that good part,**	
Lu	11:33	**man, when he h. lighted a candle,**	
Lu	12:5	**Fear him, which after he h. killed**	
Lu	12:5	**h. power to cast into hell;**	2192
Lu	12:44	**make him ruler over all that he h.**	5224
Lu	13:16	**of Abraham, whom Satan h. bound,**	
Lu	13:25	**is risen up, and h. shut to the door,**	
Lu	14:29	**after he h. laid the foundation,**	
Lu	14:33	**that forsaketh not all that he h.,**	5224
Lu	14:35	**He that h. ears to hear, let him**	2192
Lu	15:5	**when he h. found it, he layeth it**	
Lu	15:9	**when she h. found it, she calleth**	
Lu	15:27	**and thy father h. killed the fatted**	
Lu	15:27	**because he h. received him safe and**	
Lu	15:30	**which h. devoured thy living with**	
Lu	17:19	**way: thy faith h. made thee whole.**	
Lu	18:29	**man that h. left house, or parents,**	
Lu	18:42	**thy sight: thy faith h. saved thee**	
Lu	19:16	**thy pound h. gained ten pounds.**	
Lu	19:18	**thy pound h. gained five pounds.**	
Lu	19:24	**give it to him that h. ten pounds**	2192
Lu	19:25	**unto him, Lord, he h. ten pounds.**	2192
Lu	19:26	**every one which h. shall be given;**	2192
Lu	19:26	**from him that h. not, even that**	2192
Lu	19:26	**he h. shall be taken away from**	2192
Lu	19:31	**Because the Lord h. need of him**	2192
Lu	19:34	they said, The Lord h. need of him.	2192
Lu	20:24	**image and superscription h. it?**	2192
Lu	21:3	**this poor widow h. cast in more than**	
Lu	21:4	**of her penury h. cast in all the**	
Lu	22:29	**as my Father h. appointed unto me;**	
Lu	22:31	**behold, Satan h. desired to have you,**	
Lu	22:36	**he that h. a purse, let him take it,**	2192
Lu	22:36	**his scrip: and he that h. no sword,**	2192
Lu	23:22	Why, what evil h. he done?	
Lu	23:41	but this man h. done nothing amiss.	
Lu	24:34	is risen indeed, and h. appeared to	
Lu	24:39	**for a spirit h. not flesh and bones,**	2192
Joh	1:18	No man h. seen God at any time;	
Joh	1:18	of the Father, he h. declared him.	
Joh	2:17	zeal of thine house h. eaten me up.	
Joh	3:13	**And no man h. ascended up to heaven.**	
Joh	3:18	**because he h. not believed in the**	
Joh	3:29	He that h. the bride is the	2192
Joh	3:32	And what he h. seen and heard,	
Joh	3:33	He that h. received his testimony	
Joh	3:33	h. set to his seal that God is true.	
Joh	3:34	For he whom God h. sent speaketh	
Joh	3:35	and h. given all things into his hand.	
Joh	3:36	believeth on the Son h. everlasting	2192
Joh	4:33	H. any man brought him ought to	
Joh	4:44	a prophet h. no honour in his own	2192
Joh	5:22	**judgeth no man, but h. committed**	
Joh	5:23	**not the Father which h. sent him.**	
Joh	5:24	**him that sent me, h. everlasting**	2192
Joh	5:26	**For as the Father h. life in**	2192
Joh	5:26	**so h. he given to the Son to have**	
Joh	5:27	**And h. given him authority to**	
Joh	5:30	**will of the Father which h. sent me.**	
Joh	5:36	**the Father h. given me to finish,**	
Joh	5:36	**of me, that the Father h. sent me.**	
Joh	5:37	**the Father himself, which h. sent**	
Joh	5:37	**h. borne witness of me.**	
Joh	5:38	**whom he h. sent, him ye believe**	
Joh	6:9	here, which h. five barley loaves,	2192
Joh	6:27	**for him h. God the Father sealed.**	
Joh	6:29	**ye believe on him whom he h. sent.**	
Joh	6:39	**the Father's will which h. sent me,**	
Joh	6:39	**that of all which he h. given me**	
Joh	6:44	**except the Father which h. sent me.**	
Joh	6:45	**Every man therefore that h. heard,**	
Joh	6:45	**h. learned of the Father, cometh**	
Joh	6:46	**Not that any man h. seen the Father,**	
Joh	6:46	**he which is of God, he h. seen the**	
Joh	6:47	**believeth on me h. everlasting**	2192
Joh	6:54	**and drinketh my blood, h. eternal.**	2192
Joh	6:57	**As the living Father h. sent me,**	
Joh	7:29	**I am from him, and he h. sent me.**	
Joh	7:31	than these which this man h. done?	
Joh	7:38	**on me as the scripture h. said,**	
Joh	7:42	**H. not the scripture said, That Christ**	
Joh	8:10	**accusers? h. no man condemned**	
Joh	8:28	**but as my Father h. taught me, I**	
Joh	8:29	**Father h. not left me alone; for I**	
Joh	8:37	**because my word h. no place in you.**	
Joh	8:40	**a man that h. told you the truth,**	
Joh	9:3	**Neither h. this man sinned, nor his**	
Joh	9:17	that he h. opened thine eyes?	
Joh	9:21	or who h. opened his eyes, we know	
Joh	9:30	whence he is, and yet he h. opened	
Joh	10:20	He h. a devil, and is mad;	2192
Joh	10:21	not the words of him that h. a devil.	
Joh	10:36	**whom the Father h. sanctified, and**	
Joh	11:39	for he h. been dead four days.	
Joh	12:7	**the day of my burying h. she kept**	
Joh	12:38	Lord, who h. believed our report?	
Joh	12:38	and to whom h. the arm of the Lord	
Joh	12:40	He h. blinded their eyes, and	
Joh	12:48	**not my words, h. one that judgeth**	2192
Joh	13:18	**eateth bread with me h. lifted up**	
Joh	14:9	**Philip? he that h. seen me**	
Joh	14:9	**seen me h. seen the Father;**	
Joh	14:21	**He that h. my commandments,**	2192
Joh	14:30	**of this world cometh, and h.**	2192
Joh	15:9	**As the Father h. loved me, so have**	
Joh	15:13	**Greater love h. no man than this,**	2192
Joh	16:6	**you, sorrow h. filled your heart.**	
Joh	16:15	**All things that the Father h. are**	2192
Joh	16:21	**when she is in travail h. sorrow,**	2192
Joh	17:14	**and the world h. hated them,**	

Joh 17:25 **Father, the world h. not known**
Joh 18:11 **the cup which my Father h. given me,**
Joh 19:11 **me unto thee h. the greater sin** *2192*
Joh 20:21 **as my Father h. sent me, even so send**
Ac 1:7 **which the Father h. put in his own**
Ac 2:24 Whom God **h.** raised up, having
Ac 2:32 This Jesus **h.** God raised up, whereof
Ac 2:33 he **h.** shed forth this, which ye now
Ac 2:36 that God **h.** made that same Jesus,
Ac 3:13 God of our fathers, **h.** glorified his Son
Ac 3:15 whom God **h.** raised from the dead;
Ac 3:16 in his name **h.** made this man strong,
Ac 3:16 faith which is by him **h.** given him
Ac 3:18 should suffer, he **h.** so fulfilled
Ac 3:21 which God **h.** spoken by the mouth of
Ac 4:16 a notable miracle **h.** been done by
Ac 5:3 why **h.** Satan filled thine heart to lie
Ac 5:31 Him **h.** God exalted with his right
Ac 5:32 whom God **h.** given to them that obey
Ac 7:50 **H.** not my hand made all these
Ac 9:12 **And h. seen in a vision a man named**
Ac 9:13 much evil he **h.** done to thy saints
Ac 9:14 And here he **h.** authority from *2192*
Ac 9:17 way as thou camest, **h.** sent me,
Ac 10:15 What God **h.** cleansed, that call not
Ac 10:28 but God **h.** shewed me that I should
Ac 11:8 or unclean **h.** at any time entered
Ac 11:9 What God **h.** cleansed, that call not
Ac 11:18 **h.** God also to the Gentiles granted
Ac 12:11 that the Lord **h.** sent his angel,
Ac 12:11 and **h.** delivered me out of the hand
Ac 13:23 Of this man's seed **h.** God...raised
Ac 13:33 God **h.** fulfilled the same unto us
Ac 13:33 in that he **h.** raised up Jesus again;
Ac 13:47 For so **h.** the Lord commanded us,
Ac 15:14 Simeon **h.** declared how God at the
Ac 15:21 For Moses of old time **h.** in every *2192*
Ac 17:7 Whom Jason **h.** received: and these
Ac 17:26 And **h.** made of one blood all nations
Ac 17:26 face of the earth, and **h.** determined
Ac 17:31 Because he **h.** appointed a day, in
Ac 17:31 by that man whom he **h.** ordained;
Ac 17:31 whereof he **h.** given assurance unto
Ac 17:31 in that he **h.** raised him from the
Ac 19:26 this Paul **h.** persuaded and turned
Ac 20:28 the Holy Ghost **h.** made you overseers,
Ac 20:28 which he **h.** purchased with his own
Ac 21:28 and **h.** polluted this holy place
Ac 22:14 The God of our fathers **h.** chosen
Ac 23:9 but if a spirit or an angel **h.** spoken to
Ac 23:17 he **h.** a certain thing to tell him. *2192*
Ac 23:18 who **h.** something to say unto thee *2192*
Ac 24:6 Who also **h.** gone about to profane the
Ac 25:25 and that he himself **h.** appealed to
Ac 27:24 lo, God **h.** given thee all them that sail
Ac 28:4 whom, though he **h.** escaped the sea,
Ro 1:19 for God **h.** shewed it unto them
Ro 3:1 What advantage then **h.** the Jew?
Ro 3:7 if the truth of God **h.** more abounded
Ro 3:25 Whom God **h.** set forth to be
Ro 4:1 as pertaining to the flesh, **h.** found?
Ro 4:2 he **h.** whereof to glory; but not *2192*
Ro 5:15 Jesus Christ, **h.** abounded unto many.
Ro 5:21 That as sin **h.** reigned unto death,
Ro 6:9 death **h.** no more dominion over him
Ro 7:1 how that the law **h.** dominion over a
Ro 7:2 the woman which **h.** an husband 5220
Ro 8:2 in Christ Jesus **h.** made me free
Ro 8:20 of him who **h.** subjected the same in
Ro 9:6 the word of God **h.** taken none effect
Ro 9:18 Therefore **h.** he mercy on whom he
Ro 9:19 For who **h.** resisted his will?
Ro 9:21 **H.** not the potter power over the *2192*
Ro 9:24 Even us, whom he **h.** called, not of
Ro 9:31 of righteousness, **h.** not attained to
Ro 10:9 that God **h.** raised him from the dead,
Ro 10:16 Lord, who **h.** believed our report?
Ro 11:1 **H.** God cast away his people?
Ro 11:2 God **h.** not cast away his people.
Ro 11:7 Israel **h.** not obtained that which
Ro 11:7 but the election **h.** obtained it,
Ro 11:8 God **h.** given them the spirit of
Ro 11:32 For God **h.** concluded them all in
Ro 11:34 For who **h.** known the mind of the
Ro 11:34 or who **h.** been his counsellor?
Ro 11:35 Or who **h.** first given to him,

Ro 12:3 according as God **h.** dealt to every
Ro 13:8 for he that loveth another **h.** fulfilled
Ro 14:3 that eateth: for God **h.** received him.
Ro 15:18 things which Christ **h.** not wrought
Ro 15:26 For it **h.** pleased them of Macedonia
Ro 15:27 it **h.** pleased them verily; and their
Ro 16:2 whatsoever business she **h.** need of
Ro 16:2 for she **h.** been a succourer of many,
1Co 1:11 For it **h.** been declared unto me of
1Co 1:20 **h.** not God made foolish the wisdom
1Co 1:27 But God **h.** chosen the foolish things
1Co 1:27 and God **h.** chosen the weak things
1Co 1:28 which are despised, **h.** God chosen,
1Co 2:9 But as it is written, Eye **h.** not seen,
1Co 2:9 the things which God **h.** prepared for
1Co 2:10 But God **h.** revealed them unto us by
1Co 2:16 For who **h.** known the mind of the
1Co 3:14 man's work abide which he **h.** built
1Co 4:9 I think that God **h.** set forth us the
1Co 5:2 that he that **h.** done this deed might
1Co 5:3 concerning him that **h.** so done this
1Co 6:14 And God **h.** both raised up the Lord,
1Co 7:4 The wife **h.** not power of her own
1Co 7:4 also the husband **h.** not power of
1Co 7:7 But every man **h.** his proper gift *2192*
1Co 7:12 If any brother **h.** a wife that *2192*
1Co 7:13 the woman which **h.** an husband *2192*
1Co 7:15 but God **h.** called us to peace.
1Co 7:17 But as God **h.** distributed to every
1Co 7:17 as the Lord **h.** called every one, so let
1Co 7:25 as one that **h.** obtained mercy of the
1Co 7:28 if a virgin marry, she **h.** not sinned
1Co 7:37 no necessity, but **h.** power over his *2192*
1Co 7:37 and **h.** so decreed in his heart that he
1Co 9:14 Even so **h.** the Lord ordained that
1Co 10:13 There **h.** no temptation taken you but
1Co 12:12 body is one, and **h.** many members, ... *2192*
1Co 12:18 But now **h.** God set the members every
1Co 12:18 in the body, as it **h.** pleased him.
1Co 12:24 but God **h.** tempered the body
1Co 12:28 And God **h.** set some in the church,
1Co 14:26 one of you **h.** a psalm **h.** a doctrine, ... *2192*
1Co 14:26 **h.** a tongue, **h.** a revelation, ... *2192*
1Co 14:26 **h.** an interpretation. Let all things *2192*
1Co 15:25 he must reign, till he **h.** put all
1Co 15:27 he **h.** put all things under his feet
1Co 15:38 God giveth it a body as it **h.** pleased
1Co 16:2 as God **h.** prospered him, that there
2Co 1:21 you in Christ, and **h.** anointed us,
2Co 1:22 Who **h.** also sealed us, and given the
2Co 2:5 he **h.** not grieved me, but in part:
2Co 3:6 Who also **h.** made us able ministers
2Co 4:4 the god of this world **h.** blinded the
2Co 4:6 out of darkness, **h.** shined in our
2Co 5:5 Now he that **h.** wrought us for the
2Co 5:5 who also **h.** given unto us the earnest
2Co 5:10 according to that he **h.** done, whether
2Co 5:18 are of God, who **h.** reconciled us to
2Co 5:18 by Jesus Christ, and **h.** given to us
2Co 5:19 and **h.** committed unto us the word
2Co 5:21 For he **h.** made him to be sin for us.
2Co 6:14 fellowship **h.** righteousness with
2Co 6:14 communion **h.** light with darkness?
2Co 6:15 concord **h.** Christ with Belial?
2Co 6:15 **h.** he that believeth with an infidel?
2Co 6:16 And what agreement **h.** the temple of
2Co 6:16 as God **h.** said, I will dwell in them,
2Co 7:8 that the same epistle **h.** made you
2Co 8:12 according to that a man **h.**, and *2192*
2Co 8:12 not according to that he **h.** not. *2192*
2Co 9:2 and your zeal **h.** provoked very many
2Co 9:9 As it is written, He **h.** dispersed
2Co 9:9 he **h.** given to the poor:
2Co 10:8 which the Lord **h.** given us for
2Co 10:13 of the rule which God **h.** distributed
2Co 13:10 power which the Lord **h.** given me to
Ga 3:1 foolish Galatians, who **h.** bewitched
Ga 3:1 Christ **h.** been evidently set forth,
Ga 3:13 Christ **h.** redeemed us from the curse
Ga 3:22 But the scripture **h.** concluded all
Ga 4:6 God **h.** sent forth the Spirit of his Son
Ga 4:27 for the desolate **h.** many more
Ga 4:27 than she which **h.** an husband *2192*
Ga 5:1 liberty wherewith Christ **h.** made us
Eph 1:3 who **h.** blessed us with all spiritual
Eph 1:4 According as he **h.** chosen us in him

Eph 1:6 wherein he **h.** made us accepted
Eph 1:8 Wherein he **h.** abounded toward us
Eph 1:9 good pleasure which he **h.** purposed
Eph 1:22 And **h.** put all things under his feet,
Eph 2:1 And you **h.** he quickened, who were
Eph 2:5 dead in sins, **h.** quickened us together
Eph 2:6 And **h.** raised us up together, and
Eph 2:10 which God **h.** before ordained that we
Eph 2:14 he is our peace, who **h.** made both
Eph 2:14 one, and **h.** broken down the middle
Eph 3:9 beginning of the world **h.** been hid in
Eph 4:32 as God for Christ's sake **h.** forgiven
Eph 5:2 as Christ also **h.** loved us, and
Eph 5:2 **h.** given himself for us an offering
Eph 5:5 an idolater, **h.** any inheritance *2192*
Php 1:6 that he which **h.** begun a good work
Php 2:9 God also **h.** highly exalted him, and
Php 2:22 he **h.** served with me in the gospel.
Php 3:4 thinketh that he **h.** whereof he might
Php 4:10 last your care of me **h.** flourished
Col 1:12 the Father, which **h.** made us meet
Col 1:13 Who **h.** delivered us from the power
Col 1:13 of darkness, and **h.** translated us
Col 1:21 works, yet now **h.** he reconciled
Col 1:26 Even the mystery which **h.** been hid
Col 2:12 who **h.** raised him from the dead
Col 2:13 **h.** he quickened together with him,
Col 2:18 into those things which he **h.** not seen,
Col 3:25 for the wrong which he **h.** done:
Col 4:13 I bear him record, that he **h.** a zeal *2192*
1Th 2:12 who **h.** called you unto his kingdom
1Th 4:7 For God **h.** not called us unto
1Th 4:8 but God, who **h.** also given unto us
1Th 5:9 For God **h.** not appointed us to wrath,
2Th 2:13 God **h.** from the beginning chosen
2Th 2:16 even our Father, which **h.** loved us,
2Th 2:16 and **h.** given us everlasting
1Ti 1:12 Jesus our Lord, who **h.** enabled me,
1Ti 4:3 which God **h.** created to be received
1Ti 5:8 those of his own house, he **h.** denied
1Ti 6:16 Who only **h.** immortality, dwelling *2192*
1Ti 6:16 whom no man **h.** seen, nor can see:
2Ti 1:7 For God **h.** not given us the spirit of
2Ti 1:9 Who **h.** saved us, and called us with
2Ti 1:10 Jesus Christ, who **h.** abolished
2Ti 1:10 and **h.** brought life and immortality
2Ti 2:4 may please him who **h.** chosen him
2Ti 4:10 For Demas **h.** forsaken me, having
2Ti 4:15 for he **h.** greatly withstood our words.
Tit 1:3 But **h.** in due time manifested
Tit 1:9 faithful word as he **h.** been taught,
Tit 2:11 that bringeth salvation **h.** appeared
Phm 18 If he **h.** wronged thee, or oweth thee
Heb 1:2 **H.** in these last days spoken unto
Heb 1:2 whom he **h.** appointed heir of all
Heb 1:4 as he **h.** by inheritance obtained a
Heb 1:9 even thy God, **h.** anointed thee with
Heb 2:5 unto the angels **h.** he not put in
Heb 2:13 the children which God **h.** given me
Heb 2:18 in that he himself **h.** suffered being
Heb 3:3 as he who **h.** builded the house
Heb 3:3 **h.** more honour than the house *2192*
Heb 4:10 he also **h.** ceased from his own works,
Heb 7:24 **h.** an unchangeable priesthood. *2192*
Heb 8:6 But now **h.** he obtained a more
Heb 8:13 new covenant, he **h.** made the first old,
Heb 9:20 testament which God **h.** enjoined
Heb 9:26 end of the world **h.** he appeared to put
Heb 10:14 by one offering he **h.** perfected for
Heb 10:20 living way, which he **h.** consecrated
Heb 10:29 who **h.** trodden under foot the Son of
Heb 10:29 and **h.** counted the blood of the
Heb 10:29 and **h.** done despite unto the Spirit
Heb 10:30 we know him that **h.** said, Vengeance
Heb 10:35 which **h.** great recompence of *2192*
Heb 11:10 for a city which **h.** foundations, ... *2192*
Heb 11:16 for he **h.** prepared for them a city.
Heb 12:26 but now he **h.** promised, saying,
Heb 13:5 for he **h.** said, I will never leave thee,
Jas 1:12 which the Lord **h.** promised to them
Jas 1:15 Then when lust **h.** conceived, it
Jas 2:5 **H.** not God chosen the poor of this
Jas 2:5 of the kingdom which he **h.** promised
Jas 2:13 without mercy, that **h.** shewed no
Jas 2:14 though a man say he **h.** faith, and *2192*
Jas 2:17 faith, if it **h.** not works, is dead, ... *2192*

Jas 3:7 is tamed, and **h.** been tamed of
Jas 5:7 of the earth, and **h.** long patience
1Pe 1:3 to his abundant mercy **h.** begotten
1Pe 1:15 But as he which **h.** called you is holy,
1Pe 2:9 the praises of him who **h.** called you
1Pe 3:18 For Christ also **h.** once suffered for
1Pe 4:1 Forasmuch then as Christ **h.** suffered
1Pe 4:1 for he that **h.** suffered in the flesh
1Pe 4:1 in the flesh **h.** ceased from sin;
1Pe 4:10 As every man **h.** received the gift.
1Pe 5:10 who **h.** called us unto his eternal glory
2Pe 1:3 as his divine power **h.** given unto us
2Pe 1:3 knowledge of him that **h.** called us to
2Pe 1:9 and **h.** forgotten that he was purged
2Pe 1:14 our Lord Jesus Christ **h.** shewed me
2Pe 3:15 wisdom given unto him **h.** written
1Jo 2:11 because that darkness **h.** blinded
1Jo 2:23 Son, the same **h.** not the Father *2192*
1Jo 2:23 acknowledgeth the Son **h.** the Father *2192*
1Jo 2:25 is the promise that he **h.** promised
1Jo 2:27 as it **h.** taught you, ye shall abide
1Jo 3:1 of love the Father **h.** bestowed upon
1Jo 3:3 every man that **h.** this hope in *2192*
1Jo 3:6 whosoever sinneth **h.** not seen him,
1Jo 3:15 no murderer **h.** eternal life *2192*
1Jo 3:17 But whose **h.** this world's good, and *2192*
1Jo 3:24 by the Spirit which he **h.** given us.
1Jo 4:12 No man **h.** seen God at any time.
1Jo 4:13 because he **h.** given us of his Spirit.
1Jo 4:16 believed the love that God **h.** to us. *2192*
1Jo 4:18 out fear: because fear **h.** torment. *2192*
1Jo 4:20 his brother whom he **h.** seen, how
1Jo 4:20 can he love God whom he **h.** not seen?
1Jo 5:9 witness of God which he **h.** testified of
1Jo 5:10 on the Son of God **h.** the witness *2192*
1Jo 5:10 believeth not God **h.** made him a liar;
1Jo 5:11 that God **h.** given to us eternal life,
1Jo 5:12 He that **h.** the Son **h.** life; and he *2192*
1Jo 5:12 that **h.** not the Son of God **h.** not life. *2192*
1Jo 5:20 and **h.** given us an understanding, that
2Jo 9 the doctrine of Christ, **h.** not God. *2192*
2Jo 9 of Christ, he **h.** both the Father *2192*
3Jo 11 he that doeth evil **h.** not seen God.
3Jo 12 Demetrius **h.** good report of all men,
Jude 6 he **h.** reserved in everlasting chains
Re 1:6 And **h.** made us kings and priests
Re 2:7,11 **He that h. an ear, let him hear** *2192*
Re 2:12 **saith he which h. the sharp sword** *2192*
Re 2:17 **He that h. an ear, let him hear** *2192*
Re 2:18 **who h. his eyes like unto a flame** *2192*
Re 2:29 **He that h. an ear, let him hear** *2192*
Re 3:1 **saith he that h. the seven Spirits** *2192*
Re 3:6 **He that h. an ear, let him hear** *2192*
Re 3:7 **he that is true, he that h. the** *2192*
Re 3:13, 22 **He that h. an ear, let him hear** *2192*
Re 5:5 the Root of David, **h.** prevailed to open
Re 9:11 in the Greek tongue **h.** his name *2192*
Re 10:7 as he **h.** declared to his servants the
Re 12:6 where she **h.** a place prepared of *2192*
Re 12:12 knoweth that he **h.** but a short *2192*
Re 13:18 Let him that **h.** understanding *2192*
Re 16:9 the name of God, which **h.** power *2192*
Re 17:7 which **h.** the seven heads and ten *2192*
Re 17:9 here is the mind which **h.** wisdom. *2192*
Re 17:17 For God **h.** put in their hearts to fulfill
Re 18:5 and God **h.** remembered her iniquities.
Re 18:6 in the cup which she **h.** filled fill to
Re 18:7 How much she **h.** glorified herself,
Re 18:20 for God **h.** avenged you on her.
Re 19:2 for he **h.** judged the great whore,
Re 19:2 and **h.** avenged the blood of his
Re 19:7 and his wife **h.** made herself ready.
Re 19:16 And he **h.** on his vesture and on *2192*
Re 20:6 Blessed and holy is he that **h.** part *2192*
Re 20:6 such the second death **h.** no power, *2192*

HATHATH (ha'-thath)
1Ch 4:13 and the sons of Othniel; **H.** 2867

HATING
Ex 18:21 men of truth, **h.** covetousness; 8130
Tit 3:3 envy, hateful, and **h.** one another. *3404*
Jude 23 **h.** even the garment spotted by the *3404*

HATIPHA (hat'-if-ah)
Ezr 2:54 of Neziah, the children of **H.** 2412
Ne 7:56 of Neziah, the children of **H.** 2412

HATITA (hat'-it-ah)
Ezr 2:42 the children of **H.**, the children 2410
Ne 7:45 the children of **H.**, the children 2410

HATRED
Nu 35:20 But if he thrust him of **h.** 8135
2Sa 13:15 that the **h.** wherewith he hated her 8135
Ps 25:19 and they hate me with cruel **h.** 8135
Ps 109:3 me about also with words of **h.**; 8135
Ps 109:5 for good, and **h.** for my love. 8135
Ps 139:22 I hate them with perfect **h.**: 8135
Pr 10:12 **H.** stirreth up strifes: but love 8135
Pr 10:18 He that hideth **h.** with lying lips, 8135
Pr 15:17 than a stalled ox and **h.** therewith. 8135
Pr 26:26 Whose **h.** is covered by deceit, his 8135
Ec 9:1 no man knoweth either love or **h.** 8135
Ec 9:6 Also their love, and their **h.**, and 8135
Eze 25:15 to destroy it for the old **h.**; 342
Eze 35:5 thou hast had a perpetual **h.**, and 342
Eze 35:11 which thou hast used out of thy **h.** 8135
Ho 9:7 thine iniquity, and the great **h.** 4895
Ho 9:8 **h.** in the house of his God. 4895
Ga 5:20 **h.**, variance, emulations, wrath, *2189*

HATS
Da 3:21 their hosen, and their **h.**, and 3737

HATTAAVAH See KIBROTH-HATTAAVAH.

HATTICON See HAZAR-HATTICON.

HATTIL (hat'-til)
Ezr 2:57 the children of **H.**, the children 2411
Ne 7:59 of Shephatiah, the children of **H.**, 2411

HATTUSH (hat'-tush)
1Ch 3:22 **H.**, and Igeal, and Bariah, and 2407
Ezr 8:2 Daniel: of the sons of David; **H.** 2407
Ne 3:10 And next unto him repaired **H.** the 2407
Ne 10:4 **H.**, Shebaniah, Malluch, 2407
Ne 12:2 Amariah, Malluch, **H.**, 2407

HAUGHTILY
Mic 2:3 necks; neither shall ye go **h.**: 7317

HAUGHTINESS
Isa 2:11 the **h.** of men shall be bowed 7312
Isa 2:17 the **h.** of men shall be made low: 7312
Isa 13:11 will lay low the **h.** of the terrible 1346
Isa 16:6 his **h.**, and his pride, and his 1346
Jer 48:29 and the **h.** of his heart. 7312

HAUGHTY
2Sa 22:28 thine eyes are upon the **h.**, that 7311
Ps 131:1 my heart is not **h.**, nor mine eyes 1361
Pr 16:18 and an **h.** spirit before a fall. 1363
Pr 18:12 destruction the heart of man is **h.**, 1361
Pr 21:24 Proud and **h.** scorner is his name, 3093
Isa 3:16 the daughters of Zion are **h.**, 1361
Isa 10:33 and the **h.** shall be humbled. 1364
Isa 24:4 **h.** people of the earth do languish. 4791
Eze 16:50 And they were **h.**, and committed 1361
Zep 3:11 shalt no more be **h.** because of my 1361

HAUL See HALE.

HAUNT
1Sa 23:22 his place where his **h.** is, and 7272
1Sa 30:31 and his men were wont to **h.** 1980
Eze 26:17 terror to be on all that **h.** it! 3427

HAURAN (hau'-ran)
Eze 47:16 which is by the coast of **H.** 2362
Eze 47:18 ye shall measure from **H.**, and 2362

HAVE See also HAD; HAST; HATH; HAVING.
Ge 1:26 let them **h.** dominion over the fish
Ge 1:28 and **h.** dominion over the fish of
Ge 1:29 And God said, Behold, I **h.** given you
Ge 1:30 I **h.** given every green herb for meat:
Ge 4:1 said, I **h.** gotten a man from the Lord
Ge 4:20 in tents, and of such as **h.** cattle.
Ge 4:23 for I **h.** slain a man to my wounding,
Ge 6:7 whom I **h.** created from the face of
Ge 6:7 it repenteth me that I **h.** made
Ge 7:1 for thee **h.** I seen righteous before me
Ge 7:4 that I **h.** made will I destroy from
Ge 8:21 more every thing living, as I **h.** done.
Ge 9:3 as the green herb **h.** I given you.
Ge 9:17 which I **h.** established between me
Ge 11:6 and they **h.** all one language; and
Ge 11:6 from them, which they **h.** imagined
Ge 12:19 so I might **h.** taken her to me to
Ge 14:22 I **h.** lift up mine hand unto the Lord,
Ge 14:23 shouldest say, I **h.** made Abram rich:
Ge 14:24 the young men **h.** eaten, and the
Ge 15:18 Unto thy seed **h.** I given this land,
Ge 16:5 I **h.** given my maid into thy bosom;
Ge 16:13 **H.** I also here looked after him that
Ge 17:5 father of many nations **h.** I made
Ge 17:20 as for Ishmael, I **h.** heard thee:
Ge 17:20 Behold I **h.** blessed him, and will
Ge 18:3 My Lord, if now I **h.** found favour in
Ge 18:10 and lo, Sarah thy wife shall **h.** a son.
Ge 18:12 am waxed old shall I **h.** pleasure, 1961
Ge 18:14 time of life, and Sarah shall **h.** a son.
Ge 18:21 they **h.** done altogether according to
Ge 18:27 Behold now, I **h.** taken upon me to
Ge 18:31 now, I **h.** taken upon me to speak unto
Ge 19:8 Behold now, I **h.** two daughters
Ge 19:8 which **h.** not known man; let me, I
Ge 19:21 See, I **h.** accepted thee concerning
Ge 20:5 and innocency of my hands **h.** I done
Ge 20:9 and what **h.** I offended thee, that
Ge 20:16 Behold, I **h.** given thy brother a
Ge 21:7 And she said, Who would **h.** said unto
Ge 21:7 that Sarah should **h.** given children
Ge 21:7 for I **h.** borne him a son in his old age
Ge 21:23 kindness that I **h.** done unto thee,
Ge 21:30 witness unto me, that I **h.** digged this
Ge 22:16 By myself **h.** I sworn, saith the Lord,
Ge 24:19 also, until they **h.** done drinking.
Ge 24:25 We **h.** both straw and provender
Ge 24:31 for I **h.** prepared the house, and
Ge 24:33 I will not eat, until I **h.** told mine
Ge 26:10 might lightly **h.** lien with thy wife,
Ge 26:10 thou shouldest **h.** brought guiltiness
Ge 26:27 seeing ye hate me, and **h.** sent me
Ge 26:29 do us no hurt, as we **h.** not touched
Ge 26:29 and as we **h.** done unto thee nothing
Ge 26:32 said unto him, We **h.** found water.
Ge 27:19 I **h.** done according as thou badest
Ge 27:33 and I **h.** eaten of all before thou
Ge 27:33 before thou camest, and **h.** blessed him?
Ge 27:37 Behold, I **h.** made him thy lord, and
Ge 27:37 all his brethren **h.** I given to him.
Ge 27:37 and with corn and wine **h.** I sustained
Ge 27:40 when thou shalt **h.** the dominion,
Ge 28:15 I will not leave thee, until I **h.** done
Ge 28:15 that which I **h.** spoken to thee of.
Ge 28:22 And this stone, which I **h.** set for a
Ge 29:34 because I **h.** born him three sons:
Ge 30:3 that I may also **h.** children by her.
Ge 30:8 **h.** I wrestled with my sister,
Ge 30:8 with my sister, and I **h.** prevailed:
Ge 30:16 for surely I **h.** hired thee with my
Ge 30:18 because I **h.** given my maiden to my
Ge 30:20 because I **h.** born him six sons: and
Ge 30:26 for whom I **h.** served thee, and let me
Ge 30:26 knowest my service which I **h.** done
Ge 30:27 if I **h.** found favour in thine eyes,
Ge 30:27 I **h.** learned by experience that the
Ge 30:29 Thou knowest how I **h.** served thee,
Ge 31:6 with all my power I **h.** served your
Ge 31:12 for I **h.** seen all that Laban doeth unto
Ge 31:27 that I might **h.** sent thee away with
Ge 31:38 This twenty years **h.** I been with thee;
Ge 31:38 ewes and thy she goats **h.** not cast
Ge 31:38 the rams of thy flock **h.** I not eaten.
Ge 31:41 Thus **h.** I been twenty years in thy
Ge 31:43 their children which they **h.** born?
Ge 31:51 which I **h.** cast betwixt me and thee;
Ge 32:4 I **h.** sojourned with Laban and
Ge 32:5 And I **h.** oxen, and asses, flocks, 1961
Ge 32:5 and I **h.** sent to tell me Lord,
Ge 32:30 for I **h.** seen God face to face, and my
Ge 33:9 And Esau said, I **h.** enough, my 3426
Ge 33:10 if now I **h.** found grace in thy sight,
Ge 33:10 for therefore I **h.** seen thy face, as
Ge 33:11 and because I **h.** enough. And he 3426
Ge 34:30 Ye **h.** troubled me to make me to
Ge 35:17 Fear not; thou shalt **h.** this son also.
Ge 37:6 you, this dream which I **h.** dreamed:
Ge 37:8 or shalt thou indeed **h.** dominion
Ge 37:9 Behold, I **h.** dreamed a dream more;
Ge 37:32 and said, This **h.** we found: know
Ge 40:8 We **h.** dreamed a dream, and there is
Ge 40:15 and here also **h.** I done nothing that
Ge 41:15 I **h.** dreamed a dream, and there is
Ge 41:15 and I **h.** heard say of thee, that thou
Ge 41:28 This is the thing which I **h.** spoken

Ge 41:41 See, I **h.** set thee over all the land...
Ge 42:2 I **h.** heard that there is corn in Egypt: ...
Ge 42:36 Me **h.** ye bereaved of my children: ...
Ge 43:7 yet alive? **h.** ye another brother? ... 3426
Ge 43:21 and we **h.** brought it again in our ...
Ge 43:22 And other money **h.** we brought ...
Ge 44:4 Wherefore **h.** ye rewarded evil for...
Ge 44:5 indeed he diveneth? ye **h.** done evil...
Ge 44:15 What deed is this that ye **h.** done? ...
Ge 44:19 saying, **H.** ye a father, or a ... 3426
Ge 44:20 We **h.** a father, an old man, and a ... 3426
Ge 45:13 and of all that ye **h.** seen; and ye...
Ge 46:30 let me die, since I **h.** seen; and ye...
Ge 46:30 let me die, since I **h.** seen thy face, ...
Ge 46:32 and they **h.** brought their flocks, and...
Ge 46:32 and their herds, and all that they **h.** ...
Ge 47:1 and all that they **h.**, are come out of...
Ge 47:4 for thy servants **h.** no pasture for...
Ge 47:9 evil **h.** the days of the years of my life ...
Ge 47:9 and **h.** not attained unto the days of...
Ge 47:23 Behold, I **h.** bought you this day and ...
Ge 47:26 that Pharaoh should **h.** the fifth part;...
Ge 47:29 If now I **h.** found grace in thy sight, ...
Ge 48:22 Moreover I **h.** given to thee one...
Ge 49:18 I **h.** waited for thy salvation, O Lord...
Ge 49:23 The archers **h.** sorely grieved him,...
Ge 49:26 blessings of thy father **h.** prevailed ...
Ge 50:4 If now I **h.** found grace in your eyes,...
Ge 50:5 in my grave which I **h.** digged for...
Ex 1:18 and said unto them, Why **h.** ye done...
Ex 1:18 and **h.** saved the men children alive?...
Ex 2:20 why is it that ye **h.** left the man? ...
Ex 2:22 he said, I **h.** been a stranger...
Ex 3:7 I **h.** surely seen the affliction of my ...
Ex 3:7 and **h.** heard their cry by reason of...
Ex 3:9 and I **h.** also seen the oppression...
Ex 3:12 that I **h.** sent thee: When thou hast...
Ex 3:16 I **h.** surely visited you, and seen that...
Ex 3:17 And I **h.** said, I will bring you up out ...
Ex 4:11 or the seeing, or the blind? **h.** not I...
Ex 4:21 which I **h.** put in thine hand: but I...
Ex 5:14 Wherefore **h.** ye not fulfilled your...
Ex 5:21 ye **h.** made our savour to be abhorred ...
Ex 6:4 And I **h.** also established my ...
Ex 6:5 And I **h.** also heard the groaning of...
Ex 6:5 and I **h.** remembered my covenant. ...
Ex 6:12 the children of Israel **h.** not hearkened ...
Ex 7:1 See, I **h.** made thee a god to Pharaoh: ...
Ex 9:16 for this cause **h.** I raised thee up, ...
Ex 9:27 I **h.** sinned this time: the Lord is ...
Ex 10:1 for I **h.** hardened his heart, and the...
Ex 10:2 what things I **h.** wrought in Egypt...
Ex 10:2 and my signs which I **h.** done among ...
Ex 10:6 nor thy fathers' fathers **h.** seen, since ...
Ex 10:16 I **h.** sinned against the Lord your ...
Ex 12:17 for in this selfsame day **h.** I brought ...
Ex 12:31 and go, serve the Lord, as ye **h.** said. ...
Ex 12:32 and your herds, as ye **h.** said, and be ...
Ex 14:5 and they said, Why **h.** we done this,...
Ex 14:5 that we **h.** let Israel go from serving...
Ex 14:13 whom ye **h.** seen to day, ye shall see ...
Ex 14:18 when I **h.** gotten me honour upon ...
Ex 15:5 The depths **h.** covered them: they ...
Ex 15:17 which thy hands **h.** established...
Ex 15:26 which I **h.** brought upon the...
Ex 16:3 for ye **h.** brought us forth into this ...
Ex 16:12 I **h.** heard the murmurings of the ...
Ex 16:32 I **h.** fed you in the wilderness, when...
Ex 17:16 sworn that the Lord will **h.** war ...
Ex 18:3 I **h.** been an alien in a strange ...
Ex 18:16 When they **h.** a matter, they come ... 1961
Ex 19:4 Ye **h.** seen what I did unto the ...
Ex 20:2 which **h.** brought thee out of the land...
Ex 20:3 Thou shalt **h.** no other gods before...
Ex 20:22 unto the children of Israel, Ye **h.** seen ...
Ex 20:22 that I **h.** talked with you from heaven. ...
Ex 21:4 If his master **h.** given him a wife, and...
Ex 21:4 she **h.** born him sons or daughters; ...
Ex 21:8 he shall **h.** no power, seeing he ...
Ex 21:9 And if he **h.** betrothed her unto his...
Ex 21:31 Whether he **h.** gored a son, or ...
Ex 21:31 or **h.** gored a daughter, according to...
Ex 22:3 if he **h.** nothing, then he shall be...
Ex 22:8 he **h.** put his hand unto his neighbour's...
Ex 23:13 And in all things that I **h.** said unto...
Ex 23:20 into the place which I **h.** prepared...
Ex 24:12 commandments which I **h.** written; ...

Ex 24:14 if any man **h.** any matters to do, let...
Ex 26:2 every one of the curtains shall **h.** one ...
Ex 28:3 whom I **h.** filled with the spirit of...
Ex 28:7 It shall **h.** the two shoulder pieces... 1961
Ex 28:32 shall **h.** a binding of woven work... 1961
Ex 29:35 to all things which I **h.** commanded...
Ex 31:2 See, I **h.** called by name Bezaleel the ...
Ex 31:3 And I **h.** filled him with the spirit ...
Ex 31:6 And I, behold, I **h.** given with him...
Ex 31:6 that are wise hearted I **h.** put wisdom, ...
Ex 31:6 may make all that I **h.** commanded ...
Ex 31:11 according to all that I **h.** commanded...
Ex 32:7 of Egypt, **h.** corrupted themselves...
Ex 32:8 They **h.** turned aside quickly out of ...
Ex 32:8 they **h.** made them a molten calf, ...
Ex 32:8 a molten calf, and **h.** worshipped it, ...
Ex 32:8 and **h.** sacrificed thereunto, and ...
Ex 32:8 which **h.** brought thee up out of the...
Ex 32:9 I **h.** seen this people, and, behold, it is ...
Ex 32:13 and all this land that I **h.** spoken of...
Ex 32:30 Ye **h.** sinned a great sin: and now I...
Ex 32:31 and said, Oh, this people **h.** sinned a ...
Ex 32:31 a great sin, and **h.** made them gods...
Ex 32:34 the place of which I **h.** spoken unto ...
Ex 33:13 if I **h.** found grace in thy sight, ...
Ex 33:16 I and thy people **h.** found grace in thy...
Ex 34:9 If now I **h.** found grace in thy sight, ...
Ex 34:10 do marvels, such as **h.** not been done ...
Ex 34:27 I **h.** made a covenant with thee and...
Le 4:13 and they **h.** done somewhat against ...
Le 4:14 When the sin, which they **h.** sinned ...
Le 6:3 Or **h.** found that which was lost, and ...
Le 6:17 I **h.** given it unto them for their...
Le 7:7 atonement therewith shall **h.** it. ... 1961
Le 7:8 even the priest shall **h.** to himself ... 1961
Le 7:10 shall all the sons of Aaron **h.**, one ... 1961
Le 7:33 fat, shall **h.** the right shoulder ... 1961
Le 7:34 and the heave shoulder **h.** I taken of...
Le 7:34 and **h.** given them unto Aaron the ...
Le 10:17 Wherefore **h.** ye not eaten the sin...
Le 10:18 ye should indeed **h.** eaten it in the...
Le 10:19 Behold, this day **h.** they offered their...
Le 10:19 and such things **h.** befallen me: ...
Le 10:19 should it **h.** been accepted in the...
Le 11:10 And all that **h.** not fins and scales in ...
Le 11:11 shall **h.** their carcases in abomination...
Le 11:13 which ye shall **h.** in abomination ...
Le 11:21 which **h.** legs above their feet, to leap...
Le 11:23 which **h.** four feet, shall be an ...
Le 12:2 If a woman **h.** conceived seed, and...
Le 13:2 When a man shall **h.** in the skin... 1961
Le 13:10 and it **h.** turned the hair white, and ...
Le 13:13 if the leprosy **h.** covered all his flesh,...
Le 13:24 burneth **h.** a white bright spot, ... 1961
Le 13:29 If a man or a woman **h.** a plague... 1961
Le 13:38 If a man also or a woman **h.** in... 1961
Le 13:55 if the plague **h.** not changed his ...
Le 15:19 And if a woman **h.** an issue, and... 1961
Le 15:25 And if a woman **h.** an issue of her... 1961
Le 16:4 and he shall **h.** the linen breeches ... 1961
Le 16:17 and **h.** made an atonement for himself, ...
Le 17:7 after whom they **h.** gone a whoring. ...
Le 17:11 and I **h.** given it to you upon the...
Le 18:27 abominations **h.** the men of the land...
Le 19:23 and shall **h.** planted all manner of ...
Le 19:31 Regard not them that **h.** familiar...
Le 19:36 ephah, and a just hin, shall ye **h.**... 1961
Le 20:6 after such as **h.** familiar spirits, and ...
Le 20:12 they **h.** wrought confusion; their...
Le 20:13 both of them **h.** committed an...
Le 20:24 But I **h.** said unto you, Ye shall ...
Le 20:24 which **h.** separated you from other ...
Le 20:25 on the ground, which I **h.** separated ...
Le 20:26 Lord am holy, and **h.** severed you...
Le 22:13 and **h.** no child, and is returned unto...
Le 23:7 ye shall **h.** an holy convocation: ... 1961
Le 23:14 the selfsame day that ye **h.** brought...
Le 23:24 shall ye **h.** a sabbath, a memorial ... 1961
Le 23:39 when ye **h.** gathered in the fruit of...
Le 24:22 Ye shall **h.** one manner of law, as ... 1961
Le 25:26 And if the man **h.** none to redeem... 1961
Le 25:31 the villages which **h.** no wall round...
Le 25:44 bondmaids, which thou shalt **h.**, ... 1961
Le 26:9 For I will **h.** respect unto you, and...
Le 26:13 and I **h.** broken the bands of your ...
Le 26:26 And whom I **h.** broken the staff of your...

Le 26:37 and ye shall **h.** no power to stand ... 1961
Le 26:40 and that also they **h.** walked contrary...
Le 26:41 And that I also **h.** walked contrary...
Le 26:41 and **h.** brought them into the land of...
Le 27:20 or if he **h.** sold the field to another...
Nu 3:12 And I, behold, I **h.** taken the Levites ...
Nu 3:32 and **h.** the oversight of them that...
Nu 4:15 Aaron and his sons **h.** made an...
Nu 5:7 confess their sin which they **h.** done: ...
Nu 5:8 But if the man **h.** no kinsman to...
Nu 5:18 the priest shall **h.** in his hand ... 1961
Nu 5:19 If no man **h.** lain with thee, and if ...
Nu 5:20 and some man **h.** lain with thee ...
Nu 5:27 and **h.** done trespass against her...
Nu 8:16 of Israel, **h.** I taken them unto me...
Nu 8:18 And I **h.** taken the Levites for all the...
Nu 8:19 And I **h.** given the Levites as a gift to ...
Nu 9:14 ye shall **h.** one ordinance, both for ... 1961
Nu 11:11 and wherefore **h.** I not found favour...
Nu 11:12 **H.** I conceived all this people? ...
Nu 11:12 **h.** I begotten them, that thou ...
Nu 11:13 Whence should I **h.** flesh to give unto ...
Nu 11:15 if I **h.** found favour in thy sight; and...
Nu 11:18 for ye **h.** wept in the ears of the Lord, ...
Nu 11:20 because that ye **h.** despised the Lord...
Nu 11:20 and **h.** wept before him, saying, Why...
Nu 12:11 us, wherein we **h.** done foolishly, ...
Nu 12:11 foolishly, and wherein we **h.** sinned. ...
Nu 13:32 The land, through which we **h.** gone...
Nu 14:11 for all the signs which I **h.** shewed ...
Nu 14:14 for they **h.** heard that thou Lord art ...
Nu 14:15 then the nations which **h.** heard the...
Nu 14:20 I **h.** pardoned according to thy word: ...
Nu 14:22 Because all those men which **h.** seen...
Nu 14:22 in the wilderness, and **h.** tempted me ...
Nu 14:22 these ten times, and **h.** not hearkened ...
Nu 14:27 I **h.** heard the murmurings of the ...
Nu 14:28 as ye **h.** spoken in mine ears, so will I...
Nu 14:29 and upward, which **h.** murmured ...
Nu 14:31 know the land which ye **h.** despised...
Nu 14:35 I the Lord **h.** said, I will surely do it...
Nu 14:40 Lord hath promised: for we **h.** sinned. ...
Nu 15:22 And if ye **h.** erred, and not observed ...
Nu 15:29 Ye shall **h.** one law for him that... 1961
Nu 16:15 I **h.** not taken one ass from them,...
Nu 16:15 from them, neither **h.** I hurt one of...
Nu 16:28 for I **h.** not done them of mine own...
Nu 16:30 that these men **h.** provoked the Lord...
Nu 16:41 saying, Ye **h.** killed the people of the ...
Nu 18:6 And I, behold, I **h.** taken your...
Nu 18:7 I **h.** given your priest's office unto you...
Nu 18:8 Behold, I also **h.** given thee the charge ...
Nu 18:8 unto thee **h.** I given them by reason of ...
Nu 18:11 I **h.** given them unto thee, and to thy ...
Nu 18:12 offer unto the Lord, them **h.** I given...
Nu 18:19 unto the Lord, **h.** I given thee, and ...
Nu 18:20 Thou shalt **h.** no inheritance in their ...
Nu 18:20 neither shalt thou **h.** any part ... 1961
Nu 18:21 And, behold, I **h.** given the children of ...
Nu 18:23 of Israel they **h.** no inheritance. ...
Nu 18:24 I **h.** given to the Levites to inherit: ...
Nu 18:24 therefore I **h.** said unto them, Among ...
Nu 18:26 which I **h.** given you from them for ...
Nu 18:30 When ye **h.** heaved the best thereof...
Nu 18:32 when ye **h.** heaved from it the best of ...
Nu 20:4 And why **h.** ye brought up the...
Nu 20:5 And wherefore **h.** ye made us to come...
Nu 20:12 into the land which I **h.** given them. ...
Nu 20:15 and we **h.** dwelt in Egypt a long time;...
Nu 20:17 nor to the left, until we **h.** passed thy...
Nu 20:24 into the land which I **h.** given unto ...
Nu 21:5 Wherefore **h.** ye brought us up out of...
Nu 21:7 came to Moses, and said, We **h.** sinned,...
Nu 21:7 we **h.** spoken against the Lord, and...
Nu 21:30 We **h.** shot at them; Heshbon is ...
Nu 21:30 and we **h.** laid them waste even unto...
Nu 21:34 Fear him not: for I **h.** delivered him ...
Nu 22:28 What **h.** I done unto thee, that thou ...
Nu 22:34 I **h.** sinned; for I knew not that thou...
Nu 22:38 **h.** I now any power at all to say ...
Nu 23:4 him, I **h.** prepared seven altars, ...
Nu 23:4 and I **h.** offered upon every altar a...
Nu 23:20 Behold, I **h.** received commandment ...
Nu 24:19 come he that shall **h.** dominion, ...
Nu 25:13 And he shall **h.** it, and his seed ... 1961
Nu 25:18 they **h.** beguiled you in the matter of...
Nu 27:8 If a man die, and **h.** no son, then ye...

Nu 27:9 And if he **h.** no daughter, then ye............
Nu 27:10 And if he **h.** no brethren, then ye............
Nu 27:11 And if his father **h.** no brethren, then.........
Nu 27:12 which I **h.** given unto the children of..........
Nu 27:17 be not as sheep which **h.** no shepherd........
Nu 28:25, 26 ye shall **h.** an holy convocation;...... 1961
Nu 29:1 ye shall **h.** an holy convocation;.......... 1961
Nu 29:7 And ye shall **h.** on the tenth day......... 1961
Nu 29:12 ye shall **h.** an holy convocation;.......... 1961
Nu 29:35 ye shall **h.** a solemn assembly:........... 1961
Nu 30:9 they **h.** bound their souls, shall stand.........
Nu 31:15 him, **H.** ye saved all the women alive?.......
Nu 31:18 children, that **h.** not known a man.............
Nu 31:49 Thy servants **h.** taken the sum of the........
Nu 31:50 We **h.** therefore brought an oblation..........
Nu 32:4 for cattle, and thy sevants **h.** cattle:..........
Nu 32:5 if we **h.** found grace in thy sight, let..........
Nu 32:11 because they **h.** not wholly followed...........
Nu 32:12 for they **h.** wholly followed the Lord..........
Nu 32:17 until we **h.** brought them unto their...........
Nu 32:18 until the children of Israel **h.** inherited.........
Nu 32:23 behold, ye **h.** sinned against the Lord:.......
Nu 32:30 they shall **h.** possessions among.......... 270
Nu 33:53 for I **h.** given you the land to possess.........
Nu 34:6 ye shall even **h.** the great sea for........1961
Nu 34:14 fathers, **h.** received their inheritance;.........
Nu 34:14 Manasseh **h.** received...inheritance:...........
Nu 34:15 half tribe **h.** received their inheritance.........
Nu 35:3 the cities shall they **h.** to dwell in;........1961
Nu 35:8 from them that **h.** many ye shall...............
Nu 35:8 but from them that **h.** few ye shall............
Nu 35:13 six cities shall ye **h.** for refuge........... 1961
Nu 35:22 or **h.** cast upon him any thing without.........
Nu 35:28 Because he should **h.** remained in the........
De 1:6 in Horeb, saying, Ye **h.** dwelt long............
De 1:8 Behold, I **h.** set the land before you:..........
De 1:28 our brethren **h.** discouraged our................
De 1:28 and moreover we **h.** seen the sons of........
De 1:41 We **h.** sinned against the Lord, we............
De 2:3 Ye **h.** compassed this mountain long.........
De 2:5 because I **h.** given mount Seir unto...........
De 2:9 because I **h.** given Ar unto the.................
De 2:19 because I **h.** given it unto the..................
De 2:24 behold, I **h.** given into thine hand..............
De 2:31 Behold, I **h.** begun to give Sihon and.........
De 3:19 (for I know that ye **h.** much cattle,)...........
De 3:19 in your cities which I **h.** given you;............
De 3:20 Until the Lord **h.** given rest unto your.......
De 3:20 his possession, which I **h.** given you..........
De 3:21 Thine eyes **h.** seen all that the Lord.........
De 4:3 Your eyes **h.** seen what the Lord did..........
De 4:5 Behold, I **h.** taught you statutes and..........
De 4:9 things which thine eyes **h.** seen,...............
De 4:25 and ye shall **h.** remained long in the............
De 5:7 Thou shalt **h.** none other gods............1961
De 5:24 and we **h.** heard his voice out of the..........
De 5:24 we **h.** seen this day that God doth talk.......
De 5:26 out of the midst of the fire, as we **h.**,.........
De 5:28 and the Lord said unto me, I **h.** heard........
De 5:28 of this people, which they **h.** spoken..........
De 5:28 spoken unto thee: they **h.** well said............
De 5:28 well said all that they **h.** spoken.................
De 6:10 Lord thy God shall **h.** brought thee...........
De 6:11 when thou shalt **h.** eaten and be full;.........
De 7:16 thine eye shall **h.** no pity upon.................
De 7:24 thee, until thou **h.** destroyed them..............
De 9:7 ye **h.** been rebellious against the..............
De 9:8 angry with you to **h.** destroyed you...........
De 9:12 forth out of Egypt **h.** corrupted................
De 9:12 they **h.** made them a molten image.............
De 9:13 I **h.** seen this people, and, behold, it is......
De 9:20 very angry with Aaron to **h.** destroyed.......
De 9:23 which I **h.** given you; then ye rebelled.......
De 9:24 Ye **h.** been rebellious against the.............
De 10:21 things, which thine eyes **h.** seen..............
De 11:2 your children which **h.** not known,.............
De 11:2 **h.** not seen the chastisement...................
De 11:7 But your eyes **h.** seen all the great...........
De 11:28 other gods, which ye **h.** not known...........
De 12:21 as I **h.** commanded thee, and thou............
De 12:31 which he hateth, **h.** they done unto...........
De 12:31 they **h.** burnt in the fire to their gods........
De 13:13 and **h.** withdrawn the inhabitants of..........
De 13:13 other gods, which ye **h.** not known;...........
De 13:17 and **h.** compassion upon thee, and............
De 14:9 all that **h.** fins and scales shall ye.............
De 15:21 or **h.** any ill blemish, thou shalt not..........
De 17:3 heaven, which I **h.** not commanded;...........
De 17:5 woman which **h.** committed that................
De 18:1 the tribe of Levi, shall **h.** no part nor.........
De 18:2 Therefore shall they **h.** no inheritance........
De 18:8 They shall **h.** like portions to eat,.............
De 18:17 said unto me, They **h.** well spoken............
De 18:17 well spoken that which they **h.** spoken.......
De 18:20 which I **h.** not commanded him to.............
De 19:14 which they of old time **h.** set in thine.........
De 19:19 as he had thought to **h.** done unto his........
De 20:9 when the officers **h.** made an end of..........
De 20:18 which they **h.** done unto their gods;..........
De 21:7 and say, Our hands **h.** not shed this..........
De 21:7 this blood, neither **h.** our eyes seen it........
De 21:11 that thou wouldest **h.** her to thy...............
De 21:14 And it shall be, if thou **h.** no delight in........
De 21:15 If a man **h.** two wives, one beloved,.... 1961
De 21:15 and they **h.** born him children, both..........
De 21:18 If a man **h.** a stubborn and............... 1961
De 21:18 and that, when they **h.** chastened him,.......
De 21:22 And if a man **h.** committed a sin..............
De 23:12 Thou shalt **h.** a place also without....... 1961
De 23:13 and thou shalt **h.** a paddle upon thy..... 1961
De 25:5 and one of them die, and **h.** no child,.........
De 25:13 Thou shalt not **h.** in thy bag divers......1961
De 25:14 Thou shalt not **h.** in thine house......... 1961
De 25:15 But thou shalt **h.** a perfect and just..... 1961
De 25:15 and just measure shalt thou **h.**:.........1961
De 26:10 And now, behold, I **h.** brought the............
De 26:13 before the Lord thy God, I **h.** brought.......
De 26:13 out of mine house, and also **h.** given..........
De 26:13 me: I **h.** not transgressed thy..................
De 26:13 neither **h.** I forgotten them:......................
De 26:14 I **h.** not eaten thereof in my mourning.........
De 26:14 neither **h.** I taken away ought thereof........
De 26:14 but I **h.** hearkened to the voice of.............
De 26:14 and **h.** done according to all that thou.........
De 28:21 until he **h.** consumed thee from off the.......
De 28:31 and thou shalt **h.** none to rescue them.......
De 28:36 thou nor thy fathers **h.** known;.................
De 28:40 Thou shalt **h.** olive trees throughout..........
De 28:48 until he **h.** destroyed thee.......................
De 28:51 of thy sheep, until he **h.** destroyed............
De 28:64 nor thy fathers **h.** known, even wood.........
De 28:65 shall the sole of thy foot **h.** rest:.........1961
De 28:66 and shalt **h.** none assurance of thy life:.......
De 29:2 Ye **h.** seen all that the Lord did before.......
De 29:3 which thine eyes **h.** seen, the..................
De 29:5 And I **h.** led you forty years in the............
De 29:6 Ye **h.** not eaten bread, neither.................
De 29:6 **h.** ye drunk wine or strong drink: that.......
De 29:16 For ye know how we **h.** dwelt in the........
De 29:17 And ye **h.** seen their abominations, and......
De 29:19 I shall **h.** peace, though I walk in the.........
De 29:25 Because they **h.** forsaken the covenant.......
De 30:1 curse, which I **h.** set before thee,.............
De 30:3 and **h.** compassion upon thee, and............
De 30:15 See, I **h.** set before thee this day life.........
De 30:19 that I **h.** set before you life and death,.......
De 31:5 which I **h.** commanded you.....................
De 31:13 which **h.** not known anything, may............
De 31:16 break my covenant which I **h.** made..........
De 31:18 which they shall **h.** wrought, in that...........
De 31:20 For when I shall **h.** brought them into..........
De 31:20 and they shall **h.** eaten and filled..............
De 31:21 I **h.** brought them into the land which........
De 31:27 ye **h.** been rebellious against the..............
De 31:29 the way which I **h.** commanded you;..........
De 32:5 They **h.** corrupted themselves, their..........
De 32:21 They **h.** moved me to jealousy with...........
De 32:21 they **h.** provoked me to anger with...........
De 33:9 I **h.** not seen him; neither did he.............
De 33:9 for they **h.** observed thy word, and...........
De 34:4 I **h.** caused thee to see it with thine..........
Jos 1:3 that **h.** I given unto you, as I said unto......
Jos 1:8 and then thou shalt **h.** good success.........
Jos 1:9 **H.** not I commanded thee. Be strong..........
Jos 1:15 Until the Lord **h.** given your brethren........
Jos 1:15 and they also **h.** possessed the land...........
Jos 2:10 For we **h.** heard how the Lord dried...........
Jos 2:12 since I **h.** shewed you kindness, that.........
Jos 2:13 and all that they **h.**, and deliver our..........
Jos 3:4 for ye **h.** not passed this way...................
Jos 5:9 This day **h.** I rolled away the reproach.......
Jos 6:2 I **h.** given into thine hand Jericho, and........
Jos 7:11 and they **h.** also transgressed my.............
Jos 7:11 for they **h.** even taken of the accursed......
Jos 7:11 and **h.** also stolen, and dissembled............
Jos 7:11 and they **h.** put it even among their...........
Jos 7:20 Indeed I **h.** sinned against the Lord..........
Jos 7:20 of Israel, and thus and thus **h.** I done:.......
Jos 8:1 see, I **h.** given into thy hand the...............
Jos 8:6 till we **h.** drawn them from the city;..........
Jos 8:8 And it shall be, when ye **h.** taken the........
Jos 8:8 shall ye do. See, I **h.** commanded you,.......
Jos 9:9 for we **h.** heard the fame of him, and........
Jos 9:19 We **h.** sworn unto them by the Lord..........
Jos 9:22 Wherefore **h.** ye beguiled us, saying,.........
Jos 9:24 lives because of you, and **h.** done this.......
Jos 10:8 Fear them not: for I **h.** delivered them.......
Jos 11:20 and that they might **h.** no favour,.........1961
Jos 13:6 for an inheritance, as I **h.** commanded........
Jos 13:8 and the Gadites **h.** received their..............
Jos 14:9 land whereon thy feet **h.** trodden.............
Jos 17:16 in the land of the valley **h.** chariots of.......
Jos 17:17 thou shalt not **h.** one lot only:............ 1961
Jos 17:18 though they **h.** iron chariots, and.............
Jos 18:7 But the Levites **h.** no part among you;........
Jos 22:2 And said unto them, Ye **h.** kept all...........
Jos 22:2 and **h.** obeyed my voice in all that I...........
Jos 22:3 Ye **h.** not left your brethren these............
Jos 22:3 but **h.** kept the charge of the...................
Jos 22:11 tribe of Manasseh **h.** built an altar............
Jos 22:16 trespass is this that ye **h.** committed..........
Jos 22:16 in that ye **h.** builded you an altar, that.......
Jos 22:23 That we **h.** built us an altar to turn...........
Jos 22:24 And if we **h.** not rather done it for fear......
Jos 22:24 What **h.** ye to do with the Lord................
Jos 22:25 ye **h.** no part in the Lord: so shall............
Jos 22:27 in time to come, Ye **h.** no part in the.........
Jos 22:31 because ye **h.** not committed this..............
Jos 22:31 now ye **h.** delivered the children of...........
Jos 23:3 And ye **h.** seen all that the Lord your........
Jos 23:4 Behold, I **h.** divided unto you by lot..........
Jos 23:4 with all the nations that I **h.** cut off,..........
Jos 23:8 your God, as ye **h.** done unto this day.......
Jos 23:15 until he **h.** destroyed you from off this.......
Jos 23:16 When ye **h.** transgressed the..................
Jos 23:16 and **h.** gone and served other gods,..........
Jos 24:7 them; and your eyes **h.** seen....................
Jos 24:7 what I **h.** done in Egypt: and ye dwelt.........
Jos 24:13 And I **h.** given you a land for which..........
Jos 24:22 that ye **h.** chosen you the Lord, to............
Jg 1:2 behold, I **h.** delivered the land into his.......
Jg 1:7 as I **h.** done, so God hath requited me.......
Jg 2:1 and **h.** brought you unto the land.............
Jg 2:2 but ye **h.** not obeyed my voice:.................
Jg 2:2 my voice: why **h.** ye done this?.................
Jg 2:20 their fathers, and **h.** not hearkened...........
Jg 3:19 and said, I **h.** a secret errand unto............
Jg 3:20 And Ehud said, I **h.** a message from..........
Jg 5:13 that remaineth **h.** dominion.....................
Jg 5:13 the Lord made me **h.** dominion.................
Jg 5:30 **H.** they not sped?...................................
Jg 5:30 **h.** they not divided the prey; to every........
Jg 6:10 but ye **h.** not obeyed my voice.................
Jg 6:14 of the Midianites: **h.** not I sent thee?.........
Jg 6:17 If now I **h.** found grace in thy sight,..........
Jg 6:22 for because I **h.** seen an angel of the.........
Jg 7:9 unto the host; for I **h.** delivered it into.......
Jg 8:2 What **h.** I done now in comparison of.........
Jg 9:16 Now therefore, if ye **h.** done truly and.......
Jg 9:16 in that ye **h.** made Abimelech king,...........
Jg 9:16 and if ye **h.** dealt well with Jerubaal..........
Jg 9:16 and **h.** done unto him according to the.......
Jg 9:18 and **h.** slain his sons, threescore and.........
Jg 9:18 and **h.** made Abimelech, the son of his.......
Jg 9:19 If ye then **h.** dealt truly and sincerely.........
Jg 9:48 What ye **h.** seen me do, make haste,..........
Jg 9:48 me do, make haste, and do as I **h.** done......
Jg 10:10 unto the Lord, saying, We **h.** sinned.......
Jg 10:10 because we **h.** forsaken our God, and........
Jg 10:13 Yet ye **h.** forsaken me, and served............
Jg 10:14 unto the gods which ye **h.** chosen;..........
Jg 10:15 We **h.** sinned: do thou unto us.................
Jg 11:27 Wherefore I **h.** not sinned against............
Jg 11:35 for I **h.** opened my mouth unto the............
Jg 13:15 until we shall **h.** made ready a kid for.......
Jg 13:22 surely die, because we **h.** seen God.........
Jg 13:23 he would not **h.** received a burnt............
Jg 13:23 neither would he **h.** shewed us all............
Jg 13:23 nor would as at this time **h.** told us..........
Jg 14:2 and said, I **h.** seen a woman in.................

Book	Ref	Context	No.
Jg	14:6	and he rent him as he would **h.** rent a	
Jg	14:15	house with fire: **h.** ye called us to	
Jg	14:15	ye called us to take that we **h.**? is it	
Jg	14:16	Behold, I **h.** not told it my father nor	
Jg	15:7	Though ye **h.** done this, yet will I be	
Jg	15:11	As they did unto me, so **h.** I done unto	
Jg	15:16	with the jaw of an ass **h.** I slain a	
Jg	16:17	for I **h.** been a Nazarite unto God from	
Jg	17:13	good, seeing I **h.** a Levite to my	1961
Jg	18:9	for we **h.** seen the land, and, behold, it	
Jg	18:14	therefore consider what ye **h.** to do	
Jg	18:24	And he said, Ye **h.** taken away my gods	
Jg	18:24	are gone away: and what **h.** I more?	
Jg	20:5	night, and thought to **h.** slain me:	
Jg	20:5	and my concubine **h.** they forced,	
Jg	20:6	for they **h.** committed lewdness and	
Jg	20:10	all the folly that they **h.** wrought in	
Jg	21:7	seeing we **h.** sworn by the Lord that	
Jg	21:18	for the children of Israel **h.** sworn.	
Ru	1:8	as ye **h.** dealt with the dead, and with	
Ru	1:12	for I am too old to **h.** an husband	
Ru	1:12	If I should say, I **h.** hope,	
Ru	1:12	if I should **h.** an husband also to night,	
Ru	2:9	**h.** I not charged the young men that	
Ru	2:9	which the young men **h.** drawn.	
Ru	2:10	Why **h.** I found grace in thine eyes,	
Ru	2:21	until they **h.** ended all my harvest.	
Ru	3:3	until he shall **h.** done eating and	
Ru	3:18	until he **h.** finished the thing this day.	
Ru	4:9	witnesses this day, that I **h.** bought all	
Ru	4:10	the wife of Mahlon, **h.** I purchased to	
1Sa	1:15	I **h.** drunk neither wine nor strong	
1Sa	1:15	but **h.** poured out my soul before the	
1Sa	1:16	of my complaint and grief **h.** I spoken	
1Sa	1:20	Because I **h.** asked him of the Lord	
1Sa	1:23	tarry until thou **h.** weaned him; only	
1Sa	1:28	Therefore also I **h.** lent him to the	
1Sa	2:5	They that were full **h.** hired out	
1Sa	2:15	he will not **h.** sodden flesh of thee,	3947
1Sa	2:29	mine offering, which I **h.** commanded	
1Sa	3:12	all things which I **h.** spoken concerning	
1Sa	3:13	For I **h.** told him that I will judge his	
1Sa	3:14	And therefore I **h.** sworn unto the	
1Sa	4:9	as they **h.** been to you: quit yourselves	
1Sa	5:10	They **h.** brought about the ark of the	
1Sa	6:21	The Philistines **h.** brought again the	
1Sa	7:6	We **h.** sinned against the Lord. And	
1Sa	8:7	thee: for they **h.** not rejected thee,	
1Sa	8:7	but they **h.** rejected me, that I should	
1Sa	8:8	all the works which they **h.** done since	
1Sa	8:8	wherewith they **h.** forsaken me, and	
1Sa	8:18	your king which ye shall **h.** chosen	
1Sa	8:19	Nay; but we will **h.** a king over us;	1961
1Sa	9:7	bring to the man of God: what **h.** we?	
1Sa	9:8	Behold, I **h.** here at hand the	4672
1Sa	9:16	for I **h.** looked upon my people,	
1Sa	9:24	I **h.** invited the people. So Saul did	
1Sa	10:19	And ye **h.** this day rejected your God,	
1Sa	10:19	and ye **h.** said unto him, Nay, but set a	
1Sa	11:9	time the sun be hot, ye shall **h.** help	
1Sa	12:1	Israel, Behold, I **h.** hearkened unto	
1Sa	12:1	me, and **h.** made a king over you	
1Sa	12:2	and I **h.** walked before you from my	
1Sa	12:3	his anointed: whose ox **h.** I taken?	
1Sa	12:3	I taken? or whose ass **h.** I taken?	
1Sa	12:3	I taken? or whom **h.** I defrauded?	
1Sa	12:3	I defrauded? whom **h.** I oppressed?	
1Sa	12:3	whose hand **h.** I received any bribe	
1Sa	12:5	that ye **h.** not found ought in my hand	
1Sa	12:10	unto the Lord, and said, We **h.** sinned,	
1Sa	12:10	because we **h.** forsaken the Lord,	
1Sa	12:10	and **h.** served Baalim and Ashtaroth:	
1Sa	12:13	behold the king whom ye **h.** chosen.	
1Sa	12:13	and whom ye **h.** desired! and, behold,	
1Sa	12:17	which ye **h.** done in the sight of the	
1Sa	12:19	for we **h.** added unto all our sins this	
1Sa	12:20	Fear not: ye **h.** done all this	
1Sa	13:12	and I **h.** not made supplication unto	
1Sa	13:13	for now would the Lord **h.** established	
1Sa	14:29	how mine eyes **h.** been enlightened,	
1Sa	14:33	And he said, Ye **h.** transgressed:	
1Sa	15:3	destroy all that they **h.**, and spare	
1Sa	15:11	repenteth me that I **h.** set up Saul to	
1Sa	15:13	I **h.** performed the commandment of	
1Sa	15:15	Saul said, They **h.** brought them from	
1Sa	15:15	and the rest we **h.** utterly destroyed	
1Sa	15:20	I **h.** obeyed the voice of the Lord,	
1Sa	15:20	and **h.** gone the way which the Lord	
1Sa	15:20	and **h.** brought Agag the king of	
1Sa	15:20	and **h.** utterly destroyed the	
1Sa	15:21	should **h.** been utterly destroyed	
1Sa	15:24	Saul said unto Samuel, I **h.** sinned:	
1Sa	15:24	I **h.** transgressed the commandment	
1Sa	15:30	Then he said, I **h.** sinned: yet honour	
1Sa	16:1	for Saul, seeing I **h.** rejected him	
1Sa	16:1	for I **h.** provided me a king among	
1Sa	16:7	because I **h.** refused him: for the	
1Sa	16:18	Behold, I **h.** seen a son of Jesse the	
1Sa	17:25	men of Israel said, **H.** ye seen this	
1Sa	17:29	David said, What **h.** I now done? Is	
1Sa	17:39	these; for I **h.** not proved them.	
1Sa	18:8	They **h.** ascribed unto David ten	
1Sa	18:8	and to me they **h.** ascribed but	
1Sa	18:19	should **h.** been given to David, that	
1Sa	19:4	his works **h.** been to thee-ward	
1Sa	20:1	What **h.** I done? what is mine	
1Sa	20:3	certainly knoweth that I **h.** found grace	
1Sa	20:7	is well; thy servant shall **h.** peace:	
1Sa	20:12	when I **h.** sounded my father about	
1Sa	20:23	thou and I **h.** spoken of, behold, the	
1Sa	20:29	and now, if I **h.** found favour in thine	
1Sa	20:42	forasmuch as we **h.** sworn both of us	
1Sa	21:2	thee, and what I **h.** commanded thee:	
1Sa	21:2	I **h.** appointed my servants to such	
1Sa	21:4	if the young men **h.** kept themselves	
1Sa	21:5	Of a truth women **h.** been kept from	
1Sa	21:8	for I **h.** neither brought my sword	
1Sa	21:14	wherefore then **h.** ye brought him	
1Sa	21:15	**H.** I need of mad men, that ye	
1Sa	21:15	that ye **h.** brought this fellow to play	
1Sa	22:8	That all of you **h.** conspired against	
1Sa	22:13	Why **h.** ye conspired against me, thou	
1Sa	22:22	I **h.** occasioned the death of all the	
1Sa	23:21	Lord; for ye **h.** compassion on me	
1Sa	23:27	for the Philistines **h.** invaded the	
1Sa	24:10	Behold, this day thine eyes **h.** seen	
1Sa	24:11	and I **h.** not sinned again to thee; yet	
1Sa	24:17	me good, whereas I **h.** rewarded	
1Sa	25:7	And now I **h.** heard that thou hast	
1Sa	25:11	and my flesh that I **h.** killed for my	
1Sa	25:21	Surely in vain **h.** I kept all that this	
1Sa	25:30	when the Lord shall **h.** done to my	
1Sa	25:30	and shall **h.** appointed thee ruler over	
1Sa	25:31	when the Lord shall **h.** dealt well with	
1Sa	25:35	see, I **h.** harkened to thy voice,	
1Sa	25:35	thy voice, and **h.** accepted thy person.	
1Sa	26:16	because ye **h.** not kept your master,	
1Sa	26:18	for what **h.** I done? or what evil is in	
1Sa	26:19	If the Lord **h.** stirred thee up against	
1Sa	26:19	for they **h.** driven me out this day	
1Sa	26:21	Then said Saul, I **h.** sinned: return,	
1Sa	26:21	this day: behold, I **h.** played the fool,	
1Sa	26:21	the fool, and **h.** erred exceedingly.	
1Sa	27:5	if I **h.** now found grace in thine	
1Sa	27:10	Whither **h.** ye made a road to day?	
1Sa	28:9	cut off those that **h.** familiar spirits,	
1Sa	28:15	therefore I **h.** called thee, that thou	
1Sa	28:21	obeyed thy voice, and I **h.** put my life	
1Sa	28:21	and **h.** hearkened unto thy words	
1Sa	28:22	and eat, that thou mayest **h.** strength.	
1Sa	29:3	and I **h.** found no fault in him since	
1Sa	29:6	for I **h.** not found evil in thee since	
1Sa	29:8	But what **h.** I done? and what hast	
1Sa	29:8	I **h.** been with thee unto this day,	
1Sa	29:9	the Philistines **h.** said, He shall not	
1Sa	29:10	up early in the morning, and **h.** light,	
1Sa	30:22	of the spoil that we **h.** recovered, save	
2Sa	1:10	was on his arm, and **h.** brought them	
2Sa	1:16	against thee, saying, I **h.** slain the	
2Sa	2:5	that ye **h.** shewed this kindness unto	
2Sa	2:5	even unto Saul, and **h.** buried him.	
2Sa	2:6	because ye **h.** done this thing.	
2Sa	2:7	also the house of Judah **h.** anointed	
2Sa	3:8	and **h.** not delivered thee into the	
2Sa	4:6	as though they would **h.** fetched	
2Sa	4:10	Saul is dead, thinking to **h.** brought	
2Sa	4:10	who thought that I would **h.** given	
2Sa	4:11	much more, when wicked men **h.** slain	
2Sa	7:6	Whereas I **h.** not dwelt in any house	
2Sa	7:6	but **h.** walked in a tent and in a	
2Sa	7:7	all the places wherein I **h.** walked	
2Sa	7:9	and **h.** cut off all thine enemies out	
2Sa	7:9	and **h.** made thee a great name, like	
2Sa	7:11	and **h.** caused thee to rest from all	
2Sa	7:22	according to all that we **h.** heard	
2Sa	9:9	I **h.** given unto thy master's son all	
2Sa	9:10	that thy master's son may **h.** food	1961
2Sa	12:8	I would moreover **h.** given unto thee	
2Sa	12:13	David said unto Nathan, I **h.** sinned	
2Sa	12:27	to David, and said, I **h.** fought against	
2Sa	12:27	against Rabbah, and **h.** taken the city	
2Sa	13:9	And Amnon said, **H.** out all men	3318
2Sa	13:28	**h.** not I commanded you? be	
2Sa	13:32	not my lord suppose that they **h.** slain	
2Sa	14:15	because the people **h.** made me afraid:	
2Sa	14:21	Behold now, I **h.** done this thing: go	
2Sa	14:22	that I **h.** found grace in thy sight, my	
2Sa	14:29	to **h.** sent him to the king; but he	
2Sa	14:31	**h.** thy servants set my field on fire?	
2Sa	14:32	good for me to **h.** been there still:	
2Sa	15:7	pay my vow, which I **h.** vowed unto	
2Sa	15:26	But if he thus say, I **h.** no delight in	
2Sa	15:34	as I **h.** been thy father's servant	
2Sa	15:36	Behold, they **h.** there with them their	
2Sa	16:10	What **h.** I to do with you, ye sons of	
2Sa	16:19	as I **h.** served in thy father's presence,	
2Sa	17:15	and thus and thus **h.** I counselled.	
2Sa	18:11	and I would **h.** given thee ten shekels	
2Sa	18:13	Otherwise I should **h.** wrought	
2Sa	18:13	thyself wouldest **h.** set thyself against	
2Sa	18:18	I **h.** no son to keep my name in	
2Sa	19:5	this day **h.** saved thy life, and the	
2Sa	19:20	I **h.** sinned: therefore, behold, I am	
2Sa	19:22	What **h.** I to do with you, ye sons of	
2Sa	19:28	What right therefore **h.** I yet to	3426
2Sa	19:29	I **h.** said, Thou and Ziba divide the	
2Sa	19:34	How long **h.** I to live, that I should	
2Sa	19:41	Why **h.** our brethren...stolen thee	
2Sa	19:41	and **h.** brought the king, and his	
2Sa	19:42	**h.** we eaten at all of the king's cost?	
2Sa	19:43	said, We **h.** ten parts in the king,	
2Sa	19:43	and we **h.** also more right in David	
2Sa	20:1	and said, We **h.** no part in David,	
2Sa	20:1	neither **h.** we inheritance in the son	
2Sa	21:4	We will **h.** no silver nor gold of Saul,	
2Sa	21:16	sword, thought to **h.** slain David.	
2Sa	22:22	for I **h.** kept the ways of the Lord,	
2Sa	22:22	and **h.** not wickedly departed from	
2Sa	22:24	**h.** kept myself from mine iniquity.	
2Sa	22:30	for by thee I **h.** run through a troop:	
2Sa	22:30	by my God **h.** I leaped over a wall.	
2Sa	22:38	I **h.** pursued mine enemies, and	
2Sa	22:39	And I **h.** consumed them, and	
2Sa	24:10	David said unto the Lord, I **h.** sinned	
2Sa	24:10	sinned greatly in that I **h.** done:	
2Sa	24:10	servant; for I **h.** done very foolishly.	
2Sa	24:17	the people, and said, Lo, I **h.** sinned,	
2Sa	24:17	and I **h.** done wickedly: but these	
2Sa	24:17	what **h.** they done? let thine hand,	
1Ki	1:35	and I **h.** appointed him to be ruler	
1Ki	1:44	and they **h.** caused him to ride upon	
1Ki	1:45	**h.** anointed him king in Gihon:	
1Ki	1:45	This is the noise that ye **h.** heard	
1Ki	2:14	said moreover, I **h.** somewhat to say	
1Ki	2:23	if Adonijah **h.** not spoken this word	
1Ki	2:42	The word that I **h.** heard is good.	
1Ki	2:43	commandment that I **h.** charged thee	
1Ki	3:12	Behold, I **h.** done according to thy	
1Ki	3:12	lo, I **h.** given thee a wise and	
1Ki	3:13	And I **h.** also given thee that which	
1Ki	5:8	I **h.** considered the things which thou	
1Ki	8:13	I **h.** surely built thee an house to	
1Ki	8:20	and **h.** built an house for the name	
1Ki	8:21	And I **h.** set there a place for the ark.	
1Ki	8:27	less this house that I **h.** builded?	
1Ki	8:28	Yet **h.** thou respect unto the prayer	
1Ki	8:33	because they **h.** sinned against thee,	
1Ki	8:35	because they **h.** sinned against thee;	
1Ki	8:43	this house, which I **h.** builded, is	
1Ki	8:44	and toward the house that I **h.** built	
1Ki	8:47	them captives, saying, We **h.** sinned,	
1Ki	8:47	sinned, and **h.** done perversely, we	
1Ki	8:47	we **h.** committed wickedness;	
1Ki	8:48	the house which I **h.** built for thy	
1Ki	8:50	And forgive thy people that **h.** sinned	
1Ki	8:50	wherein they **h.** transgressed against	
1Ki	8:50	that they may **h.** compassion on	
1Ki	8:59	wherewith I **h.** made supplication	
1Ki	9:3	I **h.** heard thy prayer and thy	
1Ki	9:3	I **h.** hallowed this house, which thou	
1Ki	9:4	to all that I **h.** commanded thee, and	

1Ki 9:6 my statutes which I **h.** set before you,
1Ki 9:7 out of the land which I **h.** given them;
1Ki 9:7 and this house, which I **h.** hallowed for
1Ki 9:9 and **h.** taken hold on other gods,
1Ki 9:9 and **h.** worshipped them, and served
1Ki 11:11 my statutes, which I **h.** commanded
1Ki 11:13 for Jerusalem's sake which I **h.** chosen
1Ki 11:32 But he shall **h.** one tribe for my 1961
1Ki 11:32 the city which I **h.** chosen out of all
1Ki 11:33 Because that they **h.** forsaken me,
1Ki 11:33 and **h.** worshipped Ashtoreth the
1Ki 11:33 and **h.** not walked in my ways, to do
1Ki 11:36 my servant may **h.** a light away 1961
1Ki 11:36 the city which I **h.** chosen me to put
1Ki 12:9 people, who **h.** spoken to me, saying,
1Ki 12:16 saying, What portion **h.** we in David?
1Ki 12:16 neither **h.** we inheritance in the son
1Ki 14:15 because they **h.** made their groves,
1Ki 15:19 behold, I **h.** sent unto thee a present
1Ki 17:4 and I **h.** commanded the ravens to
1Ki 17:9 I **h.** commanded a widow woman
1Ki 17:12 thy God liveth, I **h.** not a cake, 3426
1Ki 17:18 What **h.** I to do with thee, O thou man
1Ki 18:9 And he said, What **h.** I sinned, that
1Ki 18:18 answered, I **h.** not troubled Israel;
1Ki 18:18 ye **h.** forsaken the commandments
1Ki 18:36 and that I **h.** done all these things at
1Ki 19:10 And he said, I **h.** been very jealous
1Ki 19:10 for the children of Israel **h.** forsaken
1Ki 19:14 And he said, I **h.** been very jealous
1Ki 19:14 the children of Israel **h.** forsaken
1Ki 19:18 Yet I **h.** left me seven thousand in
1Ki 19:18 all the knees which **h.** not bowed
1Ki 19:20 Go back again: for what **h.** I done to
1Ki 20:4 saying, I am thine, and all that I **h.**
1Ki 20:5 Although I **h.** sent unto thee, saying,
1Ki 20:28 Because the Syrians **h.** said, The
1Ki 20:31 Behold now, we **h.** heard that the
1Ki 21:2 thy vineyard, that I may **h.** it for 1961
1Ki 21:20 he answered, I **h.** found thee: because
1Ki 22:11 Syrians, until thou **h.** consumed them
1Ki 22:17 as sheep that **h.** not a shepherd:
1Ki 22:17 These **h.** no master: let them return
2Ki 2:21 Thus saith the Lord, I **h.** healed these
2Ki 3:13 What **h.** I to do with thee? get thee to
2Ki 3:23 and they **h.** smitten one another: now
2Ki 3:27 eldest son that should **h.** reigned in
2Ki 5:6 behold, I **h.** therewith sent Naaman
2Ki 5:13 wouldest thou not **h.** done it? how
2Ki 7:12 shew you what the Syrians **h.** done to
2Ki 7:17 whose hand he leaned to **h.** the charge
2Ki 9:3 I **h.** anointed thee king over Israel
2Ki 9:5 and he said, I **h.** an errand to thee, O
2Ki 9:6 I **h.** anointed thee king over the
2Ki 9:12 saith the Lord, I **h.** anointed thee king
2Ki 9:26 Surely I **h.** seen yesterday the blood
2Ki 10:8 They **h.** brought the heads of the
2Ki 10:19 wanting: for I **h.** a great sacrifice to
2Ki 10:24 any of the men whom I **h.** brought
2Ki 11:15 **H.** her forth without the ranges: 3318
2Ki 13:17 in Aphek, till thou **h.** consumed
2Ki 13:19 Thou shouldest **h.** smitted five or six
2Ki 17:38 And the covenant that I **h.** made with
2Ki 18:14 saying, I **h.** offended; return from me:
2Ki 18:20 I **h.** counsel and strength for the war
2Ki 18:34 **h.** they delivered Samaria out of
2Ki 18:35 that **h.** delivered their country out of
2Ki 19:6 of the king of Assyria **h.** blasphemed
2Ki 19:11 the kings of Assyria **h.** done at all
2Ki 19:12 **H.** the gods of the nations delivered
2Ki 19:12 which my fathers **h.** destroyed; as
2Ki 19:17 the kings of Assyria **h.** destroyed the
2Ki 19:18 And **h.** cast their gods into the fire:
2Ki 19:18 and stone: therefore they **h.** destroyed
2Ki 19:20 Sennacherib king of Assyria I **h.** heard
2Ki 19:24 **h.** digged and drunk strange waters
2Ki 19:24 and with the sole of my feet **h.** I dried
2Ki 19:25 not heard long ago how I **h.** done it,
2Ki 19:25 of ancient times that I **h.** formed it?
2Ki 19:25 now **h.** I brought it to pass, that
2Ki 20:3 remember now how I **h.** walked before
2Ki 20:3 and **h.** done that which is good in
2Ki 20:5 thy father, I **h.** heard thy prayer,
2Ki 20:5 I **h.** seen thy tears: behold, I will heal
2Ki 20:9 This sign shalt thou **h.** of the Lord,
2Ki 20:15 And he said, What **h.** they seen in
2Ki 20:15 that are in mine house **h.** they seen:
2Ki 20:15 my treasures that I **h.** not shewed
2Ki 20:17 and that which thy fathers **h.** laid up
2Ki 21:7 and in Jerusalem, which I **h.** chosen
2Ki 21:8 according to all that I **h.** commanded
2Ki 21:15 Because they **h.** done that which was
2Ki 21:15 and **h.** provoked me to anger, since the
2Ki 22:4 keepers of the door **h.** gathered of the
2Ki 22:5 that **h.** the oversight of the house of
2Ki 22:8 I **h.** found the book of the law in the
2Ki 22:9 Thy servants **h.** gathered the money
2Ki 22:9 and **h.** delivered it into the hand of
2Ki 22:9 that **h.** the oversight of the house of
2Ki 22:13 because our fathers **h.** not hearkened
2Ki 22:17 Because they **h.** forsaken me, and
2Ki 22:17 and **h.** burned incense unto other
2Ki 22:19 I also **h.** heard thee, saith the Lord
2Ki 23:27 as I **h.** removed Israel, and will cast
2Ki 23:27 city Jerusalem which I **h.** chosen,
1Ch 11:19 blood of these men that **h.** put their
1Ch 15:12 unto the place that I **h.** prepared for
1Ch 17:5 For I **h.** not dwelt in an house since the
1Ch 17:5 but **h.** gone from tent to tent, and
1Ch 17:6 Wheresoever I **h.** walked with all
1Ch 17:6 Why **h.** ye not built me an house of
1Ch 17:8 I **h.** been with thee whithersoever
1Ch 17:8 and **h.** cut off all thine enemies from
1Ch 17:8 and **h.** made thee a name like the
1Ch 17:20 to all that we **h.** heard with our ears
1Ch 21:8 And David said unto God, I **h.** sinned
1Ch 21:8 because I **h.** done this thing: but now,
1Ch 21:8 servant; for I **h.** done very foolishly
1Ch 21:17 even I it is that **h.** sinned and done
1Ch 21:17 as for these sheep, what **h.** they done?
1Ch 22:14 behold, in my trouble I **h.** prepared
1Ch 22:14 and stone **h.** I prepared; and thou
1Ch 28:6 for I **h.** chosen him to be my son, and
1Ch 29:2 Now I **h.** prepared with all my might
1Ch 29:3 because I **h.** set my affection to thee
1Ch 29:3 I **h.** of mine own proper good, of 3426
1Ch 29:3 I **h.** given to the house of my God
1Ch 29:3 all that I **h.** prepared for the holy
1Ch 29:14 and of thine own **h.** we given thee
1Ch 29:16 all this store that we **h.** prepared to
1Ch 29:17 I **h.** willingly offered all these things:
1Ch 29:17 and now **h.** I seen with joy thy people,
1Ch 29:19 for the which I **h.** made provision
2Ch 1:11 over whom I **h.** made thee king:
2Ch 1:12 such as none of the kings **h.** had
2Ch 1:12 that **h.** been before thee, either shall
2Ch 1:12 there any after thee **h.** the like, 1961
2Ch 2:13 And now I **h.** sent a cunning man,
2Ch 6:2 But I **h.** built an house of habitation
2Ch 6:6 But I **h.** chosen Jerusalem, that my
2Ch 6:6 and **h.** chosen David to be over my
2Ch 6:10 and **h.** built the house for the name of
2Ch 6:11 And in it **h.** I put the ark, wherein is
2Ch 6:18 much less this house which I **h.** built!
2Ch 6:19 **H.** respect therefore to the prayer of
2Ch 6:24, 26 because they **h.** sinned against thee;
2Ch 6:33 this house which I **h.** built is called by
2Ch 6:34 the house which I **h.** built for thy
2Ch 6:37 their captivity, saying, We **h.** sinned,
2Ch 6:37 sinned, we **h.** done amiss, and
2Ch 6:37 done amiss, and **h.** dealt wickedly;
2Ch 6:38 whither they **h.** carried them captives,
2Ch 6:38 and toward the house which I **h.** built
2Ch 6:39 forgive thy people which **h.** sinned
2Ch 7:12 and said unto him, I **h.** heard thy
2Ch 7:12 and **h.** chosen this place to myself for
2Ch 7:16 For now I **h.** chosen and sanctified
2Ch 7:17 according to all that I **h.** commanded
2Ch 7:18 according as I **h.** covenanted with
2Ch 7:19 which I **h.** set before you, and shall go
2Ch 7:20 out of my land which I **h.** given them;
2Ch 7:20 and this house, which I **h.** sanctified
2Ch 10:9 answer to this people, that **h.** spoken
2Ch 10:16 saying, What portion **h.** we in David?
2Ch 10:16 and we **h.** none inheritance in the son
2Ch 12:5 saith the Lord, Ye **h.** forsaken me,
2Ch 12:5 and therefore **h.** I also left you in
2Ch 12:7 They **h.** humbled themselves;
2Ch 13:7 **h.** strengthened themselves against
2Ch 13:9 **H.** ye not cast out the priests of the
2Ch 13:9 and **h.** made you priests after the
2Ch 13:10 our God, and we **h.** not forsaken him;
2Ch 13:11 our God; but ye **h.** forsaken him
2Ch 14:7 because we **h.** sought the Lord our
2Ch 14:7 we **h.** sought him, and he hath given
2Ch 14:11 or with them that **h.** no power: help
2Ch 16:3 behold, I **h.** sent thee silver and gold;
2Ch 16:9 henceforth thou shalt **h.** wars 3426
2Ch 18:16 as sheep that **h.** no shepherd:
2Ch 18:16 the Lord said, These **h.** no master;
2Ch 20:8 they dwelt therein, and **h.** built thee
2Ch 20:12 for we **h.** no might against this great
2Ch 21:15 And thou shalt **h.** great sickness by
2Ch 23:14 them, **H.** her forth of the ranges: 3318
2Ch 24:20 because ye **h.** forsaken the Lord, he
2Ch 25:9 hundred talents which I **h.** given to
2Ch 28:9 and ye **h.** slain them in a rage that
2Ch 28:11 which ye **h.** taken captive of your
2Ch 28:13 for whereas we **h.** offended against
2Ch 29:6 For our fathers **h.** trespassed, and
2Ch 29:6 Lord our God, and **h.** forsaken him,
2Ch 29:6 and **h.** turned away their faces from
2Ch 29:7 Also they **h.** shut up the doors of the
2Ch 29:7 and **h.** not burned incense nor offered
2Ch 29:9 For, lo, our fathers **h.** fallen by the
2Ch 29:18 We **h.** cleansed all the house of the
2Ch 29:19 **h.** we prepared and sanctified
2Ch 29:31 Now ye **h.** consecrated yourselves unto
2Ch 31:10 of the Lord, we **h.** had enough to eat,
2Ch 31:10 and **h.** left plenty: for the Lord hath
2Ch 32:13 what I and my fathers **h.** done unto all
2Ch 32:17 **h.** not delivered their people out of
2Ch 33:7 which I **h.** chosen before all the tribes
2Ch 33:8 land which I **h.** appointed for your
2Ch 33:8 to do all that I **h.** commanded them,
2Ch 34:15 I **h.** found the book of the law in the
2Ch 34:17 And they **h.** gathered together the
2Ch 34:17 and **h.** delivered it into the hand of the
2Ch 34:21 because our fathers **h.** not kept the
2Ch 34:24 book which they **h.** read before the
2Ch 34:25 Because they **h.** forsaken me, and
2Ch 34:25 and **h.** burned incense unto other gods,
2Ch 34:27 I **h.** even heard thee also, saith the
2Ch 35:21 What **h.** I to do with thee, thou king of
2Ch 35:21 against the house wherewith I **h.** war:
2Ch 35:23 **H.** me away; for I am sore 5674
Ezr 4:3 Ye **h.** nothing to do with us to build
Ezr 4:12 and **h.** set up the walls thereof, and
Ezr 4:14 Now because we **h.** maintenance
Ezr 4:14 therefore **h.** we sent and certified the
Ezr 4:15 and that they **h.** moved sedition within
Ezr 4:16 thou shalt **h.** no portion on this 383
Ezr 4:19 rebellion and sedition **h.** been made
Ezr 4:20 There **h.** been mighty kings also 1934
Ezr 4:20 which **h.** ruled over all countries
Ezr 6:9 And that which they **h.** need of, both
Ezr 6:11 Also I **h.** made a decree that whosoever
Ezr 6:12 I Darius **h.** made a decree; let it be
Ezr 7:15 and his counsellors **h.** freely offered
Ezr 7:20 which thou shalt **h.** occasion to bestow,
Ezr 9:1 and the Levites, **h.** not separated
Ezr 9:2 For they **h.** taken of their daughters
Ezr 9:2 so that the holy seed **h.** mingled
Ezr 9:7 **h.** we been in a great trespass
Ezr 9:7 iniquities **h.** we … been delivered
Ezr 9:10 for we **h.** forsaken thy commandments,
Ezr 9:11 which **h.** filled it from one end to
Ezr 10:2 said unto Ezra, We **h.** trespassed
Ezr 10:2 and **h.** taken strange wives of the
Ezr 10:10 said unto them, Ye **h.** transgressed,
Ezr 10:10 and **h.** taken strange wives, to increase
Ezr 10:13 we are many that **h.** transgressed in
Ezr 10:14 let all them which **h.** taken strange
Ne 1:6 which we **h.** sinned against thee: both
Ne 1:6 I and my father's house **h.** sinned
Ne 1:7 We **h.** dealt very corruptly against
Ne 1:7 and **h.** not kept the commandments,
Ne 1:9 the place that I **h.** chosen to set my
Ne 2:5 and if thy servant **h.** found favour in
Ne 2:20 but ye **h.** no portion, nor right, nor
Ne 4:5 for they **h.** provoked thee to anger
Ne 5:3 We **h.** mortgaged our lands,
Ne 5:4 We **h.** borrowed money for the king's
Ne 5:5 for other men **h.** our lands and
Ne 5:8 after our ability **h.** redeemed our
Ne 5:14 I and my brethren **h.** not eaten the
Ne 5:19 according to all that I **h.** done for
Ne 6:13 and that they might **h.** matter for an
Ne 6:14 the prophets, that would **h.** put me in
Ne 9:33 thou has done right, but we **h.** done
Ne 9:34 Neither **h.** our kings…kept the law,

Ne	9:35	For they **h.** not served thee in their
Ne	9:37	also they **h.** dominion over our bodies,
Ne	10:37	same Levites might **h.** the tithes
Ne	13:14	that I **h.** done for the house of my God,
Ne	13:29	because they **h.** defiled the priesthood,
Es	1:18	which **h.** heard of the deed of the
Es	3:9	of those that **h.** the charge of the
Es	4:11	but I **h.** not been called to come in
Es	5:4	the banquet that I **h.** prepared for
Es	5:8	If I **h.** found favour in the sight of the
Es	7:3	If I **h.** found favour in thy sight, O
Es	8:5	and if I **h.** found favour in his sight
Es	8:7	Behold, I **h.** given Esther the house of
Es	8:7	and him they **h.** hanged upon the
Es	9:1	enemies of the Jews hoped to **h.** power
Es	9:12	The Jews **h.** slain and destroyed five
Es	9:12	what **h.** they done in the rest of the
Job	1:5	It may be that my sons **h.** sinned, and
Job	1:15	yea, they **h.** slain the servants with
Job	1:17	fell upon the camels, and **h.** carried
Job	3:9	let it look for light, but **h.** none;
Job	3:13	For now should I **h.** lain still and
Job	3:13	I should **h.** slept: then had I been at
Job	4:4	Thy words **h.** upholden him that was
Job	4:8	Even as I **h.** seen, that they plow
Job	5:3	I **h.** seen the foolish taking root: but
Job	5:27	Lo this, we **h.** searched it, so it is;
Job	6:8	Oh that I might **h.** my request; 935
Job	6:10	Then should I yet **h.** comfort; 1961
Job	6:10	for I **h.** not concealed the words of
Job	6:15	My brethren **h.** dealt deceitfully as a
Job	6:24	me to understand wherein I **h.** erred
Job	7:20	I **h.** sinned; what shall I do unto
Job	8:4	If thy children **h.** sinned against him
Job	8:4	and he **h.** cast them away for their
Job	8:18	deny him, saying, I **h.** not seen thee
Job	10:8	Thine hands **h.** made me and
Job	10:19	I should **h.** been as though I had
Job	10:19	I should **h.** been carried from the
Job	12:3	But I **h.** understanding as well as
Job	13:18	Behold now, I **h.** ordered my cause;
Job	14:15	thou wilt **h.** a desire to the work
Job	14:22	his flesh upon him shall **h.** pain,
Job	15:17	and that which I **h.** seen I will
Job	15:18	Which wise men **h.** told from their
Job	15:18	from their fathers, and **h.** not hid it:
Job	16:2	I **h.** heard many such things:
Job	16:3	Shall vain words **h.** an end? or what
Job	16:10	They **h.** gaped upon me with their
Job	16:10	they **h.** smitted me upon the cheek
Job	16:10	they **h.** gathered themselves together
Job	16:15	I **h.** sewed sackcloth upon my skin,
Job	16:18	blood, and let my cry **h.** no place 1961
Job	17:13	I **h.** made my bed in the darkness
Job	17:14	I **h.** said to corruption, Thou art my
Job	18:17	the earth, and he shall **h.** no name in
Job	18:19	He shall neither **h.** son nor nephew
Job	19:3	These ten times **h.** ye reproached me:
Job	19:4	And be it indeed that I **h.** erred, mine
Job	19:14	my kinsfolk **h.** failed, and my
Job	19:14	and my familiar friends **h.** forgotten
Job	19:21	**H.** pity upon me, **h.** pity upon me,
Job	20:3	I **h.** heard the check of my reproach,
Job	20:7	they which **h.** seen him shall say,
Job	21:3	and after that I **h.** spoken, mock on
Job	21:15	what profit should we **h.**, if we pray
Job	21:29	**H.** ye not asked them that go by the
Job	22:9	of the fatherless **h.** been broken
Job	22:15	way which wicked men **h.** trodden?
Job	22:25	and thou shalt **h.** plenty of silver
Job	22:26	then shalt thou **h.** thy delight in the
Job	23:11	hath held his steps, his way **h.** I kept,
Job	23:12	Neither **h.** I gone back from the
Job	23:12	I **h.** esteemed the words of his mouth
Job	24:7	clothing, that they **h.** no covering
Job	24:19	the grave those which **h.** sinned
Job	27:12	Behold, all ye yourselves **h.** seen it;
Job	28:8	The lion's whelps **h.** not trodden it,
Job	28:22	We **h.** heard the fame thereof with
Job	30:1	are younger than I **h.** me in derision,
Job	30:1	whose fathers I would **h.** disdained
Job	30:1	to **h.** set with the dogs of my flock
Job	30:11	they **h.** also let loose the bridle
Job	30:13	my calamity, they **h.** no helper
Job	30:16	the days of affliction **h.** taken hold
Job	31:5	If I **h.** walked with vanity, or if my
Job	31:9	If mine heart **h.** been deceived by a
Job	31:9	or if I **h.** laid wait at my neighbour's
Job	31:16	If I **h.** withheld the poor from their
Job	31:16	or **h.** caused the eyes of the widow to
Job	31:17	Or **h.** eaten my morsel myself alone,
Job	31:18	and I **h.** guided her from my mother's
Job	31:19	If I **h.** seen any perish for want of
Job	31:20	If his loins **h.** not blessed me, and if
Job	31:21	If I **h.** lifted up my hand against the
Job	31:24	If I **h.** made gold my hope, or
Job	31:24	or **h.** said to the fine gold, Thou art
Job	31:28	for I should **h.** denied the God that is
Job	31:30	Neither **h.** I suffered my mouth to
Job	31:39	If I **h.** eaten the fruits thereof without
Job	31:39	or **h.** caused the owners thereof to
Job	32:13	should say, We **h.** found out wisdom:
Job	33:2	Behold, now I **h.** opened my mouth,
Job	33:8	and I **h.** heard the voice of thy words,
Job	33:24	to the pit: I **h.** found a ransom
Job	33:27	and if any say, I **h.** sinned, and
Job	34:2	ear unto me, ye that **h.** knowledge
Job	34:31	I **h.** borne chastisement, I will not
Job	34:32	if I **h.** done iniquity, I will do no more
Job	35:3	What profit shall I **h.**, if I be cleansed
Job	36:2	that I **h.** yet to speak on God's behalf
Job	36:9	transgressions that they **h.** exceeded
Job	36:16	Even so would he **h.** removed thee out
Job	38:17	**H.** the gates of death been opened
Job	38:23	Which I **h.** reserved against the time
Job	39:6	Whose house I **h.** made the wilderness,
Job	40:5	Once **h.** I spoken; but I will not
Job	42:3	therefore **h.** I uttered that I
Job	42:5	I **h.** heard of thee by the hearing of
Job	42:7	for ye **h.** not spoken of me the thing
Job	42:8	in that ye **h.** not spoken of me the thing
Ps	2:4	the Lord shall **h.** them in derision
Ps	2:6	Yet **h.** I set my king upon my holy
Ps	2:7	art my Son; this day **h.** I begotten
Ps	3:6	that **h.** set themselves against me
Ps	4:1	**h.** mercy upon me, and hear my
Ps	5:10	transgressions; for they **h.** rebelled
Ps	6:2	**H.** mercy upon me, O Lord; for I
Ps	7:3	O Lord my God, if I **h.** done this; if
Ps	7:4	If I **h.** rewarded evil unto him that
Ps	7:4	yea, I **h.** delivered him that without
Ps	8:6	madest him to **h.** dominion over
Ps	9:13	**H.** mercy upon me, O Lord;
Ps	10:2	in the devices that they **h.** imagined
Ps	12:4	Who **h.** said, With our tongue will we
Ps	13:4	Lest mine enemy say, I **h.** prevailed
Ps	13:5	But I **h.** trusted in thy mercy; my
Ps	14:1	they **h.** done abominable works,
Ps	14:4	**H.** all...of inquity no knowledge?
Ps	14:6	Ye **h.** shamed the counsel of the
Ps	16:6	places; yea, I **h.** a goodly heritage 5921
Ps	16:8	I **h.** set the Lord always before me:
Ps	17:4	I **h.** kept me from the paths of the
Ps	17:6	I **h.** called upon thee, for thou wilt
Ps	17:11	They **h.** now compassed us in our
Ps	17:11	they **h.** set their eyes bowing down
Ps	17:14	which **h.** their portion in this life,
Ps	18:21	For I **h.** kept the ways of the Lord,
Ps	18:21	and **h.** not wickedly departed from
Ps	18:29	For by thee I **h.** run through a troop;
Ps	18:29	and by my God **h.** I leaped over a
Ps	18:37	I **h.** pursued mine enemies, and
Ps	18:38	I **h.** wounded them that they were
Ps	18:43	a people whom I **h.** not known shall
Ps	19:13	let them not **h.** dominion over me:
Ps	22:12	Many bulls **h.** compassed me: strong
Ps	22:12	strong bulls of Bashan **h.** beset me
Ps	22:16	For dogs **h.** compassed me: the
Ps	22:16	assembly of the wicked **h.** inclosed
Ps	25:6	for they **h.** been ever of old
Ps	25:16	thee unto me, and **h.** mercy upon
Ps	26:1	Judge me, O Lord; for I **h.** walked in
Ps	26:1	I **h.** trusted also in the Lord;
Ps	26:3	before mine eyes: and I **h.** walked in
Ps	26:4	I **h.** not sat with vain persons, neither
Ps	26:5	I **h.** hated the congregation of evil
Ps	26:8	Lord, I **h.** loved the habitation of thy
Ps	27:4	One thing **h.** I desired of the Lord,
Ps	27:7	**h.** mercy also upon me, and
Ps	30:10	Hear, O Lord, and **h.** mercy upon
Ps	31:4	me out of the net that they **h.** laid
Ps	31:6	I **h.** hated them that regard lying
Ps	31:9	**H.** mercy upon me, O Lord, for I
Ps	31:13	For I **h.** heard the slander of many:
Ps	31:17	for I **h.** called upon thee: let the
Ps	32:5	thee, and mine iniquity **h.** I not hid
Ps	32:9	the mule, which **h.** no understanding:
Ps	33:21	because we **h.** trusted in his holy
Ps	35:7	For without cause **h.** they hid for me
Ps	35:7	without cause they **h.** digged for my
Ps	35:25	Ah, so would we **h.** it: let them not
Ps	35:25	say, We **h.** swallowed him up
Ps	37:14	The wicked **h.** drawn out the sword,
Ps	37:14	and **h.** bent their bow, to cast down
Ps	37:25	I **h.** been young, and now am old;
Ps	37:25	yet **h.** I not seen the righteous
Ps	37:35	I **h.** seen the wicked in great power,
Ps	38:8	I **h.** roared by reason of...disquietness
Ps	40:9	I **h.** preached righteousness in the
Ps	40:9	lo, I **h.** not refrained my lips, O Lord,
Ps	40:10	I **h.** not hid thy righteousness within
Ps	40:10	I **h.** declared thy faithfulness and thy
Ps	40:10	I **h.** not concealed thy lovingkindness
Ps	40:12	For innumerable evils **h.** compassed
Ps	40:12	mine iniquities **h.** taken hold upon
Ps	41:4	heal my soul; for I **h.** sinned against
Ps	42:3	My tears **h.** been my meat day
Ps	44:1	We **h.** heard with our ears, O God, our
Ps	44:1	our fathers **h.** told us, what work
Ps	44:17	come upon us; yet **h.** we not forgotten
Ps	44:17	neither **h.** we dealt falsely in thy
Ps	44:18	neither **h.** our steps declined from
Ps	44:20	If we **h.** forgotten the name of our
Ps	45:1	which I **h.** made touching the king:
Ps	45:8	whereby they **h.** made thee glad
Ps	48:8	As we **h.** heard, so **h.** we seen in the
Ps	48:9	We **h.** thought of thy lovingkindness,
Ps	49:14	the upright shall **h.** dominion
Ps	50:5	those that **h.** made a covenant with
Ps	50:8	to **h.** been continually before me
Ps	51:1	**H.** mercy upon me, O God,
Ps	51:4	Against thee, thee only, **h.** I sinned,
Ps	53:1	and **h.** done abominable iniquity:
Ps	53:4	**H.** the...of iniquity no knowledge?
Ps	53:4	as they eat bread: they **h.** not called
Ps	54:3	after my soul: they **h.** not set God
Ps	55:9	for I **h.** seen violence and strife in the
Ps	55:12	then I could **h.** borne it: neither was it
Ps	55:12	against me; then I would **h.** hid
Ps	55:19	Because they **h.** no changes, therefore
Ps	56:4	in God I **h.** put my trust; I will not fear
Ps	56:11	In God **h.** I put my trust: I will not be
Ps	57:6	They **h.** prepared a net for my steps;
Ps	57:6	they **h.** digged a pit before me, into
Ps	59:8	shalt **h.** all the heathen in derision,
Ps	62:11	hath spoken once; twice **h.** I heard
Ps	63:2	thy glory, so as I **h.** seen thee in the
Ps	66:14	Which my lips **h.** uttered, and my
Ps	68:13	Though we **h.** lien among the pots,
Ps	68:24	They **h.** seen thy goings, O God;
Ps	69:7	for thy sake I **h.** borne reproach;
Ps	69:22	should **h.** been for their welfare,
Ps	69:35	there, and **h.** it in possession
Ps	71:6	By thee **h.** I been holden up from the
Ps	71:17	and hitherto **h.** I declared thy
Ps	71:18	until I **h.** shewed thy strength unto
Ps	72:8	He shall **h.** dominion also from sea to
Ps	73:7	with fatness: they **h.** more than heart
Ps	73:13	Verily I **h.** cleansed my heart in vain,
Ps	73:14	For all the day long **h.** I been plagued,
Ps	73:25	Whom **h.** I in heaven but thee? and
Ps	73:28	I **h.** put my trust in the Lord God, that
Ps	74:7	They **h.** cast fire into thy sanctuary,
Ps	74:7	they **h.** defiled by casting down the
Ps	74:8	they **h.** burned up all the synagogues
Ps	74:18	that the foolish people **h.** blasphemed
Ps	74:20	**H.** respect unto the covenant: for the
Ps	76:5	are spoiled, they **h.** slept their sleep:
Ps	76:5	none of the men of might **h.** found
Ps	77:5	I **h.** considered the days of old, the
Ps	78:3	Which we **h.** heard and known, and
Ps	78:3	known, and our fathers **h.** told us
Ps	79:1	thy holy temple **h.** they defiled;
Ps	79:1	they **h.** laid Jerusalem on heaps
Ps	79:2	thy servants **h.** they given to be meat
Ps	79:3	Their blood **h.** they shed like water
Ps	79:6	the heathen that **h.** not known thee,
Ps	79:6	the kingdoms that **h.** not called upon

Ps 79:7 For they **h.** devoured Jacob, and laid
Ps 79:12 wherewith they **h.** reproached thee,
Ps 81:14 I should soon **h.** subdued their
Ps 81:15 of the Lord should **h.** submitted
Ps 81:15 but their time should **h.** endured
Ps 81:16 He should **h.** fed them also with the
Ps 81:16 the rock should I **h.** satisfied thee
Ps 82:6 I **h.** said, Ye are gods; and all of you
Ps 83:2 and they that hate thee **h.** lifted up
Ps 83:3 They **h.** taken crafty counsel against
Ps 83:4 They **h.** said, come, and let us cut
Ps 83:5 For they **h.** consulted together with
Ps 83:8 they **h.** holpen the children of Lot
Ps 85:10 righteousness and peace **h.** kissed
Ps 86:14 of violent men **h.** sought after my
Ps 86:14 and **h.** not set thee before them
Ps 86:16 O turn unto me, and **h.** mercy
Ps 88:1 I **h.** cried day and night before thee:
Ps 88:9 Lord, I **h.** called daily upon thee, I
Ps 88:9 I **h.** stretched out my hands unto thee
Ps 88:13 But unto thee **h.** I cried, O Lord: and
Ps 88:16 over me; thy terrors **h.** cut me off
Ps 89:2 For I **h.** said, mercy shall be built up
Ps 89:3 I **h.** made a covenant with my chosen,
Ps 89:3 I **h.** sworn unto David my servant,
Ps 89:19 I **h.** laid help upon one that is mighty;
Ps 89:19 I **h.** exalted one chosen out of the
Ps 89:20 I **h.** found David my servant; with my
Ps 89:20 with my holy oil **h.** I anointed him:
Ps 89:35 Once **h.** I sworn by my holiness that
Ps 89:51 thine enemies **h.** reproached, O
Ps 89:51 wherewith they **h.** reproached the
Ps 90:15 and the years wherein we **h.** seen evil
Ps 93:3 The floods **h.** lifted up, O Lord, the
Ps 93:3 the floods **h.** lifted up their voice;
Ps 94:20 the throne of iniquity **h.** fellowship
Ps 95:10 and they **h.** not known my ways:
Ps 98:3 all the ends of the earth **h.** seen the
Ps 102:9 For I **h.** eaten ashes like bread, and
Ps 102:13 Thou shall arise, and **h.** mercy
Ps 102:27 same, and thy years shall **h.** no end
Ps 104:12 fowls of the heaven **h.** their habitation,
Ps 104:33 praise to my God while I **h.** my being
Ps 106:6 We **h.** sinned with our fathers, we
Ps 106:6 we **h.** committed iniquity, we
Ps 106:6 iniquity, we have done wickedly
Ps 109:2 they **h.** spoken against me with a
Ps 109:5 And they **h.** rewarded me evil for
Ps 111:2 sought out of all them that **h.** pleasure
Ps 111:10 a good understanding **h.** all they that
Ps 115:5 They **h.** mouths, but they speak not
Ps 115:5 eye **h.** they, but they see not:
Ps 115:6 They **h.** ears, but they hear not: noses
Ps 115:6 noses **h.** they, but they smell not:
Ps 115:7 They **h.** hands, but they handle not:
Ps 115:7 feet **h.** they, but they walk not:
Ps 116:10 I believed, there **h.** I spoken: I
Ps 118:26 we **h.** blessed you out of the house of
Ps 119:6 when I **h.** respect unto all thy
Ps 119:7 when I shall **h.** learned thy righteous
Ps 119:10 With my whole heart **h.** I sought thee;
Ps 119:11 Thy word **h.** I hid in mine heart, that
Ps 119:13 With my lips **h.** I declared all the
Ps 119:14 I **h.** rejoiced in the way of thy
Ps 119:15 and **h.** respect unto thy ways
Ps 119:22 for I **h.** kept thy testimonies
Ps 119:26 I **h.** declared my ways, and thou
Ps 119:30 I **h.** chosen the way of truth: thy
Ps 119:30 thy judgments **h.** I laid before me
Ps 119:31 I **h.** stuck unto thy testimonies: O
Ps 119:40 Behold, I **h.** longed after thy precepts:
Ps 119:42 So shall I **h.** wherewith to answer him
Ps 119:43 for I **h.** hoped in thy judgments
Ps 119:47 in thy commandments.., I **h.** loved
Ps 119:48 unto thy commandments,...I **h.** loved:
Ps 119:51 proud **h.** had me greatly in derision:
Ps 119:51 yet **h.** I not declined from thy law
Ps 119:52 O Lord; and **h.** comforted myself
Ps 119:54 Thy statues **h.** been my songs in
Ps 119:55 I **h.** remembered thy name, O Lord, in
Ps 119:55 in the night, and **h.** kept thy law
Ps 119:57 I **h.** said that I would keep thy words
Ps 119:61 The bands of the wicked **h.** robbed me:
Ps 119:61 but I **h.** not forgotten thy law
Ps 119:66 for I **h.** believed thy commandments
Ps 119:67 astray; but now **h.** I kept thy word
Ps 119:69 The proud **h.** forged a lie against me:
Ps 119:71 good for me that I **h.** been afflicted;
Ps 119:73 Thy hands **h.** made me and fashioned
Ps 119:74 me; because I **h.** hoped in thy word
Ps 119:79 that **h.** known thy testimonies
Ps 119:85 The proud **h.** digged pits for me,
Ps 119:92 I should then **h.** perished in mine
Ps 119:94 me; for I **h.** sought thy precepts
Ps 119:95 The wicked **h.** waited for me to
Ps 119:96 I **h.** seen an end of all perfection:
Ps 119:99 I **h.** more understanding than all my
Ps 119:101 I **h.** refrained my feet from every evil
Ps 119:102 I **h.** not departed from thy judgments:
Ps 119:106 I **h.** sworn, and I will perform it, that
Ps 119:110 The wicked **h.** laid a snare for me:
Ps 119:111 Thy testimonies **h.** I taken as an
Ps 119:112 I **h.** inclined mine heart to perform
Ps 119:117 and I will **h.** respect unto thy statutes
Ps 119:121 I **h.** done judgment and justice:
Ps 119:126 work: for they **h.** made void thy law
Ps 119:133 let not any iniquity **h.** dominion
Ps 119:139 mine enemies **h.** forgotten thy words
Ps 119:143 Trouble and anguish **h.** taken hold on
Ps 119:152 I **h.** known of old that thou hast
Ps 119:161 Princes **h.** persecuted me without a
Ps 119:165 Great peace **h.** they which love thy
Ps 119:166 Lord, I **h.** hoped for thy salvation
Ps 119:168 I **h.** kept thy precepts and thy
Ps 119:173 help me; for I **h.** chosen thy precepts
Ps 119:174 I **h.** longed for thy salvation, O Lord;
Ps 119:176 I **h.** gone astray like a lost sheep:
Ps 123:2 until that he **h.** mercy upon us
Ps 123:3 **H.** mercy upon us, O Lord, **h.** mercy
Ps 129:1,2 Many a time **h.** they afflicted me
Ps 129:2 yet they **h.** not prevailed against me
Ps 130:1 Out of the depths **h.** I cried unto thee
Ps 131:2 Surely I **h.** behaved and quieted
Ps 132:14 here will I dwell; for I **h.** desired it
Ps 132:17 I **h.** ordained a lamp for mine
Ps 135:16 they **h.** mouths, but they speak not;
Ps 135:16 eyes **h.** they, but they see not;
Ps 135:17 They **h.** ears, but they hear not;
Ps 140:3 They **h.** sharpened their tongues like
Ps 140:4 who **h.** purposed to overthrow my
Ps 140:5 The proud **h.** hid a snare for me, and
Ps 140:5 they **h.** spread a net by the wayside;
Ps 140:5 wayside; they **h.** set gins for me
Ps 141:9 the snares which they **h.** laid for me,
Ps 142:3 I walked **h.** they privily laid a snare
Ps 143:3 as those that **h.** been long dead
Ps 146:2 unto my God while I **h.** any being
Ps 147:20 judgments, they **h.** not known them
Ps 149:9 this honour **h.** all his saints. Praise
Pr 1:14 among us; let us all **h.** one purse; 1961
Pr 1:24 Because I **h.** called, and ye refused;
Pr 1:24 I **h.** stretched out my hand, and no
Pr 1:25 But ye **h.** set at nought all my counsel,
Pr 3:30 cause, if he **h.** done thee no harm
Pr 4:11 I **h.** taught thee in the way of wisdom;
Pr 4:11 of wisdom; I **h.** led thee in right paths
Pr 4:16 sleep not, except they **h.** done mischief:
Pr 5:12 And say, How **h.** I hated instruction,
Pr 5:13 And **h.** not obeyed the voice of my
Pr 7:14 I **h.** peace offerings with me; this day
Pr 7:14 with me; this day **h.** I paid my vows
Pr 7:15 to seek thy face, and I **h.** found thee
Pr 7:16 I **h.** decked my bed with coverings of
Pr 7:17 I **h.** perfumed my bed with myrrh,
Pr 7:26 yea, many strong men **h.** been slain
Pr 8:14 I am understanding; I **h.** strength
Pr 9:5 drink of the wine which I **h.** mingled
Pr 13:3 wide his lips shall **h.** destruction
Pr 14:26 his children shall **h.** a place of 1961
Pr 17:2 A wise servant shall **h.** rule over a son
Pr 17:2 shall **h.** part of the inheritance
Pr 19:10 much less for a servent to **h.** rule over
Pr 20:4 shall he beg in harvest, and **h.** nothing
Pr 20:9 Who can say, I **h.** made my heart clean,
Pr 22:19 I **h.** made known to thee this day, even
Pr 22:20 **H.** not I written to thee excellent
Pr 22:28 landmark, which thy fathers **h.** set
Pr 23:24 begetteth a wise child shall **h.** joy
Pr 23:35 They **h.** stricken me, shalt thou say,
Pr 24:23 It is not good to **h.** respect of persons
Pr 25:7 of the prince whom thine eyes **h.** seen
Pr 27:27 And thou shalt **h.** goats' milk
Pr 28:10 but the upright shall **h.** good things
Pr 28:13 forsaketh them shall **h.** mercy
Pr 28:19 tilleth his land shall **h.** plenty of
Pr 28:19 after vain persons shall **h.** poverty
Pr 28:21 To **h.** respect of persons is not good:
Pr 28:27 hideth his eyes shall **h.** many a curse
Pr 29:21 shall **h.** him become his son at the
Pr 30:2 **h.** not the understanding of a man
Pr 30:3 wisdom, nor **h.** the knowledge of
Pr 30:7 Two things **h.** I required of thee; deny
Pr 30:20 and saith, I **h.** done no wickedness
Pr 30:27 The locusts **h.** no king, yet go they
Pr 31:11 so that he shall **h.** no need of spoil
Pr 31:29 Many daughters **h.** done virtuously,
Ec 1:14 I **h.** seen all the works that are done
Ec 1:16 and **h.** gotten more wisdom than all
Ec 1:16 that **h.** been before me in Jerusalem:
Ec 2:19 yet shall he **h.** rule over all my
Ec 2:19 all my labour wherein I **h.** laboured,
Ec 2:19 and wherein I **h.** shewed myself wise
Ec 3:10 I **h.** seen the travail, which God hath
Ec 3:19 yea, they **h.** all one breath; so that a
Ec 4:9 because they **h.** a good reward for 3426
Ec 4:11 if two lie together, then they **h.** heat:
Ec 4:16 even of all that **h.** been before them:
Ec 5:13 there is a sore evil which I **h.** seen
Ec 5:18 Behold that which I **h.** seen: it is good
Ec 6:1 There is an evil which I **h.** seen under
Ec 6:3 and also that he **h.** no burial; I 1961
Ec 7:12 giveth life to them that **h.** it 1167
Ec 7:15 All things **h.** I seen in the days of my
Ec 7:23 All this **h.** I proved by wisdom: I
Ec 7:27 Behold, this **h.** I found, saith the
Ec 7:28 one man among a thousand **h.** I found;
Ec 7:28 among all those **h.** I not found
Ec 7:29 Lo, this only **h.** I found, that God hath
Ec 7:29 they **h.** sought out many inventions
Ec 8:9 All this **h.** I seen, and applied my heart
Ec 9:5 neither **h.** they any more a reward;
Ec 9:6 neither **h.** they any more a portion for
Ec 9:13 This wisdom **h.** I seen also under the
Ec 10:5 there is an evil which I **h.** seen under
Ec 10:7 I **h.** seen servants upon horses, and
Ec 12:1 when thou shalt say, I **h.** no pleasure
Ca 1:6 but mine own vineyard **h.** I not kept
Ca 1:9 I **h.** compared thee, O my love, to a
Ca 2:15 for our vines **h.** tender grapes
Ca 5:1 I **h.** gathered my myrrh with my spice;
Ca 5:1 I **h.** eaten my honeycomb with my
Ca 5:1 I **h.** drunk my wine with my milk:
Ca 5:3 I **h.** put off my coat; how shall I
Ca 5:3 I **h.** washed my feet; how shall I
Ca 6:5 for they **h.** overcome me: thy hair is
Ca 7:13 which I **h.** laid up for thee, O my
Ca 8:8 We **h.** a little sister, and she hath no
Ca 8:12 thou, O Solomon, must **h.** a thousand,
Isa 1:2 I **h.** nourished and brought up
Isa 1:2 children, and they **h.** rebelled against
Isa 1:4 that are corrupters: they **h.** forsaken
Isa 1:4 they **h.** provoked the Holy One of
Isa 1:6 they **h.** not been closed, neither
Isa 1:9 remnant, we should **h.** been as
Isa 1:9 we should **h.** been like unto Gomorrah
Isa 1:29 of the oaks which ye **h.** desired,
Isa 1:29 for the gardens that ye **h.** chosen
Isa 2:8 that which their own fingers **h.** made:
Isa 3:9 for they **h.** rewarded evil unto
Isa 3:14 for ye **h.** eaten up the vineyard; the
Isa 4:4 When the Lord shall **h.** washed away
Isa 4:4 and shall **h.** purged the blood of
Isa 5:4 What could **h.** been done more to my
Isa 5:4 that I **h.** not done in it? wherefore
Isa 5:13 because they **h.** no knowledge: and
Isa 5:24 because they **h.** cast away the law of
Isa 6:5 for mine eyes **h.** seen the King, the
Isa 6:12 the Lord **h.** removed men far away,
Isa 7:5 **h.** taken evil counsel against thee,
Isa 7:17 days that **h.** not come, from the day
Isa 8:4 the child shall **h.** knowledge
Isa 8:19 unto them that **h.** familiar spirits,
Isa 9:2 walked in darkness **h.** seen a great
Isa 9:17 the Lord shall **h.** no joy in their
Isa 9:17 neither shall **h.** mercy on their
Isa 10:1 which they **h.** prescribed;
Isa 10:11 Shall I not, as I **h.** done unto Samaria
Isa 10:13 the strength of my hand I **h.** done it,
Isa 10:13 and I **h.** removed the bounds of the

Isa 10:13 people, and **h.** robbed their treasures,...
Isa 10:13 and I **h.** put down the inhabitants...
Isa 10:14 that are left, **h.** I gathered all the...
Isa 10:29 they **h.** taken up their lodging at...
Isa 13:3 I **h.** commanded my sanctified ones,...
Isa 13:3 I **h.** also called my mighty ones for...
Isa 13:18 and they shall **h.** no pity on the fruit...
Isa 14:1 For the Lord will **h.** mercy on...
Isa 14:24 Surely as I **h.** thought, so shall it...
Isa 14:24 and as I **h.** purposed, so shall it stand:...
Isa 15:7 the abundance they **h.** gotten, and...
Isa 15:7 and that which they **h.** laid up, shall...
Isa 16:6 We **h.** heard of the pride of Moab; he...
Isa 16:8 lords of the heathen **h.** broken down...
Isa 16:10 I **h.** made their vintage shouting to...
Isa 17:7 and his eyes shall **h.** respect to the...
Isa 17:8 which his fingers **h.** made, either the...
Isa 18:2 whose land the rivers **h.** spoiled!...
Isa 18:7 whose land the rivers **h.** spoiled, to...
Isa 19:3 to them that **h.** familiar spirits, and...
Isa 19:13 they **h.** also seduced Egypt, even they...
Isa 19:14 and they **h.** caused Egypt to err in...
Isa 21:2 the sighing thereof **h.** I made to cease...
Isa 21:3 pangs **h.** taken hold upon me, as the...
Isa 21:10 that which I **h.** heard of the Lord of...
Isa 21:10 of Israel, **h.** I declared unto you...
Isa 22:3 are bound together, which **h.** fled...
Isa 22:9 Ye **h.** seen also the breaches of the...
Isa 22:10 And ye **h.** numbered the houses of...
Isa 22:10 and the houses **h.** ye broken down to...
Isa 22:11 but ye **h.** not looked unto the maker...
Isa 23:2 that pass over the sea, **h.** replenished...
Isa 23:12 there also shalt thou **h.** no rest...
Isa 24:5 because they **h.** transgressed...
Isa 24:16 part of the earth **h.** we heard songs,...
Isa 24:16 me! the treacherous dealers **h.** dealt...
Isa 24:16 yea, the treacherous dealers **h.** dealt...
Isa 25:9 we **h.** waited for him, and he will save...
Isa 25:9 we **h.** waited for him, we will be glad...
Isa 26:1 We **h.** a strong city; salvation will...
Isa 26:8 O Lord, **h.** we waited for thee; the...
Isa 26:9 With my soul **h.** I desired thee in the...
Isa 26:13 lords beside thee **h.** had dominion...
Isa 26:16 Lord, in trouble **h.** they visited thee,...
Isa 26:17 so **h.** we been in thy sight, O Lord...
Isa 26:18 We **h.** been with child, we...
Isa 26:18 with child, we **h.** been in pain, we...
Isa 26:18 we **h.** as it were brought forth wind;...
Isa 26:18 we **h.** not wrought any deliverance in...
Isa 26:18 **h.** the inhabitants of the world fallen...
Isa 27:11 made them will not **h.** mercy on...
Isa 28:7 But they also **h.** erred through wine,...
Isa 28:7 the priest and the prophet **h.** erred...
Isa 28:15 ye **h.** said, We **h.** made a covenant...
Isa 28:15 for we **h.** made lies our refuge, and...
Isa 28:15 under falsehood **h.** we hid ourselves:...
Isa 28:22 I **h.** heard from the Lord God of hosts...
Isa 29:13 but **h.** removed their heart far from...
Isa 30:2 and **h.** not asked at my mouth; to...
Isa 30:7 therefore **h.** I cried concerning this,...
Isa 30:18 that he may **h.** mercy upon you:...
Isa 30:29 Ye shall **h.** a song, as in the night......1961
Isa 31:6 children of Israel **h.** deeply revolted...
Isa 31:7 which your own hands **h.** made unto...
Isa 33:2 unto us; we **h.** waited for thee:...
Isa 33:13 ye that are far off, what I **h.** done;...
Isa 36:5 I **h.** counsel and strength for war:...
Isa 36:19 and **h.** they delivered Samaria out of...
Isa 36:20 that **h.** delivered their land out of my...
Isa 37:6 the king of Assyria **h.** blasphemed me...
Isa 37:11 the kings of Assyria **h.** done to all...
Isa 37:12 **H.** the gods of the nations delivered...
Isa 37:12 my fathers **h.** destroyed, as Gozan,...
Isa 37:18 the kings of Assyria, **h.** laid waste all...
Isa 37:19 And **h.** cast their gods into the fire:...
Isa 37:19 and stone: therefore they **h.** destroyed...
Isa 37:25 I **h.** digged, and drunk water; and...
Isa 37:25 the sole of my feet **h.** I dried up all...
Isa 37:26 heard long ago, how I **h.** done it;...
Isa 37:26 of ancient times, that I **h.** formed it?...
Isa 37:26 now **h.** I brought it to pass, that thou...
Isa 38:3 I beseech thee, how I **h.** walked before...
Isa 38:3 and **h.** done that which is good in thy...
Isa 38:5 thy father, I **h.** heard thy prayer,...
Isa 38:5 I **h.** seen thy tears: behold, I will add...
Isa 38:12 I **h.** cut off like a weaver my life: he...
Isa 39:4 Then said he, What **h.** they seen in...
Isa 39:4 All that is in mine house **h.** they seen:...
Isa 39:4 treasures that I **h.** not shewed them...
Isa 39:6 and that which thy fathers **h.** laid up...
Isa 40:21 **H.** ye not known? **h.** ye not heard?...
Isa 40:21 **h.** ye not understood from the...
Isa 40:29 to them that **h.** no might he increaseth...
Isa 41:8 Jacob whom I **h.** chosen, the seed of...
Isa 41:9 Thou whom I **h.** taken from the ends...
Isa 41:9 I **h.** chosen thee, and not cast thee...
Isa 41:25 I **h.** raised up one from the north, and...
Isa 42:1 I **h.** put my spirit upon him: he shall...
Isa 42:4 till he **h.** set judgment in the earth:...
Isa 42:6 I the Lord **h.** called thee in...
Isa 42:14 I **h.** long time holden my peace; I...
Isa 42:14 I **h.** been still, and refrained myself:...
Isa 42:16 in paths that they **h.** not known:...
Isa 42:24 he against whom we **h.** sinned? for...
Isa 43:1 O Israel, Fear not: for I **h.** redeemed...
Isa 43:1 I **h.** called thee by thy name; thou art...
Isa 43:4 and I **h.** loved thee: therefore will I...
Isa 43:7 by my name: for I **h.** created him...
Isa 43:7 for my glory, I **h.** formed him;...
Isa 43:7 formed him; yea, I **h.** made him...
Isa 43:8 the blind people that **h.** eyes,......3426
Isa 43:8 eyes, and the deaf that **h.** ears...
Isa 43:10 and my servant whom I **h.** chosen:...
Isa 43:12 I **h.** declared, and **h.** saved, and I...
Isa 43:12 and I **h.** shewed them, when there was...
Isa 43:14 For your sake I **h.** sent to Babylon,...
Isa 43:14 and **h.** brought down all their nobles,...
Isa 43:21 This people **h.** I formed for myself;...
Isa 43:23 I **h.** not caused thee to serve with an...
Isa 43:27 and thy teachers **h.** transgressed...
Isa 43:28 Therefore I **h.** profaned the princes...
Isa 43:28 and **h.** given Jacob to the curse, and...
Isa 44:1 servant; and Israel, whom I **h.** chosen:...
Isa 44:2 thou, Jesurun, whom I **h.** chosen...
Isa 44:8 **h.** not I told thee from that time,...
Isa 44:8 and **h.** declared it? ye are even my...
Isa 44:16 Aha, I am warm, I **h.** seen the fire:...
Isa 44:18 They **h.** not known nor understood:...
Isa 44:19 to say, I **h.** burned part of it in the...
Isa 44:19 yea, also I **h.** baked bread upon the...
Isa 44:19 I **h.** roasted flesh, and eaten it: and...
Isa 44:21 I **h.** formed thee; thou art my...
Isa 44:22 I **h.** blotted out, as a thick cloud, thy...
Isa 44:22 return unto me; for I **h.** redeemed...
Isa 45:1 whose right hand I **h.** holden, to...
Isa 45:4 I **h.** even called thee by thy name; I...
Isa 45:4 I **h.** surnamed thee, though thou hast...
Isa 45:8 up together; I the Lord **h.** created it...
Isa 45:12 I **h.** made the earth, and created man...
Isa 45:12 I, even my hands, **h.** stretched out the...
Isa 45:12 all their host **h.** I commanded...
Isa 45:13 I **h.** raised him up in righteousness,...
Isa 45:19 I **h.** not spoken in secret, in a dark...
Isa 45:20 they **h.** no knowledge that set up...
Isa 45:21 **h.** not I the Lord? and there is no...
Isa 45:23 I **h.** sworn by myself, the word is gone...
Isa 45:24 in the Lord **h.** I righteousness and...
Isa 46:4 I **h.** made, and I will bear; even I will...
Isa 46:11 yea, I **h.** spoken it, I will also bring it...
Isa 46:11 I **h.** purposed it, I will also do it...
Isa 47:6 I **h.** polluted mine inheritance, and...
Isa 48:3 I **h.** declared the former things from...
Isa 48:5 **h.** even from the beginning declared...
Isa 48:6 I **h.** shewed thee new things from this...
Isa 48:10 Behold, I **h.** refined thee, but not with...
Isa 48:10 I **h.** chosen thee in the furnace of...
Isa 48:15 I, even I, **h.** spoken; yea, I **h.** called...
Isa 48:15 I **h.** brought him, and he shall make...
Isa 48:16 I **h.** not spoken in secret from the...
Isa 48:19 his name should not **h.** been cut off...
Isa 49:4 Then I said, I **h.** laboured in vain,...
Isa 49:4 I **h.** spent my strength for nought,...
Isa 49:8 In an acceptable time **h.** I heard thee,...
Isa 49:8 and in a day of salvation **h.** I helped...
Isa 49:13 will **h.** mercy upon his afflicted...
Isa 49:15 that she should not **h.** compassion...
Isa 49:16 Behold, I **h.** graven thee upon the...
Isa 49:20 children which thou shalt **h.**, after...
Isa 49:21 me these, seeing I **h.** lost my children,...
Isa 50:1 whom I **h.** put away? or which of...
Isa 50:1 creditors is it to whom I **h.** sold you?...
Isa 50:1 Behold, for your iniquities **h.** ye sold...
Isa 50:2 or **h.** I no power to deliver? behold,...
Isa 50:7 therefore **h.** I set my face like a flint,...
Isa 50:11 and in the sparks that he **h.** kindled...
Isa 50:11 This shall ye **h.** of mine hand; ye......1961
Isa 51:16 And I **h.** put my words in thy mouth,...
Isa 51:16 and I **h.** covered thee in the shadow...
Isa 51:20 Thy sons **h.** fainted, they lie at the...
Isa 51:22 Behold, I **h.** taken out of thine hand...
Isa 51:23 which **h.** said to thy soul, Bow down,...
Isa 52:3 Ye **h.** sold yourselves for nought;...
Isa 52:5 Now therefore, what **h.** I here, saith...
Isa 53:6 All we like sheep **h.** gone astray; we...
Isa 53:6 we **h.** turned every one to his own...
Isa 54:7 For a small moment **h.** I forsaken...
Isa 54:8 kindness will I **h.** mercy on thee,...
Isa 54:9 for as I **h.** sworn that the waters of...
Isa 54:9 so **h.** I sworn that I would not be...
Isa 54:16 Behold, I **h.** created the smith that...
Isa 54:16 and I **h.** created the waster to destroy...
Isa 55:4 Behold, I **h.** given him for a witness...
Isa 55:7 and he will **h.** mercy upon him:...
Isa 56:11 dogs which can never **h.** enough,......3045
Isa 57:11 **h.** not I held my peace even of old,...
Isa 57:16 and the souls which I **h.** made...
Isa 57:18 I **h.** seen his ways, and will heal him:...
Isa 58:3 Wherefore **h.** we fasted, say they, and...
Isa 58:3 wherefore **h.** we afflicted our soul,...
Isa 58:5 Is it such a fast that I **h.** chosen?...
Isa 58:6 Is not this the fast that I **h.** chosen?...
Isa 59:2 But your iniquities **h.** separated...
Isa 59:2 and your sins **h.** hid his face from...
Isa 59:3 your lips **h.** spoken lies, your tongue...
Isa 59:8 they **h.** made them crooked paths:...
Isa 59:21 and my words which I **h.** put in thy...
Isa 60:10 but in my favour **h.** I had mercy...
Isa 61:7 For your shame ye shall **h.** double;...
Isa 62:6 I **h.** set watchmen upon thy walls, O...
Isa 62:9 But they that **h.** gathered it shall eat...
Isa 62:9 and they that **h.** brought it together...
Isa 63:3 I **h.** trodden the winepress alone;...
Isa 63:18 of thy holiness **h.** possessed it...
Isa 63:18 our adversaries **h.** trodden down thy...
Isa 64:4 men **h.** not heard, nor perceived by...
Isa 64:5 for we **h.** sinned: in those is...
Isa 64:6 iniquities, like the wind, **h.** taken us...
Isa 65:2 I **h.** spread out my hands all the day...
Isa 65:7 which **h.** burned incense upon the...
Isa 65:10 in, for my people that **h.** sought me...
Isa 66:2 all those things **h.** been, saith...
Isa 66:3 Yea, they **h.** chosen their own ways,...
Isa 66:19 afar off, that **h.** not heard my fame,...
Isa 66:19 neither **h.** seen my glory; and they...
Isa 66:24 of the men that **h.** transgressed...
Jer 1:9 Behold, I **h.** put my words in thy...
Jer 1:10 See, I **h.** this day set thee over the...
Jer 1:16 all their wickedness, who **h.** forsaken...
Jer 1:16 and **h.** burned incense unto other...
Jer 1:18 For, behold, I **h.** made thee this day a...
Jer 2:5 What iniquity **h.** your fathers found in...
Jer 2:5 and **h.** walked after vanity, and are...
Jer 2:11 but my people **h.** changed their glory...
Jer 2:13 For my people **h.** committed two evils;...
Jer 2:13 they **h.** forsaken me the fountain of...
Jer 2:16 and Tahapanes **h.** broken the crown...
Jer 2:20 For of old time I **h.** broken thy yoke,...
Jer 2:23 I am not polluted, I **h.** not gone after...
Jer 2:25 for I **h.** loved strangers, and after...
Jer 2:27 for they **h.** turned their back unto me,...
Jer 2:29 ye all **h.** transgressed against me,...
Jer 2:30 In vain **h.** I smitten your children;...
Jer 2:31 **H.** I been a wilderness unto...
Jer 2:32 yet my people **h.** forgotten me days...
Jer 2:34 I **h.** not found it by secret search,...
Jer 2:35 because thou sayest, I **h.** not sinned...
Jer 3:3 the showers **h.** been withholden,...
Jer 3:13 and ye **h.** not obeyed my voice, saith...
Jer 3:18 I **h.** given for an inheritance unto...
Jer 3:20 so **h.** ye dealt treacherously with me,...
Jer 3:21 of Israel: for they **h.** perverted their...
Jer 3:21 and they **h.** forgotten the Lord their...
Jer 3:25 for we **h.** sinned against the Lord our...
Jer 3:25 and **h.** not obeyed the voice of the...
Jer 4:10 Ye shall **h.** peace; whereas the......1961
Jer 4:18 Thy way and thy doings **h.** procured...
Jer 4:22 is foolish, they **h.** not known me;...
Jer 4:22 and they **h.** none understanding: they...
Jer 4:22 to do good they **h.** no knowledge...
Jer 4:28 be black: because I **h.** spoken it, I...
Jer 4:28 I **h.** purposed it, and will not repent,...

Jer 4:31 For I **h.** heard a voice as of a woman...
Jer 5:3 them, but they **h.** not grieved;...
Jer 5:3 but they **h.** refused to receive...
Jer 5:3 they **h.** made their faces harder than...
Jer 5:3 than a rock; they **h.** refused to return...
Jer 5:5 for they **h.** known the way of the Lord...
Jer 5:5 but these **h.** altogether broken the...
Jer 5:7 thy children **h.** forsaken me, and...
Jer 5:11 and the house of Judah **h.** dealt very...
Jer 5:12 They **h.** belied the Lord, and said, It...
Jer 5:19 Like as ye **h.** forsaken me, and served...
Jer 5:21 which **h.** eyes, and see not;...
Jer 5:21 see not; which **h.** ears, and hear not:...
Jer 5:22 which **h.** placed the sand for the...
Jer 5:25 Your iniquities **h.** turned away these...
Jer 5:25 and your sins **h.** withholden good...
Jer 5:31 and my people love to **h.** it so: and...
Jer 6:2 I **h.** likened the daughter of Zion to...
Jer 6:10 they **h.** no delight in it...
Jer 6:14 They **h.** healed also the hurt of the...
Jer 6:19 because they **h.** not hearkened unto...
Jer 6:23 they are cruel, and **h.** no mercy;...
Jer 6:24 We **h.** heard the fame thereof: our...
Jer 6:27 I **h.** set thee for a tower and a fortress...
Jer 7:11 Behold, even I **h.** seen it, saith the...
Jer 7:13 And now, because ye **h.** done all these...
Jer 7:14 and to your fathers, as I **h.** done to...
Jer 7:15 as I **h.** cast out all your brethren, even...
Jer 7:23 in all the ways that I **h.** commanded...
Jer 7:25 unto this day I **h.** even sent unto you...
Jer 7:30 For the children of Judah **h.** done evil...
Jer 7:30 they **h.** set their abominations in the...
Jer 7:31 And they **h.** built the high places of...
Jer 8:2 host of heaven, whom they **h.** loved...
Jer 8:2 loved, and whom they **h.** served, and...
Jer 8:2 and after whom they **h.** walked, and...
Jer 8:2 walked, and whom they **h.** sought, and...
Jer 8:2 and whom they **h.** worshipped: they...
Jer 8:3 whither I **h.** driven them, saith the...
Jer 8:6 What **h.** I done? every one turned to...
Jer 8:9 lo, they **h.** rejected the word of the...
Jer 8:11 For they **h.** healed the hurt of the...
Jer 8:13 and the things that I **h.** given them...
Jer 8:14 because we **h.** sinned against the...
Jer 8:16 for they are come, and **h.** devoured the...
Jer 8:19 Why **h.** they provoked me to anger...
Jer 9:5 they **h.** taught their tongue to speak...
Jer 9:13 Because they **h.** forsaken my law...
Jer 9:13 and **h.** not obeyed my voice, neither...
Jer 9:14 But **h.** walked after the imagination...
Jer 9:16 they nor their fathers **h.** known:...
Jer 9:16 sword after them, till I **h.** consumed...
Jer 9:19 confounded, because we **h.** forsaken...
Jer 9:19 land, because our dwellings **h.** cast us...
Jer 10:11 The gods that **h.** not made the heavens...
Jer 10:21 are become brutish, and **h.** not sought...
Jer 10:25 for they **h.** eaten up Jacob, and...
Jer 10:25 and **h.** made his habitation desolate...
Jer 11:5 which I **h.** sworn unto your fathers,...
Jer 11:10 and the house of Judah **h.** broken my...
Jer 11:13 streets of Jerusalem **h.** ye set up altars...
Jer 11:17 which they **h.** done against themselves...
Jer 11:20 for unto thee **h.** I revealed my cause...
Jer 12:2 yea, they **h.** taken root: they grow,...
Jer 12:5 and they **h.** wearied thee, then how...
Jer 12:6 even they **h.** dealt treacherously with...
Jer 12:6 yea, they **h.** called a multitude after...
Jer 12:7 I **h.** forsaken mine house, I **h.** left...
Jer 12:7 I **h.** given the dearly beloved of my...
Jer 12:8 out against me: therefore **h.** I hated it...
Jer 12:10 Many pastors **h.** destroyed my...
Jer 12:10 they **h.** trodden my portion under foot,...
Jer 12:10 they **h.** made my pleasant portion a...
Jer 12:11 They **h.** made it desolate, and being...
Jer 12:12 end of the land: no flesh shall **h.** peace...
Jer 12:13 They **h.** sown wheat, but shall reap...
Jer 12:13 they **h.** put themselves to pain, but...
Jer 12:14 inheritance which I **h.** caused my...
Jer 12:15 after that I **h.** plucked them out I will...
Jer 12:15 and **h.** compassion on them, and...
Jer 13:11 so **h.** I caused to cleave unto me the...
Jer 13:14 pity, nor spare, nor **h.** mercy,...
Jer 13:27 I **h.** seen thine adulteries, and thy...
Jer 14:3 And their nobles **h.** sent their little...
Jer 14:7 are many; we **h.** sinned against thee...
Jer 14:10 people, Thus **h.** they loved to wander,...
Jer 14:10 they **h.** not refrained their feet,...
Jer 14:13 the sword, neither shall ye **h.** famine;...
Jer 14:14 not, neither **h.** I commanded them,...
Jer 14:16 and they shall **h.** none to bury them,...
Jer 14:20 our fathers: for we **h.** sinned against...
Jer 15:5 For who shall **h.** pity upon thee,...
Jer 15:8 I **h.** brought upon them against the...
Jer 15:8 **h.** caused him to fall upon it suddenly,...
Jer 15:10 I **h.** neither lent on usury, nor men...
Jer 15:10 nor men **h.** lent to me on usury; yet...
Jer 15:15 for thy sake I **h.** suffered rebuke...
Jer 16:2 neither shalt thou **h.** sons or...
Jer 16:5 for I **h.** taken away my peace from this...
Jer 16:10 what is our sin that we **h.** committed...
Jer 16:11 Because your fathers **h.** forsaken me,...
Jer 16:11 Lord, and **h.** walked after other gods,...
Jer 16:11 after other gods, and **h.** served them,...
Jer 16:11 served them, and **h.** worshipped them,...
Jer 16:11 worshipped them, and **h.** forsaken me,...
Jer 16:11 forsaken me, and **h.** not kept my law;...
Jer 16:12 And ye **h.** done worse than your...
Jer 16:18 sin double; because they **h.** defiled my...
Jer 16:18 they **h.** filled mine inheritance with...
Jer 16:19 Surely our fathers **h.** inherited lies,...
Jer 17:4 for ye **h.** kindled a fire in mine anger,...
Jer 17:13 because they **h.** forsaken the Lord, the...
Jer 17:16 As for me, I **h.** not hastened from...
Jer 17:16 neither **h.** I desired the woeful day;...
Jer 18:8 nation, against whom I **h.** pronounced,...
Jer 18:15 hath forgotten me, they **h.** burned...
Jer 18:15 and they **h.** caused them to stumble in...
Jer 18:20 for they **h.** digged a pit for my soul...
Jer 18:22 for they **h.** digged a pit to take me,...
Jer 19:4 Because they **h.** forsaken me, and...
Jer 19:4 me, and **h.** estranged this place, and...
Jer 19:4 and **h.** burned incense in it unto other...
Jer 19:4 they nor their fathers **h.** known...
Jer 19:4 and **h.** filled this place with the blood...
Jer 19:5 They **h.** built also the high places of...
Jer 19:13 upon whose roofs they **h.** burned...
Jer 19:13 and **h.** poured out drink offerings...
Jer 19:15 all the evil that I **h.** pronounced...
Jer 19:15 because they **h.** hardened their necks,...
Jer 20:12 for unto thee **h.** I opened my cause,...
Jer 20:17 mother might **h.** been my grave,...
Jer 21:7 neither **h.** pity, nor **h.** mercy...
Jer 21:10 For I **h.** set my face against this city...
Jer 22:9 Because they **h.** forsaken the covenant...
Jer 22:12 in the place whither they **h.** led him...
Jer 23:2 Ye **h.** scattered my flock, and driven...
Jer 23:2 them away, and **h.** not visited them:...
Jer 23:3 whither I **h.** driven them, and will...
Jer 23:11 yea, in my house **h.** I found their...
Jer 23:13 And I **h.** seen folly in the prophets of...
Jer 23:14 I **h.** seen also in the prophets of...
Jer 23:17 Ye shall **h.** peace; and they say...1961
Jer 23:20 shall not return, until he **h.** executed,...
Jer 23:20 and till he **h.** performed the thoughts...
Jer 23:21 I **h.** not sent these prophets, yet they...
Jer 23:21 I **h.** not spoken to them, yet they...
Jer 23:22 then they should **h.** turned them from...
Jer 23:25 I **h.** heard what the prophets said,...
Jer 23:25 saying, I **h.** dreamed, I **h.** dreamed...
Jer 23:27 as their fathers **h.** forgotten my name...
Jer 23:36 for ye **h.** perverted the words of the...
Jer 23:38 and I **h.** sent unto you, saying, Ye shall...
Jer 24:5 whom I **h.** sent out of this place into...
Jer 25:3 and I **h.** spoken unto you, rising...
Jer 25:3 and speaking; but ye **h.** not hearkened...
Jer 25:4 but ye **h.** not hearkened, nor inclined...
Jer 25:7 Yet ye **h.** not hearkened unto me, saith...
Jer 25:8 Because ye **h.** not heard my words,...
Jer 25:13 my words which I **h.** pronounced...
Jer 25:35 the shepherds shall **h.** no way to flee,...
Jer 26:4 to walk in my law, which I **h.** set before...
Jer 26:5 them, but ye **h.** not hearkened;...
Jer 26:11 this city, as ye **h.** heard with your ears...
Jer 26:12 this city all the words that ye **h.** heard...
Jer 27:5 I **h.** made the earth, the man and the...
Jer 27:5 and **h.** given it unto whom it seemed...
Jer 27:6 And now **h.** I given all these lands...
Jer 27:6 and the beasts of the field **h.** I given...
Jer 27:8 until I **h.** consumed them by his hand...
Jer 27:15 For I **h.** not sent them, saith the Lord,...
Jer 28:2 I **h.** broken the yoke of the king of...
Jer 28:8 The prophets that **h.** been before me...
Jer 28:14 I **h.** put a yoke of iron upon the neck...
Jer 28:14 and I **h.** given him the beasts of the...
Jer 29:4 whom I **h.** caused to be carried away...
Jer 29:7 I **h.** caused you to be carried away...
Jer 29:7 the peace thereof shall ye **h.** peace,...1961
Jer 29:9 I **h.** not sent them, saith the Lord...
Jer 29:14 whither I **h.** driven you, saith the...
Jer 29:15 Because ye **h.** said, The Lord hath...
Jer 29:18 the nations whither I **h.** driven them:...
Jer 29:19 Because they **h.** not hearkened to my...
Jer 29:20 whom I **h.** sent from Jerusalem to...
Jer 29:23 Because they **h.** committed villany in...
Jer 29:23 and **h.** committed adultery with their...
Jer 29:23 and **h.** spoken lying words in my...
Jer 29:23 which I **h.** not commanded them;...
Jer 29:32 shall not **h.** a man to dwell among...1961
Jer 30:2 the words that I **h.** spoken unto thee...
Jer 30:5 We **h.** heard a voice of trembling, of...
Jer 30:11 end of all nations whither I **h.** scattered...
Jer 30:14 All thy lovers **h.** forgotten thee; they...
Jer 30:14 for I **h.** wounded thee with the wound...
Jer 30:15 increased, I **h.** done these things unto...
Jer 30:18 and **h.** mercy on his dwellingplaces;...
Jer 30:24 shall not return, until he **h.** done it,...
Jer 30:24 and until he **h.** performed the intents...
Jer 31:3 Yea, I **h.** loved thee with an...
Jer 31:3 with lovingkindness **h.** I drawn thee...
Jer 31:18 I **h.** surely heard Ephraim bemoaning...
Jer 31:20 I will surely **h.** mercy upon him,...
Jer 31:25 For I **h.** satiated the weary soul, and...
Jer 31:25 and I **h.** replenished every sorrowful...
Jer 31:28 that like as I **h.** watched over them,...
Jer 31:29 The fathers **h.** eaten a sour grape,...
Jer 31:37 for all that they **h.** done, saith the...
Jer 32:23 they **h.** done nothing of all that thou...
Jer 32:29 upon whose roofs they **h.** offered...
Jer 32:30 children of Judah **h.** only done evil...
Jer 32:30 children of Israel **h.** only provoked...
Jer 32:32 which they **h.** done to provoke me to...
Jer 32:33 And they **h.** turned unto me the back,...
Jer 32:33 yet they **h.** not hearkened to receive...
Jer 32:37 whither I **h.** driven them in mine...
Jer 32:42 Like as I **h.** brought all this great...
Jer 32:42 all the good that I **h.** promised them...
Jer 33:5 whom I **h.** slain in mine anger and in...
Jer 33:5 wickedness I **h.** hid my face from this...
Jer 33:8 whereby they **h.** sinned against...
Jer 33:8 iniquities, whereby they **h.** sinned,...
Jer 33:8 whereby they **h.** transgressed against...
Jer 33:14 which I **h.** promised unto the house...
Jer 33:21 he should not **h.** a son to reign...1961
Jer 33:24 thou not what this people **h.** spoken,...
Jer 33:24 thus they **h.** despised my people, that...
Jer 33:25 if I **h.** not appointed the ordinances...
Jer 33:26 to return, and **h.** mercy on them...
Jer 34:5 for I **h.** pronounced the word, saith...
Jer 34:17 Ye **h.** not hearkened unto me, in...
Jer 34:18 will give the men that **h.** transgressed...
Jer 34:18 which **h.** not performed the words of...
Jer 35:7 seed, nor plant vineyard, nor **h.** any:...
Jer 35:8 Thus **h.** we obeyed the voice of...
Jer 35:9 neither **h.** we vineyard, nor field,...1961
Jer 35:10 we **h.** dwelt in tents, and **h.** obeyed,...
Jer 35:14 notwithstanding I **h.** spoken unto...
Jer 35:15 I **h.** sent also unto you all my...
Jer 35:15 which I **h.** given to you and to your...
Jer 35:15 but ye **h.** not inclined your ear, nor...
Jer 35:16 the son of Rechab **h.** performed the...
Jer 35:17 all the evil that I **h.** pronounced...
Jer 35:17 because I **h.** spoken unto them, but...
Jer 35:17 unto them, but they **h.** not heard;...
Jer 35:17 and I **h.** called unto them, but they...
Jer 35:17 unto them, but they **h.** not answered...
Jer 35:18 ye **h.** obeyed the commandment...
Jer 36:2 all the words that I **h.** spoken unto...
Jer 36:30 He shall **h.** none to sit upon the...1961
Jer 36:31 all the evil that I **h.** pronounced...
Jer 37:18 What **h.** I offended against thee, or...
Jer 37:18 people, that ye **h.** put me in prison?...
Jer 38:2 for he shall **h.** his life for a prey,...
Jer 38:9 lord the king, these men **h.** done evil...
Jer 38:9 in all that they **h.** done to Jeremiah...
Jer 38:9 whom they **h.** cast into the dungeon;...
Jer 38:22 shall say, Thy friends **h.** set thee on,...
Jer 38:22 set thee on, and **h.** prevailed against...
Jer 38:25 the princes hear that I **h.** talked...
Jer 40:3 because ye **h.** sinned against the...

Jer 40:3 and **h.** not obeyed his voice, therefore........
Jer 40:10 dwell in your cities that ye **h.** taken...........
Jer 41:8 Slay us not: for we **h.** treasures..........3426
Jer 42:4 prophet said unto them, I **h.** heard............
Jer 42:10 repent me of the evil that I **h.** done...........
Jer 42:12 that he may **h.** mercy upon you,...............
Jer 42:14 the trumpet, nor **h.** hunger of bread..........
Jer 42:19 know certainly that I **h.** admonished..........
Jer 42:21 And now I **h.** this day declared it to..........
Jer 42:21 but ye **h.** not obeyed the voice of the.........
Jer 43:10 throne upon these stones that I **h.** hid:.......
Jer 44:2 God of Israel; Ye **h.** seen all the evil.........
Jer 44:2 that I **h.** brought upon Jerusalem,..............
Jer 44:3 they **h.** committed to provoke me to..........
Jer 44:9 **H.** ye forgotten the wickedness of............
Jer 44:9 which they **h.** committed in the land..........
Jer 44:10 neither **h.** they feared, nor walked in.........
Jer 44:12 that **h.** set their faces to go into the..........
Jer 44:13 as I **h.** punished Jerusalem, by the............
Jer 44:14 they **h.** a desire to return..................5375
Jer 44:17 as we **h.** done, we, and our fathers,...........
Jer 44:18 unto her, we **h.** wanted all things,.............
Jer 44:18 and **h.** been consumed by the sword..........
Jer 44:22 abominations which you **h.** committed;.........
Jer 44:23 Because ye **h.** burned incense, and.............
Jer 44:23 because ye **h.** sinned against the..............
Jer 44:23 and **h.** not obeyed the voice of the............
Jer 44:25 Ye and your wives **h.** both spoken..............
Jer 44:25 perform our vows that we **h.** vowed,...........
Jer 44:26 Behold, I **h.** sworn by my great name,.........
Jer 45:4 Behold, that which I **h.** built will I............
Jer 45:4 and that which I **h.** planted I will..............
Jer 46:5 Wherefore **h.** I seen them dismayed...........
Jer 46:12 The nations **h.** heard of thy shame,............
Jer 46:28 the nations whither I **h.** driven thee:..........
Jer 48:2 in Heshbon they **h.** devised evil...............
Jer 48:4 little ones **h.** caused a cry to be heard........
Jer 48:5 the enemies **h.** heard a cry of...................
Jer 48:29 We **h.** heard the pride of Moab,.................
Jer 48:33 and I **h.** caused wine to fail from the..........
Jer 48:34 Jahaz, **h.** they uttered their voice,.............
Jer 48:38 for I **h.** broken Moab like a vessel..............
Jer 49:9 they will destroy till they **h.** enough............
Jer 49:10 I **h.** made Esau bare, I **h.** uncovered.........
Jer 49:12 drink of the cup **h.** assuredly drunken;........
Jer 49:13 For I **h.** sworn by myself, saith the...........
Jer 49:14 I **h.** heard a rumour from the Lord,..............
Jer 49:23 for they **h.** heard evil tidings: they are.......
Jer 49:24 anguish and sorrows **h.** taken her, as..........
Jer 49:31 which **h.** neither gates nor bars.................
Jer 49:37 sword after them, till I **h.** consumed..........
Jer 50:6 their shepherds **h.** caused them to go.........
Jer 50:6 they **h.** turned them away on the...............
Jer 50:6 they **h.** gone from mountain to hill,.............
Jer 50:6 they **h.** forgotten their restingplace............
Jer 50:7 that found them **h.** devoured them:............
Jer 50:7 because they **h.** sinned against the............
Jer 50:17 the lions **h.** driven him away: first.............
Jer 50:18 as I **h.** punished the king of Assyria...........
Jer 50:21 to all that I **h.** commanded thee................
Jer 50:24 I **h.** laid a snare for thee, and thou............
Jer 51:7 the nations **h.** drunken of her wine;...........
Jer 51:9 We would **h.** healed Babylon, but she.........
Jer 51:24 their evil that they **h.** done in Zion............
Jer 51:30 mighty men of Babylon **h.** foreborn to.........
Jer 51:30 they **h.** remained in their holds:................
Jer 51:30 they **h.** burned her dwellingplaces;............
Jer 51:32 the reeds they **h.** burned with fire,............
Jer 51:50 Ye that **h.** escaped the sword, go..............
Jer 51:51 because we **h.** heard reproach:.................
La 1:2 all her friends **h.** dealt treacherously..........
La 1:8 because they **h.** seen her nakedness:..........
La 1:11 they **h.** given their pleasant things............
La 1:18 for I **h.** rebelled against his.......................
La 1:20 for I **h.** grievously rebelled: abroad............
La 1:21 They **h.** heard that I sigh: there is............
La 1:21 all mine enemies **h.** heard of my...............
La 2:7 they **h.** made a noise in the house of.........
La 2:10 they **h.** cast up dust upon their heads;........
La 2:10 they **h.** girded themselves with..................
La 2:14 Thy prophets **h.** seen vain and foolish........
La 2:14 and they **h.** not discovered thine...............
La 2:14 but **h.** seen for thee false burdens and........
La 2:16 All thine enemies **h.** opened their...............
La 2:16 We **h.** swallowed her up: certainly..............
La 2:16 looked for; we **h.** found, we **h.** seen it........
La 2:22 those that I **h.** swaddled and brought.........
La 3:21 recall to my mind, there **h.** I hope..............
La 3:32 yet will he **h.** compassion according...........
La 3:42 We **h.** transgressed and **h.** rebelled:..........
La 3:46 All our enemies **h.** opened their.................
La 3:53 They **h.** cut off my life in the dungeon,........
La 4:10 the pitiful women **h.** sodden their own.........
La 4:12 would not **h.** believed that the.................
La 4:12 the enemy should **h.** entered into...............
La 4:13 that **h.** shed the blood of the just in...........
La 4:14 They **h.** wandered as blind men in..............
La 4:14 they **h.** polluted themselves with...............
La 4:17 in our watching we **h.** watched for a...........
La 5:4 We **h.** drunken our water for money;..........
La 5:5 persecution: we labour, and **h.** no rest........
La 5:6 We **h.** given the hand to the Egyptians,.......
La 5:7 Our fathers **h.** sinned, and are not;............
La 5:7 and we **h.** borne their iniquities.................
La 5:8 Servants **h.** ruled over us: there is............
La 5:14 The elders **h.** ceased from the gate,...........
La 5:16 woe unto us, that we **h.** sinned!...............
Eze 2:3 they and their fathers **h.** transgressed.........
Eze 3:6 they would **h.** hearkened unto thee............
Eze 3:8 Behold, I **h.** made thy face strong..............
Eze 3:9 adamant harder than flint **h.** I made...........
Eze 3:17 Son of man, I **h.** made thee a..................
Eze 4:5 For I **h.** laid upon thee the years of...........
Eze 4:6 I **h.** appointed thee each day for a.............
Eze 4:14 till now **h.** I not eaten of that which...........
Eze 4:15 Lo, I **h.** given thee cow's dung for.............
Eze 5:5 I **h.** set it in the midst of the nations.........
Eze 5:6 for they **h.** refused my judgments and.........
Eze 5:6 statutes, they **h.** not walked in them ....
Eze 5:7 and **h.** not walked in my statutes..............
Eze 5:7 neither **h.** kept my judgments,....................
Eze 5:7 neither **h.** done according to the...............
Eze 5:9 do in thee that which I **h.** not done,...........
Eze 5:11 eye spare, neither will I **h.** any pity...........
Eze 5:13 that I the Lord **h.** spoken it in my.............
Eze 5:13 when I **h.** accomplished my fury in............
Eze 5:15 furious rebukes. I the Lord **h.** spoken.........
Eze 5:17 upon thee. I the Lord **h.** spoken it..............
Eze 6:8 that ye may **h.** some that shall............1961
Eze 6:9 for the evils which they **h.** committed.........
Eze 6:10 that I **h.** not said in vain that I would..........
Eze 7:4 neither will I **h.** pity: but I will..................
Eze 7:9 will I **h.** pity: I will recompense thee...........
Eze 7:14 They **h.** blown the trumpet, even to...........
Eze 7:20 therefore **h.** I set far from them................
Eze 8:17 they **h.** filled the land with violence,..........
Eze 8:17 and **h.** returned to provoke me to...............
Eze 8:18 neither will I **h.** pity: and though................
Eze 9:1 Cause them that **h.** charge over................
Eze 9:5 your eye spare, neither **h.** ye pity:...............
Eze 9:10 neither will I **h.** pity, but I will..................
Eze 9:11 saying, I **h.** done as thou hast...................
Eze 11:5 Thus **h.** ye said, O house of Israel:.............
Eze 11:6 Ye **h.** multiplied your slain in this...............
Eze 11:6 ye **h.** filled the streets thereof with the.......
Eze 11:7 Your slain whom ye **h.** laid in the...............
Eze 11:8 Ye **h.** feared the sword; and I will..............
Eze 11:12 for ye **h.** not walked in my statutes,............
Eze 11:12 but **h.** done after the manners of the..........
Eze 11:15 of Jerusalem **h.** said, Get you far from........
Eze 11:16 I **h.** cast them far off among the...............
Eze 11:16 and although I **h.** scattered them..............
Eze 11:17 countries where ye **h.** been scattered,........
Eze 12:2 which **h.** eyes to see, and see not;............
Eze 12:2 they **h.** ears to hear, and hear not:...........
Eze 12:6 for I **h.** set thee for a sign unto the...........
Eze 12:11 like as I **h.** done, so shall it be done..........
Eze 12:22 proverb that ye **h.** in the land of................
Eze 12:28 but the word which I **h.** spoken shall..........
Eze 13:3 their own spirit, and **h.** seen nothing!..........
Eze 13:5 Ye **h.** not gone up into the gaps,...............
Eze 13:6 They **h.** seen vanity and lying...................
Eze 13:6 and they **h.** made others to hope that........
Eze 13:7 **H.** ye not seen a vain vision, and..............
Eze 13:7 **h.** ye not spoken a lying divination,............
Eze 13:7 Lord saith it; albeit I **h.** not spoken?..........
Eze 13:8 Because ye **h.** spoken vanity, and.............
Eze 13:10 because they **h.** seduced my people,...........
Eze 13:12 the daubing wherewith ye **h.** daubed..........
Eze 13:14 the wall that ye **h.** daubed with.................
Eze 13:15 and upon them that **h.** daubed it with.........
Eze 13:22 ye **h.** made the heart of the righteous........
Eze 13:22 sad, whom I **h.** not made sad;.....................
Eze 14:3 Son of man, these men **h.** set up their........
Eze 14:9 I the Lord **h.** deceived that prophet,..........
Eze 14:22 the evil that I **h.** brought upon..................
Eze 14:22 even concerning all that I **h.** brought..........
Eze 14:23 and ye shall know that I **h.** not done...........
Eze 14:23 all that I **h.** done in it, saith the Lord.........
Eze 15:6 which I **h.** given to the fire for fuel,...........
Eze 15:8 because they **h.** committed a trespass,........
Eze 16:5 to **h.** compassion upon thee; but thou.........
Eze 16:7 I **h.** caused thee to multiply as the............
Eze 16:27 Behold, therefore I **h.** stretched out..........
Eze 16:27 and **h.** diminished thine ordinary food,.........
Eze 17:21 know that I the Lord **h.** spoken it..............
Eze 17:24 I the Lord brought down the high...............
Eze 17:24 high tree, **h.** exalted the low tree,............
Eze 17:24 **h.** dried up the green tree, and................
Eze 17:24 and **h.** made the dry tree to flourish:..........
Eze 17:24 I the Lord **h.** spoken and **h.** done it..........
Eze 18:2 the fathers **h.** eaten sour grapes, and.........
Eze 18:3 ye shall not **h.** occasion any more to...........
Eze 18:23 **H.** I any pleasure at all that the..................
Eze 18:31 whereby ye **h.** transgressed; and..............
Eze 18:32 For I **h.** no pleasure in the death..............
Eze 20:27 yet in this your fathers **h.** blasphemed.........
Eze 20:27 in that they **h.** committed a trespass...........
Eze 20:41 wherein ye **h.** been scattered; and I...........
Eze 20:43 doings, wherein ye **h.** been defiled;............
Eze 20:43 for all your evils that ye **h.** committed........
Eze 20:44 when I **h.** wrought with you for my............
Eze 20:48 I the Lord **h.** kindled it: it shall not..........
Eze 21:5 that I the Lord **h.** drawn forth my.............
Eze 21:15 I **h.** set the point of the sword against........
Eze 21:17 fury to rest: I the Lord **h.** said it...............
Eze 21:23 to them that **h.** sworn oaths: but he............
Eze 21:24 Because ye **h.** made your iniquity to...........
Eze 21:25 when iniquity shall **h.** an end,...................
Eze 21:29 when their iniquity shall **h.** an end............
Eze 21:32 for I the Lord **h.** spoken it......................
Eze 22:4 therefore **h.** I made thee a reproach...........
Eze 22:7 In thee **h.** they set light by father.............
Eze 22:7 in the midst of thee **h.** they dealt by...........
Eze 22:7 in thee **h.** they vexed the fatherless...........
Eze 22:10 In thee **h.** they discovered their.................
Eze 22:10 in thee **h.** they humbled her that was..........
Eze 22:12 In thee **h.** they taken gifts to shed..............
Eze 22:13 Behold, therefore I **h.** smitten mine............
Eze 22:14 I the Lord **h.** spoken it, and will do it.........
Eze 22:22 that I the Lord **h.** poured out my...............
Eze 22:25 the prey; they **h.** devoured souls;..............
Eze 22:25 they **h.** taken the treasure and..................
Eze 22:25 they **h.** made her many widows in..............
Eze 22:26 Her priests **h.** violated my law, and............
Eze 22:26 law, and **h.** profaned mine holy things:........
Eze 22:26 they **h.** put no difference between the.........
Eze 22:26 neither **h.** they shewed difference...............
Eze 22:26 and **h.** hid their eyes from my....................
Eze 22:28 And her prophets **h.** daubed them...............
Eze 22:29 The people of the land **h.** used.................
Eze 22:29 and **h.** vexed the poor and needy:...............
Eze 22:29 yea, they **h.** oppressed the stranger...........
Eze 22:31 Therefore **h.** I poured out mine.................
Eze 22:31 I **h.** consumed them with the fire of...........
Eze 22:31 their own way **h.** I recompensed upon.........
Eze 23:9 Wherefore I **h.** delivered her into the.........
Eze 23:34 for I **h.** spoken it, saith the Lord God.........
Eze 23:37 That they **h.** committed adultery, and.........
Eze 23:37 and with their idols **h.** they committed........
Eze 23:37 **h.** also caused their sons...to pass...............
Eze 23:38 Moreover this they **h.** done unto me:..........
Eze 23:38 they **h.** defiled my sanctuary in the............
Eze 23:38 day, and **h.** profaned my sabbaths..............
Eze 23:39 thus **h.** they done in the midst of..............
Eze 23:40 furthermore, that ye **h.** sent for men..........
Eze 24:8 I **h.** set her blood upon the top of a............
Eze 24:13 because I **h.** purged thee, and thou............
Eze 24:13 till I **h.** caused my fury to rest upon...........
Eze 24:14 I the Lord **h.** spoken it: it shall come..........
Eze 24:21 whom ye **h.** left shall fall by the.................
Eze 24:22 And ye shall do as I **h.** done: ye shall.........
Eze 25:15 Because the Philistines **h.** dealt by............
Eze 25:15 and **h.** taken vengeance with a..................
Eze 26:5 for I **h.** spoken it, saith the Lord God:........
Eze 26:14 for I the Lord **h.** spoken it, saith the..........
Eze 27:4 thy builders **h.** perfected thy beauty...........
Eze 27:5 They **h.** made all thy ship boards of...........
Eze 27:5 they **h.** taken cedars from Lebanon............

Eze 27:6 Of the oaks of Bashan **h.** they made
Eze 27:6 the company of the Ashurites **h.** made
Eze 27:11 they **h.** made thy beauty perfect.
Eze 27:26 Thy rowers **h.** brought thee into great
Eze 28:10 strangers: for I **h.** spoken it, saith the
Eze 28:14 and I **h.** set thee so: thou wast upon
Eze 28:16 merchandise they **h.** filled the midst
Eze 28:22 when I shall **h.** executed judgments
Eze 28:25 When I shall **h.** gathered the house of
Eze 28:25 land that I **h.** given to my servant
Eze 28:26 when I **h.** executed judgments upon all
Eze 29:3 own, and I **h.** made it for myself.
Eze 29:5 I **h.** given thee for meat to the beasts
Eze 29:6 because they **h.** been a staff of reed to
Eze 29:9 The river is mine, and I **h.** made it
Eze 29:20 I **h.** given him the land of Egypt for
Eze 30:8 when I **h.** set a fire in Egypt, and
Eze 30:12 strangers: I the Lord **h.** spoken it.
Eze 30:16 Sin shall **h.** great pain, and No shall
Eze 30:16 and Noph shall **h.** distresses daily.
Eze 30:21 Son of man, I **h.** broken the arm of
Eze 31:9 I **h.** made him fair by the multitude
Eze 31:11 I **h.** therefore delivered him into the
Eze 31:11 I **h.** driven him out for his wickedness
Eze 31:12 **h.** cut him off, and **h.** left him:
Eze 31:12 from his shadow, and **h.** left him.
Eze 32:24 yet **h.** they borne their shame with
Eze 32:25 They **h.** set her a bed in the midst of
Eze 32:25 yet **h.** they borne their shame with
Eze 32:27 and they **h.** laid their swords under
Eze 32:32 For I **h.** caused my terror in the land
Eze 33:7 I **h.** set thee a watchman unto the
Eze 33:11 I **h.** no pleasure in the death of
Eze 33:29 when I **h.** laid the land most desolate
Eze 33:29 abominations...they **h.** committed.
Eze 34:4 The diseased **h.** ye not strengthened,
Eze 34:4 neither **h.** ye healed that which was
Eze 34:4 neither **h.** ye bound up that which
Eze 34:4 neither **h.** ye brought again that
Eze 34:4 neither **h.** ye sought that which was
Eze 34:4 and with cruelty **h.** ye ruled them.
Eze 34:12 they **h.** been scattered in the cloudy
Eze 34:18 to **h.** eaten up the good pasture,
Eze 34:18 and to **h.** drunk of the deep waters,
Eze 34:19 they eat that which ye **h.** trodden
Eze 34:19 drink that which ye **h.** fouled with
Eze 34:21 Because ye **h.** thrust with side and
Eze 34:21 with your horns, till ye **h.** scattered
Eze 34:24 among them; I the Lord **h.** spoken it.
Eze 34:27 when I **h.** broken the bands of their
Eze 35:11 among them, when I **h.** judged thee.
Eze 35:12 and that I **h.** heard all thy blasphemies
Eze 35:13 your mouth ye **h.** boasted against me,
Eze 35:13 and **h.** multiplied your words against
Eze 35:13 words against me: I **h.** heard them.
Eze 36:3 Because they **h.** made you desolate,
Eze 36:5 of my jealousy **h.** I spoken against
Eze 36:5 which **h.** appointed my land into
Eze 36:6 Behold, I **h.** spoken in my jealousy
Eze 36:6 because ye **h.** borne the shame of the
Eze 36:7 I **h.** lifted up mine hand, Surely the
Eze 36:22 which ye **h.** profaned among the
Eze 36:23 which ye **h.** profaned in the midst of
Eze 36:33 In the day that I shall **h.** cleansed
Eze 36:36 I the Lord **h.** spoken it, and I will
Eze 37:13 when I **h.** opened your graves, O my
Eze 37:14 that I the Lord **h.** spoken it, and
Eze 37:23 wherein they **h.** sinned, and will
Eze 37:24 and they all shall **h.** one shepherd: 1961
Eze 37:25 land that I **h.** given unto Jacob my
Eze 37:25 wherein your fathers **h.** dwelt; and
Eze 38:8 which **h.** been always waste: but it is
Eze 38:12 which **h.** gotten cattle and goods,
Eze 38:17 Art thou he of whom I **h.** spoken in
Eze 38:19 in the fire of my wrath **h.** I spoken,
Eze 39:5 the open field: for I **h.** spoken it,
Eze 39:8 this is the day whereof I **h.** spoken.
Eze 39:15 till the buriers **h.** buried it in the
Eze 39:19 sacrifice which I **h.** sacrificed for
Eze 39:21 see my judgment that I **h.** executed,
Eze 39:21 and my hand that I **h.** laid upon
Eze 39:24 their transgressions **h.** I done unto
Eze 39:25 and **h.** mercy upon the whole
Eze 39:26 After that they **h.** borne their shame,
Eze 39:26 they **h.** trespassed against me, when
Eze 39:27 When I **h.** brought them again from
Eze 39:28 but I **h.** gathered them unto their
Eze 39:28 and **h.** left none of them any more
Eze 39:29 for I **h.** poured out my spirit upon the
Eze 41:6 that they might **h.** hold, but they 1961
Eze 43:8 they **h.** even defiled my holy name by
Eze 43:8 abominations that they **h.** committed:
Eze 43:8 wherefore I **h.** consumed them in
Eze 43:11 ashamed of all that they **h.** done,
Eze 44:7 In that ye **h.** brought into my
Eze 44:7 and they **h.** broken my covenant
Eze 44:8 And ye **h.** not kept the charge of
Eze 44:8 but ye **h.** set keepers of my charge in
Eze 44:12 therefore **h.** I lifted up mine hand
Eze 44:13 abominations...they **h.** committed.
Eze 44:18 They shall **h.** linen bonnets upon........ 1961
Eze 44:18 and shall **h.** linen breeches upon........ 1961
Eze 45:5 house, **h.** for themselves, for a.......... 1961
Eze 45:10 Ye shall **h.** just balances, and a just 1961
Eze 45:21 ye shall **h.** the passover, a feast of..... 1961
Eze 47:13 Israel: Joseph shall **h.** two portions.
Eze 47:22 they shall **h.** inheritance with you 5307
Eze 48:11 which **h.** kept my charge, which went
Eze 48:13 the Levites shall **h.** five and twenty
Eze 48:23 side, Benjamin shall **h.** a portion.
Eze 48:24 west side, Simeon shall **h.** a portion.
Da 2:3 I **h.** dreamed a dream, and my spirit
Da 2:9 for ye **h.** prepared lying and corrupt
Da 2:25 I **h.** found a man of the captives of
Da 2:26 unto me the dream which I **h.** seen,
Da 2:30 that I **h.** more than any living,............ 383
Da 3:12 these men, O king, **h.** not regarded
Da 3:14 the golden image which I **h.** set up?
Da 3:15 worship the image which I **h.** made;
Da 3:25 of the fire, and they **h.** no hurt; 383
Da 3:28 and **h.** changed the king's word,
Da 4:9 my dream that I **h.** seen, and the
Da 4:18 dream I king Nebuchadnezzar **h.** seen.
Da 4:26 after that thou shalt **h.** known that
Da 4:30 that I **h.** built for the house of the
Da 5:7 and **h.** a chain of gold about his neck,
Da 5:14 I **h.** even heard of thee, that the spirit
Da 5:15 the astrologers, **h.** been brought in
Da 5:16 And I **h.** heard of thee, that thou canst
Da 5:16 and **h.** a chain of gold about thy neck,
Da 5:23 and they **h.** brought the vessels of his
Da 5:23 and thy concubines, **h.** drunk wine in
Da 6:2 the king should **h.** no damage. 1934
Da 6:7 and the captains, **h.** consulted
Da 6:22 mouths, that they **h.** not hurt me:
Da 6:22 before thee, O king, **h.** I done no hurt.
Da 9:5 We **h.** sinned, and **h.** committed
Da 9:5 and **h.** done wickedly, and **h.** rebelled,
Da 9:6 Neither **h.** we hearkened unto thy
Da 9:7 trespass that they **h.** trespassed
Da 9:8 to our fathers, because we **h.** sinned
Da 9:9 forgivenesses, though we **h.** rebelled
Da 9:10 Neither **h.** we obeyed the voice of the
Da 9:11 Yea, all Israel **h.** transgressed thy law,
Da 9:11 of God, because we **h.** sinned against
Da 9:15 we **h.** sinned, we **h.** done wickedly.
Da 10:16 me, and I **h.** retained no strength.
Da 11:5 and **h.** dominion; his dominion shall
Da 11:24 his fathers **h.** not done, nor his fathers'
Da 11:30 and **h.** indignation against the
Da 11:30 and **h.** intelligence with them that
Da 11:43 he shall **h.** power over the treasures
Da 12:7 and when he shall **h.** accomplished to
Ho 1:6 for I will no more **h.** mercy upon
Ho 1:7 But I will **h.** mercy upon the house
Ho 2:4 And I will not **h.** mercy upon her
Ho 2:12 rewards that my lovers **h.** given me:
Ho 2:23 and I will **h.** mercy upon her that
Ho 4:10 For they shall eat, and not **h.** enough:
Ho 4:10 because they **h.** left off to take heed to
Ho 4:12 they **h.** gone a whoring from under
Ho 4:18 they **h.** committed whoredom
Ho 5:1 because ye **h.** been a snare on Mizpah.
Ho 5:2 though I **h.** been a rebuker of them
Ho 5:4 and they **h.** not known the Lord.
Ho 5:7 They **h.** dealt treacherously against
Ho 5:7 for they **h.** begotten strange children:
Ho 5:9 the tribes of Israel **h.** I made known
Ho 6:5 Therefore **h.** I hewed them by the
Ho 6:5 I **h.** slain them by the words of my
Ho 6:7 But they like men **h.** transgressed the
Ho 6:7 there **h.** they dealt treacherously
Ho 6:10 I **h.** seen an horrible thing in the
Ho 7:1 When I would **h.** healed Israel, then
Ho 7:2 now their own doings **h.** beset them
Ho 7:5 the princes **h.** made him sick with
Ho 7:6 For they **h.** made ready their heart
Ho 7:7 and **h.** devoured their judges;
Ho 7:9 Strangers **h.** devoured his strength,
Ho 7:13 Woe unto them! for they **h.** fled from
Ho 7:13 because they **h.** transgressed against
Ho 7:13 though I **h.** redeemed them, yet they
Ho 7:13 yet they **h.** spoken lies against me.
Ho 7:14 And they **h.** not cried unto me with
Ho 7:15 Though I **h.** bound and strengthened
Ho 8:1 because they **h.** transgressed my
Ho 8:4 They **h.** set up kings, but not by me:
Ho 8:4 they **h.** made princes, and I knew it not;
Ho 8:4 their gold **h.** they made them idols,
Ho 8:7 For they **h.** sown the wind, and they
Ho 8:10 Yea, though they **h.** hired among the
Ho 8:12 I **h.** written to him the great things of
Ho 9:9 They **h.** deeply corrupted themselves,
Ho 10:1 of his land they **h.** made goodly images.
Ho 10:3 We **h.** no king, because we feared not
Ho 10:4 They **h.** spoken words, swearing
Ho 10:13 Ye **h.** plowed wickedness, ye **h.** reaped
Ho 10:13 ye **h.** eaten the fruit of lies: because
Ho 12:8 rich, I **h.** found out substance:
Ho 12:10 I **h.** also spoken by the prophets, and
Ho 12:10 and I **h.** multiplied visions, and used
Ho 13:2 and **h.** made them molten images of
Ho 13:6 therefore **h.** they forgotten me.
Ho 14:8 What **h.** I to do any more with idols?
Ho 14:8 I **h.** heard him, and observed him: I
Joe 1:18 because they **h.** no pasture;
Joe 3:2 whom they **h.** scattered among the
Joe 3:3 And they **h.** cast lots for my people;
Joe 3:3 and **h.** given a boy for an harlot, and
Joe 3:4 Yea, and what **h.** ye to do with me,
Joe 3:5 Because ye **h.** taken my silver and
Joe 3:5 and **h.** carried into your temples my
Joe 3:6 Jerusalem **h.** ye sold unto the Grecians
Joe 3:7 out of the place whither ye **h.** sold
Joe 3:19 because they **h.** shed innocent blood
Joe 3:21 their blood that I **h.** not cleansed:
Am 1:3 because they **h.** threshed Gilead with
Am 1:13 because they **h.** ripped up the women
Am 2:4 because they **h.** despised the law of
Am 2:4 and **h.** not kept his commandments,
Am 2:4 the which their fathers **h.** walked:
Am 3:2 You only **h.** I known of all the families
Am 3:4 out of his den, if he **h.** taken nothing?
Am 3:5 from the earth, and **h.** taken nothing
Am 3:15 great houses shall **h.** an end, saith
Am 4:6 And I also **h.** given you cleanness of
Am 4:6 yet **h.** ye not returned unto me, saith
Am 4:7 And also I **h.** withholden the rain
Am 4:8 yet **h.** ye not returned unto me, saith
Am 4:9 I **h.** smitten you with blasting and
Am 4:9 yet **h.** ye not returned unto me, saith
Am 4:10 I **h.** sent among you the pestilence
Am 4:10 your young men **h.** I slain with sword,
Am 4:10 and **h.** taken away your horses; and
Am 4:10 I **h.** made the stink of your camps to
Am 4:10 yet **h.** ye not returned unto me, saith
Am 4:11 I **h.** overthrown some of you, as God
Am 4:11 yet **h.** ye not returned unto me, saith
Am 5:11 ye **h.** built houses of hewn stone, but
Am 5:11 ye **h.** planted pleasant vineyards, but
Am 5:14 shall be with you, as ye **h.** spoken.
Am 5:25 **H.** ye offered unto me sacrifices and
Am 5:26 But ye **h.** borne the tabernacle of
Am 6:12 for ye **h.** turned judgment into gall,
Am 6:13 **H.** we not taken to us horns by our
Am 9:7 **H.** not I brought up Israel out of the
Am 9:15 of their land which I **h.** given them,
Ob 1 We **h.** heard a rumour from the Lord,
Ob 2 Behold, I **h.** made thee small among
Ob 5 would they not **h.** stolen till they had
Ob 7 that eat thy bread **h.** laid a wound
Ob 7 thy confederacy **h.** brought thee even
Ob 7 **h.** deceived thee, and prevailed
Ob 12 thou shouldest not **h.** looked on the
Ob 12 neither shouldest thou **h.** rejoiced
Ob 12 thou **h.** spoken proudly in the day of
Ob 13 Thou shouldest not **h.** entered into
Ob 13 thou shouldest not **h.** looked on their
Ob 13 nor **h.** laid hands on their substance
Ob 14 Neither shouldest thou **h.** stood in
Ob 14 thou **h.** delivered up those of his that

Ob 16 For as ye h. drunk upon my holy
Jon 2:9 I will pay that that I h. vowed.
Mic 2:5 therefore thou shalt h. none that 1961
Mic 2:9 The women of my people h. ye cast
Mic 2:9 from their children h. ye taken away
Mic 2:13 up before them: they h. broken up,
Mic 2:13 and h. passed through the gate, and
Mic 3:4 as they h. behaved themselves ill in
Mic 3:6 that ye shall not h. a vision; and it
Mic 4:6 driven out, and her that I h. afflicted;
Mic 4:9 for pangs h. taken thee as a woman in
Mic 5:2 whose goings forth h. been from of
Mic 5:12 shalt h. no more soothsayers: 1961
Mic 5:15 heathen, such as they h. not heard.
Mic 6:3 O my people, what h. I done unto
Mic 6:3 and wherein h. I wearied thee? testify
Mic 6:12 and the inhabitants thereof h. spoken
Mic 7:1 for I am as when they h. gathered the
Mic 7:9 because I h. sinned against him, until
Mic 7:19 he will h. compassion upon us;
Na 1:12 though I h. afflicted thee, I will afflict
Na 2:2 for the emptiers h. emptied them out,
Hab 1:14 creeping things, that h. no ruler over
Hab 3:2 O Lord, I h. heard thy speech, and
Zep 1:6 and those that h. not sought the
Zep 1:17 because they h. sinned against the
Zep 2:3 which h. wrought his judgment;
Zep 2:8 I h. heard the reproach of Moab,
Zep 2:8 whereby they h. reproached my people,
Zep 2:10 This shall they h. for their pride,
Zep 2:10 because they h. reproached and
Zep 3:4 her priests h. polluted the sanctuary,
Zep 3:4 they h. done violence to the law.
Zep 3:6 I h. cut off the nations: their towers
Zep 3:19 every land where they h. been put to
Hag 1:6 Ye h. sown much, and bring in little;
Hag 1:6 ye eat, but ye h. not enough; ye drink,
Hag 2:23 I h. chosen thee, saith the Lord of hosts
Zec 1:4 former prophets h. cried, saying,
Zec 1:11 We h. walked to and fro through the
Zec 1:12 how long wilt thou not h. mercy
Zec 1:19 These are the horns which h. scattered
Zec 1:21 These are the horns which h. scattered
Zec 2:6 for I h. spread you abroad as the four
Zec 3:4 I h. caused thine iniquity to pass
Zec 3:9 For behold the stone that I h. laid
Zec 4:2 I h. looked, and behold a candlestick
Zec 4:9 h. laid the foundations of this house;
Zec 6:8 toward the north country h. quieted
Zec 7:3 as I h. done these so many years?
Zec 8:15 So again h. I thought in these days
Zec 8:23 for we h. heard that God is with you.
Zec 9:8 any more: for now h. I seen with
Zec 9:11 I h. sent forth thy prisoners out of the
Zec 9:13 When I h. bent Judah for me, filled
Zec 10:2 For the idols h. spoken vanity, and the
Zec 10:2 vanity, and the diviners h. seen a lie,
Zec 10:2 and h. told false dreams; they comfort
Zec 10:6 for I h. mercy upon them: and
Zec 10:8 gather them; for I h. redeemed them:
Zec 10:8 shall increase as they h. increased.
Zec 12:10 look upon me whom they h. pierced,
Zec 14:12 will smite all the people that h. fought
Zec 14:18 and come not, that h. no rain; there
Mal 1:2 I h. loved you, saith the Lord. Yet ye
Mal 1:6 And ye say, Wherein h. we despised
Mal 1:7 and ye say, Wherein h. we polluted
Mal 1:10 I h. no pleasure in you, saith the Lord
Mal 1:12 But ye h. profaned it, in that ye say,
Mal 1:13 and ye h. snuffed at it, saith the
Mal 2:2 yea, I h. cursed them already, because
Mal 2:4 And ye shall know that I h. sent this
Mal 2:8 ye h. caused many to stumble at the
Mal 2:8 ye h. corrupted the covenant of Levi,
Mal 2:9 Therefore h. I also made you
Mal 2:9 according as ye h. not kept my ways,
Mal 2:9 ways, but h. been partial in the law.
Mal 2:10 H. we not all one father? hath not one
Mal 2:13 And this h. ye done again, covering
Mal 2:17 Ye h. wearied the Lord with your
Mal 2:17 Yet ye say, Wherein h. we wearied
Mal 3:7 ordinances, and h. not kept them.
Mal 3:8 man rob God? yet ye h. robbed me.
Mal 3:8 ye say, Wherein h. we robbed thee?
Mal 3:9 for ye h. robbed me, even this whole
Mal 3:13 Your words h. been stout against me,
Mal 3:13 What h. we spoken so much against
Mal 3:14 Ye h. said, It is vain to serve God:
Mal 3:14 and what profit is it that we h. kept
Mal 3:14 and that we h. walked mournfully
Mt 2:2 for we h. seen his star in the east,
Mt 2:8 and when ye h. found him, bring me
Mt 2:15 Out of Egypt h. I called my son.
Mt 3:9 We h. Abraham to our father: for *2192*
Mt 3:14 I h. need to be baptized of thee, *2192*
Mt 5:13 but if the salt h. lost his savour,
Mt 5:21, 27 Ye h. heard that it was said by
Mt 5:33 Again, ye h. heard that it hath been
Mt 5:38 Ye h. heard that it hath been said,
Mt 5:40 thy coat, let him h. thy cloke also
Mt 5:43 Ye h. heard that it hath been said,
Mt 5:46 what reward h. ye? do not even *2192*
Mt 6:1 otherwise ye h. no reward of your *2192*
Mt 6:2 that they may h. glory of men.
Mt 6:2, 5 unto you, They h. their reward *568*
Mt 6:8 what things ye h. need of, before *2192*
Mt 6:16 unto you, They h. their reward *568*
Mt 6:32 knoweth that ye h. need of all these
Mt 7:22 Lord, h. we not prophesied in thy
Mt 7:22 and in thy name h. cast out devils?
Mt 8:10 I h. not found so great faith, no, not in
Mt 8:20 unto him, The foxes h. holes, *2192*
Mt 8:20 and the birds of the air h. nests; but
Mt 8:29 What h. we to do with thee,
Mt 9:13 I will h. mercy, and not sacrifice:
Mt 9:27 Thou son of David, h. mercy on us.
Mt 10:8 freely ye h. received, freely give
Mt 10:23 Ye shall not h. gone over the cities
Mt 10:25 If they h. called the master of the
Mt 11:5 and the poor h. the gospel preached
Mt 11:17 We h. piped unto you, and ye
Mt 11:17 piped unto you, and ye h. not danced;
Mt 11:17 we h. mourned unto you, and ye
Mt 11:17 unto you, and ye h. not lamented
Mt 11:21 they would h. repented long ago in
Mt 11:23 mighty works, which h. been done in
Mt 11:23 it would h. remained until this day.
Mt 12:3 H. ye not read what David did, when
Mt 12:5 Or h. ye not read in the law, how that
Mt 12:7 meaneth, I will h. mercy, and not
Mt 12:7 ye would not h. condemned the
Mt 12:11 that shall h. one sheep, and if it *2192*
Mt 12:18 Behold my servant, whom I h. chosen;
Mt 13:12 and he shall h. more abundance: but
Mt 13:15 and their eyes they h. closed; lest at
Mt 13:17 righteous men h. desired to see
Mt 13:17 which ye hear, and h. not heard them
Mt 13:17 which ye see, and h. not seen them;
Mt 13:35 things which h. been kept secret
Mt 13:51 H. ye understood all these things?
Mt 14:4 It is not lawful for thee to h. her. *2192*
Mt 14:5 when he would h. put him to death,
Mt 14:17 We h. here but five loaves, and two *2192*
Mt 15:6 Thus h. ye made the commandment
Mt 15:22 H. mercy on me, O Lord, thou son
Mt 15:32 I h. compassion on the multitude,
Mt 15:32 three days, and h. nothing to eat: *2192*
Mt 15:33 Whence should we h. so much bread
Mt 15:34 How many loaves h. ye? And they *2192*
Mt 16:7 It is because we h. taken no bread.
Mt 16:8 because ye h. brought no bread?
Mt 17:12 but h. done unto him whatsoever they
Mt 17:15 Lord, h. mercy on my son: for he is
Mt 17:20 If ye h. faith as a grain of mustard *2192*
Mt 18:12 if a man h. an hundred sheep, and *1099*
Mt 18:26 Lord, h. patience with me, and I will
Mt 18:29 H. patience with me, and I will pay
Mt 18:33 not thou also h. had compassion
Mt 19:4 H. ye not read, that he which made
Mt 19:12 which h. made themselves eunuchs
Mt 19:16 shall I do, that I may h. eternal *2192*
Mt 19:20 All these things h. I kept from my
Mt 19:21 and thou shalt h. treasure in *2192*
Mt 19:27 Behold, we h. forsaken all, and followed
Mt 19:27 thee; what shall we h. therefore? *2701*
Mt 19:28 That ye which h. followed me, in the
Mt 20:10 that they should h. received more;
Mt 20:12 These last h. wrought but one hour,
Mt 20:12 which h. borne the burden and heat of
Mt 20:30 cried out saying, H. mercy on us,
Mt 20:31 cried the more, saying, H. mercy on
Mt 21:13 but ye h. made it a den of thieves.
Mt 21:16 h. ye never read, Out of the mouth
Mt 21:21 If ye h. faith, and doubt not, ye *2192*
Mt 22:4 I h. prepared my dinner: my oxen and
Mt 22:31 h. ye not read that which was spoken
Mt 23:23 and h. omitted the weightier matters of
Mt 23:23 these ought ye to h. done, and not to
Mt 23:30 we would not h. been partakers with
Mt 23:37 how often would I h. gathered thy
Mt 24:25 Behold, I h. told you before
Mt 24:43 would come, he would h. watched,
Mt 24:43 and would not h. suffered his house
Mt 25:20 I h. gained beside them five talents
Mt 25:22 I h. gained two other talents beside
Mt 25:26 and gather where I h. not strawed:
Mt 25:27 to h. put my money to the exchangers,
Mt 25:27 I should h. received mine own with
Mt 25:29 and he shall h. abundance: but from
Mt 25:40 Inasmuch as ye h. done it unto one of
Mt 25:40 my brethren, ye h. done it unto me.
Mt 26:9 For this ointment might h. been sold
Mt 26:11 For ye h. the poor always with *2192*
Mt 26:11 with you; but me ye h. not always. *2192*
Mt 26:65 further need h. we of witnesses? *2192*
Mt 26:65 behold, now ye h. heard his blasphemy.
Mt 27:4 Saying, I h. sinned in that I
Mt 27:4 that I h. betrayed the innocent blood.
Mt 27:19 H. thou nothing to do with that just
Mt 27:19 for I h. suffered many things this day
Mt 27:43 deliver him now, if he will h. him:
Mt 27:65 said unto them, Ye h. a watch: *2192*
Mt 28:7 there shall ye see him: lo, I h. told you.
Mt 28:20 whatsoever I h. commanded you:
Mk 1:8 I indeed h. baptized you with water:
Mk 1:24 what h. we to do with thee,
Mk 2:17 They that are whole h. no need *2192*
Mk 2:19 as long as they h. the bridegroom *2192*
Mk 2:25 H. ye never read what David did,
Mk 3:15 And to h. power to heal sicknesses, *2192*
Mk 4:15 but when they h. heard, Satan cometh
Mk 4:16 who, when they h. heard the word,
Mk 4:17 And h. no root in themselves, and *2192*
Mk 4:23 If any man h. ears to hear, let him *2192*
Mk 4:40 how is it that ye h. no faith? *2192*
Mk 5:7 What h. I to do with thee,
Mk 6:18 for thee to h. thy brother's wife, *2192*
Mk 6:19 and would h. killed him; but she
Mk 6:36 for they h. nothing to eat. *2192*
Mk 6:38 How many loaves h. ye? go and *2192*
Mk 6:48 the sea, and would h. passed by them.
Mk 7:4 which they h. received to hold, as the
Mk 7:13 tradition, which ye h. delivered: and
Mk 7:16 If any man h. ears to hear, let *2192*
Mk 7:24 and would h. no man know it: but he
Mk 8:2 I h. compassion on the multitude,
Mk 8:2 because they h. now been with me
Mk 8:2 three days, and h. nothing to eat: *2192*
Mk 8:5 How many loaves h. ye? And they *2192*
Mk 8:16 It is because we h. no bread. *2192*
Mk 8:17 reason ye, because ye h. no bread? *2192*
Mk 8:17 h. ye your heart yet hardened? *2192*
Mk 9:1 till they h. seen the kingdom of
Mk 9:13 and they h. done unto him whatsoever
Mk 9:17 Master, I h. brought unto thee my son,
Mk 9:22 h. compassion on us, and help us.
Mk 9:50 but if the salt h. lost his saltness,
Mk 9:50 ye season it? H. salt in yourselves *2192*
Mk 9:50 and h. peace with one another.
Mk 10:20 Master, all these h. I observed from
Mk 10:21 and thou shalt h. treasure in *2192*
Mk 10:23 How hardly shall they that h. *2192*
Mk 10:28 we h. left all, and h. followed thee.
Mk 10:47 Jesus, thou son of David, h. mercy
Mk 10:48 Thou son of David, h. mercy on me.
Mk 11:17 but ye h. made it a den of thieves.
Mk 11:22 saith unto them, H. faith in God *2192*
Mk 11:23 he shall h. whatsoever he saith. *2071*
Mk 11:24 receive them, and ye shall h. them *2071*
Mk 11:25 forgive, if ye h. ought against any: *2192*
Mk 12:10 And h. ye not read this scripture; The
Mk 12:26 h. ye not read in the book of Moses,
Mk 12:43 than all they which h. cast into the
Mk 13:23 But take ye heed: behold, I h. foretold
Mk 14:5 For it might h. been sold for more
Mk 14:5 and h. been given to the poor. And
Mk 14:7 For ye h. the poor with you *2192*
Mk 14:7 good: but me ye h. not always. *2192*
Mk 14:64 Ye h. heard the blasphemy: what
Lu 1:1 Forasmuch as many h. taken in hand
Lu 1:14 And thou shalt h. joy and gladness; *2071*

Lu 1:62 father, how he would h. him called
Lu 1:70 holy prophets, which h. been since the
Lu 2:30 For mine eyes h. seen thy salvation,
Lu 2:44 they, supposing him to h. been in the
Lu 2:48 and I h. sought thee sorrowing
Lu 3:8 We h. Abraham to our father: 2192
Lu 4:23 whatsoever we h. heard done in
Lu 4:34 What h. we to do with thee,
Lu 5:5 Master, we h. toiled all the night, and
Lu 5:5 and h. taken nothing: nevertheless
Lu 5:26 saying, We h. seen strange things
Lu 6:3 H. ye not read so much as this, what
Lu 6:24 for ye h. received your consolation
Lu 6:32 which love you, what thank h. ye? 2076
Lu 6:33 do good to you, what thank h. ye? 2076
Lu 6:34 hope to receive, what thank h. ye? 2076
Lu 7:9 I h. not found so great faith, no, not
Lu 7:22 tell John what things ye h. seen and
Lu 7:32 and saying, We h. piped unto you,
Lu 7:32 unto you, and ye h. not danced;
Lu 7:32 danced; we h. mourned to you,
Lu 7:32 mourned to you, and ye h. not wept,
Lu 7:39 would h. known who and what manner
Lu 7:40 I h. somewhat to say unto thee 2192
Lu 8:13 and these h. no root, which for a 2192
Lu 8:14 when they h. heard, go forth, and are
Lu 8:18 even that which he seemeth to h. 2192
Lu 8:28 What h. I to do with thee,
Lu 9:3 neither h. two coats apiece 2192
Lu 9:9 And Herod said, John h. I beheaded:
Lu 9:13 We h. no more but five loaves 2076
Lu 9:58 said unto him, Foxes h. holes, 2192
Lu 9:58 and birds of the air h. nests; but
Lu 10:13 which h. been done in you, they had
Lu 10:24 many prophets and kings h. desired
Lu 10:24 which ye see, and h. not seen them;
Lu 10:24 ye hear, and h. not heard them
Lu 11:5 Which of you shall h. a friend, 2192
Lu 11:6 and I h. nothing to set before him? 2192
Lu 11:41 give alms of such things as ye h.; 1751
Lu 11:42 these ought ye to h. done, and not to
Lu 11:52 for ye h. taken away the key of
Lu 12:3 Therefore whatsoever ye h. spoken in
Lu 12:3 and that which ye h. spoken in the
Lu 12:4 that h. no more that they can do 2192
Lu 12:17 because I h. no room where to 2192
Lu 12:24 which neither h. storehouse nor 2076
Lu 12:30 knoweth that ye h. need of these
Lu 12:33 Sell that ye h., and give alms; 5224
Lu 12:39 would h. watched, and not h. suffered
Lu 12:48 to whom men h. committed much,
Lu 12:50 But I h. a baptism to be baptized 2192
Lu 13:26 h. eaten and drunk in thy 2192
Lu 13:34 how often would I h. gathered thy
Lu 14:5 Which of you shall h. an ass or an ox
Lu 14:10 then shalt thou h. worship in the 2071
Lu 14:18 him, I h. bought a piece of ground,
Lu 14:18 see it: I pray thee h. me excused 2192
Lu 14:19 And another said, I h. bought five yoke
Lu 14:19 them: I pray thee h. me excused 2192
Lu 14:20 And another said, I h. married a wife,
Lu 14:28 the cost, whether he h. sufficient 2192
Lu 14:34 Salt is good: but if the salt h. lost
Lu 15:6 for I h. found my sheep which was
Lu 15:9 for I h. found the piece which I
Lu 15:16 And he would fain h. filled his belly
Lu 15:17 h. bread enough and to spare, and I
Lu 15:18 Father, I h. sinned against heaven,
Lu 15:21 I h. sinned against heaven, and in
Lu 15:31 with me, and all that I h. is thine 1699
Lu 16:11 If therefore ye h. not been faithful in
Lu 16:12 And if ye h. not been faithful in that
Lu 16:24 Father Abraham, h. mercy on me,
Lu 16:28 For I h. five brethren; that he 2192
Lu 16:29 They h. Moses and the prophets; 2192
Lu 17:8 serve me, till I h. eaten and drunken;
Lu 17:10 when ye shall h. done all those things
Lu 17:10 we h. done that which was our duty to
Lu 17:13 and said, Jesus, Master, h. mercy
Lu 18:21 And he said, All these h. I kept from
Lu 18:22 thou shalt h. treasure in heaven: 2192
Lu 18:24 hardly shall they that h. riches 2192
Lu 18:28 Then Peter said, Lo, we h. left all, and
Lu 18:38 Jesus, thou son of David, h. mercy
Lu 18:39 Thou son of David, h. mercy on
Lu 19:8 and if I h. taken any thing from any
Lu 19:14 We will not h. this man to reign over
Lu 19:17 h. thou authority over ten cities 2192
Lu 19:20 here is thy pound, which I h. kept 2192
Lu 19:23 I might h. required mine own with
Lu 19:46 but ye h. made it a den of thieves
Lu 21:4 all these h. of their abundance cast
Lu 22:15 With desire I h. desired to eat this
Lu 22:28 Ye are they which h. continued
Lu 22:31 Satan hath desired to h. you, that he
Lu 22:32 But I h. prayed for thee, that thy
Lu 22:37 things concerning me h. an end. 2192
Lu 22:71 for we ourselves h. heard of his
Lu 23:8 and he hoped to h. seen some miracle
Lu 23:14 Ye h. brought this man unto me, as
Lu 23:14 h. found no fault in this man
Lu 23:22 I h. found no cause of death in him:
Lu 24:17 that ye h. one to another, as ye 474
Lu 24:20 condemned to death, and h. crucified 474
Lu 24:21 he which should h. redeemed Israel: 474
Lu 24:25 believe all that the prophets h. spoken:
Lu 24:26 Ought not Christ to h. suffered these
Lu 24:28 made as though he would h. gone
Lu 24:39 flesh and bones, as ye see me h. 2192
Lu 24:41 unto them, H. ye here any meat? 2192
Joh 1:16 And of his fullness h. all we received, 2192
Joh 1:41 We h. found the Messias, which is,
Joh 1:45 We h. found him, of whom Moses in
Joh 2:3 saith unto him, They h. no wine. 2192
Joh 2:4 Woman, what h. I to do with thee?
Joh 2:10 and when men h. well drunk, then
Joh 3:11 and testify that we h. seen; and ye
Joh 3:12 If I h. told you earthly things, and ye
Joh 3:15 not perish, but h. eternal life 2192
Joh 3:16 not perish, but h. everlasting life 2192
Joh 4:9 the Jews h. no dealings with the
Joh 4:10 drink; thou wouldest h. asked of him,
Joh 4:10 and he would h. given thee living
Joh 4:17 and said, I h. no husband. 2192
Joh 4:17 hast well said, I h. no husband. 2192
Joh 4:32 I h. meat to eat that ye know not 2192
Joh 4:42 for we h. heard him ourselves, and
Joh 5:7 Sir, I h. no man, when the water 2192
Joh 5:26 given to the Son to h. life in 2192
Joh 5:29 they that h. done good, unto the
Joh 5:29 they that h. done evil, unto the
Joh 5:36 But I h. greater witness than that 2192
Joh 5:37 Ye h. neither heard his voice at any
Joh 5:38 And ye h. not his word abiding in 2192
Joh 5:39 in them ye think ye h. eternal life: 2192
Joh 5:40 come to me, that we might h. life 2192
Joh 5:42 that ye h. not the love of God in 2192
Joh 5:46 Moses, ye would h. believed me: 2192
Joh 6:36 ye also h. seen me, and believe not
Joh 6:40 may h. everlasting life: and I will 2192
Joh 6:53 drink his blood, ye h. no life in 2192
Joh 6:70 H. not I chosen you twelve, and 2192
Joh 7:21 I h. done one work, and ye all 2192
Joh 7:23 because I h. made a man every 2192
Joh 7:44 some of them would h. taken him;
Joh 7:45 them, Why h. ye not brought him.
Joh 7:48 H. any of the rulers…believed on him?
Joh 8:6 that they might h. to accuse him. 2192
Joh 8:12 but shall h. the light of life 2192
Joh 8:19 ye should h. known my Father 2192
Joh 8:26 I h. many things to say and to 2192
Joh 8:26 those things which I h. heard of 2192
Joh 8:28 When ye h. lifted up the Son of man,
Joh 8:38 I speak that which I h. seen with
Joh 8:38 that which ye h. seen with your
Joh 8:40 the truth, which I h. heard of God:
Joh 8:41 we h. one Father, even God. 2192
Joh 8:49 Jesus answered; I h. not a devil; 2192
Joh 8:55 yet ye h. not known him; but I know
Joh 9:27 He answered them, I h. told you
Joh 9:41 were blind, ye should h. no sin: 2192
Joh 10:10 I am come that they might h. life, 2192
Joh 10:10 and that they might h. it more 2192
Joh 10:16 And other sheep I h., which are 2192
Joh 10:18 I h. power to lay it down, and I 2192
Joh 10:18 and I h. power to take it again 2192
Joh 10:18 This commandment h. I received of 2192
Joh 10:32 Many good works h. I shewed you
Joh 11:34 And said, Where h. ye laid him? They
Joh 11:37 blind, h. caused that even this man
Joh 11:37 even this man should not h. died
Joh 12:8 the poor always ye h. with you; 2192
Joh 12:8 you; but me ye h. not always 2192
Joh 12:28 I h. both glorified it, and will glorify
Joh 12:34 We h. heard out of the law that
Joh 12:35 Walk while ye h. the light, lest 2192
Joh 12:36 While ye h. light, believe in the 2192
Joh 12:48 word that I h. spoken, the same 2192
Joh 12:49 For I h. not spoken of myself; but 2192
Joh 13:12 them, Know ye what I h. done to you?
Joh 13:14 Lord and Master, h. washed your feet;
Joh 13:15 For I h. given you an example, that ye
Joh 13:15 that ye should do as I h. done to you
Joh 13:18 I know whom I h. chosen: but that
Joh 13:26 I shall give a sop, when I h. dipped it
Joh 13:29 Buy those things that we h. need 2192
Joh 13:34 as I h. loved you, that ye also love
Joh 13:35 ye are my disciples, if ye h. love 2192
Joh 14:2 if it were not so, I would h. told you
Joh 14:7 ye should h. known my Father also:
Joh 14:7 henceforth ye know him, and h. seen
Joh 14:9 H. I been so long time with you, and
Joh 14:25 These things h. I spoken unto you
Joh 14:26 remembrance, whatsoever I h. said
Joh 14:28 Ye h. heard how I said unto you, I
Joh 14:29 And now I h. told you before it come
Joh 15:3 the word which I h. spoken unto
Joh 15:9 so h. I loved you: continue ye in my
Joh 15:10 even as I h. kept my Father's
Joh 15:11 These things h. I spoken unto you,
Joh 15:12 love one another, as I h. loved you
Joh 15:15 doeth: but I h. called you friends
Joh 15:15 for all things that I h. heard of my
Joh 15:15 Father I h. made known to you
Joh 15:16 h. not chosen me, but I h. chosen you,
Joh 15:19 but I h. chosen you out of the world,
Joh 15:20 If they h. persecuted me, they will
Joh 15:20 if they h. kept my saying, they will
Joh 15:22 now they h. no cloke for their sin. 2192
Joh 15:24 but now h. they both seen and hated
Joh 15:27 because ye h. been with me from the
Joh 16:1 These things h. I spoken unto you,
Joh 16:3 because they h. not known the Father,
Joh 16:4 But these things h. I told you, that
Joh 16:6 But because I h. said these things unto
Joh 16:12 I h. yet many things to say unto 2192
Joh 16:22 And ye now therefore h. sorrow: 2192
Joh 16:24 Hitherto h. ye asked nothing in my
Joh 16:25 These things h. I spoken unto you,
Joh 16:27 because ye h. loved me, and h. believed
Joh 16:33 These things I h. spoken unto you
Joh 16:33 you, that in me ye might h. peace 2192
Joh 16:33 the world ye shall h. tribulation: 2192
Joh 16:33 good cheer; I h. overcome the world
Joh 17:4 I h. glorified thee on the earth:
Joh 17:4 I h. finished the work which thou
Joh 17:6 I h. manifested thy name unto the
Joh 17:6 them me; and they h. kept thy word
Joh 17:7 Now they h. known that all things
Joh 17:8 For I h. given unto them the words
Joh 17:8 they h. received them, and h. known
Joh 17:8 and they h. believed that thou didst
Joh 17:12 those that thou gavest me I h. kept,
Joh 17:13 that they might h. my joy fulfilled 2192
Joh 17:14 I h. given them thy word; and the
Joh 17:18 even so h. I also sent them into
Joh 17:22 which thou gavest me I h. given them;
Joh 17:25 I h. known thee, and these h. known
Joh 17:26 And I h. declared unto them thy name,
Joh 18:8 Jesus answered, I h. told you that I
Joh 18:9 which thou gavest me h. I lost none.
Joh 18:20 and in secret h. I said nothing,
Joh 18:21 them which heard me, what I h. said
Joh 18:23 If I h. spoken evil, bear witness of the
Joh 18:30 we would not h. delivered him up unto
Joh 18:35 chief priests h. delivered thee unto
Joh 18:39 But ye h. a custom, that I should 2076
Joh 19:7 We h. a law, and by our law he 2192
Joh 19:10 knowest thou not that I h. power 2192
Joh 19:10 crucify thee, and h. power to 2192
Joh 19:11 Thou couldest h. no power at all 2192
Joh 19:15 answered, we h. no king but Caesar 2192
Joh 19:22 What I h. written I h. written. 2192
Joh 20:2 They h. taken away the Lord out of the
Joh 20:2 and we know not where they h. laid
Joh 20:13 Because they h. taken away my Lord,
Joh 20:13 I know not where they h. laid him
Joh 20:15 if thou h. borne him hence, tell me
Joh 20:25 said unto him, We h. seen the Lord.
Joh 20:29 that h. not seen, and yet h. believed
Joh 20:31 that believing ye might h. life 2192

Joh	21:5	**Children, h. ye any meat? They**	2192
Joh	21:10	**of the fish which ye h. now caught.**	
Ac	1:1	The former treatise **h.** I made, O	
Ac	1:4	**which, saith he, ye h. heard of me**	
Ac	1:11	come in like manner as ye **h.** seen him	
Ac	1:16	must needs **h.** been fulfilled,	
Ac	1:21	men which **h.** companied with us all	
Ac	2:23	Him, being delivered...ye **h.** taken,	
Ac	2:23	by wicked hands **h.** crucified and	
Ac	2:36	whom ye **h.** crucified, both Lord and	
Ac	3:6	silver and gold **h.** I none;	5225
Ac	3:6	but such as I **h.** give I thee:	2192
Ac	3:24	follow after, as many as **h.** spoken,	
Ac	3:24	**h.** likewise foretold of these days.	
Ac	4:7	or by what name **h.** ye done this?	
Ac	4:20	speak the things which we **h.** seen	
Ac	5:9	How is it that ye **h.** agreed together	
Ac	5:9	the feet of them which **h.** buried thy	
Ac	5:21	sent to the prison to **h.** them brought.	
Ac	5:26	lest they should **h.** been stoned.	
Ac	5:28	and, behold, ye **h.** filled Jerusalem	
Ac	6:11	We **h.** heard him speak blasphemous	
Ac	6:14	For we **h.** heard him say, that this	
Ac	7:25	his brethren would **h.** understood	
Ac	7:26	and would **h.** set them at one again,	
Ac	7:34	I **h.** seen, I...the affliction of my	
Ac	7:34	I **h.** seen the affliction of my people	
Ac	7:34	and I **h.** heard their groaning, and am	
Ac	7:42	**h.** ye offered to me slain beasts and	
Ac	7:52	**h.** not your fathers persecuted?	
Ac	7:52	and they **h.** slain them which shewed	
Ac	7:52	of whom ye **h.** been now the betrayers	
Ac	7:53	Who **h.** received the law by the	
Ac	7:53	disposition of angels, and **h.** not kept	
Ac	8:24	these things which ye **h.** spoken come	
Ac	9:6	said, Lord, what wilt thou **h.** me to	
Ac	9:13	Lord, I **h.** heard by many of this man,	
Ac	10:10	very hungry, and would **h.** eaten:	
Ac	10:14	for I **h.** never eaten any thing that is	
Ac	10:20	doubting nothing: for I **h.** sent them.	
Ac	10:29	for what intent ye **h.** sent for me?	
Ac	10:47	which **h.** received the Holy Ghost as	
Ac	12:6	And when Herod would **h.** brought	
Ac	13:2	Saul for the work whereunto I **h.** called	
Ac	13:15	if ye **h.** any word of exhortation	2076
Ac	13:22	I **h.** found David the son of Jesse, a	
Ac	13:27	they **h.** fulfilled them in condemning	
Ac	13:33	Thou art my Son, this day **h.** I begotten	
Ac	13:46	should first **h.** been spoken to you:	
Ac	13:47	I **h.** set thee to be a light of the Gentiles	
Ac	14:13	and would **h.** done sacrifice with the	
Ac	15:24	Forasmuch as we **h.** heard, that certain	
Ac	15:24	out from us **h.** troubled you with words,	
Ac	15:26	Men that **h.** hazarded their lives for the	
Ac	15:27	We **h.** sent therefore Judas and Silas,	
Ac	15:36	in every city where we **h.** preached	
Ac	16:3	Him would Paul **h.** to go forth with	
Ac	16:15	If ye **h.** judged me to be faithful to the	
Ac	16:27	and would **h.** killed himself,	
Ac	16:36	The magistrates **h.** sent to let you go:	
Ac	16:37	**h.** beaten us openly uncondemned,	
Ac	16:37	Romans, and **h.** cast us into prison;	
Ac	17:3	that Christ must needs **h.** suffered,	
Ac	17:6	These that **h.** turned the world upside	
Ac	17:28	certain also of your own poets **h.** said,	
Ac	17:28	we live, and move, and **h.** our being;	
Ac	18:10	for I **h.** much people in this city.	2076
Ac	19:2	**H.** ye received the Holy Ghost since	2076
Ac	19:2	We **h.** not so much as heard whether	2076
Ac	19:21	After I **h.** been there, I must also see	
Ac	19:25	by this craft we **h.** our wealth.	2076
Ac	19:30	And when Paul would **h.** entered in	2076
Ac	19:33	and would **h.** made his defence unto	
Ac	19:37	For ye **h.** brought hither these men,	
Ac	19:38	**h.** a matter against any man, the	2192
Ac	20:18	after what manner I **h.** been with you	2192
Ac	20:20	but **h.** shewed you, and **h.** taught	2192
Ac	20:24	which I **h.** received of the Lord Jesus,	2192
Ac	20:25	among whom I **h.** gone preaching the	2192
Ac	20:27	For I **h.** not shunned to declare	2192
Ac	20:33	I **h.** coveted no man's silver, or gold,	2192
Ac	20:34	that these hands **h.** ministered unto	2192
Ac	20:35	I **h.** shewed you all things, how	2192
Ac	21:23	We say to thee, We **h.** four men	1526
Ac	21:23	four men which **h.** a vow on them;	2192
Ac	21:25	we **h.** written and concluded that they.	2192
Ac	22:29	from him which should **h.** examined	2192
Ac	22:30	he would **h.** known the certainty	2192
Ac	23:1	I **h.** lived in all good conscience before	
Ac	23:10	Paul should **h.** been pulled in pieces	
Ac	23:14	We **h.** bound ourselves under a great	
Ac	23:14	eat nothing until we **h.** slain Paul.	
Ac	23:20	The Jews **h.** agreed to desire thee that	
Ac	23:21	which **h.** bound themselves with an	
Ac	23:21	neither eat nor drink till they **h.** killed	
Ac	23:27	and should **h.** been killed of them:	
Ac	23:28	when I would **h.** known the cause	
Ac	23:29	to **h.** nothing laid to his charge	2192
Ac	24:5	For we **h.** found this man a pestilent	
Ac	24:6	and would **h.** judged according to	
Ac	24:15	And **h.** hope toward God, which	2192
Ac	24:16	to **h.** always a conscience void of	2192
Ac	24:19	Who ought to **h.** been here before thee,	
Ac	24:20	if they **h.** found any evil doing in me,	
Ac	24:23	and to let him **h.** liberty, and	2192
Ac	24:25	when I **h.** a convenient season,	3335
Ac	24:26	that money should **h.** been given	3335
Ac	25:8	against Caesar, **h.** I offended any thing	
Ac	25:10	to the Jews **h.** I done no wrong, as	
Ac	25:11	For if I be an offender, or **h.** committed	
Ac	25:15	desiring to **h.** judgment against him	
Ac	25:16	**h.** the accusers face to face,	2192
Ac	25:16	and **h.** licence to answer for himself	2983
Ac	25:24	multitude of the Jews **h.** dealt with me,	2983
Ac	25:25	to Augustus, I **h.** determined to send	2983
Ac	25:26	Of whom I **h.** no certain thing to	2192
Ac	25:26	I **h.** brought him forth before you,	
Ac	25:26	had, I might **h.** somewhat to write.	2192
Ac	26:16	**for I h. appeared unto thee for this**	
Ac	26:32	This man might **h.** been set at liberty,	
Ac	27:21	Sirs, ye should **h.** hearkened unto me,	
Ac	27:21	unto me, and not **h.** loosed from Crete,	
Ac	27:21	and to **h.** gained this harm and loss.	
Ac	27:29	lest we should **h.** fallen upon rocks,	
Ac	27:30	they would **h.** cast anchors out of the	
Ac	27:33	that ye **h.** tarried and continued	
Ac	28:6	when he should **h.** swollen, or fallen	
Ac	28:17	I **h.** committed nothing against	
Ac	28:18	would **h.** let me go, because there	
Ac	28:20	For this cause therefore **h.** I called	
Ac	28:27	and their eyes **h.** they closed; lest	
Ro	1:5	By whom we **h.** received grace and	
Ro	1:10	I might **h.** a prosperous journey by	
Ro	1:13	Now I would not **h.** you ignorant,	
Ro	1:13	that I might **h.** some fruit among	2192
Ro	1:32	**h.** pleasure in them that do them.	2192
Ro	2:12	For as many as **h.** sinned without law	
Ro	2:12	and as many as **h.** sinned in the law	
Ro	2:14	the Gentiles, which **h.** not the law;	2192
Ro	3:9	for we **h.** before proved both Jews	2192
Ro	3:13	with their tongues they **h.** used deceit;	
Ro	3:17	the way of peace **h.** they not known:	
Ro	3:23	For all **h.** sinned, and come short of	
Ro	4:17	I **h.** made thee a father of many	
Ro	5:1	we **h.** peace with God through	2192
Ro	5:2	By whom also we **h.** access by faith	2192
Ro	5:11	by whom we **h.** now received the	
Ro	5:12	upon all men, for that all **h.** sinned:	
Ro	6:5	For if we **h.** been planted together in	
Ro	6:14	For sin shall not **h.** dominion over you:	
Ro	6:17	but ye **h.** obeyed from the heart	
Ro	6:19	for as ye **h.** yielded your members	
Ro	6:22	ye **h.** your fruit unto holiness,	2192
Ro	8:9	if any man **h.** not the Spirit of	2192
Ro	8:15	For ye **h.** not received the spirit of	2192
Ro	8:15	ye **h.** received the Spirit of adoption,	
Ro	8:23	which **h.** the firstfruits of the	2192
Ro	9:2	That I **h.** great heaviness and	2076
Ro	9:9	I come, and Sarah shall **h.** a son.	2071
Ro	9:13	Jacob **h.** I loved, but Esau **h.** I hated.	2071
Ro	9:15	saith to Moses, I will **h.** mercy on whom	
Ro	9:15	mercy on whom I will **h.** mercy, and	
Ro	9:15	and I will **h.** compassion on whom	
Ro	9:15	on whom I will **h.** compassion.	
Ro	9:17	for this same purpose **h.** I raised thee	
Ro	9:18	mercy on whom he will **h.** mercy,	
Ro	9:30	**h.** attained to righteousness, even	
Ro	10:2	record that they **h.** a zeal of God,	2192
Ro	10:3	**h.** not submitted themselves unto the	2192
Ro	10:14	on him in whom they **h.** not believed?	
Ro	10:14	in him of whom they **h.** not heard?	
Ro	10:16	But they **h.** not all obeyed the gospel.	
Ro	10:18	But I say, **H.** they not heard? Yes	
Ro	10:21	All day long I **h.** stretched forth	
Ro	11:3	Lord, they **h.** killed thy prophets, and	
Ro	11:4	I **h.** reserved to myself seven thousand	
Ro	11:4	who **h.** not bowed the knee to the	
Ro	11:11	I say then, **H.** they stumbled that	
Ro	11:30	in times past **h.** not believed God,	
Ro	11:30	yet **h.** now obtained mercy through	
Ro	11:31	so **h.** these also now not believed,	
Ro	11:32	that he might **h.** mercy upon all.	
Ro	12:4	For as we **h.** many members in	2192
Ro	12:4	members **h.** not the same office:	2192
Ro	13:3	thou shalt **h.** praise of the same:	2192
Ro	14:22	Hast thou faith? **h.** it to thyself	2192
Ro	15:4	of the scriptures might **h.** hope.	2192
Ro	15:15	I **h.** written the more boldly unto you	2192
Ro	15:17	I **h.** therefore whereof I may glory	2192
Ro	15:19	I **h.** fully preached the gospel of Christ.	
Ro	15:20	Yea, so I **h.** strived to preach the	
Ro	15:21	and they that **h.** not heard shall	
Ro	15:22	I **h.** been much hindered from coming	
Ro	15:27	if the Gentiles **h.** been made partakers	
Ro	15:28	I **h.** performed this, and **h.** sealed to	
Ro	15:31	my service which I **h.** for Jerusalem	
Ro	16:4	Who **h.** for my life laid down their	
Ro	16:17	to the doctrine which ye **h.** learned;	
Ro	16:19	but yet I would **h.** you wise unto that	
1Co	2:8	they would not **h.** crucified the Lord of	
1Co	2:9	neither **h.** entered into the heart of	
1Co	2:12	Now we **h.** received, not the spirit of	
1Co	2:16	But we **h.** the mind of Christ.	2192
1Co	3:2	I **h.** fed you with milk, and not with	2192
1Co	3:6	I **h.** planted, Apollos watered; but	2192
1Co	3:10	I **h.** laid the foundation, and another	2192
1Co	4:5	shall every man **h.** praise of God.	1096
1Co	4:6	I **h.** in a figure transferred to myself	
1Co	4:8	ye **h.** reigned as kings without us:	
1Co	4:11	and **h.** no certain dwellingplace;	
1Co	4:15	ye **h.** ten thousand instructors in	2192
1Co	4:15	yet **h.** ye not many fathers: for in	
1Co	4:17	For this cause **h.** I sent unto you	
1Co	5:1	one should **h.** his father's wife.	2192
1Co	5:2	puffed up, and **h.** not rather mourned,	2192
1Co	5:3	**h.** judged already, as though I were	
1Co	5:11	But now I **h.** written unto you not to	
1Co	5:12	For what **h.** I to do to judge them also	
1Co	6:4	If then ye **h.** judgments of things	2192
1Co	6:19	which ye **h.** of God, and ye are not	2192
1Co	7:2	let every man **h.** his own wife,	2192
1Co	7:2	every woman **h.** her own husband.	2192
1Co	7:25	virgins I **h.** no commandment of	2192
1Co	7:28	Nevertheless such shall **h.** trouble	2192
1Co	7:29	that both they that **h.** wives be as	2192
1Co	7:32	I would **h.** you without carefulness.	
1Co	7:40	I think also that I **h.** the Spirit	2192
1Co	8:1	we know that we all **h.** knowledge	2192
1Co	9:1	**h.** I not seen Jesus Christ our Lord?	
1Co	9:4	**H.** we not power to eat and to	2192
1Co	9:5	**H.** we not power to lead about a	2192
1Co	9:6	**h.** we not power to forbear	2192
1Co	9:11	If we **h.** sown unto you spiritual	2192
1Co	9:12	we **h.** not used this power;	2192
1Co	9:15	But I **h.** used none of these things:	
1Co	9:15	neither **h.** I written these things,	
1Co	9:16	gospel, I **h.** nothing to glory of:	2076
1Co	9:17	thing willingly, I **h.** a reward;	2192
1Co	9:19	yet **h.** I made myself servant unto	2192
1Co	9:27	when I **h.** preached to others, I	
1Co	10:20	that ye should **h.** fellowship with	
1Co	11:3	But I would **h.** you know, that the	
1Co	11:10	to **h.** power on her head because	2192
1Co	11:14	if a man **h.** long hair, it is a shame	
1Co	11:15	But if a woman **h.** long hair, it is a	
1Co	11:16	we **h.** no such custom, neither the	2192
1Co	11:22	**h.** ye not houses to eat and to	2192
1Co	11:22	and shame them that **h.** not?	2192
1Co	11:23	For I **h.** received of the Lord that	2192
1Co	12:1	I would not **h.** you ignorant.	
1Co	12:13	and **h.** been all made to drink into	
1Co	12:21	unto the hand, I **h.** no need of thee:	2192
1Co	12:21	to the feet, I **h.** no need of you.	2192
1Co	12:23	parts **h.** more abundant comeliness.	2192
1Co	12:24	For our comely parts **h.** no need:	2192
1Co	12:25	members should **h.** the same care	
1Co	12:30	**H.** all the gifts of healing? do all	2192
1Co	13:1	and of angels, and **h.** not charity	2192
1Co	13:2	though I **h.** the gift of prophecy,	2192
1Co	13:2	and though I **h.** all faith, so that	2192
1Co	13:2	mountains, and **h.** not charity,	2192

1Co 13:3 to be burned, and **h.** not charity, *2192*
1Co 15:1 which also ye **h.** received, and wherein *2192*
1Co 15:2 unto you, unless ye **h.** believed in vain. *2192*
1Co 15:15 because we **h.** testified of God that *2192*
1Co 15:19 If in this life only we **h.** hope in *2070*
1Co 15:24 when he shall **h.** delivered up the
1Co 15:24 when he shall **h.** put down all rule
1Co 15:31 which I **h.** in Christ Jesus our *2192*
1Co 15:32 I **h.** fought with beasts at Ephesus,
1Co 15:34 for some **h.** not the knowledge of *2192*
1Co 15:49 And as we **h.** borne the image of the
1Co 15:54 this corruptible shall **h.** put on
1Co 15:54 and this mortal shall **h.** put on
1Co 16:1 as I **h.** given order to the churches of
1Co 16:12 when he shall **h.** convenient time.
1Co 16:15 and that they **h.** addicted themselves
1Co 16:17 lacking on your part they **h.** supplied
1Co 16:18 For they **h.** refreshed my spirit and
2Co 1:8 **h.** you ignorant of our trouble which
2Co 1:12 we **h.** had our conversation in the
2Co 1:14 As also ye **h.** acknowledged us in
2Co 1:15 that ye might **h.** a second benefit; *2192*
2Co 1:24 Not for that we **h.** dominion over
2Co 2:3 I should **h.** sorrow for them of *2192*
2Co 2:4 the love which I **h.** more *2192*
2Co 2:5 But if any **h.** caused grief, he hath *2192*
2Co 3:4 And such trust **h.** we through *2192*
2Co 3:12 Seeing then that we **h.** such hope, *2192*
2Co 4:1 Therefore seeing we **h.** this *2192*
2Co 4:1 as we **h.** received mercy, we faint *2192*
2Co 4:2 But **h.** renounced the hidden things
2Co 4:7 But we **h.** this treasure in earthen *2192*
2Co 4:13 and therefore **h.** I spoken; we
2Co 5:1 we **h.** a building of God, an house *2192*
2Co 5:12 that ye may **h.** somewhat to answer *2192*
2Co 5:16 yea, though we **h.** known Christ after
2Co 6:2 For he saith, I **h.** heard thee in a
2Co 6:2 of salvation **h.** I succoured thee:
2Co 7:2 we **h.** wronged no man,
2Co 7:2 we **h.** corrupted no man,
2Co 7:2 we **h.** defrauded no man.
2Co 7:3 for I **h.** said before, that ye are in
2Co 7:11 things ye **h.** approved yourselves
2Co 7:14 For if I **h.** boasted any thing to him
2Co 7:16 rejoice therefore that I **h.** confidence
2Co 8:10 who **h.** begun before, not only to do,
2Co 8:11 also out of that which ye **h.** *2192*
2Co 8:18 And we **h.** sent with him the brother,
2Co 8:22 And we **h.** sent with him our brother,
2Co 8:22 whom we **h.** oftentimes proved
2Co 8:22 great confidence which I **h.** in you.
2Co 9:3 Yet **h.** I sent the brethren, lest our
2Co 11:2 I **h.** espoused you to one husband,
2Co 11:4 Christ, whom we **h.** not preached,
2Co 11:4 spirit, which ye **h.** not received,
2Co 11:4 gospel, which ye **h.** not accepted,
2Co 11:6 **h.** been thoroughly made manifest
2Co 11:7 **H.** I committed an offence in abasing
2Co 11:7 because I **h.** preached to you the
2Co 11:9 and in all things I **h.** kept myself
2Co 11:25 and a day I **h.** been in the deep;
2Co 12:11 in glorifying; ye **h.** compelled me:
2Co 12:11 for I ought to **h.** been commended
2Co 12:21 many which **h.** sinned already,
2Co 12:21 **h.** not repented of the uncleanness
2Co 12:21 which they **h.** committed.
2Co 13:2 which heretofore **h.** sinned, and to
Ga 1:8 than that which we **h.** preached unto
Ga 1:9 than that ye **h.** received, let him be
Ga 1:13 For ye **h.** heard of my conversation
Ga 2:4 liberty which we **h.** in Christ *2192*
Ga 2:16 even we **h.** believed in Jesus Christ, *2192*
Ga 3:4 **H.** ye suffered so many things in *2192*
Ga 3:21 a law given which could **h.** given life, *2192*
Ga 3:21 righteousness should **h.** been by the
Ga 3:27 as many of you as **h.** been baptized
Ga 3:27 into Christ **h.** put on Christ.
Ga 4:9 But now, after that ye **h.** known God,
Ga 4:11 I am afraid of you, lest I **h.** bestowed
Ga 4:12 for I am as ye are: ye **h.** not injured
Ga 4:15 would **h.** plucked out your own eyes,
Ga 4:15 own eyes, and **h.** given them to me.
Ga 5:10 I **h.** confidence in you through the
Ga 5:13 For, brethren, ye **h.** been called unto
Ga 5:21 as I **h.** also told you in time past,
Ga 5:24 And they that are Christ's **h.** crucified
Ga 6:4 and then shall he **h.** rejoicing in *2192*
Ga 6:10 As we **h.** therefore opportunity, let *2192*
Ga 6:11 Ye see how large a letter I **h.** written *2192*
Ga 6:13 but desire to **h.** you circumcised, that
Eph 1:7 In whom we **h.** redemption *2192*
Eph 1:11 In whom also we **h.** obtained an *2192*
Eph 2:18 For through him we both **h.** access *2192*
Eph 3:2 If ye **h.** heard of the dispensation of
Eph 3:12 In whom we **h.** boldness and *2192*
Eph 4:19 past feeling **h.** given themselves
Eph 4:20 But ye **h.** not so learned Christ;
Eph 4:21 ye **h.** heard him, and **h.** been taught
Eph 4:28 that he may **h.** to give to him *2192*
Eph 5:11 And **h.** no fellowship with the
Eph 6:22 Whom I **h.** sent unto you for the
Php 1:7 because I **h.** you in my heart; *2192*
Php 1:12 which happened unto me **h.** fallen out
Php 2:12 as ye **h.** always obeyed, not as in my
Php 2:16 that I **h.** not run in vain, neither
Php 2:20 For I **h.** no man likeminded, who *2192*
Php 2:27 lest I should **h.** sorrow upon *2192*
Php 3:3 and **h.** no confidence in the flesh.
Php 3:4 Though I might also **h.** confidence *2192*
Php 3:8 for whom I **h.** suffered the loss of all *2192*
Php 3:13 I count not myself to **h.** apprehended:
Php 3:16 whereto we **h.** already attained, let
Php 3:17 so as ye **h.** us for an ensample. *2192*
Php 3:18 of whom I **h.** told you often, and now *2192*
Php 4:9 things, which ye **h.** both learned, and *2192*
Php 4:11 for I **h.** learned, in whatsoever state
Php 4:14 ye **h.** well done, that ye did
Php 4:18 But I **h.** all, and abound: I am full, *568*
Col 1:4 and of the love which ye **h.** to all the
Col 1:14 In whom we **h.** redemption *2192*
Col 1:18 things he might **h.** the preeminence.
Col 1:23 gospel, which ye **h.** heard, and which
Col 2:1 what great conflict I **h.** for you, *2192*
Col 2:1 and for as many as **h.** not seen my
Col 2:6 As ye **h.** therefore received Christ
Col 2:7 in the faith, as ye **h.** been taught,
Col 2:23 Which things **h.** indeed a shew *2192*
Col 3:9 seeing that ye **h.** put off the old man
Col 3:10 And **h.** put on the new man, which is
Col 3:13 if any man **h.** a quarrel against *2192*
Col 4:1 that ye also **h.** a Master in heaven. *2192*
Col 4:8 Whom I **h.** sent unto you for the
Col 4:11 of God, which **h.** been a comfort unto
1Th 2:6 when we might **h.** been burdensome,
1Th 2:8 we were willing to **h.** imparted unto
1Th 2:14 for ye also **h.** suffered like things of
1Th 2:14 even as they **h.** of the Jews:
1Th 2:15 and **h.** persecuted us; and they
1Th 2:18 Wherefore we would **h.** come unto
1Th 3:5 the tempter **h.** tempted you, and our
1Th 3:6 and that ye **h.** good remembrance *2192*
1Th 4:1 that as ye **h.** received of us how ye *2192*
1Th 4:6 as we also **h.** forewarned you and *2192*
1Th 4:12 and that ye may **h.** lack of nothing *2192*
1Th 4:13 But I would not **h.** you to be ignorant,
1Th 4:13 even as others which **h.** no hope *2192*
1Th 5:1 brethren, ye **h.** no need that I write *2192*
2Th 2:15 traditions which ye **h.** been taught, *2192*
2Th 3:1 word of the Lord may **h.** free course, *2192*
2Th 3:2 wicked men: for all men **h.** not faith.
2Th 3:4 And we **h.** confidence in the Lord
2Th 3:9 Not because we **h.** not power, but *2192*
2Th 3:14 and **h.** no company with him, that *2192*
1Ti 1:6 some having swerved **h.** turned aside
1Ti 1:19 concerning faith **h.** made shipwreck:
1Ti 1:20 whom I **h.** delivered unto Satan, that
1Ti 2:4 Who will **h.** all men to be saved, and
1Ti 3:7 he must **h.** a good report of them *2192*
1Ti 3:13 For they that **h.** used the office of a
1Ti 5:4 But if any widow **h.** children or *2192*
1Ti 5:10 if she **h.** brought up children, *2192*
1Ti 5:10 if she **h.** lodged strangers, *2192*
1Ti 5:10 if she **h.** washed the saints' feet, *2192*
1Ti 5:10 if she **h.** relieved the afflicted, *2192*
1Ti 5:10 if she **h.** diligently followed every *2192*
1Ti 5:11 for when they **h.** begun to wax
1Ti 5:12 because they **h.** cast off their first
1Ti 5:16 woman that believeth **h.** widows, *2192*
1Ti 6:2 And they that **h.** believing masters, *2192*
1Ti 6:10 after, they **h.** erred from the faith,
1Ti 6:21 Which some professing **h.** erred
2Ti 1:3 ceasing I **h.** remembrance *2192*
2Ti 1:12 for I know whom I **h.** believed, and
2Ti 1:12 keep that which I **h.** committed unto
2Ti 2:18 Who concerning the truth **h.** erred,
2Ti 4:7 I **h.** fought a good fight, I **h.** finished
2Ti 4:7 finished my course, I **h.** kept the faith:
2Ti 4:12 And Tychicus **h.** I sent to Ephesus.
2Ti 4:20 but Trophimus **h.** I left at Miletum
Tit 3:5 righteousness which we **h.** done,
Tit 3:8 that they which **h.** believed in God
Tit 3:12 for I **h.** determined there to winter.
Phm 7 we **h.** great joy and consolation *2192*
Phm 10 Onesimus, whom I **h.** begotten in my
Phm 12 Whom I **h.** sent again: thou therefore
Phm 13 Whom I would **h.** retained with me,
Phm 13 in thy stead he might **h.** ministered
Phm 19 I Paul **h.** written it with mine own
Phm 20 Yea, brother, let me **h.** joy of thee in
Heb 1:5 my Son, this day **h.** I begotten thee?
Heb 2:1 to the things which we **h.** heard,
Heb 3:10 and they **h.** not known my ways.
Heb 4:3 For we which **h.** believed do enter
Heb 4:3 As I **h.** sworn in my wrath, if they
Heb 4:8 he not afterward **h.** spoken of
Heb 4:13 eyes of him with whom we **h.** to do.
Heb 4:14 that we **h.** a great high priest, *2192*
Heb 4:15 For we **h.** not an high priest which *2192*
Heb 5:2 Who can **h.** compassion on the *2192*
Heb 5:5 Thou art my Son, to day **h.** I begotten
Heb 5:11 Of whom we **h.** many things to say,
Heb 5:12 ye **h.** need that one teach you *2192*
Heb 5:12 and are become such as **h.** need of *2192*
Heb 5:14 of use **h.** their senses exercised to *2192*
Heb 6:4 and **h.** tasted of the heavenly gift, *2192*
Heb 6:5 And **h.** tasted the good word of God, *2192*
Heb 6:10 labour of love, which ye **h.** shewed *2192*
Heb 6:10 in that ye **h.** ministered to the saints, *2192*
Heb 6:18 we might **h.** a strong consolation, *2192*
Heb 6:18 who **h.** fled for refuge to lay hold
Heb 6:19 Which hope we **h.** as an anchor of *2192*
Heb 7:5 **h.** a commandment to take tithes *2192*
Heb 7:28 high priests which **h.** infirmity; *2192*
Heb 8:1 the things which we **h.** spoken
Heb 8:1 We **h.** such an high priest, who is *2192*
Heb 8:3 that this man **h.** somewhat also to *2192*
Heb 8:7 then should no place **h.** been sought
Heb 9:26 For then must he often **h.** suffered
Heb 10:2 For then would they not **h.** ceased
Heb 10:2 should **h.** had no more conscience *2192*
Heb 10:26 that we **h.** received the knowledge
Heb 10:34 that ye **h.** in heaven a better and *2192*
Heb 10:36 For ye **h.** need of patience,
Heb 10:36 that, after ye **h.** done the will of God,
Heb 10:38 my soul shall **h.** no pleasure
Heb 11:15 they might **h.** had opportunity *2192*
Heb 11:15 opportunity to **h.** returned.
Heb 12:4 Ye **h.** not yet resisted unto blood,
Heb 12:5 And ye **h.** forgotten the exhortation
Heb 12:9 Furthermore we **h.** had fathers *2192*
Heb 12:17 when he would **h.** inherited the *2192*
Heb 12:28 let us **h.** grace, whereby we may *2192*
Heb 13:2 for thereby some **h.** entertained
Heb 13:5 content with such things as ye **h.**: *3918*
Heb 13:7 Remember them which **h.** the rule *3918*
Heb 13:7 who **h.** spoken unto you the word of *3918*
Heb 13:9 not with meats, which **h.** not profited *3918*
Heb 13:9 them that **h.** been occupied therein. *3918*
Heb 13:10 We **h.** an altar, whereof they *2192*
Heb 13:10 they **h.** no right to eat which serve *2192*
Heb 13:14 For here we **h.** no continuing city, *2192*
Heb 13:17 Obey them that **h.** the rule over you,
Heb 13:18 trust we **h.** a good conscience, *2192*
Heb 13:22 for I **h.** written a letter unto you in
Heb 13:24 Salute all them that **h.** the rule over
Jas 1:4 But let patience **h.** her perfect *2192*
Jas 2:1 My brethren, **h.** not the faith of *2192*
Jas 2:3 ye **h.** respect to him that weareth
Jas 2:6 But ye **h.** despised the poor. Do not
Jas 2:9 But if ye **h.** respect to persons, ye
Jas 2:13 For he shall **h.** judgment without
Jas 2:14 he hath faith, and **h.** not works? *2192*
Jas 2:18 Thou hast faith, and I **h.** works: shew
Jas 3:14 But if ye **h.** bitter envying and *2192*
Jas 4:2 Ye lust, and **h.** not: ye kill, and *2192*
Jas 4:2 desire to **h.**, and cannot obtain: *2192*
Jas 4:2 ye fight and war, yet ye **h.** not, *2192*
Jas 5:3 Ye **h.** heaped treasure together for the *2192*

Jas 5:4 hire of the labourers who h. reaped.... 2192
Jas 5:4 the cries of them which h. reaped...... 2192
Jas 5:5 Ye h. lived in pleasure on the earth,.........
Jas 5:5 ye h. nourished your hearts, as in a ....
Jas 5:6 Ye h. condemned and killed the just;.........
Jas 5:10 h. spoken in the name of the Lord, ...
Jas 5:11 Ye h. heard of the patience of Job, ...
Jas 5:11 and h. seen the end of the Lord; that ....
Jas 5:15 and if he h. committed sins, they shall ......
1Pe 1:10 prophets h. enquired and searched ....
1Pe 1:12 by them that h. preached the gospel..........
1Pe 1:22 Seeing ye h. purified your souls in............
1Pe 2:3 If so be ye h. tasted that the Lord is........
1Pe 2:10 mercy, but now h. obtained mercy. ....
1Pe 4:3 may suffice us to h. wrought the will ....
1Pe 4:8 all things h. fervent charity 2192
1Pe 5:10 after that ye h. suffered a while, make......
1Pe 5:12 as I suppose, I h. written briefly,.............
2Pe 1:1 to them that h. obtained like precious ....
2Pe 1:15 to h. these things in remembrance. ....
2Pe 1:16 For we h. not followed cunningly...............
2Pe 1:19 We h. also a more sure word of 2192
2Pe 2:14 an heart they h. exercised with 2192
2Pe 2:15 Which h. forsaken the right way, and.. 2192
2Pe 2:20 For if after they h. escaped the ....
2Pe 2:21 better for them not to h. known the ....
2Pe 2:21 than, after they h. known it, to turn ....
1Jo 1:1 which we h. heard, which we h. seen.......
1Jo 1:1 which we h. looked upon, and ....
1Jo 1:1 our hand h. handled of the Word..............
1Jo 1:2 and we h. seen it, and bear witness, ...
1Jo 1:3 That which we h. seen and heard.............
1Jo 1:3 that ye also may h. fellowship 2192
1Jo 1:5 message which we h. heard of him, ...
1Jo 1:6 If we say that we h. fellowship.......... 2192
1Jo 1:7 as he is in the light, we h. fellowship.. 2192
1Jo 1:8 If we say that we h. no sin, we......... 2192
1Jo 1:10 we say that we h. not sinned, we ....
1Jo 2:1 any man sin, we h. an advocate......... 2192
1Jo 2:7 the word which ye h. heard from the.. 2192
1Jo 2:13 because ye h. known him that is from. 2192
1Jo 2:13 because ye h. overcome the wicked..........
1Jo 2:13 because ye h. known the Father. ....
1Jo 2:14 I h. written unto you, fathers, because......
1Jo 2:14 because ye h. known him that is from.......
1Jo 2:14 I h. written unto you, young men,............
1Jo 2:14 and ye h. overcome the wicked one..........
1Jo 2:18 and as ye h. heard that antichrist............
1Jo 2:19 they would no doubt h. continued.............
1Jo 2:20 But ye h. an unction from the Holy 2192
1Jo 2:21 I h. not written unto you because ye ....
1Jo 2:24 which ye h. heard from the beginning........
1Jo 2:24 If that which ye h. heard from the............
1Jo 2:26 These things h. I written unto you ....
1Jo 2:27 the anointing which ye h. received............
1Jo 2:28 we may h. confidence, and not be 2192
1Jo 3:14 We know that we h. passed from.............
1Jo 3:17 and seeth his brother h. need,........... 2192
1Jo 3:21 then h. we confidence toward God. 2192
1Jo 4:3 whereof ye h. heard that it should............
1Jo 4:4 and h. overcome them: because................
1Jo 4:14 And we h. seen and do testify that the......
1Jo 4:16 And we h. known and believed the ....
1Jo 4:17 that we may h. boldness in the.......... 2192
1Jo 4:21 this commandment h. we from him, ... 2192
1Jo 5:13 These things h. I written unto you ....
1Jo 5:13 may know that ye h. eternal life, ... 2192
1Jo 5:14 the confidence that we h. in him, ... 2192
1Jo 5:15 we know that we h. the petitions 2192
2Jo 1 also all they that h. known the truth; .. 2192
2Jo 4 as we h. received a commandment..... 2192
2Jo 6 That, as ye h. heard from the ....
2Jo 8 those things which we h. wrought, ...
3Jo 4 I h. no greater joy than to hear......... 2192
3Jo 6 Which h. borne witness of thy charity ..2192
3Jo 9 who loveth to h. the preeminence ....
Jude 11 for they h. gone in the way of Cain, ...
Jude 15 which they h. ungodly committed, and.......
Jude 15 which ungodly sinners h. spoken ....
Jude 22 And of some h. compassion, making a.......
Re 1:18 **Amen; and h. the keys of hell and..**2192
Re 2:4 **Nevertheless I h. somewhat against**2192
Re 2:10 **ye shall h. tribulation ten days**..... 2192
Re 2:14 **But I h. a few things against thee,**.2192
Re 2:20 **I h. a few things against thee,** 2192
Re 2:24 **as many as h. not this doctrine,**.... 2192
Re 2:24 **and which h. not known the depths**.....
Re 2:25 **But that which ye h. already hold.** 2192
Re 3:2 **for I h. not found thy works perfect**....
Re 3:4 **in Sardis which h. not defiled their**.....
Re 3:8 **behold, I h. set before thee an open**.....
Re 3:9 **and to know that I h. loved thee.**........
Re 3:17 **goods, and h. need of nothing;**...... 2192
Re 7:3 till we h. sealed the servants of our..........
Re 7:14 and h. washed their robes, and made........
Re 9:3 scorpions of the earth h. power.......... 2192
Re 9:4 men which h. not the seal of God 2192
Re 11:6 These h. power to shut heaven, ... 2192
Re 11:6 and h. power over waters to turn 2192
Re 11:7 And when they shall h. finished their ....
Re 12:17 and h. the testimony of Jesus............ 2192
Re 13:9 If any man h. an ear, let him hear...... 2192
Re 14:11 and they h. no rest day nor night,...... 2192
Re 16:6 For they h. shed the blood of saints ....
Re 17:2 the earth h. committed fornication, ...
Re 17:2 the earth h. been made drunk with...........
Re 17:12 which h. received no kingdom as yet; ....
Re 17:13 These h. one mind, and shall give...... 2192
Re 18:3 For all nations h. drunk of the wine..........
Re 18:3 the earth h. committed fornication.............
Re 18:5 For her sins h. reached unto heaven,.........
Re 18:9 who h. committed fornication and.............
Re 19:10 brethren that h. the testimony........... 2192
Re 21:8 shall h. their part in the lake which...........
Re 22:14 that they may h. right to the tree 2071
Re 22:16 **I Jesus h. sent mine angel to testify**....

HAVEN See also HAVENS.
Ge 49:13 shall dwell at the h. of the sea........... 2348
Ge 49:13 and he shall be for an h. of ships; 2348
Ps 107:30 them unto their desired h.................. 4231
Ac 27:12 the h. was not commodious................ 3040
Ac 27:12 which is an h. at Crete, and lieth 3040

HAVENS
Ac 27:8 place which is called The fair h.;......... 2568

HAVILAH (hav'-il-ah)
Ge 2:11 compasseth the whole land of H.,........ 2341
Ge 10:7 of Cush; Seba, and H., and Sabtah, ... 2341
Ge 10:29 Ophir, and H., and Jobab: all these..... 2341
Ge 25:18 they dwelt from H. unto Shur, that 2341
1Sa 15:7 from H. until thou comest to............... 2341
1Ch 1:9 Cush; Seba, and H., and Sabta, ... 2341
1Ch 1:23 And Ophir, and H., and Jobab. All...... 2341

HAVING
Ge 12:8 and pitched his tent, h. Bethel on the ....
Le 7:20 h. his uncleanness upon him, even............
Le 20:18 lie with a woman h. her sickness,.............
Le 22:3 the Lord, h. his uncleanness upon ....
Le 22:22 or maimed, or h. a wen, or scurvy,..........
Nu 24:4, 16 a trance, but h. his eyes open:............
De 10:3 the mount, h. the two tables in mine ....
Jg 1:7 h. their thumbs and their toes cut off,.......
Jg 19:3 h. his servant with him, and a couple.......
Ru 1:13 ye stay for them from h. husbands?..........
1Sa 22:6 in Ramah, h. his spear in his hand,...........
1Sa 26:2 of Ziph, h. three thousand chosen men......
1Ki 22:10 on his throne, h. put on their robes,..........
1Ch 4:42 h. for their captains Pelatiah, and............
1Ch 21:16 and the heaven, h. a drawn sword in ....
1Ch 26:12 men, h. wards one against another, ...
2Ch 5:12 h. cymbals and psalteries and harps, ...
2Ch 11:12 h. Judah and Benjamin on his.................
2Ch 23:10 every man h. his weapon in his hand, ...
Ezr 9:5 and h. rent my garment and my...............
Ne 10:28 h. knowledge, and h. understanding;.........
Ne 13:4 the priest, h. the oversight of 5414
Es 6:12 mourning, and h. his head covered. ....
Ps 13:2 in my soul, h. sorrow in my heart............
Pr 6:7 Which h. no guide, overseer, or ruler, ...
Pr 18:1 desire a man, h. separated himself, ...
Isa 6:6 h. a live coal in his hand,........................
Isa 41:15 threshing instrument h. teeth: 1167
Jer 41:5 h. their beards shaven, and their.............
Jer 41:5 and h. cut themselves, with offerings ....
Eze 38:11 and h. neither bars nor gates, ...
Eze 40:44 the east gate h. the prospect toward ....
Eze 44:11 my sanctuary, h. charge at the gates ....
Da 8:20 which thou sawest h. two horns......... 1167
Mic 1:11 of Saphir, h. thy shame naked: ....
Zec 9:9 he is just, and h. salvation;......................
Mt 7:29 them as one h. authority, ... 2192
Mt 8:9 authority, h. soldiers under me:......... 2192
Mt 9:36 as sheep h. no shepherd. 2192
Mt 15:30 h. with them those that were lame,.... 2192
Mt 18:8 **rather than h. two hands or two**... 2192
Mt 18:9 **rather than h. two eyes to be cast.** 2192
Mt 22:12 **hither not h. a wedding garment?**.. 2192
Mt 22:24 If a man die, h. no children, his......... 2192
Mt 22:25 deceased, and, h. no issue, left his..... 2192
Mt 26:7 a woman h. an alabaster box of 2192
Mr 6:34 were as sheep not h. a shepherd: 2192
Mk 8:1 and h. nothing to eat, Jesus called...... 2192
Mk 8:18 **H. eyes, see ye not? and h. ears,**... 2192
Mk 9:43 **than h. two hands to go into hell,**. 2192
Mk 9:45 **h. two feet to be cast into hell,**..... 2192
Mk 9:47 **h. two eyes to be cast into hell**..... 2192
Mk 11:13 a fig tree afar off h. leaves, he came, ..2192
Mk 12:6 **H. yet therefore one son, his**......... 2192
Mk 12:28 h. heard them reasoning together,............
Mk 14:3 a woman h. an alabaster box of 2192
Mk 14:51 young man, h. a linen cloth cast about.......
Lu 1:3 h. had perfect understanding of all...........
Lu 5:39 **No man also h. drunk old wine**..........
Lu 7:8 authority, h. under me soldiers,......... 2192
Lu 8:15 **heart, h. heard the word, keep it,**........
Lu 8:43 a woman h. an issue of blood..... 5607,1722
Lu 9:62 **h. put his hand to the plough,** 5607,1722
Lu 11:36 **full of light, h. no part dark, the**.. 2192
Lu 15:4 **man of you, h. an hundred sheep,**..2192
Lu 15:8 **what woman h. ten pieces of silver,**2192
Lu 17:7 **h. a servant plowing or feeding**..... 2192
Lu 19:15 **returned, h. received the kingdom,**......
Lu 20:28 If any man's brother die, h. a wife, ... 2192
Lu 23:14 h. examined him before you, have...........
Lu 23:46 and h. said thus, he gave up the ghost......
Joh 4:45 h. seen all the things that he did at..........
Joh 5:2 tongue Bethesda, h. five porches. 2192
Joh 7:15 this man letters, h. never learned? ....
Joh 13:1 h. loved his own which were in the ....
Joh 13:2 the devil now h. put into the heart of........
Joh 13:30 He then h. received the sop went ....
Joh 18:3 Judas then, h. received a band of men.......
Joh 18:10 Simon Peter h. a sword drew it,......... 2192
Ac 2:24 raised up, h. loosed the pains of death ......
Ac 2:33 h. received of the Father the promise ....
Ac 2:47 and h. favour with all the people, ... 2192
Ac 3:26 God, h. raised up his Son Jesus, sent ....
Ac 4:37 H. land, sold it, and brought........ 5225,846
Ac 12:20 h. made Blastus...their friend, ...
Ac 14:19 h. stoned Paul, drew him out of the ....
Ac 16:24 Who, h. received such a charge, ...
Ac 18:18 h. shorn his head in Cenchrea: for he ....
Ac 19:1 Paul h. passed through the upper..............
Ac 19:29 and h. caught Gaius and Aristarchus, ...
Ac 22:12 h. a good report of all the Jews ....
Ac 23:27 h. understood that he was a Roman...........
Ac 24:22 h. more perfect knowledge of that............
Ac 26:10 h. received authority from the chief..........
Ac 26:22 H. therefore obtained help of God, I.........
Ac 27:33 continued fasting, h. taken nothing............
Ro 2:14 h. not the law, are a law unto 2192
Ro 9:11 neither h. done any good or evil, that ....
Ro 12:6 H. then gifts differing according 2192
Ro 15:23 But now h. no more place in these..... 2192
Ro 15:23 h. a great desire these many years..... 2192
1Co 6:1 h. a matter against another, go.......... 2192
1Co 7:37 h. no necessity, but hath power......... 2192
1Co 11:4 prophesying, h. his head covered, ... 2192
1Co 12:24 h. given more abundant honour to ....
2Co 2:3 h. confidence in you all, that my joy ....
2Co 4:13 We h. the same spirit of faith,........... 2192
2Co 6:10 as h. nothing, and yet possessing....... 2192
2Co 7:1 H. therefore these promises, ... 2192
2Co 9:8 that ye, always h. all sufficiency......... 2192
2Co 10:6 And h. in a readiness to revenge 2192
2Co 10:15 but h. hope, when your faith is........... 2192
Ga 3:3 h. begun in the Spirit, are ye now...........
Eph 1:5 H. predestinated us unto the...................
Eph 1:9 H. made known unto us the mystery ....
Eph 2:12 h. no hope, and without God in 2192
Eph 2:15 H. abolished in his flesh the enmity, ...
Eph 2:16 cross, h. slain the enmity thereby: ....
Eph 4:18 H. the understanding darkened, ...
Eph 5:27 not h. spot, or wrinkle, or any 2192
Eph 6:13 the evil day, and h. done all, to stand. ......
Eph 6:14 Stand therefore, h. your loins girt ....
Eph 6:14 and h. on the breastplate of.............. 1746
Php 1:23 h. a desire to depart, and to be......... 2192

Php 1:25 And **h.** this confidence, I know that I........
Php 1:30 **H.** the same conflict which ye *2192*
Php 2:2 **h.** the same love, being of one *2192*
Php 3:9 not **h.** mine own righteousness, ... *2192*
Php 4:18 **h.** received of Epaphroditus the ....
Col 1:20 **h.** made peace through the blood of..........
Col 2:13 him, **h.** forgiven you all trespasses; ....
Col 2:15 **h.** spoiled principalities and powers, ...
Col 2:19 body **h.**...nourishment ministered, ...
1Th 1:6 **h.** received the word in much.................
1Ti 1:6 From which some **h.** swerved have ....
1Ti 1:19 some **h.** put away concerning faith............
1Ti 3:4 **h.** his children in subjection with *2192*
1Ti 4:2 **h.** their conscience seared with a hot ....
1Ti 4:8 **h.** promise of the life that now is, ... *2192*
1Ti 5:9 years old, **h.** been the wife of one man *2192*
1Ti 5:12 **H.** damnation, because they have *2192*
1Ti 6:8 And **h.** food and raiment let us be *2192*
2Ti 2:19 of God standeth sure, **h.** this seal, ... *2192*
2Ti 3:5 **H.** a form of godliness, but *2192*
2Ti 4:3 themselves teachers, **h.** itching ears; ....
2Ti 4:10 **h.** loved this present world, and is............
Tit 1:6 **h.** faithful children not accused.......... *2192*
Tit 2:8 **h.** no evil thing to say of you. *2192*
Phm 21 **H.** confidence in thy obedience I.............
Heb 7:3 **h.** neither beginning of days, nor.......... *2192*
Heb 9:12 **h.** obtained eternal redemption for us........
Heb 10:1 For the law **h.** a shadow of good........ *2192*
Heb 10:19 **H.** therefore, brethren, boldness to *2192*
Heb 10:21 And **h.** an high priest over the house........
Heb 10:22 **h.** our hearts sprinkled from an evil..........
Heb 11:13 but **h.** seen them afar off,......................
Heb 11:13 not **h.** received the promises, but............
Heb 11:39 all, **h.** obtained a good report through ....
Heb 11:40 God **h.** provided some better thing for ......
1Pe 1:8 Whom **h.** not seen, ye love;...................
1Pe 2:12 **H.** your conversation honest *2192*
1Pe 3:8 **h.** compassion one of another, ...
1Pe 3:16 **H.** a good conscience; that............... *2192*
2Pe 1:4 **h.** escaped the corruption that is in...........
2Pe 2:14 **H.** eyes full of adultery, and that........ *2192*
2Jo 12 **H.** many things to write unto you,...... *2192*
Jude 5 **h.** saved the people out of the land of.......
Jude 16 **h.** men's persons in admiration................
Jude 19 sensual, **h.** not the Spirit................ *2192*
Re 5:6 **h.** seven horns and seven eyes,......... *2192*
Re 5:8 **h.** every one of them harps, and........ *2192*
Re 7:2 **h.** the seal of the living God:............ *2192*
Re 8:3 at the altar, **h.** a golden censer;......... *2192*
Re 9:17 **h.** breastplates of fire, and of *2192*
Re 12:3 **h.** seven heads and ten horns, and *2192*
Re 12:12 down unto you, **h.** great wrath, ... *2192*
Re 13:1 **h.** seven heads and ten horns, and *2192*
Re 14:1 **h.** his Father's name written in.......... *2192*
Re 14:6 **h.** the everlasting gospel to preach..... *2192*
Re 14:14 **h.** on his head a golden crown, and *2192*
Re 14:17 heaven, he also **h.** a sharp sickle........ *2192*
Re 15:1 angels **h.** the seven last plagues;........ *2192*
Re 15:2 sea of glass, **h.** the harps of God. *2192*
Re 15:6 the temple, **h.** the seven plagues, ... *2192*
Re 15:6 **h.** their breasts girded with.............. *2192*
Re 17:3 **h.** seven heads and ten horns............ *2192*
Re 17:4 **h.** a golden cup in her hand full of...... *2192*
Re 18:1 from heaven, **h.** great power;........... *2192*
Re 20:1 **h.** the key of the bottomless pit......... *2192*
Re 21:11 **H.** the glory of God: and her light...... *2192*

HAVOCK
Ac 8:3 Saul, he made **h.** of the church,......... *3075*

HAVOTH-JAIR (ha''-voth-ja'-ir) See also BASHANHAVOTH.
Nu 32:41 thereof, and called them **H.**. 2334
Jg 10:4 which are called **H.** unto this day. 2334

HAWK
Le 11:16 The owl, and the night **h.**, and the..... 8464
Le 11:16 cuckow, and the **h.** after his kind, ... 5322
De 14:15 the owl, and the night **h.**, and the...... 8464
De 14:15 cuckow, and the **h.** after his kind, ... 5322
Job 39:26 Doth the **h.** fly by thy wisdom,.......... 5322

HAY
Pr 27:25 The **h.** appeareth, and the tender....... 2682
Isa 15:6 for the **h.** is withered away, the......... 2682
1Co 3:12 silver, precious stones, wood, **h.**,........ *5528*

HAZAEL (ha'-za-el)
1Ki 19:15 anoint **H.** to be king over Syria:......... 2371
1Ki 19:17 that escapeth the sword of **H.** shall 2371
2Ki 8:8 the king said unto **H.**, Take a........... 2371
2Ki 8:9 So **H.** went to meet him, and took..... 2371
2Ki 8:12 And **H.** said, Why weepeth my.......... 2371
2Ki 8:13 And **H.** said, But what, is thy........... 2371
2Ki 8:15 and **H.** reigned in his stead.............. 2371
2Ki 8:28 of Ahab to war against **H.** king of....... 2371
2Ki 8:29 Ramah, when he fought against **H.** 2371
2Ki 9:14 and all Israel, because of **H.** king 2371
2Ki 9:15 when he fought with **H.** king of 2371
2Ki 10:32 and **H.** smote them in all the............ 2371
2Ki 12:17 Then **H.** king of Syria went up, ... 2371
2Ki 12:17 and **H.** set his face to go up to.......... 2371
2Ki 12:18 and sent it to **H.** king of Syria:.......... 2371
2Ki 13:3 into the hand of **H.** king of Syria,....... 2371
2Ki 13:3 hand of Ben-hadad the son of **H.**,....... 2371
2Ki 13:22 But **H.** king of Syria oppressed.......... 2371
2Ki 13:24 So **H.** king of Syria died; and 2371
2Ki 13:25 hand of Ben-hadad the son of **H.**......... 2371
2Ch 22:5 to war against **H.** king of Syria.......... 2371
2Ch 22:6 Ramah, when he fought with **H.**.......... 2371
Am 1:4 send a fire into the house of **H.**, ... 2371

HAZAIAH (ha-za-i'-ah)
Ne 11:5 Col-hozeh, the son of **H.**, the son 2382

HAZAR See HAZAR-ADDAR; HAZAR-ENAN; HAZAR-GADDAH; HAZAR-HATTICON; HAZAR-SHUAL; HAZAR-SUSAH; HAZAR-SUSIM.

HAZAR-ADDAR (ha'-zar-ad'-dar) See also ADDAR.
Nu 34:4 and shall go on to **H.**, and pass 2692

HAZARDED
Ac 15:26 Men that have **h.** their lives for......... *3860*

HAZAR-ENAN (ha''-zar-e'-nan)
Nu 34:9 goings out of it shall be at **H.**:........... 2704
Nu 34:10 east border from **H.** to Shepham:........ 2704
Eze 47:17 border from the sea shall be **H.**, ... 2703
Eze 48:1 as one goeth to Hamath, **H.**,............. 2704

HAZAR-GADDAH (ha''-zar-gad'-dah)
Jos 15:27 **H.**, and Heshmon, and Beth-palet,...... 2693

HAZAR-HATTICON (ha''-zar-hat'-ti-con)
Eze 47:16 **H.**, which is by the coast of............. 2694

HAZARMAVETH (ha-zar-ma'-veth)
Ge 10:26 Sheleph, and **H.**, and Jerah, ... 2700
1Ch 1:20 Sheleph, and **H.**, and Jerah, ... 2700

HAZAR-SHUAL (ha''-zar-shoo'-al)
Jos 15:28 And **H.**, and Beer-sheba, and........... 2705
Jos 19:3 **H.**, and Balah, and Azem,................ 2705
1Ch 4:28 Beer-sheba, and Moladah, and **H.**,....... 2705
Ne 11:27 at **H.**, and at Beer-sheba, and in........ 2705

HAZAR-SUSAH (ha''-zar-soo'-sah) See also HAZAR-SUSIM.
Jos 19:5 and Beth-marcaboth, and **H.**.............. 2701

HAZAR-SUSIM (ha''-zar-soo'-sim) See also HAZAR-SUSAH.
1Ch 4:31 at Beth-marcaboth, and **H.**,.............. 2702

HAZAZON-TAMAR (haz''-a-zon-ta'-mar) See also HAZEZON-TAMAR.
2Ch 20:2 they be in **H.**, which is Engedi. 2688

HAZEL
Ge 30:37 and of the **h.** and chestnut tree;.......... 3869

HAZELELPONI (haz-el-el-po'-ni)
1Ch 4:3 the name of their sister was **H.**: 6753

HAZERIM (haz'-e-rim)
De 2:23 the Avims which dwelt in **H.**,............ 2699

HAZEROTH (haz'-e-roth)
Nu 11:35 from Kibroth-hattaavah unto **H.**;......... 2698
Nu 11:35 and abode at **H.**.............................. 2698
Nu 12:16 the people removed from **H.**, ... 2698
Nu 33:17 and encamped at **H.**........................ 2698
Nu 33:18 And they departed from **H.**, and 2698
De 1:1 Laban, and **H.**, and Dizahab. 2698

HAZEZON-TAMAR (haz''-e-zon-ta'-mar) See also EN-GEDI; HAZAZON-TAMAR.
GE 14:7 the Amorites, that dwelt in **H.**........... 2688

HAZIEL (ha'-ze-el)
1Ch 23:9 Shelomith, and **H.**, and Haran,........... 2381

HAZO (ha'-zo)
Ge 22:22 Chesed, and **H.**, and Pildash, ... 2375

HAZOR (ha'-zor) See also BAAL-HAZOR; EN- HAZOR; HEZRON.
Jos 11:1 when Jabin king of **H.** had heard 2674
Jos 11:10 and took **H.**, and smote the king........ 2674
Jos 11:10 for **H.** beforetime was the head 2674
Jos 11:11 and he burnt **H.** with fire.................. 2674
Jos 11:13 Israel burned none of them, save **H.**.... 2674
Jos 12:19 Madon, one; the king of **H.**, one;....... 2674
Jos 15:23 And Kedesh, and **H.**, and Ithnan,....... 2674
Jos 15:25 And **H.**, Hadattah, and.................... 2675
Jos 15:25 Kerioth, and Hezron, which is **H.**,...... 2674
Jos 19:36 And Adamah, and Ramah, and **H.**,...... 2674
Jg 4:2 king of Caanan, that reigned in **H.**;..... 2674
Jg 4:17 peace between Jabin the king of **H.** 2674
1Sa 12:9 of Sisera, captain of the host of **H.**,.... 2674
1Ki 9:15 and **H.**, and Megiddo, and Gezer. 2674
2Ki 15:29 Kedesh, and **H.**, and Gilead, ... 2674
Ne 11:33 **H.**, Ramah, Gittaim,........................ 2674
Jer 49:28 and concerning the kingdoms of **H.**,.... 2674
Jer 49:30 dwell deep, O ye inhabitants of **H.**. 2674
Jer 49:33 **H.** shall be a dwelling for dragons, ... 2674

HAZOR-HADATTAH See HAZOR and HADATTAH.

HAZZURIM See HELKATH-HAZZURIM.

HE (hay) See in the APPENDIX; also HIM; HIS.
Ps 119:33 *title* [ה] **H.**..

HEAD See also BEHEADED; FOREHEAD; GODHEAD; GRAYHEADED; HEADBANDS; HEADLONG; HEADS; HEADSTONE.
Ge 3:15 it shall bruise thy **h.**, and thou........... 7218
Ge 24:26 And the man bowed down his **h.**, and ....
Ge 24:48 And I bowed down my **h.**, and................
Ge 40:13 shall Pharaoh lift up thine **h.**, and....... 7218
Ge 40:16 I had three white baskets on my **h.**: ... 7218
Ge 40:17 them out of the basket upon my **h.**..... 7218
Ge 40:19 shall Pharaoh lift up thy **h.** from off 7218
Ge 40:20 he lifted up the **h.** of the chief........... 7218
Ge 47:31 bowed himself upon the bed's **h.**....... 7218
Ge 48:14 laid it upon Ephraim's **h.**, who was..... 7218
Ge 48:14 his left hand upon Manasseh's **h.**,....... 7218
Ge 48:17 hand upon the **h.** of Ephraim, ... 7218
Ge 48:17 Ephraim's **h.** unto Manasseh's **h.**, ... 7218
Ge 48:18 put thy right hand upon his **h.**. 7218
Ge 49:26 they shall be on the **h.** of Joseph,........ 7218
Ge 49:26 and on the crown of the **h.** of him...... 6936
Ex 12:9 his **h.** with his legs, and with the 7218
Ex 12:27 And the people bowed the **h.** and............
Ex 26:24 coupled together above the **h.** of........ 7218
Ex 29:6 put the mitre upon his **h.**, and put....... 7218
Ex 29:7 oil, and pour it upon his **h.**, and......... 7218
Ex 29:10 hands upon the **h.** of the bullock, ... 7218
Ex 29:15 their hands upon the **h.** of the ram. 7218
Ex 29:17 unto his pieces, and unto his **h.**. 7218
Ex 29:19 their hands upon the **h.** of the ram. 7218
Ex 34:8 Moses made haste, and bowed his **h.**........
Ex 36:29 coupled together at the **h.** thereof, ... 7218
Le 1:4 upon the **h.** of the burnt offering; 7218
Le 1:8 the parts, the **h.**, and the fat............ 7218
Le 1:12 pieces, with his **h.** and his fat:............ 7218
Le 1:15 wring off his **h.**, and burn it on the..... 7218
Le 3:2,8 hand upon the **h.** of his offering, ... 7218
Le 3:13 lay his hand upon the **h.** of it,............ 7218
Le 4:4 lay his hand upon the bullock's **h.**,...... 7218
Le 4:11 with his **h.**, and with his legs,........... 7218
Le 4:15 hands upon the **h.** of the bullock 7218
Le 4:24 his hand upon the **h.** of the goat, ... 7218
Le 4:29, 33 upon the **h.** of the sin offering,...... 7218
Le 5:8 wring off his **h.** from his neck,........... 7218
Le 8:9 And he put the mitre upon his **h.**; 7218
Le 8:12 the anointing oil upon Aaron's **h.**, ... 7218
Le 8:14 upon the **h.** of the bullock for the....... 7218
Le 8:18 their hands upon the **h.** of the ram. 7218
Le 8:20 Moses burnt the **h.**, and the pieces, ... 7218
Le 8:22 hands upon the **h.** of the ram. 7218
Le 9:13 with the pieces thereof, and the **h.**: 7218
Le 13:12 plague from his **h.** even to his foot, ... 7218
Le 13:29 a plague upon the **h.** or the beard; 7218
Le 13:30 a leprosy upon the **h.** or beard. 7218
Le 13:40 whose hair is fallen off his **h.**,............ 7218
Le 13:41 the part of his **h.** toward his face, ... 7218
Le 13:42 if there be in the bald **h.**, or bald ....
Le 13:42 leprosy sprung up in his bald **h.**, ...
Le 13:43 sore be white reddish in his bald **h.**, ...
Le 13:44 unclean; his plague is in his **h.**. 7218
Le 13:45 shall be rent, and his **h.** bare,............ 7218
Le 14:9 shall shave all his hair off his **h.** 7218
Le 14:18 the **h.** of him that is to be cleaned:...... 7218
Le 14:29 the **h.** of him that is to be cleansed, ... 7218
Le 16:21 hands upon the **h.** of the live goat, ... 7218
Le 16:21 them upon the **h.** of the goat,............ 7218

Le 19:32 rise up before the hoary **h.**, and...
Le 21:5 not make baldness upon their **h.**, ... 7218
Le 21:10 upon whose **h.** the anointing oil... 7218
Le 21:10 shall not uncover his **h.**, nor rend... 7218
Le 24:14 lay their hands upon his **h.**, and... 7218
Nu 1:4 one **h.** of the house of his fathers... 7218
Nu 5:18 uncover the woman's **h.**, and put ... 7218
Nu 6:5 shall no rasor come upon his **h.**: ... 7218
Nu 6:5 the locks of the hair of his **h.** grow... 7218
Nu 6:7 of his God is upon his **h.**... 7218
Nu 6:9 defiled the **h.** of his consecration;... 7218
Nu 6:9 shall shave his **h.** in the day... 7218
Nu 6:11 and shall hallow his **h.** that same... 7218
Nu 6:18 Nazarite shall shave the **h.** of his ... 7218
Nu 6:18 the hair of the **h.** of his separation,... 7218
Nu 17:3 **h.** of the house of their fathers... 7218
Nu 22:31 and he bowed down his **h.**, and fell...
Nu 25:15 he was **h.** over a people, and of a... 7218
De 19:5 the **h.** slippeth from the helve, and... 1270
De 21:12 she shall shave her **h.**, and pare ... 7218
De 28:13 the Lord shall make thee the **h.**,... 7218
De 28:23 thy heaven that is over thy **h.** ... 7218
De 28:35 of thy foot unto the top of thy **h.**. ... 6936
De 28:44 he shall be the **h.**, and thou shalt... 7218
De 33:16 come upon the **h.** of Joseph, ... 7218
De 33:16 and upon the top of the **h.** of him... 6936
De 33:20 the arm with the crown of the **h.**. ... 6936
Jos 2:19 his blood shall be upon his **h.**, ... 7218
Jos 2:19 his blood shall be on our **h.**,... 7218
Jos 11:10 was the **h.** of all those kingdoms... 7218
Jos 22:14 each one was an **h.** of the house of... 7218
Jg 5:26 Sisera, she smote off his **h.**, ... 7218
Jg 9:53 of a millstone upon Abimelech's **h.**,... 7218
Jg 10:18 **h.** over all the inhabitants of... 7218
Jg 11:8 be our **h.** over all the inhabitants... 7218
Jg 11:9 before me, shall I be your **h.**? ... 7218
Jg 11:11 the people made him **h.** and captain... 7218
Jg 13:5 no rasor shall come on his **h.**: ... 7218
Jg 16:13 weavest the seven locks of my **h.** ... 7218
Jg 16:17 hath not come a rasor upon mine **h.**; .. 7218
Jg 16:19 shave off the seven locks of his **h.**; ... 7218
Jg 16:22 the hair of his **h.** began to grow... 7218
1Sa 1:11 shall no rasor come upon his **h.**, ... 7218
1Sa 4:12 rent, and with earth upon his **h.**... 7218
1Sa 5:4 and the **h.** of Dagon and both the... 7218
1Sa 10:1 vial of oil, and poured it upon his **h.**,... 7218
1Sa 14:45 one hair of his **h.** fall to the ground; ... 7218
1Sa 15:17 made the **h.** of the tribes of Israel,... 7218
1Sa 17:5 had an helmet of brass upon his **h.**,... 7218
1Sa 17:7 and his spear's **h.** weighed six... 3852
1Sa 17:38 an helmet of brass upon his **h.**;... 7218
1Sa 17:46 take thine **h.** from thee; and I will... 7218
1Sa 17:51 him, and cut off his **h.** therewith... 7218
1Sa 17:54 David took the **h.** of the Philistine, ... 7218
1Sa 17:57 with the **h.** of the Philistine in his... 7218
1Sa 25:39 of Nabal upon his own **h.**... 7218
1Sa 28:2 thee keeper of mine **h.** for ever... 7218
1Sa 31:9 they cut off his **h.**, and stripped off... 7218
2Sa 1:2 rent, and earth upon his **h.**: and so... 7218
2Sa 1:10 the crown that was upon his **h.**,... 7218
2Sa 1:16 Thy blood be upon thy **h.**; for ... 7218
2Sa 2:16 every one his fellow by the **h.**,... 7218
2Sa 3:8 Am I a dog's **h.**, which against ... 7218
2Sa 3:29 Let it rest on the **h.** of Joab... 7218
2Sa 4:7 beheaded him, and took his **h.**,... 7218
2Sa 4:8 they brought the **h.** of Ish-bosheth ... 7218
2Sa 4:8 Behold the **h.** of Ish-bosheth the... 7218
2Sa 4:12 they took the **h.** of Ish-bosheth,... 7218
2Sa 12:30 their king's crown from off his **h.**, ... 7218
2Sa 12:30 and it was set on David's **h.**... 7218
2Sa 13:19 Tamar put ashes on her **h.**, and... 7218
2Sa 13:19 laid her hand on her **h.**, and went ... 7218
2Sa 14:25 his foot even to the crown of his **h.**... 6936
2Sa 14:26 And when he polled his **h.**, (for it... 7218
2Sa 14:26 he weighed the hair of his **h.** at two ... 7218
2Sa 15:30 and had his **h.** covered, and he... 7218
2Sa 15:30 covered every man his **h.**, and they... 7218
2Sa 15:32 coat rent, and earth upon his **h.**:... 7218
2Sa 16:9 I pray thee, and take off his **h.**... 7218
2Sa 18:9 and his **h.** caught hold of the oak, ... 7218
2Sa 20:21 his **h.** shall be thrown to thee over... 7218
2Sa 20:22 they cut off the **h.** of Sheba ... 7218
2Sa 22:44 kept me to be **h.** of the heathen: ... 7218
1Ki 2:6 let not his hoar **h.** go down to the grave...
1Ki 2:9 his hoar **h.** bring thou down to the ...
1Ki 2:32 return his blood upon his own **h.**, ... 7218
1Ki 2:33 return upon the **h.** of Joab, and... 7218
1Ki 2:33 and upon the **h.** of his seed for ever;.. 7218
1Ki 2:37 blood shall be upon thine own **h.**. ... 7218
1Ki 2:44 thy wickedness upon thine own **h.**;... 7218
1Ki 8:32 to bring his way upon his **h.**;... 7218
1Ki 19:6 and a cruse of water at his **h.**... 4763
2Ki 2:3,5 thy master from thy **h.** to-day? ... 7218
2Ki 2:23 thou bald **h.**; go up, thou bald **h.**...
2Ki 4:19 said unto his father, My **h.**, my **h.**. ... 7218
2Ki 6:5 the axe **h.** fell into the water:... 1270
2Ki 6:25 an ass's **h.** was sold for fourscore ... 7218
2Ki 6:31 the **h.** of Elisha the son of Shaphat... 7218
2Ki 6:32 hath sent to take away mine **h.**? ... 7218
2Ki 9:3 the box of oil, and pour it on his **h.**, ... 7218
2Ki 9:6 he poured the oil on his **h.**,... 7218
2Ki 9:30 painted her face, and tired her **h.**, ... 7218
2Ki 19:21 Jerusalem hath shaken her **h.** at... 7218
2Ki 25:27 did lift up the **h.** of Jehoiachin... 7218
1Ch 10:9 they took his **h.**, and his armour, ... 7218
1Ch 10:10 fastened his **h.** in the temple of ... 1538
1Ch 20:2 crown of their king from off his **h.**,... 7218
1Ch 20:2 and it was set upon David's **h.**:... 7218
1Ch 29:11 thou art exalted as **h.** above all... 7218
2Ch 6:23 his way upon his own **h.**;... 7218
2Ch 20:18 And Jehoshaphat bowed his **h.** with...
Ezr 9:3 plucked off the hair of my **h.** and ... 7218
Ezr 9:6 iniquities are increased over our **h.**,... 7218
Ne 4:4 their reproach upon their own **h.**,... 7218
Es 2:17 he set the royal crown upon her **h.**, ... 7218
Es 6:8 royal which is set upon his **h.**:... 7218
Es 6:12 and having his **h.** covered... 7218
Es 9:25 should return upon his own **h.**, ... 7218
Job 1:20 rent his mantle, and shaved his **h.**,... 7218
Job 10:15 yet will I not lift up my **h.**. ... 7218
Job 16:4 you, and shake mine **h.** at you... 7218
Job 19:9 and taken the crown from my **h.**... 7218
Job 20:6 and his **h.** reach unto the clouds; ... 7218
Job 29:3 When his candle shined upon my **h.**,... 7218
Job 41:7 irons? or his **h.** with fish spears?... 7218
Ps 3:3 glory, and the lifter up of mine **h.**. ... 7218
Ps 7:16 shall return upon his own **h.**,... 7218
Ps 18:43 made me the **h.** of the heathen:... 7218
Ps 21:3 a crown of pure gold on his **h.**... 7218
Ps 22:7 the lip, they shake the **h.**, saying, ... 7218
Ps 23:5 thou anointest my **h.** with oil;... 7218
Ps 27:6 now shall mine **h.** be lifted up... 7218
Ps 38:4 iniquities are gone over mine **h.**:... 7218
Ps 40:12 more than the hairs of mine **h.**:... 7218
Ps 44:14 shaking of the **h.** among the people. ... 7218
Ps 60:7 also is the strength of mine **h.**;... 7218
Ps 68:21 shall wound the **h.** of his enemies,... 7218
Ps 69:4 more than the hairs of mine **h.**: ... 7218
Ps 83:2 that hate thee have lifted up the **h.**... 7218
Ps 108:8 also is the strength of mine **h.**;... 7218
Ps 110:7 therefore shall he lift up the **h.**... 7218
Ps 118:22 become the **h.** stone of the corner. ... 7218
Ps 133:2 the precious ointment upon the **h.**, ... 7218
Ps 140:7 covered my **h.** in the day of battle... 7218
Ps 140:9 the **h.** of those that compass me... 7218
Ps 141:5 oil, which shall not break my **h.**: ... 7218
Pr 1:9 an ornament of grace unto thy **h.**, ... 7218
Pr 4:9 shall give to thine **h.** an ornament ... 7218
Pr 10:6 Blessings are upon the **h.** of the ... 7218
Pr 11:26 blessing shall be upon the **h.** of him... 7218
Pr 16:31 The hoary **h.** is a crown of glory,...
Pr 20:29 the beauty of old men is the gray **h.**...
Pr 25:22 heap coals of fire upon his **h.**,... 7218
Ec 2:14 The wise man's eyes are in his **h.**;... 7218
Ec 9:8 and let thy **h.** lack no ointment... 7218
Ca 2:6 His left hand is under my **h.**,... 7218
Ca 5:2 for my **h.** is filled with dew,... 7218
Ca 5:11 His **h.** is as the most fine gold,... 7218
Ca 7:5 Thine **h.** upon thee is like Carmel, ... 7218
Ca 7:5 and the hair of thine **h.** like purple;... 7218
Ca 8:3 left hand should be under my **h.**,... 7218
Isa 1:5 the whole **h.** is sick, and the whole ... 7218
Isa 1:6 the sole of the foot even unto the **h.** .. 7218
Isa 3:17 with a scab the crown of the **h.** of... 6936
Isa 7:8 the **h.** of Syria is Damascus, and... 7218
Isa 7:8 the **h.** of Damascus is Rezin;... 7218
Isa 7:9 And the **h.** of Ephraim is Samaria,... 7218
Isa 7:9 the **h.** of Samaria is Remaliah's son... 7218
Isa 7:20 the **h.**, and the hair of the feet:... 7218
Isa 9:14 will cut off from Israel **h.** and tail, ... 7218
Isa 9:15 ancient and honourable, he is the **h.**;... 7218
Isa 19:15 the **h.** or tail, branch or rush,... 7218
Isa 28:1 are on the **h.** of the fat valleys ... 7218
Isa 28:4 which is on the **h.** of the fat valley, ... 7218
Isa 37:22 of Jerusalem hath shaken her **h.**... 7218
Isa 51:11 joy shall be upon their **h.**:... 7218
Isa 51:20 they lie at the **h.** of all the streets,... 7218
Isa 58:5 to bow down his **h.** as a bulrush, ... 7218
Isa 59:17 an helmet of salvation upon his **h.**: ... 7218
Jer 2:16 have broken the crown of thy **h.**. ... 6936
Jer 2:37 and thine hands upon thine **h.**:... 7218
Jer 9:1 Oh that my **h.** were waters,... 7218
Jer 18:16 shall be astonished, and wag his **h.**... 7218
Jer 22:6 unto me, and the **h.** of Lebanon:... 7218
Jer 23:19 grievously upon the **h.** of the wicked... 7218
Jer 30:23 with pain upon the **h.** of the wicked... 7218
Jer 48:37 every **h.** shall be bald, and every ... 7218
Jer 48:45 of the **h.** of the tumultuous ones. ... 6936
Jer 52:31 **h.** of Jehoiachin king of Judah, ... 7218
La 2:15 they hiss and wag their **h.** at the ... 7218
La 3:54 Waters flowed over mine **h.**; then I... 7218
La 5:16 The crown is fallen from our **h.**: ... 7218
Eze 5:1 upon thine **h.** and upon thy beard:... 7218
Eze 8:3 took me by a lock of mine **h.**; ... 7218
Eze 9:10 recompense their way upon their **h.**... 7218
Eze 10:1 above the **h.** of the cherubims there ... 7218
Eze 10:11 whither the **h.** looked they followed... 7218
Eze 13:18 upon the **h.** of every stature to hunt... 7218
Eze 16:12 a beautiful crown upon thine **h.**... 7218
Eze 16:25 high place at every **h.** of the way,... 7218
Eze 16:31 eminent place the **h.** of every way,... 7218
Eze 16:43 recompense thy way upon thine **h.**,... 7218
Eze 17:19 will I recompense upon his own **h.**. ... 7218
Eze 21:19 at the **h.** of the way to the city... 7218
Eze 21:21 at the **h.** of the two ways,... 7218
Eze 24:17 bind the tire of thine **h.** upon thee,...
Eze 29:18 every **h.** was made bald, and every ... 7218
Eze 33:4 his blood shall be upon his own **h.**... 7218
Eze 42:12 was a door in the **h.** of the way,... 7218
Da 1:10 me endanger my **h.** to the king... 7218
Da 2:28 the visions of thy **h.** upon thy bed... 7217
Da 2:32 This image's **h.** was of fine gold,... 7217
Da 2:38 Thou art this **h.** of gold... 7217
Da 3:27 nor was an hair of their **h.** singed,... 7217
Da 4:5 the visions of my **h.** troubled me... 7217
Da 4:10 the visions of mine **h.** in my bed;... 7217
Da 4:13 I saw in the visions of my **h.** upon ... 7217
Da 7:1 and visions of his **h.** upon his bed:... 7217
Da 7:9 hair of his **h.** like the pure wool:... 7217
Da 7:15 the visions of my **h.** troubled me... 7217
Da 7:20 of the ten horns that were in his **h.**,... 7217
Ho 1:11 and appoint themselves one **h.**,... 7218
Joe 3:4 recompence upon your own **h.**;... 7218
Joe 3:7 your recompence upon your own **h.**:... 7218
Am 2:7 of the earth on the **h.** of the poor,... 7218
Am 8:10 loins, and baldness upon every **h.**;... 7218
Am 9:1 cut them in the **h.**, all of them:... 7218
Ob 15 shall return upon thine own **h.**... 7218
Jon 2:5 weeds were wrapped about my **h.**... 7218
Jon 4:6 a shadow over his **h.**, to deliver... 7218
Jon 4:8 the sun beat upon the **h.** of Jonah. ... 7218
Mic 2:13 and the Lord on the **h.** of them. ... 7218
Hab 3:13 woundedst the **h.** out of the house ... 7218
Hab 3:14 his staves the **h.** of his villages:... 7218
Zec 1:21 so that no man did lift up his **h.**:... 7218
Zec 3:5 men set a fair mitre upon his **h.**... 7218
Zec 3:5 they set a fair mitre upon his **h.**, ... 7218
Zec 6:11 set them upon the **h.** of Joshua... 7218
Mt 5:36 **Neither shalt thou swear by thy h.**, *2776*
Mt 6:17 **when thou fastest, anoint thine h.**, *2776*
Mt 8:20 **hath not where to lay his h.** ... *2776*
Mt 10:30 **hairs of your h. are all numbered** .. *2776*
Mt 14:8 Give me here John Baptist's **h.** in... *2776*
Mt 14:11 And his **h.** was brought in a... *2776*
Mt 21:42 **is become the h. of the corner:**... *2776*
Mt 26:7 ointment, and poured it on his **h.**, ... *2776*
Mt 27:29 of thorns, they put it upon his **h.**, ... *2776*
Mt 27:30 the reed, and smote him on the **h.**... *2776*
Mt 27:37 set up over his **h.** his accusation... *2776*
Mk 6:24 she said, The **h.** of John the Baptist. .. *2776*
Mk 6:25 in a charger the **h.** of John the... *2776*
Mk 6:27 commanded his **h.** to be brought:... *2776*
Mk 6:28 brought his **h.** in a charger, and... *2776*
Mk 12:4 **and wounded him in the h., and**... *2775*
Mk 12:10 **is become the h. of the corner:**... *2776*
Mk 14:3 the box, and poured it on his **h.**... *2776*
Mk 15:17 thorns, and put it about his **h.**,...
Mk 15:19 they smote him on the **h.** with a... *2776*
Lu 7:38 wipe them with the hairs of her **h.**, ... *2776*
Lu 7:44 **them with the hairs of her h.**... *2776*

Lu 7:46 **My h. with oil thou didst not**........ *2776*
Lu 9:58 **hath not where to lay his h.**........ *2776*
Lu 12:7 **hairs of your h. are all numbered**.. *2776*
Lu 20:17 **is become the h. of the corner?**..... *2776*
Lu 21:18 **shall not an hair of your h. perish.** *2776*
Joh 13:9 but also my hands and my **h.**............ *2776*
Joh 19:2 of thorns, and put it on his **h.**, and..... *2776*
Joh 19:30 and he bowed his **h.**, and gave up...... *2776*
Joh 20:7 the napkin, that was about his **h.**, ... *2776*
Joh 20:12 the one at the **h.**, and the other *2776*
Ac 4:11 is become the **h.** of the corner. *2776*
Ac 18:18 having shorn his **h.** in Cenchrea: *2776*
Ac 27:34 shall not an hair fall from the **h.** of..... *2776*
Ro 12:20 shalt heap coals of fire on his **h.**. *2776*
1Co 11:3 the **h.** of every man is Christ; and....... *2776*
1Co 11:3 the **h.** of the woman is the man;........ *2776*
1Co 11:3 and the **h.** of Christ is God.............. *2776*
1Co 11:4 prophesying, having his **h.** covered, ... *2776*
1Co 11:4 covered, dishonoureth his **h.**. *2776*
1Co 11:5 prophesieth with her **h.** uncovered....... *2776*
1Co 11:5 uncovered dishonoureth her **h.**:.......... *2776*
1Co 11:7 indeed ought not to cover his **h.**, ... *2776*
1Co 11:10 woman to have power on her **h.** *2776*
1Co 12:21 nor again the **h.** to the feet, I have *2776*
Eph 1:22 gave him to be **h.** over all things........ *2776*
Eph 4:15 which is the **h.**, even Christ:............ *2776*
Eph 5:23 the husband is the **h.** of the wife,....... *2776*
Eph 5:23 as Christ is the **h.** of the church: *2776*
Col 1:18 he is the **h.** of the body, the church: .. *2776*
Col 2:10 the **h.** of all principality and power:..... *2776*
Col 2:19 And not holding the **H.**, from *2776*
1Pe 2:7 same is made the **h.** of the corner,..... *2776*
Re 1:14 His **h.** and his hairs were white *2776*
Re 10:1 and a rainbow was upon his **h.**,.......... *2776*
Re 12:1 her **h.** a crown of twelve stars: *2776*
Re 14:14 having on his **h.** a golden crown,........ *2776*
Re 19:12 and on his **h.** were many crowns;....... *2776*

HEADBANDS
Isa 3:20 and the **h.**, and the tablets, and......... 7196

HEADED See BEHEADED; GRAYHEADED.

HEADLONG
Job 5:13 counsel of the froward is carried **h.**. ....
Lu 4:29 that they might cast him down **h.**....... *2630*
Ac 1:18 of iniquity; and falling **h.**, he burst...... *4248*

HEADS
Ge 2:10 parted, and became into four **h.**. 7218
Ge 43:28 And they bowed down their **h.**, and..........
Ex 4:31 then they bowed their **h.** and ....
Ex 6:14 the **h.** of their fathers' houses: 7218
Ex 6:25 the **h.** of the fathers of the Levites...... 7218
Ex 18:25 and made them **h.** over the people, ... 7218
Le 10:6 Uncover not your **h.**, neither rend...... 7218
Le 19:27 not round the corners of your **h.**,....... 7218
Nu 1:16 fathers, **h.** of thousands in Israel. 7218
Nu 7:2 **h.** of the house of their fathers, ... 7218
Nu 8:12 hands upon the **h.** of the bullocks:...... 7218
Nu 10:4 are **h.** of the thousands of Israel, ... 7218
Nu 13:3 were **h.** of the children of Israel......... 7218
Nu 25:4 Take all the **h.** of the people............ 7218
Nu 30:1 spake unto the **h.** of the tribes 7218
De 1:15 and made them **h.** over you, ... 7218
De 5:23 even all the **h.** of your tribes, and...... 7218
De 33:5 when the **h.** of the people and the...... 7218
De 33:21 he came with the **h.** of the people, ... 7218
Jos 7:6 Israel, and put dust upon their **h.**........ 7218
Jos 14:1 the **h.** of the fathers of the tribes....... 7218
Jos 19:51 the **h.** of the fathers of the tribes....... 7218
Jos 21:1 the **h.** of the fathers of the Levites..... 7218
Jos 21:1 the **h.** of the fathers of the tribes....... 7218
Jos 22:21 the **h.** of the thousands of Israel, ... 7218
Jos 22:30 and **h.** of the thousands of Israel......... 7218
Jos 23:2 for their **h.**, and for their judges, ... 7218
Jos 24:1 for their **h.**, and for their judges, ... 7218
Jg 7:25 brought the **h.** of Oreb and Zeeb to.... 7218
Jg 8:28 they lifted up their **h.** no more. 7218
Jg 9:57 did God render upon their **h.**:............ 7218
1Sa 29:4 it not be with the **h.** of these men? 7218
1Ki 8:1 all the **h.** of the tribes, the chief of..... 7218
1Ki 20:31 on our loins, and ropes upon our **h.**,.... 7218
1Ki 20:32 and put ropes on their **h.**, and came ... 7218
2Ki 10:6 take ye the **h.** of the men your.......... 7218
2Ki 10:7 put their **h.** in baskets, and sent......... 7218
2Ki 10:8 have brought the **h.** of the king's 7218
1Ch 5:24 **h.** of the house of their fathers, ... 7218
1Ch 7:2 **h.** of their father's house, to wit, of.... 7218
1Ch 7:7, 9 **h.** of the house of their fathers, ... 7218
1Ch 7:11 by the **h.** of their fathers, mighty....... 7218
1Ch 7:40 **h.** of their father's house, choice........ 7218
1Ch 8:6 the **h.** of the fathers of the 7218
1Ch 8:10 were his sons, **h.** of the fathers......... 7218
1Ch 8:13 **h.** of the fathers of the inhabitants...... 7218
1Ch 8:28 These were **h.** of the fathers, by 7218
1Ch 9:13 **h.** of the house of their fathers, ... 7218
1Ch 12:19 Saul to the jeopardy of our **h.**............ 7218
1Ch 12:32 the **h.** of them were two hundred;...... 7218
1Ch 29:20 and bowed down their **h.**, and 7218
2Ch 3:16 put them on the **h.** of the pillars; 7218
2Ch 5:2 all the **h.** of the tribes, the chief of..... 7218
2Ch 28:12 the **h.** of the children of Ephraim, ... 7218
2Ch 29:30 bowed their **h.** and worshipped. ....
Ne 8:6 bowed their **h.**, and worshipped ....
Job 2:12 sprinkled dust upon their **h.** 7218
Ps 24:7 Lift up your **h.**, O ye gates; and........ 7218
Ps 24:9 Lift up your **h.**, O ye gates; even 7218
Ps 66:12 caused men to ride over our **h.**; 7218
Ps 74:13 thou brakest the **h.** of the dragons 7218
Ps 74:14 Thou brakest the **h.** of leviathan 7218
Ps 109:25 upon me they shaked their **h.**............ 7218
Ps 110:6 wound the **h.** over many countries...... 7218
Isa 15:2 on all their **h.** shall be baldness,........ 7218
Isa 35:10 and everlasting joy upon their **h.**: 7218
Jer 14:3 confounded, and covered their **h.**. 7218
Jer 14:4 ashamed, they covered their **h.**.......... 7218
La 2:10 have cast up dust upon their **h.**; 7218
La 2:10 of Jerusalem hang down their **h.**......... 7218
Eze 1:22 upon the **h.** of the living creature 7218
Eze 1:22 stretched forth over their **h.** above..... 7218
Eze 1:25 firmament that was over their **h.**,....... 7218
Eze 1:26 firmament that was over their **h.**........ 7218
Eze 7:18 and baldness upon all their **h.**........... 7218
Eze 11:21 their way upon their own **h.**, saith...... 7218
Eze 22:31 have I recompensed upon their **h.**, ... 7218
Eze 23:15 in dyed attire upon their **h.**, all of....... 7218
Eze 23:42 beautiful crowns upon their **h.**. 7218
Eze 24:23 your tires shall be upon your **h.**,........ 7218
Eze 27:30 shall cast up dust upon their **h.**,......... 7218
Eze 32:27 laid their swords under their **h.**,......... 7218
Eze 44:18 have linen bonnets upon their **h.**, ... 7218
Eze 44:20 Neither shall they shave their **h.**, ... 7218
Eze 44:20 they shall only poll their **h.**. 7218
Da 7:6 the beast had also four **h.**; and 7217
Mic 3:1 Hear, I pray you, O **h.** of Jacob, ... 7218
Mic 3:9 ye **h.** of the house of Jacob,............... 7218
Mic 3:11 The **h.** thereof judge for reward,........ 7218
Mt 27:39 by reviled him, wagging their **h.**,........ *2776*
Mk 15:29 railed on him, wagging their **h.**, ... *2776*
Lu 21:28 **look up, and lift up your h.**; *2776*
Ac 18:6 Your blood be upon your own **h.**; *2776*
Ac 21:24 that they may shave their **h.**: *2776*
Re 4:4 they had on their **h.** crowns of gold. ... *2776*
Re 9:7 on their **h.** were as it were crowns *2776*
Re 9:17 and the **h.** of the horses were as the .. *2776*
Re 9:17 horses were as the **h.** of lions; *2776*
Re 9:19 like unto serpents, and had **h.**, ... *2776*
Re 12:3 having seven **h.** and ten horns, and *2776*
Re 12:3 and seven crowns upon his **h.**. *2776*
Re 13:1 having seven **h.** and ten horns, ... *2776*
Re 13:1 upon his **h.** the name of blasphemy..... *2776*
Re 13:3 And I saw one of his **h.** as it were..... *2776*
Re 17:3 having seven **h.** and ten horns........... *2776*
Re 17:7 hath the seven **h.** and ten horns. *2776*
Re 17:9 The seven **h.** are seven mountains, ... *2776*
Re 18:19 they cast dust on their **h.**, and cried, .. *2776*

HEADSTONE See also HEAD and STONE.
Zec 4:7 he shall bring forth the **h.**............. 68,7222

HEADY
2Ti 3:4 Traitors, **h.**, highminded, lovers......... *4312*

HEAL See also HEALED; HEALETH; HEALING.
Nu 12:13 **H.** her now, O God, I beseech.......... 7495
De 32:39 I make alive; I wound, and I **h.**: 7495
2Ki 20:5 I will **h.** thee: on the third day.......... 7495
2Ki 20:8 the sign that the Lord will **h.** me, ... 7495
2Ch 7:14 their sin, and will **h.** their land........... 7495
Ps 6:2 O Lord, **h.** me; for my bones are........ 7495
Ps 41:4 be merciful unto me: **h.** my soul; 7495
Ps 60:2 **h.** the breaches thereof; for it 7495
Ec 3:3 A time to kill, and a time to **h.**; 7495
Isa 19:22 he shall smite and **h.** it: and they 7495
Isa 19:22 of them, and shall **h.** them. 7495
Isa 57:18 I have seen his ways, and will **h.** 7495
Isa 57:19 saith the Lord; and I will **h.** him. 7495
Jer 3:22 and I will **h.** your backslidings........... 7495
Jer 17:14 **H.** me, O Lord, and I shall be........... 7495
Jer 30:17 I will **h.** thee of thy wounds, ... 7495
La 2:13 great like the sea: who can **h.** thee? ... 7495
Ho 5:13 yet could he not **h.** you, nor cure....... 7495
Ho 6:1 he hath torn, and he will **h.** us; he 7495
Ho 14:4 I will **h.** their backsliding, I will.......... 7495
Zec 11:16 nor **h.** that that is broken, ... 7495
Mt 8:7 unto him, **I will come and h. him**.... *2323*
Mt 10:1 and to **h.** all manner of sickness......... *2323*
Mt 10:8 **H. the sick, cleanse the lepers,**...... *2323*
Mt 12:10 lawful to **h.** on the sabbath days? *2323*
Mt 13:15 **converted, and I should h. them**.... *2390*
Mk 3:2 he would **h.** on the sabbath day; *2323*
Mk 3:15 to have power to **h.** sicknesses,......... *2323*
Lu 4:18 **sent me to h. the brokenhearted,**... *2390*
Lu 4:23 **proverb, Physician, h. thyself:**....... *2323*
Lu 5:17 the Lord was present to **h.** them. *2390*
Lu 6:7 he would **h.** on the sabbath day; *2323*
Lu 7:3 would come and **h.** his servant. *1295*
Lu 9:2 of God, and to **h.** the sick. *2390*
Lu 10:9 **h. the sick that are therein, and**.... *2323*
Lu 14:3 **lawful to h. on the sabbath day?** ... *2323*
Joh 4:47 would come down, and **h.** his son:...... *2390*
Joh 12:40 be converted, and I should **h.** them. ... *2390*
Ac 4:30 stretching forth thine hand to **h.**;........ *2392*
Ac 28:27 be converted, and I should **h.** them. ... *2392*

HEALED
Ge 20:17 and God **h.** Abimelech, and his 7495
Ex 21:19 cause him to be thoroughly **h.**. 7495
Le 13:18 skin thereof, was a boil, and is **h.**, ... 7495
Le 13:37 the scall is **h.**, he is clean: 7495
Le 14:3 if the plague of leprosy be **h.** in 7495
Le 14:48 clean, because the plague is **h.**. 7495
De 28:27 itch, whereof thou canst not be **h.**....... 7495
De 28:35 a sore botch that cannot be **h.**,.......... 7495
1Sa 6:3 then ye shall be **h.**, and it shall be...... 7495
2Ki 2:21 the Lord, I have **h.** these waters; 7495
2Ki 2:22 So the waters were **h.** unto this 7495
2Ki 8:29 king Joram went back to be **h.** in 7495
2Ki 9:15 king Joram was returned to be **h.**....... 7495
2Ch 22:6 he returned to be **h.** in Jezreel 7495
2Ch 30:20 to Hezekiah, and **h.** the people. 7495
Ps 30:2 cried unto thee, and thou hast **h.** me. ..7495
Ps 107:20 He sent his word, and **h.** them, ... 7495
Isa 6:10 their heart, and convert, and be **h.**..... 7495
Isa 53:5 and with his stripes we are **h.**. 7495
Jer 6:14 They have **h.** also the hurt of the....... 7495
Jer 8:11 For they have **h.** the hurt of the......... 7495
Jer 15:18 incurable, which refuseth to be **h.**? 7495
Jer 17:14 Heal me, O Lord, and I shall be **h.**;..... 7495
Jer 51:8 her pain, if so be she may be **h.**. 7495
Jer 51:9 We would have **h.** Babylon,.............. 7495
Jer 51:9 Babylon, but she is not **h.**: 7495
Eze 30:21 not be bound up to be **h.**, ... 5414,7499
Eze 34:4 have ye **h.** that which was sick, ... 7495
Eze 47:8 the sea, the waters shall be **h.**. 7495
Eze 47:9 for they shall be **h.**; and every 7495
Eze 47:11 marishes thereof shall not be **h.**; 7495
Ho 7:1 When I would have **h.** Israel, then...... 7495
Ho 11:3 they knew not that I **h.** them. 7495
Mt 4:24 had the palsy; and he **h.** them. *2323*
Mt 8:8 only, and my servant shall be **h.**. *2390*
Mt 8:13 servant was **h.** in the selfsame *2390*
Mt 8:16 his word, and **h.** all that were sick: *2323*
Mt 12:15 followed him, and he **h.** them all; *2323*
Mt 12:22 blind, and dumb: and he **h.** him,......... *2323*
Mt 14:14 toward them, and he **h.** their sick. *2323*
Mt 15:30 at Jesus' feet; and he **h.** them: *2323*
Mt 19:2 followed him; and he **h.** them there. ... *2323*
Mt 21:14 him in the temple; and he **h.** them. *2323*
Mk 1:34 he **h.** many that were sick of............. *2323*
Mk 3:10 For he had **h.** many; insomuch *2323*
Mk 5:23 hands on her, that she may be **h.**;...... *4982*
Mk 5:29 that she was **h.** of that plague. *2390*
Mk 6:5 upon a few sick folk, and **h.** them. *2323*
Mk 6:13 many that were sick, and **h.** them. *2323*
Lu 4:40 on every one of them, and **h.** them. ... *2323*
Lu 5:15 hear, and to be **h.** by him of their *2323*
Lu 6:17 and to be **h.** of their diseases; *2390*
Lu 6:18 unclean spirits: and they were **h.**. *2323*
Lu 6:19 virtue out of him, and **h.** them all. *2390*
Lu 7:7 word, and my servant shall be **h.**. *2390*
Lu 8:2 women, which had been **h.** of evil *2390*

Lu 8:36 possessed of the devils was **h.**. *4982*
Lu 8:43 neither could be **h.** of any, ... *2323*
Lu 8:47 and how she was **h.** immediately. *2390*
Lu 9:11 **h.** them that had need of healing. *2390*
Lu 9:42 and **h.** the child, and delivered *2390*
Lu 13:14 Jesus had **h.** on the sabbath day, ... *2323*
Lu 13:14 in them therefore come and be **h.**, ... *2323*
Lu 14:4 him, and **h.** him, and let him go; *2323*
Lu 17:15 when he saw that he was **h.**, ... *2390*
Lu 22:51 he touched his ear, and **h.** him. *2390*
Joh 5:13 And he that was **h.** wist not who *2390*
Ac 3:11 man which was **h.** held Peter and *2390*
Ac 4:14 beholding the man which was **h.** *2323*
Ac 5:16 and they were **h.** every one. *2323*
Ac 8:7 and that were lame, were **h.**. *2323*
Ac 14:9 that he had faith to be **h.**, ... *4982*
Ac 28:8 his hands on him and **h.** him. *2390*
Ac 28:9 in the island, came, and were **h.**: *2323*
Heb 12:13 the way; but let it rather be **h.** *2390*
Jas 5:16 one for another, that ye may be **h.** *2390*
1Pe 2:24 by whose stripes ye were **h.** *2390*
Re 13:3 his deadly wound was **h.**: and all *2323*
Re 13:12 beast, whose deadly wound was **h.** *2323*

HEALER
Isa 3:7 swear, saying, I will not be an **h.**; 2280

HEALETH
Ex 15:26 for I am the Lord that **h.** thee. 7495
Ps 103:3 iniquities; who **h.** all thy diseases; 7495
Ps 147:3 He **h.** the broken in heart, and 7495
Isa 30:26 and **h.** the stroke of their wound. 7495

HEALING See also HEALINGS.
Jer 14:19 us, and there is no **h.** for us? 4832
Jer 14:19 and for the time of **h.**, and behold 4832
Jer 30:13 up: thou hast no **h.** medicines. 8585
Na 3:19 There is no **h.** of thy bruise; 3545
Mal 4:2 arise with **h.** in his wings; 4832
Mt 4:23 **h.** all manner of sickness and all *2323*
Mt 9:35 **h.** every sickness and every disease ... *2323*
Lu 9:6 the gospel, and **h.** every where. *2323*
Lu 9:11 healed them that had need of **h.** *2322*
Ac 4:22 this miracle of **h.** was shewed. *2392*
Ac 10:38 and **h.** all that were oppressed of *2390*
1Co 12:9 gifts of **h.** by the same Spirit; *2386*
1Co 12:30 Have all the gifts of **h.**? do all *2386*
Re 22:2 were for the **h.** of the nations. *2322*

HEALINGS
1Co 12:28 miracles, then gift of **h.**, helps, ... *2386*

HEALTH
Ge 43:28 servant our father is in good **h.**. 7965
2Sa 20:9 Art thou in **h.**, my brother? 7965
Ps 42:11 who is the **h.** of my countenance, ... 3444
Ps 43:5 who is the **h.** of my countenance, ... 3444
Ps 67:2 thy saving **h.** among all nations. 3444
Pr 3:8 It shall be **h.** to thy navel, and 7500
Pr 4:22 find them, and **h.** to all their flesh. 4832
Pr 12:18 but the tongue of the wise is **h.**. 4832
Pr 13:17 but a faithful ambassador is **h.**. 4832
Pr 16:24 the soul, and **h.** to the bones. 4832
Isa 58:8 and thine **h.** shall spring forth. 724
Jer 8:15 and for a time of **h.**, and behold 4832
Jer 8:22 the **h.** of the daughter of my 724
Jer 30:17 For I will restore **h.** unto thee, ... 724
Jer 33:6 I will bring it **h.** and cure, and I 724
Ac 27:34 some meat: for this is for your **h.**: *4991*
3Jo 2 thou mayest prosper and be in **h.**, ... *5198*

HEAP See also HEAPED; HEAPETH; HEAPS.
Ge 31:46 they took stones, and made an **h.**: 1530
Ge 31:46 they did eat there upon the **h.**. 1530
Ge 31:48 This **h.** is a witness between me. 1530
Ge 31:51 Behold this **h.**, and behold this 1530
Ge 31:52 This **h.** be witness, and this pillar. 1530
Ge 31:52 I will not pass over this **h.** to thee, ... 1530
Ge 31:52 thou shalt not pass over this **h.** and 1530
Ex 15:8 the floods stood upright as an **h.**, ... 5067
De 13:16 and it shall be an **h.** for ever; 8510
De 32:23 I will **h.** mischiefs upon them; 5595
Jos 3:13 and they shall stand upon an **h.** 5067
Jos 3:16 rose up upon an **h.** very far from 5067
Jos 7:26 over him a great **h.** of stones 1530
Jos 8:28 Ai, and made it an **h.** for ever, even ... 8510
Jos 8:29 raise thereon a great **h.** of stones, ... 1530
Ru 3:7 down at the end of the **h.** of corn: 6194
2Sa 18:17 very great **h.** of stones upon him: 1530
Job 8:17 roots are wrapped about the **h.**, ... 1530
Job 16:4 I could **h.** up words against you, ... 2266
Job 27:16 Though he **h.** up silver as the dust, ... 6651
Job 36:13 hypocrites in heart **h.** up wrath: 7760
Ps 33:7 waters of the sea together as an **h.**: ... 5067
Ps 78:13 made the waters to stand as an **h.**. 5067
Pr 25:22 shalt **h.** coals of fire upon his head, ... 2846
Ec 2:26 gather and to **h.** up, that he may 3664
Ca 7:2 thy belly is like an **h.** of wheat. 6194
Isa 17:1 city, and it shall be a ruinous **h.**. 4596
Isa 17:11 the harvest shall be a **h.** in the day 5067
Isa 25:2 thou hast made of a city an **h.**; 1530
Jer 30:18 shall be builded on her own **h.**, ... 8510
Jer 49:2 it shall be a desolate **h.**, and her 8510
Eze 24:10 **H.** on wood, kindle the fire, ... 7235
Mic 1:6 make Samaria as an **h.** of the field, ... 5856
Hab 1:10 for they shall **h.** dust, and take it. 6651
Hab 3:15 through the **h.** of great waters. 2563
Hag 2:16 came to an **h.** of twenty measures, ... 6194
Ro 12:20 shalt **h.** coals of fire on his head. *4987*
2Ti 4:3 they **h.** to themselves teachers, ... *2002*

HEAPED
Zec 9:3 and **h.** up silver as the dust, and 6651
Jas 5:3 Ye have **h.** treasures together for *2343*

HEAPETH
Ps 39:6 he **h.** up riches, and knoweth not 6651
Hab 2:5 and **h.** unto him all people: 6908

HEAPS
Ex 8:14 gathered them together upon **h.**: 2563
Jg 15:16 the jawbone of an ass, **h.** upon **h.**, ... 2565
2Ki 10:8 Lay ye them in two **h.** at the 6652
2Ki 19:25 waste fenced cities into ruinous **h.**. 1530
2Ch 31:6 their God, and laid them by **h.** 6194
2Ch 31:7 to lay the foundation of the **h.**, ... 6194
2Ch 31:8 the princes came and saw the **h.**, ... 6194
2Ch 31:9 and the Levites concerning the **h.** 6194
Ne 4:2 stones out of the **h.** of the rubbish 6194
Job 15:28 which are ready to become **h.**, ... 1530
Ps 79:1 they have laid Jerusalem on **h.** 5856
Isa 37:26 defenced cities into ruinous **h.**. 1530
Jer 9:11 I will make Jerusalem **h.**, and a 1530
Jer 26:18 Jerusalem shall become **h.**, and 5856
Jer 31:21 up waymarks, make thee high **h.**: 8564
Jer 50:26 cast her up as **h.**, and destroy her 6194
Jer 51:37 And Babylon shall become **h.**, a 1530
Ho 12:11 their altars are as **h.** in the furrows 1530
Mic 3:12 Jerusalem shall become **h.**, and 5856

HEAR See also HEARD; HEAREST; HEARETH; HEARING.
Ge 4:23 **H.** my voice; ye wives of Lamech, ... 8085
Ge 21:6 that all that **h.** will laugh with me. 8085
Ge 23:6 **H.** us, my lord: thou art a mighty 8085
Ge 23:8 **h.** me, and intreat for me to Ephron ... 8085
Ge 23:11 Nay, my lord, **h.** me: the field give 8085
Ge 23:13 I pray thee, **h.** me: I will give thee 8085
Ge 37:6 **H.**, I pray you, this dream which 8085
Ge 42:21 besought us, and we would not **h.**; 8085
Ge 42:22 the child; and ye would not **h.**? 8085
Ge 49:2 together, and **h.**, ye sons of Jacob; 8085
Ex 6:12 how then shall Pharaoh **h.** me, ... 8085
Ex 7:16 hitherto thou wouldest not **h.**. 8085
Ex 15:14 The people shall **h.**, and be afraid: 8085
Ex 19:9 the people may **h.** when I speak 8085
Ex 20:19 Speak thou with us, and we will **h.**: 8085
Ex 22:23 unto me, I will surely **h.** their cry; 8085
Ex 22:27 he crieth unto me, that I will **h.**; 8085
Ex 32:18 the noise of them that sing do I **h.**. 8085
Le 5:1 sin and **h.** the voice of swearing, ... 8085
Nu 9:8 **h.** what the Lord will command. 8085
Nu 12:6 **H.** now my words: If there be a 8085
Nu 14:13 Then the Egyptians shall **h.** it, ... 8085
Nu 16:8 **H.**, I pray you, ye sons of Levi: 8085
Nu 20:10 said unto them, **H.** now, ye rebels; 8085
Nu 23:18 Rise up, Balak, and **h.**; hearken 8085
Nu 30:4 And her father **h.** her vow, and 8085
De 1:16 **h.** the causes between your 8085
De 1:17 ye shall **h.** the small as well as the 8085
De 1:17 bring it unto me, and I will **h.** it. 8085
De 1:43 and ye would not **h.**, but rebelled 8085
De 2:25 who shall **h.** report of thee, and 8085
De 3:26 your sakes, and would not **h.** me: 8085
De 4:6 which shall **h.** all these statutes, ... 8085
De 4:10 and I will make them **h.** my words, ... 8085
De 4:28 which neither see, nor **h.**, nor eat, ... 8085
De 4:33 Did ever people **h.** the voice of God ... 8085
De 4:36 of heaven he made thee to **h.** his 8085
De 5:1 **H.**, O Israel, the statutes and 8085
De 5:25 if we **h.** the voice of the Lord our 8085
De 5:27 and **h.** all that the Lord our God 8085
De 5:27 thee; and we will **h.** it, and do it. 8085
De 6:3 **H.** therefore, O Israel, and observe 8085
De 6:4 **H.**, O Israel: The Lord our God is 8085
De 9:1 **H.**, O Israel: Thou art to pass over 8085
De 12:28 Observe and **h.** all these words 8085
De 13:11 all Israel shall **h.**, and fear, and 8085
De 13:12 shalt **h.** say in one of thy cities, ... 8085
De 17:13 all the people shall **h.**, and fear 8085
De 18:16 Let me not **h.** again the voice of 8085
De 19:20 which remain shall **h.**, and fear, ... 8085
De 20:3 **H.**, O Israel, ye approach this day 8085
De 21:21 and all Israel shall **h.**, and fear. 8085
De 29:4 eyes to see, and ears to **h.**, unto this . 8085
De 30:12, 13 that we may **h.** it, and do it? 8085
De 30:17 turn away, so that thou wilt not **h.**, ... 8085
De 31:12 that they may **h.**, and that they may ... 8085
De 31:13 may **h.**, and learn to fear the 8085
De 32:1 and **h.**, O earth, the words of my 8085
De 33:7 said, **H.**, Lord, the voice of Judah, ... 8085
Jos 3:9 hither, and **h.** the words of the Lord ... 8085
Jos 6:5 ye **h.** the sound of the trumpet, ... 8085
Jos 7:9 inhabitants of the land shall **h.** of 8085
Jg 5:3 **H.**, O ye kings; give ear, O ye 8085
Jg 5:16 to **h.** the bleatings of the flocks? 8085
Jg 7:11 And thou shalt **h.** what they say: 8085
Jg 14:13 forth thy riddle, that we may **h.** it. 8085
1Sa 2:23 I **h.** of your evil dealings by all 8085
1Sa 2:24 for it is no good report that I **h.**: 8085
1Sa 8:18 the Lord will not **h.** you in that. 6030
1Sa 13:3 land, saying, Let the Hebrews **h.**. 8085
1Sa 15:14 the lowing of the oxen which I **h.**? 8085
1Sa 16:2 can I go? if Saul **h.** it, he will kill me. . 8085
1Sa 22:7 **H.** now, ye Benjamites; will the 8085
1Sa 22:12 said, **H.** now, thou son of Ahitub. 8085
1Sa 25:24 **h.** the words of thine handmaid. 8085
1Sa 26:19 let my lord the king **h.** the words. 8085
2Sa 14:16 For the king will **h.**, to deliver his 8085
2Sa 15:3 man deputed of the king to **h.** thee. 8085
2Sa 15:10 as ye **h.** the sound of the trumpet, ... 8085
2Sa 15:35 thing soever thou shalt **h.** out of the ... 8085
2Sa 15:36 unto me every thing that ye can **h.** 8085
2Sa 16:21 shall **h.** that thou art abhorred of 8085
2Sa 17:5 let us **h.** likewise what he saith. 8085
2Sa 19:35 I **h.** any more the voice of singing 8085
2Sa 20:16 **H.**, **h.**; say, I pray you, unto Joab, ... 8085
2Sa 20:17 **H.** the words of thine handmaid. 8085
2Sa 20:17 And he answered, I do **h.**. 8085
2Sa 22:7 did **h.** my voice out of his temple, ... 8085
2Sa 22:45 as soon as they **h.**, they shall be 8085
1Ki 4:34 people to **h.** the wisdom of Solomon, .. 8085
1Ki 8:30 and **h.** thou in heaven thy dwelling 8085
1Ki 8:32 Then **h.** thou in heaven, and do, ... 8085
1Ki 8:34, 36 **h.** thou in heaven, and forgive 8085
1Ki 8:39 Then **h.** thou in heaven thy 8085
1Ki 8:42 For they shall **h.** of thy great name, ... 8085
1Ki 8:43 **H.** thou in heaven thy dwelling 8085
1Ki 8:45 **h.** thou in heaven their prayer 8085
1Ki 8:49 Then **h.** thou their prayer and 8085
1Ki 10:8 before thee, and that **h.** thy wisdom. .. 8085
1Ki 10:24 sought to Solomon, to **h.** his wisdom, . 8085
1Ki 18:26 O Baal, **h.** us. But there was no 6030
1Ki 18:37 **H.** me, O Lord, **h.** me, that this 6030
1Ki 22:19 **H.** thou therefore the word of 8085
2Ki 7:1 said, **H.** ye the word of the Lord; 8085
2Ki 7:6 Syrians to **h.** a noise of chariots, ... 8085
2Ki 14:11 But Amaziah would not **h.** 8085
2Ki 17:14 they would not **h.**, but hardened 8085
2Ki 18:12 would not **h.** them, nor do them. 8085
2Ki 18:28 **H.** the word of the great king, the 8085
2Ki 19:4 thy God will **h.** all the words of 8085
2Ki 19:7 and he shall **h.** a rumour, and shall 8085
2Ki 19:16 Lord, bow down thine ear, and **h.**: 8085
2Ki 19:16 and **h.** the words of Sennacherib, ... 8085
2Ki 20:16 Hezekiah, **H.** the word of the Lord. 8085
1Ch 14:15 thou shalt **h.** a sound of going 8085
1Ch 28:2 **H.** me, my brethren, and my 8085
2Ch 6:21 **h.** thou from thy dwelling place, ... 8085
2Ch 6:23 Then **h.** thou from heaven, and 8085
2Ch 6:25 Then **h.** thou from the heavens, ... 8085
2Ch 6:27 Then **h.** thou from heaven, and 8085
2Ch 6:30 Then **h.** thou from heaven thy 8085
2Ch 6:33 Then **h.** thou from the heavens, ... 8085
2Ch 6:35 Then **h.** thou from the heavens 8085

2Ch 6:39 Then **h.** thou from the heavens,......... 8085
2Ch 7:14 then will I **h.** from heaven, and.......... 8085
2Ch 9:7 before thee, and **h.** thy wisdom. 8085
2Ch 9:23 Solomon, to **h.** his wisdom, that......... 8085
2Ch 13:4 **H.** me, thou Jeroboam, and all........... 8085
2Ch 15:2 **H.** ye me, Asa, and all Judah and....... 8085
2Ch 18:18 Therefore **h.** the word of the Lord; 8085
2Ch 20:9 then thou wilt **h.** and help................ 8085
2Ch 20:20 and said, **H.** me, O Judah, and ye 8085
2Ch 25:20 But Amaziah would not **h.**; for it........ 8085
2Ch 28:11 Now **h.** me therefore, and deliver 8085
2Ch 29:5 **H.** me, ye Levites, sanctify now 8085
Ne 1:6 that thou mayest **h.** the prayer of....... 8085
Ne 4:4 **H.**, O our God: for we are despised: .. 8085
Ne 4:20 ye **h.** the sound of the trumpet,......... 8085
Ne 8:2 that could **h.** with understanding,....... 8085
Ne 9:29 their neck, and would not **h.**. 8085
Job 3:18 **h.** not the voice of the oppressor. 8085
Job 5:27 **h.** it, and know thou it for thy good.... 8085
Job 13:6 **H.** now my reasoning, and hearken..... 8085
Job 13:17 **H.** diligently my speech, and my 8085
Job 15:17 I will shew thee, **h.** me; and that 8085
Job 21:2 **H.** diligently my speech, and let......... 8085
Job 22:27 prayer unto him, and he shall **h.** 8085
Job 27:9 Will God **h.** his cry when trouble........ 8085
Job 30:20 thee, and thou dost not **h.** me: 6030
Job 31:35 Oh that one would **h.** me! behold 8085
Job 33:1 Job, I pray thee, **h.** my speeches, ... 8085
Job 34:2 **H.** my words, O ye wise men; 8085
Job 34:16 thou hast understanding, **h.** this: 8085
Job 35:13 God will not **h.** vanity, neither will...... 8085
Job 37:2 **H.** attentively the noise of his 8085
Job 42:4 **H.**, I beseech thee, and I will speak: .. 8085
Ps 4:1 **H.** me when I call, O God of my 6030
Ps 4:1 mercy upon me, and **h.** my prayer. 8085
Ps 4:3 the Lord will **h.** when I call unto........ 8085
Ps 5:3 voice shalt thou **h.** in the morning, ... 8085
Ps 10:17 thou wilt cause thine ear to **h.**: 7181
Ps 13:3 Consider and **h.** me, O Lord my 6030
Ps 17:1 **H.** the right, O Lord, attend unto 8085
Ps 17:6 for thou wilt **h.** me, O God:............. 6030
Ps 17:6 ear unto me, and **h.** my speech. 8085
Ps 18:44 As soon as they **h.** of me, they 8085
Ps 20:1 **h.** thee in the day of trouble; 6030
Ps 20:6 will **h.** him from his holy heaven 6030
Ps 20:9 let the king **h.** us when we call.......... 6030
Ps 27:7 **H.**, O Lord, when I cry with my.......... 8085
Ps 28:2 **H.** the voice of my supplications, ... 8085
Ps 30:10 **H.**, O Lord, and have mercy upon...... 8085
Ps 34:2 the humble shall **h.** thereof, and be..... 8085
Ps 38:15 thou wilt **h.**, O Lord my God. 6030
Ps 38:16 For I said, **H.** me, lest otherwise....... 6030
Ps 39:12 **H.** my prayer, O Lord, and give 8085
Ps 49:1 **H.** this, all ye people; give ear, ... 8085
Ps 50:7 **H.**, O my people, and I will speak;..... 8085
Ps 51:8 Make me to **h.** joy and gladness; 8085
Ps 54:2 **H.** my prayer, O God; give ear to...... 8085
Ps 55:2 Attend unto me, and **h.** me:............. 6030
Ps 55:17 aloud: and he shall **h.** my voice.......... 8085
Ps 55:19 God shall **h.**, and afflict them, even 8085
Ps 59:7 lips: for who, say they, doth **h.**? 8085
Ps 60:5 with thy right hand, and **h.** me. 6030
Ps 61:1 **H.** my cry, O God; attend unto my 8085
Ps 64:1 **H.** my voice, O God, in my prayer..... 8085
Ps 66:16 Come and **h.**, all ye that fear God, ... 8085
Ps 66:18 in my heart, the Lord will not **h.** me:.. 8085
Ps 69:13 the multitude of thy mercy **h.** me, ... 6030
Ps 69:16 **H.** me, O Lord; for thy.................... 6030
Ps 69:17 I am in trouble: **h.** me speedily.......... 6030
Ps 81:8 **H.**, O my people, and I will testify..... 8085
Ps 84:8 O Lord God of hosts, **h.** my prayer:.... 8085
Ps 85:8 **h.** what God the Lord will speak: 8085
Ps 86:1 down thine ear, O Lord, **h.** me:......... 6030
Ps 92:11 shall **h.** my desire of the wicked 8085
Ps 94:9 planted the ear, shall he not **h.**?......... 8085
Ps 95:7 To day if ye will **h.** his voice,........... 8085
Ps 102:1 **H.** my prayer, O Lord, and let my..... 8085
Ps 102:20 To **h.** the groaning of the prisoner;..... 8085
Ps 115:6 They have ears, but they **h.** not: 8085
Ps 119:145 my whole heart; **h.** me, O Lord:........ 6030
Ps 119:149 **H.** my voice according unto thy 8085
Ps 130:2 Lord, **h.** my voice: let thine ears 8085
Ps 135:17 They have ears, but they **h.** not;......... 238
Ps 138:4 they **h.** the words of thy mouth. 8085
Ps 140:6 **h.** the voice of my supplications,.......... 238
Ps 141:6 **h.** my words; for they are sweet. 8085
Ps 143:1 **H.** my prayer, O Lord, give ear to...... 8085
Ps 143:7 **H.** me speedily, O Lord: my............ 6030
Ps 143:8 Cause me to **h.** thy lovingkindness 8085
Ps 145:19 he also will **h.** their cry, and will........ 8085
Pr 1:5 wise man will **h.**, and will increase...... 8085
Pr 1:8 **h.** the instruction of thy father,.......... 8085
Pr 4:1 **H.**, ye children, the instruction of a.... 8085
Pr 4:10 **H.**, O my son, and receive my 8085
Pr 5:7 **H.** me now therefore, O ye 8085
Pr 8:6 **H.**; for I will speak of excellent 8085
Pr 8:33 **H.** instruction, and be wise, and 8085
Pr 19:20 **H.** counsel, and receive instruction, ... 8085
Pr 19:27 Cease, my son, to **h.** the instruction... 8085
Pr 22:17 ear, and **h.** the words of the wise, ... 8085
Pr 23:19 **H.** thou, my son, and be wise, ... 8085
Ec 5:1 be more ready to **h.**, than to give 8085
Ec 7:5 better to **h.** the rebuke of the wise, ... 8085
Ec 7:5 for a man to **h.** the song of fools........ 8085
Ec 7:21 lest thou **h.** thy servant curse thee:.... 8085
Ec 12:13 us **h.** the conclusion of the whole 8085
Ca 2:14 let me **h.** thy voice; for sweet is thy... 8085
Ca 8:13 to thy voice: cause me to **h.** it. 8085
Isa 1:2 **H.**, O heavens, and give ear, O......... 8085
Isa 1:10 **H.** the word of the Lord, ye rulers..... 8085
Isa 1:15 make many prayers, I will not **h.**: 8085
Isa 6:9 **H.** ye indeed, but understand not; 8085
Isa 6:10 **h.** with their ears, and understand...... 8085
Isa 7:13 said, **H.** ye now, O house of David;.... 8085
Isa 18:3 when he bloweth a trumpet, **h.** ye...... 8085
Isa 28:12 refreshing: yet they would not **h.**. 8085
Isa 28:14 **h.** the word of the Lord, ye scornful... 8085
Isa 28:23 Give ye ear, and **h.** my voice; 8085
Isa 28:23 voice; hearken, and **h.** my speech. 8085
Isa 29:18 And in that day shall the deaf **h.** the... 8085
Isa 30:9 children that will not **h.** the law of...... 8085
Isa 30:19 when he shall **h.** it, he will answer 8085
Isa 30:21 ears shall **h.** a word behind thee, ... 8085
Isa 32:3 ears of them that **h.** shall hearken, ... 8085
Isa 32:9 **h.** my voice, ye careless daughters;.... 8085
Isa 33:13 **H.**, ye that are far off, what I have 8085
Isa 34:1 Come near, ye nations, to **h.**; and...... 8085
Isa 34:1 the earth **h.**, and all that is therein; 8085
Isa 36:13 **H.** ye the words of the great king, ... 8085
Isa 37:4 the Lord thy God will **h.** the words 8085
Isa 37:7 and he shall **h.** a rumour, and............ 8085
Isa 37:17 Incline thine ear, O Lord, and **h.**;........ 8085
Isa 37:17 and **h.** all the words of Sennacherib, ... 8085
Isa 39:5 **H.** the word of the Lord of hosts: 8085
Isa 41:17 I the Lord will **h.** them, I the God 6030
Isa 42:18 **H.**, ye deaf; and look, ye blind, ... 8085
Isa 42:23 and **h.** for the time to come?............ 8085
Isa 43:9 or let them **h.**, and say, It is truth. 8085
Isa 44:1 Yet now **h.**, O Jacob my servant; 8085
Isa 47:8 Therefore **h.** now this, thou that art ... 8085
Isa 48:1 **H.** ye this, O house of Jacob, which ... 8085
Isa 48:14 All ye, assemble yourselves, and **h.**; ... 8085
Isa 48:16 Come ye near unto me, **h.** ye this;..... 8085
Isa 50:4 mine ear to **h.** as the learned. 8085
Isa 51:21 Therefore **h.** now this, thou afflicted, .. 8085
Isa 55:3 **h.**, and your soul shall live; and I 8085
Isa 59:1 his ear heavy, that it cannot **h.**: 8085
Isa 59:2 face from you, that he will not **h.**. 8085
Isa 65:12 when I spake, ye did not **h.**; but......... 8085
Isa 65:24 while they are yet speaking, I will **h.**. ..8085
Isa 66:4 when I spake, they did not **h.**: but 8085
Isa 66:5 **H.** the word of the Lord, ye that 8085
Jer 2:4 **H.** ye the word of the Lord, O house . 8085
Jer 4:21 and **h.** the sound of the trumpet?....... 8085
Jer 5:21 **H.** now this, O foolish people, and 8085
Jer 5:21 which have ears, and **h.** not: 8085
Jer 6:10 and give warning, that they may **h.**? ... 8085
Jer 6:18 Therefore **h.**, ye nations, and know, ... 8085
Jer 6:19 **H.**, O earth: behold, I will bring 8085
Jer 7:2 **H.** the word of the Lord, all ye of...... 8085
Jer 7:16 to me: for I will not **h.** thee. 8085
Jer 9:10 can men **h.** the voice of the cattle; 8085
Jer 9:20 **h.** the word of the Lord, O ye women, 8085
Jer 10:1 **H.** ye the word which the Lord 8085
Jer 11:2,6 **H.** ye the words of this covenant, ... 8085
Jer 11:10 which refused to **h.** my words, ... 8085
Jer 11:14 for I will not **h.** them in the time 8085
Jer 13:10 people, which refuse to **h.** my words, ..8085
Jer 13:11 for a glory: but they would not **h.**. 8085
Jer 13:15 **H.** ye, and give ear; be not proud: 8085
Jer 13:17 But if ye will not **h.** it, my soul shall... 8085
Jer 14:12 they fast, I will not **h.** their cry; 8085
Jer 17:20 **H.** ye the word of the Lord, ye kings . 8085
Jer 17:23 neck stiff, that they might not **h.**,........ 8085
Jer 18:2 I will cause thee to **h.** my words........ 8085
Jer 19:3 **H.** ye the word of the Lord, O kings .. 8085
Jer 19:15 that they might not **h.** my words........ 8085
Jer 20:16 let him **h.** the cry in the morning, ... 8085
Jer 21:11 say, **H.** ye the word of the Lord; 8085
Jer 22:2 **H.** the word of the Lord, O king of.... 8085
Jer 22:5 But if ye will not **h.** these words,....... 8085
Jer 22:21 but thou saidst, I will not **h.**............. 8085
Jer 22:29 O earth, earth, earth, **h.** the word 8085
Jer 23:22 caused my people to **h.** my words, ... 8085
Jer 25:4 nor inclined your ear to **h.**. 8085
Jer 28:7 **h.** thou now this word that I speak..... 8085
Jer 28:15 **H.** now, Hananiah; the Lord hath 8085
Jer 29:19 but ye would not **h.**, saith the Lord. ... 8085
Jer 29:20 **H.** ye therefore the word of the 8085
Jer 31:10 **H.** the word of the Lord, O ye.......... 8085
Jer 33:9 which shall **h.** all the good that I do.... 8085
Jer 34:4 Yet **h.** the word of the Lord, O 8085
Jer 36:3 Judah will **h.** all the evil which I 8085
Jer 36:25 the roll: but he would not **h.** them....... 8085
Jer 37:20 **h.** now, I pray thee, O my lord the 8085
Jer 38:25 if the princes **h.** that I have talked...... 8085
Jer 42:14 nor **h.** the sound of the trumpet,........ 8085
Jer 42:15 therefore **h.** the word of the Lord, ... 8085
Jer 44:24 **H.** the word of the Lord, all Judah 8085
Jer 44:26 **h.** ye the word of the Lord, all 8085
Jer 49:20 **h.** the counsel of the Lord, that the.... 8085
Jer 50:45 **h.** ye the counsel of the Lord, that..... 8085
La 1:18 **h.**, I pray you, all people, and 8085
Eze 2:5,7 whether they will **h.**, or whether........ 8085
Eze 2:8 **h.** what I say unto thee; Be not......... 8085
Eze 3:10 thine heart, and **h.** with thine ears...... 8085
Eze 3:11 whether they will **h.**, or whether........ 8085
Eze 3:17 therefore **h.** the word at my mouth, ... 8085
Eze 3:27 He that heareth, let him **h.**; and he 8085
Eze 6:3 **h.** the word of the Lord God: Thus 8085
Eze 8:18 a loud voice, yet will I not **h.** them..... 8085
Eze 12:2 they have ears to **h.**, and **h.** not: 8085
Eze 13:2 hearts, **H.** ye the word of the Lord; ... 8085
Eze 13:19 lying to my people that **h.** your lies? ... 8085
Eze 16:35 O harlot, **h.** the word of the Lord: 8085
Eze 18:25 **H.** now, O house of Israel; Is not 8085
Eze 20:47 **H.** the word of the Lord; Thus.......... 8085
Eze 24:26 to cause thee to **h.** it with thine......... 2045
Eze 25:3 **H.** the word of the Lord God;........... 8085
Eze 33:7 thou shalt **h.** the word at my mouth,... 8085
Eze 33:30 **h.** what is the word that cometh 8085
Eze 33:31 and they **h.** thy words, but they will... 8085
Eze 33:32 for they **h.** thy words, but they do..... 8085
Eze 34:7,9 ye shepherds, **h.** the word of the...... 8085
Eze 36:1 Ye mountains of Israel, **h.** the word.... 8085
Eze 36:4 **h.** the word of the Lord God; Thus 8085
Eze 36:15 Neither will I cause men to **h.** in......... 8085
Eze 37:4 O ye dry bones, **h.** the word of the...... 8085
Eze 40:4 **h.** with thine ears, and set thine 8085
Eze 44:5 **h.** with thine ears all that I say unto ... 8085
Da 3:5 time ye **h.** the sound of the cornet, ... 8086
Da 3:10 shall **h.** the sound of the cornet, ... 8086
Da 3:15 time ye **h.** the sound of the cornet, ... 8086
Da 5:23 which see not, nor **h.**, nor know: 8086
Da 9:17 **h.** the prayer of thy servant, and 8085
Da 9:18 O my God, incline thine ear, and **h.**;.... 8085
Da 9:19 O Lord, **h.**; O Lord, forgive; O Lord, . 8085
Ho 2:21 to pass in that day, I will **h.**, saith...... 6030
Ho 2:21 the Lord, I will **h.** the heavens, ... 6030
Ho 2:21 and they shall **h.** the earth;.............. 6030
Ho 2:22 And the earth shall **h.** the corn, ... 6030
Ho 2:22 the oil; and they shall **h.** Jezreel......... 6030
Ho 4:1 **H.** the word of the Lord, ye 8085
Ho 5:1 **H.** ye this, O priests; and hearken, ... 8085
Joe 1:2 **H.** this, ye old men, and give ear,...... 8085
Am 3:1 **H.** this word that the Lord hath......... 8085
Am 3:13 **H.** ye, and testify in the house of........ 8085
Am 4:1 **H.** this word, ye kine of Bashan, ... 8085
Am 5:1 **H.** ye this word which I take up 8085
Am 5:23 I will not **h.** the melody of thy viols, ... 8085
Am 7:16 **h.** thou the word of the Lord: Thou.... 8085
Am 8:4 **H.** this, O ye that swallow up the 8085
Mic 1:2 **H.**, all ye people; hearken, O earth, ... 8085
Mic 3:1 **H.**, I pray you, O heads of Jacob, ... 8085
Mic 3:4 the Lord, but he will not **h.** them:...... 6030
Mic 3:9 **H.** this, I pray you, ye heads of......... 8085
Mic 6:1 **H.** ye now what the Lord saith;.......... 8085
Mic 6:1 and let the hills **h.** thy voice............. 8085
Mic 6:2 **H.** ye, O mountains, the Lord's 8085
Mic 6:9 **h.** ye the rod, and who hath............. 8085
Mic 7:7 my salvation: my God will **h.** me........ 8085

Na 3:19 all that h. the bruit of thee shall 8085
Hab 1:2 shall I cry, and thou wilt not h.! 8085
Zec 1:4 but they did not h., nor hearken 8085
Zec 3:8 H. now, O Joshua the high priest, 8085
Zec 7:7 Should ye not h. the words which
Zec 7:11 their ears, that they should not h. 8085
Zec 7:12 lest they should h. the law, and the 8085
Zec 7:13 as he cried, and they would not h.; 8085
Zec 7:13 so they cried, and I would not h., 8085
Zec 8:9 be strong, ye that h. in these days 8085
Zec 10:6 Lord their God, and will h. them 6030
Zec 13:9 call on my name, and I will h. them: 6030
Mal 2:2 If ye will not h., and if ye will not 8085
Mt 10:14 not receive you, nor h. your words, 191
Mt 10:27 what ye h. in the ear, that preach 191
Mt 11:4 those things which ye do h. and see: 191
Mt 11:5 lepers are cleansed, and the deaf h., 191
Mt 11:15 He that ears to h., let him h. 191
Mt 12:19 any man h. his voice in the streets. 191
Mt 12:42 to h. the wisdom of Solomon; and, 191
Mt 13:9 Who hath ears to h., let him 191
Mt 13:9 Who hath ears...let him h. 191
Mt 13:13 see not; and hearing they h. not, 191
Mt 13:14 hearing ye shall h., and shall not 191
Mt 13:15 their eyes, and h. with their ears, 191
Mt 13:16 they see: and your ears, for they h. 191
Mt 13:17 and to h. those things which ye h., 191
Mt 13:18 H. ye therefore the parable of the 191
Mt 13:43 Who hath ears to h., let him 191
Mt 13:43 Who hath ears...let him h. 191
Mt 15:10 said unto them, H., and understand: 191
Mt 17:5 whom I am well pleased; h. ye him. 191
Mt 18:15 if he shall h. thee, thou hast gained. 191
Mt 18:16 if he will not h. thee, then take 191
Mt 18:17 And if he shall neglect to h. them, 3878
Mt 18:17 but if he neglect to h. the church, 3878
Mt 21:33 H. another parable: There was a 191
Mt 24:6 ye shall h. of wars and rumours of 191
Mk 4:9 He that hath ears to h., let him h. 191
Mk 4:12 they may h., and not understand; 191
Mk 4:18 among thorns; such as h. the word, 191
Mk 4:20 such as h. the word, and receive it, 191
Mk 4:23 any man have ears to h., let him h. 191
Mk 4:24 Take heed what ye h.: with what 191
Mk 4:24 you that h. shall more be given. 191
Mk 4:33 unto them, as they were able to h. it. 191
Mk 6:11 shall not receive you, nor h. you, 191
Mk 7:16 any man have ears to h., let him h. 191
Mk 7:37 he maketh both the deaf to h., and 191
Mk 8:18 see ye not? having ears, h. ye not? 191
Mk 9:7 This is my beloved Son: h. him. 191
Mk 12:29 H., O Israel; the Lord our God is 191
Mk 13:7 ye shall h. of wars and rumours of 191
Lu 5:1 upon him to h. the word of God, 191
Lu 5:15 multitudes came together to h., and 191
Lu 6:17 came to h. him, and to be healed of 191
Lu 6:27 I say unto you which h., Love your 191
Lu 7:22 lepers are cleansed, the deaf h., the 191
Lu 8:8 He that hath ears to h., let him h. 191
Lu 8:12 by the way side are they that h.; 191
Lu 8:13 they h., receive the word with 191
Lu 8:18 Take heed therefore how ye h.: for 191
Lu 8:21 which h. the word of God, and do it 191
Lu 9:9 is this, of whom I h. such things? 191
Lu 9:35 This is my beloved Son: h. him. 191
Lu 10:24 to h. those things which ye h., and 191
Lu 11:28 blessed are they that h. the word of 191
Lu 11:31 to h. the wisdom of Solomon; and, 191
Lu 14:35 He that hath ears to h., let him h. 191
Lu 15:1 publicans and sinners for to h. him. 191
Lu 16:2 How is it that I h. this of thee? 191
Lu 16:29 and the prophets; let them h. them. 191
Lu 16:31 they h. not Moses and the prophets, 191
Lu 18:6 said, H. what the unjust judge saith. 191
Lu 19:48 people were very attentive to h. him. 191
Lu 21:9 ye shall h. of wars and commotions, 191
Lu 21:38 to him in the temple, for to h. him. 191
Joh 5:25 the dead shall h. the voice of God: 191
Joh 5:25 God: and they that h. shall live. 191
Joh 5:28 are in the graves shall h. his voice, 191
Joh 5:30 as I h., I judge; and my judgment is 191
Joh 6:60 This is an hard saying; who can h. it? 191
Joh 7:51 law judge any man, before it h. him, 191
Joh 8:43 even because ye cannot h. my word. 191
Joh 8:47 ye therefore h. them not, because ye 191
Joh 9:27 told you already, and ye did not h.: 191
Joh 9:27 wherefore would ye h. it again? 191
Joh 10:3 and the sheep h. his voice: and he 191
Joh 10:8 but the sheep did not h. them. 191
Joh 10:16 and they shall h. my voice; and they 191
Joh 10:20 a devil, and is mad; why h. ye him? 191
Joh 10:27 My sheep h. my voice, and I know 191
Joh 12:47 if any man h. my words, and believe 191
Joh 14:24 the word which ye h. is not mine, 191
Joh 16:13 whatsoever he shall h., that shall he 191
Ac 2:8 h. we every man in our own tongue, 191
Ac 2:11 we do h. them speak in our tongues, 191
Ac 2:22 Ye men of Israel, h. these words; 191
Ac 2:33 forth this, which ye now see and h. 191
Ac 3:22 shall ye h. in all things whatsoever 191
Ac 3:23 which will not h. that prophet, 191
Ac 7:37 like unto me; him shall ye h. 191
Ac 10:22 his house, and to h. words of thee. 191
Ac 10:33 to h. all things that are commanded 191
Ac 13:7 and desired to h. the word of God. 191
Ac 13:44 city together, to h. the word of God. 191
Ac 15:7 should h. the word of the gospel, 191
Ac 17:21 either to tell, or to h. some new thing. 191
Ac 17:32 We will h. thee again of this matter. 191
Ac 19:26 see and h., that not alone at Ephesus, 191
Ac 21:22 for they will h. that thou art come. 191
Ac 22:1 h. ye my defence which I make 191
Ac 22:14 shouldest h. the voice of his mouth. 191
Ac 23:35 I will h. thee, said he, when thine 1251
Ac 24:4 wouldest h. us of thy clemency a 191
Ac 25:22 I would also h. the man myself. 191
Ac 25:22 morrow, said he, thou shalt h. him. 191
Ac 26:3 I beseech thee to h. me patiently. 191
Ac 26:29 thou, but also all that h. me this day, 191
Ac 28:22 to h. of thee what thou thinkest: 191
Ac 28:26 Hearing ye shall h., and shall not 191
Ac 28:27 their eyes, and h. with their ears, 191
Ac 28:28 the Gentiles, and that they will h. it. 191
Ro 10:14 shall they h. without a preacher? 191
Ro 11:8 see, and ears that they should not h.; 191
1Co 11:18 I h. that there be divisions among 191
1Co 14:21 yet for all that will they not h. me, 1522
Ga 4:21 under the law, do ye not h. the law? 191
Php 1:27 be absent, I may h. of your affairs, 191
Php 1:30 saw in me, and now h. to be in me. 191
2Th 3:11 h. that there are some which walk 191
1Ti 4:16 save thyself, and them that h. thee. 191
2Ti 4:17 and that all the Gentiles might h.: 191
Heb 3:7, 15 to day if ye will h. his voice, 191
Heb 4:7 said, To day if ye will h. his voice, 191
Jas 1:19 let every man be swift to h., slow to 191
1Jo 5:15 that he h. us, whatsoever we ask, 191
3Jo 4 no greater joy than to h. that my 191
Re 1:3 that h. the words of this prophecy, 191
Re 2:7, 11,17,29 that hath an ear, let him h. 191
Re 3:6, 13 He that hath an ear, let him h. 191
Re 3:20 if any man h. my voice, and open 191
Re 3:22 He that hath an ear, let him h. 191
Re 9:20 neither can see, nor h., nor walk: 191
Re 13:9 If any man have an ear, let him h. 191

HEARD See also HEARDEST.

Ge 3:8 And they h. the voice of the Lord 8085
Ge 3:10 I h. thy voice in the garden, and I 8085
Ge 14:14 Abraham h. that his brother was 8085
Ge 16:11 the Lord hath h. thy affliction. 8085
Ge 17:20 And as for Ishmael, I have h. thee: 8085
Ge 18:10 Sarah h. it in the tent door, which 8085
Ge 21:17 And God h. the voice of the lad; 8085
Ge 21:17 God hath h. the voice of the lad 8085
Ge 21:26 thou tell me, neither yet h. I of it, 8085
Ge 24:30 when he h. the words of Rebekah 8085
Ge 24:52 Abraham's servant h. their words, 8085
Ge 27:5 Rebekah h. when Isaac spake to 8085
Ge 27:6 I h. thy father speak unto Esau thy 8085
Ge 27:34 And when Esau h. the words of his 8085
Ge 29:13 when Laban h. the tidings of Jacob 8085
Ge 29:33 the Lord hath h. that I was hated, 8085
Ge 30:6 and hath also h. my voice, and hath 8085
Ge 31:1 he h. the words of Laban's sons, 8085
Ge 34:5 And Jacob h. that he had defiled 8085
Ge 34:7 came out of the field when they h. it: 8085
Ge 35:22 father's concubine: and Israel h. it. 8085
Ge 37:17 I h. them say, Let us go to Dothan. 8085
Ge 37:21 And Reuben h. it, and he delivered 8085
Ge 39:15 when he h. that I lifted up my voice 8085
Ge 39:19 his master h. the words of his wife, 8085
Ge 41:15 have h. say of thee, that thou canst 8085
Ge 42:2 have h. that there is corn in Egypt: 8085
Ge 43:25 they h. that they should eat bread 8085
Ge 45:2 and the house of Pharaoh h. 8085
Ge 45:16 fame thereof was h. in Pharaoh's 8085
Ex 2:15 Now when Pharaoh h. this thing, he 8085
Ex 2:24 And God h. their groaning, and 8085
Ex 3:7 have h. their cry by reason of their 8085
Ex 4:31 they h. that the Lord had visited 8085
Ex 6:5 I have also h. the groaning of the 8085
Ex 16:9 for he hath h. your murmurings. 8085
Ex 16:12 I have h. the murmurings of the 8085
Ex 18:1 Midian, Moses' father in law, h. of all 8085
Ex 23:13 neither let it be h. out of thy mouth. 8085
Ex 28:35 be h. when he goeth into the holy 8085
Ex 32:17 Joshua h. the noise of the people 8085
Ex 33:4 the people h. these evil tidings, 8085
Le 10:20 when Moses h. that, he was content. 8085
Le 24:14 let all that h. him lay their hands 8085
Nu 7:89 then he h. the voice of one speaking 8085
Nu 11:1 and the Lord h. it; and his anger 8085
Nu 11:10 Then Moses h. the people weep 8085
Nu 12:2 also by us? And the Lord h. it. 8085
Nu 14:14 have h. that thou Lord art seen face 8085
Nu 14:15 the nations which have h. the fame 8085
Nu 14:27 I have h. the murmurings of the 8085
Nu 16:4 Moses h. it, he fell upon his face: 8085
Nu 20:16 he h. our voice, and sent an angel, 8085
Nu 21:1 h. tell that Israel came by the way 8085
Nu 22:36 Balak h. that Balaam was come, 8085
Nu 24:4 which h. the words of God, which 8085
Nu 24:16 which h. the words of God, and 8085
Nu 30:7 husband h. it, and held his peace 8085
Nu 30:7 at her in the day that he h. it: 8085
Nu 30:8 the day that he h. it; then he shall 8085
Nu 30:11 husband h. it, and held his peace 8085
Nu 30:12 them void on the day he h. them; 8085
Nu 30:14 at her in the day that he h. them. 8085
Nu 30:15 void after that he hath h. them; 8085
Nu 33:40 h. of the coming of the children of 8085
De 1:34 the Lord h. the voice of your words, 8085
De 4:12 ye h. the voice of the words, but saw 8085
De 4:12 no similitude; only ye h. a voice. 8085
De 4:32 thing is, or hath been h. like it? 8085
De 4:33 of the fire, as thou hast h., and live? 8085
De 5:23 ye h. the voice out of the midst 8085
De 5:24 have h. his voice out of the midst 8085
De 5:26 hath h. the voice of the living God 8085
De 5:28 the Lord h. the voice of your words, 8085
De 5:28 I have h. the voice of the words of 8085
De 9:2 and of whom thou hast h. say, 8085
De 17:4 be told thee, and thou hast h. of it, 8085
De 26:7 the Lord h. our voice, and looked 8085
Jos 2:10 we have h. how the Lord dried up 8085
Jos 2:11 as soon as we had h. these things, 8085
Jos 5:1 h. that the Lord had dried up 8085
Jos 6:20 people h. the sound of the trumpet, 8085
Jos 9:1 Hivite, and the Jebusite, h. thereof; 8085
Jos 9:3 when the inhabitants of Gibeon h. 8085
Jos 9:9 for we have h. the fame of him, 8085
Jos 9:16 h. that they were their neighbours, 8085
Jos 10:1 had h. how Joshua had taken Ai, 8085
Jos 11:1 when Jabin king of Hazor had h. 8085
Jos 22:11 And the children of Israel h. say, 8085
Jos 22:12 when the children of Israel h. of it, 8085
Jos 22:30 h. the words that the children of 8085
Jos 24:27 it hath h. all the words of the Lord 8085
Jg 7:15 Gideon h. the telling of the dream, 8085
Jg 9:30 ruler of the city h. the words of Gaal 8085
Jg 9:46 the men of the tower of Shechem h. 8085
Jg 18:25 Let not thy voice be h. among us. 8085
Jg 20:3 Now the children of Benjamin h. 8085
Ru 1:6 she had h. in the country of Moab 8085
1Sa 1:13 lips moved, but her voice was not h.; 8085
1Sa 2:22 and h. all that his sons did unto all 8085
1Sa 4:6 Philistines h. the noise of the shout, 8085
1Sa 4:14 when Eli h. the noise of the crying, 8085
1Sa 4:19 h. the tidings that the ark of God 8085
1Sa 7:7 when the Philistines h. that the 8085
1Sa 7:7 when the children of Israel h. it, 8085
1Sa 7:9 for Israel; and the Lord h. him. 6030
1Sa 8:21 And Samuel h. all the words of the 8085
1Sa 11:6 upon Saul when he h. those tidings, 8085
1Sa 13:3 in Geba, and the Philistines h. of it. 8085
1Sa 13:4 Israel h. say that Saul had smitten 8085
1Sa 14:22 they h. that the Philistines fled, 8085
1Sa 14:27 Jonathan h. not when his father 8085
1Sa 17:11 Saul and all Israel h. those words 8085
1Sa 17:23 the same words: and David h. them, 8085

1Sa 17:28 And Eliab his eldest brother **h.** 8085
1Sa 17:31 And when the words were **h.** 8085
1Sa 22:1 all his father's house **h.** it, they 8085
1Sa 22:6 Saul **h.** that David was discovered, ... 8085
1Sa 23:10 hath certainly **h.** that Saul seeketh...... 8085
1Sa 23:11 come down, as thy servant hath **h.**? ... 8085
1Sa 23:25 And when Saul **h.** that, he pursued...... 8085
1Sa 25:4 And David **h.** in the wilderness.......... 8085
1Sa 25:7 I have **h.** that thou hast shearers: 8085
1Sa 25:39 David **h.** that Nabal was dead, ... 8085
1Sa 31:11 inhabitants of Jabesh-gilead **h.** of 8085
2Sa 3:28 afterward when David **h.** it, he 8085
2Sa 4:1 Saul's son **h.** that Abner was dead....... 8085
2Sa 5:17 Philistines **h.** that they had anointed.... 8085
2Sa 5:17 and David **h.** of it, and went down...... 8085
2Sa 7:22 to all that we have **h.** with our ears.... 8085
2Sa 8:9 Toi king of Hamath **h.** that David 8085
2Sa 10:7 when David **h.** of it, he sent Joab, ... 8085
2Sa 11:26 the wife of Uriah **h.** that Uriah 8085
2Sa 13:21 But when king David **h.** of all these.... 8085
2Sa 18:5 the people **h.** when the king gave....... 8085
2Sa 19:2 people **h.** say that day how the king ... 8085
1Ki 1:11 hast thou not **h.** that Adonijah 8085
1Ki 1:41 **h.** it as they had made an end of........ 8085
1Ki 1:41 Joab **h.** the sound of the trumpet, ... 8085
1Ki 1:45 This is the noise that ye have **h.**........ 8085
1Ki 2:42 The word that I have **h.** is good. 8085
1Ki 3:28 And all Israel **h.** of the judgment......... 8085
1Ki 4:34 earth, which had **h.** of his wisdom. 8085
1Ki 5:1 he had **h.** that they had anointed........ 8085
1Ki 5:7 Hiram **h.** the words of Solomon, ... 8085
1Ki 6:7 nor any tool of iron **h.** in the house, ... 8085
1Ki 9:3 I have **h.** thy prayer and thy 8085
1Ki 10:1 the queen of Sheba **h.** of the fame...... 8085
1Ki 10:6 report that I **h.** in mine own land 8085
1Ki 10:7 exceedeth the fame which I **h.**........... 8085
1Ki 11:21 when Hadad **h.** in Egypt that David 8085
1Ki 12:2 Jeroboam the son of Nebat,...**h.** of it, . 8085
1Ki 12:20 when all Israel **h.** that Jeroboam......... 8085
1Ki 13:4 when king Jeroboam **h.** the saying...... 8085
1Ki 13:26 him back from the way **h.** thereof, ... 8085
1Ki 14:6 Ahijah **h.** the sound of her feet, ... 8085
1Ki 15:21 when Baasha **h.** thereof, that he 8085
1Ki 16:16 people that were encamped **h.** say,..... 8085
1Ki 17:22 the Lord **h.** the voice of Elijah;.......... 8085
1Ki 19:13 when Elijah **h.** it, that he wrapped...... 8085
1Ki 20:12 when Ben-hadad **h.** this message,....... 8085
1Ki 20:31 we have **h.** that the kings of the 8085
1Ki 21:15 Jezebel **h.** that Naboth was stoned,..... 8085
1Ki 21:16 when Ahab **h.** that Naboth was dead, .. 8085
1Ki 21:27 to pass, when Ahab **h.** those words, ... 8085
2Ki 3:21 Moabites **h.** that the kings were 8085
2Ki 5:8 when Elisha the man of God had **h.**..... 8085
2Ki 6:30 the king **h.** the words of the woman, .. 8085
2Ki 9:30 come to Jezreel, Jezebel **h.** of it;....... 8085
2Ki 11:13 Athaliah **h.** the noise of the guard....... 8085
2Ki 19:1 to pass, when king Hezekiah **h.** it, ... 8085
2Ki 19:4 which the Lord thy God hath **h.**:......... 8085
2Ki 19:6 of the words which thou hast **h.**,......... 8085
2Ki 19:8 for he had **h.** that he was departed..... 8085
2Ki 19:9 And when he **h.** say of Tirhakah 8085
2Ki 19:11 hast **h.** what the kings of Assyria 8085
2Ki 19:20 king of Assyria I have **h.**.................. 8085
2Ki 19:25 Hast thou not **h.** long ago how I 8085
2Ki 20:5 **h.** thy prayer, I have seen thy tears, .. 8085
2Ki 20:12 had **h.** that Hezekiah had been sick..... 8085
2Ki 22:11 king had **h.** the words of the book...... 8085
2Ki 22:18 the words which thou hast **h.**; 8085
2Ki 22:19 I also have **h.** thee, saith the Lord. 8085
2Ki 25:23 **h.** that the king of Babylon had.......... 8085
1Ch 10:11 when all Jabesh-gilead **h.** all that 8085
1Ch 14:8 **h.** that David was anointed king.......... 8085
1Ch 14:8 David **h.** of it, and went out against.... 8085
1Ch 17:20 to all that we have **h.** with our ears.... 8085
1Ch 18:9 Tou king of Hamath **h.** how David....... 8085
1Ch 19:8 when David **h.** of it, he sent Joab,...... 8085
2Ch 5:13 make one sound to be **h.** in praising ... 8085
2Ch 7:12 have **h.** thy prayer, and have chosen... 8085
2Ch 9:1 the queen of Sheba **h.** of the fame...... 8085
2Ch 9:5 report which I **h.** in mine own land..... 8085
2Ch 9:6 thou exceedest the fame that I **h.**. 8085
2Ch 10:2 Jeroboam the son of Nebat,...**h.** it, ... 8085
2Ch 15:8 And when Asa **h.** these words, and 8085
2Ch 16:5 when Baasha **h.** it, that he left off...... 8085
2Ch 20:29 they had **h.** that the Lord fought........ 8085
2Ch 23:12 Athaliah **h.** the noise of the people 8085
2Ch 30:27 and their voice was **h.**, and their........ 8085
2Ch 33:13 and **h.** his supplication, and brought 8085
2Ch 34:19 king had **h.** the words of the law,....... 8085
2Ch 34:26 the words which thou hast **h.**; 8085
2Ch 34:27 I have even **h.** thee also, saith the 8085
Ezr 3:13 shout, and the noise was **h.** afar off.... 8085
Ezr 4:1 of Judah and Benjamin **h.** that the....... 8085
Ezr 9:3 And when I **h.** this thing, I rent my.... 8085
Ne 1:4 when I **h.** these words, that I sat....... 8085
Ne 2:10 Ammonite, **h.** of it, it grieved them 8085
Ne 2:19 Arabian, **h.** it, they laughed us to....... 8085
Ne 4:1 when Sanballat **h.** that we builded....... 8085
Ne 4:7 **h.** that the walls of Jerusalem were 8085
Ne 4:15 our enemies **h.** that it was known 8085
Ne 5:6 I was very angry when I **h.** their cry .. 8085
Ne 6:1 **h.** that I had builded the wall,........... 8085
Ne 6:16 when all our enemies **h.** thereof,......... 8085
Ne 8:9 when they **h.** the words of the law..... 8085
Ne 12:43 joy of Jerusalem was **h.** even afar off. ..8085
Ne 13:3 when they had **h.** the law, that they ...8085
Es 1:18 have **h.** of the deed of the queen. 8085
Es 2:8 commandment and...decree was **h.**,.... 8085
Job 2:11 when Job's three friends **h.** of all........ 8085
Job 4:16 there was silence, and I **h.** a voice, ... 8085
Job 13:1 mine ear hath **h.** and understood it..... 8085
Job 15:8 Hast thou **h.** the secret of God? 8085
Job 16:2 I have **h.** many such things: 8085
Job 19:7 I cry out of wrong, but I am not **h.**: ... 6030
Job 20:3 have **h.** the check of my reproach, ... 8085
Job 26:14 how little a portion is **h.** of him? 8085
Job 28:22 We have **h.** the fame thereof with...... 8085
Job 29:11 When the ear **h.** me, then it blessed... 8085
Job 33:8 and I have **h.** the voice of thy words, ..8085
Job 37:4 not stay them when his voice is **h.**..... 8085
Job 42:5 I have **h.** of thee by the hearing of..... 8085
Ps 3:4 and he **h.** me out of his holy hill. 6030
Ps 6:8 hath **h.** the voice of my weeping. 8085
Ps 6:9 The Lord hath **h.** my supplication;...... 8085
Ps 10:17 hast **h.** the desire of the humble: 8085
Ps 18:6 he **h.** my voice out of his temple,....... 8085
Ps 19:3 language, where their voice is not **h.**, . 8085
Ps 22:21 thou hast **h.** me from the horns of...... 6030
Ps 22:24 when he cried unto him, he **h.**........... 8085
Ps 28:6 **h.** the voice of my supplications. 8085
Ps 31:13 For I have **h.** the slander of many: 8085
Ps 34:4 I sought the Lord, and he **h.** me,...... 6030
Ps 34:6 poor man cried, and the Lord **h.** 8085
Ps 38:13 But I, as a deaf man, **h.** not;.............. 8085
Ps 40:1 he inclined unto me, and **h.** my cry 8085
Ps 44:1 We have **h.** with our ears, O God, ... 8085
Ps 48:8 As we have **h.**, so have we seen in.... 8085
Ps 61:5 For thou, O God, hast **h.** my vows: ... 8085
Ps 62:11 twice have I **h.** this; that power......... 8085
Ps 66:8 make the voice of his praise to be **h.**: . 8085
Ps 66:19 But verily God hath **h.** me; he hath.... 8085
Ps 76:8 didst cause judgment to be **h.** from..... 8085
Ps 78:3 Which we have **h.** and known, and 8085
Ps 78:21 the Lord **h.** this, and was wroth: 8085
Ps 78:59 When God h. this, he was wroth, ... 8085
Ps 81:5 **h.** a language that I understood not. ... 8085
Ps 97:8 Zion **h.**, and was glad; and the........... 8085
Ps 106:44 their affliction, when he **h.** their cry:... 8085
Ps 116:1 because he hath **h.** my voice and 8085
Ps 118:21 **h.** me, and...become my salvation. 6030
Ps 120:1 cried unto the Lord, and he **h.** me. 6030
Ps 132:6 Lo, we **h.** of it at Ephratah:.............. 8085
Pr 21:13 cry himself, but shall not be **h.**. 6030
Ec 9:16 despised, and his words are not **h.**. 8085
Ec 9:17 words of wise men are **h.** in quiet...... 8085
Ca 2:12 voice of the turtle is **h.** in our land; 8085
Isa 6:8 Also I **h.** the voice of the Lord, ... 8085
Isa 10:30 cause it to be **h.** unto Laish, ... 7181
Isa 15:4 voice shall be **h.** even unto Jahaz: 8085
Isa 16:6 We have **h.** of the pride of Moab; 8085
Isa 21:10 that which I have **h.** of the Lord of...... 8085
Isa 24:16 part of the earth have we **h.** songs,.... 8085
Isa 28:22 for I have **h.** from the Lord of hosts... 8085
Isa 30:30 cause his glorious voice to be **h.**, ... 8085
Isa 37:1 to pass, when king Hezekiah **h.** it, ... 8085
Isa 37:4 which the Lord thy God hath **h.**:......... 8085
Isa 37:6 afraid of the words that thou hast **h.**,.. 8085
Isa 37:8 he had **h.** that he was departed 8085
Isa 37:9 And he **h.** say concerning Tirhakah..... 8085
Isa 37:9 when he **h.** it, he sent messengers...... 8085
Isa 37:11 hast **h.** what the kings of Assyria 8085
Isa 37:26 Hast thou not **h.** long ago, how I 8085
Isa 38:5 I have **h.** thy prayer, I have seen....... 8085
Isa 39:1 for he had **h.** that he had been sick, ... 8085
Isa 40:21 have ye not known? have ye not **h.**?... 8085
Isa 40:28 hast thou not **h.**, that the everlasting .. 8085
Isa 42:2 cause his voice to be **h.** in the street...8085
Isa 48:6 Thou hast **h.**, see all this; and will...... 8085
Isa 49:8 In an acceptable time have I **h.**.......... 6030
Isa 52:15 had not **h.** shall they consider............ 8085
Isa 58:4 to make your voice to be **h.** on high. .. 8085
Isa 60:18 Violence shall no more be **h.** in thy 8085
Isa 64:4 men have not **h.**, nor perceived by..... 8085
Isa 65:19 voice of weeping shall be no more **h.** .. 8085
Isa 66:8 Who hath **h.** such a thing? who.......... 8085
Isa 66:19 isles...that have not **h.** my fame,........ 8085
Jer 3:21 voice was **h.** upon the high places, ... 8085
Jer 4:19 thou hast **h.**, O my soul, the sound 8085
Jer 4:31 For I have **h.** a voice as of a woman... 8085
Jer 6:7 violence and spoil is **h.** in her; 8085
Jer 6:24 We have **h.** the fame thereof: our 8085
Jer 7:13 early and speaking, but ye **h.** not; 8085
Jer 8:6 I hearkened and **h.**, but they spake 8085
Jer 8:16 The snorting of his horses was **h.** 8085
Jer 9:19 a voice of wailing is **h.** out of Zion,..... 8085
Jer 18:13 heathen, who hath **h.** such things; 8085
Jer 18:22 Let a cry be **h.** from their houses, ... 8085
Jer 20:1 **h.** that Jeremiah prophesied these 8085
Jer 20:10 For I **h.** the defaming of many,.......... 8085
Jer 23:18 hath perceived and **h.** his word?......... 8085
Jer 23:18 hath marked his word, and **h.** it?........ 8085
Jer 23:25 I have **h.** what the prophets said,....... 8085
Jer 25:8 Because ye have not **h.** my words,...... 8085
Jer 25:36 principal of the flock, shall be **h.**: 8085
Jer 26:7 the prophets and all the people **h.** 8085
Jer 26:10 When the princes of Judah **h.** these 8085
Jer 26:11 city, as ye have **h.** with your ears. 8085
Jer 26:12 all the words that ye have **h.**............ 8085
Jer 26:21 and all the princes, **h.** his words, ... 8085
Jer 26:21 but when Urijah **h.** it, he was afraid,... 8085
Jer 30:5 We have **h.** a voice of trembling, ... 8085
Jer 31:15 voice was **h.** in Ramah, lamentation, ... 8085
Jer 31:18 have surely **h.** Ephraim bemoaning 8085
Jer 33:10 Again there shall be **h.** in this place, ... 8085
Jer 34:10 **h.** that every one should let his 8085
Jer 35:17 unto them, but they have not **h.**; 8085
Jer 36:11 had **h.** out of the book all the words ... 8085
Jer 36:13 them all the words that he had **h.**, ... 8085
Jer 36:16 pass, when they had **h.** all the words,. 8085
Jer 36:24 his servants that **h.** all these words. ... 8085
Jer 37:5 that besieged Jerusalem **h.** tidings 8085
Jer 38:1 **h.** the words that Jeremiah had.......... 8085
Jer 38:7 **h.** that they had put Jeremiah in......... 8085
Jer 40:7 **h.** that the king of Babylon had.......... 8085
Jer 40:11 **h.** that the king of Babylon had left..... 8085
Jer 41:11 **h.** of all the evil that Ishmael............ 8085
Jer 42:4 said unto them, I have **h.** you; 8085
Jer 46:12 The nations have **h.** of thy shame, ... 8085
Jer 48:4 little ones have caused a cry to be **h.**.. 8085
Jer 48:5 enemies have **h.** a cry of destruction... 8085
Jer 48:29 We have **h.** the pride of Moab, ... 8085
Jer 49:2 will cause an alarm of war to be **h.**..... 8085
Jer 49:14 I have **h.** a rumour from the Lord, ... 8085
Jer 49:21 noise thereof was **h.** in the Red sea.... 8085
Jer 49:23 for they have **h.** evil tidings; 8085
Jer 50:43 king of Babylon hath **h.** the report...... 8085
Jer 50:46 and the cry is **h.** among the nations.... 8085
Jer 51:46 rumour that shall be **h.** in the land:..... 8085
Jer 51:51 because we have **h.** reproach: 8085
La 1:21 They have **h.** that I sigh: there is 8085
La 1:21 mine enemies have **h.** of my trouble; .. 8085
La 3:56 Thou hast **h.** my voice; hide not 8085
La 3:61 Thou hast **h.** their reproach, O lord,.... 8085
Eze 1:24 went, I **h.** the noise of their wings, ... 8085
Eze 1:28 and I **h.** a voice of one that spake. 8085
Eze 2:2 that I **h.** him that spake unto me........ 8085
Eze 3:12 I **h.** behind me a voice of great.......... 8085
Eze 3:13 I **h.** also the voice of the wings of...... 8085
Eze 10:5 the cherubims' wings was **h.** even...... 8085
Eze 19:4 The nations also **h.** of him; he was..... 8085
Eze 19:9 no more be **h.** upon the mountains 8085
Eze 26:13 of thy harps shall be no more **h.**. 8085
Eze 27:30 And shall cause their voice to be **h.**.... 8085
Eze 33:5 He **h.** the sound of the trumpet, ... 8085
Eze 35:12 I have **h.** all thy blasphemies which..... 8085
Eze 35:13 words against me: I have **h.** them. 8085
Eze 43:6 And I **h.** him speaking unto me out..... 8085
Da 3:7 people **h.** the sound of the cornet,...... 8086
Da 5:14 have even **h.** of thee, that the spirit ... 8086
Da 5:16 I have **h.** of thee, that thou canst....... 8086
Da 6:14 the king, when he **h.** these words, ... 8086

Book	Ref	Context	No.
Da	8:13	Then I **h.** one saint speaking, and......	8085
Da	8:16	And I **h.** a man's voice between the....	8085
Da	10:9	Yet **h.** I the voice of his words:.........	8085
Da	10:9	and when I **h.** the voice of his words, .	8085
Da	10:12	thy words were **h.**, and I am come......	8085
Da	12:7	And I **h.** the man clothed in linen,......	8085
Da	12:8	And I **h.**, but I understood not:	8085
Ho	7:12	them, as their congregation hath **h.**. ...	8085
Ho	14:8	I have **h.** him, and observed him:.......	6030
Ob	1	We have **h.** a rumour from the..........	8085
Jon	2:2	unto the Lord, and he **h.** me;............	6030
Mic	5:15	heathen, such as they have not **h.**......	8085
Na	2:13	thy messengers shall no more be **h.**. ..	8085
Hab	3:2	O Lord, I have **h.** thy speech, and.....	8085
Hab	3:16	When I **h.**, my belly trembled; my......	8085
Zep	2:8	I have **h.** the reproach of Moab, ...	8085
Zec	8:23	for we have **h.** that God is with you....	8085
Mal	3:16	and the Lord hearkened, and **h.** it, ...	8085
Mt	2:3	When Herod the king had **h.** these.......	*191*
Mt	2:9	When they had **h.** the king, they	*191*
Mt	2:18	In Rama was there a voice **h.**, ...	*191*
Mt	2:22	when he **h.** that Archelaus did reign.....	*191*
Mt	4:12	Jesus had **h.** that John was cast into.....	*191*
Mt	5:21,	27 **Ye have h. that it was said by**....	*191*
Mt	5:33	**ye have h. that it hath been said by.**	*191*
Mt	5:38,	43 **Ye have h. that it hath been**......	*191*
Mt	6:7	**be h. for their much speaking**......	*1522*
Mt	8:10	When Jesus **h.** it, he marvelled, and.....	*191*
Mt	9:12	But when Jesus **h.** that, he said unto....	*191*
Mt	11:2	when John had **h.** in the prison the	*191*
Mt	12:24	when the Pharisees **h.** it, they said, ...	*191*
Mt	13:17	**ye hear, and have not h. them**........	*191*
Mt	14:1	Herod the tetrarch **h.** of the fame of....	*191*
Mt	14:13	When Jesus **h.** of it, he departed.........	*191*
Mt	14:13	people had **h.** thereof, they followed.....	*191*
Mt	15:12	offended, after they **h.** this saying?	*191*
Mt	17:6	when the disciples **h.** it, they fell on.....	*191*
Mt	19:22	when the young man **h.** that saying,.....	*191*
Mt	19:25	When his disciples **h.** it, they were	*191*
Mt	20:24	when the ten **h.** it, they were moved....	*191*
Mt	20:30	when they **h.** that Jesus passed by,......	*191*
Mt	21:45	chief priests and Pharisees had **h.**........	*191*
Mt	22:7	**the king h. thereof, he was wroth:**..	*191*
Mt	22:22	had **h.** these words, they marvelled,......	*191*
Mt	22:33	when the multitude **h.** this, they were ..	*191*
Mt	22:34	had **h.** that he had put the Sadducees...	*191*
Mt	26:65	now ye have **h.** his blasphemy.	*191*
Mt	27:47	they **h.** that, said, This man calleth......	*191*
Mk	2:17	When Jesus **h.** it, he saith unto them,...	*191*
Mk	3:8	when they had **h.** what great things.....	*191*
Mk	3:21	when his friends **h.** of it, they went	*191*
Mk	4:15	**when they have h., Satan cometh**...	*191*
Mk	4:16	**who, when they have h. the word,**..	*191*
Mk	5:27	When she had **h.** of Jesus, came..........	*191*
Mk	5:36	As soon as Jesus **h.** the word that........	*191*
Mk	6:14	king Herod **h.** of him; for his name	*191*
Mk	6:16	Herod **h.** thereof, he said, It is John,....	*191*
Mk	6:20	when he **h.** him, he did many things,....	*191*
Mk	6:20	did many things, and **h.** him gladly.......	*191*
Mk	6:29	when his disciples **h.** of it, they came....	*191*
Mk	6:55	that were sick, where they **h.** he was...	*191*
Mk	7:25	had an unclean spirit, **h.** of him, ...	*191*
Mk	10:41	when the ten **h.** it, they began to be....	*191*
Mk	10:47	when he **h.** that it was Jesus of..........	*191*
Mk	11:14	**for ever.** And his disciples **h.** it.	*191*
Mk	11:18	the scribes and chief priests **h.** it,.........	*191*
Mk	12:28	having **h.** them reasoning together, ...	*191*
Mk	12:37	the common people **h.** him gladly.........	*191*
Mk	14:11	And when they **h.** it, they were glad, ...	*191*
Mk	14:58	We **h.** him say, I will destroy this........	*191*
Mk	14:64	Ye have **h.** the blasphemy: what..........	*191*
Mk	15:35	**h.** it, said, Behold, he calleth Elias.......	*191*
Mk	16:11	when they had **h.** that he was alive, ...	*191*
Lu	1:13	for thy prayer is **h.**; and thy wife.........	*1522*
Lu	1:41	when Elisabeth **h.** the salutation of.........	*191*
Lu	1:58	cousins **h.** how the Lord had shewed....	*191*
Lu	1:66	**h.** them laid them up in their hearts, ...	*191*
Lu	2:18	all they that **h.** it, wondered at those....	*191*
Lu	2:20	things that they had **h.** and seen,.........	*191*
Lu	2:47	all that **h.** him were astonished at his ...	*191*
Lu	4:23	**we have h. done in Capernaum, do**..	*191*
Lu	4:28	when they **h.** these things, were filled ..	*191*
Lu	7:3	when he **h.** of Jesus, he sent unto	*191*
Lu	7:9	Jesus **h.** these things, he marvelled	*191*
Lu	7:22	**what things ye have seen and h.;**....	*191*
Lu	7:29	all the people that **h.** him, and the	*191*
Lu	8:14	**which, when they have h., go forth,**	*191*
Lu	8:15	**having h. the word, keep it, and**.....	*191*
Lu	8:50	when Jesus **h.** it, he answered him, ...	*191*
Lu	9:7	Herod the tetrarch **h.** of all that was	*191*
Lu	10:24	**ye hear, and have not h. them**.........	*191*
Lu	10:39	sat at Jesus' feet, and **h.** his word.	*191*
Lu	12:3	**in darkness shall be h. in the light;**	*191*
Lu	14:15	sat at meat with him **h.** these things, ...	*191*
Lu	15:25	**house, he h. musick and dancing**...	*191*
Lu	16:14	were covetous, **h.** all these things:.......	*191*
Lu	18:22	when Jesus **h.** these things, he said	*191*
Lu	18:23	he **h.** this, he was very sorrowful:	*191*
Lu	18:26	**h.** it said, Who then can be saved?	*191*
Lu	19:11	as they **h.** these things, he added........	*191*
Lu	20:16	they **h.** it, they said, God forbid.	*191*
Lu	22:71	ourselves have **h.** of his own mouth.	*191*
Lu	23:6	When Pilate **h.** of Galilee, he asked......	*191*
Lu	23:8	he had **h.** many things of him;............	*191*
Joh	1:37	the two disciples **h.** him speak, and......	*191*
Joh	1:40	One of the two which **h.** John speak,.....	*191*
Joh	3:32	hath seen and **h.**, that he testifieth;......	*191*
Joh	4:1	Pharisees had **h.** that Jesus made	*191*
Joh	4:42	for we have **h.** him ourselves, and	*191*
Joh	4:47	When he **h.** that Jesus was come out....	*191*
Joh	5:37	**Ye have neither h. his voice at any**..	*191*
Joh	6:45	**Every man therefore that hath h.,**..	*191*
Joh	6:60	disciples, when they had **h.** this, said,...	*191*
Joh	7:32	The Pharisees **h.** that the people	*191*
Joh	7:40	when they **h.** this saying, said, Of a	*191*
Joh	8:6	the ground, as though he **h.** them not...	*191*
Joh	8:9	they which **h.** it, being convicted by	*191*
Joh	8:26	**those things which I have h. of him**	*191*
Joh	8:40	**the truth, which I have h. of God:**..	*191*
Joh	9:32	world began was it not **h.** that any.......	*191*
Joh	9:35	Jesus **h.** that they had cast him out;.....	*191*
Joh	9:40	Pharisees which were with him **h.**........	*191*
Joh	11:4	Jesus **h.** that, he said, **This sickness**..	*191*
Joh	11:6	had **h.** therefore that he was sick, ...	*191*
Joh	11:20	soon as she **h.** that Jesus was coming,..	*191*
Joh	11:29	As soon as she **h.** that, she arose........	*191*
Joh	11:41	**I thank thee that thou hast h. me**..	*191*
Joh	12:12	when they **h.** that Jesus was coming.....	*191*
Joh	12:18	**h.** that he had done this miracle.	*191*
Joh	12:29	and **h.** it, said that it thundered:	*191*
Joh	12:34	have **h.** out of the law that Christ........	*191*
Joh	14:28	**Ye have h. how I said unto you, I**..	*191*
Joh	15:15	**things that I have h. of my Father**..	*191*
Joh	18:21	**ask them which h. me, what I have**	*191*
Joh	19:8	When Pilate...**h.** that saying, he was	*191*
Joh	19:13	Pilate...**h.** that saying, he brought.......	*191*
Joh	21:7	Simon Peter **h.** that it was the Lord,....	*191*
Ac	1:4	**which,** saith he, **ye have h. of me**....	*191*
Ac	2:6	every man **h.** them speak in his own....	*191*
Ac	2:37	when they **h.** this, they were pricked....	*191*
Ac	4:4	of them which **h.** the word believed;	*191*
Ac	4:20	things which we have seen and **h.**........	*191*
Ac	4:24	they **h.** that, they lifted up their voice ..	*191*
Ac	5:5	fear came on all them that **h.** these......	*191*
Ac	5:11	upon as many as **h.** these things..........	*191*
Ac	5:21	when they **h.** that, they entered into....	*191*
Ac	5:24	priests **h.** these things, they doubted....	*191*
Ac	5:33	When they **h.** that, they were cut to....	*191*
Ac	6:11	We have **h.** him speak blasphemous	*191*
Ac	6:14	have **h.** him say, that this Jesus	*191*
Ac	7:12	when Jacob **h.** that there was corn in ...	*191*
Ac	7:34	have **h.** their groaning, and am come....	*191*
Ac	7:54	they **h.** these things, they were cut	*191*
Ac	8:14	at Jerusalem **h.** that Samaria had	*191*
Ac	8:30	and **h.** him read the prophet Esaias, ...	*191*
Ac	9:4	he fell to the earth, and **h.** a voice.......	*191*
Ac	9:13	I have **h.** by many of this man, how.....	*191*
Ac	9:21	all that **h.** him were amazed, and.........	*191*
Ac	9:38	the disciples had **h.** that Peter was	*191*
Ac	10:31	said, Cornelius, thy prayer is **h.**,........	*1522*
Ac	10:44	fell on all them which **h.** the word.........	*191*
Ac	10:46	they **h.** them speak with tongues, ...	*191*
Ac	11:1	in Judaea **h.** that the Gentiles had.........	*191*
Ac	11:7	I **h.** a voice saying unto me, Arise, ...	*191*
Ac	11:18	When they **h.** these things, they held...	*191*
Ac	13:48	the Gentiles **h.** this, they were glad	*191*
Ac	14:9	The same **h.** Paul speak: who............	*191*
Ac	14:14	Barnabas and Paul, **h.** of, they rent......	*191*
Ac	15:24	Forasmuch as we have **h.**, that	*191*
Ac	16:14	which worshipped God, **h.** us: whose....	*191*
Ac	16:25	God: and the prisoners **h.** them.	*1874*
Ac	16:38	when they **h.** that they were Romans. ..	*191*
Ac	17:8	of the city, when they **h.** these things. ..	*191*
Ac	17:32	when they **h.** of the resurrection of......	*191*
Ac	18:26	when Aquila and Priscilla had **h.**, ...	*191*
Ac	19:2	We have not so much as **h.** whether	*191*
Ac	19:5	they **h.** this, they were baptized..........	*191*
Ac	19:10	dwelt in Asia **h.** the word of the Lord...	*191*
Ac	19:28	**h.** these sayings, they were full of.......	*191*
Ac	21:12	when we **h.** these things, both we, ...	*191*
Ac	21:20	when they **h.** it, they glorified the........	*191*
Ac	22:2	they **h.** that he spake in the Hebrew	*191*
Ac	22:7	**h.** a voice saying unto me, **Saul, Saul,**	*191*
Ac	22:9	**h.** not the voice of him that spake to....	*191*
Ac	22:15	men of what thou hast seen and **h.**.	*191*
Ac	22:26	When the centurion **h.** that, he went....	*191*
Ac	23:16	Paul's sister's son **h.** of their lying	*191*
Ac	24:22	when Felix **h.** these things, having........	*191*
Ac	24:24	sent for Paul, and **h.** him concerning	*191*
Ac	26:14	I **h.** a voice speaking unto me, and	*191*
Ac	28:15	brethren **h.** of us, they came to meet...	*191*
Ro	10:14	in him of whom they have not **h.**?........	*191*
Ro	10:18	I say, Have they not **h.**? Yes verily,......	*191*
Ro	15:21	that have not **h.** shall understand.	*191*
1Co	2:9	Eye hath not seen, nor ear **h.**,............	*191*
2Co	6:2	I have **h.** thee in a time accepted, ...	*1873*
2Co	12:4	into paradise, and **h.** unspeakable.........	*191*
Ga	1:13	ye have **h.** of my conversation in..........	*191*
Ga	1:23	**h.** only, That he which persecuted	*191*
Eph	1:13	after that ye **h.** the word of truth, ...	*191*
Eph	1:15	after I **h.** of your faith in the Lord	*191*
Eph	3:2	If ye have **h.** of the dispensation of........	*191*
Eph	4:21	If so be that ye have **h.** him, and.........	*191*
Php	2:26	that ye had **h.** that he had been sick	*191*
Php	4:9	both learned, and received, and **h.**, ...	*191*
Col	1:4	Since we **h.** of your faith in Christ	*191*
Col	1:5	whereof ye **h.** before in the word of	*4257*
Col	1:6	since the day ye **h.** of it, and knew......	*191*
Col	1:9	since the day we **h.** it, do not cease.....	*191*
Col	1:23	the gospel, which ye have **h.**, and........	*191*
1Th	2:13	the word of God which ye **h.** of us, ...	*189*
2Ti	1:13	words, which thou hast **h.** of me, ...	*191*
2Ti	2:2	the things that thou hast **h.** of me........	*191*
Heb	2:1	heed to the things which we have **h.**, ...	*191*
Heb	2:3	confirmed unto us by them that **h.**	*191*
Heb	3:16	when they had **h.**, did provoke:...........	*191*
Heb	4:2	mixed with faith in them that **h.** it........	*191*
Heb	5:7	and was **h.** in that he feared;............	*1522*
Heb	12:19	which voice they that **h.** intreated........	*191*
Jas	5:11	Ye have **h.** of the patience of Job,........	*191*
2Pe	1:18	voice which came from heaven we **h.**, ..	*191*
1Jo	1:1	which we have **h.**, which we have seen.	*191*
1Jo	1:3	we have seen and **h.** declare we..........	*191*
1Jo	1:5	message which we have **h.** of him,.......	*191*
1Jo	2:7	the word which ye have **h.** from..........	*191*
1Jo	2:18	have **h.** that antichrist shall come,.......	*191*
1Jo	2:24	which ye have **h.** from the beginning. ...	*191*
1Jo	2:24	which ye have **h.** from the beginning	*191*
1Jo	3:11	that ye **h.** from the beginning,.............	*191*
1Jo	4:3	ye have **h.** that it should come;...........	*191*
2Jo	6	as ye have **h.** from the beginning,.........	*191*
Re	1:10	**h.** behind me a great voice, as of a	*191*
Re	3:3	**how hast thou received and h., and**.	*191*
Re	4:1	first voice which I **h.** was as it were	*191*
Re	5:11	I **h.** the voice of many angels round	*191*
Re	5:13	and all that are in them, **h.** I saying, ...	*191*
Re	6:1	I **h.**, as it were, the noise of thunder, ..	*191*
Re	6:3	I **h.** the second beast say, Come	*191*
Re	6:5	I **h.** the third beast say, Come and	*191*
Re	6:6	I **h.** a voice in the midst of the four	*191*
Re	6:7	I **h.** the voice of the fourth beast say, ..	*191*
Re	7:4	I **h.** the number of them which were....	*191*
Re	8:13	I beheld, and **h.** an angel flying............	*191*
Re	9:13	I **h.** a voice from the four horns of.......	*191*
Re	9:16	and I **h.** the number of them...............	*191*
Re	10:4	I **h.** a voice from heaven saying unto....	*191*
Re	10:8	the voice which I **h.** from heaven..........	*191*
Re	11:12	they **h.** a great voice from heaven	*191*
Re	12:10	I **h.** a loud voice saying in heaven, ...	*191*
Re	14:2	I **h.** a voice from heaven, as the voice..	*191*
Re	14:2	I **h.** the voice of harpers harping	*191*
Re	14:13	I **h.** a voice from heaven saying unto....	*191*
Re	16:1	I **h.** a great voice out of the temple	*191*
Re	16:5	I **h.** the angel of the waters say, ...	*191*
Re	16:7	I **h.** another out of the altar say, ...	*191*
Re	18:4	I **h.** another voice from heaven, ...	*191*
Re	18:22	trumpeters, shall be **h.** no more at all...	*191*
Re	18:22	millstone shall be **h.** no more at all.......	*191*
Re	18:23	the bride shall be **h.** no more at all	*191*
Re	19:1	I **h.** a great voice of much people	*191*
Re	19:6	I **h.**, as it were, the voice of a great....	*191*

Re 21:3 I **h.** a great voice out of heaven.......... *191*
Re 22:8 I John saw these things, and **h.**.......... *191*
Re 22:8 them. And when I had **h.** and seen,..... *191*

HEARDEST
De 4:36 thou **h.** his words out of the midst..... 8085
Jos 14:12 thou **h.** in that day how the Anakims... 8085
2Ki 22:19 **h.** what I spake against this place,...... 8085
2Ch 34:27 thou **h.** his words against this place,... 8085
Ne 9:9 and **h.** their cry by the Red sea;........ 8085
Ne 9:27, 28 thee, thou **h.** them from heaven;... 8085
Ps 31:22 thou **h.** the voice of my supplications.. 8085
Ps 119:26 declared my ways, and thou **h.** me:.... 6030
Isa 48:7 the day when thou **h.** them not;......... 8085
Isa 48:8 Yea, thou **h.** not; yea, thou knewest... 8085
Jon 2:2 hell cried I, and thou **h.** my voice....... 8085

HEARER See also HEARERS.
Jas 1:23 if any be a **h.** of the word, and not...... *202*
Jas 1:25 he being not a forgetful **h.**, but........... *202*

HEARERS
Ro 2:13 For not the **h.** of the law are just........ *202*
Eph 4:29 may minister grace unto the **h.**.......... *191*
2Ti 2:14 but to the subverting of the **h.**........... *191*
Jas 1:22 doers of the word, and not **h.** only,...... *202*

HEAREST
Ru 2:8 Boaz unto Ruth, **H.** thou not, my....... 8085
1Sa 24:9 Wherefore **h.** thou men's words,........ 8085
2Sa 5:24 when thou **h.** the sound of a going..... 8085
1Ki 8:30 and when thou **h.**, forgive................ 8085
2Ch 6:21 and when thou **h.**, forgive................ 8085
Ps 22:2 in the daytime, but thou **h.** not;......... 6030
Ps 65:2 O thou that **h.** prayer, unto thee........ 8085
Mt 21:16 unto him, **H.** thou what these say?...... *191*
Mt 27:13 **H.** thou not how many things they....... *191*
Joh 3:8 and thou h. the sound thereof, but.. *191*
Joh 11:42 I knew that thou h. me always:...... *191*

HEARETH
Ex 16:7 for that he **h.** your murmurings.......... 8085
Ex 16:8 that the Lord **h.** your murmurings...... 8085
Nu 30:5 disallow her in the day that he **h.**;...... 8085
De 29:19 when he **h.** the words of this curse,... 8085
1Sa 3:9 Speak, Lord; for thy servant **h.**......... 8085
1Sa 3:10 answered, Speak; for thy servant **h.**.. 8085
1Sa 3:11 of every one that **h.** it shall tingle...... 8085
2Sa 17:9 first, that whosoever **h.** it will say,..... 8085
2Ki 21:12 that whosoever **h.** of it, both his ears..8085
Job 34:28 and he **h.** the cry of the afflicted........ 8085
Ps 34:17 and the Lord **h.** and delivereth.......... 8085
Ps 38:14 I was as a man that **h.** not,............... 8085
Ps 69:33 for the Lord **h.** the poor, and............ 8085
Pr 8:34 Blessed is the man that **h.** me,.......... 8085
Pr 13:1 wise son **h.** his father's instruction:..... 8085
Pr 13:1 but a scorner **h.** not rebuke............. 8085
Pr 13:8 riches: but the poor **h.** not rebuke...... 8085
Pr 15:29 he **h.** the prayer of the righteous....... 8085
Pr 15:31 The ear that **h.** the reproof of life...... 8085
Pr 15:32 **h.** reproof getteth understanding........ 8085
Pr 18:13 answereth a matter before he **h.** it,.... 8085
Pr 21:28 man that **h.** speaketh constantly......... 8085
Pr 25:10 Lest he that **h.** it put thee to shame,.. 8085
Pr 29:24 he **h.** cursing, and bewrayeth it not.... 8085
Isa 41:26 there is none that **h.** your words........ 8085
Isa 42:20 opening the ears, but he **h.** not......... 8085
Jer 19:3 whosoever **h.**, his ears shall tingle...... 8085
Eze 3:27 He that **h.**, let him hear; and he........ 8085
Eze 33:4 Then whosoever **h.** the sound of the... 8085
Mt 7:24 whosoever h. these sayings of mine,.*191*
Mt 7:26 every one that h. these sayings of... *191*
Mt 13:19 one h. the word of the kingdom,..... *191*
Mt 13:20 the same is he that h. the word,..... *191*
Mt 13:22 the thorns is he that h. the word;... *191*
Mt 13:23 good ground is he that h. the word,.*191*
Lu 6:47 cometh to me, and h. my sayings,... *191*
Lu 6:49 he that h., and doeth not, is like.... *191*
Lu 10:16 He that h. you h. me; and he that.. *191*
Joh 3:29 bridegroom, which standeth and **h.**........ *191*
Joh 5:24 He that h. my word, and believeth.. *191*
Joh 8:47 He that is of God h. God's words:... *191*
Joh 9:31 we know that God **h.** not sinners:........ *191*
Joh 9:31 of God, and doeth his will, him he **h.**.... *191*
Joh 18:37 one that is of the truth h. my voice. *191*
2Co 12:6 seeth me to be, or that he **h.** of me..... *191*
1Jo 4:5 of the world, and the world **h.** them..... *191*
1Jo 4:6 he that knoweth God **h.** us; he that..... *191*
1Jo 4:6 he that is not of God **h.** not us........... *191*
1Jo 5:14 thing according to his will, he **h.** us:..... *191*
Re 22:17 And let him that **h.** say, Come........... *191*
Re 22:18 that **h.** the words of the prophecy of.... *191*

HEARING
De 31:11 this law before all Israel in their **h.**..... 241
2Sa 18:12 for in our **h.** the king charged thee...... 241
2Ki 4:31 there was neither voice, nor **h.**........... 7182
Job 33:8 Surely thou hast spoken in mine **h.**,..... 241
Job 42:5 heard of thee by the **h.** of the ear:..... 8088
Pr 20:12 The **h.** ear, and the seeing eye,.......... 8085
Pr 28:9 turneth away his ear from **h.** the law,..8085
Ec 1:8 seeing, nor the ear filled with **h.**........ 8085
Isa 11:3 reprove after the **h.** of his ears:......... 4926
Isa 21:3 I was bowed down at the **h.** of it;...... 8085
Isa 33:15 stoppeth his ears from **h.** of blood,..... 8085
Eze 9:5 to the others he said in mine **h.**,......... 241
Eze 10:13 it was cried unto them in my **h.**,......... 241
Am 8:11 but of **h.** the words of the Lord:........ 8085
Mt 13:13 seeing see not; and h. they hear not.*191*
Mt 13:14 By h. ye shall hear, and shall not... *189*
Mt 13:15 and their ears are dull of h.,.......... *191*
Mk 4:12 and h. they may hear, and not....... *191*
Mk 6:2 and many **h.** him were astonished,....... *191*
Lu 2:46 both **h.** them, and asking them........... *191*
Lu 8:10 and h. they might not understand... *191*
Lu 18:36 **h.** the multitude pass by, he asked....... *191*
Ac 5:5 Ananias **h.** these words fell down,....... *191*
Ac 8:6 Philip spake, **h.** and seeing the............ *191*
Ac 9:7 **h.** a voice, but seeing no man............. *191*
Ac 18:8 many of the Corinthians **h.** believed,..... *191*
Ac 25:21 reserved unto the **h.** of Augustus,...... *1233*
Ac 25:23 and was entered into the place of **h.**,..... *201*
Ac 28:26 **H.** ye shall hear, and shall not............ *189*
Ac 28:27 and their ears are dull of **h.**,............... *191*
Ro 10:17 So then faith cometh by **h.**,............... *189*
Ro 10:17 and **h.** by the word of God.................. *189*
1Co 12:17 body were an eye, where were the **h.**?. *189*
1Co 12:17 whole were **h.**, where...the smelling?... *189*
Ga 3:2,5 of the law, or by the **h.** of faith?.......... *189*
Phm 5 **H.** of thy love and faith, which thou..... *191*
Heb 5:11 to be uttered, seeing ye are dull of **h.**.. *189*
2Pe 2:8 them, in seeing and **h.**, vexed his........ *189*

HEARKEN See also HEARKENED; HEARKENETH; HEARKENING.
Ge 4:23 wives of Lamech, **h.** unto...speech:...... 238
Ge 21:12 said unto thee, **h.** unto her voice;...... 8085
Ge 23:15 My lord, **h.** unto me: the land is........ 8085
Ge 34:17 not **h.** unto us, to be circumcised;...... 8085
Ge 49:2 and **h.** unto Israel your father............ 8085
Ex 3:18 And they shall **h.** to thy voice:.......... 8085
Ex 4:1 they will not believe me, nor **h.** unto.. 8085
Ex 4:8 neither **h.** to the voice of the first...... 8085
Ex 4:9 two signs, neither **h.** unto thy voice,.... 8085
Ex 6:30 and how shall Pharaoh **h.** unto me?..... 8085
Ex 7:4 But Pharaoh shall not **h.** unto you,..... 8085
Ex 7:22 neither did he **h.** unto them; as......... 8085
Ex 11:9 Pharaoh shall not **h.** unto you:........... 8085
Ex 15:26 If thou wilt diligently **h.** to the voice... 8085
Ex 18:19 **H.** now unto my voice, I will give...... 8085
Le 26:14 But if ye will not **h.** unto me,........... 8085
Le 26:18 ye will not yet for all this **h.** unto....... 8085
Le 26:21 will not **h.** unto me; I will bring......... 8085
Le 26:27 if ye will not for all this **h.** unto me,... 8085
Nu 23:18 **h.** unto me, thou son of Zippor:.......... 238
De 1:45 Lord would not **h.** to your voice,....... 8085
De 4:1 Now therefore **h.**, O Israel, unto the.. 8085
De 7:12 if ye **h.** to these judgments, and........ 8085
De 11:13 if ye shall **h.** diligently unto my.......... 8085
De 13:3 Thou shalt not **h.** unto the words....... 8085
De 13:8 consent unto him, nor **h.** unto him;..... 8085
De 13:18 shalt **h.** to the voice of the Lord........ 8085
De 15:5 if thou carefully **h.** unto the voice....... 8085
De 17:12 **h.** unto the priest that standeth.......... 8085
De 18:15 like unto me; unto him ye shall **h.**;..... 8085
De 18:19 whosoever will not **h.** unto my words.. 8085
De 21:18 chastened him, will not **h.** unto.......... 8085
De 23:5 thy God would not **h.** unto Balaam;.... 8085
De 26:17 judgments, and to **h.** unto his voice:... 8085
De 27:9 Take heed, and **h.**, O Israel; this day.. 8085
De 28:1 shalt **h.** diligently unto the voice of..... 8085
De 28:2 if thou shalt **h.** unto the voice of the... 8085
De 28:13 thou **h.** unto the commandments......... 8085
De 28:15 if thou wilt not **h.** unto the voice of.... 8085
De 30:10 If thou shalt **h.** unto the voice of........ 8085
Jos 1:17 in all things, so will we **h.** unto thee:.. 8085
Jos 1:18 will not **h.** unto thy words in all that... 8085
Jos 24:10 But I would not **h.** unto Balaam;........ 8085
Jg 2:17 would not **h.** unto their judges,.......... 8085
Jg 3:4 would **h.** unto the commandments...... 8085
Jg 9:7 **H.** unto me, ye men of Shechem,...... 8085
Jg 9:7 Shechem, that God may **h.** unto you... 8085
Jg 11:17 king of Edom would not **h.** thereto..... 8085
Jg 19:25 But the men would not **h.** to him:...... 8085
Jg 20:13 Benjamin would not **h.** to the voice..... 8085
1Sa 8:7 **H.** unto the voice of the people in all.. 8085
1Sa 8:9 Now therefore **h.** unto their voice:..... 8085
1Sa 8:22 **H.** unto their voice, and make them.... 8085
1Sa 15:1 therefore **h.** thou unto the voice of..... 8085
1Sa 15:22 better...to **h.** than the fat of rams...... 7181
1Sa 28:22 **h.** thou also unto the voice of thine.... 8085
1Sa 30:24 For who will **h.** unto you in this......... 8085
2Sa 12:18 he would not **h.** unto our voice:......... 8085
2Sa 13:14 he would not **h.** unto her voice:......... 8085
2Sa 13:16 But he would not **h.** unto her........... 8085
1Ki 8:28 to **h.** unto the cry and to the prayer,.. 8085
1Ki 8:29 that thou mayest **h.** unto the prayer,.. 8085
1Ki 8:30 And **h.** thou to the supplication of....... 8085
1Ki 8:52 to **h.** unto them in all that they call...... 8085
1Ki 11:38 thou wilt **h.** unto all that I command... 8085
1Ki 20:8 **H.** not unto him, nor consent........... 8085
1Ki 22:28 **H.**, O people, every one of you.......... 8085
2Ki 10:6 if ye will **h.** unto my voice, take ye.... 8085
2Ki 17:40 Howbeit they did not **h.**, but they...... 8085
2Ki 18:31 **H.** not to Hezekiah: for thus saith...... 8085
2Ki 18:32 and **h.** not unto Hezekiah, when he.... 8085
2Ch 6:19 to **h.** unto the cry and the prayer....... 8085
2Ch 6:20 to **h.** unto the prayer which thy......... 8085
2Ch 6:21 **H.** therefore unto the supplications..... 8085
2Ch 10:16 the king would not **h.** unto them,....... 8085
2Ch 18:27 And he said, **H.**, all ye people........... 8085
2Ch 20:15 **H.** ye, all Judah, and ye.................. 7181
2Ch 33:10 his people: but they would not **h.**........ 7181
Ne 13:27 Shall we then **h.** unto you to do all..... 8085
Job 13:6 and **h.** to the pleadings of my lips....... 7181
Job 32:10 **H.** to me; I also will shew mine......... 8085
Job 33:1 speeches, and **h.** to all my words........ 238
Job 33:31 Mark well, O Job, **h.** unto me:.......... 8085
Job 33:33 If not, **h.** unto me: hold thy peace,..... 8085
Job 34:10 Therefore **h.** unto me, ye men of....... 8085
Job 34:16 this; **h.** to the voice of my words......... 238
Job 34:34 and let a wise man **h.** unto me.......... 8085
Job 37:14 **H.** unto this, O Job: stand still,.......... 238
Ps 5:2 **H.** unto the voice of my cry,............. 7181
Ps 34:11 Come, ye children, **h.** unto me: I....... 8085
Ps 45:10 **H.**, O daughter, and consider, and...... 8085
Ps 58:5 not **h.** to the voice of charmers,........ 8085
Ps 81:8 O Israel, if thou wilt **h.** unto me;........ 8085
Ps 81:11 But my people would not **h.** to my..... 8085
Pr 7:24 **H.** unto me now therefore, O ye....... 8085
Pr 8:32 Now therefore **h.** unto me, O ye........ 8085
Pr 23:22 **H.** unto thy father that begat thee,..... 8085
Pr 29:12 If a ruler **h.** to lies, all his servants.... 7181
Ca 8:13 the companions **h.** to thy voice:......... 7181
Isa 28:23 my voice; **h.**, and hear my speech...... 7181
Isa 32:3 the ears of them that hear shall **h.**..... 7181
Isa 34:1 **h.**, ye people: let the earth hear,....... 7181
Isa 36:16 **H.** not to Hezekiah: for thus saith...... 8085
Isa 42:23 who will **h.** and hear for the time....... 7181
Isa 46:3 **H.** unto me, O house of Jacob,.......... 8085
Isa 46:12 **H.** unto me, ye stouthearted, that...... 8085
Isa 48:12 **H.** unto me, O Jacob and Israel,........ 8085
Isa 49:1 and **h.**, ye people, from far; The......... 7181
Isa 51:1 **H.** to me, ye that follow after........... 8085
Isa 51:4 **H.** unto me, my people; and give....... 7181
Isa 51:7 **H.** unto me, ye that know................ 8085
Isa 55:2 **h.** diligently unto me, and eat ye....... 8085
Jer 6:10 uncircumcised, and they cannot **h.**:...... 7181
Jer 6:17 **H.** to the sound of the trumpet. But... 7181
Jer 6:17 But they said, We will not **h.**............ 7181
Jer 7:27 but they will not **h.** to thee: thou....... 8085
Jer 11:11 cry unto me, I will not **h.** unto them.... 8085
Jer 16:12 heart, that they may not **h.** unto me:.. 8085
Jer 17:24 to pass, if ye diligently **h.** unto me,.... 8085
Jer 17:27 **h.** unto me to hallow the sabbath....... 8085
Jer 18:19 **h.** to the voice of them that contend... 8085
Jer 23:16 **H.** not unto the words of the............ 8085
Jer 26:3 If so be they will **h.**, and turn every... 8085
Jer 26:4 If ye will not **h.** to me, to walk in...... 8085
Jer 26:5 To **h.** to the words of my servants..... 8085
Jer 27:9 **h.** not ye to your prophets, nor to...... 8085
Jer 27:14 **h.** not unto the words of the............ 8085
Jer 27:16 **H.** not to the words of your............. 8085
Jer 27:17 **H.** not unto them; serve the king of... 8085

Jer 29:8 neither **h.** to your dreams which ye.... 8085
Jer 29:12 pray unto me, and I will **h.** unto you... 8085
Jer 35:13 Will ye not receive instruction to **h.**.... 8085
Jer 37:2 did **h.** unto the words of the Lord, ... 8085
Jer 38:15 counsel, wilt thou not **h.** unto me? 8085
Jer 44:16 of the Lord, we will not **h.** unto thee. ..8085
Eze 3:7 the house of Israel will not **h.** unto..... 8085
Eze 3:7 thee; for they will not **h.** unto me: 8085
Eze 20:8 me, and would not **h.** unto me: they... 8085
Eze 20:39 also, if ye will not **h.** unto me:........... 8085
Da 9:19 O Lord, **h.** and do; defer not,............ 7181
Ho 5:1 **h.**, ye house of Israel; and give ye..... 7181
Ho 9:17 because they did not **h.** unto him: 8085
Mic 1:2 **h.**, O earth, and all that therein is:..... 7181
Zec 1:4 did not hear, nor **h.** unto me,............ 7181
Zec 7:11 they refused to **h.** and pulled away..... 7181
Mk 4:3 **H.; Behold, there went out a sower** .*191*
Mk 7:14 **H. unto me every one of you,**......... *191*
Ac 2:14 unto you, and **h.** to my words: *1801*
Ac 4:19 right in the sight of God to **h.** unto...... *191*
Ac 7:2 Men, brethren, and fathers, **h.**; The..... *191*
Ac 12:13 damsel came to **h.**, named Rhoda,...... *5219*
Ac 15:13 Men and brethren, **h.** unto me: *191*
Jas 2:5 **H.**, my beloved brethren, Hath not...... *191*

HEARKENED See also HEARKENEDST.

Ge 3:17 hast **h.** unto the voice of thy wife,....... 8085
Ge 16:2 And Abram **h.** to the voice of Sarai. ... 8085
Ge 23:16 And Abraham **h.** unto Ephron; and 8085
Ge 30:17 And God **h.** unto Leah, and she.......... 8085
Ge 30:22 and God **h.** to her, and opened her..... 8085
Ge 34:24 and unto Shechem his son **h.** all......... 8085
Ge 39:10 that he **h.** not unto her, to lie by her, ..8085
Ex 6:9 they **h.** not unto Moses for anguish 8085
Ex 6:12 Israel have not **h.** unto me; how 8085
Ex 7:13 Pharaoh's heart, that he **h.** not.......... 8085
Ex 8:15 hardened his heart, and **h.** not........... 8085
Ex 8:19 heart was hardened, and he **h.** not 8085
Ex 9:12 heart of Pharaoh, and he **h.** not.......... 8085
Ex 16:20 they **h.** not unto Moses; but some 8085
Ex 18:24 So Moses **h.** to the voice of his father .8085
Nu 14:22 and have not **h.** to my voice;............. 8085
Nu 21:3 the Lord **h.** to the voice of Israel,....... 8085
De 9:19 Lord **h.** unto me at that time also. 8085
De 9:23 believed him not, nor **h.** to his voice... 8085
De 10:10 Lord **h.** unto me at that time also. 8085
De 18:14 **h.** unto observers of times, and unto 8085
De 26:14 I have **h.** to the voice of the Lord...... 8085
De 34:9 the children of Israel **h.** unto him, ... 8085
Jos 1:17 as we **h.** unto Moses in all things,....... 8085
Jos 10:14 the Lord **h.** unto the voice of a man: .. 8085
Jg 2:20 and have not **h.** unto my voice; 8085
Jg 11:28 Ammon **h.** not unto the words of 8085
Jg 13:9 And God **h.** to the voice of Manoah; ... 8085
1Sa 2:25 **h.** not unto the voice of their father,.... 8085
1Sa 12:1 I have **h.** unto your voice in all that.... 8085
1Sa 19:6 Saul **h.** unto the voice of Jonathan: 8085
1Sa 25:35 I have **h.** to thy voice, and have 8085
1Sa 28:21 and have **h.** unto thy words which....... 8085
1Sa 28:23 him; and he **h.** unto their voice.......... 8085
1Ki 12:15 the king **h.** not unto the people;......... 8085
1Ki 12:16 Israel saw that the king **h.** not........... 8085
1Ki 12:24 They **h.** therefore to the word of the.. 8085
1Ki 15:20 So Ben-hadad **h.** unto king Asa, ... 8085
1Ki 20:25 and he **h.** unto their voice, and did 8085
2Ki 13:4 and the Lord **h.** unto him: for he saw ..8085
2Ki 16:9 And the king of Assyria **h.** unto him: .. 8085
2Ki 20:13 And Hezekiah **h.** unto them, and........ 8085
2Ki 21:9 But they **h.** not: and Manasseh............ 8085
2Ki 22:13 because our fathers have not **h.** unto .. 8085
2Ch 10:15 So the king **h.** not unto the people: 8085
2Ch 16:4 And Ben-hadad **h.** unto king Asa, ... 8085
2Ch 24:17 Then the king **h.** unto them. 8085
2Ch 25:16 and hast not **h.** unto my counsel. 8085
2Ch 30:20 Lord **h.** to Hezekiah, and healed 8085
2Ch 35:22 and **h.** not unto the words of Necho ... 8085
Ne 9:16 and **h.** not to thy commandments, ... 8085
Ne 9:29 **h.** not unto thy commandments, but.... 8085
Ne 9:34 nor **h.** unto thy commandments.......... 7181
Es 3:4 unto him, he **h.** not unto them, that.... 8085
Job 9:16 that he had **h.** unto my voice. 238
Ps 81:13 Oh that my people had **h.** unto me, ... 8085
Ps 106:25 **h.** not unto the voice of the Lord. 8085
Isa 21:7 he **h.** diligently with much heed: 7181
Isa 48:18 hadst **h.** to my commandments! 7181
Jer 6:19 they have not **h.** unto my words, ... 7181
Jer 7:24 But they **h.** not, nor inclined their 8085
Jer 7:26 Yet they **h.** not unto me, nor inclined.. 8085
Jer 8:6 I **h.** and heard, but they spake not 8085
Jer 25:3 and speaking; but ye have not **h.**. 8085
Jer 25:4 but ye have not **h.**, nor inclined 8085
Jer 25:7 Yet ye have not **h.** unto me, saith...... 8085
Jer 26:5 sending them, but ye have not **h.**;...... 8085
Jer 29:19 they have not **h.** to my words, saith... 8085
Jer 32:33 have not **h.** to receive instruction. 8085
Jer 34:14 but your fathers **h.** not unto me,......... 8085
Jer 34:17 have not **h.** unto me, in proclaiming.... 8085
Jer 35:14 speaking; but ye **h.** not unto me. 8085
Jer 35:15 inclined your ear, nor **h.** unto me. 8085
Jer 35:16 but this people hath not **h.** unto me:... 8085
Jer 36:31 against them; but they **h.** not. 8085
Jer 37:14 But he **h.** not to him: so Irijah took.... 8085
Jer 44:5 But they **h.** not, nor inclined their...... 8085
Eze 3:6 them, they would have **h.** unto thee. .. 8085
Da 9:6 have we **h.** unto thy servants the....... 8085
Mal 3:16 and the Lord **h.**, and heard it, and...... 7181
Ac 27:21 Sirs, ye should have **h.** unto me, ... *3980*

HEARKENEDST

De 28:45 because thou **h.** not unto the voice..... 8085

HEARKENETH

Pr 1:33 But whoso **h.** unto me shall dwell....... 8085
Pr 12:15 but he that **h.** unto counsel is wise. 8085

HEARKENING

Ps 103:20 **h.** unto the voice of his word. 8085

HEART See also HEARTED; HEART'S; HEARTS.

Ge 6:5 thoughts of his **h.** was only evil 3820
Ge 6:6 earth, and it grieved him at his **h.**. 3820
Ge 8:21 Lord said in his **h.**, I will not again..... 3820
Ge 8:21 the imagination of man's **h.** is evil....... 3820
Ge 17:17 said in his **h.**, Shall a child be born..... 3820
Ge 20:5 integrity of my **h.** and innocency 3824
Ge 20:6 didst this in the integrity of thy **h.**;...... 3824
Ge 24:45 I had done speaking in mine **h.**. 3820
Ge 27:41 Esau said in his **h.**, The days of.......... 3820
Ge 42:28 their **h.** failed them, and they were..... 3820
Ge 45:26 Jacob's **h.** fainted, for he believed........ 3820
Ex 4:14 seeth thee, he will be glad in his **h.**.... 3820
Ex 4:21 I will harden his **h.**, that he shall........ 3820
Ex 7:3 harden Pharaoh's **h.**, and multiply....... 3820
Ex 7:13 hardened Pharaoh's **h.**, that he 3820
Ex 7:14 Pharaoh's **h.** is hardened, he 3820
Ex 7:22 Pharaoh's **h.** was hardened, neither 3820
Ex 7:23 neither did he set his **h.** to this also. .. 3820
Ex 8:15 was respite, he hardened his **h.**, ... 3820
Ex 8:19 and Pharaoh's **h.** was hardened, ... 3820
Ex 8:32 Pharaoh hardened his **h.** at this.......... 3820
Ex 9:7 the **h.** of Pharaoh was hardened,......... 3820
Ex 9:12 Lord hardened the **h.** of Pharaoh,....... 3820
Ex 9:14 send all my plagues upon thine **h.**,....... 3820
Ex 9:34 and hardened his **h.**, he and his 3820
Ex 9:35 the **h.** of Pharaoh was hardened,......... 3820
Ex 10:1 for I have hardened his **h.**, and.......... 3820
Ex 10:1 and the **h.** of his servants, that I........ 3820
Ex 10:20 hardened Pharaoh's **h.**, so that he 3820
Ex 10:27 Lord hardened Pharaoh's **h.**, and he.... 3820
Ex 11:10 hardened Pharaoh's **h.**, so that he 3820
Ex 14:4 will harden Pharaoh's **h.**, that he....... 3820
Ex 14:5 **h.** of Pharaoh and of his servants 3824
Ex 14:8 Lord hardened the **h.** of Pharaoh........ 3820
Ex 15:8 were congealed in the **h.** of the sea. 3820
Ex 23:9 for ye know the **h.** of a stranger, ... 5315
Ex 25:2 giveth it willingly with his **h.** ye 3820
Ex 28:29 breastplate of judgment upon his **h.**, ... 3820
Ex 28:30 and they shall be upon Aaron's **h.**,....... 3820
Ex 28:30 Israel upon his **h.** before the Lord...... 3820
Ex 35:5 whosoever is of a willing **h.**, let him 3820
Ex 35:21 every one whose **h.** stirred him up, ... 3820
Ex 35:26 the women whose **h.** stirred them up.. 3820
Ex 35:29 whose **h.** made them willing to bring... 3820
Ex 35:34 hath put in his **h.** that he may teach, .. 3820
Ex 35:35 hath he filled with wisdom of **h.**,......... 3820
Ex 36:2 whose **h.** the Lord had put wisdom,..... 3820
Ex 36:2 every one whose **h.** stirred him up..... 3820
Le 19:17 not hate thy brother in thine **h.**: 3824
Le 26:16 the eyes, and cause sorrow of **h.**: 5315
Nu 15:39 that ye seek not after your own **h.**...... 3824
Nu 32:7 discourage ye the **h.** of the children.... 3820
Nu 32:9 discouraged the **h.** of the children....... 3820
De 1:28 brethren have discouraged our **h.**........ 3824
De 2:30 spirit, and made his **h.** obstinate, ... 3824
De 4:9 lest they depart form thy **h.** all the..... 3824
De 4:29 if thou seek him with all thy **h.** and 3824
De 4:39 consider it in thine **h.**, that the Lord... 3824
De 5:29 that there were such an **h.** in them, ... 3824
De 6:5 the Lord thy God with all thine **h.**, ... 3824
De 6:6 thee this day, shall be in thine **h.**: 3824
De 7:17 say in thine **h.**, These nations are 3824
De 8:2 to know what was in thine **h.**: 3824
De 8:5 Thou shalt also consider in thine **h.**, ... 3824
De 8:14 thine **h.** be lifted up, and thou forget... 3824
De 8:17 And thou say in thine **h.**, My power ... 3824
De 9:4 Speak not thou in thine **h.**, after 3824
De 9:5 or for the uprightness of thine **h.**, ... 3824
De 10:12 the Lord thy God with all thy **h.** and... 3824
De 10:16 the foreskin of your **h.**, and be no...... 3824
De 11:13 serve him with all your **h.** and with 3824
De 11:16 that your **h.** be not deceived, and ye .. 3824
De 11:18 lay up these my words in your **h.**........ 3824
De 13:3 the Lord your God with all your **h.**........ 3824
De 15:7 thou shalt not harden thine **h.**, nor 3824
De 15:9 be not a thought in thy wicked **h.**,....... 3824
De 15:10 thine **h.** shall not be grieved when...... 3824
De 17:17 that his **h.** turn not away: neither....... 3824
De 17:20 That his **h.** be not lifted up above 3824
De 18:21 if thou say in thine **h.**, How shall we... 3824
De 19:6 the slayer, while his **h.** is hot, and 3824
De 20:8 brethren's **h.** faint as well as his **h.**, .. 3824
De 24:15 he is poor,...setteth his **h.** upon it:..... 5313
De 26:16 keep and do them with all thine **h.**, ... 3824
De 28:28 blindness, and astonishment of **h.**: 3824
De 28:47 joyfulness, and with gladness of **h.**,..... 3824
De 28:65 a trembling **h.**, and failing of eyes,...... 3820
De 28:67 for the fear of thine **h.** wherewith 3824
De 29:4 not given you an **h.** to perceive, ... 3820
De 29:18 whose **h.** turneth away this day 3824
De 29:19 he bless himself in his **h.**, saying, I..... 3824
De 29:19 walk in the imagination of mine **h.**, ... 3820
De 30:2 all thine **h.**, and with all thy soul; 3824
De 30:6 thy God will circumcise thine **h.**,......... 3824
De 30:6 and the **h.** of thy seed, to love the..... 3824
De 30:6 Lord thy God with all thine **h.**, and..... 3824
De 30:10 the Lord thy God with all thine **h.**,..... 3824
De 30:14 thy mouth, and in thy **h.**, that thou..... 3824
De 30:17 if thine **h.** turn away, so that thou...... 3824
Jos 5:1 their **h.** melted, neither was there...... 3824
Jos 14:7 word again as it was in mine **h.**. 3824
Jos 14:8 made the **h.** of the people melt:......... 3820
Jos 22:5 to serve him with all your **h.** and 3824
Jos 24:23 incline your **h.** unto the Lord God 3824
Jg 5:9 My **h.** is toward the governors of....... 3820
Jg 5:15 there were great thoughts of **h.**......... 3820
Jg 5:16 there were great searchings of **h.**........ 3820
Jg 16:15 thee, when thine **h.** is not with me? ... 3820
Jg 16:17 That he told her all his **h.**, and said.... 3820
Jg 16:18 saw that he had told her all his **h.**, ... 3820
Jg 16:18 for he hath shewed me all his **h.**. 3820
Jg 18:20 the priest's **h.** was glad, and he took .. 3820
Jg 19:5 Comfort thine **h.** with a morsel of 3820
Jg 19:6 all night, and let thine **h.** be merry. 3820
Jg 19:8 said, Comfort thine **h.**, I pray thee. 3824
Jg 19:9 here, that thine **h.** may be merry;...... 3824
Ru 3:7 his **h.** was merry, he went to lie........ 3820
1Sa 1:8 not? and why is thy **h.** grieved?.......... 3824
1Sa 1:13 Now Hannah, she spake in her **h.**: 3820
1Sa 2:1 My **h.** rejoiceth in the Lord, mine 3820
1Sa 2:33 thine eyes, and to grieve thine **h.**:...... 5315
1Sa 2:35 is in mine **h.** and in my mind:.......... 3824
1Sa 4:13 his **h.** trembled for the ark of God...... 3820
1Sa 9:19 will tell thee all that is in thine **h.**........ 3824
1Sa 10:9 Samuel, God gave him another **h.**:...... 3820
1Sa 12:20 serve the Lord with all your **h.**; 3824
1Sa 12:24 serve him in truth with all your **h.**: 3824
1Sa 13:14 sought him a man after his own **h.**, ... 3824
1Sa 14:7 Do all that is in thine **h.**: turn thee; 3824
1Sa 14:7 I am with thee according to thy **h.**. 3824
1Sa 16:7 but the Lord looketh on the **h.**. 3824
1Sa 17:28 the naughtiness of thine **h.**; for thou ... 3824
1Sa 17:32 Let no man's **h.** fail because of.......... 3820
1Sa 21:12 David laid up these words in his **h.**,.... 3824
1Sa 24:5 David's **h.** smote him, because he 3820
1Sa 25:31 nor offence of **h.** unto my lord,.......... 3820
1Sa 25:36 and Nabal's **h.** was merry within 3820
1Sa 25:37 that his **h.** died within him, and he 3820
1Sa 27:1 David said in his **h.**, I shall now......... 3820
1Sa 28:5 afraid, and his **h.** greatly trembled. 3820
2Sa 3:21 over all that thine **h.** desireth. 5315
2Sa 6:16 and she despised him in her **h.**. 3820
2Sa 7:3 king, Go, do all that is in thine **h.**; 3824
2Sa 7:21 to thine own **h.**, hast thou done......... 3820
2Sa 7:27 thy servant found in his **h.** to pray 3820

2Sa 13:28 when Amnon's **h.** is merry with wine, .. 3820
2Sa 13:33 the king take the thing to his **h.**, 3820
2Sa 14:1 the king;s **h.** was toward Absalom. 3820
2Sa 17:10 whose **h.** is as the **h.** of a lion, 3820
2Sa 18:14 them through the **h.** of Absalom, 3820
2Sa 19:14 the **h.** of all the men of Judah, 3824
2Sa 19:14 of Judah, even as the **h.** of one man; .. 3824
2Sa 19:19 the king should take it to his **h.**. 3820
2Sa 24:10 David's **h.** smote him after that he 3820
1Ki 2:4 all their **h.** and with all their soul, 3824
1Ki 2:44 wickedness which thine **h.** is privy to, . 3824
1Ki 3:6 and in uprightness of **h.** with thee; 3824
1Ki 3:9 an understanding **h.** to judge thy 3820
1Ki 3:12 wise and an understanding **h.**; 3820
1Ki 4:29 largeness of **h.**, even as the sand 3820
1Ki 8:17 the **h.** of David my father to build 3824
1Ki 8:18 it was in thine **h.** to build an house 3824
1Ki 8:18 didst well that it was in thine **h.** 3824
1Ki 8:23 walk before thee with all their **h.**: 3824
1Ki 8:38 every man the plague of his own **h.**, 3824
1Ki 8:39 to his ways, whose **h.** thou knowest; .. 3824
1Ki 8:48 return unto thee with all their **h.**, 3824
1Ki 8:61 Let your **h.** therefore be perfect 3824
1Ki 8:66 and glad of **h.** for all the goodness 3824
1Ki 9:3 mine eyes and mine **h.** shall be there .. 3824
1Ki 9:4 integrity of **h.**, and in uprightness, 3824
1Ki 10:2 with him of all that was in her **h.**. 3824
1Ki 10:24 wisdom...God had put in his **h.** 3820
1Ki 11:2 they will turn away your **h.** after 3824
1Ki 11:3 and his wives turned away his **h.**. 3820
1Ki 11:4 wives turned away his **h.** after 3824
1Ki 11:4 and his **h.** was not perfect with 3824
1Ki 11:4 was the **h.** of David his father, 3824
1Ki 11:9 his **h.** was turned from the Lord 3824
1Ki 12:26 And Jeroboam said in his **h.**, 3820
1Ki 12:27 the **h.** of this people turn again 3820
1Ki 12:33 which he had devised of his own **h.**; 3820
1Ki 14:8 followed me with all his **h.**, to do 3824
1Ki 15:3 his **h.** was not perfect with the Lord 3824
1Ki 15:3 God, as the **h.** of David his father. 3824
1Ki 15:14 Asa's **h.** was perfect with the Lord 3824
1Ki 18:37 has turned their **h.** back again. 3820
1Ki 21:7 eat bread, and let thine **h.** be merry: .. 3820
2Ki 5:26 Went not mine **h.** with thee, when 3820
2Ki 6:11 the **h.** of the king of Syria was sore 3820
2Ki 9:24 and the arrow went out at his **h.**, 3820
2Ki 10:15 **h.** right, as my **h.** is with thy **h.**? 3824
2Ki 10:30 according to all that was in mine **h.**, 3824
2Ki 10:31 Lord God of Israel with all his **h.**: 3824
2Ki 12:4 cometh into any man's **h.** to bring 3820
2Ki 14:10 and thine **h.** hath lifted thee up: 3820
2Ki 20:3 in truth and with a perfect **h.**, 3824
2Ki 22:19 thine **h.** was tender, and thou hast 3824
2Ki 23:3 with all their **h.** and all their soul, 3820
2Ki 23:25 turned to the Lord with all his **h.**, 3824
1Ch 12:17 mine **h.** shall be knit unto you: 3824
1Ch 12:33 rank: they were not of double **h.** 3820
1Ch 12:38 came with a perfect **h.** to Hebron, 3820
1Ch 12:38 were of one **h.** to make David king 3824
1Ch 15:29 and she despised him in her **h.**. 3820
1Ch 16:10 the **h.** of them rejoice that seek the 3820
1Ch 17:2 David, Do all that is in thine **h.**; 3824
1Ch 17:19 according to thine own **h.**, hast thou 3820
1Ch 17:25 found in his **h.** to pray before thee. 3820
1Ch 22:19 set your **h.** and your soul to seek 3824
1Ch 28:2 I had in mine **h.** to build an house 3824
1Ch 28:9 serve him with a perfect **h.** and 3820
1Ch 29:9 with perfect **h.** they offered willingly 3820
1Ch 29:17 triest the **h.**, and hast pleasure in 3824
1Ch 29:17 the uprightness of mine **h.** I have 3824
1Ch 29:18 the thoughts of the **h.** of thy people, 3824
1Ch 29:18 and prepare their **h.** unto thee: 3824
1Ch 29:19 give...Solomon my son a perfect **h.**, 3824
2Ch 1:11 Because this was in thine **h.**, and 3824
2Ch 6:7 was in the **h.** of David my father 3824
2Ch 6:8 as it was in thine **h.** to build an 3824
2Ch 6:8 didst well in that it was in thine **h.** 3824
2Ch 6:30 his ways, whose **h.** thou knowest; 3824
2Ch 6:38 they return to thee with all their **h.** 3820
2Ch 7:10 and merry in **h.** for the goodness 3820
2Ch 7:11 came in Solomon's **h.** to make in 3820
2Ch 7:16 mine eyes and mine **h.** to make in 3820
2Ch 9:1 with him of all that was in her **h.** 3824
2Ch 9:23 wisdom, that God had put in his **h.** 3820
2Ch 12:14 prepared not his **h.** to seek the Lord. ..3820
2Ch 15:12 all their **h.** and with all their soul; 3824
2Ch 15:15 for they had sworn with all their **h.**, 3824
2Ch 15:17 **h.** of Asa was perfect all his days 3824
2Ch 16:9 whose **h.** is perfect toward him 3824
2Ch 17:6 his **h.** was lifted up in the ways 3820
2Ch 19:3 hast prepared thine **h.** to seek God. 3824
2Ch 19:9 faithfully, and with a perfect **h.**. 3824
2Ch 22:9 who sought the Lord with all his **h.**. 3824
2Ch 25:2 the Lord, but not with a perfect **h.** 3824
2Ch 25:19 thine **h.** lifteth thee up to boast: 3820
2Ch 26:16 **h.** was lifted up to his destruction: 3820
2Ch 29:10 it is in mine **h.** to make a covenant 3824
2Ch 29:31 as many as were of a free **h.** burnt 3820
2Ch 29:34 Levites were more upright in **h.** 3824
2Ch 30:12 one **h.** to do the commandment of 3820
2Ch 30:19 That prepareth his **h.** to seek God, 3824
2Ch 31:21 did it with all his **h.**, and prospered. 3824
2Ch 32:25 for his **h.** was lifted up: therefore 3820
2Ch 32:26 himself for the pride of his **h.**, 3820
2Ch 32:31 might know all that was in his **h.** 3824
2Ch 34:27 Because thine **h.** was tender, and 3824
2Ch 34:31 and his statutes, with all his **h.**, 3824
2Ch 36:13 hardened his **h.** from turning unto 3824
Ezr 6:22 turned the **h.** of the king of Assyria 3820
Ezr 7:10 Ezra had prepared his **h.** to seek 3824
Ezr 7:27 a thing as this in the king's **h.**, 3820
Ne 2:2 nothing else but sorrow of **h.** 3820
Ne 2:12 had put in my **h.** to do at Jerusalem: 3820
Ne 6:8 feignest them out of thine own **h.** 3820
Ne 7:5 my God put into mine **h.** to gather 3820
Ne 9:8 foundest his **h.** faithful before thee, 3824
Es 1:10 the **h.** of the king was merry with 3820
Es 5:9 that day joyful and with a glad **h.**: 3820
Es 6:6 Haman thought in his **h.**, For whom 3820
Es 7:5 durst presume in his **h.** to do so? 3820
Job 7:17 shouldest set thine **h.** upon him? 3820
Job 8:10 and utter words out of their **h.**? 3820
Job 9:4 He is wise in **h.**, and mighty in 3824
Job 10:13 things hast thou hid in thine **h.**: 3824
Job 11:13 thou prepare thine **h.**, and stretch 3820
Job 12:24 the **h.** of the chief of the people 3820
Job 15:12 Why doth thine **h.** carry thee away? 3820
Job 17:4 hid their **h.** from understanding: 3820
Job 17:11 off, even the thoughts of my **h.**. 3824
Job 22:22 and lay up his words in thine **h.**. 3824
Job 23:16 God maketh my **h.** soft, and the 3820
Job 27:6 my **h.** shall not reproach me so 3824
Job 29:13 and I caused the widow's **h.** to sing 3820
Job 31:7 mine **h.** walked after mine eyes, 3820
Job 31:9 If mine **h.** have been deceived by a 3820
Job 31:27 my **h.** hath been secretly enticed, 3820
Job 33:3 be of the uprightness of my **h.**: 3820
Job 34:14 If he set his **h.** upon man, 3820
Job 36:13 hypocrites in **h.** heap up wrath: 3820
Job 37:1 At this also my **h.** trembleth, and is 3820
Job 37:24 not any that are wise of **h.**. 3820
Job 38:36 given understanding to the **h.**? 7907
Job 41:24 His **h.** is as firm as a stone: 3820
Ps 4:4 commune with your own **h.** upon 3824
Ps 4:7 Thou has put gladness in my **h.**, 3820
Ps 7:10 God, which saveth the upright in **h.** 3820
Ps 9:1 thee, O Lord, with my whole **h.**; 3820
Ps 10:6 said in his **h.**, I shall not be moved: 3820
Ps 10:11 said in his **h.**, God hath forgotten: 3820
Ps 10:13 said in his **h.**, Thou wilt not require 3820
Ps 10:17 thou wilt prepare their **h.**, thou wilt 3820
Ps 11:2 privily shoot at the upright in **h.** 3820
Ps 12:2 and with a double **h.** do they speak. 3820
Ps 13:2 soul, having sorrow in my **h.** daily? 3824
Ps 13:5 **h.** shall rejoice in thy salvation. 3820
Ps 14:1 The fool hath said in his **h.**, There 3820
Ps 15:2 and speaketh the truth in his **h.** 3824
Ps 16:9 Therefore my **h.** is glad, and my 3820
Ps 17:3 Thou hast proved mine **h.**; thou 3820
Ps 19:8 Lord are right, rejoicing the **h.**: 3820
Ps 19:14 mouth, and the meditation of my **h.**, 3820
Ps 20:4 thee according to thine own **h.**, 3824
Ps 22:14 my **h.** is like wax; it is melted in 3820
Ps 22:26 him: your **h.** shall live for ever. 3824
Ps 24:4 hath clean hands, and a pure **h.**; 3824
Ps 25:17 The troubles of my **h.** are enlarged: 3824
Ps 26:2 prove me; try my reins and my **h.**. 3820
Ps 27:3 against me, my **h.** shall not fear: 3820
Ps 27:8 my **h.** said unto thee, Thy face, 3820
Ps 27:14 and he shall strengthen thine **h.**: 3820
Ps 28:7 **h.** trusted in him, and I am helped: 3820
Ps 28:7 therefore my **h.** greatly rejoiceth; 3820
Ps 31:24 he shall strengthen your **h.**, all ye 3824
Ps 32:11 joy, all ye that are upright in **h.**, 3820
Ps 33:11 of his **h.** to all generations. 3820
Ps 33:21 our **h.** shall rejoice in him, because 3820
Ps 34:18 unto them that are of a broken **h.**; 3820
Ps 36:1 saith within my **h.**, that there is no 3820
Ps 36:10 righteousness to the upright in **h.** 3820
Ps 37:4 give thee the desires of thine **h.**. 3820
Ps 37:15 sword shall enter into their own **h.**, 3820
Ps 37:31 The law of his God is in his **h.**; 3820
Ps 38:8 reason of the disquietness of my **h.**. 3820
Ps 38:10 My **h.** panteth, my strength faileth 3820
Ps 39:3 My **h.** was hot within me, while I 3820
Ps 40:8 God: yea, thy law is within my **h.** 4578
Ps 40:10 thy righteousness within my **h.**; 3820
Ps 40:12 head: therefore my **h.** faileth me. 3820
Ps 41:6 his **h.** gathereth iniquity to itself; 3820
Ps 44:18 Our **h.** is not turned back, neither 3820
Ps 44:21 he knoweth the secrets of the **h.**. 3820
Ps 45:1 My **h.** is inditing a good matter: 3820
Ps 45:5 in the **h.** of the king's enemies; 3820
Ps 49:3 the meditation of my **h.** shall be of 3820
Ps 51:10 Create in me a clean **h.**, O God; 3820
Ps 51:17 a broken and a contrite **h.**, O God, 3820
Ps 53:1 The fool hath said in his **h.**, There 3820
Ps 55:4 My **h.** is sore pained within me: 3820
Ps 55:21 than butter, but war was in his **h.**: 3820
Ps 57:7 My **h.** is fixed, O God, my **h.** is fixed: .3820
Ps 58:2 in **h.** ye work wickedness; ye weigh 3820
Ps 61:2 thee, when my **h.** is overwhelmed: 3820
Ps 62:8 pour out your **h.** before him: 3824
Ps 62:10 increase, set not your **h.** upon them. .. 3820
Ps 64:6 one of them, and the **h.**, is deep. 3820
Ps 64:10 and all the upright in **h.** shall glory. 3820
Ps 66:18 I regard iniquity in my **h.**, the Lord 3820
Ps 69:20 Reproach hath broken my **h.**; and 3820
Ps 69:32 your **h.** shall live that seek God. 3824
Ps 73:1 even to such as are of a clean **h.**. 3824
Ps 73:7 they have more than **h.** could wish. 3824
Ps 73:13 I have cleansed my **h.** in vain, 3824
Ps 73:21 Thus my **h.** was grieved, and I was 3824
Ps 73:26 My flesh and my **h.** faileth: but God 3824
Ps 73:26 but God is the strength of my **h.**, 3824
Ps 77:6 I commune with mine own **h.**: and 3824
Ps 78:8 that set not their **h.** aright, and 3820
Ps 78:18 they tempted God in their **h.** by 3824
Ps 78:37 their **h.** was not right with him, 3820
Ps 78:72 to the integrity of his **h.**; and 3824
Ps 84:2 my **h.** and my flesh crieth out for 3820
Ps 84:5 in whose **h.** are the ways of them. 3824
Ps 86:11 truth: unite my **h.** to fear thy name. 3824
Ps 86:12 O Lord my God, with all my **h.**: 3824
Ps 94:15 all the upright in **h.** shall follow it. 3820
Ps 95:8 Harden not your **h.**, as in the 3824
Ps 95:10 It is a people that do err in their **h.**, 3824
Ps 97:11 and gladness for the upright in **h.** 3820
Ps 101:2 within my house with a perfect **h.** 3824
Ps 101:4 A froward **h.** shall depart from me: 3820
Ps 101:5 hath an high look and a proud **h.** 3824
Ps 102:4 My **h.** is smitten, and withered like 3824
Ps 104:15 that maketh glad the **h.** of man, 3824
Ps 104:15 which strengtheneth man's **h.** 3824
Ps 105:3 let the **h.** of them rejoice that seek 3820
Ps 105:25 turned their **h.** to hate his people, 3820
Ps 107:12 brought down their **h.** with labour; 3820
Ps 108:1 O God, my **h.** is fixed; I will sing 3820
Ps 109:16 might even slay the broken in **h.** 3824
Ps 109:22 and my **h.** is wounded within me. 3820
Ps 111:1 praise the Lord with my whole **h.**, 3824
Ps 112:7 his **h.** is fixed, trusting in the Lord. 3820
Ps 112:8 His **h.** is established, he shall not 3820
Ps 119:2 that seek him with the whole **h.** 3820
Ps 119:7 praise thee with uprightness of **h.**, 3824
Ps 119:10 With my whole **h.** have I sought 3820
Ps 119:11 Thy word have I hid in mine **h.**, 3820
Ps 119:32 when thou shalt enlarge my **h.** 3820
Ps 119:34 I shall observe it with my whole **h.** 3820
Ps 119:36 Incline my **h.** unto thy testimonies, 3820
Ps 119:58 thy favour with my whole **h.**: but 3820
Ps 119:69 keep thy precepts with my whole **h.**. 3820
Ps 119:70 Their **h.** is as fat as grease; but I 3820
Ps 119:80 Let my **h.** be sound in thy statutes; 3820
Ps 119:111 for they are the rejoicing of my **h.** 3820
Ps 119:112 I have inclined mine **h.** to perform 3820
Ps 119:145 I cried with my whole **h.**; hear me, 3820
Ps 119:161 my **h.** standeth in awe of thy word. 3820
Ps 131:1 my **h.** is not haughty, nor mine eyes 3820
Ps 138:1 will praise thee with my whole **h.** 3820
Ps 139:23 Search me...and know my **h.** 3824

Ps 140:2 imagine mischiefs in their **h.**; 3820
Ps 141:4 Incline not my **h.** to any evil thing, 3820
Ps 143:4 me; my **h.** within me is desolate. 3820
Ps 147:3 He healeth the broken in **h.**, and 3820
Pr 2:2 apply thine **h.** to understanding; 3820
Pr 2:10 wisdom entereth into thine **h.**, and 3820
Pr 3:1 thine **h.** keep my commandments: 3820
Pr 3:3 them upon the table of thine **h.**: 3820
Pr 3:5 Trust in the Lord with all thine **h.**; 3820
Pr 4:4 Let thine **h.** retain my words: keep 3820
Pr 4:21 keep them in the midst of thine **h.**, 3824
Pr 4:23 Keep thy **h.** with all diligence; for 3820
Pr 5:12 and my **h.** despised reproof; 3820
Pr 6:14 Frowardness is in his **h.**, he deviseth 3820
Pr 6:18 An **h.** that deviseth wicked 3820
Pr 6:21 Bind them continually upon thine **h.**, 3820
Pr 6:25 not after her beauty in thine **h.**; 3824
Pr 7:3 them upon the table of thine **h.** 3820
Pr 7:10 attire of an harlot, and subtil of **h.** 3820
Pr 7:25 Let not thine **h.** decline to her ways, 3820
Pr 8:5 fools, be ye of an understanding **h.** 3820
Pr 10:8 The wise in **h.** will receive 3820
Pr 10:20 the **h.** of the wicked is little worth. 3820
Pr 11:20 They that are of a froward **h.** are 3820
Pr 11:29 shall be servant to the wise of **h.** 3820
Pr 12:8 of a perverse **h.** shall be despised. 3820
Pr 12:20 Deceit is in the **h.** of them that 3820
Pr 12:23 but the **h.** of fools proclaimeth 3820
Pr 12:25 Heaviness in the **h.** of man maketh 3820
Pr 13:12 Hope deferred maketh the **h.** sick: 3820
Pr 14:10 The **h.** knoweth his own bitterness; 3820
Pr 14:13 in laughter the **h.** is sorrowful; 3820
Pr 14:14 The backslider in **h.** shall be filled 3820
Pr 14:30 A sound **h.** is the life of the flesh: 3820
Pr 14:33 Wisdom resteth in the **h.** of him 3820
Pr 15:7 the **h.** of the foolish doeth not so. 3820
Pr 15:13 A merry **h.** maketh a cheerful 3820
Pr 15:13 but by sorrow of the **h.** the spirit 3820
Pr 15:14 **h.** of him that hath understanding 3820
Pr 15:15 is of a merry **h.** hath a continual 3820
Pr 15:28 The **h.** of the righteous studieth to 3820
Pr 15:30 The light of the eyes rejoiceth the **h.**: 3820
Pr 16:1 The preparations of the **h.** in man, 3820
Pr 16:5 Every one that is proud in **h.** is an 3820
Pr 16:9 A man's **h.** deviseth his way; but 3820
Pr 16:21 wise in **h.** shall be called prudent: 3820
Pr 16:23 **h.** of the wise teacheth his mouth, 3820
Pr 17:16 wisdom, seeing he hath no **h.** to it? 3820
Pr 17:20 He that hath a froward **h.** findeth 3820
Pr 17:22 A merry **h.** doeth good like a 3820
Pr 18:2 but that his **h.** may discover itself. 3820
Pr 18:12 the **h.** of man is haughty, and 3820
Pr 18:15 The **h.** of the prudent getteth 3820
Pr 19:3 his **h.** fretteth against the Lord. 3820
Pr 19:21 are many devices in a man's **h.**; 3820
Pr 20:5 Counsel in the **h.** of man is like 3820
Pr 20:9 I have made my **h.** clean, I am pure 3820
Pr 21:1 The king's **h.** is in the hand of the 3820
Pr 21:4 An high look, and a proud **h.** 3820
Pr 22:11 He that loveth pureness of **h.**, 3820
Pr 22:15 Foolishness is bound in the **h.** of a 3820
Pr 22:17 apply thine **h.** unto my knowledge. 3820
Pr 23:7 as he thinketh in his **h.**, so is he: 5315
Pr 23:7 but his **h.** is not with thee. 3820
Pr 23:12 Apply thine **h.** unto instruction, 3820
Pr 23:15 thine **h.** be wise, my **h.** shall rejoice, 3820
Pr 23:17 Let not thine **h.** envy sinners: 3820
Pr 23:19 wise, and guide thine **h.** in the way. 3820
Pr 23:26 My son, give me thine **h.**, and 3820
Pr 23:33 and thine **h.** shall utter perverse 3820
Pr 24:2 For their **h.** studieth destruction, 3820
Pr 24:12 he that pondereth the **h.** consider 3826
Pr 24:17 let not thine **h.** be glad when he 3820
Pr 25:3 the **h.** of kings is unsearchable 3820
Pr 25:20 he that singeth songs to an heavy **h.** 3820
Pr 26:23 Burning lips and a wicked **h.** are 3820
Pr 26:25 are seven abominations in his **h.** 3820
Pr 27:9 Ointment...perfume rejoice the **h.**: 3820
Pr 27:11 son, be wise, and make my **h.** glad, 3820
Pr 27:19 to face, so the **h.** of man to man 3820
Pr 28:14 he that hardeneth his **h.** shall fall 3820
Pr 28:25 He that is of proud **h.** stirreth up 5315
Pr 28:26 trusteth in his own **h.** is a fool: 3820
Pr 31:11 The **h.** of her husband doth safely 3820
Ec 1:13 I gave my **h.** to seek and search out 3820
Ec 1:16 I communed with mine own **h.**, 3820
Ec 1:16 yea, my **h. and great experience of.** 3820
Ec 1:17 And I gave my h. to know wisdom, 3820
Ec 2:1 I said in mine **h.**, Go to now, I will 3820
Ec 2:3 I sought in mine **h.** to give myself 3820
Ec 2:3 acquainting mine **h.** with wisdom; 3820
Ec 2:10 I withheld not my **h.** from any joy; 3820
Ec 2:10 for my **h.** rejoiced in all my labour: 3820
Ec 2:15 said I in my **h.**, As it happeneth 3820
Ec 2:15 Then I said in my **h.**, that this also 3820
Ec 2:20 to cause my **h.** to despair of all the 3820
Ec 2:22 labour, and the vexation of his **h.**, 3820
Ec 2:23 his **h.** taketh not rest in the night 3820
Ec 3:11 he hath set the world in their **h.**, 3820
Ec 3:17 I said in mine **h.**, God shall judge 3820
Ec 3:18 in mine **h.** concerning the estate of 3820
Ec 5:2 and let not thine **h.** be nasty to utter 3820
Ec 5:20 answereth him in the joy of his **h.** 3820
Ec 7:2 and the living will lay it to his **h.** 3820
Ec 7:3 countenance the **h.** is made better 3820
Ec 7:4 The **h.** of the wise is in the house of 3820
Ec 7:4 **h.** of fools is in the house of mirth. 3820
Ec 7:7 mad; and a gift destroyeth the **h.** 3820
Ec 7:22 oftentimes...thine own **h.** knoweth 3820
Ec 7:25 I applied mine **h.** to know, and to 3820
Ec 7:26 woman, whose **h.** is snares and nets, 3820
Ec 8:5 wise man's **h.** discerneth both time 3820
Ec 8:9 and applied my **h.** unto every work 3820
Ec 8:11 the **h.** of the sons of men is fully set 3820
Ec 8:16 I applied mine **h.** to know wisdom, 3820
Ec 9:1 For all this I considered in my **h.** 3820
Ec 9:3 the **h.** of the sons of men is full of 3820
Ec 9:3 and madness is in their **h.** while 3824
Ec 9:7 drink thy wine with a merry **h.**; 3820
Ec 10:2 wise man's **h.** is at his right hand; 3820
Ec 10:2 hand; but a fool's **h.** at his left 3820
Ec 11:9 let thy **h.** cheer thee in the days of 3820
Ec 11:9 and walk in the ways of thine **h.**, 3820
Ec 11:10 remove sorrow from thy **h.**, and put 3820
Ca 3:11 in the day of the gladness of his **h.** 3820
Ca 4:9 Thou hast ravished my **h.**, my 3823
Ca 4:9 thou hast ravished my **h.** with one 3823
Ca 5:2 I sleep, but my **h.** waketh: it is 3820
Ca 8:6 Set me as a seal upon thine **h.**, 3820
Isa 1:5 head is sick, and the whole **h.** faint 3824
Isa 6:10 Make the **h.** of this people fat, 3820
Isa 6:10 and understand with their **h.**, and 3824
Isa 7:2 And his **h.** was moved, and the **h.** of 3824
Isa 9:9 say in the pride and stoutness of **h.**, 3824
Isa 10:7 neither doth his **h.** think so; 3824
Isa 10:7 but it is in his **h.** to destroy and 3824
Isa 10:12 the stout **h.** of the king of Assyria, 3824
Isa 13:7 faint, and every man's **h.** shall melt: 3824
Isa 14:13 hast said in thine **h.**, I will ascend 3824
Isa 15:5 My **h.** shall cry out for Moab; 3820
Isa 19:1 and the **h.** of Egypt shall melt in 3824
Isa 21:4 **h.** panted, fearfulness affrighted 3824
Isa 29:13 have removed their **h.** far from me, 3820
Isa 30:29 gladness of **h.**, as when one goeth 3824
Isa 32:4 The **h.** also of the rash shall 3824
Isa 32:6 and his **h.** shall work iniquity, to 3820
Isa 33:18 Thine **h.** shall meditate terror. 3820
Isa 35:4 Say to them that are of a fearful **h.**, 3820
Isa 38:3 in truth and with a perfect **h.**, 3820
Isa 42:25 burned him, yet he laid it not to **h.** 3820
Isa 44:19 none considereth in his **h.**, neither 3820
Isa 44:20 deceived **h.** hath turned him aside, 3820
Isa 47:7 didst not lay these things to thy **h.**, 3820
Isa 47:8 that sayest in thine **h.**, I am, and 3824
Isa 47:10 thou hast said in thine **h.**, I am 3820
Isa 49:21 Then shalt thou say in thine **h.**, 3824
Isa 51:7 the people in whose **h.** is my law; 3820
Isa 57:1 and no man layeth it to **h.**: 3820
Isa 57:11 remembered...nor laid it to thy **h.**? 3820
Isa 57:15 revive the **h.** of the contrite ones. 3820
Isa 57:17 on frowardly in the way of his **h.** 3820
Isa 59:13 from the **h.** words of falsehood. 3820
Isa 60:5 and thine **h.** shall fear, and be 3824
Isa 63:4 the day of vengeance is in mine **h.**, 3820
Isa 63:17 and hardened our **h.** from thy fear? 3820
Isa 65:14 my servants shall sing for joy of **h.**, 3820
Isa 65:14 but ye shall cry for sorrow of **h.**, 3820
Isa 66:14 ye see this, your **h.** shall rejoice 3820
Jer 3:10 turned unto me with her whole **h.**, 3820
Jer 3:15 you pastors according to mine **h.**, 3820
Jer 3:17 the imagination of their evil **h.**, 3820
Jer 4:4 take away the foreskins of your **h.**, 3824
Jer 4:9 that the **h.** of the king shall perish, 3820
Jer 4:9 perish, and the **h.** of the princes; 3820
Jer 4:14 wash thine **h.** from wickedness, 3820
Jer 4:18 because it reacheth unto thine **h.** 3820
Jer 4:19 I am pained at my very **h.**; 3820
Jer 4:19 my **h.** maketh a noise in me; 3820
Jer 5:23 hath a revolting and a rebellious **h.**; 3820
Jer 5:24 Neither say they in their **h.**, Let 3824
Jer 7:24 in the imagination of their evil **h.**, 3820
Jer 7:31 not, neither came it into my **h.**, 3820
Jer 8:18 against sorrow, my **h.** is faint in me. 3820
Jer 9:8 but in **h.** he layeth his wait. 7130
Jer 9:14 the imagination of their own **h.**, 3820
Jer 9:26 Israel are uncircumcised in the **h.** 3820
Jer 11:8 in the imagination of their evil **h.**: 3820
Jer 11:20 that triest the reins and the **h.**, 3820
Jer 12:3 and tried mine **h.** toward thee: 3820
Jer 12:11 because no man layeth it to **h.** 3820
Jer 13:10 walk in the imagination of their **h.**, 3820
Jer 13:22 if thou say in thine **h.**, Wherefore 3824
Jer 14:14 nought, and the deceit of their **h.** 3820
Jer 15:16 me the joy and rejoicing of mine **h.**: 3824
Jer 16:12 after the imagination of his evil **h.**, 3820
Jer 17:1 graven upon the table of their **h.**, 3820
Jer 17:5 whose **h.** departeth from the Lord. 3820
Jer 17:9 The **h.** is deceitful above all things, 3820
Jer 17:10 I the Lord search the **h.**, I try the 3820
Jer 18:12 do the imagination of his evil **h.** 3820
Jer 20:9 word was in mine **h.** as a burning 3820
Jer 20:12 seest the reins and the **h.**, let me see. 3820
Jer 22:17 thine eyes and thine **h.** are not but 3820
Jer 23:9 Mine **h.** within me is broken 3820
Jer 23:16 they speak a vision of their own **h.**, 3820
Jer 23:17 after the imagination of his own **h.**, 3820
Jer 23:20 performed the thoughts of his **h.**: 3820
Jer 23:26 the **h.** of the prophets that prophesy 3820
Jer 23:26 of the deceit of their own **h.**; 3820
Jer 24:7 I will give them an **h.** to know me, 3820
Jer 24:7 return unto me with their whole **h.** 3820
Jer 29:13 shall search for me with all your **h.** 3824
Jer 30:21 engaged his **h.** to approach unto 3820
Jer 30:24 performed the intents of his **h.**: 3820
Jer 31:21 set thine **h.** toward the highway, 3820
Jer 32:39 will give them one **h.**, and one way, 3820
Jer 32:41 with my whole **h.** and with my whole 3820
Jer 48:29 pride, and the haughtiness of his **h.** 3820
Jer 48:31 mine **h.** shall mourn for the men
Jer 48:36 mine **h.** shall sound for Moab like 3820
Jer 48:36 and mine **h.** shall sound like pipes 3820
Jer 48:41 as the **h.** of a woman in her pangs. 3820
Jer 49:16 the pride of thine **h.**, O thou that 3820
Jer 49:22 the **h.** of the mighty men of Edom 3820
Jer 49:22 as the **h.** of a woman in her pangs. 3820
Jer 51:46 And lest your **h.** faint, and ye fear 3824
La 1:20 mine **h.** is turned within me; for I 3820
La 1:22 my sighs are many, and my **h.** is 3820
La 2:18 Their **h.** cried unto the Lord, O wall 3820
La 2:19 pour out thine **h.** like water before 3820
La 3:41 Let us lift up our **h.** with our hands 3824
La 3:51 eye affecteth mine **h.** because of 5315
La 3:65 Give them sorrow of **h.**, thy curse 3820
La 5:15 The joy of our **h.** is ceased; our 3820
La 5:17 For this our **h.** is faint; for these 3820
Eze 3:10 receive in thine **h.**, and hear with 3824
Eze 6:9 am broken with their whorish **h.**, 3820
Eze 11:19 I will give them one **h.**, and I will 3820
Eze 11:19 I will take the stony **h.** out of their 3820
Eze 11:19 and will give them an **h.** of flesh: 3820
Eze 11:21 But as for them whose **h.** walketh 3820
Eze 11:21 after the **h.** of their detestable things 3820
Eze 13:17 which prophesy out of their own **h.**; 3820
Eze 13:22 have made the **h.** of the righteous 3820
Eze 14:3 have set up their idols in their **h.**, 3820
Eze 14:4 that setteth up his idols in his **h.**, 3820
Eze 14:5 the house of Israel in their own **h.**, 3820
Eze 14:7 and setteth up his idols in his **h.**, 3820
Eze 16:30 weak is thine **h.**, saith the Lord 3826
Eze 18:31 and make you a new **h.** and a new 3820
Eze 20:16 for their **h.** went after their idols 3820
Eze 21:7 every **h.** shall melt, and all hands 3820
Eze 21:15 that their **h.** may faint, and their 3820
Eze 22:14 can thine **h.** endure, or can thine 3820
Eze 25:6 rejoiced in **h.** with all thy despite 5315
Eze 25:15 vengeance with a despiteful **h.**, 5315
Eze 27:31 weep for thee with bitterness of **h.** 5315
Eze 28:2 thine **h.** is lifted up, and thou hast 3820
Eze 28:2 thou set thine **h.** as the **h.** of God: 3820
Eze 28:5 thine **h.** is lifted up because of thy 3824

Eze 28:6 set thine **h.** as the **h.** of God; 3820
Eze 28:17 Thine **h.** was lifted up because of 3820
Eze 31:10 his **h.** is lifted up in his height; 3824
Eze 33:31 **h.** goeth after their covetousness. 3820
Eze 36:5 with the joy of all their **h.**, 3824
Eze 36:26 A new **h.** also will I give you, and 3820
Eze 36:26 I will take away the stony **h.** out of 3820
Eze 36:26 and I will give you an **h.** of flesh. 3820
Eze 40:4 set thine **h.** upon all that I shall 3820
Eze 44:7 strangers, uncircumcised in **h.**, and 3820
Eze 44:9 No stranger, uncircumcised in **h.**, 3820
Da 1:8 Daniel purposed in his **h.** that he 3820
Da 2:30 know the thoughts of thy **h.**. 3825
Da 4:16 Let his **h.** be changed from man's, 3825
Da 4:16 let a beast's **h.** be given unto him; 3825
Da 5:20 But when his **h.** was lifted up, 3825
Da 5:21 and his **h.** was made like the beasts, 3825
Da 5:22 hast not humbled thine **h.**, though 3825
Da 6:14 set his **h.** on Daniel to deliver him: 1079
Da 7:4 and a man's **h.** was given to it. 3825
Da 7:28 but I kept the matter in my **h.** 3821
Da 8:25 he shall magnify himself in his **h.**, 3824
Da 10:12 didst set thine **h.** to understand, 3820
Da 11:12 multitude, his **h.** shall be lifted up; 3824
Da 11:28 and his **h.** shall be against the holy 3824
Ho 4:8 they set their **h.** on their iniquity. 5315
Ho 4:11 and new wine take away the **h.**. 3820
Ho 7:6 made ready their **h.** like an oven, 3820
Ho 7:11 is like a silly dove with out **h.**: 3820
Ho 7:14 have not cried unto me with their **h.**, 3820
Ho 10:2 Their **h.** is divided; now shall they 3820
Ho 11:8 mine **h.** is turned within me, my 3820
Ho 13:6 were filled, and their **h.** was exalted; 3820
Ho 13:8 and will rend the caul of their **h.**, 3820
Joe 2:12 turn ye even to me with all your **h.**, 3824
Joe 2:13 And rend your **h.**, and not your 3824
Ob 3 The pride of thine **h.** hath deceived 3820
Ob 3 that saith in his **h.**, Who shall 3820
Na 2:10 and the **h.** melteth, and the knees 3820
Zep 1:12 that say in their **h.**, The Lord will 3824
Zep 2:15 that said in her **h.**, I am, and there 3824
Zep 3:14 be glad and rejoice with all the **h.**, 3820
Zec 7:10 evil against his brother in your **h.** 3824
Zec 10:7 **h.** shall rejoice as through wine: 3820
Zec 10:7 their **h.** shall rejoice in the Lord. 3820
Zec 12:5 of Judah shall say in their **h.**, 3820
Mal 2:2 if ye will not lay it to **h.**, to give glory 3820
Mal 2:2 because ye do not lay it to **h.** 3820
Mal 4:6 he shall turn the **h.** of the fathers to 3820
Mal 4:6 and the **h.** of the children to their 3820
Mt 5:8 **Blessed are the pure in h.; for they** *2588*
Mt 5:28 **adultery with her already in his h.** *2588*
Mt 6:21 **treasure is, there will your h. be** *2588*
Mt 11:29 **for I am meek and lowly in h.:** *2588*
Mt 12:34 **the abundance of the h. the mouth** *2588*
Mt 12:35 **out of the good treasure of the h** *2588*
Mt 12:40 **three nights in the h. of the earth.** *2588*
Mt 13:15 **this people's h. is waxed gross, and** *2588*
Mt 13:15 **should understand with their h.,** *2588*
Mt 13:19 **that which was sown in his h.;** *2588*
Mt 15:8 **lips; but their h. is far from me.** *2588*
Mt 15:18 **the mouth come forth from the h.;** *2588*
Mt 15:19 **out of the h. proceed evil thoughts,** *2588*
Mt 22:37 **the Lord thy God with all thy h.,** *2588*
Mt 24:48 **evil servant shall say in his h.,** *2588*
Mk 6:52 loaves: for their **h.** was hardened. *2588*
Mk 7:6 **lips,but their h. is far from me.** *2588*
Mk 7:19 **Because it entereth not into his h.,** *2588*
Mk 7:21 **out of the h. of men, proceed evil** *2588*
Mk 8:17 **have ye your h. yet hardened?** *2588*
Mk 10:5 **the hardness of your h. he wrote** *4641*
Mk 11:23 **and shall not doubt in his h., but** *2588*
Mk 12:30 **the Lord thy God with all thy h.,** *2588*
Mk 12:33 And to love him with all the **h.**, *2588*
Mk 16:14 their unbelief and hardness of **h.**, *4641*
Lu 2:19 and pondered them in her **h.** *2588*
Lu 2:51 kept all these sayings in her **h.** *2588*
Lu 6:45 **out of the good treasure of his h** *2588*
Lu 6:45 **out of the evil treasure of his h** *2588*
Lu 6:45 **abundance of the h. his mouth** *2588*
Lu 8:15 **which in an honest and good h.,** *2588*
Lu 9:47 perceiving the thought of their **h.**, *2588*
Lu 10:27 the Lord thy God with all thy **h.**, *2588*
Lu 12:34 **treasure is, there will your h. be** *2588*
Lu 12:45 **and if that servant say in his h.,** *2588*
Lu 24:25 **and slow of h. to believe all that** *2588*
Lu 24:32 Did not our **h.** burn within us, while *2588*
Joh 12:40 their eyes, and hardened their **h.**; *2588*
Joh 12:40 eyes, nor understand with their **h.**, *2588*
Joh 13:2 having now put into the **h.** of Judas *2588*
Joh 14:1 **Let not your h. be troubled: ye** *2588*
Joh 14:27 **Let not your h. be troubled,** *2588*
Joh 16:6 **you, sorrow hath filled your h.** *2588*
Joh 16:22 **and your h. shall rejoice, and your** *2588*
Ac 2:26 Therefore did my **h.** rejoice, and my *2588*
Ac 2:37 they were pricked in their **h.**, and *2588*
Ac 2:46 with gladness and singleness of **h.**, *2588*
Ac 4:32 were of one **h.**, and of one soul: *2588*
Ac 5:3 why hath Satan filled thine **h.** to lie *2588*
Ac 5:4 conceived this thing in thine **h.**? *2588*
Ac 5:33 heard that, they were cut to the **h.**, *2588*
Ac 7:23 into his **h.** to visit his brethren *2588*
Ac 7:51 and uncircumcised in **h.** and ears, *2588*
Ac 7:54 they were cut to the **h.**, and they *2588*
Ac 8:21 thy **h.** is not right in the sight of *2588*
Ac 8:22 the thought of thine **h.** may be *2588*
Ac 8:37 If thou believest with all thine **h.**, *2588*
Ac 11:23 with purpose of **h.** they would cleave *2588*
Ac 13:22 Jesse, a man after mine own **h.**, *2588*
Ac 16:14 whose **h.** the Lord opened, that she *2588*
Ac 21:13 ye to weep and to break mine **h.**? *2588*
Ac 28:27 For the **h.** of this people is waxed *2588*
Ac 28:27 understand with their **h.**, and should *2588*
Ro 1:21 and their foolish **h.** was darkened. *2588*
Ro 2:5 after thy hardness and impenitent **h.** *2588*
Ro 2:29 and circumcision is that of the **h.**, *2588*
Ro 6:17 have obeyed from the **h.** that form *2588*
Ro 9:2 and continual sorrow in my **h.** *2588*
Ro 10:6 Say not in thine **h.**, Who shall ascend *2588*
Ro 10:8 even in thy mouth, and in thy **h.**: *2588*
Ro 10:9 shalt believe in thine **h.** that God *2588*
Ro 10:10 For with the **h.** man believeth unto *2588*
1Co 2:9 have entered in to the **h.** of man, *2588*
1Co 7:37 he that standeth stedfast in his **h.**, *2588*
1Co 7:37 and hath so decreed in his **h.** that *2588*
1Co 14:25 the secrets of his **h.** made manifest; *2588*
2Co 2:4 and anguish of **h.** I wrote unto you *2588*
2Co 3:3 stone, but in fleshy tables of the **h.** *2588*
2Co 3:15 is read, the vail is upon their **h.** *2588*
2Co 5:12 glory in appearance, and not in **h.**. *2588*
2Co 6:11 open unto you, our **h.** is enlarged. *2588*
2Co 8:16 care into the **h.** of Titus for you. *2588*
2Co 9:7 as he purposeth in his **h.**, so let him *2588*
Eph 4:18 because of the blindness of their **h.**: *2588*
Eph 5:19 making melody in your **h.** to the *2588*
Eph 6:5 in singleness of your **h.**, as unto *2588*
Eph 6:6 doing the will of God from the **h.**; *5590*
Php 1:7 all, because I have you in my **h.**; *2588*
Col 3:22 but in singleness of **h.**, fearing God: *2588*
1Th 2:17 short time in presence, not in **h.**, *2588*
1Ti 1:5 is charity out of a pure **h.**, and of a *2588*
2Ti 2:22 call on the Lord out of a pure **h.** *2588*
Heb 3:10 They do alway err in their **h.**; *2588*
Heb 3:12 be in any of you an evil **h.** of *2588*
Heb 4:12 of thoughts and intents of the **h.** *2588*
Heb 10:22 Let us draw near with a true **h.** in *2588*
Heb 13:9 thing that the **h.** be established. *2588*
Jas 1:26 his tongue, but deceiveth his own **h.**, *2588*
1Pe 1:22 ye love one another with a pure **h.** *2588*
1Pe 3:4 let it be the hidden man of the **h.**, *2588*
2Pe 2:14 an **h.** they have exercised with *2588*
1Jo 3:20 For if our **h.** condemn us, God is *2588*
1Jo 3:20 God is greater than our **h.**, and *2588*
1Jo 3:21 if our **h.** condemn us not, then have *2588*
Re 18:7 for she saith in her **h.**, I sit a queen, *2588*

HEARTED See also BROKENHEARTED; FAINTHEARTED; HARDHEARTED; MERRYHEARTED; STIFFHEARTED; STOUTHEARTED; TENDERHEARTED.

Ex 28:3 speak unto all that are wise **h.**, 3820
Ex 31:6 in the hearts of all that are wise **h.** 3820
Ex 35:10 And every wise **h.** among you shall 3820
Ex 35:22 as many as were willing **h.**, and 3820
Ex 35:25 And all the women that were wise **h.** 3820
Ex 36:1 and every wise **h.** man, in whom 3820
Ex 36:2 and every wise **h.** man, in whose 3820
Ex 36:8 And every wise **h.** man among them 3820

HEARTH

Ge 18:6 knead it and make cakes upon the **h.** 3820
Ps 102:3 my bones are burned as an **h.** 4168
Isa 30:14 a sherd to take fire from the **h.**, or 3344
Jer 36:22 fire on the **h.** burning before him. 254
Jer 36:23 it into the fire that was on the **h.**, 254
Jer 36:23 in the fire that was on the **h.** 254
Zec 12:6 like an **h.** of fire among the wood, 3595

HEARTILY

Col 3:23 whatsoever ye do, do it **h.**, as to *1537,5590*

HEART'S

Ps 10:3 wicked boasteth of his **h.** desire, 5315
Ps 21:2 Thou hast given him his **h.** desire, 3820
Ro 10:1 my **h.** desire and prayer to God *2588*

HEARTS

Ge 18:5 of bread, and comfort ye your **h.**; 3820
Ex 14:17 will harden the **h.** of the Egyptians, 3820
Ex 31:6 the **h.** of all that are wise hearted 3820
Le 26:36 will send a faintness into their **h.** 3824
Le 26:41 uncircumcised **h.** be humbled, 3824
De 20:3 let not your **h.** faint, fear not, and 3824
De 32:46 Set your **h.** unto all the words 3824
Jos 2:11 our **h.** did melt, neither did there 3824
Jos 7:5 the **h.** of the people melted, and 3824
Jos 11:20 was of the Lord to harden their **h.**, 3820
Jos 23:14 ye know in all your **h.** and in all 3824
Jg 9:3 **h.** inclined to follow Abimelech; 3820
Jg 16:25 to pass, when their **h.** were merry, 3820
Jg 19:22 they were making their **h.** merry, 3820
1Sa 6:6 then do ye harden your **h.**, as the 3824
1Sa 6:6 and Pharaoh hardened their **h.**? 3820
1Sa 7:3 unto the Lord with all your **h.**, 3824
1Sa 7:3 and prepare your **h.** unto the Lord, 3824
1Sa 10:26 men, whose **h.** God had touched. 3820
2Sa 15:6 Absalom stole the **h.** of the men of 3820
2Sa 15:13 The **h.** of the men of Israel are 3820
1Ki 8:39 thou only, knowest the **h.** of all 3824
1Ki 8:58 he may incline our **h.** unto him, 3824
1Ch 28:9 for the Lord searcheth all **h.**, and 3824
2Ch 6:14 walk before thee with all their **h.**: 3820
2Ch 6:30 for thou only knowest the **h.** of the 3824
2Ch 11:16 such as set their **h.** to seek the Lord 3824
2Ch 20:33 the people had not prepared their **h.** 3824
Job 1:5 sinned, and cursed God in their **h.** 3824
Ps 7:9 the righteous God trieth the **h.** and 3826
Ps 28:3 but mischief is in their **h.** 3824
Ps 33:15 He fashioneth their **h.** alike; he 3820
Ps 35:25 Let them not say in their **h.**, Ah, so 3820
Ps 74:8 said in their **h.**, Let us destroy 3820
Ps 90:12 may apply our **h.** unto wisdom. 3824
Ps 125:4 them that are upright in their **h.** 3826
Pr 15:11 then the **h.** of the children of men? 3826
Pr 17:3 for gold: but the Lord trieth the **h.** 3826
Pr 21:2 eyes: but the Lord pondereth the **h.** 3826
Pr 31:6 unto those that be of heavy **h.** 5315
Isa 44:18 see; and their **h.**, that they cannot 3826
Jer 31:33 and write it in their **h.**; and will 3820
Jer 32:40 but I will put my fear in their **h.**, 3824
Jer 42:20 ye dissembled in your **h.**, when ye 5315
Jer 48:41 the mighty men's **h.** in Moab at 3820
Eze 13:2 that prophesy out of their own **h.**, 3820
Eze 32:9 will also vex the **h.** of many people, 3820
Da 11:27 both these kings' **h.** shall be to do 3824
Ho 7:2 they consider not in their **h.** that I 3824
Zec 7:12 they made their **h.** as an adamant 3820
Zec 8:17 none of you imagine evil in your **h.** 3820
Mt 9:4 **Wherefore think ye evil in your h.?** *2588*
Mt 18:35 **from your h. forgive not every one** *2588*
Mt 19:8 **because of the hardness of your h.** *4641*
Mk 2:6 there, and reasoning in their **h.**, *2588*
Mk 2:8 **reason ye these things in your h.?** *2588*
Mk 3:5 grieved for the hardness of their **h.**, *2588*
Mk 4:15 **word that was sown in their h.** *2588*
Lu 1:17 to turn the **h.** of the fathers to the *2588*
Lu 1:51 in the imagination of their **h.** *2588*
Lu 1:66 laid them up in their **h.**, saying, *2588*
Lu 2:35 the thoughts of many **h.** may be *2588*
Lu 3:15 all men mused in their **h.** of John, *2588*
Lu 5:22 them, **What reason ye in your h.?** *2588*
Lu 8:12 **away the word out of their h.,** *2588*
Lu 16:15 **but God knoweth your h.: for** *2588*
Lu 21:14 **Settle it therefore in your h., not** *2588*
Lu 21:26 **Men's h. failing them for fear, and** *674*
Lu 21:34 **any time your h. be overcharged** *2588*
Lu 24:38 **why do thoughts arise in your h.?** *2588*
Ac 1:24 which knowest the **h.** of all men, *2589*
Ac 7:39 in their **h.** turned back again into *2588*
Ac 14:17 filling our **h.** with food and gladness, *2588*
Ac 15:8 And God, which knoweth the **h.**, *2589*
Ac 15:9 them, purifying their **h.** by faith. *2588*

Ro 1:24 through the lusts of their own **h.**, *2588*
Ro 2:15 work of the law written in their **h.**, *2588*
Ro 5:5 love of God is shed abroad in our **h.** *2588*
Ro 8:27 he that searcheth the **h.** knoweth *2588*
Ro 16:18 deceive the **h.** of the simple. *2588*
1Co 4:5 manifest the counsels of the **h.**: *2588*
2Co 1:22 the earnest of the Spirit in our **h.** *2588*
2Co 3:2 written in our **h.**, known and read *2588*
2Co 4:6 hath shined in our **h.**, to give the *2588*
2Co 7:3 that ye are in our **h.** to die and live *2588*
Ga 4:6 the Spirit of his Son into your **h.**, *2588*
Eph 3:17 That Christ may dwell in your **h.** by *2588*
Eph 6:22 and that he might comfort your **h.** *2588*
Php 4:7 shall keep your **h.** and minds *2588*
Col 2:2 That their **h.** might be comforted, *2588*
Col 3:15 let the peace of God rule in your **h.**, *2588*
Col 3:16 singing with grace in your **h.** to the *2588*
Col 4:8 your estate, and comfort your **h.**; *2588*
1Th 2:4 men, but God, which trieth our **h.** *2588*
1Th 3:13 he may stablish your **h.** unblamable *2588*
2Th 2:17 Comfort your **h.**, and stablish you *2588*
2Th 3:5 And the Lord direct your **h.** into the *2588*
Heb 3:8 Harden not your **h.**, as in the *2588*
Heb 3:15 voice, harden not your **h.**, as in the *2588*
Heb 4:7 hear his voice, harden not your **h.** *2588*
Heb 8:10 mind, and write them in their **h.**: *2588*
Heb 10:16 I will put my laws into their **h.**, *2588*
Heb 10:22 having our **h.** sprinkled from an evil *2588*
Jas 3:14 envying and strife in your **h.**, *2588*
Jas 4:8 purify your **h.**, ye double minded *2588*
Jas 5:5 ye have nourished your **h.**, as in a *2588*
Jas 5:8 ye also patient; stablish your **h.**: *2588*
1Pe 3:15 sanctify the Lord God in your **h.**: *2588*
2Pe 1:19 and the day star arise in your **h.**: *2588*
1Jo 3:19 and shall assure our **h.** before him *2588*
Re 2:23 **which searcheth the reins and h.:** *2588*
Re 17:17 God hath put in their **h.** fulfil *2588*

HEARTS'
Ps 81:12 them up unto their own **h.** lust: 3820

HEARTY
Pr 27:9 of a man's friend by **h.** counsel. 5315

HE-ASSES See ASSES.

HEAT See also HEATED.
Ge 8:22 and cold and **h.**, and summer and 2527
Ge 18:1 in the tent door in the **h.** of the day; 2527
De 29:24 meaneth the **h.** of this great anger? 2750
De 32:34 devoured with burning **h.**, and 7565
1Sa 11:11 Ammonites until the **h.** of the day: 2527
2Sa 4:5 came about the **h.** of the day to her 2527
1Ki 1:1 him with clothes, but he gat no **h.** 3179
1Ki 1:2 that my lord the king may get **h.** 2552
Job 24:19 Drought and **h.** consume the snow 2527
Job 30:30 and my bones are burned with **h.** 2721
Ps 19:6 nothing hid from the **h.** thereof. 2535
Ec 4:11 lie together, then they have **h.**: 2552
Isa 4:6 shadow in the daytime from the **h.**, 2721
Isa 18:4 like a clear **h.** upon herbs, and like 2527
Isa 18:4 a cloud of dew in the **h.** of harvest. 2527
Isa 25:4 the storm, a shadow from the **h.**, 2721
Isa 25:5 strangers, as the **h.** in a dry place; 2721
Isa 25:5 the **h.** with the shadow of a cloud: 2721
Isa 49:10 neither shall the **h.** nor sun smite 8273
Jer 17:8 and shall not see when **h.** cometh, 2527
Jer 36:30 be cast out in the day to the **h.**, 2721
Jer 51:39 their **h.** I will make their feasts, 2527
Eze 3:14 bitterness, in the **h.** of my spirit; 2534
Da 3:19 that they should **h.** the furnace 228
Mt 20:12 **borne the burden and h. of the** *2742*
Lu 12:55 **ye say, There will be h.; and it** *2742*
Ac 28:3 there came a viper out of the **h.**, *2329*
Jas 1:11 no sooner risen with a burning **h.**, *2742*
2Pe 3:10 elements shall melt with fervent **h.**, *2741*
2Pe 3:12 elements shall melt with fervent **h.**? *2741*
Re 7:16 the sun light on them, nor any **h.** *2738*
Re 16:9 men were scorched with great **h.**, *2738*

HEATED
Da 3:19 more than it was wont to be **h.** 228
Ho 7:4 as an oven **h.** by the baker, 1197

HEATH
Jer 17:6 shall be like the **h.** in the desert, 6176
Jer 48:6 be like the **h.** in the wilderness. 6176

HEATHEN
Le 25:44 the **h.** that are round about you; 1471
Le 26:33 I will scatter you among the **h.**, 1471
Le 26:38 And ye shall perish among the **h.**, 1471
Le 26:45 land of Egypt in the sight of the **h.**, 1471
De 4:27 left few in number among the **h.**, 1471
2Sa 22:44 hast kept me to be head of the **h.**: 1471
2Sa 22:50 unto thee, O Lord, among the **h.**, 1471
2Ki 16:3 to the abominations of the **h.**, 1471
2Ki 17:8 walked in the statutes of the **h.**, 1471
2Ki 17:11 did the **h.** whom the Lord carried 1471
2Ki 17:15 went after the **h.** that were round 1471
2Ki 21:2 after the abominations of the **h.**, 1471
1Ch 16:24 Declare his glory among the **h.**; 1471
1Ch 16:35 deliver us from the **h.**, that we may 1471
2Ch 20:6 over all the kingdoms of the **h.**? 1471
2Ch 28:3 after the abominations of the **h.** 1471
2Ch 33:2 unto the abominations of the **h.**, 1471
2Ch 33:9 to do worse than the **h.**, whom the 1471
2Ch 36:14 all the abominations of the **h.**; 1471
Ezr 6:21 the filthiness of the **h.** of the land, 1471
Ne 5:8 Jews, which were sold unto the **h.**; 1471
Ne 5:9 because of the reproach of the **h.** 1471
Ne 5:17 came unto us from among the **h.** 1471
Ne 6:6 It is reported among the **h.**, and 1471
Ne 6:16 all the **h.** that were about us saw 1471
Ps 2:1 Why do the **h.** rage, and the people 1471
Ps 2:8 I shall give thee the **h.** for thine 1471
Ps 9:5 Thou hast rebuked the **h.**, thou 1471
Ps 9:15 The **h.** are sunk down in the pit 1471
Ps 9:19 let the **h.** be judged in thy sight. 1471
Ps 10:16 the **h.** are perished out of his land. 1471
Ps 18:43 hast made me the head of the **h.**: 1471
Ps 18:49 unto thee, O Lord, among the **h.**, 1471
Ps 33:10 the counsel of the **h.** to nought: 1471
Ps 44:2 thou didst drive out the **h.** with 1471
Ps 44:11 hast scattered us among the **h.** 1471
Ps 44:14 us a byword among the **h.**, a 1471
Ps 46:6 The **h.** raged, the kingdoms were 1471
Ps 46:10 I will be exalted among the **h.**, 1471
Ps 47:8 God reigneth over the **h.**: God 1471
Ps 59:5 of Israel, awake to visit all the **h.**: 1471
Ps 59:8 shalt have all the **h.** in derision. 1471
Ps 78:55 cast out the **h.** also before them, 1471
Ps 79:1 **h.** are come into thine inheritance; 1471
Ps 79:6 Pour out thy wrath upon the **h.** that 1471
Ps 79:10 Wherefore should the **h.** say, Where 1471
Ps 79:10 let him be known among the **h.** in 1471
Ps 80:8 hast cast out the **h.**, and planted 1471
Ps 94:10 He that chastiseth the **h.**, shall not 1471
Ps 96:3 Declare his glory among the **h.**, 1471
Ps 96:10 Say among the **h.** that the Lord 1471
Ps 98:2 shewed in the sight of the **h.** 1471
Ps 102:15 So the **h.** shall fear the name of 1471
Ps 105:44 And gave them the lands of the **h.**: 1471
Ps 106:35 But were mingled among the **h.**, 1471
Ps 106:41 gave them into the hand of the **h.**; 1471
Ps 106:47 and gather us from among the **h.**, 1471
Ps 110:6 He shall judge among the **h.**, he 1471
Ps 111:6 give them the heritage of the **h.** 1471
Ps 115:2 Wherefore should the **h.** say, 1471
Ps 126:2 then said they among the **h.**, The 1471
Ps 135:15 The idols of the **h.** are silver and 1471
Ps 149:7 To execute vengeance upon the **h.**, 1471
Isa 16:8 lords of the **h.** have broken down 1471
Jer 9:16 scatter them also among the **h.**, 1471
Jer 10:2 Learn not the way of the **h.**, and 1471
Jer 10:2 for the **h.** are dismayed at them. 1471
Jer 10:25 Pour out thy fury upon the **h.** that 1471
Jer 18:13 Ask ye now among the **h.**, who 1471
Jer 49:14 an ambassador is sent unto the **h.**, 1471
Jer 49:15 make thee small among the **h.**, 1471
La 1:3 she dwelleth among the **h.**, she 1471
La 1:10 she hath seen that the **h.** entered 1471
La 4:15 they said among the **h.**, They shall 1471
La 4:20 shadow we shall live among the **h.** 1471
Eze 7:24 I will bring the worst of the **h.**, 1471
Eze 11:12 after the manners of the **h.** that 1471
Eze 11:16 cast them far off among the **h.**, and 1471
Eze 12:16 their abominations among the **h.** 1471
Eze 16:14 renown went forth among the **h.** 1471
Eze 20:9 be polluted before the **h.**, among 1471
Eze 20:14 be polluted before the **h.**, in 1471
Eze 20:22 be polluted in the sight of the **h.**, 1471
Eze 20:23 would scatter them among the **h.**, 1471
Eze 20:32 say, We will be as the **h.**, as the 1471
Eze 20:41 be sanctified in you before the **h.** 1471
Eze 22:4 made thee a reproach unto the **h.**, 1471
Eze 22:15 will scatter thee among the **h.**, 1471
Eze 22:16 in thyself in the sight of the **h.**, 1471
Eze 23:30 hast gone a whoring after the **h.**, 1471
Eze 25:7 deliver thee for a spoil to the **h.**; 1471
Eze 25:8 of Judah is like unto all the **h.**; 1471
Eze 28:25 sanctified…in the sight of the **h.**, 1471
Eze 30:3 it shall be the time of the **h.**, 1471
Eze 31:11 hand of the mighty one of the **h.**; 1471
Eze 31:17 shadow in the midst of the **h.** 1471
Eze 34:28 shall no more be a prey to the **h.**, 1471
Eze 34:29 neither bear the shame of the **h.** 1471
Eze 36:3 unto the residue of the **h.**, and ye 1471
Eze 36:4 to the residue of the **h.** that are 1471
Eze 36:5 against the residue of the **h.**, and 1471
Eze 36:6 ye have born the shame of the **h.**: 1471
Eze 36:7 Surely the **h.** that are about you, 1471
Eze 36:15 the shame of the **h.** any more, 1471
Eze 36:19 I scattered them among the **h.**, 1471
Eze 36:20 And when they entered unto the **h.**, 1471
Eze 36:21 Israel had profaned among the **h.**, 1471
Eze 36:22 ye have profaned among the **h.**, 1471
Eze 36:23 which was profaned among the **h.**, 1471
Eze 36:23 **h.** shall know that I am the Lord, 1471
Eze 36:24 will take you from among the **h.**, 1471
Eze 36:30 reproach of famine among the **h.** 1471
Eze 36:36 Then the **h.** that are left round 1471
Eze 37:21 Israel from among the **h.**, whither 1471
Eze 37:28 **h.** shall know that I the Lord do 1471
Eze 38:16 that the **h.** may know me, when 1471
Eze 39:7 **h.** shall know that I am the Lord, 1471
Eze 39:21 I will set my glory among the **h.** 1471
Eze 39:21 all the **h.** shall see my judgment 1471
Eze 39:23 the **h.** shall know that the house 1471
Eze 39:28 led into captivity among the **h.**: 1471
Joe 2:17 that the **h.** should rule over them: 1471
Joe 2:19 you a reproach among the **h.**: 1471
Joe 3:11 and come, all ye **h.**, and gather 1471
Joe 3:12 Let the **h.** be wakened, and come 1471
Joe 3:12 to judge all the **h.** round about. 1471
Am 9:12 of all the **h.**, which are called by 1471
Ob 1 ambassador is sent among the **h.**, 1471
Ob 2 made thee small among the **h.**: 1471
Ob 15 the Lord is near upon all the **h.**: 1471
Ob 16 shall all the **h.** drink continually, 1471
Mic 5:15 in anger and fury upon the **h.**, 1471
Hab 1:5 Behold ye among the **h.**, and 1471
Hab 3:12 thou didst thresh the **h.** in anger. 1471
Zep 2:11 even all the isles of the **h.** 1471
Hag 2:22 of the kingdoms of the **h.**; and I 1471
Zec 1:15 sore displeased with the **h.** that 1471
Zec 8:13 as ye were a curse among the **h.**, 1471
Zec 9:10 he shall speak peace unto the **h.**: 1471
Zec 14:14 the wealth of all the **h.** round 1471
Zec 14:18 smite the **h.** that come not up 1471
Mal 1:11 name shall be great among the **h.**, 1471
Mal 1:14 name is dreadful among the **h.** 1471
Mt 6:7 **not vain repetitions, as the h. do:** *1482*
Mt 18:17 **let him be unto thee as an h. man.** *1482*
Ac 4:25 Why did the **h.** rage, and the *1484*
2Co 11:26 in perils by the **h.**, in perils in the *1484*
Ga 1:16 I might preach him among the **h.**; *1484*
Ga 2:9 that we should go unto the **h.**, and *1484*
Ga 3:8 that God would justify the **h.** *1484*

HEAVE See also HEAVED.
Ex 29:27 the shoulder of the **h.** offering, 8641
Ex 29:28 for it is an **h.** offering: and it shall 8641
Ex 29:28 be an **h.** offering from the children 8641
Ex 29:28 their **h.** offering unto the Lord. 8641
Le 7:14 an **h.** offering unto the Lord, and it 8641
Le 7:32 an **h.** offering of the sacrifices of 8641
Le 7:34 and the **h.** shoulder have I taken of 8641
Le 10:14 the wave breast and **h.** shoulder 8641
Le 10:15 The **h.** shoulder and the wave 8641
Nu 6:20 the wave breast and **h.** shoulder: 8641
Nu 15:19 shall offer up an **h.** offering unto the 8641
Nu 15:20 of your dough for an **h.** offering: 8641
Nu 15:20 **h.** offering of the threshingfloor, 8641
Nu 15:20 threshingfloor, so shall ye **h.** it. 7311
Nu 15:21 the Lord an **h.** offering in your 8641
Nu 18:8 the charge of mine **h.** offerings of 8641
Nu 18:11 the **h.** offering of their gift, with all 8641
Nu 18:19 the **h.** offerings of the holy things, 8641
Nu 18:24 which they offer as an **h.** offering 8641
Nu 18:26 ye shall offer up an **h.** offering of 8641
Nu 18:27 your **h.** offering shall be reckoned 8641
Nu 18:28 offer an **h.** offering unto the Lord 8641

Nu	18:28	the Lord's **h.** offering to Aaron the	8641
Nu	18:29	offer every **h.** offering of the Lord,	8641
Nu	31:29	for an **h.** offering of the Lord.	8641
Nu	31:41	which was the Lord's **h.** offering,	8641
De	12:6	**h.** offerings of your hand, and your	8641
De	12:11	and the **h.** offering of your hand,	8641
De	12:17	or **h.** offering of thine hand:	8641

HEAVED

Ex	29:27	is waved, and which is **h.** up, of	7311
Nu	18:30	When ye have **h.** the best thereof	7311
Nu	18:32	when ye have **h.** from it the best of	7311

HEAVEN See also HEAVEN'S; HEAVENS.

Ge	1:1	the beginning God created the **h.**	8064
Ge	1:8	And God called the firmament **H.**	8064
Ge	1:9	waters under the **h.** be gathered	8064
Ge	1:14,	15 lights in the firmament of the **h.**	8064
Ge	1:17	set them in the firmament of the **h.**	8064
Ge	1:20	earth in the open firmament of **h.**	8064
Ge	6:17	the breath of life, from under **h.**;	8064
Ge	7:11	and the windows of **h.** were opened	8064
Ge	7:19	hills, that were under the whole **h.**,	8064
Ge	7:23	things, and the fowl of the **h.**; and	8064
Ge	8:2	the windows of **h.** were stopped, and	8064
Ge	8:2	the rain from **h.** was restrained,	8064
Ge	11:4	whose top may reach unto **h.**; and	8064
Ge	14:19	high God, possessor of **h.** and earth:	8064
Ge	14:22	God, the possessor of **h.** and earth,	8064
Ge	15:5	Look now toward **h.**, and tell the	8064
Ge	19:24	and fire from the Lord out of **h.**;	8064
Ge	21:17	of God called to Hagar out of **h.**,	8064
Ge	22:11	the Lord called unto him out of **h.**,	8064
Ge	22:15	Lord called unto Abraham out of **h.**	8064
Ge	22:17	thy seed as the stars of the **h.**,	8064
Ge	24:3	the Lord, the God of **h.**, and the God	8064
Ge	24:7	The Lord God of **h.**, which took me	8064
Ge	26:4	seed to multiply as the stars of **h.**,	8064
Ge	27:28	God give thee of the dew of **h.**, and	8064
Ge	27:39	and of the dew of **h.** from above;	8064
Ge	28:12	and the top of it reached to **h.**: and	8064
Ge	28:17	of God, and this is the gate of **h.**	8064
Ge	49:25	bless thee with blessings of **h.** above,	8064
Ex	9:8	sprinkle it toward the **h.** in the sight	8064
Ex	9:10	Moses sprinkled it up toward **h.**;	8064
Ex	9:22	Stretch forth thine hand toward **h.**,	8064
Ex	9:23	stretched forth his rod toward **h.**:	8064
Ex	10:21	Stretch out thine hand toward **h.**,	8064
Ex	10:22	stretched forth his hand toward **h.**;	8064
Ex	16:4	I will rain bread from **h.** for you;	8064
Ex	17:14	of Amalek from under **h.**	8064
Ex	20:4	likeness of any thing that is in **h.**	8064
Ex	20:11	days the Lord made **h.** and earth,	8064
Ex	20:22	that I have talked with you from **h.**	8064
Ex	24:10	were the body of **h.** in his clearness.	8064
Ex	31:17	days the Lord made **h.** and earth,	8064
Ex	32:13	multiply your seed as the stars of **h.**,	8064
Le	26:19	and I will make your **h.** as iron, and	8064
De	1:10	as the stars of **h.** for multitude.	8064
De	1:28	cities are great and walled up to **h.**;	8064
De	2:25	nations that are under the whole **h.**,	8064
De	3:24	what God is there in **h.** or in earth,	8064
De	4:11	with fire unto the midst of **h.**, with	8064
De	4:19	lest thou lift up thine eyes unto **h.**,	8064
De	4:19	and the stars, even all the host of **h.**,	8064
De	4:19	unto all nations under the whole **h.**	8064
De	4:26	I call **h.** and earth to witness against	8064
De	4:32	the one side of **h.** unto the other,	8064
De	4:36	Out of **h.** he made thee to hear his	8064
De	4:39	he is God in **h.** above, and upon the	8064
De	5:8	likeness of any thing that is in **h**,	8064
De	7:24	destroy their name from under **h.**:	8064
De	9:1	cities great and fenced up to **h.**,	8064
De	9:14	blot out their name from under **h.**:	8064
De	10:14	the **h.** and the **h.** of heavens is the	8064
De	10:22	thee as the stars of **h.** for multitude.	8064
De	11:11	and drinketh water of the rain of **h.**:	8064
De	11:17	and he shut up the **h.**, that there be	8064
De	11:21	as the days of **h.** upon the earth.	8064
De	17:3	or moon, or any of the host of **h.**,	8064
De	25:19	of Amalek from under **h.**; thou	8064
De	26:15	from thy holy habitation, from **h.**,	8064
De	28:12	the **h.** to give the rain unto thy land	8064
De	28:23	thy **h.** that is over thy head shall be	8064
De	28:24	**h.** shall it come down upon thee,	8064
De	28:62	as the stars of **h.** for multitude;	8064
De	29:20	blot out his name from under **h.**	8064
De	30:4	out unto the uttermost parts of **h.**,	8064
De	30:12	It is not in **h.**, that thou shouldest	8064
De	30:12	say, Who shall go up for us to **h.**,	8064
De	30:19	I call **h.** and earth to record this day	8064
De	31:28	call **h.** and earth to record against	8064
De	32:40	For I lift up my hand to **h.**, and say,	8064
De	33:13	precious things of **h.**, for the dew,	8064
De	33:26	who rideth upon the **h.** in thy help,	8064
Job	2:11	he is God in **h.** above, and in earth	8064
Job	8:20	smoke of the city ascended up to **h.**,	8064
Job	10:11	Lord cast down great stones from **h.**	8064
Job	10:13	the sun stood still in the midst of **h.**,	8064
Jg	5:20	They fought from **h.**; the stars in	8064
Jg	13:20	the flame went up toward **h.** from	8064
Jg	20:40	flame of the city ascended up to **h.**	8064
1Sa	2:10	of **h.** shall he thunder upon them:	8064
1Sa	5:12	they cry of the city went up to **h.**	8064
2Sa	18:9	taken up between the **h.** and the	8064
2Sa	21:10	water dropped upon them out of **h.**,	8064
2Sa	22:8	foundations of **h.** moved and shook,	8064
2Sa	22:14	The Lord thundered from **h.**, and	8064
1Ki	8:22	spread forth his hands toward **h.**:	8064
1Ki	8:23	is no God like thee, in **h.** above, or	8064
1Ki	8:27	**h.** and **h.** of heavens cannot contain	8064
1Ki	8:30	hear thou in **h.** thy dwelling place:	8064
1Ki	8:32	hear thou in **h.**, and do, and judge	8064
1Ki	8:34	Then hear thou in **h.**, and forgive	8064
1Ki	8:35	When **h.** is shut up, and there is no	8064
1Ki	8:36	Then hear thou in **h.**, and forgive	8064
1Ki	8:39,	43 hear thou in **h.** thy dwelling place,	8064
1Ki	8:45	hear thou in **h.** their prayer and	8064
1Ki	8:49	in **h.** thy dwelling place, and	8064
1Ki	8:54	with his hands spread up to **h.**	8064
1Ki	18:45	that the **h.** was black with clouds	8064
1Ki	22:19	all the host of **h.** standing by him	8064
2Ki	1:10	then let fire come down from **h.**,	8064
2Ki	1:10	And there came down fire from **h.**,	8064
2Ki	1:12	of God, let fire come down from **h.**,	8064
2Ki	1:12	the fire of God came down from **h.**,	8064
2Ki	1:14	came fire down from **h.**, and burnt	8064
2Ki	2:1	Lord would take up Elijah into **h.**	8064
2Ki	2:11	went up by a whirlwind into **h.**	8064
2Ki	7:2	Lord would make windows in **h.**,	8064
2Ki	7:19	Lord should make windows in **h.**,	8064
2Ki	14:27	the name of Israel from under **h.**:	8064
2Ki	17:16	and worshipped all the host of **h.**,	8064
2Ki	19:15	thou hast made **h.** and earth.	8064
2Ki	21:3	all the host of **h.**, and served them.	8064
2Ki	21:5	he built altars for all the host of **h.**	8064
2Ki	23:4	the grove, and for all the host of **h.**;	8064
2Ki	23:5	planets, and to all the host of **h.**	8064
1Ch	21:16	stand between the earth and the **h.**,	8064
1Ch	21:26	he answered him from **h.** by fire	8064
1Ch	29:11	all that is in the **h.** and in the earth	8064
2Ch	2:6	**h.** and **h.** of heavens cannot contain	8064
2Ch	2:12	of Israel, that made **h.** and earth,	8064
2Ch	6:13	spread forth his hands toward **h.**,	8064
2Ch	6:14	no God like thee in the **h.**, nor in the	8064
2Ch	6:18	**h.** and the **h.** of heavens cannot	8064
2Ch	6:21	thy dwelling place, even from **h.**;	8064
2Ch	6:23	Then hear thou from **h.**, and do, and	8064
2Ch	6:26	the **h.** is shut up, and there is no	8064
2Ch	6:27	hear thou from **h.**, and forgive the	8064
2Ch	6:30	hear thou from **h.** thy dwelling	8064
2Ch	7:1	the fire came down from **h.**, and	8064
2Ch	7:13	If I shut up **h.** that there be no rain,	8064
2Ch	7:14	then will I hear from **h.**, and will	8064
2Ch	18:18	the host of **h.** standing on his right	8064
2Ch	20:6	our fathers, art not thou God in **h.**?	8064
2Ch	28:9	in a rage that reacheth up unto **h.**	8064
2Ch	30:27	holy dwelling place, even unto **h.**	8064
2Ch	32:20	son of Amoz, prayed and cried to **h.**	8064
2Ch	33:3	and worshipped all the host of **h.**,	8064
2Ch	33:5	he built altars for all the host of **h.**	8064
2Ch	36:23	hath the Lord God of **h.** given me;	8064
Ezr	1:2	The Lord God of **h.** hath given me	8064
Ezr	5:11	We are the servants of the God of **h.**	8065
Ezr	5:12	fathers had provoked the God of **h.**	8065
Ezr	6:9	the burnt offerings of the God of **h.**,	8065
Ezr	6:10	sweet savours unto the God of **h.**,	8065
Ezr	7:12,	21 scribe of the law of the God of **h.**,	8065
Ezr	7:23	is commanded by the God of **h.**, let	8065
Ezr	7:23	done for the house of the God of **h.**:	8065
Ne	1:4	and prayed before the God of **h.**,	8064
Ne	1:5	O Lord God of **h.**, the great and	8064
Ne	1:9	unto the uttermost part of the **h.**,	8064
Ne	2:4	So I prayed to the God of **h.**	8064
Ne	2:20	The God of **h.**, he will prosper us;	8064
Ne	9:6	thou hast made **h.**, the **h.** of heavens,	8064
Ne	9:6	and the host of **h.** worshippeth thee	8064
Ne	9:13	and spakest with them from **h.**,	8064
Ne	9:15	gavest them bread from **h.** for their	8064
Ne	9:23	mutipliedst thou as the stars of **h.**,	8064
Ne	9:27,	28 thou heardest them from **h.**; and	8064
Job	1:16	The fire of God is fallen from **h.**,	8064
Job	2:12	dust upon their heads toward **h.**	8064
Job	11:8	It is as high as **h.**; what canst thou	8064
Job	16:19	behold, my witness is in **h.**, and my	8064
Job	20:27	The **h.** shall reveal his iniquity;	8064
Job	22:12	Is not God in the height of **h.**?	8064
Job	22:14	and he walketh in the circuit of **h.**	8064
Job	26:11	The pillars of **h.** tremble and are	8064
Job	28:24	earth, and seeth under the whole **h.**;	8064
Job	35:11	maketh us wiser than the fowls of **h.**?	8064
Job	37:3	He directeth it under the whole **h.**,	8064
Job	38:29	and the hoary frost of **h.**, who hath	8064
Job	38:33	Knowest thou the ordinances of **h.**?	8064
Job	38:37	or who can stay the bottles of **h.**,	8064
Job	41:11	is under the whole **h.** is mine.	8064
Ps	11:4	temple, the Lord's throne is in **h.**:	8064
Ps	14:2	The Lord looked down from **h.** upon	8064
Ps	19:6	forth is from the end of the **h.**, and	8064
Ps	20:6	he will hear him from his holy **h.**	8064
Ps	33:13	Lord looketh from **h.**; he beholdeth	8064
Ps	53:2	God looked down from **h.** upon the	8064
Ps	57:3	He shall send from **h.**, and save me	8064
Ps	69:34	Let the **h.** and earth praise him,	8064
Ps	73:25	Whom have I in **h.** but thee? and	8064
Ps	76:8	judgment to be heard from **h.**;	8064
Ps	77:18	of thy thunder was in the **h.**; the	1534
Ps	78:23	above, and opened the doors of **h.**,	8064
Ps	78:24	had given them of the corn of **h.**	8064
Ps	78:26	an east wind to blow in the **h.**;	8064
Ps	79:2	be meat unto the fowls of the **h.**,	8064
Ps	80:14	look down from **h.**, and behold, and	8064
Ps	85:11	righteousness shall look...from **h.**	8064
Ps	89:6	who in the **h.** can be compared	7834
Ps	89:29	and his throne as the days of **h.**	8064
Ps	89:37	and as a faithful witness in **h.**	7834
Ps	102:19	from **h.** did the Lord behold the	8064
Ps	103:11	as the **h.** is high above the earth,	8064
Ps	104:12	shall the fowls of the **h.** have their	8064
Ps	105:40	them with the bread of **h.**	8064
Ps	107:26	They mount up to the **h.**, they go	8064
Ps	113:6	the things that are in **h.**, and in the	8064
Ps	115:15	the Lord which made **h.** and earth.	8064
Ps	115:16	The **h.**, even the heavens, are the	8064
Ps	119:89	O Lord, thy work is settled in **h.**	8064
Ps	121:2	the Lord, which made **h.** and earth.	8064
Ps	124:8	the Lord, who made **h.** and earth.	8064
Ps	134:3	The Lord that made **h.** and earth	8064
Ps	135:6	the Lord pleased, that did he in **h.**,	8064
Ps	136:26	O give thanks unto the God of **h.**:	8064
Ps	139:8	If I ascend up into **h.**, thou art there:	8064
Ps	146:6	Which made **h.**, and earth, the sea,	8064
Ps	147:8	Who covereth the **h.** with clouds,	8064
Ps	148:13	his glory is above the earth and **h.**	8064
Pr	23:5	they fly away as an eagle toward **h.**	8064
Pr	25:3	The **h.** for height, and the earth for	8064
Pr	30:4	Who hath ascended up into **h.**, or	8064
Ec	1:13	all things that are done under **h.**:	8064
Ec	2:3	should do under the **h.** all the days	8064
Ec	3:1	time to every purpose under the **h.**;	8064
Ec	5:2	God is in **h.**, and thou upon earth:	8064
Isa	13:5	a far country, from the end of **h.**,	8064
Isa	13:10	the stars of **h.** and the constellations	8064
Isa	14:12	How art thou fallen from **h.**, O	8064
Isa	14:13	I will ascend into **h.**, I will exalt	8064
Isa	34:4	all the host of **h.** shall be dissolved,	8064
Isa	34:5	for my sword shall be bathed in **h.**:	8064
Isa	37:16	earth: thou hast made **h.** and earth.	8064
Isa	40:12	and meted out **h.** with the span,	8064
Isa	55:10	cometh down, and the snow from **h.**,	8064
Isa	63:15	Look down from **h.**, and behold	8064
Isa	66:1	The **h.** is my throne, and the earth	8064
Jer	7:18	to make cakes to the queen of **h.**,	8064
Jer	7:33	shall be meat for the fowls of the **h.**,	8064
Jer	8:2	the moon, and all the host of **h.**,	8064
Jer	8:7	Yea, the stork in the **h.** knoweth her	8064
Jer	10:2	be not dismayed at the signs of **h.**;	8064
Jer	15:3	the fowls of the **h.**, and the beasts	8064
Jer	16:4	shall be meat for the fowls of **h.**,	8064

Jer 19:7 to be meat for the fowls of the h., ... 8064
Jer 19:13 incense unto all the host of h., and..... 8064
Jer 23:24 Do not I fill h. and earth? saith......... 8064
Jer 31:37 If h. above can be measured, and....... 8064
Jer 32:17 thou hast made the h. and the earth... 8064
Jer 33:22 the host of h. cannot be numbered, ... 8064
Jer 33:25 the ordinances of h. and earth; 8064
Jer 34:20 be for meat unto the fowls of the h., .. 8064
Jer 44:17 burn incense unto the queen of h., ... 8064
Jer 44:18 to burn incense to the queen of h., ... 8064
Jer 44:19 burned incense to the queen of h., ... 8064
Jer 44:25 to burn incense to the queen of h., ... 8064
Jer 49:36 winds from the four quarters of h.,..... 8064
Jer 51:9 for her judgment reacheth unto h., ... 8064
Jer 51:15 hath stretched out the h. by his........ 8064
Jer 51:48 the h. and the earth, and all that is 8064
Jer 51:53 Babylon should mount up to h., ... 8064
La 2:1 cast down from h. unto the earth....... 8064
La 3:50 Lord look down, and behold from h.. .. 8064
La 4:19 swifter than the eagles of the h.: 8064
Eze 8:3 up between the earth and the h., ... 8064
Eze 29:5 of the field and to the fowls of the h.,. 8064
Eze 31:6 All the fowls of h. made their nests.... 8064
Eze 31:13 shall all the fowls of the h. remain,.... 8064
Eze 32:4 all the fowls of the h. to remain......... 8064
Eze 32:7 I will cover the h. and make the 8064
Eze 32:8 All the bright lights of h. will I........... 8064
Eze 38:20 the fowls of the h., and the beasts 8064
Da 2:18 desire mercies of the God of h. 8065
Da 2:19 Then Daniel blessed the God of h.. 8065
Da 2:28 there is a God in h. that revealeth 8065
Da 2:37 for the God of h. hath given thee a 8065
Da 2:38 the fowls of the h. hath he given 8065
Da 2:44 shall the God of h. set up a kingdom, ..8065
Da 4:11 height thereof reached unto h., and 8065
Da 4:12 and the fowls of the h. dwelt in the.... 8065
Da 4:13 and an holy one came down from h.; .. 8065
Da 4:15 let it be wet with the dew of h., and .. 8065
Da 4:20 whose height reached unto the h.,....... 8065
Da 4:21 branches the fowls of the h. had 8065
Da 4:22 is grown, and reacheth unto h., and.... 8065
Da 4:23 an holy one coming down from h.,...... 8065
Da 4:23 and let it be wet with the dew of h., .. 8065
Da 4:25 shall wet thee with the dew of h.,...... 8065
Da 4:31 there fell a voice from h., saying,....... 8065
Da 4:33 his body was wet with the dew of h., . 8065
Da 4:34 lifted up mine eyes unto h., and.......... 8065
Da 4:35 to his will in the army of h., and........ 8065
Da 4:37 and extol and honour the King of h.,.... 8065
Da 5:21 his body was wet with the dew of h.; . 8065
Da 5:23 up thyself against the Lord of h.: 8065
Da 6:27 he worketh signs and wonders in h...... 8065
Da 7:2 the four winds of the h. strove.......... 8065
Da 7:13 of man came with the clouds of h.,..... 8065
Da 7:27 of the kingdom under the whole h., ... 8065
Da 8:8 ones toward the four winds of h., ... 8064
Da 8:10 waxed great, even to the host of h.; 8064
Da 9:12 under the whole h. hath not been....... 8064
Da 11:4 divided toward the four winds of h.; ... 8064
Da 12:7 right hand and his left hand unto h., ... 8064
Ho 2:18 and with the fowls of h., and with...... 8064
Ho 4:3 the field, and with the fowls of h.;...... 8064
Ho 7:12 them down as the fowls of the h.;....... 8064
Am 9:2 though they climb up to h., thence..... 8064
Am 9:6 that buildeth his stories in the h.,....... 8064
Jon 1:9 the Lord, the God of h., which hath ... 8064
Na 3:16 thy merchants above the stars of h.:... 8064
Zep 1:3 I will consume the fowls of the h.. 8064
Zep 1:5 them that worship the host of h.......... 8064
Hag 1:10 the h. over you is stayed from dew.... 8064
Zec 2:6 abroad as the four winds of the h.,..... 8064
Zec 5:2 ephah between the earth and the h...... 8064
Mal 3:10 will not open you the windows of h., .. 8064
Mt 3:2 for the kingdom of h. is at hand......... 3772
Mt 3:17 And lo a voice from h., saying,.......... 3772
Mt 4:17 for the kingdom of h. is at hand... 3772
Mt 5:3, 10 theirs is the kingdom of h. 3772
Mt 5:12 for great is your reward in h.: for. 3772
Mt 5:16 glorify your Father which is in h...3772
Mt 5:18 Till h. and earth pass, one jot or .. 3772
Mt 5:19 the least in the kingdom of h.: 3772
Mt 5:19 called great in the kingdom of h. ... 3772
Mt 5:20 case enter into the kingdom of h.... 3772
Mt 5:34 Swear not at all; neither by h.; for.3772
Mt 5:45 of your Father which is in h.:....... 3772
Mt 5:48 Father which is in h. is perfect..... 3772
Mt 6:1 of your Father which is in h......... 3772
Mt 6:9 ye: Our Father which art in h.,..... 3772
Mt 6:10 will be done in earth, as it is in h..3772
Mt 6:20 up for yourselves treasures in h. ... 3772
Mt 7:11 Father which is in h. give good..... 3772
Mt 7:21 shall enter into the kingdom of h.. 3772
Mt 7:21 will of my Father which is in h., .. 3772
Mt 8:11 and Jacob, in the kingdom of h...... 3772
Mt 10:7 saying, The kingdom of h. is at..... 3772
Mt 10:32 before my Father which is in h..... 3772
Mt 10:33 before my Father which is in h..... 3772
Mt 11:11 that is least in the kingdom of h.... 3772
Mt 11:12 kingdom of h. suffereth violence... 3772
Mt 11:23 which art exalted unto h., shalt be.3772
Mt 11:25 O Father, Lord of h. and earth,.... 3772
Mt 12:50 will of my Father which is in h., .. 3772
Mt 13:11 the mysteries of the kingdom of h.,3772
Mt 13:24 kingdom of h. is likened unto a 3772
Mt 13:31 kingdom of h. is like to a grain 3772
Mt 13:33 kingdom of h. is like unto leaven,..3772
Mt 13:44, 45 Again, the kingdom of h. is like.3772
Mt 13:47 kingdom of h. is like unto a net.... 3772
Mt 13:52 instructed unto the kingdom of h. ..3772
Mt 14:19 and looking up to h., he blessed, and.. 3772
Mt 16:1 he would shew them a sign from h..... 3772
Mt 16:17 but thy Father which is in h......... 3772
Mt 16:19 thee the keys of the kingdom of h... 3772
Mt 16:19 bind on earth shall be bound in h.:3772
Mt 16:19 loose on earth shall be loosed in h. 3772
Mt 18:1 the greatest in the kingdom of h.?...... 3772
Mt 18:3 not enter into the kingdom of h.... 3772
Mt 18:4 is greatest in the kingdom of h. ... 3772
Mt 18:10 h. their angels do always behold ... 3772
Mt 18:10 face of my Father which is in h.... 3772
Mt 18:14 of your Father which is in h......... 3772
Mt 18:18 bind on earth shall be bound in h...3772
Mt 18:18 on earth shall be loosed in h......... 3772
Mt 18:19 them of my Father which is in h... 3772
Mt 18:23 the kingdom of h. is likened unto.. 3772
Mt 19:14 for of such is the kingdom of h..... 3772
Mt 19:21 and thou shalt have treasure in h.. 3772
Mt 19:23 enter into the kingdom of h.......... 3772
Mt 20:1 kingdom of h. is like unto a man.. 3772
Mt 21:25 whence was it? from h., or of men?3772
Mt 21:25 If we shall say, From h.; he will say... 3772
Mt 22:2 The kingdom of h. is like unto a... 3772
Mt 22:30 but are as the angels of God in h.. 3772
Mt 23:9 one is your Father, which is in h.. 3772
Mt 23:13 shut up the kingdom of h. against. 3772
Mt 23:22 that shall swear by h., sweareth by3772
Mt 24:29 the stars shall fall from h., and 3772
Mt 24:30 the sign of the Son of man in h. ... 3772
Mt 24:30 of man coming of the clouds of h...3772
Mt 24:31 from one end of h. to the other..... 3772
Mt 24:35 H. and earth shall pass away, but ..3772
Mt 24:36 the angels of h., but my Father 3772
Mt 25:1 the kingdom of h. be likened unto. 3772
Mt 25:14 For the kingdom of h. is as a man.3772
Mt 26:64 and coming in the clouds of h....... 3772
Mt 28:2 of the Lord descended from h., and.... 3772
Mt 28:18 given unto me in h. and in earth... 3772
Mk 1:11 there came a voice from h., saying,.... 3772
Mk 6:41 he looked up to h., and blessed, and... 3772
Mk 7:34 And looking up to h., he sighed, and... 3772
Mk 8:11 him, seeking of him a sign from h., ... 3772
Mk 10:21 and thou shalt have treasure in h.:3772
Mk 11:25 your Father also which is in h. ... 3772
Mk 11:26 your Father which is in h. forgive. 3772
Mk 11:30 John, was it from h., or of men? ... 3772
Mk 11:31 If we shall say, From h.; he will say,.. 3772
Mk 12:25 are as the angels which are in h. .. 3772
Mk 13:25 the stars of h. shall fall, and the... 3772
Mk 13:25 the powers that are in h. shall be.. 3772
Mk 13:27 earth to the uttermost part of h.... 3772
Mk 13:31 H. and earth shall pass away: but ..3772
Mk 13:32 no, not the angels which are in h...3772
Mk 14:62 and coming in the clouds of h....... 3772
Mk 16:19 he was received up into h., and sat.... 3772
Lu 2:15 were gone away from them into h., ... 3772
Lu 3:21 and praying, the h. was opened, And.. 3772
Lu 3:22 and a voice came from h., which....... 3772
Lu 4:25 the h. was shut up three years 3772
Lu 6:23 your reward is great in h.: for in .. 3772
Lu 9:16 and looking up to h., he blessed 3772
Lu 9:54 command fire to come down from h.,... 3772
Lu 10:15 which art exalted to h., shalt be.... 3772
Lu 10:18 Satan as lightning fall from h....... 3772
Lu 10:20 your names are written in h., ... 3772
Lu 10:21 O Father, Lord of h. and earth,..... 3772
Lu 11:2 say, Our Father which art in h.,.... 3772
Lu 11:2 will be done as in h., so in earth... 3772
Lu 11:16 him, sought of him a sign from h. 3772
Lu 15:7 joy shall be in h. over one sinner.. 3772
Lu 15:18 I have sinned against h., and........ 3772
Lu 15:21 Father, I have sinned against h.,... 3772
Lu 16:17 is easier for h. and earth to pass... 3772
Lu 17:24 out of the one part under h., ... 3772
Lu 17:24 unto the other part under h.;........ 3772
Lu 17:29 rained fire and brimstone from h., .3772
Lu 18:13 lift up so much as his eyes unto h.,3772
Lu 18:22 and thou shalt have treasure in h.:.3772
Lu 19:38 peace in h., and glory in the highest... 3772
Lu 20:4 baptism of John, was it from h., or3772
Lu 20:5 If we shall say, From h.; he will........ 3772
Lu 21:11 great signs shall there be from h... 3772
Lu 21:26 the powers of h. shall be shaken. .. 3772
Lu 21:33 H. and earth shall pass away: but ..3772
Lu 22:43 appeared an angel unto him from h.,... 3772
Lu 24:51 from them, and carried up into h........ 3772
Joh 1:32 descending from h. like a dove, and.... 3772
Joh 1:51 Hereafter ye shall see h. open, and 3772
Joh 3:13 no man hath ascended up to h.,.... 3772
Joh 3:13 but he that came down from h.,.... 3772
Joh 3:13 the Son of man which is in h........ 3772
Joh 3:27 except it be given him from h. 3772
Joh 3:31 he that cometh from h. is above all. ... 3772
Joh 6:31 He gave them bread from h. to eat 3772
Joh 6:32 gave you not that bread from h.;... 3772
Joh 6:32 giveth you the true bread from h... 3772
Joh 6:33 is he which cometh down from h., .3772
Joh 6:38 I came down from h., not to do 3772
Joh 6:41 the bread which came down from h. ... 3772
Joh 6:42 that he saith, I came down from h.? ... 3772
Joh 6:50 bread which cometh down from h., 3772
Joh 6:51, 58 which came down from h.: 3772
Joh 12:28 Then came there a voice from h., ... 3772
Joh 17:1 and lifted up his eyes to h., and said,.. 3772
Ac 1:10 looked stedfastly toward h. as he 3772
Ac 1:11 why stand ye gazing up into h.? 3772
Ac 1:11 which is taken up from you into h., ... 3772
Ac 1:11 as ye have seen him go into h........... 3772
Ac 2:2 there came a sound from h. as of a 3772
Ac 2:5 men, out of every nation under h. 3772
Ac 2:19 I will shew wonders in h. above, and.. 3772
Ac 3:21 Whom the h. must receive until the.... 3772
Ac 4:12 none other name under h. given 3772
Ac 4:24 which hast made h., and earth, and 3772
Ac 7:42 them up to worship the host of h.; 3772
Ac 7:49 H. is my throne, and earth is my....... 3772
Ac 7:55 looked up stedfastly into h., and saw .. 3772
Ac 9:3 round about him a light from h.: 3772
Ac 10:11 And saw h. opened, and a certain 3772
Ac 10:16 vessel was received up again into h. ... 3772
Ac 11:5 let down from h. by four corners; 3772
Ac 11:9 voice answered me again from h., ... 3772
Ac 11:10 and all were drawn up again into h., ... 3772
Ac 14:15 which made h., and earth, and the 3772
Ac 14:17 gave us rain from h., and fruitful......... 3771
Ac 17:24 that he is Lord of h. and earth, ... 3772
Ac 22:6 there shone from h. a great light 3772
Ac 26:13 I saw in the way a light from h.,......... 3771
Ro 1:18 wrath of God is revealed from h. 3772
Ro 10:6 heart, Who shall ascend into h.? 3772
1Co 8:5 gods, whether in h. or in earth, as...... 3772
1Co 15:47 the second man is the Lord from h..... 3772
2Co 5:2 with our house which is from h.:........ 3772
2Co 12:2 an one caught up to the third h. 3772
Ga 1:8 we, or an angel from h., preach any ... 3772
Eph 1:10 both which are in h., and which 3772
Eph 3:15 family in h. and earth is named, ... 3772
Eph 6:9 your Master also is in h.; neither........ 3772
Php 2:10 of things in h., and things in earth...... 2032
Php 3:20 For our conversation is in h.; from..... 3772
Col 1:5 hope which is laid up for you in h.,...... 3772
Col 1:16 that are in h., and that are in earth, ... 3772
Col 1:20 be things in earth, or things in h......... 3772
Col 1:23 every creature which is under h.;........ 3772
Col 4:1 knowing ye also have a Master in h..... 3772
1Th 1:10 And to wait for his Son from h., ... 3772
1Th 4:16 shall descend from h. with a shout, ... 3772
2Th 1:7 Jesus shall be revealed from h. 3772
Heb 9:24 but into h. itself, now to appear in 3772
Heb 10:34 that ye have in h. a better and an 3772
Heb 12:23 firstborn, which are written in h., ... 3772
Heb 12:25 from him that speaketh from h.: 3772

Heb 12:26 shake not the earth only, but also **h.** *3772*
Jas 5:12 swear not neither by **h.**, neither *3772*
Jas 5:18 and the **h.** gave rain, and the earth *3772*
1Pet 1:4 not away, reserved in **h.** for you, *3772*
1Pet 1:12 the Holy Ghost sent down from **h.**; *3772*
1Pet 3:22 Who is gone into **h.**, and is on the *3772*
2Pe 1:18 this voice which came from **h.** we *3772*
1Jo 5:7 are three that bear record in **h.**, the *3772*
Re 3:12 **down out of h. from my God:** *3772*
Re 4:1 behold, a door was opened in **h.**: *3772*
Re 4:2 a throne was set in **h.**, and one sat *3772*
Re 5:3 And no man in **h.**, nor in earth, *3772*
Re 5:13 every creature which is in **h.**, and *3772*
Re 6:13 the stars of **h.** fell unto the earth, *3772*
Re 6:14 And the **h.** departed as a scroll when *3772*
Re 8:1 was silence in **h.** about the space of *3772*
Re 8:10 and there fell a great star from **h.**, *3772*
Re 8:13 flying through the midst of **h.**, *3321*
Re 9:1 I was a star fall from **h.** unto the *3772*
Re 10:1 angel come down from **h.**, clothed *3772*
Re 10:4 I heard a voice from **h.** saying unto *3772*
Re 10:5 the earth lifted up his hand to **h.**, *3772*
Re 10:6 who created **h.**, and the things that *3772*
Re 10:8 voice which I heard from **h.** spake *3772*
Re 11:6 These have power to shut **h.**, that it *3772*
Re 11:12 heard a great voice from **h.** saying *3772*
Re 11:12 they ascended up to **h.** in a cloud; *3772*
Re 11:13 and gave glory to the God of **h.** *3772*
Re 11:15 were great voices in **h.**, saying, The *3772*
Re 11:19 the temple of God was opened in **h.**, *3772*
Re 12:1 appeared a great wonder in **h.**; *3772*
Re 12:3 appeared another wonder in **h.**; *3772*
Re 12:4 third part of the stars of **h.**, and did *3772*
Re 12:7 And there was war in **h.**: Michael *3772*
Re 12:8 was their place found any more in **h.** *3772*
Re 12:10 heard a loud voice saying in **h.**, Now *3772*
Re 13:6 and them that dwell in **h.** *3772*
Re 13:13 fire come down from **h.** on the earth *3772*
Re 14:2 I heard a voice from **h.**, as the voice *3772*
Re 14:6 another angel fly in the midst of **h.**, *3321*
Re 14:7 that made **h.**, and earth, and the *3772*
Re 14:13 I heard a voice from **h.** saying unto *3772*
Re 14:17 out of the temple which is in **h.**, he *3772*
Re 15:1 I saw another sign in **h.**, great and *3772*
Re 15:5 the tabernacle of the testimony in **h.** *3772*
Re 16:11 blasphemed the God of **h.** because *3772*
Re 16:17 great voice out of the temple of **h.**, *3772*
Re 16:21 fell upon men a great hail out of **h.**, *3772*
Re 18:1 another angel come down from **h.**, *3772*
Re 18:4 and I heard another voice from **h.**, *3772*
Re 18:5 For her sins have reached unto **h.**, *3772*
Re 18:20 Rejoice over her, thou **h.**, and ye *3772*
Re 19:1 a great voice of much people in **h.**, *3321*
Re 19:11 And I saw **h.** opened, and behold a *3321*
Re 19:14 armies which were in **h.** followed *3321*
Re 19:17 the fowls that fly in the midst of **h.**, *3321*
Re 20:1 angel came down from **h.**, having *3772*
Re 20:9 fire came down from God out of **h.**, *3772*
Re 20:11 face the earth and the **h.** fled away; *3772*
Re 21:1 I saw a new **h.** and a new earth: *3772*
Re 21:1 for the first **h.** and the first earth *3772*
Re 21:2 coming down from God out of **h.**, *3772*
Re 21:3 heard a great voice out of **h.** saying, *3772*
Re 21:10 holy Jerusalem, descending out of **h.** *3772*

HEAVENLY
Mt 6:14 **your h. Father will also forgive** *3770*
Mt 6:26 **yet your h. Father feedeth them** *3770*
Mt 6:32 **h. Father knoweth that ye have** *3770*
Mt 15:13 **my h. Father hath not planted,** *3770*
Mt 18:35 **shall my h. Father do also unto** *2032*
Lu 2:13 a multitude of the **h.** host praising *3770*
Lu 11:13 **your h. Father give the Holy** *1537,3772*
Joh 3:12 **believe, if I tell you of h. things?** *2032*
Ac 26:19 disobedient unto the **h.** vision: *3770*
1Co 15:48 and as is the **h.**, such are they also *2032*
1Co 15:48 such are they also that are **h.**, *2032*
1Co 15:49 shall also bear the image of the **h.** *2032*
Eph 1:3 spiritual blessings in **h.** places in *2032*
Eph 1:20 own right hand in the **h.** places, *2032*
Eph 2:6 together in **h.** places in Christ Jesus: *2032*
Eph 3:10 powers in **h.** places might be known *2032*
2Ti 4:18 preserve me unto his **h.** kingdom: *2032*
Heb 3:1 brethren, partakers of the **h.** calling, *2032*
Heb 6:4 tasted of the **h.** gift, and were made *2032*
Heb 8:5 example and shadow of **h.** things *2032*
Heb 9:23 but the **h.** things themselves with *2032*
Heb 11:16 a better country, that is, an **h.**; *2032*
Heb 12:22 of the living God, the **h.** Jerusalem, *2032*

HEAVEN'S
Mt 19:12 **eunuchs for the kingdom of h.** *3772*

HEAVENS
Ge 2:1 the **h.** and the earth were finished, 8064
Ge 2:4 the generations of the **h.** and of 8064
Ge 2:4 God made the earth and the **h.**, 8064
De 10:14 and the heaven of **h.** is the Lord's 8064
De 32:1 Give ear, O ye **h.**, and I will speak; 8064
De 33:28 also his **h.** shall drop down dew 8064
Jg 5:4 and the **h.** dropped the clouds also 8064
2Sa 22:10 He bowed the **h.** also, and came 8064
1Ki 8:27 heaven of **h.** cannot contain thee; 8064
1Ch 16:26 are idols: but the Lord made the **h.** 8064
1Ch 16:31 Let the **h.** be glad, and let the earth 8064
1Ch 27:23 Israel like to the stars of the **h.** 8064
2Ch 2:6 heaven of **h.** cannot contain him? 8064
2Ch 6:18 heaven of **h.** cannot contain thee; 8064
2Ch 6:25 Then hear thou from the **h.**, and 8064
2Ch 6:33 Then hear thou from the **h.**, even 8064
2Ch 6:35 hear thou from the **h.** their prayer 8064
2Ch 6:39 Then hear thou from the **h.**, even 8064
Ezr 9:6 our trespass is grown up unto the **h.** 8064
Ne 9:6 hast made heaven, the heaven of **h.**, 8064
Job 9:8 Which alone spreadeth out the **h.**, 8064
Job 14:12 till the **h.** be no more, they shall not 8064
Job 15:15 yea, the **h.** are not clean in his sight 8064
Job 20:6 his excellency mount up to the **h.**, 8064
Job 26:13 his spirit he hath garnished the **h.**; 8064
Job 35:5 Look unto the **h.**, and see; and 8064
Ps 2:4 He that sitteth in the **h.** shall laugh: 8064
Ps 8:1 who hast set thy glory above the **h.** 8064
Ps 8:3 When I consider thy **h.**, the work of 8064
Ps 18:9 He bowed the **h.** also, and came 8064
Ps 18:13 The Lord also thundered in the **h.**, 8064
Ps 19:1 The **h.** declare the glory of God; 8064
Ps 33:6 word of the Lord were the **h.** made; 8064
Ps 36:5 Thy mercy, O Lord, is in the **h.**; 8064
Ps 50:4 He shall call to the **h.** from above, 8064
Ps 50:6 **h.** shall declare his righteousness: 8064
Ps 57:5 Be thou exalted, O God, above the **h.**; 8064
Ps 57:10 For thy mercy is great unto the **h.**, 8064
Ps 57:11 Be thou exalted, O God, above the **h.**: 8064
Ps 68:4 extol him that rideth upon the **h.** 6160
Ps 68:8 **h.** also dropped at the presence 8064
Ps 68:33 To him that rideth upon the **h.** of **h.**, 8064
Ps 73:9 They set their mouth against the **h.**, 8064
Ps 89:2 shalt thou establish in the very **h.** 8064
Ps 89:5 And the **h.** shall praise thy wonders, 8064
Ps 89:11 The **h.** are thine, the earth also is 8064
Ps 96:5 are idols: but the Lord made the **h.**, 8064
Ps 96:11 Let the **h.** rejoice, and let the earth 8064
Ps 97:6 The **h.** declare his righteousness, 8064
Ps 102:25 and the **h.** are the work of thy hands 8064
Ps 103:19 hath prepared his throne in the **h.**; 8064
Ps 104:2 stretchest out the **h.** like a curtain: 8064
Ps 108:4 For thy mercy is great above the **h.**: 8064
Ps 108:5 Be thou exalted, O God, above the **h.**: 8064
Ps 113:4 nations, and his glory above the **h.** 8064
Ps 115:3 our God is in the **h.**: he hath done 8064
Ps 115:16 heaven, even the **h.**, are the Lord's: 8064
Ps 123:1 eyes, O thou that dwellest in the **h.** 8064
Ps 136:5 To him that by wisdom made the **h.**: 8064
Ps 144:5 Bow thy **h.**, O Lord, and come down: 8064
Ps 148:1 Praise ye the Lord from the **h.**: 8064
Ps 148:4 Praise him, ye **h.** of **h.**, and ye waters 8064
Ps 148:4 and ye waters that be above the **h.** 8064
Pr 3:19 hath he established the **h.** 8064
Pr 8:27 he prepared the **h.**, I was there: 8064
Isa 1:2 Hear, O **h.**, and give ear, O earth: 8064
Isa 5:30 light is darkened in the **h.** thereof. 6183
Isa 13:13 Therefore I will shake the **h.**, and 8064
Isa 34:4 the **h.** shall be rolled together as a 8064
Isa 40:22 stretcheth out the **h.** as a curtain, 8064
Isa 42:5 he that created the **h.**, and stretched 8064
Isa 44:23 Sing, O ye **h.**; for the Lord hath 8064
Isa 44:24 that stretcheth forth the **h.** alone; 8064
Isa 45:8 Drop down, ye **h.**, from above, and 8064
Isa 45:12 have stretched out the **h.**, and all 8064
Isa 45:18 saith the Lord that created the **h.**; 8064
Isa 48:13 my right hand hath spanned the **h.**; 8064
Isa 49:13 Sing, O **h.**; and be joyful, O earth; 8064
Isa 50:3 I clothe the **h.** with blackness, and 8064
Isa 51:6 Lift up your eyes to the **h.**, and look 8064
Isa 51:6 the **h.** shall vanish away like smoke, 8064
Isa 51:13 hath stretched forth the **h.**, and laid 8064
Isa 51:16 that I may plant the **h.**, and lay the 8064
Isa 55:9 as the **h.** are higher than the earth, 8064
Isa 64:1 Oh that thou wouldest rend the **h.**, 8064
Isa 65:17 I create new **h.** and a new earth: 8064
Isa 66:22 as the new **h.** and the new earth, 8064
Jer 2:12 Be astonished, O ye **h.**, at this, and 8064
Jer 4:23 and the **h.**, and thy had no light. 8064
Jer 4:25 and all the birds of the **h.** were fled 8064
Jer 4:28 mourn, and the **h.** above be black: 8064
Jer 9:10 the fowl of the **h.** and the beast are 8064
Jer 10:11 gods that have not made the **h.** 8065
Jer 10:11 the earth, and from under these **h.** 8065
Jer 10:12 hath stretched out the **h.** by his 8064
Jer 10:13 is a multitude of waters in the **h.**, 8064
Jer 14:22 rain? or can the **h.** give showers? 8064
Jer 51:16 is a multitude of waters in the **h.**; 8064
La 3:41 with our hands unto God in the **h.** 8064
La 3:66 in anger from under the **h.** of the 8064
Eze 1:1 that the **h.** were opened, and I saw 8064
Da 4:26 have known that the **h.** do rule 8065
Ho 2:21 I will hear the **h.**, and they shall 8064
Joe 2:10 the **h.** shall tremble: the sun and 8064
Joe 2:30 I will shew wonders in the **h.** and in 8064
Joe 3:16 the **h.** and the earth shall shake: 8064
Hab 3:3 His glory covered the **h.**, and the 8064
Hag 2:6 I will shake the **h.**, and the earth, 8064
Hag 2:21 I will shake the **h.** and the earth; 8064
Zec 6:5 These the four spirits of the **h.**, 8064
Zec 8:12 and the **h.** shall give their dew; 8064
Zec 12:1 stretcheth forth the **h.**, and layeth 8064
Mt 3:16 lo, the **h.** were opened unto him, *3772*
Mt 24:29 **powers of the h. shall be shaken:** *3772*
Mk 1:10 he saw the **h.** opened, and the Spirit *3772*
Lu 12:33 **a treasure in the h. that faileth not** *3772*
Ac 2:34 David is not ascended into the **h.**: *3772*
Ac 7:56 Behold, I see the **h.** opened, and the *3772*
2Co 5:1 made with hands, eternal in the **h.** *3772*
Eph 4:10 that ascended up far above all **h.**, *3772*
Heb 1:10 and the **h.** are the works of thine *3772*
Heb 4:14 priest, that is passed into the **h.**, *3772*
Heb 7:26 and made higher than the **h.**; *3772*
Heb 8:1 the throne of the Majesty in the **h.**; *3772*
Heb 9:23 patterns of things in the **h.** should *3772*
2Pe 3:5 the word of God the **h.** were of old, *3772*
2Pe 3:7 But the **h.** and the earth, which are *3772*
2Pe 3:10 the **h.** shall pass away with a great *3772*
2Pe 3:12 **h.** being on fire shall be dissolved, *3772*
2Pe 3:13 look for new **h.** and a new earth, *3772*
Re 12:12 Therefore rejoice, ye **h.**, and ye that *3772*

HEAVE-OFFERING See HEAVE and OFFERING.

HEAVE-SHOULDER See HEAVE and SHOULDER.

HEAVIER
Job 6:3 now it would be **h.** than the sand 3513
Job 23:2 my stroke is **h.** than my groaning 3513
Pr 27:3 a fool's wrath is **h.** than them both. 3513

HEAVILY
Ex 14:25 wheels, that they drave them **h.**: 3517
Ps 35:14 I bowed down **h.**, as one that 6957
Isa 47:6 hast thou very **h.** laid thy yoke. 3513

HEAVINESS
Ezr 9:5 sacrifice I arose up from my **h.**; 8589
Job 9:27 I will leave off my **h.**, and comfort 6440
Ps 69:20 and I am full of **h.**: and I looked 5136
Ps 119:28 My soul melteth for **h.**: strengthen 8424
Pr 10:1 foolish son is the **h.** of his mother. 8424
Pr 12:25 **H.** in the heart of man maketh it 1674
Pr 14:13 but the end of that mirth is **h.** 8424
Isa 29:2 and there shall be **h.** and sorrow: 8386
Isa 61:3 of praise for the spirit of **h.**; 3544
Ro 9:2 great **h.** and continual sorrow *3077*
2Co 2:1 would not come again to you in **h.** *3077*
Php 2:26 and was full of **h.**, because that *85*
Jas 4:9 to mourning, and your joy to **h.** *2726*
1Pe 1:6 ye are in **h.** through manifold *3076*

HEAVY See also HEAVIER.
Ex 17:12 Moses' hands were **h.**; and they 3515
Ex 18:18 for this thing is too **h.** for thee; 3515
Nu 11:14 alone, because it is too **h.** for me. 3515
1Sa 4:18 for he was an old man, and **h.** 3513
1Sa 5:6 But the hand of the Lord was **h.** 3513
1Sa 5:11 the hand of God was very **h.** there. 3513
2Sa 14:26 because the hair was **h.** on him, 3513
1Ki 12:4 his **h.** yoke which he put upon us, 3515
1Ki 12:10 Thy father made our yoke **h.**, but 3513

1Ki 12:11 father did lade you with a **h.** yoke, ... 3515
1Ki 12:14 My father make your yoke **h.**, and 3513
1Ki 14:6 I am sent to thee with **h.** tidings, ... 7186
1Ki 20:43 went to his house **h.** and displeased, ... 5620
1Ki 21:4 Ahab came into his house **h.**,and 5620
2Ch 10:4 his **h.** yoke that he put upon us, ... 3515
2Ch 10:10 Thy father made our yoke **h.**, but 3513
2Ch 10:11 my father put a **h.** yoke upon you, ... 3515
2Ch 10:14 my father make your yoke **h.**, but 3513
Ne 5:18 bondage was **h.** upon this people. 3513
Job 33:7 neither shall my hand be **h.** upon 3513
Ps 32:4 night thy hand was **h.** upon me: 3513
Ps 38:4 over mine head: as an **h.** burden 3515
Ps 38:4 burden they are too **h.** for me. 3513
Pr 25:20 that singeth songs to an **h.** heart 7451
Pr 27:3 stone is **h.**, and the sand weighty: 3514
Pr 31:6 unto those that be of **h.** hearts. 4751
Isa 6:10 make their ears **h.**, and shut their 3513
Isa 24:20 transgression thereof shall be **h.** 3513
Isa 30:27 and the burden thereof is **h.**: 3514
Isa 46:1 your carriages were **h.** loaden: 3514
Isa 58:6 to undo the **h.** burdens, and to let 4133
Isa 59:1 neither his ear **h.**, that it cannot 3513
La 3:7 get out: he hath made my chain **h.**, ... 3513
Mt 11:28 **all ye that labour and are h. laden.** .....
Mt 23:4 **For they bind h. burdens and** *926*
Mt 26:37 began to be sorrowful and very **h.** *85*
Mt 26:43 asleep again: for their eyes were **h.** *916*
Mk 14:33 be sore amazed, and to be very **h.**; *85*
Mk 14:40 asleep again, for their eyes were **h.**, ... *916*
Lu 9:32 were with him were **h.** with sleep: *916*

HEBER (he'-bur) See also EBER; HEBER'S; HEBERITES.
Ge 46:17 and the sons of Beriah; **H.**, and 2268
Nu 26:45 the sons of Beriah: of **H.**, the 2268
Jg 4:11 Now **H.** the Kenite, which was of 2268
Jg 4:17 the tent of Jael the wife of **H.** the 2268
Jg 4:17 and the house of **H.** of Kenite. 2268
Jg 5:24 Jael the wife of **H.** the Kenite be, ... 2268
1Ch 4:18 and **H.** the father of Socho, and 2268
1Ch 5:13 Jachan, and Zia and **H.**, seven 5677
1Ch 7:31 And the sons of Beriah; **H.**, ... 2268
1Ch 7:32 And **H.** begat Japhlet, and Shomer, ... 2268
1Ch 8:17 Meshullam, and Hezeki, and **H.**, ... 2268
1Ch 8:22 And Ishpan, and **H.**, and Eliel, ... 5677
Lu 3:35 Phalec, which was the son of **H.**, ... *1443*

HEBERITES (he'-bur-ites)
Nu 26:45 of Heber, the family of the **H.**: of 2277

HEBER'S (he'-burs)
Jg 4:21 Then Jael **H.** wife took a nail of 2268

HEBREW (he'-broo) See also HEBREWESS; HEBREWS.
Ge 14:13 escaped, and told Abram the **H.**; 5680
Ge 39:14 he hath brought in a **H.** unto us 5680
Ge 39:17 the **H.** servant, which thou hast 5680
Ge 41:12 with us a young man, an **H.**, ... 5680
Ex 1:15 Egypt spake to the **H.** midwives, ... 5680
Ex 1:16 of a midwife to the **H.** women, ... 5680
Ex 1:19 Because the **H.** women are not as 5680
Ex 2:7 to thee a nurse of the **H.** women, ... 5680
Ex 2:11 spied an Egyptian smiting a **H.**, ... 5680
Ex 21:2 If thou buy an **H.** servant, six years ... 5680
De 15:12 and **H.** man, or an **H.** woman, ... 5680
Jer 34:9 being an **H.** or an Hebrewess, go 5680
Jer 34:14 every man his brother an **H.**, which 5680
Jon 1:9 And he said unto them, I am a **H.**; 5680
Lu 23:28 of Greek, and Latin, and **H.**, ... *1444*
Joh 5:2 called in the **H.** tongue Bethesda, ... *1447*
Joh 19:13 Pavement, but in the **H.**, Gabbatha *1447*
Joh 19:17 which is called in the **H.** Golgotha: *1447*
Joh 19:20 written in **H.**, and Greek, and Latin *1447*
Ac 21:40 spake unto them in the **H.** tongue, ... *1446*
Ac 22:2 that he spake in the **H.** tongue to *1446*
Ac 26:14 saying in the **H.** tongue, **Saul, Saul,** .. *1446*
Php 3:5 of Benjamin, an **H.** of the Hebrews; ... *1446*
Re 9:11 name in the **H.** tongue is Abaddon, ... *1447*
Re 16:16 in the **H.** tongue Armageddon *1447*

HEBREWESS (he'-broo-ess)
Jer 34:9 being an Hebrew or an **H.**, go free; 5680

HEBREWS (he'-brooz) See also HEBREWS'.
Ge 40:15 away out of the land of the **H.** 5680
Ge 43:32 might not eat bread with the **H.**; 5680
Ex 2:13 two men of the **H.** strove together 5680
Ex 3:18 God of the **H.** hath met with us: 5680
Ex 5:3 God of the **H.** hath met with us: 5680
Ex 7:16 The Lord God of the **H.** hath sent 5680
Ex 9:1, 13 saith the Lord God of the **H.**, ... 5680
Ex 10:3 Thus saith the Lord God of the **H.**, ... 5680
1Sa 4:6 great shout in the camp of the **H.**? 5680
1Sa 4:9 that ye be not servants unto the **H.** 5680
1Sa 13:3 all the land, saying, Let the **H.** hear. .. 5680
1Sa 13:7 some of the **H.** went over Jordan 5680
1Sa 13:19 the **H.** make them swords or spears: .. 5680
1Sa 14:11 the **H.** come forth out of the holes 5680
1Sa 14:21 **H.** that were with the Philistines 5680
1Sa 29:3 What do these **H.** here? And 5680
Ac 6:1 of the Grecians against the **H.**, ... *1445*
2Co 11:22 Are they **H.**? so am I. Are they *1445*
Php 3:5 of Benjamin, and Hebrew of the **H.**; ... *1445*
Heb *title* Paul The Apostle To The **H.** *1445*
Heb *subscr.* Written to the **H.** from Italy *1445*

HEBREWS' (he'-brooz)
Ex 2:6 This is one of the **H.** children 5680

HEBRON (he'-brun) See also HEBRONITES.
Ge 13:18 plain of Mamre, which is in **H.**, ... 2275
Ge 23:2 same is **H.** in the land of Canaan: 2275
Ge 23:19 same is **H.** in the land of Canaan. 2275
Ge 35:27 unto the city of Arbah, which is **H.**, ... 2275
Ge 37:14 So he sent him out of the vale of **H.**, .. 2275
Ex 6:18 Amram, and Izhar, and **H.**, and 2275
Nu 3:19 Amram, and Izehar, **H.**, and Uzziel 2275
Nu 13:22 by the south, and came unto **H.**; 2275
Nu 13:22 Now **H.** was built seven years before .. 2275
Jos 10:3 sent unto Hoham king of **H.**, and 2275
Jos 10:5 king of Jerusalem, the king of **H.**, ... 2275
Jos 10:23 king of Jerusalem the king of **H.**, ... 2275
Jos 10:36 and all Israel with him, unto **H.**; 2275
Jos 10:39 as he had done to **H.**, so he did to 2275
Jos 11:21 from the mountains, from **H.**, from 2275
Jos 12:10 Jerusalem, one; the king of **H.**, one; ... 2275
Jos 14:13 Jephunneh **H.** for an inheritance. 2275
Jos 14:14 **H.** therefore became the 2275
Jos 14:15 name of **H.** before was Kirjath-arba; ... 2275
Jos 15:13 father of Anak, which city is **H.** 2275
Jos 15:54 and Kirjath-arba, which is **H.**, and 2275
Jos 19:28 And **H.**, and Rehob, and Hammon, ... 2275
Jos 20:7 and Kirjath-arba, which is **H.**, ... 2275
Jos 21:11 **H.**, in the hill country of Judah, ... 2275
Jos 21:13 **H.** with her suburbs, to be a city 2275
Jg 1:10 the Canaanites that dwelt in **H.**, ... 2275
Jg 1:10 now the name of **H.** before was 2275
Jg 1:20 And they gave **H.** unto Caleb, as 2275
Jg 16:3 the top of an hill that is before **H.** 2275
1Sa 30:31 to them which were in **H.**, and to 2275
2Sa 2:1 I go up? And he said, Unto **H.** 2275
2Sa 2:3 and they dwelt in the cities of **H.**, ... 2275
2Sa 2:11 David was king in **H.** over the house .. 2275
2Sa 2:32 they came to **H.** at break of day. 2275
2Sa 3:2 unto David were sons born in **H.** 2275
2Sa 3:5 These were born to David in **H.** 2275
2Sa 3:19 to speak in the ears of David in **H.** 2275
2Sa 3:20 So Abner came to David to **H.**, and 2275
2Sa 3:22 Abner was not with David in **H.**; 2275
2Sa 3:27 when Abner was returned to **H.**, ... 2275
2Sa 3:32 And they buried Abner in **H.**: and 2275
2Sa 4:1 heard that Abner was dead in **H.**, ... 2275
2Sa 4:8 of Ish-bosheth unto David to **H.**, ... 2275
2Sa 4:12 hanged them up over the pool in **H.** .. 2275
2Sa 4:12 it in the sepulchre of Abner of **H.** 2275
2Sa 5:1 tribes of Israel to David unto **H.**, ... 2275
2Sa 5:3 of Israel came to the king to **H.**; 2275
2Sa 5:3 made a league with them in **H.** 2275
2Sa 5:5 In **H.** he reigned over Judah seven 2275
2Sa 5:13 after he was come from **H.**: and 2275
2Sa 15:7 I have vowed unto the Lord, in **H.** 2275
2Sa 15:9 peace. So he arose, and went to **H.** .. 2275
2Sa 15:10 shall say, Absalom reigneth in **H.** 2275
1Ki 2:11 seven years reigned he in **H.**, and 2275
1Ch 2:42 sons of Mareshah the father of **H.** 2275
1Ch 2:43 And the sons of **H.**; Korah, and 2275
1Ch 3:1 which were born unto him in **H.**; 2275
1Ch 3:4 These six were born unto him in **H.**; .. 2275
1Ch 6:2 Kohath; Amram, Izhar, and **H.**, and 2275
1Ch 6:18 were, Amram, and Izhar, and **H.**, ... 2275
1Ch 6:55 gave them **H.** in the land of Judah, ... 2275
1Ch 6:57 namely, **H.**, the city of refuge, ... 2275
1Ch 11:1 themselves to David unto **H.**, ... 2275
1Ch 11:3 elders of Israel to the king to **H.**; 2275
1Ch 11:3 made a covenant with them in **H.** 2275
1Ch 12:23 came to David to **H.**, to turn the 2275
1Ch 12:38 came with a perfect heart to **H.**, to 2275
1Ch 15:9 Of the sons of **H.**; Eliel the chief, ... 2275
1Ch 23:12 Amram, Izhar, **H.**, and Uzziel, four. ... 2275
1Ch 23:12 Of the sons of **H.**; Jeriah the first, ... 2275
1Ch 24:23 And the sons of **H.**; Jeriah the ....
1Ch 29:27 seven years reigned he in **H.**, and 2275
2Ch 11:10 Zorah, and Aijalon, and **H.**, which 2275

HEBRONITES (he-brun-ites)
Nu 3:27 and the family of the **H.**, and the 2276
Nu 26:58 the family of the **H.**, the family of 2276
1Ch 26:23 and the Izharites, the **H.**, and the 2276
1Ch 26:30 And of the **H.**, Hashabiah and his 2276
1Ch 26:31 Among the **H.** was Jerijah the chief, ... 2276
1Ch 26:31 even among the **H.**, according to 2276

HEDGE See also HEDGED; HEDGES.
Job 1:10 not thou made an **h.** about him, ... 7753
Pr 15:19 slothful man is as an **h.** thorns of 4881
Ec 10:8 whoso breaketh an **h.**, a serpent 1447
Isa 5:5 I will take away the **h.** thereof, ... 4881
Eze 13:5 the **h.** for the house of Israel 1447
Eze 22:30 them, that should make up the **h.**, ... 1447
Ho 2:6 I will **h.** up thy way with thorns, ... 7753
Mic 7:4 upright is sharper than a thorn **h.**: 4534
Mk 12:1 **and set an h. about it, and digged** . *5418*

HEDGED
Job 3:23 is hid, and whom God hath **h.** in? 5526
La 3:7 He hath **h.** me about, that I cannot 1443
Mt 21:33 **a vineyard, and h. it round** *5418,4060*

HEDGES
1Ch 4:23 that dwelt among plants and **h.**: 1448
Ps 80:12 thou then broken down her **h.**, ... 1447
Ps 89:40 Thou hast broken down all his **h.**; 1448
Jer 49:3 and run to and fro by the **h.**; for 1448
Na 3:17 which camp in the **h.** in the cold 1448
Lu 14:23 **Go out into the highways and h.,** .. *5418*

HEED
Ge 31:24 Tahe **h.** that thou speak not to 8104
Ge 31:29 Take thou **h.** that thou speak not 8104
Ex 10:28 Get thee from me, take **h.** to thyself, .. 8104
Ex 19:12 Take **h.** to yourselves, that ye go not . 8104
Ex 34:12 Take **h.** to thyself, lest thou make 8104
Nu 23:12 Must I not take **h.** to speak that 8104
De 2:4 take ye good **h.** unto yourselves 8104
De 4:9 Only take **h.** to thyself, and keep thy .. 8104
De 4:15 Take ye therefore good **h.** unto 8104
De 4:23 Take **h.** unto yourselves, lest ye 8104
De 11:16 Take **h.** to yourselves, that your 8104
De 12:13 Take **h.** to thyself that thou offer not .. 8104
De 12:19 Take **h.** to thyself that thou forsake 8104
De 12:30 Take **h.** to thyself that thou be not 8104
De 24:8 Take **h.** in the plague of leprosy, ... 8104
De 27:9 Take **h.**, and hearken, O Israel: 5535
Jos 22:5 But take diligent **h.** to do the 8104
Jos 23:11 Take good **h.** therefore unto your 8104
1Sa 19:2 take **h.** to thyself until the morning, ... 8104
2Sa 20:10 Amasa took no **h.** to the sword that ... 8104
1Ki 2:4 If thy children take **h.** to their way, ... 8104
1Ki 8:25 thy children take **h.** to their way, ... 8104
2Ki 10:31 Jehu took no **h.** to walk in the law 8104
1Ch 22:13 prosper if thou takest **h.** to fulfil 8104
1Ch 28:10 Take **h.** now; for the Lord hath 7200
2Ch 6:16 thy children take **h.** to their way 8104
2Ch 19:6 Take **h.** what ye do: for ye judge 7200
2Ch 19:7 take **h.** and do it: for there is no 8104
2Ch 33:8 so that they will take **h.** to do all 8104
Ezr 4:22 Take **h.** now that ye fail not to do 2095
Job 36:21 Take **h.**, regard not iniquity: for 8104
Ps 39:1 I said, I will take **h.** to my ways, ... 8104
Ps 119:9 by taking **h.** thereto according to 8104
Pr 17:4 wicked doer giveth **h.** to false lips; 7181
Ec 7:21 Also take no **h.** unto all words 5414,3820
Ec 12:9 he gave good **h.**, and sought out, ... 238
Isa 7:4 Take **h.**, and be quiet; fear him, ... 8104
Isa 21:7 hearkened diligently with much **h.** 7182
Jer 9:4 Take ye **h.** every one of his 8104
Jer 17:21 Take **h.** to yourselves, and bear no 8104
Jer 18:18 us not give **h.** to any of his words 7181
Jer 18:19 Give **h.** to me, O Lord, and hearken ... 7181
Ho 4:10 have left off to take **h.** to the Lord 8104
Mal 2:15 Therefore take **h.** to your spirit, and ... 8104
Mal 2:16 therefore take **h.** to your spirit, that ... 8104
Mt 6:1 **Take h. that ye do not your alms** .. *4337*
Mt 16:6 **Take h. and beware of the leaven** .. *3708*
Mt 18:10 **Take h. that ye despise not one of** . *3708*
Mt 24:4 **Take h. that no man deceive you.** ... *991*

Mk 4:24 **Take h. what ye hear: with what**.... *991*
Mk 8:15 **Take h., beware of the leaven of**... *3708*
Mk 13:5 **Take h. lest any man deceive you:**.. *991*
Mk 13:9 **take h. to yourselves: for they shall**. *991*
Mk 13:23 **take ye h.: behold, I have foretold**.. *991*
Mk 13:33 **Take ye h., watch and pray: for ye**. *991*
Lu 8:18 **Take h. therefore how ye hear: for**.. *991*
Lu 11:35 **Take h. therefore that the light**..... *4648*
Lu 12:15 **Take h.,...beware of covetousness:**. *3708*
Lu 17:3 **Take h. to yourselves: if thy**......... *4337*
Lu 21:8 **Take h. that ye be not deceived;**..... *991*
Lu 21:34 **take h. to yourselves, lest at any**... *4337*
Ac 3:5 he gave **h.** unto them, expecting to.... *1907*
Ac 5:35 take **h.** to yourselves what ye........... *4337*
Ac 8:6 accord gave **h.** unto those things........ *4337*
Ac 8:10 To whom they all gave **h.**, from the... *4337*
Ac 20:28 Take **h.** therefore unto yourselves,..... *4337*
Ac 22:26 Take **h.** what thou doest: for this....... *3708*
Ro 11:21 take **h.** lest he also spare not thee. *3708*
1Co 3:10 every man take **h.** how he buildeth...... *991*
1Co 8:9 But take **h.** lest by any means this....... *991*
1Co 10:12 thinketh he standeth take **h.** lest he..... *991*
Ga 5:15 take **h.** that ye be not consumed one.... *991*
Col 4:17 Take **h.** to the ministry which thou...... *991*
1Ti 1:4 give **h.** to fables and endless............. *4337*
1Ti 4:1 giving **h.** to seducing spirits, and........ *4337*
1Ti 4:16 Take **h.** unto thyself, and unto the..... *1907*
Tit 1:14 Not giving **h.** to Jewish fables, and..... *4337*
Heb 2:1 the more earnest **h.** to the things......... *4337*
Heb 3:12 Take **h.** brethren, lest there be in....... *991*
2Pe 1:19 ye do well that ye take **h.**, as unto..... *4337*

HEEL See also HEELS.
Ge 3:15 head, and thou shalt bruise his **h.**........ 6119
Ge 25:26 his hand took hold on Esau's **h.**;........ 6119
Job 18:9 The gin shall take him by the **h.**,....... 6119
Ps 41:9 hath lifted up his **h.** against me.......... 6119
Ho 12:3 He took his brother by the **h.** in the... 6117
Joh 13:18 **hath lifted up his h. against me**.... *4418*

HEELS
Ge 49:17 adder... that biteth the horse **h.**,........ 6119
Job 13:27 thou settest a print upon the **h.** of...... 8328
Ps 49:5 iniquity of my **h.** shall compass.......... 6120
Jer 13:22 discovered and thy **h.** made bare........ 6119

HEGAI (he'-gahee) See also HEGE.
Es 2:8 the palace, to the custody of **H.**,........ 1896
Es 2:8 custody of **H.**, keeper of the women... 1896
Es 2:15 **H.** the kin's chamberlain, the............. 1896

HEGE (he'-ghe) See also HEGAI.
Es 2:3 unto the custody of **H.** the king's....... 1896

HEIFER See also HEIFER'S.
Ge 15:9 Take me an **h.** of three years old,...... 5697
Nu 19:2 bring thee a red **h.** without spot,....... 6510
Nu 19:5 one shall burn the **h.** in his sight;....... 6510
Nu 19:6 the midst of the burning of the **h.**....... 6510
Nu 19:9 shall gather up the ashes of the **h.**,.... 6510
Nu 19:10 gathereth the ashes of the **h.** shall...... 6510
Nu 19:17 ashes of the burnt **h.** of purification.... 6510
De 21:3 elders of that city shall take an **h.**,..... 5697
De 21:4 down the **h.** unto a rough valley,........ 5697
De 21:6 shall wash their hands over the **h.**....... 5697
Jg 14:18 If ye had not plowed with my **h.**, ye.... 5697
1Sa 16:2 Take an **h.** with thee, and way, I am.. 5697
Isa 15:5 unto Zoar, an **h.** of three years old:..... 5697
Jer 46:20 Egypt is like a very fair **h.**, but......... 5697
Jer 48:34 voice,...as an **h.** of three years old:.... 5697
Jer 50:11 ye are grown fat as the **h.** at grass,... 5697
Ho 4:16 slideth back as a backsliding **h.**:......... 6510
Ho 10:11 Ephraim is as an **h.** that is taught,...... 5697
Heb 9:13 the ashes of an **h.** sprinkling the........ *1151*

HEIFER'S
De 21:4 shall strike off the **h.** neck there........ 5697

HEIGHT See also HEIGHTS.
Ge 6:15 and the **h.** of it thirty cubits............. 6967
Ex 25:10, 23 a cubit and a half the **h.** thereof..... 6967
Ex 27:1 the **h.** thereof shall be three cubits..... 6967
Ex 27:18 and the **h.** five cubits of fine twined.... 6967
Ex 30:2 two cubits shall be the **h.** thereof:....... 6967
Ex 37:1 and a cubit and a half the **h.** of it:...... 6967
Ex 37:10 a cubit and a half the **h.** thereof:........ 6967
Ex 37:25 and two cubits was the **h.** of it; the.... 6967
Ex 38:1 and three cubits the **h.** thereof.......... 6967
Ex 38:18 the **h.** in the breadth was five cubits... 6967
1Sa 16:7 or on the **h.** of his stature:............... 1364
1Sa 17:4 whose **h.** was six cubits and a span.... 1363
1Ki 6:2 and the **h.** thereof thirty cubits.......... 6967
1Ki 6:20 and twenty cubits in the **h.** thereof:.... 6967
1Ki 6:26 The **h.** of the one cherub was ten...... 6967
1Ki 7:2 the **h.** thereof thirty cubits, upon....... 6967
1Ki 7:16 the **h.** of the one chapiter was five..... 6967
1Ki 7:16 the **h.** of the other chapiter was five... 6967
1Ki 7:23 all about, his **h.** was five cubits: and... 6967
1Ki 7:27 thereof, and three cubits the **h.** of it... 6967
1Ki 7:32 the **h.** of a wheel was a cubit and....... 6967
2Ki 19:23 come up to the **h.** of the mountains,... 4791
2Ki 25:17 **h.** of the one pillar was eighteen....... 6967
2Ki 25:17 the **h.** of the chapiter three cubits;..... 6967
2Ch 3:4 the **h.** was an hundred and twenty:..... 1363
2Ch 4:1 and ten cubits the **h.** thereof............ 6967
2Ch 4:2 and five cubits the **h.** thereof; and a... 6967
2Ch 33:14 and raised it up a very great **h.**,........ 1361
Ezr 6:3 the **h.** thereof threescore cubits,........ 7312
Job 22:12 Is not God in the **h.** of heaven? and.... 1363
Job 22:12 behold the **h.** of the stars, how high... 7218
Ps 102:19 down from the **h.** of his sanctuary;..... 4791
Pr 25:3 The heaven for **h.**, and the earth....... 7312
Isa 7:11 in the depth; or in the **h.** above......... 1361
Isa 37:24 come up to the **h.** of the mountains,... 4791
Isa 37:24 will enter into the **h.** of his border,..... 4791
Jer 31:12 come and sing in the **h.** of Zion, and... 4791
Jer 49:16 rock, that holdest the **h.** of the hill;.... 4791
Jer 51:53 should fortify the **h.** of her strength,... 4791
Jer 52:21 the **h.** of one pillar was eighteen........ 6967
Jer 52:22 and the **h.** of one chapiter was five..... 6967
Eze 17:23 In the mountain of the **h.** of Israel...... 4791
Eze 19:11 and she appeared in her **h.** with the.... 1363
Eze 20:40 in the mountain of the **h.** of Israel,..... 4791
Eze 31:5 his **h.** was exalted above all the......... 6967
Eze 31:10 thou hast lifted up thyself in **h.**,......... 6967
Eze 31:10 and his heart is lifted up in his **h.**;...... 1363
Eze 31:14 exalt themselves for their **h.**,............ 6967
Eze 31:14 their trees stand up in their **h.**,......... 1363
Eze 32:5 and fill the valleys with thy **h.**,.......... 7419
Eze 40:5 one reed; and the **h.**, one reed........... 6967
Eze 41:8 I saw also the **h.** of the house.......... 1364
Da 3:1 whose **h.** was threescore cubits,........ 7314
Da 4:10 earth, and the **h.** thereof was great.... 7314
Da 4:11 the **h.** thereof reached unto heaven,... 7314
Da 4:20 whose **h.** reached unto the heaven,.... 7314
Am 2:9 Amorite before them, whose **h.** was.... 1363
Am 2:9 was like the **h.** of the cedars, and...... 1363
Ro 8:39 Nor **h.**, nor depth, nor any other....... *5313*
Eph 3:18 and length, and depth, and **h.**;........... *5311*
Re 21:16 breadth and the **h.** of it are equal....... *5311*

HEIGHTS
Ps 148:1 the heavens: praise him in the **h.**....... 4791
Isa 14:14 ascend above the **h.** of the clouds:..... 1116

HEINOUS
Job 31:11 For this is an **h.** crime; yea, it is an... 2154

HEIR See also HEIRS.
Ge 15:3 one born in my house is mine **h.**........ 3423
Ge 15:4 this shall not be thine **h.**; but he........ 3423
Ge 15:4 thine own bowels shall be thine **h.**....... 3423
Ge 21:10 of this bondwoman shall not be **h.**....... 3423
2Sa 14:7 and we will destroy the **h.** also;.......... 3423
Pr 30:23 handmaid that is **h.** to her mistress...... 3423
Jer 49:1 Hath Israel no sons? hath he no **h.**?.... 3423
Jer 49:2 then shall Israel be **h.** unto them........ 3423
Mic 1:15 Yet will I bring an **h.** unto thee,......... 3423
Mt 21:38 **is the h.; come, let us kill him,**..... *2818*
Mk 12:7 **is the h.; come, let us kill him,**..... *2818*
Lu 20:14 **is the h.; come, let us kill him,**..... *2818*
Ro 4:13 he should be the **h.** of the world,....... *2818*
Ga 4:1 That the **h.**, as long as he is a child,... *2818*
Ga 4:7 then an **h.** of God through Christ....... *2818*
Ga 4:30 shall not be **h.** with the son of the...... *2816*
Heb 1:2 whom...appointed **h.** of all things,...... *2818*
Heb 11:7 and became **h.** of the righteousness.... *2818*

HEIRS See also FELLOWHEIRS; JOINT-HEIRS.
Jer 49:2 unto them that were his **h.**, saith....... 3423
Ro 4:14 if they which are of the law be **h.**,..... *2818*
Ro 8:17 And if children, then **h.**; **h.** of God,.... *2818*
Ga 3:29 and **h.** according to the promise......... *2818*
Tit 3:7 by his grace, we should be made **h.**.... *2818*
Heb 1:14 them who shall be **h.** of salvation?...... *2816*
Heb 6:17 to shew unto the **h.** of promise.......... *2818*
Heb 11:9 **h.** with him of the same promise:....... *4789*
Jas 2:5 rich in faith, and **h.** of the kingdom..... *2818*
1Pe 3:7 **h.** together of the grace of life;.......... *4789*

HELAH (he'-lah)
1Ch 4:5 had two wives, **H.** and Naarah.......... 2458
1Ch 4:7 the sons of **H.** were, Zereth, and....... 2458

HELAM (he'-lam)
2Sa 10:16 the river: and they came to **H.**: and... 2431
2Sa 10:17 passed over Jordan, and came to **H.**... 2431

HELBAH (hel'-bah)
Jg 1:31 nor of **H.**, nor of Aphik, nor of.......... 2462

HELBON (hel'-bon)
Eze 27:18 in the wine of **H.**, and white wool...... 2463

HELD See also BEHELD; HOLDEN; UPHELD; WITHHELD.
Ge 24:21 wondering at her **h.** his peace, to....... 2790
Ge 34:5 and Jacob **h.** his peace until they........ 2790
Ge 48:17 and he **h.** up his father's hand, to....... 8557
Ex 17:11 when Moses **h.** up his hand, that....... 7311
Ex 36:12 the loops **h.** one curtain to another..... 6901
Le 10:3 glorified. And Aaron **h.** his peace....... 1826
Nu 30:7 and **h.** his peace at her in the day...... 2790
Nu 30:11 heard it, and **h.** his peace at her,....... 2790
Nu 30:14 he **h.** his peace at her in the day he... 2790
Jg 7:20 **h.** the lamps in their left hands,......... 2388
Jg 16:26 unto the lad that **h.** him by the hand,.. 2388
Ru 3:15 And when she **h.** it, he measured........ 270
1Sa 10:27 no presents. But he **h.** his peace....... 2790
1Sa 25:36 behold, he **h.** a feast in his house,...... 2790
2Sa 18:16 Israel: for Joab **h.** back the people...... 2820
1Ki 8:65 at that time Solomon **h.** a feast,.......... 6213
2Ki 18:36 But the people **h.** their peace, and..... 2790
2Ch 4:5 received and **h.** three thousand.......... 3557
Ne 4:16 half of them **h.** both the spears,......... 2388
Ne 4:17 with the other hand **h.** a weapon......... 2388
Ne 4:21 half of them **h.** the spears from.......... 2388
Ne 5:8 Then **h.** they their peace, and........... 2790
Es 5:2 king **h.** out to Esther the golden........ 3447
Es 7:4 I had **h.** my tongue, although............ 2790
Es 8:4 the king **h.** out the golden sceptre...... 3447
Job 23:11 My foot hath **h.** his steps, his............ 270
Job 29:10 The nobles **h.** their peace, and.......... 2244
Ps 32:9 whose mouth must be **h.** in with........ 1102
Ps 39:2 I **h.** my peace, even from good;......... 2814
Ps 94:18 thy mercy, O Lord, **h.** me up............ 5582
Ca 3:4 I **h.** him, and would not let him go,....... 270
Ca 7:5 the king is **h.** in the galleries............. 631
Isa 36:21 they **h.** their peace, and answered...... 2790
Isa 57:11 have not I **h.** my peace even of old,... 2814
Jer 50:33 took them captives **h.** them fast;........ 2388
Da 12:7 when he **h.** up his right hand and....... 7311
Mt 12:14 and **h.** a council against him, how...... *2983*
Mt 26:63 But Jesus **h.** his peace. And the......... *4623*
Mt 28:9 they came and **h.** him by the feet,...... *2902*
Mk 3:4 **or to kill?** But they **h.** their peace.... *4623*
Mk 9:34 But they **h.** their peace: for by the..... *4623*
Mk 14:61 But he **h.** his peace, and answered..... *4623*
Mk 15:1 the chief priests **h.** a consultation....... *4160*
Lu 14:4 And they **h.** their peace. And he......... *2270*
Lu 20:26 at his answer, and **h.** their peace....... *4601*
Lu 22:63 the men that **h.** Jesus mocked him,.... *4912*
Ac 3:11 man which was healed **h.** Peter.......... *2902*
Ac 11:18 they **h.** their peace, and glorified........ *2270*
Ac 14:4 and part **h.** with the Jews, and part.... *2258*
Ac 15:13 and after they had **h.** their peace,...... *4601*
Ro 7:6 being dead wherein we were **h.**,......... *2722*
Re 6:9 for the testimony which they **h.**:......... *2192*

HELDAI (hel'-dahee) See also HELED; HELEM.
1Ch 27:15 **H.** the Netophathite, of Othniel:......... 2469
Zec 6:10 of them of the captivity, even of **H.**,.... 2469

HELDEST See WITHHELDEST.

HELEB (he'-leb) See also HELED.
2Sa 23:29 **H.** the son of Baanah, a.................... 2460

HELED (he'-led) See also HELEB; HELDAI.
1Ch 11:30 **H.** the son of Baanah the................. 2466

HELEK (he'-lek) See also HELEKITES.
Nu 26:30 of **H.**, the family of the Helekites:...... 2507
Jos 17:2 and for the children of **H.**, and for...... 2507

HELEKITES (he'-lek-ites)
Nu 26:30 of Helek, the family of the **h.**:........... 2516

HELEM (he'-lem) See also HELDAI.
1Ch 7:35 And the sons of his brother **H.**;......... 2494
Zec 6:14 And the crowns shall be to **H.**,........... 2494

HELEPH (he'-lef)
Jos 19:33 And their coast was from **H.**,........... 2501

HELEZ (he'-lez)
2Sa 23:26 H. the Paltite, Ira the son of 2503
1Ch 2:39 Azariah begat H., and H. begat 2503
1Ch 11:27 the Harorite, H. the Pelonite, 2503
1Ch 27:10 seventh month was H. the Pelonite, 2503

HELI (he'-li) See also ELI.
Lu 3:23 Joseph, which was the son of H., *2242*

HELKAI (hel'-kahee)
Ne 12:15 Of Harim, Adna; of Meraioth, H.; 2517

HELKATH (hel'-kath) See also HELKATH-HAZZURIM; HUKOK.
Jos 19:25 their border was H., and Hali, and 2520
Jos 21:31 H. with her suburbs, and Rehob 2520

HELKATH-HAZZURIM (hel'-kath-haz'-zu-rim)
2Sa 2:16 that place was called H., which is 2521

HELL
De 32:22 shall burn unto the lowest h., 7585
2Sa 22:6 The sorrows of h. compassed me 7585
Job 11:8 deeper than h.; what canst thou 7585
Job 26:6 H. is naked before him, and 7585
Ps 9:17 The wicked shall be turned into h., 7585
Ps 16:10 thou wilt not leave my soul in h.; 7585
Ps 18:5 The sorrows of h. compassed me 7585
Ps 55:15 let them go down quick into h.: 7585
Ps 86:13 my soul from the lowest h. 7585
Ps 116:3 the pains of h. gat hold upon me: 7585
Ps 139:8 if I make my bed in h., behold, 7585
Pr 5:5 death; her steps take hold on h. 7585
Pr 7:27 Her house is the way to h., going 7585
Pr 9:18 her guests are in the depths of h. 7585
Pr 15:11 H. and destruction are before the 7585
Pr 15:24 he may depart from h. beneath 7585
Pr 23:14 and shalt deliver his soul from h. 7585
Pr 27:20 H. and destruction are never full; 7585
Isa 5:14 Therefore h. hath enlarged herself, 7585
Isa 14:9 H. from beneath is moved for thee 7585
Isa 14:15 thou shalt be brought down to h., 7585
Isa 28:15 and with h. are we at agreement; 7585
Isa 28:18 agreement with h. shall not stand; 7585
Isa 57:9 didst debase thyself even unto h. 7585
Eze 31:16 I cast him down to h. with them 7585
Eze 31:17 They also went down into h. with 7585
Eze 32:21 speak to him out of the midst of h. 7585
Eze 32:27 gone down to h. with their weapons 7585
Am 9:2 Though they dig into h., thence 7585
Jon 2:2 out of the belly of h. cried I, and 7585
Hab 2:5 who enlargeth his desire as h., and 7585
Mt 5:22 **fool, shall be in danger of h. fire** *1067*
Mt 5:29, 30 **body should be cast into h.** *1067*
Mt 10:28 **destroy both soul and body in h.** *1067*
Mt 11:23 **shalt be brought down to h.: for if** *86*
Mt 16:18 **and the gates of h. shall not prevail** *86*
Mt 18:9 **two eyes to be cast into h. fire** *1067*
Mt 23:15 **the child of h. than yourselves** *1067*
Mt 23:33 **can ye escape the damnation of h.?** *1067*
Mk 9:43 **having two hands to go into h.** *1067*
Mk 9:45 **having two feet to be cast into h.,** *1067*
Mk 9:47 **having two eyes to be cast into h.** *1067*
Lu 10:15 **heaven, shalt be thrust down to h.** *86*
Lu 12:5 **killed hath power to cast into h.;** *1067*
Lu 16:23 **in h. he lift up his eyes, being in** *86*
Ac 2:27 thou wilt not leave my soul in h. *86*
Ac 2:31 that his soul was not left in h., *86*
Jas 3:6 nature; and it is set on fire of h. *1067*
2Pe 2:4 sinned, but cast them down to h. *5020*
Re 1:18 **have the keys of h. and of death** *86*
Re 6:8 Death, and H. followed with him *86*
Re 20:13 death and h. delivered up the dead *86*
Re 20:14 death and h. were cast into the lake *86*

HELL-FIRE See HELL and FIRE.

HELM
Jas 3:4 turned about with a very small h., *4079*

HELMET See also HELMETS.
1Sa 17:5 had an h. of brass upon his head, 3553
1Sa 17:38 put an h. of brass upon his head; 6959
Isa 59:17 an h. of salvation upon his head; 3553
Eze 23:24 buckler and shield and h. round 6959
Eze 27:10 hanged the shield and h. in thee; 3553
Eze 38:5 all of them with shield and h.: 3553
Eph 6:17 And take the h. of salvation, and *4030*
1Th 5:8 and for an h., the hope of salvation. *4030*

HELMETS
2Ch 26:14 spears, and h., and habergeons, 3553
Jer 46:4 stand forth with your h.; furbish 3553

HELON (he'-lon)
Nu 1:9 of Zebulun; Eliab the son of H. 2497
Nu 2:7 Eliab the son H. shall be captain 2497
Nu 7:24 Eliab the son of H., prince of the 2497
Nu 7:29 the offering of Eliab the son of H. 2497
Nu 10:16 of Zebulun was Eliab the son of H. 2497

HELP See also HELPED; HELPETH; HELPING; HELPS; HOLPEN.
Ge 2:18 will make him an h. meet for him 5828
Ge 2:20 was not found an h. meet for him. 5828
Ge 49:25 of thy father, who shall h. thee; 5826
Ex 18:4 of my father, said he, was mine h., 5828
Ex 23:5 and wouldest forbear to h. him, 5800
Ex 23:5 thou shalt surely h. with him 5800
De 22:4 shalt surely h. him to lift them up 6965
De 32:38 let them rise up and h. you, and 5826
De 33:7 an h. to him from his enemies 5828
De 33:26 rideth upon the heaven in thy h. 5828
De 33:29 Lord, the shield of thy h., and who is 5828
Jos 1:14 men of valour, and h. them; 5826
Jos 10:4 Come up unto me, and h. me, that 5826
Jos 10:6 us quickly, and save us, and h. us: 5826
Jos 10:33 of Gezer came up to h. Lachish; 5826
Jg 5:23 came not to the h. of the Lord, 5833
Jg 5:23 h. of the Lord against the mighty 5833
1Sa 11:9 the sun be hot, ye shall have h. 8668
2Sa 10:11 for me, then thou shalt h. me: 3447
2Sa 10:11 thee, then I will come and h. thee 3467
2Sa 10:19 Syrians feared to h. the children of 3467
2Sa 14:4 did obeisance, and said, H., O king. 3467
2Ki 6:26 him, saying, H., my lord, O king. 3467
2Ki 6:27 not h. thee, whence shall I h. thee? 3467
1Ch 12:17 come peaceably unto me to h. me, 5826
1Ch 12:22 day there came to David to h. him, 5826
1Ch 18:5 Syrians of Damascus came to h. 5826
1Ch 19:12 for me, then thou shalt h. me: but 8668
1Ch 19:12 strong for thee, then I will h. thee 3467
1Ch 19:19 Syrians h. the children of Ammon 3467
1Ch 22:17 princes of Israel to h. Solomon 5826
2Ch 14:11 Lord, it is nothing with thee to h., 5826
2Ch 14:11 no power: h. us, O Lord our God; 5826
2Ch 19:2 Shouldest thou h. the ungodly, 5826
2Ch 20:4 together, to ask h. of the Lord: even 5826
2Ch 20:9 then thou wilt hear and h. 3467
2Ch 25:8 God hath power to h., and to cast 5826
2Ch 26:13 to h. the king against the enemy 5826
2Ch 28:16 unto the kings of Assyria to h. him 5826
2Ch 28:23 the gods of the kings of Syria to h. 5826
2Ch 28:23 I sacrifice to them, that they may h. 5826
2Ch 29:34 brethren the Levites did h. them, 2388
2Ch 32:3 the city: and they did h. him 5826
2Ch 32:8 with us is the Lord our God to h. us, 5826
Ezr 1:4 of his place h. him with silver, 5375
Ezr 8:22 of soldiers and horsemen to h. us 5826
Job 6:13 Is not my h. in me? and is wisdom 5833
Job 8:20 neither will he h. the evil doers: 2388
Job 29:12 and him that had none to h. him 5826
Job 31:21 when I saw my h. in the gate: 5833
Ps 3:2 soul, There is no h. for him in God. 3444
Ps 12:1 H., Lord; for the godly man 3467
Ps 20:2 Send thee h. from the sanctuary, 5828
Ps 22:11 trouble is near; there is none to h. 5826
Ps 22:19 O my strength, haste thee to h. me. 5833
Ps 27:9 thou hast been my h.; leave me not, 5833
Ps 33:20 Lord: he is our h. and our shield. 5828
Ps 35:2 buckler, and stand up for mine h. 5833
Ps 37:40 And the Lord shalt h. them, and 5826
Ps 38:22 Make haste to h. me, O Lord my 5833
Ps 40:13 me: O Lord, make haste to h. me 5833
Ps 40:17 thou art my h. and my deliverer; 5833
Ps 42:5 for the h. of his countenance 3444
Ps 44:26 Arise for our h., and redeem us 5833
Ps 46:1 a very present h. in trouble 5833
Ps 46:5 God shall h. her, and that right 5826
Ps 59:4 fault: awake to h. me, and behold. 7125
Ps 60:11 Give us h. from trouble: for vain 5833
Ps 60:11 trouble: for vain is the h. of man 8668
Ps 63:7 Because thou hast been my h., 5833
Ps 70:1 me: make hast to h. me, O Lord 5833
Ps 70:5 thou art my h. and my deliverer; 5828
Ps 71:12 O my God, make haste for my h., 5833
Ps 79:9 H. us, O God of our salvation, for 5826
Ps 89:19 I have laid h. upon one that is 5828
Ps 94:17 Unless the Lord had been my h., 5833
Ps 107:12 fell down, and there was none to h. 5826
Ps 108:12 Give us h. from trouble: for vain 5833
Ps 108:12 trouble: for vain is the h. of man. 8668
Ps 109:26 H. me, O Lord my God: O save me 5826
Ps 115:9, 10,11 is their h. and their shield 5828
Ps 118:7 my part with them that h. me: 5826
Ps 119:86 persecute me wrongfully; h. thou 5826
Ps 119:173 Let thine hand h. me; for I have 5826
Ps 119:175 thee; and let thy judgments h. me 5826
Ps 121:1 hills, from which cometh my h. 5828
Ps 121:2 My h. cometh from the Lord, which 5828
Ps 124:8 our h. is in the name of the Lord, 5828
Ps 146:3 son of man, in whom there is no h. 8668
Ps 146:5 hath the God of Jacob for his h., 5828
Ec 4:10 he hath not another to h. him up. 6965
Isa 10:3 to whom will ye flee for h.? and 5833
Isa 20:6 whither we flee for h. to be delivered. 5833
Isa 30:5 be an h. nor profit, but a shame, 5828
Isa 30:7 For the Egyptians shall h. in vain, 5826
Isa 31:1 them that go down to Egypt for h.; 5833
Isa 31:2 the h. of them that work iniquity 5833
Isa 41:10 I will h. thee; yea, I will uphold 5826
Isa 41:13 unto thee, Fear not; I will h. thee 5826
Isa 41:14 I will h. thee, saith the Lord, and 5826
Isa 44:2 from the womb, which will h. thee; 5826
Isa 50:7 the Lord God will h. me; therefore 5826
Isa 50:9 Behold, the Lord God will h. me; 5826
Isa 63:5 I looked, and there was none to h.; 5826
Jer 37:7 which is come forth to h. you 5833
La 1:7 the enemy, and none did h. her: 5826
La 4:17 eyes as yet failed for our vain h.: 5833
Eze 12:14 all that are about him to h. him, 5828
Eze 32:21 midst of hell with them that h. him: 5826
Da 10:13 of the chief princes, came to h. me; 5826
Da 11:34 they shall be holpen with a little h.: 5828
Da 11:45 to his end, and none shall h. him. 5826
Ho 13:9 thyself; but in me is thine h. 5828
Mt 15:25 worshipped him, saying, Lord, h. me. *997*
Mk 9:22 have compassion on us, and h. us. *997*
Mk 9:24 I believe; h. thou mine unbelief. *997*
Lu 5:7 that they should come and h. them. *4815*
Lu 10:40 bid her therefore that she H. me. *4878*
Ac 16:9 over into Macedonia, and h. us *997*
Ac 21:28 Crying out, Men of Israel, h.: This *997*
Ac 26:22 Having therefore obtained h. of *1947*
Php 4:3 h. those women which laboured *4815*
Heb 4:16 find grace to h. in time o need *996*

HELPED See also HOLPEN.
Ex 2:17 Moses stood up and h. them, and 3467
1Sa 7:12 Hitherto hath the Lord h. us 5826
1Ki 1:7 and they following Adonijah h. him 5826
1Ki 20:16 the thirty and two kings that h. him 5826
1Ch 5:20 And they were h. against them, and 5826
1Ch 12:19 Saul to battle: but they h. them not: 5826
1Ch 12:21 And they h. David against the band 5826
1Ch 15:26 when God h. the Levites that bare 5826
2Ch 18:31 cried out, and the Lord h. him; and 5826
2Ch 20:23 every one h. to destroy another. 5826
2Ch 26:7 God h. him against the Philistines, 5826
2Ch 26:15 marvellously h., till he was strong. 5826
2Ch 28:21 king of Assyria: but he h. him not. 5833
Ezr 10:15 and Shabbethai the Levite h. them. 5826
Es 9:3 officers of the king, h. the Jews; 5375
Job 26:2 thou h. him that is without power? 5826
Ps 28:7 heart trusted in him, and I am h.: 5826
Ps 116:6 I was brought low, and he h. me. 3467
Ps 118:13 I might fall: but the Lord h. me. 5826
Isa 41:6 They h. every one his neighbour; 5826
Isa 49:8 in a day of salvation have I h. thee: 5826
Zec 1:15 and they h. forward the affliction 5826
Ac 18:27 h. them much which had believed *4820*
Re 12:16 the earth h. the woman, and the *997*

HELPER See also HELPERS.
2Ki 14:26 nor any left, nor any h. for Israel 5826
Job 30:13 my calamity, they have no h. 5826
Ps 10:14 thou art the h. of the fatherless 5826
Ps 30:10 upon me: Lord, be thou my h. 5826
Ps 54:4 Behold, God is mine h.: the Lord is 5826
Ps 72:12 poor also, and him that hath no h. 5826
Jer 47:4 and Zidon every h. that remaineth: 5826
Ro 16:9 Salute Urbane, our h. in Christ, *4904*
Heb 13:6 Lord is my h., and I will not fear *998*

HELPERS See also FELLOWHELPERS.
1Ch 12:1 the mighty men, h. of the war 5826

1Ch 12:18 unto thee, and peace be to thine **h.**;... 5826
Job 9:13 the proud **h.** do stoop under him........ 5826
Eze 30:8 when all her **h.** shall be destroyed...... 5826
Na 3:9 Put and Lubim were thy **h.**.................. 5833
Ro 16:3 and Aquila my **h.** in Christ Jesus: *4904*
2Co 1:24 your faith, but are **h.** of your joy:....... *4904*

HELPETH
1Ch 12:18 thine helpers; for thy God **h.** thee...... 5826
Isa 31:3 both he that **h.** shall fall, and he......... 5826
Ro 8:26 the Spirit also **h.** our infirmities:......... *4878*
1Co 16:16 and to every one that **h.** with us,....... *4903*

HELPING
Ezr 5:2 were the prophets of God **h.** them...... 5582
Ps 22:1 why art thou so far from **h.** me, ... 3467
2Co 1:11 Ye also **h.** together by prayer for us... *4943*

HELPS
Ac 27:17 they used **h.**, undergirding the ship,..... *996*
1Co 12:28 gifts of healings, **h.**, governments, ... *484*

HELVE
De 19:5 and the head slippeth from the **h.**,....... 6086

HEM See also HEMS.
Ex 28:33 upon the **h.** of it thou shalt make........ 7757
Ex 28:33 scarlet, round about the **h.** thereof; 7757
Ex 28:34 upon the **h.** of the robe round........... 7757
Ex 39:25 upon the **h.** of the robe, round........... 7757
Ex 39:26 round about the **h.** of the robe to........ 7757
Mt 9:20 touched the **h.** of his garment:........... *2899*
Mt 14:36 only touch the **h.** of his garment: *2899*

HEMAM (he'-mam) See also HOMAM.
Ge 36:22 of Lotan were Hori and **H.**; 1967

HEMAN (he'-man)
1Ki 4:31 than Ethan the Ezrahite, and **H.**, ... 1968
1Ch 2:6 of Zerah; Zimri, and Ethan, and **H.**,.... 1968
1Ch 6:33 **H.** a singer, the son of Joel, the son.... 1968
1Ch 15:17 So the Levites appointed **H.** the son.... 1968
1Ch 15:19 the singers, **H.**, Asaph, and Ethan,...... 1968
1Ch 16:41 And with them **H.** and Jeduthun,......... 1968
1Ch 16:42 **H.** and Jeduthun with trumpets.......... 1968
1Ch 25:1 of the sons of Asaph, and of **H.**, and .. 1968
1Ch 25:4 Of **H.**: the son of **H.**; Bukkiah,.......... 1968
1Ch 25:5 **H.** the king's seer in the words of...... 1968
1Ch 25:5 And God gave to **H.** fourteen sons...... 1968
1Ch 25:6 order to Asaph, Jeduthun, and **H.**........ 1968
2Ch 5:12 of Asaph, of **H.**, of Jeduthun, with...... 1968
2Ch 29:14 the sons of **H.**; Jehiel, and Shimei; 1968
2Ch 35:15 and Asaph, and **H.**, and Jeduthun....... 1968
Ps 88:*title* Mashchil of **H.** the Ezrahite. 1968

HEMATH (he'-math) See also HAMATH.
1Ch 2:55 the Kenites that came of **H.**, the 2574
1Ch 13:5 even unto the entering of **H.**,............ 2574
Am 6:14 the entering in of **H.** unto the............ 2574

HEMDAN (hem'-dan) See also AMRAM.
Ge 36:26 **H.**, and Eshban, and Ithran, and 2533

HEMLOCK
Ho 10:4 as **h.** in the furrows of the field. 7219
Am 6:12 the fruit of righteousness into **h.**: 3939

HEMS
Ex 39:24 they made upon the **h.** of the robe..... 7757

HEN
Mt 23:37 **as a h. gathereth her chickens**...... *3733*
Lu 13:34 **as a h. doth gather her brood**....... *3733*

HEN (hen)
Zec 6:14 and to **H.** the son of Zephaniah,......... 2581

HENA (he'-nah)
2Ki 18:34 gods of Sepharvaim, **H.**, and Ivah? 2012
2Ki 19:13 city of Sepharvaim, of **H.**, and Ivah? 2012
Isa 37:13 city of Sepharvaim, **H.**, and Ivah? 2012

HENADAD (hen'-a-dad)
Ezr 3:9 the sons of **H.**, with their sons and 2582
Ne 3:18 Bavai the son of **H.**, the ruler of the... 2582
Ne 3:24 him repaired Binnui the son of **H.** 2582
Ne 10:9 Binnui of the sons of **H.**, Kadmiel; 2582

HENCE See also HENCEFORTH; HENCEFORWARD.
Ge 37:17 They are departed **h.**; for I heard 2088
Ge 42:15 ye shall not go forth **h.**, except your... 2088
Ge 50:25 ye shall carry up my bones from **h.**. ... 2088
Ex 11:1 afterwards he will let you go **h.**: 2088
Ex 11:1 surely thrust you out **h.** altogether. 2088
Ex 13:19 carry up my bones away **h.** with you. ..2088
Ex 33:1 and go up **h.**, thou and the people...... 2088
Ex 33:15 go not with me, carry us not up **h.**...... 2088
De 9:12 Arise, get thee down quickly from **h.**, ..2088
Jos 4:3 you **h.** out of the midst of Jordan, ... 2088
Jg 6:18 Depart not **h.**, I pray thee, until I 2088
Ru 2:8 neither go from **h.**, but abide here...... 2088
1Ki 17:3 Get thee **h.**, and turn thee eastward,.. 2088
Ps 39:13 strength, before I go **h.**, and be no 2088
Isa 30:22 thou shalt say unto it, Get thee **h.** 3318
Jer 38:10 Take from **h.** thirty men with thee, ... 2088
Zec 6:7 Get you **h.**, walk to and fro through ... 3212
Mt 4:10 **Get thee h., Satan: for it is written***5217*
Mt 17:20 **Remove h. to yonder place; and it**..*1782*
Lu 4:9 of God, cast thyself down from **h.**: *1782*
Lu 13:31 Get thee out, and depart **h.**: for *1782*
Lu 16:26 **would pass from h. to you cannot;** .*1782*
Joh 2:16 **Take these things h.; make not my** *1782*
Joh 7:3 Depart **h.**, and go into Judaea, that..... *1782*
Joh 14:31 **even so I do. Arise, let us go h.**...... *1782*
Joh 18:36 **now is my kingdom not from h.**....... *1782*
Joh 20:15 Sir, if thou have borne him **h.**, tell me ......
Ac 1:5 **Holy Ghost not many days h.**. *3326,5025*
Ac 22:21 **send thee far h., unto the Gentiles.** *1821*
Jas 4:1 come they not **h.**, even of your lusts .. *1782*

HENCEFORTH
Ge 4:12 it shall not **h.** yield unto thee her....... 3254
Nu 18:22 Israel **h.** come nigh the tabernacle...... 5750
De 17:16 Ye shall **h.** return no more that 3254
De 19:20 shall **h.** commit no more any such 3254
Jg 2:21 will not **h.** drive out any from before... 3254
2Ki 5:17 for thy servant will **h.** offer neither..... 5750
2Ch 16:9 from **h.** shalt have wars. 6258
Ps 125:2 his people from **h.** even for ever........ 6258
Ps 131:3 in the Lord from **h.** and for ever......... 6258
Isa 9:7 with justice from **h.** even for ever. 6258
Isa 52:1 for **h.** there shall no more come into... 6258
Isa 59:21 saith the Lord, from **h.** and for ever... 3254
Eze 36:12 shalt no more **h.** bereave them of men. ......
Mic 4:7 over them in mount Zion from **h.** 6258
Mt 23:39 **Ye shall not see me h., till ye**... *575,737*
Mt 26:29 **I will not drink h. of this fruit**.. *575,737*
Lu 1:48 from **h.** all generations shall call me.... *3568*
Lu 5:10 **not; from h. thou shalt catch men**..*3568*
Lu 12:52 **h. there shall be five in one house**..*3568*
Joh 14:7 **from h. ye know him, and have seen***737*
Joh 15:15 **H. I call you not servants; for the**. *3765*
Ac 4:17 speak **h.** to no man in this name. *3371*
Ac 18:6 from **h.** I will go unto the Gentiles. *3568*
Ro 6:6 that **h.** we should not serve sin. *3371*
2Co 5:15 should not **h.** live unto themselves,..... *3371*
2Co 5:16 **h.** know we no man after..... *575,3588,3568*
2Co 5:16 yet now **h.** know we him no more....... *2089*
Ga 6:17 From **h.** let no man trouble me:......... *3063*
Eph 4:14 That we **h.** be no more children,......... *3063*
Eph 4:17 ye **h.** walk not as other Gentiles........ *3371*
2Ti 4:8 **H.** there is laid up for me a crown...... *3063*
Heb 10:13 From **h.** expecting till his enemies...... *3063*
Re 14:13 dead which die in the Lord from **h.**: *534*

HENCEFORWARD
Nu 15:23 and **h.** among your generations; 1973
Mt 21:19 **no fruit grow on thee h. for ever**... *3371*

HENOCH (he'-nok) See also ENOCH.
1Ch 1:3 **H.**, Methuselah, Lamech, Noah 2585
1Ch 1:33 Epher, and **H.**, and Abido, and.......... 2585

HEPHER (he'-fer) See also GATH-HEPHER; HEPHERITES.
Nu 26:32 of **H.**, the family of the Hepherites..... 2660
Nu 26:33 Zelophehad the son of **H.** had no........ 2660
Nu 27:1 the son of **H.**, the son of Gilead, ... 2660
Jos 12:17 Tappuah, one; the king of **H.**, one;...... 2660
Jos 17:2 for the children of **H.**, and for the...... 2660
Jos 17:3 But Zelophehad, the son of **H.**, the 2660
1Ki 4:10 Sochoh, and all the land of **H.**: 2660
1Ch 4:6 Naarah bare him Ahuzam, and **H.**,....... 2660
1Ch 11:36 **H.** the Mecherathite, Ahijah the......... 2660

HEPHERITES (he'-fer-ites)
Nu 26:32 of Hepher, the family of the **H.**. 2662

HEPHZI-BAH (hef'-zi-bah)
2Ki 21:1 And his mother's name was **H.**........... 2657
Isa 62:4 but thou shalt be called **H.**, and......... 2657

HER See in the APPENDIX; also HERS; HERSELF.

HERALD
Da 3:4 Then an **h.** cried aloud. To you it is ... 3744

HERB See also HERBS.
Ge 1:11 the **h.** yielding seed, and the fruit...... 6212
Ge 1:12 **h.** yielding seed after his kind, and..... 6212
Ge 1:29 I have given you every **h.** bearing 6212
Ge 1:30 have given every green **h.** for meat:... 6212
Ge 2:5 every **h.** of the field before it grew:.... 6212
Ge 3:18 and thou shalt eat the **h.** of the field;.. 6212
Ge 9:3 even as the green **h.** have I given....... 6212
Ex 9:22 every **h.** of the field, throughout 6212
Ex 9:25 the hail smote every **h.** of the field,.... 6212
Ex 10:12 and eat every **h.** of the land, even all.. 6212
Ex 10:15 and they did eat every **h.** of the land, . 6212
De 32:2 the small rain upon the tender **h.**, ... 1877
2Ki 19:26 and as the green **h.**. as the grass on... 1877
Job 8:12 it withereth before any other **h.**.......... 2682
Job 38:27 the bud of the tender **h.** to spring...... 1877
Ps 37:2 grass, and wither as the green **h.**........ 1877
Ps 104:14 and **h.** for the service of man: that..... 6212
Isa 37:27 of the field, and as the green **h.**, as..... 1877
Isa 66:14 your bones shall flourish like an **h.**:..... 1877

HERBS
Ex 10:15 the trees, or in the **h.** of the field, ... 6212
Ex 12:8 and with bitter **h.** they shall eat it. ....
Nu 9:11 with unleavened bread and bitter **h.**.........
De 11:10 it with thy foot, as a garden of **h.**: 3419
1Ki 21:2 I may have it for a garden of **h.**,......... 3419
2Ki 4:39 went out into the field to gather **h.**, ... 219
Ps 105:35 did eat up all the **h.** in their land,........ 6212
Pr 15:17 Better is a dinner of **h.** where love..... 3419
Pr 27:25 **h.** of the mountains are gathered........ 6212
Isa 18:4 like a clear heat upon **h.**, and like........ 216
Isa 26:19 thy dew is as the dew of **h.**. and the.... 219
Isa 42:15 and hills, and dry up all their **h.**; 6212
Jer 12:4 and the **h.** of every field wither, for.... 6212
Mt 13:32 **grown, it is the greatest among h.**,.*3001*
Mk 4:32 **and becometh greater than all h.**, .*3001*
Lu 11:42 **mint and rue and all manner of h.**,*3001*
Ro 14:2 another, who is weak, eateth **h.**.......... *3001*
Heb 6:7 and bringeth forth **h.** meet for them.... *1008*

HERD See also HERDMAN; HERDS; SHEPHERD.
Ge 18:7 And Abraham ran unto the **h.**,........... 1241
Le 1:2 even of the **h.**, and of the flock. 1241
Le 1:3 offering be a burnt sacrifice of the **h.**, ..1241
Le 3:1 peace offering, if he offer it of the **h.**;. 1241
Le 27:32 concerning the tithe of the **h.**, or of.... 1241
Nu 15:3 the Lord, of the **h.**, or of the flock: 1241
De 12:21 shalt kill of thy **h.** and of thy flock, ... 1241
De 15:19 that come of thy **h.** and of thy flock.... 1241
De 16:2 of the flock and the **h.**, in the place..... 1241
1Sa 11:5 came after the **h.** out of the field 1241
2Sa 12:4 of his own flock and of his own **h.**...... 1241
Jer 31:12 the young of the flock and of the **h.**:.... 1241
Jon 3:7 man nor beast, **h.** nor flock, taste 1241
Hab 3:17 and there shall be no **h.** in the stalls:.. 1241
Mt 8:30 them an **h.** of many swine feeding. *34*
Mt 8:31 us to go away into the **h.** of swine. *34*
Mt 8:32 they went into the **h.** of swine: and, ... *34*
Mt 8:32 they whole **h.** of swine ran violently........ *34*
Mk 5:11 mountains a great **h.** of swine feeding *34*
Mk 5:13 the **h.** ran violently down a steep place... *34*
Lu 8:32 an **h.** of many swine feeding on the *34*
Lu 8:33 the **h.** ran violently down a steep place...... *34*

HERDMAN See also HERDMEN.
Am 7:14 but I was an **h.**, and a gatherer of....... 951

HERDMEN
Ge 13:7 between the **h.** of Abram's cattle 7462
Ge 13:7 cattle and the **h.** of Lot's cattle:.......... 7462
Ge 13:8 between my **h.** and thy **h.**; for we be . 7462
Ge 26:20 And the **h.** of Gerar did strive with 7462
Ge 26:20 of Gerar did strive with Isaac's **h.**,..... 7462
1Sa 21:7 the chiefest of the **h.** that belonged to..7462
Am 1:1 who was among the **h.** of Tekoa, ... 5349

HERDS See also SHEPHERDS.
Ge 13:5 with Abram, had flocks, and **h.**, and.... 1241
Ge 24:35 hath given him flocks, and **h.**, and...... 1241
Ge 26:14 and possession of **h.**, and great store.. 1241
Ge 32:7 the flocks, and **h.**, and the camels, ... 1241
Ge 33:13 and the flocks and **h.** with young are... 1241
Ge 45:10 and thy **h.**, and all that thou hast: 1241
Ge 46:32 and their **h.**, and all that they have...... 1241
Ge 47:1 and their **h.**, and all that they have,..... 1241
Ge 47:17 for the cattle of the **h.**, and for the..... 1241
Ge 47:18 my lord also hath our **h.** of cattle; 4735
Ge 50:8 their flocks, and their **h.**, they left...... 1241
Ex 10:9 flocks and with our **h.** will we go: 1241

Ex 10:24 your flocks and your **h.** be stayed: 1241
Ex 12:32 take your flocks and your **h.**, as ye 1241
Ex 12:38 flocks, and **h.**, even very much cattle.. 1241
Ex 34:3 flocks nor **h.** feed before that mount... 1241
Nu 11:22 Shall the flocks and the **h.** be slain 1241
De 8:13 when thy **h.** and thy flocks multiply, ... 1241
De 12:6 firstlings of your **h.** and of your 1241
De 12:17 firstlings of thy **h.** or of thy flock, ... 1241
De 14:23 the firstlings of thy **h.** and of thy....... 1241
1Sa 30:20 David took all the flocks and the **h.**, ... 1241
2Sa 12:2 had exceeding many flocks and **h.**....... 1241
1Ch 27:29 And over the **h.** that fed in Sharon..... 1241
1Ch 27:29 over the **h.** that were in the valleys.... 1241
2Ch 32:29 and possessions of flocks and **h.** in..... 1241
Ne 10:36 firstlings of our **h.** and of our flocks, ... 1241
Pr 27:23 thy flocks, and look well to thy **h.**. 5739
Isa 65:10 a place for the **h.** to lie down in,........ 1241
Jer 3:24 their flocks and their **h.**, their sons..... 1241
Jer 5:17 shall eat up thy flocks and thine **h.**: 1241
Ho 5:6 and with their **h.** to seek the Lord; 1241
Joe 1:18 the **h.** of cattle are preplexed, ... 5739

HERE See also HEREAFTER; HEREBY; HEREIN; HEREOF; HERETOFORE; HEREUNTO; HEREWITH.

Ge 16:13 Have I also **h.** looked after him that.... 1988
Ge 19:12 unto Lot, Hast thou **h.** any besides? ... 6311
Ge 19:15 thy two daughters, which are **h.**; 4672
Ge 21:23 swear unto me **h.** by God that thou.... 2008
Ge 22:1 Abraham: and he said, Behold, **h.** I am......
Ge 22:5 Abide ye **h.** with the ass; and I and.... 6311
Ge 22:7 and he said, **H.** am I, my son........... 2009
Ge 22:11 Abraham: and he said, **H.** am I......... 2009
Ge 24:13 Behold, I stand **h.** by the well of water; ....
Ge 27:1 and he said unto him, Behold, **h.** am I.......
Ge 27:18 **H.** am I; who art thou, my son? 2009
Ge 31:11 saying, Jacob: And I said, **H.** am I...... 2009
Ge 31:37 set it **h.** before my brethren and thy... 3541
Ge 37:13 And he said to him, **H.** am I. 2009
Ge 40:15 and **h.** also have I done nothing 6311
Ge 42:33 leave one of your brethren **h.** with me. .....
Ge 46:2 Jacob, Jacob. And he said, **H.** am I..... 2009
Ge 47:23 **h.** is seed for you, and ye shall sow the ....
Ex 3:4 Moses. And he said, **H.** am I. 2009
Ex 24:14 Tarry ye **h.** for us, until we come....... 2088
Ex 33:16 wherein shall it be known **h.** that I....... 645
Nu 14:40 Lo we be **h.**, and will go up unto the........
Nu 22:8 said unto them, Lodge **h.** this night. ... 6311
Nu 22:19 pray you, tarry ye also **h.** this night,.... 2088
Nu 23:1 unto Balak, Build me **h.** seven altars,.. 2088
Nu 23:1 and prepare me **h.** seven oxen and..... 2088
Nu 23:15 Stand **h.** by thy burnt-offering,........... 3541
Nu 23:29 Balak, Build me **h.** seven altars, ... 2088
Nu 23:29 and prepare me **h.** seven bullocks 2088
Nu 32:6 go to war, and shall ye sit **h.**? 6311
Nu 32:16 will build sheepfolds **h.** for our cattle,.. 6311
De 5:3 who are all of us **h.** alive this day....... 6311
De 5:31 But as for thee, stand thou **h.** by me,..6311
De 12:8 the things that we do **h.** this day, ... 6311
De 29:15 him that standeth **h.** with us this day.. 6311
De 29:15 him that is not **h.** with us this day:...... 6311
Jos 18:6 cast lots for you **h.** before the Lord.... 6311
Jos 18:8 that I may **h.** cast lots for you before.. 6311
Jos 21:9 cities which are **h.** mentioned by name, ...
Jg 4:20 thee, and say, Is there any man **h.**? ... 6311
Jg 18:3 this place? and what hast thou **h.**? 6311
Jg 19:9 lodge **h.**, that thine heart may be 6311
Jg 19:24 Behold, **h.** is my daughter a maiden,.........
Jg 20:7 give **h.** your advice and counsel. 1988
Ru 2:8 but abide **h.** fast by my maidens: 3541
Ru 4:1 turn aside, sit down **h.**. And he 6311
Ru 4:2 Sit ye down **h.**. And they sat down. ... 6311
1Sa 1:26 the woman that stood by thee **h.**, ... 2088
1Sa 3:4 Samuel: and he answered, **H.** am I....... 2009
1Sa 3:5 he said, **H.** am I; for thou calledst...... 2005
1Sa 3:6,8 **H.** am I; for thou didst call me. 2005
1Sa 3:16 my son. And he answered, **H.** am I.... 2009
1Sa 9:8 I have **h. at hand the fourth part of .....**
1Sa 9:11 and said unto them, Is the seer h.?.2088
1Sa 12:3 behold, **h.** I am: witness against me.........
1Sa 14:34 sheep, and slay them **h.**, and eat; 2088
1Sa 16:11 Jesse, Are **h.** all thy children? 8552
1Sa 21:8 not **h.** under thine hand spear or......... 6311
1Sa 21:9 behold, it is **h.** wrapped in a cloth ....
1Sa 21:9 for there is no other save that **h.**....... 2088
1Sa 22:12 he answered, **H.** I am, my lord. 2005
1Sa 23:3 Behold, we be afraid **h.** in Judah: 6311
1Sa 29:3 What do these Hebrews **h.**? And.............
2Sa 1:7 And I answered, **H.** am I. 2009
2Sa 11:12 Tarry **h.** to day also, and to-morrow... 2088
2Sa 15:26 behold, **h.** am I, let him do to me as.........
2Sa 18:30 Turn aside, and stand **h.**. And he....... 3541
2Sa 20:4 three days, and be thou **h.** present..... 6311
2Sa 24:22 behold, **h.** be oxen for burnt sacrifice, ...
1Ki 2:30 And he said, Nay: but I will die **h.**. 6311
1Ki 18:8, 11 tell thy lord, Behold, Elijah is **h.**.........
1Ki 18:14 tell thy lord, Behold, Elijah is **h.**. ....
1Ki 19:9, 13 What doest thou **h.**, Elijah?........... 6311
1Ki 20:40 thy servant was busy **h.** and there, ... 2008
1Ki 22:7 Is there not **h.** a prophet of the......... 6311
2Ki 2:2 Tarry **h.**, I pray thee; for the Lord..... 6311
2Ki 2:4 tarry **h.**, I pray thee; for the Lord....... 6311
2Ki 2:6 Tarry, I pray thee, **h.**; for the Lord...... 6311
2Ki 3:11 Is there not **h.** a prophet of the Lord,..6311
2Ki 3:11 **H.** is Elisha, the son of Shaphat,........ 6311
2Ki 7:3 Why sit we **h.**, until we die? 6311
2Ki 7:4 and if we sit still **h.**, we die also. 6311
2Ki 10:23 be **h.** with you none of the servants ... 6311
1Ch 29:17 joy thy people, which are present **h.**,.. 6311
2Ch 18:6 there not **h.** a prophet of the Lord 6311
Job 38:11 **h.** shall thy proud waves be stayed? ... 6311
Job 38:35 and say unto thee, **H.** we are? 2009
Ps 132:14 **h.** will I dwell; for I have desired it. ... 6311
Isa 6:8 Then said I, **H.** am I; send me.......... 2005
Isa 21:9 behold, **h.** cometh a chariot of men,..... 2088
Isa 22:16 What hast thou **h.**? and whom 6311
Isa 22:16 and whom hast thou **h.**, that thou........ 6311
Isa 22:16 hast hewed thee out a sepulchre **h.**, ... 6311
Isa 28:10 line; **h.** a little, and there a little: 8033
Isa 28:13 line; **h.** a little, and there a little; 8033
Isa 52:5 what have I **h.**, saith the Lord, that.... 6311
Isa 58:9 shalt cry, and he shall say, **H.** I am.... 2009
Eze 8:6 house of Israel committeth **h.**, ... 6311
Eze 8:9 wicked abominations that they do **h.**. .. 6311
Eze 8:17 abominations which they commit **h.**? ... 6311
Ho 7:9 gray hairs are **h.** and there upon........ 2236
Mt 12:41 **behold, a greater than Jonas is h.** .. *5602*
Mt 12:42 **a greater than Solomon is h.**.......... *5602*
Mt 14:8 Give me **h.** John Baptist's head in a.... *5602*
Mt 14:17 We have **h.** but five loaves, and two... *5602*
Mt 16:28 **standing h., which shall not taste** ..*5602*
Mt 17:4 Lord, it is good for us to be **h.**:......... *5602*
Mt 17:4 let us make **h.** three tabernacles; *5602*
Mt 20:6 **Why stand ye h. all the day idle?** .. *5602*
Mt 24:2 **shall not be left h. one stone upon** .*5602*
Mt 24:23 **you, Lo, h. is Christ, or there;** *5602*
Mt 26:36 **Sit ye h., while I go and pray**......... *848*
Mt 26:38 **tarry ye h., and watch with me**..... *5602*
Mt 28:6 He is not **h.**: for he is risen, as *5602*
Mk 6:3 and are not his sisters **h.** with us?...... *5602*
Mk 8:4 with bread **h.** in the wilderness? *5602*
Mk 9:1 **be some of them that stand h.**,........ *5602*
Mk 9:5 Master, it is good for us to be **h.**:........ *5602*
Mk 13:1 of stones and what buildings are **h.**!.... *5602*
Mk 13:21 **Lo, h. is Christ; or, lo, he is there;** *5602*
Mk 14:32 **Sit ye h., while I shall pray.**......... 5602
Mk 14:34 **unto death: tarry ye h., and watch.** 5602
Mk 16:6 he is risen; he is not **h.**: behold the.... 5602
Lu 4:23 **Capernaum, do...h. in thy country.** 5602
Lu 9:12 for we are **h.** in a desert place. 5602
Lu 9:27 **standing h., which shall not taste** ..5602
Lu 9:33 Master, it is good for us to be **h.**:........ 5602
Lu 11:31 **a greater than Solomon is h.**......... 5602
Lu 11:32 **behold, a greater than Jonas is h.** ..5602
Lu 17:21 **shall they way, Lo h.! or, lo there!**.5602
Lu 17:23 **they shall say to you, See h.; or**.... 5602
Lu 19:20 **Lord, behold, h. is thy pound, which I**..
Lu 22:38 Lord, behold, **h.** are two swords........ *5602*
Lu 24:6 He is not **h.**, but is risen: remember .. *5602*
Lu 24:41 unto them, **Have ye h. any meat?**.... 1759
Joh 6:9 There is a lad **h.**, which hath five......... *5602*
Joh 11:21, 32 if thou hadst been **h.**, my brother .. *5602*
Ac 4:10 doth this man stand **h.** before you...... *3936*
Ac 8:36 See, **h.** is water; what doth hinder...........
Ac 9:10 And he said, Behold, I am **h.**, Lord. ....
Ac 9:14 And **h.** he hath authority from the...... *5602*
Ac 10:33 Now therefore are we all **h.** present... *3918*
Ac 16:28 thyself no harm: for we are all **h.**....... *1759*
Ac 24:19 ought to have been **h.** before thee,..... *3918*
Ac 24:20 Or else let these same **h.** say, if they.......
Ac 25:24 men which are **h.** present with us, ... *4840*
Ac 25:24 me, both at Jerusalem, and also **h.**, ... *1759*
Col 4:9 you all things which are done **h.**......... *5602*
Heb 7:8 And **h.** men that die receive tithes; *5602*
Heb 13:14 For **h.** have we no continuing city, ... *5602*
Jas 2:3 unto him, Sit thou **h.** in a good place: ..*5602*
Jas 2:3 there, or sit **h.** under my footstool: *5602*
1Pe 1:17 the time of your sojourning **h.** in fear........
Re 13:10 **H.** is the patience and the faith of...... *5602*
Re 13:18 **H.** is wisdom. Let him that hath *5602*
Re 14:12 **H.** is the patience of the saints: *5602*
Re 14:12 **h.** are they that keep the *5602*
Re 17:9 **h.** is the mind which hath wisdom. *5602*

HEREAFTER

Isa 41:23 Shew the things that are to come **h.**, ... 268
Eze 20:39 and **h.** also, if ye will not hearken........ 310
Da 2:29 what should come to pass **h.** 311,1836
Da 2:45 what shall come to pass **h.**............. 311,1836
Mt 26:64 **H. shall ye see the Son of man** .*575,737*
Mk 11:14 **man eat fruit of thee h. for ever.** .. *3370*
Lu 22:69 **H. shall the Son of man sit on** .*575,3568*
Joh 1:51 **H. ye shall see heaven open,**........... *737*
Joh 13:7 **now; but thou shalt know h.**,. *3326,5028*
Joh 14:30 **H. I will not talk much with you:** ..*2089*
1Ti 1:16 should **h.** believe on him to life.......... *3195*
Re 1:19 **the things which shall be h.**;.. *3326,5023*
Re 4:1 thee things which must be **h.**. *3326,5023*
Re 9:12 there come two woes more **h.**..... *3326,5023*

HEREBY

Ge 42:15 **H.** ye shall be proved: By the life 2063
Ge 42:33 **H.** shall I know that ye are true men;..2063
Nu 16:28 And Moses said, **H.** ye shall know 2063
Jos 3:10 And Joshua said, **H.** ye shall know....... 2063
1Co 4:4 yet am I not **h.** justified: but...... *1722,5129*
1Jo 2:3 And **h.** we do know that we do .. *1722,5129*
1Jo 2:5 **h.** know we that we are in him.. *1722,5129*
1Jo 3:16 **H.** perceive we the love of God,..*1722,5129*
1Jo 3:19 And **h.** we know that we are of.. *1722,5129*
1Jo 3:24 **h.** we know that he abideth in.... *1722,5129*
1Jo 4:2 **H.** know ye the Spirit of God:.... *1722,5129*
1Jo 4:6 **H.** know we the spirit of truth,... *1537,5124*
1Jo 4:13 **H.** know we that we dwell in..... *1722,5129*

HEREIN

Ge 34:22 Only **h.** will the men consent unto...... 2063
2Ch 16:9 **H.** thou hast done foolishly: 5921
Joh 4:37 **h. is that saying true, One**..... *1722,5129*
Joh 9:30 Why **h.** is a marvellous thing,...... *1722,5129*
Joh 15:8 **H. is my Father glorified, that***1722,5129*
Ac 24:16 And **h.** do I exercise myself, to.. *1722,5129*
2Co 8:10 And **h.** I give my advice: for...... *1722,5129*
1Jo 4:10 **H.** is love, not that we loved God*1722,5129*
1Jo 4:17 **H.** is our love made perfect,...... *1722,5129*

HEREOF

Mt 9:26 the fame **h.** went abroad into all......... *3778*
Heb 5:3 And by reason **h.** he ought, as for...... *5026*

HERES (he'-res) See also KIR-HERES; TIMMATH-HERES.

Jg 1:35 Amorites would dwell in mount **H.**....... 2776

HERESH (he'-resh)

1Ch 9:15 Bakbakkar, **H.**, and Galal, and........... 2792

HERESIES

1Co 11:19 there must be also **h.** among you,........ *139*
Ga 5:20 wrath, strife, seditions, **h.**, envyings, ... *139*
2Pe 2:1 shall bring in damnable **h.**, even *139*

HERESY See also HERESIES.

Ac 24:14 after the way which they call **h.**, so *139*

HERETICK

Tit 3:10 A man that is an **h.** after the first........ *141*

HERETOFORE

Ex 4:10 not eloquent, neither **h.**, nor since...... 8543
Ex 5:7 people straw to make brick, as **h.**: 8543
Ex 5:8 the bricks, which they did make **h.**, ... 8543
Ex 5:14 both yesterday and to day, as **h.**? 8543
Jos 3:4 for ye have not passed this way **h.**..... 8543
Ru 2:11 a people which thou knewest not **h.**..... 8543
1Sa 4:7 hath not been such a thing **h.**.............. 865
2Co 13:2 write to them which **h.** have sinned, ... *4258*

HEREUNTO

Ec 2:25 who else can hasten **h.**, more than I?........
1Pe 2:21 For even **h.** were ye called:........ *1519,5124*

HEREWITH

Eze 16:29 and yet thou wast not satisfied **h.**....... 2063
Mal 3:10 prove me now **h.**, saith the Lord of.... 2063

HERITAGE See also HERITAGES.
Ex 6:8 and I will give it you for an **h.** 4181
Job 20:29 the **h.** appointed unto him by God. 5159
Job 27:13 and the **h.** of oppressors, which they 5159
Ps 16:6 places; yea, I have a goodly **h.** 5159
Ps 61:5 the **h.** of those that fear thy name. 3425
Ps 94:5 people, O Lord, and afflict thine **h.** 5159
Ps 111:6 may give them the **h.** of the heathen. 5159
Ps 119:111 testimonies have I taken as an **h.** 5157
Ps 127:3 Lo, children are an **h.** of the Lord: 5159
Ps 135:12 And gave their land for an **h.**, 5159
Ps 135:12 and **h.** unto Israel his people. 5159
Ps 136:21 And gave their land for an **h.**: for his 5159
Ps 136:22 Even an **h.** unto Israel his servant: 5159
Isa 54:17 the **h.** of the servants of the Lord, 5159
Isa 58:14 thee with the **h.** of Jacob thy father: 5159
Jer 2:7 and made mine **h.** an abomination. 5159
Jer 3:19 a goodly **h.** of the hosts of nations? 5159
Jer 12:7 I have left mine **h.**; I have given the 5159
Jer 12:8 Mine **h.** is unto me as a lion in the 5159
Jer 12:9 Mine **h.** is unto me as a speckled 5159
Jer 12:15 every man to his **h.**, and every man 5159
Jer 17:4 discontinue from thine **h.** that I gave 5159
Jer 50:11 O ye destroyers of mine **h.**, because 5159
Joe 2:17 give not thine **h.** to reproach, that 5159
Joe 3:2 for my people and for my **h.** Israel, 5159
Mic 2:2 his house, even a man and his **h.** 5159
Mic 7:14 the flock of thine **h.**, which dwell 5159
Mic 7:18 the remnant of his **h.**? he retaineth 5159
Mal 1:3 laid his mountains and his **h.** waste 5159
1Pe 5:3 as being lords over God's **h.**, but *2819*

HERITAGES
Isa 49:8 to cause to inherit the desolate **h.**; 5159

HERMAS (her'-mas)
Ro 16:14 Phlegon, **H.**, Patrobas, Hermes, *2057*

HERMES (her'-mees)
Ro 16:14 **H.**, and the brethren which are *2060*

HERMOGENES (her-moj'-e-nees)
2Ti 1:15 of whom are Phygellus and **H.** *2061*

HERMON (her'-mon) See also BAAL-HERMON; HERMONITES.
De 3:8 the river of Arnon unto mount **H.**; 2768
De 3:9 which **H.** the Sidonians call Sirion; 2768
De 4:48 even unto mount Sion, which is **H.**, 2768
Jos 11:3 under **H.** in the land of Mizpeh. 2768
Jos 11:17 valley of Lebanon under mount **H.**: 2768
Jos 12:1 unto mount **H.**, and all the plain on 2768
Jos 12:5 And reigned in mount **H.**, and in 2768
Jos 13:5 from Baal-gad under mount **H.** unto 2768
Jos 13:11 and all mount **H.**, and all Bashan 2768
1Ch 5:23 and Senir, and unto mount **H.** 2768
Ps 89:12 Tabor and **H.** shall rejoice in thy 2768
Ps 133:3 As the dew of **H.**, and as the dew 2768
Ca 4:8 from the top of Shenir and **H.**, 2768

HERMONITES her'-mon-ites) See also HERMON.
Ps 42:6 land of Jordan, and of the **H.**, 2769

HEROD (her'-od) See also HERODIANS; HEROD'S.
Mt 2:1 in the days of **H.** the king, behold, *2264*
Mt 2:3 When **H.** the king had heard these *2264*
Mt 2:7 Then **H.**, when he had privily *2264*
Mt 2:12 that they should not return to **H.**, *2264*
Mt 2:13 for **H.** will seek the young child to *2264*
Mt 2:15 was there until the death of **H.** *2264*
Mt 2:16 Then **H.**, when he saw that he was *2264*
Mt 2:19 But when **H.** was dead, behold, an *2264*
Mt 2:22 in the room of his father **H.**, he *2264*
Mt 14:1 At that time **H.** the tetrarch heard *2264*
Mt 14:3 For **H.** had laid hold on John, and *2264*
Mt 14:6 danced before them, and pleased **H.** *2264*
Mk 6:14 king **H.** heard of him; for his name *2264*
Mk 6:16 But when **H.** heard thereof, he said, *2264*
Mk 6:17 **H.** himself had sent forth and laid *2264*
Mk 6:18 For John had said unto **H.**, It is not *2264*
Mk 6:20 For **H.** feared John, knowing that *2264*
Mk 6:21 **H.** on his birthday made a supper *2264*
Mk 6:22 came in, and danced, and pleased **H.** *2264*
Mk 8:15 **Pharisees, and the of leaven of H.** *2264*
Lu 1:5 There was in the days of **H.**, the *2264*
Lu 3:1 and **H.** being tetrarch of Galilee, *2264*
Lu 3:19 **H.** the tetrarch, being reproved *2264*
Lu 3:19 for all the evils which **H.** had done, *2264*
Lu 9:7 **H.** the tetrarch heard of all that was *2264*
Lu 9:9 And **H.** said, John have I beheaded: *2264*
Lu 13:31 depart hence: for **H.** will kill thee. *2264*
Lu 23:7 he sent him to **H.**, who himself also *2264*
Lu 23:8 And when **H.** saw Jesus, he was *2264*
Lu 23:11 and **H.** with his men of war set him *2264*
Lu 23:12 Pilate and **H.** were made friends *2264*
Lu 23:15 nor yet **H.**: for I sent you to him; *2264*
Ac 4:27 whom thou hast anointed, both **H.** *2264*
Ac 12:1 Now about that time **H.** the king *2264*
Ac 12:6 **H.** would have brought him forth, *2264*
Ac 12:11 delivered me out of the hand of **H.**, *2264*
Ac 12:19 And when **H.** had sought for him, *2264*
Ac 12:20 **H.** was highly displeased with them *2264*
Ac 12:21 And upon a set day **H.**, arrayed in *2264*
Ac 13:1 brought up with **H.** the tetrarch, *2264*

HERODIANS (he-ro'-de-uns)
Mt 22:16 their disciples with the **H.**, saying, *2265*
Mk 3:6 took counsel with the **H.** against *2265*
Mk 12:13 of the Pharisees and of the **H.**, to *2265*

HERODIAS (he-ro'-de-as) See also HERODIAS'.
Mt 14:6 the daughter of **H.** danced before *2266*
Mk 6:19 Therefore **H.** had a quarrel against *2266*
Mk 6:22 when the daughter of the said **H.** *2266*
Lu 3:19 being reproved by him for **H.** his *2266*

HERODIAS' (he-ro'-de-as)
Mt 14:3 and put him in prison for **H.** sake, *2266*
Mk 6:17 bound him in prison for **H.** sake, *2266*

HERODION (he-ro'-de-on)
Ro 16:11 Salute **H.** my kinsman. Greet *2267*

HEROD'S (her'-ods)
Mt 14:6 when **H.** birthday was kept, the *2264*
Lu 8:3 the wife of Chuza **H.** steward, and *2264*
Lu 23:7 he belonged unto **H.** jurisdiction, *2264*
Ac 23:35 him to be kept in **H.** judgment hall. *2264*

HERON
Le 11:19 stork, the **H.** after her kind, and the 601
De 14:18 and the **h.** after her kind, and the 601

HERS See also HERSELF.
De 21:15 if the firstborn be **h.** that was hated:
1Sa 25:42 with five damsels of **h.** that went after
2Ki 8:6 Restore all that was **h.**, and all the
Job 39:16 ones, as though they were not **h.**: her

HERSELF
Ge 18:12 Therefore Sarah laughed within **h.**
Ge 20:5 even she **h.**, said, He is my brother:
Ge 24:65 she took a vail, and covered **h.**
Ge 38:14 covered...with a vail, and wrapped **h.**,
Ex 2:5 came down to wash **h.** at the river;
Le 15:28 she shall number to **h.** seven days,
Le 21:9 if she profane **h.** by playing the whore,
Nu 22:25 she thrust **h.** unto the wall: and
Nu 30:3 and bind **h.** by a bond, being in her
Jg 5:29 her, yea, she returned answer to **h.**,
Ru 2:10 her face, and bowed **h.** to the ground,
1Sa 4:19 husband were dead, she bowed **h.** and
1Sa 25:23 on her face, and bowed **h.** to the ground,
1Sa 25:41 she arose, and bowed **h.** on her face
2Sa 11:2 the roof he saw a woman washing **h.**;
1Ki 14:5 she shall feign **h.** to be another woman.
2Ki 4:37 and bowed **h.** to the ground, and took
Job 39:18 What time she lifteth up **h.** on high,
Ps 84:3 and the swallow a nest for **h.**, where
Pr 31:22 She maketh **h.** coverings of tapestry;
Isa 5:14 Therefore hell hath enlarged **h.**, 5315
Isa 34:14 there, and find for **h.** a place of rest.
Isa 61:10 as a bride adorneth **h.** with her jewels.
Jer 3:11 backsliding Israel hath justified **h.**
Jer 4:31 Zion, that bewaileth **h.**, that spreadeth
Jer 49:24 and turneth **h.** to flee, and fear hath
Eze 22:3 maketh idols against **h.** to defile
Eze 22:3 maketh idols against...to defile **h.**
Eze 23:7 with all their idols she defiled **h.**
Eze 24:12 She hath wearied **h.** with lies, and her
Ho 2:13 she decked **h.** with her earrings and
Zec 9:3 And Tyrus did build **h.** a strong hold,
Mt 9:21 For she said within **h.**, if I may but *1438*
Mk 4:28 **the earth bringeth forth fruit of h.**; *844*
Lu 1:24 and hid **h.** five months, saying, *1433*
Lu 13:11 together, and could in no wise lift up **h.**
Joh 20:14 she turned **h.** back, and saw Jesus.
Joh 20:16 She turned **h.**, and saith unto him,
Heb 11:11 Through faith also Sara **h.** received *846*
Re 2:20 **woman Jezebel, which calleth h. a** *1433*
Re 18:7 How much she hath glorified **h.**, and *1433*
Re 19:7 and his wife hath made **h.** ready. *1433*

HESED (he'-sed) See also JUSHAB-HESED.
1Ki 4:10 The son of **H.**, in Aruboth; to him 2618

HESHBON (hesh'-bon)
Nu 21:25 in **H.**, and in all the villages thereof. 2809
Nu 21:26 for **H.** was the city of Sihon the king 2809
Nu 21:27 Come in to **H.** let the city of Sihon 2809
Nu 21:28 For there is a fire gone out of **H.**, 2809
Nu 21:30 **H.** is perished even unto Dibon, and 2809
Nu 21:34 of the Amorites, which dwelt at **H.** 2809
Nu 32:3 Nimrah, and **H.**, and Elealeh, and 2809
Nu 32:37 the children of Reuben built **H.**, 2809
De 1:4 of the Amorites, which dwelt in **H.**, 2809
De 2:24 hand Sihon the Amorite, king of **H.**, 2809
De 2:26 unto Sihon king of **H.** with words 2809
De 2:30 Sihon king of **H.** would not let us 2809
De 3:2 of the Amorites, which dwelt at **H.**, 2809
De 3:6 as we did unto Sihon king of **H.**, 2809
De 4:46 of the Amorites, who dwelt at **H.**, 2809
De 29:7 unto this place, Sihon the king of **H.**, 2809
Jos 9:10 beyond Jordan, to Sihon king of **H.**, 2809
Jos 12:2 of the Amorites, who dwelt in **H.**, 2809
Jos 12:5 the border of Sihon king of **H.** 2809
Jos 13:10 the Amorites, which reigned in **H.**, 2809
Jos 13:17 **H.**, and all her cities that are in the 2809
Jos 13:21 the Amorites, which reigned in **H.**, 2809
Jos 13:26 And from **H.** unto Ramath-mizpeh, 2809
Jos 13:27 the kingdom of Sihon king of **H.**, 2809
Jos 21:39 **H.** with her suburbs, Jazer with her 2809
Jg 11:19 of the Amorites, the king of **H.**; 2809
Jg 11:26 While Israel dwelt in **H.** and her 2809
1Ch 6:81 **H.** with her suburbs, and Jazer with 2809
Ne 9:22 and the land of the king of **H.**, and 2809
Ca 7:4 thine eyes like the fishpools in **H.**, 2809
Isa 15:4 And **H.** shall cry, and Elealeh: their 2809
Isa 16:8 fields of **H.** languish, and the vine 2809
Isa 16:9 will water thee with my tears, O **H.**, 2809
Jer 48:2 in **H.** they have devised evil against 2809
Jer 48:34 the cry of **H.**, even unto Elealeh, 2809
Jer 48:45 fled stood under the shadow of **H.** 2809
Jer 48:45 but a fire shall come forth out of **H.**, 2809
Jer 49:3 Howl, O **H.**, for Ai is spoiled: cry, 2809

HESHMON (hesh'-mon) See also AZMON.
Jos 15:27 And Hazar-gaddah, and **H.**, and 2829

HETH (heth)
Ge 10:15 begat Sidon his firstborn, and **H.**, 2845
Ge 23:3 spake unto the sons of **H.**, saying, 2845
Ge 23:5 And the children of **H.** answered 2845
Ge 23:7 the land, even to the children of **H.** 2845
Ge 23:10 dwelt among the children of **H.**: 2845
Ge 23:10 the audience of the children of **H.**, 2845
Ge 23:16 in the audience of the sons of **H.**, 2845
Ge 23:18 the presence of the children of **H.**, 2845
Ge 23:20 of a buryingplace by the sons of **H.** 2845
Ge 25:10 purchased of the sons of **H.**: 2845
Ge 27:46 because of the daughters of **H.**: 2845
Ge 27:46 take a wife of the daughters of **H.**, 2845
Ge 49:32 therein was from the children of **H.** 2845
1Ch 1:13 begat Zidon his firstborn, and **H.**, 2845

HETHLON (heth'-lon)
Eze 47:15 way of **H.**, as men go to Zedad; 2855
Eze 48:1 end to the coast of the way of **H.**, 2855

HEW See also HEWED; HEWETH; HEWN.
Ex 34:1 **H.** thee two tables of stone like 6458
De 10:1 **H.** thee two tables of stone like 6458
De 12:3 shall **h.** down the graven images of 1438
De 19:5 with his neighbour to **h.** wood, and 2404
1Ki 5:6 that they **h.** me cedar trees out of 3772
1Ki 5:6 to **h.** timber like unto the Sidonions. 3772
1Ki 5:18 and Hiram's builders did **h.** them, 6458
1Ch 22:2 set masons to **h.** wrought stones 2672
2Ch 2:2 thousand to **h.** in the mountain, 2672
Jer 6:6 **H.** ye down trees, and cast them 3772
Da 4:14 **H.** down the tree, and cut off his 1414
Da 4:23 **H.** the tree down, and destroy it; 1414

HEWED See also HEWN.
Ex 34:4 And he **h.** two tables of stone like 6458
De 10:3 and **h.** two tables of stone like unto 6458
1Sa 11:7 of oxen, and **h.** them in pieces, 5408
1Sa 15:33 And Samuel **h.** Agag in pieces 8158
1Ki 5:17 costly stones, and **h.** stones, to lay 1496
1Ki 6:36 with three rows of **h.** stone, and a 1496
1Ki 7:9 to the measures of **h.** stones, sawed 1496
1Ki 7:11 after the measures of **h.** stones, 1496
1Ki 7:12 with three rows of **h.** stones, and a 1496

2Ki 12:12 and to buy timber and **h.** stone to...... 4274
Isa 22:16 thou hast **h.** thee out a sepulchre....... 2672
Jer 2:13 and **h.** them out cisterns, broken....... 2672
Ho 6:5 have I **h.** them by the prophets;........ 2672

HEWER See also HEWERS.
De 29:11 the **h.** of thy wood unto the drawer.... 2404

HEWERS
Jos 9:21 let them be **h.** of wood and drawers... 2404
Jos 9:23 bondmen, and **h.** of wood and........... 2404
Jos 9:27 make them that day **h.** of wood and.... 2404
1Ki 5:15 thousand **h.** in the mountains;........... 2672
2Ki 12:12 masons, and **h.** of stone, and to buy... 2672
1Ch 22:15 **h.** and workers of stone and timber,... 2672
2Ch 2:10 thy servants, the **h.** that cut timber,... 2404
2Ch 2:18 thousand to be **h.** in the mountain...... 2672
Jer 46:22 her with axes, as **h.** of wood............ 2404

HEWETH
Isa 10:15 axe boast itself against him that **h.**..... 2672
Isa 22:16 as he that **h.** him out a sepulchre....... 2672
Isa 44:14 He **h.** him down cedars, and taketh.... 3772

HEWN See also HEWED.
Ex 20:25 thou shalt not build it of **h.** stone:...... 1496
2Ki 22:6 timber and **h.** stone to repair the....... 4274
2Ch 34:11 to buy **h.** stone, and timber for.......... 4274
Pr 9:1 she hath **h.** out her seven pillars:....... 2672
Isa 9:10 but we will build with **h.** stones:........ 1496
Isa 10:33 ones of stature shall be **h.** down......... 1438
Isa 33:9 Lebanon is ashamed and **h.** down:...... 7060
Isa 51:1 unto the rock whence ye are **h.**,........ 2672
La 3:9 inclosed my ways with **h.** stone,........ 1496
Eze 40:42 four tables were of **h.** stone for the.... 1496
Am 5:11 ye have built houses of **h.** stone,....... 1496
Mt 3:10 is **h.** down, and cast into the fire....... *1581*
Mt 7:19 **is h. down, and cast into the fire.** ..*1581*
Mt 27:60 which he had **h.** out in the rock;........ *2998*
Mk 15:46 in a sepulchre which was **h.** out of a... *2998*
Lu 3:9 is **h.** down, and cast into the fire....... *1581*
Lu 23:53 a sepulchre that was **h.** in stone,....... *2991*

HEZEKI (hez'-e-ki)
1Ch 8:17 and Meshullam, and **H.**, and............. 2395

HEZEKIAH (hez-e-ki'-ah) See also EZEKIAS; HIZKIAH.
2Ki 16:20 **H.** his son reigned in his stead......... 2396
2Ki 18:1 that **H.** the son of Ahaz king of.......... 2396
2Ki 18:9 pass in the fourth year of king **H.**,..... 2396
2Ki 18:10 even in the sixth year of **H.**, that....... 2396
2Ki 18:13 fourteenth year of king **H.** did........... 2396
2Ki 18:14 And **H.** king of Judah sent to the........ 2396
2Ki 18:14 king of Assyria appointed unto **H.**....... 2396
2Ki 18:15 And **H.** gave him all the silver that..... 2396
2Ki 18:16 At that time did **H.** cut off the gold.... 2396
2Ki 18:16 pillars which **H.** king of Judah had....... 2396
2Ki 18:17 from Lachish to king **H.** with a........... 2396
2Ki 18:19 Speak ye now to **H.**, Thus saith......... 2396
2Ki 18:22 whose altars **H.** hath taken away,........ 2396
2Ki 18:29 saith the king, Let not **H.** decieve...... 2396
2Ki 18:30 Neither let **H.** make you trust in the... 2396
2Ki 18:31 Hearken not to **H.**: for thus saith........ 2396
2Ki 18:32 and hearken not unto **H.**, when he..... 2396
2Ki 18:37 to **H.** with their clothes rent, and....... 2396
2Ki 19:1 when king **H.** heard it, that he rent.... 2396
2Ki 19:3 Thus saith **H.**, This day is a day of.... 2396
2Ki 19:5 servants of king **H.** came to Isaiah..... 2396
2Ki 19:9 he sent messengers again unto **H.**,...... 2396
2Ki 19:10 Thus shall ye speak to **H.** king of....... 2396
2Ki 19:14 And **H.** received the letter of the....... 2396
2Ki 19:14 and **H.** went up into the house of........ 2396
2Ki 19:15 And **H.** prayed before the Lord,......... 2396
2Ki 19:20 Isaiah the son of Amoz sent to **H.**,...... 2396
2Ki 20:1 those days was **H.** sick unto death..... 2396
2Ki 20:3 in thy sight. And **H.** wept sore........... 2396
2Ki 20:5 Turn again, and tell **H.** the captain..... 2396
2Ki 20:8 And **H.** said unto Isaiah, What.......... 2396
2Ki 20:10 **H.** answered, It is a light thing for..... 2396
2Ki 20:12 sent letters and a present unto **H.**:...... 2396
2Ki 20:12 he had heard that **H.** had been sick.... 2396
2Ki 20:13 And **H.** hearkened unto them, and...... 2396
2Ki 20:13 dominion, that **H.** shewed them not.... 2396
2Ki 20:14 Isaiah the prophet unto king **H.**,........ 2396
2Ki 20:14 And **H.** said, They are come from....... 2396
2Ki 20:15 And **H.** answered, All the things......... 2396
2Ki 20:16 Isaiah said unto **H.**, Hear the word..... 2396
2Ki 20:19 Then said **H.** unto Isaiah, Good is...... 2396
2Ki 20:20 And the rest of the acts of **H.**, and.... 2396
2Ki 20:21 And **H.** slept with his fathers: and...... 2396
2Ki 21:3 high places which **H.** his father had..... 2396
1Ch 3:13 Ahaz his son, **H.** his son, Manasseh... 2396
1Ch 3:23 of Neariah: Elioenai, and **H.**, and....... 2396
1Ch 4:41 came in the days of **H.** king of........... 2396
2Ch 28:27 **H.** his son reigned in his stead.......... 2396
2Ch 29:1 **H.** began to reign when he was five... 2396
2Ch 29:18 Then they went into **H.** the king,....... 2396
2Ch 29:20 Then **H.** the king rose early, and....... 2396
2Ch 29:27 And **H.** commanded to offer the......... 2396
2Ch 29:30 **H.** the king and the princes.............. 2396
2Ch 29:31 Then **H.** answered and said, Now...... 2396
2Ch 29:36 and **H.** rejoiced, and all the people,.... 2396
2Ch 30:1 And **H.** sent to all Israel and Judah,.... 2396
2Ch 30:18 But **H.** prayed for them, saying, The.. 2396
2Ch 30:20 Lord hearkened to **H.**, and healed...... 2396
2Ch 30:22 **H.** spake comfortably unto all the....... 2396
2Ch 30:24 For **H.** king of Judah did give to........ 2396
2Ch 31:2 **H.** appointed the courses of the......... 2396
2Ch 31:8 when **H.** and the princes came and..... 2396
2Ch 31:9 **H.** questioned with the priests........... 2396
2Ch 31:11 Then **H.** commanded to prepare......... 2396
2Ch 31:13 the commandment of **H.** the king,...... 2396
2Ch 31:20 thus did **H.** throughout all Judah......... 2396
2Ch 32:2 when **H.** saw that Sennacherib was..... 2396
2Ch 32:8 themselves upon the words of **H.**........ 2396
2Ch 32:9 unto **H.** king of Judah, and unto all..... 2396
2Ch 32:11 Doth not **H.** persuade you to give...... 2396
2Ch 32:12 Hath not the same **H.** taken away...... 2396
2Ch 32:15 therefore let not **H.** deceive you,....... 2396
2Ch 32:16 God, and against his servant **H.**......... 2396
2Ch 32:17 so shall not the God **H.** deliver.......... 2396
2Ch 32:20 And for this cause **H.** the king,.......... 2396
2Ch 32:22 Lord saved **H.** and the inhabitants...... 2396
2Ch 32:23 and presents to **H.** king of Judah:....... 2396
2Ch 32:24 those days **H.** was sick to the death,.. 2396
2Ch 32:25 **H.** rendered not again according......... 2396
2Ch 32:26 **H.** humbled himself for the pride........ 2396
2Ch 32:26 not upon them in the days of **H.**........ 2396
2Ch 32:27 **H.** had exceeding much riches and...... 2396
2Ch 32:30 same **H.** also stopped the upper......... 2396
2Ch 32:30 And **H.** prospered in all his works...... 2396
2Ch 32:32 the rest of the acts of **H.**, and his...... 2396
2Ch 32:33 **H.** slept with his fathers, and they..... 2396
2Ch 33:3 high places which **H.** his father had..... 2396
Ezr 2:16 The children of Ater of **H.**, ninety...... 2396
Ne 7:21 The children of Ater of **H.**, ninety...... 2396
Pr 25:1 men of **H.** king of Judah copied out..... 2396
Isa 1:1 Ahaz, and **H.**, kings of Judah............ 2396
Isa 36:1 in the fourteenth year of king **H.**,....... 2396
Isa 36:2 unto king **H.** with a great army.......... 2396
Isa 36:4 Say ye now to **H.**, Thus saith the...... 2396
Isa 36:7 whose altars **H.** hath taken away,....... 2396
Isa 36:14 saith the king, Let not **H.** deceive...... 2396
Isa 36:15 Neither let **H.** make you trust in the... 2396
Isa 36:16 Hearken not to **H.**: for thus saith....... 2396
Isa 36:18 Beware lest **H.** persuade you,........... 2396
Isa 36:22 to **H.** with their clothes rent, and....... 2396
Isa 37:1 when king **H.** heard it, that he rent..... 2396
Isa 37:3 Thus saith **H.**. This day is a day of..... 2396
Isa 37:5 servants of king **H.** came to Isaiah..... 2396
Isa 37:9 he sent messengers to **H.**, saying,...... 2396
Isa 37:10 Thus shall ye speak to **H.** king of....... 2396
Isa 37:14 And **H.** received the letter from the... 2396
Isa 37:14 and **H.** went up unto the house of...... 2396
Isa 37:15 **H.** prayed unto the Lord, saying,....... 2396
Isa 37:21 Isaiah the son of Amoz sent unto **H.**,.. 2396
Isa 38:1 those days was **H.** sick unto death..... 2396
Isa 38:2 Then **H.** turned his face toward the.... 2396
Isa 38:3 in thy sight. And **H.** wept sore.......... 2396
Isa 38:5 Go, and say to **H.**, Thus saith the...... 2396
Isa 38:9 The writing of **H.** king of Judah,........ 2396
Isa 38:22 **H.** also had said, What is the sign...... 2396
Isa 39:1 sent letters and a present to **H.**......... 2396
Isa 39:2 **H.** was glad of them, and shewed...... 2396
Isa 39:2 dominion, that **H.** shewed them not.... 2396
Isa 39:3 Isaiah the prophet unto king **H.**......... 2396
Isa 39:3 And **H.** said, They are come from....... 2396
Isa 39:4 And **H.** answered, All that is in mine.. 2396
Isa 39:5 Then said Isaiah to **H.**, Hear the........ 2396
Isa 39:8 Then said **H.** to Isaiah, Good is the.... 2396
Jer 15:4 because of Manasseh the son of **H.**.... 2396
Jer 26:18 prophesied in the days of **H.** king....... 2396
Jer 26:19 Did **H.** king of Judah and all Judah...... 2396
Ho 1:1 Uzziah, Jotham, Ahaz, and **H.**, kings... 2396
Mic 1:1 the days of Jotham, Ahaz, and **H.**....... 2396

HEZION (he'-zi-on)
1Ki 15:18 the son of **H.**, king of Syria, that....... 2383

HEZIR (he'-zur)
1Ch 24:15 seventeenth to **H.**, the eighteenth...... 2387
Ne 10:20 Magpiash, Meshullam, **H.**,................ 2387

HEZRAI (hez'-rahee) See also HEZRO.
2Sa 23:35 **H.** the Carmelite, Paarai the............ 2695

HEZRO (hez'-ro) See also HEZRAI.
1Ch 11:37 **H.** the Carmelite, Naarai the son....... 2695

HEZRON (hez'-ron) See also HAZOR; HEZRONITES; HEZRON'S.
Ge 46:9 Hanoch, and Phallu, and **H.**, and........ 2696
Ge 46:12 sons of Pharez were **H.** and Hamul.... 2696
Ex 6:14 Hanoch, and Pallu, **H.**, and Carmi:..... 2696
Nu 26:6 Of **H.**, the family of the Hezronites:... 2696
Nu 26:21 of **H.**, the family of the Hezronites:.... 2696
Jos 15:3 and passed along to **H.**, and went...... 2696
Jos 15:25 Kerioth, and **H.**, which is Hazor,....... 2696
Ru 4:18 of Pharez: Pharez begat **H.**,.............. 2696
Ru 4:19 And **H.** begat Ram, and Ram begat..... 2696
1Ch 2:5 The sons of Pharez; **H.**, and Hamul.... 2696
1Ch 2:9 The sons also of **H.**, that were born... 2696
1Ch 2:18 Caleb the son of **H.** begat children..... 2696
1Ch 2:21 **H.** went in to the daughter of Machir.. 2696
1Ch 2:24 And after that **H.** was dead in.......... 2696
1Ch 2:25 Jerahmeel the firstborn of **H.** were,.... 2696
1Ch 4:1 The sons of Judah; Pharez, **H.**, and.... 2696
1Ch 5:3 were, Hanoch, and Pallu, **H.**, and....... 2696

HEZRONITES (hez'-ron-ites)
Nu 26:6 Of Hezron, the family of the **H.**;........ 2697
Nu 26:21 of Hezron, the family of the **H.**.......... 2697

HEZRON'S (hez'-ronz)
1Ch 2:24 Abiah **H.** wife bare him Ashur........... 2696

HID See also HIDDEN.
Ge 3:8 Adam and his wife **H.** themselves....... 2244
Ge 3:10 I was naked; and I **h.** myself............ 2244
Ge 4:14 and from thy face shall I be **h.**;......... 5641
Ge 35:4 and Jacob **h.** them under the oak........ 2934
Ex 2:2 child, she **h.** him three months.......... 6845
Ex 2:12 Egyptian, and **h.** him in the sand........ 2934
Ex 3:6 And Moses **h.** his face; for he was...... 5641
Le 4:13 and the thing be **h.** from the eyes...... 5956
Le 5:3 defiled withal, and it be **h.** from him;.. 5956
Le 5:4 with an oath, and it be **h.** from him;.. 5956
Nu 5:13 be **h.** from the eyes of her husband,... 5956
De 33:19 and of treasures **h.** in the sand.......... 2934
Jos 2:4 took the two men, and **h.** them,........ 6845
Jos 2:6 **h.** them with the stalks of flax,.......... 2934
Jos 6:17 because she **h.** the messengers......... 2244
Jos 6:25 because she **h.** the messengers,........ 2244
Jos 7:21 are **h.** in the earth in the midst......... 2934
Jos 7:22 behold, it was **h.** in his tent, and the.. 2934
Jos 10:16 five kings fled, and **h.** themselves....... 2244
Jos 10:17 five kings are found **h.** in a cave........ 2244
Jos 10:27 cave wherein they had been **h.**,......... 2244
Jg 9:5 Jerubbaal was left; for he **h.** himself.... 2244
1Sa 3:18 whit, and **h.** nothing from him........... 3582
1Sa 10:22 hath **h.** himself among the stuff.......... 2244
1Sa 14:11 holes where they had **h.** themselves... 2244
1Sa 14:22 which had **h.** themselves in mount...... 2244
1Sa 20:24 So David **h.** himself in the field:......... 5641
2Sa 17:9 he is **h.** now in some pit, or in some.. 2244
2Sa 18:13 there is no matter **h.** from the king,... 3582
1Ki 10:3 was not any thing **h.** from the king,.... 5956
1Ki 18:4 and **h.** them by fifty in a cave, and..... 2244
1Ki 18:13 how I **h.** an hundred men of the........ 2244
2Ki 4:27 and the Lord hath **h.** it from me,........ 5956
2Ki 6:29 eat him: and she hath **h.** her son....... 2244
2Ki 7:8 and raiment, and went and **h.** it;........ 2934
2Ki 7:8 thence also, and went and **h.** it.......... 2934
2Ki 11:2 and they **h.** him, even him and his..... 5641
2Ki 11:3 he was with her **h.** in the house of...... 2244
1Ch 21:20 four sons with him **h.** themselves....... 2244
2Ch 9:2 nothing **h.** from Solomon which........... 5956
2Ch 22:9 for he was **h.** in Samaria, and........... 2244
2Ch 22:11 of Ahaziah, **h.** him from Athaliah,....... 5641
2Ch 22:12 **h.** in the house of God six years:....... 2244
Job 3:10 nor **h.** sorrow from mine eyes........... 5641
Job 3:21 for it more than for **h.** treasures;........ 4301
Job 3:23 given to a man whose way is **h.**,........ 5641
Job 5:21 Thou shalt be **h.** from the scourge...... 2244
Job 6:16 ice, and wherein the snow is **h.**:......... 5956
Job 10:13 things hast thou **h.** in thine heart:...... 6845
Job 15:18 their fathers, and have not **h.** it:........ 3582

Job 17:4 For thou hast **h.** their heart from....... 6845
Job 20:26 darkness shall be **h.** in his secret....... 2244
Job 28:11 thing that is **h.** bringeth he forth........ 8587
Job 28:21 Seeing it is **h.** from the eyes of all..... 5956
Job 29:8 men saw me, and **h.** themselves:....... 2244
Job 38:30 The waters are **h.** as with a stone,...... 2244
Ps 9:15 net which they **h.** is their own foot..... 2934
Ps 17:14 thou fillest with thy **h.** treasure:........ 6845
Ps 19:6 there is nothing **h.** from the heat........ 5641
Ps 22:24 neither hath he **h.** his face from him; .. 5641
Ps 32:5 and mine iniquity have I not **h.**.......... 3680
Ps 35:7 have they **h.** for me their net in a....... 2934
Ps 35:8 net that he hath **h.** catch himself:....... 2934
Ps 38:9 my groaning is not **h.** from thee......... 5641
Ps 40:10 I have not **h.** thy righteousness 3680
Ps 55:12 then I would have **h.** myself from....... 5641
Ps 69:5 and my sins are not **h.** from thee....... 3582
Ps 119:11 Thy word have I **h.** in mine heart, ... 6845
Ps 139:15 My substance was not **h.** from 3582
Ps 140:5 The proud have **h.** a snare for me,...... 2934
Pr 2:4 for her as for **h.** treasures;.............. 4301
Isa 28:15 falsehood have we **h.** ourselves:......... 5641
Isa 29:14 of their prudent men shall be **h.**......... 5641
Isa 40:27 My way is **h.** from the Lord, and my.. 5641
Isa 42:22 and they are **h.** in prison houses:....... 2244
Isa 49:2 shadow of his hand hath he **h.** me...... 2244
Isa 49:2 in his quiver hath he **h.** me;............. 5641
Isa 50:6 I **h.** not my face from shame and........ 5641
Isa 53:3 and we **h.** as it were our faces from... 5641
Isa 54:8 In a little wrath I **h.** my face from...... 5641
Isa 57:17 I **h.** me, and was wroth, and he went . 5641
Isa 59:2 your sins have **h.** his face from you, ... 5641
Isa 64:7 for thou hast **h.** thy face from us, ... 5641
Isa 65:16 because they are **h.** from mine eyes. .. 5641
Jer 13:5 So I went, and **h.** it by Euphrates, ... 2934
Jer 13:7 from the place where I had **h.** it: 2934
Jer 16:17 they are not **h.** from my face, ... 5641
Jer 16:17 is their iniquity **h.** from mine eyes...... 6845
Jer 18:22 take me, and **h.** snares for my feet. ... 2934
Jer 33:5 I have **h.** my face from this city......... 5641
Jer 36:26 the prophet: but the Lord **h.** them. 5641
Jer 43:10 upon these stones that I have **h.**;....... 2934
Eze 22:26 **h.** their eyes from my sabbaths, ... 5956
Eze 39:23 therefore **h.** I my face from them,....... 5641
Eze 39:24 them, and **h.** my face from them......... 5641
Ho 5:3 and Israel is not **h.** from me:............ 3582
Ho 13:12 is bound up; his sin is **h.**................ 6845
Ho 13:14 repentance shall be **h.** from mine 5641
Am 9:3 be **h.** from my sight in the bottom...... 5641
Na 3:11 thou shalt be **h.**, thou also shalt.......... 5956
Zep 2:3 it may be ye shall be **h.** in the day...... 5641
Mt 5:14 **that is set on an hill cannot be h.** . *2928*
Mt 10:26 **and h., that shall not be known.** ... *2927*
Mt 11:25 **because thou hast h. these things**... *613*
Mt 13:33 **and h. in three measures of meal,** ..*1470*
Mt 13:44 **is like unto treasure h. in a field;** .. *2928*
Mt 25:18 **the earth, and h. his lord's money.** ..*613*
Mt 25:25 **and h. thy talent in the earth:** *2928*
Mk 4:22 **For there is nothing h., which**...... *2927*
Mk 7:24 know it: but he could not be **h.**........ *2990*
Lu 1:24 and **h.** herself five months, saying, ... *4032*
Lu 8:17 **neither any thing h., that shall not** .*614*
Lu 8:47 saw that she was not **h.**, she came..... *2990*
Lu 9:45 and it was **h.** from them, that they..... *3871*
Lu 10:21 **that thou hast h. these things from** .*613*
Lu 12:2 **neither h., that shall not be known***2927*
Lu 13:21 **and h. in three measures of meal,** ..*1470*
Lu 18:34 and this saying was **h.** from them,...... *2928*
Lu 19:42 **now they are h. from thine eyes**.... *2928*
Joh 8:59 but Jesus **h.** himself, and went out *2928*
2Co 4:3 if our gospel be **h.**, it is **h.** to them.... *2572*
Eph 3:9 hath been **h.** in God, who created........ *618*
Col 1:26 which hath been **h.** from ages and........ *618*
Col 2:3 In whom are **h.** all the treasures *614*
Col 3:3 your life is **h.** with Christ in God........ *2928*
1Ti 5:25 that are otherwise cannot be **h.** *2928*
Heb 11:23 was **h.** three months of his parents,.... *2928*
Re 6:15 **h.** themselves in the dens and in........ *2928*

HIDDAI (hid'-dahee) See also HURAI.
2Sa 23:30 **H.** of the brooks of Gaash, ... 1914

HIDDEKEL (hid'-de-kel)
Ge 2:14 the name of the third river is **H.**:....... 2313
Da 10:4 side of the great river, which is **H.**..... 2313

HIDDEN See also HID.
Le 5:2 and if it be **h.** from him; he also........ 5956
De 30:11 it is not **h.** from thee, neither is 6381
Job 3:16 Or as an **h.** untimely birth I had......... 2934
Job 15:20 of years is **h.** to the oppressor. 6845
Job 24:1 times are not **h.** from the Almighty,.... 6845
Ps 51:6 in the **h.** part thou shalt make me 5640
Ps 83:3 and consulted against thy **h.** ones. 6845
Pr 28:12 when the wicked rise, a man is **h.**...... 2664
Isa 45:3 and **h.** riches of secret places, that..... 4301
Isa 48:6 from this time, even **h.** things, and..... 5341
Ob 6 how are his **h.** things sought up!......... 4710
Ac 26:26 none of these things are **h.** from........ *2990*
1Co 2:7 the **h.** wisdom, which God ordained...... *613*
1Co 4:5 bring to the light the **h.** things of....... *2927*
2Co 4:2 the **h.** things of dishonesty, not *2927*
1Pe 3:4 But let it be the **h.** man of the heart,.. *2927*
Re 2:17 **will I give to eat of the h. manna,**. *2928*

HIDE See also HID; HIDDEN; HIDEST; HIDETH; HIDING.
Ge 18:17 Shall I **h.** from Abraham that thing...... 3680
Ge 47:18 We will not **h.** it from my lord, how ... 3582
Ex 2:3 when she could not longer **h.** him,...... 6845
Le 8:17 the bullock, and his **h.**, his flesh,........ 5785
Le 9:11 flesh and the **h.** he burnt with fire...... 5785
Le 20:4 ways **h.** their eyes from the man, ... 5956
De 7:20 left, and **h.** themselves from thee,...... 5641
De 22:1 astray, and **h.** myself from them: 5956
De 22:3 likewise thou mayest not **h.** thyself..... 5956
De 22:4 the way, and **h.** thyself from them:..... 5956
De 31:17 and I will **h.** my face from them......... 5641
De 31:18 I will surely **h.** my face in that day..... 5641
De 32:20 said, I will **h.** my face from them. 5641
Jos 2:16 **h.** yourselves there three days. 2247
Jos 7:19 thou hast done; **h.** it not from me. 3582
Jg 6:11 to **h.** it from the Midianites............... 5127
1Sa 3:17 I pray thee **h.** it not from me: God..... 3582
1Sa 3:17 if thou **h.** any thing from me of all..... 3582
1Sa 13:6 people did **h.** themselves in caves, ... 2244
1Sa 19:2 in a secret place, and **h.** thyself: 2244
1Sa 20:2 why should my father **h.** this thing 5641
1Sa 20:5 that I may **h.** myself in the field.......... 5641
1Sa 20:19 the place where thou didst **h.** thyself .. 5641
1Sa 23:19 Doth not David **h.** himself with us 5641
1Sa 26:1 Doth not David **h.** himself in the......... 5641
2Sa 14:18 **H.** not from me, I pray thee, the........ 3582
1Ki 17:3 **h.** thyself by the brook Cherith,.......... 5641
1Ki 22:25 an inner chamber to **h.** thyself........... 2247
2Ki 7:12 out of the camp to **h.** themselves........ 2247
2Ch 18:24 an inner chamber to **h.** thyself. 2244
Job 13:20 then will I not **h.** myself from thee. 5641
Job 14:13 thou wouldest **h.** me in the grave,...... 6845
Job 20:12 though he **h.** it under his tongue; 3582
Job 24:4 poor of the earth **h.** themselves......... 2244
Job 33:17 purpose, and **h.** pride from man.......... 3680
Job 34:22 of iniquity may **h.** themselves. 5641
Job 40:13 **H.** them in the dust together; 2934
Ps 13:1 how long wilt thou **h.** thy face 5641
Ps 17:8 **h.** me under the shadow of thy.......... 5641
Ps 27:5 the time of trouble he shall **h.** me 6845
Ps 27:5 of his tabernacle shall he **h.** me; 5641
Ps 27:9 **H.** not thy face far from me; put........ 5641
Ps 30:7 thou didst **h.** thy face, and I was........ 5641
Ps 31:20 Thou shalt **h.** them in the secret........ 5641
Ps 51:9 **H.** thy face from my sins, and blot 5641
Ps 54:*title* Doth not David **h.** himself with 5641
Ps 55:1 O God, and **h.** not thyself from my..... 5956
Ps 56:6 they **h.** themselves, they mark my 6845
Ps 64:2 **H.** me from the secret counsel of....... 5641
Ps 69:17 **h.** not thy face from thy servant; 5641
Ps 78:4 not **h.** them from their children,......... 3582
Ps 89:46 Lord? wilt thou **h.** thyself for ever? 5641
Ps 102:2 **H.** not thy face from me in the day 5641
Ps 119:19 **h.** not thy commandments from me. ... 5641
Ps 143:7 **h.** not thy face from me, lest I be...... 5641
Ps 143:9 enemies: I flee unto thee to **h.** me. 3680
Pr 2:1 **h.** my commandments with thee;......... 6845
Pr 28:28 wicked rise, men **h.** themselves:......... 5641
Isa 1:15 will **h.** mine eyes from you: yea,........ 5956
Isa 2:10 and **h.** thee in the dust, for fear of..... 2934
Isa 3:9 their sin as Sodom, they **h.** it not....... 3582
Isa 16:3 **h.** the outcasts; bewray not him......... 5641
Isa 26:20 **h.** thyself as it were for a little.......... 2247
Isa 29:15 that seek deep to **h.** their counsel...... 5641
Isa 58:7 thou **h.** not thyself from thine own 5956
Jer 13:4 Euphrates, and **h.** it there in a hole.... 2934
Jer 13:6 which I commanded thee to **h.** there.... 2934
Jer 23:24 Can any **h.** himself in secret places..... 5641
Jer 36:19 Go, **h.** thee, thou and Jeremiah; and... 5641
Jer 38:14 thee a thing; **h.** nothing from me........ 3582
Jer 38:25 **h.** it not from us, and we will not....... 3582
Jer 43:9 and **h.** them in the clay in the............ 2934
Jer 49:10 he shall not be able to **h.** himself: 2247
La 3:56 **h.** not thine ear at my breathing, ... 5956
Eze 28:3 no secret that they can **h.** from 6004
Eze 31:8 the garden of God could not **h.** him: ... 6004
Eze 39:29 Neither will I **h.** face any more.......... 5641
Da 10:7 so that they fled to **h.** themselves. 2244
Am 9:3 they **h.** themselves in the top............ 2244
Mic 3:4 he will even **h.** his face from them 5641
Joh 12:36 and did **h.** himself from them............ *2928*
Jas 5:20 and shall **h.** a multitude of sins. *2572*
Re 6:16 **h.** us from the face of him that.......... *2928*

HIDEST
Job 13:24 Wherefore **h.** thou thy face, and 5641
Ps 10:1 why **h.** thou thyself in times of.......... 5956
Ps 44:24 Wherefore **h.** thou thy face, and 5641
Ps 88:14 why **h.** thou thy face from me?.......... 5641
Ps 104:29 Thou **h.** thy face, they are troubled: ... 5641
Isa 45:15 thou art a God that **h.** thyself, O 5641

HIDETH
1Sa 23:23 places where he **h.** himself, and......... 2244
Job 23:9 he **h.** himself on the right hand,......... 5848
Job 34:29 and when he **h.** his face, who then..... 5641
Job 42:3 Who is he that **h.** counsel without 5956
Ps 10:11 he **h.** his face; he will never see it. 5641
Ps 139:12 the darkness **h.** not from thee; 2821
Pr 10:18 He that **h.** hatred with lying lips,........ 3680
Pr 19:24 man **h.** his hand in his bosom, ... 2934
Pr 22:3 foreseeth the evil, and **h.** himself: 5641
Pr 26:15 slothful **h.** his hand in his bosom; 2934
Pr 27:12 foreseeth the evil, and **h.** himself; 5641
Pr 27:16 Whosoever **h.** her **h.** the wind, and.... 6845
Pr 28:27 that **h.** his eyes shall have many a...... 5956
Isa 8:17 that **h.** his face from the house of...... 5641
Mt 13:44 **when a man hath found, he h.**...... *2928*

HIDING
Job 31:33 by **h.** mine iniquity in my bosom: 2934
Ps 32:7 Thou art my **h.** place; thou shalt......... 5643
Ps 119:114 art my **h.** place and my shield: 5643
Isa 28:17 waters shall overflow the **h.** place. 5643
Isa 32:2 be as an **h.** place from the wind,........ 4224
Hab 3:4 and there was the **h.** of his power...... 2253

HIDING-PLACE See HIDING and PLACE.

HIEL (hi'-el)
1Ki 16:34 **H.** the Beth-elite build Jericho: 2419

HIERAPOLIS (hi-e-rap'-o-lis)
Col 4:13 are in Laodicea, and them in **H.**........ *2404*

HIGGAION (hig-gah'-yon)
Ps 9:16 work of his own hands. **H.** Selah....... 1902

HIGH See also HIGHER; HIGHEST; HIGHMINDED; HIGHWAY.
Ge 7:19 all the **h.** hills, that were under the 1364
Ge 14:18 was the priest of the most **h.** God...... 5945
Ge 14:19 be Abram of the most **h.** God, ... 5945
Ge 14:20 And blessed be the most **h.** God,......... 5945
Ge 14:22 unto the Lord, the most **h.** God,......... 5945
Ge 29:7 Lo, it is yet **h.** day, neither is it 1419
Ex 14:8 of Israel went out with an **h.** hand...... 7311
Ex 25:20 stretch forth their wings on **h.**,.......... 4605
Ex 37:9 spread out their wings on **h.**, and........ 4605
Ex 39:31 to fasten it on **h.** upon the mitre;...... 4605
Le 21:10 And he that is the **h.** priest among...... 1419
Le 26:22 and your **h.** ways shall be desolate. ....
Le 26:30 I will destroy your **h.** places, and....... 1116
Nu 11:31 it were two cubits **h.** upon the face of.......
Nu 20:17 we will go by the king's **h.** way, ...
Nu 20:19 We will go by the **h.** way: and if I....... 4546
Nu 21:22 we will go along by the king's **h.** way,.......
Nu 21:28 the lords of the **h.** places of Arnon. 1116
Nu 22:41 him up into the **h.** places of Baal,....... 1116
Nu 23:3 thee. And he went to an **h.** place......... 8205
Nu 24:16 the knowledge of the most **H.**, ... 5945
Nu 33:3 of Israel went out with an **h.** hand...... 7311
Nu 33:52 pluck down all their **h.** places: 1116
Nu 35:25 in it unto the death of the **h.** priest, ... 1419
Nu 35:28 until the death of the **h.** priest: but..... 1419
Nu 35:28 after the death of the **h.** priest the..... 1419
De 2:27 I will go along by the **h.** way, I will.... 1870
De 3:5 cities were fenced with **h.** walls, ... 1364
De 12:2 upon the **h.** mountains, and upon........ 7311
De 26:19 to make thee **h.** above all nations........ 5945
De 28:1 thy God will set thee on **h.** above all .. 5945

De 28:43 shall get up above thee very **h.**; 4605
De 28:52 thy **h.** and fenced walls come down, ... 1364
De 32:8 When the most **H.** divided to the....... 5945
De 32:13 He made him ride on the **h.** places..... 1116
De 32:27 Our hands is **h.**, and the Lord hath..... 7311
De 33:29 shalt tread upon their **h.** places.......... 1116
Jos 20:6 and until the death of the **h.** priest..... 1419
Jg 5:18 death in the **h.** places of the field....... 4791
1Sa 9:12 of the people to day in the **h.** place: ... 1116
1Sa 9:13 before he go up to the **h.** place to eat;.1116
1Sa 9:14 them, for to go up to the **h.** place...... 1116
1Sa 9:19 go up before me unto the **h.** place;..... 1116
1Sa 9:25 from the **h.** place into the city, ... 1116
1Sa 10:5 coming down from the **h.** place with ... 1116
1Sa 10:13 prophesying, he came to the **h.** place.. 1116
1Sa 13:6 in rocks, and in **h.** places, and in....... 6877
2Sa 1:19 Israel is slain upon thy **h.** places: 1116
2Sa 1:25 thou wast slain in thine **h.** places........ 1116
2Sa 22:3 my **h.** tower, and my refuge, my 4869
2Sa 22:14 and the most **H.** uttered his voice...... 5845
2Sa 22:34 and setteth me upon my **h.** places........ 1116
2Sa 22:49 hast lifted me up on **h.** above them 7311
2Sa 23:1 the man who was raised up on **h.**,....... 5920
1Ki 3:2 the people sacrificed in **h.** places,....... 1116
1Ki 3:3 and burnt incense in **h.** places. 1116
1Ki 3:4 for that was the great **h.** place: 1116
1Ki 6:10 all the house, five cubits **h.**: and 6967
1Ki 6:23 of olive tree, each ten cubits **h.**. 6967
1Ki 7:15 brass, of eighteen cubits **h.** apiece:..... 6967
1Ki 7:35 a round compass of half a cubit **h.**: 6967
1Ki 9:8 this house, which is **h.**, every one...... 5945
1Ki 11:7 Solomon build an **h.** place for 1116
1Ki 12:31 he made an house of **h.** places, and.... 1116
1Ki 12:32 the priests of the **h.** places which....... 1116
1Ki 13:2 he offer the priests of the **h.** places.... 1116
1Ki 13:32 all the houses of the **h.** places which... 1116
1Ki 13:33 the people priests of the **h.** places:..... 1116
1Ki 13:33 one of the priests of the **h.** places...... 1116
1Ki 14:23 For they also built them **h.** places, ... 1364
1Ki 14:23 on every **h.** hill, and under every....... 1364
1Ki 15:14 the **h.** places were not removed:......... 1116
1Ki 21:9 set Naboth on **h.** among the people: ... 7218
1Ki 21:12 set Naboth on **h.** among the people. ... 7218
1Ki 22:43 the **h.** places were not taken away; 1116
1Ki 22:43 burnt incense yet in the **h.** places....... 1116
2Ki 12:3 the **h.** places were not taken away: 1116
2Ki 12:3 and burnt incense in the **h.** places. 1116
2Ki 12:10 scribe and the **h.** priest came up,....... 1419
2Ki 14:4 Howbeit the **h.** places were not......... 1116
2Ki 14:4 and burnt incense on the **h.** places. 1116
2Ki 15:4 the **h.** places were not removed: the .. 1116
2Ki 15:4 burnt incense still on the **h.** places. 1116
2Ki 15:35 the **h.** places were not removed: the .. 1116
2Ki 15:35 burned incense still in the **h.** places. ... 1116
2Ki 16:4 burnt incense in the **h.** places, and..... 1116
2Ki 17:9 they built them **h.** places in all their.... 1116
2Ki 17:10 groves in every **h.** hill, and under....... 1364
2Ki 17:11 burnt incense in all the **h.** places,....... 1116
2Ki 17:29 them in the houses of the **h.** places 1116
2Ki 17:32 of them priests of the **h.** places, ... 1116
2Ki 17:32 them in the houses of the **h.** places. ... 1116
2Ki 18:4 He removed the **h.** places, and brake.. 1116
2Ki 18:22 whose **h.** places and whose altars....... 1116
2Ki 19:22 and lifted up thine eyes on **h.**?.......... 4791
2Ki 21:3 For he built up again the **h.** places 1116
2Ki 22:4 Go up to Hilkiah the **h.** priest, that..... 1419
2Ki 22:8 And Hilkiah the **h.** priest said unto 1419
2Ki 23:4 commmanded Hilkiah th **h.** priest, ... 1419
2Ki 23:5 to burn incense in the **h.** places in...... 1116
2Ki 23:8 and defiled the **h.** places where the 1116
2Ki 23:8 down the **h.** places of the gates 1116
2Ki 23:9 the priests of the **h.** places came not .. 1116
2Ki 23:13 And the **h.** places that were before..... 1116
2Ki 23:15 and the **h.** place which Jeroboam........ 1116
2Ki 23:15 both that altar and the **h.** place he...... 1116
2Ki 23:15 brake down, and burned the **h.** place, . 1116
2Ki 23:19 all the houses also of the **h.** places..... 1116
2Ki 23:20 slew all the priests of the **h.** places 1116
1Ch 11:23 man of great stature, five cubits **h.**..........
1Ch 14:2 his kingdom was lifted up on **h.**, ... 4605
1Ch 16:39 in the **h.** place that was at Gibeon,..... 1116
1Ch 17:17 to the estate of a man of **h.** degree, ... 4608
1Ch 21:29 season in the **h.** place at Gibeon. 1116
2Ch 1:3 to the **h.** place that was at Gibeon;..... 1116
2Ch 1:13 to the **h.** place that was at Gibeon...... 1116
2Ch 3:15 pillars of thirty and five cubits **h.**, ... 753
2Ch 6:13 and three cubits **h.**, and had set it...... 6967
2Ch 7:21 this house, which is **h.**, shall be......... 5945
2Ch 11:15 priests for the **h.** places, and for........ 1116
2Ch 14:3 and the **h.** places, and brake down 1116
2Ch 14:5 the **h.** places and the images: and 1116
2Ch 15:17 the **h.** places were not taken away 1116
2Ch 17:6 took away the **h.** places and groves 1116
2Ch 20:19 of Israel with a loud voice on **h.**......... 4605
2Ch 20:33 the **h.** places were not taken away; 1116
2Ch 21:11 made **h.** places in the mountains 1116
2Ch 23:20 through the **h.** gate into the king's....... 5945
2Ch 24:11 and the **h.** priest's officer came and 7218
2Ch 27:3 He built the **h.** gate of the house 5945
2Ch 28:4 and burnt incense in the **h.** places, ... 1116
2Ch 28:25 he made **h.** places to burn incense...... 1116
2Ch 31:1 threw down the **h.** places and the 1116
2Ch 32:12 taken away his **h.** places and his 1116
2Ch 33:3 he built again the **h.** places which....... 1116
2Ch 33:17 did sacrifice still in the **h.** places, ... 1116
2Ch 33:19 places wherein he built **h.** places, ... 1116
2Ch 34:3 Jerusalem from the **h.** places, and 1116
2Ch 34:4 the images, that were on **h.** above 4605
2Ch 34:9 they came to Hilkiah the **h.** priest, ... 1419
Ne 3:1 Eliashib the **h.** priest rose up with...... 1419
Ne 3:20 the house of Eliashib the **h.** priest...... 1419
Ne 3:25 lieth out from the king's **h.** house,...... 5945
Ne 13:28 the son of Eliashib the **h.** priest,....... 1419
Es 5:14 gallows be made of fifty cubits **h.**, ... 1364
Es 7:9 the gallows fifty cubits **h.**, which........ 1364
Job 5:11 To set up on **h.** those that be low;..... 4791
Job 11:8 It is as **h.** as heaven; what canst........ 1363
Job 16:19 in heaven, and my record is on **h.**....... 4791
Job 21:22 seeing he judgeth those that are **h.**...... 7311
Job 22:12 height of the stars, how **h.** they are! .. 7311
Job 25:2 he maketh peace in his **h.** places........ 4791
Job 31:2 of the Almighty from on **h.**?............. 4791
Job 38:15 and the **h.** arm shall be broken. 7311
Job 39:18 time she lifteth up herself on **h.**, ... 4791
Job 39:27 command, and make her nest on **h.**?... 7311
Job 41:34 He beholdeth all **h.** things: he is 1364
Ps 7:7 sakes therefore return thou on **h.**......... 4791
Ps 7:17 to the name of the Lord most **h.**........ 5945
Ps 9:2 praise to thy name O thou most **H.**. ... 5945
Ps 18:2 of my salvation, and my **h.** tower....... 4869
Ps 18:27 but wilt bring down **h.** looks............. 7311
Ps 18:33 and setteth me upon my **h.** places........ 1116
Ps 21:7 through the mercy of the most **H.**...... 5945
Ps 46:4 of the tabernacles of the most **H.**....... 5945
Ps 47:2 the Lord most **h.** is terrible; he is...... 5945
Ps 49:2 Both low and **h.**, rich and poor,........... 376
Ps 50:14 pay thy vows unto the most **H.**: 5945
Ps 56:2 fight against me, O thou most **H.**......... 4791
Ps 57:2 I will cry unto God most **h.**; unto....... 5945
Ps 62:9 and men of **h.** degree are a lie: 376
Ps 68:15 an **h.** hill as the hill of Bashan........... 1386
Ps 68:16 Why leap ye, ye **h.** hills? this is the.... 1386
Ps 68:18 Thou hast ascended on **h.**, thou.......... 4791
Ps 69:29 salvation, O God, set me up on **h.**. 7682
Ps 71:19 also, O God, is very **h.**, who hast...... 4791
Ps 73:11 is there knowledge in the most **H.**? 5945
Ps 75:5 Lift not up your horn on **h.**: speak 4791
Ps 77:10 of the right hand of the most **H.**......... 5945
Ps 78:17 by provoking the most **H.** in the 5945
Ps 78:35 and the **h.** God their redeemer. 5945
Ps 78:56 and provoked the most **h.** God, and..... 5945
Ps 78:58 to anger with their **h.** places, and....... 1116
Ps 78:69 built his sanctuary like **h.** palaces, ... 7311
Ps 82:6 of you are children of the most **H.**. 5945
Ps 83:18 art the most **h.** over all the earth....... 5945
Ps 89:13 thy hand, and **h.** is thy right hand. 7311
Ps 91:1 in the secret place of the most **H.**....... 5945
Ps 91:9 even the most **H.**, thy habitation;....... 5945
Ps 91:14 I will set him on **h.**, because he......... 7682
Ps 92:1 praises unto thy name, O most **H.**: 5945
Ps 92:8 Lord, art most **h.** for evermore. 4791
Ps 93:4 The Lord on **h.** is mightier than the.... 4791
Ps 97:9 Lord, art **h.** above all the earth: 5945
Ps 99:2 and he is **h.** above all the people........ 7311
Ps 101:5 hath an **h.** look and a proud heart....... 1362
Ps 103:11 the heaven is **h.** above the earth,....... 1361
Ps 104:18 The **h.** hills are a refuge for the......... 1364
Ps 107:11 the counsel of the most **H.**: 5945
Ps 107:41 Yet setteth he the poor on **h.** from..... 7682
Ps 113:4 The Lord is **h.** above all nations,........ 7311
Ps 113:5 out God, who dwelleth on **h.**,............. 1361
Ps 131:1 matters, or in things too **h.** for me..... 6381
Ps 138:6 Though the Lord be **h.**, yet hath........ 7311
Ps 139:6 it is **h.**, I cannot attain unto it........... 7682
Ps 144:2 my **h.** tower, and my deliverer; 4869
Ps 149:6 the **h.** praises of God be in their........ 7319
Ps 150:5 him upon the **h.** sounding cymbals...... 8643
Pr 8:2 standeth in the top of the **h.** places, ... 4791
Pr 9:14 a seat in the **h.** places of the city. 4791
Pr 18:11 as an **h.** wall in his own conceit. 7682
Pr 21:4 An **h.** look, and a proud heart, and...... 7312
Pr 24:7 Wisdom is too **h.** for a fool: he.......... 7311
Ec 12:5 shall be afraid of that which is **h.**,....... 1364
Isa 2:13 the cedars of Lebanon, that are **h.** 7311
Isa 2:14 upon all the **h.** mountains, and upon.... 7311
Isa 2:15 upon every **h.** tower, and upon........... 1364
Isa 6:1 upon a throne, **h.** and lifted up, ... 7311
Isa 10:12 and the glory of his **h.** looks.............. 7312
Isa 10:33 the **h.** ones of stature shall be hewn... 7312
Isa 13:2 a banner upon the **h.** mountain, ... 8192
Isa 14:14 clouds; I will be like the most **H.**. 5945
Isa 15:2 gone up to...the **h.** places, to weep: ... 1116
Isa 16:12 that Moab is weary on the **h.** place, ... 1116
Isa 22:16 heweth him out a sepulchre on **h.**, ... 4791
Isa 24:18 the windows from on **h.** are open,....... 4791
Isa 24:21 the host of the **h.** ones that are on **h.**,.4791
Isa 25:12 fortress of the **h.** fort of thy walls...... 4869
Isa 26:5 down them that dwell on **h.**; the........ 4791
Isa 30:13 swelling out in a **h.** wall, whose......... 7682
Isa 30:25 upon every **h.** mountain, and upon....... 1364
Isa 30:25 and upon every **h.** hill, rivers and....... 4791
Isa 32:15 spirit be poured upon us from on **h.**,... 4791
Isa 33:5 is exalted; for he dwelleth on **h.**: 4791
Isa 33:16 He shall dwell on **h.**: his place of 4791
Isa 36:7 whose **h.** places and whose altars....... 1111
Isa 37:23 and lifted up thine eyes on **h.**? even ... 4796
Isa 40:9 get thee up into the **h.** mountain;....... 1364
Isa 40:26 Lift up your eyes on **h.**, and behold.... 4791
Isa 41:18 I will open rivers in **h.** places, and...... 8203
Isa 49:9 pastures shall be in all **h.** places......... 8203
Isa 52:13 and extolled, and be very **h.**. 1361
Isa 57:7 Upon a lofty and **h.** mountain hast...... 5375
Isa 57:15 the **h.** and lofty One that inhabiteth 7311
Isa 57:15 I dwell in the **h.** and holy place,......... 4791
Isa 58:4 make your voice to be heard on **h.**..... 4791
Isa 58:14 ride upon the **h.** places of the earth, ... 1116
Jer 2:20 when upon every **h.** hill and under...... 1364
Jer 3:2 up thine eyes unto the **h.** places, ... 8205
Jer 3:6 upon every **h.** mountain and under....... 1364
Jer 3:21 was heard upon the **h.** places, ... 8205
Jer 4:11 A dry wind of the **h.** places in the...... 8205
Jer 7:29 take up a lamentation on **h.** places;..... 8205
Jer 7:31 have built the **h.** places of Tophet, ... 1116
Jer 12:12 are come upon all **h.** places.............. 8205
Jer 14:6 asses did stand in the **h.** places, ... 8205
Jer 17:2 by the green trees upon the **h.** hills.... 1364
Jer 17:3 thy **h.** places for sin, throughout 1116
Jer 17:12 A glorious **h.** throne from the........... 4791
Jer 19:5 built also the **h.** places of Baal,......... 1116
Jer 20:2 were in the **h.** gate of Benjamin,........ 5945
Jer 25:30 The Lord shall roar from on **h.**,......... 4791
Jer 26:18 house as the **h.** places of a forest....... 1116
Jer 31:21 up waymarks, make thee **h.** heaps:...... 8564
Jer 32:35 they built the **h.** places of Baal, ... 1116
Jer 48:35 him that offereth in the **h.** places, ... 1116
Jer 49:16 make thy nest as **h.** as the eagle, ... 1361
Jer 51:58 her **h.** gates shall be burned with....... 1364
La 3:35 before the face of the most **H.**, ... 5945
La 3:38 Out of the mouth of the most **H.** 5945
Eze 1:18 were so **h.** that they were dreadful;.... 1362
Eze 6:3 and I will destroy your **h.** places. 1116
Eze 6:6 and the **h.** places shall be desolate;..... 1116
Eze 6:13 upon every **h.** hill, in all the tops 7311
Eze 16:16 deckedst thy **h.** places with divers...... 1116
Eze 16:24 thee an **h.** place in every street. 7413
Eze 16:25 built thy **h.** place at every head of...... 7413
Eze 16:31 and makest thine **h.** place in every 7413
Eze 16:39 shall break down thy **h.** places:.......... 7413
Eze 17:22 highest branch of the **h.** cedar, ... 7311
Eze 17:22 will plant it upon an **h.** mountain 1364
Eze 17:24 Lord have brought down the **h.** tree, .. 1364
Eze 20:28 then they saw every **h.** hill, and all..... 7311
Eze 20:29 What is the **h.** place whereunto ye 1116
Eze 21:26 is low, and abase him that is **h.**. 1364
Eze 31:3 and of an **h.** stature; and his top 1362
Eze 31:4 the deep set him up on **h.** with her 7311
Eze 34:6 mountains, and upon every **h.** hill: 7311
Eze 34:14 the **h.** mountains of Israel shall 4791
Eze 36:2 even the ancient **h.** places are ours 1116
Eze 40:2 set me upon a very **h.** mountain, ... 1364
Eze 40:42 and one cubit **h.**: whereupon also 1363

Eze 41:22 altar of wood was three cubits h., ... 1364
Eze 43:7 of their kings in their h. places. 1116
Da 3:26 ye servants of the most h. God, ... 5943
Da 4:2 and wonders that the h. God hath 5943
Da 4:17 the most H. ruleth in the kingdom...... 5943
Da 4:24 this is the decree of the most H., ... 5943
Da 4:32 most H. ruleth in the kingdom........... 5943
Da 4:34 and I blessed the most H., and I 5943
Da 5:18 most h. God gave Nebuchadnezzar..... 5943
Da 5:21 most h. God ruled in the kingdom 5943
Da 7:18 But the saints of the most H. shall..... 5946
Da 7:22 given to the saints of the most H.;..... 5946
Da 7:25 great words against the most H......... 5943
Da 7:25 wear out the saints of the most H.,..... 5946
Da 7:27 people of the saints of the most H., ... 5946
Da 8:3 and the two horns were h.; but one ... 1364
Ho 7:16 return, but not to the most H. 5920
Ho 10:8 The h. places also of Aven, the sin 1116
Ho 11:7 they called them to the most H., ... 5920
Am 4:13 treadeth upon the h. places of the...... 1116
Am 7:9 h. places of Isaac shall be desolate, ... 1116
Ob 3 whose habitation is h.; that saith........ 4791
Mic 1:3 and tread upon the h. places of the 1116
Mic 1:5 what are the h. places of Judah? 1116
Mic 3:12 house as the h. places of the forest.... 1116
Mic 6:6 and bow myself before the h. God? 4791
Hab 2:9 that he may set his nest on h., that.... 4791
Hab 3:10 voice, and lifted up his hands on h...... 7315
Hab 3:19 me to walk upon mine h. places. 1116
Zep 1:16 cities, and against the h. towers. 1364
Hag 1:1, 12,14 of Josedech, the h. priest, ... 1419
Hag 2:2 the son of Josedech, the h. priest, ... 1419
Hag 2:4 the son of Josedech, the h. priest; 1419
Zec 3:1 he shewed me Joshua the h. priest...... 1419
Zec 3:8 Hear now, O Joshua the h. priest,...... 1419
Zec 6:11 the son of Josedech, the h. priest; 1419
Mt 4:8 up into an exceeding h. mountain, ... 5308
Mt 17:1 them up into an h. mountain apart, ... 5308
Mt 26:3 the palace of the h. priest, who was..... 749
Mt 26:51 struck a servant of the h. priest's........ 749
Mt 26:57 him away to Caiaphas the h. priest, ... 749
Mt 26:58 afar off unto the h. priest's palace, ... 749
Mt 26:62 And the h. priest arose, and said unto.. 749
Mt 26:63 And the h. priest answered and said..... 749
Mt 26:65 Then the h. priest rent his clothes,....... 749
Mk 2:26 **days of Abiathar the h. priest, and..** 749
Mk 5:7 Jesus, thou Son of the most h. God? .. 5310
Mk 6:21 supper to his lords, h. captains, and ... 5310
Mk 9:2 them up into an h. mountain apart...... 5308
Mk 14:47 and smote a servant of the h. priest,.... 749
Mk 14:53 led Jesus away to the h. priest: and..... 749
Mk 14:54 into the palace of the h. priest: and...... 749
Mk 14:60 the h. priest stood up in the midst,...... 749
Mk 14:61 Again the h. priest asked him, and....... 749
Mk 14:63 Then the h. priest rent his clothes,....... 749
Mk 14:66 one of the maids of the h. priest: 749
Lu 1:78 dayspring from on h. hath visited 5311
Lu 3:2 and Caiaphas being the h. priests,......... 749
Lu 4:5 taking him up into an h. mountain,....... 5308
Lu 8:28 Jesus, thou son of God most h.? 5310
Lu 22:50 smote the servant of the h. priest, ... 749
Lu 22:54 him into the h. priest's house. And 749
Lu 24:49 **be endued with power from on h....**5311
Joh 11:49 being the h. priest that same year, ... 749
Joh 11:51 but being h. priest that year, he......... 749
Joh 18:10 and smote the h. priest's servant, and.. 749
Joh 18:13 which was the h. priest that same 749
Joh 18:15 was known unto the h. priest, and....... 749
Joh 18:15 Jesus into the palace of the h. priest. ... 749
Joh 18:16 which was known unto the h. priest, ... 749
Joh 18:19 The h. priest then asked Jesus of his ... 749
Joh 18:22 Answerest thou the h. priest so?......... 749
Joh 18:24 bound unto Caiaphas the h. priest......... 749
Joh 18:26 of the servants of the h. priest, ... 749
Joh 19:31 that sabbath day was an h. day,......... 3173
Ac 4:6 Annas the h. priest, and Caiaphas,....... 749
Ac 4:6 were of the kindred of the h. priest, ... 749
Ac 5:17 the h. priest rose up, and all they......... 749
Ac 5:21 But the h. priest came, and they that... 749
Ac 5:24 the h. priest and the captain of the..... 2409
Ac 5:27 and the h. priest asked them, ... 749
Ac 7:1 said the h. priest, Are these things...... 749
Ac 7:48 most H. dwelleth not in temples 5310
Ac 9:1 And Saul...went unto the h. priest, ... 749
Ac 13:17 with an h. arm brought he them 5308
Ac 16:17 are the servants of the most h. God,.. 5310
Ac 22:5 the h. priest doth bear me witness, ... 749
Ac 23:2 the h. priest Ananias commanded......... 749
Ac 23:4 said, Revilest thou God's h. priest?...... 749
Ac 23:5 wist not...that he was the h. priest;..... 749
Ac 24:1 Ananias the h. priest descended with.... 749
Ac 25:2 Then the h. priest and the chief of....... 749
Ro 12:16 Mind not h. things, but condescend 5308
Ro 13:11 it is h. time to awake out of sleep:...........
2Co 10:5 and every h. thing that exalteth......... 5313
Eph 4:8 When he ascended up on h., he led..... 5311
Eph 6:12 spiritual wickedness in h. places......... 2032
Php 3:14 the prize of the h. calling of God in...... 507
Heb 1:3 the right hand of the Majesty on h.; ... 5308
Heb 2:17 a merciful and faithful h. priest in......... 749
Heb 3:1 consider the Apostle and H. Priest of... 749
Heb 4:14 that we have a great h. priest, that is .. 749
Heb 4:15 we have not an h. priest which cannot.. 749
Heb 5:1 For every h. priest taken from among.. 749
Heb 5:5 not himself to be made an h. priest;..... 749
Heb 5:10 of God an h. priest after the order of... 749
Heb 6:20 an h. priest for ever after the order..... 749
Heb 7:1 of Salem, priest of the most h. God,... 5310
Heb 7:26 For such an h. priest became............. 749
Heb 7:27 not daily, as those h. priests, to offer... 749
Heb 7:28 the law maketh men h. priests which.... 749
Heb 8:1 We have such an h. priest, who is set.. 749
Heb 8:3 every h. priest is ordained to offer....... 749
Heb 9:7 went the h. priest alone once every...... 749
Heb 9:11 an h. priest of good things to come,..... 749
Heb 9:25 as the h. priest entereth into the holy .. 749
Heb 10:21 having an h. priest over the house 3173
Heb 13:11 sanctuary by the h. priest for sin,........ 749
Re 21:10 spirit to a great and h. mountain, ... 5308
Re 21:12 And had a wall great and h., and had.. 5308

HIGHER
Nu 24:7 and his king shall be h. than Agag, ... 7311
1Sa 9:2 he was h. than any of the people. 1364
1Sa 10:23 he was h. than any of the people 1361
2Ki 15:35 He built the h. gate of the house 5945
Ne 4:13 the wall, and on the h. places, I 6706
Job 35:5 the clouds which are h. than thou....... 1361
Ps 61:2 me to the rock that is h. than I. 7311
Ps 89:27 h. than the kings of the earth............ 5945
Ec 5:8 for he that is h. than the highest........ 1364
Ec 5:8 and there be h. than they................. 1364
Isa 55:9 the heavens are h. than the earth, ... 1361
Isa 55:9 so are my ways h. than your ways,..... 1361
Jer 36:10 in the h. court, at the entry of the..... 5945
Eze 9:2 came from the way of the h. gate, ... 5945
Eze 42:5 the galleries were h. than these,......... 3201
Eze 43:13 shall be the h. place of the altar......... 1354
Da 8:3 but one was h. than the other, and..... 1364
Da 8:3 the other, and the h. came up last. 1364
Lu 14:10 **say unto thee, Friend, go up h.** 511
Ro 13:1 soul be subject unto the h. powers..... 5242
Heb 7:26 and made h. than the heavens; 5308

HIGHEST
Ps 18:13 and the H. gave his voice;................ 5945
Ps 87:5 the h. himself shall establish her. 5945
Pr 8:26 h. part of the dust of the world. 7218
Pr 9:3 upon the h. places of the city,........... 4791
Ec 5:8 for he that is higher than the h.......... 1364
Eze 17:3 took the h. branch of the cedar: 6788
Eze 17:22 of the h. branch of the high cedar, ... 6788
Eze 41:7 from the lowest chamber to the h. 5945
Mt 21:9 of the Lord; Hosanna in the h.. 5310
Mk 11:10 of the Lord: Hosanna in the h.. 5310
Lu 1:32 shall be called the Son of the H. 5310
Lu 1:35 power of the H. shall overshadow 5310
Lu 1:76 be called the prophet of the H........... 5310
Lu 2:14 Glory to God in the h., and on earth .. 5310
Lu 6:35 **ye shall be the children of the H..** 5310
Lu 14:8 **sit not down in the h. room; lest** .. 4411
Lu 19:38 peace in heaven, and glory in the h. ... 5310
Lu 20:46 **the h. seats in the synagogues,**...... 4410

HIGHLY
Lu 1:28 said, Hail, thou that art h. favoured, ...
Lu 16:15 **which is h. esteemed among men** .. 5308
Ac 12:20 Herod was h. displeased with them 2371
Ro 12:3 not to think of himself more h. tham... 5252
Php 2:9 God also hath h. exalted him, and 5251
1Th 5:13 to esteem them very h. in love .. 1537,4053

HIGHMINDED
Ro 11:20 by faith. Be not h., but fear:............ 5309
1Ti 6:17 they be not h., nor trust in uncertain.. 5309
2Ti 3:4 heady, h., lovers of pleasures more.... 5187

HIGHNESS
Job 31:23 by reason of his h. I could not........... 7613
Isa 13:3 even them that rejoice in my h.. 1346

HIGH-PLACE See HIGH and PLACE.

HIGH-PRIEST See HIGH and PRIEST.

HIGHWAY See also HIGH; HIGHWAYS.
Jg 21:19 on the east side of the h. that goeth... 4546
1Sa 6:12 went along the h., lowing as they....... 4546
2Sa 20:12 in blood in the midst of the h.. And.... 4546
2Sa 20:12 he removed Amasa out of the h. into.. 4546
2Sa 20:13 When he was removed out of the h.,.. 4546
2Ki 18:17 which is in the h. of the fuller's field... 4546
Pr 16:17 The h. of the upright is to depart....... 4546
Isa 7:3 pool in the h. of the fuller's field; 4546
Isa 11:16 there shall be an h. for the remnant ... 4546
Isa 19:23 day shall there be a h. out of Egypt ... 4546
Isa 35:8 And an h. shall be there, and a way, .. 4547
Isa 36:2 pool in the h. of the fuller's field. 4546
Isa 40:3 in the desert a h. for our God. 4546
Isa 62:10 cast up, cast up the h.; gather out 4546
Jer 31:21 set thine heart toward the h., even 4546
Mk 10:46 Timaeus, sat by the h. side begging. .. 3598

HIGHWAYS
Jg 5:6 the h. were unoccupied, and the.......... 734
Jg 20:31 in the h., of which one goeth up 4546
Jg 20:32 draw them from the city unto the h.... 4546
Jg 20:45 they gleaned of them in the h. five..... 4546
Isa 33:8 The h. lie waste, the warfaring man ... 4546
Isa 49:11 a way, and my h. shall be exalted. 4546
Am 5:16 they shall say in all the h., Alas!......... 2351
Mt 22:9 **Go ye therefore into the h., ...** 1327,3598
Mt 22:10 **servants went out into the h., .**1327,3598
Lu 14:23 **Go out into the h. and hedges,** 1327,3598

HILEN (hi'-len) See also HOLON.
1Ch 6:58 And H. with her suburbs, Debir......... 2432

HILKIAH (hil-ki'-ah) See also HELKAI; HILKIAH'S.
2Ki 18:18 out to them Eliakim the son of H., ... 2518
2Ki 18:26 Then said Eliakim the son of H.,........ 2518
2Ki 18:37 Then came Eliakim the son of H.,....... 2518
2Ki 22:4 Go up to H. the high priest, that he ... 2518
2Ki 22:8 And H. the high priest said unto........ 2518
2Ki 22:8 And H. gave the book to Shaphan, ... 2518
2Ki 22:10 H. the priest hath delivered me a....... 2518
2Ki 22:12 the king commanded H. the priest,..... 2518
2Ki 22:14 So H. the priest, and Ahikam, and 2518
2Ki 23:4 the king commanded H. the high........ 2518
2Ki 23:24 the book that H. the priest found in.... 2518
1Ch 6:13 Shallum begat H., and H. begat......... 2518
1Ch 6:45 the son of Amaziah, the son of H.,..... 2518
1Ch 9:11 Azariah the son of H., the son of....... 2518
1Ch 26:11 H. the second, Tebaliah the third,...... 2518
2Ch 34:9 they came to H. the high priest,......... 2518
2Ch 34:14 H. the priest found a book of the....... 2518
2Ch 34:15 H. answered and said to Shaphan....... 2518
2Ch 34:15 H. delivered the book to Shaphan....... 2518
2Ch 34:18 H. the priest hath given me a book. ... 2518
2Ch 34:20 And the king commanded H., and....... 2518
2Ch 34:22 H.,...went to Huldah the prophetess,.. 2518
2Ch 35:8 H. and Zechariah and Jehiel, rulers..... 2518
Ezr 7:1 the son of Azariah, the son of H.,...... 2518
Ne 8:4 and Urijah, and H., and Maaseiah,...... 2518
Ne 11:11 Seraiah the son of H., the son of....... 2518
Ne 12:7 Sallu, Amok, H., Jedaiah. These 2518
Ne 12:21 of H., Hashabiah; of Jedaiah, ... 2518
Isa 22:20 my servant Eliakim the son of H.:...... 2518
Isa 36:22 Then came Eliakim, the son of H., ... 2518
Jer 1:1 words of Jeremiah the son of H., ... 2518
Jer 29:3 and Gemariah the son of H., whom 2518

HILKIAH'S (hil-ki'ahs)
Isa 36:3 H. son, which was over the house, ... 2518

HILL See also DUNGHILL; HILL'S; HILLS.
Ex 17:9 I will stand on the top of the h. with .. 1389
Ex 17:10 and Hur went up to the top of the h... 1389
Ex 24:4 builded an altar under the h., and....... 2022
Nu 14:44 presumed to go up unto the h. top: 2022
Nu 14:45 which dwelt in that h., and smote 2022
De 1:41 ye were ready to go up into the h. 2022
De 1:43 went presumptuously up into the h..... 2022
Jos 5:3 of Israel at the h. of the foreskins. 1389
Jos 13:6 the inhabitants of the h. country 2022

Jos 15:9 drawn from the top of the **h.** unto...... 2022
Jos 17:16 The **h.** is not enough for us: and........ 2022
Jos 18:13 near the **h.** that lieth on the south...... 2022
Jos 18:14 the **h.** that lieth before Beth-horon..... 2022
Jos 21:11 Hebron, in the **h.** country of Judah,.... 2022
Jos 24:30 on the north side of the **h.** of Gaash... 2022
Jos 24:33 buried him in a **h.** that pertained........ 1389
Jg 2:9 on the north side of the **h.** Gaash....... 2022
Jg 7:1 by the **h.** of Moreh, in the valley....... 1389
Jg 16:3 carried them up to the top of an **h.** 2022
1Sa 7:1 the house of Abinadab in the **h.**, ... 1389
1Sa 9:11 they went up to the **h.** to the city,..... 4608
1Sa 10:5 thou shalt come to the **h.** of God, ... 1389
1Sa 10:10 they came thither to the **h.**, behold, ... 1389
1Sa 23:19 in the **h.** of Hachilah, which is on....... 1389
1Sa 25:20 came down by the covert of the **h.**,..... 2022
1Sa 26:1 not David hide himself in the **h.** of...... 1389
1Sa 26:3 Saul pitched in the **h.** of Hachilah, ... 1389
1Sa 26:13 stood on the top of an **h.** afar off; 2022
2Sa 2:24 they were come to the **h.** of Ammah, ..1389
2Sa 2:25 troop, and stood on the top of an **h.**... 1389
2Sa 13:34 the way of the **h.** side behind him. 2022
2Sa 16:1 was a little past the top of the **h.**, ...
2Sa 21:9 they hanged them in the **h.** before...... 2022
1Ki 11:7 in the **h.** that is before Jerusalem,...... 2022
1Ki 14:23 groves, on every high **h.**, and under... 1389
1Ki 16:24 bought the **h.** Samaria of Shemer....... 2022
1Ki 16:24 and built on the **h.**, and called........... 2022
1Ki 16:24 of Shemer, owner of the **h.**, Samaria. . 2022
2Ki 1:9 behold, he sat on the top of an **h.**. 2022
2Ki 4:27 she came to the man of God to the **h.**, 2022
2Ki 17:10 groves in every high **h.**, and under..... 1389
Ps 2:6 my king upon my holy **h.** of Zion........ 2022
Ps 3:4 and he heard me out of his holy **h.**. 2022
Ps 15:1 who shall dwell in thy holy **h.**?.......... 2022
Ps 24:3 Who shall ascend into the **h.** of the..... 2022
Ps 42:6 the Hermonites, from the **h.** Mizar..... 2022
Ps 43:3 let them bring me unto thy holy **h.**, ... 2022
Ps 68:15 **h.** of God is as the **h.** of Bashan;....... 2022
Ps 68:15 an high **h.** as the **h.** of Bashan. 2022
Ps 68:16 this is the **h.** which God desireth to.... 2022
Ps 99:9 our God, and worship at his holy **h.**;... 2022
Ca 4:6 and to the **h.** of frankincense............ 1389
Isa 5:1 a vineyard in a very fruitful **h.**: 7161
Isa 10:32 of Zion, the **h.** of Jerusalem. 1389
Isa 30:17 mountain, and as an ensign on an **h.**... 1389
Isa 30:25 and upon every high **h.**, rivers and..... 1389
Isa 31:4 mount Zion, and for the **h.** thereof. 1389
Isa 40:4 mountain and **h.** shall be made low: 1389
Jer 2:20 when upon every high **h.** and under.... 1389
Jer 16:16 from every **h.**, and out of the holes.... 1389
Jer 31:39 over against it upon the **h.** Gareb,...... 1389
Jer 49:16 that holdest the height of the **h.**:........ 1389
Jer 50:6 they have gone from mountain to **h.**, .. 1389
Eze 6:13 altars, upon every high **h.**, in all the.... 1389
Eze 20:28 they saw every high **h.**, and all the..... 1389
Eze 34:6 mountains, and upon every high **h.**: 1389
Eze 34:26 round about my **h.** a blessing; 1389
Mt 5:14 **A city that is set on an h. cannot** *3735*
Lu 1:39 went into the **h.** country with haste,... *3714*
Lu 1:65 throughout all the **h.** country of *3714*
Lu 3:5 mountain and **h.** shall be brought........ *1015*
Lu 4:29 led him unto the brow of the **h.**......... *3735*
Lu 9:37 they were come down from the **h.**, ... *3735*
Ac 17:22 Paul stood in the midst of Mars' **h.**, ... *697*

HILL-COUNTRY See HILL and COUNTRY.

HILLEL (hil'-lel)
Jg 12:13 And after him Abdon the son of **H.**,..... 1985
Jg 12:15 the son of **H.** the Pirathonite died, ... 1985

HILL'S
2Sa 16:13 Shimei went along on the **h.** side 2022

HILLS
Ge 7:19 all the high **h.**, that were under 2022
Ge 49:26 utmost bound of the everlasting **h.** 1389
Nu 23:9 him, and from the **h.** I behold him: 1389
De 1:7 in the **h.**, and in the vale, and in........ 2022
De 8:7 that spring out of valleys and **h.**;........ 2022
De 8:9 out of whose **h.** thou mayest dig........ 2042
De 11:11 it, is a land of **h.** and valleys, and....... 2022
De 12:2 upon the **h.**, and under every green.... 1389
De 33:15 the precious things of the lasting **h.**, ... 1389
Jos 9:1 on this side Jordan, in the **h.**,and 2022
Jos 10:40 smote all the country of the **h.**, and.... 2022
Jos 11:16 the **h.**, and all the south country, ... 2022
1Ki 20:23 Their gods are gods of the **h.**........... 2022
1Ki 20:28 The Lord is God of the **h.**, but he is .. 2022
1Ki 22:17 saw all Israel scattered upon the **h.**, ... 2022
2Ki 16:4 on the **h.**, and under every green....... 1389
2Ch 28:4 on the **h.**, and under every green........ 1389
Job 15:7 wast thou made before the **h.**? 1389
Ps 18:7 foundations also of the **h.** moved........ 2022
Ps 50:10 and the cattle upon a thousand **h.**....... 2042
Ps 65:12 and the little **h.** rejoice on every........ 1389
Ps 68:16 Why leap ye, ye high **h.**? this is......... 2022
Ps 72:3 and the little **h.**, by righteousness. 1389
Ps 80:10 The **h.** were covered with the........... 2022
Ps 95:4 the strength of the **h.** is his also. 2022
Ps 97:5 **h.** melted like wax at the presence..... 2022
Ps 98:8 hands: let the **h.** be joyful together..... 2022
Ps 104:10 valleys, which run among the **h.**......... 2022
Ps 104:13 watereth the **h.** from his chambers: 2022
Ps 104:18 The high **h.** are a refuge for the 2022
Ps 104:32 he toucheth the **h.**, and they smoke.... 2022
Ps 114:4 rams, and the little **h.** like lambs........ 1389
Ps 114:6 rams; and ye little **h.**, like lambs?....... 1389
Ps 121:1 I will lift up mine eyes unto the **h.**, ... 2022
Ps 148:9 Mountains, and all **h.**; fruitful............. 1389
Pr 8:25 before the **h.** was I brought forth:...... 1389
Ca 2:8 mountains, skipping upon the **h.**......... 1389
Isa 2:2 shall be exalted above the **h.**; and...... 1389
Isa 2:14 upon all the **h.** that are lifted up,........ 1389
Isa 5:25 the **h.** did tremble, and their 2022
Isa 7:25 all **h.** that shall be digged with the...... 2022
Isa 40:12 in scales, and the **h.** in a balance? 1389
Isa 41:15 and shalt make the **h.** as chaff. 1389
Isa 42:15 make waste mountains and **h.**, and..... 1389
Isa 54:10 depart, and the **h.** be removed; but.... 1389
Isa 55:12 the mountains and the **h.** shall break... 1389
Isa 65:7 and blasphemed me upon the **h.**:........ 1389
Jer 3:23 salvation is hoped for from the **h.**,...... 1389
Jer 4:24 and all the **h.** moved lightly.............. 1389
Jer 13:27 abominations on the **h.** in the fields..... 1389
Jer 17:2 by the green trees upon the high **h.**. .. 1389
Eze 6:3 and to the **h.**, to the rivers, and to..... 1389
Eze 35:8 in thy **h.**, and in thy valleys, and in 1389
Eze 36:4, 6 and to the **h.**, to the rivers, and to.. 1389
Ho 4:13 and burn incense upon the **h.**, under... 1389
Ho 10:8 Cover us; and to the **h.**, Fall on us. ... 1389
Joe 3:18 and the **h.** shall flow with milk, and 1389
Am 9:13 sweet wine, and all the **h.** shall melt... 1389
Mic 4:1 it shall be exalted above the **h.**; and ... 1389
Mic 6:1 and let the **h.** hear thy voice. 1389
Na 1:5 the **h.** melt, and the earth is burned... 1389
Hab 3:6 the perpetual **h.** did bow: his ways..... 1389
Zep 1:10 and a great crashing from the **h.**. 1389
Lu 23:30 **Fall on us; and to the h., Cover us** *1015*

HILL-TOP See HILL and TOP.

HIM See in the APPENDIX; also HIMSELF.

HIMSELF
Ge 14:15 And he divided **h.** against them, he..........
Ge 18:2 door, and bowed **h.** toward the ground,.....
Ge 19:1 and he bowed **h.** with his face toward ......
Ge 22:8 My son, God will provide **h.** a lamb for .....
Ge 23:7 And Abraham stood up, and bowed **h.**........
Ge 23:12 And Abraham bowed down **h.** before.........
Ge 24:52 worshipped the Lord, bowing **h.** to the......
Ge 27:42 doth comfort **h.**, purposing to kill ....
Ge 30:36 three days' journey betwixt **h.** and...........
Ge 32:21 **h.** lodged that night in...company. 1931
Ge 33:3 bowed **h.** to the ground seven times,........
Ge 41:14 shaved **h.**, and changed his raiment, ...
Ge 42:7 but made **h.** strange unto them,...............
Ge 42:24 And he turned **h.** about from them, ...
Ge 43:31 refrained **h.**, and said, Set on bread..........
Ge 43:32 And they set on for him by **h.**, and for......
Ge 45:1 Then Joseph could not refrain **h.** before.....
Ge 45:1 while Joseph made **h.** known unto his........
Ge 46:29 to Goshen, and presented **h.** unto him;......
Ge 47:31 Israel bowed **h.** upon the bed's head.........
Ge 48:2 and Israel strengthened **h.**, and sat..........
Ge 48:12 and he bowed **h.** with his face to the ....
Ex 10:6 and he turned **h.**, and went out from ....
Ex 21:3 If he came in by **h.**, he shall go out.... 1610
Ex 21:3 he shall go out by **h.**: if he were........ 1610
Ex 21:4 master's, and he shall go out by **h.**..... 1610
Ex 21:8 master, who hath betrothed her to **h.**, ...
Le 7:8 the priest shall have to **h.** the skin of.........
Le 9:8 of the sin offering, which was for **h.**. ....
Le 14:8 wash **h.** in water, that he may be clean: ....
Le 15:13 shall number to **h.** seven days for his........
Le 15:5, 6,7,8,10,11,22,27 bathe **h.** in water, ...
Le 15:21 bathe **h.** in water, and be unclean............
Le 16:6 of the sin offering, which is for **h.**, ...
Le 16:6 and make an atonement for **h.**, and for......
Le 16:11 of the sin offering, which is for **h.**, ...
Le 16:11 and shall make an atonement for **h.**, ...
Le 16:11 of the sin offering which is for **h.**: ....
Le 16:17 and have made an atonement for **h.**, ...
Le 16:24 an atonement for **h.**, and for the people,....
Le 17:15 and bathe **h.** in water, and be unclean.......
Le 21:4 he shall not defile **h.**, being a chief ....
Le 21:4 man among his people, to profane **h.**.........
Le 21:11 nor defile **h.** for his father, or for his ....
Le 22:8 he shall not eat to defile **h.** therewith:.......
Le 25:26 it, and **h.** be able to redeem it;.......... 3027
Le 25:47 wax poor, and sell **h.** unto the stranger.....
Le 25:49 or if he be able, he may redeem **h.**. ... 3027
Le 27:8 then he will present **h.** before the ....
Nu 6:3 He shall separate **h.** from wine and...........
Nu 6:5 in the which he separateth **h.** unto the ......
Nu 6:6 All the days that he separateth **h.** unto......
Nu 6:7 He shall not make **h.** unclean for his.........
Nu 16:9 bring you near to **h.** to do the service.........
Nu 19:12 shall purify **h.** with it on the third....... 1931
Nu 19:12 but if he purfy not **h.** the third day, ...
Nu 19:13 purifieth not **h.**, defileth the tabernacle ......
Nu 19:19 on the seventh day he shall purify **h.**, ...
Nu 19:19 wash his clothes, and bathe **h.** in water, ...
Nu 19:20 and shall not purify **h.**, that soul shall........
Nu 23:24 lion, and lift up **h.** as a young lion:............
Nu 25:3 And Israel, joined **h.** unto Baal-peor:.........
Nu 31:53 was had taken spoil, every man for **h.**........
Nu 35:19 revenger of blood **h.** shall slay the...... 1931
Nu 36:7 Israel shall keep **h.** to the inheritance........
Nu 36:9 shall keep **h.** to his own inheritance. ....
De 7:6 thee to be a special people unto **h.**, ...
De 14:2 thee to be a peculiar people unto **h.**,.........
De 17:16 But he shall not multiply horses to **h.**,.......
De 17:17 Neither shall he multiply wifes to **h.**,.........
De 17:17 shall he greatly multiply to **h.** silver ....
De 23:11 cometh on, he shall wash **h.** with water:....
De 28:9 establish thee a holy people unto **h.**, ...
De 29:13 thee to day for a people unto **h.**, and........
De 29:19 that he bless **h.** in his heart, saying, I.......
De 32:36 and repent **h.** for his servants, when he ....
De 33:21 And he provided the first part for **h.**, ...
Jos 22:23 thereon, let the Lord **h.** require it; ....
Jg 3:19 he **h.** turned again from the quarries... 1931
Jg 3:20 parlour, which he had for **h.** alone. ....
Jg 4:11 in law of Moses, had severed **h.** from.......
Jg 6:31 if he be a god, let him plead for **h.**, ...
Jg 7:5 a dog lappeth, him shalt thou set by **h.**;.....
Jg 9:5 son of Jerubbaal was left ; for he hid **h.**.....
Jg 16:30 And he bowed **h.** with all his might;..........
Ru 3:8 the man was afraid, and turned **h.**: ....
1Sa 2:14 brought up the priest took for **h.**.............
1Sa 3:21 Lord revealed **h.** to Samuel in Shiloh.........
1Sa 8:11 your sons, and appoint them for **h.**, ...
1Sa 10:19 your God, who **h.** saved you out of all ......
1Sa 10:22 he hath hid **h.** among the stuff........... 1931
1Sa 14:47 whithersoever he turned **h.**, he vexed.......
1Sa 17:16 evening, and presented **h.** forty days. ....
1Sa 18:4 And Jonathan stripped **h.** of the robe.........
1Sa 18:5 Saul sent him, and behaved **h.** wisely: ....
1Sa 18:14 And David behaved **h.** wisely in all his.......
1Sa 18:15 Saul saw that he behaved **h.** very wisely,...
1Sa 18:30 that David behaved **h.** more wisely than ....
1Sa 20:24 So David hid **h.** in the field: and when.......
1Sa 20:41 the ground, and bowed **h.** three times:......
1Sa 21:13 and feigned **h.** mad in their hands, and ......
1Sa 23:19 Doth not David hide **h.** with us in the ....
1Sa 23:23 the lurking places where he hideth **h.**,........
1Sa 24:8 with his face to the earth, and bowed **h.**.....
1Sa 25:31 or that my lord hath avenged **h.**: but ....
1Sa 26:1 Doth not David hide **h.** in the hill of..........
1Sa 28:8 And Saul disguised **h.**, and put on other.....
1Sa 28:14 his face to the ground, and bowed **h.**. ....
1Sa 29:4 he reconcile **h.** unto his master?..............
1Sa 30:6 but David encouraged **h.** in the Lord.........
1Sa 30:31 David **h.** and his men were wont to..........
2Sa 3:6 Abner made **h.** strong for the house ....
2Sa 3:31 And king David **h.** followed the bier..........
2Sa 6:20 who uncovered **h.** to day in the eyes of.....
2Sa 6:20 fellows shamelessly uncovereth **h.**! ....
2Sa 7:23 God went to redeem for a people to **h.**, ...
2Sa 9:8 And he bowed **h.**, and said, What is thy ....
2Sa 12:18 how will he then vex **h.**, if we tell him......

2Sa 12:20 anointed **h.**, and changed his apparel,
2Sa 13:6 Amnon lay down, and made **h.** sick:
2Sa 14:22 and bowed **h.**, and thanked the king:
2Sa 14:33 bowed **h.** on his face to the ground
2Sa 15:23 the king also **h.** passed over the brook
2Sa 17:23 hanged **h.**, and died, and was buried
2Sa 18:21 And Cushi bowed **h.** unto Joab, and ran.
2Sa 24:20 bowed **h.** before the king on his face
1Ki 1:5 the son of Haggith exalted **h.**, saying, I
1Ki 1:23 he bowed **h.** before the king with his
1Ki 1:47 And the king bowed **h.** upon the bed.
1Ki 1:52 said, If he will shew **h.** a worthy man,
1Ki 1:53 and bowed **h.** to king Solomon: and
1Ki 2:19 and bowed **h.** unto her, and sat down
1Ki 11:29 he had clad **h.** with a new garment; 1931
1Ki 15:15 and the things which **h.** had dedicated,
1Ki 16:9 drinking **h.** drunk in the house of Azra
1Ki 17:21 And he stretched **h.** upon the child
1Ki 18:2 And Elijah went to shew **h.** unto Ahab.
1Ki 18:6 Ahab went one way by **h.**, and Obadiah
1Ki 18:6 and Obadiah went another way by **h.**.
1Ki 18:42 And he cast **h.** down upon the earth,
1Ki 19:4 But he **h.** went a day's journey into 1931
1Ki 19:4 requested for **h.** that he might die; 5315
1Ki 20:11 that girdeth on his harness boast **h.** as
1Ki 20:16 Ben-hadad was drinking **h.** drunk in
1Ki 20:38 disguised **h.** with ashes upon his face.
1Ki 21:25 which did sell **h.** to work wickedness
1Ki 21:29 how Ahab humbleth **h.** before me?
1Ki 21:29 he humbleth **h.** before me, I will not
1Ki 22:30 king of Israel disguised **h.**, and went
2Ki 4:34 and he stretched **h.** upon the child;
2Ki 4:35 and stretched **h.** upon him: and the
2Ki 5:14 and dipped **h.** seven times in Jordan,
2Ki 6:10 and saved **h.** there, not once nor twice.
2Ki 19:1 covered **h.** with sackcloth, and went
2Ki 23:16 And as Josiah turned **h.**, he spied the
1Ch 12:1 he yet kept **h.** close because of Saul
1Ch 13:13 brought not the ark home to **h.** to
1Ch 21:21 and bowed **h.** to David with his face to
2Ch 12:1 and had strengthened **h.**, he forsook
2Ch 12:12 And when he humbled **h.**, the wrath of
2Ch 12:13 So king Rehoboam strengthened **h.** in
2Ch 13:9 cometh to consecrate **h.** with a 3027
2Ch 13:12 God **h.** is with us for our captain, and
2Ch 15:18 and that he **h.** had dedicated, silver,
2Ch 16:9 to shew **h.** strong in the behalf of them
2Ch 16:14 sepulchres, which he had made for **h.**
2Ch 17:1 and strengthened **h.** against Israel
2Ch 17:16 Zichri, who willingly offered **h.** unto
2Ch 18:29 So the king of Israel disguised **h.**; and
2Ch 18:34 of Israel stayed **h.** up in his chariot
2Ch 20:3 and set **h.** to seek the Lord, and 6440
2Ch 20:35 Jehoshaphat king of Judah join **h.** with
2Ch 20:36 he joined **h.** with him to make ships
2Ch 21:4 he strengthened **h.**, and slew all his
2Ch 23:1 Jehoiada strengthened **h.**, and took
2Ch 25:11 And Amaziah strengthened **h.**, and
2Ch 25:14 and bowed down **h.** before them, and
2Ch 26:8 for he strengthened **h.** exceedingly.
2Ch 26:20 yea, **h.** hasted also to go out, 1931
2Ch 32:1 cities, and thought to win them for **h.**.
2Ch 32:5 Also he strengthened **h.**, and built up
2Ch 32:9 he **h.** laid siege against Lachish, 1931
2Ch 32:26 Hezekiah humbled **h.** for the pride of
2Ch 32:27 he made **h.** treasuries for silver, and
2Ch 33:12 and humbled **h.** greatly before the God
2Ch 33:23 And humbled not **h.** before the Lord,
2Ch 33:23 Manasseh his father had humbled **h.**;
2Ch 35:22 but disguised **h.**, that he might fight
2Ch 36:12 and humbled not **h.** before Jeremiah
Ezr 10:1 weeping and casting **h.** down before
Ezr 10:8 forfeited, and **h.** separated from 1931
Es 5:10 Nevertheless Haman refrained **h.**: and
Job 1:12 only upon **h.** put not forth thine hand.
Job 2:1 among them to present **h.** before the
Job 2:8 a potsherd to scrape **h.** withal; and he
Job 4:2 who can withhold **h.** from speaking?
Job 9:4 who hath hardened **h.** against him,
Job 15:25 strengthened **h.** against the Almighty.
Job 17:8 shall stir up **h.** against the hypocrite.
Job 18:4 He teareth **h.** in his anger: shall *5315*
Job 22:2 that is wise may be profitable unto **h.**? *5315*
Job 23:9 he hideth **h.** on the right hand, that I *5315*
Job 27:10 Will he delight **h.** in the Almighty?
Job 32:2 he justified **h.** rather than God 5315
Job 34:9 that he should delight **h.** with God.

Job 34:14 gather unto **h.** his spirit and his breath;
Job 41:25 When he raiseth up **h.**, the mighty are
Ps 4:3 hath set apart him that is godly for **h.**:
Ps 10:10 He croucheth, and humbleth h., that
Ps 10:14 the poor committeth **h.** unto thee; thou
Ps 35:8 let his net that he hath hid catch **h.**:
Ps 36:2 For he flattereth **h.** in his own eyes,
Ps 36:4 he setteth **h.** in a way that is not good;
Ps 37:35 and spreading **h.** like a green bay tree.
Ps 50:6 righteousness: for God is judge **h.**. 1931
Ps 52:7 and strengthened **h.** in his wickedness,
Ps 54:*title* Doth not David hide **h.** with us?
Ps 55:12 me that did magnify **h.** against me;
Ps 68:30 one submit **h.** with pieces of silver:
Ps 87:5 the Highest **h.** shall establish her. 1931
Ps 93:1 strength, wherewith he hath girded **h.**:
Ps 109:18 As he clothed **h.** with cursing like as
Ps 113:6 Who humbleth **h.** to behold the things
Ps 132:18 But upon **h.** shall his crown flourish.
Ps 135:4 the Lord hath chosen Jacob unto **h.**,
Ps 135:14 will repent **h.** concerning his servants
Pr 5:22 own iniquities shall take the wicked **h.**,
Pr 9:7 a scorner getteth to **h.** shame: and he
Pr 9:7 a wicked man getteth **h.** a blot.
Pr 11:25 watereth shall be watered also **h.**. 1931
Pr 12:9 better than he that honoureth **h.**, and
Pr 13:7 that maketh **h.** rich, yet hath nothing:
Pr 13:7 maketh **h.** poor, yet hath great riches.
Pr 14:14 a good man shall be satisfied from **h.**.
Pr 16:4 Lord hath made all things for **h.**: 4617
Pr 16:26 He that laboureth laboureth for **h.**;
Pr 18:1 a man, having separated **h.**, seeketh
Pr 18:24 hath friends must shew **h.** friendly:
Pr 21:13 shall cry **h.**, but shall not be heard. 1931
Pr 22:3 man foreseeth the evil, and hideth **h.**:
Pr 25:9 Debate thy cause with thy neighbour **h.**;
Pr 25:14 Whoso boasteth **h.** of a false gift is
Pr 27:12 man foreseeth the evil, and hideth **h.**;
Pr 28:10 he shall fall **h.** into his own pit: 1931
Pr 29:15 child left to **h.** bringeth his mother to
Ec 5:9 the king **h.** is served by the field
Ec 10:12 but the lips of a fool will swallow up **h.**
Ca 2:9 shewing **h.** through the lattice
Ca 3:9 King Solomon made **h.** a chariot of the
Ca 5:6 but my beloved had withdrawn **h.**, and
Isa 2:9 and the great man humbleth **h.**:
Isa 2:20 they made each one for **h.** to worship,
Isa 3:5 the child shall behave **h.** proudly
Isa 7:14 the Lord **h.** shall give you a sign; 1931
Isa 8:13 Sanctify the Lord of hosts **h.**; and let
Isa 19:17 mention thereof shall be afraid in **h.**,
Isa 22:16 graveth a habitation for **h.** in a rock?
Isa 28:20 than that a man can stretch **h.** on it:
Isa 28:20 narrower than that he can wrap **h.** in
Isa 31:4 nor abase **h.** for the noise for them:
Isa 37:1 clothes, and covered **h.** with sackcloth,
Isa 38:15 both spoken...and **h.** hath done it: 1931
Isa 44:5 and another shall call **h.** by the name
Isa 44:5 and surname **h.** by the name of Israel.
Isa 44:14 oak, which he strengtheneth for **h.**
Isa 44:15 for he will take thereof, and warm **h.**;
Isa 44:16 yea, he warmeth **h.**, and saith, Aha,
Isa 44:23 Jacob, and glorified **h.** in Israel
Isa 45:18 God **h.** that formed the earth and 1931
Isa 56:3 that hath joined **h.** to the Lord, speak,
Isa 59:15 departeth from evil maketh **h.** a prey:
Isa 61:10 as a bridegroom decketh **h.** with
Isa 63:12 them, to make **h.** an everlasting name?
Isa 64:7 that stirreth up **h.** to take hold of thee:
Isa 65:16 That he who blesseth **h.** in the earth
Isa 65:16 shall bless **h.** in the God of truth; and
Jer 10:23 know that the way of man is not in **h.**:
Jer 16:20 Shall a man make gods unto **h.**, and
Jer 23:24 Can any hide **h.** in secret places that I
Jer 29:26 that is mad, and maketh **h.** a prophet,
Jer 29:27 which maketh **h.** a prophet to you?
Jer 31:18 heard Ephraim bemoaning **h.** thus;
Jer 34:9 none should serve **h.** of them, to wit, of
Jer 37:12 to separate **h.** thence in the midst of
Jer 43:12 shall array **h.** with the land of Egypt,
Jer 48:26 for he magnified **h.** against the Lord:
Jer 48:42 because he hath magnified **h.** against
Jer 49:10 he shall not be able to hide **h.**: his seed
Jer 51:3 and against him that lifteth **h.** up in his
Jer 51:14 The Lord of hosts hath sworn by **h.**, 5315
La 1:9 for the enemy hath magnified **h.**
Eze 7:13 neither shall any strengthen **h.** in the

Eze 14:7 Israel, which separateth **h.** from me,
Eze 24:2 the king of Babylon set **h.** against
Eze 25:12 offended, and revenged **h.** upon them;
Eze 45:22 prepare for **h.** and for all the people
Da 1:8 not defile **h.** with the portion of the
Da 1:8 eunuchs that he might not defile **h.**.
Da 6:14 was sore displeased with **h.**, and set
Da 8:11 he magnified **h.** even to the prince
Da 8:25 and he shall magnify **h.** in his heart,
Da 9:26 Messiah be cut off, but not for **h.**:
Da 11:36 to his will; and he shall exalt **h.**, and
Da 11:36 and magnify **h.** above every god, and
Da 11:37 for he shall magnify **h.** above all,
Ho 5:6 he hath withdrawn **h.** from them.
Ho 7:8 hath mixed **h.** among the people; 1931
Ho 8:9 up to Assyria, a wild ass alone by **h.**:
Ho 10:1 vine, he bringeth forth fruit unto **h.**:
Ho 13:1 he exalted **h.** in Israel; but when 1931
Am 2:14 neither shall the mighty deliver **h.**: 5315
Am 2:15 is swift of foot shall not deliver **h.**: 5313
Am 2:15 he that rideth the horse deliver **h.**. 5313
Am 6:8 The Lord God hath sworn by **h.**, 5313
Jon 4:8 he fainted, and wished in **h.** to die, and
Hab 2:6 him that ladeth **h.** with thick clay!
Mt 6:4 **secret h. shall reward thee openly** *846*
Mt 8:17 **H.** took our infirmities, and bare our *846*
Mt 12:15 knew it, he withdrew **h.** from thence:
Mt 12:26 **out Satan, he is divided against h.;** *1438*
Mt 12:45 **taketh with h. seven other spirits** *1438*
Mt 12:45 **other spirits more wicked than h.,** *1438*
Mt 13:21 **Yet hath he not root in h., but** *1438*
Mt 16:24 **come after me, let him deny h.,** *1438*
Mt 18:4 **shall humble h. as this little child,** *1438*
Mt 23:12 **shall exalt h. shall be abased; and** *1438*
Mt 23:12 **shall humble h. shall be exalted.** *1438*
Mt 27:3 repented **h.**, and brought again the
Mt 27:5 departed, and went and hanged **h.**
Mt 27:42 He saved others; **h.** he cannot save. *1438*
Mt 27:57 who also **h.** was Jesus' disciple: *846*
Mk 3:7 Jesus withdrew **h.** with his disciples
Mk 3:21 on him: for they said, He is beside **h.**.
Mk 3:26 **If Satan rise up against h., and be** *1438*
Mk 5:5 crying, and cutting **h.** with stones. *1438*
Mk 5:30 knowing in **h.** that virtue had gone *1438*
Mk 6:17 For Herod **h.** had sent forth and laid *846*
Mk 8:34 **let him deny h., and take up his** *1438*
Mk 12:33 and to love his neighbour as **h.**, is *1438*
Mk 12:36 **David h. said by the Holy Ghost,** *846*
Mk 12:37 **David therefore h. calleth him Lord;** *846*
Mk 14:54 the servants, and warmed **h.** at the fire. *846*
Mk 14:67 saw Peter warming **h.**, she looked upon. *846*
Mk 15:31 He saved others; **h.** he cannot save. *1438*
Lu 3:23 Jesus **h.** began to be about thirty *846*
Lu 5:16 And he withdrew **h.** into the wilderness,
Lu 6:3 **David did, when h. was an hungred,** *846*
Lu 7:39 he spake within **h.**, saying, This *1438*
Lu 9:23 **let him deny h., and take up his** *1438*
Lu 9:25 **and lose h., or be cast away?** *1438*
Lu 10:1 place, whither he **h.** would come. *846*
Lu 10:29 he, willing to justify **h.**, said unto *1438*
Lu 11:18 **If Satan also be divided against h.,** *1438*
Lu 11:26 **other spirits more wicked than h.;** *1438*
Lu 12:17 **And he thought within h., saying,** *1438*
Lu 12:21 **layeth up treasure for h., and is** *1438*
Lu 12:37 **he shall gird h., and make them to sit**
Lu 12:47 **will, and prepared not h., neither did**
Lu 14:11 **whosoever exalteth h. shall be** *1438*
Lu 14:11 **and he that humbleth h. shall be** *1438*
Lu 15:15 **he went and joined h. to a citizen** *1438*
Lu 15:17 **And when he came to h., he said,** *1438*
Lu 16:3 **the steward said within h., What** *1438*
Lu 18:4 **said within h., Though I fear not** *1438*
Lu 18:11 **and prayed thus with h., God** *1438*
Lu 18:14 **that exalteth h. shall be abased;** *1438*
Lu 18:14 **that humbleth h. shall be exalted.** *1438*
Lu 19:12 **to receive for h. a kingdom, and to** *1438*
Lu 20:42 **And David h. saith in the book of** *846*
Lu 23:2 saying that he **h.** is Christ a King. *1438*
Lu 23:7 who **h.** also was at Jerusalem at *846*
Lu 23:35 let him save **h.**, if he be Christ, the *1438*
Lu 23:51 who also **h.** waited for the kingdom *846*
Lu 24:12 wondering in **h.** at that which was *1438*
Lu 24:15 Jesus **h.** drew near, and went with *846*
Lu 24:27 the things concerning **h.**, *1438*
Lu 24:36 Jesus **h.** stood in the midst of them, *846*
Joh 2:24 Jesus did not commit **h.** unto them, *1438*

Joh 4:2 Though Jesus **h.** baptized not, but........ *846*
Joh 4:12 drank thereof **h.**, and his children, ... *846*
Joh 4:44 For Jesus **h.** testified, that a prophet.... *846*
Joh 4:53 and **h.** believed, and his whole house.... *846*
Joh 5:13 for Jesus had conveyed **h.** away, a...........
Joh 5:18 Father, making **h.** equal wih God. *1438*
Joh 5:19 **Son can do nothing of h., but what** *1438*
Joh 5:20 **him all things that h. doeth:** *846*
Joh 5:26 **For as the Father hath life in h.;** .. *1438*
Joh 5:26 **given to the Son to have life in h.;** . *1438*
Joh 5:37 **And the Father h., which hath sent** . *846*
Joh 6:6 for he **h.** knew what he would do. *846*
Joh 6:15 again into a mountain **h.** alone............ *846*
Joh 6:61 Jesus knew in **h.** that his disciples *1438*
Joh 7:4 he **h.** seeketh to be known openly. *846*
Joh 7:18 **He that speaketh of h. seeketh his** . *1438*
Joh 8:7 he lifted up **h.**, and said unto them, ...
Joh 8:10 When Jesus had lifted up **h.**, and saw........
Joh 8:22 Will he kill **h.**? because he saith, ... *1438*
Joh 8:59 Jesus hid **h.**, and went out of the temple, ..
Joh 9:21 age; ask him; he shall speak for **h.**....... *848*
Joh 11:38 groaning in **h.** cometh to the grave..... *1438*
Joh 11:51 this spake he not of **h.**: but being....... *1438*
Joh 12:36 departed, and did hide **h.** from them. ....
Joh 13:4 and took a towel, and girded **h.**. *1438*
Joh 13:32 **God shall also glorify him in h.,** ... *1438*
Joh 16:13 **for he shall not speak of h.; but** *1438*
Joh 16:27 **the Father h. loveth you, because** ... *846*
Joh 18:18 Peter stood with them, and warmed **h.**......
Joh 18:25 And Simon Peter stood and warmed **h.**,......
Joh 19:7 because he made **h.** the Son of God. .. *1438*
Joh 19:12 whosoever maketh **h.** a king............... *848*
Joh 21:1 things Jesus shewed **h.** again to the..... *1438*
Joh 21:1 and on this wise shewed he **h.**.................
Joh 21:7 naked, and did cast **h.** into the sea. *1438*
Joh 21:14 that Jesus shewed **h.** to his disciples, ...
Ac 1:3 To whom also he shewed **h.** alive *1438*
Ac 2:34 he saith **h.**, The Lord said unto my...... *846*
Ac 5:13 rest durst no man join **h.** to them:...........
Ac 5:36 boasting **h.** to be somebody; to.......... *1438*
Ac 7:26 next day he shewed **h.** unto them as ....
Ac 8:9 out that he **h.** was some great one:..... *1448*
Ac 8:13 Then Simon **h.** believed also: and *846*
Ac 8:34 this? of **h.**, or of some other man? *1438*
Ac 9:26 he assayed to join **h.** to the disciples:........
Ac 10:17 while Peter doubted in **h.** what this *1438*
Ac 12:11 when Peter was come to **h.**, he said,.. *1438*
Ac 14:17 he left not **h.** without witness, in that .. *1438*
Ac 16:27 and would have killed **h.**, supposing *1438*
Ac 18:19 be **h.** entered into the synagogue,......... *846*
Ac 19:22 but he stayed in Asia for a season......... *846*
Ac 19:31 not adventure **h.** into the theatre. *1438*
Ac 20:13 he appointed, minding **h.** to go afoot...... *846*
Ac 21:26 the next day purifying **h.** with them ....
Ac 25:4 he **h.** would depart shortly thither. *1438*
Ac 25:8 he answered for **h.**, Neither against..........
Ac 25:16 to answer for **h.** concerning the crime.......
Ac 25:25 he **h.** hath appealed to Augustus,.......... *848*
Ac 26:1 forth the hand, and answered for **h.**..........
Ac 26:24 And as he thus spake for **h.**, Festus, ...
Ac 27:3 to go unto his friends to refresh **h.**...........
Ac 28:16 suffered to dwell by **h.** with a soldier .. *1438*
Ro 12:3 not to think of **h.** more highly than he ....
Ro 14:7 liveth to **h.**, and no man dieth to **h.**...... *1438*
Ro 14:12 shall give an account of **h.** to God. *1438*
Ro 14:22 Happy is he that condemneth not **h.** ... *1438*
Ro 15:3 For even Christ pleased not **h.**; but, ... *1438*
1Co 2:15 things, yet he **h.** is judged of no man. .. *846*
1Co 3:15 he **h.** shall be saved; yet so as by fire. .. *846*
1Co 3:18 Let no man deceive **h.**. If any man..... *1438*
1Co 7:36 that he behaveth **h.** uncomely toward........
1Co 11:28 But let a man examine **h.**, and so....... *1438*
1Co 11:29 eateth and drinketh damnation to **h.**,... *1438*
1Co 14:4 in an unknown tongue edifieth **h.**;......... *1438*
1Co 14:8 who shall prepare **h.** to the battle? ....
1Co 14:28 and let him speak to **h.**, and to God. .. *1438*
1Co 14:37 If any man think **h.** to be a prophet, ...
1Co 15:28 then shall the Son also **h.** be subject *846*
2Co 5:18 who hath reconciled us to **h.** by......... *1438*
2Co 5:19 reconciling the world unto **h.**, not........ *1438*
2Co 10:7 man trust to **h.** that he is Christ's, ... *1438*
2Co 10:7 let him of **h.** think this again, that, ... *1438*
2Co 10:18 For not he that commendeth **h.** is *1438*
2Co 11:14 Satan **h.** is transformed into an angel.... *846*
2Co 11:20 if a man exalt **h.**, if a man smite you.........
Ga 1:4 Who gave **h.** for our sins, that he *1438*
Ga 2:12 withdrew and separated **h.**, fearing..... *1438*
Ga 2:20 who loved me, and gave **h.** for me. *1438*
Ga 6:3 if a man think **h.** to be something, ...
Ga 6:3 when he is nothing, he deceiveth **h.**...... *1438*
Ga 6:4 shall he have rejoicing in **h.** alone, ... *1438*
Eph 1:5 of children by Jesus Christ to **h.**,......... *848*
Eph 1:9 which he hath purposed in **h.**:............. *848*
Eph 2:15 make in **h.** of twain one new man,...... *1438*
Eph 2:20 Jesus Christ **h.** being the chief corner... *846*
Eph 5:2 loved us, and hath given **h.** for us...... *1438*
Eph 5:25 loved the church, and gave **h.** for it; ... *1438*
Eph 5:27 present it to **h.** a glorious church, ... *1438*
Eph 5:28 He that loveth his wife loveth **h.**. *1438*
Eph 5:33 so love his wife even as **h.**; and the ... *1438*
Php 2:7 But made **h.** of no reputation, and...... *1438*
Php 2:8 in fashion as a man, he humbled **h.**,..... *1438*
Php 3:21 even to subdue all things unto **h.**. *1438*
Col 1:20 him to reconcile all things unto **h.**;........ *848*
1Th 3:11 Now God **h.** and our Father, and......... *846*
1Th 4:16 Lord **h.** shall descend from heaven....... *846*
2Th 2:4 opposeth and exalteth **h.** above all...... *1438*
2Th 2:4 of God, shewing **h.** that he is God...... *1438*
2Th 2:16 Now our Lord Jesus Christ **h.**, and *846*
2Th 3:16 Now the Lord of peace **h.** give you...... *846*
1Ti 2:6 Who gave **h.** a ransom for all, to be ... *1438*
2Ti 2:4 No man that warreth entangleth **h.**...........
2Ti 2:13 abideth faithful: he cannot deny **h.**...... *1438*
2Ti 2:21 If a man therefore purge **h.** from *1438*
Tit 2:14 Who gave **h.** for us, that he might...... *1438*
Tit 2:14 and purify unto **h.** a peculiar people, ... *1438*
Tit 3:11 sinneth, being condemned of **h.**. *848*
Heb 1:3 when he had by **h.** purged our sins,..... *1438*
Heb 2:14 **h.** likewise took part of the same;........ *846*
Heb 2:18 For in that he **h.** hath suffered being.... *846*
Heb 5:2 for that he **h.** is also compassed with..... *846*
Heb 5:3 so also for **h.**, to offer for sins. *1438*
Heb 5:4 no man taketh this honour unto **h.**,...... *1438*
Heb 5:5 So also Christ glorified not **h.** to be.... *1438*
Heb 6:13 swear by no greater, he sware by **h.**,. *1438*
Heb 7:27 he did once, when he offered up **h.**. ... *1438*
Heb 9:7 blood, which he offered for **h.**, and..... *1438*
Heb 9:14 eternal Spirit offered **h.** without spot... *1438*
Heb 9:25 Nor yet that he should offer **h.** often, .. *1438*
Heb 9:26 put away sin by the sacrifice of **h.**. *848*
Heb 12:3 contradiction of sinners against **h.**,........ *848*
Jas 1:24 For he beholdeth **h.**, and goeth his...... *1438*
Jas 1:27 and to keep **h.** unspotted from the *1438*
1Pe 2:23 but committed **h.** to him that judgeth ....
1Jo 2:6 ought **h.** also so to walk, even as he *846*
1Jo 3:3 hath this hope in him purifieth **h.**,....... *1438*
1Jo 5:10 Son of God hath the witness in **h.**....... *1438*
1Jo 5:18 that is begotten of God keepeth **h.**, ... *1438*
3Jo 10 doth he **h.** receive the brethren,.......... *846*
Re 19:12 written, that no man knew, but he **h.**.........
Re 21:3 God **h.** shall be with them, and be *846*

HIN
Ex 29:40 fourth part of an **h.** of beaten oil; 1969
Ex 29:40 the fourth part of an **h.** of wine for...... 1969
Ex 30:24 the sanctuary, and of oil olive an **h.** 1969
Le 19:36 ephah, and a just **h.**, shall ye have: 1969
Le 23:13 be of wine, the fourth part of an **h.**. ... 1969
Nu 15:4 with the fourth part of an **h.** of oil. 1969
Nu 15:5 the fourth part of an **h.** of wine for..... 1969
Nu 15:6 with the third part of an **h.** of oil........ 1969
Nu 15:7 offer the third part of an **h.** of wine, ... 1969
Nu 15:9 flour mingled with half an **h.** of oil, ... 1969
Nu 15:10 half an **h.** of wine, for an offering 1969
Nu 28:5 fourth part of an **h.** of beaten oil. 1969
Nu 28:7 part of an **h.** for the one lamb: 1969
Nu 28:14 be half an **h.** of wine unto a bullock, ... 1969
Nu 28:14 the third part of an **h.** unto a ram, ... 1969
Nu 28:14 a fourth part of an **h.** unto a lamb: 1969
Eze 4:11 by measure; the sixth part of an **h.**: ... 1969
Eze 45:24 for a ram, an **h.** of oil for an ephah..... 1969
Eze 46:5 to give, and an **h.** of oil to an ephah. .. 1969
Eze 46:7 unto, and an **h.** of oil to an ephah....... 1969
Eze 46:11 to give, and an **h.** of oil to an ephah. .. 1969
Eze 46:14 and the third part of an **h.** of oil, to..... 1969

HIND See also HINDS; HINDER; HINDMOST; HINDS.
Ge 49:21 Naphtali is a **h.** let loose: he giveth...... 355
Pr 5:19 Let her be as the loving **h.** and........... 365
Jer 14:5 the **h.** also calved in the field, and 365

HINDER See also HINDERED; HINDERETH; HINDERMOST.
Ge 24:56 And he said unto them, **H.** me not,...... 309
Nu 22:16 thee, **h.** thee from coming unto me: ... 4513
2Sa 2:23 the **h.** end of the spear smote him....... 310
1Ki 7:25 and all their **h.** parts were inward........ 268
2Ch 4:4 and all their **h.** parts were inward.......... 268
Ne 4:8 against Jersualem, and to **h.**........ 6213,8442
Job 9:12 he taketh away, who can **h.** him?........ 7725
Job 11:10 together, then who can **h.** him? 7725
Ps 78:66 smote his enemies in the **h.** parts:........ 268
Joe 2:20 his **h.** part toward the utmost sea, ... 5490
Zec 14:8 and half of them toward the **h.** sea:...... 314
Mk 4:38 he was in the **h.** part of the ship,......... *4403*
Ac 8:36 what doth **h.** me to be baptized? *2967*
Ac 27:41 but the **h.** part was broken with.......... *4403*
1Co 9:12 we should **h.** the gospel..... *5100,1464,1325*
Ga 5:7 did **h.** you that ye should not obey....... *848*

HINDERED
Ezr 6:8 unto these men, that they be not **h.**..... 989
Lu 11:52 **them that were entering in ye h.**... *2967*
Ro 15:22 been much **h.** from coming to you. *1465*
1Th 2:18 once and again; but Satan **h.** us. *1465*
1Pe 3:7 of life; that your prayers be not **h.**. *1581*

HINDERETH
Isa 14:6 anger is persecuted, and none **h.**. 2820

HINDERMOST See also HINDMOST.
Ge 33:2 after, and Rachel and Joseph **h.**........... 314
Jer 50:12 the **h.** of the nations shall be a............ 319

HINDMOST See also HINDERMOST.
Nu 2:31 They shall go **h.** with their standards.... 314
De 25:18 and smote the **h.** of thee, even all...... 2179
Jos 10:19 enemies, and smite the **h.** of them; 2179

HINDS See also HINDS'.
Job 39:1 thou mark when the **h.** do calve?......... 355
Ps 29:9 of the Lord maketh the **h.** to calve, ... 355
Ca 2:7 the **h.** of the field, that ye stir not up, .. 355
Ca 3:5 the **h.** of the field that ye stir not up, ... 355

HINDS'
2Sa 22:34 He maketh my feet like **h.** feet: 355
Ps 18:33 He maketh my feet like **h.** feet, and...... 355
Hab 3:19 and he will make my feet like **h.** feet,... 355

HINGES
1Ki 7:50 and the **h.** of gold, both for the 6596
Pr 26:14 As the door turneth upon its **h.**, so 6735

HINNOM (hin'-nom)
Jos 15:8 up by the valley of the son of **H.**....... 2011
Jos 15:8 before the valley of **H.** westward, ... 2011
Jos 18:16 before the valley of the son of **H.**, ... 2011
Jos 18:16 and descended to the valley of **H.**, ... 2011
2Ki 23:10 in the valley of the children of **H.**,........ 2011
2Ch 28:3 incense in the valley of the son of **H.**,..2011
2Ch 33:6 the fire in the valley of the son of **H.**... 2011
Ne 11:30 Beer-sheba unto the valley of **H.**......... 2011
Jer 7:31 is in the valley of the son of **H.**, ... 2011
Jer 7:32 nor the valley of the son of **H.**, but 2011
Jer 19:2 forth unto the valley of the son of **H.**,..2011
Jer 19:6 nor The valley of the son of **H.**, but.... 2011
Jer 32:35 are in the valley of the son of **H.**, ... 2011

HIP
Jg 15:8 he smote them **h.** and thigh with a 7785

HIRAH (hi'-rah)
Ge 38:1 Adullamite, whose name was **H.**.......... 2437
Ge 38:12 he and his friend **H.** the Adullamite..... 2437

HIRAM (hi'-ram) See also HIRAM'S; HURAM.
2Sa 5:11 **H.** king of Tyre sent messengers......... 2438
1Ki 5:1 **H.** king of Tyre sent his servants....... 2438
1Ki 5:1 for **H.** was ever a lover of David. 2438
1Ki 5:2 And Solomon sent to **H.**, saying,......... 2438
1Ki 5:7 **H.** heard the words of Solomon, ... 2438
1Ki 5:8 And **H.** sent to Solomon, saying,......... 2438
1Ki 5:10 **H.** gave Solomon cedar trees and........ 2438
1Ki 5:11 Solomon gave **H.** twenty thousand....... 2438
1Ki 5:11 gave Solomon to **H.** year by year........ 2438
1Ki 5:12 was peace between **H.** and Solomon; .. 2438
1Ki 7:13 sent and fetched **H.** out of Tyre. 2438
1Ki 7:40 **H.** made the lavers, and the shovels, .. 2438
1Ki 7:40 **H.** made an end of...all the work 2438
1Ki 7:45 which **H.** made to king Solomon.......... 2438
1Ki 9:11 **H.** the king of Tyre had furnished 2438
1Ki 9:11 king Solomon gave **H.** twenty cities..... 2438
1Ki 9:12 **H.** came out from Tyre to see the 2438
1Ki 9:14 And **H.** sent to the king sixscore 2438
1Ki 9:27 **H.** sent in the navy his servants, ... 2438
1Ki 10:11 navy also of **H.**, that brought gold 2438

1Ki 10:22 of Tharshish with the navy of **H.**:....... 2438
1Ch 14:1 **H.** king of Tyre sent messengers to ... 2438

HIRAM'S (hi'-rams)
1Ki 5:18 Solomon's builders and **H.** builders 2438

HIRE See also HIRED; HIRES; HIREST.
Ge 30:18 God hath given me my **h.**, because..... 7939
Ge 30:32 Goats: and of such shall be my **h.**. 7939
Ge 30:33 shall come for my **h.** before thy face: .. 7939
Ge 31:8 The ringstraked shall be thy **h.**; 7939
Ex 22:15 an hired thing, it came for his **h.**........ 7939
De 23:18 shalt not bring the **h.** of a whore, ... 868
De 24:15 At his day thou shalt give him his **h.**.... 7939
1Ki 5:6 thee will I give **h.** for thy servants 7939
1Ch 19:6 to **h.** them chariots and horsemen 7936
Isa 23:17 Tyre, and she shall turn to her **h.**,........ 868
Isa 23:18 her **h.** shall be holiness to the Lord:..... 868
Isa 46:6 the balance, and **h.** a goldsmith;.......... 7936
Eze 16:31 an harlot, in that thou scornest **h.**;....... 868
Eze 16:41 thou also shalt give no **h.** any more...... 868
Mic 1:7 she gathered it of the **h.** of an harlot, ... 868
Mic 1:7 shall return to the **h.** of an harlot......... 868
Mic 3:11 the priests thereof teach for **h.**, and ... 4242
Zec 8:10 no **h.** for man, nor any **h.** for beast; ... 7939
Mt 20:1 **to h. labourers into his vineyard.** .. *3409*
Mt 20:8 **give them their h., beginning from.** *3408*
Lu 10:7 **the labourer is worthy of his h.**..... *3408*
Jas 5:4 **h.** of the labourers who have reaped... *3408*

HIRED
Ge 30:16 surely I have **h.** thee with my son's.... 7936
Ex 12:45 an **h.** servant shall not eat thereof. 7916
Ex 22:15 be an **h.** thing, it came for his hire. 7916
Le 19:13 the wages of him that is **h.** shall not ... 7916
Le 22:10 **h.** servant, shall not eat of the holy ... 7916
Le 25:6 thy **h.** servant and for thy stranger..... 7916
Le 25:40 as an **h.** servant, and as a sojourner, .. 7916
Le 25:50 to the time of an **h.** servant shall it 7916
Le 25:53 as a yearly **h.** servant shall he be....... 7916
De 15:18 worth a double **h.** servant to thee, ... 7916
De 23:4 **h.** against thee Balaam the son of....... 7936
De 24:14 oppress an **h.** servant that is poor...... 7916
Jg 9:4 wherewith Abimelech **h.** vain and 7936
Jg 18:4 Micah with me, and hath **h.** me, and... 7936
1Sa 2:5 full have **h.** out themselves for bread; ..7936
2Sa 10:6 Ammon sent and **h.** the Syrians of...... 7936
2Ki 7:6 Israel hath **h.** against us the kings 7936
1Ch 19:7 So they **h.** thirty and two thousand..... 7936
2Ch 24:12 **h.** masons and carpenters to repair..... 7936
2Ch 25:6 he **h.** also an hundred thousand.......... 7936
Ezr 4:5 And **h.** counsellers against them, to 7936
Ne 6:12 for Tobiah and Sanballat had **h.** him. ... 7936
Ne 6:13 Therefore was he **h.**, that I should..... 7936
Ne 13:2 but **h.** Balaam against them, that he.... 7936
Isa 7:20 Lord shave with a rasor that is **h.**, ... 7917
Jer 46:21 her **h.** men are in the midst of her..... 7916
Ho 8:9 himself: Ephraim hath **h.** lovers. 8566
Ho 8:10 they have **h.** among the nations, ... 8566
Mt 20:7 **him, Because no man hath h., us.** . *3409*
Mt 20:9 **were h. about the eleventh hour,**... *3409*
Mk 1:20 the ship with the **h.** servants, and....... *3411*
Lu 15:17 **many h. servants of my father's**.... *3407*
Lu 15:19 **make me as one of thy h. servants.** *3407*
Ac 28:30 whole years in his own **h.** house, ... *3410*

HIRELING
Job 7:1 days also like the days of an **h.**? 7916
Job 7:2 and as an **h.** looketh for the reward.... 7916
Job 14:6 shall accomplish, as an **h.**, his day. 7916
Isa 16:14 three years, as the years of an **h.**, ... 7916
Isa 21:16 year, according to the years of an **h.**, ..7916
Mal 3:5 that oppress the **h.** in his wages, ... 7916
Joh 10:12 **is an h., and not the shepherd,**....... *3411*
Joh 10:13 **The h. fleeth, because he is an**...... *3411*
Joh 10:13 **because he is an h., and careth not** *3411*

HIRES
Mic 1:7 all the **h.** thereof shall be burned 868

HIREST
Eze 16:33 gifts to all thy lovers, and **h.** them, ... 7806

HIS See in the APPENDIX.

HISS See also HISSING.
1Ki 9:8 shall be astonished, and shall **h.**; 8319
Job 27:23 and shall **h.** him out of his place......... 8319
Isa 5:26 will **h.** unto them from the end of....... 8319
Isa 7:18 the Lord shall **h.** for the fly that is 8319
Jer 19:8 shall be astonished and **h.** because...... 8319
Jer 49:17 shall **h.** at all the plagues thereof........ 8319
Jer 50:13 astonished and **h.** at all her plagues. ... 8319
La 2:15 they **h.** and wag their head at the 8319
La 2:16 they **h.** and gnash the teeth: they 8319
Eze 27:36 merchants among the people shall **h.**... 8319
Zep 2:15 one that passeth by her shall **h.**, ... 8319
Zec 10:8 I will **h.** for them and gather them;..... 8319

HISSING
2Ch 29:8 to astonishment, and to **h.**, as ye....... 8322
Jer 18:16 land desolate, and a perpetual **h.**; 8292
Jer 19:8 make this city desolate, and an **h.**; 8322
Jer 25:9 an astonishment, and an **h.**, and......... 8322
Jer 25:18 astonishment, an **h.**, and a curse;....... 8322
Jer 29:18 an astonishment, and an **h.**, and a 8322
Jer 51:37 an astonishment, and an **h.**, without.... 8322
Mic 6:16 and the inhabitants thereof an **h.**: 8322

HIT
1Sa 31:3 Saul, and the archers **h.** him: 4672
1Ch 10:3 Saul, and the archers **h.** him, ... 4672

HITHER See also HITHERTO.
Ge 15:16 they shall come **h.** again: for the 2008
Ge 42:15 except your youngest brother come **h.**. .....
Ge 45:5 with yourselves, that ye sold me **h.**: ....
Ge 45:8 was not you that sent me **h.**, but God:......
Ge 45:13 haste and bring down my father **h.**. ....
Ex 3:5 Draw not nigh **h.**: put off thy shoes 1988
Jos 2:2 Behold, there came men in **h.** to night ......
Jos 3:9 Come **h.**, and hear the words of 5066
Jos 18:6 and bring the description **h.** to me, ...
Jg 16:2 Gazites, saying, Samson is come **h.**. ....
Jg 18:3 Who brought thee **h.**? and what 1988
Jg 19:12 We will not turn aside **h.** into the city ....
Ru 2:14 At mealtime come thou **h.**, and eat..... 1988
1Sa 13:9 Bring **h.** a burnt offering to me,......... 5066
1Sa 14:18 Bring **h.** the ark of God. For the ark .. 5066
1Sa 14:34 Bring me **h.** every man his ox, and 5066
1Sa 14:36 Let us draw near **h.** unto God........... 1988
1Sa 14:38 Draw ye near **h.**, all the chief of the... 1988
1Sa 15:32 Bring ye **h.** to me Agag the king of 5066
1Sa 16:11 we will not sit down till he come **h.**..... 6311
1Sa 17:28 he said, Why camest thou down **h.**?.........
1Sa 23:9 the priest, Bring **h.** the ephod. 5066
1Sa 30:7 I pray thee, bring me **h.** the ephod..... 5066
2Sa 1:10 Have brought them **h.** unto my lord..........
2Sa 5:6 the lame, thou shalt not come in **h.**: ....
2Sa 5:6 thinking, David cannot come in **h.**.............
2Sa 14:32 Come **h.**, that I may send thee unto the....
2Sa 20:16 Come near **h.**, that I may speak with........
1Ki 22:9 Hasten **h.** Micaiah the son of Imlah..........
2Ki 2:8 and they were divided **h.** and thither,.........
2Ki 2:14 the waters, they parted **h.** and thither:......
2Ki 8:7 saying, The man of God is come **h.**.... 2008
1Ch 11:5 said to David, Thou shalt not come **h.**........
2Ch 28:13 Ye shall not bring in the captives **h.**: ....
Ezr 4:2 king of Assur, which brought us up **h.**........
Ps 73:10 Therefore his people return **h.**:.......... 1988
Ps 81:2 Take a psalm, and bring **h.** the timbrel......
Pr 9:4,16 Whoso is simple, let him turn in **h.**:..........
Pr 25:7 it be said unto thee, Come up **h.**........... 20
Isa 57:3 draw near **h.** ye sons of the sorceress, ...
Eze 40:4 them unto thee art thou brought **h.** ....
Da 3:26 high God, come forth, and come **h.**. ....
Mt 8:29 art thou come **h.** to torment us *5602*
Mt 14:18 he said, **Bring them h. to me.** *5602*
Mt 17:17 **I suffer you? bring him h. to me.**.. *5602*
Mt 22:12 **thou in h. not having a wedding**.... *5602*
Mk 11:3 **straightway he will send him h.** ... *5602*
Lu 9:41 **and suffer you? Bring thy son h.**... *5602*
Lu 14:21 **bring in h. the poor, and...maimed.** *5602*
Lu 15:23 **bring h. the fatted calf, and kill**.... *5602*
Lu 19:27 **bring h., and slay them before me.** .*5602*
Lu 19:30 **man sat: loose him, and bring him h.**..
Joh 4:15 thirst not, neither come **h.** to draw..... *1759*
Joh 4:16 **Go, call thy husband, and come h.** . *1759*
Joh 6:25 him, Rabbi, when camest thou **h.**?...... *5602*
Joh 20:27 **Reach h. thy finger, and behold**.... *5602*
Joh 20:27 **and reach h. thy hand, and thrust.** *5602*
Ac 9:21 and came **h.** for that intent, that he.... *5602*
Ac 10:32 and call **h.** Simon, whose surname...... *3333*
Ac 17:6 upside down are come **h.** also; *1759*
Ac 19:37 For ye have brought **h.** these men, ...
Ac 25:17 when they were come **h.**, without...... *1759*
Re 4:1 Come up **h.**, and I will shew thee *5602*
Re 11:12 saying unto them, Come up **h.**. And ... *5602*
Re 17:1 Come **h.**; I will shew unto thee the *1204*
Re 21:9 Come **h.**, I will shew thee the bride, .. *1204*

HITHERTO
Ex 7:16 **h.** thou wouldest not hear.......... 5704,3541
Jos 17:14 as the Lord hath blessed me **h.**?..5704,3541
Jg 16:13 **H.** thou hast mocked me, and 5704,2008
1Sa 1:16 and grief have I spoken **h.**......... 5704,2008
1Sa 7:12 **H.** hath the Lord helped us........ 5704,2008
2Sa 7:18 that thou hast brought me **h.**? 1988
2Sa 15:34 have been thy father's servant **h.**,........ 227
1Ch 9:18 Who **h.** waited in...king's gate 5704,2008
1Ch 12:29 **h.** the greatest part of them had. 5704,2008
1Ch 17:16 that thou hast brought me **h.**? 1988
Job 38:11 **H.** shalt thou come, but no........ 5704,6311
Ps 71:17 **h.** have I declared thy wondrous. 5704,2008
Isa 18:2,7 terrible from their beginning **h.**;.......... 1973
Da 7:28 **H.** is the end of the matter......... 5705,3542
Joh 5:17 **My father worketh h., and I**.... *2193,737*
Joh 16:24 **H. have ye asked nothing in**.... *2193,737*
Ro 1:13 to come unto you, but was let **h.**,..*891,1204*
1Co 3:2 for **h.** ye were not able to bear it,...... *3768*

HITTITE (hit'-tite) See also HITTITES.
Ge 23:10 and Ephron the **H.** answered............. 2850
Ge 25:9 of Ephron the son of Zohar the **H.**, ... 2850
Ge 26:34 Judith the daughter of Beeri the **H.**, ... 2850
Ge 26:34 the daughter of Elon the **H.**.............. 2850
Ge 36:2 Adah the daughter of Elon the **H.**. 2850
Ge 49:29 is in the field of Ephron the **H.**,.......... 2850
Ge 49:30 with the field of Ephron the **H.** for..... 2850
Ge 50:13 a buryingplace of Ephron the **H.**, ... 2850
Ex 23:28 and the **H.**, from before thee. 2850
Ex 33:2 Canaanite, the Amorite, and the **H.**, ... 2850
Ex 34:11 and the Canaanite, and the **H.**, and..... 2850
Jos 9:1 sea over against Lebanon, the **H.**,...... 2850
Jos 11:3 and to the Amorite, and the **H.**, and... 2850
1Sa 26:6 David and said to Ahimelech the **H.**,... 2850
2Sa 11:3 of Eliam, the wife of Uriah the **H.**?..... 2850
2Sa 11:6 Joab, saying, Send me Uriah the **H.**..... 2850
2Sa 11:17 and Uriah the **H.** died also................ 2850
2Sa 11:21, 24 servant Uriah the **H.** is dead also... 2850
2Sa 12:9 killed Uriah the **H.** with the sword, ... 2850
2Sa 12:10 wife of Uriah the **H.** to be thy wife. 2850
2Sa 23:39 Uriah the **H.**: thirty and seven in all. .. 2850
1Ki 15:5 only in the matter of Uriah the **H.**....... 2850
1Ch 11:41 Uriah the **H.**, Zabad the son of.......... 2850
Eze 16:3 an Amorite, and thy mother an **H.**....... 2850
Eze 16:45 your mother was an **H.**, and your 2850

HITTITES (hit'-tites)
Ge 15:20 And the **H.**, and the Perizzites, ... 2850
Ex 3:8 place of the Canaanites, and the **H.**, ... 2850
Ex 3:17 land of the Canaanites, and the **H.**,..... 2850
Ex 13:5 land of the Canaanites, and the **H.**,...... 2850
Ex 23:23 in unto the Amorites and the **H.**, ... 2850
Nu 13:29 and the **H.**, and the Jebusites, and 2850
De 7:1 many nations before thee, the **H.**, ... 2850
De 20:17 destroy them: namely, the **H.**, and..... 2850
Jos 1:4 all the land of the **H.**, and unto the..... 2850
Jos 3:10 you the Canaanites, and the **H.**,......... 2850
Jos 12:8 and the south country; the **H.**, ... 2850
Jos 24:11 and the Canaanites, and the **H.**,......... 2850
Jg 1:26 man went into the land of the **H.**,....... 2850
Jg 3:5 dwelt among the Canaanites, **H.**,......... 2850
1Ki 9:20 that were left of the Amorites, **H.**,..... 2850
1Ki 10:29 and so for all the kings of the **H.**, ... 2850
1Ki 11:1 Edomites, Zidonians, and **H.**; 2850
2Ki 7:6 hired against us the kings of the **H.**,... 2850
2Ch 1:17 horses for all the kings of the **H.**, ... 2850
2Ch 8:7 the people that were left of the **H.**,.... 2850
Ezr 9:1 even of the Canaanites, the **H.**, the.... 2850
Ne 9:8 the land of the Canaanites, the **H.**,..... 2850

HIVITE (hi'-vite) See also HIVITES.
Ge 10:17 And the **H.**, and the Arkite, and........ 2340
Ge 34:2 Shechem the son of Hamor the **H.**, ... 2340
Ge 36:2 Anah the daughter of Zibeon the **H.**;... 2340
Ex 23:28 which shall drive out the **H.**, the........ 2340
Ex 33:2 Hittite, and the Perizzite, the **H.**,........ 2340
Ex 34:11 and the Perizzite, and the **H.**, and....... 2340
Jos 9:1 Perizzite, the **H.**, and the Jebusite,..... 2340
Jos 11:3 and to the **H.** under Hermon in the 2340
1Ch 1:15 And the **H.**, and the Arkite, and 2340

HIVITES (hi'-vites)
Ex 3:8 and the **H.**, and the Jebusites. 2340
Ex 3:17 and the **H.**, and the Jebusites, ... 2340

Ex 13:5 and the **H.**, and the Jebusites, 2340
Ex 23:23 and the Canaanites, the **H.**, and the 2340
De 7:1 and the **H.**, and the Jebusites, 2340
De 20:17 the **H.**, and the Jebusites; as the 2340
Jos 3:10 **H.**, and the Perizzites, and the 2340
Jos 9:7 the men of Israel said unto the **H.**, 2340
Jos 11:19 Israel, save the **H.** the inhabitants 2340
Jos 12:8 the Perizzites, the **H.**, and the 2340
Jos 24:11 and the Girgashites, the **H.**, and 2340
Jg 3:3 **H.** that dwelt in mount Lebanon; 2340
Jg 3:5 Amorites, and Perizzites, and **H.**, 2340
2Sa 24:7 and to all the cities of the **H.**, and 2340
1Ki 9:20 **H.**, and Jebusites, which were not 2340
2Ch 8:7 the **H.**, and the Jebusites, which 2340

HIZKIAH (hiz-ki'-ah) See also HEZEKIAH; HIZKIJAH.
Zep 1:1 the son of **H.**, in the days of Josiah 2396

HIZKIJAH (hiz-ki'-jah) See also HIZKIAH.
Ne 10:17 Aer, **H.**, Azzur, Hodijah, Bani, 2396

HO
Ru 4:1 unto whom he said, **H.** such a one!
Isa 55:1 **H.** every one that thirsteth, come 1945
Zec 2:6 **H.**, **h.**, come forth, and flee from the 1945

HOAR See also HOARFROST; HOARY.
Ex 16:14 small as the **h.** frost on the ground 3713
1Ki 2:6 let not his **h.** head go down to the 7872
1Ki 2:9 his **h.** head bring thou down to the 7872
Isa 46:4 even to **h.** hairs will I carry you: 7872

HOARFROST See also HOAR; HOARY; and FROST.
Ps 147:16 he scattereth the **h.** like ashes 3713

HOARY
Le 19:32 shalt rise up before the **h.** head, 7872
Job 38:29 and the **h.** frost of heaven, who hath 3713
Job 41:32 one would think the deep to be **h.** 7872
Pr 16:31 The **h.** head is a crown of glory, if 7872

HOBAB (ho'-bab) See also JETHRO.
Nu 10:29 And Moses said unto **H.**, the son of 2246
Jg 4:11 the children of **H.** the father in law 2246

HOBAH (ho'-bah)
Ge 14:15 and pursued them unto **H.**, which 2327

HOD (hod)
1Ch 7:37 Bezer, and **H.**, and Shamma, and 1963

HODAIAH (ho-da-i'-ah) See also HODAVIAH.
1Ch 3:24 the sons of Elioenai were, **H.**, and 1939

HODAVIAH (ho-da-vi'ah) See also HODAIAH; HODEVAH.
1Ch 5:24 and Jeremiah, and **H.**, and Jahdiel, 1938
1Ch 9:7 the son of **H.**, the son of Hasenuah, 1938
Ezr 2:40 children of **H.**, seventy and four. 1938

HODESH (ho'-desh)
1Ch 8:9 begat of **H.** his wife, Jobab, and 2321

HODEVAH (ho-de'-vah) See also HODAVIAH.
Ne 7:43 children of **H.**, seventy and four. 1937

HODIAH (ho-di'-ah) See also HODIJAH.
1Ch 4:19 the sons of his wife **H.** the sister 1940

HODIJAH (ho-di'-jah) See also HODIAH.
Ne 8:7 Shabbethai, **H.**, Maaseiah, Kelita, 1940
Ne 9:5 Sherebiah, **H.**, Shebaniah, and 1940
Ne 10:10 Shebaniah, **H.**, Kelita, Pelaiah, 1940
Ne 10:13 **H.**, Bani, Beninu. 1940
Ne 10:18 **H.**, Hashum, Bezai, 1940

HODSHI See TAHTIM-HODSHI.

HOGLAH (hog'-lah) See also BETH-HOGLAH.
Nu 26:33 were Mahlah, and Noah, **H.**, 2295
Nu 27:1 daughters; Mahlah, Noah, and **H.**, 2295
Nu 36:11 and **H.**, and Milcah, and Noah, the 2295
Jos 17:3 daughters, Mahlah, and Noah, **H.**, 2295

HOHAM (ho'-ham)
Jos 10:3 sent unto **H.** king of Hebron, and 1944

HOISED
Ac 27:40 and **h.** up the mainsail to the wind, *1869*

HOIST See HOISED.

HOLD See also BEHOLD; HELD; HOLDEN; HOLDEST; HOLDETH; HOLDING; HOLDS; HOUSEHOLD; UPHOLD; WITHHOLD.
Ge 19:16 the men laid **h.** upon his hand, 2388
Ge 21:18 up the lad, and **h.** him in thine hand; 2388
Ge 25:26 his hand took **h.** on Esau's heel; 270
Ex 5:1 that they may **h.** a feast unto me
Ex 9:2 let them go, and wilt **h.** them still, 2388
Ex 10:9 we must **h.** a feast unto the Lord
Ex 14:14 for you, and ye shall **h.** your peace 2790
Ex 15:14 sorrow shall take **h.** on the 270
Ex 15:15 trembling shall take **h.** upon them; 270
Ex 20:7 the Lord will not **h.** him guiltless
Ex 26:5 loops may take **h.** one of another. 6901
Nu 30:4 and her father shall **h.** his peace 2790
Nu 30:14 **h.** his peace at her from day to day; 2790
De 5:11 the Lord will not **h.** him guiltless
De 21:19 father and his mother lay **h.** on him, 8610
De 22:28 and lay **h.** on her, and lie wih her, 8610
De 32:41 and mine hand take **h.** on judgment; 270
Jg 9:46 entered into an **h.** of the house 6877
Jg 9:49 Abimelech, and put them to the **h.**, 6877
Jg 9:49 and set the **h.** on fire upon them; 6877
Jg 16:29 Samson took **h.** of the two middle 3943
Jg 18:19 they said unto him, **H.** thy peace, 2790
Jg 19:29 knife, and laid **h.** on his concubine, 2388
Ru 3:15 that thou hast upon thee, and **h.** it 270
1Sa 15:27 laid **h.** upon the skirt of his mantle, 2388
1Sa 22:4 the while that David was in the **h.** 4686
1Sa 22:5 said unto David, Abide not in the **h.** 4686
1Sa 24:22 his men gat them up unto the **h.** 4686
2Sa 1:11 then David took **h.** on his clothes, 2388
2Sa 2:21 lay thee **h.** on one of the young men, 270
2Sa 2:22 I **h.** up my face to Joab my brother? 5375
2Sa 4:10 I took **h.** of him, and slew him in 270
2Sa 5:7 David took the strong **h.** of Zion: 4686
2Sa 5:17 heard of it; and went down to the **h.** 4686
2Sa 6:6 to the ark of God, and took **h.** of it; 270
2Sa 13:11 he took **h.** of her, and said unto her, 2388
2Sa 13:20 but **h.** now thy peace, my sister: 2790
2Sa 18:9 and his head caught **h.** of the oak, 2388
2Sa 23:14 David was then in an **h.**, and the 4686
2Sa 24:7 And came to the strong **h.** of Tyre, 4013
1Ki 1:50 caught **h.** on the horns of the altar. 2388
1Ki 1:51 caught **h.** on the horns of the altar, 270
1Ki 2:9 **h.** him not guiltless: for thou art
1Ki 2:28 caught **h.** on the horns of the altar. 2388
1Ki 9:9 and have taken **h.** upon other gods, 2388
1Ki 13:4 the altar, saying, Lay **h.** on him. 8610
2Ki 2:3,5 Yea, I know it; **h.** ye your peace. 2814
2Ki 2:12 and he took **h.** of his own clothes, 2388
2Ki 6:32 door, and **h.** him fast at the door: 3905
2Ki 7:9 good tidings, and we **h.** our peace: 2814
1Ch 11:16 David was then in the **h.**, and the 4686
1Ch 12:8 David into the **h.** to the wilderness 4679
1Ch 12:16 and Judah to the **h.** unto David. 4679
1Ch 13:9 put forth his hand to **h.** to ark; 270
2Ch 7:22 Egypt, and laid **h.** on other gods, 2388
Ne 8:11 saying, **H.** your peace, for the day 2013
Es 4:11 the king shall **h.** out the golden 3447
Job 6:24 Teach me, and I will **h.** my tongue: 2790
Job 8:15 he shall **h.** it fast, but it shall not 2388
Job 9:28 that thou wilt not **h.** me innocent.
Job 11:3 thy lies make men **h.** their peace? 2790
Job 13:5 ye would altogether **h.** your peace! 2790
Job 13:13 **H.** your peace, let me alone, that 2790
Job 13:19 for now, if I **h.** my tongue, I shall 2790
Job 17:9 righteous shall also **h.** on his way, 270
Job 21:6 am afraid, and trembling taketh **h.** 270
Job 27:6 My righteousness I **h.** fast, and 2388
Job 27:20 Terrors take **h.** on him as waters, 5381
Job 30:16 days of affliction have taken **h.** upon 270
Job 33:31 **h.** thy peace, and I will speak. 2790
Job 33:33 **h.** thy peace, and I shall teach thee 2790
Job 36:17 judgment and justice take **h.** on 8551
Job 38:13 take **h.** of the ends of the earth, 270
Job 41:26 him that layeth at him cannot **h.**: 6965
Ps 17:5 **H.** up my goings in thy paths, 8551
Ps 35:2 Take **h.** of shield and buckler, and 2388
Ps 39:12 **h.** not thy peace at my tears: for I 2790
Ps 40:12 iniquities have taken **h.** upon me, 5381
Ps 48:6 Fear took **h.** upon them there, and 270
Ps 69:24 wrathful anger take **h.** of them. 5381
Ps 83:1 **h.** not thy peace, and be not still, 2790
Ps 109:1 **H.** not thy peace, O God of my 2790
Ps 116:3 the pains of hell gat **h.** upon me: 4672
Ps 119:53 Horror hath taken **h.** upon me 270
Ps 119:117 **H.** thou me up, and I shall be safe: 5582
Ps 119:143 and anguish have taken **h.** on me: 4672
Ps 139:10 me, and thy right hand shall **h.** me. 270
Pr 2:19 neither take they **h.** of the paths 5381
Pr 3:18 life to them that lay **h.** upon her: 2388
Pr 4:13 Take fast **h.** of instruction; let her 2388
Pr 5:5 to death; her steps take **h.** on hell. 8551
Pr 30:28 spider taketh **h.** with her hands, 8610
Pr 31:19 and her hands **h.** the distaff 8551
Ec 2:3 and to lay **h.** on folly, till I might 270
Ec 7:18 that thou shouldest take **h.** of this; 270
Ca 3:8 They all **h.** swords, being expert 270
Ca 7:8 I will take **h.** of the boughs thereof: 270
Isa 3:6 a man shall take **h.** of his brother 8610
Isa 4:1 seven women shall take **h.** of one 2388
Isa 5:29 shall roar, and lay **h.** of the prey, 270
Isa 13:8 and sorrows shall take **h.** of them; 270
Isa 21:3 pangs have taken **h.** upon me, as 270
Isa 27:5 Or let him take **h.** of my strength, 2388
Isa 31:9 pass over to his strong **h.** for fear, 5553
Isa 41:13 Lord thy God will **h.** thy right hand, 2388
Isa 42:6 and will **h.** thine hand, and will keep 2388
Isa 56:2 the son of man that layeth **h.** on it; 2388
Isa 56:4 me, and take **h.** of my covenant; 2388
Isa 56:6 it, and taketh **h.** of my covenant; 2388
Isa 62:1 Zion's sake will I not **h.** my peace, 2814
Isa 62:6 never **h.** their peace day nor night: 2814
Isa 64:7 stirreth up himself to take **h.** of 2388
Isa 64:12 wilt thou **h.** thy peace, and afflict 2814
Jer 2:13 cisterns, that can **h.** no water. 3557
Jer 4:19 I cannot **h.** my peace, because thou 2790
Jer 6:23 They shall lay **h.** on bow and spear; 2388
Jer 6:24 anguish hath taken **h.** of us, and 2388
Jer 8:5 **h.** fast deceit, they refuse to return. 2388
Jer 8:21 astonishment hath taken **h.** on me. 2388
Jer 50:42 They shall **h.** the bow and the lance: 2388
Jer 50:43 feeble: anguish took **h.** of him, 2388
Eze 29:7 they took **h.** of thee by thy hand, 8610
Eze 30:21 to make it strong to **h.** the sword. 8610
Eze 41:6 round about that they might have **h.**, 270
Eze 41:6 had not **h.** in the wall of the house. 270
Am 6:10 Then shall he say, **H.** thy tongue: 2013
Mic 4:8 strong **h.** of the daughter of Zion, 6076
Mic 6:14 take **h.**, but shalt not deliver; 5253
Na 1:7 a strong **h.** in the day of trouble; 4581
Hab 1:10 they shall deride every strong **h.**: 4013
Zep 1:7 **H.** thy peace at the presence of the
Zec 1:6 they not take **h.** of your fathers? 5381
Zec 8:23 ten men shall take **h.** out of all 2388
Zec 8:23 even shall take **h.** of the skirt of 2388
Zec 9:3 Tyrus did build herself a strong **h.**, 4692
Zec 9:12 Turn you to the strong **h.**, ye 1225
Zec 11:5 and **h.** themselves not guilty; and 816
Zec 14:13 shall lay **h.** every one on the hand 2388
Mt 6:24 **or else he will h. to the one, and** *472*
Mt 12:11 **he not lay h. on it, and lift it out?** *2902*
Mt 14:3 For Herod had laid **h.** on John, and *2902*
Mt 20:31 because they should **h.** their peace: *4623*
Mt 21:26 for all **h.** John as a prophet. *2192*
Mt 26:48 kiss, that same is he: **h.** him fast. *2902*
Mt 26:55 **temple, and ye laid no h. on me.** *2902*
Mt 26:57 they that had laid **h.** on Jesus led *2902*
Mk 1:25 **H. thy peace, and come out of him.** *5392*
Mk 3:21 they went out to lay **h.** on him: *2902*
Mk 6:17 and laid **h.** upon John, and bound *2902*
Mk 7:4 which they have received to **h.**, as *2902*
Mk 7:8 **ye h. the tradition of men, as the** *2902*
Mk 10:48 that he should **h.** his peace: but *4623*
Mk 12:12 and they sought to lay **h.** on him, *2902*
Mk 14:51 and the youn men laid **h.** on him: *2902*
Lu 4:35 **H. thy peace, and come out of him.** *5392*
Lu 16:13 **or else he will h. to the one, and** *472*
Lu 18:39 him, that he should **h.** his peace: *4623*
Lu 19:40 **if these should h. their peace, the** *4623*
Lu 20:20 that they might take **h.** of his words, *1949*
Lu 20:26 they could not take **h.** of his words *1949*
Lu 23:26 they laid **h.** upon one Simon, a *1949*
Ac 4:3 put them in **h.** unto the next day: 5084
Ac 12:17 with the hand to **h.** their peace, *4601*
Ac 18:9 **but speak, and h. not thy peace:** *4623*
Ro 1:18 **h.** the truth in unrighteousness; *2722*
1Co 14:30 sitteth by, let the first **h.** his peace. *4601*
Php 2:29 gladness; and **h.** such in reputation *2192*
1Th 5:21 things; **h.** fast that which is good. *2722*
2Th 2:15 stand fast, and **h.** the traditions *2902*
1Ti 6:12 of faith, lay **h.** on eternal life, *1949*
1Ti 6:19 that they may lay **h.** on eternal life. *1949*
2Ti 1:13 **H.** fast the form of sound words, *2192*
Heb 3:6 if we **h.** fast the confidence and the *2722*
Heb 3:14 Christ, if we **h.** the beginning of our *2722*
Heb 4:14 of God, let us **h.** fast our profession. *2902*
Heb 6:18 lay **h.** upon the hope set before us: *2902*
Heb 10:23 Let us **h.** fast the profession of our *2722*
Re 2:14 **that h. the doctrine of Balaam,** *2902*

Re 2:15 **h. the doctrine of the Nicolaitanes,** *2902*
Re 2:25 **ye have already h. fast till I come.** *2902*
Re 3:3 **and heard, and h. fast, and repent.** *5083*
Re 3:11 **h. that fast which thou hast, that** *2902*
Re 18:2 and the **h.** of every foul spirit, and *5438*
Re 20:2 And he laid **h.** on the dragon, that...... *2902*

HOLDEN See also HELD; UPHOLDEN; WITHHOLDEN.
2Ki 23:22 there was not **h.** such a passover....... 6213
2Ki 23:23 this passover was **h.** to the Lord 6213
Job 36:8 and be **h.** in cords of affliction; 3920
Ps 18:35 and thy right hand hath **h.** me up, ... 5582
Ps 71:6 By thee have I been **h.** up from the ... 5564
Ps 73:23 thou hast **h.** me by my right hand........ 270
Pr 5:22 be **h.** with the cords of his sins. 8551
Isa 42:14 I have long time **h.** my peace; I......... 2814
Isa 45:1 Cyrus, whose right hand I have **h.**, ... 2388
Lu 24:16 But their eyes were **h.** that they........ *2902*
Ac 2:24 possible that he should be **h.** of it. *2902*
Ro 14:4 Yea, he shall be **h.** up: for God is *2676*

HOLDER See HOUSEHOLDER.

HOLDEST See BEHOLDEST; UPHOLDEST.
Es 4:14 if thou altogether **h.** thy peace at 2790
Job 13:24 face, and **h.** me for thine enemy?........ 2803
Ps 77:4 Thou **h.** mine eyes waking: I am so..... 270
Jer 49:16 rock, that **h.** the height of the hill: 8610
Hab 1:13 **h.** thy tongue when the wicked.......... 2790
Re 2:13 **and thou h. fast my name and** *2902*

HOLDETH See also BEHOLDETH; UPHOLDETH; WITHHOLDETH.
Job 2:3 and still he **h.** fast his integrity, ... 2388
Job 26:9 He **h.** back the face of his throne, ... 270
Ps 66:9 Which **h.** our soul in life, and............. 7760
Pr 11:12 man of understanding **h.** his peace...... 2790
Pr 17:28 a fool, when he **h.** his peace 2790
Da 10:21 none that **h.** with me in these........... 2388
Am 1:5 that **h.** the sceptre from the house 8551
Am 1:8 that **h.** the sceptre from Ashkelon, ... 8551
Re 2:1 **saith he that h. the seven stars in** *2902*

HOLDING See also BEHOLDING; UPHOLDING.
Isa 33:15 his hands from **h.** of bribes, ... 8551
Jer 6:11 I am weary with **h.** in: I will pour 3557
Mk 7:3 not, **h.** the tradition of the elders. *2902*
Php 2:16 **H.** forth the word of life; that I *1907*
Col 2:19 And not **h.** the Head, from which........ *2902*
1Ti 1:19 **H.** faith, and a good conscience; *2192*
1Ti 3:9 **H.** the mystery of the faith in a *2192*
Tit 1:9 **H.** fast the faithful word as he............ *472*
Re 7:1 **h.** the four winds of the earth, ... *2902*

HOLDS See also HOUSEHOLDS.
Nu 13:19 whether in tents, or in strong **h.**;....... 4013
Jg 6:2 mountains...caves and strong **h.**......... 4679
1Sa 23:14 abode in the wilderness in strong **h.**, .. 4679
1Sa 23:19 hide himself with us in strong **h.** 4679
1Sa 23:29 and dwelt in strong **h.** at En-gedi. 4679
2Ki 8:12 their strong **h.** wilt thou set on fire, ... 4013
2Ch 11:11 he fortified the strong **h.**, and put 4694
Ps 89:40 hast brought his strong **h.** to ruin....... 4013
Isa 23:11 to destroy the strong **h.** thereof......... 4581
Jer 48:18 and he shall destroy thy strong **h.**...... 4013
Jer 48:41 and the strong **h.** are surprised,......... 4679
Jer 51:30 they have remained in their **h.**:......... 4679
La 2:2 strong **h.** of the daughter of Judah;...... 4013
La 2:5 he hath destroyed his strong **h.**, ... 4013
Eze 19:9 they brought him into **h.**, that his....... 4686
Da 11:24 his devices against the strong **h.**, ... 4013
Da 11:39 shall he do in the most strong **h.** 4013
Mic 5:11 and throw down all thy strong **h.**: 4013
Na 3:12 All thy strong **h.** shall be like fig........ 4013
Na 3:14 fortify thy strong **h.**: go into clay, ... 4013
2Co 10:4 to the pulling down of strong **h.**;......... *3794*

HOLE See also HOLE'S; HOLES.
Ex 28:32 there shall be an **h.** in the top of it,.... 6310
Ex 28:32 woven work round about the **h.** of it,.. 6310
Ex 28:32 as it were the **h.** of an habergeon, ... 6310
Ex 39:23 And there was an **h.** in the midst of 6310
Ex 39:23 the robe, as the **h.** of an habergeon,.... 6310
Ex 39:23 with a band round about the **h.**, ... 6310
2Ki 12:9 a chest, bored a **h.** in the lid of it, ... 2356
Ca 5:4 put in his hand by the **h.** of the door, . 2356
Isa 11:8 shall play on the **h.** of the asp, ... 2356
Isa 51:1 **h.** of the pit whence ye are digged. 4718
Jer 13:4 and hid it there in a **h.** of the rock. 5357
Eze 8:7 I looked, behold a **h.** in the wall......... 2356

HOLE'S
Jer 48:28 nest in the sides of the **h.** mouth. 6354

HOLES See also ARMHOLES.
1Sa 14:11 Hebrews come forth out of the **h.**...... 2356
Isa 2:19 shall go into the **h.** of the rocks, ... 4631
Isa 7:19 valleys, and in the **h.** of the rocks, ... 5357
Isa 42:22 all of them snared in **h.**, and they....... 2356
Jer 16:16 hill, and out of the **h.** of the rocks...... 5357
Mic 7:17 they shall move out of their **h.** 4526
Na 2:12 filled his **h.** with prey, and his dens 2356
Hag 1:6 wages to put it into a bag with **h.**. 5344
Zec 14:12 shall consume away in their **h.**,......... 2356
Mt 8:20 **The foxes have h., and the birds....** *5454*
Lu 9:58 **Foxes have h., and the birds of ....** *5454*

HOLIDAY See HOLYDAY.

HOLIER
Isa 65:5 near to me; for I am **h.** than thou. 6942

HOLIEST
Heb 9:3 which is called the **H.** of all:................ *39*
Heb 9:8 the way into the **h.** of all was not.......... *39*
Heb 10:19 into the **h.** by the blood of Jesus, ... *39*

HOLILY
1Th 2:10 how **h.** and justly and unblameably...... *3743*

HOLINESS
Ex 15:11 who is like thee, glorious in **h.**, ... 6944
Ex 28:36 of a signet, **H.** to the Lord. 6944
Ex 39:30 of a signet, **H.** to the Lord. 6944
1Ch 16:29 worship the Lord in the beauty of **h.**... 6944
2Ch 20:21 that should praise the beauty of **h.**, ... 6944
2Ch 31:18 they sanctified themselves in **h.**: 6944
Ps 29:2 worship the Lord in the beauty of **h.**... 6944
Ps 30:4 at the remembrance of his **h.**. 6944
Ps 47:8 sitteth upon the throne of his **h.**. 6944
Ps 48:1 our God, in the mountain of his **h.**....... 6944
Ps 60:6 God hath spoken in his **h.**; I will........ 6944
Ps 89:35 Once have I sworn by my **h.** that I 6944
Ps 93:5 **h.** becometh thine house, O Lord,...... 6944
Ps 96:9 worship the Lord in the beauty of **h.**:.. 6944
Ps 97:12 thanks at the remembrance of his **h.**... 6944
Ps 108:7 God hath spoken in his **h.**; I will........ 6944
Ps 110:3 in the beauties of **h.** from the........... 6944
Isa 23:18 and her hire shall be **h.** to the Lord:... 6944
Isa 35:8 and it shall be called The way of **h.**, ... 6944
Isa 62:9 shall drink it in the courts of my **h.**. ... 6944
Isa 63:15 behold from the habitation of thy **h.**.... 6944
Isa 63:18 people of thy **h.** have possessed it...... 6944
Jer 2:3 Israel was **h.** unto the Lord, and the... 6944
Jer 23:9 and because of the words of his **h.**.... 6944
Jer 31:23 of justice, and mountain of **h.**. 6944
Am 4:2 The Lord God hath sworn by his **h.**.... 6944
Ob 17 deliverance, and there shall be **h.**;...... 6944
Zec 14:20 of the horses, **H.** unto the Lord;........ 6944
Zec 14:21 shall be **h.** unto the Lord of hosts: 6944
Mal 2:11 Judah hath profaned the **h.** of the 6944
Lu 1:75 In **h.** and righteousness before him, ... *3742*
Ac 3:12 though by our own power or **h.** we *2150*
Ro 1:4 power, according to the spirit of **h.**,........ *42*
Ro 6:19 srvants to righteousness unto **h.**. *38*
Ro 6:22 have your fruit unto **h.**, and the end *38*
2Co 7:1 perfecting **h.** in the fear of God............ *42*
Eph 4:24 in righteousness and true **h.**.............. *3742*
1Th 3:13 hearts unblameable in **h.** before God, ... *42*
1Th 4:7 us unto uncleanness, but unto **h.**........... *38*
1Ti 2:15 faith...chairty and **h.** with sobriety. *38*
Tit 2:3 be in behaviour as becometh **h.**, ... *2412*
Heb 12:10 that we might be partakers of his **h.**. *41*
Heb 12:14 Follow peace with all men, and **h.**, ... *38*

HOLLOW
Ge 32:25 him, he touched the **h.** of his thigh;.... 3709
Ge 32:25 and the **h.** of Jacob's thigh was out..... 3709
Ge 32:32 the **h.** of the thigh, unto this day: 3709
Ge 32:32 because he touched the **h.** of Jacob's... 3709
Ex 27:8 **H.** with boards shalt thou make it: 5014
Ex 38:7 he made the altar **h.** with boards........ 5014
Le 14:37 walls of the house with **h.** strakes, ... 8258
Jg 15:19 God clave an **h.** place that was.......... 4388
Isa 40:12 the waters in the **h.** of his hand, ... 8168
Jer 52:21 thereof was four fingers: it was **h.**....... 5014

HOLON (ho'-lon) See also HILEN.
Jos 15:51 And Goshen, and **H.**, and Giloh; 2473
Jos 21:15 And **H.** with her suburbs, and Debir ... 2473
Jer 48:21 upon **H.**, and upon Jahazah, and......... 2473

HOLPEN See also HELPED.
Ps 83:8 they have **h.** the children of Lot......... 2220
Ps 86:17 because thou, Lord, hast **h.** me, ... 5826
Isa 31:3 he that is **h.** shall fall down, and 5826
Da 11:34 they shall be **h.** with a little help: 5826
Lu 1:54 He hath **h.** his servant Israel, in.......... *482*

HOLY See also HOLIER; HOLIEST; HOLYDAY; UNHOLY.
Ex 3:5 whereon thou standest is **h.** ground. ... 6944
Ex 12:16 there shall be an **h.** convocation, ... 6944
Ex 12:16 shall be an **h.** convocation to you; 6944
Ex 15:13 thy strength unto thy **h.** habitation...... 6944
Ex 16:23 of the **h.** sabbath unto the Lord: 6944
Ex 19:6 of priests, and an **h.** nation. 6918
Ex 20:8 the sabbath day, to keep it **h.**. 6942
Ex 22:31 And ye shall be **h.** men unto me: 6944
Ex 26:33 between the **h.** place and the most **h.**.. 6944
Ex 26:34 of the testimony in the most **h.** place. . 6944
Ex 28:2 shalt make **h.** garments for Aaron 6944
Ex 28:4 shall make **h.** garments for Aaron....... 6944
Ex 28:29 when he goeth in unto the **h.** place,.... 6944
Ex 28:35 when he goeth in unto the **h.** place..... 6944
Ex 28:38 bear the inquity of the **h.** things,........ 6944
Ex 28:38 shall hallow in all their **h.** gifts; 6944
Ex 28:43 the altar to minister in the **h.** place;.... 6944
Ex 29:6 and put the crown upon the mitre....... 6944
Ex 29:29 the **h.** garments of Aaron shall be 6944
Ex 29:30 cometh...to minister in the **h.** place. ... 6944
Ex 29:31 seethe his flesh in the **h.** place. 6918
Ex 29:33 eat thereof, because they are **h.**. 6944
Ex 29:34 shall not be eaten, because it is **h.**, ... 6944
Ex 29:37 it; and it shall be an altar most **h.**; 6944
Ex 29:37 toucheth the altar shall be **h.**............ 6944
Ex 30:10 it is most **h.** unto the Lord. 6944
Ex 30:25 shalt make it an oil of **h.** ointment, ... 6944
Ex 30:25 it shall be an **h.** anointing oil............. 6944
Ex 30:29 them, that they may be most **h.**: 6944
Ex 30:29 whatsoever toucheth them...be **h.**. 6942
Ex 30:31 This shall be an **h.** anointing oil......... 6944
Ex 30:32 it is **h.**, and it shall be **h.** unto you. 6944
Ex 30:35 tempered together, pure and **h.**: 6944
Ex 30:36 thee: it shall be unto you most **h.**. 6944
Ex 30:37 shall be unto thee **h.** for the Lord. 6944
Ex 31:10 the **h.** garments for Aaron the priest,.. 6944
Ex 31:11 and sweet incense for the **h.** place: 6944
Ex 31:14 sabbath therefore; for it is **h.** unto...... 6944
Ex 31:15 sabbath to rest, **h.** to the Lord: 6944
Ex 35:2 day there shall be to you an **h.** day, ... 6944
Ex 35:19 service, to do service in the **h.** place, ..6944
Ex 35:19 the **h.** garments for Aaron the priest,.. 6944
Ex 35:21 service, and for the **h.** garments. 6944
Ex 37:29 And he made the **h.** anointing oil,....... 6944
Ex 38:24 work in all the work of the **h.** place,... 6944
Ex 39:1 to do service in the **h.** place, and........ 6944
Ex 39:1 made the **h.** garments for Aaron; 6944
Ex 39:30 plate of the **h.** crown of pure gold, ... 6944
Ex 39:41 to do service in the **h.** place, and........ 6944
Ex 39:41 the **h.** garments for Aaron the priest,.. 6944
Ex 40:9 vessels thereof: and it shall be **h.**....... 6944
Ex 40:10 altar: and it shall be an altar most **h.**... 6944
Ex 40:13 put upon Aaron the **h.** garments, ... 6944
Le 2:3,10 is a thing most **h.** of the offerings 6944
Le 5:15 in the **h.** things of the Lord; then....... 6944
Le 5:16 that he hath done in the **h.** things 6944
Le 6:16 shall it be eaten in the **h.** place;......... 6918
Le 6:17 it is most **h.**, as is the sin offering,..... 6944
Le 6:18 one that toucheth them shall be **h.**. 6942
Le 6:25 before the Lord: it is most **h.**............ 6944
Le 6:26 in the **h.** place shall it be eaten, in 6918
Le 6:27 touch the flesh thereof shall be **h.**: 6942
Le 6:27 it was sprinkled in the **h.** place. 6918
Le 6:29 shall eat thereof: it is most **h.**. 6944
Le 6:30 to reconcile withal in the **h.** place, ... 6944
Le 7:1 trespass offering: it is most **h.**........... 6944
Le 7:6 it shall be eaten in the **h.** place.......... 6918
Le 7:6 eaten in the...place: it is most **h.**. 6944
Le 8:9 put the golden plate, the **h.** crown;..... 6944
Le 10:10 difference between **h.** and unholy, ... 6944
Le 10:12 beside the altar: for it is most **h.**: 6944
Le 10:13 And ye shall eat it in the **h.** place,...... 6918
Le 10:17 have ye not eaten...in the **h.** place, ... 6944
Le 10:17 seeing it is most **h.**, and God hath...... 6944
Le 10:18 not brought in within the **h.** place:..... 6944
Le 10:18 indeed have eaten it in the **h.** place, ... 6944
Le 11:44 and ye shall be **h.**; for I am **h.**: 6918
Le 11:45 ye shall therefore be **h.**, for I am **h.**... 6918
Le 14:13 the burnt offering, in the **h.** place:...... 6944

Le 14:13 the trespass offering: it is most **h.**...... 6944
Le 16:2 not at all times into the **h.** place 6944
Le 16:3 shall Aaron come into the **h.** place:...... 6944
Le 16:4 He shall put on the **h.** linen coat, ... 6944
Le 16:4 these are **h.** garments; be attired:...... 6944
Le 16:16 make an atonement for the **h.** place, ... 6944
Le 16:17 make an atonement in the **h.** place, ... 6944
Le 16:20 an end of reconciling the **h.** place, ... 6944
Le 16:23 when he went into the **h.** place,.......... 6944
Le 16:24 his flesh with water in the **h.** place, ... 6918
Le 16:27 to make atonement in the **h.** place,..... 6944
Le 16:32 linen clothes, even the **h.** garments: ... 6944
Le 16:33 an atonement for the **h.** sanctuary, ... 6944
Le 19:2 and say unto them, Ye shall be **h.**...... 6918
Le 19:2 for I the Lord your God am **h.** 6918
Le 19:24 fruit thereof shall be **h.** to praise........ 6944
Le 20:3 and to profane my **h.** name............... 6944
Le 20:7 be ye **h.**: for I am the Lord your 6918
Le 20:26 **h.** unto me: for I am the Lord am **h.**, ..6918
Le 21:6 They shall be **h.** unto their God, and .. 6918
Le 21:6 do offer: therefore they shall be **h.**..... 6944
Le 21:7 husband: for he is **h.** unto his God. 6918
Le 21:8 thy God: he shall be **h.** unto thee:...... 6918
Le 21:8 the Lord which sanctify you, am **h.**...... 6918
Le 21:22 both of the most **h.**, and of the **h.**...... 6944
Le 22:2 themselves from the **h.** things of........ 6944
Le 22:2 that they profane not my **h.** name 6944
Le 22:3 that goeth unto the **h.** things, which ... 6944
Le 22:4 he shall not eat of the **h.** things, ... 6944
Le 22:6 and shall not eat of the **h.** things,....... 6944
Le 22:7 shall afterward eat of the **h.** things; 6944
Le 22:10 shall no stranger eat of the **h.** thing: ... 6944
Le 22:10 servant, shall not eat of the **h.** thing. .. 6944
Le 22:12 eat of an offering of the **h.** things....... 6944
Le 22:14 man eat of the **h.** thing unwittingly, ... 6944
Le 22:14 it unto the priest with the **h.** thing. 6944
Le 22:15 they shall not profane the **h.** things..... 6944
Le 22:16 when they eat their **h.** things: for....... 6944
Le 22:32 Neither shall ye profane my **h.** name;.. 6944
Le 23:2 which ye shall proclaim to be **h.**......... 6944
Le 23:3 sabbath of rest, an **h.** convocation; 6944
Le 23:4 even **h.** convocations, which ye.......... 6944
Le 23:7 day ye shall have an **h.** convocation: ... 6944
Le 23:8 seventh day is an **h.** convocation:........ 6944
Le 23:20 shall be **h.** to the Lord for the priest. ..6944
Le 23:21 may be an **h.** convocation unto you:.... 6944
Le 23:24 of trumpets, an **h.** convocation.......... 6944
Le 23:27 shall be an **h.** convocation unto you; ... 6944
Le 23:35 first day shall be an **h.** convocation: 6944
Le 23:36 eighth day shall be an **h.** convocation .. 6944
Le 23:37 shall proclaim to be **h.** convocations, ... 6944
Le 24:9 and they shall eat it in the **h.** place:.... 6918
Le 24:9 is most **h.** unto him of the offerings..... 6944
Le 25:12 it shall be **h.** unto you: ye shall eat..... 6944
Le 27:9 of such unto the Lord shall be **h.**....... 6944
Le 27:10 and the exchange thereof shall be **h.**..... 6944
Le 27:14 man shall sanctify his house to be **h.**.... 6944
Le 27:21 shall be **h.** unto the Lord, as a field.... 6944
Le 27:23 that day, as a **h.** thing uno the Lord. .. 6944
Le 27:28 every devoted thing is most **h.** unto ... 6944
Le 27:30 is the Lord's: it is **h.** unto the Lord.... 6944
Le 27:32 the tenth shall be **h.** unto the Lord..... 6944
Le 27:33 it the change thereof shall be **h.**;........ 6944
Nu 4:4 about the most **h.** things: 6944
Nu 4:15 they shall not touch any **h.** thing, ... 6944
Nu 4:19 approach nto the most **h.** things:........ 6944
Nu 4:20 see when the **h.** things are covered, ... 6944
Nu 5:9 every offering of the **h.** things of the .. 6944
Nu 5:17 the priest shall take **h.** water in an..... 6918
Nu 6:5 he shall be **h.**, and shall let the locks .. 6918
Nu 6:8 separation he is **h.** unto the Lord. 6918
Nu 6:20 this is **h.** for the priest, with the....... 6944
Nu 15:40 and be **h.** unto your God. 6918
Nu 16:3 seeing all the congregation are **h.**,........ 6918
Nu 16:5 will shew who are his, and who is **h.**; . 6918
Nu 16:7 Lord doth choose, he shall be **h.**:........ 6918
Nu 18:9 shall be thine of the most **h.** things,..... 6944
Nu 18:9 be most **h.** for thee and for thy sons. ..6944
Nu 18:10 In the most **h.** place shalt thou eat..... 6944
Nu 18:10 shall eat it: it shall be **h.** unto thee..... 6944
Nu 18:17 they are **h.**: thou shalt sprinkle.......... 6944
Nu 18:19 the heave offerings of the **h.** things, ... 6944
Nu 18:32 neither shall ye pollute the **h.** things ... 6944
Nu 28:7 in the **h.** place shalt thou cause the 6944
Nu 28:18 first day shall be an **h.** convocation; 6944
Nu 28:25, 26 ye shall have an **h.** convocation;..... 6944
Nu 29:1 ye shall have an **h.** convocation;......... 6944
Nu 29:7 seventh month an **h.** convocation;....... 6944
Nu 29:12 ye shall have an **h.** convocation; ye...... 6944
Nu 31:6 to the war, with the **h.** instruments, ... 6944
Nu 35:25 which was anointed with the **h.** oil..... 6944
De 7:6 thou art an **h.** people unto the Lord.... 6918
De 12:26 Only thy **h.** things which thou hast; 6944
De 14:2 for thou art an **h.** people unto the 6918
De 14:21 For thou art an **h.** people unto the 6918
De 23:14 therefore shall thy camp be **h.**: that.... 6918
De 26:15 Look down from thy **h.** habitation,...... 6944
De 26:19 thou mayest be an **h.** people unto 6918
De 28:9 shall establish thee an **h.** people......... 6918
De 33:8 Urim be with thy **h.** one, whom......... 2623
Jos 5:15 place whereon thou standest is **h.**. 6944
Jos 24:19 serve the Lord: for he is an **h.** God;... 6918
1Sa 2:2 There is none **h.** as the Lord: for 6918
1Sa 6:20 to stand before this **h.** Lord God? 6918
1Sa 21:5 vessels of the young men are **h.**, ... 6944
1Ki 6:16 oracle, even for the most **h.** place...... 6944
1Ki 7:50 the inner house, the most **h.** place, ... 6944
1Ki 8:4 all the **h.** vessels that were in the...... 6944
1Ki 8:6 of the house, to the most **h.** place,..... 6944
1Ki 8:8 out in the **h.** place before the oracle, .. 6944
1Ki 8:10 priests were come out of the **h.** place, .6944
2Ki 4:9 I perceive that is an **h.** man............. 6918
2Ki 19:22 even against the **H.** One of Israel....... 6918
1Ch 6:49 all the work of the place most **h.**, ... 6944
1Ch 16:10 Glory ye in his **h.** name: let the......... 6944
1Ch 16:35 we may give thanks to thy **h.** name, ... 6944
1Ch 22:19 the **h.** vessels of God, into the house.. 6944
1Ch 23:13 should sanctify the most **h.** things, ... 6944
1Ch 23:28 in the purifying of all **h.** things,.......... 6944
1Ch 23:32 and the charge of the **h.** place, ... 6944
1Ch 29:3 I have prepared for the **h.** house,....... 6944
1Ch 29:16 build thee an house for thine **h.** name ..6944
2Ch 3:8 and he made the most **h.** house, the... 6944
2Ch 3:10 in the most **h.** house he made two 6944
2Ch 4:22 doors thereof for the most **h.** place, ... 6944
2Ch 5:5 all the **h.** vessels that were in the...... 6944
2Ch 5:7 into the most **h.** place, even under..... 6944
2Ch 5:11 were come out of the **h.** place:.......... 6944
2Ch 8:11 of Israel, because the places are **h.**, ... 6944
2Ch 23:6 they shall go in, for they are **h.**: but... 6944
2Ch 29:5 the filthiness out of the **h.** place......... 6944
2Ch 29:7 burnt offerings in the **h.** place unto..... 6944
2Ch 30:27 came up to his **h.** dwelling place, ... 6944
2Ch 31:6 the tithe of **h.** things which were 6944
2Ch 31:14 of the Lord, and the most **h.** things.... 6944
2Ch 35:3 which were **h.** unto the Lord,........... 6918
2Ch 35:3 Put the **h.** ark in the house which 6944
2Ch 35:5 stand in the **h.** place according to....... 6944
2Ch 35:13 but the other **h.** offerings sod they...... 6944
Ezr 2:63 should not eat of the most **h.** things, .. 6944
Ezr 8:28 unto them Ye are **h.** unto the Lord;...... 6944
Ezr 8:28 Lord; the vessels are **h.** also; and...... 6944
Ezr 9:2 **h.** seed have mingled themselves 6944
Ezr 9:8 to give us a nail in his **h.** place, ... 6944
Ne 7:65 should not eat of the most **h.** things, .. 6944
Ne 8:9 This day is **h.** unto the Lord your 6918
Ne 8:10 for this day is **h.** unto our Lord: 6918
Ne 8:11 Hold your peace, for the day is **h.**;..... 6918
Ne 9:14 known unto them thy **h.** sabbath,........ 6944
Ne 10:31 on the sabbath, or on the **h.** day:....... 6944
Ne 10:33 the set feasts, and for the **h.** things,... 6944
Ne 11:1 to dwell in Jerusalem the **h.** city, ... 6944
Ne 11:18 All the Levites in the **h.** city............ 6944
Ne 12:47 and they sanctified **h.** things unto......... 6944
Job 6:10 concealed the words of the **H.** One. ... 6918
Ps 2:6 my king upon my **h.** hill of Zion. 6944
Ps 3:4 and he heard me out of his **h.** hill....... 6944
Ps 5:7 will I worship toward thy **h.** temple. ... 6944
Ps 11:4 The Lord is in his **h.** temple, the....... 6944
Ps 15:1 who shalll dwell in thy **h.** hill?............ 6944
Ps 16:10 thou suffer thine **H.** One to see......... 2623
Ps 20:6 will hear him from his **h.** heaven 6944
Ps 22:3 thou art **h.**, O thou that inhabitest...... 6918
Ps 24:3 or who shall stanad in his **h.** place?..... 6944
Ps 28:2 up my hands toward thy **h.** oracle. 6944
Ps 33:21 we have trusted in his **h.** name......... 6944
Ps 43:3 let them bring me unto thy **h.** hill,...... 6944
Ps 46:4 the **h.** place of the tabernacles of....... 6918
Ps 51:11 take not thy **h.** spirit from me........... 6944
Ps 65:4 thy house, even of thy **h.** temple. 6918
Ps 68:5 widows, is God in his **h.** habitation. 6944
Ps 68:17 them, as in Sinai, in the **h.** place........ 6944
Ps 68:35 art terrible out of thy **h.** places:......... 4720
Ps 71:22 the harp, O thou **H.** One of Israel...... 6918
Ps 78:41 and limited the **H.** One of Israel......... 6918
Ps 79:1 thy **h.** temple have they defiled;......... 6944
Ps 86:2 Preserve my soul; for I am **h.**: O....... 2623
Ps 87:1 foundation is in the **h.** mountains........ 6944
Ps 89:18 the **H.** One of Israel is our king......... 6918
Ps 89:19 spakest in vision to thy **h.** one,.......... 2623
Ps 89:20 with my **h.** oil have I anointed him: 6944
Ps 98:1 his right hand, and his **h.** arm,........... 6944
Ps 99:3 and terrible name; for it is **h.**. 6918
Ps 99:5 at his footstool; for he is **h.**. 6918
Ps 99:9 our God, and worship at his **h.** hill; 6944
Ps 99:9 hill; for the Lord our God is **h.**. 6918
Ps 103:1 is within me, bless his **h.** name.......... 6944
Ps 105:3 Glory ye in his **h.** name: let the......... 6944
Ps 105:42 For he remembererd his **h.** promise, .. 6944
Ps 106:47 to give thanks unto thy **h.** name, ... 6944
Ps 111:9 ever: **h.** and reverend is his name....... 6918
Ps 138:2 will worship toward thy **h.** temple, ... 6944
Ps 145:17 his ways, and **h.** in all his works. 2623
Ps 145:21 bless his **h.** name for ever and ever.... 6944
Pr 9:10 and the knowledge of the **h.** is 6918
Pr 20:25 who devoureth that which is **h.**,......... 6944
Pr 30:3 nor have the knowledge of the **h.**....... 6918
Ec 8:10 and gone from the place of the **h.**, ... 6918
Isa 1:4 have provoked the **H.** One of Israel.... 6918
Isa 4:3 in Jerusalem, shall be called **h.**,.......... 6918
Isa 5:16 God that is **h.** shall be sanctified 6918
Isa 5:19 counsel of the **H.** One of Israel draw .. 6918
Isa 5:24 despised the word of the **H.** One....... 6918
Isa 6:3 said, **H.**, **h.**, **h.**, is the Lord of hosts: ..6918
Isa 6:13 the **h.** seed shall be the substance...... 6944
Isa 10:17 fire, and his **H.** One for a flame: 6918
Isa 10:20 stay uon the Lord, the **H.** One of 6918
Isa 11:9 nor destroy in all my **h.** mountain:...... 6944
Isa 12:6 great is the **H.** One of Israel in the 6918
Isa 17:7 shall have respect to the **H.** One 6918
Isa 27:13 worship the Lord in the **H.** mount...... 6944
Isa 29:19 rejoice in the **H.** One of Israel........... 6918
Isa 29:23 sanctify the **H.** One of Jacob, and....... 6918
Isa 30:11 cause the **H.** One of Israel to cease.... 6918
Isa 30:12 thus saith the **H.** One of Israel, ... 6918
Isa 30:15 the Lord God, the **H.** One of Israel;... 6918
Isa 30:29 night when a **h.** solemnity is kept;...... 6942
Isa 31:1 look not unto the **H.** One of Israel, ... 6918
Isa 37:23 even against the **H.** One of Israel...... 6918
Isa 40:25 shall I be equal? saith the **H.** One. 6918
Isa 41:14 thy redeemer, the **H.** One of Israel. 6918
Isa 41:16 shalt glory in the **H.** One of Israel..... 6918
Isa 41:20 the **H.** One of Israel hath created it.... 6918
Isa 43:3 Lord thy God, the **H.** One of Israel, ... 6918
Isa 43:14 your redeemer, the **H.** One of Israel; . 6918
Isa 43:15 I am the Lord, your **H.** One, the 6918
Isa 45:11 saith the Lord, the **H.** One of Israel, .. 6918
Isa 47:4 is his name, the **H.** One of Israel....... 6918
Isa 48:2 they call themselves of the **h.** city,..... 6944
Isa 48:17 Redeemer, the **H.** One of Israel; 6918
Isa 49:7 Redeemer of Israel, and his **H.** One, ... 6918
Isa 49:7 the **H.** One of Israel, and he shall 6918
Isa 52:1 garments, O Jerusalem, the **h.** city: 6944
Isa 52:10 The Lord hath made bare his **h.** arm .. 6944
Isa 54:5 Redeemer the **H.** One of Israel; 6918
Isa 55:5 God, and for the **H.** One of Israel; 6918
Isa 56:7 will I bring to my **H.** mountain,.......... 6944
Isa 57:13 and shall inherit my **h.** mountain;........ 6944
Isa 57:15 eternity, whose name is **H.**; I dwell.... 6918
Isa 57:15 I dwell in the high and **h.** place,......... 6918
Isa 58:13 doing thy pleasure on my **h.** day 6944
Isa 58:13 the **h.** of the Lord, honourable;.......... 6918
Isa 60:9 God, and to the **H.** One of Israel, ... 6918
Isa 60:14 The Zion of the **H.** One of Israel. 6918
Isa 62:12 they shall call them, The **h.** people, ... 6944
Isa 63:10 rebelled, and vexed his **h.** Spirit:........ 6944
Isa 63:11 he that put his **h.** Spirit within him?.... 6944
Isa 64:10 Thy **h.** cities are a wilderness, Zion.... 6944
Isa 64:11 Our **h.** and our beautiful house, ... 6944
Isa 65:11 Lord, that forget my **h.** mountain, ... 6944
Isa 65:25 nor destroy in all my **h.** mountain,...... 6944
Isa 66:20 to my **h.** mountain Jerusalem, saith..... 6944
Jer 11:15 the **h.** flesh is passed from thee? 6944
Jer 25:30 his voice from his **h.** habitation; 6944
Jer 31:40 shall be **h.** unto the Lord; it shall....... 6944
Jer 50:29 Lord, against the **H.** One of Israel...... 6918
Jer 51:5 sin against the **H.** One of Israel. 6918
Eze 7:24 and their **h.** places shall be defiled...... 6942
Eze 20:39 but pollute ye my **h.** name no more.... 6944
Eze 20:40 mine **h.** mountain, in the mountain...... 6944

Ref	Context	No.
Eze 20:40	oblations, with all your **h.** things	
Eze 21:2	drop thy word toward the **h.** place,	4720
Eze 22:8	Thou hast despised mine **h.** things	6944
Eze 22:26	and have profaned mine **h.** things,	6944
Eze 22:26	between the **h.** and profane,	6944
Eze 28:14	thou wast upon the **h.** mountain	6944
Eze 36:20	they profaned my **h.** name, when	6944
Eze 36:21	I had pity for mine **h.** name, which	6944
Eze 36:22	but for mine **h.** name's sake, which	6944
Eze 36:38	As the **h.** flock, as the flock of	6944
Eze 39:7	So will I make my **h.** name known	6944
Eze 39:7	will not let them pollute my **h.** name	6944
Eze 39:7	I am the Lord, the **H.** One in Israel.	6918
Eze 39:25	will be jealous for my **h.** name;	6944
Eze 41:4	unto me, This is the most **h.** place.	6944
Eze 42:13	separate place, they be **h.** chambers,	6944
Eze 42:13	shall eat the most **h.** things:	6944
Eze 42:13	shall they lay the most **h.** things,	6944
Eze 42:13	trespass offering...the place is **h.**.	6918
Eze 42:14	shall they not go out of the **h.** place	6944
Eze 42:14	wherein they minister; for they are **h.**;	
Eze 43:7	and my **h.** name, shall the house of	6944
Eze 43:8	they have even defiled my **h.** name	6944
Eze 43:12	round about shall be most **h.**.	6944
Eze 44:8	kept the charge of mine **h.** things:	6944
Eze 44:13	to come near to any of my **h.** things,	6944
Eze 44:13	in the most **h.** place: but they shall	6944
Eze 44:19	lay them in the **h.** chambers, and	6944
Eze 44:23	between the **h.** and profane,	6944
Eze 45:1	the Lord, an **h.** portion of the land:	6944
Eze 45:1	This shall be **h.** in all the borders	6944
Eze 45:3	sanctuary and the most **h.** place	6944
Eze 45:4	The **h.** portion of the land shall be	6944
Eze 45:4	and an **h.** place for the sanctuary.	4720
Eze 45:6	the oblation of the **h.** portion:	6944
Eze 45:7	of the oblation of the **h.** portion,	6944
Eze 45:7	before the oblation of the **h.** portion,	6944
Eze 46:19	into the **h.** chambers of the priests,	6944
Eze 48:10	the priests, shall be this **h.** oblation;	6944
Eze 48:12	shall be unto them a thing most **h.**	6944
Eze 48:14	the land: for it is **h.** unto the Lord.	6944
Eze 48:18	the oblation of the **h.** portion shall	6944
Eze 48:18	the oblation of the **h.** portion;	6944
Eze 48:20	ye shall offer the **h.** oblation	6944
Eze 48:21	and on the other of the **h.** oblation,	6944
Eze 48:21	and it shall be the **h.** oblation;	6944
Da 4:8	in whom is the spirit of the **h.** gods:	6922
Da 4:9	the spirit of the **h.** gods is in thee,	6922
Da 4:13	a watcher and an **h.** one came down	6922
Da 4:17	demand by the word of the **h.** ones:	6922
Da 4:18	the spirit of the **h.** gods is in thee.	6922
Da 4:23	a watcher and an **h.** one coming	6922
Da 5:11	whom is the spirit of the **h.** gods;	6922
Da 8:24	destroy the mighty...**h.** people	6918
Da 9:16	city Jerusalem, thy **h.** mountain:	6944
Da 9:20	God for the **h.** mountain of my God;	6944
Da 9:24	thy people and upon thy **h.** city,	6944
Da 9:24	prophecy, and to anoint the most **H.**	6944
Da 11:28	shall be against the **h.** covenant;	6944
Da 11:30	indignation against the **h.** covenant:	6944
Da 11:30	them that forsake the **h.** covenant.	6944
Da 11:45	seas in the glorious **h.** mountain;	6944
Da 12:7	scatter the power of the **h.** people,	6944
Ho 11:9	the **H.** One in the midst of thee:	6918
Joe 2:1	sound an alarm in my **h.** mountain:	6944
Joe 3:17	dwelling in Zion, my **h.** mountain:	6944
Joe 3:17	then shall Jerusalem be **h.**, and	6944
Am 2:7	same maid, to profane my **h.** name:	6944
Ob 16	have drunk upon my **h.** mountain,	6944
Jon 2:4	look again toward thy **h.** temple.	6944
Jon 2:7	unto thee, into thine **h.** temple.	6944
Mic 1:2	you, the Lord from his **h.** temple.	6944
Hab 1:12	O Lord my God, mine **H.** One?	6918
Hab 2:20	but the Lord is in his **h.** temple:	6944
Hab 3:3	and the **H.** One from mount Paran.	6918
Zep 3:11	because of my **h.** mountain.	6944
Hag 2:12	If one bear **h.** flesh in the skirt of	6944
Hag 2:12	oil, or any meat, shall it be **h.**?	6942
Zec 2:12	Judah his portion in the **h.** land,	6944
Zec 2:13	raised up out of his **h.** habitation.	6944
Zec 8:3	the Lord of hosts the **h.** mountain.	6944
Mt 1:18	found with child of the **H.** Ghost.	*40*
Mt 1:20	in her is of the **H.** Ghost.	*40*
Mt 3:11	baptize you with the **H.** Ghost,	*40*
Mt 4:5	devil taketh him up into the **h.** city,	*40*
Mt 7:6	**not that which is h. unto the dogs,**	*40*
Mt 12:31	**the blasphemy against the H. Ghost**	
Mt 12:32	**speaketh against the H. Ghost,**	*40*
Mt 24:15	**of desolation...stand in the h. place,**	*40*
Mt 25:31	**glory, and all the h. angels with**	*40*
Mt 27:53	went into the **h.** city, and appeared	*40*
Mt 28:19	**of the Son, and of the H. Ghost:**	*40*
Mk 1:8	baptize you with the **H.** Ghost.	*40*
Mk 1:24	who thou art, the **H.** One of God.	*40*
Mk 3:29	**blaspheme against the H. Ghost**	*40*
Mk 6:20	that he was a just man and an **h.**,	*40*
Mk 8:38	**of his Father with the h. angels**	*40*
Mk 12:36	**himself said by the H. Ghost,**	*40*
Mk 13:11	**not ye that speak, but the H. Ghost**	*40*
Lu 1:15	shall be filled with the **H.** Ghost,	*40*
Lu 1:35	The **H.** Ghost shall come upon	*40*
Lu 1:35	that **h.** thing which shall be born	*40*
Lu 1:41	was filled with the **H.** Ghost:	*40*
Lu 1:49	great things; and **h.** is his name.	*40*
Lu 1:67	was filled with the **H.** Ghost,	*40*
Lu 1:70	the mouth of his **h.** prophets, which	*40*
Lu 1:72	and to remember his **h.** covenant;	*40*
Lu 2:23	womb shall be called **h.** to the Lord;	*40*
Lu 2:25	and the **H.** Ghost was upon him.	*40*
Lu 2:26	unto him by the **H.** Ghost, that	*40*
Lu 3:16	baptize you with the **H.** Ghost	*40*
Lu 3:22	the **H.** Ghost descended in a bodily	*40*
Lu 4:1	Jesus being full of the **H.** Ghost	*40*
Lu 4:34	who thou art; the **H.** One of God.	*40*
Lu 9:26	**in his Father's, and of the h. angels**	*40*
Lu 11:13	**give the H. Spirit to them that ask**	*40*
Lu 12:10	**against the H. Ghost it shall**	*40*
Lu 12:12	**For the H. Ghost shall teach you**	*40*
Joh 1:33	which baptizeth with the **H.** Ghost.	*40*
Joh 7:39	for the **H.** Ghost was not yet given;	*40*
Joh 14:26	**Comforter, which is the H. Ghost,**	*40*
Joh 17:11	**H. Father, keep through thine own**	*40*
Joh 20:22	**them, Receive ye the H. Ghost:**	*40*
Ac 1:2	he through the **H.** Ghost had given	*40*
Ac 1:5	**be baptized with the H. Ghost not**	*40*
Ac 1:8	**that the H. Ghost is come upon**	*40*
Ac 1:16	the **H.** Ghost by the mouth of David	*40*
Ac 2:4	were all filled with the **H.** Ghost,	*40*
Ac 2:27	thine **H.** One to see corruption.	*3741*
Ac 2:33	the promise of the **H.** Ghost, he	*40*
Ac 2:38	receive the gift of the **H.** Ghost.	*40*
Ac 3:14	ye denied the **H.** One and the Just,	*40*
Ac 3:21	by the mouth of all his **h.** prophets	*40*
Ac 4:8	Peter, filled with the **H.** Ghost, said	*40*
Ac 4:27	of a truth against thy **h.** child Jesus,	*40*
Ac 4:30	by the name of thy **h.** child Jesus.	*40*
Ac 4:31	were all filled with the **H.** Ghost,	*40*
Ac 5:3	heart to lie to the **H.** Ghost, and	*40*
Ac 5:32	so is also the **H.** Ghost, whom	*40*
Ac 6:3	full of the **H.** Ghost and wisdom,	*40*
Ac 6:5	full of faith and of the **H.** Ghost,	*40*
Ac 6:13	words against this **h.** place, and the	*40*
Ac 7:33	where thou standest is **h.** ground.	*40*
Ac 7:51	do always resist the **H.** Ghost:	*40*
Ac 7:55	he, being full of the **H.** Ghost,	*40*
Ac 8:15	they might receive the **H.** Ghost:	*40*
Ac 8:17	and they received the **H.** Ghost.	*40*
Ac 8:18	hands the **H.** Ghost was given, he	*40*
Ac 8:19	he may receive the **H.** Ghost.	*40*
Ac 9:17	and be filled with the **H.** Ghost.	*40*
Ac 9:31	in the comfort of the **H.** Ghost,	*40*
Ac 10:22	was warned from God by an **h.** angel	*40*
Ac 10:38	with the **H.** Ghost and with power:	*40*
Ac 10:44	the **H.** Ghost fell on all them	*40*
Ac 10:45	out the gift of the **H.** Ghost	*40*
Ac 10:47	have received the **H.** Ghost as well	*40*
Ac 11:15	the **H.** Ghost fell on them, as on	*40*
Ac 11:16	**shall be baptized with the H. Ghost**	*40*
Ac 11:24	full of the **H.** Ghost and of faith:	*40*
Ac 13:2	the **H.** Ghost said, Separate me	*40*
Ac 13:4	being sent forth by the **H.** Ghost,	*40*
Ac 13:9	filled with the **H.** Ghost, set his	*40*
Ac 13:35	thine **H.** One to see corruption.	*3741*
Ac 13:52	with joy, and with the **H.** Ghost.	*40*
Ac 15:8	giving them the **H.** Ghost, even	*40*
Ac 15:28	it seemed good to the **H.** Ghost,	*40*
Ac 16:6	were forbidden of the **H.** Ghost	*40*
Ac 19:2	Have ye received the **H.** Ghost	*40*
Ac 19:2	whether there be any **H.** Ghost.	*40*
Ac 19:6	the **H.** Ghost came on them;	*40*
Ac 20:23	Save that the **H.** Ghost witnesseth	*40*
Ac 20:28	**H.** Ghost hath made you overseers,	*40*
Ac 21:11	said, Thus saith the **H.** Ghost, So	*40*
Ac 21:28	and hath polluted this **h.** place.	*40*
Ac 28:25	Well spake the **H.** Ghost by Esaias	*40*
Ro 1:2	by his prophets in the **h.** scriptures,	*40*
Ro 5:5	in our hearts by the **H.** Ghost	*40*
Ro 7:12	law is **h.**, and the commandment **h.**,	*40*
Ro 9:1	me witness in the **H.** Ghost,	*40*
Ro 11:16	For if the firstfruit be **h.**, the lump is	*40*
Ro 11:16	the lump is also **h.**: and if the lump	*40*
Ro 11:16	if the root be **h.**, so are the branches.	*40*
Ro 12:1	a living sacrifice, **h.**, acceptable unto	*40*
Ro 14:17	peace, and joy in the **H.** Ghost.	*40*
Ro 15:13	through the power of the **H.** Ghost.	*40*
Ro 15:16	being sanctified by the **H.** Ghost.	*40*
Ro 16:16	Salute one another with an **h.** kiss.	*40*
1Co 2:13	which the **H.** Ghost teacheth;	*40*
1Co 3:17	for the temple of God is **h.**, which	*40*
1Co 6:19	is the temple of the **H.** Ghost	*40*
1Co 7:14	children unclean; but now are they **h.**,	*40*
1Co 7:34	may be **h.** both in body and in spirit:	*40*
1Co 9:13	which minister about **h.** things	*2413*
1Co 12:3	is the Lord, but by the **H.** Ghost.	*40*
1Co 16:20	Greet ye one another with an **h.** kiss.	*40*
2Co 6:6	by kindness, by the **H.** Ghost, by	*40*
2Co 13:12	Greet one another with an **h.** kiss.	*40*
2Co 13:14	communion of the **H.** Ghost, be	*40*
Eph 1:4	we should be **h.** and without blame	*40*
Eph 1:13	sealed with that **h.** Spirit of promise,	*40*
Eph 2:21	groweth unto an **h.** temple in the	*40*
Eph 3:5	unto his **h.** apostles and prophets	*40*
Eph 4:30	And grieve not the **h.** Spirit of God,	*40*
Eph 5:27	it should be **h.** and without blemish.	*40*
Col 1:22	to present you **h.** and unblameable	*40*
Col 3:12	as the elect of God, **h.** and beloved,	*40*
1Th 1:5	in power, and in the **H.** Ghost,	*40*
1Th 1:6	affliction with joy of the **H.** Ghost:	*40*
1Th 4:8	hath also given unto us his **h.** Spirit.	*40*
1Th 5:26	Greet all the brethren with an **h.** kiss.	*40*
1Th 5:27	be read unto all the **h.** brethren.	*40*
1Ti 2:8	lifting up **h.** hands, without wrath	*3741*
2Ti 1:9	us, and called us with an **h.** calling,	*40*
2Ti 1:14	by the **H.** Ghost which dwelleth	*40*
2Ti 3:15	thou hast known the **h.** scriptures,	*2413*
Tit 1:8	sober, just, **h.**, temperate; Holdings	*3741*
Tit 3:5	and renewing of the **H.** Ghost;	*40*
Heb 2:4	miracles and gifts of the **H.** Ghost,	*40*
Heb 3:1	Wherefore, **h.** brethren, partakers of	*40*
Heb 3:7	as the **H.** Ghost saith, To day if	*40*
Heb 6:4	made partakers of the **H.**, Ghost,	*40*
Heb 7:26	who is **h.**, harmless, undefiled,	*3741*
Heb 9:8	The **H.** Ghost this signifying,	*40*
Heb 9:12	he entered in once into the **h.** place,	*39*
Heb 9:24	into the **h.** places made with hands,	*39*
Heb 9:25	entereth into the **h.** place every year	*39*
Heb 10:15	the **H.** Ghost also is a witness to	*40*
1Pe 1:12	you with the **H.** Ghost sent down	*40*
1Pe 1:15	hath called you is **h.**, so be ye **h.** in all	*40*
1Pe 1:16	it is written, Be ye **h.**; for I am **h.**	*40*
1Pe 2:5	spiritual house, an **h.** priesthood, to	*40*
1Pe 2:9	a royal priesthood, an **h.** nation, a	*40*
1Pe 3:5	in the old time the **h.** women also,	*40*
2Pe 1:18	we were with him in the **h.** mount.	*40*
2Pe 1:21	**h.** men of God spake as they were	*40*
2Pe 1:21	were moved by the **H.** Ghost.	*40*
2Pe 2:21	from the **h.** commandment delivered	*40*
2Pe 3:2	spoken before by the **h.** prophets,	*40*
2Pe 3:11	in all **h.** conversation and godliness,	*40*
1Jo 2:20	ye have an unction from the **H.** One.	*40*
1Jo 5:7	the Word, and the **H.**, Ghost:	*40*
Jude 20	yourselves in your most **h.** faith,	*40*
Jude 20	faith, praying in the **H.** Ghost,	*40*
Re 3:7	**saith he that is h., he that is true,**	*40*
Re 4:8	night, saying, **H.**, **h.**,**h.**, Lord God	*40*
Re 6:10	How long, O Lord, **h.** and true, dost	*40*
Re 11:2	the **h.** city shall they tread under foot	*40*
Re 14:10	the presence of the **h.** angels, and in	*40*
Re 15:4	for thou only art **h.**: for all nations	*3741*
Re 18:20	and ye **h.** apostles and prophets;	*40*
Re 20:6	Blessed and **h.** is he that hath part	*40*
Re 21:2	John saw the **h.** city, new Jerusalem,	*40*
Re 21:10	me that great city, the **h.** Jerusalem.	*40*
Re 22:6	God of the **h.** prophets sent his angel	*40*
Re 22:11	and that is **h.**, let him be...still.	*40*
Re 22:11	and he that is...let him be **h.** still.	*37*
Re 22:19	book of life, and out of the **h.** city,	*40*

HOLYDAY See also HOLY and DAY.

Ref	Context	No.
Ps 42:4	with a multitude that kept **h.**.	2287
Col 2:16	in respect of an **h.**, or of the new	*1859*

HOLY GHOST See HOLY and GHOST.

HOLY ONE See HOLY and ONE.

HOLY PLACE See HOLY and PLACE.

HOLY SPIRIT See HOLY and SPIRIT.

HOMAM (ho'-mam) See also HEMAM.
1Ch 1:39 the sons of Lotan; Hori and **H.**:......... 1950

HOME See also HOMEBORN.
Ge 39:16 by her, until his lord came **h.**........... 1004
Ge 43:16 Bring these men **h.**, and slay, and...... 1004
Ge 43:26 And when Joseph came **h.**, they......... 1004
Ex 9:19 the field, and shall not be brought **h.**,.. 1004
Le 18:9 she be born at **h.**, or born abroad, ... 1004
De 21:12 shalt bring her **h.** to thine house; 8432
De 24:5 but he shall be free at **h.** one year. 1004
Jos 2:18 father's household, **h.** unto thee.......... 1004
Jg 11:9 If ye bring me **h.** again to fight.......... 7725
Jg 19:9 your way, that thou mayest go **h.**........ 168
Ru 1:21 hath brought me **h.** again empty:........ 7725
1Sa 2:20 And they went unto their own **h.**. 4725
1Sa 6:7 bring their calves **h.** from them:......... 1004
1Sa 6:10 cart, and shut up their calves at **h.**: 1004
1Sa 10:26 And Saul also went **h.** to Gibeah; 1004
1Sa 18:2 go no more **h.** to his father's house. ... 7725
1Sa 24:22 And Saul went **h.**; but David and........ 1004
2Sa 13:7 David sent **h.** to Tamar, saying,......... 1004
2Sa 14:13 not fetch **h.** again his banished............ 7725
2Sa 17:23 and gat him **h.** to his house, to his 1004
1Ki 5:14 in Lebanon, and two months at **h.**: 1004
1Ki 13:7 Come **h.** with me, and refresh thyself..1004
1Ki 13:15 Come **h.** with me, and eat bread........ 1004
2Ki 14:10 glory of this, and tarry at **h.**: for......... 1004
1Ch 13:12 shall I bring the ark of God **h.** to me? ....
1Ch 13:13 So David brought not the ark **h.** to...........
2Ch 25:10 our of Ephraim, to go **h.** again:.......... 4725
2Ch 25:10 and they returned **h.** in great anger. ... 4725
2Ch 25:19 abide now at **h.**; why shouldest.......... 1004
Es 5:10 and when he came **h.**, he sent and...... 1004
Job 39:12 him, that he will bring **h.** thy seed,..... 7725
Ps 68:12 that tarried at **h.** divided the spoil. 1004
Pr 7:19 For the goodman is not at **h.**, he is 1004
Pr 7:20 will come **h.** at the day appointed........ 1004
Ec 12:5 man goeth to his long **h.**, and the....... 1004
Jer 39:14 that he should carry him **h.**: so he....... 1004
La 1:20 bereaveth, at **h.** there is as death. 1004
Hab 2:5 proud man, neither keepeth at **h.**, ... 5115
Hag 1:9 when ye brought it **h.**, I did blow....... 1004
Mt 8:6 my servant lieth at **h.** sick of the *3614*
Mk 5:19 **Go h. to thy friends, and tell them** *3624*
Lu 9:61 bid them farewell, which are at **h.** at.........
Lu 15:6 **And when he cometh h., he calleth** *3624*
Joh 19:27 that disciple took her unto his own **h.**. *3624*
Joh 20:10 went away again unto their own **h.**. *1438*
Ac 21:6 ship; and they returned **h.** again........ *2398*
1Co 11:34 any man hunger, let him eat at **h.**........ *3624*
1Co 14:35 let them ask their husbands at **h.**........ *3624*
2Co 5:6 whilst we are at **h.** in the body, we *1736*
1Ti 5:4 learn first to shew piety at **h.**, and *2398*
Tit 2:5 be discreet, chaste, keepers at **h.**, ... *3626*

HOMEBORN
Ex 12:49 One law shall be to him that is **h.**, ... 249
Jer 2:14 Israel a servant? is he a **h.** slave? 1004

HOMER (ho'-mer) See also HOLMERS.
Le 27:16 an **h.** of barley seed shall be valued 2563
Isa 5:10 seed of an **h.** shall yield an ephah....... 2563
Eze 45:11 may contain the tenth part of an **h.**,.... 2563
Eze 45:11 the ephah the tenth part of an **h.** 2563
Eze 45:11 measure thereof shall be after the **h.**. . 2563
Eze 45:13 part of an ephah of an **h.** of wheat,..... 2563
Eze 45:13 part of an ephah of an **h.** of barley: 2563
Eze 45:14 the cor, which is an **h.** of ten baths; ... 2563
Eze 45:14 ten baths; for ten baths are an **h.**....... 2563
Ho 3:2 of silver, and for an **h.** of barley, ... 2563
Ho 3:2 of barley, and an half **h.** of barley:...... 3963

HOMERS (ho'-mers)
Nu 11:32 gathered least gathered ten **h.**........... 2563

HONEST See also DISHONEST.
Lu 8:15 **which in an h. and good heart**...... *2570*
Ac 6:3 you seven men of **h.** report, full of the......
Ro 12:17 things **h.** in the sight of all men. *2570*
2Co 8:21 Providing for **h.** things, not only in..... *2570*
2Co 13:7 but ye should do that which is **h.**, ... *2570*
Php 4:8 are true, whatsoever things are **h.**, ... *4586*
1Pe 2:12 your conversation **h.** among the......... *2570*

HONESTLY
Ro 13:13 Let us walk **h.**, as in the day; not *2156*
1Th 4:12 That ye may walk **h.** toward them...... *2156*
Heb 13:18 in all things willing to live **h.**............. *2573*

HONESTY See also DISHONESTY.
1Ti 2:2 quiet...life in all godliness and **h.**. *4587*

HONEY See also HONEYCOMB.
Ge 43:11 a little balm, and a little **h.**, spices,..... 1706
Ex 3:8 a land flowing with milk and **h.**; 1706
Ex 3:17 a land flowing with milk and **h.**. 1706
Ex 13:5 a land flowing with milk and **h.**, ... 1706
Ex 16:31 of it was like wafers made with **h.**...... 1706
Ex 33:3 a land flowing with milk and **h.** 1706
Le 2:11 burn no leaven, nor any **h.**, in any...... 1706
Le 20:24 land that floweth with milk and **h.**:...... 1706
Nu 13:27 surely it floweth with milk and **h.**; 1706
Nu 14:8 land which floweth with milk and **h.**. ... 1706
Nu 16:13, 14 that floweth with milk and **h.**,........ 1706
De 6:3 land that floweth with milk and **h.**........ 1706
De 8:8 a land of oil olive, and **h.**; 1706
De 11:9 land that floweth with milk and **h.**........ 1706
De 26:9, 15 that floweth with milk and **h.**........ 1706
De 27:3 land that floweth with milk and **h.**;....... 1706
De 31:20 that floweth with milk and **h.**; and 1706
De 32:13 made him to suck **h.** out of the rock, .. 1706
Jos 5:6 land that floweth with milk and **h.**........ 1706
Jg 14:8 was a swarm of bees and **h.** in the 1706
Jg 14:9 had taken the **h.** out of the carcase 1706
Jg 14:18 What is sweeter than **h.**? and what..... 1706
1Sa 14:25 and there was **h.** upon the ground...... 1706
1Sa 14:26 the **h.** dropped; but no man put his 1706
1Sa 14:29 because I tasted a little of this **h.**. 1706
1Sa 14:43 I did but taste a little **h.** with the 1706
2Sa 17:29 And **h.**, and butter, and sheep, and 1706
1Ki 14:3 and cracknels, and a cruse of **h.**,........ 1706
2Ki 18:32 a land of oil olive and of **h.**, that ye 1706
2Ch 31:5 wine, and oil, and **h.**, and of all the 1706
Job 20:17 floods, the brooks of **h.** and butter. 1706
Ps 19:10 gold: sweeter also than **h.** and the...... 1706
Ps 81:16 and with **h.** out of the rock should I.... 1706
Ps 119:103 yea, sweeter than **h.** to my mouth! 1706
Pr 24:13 son, eat thou **h.**, because it is good;... 1706
Pr 25:16 Hast thou found **h.**? eat so much as.... 1706
Pr 25:27 It is not good to eat much **h.**: so for.... 1706
Ca 4:11 **h.** and milk are under thy tongue; 1706
Ca 5:1 eaten my honeycomb with my **h.**;........ 1706
Isa 7:15 Butter and **h.** shall he eat, that he...... 1706
Isa 7:22 for butter and **h.** shall every one eat... 1706
Jer 11:5 a land flowing with milk and **h.**, as...... 1706
Jer 32:22 a land flowing with milk and **h.**; 1706
Jer 41:8 and of barley, and of oil, and of **h.**...... 1706
Eze 3:3 in my mouth as **h.** for sweetness. 1706
Eze 16:13 didst eat fine flour, and **h.**, and oil:..... 1706
Eze 16:19 gave thee, fine flour, and oil, and **h.**, .. 1706
Eze 20:6, 15 flowing with milk and **h.**, which...... 1706
Eze 27:17 Pannag, and **h.**, and oil, and balm....... 1706
Mt 3:4 his meat was locusts and wild **h.**........ *3192*
Mk 1:6 and he did eat locusts and wild **h.**; *3192*
Re 10:9 it shall be in thy mouth sweet as **h.**.... *3192*
Re 10:10 it was in my mouth sweet as **h.**:......... *3192*

HONEYCOMB
1Sa 14:27 and dipped it in an **h.**, and put.... 3295,1706
Ps 19:10 also than honey and the **h.**.......... 5317,6688
Pr 5:3 a strange woman drop as an **h.**,.......... 5317
Pr 16:24 Pleasant words are as an **h.**,....... 6688,1706
Pr 24:13 the **h.**, which is sweet to thy taste: 5317
Pr 27:7 The full soul loatheth an **h.**; but to 5317
Ca 4:11 lips, O my spouse, drop as the **h.**....... 5317
Ca 5:1 have eaten my **h.** with my honey; 3293
Lu 24:42 a broiled fish, and of an **h.**.......... *3193,2781*

HONOUR See also DISHONOUR; HONOURABLE; HONOURED; HONOURETH; HONOURS.
Ge 49:6 mine **h.**, be not thou united: for......... 3519
Ex 14:17 and I will get me **h.** upon Pharaoh,..... 3513
Ex 14:18 I have gotten me **h.** upon Pharaoh,..... 3513
Ex 20:12 **H.** thy father and thy mother: that...... 3513
Le 19:15 nor **h.** the person of the mighty:.......... 1921
Le 19:32 and **h.** the face of the old man, and..... 1921
Nu 22:17 promote thee unto very great **h.**,........ 3513
Nu 22:37 able indeed to promote thee to **h.**?..... 3513
Nu 24:11 to promote thee unto great **h.**: but,..... 3513
Nu 24:11 Lord hath kept thee back from **h.**........ 3519
Nu 27:20 put some of thine **h.** upon him,.......... 1935
De 5:16 **H.** thy father and thy mother, as 3513
De 26:19 in praise, and in name, and in **h.**;....... 8597
Jg 4:9 thou takest shall not be for thine **h.**;... 8597
Jg 9:9 by me they **h.** God and man, and......... 3513
Jg 13:17 come to pass we may do thee **h.**?...... 3513
1Sa 2:30 them that **h.** me I will **h.**, and they 3513
1Sa 15:30 sinned: yet **h.** me now, I pray thee, ... 3513
2Sa 6:22 of, of them shall I be had in **h.**. 3513
2Sa 10:3 thou that David doth **h.** thy father, ... 3513
1Ki 3:13 hast not asked, both riches, and **h.**;.... 3519
1Ch 16:27 Glory and **h.** are in his presence: 1926
1Ch 17:18 to thee, for the **h.** of thy servant?...... 3519
1Ch 19:3 thou that David doth **h.** thy father, ... 3513
1Ch 29:12 Both riches and **h.** come of thee, ... 3519
1Ch 29:28 old age, full of days, riches, and **h.**..... 3519
2Ch 1:11 hast not asked riches, wealth, or **h.**,... 3519
2Ch 1:12 give thee riches, and wealth, and **h.**, .. 3519
2Ch 17:5 he had riches and **h.** in abundance. 3519
2Ch 18:1 had riches and **h.** in abundance, and.... 3519
2Ch 26:18 neither shall it be for thine **h.** from..... 3519
2Ch 32:27 exceeding much riches and **h.**: and 3519
2Ch 32:33 inhabitants of Jerusalem did him **h.** 3519
Es 1:4 and the **h.** of his excellent majesty 3366
Es 1:20 shall give to their husbands **h.**, both ... 3366
Es 6:3 What **h.** and dignity hath been done.... 3366
Es 6:6 whom the king delighteth to **h.**?........ 3366
Es 6:6 would the king delight to do **h.** more .. 3366
Es 6:7, 9 whom the king delighteth to **h.**, ... 3366
Es 6:9, 11 whom the king delighteth to **h.**. 3366
Es 8:16 light, and gladness, and joy, and **h.**...... 3366
Job 14:21 sons come to **h.**, and he knoweth....... 3513
Ps 7:5 earth, and lay mine **h.** in the dust. 3519
Ps 8:5 crowned him with glory and **h.**. 1926
Ps 21:5 **h.** and majesty hast thou laid upon...... 1935
Ps 26:8 the place where thine **h.** dwelleth....... 3519
Ps 49:12 man being in **h.** abideth not: he is 3366
Ps 49:20 that is in **h.**, and understandeth not, ... 3366
Ps 66:2 Sing forth the **h.** of his name:............ 3519
Ps 71:8 praise and with thy **h.** all the day. 8597
Ps 91:15 I will deliver him, and **h.** him............ 3515
Ps 96:6 **H.** and majesty are before him: 1935
Ps 104:1 art clothed with **h.** and majesty.......... 1935
Ps 112:9 his horn shall be exalted with **h.**. 3519
Ps 145:5 the glorious **h.** of thy majesty, and 1926
Ps 149:9 written: this **h.** have all his saints...... 1926
Pr 3:9 **H.** the Lord with thy substance. 3513
Pr 3:16 and in her left hand riches and **h.**. 3519
Pr 4:8 she shall bring thee to **h.**, when......... 3513
Pr 5:9 Lest thou give thine **h.** unto others, ... 1935
Pr 8:18 Riches and **h.** are with me; yea, ... 3519
Pr 11:16 A gracious woman retaineth **h.** 3519
Pr 14:28 multitude of people is the king's **h.**...... 1927
Pr 15:33 wisdom; and before **h.** is humility....... 3519
Pr 18:12 haughty, and before **h.** is humility....... 3519
Pr 20:3 It is an **h.** for a man to cease from...... 3519
Pr 21:21 findeth life, righteousness, and **h.**....... 3519
Pr 22:4 the Lord are riches, and **h.**, and life. .. 3519
Pr 25:2 but the **h.** of kings is to search out..... 3519
Pr 26:1 harvest, so **h.** is not seemly for a fool..3519
Pr 26:8 so is he that giveth **h.** to a fool.......... 3519
Pr 29:23 **h.** shall uphold the humble in spirit. 3519
Pr 31:25 Strength and **h.** are her clothing;........ 1926
Ec 6:2 riches, wealth, and **h.**, so that he......... 3519
Ec 10:1 is in reputation for wisdom and **h.**. 3519
Isa 29:13 with their lips do **h.** me, but have 3513
Isa 43:20 The beast of the field shall **h.** me,....... 3513
Isa 58:13 and shalt **h.** him, not doing thine........ 3513
Jer 33:9 a praise and an **h.** before all the......... 8597
Da 2:6 me gifts and rewards and great **h.**....... 3367
Da 4:30 of my power, and for the **h.** of my 3367
Da 4:36 mine **h.** and brightness returned......... 1923
Da 4:37 extol and **h.** the King of heaven, all.... 1922
Da 5:18 and majesty, and glory, and **h.**:.......... 1923
Da 11:21 not give the **h.** of the kingdom: 1935
Da 11:38 shall he **h.** the God of forces: and 3513
Da 11:38 his fathers knew not shall he **h.** 3513
Mal 1:6 I be a father, where is mine **h.**? 3519
Mt 13:57 **A prophet is not without h., save in** *820*
Mt 15:4 **H. thy father and mother: and he** *5091*
Mt 15:6 **h. not his father or his mother, he** *5091*
Mt 19:19 **H. thy father and thy mother:** *5091*
Mk 6:4 **A prophet is not without h., but in** *820*
Mk 7:10 **H. thy father and thy mother';** *5091*
Mk 10:19 **not; H. thy father and mother** *5091*
Lu 18:20 **h. thy father and thy mother** *5091*
Joh 4:44 hath no **h.** in his own country............ *5092*

Joh 5:23 all men should h. the Son, father.. 5091
Joh 5:23 the Son, even as they h. the......... 5091
Joh 5:41 I receive not h. from men............ 1391
Joh 5:44 which receive h. one of another, ... 1391
Joh 5:44 the h. that cometh from God only?.1391
Joh 8:49 but I h. my Father, and ye do....... 5091
Joh 8:54 Jesus answered, If I h. myself........ 1392
Joh 8:54 if I...myself, my h. is nothing:...... 1391
Joh 12:26 serve me, him will my Father h.... 5091
Ro 2:7 for glory and h. and immortality,........ 5092
Ro 2:10 But glory, h., and peace, to every..... 5092
Ro 9:21 to make one vessel unto h., and......... 5092
Ro 12:10 love; in h. preferring one another;....... 5092
Ro 13:7 fear to whom fear; h. to whom h....... 5092
1Co 12:23 these we bestow more abundant h.; ... 5092
1Co 12:24 given more abundant h. to that.......... 5092
2Co 6:8 h. and dishonour, by evil report........... 1391
Eph 6:2 H. thy father and mother; which........ 5091
Col 2:23 not in any h. to the satisfying of........ 5092
1Th 4:4 his vessel in sanctifiction and h.;........ 5092
1Ti 1:17 be h. and glory for ever and ever...... 5092
1Ti 5:3 H. widows that are widows indeed..... 5091
1Ti 5:17 be counted worthy of double h.,......... 5092
1Ti 6:1 their own masters worthy of all h.,...... 5092
1Ti 6:16 whom be h. and power everlasting:.... 5092
2Ti 2:20 some to h., and some to dishonour..... 5092
2Ti 2:21 be a vessel unto h., sanctified, and..... 5092
Heb 2:7 crownedst him with glory and h........ 5092
Heb 2:9 death, crowned with glory and h.;....... 5092
Heb 3:3 builded the house hath more h........... 5092
Heb 5:4 no man taketh this h. unto himself,..... 5092
1Pe 1:7 might be found unto praise and h....... 5092
1Pe 2:17 H. all men. Love the brotherhood...... 5091
1Pe 2:17 Fear God. H. the king...................... 5091
1Pe 3:7 giving h. unto the wife, as unto......... 5092
2Pe 1:17 from God the Father h. and glory,..... 5092
Re 4:9 beasts give glory and h. and thanks.... 5092
Re 4:11 to receive glory and h. and power:..... 5092
Re 5:12 and h., and glory, and blessing........... 5092
Re 5:13 Blessing, and h., and glory, and......... 5092
Re 7:12 h., and power, and might, be unto..... 5092
Re 19:1 Salvation, and glory, and h., and........ 5092
Re 19:7 and rejoice, and give h. to him:.......... 1391
Re 21:24 do bring their glory and h. into it........ 5092
Re 21:26 bring the glory and h. of the nations... 5092

HONOURABLE
Ge 34:19 was more h. than all the house of...... 3513
Nu 22:15 more, and more h. than they........... 3513
1Sa 9:6 man of God, and he is an h. man;...... 3513
1Sa 22:14 bidding, and is h. in thine house?...... 3513
2Sa 23:19 Was he not most h. of three?........... 3513
2Sa 23:23 He was more h. than the thirty.......... 3513
2Ki 5:1 man with his master, and h.,...... 5375,6440
1Ch 4:9 was more h. than his brethren:............ 3513
1Ch 11:21 three, he was more h. than the two;.. 3513
1Ch 11:25 he was h. among the thirty, but......... 3513
Job 22:8 and the h. man dwelt in it........ 5375,6440
Ps 45:9 were among thy h. women: upon........ 3368
Ps 111:3 His work is h. and glorious: and........ 1935
Isa 3:3 of fifty, and the h. man, and...... 5375,6440
Isa 3:5 ancient, and...base against the h....... 3519
Isa 5:13 and their h. men are famished, and..... 3519
Isa 9:15 ancient and h., he is the head;... 5375,6440
Isa 23:8 traffickers are the h. of the earth?...... 1935
Isa 23:9 contempt all the h. of the earth......... 3513
Isa 42:21 magnify the law, and make it h......... 142
Isa 43:4 thou hast been h., and I have loved.... 3513
Isa 58:13 delight, the holy of the Lord, h.; and... 3513
Na 3:10 and they cast lots for her h. men,........ 3513
Mk 15:43 of Arimathaea, an h. counsellor,......... 2158
Lu 14:8 more h. man than thou be bidden.. 1784
Ac 13:50 up the devout and h. women,............ 2158
Ac 17:12 of h. women which were Greeks,........ 2158
1Co 4:10 ye are h., but we are despised........... 1741
1Co 12:23 body, which we think to be less h.,..... 820
Heb 13:4 Marriage is h. in all, and the bed....... 5093

HONOURED
Ex 14:4 and I will be h. upon Pharaoh,........... 3513
Pr 13:18 that regardeth reproof shall be h........ 3513
Pr 27:18 waiteth on his master shall be h......... 3513
Isa 43:23 hast thou h. me with thy sacrifices..... 3513
La 1:8 all that h. her despise her, because.... 3513
La 5:12 the faces of elders were not h........... 1921
Da 4:34 and h. him that liveth for ever,........... 1922
Ac 28:10 also h. us with many honours;.......... 5092
1Co 12:26 one member be h., all the members... 1392

HONOUREST See also DISHONOUREST.
1Sa 2:29 and h. thy sons above me, to make.... 3513

HONOURETH See also DISHONOURETH.
Ps 15:4 but he h. them that fear the Lord...... 3513
Pr 12:9 better than he that h. himself, and...... 3513
Pr 14:31 that h. him hath mercy on the poor..... 3513
Mal 1:6 A son h. his father, and a servant...... 3513
Mt 15:8 mouth, and h. me with their lips;.. 5091
Mk 7:6 This people h. me with their lips,.. 5091
Joh 5:23 that h. not the Son h. not the....... 5091
Joh 8:54 it is my Father that h. me; of....... 1392

HONOURS
Ac 28:10 also honoured us with many h.;......... 5091

HOODS
Isa 3:23 linen, and the h., and the vails.......... 6797

HOOF See also HOOFS.
Ex 10:26 shall not an h. be left behind;............ 6541
Le 11:3 Whatsoever parteth the h., and is....... 6541
Le 11:4 cud, or of them that divide the h.:...... 6541
Le 11:4, 5,6 cud, but divideth not the h.;......... 6541
Le 11:7 the swine, though he divide the h....... 6541
Le 11:26 every beast which divideth the h.,....... 6541
De 14:6 And every beast that parteth the h.,.... 6541
De 14:7 of them that divide the cloven h.;....... 6541
De 14:7 chew the cud, but divide not the h.;... 6541
De 14:8 swine, because it divideth the h.,........ 6541

HOOFS See also HORSEHOOFS.
Ps 69:31 or bullock that hath horns and h......... 6536
Isa 5:28 horses' h. shall be counted like.......... 6541
Jer 47:3 the noise of the stamping of the h...... 6541
Eze 26:11 the h. of his horses shall he tread....... 6541
Eze 32:13 nor the h. of beasts trouble them....... 6541
Mic 4:13 iron, and I will make thy h. brass:...... 6541

HOOK See also HOOKS.
2Ki 19:28 I will put my h. in thy nose,............. 2397
Job 41:1 draw out leviathan with an h.?............ 100
Job 41:2 thou put an h. into his nose?............. 2443
Isa 37:29 will I put my h. in thy nose,............. 2397
Mt 17:27 go thou to the sea, and cast an h.,... 44

HOOKS See also FISHHOOKS; PRUNINGHOOKS.
Ex 26:32 their h. shall be of gold, upon the...... 2053
Ex 26:37 gold, and their h. shall be of gold:...... 2053
Ex 27:10, 11 h. of the pillars and their fillets...... 2053
Ex 27:17 their h. shall be of silver, and their..... 2053
Ex 36:36 with gold: their h. were of gold;........ 2053
Ex 36:38 the five pillars of it with their h.:....... 2053
Ex 38:10, 11,12,17, the h. of the pillars and....... 2053
Ex 38:19 their h. of silver, and the overlaying... 2053
Ex 38:28 shekels he made h. for the pillars,....... 2053
Isa 18:5 cut off the sprigs with pruning h.,............
Eze 29:4 But I will put h. in thy jaws, and........ 2397
Eze 38:4 thee back, and put h. into thy jaws,.... 2397
Eze 40:43 And within were h., an hand broad,.... 8240
Am 4:2 that he will take you away with h.,...... 6793

HOPE See also HOPED; HOPE'S; HOPETH; HOPING.
Ru 1:12 if I should say, I have h., if I............ 8615
Ezr 10:2 yet now there is h. in Israel.............. 4723
Job 4:6 thy fear, thy confidence, thy h.,......... 8615
Job 5:16 So the poor hath h., and iniquity......... 8615
Job 6:11 is my strength, that I should h.?......... 3176
Job 7:6 shuttle, and are spent without h......... 8615
Job 8:13 and the hypocrite's h. shall perish:..... 8615
Job 8:14 Whose h. shall be cut off; and........... 3689
Job 11:18 be secure, because there is h.:........... 8615
Job 11:20 their h. shall be as the giving up......... 8615
Job 14:7 there is h. of a tree, if it be cut down,. 8615
Job 14:19 and thou destroyest the h. of man...... 8615
Job 17:15 And where is now my h.? as for......... 8615
Job 17:15 as for my h., who shall see it?.......... 8615
Job 19:10 mine h. hath he removed like a tree... 8615
Job 27:8 For what is the h. of the hypocrite,.... 8615
Job 31:24 If I have made gold my h., or have..... 3689
Job 41:9 Behold, the h. of him is in vain:.......... 8431
Ps 16:9 my flesh also shall rest in h............ 983
Ps 22:9 didst make me h. when I was upon...... 982
Ps 31:24 heart, all ye that h. in the Lord.......... 3176
Ps 33:18 upon them that h. in his mercy;.......... 3176
Ps 33:22 upon us, according as we h. in thee..... 3176
Ps 38:15 in thee, O Lord, do I h.: thou wilt..... 3176
Ps 39:7 what wait I for? my h. is in thee........ 8431
Ps 42:5 disquieted in me? h. thou in God:........ 3176
Ps 42:11 within me? h. thou in God:............... 3176
Ps 43:5 disquieted within me? h. in God:........ 3176
Ps 71:5 For thou art my h., O Lord God:........ 8615
Ps 71:14 But I will h. continually, and will......... 3176
Ps 78:7 they might set their h. in God,............ 3689
Ps 119:49 which thou hast caused me to h.......... 3176
Ps 119:81 salvation: but I h. in thy word............ 3176
Ps 119:114 and my shield: I h. in thy word........... 3176
Ps 119:116 let me not be ashamed of my h......... 7664
Ps 130:5 doth wait, and in his word do I h....... 3176
Ps 130:7 Let Israel h. in the Lord: for with....... 3176
Ps 131:3 Let Israel h. in the Lord from............ 3176
Ps 146:5 whose h. is in the Lord his God:........ 7664
Ps 147:11 him, in those that h. in his mercy...... 3176
Pr 10:28 The h. of the righteous shall be......... 8431
Pr 11:7 and the h. of unjust men perisheth...... 8431
Pr 13:12 H. deferred maketh the heart sick:..... 8431
Pr 14:32 the righteous hath h. in his death....... 2620
Pr 19:18 Chasten thy son while there is h.,...... 8615
Pr 26:12 is more h. of a fool than of him......... 8615
Pr 29:20 is more h. of a fool than of him......... 8615
Ec 9:4 joined to all the living there is h.:......... 986
Isa 38:18 into the pit cannot h. for thy truth...... 7663
Isa 57:10 saidst thou not, There is no h.:.......... 2976
Jer 2:25 but thou saidst, There is no h.:......... 2976
Jer 14:8 O the h. of Israel, the saviour............ 4723
Jer 17:7 Lord, and whose h. the Lord is,........ 4009
Jer 17:13 O Lord, the h. of Israel, all that........ 4723
Jer 17:17 thou art my h. in the day of evil......... 4268
Jer 18:12 And they said, There is no h.:.......... 2976
Jer 31:17 And there is h. in thine end, saith....... 8615
Jer 50:7 the Lord, the h. of their fathers........ 4723
La 3:18 strength and my h. is perished.......... 8431
La 3:21 to my mind, therefore have I h........... 3176
La 3:24 soul; therefore will I h. in him........... 3176
La 3:26 good that a man should both h.......... 2342
La 3:29 the dust; if so be there may be h....... 8615
Eze 13:6 and they have made othes to h.......... 3176
Eze 19:5 had waited, and her h. was lost,........ 8615
Eze 37:11 bones are dried, and our h. is lost:...... 8615
Ho 2:15 the valley of Achor for a door of h.:... 8615
Joe 3:16 Lord will be the h. of his people,........ 4268
Zec 9:12 the strong hold, ye prisoners of h.:.... 8615
Lu 6:34 to them of whom ye h. to receive.. 1679
Ac 2:26 also my flesh shall rest in h.:............ 1680
Ac 16:19 that the h. of their gains was gone,..... 1680
Ac 23:6 the h. and resurrection of the dead..... 1680
Ac 24:15 And have h. toward God, which......... 1680
Ac 26:6 am judged for the h. of the promise.... 1680
Ac 26:7 God day and night, h. to come.......... 1679
Ac 27:20 all h. that we should be saved was...... 1680
Ac 28:20 that for the h. of Israel I am bound.... 1680
Ro 4:18 Who against h. believed in h., that...... 1680
Ro 5:2 and rejoice in h. of the glory of God.. 1680
Ro 5:4 experience; and experience, h.:.......... 1680
Ro 5:5 And h. maketh not ashamed:............. 1680
Ro 8:20 who hath subjected the same in h.,.... 1680
Ro 8:24 for we are saved by h.:................... 1680
Ro 8:24 but h. that is seen is not h.:............. 1680
Ro 8:24 man seeth, why doth he yet h. for?.... 1679
Ro 8:25 But if we h. for that we see not,....... 1679
Ro 12:12 Rejoicing in h.; patient in................. 1680
Ro 15:4 of the scriptures might have h.......... 1680
Ro 15:13 the God of h. fill you with all joy and.. 1680
Ro 15:13 that ye may abound in h., through...... 1680
1Co 9:10 he that ploweth should plow in h.;...... 1680
1Co 9:10 and that he that thresheth in h.......... 1680
1Co 9:10 should be partaker of his h.............. 1680
1Co 13:13 And now abideth faith, h., charity,...... 1680
1Co 15:19 If in this life only we have h. in......... 1679
2Co 1:7 And our h. of you is stedfast,........... 1680
2Co 3:12 Seeing then that we have such h.,...... 1680
2Co 10:15 but having h., when your faith is........ 1680
Ga 5:5 wait for the h. of righteousness by..... 1680
Eph 1:18 know what is the h. of his calling,...... 1680
Eph 2:12 having no h., and without God in....... 1680
Eph 4:4 are called in one h. of your calling;..... 1680
Php 1:20 my earnest expectation and my h.,..... 1680
Php 2:23 Him therefore I h. to send................ 1679
Col 1:5 the h. which is laid up for you in........ 1680
Col 1:23 away from the h. of the gospel,......... 1680
Col 1:27 Christ in you, the h. of glory:............ 1680
1Th 1:3 patience of h. in our Lord Jesus......... 1680
1Th 2:19 For what is our h., or joy, or crown... 1680
1Th 4:13 even as others which have no h......... 1680
1Th 5:8 for an helmet, the h. of salvation........ 1680
2Th 2:16 and good h. through grace,............... 1680
1Ti 1:1 Lord Jesus Christ, which is our h.;..... 1680

Tit 1:2 In **h.** of eternal life, which God, ... *1680*
Tit 2:13 Looking for that blessed **h.**, and......... *1680*
Tit 3:7 according to the **h.** of eternal life. *1680*
Heb 3:6 confidence and rejoicing of the **h.** *1680*
Heb 6:11 full assurance of **h.** unto the end: *1680*
Heb 6:18 lay hold upon the **h.** set before us: *1680*
Heb 6:19 which **h.** we have as an anchor of............
Heb 7:19 the bringing in of a better **h.** did; *1680*
1Pe 1:3 begotten us again unto a lively **h.** *1680*
1Pe 1:13 and **h.** to the end for the grace that.... *1679*
1Pe 1:21 your faith and **h.** might be in God....... *1680*
1Pe 3:15 a reason of the **h.** that is in you......... *1680*
1Jo 3:3 every man that hath this **h.** in him...... *1680*

HOPED
Es 9:1 the enemies of the Jews **h.** to have 7663
Job 6:20 confounded because they had **h.**; 982
Ps 119:43 for I have **h.** in thy judgments. 3176
Ps 119:74 because I have **h.** in thy word. 3176
Ps 119:147 and cried: I **h.** in thy word................ 3176
Ps 119:166 Lord, I have **h.** for thy salvation, ... 7663
Jer 3:23 Truly in vain is salvation **h.** for from.........
Lu 23:8 he **h.** to have seen some miracle........ *1679*
Ac 24:26 He **h.** also that the money should........ *1679*
2Co 8:5 And this they did, not as we **h.**, but... *1679*
Heb 11:1 is the substance of things **h.** for, ... *1679*

HOPE'S
Ac 26:7 For which **h.** sake, king Agrippa, I..... *1679*

HOPETH
1Co 13:7 believeth all things, **h.** all things, ... *1679*

HOPHNI (hof'-ni)
1Sa 1:3 two sons of Eli, **H.** and Phinehas, ... 2652
1Sa 2:34 thy two sons, on **H.** and Phinehas; 2652
1Sa 4:4 **H.** and Phinehas, were there with...... 2652
1Sa 4:11 two sons of Eli, **H.** and Phinehas, ... 2652
1Sa 4:17 **H.** and Phinehas are dead, and 2652

HOPHRA See PHARAOH-HOPHRA.

HOPING
Lu 6:35 **and lend, h. for nothing again;** *560*
1Ti 3:14 thee, **h.** to come unto thee shortly: *1679*

HOPPER See GRASSHOPPER.

HOR (hor) See also HOR-HAGIDGAD.
Nu 20:22 Kadesh, and came unto mount **H.** 2023
Nu 20:23 unto Moses and Aaron in mount **H.**,..... 2023
Nu 20:25 and bring them up unto mount **H.** 2023
Nu 20:27 and they went up into mount **H.** 2023
Nu 21:4 And they journeyed from mount **H.** 2023
Nu 33:37 Kadesh, and pitched in mount **H.**, ... 2023
Nu 33:38 the priest went up into mount **H.**......... 2023
Nu 33:39 years old when he died in mount **H.**.. . 2023
Nu 33:41 And they departed from mount **H.**,...... 2023
Nu 34:7 ye shall point out for you mount **H.** 2023
Nu 34:8 From mount **H.** ye shall point out 2023
De 32:50 thy brother died in mount **H.**, and........ 2023

HORAM (ho'-ram)
Jos 10:33 Then **H.** king of Gezer came up......... 2036

HOREB (ho'-reb) See also SINAI.
Ex 3:1 the mountain of God, even to **H.**. 2722
Ex 17:6 thee there upon the rock in **H.**; 2722
Ex 33:6 their ornaments by the mount **H.**. 2722
De 1:2 are eleven days' journey from **H.** 2722
De 1:6 Lord our God spake unto us in **H.**,..... 2722
De 1:19 And when we departed from **H.**, we... 2722
De 4:10 before the Lord thy God in **H.**, ... 2722
De 4:15 Lord spake unto you in **H.** out of....... 2722
De 5:2 God made a covenant with us in **H.**, ... 2722
De 9:8 Also in **H.** ye provoked the Lord to.... 2722
De 18:16 desiredst of the Lord thy God in **H.** ... 2722
De 29:1 which he made with them in **H.**. 2722
1Ki 8:9 stone, which Moses put there at **H.**, .. 2722
1Ki 19:8 nights unto **H.** the mount of God. 2722
2Ch 5:10 which Moses put therein at **H.**, ... 2722
Ps 106:19 made a calf in **H.**, and worshipped........ 2722
Mal 4:4 which I commanded unto him in **H.**..... 2722

HOREM (ho'-rem)
Jos 19:38 And Iron, and Migdal-el, **H.**,and........ 2765

HOR-HAGIDGAD (hor-hag-id'-gad) See also GUDGODAH.
Nu 33:32 Bene-jaakan,and encamped at **H.**........ 2735
Nu 33:33 they went from **H.**, and pitched 2735

HORI (ho'-ri) See also HORITE.
Ge 36:22 of Lotan were **H.** and Hemam; 2753
Ge 36:30 are the dukes that came of **H.**,.......... 2753
Nu 13:5 of Simeon, Shaphat, the son of **H.**..... 2753
1Ch 1:39 the sons of Lotan; **H.**, and Homam: 2753

HORIMS (ho'-rims) See also HORITES.
De 2:12 The **H.** also dwelt in Seir 2752
De 2:22 when he destroyed the **H.** from 2752

HORITE (ho'-rite) See also HORI; HORITES.
Ge 36:20 These are the sons of Seir the **H.**, ... 2752

HORITES (ho'-rites) See also HORIMS.
Ge 14:6 And the **H.** in their mount Seir, ... 2752
Ge 36:21 these are the dukes of the **H.**, the 2752
Ge 36:29 are the dukes that came of the **H.**;..... 2752

HORMAH (hor'-mah) See also ZEPHATH.
Nu 14:45 discomfited them, even unto **H.**. 2767
Nu 21:3 he called the name of the place **H.**. 2767
De 1:44 destroyed you in Seir, even unto **H.**.. . 2767
Jos 12:14 The king of **H.**, one; the king of........ 2767
Jos 15:30 And Eltolad, and Chesil, and **H.**,......... 2767
Jos 19:4 And Eltolad, and Bethul, and **H.**, ... 2767
Jg 1:17 the name of the city was called **H.**. 2767
1Sa 30:30 And to them which were in **H.**, ... 2767
1Ch 4:30 And at Bethuel, and at **H.**, and at 2767

HORN See also HORNS; INKHORN.
Ex 21:29 ox were wont to push with his **h.**........ 2767
Jos 6:5 a long blast with the ram's **h.**, ... 7161
1Sa 2:1 mine **h.** is exalted in the Lord: my 7161
1Sa 2:10 and exalt the **h.** of his anointed.......... 7161
1Sa 16:1 fill thine **h.** with oil, and go, I will 7161
1Sa 16:13 Then Samuel took the **h.** of oil, and.... 7161
2Sa 22:3 shield, and the **h.** of my salvation, ... 7161
1Ki 1:39 Zadok the priest took an **h.** of oil 7161
1Ch 25:5 the words of God, to lift up the **h.**. 7161
Job 16:15 skin, and defiled my **h.** in the dust. 7161
Ps 18:2 buckler, and the **h.** of my salvation, ... 7161
Ps 75:4 to the wicked, Lift not up the **h.**:........ 7161
Ps 75:5 Lift not up your **h.** on high: speak 7161
Ps 89:17 thy favour our **h.** shall be exalted. 7161
Ps 89:24 in my name shall his **h.** be exalted...... 7161
Ps 92:10 But my **h.** shalt thou exalt like 7161
Ps 92:10 thou exalt like the **h.** of an unicorn: ....
Ps 112:9 his **h.** shalt be exalted with honour. 7161
Ps 132:17 will I make the **h.** of David to bud:..... 7161
Ps 148:14 also exalteth the **h.** of his people,........ 7161
Jer 48:25 The **h.** of Moab is cut off,and his 7161
La 2:3 his fierce anger all the **h.** of Israel:..... 7161
La 2:17 set up the **h.** of thine adversaries....... 7161
Eze 29:21 the **h.** of the house of Israel to bud 7161
Da 7:8 up among them another little **h.**, ... 7162
Da 7:8 in this **h.** were eyes like the eyes of... 7162
Da 7:11 great words which the **h.** spake: 7162
Da 7:20 even of that **h.** that had eyes, and...... 7162
Da 7:21 same **h.** made war with the saints, ... 7162
Da 8:5 the goat had a notable **h.** between...... 7161
Da 8:8 strong, the great **h.** was broken;......... 7161
Da 8:9 one of them came forth a little **h.**,....... 7161
Da 8:21 great **h.** that is between his eyes 7161
Mic 4:13 I will make thine **h.** iron, and I will...... 7161
Zec 1:21 the Gentiles, which lifted up their **h.**.... 7161
Lu 1:69 hath raised up an **h.** of salvation......... *2768*

HORNET See also HORNETS.
De 7:20 God will send the **h.** among them,...... 6880
Jos 24:12 I sent the **h.** before you, which drave ..6880

HORNETS
Ex 23:28 And I will send **h.** before thee, ... 6880

HORNS
Ge 22:13 ram caught in a thicket by his **h.**........ 7161
Ex 27:2 And thou shalt make the **h.** of it 7161
Ex 27:2 his **h.** shall be of the same: and......... 7161
Ex 29:12 and put it upon the **h.** of the altar 7161
Ex 30:2 the **h.** thereof shall be of the same..... 7161
Ex 30:3 round about, and the **h.** thereof: 7161
Ex 30:10 an atonement upon the **h.** of it once ... 7161
Ex 37:25 the **h.** thereof were of the same. 7161
Ex 37:26 round about, and the **h.** of it: also 7161
Ex 38:2 he made the **h.** thereof on the four..... 7161
Ex 38:2 it: the **h.** thereof were of the same: ... 7161
Le 4:7 blood upon the **h.** of the altar of 7161
Le 4:18 blood upon the **h.** of the altar which.... 7161
Le 4:25, 30,34 upon the **h.** of the altar of........ 7161
Le 8:15 and put it upon the **h.** of the altar 7161
Le 9:9 and put it upon the **h.** of the altar, ... 7161
Le 16:18 and put it upon the **h.** of the altar 7161
De 33:17 his **h.** are like the **h.** of unicorns: 7161
Jos 6:4 ark seven trumpets of rams' **h.**: 3104
Jos 6:6 bear seven trumpets of rams' **h.** 3104
Jos 6:8 the seven trumpets of rams' **h.**........... 3104
Jos 6:13 seven trumpets of rams' **h.** before...... 3104
1Ki 1:50 caught hold on the **h.** of the altar. 7161
1Ki 1:51 caught hold on the **h.** of the altar, ... 7161
1Ki 2:28 caught hold on the **h.** of the altar. 7161
1Ki 22:11 And Zedekiah...made him **h.** of iron: ... 7161
2Ch 18:10 And Zedekiah...made him **h.** of iron, ... 7161
Ps 22:21 me from the **h.** of the unicorns. 7161
Ps 69:31 or bullock that hath **h.** and hoofs. 7160
Ps 75:10 the **h.** of the wicked also will I cut 7161
Ps 75:10 **h.** of the righteous shall be exalted. 7161
Ps 118:27 even unto the **h.** of the altar. 7161
Jer 17:1 and upon the **h.** of your altars; 7161
Eze 27:15 for a present **h.** of ivory and ebony. 7161
Eze 34:21 pushed all the diseased with your **h.**, .. 7161
Eze 43:15 altar and upward shall be four **h.**. 7161
Eze 43:20 thereof, and on the four **h.** of it, ... 7161
Da 7:7 were before it; and it had ten **h.**. 7162
Da 7:8 I considered the **h.**, and behold.......... 7162
Da 7:8 three of the first **h.** plucked up by...... 7162
Da 7:20 the ten **h.** that were in his head,........ 7162
Da 7:24 And the ten **h.** out of this kingdom...... 7162
Da 8:3 the river a ram which had two **h.**: 7161
Da 8:3 and the two **h.** were high; but one 7161
Da 8:6 came to the ram that had two **h.**,....... 7161
Da 8:7 smote the ram, and brake his two **h.**... 7161
Da 8:20 sawest having two **h.** are the kings..... 7161
Am 3:14 the **h.** of the altar shall be cut off, ... 7161
Am 6:13 Have we not taken to us **h.** by our..... 7161
Hab 3:4 he had **h.** coming out of his hand: 7161
Zec 1:18 eyes, and saw, and behold four **h.**. 7161
Zec 1:19, 21 **h.** which have scattered Judah, ... 7161
Zec 1:21 to cast out the **h.** of the Gentiles, ... 7161
Re 5:6 having seven **h.** and seven eyes, ... *2768*
Re 9:13 from the four **h.** of the golden altar *2768*
Re 12:3 having seven heads and ten **h.**,......... *2768*
Re 13:1 sea, having seven heads and ten **h.**, ... *2768*
Re 13:1 and upon his **h.** ten crowns, and *2768*
Re 13:11 he had two **h.** like a lamb, and he *2768*
Re 17:3 having seven heads and ten **h.** *2768*
Re 17:7 hath the seven heads and ten **h.**. *2768*
Re 17:12 the ten **h.** which thou sawest are *2768*
Re 17:16 the ten **h.** which thou sawest upon *2768*

HORON See BETH-HORON; HORONITE.

HORONAIM (hor-o-na'-im) See also HOLON.
Isa 15:5 in the way of **H.** they shall raise 2773
Jer 48:3 A voice of crying shall be from **H.**,..... 2773
Jer 48:5 for in the going down of **H.** the 2773
Jer 48:34 voice, from Zoar even unto **H.**, ... 2773

HORONITE (ho'-ron-ite)
Ne 2:10 When Sanballat the **H.**, and.............. 2772
Ne 2:19 But when Sanballat the **H.**, and 2772
Ne 13:28 was son in law to Sanballat the **H.**:...... 2772

HORRIBLE
Ps 11:6 brimstone,and an **h.** tempest: 2152
Ps 40:2 brought me up also out of an **h.** pit, ... 7588
Jer 5:30 A wonderful and **h.** thing is............... 8186
Jer 18:13 Israel hath done a very **h.** thing.......... 8186
Jer 23:14 prophets of Jerusalem an **h.** thing: 8186
Ho 6:10 I have seen an **h.** thing in the house... 8186

HORRIBLY
Jer 2:12 heavens, at this, and be **h.** afraid, ... 8175
Eze 32:10 their kings shall be **h.** afraid for 8178

HORROR
Ge 15:12 an **h.** of great darkness fell upon 367
Ps 55:5 and **h.** hath overwhelmed me. 6427
Ps 119:53 **H.** hath takenhold upon me.............. 2152
Eze 7:18 **h.** shall cover them; and shame 6427

HORSE See also HORSEBACK; HORSEHOOFS; HORSE-LEACH; HORSEMAN; HORSES.
Ge 49:17 the path, that biteth the **h.** heels,....... 5483
Ex 15:1 the **h.** and his rider hath he thrown 5483
Ex 15:19 For the **h.** of Pharaoh went in with..... 5483
Ex 15:21 the **h.** and his rider hath he thrown 5483
1Ki 10:29 and an **h.** for an hundred and fifty: 5483
1Ki 20:20 king of Syria escaped on an **h.** with 5483
1Ki 20:25 **h.** for **h.**, and chariot for chariot: 5483
2Ch 1:17 and an **h.** for an hundred and fifty: 5483
2Ch 23:15 come to the entering of the **h.** gate 5483
Ne 3:28 From above the **h.** gate repaired........ 5483

Es 6:8 the **h.** that the king rideth upon, 5483
Es 6:9 this apparel and **h.** be delivered 5483
Es 6:10 and take the apparel and the **h.**, 5483
Es 6:11 took Haman the apparel and the **h.**, 5483
Job 39:18 she scorneth the **h.** and his rider. 5483
Job 39:19 Hast thou given the **h.** strength? 5483
Ps 32:9 Be ye not as the **h.**, or as the mule, 5483
Ps 33:17 An **h.** is a vain thing for safety: 5483
Ps 76:6 both the chariot and **h.** are cast 5483
Ps 147:10 not in the strength of the **h.**: 5483
Pr 21:31 The **h.** is prepared against the day 5483
Pr 26:3 A whip for the **h.**, a bridle for the 5483
Isa 43:17 bringeth forth the chariot and **h.**, 5483
Isa 63:13 the deep, as an **h.** in the wilderness, 5483
Jer 8:6 as the **h.** rusheth into the battle 5483
Jer 31:40 unto the corner of the **h.** gate toward 5483
Jer 51:21 break in pieces the **h.** and his rider; 5483
Am 2:15 he that rideth the **h.** deliver himself 5483
Zec 1:8 behold a man riding upon a red **h.**, 5483
Zec 9:10 and the **h.** from Jerusalem, 5483
Zec 10:3 them as his goodly **h.** in the battle. 5483
Zec 12:4 smite every **h.** with astonishment, 5483
Zec 12:4 smite every **h.** of the people with 5483
Zec 14:15 And so shall be the plague of the **h.**, 5483
Re 6:2 I saw, and behold a white **h.**: and *2462*
Re 6:4 went out another **h.** that was red: *2462*
Re 6:5 I beheld, and lo a black **h.**; and he *2462*
Re 6:8 And I looked, and behold a pale **h.**: *2462*
Re 14:20 winepress, even unto the **h.** bridles, *2462*
Re 19:11 opened, and behold a white **h.**; *2462*
Re 19:19 war against him that sat on the **h.**, *2462*
Re 19:21 sword of him that sat upon the **h.**, *2462*

HORSEBACK
2Ki 9:18 there went one on **h.** to meet 7392,5483
2Ki 9:19 Then he sent out a second on **h.**; 5483
Es 6:9 on **h.** through the street of the 7392
Es 6:11 on **h.** through the street of the city, 7392
Es 8:10 and sent letters by posts on **h.**, 5483

HORSE-GATE See HORSE and GATE.

HORSE-HEELS See HORSE and HEELS.

HORSEHOOFS
Jg 5:22 Then were the **h.** broken by 6119,5483

HORSELEACH
Pr 30:15 the **h.** hath two daughters, 5936

HORSEMAN See also HORSEMEN.
2Ki 9:17 Joram said, Take an **h.**, and send 7395
Na 3:3 The **h.** lifteth up both the bright 6571

HORSEMEN
Ge 50:9 up with him both chariots and **h.** 6571
Ex 14:9 chariots of Pharaoh, and his **h.**, 6571
Ex 14:17 18 his chariots, and upon his **h.** 6571
Ex 14:23 horses, his chariots, and his **h.** 6571
Ex 14:26 their chariots, and upon their **h.** 6571
Ex 14:28 covered the chariots, and the **h.**, 6571
Ex 15:19 in with his chariots, and with his **h.** 6571
Jos 24:6 with chariots and **h.** unto the Red 6571
1Sa 8:11 for his chariots, and to be his **h.**; 6571
1Sa 13:5 chariots, and six thousand **h.**, 6571
2Sa 1:6 **h.** followed hard after him 1167,6571
2Sa 8:4 chariots,and seven hundred **h.**, 6571
2Sa 10:18 the Syrians, and forty thousand **h.**, 6571
1Ki 1:5 he prepared him chariots and **h.**, 6571
1Ki 4:26 chariots, and twelve thousand **h.** 6571
1Ki 9:19 for his chariots, and cities for his **h.**, 6571
1Ki 9:22 rulers of his chariots, and his **h.** 6571
1Ki 10:26 gathered together chariots and **h.** 6571
1Ki 10:26 chariots, and twelve thousand **h.**, 6571
1Ki 20:20 escaped on an horse with the **h.** 6571
2Ki 2:12 chariot of Israel, and the **h.** thereof. 6571
2Ki 13:7 he leave of the people...but fifty **h.**, 6571
2Ki 13:14 chariot of Israel, and the **h.** thereof. 6571
2Ki 18:24 on Egypt for chariots and for **h.**? 6571
1Ch 18:4 chariots, and seven thousand **h.**, 6571
1Ch 19:6 silver to hire them chariots and **h.** 6571
2Ch 1:14 Solomon gathered chariots and **h.**: 6571
2Ch 1:14 chariots, and twelve thousand **h.**, 6571
2Ch 8:6 cities, and the cities of the **h.**, and 6571
2Ch 8:9 and captains of his chariots and **h.** 6571
2Ch 9:25 chariots, and twelve thousand **h.**; 6571
2Ch 12:3 and threescore thousand **h.**: 6571
2Ch 16:8 with very many chariots and **h.**? 6571
Ezr 8:22 a band of soldiers and **h.** to help us 6571
Ne 2:9 had sent captains of the army and **h.** 6571
Isa 21:7 he saw a chariot with a couple of **h.**, 6571
Isa 21:9 chariot of men, with a couple of **h.** 6571
Isa 22:6 quiver with chariots of men and **h.**, 6571
Isa 22:7 the **h.** shall set themselves in array 6571
Isa 28:28 his cart, nor bruise it with his **h.** 6571
Isa 31:1 in **h.**, because they are very strong 6571
Isa 36:9 on Egypt for chariots and for **h.**? 6571
Jer 4:29 for the noise of the **h.** and bowmen; 6571
Jer 46:4 get up, ye **h.**, and stand forth with 6571
Eze 23:6 young men, **h.** riding upon horses. 6571
Eze 23:12 **h.** riding upon horses, all of them 6571
Eze 26:7 with chariots, and with **h.**, and 6571
Eze 26:10 shall shake at the noise of the **h.**, 6571
Eze 27:14 in thy fairs with horses and **h.** and 6571
Eze 38:4 and all thine army, horses and **h.**, 6571
Da 11:40 with chariots, and with **h.**, and with 6571
Ho 1:7 nor by battle, by horses, nor by **h.** 6571
Joe 2:4 and as **h.**, so shall they run 6571
Hab 1:8 their **h.** shall spread themselves, 6571
Hab 1:8 and their **h.** shall come from far; 6571
Ac 23:23 and **h.** threescore and ten, and *2460*
Ac 23:32 they left the **h.** to go with him, *2460*
Re 9:16 the number of the army of the **h.** *2461*

HORSES See also HORSES'.
Ge 47:17 them bread in exchange for **h.**, 5483
Ex 9:3 field, upon the **h.**, upon the asses, 5483
Ex 14:9 all the **h.** and chariots of Pharaoh, 5483
Ex 14:23 even all Pharaoh's **h.**, his chariots, 5483
De 11:4 unto their **h.**, and to their chariots; 5483
De 17:16 he shall not multiply **h.** to himself, 5483
De 17:16 the end that he should multiply **h.** 5483
De 20:1 and seest **h.**, and chariots, and a 5483
Jos 11:4 with **h.** and chariots very many 5483
Jos 11:6 thou shalt hough their **h.**, and burn 5483
Jos 11:9 he houghed their **h.**, and burnt 5483
2Sa 8:4 David houghed all the chariot **h.** but
2Sa 15:1 prepared him chariots and **h.**, 5483
1Ki 4:26 had forty thousand stalls of **h.** for 5483
1Ki 4:28 Barley also and straw for the **h.** and 5483
1Ki 10:25 armour, and spices, **h.**, and mules, 5483
1Ki 10:28 had **h.** brought out of Egypt, 5483
1Ki 18:5 grass to save the **h.** and mules alive, 5483
1Ki 20:1 with him, and **h.**, and chariots: 5483
1Ki 20:21 and smote the **h.** and chariots, and 5483
1Ki 22:4 people as thy people, my **h.** as thy **h.** 5483
2Ki 2:11 a chariot of fire, and **h.** of fire, and 5483
2Ki 3:7 as thy people, and my **h.** as thy **h.** 5483
2Ki 5:9 Naaman came with his **h.** and with 5483
2Ki 6:14 sent he thither **h.**, and chariots, 5483
2Ki 6:15 the city both with **h.** and chariots. 5483
2Ki 6:17 was full of **h.** and chariots of fire 5483
2Ki 7:6 noise of chariots, and a noise of **h.**, 5483
2Ki 7:7 left their tents, and their **h.**, and 5483
2Ki 7:10 but **h.** tied, and asses tied, and the 5483
2Ki 7:13 five of the **h.** that remain, which 5483
2Ki 7:14 They took therefore two chariot **h.** 5483
2Ki 9:33 sprinkled on the wall, and on the **h.** 5483
2Ki 10:2 there are with you chariots and **h.**, 5483
2Ki 11:16 way by the which the **h.** came into 5483
2Ki 14:20 And they brought him on **h.**: and 5483
2Ki 18:23 I will deliver thee two thousand **h.**, 5483
2Ki 23:11 he took away the **h.** that the kings 5483
1Ch 18:4 also houghed all the chariot **h.**, but 5483
2Ch 1:16 had **h.** brought out of Egypt, 5483
2Ch 1:17 so brought they out **h.** for all the 5483
2Ch 9:24 harness and spices, **h.**, and mules, 5483
2Ch 9:25 had four thousand stalls for **h.** and 5483
2Ch 9:28 unto Solomon **h.** out of Egypt, 5483
2Ch 25:28 And they brought him upon **h.**, and 5483
Ezr 2:66 Their **h.** were seven hundred thirty 5483
Ne 7:68 Their **h.**, seven hundred thirty and 5483
Ps 20:7 trust in chariots, and some in **h.**: 5483
Ec 10:7 I have seen servants upon **h.**, and 5483
Ca 1:9 to a company of **h.** in Pharaoh's 5484
Isa 2:7 thier land is also full of **h.**, neither 5483
Isa 30:16 said, No; for we will flee upon **h.**; 5483
Isa 31:1 stay on **h.**, and trust in chariots, 5483
Isa 31:3 and their **h.** flesh, and not spirit. 5483
Isa 36:8 I will give thee two thousand **h.**, 5483
Isa 66:20 the Lord out of all nations upon **h.**, 5483
Jer 4:13 his **h.** are swifter than eagles. 5483
Jer 5:8 They were as fed **h.** in the morning: 5483
Jer 6:23 they ride upon **h.**, set in array as 5483
Jer 8:16 The snorting of his **h.** was heard 5483
Jer 12:5 how canst thou contend with **h.**? 5483
Jer 17:25 riding in chariots and on **h.**, they, 5483
Jer 22:4 riding in chariots and on **h.**, he, 5483
Jer 46:4 Harness the **h.**; and get up, ye 5483
Jer 46:9 Come up, ye **h.**; and rage, ye 5483
Jer 47:3 stamping of...hoofs of his strong **h.**, 5483
Jer 50:37 A sword is upon their **h.**, and upon 5483
Jer 50:42 they shall ride upon **h.**, every one 5483
Jer 51:27 cause the **h.** to come up as the rough 5483
Eze 17:15 that they might give him **h.** and 5483
Eze 23:6 men, horsemen riding upon **h.** 5483
Eze 23:12 horsemen riding upon **h.**, all of 5483
Eze 23:20 whose issue is like the issue of **h.** 5483
Eze 23:23 renowned, all of them riding upon **h.** 5483
Eze 26:7 with **h.**, and with chariots, and with 5483
Eze 26:10 By reason of the abundance of his **h.** 5483
Eze 26:11 the hoofs of his **h.** shall he tread 5483
Eze 27:14 with **h.** and horsemen and mules. 5483
Eze 38:4 all thine army, **h.** and horsemen, 5483
Eze 38:15 all of them riding upon **h.**, a great 5483
Eze 39:20 at my table with **h.** and chariots, 5483
Ho 1:7 by battle, by **h.**, nor by horsemen. 5483
Ho 14:3 save us; we will not ride upon **h.** 5483
Joe 2:4 of them is as the appearance of **h.**; 5483
Am 4:10 and have taken away your **h.**; 5483
Am 6:12 Shall **h.** run upon the rock? will one 5483
Mic 5:10 that I will cut off thy **h.** out of the 5483
Na 3:2 of the wheels and of the pransing **h.**, 5483
Hab 1:8 Their **h.** are also swifter than the 5483
Hab 3:8 that thou didst ride upon thine **h.** 5483
Hab 3:15 walk through the sea with thine **h.**, 5483
Hag 2:22 the **h.** and their riders shall come 5483
Zec 1:8 and behind him were there red **h.**, 5483
Zec 6:2 In the first chariot were red **h.**; 5483
Zec 6:2 and in the second chariot black **h.**; 5483
Zec 6:3 And in the third chariot white **h.**; 5483
Zec 6:3 fourth chariot grisled and bay **h.** 5483
Zec 6:6 The black **h.** which are therein go 5483
Zec 10:5 riders on **h.** shall be confounded 5483
Zec 14:20 there be upon the bells of the **h.**, 5483
Re 9:7 of the locusts were like unto **h.** *2462*
Re 9:9 the chariots of many **h.** running to *2462*
Re 9:17 And thus I saw the **h.** in the vision, *2462*
Re 9:17 heads of the **h.** were as the heads *2462*
Re 18:13 and **h.**, and chariots, and slaves, *2462*
Re 19:14 heaven followed him upon white **h.**, *2462*
Re 19:18 of mighty men, and the flesh of **h.**, *2462*

HORSES'
Isa 5:28 their **h.** hoofs shall be counted 5483
Jas 3:3 we put bits in the **h.** mouths, that *2462*

HOSAH (ho'-sah)
Jos 19:29 and the coast turneth to **H.**; 2621
1Ch 16:38 of Jeduthun and **H.** to be porters: 2621
1Ch 26:10 Also **H.**, of the children of Merari, 2621
1Ch 26:11 and brethren of **H.** were thirteen. 2621
1Ch 26:16 To Shuppim and **H.** the lot came 2621

HOSANNA (ho-zan'-nah)
Mt 21:9 **H.** to the son of David: Blessed *5614*
Mt 21:9 name of the Lord; **H.** in the highest. *5614*
Mt 21:15 and saying, **H.** to the son of David; *5614*
Mk 11:9 **H.**; Blessed is he that cometh in *5614*
Mk 11:10 name of the Lord; **H.** in the highest. *5614*
Joh 12:13 **H.**: Blessed is the King of Israel *5614*

HOSEA (ho-se'-ah) See also HOSHEA; OSEE; OSHEA.
Ho *general* title **H.** 1954
Ho 1:1 of the Lord that came unto **H.**, 1954
Ho 1:2 of the word of the Lord by **H.** 1954
Ho 1:2 Lord said to **H.**, Go, take unto thee 1954

HOSEN
Da 3:21 were bound in their coats, their **h.**, 6361

HOSHAIAH (ho-sha-i'-ah)
Ne 12:32 And after them went **H.**, and half 1955
Jer 42:1 and Jezaniah the son of **H.**, 1955
Jer 43:2 Then spake Azariah the son of **H.**, 1955

HOSHAMA (ho-sha'-mah)
1Ch 3:18 Jecamiah, **H.**, and Nedabiah. 1953

HOSHEA (ho-she'-ah) See also HOSEA.
De 32:44 people, he, and **H.** the son of Nun. 1954
2Ki 15:30 And **H.** the son of Elah made a 1954
2Ki 17:1 began **H.** the son of Elah to reign 1954
2Ki 17:3 and **H.** became his servant, and 1954
2Ki 17:4 of Assyria found conspiracy in **H.** 1954
2Ki 17:6 In the ninth year of **H.** the king of 1954
2Ki 18:1 in the third year of **H.** son of Elah 1954

2Ki 18:9 which was the seventh year of **H.**...... 1954
2Ki 18:10 that is the ninth year of **H.** king of..... 1954
1Ch 27:20 of Ephraim, **H.** the son of Azaziah:..... 1954
Ne 10:23 **H.**, Hananiah, Hashub,..................... 1954

HOSPITALITY
Ro 12:13 necessity of saints; given to **h.**......... *5381*
1Ti 3:2 given to **h.**, apt to teach;.................. *5382*
Tit 1:8 But a lover of **h.**, a lover of good....... *5382*
1Pe 4:9 Use **h.** one to another without........... *5382*

HOST See also HOSTS.
Ge 2:1 finished, and all the **h.** of them......... 6635
Ge 21:22 chief captain of his **h.** spake unto....... 6635
Ge 21:32 Phichol the chief captain of his **h.**,...... 6635
Ge 32:2 them, he said, This is God's **h.**:......... 4264
Ex 14:4 upon Pharaoh, and upon all his **h.**;...... 2428
Ex 14:17 upon Pharaoh, and upon all his **h.**,...... 2428
Ex 14:24 unto the **h.** of the Egyptians,........... 4264
Ex 14:24 troubled the **h.** of the Egyptians,....... 4264
Ex 14:28 all the **h.** of Pharaoh that came.......... 2428
Ex 15:4 Pharaoh's chariots and his **h.** hath...... 2428
Ex 16:13 the dew lay round about the **h.**.......... 4264
Nu 2:4, 6,8,11,13,15,19,21,23,26,28,30 And his **h.**, and those that were.................... 6635
Nu 4:3 all that enter into the **h.**, to do the..... 6635
Nu 10:14 and over his **h.** was Nahshon the son of....
Nu 10:15, 16 over the **h.** of the tribe of the....... 6635
Nu 10:18 and over his **h.** was Elizur the son..... 6635
Nu 10:19, 20 over the **h.** of the tribe of the....... 6635
Nu 10:22 and over his **h.** was Elishama the....... 6635
Nu 10:23, 24 over the **h.** of the tribe of the....... 6635
Nu 10:25 and over his **h.** was Ahiezer the........ 6635
Nu 10:26, 27 over the **h.** of the tribe of the....... 6635
Nu 31:14 wroth with the officers of the **h.**,....... 2428
Nu 31:48 were over thousands of the **h.**,.......... 6635
De 2:14 wasted out from among the **h.**,......... 4264
De 2:15 destroy them from among the **h.**,........ 4264
De 4:19 stars, even all the **h.** of heaven,........ 6635
De 17:3 moon, or any of the **h.** of heaven,...... 6635
De 23:9 When the **h.** goeth forth against......... 4264
Jos 1:11 Pass through the **h.**, and command..... 4264
Jos 3:2 the officers went through the **h.**;........ 4264
Jos 5:14 captain of the **h.** of the Lord am........ 6635
Jos 5:15 captain of the Lord's **h.** said unto....... 6635
Jos 8:13 all the **h.** that was on the north of...... 4264
Jos 18:9 came again to Joshua to the **h.** at....... 4264
Jg 4:2 captain of whose **h.** was Sisera,......... 6635
Jg 4:15 all his chariots, and all his **h.**,........... 4264
Jg 4:16 after the chariots, and after the **h.**,..... 4264
Jg 4:16 all the **h.** of Sisera fell upon the......... 4264
Jg 7:1 so that the **h.** of the Midianites.......... 4264
Jg 7:8 and the **h.** of Midian was beneath....... 4264
Jg 7:9 Arise, get thee down unto the **h.**;...... 4264
Jg 7:10 thy servant down to the **h.**:............. 4264
Jg 7:11 strengthened to go...unto the **h.**:....... 4264
Jg 7:11 armed men that were in the **h.**......... 4264
Jg 7:13 bread tumbled into the **h.** of............. 4264
Jg 7:14 delivered Midian, and all the **h.**.......... 4264
Jg 7:15 and returned into the **h.** of Israel,...... 4264
Jg 7:15 into your hand the **h.** of Midian.......... 4264
Jg 7:21 the **h.** ran, and cried, and fled........... 4264
Jg 7:22 even throughout all the **h.**: and the..... 4264
Jg 7:22 and the **h.** fled to Beth-shittah in........ 4264
Jg 8:11 smote the **h.**: for the **h.** was secure... 4264
Jg 8:12 Zalmunna, discomfited all the **h.**........ 4264
1Sa 11:11 came into the midst of the **h.**............ 4264
1Sa 12:9 captain of the **h.** of Hazor, and.......... 6635
1Sa 14:15 there was trembling in the **h.**, in........ 4264
1Sa 14:19 the noise that was in the **h.** of the..... 4264
1Sa 14:48 And he gathered an **h.**, and smote...... 2428
1Sa 14:50 the captain of his **h.** was Abner,........ 6635
1Sa 17:20 as the **h.** was going forth to the......... 2428
1Sa 17:46 the carcases of the **h.** of the............. 4264
1Sa 17:55 unto Abner, the captain of the **h.**,...... 6635
1Sa 26:5 son of Ner, the captain of his **h.**:....... 6635
1Sa 28:5 Saul saw the **h.** of the Philistines,...... 4264
1Sa 28:19 also shall deliver the **h.** of Israel....... 4264
1Sa 29:6 thy coming in with me in the **h.** is...... 4264
2Sa 2:8 Son of Ner, captain of Saul's **h.**,........ 6635
2Sa 3:23 Joab and all the **h.** that was with........ 6635
2Sa 5:24 to smite the **h.** of the Philistines....... 4264
2Sa 8:9 David had smitten all the **h.** of.......... 2428
2Sa 8:16 son of Zeruiah was over the **h.**;......... 6635
2Sa 10:7 and all the **h.** of the mighty men......... 6635
2Sa 10:16 Shobach the captain of the **h.** of......... 6635
2Sa 10:18 Shobach the captain of their **h.**,......... 6635
2Sa 17:25 Amasa captain of the **h.** instead of...... 6635
2Sa 19:13 be not captain of the **h.** before me..... 6635
2Sa 20:23 Joab was over all the **h.** of Israel:...... 6635
2Sa 23:16 through the **h.** of the Philistines,........ 4264
2Sa 24:2 said to Joab the captain of the **h.**,....... 2428
2Sa 24:4 and against the captains of the **h.**....... 2428
2Sa 24:4 and the captain of the **h.** went.......... 2428
1Ki 1:19 Joab the captain of the **h.**:................ 6635
1Ki 1:25 and the captains of the **h.**, and.......... 6635
1Ki 2:32 of Ner, captain of the **h.** of Israel,...... 6635
1Ki 2:32 Jether, captain of the **h.** of Judah........ 6635
1Ki 2:35 Jehoiada in his room over the **h.**:........ 6635
1Ki 4:4 son of Jehoiada was over the **h.**:........ 6635
1Ki 11:15 and Joab the captain of the **h.** was...... 6635
1Ki 11:21 Joab the captain of the **h.** was.......... 6635
1Ki 16:16 made Omri, the captain of the **h.**,...... 6635
1Ki 20:1 Syria gathered all his **h.** together:...... 2428
1Ki 22:19 And all the **h.** of heaven standing....... 6635
1Ki 22:34 hand, and carry me out of the **h.**;...... 4264
1Ki 22:36 a proclamation throughout the **h.**........ 4264
2Ki 3:9 there was no water for the **h.**, and..... 4264
2Ki 4:13 king, or to the captain of the **h.**?........ 6635
2Ki 5:1 Naaman, captain of the **h.** of the........ 6635
2Ki 6:14 and chariots, and a great **h.**:............ 2428
2Ki 6:15 an **h.** compassed the city both with..... 2428
2Ki 6:24 king of Syria gathered all his **h.**,................
2Ki 7:4 let us fall unto the **h.** of the............. 4264
2Ki 7:6 had made the **h.** of the Syrians.......... 4264
2Ki 7:6 even the noise of a great **h.**:............ 2428
2Ki 7:14 sent after the **h.** of the Syrians,......... 4264
2Ki 9:5 the captains of the **h.** were sitting;..... 2428
2Ki 11:15 the hundreds, the officers of the **h.**,... 2428
2Ki 17:16 worshipped all the **h.** of heaven,........ 6635
2Ki 18:17 Hezekiah with a great **h.** against........ 2426
2Ki 21:3 worshipped all the **h.** of heaven,......... 6635
2Ki 21:5 built altars for all the **h.** of heaven...... 6635
2Ki 23:4 grove, and for all the **h.** of heaven:.... 6635
2Ki 23:5 planets, and to all the **h.** of heaven..... 6635
2Ki 25:1 Babylon came, he, and all his **h.**,....... 2428
2Ki 25:19 the principal scribe of the **h.**,............ 6635
1Ch 9:19 being over the **h.** of the Lord,........... 4264
1Ch 11:15 the **h.** of the Philistines encamped...... 4264
1Ch 11:18 brake through the **h.** of the.............. 4264
1Ch 12:14 sons of Gad, captains of the **h.**:......... 6635
1Ch 12:21 valour, and were captains in the **h.**..... 6635
1Ch 12:22 was a great **h.**, like the **h.** of God...... 4264
1Ch 14:15 to smite the **h.** of the Philistines........ 4264
1Ch 14:16 they smote the **h.** of the Philistines.... 4264
1Ch 18:9 smitten all the **h.** of Hadarezer.......... 2428
1Ch 18:15 the son of Zeruiah was over the **h.**;.... 6635
1Ch 19:8 and all the **h.** of the mighty men,....... 6635
1Ch 19:16 Shophach the captain of the **h.** of....... 6635
1Ch 19:18 Shophach the captain of the **h.**.......... 6635
1Ch 25:1 David and the captains of the **h.**......... 6635
1Ch 26:26 captains of the **h.**, had dedicated,...... 6635
1Ch 27:3 of all the captains of the **h.** for the..... 6635
1Ch 27:5 The third captain of the **h.** for the...... 6635
2Ch 14:9 an **h.** of a thousand thousand,........... 2428
2Ch 14:13 before the Lord, and before his **h.**;..... 4264
2Ch 16:7 the **h.** of the king of Syria escaped..... 2428
2Ch 16:8 and the Lubims a huge **h.**,................ 2428
2Ch 18:18 all the **h.** of heaven standing on......... 6635
2Ch 18:33 thou mayest carry me out of the **h.**;... 4264
2Ch 23:14 hundreds that were set over the **h.**,... 2428
2Ch 24:23 the **h.** of Syria came up against.......... 2428
2Ch 24:24 the Lord delivered a very great **h.**...... 2428
2Ch 26:11 Uzziah had an **h.** of fighting men,....... 2428
2Ch 26:14 for them throughout all the **h.**.......... 6635
2Ch 28:9 before the **h.** that came to Samaria,.... 6635
2Ch 33:3 worshipped all the **h.** of heaven,........ 6635
2Ch 33:5 built altars for all the **h.** of heaven...... 6635
2Ch 33:11 the captains of the **h.** of the king of.... 6635
Ne 9:6 heaven of heavens, with all their **h.**,... 6635
Ne 9:6 the **h.** of heaven worshippeth thee...... 6635
Ps 27:3 Though an **h.** should encamp............ 4264
Ps 33:6 and all the **h.** of them by the............ 6635
Ps 33:16 saved by the multitude of an **h.**:........ 2428
Ps 136:15 overthrew Pharaoh and his **h.** in........ 2428
Isa 13:4 mustereth the **h.** of the battle........... 6635
Isa 24:21 shall punish the **h.** of the high ones.... 6635
Isa 34:4 all the **h.** of heaven shall be............. 6635
Isa 34:4 all their **h.** shall fall down, as the....... 6635
Isa 40:26 bringeth out their **h.** by number:........ 6635
Isa 45:12 and all their **h.** have I commanded...... 6635
Jer 8:2 the moon, and all the **h.** of heaven,..... 6635
Jer 19:13 incense unto all the **h.** of heaven,....... 6635
Jer 33:22 **h.** of heaven cannot be numbered,...... 6635
Jer 51:3 men; destroy ye utterly all her **h.**...... 6635
Jer 52:25 the principal scribe of the **h.**, who...... 6635
Eze 1:24 of speech, as the noise of an **h.**:........ 4264
Da 8:10 great, even to the **h.** of heaven;........ 6635
Da 8:10 some of the **h.** and of the stars.......... 6635
Da 8:11 himself even to the prince of the **h.**,... 6635
Da 8:12 And an **h.** was given him against........ 6635
Da 8:13 give both the sanctuary and the **h.**..... 6635
Ob 20 captivity of this **h.** of the children....... 2426
Zep 1:5 that worship the **h.** of heaven........... 6635
Lu 2:13 a multitude of the heavenly **h.**........... *4756*
Lu 10:35 pence, and gave them to the **h.**,.... *3830*
Ac 7:42 up to worship the **h.** of heaven;......... *4756*
Ro 16:23 Gaius mine **h.**, and of the whole........ *3581*

HOSTAGES
2Ki 14:14 house,and **h.**, and returned........ 1121,8594
2Ch 25:24 house, the **h.** also, and returned..1121,8594

HOSTS
Ex 12:41 the **h.** of the Lord went out from....... 6635
Nu 1:52 standard, throughout their **h.**............ 6635
Nu 2:32 of the camps throughout their **h.**........ 6635
Nu 10:25 all the camps throughout their **h.**:....... 6635
Jos 10:5 and went up, they and all their **h.**,..... 4264
Jos 11:4 went out, they and all their **h.** with.... 4264
Jg 8:10 in Karkor, and their **h.** with them,...... 4264
Jg 8:10 that were left of all the **h.** of the....... 4264
1Sa 1:3 unto the Lord of **h.** in Shiloh............ 6635
1Sa 1:11 O Lord of **h.**, if thou wilt indeed........ 6635
1Sa 4:4 of the covenant of the Lord of **h.**,...... 6635
1Sa 15:2 Thus saith the Lord of **h.**, I............. 6635
1Sa 17:45 thee in the name of the Lord of **h.**,.... 6635
2Sa 5:10 the Lord God of **h.** was with him......... 6635
2Sa 6:2 called by the name of the Lord of **h.**.... 6635
2Sa 6:18 in the name of the Lord of **h.**............ 6635
2Sa 7:8 Thus saith the Lord of **h.**, I took....... 6635
2Sa 7:26 The Lord of **h.** is the God over......... 6635
2Sa 7:27 For thou, O Lord of **h.**, God of.......... 6635
1Ki 2:5 did to the two captains of the **h.** of..... 6635
1Ki 15:20 sent the captains of the **h.** with......... 2428
1Ki 18:15 As the Lord of **h.** liveth, before......... 6635
1Ki 19:10, 14 jealous for the Lord God of **h.**:...... 6635
2Ki 3:14 As the Lord of **h.** liveth, before......... 6635
2Ki 19:31 zeal of the Lord of **h.** shall do this............
1Ch 11:9 and greater; for the Lord of **h.**........... 6635
1Ch 17:7 Thus saith the Lord of **h.**, I took....... 6635
1Ch 17:24 The Lord of **h.** is the God of Israel,.... 6635
Ps 24:10 Lord of **h.**, he is the King of glory..... 6635
Ps 46:7, 11 The Lord of **h.** is with us; the....... 6635
Ps 48:8 seen in the city of the Lord of **h.**,...... 6635
Ps 59:5 O Lord God of **h.**, the God of Israel,.. 6635
Ps 69:6 that wait on thee, O Lord God of **h.**,.. 6635
Ps 80:4 O Lord God of **h.**, how long wilt........ 6635
Ps 80:7 Turn us again, O God of **h.**, and........ 6635
Ps 80:14 we beseech thee, O God of **h.**:......... 6635
Ps 80:19 Turn us again, O Lord God of **h.**,...... 6635
Ps 84:1 are thy tabernacles, O Lord of **h.**!..... 6635
Ps 84:3 O Lord of **h.**, my King, and my God... 6635
Ps 84:8 O Lord God of **h.**, hear my prayer:.... 6635
Ps 84:12 O Lord of **h.**, blessed is the man....... 6635
Ps 89:8 O Lord God of **h.**, who is a strong..... 6635
Ps 103:21 Bless ye the Lord, all ye his **h.**; ye.... 6635
Ps 108:11 thou, O God, go forth with our **h.**?..... 6635
Ps 148:2 angels: praise ye him, all his **h.**........ 6635
Isa 1:9 Except the Lord of **h.** had left unto.... 6635
Isa 1:24 saith the Lord, the Lord of **h.**,.......... 6635
Isa 2:12 For the day of the Lord of **h.** shall..... 6635
Isa 3:1 the Lord, the Lord of **h.**, doth take.... 6635
Isa 3:15 the poor? saith the Lord God of **h.**..... 6635
Isa 5:7 For the vineyard of the Lord of **h.**..... 6635
Isa 5:9 In mine ears said the Lord of **h.**,....... 6635
Isa 5:16 But the Lord of **h.** shall be exalted..... 6635
Isa 5:24 cast away the law of the Lord of **h.**,.... 6635
Isa 6:3 Holy, holy, holy, is the Lord of **h.**:..... 6635
Isa 6:5 have seen the King, the Lord of **h.**..... 6635
Isa 8:13 Sanctify the Lord of **h.** himself;.......... 6635
Isa 8:18 in Israel from the Lord of **h.**, which.... 6635
Isa 9:7 The zeal of the Lord of **h.** will.......... 6635
Isa 9:13 neither do they seek the Lord of **h.**.... 6635
Isa 9:19 Through the wrath of the Lord of **h.**.... 6635
Isa 10:16 shall the Lord, the Lord of **h.**,.......... 6635
Isa 10:23 For the Lord God of **h.** shall make...... 6635
Isa 10:24 thus saith the Lord God of **h.**, O my.. 6635
Isa 10:26 And the Lord of **h.** shall stir up a....... 6635
Isa 10:33 Behold, the Lord, the Lord of **h.**,...... 6635

Isa 13:4 the Lord of **h.** mustereth the **h.** of..... 6635
Isa 13:13 in the wrath of the Lord of **h.**, and..... 6635
Isa 14:22 against them, saith the Lord of **h.**, ... 6635
Isa 14:23 of destruction, saith the Lord of **h.**..... 6635
Isa 14:24 The Lord of **h.** hath sworn, saying, ... 6635
Isa 14:27 For the Lord of **h.** hath purposed,...... 6635
Isa 17:3 of Israel, saith the Lord of **h.**.......... 6635
Isa 18:7 be brought unto the Lord of **h.**.......... 6635
Isa 18:7 place of the name of the Lord of **h.**, ... 6635
Isa 19:4 saith the Lord, the Lord of **h.**. 6635
Isa 19:12 what the Lord of **h.** hath purposed..... 6635
Isa 19:16 of the hand of the Lord of **h.**, which... 6635
Isa 19:17 of the counsel of the Lord of **h.**,........ 6635
Isa 19:18 and swear to the Lord of **h.**; one....... 6635
Isa 19:20 for a witness unto the Lord of **h.**........ 6635
Isa 19:25 Whom the Lord of **h.** shall bless, ... 6635
Isa 21:10 I have heard of the Lord of **h.**, the..... 6635
Isa 22:5 perplexity by the Lord God of **h.**........ 6635
Isa 22:12 that day did the Lord God of **h.** call.... 6635
Isa 22:14 in mine ears by the Lord of **h.**, ... 6635
Isa 22:14 till ye die, saith the Lord God of **h.**. ... 6635
Isa 22:15 Thus saith the Lord God of **h.**, Go,..... 6635
Isa 22:25 In that day, saith the Lord of **h.**, ... 6635
Isa 23:9 The Lord of **h.** hath purposed it, to.... 6635
Isa 24:23 Lord of **h.** shall reign in mount Zion,... 6635
Isa 25:6 this mountain shall the Lord of **h.**........ 6635
Isa 28:5 Lord of **h.** be for a crown of glory,...... 6635
Isa 28:22 have heard from the Lord God of **h.**.... 6635
Isa 28:29 cometh forth from the Lord of **h.**, ... 6635
Isa 29:6 be visited of the Lord of **h.** with........ 6635
Isa 31:4 the Lord of **h.** come down to fight...... 6635
Isa 31:5 the Lord of **h.** defend Jerusalem;........ 6635
Isa 37:16 O Lord of **h.**, God of Israel, that 6635
Isa 37:32 zeal of the Lord of **h.** shall do this...... 6635
Isa 39:5 Hear the word of the Lord of **h.**: 6635
Isa 44:6 and his redeemer the Lord of **h.**; 6635
Isa 45:13 nor reward, saith the Lord of **h.**. 6635
Isa 47:4 the Lord of **h.** is his name, the.......... 6635
Isa 48:2 Israel; the Lord of **h.** is his name....... 6635
Isa 51:15 roared: The Lord of **h.** is his name..... 6635
Isa 54:5 husband; the Lord of **h.** is his name;... 6635
Jer 2:19 in thee, saith the Lord God of **h.**. 6635
Jer 3:19 goodly heritage of the **h.** of nations? ... 6635
Jer 5:14 thus saith the Lord God of **h.**,........... 6635
Jer 6:6 For thus hath the Lord of **h.** said....... 6635
Jer 6:9 Thus saith the Lord of **h.**, They 6635
Jer 7:3 the Lord of **h.**, the God of Israel,...... 6635
Jer 7:21 the Lord of **h.**, the God of Israel; 6635
Jer 8:3 driven them, saith the Lord of **h.**. 6635
Jer 9:7 Therefore saith the Lord of **h.**,.......... 6635
Jer 9:15 the Lord of **h.**, the God of Israel; 6635
Jer 9:17 Thus saith the Lord of **h.**, Consider.... 6635
Jer 10:16 The Lord of **h.** is his name. 6635
Jer 11:17 For the Lord of **h.**, that planted......... 6635
Jer 11:20 Lord of **h.**, that judgest righteously,.... 6635
Jer 11:22 Therefore thus saith the Lord of **h.**, ... 6635
Jer 15:16 by thy name, O Lord God of **h.**......... 6635
Jer 16:9 the Lord of **h.**, the God of Israel; 6635
Jer 19:3 the Lord of **h.**, the God of Israel; 6635
Jer 19:11 Thus saith the Lord of **h.**; Even so 6635
Jer 19:15 the Lord of **h.**, the God of Israel; 6635
Jer 20:12 Lord of **h.**, that triest the righteous,.... 6635
Jer 23:15 Therefore thus saith the Lord of **h.** 6635
Jer 23:16 Thus saith the Lord of **h.**, Hearken 6635
Jer 23:36 living God, of the Lord of **h.** our God. .6635
Jer 25:8 Therefore thus saith the Lord of **h.**; ... 6635
Jer 25:27 the Lord of **h.**, the God of Israel; 6635
Jer 25:28 Thus saith the Lord of **h.**; Ye shall..... 6635
Jer 25:29 of the earth, saith the Lord of **h.**. 6635
Jer 25:32 Thus saith the Lord of **h.**, Behold, ... 6635
Jer 26:18 Thus saith the Lord of **h.**; Zion......... 6635
Jer 27:4 the Lord of **h.**, the God of Israel; 6635
Jer 27:18 make intercession to the Lord of **h.**,.... 6635
Jer 27:19 For thus saith the Lord of **h.**............ 6635
Jer 27:21 the Lord of **h.**, the God of Israel, ... 6635
Jer 28:2 the Lord of **h.**, the God of Israel, ... 6635
Jer 28:14 the Lord of **h.**, the God of Israel; 6635
Jer 29:4 the Lord of **h.**, the God of Israel, ... 6635
Jer 29:8 the Lord of **h.**, the God of Israel; 6635
Jer 29:17 Thus saith the Lord of **h.**; Behold, ... 6635
Jer 29:21, 25 the Lord of **h.**, the God of Israel, .. 6635
Jer 30:8 saith the Lord of **h.**, that I will break.. 6635
Jer 31:23 the Lord of **h.**, the God of Israel; 6635
Jer 31:35 The Lord of **h.** is his name: 6635
Jer 32:14, 15 the Lord of **h.**, the God of Israel; .. 6635
Jer 32:18 the Mighty God, the Lord of **h.**, is..... 6635
Jer 33:11 Praise the Lord of **h.**: for the Lord..... 6635
Jer 33:12 Thus saith the Lord of **h.**; Again........ 6635
Jer 35:13, 17,18,19, the Lord of **h.**,the God of.... 6635
Jer 38:17 the God of **h.**, the God of Israel; 6635
Jer 39:16 the Lord of **h.**, the God of Israel; 6635
Jer 42:15, 18 the Lord of **h.**, the God of Israel; .. 6635
Jer 43:10 the Lord of **h.**, the God of Israel; 6635
Jer 44:2 the Lord of **h.**, the God of Israel; 6635
Jer 44:7 thus saith the Lord, the God of **h.**,..... 6635
Jer 44:11 the Lord of **h.**, the God of Israel; 6635
Jer 44:25 the Lord of **h.**, the God of Israel, ... 6635
Jer 46:10 is the day of the Lord God of **h.**,....... 6635
Jer 46:10 the Lord God of **h.** hath a sacrifice..... 6635
Jer 46:18 King, whose name is the Lord of **h.**, .. 6635
Jer 46:25 The Lord of **h.**, the God of Israel, ... 6635
Jer 48:1 the Lord of **h.**, the God of Israel; 6635
Jer 48:15 King, whose name is the Lord of **h.**. .. 6635
Jer 49:5 upon thee, saith the Lord God of **h.**, .. 6635
Jer 49:7 Edom, thus saith the Lord of **h.**;........ 6635
Jer 49:26 off in that day, saith the Lord of **h.**. ... 6635
Jer 49:35 Thus saith the Lord of **h.**; Behold, ... 6635
Jer 50:18 the Lord of **h.**, the God of Israel; 6635
Jer 50:25 the work of the Lord Gof of **h.** in 6635
Jer 50:31 proud, saith the Lord God of **h.**:......... 6635
Jer 50:33 Thus saith the Lord of **h.**; The.......... 6635
Jer 50:34 strong; the Lord of **h.** is his name:..... 6635
Jer 51:5 Judah of his God, of the Lord of **h.**;..... 6635
Jer 51:14 The Lord of **h.** hath sworn by........... 6635
Jer 51:19 the Lord of **h.** is his name. 6635
Jer 51:33 the Lord of **h.**, the God of Israel; 6635
Jer 51:57 King, whose name is the Lord of **h.**. ... 6635
Jer 51:58 Thus saith the Lord of **h.**; The.......... 6635
Ho 12:5 Even the Lord God of **h.**; the Lord.... 6635
Am 3:13 saith the Lord God, the God of **h.**,..... 6635
Am 4:13 Lord, the God of **h.**, is his name........ 6635
Am 5:14 the Lord, the God of **h.**, shall be 6635
Am 5:15 Lord God of **h.** will be gracious 6635
Am 5:16 Therefore the Lord, the God of **h.**, ... 6635
Am 5:27 Lord, whose name is The God of **h.**. ... 6635
Am 6:8 saith the Lord the God of **h.**, I.......... 6635
Am 6:14 Israel, saith the Lord the God of **h.**; ... 6635
Am 9:5 Lord God of **h.** is he that toucheth..... 6635
Mic 4:4 of the Lord of **h.** hath spoken it......... 6635
Na 2:13 against thee, saith the Lord of **h.**, ... 6635
Na 3:5 against thee, saith the Lord of **h.**; 6635
Hab 2:13 not of the Lord of **h.** that the people .. 6635
Zep 2:9 the Lord of **h.**, the God of Israel, ... 6635
Zep 2:10 against the people of the Lord of **h.**.... 6635
Hag 1:2 Thus speaketh the Lord of **h.**,.......... 6635
Hag 1:5 therefore thus saith the Lord of **h.**; 6635
Hag 1:7 saith the Lord of **h.**; Consider your 6635
Hag 1:9 Why? saith the Lord of **h.**. Because.... 6635
Hag 1:14 work in the house of the Lord of **h.**,.... 6635
Hag 2:4 I am with you, saith the Lord of **h.**: 6635
Hag 2:6 For thus saith the Lord of **h.**; Yet...... 6635
Hag 2:7 with glory, saith the Lord of **h.**.......... 6635
Hag 2:8 gold is mine, saith the Lord of **h.**........ 6635
Hag 2:9 of the former, saith the Lord of **h.**: 6635
Hag 2:9 I give peace, saith the Lord of **h.**........ 6635
Hag 2:11 Thus saith the Lord of **h.**; Ask now.... 6635
Hag 2:23 In that day, saith the Lord of **h.**, ... 6635
Hag 2:23 chosen thee, saith the Lord of **h.**. 6635
Zec 1:3 them, Thus saith the Lord of **h.**;......... 6635
Zec 1:3 ye unto me, saith the Lord of **h.**,........ 6635
Zec 1:3 turn unto you, saith the Lord of **h.**..... 6635
Zec 1:4 Thus saith the Lord of **h.**; Turn ye..... 6635
Zec 1:6 Like as the Lord of **h.** thought to do... 6635
Zec 1:12 O Lord of **h.**, how long wilt thou not .. 6635
Zec 1:14 Thus saith the Lord of **h.**; I am........ 6635
Zec 1:16 be built in it, saith the Lord of **h.**,....... 6635
Zec 1:17 Thus saith the Lord of **h.**; My cities ... 6635
Zec 2:8 For thus saith the Lord of **h.**;........... 6635
Zec 2:9 that the Lord of **h.** hath sent me........ 6635
Zec 2:11 that the Lord of **h.** hath sent me unto..6635
Zec 3:7 Thus saith the Lord of **h.**; If thou 6635
Zec 3:9 thereof, saith the Lord of **h.**, ... 6635
Zec 3:10 In that day, saith the Lord of **h.**, ... 6635
Zec 4:6 by my spirit, saith the Lord of **h.**........ 6635
Zec 4:9 that the Lord of **h.** hath sent me unto..6635
Zec 5:4 bring it forth, saith the Lord of **h.**, ... 6635
Zec 6:12 Thus speaketh the Lord of **h.**,.......... 6635
Zec 6:15 that the Lord of **h.** hath sent me unto..6635
Zec 7:3 were in the house of the Lord of **h.**,.... 6635
Zec 7:4 came the word of the Lord of **h.**........ 6635
Zec 7:9 Thus speaketh the Lord of **h.**,.......... 6635
Zec 7:12 which the Lord of **h.** hath sent in....... 6635
Zec 7:12 a great wrath from the Lord of **h.**. 6635
Zec 7:13 would not hear, saith the Lord of **h.** ... 6635
Zec 8:1 the word of the Lord of **h.** came to 6635
Zec 8:2 Thus saith the Lord of **h.**; I was........ 6635
Zec 8:3 the mountain of the Lord of **h.** the 6635
Zec 8:4 Thus saith the Lord of **h.**; There 6635
Zec 8:6 Thus saith the Lord of **h.**; If it be 6635
Zec 8:6 in mine eyes? saith the Lord of **h.**...... 6635
Zec 8:7 Thus saith the Lord of **h.**; Behold, ... 6635
Zec 8:9 Thus saith the Lord of **h.**; Let your.... 6635
Zec 8:9 the house of the Lord of **h.** was laid, .. 6635
Zec 8:11 former days, saith the Lord of **h.**. 6635
Zec 8:14 For thus saith the Lord of **h.**; As I..... 6635
Zec 8:14 saith the Lord of **h.**, and I repented.... 6635
Zec 8:18 the word of the Lord of **h.** came........ 6635
Zec 8:19 Thus saith the Lord of **h.**; The fast 6635
Zec 8:20 Thus saith the Lord of **h.**; It shall 6635
Zec 8:21 and to seek the Lord of **h.**: I will....... 6635
Zec 8:22 shall come to seek the Lord of **h.** in.... 6635
Zec 8:23 Thus saith the Lord of **h.**; In those 6635
Zec 9:15 The Lord of **h.** shall defend them;...... 6635
Zec 10:3 the Lord of **h.** hath visited his flock.... 6635
Zec 12:5 strength in the Lord of **h.** their God. .. 6635
Zec 13:2 in that day, saith the Lord of **h.**,........ 6635
Zec 13:7 is my fellow, saith the Lord of **h.**........ 6635
Zec 14:16, 17 worship the King, the Lord of **h.**, .. 6635
Zec 14:21 be holiness unto the Lord of **h.**.......... 6635
Zec 14:21 in the house of the Lord of **h.**. 6635
Mal 1:4 thus saith the Lord of **h.**, They 6635
Mal 1:6 saith the Lord of **h.** unto you, O 6635
Mal 1:8 thy person? saith the Lord of **h.**. 6635
Mal 1:9 your persons? saith the Lord of **h.**. 6635
Mal 1:10 pleasure in you, saith...Lord of **h.**, ... 6635
Mal 1:11 the heathen, saith the Lord of **h.**. 6635
Mal 1:13 snuffed at it, saith the Lord of **h.**; 6635
Mal 1:14 a great King, saith the Lord of **h.**, ... 6635
Mal 2:2 unto my name, saith the Lord of **h.**, ... 6635
Mal 2:4 be with Levi, saith the Lord of **h.**. 6635
Mal 2:7 is the messenger of the Lord of **h.**,..... 6635
Mal 2:8 of Levi, saith the Lord of **h.**.............. 6635
Mal 2:12 an offering unto the Lord of **h.**. 6635
Mal 2:16 his garment, saith the Lord of **h.** 6635
Mal 3:1 he shall come, saith the Lord of **h.**...... 6635
Mal 3:5 fear not me, saith the Lord of **h.**. 6635
Mal 3:7 unto you, saith the Lord of **h.**. 6635
Mal 3:10 now herewith, saith the Lord of **h.**, ... 6635
Mal 3:11 in the field, saith the Lord of **h.**......... 6635
Mal 3:12 delightsome land, saith...Lord of **h.**. ... 6635
Mal 3:14 mournfully before the Lord of **h.**?....... 6635
Mal 3:17 shall be mine, saith the Lord of **h.**,..... 6635
Mal 4:1 burn them up, saith the Lord of **h.**, ... 6635
Mal 4:3 I shall do this, saith the Lord of **h.**..... 6635

HOT See also HOTTEST.
Ex 16:21 when the sun waxed **h.**, it melted. 2552
Ex 22:24 And my wrath shall wax **h.**, and I 2734
Ex 32:10 that my wrath may wax **h.** against...... 2734
Ex 32:11 why doth thy wrath wax **h.** against..... 2734
Ex 32:19 and Moses' anger waxed **h.**, and he..... 2734
Ex 32:22 not the anger of my lord wax **h.**: 2734
Le 13:24 skin whereof there is a **h.** burning, ... 784
De 9:19 of the anger and **h.** displeasure,......... 2534
De 19:6 the slayer, while his heart is **h.**, ... 3179
Jos 9:12 This our bread we took **h.** for our....... 2525
Jg 2:14, 20 the anger of the Lord was **h.**......... 2734
Jg 3:8 anger of the Lord was **h.** against......... 2734
Jg 6:39 Let not thine anger be **h.** against 2734
Jg 10:7 anger of the Lord was **h.** against........ 2734
1Sa 11:9 by that time the sun be **h.**, ye shall..... 2527
1Sa 21:6 to put **h.** bread in the day when it....... 2527
Ne 7:3 be opened until the sun be **h.**;............ 2527
Job 6:17 when it is **h.**, they are consumed........ 2527
Ps 6:1 chasten me in thy **h.** displeasure. 2534
Ps 38:1 chasten me in thy **h.** displeasure. 2534
Ps 39:3 My heart was **h.** within me, while 2552
Ps 78:48 their flocks to **h.** thunderbolts............ 7565
Pr 6:28 Can one go upon **h.** coals, and his feet......
Eze 24:11 that the brass of it may be **h.**, and..... 3179
Da 3:22 and the furnace exceeding **h.**, the 228
Ho 7:7 They are all **h.** as an oven, and 2552
1Ti 4:2 conscience seared with a **h.** iron; *2743*
Re 3:15 **that thou art neither cold nor h.**: .. *2200*
Re 3:15 **I would thou wert cold or h.** *2200*
Re 3:16 **lukewarm, and neither cold nor h.**, *2200*

HOTHAM (ho'-tham) See also HOTHAN.
1Ch 7:32 Japhlet, and Shomer, and **H.**, ... 2369

HOTHAN (ho'-than) See also HOTHAM.
1Ch 11:44 Shama and Jehiel the sons of **H.** 2369

HOTHIR (ho'-thir)
1Ch 25:4 Mallothi, H., and Mahazioth: ... 1956
1Ch 25:28 The one and twentieth to H., he, ... 1956

HOTLY
Ge 31:36 thou hast so h. pursued after me? ... 1814

HOTTEST
2Sa 11:15 in the forefront of the h. battle, ... 2389

HOUGH See also HOUGHED.
Jos 11:6 shalt h. their horses, and burn ... 6131

HOUGHED
Jos 11:9 he h. their horses, and burnt their ... 6131
2Sa 8:4 David h. all the chariot horses, but ... 6131
1Ch 18:4 David also h. all the chariot horses, ... 6131

HOUND See GREYHOUND.

HOUR See also HOURS.
Da 3:6 the same h. be cast into the midst ... 8160
Da 3:15 be cast the same h. into the midst ... 8160
Da 4:19 was astonied for one h., and his ... 8160
Da 4:33 The same h. was the thing fulfilled ... 8160
Da 5:5 In the same h. came forth fingers ... 8160
Mt 8:13 was healed in the selfsame h.. ... 5610
Mt 9:22 was made whole from that h., ... 5610
Mt 10:19 **that same h. what ye shall speak.** ... 5610
Mt 15:28 was made whole from that very h.. ... 5610
Mt 17:18 child was cured from that very h. ... 5610
Mt 20:3 **he went out about the third h.,** ... 5610
Mt 20:5 **out about the sixth and ninth h.,** ... 5610
Mt 20:6 **about the eleventh h. he went out,** ... 5610
Mt 20:9 **were hired about the eleventh h.,** ... 5610
Mt 20:12 **these last have wrought but one h.,** 5610
Mt 24:36 **that day and h. knoweth no man** ... 5610
Mt 24:42 **not what h. your Lord doth come** ... 5610
Mt 24:44 **such an h. as ye think not the Son** 5610
Mt 24:50 **and in an h. that he is not aware** ... 5610
Mt 25:13 **ye know neither the day nor the h.** 5610
Mt 26:40 **ye not watch with me one h.?** ... 5610
Mt 26:45 **the h. is at hand, and the Son of** ... 5610
Mt 26:55 In that same h. said Jesus to the ... 5610
Mt 27:45 the sixth h. there was darkness ... 5610
Mt 27:45 over all the land unto the ninth h., ... 5610
Mt 27:46 about the ninth h. Jesus cried with ... 5610
Mk 13:11 **given you in that h., that speak** ... 5610
Mk 13:32 **day and that h. knoweth no man,** ... 5610
Mk 14:35 possible, the h. might pass from ... 5610
Mk 14:37 **couldest not thou watch one h.?** ... 5610
Mk 14:41 **it is enough, the h. is come;** ... 5610
Mk 15:25 was the third h., and they crucified ... 5610
Mk 15:33 And when the sixth h. was come, ... 5610
Mk 15:33 the whole land until the ninth h. ... 5610
Mk 15:34 the ninth h. Jesus cried with a loud ... 5610
Lu 7:21 And in that same h. he cured many ... 5610
Lu 10:21 In that h. Jesus rejoiced in spirit, ... 5610
Lu 12:12 **in the same h. what ye ought to** ... 5610
Lu 12:39 **known what h. the thief would** ... 5610
Lu 12:40 **cometh at an h. when ye think** ... 5610
Lu 12:46 **at an h. when he is not aware,** ... 5610
Lu 20:19 the same h. sought to lay hands ... 5610
Lu 22:14 when the h. was come, he sat down, ... 5610
Lu 22:53 **this is your h., and the power of** ... 5610
Lu 22:59 And about the space of one h. after ... 5610
Lu 23:44 it was about the sixth h., and there ... 5610
Lu 23:44 over all the earth until the ninth h.. ... 5610
Lu 24:33 rose up the same h., and returned ... 5610
Joh 1:39 day: for it was about the tenth h. ... 5610
Joh 2:4 **with thee? mine h. is not yet come** 5610
Joh 4:6 well: and it was about the sixth h. ... 5610
Joh 4:21 **Woman, believe me, the h. cometh,** 5610
Joh 4:23 **the h. cometh, and now is, when** ... 5610
Joh 4:52 enquired he of them the h. when he ... 5610
Joh 4:52 Yesterday at the seventh h. the ... 5610
Joh 4:53 knew that it was at the same h., ... 5610
Joh 5:25 **The h. is coming, and now is,** ... 5610
Joh 5:28 **the h. is coming, in the which all** ... 5610
Joh 7:30 because his h. was not yet come. ... 5610
Joh 8:20 on him; for his h. was not yet come. ... 5610
Joh 12:23 **h. is come, that the Son of man** ... 5610
Joh 12:27 **I say Father, save me from this h.** 5610
Joh 12:27 **for this cause came I unto this h.** 5610
Joh 13:1 when Jesus knew that his h. was ... 5610
Joh 16:21 **sorrow, because her h. is come:** ... 5610
Joh 16:32 **the h. cometh, yea, is now come** ... 5610
Joh 17:1 and said, **Father, the h. is come:** ... 5610
Joh 19:14 the passover, and about the sixth h. ... 5610
Joh 19:27 from that h. that disciple took her ... 5610
Ac 2:15 seeing it is but the third h. of the ... 5610
Ac 3:1 into the temple at the h. of prayer, ... 5610
Ac 3:1 of prayer, being the ninth h.. ... 5610
Ac 10:3 the ninth h. of the day an angel ... 5610
Ac 10:9 housetop to pray about the sixth h.: ... 5610
Ac 10:30 days ago I was fasting until this h.; ... 5610
Ac 10:30 the ninth h. I prayed in my house, ... 5610
Ac 16:18 her. And he came out the same h.. ... 5610
Ac 16:33 took them the same h. of the night, ... 5610
Ac 22:13 And the same h. I looked up upon ... 5610
Ac 23:23 hundred, at the third h. of the night; ... 5610
1Co 4:11 this present h. we both hunger, ... 5610
1Co 8:7 of the idol unto this h. eat it as a ... 734
1Co 15:30 stand we in jeopardy every h.? ... 5610
Ga 2:5 by subjection, no, not for an h.; ... 5610
Re 3:3 **shalt not know what h. I will come** 5610
Re 3:10 **thee from the h. of temptation** ... 5610
Re 8:1 about the space of half an h.. ... 2256
Re 9:15 prepared for an h., and a day, and ... 5610
Re 11:13 same h. was there a great ... 5610
Re 14:7 for the h. of his judgment is come: ... 5610
Re 17:12 power as kings one h. with the ... 5610
Re 18:10 for in one h. is thy judgment come. ... 5610
Re 18:17 in one h. so great riches is come ... 5610
Re 18:19 for in one h. is she made desolate. ... 5610

HOURS
Joh 11:9 **Are there not twelve h. in the** ... 5610
Ac 5:7 about the space of three h. after, ... 5610
Ac 19:34 about the space of two h. cried out, ... 5610

HOUSE See also HOUSEHOLD; HOUSES; HOUSETOP; STOREHOUSES.
Ge 7:1 thou and all thy h. into the ark; ... 1004
Ge 12:1 kindred, and from thy father's h., ... 1004
Ge 12:15 woman was taken into Pharaoh's h., ... 1004
Ge 12:17 plagued Pharaoh and his h. with ... 1004
Ge 14:14 trained servants, born in his own h., ... 1004
Ge 15:2 the steward of my h. is this Eliezer ... 1004
Ge 15:3 one born in my h. is mine heir. ... 1004
Ge 17:12 he that is born in the h., or bought ... 1004
Ge 17:13 He that is born in thy h., and he ... 1004
Ge 17:23 son, and all that were born in his h., ... 1004
Ge 17:23 among the men of Abraham's h.; ... 1004
Ge 17:27 all the men of his h., born in the h., ... 1004
Ge 19:2 I pray you, into your servant's h. ... 1004
Ge 19:3 unto him, and entered into his h.; ... 1004
Ge 19:4 of Sodom, compassed the h. round, ... 1004
Ge 19:10 pulled Lot into the h. to them, ... 1004
Ge 19:11 at the door of the h. with blindnes, ... 1004
Ge 20:13 me to wander from my father's h. ... 1004
Ge 20:18 the wombs of the h. of Abimelech, ... 1004
Ge 24:2 unto his eldest servant of his h.. ... 1004
Ge 24:7 which took me from my father's h., ... 1004
Ge 24:23 is there room in thy father's h. for ... 1004
Ge 24:27 to the h. of my master's brethren. ... 1004
Ge 24:28 told them of her mother's h. these ... 1004
Ge 24:31 for I have prepared the h., and room ... 1004
Ge 24:32 the man came into the h.: and he ... 1004
Ge 24:38 go unto my father's h., and to my ... 1004
Ge 24:40 my kindred, and of my father's h.: ... 1004
Ge 27:15 which were with her in the h., ... 1004
Ge 28:2 to the h. of Bethuel thy mother's ... 1004
Ge 28:17 none other but the h. of God, and ... 1004
Ge 28:21 again to my father's h. in peace; ... 1004
Ge 28:22 set for a pillar, shall be God's h.: ... 1004
Ge 29:13 him, and brought him to his h.. ... 1004
Ge 30:30 I provide for mine own h. also? ... 1004
Ge 31:14 inheritance for us in our father's h.? ... 1004
Ge 31:30 sore longedst after thy father's h., ... 1004
Ge 31:41 have I been twenty years in thy h.; ... 1004
Ge 33:17 built him an h., and made booths ... 1004
Ge 34:19 than all the h. of his father. ... 1004
Ge 34:26 took Dinah out of Shechem's h., ... 1004
Ge 34:29 spoiled even all that was in the h.. ... 1004
Ge 34:30 I shall be desroyed, I and my h.. ... 1004
Ge 36:6 and all the persons of his h., ... 1004
Ge 38:11 Remain a widow ath thy father's h., ... 1004
Ge 38:11 went and dwelt in her father's h.. ... 1004
Ge 39:2 he was in the h. of his master the ... 1004
Ge 39:4 he made him overseer over his h., ... 1004
Ge 39:5 he had made him overseer in his h., ... 1004
Ge 39:5 Lord blessed the Egyptian's h. ... 1004
Ge 39:5 was upon all that he had in the h., ... 1004
Ge 39:8 not what is with me in the h., ... 1004
Ge 39:9 is none greater in this h. than I; ... 1004
Ge 39:11 that Joseph went into the h. to do ... 1004
Ge 39:11 was none of the men of the h. there ... 1004
Ge 39:14 she called unto the men of her h., ... 1004
Ge 40:3 in ward in the h. of the captain of ... 1004
Ge 40:7 with him in the ward of his lord's h., ... 1004
Ge 40:14 and bring me out of this h. ... 1004
Ge 41:10 in the captain of the guard's h., ... 1004
Ge 41:40 Thou shalt be over my h., and ... 1004
Ge 41:51 all my toil, and all my father's h.. ... 1004
Ge 42:19 be bound in the h. of your prison: ... 1004
Ge 43:16 he said to the ruler of his h.. ... 1004
Ge 43:17 brought the men into Joseph's h.. ... 1004
Ge 43:18 they were brought into Joseph's h.; ... 1004
Ge 43:19 near to the steward of Joseph's h., ... 1004
Ge 43:19 with him at the door of the h., ... 1004
Ge 43:24 brought the men into Joseph's h., ... 1004
Ge 43:26 which was in their hand into the h., ... 1004
Ge 44:1 commanded the steward of his h.. ... 1004
Ge 44:8 should we steal out of thy lord's h. ... 1004
Ge 44:14 his brethren came to Joseph's h.; ... 1004
Ge 45:2 and the h. of Pharaoh heard. ... 1004
Ge 45:8 to Pharaoh, and lord of all his h., ... 1004
Ge 45:16 thereof was heard in Pharaoh's h., ... 1004
Ge 46:27 all the souls of the h. of Jacob, ... 1004
Ge 46:31 brethren, and unto his father's h., ... 1004
Ge 46:31 My brethren, and my father's h., ... 1004
Ge 47:14 the money into Pharaoh's h. ... 1004
Ge 50:4 spake unto the h. of Pharaoh, ... 1004
Ge 50:7 the elders of his h., and all the ... 1004
Ge 50:8 and all the h. of Joseph, and his ... 1004
Ge 50:8 and his father's h.: only their little ... 1004
Ge 50:22 in Egypt, he, and his father's h. ... 1004
Ex 2:1 there went a man of the h. of Levi, ... 1004
Ex 3:22 of her that sojourneth in her h., ... 1004
Ex 7:23 Pharaoh turned and went into his h., ... 1004
Ex 8:3 shall go up and come into thine h., ... 1004
Ex 8:3 and into the h. of thy servants, and ... 1004
Ex 8:24 of flies into the h. of Pharaoh, ... 1004
Ex 12:3 according to the h. of their fathers, ... 1004
Ex 12:3 of their fathers, a lamb for an h.: ... 1004
Ex 12:4 and his neighbour next unto his h. ... 1004
Ex 12:22 go out at the door of his h. until ... 1004
Ex 12:30 there was not a h. where there was ... 1004
Ex 12:46 In one h. shall it be eaten; thou ... 1004
Ex 12:46 of the flesh abroad out of the h.; ... 1004
Ex 13:3 Egypt, out of the h. of bondage; ... 1004
Ex 13:14 Egypt, from the h. of bondage: ... 1004
Ex 16:31 the h. of Israel called the name ... 1004
Ex 19:3 shalt thou say to the h. of Jacob, ... 1004
Ex 20:2 Egypt out of the h. of bondage. ... 1004
Ex 20:17 shalt not covet thy neighbour's h., ... 1004
Ex 22:7 and it be stolen out of the man's h.; ... 1004
Ex 22:8 then the master of the h. shall be ... 1004
Ex 23:19 bring into the h. of the Lord thy ... 1004
Ex 34:26 bring unto the h. of the Lord thy ... 1004
Ex 40:38 in the sight of all the h. of Israel, ... 1004
Le 10:6 the whole h. of Israel, bewail the ... 1004
Le 14:34 the plague of leprosy in a h. of the ... 1004
Le 14:35 And he that owneth the h. shall ... 1004
Le 14:35 is as it were a plague in the h.: ... 1004
Le 14:36 that they empty the h., before the ... 1004
Le 14:36 all that is in the h. be not made ... 1004
Le 14:36 priest shall go in to see the h.: ... 1004
Le 14:37 in the walls of the h. with hollow ... 1004
Le 14:38 out of the h. to the door of the h., ... 1004
Le 14:38 and shut up the h. seven days: ... 1004
Le 14:39 be spread in the walls of the h.; ... 1004
Le 14:41 shall cause the h. to be scraped ... 1004
Le 14:42 mortar, and shall plaister the h.. ... 1004
Le 14:43 again, and break out in the h., ... 1004
Le 14:43 and after he hath scraped the h., ... 1004
Le 14:44 if the plague be spread in the h., ... 1004
Le 14:44 it is a fretting leprosy in the h.: ... 1004
Le 14:45 he shall break down the h., the ... 1004
Le 14:45 thereof, and all the mortar of the h.; ... 1004
Le 14:46 he that goeth into the h. all the ... 1004
Le 14:47 he that lieth in the h. shall wash ... 1004
Le 14:47 he that eateth in the h. shall wash ... 1004
Le 14:48 plague hath not spread in the h., ... 1004
Le 14:48 after the h. was plaistered: then the ... 1004
Le 14:48 priest shall pronounce the h. clean ... 1004
Le 14:49 take to cleanse the h. two birds, ... 1004
Le 14:52 water, sprinkle the h. seven times: ... 1004
Le 14:52 cleanse the h. with the blood of the ... 1004
Le 14:53 make an atonement for the h.: and ... 1004
Le 14:55 leprosy of a garment, and of a h., ... 1004

Le	16:6	atonement for himself, and for his **h.**	1004
Le	16:11	atonement for himself, and for his **h.**,	1004
Le	17:3	be of the **h.** of Israel, that killeth	1004
Le	17:8	the **h.** of Israel, or of the strangers	1004
Le	17:10	man there be of the **h.** of Israel,	1004
Le	22:11	of it, and he that is born in his **h.**:	1004
Le	22:13	is returned unto her father's **h.**, as	1004
Le	22:18	he be of the **h.** of Israel, or of the	1004
Le	25:29	if a man sell a dwelling **h.** in a	1004
Le	25:30	then the **h.** that is in the walled city	1004
Le	25:33	then the **h.** that was sold, and the	1004
Le	27:14	man shall sanctify his **h.** to be holy	1004
Le	27:15	that sanctified it will redeem his **h.**,	1004
Nu	1:2	families, by the **h.** of their fathers,	1004
Nu	1:4	every one head of the **h.** of his	1004
Nu	1:18,	20,22,24,26,28,30,32,34,36,38,40,42 by the **h.** of their fathers,	1004
Nu	1:44	one was for the **h.** of his fathers.	1004
Nu	1:45	Israel, by the **h.** of their fathers,	1004
Nu	2:2	the ensign of their father's **h.**:	1004
Nu	2:32	Israel by the **h.** of their fathers:	1004
Nu	2:34	according to the **h.** of their fathers.	1004
Nu	3:15	after the **h.** of their fathers, by	1004
Nu	3:20	according to the **h.** of their fathers.	1004
Nu	3:24	the chief of the **h.** of the father of	1004
Nu	3:30	the **h.** of the father of the families	1004
Nu	3:35	the chief of the **h.** of the father of	1004
Nu	4:2	families, by the **h.** of their fathers,	1004
Nu	4:29	families, by the **h.** of their fathers;	1004
Nu	4:34	and after the **h.** of their fathers,	1004
Nu	4:38	and by the **h.** of their fathers,	1004
Nu	4:40,	42 families, by the **h.** of...fathers,	1004
Nu	4:46	and after the **h.** of their fathers,	1004
Nu	7:2	heads of the **h.** of their fathers,	1004
Nu	12:7	so, who is faithful in all mine **h.**.	1004
Nu	17:2	according to the **h.** of their fathers,	1004
Nu	17:2	according to the **h.** of their fathers	1004
Nu	17:3	head of the **h.** of their fathers.	1004
Nu	17:8	the rod of Aaron for the **h.** of Levi.	1004
Nu	18:1	and thy sons, and thy father's **h.**	1004
Nu	18:11	every one that is clean in thy **h.**	1004
Nu	18:13	every one that is clean in thine **h.**	1004
Nu	20:29	thirty days, even all the **h.** of Israel.	1004
Nu	22:18	give me his **h.** full of silver and gold,	1004
Nu	24:13	give me his **h.** full of silver and gold,	1004
Nu	25:14	a prince of a chief **h.** among the	1004
Nu	25:15	people, and of a chief **h.** in Midian.	1004
Nu	26:2	throughout their fathers' **h.**, all	1004
Nu	30:3	in her father's **h.** in her youth;	1004
Nu	30:10	if she vowed in her husband's **h.**,	1004
Nu	30:16	yet in her youth in her father's **h.**.	1004
Nu	34:14	according to the **h.** of their fathers,	1004
Nu	34:14	according to the **h.** of their fathers,	1004
De	5:16	of Egypt, from the **h.** of bondage.	1004
De	5:21	thou covet thy neighbour's **h.**, his	1004
De	6:7	when thou sittest in thine **h.**, and	1004
De	6:9	write them upon the posts of thy **h.**,	1004
De	6:12	of Egypt, from the **h.** of bondage.	1004
De	7:8	you out of the **h.** of bondmen,	1004
De	7:26	bring an abomination into thine **h.**,	1004
De	8:14	of Egypt, from the **h.** of bondage;	1004
De	11:19	them when thou sittest in thine **h.**,	1004
De	11:20	upon the door posts of thine **h.**,	1004
De	13:5	you out of the **h.** of bondage,	1004
De	13:10	of Egypt, from the **h.** of bondage.	1004
De	15:16	because he loveth thee and thine **h.**,	1004
De	20:5	is there that hath built a new **h.**,	1004
De	20:5	let him go and return to his **h.**, lest	1004
De	20:6	him also go and return unto his **h.**,	1004
De	20:7,	8 let him go and return unto his **h.**,	1004
De	21:12	shalt bring her home to thine **h.**;	1004
De	21:13	shall remain in thine **h.**, and bewail	1004
De	22:2	shalt bring it unto thine own **h.**,	1004
De	22:8	When thou buildest a new **h.**, then	1004
De	22:8	thou bring not blood upon thine **h.**,	1004
De	22:21	damsel to the door of her father's **h.**,	1004
De	22:21	to play the whore in her father's **h.**:	1004
De	23:18	into the **h.** of the Lord thy God	1004
De	24:1	hand, and send her out of his **h.**.	1004
De	24:2	when she is departed out of his **h.**,	1004
De	24:3	hand, and sendeth her out of his **h.**;	1004
De	24:10	not go into his **h.** to fetch his pledge	1004
De	25:9	will not build up his brother's **h.**	1004
De	25:10	The **h.** of him that hath his shoe	1004
De	25:14	Thou shalt not have in thine **h.**	1004
De	26:11	given unto thee, and unto thine **h.**,	1004
De	26:13	the hallowed things out of mine **h.**,	1004
De	28:30	thou shalt build an **h.**, and thou	1004
Jos	2:1	went, and came into an harlot's **h.**,	1004
Jos	2:3	which are entered into thine **h.**:	1004
Jos	2:6	brought them up to the roof of the **h.**,	
Jos	2:12	shew kindness unto my father's **h.**,	1004
Jos	2:15	for her **h.** was upon the town wall,	1004
Jos	2:19	shall go out of the doors of thy **h.**	1004
Jos	2:19	shall be with thee in the **h.**,	1004
Jos	6:17	and all that are with her in the **h.**,	1004
Jos	6:22	Go into the harlot's **h.**, and bring	1004
Jos	6:24	the treasury of the **h.** of the Lord.	1004
Jos	9:23	of water for the **h.** of my God.	1004
Jos	17:17	Joshua spake unto the **h.** of Joseph,	1004
Jos	18:5	and the **h.** of Joseph shall abide in	1004
Jos	20:6	his own city, and unto his own **h.**,	1004
Jos	21:45	had spoken unto the **h.** of Israel;	1004
Jos	22:14	of each chief **h.** a prince throughout	1004
Jos	22:14	an head of the **h.** of their fathers	1004
Jos	24:15	as for me and my **h.**, we will serve	1004
Jos	24:17	of Egypt, from the **h.** of bondage,	1004
Jg	1:22	the **h.** of Joseph, they also went up	1004
Jg	1:23	And the **h.** of Joseph sent to descry	1004
Jg	1:35	hand of the **h.** of Joseph prevailed,	1004
Jg	4:17	and the **h.** of Heber the Kenite	1004
Jg	6:8	you forth out of the **h.** of bondage;	1004
Jg	6:15	I am the least in my father's **h.**.	1004
Jg	8:27	a snare unto Gideon, and to his **h.**.	1004
Jg	8:29	Joash went and dwelt in his own **h.**.	1004
Jg	8:35	kindness to the **h.** of Jerubbaal,	1004
Jg	9:1	of the **h.** of his mother's father,	1004
Jg	9:4	silver out of the **h.** of Baal-berith,	1004
Jg	9:5	And he went unto his father's **h.**	1004
Jg	9:6	all the **h.** of Millo, and went, and	1004
Jg	9:16	well with Jerubbaal and his **h.**,	1004
Jg	9:18	are risen up against my father's **h.**	1004
Jg	9:19	with Jerubbaal and with his **h.** this	1004
Jg	9:20	of Shechem, and the **h.** of Millo;	1004
Jg	9:20	Shechem, and from the **h.** of Millo,	1004
Jg	9:27	and went into the **h.** of their god,	1004
Jg	9:46	an hold of the **h.** of the god Berith.	1004
Jg	10:9	and against the **h.** of Ephraim;	1004
Jg	11:2	shalt not inherit in our father's **h.**;	1004
Jg	11:7	and expel me out of my father's **h.**?	1004
Jg	11:31	cometh forth of the doors of my **h.**	1004
Jg	11:34	came to Mizpeh unto his **h.**, and,	1004
Jg	12:1	we will burn thine **h.** upon thee	1004
Jg	14:15	we burn thee and thy father's **h.**	1004
Jg	14:19	and he went up to his father's **h.**.	1004
Jg	16:21	and he did grind in the prison **h.**.	1004
Jg	16:25	for Samson out of the prison **h.**;	1004
Jg	16:26	pillars whereupon the **h.** standeth,	1004
Jg	16:27	Now the **h.** was full of men and	1004
Jg	16:29	pillars upon which the **h.** stood,	1004
Jg	16:30	and the **h.** fell upon the lords, and	1004
Jg	16:31	and all the **h.** of his father came	1004
Jg	17:4	and they were in the **h.** of Micah.	1004
Jg	17:5	the man Micah had an **h.** of gods,	1004
Jg	17:8	to the **h.** of Micah, as he journeyed.	1004
Jg	17:12	priest, and was in the **h.** of Micah.	1004
Jg	18:2	to the **h.** of Micah, they lodged	1004
Jg	18:3	When they were by the **h.** of Micah,	1004
Jg	18:13	and came unto the **h.** of Micah.	1004
Jg	18:15	came to the **h.** of the young man	1004
Jg	18:15	Levite, even unto the **h.** of Micah,	1004
Jg	18:18	these went into Micah's **h.**, and	1004
Jg	18:19	be a priest unto the **h.** of one man,	1004
Jg	18:22	good way from the **h.** of Micah,	1004
Jg	18:22	in the houses near to Micah's **h.**	1004
Jg	18:26	turned and went back unto his **h.**	1004
Jg	18:31	that the **h.** of God was in Shiloh.	1004
Jg	19:2	away from him unto her father's **h.**	1004
Jg	19:3	brought him into her father's **h.**:	1004
Jg	19:15	took them into his **h.** to lodging.	1004
Jg	19:18	am now going to the **h.** of the Lord;	1004
Jg	19:18	is no man that receiveth me to **h.**.	1004
Jg	19:21	So he brought him into his **h.**, and	1004
Jg	19:22	of Belial, beset the **h.** round about,	1004
Jg	19:22	spake to the master of the **h.**, the	1004
Jg	19:22	the man that came into thine **h.**,	1004
Jg	19:23	man, the master of the **h.**, went out	1004
Jg	19:23	that this man is come into mine **h.**,	1004
Jg	19:26	fell down at the door of the man's **h.**	1004
Jg	19:27	opened the doors of the **h.**, and	1004
Jg	19:27	fallen down at the door of the **h.**	1004
Jg	19:29	when he was come into his **h.**, he	1004
Jg	20:5	beset the **h.** round about upon me	1004
Jg	20:8	will we any of us turn into his **h.**.	1004
Jg	20:18	and went up to the **h.** of God,	1008
Jg	20:26	came unto the **h.** of God, and wept,	1008
Jg	20:31	one goeth up to the **h.** of God,	1008
Jg	21:2	the people came to the **h.** of God,	1008
Ru	1:8	Go, return each to her mother's **h.**:	1004
Ru	1:9	each of you in the **h.** of her husband.	1004
Ru	2:7	that she tarried a little in the **h.**	1004
Ru	4:11	is come into thine **h.** like Rachel	1004
Ru	4:11	which two did build the **h.** of Israel:	1004
Ru	4:12	let thy **h.** be like the **h.** of Pharez,	1004
1Sa	1:7	she went up to the **h.** of the Lord,	1004
1Sa	1:19	and came to their **h.** to Ramah:	1004
1Sa	1:21	the man Elkanah, and all his **h.**,	1004
1Sa	1:24	unto the **h.** of the Lord in Shiloh:	1004
1Sa	2:11	Elkanah went to Ramah to his **h.**.	1004
1Sa	2:27	appear unto the **h.** of thy father,	1004
1Sa	2:27	were in Egypt in Pharaoh's **h.**?	1004
1Sa	2:28	I give unto the **h.** of thy father all	1004
1Sa	2:30	that thy **h.**, and the **h.** of thy father,	1004
1Sa	2:31	and the arm of thy father's **h.**,	1004
1Sa	2:31	shall not be an old man in thine **h.**	1004
1Sa	2:32	an old man in thine **h.** for ever.	1004
1Sa	2:33	the increase of thine **h.** shall die in	1004
1Sa	2:35	I will build him a sure **h.**; and he	1004
1Sa	2:36	every one that is left in thine **h.**	1004
1Sa	3:12	I have spoken concerning his **h.**:	1004
1Sa	3:13	that I will judge his **h.**, for ever for	1004
1Sa	3:14	I have sworn unto the **h.** of Eli,	1004
1Sa	3:14	iniquity of Eli's **h.** shall not be	1004
1Sa	3:15	the doors of the **h.** of the Lord.	1004
1Sa	5:2	brought it into the **h.** of Dagon,	1004
1Sa	5:5	nor any that come into Dagon's **h.**,	1004
1Sa	7:1	brought it into the **h.** of Abinadab	1004
1Sa	7:2	all the **h.** of Israel lamented after	1004
1Sa	7:3	spake unto all the **h.** of Israel,	1004
1Sa	7:17	for there was his **h.**; and there he	1004
1Sa	9:18	I pray thee, where the seer's **h.** is.	1004
1Sa	9:20	on thee, and on all thy father's **h.**?	1004
1Sa	9:25	with Saul upon the top of the **h.**	
1Sa	9:26	called Saul to the top of the **h.**,	
1Sa	10:25	people away, every man to his **h.**	1004
1Sa	15:34	Saul went up to his **h.** to Gibeah	1004
1Sa	17:25	make his father's **h.** free in Israel.	1004
1Sa	18:2	go no more home to his father's **h.**	1004
1Sa	18:10	prophesied in the midst of the **h.**:	1004
1Sa	19:9	he sat in his **h.** with his javelin in	1004
1Sa	19:11	sent messengers unto David's **h.**,	1004
1Sa	20:15	thy kindness from my **h.** for ever:	1004
1Sa	20:16	a covenant with the **h.** of David,	1004
1Sa	21:15	shall this fellow come into my **h.**?	1004
1Sa	22:1	and all his father's **h.** heard it,	1004
1Sa	22:11	son of Ahitub, and all his father's **h.**,	1004
1Sa	22:14	and is honourable in thine **h.**?	1004
1Sa	22:15	nor to all the **h.** of my father:	1004
1Sa	22:16	thou, and all thy father's **h.**	1004
1Sa	22:22	of all the persons of thy father's **h.**	1004
1Sa	23:18	wood, and Jonathan went to his **h.**	1004
1Sa	24:21	my name out of my father's **h.**.	1004
1Sa	25:1	and buried him in his **h.** at Ramah.	1004
1Sa	25:3	and he was of the **h.** of Caleb.	1004
1Sa	25:6	to thee, and peace be to thne **h.**,	1004
1Sa	25:28	certainly make my lord a sure **h.**;	1004
1Sa	25:35	unto her, Go up in peace to thine **h.**;	1004
1Sa	25:36	he held a feast in his **h.**, like the	1004
1Sa	28:24	the woman had a fat calf in the **h.**;	1004
1Sa	31:9	to publish it in the **h.** of their idols,	1004
1Sa	31:10	his armour in the **h.** of Ashtaroth:	1004
2Sa	1:12	the Lord, and for the **h.** of Israel;	1004
2Sa	2:4	David king over the **h.** of Judah.	1004
2Sa	2:7	the **h.** of Judah have anointed me	1004
2Sa	2:10	But the **h.** of Judah followed David.	1004
2Sa	2:11	king in Hebron over the **h.** of Judah.	1004
2Sa	3:1	the **h.** of Saul and the **h.** of David:	1004
2Sa	3:1	the **h.** of Saul waxed weaker and	1004
2Sa	3:6	the **h.** of Saul and the **h.** of David,	1004
2Sa	3:6	himself strong for the **h.** of Saul.	1004
2Sa	3:8	day unto the **h.** of Saul thy father,	1004
2Sa	3:10	the kingdom from the **h.** of Saul,	1004
2Sa	3:19	good to the whole **h.** of Benjamin.	1004
2Sa	3:29	of Joab, and on all his father's **h.**;	1004
2Sa	3:29	there not fail from the **h.** of Joab	1004
2Sa	4:5	of the day to the **h.** of Ish-bosheth,	1004
2Sa	4:6	thither into the midst of the **h.**,	1004
2Sa	4:7	For when they came into the **h.**, he	1004
2Sa	4:11	a righteous person in his own **h.**	1004
2Sa	5:8	the lame shall not come into the **h.**	1004
2Sa	5:11	masons; and they built David an **h.**.	1004

Book	Ref.	Context	No.
2Sa	6:3,4	it out of the **h.** of Abinadab	1004
2Sa	6:5	and all the **h.** of Israel played	1004
2Sa	6:10	aside into the **h.** of Obed-edom	1004
2Sa	6:11	continued in the **h.** of Obed-edom	1004
2Sa	6:12	hath blessed the **h.** of Obed-edom,	1004
2Sa	6:12	ark of God from the **h.** of Obed-edom.	1004
2Sa	6:15	David and all the **h.** of Israel	1004
2Sa	6:19	people departed every one to his **h.**	1004
2Sa	6:21	thy father, and before all his **h.**,	1004
2Sa	7:1	to pass, when the king sat in his **h.**.	1004
2Sa	7:2	I dwell in an **h.** of cedar, but the ark	1004
2Sa	7:5	Shalt thou build me an **h.** for me	1004
2Sa	7:6	I have not dwelt in any **h.** since	1004
2Sa	7:7	Why build ye not me an **h.** of cedar?	1004
2Sa	7:11	thee that he will make thee an **h.**	1004
2Sa	7:13	He shall build an **h.** for my name,	1004
2Sa	7:16	And thine **h.** and thy kingdom shall	1004
2Sa	7:18	and what is my **h.**, that thou hast	1004
2Sa	7:19	hast spoken also of thy servant's **h.**	1004
2Sa	7:25	thy servant, and concerning his **h.**,	1004
2Sa	7:26	and let the **h.** of thy servant David	1004
2Sa	7:27	saying, I will build thee an **h.**:	1004
2Sa	7:29	thee to bless the **h.** of thy servant,	1004
2Sa	7:29	let the **h.** of thy servant be blessed	1004
2Sa	9:1	any that is left of the **h.** of Saul.	1004
2Sa	9:2	there was of the **h.** of Saul a servant	1004
2Sa	9:3	there not yet any of the **h.** of Saul,	1004
2Sa	9:4	Behold, he is in the **h.** of Machir,	1004
2Sa	9:5	fetched him out of the **h.** of Machir,	1004
2Sa	9:9	pertained to Saul and to all his **h.**	1004
2Sa	9:12	in the **h.** of Ziba were servants	1004
2Sa	11:2	upon the roof of the king's **h.**:	1004
2Sa	11:4	and she returned unto her **h.**.	1004
2Sa	11:8	Go down to thy **h.**, and wash thy	1004
2Sa	11:8	Uriah departed out of the king's **h.**,	1004
2Sa	11:9	slept at the door of the king's **h.**	1004
2Sa	11:9	lord, and went not down to his **h.**	1004
2Sa	11:10	Uriah went not down unto his **h.**,	1004
2Sa	11:10	thou not go down unto thine **h.**?	1004
2Sa	11:11	shall I then go into mine **h.**, to eat	1004
2Sa	11:13	lord, but went not down to his **h.**	1004
2Sa	11:27	David sent and fetched her to his **h.**,	1004
2Sa	12:8	I gave thee thy master's **h.**, and	1004
2Sa	12:8	and gave thee the **h.** of Israel and	1004
2Sa	12:10	shall never depart from thine **h.**;	1004
2Sa	12:11	against thee out of thine own **h.**,	1004
2Sa	12:15	And Nathan departed unto his **h.**.	1004
2Sa	12:17	And the elders of his **h.** arose,	1004
2Sa	12:20	came into the **h.** of the Lord, and	1004
2Sa	12:20	then he came to his own **h.**; and	1004
2Sa	13:7	Go now to thy brother Amnon's **h.**,	1004
2Sa	13:8	went to her brother Amnon's **h.**;	1004
2Sa	13:20	in her brother Absalom's **h.**.	1004
2Sa	14:8	Go to thine **h.**, and I will give	1004
2Sa	14:9	be on me, and on my father's **h.**:	1004
2Sa	14:24	Let him turn to his own **h.**, and	1004
2Sa	14:24	So Absalom returned to his own **h.**,	1004
2Sa	14:31	and came to Absalom unto his **h.**,	1004
2Sa	15:16	were concubines, to keep the **h.**.	1004
2Sa	15:35	thou shalt hear out of the king's **h.**,	1004
2Sa	16:3	To day shall the **h.** of Israel restore	1004
2Sa	16:5	man of the family of the **h.** of Saul,	1004
2Sa	16:8	thee all the blood of the **h.** of Saul,	1004
2Sa	16:21	which he hath left to keep the **h.**;	1004
2Sa	16:22	a tent upon the top of the **h.**;	1004
2Sa	17:18	quickly, and came to a man's **h.** in	1004
2Sa	17:20	came to the woman to the **h.**,	1004
2Sa	17:23	arose, and gat him home to his **h.**,	1004
2Sa	19:5	Joab came into the **h.** to the king,	1004
2Sa	19:11	to bring the king back to his **h.**?	1004
2Sa	19:11	is come to the king, even to his **h.**	1004
2Sa	19:17	Ziba the servant of the **h.** of Saul,	1004
2Sa	19:20	of all the **h.** of Joseph to go down	1004
2Sa	19:28	my father's **h.** were but dead men	1004
2Sa	19:30	again in peace unto his own **h.**	1004
2Sa	20:3	David came to his **h.** at Jerusalem;	1004
2Sa	20:3	whom he had left to keep the **h.**	1004
2Sa	21:1	It is for Saul, and for his bloody **h.**,	1004
2Sa	21:4	silver nor gold of Saul, nor of his **h.**;	1004
2Sa	23:5	Although my **h.** be not so with God;	1004
2Sa	24:17	me, and against my father's **h.**	1004
1Ki	1:53	said unto him, Go to thine **h.**.	1004
1Ki	2:24	and who hath made me an **h.**, as	1004
1Ki	2:27	he spake concerning the **h.** of Eli	1004
1Ki	2:31	me, and from the **h.** of my father	1004
1Ki	2:33	upon his **h.**, and upon his throne,	1004
1Ki	2:34	he was buried in his own **h.** in the	1004
1Ki	2:36	Build thee an **h.** in Jerusalem,	1004
1Ki	3:1	made an end of building his own **h.**,	1004
1Ki	3:1	the **h.** of the Lord, and the wall of	1004
1Ki	3:2	because there was no **h.** built unto	1004
1Ki	3:17	I and this woman dwell in one **h.**;	1004
1Ki	3:17	delivered of a child...in the **h.**	1004
1Ki	3:18	us in the **h.**, save we two in the **h.**.	1004
1Ki	5:3	my father could not build an **h.**	1004
1Ki	5:5	I purpose to build an **h.** unto the	1004
1Ki	5:5	he shall build an **h.** unto my name.	1004
1Ki	5:17	to lay the foundation of the **h.**.	1004
1Ki	5:18	timber and stones to build the **h.**.	1004
1Ki	6:1	he began to build the **h.** of the Lord.	1004
1Ki	6:2	the **h.** which king Solomon built	1004
1Ki	6:3	porch before the temple of the **h.**,	1004
1Ki	6:3	according to the breadth of the **h.**;	1004
1Ki	6:3	the breadth thereof before the **h.**.	1004
1Ki	6:4	for the **h.** he made windows of	1004
1Ki	6:5	And against the wall of the **h.** he	1004
1Ki	6:5	against the walls of the **h.** round	1004
1Ki	6:6	wall of the **h.** he made narrowed	1004
1Ki	6:6	not be fastened in the wall of the **h.**.	1004
1Ki	6:7	And the **h.**, when it was in building,	1004
1Ki	6:7	nor any tool of iron heard in the **h.**,	1004
1Ki	6:8	was in the right side of the **h.**:	1004
1Ki	6:9	So he built the **h.**, and finished it;	1004
1Ki	6:9	covered the **h.** with beams and	1004
1Ki	6:10	he built chambers against all the **h.**,	1004
1Ki	6:10	rested on the **h.** with timber of cedar	1004
1Ki	6:12	this **h.** which thou art in building,	1004
1Ki	6:14	built the **h.**, and finished it.	1004
1Ki	6:15	he built the walls of the **h.** within	1004
1Ki	6:15	floor of the **h.**, and the walls of the	1004
1Ki	6:15	covered the floor of the **h.** with	1004
1Ki	6:16	twenty cubits on the sides of the **h.**,	1004
1Ki	6:17	And the **h.**, that is, the temple	1004
1Ki	6:18	And the cedar of the **h.** within	1004
1Ki	6:19	the oracle he prepared in the **h.**	1004
1Ki	6:21	overlaid the **h.** within with pure	1004
1Ki	6:22	the whole **h.** he overlaid with gold,	1004
1Ki	6:22	until he had finished all the **h.**:	1004
1Ki	6:27	the cherubims within the inner **h.**	1004
1Ki	6:27	one another in the midst of the **h.**	1004
1Ki	6:29	And he carved all the walls of the **h.**	1004
1Ki	6:30	the floor of the **h.** he overlaid with	1004
1Ki	6:37	the foundation of the **h.** of the Lord	1004
1Ki	6:38	was the **h.** finished throughout	1004
1Ki	7:1	Solomon was building his own **h.**	1004
1Ki	7:1	years, and he finished all his **h.**	1004
1Ki	7:2	He built alo the **h.** of the forest	1004
1Ki	7:8	And his **h.** where he dwelt had	1004
1Ki	7:8	also an **h.** for Pharaoh's daughter,	1004
1Ki	7:12	inner court of the **h.** of the Lord,	1004
1Ki	7:12	and for the porch of the **h.**.	1004
1Ki	7:39	bases on the right side of the **h.**,	1004
1Ki	7:39	and five on the left side of the **h.**	1004
1Ki	7:39	set the sea on the right side of the **h.**.	1004
1Ki	7:40	king Solomon for the **h.** of the Lord:	1004
1Ki	7:45	vessels...for the **h.** of the Lord,	1004
1Ki	7:48	pertained unto the **h.** of the Lord:	1004
1Ki	7:50	of the inner **h.**, the most holy place,	1004
1Ki	7:50	and for the doors of the **h.**, to wit,	1004
1Ki	7:51	all the work...for the **h.** of the Lord.	1004
1Ki	7:51	the treasures of the **h.** of the Lord.	1004
1Ki	8:6	into the oracle of the **h.**, to the	1004
1Ki	8:10	the cloud filled the **h.** of the Lord,	1004
1Ki	8:11	glory of the Lord had filled the **h.**	1004
1Ki	8:13	surely built thee an **h.** to dwell in,	1004
1Ki	8:16	all the tribes of Israel to build an **h.**,	1004
1Ki	8:17	David my father to build an **h.** for	1004
1Ki	8:18	heart to build an **h.** unto my name,	1004
1Ki	8:19	thou shalt not build the **h.**; but thy	1004
1Ki	8:19	of thy loins, he shall build the **h.**	1004
1Ki	8:20	built an **h.** for the name of the Lord	1004
1Ki	8:27	how much less this **h.** that I have	1004
1Ki	8:29	eyes may be open toward this **h.**	1004
1Ki	8:31	come before thine altar in this **h.**	1004
1Ki	8:33	supplication unto thee in this **h.**	1004
1Ki	8:38	forth his hands toward this **h.**	1004
1Ki	8:42	shall come and pray toward this **h.**;	1004
1Ki	8:43	that this **h.**, which I have builded,	1004
1Ki	8:44	toward the **h.** that I have built	1004
1Ki	8:48	and the **h.** which I have built for	1004
1Ki	8:63	Israel, dedicated the **h.** of the Lord.	1004
1Ki	8:64	that was before the **h.** of the Lord:	1004
1Ki	9:1	had finished the building of the **h.**	1004
1Ki	9:1	king's **h.**, and all Solomon's desire	1004
1Ki	9:3	I have hallowed this **h.**, which thou	1004
1Ki	9:7	and this **h.**, which I have hallowed	1004
1Ki	9:8	And at this **h.**, which is high, every	1004
1Ki	9:8	thou unto this land, and to this **h.**?	1004
1Ki	9:10	the **h.** of the Lord, and the king's **h.**,	1004
1Ki	9:15	the **h.** of the Lord, and his own **h.**,	1004
1Ki	9:24	unto her **h.** which Solomon had	1004
1Ki	9:25	the Lord. So he finished the **h.**	1004
1Ki	10:4	wisdom, and the **h.** that he had built,	1004
1Ki	10:5	he went up unto the **h.** of the Lord;	1004
1Ki	10:12	trees pillars for the **h.** of the Lord,	1004
1Ki	10:12	and for the king's **h.**, harps also	1004
1Ki	10:17	in the **h.** of the forest of Lebanon.	1004
1Ki	10:21	of the **h.** of the forest of Lebanon	1004
1Ki	11:18	which gave him an **h.**, and appointed	1004
1Ki	11:20	Tahpenes weaned in Pharaoh's **h.**	1004
1Ki	11:28	all the charge of the **h.** of Joseph.	1004
1Ki	11:38	with thee, and build thee a sure **h.**	1004
1Ki	12:16	now see to thine own **h.**, David.	1004
1Ki	12:19	rebelled against the **h.** of David	1004
1Ki	12:20	none that followed the **h.** of David,	1004
1Ki	12:21	he assembled all the **h.** of Judah,	1004
1Ki	12:21	to fight against the **h.** of Israel,	1004
1Ki	12:23	all the **h.** of Judah and Benjamin,	1004
1Ki	12:24	return every man to his **h.**: for this	1004
1Ki	12:26	kingdom return to the **h.** of David:	1004
1Ki	12:27	sacrifice in the **h.** of the Lord at	1004
1Ki	12:31	he made an **h.** of high places, and	1004
1Ki	13:2	shall be born unto the **h.** of David,	1004
1Ki	13:8	If thou wilt give me half thine **h.**,	1004
1Ki	13:18	him back with thee into thine **h.**,	1004
1Ki	13:19	eat bread in his **h.**, and drank water,	1004
1Ki	13:34	became sin unto the **h.** of Jeroboam,	1004
1Ki	14:4	and came to the **h.** of Ahijah.	1004
1Ki	14:8	kingdom away from the **h.** of David,	1004
1Ki	14:10	bring evil upon the **h.** of Jeroboam	1004
1Ki	14:10	remnant of the **h.** of Jeroboam,	1004
1Ki	14:12	get thee to thine own **h.**: and	1004
1Ki	14:13	God of Israel in the **h.** of Jeroboam.	1004
1Ki	14:14	cut off the **h.** of Jeroboam that day:	1004
1Ki	14:26	the treasures of the **h.** of the Lord,	1004
1Ki	14:26	and the treasures of the king's **h.**:	1004
1Ki	14:27	which kept the door of the king's **h.**.	1004
1Ki	14:28	king went into the **h.** of the Lord,	1004
1Ki	15:15	into the **h.** of the Lord, silver, and	1004
1Ki	15:18	the treasures of the **h.** of the Lord,	1004
1Ki	15:18	and the treasures of the king's **h.**,	1004
1Ki	15:27	son of Abijah, of the **h.** of Issachar,	1004
1Ki	15:29	he smote all the **h.** of Jeroboam;	1004
1Ki	16:3	and the posterity of his **h.**; and will	1004
1Ki	16:3	make thy **h.** like the **h.** of Jeroboam	1004
1Ki	16:7	against Baasha, and against his **h.**,	1004
1Ki	16:7	in being like the **h.** of Jeroboam;	1004
1Ki	16:9	drinking himself drunk in the **h.** of	1004
1Ki	16:9	of Arza steward of his **h.** in Tirzah.	1004
1Ki	16:11	that he slew all the **h.** of Baasha:	1004
1Ki	16:12	Zimri destroy all the **h.** of Baasha,	1004
1Ki	16:18	went into the palace of the king's **h.**,	1004
1Ki	16:18	burnt the king's **h.** over him with	1004
1Ki	16:32	an altar to Baal in the **h.** of Baal,	1004
1Ki	17:15	he and her **h.**, did eat many days.	1004
1Ki	17:17	the mistress of the **h.**, fell sick;	1004
1Ki	17:23	down out of the chamber into the **h.**,	1004
1Ki	18:3	which was the governor of his **h.**.	1004
1Ki	18:18	but thou, and thy father's **h.**, in that	1004
1Ki	20:6	they shall search thine **h.**, and the	1004
1Ki	20:31	the **h.** of Israel are merciful kings:	1004
1Ki	20:43	king of Israel went to his **h.** heavy	1004
1Ki	21:2	because it is near unto my **h.**:	1004
1Ki	21:4	And Ahab came into his **h.** heavy	1004
1Ki	21:22	make thine **h.** like the **h.** of Jeroboam.	1004
1Ki	21:22	and like the **h.** of Baasha the son of	1004
1Ki	21:29	will I bring the evil upon his **h.**.	1004
1Ki	22:17	return every man to his **h.** in peace.	1004
1Ki	22:39	and the ivory **h.** which he made,	1004
2Ki	4:2	tell me, what hast thou in the **h.**?	1004
2Ki	4:2	hath not any thing in the **h.**, save	1004
2Ki	4:32	Elisha was come into the **h.**, behold,	1004
2Ki	4:35	and walked in the **h.** to and fro;	1004
2Ki	5:9	stood at the door of the **h.** of Elisha.	1004
2Ki	5:18	into the **h.** of Rimmon to worship	1004
2Ki	5:18	I bow myself in the **h.** of Rimmon:	1004
2Ki	5:18	down myself in the **h.** of Rimmon,	1004
2Ki	5:24	hand, and bestowed them in the **h.**	1004
2Ki	6:32	But Elisha sat in his **h.**, and the	1004
2Ki	7:11	they told it to the king's **h.** within.	1004
2Ki	8:3	to cry unto the king for her **h.** and	1004

2Ki 8:5 cried to the king for her **h.** and for..... 1004
2Ki 8:18 of Israel, as did the **h.** of Ahab:......... 1004
2Ki 8:27 walked in the way of the **h.** of Ahab, .. 1004
2Ki 8:27 of the Lord, as did the **h.** of Ahab:..... 1004
2Ki 8:27 was the son in law of the **h.** of Ahab. . 1004
2Ki 9:6 And he arose, and went into the **h.**; ... 1004
2Ki 9:7 smite the **h.** of Ahab thy master, ... 1004
2Ki 9:8 the whole **h.** of Ahab shall perish: 1004
2Ki 9:9 **h.** of Ahab like the **h.** of Jeroboam 1004
2Ki 9:9 and like the **h.** of Baasha the son....... 1004
2Ki 9:27 he fled by the way of the garden **h.**..... 1004
2Ki 10:3 and fight for your master's **h.**............. 1004
2Ki 10:5 And he that was over the **h.**, and....... 1004
2Ki 10:10 spake concerning the **h.** of Ahab: 1004
2Ki 10:11 all that remained of the **h.** of Ahab 1004
2Ki 10:12 was at the shearing **h.** in the way, ... 1004
2Ki 10:14 them at the pit of the shearing **h.**....... 1004
2Ki 10:21 And they came into the **h.** of Baal;..... 1004
2Ki 10:21 and the **h.** of Baal was full from......... 1004
2Ki 10:23 And Jehu went...into the **h.** of Baal, ... 1004
2Ki 10:25 went to the city of the **h.** of Baal. 1004
2Ki 10:26 images out of the **h.** of Baal, and 1004
2Ki 10:27 and brake down the **h.** of Baal,.......... 1004
2Ki 10:27 and made it a draught **h.** unto this day. .....
2Ki 10:30 eyes, hast done unto the **h.** of Ahab ... 1004
2Ki 11:3 hid in the **h.** of the Lord six years...... 1004
2Ki 11:4 them to him into the **h.** of the Lord,... 1004
2Ki 11:4 oath of them in the **h.** of the Lord,..... 1004
2Ki 11:5 of the watch of the king's **h.**;............ 1004
2Ki 11:6 so shall ye keep the watch of the **h.**, .. 1004
2Ki 11:7 keep the watch of the **h.** of the Lord .. 1004
2Ki 11:15 not be slain in the **h.** of the Lord. 1004
2Ki 11:16 the horses came into the king's **h.**....... 1004
2Ki 11:18 went into the **h.** of Baal, and brake 1004
2Ki 11:18 officers over the **h.** of the Lord. 1004
2Ki 11:19 the king from the **h.** of the Lord, ... 1004
2Ki 11:19 gate of the guard to the king's **h.**....... 1004
2Ki 11:20 with the sword beside the king's **h.** ... 1004
2Ki 12:4 is brought into the **h.** of the Lord,...... 1004
2Ki 12:4 to bring into the **h.** of the Lord, ... 1004
2Ki 12:5 them repair the breaches of the **h.**, ... 1004
2Ki 12:6 not repaired the breaches of the **h.**...... 1004
2Ki 12:7 repair ye not the breaches of the **h.**? .. 1004
2Ki 12:7 deliver it for the breaches of the **h.** ... 1004
2Ki 12:8 to repair the breaches of the **h.**......... 1004
2Ki 12:9 one cometh into the **h.** of the Lord:.... 1004
2Ki 12:9 was brought into the **h.** of the Lord.... 1004
2Ki 12:10 was found in the **h.** of the Lord. 1004
2Ki 12:11 the oversight of the **h.** of the Lord: 1004
2Ki 12:11 wrought upon the **h.** of the Lord........ 1004
2Ki 12:12 the breaches of the **h.** of the Lord, ... 1004
2Ki 12:12 was laid out for the **h.** to repair it. 1004
2Ki 12:13 the **h.** of the Lord bowls of silver,...... 1004
2Ki 12:13 was brought into the **h.** of the Lord:... 1004
2Ki 12:14 repaired therewith the **h.** of the......... 1004
2Ki 12:16 not brought into the **h.** of the Lord:.... 1004
2Ki 12:18 the treasures of the **h.** of the Lord,.... 1004
2Ki 12:18 and in the king's **h.**, and sent it 1004
2Ki 12:20 and slew Joash in the **h.** of Millo, ... 1004
2Ki 13:6 from the sins of the **h.** of Jeroboam, ... 1004
2Ki 14:14 were found in the **h.** of the Lord........ 1004
2Ki 14:14 in the treasures of the king's **h.**,........ 1004
2Ki 15:5 his death, and dwelt in a several **h.** 1004
2Ki 15:5 the king's son was over the **h.**, ... 1004
2Ki 15:25 in the palace of the king's **h.**, with...... 1004
2Ki 15:35 higher gate of the **h.** of the Lord, ... 1004
2Ki 16:8 gold that was found in the **h.** of......... 1004
2Ki 16:8 in the treasures of the king's **h.**,........ 1004
2Ki 16:14 Lord, from the forefront of the **h.**, ... 1004
2Ki 16:14 the altar and the **h.** of the Lord, ... 1004
2Ki 16:18 sabbath that they had built in the **h.**,... 1004
2Ki 16:18 turned he from the **h.** of the Lord...... 1004
2Ki 17:21 rent Israel from the **h.** of David;........ 1004
2Ki 18:15 silver that was found in the **h.** of 1004
2Ki 18:15 in the treasures of the king's **h.**......... 1004
2Ki 19:1 and went into the **h.** of the Lord........ 1004
2Ki 19:14 went up into the **h.** of the Lord, ... 1004
2Ki 19:26 as the grass on the **h.** tops, and as corn....
2Ki 19:30 that is escaped of the **h.** of Judah........ 1004
2Ki 19:37 worshipping in the **h.** of Nisroch 1004
2Ki 20:1 Set thine **h.** in order; for thou shalt.... 1004
2Ki 20:5 shalt go up unto the **h.** of the Lord. ... 1004
2Ki 20:8 I shall go up into the **h.** of the Lord ... 1004
2Ki 20:13 and all the **h.** of his precious things, ... 1004
2Ki 20:13 and all the **h.** of his armour, and all.... 1004
2Ki 20:13 there was nothing in his **h.**, nor in...... 1004
2Ki 20:15 What have they seen in thine **h.**? 1004
2Ki 20:15 that are in mine **h.** have they seen: 1004
2Ki 20:17 that all that is in thine **h.**, and that 1004
2Ki 21:4 he built altars in the **h.** of the Lord, ... 1004
2Ki 21:5 the two courts of the **h.** of the Lord .. 1004
2Ki 21:7 grove that he had made in the **h.**, ... 1004
2Ki 21:7 In this **h.**, and in Jerusalem, which 1004
2Ki 21:13 and the plummet of the **h.** of Ahab: ... 1004
2Ki 21:18 buried in the garden of his own **h.**,...... 1004
2Ki 21:23 and slew the king in his own **h.**. 1004
2Ki 22:3 the scribe, to the **h.** of the Lord, ... 1004
2Ki 22:4 is brought into the **h.** of the Lord,...... 1004
2Ki 22:5 the oversight of the **h.** of the Lord:.... 1004
2Ki 22:5 work which is in the **h.** of the Lord, ... 1004
2Ki 22:5 to repair the breaches of the **h.**, ... 1004
2Ki 22:6 and hewn stone to repair the **h.**.......... 1004
2Ki 22:8 found the book of the law in the **h.**..... 1004
2Ki 22:9 the money that was found in the **h.**, ... 1004
2Ki 22:9 the oversight of the **h.** of the Lord. 1004
2Ki 23:2 king went up into the **h.** of the Lord,.. 1004
2Ki 23:2 was found in the **h.** of the Lord. 1004
2Ki 23:6 the grove from the **h.** of the Lord, ... 1004
2Ki 23:7 that were by the **h.** of the Lord......... 1004
2Ki 23:11 entering in of the **h.** of the Lord, ... 1004
2Ki 23:12 the two courts of the **h.** of the Lord,.. 1004
2Ki 23:24 priest found in the **h.** of the Lord....... 1004
2Ki 23:27 and the **h.** of which I said, My name... 1004
2Ki 24:13 the treasures of the **h.** of the Lord,.... 1004
2Ki 24:13 and the treasures of the king's **h.**,....... 1004
2Ki 25:9 the **h.** of the Lord, and the king's **h.**, ..1004
2Ki 25:9 great man's **h.** burnt he with fire........ 1004
2Ki 25:13 brass that were in the **h.** of the......... 1004
2Ki 25:13 sea that was in the **h.** of the Lord,..... 1004
2Ki 25:16 had made for the **h.** of the Lord; 1004
1Ch 2:54 Ataroth, the **h.** of Joab, and half......... 5854
1Ch 2:55 the father of the **h.** of Rechab. 1004
1Ch 4:21 the families of the **h.** of them that...... 1004
1Ch 4:21 fine linen, of the **h.** of Ashbea, ... 1004
1Ch 4:38 the **h.** of their fathers increased......... 1004
1Ch 5:13 brethren of the **h.** of their fathers 1004
1Ch 5:15 Guni, chief of the **h.** of their 1004
1Ch 5:24 heads of the **h.** of their fathers, ... 1004
1Ch 5:24 heads of the **h.** of their fathers. 1004
1Ch 6:31 service of song in the **h.** of the Lord, ..1004
1Ch 6:32 Solomon had built the **h.** of the......... 1004
1Ch 6:48 of the tabernacle of the **h.** of God. 1004
1Ch 7:2 heads of their father's **h.**, to wit, ... 1004
1Ch 7:4 generations, after the **h.** of their........ 1004
1Ch 7:7, 9 heads of the **h.** of their fathers, ... 1004
1Ch 7:23 because it went evil with his **h.** 1004
1Ch 7:40 heads of their fathers' **h.**, choice........ 1004
1Ch 9:9 fathers in the **h.** of their fathers......... 1004
1Ch 9:11 Ahitub, the ruler of the **h.** of God; 1004
1Ch 9:13 heads of the **h.** of their fathers, ... 1004
1Ch 9:13 work of the service of the **h.** of God... 1004
1Ch 9:19 his brethren, of the **h.** of his father, ... 1004
1Ch 9:23 of the gates of the **h.** of the Lord, ... 1004
1Ch 9:23 namely, the **h.** of the tabernacle, by ... 1004
1Ch 9:26 and treasuries of the **h.** of God.......... 1004
1Ch 9:27 lodged round about the **h.** of God,....... 1004
1Ch 10:6 sons, and all his **h.** died together. 1004
1Ch 10:10 his armour in the **h.** of their gods,...... 1004
1Ch 12:28 of his father's **h.** twenty and two........ 1004
1Ch 12:29 had kept the ward of the **h.** of Saul. ... 1004
1Ch 12:30 famous throughout the **h.** of their........ 1004
1Ch 13:7 new cart out of the **h.** of Abinadab: 1004
1Ch 13:13 it aside into the **h.** of Obed-edom....... 1004
1Ch 13:14 Obed-edom in his **h.** three months...... 1004
1Ch 13:14 Lord blessed the **h.** of Obed-edom, ... 1004
1Ch 14:1 and carpenters, to build him an **h.**....... 1004
1Ch 15:25 out of the **h.** of Obed-edom with joy. .. 1004
1Ch 16:43 departed every man to his **h.**: 1004
1Ch 16:43 and David returned to bless his **h.**...... 1004
1Ch 17:1 came to pass, as David sat in his **h.**, .. 1004
1Ch 17:1 Lo, I dwell in an **h.** of cedars but....... 1004
1Ch 17:4 Thou shalt not build me an **h.** to........ 1004
1Ch 17:5 For I have not dwelt in an **h.** since..... 1004
1Ch 17:6 ye not built me an **h.** of cedars? 1004
1Ch 17:10 that the Lord will build thee an **h.**...... 1004
1Ch 17:12 He shall build me an **h.**, and I will....... 1004
1Ch 17:14 But I will settle him in mine **h.**, and ... 1004
1Ch 17:16 I, O Lord God, and what is mine **h.**, .. 1004
1Ch 17:17 spoken of thy servant's **h.** for a......... 1004
1Ch 17:23 thy servant and concerning his **h.**........ 1004
1Ch 17:24 and let the **h.** of David thy servant..... 1004
1Ch 17:25 that thou wilt build him an **h.**:........... 1004
1Ch 17:27 thee to bless the **h.** of thy servant, ... 1004
1Ch 21:17 be on me, and on my father's **h.**; 1004
1Ch 22:1 said, This is the **h.** of the Lord God, .. 1004
1Ch 22:2 stones to build the **h.** of God............ 1004
1Ch 22:5 the **h.** that is to be builded for the 1004
1Ch 22:6 him to build an **h.** for the Lord God.... 1004
1Ch 22:7 it was in my mind to build an **h.**......... 1004
1Ch 22:8 shalt not build an **h.** unto my name,.... 1004
1Ch 22:10 He shall build an **h.** for my name; 1004
1Ch 22:11 build the **h.** of the Lord thy God, ... 1004
1Ch 22:14 I have prepared for the **h.** of the 1004
1Ch 22:19 into the **h.** that is to be built to the.... 1004
1Ch 23:4 to set forward the work of the **h.** of... 1004
1Ch 23:11 according to their father's **h.**. 1004
1Ch 23:24 Levi after the **h.** of their fathers; 1004
1Ch 23:24 for the service of the **h.** of the Lord, .. 1004
1Ch 23:28 for the service of the **h.** of the Lord, .. 1004
1Ch 23:28 work of the service of the **h.** of God;.. 1004
1Ch 23:32 in the service of the **h.** of the Lord, ... 1004
1Ch 24:4 chief men of the **h.** of their fathers,.... 1004
1Ch 24:4 according to the **h.** of their fathers. 1004
1Ch 24:5 and governors of the **h.** of God,..............
1Ch 24:19 to come into the **h.** of the Lord, ... 1004
1Ch 24:30 after the **h.** of their fathers. 1004
1Ch 25:6 for song in the **h.** of the Lord,........... 1004
1Ch 25:6 for the service of the **h.** of God, ... 1004
1Ch 26:6 ruled throughout the **h.** of their 1004
1Ch 26:12 to minister in the **h.** of the Lord. 1004
1Ch 26:13 according to the **h.** of their.............. 1004
1Ch 26:15 and to his sons the **h.** of Asuppim. 1004
1Ch 26:20 over the treasures of the **h.** of God,... 1004
1Ch 26:22 the treasures of the **h.** of the Lord..... 1004
1Ch 26:27 to maintain the **h.** of the Lord. 1004
1Ch 28:2 to build an **h.** of rest for the ark........ 1004
1Ch 28:3 shalt not build an **h.** for my name,...... 1004
1Ch 28:4 chose me before all the **h.** of my 1004
1Ch 28:4 the **h.** of Judah, the **h.** of my father;... 1004
1Ch 28:6 thy son, he shall build my **h.** and 1004
1Ch 28:10 to build an **h.** for the sanctuary:......... 1004
1Ch 28:12 of the courts of the **h.** of the Lord. 1004
1Ch 28:12 of the treasuries of the **h.** of God,...... 1004
1Ch 28:13 of the service of the **h.** of the Lord, .. 1004
1Ch 28:13 of service in the **h.** of the Lord. 1004
1Ch 28:20 for the service of the **h.** of the Lord.. 1004
1Ch 28:21 for all the service of the **h.** of God: 1004
1Ch 29:2 for the **h.** of my God the gold for....... 1004
1Ch 29:3 my affection to the **h.** of my God, ... 1004
1Ch 29:3 which I have given to the **h.** of God, .. 1004
1Ch 29:3 all I have prepared for the holy **h.**,..... 1004
1Ch 29:7 gave for the service of the **h.** of God.. 1004
1Ch 29:8 to the treasure of the **h.** of the Lord, ..1004
1Ch 29:16 have prepared to build thee an **h.**........ 1004
2Ch 2:1 Solomon determined to build an **h.**....... 1004
2Ch 2:1 Lord, and an **h.** for his kingdom......... 1004
2Ch 2:3 to build him an **h.** to dwell therein,..... 1004
2Ch 2:4 build an **h.** to the name of the Lord.... 1004
2Ch 2:5 And the **h.** which I build is great:...... 1004
2Ch 2:6 But who is able to build him an **h.**,..... 1004
2Ch 2:6 then, that I should build him an **h.**,..... 1004
2Ch 2:9 the **h.** which I am about to build 1004
2Ch 2:12 that might build an **h.** for the Lord, ... 1004
2Ch 2:12 Lord, and an **h.** for his kingdom......... 1004
2Ch 3:1 began to build the **h.** of the Lord 1004
2Ch 3:3 for the building of the **h.** of God. 1004
2Ch 3:4 porch that was in front of the **h.**, ...
2Ch 3:4 according to the breadth of the **h.**, ... 1004
2Ch 3:5 And the greater **h.** he cieled with........ 1004
2Ch 3:6 he garnished the **h.** with precious....... 1004
2Ch 3:7 He overlaid also the **h.**, the beams, ... 1004
2Ch 3:8 he made the most holy **h.**, the length.. 1004
2Ch 3:8 according to the breadth of the **h.**, ... 1004
2Ch 3:10 in the most holy **h.**, he made two 1004
2Ch 3:11, 12 reaching to the wall of the **h.**......... 1004
2Ch 3:15 he made before the **h.** two pillars....... 1004
2Ch 4:11 king Solomon for the **h.** of God;......... 1004
2Ch 4:16 Solomon for the **h.** of the Lord of 1004
2Ch 4:19 all the vessels that were for the **h.**...... 1004
2Ch 4:22 the entry of the **h.**, the inner doors.... 1004
2Ch 4:22 the doors of the **h.** of the temple, ... 1004
2Ch 5:1 Solomon made for the **h.** of the 1004
2Ch 5:1 among the treasures of the **h.** of........ 1004
2Ch 5:7 to the oracle of the **h.**, into the most.. 1004
2Ch 5:13 **h.** was filled with a cloud, even the **h.** .1004
2Ch 5:14 glory of the Lord had filled the **h.** of... 1004
2Ch 6:2 I have built an **h.** of habitation for 1004
2Ch 6:5 the tribes of Israel to build an **h.** in, ... 1004
2Ch 6:7 David my father to build an **h.** for 1004
2Ch 6:8 heart to build an **h.** for my name,....... 1004
2Ch 6:9 thou shalt not build the **h.**; but thy..... 1004

2Ch 6:9 he shall build the **h.** for my name....... 1004
2Ch 6:10 have built the **h.** for the name of........ 1004
2Ch 6:18 how much less this **h.** which I have..... 1004
2Ch 6:20 eyes may be open upon this **h.** day 1004
2Ch 6:22 come before thine altar in this **h.**; 1004
2Ch 6:24 supplication before thee in this **h.**; 1004
2Ch 6:29 spread forth his hands in this **h.**: 1004
2Ch 6:32 if they come and pray in this **h.**; 1004
2Ch 6:33 may know that this **h.** which I have 1004
2Ch 6:34 and the **h.** which I have built for 1004
2Ch 6:38 toward the **h.** which I have built for.... 1004
2Ch 7:1 the glory of the Lord filled the **h.**....... 1004
2Ch 7:2 priests could not enter into the **h.**....... 1004
2Ch 7:2 of the Lord had filled the Lord's **h.**...... 1004
2Ch 7:3 the glory of the Lord upon the **h.**,...... 1004
2Ch 7:5 the people dedicated the **h.** of God..... 1004
2Ch 7:7 that was before the **h.** of the Lord: 1004
2Ch 7:11 the **h.** of the Lord, and the king's **h.**: ..1004
2Ch 7:11 the **h.** of the Lord, and in his own **h.**,. 1004
2Ch 7:12 place to myself for an **h.** of sacrifice. .. 1004
2Ch 7:16 have I chosen and sanctified this **h.**, ... 1004
2Ch 7:20 and this **h.**, which I have sanctified..... 1004
2Ch 7:21 And this **h.**, which is high, shall be..... 1004
2Ch 7:21 unto this land, and unto this **h.**?........ 1004
2Ch 8:1 the **h.** of the Lord, and his own **h.**,..... 1004
2Ch 8:11 unto the **h.** that he had built for her: .. 1004
2Ch 8:11 My wife shall not dwell in the **h.** of 1004
2Ch 8:16 the foundation of the **h.** of the Lord,... 1004
2Ch 8:16 So the **h.** of the Lord was perfected. .. 1004
2Ch 9:3 Solomon, and the **h.** that he had 1004
2Ch 9:4 he went up into the **h.** of the Lord;.... 1004
2Ch 9:11 trees terraces to the **h.** of the Lord,... 1004
2Ch 9:16 in the **h.** of the forest of Lebanon. 1004
2Ch 9:20 of the **h.** of the forest of Lebanon 1004
2Ch 10:16 and now, David, see to thine own **h.**. ..1004
2Ch 10:19 rebelled against the **h.** of David 1004
2Ch 11:1 he gathered of the **h.** of Judah and 1004
2Ch 11:4 return every man to his **h.**: for......... 1004
2Ch 12:9 the treasures of the **h.** of the Lord,.... 1004
2Ch 12:9 and the treasures of the king's **h.**;...... 1004
2Ch 12:10 kept the entrance of the king's **h.**....... 1004
2Ch 12:11 king entered into the **h.** of the Lord, .. 1004
2Ch 15:18 he brought into the **h.** of God the 1004
2Ch 16:2 **h.** of the Lord, and of the king's **h.**, ... 1004
2Ch 16:10 seer, and put him in a prison **h.**;........ 1004
2Ch 17:14 according to the **h.** of their fathers: 1004
2Ch 18:16 every man to his **h.** in peace............ 1004
2Ch 19:1 Judah returned to his **h.** in peace 1004
2Ch 19:11 the ruler of the **h.** of Judah,............. 1004
2Ch 20:5 in the **h.** of the Lord, before the new ..1004
2Ch 20:9 we stand before this **h.**, and in thy..... 1004
2Ch 20:9 for thy name is in this **h.**, and cry...... 1004
2Ch 20:28 trumpets unto the **h.** of the Lord. 1004
2Ch 21:6 of Israel, like as did the **h.** of Ahab: ... 1004
2Ch 21:7 would not destroy the **h.** of David,...... 1004
2Ch 21:13 to the whoredoms of the **h.** of Ahab, .. 1004
2Ch 21:13 slain thy brethren of thy father's **h.**, ... 1004
2Ch 21:17 that was found in the king's **h.**,.......... 1004
2Ch 22:3 also in the ways of the **h.** of Ahab:..... 1004
2Ch 22:4 of the Lord like the **h.** of Ahab:......... 1004
2Ch 22:7 anointed to cut off the **h.** of Ahab....... 1004
2Ch 22:8 judgment upon the **h.** of Ahab, ... 1004
2Ch 22:9 So the **h.** of Ahaziah had no power..... 1004
2Ch 22:10 all the seed royal of the **h.** of Judah.... 1004
2Ch 22:12 them hid in the **h.** of God six years:... 1004
2Ch 23:3 with the king in the **h.** of God.......... 1004
2Ch 23:5 third part shall be at the king's **h.**; 1004
2Ch 23:5 in the courts of the **h.** of the Lord. 1004
2Ch 23:6 none come into the **h.** of the Lord,...... 1004
2Ch 23:7 cometh into the **h.**, he shall be put..... 1004
2Ch 23:9 David's which were in the **h.** of God... 1004
2Ch 23:12 the people into the **h.** of the Lord: 1004
2Ch 23:14 Slay her not in the **h.** of the Lord. 1004
2Ch 23:15 of the horse gate by the king's **h.**, ... 1004
2Ch 23:17 went to the **h.** of Baal, and brake it.... 1004
2Ch 23:18 the offices of the **h.** of the Lord......... 1004
2Ch 23:18 distributed in the **h.** of the Lord,........ 1004
2Ch 23:19 at the gates of the **h.** of the Lord, ... 1004
2Ch 23:20 the king from the **h.** of the Lord:....... 1004
2Ch 23:20 the high gate into the king's **h.**, ... 1004
2Ch 24:4 minded to repair the **h.** of the Lord. ... 1004
2Ch 24:5 repair the **h.** of your God from year ... 1004
2Ch 24:7 had broken up the **h.** of God; and 1004
2Ch 24:7 dedicated things of the **h.** of the 1004
2Ch 24:8 at the gate of the **h.** of the Lord....... 1004
2Ch 24:12 of the service of the **h.** of the Lord, ... 1004
2Ch 24:12 to repair the **h.** of the Lord, ... 1004
2Ch 24:12 brass to mend the **h.** of the Lord...... 1004
2Ch 24:13 they set the **h.** of God in his state, ... 1004
2Ch 24:14 made vessels for the **h.** of the Lord,.... 1004
2Ch 24:14 burnt offerings in the **h.** of the Lord... 1004
2Ch 24:16 both toward God, and toward his **h.**.... 1004
2Ch 24:18 And they left the **h.** of the Lord God.. 1004
2Ch 24:21 in the court of the **h.** of the Lord...... 1004
2Ch 24:27 and the repairing of the **h.** of God, ... 1004
2Ch 25:24 that were found in the **h.** of God........ 1004
2Ch 25:24 and the treasures of the king's **h.**,...... 1004
2Ch 26:19 before the priests in the **h.** of the 1004
2Ch 26:21 dwelt in a several **h.**, being a leper;.... 1004
2Ch 26:21 was cut off from the **h.** of the Lord: ... 1004
2Ch 26:21 his sons was over the king's **h.**,......... 1004
2Ch 27:3 the high gate of the **h.** of the Lord, ... 1004
2Ch 28:7 Azrikam the governor of the **h.**, and... 1004
2Ch 28:21 a portion out of the **h.** of the Lord, ... 1004
2Ch 28:21 and out of the **h.** of the king, and of... 1004
2Ch 28:24 together the vessels of the **h.** of God,..1004
2Ch 28:24 pieces the vessels of the **h.** of God, ... 1004
2Ch 28:24 up the doors of the **h.** of the Lord, ... 1004
2Ch 29:3 the doors of the **h.** of the Lord,......... 1004
2Ch 29:5 sanctify the **h.** of the Lord God of...... 1004
2Ch 29:15 Lord, to cleanse the **h.** of the Lord. ... 1004
2Ch 29:16 the inner part of the **h.** of the Lord, ... 1004
2Ch 29:16 into the court of the **h.** of the Lord. ... 1004
2Ch 29:17 so they sanctified the **h.** of the Lord... 1004
2Ch 29:18 We have cleansed all the **h.** of the...... 1004
2Ch 29:20 and went up to the **h.** of the Lord...... 1004
2Ch 29:25 set the Levites in the **h.** of the Lord .. 1004
2Ch 29:31 offerings into the **h.** of the Lord......... 1004
2Ch 29:35 the service of the **h.** of the Lord was.. 1004
2Ch 30:1 should come to the **h.** of the Lord...... 1004
2Ch 30:15 offerings into the **h.** of the Lord......... 1004
2Ch 31:10 the chief priest of the **h.** of Zadok...... 1004
2Ch 31:10 the offerings into the **h.** of the Lord, .. 1004
2Ch 31:11 chambers in the **h.** of the Lord; 1004
2Ch 31:13 Azariah the ruler of the **h.** of God. 1004
2Ch 31:16 that entereth into the **h.** of the Lord,.. 1004
2Ch 31:17 priests by the **h.** of their fathers, ... 1004
2Ch 31:21 began in the service of the **h.** of God,..1004
2Ch 32:21 he was come into the **h.** of his god,.... 1004
2Ch 33:4 he build altars in the **h.** of the Lord, .. 1004
2Ch 33:5 the two courts of the **h.** of the Lord.. 1004
2Ch 33:7 idol...he had made, in the **h.** of God, .. 1004
2Ch 33:7 In this **h.**, and in Jerusalem, which 1004
2Ch 33:15 the idol out of the **h.** of the Lord, ... 1004
2Ch 33:15 in the mount of the **h.** of the Lord, ... 1004
2Ch 33:20 and they buried him in his own **h.**: 1004
2Ch 33:24 him, and slew him in his own **h.**. 1004
2Ch 34:8 he had purged the land, and the **h.**,.... 1004
2Ch 34:8 to repair the **h.** of the Lord his God. .. 1004
2Ch 34:9 that was brought into the **h.** of God,... 1004
2Ch 34:10 the oversight of the **h.** of the Lord,.... 1004
2Ch 34:10 workmen that wrought in the **h.** of..... 1004
2Ch 34:10 Lord, to repair and amend the **h.**; 1004
2Ch 34:14 was brought into the **h.** of the Lord.... 1004
2Ch 34:15 book of the law in the **h.** of the Lord...1004
2Ch 34:17 money that was found in the **h.** of...... 1004
2Ch 34:30 king went up into the **h.** of the Lord,.. 1004
2Ch 34:30 that was found in the **h.** of the Lord. .. 1004
2Ch 35:2 to the service of the **h.** of the Lord,... 1004
2Ch 35:3 Put the holy ark in the **h.** which 1004
2Ch 35:8 and Jehiel, rulers of the **h.** of God,..... 1004
2Ch 35:21 against the **h.** wherewith I have war: .. 1004
2Ch 36:7 of the vessels of the **h.** of the Lord.... 1004
2Ch 36:10 goodly vessels of the **h.** of the Lord, .. 1004
2Ch 36:14 polluted the **h.** of the Lord which....... 1004
2Ch 36:17 sword in the **h.** of their sanctuary, ... 1004
2Ch 36:18 all the vessels of the **h.** of God,......... 1004
2Ch 36:18 the treasures of the **h.** of the Lord,.... 1004
2Ch 36:19 And they burnt the **h.** of God, and..... 1004
2Ch 36:23 charged me to build him an **h.** in........ 1004
Ezr 1:2 charged me to build him an **h.** at........ 1004
Ezr 1:3 and build the **h.** of the Lord God of.... 1004
Ezr 1:4 freewill offering for the **h.** of God....... 1004
Ezr 1:5 to go up to build the **h.** of the Lord.... 1004
Ezr 1:7 the vessels of the **h.** of the Lord, ... 1004
Ezr 1:7 had put them in the **h.** of his gods;..... 1004
Ezr 2:36 of the **h.** of Jeshua, nine hundred....... 1004
Ezr 2:59 could not shew their father's **h.**, ... 1004
Ezr 2:68 when they came to the **h.** of the Lord. 1004
Ezr 2:68 offered freely for the **h.** of God 1004
Ezr 3:8 of their coming unto the **h.** of God..... 1004
Ezr 3:8 the work of the **h.** of the Lord. 1004
Ezr 3:9 the workmen in the **h.** of God: 1004
Ezr 3:11 foundation of the **h.** of the Lord was... 1004
Ezr 3:12 men, that had seen the first **h.**, ... 1004
Ezr 3:12 the foundation of this **h.** was laid........ 1004
Ezr 4:3 nothing to do with us to build an **h.**..... 1004
Ezr 4:24 ceased the work of the **h.** of God....... 1005
Ezr 5:2 and began to build the **h.** of God........ 1005
Ezr 5:3 commanded you to build this **h.**, ... 1005
Ezr 5:8 to the **h.** of the great God, which is ... 1005
Ezr 5:9 commanded you to build this **h.**, ... 1005
Ezr 5:11 and build the **h.** that was builded........ 1005
Ezr 5:12 who destroyed this **h.**, and carried 1005
Ezr 5:13 a decree to build this **h.** of God. 1005
Ezr 5:14 of gold and silver of the **h.** of God,..... 1005
Ezr 5:15 let the **h.** of God be builded in his...... 1005
Ezr 5:16 laid the foundation of the **h.** of God 1005
Ezr 5:17 made in the king's treasure **h.**, ... 1005
Ezr 5:17 to build this **h.** of God at Jerusalem, ... 1005
Ezr 6:1 was made in the **h.** of the rolls, ... 1005
Ezr 6:3 a decree concerning the **h.** of God...... 1005
Ezr 6:3 Let the **h.** be builded, the place......... 1005
Ezr 6:4 be given out of the king's **h.**: 1005
Ezr 6:5 and silver vessels of the **h.** of God, ... 1005
Ezr 6:5 and place them in the **h.** of God......... 1005
Ezr 6:7 Let the work of this **h.** of God alone;.. 1005
Ezr 6:7 elders of the Jews build this **h.** of....... 1005
Ezr 6:8 for the building of this **h.** of God: 1005
Ezr 6:11 timber be pulled down from his **h.**,..... 1005
Ezr 6:11 and let his **h.** be made a dunghill........ 1005
Ezr 6:12 alter and to destroy this **h.** of God 1005
Ezr 6:15 And this **h.** was finished on the.......... 1005
Ezr 6:16 kept the dedication of this **h.** of God... 1005
Ezr 6:17 at the dedication of this **h.** of God...... 1005
Ezr 6:22 hands in the work of the **h.** of God,..... 1004
Ezr 7:16 willingly for the **h.** of their God.......... 1005
Ezr 7:17 upon the altar of the **h.** of your God... 1005
Ezr 7:19 for the service of the **h.** of thy God,... 1005
Ezr 7:20 be needful for the **h.** of thy God, ... 1005
Ezr 7:20 it out of the king's treasure **h.**.......... 1005
Ezr 7:23 done for the **h.** of the God of heaven:..1005
Ezr 7:24 or ministers of this **h.** of God, ... 1005
Ezr 7:27 to beautify the **h.** of the Lord........... 1004
Ezr 8:17 us ministers for the **h.** of our God...... 1004
Ezr 8:25 the offering of the **h.** of our God,....... 1004
Ezr 8:29 the chambers of the **h.** of the Lord..... 1004
Ezr 8:30 to Jerusalem unto the **h.** of our God. .. 1004
Ezr 8:33 vessels weighed in the **h.** of our God.. 1004
Ezr 8:36 the people, and the **h.** of God. 1004
Ezr 9:9 reviving, to set up the **h.** of our God, . 1004
Ezr 10:1 himself down before the **h.** of God, ... 1004
Ezr 10:6 rose up from before the **h.** of God, ... 1004
Ezr 10:9 sat in the street of the **h.** of God,...... 1004
Ezr 10:16 after the **h.** of their fathers, and all,.... 1004
Ne 1:6 I and my father's **h.** have sinned. 1004
Ne 2:8 palace which appertained to the **h.**,...... 1004
Ne 2:8 and for the **h.** that I shall enter into.... 1004
Ne 3:10 Harumaph, even over against his **h.**.... 1004
Ne 3:16 and unto the **h.** of the mighty............. 1004
Ne 3:20 unto the door of the **h.** of Eliashib...... 1004
Ne 3:21 from the door of the **h.** of Eliashib 1004
Ne 3:21 even to the end of the **h.** of Eliashib... 1004
Ne 3:23 and Hashub over against their **h.**......... 1004
Ne 3:23 the son of Ananiah by his **h.**.............. 1004
Ne 3:24 from the **h.** of Azariah unto the 1004
Ne 3:25 lieth out from the king's high **h.**, ... 1004
Ne 3:28 every one over against his **h.**............ 1004
Ne 3:29 son of Immer over against his **h.**......... 1004
Ne 4:16 were behind all the **h.** of Judah. 1004
Ne 5:13 shake out every man from his **h.**,......... 1004
Ne 6:10 I came unto the **h.** of Shemaiah 1004
Ne 6:10 us meet together in the **h.** of God,...... 1004
Ne 7:3 every one to be over against his **h.**. ... 1004
Ne 7:39 of the **h.** of Jeshua, nine hundred 1004
Ne 7:61 could not shew their father's **h.**, ... 1004
Ne 8:16 every one upon the roof of his **h.**,...........
Ne 8:16 and in the courts of the **h.** of God, ... 1004
Ne 10:32 for the service of the **h.** of our God;... 1004
Ne 10:33 for all the work of the **h.** of our God. . 1004
Ne 10:34 to bring it into the **h.** of our God, ... 1004
Ne 10:35 by year, unto the **h.** of the Lord: 1004
Ne 10:36 flocks, to bring to the **h.** of our God. .. 1004
Ne 10:36 that minister in the **h.** of our God: 1004
Ne 10:37 the chambers of the **h.** of our God; 1004
Ne 10:38 of the tithes unto the **h.** of our God,... 1004
Ne 10:38 the chambers, into the treasure **h.** 1004
Ne 10:39 will not forsake the **h.** of our God. 1004
Ne 11:11 was the ruler of the **h.** of God.......... 1004
Ne 11:12 brethren that did the work of the **h.** ... 1004

Book	Ref	Context	No.
Ne	11:16	outward business of the **h.** of God	1004
Ne	11:22	over the business of the **h.** of God.	1004
Ne	12:29	Also from the **h.** of Gilgal, and out	1004
Ne	12:37	above the **h.** of David, even unto	1004
Ne	12:40	that gave thanks in the **h.** of God,	1004
Ne	13:4	the chamber of the **h.** of our God,	1004
Ne	13:7	in the courts of the **h.** of God	1004
Ne	13:9	again the vessels of the **h.** of God,	1004
Ne	13:11	Why is the **h.** of God forsaken?	1004
Ne	13:14	I have done for the **h.** of my God,	1004
Es	1:8	appointed to all the officers of his **h.**,	1004
Es	1:9	feast for the women in the royal **h.**	1004
Es	1:22	man should bear rule in his own **h.**,	1004
Es	2:3	the palace, to the **h.** of the women.	1004
Es	2:8	was brought also unto the king's **h.**,	1004
Es	2:9	be given her, out of the king's **h.**:	1004
Es	2:9	best place of the **h.** of the women.	1004
Es	2:11	before the court of the women's **h.**,	1004
Es	2:13	her out of the **h.** of the women	1004
Es	2:13	of the women unto the king's **h.**.	1004
Es	2:14	into the second **h.** of the women,	1004
Es	2:16	king Ahasuerus into his **h.** royal	1004
Es	4:13	thou shalt escape in the king's **h.**,	1004
Es	4:14	thy father's **h.** shall be destroyed:	1004
Es	5:1	in the inner court of the king's **h.**,	1004
Es	5:1	over against the king's **h.**:	1004
Es	5:1	upon his royal throne in the royal **h.**,	1004
Es	5:1	over against the gate of the **h.**.	1004
Es	6:4	the outward court of the king's **h.**,	1004
Es	6:12	Haman hasted to his **h.** mourning.	1004
Es	7:8	the queen also before me in the **h.**?	1004
Es	7:9	king, standeth in the **h.** of Haman.	1004
Es	8:1	give the **h.** of Haman the Jews'	1004
Es	8:2	set Mordecai over the **h.** of Haman.	1004
Es	8:7	have given Esther the **h.** of Haman,	1004
Es	9:4	Mordecai was great in the king's **h.**,	1004
Job	1:10	hedge about him, and about his **h.**,	1004
Job	1:13,	18 wine in their eldest brother's **h.**:	1004
Job	1:19	smote the four corners of the **h.**,	1004
Job	7:10	He shall return no more to his **h.**,	1004
Job	8:15	He shall lean upon his **h.**, but it	1004
Job	17:13	If I wait, the grave is mine **h.**:	1004
Job	19:15	They that dwell in mine **h.**, and my	1004
Job	20:19	violently taken away an **h.** which	1004
Job	20:28	The increase of his **h.** shall depart,	1004
Job	21:21	pleasure hath he in his **h.** after him,	1004
Job	21:28	say, Where is the **h.** of the prince?	1004
Job	27:18	He buildeth his **h.** as a moth, and as	1004
Job	30:23	to the **h.** appointed for all living.	1004
Job	38:20	know the paths to the **h.** thereof?	1004
Job	39:6	**h.** I have made the wilderness,	1004
Job	42:11	did eat bread with him in his **h.**:	1004
Ps	5:7	as for me, I will come into thy **h.** in	1004
Ps	23:6	dwell in the **h.** of the Lord for ever.	1004
Ps	26:8	have loved the habitation of thy **h.**	1004
Ps	27:4	I may dwell in the **h.** of the Lord all	1004
Ps	30:*title*	at the dedication of the **h.** of	1004
Ps	31:2	for an **h.** of defence to save me.	1004
Ps	36:8	satisfied with the fatness of thy **h.**;	1004
Ps	42:4	I went with them to the **h.** of God,	1004
Ps	45:10	own people, and thy father's **h.**;	1004
Ps	49:16	the glory of his **h.** is increased;	1004
Ps	50:9	I will take no bullock out of thy **h.**,	1004
Ps	52:*title*	come to the **h.** of Abimelech.	1004
Ps	50:8	a green olive tree in the **h.** of God:	1004
Ps	55:14	and walked unto the **h.** of God in	1004
Ps	59:*title*	they watched the **h.** to kill him.	1004
Ps	65:4	satisfied with the goodness of thy **h.**,	1004
Ps	66:13	I will go into thy **h.** with burnt	1004
Ps	69:9	the zeal of thine **h.** hath eaten me	1004
Ps	84:3	the sparrow hath found an **h.**, and	1004
Ps	84:4	are they that dwell in thy **h.**: they	1004
Ps	84:10	a doorkeeper in the **h.** of my God,	1004
Ps	92:13	be planted in the **h.** of the Lord	1004
Ps	93:5	holiness becometh thine **h.**, O Lord,	1004
Ps	98:3	his truth toward the **h.** of Israel:	1004
Ps	101:2	walk within my **h.** with a perfect	1004
Ps	101:7	deceit shall not dwell within my **h.**:	1004
Ps	102:7	a sparrow alone upon the **h.** top	
Ps	104:17	the stork, the fir trees are her **h.**.	1004
Ps	105:21	He made him lord of his **h.**, and	1004
Ps	112:3	Wealth and riches shall be in his **h.**:	1004
Ps	113:9	the barren woman to keep **h.**, and	1004
Ps	114:1	the **h.** of Jacob from a people of	1004
Ps	115:10	O **h.** of Aaron, trust in the Lord:	1004
Ps	115:12	he will bless the **h.** of Israel;	1004
Ps	115:12	he will bless the **h.** of Aaron.	1004
Ps	116:9	In the courts of the Lord's **h.**, in	1004
Ps	118:3	Let the **h.** of Aaron now say, that	1004
Ps	118:26	blessed you out of the **h.** of the	1004
Ps	119:54	songs in the **h.** of my pilgrimage.	1004
Ps	122:1	Let us go into the **h.** of the Lord.	1004
Ps	122:5	the thrones of the **h.** of David.	1004
Ps	122:9	Because of the **h.** of the Lord our	1004
Ps	127:1	Except the Lord build the **h.**, they	1004
Ps	128:3	vine by the sides of thine **h.**:	1004
Ps	132:3	come into the tabernacle of my **h.**,	1004
Ps	134:1	night stand in the **h.** of the Lord.	1004
Ps	135:2	Ye that stand in the **h.** of the Lord,	1004
Ps	135:2	in the courts of the **h.** of our God,	1004
Ps	135:19	Bless the Lord, O **h.** of Israel:	1004
Ps	135:19	bless the Lord, O **h.** of Aaron:	1004
Ps	135:20	Bless the Lord, O **h.** of Levi: ye	1004
Pr	2:18	For her **h.** inclineth unto death,	1004
Pr	3:33	the Lord is in the **h.** of the wicked:	1004
Pr	5:8	come not nigh the door of her **h.**:	1004
Pr	5:10	labours be in the **h.** of a stranger;	1004
Pr	6:31	give all the substance of his **h.**.	1004
Pr	7:6	For at the window of my **h.** I looked	1004
Pr	7:8	he went the way to her **h.**, and	1004
Pr	7:11	her feet abide not in her **h.**:	1004
Pr	7:27	Her **h.** is the way to hell, going	1004
Pr	9:1	Wisdom hath builded her **h.**, she	1004
Pr	9:14	she sitteth at the door of her **h.**,	1004
Pr	11:29	He that troubleth his own **h.** shall	1004
Pr	12:7	the **h.** of the righteous shall stand.	1004
Pr	14:1	wise woman buildeth her **h.**: but	1004
Pr	14:11	The **h.** of the wicked shall be	1004
Pr	15:6	In the **h.** of the righteous is much	1004
Pr	15:25	will destroy the **h.** of the proud:	1004
Pr	15:27	greedy of gain troubleth his own **h.**;	1004
Pr	17:1	than an **h.** full of sacrifices with	1004
Pr	17:13	evil shall not depart from his **h.**.	1004
Pr	19:14	**H.** and riches are the inheritance	1004
Pr	21:9	a brawling woman in a wide **h.**.	1004
Pr	21:12	considereth the **h.** of the wicked:	1004
Pr	24:3	Through wisdom is an **h.** builded;	1004
Pr	24:27	and afterwards build thine **h.**.	1004
Pr	25:17	thy foot from thy neighbour's **h.**;	1004
Pr	25:24	brawling woman and in a wide **h.**.	1004
Pr	27:10	neither go into thy brother's **h.** in	1004
Ec	2:7	and had servant born in my **h.**;	1004
Ec	5:1	when thou goest to the **h.** of God,	1004
Ec	7:2	better to go to the **h.** of mourning,	1004
Ec	7:2	that to go to the **h.** of feasting:	1004
Ec	7:4	the wise is in the **h.** of mourning;	1004
Ec	7:4	heart of fools is in the **h.** of mirth.	1004
Ec	10:18	of the hands the **h.** droppeth	1004
Ec	12:3	the keepers of the **h.** shall tremble,	1004
Ca	1:17	The beams of our **h.** are cedar, and	1004
Ca	2:4	brought me to the banqueting **h.**,	1004
Ca	3:4	brought him into my mother's **h.**.	1004
Ca	8:2	bring thee into my mother's **h.**,	1004
Ca	8:7	all the substance of his **h.** for love.	1004
Isa	2:2	the mountain of the Lord's **h.** shall	1004
Isa	2:3	Lord, to the **h.** of the God of Jacob;	1004
Isa	2:5	O **h.** of Jacob, come ye, and let us	1004
Isa	2:6	forsaken thy people the **h.** of Jacob,	1004
Isa	3:6	his brother of the **h.** of his father,	1004
Isa	3:7	for in my **h.** is neither bread nor	1004
Isa	5:7	Lord of hosts is the **h.** of Israel,	1004
Isa	5:8	Woe unto them that join **h.** to **h.**,	1004
Isa	6:4	and the **h.** was filled with smoke.	1004
Isa	7:2	it was told the **h.** of David, saying,	1004
Isa	7:13	said, Hear ye now, O **h.** of David;	1004
Isa	7:17	and upon thy father's **h.**, days that	1004
Isa	8:17	hideth his face from the **h.** of Jacob,	1004
Isa	10:20	as are escaped of the **h.** of Jacob,	1004
Isa	14:1	they shall cleave to the **h.** of Jacob.	1004
Isa	14:2	the **h.** of Israel shall possess them	1004
Isa	14:17	opened not the **h.** of his prisoners?	1004
Isa	14:18	in glory, every one in his own **h.**.	1004
Isa	22:8	the armour of the **h.** of the forest.	1004
Isa	22:15	Shebna, which is over the **h.**, and	1004
Isa	22:18	shall be the shame of thy Lord's **h.**.	1004
Isa	22:21	Jerusalem, and to the **h.** of Judah.	1004
Isa	22:22	the key of the **h.** of David will I lay	1004
Isa	22:23	a glorious throne to his father's **h.**	1004
Isa	22:24	him all the glory of his father's **h.**,	1004
Isa	23:1	is laid waste, so that there is no **h.**,	1004
Isa	24:10	every **h.** is shut up, that no man	1004
Isa	29:22	concerning the **h.** of Jacob, Jacob	1004
Isa	31:2	arise against the **h.** of the evildoers,	1004
Isa	36:3	son, which was over the **h.**, and	1004
Isa	37:1	and went into the **h.** of the Lord.	1004
Isa	37:14	went up unto the **h.** of the Lord,	1004
Isa	37:31	escaped of the **h.** of Judah shall	1004
Isa	37:38	worshipping in the **h.** of Nisroch	1004
Isa	38:1	Set thine **h.** in order: for thou shalt	1004
Isa	38:20	days of our life in the **h.** of the Lord	1004
Isa	38:22	I shall go up to the **h.** of the Lord?	1004
Isa	39:2	them the **h.** of his precious things,	1004
Isa	39:2	and all the **h.** of his armour, and all	1004
Isa	39:2	there was nothing in his **h.**, nor in	1004
Isa	39:4	What have they seen in thy **h.**? And	1004
Isa	39:4	All that is in mine **h.** have they	1004
Isa	39:6	all that is in thine **h.**, and that	1004
Isa	42:7	in darkness out of the prison **h.**.	1004
Isa	44:13	man; that it may remain in the **h.**.	1004
Isa	46:3	Hearken unto me, O **h.** of Jacob,	1004
Isa	46:3	all the remnant of the **h.** of Israel,	1004
Isa	48:1	Hear ye this O **h.** of Jacob, which	1004
Isa	56:5	will I give in mine **h.** and within	1004
Isa	56:7	them joyful in my **h.** of prayer:	1004
Isa	56:7	mine **h.** shall be called an **h.** of	1004
Isa	58:1	and the **h.** of Jacob their sins	1004
Isa	58:7	the poor that are cast out to thy **h.**?	1004
Isa	60:7	I will glorify the **h.** of my glory.	1004
Isa	63:7	goodness toward the **h.** of Israel,	1004
Isa	64:11	Our holy and our beautiful **h.**,	1004
Isa	66:1	where is the **h.** that ye build unto	1004
Isa	66:20	clean vessel into the **h.** of the Lord.	1004
Jer	2:4	word of the Lord, O **h.** of Jacob,	1004
Jer	2:4	all the families of the **h.** of Israel:	1004
Jer	2:26	so is the **h.** of Israel ashamed; they,	1004
Jer	3:18	In those days the **h.** of Judah shall	1004
Jer	3:18	walk with the **h.** of Israel, and they	1004
Jer	3:20	with me, O **h.** of Israel,	1004
Jer	5:11	the **h.** of Israel and the **h.** of Judah	1004
Jer	5:15	upon you from far, O **h.** of Israel,	1004
Jer	5:20	Declare this in the **h.** of Jacob,	1004
Jer	7:2	Stand in the gate of the Lord's **h.**,	1004
Jer	7:10	come and stand before me in this **h.**,	1004
Jer	7:11	Is this **h.**, which is called by my	1004
Jer	7:14	will I do unto this **h.**, which is	1004
Jer	7:30	the **h.** which is called by my name,	1004
Jer	9:26	**h.** of Israel are uncircumcised in	1004
Jer	10:1	speaketh unto you, O **h.** of Israel:	1004
Jer	11:10	the **h.** of Israel and the **h.** of Judah	1004
Jer	11:15	hath my beloved to do in mine **h.**,	1004
Jer	11:17	**h.** of Israel and of the **h.** of Judah,	1004
Jer	12:6	brethren, and the **h.** of thy father,	1004
Jer	12:7	I have forsaken mine **h.**, I have left	1004
Jer	12:14	pluck out the **h.** of Judah from	1004
Jer	13:11	to cleave unto me the whole **h.** of	1004
Jer	13:11	whole **h.** of Judah, saith the Lord;	1004
Jer	16:5	enter not into the **h.** of mourning,	1004
Jer	16:8	not also go into the **h.** of feasting,	1004
Jer	17:26	of praise, unto the **h.** of the Lord.	1004
Jer	18:2	go down to the potter's **h.**, and	1004
Jer	18:3	Then I went down to the potter's **h.**,	1004
Jer	18:6	O **h.** of Israel, cannot I do with you.	1004
Jer	18:6	are ye in mine hand, O **h.** of Israel.	1004
Jer	19:14	stood in the court of the Lord's **h.**;	1004
Jer	20:1	chief governor in the **h.** of the Lord,	1004
Jer	20:2	which was by the **h.** of the Lord.	1004
Jer	20:6	all that dwell in thine **h.** shall go	1004
Jer	21:11	and touching the **h.** of the king of	1004
Jer	21:12	O **h.** of David, thus saith the Lord;	1004
Jer	22:1	down to the **h.** of the king of Judah,	1004
Jer	22:4	enter in by the gates of this **h.**	1004
Jer	22:5	Lord, that this **h.** shall become a	1004
Jer	22:6	Lord unto the king's **h.** of Judah;	1004
Jer	22:13	buildeth his **h.** by unrighteousness,	1004
Jer	22:14	I will build me a wide **h.** and large	1004
Jer	23:8	led the seed of the **h.** of Israel out	1004
Jer	23:11	in my **h.** have I found their	1004
Jer	23:34	will even punish the man and his **h.**.	1004
Jer	26:2	Stand in the court of the Lord's **h.**,	1004
Jer	26:2	come to worship in the Lord's **h.**,	1004
Jer	26:6	Then will I make this **h.** like Shiloh,	1004
Jer	26:7	these words in the **h.** of the Lord.	1004
Jer	26:9	saying, This **h.** shall be like Shiloh,	1004
Jer	26:9	Jeremiah in the **h.** of the Lord.	1004
Jer	26:10	from the king's **h.** unto the **h.** of the	1004
Jer	26:10	entry of the new gate of the Lord's **h.**	
Jer	26:12	to prophesy against this **h.** and	1004
Jer	26:18	**h.** as the high places of a forest.	1004
Jer	27:16	the vessels of the Lord's **h.** shall	1004
Jer	27:18	which are left in the **h.** of the Lord,	1004
Jer	27:18	and in the **h.** of the king of Judah,	1004

Book	Ref	Context	No.
Jer	27:21	that remain in the **h.** of the Lord,	1004
Jer	27:21	and in the **h.** of the king of Judah	1004
Jer	28:1	spake unto me in the **h.** of the Lord,	1004
Jer	28:3	lace all the vessels of the Lord's **h.**,	1004
Jer	28:5	that stood in the **h.** of the Lord,	1004
Jer	28:6	again the vessels of the Lord's **h.**,	1004
Jer	29:26	officers in the **h.** of the Lord, for	1004
Jer	31:27	that I will sow the **h.** of Israel	1004
Jer	31:27	and the **h.** of Judah with the seed	1004
Jer	31:31	new covenant with the **h.** of Israel,	1004
Jer	31:31	and with the **h.** of Judah:	1004
Jer	31:33	I will make with the **h.** of Israel;	1004
Jer	32:2	which was in the king of Judah's **h.**	1004
Jer	32:34	set their abominations in the **h.**,	1004
Jer	33:11	of praise into the **h.** of the Lord.	1004
Jer	33:14	the **h.** of Israel...to the **h.** of Judah.	1004
Jer	33:17	upon the throne of the **h.** of Israel;	1004
Jer	34:13	out of the **h.** of bondmen, saying,	1004
Jer	34:15	before me in the **h.** which is called	1004
Jer	35:2	Go unto the **h.** of the Rechabites,	1004
Jer	35:2	bring them into the **h.** of the Lord,	1004
Jer	35:3	and the whole **h.** of the Rechabites;	1004
Jer	35:4	brought them into the **h.** of the Lord,	1004
Jer	35:5	the sons of the **h.** of the Rechabites	1004
Jer	35:7	shall ye build **h.**, nor sow seed, nor	1004
Jer	35:18	said unto the **h.** of the Rechabites,	1004
Jer	36:3	that the **h.** of Judah will hear all the	1004
Jer	36:5	cannot go into the **h.** of the Lord:	1004
Jer	36:6	in the Lord's **h.** upon the fasting	1004
Jer	36:8	words of the Lord in the Lord's **h.**,	1004
Jer	36:10	of Jeremiah in the **h.** of the Lord,	1004
Jer	36:10	the new gate of the Lord's **h.**, in	1004
Jer	36:12	he went down into the king's **h.**,	1004
Jer	37:15	in prison in the **h.** of Jonathan the	1004
Jer	37:17	king asked him secretly in his **h.**,	1004
Jer	37:20	not to return to the **h.** of Jonathan	1004
Jer	38:7	eunuchs which was in the king's **h.**,	1004
Jer	38:8	went forth out of the king's **h.**, and	1004
Jer	38:11	went into the **h.** of the king under	1004
Jer	38:14	the third entry that is in the **h.** of	1004
Jer	38:17	and thou shalt live, and thine **h.**:	1004
Jer	38:22	are left in the king of Judah's **h.**	1004
Jer	38:26	to return to Jonathan's **h.**, to die	1004
Jer	39:8	Chaldeans burned the king's **h.**,	1004
Jer	41:5	bring them to the **h.** of the Lord.	1004
Jer	43:9	at the entry of Pharaoh's **h.** in	1004
Jer	48:13	as the **h.** of Israel was ashamed of	1004
Jer	51:51	the sanctuaries of the Lord's **h.**	1004
Jer	52:13	the **h.** of the Lord, and the king's **h.**;	1004
Jer	52:17	brass that were in the **h.** of the Lord,	1004
Jer	52:17	sea that was in the **h.** of th Lord,	1004
Jer	52:20	had made in the **h.** of the Lord:	1004
La	2:7	made a noise in the **h.** of the Lord,	1004
Eze	2:5	for they are a rebellious **h.**, yet	1004
Eze	2:6	looks, though they be a rebellious **h.**	
Eze	2:8	rebellious like that rebellious **h.**:	1004
Eze	3:1	and go speak unto the **h.** of Israel.	1004
Eze	3:4	go, get thee unto the **h.** of Israel,	1004
Eze	3:5	language, but to the **h.** of Israel;	1004
Eze	3:7	the **h.** of Israel will not hearken	1004
Eze	3:7	all the **h.** of Israel are impudent	1004
Eze	3:9	though they be a rebellious **h.**.	1004
Eze	3:17	a watchman unto the **h.** of Israel:	1004
Eze	3:24	me, Go, shut thyself within thine **h.**	1004
Eze	3:26	reprover: for they are a rebellious **h.**	1004
Eze	3:27	forbear: for they are a rebellious **h.**.	1004
Eze	4:3	shall be a sign to the **h.** of Israel.	1004
Eze	4:4	iniquity of the **h.** of Israel upon it:	1004
Eze	4:5	bear the iniquity of the **h.** of Israel.	1004
Eze	4:6	the iniquity of the **h.** of Judah forty	1004
Eze	5:4	come forth into all the **h.** of Israel.	1004
Eze	6:11	abominations of the **h.** of Israel!	1004
Eze	8:1	I sat in mine **h.**, and the elders of	1004
Eze	8:6	that the **h.** of Israel committeth	1004
Eze	8:10	and all the idols of the **h.** of Israel,	1004
Eze	8:11	of the ancients of the **h.** of Israel,	1004
Eze	8:12	the ancients of the **h.** of Israel do	1004
Eze	8:14	door of the gate of the Lord's **h.**	1004
Eze	8:16	the inner court of the Lord's **h.**,	1004
Eze	8:17	Is it a light thing to the **h.** of Judah	1004
Eze	9:3	he was, to the threshold of the **h.**.	1004
Eze	9:6	men which were before the **h.**	1004
Eze	9:7	Defile the **h.**, and fill the courts	1004
Eze	9:9	The iniquity of the **h.** of Israel and	1004
Eze	10:3	stood on the right side of the **h.**.	1004
Eze	10:4	stood over the threshold of the **h.**;	1004
Eze	10:4	the **h.** was filled with the cloud,	1004
Eze	10:18	from off the threshold of the **h.**,	1004
Eze	10:19	of the east gate of the Lord's **h.**;	1004
Eze	11:1	unto the east gate of the Lord's **h.**,	1004
Eze	11:5	Thus have ye said, O **h.** of Israel:	1004
Eze	11:15	and all the **h.** of Israel wholly, are	1004
Eze	12:2	in the midst of a rebellious **h.**,	1004
Eze	12:2	not: for they are a rebellious **h.**.	1004
Eze	12:3	though they be a rebellious **h.**.	1004
Eze	12:6	thee for a sign unto the **h.** of Israel.	1004
Eze	12:9	the **h.** of Israel, the rebellious **h.**,	1004
Eze	12:10	all the **h.** of Israel that are among	1004
Eze	12:24	divination within the **h.** of Israel.	1004
Eze	12:25	O rebellious **h.**, will I say the word,	1004
Eze	12:27	they of the **h.** of Israel say, The	1004
Eze	13:5	hedge for the **h.** of Israel to stand	1004
Eze	13:9	in the writing of the **h.** of Israel,	1004
Eze	14:4	Every man of the **h.** of Israel that	1004
Eze	14:5	I may take the **h.** of Israel in their	1004
Eze	14:6	say unto the **h.** of Israel, Thus saith	1004
Eze	14:7	every one of the **h.** of Israel, or of	1004
Eze	14:11	That the **h.** of Israel may go no	1004
Eze	17:2	a parable unto the **h.** of Israel;	1004
Eze	17:12	Say now to the rebellious **h.**, Know	1004
Eze	18:6, 15	to the idols of the **h.** of Israel,	1004
Eze	18:25	Hear now, O **h.** of Israel; Is not my	1004
Eze	18:29	Yet saith the **h.** of Israel, The way	1004
Eze	18:29	O **h.** of Israel, are not my ways	1004
Eze	18:30	I will judge you, O **h.** of Israel,	1004
Eze	18:31	for why will ye die, O **h.** of Israel?	1004
Eze	20:5	unto the seed of the **h.** of Jacob,	1004
Eze	20:13	But the **h.** of Israel rebelled against	1004
Eze	20:27	speak unto the **h.** of Israel, and say	1004
Eze	20:30	Wherefore say unto the **h.** of Israel,	1004
Eze	20:31	enquired of by you, O **h.** of Israel?	1004
Eze	20:39	As for you, O **h.** of Israel, thus	1004
Eze	20:40	there shall all the **h.** of Israel, all of	1004
Eze	20:44	corrupt doings, O ye **h.** of Israel,	1004
Eze	22:18	the **h.** of Israel is to me become	1004
Eze	23:39	they done in the midst of mine **h.**.	1004
Eze	24:3	a parable unto the rebellious **h.**,	1004
Eze	24:21	Speak unto the **h.** of Israel, Thus	1004
Eze	25:3	against the **h.** of Judah, when they	1004
Eze	25:8	the **h.** of Judah is like unto all the	1004
Eze	25:12	against the **h.** of Judah by taking	1004
Eze	27:14	They of the **h.** of Togarmah traded	1004
Eze	28:24	pricking brier unto the **h.** of Israel,	1004
Eze	28:25	shall have gathered the **h.** of Israel	1004
Eze	29:6	a staff of reed to the **h.** of Israel.	1004
Eze	29:16	the confidence of the **h.** of Israel,	1004
Eze	29:21	the horn of the **h.** of Israel to bud	1004
Eze	33:7	watchman unto the **h.** of Israel;	1004
Eze	33:10	man, speak unto the **h.** of Israel;	1004
Eze	33:11	for why will ye die, O **h.** of Israel?	1004
Eze	33:20	O ye **h.** of Israel, I will judge you	1004
Eze	34:30	the **h.** of Israel, are my people,	1004
Eze	35:15	the inheritance of the **h.** of Israel,	1004
Eze	36:10	all the **h.** of Israel, even all of it:	1004
Eze	36:17	when the **h.** of Israel dwelt in their	1004
Eze	36:21	the **h.** of Israel had profaned among	1004
Eze	36:22	say unto the **h.** of Israel, Thus saith	1004
Eze	36:22	this for your sakes, O **h.** of Israel,	1004
Eze	36:32	for your own ways, O **h.** of Israel.	1004
Eze	36:37	be enquired of by the **h.** of Israel,	1004
Eze	37:11	bones are the whole **h.** of Israel:	1004
Eze	37:16	all the **h.** of Israel his companions:	1004
Eze	38:6	the **h.** of Togarmah of the north	1004
Eze	39:12	shall the **h.** of Israel be burying of	1004
Eze	39:22	So the **h.** of Israel shall know that	1004
Eze	39:23	the **h.** of Israel went into captivity	1004
Eze	39:25	mercy upon the whole **h.** of Israel,	1004
Eze	39:29	out of my spirit upon the **h.** of Israel,	1004
Eze	40:4	that thou seest to the **h.** of Israel.	1004
Eze	40:5	wall on the outside of the **h.** round	1004
Eze	40:45	the keepers of the charge of the **h.**.	1004
Eze	40:47	the altar that was before the **h.**.	1004
Eze	40:48	brought me to the porch of the **h.**,	1004
Eze	41:5	he measured the wall of the **h.**, six	1004
Eze	41:5	round about the **h.** on every side.	1004
Eze	41:6	into the wall which was of the **h.**	1004
Eze	41:6	had not hold in the wall of the **h.**.	1004
Eze	41:7	the winding about of the **h.** went	1004
Eze	41:7	still upward round about the **h.**:	1004
Eze	41:7	breadth of the **h.** was still upward,	1004
Eze	41:8	I saw also the height of the **h.** round	1004
Eze	41:10	round about the **h.** on every side.	1004
Eze	41:13	So he measured the **h.**, an hundred	1004
Eze	41:14	the breadth of the face of the **h.**,	1004
Eze	41:17	the door, even unto the inner **h.**,	1004
Eze	41:19	through all the **h.** round about.	1004
Eze	41:26	the side chambers of the **h.**, and	1004
Eze	42:15	an end of measuring the inner **h.**,	1004
Eze	43:4	glory of the Lord came into the **h.**	1004
Eze	43:5	the glory of the Lord filled the **h.**.	1004
Eze	43:6	speaking unto me out of the **h.**;	1004
Eze	43:7	shall the **h.** of Israel no more defile	1004
Eze	43:10	shew the **h.** to the **h.** of Israel, that	1004
Eze	43:11	shew them the form of the **h.**, and	1004
Eze	43:12	This is the law of the **h.**; upon the	1004
Eze	43:12	Behold, this is the law of the **h.**	1004
Eze	43:21	it in the appointed place of the **h.**,	1004
Eze	44:4	way of the north gate before the **h.**:	1004
Eze	44:4	the Lord filled the **h.** of the Lord:	1004
Eze	44:5	ordinances of the **h.** of the Lord,	1004
Eze	44:5	mark well the entering in of the **h.**,	1004
Eze	44:6	rebellious, even to the **h.** of Israel,	1004
Eze	44:6	the Lord God; O ye **h.** of Israel,	1004
Eze	44:7	sanctuary, to pollute it, even my **h.**,	1004
Eze	44:11	having charge at the gates of the **h.**,	1004
Eze	44:11	and ministering to the **h.**:	1004
Eze	44:12	the **h.** of Israel to fall into iniquity;	1004
Eze	44:14	keepers of the charge of the **h.**,	1004
Eze	44:22	of the seed of the **h.** of Israel,	1004
Eze	44:30	the blessing to rest in thine **h.**	1004
Eze	45:5	the Levites, the ministers of the **h.**,	1004
Eze	45:6	shall be for the whole **h.** of Israel.	1004
Eze	45:8	shall they give to the **h.** of Israel	1004
Eze	45:17	all solemnities of the **h.** of Israel:	1004
Eze	45:17	reconciliation for the **h.** of Israel.	1004
Eze	45:19	upon the posts of the **h.**, and upon	1004
Eze	45:20	so shall ye reconcile the **h.**.	1004
Eze	46:24	the ministers of the **h.** shall boil the	1004
Eze	47:1	me again unto the door of the **h.**;	1004
Eze	47:1	the threshold of the **h.** eastward:	1004
Eze	47:1	forefront of the **h.** stood toward the	1004
Eze	47:1	under from the right side of the **h.**,	1004
Eze	48:21	the sanctuary of the **h.** shall be in	1004
Da	1:2	part of the vessels of the **h.** of God:	1004
Da	1:2	land of Shinar to the **h.** of his god;	1004
Da	1:2	into the treasure **h.** of his god.	1004
Da	2:17	Daniel went to his **h.**, and made	1005
Da	4:4	was at rest in mine **h.**,	1005
Da	4:30	built for the **h.** of the kingdom	1005
Da	5:3	out of the temple of the **h.** of God	1005
Da	5:10	his lords came into the banquet **h.**:	1005
Da	5:23	brought the vessels of his **h.** before	1005
Da	6:10	was signed, he went into his **h.**;	1005
Ho	1:4	of Jezreel upon the **h.** of Jehu,	1004
Ho	1:4	the kingdom of the **h.** of Israel.	1004
Ho	1:6	have mercy upon the **h.** of Israel;	1004
Ho	1:7	have mercy upon the **h.** of Judah,	1004
Ho	5:1	and hearken, ye **h.** of Israel;	1004
Ho	5:1	and give ye ear, O **h.** of the king;	1004
Ho	5:12	to the **h.** of Judah as rottenness.	1004
Ho	5:14	as a young lion to the **h.** of Judah:	1004
Ho	6:10	horrible thing in the **h.** of Israel:	1004
Ho	8:1	an eagle against the **h.** of the Lord,	1004
Ho	9:4	not come into the **h.** of the Lord.	1004
Ho	9:8	and hatred in the **h.** of his God.	1004
Ho	9:15	I will drive them out of mine **h.**,	1004
Ho	11:12	and the **h.** of Israel with deceit:	1004
Joe	1:9	is cut off from the **h.** of the Lord;	1004
Joe	1:13	withholden from the **h.** of your God.	1004
Joe	1:14	into the **h.** of the Lord your God,	1004
Joe	1:16	gladness from the **h.** of our God?	1004
Joe	3:18	come forth of the **h.** of the Lord,	1004
Am	1:4	will send a fire into the **h.** of Hazael,	1004
Am	1:5	the sceptre from the **h.** of Eden:	1004
Am	2:8	condemned in the **h.** of their god.	1004
Am	3:13	ye, and testify in the **h.** of Jacob,	1004
Am	3:15	the winter **h.** with the summer **h.**;	1004
Am	5:1	even a lamentation, O **h.** of Israel.	1004
Am	5:3	shall leave ten, to the **h.** of Israel.	1004
Am	5:4	saith the Lord unto the **h.** of Israel,	1004
Am	5:6	out like fire in the **h.** of Joseph,	1004
Am	5:19	or went into the **h.**, and leaned his	1004
Am	5:25	forty years, O **h.** of Israel?	1004
Am	6:1	to whom the **h.** of Israel came!	1004
Am	6:9	remain ten men in one **h.**, that they	1004
Am	6:10	to bring out the bones out of the **h.**,	1004
Am	6:10	him that is by the sides of the **h.**,	1004
Am	6:11	smite the great **h.** with breaches,	1004
Am	6:11	and the little **h.** with clefts.	1004
Am	6:14	against you a nation, O **h.** of Israel,	1004
Am	7:9	will rise against the **h.** of Jeroboam	1004

Am 7:10 thee in the midst of the h. of Israel: 1004
Am 7:16 not thy word against the h. of Isaac 1004
Am 9:8 not utterly destroy the h. of Jacob, 1004
Am 9:9 I will sift the h. of Israel among all 1004
Ob 17 and the h. of Jacob shall possess 1004
Ob 18 And the h. of Jacob shall be a fire, 1004
Ob 18 and the h. of Joseph a flame, 1004
Ob 18 and the h. of Esau for stubble, 1004
Ob 18 be any remaining of the h. of Easu; 1004
Mic 1:5 and for the sins of the h. of Israel, 1004
Mic 1:10 in the h. of Aphrah roll thyself in 1035
Mic 2:2 so they oppress a man and his h., 1004
Mic 2:7 thou that art named the h. of Jacob, 1004
Mic 3:1 and ye princes of the h. of Israel; 1004
Mic 3:9 and you, ye heads of the h. of Jacob, 1004
Mic 3:9 and princes of the h. of Israel, that 1004
Mic 3:12 mountain of the h. as the high 1004
Mic 4:1 the mountain of the h. of the Lord 1004
Mic 4:2 and to the h. of the God of Jacob; 1004
Mic 6:4 thee out of the h. of servants; 1004
Mic 6:10 wickedness in the h. of the wicked, 1004
Mic 6:16 all the works of the h. of Ahab, and 1004
Mic 7:6 enemies are the men of his own h. 1004
Na 1:14 out of the h. of thy gods will I cut 1004
Hab 2:9 an evil covetousness to his h., 1004
Hab 2:10 hast consulted shame to thy h. by 1004
Hab 3:13 head out of the h. of the wicked, by 1004
Zep 2:7 for the remnant of the h. of Judah; 1004
Hag 1:2 that the Lord's h. should be built. 1004
Hag 1:4 cieled houses, and this h. lie waste? 1004
Hag 1:8 and bring wood, and build the h.; 1004
Hag 1:9 Because of mine h. that is waste, 1004
Hag 1:9 ye run every man unto his own h. 1004
Hag 1:14 work in the h. of the Lord of hosts, 1004
Hag 2:3 among you that saw this h. in her 1004
Hag 2:7 and I will fill this h. with glory, 1004
Hag 2:9 The glory of this latter h. shall be 1004
Zec 1:16 my h. shall be built in it, saith the 1004
Zec 3:7 thou shalt also judge my h., and 1004
Zec 4:9 have laid the foundation of this h.; 1004
Zec 5:4 shall enter into the h. of the thief, 1004
Zec 5:4 the h. of him that sweareth falsely 1004
Zec 5:4 shall remain in the midst of his h., 1004
Zec 5:11 build it an h. in the land of Shinar: 1004
Zec 6:10 go into the h. of Josiah the son of 1004
Zec 7:2 they had sent unto the h. of God 1008
Zec 7:3 priests which were in the h. of the 1004
Zec 8:9 the foundation of the h. of the Lord 1004
Zec 8:13 O h. of Judah, and h. of Israel; 1004
Zec 8:15 Jerusalem and to the h. of Judah: 1004
Zec 8:19 to the h. of Judah joy and gladness, 1004
Zec 9:8 And I will encamp about mine h. 1004
Zec 10:3 visited his flock the h. of Judah, 1004
Zec 10:6 I will strengthen the h. of Judah, 1004
Zec 10:6 and I will save the h. of Joseph, 1004
Zec 11:13 to the potter in the h. of the Lord. 1004
Zec 12:4 mine eyes upon the h. of Judah, 1004
Zec 12:7 that the glory of the h. of David 1004
Zec 12:8 and the h. of David shall be as God, 1004
Zec 12:10 I will pour upon the h. of David, 1004
Zec 12:12 the family of the h. of David apart, 1004
Zec 12:12 family of the h. of Nathan apart, 1004
Zec 12:13 The family of the h. of Levi apart, 1004
Zec 13:1 fountain opened to the h. of David 1004
Zec 13:6 wounded in the h. of my friends. 1004
Zec 14:20 the pots in the Lord's h. shall be 1004
Zec 14:21 in the h. of the Lord of hosts. 1004
Mal 3:10 there may be meat in mine h., and 1004
Mt 2:11 when they were come into the h., 3614
Mt 5:15 light unto all that are in the h., 3614
Mt 7:24 which build his h. upon a rock: 3614
Mt 7:25 winds blew, and beat upon that h.; 3614
Mt 7:26 which built his h. upon the sand: 3614
Mt 7:27 winds blew, and beat upon that h.; 3614
Mt 8:14 Jesus was come into Peter's h., he 3614
Mt 9:6 up thy bed, and go unto thine h. 3624
Mt 9:7 he arose, and departed to his h. 3624
Mt 9:10 as Jesus sat at meat in the h., 3614
Mt 9:23 when Jesus came into the ruler's h., 3614
Mt 9:28 And when he was come into the h. 3614
Mt 10:6 the lost sheep of the h. of Israel. 3624
Mt 10:12 when ye come into an h., salute it 3614
Mt 10:13 And if the h. be worthy, let your 3614
Mt 10:14 when ye depart out of that h. or 3614
Mt 10:25 call the master of the h. 3617
Mt 12:4 How he entered into the h. of God, 3624
Mt 12:25 city or h. divided against itself 3614

Mt 12:29 one enter into a strong man's h. 3614
Mt 12:29 man? and then he will spoil his h. 3614
Mt 12:44 return into my h. from whence I 3624
Mt 13:1 same day went Jesus out of the h., 3614
Mt 13:36 away, and went into the h.: 3614
Mt 13:57 own country, and in his own h. 3614
Mt 15:24 the lost sheep of the h. of Israel. 3624
Mt 17:25 And when he was come into the h., 3614
Mt 20:11 against the goodman of the h. 3617
Mt 21:13 My h. shall be called the h. of 3624
Mt 23:38 your h. is left unto you desolate 3624
Mt 24:17 to take any thing out of his h.: 3614
Mt 24:43 goodman of the h. had known in 3617
Mt 24:43 suffered his h. to be broken up. 3614
Mt 26:6 in the h. of Simon the leper, 3614
Mt 26:18 I will keep the passover at thy h.
Mk 1:29 entered into the h. of Simon and 3614
Mk 2:1 was noised that he was in the h. 3624
Mk 2:11 bed, and go thy way into thine h. 3624
Mk 2:15 that, as Jesus sat at meat in his h., 3614
Mk 2:26 How he went into the h. of God in 3624
Mk 3:19 him; and they went into an h. 3624
Mk 3:25 if a h. be divided against itself, 3614
Mk 3:25 itself, that h. cannot stand. 3614
Mk 3:27 can enter into a strong man's h., 3614
Mk 3:27 man; and then he will spoil his h. 3614
Mk 5:35 from the ruler of the synagogue's h.
Mk 5:38 cometh to the h. of the ruler of the 3624
Mk 6:4 his own kin, and in his own h. 3614
Mk 6:10 ye enter into a h., there abide till 3614
Mk 7:17 when he was entered into the h. 3624
Mk 7:24 and Sidon, and entered into an h., 3614
Mk 7:30 when she was come to her h., she 3624
Mk 8:26 And he sent him away to his h., 3624
Mk 9:28 when he was come into the h., his 3624
Mk 9:33 and being in the h. he asked them, 3614
Mk 10:10 And in the h. his disciples asked 3614
Mk 10:29 There is no man that hath left h., 3614
Mk 11:17 not written, My h. shall be called 3624
Mk 11:17 of all nations the h. of prayer? 3624
Mk 13:15 housetop not go down into the h., 3614
Mk 13:15 to take any thing out of his h.: 3614
Mk 13:34 a far journey, who left his h., 3614
Mk 13:35 when the master of the h. cometh, 3614
Mk 14:3 Bethany in the h. of Simon the leper, 3614
Mk 14:14 say ye to the goodman of the h., 3617
Lu 1:23 he departed to his own h. 3624
Lu 1:27 was Joseph, of the h. of David; 3624
Lu 1:33 reign over the h. of Jacob for ever; 3624
Lu 1:40 entered into the h. of Zacharias, 3624
Lu 1:56 months, and returned to her own h. 3624
Lu 1:69 us in the h. of his servant David: 3624
Lu 2:4 was of the h. and lineage of David: 3624
Lu 4:38 and entered into Simon's h. 3614
Lu 5:24 up thy couch, and go into thine h.; 3624
Lu 5:25 he lay, and departed to his own h., 3624
Lu 5:29 him a great feast in his own h.: 3614
Lu 6:4 How he went into the h. of God, 3624
Lu 6:48 He is like a man which built an h. 3614
Lu 6:48 beat vehemently upon that h., 3614
Lu 6:49 built an h. upon the earth; against 3614
Lu 6:49 and the ruin of that h. was great. 3614
Lu 7:6 he was now not far from the h., 3614
Lu 7:10 that were sent, returning to the h., 3624
Lu 7:36 he went into the Pharisee's h., and 3614
Lu 7:37 sat at meat in the Pharisee's h., 3614
Lu 7:44 I entered into thine h., thou gavest 3614
Lu 8:27 neither abode in any h., but in the 3614
Lu 8:39 Return to thine own h., and shew 3624
Lu 8:41 him that he would come into his h.: 3624
Lu 8:49 from the ruler of the synagogue's h., 3614
Lu 8:51 And when he came into the h., he 3614
Lu 9:4 whatsoever h. ye enter into, there 3614
Lu 9:61 which are at home at my h. 3624
Lu 10:5 into whatsoever h. ye enter, first 3614
Lu 10:5 first say, Peace be to this h. 3624
Lu 10:7 in the same h. remain, eating and 3614
Lu 10:7 of his hire. Go not from h. to h. 3614
Lu 10:38 Martha received him into her h. 3624
Lu 11:17 a h. divided against a h. falleth 3624
Lu 11:24 I will return unto my h. whence I 3624
Lu 12:39 the goodman of the h. had known 3617
Lu 12:39 have suffered his h. to be broken 3624
Lu 12:52 there shall be five in one h. 3624
Lu 13:25 the master of the h. is risen up, 3617
Lu 13:35 your h. is left unto you desolate: 3624

Lu 14:1 the h. of one of the chief Pharisees 3624
Lu 14:21 the master of the h. being angry 3617
Lu 14:23 to come in, that my h. may be 3624
Lu 15:8 sweep the h., and seek diligently 3614
Lu 15:25 he came and drew nigh to the h., 3614
Lu 16:27 send him to my father's h.: 3624
Lu 17:31 housetop, and his stuff in the h., 3614
Lu 18:14 man went down to his h. justified 3624
Lu 18:29 no man that hath left h., or 3614
Lu 19:5 for to day I must abide at thy h. 3624
Lu 19:9 day is salvation come to this h., 3624
Lu 19:46 written, My h. is the h. of prayer: 3624
Lu 22:10 follow him into the h. where he 3614
Lu 22:11 say unto the goodman of the h., 3614
Lu 22:54 him into the high priest's h. 3624
Joh 2:16 Father's h. an h. of merchandise. 3624
Joh 2:17 zeal of thine h. hath eaten me up. 3624
Joh 4:53 himself believed, and his whole h. 3614
Joh 7:53 every man went unto his own h. 3624
Joh 8:35 abideth not in the h. for ever: 3614
Joh 11:20 him: but Mary sat still in the h. 3624
Joh 11:31 which were with her in the h., 3614
Joh 12:3 the h. was filled with the odour of 3614
Joh 14:2 my Father's h. are many mansions: 3614
Ac 2:2 all the h. where they were sitting. 3624
Ac 2:36 let all the h. of Israel know 3624
Ac 2:46 breaking bread from h. to h., 3624
Ac 5:42 in the temple, and in every h., 3624
Ac 7:10 govenor over Egypt and all his h. 3624
Ac 7:20 up in his father's h. three months: 3624
Ac 7:42 O ye h. of Israel, have ye offered to 3624
Ac 7:47 But Solomon built him an h. 3624
Ac 7:49 what h. will ye build me? saith 3624
Ac 8:3 entering into every h., and 3624
Ac 9:11 enquire in the h. of Judas for one 3614
Ac 9:17 his way, and entered into the h.; 3614
Ac 10:2 one that feared God with all his h., 3624
Ac 10:6 tanner, whose h. is by the sea side: 3614
Ac 10:17 had made enquiry for Simon's h., 3614
Ac 10:22 angel to send for thee into his h., 3624
Ac 10:30 ninth hour I prayed in my h., and, 3624
Ac 10:32 he is lodged in the h. of one Simon 3614
Ac 11:11 three men already come unto the h. 3614
Ac 11:12 and we entered into the man's h.: 3624
Ac 11:13 how he had seen an angel in his h., 3624
Ac 11:14 thou and all thy h. shall be saved. 3624
Ac 12:12 came to the h. of Mary the mother 3614
Ac 16:15 Lord, come into my h., and abide 3624
Ac 16:31 and thou shalt be saved, and thy h. 3624
Ac 16:32 Lord, and to all that were in his h. 3614
Ac 16:34 he had brought them into his h., 3624
Ac 16:34 believing in God with all his h. 3832
Ac 16:40 and entered into the h. of Lydia:
Ac 17:5 and assaulted the h. of Jason, 3614
Ac 18:7 a certain man's h., named Justus, 3614
Ac 18:7 h. joined hard to the synagogue. 3614
Ac 18:8 believed on the Lord with all his h.; 3624
Ac 19:16 they fled out of the h. naked and 3624
Ac 20:20 you publickly, and from h. to h., 3624
Ac 21:8 we entered into the h. of Philip the 3624
Ac 28:30 whole years in his own hired h.,
Ro 16:5 greet the church that is in their h. 3624
1Co 1:11 them which are of the h. of Chloe,
1Co 16:15 ye know the h. of Stephanas, that 3614
1Co 16:19 with the church that is in their h. 3624
2Co 5:1 we know that if our earthly h. of 3614
2Co 5:1 an h. not made with hands, eternal 3614
2Co 5:2 with our h. which is from heaven: 3613
Col 4:15 and the church which is in his h. 3624
1Ti 3:4 One that ruleth well his own h., 3624
1Ti 3:5 know not how to rule his own h., 3624
1Ti 3:15 to behave thyself in the h. of God, 3624
1Ti 5:8 specially for those of his own h., 3609
1Ti 5:13 wandering about from h. to h.; 3614
1Ti 5:14 bear children, guide the h., give 3616
2Ti 1:16 mercy unto the h. of Onesiphorus; 3624
2Ti 2:20 But in a great h. there are not only 3614
Phm 2 and to the church in thy h.: 3624
Heb 3:2 also Moses was faithful in all his h. 3624
Heb 3:3 as he who hath builded the h. 3624
Heb 3:3 hath more honour than the h. 3624
Heb 3:4 every h. is builded by some man; 3624
Heb 3:5 verily was faithful in all his h., 3624
Heb 3:6 But Christ as a son over his own h.; 3624
Heb 3:6 whose h. are we, if we hold fast the 3624
Heb 8:8 h. of Israel and with the h. of Judah: 3624
Heb 8:10 I will make with the h. of Israel 3624

Heb 10:21 an high priest over the **h.** of God;...... *3624*
Heb 11:7 an ark to the saving of his **h.**;.......... *3624*
1Pe 2:5 stones, are built up a spiritual **h.**,....... *3624*
1Pe 4:17 must begin at the **h.** of God:............ *3624*
2Jo 10 receive him not into your **h.**,............ *3614*

HOUSE-FULL See HOUSE and FULL.

HOUSEHOLD See also HOUSEHOLDS.
Ge 18:19 his children and his **h.** after him,....... 1004
Ge 31:37 hast thou found of all thy **h.** stuff?....... 1004
Ge 35:2 Jacob said unto his **h.**, and to all........ 1004
Ge 45:11 lest thou, and thy **h.**, and all that....... 1004
Ge 47:12 and all his father's **h.**, with bread,...... 1004
Ex 1:1 man and his **h.** came with Jacob......... 1004
Ex 12:4 if the **h.** be too little for the lamb,....... 1004
Le 16:17 for himself, and for his **h.**, and for...... 1004
De 6:22 upon Pharaoh, and upon all his **h.**,....... 1004
De 14:26 thou shalt rejoice, thou, and thine **h.**,.. 1004
De 15:20 Lord shall choose, thou and thy **h.**..... 1004
Jos 2:18 all thy father's **h.**, home unto thee....... 1004
Jos 6:25 harlot alive, and her father's **h.**,........ 1004
Jos 7:14 the **h.** which the Lord shall take......... 1004
Jos 7:18 And he brought his **h.** man by man;..... 1004
Jg 6:27 because he feared his father's **h.**,....... 1004
Jg 18:25 lose thy life, with the lives of thy **h.**.. 1004
1Sa 25:17 our master, and against all his **h.**:...... 1004
1Sa 27:3 and his men, every man with his **h.**,..... 1004
2Sa 2:3 bring up, every man with his **h.**:........ 1004
2Sa 6:11 blessed Obed-edom, and all his **h.**...... 1004
2Sa 6:20 Then David returned to bless his **h.**...... 1004
2Sa 15:16 went forth, and all his **h.** after him...... 1004
2Sa 16:2 asses be for the king's **h.** to ride on;.. 1004
2Sa 17:23 put his **h.** in order, and hanged.......... 1004
2Sa 19:18 ferry boat to carry over the king's **h.**,. 1004
2Sa 19:41 have brought the king, and his **h.**,....... 1004
1Ki 4:6 Ahishar was over the **h.**: and........... 1004
1Ki 4:7 victuals for the king and his **h.**:......... 1004
1Ki 5:9 my desire, in giving food for my **h.**...... 1004
1Ki 5:11 measures of wheat for food to his **h.**,... 1004
1Ki 11:20 and Genubath was in Pharaoh's **h.**....... 1004
2Ki 7:9 we may go and tell the king's **h.**......... 1004
2Ki 8:1 go thou and thine **h.**, and sojourn....... 1004
2Ki 8:2 she went with her **h.**, and sojourned..... 1004
2Ki 18:18, 37 Hilkiah, which was over the **h.**,...... 1004
2Ki 19:2 sent Eliakim, which was over the **h.**,.. 1004
1Ch 24:6 one principal **h.** being taken for.......... 1004
Ne 13:8 I cast forth all the **h.** stuff of Tobiah... 1004
Job 1:3 she asses, and a very great **h.**;.......... 5657
Pr 27:27 for the food of thy **h.**, and for the...... 1004
Pr 31:15 giveth meat to her **h.**, and a portion.... 1004
Pr 31:21 not afraid of the snow for her **h.**:....... 1004
Pr 31:21 for all her **h.** are clothed with scarlet...1004
Pr 31:27 looketh well to the ways of her **h.**,...... 1004
Isa 36:22 son of Hilkiah, that was over the **h.**,..... 1004
Isa 37:2 sent Eliakim, who was over the **h.**,.... 1004
Mt 10:25 **shall they call them of his h.?**....... *3615*
Mt 10:36 **foes shall be they of his own h.**...... *3615*
Mt 24:45 **lord hath made ruler over his h.**,..... *2322*
Lu 12:42 **lord shall make ruler over his h.**,.... *2322*
Ac 10:7 he called two of his **h.** servants,........ *3610*
Ac 16:15 when she was baptized, and her **h.**,....... *3624*
Ro 16:10 them which are of Aristobulus' **h.**.............
Ro 16:11 them that be of the **h.** of Narcissus,.........
1Co 1:16 baptized also the **h.** of Stephanas:...... *3624*
Ga 6:10 unto them who are of the **h.** of faith..... *3609*
Eph 2:19 with the saints, and of the **h.** of God;...*3609*
Php 4:22 chiefly they that are of Caesar's **h.**...... *3614*
2Ti 4:19 and the **h.** of Onesiphorus................ *3624*

HOUSEHOLDER
Mt 13:27 **servants of the h. came and said**... *3617*
Mt 13:52 **is like unto a man that is an h.**,.... *3617*
Mt 20:1 **is like unto a man that is an h.**,.... *3617*
Mt 21:33 **was a certain h., which planted a**.. *3617*

HOUSEHOLDS
Ge 42:33 food for the famine of your **h.**,.......... 1004
Ge 45:18 take your father and your **h.**, and....... 1004
Ge 47:24 your food, and for them of your **h.**,..... 1004
Nu 18:31 eat it in every place, ye and your **h.**:.. 1004
De 11:6 swallowed them up, and their **h.**,....... 1004
De 12:7 put your hand unto, ye and your **h.**,... 1004
Jos 7:14 Lord shall take shall come by **h.**;....... 1004

HOUSES See also STOREHOUSES.
Ge 42:19 corn for the famine of your **h.**:.......... 1004
Ex 1:21 feared God, that he made them **h.**....... 1004
Ex 6:14 be the heads of their fathers' **h.**:........ 1004
Ex 8:9 the frogs from thee and thy **h.**,......... 1004
Ex 8:11 depart from thee, and from thy **h.**,... 1004
Ex 8:13 the frogs died out of the **h.**, out of..... 1004
Ex 8:21 upon thy people, and into thy **h.**:....... 1004
Ex 8:21 **h.** of the Egyptians shall be full of..... 1004
Ex 8:24 into his servants' **h.**, and into all the... 1004
Ex 9:20 and his cattle flee into the **h.**:........... 1004
Ex 10:6 And they shall fill thy **h.**, and the....... 1004
Ex 10:6 and the **h.** of all thy servants, and....... 1004
Ex 10:6 and the **h.** of all the Egyptians;.......... 1004
Ex 12:7 on the upper door post of the **h.**,........ 1004
Ex 12:13 for a token upon the **h.** where ye are: .1004
Ex 12:15 put away leaven out of your **h.**:.......... 1004
Ex 12:19 be no leaven found in your **h.**: for....... 1004
Ex 12:23 destroyer to come in unto your **h.** to.. 1004
Ex 12:27 over the **h.** of the children of Israel.... 1004
Ex 12:27 the Egyptians, and delivered our **h.**... 1004
Le 25:31 But the **h.** of the villages which no..... 1004
Le 25:32 and the **h.** of the cities of their.......... 1004
Le 25:33 the **h.** of the cities of the Levites....... 1004
Nu 4:22 throughout the **h.** of their fathers,...... 1004
Nu 16:32 swallowed them up, and their **h.**,....... 1004
Nu 17:6 according to their fathers' **h.**, even...... 1004
Nu 32:18 We will not return unto our **h.**, until... 1004
De 6:11 and **h.** full of all good things, which..... 1004
De 8:12 and hast built goodly **h.**, and dwelt..... 1004
De 19:1 in their cities, and in their **h.**;........... 1004
Jos 9:12 hot for our provision out of our **h.**....... 1004
Jg 18:14 that there is in these **h.** an ephod,..... 1004
Jg 18:22 that were in the **h.** near to Micah's.... 1004
1Ki 9:10 Solomon had built the two **h.**, the...... 1004
1Ki 13:32 against all the **h.** of the high places..... 1004
1Ki 20:6 house, and the **h.** of thy servants;...... 1004
2Ki 17:29 for them in the **h.** of the high places.... 1004
2Ki 17:32 for them in the **h.** of the high places... 1004
2Ki 23:7 brake down the **h.** of the sodomites,... 1004
2Ki 23:19 all the **h.** also of the high places........ 1004
2Ki 25:9 and all the **h.** of Jerusalem, and......... 1004
1Ch 15:1 David made him **h.** in the city of........ 1004
1Ch 28:11 and of the **h.** thereof, and of the........ 1004
1Ch 29:4 to overlay the walls of the **h.** withal:... 1004
2Ch 25:5 according to the **h.** of their fathers,.... 1004
2Ch 34:11 floor the **h.** which the kings of Judah... 1004
2Ch 35:4 yourselves by the **h.** of your fathers,.. 1004
Ne 4:14 daughters, your wives, and your **h.**... 1004
Ne 5:3 our lands, vineyards, and **h.**, that....... 1004
Ne 5:11 their oliveyards, and their **h.**, also...... 1004
Ne 7:4 therein, and the **h.** were not builded.... 1004
Ne 9:25 and possessed **h.** full of all goods,...... 1004
Ne 10:34 our God, after the **h.** of our fathers,... 1004
Job 1:4 sons went and feasted in their **h.**,....... 1004
Job 3:15 gold, who filled their **h.** with silver:.... 1004
Job 4:19 less in them that dwell in **h.** of clay,... 1004
Job 15:28 and in **h.** which no man inhabiteth,..... 1004
Job 21:9 Their **h.** are safe from fear, neither.... 1004
Job 22:18 he filled their **h.** with good things:...... 1004
Job 24:16 In the dark they dig through **h.**,......... 1004
Ps 49:11 that their **h.** shall continue for ever,..... 1004
Ps 83:12 us take to ourselves the **h.** of God..... 4999
Pr 1:13 we shall fill our **h.** with spoil:........... 1004
Pr 30:26 yet make they their **h.** in the rocks;... 1004
Ec 2:4 I builded me **h.**; I planted me............ 1004
Isa 3:14 the spoil of the poor is in your **h.**....... 1004
Isa 5:9 a truth many **h.** shall be desolate,...... 1004
Isa 6:11 and the **h.** without man, and the........ 1004
Isa 8:14 of offence to both the **h.** of Israel,....... 1004
Isa 13:16 their **h.** shall be spoiled, and their...... 1004
Isa 13:21 and their **h.** shall be full of doleful..... 1004
Isa 13:22 shall cry in their desolate **h.**,.............. 490
Isa 15:3 on the tops of their **h.**, and in their.........
Isa 22:10 numbered the **h.** of Jerusalem,........... 1004
Isa 22:10 **h.** have ye broken down to fortify...... 1004
Isa 32:13 upon all the **h.** of joy in the joyous.... 1004
Isa 42:22 and they are hid in the prison **h.**:...... 1004
Isa 65:21 And they shall build **h.**, and inhabit.... 1004
Jer 5:7 by troops in the harlots' **h.**............ 1004
Jer 5:27 birds, so are their **h.** full of deceit:...... 1004
Jer 6:12 their **h.** shall be turned unto others,... 1004
Jer 17:22 carry forth a burden out of your **h.**..... 1004
Jer 18:22 Let a cry be heard from their **h.**,........ 1004
Jer 19:13 And the **h.** of Jerusalem, and the **h.**... 1004
Jer 19:13 because of all the **h.** upon whose........ 1004
Jer 29:5 Build ye **h.**, and dwell in them; and.... 1004
Jer 29:28 build ye **h.**, and dwell in them; and..... 1004
Jer 32:15 **H.** and fields and vineyards shall be.... 1004
Jer 32:29 on this city, and burn it with the **h.**,... 1004
Jer 33:4 concerning the **h.** of this city, and...... 1004
Jer 33:4 the **h.** of the kings of Judah, which..... 1004
Jer 35:9 Nor to build **h.** for us to dwell in:...... 1004
Jer 39:8 and the **h.** of the people, with fire,...... 1004
Jer 43:12 fire in the **h.** of the gods of Egypt;..... 1004
Jer 43:13 the **h.** of the gods of the Egyptians.... 1004
Jer 52:13 and all the **h.** of Jerusalem, and all...... 1004
Jer 52:13 the **h.** of the great men, burned he.... 1004
La 5:2 turned to strangers, our **h.** to aliens... 1004
Eze 7:24 then, and they shall possess their **h.**:.. 1004
Eze 11:3 say, It is not near; let us build **h.**:...... 1004
Eze 16:41 they shall burn thine **h.** with fire,....... 1004
Eze 23:47 and burn up their **h.** with fire........... 1004
Eze 26:12 walls and destroy thy pleasant **h.**:...... 1004
Eze 28:26 therein, and shall build **h.**, and plant.... 1004
Eze 33:30 the walls and in the doors of the **h.**,... 1004
Eze 45:4 It shall be a place for their **h.**, and..... 1004
Da 2:5 your **h.** shall be made a dunghill......... 1005
Da 3:29 their **h.** shall be made a dunghill:....... 1005
Ho 11:11 I will place them in their **h.**, saith....... 1004
Joe 2:9 they shall climb up upon the **h.**;......... 1004
Am 3:15 and the **h.** of ivory shall perish, and.... 1004
Am 3:15 and the great **h.** shall have an end,..... 1004
Am 5:11 ye have built **h.** of hewn stone, but.... 1004
Mic 1:14 the **h.** of Achzib shall be a lie to the.... 1004
Mic 2:2 and **h.**, and take them away: so they.. 1004
Mic 2:9 cast out from their pleasant **h.**;.......... 1004
Zep 1:9 fill their master's **h.** with violence....... 1004
Zep 1:13 a booty, and their **h.** a desolation:...... 1004
Zep 1:13 they shall also build **h.**, but not.......... 1004
Zep 2:7 in the **h.** of Ashkelon shall they lie..... 1004
Hag 1:4 to dwell in your cieled **h.**, and this..... 1004
Zec 14:2 city shall be taken, and the **h.** rifled,... 1004
Mt 11:8 **wear soft clothing are in kings' h.**. *3624*
Mt 19:29 **that hath forsaken h., or brethren,**. *3614*
Mt 23:14 **ye devour widows' h., and for a**..... *3614*
Mk 8:3 **away, fasting to their own h., they** *3624*
Mk 10:30 **h., and brethren, and sisters, and**.. *3614*
Mk 12:40 **Which devour widows' h., and**....... *3614*
Lu 16:4 **they may receive me into their h.**... *3624*
Lu 20:47 **Which devour widows' h., and for**. *3614*
Ac 4:34 possessors of lands or **h.** sold them,... *3614*
1Co 11:22 ye not **h.** to eat and to drink in?........ *3614*
1Ti 3:12 their children and their own **h.** well.... *3624*
2Ti 3:6 sort are they which creep into **h.**,...... *3614*
Tit 1:11 who subvert whole **h.**, teaching........ *3624*

HOUSETOP See also HOUSE and TOP; HOUSETOPS.
Pr 21:9 better to dwell in a corner of the **h.**,.. 1406
Pr 25:24 better to dwell in the corner of the **h.**,.1406
Mt 24:17 **Let him which is on the h. not**..... *1430*
Mk 13:15 **him that is on the h. not go down**..*1430*
Lu 5:19 they went upon the **h.**, and let him..... *1430*
Lu 17:31 **he which shall be upon the h., and**.*1430*
Ac 10:9 Peter went up upon the **h.** to pray..... *1430*

HOUSETOPS
Ps 129:6 them be as the grass upon the **h.**,...... 1406
Isa 22:1 thou art wholly gone up to the **h.**?..... 1406
Isa 37:27 as the grass on the **h.**, and as corn..... 1406
Jer 48:38 upon all the **h.** of Moab, and in the..... 1406
Zep 1:5 the host of heaven upon the **h.**;......... 1406
Mt 10:27 **the ear, that preach ye upon the h.** *1430*
Lu 12:3 **shall be proclaimed upon the h.**.... *1430*

HOUSHOLD See HOUSEHOLD.

HOW See also HOWBEIT; HOWSOEVER.
Ge 26:9 **h.** saidst thou, She is my sister?........ 349
Ge 27:20 **H.** is it that thou hast found it so........ 4100
Ge 28:17 **H.** dreadful is this place! this is......... 4100
Ge 30:29 knowest **h.** I have served thee,..... 854,834
Ge 30:29 and **h.** thy cattle was with me....... 854,834
Ge 38:29 said, **H.** hast thou broken forth?........ 4100
Ge 39:9 his wife: **h.** then can I do this great..... 349
Ge 44:8 **h.** then should we steal out of thy....... 349
Ge 44:16 or **h.** shall we clear ourselves?.......... 4100
Ge 44:34 **h.** shall I go up to my father, and........ 349
Ge 47:8 said unto Jacob, **H.** old art thou?......... 4100
Ge 47:18 lord, **h.** that our money is spent;.............
Ex 2:18 **h.** is it that ye are come so soon....... 4069
Ex 6:12 **h.** then shall Pharaoh hear me,............ 349
Ex 6:30 **h.** shall Pharaoh hearken unto me?....... 349
Ex 9:29 **h.** that the earth is the Lord's..............
Ex 10:2 may know **h.** that I am the Lord,.............
Ex 10:3 **H.** long wilt thou refuse to humble..... 5704
Ex 10:7 **H.** long shall this man be a snare....... 4970
Ex 11:7 may know **h.** that the Lord doth put a..........
Ex 16:28 **H.** long refuse ye to keep my........... 5704

Ex 18:8 way, and **h.** the Lord delivered them.
Ex 19:4 **h.** I bare you on eagles' wings, and
Ex 36:1 know **h.** to work all manner of work
Nu 10:31 **h.** we are to encamp in the wilderness,
Nu 14:11 **H.** long will this people provoke 5704
Nu 14:11 **h.** long will it be ere they believe 5704
Nu 14:27 **H.** long shall I bear with this evil 5704
Nu 20:15 **H.** our fathers went down into Egypt,
Nu 23:8 **H.** shall I curse, whom God hath 4100
Nu 23:8 **h.** shall I defy, whom the Lord hath 4100
Nu 24:5 **H.** goodly are thy tents, O Jacob, 4100
De 1:12 **H.** can I myself alone bear your 349
De 1:31 **h.** that the Lord thy God bare thee,
De 7:17 than I; **h.** can I dispossess them? 349
De 9:7 not, **h.** thou provokedst the Lord 834
De 11:4 **h.** he made the water of the Red 834
De 11:4 and **h.** the Lord hath destroyed them
De 11:6 **h.** the earth opened her mouth, and, 834
De 12:30 **H.** did these nations serve their 349
De 18:21 **H.** shall we know the word which 349
De 25:18 **H.** he met thee by the way, and 834
De 29:16 **h.** we have dwelt in the land of 834
De 29:16 and **h.** we came through the nations 834
De 31:27 and **h.** much more after my death? 637
De 32:30 **H.** should one chase a thousand, 349
Jos 2:10 **h.** the Lord dried up the water of 834
Jos 9:7 **h.** shall we make a league with you? 349
Jos 9:24 **h.** that the Lord...commanded his
Jos 10:1 **h.** Joshua had taken Ai, and had 3588
Jos 10:1 **h.** the inhabitants of Gibeon had 3588
Jos 14:12 that day **h.** the Anakims were there, 3588
Jos 18:3 **H.** long are ye slack to go to 5704
Jg 13:12 **H.** shall we order the child, and 4100
Jg 13:12 and **h.** shall we do unto him?
Jg 16:15 **H.** canst thou say, I love thee, 349
Jg 18:7 **h.** they dwelt careless, after the
Jg 20:3 Tell us, **h.** was this wickedness? 349
Jg 21:7, 16 **H.** shall we do for wives for 4100
Ru 1:6 **h.** that the Lord had visited his
Ru 2:11 **h.** thou hast left thy father and thy
Ru 3:18 thou know **h.** the matter will fall 5704
1Sa 1:14 **H.** long wilt thou be drunken? put 5704
1Sa 2:22 **h.** they lay with the women that 434
1Sa 10:27 said, **H.** shall this man save us? 4100
1Sa 12:24 **h.** great things he hath done for 834
1Sa 14:29 **h.** mine eyes have been enlightened 3588
1Sa 14:30 **H.** much more, if haply the 637
1Sa 15:2 **h.** he laid wait for him in the way, 834
1Sa 16:1 **H.** long wilt thou mourn for Saul, 5704
1Sa 16:2 **H.** can I go? if Saul hear it, he will 349
1Sa 17:18 and look **h.** thy brethren fare, and
1Sa 23:3 **h.** much more then if we come to 637
1Sa 24:10 **h.** that the Lord had delivered thee 834
1Sa 24:18 **h.** that thou hast dealt well with
1Sa 28:9 **h.** he hath cut off those that have
2Sa 1:4 unto him, **H.** went the matter? 4100
2Sa 1:5 **H.** knowest thou that Saul and 349
2Sa 1:14 **H.** wast thou not afraid to stretch 349
2Sa 1:19 places: **h.** are the mighty fallen! 349
2Sa 1:25 **H.** are the mighty fallen in the 349
2Sa 1:27 **H.** are the mighty fallen, and the 349
2Sa 2:22 **h.** then should I hold up my face to 349
2Sa 2:26 **h.** long shall it be then, ere thou 5704
2Sa 4:11 **H.** much more, when wicked men 637
2Sa 6:9 **H.** shall the ark of the Lord come 349
2Sa 6:20 **H.** glorious was the king of Israel 4100
2Sa 11:7 demanded of him **h.** Joab did, and
2Sa 11:7 and **h.** the people did, and **h.** the war
2Sa 12:18 **h.** will he then vex himself, if we 349
2Sa 16:11 **h.** much more now may this 637
2Sa 18:19 **h.** that the Lord hath avenged him
2Sa 19:2 **h.** the king was grieved for his son
2Sa 19:34 **H.** long have I to live, that I should 4100
2Sa 24:3 people, **h.** many soever they be, an
1Ki 3:7 I know not **h.** to go out or come in.
1Ki 5:3 **h.** that David my father could not
1Ki 8:27 **h.** much less this house that I 637
1Ki 12:6 **H.** do ye advise that I may answer 349
1Ki 14:19 **h.** he warred, and **h.** he reigned, 834
1Ki 18:13 **h.** I hid an hundred men of the Lord's
1Ki 18:21 **H.** long halt ye between two 5704
1Ki 19:1 **h.** he had slain all the prophets 834
1Ki 20:7 see **h.** this man seeketh mischief: 3588
1Ki 21:29 thou **h.** Ahab humbleth himself 3588
1Ki 22:16 **H.** many times shall I adjure 5704
1Ki 22:45 of Jehoshaphat,...and **h.** he warred, 834
2Ki 5:7 **h.** he seeketh a quarrel against me 3588
2Ki 5:13 **h.** much rather then, when he 637
2Ki 6:15 Alas, my master! **h.** shall we do? 349
2Ki 6:32 **h.** this son of a murderer hath sent 3588
2Ki 8:5 **h.** he had restored a dead body to 834
2Ki 9:25 **h.** that, when I and thou rode together
2Ki 10:4 before him: **h.** then shall we stand? 349
2Ki 14:15 **h.** he fought with Amaziah king of 834
2Ki 14:28 **h.** he warred, and **h.** he recovered 834
2Ki 17:28 them **h.** they should fear the Lord 349
2Ki 18:24 **H.** then wilt thou turn away the face 349
2Ki 19:25 not heard long ago **h.** I have done it,
2Ki 20:3 **h.** I have walked before thee in 834
2Ki 20:20 and **h.** he made a pool, and a conduit, 834
1Ch 13:12 **H.** shall I bring the ark of God 1963
1Ch 18:9 **h.** David had smitten all the host 3588
1Ch 19:5 told David **h.** the men were served
2Ch 6:18 **h.** much less this house which I 637
2Ch 7:3 saw **h.** the fire came down, and the
2Ch 18:15 **H.** many times shall I adjure 5704
2Ch 20:11 Behold, I say, **h.** they reward us,
2Ch 32:15 **h.** much less shall your God 637
2Ch 33:19 also, and **h.** God was intreated of him,
Ezr 7:22 and salt without prescribing **h.** much.
Ne 2:6 For **h.** long shall thy journey be? 5704
Ne 2:17 **h.** Jerusalem lieth waste, and the 834
Es 2:11 to know **h.** Esther did, and what should
Es 5:11 **h.** he had advanced him above the 834
Es 8:6 **h.** can I endure to see the evil that 346
Es 8:6 **h.** can I endure to see the destruction 346
Job 4:19 **H.** much less in them that dwell in 637
Job 6:25 **H.** forcible are right words! but 4100
Job 7:19 **H.** long wilt thou not depart 5704
Job 8:2 **H.** long wilt thou speak these 5704
Job 8:2 **h.** long shall the words of thy mouth
Job 9:2 **h.** should man be just with God? 4100
Job 9:14 **H.** much less shall I answer him, 637
Job 13:23 **H.** many are mine iniquities and 4100
Job 15:16 **H.** much more abominable 637
Job 18:2 **H.** long will it be ere ye make 5704
Job 19:2 **H.** long will ye vex my soul, and 5704
Job 21:17 **H.** oft is the candle of the wicked 4100
Job 21:17 and **h.** oft cometh their destruction
Job 21:34 **H.** then comfort ye me in vain, 349
Job 22:12 the height of the stars, **h.** high 3588
Job 22:13 thou sayest, **H.** doth God know? 4100
Job 25:4 **H.** then can man be justified with 4100
Job 25:4 or **h.** can he be clean that is born of 4100
Job 25:4 **H.** much less man, that is a 637
Job 26:2 **H.** hast thou helped him that is 4100
Job 26:2 **h.** savest thou the arm that hath no
Job 26:3 **H.** hast thou counselled him that 4100
Job 26:3 **h.** hast thou plentifully declared the
Job 26:14 **h.** little a portion is heard of him? 4100
Job 34:19 **H.** much less to him that accepted 834
Job 37:17 **H.** thy garments are warm, when he 834
Ps 3:1 **h.** are they increased that trouble 4100
Ps 4:2 **h.** long will ye turn my glory 5704
Ps 4:2 **h.** long will ye love vanity, and seek
Ps 6:3 vexed: but thou, O Lord, **h.** long? 5704
Ps 8:1,9 **h.** excellent is thy name in all the 4100
Ps 11:1 **h.** say ye to my soul, Flee as a bird 349
Ps 13:1 **H.** long wilt thou forget me, O 5704
Ps 13:1 **h.** long wilt thou hide thy face from 5704
Ps 13:2 **H.** long shall I take counsel in my 5704
Ps 13:2 **h.** long shall mine enemy be exalted 5704
Ps 21:1 **h.** greatly shall he rejoice! 4100
Ps 31:19 Oh **h.** great is thy goodness, which 4100
Ps 35:17 Lord, **h.** long wilt thou look on? 4100
Ps 36:7 **H.** excellent is thy lovingkindness, 4100
Ps 39:4 it is; that I may know **h.** frail I am. 4100
Ps 44:2 **H.** thou didst drive out the heathen
Ps 44:2 **h.** thou didst afflict the people, and
Ps 62:3 **H.** long will ye imagine mischief 5704
Ps 66:3 **H.** terrible art thou in thy works! 4100
Ps 73:11 **H.** doth God know? and is there 349
Ps 73:19 **H.** are they brought into desolation, 349
Ps 74:9 us any that knoweth **h.** long. 5704
Ps 74:10 God, **h.** long shall the adversary 5704
Ps 74:22 **h.** the foolish man reproacheth thee
Ps 78:40 **H.** oft did they provoke him in the 4101
Ps 78:43 **H.** he had wrought his signs in 834
Ps 79:5 **H.** long, Lord? wilt thou be angry 5704
Ps 80:4 hosts, **h.** long wilt thou be angry 5704
Ps 82:2 **H.** long will ye judge unjustly, and 5704
Ps 84:1 **H.** amiable are thy tabernacles, O 4100
Ps 89:46 **H.** long, Lord? wilt thou hide 5704
Ps 89:47 Remember **h.** short my time is: 4100
Ps 89:50 **h.** I do bear in my bosom the reproach
Ps 90:13 Return, O Lord, **h.** long? and let it 5704
Ps 92:5 O Lord, **h.** great are thy works! 4100
Ps 94:3 **h.** long shall the wicked, **h.** long 5704
Ps 94:4 **H.** long shall they utter and speak hard
Ps 104:24 **h.** manifold are thy works! in 4100
Ps 119:84 **H.** many are the days of thy 4100
Ps 119:97 O **h.** love I thy law! it is my 4100
Ps 119:103 **H.** sweet are thy words unto my 4100
Ps 119:159 Consider **h.** I love thy precepts: 3588
Ps 132:2 **H.** he sware unto the Lord, and 834
Ps 133:1 **h.** good and **h.** pleasant it is for 4100
Ps 137:4 **H.** shall we sing the Lord's song in 349
Ps 139:17 **H.** precious also are thy thoughts 4100
Ps 139:17 O God! **h.** great is the sum of them! 4100
Pr 1:22 **H.** long, ye simple ones, will ye 5704
Pr 5:12 **H.** have I hated instruction, and 349
Pr 6:9 **H.** long wilt thou sleep, O 5704
Pr 15:11 **h.** much more then the hearts 637
Pr 15:23 spoken in due season, **h.** good is it! 4100
Pr 16:16 **H.** much better is it to get wisdom 4100
Pr 19:7 **h.** much more do his friends 637
Pr 20:24 **h.** can a man then understand his 4100
Pr 21:27 **h.** much more, when he 637
Pr 30:13 O **h.** lofty are their eyes! 4100
Ec 2:16 And **h.** dieth the wise man? as the 349
Ec 4:11 but **h.** can one be warm alone? 349
Ec 10:15 he knoweth not **h.** to go to the city. 834
Ec 11:5 **h.** the bones do grow in the womb of
Ca 4:10 **H.** fair is thy love, my sister, my 4100
Ca 4:10 **h.** much better is thy love than 4100
Ca 5:3 off my coat; **h.** shall I put it on? 349
Ca 5:3 my feet; **h.** shall I defile them? 349
Ca 7:1 **H.** beautiful are thy feet with 4100
Ca 7:6 **H.** fair and **h.** pleasant art thou, 4100
Isa 1:21 **H.** is the faithful city become an 349
Isa 6:11 Then said I, Lord, **h.** long? And 5704
Isa 14:4 **H.** hath the oppressor ceased! the 349
Isa 14:12 **h.** art thou cut down to the ground,
Isa 14:12 **H.** art thou fallen from heaven, O 349
Isa 19:11 **h.** say ye unto Pharaoh, I am the son 349
Isa 20:6 Assyria: and **h.** shall we escape? 349
Isa 36:9 **H.** then wilt thou turn away the face 349
Isa 37:26 heard long ago, **h.** I have done it;
Isa 38:3 **h.** I have walked before thee in 834
Isa 48:11 **h.** should my name be polluted? 349
Isa 50:4 know **h.** to speak a word in season
Isa 52:7 **H.** beautiful upon the mountains 4100
Jer 2:21 **h.** then art thou turned into the 349
Jer 2:23 **H.** canst thou say, I am not polluted, 349
Jer 3:19 **H.** shall I put thee among the 349
Jer 4:14 **H.** long shall thy vain thoughts 5704
Jer 4:21 **H.** long shall I see the standard, 5704
Jer 5:7 **H.** shall I pardon thee for this? 335
Jer 8:8 **H.** do ye say, We are wise, and the 349
Jer 9:7 **h.** shall I do for the daughter of my 349
Jer 9:19 **H.** are we spoiled! we are greatly 349
Jer 12:4 **H.** long shall the land mourn, and 5704
Jer 12:5 **h.** canst thou contend with horses? 349
Jer 12:5 **h.** wilt thou do in the swelling of 349
Jer 15:5 shall go aside to ask **h.** thou doest?
Jer 22:23 **h.** gracious shalt thou be when 4100
Jer 23:26 **H.** long shall this be in the heart 5704
Jer 31:22 **H.** long wilt thou go about, O thou 5704
Jer 36:17 **H.** didst thou write all these words 349
Jer 46:13 **h.** Nebuchadrezzar king of Babylon
Jer 47:5 **h.** long wilt thou cut thyself? 5704
Jer 47:6 **h.** long will it be ere thou be quiet? 5704
Jer 47:7 **H.** can it be quiet, seeing the Lord 349
Jer 48:14 **H.** say ye, We are mighty and strong 349
Jer 48:17 **H.** is the strong staff broken, and 349
Jer 48:39 howl, saying, **H.** is it broken down! 349
Jer 48:39 **h.** hath Moab turned the back 349
Jer 49:25 **H.** is the city of praise not left, the 349
Jer 50:23 **H.** is the hammer of the whole earth 349
Jer 50:23 **h.** is Babylon become a desolation 349
Jer 51:41 **H.** is Sheshach taken! and 349
Jer 51:41 **h.** is the praise of the whole earth
Jer 51:41 **h.** is Babylon...an astonishment 349
La 1:1 **H.** doth the city sit solitary, that 349
La 1:1 **h.** is she become as a widow! she that
La 1:1 provinces, **h.** is she become tributary!
La 2:1 **H.** hath the Lord covered the 349
La 4:1 **H.** is the gold become dim! 349
La 4:1 **h.** is the fine gold changed!
La 4:2 **h.** are they esteemed as earthen 349
Eze 14:21 **H.** much more when I send 637

Eze 15:5 h. much less shall it be meet 637
Eze 16:30 h. weak is thine heart, saith the 4100
Eze 26:17 H. are thou destroyed, that wast 349
Eze 33:10 in them, h. should we then live? 349
Da 4:3 H. great are his signs! and 4101
Da 4:3 and how mighty are his wonders! 4101
Da 8:13 H. long shall be the vision 5704
Da 10:17 For h. can the servant of this my 1963
Da 12:6 H. long shall it be to the end of 5704
Ho 8:5 h. long will it be ere they attain to 349
Ho 11:8 H. shall I give thee up, Ephraim? 349
Ho 11:8 h. shall I deliver thee, Israel?
Ho 11:8 h. shall I make thee as Adinah? 349
Ho 11:8 h. shall I set thee as Zeboim? mine
Joe 1:18 H. do the beasts groan! the 4100
Ob 5 h. art thou cut off! would they not 349
Ob 6 H. are the things of Esau searched 349
Ob 6 h. are his hidden things sought up!
Mic 2:4 h. hath he removed it from me! 349
Hab 1:2 O Lord, h. long shall I cry, and 5704
Hab 2:6 that which is not his! h. long? 5704
Zep 2:15 h. is she become a desolation, a 349
Hag 2:3 and h. do ye see it now? it is not 4100
Zec 1:12 h. long wilt thou not have mercy 5704
Zec 9:17 For h. great is his goodness, and 4100
Zec 9:17 and h. great is his beauty! 4100
Mt 6:23 **h. great is that darkness!** *4214*
Mt 6:28 **lilies of the field, h. they grow;** *4459*
Mt 7:4 **Or h. wilt thou say to thy brother,** *4459*
Mt 7:11 **h. to give good gifts unto your**
Mt 7:11 **h. much more shall your Father** *4214*
Mt 10:19 **thought h. or what ye shall speak:** *4459*
Mt 10:25 **h. much more shall they call them** *4214*
Mt 12:4 **H. he entered into the house of** *4459*
Mt 12:5 **h. that on the sabbath days the**
Mt 12:12 **H. much then is a man better** *4214*
Mt 12:14 him, h. they might destroy him *3704*
Mt 12:26 **h. shall then his kingdom stand?** *4459*
Mt 12:29 **h. can one enter into a strong** *4459*
Mt 12:34 **h. can ye, being evil, speak good** *4459*
Mt 15:34 them, **H. many loaves have ye?** *4214*
Mt 16:9, 10 **and h. many baskets ye took** *4214*
Mt 16:11 **H. is it that ye do not understand** *4459*
Mt 16:12 h. that he bade them not beware
Mt 16:21 h. that he must go unto Jerusalem,
Mt 17:17 **h. long shall I be with you?** *2193*
Mt 17:17 **h. long shall I suffer you? bring** *4219*
Mt 18:12 **H. think ye? if a man have an** *5101*
Mt 18:21 Lord, h. oft shall my brother sin *4212*
Mt 21:20 H. soon is the fig tree withered *4459*
Mt 22:12 **h. camest thou in hither not** *4459*
Mt 22:15 h. they might entangle him in his *3704*
Mt 22:43 **H. then doth David in spirit call** *4459*
Mt 22:45 **call him Lord, h. is he his son?** *4459*
Mt 23:33 **h. can ye escape the damnation** *4459*
Mt 23:37 **h. often would I have gathered thy**
Mt 26:54 **h. then shall the scriptures be** *4459*
Mt 27:13 not h. many things they witness *4214*
Mk 2:16 H. is it that he eateth and *5101*
Mk 2:26 **H. he went into the house of God** *4459*
Mk 3:6 him, h. they might destroy him *3704*
Mk 3:23 **H. can Satan cast out Satan?** *4459*
Mk 4:13 **h. then will ye know all parables?** *4459*
Mk 4:27 **and grow up, he knoweth not h.** *5613*
Mk 4:40 **h. is it that ye have no faith?** *4459*
Mk 5:16 h. it befell to him that was possessed *4459*
Mk 5:19 **h. great things the Lord hath done** *3745*
Mk 5:20 h. great things Jesus had done for *3745*
Mk 6:38 **H. many loaves have ye? go and** *4214*
Mk 8:5 **H. many loaves have ye? And they** *4214*
Mk 8:19, 20 **h. many baskets full of** *4214*
Mk 8:21 **H. is it that ye do not understand?** *4459*
Mk 9:12 **h. it is written of the Son of man,** *4459*
Mk 9:19 **h. long shall I be with you?** *2193*
Mk 9:19 **h. long shall I suffer you? bring** *2193*
Mk 9:21 **H. long is it ago since this came** *4214*
Mk 10:23 **H. hardly shall they that have** *4459*
Mk 10:24 **h. hard is it for them that trust in** *4459*
Mk 11:18 sought h. they might destroy him: *4459*
Mk 12:26 **h. in the bush God spake unto** *5613*
Mk 12:35 **H. say the scribes that Christ is** *4459*
Mk 12:41 h. the people cast money into the *4459*
Mk 14:1 h. they might take him by craft *4459*
Mk 14:11 h. he might conveniently betray *4459*
Mk 15:4 h. many things they witness *4214*
Lu 1:34 H. shall this be, seeing I know not *4459*
Lu 1:58 h. the Lord had shewed great *3754*
Lu 1:62 h. he would have him called *5105*
Lu 2:49 them, **H. is it that ye sought me?** *5105*
Lu 6:4 **H. he went into the house of God,** *5613*
Lu 6:42 **h. canst thou say to thy brother,** *4459*
Lu 7:22 **h. that the blind see, the lame** *3754*
Lu 8:18 **Take heed therefore h. ye hear:** *4459*
Lu 8:39 **h. great things God hath done** *3745*
Lu 8:39 h. great things Jesus had done *3745*
Lu 8:47 h. she was healed immediately *5613*
Lu 9:41 **h. long shall I be with you,** *2193*
Lu 10:26 **written in the law? h. readest** *4459*
Lu 11:13 **h. to give good gifts unto your**
Lu 11:13 **h. much more shall your heavenly** *4214*
Lu 11:18 **h. shall his kingdom stand?** *4559*
Lu 12:11 **h. or what thing ye shall answer,** *4559*
Lu 12:24 **h. much more are ye better than** *4214*
Lu 12:27 **Consider the lilies h. they grow:** *4459*
Lu 12:28 **h. much more will he clothe you,** *4214*
Lu 12:50 **and h. am I straitened till it be** *4459*
Lu 12:56 **h. is it that ye do not discern this** *4459*
Lu 13:34 **h. often would I have gathered** *4212*
Lu 14:7 h. they chose out the chief rooms; *4459*
Lu 15:17 **H. many hired servants of my** *4214*
Lu 16:2 **H. is it that I hear this of thee?** *5101*
Lu 16:5 **H. much owest thou unto my** *4214*
Lu 16:7 **another, And h. much owest thou?** *4214*
Lu 18:24 **H. hardly shall they that have** *4459*
Lu 19:15 **h. much every man had gained by** *5101*
Lu 20:41 **H. say they that Christ is David's** *4459*
Lu 20:44 **him Lord, h. is he then his son?** *4459*
Lu 21:5 h. it was adorned with goodly *3754*
Lu 22:2 scribes sought h. they might kill *4459*
Lu 22:4 h. he might betray him unto them *4459*
Lu 22:61 h. he had said unto him, Before *5613*
Lu 23:55 sepulchre, and h. his body was laid *5613*
Lu 24:6 h. he spake unto you when he was *5613*
Lu 24:20 h. the chief priests and our rulers *3704*
Lu 24:35 and h. he was known of them in *5613*
Joh 3:4 H. can a man be born when he is *4459*
Joh 3:9 unto him, H. can these things be? *4459*
Joh 3:12 **h. shall ye believe, if I tell you of** *4459*
Joh 4:1 h. the Pharisees had heard that *3754*
Joh 4:9 H. is it that thou, being a Jew, *4459*
Joh 5:44 **H. can ye believe, which receive** *4459*
Joh 5:47 **h. shall ye believe my words?** *4459*
Joh 6:42 h. is it then that he saith, I came *4459*
Joh 6:52 H. can this man give us of his flesh *4459*
Joh 7:15 H. knoweth this man letters, *4459*
Joh 8:33 h. sayest thou, Ye shall be made *4459*
Joh 9:10 him, H. were thine eyes opened? *4459*
Joh 9:15 him h. he had received his sight *4459*
Joh 9:16 H. can a man that is a sinner do *4459*
Joh 9:19 blind? h. then doth he now see? *4459*
Joh 9:26 to thee? h. opened he thine eyes? *4459*
Joh 10:24 H. long dost thou make us to *2193*
Joh 11:36 the Jews, Behold h. he loved him! *4459*
Joh 12:19 Perceive ye h. ye prevail nothing? *3754*
Joh 12:34 h. sayest thou, The Son of man *4459*
Joh 14:5 goest; and h. can we know the way? *4459*
Joh 14:9 **h. sayest thou then, Shew us the** *4459*
Joh 14:22 h. is it that thou wilt manifest *5101*
Joh 14:28 **h. I said unto you, I go away, and** *3754*
Ac 2:8 h. hear we every man in our own *4459*
Ac 4:21 nothing h. they might punish them, *4459*
Ac 5:9 H. is it that ye have agreed *5101*
Ac 7:25 h. that God by his hand would
Ac 8:31 H. can I, except some man should *4459*
Ac 9:13 h. much evil he hath done to thy *3745*
Ac 9:16 **him h. great things he must suffer** *3745*
Ac 9:27 h. he had seen the Lord in the way, *4459*
Ac 9:27 and h. he had preached boldly at *4459*
Ac 10:28 h. that it is an unlawful thing for *5613*
Ac 10:38 H. God anointed Jesus of Nazareth *5613*
Ac 11:13 h. he had seen an angel in his *4459*
Ac 11:16 h. that he said, **John indeed** *5613*
Ac 12:14 h. Peter stood before the gate
Ac 12:17 h. the Lord had brought him out *4459*
Ac 13:32 h. that the promise which was
Ac 14:27 h. he had opened the door of faith
Ac 15:7 h. that a good while ago God made
Ac 15:14 h. God at the first did visit the *2531*
Ac 15:36 of the Lord, and see h. they do *4459*
Ac 19:35 knoweth not h. that the city of the
Ac 20:20 And h. I kept back nothing that *5613*
Ac 20:35 h. that so labouring ye ought to
Ac 20:35 h. he said, **It is more blessed to** *3754*
Ac 21:20 h. many thousands of Jews there *4214*
Ac 23:30 h. that the Jews laid wait for the
Ro 3:6 h. then shall God judge the world? *4459*
Ro 4:10 H. was it then reckoned? when *4459*
Ro 6:2 H. shall we, that are dead to sin, *4459*
Ro 7:1 h. that the law hath dominion over
Ro 7:18 h. to perform that which is good
Ro 8:32 h. shall he not with him also freely *4459*
Ro 10:14 H. then shall they call on him in *4459*
Ro 10:14 h. shall they believe in him of whom *4459*
Ro 10:14 h. shall they hear without a *4459*
Ro 10:15 h. shall they preach, except they *5613*
Ro 10:15 H. beautiful are the feet of them
Ro 11:2 h. he maketh intercession to God *5613*
Ro 11:12 h. much more their fulness? *4214*
Ro 11:24 h. much more shall these, which *4214*
Ro 11:33 h. unsearchable are his judgments, *5613*
1Co 1:26 h. that not many wise men after
1Co 3:10 heed h. he buildeth thereupon *4459*
1Co 6:3 h. much more things that pertain *3386*
1Co 7:16 or h. knowest thou, O man, *5101*
1Co 7:32 Lord, h. he may please the Lord: *4459*
1Co 7:33 world, h. he may please his wife *4459*
1Co 7:34 h. she may please her husband *4459*
1Co 10:1 h. that all our fathers were under
1Co 14:7 h. shall it be known what is piped *4459*
1Co 14:9 h. shall it be known what is spoken? *4459*
1Co 14:16 h. shall he that occupieth the room *4459*
1Co 14:26 H. is it then, brethren? when ye *5101*
1Co 15:3 h. that Christ died for our sins
1Co 15:12 h. say some among you that there *4459*
1Co 15:35 H. are the dead raised up? and *4459*
2Co 3:8 H. shall not the ministration of the *4459*
2Co 7:15 h. with fear and trembling ye *5613*
2Co 8:2 H. that in a great trial of affliction
2Co 12:4 H. that he was caught up into
2Co 13:5 h. that Jesus Christ is in you,
Ga 1:13 h. that beyond measure I persecuted
Ga 4:9 h. turn ye again to the weak and *4459*
Ga 4:13 h. through infirmity of the flesh *3754*
Ga 6:11 Ye see h. large a letter I have *4080*
Eph 3:3 H. that by revelation he made
Eph 6:21 may know my affairs, and h. I do, *5101*
Php 1:8 h. greatly I long after you all in *5613*
Php 2:23 as I shall see h. it will go with me. *4012*
Php 4:12 h. to be abased, and I know how to
Col 4:6 h. ye ought to answer every man *4459*
1Th 1:9 h. ye turned to God from idols to *4459*
1Th 2:10 God also, h. holily and justly and *5613*
1Th 2:11 h. we exhorted and comforted and *5613*
1Th 4:1 h. ye ought to walk and to please *4459*
1Th 4:4 know h. to possess his vessel in
2Th 3:7 know h. ye ought to follow us: *4459*
1Ti 3:5 know not h. to rule his own house,
1Ti 3:5 h. shall he take care of the church *4459*
1Ti 3:15 h. thou oughtest to behave thyself *4459*
2Ti 1:18 h. many things he ministered unto *3745*
Phm 16 me, but h. much more unto thee, *4214*
Phm 19 h. thou owest unto me even thine *3754*
Heb 2:3 H. shall we escape, if we neglect *4459*
Heb 7:4 consider h. great this man was, *4080*
Heb 8:6 by h. much also he is the mediator *3745*
Heb 9:14 H. much more shall the blood of *4214*
Heb 10:29 Of h. much sorer punishment, *4214*
Heb 12:17 For ye know h. that afterward, *3754*
Jas 2:22 h. faith wrought with his works, *3754*
Jas 2:24 h. that by works a man is justified,
Jas 3:5 h. great a matter a little fire *2245*
2Pe 2:9 knoweth h. to deliver the godly out
1Jo 3:17 h. dwelleth the love of God in him? *4459*
1Jo 4:20 h. can he love God whom he hath *4459*
Jude 5 h. that the Lord, having saved the
Jude 18 H. that they told you there should
Re 2:2 **h. thou canst not bear them which** *3754*
Re 3:3 **h. thou hast received and heard,** *4459*
Re 6:10 H. long, O Lord, holy and *2193*
Re 18:7 H. much she hath glorified herself, *3745*

HOWBEIT

Jg 4:17 H. Sisera fled away on his feet to the
Jg 11:28 H. the king of the children of Ammon
Jg 16:22 H. the hair of his head began to grown
Jg 18:29 H. the name of the city was Laish 199
Jg 21:18 H. we may not give them wives of our
Ru 3:12 h. there is a kinsman nearer than I
1Sa 8:9 h. yet protest solemnly unto them 389

2Sa 2:23 **H.** he refused to turn aside: wherefore......
2Sa 12:14 **H.**, because by this deed thou hast...... 657
2Sa 13:14 **H.** he would not hearken unto her..........
2Sa 13:25 **h.** he would not go, but blessed him. ....
2Sa 23:19 **h.** he attained not unto the first three. ......
1Ki 2:15 **h.** the kingdom is turned about, and is ......
1Ki 10:7 **H.** I believed not the words, until I..........
1Ki 11:13 **H.** I will not rend away all the.......... 7535
1Ki 11:22 Nothing: **h.** let me go in any wise. ....
1Ki 11:34 **H.** I will not take the whole kingdom........
2Ki 3:25 **h.** the slingers went about it, and............
2Ki 8:10 **h.** the Lord hath shewed me that he.........
2Ki 10:29 **H.** from the sins of Jeroboam the son ....
2Ki 12:13 **H.** there were not made for the house......
2Ki 14:4 **H.** the high places were not taken............
2Ki 15:35 **H.** the high places were not removed:........
2Ki 17:29 **H.** every nation made gods of their ....
2Ki 17:40 **H.** they did not hearken, but they did.......
2Ki 22:7 **H.** there was no reckoning made with.......
1Ch 11:21 **h.** he attained not to the first three. ....
1Ch 28:4 **H.** the Lord God of Israel chose me.........
2Ch 9:6 **H.** I believed not their words, until I........
2Ch 18:34 **h.** the king of Israel stayed himself up.......
2Ch 20:33 **H.** the high places were not taken...........
2Ch 21:7 **H.** the Lord would not destroy the...........
2Ch 21:20 **H.** they buried him in the city of.............
2Ch 24:5 **H.** the Levites hastened it not.................
2Ch 27:2 **h.** he entered not into the temple of..........
2Ch 32:31 **H.** in the business of the.................. 3651
Ne 9:33 **H.** thou art just in all that is brought.........
Ne 13:2 **h.** our God turned the cursed into a ....
Job 30:24 **H.** he will not stretch out his hand to........
Isa 10:7 **H.** he meaneth not so, neither doth his .....
Jer 44:4 **H.** I sent unto you all my servants the......
Mt 17:21 **H. this kind goeth not out but by**........
Mk 5:19 **H.** Jesus suffered him not, but saith..........
Mk 7:7 **H. in vain do they worship me,**............
Joh 6:23 **H.** there came other boats from......... *1161*
Joh 7:13 **H.** no man spaked openly of him.......... *3305*
Joh 7:27 **H.** we know this man whence he is:..... *235*
Joh 11:13 **H.** Jesus spake of his death: but they.........
Joh 16:13 **H. when he, the Spirit of truth, is**.......
Ac 4:4 **H.** many of them which heard the ....
Ac 7:48 **H.** the most High dwelleth not in......... *235*
Ac 14:20 **H.**, as the disciples stood round.............
Ac 17:34 **H.** certain men clave unto him, and ....
Ac 27:26 **H.** we must be cast upon a certain............
Ac 28:6 **H.** they looked when he should have.........
1Co 2:6 **H.** we speak wisdom among them ....
1Co 8:7 **H.** there is not in every man that........ *235*
1Co 14:2 **h.** in the spirit he speaketh mysteries. ......
1Co 14:20 **h.** in malice be ye children, but in........ *235*
1Co 15:46 **H.** that was not first which is............. *235*
2Co 11:21 **H.** whereinsoever any is bold, ...
Ga 4:8 **H.** then, when ye know not God, ... *235*
1Ti 1:16 **H.** for this cause I obtained mercy,...... *235*
Heb 3:16 **h.** not all that came out of Egypt............ *235*

HOWL See also HOWLED; HOWLING.
Isa 13:6 **H.** ye; for the day of the Lord.......... 3213
Isa 14:31 **H.**, O gate; cry, O city; thou, ... 3213
Isa 15:2 Moab shall **h.** over Nebo, and 3213
Isa 15:3 every one shall **h.**, weeping 3213
Isa 16:7 **h.** for Moab, every one shall **h.**:....... 3213
Isa 23:1 **H.**, ye ships of Tarshish; for it.......... 3213
Isa 23:6 **h.**, ye inhabitants of the isle............ 3213
Isa 23:14 **H.**, ye ships of Tarshish, for your...... 3213
Isa 52:5 rule over them make them to **h.**, ... 3213
Isa 65:14 and shall **h.** for vexation of spirit........ 3213
Jer 4:8 you with sackcloth, lament and **h.**:...... 3213
Jer 25:34 **H.**, ye shepherds, and cry; and 3213
Jer 47:2 the inhabitants of the land shall **h.**. 3213
Jer 48:20 **h.** and cry; tell ye it in Arnon,.......... 3213
Jer 48:31 Therefore will I **h.** for Moab, and....... 3213
Jer 48:39 They shall **h.**, saying, How is it......... 3213
Jer 49:3 **H.**, O Heshbon, for Ai is spoiled:....... 3213
Jer 51:8 fallen and destroyed: **h.** for her:......... 3213
Eze 21:12 Cry and **h.**, son of man: for it 3213
Eze 30:2 Thus saith the Lord God; **H.** ye, ... 3213
Joe 1:5 and **h.**, all ye drinkers of wine, ... 3213
Joe 1:11 **h.**, O ye vinedressers, for the........... 3213
Joe 1:13 **h.**, ye ministers of the altar; come 3213
Mic 1:8 I will wail and **h.**, I will go stripped 3213
Zep 1:11 **H.**, ye inhabitants of Maktesh,.......... 3213
Zec 11:2 **H.**, fir tree; for the cedar is fallen;..... 3213
Zec 11:2 **h.**, O ye oaks of Bashan; for the........ 3213
Jas 5:1 weep and **h.** for your miseries that..... *3649*

HOWLED
Ho 7:14 when they **h.** upon their beds:........... 3213

HOWLING See also HOWLINGS.
De 32:10 and in the waste **h.** wilderness; he..... 3214
Isa 15:8 Moab; the **h.** thereof unto Eglaim,...... 3213
Isa 15:8 and the **h.** thereof unto Beer-elim. 3213
Jer 25:36 an **h.** of the principal of the flock,....... 3213
Zep 1:10 and an **h.** from the second, and 3213
Zec 11:3 voice of the **h.** of the shepherds; 3213

HOWLINGS
Am 8:3 songs of the temple shall be **h.**........... 3213

HOWSOEVER
Jg 19:20 **h.** let all thy wants lie upon me; 7535
2Sa 18:22 **h.**, let me, I pray thee, also....... 1961,4101
2Sa 18:23 But **h.**, said he let me run. And he..........
Zep 3:7 be cut off, **h.** I punished them:..... 3605,834

HOZEH See COL-HOZEH.

HUGE
2Ch 16:8 and the Lubims a **h.** host, with.......... 7230

HUKKOK (huk'-kok) See also HELKATH; HUKOK.
Jos 19:34 and goeth out from thence to **H.**,....... 2712

HUKOK (hu'-kok) See also HUKKOK.
1Ch 6:75 And **H.** with her suburbs, and.......... 2712

HUL (hul)
Ge 10:23 Uz, and **H.**, and Gether, and Mash..... 2343
1Ch 1:17 and Aram, Uz, and **H.**, and Gether,..... 2343

HULDAH (hul'-dah)
2Ki 22:14 went unto **H.** the prophetess, the 2468
2Ch 34:22 went to **H.** the prophetess, the 2468

HUMBLE See also HUMBLED; HUMBLETH.
Ex 10:3 long wilt thou refuse to **h.** thyself....... 6031
De 8:2 to **h.** thee, and to prove thee,........... 6031
De 8:16 that he might **h.** thee, and that he...... 6031
Jg 19:24 and **h.** ye them, and do with them...... 6031
2Ch 7:14 If my people,...shall **h.** themselves, ... 3665
2Ch 34:27 thou didst **h.** thyself before God,....... 3665
Job 22:29 and he shall save the **h.**..... 7807,5869,3665
Ps 9:12 he forgetteth not the cry of the **h.**. 6041
Ps 10:12 up thine hand: forget not the **h.**.......... 6041
Ps 10:17 hast heard the desire of the **h.**: 6041
Ps 34:2 the **h.** shall hear thereof, and be 6041
Ps 69:32 The **h.** shall see this, and be glad........ 6041
Pr 6:3 go, **h.** thyself, and make sure thy....... 7511
Pr 16:19 Better it is to be of an **h.** spirit 8213
Pr 29:23 but honour shall uphold the **h.** in......... 8217
Isa 57:15 that is of a contrite and **h.** spirit, ... 8217
Isa 57:15 to revive the spirit of the **h.**, and......... 8217
Jer 13:18 the queen, **H.** yourselves, sit down: ... 8213
Mt 18:4 **Whosoever therefore shall h.**.......... *5013*
Mt 23:12 **and he that shall h. himself shall**.. *5013*
2Co 12:21 my God will **h.** me among you,.......... *5013*
Jas 4:6 but giveth grace unto the **h.**............. *5011*
Jas 4:10 **H.** yourselves in the sight of the........ *5013*
1Pe 5:5 proud, and giveth grace to the **h.**. *5011*
1Pe 5:6 **H.** yourselves therefore under........... *5013*

HUMBLED See also HUMBLEDST.
Le 26:41 their uncircumcised hearts be **h.**, ... 3665
De 8:3 And he **h.** thee, and suffered thee...... 6031
De 21:14 her, because thou hast **h.** her........... 6031
De 22:24 he hath **h.** his neighbour's wife: 6031
De 22:29 because he hath **h.** her, he may not..... 6031
2Ki 22:19 and thou hast **h.** thyself before 3665
2Ch 12:6 Israel and the king **h.** themselves;...... 3665
2Ch 12:7 Lord saw that they **h.** themselves, ... 3665
2Ch 12:7 saying, They have **h.** themselves; 3665
2Ch 12:12 And when he **h.** himself, the wrath...... 3665
2Ch 30:11 and of Zebulun **h.** themselves, and...... 3665
2Ch 32:26 Hezekiah **h.** himself for the pride 3665
2Ch 33:12 and **h.** himself greatly before the........ 3665
2Ch 33:19 graven images, before he was **h.**:...... 3665
2Ch 33:23 And **h.** not himself before the Lord,..... 3665
2Ch 33:23 Manasseh his father had **h.** himself;.... 3665
2Ch 36:12 **h.** not himself before Jeremiah........... 3665
Ps 35:13 I **h.** my soul with fasting; and............ 6031
Isa 2:11 The lofty looks of man shall be **h.**, ... 8213
Isa 5:15 and the mighty man shall be **h.**,......... 8213
Isa 5:15 the eyes of the lofty shall be **h.**: 8213
Isa 10:33 down, and the haughty shall be **h.**. 8213
Jer 44:10 They are not **h.** even unto this.......... 1792
La 3:20 remembrances, and is **h.** in me......... 7743
Eze 22:10 thee have they **h.** her that was set..... 6031
Eze 22:11 another in thee hath **h.** his sister, ... 6031
Da 5:22 Belshazzar, hast not **h.** thine heart, ... 8214
Php 2:8 he **h.** himself, and became obedient.... *5013*

HUMBLEDST
2Ch 34:27 and **h.** thyself before me, and........... 3665

HUMBLENESS
Col 3:12 kindness, **h.** of mind, meekness, ... *5012*

HUMBLETH
1Ki 21:29 how Ahab **h.** himself before me? 3665
1Ki 21:29 because he **h.** himself before me, ... 3665
Ps 10:10 He croucheth, and **h.** himself,............ 7817
Ps 113:6 Who **h.** himself to behold the 8213
Isa 2:9 and the great man **h.** himself:............ 8213
Lu 14:11 **that h. himself shall be exalted.**.... *5013*
Lu 18:14 **that h. himself shall be exalted.**.... *5013*

HUMBLY
2Sa 16:4 I **h.** beseech thee that I may find....... 7812
Mic 6:8 love mercy, and to walk **h.** with......... 6800

HUMILIATION
Ac 8:33 In his **h.** his judgment was taken........ 5014

HUMILITY
Pr 15:33 wisdom; and before honour is **h.**. 6038
Pr 18:12 haughty, and before honour is **h.**......... 6038
Pr 22:4 By **h.** and the fear of the Lord are..... 6038
Ac 20:19 Serving the Lord with all **h.** of.......... *5012*
Col 2:18 your reward in a voluntary **h.** and *5012*
Col 2:23 and **h.**, and neglecting of the body;..... *5012*
1Pe 5:5 another and be clothed with **h.**: *5012*

HUMTAH (hum'-tah)
Jos 15:54 And **H.**, and Kirjath-arba, which......... 2547

HUNDRED See also HUNDREDFOLD; HUNDREDS.
Ge 5:3 Adam lived an **h.** and thirty years,...... 3967
Ge 5:4 begotten Seth were eight **h.** years:..... 3967
Ge 5:5 lived were nine **h.** and thirty years: 3967
Ge 5:6 And Seth lived an **h.** and five years, ... 3967
Ge 5:7 Enos eight **h.** and seven years,.......... 3967
Ge 5:8 were nine **h.** and twelve years:.......... 3967
Ge 5:10 Cainan eight **h.** and fifteen years, ... 3967
Ge 5:11 Enos were nine **h.** and five years:....... 3967
Ge 5:13 Mahalaleel eight **h.** and forty years, ... 3967
Ge 5:14 Cainan were nine **h.** and ten years: 3967
Ge 5:16 Jared eight **h.** and thirty years,.......... 3967
Ge 5:17 were eight **h.** ninety and five years:.... 3967
Ge 5:18 Jared lived an **h.** sixty and two 3967
Ge 5:19 he begat Enoch eight **h.** years, ... 3967
Ge 5:20 were nine **h.** sixty and two years: 3967
Ge 5:22 he begat Methuselah three **h.** years,... 3967
Ge 5:23 were three **h.** sixty and five years:....... 3967
Ge 5:25 Methuselah lived an **h.** eighty and 3967
Ge 5:26 seven **h.** eighty and two years,.......... 3967
Ge 5:27 were nine **h.** sixty and nine years:....... 3967
Ge 5:28 Lamech lived an **h.** eighty and two..... 3967
Ge 5:30 Noah five **h.** ninety and five years, ... 3967
Ge 5:31 seven **h.** seventy and seven years:...... 3967
Ge 5:32 And Noah was five **h.** years old: 3967
Ge 6:3 his days shall be an **h.** and twenty....... 3967
Ge 6:15 of the ark shall be three **h.** cubits, ... 3967
Ge 7:6 And Noah was six **h.** years old 3967
Ge 7:24 upon the earth an **h.** and fifty days 3967
Ge 8:3 after the end of the **h.** and fifty days... 3967
Ge 9:28 flood three **h.** and fifty years. 3967
Ge 9:29 of Noah nine **h.** and fifty years: 3967
Ge 11:10 Shem was an **h.** years old, and......... 3967
Ge 11:11 he begat Arphaxad five **h.** years,........ 3967
Ge 11:13 begat Salah four **h.** and three years, ... 3967
Ge 11:15 begat Eber four **h.** and three years,..... 3967
Ge 11:17 begat Peleg four **h.** and thirty years,... 3967
Ge 11:19 begat Reu two **h.** and nine years,........ 3967
Ge 11:21 begat Serug two **h.** and seven years... 3967
Ge 11:23 after he begat Nahor two **h.** years,...... 3967
Ge 11:25 Terah an **h.** and nineteen years, ... 3967
Ge 11:32 Terah were two **h.** and five years: 3967
Ge 14:14 own house, three **h.** and eighteen, ... 3967
Ge 15:13 shall afflict them four **h.** years; 3967
Ge 17:17 unto him that is an **h.** years old?........ 3967
Ge 21:5 Abraham was an **h.** years old, ... 3967
Ge 23:1 an **h.** and seven and twenty years 3967
Ge 23:15 land is worth four **h.** shekels of 3967
Ge 23:16 four **h.** shekels of silver, current......... 3967
Ge 25:7 an **h.** threescore and fifteen years. 3967
Ge 25:17 an **h.** and thirty and seven years: 3967
Ge 32:6 thee, and four **h.** men with him. 3967

Ge 32:14 Two **h.** she goats and twenty he........ 3967
Ge 32:14 two **h.** ewes, and twenty rams, ... 3967
Ge 33:1 Esau came, and with him four **h.**......... 3967
Ge 33:19 father, for an **h.** pieces of money. 3967
Ge 35:28 Isaac were an **h.** and fourscore.......... 3967
Ge 45:22 gave three **h.** pieces of silver, ... 3967
Ge 47:9 of my pilgrimage are an **h.** and......... 3967
Ge 47:28 was an **h.** forty and seven years. 3967
Ge 50:22 Joseph lived an **h.** and ten years. 3967
Ge 50:26 being an **h.** and ten years old: 3967
Ex 6:16 were an **h.** thirty and seven years...... 3967
Ex 6:18 were an **h.** thirty and three years....... 3967
Ex 6:20 Amram were an **h.** and thirty and....... 3967
Ex 12:37 about six **h.** thousand on foot that...... 3967
Ex 12:40 was four **h.** and thirty years............. 3967
Ex 12:41 end of the four **h.** and thirty years, ... 3967
Ex 14:7 And he took six **h.** chosen chariots,.... 3967
Ex 27:9 fine twined linen of an **h.** cubits 3967
Ex 27:11 be hangings of an **h.** cubits long, ... 3967
Ex 27:18 the court shall be an **h.** cubits, ... 3967
Ex 30:23 of pure myrrh five **h.** shekels, and...... 3967
Ex 30:23 two **h.** and fifty shekels, and of......... 3967
Ex 30:23 calamus two **h.** and fifty shekels,........ 3967
Ex 30:24 And of cassia five **h.** shekels, ... 3967
Ex 38:9 fine twined linen, an **h.** cubits:.......... 3967
Ex 38:11 the hangings were an **h.** cubits, ... 3967
Ex 38:24 seven **h.** and thirty shekels, after....... 3967
Ex 38:25 congregation was an **h.** talents,.......... 3967
Ex 38:25 seven **h.** and threescore and fifteen...... 3967
Ex 38:26 old and upward, for six **h.** thousand.... 3967
Ex 38:26 thousand and five **h.** and fifty men...... 3967
Ex 38:27 of the **h.** talents of silver were cast.... 3967
Ex 38:27 an **h.** sockets of the **h.** talents,.......... 3967
Ex 38:28 seven **h.** seventy and five shekels 3967
Ex 38:29 two thousand and four **h.** shekels. 3967
Le 26:8 five of you shall chase an **h.**, and an ... 3967
Le 26:8 **h.** of you shall put ten thousand to 3967
Nu 1:21 forty and six thousand and five **h.**....... 3967
Nu 1:23 fifty and nine thousand and three **h.**.... 3967
Nu 1:25 and five thousand six **h.** and fifty........ 3967
Nu 1:27 and fourteen thousand and six **h.**......... 3967
Nu 1:29 fifty and four thousand and four **h.**...... 3967
Nu 1:31 and seven thousand and four **h.**. 3967
Nu 1:33 were forty thousand and five **h.**. 3967
Nu 1:35 thirty and two thousand and two **h.**. ... 3967
Nu 1:37 and five thousand and four **h.**. 3967
Nu 1:39 and two thousand and seven **h.**.......... 3967
Nu 1:41 forty and one thousand and five **h.**...... 3967
Nu 1:43 fifty and three thousand and four **h.**...... 3967
Nu 1:46 numbered were six **h.** thousand and.... 3967
Nu 1:46 three thousand and five **h.** and fifty..... 3967
Nu 2:4 and fourteen thousand and six **h.**......... 3967
Nu 2:6 fifty and four thousand and four **h.**....... 3967
Nu 2:8 and seven thousand and four **h.**. 3967
Nu 2:9 an **h.** thousand and fourscore............. 3967
Nu 2:9 and four **h.**, throughout their armies. .. 3967
Nu 2:11 forty and six thousand and five **h.**....... 3967
Nu 2:13 fifty and nine thousand and three **h.**.... 3967
Nu 2:15 forty and five thousand and six **h.**........ 3967
Nu 2:16 of Reuben were an **h.** thousand 3967
Nu 2:16 one thousand and four **h.** and fifty, ... 3967
Nu 2:19 were forty thousand and five **h.**. 3967
Nu 2:21 thirty and two thousand and two **h.**. ... 3967
Nu 2:23 thirty and five thousand and four **h.**. ... 3967
Nu 2:24 of Ephraim were an **h.** thousand 3967
Nu 2:24 and eight thousand and an **h.**,............ 3967
Nu 2:26 and two thousand and seven **h.**........... 3967
Nu 2:28 forty and one thousand and five **h.**....... 3967
Nu 2:30 fifty and three thousand and four **h.**.... 3967
Nu 2:31 camp of Dan were an **h.** thousand...... 3967
Nu 2:31 fifty and seven thousand and six **h.**..... 3967
Nu 2:32 their hosts were six **h.** thousand........ 3967
Nu 2:32 three thousand and five **h.** and fifty..... 3967
Nu 3:22 were seven thousand and five **h.**........ 3967
Nu 3:28 eight thousand and six **h.**, keeping...... 3967
Nu 3:34 were six thousand and two **h.**............ 3967
Nu 3:43 two thousand two **h.** and threescore ... 3967
Nu 3:46 two **h.** and threescore and thirteen...... 3967
Nu 3:50 a thousand three **h.** and threescore..... 3967
Nu 4:36 two thousand seven **h.** and fifty. 3967
Nu 4:40 two thousand and six **h.** and thirty...... 3967
Nu 4:44 were three thousand and two **h.**, ... 3967
Nu 4:48 thousand and five **h.** and fourscore. 3967
Nu 7:13, 19,25,31,37,43,49,55,61,67,73,79,85 an
h. and thirty shekels,....................... 3967
Nu 7:85 two thousand and four **h.** shekels, ... 3967
Nu 7:86 spoons was an **h.** and twenty shekels.. 3967

Nu 11:21 I am, are six **h.** thousand footmen;..... 3967
Nu 16:2 two **h.** and fifty princes of the 3967
Nu 16:17 his censer, two **h.** and fifty censers;... 3967
Nu 16:35 consumed the two **h.** and fifty men..... 3967
Nu 16:49 were fourteen thousand and seven **h.**,..3967
Nu 26:7 thousand and seven **h.** and thirty........ 3967
Nu 26:10 fire devoured two **h.** and fifty men: 3967
Nu 26:14 twenty and two thousand and two **h.**.... 3967
Nu 26:18 of them, forty thousand and five **h.**.... 3967
Nu 26:22 and sixteen thousand and five **h.**. 3967
Nu 26:25 and four thousand and three **h.**. 3967
Nu 26:27 threescore thousand and five **h.**. 3967
Nu 26:34 fifty and two thousand and seven **h.**.... 3967
Nu 26:37 thirty and two thousand and five **h.**..... 3967
Nu 26:41 forty and five thousand and six **h.**........ 3967
Nu 26:43 and four thousand and four **h.**............ 3967
Nu 26:47 fifty and three thousand and four **h.**. ... 3967
Nu 26:50 forty and five thousand and four **h.**. ... 3967
Nu 26:51 children of Israel, six **h.** thousand....... 3967
Nu 26:51 and a thousand seven **h.** and thirty. 3967
Nu 81:28 one soul of five **h.**, both of the 3967
Nu 81:32 six **h.** thousand and seventy.............. 3967
Nu 81:36 number three **h.** thousand and seven... 3967
Nu 81:36 thirty thousand and five **h.** sheep: 3967
Nu 81:37 six **h.** and threescore and fifteen. 3967
Nu 81:39 were thirty thousand and five **h.**; 3967
Nu 81:43 three **h.** thousand and thirty............. 3967
Nu 81:43 seven thousand and five **h.** sheep, ... 3967
Nu 81:45 thirty thousand asses and five **h.**, ... 3967
Nu 81:52 thousand seven **h.** and fifty shekels..... 3967
Nu 33:39 Aaron was an **h.** and twenty and........ 3967
De 22:19 amerce him in an **h.** shekels of.......... 3967
De 31:2 I am an **h.** and twenty years 3967
De 34:7 Moses was an **h.** and twenty years..... 3967
Jos 7:21 and two **h.** shekels of silver, ... 3967
Jos 24:29 died, being an **h.** and ten years old..... 3967
Jos 24:32 Shechem for an **h.** pieces of silver:..... 3967
Jg 2:8 died, being an **h.** and ten years old..... 3967
Jg 3:31 slew of the Philistines six **h.** men........ 3967
Jg 4:3 for he had nine **h.** chariots of iron; 3967
Jg 4:13 nine **h.** chariots of iron, and all the..... 3967
Jg 7:6 to their mouth, were three **h.** men: 3967
Jg 7:7 By the three **h.** men that lapped will... 3967
Jg 7:8 and retained those three **h.** men: 3967
Jg 7:16 he divided the three **h.** men into........ 3967
Jg 7:19 Gideon, and the **h.** men that were...... 3967
Jg 7:22 And the three **h.** blew the trumpets,... 3967
Jg 8:4 three **h.** men that were with him, ... 3967
Jg 8:10 an **h.** and twenty thousand men that ... 3967
Jg 8:26 a thousand and seven **h.** shekels of..... 3967
Jg 11:26 coasts of Arnon, three **h.** years?........ 3967
Jg 15:4 went and caught three **h.** foxes,......... 3967
Jg 16:5 one of us eleven **h.** pieces of silver 3967
Jg 17:2 The eleven **h.** shekels of silver that.... 3967
Jg 17:3 restored the eleven **h.** shekels of....... 3967
Jg 17:4 his mother took two **h.** shekels of...... 3967
Jg 18:11 six **h.** men appointed with weapons..... 3967
Jg 18:16 six **h.** men appointed with their.......... 3967
Jg 18:17 six **h.** men that were appointed with... 3967
Jg 20:2 four **h.** thousand footmen that drew.... 3967
Jg 20:10 And we will take ten men of an **h.** 3967
Jg 20:10 of Israel, and an **h.** of a thousand,...... 3967
Jg 20:15 numbered seven **h.** chosen men. 3967
Jg 20:16 there were seven **h.** chosen men 3967
Jg 20:17 four **h.** thousand men that drew......... 3967
Jg 20:35 and five thousand an an **h.** men: 3967
Jg 20:47 But six **h.** men turned and fled to 3967
Jg 21:12 four **h.** young virgins, that had.......... 3967
1Sa 11:8 of Israel were three **h.** thousand, ... 3967
1Sa 13:15 present with him, about six **h.** men. ... 3967
1Sa 14:2 with him were about six **h.** men;.......... 3967
1Sa 15:4 Telaim, two **h.** thousand footmen, ... 3967
1Sa 17:7 weighed six **h.** shekels of iron: 3967
1Sa 18:25 an **h.** foreskins of the Philistines, ... 3967
1Sa 18:27 slew of the Philistines two **h.** men;..... 3967
1Sa 22:2 were with him about four **h.** men. 3967
1Sa 23:13 his men, which were about six **h.**,...... 3967
1Sa 25:13 up after David about four **h.** men; 3967
1Sa 25:13 and two **h.** abode by the stuff........... 3967
1Sa 25:18 made haste, and took two **h.** loaves,... 3967
1Sa 25:18 corn, and an **h.** clusters of raisins,...... 3967
1Sa 25:18 and two **h.** cakes of figs, and laid....... 3967
1Sa 27:2 he passed over with the six **h.** men.... 3967
1Sa 30:9 David went, he and the six **h.** men..... 3967
1Sa 30:10 David pursued, he and four **h.** men:.... 3697
1Sa 30:10 for two **h.** abode behind, which were .. 3967
1Sa 30:17 four **h.** young men, which rode upon... 3967

1Sa 30:21 And David came to the two **h.** men, ... 3967
2Sa 2:31 three **h.** and threescore men died....... 3967
2Sa 3:14 I espoused to me for an **h.** foreskins... 3967
2Sa 8:4 chariots, and seven **h.** horsemen,....... 3967
2Sa 8:4 reserved of them for an **h.** chariots. ... 3967
2Sa 10:18 slew the men of seven **h.** chariots...... 3967
2Sa 14:26 hair of his head at two **h.** shekels...... 3967
2Sa 15:11 with Absalom went two **h.** men out 3967
2Sa 15:18 six **h.** men which came after him........ 3967
2Sa 16:1 upon them two **h.** loaves of bread, ... 3967
2Sa 16:1 and an **h.** bunches of raisins,............. 3967
2Sa 16:1 and an **h.** of summer fruits, and a 3967
2Sa 21:16 weighed three **h.** shekels of brass 3967
2Sa 23:8 lift up his spear against eight **h.**, ... 3967
2Sa 23:18 lifted up his spear against three **h.**,...... 3967
2Sa 24:9 Israel eight **h.** thousand valiant men.... 3967
2Sa 24:9 of Judah were five **h.** thousand men.... 3967
1Ki 4:23 and an **h.** sheep, beside harts, and..... 3967
1Ki 5:16 three thousand and three **h.**, which..... 3967
1Ki 6:1 in the four **h.** and eightieth year......... 3967
1Ki 7:2 the length thereof was an **h.** cubits,.... 3967
1Ki 7:20 the pomegranates were two **h.** in........ 3967
1Ki 7:42 And four **h.** pomegranates for the....... 3967
1Ki 8:63 an **h.** and twenty thousand sheep. 3967
1Ki 9:23 five **h.** and fifty, which bare rule 3967
1Ki 9:28 gold, four **h.** and twenty talents, ... 3967
1Ki 10:10 an **h.** and twenty talents of gold,........ 3967
1Ki 10:14 six **h.** threescore and six talents of..... 3967
1Ki 10:16 six **h.** shekels of gold went to one...... 3967
1Ki 10:16 made two **h.** targets of beaten gold: ... 3967
1Ki 10:17 he made three **h.** shields of beaten..... 3967
1Ki 10:26 had a thousand and four **h.** chariots, ... 3967
1Ki 10:29 of Egypt for six **h.** shekels of silver, ... 3967
1Ki 10:29 and an horse for an **h.** and fifty: and ... 3967
1Ki 11:3 he had seven **h.** wives, princesses,..... 3967
1Ki 11:3 and three **h.** concubines: and his 3967
1Ki 12:21 an **h.** and fourscore thousand chosen... 3967
1Ki 18:4 Obadiah took an **h.** prophets, and....... 3967
1Ki 18:13 how I hid an **h.** men of the Lord's...... 3967
1Ki 18:19 prophets of Baal four **h.** and fifty,........ 3967
1Ki 18:19 the prophets of the groves four **h.**,...... 3967
1Ki 18:22 prophets are four **h.** and fifty men. 3967
1Ki 20:15 and they were two **h.** and thirty two:... 3967
1Ki 20:29 an **h.** thousand footmen in one day. 3967
1Ki 22:6 the prophets together, about four **h.**.... 3967
2Ki 3:4 of Israel an **h.** thousand lambs, and..... 3967
2Ki 3:4 an **h.** thousand rams, with the wool. ... 3967
2Ki 3:26 he took with him seven **h.** men that ... 3967
2Ki 4:43 should I set this before an **h.** men? 3967
2Ki 14:13 unto the corner gate, four **h.** cubits. ... 3967
2Ki 18:14 of Judah three **h.** talents of silver 3967
2Ki 19:35 an **h.** fourscore and five thousand:....... 3967
2Ki 23:33 a tribute of an **h.** talents of silver, ... 3967
1Ch 4:42 of the sons of Simeon, five **h.** men, ... 3967
1Ch 5:18 thousand seven **h.** and threescore, ... 3967
1Ch 5:21 of sheep two **h.** and fifty thousand,..... 3967
1Ch 5:21 and of men an **h.** thousand................ 3967
1Ch 7:2 two and twenty thousand and six **h.**..... 3967
1Ch 7:9 was twenty thousand and two **h.**......... 3967
1Ch 7:11 thousand and two **h.** soldiers, fit to..... 3967
1Ch 8:40 sons, and sons's sons, an **h.** and fifty.. 3967
1Ch 9:6 their brethren, six **h.** and ninety. 3967
1Ch 9:9 generations, nine **h.** and fifty and six.... 3967
1Ch 9:13 and seven **h.** and threescore; 3967
1Ch 9:22 in the gates were two **h.** and twelve... 3967
1Ch 11:11 up his spear against three **h.** slain 3967
1Ch 11:20 lifting up his spear against three **h.**,..... 3967
1Ch 12:14 one of the least was over an **h.**, and... 3967
1Ch 12:24 six thousand and eight **h.**, ready 3967
1Ch 12:25 the war, seven thousand and one **h.**. .. 3967
1Ch 12:26 of Levi four thousand and six **h.**......... 3967
1Ch 12:27 were three thousand and seven **h.**;..... 3967
1Ch 12:30 twenty thousand and eight **h.**, ... 3967
1Ch 12:32 the heads of them were two **h.**; and... 3967
1Ch 12:35 and eight thousand and six **h.**. 3967
1Ch 12:37 battle, an **h.** and twenty thousand....... 3967
1Ch 15:5 and his brethren an **h.** and twenty:...... 3967
1Ch 15:6 and his brethren two **h.** and twenty: ... 3967
1Ch 15:7 his brethren an **h.** and thirty: and....... 3967
1Ch 15:8 the chief, and his brethren two **h.**: 3967
1Ch 15:10 his brethren an **h.** and twelve, and 3967
1Ch 18:4 but reserved of them an **h.** chariots.... 3967
1Ch 21:3 Lord make his people an **h.** times 3967
1Ch 21:5 an **h.** thousand men that drew........... 3967
1Ch 21:5 Judah was four **h.** threescore and....... 3967
1Ch 21:25 for the place six **h.** shekels of gold..... 3967
1Ch 22:14 Lord an **h.** thousand talents of gold,.... 3967

1Ch 25:7 was two **h.** fourscore and eight. 3967
1Ch 26:30 of valour, a thousand and seven **h.**, 3967
1Ch 26:32 thousand and seven **h.** chief fathers, 3967
1Ch 29:7 and one **h.** thousand talents of iron. 3967
2Ch 1:14 had a thousand and four **h.** chariots, 3967
2Ch 1:17 a chariot for six **h.** shekels of silver, 3967
2Ch 1:17 and an horse for an **h.** and fifty: 3967
2Ch 2:2 three thousand and six **h.** to oversee 3967
2Ch 2:17 were found an **h.** and fifty thousand 3967
2Ch 2:17 and three thousand and six **h.** 3967
2Ch 2:18 thousand and six **h.** overseers to set 3967
2Ch 3:4 the height was an **h.** and twenty: 3967
2Ch 3:8 gold, amounting to six **h.** talents. 3967
2Ch 3:16 and made an **h.** pomegranates, and 3967
2Ch 4:8 And he made an **h.** basons of gold. 3967
2Ch 4:13 four **h.** pomegranates on the two 3967
2Ch 5:12 an **h.** and twenty priests sounding 3967
2Ch 7:5 an **h.** and twenty thousand sheep: 3967
2Ch 8:10 officers, even two **h.** and fifty, that 3967
2Ch 8:18 four **h.** and fifty talents of gold, 3967
2Ch 9:9 an **h.** and twenty talents of gold, 3967
2Ch 9:13 six **h.** and threescore and six talents 3967
2Ch 9:15 Solomon made two **h.** targets of 3967
2Ch 9:15 six **h.** shekels of beaten gold went 3967
2Ch 9:16 three **h.** shields made he of beaten 3967
2Ch 9:16 three **h.** shekels of gold went to one 3967
2Ch 11:1 an **h.** and fourscore thousand 3967
2Ch 12:3 With twelve **h.** chariots, and 3967
2Ch 13:3 even four **h.** thousand chosen men: 3967
2Ch 13:3 with eight **h.** thousand chosen men, 3967
2Ch 13:17 Israel five **h.** thousand chosen men. 3967
2Ch 14:8 out of Judah three **h.** thousand; 3967
2Ch 14:8 two **h.** and fourscore thousand: 3967
2Ch 14:9 thousand, and three **h.** chariots; 3967
2Ch 15:11 brought, seven **h.**, oxen and seven 3967
2Ch 17:11 seven thousand and seven **h.** rams, 3967
2Ch 17:11 thousand and seven **h.** he goats. 3967
2Ch 17:14 men of valour three **h.** thousand. 3967
2Ch 17:15 him two **h.** and fourscore thousand. 3967
2Ch 17:16 him two **h.** thousand mighty men 3967
2Ch 17:17 bow and shield two **h.** thousand. 3967
2Ch 17:18 an **h.** and fourscore thousand ready 3967
2Ch 18:5 together of prophets four **h.** men, 3967
2Ch 24:15 an **h.** and thirty years old was he 3967
2Ch 25:5 three **h.** thousand choice men, able 3967
2Ch 25:6 hired...an **h.** thousand mighty men 3967
2Ch 25:6 of Israel for an **h.** talents of silver. 3967
2Ch 25:9 the **h.** talents which I have given to 3967
2Ch 25:23 to the corner gate, four **h.** cubits. 3967
2Ch 26:12 valour were two thousand and six **h.** 3967
2Ch 26:13 army, three **h.** thousand and seven 3967
2Ch 26:13 thousand and five **h.**, that made war 3967
2Ch 27:5 same year an **h.** talents of silver, 3967
2Ch 28:6 an **h.** and twenty thousand in one 3967
2Ch 28:8 of their brethren two **h.** thousand, 3967
2Ch 29:32 an **h.** rams, and two **h.** lambs: 3967
2Ch 29:33 consecrated things were six **h.** oxen 3967
2Ch 35:8 thousand and six **h.** small cattle, 3967
2Ch 35:8 small cattle, and three **h.** oxen. 3967
2Ch 35:9 small cattle, and five **h.** oxen. 3967
2Ch 36:3 condemned the land in an **h.** talents 3967
Ezr 1:10 of a second sort four **h.** and ten, 3967
Ezr 1:11 were five thousand and four **h.** 3967
Ezr 2:3 thousand an **h.** seventy and two, 3967
Ezr 2:4 Shephatiah, three **h.** seventy and 3967
Ezr 2:5 of Arah, seven **h.** seventy and five. 3967
Ezr 2:6 two thousand eight **h.** and twelve. 3967
Ezr 2:7 a thousand two **h.** fifty and four. 3967
Ezr 2:8 of Zattu, nine **h.** forty and five. 3967
Ezr 2:9 of Zaccai, seven **h.** and threescore. 3967
Ezr 2:10 children of Bani, six **h.** forty and two. 3967
Ezr 2:11 of Bebai, six **h.** twenty and three. 3967
Ezr 2:12 a thousand two **h.** twenty and two. 3967
Ezr 2:13 of Adonikam, six **h.** sixty and six. 3967
Ezr 2:15 of Adin, four **h.** fifty and four. 3967
Ezr 2:17 of Bezai, three **h.** twenty and three. 3967
Ezr 2:18 children of Jorah, an **h.** and twelve. 3967
Ezr 2:19 of Hashum, two **h.** twenty and three. 3967
Ezr 2:21 Beth-lehem, an **h.** twenty and three. 3967
Ezr 2:23 of Anathoth, an **h.** twenty and eight. 3967
Ezr 2:25 Beeroth, seven **h.** and forty and three. 3967
Ezr 2:26 and Gaba, six **h.** twenty and one. 3967
Ezr 2:27 of Michmas, an **h.** twenty and two. 3967
Ezr 2:28 and Ai, two **h.** twenty and three. 3967
Ezr 2:30 of Magbish, an **h.** fifty and six. 3967
Ezr 2:31 a thousand two **h.** fifty and four, 3967
Ezr 2:32 of Harim, three **h.** and twenty. 3967
Ezr 2:33 and Ono, seven **h.** twenty and five. 3967
Ezr 2:34 of Jericho, three **h.** forty and five. 3967
Ezr 2:35 three thousand and six **h.** and thirty. 3967
Ezr 2:36 of Jeshua, nine **h.** seventy and three. 3967
Ezr 2:38 a thousand two **h.** forty and seven. 3967
Ezr 2:41 of Asaph, an **h.** twenty and eight. 3967
Ezr 2:42 Shobai, in all an **h.** thirty and nine. 3967
Ezr 2:58 were three **h.** ninety and two. 3967
Ezr 2:60 of Nekoda, six **h.** fifty and two. 3967
Ezr 2:64 thousand three **h.** and threescore, 3967
Ezr 2:65 thousand three **h.** thirty and seven: 3967
Ezr 2:65 two **h.** singing men and singing 3967
Ezr 2:66 horses were seven **h.** thirty and six; 3967
Ezr 2:66 their mules, two **h.** forty and five; 3967
Ezr 2:67 their camels, four **h.** thirty and five; 3967
Ezr 2:67 six thousand seven **h.** and twenty. 3967
Ezr 2:69 silver, and one **h.** priests' garments. 3967
Ezr 6:17 an **h.** bullocks, two **h.** rams, four **h.** 3969
Ezr 7:22 Unto an **h.** talents of silver, 3969
Ezr 7:22 and to an **h.** measures of wheat, 3969
Ezr 7:22 and to an **h.** baths of wine, 3969
Ezr 7:22 and to an **h.** baths of oil, and salt 3969
Ezr 8:3 of the males an **h.** and fifty. 3967
Ezr 8:4 and with him two **h.** males. 3967
Ezr 8:5 and with him three **h.** males. 3967
Ezr 8:9 with him two **h.** and eighteen males. 3967
Ezr 8:10 him an **h.** and threescore males. 3967
Ezr 8:12 and with him an **h.** and ten males. 3967
Ezr 8:20 two **h.** and twenty Nethinims: all of 3967
Ezr 8:26 six **h.** and fifty talents of silver, 3967
Ezr 8:26 and silver vessels an **h.** talents, 3967
Ezr 8:26 and of gold an **h.** talents; 3967
Ne 5:17 my table an **h.** and fifty of the Jews 3967
Ne 7:8 thousand an **h.** seventy and two. 3967
Ne 7:9 three **h.** seventy and two. 3967
Ne 7:10 of Arah, six **h.** fifty and two, 3967
Ne 7:11 thousand and eight **h.** and eighteen. 3967
Ne 7:12 a thousand two **h.** fifty and four. 3967
Ne 7:13 of Zattu, eight **h.** forty and five. 3967
Ne 7:14 of Zaccai, seven **h.** and threescore. 3967
Ne 7:15 of Binnui, six **h.** forty and eight. 3967
Ne 7:16 of Bebai, six **h.** twenty and eight. 3967
Ne 7:17 thousand three **h.** twenty and two. 3967
Ne 7:18 six **h.** threescore and seven. 3967
Ne 7:20 children of Adin, six **h.** fifty and five. 3967
Ne 7:22 Hashum, three **h.** twenty and eight. 3967
Ne 7:23 of Bezai, three **h.** twenty and four. 3967
Ne 7:24 children of Hariph, an **h.** and twelve. 3967
Ne 7:26 an **h.** fourscore and eight. 3967
Ne 7:27 Anathoth, an **h.** twenty and eight. 3967
Ne 7:29 Beeroth, seven **h.** forty and three. 3967
Ne 7:30 and Gaba, six **h.** twenty and one. 3967
Ne 7:31 Michmas, an **h.** and twenty and two. 3967
Ne 7:32 and Ai, an **h.** twenty and three. 3967
Ne 7:34 a thousand two **h.** fifty and four. 3967
Ne 7:35 of Harim, three **h.** and twenty. 3967
Ne 7:36 of Jericho, three **h.** forty and five. 3967
Ne 7:37 and Ono, seven **h.** twenty and one. 3967
Ne 7:38 three thousand nine **h.** and thirty. 3967
Ne 7:39 Jeshua, nine **h.** seventy and three. 3967
Ne 7:41 a thousand two **h.** forty and seven. 3967
Ne 7:44 of Asaph, an **h.** forty and eight. 3967
Ne 7:45 of Shobai, an **h.** thirty and eight. 3967
Ne 7:60 were three **h.** ninety and two. 3967
Ne 7:62 of Nekoda, six **h.** forty and two. 3967
Ne 7:66 thousand three **h.** and threescore, 3967
Ne 7:67 thousand three **h.** thirty and seven: 3967
Ne 7:67 two **h.** forty and five singing men 3967
Ne 7:68 horses, seven **h.** thirty and six: 3967
Ne 7:68 their mules, two **h.** forty and five: 3967
Ne 7:69 their camels, four **h.** thirty and five: 3967
Ne 7:69 thousand seven **h.** and twenty asses. 3967
Ne 7:70 five **h.** and thirty priests' garments. 3967
Ne 7:71 thousand and two **h.** pound of silver. 3967
Ne 11:6 four **h.** threescore and eight valiant. 3967
Ne 11:8 Sallai, nine **h.** twenty and eight. 3967
Ne 11:12 were eight **h.** twenty and two: 3967
Ne 11:13 of the fathers, two **h.** forty and two: 3967
Ne 11:14 of valour, an **h.** twenty and eight: 3967
Ne 11:18 city were two **h.** fourscore and two: 3967
Ne 11:19 gates, were an **h.** seventy and two. 3967
Es 1:1 **h.** and seven and twenty provinces: 3967
Es 1:4 days, even an **h.** and fourscore days 3967
Es 8:9 an **h.** twenty and seven provinces, 3967
Es 9:6 Jews slew and destroyed five **h.** men. 3967
Es 9:12 have slain and destroyed five **h.** men 3967
Es 9:15 and slew three **h.** men at Shushan; 3967
Es 9:30 the **h.** twenty and seven provinces 3967
Job 1:3 five **h.** yoke of oxen, and five **h.** she 3967
Job 42:16 this lived Job an **h.** and forty years, 3967
Pr 17:10 man than an **h.** stripes into a fool. 3967
Ec 6:3 If a man beget an **h.** children, and 3967
Ec 8:12 Though a sinner do evil an **h.** times, 3967
Ca 8:12 that keep the fruit thereof two **h.** 3967
Isa 37:36 a **h.** and fourscore and five thousand: 3967
Isa 65:20 the child shall die an **h.** years old; 3967
Isa 65:20 sinner being an **h.** years old shall 3967
Jer 52:23 upon the network were an **h.** round. 3967
Jer 52:29 eight **h.** thirty and two persons: 3967
Jer 52:30 seven **h.** forty and five persons: 3967
Jer 52:30 were four thousand and six **h.** 3967
Eze 4:5 the days, three **h.** and ninety days: 3967
Eze 4:9 three **h.** and ninety days shalt thou 3967
Eze 40:19 **h.** cubits eastward and northward. 3967
Eze 40:23 from gate to gate an **h.** cubits. 3967
Eze 40:27 gate toward the south an **h.** cubits. 3967
Eze 40:47 an **h.** cubits long, and an **h.** cubits. 3967
Eze 41:13 the house, an **h.** cubits long; 3967
Eze 41:13 the walls thereof, an **h.** cubits long; 3967
Eze 41:14 place toward the east, an **h.** cubits. 3967
Eze 41:15 and on the other side, an **h.** cubits, 3967
Eze 42:2 length of an **h.** cubits was the north. 3967
Eze 42:8 before the temple were an **h.** cubits. 3967
Eze 42:16 measuring reed, five **h.** reeds, 520
Eze 42:17 the north side, five **h.** reeds, 3967
Eze 42:18 the south side, five **h.** reeds, 3967
Eze 42:19 and measured five **h.** reeds with the 3967
Eze 42:20 five **h.** reeds long, and five **h.** broad, 3967
Eze 45:2 for the sanctuary five **h.** in length, 3967
Eze 45:2 with five **h.** in breadth, square round 3967
Eze 45:15 lamb out of the flock, out of two **h.**, 3967
Eze 48:16 north side four thousand and five **h.**, 3967
Eze 48:16 south side four thousand and five **h.**, 3967
Eze 48:16 east side four thousand and five **h.**, 3967
Eze 48:16 west side four thousand and five **h.** 3967
Eze 48:17 toward the north two **h.** and fifty, 3967
Eze 48:17 toward the south two **h.** and fifty, 3967
Eze 48:17 toward the east two **h.** and fifty, 3967
Eze 48:17 toward the west two **h.** and fifty. 3967
Eze 48:30 four thousand and five **h.** measures. 3967
Eze 48:32 east side four thousand and five **h.**: 3967
Eze 48:33 four thousand and five **h.** measures: 3967
Eze 48:34 west side four thousand and five **h.**, 3967
Da 6:1 kingdom an **h.** and twenty princes, 3969
Da 8:14 two thousand and three **h.** days; 3967
Da 12:11 a thousand two **h.** and ninety days. 3967
Da 12:12 three **h.** and five and thirty days. 3967
Am 5:3 out by a thousand shall leave an **h.**, 3967
Am 5:3 went forth by an **h.** shall leave ten, 3967
Mt 18:12 **if a man have an h. sheep, and one** *1540*
Mt 18:28 **which owed him an h. pence;** *1540*
Mk 4:8 **and some sixty, and some an h.** *1540*
Mk 4:20 **some sixty, and some an h.** *1540*
Mk 6:37 buy two **h.** pennyworth of bread, *1250*
Mk 14:5 sold for more than three **h.** pence, *5145*
Lu 7:41 **the one owed five h. pence, and** *4001*
Lu 15:4 **man of you, having an h. sheep,** *1540*
Lu 16:6 **And he said, An h. measures of oil.** *1540*
Lu 16:7 **he said, An h. measures of wheat.** *1540*
Joh 6:7 Two **h.** pennyworth of bread is not *1250*
Joh 12:5 ointment sold for three **h.** pence, *5145*
Joh 19:39 aloes, about an **h.** pound weight. *1540*
Joh 21:8 land, but as it were two **h.** cubits, *1250*
Joh 21:11 great fishes, an **h.** and fifty and *1540*
Ac 1:15 were about an **h.** and twenty, *1540*
Ac 5:36 a number of men, about four **h.**, *5071*
Ac 7:6 and entreat them evil four **h.** years. *5071*
Ac 13:20 the space of four **h.** and fifty years, *5071*
Ac 23:23 Make ready two **h.** soldiers to go *1250*
Ac 23:23 and spearmen two **h.**, at the third *1250*
Ac 27:37 two **h.** threescore and sixteen souls. *1250*
Ro 4:19 when he was about an **h.** years old, *1541*
1Co 15:6 of above five **h.** brethren at once; *4001*
Ga 3:17 was four **h.** and thirty years after, *5071*
Re 7:4 an **h.** and forty and four thousand *1540*
Re 9:16 were two **h.** thousand thousand: *3461*
Re 11:3 a thousand two **h.** and threescore *1250*
Re 12:6 a thousand two **h.** and threescore *1250*
Re 13:18 number is Six **h.** threescore and six. *5516*
Re 14:1 him an **h.** forty and four thousand, *1540*
Re 14:3 the **h.** and forty and four thousand, *1540*
Re 14:20 of a thousand and six **h.** furlongs, *5516*
Re 21:17 an **h.** and forty and four cubits, *1540*

HUNDREDFOLD
Ge 26:12 in the same year an h.............. 3967,8180
2Sa 24:3 many soever they be, an h., ... 3967,6471
Mt 13:8 some an h., some sixtyfold, some .. 1540
Mt 13:23 bringeth forth, some an h., some... 1540
Mt 19:29 shall receive an h., and shall 1542
Mk 10:30 he shall receive an h. now in this.. 1542
Lu 8:8 sprang up, and bare fruit an h...... 1542

HUNDREDS
Ex 18:21, 25 rulers of h., rulers of fifties, ... 3967
Nu 31:14 thousands, and captains over h., ... 3967
Nu 31:48 and captains of h., came near unto 3967
Nu 31:52 thousands, and of the captains of h., ... 3967
Nu 31:54 the captains of thousands and of h., ... 3967
De 1:15 captains over h., and captains over..... 3967
1Sa 22:7 of thousands, and captains of h.; 3967
1Sa 29:2 of the Philistines passed on by h., ... 3967
2Sa 18:1 thousands and captains of h. over....... 3967
2Sa 18:4 all the people came out by h. and....... 3967
2Ki 11:4 sent and fetched the rulers over h., ... 3967
2Ki 11:9 captains over the h. did according 3967
2Ki 11:10 the captains over h. did the priest...... 3967
2Ki 11:15 commanded the captains of the h., ... 3967
2Ki 11:19 he took the rulers over h., and the 3967
1Ch 13:1 the captains of thousands and h., ... 3967
1Ch 26:26 the captains over thousands and h., ... 3967
1Ch 27:1 and captains of thousands and h., ... 3967
1Ch 28:1 captains over the h., and the............ 3967
1Ch 29:6 the captains of thousands and of h., ... 3967
2Ch 1:2 the captains of thousands and of h., ... 3967
2Ch 23:1 himself, and the captains of h., ... 3967
2Ch 23:9 to the captains of h. spears, and 3967
2Ch 23:14 the captains of h. that were set.......... 3967
2Ch 23:20 And he took the captains of h., and.... 3967
2Ch 25:5 captains over h., according to the....... 3967
Mk 6:40 in ranks, by h., and by fifties. 1540

HUNDREDTH
Ge 7:11 In the six h. year of Noah's life, in..... 3967
Ge 8:13 in the six h. and first year, in the 3967
Ne 5:11 also the h. part of the money, and 3967

HUNDRED THOUSAND See HUNDRED and THOUSAND.

HUNG see HANGED.

HUNGER See also HUNGERBITTEN; HUNGERED.
Ex 16:3 to kill the whole assembly with h.. 7457
De 8:3 thee, and suffered thee to h.,............ 7456
De 28:48 in h., and in thirst, and in............... 7457
De 32:24 They shall be burnt with h., and........ 7457
Ne 9:15 bread from heaven for their h.,........... 7457
Ps 34:10 young lions do lack, and suffer h.:....... 7456
Pr 19:15 sleep; and idle soul shall suffer h........ 7456
Isa 49:10 They shall not h. nor thirst;.............. 7456
Jer 38:9 he is like to die for h. in the place 7457
Jer 42:14 trumpet, nor have h. of bread; 7456
La 2:19 young children, that faint for h........... 7457
La 4:9 than they that be slain with h.:.......... 7457
Eze 34:29 shall be no more consumed with h....... 7457
Mt 5:6 Blessed are they which do h. and .. 3983
Lu 6:21 Blessed are ye that h. now: for ye . 3983
Lu 6:25 you that are full! for ye shall h..... 3983
Lu 15:17 and to spare, and I perish with h.! .3042
Joh 6:35 that cometh to me shall never h.;.. 3983
Ro 12:20 Therefore if thine enemy h., feed....... 3983
1Co 4:11 we both h., and thirst, and are.......... 3983
1Co 11:34 And if any man h., let him eat at 3983
2Co 11:27 often, in h. and thirst, in fastings 3042
Re 6:8 to kill with sword, and with h., ... 3042
Re 7:16 They shall h. no more, neither 3983

HUNGERBITTEN
Job 18:12 His strength shall be h., and 7457

HUNGERED See also HUNGRED; HUNGRY.
Mt 21:18 as he returned into the city, he h....... 3983
Lu 4:2 they were ended, he afterward h.. 3983

HUNGRED See also HUNGERED.
Mt 4:2 nights, he was afterward an h.. 3983
Mt 12:1 his disciples were an h., and began..... 3983
Mt 12:3 David did, when he was an h., ... 3983
Mt 25:35 I was an h., and ye gave me meat: .3983
Mt 25:37 when saw we thee an h., and fed... 3983
Mt 25:42 For I was an h., and ye gave me... 3983
Mt 25:44 Lord, when saw we thee an h., or ..3983
Mk 2:25 when he had need, and was an h.,..3983
Lu 6:3 David did, when himself was an h.,3983

HUNGRY See also HUNGERED.
1Sa 2:5 and they that were h. ceased: 7456
2Sa 17:29 The people is h., and weary, and....... 7456
2Ki 7:12 They know that we be h.; therefore... 7456
Job 5:5 Whose harvest the h. eateth up, ... 7456
Job 22:7 hast withholden bread from the h.. 7456
Job 24:10 take away the sheaf from the h.; 7456
Ps 50:12 If I were h., I would not tell thee: 7456
Ps 107:5 H. and thirsty, their soul fainted 7456
Ps 107:9 filleth the h. soul with goodness......... 7456
Ps 107:36 there he maketh the h. to dwell,........ 7456
Ps 146:7 which giveth food to the h............... 7456
Pr 6:30 to satisfy his soul when he is h.;........ 7456
Pr 25:21 If thine enemy be h., give him bread .. 7456
Pr 27:7 to the h. soul every bitter thing is...... 7456
Isa 8:21 through it, hardly bestead and h.:....... 7456
Isa 8:21 that when they shall be h., they 7456
Isa 9:20 snatch on the right hand, and be h.; ... 7456
Isa 29:8 be as when an h. man dreameth, ... 7456
Isa 32:6 to make empty the soul of the h., ... 7456
Isa 44:12 he is h., and his strength faileth:........ 7456
Isa 58:7 Is it not to deal thy bread to the h., ... 7456
Isa 58:10 if thou draw out thy soul to the h., ... 7456
Isa 65:13 servants shall eat, but ye shall be h.:.. 7456
Eze 18:7, 16 hath given his bread to the h., ... 7456
Mk 11:12 come from Bethany, he was h.:......... 3983
Lu 1:53 He hath filled the h. with good 3983
Ac 10:10 And he became very h., and would..... 4361
1Co 11:21 one is h., and another is drunken, ... 3983
Ph 4:12 both to be full and to be h., both 3983

HUNT See also HUNTED; HUNTEST; HUNTETH; HUNTING.
Ge 27:5 went to the field to h. for venison, ... 6679
1Sa 26:20 h. a partridge in the mountains. 7291
Job 38:39 Wilt thou h. the prey for the lion? 6679
Ps 140:11 evil shall h. the violent man to........... 6679
Pr 6:26 adulteress will h. for the precious....... 6679
Jer 16:16 shall h. them from every mountain, ... 6679
La 4:18 They h. our steps, that we cannot 6679
Eze 13:18 head of every stature to h. souls! 6679
Eze 13:18 Will ye h. the souls of my people, ... 6679
Eze 13:20 wherewith ye there h. the souls to..... 6679
Eze 13:20 even the souls that ye h. to make 6679
Mic 7:2 they h. every man his brother with 6679

HUNTED
Eze 13:21 be no more in your hand to be h.; 4686

HUNTER See also HUNTERS.
Ge 10:9 was a mighty h. before the Lord: 6718
Ge 10:9 Even as Nimrod the mighty h............ 6718
Ge 25:27 Esau was a cunning h., a man of........ 6718
Pr 6:5 as a roe from the hand of the h., ... 6718

HUNTERS
Jer 16:16 and after will I send for many h., ... 6719

HUNTEST
1Sa 24:11 thee; yet thou h. my soul to take it.... 6658
Job 10:16 Thou h. me as a fierce lion: and 6679

HUNTETH
Le 17:13 which h. and catcheth any beast......... 6679

HUNTING
Ge 27:30 his brother came in from his h........... 6718
Pr 12:27 roasteth not that...he took in h........... 6718

HUPHAM (hu'-fam) See also HUPPIM; HUPHAMITES.
Nu 26:39 H., the family of the Huphamites. 2349

HUPHAMITES (hu'-fam-ites)
Nu 26:39 of Hupham, the family of the H.. 2350

HUPPAH (hup'-pah)
1Ch 24:13 thirteenth to H., the fourteenth 2647

HUPPIM (hup'-pim) See also HUPHAM.
Ge 46:21 Rosh, Muppim, and H., and Ard. 2650
1Ch 7:12 Shuppim also, and H., the children 2650
1Ch 7:15 Machir took to wife the sister of H. ... 2650

HUR (hur)
Ex 17:10 Moses, Aaron, and H. went up to...... 2354
Ex 17:12 Aaron and H. stayed up his hands, ... 2354
Ex 24:14 behold, Aaron and H. are with you: 2354
Ex 31:2 the son of Uri, the son of H., of the... 2354
Ex 35:30 the son of Uri, the son of H., of the... 2354
Ex 38:22 the son of Uri, the son of H., of the... 2354
Nu 31:8 Zur, and H., and Reba, five kings 2354
Jos 13:21 Zur, and H., and Reba, which were.... 2354
1Ki 4:8 The son of H., in mount Ephraim:...... 2354
1Ch 2:19 him Ephrath, which bare him H. 2354
1Ch 2:20 And H. begat Uri, and Uri begat........ 2354
1Ch 2:50 were the sons of Caleb the son of H., .2354
1Ch 4:1 and Carmi, and H., and Shobal. 2354
1Ch 4:4 are sons of H., the firstborn of.......... 2354
2Ch 1:5 the son of Uri, the son of H., had...... 2354
Ne 3:9 repaired Rephaiah the son of H.,......... 2354

HURAI (hu'-rahee) see also HIDDAI.
1Ch 11:32 H. of the brooks of Gaash, Abiel........ 2360

HURAM (hu'-ram) See also HIRAM.
1Ch 8:5 Gera, and Shephuphan, and H.. 2361
2Ch 2:3 Solomon sent to H. the king of Tyre, ..2361
2Ch 2:11 H. the king of Tyre answered 2438
2Ch 2:12 H. said moreover, Blessed be the...... 2361
2Ch 2:13 understanding, of H. my father's, ... 2438
2Ch 4:11 And H. made the pots, and the 2361
2Ch 4:11 And H. finished the work that he 2361
2Ch 4:16 did H. his father make to king........... 2361
2Ch 8:2 cities which H. had restored to.......... 2438
2Ch 8:18 And H. sent him by the hands of 2438
2Ch 9:10 And the servants also of H., and........ 2438
2Ch 9:21 to Tarshish with the servants of H.: ... 2438

HURI (hu'-ri)
1Ch 5:14 Abihail the son of H., the son of........ 2359

HURL See also HURLETH; HURLING.
Nu 35:20 or h. at him by laying of wait, ... 7993

HURLETH
Job 27:21 as a storm h. him out of his place. 8175

HURLING
1Ch 12:2 in h. stones and shooting arrows out.........

HURT See also HURTFUL; HURTING.
Ge 4:23 and a young man to my h.. 2250
Ge 26:29 That thou wilt do us no h., as we 7451
Ge 31:7 but God suffered him not to h. me. 7489
Ge 31:29 the power of my hand to do you h.: ... 7451
Ex 21:22 strive, and h. a woman with child,...... 5062
Ex 21:35 if one man's ox h. another's, that he... 5062
Ex 22:10 and it die, or be h., or driven away,... 7665
Ex 22:14 ought of his neighbour, and it be h., ... 7665
Nu 16:15 neither have I h. one of them............ 7489
Jos 24:20 then he will turn and do you h.,.......... 7489
1Sa 20:21 there is peace to thee, and no h.; 1697
1Sa 24:9 Behold, David seeketh thy h.?........... 7451
1Sa 25:7 which were with us, we h. them not,.. 3637
1Sa 25:15 good unto us, and we were not h.,..... 3637
2Sa 18:32 rise against thee to do thee h.,.......... 7451
2Ki 14:10 shouldest thou meddle to thy h.,........ 7451
2Ch 25:19 shouldest thou meddle to thine h.,...... 7451
Ezr 4:22 grow to the h. of the kings?.............. 5142
Es 9:2 hand on such as sought their h.: 7451
Job 35:8 Thy wickedness may h. a man as thou ......
Ps 15:4 He that sweareth to his own h., ... 7489
Ps 35:4 to confusion that devise my h............ 7451
Ps 35:26 together that rejoice at mine h.: 7451
Ps 38:12 that seek my h. speak mischievous..... 7451
Ps 41:7 against me do they devise my h......... 7451
Ps 70:2 put to confusion, that desire my h.. 7451
Ps 71:13 and dishonour that seek my h............ 7451
Ps 71:24 unto shame, that seek my h............. 7451
Ps 105:18 Whose feet they h. with fetters: 6031
Ec 5:13 for the owners thereof to their h.. 7451
Ec 8:9 ruleth over another to his own h......... 7451
Ec 10:9 Whoso removeth stones shall be h. 6087
Isa 11:9 They shall not h. nor destroy in all..... 7489
Isa 27:3 lest any h. it, I will keep it night........ 6485
Isa 65:25 They shall not h. nor destroy in all..... 7489
Jer 6:14 healed also the h. of the daughter 7667
Jer 7:6 walk after other gods to your h.: 7451
Jer 8:11 healed the h. of the daughter of......... 7667
Jer 8:21 the h. of the daughter of my people.... 7667
Jer 8:21 the daughter of my people am I h.; 7665
Jer 10:19 Woe is me for my h.! my wound is 7667
Jer 24:9 kingdoms of the earth for their h., ... 7451
Jer 25:6 hands; and I will do you no h.. 7489
Jer 25:7 works of your hands to your own h.. .. 7451
Jer 38:4 welfare of this people, but the h. 7451
Da 3:25 of the fire, and they have no h.; 2257
Da 6:22 mouths, that they have not h. me: 2255
Da 6:22 thee, O king, have I done no h.......... 2248
Da 6:23 no manner of h. was found upon 2257
Mk 16:18 deadly thing, it shall not h. them; .. 984
Lu 4:35 he came out of him, and h. him not. 984
Lu 10:19 nothing shall by any means h. you... 91

Ac 18:10 **no man shall set on thee to h.** *2559*
Ac 27:10 will be with **h.** and much damage, ... *5196*
Re 2:11 **shall not be h. of the second death**... *91*
Re 6:6 see thou **h.** not the oil and the wine. *91*
Re 7:2 it was given to **h.** the earth and the....... *91*
Re 7:3 **H.** not the earth, neither the sea, ... *91*
Re 9:4 should not **h.** the grass of the earth,....... *91*
Re 9:10 power was to **h.** men five months. *91*
Re 9:19 had heads, and with them they do **h.**. *91*
Re 11:5 any man will **h.** them, fire proceedeth.... *91*
Re 11:5 if any man will **h.** them, he must in....... *91*

HURTFUL
Ezr 4:15 rebellious city, and **h.** unto kings........ 5142
Ps 144:10 his servant from the **h.** sword. 7451
1Ti 6:9 and into many foolish and **h.** lusts, ... *983*

HURTING
1Sa 25:34 hath kept me back from **h.** thee,........ 7489

HUSBAND See also HUSBANDMAN; HUSBAND'S; HUSBANDS.
Ge 3:6 and gave also unto her **h.** with her;...... 376
Ge 3:16 and thy desire shall be to thy **h.**,......... 376
Ge 16:3 gave her to her **h.** Abram to be his...... 376
Ge 29:32 now therefore my **h.** will love me. 376
Ge 29:34 time will my **h.** be joined unto me,....... 376
Ge 30:15 matter that thou hast taken my **h.**? 376
Ge 30:18 I have given my maiden to my **h.**: 376
Ge 30:20 now will my **h.** dwell with me, ... 376
Ex 4:25 Surely a bloody **h.** art thou to me. 2860
Ex 4:26 A bloody **h.** thou art, because of........ 2860
Ex 21:22 as the woman's **h.** will lay upon 1167
Le 19:20 is a bondmaid, betrothed to an **h.**, ... 376
Le 21:3 nigh unto him, which hath had no **h.**;..... 376
Le 21:7 take a woman put away from her **h.**:.... 376
Nu 5:13 and it be hid from the eyes of her **h.**,... 376
Nu 5:19 with another instead of thy **h.**; 376
Nu 5:20 aside to another, instead of thy **h.**, ... 376
Nu 5:20 have lain with thee beside thine **h.**: 376
Nu 5:27 have done trespass against her **h.**, ... 376
Nu 5:29 aside to another instead of her **h.**, ... 376
Nu 30:6 had at all an **h.**, when she vowed, ... 376
Nu 30:7 her **h.** heard it, and held his peace........ 376
Nu 30:8 if her **h.** disallowed her on the day....... 376
Nu 30:11 her **h.** heard it, and held his peace....... 376
Nu 30:12 if her **h.** hath utterly made them void ... 376
Nu 30:12 her **h.** hath made them void;............... 376
Nu 30:13 afflict the soul, her **h.** may establish...... 376
Nu 30:13 it, or her **h.** may make it void............. 376
Nu 30:14 if her **h.** altogether hold his peace........ 376
De 21:13 and be her **h.**, and she shall be thy 1167
De 22:22 with a woman married to an **h.**, then... 1167
De 22:23 is a virgin be betrothed unto an **h.**,...... 376
De 24:3 if the latter **h.** hate her, and write 376
De 24:3 or if the latter **h.** die, which took her ... 376
De 24:4 former **h.**, which sent her away, ... 1167
De 25:11 to deliver her **h.** out of the hand of....... 376
De 28:56 be evil toward the **h.** of her bosom, ... 376
Jg 13:6 the woman came and told her **h.**, ... 376
Jg 13:9 but Manoah her **h.** was not with her. 376
Jg 13:10 haste, and ran, and shewed her **h.**,....... 376
Jg 14:15 Entice thy **h.**, that he may declare........ 376
Jg 19:3 And her **h.** arose, and went after her, .. 376
Jg 20:4 And the Levite, the **h.** of the woman.... 376
Ru 1:3 Elimelech Naomi's **h.** died; and she...... 376
Ru 1:5 was left of her two sons and her **h.**. 376
Ru 1:9 each of you in the house of her **h.**. 376
Ru 1:12 way; for I am too old to have a **h.**......... 376
Ru 1:12 I should have an **h.** also to night,......... 376
Ru 2:11 in law since the death of thine **h.**:......... 376
1Sa 1:8 Then said Elkanah her **h.** to her, ... 376
1Sa 1:22 for she said unto her **h.**, I will not 376
1Sa 1:23 And Elkanah her **h.** said unto her, ... 376
1Sa 2:19 she came up with her **h.** to offer 376
1Sa 4:19 father in law and her **h.** were dead, ... 376
1Sa 4:21 of her father in law and her **h.**. 376
1Sa 25:19 But she told not her **h.** Nabal. 376
2Sa 3:15 and took her from her **h.**, even from.... 376
2Sa 3:16 her **h.** went with her along weeping..... 376
2Sa 11:26 heard that Uriah her **h.** was dead. 376
2Sa 11:26 was dead, she mourned for her **h.**....... 1167
2Sa 14:5 widow woman, and mine **h.** is dead...... 376
2Sa 14:7 shall not leave to my **h.** neither name... 376
2Ki 4:1 Thy servant my **h.** is dead; and thou.... 376
2Ki 4:9 she said unto her **h.**, Behold now, I..... 376
2Ki 4:14 she hath no child, and her **h.** is old...... 376
2Ki 4:22 And she called unto her **h.**, and said,.... 376
2Ki 4:26 Is it well with thy **h.**? is it well with..... 376
Pr 12:4 woman is a crown to her **h.**.............. 1167
Pr 31:11 The heart of her **h.** doth safely trust... 1167
Pr 31:23 Her **h.** is known in the gates,............ 1167
Pr 31:28 her **h.** also, and he praiseth her......... 1167
Isa 54:5 For thy Maker is thine **h.**; the Lord ... 1167
Jer 3:20 treacherously departeth from her **h.**,... 1167
Jer 6:11 the **h.** with the wife shall be taken, ... 376
Jer 31:32 an **h.** unto them, saith the Lord: 1167
Eze 16:32 taketh strangers instead of her **h.**! 376
Eze 16:45 that lotheth her **h.** and her children;..... 376
Eze 44:25 or for sister than hath had no **h.**,......... 376
Ho 2:2 is not my wife, neither am I her **h.**:...... 376
Ho 2:7 I will go and return to my first **h.**; 376
Joe 1:8 sackcloth for the **h.** of her youth. 1167
Mt 1:16 begat Joseph the **h.** of Mary, of *435*
Mt 1:19 Then Joseph her **h.**, being a just man, .. *435*
Mk 10:12 **a woman shall put away her h.**,....... *435*
Lu 2:36 had lived with an **h.** seven years *435*
Lu 16:18 **her that is put away from her h.** *435*
Joh 4:16 **Go, call thy h., and come hither**..... *435*
Joh 4:17 answered and said, I have no **h.**. *435*
Joh 4:17 **Thou hast well said, I have no h.**... *435*
Joh 4:18 **whom thou now hast is not thy h.** .. *435*
Ac 5:9 which have buried thy **h.** are at the...... *435*
Ac 5:10 her forth, buried her by her **h.**............ *435*
Ro 7:2 woman which hath an **h.** is bound....... *5220*
Ro 7:2 by the law to her **h.** so long as he....... *435*
Ro 7:2 if the **h.** be dead, she is loosed from.... *435*
Ro 7:2 she is loosed from the law of her **h.**..... *435*
Ro 7:3 while her **h.** liveth, she be married *435*
Ro 7:3 if her **h.** be dead, she is free from *435*
1Co 7:2 let every woman have her own **h.**......... *435*
1Co 7:3 Let the **h.** render unto the wife due..... *435*
1Co 7:3 likewise also the wife unto the **h.** *435*
1Co 7:4 power of her own body, but the **h.**: *435*
1Co 7:4 likewise also the **h.** hath not power...... *435*
1Co 7:10 Let not the wife depart from her **h.**: *435*
1Co 7:11 or be reconciled to her **h.**: and let *435*
1Co 7:11 and let not the **h.** put away his wife. *435*
1Co 7:13 which hath an **h.** that believeth not, ... *435*
1Co 7:14 the unbelieving **h.** is sanctified by *435*
1Co 7:14 wife is sanctified by the **h.**: *435*
1Co 7:16 whether thou shalt save thy **h.**? or....... *435*
1Co 7:34 world, how she may please her **h.**. *435*
1Co 7:39 by the law as long as her **h.** liveth; *435*
1Co 7:39 if her **h.** be dead, she is at liberty *435*
2Co 11:2 for I have espoused you to one **h.** *435*
Ga 4:27 children than she which hath an **h.** *435*
Eph 5:23 For the **h.** is the head of the wife,....... *435*
Eph 5:33 wife see that she reverence her **h.** *435*
1Ti 3:2 the **h.** of one wife, vigilant, sober, ... *435*
Tit 1:6 the **h.** of one wife, having faithful......... *435*
Re 21:2 as a bride adorned for her **h.**. *435*

HUSBANDMAN See also HUSBANDMEN.
Ge 9:20 Noah began to be an **h.**, and he..... 376,127
Jer 51:23 I break in pieces the **h.** and his yoke.... 406
Am 5:16 they shall call the **h.** to mourning,........ 406
Zec 13:5 I am no prophet, I am an **h.**;............ 5647
Joh 15:1 **true vine, and my Father is the h.**...*1092*
2Ti 2:6 The **h.** that laboureth must be first...... *1092*
Jas 5:7 the **h.** waiteth for the precious fruit.... *1092*

HUSBANDMEN
2Ki 25:12 the land to be vine dressers and **h.**. ... 1461
2Ch 26:10 **h.** also, and vine dressers in the.......... 406
Jer 31:24 **h.**, and they that go with flocks........... 406
Jer 52:16 land for vinedressers and for **h.**. 3009
Joe 1:11 Be ye ashamed, O ye **h.**; howl, O 406
Mt 21:33 **let it out to h., and went into a far** *1092*
Mt 21:34 **he sent his servants to the h., that** .*1092*
Mt 21:35 **the h. took his servants, and beat**.. *1092*
Mt 21:38 **when the h. saw the son, they said**.*1092*
Mt 21:40 **what will he do unto those h.?** *1092*
Mt 21:41 let out his vineyard unto other **h.**,...... *1092*
Mk 12:1 **let it out to h., and went into a far** *1092*
Mk 12:2 **he sent to the h. a servant, that he** *1092*
Mk 12:2 **receive from the h. of the fruit of** ..*1092*
Mk 12:7 **those h. said among themselves,**.... *1092*
Mk 12:9 **will come and destroy the h., and**.. *1092*
Lu 20:9 **a vineyard and let it forth to h.,** ... *1092*
Lu 20:10 **sent a servant to the h., that they** . *1092*
Lu 20:10 **the h. beat him, and sent him** *1092*
Lu 20:14 **when the h. saw him, they**............ *1092*
Lu 20:16 **shall come and destroy these h.,**..... *1092*

HUSBANDRY
2Ch 26:10 and in Carmel: for he loved **h.**. 127
1Co 3:9 with God: ye are God's **h.**, ye are...... *1091*

HUSBAND'S
Nu 30:10 vowed in her **h.** house, or bound......... 376
De 25:5 her **h.** brother shall go in unto her, ... 2993
De 25:5 perform the duty of an **h.** brother 2992
De 25:7 My **h.** brother refuseth to raise up..... 2993
De 25:7 perform the duty of my **h.** brother. 2992
Ru 2:1 kinsman of her **h.**, a mighty man 376

HUSBANDS
Ru 1:11 womb, that they may be your **h.**? 582
Ru 1:13 ye stay for them from having **h.**? 376
Es 1:17 they shall despise their **h.** in their...... 1167
Es 1:20 wives shall give to their **h.** honour,..... 1167
Jer 29:6 and give your daughters to **h.**, that...... 582
Eze 16:45 lothed their **h.** and their children:......... 582
Joh 4:18 **For thou hast had five h.; and he** ... *435*
1Co 14:35 let them ask their **h.** at home: for it..... *435*
Eph 5:22 submit yourselves unto your own **h.**,..... *435*
Eph 5:24 be to their own **h.** in every thing........ *435*
Eph 5:25 **H.**, love your wives, even as Christ....... *435*
Col 3:18 submit yourselves unto your own **h.**,..... *435*
Col 3:19 **H.**, love your wives, and be not bitter.. *435*
1Ti 3:12 deacons be the **h.** of one wife, ruling.... *435*
Tit 2:4 love their **h.**, to love their children, ... *5362*
Tit 2:5 obedient to their own **h.**, that the........ *435*
1Pe 3:1 wives, in subjection to your own **h.**;...... *435*
1Pe 3:5 in subjection unto their own **h.**: *435*
1Pe 3:7 Likewise, ye **h.**, dwell with them......... *435*

HUSHAH (hu'-shah) See also HUSHATHITE; SHUAH.
1Ch 4:4 Gedor, and Ezer the father of **H.**. 2364

HUSHAI (hu'-shahee)
2Sa 15:32 **H.** the Archite came to meet him....... 2365
2Sa 15:37 So **H.** David's friend came into the..... 2365
2Sa 16:16 when **H.** the Archite, David's friend,... 2365
2Sa 16:16 that **H.** said unto Absalom, God.......... 2365
2Sa 16:17 Absalom said to **H.**, Is this thy.......... 2365
2Sa 16:18 **H.** said unto Absalom, Nay; but......... 2365
2Sa 17:5 Call now **H.** the Archite also, and........ 2365
2Sa 17:6 when **H.** was come to Absalom,.......... 2365
2Sa 17:7 And **H.** said unto Absalom, The.......... 2365
2Sa 17:8 For, said **H.**, thou knowest thy.......... 2365
2Sa 17:14 The counsel of **H.** the Archite is......... 2365
2Sa 17:15 Then said **H.** unto Zadok and to......... 2365
1Ki 4:16 Baanah the son of **H.** was in Asher 2365
1Ch 27:33 and **H.** the Archite was the king's 2365

HUSHAM (hu'-sham)
Ge 36:34 and **H.** of the land of Temani............. 2367
Ge 36:35 And **H.** died, and Hadad the son of..... 2367
1Ch 1:45 **H.** of the land of the Temanites.......... 2367
1Ch 1:46 when **H.** was dead, Hadad the son 2367

HUSHATHITE (hu'-shath-ite)
2Sa 21:18 then Sibbechai the **H.** slew Saph, ... 2843
2Sa 23:27 the Anethothite, Mebunnai the **H.**, ... 2843
1Ch 11:29 Sibbecai the **H.**, Ilai the Ahohite, ... 2843
1Ch 20:4 time Sibbechai the **H.** slew Sippai,...... 2843
1Ch 27:11 eighth month was Sibbecai the **H.**, ... 2843

HUSHIM (hu'-shim) See also SHUHAM.
Ge 46:23 And the sons of Dan; **H.**.................. 2366
1Ch 7:12 the children of Ir, and **H.**, the sons 2366
1Ch 8:8 **H.** and Baara were his wives. 2366
1Ch 8:11 And of **H.** he begat Abitub, and......... 2366

HUSK See also HUSKS.
Nu 6:4 from the kernels even to the **h.**. 2085
2Ki 4:42 ears of corn in the **h.** thereof. 6861

HUSKS
Lu 15:16 **filled his belly with the h. that** *2769*

HUZ (huz)
Ge 22:21 **H.** his firstborn, and Buz his 5780

HUZOTH See KIRJATH-HUZOTH.

HUZZAB (huz'-zab)
Na 2:7 And **H.** shall be led away captive, ... 5324

HYACINTH See JACINTH.

HYMENAEUS (hy-men-e'-us)
1Ti 1:20 Of whom is **H.** and Alexander; *5211*
2Ti 2:17 Of whom is **H.** and Philetus;............. *5211*

HYMN See also HYMNS.
Mt 26:30 they had sung an **h.**, they went out.... *5214*
Mk 14:26 they had sung an **h.**, they went out..........

HYMNS
Eph 5:19 in psalms and **h.** and spiritual *5215*
Col 3:16 in psalms and **h.** and spiritual *5215*

HYPOCRISIES
1Pe 2:1 and all guile, and **h.**, and envies, ... *5272*

HYPOCRISY See also HYPOCRISIES.
Isa 32:6 work iniquity, to practise **h.**, and........ 2612
Mt 23:28 **within ye are full of h. and**........... *5272*
Mk 12:15 knowing their **h.**, said unto them,........ *5272*
Lu 12:1 **of the Pharisees, which is h.**.......... *5272*
1Ti 4:2 Speaking lies in **h.**; having their *5272*
Jas 3:17 without partiality, and without **h.**. *505*

HYPOCRITE See also HYPOCRITE'S; HYPOCRITES.
Job 13:16 for an **h.** shall not come before.......... 2611
Job 17:8 stir up himself against the **h.**............. 2611
Job 20:5 the joy of the **h.** but for a moment?.... 2611
Job 27:8 For what is the hope of the **h.**, ... 2611
Job 34:30 That the **h.** reign not, lest 120,2611
Pr 11:9 An **h.** with his mouth destroyeth........ 2611
Isa 9:17 for every one is a **h.** and an............. 2611
Mt 7:5 **Thou h., first cast out the beam**.... *5273*
Lu 6:42 **Thou h., cast out first the beam**.... *5273*
Lu 13:15 **Thou h., doth not each one of you** .*5273*

HYPOCRITE'S
Job 8:13 and the **h.** hope shall perish; 2611

HYPOCRITES
Job 15:34 the congregation of **h.** shall be.......... 2611
Job 36:13 But the **h.** in heart heap up wrath;..... 2611
Isa 33:14 hath surprised the **h.**.................. 120,2611
Mt 6:2 **as the h. do in the synagogues**....... *5273*
Mt 6:5 **thou shalt not be as the h. are: for**.*5273*
Mt 6:16 **when ye fast, be not, as the h., of**..*5273*
Mt 15:7 **Ye h., well did Esaias prophesy of** .*5273*
Mt 16:3 **O ye h., ye can discern the face**.... *5273*
Mt 22:18 and said, **Why tempt ye me, ye h.?**.. *5273*
Mt 23:13 **scribes and Pharisees, h.! for ye**.... *5273*
Mt 23:14 **scribes and Pharisees, h.! for ye**.... *5273*
Mt 23:15, 23,25,27 **scribes and Pharisees, h.!**. *5273*
Mt 23:29 **scribes and Pharisees, h.! because**. *5273*
Mt 24:51 **him his portion with the h.**........... *5273*
Mk 7:6 **Esaias prophesied of you h., as**..... *5273*
Lu 11:44 **scribes and Pharisees, h.! for ye**.... *5273*
Lu 12:56 **Ye h., ye can discern the face**....... *5273*

HYPOCRITICAL
Ps 35:16 With **h.** mockers in feasts, they......... 2611
Isa 10:6 will send him against an **h.** nation,...... 2611

HYSSOP
Ex 12:22 ye shall take a bunch of **h.**, and dip...... 231
Le 14:4 cedar wood, and scarlet, and **h.**........... 231
Le 14:6 wood, and the scarlet, and the **h.**, ... 231
Le 14:49 cedar wood, and scarlet, and **h.**:........ 231
Le 14:51 the cedar wood, and the **h.**, and the..... 231
Le 14:52 cedar wood, and with the **h.**, and 231
Nu 19:6 cedar wood, and **h.**, and scarlet,.......... 231
Nu 19:18 a clean person shall take **h.**, and......... 231
1Ki 4:33 the **h.** that springeth out of the 231
Ps 51:7 Purge me with **h.**, and I shall be 231
Joh 19:29 with vinegar, and put it upon **h.**, ... *5301*
Heb 9:19 water, and scarlet wool, and **h.**, and... *5301*

I.

I See in the APPENDIX; also I-CHABOD; ME; MY.

I AM See AM.

IBHAR (ib'-har)
2Sa 5:15 **I.** also, and Elishua, and Nepheg,....... 2984
1Ch 3:6 **I.** also, and Elishama,and................. 2984
1Ch 14:5 And **I.**, and Elishua, and Elpalet,.......... 2984

IBLEAM (ib'-le-am)
Jos 17:11 and **I.** and her towns, and the 2991
Jg 1:27 nor the inhabitants of **I.** and her......... 2991
2Ki 9:27 going up to Gur, which is by **I.**........... 2991

IBENEIAH (ib-ne-i'-ah)
1Ch 9:8 And **I.** the son of Jeroham, and.......... 2997

IBNIJAH (ib-ni'-jah)
1Ch 9:8 the son of Reuel, the son of **I.**: 2998

IBRI (ib'-ri)
1Ch 24:27 and Shoham, and Zaccur, and **I.**, ... 5681

IBZAN (ib'-zan)
Jg 12:8 And after him **I.** of Bethlehem.............. 78
Jg 12:10 Then died **I.**, and was buried at............ 78

ICE
Job 6:16 are blackish by reason of the **i.**,.......... 7140
Job 38:29 Out of whose womb came the **i.**?......... 7140
Ps 147:17 He casteth forth his **i.** like morsels:.... 7140

I-CHABOD (ik'-a-bod) See also I-CHABOD'S.
1Sa 4:21 she named the child **I.**, saying,............ 350

I-CHABOD'S (ik'-a-bods)
Isa 14:3 the son of Ahitub, **I.** brother,.............. 350

ICONIUM (i-co'-ne-um)
Ac 13:51 against them, and came unto **I.**.......... *2430*
Ac 14:1 And it came to pass in **I.**, that they.... *2430*
Ac 14:19 certain Jews from Antioch and **I.**........ *2430*
Ac 14:21 to Lystra, and to **I.**, and Antioch,........ *2430*
Ac 16:2 brethren that were at Lystra and **I.**.... *2430*
2Ti 3:11 unto me at Antioch, at **I.**, at Lystra;... *2430*

IDALAH (id'-a-lah)
Jos 19:15 and Shimron, and **I.**, and.................. 3030

IDBASH (id'-bash)
1Ch 4:3 Jezreel, and Ishma, and **I.**: and........... 3031

IDDO (id'-do)
1Ki 4:14 Ahinadab the son of **I.** had............... 5714
1Ch 6:21 Joah his son, **I.** his son, Zerah his...... 5714
1Ch 27:21 **I.** the son of Zechariah: of................ 3035
2Ch 9:29 and in the visions of **I.** the seer......... 3260
2Ch 12:15 and of **I.** the seer concerning 5714
2Ch 13:22 written in the story of the prophet **I.**.. 5714
Ezr 5:1 and Zechariah the son of **I.**, ... 5714
Ezr 6:14 and Zechariah the son of **I.**.............. 5714
Ezr 8:17 with commandment unto **I.** the........... 112
Ezr 8:17 what they should say unto **I.**, and........ 112
Ne 12:4 **I.**, Ginnetho, Abijah,........................ 5714
Ne 12:16 Of **I.**, Zechariah; of Ginnethon, ... 5714
Zec 1:1 the son of Berechiah, the son of **I.**....... 5714
Zec 1:7 the son of **I.** the prophet, saying,....... 5714

IDLE
Ex 5:8 for they be **i.**: therefore they cry, ... 7504
Ex 5:17 But he said, Ye are **i.**, ye are **i.**: 7504
Pr 19:15 and an **i.** soul shall suffer hunger......... 7423
Mt 12:36 **That every i. word that men shall**.... *692*
Mt 20:3 **and saw others standing i. in the**.... *692*
Mt 20:6 **found others standing i., and saith** . *692*
Mt 20:6 **Why stand ye here all the day i.?**.... *692*
Lu 24:11 words seemed to them as **i.** tales,...... *3026*
1Ti 5:13 And withal they learn to be **i.**, ... *692*
1Ti 5:13 not only **i.**, but tattlers also and *692*

IDLENESS
Pr 31:27 and eateth not the bread of **i.**.......... 6104
Ec 10:18 and through **i.** of the hands the.......... 8220
Eze 16:49 and abundance of **i.** was in her 8252

IDOL See also IDOL'S; IDOLS.
1Ki 15:13 she had made an **i.** in a grove; 4656
1Ki 15:13 Asa destroyed her **i.**, and burnt it 4656
2Ch 15:16 because she had made an **i.** in a 4656
2Ch 15:16 grove: and Asa cut down her **i.**, ... 4656
2Ch 33:7 image, the **i.** which he had made,....... 5566
2Ch 33:15 the **i.** out of the house of the Lord, ... 5566
Isa 48:5 Mine **i.** hath done them, and my 6090
Isa 66:3 incense, as if he blessed an **i.**............. 205
Jer 22:28 man Coniah a despised broken **i.**?....... 6089
Zec 11:17 Woe to the **i.** shepherd that leaveth 457
Ac 7:41 and offered a sacrifice unto the **i.**,...... *1497*
1Co 8:4 we know that an **i.** is nothing in......... *1497*
1Co 8:7 with conscience of the **i.** unto this...... *1497*
1Co 8:7 eat it as a thing offered unto an **i.**; *1494*
1Co 10:19 say I then? that the **i.** is anything,...... *1497*

IDOLATER See also IDOLATERS.
1Co 5:11 a fornicator, or covetous, or an **i.**,....... *1496*
Eph 5:5 nor covetous man, who is an **i.**,....... *1496*

IDOLATERS
1Co 5:10 or extortioners, or with **i.**;............... *1496*
1Co 6:9 neither fornicators, nor **i.**, nor *1496*
1Co 10:7 Neither be **i.**, as were some of.......... *1496*
Re 21:8 **i.**, and all liars, shall have their......... *1496*
Re 22:15 and murderers, and **i.**, and................ *1496*

IDOLATRIES
1Pe 4:3 banquetings, and abominable **i.**:.......... *1495*

IDOLATROUS
2Ki 23:5 he put down the **i.** priests, whom....... 3649

IDOLATRY See also IDOLATRIES.
1Sa 15:23 stubbornness is as iniquity and **i.**........ 8655
Ac 17:16 he saw the city wholly given to **i.**........ *2712*
1Co 10:14 my dearly beloved, flee from **i.**.......... *1495*
Ga 5:20 **I.**, witchcraft, hatred, variance,.......... *1495*
Col 3:5 and covetousness, which is **i.**: *1495*

IDOL'S
1Co 8:10 sit at meat in the **i.** temple, shall *1493*

IDOLS
Le 19:4 Turn ye not unto **i.**, nor make 457
Le 26:1 Ye shall make you no **i.** nor graven...... 457
Le 26:30 upon the carcases of your **i.**,............. 1544
De 29:17 and their **i.**, wood and stone, silver 1544
1Sa 31:9 publish it in the house of their **i.**,....... 6091
1Ki 15:12 and removed all the **i.** that his........... 1544
1Ki 21:26 did very abominably in following **i.**,..... 1544
2Ki 17:12 For they served **i.**, whereof the.......... 1544
2Ki 21:11 made Judah also to sin with his **i.**:...... 1544
2Ki 21:21 served the **i.** that his father served,.... 1544
2Ki 23:24 and the images, and the **i.**, and all...... 1544
1Ch 10:9 to carry tidings unto their **i.**, and 6091
1Ch 16:26 all the gods of the people are **i.**:.......... 457
2Ch 15:8 put away the abominable **i.** out 8251
2Ch 24:18 and served groves and **i.**: and 6091
2Ch 34:7 cut down all the **i.** throughout all........ 2553
Ps 96:5 the gods of the nations are **i.**: but........ 457
Ps 97:7 that boast themselves of **i.**: worship..... 457
Ps 106:36 And they served their **i.**: which 6091
Ps 106:38 sacrificed unto the **i.** of Canaan:......... 6091
Ps 115:4 Their **i.** are silver and gold, the......... 6091
Ps 135:15 The **i.** of the heathen are silver and..... 6091
Isa 2:8 Their land also is full of **i.**: they........... 457
Isa 2:18 and the **i.** he shall utterly abolish. 457
Isa 2:20 day a man shall cast his **i.** of silver, ... 457
Isa 2:20 and his **i.** of gold, which they made...... 457
Isa 10:10 hath found the kingdoms of the **i.**, ... 457
Isa 10:11 have done unto Samaria and her **i.**, ... 457
Isa 10:11 so do to Jerusalem and her **i.**?........... 6091
Isa 19:1 the **i.** of Egypt shall be moved at......... 457
Isa 19:3 and they shall seek to the **i.**, and to..... 457
Isa 31:7 man shall cast away his **i.** of silver,...... 457
Isa 31:7 and his **i.** of gold, which your own 457
Isa 45:16 together that are makers of **i.**. 6736
Isa 46:1 their **i.** were upon the beasts, and...... 6091
Isa 57:5 Enflaming yourselves with **i.** under....... 410
Jer 50:2 her **i.** are confounded, her images 6091
Jer 50:38 and they are mad upon their **i.**............ 367
Eze 6:4 your slain men before your **i.**.............. 1544
Eze 6:5 children of Israel before their **i.**: 1544
Eze 6:6 your **i.** may be broken and cease, ... 1544
Eze 6:9 which go a whoring after their **i.**: 1544
Eze 6:13 shall be among their **i.** round about..... 1544
Eze 6:13 offer sweet savour to all their **i.**.......... 1544
Eze 8:10 and all the **i.** of the house of Israel, ... 1544
Eze 14:3 man, these men have set up their **i.** 1544
Eze 14:4 that setteth up his **i.** in his heart........ 1544
Eze 14:4 according to the multitude of his **i.**: 1544
Eze 14:5 estranged from me through their **i.**...... 1544
Eze 14:6 turn yourselves from your **i.**: and........ 1544
Eze 14:7 setteth up his **i.** in his heart, and 1544
Eze 16:36 with all the **i.** of thy abominations....... 1544
Eze 18:6 eyes to the **i.** of the house of Israel,... 1544
Eze 18:12 hath lifted up his eyes to the **i.**,.......... 1544
Eze 18:15 eyes to the **i.** of the house of Israel,.... 1544
Eze 20:7 not yourselves with the **i.** of Egypt;.... 1544
Eze 20:8 did they forsake the **i.** of Egypt: 1544
Eze 20:16 for their heart went after their **i.**........ 1544
Eze 20:18 nor defile yourselves with their **i.**: 1544
Eze 20:24 eyes were after their fathers' **i.**. 1544
Eze 20:31 pollute yourselves with all your **i.**,...... 1544
Eze 20:39 Go ye, serve ye every one his **i.**, and..1544

Eze 20:39 with your gifts, and with your **i.**........ 1544
Eze 22:3 maketh **i.** against herself to defile....... 1544
Eze 22:4 defiled thyself in thine **i.** which 1544
Eze 23:7 with all their **i.** she defiled herself. 1544
Eze 23:30 thou are polluted with their **i.**........... 1544
Eze 23:37 with their **i.** have they committed....... 1544
Eze 23:39 had slain their children to their **i.**, ... 1544
Eze 23:49 you, and ye bear the sins of your **i.**:... 1544
Eze 30:13 I will also destroy the **i.**, and I will..... 1544
Eze 33:25 lift up your eyes toward your **i.**, ... 1544
Eze 36:18 shed upon the land, and for their **i.**..... 1544
Eze 36:25 from all your **i.**, will I cleanse you. 1544
Eze 37:23 themselves any more with their **i.**, ... 1544
Eze 44:10 astray away from me after their **i.**:..... 1544
Eze 44:12 unto them before their **i.**, and 1544
Ho 4:17 Ephraim is joined to **i.**: let him 6091
Ho 8:4 their gold have they made them **i.**,..... 6091
Ho 13:2 and **i.** according to their own............ 6091
Ho 14:8 have I to do any more with **i.**? I........ 6091
Mic 1:7 all the **i.** thereof will I lay desolate: 6091
Hab 2:18 trusteth therein, to make dumb **i.**?...... 457
Zec 10:2 For the **i.** have spoken vanity,........... 8655
Zec 13:2 cut off the names of the **i.** out of......... 6091
Ac 15:20 they abstain from pollutions of **i.**, ... *1497*
Ac 15:29 abstain from meats offered to **i.**. *1494*
Ac 21:25 from things offered to **i.**, and from *1494*
Ro 2:22 thou that abhorrest **i.**, dost thou *1497*
1Co 8:1 as touching things offered to **i.**, we..... *1494*
1Co 8:4 that are offered in sacrifice unto **i.**,..... *1494*
1Co 8:10 those things which are offered to **i.**: ... *1494*
1Co 10:19 which is offered in sacrifice to **i.** is *1494*
1Co 10:28 offered in sacrifice unto **i.**, eat not...... *1494*
1Co 12:2 carried away unto these dumb **i.**, ... *1497*
2Co 6:16 hath the temple of God with **i.**? *1497*
1Th 1:9 ye turned to God from **i.** to serve...... *1497*
1Jo 5:21 children, keep yourselves from **i.**. *1497*
Re 2:14 eat things sacrificed unto **i.**, and... *1494*
Re 2:20 and to eat things sacrificed unto **i.**.*1494*
Re 9:20 **i.** of gold, and silver, and brass,......... *1497*

IDUMAEA (i-doo-me'-ah) See also IDUMEA.
Mk 3:8 from Jerusalem, and from **I.**, and *2401*

IDUMEA (i-doo-me'-ah) See also EDOM; IDUMAEA.
Isa 34:5 it shall come down upon **I.**, and.......... 123
Isa 34:6 great slaughter in the land of **I.**......... 123
Eze 35:15 O Mount Seir, and all **I.**, even all 123
Eze 36:5 of the heathen, and against all **I.**,......... 123

IF
Ge 4:7 **I.** thou doest well, shalt thou not......... 518
Ge 4:7 **i.** thou doest not well, sin lieth at 518
Ge 4:24 **I.** Cain should be avenged................ 3588
Ge 8:8 to see **i.** the waters were abated from ......
Ge 13:9 **i.** thou wilt take the left hand, then...... 518
Ge 13:9 or **i.** thou depart to the right hand, ... 518
Ge 13:16 so that **i.** a man can number the......... 518
Ge 15:5 **i.** thou be able to number them: 518
Ge 18:3 My Lord, **i.** now I have found favour.... 518
Ge 18:21 unto me; and **i.** not, I will know. 518
Ge 18:26 **I.** I find in Sodom fifty righteous......... 518
Ge 18:28 **I.** I find there forty and five, I will...... 518
Ge 18:30 I will not do it, **i.** I find thirty there. 518
Ge 20:7 and **i.** thou restore her not, know........ 518
Ge 23:8 **I.** it be your mind that I should bury.........
Ge 23:13 But **i.** thou wilt give it, I pray thee..........
Ge 24:8 and **i.** the woman will not be willing.........
Ge 24:41 and **i.** they give not thee one, thou...... 518
Ge 24:42 **i.** now thou do prosper my way........... 518
Ge 24:49 **i.** ye will deal kindly and truly with....... 518
Ge 24:49 and **i.** not, tell me; that I may turn 518
Ge 25:22 **I.** it be so, why am I thus! And she..... 518
Ge 27:46 **i.** Jacob take a wife of the daughters 518
Ge 28:20 **I.** God will be with me, and will 518
Ge 30:27 **i.** I have found favour in thine eyes,..... 518
Ge 30:31 **i.** thou wilt do this thing for me, I 518
Ge 31:8 **I.** he said thus, The speckled shall....... 518
Ge 31:8 and **i.** he said thus, The ringstraked..... 518
Ge 31:50 **I.** thou shalt afflict my daughters, ... 518
Ge 31:50 or **i.** thou shalt take other wives.......... 518
Ge 32:8 **I.** Esau come to the one company,........ 518
Ge 33:10 **i.** now I have found grace in thy......... 518
Ge 33:13 and **i.** men shall overdrive them one...... 518
Ge 34:15 **I.** ye will be as we be, that every........ 518
Ge 34:17 But **i.** ye will not hearken unto us,....... 518
Ge 34:22 **i.** every male among us be................ 518
Ge 37:26 What profit is it **i.** we slay our........... 3588
Ge 42:19 **I.** ye be true men, let one of your....... 518
Ge 42:37 my two sons, **i.** I bring him not to thee:....
Ge 42:38 **i.** mischief befall him by the way in..........
Ge 43:4 **I.** thou wilt send our brother with........ 518
Ge 43:5 But **i.** thou wilt not send him, we 518
Ge 43:9 **i.** I bring him not unto thee, and set 518
Ge 43:11 **I.** it must be so now, do this; take 518
Ge 43:14 **I.** I be bereaved of my children, I........ 834
Ge 44:22 for **i.** he should leave his father, his.........
Ge 44:26 **i.** our youngest brother be with us,...... 518
Ge 44:29 And **i.** ye take this also from me, ... 518
Ge 44:32 **I.** I bring him not unto thee, then........ 518
Ge 47:6 and **i.** thou knowest any man of.......... 518
Ge 47:16 you for your cattle, **i.** money fail. 518
Ge 47:29 **I.** now I have found grace in thy 518
Ge 50:4 **I.** now I have found grace in your........ 518
Ex 1:16 but **i.** it be a daughter, then she ....
Ex 1:16 **i.** it be a son, then ye shall kill............ 518
Ex 4:8 **i.** they will not believe thee, neither..... 518
Ex 4:9 **i.** they will not believe also these........ 518
Ex 4:23 and **i.** thou refuse to let him go, ...
Ex 8:2 and **i.** thou refuse to let them go,............
Ex 8:21 Else, **i.** thou wilt not let my people...... 518
Ex 9:2 For **i.** thou refuse to let them go,......... 518
Ex 10:4 Else, **i.** thou refuse to let my people 518
Ex 12:4 And **i.** the household be too little for 518
Ex 13:13 **i.** thou wilt not redeem it, then thou 518
Ex 15:26 **I.** thou wilt diligently hearken to.......... 518
Ex 18:23 **I.** thou shalt do this thing, and God....... 518
Ex 19:5 **i.** ye will obey my voice indeed, and..... 518
Ex 20:25 And **i.** thou wilt make me an altar........ 518
Ex 20:25 for **i.** thou lift up thy tool upon it,............
Ex 21:2 **I.** thou buy an Hebrew servant, ... 3588
Ex 21:3 **I.** he came in by himself, he shall 518
Ex 21:3 **i.** he were married, then his wife......... 518
Ex 21:4 **I.** his master have given him a wife,...... 518
Ex 21:5 **i.** the servant shall plainly say, I.......... 518
Ex 21:7 **i.** a man sell his daughter to be a....... 3588
Ex 21:8 **I.** she please not her master, who 518
Ex 21:9 And **i.** he have betrothed her unto....... 518
Ex 21:10 **I.** he take him another wife; her......... 518
Ex 21:11 **i.** he do not these three unto her, ... 518
Ex 21:13 **i.** a man lie not in wait, but God.......... 834
Ex 21:14 **i.** a man come presumptuously........... 3588
Ex 21:16 **i.** he be found in his hand, he shall...........
Ex 21:18 **i.** men strive together, and one 3588
Ex 21:19 **I.** he rise again, and walk abroad 518
Ex 21:20 **i.** a man smite his servant, or his....... 3588
Ex 21:21 **i.** he continue a day or two, he 518
Ex 21:22 **I.** men strive, and hurt a woman 518
Ex 21:23 **i.** any mischief follow, then thou 518
Ex 21:26 **i.** any man smite the eye of his 3588
Ex 21:27 **i.** he smite out his manservant's.......... 518
Ex 21:28 **I.** an ox gore a man or a woman,....... 3588
Ex 21:29 **i.** the ox were wont to push with 518
Ex 21:30 **I.** there be laid on him a sum of.......... 518
Ex 21:32 **I.** the ox shall push a manservant 518
Ex 21:33 **i.** a man shall open a pit, or **i.** a man ... 518
Ex 21:35 **i.** one man's ox hurt another's, ... 3588
Ex 21:36 Or **i.** it be known that the ox ....
Ex 22:1 **I.** a man shall steal an ox, or a.......... 3588
Ex 22:2 **I.** a thief be found breaking up, ... 518
Ex 22:3 **I.** the sun be risen upon him, there...... 518
Ex 22:3 **i.** he have nothing, then he shall be...... 518
Ex 22:4 **I.** the theft be certainly found in.......... 518
Ex 22:5 **I.** a man shall cause a field or 518
Ex 22:6 **I.** fire break out, and catch in............ 3588
Ex 22:7 **I.** a man shall deliver unto his............ 3588
Ex 22:7 **i.** the thief be found, let him pay 518
Ex 22:8 **I.** the thief be not found, then the 518
Ex 22:10 **I.** a man deliver unto his 3588
Ex 22:12 **i.** it be not stolen from him, he 518
Ex 22:13 **I.** it be torn in pieces, then let him...... 518
Ex 22:14 And **i.** a man borrow ought of his....... 3588
Ex 22:15 **i.** the owner thereof be with it, he....... 518
Ex 22:15 **i.** it be an hired thing, it came for........ 518
Ex 22:16 **i.** a man entice a maid that is not....... 3588
Ex 22:17 **I.** her father utterly refuse to give 518
Ex 22:23 **I.** thou afflict them in any wise,........... 518
Ex 22:25 **I.** thou lend money to any of my 518
Ex 22:26 **I.** thou at all take thy neighbour's 518
Ex 23:4 **I.** thou meet thine enemy's ox or........ 3588
Ex 23:5 **I.** thou see the ass of him that 3588
Ex 23:22 **i.** thou shalt indeed obey his voice, ... 518
Ex 23:33 **i.** thou serve their gods, it will surely ....
Ex 24:14 **i.** any man have any matters to do, ...
Ex 29:34 And **i.** ought of the flesh of the........... 518
Ex 32:32 now, **i.** thou wilt forgive their sin;........ 518
Ex 32:32 and **i.** not, blot me, I pray thee, out..... 518
Ex 33:13 **i.** I have found grace in thy sight, ... 518
Ex 33:15 **I.** thy presence go not with me, ... 518
Ex 34:9 **I.** now I have found grace in thy 518
Ex 34:20 and **i.** thou redeem him not, then 518
Ex 40:37 But **i.** the cloud were not taken up 518
Le 1:2 **I.** any man of you bring an................ 3588
Le 1:3 **I.** his offering be a burnt sacrifice 518
Le 1:10 And **i.** his offering be of the flocks, ... 518
Le 1:14 And **i.** the burnt sacrifice for his.......... 518
Le 2:4 And **i.** thou bring an oblation of........... 518
Le 2:5, 7 And **i.** thy oblation be a meat.......... 518
Le 2:14 And **i.** thou offer a meat offering of...... 518
Le 3:1 And **i.** his oblation be a sacrifice of....... 518
Le 3:1 **i.** he offer it of the herd; whether it..... 518
Le 3:6 And **i.** his offering for a sacrifice of...... 518
Le 3:7 **I.** he offer a lamb for his offering,........ 518
Le 3:12 And **i.** his offering be a goat, then 518
Le 4:2 **I.** a soul shall sin through 3588
Le 4:3 **I.** the priest that is anointed do........... 518
Le 4:13 And **i.** the whole congregation of 518
Le 4:23 Or **i.** his sin, wherein he hath..................
Le 4:27 And **i.** any one of the common 518
Le 4:28 Or **i.** his sin, which he hath sinned,...... 176
Le 4:32 And **i.** he bring a lamb for a sin........... 518
Le 5:1 And **i.** a soul sin, and hear the........... 3588
Le 5:1 **i.** he do not utter it, then he shall........ 518
Le 5:2 Or **i.** a soul touch any unclean............. 834
Le 5:2 things, and **i.** it be hidden from him; ....
Le 5:3 Or **i.** he touch the uncleanness of....... 3588
Le 5:4 Or **i.** a soul swear, pronouncing.......... 3588
Le 5:7 And **i.** he be not able to bring a 518
Le 5:11 But **i.** he be not able to bring two 518
Le 5:15 **I.** a soul commit a trespass, and 3588
Le 5:17 And **i.** a soul sin, and commit any 3588
Le 6:2 **I.** a soul sin, and commit a 3588
Le 6:28 and **i.** it be sodden in a brasen pot,...... 518
Le 7:12 **I.** he offer it for a thanksgiving,........... 518
Le 7:16 But **i.** the sacrifice of his offering......... 518
Le 7:18 And **i.** any of the flesh of the............. 518
Le 10:19 and **i.** I had eaten the sin offering............
Le 11:37 And **i.** any part of their carcase 3588
Le 11:38 But **i.** any water be put upon the 3588
Le 11:39 And **i.** any beast, of which ye may 3588
Le 12:2 **I.** a woman have conceived seed,....... 3588
Le 12:5 But **i.** she bear a maid child, then........ 518
Le 12:8 And **i.** she be not able to bring a........ 518
Le 13:4 **I.** the bright spot be white in the......... 518
Le 13:5 behold, **i.** the plague in his sight be at.......
Le 13:6 behold, **i.** the plague be somewhat............
Le 13:7 But **i.** the scab spread much abroad 518
Le 13:8 And **i.** the priest see that, behold, the.......
Le 13:10 behold, **i.** the rising be white in the ....
Le 13:12 And **i.** a leprosy break out abroad........ 518
Le 13:13 **i.** the leprosy have covered all his ....
Le 13:16 Or **i.** the raw flesh turn again,........... 3588
Le 13:17 **i.** the plague be turned into white;............
Le 13:20 And **i.**, when the priest seeth it, ...
Le 13:21 But **i.** the priest look on it, and,.......... 518
Le 13:21 and **i.** it be not lower than the skin, ... 518
Le 13:22 And **i.** it spread much abroad in.......... 518
Le 13:23 But **i.** the bright spot stay in his.......... 518
Le 13:24 Or **i.** there be any flesh, in the.......... 3588
Le 13:25 behold, **i.** the hair in the bright spot ....
Le 13:26 But **i.** the priest look on it, and, ...
Le 13:27 and **i.** it be spread much abroad in 518
Le 13:28 And **i.** the bright spot stay in his 518
Le 13:29 **I.** a man or woman have a................ 3588
Le 13:30 behold, **i.** it be in sight deeper than.... 3588
Le 13:31 And **i.** the priest look on the............. 3588
Le 13:32 **i.** the scall spread not, and there be in......
Le 13:34 **i.** the scall be not spread in the skin. ....
Le 13:35 But **i.** the scall spread much in 3588
Le 13:36 **i.** the scall be spread in the skin, the ....
Le 13:37 But **i.** the scall be in his sight at a 518
Le 13:38 **I.** a man also or a woman have in the 518
Le 13:39 behold, **i.** the bright spots in the skin, ...
Le 13:42 And **i.** there be in the bald head, ... 3588
Le 13:43 **i.** the rising of the sore be white..............
Le 13:49 And **i.** the plague be greenish or.............
Le 13:51 **i.** the plague be spread in the........... 3588
Le 13:53 And **i.** the priest shall look, and,.......... 518
Le 13:55 **i.** the plague have not changed his............
Le 13:56 And **i.** the priest look, and, behold, ...
Le 13:57 And **i.** it appear still in the 518
Le 13:58 **i.** the plague be departed from them, ...

Le 14:3 **i.** the plague of leprosy be healed in ....
Le 14:21 And **i.** he be poor, and cannot get 518
Le 14:37 **i.** the plague be in the walls of the ....
Le 14:39 **i.** the plague be spread in the walls of.......
Le 14:43 And **i.** the plague come again, and 518
Le 14:44 **i.** the plague be spread in the house, it .....
Le 14:48 And **i.** the priest shall come in, and...... 518
Le 15:8 And **i.** he that hath the issue spit....... 3588
Le 15:16 And **i.** any man's seed of copulation.... 3588
Le 15:19 And **i.** a woman have an issue, and..... 3588
Le 15:23 And **i.** it be on her bed, or on............ 518
Le 15:24 And **i.** any man lie with her at all,......... 518
Le 15:25 And **i.** a woman have an issue of........ 3588
Le 15:25 or **i.** it run beyond the time of her 3588
Le 15:28 But **i.** she be cleansed of her issue, ... 518
Le 17:16 But **i.** he wash them not, nor bathe 518
Le 18:5 which **i.** a man do, he shall live in ....
Le 19:5 And **i.** ye offer a sacrifice of peace 3588
Le 19:6 and **i.** ought remain until the third ....
Le 19:7 and **i.** it be eaten at all on the third...... 518
Le 19:33 And **i.** a stranger sojourn with........... 3588
Le 20:4 And **i.** the people of the land do.......... 518
Le 20:12 And **i.** a man lie with his daughter 834
Le 20:13 **I.** a man also lie with mankind, as........ 834
Le 20:14 And **i.** a man take a wife and her......... 834
Le 20:15 And **i.** a man lie with a beast, he......... 834
Le 20:16 And **i.** a woman approach unto any....... 834
Le 20:17 And **i.** a man shall take his sister,......... 834
Le 20:18 And **i.** a man shall lie with a woman..... 834
Le 20:20 And **i.** a man shall lie with his............ 834
Le 20:21 And **i.** a man shall take his brother's 834
Le 21:9 **i.** she profane herself by playing......... 3588
Le 22:9 **i.** they profane it: I the Lord do......... 3588
Le 22:11 But **i.** the priest buy any soul with..... 3588
Le 22:12 **I.** the priest's daughter also be.......... 3588
Le 22:13 But **i.** the priest's daughter also be..... 3588
Le 22:14 And **i.** a man eat of the holy thing...... 3588
Le 24:19 And **i.** a man cause a blemish in......... 3588
Le 25:14 And **i.** thou sell ought unto thy.......... 3588
Le 25:20 And **i.** ye shall say, What shall we...... 3588
Le 25:25 **I.** thy brother be waxen poor, and...... 3588
Le 25:25 and **i.** any of his kin come to redeem........
Le 25:26 And **i.** the man have none to............ 3588
Le 25:28 But **i.** he be not able to restore it........ 518
Le 25:29 And **i.** a man sell a dwelling house...... 3588
Le 25:30 And **i.** it be not redeemed within........ 518
Le 25:33 And **i.** a man purchase of the............. 834
Le 25:35 And **i.** thy brother be waxen poor, ... 3588
Le 25:39 And **i.** thy brother that dwelleth by..... 3588
Le 25:47 And **i.** a sojourner or stranger wax..... 3588
Le 25:49 or **i.** he be able, he may redeem..............
Le 25:51 **I.** there be yet many years behind, ... 518
Le 25:52 And **i.** there remain but few years 518
Le 25:54 And **i.** he be not redeemed in these..... 518
Le 26:3 **I.** ye walk in my statutes, and keep..... 518
Le 26:14 But **i.** ye will not hearken unto me,...... 518
Le 26:15 And **i.** ye shall despise my statutes, ... 518
Le 26:15 or **i.** your soul abhor my judgements,........
Le 26:18 And **i.** ye will not yet for all this.......... 518
Le 26:21 And **i.** ye walk contrary unto me, ... 518
Le 26:23 And **i.** ye will not be reformed by........ 518
Le 26:27 And **i.** ye will not for all this.............. 518
Le 26:40 **i.** they shall confess their iniquity, ...
Le 26:41 **i.** then their uncircumcised hearts........ 176
Le 27:4 And **i.** it be a female, then thy........... 518
Le 27:5 **i.** it be from five years old even unto ... 518
Le 27:6 **i.** it be from a month old even unto...... 518
Le 27:7 **i.** it be from sixty years old and 518
Le 27:7 **i.** it be a male, then thy estimation 518
Le 27:8 **i.** he be poorer than thy estimation...... 518
Le 27:9 **i.** it be a beast, whereof men bring....... 518
Le 27:10 **i.** he shall at all change beast for 518
Le 27:11 And **i.** it be any unclean beast, of........ 518
Le 27:13 But **i.** he will at all redeem it, then...... 518
Le 27:15 And **i.** he that sanctified it will............ 518
Le 27:16 And **i.** a man shall sanctify unto.......... 518
Le 27:17 **I.** he sanctify his field from the........... 518
Le 27:18 But **i.** he sanctify his field after 518
Le 27:19 And **i.** he that sanctified the field........ 518
Le 27:20 And **i.** he will not redeem the field,...... 518
Le 27:20 **i.** he have sold the field to another...... 518
Le 27:22 And **i.** a man sanctify unto the 518
Le 27:27 And **i.** it be of an unclean beast,.......... 518
Le 27:27 or **i.** it be not redeemed, then it.......... 518
Le 27:31 And **i.** a man will at all redeem........... 518
Le 27:33 and **i.** he change it all, then both it 518
Nu 5:8 But **i.** the man have no kinsman.......... 518

Nu 5:12 **I.** any man's wife go aside, and.......... 3588
Nu 5:14 or **i.** the spirit of jealousy come upon........
Nu 5:19 **I.** no man have lain with thee,............ 518
Nu 5:19 and **i.** thou hast not gone aside to........ 518
Nu 5:20 But **i.** thou hast gone aside to 3588
Nu 5:20 and **i.** thou be defiled, and some 3588
Nu 5:27 **i.** she be defiled, and have done 518
Nu 5:28 And **i.** the woman be not defiled,......... 518
Nu 6:9 And **i.** any man die very suddenly 3588
Nu 9:10 **I.** any man of you or your posterity.... 3588
Nu 9:14 And **i.** a stranger shall sojourn........... 3588
Nu 10:4 And **i.** they blow but with one............. 518
Nu 10:9 And **i.** ye go to war in your land........ 3588
Nu 10:32 **i.** thou go with us, yea, it shall be,..... 3588
Nu 11:15 And **i.** thou deal thus with me,............ 518
Nu 11:15 **i.** I have found favour in thy sight;....... 518
Nu 12:6 **I.** there be a prophet among you, ... 518
Nu 12:14 **I.** her father had but spit in her face,........
Nu 14:8 **I.** the Lord delight in us, then............. 518
Nu 14:15 Now **i.** thou shalt kill all this people as ......
Nu 15:14 And **i.** a stranger sojourn with........... 3588
Nu 15:22 And **i.** ye have erred, and not 3588
Nu 15:24 **i.** ought be committed by ignorance...... 518
Nu 15:27 **i.** any soul sin through ignorance, ... 518
Nu 16:29 **I.** these men die the common death..... 518
Nu 16:29 or **i.** they be visited after the visitation......
Nu 16:30 But **i.** the Lord make a new thing........ 518
Nu 19:12 **i.** he purify not himself the third.......... 518
Nu 20:19 and **i.** I and my cattle drink of thy 518
Nu 21:2 **I.** thou wilt indeed deliver this 518
Nu 21:9 that **i.** a serpent had bitten any man..... 518
Nu 22:18 **I.** Balak would give me his house 518
Nu 22:20 **I.** the men come to call thee, rise........ 518
Nu 22:34 **i.** it displease thee, I will get me 518
Nu 24:13 **I.** Balak would give me his house 518
Nu 27:8 **I.** a man die, and have no son, ... 3588
Nu 27:9 And **i.** he have no daughter, then 518
Nu 27:10 And **i.** he have no brethren, then......... 518
Nu 27:11 And **i.** his father have no brethren, ... 518
Nu 30:2 **I.** a man vow a vow unto the 3588
Nu 30:3 **I.** a woman also vow a vow unto the.........
Nu 30:5 But **i.** her father disallow her in.......... 518
Nu 30:6 And **i.** she had at all an husband, ... 518
Nu 30:8 But **i.** her husband disallowed her....... 518
Nu 30:10 And **i.** she vowed in her husband's...... 518
Nu 30:12 But **i.** her husband hath utterly 518
Nu 30:14 But **i.** her husband altogether hold 518
Nu 30:15 **i.** he shall any ways make them void 518
Nu 32:5 **i.** we have found grace in thy sight, ... 518
Nu 32:15 For **i.** ye turn away from after.................
Nu 32:20 **I.** ye will do this thing, **i.** ye will go..... 518
Nu 32:23 But **i.** ye will not do so, behold, ye...... 518
Nu 32:29 **I.** the children of God and the............. 518
Nu 32:30 But **i.** they will not pass over with....... 518
Nu 33:55 But **i.** ye will not drive out the........... 518
Nu 35:16 **i.** he smite him with an instrument....... 518
Nu 35:17 And **i.** he smite him with throwing....... 518
Nu 35:18 Or **i.** he smite him with an hand.......... 518
Nu 35:20 But **i.** he thrust him of hatred, or........ 518
Nu 35:22 But **i.** he thrust him suddenly............. 518
Nu 35:26 But **i.** the slayer shall at any time........ 518
Nu 36:3 And **i.** they be married to any of the.........
De 4:29 But **i.** from thence thou shalt seek the ......
De 4:29 **i.** thou seek him with all thy heart...... 3588
De 4:30 **i.** thou turn to the Lord thy God, and ....
De 5:25 **i.** we hear the voice of the Lord.......... 518
De 6:25 **i.** we observe to do all these............ 3588
De 7:12 **i.** ye hearken to these judgments, ... 6112
De 7:17 **I.** thou shalt say in thine heart,.......... 3588
De 8:19 **i.** thou do at all forget the Lord........... 518
De 11:13 **i.** ye shall hearken diligently unto......... 518
De 11:22 For **i.** ye shall diligently keep all.......... 518
De 11:27 **i.** ye obey the commandments of......... 834
De 11:28 **i.** ye will not obey the 518
De 12:21 **I.** the place which the Lord thy 3588
De 13:1 **I.** there arise among you a prophet,.... 3588
De 13:6 **I.** thy brother, the son of thy 3588
De 13:12 **I.** thou shalt hear say in one of thy..... 3588
De 13:14 **i.** it be truth, and the thing certain, ...
De 14:24 **i.** the way be too long for thee, ... 3588
De 14:24 or **i.** the place be too far from thee 3588
De 15:5 Only **i.** thou carefully hearken 518
De 15:7 **I.** there be among you a poor man 3588
De 15:12 And **i.** thy brother, an Hebrew man, ... 3588
De 15:16 **i.** he say unto thee, I will not go........ 3588
De 15:21 And **i.** there be any blemish therein, ... 3588
De 15:21 as **i.** it be lame, or blind, or have any ....

De 17:2 **I.** there be found among you, ... 3588
De 17:8 **I.** there arise a matter too hard for 3588
De 18:6 And **i.** a Levite come from any of....... 3588
De 18:21 And **i.** thou say in thine heart,.......... 3588
De 18:22 **i.** the thing follow not, nor come to ....
De 19:8 And **i.** the Lord thy God enlarge 518
De 19:9 **I.** thou shalt keep all these 3588
De 19:11 But **i.** any man hate his neighbour, ... 3588
De 19:16 **I.** a false witness rise up against 3588
De 19:18 and, behold, **i.** the witness be a false........
De 20:11 **i.** it make thee answer of peace, and.... 518
De 20:12 And **i.** it will make no peace with......... 518
De 21:1 **I.** one be found slain in the land......... 3588
De 21:14 **i.** thou have no delight in her, then...... 518
De 21:15 **I.** a man have two wives, one 3588
De 21:15 and **i.** the firstborn son be hers that ....
De 21:18 **I.** a man have a stubborn and............ 3588
De 21:22 And **i.** a man have committed a sin..... 3588
De 22:2 And **i.** thy brother be not nigh 518
De 22:2 or **i.** thou know him not, then thou...........
De 22:6 **I.** a bird's nest chance to be.............. 3588
De 22:8 house, **i.** any man fall from thence...... 3588
De 22:13 **I.** any man take a wife, and go in....... 3588
De 22:20 But **i.** this thing be true,and the 518
De 22:22 **I.** a man be found lying with a........... 3588
De 22:23 **I.** a damsel that is a virgin be............ 3588
De 22:25 But **i.** a man find a betrothed............. 518
De 22:28 **I.** a man find a damsel that is a.......... 3588
De 23:10 **I.** there be among you any man, ... 3588
De 23:22 But **i.** thou shalt forbear to vow, it..... 3588
De 24:3 And **i.** the latter husband hate her, ...
De 24:3 or **i.** the latter husband die, ... 3588
De 24:7 **I.** a man be found stealing any of 3588
De 24:12 And **i.** the man be poor, thou shalt 518
De 25:1 **I.** there be a controversy between 3588
De 25:2 **i.** the wicked man be worthy to be 518
De 25:3 lest, **i.** he should exceed, and beat ....
De 25:5 **I.** brethren dwell together, and.......... 3588
De 25:7 And **i.** the man like not to take 518
De 25:8 and **i.** he stand to it, and say, I like..........
De 28:1 **i.** thou shalt hearken diligently............. 518
De 28:2 **i.** thou shalt hearken unto the........... 3588
De 28:9 **i.** thou shalt keep...commandments.... 3588
De 28:13 **i.** that thou hearken unto the............. 3588
De 28:15 **i.** thou wilt not hearken unto the 518
De 28:58 **I.** thou wilt not observe to do all 518
De 30:4 **I.** any of thine be driven out unto 518
De 30:10 **I.** thou shalt hearken unto the 3588
De 30:10 and **i.** thou turn unto the Lord thy...... 3588
De 30:17 But **i.** thine heart turn away, so that 518
De 32:41 **I.** I whet my glittering sword, and 518
Jos 2:14 **i.** ye utter not this our business. 518
Jos 2:19 our head, **i.** any hand be upon him......... 518
Jos 2:20 And **i.** thou utter this our business,...... 518
Jos 8:15 as **i.** they were beaten before them, ...
Jos 9:4 as **i.** they had been ambassadors, and ....
Jos 14:12 **i.** so be the Lord will be with me, ... 194
Jos 17:15 **I.** thou be a great people, then............ 518
Jos 17:15 **i.** mount Ephraim be too narrow 3588
Jos 20:5 And **i.** the avenger of blood pursue..... 3588
Jos 22:19 **i.** the land of your possession be 518
Jos 22:22 **i.** it be in rebellion, or **i.** in 518
Jos 22:23 or **i.** to offer thereon burnt offering...... 518
Jos 22:23 or **i.** to offer peace offerings thereon, ... 518
Jos 22:24 And **i.** we have not rather done it for... 518
Jos 24:15 And **i.** it seem evil unto you to serve ... 518
Jos 24:20 **I.** ye forsake the Lord, and serve 3588
Jg 4:8 **I.** thou wilt go with me, then I............ 518
Jg 4:8 but **i.** thou wilt not go with me,........... 518
Jg 6:13 **i.** the Lord be with us, why then is all ......
Jg 6:17 **I.** now I have found grace in thy 518
Jg 6:31 **i.** he be a god, let him plead for.......... 518
Jg 6:36 **I.** thou wilt save Israel by mine........... 518
Jg 6:37 and **i.** the dew be on the fleece........... 518
Jg 7:10 But **i.** thou fear to go down, go thou.... 518
Jg 8:19 **i.** ye had saved them alive, I would 3863
Jg 9:15 **I.** in truth ye anoint me king over........ 518
Jg 9:15 and **i.** not, let fire come out of the....... 518
Jg 9:16 **i.** ye have done truly and sincerely,...... 518
Jg 9:16 and **i.** ye have dealt well with 518
Jg 9:19 **I.** ye then have dealt truly and............ 518
Jg 9:20 But **i.** not, let fire come out from 518
Jg 9:36 of the mountains as **i.** they were men. ......
Jg 11:9 **I.** ye bring me home again to fight....... 518
Jg 11:10 **i.** we do not so according to thy.......... 518
Jg 11:30 **I.** thou shalt without fail deliver........... 518

Jg 11:36 **i.** thou hast opened thy mouth unto..........
Jg 12:5 thou an Ephraimite? **I.** he said, Nay;.........
Jg 13:16 **i.** thou wilt offer a burnt offering, ... 518
Jg 13:23 **I.** the Lord were pleased to kill......... 3863
Jg 14:12 **i.** ye can certainly declare it me 518
Jg 14:13 **i.** ye cannot declare it me, then........... 518
Jg 14:18 **I.** ye had not ploughed with my 3883
Jg 16:7 **I.** they bind me with seven green........ 518
Jg 16:11 **I.** they bind me fast with new ropes...... 518
Jg 16:13 **I.** thou weavest the seven locks of...... 518
Jg 16:17 **i.** I be shaven, then my strength will.... 518
Jg 21:21 **i.** the daughters of Shiloh come out...... 518
Ru 1:12 **I.** I should say, I have hope, **i.** I........ 3588
Ru 1:17 also, **i.** ought but death part thee....... 3588
Ru 3:13 that **i.** he will perform unto thee......... 518
Ru 3:13 but **i.** he will not do the part of a......... 518
Ru 4:4 **I.** thou wilt redeem it, redeem it: 518
Ru 4:4 but **i.** thou wilt not redeem it, then...... 518
1Sa 1:11 **i.** thou wilt indeed look on the............ 518
1Sa 2:16 And **i.** any man said unto him, Let...........
1Sa 2:16 me now: and **i.** not, I will take it......... 518
1Sa 2:25 **I.** one man sin against another, the...... 518
1Sa 2:25 but **i.** a man sin against the Lord,........ 518
1Sa 3:9 **i.** he call thee, that thou shalt say,....... 518
1Sa 3:17 also, **i.** thou hide anything from me....... 518
1Sa 6:3 **I.** ye send away the ark of the God..... 518
1Sa 6:9 **i.** it goeth up by the way of his own..... 518
1Sa 6:9 but **i.** not, then we shall know that...... 518
1Sa 7:3 **I.** ye do return unto the Lord with....... 518
1Sa 9:7 behold, **i.** we go, what shall we ....
1Sa 10:22 **i.** the man should yet come thither...........
1Sa 11:3 **i.** there be no man to save us, we....... 518
1Sa 12:14 **I.** ye will fear the Lord, and serve....... 518
1Sa 12:15 But **i.** ye will not obey the voice of...... 518
1Sa 12:25 But **i.** ye shall still do wickedly, ye...... 518
1Sa 14:9 **I.** they say thus unto us, Tarry........... 518
1Sa 14:10 But **i.** they say thus, Come up unto...... 518
1Sa 14:30 **i.** haply the people had eaten freely.... 3863
1Sa 16:2 **i.** Saul hear it, he will kill me. And the......
1Sa 17:9 **I.** he be able to fight with me, and....... 518
1Sa 17:9 but **i.** I prevail against him, and kill...... 518
1Sa 19:11 saying, **I.** thou save not thy life.......... 518
1Sa 20:6 **I.** thy father at all miss me, then......... 518
1Sa 20:7 **I.** he say thus, It is well; thy............. 518
1Sa 20:7 but **i.** he be very wroth, then be sure .. 518
1Sa 20:8 **i.** there be in me iniquity, slay me....... 518
1Sa 20:9 for **i.** I knew certainly that evil............ 518
1Sa 20:10 or what **i.** thy father answer thee........ 176
1Sa 20:12 behold, **i.** there be good toward..............
1Sa 20:13 but **i.** it please my father to do.......... 3588
1Sa 20:21 **I.** I expressly say unto the lad, ... 518
1Sa 20:22 But **i.** I say thus unto the young.......... 518
1Sa 20:29 **i.** I have found favour in thine eyes,..... 518
1Sa 21:4 **i.** the young men have kept................ 518
1Sa 21:9 **i.** thou wilt take that, take it; for......... 518
1Sa 23:3 **i.** we come to Keilah against the........ 3588
1Sa 23:23 **i.** he be in the land, that I will............ 518
1Sa 24:19 For **i.** a man find his enemy, will........ 3588
1Sa 25:22 **i.** I leave of all that pertain to him....... 518
1Sa 26:19 **I.** the Lord have stirred thee up.......... 518
1Sa 26:19 but **i.** they be the children of men,....... 518
1Sa 27:5 **I.** I have now found grace in thine....... 518
2Sa 3:35 **i.** I taste bread, or ought else,..... 3588,518
2Sa 7:14 **I.** he commit iniquity, I will chasten...... 834
2Sa 10:11 **I.** the Syrians be too strong for........... 518
2Sa 10:11 **i.** the children of Ammon be too.......... 518
2Sa 11:20 And **i.** so be that the king's wrath........ 518
2Sa 12:8 and **i.** that had been too little, I........... 518
2Sa 12:18 **i.** we tell him that the child is dead? ....
2Sa 13:26 **I.** not, I pray thee, let my brother..... 3808
2Sa 14:32 and **i.** there be any iniquity in me,....... 518
2Sa 15:8 **I.** the Lord shall bring me again 518
2Sa 15:25 **i.** I shall find favour in the eyes of....... 518
2Sa 15:26 But **i.** he thus say, I have no delight.... 518
2Sa 15:33 **i.** thou passest on with me, then......... 518
2Sa 15:34 But **i.** thou return to the city, and 518
2Sa 16:23 was as **i.** a man had enquired at..............
2Sa 17:3 whom thou seekest is as **i.** all returned: ....
2Sa 17:6 after his saying? **i.** not; speak thou,...... 518
2Sa 17:13 Moreover, **i.** he be gotten into a city,... 518
2Sa 18:3 for **i.** we flee away, they will not......... 518
2Sa 18:3 neither **i.** half of us, will they care....... 518
2Sa 18:25 **I.** he be alone, there is tidings in........ 518
2Sa 19:6 that **i.** Absalom had lived, and all........ 3863
2Sa 19:7 **i.** thou go not forth, there will not...... 3588
2Sa 19:13 **i.** thou be not captain of the host......... 518

1Ki 1:52 **I.** he will shew himself a worthy......... 518
1Ki 1:52 **i.** wickedness shall be found in him, ... 518
1Ki 2:4 **I.** thy children take heed to their........ 518
1Ki 2:23 **i.** Adonijah have not spoken this......... 3588
1Ki 3:14 And **i.** thou wilt walk in my ways,......... 518
1Ki 6:12 **i.** thou will walk in my statutes, ... 518
1Ki 8:31 **I.** any man trespass against his................
1Ki 8:35 **i.** they pray toward this place, and............
1Ki 8:37 **I.** there be in the land famine, ... 3588
1Ki 8:37 **i.** there be pestilence, blasting, ... 3588
1Ki 8:37 or **i.** there be caterpiller; **i.** their........ 3588
1Ki 8:44 **I.** thy people go out to battle 3588
1Ki 8:46 **I.** they sin against thee, (for there...... 3588
1Ki 8:47 Yet **i.** they shall bethink themselves..........
1Ki 9:4 And **i.** thou wilt walk before me, as..... 518
1Ki 9:6 But **i.** ye shall at all turn from............. 518
1Ki 11:38 **i.** thou wilt hearken unto all that I........ 518
1Ki 12:7 **I.** thou wilt be a servant unto this........ 518
1Ki 12:27 **I.** this people go up to do sacrifice....... 518
1Ki 13:8 **I.** thou wilt give me half thine............ 518
1Ki 16:31 as **i.** it had been a light thing for him to.....
1Ki 18:21 **i.** the Lord be God, follow him: but...... 518
1Ki 18:21 but **i.** Baal, then follow him. And......... 518
1Ki 19:2 **i.** I make not thy life as the life of one .....
1Ki 20:10 **i.** the dust of Samaria shall suffice ....
1Ki 20:39 **i.** by any means he be missing, ... 518
1Ki 21:2 or, **i.** it seem good to thee, I will 518
1Ki 21:6 or else, **i.** it please thee, I will give 518
1Ki 22:28 **I.** thou return at all in peace, the......... 518
2Ki 1:10 **I.** I be a man of God, then let fire 518
2Ki 1:12 **I.** I be a man of God, let fire come...... 518
2Ki 2:10 **i.** thou see me when I am taken........... 518
2Ki 2:10 unto thee; but **i.** not, it shall not be..... 518
2Ki 4:29 **i.** thou meet any man, salute him....... 3588
2Ki 4:29 and **i.** any salute thee, answer him..... 3588
2Ki 5:13 **i.** the prophet had bid thee do some.........
2Ki 6:27 **I.** the Lord do not help thee, whence........
2Ki 6:31 **i.** the head of Elisha the son of........... 518
2Ki 7:2 **i.** the Lord would make windows..............
2Ki 7:4 **I.** we say, We will enter into the......... 518
2Ki 7:4 and **i.** we sit still here, we die also. 518
2Ki 7:4 **i.** they save us alive, we shall live; 518
2Ki 7:4 and **i.** they kill us, we shall but die: 518
2Ki 7:9 **i.** we tarry till the morning light, ...
2Ki 7:19 **i.** the Lord shall make windows in............
2Ki 9:15 **I.** it be your minds, then let none........ 518
2Ki 10:6 time to them, saying, **I.** ye be mine, ... 518
2Ki 10:6 and **i.** ye will hearken unto my voice,........
2Ki 10:15 **I.** it be, give me thine hand. And he.........
2Ki 10:24 **I.** any of the men whom I have................
2Ki 18:21 on which **i.** a man lean, it will go......... 834
2Ki 18:22 But **i.** ye say unto me, We trust in..... 3588
2Ki 18:23 **i.** thou be able on thy part to set......... 518
2Ki 20:19 **i.** peace and truth be in my days?......... 518
2Ki 21:8 only **i.** they will observe to do............. 518
1Ch 12:17 **I.** ye be come peaceably unto me to..... 518
1Ch 12:17 but **i.** ye be come to betray me to....... 518
1Ch 13:2 **I.** it seen good unto you, and that........ 518
1Ch 19:12 he said, **I.** the Syrians be too strong.... 518
1Ch 19:12 but **i.** the children of Ammon be too..... 518
1Ch 22:13 **i.** thou takest heed to fulfill the 518
1Ch 28:7 **i.** he be constant to do my................. 518
1Ch 28:9 **i.** thou seek him, he will be found......... 518
1Ch 28:9 but **i.** thou forsake him, he will cast 518
2Ch 6:22 **I.** a man sin against his neighbour,....... 518
2Ch 6:24 And **i.** thy people Israel be put to........ 518
2Ch 6:26 yet **i.** they pray toward this place, and......
2Ch 6:28 **I.** there be a dearth in the land,......... 3588
2Ch 6:28 **I.** there be pestilence, **i.** there be...... 3588
2Ch 6:28 **i.** their enemies besiege them in........ 3588
2Ch 6:32 **i.** they come and pray in this house; ....
2Ch 6:34 **I.** thy people go out to war against..... 3588
2Ch 6:36 **I.** they sin against thee, (for there...... 3588
2Ch 6:37 Yet **i.** they bethink themselves in the........
2Ch 6:38 **I.** they return to thee with all their..........
2Ch 7:13 **I.** I shut up heaven that there be....... 2005
2Ch 7:13 or **i.** I command the locust to............ 2005
2Ch 7:13 or **i.** I send pestilence among my......... 518
2Ch 7:14 **I.** my people, which are called by my........
2Ch 7:17 **i.** thou wilt walk before me, as............ 518
2Ch 7:19 But **i.** ye turn away, and forsake my.... 518
2Ch 10:7 **I.** thou be kind to this people, and....... 518
2Ch 15:2 and **i.** ye seek him, he will be found...... 518
2Ch 15:2 but **i.** ye forsake him, he will forsake.... 518
2Ch 18:27 **I.** thou certainly return in peace, ... 518
2Ch 20:9 **I.**, when evil cometh upon us, as the.... 518

2Ch 25:8 But **i.** thou wilt go, do it, be strong..... 518
2Ch 30:9 For **i.** ye turn again unto the Lord,...........
2Ch 30:9 from you, **i.** ye return unto him........... 518
Ezr 4:13 **i.** this city be builded, and the........... 2006
Ezr 4:16 **i.** this city be builded again, and........ 2006
Ezr 5:17 **i.** it seem good to the king, let there .. 2006
Ne 1:8 **I.** ye transgress, I will scatter you...........
Ne 1:9 But **i.** ye turn unto me, and keep my........
Ne 2:5 **I.** it please the king, and if thy............ 518
Ne 2:7 **I.** it please the king, let letters be............
Ne 4:3 **i.** a fox go up, he shall even break....... 518
Ne 9:29 (which **i.** a man do, he shall live in...........
Ne 10:31 And **i.** the people of the land bring...........
Ne 13:21 **i.** ye do so again, I will lay hands......... 518
Es 1:19 **I.** it please the king, let there go a...... 518
Es 3:9 **I.** it please the king, let it be............. 518
Es 4:14 For **i.** thou altogether holdest thy......... 518
Es 4:16 the law: and **i.** I perish, I perish.......... 834
Es 5:4 **I.** it seem good unto the king, let........ 518
Es 5:8 **I.** I have found favour in the sight........ 518
Es 5:8 and **i.** it please the king to grant my..... 518
Es 6:13 **I.** Mordecai be of the seed of the........ 518
Es 7:3 and said, **I.** I have found favour in 518
Es 7:3 and **i.** it please the king, let my life...... 518
Es 7:4 But **i.** we had been sold for................. 432
Es 8:5 **I.** it please the king, and **i.** I have 518
Es 9:13 **I.** it please the king, let it be............. 518
Job 4:2 **I.** we assay to commune with thee, ...
Job 5:1 **i.** there be any that will answer thee;........
Job 6:28 for it is evident unto you **i.** I lie. 518
Job 8:4 **I.** thy children have sinned against 518
Job 8:5 **I.** thou wouldest seek unto God 518
Job 8:6 **I.** thou wert pure and upright; 518
Job 8:18 **I.** he destroy him from his place,.......... 518
Job 9:3 **I.** he will contend with him, he............ 518
Job 9:13 **I.** God will not withdraw his anger,...........
Job 9:16 **I.** I had called, and he had.................. 518
Job 9:19 **I.** I speak of strenth, lo, he is............. 518
Job 9:19 and **i.** of judgment, who shall set......... 518
Job 9:20 **I.** I justify myself, mine own mouth...... 518
Job 9:20 **i.** I say, I am perfect, it shall also ....
Job 9:23 **I.** the scourge slay suddenly, he.......... 518
Job 9:24 thereof; **i.** not, where, and who is he?.. 518
Job 9:27 **I.** I say, I will forget my complaint,...... 518
Job 9:29 **I.** I be wicked, why then labour I in..........
Job 9:30 **I.** I wash myself with snow water,........ 518
Job 10:14 **I.** I sin, then thou markest me, and 518
Job 10:15 **I.** I be wicked, woe unto me; 518
Job 10:15 and **i.** I be righteous, yet will I not...... 518
Job 11:10 **I.** he cut off, and shut up, or gather..... 518
Job 11:13 **I.** thou prepare thine heart, and 518
Job 11:14 **I.** iniquity be in thine hand, put it 518
Job 13:10 **i.** ye do secretly accept persons........... 518
Job 13:19 now, **i.** I hold my tongue, I shall........ 3588
Job 14:7 hope of a tree, **i.** it be cut down.............
Job 14:14 **I.** a man die, shall he live again?.......... 518
Job 16:4 **i.** your soul were in my soul's 3863
Job 17:13 **I.** I wait, the grave is mine house:....... 518
Job 19:5 **I.** indeed ye will magnify yourselves..... 518
Job 21:4 and **i.** it were so, why should not my.... 518
Job 21:15 we have, **i.** we pray unto him? 3588
Job 22:23 **I.** thou return to the Almighty,............ 518
Job 24:17 **i.** one know them, they are in the...... 3588
Job 24:25 And **i.** it be not so now, who will......... 518
Job 27:14 **I.** his children be multiplied, it is 518
Job 29:24 **I.** I laughed on them, they believed ....
Job 31:5 **I.** I have walked with vanity, ... 518
Job 31:5 **i.** my foot hath hasted to deceit; ....
Job 31:7 **I.** my step hath turned out of the 518
Job 31:7 and **i.** any blot hath cleaved to mine..........
Job 31:9 **I.** mine heart have been deceived........ 518
Job 31:9 or **i.** I have laid wait at my neighbour's......
Job 31:13 **I.** I did despise the cause of my.......... 518
Job 31:16 **I.** have withheld the poor from their..... 518
Job 31:19 **I.** I have seen any perish for want....... 518
Job 31:20 **I.** his loins have not blessed me, ... 518
Job 31:20 and **i.** he were not warmed with the ....
Job 31:21 **I.** I have lifted up my hand against....... 518
Job 31:24 **I.** I have made gold my hope, or......... 518
Job 31:25 **I.** I rejoiced because my wealth was..... 518
Job 31:26 **I.** I beheld the sun when it shined, ... 518
Job 31:29 **I.** I rejoiced at the destruction of......... 518
Job 31:31 **I.** the men of my tabernacle said 518
Job 31:33 **I.** I covered my transgressions as......... 518
Job 31:38 **I.** my land cry against me, or that 518
Job 31:39 **I.** I have eaten the fruits thereof 518

Job 33:5 **I.** thou canst answer me, set thy......... 518
Job 33:23 **I.** there be a messenger with him,....... 518
Job 33:27 and **i.** any say, I have sinned, and...........
Job 33:32 **I.** thou hast anything to say,............. 518
Job 33:33 **I.** not, hearken unto me: hold thy........ 518
Job 34:14 **I.** he set his heart upon man,............. 518
Job 34:14 **i.** he gather unto himself his spirit...........
Job 34:16 **I.** now thou hast understanding, ... 518
Job 34:32 **i.** I have done iniquity, I will do no 518
Job 35:3 I have, **i.** I be cleansed from my sin?........
Job 35:6 **I.** thou sinnest, what doest thou.......... 518
Job 35:6 or **i.** thy transgressions be multiplied,........
Job 35:7 **I.** thou be righteous, what givest......... 518
Job 36:8 And **i.** they be bound in fetters, and..... 518
Job 36:11 **I.** they obey and serve him, they......... 518
Job 36:12 But **i.** they obey not, they shall........... 518
Job 37:20 **i.** a man speak, surely he shall be........ 518
Job 38:4 declare, **i.** thou hast understanding...........
Job 38:5 measures thereof, **i.** thou knowest? 3588
Job 38:8 as **i.** it had issued out of the womb? ....
Job 38:18 the earth? declare **i.** thou knowest....... 518
Ps 7:3 O Lord my God, **i.** I have done this;.... 518
Ps 7:3 **i.** there be iniquity in my hands;.......... 518
Ps 7:4 **I.** I have rewarded evil unto him 518
Ps 7:12 **I.** he turn not, he will whet his 518
Ps 11:3 **I.** the foundations be destroyed,......... 3588
Ps 14:2 to see **i.** there were any that did.............
Ps 28:1 **i.** thou be silent to me, I become like ....
Ps 40:5 **i.** I would declare and speak of them,........
Ps 41:6 And **i.** he come to see me, he 518
Ps 44:20 **I.** we have forgotten the name of 518
Ps 50:12 **I.** I were hungry, I would not tell........ 518
Ps 53:2 to see **i.** there were any that did.............
Ps 59:15 and grudge **i.** they be not satisfied. 518
Ps 62:10 **i.** riches increase, set not your 3588
Ps 66:18 **I.** I regard iniquity in my heart, the...... 518
Ps 73:15 **I.** I say, I will speak thus; behold, ... 518
Ps 81:8 Israel, **i.** thou wilt hearken unto me; 518
Ps 89:30 **I.** his children forsake my law, and....... 518
Ps 89:31 **I.** they break my statutes, and keep..... 518
Ps 90:10 and **i.** by reason of strength they be..... 518
Ps 95:7 To day **i.** ye will hear his voice, ... 518
Ps 124:1, 2 **I.** it had not been the Lord who...... 3884
Ps 130:3 **I.** thou, Lord, shouldest mark............ 518
Ps 132:12 **I.** thy children will keep my............. 518
Ps 137:5 **I.** I forget thee, O Jerusalem, let my.... 518
Ps 137:6 **I.** I do not remember thee, let my....... 518
Ps 137:6 **I.** I prefer not Jerusalem above my....... 518
Ps 139:8 **I.** I ascend up into heaven, thou art..... 518
Ps 139:8 **i.** I make my bed in hell, behold,............
Ps 139:9 **I.** I take the wings of the morning,...........
Ps 139:11 **I.** I say, Surely the darkness shall............
Ps 139:18 **I.** I should count them, they are more.......
Ps 139:24 And see **i.** there be any wicked way..... 518
Pr 1:10 **i.** sinners entice thee, consent thou...... 518
Pr 1:11 **I.** they say, Come with us, let us lay ... 518
Pr 2:1 **i.** thou wilt receive my words, and....... 518
Pr 2:3 Yea, **i.** thou criest after knowledge,....... 518
Pr 2:4 **I.** thou seekest her as silver, and........ 518
Pr 3:30 without cause, **i.** he have done thee..... 518
Pr 6:1 **i.** thou be surety for thy friend,........... 518
Pr 6:1 **i.** thou hast stricken thy hand with...........
Pr 6:30 do not despise a thief, **i.** he steal....... 3588
Pr 6:31 But **i.** he be found, he shall restore ....
Pr 9:12 **I.** thou be wise, thou shalt be wise...... 518
Pr 9:12 but **i.** thou scornest, thou alone shall.........
Pr 16:31 **i.** it be found in...way of righteousness......
Pr 19:19 for **i.** thou deliver him, yet thou 518
Pr 22:18 pleasant thing **i.** thou keep them 3588
Pr 22:27 **I.** thou hast nothing to pay, why......... 518
Pr 23:2 **i.** thou be a man given to appetite. 518
Pr 23:13 for **i.** thou beatest him with the rod,.........
Pr 23:15 **i.** thine heart be wise, my heart shall ... 518
Pr 24:10 **I.** thou faint in the day of adversity,..........
Pr 24:11 **I.** thou forbear to deliver them that ....
Pr 24:12 **I.** thou sayest, Behold, we knew it..... 3588
Pr 25:21 **I.** thine enemy be hungry, give 518
Pr 25:21 and **i.** he be thirsty, give him water 518
Pr 29:9 **I.** a wise man contendeth with a foolish.....
Pr 29:12 **I.** a ruler hearken to lies, all his servants...
Pr 30:4 is his son's name, **i.** thou canst tell? ....
Pr 30:32 **I.** thou hast done foolishly in lifting....... 518
Pr 30:32 or **i.** thou hast thought evil, lay thine..... 518
Ec 4:10 For **i.** they fall, the one will lift up 518
Ec 4:11 Again, **i.** two lie together, then 518
Ec 4:12 And **i.** one prevail against him, two...... 518
Ec 5:8 **I.** thou seest the oppression of the 518
Ec 6:3 **I.** a man beget an hundred children, ... 518
Ec 10:4 **I.** the spirit of the ruler rise up........... 518
Ec 10:10 **I.** the iron be blunt, and he do not........ 518
Ec 11:3 And **i.** the tree fall toward the south, ... 518
Ec 11:3 **I.** the clouds be full of rain, they 518
Ec 11:8 But **i.** a man live many years, and 518
Ca 1:8 **I.** thou know not, O thou fairest.......... 518
Ca 8:7 **i.** a man would give all the substance.... 518
Ca 8:9 **I.** she be a wall, we will build upon...... 518
Ca 7:12 let us see **i.** the vine flourish, ... 518
Ca 8:9 and **i.** she be a door, we will inclose 518
Isa 1:19 **I.** ye be willing and obedient, ye.......... 518
Isa 1:20 But **i.** ye refuse and rebel, ye shall..........
Isa 5:30 and **i.** one look unto the land, behold ....
Isa 7:9 **I.** ye will not believe, surely ye........... 518
Isa 8:20 **i.** they speak not according to this 518
Isa 10:15 as **i.** the rod should shake itself ....
Isa 10:15 or as **i.** the staff should lift up itself..........
Isa 10:15 itself, as **i.** it were no wood. ....
Isa 21:12 **i.** ye will enquire, enquire ye: 518
Isa 36:6 whereon **i.** a man lean, it will go.............
Isa 36:7 **i.** thou say to me, We trust in the Lord ....
Isa 36:8 **i.** thou be able on thy part to set......... 518
Isa 47:12 **i.** so be thou shalt be able to profit, ... 194
Isa 47:12 **i.** so be thou mayest prevail. 194
Isa 51:13 as **i.** he were ready to destroy? 834
Isa 58:9 **I.** thou take away from the midst of.........
Isa 58:10 And **i.** thou draw out thy soul to the.........
Isa 58:13 **I.** thou turn away thy foot from........... 518
Isa 59:10 and we grope as **i.** we had no eyes: ....
Isa 66:3 killeth an ox is as **i.** he slew a man;..........
Isa 66:3 lamb, as **i.** he cut off a dog's neck;...........
Isa 66:3 as **i.** he offered swine's blood; he............
Isa 66:3 incense, as **i.** he blessed an idol...............
Jer 2:10 and see **i.** there be such a thing,........ 2005
Jer 2:28 **i.** they can save thee in the time of...... 518
Jer 3:1 **I.** a man put away his wife, and......... 2005
Jer 4:1 and **i.** thou wilt put away thine........... 518
Jer 4:1 **I.** thou wilt return, O Israel, saith........ 518
Jer 5:1 places thereof, **i.** ye can find a man,..... 518
Jer 5:1 **i.** there be any that executeth............ 518
Jer 7:5 For **i.** ye throughly amend your.......... 518
Jer 7:5 **i.** ye throughly execute judgment.......... 518
Jer 7:6 **I.** ye oppress not the stranger, the..........
Jer 12:5 **I.** thou hast run with thy footmen,...... 3588
Jer 12:5 **i.** in the land of peace, wherein thou.........
Jer 12:16 **i.** they will diligently learn the............ 518
Jer 12:17 But **i.** they will not obey, I will 518
Jer 13:17 But **i.** ye will not hear it, my soul........ 518
Jer 13:22 And **i.** thou say in thine heart,........... 3588
Jer 14:18 **I.** I go forth into the field, then........... 518
Jer 14:18 and **i.** I enter into the city, then.......... 518
Jer 15:2 **i.** they say unto thee, Whither.......... 3588
Jer 15:19 **I.** thou return, then will I bring........... 518
Jer 15:19 and **i.** thou take forth the precious....... 518
Jer 17:24 **i.** ye diligently hearken unto me, ... 518
Jer 17:27 But **i.** ye will not hearken unto me......... 518
Jer 18:8 **I.** that nation, against whom I have...........
Jer 18:10 **I.** it do evil in my sight, that it obey.........
Jer 21:2 **i.** so be that the Lord will deal........... 194
Jer 22:4 For **i.** ye do this thing indeed, then...... 518
Jer 22:5 But **i.** ye will not hear these words, ... 518
Jer 23:22 But **i.** they had stood in my counsel,.........
Jer 25:28 **i.** they refuse to take the cup..................
Jer 26:3 **I.** so be they will hearken, and........... 194
Jer 26:4 **I.** ye will not hearken to me, ... 518
Jer 26:15 that **i.** ye put me to death, ye shall...... 518
Jer 27:18 But **i.** they be prophets, and **i.** the 518
Jer 31:36 **I.** those ordinances depart from........... 518
Jer 31:37 **I.** heaven above can be measured, ... 518
Jer 33:20 **I.** ye can break my covenant of the...... 518
Jer 33:25 **I.** my covenant be not with day........... 518
Jer 33:25 and **i.** I have not appointed the ....
Jer 38:15 **I.** I declare it unto thee, wilt thou........ 518
Jer 38:15 **i.** I give thee counsel, wilt thou not...... 518
Jer 38:17 **I.** thou wilt assuredly go forth unto...... 518
Jer 38:18 But **i.** thou wilt not go forth to............ 518
Jer 38:25 But **i.** the princes hear that I............ 3588
Jer 40:4 **I.** it seem good unto thee to come....... 518
Jer 40:4 but **i.** it seem ill unto thee to come...... 518
Jer 42:5 **i.** we do not even according to all........ 518
Jer 42:10 **I.** ye will still abide in this land,......... 518
Jer 42:13 But **i.** ye say, We will not dwell in......... 518
Jer 42:15 **I.** ye wholly set your faces to enter..... 518
Jer 49:9 **I.** grapegatherers come to thee, ... 518
Jer 49:9 **i.** thieves by night, they will destroy 518
Jer 51:8 pain, **i.** so be she may be healed. 194
La 1:12 and see **i.** there be any sorrow like...... 518
La 2:6 tabernacle, as **i.** it were of a garden: ....
La 3:29 dust; **i.** so be there may be hope......... 194
Eze 3:19 Yet **i.** thou warn the wicked, and 3588
Eze 3:21 Nevertheless **i.** thou warn the 3588
Eze 10:10 as **i.** a wheel had been in the............. 834
Eze 14:9 And **i.** the prophet be deceived........... 3588
Eze 14:15 **I.** I cause noisome beasts to pass....... 3863
Eze 14:17 Or **i.** I bring a sword upon that land,.........
Eze 14:19 Or **i.** I send a pestilence into that............
Eze 16:47 but, as **i.** that were a very little thing, ...
Eze 18:5 But **i.** a man be just, and do that 3588
Eze 18:10 **I.** he beget a son that is a robber,...........
Eze 18:14 Now, lo, **i.** he beget a son, that...............
Eze 18:21 But **i.** the wicked will turn from......... 3588
Eze 20:11, 13,21 which **i.** a man do, he shall.............
Eze 20:39 **i.** ye will not hearken unto me: 518
Eze 21:13 and what **i.** the sword contemn 518
Eze 33:2 **i.** the people of the land take a man..........
Eze 33:3 **I.** when he seeth the sword come ....
Eze 33:4 **i.** the sword come, and take him.............
Eze 33:6 But **i.** the watchman see the............ 3588
Eze 33:6 **i.** the sword come, and take any.............
Eze 33:8 **i.** thou dost not speak to warn the............
Eze 33:9 **i.** thou warn the wicked of his 3588
Eze 33:9 **i.** he do not turn from his way,................
Eze 33:10 **I.** our transgressions and our 3588
Eze 33:13 **i.** he trust to his own righteousness,.........
Eze 33:14 **i.** he turn from his sin, and do that..........
Eze 33:15 **I.** the wicked restore the pledge, ...
Eze 33:19 But **i.** the wicked turn from his................
Eze 43:11 And **i.** they be ashamed of all that 518
Eze 46:16 **I.** the prince give a gift unto any........ 3588
Eze 46:17 But **i.** he give a gift of his 3588
Da 2:5 **i.** ye will not make known unto.......... 2006
Da 2:6 But **i.** ye shew the dream, and the..... 2006
Da 2:9 But **i.** ye will not make known........... 2006
Da 3:15 Now **i.** ye be ready that at what........ 2006
Da 3:15 but **i.** ye worship not, ye shall be 2006
Da 3:17 **I.** it be so, our God whom we serve... 2006
Da 3:18 But **i.** not, be it known unto thee,...... 2006
Da 4:27 **i.** it may be the lengthening of thy...... 2006
Da 5:16 now **i.** thou canst read the writing,..... 2006
Ho 6:3 **i.** we follow on to know the Lord:............
Ho 8:7 **i.** so be it yield, the strangers shall...... 194
Joe 2:14 Who knoweth **i.** he will return and............
Joe 3:4 and **i.** ye recompense me, swiftly 518
Am 3:4 out of his den, **i.** he have taken........... 518
Am 5:19 As **i.** a man did flee from a lion, ... 834
Am 6:9 **i.** there remain ten men in one........... 518
Ob 5 **I.** thieves came to thee, ... 518
Ob 5 **i.** robbers by night, how art thou......... 518
Ob 5 **i.** the grapegatherers came to thee, ... 518
Jon 1:6 **i.** so be that God will think upon 194
Jon 3:9 Who can tell **i.** God will turn and.............
Mic 2:11 **I.** a man walking in the spirit............ 3863
Mic 5:8 who, **i.** he go through, both................ 518
Na 3:12 **i.** they be shaken, they shall even........ 518
Hag 2:12 **I.** one bear holy flesh in the skirt....... 2005
Hag 2:13 **I.** one that is unclean by a dead.......... 518
Zec 3:7 **I.** thou wilt walk in my ways, and......... 518
Zec 3:7 and **i.** thou wilt keep my charge, ... 518
Zec 6:15 **i.** ye will diligently obey the voice.............
Zec 8:6 **I.** it be marvellous in the eyes of 3588
Zec 11:12 **I.** ye think good, give me my price; 518
Zec 11:12 and **i.** not forbear. So they weighed 518
Zec 14:18 And **i.** the family of Egypt go not up,........
Mal 1:6 **i.** then I be a father, where is mine 518
Mal 1:6 and **i.** I be a master, where is my 518
Mal 1:8 And **i.** ye offer the blind for............. 3588
Mal 1:8 and **i.** ye offer the lame and sick, ... 3588
Mal 2:2 **I.** ye will not hear, and **i.** ye will......... 518
Mal 3:10 **i.** I will not open you the windows of........
Mt 4:3 **I.** thou be the Son of God, command .. *1487*
Mt 4:6 **I.** thou be the Son of God, cast *1487*
Mt 4:9 **i.** thou wilt fall down and worship........ *1437*
Mt 5:13 **but i. the salt have lost his savour,** *1437*
Mt 5:23 **Therefore i. thou bring thy gift to**.......
Mt 5:29 **And i. thy right eye offend thee,** ... *1487*
Mt 5:30 **i. thy right hand offend thee, cut**.........
Mt 5:40 **i. any man will sue thee at law,**.........
Mt 5:46 **For i. ye love them which love**...... *1437*
Mt 5:47 **And i. ye salute your brethren** *1437*
Mt 6:14 **For i. ye forgive men their** *1437*
Mt 6:15 **But i. ye forgive not men their** *1437*

Mt 6:22 i. therefore thine eye be single, 1437
Mt 6:23 But i. thine eye be evil, thy whole 1487
Mt 6:23 I. therefore the light that is in 1487
Mt 6:30 wherefore, i. God so clothed the 1487
Mt 7:9 i. his son ask bread, will he give 1437
Mt 7:10 Or i. he ask a fish, will he give 1437
Mt 7:11 I. ye then, being evil, know how to 1487
Mt 8:2 i. thou wilt, thou canst make me 1437
Mt 8:31 I. thou cast us out, suffer us to 1487
Mt 9:21 I. I may but touch his garment, 1437
Mt 10:13 And i. the house be worthy, let 1437
Mt 10:13 but i. it be not worthy, let your 1437
Mt 10:25 I. they have called the master of 1487
Mt 11:14 And i. ye will receive it, this is 1487
Mt 11:21 for i. the mighty works, which 1487
Mt 11:23 for i. the mighty works, which 1487
Mt 12:7 But i. ye had known what this 1487
Mt 12:11 and i. it fall into a pit on the 1437
Mt 12:26 And i. Satan cast out Satan, he 1487
Mt 12:27 And i. I by Beelzebub cast out 1487
Mt 12:28 But i. I cast out devils by the 1487
Mt 14:28 Lord, i. it be thou, bid me come 1487
Mt 15:14 And i. the blind lead the blind, 1437
Mt 16:24 I. any man will come after me, let 1487
Mt 16:26 i. he shall gain the whole world, 1437
Mt 17:4 i. thou wilt, let us make here three 1487
Mt 17:20 I. ye have faith as a grain of 1437
Mt 18:8 Wherefore i. thy hand or thy foot 1487
Mt 18:9 And i. thine eye offend thee, pluck 1487
Mt 18:12 i. a man have an hundred sheep 1437
Mt 18:13 And i. so be that he find it, verily 1437
Mt 18:15 Moreover i. thy brother shall 1437
Mt 18:15 i. he shall hear thee, thou hast 1437
Mt 18:16 But i. he will not hear thee, then 1437
Mt 18:17 And i. he shall neglect to hear 1437
Mt 18:17 but i. he neglect to hear the 1437
Mt 18:19 That i. two of you shall agree on 1437
Mt 18:35 i. ye from your hearts forgive not 1437
Mt 19:10 I. the case of the man be so with 1487
Mt 19:17 but i. thou wilt enter into life,keep 1487
Mt 19:21 I. thou wilt be perfect, go and sell 1487
Mt 21:3 And i. any man say ought unto 1437
Mt 21:21 I. ye have faith, and doubt not, ye 1437
Mt 21:21 but also i. ye shall say unto this 2579
Mt 21:24 which i. ye tell me, I in like wise 1437
Mt 21:25 I. we shall say, From heaven; he 1437
Mt 21:26 But i. we shall say, Of men; we 1437
Mt 22:24 Moses said, I. a man die, having 1437
Mt 22:45 I. David then call him Lord, how 1487
Mt 23:30 I. we had been in the days of our 1487
Mt 24:23 Then i. any man shall say unto 1437
Mt 24:24 i. it were possible, they shall 1487
Mt 24:26 Wherefore i. they shall say unto 1437
Mt 24:43 that i. the goodman of the house 1487
Mt 24:48 But and i. that evil servant shall 1437
Mt 26:24 good for that man i. he had not 1487
Mt 26:39 i. it be possible, let this cup pass 1487
Mt 26:42 i. this cup may not pass away from 1487
Mt 27:40 I. thou be the Son of God, come 1487
Mt 27:42 I. he be the King of Israel, let 1487
Mt 27:43 i. he will have him: for he said, I 1487
Mt 28:14 And i. this come to the governor's 1437
Mk 1:40 I. thou wilt, thou canst make me 1437
Mk 3:24 i. a kingdom be divided against 1437
Mk 3:25 And i. a house be divided against 1437
Mk 3:26 i. Satan rise up against himself, 1487
Mk 4:23 I. any man have ears to hear, let him
Mk 4:26 as i. a man should cast seed into 1487
Mk 5:28 I. I may touch but his clothes, I 2579
Mk 6:56 touch i. it were but the border of 2579
Mk 7:11 I. a man shall say to his father or 1437
Mk 7:16 I. any man have ears to hear, 1487
Mk 8:3 And i. I send them away fasting to 1437
Mk 8:23 he asked him i. he saw ought 1487
Mk 8:36 i. he shall gain the whole world, 1437
Mk 9:22 i. thou canst do any thing, have compassion
Mk 9:23 I. thou canst believe, all things 1487
Mk 9:35 I. any man desire to be first, the 1487
Mk 9:43 i. thy hand offend thee, cut it off: 1437
Mk 9:45 And i. thy foot offend thee, cut it 1437
Mk 9:47 i. thine eye offend thee, pluck it 1437
Mk 9:50 i. the salt have lost his saltness, 1437
Mk 10:12 And i. a woman shall put away her 1437
Mk 11:3 i. any man say unto you, Why do 1437
Mk 11:13 i. haply he might find any thing 1487
Mk 11:25 forgive, i. ye have ought against 1487
Mk 11:26 But i. ye do not forgive, neither 1487
Mk 11:31 I. we shall say, From heaven; he 1487
Mk 11:32 i. we shall say, Of men; they feared 1437
Mk 12:19 I. a man's brother die, and leave 1437
Mk 13:21 then i. any man shall say to you, 1437
Mk 13:22 to seduce, i. it were possible, even 1487
Mk 14:21 that man i. he had never been 1487
Mk 14:31 I. I should die with thee, I will not 1437
Mk 14:35 and prayed that, i. it were possible, 1487
Mk 15:44 marvelled i. he were already dead: 1487
Mk 16:18 and i. they drink any deadly thing, 2579
Lu 4:3 I. thou be the Son of God, 1487
Lu 4:7 I. thou therefore wilt worship me, 1437
Lu 4:9 I. thou be the Son of God, cast 1487
Lu 5:12 i. thou wilt, thou canst make me 1437
Lu 5:36 i. otherwise, then both the new 1490
Lu 6:32 For i. ye love them which love 1487
Lu 6:33 And i. ye do good to them which 1437
Lu 6:34 i. ye lend to them of whom ye hope 1437
Lu 7:39 This man, i. he were a prophet, 1487
Lu 9:23 I. any man will come after me, let 1487
Lu 9:25 i. he gain the whole world, and lose
Lu 10:6 And i. the son of peace be there, 1437
Lu 10:6 i. not, it shall turn to you again 1490
Lu 10:13 i. the mighty works had been done 1487
Lu 11:11 I. a son shall ask bread of any of you
Lu 11:11 i. he ask a fish, will he for a fish give
Lu 11:12 i. he shall ask an egg, will he offer 1437
Lu 11:13 I. ye then, being evil, know how to 1487
Lu 11:18 I. Satan also be divided against 1499
Lu 11:19 i. I by Beelzebub cast out devils, 1487
Lu 11:20 But i. I with the finger of God cast 1487
Lu 11:36 I. thy whole body therefore be full 1487
Lu 12:26 I. ye then be not able to do that 1487
Lu 12:28 I. then God so clothe the grass, 1487
Lu 12:38 And i. he shall come in the second 1437
Lu 12:39 that i. the goodman of the house 1487
Lu 12:45 But and i. that sevant say in his 1437
Lu 12:49 will I, i. it be already kindled? 1487
Lu 13:9 And i. it bear fruit, well: and 2579
Lu 13:9 and i. not, then after that thou 1487
Lu 14:26 I. any man come to me, and hate 1487
Lu 14:34 but i. the salt have lost his savour, 1437
Lu 15:4 i. he lose one of them, doth not leave
Lu 15:8 i. she lose one piece, doth not light 1437
Lu 16:11 I. therefore ye have not been 1487
Lu 16:12 And i. ye have not been faithful in 1487
Lu 16:30 but i. one went unto them from 1437
Lu 16:31 I. they hear not Moses and the 1487
Lu 17:3 I. thy brother trespass against 1437
Lu 17:3 and i. he repent, forgive him 1437
Lu 17:4 i. he trespass against thee seven 1437
Lu 17:6 I. ye had faith as a grain of 1487
Lu 19:8 and i. I have taken any thing from 1487
Lu 19:31 And i. any man ask you, Why do 1437
Lu 19:40 i. these should hold their peace, 1437
Lu 19:42 I thou hadst known, even thou, 1487
Lu 20:5 I. we shall say, From heaven; he 1437
Lu 20:6 But and i. we say, Of men; all the 1437
Lu 20:28 I. any man's brother die, having a 1437
Lu 22:42 i. thou be willing, remove this cup 1487
Lu 22:67 I. I tell you, ye will not believe: 1437
Lu 22:68 And i. I also ask you, ye will not 1437
Lu 23:31 i. they do these things in a green 1487
Lu 23:35 himself, i. he be Christ, the chosen 1487
Lu 23:37 I. thou be the king of the Jews, save 1487
Lu 23:39 I. thou be Christ, save thyself and 1487
Joh 1:25 i. thou be not that Christ, nor Elias, 1487
Joh 3:12 I. I have told you earthly things, 1487
Joh 3:12 i. I tell you of heavenly things? 1437
Joh 4:10 I. thou knewest the gift of God, 1487
Joh 5:31 I. I bear witness of myself, my 1437
Joh 5:43 i. another shall come in his own 1437
Joh 5:47 But i. ye believe not his writings, 1487
Joh 6:51 i. any man eat of this bread, he 1437
Joh 6:62 What and i. ye shall see the Son 1437
Joh 7:4 I. thou do these things, shew 1487
Joh 7:17 I. any man will do his will, he 1437
Joh 7:23 I. a man on the sabbath day 1487
Joh 7:37 I. any man thirst, let him come 1437
Joh 8:16 And yet i. I judge, my judgment is 1437
Joh 8:19 i. ye had known me, ye should 1487
Joh 8:24 for i. ye believe not that I am he, 1437
Joh 8:31 I. ye continue in my word, then 1437
Joh 8:36 I. the Son therefore shall make 1437
Joh 8:39 I. ye were Abraham's children, 1487
Joh 8:42 I. God were your Father, ye would 1487
Joh 8:46 i. I say the truth, why do ye not 1487
Joh 8:51, 52 I. a man keep my saying, he 1437
Joh 8:54 I. I honour myself, my honour is 1437
Joh 8:55 and i. I should say, I know him 1437
Joh 9:22 that i. any man did confess that he 1437
Joh 9:31 but i. any man be a worshipper of 1437
Joh 9:33 I. this man were not of God, he 1487
Joh 9:41 I. ye were blind, ye should have 1487
Joh 10:9 by me i. any man enter in, he shall 1437
Joh 10:24 I. thou be the Christ, tell us 1487
Joh 10:35 I. he called them gods, unto whom 1487
Joh 10:37 I. I do not the works of my 1487
Joh 10:38 But i. I do, though ye believe not 1487
Joh 11:9 I. any man walk in the day, he 1437
Joh 11:10 But i. a man walk in the night, he 1437
Joh 11:12 Lord, i. he sleep, he shall do well 1487
Joh 11:21, 32 i. thou hadst been here, my brother 1487
Joh 11:40 i. thou wouldest believe, thou 1437
Joh 11:48 I. we let him thus alone, all men 1437
Joh 11:57 i. any man knew where he were, he 1437
Joh 12:24 but i. it die, it bringeth forth much 1437
Joh 12:26 I. any man serve me, let him 1437
Joh 12:26 i. any man serve me, him will my 1437
Joh 12:32 I, i. I be lifted up from the earth, 1437
Joh 12:47 And i. any man hear my words, 1437
Joh 13:8 I. I wash thee not, thou hast no 1437
Joh 13:14 I. I then, your Lord and Master, 1487
Joh 13:17 I. ye know these things, 1487
Joh 13:17 happy are ye i. ye do them 1437
Joh 13:32 I. God be glorified in him, God 1487
Joh 13:35 disciples, i. ye have love one to 1437
Joh 14:2 i. it were not so, I would have told 1490
Joh 14:3 And i. I go and prepare a place 1437
Joh 14:7 I. ye had known me, ye should 1487
Joh 14:14 I. ye shall ask any thing in my 1437
Joh 14:15 I. ye love me, keep my 1437
Joh 14:23 I. a man love me, he will keep my 1437
Joh 14:28 I. ye loved me, ye would rejoice, 1487
Joh 15:6 I. a man abide not in me, he is 1437
Joh 15:7 I. ye abide in me, and my words 1437
Joh 15:10 I. ye keep my commandments, ye 1437
Joh 15:14 my friends, i. ye do whatsoever I 1437
Joh 15:18 I. the world hate you, ye know 1487
Joh 15:19 I. ye were of the world, the world 1487
Joh 15:20 I. they have persecuted me, they 1487
Joh 15:20 i. they have kept my saying, they 1487
Joh 15:22 I. I had not come and spoken unto 1487
Joh 15:24 I. I had not done among them the 1487
Joh 16:7 for i. I go not away, the Comforter 1437
Joh 16:7 i. I depart, I will send him unto 1437
Joh 18:8 i. therefore ye seek me, let these 1487
Joh 18:23 I. I have spoken evil, bear witness 1487
Joh 18:23 but i. well, why smitest thou me? 1487
Joh 18:30 I. he were not a malefactor, we 1487
Joh 18:36 i. my kingdom were of this world, 1487
Joh 19:12 I. thou let this man go,thou art 1437
Joh 20:15 i. thou have borne him hence, tell 1487
Joh 21:22 I. I will that he tarry till I come, 1437
Joh 21:23 but, I. I will that he tarry till I 1437
Joh 21:25 i. they should be written every one, 1437
Ac 4:9 I. we this day be examined of the 1487
Ac 5:38 for i. this counsel or this work be 1437
Ac 5:39 But i. it be of God, ye cannot 1487
Ac 8:22 i. perhaps the thought of thine 1487
Ac 8:37 I. thou believest with all thine 1487
Ac 9:2 that i. he found any of this way, 1437
Ac 13:15 i. ye have any word of exhortation 1487
Ac 15:29 from which i. ye keep yourselves, ye
Ac 16:15 I. ye have judged me to be faithful 1487
Ac 17:27 i. haply they might feel after him, 1487
Ac 18:14 I. it were a matter of wrong or 1487
Ac 18:15 But i. it be a question of words and 1487
Ac 18:21 will return again unto you, i. God will
Ac 19:38 Wherefore i. Demetrius, and the 1487
Ac 19:39 i. ye enquire any thing concerning 1487
Ac 20:16 i. it were possible for him, to be at 1487
Ac 23:9 i. a spirit or an angel hath spoken 1487
Ac 24:19 i. they had ought against me 1487
Ac 24:20 i. they have found any evil doing 1487
Ac 25:5 i. there be any wickedness in him 1487
Ac 25:11 For i. I be an offender, or have 1487
Ac 25:11 but i. there be none of these things 1487
Ac 26:5 i. they would testify, that after 1437
Ac 26:32 i. he had not appealed unto Caesar 1487
Ac 27:12 i. by any means they might attain 1513

Ac 27:39 **i.** it were possible, to thrust in.......... *1487*
Ro 1:10 **i.** by any means now at length I.......... *1513*
Ro 2:25 profiteth, **i.** thou keep the law: *1437*
Ro 2:25 but **i.** thou be a breaker of the law, ... *1437*
Ro 2:26 Therefore **i.** the uncircumcision.......... *1437*
Ro 2:27 **i.** it fulfil the law, judge thee, who..........
Ro 3:3 For what **i.** some do not believe?....... *1487*
Ro 3:5 **i.** our unrighteousness commend *1487*
Ro 3:7 For **i.** the truth of God hath more *1487*
Ro 4:2 For **i.** Abraham were justified by........ *1487*
Ro 4:14 For **i.** they which are of the law be *1487*
Ro 4:24 **i.** we believe on him that raised up..........
Ro 5:10 For **i.**, when we were enemies, we *1477*
Ro 5:15 For **i.** through the offence of one *1477*
Ro 5:17 For **i.** by one man's offence death *1477*
Ro 6:5 **i.** we have been planted together *1477*
Ro 6:8 Now **i.** we be dead with Christ, we *1477*
Ro 7:2 but **i.** the husband be dead, she......... *1437*
Ro 7:3 So then **i.**, while her husband liveth, ... *1437*
Ro 7:3 but **i.** her husband be dead, she is...... *1437*
Ro 7:16 **I.** then I do that which I would.......... *1487*
Ro 7:20 Now **i.** I do that I would not, it is...... *1487*
Ro 8:9 **i.** so be that the Spirit of God........... *1512*
Ro 8:9 Now **i.** any man have not the Spirit *1487*
Ro 8:10 And **i.** Christ be in you, the body....... *1487*
Ro 8:11 But **i.** the Spirit of him that raised...... *1437*
Ro 8:13 For **i.** ye live after the flesh, ye......... *1437*
Ro 8:13 but **i.** ye through the Spirit do........... *1487*
Ro 8:17 And **i.** children, then heirs; heirs........ *1487*
Ro 8:17 **i.** so be that we suffer with him,........ *1512*
Ro 8:25 But **i.** we hope for that we see not, ... *1487*
Ro 8:31 **I.** God be for us, who can be........... *1487*
Ro 9:22 What **i.** God, willing to shew his *1487*
Ro 10:9 That **i.** thou shalt confess with.......... *1437*
Ro 11:6 And **i.** by grace, then is it no more *1487*
Ro 11:6 But **i.** it be of works, then is it no *1487*
Ro 11:12 Now **i.** the fall of them be the riches .. *1487*
Ro 11:14 **I.** by any means I may provoke *1513*
Ro 11:15 For **i.** the casting away of them be...... *1487*
Ro 11:16 For **i.** the firstfruit be holy, the *1487*
Ro 11:16 and **i.** the root be holy, so are the *1487*
Ro 11:17 And **i.** some of the branches be......... *1487*
Ro 11:18 But **i.** thou boast, thou bearest.......... *1487*
Ro 11:21 For **i.** God spared not the natural....... *1487*
Ro 11:22 **i.** thou continue in his goodness: *1437*
Ro 11:23 **i.** they abide not still in unbelief, ... *1437*
Ro 11:24 For **i.** thou wert cut out of the *1487*
Ro 12:18 **I.** it be possible, as much as lieth....... *1487*
Ro 12:20 Therefore **i.** thine enemy hunger,....... *1437*
Ro 12:20 **i.** he thirst, give him drink: for in....... *1437*
Ro 13:4 But **i.** thou do that which is evil,........ *1437*
Ro 13:9 and **i.** there be any other................. *1487*
Ro 14:15 But **i.** thy brother be grieved with...... *1487*
Ro 14:23 is damned **i.** he eat, because he.......... *1437*
Ro 15:24 **i.** first I be somewhat filled with *1437*
Ro 15:27 For **i.** the Gentiles have been made.... *1487*
1Co 3:12 Now **i.** any man build upon this.......... *1487*
1Co 3:14 **I.** any man's work abide which........... *1487*
1Co 3:15 **I.** any man's work shall be burned, ... *1487*
1Co 3:17 **I.** any man defile the temple of.......... *1487*
1Co 3:18 **I.** any man among you seemeth to....... *1487*
1Co 4:7 now **i.** thou didst receive it, why......... *1499*
1Co 4:7 glory, as **i.** thou hadst not received it? ......
1Co 4:19 to you shortly, **i.** the Lord will, ... *1437*
1Co 5:11 **i.** any man that is called a brother...... *1437*
1Co 6:2 and **i.** the world shall be judged *1487*
1Co 6:4 **I.** then ye have judgments of............. *1437*
1Co 7:8 It is good for them **i.** they abide *1437*
1Co 7:9 But **i.** they cannot contain, let *1487*
1Co 7:11 But and **i.** she depart, let her........... *1437*
1Co 7:12 **i.** any brother hath a wife that........... *1487*
1Co 7:13 and **i.** he be pleased to dwell with her,......
1Co 7:15 But **i.** the unbelieving depart, let........ *1487*
1Co 7:21 but **i.** thou mayest be made free, ... *1499*
1Co 7:28 But and **i.** thou marry, thou hast........ *1437*
1Co 7:28 and **i.** a virgin marry, she hath not..... *1437*
1Co 7:36 But **i.** any man think that he *1487*
1Co 7:36 **i.** she pass the flower of her age,........ *1437*
1Co 7:39 but **i.** her husband be dead, she is...... *1437*
1Co 7:40 But she is happier **i.** she so abide, ... *1437*
1Co 8:2 And **i.** any man think that he............ *1487*
1Co 8:3 But **i.** any man love God, the same *1487*
1Co 8:8 for neither, **i.** we eat, are we the....... *1437*
1Co 8:8 neither, **i.** we eat not, are we the....... *1437*
1Co 8:10 For **i.** any man see thee which hast.... *1437*
1Co 8:13 **i.** meat make my brother to offend, ... *1487*
1Co 9:2 **I.** I be not an apostle unto others,...... *1487*
1Co 9:11 **I.** we have sown unto you spiritual..... *1487*
1Co 9:11 **i.** we shall reap your carnal things?..... *1487*
1Co 9:12 **I.** others be partakers of this *1487*
1Co 9:16 unto me, **i.** I preach not the gospel! ... *1437*
1Co 9:17 For **i.** I do this thing willingly, I......... *1487*
1Co 9:17 **i.** against my will, a dispensation......... *1487*
1Co 10:27 **I.** any of them that believe not *1487*
1Co 10:28 But **i.** any man say unto you, This *1437*
1Co 10:30 For **i.** I by grace be a partaker, ... *1487*
1Co 11:5 is even all one as **i.** she were shaven........
1Co 11:6 For **i.** the woman be not covered,...... *1487*
1Co 11:6 but **i.** it be a shame for a woman *1487*
1Co 11:14 **i.** a man have long hair, it is a........... *1437*
1Co 11:15 But **i.** a woman have long hair, it is.... *1437*
1Co 11:16 But **i.** any man seem to be *1487*
1Co 11:31 For **i.** we would judge ourselves, ... *1487*
1Co 11:34 **i.** any man hunger, let him eat at *1487*
1Co 12:15 **I.** the foot shall say, Because I.......... *1437*
1Co 12:16 And **i.** the ear shall say, Because I..... *1437*
1Co 12:17 **I.** the whole body were an eye, ... *1487*
1Co 12:17 **I.** the whole were hearing, where *1487*
1Co 12:19 And **i.** they were all one member,...... *1487*
1Co 14:6 **i.** I come unto you speaking with *1437*
1Co 14:8 **i.** the trumpet give an uncertain......... *1437*
1Co 14:11 Therefore **i.** I know not the meaning... *1437*
1Co 14:14 For **i.** I pray in an unknown tongue, ... *1437*
1Co 14:23 **I.** therefore the whole church be........ *1437*
1Co 14:24 But **i.** all prophesy, and there come.... *1437*
1Co 14:27 **I.** any man speak in an unknown *1535*
1Co 14:28 But **i.** there be no interpreter,........... *1437*
1Co 14:30 **I.** any thing be revealed to another..... *1437*
1Co 14:35 And **i.** they will learn any thing, ... *1487*
1Co 14:37 **I.** any man think himself to be a *1487*
1Co 14:38 But **i.** any man be ignorant, ... *1487*
1Co 15:2 saved, **i.** ye keep in memory what I ... *1487*
1Co 15:12 Now **i.** Christ be preached that he...... *1487*
1Co 15:13 But **i.** there be no resurrection of *1487*
1Co 15:14 And **i.** Christ be not risen, then is...... *1487*
1Co 15:15 **i.** so be that the dead rise not........... *1512*
1Co 15:16 For **i.** the dead rise not,then is.......... *1487*
1Co 15:17 And **i.** Christ be not raised, your *1487*
1Co 15:19 **I.** in this life only we have hope in *1487*
1Co 15:29 the dead, **i.** the dead rise not at all? ... *1487*
1Co 15:32 **I.** after the manner of men I have *1487*
1Co 15:32 what advantageth it me, **i.** the dead.... *1487*
1Co 16:4 And **i.** it be meet that I go also, ... *1437*
1Co 16:7 while with you, **i.** the Lord permit..... *1437*
1Co 16:10 now **i.** Timotheus come, see that......... *1437*
1Co 16:22 **I.** any man love not the Lord Jesus *1487*
2Co 2:2 For **i.** I make you sorry, who is he *1487*
2Co 2:5 But **i.** any have caused grief,............. *1487*
2Co 2:10 for **i.** I forgave any thing, to whom..... *1487*
2Co 3:7 But **i.** the ministration of death, ... *1487*
2Co 3:9 For **i.** the ministration of................. *1487*
2Co 3:11 For **i.** that which is done away was *1487*
2Co 4:3 But **i.** our gospel be hid, it is hid *1499*
2Co 5:1 For we know that **i.** our earthly.......... *1437*
2Co 5:3 **I.** so be that being clothed we........... *1489*
2Co 5:14 that **i.** one died for all, then were....... *1487*
2Co 5:17 Therefore **i.** any man be in Christ, ... *1487*
2Co 7:14 For **i.** I have boasted any thing to *1487*
2Co 8:12 For **i.** there be first a willing mind,..... *1487*
2Co 9:4 Lest haply **i.** they of Macedonia *1437*
2Co 10:2 as **i.** we walked according to the flesh......
2Co 10:7 **I.** any man trust to himself that *1487*
2Co 10:9 as **i.** I would terrify you by letters...........
2Co 11:4 For **i.** he that cometh preacheth.......... *1487*
2Co 11:4 or **i.** ye receive another spirit, which ....
2Co 11:15 **i.** his ministers also be transformed *1499*
2Co 11:16 **i.** otherwise, yet as a fool receive *1490*
2Co 11:20 **i.** a man bring you into bondage,........ *1487*
2Co 11:20 **i.** a man devour you, **i.** a man take *1487*
2Co 11:20 **i.** a man exalt himself, **i.** a man *1487*
2Co 11:30 **I.** I must needs glory, I will glory *1487*
2Co 13:2 as **i.** I were present, the second *1437*
2Co 13:2 that, **i.** I come again, I will not spare: ....
Ga 1:9 **I.** any man preach any other gospel.... *1487*
Ga 1:10 for **i.** I yet pleased men, I should....... *1487*
Ga 2:14 **I.** thou, being a Jew, livest after *1487*
Ga 2:17 But **i.**, while we seek to be justified ... *1487*
Ga 2:18 For **i.** I build again the things which.... *1487*
Ga 2:21 **i.** righteousness come by the law, ... *1487*
Ga 3:4 in vain? **i.** it be yet in vain............. *1489*
Ga 3:15 yet **i.** it be confirmed, no man ....
Ga 3:18 For **i.** the inheritance be of the law *1487*
Ga 3:21 for **i.** there had been a law given *1487*
Ga 3:29 And **i.** ye be Christ's, then are ye...... *1487*
Ga 4:7 and **i.** a son, then an heir of God *1487*
Ga 4:15 that, **i.** it had been possible, ye *1487*
Ga 5:2 that **i.** ye be circumcised, Christ *1437*
Ga 5:11 **i.** I yet preach circumcision, why........ *1487*
Ga 5:15 But **i.** ye bite and devour one........... *1487*
Ga 5:18 But **i.** ye be led of the Spirit, ye are... *1487*
Ga 5:25 **I.** we live in the Spirit, let us also...... *1487*
Ga 6:1 **i.** a man be overtaken in a fault, ... *1437*
Ga 6:3 For **i.** a man think himself to be......... *1487*
Ga 6:9 season we shall reap, **i.** we faint not..........
Eph 3:2 **I.** ye have heard of the..................... *1489*
Eph 4:21 **I.** so be that ye have heard him,........ *1489*
Php 1:22 But **i.** I live in the flesh, this is.......... *1487*
Php 2:1 **I.** there be...any consolation in *1487*
Php 2:1 **i.** any comfort of love, ... *1487*
Php 2:1 **i.** any fellowship of the Spirit,............ *1487*
Php 2:1 **i.** any bowels and mercies,................ *1487*
Php 2:17 Yea, and **i.** I be offered upon the *1487*
Php 3:4 **I.** any other man thinketh that he....... *1487*
Php 3:11 **I.** by any means I might attain........... *1513*
Php 3:12 **i.** that I may apprehend that for......... *1499*
Php 3:15 **i.** in any thing ye be otherwise *1487*
Php 4:8 good report; **i.** there be any virtue, ... *1487*
Php 4:8 and **i.** there be any praise, think on *1487*
Col 1:23 **I.** ye continue in the faith *1489*
Col 2:20 Wherefore **i.** ye be dead with........... *1487*
Col 3:1 **I.** ye then be risen with Christ, ... *1487*
Col 3:13 **i.** any man have a quarrel against *1437*
Col 4:10 **i.** he come unto you, receive him;...... *1437*
1Th 3:8 For now we live, **i.** ye stand fast in.... *1437*
1Th 4:14 For **i.** we believe that Jesus died........ *1487*
2Th 3:10 that **i.** any would not work, neither..... *1487*
2Th 3:14 And **i.** any man obey not our word *1487*
1Ti 1:8 is good, **i.** a man use it lawfully: *1437*
1Ti 1:10 and **i.** there be any other thing *1487*
1Ti 2:15 **i.** they continue in faith and.............. *1437*
1Ti 3:1 **I.** a man desire the office of a *1487*
1Ti 3:5 For **i.** a man know not how to........... *1487*
1Ti 3:15 But **i.** I tarry long, that thou mayest... *1437*
1Ti 4:4 **i.** it be received with thanksgiving: ....
1Ti 4:6 **I.** thou put the brethren in.....................
1Ti 5:4 **i.** any widow have children or............ *1487*
1Ti 5:8 But **i.** any provide not for his own,..... *1487*
1Ti 5:10 **i.** she have brought up children.......... *1487*
1Ti 5:10 **i.** she have lodged strangers, ... *1487*
1Ti 5:10 **i.** she have washed the saints' feet, ... *1487*
1Ti 5:10 **i.** she have relieved the afflicted,........ *1487*
1Ti 5:10 **i.** she have diligently followed every.... *1487*
1Ti 5:16 **I.** any man or woman that *1487*
1Ti 6:3 **I.** any man teach otherwise, and *1487*
2Ti 2:5 **i.** a man also strive for masteries, ... *1437*
2Ti 2:11 For **i.** we be dead with him, we......... *1487*
2Ti 2:12 **I.** we suffer, we shall also reign.......... *1487*
2Ti 2:12 **i.** we deny him, he also will deny *1487*
2Ti 2:13 **I.** we believe not, yet he abideth *1487*
2Ti 2:21 **I.** a man therefore purge himself........ *1437*
2Ti 2:25 **i.** God peradventure will give them..... *3379*
Tit 1:6 **I.** any be blameless, the husband of.... *1487*
Phm 17 **I.** thou count me therefore a............ *1487*
Phm 18 **I.** he hath wronged thee, or oweth..... *1487*
Heb 2:2 For **i.** the word spoken by angels....... *1487*
Heb 2:3 **i.** we neglect so great salvation;...............
Heb 3:6 **i.** we hold fast the confidence and *1437*
Heb 3:7 To day **i.** ye will hear his voice,......... *1437*
Heb 3:14 **i.** we hold the beginning of our *1437*
Heb 3:15 To day **i.** ye will hear his voice,......... *1437*
Heb 4:3 **i.** they shall enter into my rest: *1487*
Heb 4:5 **I.** they shall enter into my rest.......... *1487*
Heb 4:7 To day **i.** ye will hear his voice,......... *1437*
Heb 4:8 For **i.** Jesus had given them rest,...... *1487*
Heb 6:3 And this will we do, **i.** God permit. *1437*
Heb 6:6 **I.** they shall fall away, to renew..............
Heb 7:11 **I.** therefore perfection were by.......... *1487*
Heb 8:4 For **i.** he were on earth, he should..... *1487*
Heb 8:7 For **i.** that first covenant had been *1487*
Heb 9:13 For **i.** the blood of bulls and of *1487*
Heb 10:26 For **i.** we sin wilfully after that we...........
Heb 10:38 but **i.** any man draw back, my soul..... *1437*
Heb 11:15 **i.** they had been mindful of that *1487*
Heb 12:7 **I.** ye endure chastening, God *1487*
Heb 12:8 But **i.** ye be without chastisement, ... *1487*
Heb 12:20 And **i.** so much as a beast touch the.........
Heb 12:25 for **i.** they escaped not who refused.... *1487*
Heb 12:25 **i.** we turn away from him that................
Heb 13:23 **i.** he come shortly, I will see you........ *1437*
Jas 1:5 **I.** any of you lack wisdom, let him...... *1487*

Jas 1:23 For i. any be a hearer of the word,.... 1487
Jas 1:26 I. any man among you seem to be 1487
Jas 2:2 i. there come unto your assembly 1437
Jas 2:8 I. ye fulfil the royal law according....... 1487
Jas 2:9 But i. ye have respect to persons, ... 1487
Jas 2:11 Now i. thou commit no adultery,........ 1487
Jas 2:11 yet i. thou kill, thou art become a...........
Jas 2:15 I. a brother or sister be naked, ... 1437
Jas 2:17 i. it hath not works, is dead,............ 1437
Jas 3:2 I. any man offend not in word, ... 1487
Jas 3:14 But i. ye have bitter envying and....... 1487
Jas 4:11 but i. thou judge the law, thou art....... 1487
Jas 4:15 I. the Lord will, we shall live, and...... 1437
Jas 5:15 and i. he have committed sins, they.........
Jas 5:19 Brethren, i. any of you do err from.... 1437
1Pe 1:6 i. need be, ye are in heaviness.......... 1487
1Pe 1:17 And i. ye call on the Father, who....... 1487
1Pe 2:3 I. so be ye have tasted that the......... 1512
1Pe 2:19 i. a man for conscience toward God...... 1487
1Pe 2:20 i., when ye be buffeted for your 1487
1Pe 2:20 i., when ye do well, and suffer for 1487
1Pe 3:1 that, i. any obey not the word, they... 1487
1Pe 3:13 i. ye be followers of that which is 1437
1Pe 3:14 and i. ye suffer for righteousness' sake,.....
1Pe 3:17 i. the will of God be so, that ye.......... 1487
1Pe 4:11 I. any man speak, let him speak 1487
1Pe 4:11 i. any man minister, let him do it....... 1487
1Pe 4:14 I. ye be reproached for the name........ 1487
1Pe 4:16 Yet i. any man suffer as a Christian,... 1487
1Pe 4:17 and i. it first begin at us, what 1487
1Pe 4:18 And i. the righteous scarcely be.......... 1487
2Pe 1:8 For i. these things be in you, and ....
2Pe 1:10 for i. ye do these things, ye shall never ....
2Pe 2:4 For i. God spared not the angels 1487
2Pe 2:20 For i. after they have escaped the........ 1487
1Jo 1:6 I. we say that we have fellowship 1437
1Jo 1:7 But i. we walk in the light, as he is.... 1437
1Jo 1:8 I. we say that we have no sin, we 1437
1Jo 1:9 I. we confess our sins, he is............. 1437
1Jo 1:10 I. we say that we have not sinned,....... 1437
1Jo 2:1 And i. any man sin, we have an......... 1437
1Jo 2:3 i. we keep his commandments........... 1437
1Jo 2:15 I. any man love the world, the love.... 1437
1Jo 2:19 for i. they had been of us, they 1487
1Jo 2:24 I. that which ye have heard from 1437
1Jo 2:29 I. ye know that he is righteous, ye..... 1437
1Jo 3:13 my brethren, i. the world hate you....... 1487
1Jo 3:20 For i. our heart condemn us, God...... 1437
1Jo 3:21 i. our heart condemn us not,............ 1437
1Jo 4:11 Beloved, i. God so loved us, we........... 1487
1Jo 4:12 I. we love one another, God............. 1437
1Jo 4:20 I. a man say, I love God, and............ 1437
1Jo 5:9 I. we receive the witness of men,...... 1487
1Jo 5:14 i. we ask any thing according to......... 1437
1Jo 5:15 And i. we know that he hear us,......... 1437
1Jo 5:16 I. any man see his brother sin a 1437
2Jo 10 I. there come any unto you, and.......... 1487
3Jo 6 whom i. thou bring forward on their ....
3Jo 10 i. I come, I will remember his.......... 1437
Re 1:15 brass, as i. they burned in a furnace;........
Re 3:3 I. therefore thou shalt not........... 1437
Re 3:20 i. any man hear my voice, and...... 1437
Re 11:5 And i. any man will hurt them, ... 1487
Re 11:5 and i. any man will hurt them, he....... 1487
Re 13:9 I. any man have an ear, let him........ 1487
Re 14:9 I. any man worship the beast and....... 1487
Re 22:18 I. any man shall add unto these 1437
Re 22:19 And i. any man shall take away.......... 1437

IGAL (i'-gal) See also IGEAL.
Nu 13:7 Issachar, I. the son of Joseph........... 3008
2Sa 23:36 I. the son of Nathan of Zobah,.......... 3008

IGDALIAH (ig-da-li'-ah)
Jer 35:4 of I., a man of God, which was 3012

IGEAL (ig'-e-al) See also IGAL.
1Ch 3:22 Hattush, and I., and Bariah, and 3008

IGNOMINY
Pr 18:3 contempt, and with i. reproach. 7036

IGNORANCE
Le 4:2 If a soul shall sin through i.................. 7684
Le 4:13 of Israel sin through i.,......................... 7686
Le 4:22 done somewhat through i..................... 7684
Le 4:27 common people sin through i.,............. 7684
Le 5:15 a trespass, and sin through i.,........... 7684
Le 5:18 his i. wherein he erred and wist it...... 7684
Nu 15:24 if ought be committed by i.............. 7684
Nu 15:25 shall be forgiven them; for it is i........ 7684
Nu 15:25 before the Lord, for their i.:............ 7684
Nu 15:26 seeing all the people were in i......... 7684
Nu 15:27 if any soul sin through i., then he....... 7684
Nu 15:28 he sinneth by i. before the Lord, ... 7684
Nu 15:29 for him that sinneth through i.,.......... 7684
Ac 3:17 brethen, I wot that through i. ye did...... 52
Ac 17:30 the times of this i. God winked at; 52
Eph 4:18 God through the i. that is in them, ... 52
1Pe 1:14 to the former lusts in your i.:.............. 52
1Pe 2:15 to silence the i. of foolish men:............ 56

IGNORANT
Ps 73:22 So foolish was I, and i.: I was.... 3808,3045
Isa 56:10 they are all i., they are all........ 3808,3045
Isa 63:16 though Abraham be i. of us,........ 3808,3045
Ac 4:13 they were unlearned and i. men,........ 2399
Ro 1:13 Now I would not have you i.,.............. 50
Ro 10:3 For they being i. of God's.................. 50
Ro 11:25 that ye should be i. of this mystery,...... 50
1Co 10:1 I would not that ye should be i.,........... 50
1Co 12:1 brethren, I would not have you i........... 50
1Co 14:38 if any man be i., let him be i.............. 50
2Co 1:8 would not, brethren, have you i. of....... 50
2Co 2:11 of us: for we are not i. of his devices. ... 50
1Th 4:13 But I would not have you to be i., ... 50
Heb 5:2 Who can have compassion on the i.,...... 50
2Pe 3:5 For this they willingly are i. of 2990
2Pe 3:8 beloved, be not i. of this one thing,.... 2990

IGNORANTLY
Nu 15:28 for the soul that sinneth i., when 7683
De 19:4 Whoso killeth...neighbour i., ... 1097,1847
Ac 17:23 Whom therefore ye i. worship, him 50
1Ti 1:13 mercy, because I did it i. in unbelief. 50

IIM (i'-im) See also IJE-ABARIM.
Nu 33:45 And they departed from I., and 5864
Jos 15:29 Baalah, and I., and Azem, ... 5864

IJE-ABARIM (i''-je-ab'-a-rim) See also IIM.
Nu 21:11 and pitched at I., in the 5863
Nu 33:44 and pitched in I., in the border.......... 5863

IJON (i'-jon)
1Ki 15:20 and smote I., and Dan, and.............. 5859
2Ki 15:29 took I., and Abel-beth-maachah,......... 5859
2Ch 16:4 and they smote I., and Dan, and........ 5859

IKKESH ik'-kesh)
2Sa 23:26 Ira the son of I. the Tekoite, ... 6142
1Ch 11:28 Ira the son of I. the Tekoite, ... 6142
1Ch 27:9 sixth month was Ira the son of I........ 6142

ILAI (i'-lahee) See also ZALMON.
1Ch 11:29 the Hushathite, I. the Ahohite, ... 5866

ILL
Ge 41:3 them out of the river, i. favoured....... 7451
Ge 41:4 the i. favoured and lean fleshed kine... 7451
Ge 41:19 up after them, poor and very i. 7451
Ge 41:20 the lean and the i. favoured kine........ 7451
Ge 41:21 they were still i. favoured, as at 7451
Ge 41:27 the seven thin and i. favoured kine..... 7451
Ge 43:6 dealt so i. with me, as to tell........... 7489
De 15:21 blind, or have any i. blemish, ... 7451
Job 20:26 it shall go i. with him that is left........ 3415
Ps 106:32 so that it went i. with Moses for 3415
Isa 3:11 it shall be i. with him: for the........... 7451
Jer 40:4 if it seem i. unto thee to come.......... 7489
Joel 2:20 and his i. savour shall come up,......... 6709
Mic 3:4 they have behaved themselves i.......... 7489
Ro 13:10 Love worketh no i. to his................ 2556

ILL-FAVOURED See ILL and FAVOURED.

ILLUMINATED
Heb 10:32 in which, after ye were i., ye............ 5461

ILLYRICUM (il-lir'-ic-um)
Ro 15:19 and round about unto I., I have 2437

IMAGE See also IMAGE'S; IMAGES.
Ge 1:26 said, Let us make man in our i., ... 6754
Ge 1:27 God created man in his own i.,........... 6754
Ge 1:27 in the i. of God created he him;.......... 6754
Ge 5:3 in his own likeness, after his i. 6754
Ge 9:6 for in the i. of God made he man, ... 6754
Ex 20:4 not make unto thee any graven i.,...... 6754
Le 26:1 make you no idols nor graven i.,........ 6754
Le 26:1 neither rear you up a standing i., ... 6676
Le 26:1 neither shall ye set up any i. of 4906
De 4:16 and make you a graven i., the.................
De 4:23 and make you a graven i., or the ....
De 4:25 and make a graven i., or the..................
De 5:8 shalt not make thee any graven i.,............
De 9:12 they have made them a molten i.. ....
De 16:22 shalt thou set thee up any i. 4676
De 27:15 maketh any graven or molten i., ...
Jg 17:3 for my son, to make a graven i................
Jg 17:3 and a molten i.: now therefore I ....
Jg 17:4 thereof a graven i., and a molten i. ....
Jg 18:14 and a graven i. and a molten i.?..............
Jg 18:17 and took the graven i., and the...............
Jg 18:17 teraphim, and the molten i.: and the ....
Jg 18:18 and fetched the carved i., the ephod, ...
Jg 18:18 the teraphim, and the molten i.................
Jg 18:20 the teraphim, and the graven i.,...............
Jg 18:30 children of Dan set up the graven i.:.........
Jg 18:31 them up Micah's graven i., which.............
1Sa 19:13 Michal took an i., and laid it in 8655
1Sa 19:16 behold, there was an i. in the bed,..... 8655
2Ki 3:2 he put away the i. of Baal that 4676
2Ki 10:27 they brake down the i. of Baal, and.... 4676
2Ki 21:7 he set a graven i. of the grove that he......
2Ch 3:10 he made two cherubims of i. work, ... 6816
2Ch 33:7 And he set a carved i., the idol ....
Job 4:16 an i. was before mine eyes, there...... 8544
Ps 73:20 thou shalt despise their i.................. 6754
Ps 106:19 Horeb, and worshipped the molten i.. ....
Isa 40:19 The workman melteth a graven i.,............
Isa 40:20 workman to prepare a graven i., ...
Isa 44:9 They that make a graven i. are all............
Isa 44:10 formed a god, or molten a graven i. ....
Isa 44:15 he maketh it a graven i., and falleth.........
Isa 44:17 he maketh a god, even his graven i. ....
Isa 45:20 set up the wood of their graven i., ...
Isa 48:5 hath done them, and my graven i.,............
Isa 48:5 and my molten i., hath commanded...........
Jer 10:14 is confounded by the graven i........... 6459
Jer 10:14 for his molten i. is falsehood, and...........
Jer 51:17 is confounded by the graven i.:.......... 6459
Jer 51:17 for his molten i. is falsehood, and............
Eze 8:3 was the seat of the i. of jealousy, ... 5566
Eze 8:5 altar this i. of jealousy in the entry..... 5566
Da 2:31 king, sawest, and behold a great i.. 6755
Da 2:31 This great i., whose brightness was.... 6755
Da 2:34 which smote the i. upon his feet, ... 6755
Da 2:35 and the stone that smote the i........... 6755
Da 3:1 the king made an i. of gold, whose..... 6755
Da 3:2 to the dedication of the i. which........ 6755
Da 3:3 unto the dedication of the i. that........ 6755
Da 3:3 set up; and they stood before the i...... 6755
Da 3:5 fall down and worship the golden i...... 6755
Da 3:7 down and worshipped the golden i....... 6755
Da 3:10 fall down and worship the golden i....... 6755
Da 3:12 nor worship the golden i. which......... 6755
Da 3:14 nor worship the golden i. which I........ 6755
Da 3:15 fall down and worship the i. which...... 6755
Da 3:18 nor worship the golden i. which 6755
Ho 3:4 and without an i., and without an 6755
Na 1:14 cut off the graven i. and the molten i.. 6755
Hab 2:18 What profiteth the graven i. that........ 6755
Hab 2:18 the molten i., and a teacher of lies, ... 6755
Mt 22:20 Whose is this i. and superscription? 1504
Mk 12:16 Whose is this i. and superscription? 1504
Lu 20:24 Whose i. and superscription hath .. 1504
Ac 19:35 i. which fell down from Jupiter?................
Ro 1:23 into an i. made like to corruptible....... 1504
Ro 8:29 conformed to the i. of his Son, that 1504
Ro 11:4 not bowed the knee to the i. of Baal........
1Co 11:7 as he is the i. and glory of God: 1504
1Co 15:49 as we have borne the i. of the earthy, .1504
1Co 15:49 also bear the i. of the heavenly...............
2Co 3:18 changed into the same i. from glory.... 1504
2Co 4:4 gospel of Christ, who is the i. of God, .1504
Col 1:15 Who is the i. of the invisible God, ... 1504
Col 3:10 after the i. of him that created him:.... 1504
Heb 1:3 and the express i. of his person,........ 5481
Heb 10:1 not the very image of the things, ... 1504
Re 13:14 they should make an i. to the beast,... 1504
Re 13:15 to give life unto the i. of the beast, ... 1504
Re 13:15 i. of the beast should both speak,....... 1504
Re 13:15 not worship the i. of the beast 1504
Re 14:9 man worship the beast and his i.,....... 1504
Re 14:11 who worship the beast and his i.,....... 1504
Re 15:2 victory over the beast, and over his i.,.1504

Re 16:2 upon them which worshipped his **i.** *1504*
Re 19:20 and them that worshipped his **i.** *1504*
Re 20:4 worshipped the beast, neither his **i.** *1504*

IMAGERY
Eze 8:12 man in the chambers of his **i.**? 4906

IMAGE'S
Da 2:32 This **i.** head was of fine gold, 6755

IMAGES
Ge 31:19 Rachel had stolen the **i.** that were 8655
Ge 31:34 Rachel had taken the **i.**, and put 8655
Ge 31:35 he searched, but found not the **i.** 8655
Ex 23:24 and quite break down their **i.** 4676
Ex 34:13 break their **i.**, and cut down their 4676
Le 26:30 cut down your **i.**, and cast your 2553
Nu 33:52 destroy all their molten **i.**, and
De 7:5 and break down their **i.**, and cut 4676
De 7:5 and burn their graven **i.** with fire
De 7:25 The graven **i.** of their gods shall ye
De 12:3 ye shall hew down the graven **i.** of
1Sa 6:5 ye shall make **i.** of your emerods, 6754
1Sa 6:5 and **i.** of your mice that mar the 6754
1Sa 6:11 of gold and the **i.** of their emerods, 6754
2Sa 5:21 And there they left their **i.**, and 6091
1Ki 14:9 made thee other gods, and molten **i.**,
1Ki 14:23 built them high places, and **i.**, 4676
2Ki 10:26 forth the **i.** out of the house of Baal, 4676
2Ki 11:18 and his **i.** brake they in pieces 6754
2Ki 17:10 they set them up **i.** and groves 4676
2Ki 17:16 made them molten **i.**, even two calves,
2Ki 17:41 and served their graven **i.**, both
2Ki 18:4 brake the **i.**, and cut down the 4676
2Ki 23:14 And he brake in pieces the **i.**, 4676
2Ki 23:24 wizards, and the **i.**, and the idols, 8655
2Ch 14:3 and brake down the **i.**, and cut 4676
2Ch 14:5 away...the high places and the **i.**:
2Ch 23:17 his altars and his **i.** in pieces, 6754
2Ch 28:2 and made also molten **i.** for Baalim.
2Ch 31:1 Judah, and brake the **i.** in pieces, 4676
2Ch 33:19 and set up groves and graven **i.**,
2Ch 33:22 sacrificed unto all the the carved **i.**
2Ch 34:3 and the groves, and the carved **i.**,
2Ch 34:3 the groves...and the molten **i.**,
2Ch 34:4 and the **i.**, that were on high above 2553
2Ch 34:4 and the groves, and the carved **i.**,
2Ch 34:4 the groves...and the molten **i.**
2Ch 34:7 beaten the graven **i.** into powder, 6456
Ps 78:58 him to jealousy with their graven **i.** 6456
Ps 97:7 be all they that serve graven **i.**,
Isa 10:10 and whose graven **i.** did excel
Isa 17:8 made, either the groves, or the **i.** 2553
Isa 21:9 and all the graven **i.** of her gods
Isa 27:9 the groves and **i.** shall not stand 2553
Isa 30:22 covering of thy graven **i.** of silver,
Isa 30:22 ornament of thy molten **i.** of gold:
Isa 41:29 their molten **i.** are wind and confusion.
Isa 42:8 neither my praise to graven **i.**
Isa 42:17 ashamed, that trust in graven **i.**,
Isa 42:17 that say to the molten **i.**, Ye are our
Jer 8:19 me to anger with their graven **i.**,
Jer 43:13 He shall break also the **i.** of 4676
Jer 50:2 confounded, her **i.** are broken in 1544
Jer 50:38 for it is the land of graven **i.**, and
Jer 51:47 upon the graven **i.** of Babylon:
Jer 51:52 do judgment upon her graven **i.**:
Eze 6:4 your **i.** shall be broken: and I will 2553
Eze 6:6 and your **i.** may be cut down, and 2553
Eze 7:20 made the **i.** of their abominations 6754
Eze 16:17 and madest to thyself **i.** of men, and 6754
Eze 21:21 he consulted with **i.**, he looked in 8655
Eze 23:14 the **i.** of the Chaldeans pourtrayed 6754
Eze 30:13 cause their **i.** to cease out of Noph; 457
Ho 10:1 his land they have made goodly **i.** 4676
Ho 10:2 their altars, he shall spoil their **i.** 4676
Ho 11:2 and burned incense to graven **i.**
Ho 13:2 and have made them molten **i.** of their
Am 5:26 Moloch and Chiun your **i.**, the 6754
Mic 1:7 all the graven **i.** thereof shall be
Mic 5:13 Thy graven **i.** also will I cut off, 4676
Mic 5:13 and thy standing **i.** out of the midst

IMAGE-WORK See IMAGE and WORK.

IMAGINATION See also IMAGINATIONS.
Ge 6:5 every **i.** of the thoughts of his 3336
Ge 8:21 the **i.** of man's heart is evil from 3336
De 29:19 I walk in the **i.** of mine heart, 8307
De 31:21 for I know their **i.** which they go 3336
1Ch 29:18 keep this for ever in the **i.** of the 3336
Jer 3:17 after the **i.** of their evil heart 8307
Jer 7:24 and in the **i.** of their evil heart, 8307
Jer 9:14 the **i.** of their own heart, and after 8307
Jer 11:8 one in the **i.** of their evil heart: 8307
Jer 13:10 walk in the **i.** of their heart, and 8307
Jer 16:12 one after the **i.** of his evil heart, 8307
Jer 18:12 every one do the **i.** of his evil heart 8307
Jer 23:17 after the **i.** of his own heart, 8307
Lu 1:51 proud in the **i.** of their hearts. *1271*

IMAGINATIONS
1Ch 28:9 all the **i.** of the thoughts: if thou 3336
Pr 6:18 An heart that deviseth wicked **i.**, 4284
La 3:60 and all their **i.** against me. 4284
La 3:61 Lord, and all their **i.** against me; 4284
Ro 1:21 became vain in their **i.**, and their *1261*
2Co 10:5 Casting down **i.**, and every high *3053*

IMAGINE See also IMAGINED; IMAGINETH.
Job 6:26 Do ye **i.** to reprove words, and 2803
Job 21:27 the devices which ye wrongfully **i.** 2554
Ps 2:1 and the people **i.** a vain thing? 1897
Ps 38:12 and **i.** deceits all the day long. 1897
Ps 62:3 will ye **i.** mischief against a man? 2050
Ps 140:2 Which **i.** mischiefs in their heart; 2803
Pr 12:20 in the heart of them that **i.** evil: 2790
Ho 7:15 yet do they **i.** mischief against 2803
Na 1:9 What do ye **i.** against the Lord? 2803
Zec 7:10 you **i.** evil against his brother 2803
Zec 8:17 none of you **i.** evil in your hearts
Ac 4:25 rage, and the people **i.** vain things? *3191*

IMAGINED
Ge 11:6 them, which they have **i.** to do. 2161
Ps 10:2 in the devices that they have **i.** 2803
Ps 21:11 they **i.** a mischievous device, 2803

IMAGINETH
Na 1:11 that **i.** evil against the Lord, 2803

IMLA (im'-lah) See also IMLAH.
2Ch 18:7 the same is Micaiah the son of **I.** 3229
2Ch 18:8 quickly Micaiah the son of **I.** 3229

IMLAH (im'-lah) See also IMLA.
1Ki 22:8 one man, Micaiah the son of **I.**, 3229
1Ki 22:9 hither Micaiah the son of **I.** 3229

IMMANUEL (im-man'-u-el) See also EMMANUEL.
Isa 7:14 a son, and shall call his name **I.** 6005
Isa 8:8 fill the breadth of the land, O **I.** 6005

IMMEDIATELY
Mt 4:22 And they **i.** left the ship, and *2112*
Mt 8:3 And **i.** his leprosy was cleansed. *2112*
Mt 14:31 And **i.** Jesus stretched forth his *2112*
Mt 20:34 **i.** their eyes received sight, and *2112*
Mt 24:29 **i. after the tribulation of those** *2112*
Mt 26:74 the man. And **i.** the cock crew. *2112*
Mk 1:12 **i.** the spirit driveth him into the *2117*
Mk 1:28 **i.** his fame spread abroad *2117*
Mk 1:31 **i.** the fever left her, and she *2112*
Mk 1:42 **i.** the leprosy departed from him, *2112*
Mk 2:8 **i.** when Jesus perceived in his *2112*
Mk 2:12 And **i.** he arose, took up the bed, *2112*
Mk 4:5 **and i. it sprang up, because it** *2112*
Mk 4:15 **Satan cometh i., and taketh away** *2112*
Mk 4:16 **word, i. receive it with gladness;** *2112*
Mk 4:17 **word's sake, i. they are offended** *2112*
Mk 4:26 **i. he putteth in the sickle,** *2112*
Mk 5:2 **i.** there met him out of the tombs *2112*
Mk 5:30 Jesus, **i.** knowing in himself that *2112*
Mk 6:27 **i.** the king sent an executioner, *2112*
Mk 6:50 **i.** he talked with them, and saith *2112*
Mk 10:52 And **i.** he received his sight, and *2112*
Mk 14:43 And **i.**, while he yet spake, *2112*
Lu 1:64 And his mouth was opened **i.**, and *3916*
Lu 4:39 **i.** she arose and ministered unto *3916*
Lu 5:13 **i.** the leprosy departed from him. *2112*
Lu 5:25 And **i.** he rose up before them, *3916*
Lu 6:49 **beat vehemently, and i. it fell;** *2112*
Lu 8:44 and **i.** her issue of blood stanched. *3916*
Lu 8:47 him, and how she was healed **i.** *3916*
Lu 12:36 **they may open unto him i** *2112*
Lu 13:13 and **i.** she was made straight, *3916*
Lu 18:43 And **i.** he received his sight, and *3916*
Lu 19:11 kingdom of God should **i.** appear. *3916*
Lu 19:40 **peace, the stones would i. cry out.**
Lu 22:60 And **i.**, while he yet spake, the *3916*
Joh 5:9 **i.** the man was made whole, and *2112*
Joh 6:21 **i.** the ship was at the land *2112*
Joh 13:30 received the sop went **i.** out: *2112*
Joh 18:27 again: and **i.** the cock crew. *2112*
Joh 21:3 forth, and entered into a ship **i.** *2117*
Ac 3:7 and **i.** his feet and ancle bones *3916*
Ac 9:18 **i.** there fell from his eyes as it *2112*
Ac 9:34 make thy bed. And he arose **i.** *2112*
Ac 10:33 **I.** therefore I sent to thee; and *1824*
Ac 11:11 **i.** there were three men already *1824*
Ac 12:23 And **i.** the angel of the Lord smote *3916*
Ac 13:11 And **i.** there fell on him a mist and *3916*
Ac 16:10 **i.** we endeavoured to go into *2112*
Ac 16:26 and **i.** all the doors were opened, *3916*
Ac 17:10 the brethren **i.** sent away Paul *2112*
Ac 17:14 **i.** the brethren sent away Paul *2112*
Ac 21:32 Who **i.** took soldiers and *1824*
Ga 1:16 **i.** I conferred not with flesh and *2112*
Re 4:2 And **i.** I was in the spirit: and *2112*

IMMER (im'-mur)
1Ch 9:12 son of Meshillemith, the son of **I.**; 564
1Ch 24:14 to Bilgah, the sixteenth to **I.**, 564
Ezr 2:37 The children of **I.**, a thousand fifty 564
Ezr 2:59 Tel-harsa, Cherub, Addan, and **I.** 564
Ezr 10:20 of the sons of **I.**: Hanani, and 564
Ne 3:29 them repaired Zadok the son of **I.** 564
Ne 7:40 The children of **I.**, a thousand fifty 564
Ne 7:61 Tel-haresha, Cherub, Addon, and **I.** 564
Ne 11:13 son of Meshillemoth, the son of **I.**, 564
Jer 20:1 Now Pashur the son of **I.** the priest, 564

IMMORTAL
1Ti 1:17 Now unto the King eternal, **i.**, *862*

IMMORTALITY
Ro 2:7 glory and honour and **i.**, eternal *861*
1Co 15:53 and this mortal must put on **i.** *110*
1Co 15:54 this mortal shall have put on **i.**, *110*
1Ti 6:16 Who only hath **i.**, dwelling in the *110*
2Ti 1:10 hath brought life and **i.** to light *861*

IMMOVABLE See UNMOVABLE.

IMMUTABILITY
Heb 6:17 The **i.** of his counsel, confirmed it *276*

IMMUTABLE
Heb 6:18 That by two **i.** things, in which it *276*

IMNA (im'-nah) See also IMNAH; JIMNA.
1Ch 7:35 Zophah, and **I.**, and Shelesh, and 3234

IMNAH (im'-nah) see also IMNA; JIMNAH.
1Ch 7:30 sons of Asher; **I.**, and Ishuah, 3232
2Ch 31:14 And Kore the son of **I.** the Levite, 3232

IMPART See also IMPARTED.
Lu 3:11 let him **i.** to him that hath none; *3330*
Ro 1:11 **i.** unto you some spiritual gift, *3330*

IMPARTED
Job 39:17 hath he **i.** to her understanding. 2505
1Th 2:8 were willing to have **i.** unto you, *3330*

IMPEDIMENT
Mk 7:32 deaf, and had an **i.** in his speech; *3424*

IMPENITENT
Ro 2:5 But, after thy hardness and **i.** heart *279*

IMPERFECT See UNPERFECT.

IMPERIOUS
Eze 16:30 the work of an **i.** whorish woman; 7986

IMPLACABLE
Ro 1:31 without natural affection, **i.**, *786*

IMPLEAD
Ac 19:38 deputies: let them **i.** one another. *1458*

IMPORTUNITY
Lu 11:8 **yet because of his i. he will rise** *335*

IMPOSE See also IMPOSED.
Ezr 7:24 it shall not be lawful to **i.** toll, 7412

IMPOSED
Heb 9:10 **i.** on them until the time of *1945*

IMPOSSIBLE
Mt 17:20 **and nothing shall be i. unto you** *101*
Mt 19:26 **With men this is i.: but with God** *102*
Mk 10:27 **With men it is i., but not with God** *102*
Lu 1:37 with God nothing shall be **i.** *101*

Lu 17:1 **is i. but that offences will come:**..... *418*
Lu 18:27 **things which are i. with men are**.... *102*
Heb 6:4 For it is **i.** for those who were once..... *102*
Heb 6:18 in which it was **i.** for God to lie,.......... *102*
Heb 11:6 without faith it is **i.** to please him: *102*

IMPOTENT
Joh 5:3 lay a great multitude of **i.** folk,............ *770*
Joh 5:7 The **i.** man answered him, Sir, I.......... *770*
Ac 4:9 the good deed done to the **i.** man,....... *772*
Ac 14:8 certain man at Lystra, **i.** in his feet,..... *102*

IMPOVERISH See also IMPOVERISHED.
Jer 5:17 they shall **i.** thy fenced cities,........... 7567

IMPOVERISHED
Jg 6:6 And Israel was greatly **i.** because....... 1809
Isa 40:20 is so **i.** that he hath no oblation 5533
Mal 1:4 Whereas, Edom saith, We are **i.**,....... 7567

IMPRISONED
Ac 22:19 know that I **i.** and beat in every......... *5439*

IMPRISONMENT See also IMPRISONMENTS.
Ezr 7:26 or to confiscation of goods, or to **i.**..... 613
Heb 11:36 yea, moreover of bonds and **i.**:.......... *5438*

IMPRISONMENTS
2Co 6:5 In stripes, in **i.**, in tumults, in........... *5438*

IMPUDENT
Pr 7:13 kissed him, and with an **i.** face 5810
Eze 2:4 **i.** children and stiff hearted. 7186,6440
Eze 3:7 all the house of Israel are **i.**....... 2389,4696

IMPUTE See also IMPUTED;IMPUTETH;IMPUTING.
1Sa 22:15 king **i.** any thing unto his servant, ... 7760
2Sa 19:19 Let not my lord **i.** iniquity unto.......... 2803
Ro 4:8 to whom the Lord will not **i.** sin. *3049*

IMPUTED
Le 7:18 it be **i.** unto him that offereth it: 2803
Le 17:4 blood shall be **i.** unto that man; he 2803
Ro 4:11 might be **i.** unto them also:............... *3049*
Ro 4:22 therefore it was **i.** to him for............ *3049*
Ro 4:23 sake alone, that it was **i.** to him;........ *3049*
Ro 4:24 to whom it shall be **i.**, if we believe.... *3049*
Ro 5:13 sin is not **i.** when there is no law....... *1677*
Jas 2:23 and it was **i.** unto him for................ *3049*

IMPUTETH
Ps 32:2 whom the Lord **i.** not iniquity,........... 2803
Ro 4:6 unto whom God **i.** righteousness........ *3049*

IMPUTING
Hab 1:11 offend, **i.** this his power unto his God. ......
2Co 5:19 not **i.** their trespasses unto them; *3049*

IMRAH (im'-rah)
1Ch 7:36 and Shual, and Beri, and **I.**,.............. 3236

IMRI (im'-ri)
1Ch 9:4 the son of **I.**, the son of Bani,............ 556
Ne 3:2 them builded Zaccur the son of **I.**....... 556

IN See in the APPENDIX; also INASMUCH; INDEED; INGATHERING; INNER; INSIDE; INSOMUCH; INTO; INWARD; HEREIN; THEREIN; WHEREIN; WITHIN.

INASMUCH
De 19:6 of death, **i.** as he hated him not......... 3588
Ru 3:10 **i.** as thou followedst not young.......... 1115
Mt 25:40 **I. as ye have done it unto one**.*1909,3745*
Mt 25:45 **I. as ye did it not to one**........ *1909,3745*
Ro 11:13 **i.** as I am the apostle of the....... *1909,3745*
Php 1:7 **i.** as both in my bonds, and in.... *1909,3745*
Heb 3:3 **i.** as he who hath builded the..... *2596,3745*
Heb 7:20 And **i.** as not without an oath..... *2596,3745*
1Pe 4:13 **i.** as ye are partakers of Christ's........ *2526*

INCENSE See also FRANKINCENSE; INCENSED.
Ex 25:6 for anointing oil, and for sweet **i.**, ... 7004
Ex 30:1 make an altar to burn **i.** upon: 7004
Ex 30:7 shall burn thereon sweet **i.** every....... 7004
Ex 30:7 the lamps, he shall burn **i.** upon it. ....
Ex 30:8 at even, he shall burn **i.** upon it,........ 6999
Ex 30:8 a perpetual **i.** before the Lord 7004
Ex 30:9 Ye shall offer no strange **i.** thereon,..... 7004
Ex 30:27 and his vessels, and the altar of **i.**,...... 7004
Ex 31:8 all his furniture, and the altar of **i.**,..... 7004
Ex 31:11 and sweet **i.** for the holy place: 7004
Ex 35:8 anointing oil, and for the sweet **i.**,....... 7004
Ex 35:15 And the **i.** altar, and his staves,........... 7004
Ex 35:15 the anointing oil, and the sweet **i.**, ... 7004
Ex 35:28 anointing oil, and for the sweet **i.**....... 7004
Ex 37:25 made the **i.** altar of shittim wood:....... 7004
Ex 37:29 and the pure **i.** of sweet spices,........ 7004
Ex 39:38 the anointing oil, and the sweet **i.**, ... 7004
Ex 40:5 altar of gold for the **i.** before the ark .. 7004
Ex 40:27 And he burnt sweet **i.** thereon; as...... 7004
Le 4:7 the horns of the altar of sweet **i.** 7004
Le 10:1 put fire therein, and put **i.** thereon, ... 7004
Le 16:12 and his hands full of sweet **i.** beaten... 7004
Le 16:13 he shall put the **i.** upon the fire 7004
Le 16:13 of the **i.** may cover the mercy seat..... 7004
Nu 4:16 light, and the sweet **i.**, and the daily... 7004
Nu 7:14 of ten shekels of gold, full of **i.**.......... 7004
Nu 7:20 of gold of ten shekels, full of **i.**.......... 7004
Nu 7:26, 32,38,44,50,56,62,68,74,80 One golden spoon of ten shekels, full of **i.** 7004
Nu 7:86 golden spoons were twelve, full of **i.**,.. 7004
Nu 16:7 put **i.** in them before the Lord to....... 7004
Nu 16:17 man his censer, and put **i.** in them, ... 7004
Nu 16:18 fire in them, and laid **i.** thereon, ... 7004
Nu 16:35 hundred and fifty men that offered **i.**... 7004
Nu 16:40 near to offer **i.** before the Lord; 7004
Nu 16:46 from off the altar, and put on **i.**, ... 7004
Nu 16:47 put on **i.**, and made an atonement 7004
De 33:10 they shall put **i.** before thee, and 7004
1Sa 2:28 burn **i.**, to wear an ephod before......... 7004
1Ki 3:3 he sacrificed and burnt **i.** in high........ 6999
1Ki 9:25 and he burnt **i.** upon the altar that...... 6999
1Ki 11:8 wives, which burnt **i.** and sacrificed 6999
1Ki 12:33 offered upon the altar, and burnt **i.**..... 6999
1Ki 13:1 stood by the altar to burn **i.**.............. 6999
1Ki 13:2 high places that burn **i.** upon thee, ... 6999
1Ki 22:43 the people offered and burnt **i.** yet 6999
2Ki 12:3 people still sacrificed and burnt **i.** 6999
2Ki 14:4 people did sacrifice and burnt **i.** on 6999
2Ki 15:4 people sacrificed and burnt **i.** still 6999
2Ki 15:35 and burned **i.** still in the high............ 6999
2Ki 16:4 and burnt **i.** in the high places, ... 6999
2Ki 17:11 they burnt **i.** in all the high places, ... 6999
2Ki 18:4 children of Israel did burn **i.** to it: 6999
2Ki 22:17 and have burned **i.** unto other gods, ... 6999
2Ki 23:5 had ordained to burn **i.** in the high...... 6999
2Ki 23:5 them also that burned **i.** unto Baal,..... 6999
2Ki 23:8 where the priests had burned **i.**, ... 6999
1Ch 6:49 offering, and on the altar of **i.**,........... 7004
1Ch 23:13 for ever, to burn **i.** before the Lord,... 6999
1Ch 28:18 for the altar of **i.** refined gold by........ 7004
2Ch 2:4 and to burn before him sweet **i.**,......... 7004
2Ch 13:11 burnt sacrifices and sweet **i.**:............ 7004
2Ch 25:14 before them, and burned **i.** to them. ... 6999
2Ch 26:16 to burn **i.** upon the altar of 6999
2Ch 26:16 to burn...upon the altar of **i.**. 7004
2Ch 26:18 Uzziah, to burn **i.** unto the Lord, ... 6999
2Ch 26:18 that are consecrated to burn **i.**: 6999
2Ch 26:19 had a censer in his hand to burn **i.**: 6999
2Ch 26:19 the Lord, from beside the **i.** altar....... 7004
2Ch 28:3 he burnt **i.** in the valley of the son 6999
2Ch 28:4 also and burnt **i.** in the high places, ... 6999
2Ch 28:25 places to burn **i.** unto other gods, ... 6999
2Ch 29:7 not burned **i.** nor offered burnt.......... 7004
2Ch 29:11 minister unto him, and burn **i.**........... 6999
2Ch 30:14 all the altars for **i.** took they away,..... 6999
2Ch 32:12 one altar, and burn **i.** upon it? 6999
2Ch 34:25 and have burned **i.** unto other gods, ... 6999
Ps 66:15 of fatlings, with the **i.** of rams; 7004
Ps 141:2 prayer be set forth before thee as **i.** ... 7004
Isa 1:13 **i.** is an abomination unto me; 7004
Isa 43:23 offering, nor wearied thee with **i.**....... 3828
Isa 60:6 they shall bring gold and **i.**:and 3828
Isa 65:3 burneth **i.** upon altars of brick; 6999
Isa 65:7 burned **i.** upon the mountains, ... 6999
Isa 66:3 he that burneth **i.**, as if he blessed..... 3828
Jer 1:16 have burned **i.** unto other gods,........... 6999
Jer 6:20 cometh there to me **i.** from Sheba,..... 3828
Jer 7:9 and burn **i.** unto Baal, and walk 6999
Jer 11:12 the gods unto whom they offer **i.** 6999
Jer 11:13 even altars to burn **i.** unto Baal. 6999
Jer 11:17 me to anger in offering **i.** unto Baal. ... 6999
Jer 17:26 and meat offerings, and **i.**, and 3828
Jer 18:15 they have burned **i.** to vanity, and...... 6999
Jer 19:4 have burned **i.** in it unto other gods,... 6999
Jer 19:13 **i.** unto all the host of heaven,........... 6999
Jer 32:29 roofs they have offered **i.** unto Baal,... 6999
Jer 41:5 with offerings and **i.** in their hand,...... 3828
Jer 44:3 in that they went to burn **i.**, and........ 6999
Jer 44:5 to burn no **i.** unto other gods. 6999
Jer 44:8 burning **i.** unto other gods in the........ 6999
Jer 44:15 wives had burned **i.** unto other gods, .. 6999
Jer 44:17 to burn **i.** unto the queen of............. 6999
Jer 44:18 to burn **i.** to the queen of heaven,...... 6999
Jer 44:19 burned **i.** to the queen of heaven, ... 6999
Jer 44:21 The **i.** that ye burned in the cities...... 7002
Jer 44:23 Because ye have burned **i.**, and......... 6999
Jer 44:25 to burn **i.** to the queen of heaven,...... 6999
Jer 48:35 and him that burneth **i.** to his gods..... 6999
Eze 8:11 and a thick cloud of **i.** went up. 7004
Eze 16:18 set mine oil and mine **i.** before 7004
Eze 23:41 thou hast set mine **i.** and mine oil. 7004
Ho 2:13 wherein she burned **i.** to them,.......... 6999
Ho 4:13 burn **i.** upon the hills, under oaks........ 6999
Ho 11:2 and burned **i.** to graven images,......... 6999
Hab 1:16 and burn **i.** unto their drag;.............. 6999
Mal 1:11 in every place **i.** shall be offered 6999
Lu 1:9 his lot was to burn **i.** when he went ... *2370*
Lu 1:10 praying without at the time of **i.**......... *2368*
Lu 1:11 on the right side of the altar of **i.**........ *2368*
Re 8:3 there was given unto him much **i.**, ... *2368*
Re 8:4 the smoke of the **i.**, which came *2368*

INCENSED
Isa 41:11 all they that were **i.** against thee........ 2734
Isa 45:24 and all that are **i.** against him shall...... 2734

INCLINE See also INCLINED; INCLINETH.
Jos 24:23 and **i.** your heart unto the Lord 5186
1Ki 8:58 That he may **i.** our hearts unto him, ... 5186
Ps 17:6 **i.** thine ear unto me, and hear my...... 5186
Ps 45:10 and consider, and **i.** thine ear; 5186
Ps 49:4 I will **i.** mine ear to a parable: 5186
Ps 71:2 escape: **i.** thine ear unto me, and....... 5186
Ps 78:1 **i.** your ears to the words of my......... 5186
Ps 88:2 thee: **i.** thine ear unto my cry; 5186
Ps 102:2 **i.** thine ear unto me: in the day 5186
Ps 119:36 **I.** my heart unto thy testimonies,....... 5186
Ps 141:4 **I.** not my heart to any evil thing, ... 5186
Pr 2:2 thou **i.** thine ear unto wisdom,........... 7181
Pr 4:20 **i.** thine ear unto my sayings............. 5186
Isa 37:17 **I.** thine ear, O Lord, and hear;.......... 5186
Isa 55:3 **I.** your ear, and come unto me:......... 5186
Da 9:18 O my God, **i.** thine ear, and hear;...... 5186

INCLINED
Jg 9:3 and their hearts **i.** to follow.............. 5186
Ps 40:1 and he **i.** unto me, and heard my 5186
Ps 116:2 Because he hath **i.** his ear unto me, ... 5186
Ps 119:112 I have **i.** mine heart to perform 5186
Pr 5:13 nor **i.** mine ear to them that............. 5186
Jer 7:24 hearkened not, nor **i.** their ear, ... 5186
Jer 7:26 not unto me, nor **i.** their ear,............. 5186
Jer 11:8 they obeyed not, nor **i.** their ear,......... 5186
Jer 17:23 obeyed not, neither **i.** their ear,......... 5186
Jer 25:4 hearkened, nor **i.** your ear to hear. 5186
Jer 34:14 not unto me, neither **i.** their ear. 5186
Jer 35:15 ye have not **i.** your ear, nor............. 5186
Jer 44:5 nor **i.** their ear to turn from their....... 5186

INCLINETH
Pr 2:18 her house **i.** unto death, and her........ 7743

INCLOSE See also INCLOSED; INCLOSINGS.
Ca 8:9 we will **i.** her with boards of cedar. 6696

INCLOSED
Ex 39:6 onyx stones **i.** in ouches of gold,........ 4142
Ex 39:13 they were **i.** in ouches of gold in........ 4142
Jg 20:43 Thus they **i.** the Benjamites.............. 3803
Ps 17:10 They are **i.** in their own fat: with....... 5462
Ps 22:16 assembly of the wicked have **i.** me: 5362
Ca 4:12 A garden **i.** is my sister, my............. 5274
La 3:9 He hath **i.** my ways with hewn.......... 1443
Lu 5:6 they **i.** a great multitude of fishes:...... *4788*

INCLOSINGS.
Ex 28:20 shall be set in gold in their **i.**............. 4396
Ex 39:13 in ouches of gold in their **i.**............. 4396

INCONTINENCY
1Co 7:5 Satan tempt you not for your **i.**.......... *192*

INCONTINENT
2Ti 3:3 false accusers, **i.**, fierce, despisers....... *193*

INCORRUPTIBLE See also UNCORRUPTIBLE.
1Co 9:25 corruptible crown; but we an **i.**........... *862*
1Co 15:52 and the dead shall be raised **i.**,............ *862*
1Pe 1:4 To an inheritance **i.**, and undefiled, ... *862*
1Pe 1:23 corruptible seed, but of **i.**,................. *862*

INCORRUPTION
1Co 15:42 in corruption; it is raised in **i.** 861
1Co 15:50 neither doth corruption inherit **i.** 861
1Co 15:53 must put on **i.**, and this mortal 861
1Co 15:54 corruptible shall have put on **i.**, 861

INCREASE See also INCREASED; INCREASEST; INCREASETH; INCREASING.
Ge 47:24 to pass in the **i.**, that ye shall give 8393
Le 19:25 may yield unto you the **i.** thereof: 8393
Le 25:7 shall all the **i.** thereof be meat 8393
Le 25:12 ye shall eat the **i.** thereof out of 8393
Le 25:16 thou shalt **i.** the price thereof, and 7235
Le 25:20 shall not sow, nor gather in our **i.**: 8393
Le 25:36 Take thou no usury of him, or **i.**: 8635
Le 25:37 nor lend him thy victuals for **i.** 4768
Le 26:4 the land shall yield her **i.**, and the 2981
Le 26:20 your land shall not yield her **i.**, 2981
Nu 18:30 as the **i.** of the threshing floor, 8393
Nu 18:30 and as the **i.** of the winepress. 8393
Nu 32:14 an **i.** of sinful men, to augment 8635
De 6:3 that ye may **i.** mightily, as the 7235
De 7:13 the **i.** of thy kine, and the flocks 7698
De 7:22 once, lest the beasts of the field **i.** 7235
De 14:22 truly tithe all the **i.** of thy seed, 8393
De 14:28 bring forth all the tithe of thine **i.** 8393
De 16:15 God shall bless thee in all thine **i.**, 8393
De 26:12 tithing all the tithes of thine **i.** the 8393
De 28:4 thy cattle, the **i.** of thy kine, 7698
De 28:18 the **i.** of thy kine, and the flocks of 7698
De 28:51 or the **i.** of thy kine, or flocks of thy 7698
De 32:13 he might eat the **i.** of the fields; 8570
De 32:22 consume the earth with her **i.**, 2981
Jg 6:4 and destroyed the **i.** of the earth, 2981
Jg 9:29 **I.** thine army, and come out 7239
1Sa 2:33 all the **i.** of thine house shall die 4768
1Ch 27:23 Lord had said he would **i.** Israel 7235
1Ch 27:27 over the **i.** of the vineyards for the
2Ch 31:5 and of all the **i.** of the field; 8393
2Ch 32:28 Storehouses also for the **i.** of corn, 8393
Ezr 10:10 wives, to **i.** the trespass of Israel 3254
Ne 9:37 yieldeth much **i.** unto the kings 8393
Job 8:7 thy latter end should greatly **i.** 7685
Job 20:28 The **i.** of his house shall depart, 2981
Job 31:12 and would root out all mine **i.** 8393
Ps 44:12 not **i.** thy wealth by their price. 7235
Ps 62:10 if riches **i.**, set not your heart upon 5107
Ps 67:6 Then shall the earth yield her **i.**; 2981
Ps 71:21 Thou shalt **i.** my greatness, and 7235
Ps 73:12 in the world; they **i.** in riches. 7685
Ps 78:46 also their **i.** unto the caterpiller, 2981
Ps 85:12 and our land shall yield her **i.** 2981
Ps 107:37 which may yield fruits of **i.** 8393
Ps 115:14 The Lord shall **i.** you more and 3254
Pr 1:5 man will hear, and will **i.** learning; 3254
Pr 3:9 with the firstfruits of all thine **i.** 8393
Pr 9:9 man, and he will **i.** in learning. 3254
Pr 13:11 that gathereth by labour shall **i.** 7235
Pr 14:4 much **i.** is by the strength of the ox. 8393
Pr 18:20 the **i.** of his lips shall he be filled 8393
Pr 22:16 oppresseth the poor to **i.** his riches, 7235
Pr 28:28 when they perish, the righteous **i.** 7235
Ec 5:10 he that loveth abundance with **i.**: 8393
Ec 5:11 When goods **i.**, they are increased 7235
Ec 6:11 there be many things that **i.** vanity, 7235
Isa 9:7 Of the **i.** of his government and 4768
Isa 29:19 The meek also shall **i.** their joy 3254
Isa 30:23 and bread of the **i.** of the earth, 8393
Isa 57:9 and didst **i.** thy perfumes, and 7235
Jer 2:3 and the firstfruits of his **i.**: all that 8393
Jer 23:3 and they shall be fruitful and **i.** 7235
Eze 5:16 I will **i.** the famine upon you, and 3254
Eze 18:8 usury, neither hath taken any **i.**, 8635
Eze 18:13 upon usury, and hath taken **i.**: 8635
Eze 18:17 that hath not received usury nor **i.**, 8635
Eze 22:12 thou hast taken usury and **i.**, and 8635
Eze 34:27 and the earth shall yield her **i.**, 2981
Eze 36:11 and they shall **i.** and bring fruit: 7235
Eze 36:29 I will call for the corn, and will **i.** it, 7235
Eze 36:30 of the tree, and the **i.** of the field, 8570
Eze 36:37 I will **i.** them with men like a flock. 7235
Eze 48:18 and the **i.** thereof shall be for food 8393
Da 11:39 acknowledge and **i.** with glory: 7235
Ho 4:10 whoredom, and shall not **i.**: 6555
Zec 8:12 and the ground shall give her **i.**, 2981
Zec 10:8 shall **i.** as they have increased. 7235
Lu 17:5 said unto the Lord, **I.** our faith. 4369
Joh 3:30 He must **i.**, but I must decrease 837
1Co 3:6 Apollos watered; but God gave the **i.** 837
1Co 3:7 watereth; but God that giveth the **i.** 837
2Co 9:10 **i.** the fruits of your righteousness; 837
Eph 4:16 **i.** of the body unto the edifying 838
Col 2:19 increaseth with the **i.** of God. 838
1Th 3:12 the Lord make you to **i.** and abound 4121
1Th 4:10 that ye **i.** more and more; 4052
2Ti 2:16 they will **i.** unto more ungodliness. 4298

INCREASED
Ge 7:17 and the waters **i.**, and bare up the 7235
Ge 7:18 and were **i.** greatly upon the earth; 7235
Ge 30:30 and it is now **i.** unto a multitude; 6555
Ge 30:43 And the man **i.** exceedingly, and 6555
Ex 1:7 were fruitful, and **i.** abundantly, 8317
Ex 23:30 thou be **i.**, and inherit the land, 6509
1Sa 14:19 of the Philistines went on and **i.**: 7227
2Sa 15:12 for the people **i.** continually with 7227
1Ki 22:35 And the battle **i.** that day: and 5927
1Ch 4:38 house of their fathers **i.** greatly. 6555
1Ch 5:23 they **i.** from Bashan unto 7235
2Ch 18:34 And the battle **i.** that day: howbeit 5927
Ezr 9:6 for our iniquities are **i.** over our 7235
Job 1:10 and his substance is **i.** in the land. 6555
Ps 3:1 Lord, how are they **i.** that trouble 7231
Ps 4:7 that their corn and their wine **i.** 7231
Ps 49:16 when the glory of his house is **i.**; 7235
Ps 105:24 And he **i.** his people greatly; and 6509
Pr 9:11 and the years of thy life shall be **i.** 3254
Ec 2:9 So I was great, and **i.** more than 3254
Ec 5:11 increase, they are **i.** that eat them: 7231
Isa 9:3 the nation, and not **i.** the joy: 1431
Isa 26:15 Thou hast **i.** the nation, O Lord, 3254
Isa 26:15 thou hast **i.** the nation: thou art 3254
Isa 51:2 and blessed him, and **i.** him 7235
Jer 3:16 ye be multiplied and **i.** in the land, 6509
Jer 5:6 and their backslidings are **i.** 6105
Jer 15:8 Their widows are **i.** to me above 6105
Jer 29:6 that ye may be **i.** there, and not 7235
Jer 30:14 iniquity; because thy sins were **i.** 6105
Jer 30:15 because thy sins were **i.**, I have 6105
La 2:5 hath **i.** in the daughter of Judah 7235
Eze 16:7 and thou hast **i.** and waxen great, 7235
Eze 16:26 and hast **i.** thy whoredoms, to 7235
Eze 23:14 And that she **i.** her whoredoms: 3254
Eze 28:5 thy traffick hast thou **i.** thy riches, 7235
Eze 41:7 so **i.** from the lowest chamber 5927
Da 12:4 and fro, and knowledge shall be **i.** 7235
Ho 4:7 As they were **i.**, so they sinned 7230
Ho 10:1 of his fruit he hath **i.** the altars; 7235
Am 4:9 fig trees and your olive trees **i.**, 7235
Zec 10:8 they shall increase as they have **i.** 7235
Mk 4:8 **yield fruit that sprang up and i.** 837
Lu 2:52 Jesus **i.** in wisdom and stature, 4298
Ac 6:7 And the word of God **i.**; and the 837
Ac 9:22 Saul **i.** the more in strength, and 1743
Ac 16:5 the faith, and **i.** in number daily. 4052
2Co 10:15 having hope, when your faith is **i.**, 837
Re 3:17 **I am rich, and i. with goods, and** 4147

INCREASEST
Job 10:17 and **i.** thine indignation upon me; 7235

INCREASETH
Job 10:16 For it **i.** Thou huntest me as a 1342
Job 12:23 He **i.** the nations, and destroyeth 7679
Ps 74:23 rise up against thee **i.** continually. 5927
Pr 11:24 is that scattereth, and yet **i.**; 3254
Pr 16:21 sweetness of the lips **i.** learning. 3254
Pr 23:28 **i.** the transgressors among men. 3254
Pr 24:5 yea, a man of knowledge **i.** strength. 553
Pr 28:8 that by usury and unjust gain **i.** 7235
Pr 29:16 are multiplied, transgression **i.** 7235
Ec 1:18 he that **i.** knowledge, **i.** sorrow. 3254
Isa 40:29 that have no might he **i.** strength. 7235
Ho 12:1 he daily **i.** lies and desolation; 7235
Hab 2:6 to him that **i.** that which is not his 7235
Col 2:19 together, **i.** with the increase of God. 837

INCREASING
Col 1:10 and **i.** in the knowledge of God; 837

INCREDIBLE
Ac 26:8 it be thought a thing **i.** with you, 571

INCURABLE
2Ch 21:18 his bowels with an **i.** disease. 369,4832
Job 34:6 wound is **i.** without transgression. 605
Jer 15:18 my wound **i.**, which refuseth to be 605
Jer 30:12 Thy bruise is **i.**, and thy wound is 605
Jer 30:15 thy sorrow is **i.** for the multitude 605
Mic 1:9 For her wound is **i.**: for it is come 605

INDEBTED
Lu 11:4 **forgive every one that is i. to us** 3784

INDEED
Ge 17:19 thy wife shall bear thee a son **i.**; 61
Ge 20:12 And yet **i.** she is my sister; she is 546
Ge 37:8 to him. Shalt thou **i.** reign over us?
Ge 37:8 or shalt thou **i.** have dominion over us?
Ge 37:10 thy brethren **i.** come to bow down
Ge 40:15 For **i.** I was stolen away out of the
Ge 43:20 And said, O sir, we came **i.** down at
Ge 44:5 drinketh, and whereby **i.** he divineth?
Ex 19:5 if ye will obey my voice **i.**, and keep
Ex 23:22 But if thou shalt **i.** obey his voice, and
Le 10:18 ye should **i.** have eaten it in the holy
Nu 12:2 Hath the Lord **i.** spoken only by
Nu 21:2 If thou wilt **i.** deliver this people 389
Nu 22:37 am I not able **i.** to promote thee to 552
De 2:15 For **i.** the hand of the Lord was 1571
De 21:16 of the hated, which is **i.** the firstborn:
Jos 7:20 **I.** I have sinned against the Lord 546
1Sa 1:11 if thou wilt **i.** look on the affliction of
1Sa 2:30 I said **i.** that thy house, and the house
2Sa 14:5 I am **i.** a widow woman, and mine 61
2Sa 15:8 shall bring me again **i.** to Jerusalem,
1Ki 8:27 But will God **i.** dwell on the earth? 552
2Ki 14:10 Thou hast **i.** smitten Edom, and thine
1Ch 4:10 Oh that thou wouldest bless me **i.**, and
1Ch 21:17 I it is that have sinned and done evil **i.**:
Job 19:4 And be it **i.** that I have erred, 551
Job 19:5 If **i.** ye will magnify yourselves 551
Ps 58:1 Do ye **i.** speak righteousness, O 552
Isa 6:9 people, Hear ye **i.**, but understand not;
Isa 6:9 and see ye **i.**, but perceive not.
Jer 22:4 For if ye do this thing **i.**, then shall
Mt 3:11 I **i.** baptize you with water unto 3303
Mt 13:32 **Which i. is the least of all seeds:** 3303
Mt 20:23 them, **Ye shall drink i. of my cup,** 3303
Mt 23:27 **which i. appear beautiful outward,** 3303
Mt 26:41 **spirit i. is willing, but the flesh** 3303
Mk 1:8 I **i.** have baptized you with water: 3303
Mk 9:13 **That Elias is i. come, and they** 2532
Mk 10:39 **Ye shall i. drink of the cup that** 3303
Mk 11:32 John, that he was a prophet **i.** 3689
Mk 14:21 **The Son of man i. goeth, as it is** 3303
Lu 3:16 I **i.** baptize you with water; but 3303
Lu 11:48 **for they i. killed them, and ye** 3303
Lu 23:41 And we **i.** justly; for we receive the 3303
Lu 24:34 Saying, The Lord is risen **i.**, and 3689
Joh 1:47 **Behold an Israelite i., in whom is** 230
Joh 4:42 this is **i.** the Christ, the Saviour of 230
Joh 6:55 **For my flesh is meat i.,** 230
Joh 6:55 **and my blood is drink i.** 230
Joh 7:26 know **i.** that this is the very Christ? 230
Joh 8:31 **word, then are ye my disciples i.** 230
Joh 8:36 **make you free, ye shall be free i.** 3689
Ac 4:16 for that **i.** a noble miracle hath 3303
Ac 11:16 **John i. baptized with water; but** 3303
Ac 22:9 that were with me saw **i.** the light, 3303
Ro 6:11 to be dead **i.** unto sin, but alive 3303
Ro 8:7 the law of God, neither **i.** can be. 1063
Ro 14:20 All things **i.** are pure; but it is evil 3303
1Co 11:7 For a man **i.** ought not to cover his 3303
2Co 8:17 For **i.** he accepted the exhortation; 3303
2Co 11:1 in my folly: and **i.** bear with me. 235
Php 1:15 Some **i.** preach Christ even of envy 3303
Php 2:27 For **i.** he was sick nigh unto death: 2532
Php 3:1 to me **i.** is not grievous, but for you 3303
Col 2:23 Which things have **i.** a shew of 3303
1Th 4:10 And **i.** ye do it toward all the 1063
1Ti 5:3 Honour widows that are widows **i.** 3689
1Ti 5:5 Now she that is a widow **i.**, and 3689
1Ti 5:16 relieve them that are widows **i.** 3689
1Pe 2:4 disallowed **i.** of men, but chosen of 3303

INDIA (in'-de-ah)
Es 1:1 from **I.** even unto Ethiopia, 1912
Es 8:9 which are from **I.** unto Ethiopia, 1912

INDIGNATION
De 29:28 and in wrath, and in great **i.**, and 7110
2Ki 3:27 there was great **i.** against Israel: 7110
Ne 4:1 was wroth, and took great **i.**, and 3707
Es 5:9 he was full of **i.** against Mordecai. 2534

Job 10:17 and increasest thine **i.** upon me; 3708
Ps 69:24 Pour out thine **i.** upon them, and 2195
Ps 78:49 anger, wrath, and **i.**, and trouble, ... 2195
Ps 102:10 Because of thine **i.** and thy wrath: 2195
Isa 10:5 the staff in their hand is mine **i.** 2195
Isa 10:25 the **i.** shall cease, and mine anger 2195
Isa 13:5 the weapons of his **i.**, to destroy the .. 2195
Isa 26:20 moment, until the **i.** be overpast. 2195
Isa 30:27 his lips are full of **i.**, and his tongue 2195
Isa 30:30 with the **i.** of his anger, and with 2197
Isa 34:2 **i.** of the Lord is upon all nations, ... 7110
Isa 66:14 and his **i.** toward his enemies. 2194
Jer 10:10 shall not be able to abide his **i.** 2195
Jer 15:17 hand: for thou hast filled me with **i.** 2195
Jer 50:25 brought forth the weapons of his **i.** 2195
La 2:6 hath despised in the **i.** of his anger 2195
Eze 21:31 I will pour out mine **i.** upon thee, ... 2195
Eze 22:24 nor rained upon in the day of **i.**. 2195
Eze 22:31 I poured out mine **i.** upon them; 2195
Da 8:19 shall be in the last end of the **i.**: 2195
Da 11:30 have **i.** against the holy covenant. 2194
Da 11:36 prosper till the **i.** be accomplished: 2195
Mic 7:9 I will bear the **i.** of the Lord, ... 2197
Na 1:6 Who can stand before his **i.**? and 2195
Hab 3:12 didst march through the land in **i.**, ... 2195
Zep 3:8 to pour upon them mine **i.**, even all 2195
Zec 1:12 hast had **i.** these threescore and 2194
Mal 1:4 whom the Lord hath **i.** for ever. 2194
Mt 20:24 were moved with **i.** against the two *23*
Mt 26:8 they had **i.**, saying, To what purpose *23*
Mk 14:4 some that had **i.** within themselves, ... *23*
Lu 13:14 of the synagogue answered with **i.**, ... *23*
Ac 5:17 Sadducees, and were filled with **i.**, ... *2205*
Ro 2:8 unrighteousness, **i.**, and wrath, ... *2372*
2Co 7:11 yea, what **i.**, yea, what fear, yea, ... *24*
Heb 10:27 of judgment and fiery **i.**, which *2205*
Re 14:10 mixture into the cup of his **i.**; *3709*

INDITING
Ps 45:1 My heart is **i.** a good matter: I 7370

INDUSTRIOUS
1Ki 11:28 young man that he was **i.**, he 6213,4399

INEXCUSABLE
Ro 2:1 Therefore thou art **i.**, O man, ... *379*

INFALLIBLE
Ac 1:3 by many **i.** proofs, being seen of them ......

INFAMOUS
Eze 22:5 shall mock thee, which art **i.** 2931,8034

INFAMY
Pr 25:10 shame, and thine **i.** turn not away. 1681
Eze 36:3 talkers, and are an **i.** of the people: 1681

INFANT See also INFANTS.
1Sa 15:3 slay both man and woman, **i.** and 5768
Isa 65:20 be no more thence an **i.** of days, ... 5764

INFANTS
Job 3:16 been; as **i.** which never saw light. 5768
Ho 13:16 their **i.** shall be dashed in pieces, ... 5768
Lu 18:15 they brought unto him also **i.**, that *1025*

INFERIOR
Job 12:3 I am not **i.** to you: yea, who 5307
Job 13:2 I know also: I am not **i.** unto you. 5307
Da 2:39 arise another kingdom **i.** to thee, ... 772
2Co 12:13 you were **i.** to other churches, ... *2274*

INFIDEL
2Co 6:15 hath he that believeth with an **i.**? *571*
1Ti 5:8 the faith, and is worse than an **i.** *571*

INFINITE
Job 22:5 great? and thine iniquities **i.**? 369,7093
Ps 147:5 power: his understanding is **i.** 369,4557
Na 3:9 her strength, and it was **i.**; 7097

INFIRMITIES
Mt 8:17 Himself took our **i.**, and bare our *769*
Lu 5:15 and to be healed by him of their **i.** *769*
Lu 7:21 cured many of their **i.** and plagues, ... *3554*
Lu 8:2 been healed of evil spirits and **i.**, ... *769*
Ro 8:26 the Spirit also helpeth our **i.**: for *769*
Ro 15:1 to bear the **i.** of the weak, and not *771*
2Co 11:30 of the things which concern my **i.** *769*
2Co 12:5 I will not glory, but in mine **i.** *769*
2Co 12:9 will I rather glory in my **i.**, that the *769*
2Co 12:10 Therefore I take pleasure in **i.**, in *769*
1Ti 5:23 stomach's sake and thine often **i.** *769*
Heb 4:15 touched with the feeling of our **i.**; *769*

INFIRMITY See also INFIRMITIES.
Le 12:2 days of the separation for her **i.** 1738
Ps 77:10 And I said, This is my **i.**: but I 2470
Pr 18:14 spirit of a man will sustain his **i.**; 4245
Lu 13:11 a woman which had a spirit of **i.** *769*
Lu 13:12 **thou art loosed from thine i.** *769*
Joh 5:5 had an **i.** thirty and eight years. *769*
Ro 6:19 men because of the **i.** of your flesh: *769*
Ga 4:13 Ye know how through **i.** of the flesh *769*
Heb 5:2 himself also is compassed with **i.** *769*
Heb 7:28 men high priests which have **i.**; *769*

INFLAME See also ENFLAME.
Isa 5:11 until night, till wine **i.** them! 1814

INFLAMMATION
Le 13:28 clean: for it is an **i.** of the burning. 6867
De 28:22 and with a fever, and with an **i.**, ... 1816

INFLICTED
2Co 2:6 this punishment, which was **i.** of many. .....

INFLUENCES
Job 38:31 bind the sweet **i.** of Pleiades, ... 4575

INFOLDING
Eze 1:4 a fire **i.** itself, and a brightness 3947

INFORM See also INFORMED.
De 17:10 according to all that they **i.** thee: 3384

INFORMED
Da 9:22 And he **i.** me, and talked with me, ... 995
Ac 21:21 are **i.** of thee, that thou teachest *2727*
Ac 21:24 they were **i.** concerning thee, ... *2727*
Ac 24:1 who **i.** the governor against Paul. *1718*
Ac 25:2 of the Jews **i.** him against Paul, and *1718*
Ac 25:15 and the elders of the Jew **i.** me, ... *1718*

INGATHERING
Ex 23:16 and the feast of **i.**, which is in the 614
Ex 34:22 the feast of **i.** at the year's end. 614

INHABIT See also INHABITED; INHABITEST; INHABITETH; INHABITING.
Nu 35:34 the land which ye shall **i.**, wherein 3427
Pr 10:30 the wicked shall not **i.** the earth. 7931
Isa 42:11 the villages that Kedar doth **i.** 3427
Isa 65:21 shall build houses, and **i.** them; 3427
Isa 65:22 shall not build and another **i.**; they 3427
Jer 17:6 but shall **i.** the parched places in 7931
Jer 48:18 Thou daughter that dost **i.** Dibon, ... 3427
Eze 33:24 they that **i.** those wastes of the land ... 3427
Am 9:14 build the waste cities, and **i.** them; 3427
Zep 1:13 also build houses, but not **i.** them; 3427

INHABITANT See also INHABITANTS.
Job 28:4 flood breaketh out from the **i.**; 1481
Isa 5:9 even great and fair, without **i.** 3427
Isa 6:11 Until the cities be wasted without **i.**, ... 3427
Isa 9:9 and the **i.** of Samaria that say in 3427
Isa 12:6 Cry out and shout, thou **i.** of Zion: 3427
Isa 20:6 And the **i.** of this isle shall say in 3427
Isa 24:17 are upon thee, O **i.** of the earth. 3427
Isa 33:24 And the **i.** shall not say, I am sick: 7934
Jer 2:15 his cities are burned without **i.** 3427
Jer 4:7 shall be laid waste, without an **i.** 3427
Jer 9:11 of Judah desolate, without an **i.** 3427
Jer 10:17 out of the land, O **i.** of the fortress. ... 3427
Jer 21:13 I am against thee, O **i.** of the valley, .. 3427
Jer 22:23 O **i.** of Lebanon, that makest thy 3427
Jer 26:9 city shall be desolate without an **i.**? 3427
Jer 33:10 without man, and without **i.**, and 3427
Jer 34:22 of Judah a desolation without an **i.** 3427
Jer 44:22 and a curse, without an **i.**, as at 3427
Jer 46:19 waste and desolate without an **i.** 3427
Jer 48:19 O **i.** of Aroer, stand by the way, and .. 3427
Jer 48:43 thee, O **i.** of Moab, saith the Lord. 3427
Jer 51:29 Babylon a desolation without an **i.** 3427
Jer 51:35 Babylon, shall the **i.** of Zion say; 3427
Jer 51:37 and an hissing, without an **i.** 3427
Am 1:5 cut off the **i.** from the plain of Aven, ... 3427
Am 1:8 I will cut off the **i.** from Ashdod, ... 3427
Mic 1:11 Pass ye away, thou **i.** of Saphir, ... 3427
Mic 1:11 the **i.** of Zaanan came not forth in 3427
Mic 1:12 the **i.** of Maroth waited carefully for 3427
Mic 1:13 O thou **i.** of Lachish, bind the 3427
Mic 1:15 heir unto thee, O **i.** of Mareshah: 3427
Zep 2:5 thee, that there shall be no **i.** 3427
Zep 3:6 is no man, that there is none **i.** 3427

INHABITANTS See also INHABITERS.
Ge 19:25 and all the **i.** of the cities, and all 3427
Ge 34:30 to stink among the **i.** of the land, ... 3427
Ge 50:11 the **i.** of the land, the Canaanites, ... 3427
Ex 15:14 take hold on the **i.** of Palestina. 3427
Ex 15:15 all the **i.** of Canaan shall melt away 3427
Ex 23:31 I will deliver the **i.** of the land into 3427
Ex 34:12 with the **i.** of the land whither thou 3427
Ex 34:15 a covenant with the **i.** of the land, ... 3427
Le 18:25 the land itself vomiteth out her **i.** 3427
Le 25:10 all the land unto all the **i.** thereof: 3427
Nu 13:32 land that eateth up the **i.** thereof; 3427
Nu 14:14 they will tell it to the **i.** of this land: .. 3427
Nu 32:17 cities because of the **i.** of the land. 3427
Nu 33:52 ye shall drive out the **i.** of the land 3427
Nu 33:53 ye shall dispossess the **i.** of the land, ...
Nu 33:55 will not drive out the **i.** of the land 3427
De 13:13 have withdrawn the **i.** of their city, ... 3427
De 13:15 shalt surely smite the **i.** of that city 3427
Jos 2:9 all the **i.** of the land faint because 3427
Jos 2:24 all the **i.** of the country do faint 3427
Jos 7:9 all the **i.** of the land shall hear of it, ... 3427
Jos 8:24 of slaying all the **i.** of Ai in the field, ... 3427
Jos 8:26 had utterly destroyed all the **i.** of Ai. .. 3427
Jos 9:3 And when the **i.** of Gibeon heard 3427
Jos 9:11 all the **i.** of our country spake to us, ... 3427
Jos 9:24 to destroy all the **i.** of the land from ... 3427
Jos 10:1 the **i.** of Gibeon had made peace 3427
Jos 11:19 save the Hivites the **i.** of Gibeon: 3427
Jos 13:6 All the **i.** of the hill country from 3427
Jos 15:15 he went up thence to the **i.** of Debir: .. 3427
Jos 15:63 the Jebusites the **i.** of Jerusalem, ... 3427
Jos 17:7 hand unto the **i.** of En-tappuah. 3427
Jos 17:11 and the **i.** of Dor and her towns, ... 3427
Jos 17:11 and the **i.** of En-dor and her towns, ... 3427
Jos 17:11 the **i.** of Taanach and her towns, ... 3427
Jos 17:11 the **i.** of Megiddo and her towns, ... 3427
Jos 17:12 not drive out the **i.** of those cities; ....
Jg 1:11 he went against the **i.** of Debir: 3427
Jg 1:19 he drave out the **i.** of the mountain; ....
Jg 1:19 not drive out the **i.** of the valley, ... 3427
Jg 1:27 the **i.** of Beth-shean and her towns, ...
Jg 1:27 nor the **i.** of Dor and her towns, ... 3427
Jg 1:27 nor the **i.** of Ibleam and her towns, ... 3427
Jg 1:27 the **i.** of Megiddo and her towns: 3427
Jg 1:30 Zebulun drive out the **i.** of Kitron, ... 3427
Jg 1:30 nor the **i.** of Nahalol; but the 3427
Jg 1:31 did Asher drive out the **i.** of Accho, ... 3427
Jg 1:31 nor the **i.** of Zidon, nor of Ahlab, ... 3427
Jg 1:32 the Canaanites, the **i.** of the land: 3427
Jg 1:33 drive out the **i.** of Beth-shemesh, ... 3427
Jg 1:33 nor the **i.** of Beth-anath; 3427
Jg 1:33 the Canaanites, the **i.** of the land: 3427
Jg 1:33 nevertheless the **i.** of Beth-shemesh ... 3427
Jg 2:2 no league with the **i.** of this land; 3427
Jg 5:7 The **i.** of the villages ceased, they ....
Jg 5:11 toward the **i.** of his villages in Israel: ....
Jg 5:23 curse ye bitterly the **i.** thereof; 3427
Jg 10:18 be head over all the **i.** of Gilead. 3427
Jg 11:8 our head over all the **i.** of Gilead. 3427
Jg 11:21 the Amorites, the **i.** of that country. ... 3427
Jg 20:15 **i.** of Gibeah, which were numbered 3427
Jg 21:9 none of the **i.** of Jabesh-gilead there 3427
Jg 21:10 Go and smite the **i.** of Jabesh-gilead ... 3427
Jg 21:12 found among the **i.** of Jabesh-gilead 3427
Ru 4:4 Buy it before the **i.**, and before the 3427
1Sa 6:21 to the **i.** of Kirjath-jearim, saying, ... 3427
1Sa 23:5 So David saved the **i.** of Keilah. 3427
1Sa 27:8 nations were of old the **i.** of the land, .. 3427
1Sa 31:11 when the **i.** of Jabesh-gilead heard 3427
2Sa 5:6 the Jebusites, the **i.** of the land: 3427
1Ki 17:1 who was of the **i.** of Gilead, ... 8453
1Ki 21:11 nobles who were the **i.** in his city, ... 3427
2Ki 19:26 their **i.** were of small power, ... 3427
2Ki 22:16 this place, and upon the **i.** thereof, ... 3427
2Ki 22:19 place, and against the **i.** thereof, ... 3427
2Ki 23:2 and all the **i.** of Jerusalem with him, ... 3427
1Ch 8:6 of the fathers of the **i.** of Geba, and 3427
1Ch 8:13 of the fathers of the **i.** of Aijalon, ... 3427
1Ch 8:13 who drove away the **i.** of Gath: 3427
1Ch 9:2 Now the first **i.** that dwelt in their 3427
1Ch 11:4 Jebusites were, the **i.** of the land. 3427
1Ch 11:5 And the **i.** of Jebus said to David, ... 3427
1Ch 22:18 the **i.** of the land into mine hand; 3427

2Ch 15:5 were upon all the **i.** of the countries. .. 3427
2Ch 20:7 the **i.** of this land before thy people 3427
2Ch 20:15 all Judah, and ye **i.** of Jerusalem, ... 3427
2Ch 20:18 and the **i.** of Jerusalem fell before......... 3427
2Ch 20:20 O Judah, and ye **i.** of Jerusalem; 3427
2Ch 20:23 up against the **i.** of mount Seir, ... 3427
2Ch 20:23 had made an end of the **i.** of Seir, ... 3427
2Ch 21:11 caused the **i.** of Jerusalem to commit .. 3427
2Ch 21:13 the **i.** of Jerusalem to go a whoring,..... 3427
2Ch 22:1 **i.** of Jerusalem made Ahaziah king 3427
2Ch 32:22 the **i.** of Jerusalem from the hand of ... 3427
2Ch 32:26 both he and the **i.** of Jerusalem, so..... 3427
2Ch 32:33 the **i.** of Jerusalem did him honour...... 3427
2Ch 33:9 Judah and the **i.** of Jerusalem to err, ... 3427
2Ch 34:24 this place, and upon the **i.** thereof, ... 3427
2Ch 34:27 place, and against the **i.** thereof, ... 3427
2Ch 34:28 place, and upon the **i.** of the same...... 3427
2Ch 34:30 of Judah, and the **i.** of Jerusalem, ... 3427
2Ch 34:32 the **i.** of Jerusalem did according to..... 3427
2Ch 35:18 present, and the **i.** of Jerusalem. 3427
Ezr 4:6 the **i.** of Judah and Jerusalem............ 3427
Ne 3:13 and the **i.** of Zanoah; they build it,...... 3427
Ne 7:3 watches of the **i.** of Jerusalem, ... 3427
Ne 9:24 the **i.** of the land, the Canaanites, ... 3427
Job 26:5 the waters, and the **i.** thereof............ 7934
Ps 33:8 all the **i.** of the world stand in awe 3427
Ps 33:14 looketh upon all the **i.** of the earth. 3427
Ps 49:1 give ear, all ye **i.** of the world: 3427
Ps 75:3 and all the **i.** thereof are dissolved:...... 3427
Ps 83:7 the Philistines with the **i.** of Tyre;...... 3427
Isa 5:3 O **i.** of Jerusalem, and men of Judah, .. 3427
Isa 8:14 for a snare to the **i.** of Jerusalem. 3427
Isa 10:13 have put down the **i.** like a valiant...... 3427
Isa 10:31 the **i.** of Gebim gather themselves....... 3427
Isa 18:3 All ye **i.** of the world, and dwellers..... 3427
Isa 21:14 The **i.** of the land of Tema brought...... 3427
Isa 22:21 be a father to the **i.** of Jerusalem, ... 3427
Isa 23:2 Be still, ye **i.** of the isle; thou whom... 3427
Isa 23:6 to Tarshish; howl, ye **i.** of the isle. 3427
Isa 24:1 scattereth abroad the **i.** thereof......... 3427
Isa 24:5 also is defiled under the **i.** thereof; 3427
Isa 24:6 the **i.** of the earth are burned, and 3427
Isa 26:9 the **i.** of the world will learn.............. 3427
Isa 26:18 have the **i.** of the world fallen............ 3427
Isa 26:21 to punish the **i.** of the earth for 3427
Isa 37:27 their **i.** were of small power, ... 3427
Isa 38:11 no more with the **i.** of the world. 3427
Isa 40:22 the **i.** thereof are as grasshoppers; 3427
Isa 42:10 therein; the isles, and the **i.** thereof.... 3427
Isa 42:11 let the **i.** of the rock sing, let them 3427
Isa 49:19 be too narrow by reason of the **i.**,....... 3427
Jer 1:14 forth upon all the **i.** of the land. 3427
Jer 4:4 men of Judah and **i.** of Jerusalem:........ 3427
Jer 6:12 out my hand upon the **i.** of the land,... 3427
Jer 8:1 the bones of the **i.** of Jerusalem, ... 3427
Jer 10:18 I will sling out the **i.** of the land......... 3427
Jer 11:2 Judah, and to the **i.** of Jerusalem;......... 3427
Jer 11:9 and among the **i.** of Jerusalem. 3427
Jer 11:12 of Judah and **i.** of Jerusalem go, ... 3427
Jer 13:13 I will fill all the **i.** of this land even 3427
Jer 13:13 prophets, and all the **i.** of Jerusalem, ... 3427
Jer 17:20 Judah, and all the **i.** of Jerusalem,....... 3427
Jer 17:25 of Judah, and the **i.** of Jerusalem: 3427
Jer 18:11 Judah, and to the **i.** of Jerusalem, ... 3427
Jer 19:3 of Judah, and **i.** of Jerusalem; 3427
Jer 19:12 this place...and to the **i.** thereof, ... 3427
Jer 21:6 I will smite the **i.** of this city, both 3427
Jer 23:14 and the **i.** thereof as Gomorrah. 3427
Jer 25:2 Judah, and to all the **i.** of Jerusalem, ... 3427
Jer 25:9 against the **i.** thereof, and against........ 3427
Jer 25:29 sword upon all the **i.** of the earth, ... 3427
Jer 25:30 grapes, against all the **i.** of the earth... 3427
Jer 26:15 this city, and upon the **i.** thereof: 3427
Jer 32:32 of Judah, and the **i.** of Jerusalem. 3427
Jer 35:13 of Judah and the **i.** of Jerusalem, ... 3427
Jer 35:17 all the **i.** of Jerusalem all the evil........ 3427
Jer 36:31 upon the **i.** of Jerusalem, and upon 3427
Jer 42:18 forth upon the **i.** of Jerusalem;........... 3427
Jer 46:8 I will destroy the city and the **i.**............ 3427
Jer 47:2 and all the **i.** of the land shall howl. 3427
Jer 49:8 back, dwell deep, O **i.** of Dedan;......... 3427
Jer 49:20 purposed against the **i.** of Teman: 3427
Jer 49:30 far off, dwell deep, O ye **i.** of Hazor, .. 3427
Jer 50:21 it, and against the **i.** of Pekod: 3427
Jer 50:34 and disquiet the **i.** of Babylon. 3427
Jer 50:35 upon the **i.** of Babylon, and upon........ 3427
Jer 51:12 he spake against the **i.** of Babylon. 3427
Jer 51:24 to all the **i.** of Chaldea all their evil..... 3427
Jer 51:35 my blood upon the **i.** of Chaldea,......... 3427
La 4:12 the earth and all the **i.** of the world, ... 3427
Eze 11:15 whom the **i.** of Jerusalem have said, ... 3427
Eze 12:19 Lord God of the **i.** of Jerusalem, ... 3427
Eze 15:6 so will I give the **i.** of Jerusalem. 3427
Eze 26:17 she and her **i.**, which cause their 3427
Eze 27:8 The **i.** of Zidon and Arvad were thy.... 3427
Eze 27:35 the **i.** of the isles shall be astonished... 3427
Eze 29:6 all the **i.** of Egypt shall know that I 3427
Da 4:35 all the **i.** of the earth are reputed 1753
Da 4:35 and among the **i.** of the earth: and 1753
Da 9:7 Judah, and to the **i.** of Jerusalem, ... 3427
Ho 4:1 controversy with the **i.** of the land,..... 3427
Ho 10:5 The **i.** of Samaria shall fear.............. 7934
Joe 1:2 and give ear, all ye **i.** of the land. 3427
Joe 1:14 the **i.** of the land into the house of 3427
Joe 2:1 let all the **i.** of the land tremble: 3427
Mic 6:12 and the **i.** thereof have spoken lies, ... 3427
Mic 6:16 and the **i.** thereof an hissing: 3427
Zep 1:4 and upon all the **i.** of Jerusalem;......... 3427
Zep 1:11 Howl, ye **i.** of Maktesh, for all the 3427
Zep 2:5 Woe unto the **i.** of the sea coast, ... 3427
Zec 8:20 people, and the **i.** of many cities: 3427
Zec 8:21 the **i.** of one city shall go to another, .. 3427
Zec 11:6 I will no more pity the **i.** of the land, .. 3427
Zec 12:5 The **i.** of Jerusalem shall be my 3427
Zec 12:7 the **i.** of Jerusalem do not magnify...... 3427
Zec 12:8 the Lord defend the **i.** of Jerusalem; ... 3427
Zec 12:10 David, and upon the **i.** of Jerusalem, ... 3427
Zec 13:1 of David and to the **i.** of Jerusalem..... 3427
Re 17:2 the **i.** of the earth have been made..... *2730*

INHABITED
Ge 36:20 of Seir the Horite, who **i.** the land;..... 3427
Ex 16:35 years, until they came to a land **i.**; 3427
Le 16:22 their iniquities unto a land not **i.**:........ 1509
Jg 1:17 the Canaanites that **i.** Zephath, ... 3427
Jg 1:21 out the Jebusites that **i.** Jerusalem; 3427
1Ch 5:9 eastward he **i.** unto the entering in..... 3427
Isa 13:20 It shall never be **i.**, neither shall it 3427
Isa 44:26 saith to Jerusalem, Thou shalt be **i.**; ... 3427
Isa 45:18 it not in vain, he formed it to be **i.**: 3427
Isa 54:3 make the desolate cities to be **i.**. 3427
Jer 6:8 make thee desolate, a land not **i.**. 3427
Jer 17:6 wilderness, in a salt land and not **i.**..... 3427
Jer 22:6 and cities which are not **i.**................ 3427
Jer 46:26 and afterward it shall be **i.**, as in........ 7931
Jer 50:13 it shall not be **i.**, but it shall be.......... 3427
Jer 50:39 it shall be no more **i.** for ever; 3427
Eze 12:20 cities that are **i.** shall be laid waste...... 3427
Eze 26:17 that wast **i.** of seafaring men, ... 3427
Eze 26:19 city, like the cities that are not **i.**; 3427
Eze 26:20 down to the pit, that thou be not **i.**; ... 3427
Eze 29:11 it, neither shall it be **i.** forty years...... 3427
Eze 34:13 in all the **i.** places of the country......... 4186
Eze 36:10 and the cities shall be **i.**, and the 3427
Eze 36:35 cities are become fenced, and are **i.**.... 3427
Eze 38:12 the desolate places that are now **i.**, ... 3427
Zec 2:4 Jerusalem shall be **i.** as towns 3427
Zec 7:7 when Jerusalem was **i.** and in............ 3427
Zec 7:7 men **i.** the south and the plain?.......... 3427
Zec 9:5 Gaza, and Ashkelon shall not be **i.**..... 3427
Zec 12:6 and Jerusalem shall be **i.** again in........ 3427
Zec 14:10 be lifted up, and **i.** in her place,......... 3427
Zec 14:11 but Jerusalem shall be safely **i.**. 3427

INHABITERS See also INHABITANTS.
Re 8:13 woe, woe, to the **i.** of the earth *2730*
Re 12:12 Woe to the **i.** of the earth and of *2730*

INHABITEST
Ps 22:3 O thou that **i.** the praises of Israel. 3427

INHABITETH
Job 15:28 and in houses which no man **i.**,.......... 3427
Isa 57:15 high and lofty One that **i.** eternity, ... 7931

INHABITING
Ps 74:14 to the people **i.** the wilderness. 6728

INHERIT See also DISINHERIT; INHERITED; INHERITETH.
Ge 15:7 to give thee this land to **i.** it. 3423
Ge 15:8 shall I know that I shall **i.** it?............ 3423
Ge 28:4 that thou mayest **i.** the land 3423
Ex 23:30 thou be increased,and **i.** the land........ 5157
Ex 32:13 seed, and they shall **i.** it for ever. 5157
Le 20:24 Ye shall **i.** their land, and I will........... 3423
Le 25:46 you, to **i.** them for a possession;........ 3423
Nu 18:24 I have given to the Levites to **i.**: 5159
Nu 26:55 tribes of their fathers they shall **i.**. 5157
Nu 32:19 we will not **i.** with them on yonder..... 5157
Nu 33:54 the tribes of your fathers ye shall **i.**.... 5157
Nu 34:13 is the land which ye shall **i.** by lot, ... 5157
De 1:38 for he shall cause Israel to **i.** it. 5157
De 2:31 that thou mayest **i.** his land.............. 3423
De 3:28 he shall cause them to **i.** the land....... 5157
De 12:10 the Lord your God giveth you to **i.**,..... 5157
De 16:20 thou mayest live, and **i.** the land........ 3423
De 19:3 the Lord thy God giveth thee to **i.**, ... 5157
De 19:14 which thou shalt **i.** in the land that...... 5157
De 21:16 his sons to **i.** that which he hath, ... 5157
De 31:7 and thou shalt cause them to **i.** it. 5157
Jos 17:14 but one lot and one portion to **i.**, ... 5159
Jg 11:2 shalt not **i.** in our father's house, ... 5157
1Sa 2:8 to make them **i.** the throne of glory:... 5157
2Ch 20:11 which thou hast given us to **i.**. 3423
Ps 25:13 and his seed shall **i.** the earth............ 3423
Ps 37:9 the Lord, they shall **i.** the earth. 3423
Ps 37:11 But the meek shall **i.** the earth; 3423
Ps 37:22 blessed of him shall **i.** the earth; 3423
Ps 37:29 The righteous shall **i.** the land, ... 3423
Ps 37:34 he shall exalt thee to **i.** the land:......... 3423
Ps 69:36 seed also of his servants shall **i.** it:..... 5157
Ps 82:8 earth: for thou shalt **i.** all nations. 5157
Pr 3:35 The wise shall **i.** glory: but shame...... 5157
Pr 8:21 those that love me to **i.** substance;..... 5157
Pr 11:29 his own house shall **i.** the wind: 5157
Pr 14:18 The simple **i.** folly: but the prudent 5157
Isa 49:8 to cause to **i.** the desolate heritages; .. 5157
Isa 54:3 and thy seed shall **i.** the Gentiles, ... 3423
Isa 57:13 and shall **i.** my holy mountain; 3423
Isa 60:21 they shall **i.** the land for ever, the...... 3423
Isa 65:9 and mine elect shall **i.** it, and my 3423
Jer 8:10 fields to them that shall **i.** them: 3423
Jer 12:14 caused my people Israel to **i.**: 5157
Jer 49:1 why then doth their king **i.** Gad, ... 3423
Eze 47:13 whereby ye shall **i.** the land 5157
Eze 47:14 shall **i.** it, one as well as another:........ 3423
Zec 2:12 And the Lord shall **i.** Judah his 5157
Mt 5:5 **meek: for they shall i. the earth**.... *2816*
Mt 19:29 **and shall i. everlasting life**. *2816*
Mt 25:34 **i. the kingdom prepared for you**..... *2816*
Mk 10:17 shall I do that I may **i.** eternal life?..... *2816*
Lu 10:25 what shall I do to **i.** eternal life? *2816*
Lu 18:18 what shall I do to **i.** eternal life? *2816*
1Co 6:9 shall not **i.** the kingdom of God? *2816*
1Co 6:10 shall **i.** the kingdom of God. *2816*
1Co 15:50 and blood cannot **i.** the kingdom......... *2816*
1Co 15:50 doth corruption **i.** incorruption. *2816*
Ga 5:21 shall not **i.** the kingdom of God. *2816*
Heb 6:12 faith and patience **i.** the promises. *2816*
1Pe 3:9 called, that ye should **i.** a blessing. *2816*
Rev 21:7 that overcometh shall **i.** all things; *2816*

INHERITANCE See also INHERITANCES.
Ge 31:14 yet any portion or **i.** for us in our 5159
Ge 48:6 name of their brethren in their **i.**......... 5159
Ex 15:17 in the mountain of thine **i.**, in the....... 5159
Ex 34:9 our sin, and take us for thine **i.**........ 5157
Le 25:46 them as an **i.** for your children 5157
Nu 16:14 given us **i.** of fields and vineyards:...... 5159
Nu 18:20 Thou shalt have no **i.** in their land,..... 5157
Nu 18:20 I am thy part and thine **i.** among........ 5159
Nu 18:21 Levi all the tenth in Israel for an **i.**,.... 5159
Nu 18:23 children of Israel they have no **i.**........ 5159
Nu 18:24 of Israel they shall have no **i.**. 5159
Nu 18:26 given you from them for your **i.**,........ 5159
Nu 26:53 the land shall be divided for an **i.** 5159
Nu 26:54 many thou shalt give the more **i.**, ... 5159
Nu 26:54 and to few thou shalt give the less **i.**: . 5159
Nu 26:54 to every one shall his **i.** be given 5159
Nu 26:62 because there was no **i.** given 5159
Nu 27:7 an **i.** among their father's brethren; 5159
Nu 27:7 **i.** of their father to pass unto them..... 5159
Nu 27:8 his **i.** to pass unto his daughter........... 5159
Nu 27:9 shall give his **i.** unto his brethren. 5159
Nu 27:10 his **i.** unto his father's brethren.......... 5159
Nu 27:11 shall give his **i.** unto his kinsman........ 5159
Nu 32:18 have inherited every man his **i.**.......... 5159
Nu 32:19 our **i.** is fallen to us on this side.......... 5159
Nu 32:32 the possession of our **i.** on this side.... 5159
Nu 33:54 divide the land by lot for an **i.** 5157
Nu 33:54 the more ye shall give the more **i.**, ... 5159
Nu 33:54 to the fewer ye shall give the less **i.**:.. 5159
Nu 33:54 every man's **i.** shall be in the place...........

Nu 34:2 that shall fall unto you for an **i.**, ... 5159
Nu 34:14 fathers, have received their **i.**; ....
Nu 34:14 of Manasseh have received their **i.**: 5159
Nu 34:15 have received their **i.** on this side 5159
Nu 34:18 every tribe, to divide the land by **i.** ... 5157
Nu 34:29 Lord commanded to divide the **i.** 5157
Nu 35:2 the **i.** of their possession cities to....... 5159
Nu 35:8 to his **i.** which he inheriteth. 5159
Nu 36:2 to give the land for an **i.** by lot to 5159
Nu 36:2 the **i.** of Zelophehad our brother 5159
Nu 36:3 their **i.** be taken from the **i.** of our..... 5159
Nu 36:3 shall be put to the **i.** of the tribe........ 5159
Nu 36:3 it be taken from the lot of our **i.** 5159
Nu 36:4 their **i.** be put unto the **i.** of the 5159
Nu 36:4 their **i.** be taken away from the **i.** 5159
Nu 36:7 not the **i.** of the children of Israel....... 5159
Nu 36:7 to the **i.** of the tribe of his fathers...... 5159
Nu 36:8 daughter, that possesseth an **i.** in........ 5159
Nu 36:8 enjoy every man the **i.** of his fathers... 5159
Nu 36:9 Neither shall the **i.** remove from 5159
Nu 36:9 shall keep himself to his own **i.** 5159
Nu 36:12 and their **i.** remained in the tribe........ 5159
De 4:20 to be unto him a people of **i.**, as ye.... 5159
De 4:21 Lord thy God giveth thee for an **i.**: 5159
De 4:38 to give thee their land for an **i.**, as it.. 5159
De 9:26 destroy not thy people and thine **i.**, ... 5159
De 9:29 they are thy people and thine **i.**, ... 5159
De 10:9 no part nor **i.** with his brethren; 5159
De 10:9 the Lord is his **i.**, according as the 5159
De 12:9 as yet come to the rest and to the **i.**, ..5159
De 12:12 as he hath no part nor **i.** with you. 5159
De 14:27 for he hath no part nor **i.** with thee. ... 5159
De 14:29 he hath no part nor **i.** with thee, ... 5159
De 15:4 Lord thy God giveth thee for an **i.** 5159
De 18:1 have no part nor **i.** with Israel: 5159
De 18:1 the Lord made by fire, and his **i.** 5159
De 18:2 Therefore shall they have no **i.** 5159
De 18:2 the Lord is their **i.**, as he hath said 5159
De 19:10 Lord thy God giveth thee for an **i.**, ... 5159
De 19:14 they of old time have set in thine **i.**, ... 5159
De 20:16 thy God doth give thee for an **i.**, ... 5159
De 21:23 Lord thy God giveth thee for an **i.** 5159
De 24:4 Lord thy God giveth thee for an **i.** 5159
De 25:19 giveth thee for an **i.** to possess it,...... 5159
De 26:1 Lord thy God giveth thee for an **i.**, ... 5159
De 29:8 it for an **i.** unto the Reubenites, ... 5159
De 32:8 divided to the nations their **i.**, ... 5157
De 32:9 people; Jacob is the lot of his **i.** 5159
De 33:4 the **i.** of the congregation of Jacob...... 4181
Jos 1:6 shalt thou divide for an **i.** the land, ... 5157
Jos 11:23 and Joshua gave it for an **i.** unto 5159
Jos 13:6 by lot unto the Israelites for an **i.**,....... 5159
Jos 13:7 land for an **i.** unto the nine tribes, ... 5159
Jos 13:8 the Gadites have received their **i.**,...... 5159
Jos 13:14 the tribe of Levi he gave none **i.**;....... 5159
Jos 13:14 of Israel made by fire are their **i.**, ... 5159
Jos 13:15 the children of Reuben **i.** according..........
Jos 13:23 the **i.** of the children of Reuben 5159
Jos 13:24 Moses gave **i.** unto the tribe of Gad ....
Jos 13:28 is the **i.** of the children of Gad........... 5159
Jos 13:29 And Moses gave the **i.** unto the half.........
Jos 13:32 which Moses did distribute for **i.** 5157
Jos 13:33 of Levi Moses gave not any **i.**: 5159
Jos 13:33 the Lord God of Israel was their **i.**, ... 5159
Jos 14:1 Israel, distributed for **i.** to them......... 5157
Jos 14:2 By lot was their **i.**, as the Lord 5159
Jos 14:3 Moses had given the **i.** of two tribes... 5159
Jos 14:3 unto the Levites he gave none **i.** 5159
Jos 14:9 feet have trodden shall be thine **i.**, ... 5159
Jos 14:13 son of Jephunneh Hebron for an **i.** 5159
Jos 14:14 Hebron therefore became the **i.** of...... 5159
Jos 15:20 **i.** of the tribe of..children of Judah...... 5159
Jos 16:4 and Ephraim, took their **i.** 5157
Jos 16:5 the border of their **i.** on the east 5159
Jos 16:8 the **i.** of the tribe of the children of 5159
Jos 16:9 the **i.** of the children of Manasseh, ... 5159
Jos 17:4 to give us an **i.** among our brethren.... 5159
Jos 17:4 them an **i.** among the brethren of........ 5159
Jos 17:6 daughters of Manasseh had an **i.** 5157
Jos 18:2 which had not yet received their **i.** 5159
Jos 18:4 it according to the **i.** of them;........... 5159
Jos 18:7 priesthood of the Lord is their **i.**: 5159
Jos 18:7 received their **i.** beyond Jordan 5159
Jos 18:20 the **i.** of the children of Benjamin, ... 5159
Jos 18:28 the **i.** of the children of Benjamin 5159
Jos 19:1 **i.** was within the **i.** of the children...... 5159
Jos 19:2 and they had in their **i.** Beer-sheba, ... 5159
Jos 19:8 This is the **i.** of the tribe of the 5159
Jos 19:9 the **i.** of the children of Simeon: 5159
Jos 19:9 the children of Simeon had their **i.** 5157
Jos 19:9 had their...within the **i.** of them. 5159
Jos 19:10 border of their **i.** was unto Sarid: 5159
Jos 19:16 is the **i.** of the children of Zebulun...... 5159
Jos 19:23, 31,39 This is the **i.** of the tribe of........ 5159
Jos 19:41 And the coast of their **i.** was Zorah, ... 5159
Jos 19:48 This is the **i.** of the tribe of the 5159
Jos 19:49 an end of dividing the land for **i.** 5157
Jos 19:49 of Israel gave an **i.** to Joshua the 5159
Jos 19:51 divided for an **i.** by lot in Shiloh 5157
Jos 21:3 unto the Levites out of their **i.**, ... 5159
Jos 23:4 to be an **i.** for your tribes, from......... 5159
Jos 24:28 depart, every man unto his **i.** 5159
Jos 24:30 buried him in the border of his **i.** 5159
Jos 24:32 the **i.** of the children of Joseph. 5159
Jg 2:6 every man unto his **i.** to possess........ 5159
Jg 2:9 buried him in the border of his **i.** 5159
Jg 18:1 the Danites sought them an **i.** to......... 5159
Jg 18:1 all their **i.** had not fallen unto them..... 5159
Jg 20:6 all the country of the **i.** of Israel: 5159
Jg 21:17 There must be an **i.** for them that...... 3425
Jg 21:23 went and returned unto their **i.**,......... 5159
Jg 21:24 from thence every man unto his **i.** 5159
Ru 4:5 up the name of the dead upon his **i.** 5159
Ru 4:6 for myself, lest I mar mine own **i.**: 5159
Ru 4:10 up the name of the dead upon his **i.**.... 5159
1Sa 10:1 thee to be captain over his **i.**? 5159
1Sa 26:19 from abiding in the **i.** of the Lord, ... 5159
2Sa 14:16 my son together out of the **i.** of God. . 5159
2Sa 20:1 have we **i.** in the son of Jesse: 5159
2Sa 20:19 thou swallow up the **i.** of the Lord? 5159
2Sa 21:3 ye may bless the **i.** of the Lord? 5159
1Ki 8:36 hast given to thy people for an **i.** 5159
1Ki 8:51 For they be thy people, and thine **i.**, .. 5159
1Ki 8:53 people of the earth to be thine **i.**, ... 5159
1Ki 12:16 have we **i.** in the son of Jesse: 5159
1Ki 21:3 I should give the **i.** of my fathers 5159
1Ki 21:4 not give thee the **i.** of my fathers....... 5159
2Ki 21:14 will forsake the remnant of mine **i.**, ... 5159
1Ch 16:18 land of Canaan, the lot of your **i.**;....... 5159
1Ch 28:8 leave it for an **i.** for your children....... 5157
2Ch 6:27 given unto thy people for an **i.** 5159
2Ch 10:16 we have none **i.** in the son of Jesse: ... 5159
Ezr 9:12 leave it for an **i.** to your children........ 3423
Ne 11:20 cities of Judah, every one in his **i.** 5159
Job 31:2 **i.** of the Almighty from on high? 5159
Job 42:15 gave them **i.** among their brethren. 5159
Ps 2:8 give thee the heathen for thine **i.**, ... 5159
Ps 16:5 The Lord is the portion of mine **i.** 2506
Ps 28:9 Save thy people, and bless thine **i.**: 5159
Ps 33:12 whom he hath chosen for his own **i.** .. 5159
Ps 37:18 and their **i.** shall be for ever............... 5159
Ps 47:4 He shall choose our **i.** for us, ... 5159
Ps 68:9 whereby thou didst confirm thine **i.**,..... 5159
Ps 74:2 the rod of thine **i.**, which thou hast..... 5159
Ps 78:55 and divided them an **i.** by line, and..... 5159
Ps 78:62 and was wroth with his **i.** 5159
Ps 78:71 Jacob his people, and Israel his **i.** 5159
Ps 79:1 the heathen are come into thine **i.**; 5159
Ps 94:14 people, neither will he forsake his **i.** .. 5159
Ps 105:11 land of Canaan, the lot of your **i.**: 5159
Ps 106:5 that I may glory with thine **i.** 5159
Ps 106:40 that he abhorred his own **i.** 5159
Pr 13:22 A good man leaveth an **i.** to his 5157
Pr 17:2 part of the **i.** among the brethren 5159
Pr 19:14 and riches are the **i.** of fathers: 5159
Pr 20:21 An **i.** may be gotten hastily at the 5159
Ec 7:11 Wisdom is good with an **i.**: and by...... 5159
Isa 19:25 of my hands, and Israel mine **i.** 5159
Isa 47:6 I have polluted mine **i.**, and given....... 5159
Isa 63:17 servants' sake, the tribes of thine **i.** 5159
Jer 3:18 given for an **i.** unto your fathers. 5157
Jer 10:16 and Israel is the rod of his **i.**: The...... 5159
Jer 12:14 evil neighbours, that touch the **i.** 5159
Jer 16:18 filled mine **i.** with the carcases of....... 5159
Jer 32:8 for the right of **i.** is thine, and the...... 3425
Jer 51:19 and Israel is the rod of his **i.**: The...... 5159
La 5:2 Our **i.** is turned to strangers, our....... 5159
Eze 22:16 And thou shalt take thine **i.** in 2490
Eze 33:24 many; the land is given us for **i.** 4181
Eze 35:15 at the **i.** of the house of Israel,........... 5159
Eze 36:12 and thou shalt be their **i.**, and thou..... 5159
Eze 44:28 be unto them for an **i.**: I am their **i.**: .. 5159
Eze 45:1 shall divide by lot the land for **i.**,........ 5159
Eze 46:16 the **i.** thereof shall be his sons'; 5159
Eze 46:16 it shall be their possession by **i.** 5159
Eze 46:17 gift of his **i.** to one of his servants,..... 5159
Eze 46:17 his **i.** shall be his sons' for them. 5159
Eze 46:18 shall not take of the people's **i.** by...... 5159
Eze 46:18 shall give his sons **i.** out of his own.... 5157
Eze 47:14 this land shall fall unto you for **i.** 5159
Eze 47:22 divide it by lot for an **i.** unto you, ... 5159
Eze 47:22 they shall have **i.** with you among 5159
Eze 47:23 there shall ye give him his **i.**, saith..... 5159
Eze 48:29 lot unto the tribes of Israel for **i.**, ... 5159
Mt 21:38 **kill him, and let us seize on his i...** *2817*
Mk 12:7 **kill him, and the i. shall be ours...** *2817*
Lu 12:13 that he divide the **i.** with me. *2817*
Lu 20:14 **kill him, that the i. may be ours...** *2817*
Ac 7:5 And he gave him none **i.** in it, ... *2817*
Ac 20:32 to give you an **i.** among all them *2817*
Ac 26:18 **i. among them which are sanctified** *2819*
Ga 3:18 if the **i.** be of the law, it is no more ... *2817*
Eph 1:11 In whom...we...obtained an **i.**,........... *2820*
Eph 1:14 is the earnest of our **i.** until the......... *2817*
Eph 1:18 of the glory of his **i.** in the saints. *2817*
Eph 5:5 hath any **i.** in the kingdom of Christ.... *2817*
Col 1:12 be partakers of the **i.** of the saints *2819*
Col 3:24 shall receive the reward of the **i.**: *2817*
Heb 1:4 as he hath by **i.** obtained a more........ *2820*
Heb 9:15 receive the promise of eternal **i.** *2817*
Heb 11:8 he should after receive for an **i.**, ... *2817*
1Pe 1:4 an **i.** incorruptible, and undefiled,........ *2817*

INHERITANCES

Jos 19:51 These are the **i.**, which Eleazer......... 5159

INHERITED

Nu 32:18 have **i.** every man his inheritance. 5157
Jos 14:1 of Israel **i.** in the land of Canaan, ... 5157
Ps 105:44 they **i.** the labour of the people;......... 3423
Jer 16:19 Surely our fathers have **i.** lies,........... 5157
Eze 33:24 and he **i.** the land: but we are 3423
Heb 12:17 he would have **i.** the blessing. *2816*

INHERITETH

Nu 35:8 to his inheritance which he **i.** 5157

INHERITOR

Isa 65:9 of Judah an **i.** of my mountains: 3423

INIQUITIES

Le 16:21 all the **i.** of the children of Israel, ... 5771
Le 16:22 goat shall bear upon him all their **i.** 5771
Le 26:39 **i.** of their fathers shall they pine 5771
Nu 14:34 day for a year, shall ye bear your **i.**,.... 5771
Ezr 9:6 our **i.** are increased over our head,..... 5771
Ezr 9:7 for our **i.** have we, our kings, and....... 5771
Ezr 9:13 punished us less than our **i.** deserve, .. 5771
Ne 9:2 sins, and the **i.** of their fathers. 5771
Job 13:23 How many are mine **i.** and sins? 5771
Job 13:26 me to possess the **i.** of my youth. 5771
Job 22:5 great? and thine **i.** infinite? 5771
Ps 38:4 mine **i.** are gone over mine head: as... 5771
Ps 40:12 mine **i.** have taken hold upon me,....... 5771
Ps 51:9 my sins, and blot out all mine **i.** 5771
Ps 64:6 They search out **i.**:they.................... 5766
Ps 65:3 **I.** prevail against me: as for 1697,5771
Ps 79:8 not against us former **i.**: 5771
Ps 90:8 Thou hast set our **i.** before thee, ... 5771
Ps 103:3 Who forgiveth all thine **i.**; who........... 5771
Ps 103:10 rewarded us according to our **i.** 5771
Ps 107:17 and because of their **i.**, are 5771
Ps 130:3 If thou, Lord, shouldest mark **i.**, ... 5771
Ps 130:8 shall redeem Israel from all his **i.**,....... 5771
Pr 5:22 His own **i.** shall take the wicked......... 5771
Isa 43:24 hast wearied me with thine **i.** 5771
Isa 50:1 for your **i.** have ye sold.................... 5771
Isa 53:5 he was bruised for our **i.**: 5771
Isa 53:11 many; for he shall bear their **i.** 5771
Isa 59:2 But your **i.** have separated 5771
Isa 59:12 and as for our **i.**, we know them; 5771
Isa 64:6 our **i.**, like the wind, have taken......... 5771
Isa 64:7 consumed us, because of our **i.** 5771
Isa 65:7 Your **i.**, and the **i.** of your fathers 5771
Jer 5:25 Your **i.** have turned away these 5771
Jer 11:10 back to the **i.** of their forefathers,....... 5771
Jer 14:7 though our **i.** testify against us,......... 5771
Jer 33:8 and I will pardon all their **i.**, ... 5771
La 4:13 the **i.** of her priests, that have........... 5771
La 5:7 not; and we have borne their **i.** 5771
Eze 24:23 but ye shall pine away for your **i.**, ... 5771
Eze 28:18 by the multitude of thine **i.**, by 5771
Eze 32:27 their **i.** shall be upon their bones,....... 5771

Eze 36:31 in your own sight for your **i.** and ... 5771
Eze 36:33 have cleansed you from all your **i.** ... 5771
Eze 43:10 they may be ashamed of their **i.**: ... 5771
Da 4:27 and thine **i.** by shewing mercy to ... 5758
Da 9:13 that we might turn from our **i.**, ... 5771
Da 9:16 sins, and for the **i.** of our fathers, ... 5771
Am 3:2 I will punish you for all your **i.** ... 5771
Mic 7:19 he will subdue our **i.**; and thou ... 5771
Ac 3:26 away every one of you from his **i.** ... *4189*
Ro 4:7 are they whose **i.** are forgiven, ... *458*
Heb 8:12 their **i.** will I remember no more. ... *458*
Heb 10:17 sins and **i.** will I remember no more. ... *458*
Re 18:5 and God hath remembered her **i.** ... *92*

INIQUITY See also INIQUITIES.
Ge 15:16 **i.** of the Amorites is not yet full ... 5771
Ge 19:15 be consumed in the **i.** of the city ... 5771
Ge 44:16 found out the **i.** of thy servants: ... 5771
Ex 20:5 visiting the **i.** of the fathers upon ... 5771
Ex 28:38 may bear the **i.** of the holy thngs, ... 5771
Ex 28:43 that they bear not **i.**, and die: ... 5771
Ex 34:7 forgiving **i.** and transgression and ... 5771
Ex 34:7 visiting the **i.** of the fathers upon ... 5771
Ex 34:9 and pardon our **i.** and our sin, and ... 5771
Le 5:1 utter it, then he shall bear his **i.** ... 5771
Le 5:17 is he guilty, and shall bear his **i.** ... 5771
Le 7:18 that eateth of it shall bear his **i.** ... 5771
Le 10:17 to bear the **i.** of the congregation, ... 5771
Le 17:16 his flesh; then he shall bear his **i.** ... 5771
Le 18:25 I do visit the **i.** thereof upon it, ... 5771
Le 19:8 one that eateth it shall bear his **i.**, ... 5771
Le 20:17 nakedness; he shall bear his **i.** ... 5771
Le 20:19 near kin: they shall bear their **i.** ... 5771
Le 22:16 them to bear the **i.** of trespass, ... 5771
Le 26:39 of you shall pine away in their **i.** in ... 5771
Le 26:40 confess their **i.**, and the **i.** of their ... 5771
Le 26:41 43 of the punishment of their **i.**: ... 5771
Nu 5:15 bringing **i.** to remembrance. ... 5771
Nu 5:31 shall the man be guiltless from **i.**, ... 5771
Nu 5:31 and this woman shall bear her **i.** ... 5771
Nu 14:18 forgiving **i.** and transgression, ... 5771
Nu 14:18 visiting the **i.** of the fathers upon ... 5771
Nu 14:19 I beseech thee, the **i.** of this people ... 5771
Nu 15:31 cut off; his **i.** shall be upon him. ... 5771
Nu 18:1 shall bear the **i.** of the sanctuary: ... 5771
Nu 18:1 shall bear the **i.** of your priesthood. ... 5771
Nu 18:23 and they shall bear their **i.**: it shall ... 5771
Nu 23:21 He hath not beheld **i.** in Jacob, ... 205
Nu 30:15 them; then he shall bear her **i.** ... 5771
De 5:9 visiting the **i.** of the fathers upon ... 5771
De 19:15 not rise up against a man for any **i.**, ... 5771
De 32:4 a God of truth and without **i.**, ... 5766
Jos 22:17 Is the **i.** of Peor too little for us, ... 5771
Jos 22:20 man perished not alone in his **i.** ... 5771
1Sa 3:13 ever for the **i.** which he knoweth; ... 5771
1Sa 3:14 **i.** of Eli's house shall not be purged ... 5771
1Sa 15:23 stubbornness is as **i.** and idolatry. ... 205
1Sa 20:1 have I done? what is mine **i.**? ... 5771
1Sa 20:8 if there be in me **i.**, slay me ... 5771
1Sa 25:24 me, my lord, upon me let this **i.** be; ... 5771
2Sa 7:14 If he commit **i.**, I will chasten him ... 5753
2Sa 14:9 the **i.** be on me, and on my father's ... 5771
2Sa 14:32 if there be any **i.** in me, let him kill ... 5771
2Sa 19:19 Let not my lord impute **i.** unto me, ... 5771
2Sa 22:24 and have kept myself from mine **i.** ... 5771
2Sa 24:10 take away the **i.** of thy servant; ... 5771
1Ch 21:8 do away the **i.** of thy servant; for ... 5771
2Ch 19:7 is no **i.** with the Lord our God, ... 5766
Ne 4:5 And cover not their **i.**, and let not ... 5771
Job 4:8 that plow **i.**, and sow wickedness, ... 205
Job 5:16 hope, and **i.** stoppeth her mouth. ... 5766
Job 6:29 Return, I pray you, let it not be **i.**; ... 5766
Job 6:30 Is there **i.** in my tongue? cannot ... 5766
Job 7:21 and take away mine **i.**? ... 5771
Job 10:6 That thou enquirest after thine **i.**, ... 5771
Job 10:14 wilt not acquit me from mine **i.** ... 5771
Job 11:6 thee less than thine **i.** deserveth. ... 5771
Job 11:14 If **i.** be in thine hand, put it far ... 205
Job 14:17 a bag, and thou sewest up mine **i.** ... 5771
Job 15:5 thy mouth uttereth thine **i.**, and ... 5771
Job 15:16 man, which drinketh **i.** like water? ... 5766
Job 20:27 The heaven shall reveal his **i.**:and ... 5771
Job 21:19 God layeth up his **i.** for his children: ... 205
Job 22:23 away **i.** far from thy tabernacles. ... 5766
Job 31:3 punishment to the workers of **i.**? ... 205
Job 31:11 an **i.** to be punished by the judges. ... 5771
Job 31:28 an **i.** to be punished by the judge: ... 5771
Job 31:33 by hiding mine **i.** in my bosom: ... 5771
Job 33:9 innocent; neither is there **i.** in me. ... 5771
Job 34:8 in company with the workers of **i.**, ... 205
Job 34:10 that he should commit **i.** ... 5766
Job 34:22 where the workers of **i.** may hide ... 205
Job 34:32 if I have done **i.**, I will do no more. ... 5766
Job 36:10 that they return from **i.** ... 205
Job 36:21 Take heed, regard not **i.**: for this ... 205
Job 36:23 can say, Thou hast wrought **i.**? ... 5766
Ps 5:5 sight: thou hatest all workers of **i.** ... 205
Ps 6:8 Depart from me, all ye workers of **i.**; ... 205
Ps 7:3 this; if there be **i.** in my hands; ... 5766
Ps 7:14 Behold, he travaileth with **i.**, and ... 205
Ps 14:4 all the workers of **i.** no knowledge? ... 205
Ps 18:23 and I kept myself from mine **i.** ... 5771
Ps 25:11 O Lord, pardon mine **i.**; for it is ... 5771
Ps 28:3 with the workers of **i.**, which speak ... 205
Ps 31:10 strength faileth because of mine **i.**, ... 5771
Ps 32:2 whom the Lord imputeth not **i.**, ... 5771
Ps 32:5 thee, and mine **i.** have I not hid. ... 5771
Ps 32:5 and thou forgavest the **i.** of my sin. ... 5771
Ps 36:2 until his **i.** be found to be hateful. ... 5771
Ps 36:3 The words of his mouth are **i.** and ... 205
Ps 36:12 There are the workers of **i.** fallen: ... 205
Ps 37:1 envious against the workers of **i.** ... 5766
Ps 38:18 For I will declare mine **i.**:I will ... 5771
Ps 39:11 with rebukes dost correct man for **i.**, ... 5771
Ps 41:6 his heart gathereth **i.** to itself; ... 205
Ps 49:5 the **i.** of my heels shall compass ... 5771
Ps 51:2 Wash me thoroughly from mine **i.**, ... 5771
Ps 51:5 I was shapen in **i.**; and in sin ... 5771
Ps 53:1 and have done abominable **i.**: ... 5766
Ps 53:4 the workers of **i.** no knowledge? ... 205
Ps 55:3 for they cast **i.** upon me, and in ... 205
Ps 56:7 Shall they escape by **i.**? in thine ... 205
Ps 59:2 Deliver me from the workers of **i.**, ... 205
Ps 64:2 insurrection of the workers of **i.**: ... 205
Ps 66:18 If I regard **i.** in my heart, the Lord ... 205
Ps 69:27 Add **i.** unto their **i.**: and let them ... 5771
Ps 78:38 full of compassion, forgave their **i.**, ... 5771
Ps 85:2 hast forgiven the **i.** of thy people, ... 5771
Ps 89:32 the rod, and their **i.** with stripes. ... 5771
Ps 92:7 all the workers of **i.** do flourish; ... 205
Ps 92:9 the workers of **i.** shall be scattered. ... 205
Ps 94:4 the workers of **i.** boast themselves. ... 205
Ps 94:16 up for me against the workers of **i.**? ... 205
Ps 94:20 the throne of **i.** have fellowship ... 1942
Ps 94:23 shall bring upon them their own **i.**, ... 205
Ps 106:6 we have committed **i.**, we have ... 5753
Ps 106:43 and were brought low for their **i.** ... 5771
Ps 107:42 and all **i.** shall stop her mouth. ... 5766
Ps 109:14 **i.** of his fathers be remembered ... 5771
Ps 119:3 They also do no **i.**: they walk in ... 5766
Ps 119:133 let not any **i.** have dominion over ... 205
Ps 125:3 put forth their hands unto **i.** ... 5766
Ps 125:5 them forth with the workers of **i.**: ... 205
Ps 141:4 wicked works with men that work **i.**: ... 205
Ps 141:9 and the gins of the workers of **i.** ... 205
Pr 10:29 shall be to the workers of **i.** ... 205
Pr 16:6 By mercy and truth **i.** is purged: ... 5771
Pr 19:28 mouth of the wicked devoureth **i.** ... 205
Pr 21:15 shall be to the workers of **i.** ... 205
Pr 22:8 that soweth **i.** shall reap vanity: ... 5766
Ec 3:16 righteousness, that **i.** was there. ... 7562
Isa 1:4 nation, a people laden with **i.**, ... 5771
Isa 1:13 it is **i.**, even the solemn meeting. ... 205
Isa 5:18 unto them that draw **i.** with cords ... 5771
Isa 6:7 thine **i.** is taken away, and thy sin ... 5771
Isa 13:11 evil, and the wicked for their **i.**; and ... 5771
Isa 14:21 children for the **i.** of their fathers; ... 5771
Isa 22:14 Surely this **i.** shall not be purged ... 5771
Isa 26:21 inhabitants of the earth for their **i.**: ... 5771
Isa 27:9 shall the **i.** of Jacob be purged; ... 5771
Isa 29:20 all that watch for **i.** are cut off: ... 205
Isa 30:13 this **i.** shall be to you as a breach ... 5771
Isa 31:2 the help of them that work **i.** ... 205
Isa 32:6 his heart will work **i.**, to practice ... 205
Isa 33:24 therein shall be forgiven their **i.** ... 5771
Isa 40:2 her **i.** is pardoned: for she hath ... 5771
Isa 53:6 hath laid on him the **i.** of us all. ... 5771
Isa 57:17 For the **i.** of his covetousness was I ... 5771
Isa 59:3 with blood,and your fingers with **i.**; ... 5771
Isa 59:4 conceive mischief, and bring forth **i.** ... 205
Isa 59:6 their works are works of **i.**, and the ... 205
Isa 59:7 their thoughts are thoughts of **i.**; ... 205
Isa 64:9 neither remember **i.** for ever: ... 5771
Jer 2:5 What **i.** have your fathers found ... 5766
Jer 2:22 yet thine **i.** is marked before me, ... 5771
Jer 3:13 Only acknowledge thine **i.**, that ... 5771
Jer 9:5 weary themselves to commit **i.** ... 5753
Jer 13:22 For the greatness of thine **i.** are ... 5771
Jer 14:10 he will now remember their **i.**, ... 5771
Jer 14:20 wickedness, and the **i.** of our fathers: ... 5771
Jer 16:10 or what is our **i.**? or what is our sin ... 5771
Jer 16:17 neither is their **i.** hid from mine ... 5771
Jer 16:18 I will recompense their **i.** and their ... 5771
Jer 18:23 forgive not their **i.**, neither blot out ... 5771
Jer 25:12 nation, saith the Lord, for their **i.**, ... 5771
Jer 30:14 for the multitude of thine **i.**; ... 5771
Jer 30:15 for the multitude of thine **i.**: ... 5771
Jer 31:30 every one shall die for his own **i.**: ... 5771
Jer 31:34 for I will forgive their **i.**, and I will ... 5771
Jer 32:18 recompensest the **i.** of the fathers ... 5771
Jer 33:8 I will cleanse them from all their **i.**, ... 5771
Jer 36:3 I may forgive their **i.** and their sin. ... 5771
Jer 36:31 seed and his servants for their **i.**: ... 5771
Jer 50:20 the **i.** of Israel shall be sought for, ... 5771
Jer 51:6 be not cut off in her **i.**; for this ... 5771
La 2:14 they have not discovered thine **i.**, ... 5771
La 4:6 punishment of the **i.** of the daughter ... 5771
La 4:22 The punishment of thine **i.** is ... 5771
La 4:22 he will visit thine **i.**, O daughter of ... 5771
Eze 3:18 same wicked man shall die in his **i.**; ... 5771
Eze 3:19 wicked way, he shall die in his **i.**; ... 5771
Eze 3:20 his righteousness, and commit **i.** ... 5766
Eze 4:4 lay the **i.** of the house of Israel ... 5771
Eze 4:4 lie upon it thou shalt bear their **i.** ... 5771
Eze 4:5 laid upon thee the years of their **i.**, ... 5771
Eze 4:5 shalt thou bear the **i.** of the house ... 5771
Eze 4:6 thou shalt bear the **i.** of the house ... 5771
Eze 4:17 and consume away for their **i.** ... 5771
Eze 7:13 himself in the **i.** of his life, ... 5771
Eze 7:16 mourning, every one for his **i.** ... 5771
Eze 7:19 it is the stumblingblock of their **i.** ... 5771
Eze 9:9 **i.** of the house of Israel and Judah ... 5771
Eze 14:3 the stumblingblock of their **i.** ... 5771
Eze 14:4, 7 the stumblingblock of his **i.** ... 5771
Eze 14:10 bear the punishment of their **i.**: ... 5771
Eze 16:49 this was the **i.** of thy sister Sodom, ... 5771
Eze 18:8 hath withdrawn his hand from **i.**, ... 5766
Eze 18:17 not die for the **i.** of his father, he ... 5771
Eze 18:18 lo, even he shall die in his **i.** ... 5771
Eze 18:19 not the son bear the **i.** of the father? ... 5771
Eze 18:20 shall not bear the **i.** of the father, ... 5771
Eze 18:20 the father bear the **i.** of the son: ... 5771
Eze 18:24 and committeth **i.**, and doeth ... 5766
Eze 18:26 committeth **i.**, and dieth in them; ... 5766
Eze 18:26 his **i.** that he hath done shall he die. ... 5766
Eze 18:30 so **i.** shall not be your ruin. ... 5771
Eze 21:23 he will call to remembrance the **i.**, ... 5771
Eze 21:24 made your **i.** to be remembered, ... 5771
Eze 21:25 is come, when **i.** shall have an end, ... 5771
Eze 21:29 when their **i.** shall have an end. ... 5771
Eze 28:15 created, till **i.** was found in thee. ... 5766
Eze 28:18 by the **i.** of thy traffick; ... 5766
Eze 29:16 bringeth their **i.** to remembrance, ... 5771
Eze 33:6 them, he is taken away in his **i.**; ... 5771
Eze 33:8 that wicked man shall die in his **i.**; ... 5771
Eze 33:9 from his way, he shall die in his **i.**; ... 5771
Eze 33:13 own righteousness, and commit **i.**, ... 5766
Eze 33:13 for his **i.** that he hath committed, ... 5766
Eze 33:15 of life, without committing **i.**; ... 5766
Eze 33:18 righteousness, and committeth **i.**, ... 5766
Eze 35:5 the time that their **i.** had an end: ... 5771
Eze 39:23 went into captivity for their **i.**: ... 5771
Eze 44:10 idols; they shall even bear their **i.** ... 5771
Eze 44:12 the house of Israel to fall into **i.**; ... 5771
Eze 44:12 God, and they shall bear their **i.** ... 5771
Da 9:5 sinned, and have committed **i.**, ... 5753
Da 9:24 and to make reconciliation for **i.**, ... 5771
Ho 4:8 and they set their heart on their **i.** ... 5771
Ho 5:5 Israel and Ephraim fall in their **i.**; ... 5771
Ho 6:8 Gilead is a city of them that work **i.**, ... 205
Ho 7:1 the **i.** of Ephraim was discovered, ... 5771
Ho 8:13 now will he remember their **i.**, ... 5771
Ho 9:7 for the multitude of thine **i.**, and ... 5771
Ho 9:9 he will remember their **i.**, he will ... 5771
Ho 10:9 battle...against the children of **i.** ... 5932
Ho 10:13 wickedness, ye have reaped **i.**;ye ... 5766
Ho 12:8 find none **i.** in me that were sin. ... 5771
Ho 12:11 Is there **i.** in Gilead? surely they ... 205
Ho 13:12 The **i.** of Ephraim is bound up; ... 5771

Ho 14:1 for thou hast fallen by thine **i.**. 5771
Ho 14:2 Take away all **i.**, and receive us 5771
Mic 2:1 Woe to them that devise **i.**, and 205
Mic 3:10 with blood, and Jerusalem with **i.**. 5766
Mic 7:18 like unto thee, that pardoneth **i.**, 5771
Hab 1:3 Why dost thou shew me **i.**, and 205
Hab 1:13 evil, and canst not look on **i.**: 5999
Hab 2:12 blood, and stablisheth a city by **i.**! 5766
Zep 3:5 the midst thereof; he will not do **i.**: 5766
Zep 3:13 remnant of Israel shall not do **i.**, 5766
Zec 3:4 I have caused thine **i.** to pass 5771
Zec 3:9 will remove the **i.** of that land in one 5771
Mal 2:6 and **i.** was not found in his lips: 5766
Mal 2:6 and did turn many away from **i.**. 5771
Mt 7:23 **depart from me, ye that work i.** *458*
Mt 13:41 **that offend, and them which do i.:** *458*
Mt 23:28 **ye are full of hypocrisy and i.** *458*
Mt 24:12 **because i. shall abound, the love of** *458*
Lu 13:27 **depart from me, all ye workers of i.** *93*
Ac 1:18 a field with the reward of **i.**: *93*
Ac 8:23 of bitterness, and in the bond of **i.**. *93*
Ro 6:19 to uncleanness and to **i.** unto **i.**; *458*
1Co 13:6 Rejoiceth not in **i.**, but rejoiceth in *93*
2Th 2:7 mystery of **i.** doth already work: *458*
2Ti 2:19 the name of Christ depart from **i.**. *93*
Tit 2:14 might redeem us from all **i.**, and *458*
Heb 1:9 loved righteousness, and hated **i.**; *458*
Jas 3:6 And the tongue is a fire, a world of **i.**: *93*
2Pe 2:16 But was rebuked for his **i.**: the *3892*

INJOIN See ENJOIN.

INJURED
Ga 4:12 as ye are: ye have not **i.** me at all. *91*

INJURIOUS
1Ti 1:13 and a persecutor, and **i.**: but I *5197*

INJUSTICE
Job 16:17 Not for any **i.** in mine hands: also 2555

INK See also INKHORN.
Jer 36:18 and I wrote them with **i.** in the 1773
2Co 3:3 written not with **i.**, but with the *3188*
2Jo 12 would not write with paper and **i.**: *3188*
3Jo 13 I will not with **i.** and pen write unto *3188*

INKHORN
Eze 9:2 with a writer's **i.** by his side: 7083
Eze 9:3 had the writer's **i.** by his side; 7083
Eze 9:11 linen, which had the **i.** by his side, 7083

INN
Ge 42:27 to give his ass provender in the **i.**, 4411
Ge 43:21 when we came to the **i.**, that we 4411
Ex 4:24 came to pass by the way in the **i.**, 4411
Lu 2:7 was no room for them in the **i.**. *2646*
Lu 10:34 **and brought him to an i., and took** *3829*

INNER See also INNERMOST.
1Ki 6:27 the cherubims within the **i.** house: 6442
1Ki 6:36 he built the **i.** court with three rows 6442
1Ki 7:12 for the **i.** court of the house of the 6442
1Ki 7:50 the doors of the **i.** house, the most 6442
1Ki 20:30 into the city, into an **i.** chamber. 2315
1Ki 22:25 shalt go into an **i.** chamber to hide 2315
2Ki 9:2 and carry him to an **i.** chamber; 2315
1Ch 28:11 and of the **i.** parlours thereof, and 6442
2Ch 4:22 the **i.** doors thereof for the most 6442
2Ch 18:24 shalt go into an **i.** chamber to hide 2315
2Ch 29:16 went into the **i.** part of the house 6441
Es 4:11 unto the king into the **i.** court, 6442
Es 5:1 stood in the **i.** court of the king's 6442
Eze 8:3 the door of the **i.** gate that looketh 6442
Eze 8:16 he brought me into the **i.** court 6442
Eze 10:3 and the cloud filled the **i.** court. 6442
Eze 40:15 the porch of the **i.** gate were fifty 6442
Eze 40:19 unto the forefront of the **i.** court 6442
Eze 40:23 the gate of the **i.** court was over 6442
Eze 40:27 a gate in the **i.** court toward the 6442
Eze 40:28 he brought me to the **i.** court by 6442
Eze 40:32 he brought me into the **i.** court 6442
Eze 40:44 the **i.** gate were the chambers 6442
Eze 40:44 of the singers in the **i.** court, which 6442
Eze 41:15 with the **i.** temple, and the porches 6442
Eze 41:17 the door, even unto the **i.** house, 6442
Eze 42:3 cubits which were for the **i.** court, 6442
Eze 42:15 an end of measuring the **i.** house, 6442
Eze 43:5 and brought me into the **i.** court; 6442
Eze 44:17 enter in at the gates of the **i.** court, 6442
Eze 44:17 minister in the gates of the **i.** court, 6442
Eze 44:21 when they enter into the **i.** court. 6442
Eze 44:27 into the sanctuary, unto the **i.** court, 6442
Eze 45:19 the posts of the gate of the **i.** court 6442
Eze 46:1 The gate of the **i.** court that looketh 6442
Ac 16:24 thrust them into the **i.** prison, and *2082*
Eph 3:16 might by his Spirit in the **i.** man; *2080*

INNERMOST
Pr 18:8 down into the **i.** parts of the belly. 2315
Pr 26:22 down into the **i.** parts of the belly. 2315

INNOCENCY
Ge 20:5 and **i.** of my hands have I done 5356
Ps 26:6 I will wash mine hands in **i.**: so will 5356
Ps 73:13 in vain, and washed my hands in **i.** 5356
Da 6:22 as before him **i.** was found in me; 2136
Ho 8:5 long will it be ere they attain to **i.**? 5356

INNOCENT See also INNOCENTS.
Ex 23:7 the **i.** and righteous slay thou not: 5355
De 19:10 That **i.** blood be not shed in thy 5355
De 19:13 the guilt of **i.** blood from Israel, 5355
De 21:8 and lay not **i.** blood unto thy people 5355
De 21:9 put away the guilt of **i.** blood from 5355
De 27:25 taketh reward to slay an **i.** person. 5355
1Sa 19:5 then wilt thou sin against **i.** blood, 5355
1Ki 2:31 mayest take away the **i.** blood, 2600
2Ki 21:16 Manasseh shed **i.** blood very much, 5355
2Ki 24:4 also for the **i.** blood that he shed: 5355
2Ki 24:4 he filled Jerusalem with **i.** blood; 5355
Job 4:7 thee, who ever perished, being **i.**? 5355
Job 9:23 he will laugh at the trial of the **i.**. 5355
Job 9:28 know that thou wilt not hold me **i.** 5352
Job 17:8 the **i.** shall stir up himself against 5355
Job 22:19 and the **i.** laugh them to scorn. 5355
Job 22:30 He shall deliver the island of the **i.**: 5355
Job 27:17 on, and the **i.** shall divide the silver. 5355
Job 33:9 without transgression, I am **i.**: 2643
Ps 10:8 places doth he murder the **i.**: 5355
Ps 15:5 nor taketh reward against the **i.**. 5355
Ps 19:13 **i.** from the great transgression. 5352
Ps 94:21 and condemn the **i.** blood. 5355
Ps 106:38 And shed **i.** blood, even the blood 5355
Pr 1:11 let us lurk privily for the **i.** without 5355
Pr 6:17 and hands that shed **i.** blood, 5355
Pr 6:29 toucheth her shall not be **i.**. 5352
Pr 28:20 haste to be rich shall not be **i.** 5352
Isa 59:7 they make haste to shed **i.** blood: 5355
Jer 2:35 Yet thou sayest, Because I am **i.**, 5352
Jer 7:6 and shed not **i.** blood in this place, 5355
Jer 22:3 neither shed **i.** blood in this place. 5355
Jer 22:17 and for to shed **i.** blood, and for 5355
Jer 26:15 ye shall surely bring **i.** blood upon 5355
Joe 3:19 they have shed **i.** blood in their land. 5355
Jon 1:14 and lay not upon us **i.** blood: for 5355
Mt 27:4 in that I have betrayed the **i.** blood. *121*
Mt 27:24 I am **i.** of the blood of this just *121*

INNOCENTS
Jer 2:34 blood of the souls of the poor **i.**: 5355
Jer 19:4 filled this place with the blood of **i.**; 5355

INNUMERABLE
Job 21:33 as there are **i.** before him. 369,4557
Ps 40:12 For **i.** evils have compassed me 369,4557
Ps 104:25 wherein are things creeping **i.**, 369,4557
Jer 46:23 the grasshoppers, and are **i.**. 369,4557
Lu 12:1 an **i.** multitude of people; *3461*
Heb 11:12 sand which is by the sea shore **i.** *382*
Heb 12:22 and to an **i.** company of angels, *3461*

INORDINATE
Eze 23:11 was more corrupt in her **i.** love 5691
Col 3:5 uncleanness, **i.** affection, evil *3806*

INQUIRE See ENQUIRE.

INQUISITION
De 19:18 the judges shall make diligent **i.**: 1875
Es 2:23 when **i.** was made of the matter, 1245
Ps 9:12 When he maketh **i.** for blood, he 1875

INSATIABLE See UNSATIABLE.

INSCRIPTION
Ac 17:23 altar with this **i.**, To The Unknown *1924*

INSIDE
1Ki 6:15 covered them on the **i.** with wood, 1004

INSOMUCH See also FORASMUCH; INASMUCH.
Ps 106:40 **i.** that he abhorred his own 599
Mal 2:13 **i.** that he regardeth not the offering
Mt 8:24 **i.** that the ship was covered with *5620*
Mt 12:22 **i.** that the blind and dumb both *5620*
Mt 13:54 **i.** that they were astonished, and *5620*
Mt 15:31 **I.** that the multitude wondered, *5620*
Mt 24:24 **i. that, if it were possible, they** *5620*
Mt 27:14 **i.** that the governor marvelled *5620*
Mk 1:27 **i.** that they questioned among *5620*
Mk 1:45 **i.** that Jesus could no more openly *5620*
Mk 2:2 **i.** that there was no room to receive *5620*
Mk 2:12 **i.** that they were all amazed, and *5620*
Mk 3:10 **i.** that they pressed upon him for to *5620*
Mk 9:26 dead; **i.** that many said, He is dead. *5620*
Lu 12:1 **i.** that they trode one upon another, *5620*
Ac 1:19 **i.** as that field is called in their *5620*
Ac 5:15 **I.** that they brought forth the sick *5620*
2Co 1:8 **i.** that we despaired even of life: *5620*
2Co 8:6 **I.** that we desired Titus, that as *1519*
Ga 2:13 **i.** that Barnabas also was carried *5620*

INSPIRATION
Job 32:8 the **i.** of the Almighty giveth them 5397
2Ti 3:16 scripture is given by **i.** of God, *2315*

INSTANT
Isa 29:5 yea, it shall be at an **i.** suddenly. 6621
Isa 30:13 breaking cometh suddenly at an **i.**. 6621
Jer 18:7 At what **i.** I shall speak concerning 7281
Jer 18:9 at what **i.** I shall speak concerning 7281
Lu 2:38 she coming in that **i.** gave thanks *5610*
Lu 23:23 And they were **i.** with loud voices, *1945*
Ro 12:12 continuing **i.** in prayer; *4342*
2Ti 4:2 be **i.** in season, out of season; *2186*

INSTANTLY
Lu 7:4 they besought him **i.**, saying, *4705*
Ac 26:7 **i.** serving God day and night, *1722,1616*

INSTEAD
Ge 2:21 and closed up the flesh **i.** thereof; 8478
Ge 4:25 me another seed **i.** of Abel, 8478
Ge 44:33 let thy servant abide **i.** of the lad a 8478
Ex 4:16 even he shall be to thee **i.** of a mouth,
Ex 4:16 and thou shalt be to him **i.** of God.
Ex 5:12 of Egypt to gather stubble **i.** of straw.
Nu 3:12 of Israel **i.** of all the firstborn 8478
Nu 3:41 **i.** of all the firstborn among the 8478
Nu 3:41 **i.** of all the firstlings among the 8478
Nu 3:45 the Levites **i.** of all the firstborn 8478
Nu 3:45 of the Levites **i.** of their cattle; 8478
Nu 5:19 with another **i.** of thy husband, 8478
Nu 5:20 aside to another **i.** of thy husband, 8478
Nu 5:29 aside to another **i.** of her husband, 8478
Nu 8:16 **i.** of such as open every womb, 8478
Nu 8:16 even **i.** of the firstborn of all the
Nu 10:31 thou mayest be to us **i.** of eyes. 8478
Jg 15:2 she? take her, I pray thee, **i.** of her. 8478
2Sa 17:25 captain of the host **i.** of Joab: 8478
1Ki 3:7 made thy servant king **i.** of David 8478
2Ki 14:21 him king **i.** of his father Amaziah. 8478
2Ki 17:24 of Samaria **i.** of the children of 8478
1Ch 29:23 as king **i.** of David his father, and 8478
2Ch 12:10 **I.** of which king Rehoboam made 8478
Es 2:4 the king be queen **i.** of Vashti. 8478
Es 2:17 and made her queen **i.** of Vashti. 8478
Job 31:40 **i.** of wheat, and cockle **i.** of barley. 8478
Ps 45:16 **I.** of thy fathers shall be thy 8478
Isa 3:24 **i.** of sweet smell there shall be 8478
Isa 3:24 stink; and **i.** of a girdle a rent; 8478
Isa 3:24 and **i.** of well set hair baldness; 8478
Isa 3:24 and **i.** of a stomacher a girding of 8478
Isa 3:24 sackcloth; and burning **i.** of beauty. 8478
Isa 55:13 **I.** of the thorn shall come up the fir 8478
Isa 55:13 **i.** of the brier shall come up the 8478
Jer 22:11 which reigned **i.** of Josiah his father, 8478
Jer 37:1 son of Josiah reigned **i.** of Coniah 8478
Eze 16:32 taketh strangers **i.** of her husband! 8478

INSTRUCT See also INSTRUCTED; INSTRUCTING.
De 4:36 his voice, that he might **i.** thee: 3256
Ne 9:20 also thy good spirit to **i.** them, 7919
Job 40:2 with the Almighty **i.** him? 3250
Ps 16:7 my reins also **i.** me in the night 3256
Ps 32:8 I will **i.** thee and teach thee in the 7919
Ca 8:2 mother's house, who would **i.** me: 3925
Isa 28:26 his God doth **i.** him to discretion, 3256
Da 11:33 among the people shall **i.** many: 995
1Co 2:16 of the Lord, that he may **i.** him? *4822*

INSTRUCTED
De 32:10 he **i.** him, he kept him as the 995
2Ki 12:2 Jehoiada the priest **i.** him 3384
1Ch 15:22 he **i.** about the song, because he 3256
1Ch 25:7 brethren that were **i.** in the songs 3925
2Ch 3:3 Solomon was **i.** for the building 3245
Job 4:3 Behold, thou hast **i.** many, and 3256
Ps 2:10 be **i.**, ye judges of the earth 3256
Pr 5:13 mine ear to them that **i.** me! 3925
Pr 21:11 when the wise is **i.**, he receiveth 7919
Isa 8:11 and **i.** me that I should not walk 3256
Isa 40:14 and who **i.** him, and taught him 995
Jer 6:8 Be thou **i.**, O Jerusalem, lest my 3256
Jer 31:19 and after that I was **i.**, I smote 3045
Mt 13:52 **is i. unto the kingdom of heaven** *3100*
Mt 14:8 being before **i.** of her mother, *4264*
Lu 1:4 things, wherein thou hast been **i.** *2727*
Ac 18:25 man was **i.** in the way of the Lord; *2727*
Ro 2:18 excellent, being **i.** out of the law; *2727*
Php 4:12 all things I am **i.** both to be full *3453*

INSTRUCTER See also INSTRUCTERS; INSTRUCTOR.
Ge 4:22 an **i.** of every artificer in brass 3913

INSTRUCTERS
1Co 4:15 ye have ten thousand **i.** in Christ, *3807*

INSTRUCTING
2Ti 2:25 In meekness **i.** those that oppose *3811*

INSTRUCTION
Job 33:16 ears of men, and sealeth their **i.**, 4561
Ps 50:17 Seeing thou hatest **i.**, and castest 4148
Pr 1:2 To know wisdom and **i.**; to 4148
Pr 1:3 To receive the **i.** of wisdom, 4148
Pr 1:7 but fools despise wisdom and **i.** 4148
Pr 1:8 My son, hear the **i.** of thy father, 4148
Pr 4:1 Hear, ye children, the **i.** of a father, 4148
Pr 4:13 Take fast hold of **i.**; let her not go: 4148
Pr 5:12 How have I hated **i.**, and my heart 4148
Pr 5:23 He shall die without **i.**; and in the 4148
Pr 6:23 reproofs of **i.** are the way of life: 4148
Pr 8:10 Receive my **i.**, and not silver; and 4148
Pr 8:33 Hear **i.**, and be wise, and refuse it 4148
Pr 9:9 Give **i.** to a wise man, and he will be
Pr 10:17 in the way of life that keepeth **i.**: 4148
Pr 12:1 Whoso loveth **i.** loveth knowledge: 4148
Pr 13:1 A wise son heareth his father's **i.**: 4148
Pr 13:18 shall be to him that refuseth **i.**: 4148
Pr 15:5 A fool despiseth his father's **i.**: 4148
Pr 15:32 refuseth **i.** despiseth his own soul: 4148
Pr 15:33 fear of the Lord is the **i.** of wisdom; 4148
Pr 16:22 hath it: but the **i.** of fools is folly 4148
Pr 19:20 Hear counsel, and receive **i.**, that 4148
Pr 19:27 to hear the **i.** that causeth to err 4148
Pr 23:12 Apply thine heart unto **i.**, and 4148
Pr 23:23 wisdom, and **i.**, and understanding 4148
Pr 24:32 I looked upon it, and received **i.** 4148
Jer 17:23 they might not hear, nor receive **i.** 4148
Jer 32:33 have not hearkened to receive **i.** 4148
Jer 35:13 Will ye not receive **i.** to hearken to 4148
Eze 5:15 an **i.** and an astonishment unto 4148
Zep 3:7 wilt fear me, thou wilt receive **i.**: 4148
2Ti 3:16 correction, for **i.** in righteousness: *3809*

INSTRUCTOR See also INSTRUCTER.
Ro 2:20 An **i.** of the foolish, a teacher of *3810*

INSTRUMENT See also INSTRUMENTS.
Nu 35:16 if he smite him with an **i.** of iron, 3627
Ps 33:2 the psaltery and an **i.** of ten strings.
Ps 92:3 Upon an **i.** of ten strings, and upon
Ps 144:9 upon a psaltery and an **i.** of ten strings
Isa 28:27 are not threshed with a threshing **i.**,
Isa 41:15 make thee a new sharp threshing **i.**
Isa 54:16 bringeth forth an **i.** for his work; 3627
Eze 33:32 voice, and can play well on an **i.**:

INSTRUMENTS
Ge 49:5 **i.** of cruelty are in their 3627
Ex 25:9 the pattern of all the **i.** thereof, 3627
Nu 3:8 keep all the **i.** of the tabernacle 3627
Nu 4:12 shall take all the **i.** of ministry, 3627
Nu 4:26 cords, and all the **i.** of their service, 3627
Nu 4:32 with all their **i.**, and with all their 3627
Nu 4:32 ye shall reckon the **i.** of the charge 3627
Nu 7:1 sanctified it, and all the **i.** thereof, 3627
Nu 31:6 with the holy **i.**, and the trumpets 3627
1Sa 8:12 his **i.** of war, and **i.** of his chariots. 3627
1Sa 18:6 with joy, and with **i.** of musick 7991
2Sa 6:5 on all manner of **i.** made of fir wood,
2Sa 24:22 burnt sacrifice, and threshing **i.**
2Sa 24:22 and other **i.** of the oxen for wood 3627
1Ki 19:21 their flesh with the **i.** of the oxen, 3627
1Ch 9:29 and all the **i.** of the sanctuary, 3627
1Ch 12:33 with all **i.** of war, fifty thousand, 3627
1Ch 12:37 with all manner of **i.** of war for the 3627
1Ch 15:16 to be the singers with **i.** of musick, 3627
1Ch 16:42 sound, and with musical **i.** of God 3627
1Ch 21:23 and the threshing **i.** for wood, and the
1Ch 23:5 Lord with the **i.** which I made, 3627
1Ch 28:14 for all **i.** of all manner of service; 3627
1Ch 28:14 silver also for all **i.** of silver by 3627
1Ch 28:14 for all **i.** of every kind of service: 3627
2Ch 4:16 and all their **i.**, did Huram his 3627
2Ch 5:1 and all the **i.**, put he among the 3627
2Ch 5:13 and cymbals and **i.** of musick, and 3627
2Ch 7:6 also with **i.** of musick of the Lord, 3627
2Ch 23:13 the singers with **i.** of musick, and 3627
2Ch 29:26 Levites stood with the **i.** of David, 3627
2Ch 29:27 with the **i.** ordained by David king 3627
2Ch 30:21 singing with loud **i.** unto the Lord 3627
2Ch 34:12 all that could skill of **i.** of musick 3627
Ne 12:36 with the musical **i.** of David the 3627
Ps 7:13 prepared for him the **i.** of death; 3627
Ps 68:25 the players on **i.** followed after;
Ps 87:7 as the players on **i.** shall be there:
Ps 150:4 him with stringed **i.** and organs 4482
Ec 2:8 as musical **i.**, and that of all sorts
Isa 32:7 The **i.** also of the churl are evil: 3627
Isa 38:20 sing my songs to the stringed **i.**
Eze 40:42 **i.** wherewith they slew the burnt 3627
Da 6:18 neither were **i.** of musick brought 1761
Am 1:3 Gilead with threshing **i.** of iron:
Am 6:5 invent to themselves **i.** of musick, 3627
Hab 3:19 chief singer on my stringed **i.**
Zec 11:15 yet the **i.** of a foolish shepherd. 3627
Ro 6:13 as **i.** of unrighteousness unto sin: *3696*
Ro 6:13 as **i.** of righteousness unto God. *3696*

INSURRECTION
Ezr 4:19 time hath made **i.** against kings, 5376
Ps 64:2 the **i.** of the workers of iniquity: 7285
Mk 15:7 bound with them that had made **i.** *4955*
Mk 15:7 had committed murder in the **i.** *4714*
Ac 18:12 the Jews made **i.** with one accord *2721*

INTANGLE See ENTANGLE.

INTEGRITY
Ge 20:5 the **i.** of my heart and innocency 8537
Ge 20:6 didst this in the **i.** of thy heart; 8537
1Ki 9:4 thy father walked, in **i.** of heart, 8537
Job 2:3 and still he holdeth fast his **i.**, 8538
Job 2:9 him, Dost thou still retain thine **i.**? 8538
Job 27:5 till I die I will not remove mine **i.** 8538
Job 31:6 that God may know mine **i.** 8538
Ps 7:8 according to mine **i.** that is in me. 8537
Ps 25:21 Let **i.** and uprightness preserve 8537
Ps 26:1 Lord; for I have walked in mine **i.**: 8537
Ps 26:11 as for me, I will walk in mine **i.**: 8537
Ps 41:12 me, thou upholdest me in mine **i.**, 8537
Ps 78:72 according to the **i.** of his heart; 8537
Pr 11:3 The **i.** of the upright shall guide 8538
Pr 19:1 is the poor that walketh in his **i.**, 8537
Pr 20:7 The just man walketh in his **i.**: his 8537

INTELLIGENCE
Da 11:30 and have **i.** with them that forsake 995

INTEND See also INTENDED; INTENDEST; INTENDING.
Jos 22:33 and did not **i.** to go up against 559
2Ch 28:13 ye **i.** to add more to our sins and to 559
Ac 5:28 and **i.** to bring this man's blood *1014*
Ac 5:35 what ye **i.** to do as touching these *3195*

INTENDED
Ps 21:11 For they **i.** evil against thee: they 5186

INTENDEST
Ex 2:14 **i.** thou to kill me, as thou killedst 559

INTENDING
Lu 14:28 **which of you, i. to build a tower,** *2309*
Ac 12:4 **i.** after Easter to bring him forth *1011*
Ac 20:13 Assos, there **i.** to take in Paul: *3195*

INTENT See also INTENTS.
2Sa 17:14 **i.** that the Lord might bring evil 5668
2Ki 10:19 to the **i.** that he might destroy the 4616
2Ch 16:1 to the **i.** that he might let none go out
Eze 40:4 the **i.** that I might shew them unto 4616
Da 4:17 to the **i.** that the living may know 1701
Joh 11:15 not there, to the **i.** ye may believe; *2443*
Joh 13:28 for what **i.** he spake this unto
Ac 9:21 and came hither for that **i.**,
Ac 10:29 for what **i.** ye have sent for me? *3056*
1Co 10:6 to the **i.** we should not lust after
Eph 3:10 To the **i.** that now unto the *2443*

INTENTS
Jer 30:24 have performed the **i.** of his heart: 4209
Heb 4:12 of the thoughts and **i.** of the heart. *1771*

INTERCESSION See also INTERCESSIONS.
Isa 53:12 and made **i.** for the transgressors 6293
Jer 7:16 for them, neither make **i.** to me: 6293
Jer 27:18 let them now make **i.** to the Lord 6293
Jer 36:25 Gemariah had made **i.** to the king 6293
Ro 8:26 the Spirit itself maketh **i.** for us *5241*
Ro 8:27 maketh **i.** for the saints according *1793*
Ro 8:34 of God, who also maketh **i.** for us. *1793*
Ro 11:2 he maketh **i.** to God against Israel, *1793*
Heb 7:25 he ever liveth to make **i.** for them *1793*

INTERCESSIONS
1Ti 2:1 prayers, **i.**, and giving of thanks, *1783*

INTERCESSOR
Isa 59:16 wondered that there was no **i.**: 6293

INTERMEDDLE See also INTERMEDDLETH.
Pr 14:10 a stranger doth not **i.** with his joy. 6148

INTERMEDDLETH
Pr 18:1 seeketh and **i.** with all wisdom 1566

INTERMISSION
La 3:49 and ceaseth not, without any **i.**, 2014

INTERPRET See also INTERPRETED; INTERPRETING.
Ge 41:8 there was none that could **i.** them 6622
Ge 41:12 according to his dream he did **i.** 6622
Ge 41:15 and there is none that can **i.** it: 6622
Ge 41:15 canst understand a dream to **i.** it. 6622
1Co 12:30 all speak with tongues? do all **i.**? *1329*
1Co 14:5 speaketh with tongues, except he **i.**, *1329*
1Co 14:13 tongue pray that he may **i.** *1329*
1Co 14:27 and that by course; and let one **i.** *1329*

INTERPRETATION See also INTERPRETATIONS.
Ge 40:5 according to the **i.** of his dream, 6623
Ge 40:12 This is the **i.** of it: The three 6623
Ge 40:16 baker saw that the **i.** was good, 6623
Ge 40:18 This is the **i.** thereof: The three 6623
Ge 41:11 according to the **i.** of his dream. 6623
Jg 7:15 of the dream, and the **i.** thereof, 7667
Pr 1:6 understand a proverb, and the **i.**; 4426
Ec 8:1 who knoweth the **i.** of a thing? 6592
Da 2:4 the dream, and we will shew the **i.** 6591
Da 2:5 me the dream, with the **i.** thereof, 6591
Da 2:6 shew the dream and the **i.** thereof, 6591
Da 2:6 me the dream, and the **i.** thereof. 6591
Da 2:7 dream, and we will shew the **i.** of it. 6591
Da 2:9 that ye can shew me the **i.** thereof. 6591
Da 2:16 that he would shew the king the **i.** 6591
Da 2:24 I will shew unto the king the **i.** 6591
Da 2:25 make known unto the king the **i.** 6591
Da 2:26 I have seen, and the **i.** thereof? 6591
Da 2:30 make known the **i.** to the king, 6591
Da 2:36 and we will tell the **i.** thereof before 6591
Da 2:45 is certain, and the **i.** thereof sure. 6591
Da 4:6 known unto me the **i.** of the dream. 6591
Da 4:7 make known unto me the **i.** thereof. 6591
Da 4:9 that I have seen, and the **i.** thereof. 6591
Da 4:18 declare the **i.** thereof, forasmuch 6591
Da 4:18 able to make known unto me the **i.**: 6591
Da 4:19 dream or the **i.** thereof, trouble 6591
Da 4:19 and the **i.** thereof to thine enemies. 6591
Da 4:24 This is the **i.**, O king, and this is 6591
Da 5:7 writing, and shew me the **i.** thereof, 6591
Da 5:8 known to the king the **i.** thereof. 6591
Da 5:12 be called, and he will shew the **i.** 6591
Da 5:15 make known unto me the **i.** thereof: 6591
Da 5:15 could not shew the **i.** of the thing: 6591
Da 5:16 known to me the **i.** thereof, thou 6591
Da 5:17 and make known to him the **i.** 6591
Da 5:26 This is the **i.** of the thing: Mene; 6591
Da 7:16 made me know the **i.** of the things. 6591
Joh 1:42 Cephas, which is by **i.**, A stone. *2059*
Joh 9:7 **pool of Siloam,** which is by **i.**, Sent *2059*
Ac 9:36 which by **i.** is called Dorcas; this *1329*

Ac 13:8 sorcerer (for so is his name by **i.**)...... *3177*
1Co 12:10 to another the **i.** of tongues: *2058*
1Co 14:26 tongue, hath a revelation, hath an **i.**.... *2058*
Heb 7:2 being by **i.** King of righteousness, ... *2059*
2Pe 1:20 the scripture is of any private **i.**......... *1955*

INTERPRETATIONS
Ge 40:8 Do not **i.** belong to God? tell me........ 6623
Da 5:16 that thou canst make **i.**, and............. 6591

INTERPRETED
Ge 40:22 baker: as Joseph had **i.** to them. 6622
Ge 41:12 him, and he **i.** to us our dreams;........ 6622
Ge 41:13 to pass, as he **i.** to us, so it was; 6622
Ezr 4:7 and **i.** in the Syrian tongue............... 8638
Mt 1:23 which being **i.** is, God with us. *3177*
Mk 5:41 cumi; which is, being **i.**, Damsel, ... *3177*
Mk 15:22 is, being **i.**, The place of a skull......... *3177*
Mk 15:34 which is, being **i.**, My God, my God,.. *3177*
Joh 1:38 which is to say, being **i.**, Master,....... *2059*
Joh 1:41 which is, being **i.**, the Christ............ *3177*
Ac 4:36 being **i.**, The son of consolation, ... *3177*

INTERPRETER
Ge 40:8 a dream, and there is no **i.** of it........ 6622
Ge 42:23 for he spake unto them by an **i.**......... 3887
Job 33:23 an **i.**, one among a thousand, to......... 3887
1Co 14:28 if there be no **i.**, let him keep *1328*

INTERPRETING
Da 5:12 understanding, **i.** of dreams, and........ 6591

INTO See also THEREINTO.
Ge 2:7 breathed **i.** his nostrils the breath of.........
Ge 2:10 parted, and became **i.** four heads. ....
Ge 2:15 and put him **i.** the garden of Eden...........
Ge 6:18 and thou shalt come **i.** the ark,........... 413
Ge 6:19 sort shalt thou bring **i.** the ark, ... 413
Ge 7:1 thou and all thy house **i.** the ark;......... 413
Ge 7:7 his sons' wives with him, **i.** the ark,..... 413
Ge 7:9 two and two unto Noah **i.** the ark,....... 413
Ge 7:13 of his sons with them, **i.** the ark, ... 413
Ge 7:15 went in unto Noah **i.** the ark,.............. 413
Ge 8:9 she returned unto him **i.** the ark,......... 413
Ge 8:9 pulled her in unto him **i.** the ark,......... 413
Ge 9:2 sea; **i.** your hands are they delivered. ....
Ge 11:31 Chaldees, to go **i.** the land of Canaan;.......
Ge 12:5 went forth to go **i.** the land of Canaan;......
Ge 12:5 and **i.** the land of Canaan they came. ....
Ge 12:10 Abram went down **i.** Egypt to sojourn.......
Ge 12:11 he was come near to enter **i.** Egypt,.... 935
Ge 12:14 that, when Abram was come **i.** Egypt, ...
Ge 12:15 woman was taken **i.** Pharaoh's house. ....
Ge 13:1 he had, and Lot with him, **i.** the south. .....
Ge 14:20 delivered thine enemies **i.** thy hand..........
Ge 16:5 I have given my maid **i.** thy bosom;..........
Ge 18:6 And Abraham hastened **i.** the tent ....
Ge 19:2 I pray you, **i.** your servant's house, ... 413
Ge 19:3 unto him, and entered **i.** his house;...... 413
Ge 19:10 and pulled Lot **i.** the house to them, ...
Ge 19:23 the earth when Lot entered **i.** Zoar. ....
Ge 21:32 **i.** the land of the Philistines. 413
Ge 22:2 and get thee **i.** the land of Moriah;....... 413
Ge 24:20 emptied her pitcher **i.** the trough,........ 413
Ge 24:32 And the man came **i.** the house: and.........
Ge 24:67 Isaac brought her **i.** his mother...............
Ge 26:2 Go not down **i.** Egypt; dwell in the...........
Ge 27:17 prepared, **i.** the hand of her son Jacob.......
Ge 28:15 will bring thee again **i.** this land;.......... 413
Ge 29:1 came **i.** the land of the people of the.........
Ge 30:35 gave them **i.** the hand of his sons...........
Ge 31:33 went **i.** Jacob's tent, and **i.** Leah's tent,.....
Ge 31:33 and **i.** the two maidservants' tents;...........
Ge 31:33 tent, and entered **i.** Rachel's tent. ....
Ge 32:7 herds, and the camels, **i.** two bands;.........
Ge 32:16 delivered them **i.** the hand of his.............
Ge 36:6 went **i.** the country from the face 413
Ge 37:20 us slay him, and cast him **i.** some pit, ...
Ge 37:22 cast him **i.** this pit that is in the 413
Ge 37:24 they took him, and cast him **i.** a pit: ....
Ge 37:28 and they brought Joseph **i.** Egypt. ....
Ge 37:35 I will go down **i.** the grave unto my..........
Ge 37:36 Midianites sold him **i.** Egypt unto......... 413
Ge 39:4 and all that he had he put **i.** his hand. ....
Ge 39:11 that Joseph went **i.** the house to do..........
Ge 39:20 took him, and put him **i.** the prison, ... 413
Ge 40:3 **i.** the prison, the place where Joseph.... 413
Ge 40:11 and pressed them **i.** Pharaoh's cup, ... 413
Ge 40:11 I gave the cup **i.** Pharaoh's hand. 5921
Ge 40:13 deliver Pharaoh's cup **i.** his hand, ...
Ge 40:15 they should put me **i.** the dungeon. ....
Ge 40:21 gave the cup **i.** Pharaoh's hand: 5921
Ge 41:57 And all countries came **i.** Egypt to............
Ge 42:17 all together **i.** ward three days. 413
Ge 42:25 every man's money **i.** his sack, ... 413
Ge 42:37 deliver him **i.** my hand, and I will....... 5921
Ge 43:17 brought the men **i.** Joseph's house...........
Ge 43:18 they were brought **i.** Joseph's.................
Ge 43:24 brought the men **i.** Joseph's house,...........
Ge 43:26 which was in their hand **i.** the house, ...
Ge 43:30 he entered **i.** his chamber, and wept.........
Ge 45:4 your brother, whom ye sold **i.** Egypt. ....
Ge 45:25 and came **i.** the land of Canaan unto ....
Ge 46:3 fear not to go down **i.** Egypt; for I will.....
Ge 46:4 I will go down with thee **i.** Egypt; for ....
Ge 46:6 and came **i.** Egypt, Jacob, and all his.........
Ge 46:7 seed brought he with him **i.** Egypt. ....
Ge 46:8 of Israel, which came **i.** Egypt, ...
Ge 46:26 the souls that came with Jacob **i.** Egypt, 600
Ge 46:27 house of Jacob, which came **i.** Egypt,........
Ge 46:28 they came **i.** the land of Goshen...............
Ge 47:14 brought the money **i.** Pharaoh's house.......
Ge 48:5 I came unto thee **i.** Egypt, are mine; ....
Ge 48:16 let them grow **i.** a multitude in the ....
Ge 49:6 my soul, come not thou **i.** their secret; .....
Ge 49:33 he gathered up his feet **i.** the bed,....... 413
Ge 50:13 his sons carried him **i.** the land of..........
Ge 50:14 And Joseph returned **i.** Egypt, he, and ......
Ex 1:1 of Israel, which came **i.** Egypt;................
Ex 1:22 son that is born ye shall cast **i.** the..........
Ex 3:18 three days' journey **i.** the wilderness,........
Ex 4:6 him, Put now thine hand **i.** thy bosom. ......
Ex 4:6 he put his hand **i.** his bosom: and............
Ex 4:7 Put thine hand **i.** thy bosom again........ 413
Ex 4:7 put his hand **i.** his bosom again; 413
Ex 4:19 Moses in Midian, Go, return **i.** Egypt: ......
Ex 4:21 When thou goest to return **i.** Egypt, ...
Ex 4:27 Go **i.** the wilderness to meet Moses. ....
Ex 5:3 thee, three days' journey **i.** the desert, ...
Ex 7:23 turned and went **i.** his house,.............. 413
Ex 8:3 shall go up and come **i.** thine house, ...
Ex 8:3 and **i.** thy bedchamber, and upon thy ....
Ex 8:3 and **i.** the house of thy servants, and........
Ex 8:3 upon thy people and **i.** thine ovens, ...
Ex 8:3 and **i.** thy kneading troughs:....................
Ex 8:21 upon thy people, and **i.** thy houses: ....
Ex 8:24 grievous swarm of flies **i.** the house of......
Ex 8:24 **i.** his servants' houses, and **i.** all the.......
Ex 8:27 three days' journey **i.** the wilderness,........
Ex 9:20 and his cattle flee **i.** the houses:.......... 413
Ex 10:4 will I bring the locusts **i.** thy coast:...........
Ex 10:19 locusts, and cast them **i.** the Red sea;.......
Ex 11:4 midnight will I go out **i.** the midst............
Ex 13:5, 11 thee **i.** the land of the Canaanites, ... 413
Ex 14:22 of Israel went **i.** the midst of the sea ....
Ex 14:28 that came **i.** the sea after them;...............
Ex 15:1 his rider hath he thrown **i.** the sea. ....
Ex 15:4 and his host hath he cast **i.** the sea: ....
Ex 15:5 they sank **i.** the bottom as a stone. ....
Ex 15:19 and with his horsemen **i.** the sea,............
Ex 15:21 his rider hath he thrown **i.** the sea. ....
Ex 15:22 went out **i.** the wilderness of Shur; 413
Ex 15:25 when he had cast **i.** the waters, ... 413
Ex 16:3 brought us forth **i.** this wilderness,....... 413
Ex 18:5 his wife unto Moses **i.** the wilderness,.. 413
Ex 18:7 welfare; and they came **i.** the tent...........
Ex 18:27 he went his way **i.** his own land. 413
Ex 19:1 came they **i.** the wilderness of Sinai.........
Ex 19:12 that ye go not up **i.** the mount, or............
Ex 21:13 but God deliver him **i.** his hand;..............
Ex 23:19 shalt bring **i.** the house of the Lord thy.....
Ex 23:20 bring thee **i.** the place which I have 413
Ex 23:31 inhabitants of the land **i.** your hand; ....
Ex 24:12 Come up to me **i.** the mount,..................
Ex 24:13 Moses went up **i.** the mount of God..... 413
Ex 24:15 Moses went up **i.** the mount, and a...... 413
Ex 24:18 Moses went **i.** the midst of the cloud, ...
Ex 24:18 and gat him **i.** the mount: and............ 413
Ex 25:14 thou shalt put the staves **i.** the rings.........
Ex 25:16 shalt put **i.** the ark the testimony......... 413
Ex 26:11 put the taches **i.** the loops, and couple ......
Ex 27:7 the staves shall be put **i.** the rings, and.....
Ex 29:3 thou shalt put them **i.** one basket, ... 5921
Ex 29:30 **i.** the tabernacle of...congregation 413
Ex 30:20 **i.** the tabernacle of the congregation,.... 413
Ex 32:24 then I cast it **i.** the fire, and there...........
Ex 33:5 I will come up **i.** the midst of thee...........
Ex 33:8 until he was gone **i.** the tabernacle. ....
Ex 33:9 as Moses entered **i.** the tabernacle, ...
Ex 33:11 And he turned again **i.** the camp:......... 413
Ex 37:5 And he put the staves **i.** the rings by........
Ex 38:7 And he put the staves **i.** the rings on........
Ex 39:3 did beat the gold **i.** thin plates, ...
Ex 39:3 and cut it **i.** wires, to work it in the..........
Ex 40:20 and put the testimony **i.** the ark, ... 413
Ex 40:21 brought the ark **i.** the tabernacle, ... 413
Ex 40:32 went **i.** the tent of the congregation, ... 413
Ex 40:35 was not able to enter **i.** the tent.......... 413
Le 1:6 burnt offering, and cut it **i.** his pieces........
Le 1:12 And he shall cut it **i.** his pieces, with ....
Le 6:30 blood is brought **i.** the tabernacle......... 413
Le 8:20 he cut the ram **i.** pieces; and Moses........
Le 9:23 and Aaron went **i.** the tabernacle 413
Le 10:9 with ye, when ye go **i.** the tabernacle... 413
Le 11:32 it must be put **i.** water, and it shall..........
Le 12:4 thing, nor come **i.** the sanctuary, ... 413
Le 13:17 if the plague be turned **i.** white;..............
Le 14:7 living bird loose **i.** the open field. 5921
Le 14:8 that he shall come **i.** the camp, ... 413
Le 14:15 pour it **i.** the palm of his own left....... 5921
Le 14:26 oil **i.** the palm of his own left hand: 5921
Le 14:34 ye be come **i.** the land of Canaan,........ 413
Le 14:36 the priest go **i.** it to see the plague, ...
Le 14:40 shall cast them **i.** an unclean place 413
Le 14:41 without the city **i.** an unclean place: 413
Le 14:45 out of the city **i.** an unclean place. 413
Le 14:46 he that goeth **i.** the house all the......... 413
Le 14:53 bird out of the city **i.** the open fields, ... 413
Le 16:2 not at all times **i.** the holy place 413
Le 16:3 shall Aaron come **i.** the holy place:......... 413
Le 16:10 go for a scapegoat **i.** the wilderness.........
Le 16:21 hand of a fit man **i.** the wilderness:...........
Le 16:23 Aaron shall come **i.** the tabernacle 413
Le 16:23 on when he went **i.** the holy place, ... 413
Le 16:26 and afterward come **i.** the camp. 413
Le 16:28 afterward he shall come **i.** the camp. 413
Le 19:23 when ye shall come **i.** the land, and 413
Le 23:10 ye be come **i.** the land which I give 413
Le 25:2 ye come **i.** the land which I give you,... 413
Le 26:25 be delivered **i.** the hand of the enemy. ......
Le 26:32 will bring the land **i.** desolation:................
Le 26:36 send a faintness **i.** their hearts in the........
Le 26:41 them **i.** the land of their enemies;.............
Nu 4:3 all that enter **i.** the host, to do the 601
Nu 4:30, 35,39,43 that entereth **i.** the service, ...
Nu 5:17 shall take, and put it **i.** the water:........ 413
Nu 5:22 the curse shall go **i.** thy bowels,.......... 602
Nu 5:24 shall enter **i.** her and become bitter...... 603
Nu 5:27 causeth the curse shall enter **i.** her,..........
Nu 7:89 Moses was gone **i.** the tabernacle 413
Nu 11:30 Moses gat him **i.** the camp, he and...... 413
Nu 13:17 and go up **i.** the mountain: ....
Nu 14:3 it not better for us to return **i.** Egypt? ......
Nu 14:4 captain, and let us return **i.** Egypt............
Nu 14:8 he will bring us **i.** this land, and.......... 413
Nu 14:16 able to bring this people **i.** the land........ 413
Nu 14:24 him will I bring **i.** the land whereinto..... 413
Nu 14:25 get you **i.** the wilderness by the way ....
Nu 14:30 ye shall not come **i.** the land,.............. 413
Nu 14:40 them up **i.** the top of the mountain,...... 413
Nu 15:2 come **i.** the land of your habitations,..... 413
Nu 15:18 ye come **i.** the land whither I bring...... 413
Nu 16:14 **i.** a land that floweth with milk and...........
Nu 16:30 they go down quick **i.** the pit; then ye.......
Nu 16:33 went down alive **i.** the pit, and the ....
Nu 16:47 ran **i.** the midst of the congregation;...... 413
Nu 17:8 went **i.** the tabernacle of witness; 413
Nu 19:6 **i.** the midst of the burning of the......... 413
Nu 19:7 he shall come **i.** the camp, and the....... 413
Nu 19:14 all that come **i.** the tent, and all that 413
Nu 20:1 congregation, **i.** the desert of Zin in the.....
Nu 20:4 of the Lord **i.** this wilderness,............ 413
Nu 20:12 **i.** the land which I have given them...... 413
Nu 20:15 How our fathers went down **i.** Egypt, ...
Nu 20:24 he shall not enter **i.** the land which 413
Nu 20:27 they went up **i.** mount Hor in the 413
Nu 21:2 indeed deliver this people **i.** my hand, ...
Nu 21:22 turn **i.** the fields, or **i.** the vineyards;........
Nu 21:23 out against Israel **i.** the wilderness: ....
Nu 21:27 Come **i.** Heshbon, let the city of Sihon......
Nu 21:29 **i.** captivity unto Sihon king of the............

Nu 21:34 I have delivered him **i.** thy hand, and........
Nu 22:13 Get you **i.** your land: for the Lord....... 413
Nu 22:23 out of the way, and went **i.** the field:........
Nu 22:23 smote the ass, to turn her **i.** the way. ......
Nu 22:41 brought him up **i.** the high places of.........
Nu 23:14 he brought him **i.** the field of Zophim, ...
Nu 24:4, 16 falling **i.** a trance, but having his ....
Nu 25:8 after the man of Israel **i.** the tent, ... 413
Nu 27:12 Get thee up **i.** this mount Abarim, ... 413
Nu 31:24 afterward ye shall come **i.** the camp..........
Nu 31:27 And divide the prey **i.** two parts;......... 413
Nu 31:54 brought it **i.** the tabernacle of the 413
Nu 32:7 from going over **i.** the land which........ 413
Nu 32:9 they should not go **i.** the land which..... 413
Nu 32:32 before the Lord **i.** the land of Canaan,.......
Nu 33:8 midst of the sea **i.** the wilderness,............
Nu 33:38 the priest went up **i.** mount Hor.......... 413
Nu 33:51 over Jordan **i.** the land of Canaan;........ 413
Nu 34:2 ye come **i.** the land of Canaan;........... 413
Nu 35:10 over jordan **i.** the land of Canaan;............
Nu 35:28 slayer shall return **i.** the land of his...... 413
Nu 36:12 married **i.** the families of the sons of.........
De 1:22 and **i.** what cities we shall come..............
De 1:24 turned and went up **i.** the mountain, ...
De 1:27 deliver us **i.** the hand of the Amorites, ...
De 1:31 went, until ye came **i.** this place. 5704
De 1:40 take your journey **i.** the wilderness...........
De 1:41 war, ye were ready to go up **i.** the hill.....
De 1:43 went presumptuously up **i.** the hill...........
De 2:1 took our journey **i.** the wilderness by........
De 2:24 behold, I have given **i.** thine hand Sihon.....
De 2:29 **i.** the land which the Lord our God...... 413
De 2:30 that he might deliver him **i.** thy hand, ...
De 3:2 his people, and his land, **i.** thy hand;.........
De 3:3 God delivered **i.** our hands Og also,..........
De 3:27 Get thee up **i.** the top of Pisgah, and.........
De 5:5 and went not up **i.** the mount: saying,.......
De 5:30 to them, Get you **i.** your tents again.........
De 6:10 **i.** the land which he sware unto thy..... 413
De 7:1 thy God shall bring thee **i.** the land...... 413
De 7:24 shall deliver their kings **i.** thine hand,........
De 7:26 an abomination **i.** thine house,............ 413
De 8:7 God bringeth thee **i.** a good land, ... 413
De 9:9 **i.** the mount to receive the tables of........
De 9:21 I cast the dust thereof **i.** the brook...... 413
De 9:28 not able to bring them **i.** the land 413
De 10:1 and come up unto me **i.** the mount, ...
De 10:3 and went up **i.** the mount, having the........
De 10:22 Thy fathers went down **i.** Egypt with........
De 11:5 until ye came **i.** this place;............... 5704
De 13:16 spoil of it **i.** the midst of the street...... 413
De 14:6 and cleveth the cleft **i.** two claws, ...
De 14:25 turn it **i.** money, and bind up the.............
De 17:8 get thee up **i.** the place which the........ 413
De 18:9 thou art come **i.** the land which.......... 413
De 19:3 **i.** three parts, that every slayer may.........
De 19:5 **i.** the wood with his neighbour to.............
De 19:11 die, and fleeth **i.** one of these cities: 413
De 19:12 deliver him **i.** the hand of the avenger......
De 20:13 thy God hath delivered it **i.** thine hands, ...
De 21:10 God hath delivered them **i.** thine hands,.....
De 23:1 off, shall not enter **i.** the congregation.........
De 23:2 shall not enter **i.** the congregation of.........
De 23:2 shall he not enter **i.** the congregation........
De 23:3 shall not enter **i.** the congregation of.........
De 23:3 they not enter **i.** the congregation of.........
De 23:5 turned the curse **i.** a blessing unto...........
De 23:8 shall enter **i.** the congregation of the.........
De 23:11 he shall come **i.** the camp again. 8432
De 23:18 **i.** the house of the Lord thy God for.........
De 23:24 When thou comest **i.** thy neighbour's ....
De 23:25 When thou comest **i.** the standing corn......
De 24:10 not go **i.** his house to fetch his........... 413
De 26:5 he went down **i.** Egypt, and sojourned ......
De 26:9 and he hath brought us **i.** this land, ... 413
De 28:25 shalt be removed **i.** all the kingdoms?........
De 28:38 shalt carry much seed out **i.** the field, ...
De 28:41 them; for they shall go **i.** captivity...........
De 28:68 Lord shall bring thee **i.** Egypt again..........
De 29:12 enter **i.** covenant with the Lord thy ....
De 29:12 **i.** his oath, which the Lord thy God..........
De 29:28 and cast them **i.** another land,............. 413
De 30:5 thy God will bring thee **i.** the land 413
De 31:20 shall have brought them **i.** the land 413
De 31:21 them **i.** the land which I sware........... 413
De 31:23 the children of Israel **i.** the land.......... 413
De 32:26 I said, I would scatter them **i.** corners, ...
De 32:49 Get thee up **i.** this mountain.............. 413
Jos 2:1 and came **i.** an harlot's house, named........
Jos 2:3 thee, which are entered **i.** thine house: .....
Jos 2:18 when we come **i.** the land, thou shalt........
Jos 2:19 of the doors of thy house **i.** the street, ...
Jos 2:24 Lord hath delivered **i.** our hands all ....
Jos 3:11 passeth over before you **i.** Jordan............
Jos 4:5 your God **i.** the midst of Jordan,.......... 413
Jos 6:2 I have given **i.** thine hand Jericho, ...
Jos 6:11 and they came **i.** the camp, and...............
Jos 6:14 city once, and returned **i.** the camp. ....
Jos 6:19 shall come **i.** the treasury of the Lord. ......
Jos 6:20 so that the people went up **i.** the city, ...
Jos 6:22 Go **i.** the harlot's house, and bring out ......
Jos 6:24 put **i.** the treasury of the house of the ......
Jos 7:7 deliver us **i.** the hand of the Amorites, ...
Jos 8:1 given **i.** thy hand the king of Ai, and.........
Jos 8:7 your God will deliver it **i.** your hand. ....
Jos 8:13 Joshua went that night **i.** the midst of........
Jos 8:18 Ai; for i will give it **i.** thine hand. ....
Jos 8:19 and they entered **i.** the city, and took ....
Jos 10:8 for I have delivered them **i.** thine hand;.....
Jos 10:19 suffer them not to enter **i.** their 413
Jos 10:19 God hath delivered them **i.** your hand. ......
Jos 10:20 of them entered **i.** fenced cities........... 413
Jos 10:27 and cast them **i.** the cave wherein 413
Jos 10:30 king thereof, **i.** the hand of Israel;...........
Jos 10:32 delivered Lachish **i.** the hand of Israel. ......
Jos 11:8 delivered them **i.** the hand of Israel, ...
Jos 13:5 Hermon unto the entering **i.** Hamath.........
Jos 18:5 shall divide it **i.** seven parts: Judah ....
Jos 18:6 describe the land **i.** seven parts, ...
Jos 18:9 described it by cities **i.** seven parts ....
Jos 20:4 take him **i.** the city unto them, and..........
Jos 20:5 not deliver the slayer up **i.** his hand;.........
Jos 21:44 delivered all their enemies **i.** their ....
Jos 22:13 of Manasseh, **i.** the land of Gilead,....... 413
Jos 24:4 and his children went down **i.** Egypt. ....
Jos 24:8 And I brought you **i.** the land of the..........
Jos 24:8 And I gave them **i.** your hand, that ye ....
Jos 24:11 and I delivered them **i.** your hand............
Jg 1:2 I have delivered the land **i.** his hand. ....
Jg 1:3 Come up with me **i.** my lot, that we.........
Jg 1:3 I likewise will go with thee **i.** thy lot........
Jg 1:4 and the Perizzites **i.** their hand: ....
Jg 1:16 of Judah **i.** the wilderness of Judah,...........
Jg 1:24 we pray thee, the entrance **i.** the city. ......
Jg 1:25 he shewed them the entrance **i.** the..........
Jg 1:26 man went **i.** the land of the Hittites, ...
Jg 1:34 the children of Dan **i.** the mountain:..........
Jg 2:14 he delivered them **i.** the hands of............
Jg 2:14 he sold them **i.** the hands of their............
Jg 2:23 he them **i.** the hand of Joshua..................
Jg 3:8 and he sold them **i.** the hand of ....
Jg 3:10 king of Mesopotamia **i.** his hand; and ....
Jg 3:21 right thigh, and thrust it **i.** his belly: ....
Jg 3:28 your enemies the Moabites **i.** your ....
Jg 4:2 sold them **i.** the hand of Jabin king of........
Jg 4:7 and I will deliver him **i.** thine hand...........
Jg 4:9 sell Sisera **i.** the hand of a woman............
Jg 4:14 hath delivered Sisera **i.** thine hand: ....
Jg 4:18 had turned in unto her **i.** the tent, she ......
Jg 4:21 and smote the nail **i.** his temples,............
Jg 4:21 fastened it **i.** the ground: for he was..........
Jg 4:22 And when he came **i.** her tent, behold,......
Jg 5:15 he was sent on foot **i.** the valley.............
Jg 6:1 delivered them **i.** the hand of Midian.........
Jg 6:5 they entered **i.** the land to destroy it. ....
Jg 6:13 delivered us **i.** the hands of the...............
Jg 7:2 to give the Midianites **i.** their hands,.........
Jg 7:7 deliver the Midianites **i.** thine hand: ....
Jg 7:9 for I have delivered it **i.** thine hand..........
Jg 7:13 of barley bread tumbeled **i.** the host ....
Jg 7:14 for **i.** his hand hath God delivered............
Jg 7:15 returned **i.** the host of Israel, and........ 413
Jg 7:15 delivered **i.** your hand the host of............
Jg 7:16 three hundred men **i.** three companies,......
Jg 8:3 delivered **i.** your hands the princes...........
Jg 8:7 Zebah and Zalmunna **i.** mine hand,...........
Jg 9:27 And they went out **i.** the fields, and..........
Jg 9:27 and went **i.** the house of their God, ...
Jg 9:42 that the people went out **i.** the field;.........
Jg 9:43 and divided them **i.** three companies, ...
Jg 9:46 entered **i.** an hold of the house of........ 413
Jg 10:7 them **i.** the hands of the Philistines,..........
Jg 10:7 **i.** the hands of the children of Ammon.......
Jg 11:19 thee, through my land **i.** my place...... 5704
Jg 11:21 and all his people **i.** the hand of Israel. ......
Jg 11:30 the children of Ammon **i.** mine hands, ...
Jg 11:32 the Lord delivered them **i.** his hands.........
Jg 12:3 the Lord delivered them **i.** my hand:..........
Jg 13:1 them **i.** the hand of the Philistines ....
Jg 15:1 I will go in to my wife **i.** the chamber. ......
Jg 15:5 them go **i.** the standing corn of the...........
Jg 15:12 thee **i.** the hand of the Philistines.............
Jg 15:13 fast, and deliver thee **i.** their hand:...........
Jg 15:18 deliverance **i.** the hand of thy servant:.......
Jg 15:18 fall **i.** the hand of the uncircumcised?.........
Jg 16:23 Samson our enemy **i.** our hand. ....
Jg 16:24 hath delivered **i.** our hands our enemy,......
Jg 18:10 for God hath given it **i.** your hands; ....
Jg 18:18 these went **i.** Micah's house, and ....
Jg 19:3 she brought him **i.** her father's house: ....
Jg 19:11 turn in **i.** this city of the Jebusites,....... 413
Jg 19:12 aside hither **i.** the city of a stranger, ... 413
Jg 19:15 took them **i.** his house to lodgng. ....
Jg 19:21 So he brought him **i.** his house, and..........
Jg 19:22 the man that came **i.** thine house,........ 413
Jg 19:23 that this man is come **i.** mine house, ... 413
Jg 19:29 when he was come **i.** his house, he...... 413
Jg 19:29 with her bones, **i.** twelve pieces,..............
Jg 19:29 and sent her **i.** all the coasts of Israel. ......
Jg 20:4 **i.** Gibeah that belongeth to Benjamin,........
Jg 20:8 will we any of us turn **i.** his house...........
Jg 20:28 I will deliver them **i.** thine hand. ....
Ru 1:2 And they came **i.** the country of Moab, ...
Ru 2:18 she took it up, and went **i.** the city:..........
Ru 3:14 known that a woman came **i.** the floor.......
Ru 3:15 it on her: and she went **i.** the city............
Ru 4:11 woman that is come **i.** thine house....... 413
1Sa 2:14 And he struck it **i.** the pan, or kettle, or ...
1Sa 2:36 thee, **i.** one of the priests' offices, ... 413
1Sa 4:3 the people were come **i.** the camp, ... 413
1Sa 4:5 ark...of the Lord came **i.** the camp, ... 413
1Sa 4:6 of the Lord was come **i.** the camp. 413
1Sa 4:7 they said, God is come **i.** the camp...... 413
1Sa 4:10 and they fled every man **i.** his tent: ....
1Sa 4:13 when the man came **i.** the city, and.........
1Sa 5:2 they brought it **i.** the house of Dagon,.......
1Sa 5:5 nor any that come **i.** Dagon's house, ...
1Sa 6:14 the cart came **i.** the field of Joshua,...... 413
1Sa 6:19 they had looked **i.** the ark of the Lord,......
1Sa 7:1 brought it **i.** the house of Abinadab 413
1Sa 7:13 came no more **i.** the coast of Israel: ....
1Sa 9:13 As soon as ye be come **i.** the city, ye.......
1Sa 9:14 And they went up **i.** the city: 8432
1Sa 9:14 and when they were come **i.** the city, ...
1Sa 9:22 and brought them **i.** the parlour, and.........
1Sa 9:25 down from the high place **i.** the city,.........
1Sa 10:6 and shalt be turned **i.** another man. ....
1Sa 11:11 they came **i.** the midst of the host in ....
1Sa 12:8 When Jacob was come **i.** Egypt, and.........
1Sa 12:9 he sold them **i.** the hand of Sisera, ...
1Sa 12:9 and **i.** the hand of the Philistines. ....
1Sa 12:9 and **i.** the hand of the king of Moab, ...
1Sa 4:10 Lord hath delivered them **i.** our hand: ....
1Sa 4:12 delivered them **i.** the hand of Israel. ....
1Sa 4:21 went up with them **i.** the camp from.........
1Sa 4:26 the people were come **i.** the wood,...... 413
1Sa 4:37 deliver them **i.** the hand of Israel?............
1Sa 17:22 and ran **i.** the army, and came and ....
1Sa 17:46 the Lord deliver thee **i.** mine hand; ....
1Sa 17:47 and he will give you **i.** our hands..............
1Sa 17:49 that the stone sunk **i.** his forehead; ....
1Sa 19:10 and he smote the javelin **i.** the wall: ....
1Sa 20:8 hast brought thy servant **i.** a covenant.......
1Sa 20:11 Come, and let us go out **i.** the field...... 604
1Sa 20:11 they went out both of them **i.** the field......
1Sa 20:35 that Jonathan went out **i.** the field at.........
1Sa 20:42 and Jonathan went **i.** the city..................
1Sa 21:15 shall this fellow come **i.** my house? 413
1Sa 22:5 and get thee **i.** the land of Judah. ....
1Sa 22:5 and came **i.** the forest of Hareth. ....
1Sa 23:4 deliver the Philistines **i.** thine hand. ....
1Sa 23:7 God hath delivered him **i.** mine hand;.........
1Sa 23:7 by entering **i.** a town that hath gates ....
1Sa 23:11 of Keilah deliver me up **i.** his hand? ....
1Sa 23:12 me and my men **i.** the hand of Saul? ....
1Sa 23:14 but God delivered him not **i.** his hand........
1Sa 23:16 and went to David **i.** the wood, and..........
1Sa 23:20 be to deliver him **i.** the king's hand..........

1Sa 23:25 he came down **i.** a rock, and abode in
1Sa 24:4 deliver thine enemy **i.** thine hand,
1Sa 24:10 thee to day **i.** mine hand in the cave:
1Sa 24:18 Lord had delivered me **i.** thine hand,
1Sa 26:3 Saul came after him **i.** the wilderness.
1Sa 26:8 thine enemy **i.** thine hand this day:
1Sa 26:10 or he shall descend **i.** battle, and
1Sa 26:23 Lord delivered thee **i.** my hand to day,
1Sa 27:1 **i.** the land of the Philistines; 413
1Sa 28:19 with thee **i.** the hand of the Philistines:
1Sa 28:19 of Israel **i.** the hand of the Philistines.
1Sa 29:11 return **i.** the land of the Philistines. 413
1Sa 30:15 deliver me **i.** the hands of my master,
1Sa 30:23 that came against us **i.** our hand
1Sa 31:9 and sent **i.** the land of the Philistines
2Sa 2:1 I go up **i.** any of the cities of Judah?
2Sa 3:8 delivered thee **i.** the hand of David,
2Sa 3:34 not bound, nor thy feet put **i.** fetters:
2Sa 4:6 thither **i.** the midst of the house, 5704
2Sa 4:7 For when they came **i.** the house, he
2Sa 5:8 lame shall not come **i.** the house. 413
2Sa 5:19 wilt thou deliver them **i.** mine hand?
2Sa 5:19 deliver the Philistines **i.** thine hand.
2Sa 6:10 Lord unto him **i.** the city of David: 5921
2Sa 6:10 it aside **i.** the house of Obed-edom
2Sa 6:12 the house of Obed-edom **i.** the city of
2Sa 6:16 of the Lord came **i.** the city of David,
2Sa 10:2 servants came **i.** the land of the
2Sa 10:10 he delivered **i.** the hand of Abishai
2Sa 10:14 before Abishai, and entered **i.** the city.
2Sa 11:11 I then go **i.** mine house, to eat and to 413
2Sa 11:23 us, and came out unto us **i.** the field,
2Sa 12:8 and thy master's wives **i.** thy bosom,
2Sa 12:20 came **i.** the house of the Lord, and
2Sa 13:10 Bring the meat **i.** the chamber, that I
2Sa 13:10 brought them **i.** the chamber to Amnon
2Sa 15:25 Carry back the ark of God **i.** the city:
2Sa 15:27 return **i.** the city in peace, and your
2Sa 15:31 the counsel of Ahithophel **i.** foolishness
2Sa 15:37 Hushai David's friend came **i.** the city,
2Sa 15:37 and Absalom came **i.** Jerusalem.
2Sa 16:8 the kingdom **i.** the hand of Absalom
2Sa 17:13 if he be gotten **i.** a city, then shall 413
2Sa 17:13 and we will draw it **i.** the river, 5704
2Sa 17:17 might not be seen to come **i.** the city:
2Sa 18:6 went out **i.** the field against Israel:
2Sa 18:17 cast him **i.** a great pit in the wood, 413
2Sa 19:2 that day was turned **i.** mourning
2Sa 19:3 them by stealth that day **i.** the city,
2Sa 19:5 Joab came **i.** the house to the king,
2Sa 20:12 Amasa out of the highway **i.** the field,
2Sa 21:9 them **i.** the hands of the Gibeonites,
2Sa 22:7 temple, and my cry did enter **i.** his ears.
2Sa 22:20 brought me forth also **i.** a large place:
2Sa 23:11 were gathered together **i.** a troop,
2Sa 24:14 let us fall now **i.** the hand of the Lord;
2Sa 24:14 and let me not fall **i.** the hand of man.
1Ki 1:15 went in unto the king **i.** the chamber:
1Ki 1:28 she came **i.** the king's presence, and
1Ki 3:1 brought her **i.** the city of David, 413
1Ki 6:8 with winding stairs **i.** the middle 5921
1Ki 6:8 and out of the middle **i.** the third. 413
1Ki 8:6 **i.** the oracle of the house, to the 413
1Ki 11:17 servants with him, to go **i.** Egypt;
1Ki 11:40 and fled **i.** Egypt, unto Shishak king of
1Ki 13:18 him back with thee **i.** thine house, 413
1Ki 14:12 and when thy feet enter **i.** the city, the
1Ki 14:28 the king went **i.** the house of the Lord,
1Ki 14:28 them back **i.** the guard chamber. 413
1Ki 15:15 dedicated, **i.** the house of the Lord,
1Ki 15:18 them **i.** the hand of his servants;
1Ki 16:18 **i.** the palace of the king's house, 413
1Ki 16:21 the people of Israel divided **i.** two parts:
1Ki 17:19 and carried him up **i.** a loft, where 413
1Ki 17:21 this child's soul come **i.** him again. 5921
1Ki 17:22 soul of the child came **i.** him again, 5921
1Ki 17:23 down out of the chamber **i.** the house,
1Ki 18:5 Go **i.** the land, unto all fountains of
1Ki 18:9 deliver thy servant **i.** the hand of Ahab,
1Ki 19:4 went a day's journey **i.** the wilderness,
1Ki 20:2 to Ahab king of Israel **i.** the city, and
1Ki 20:13 I will deliver it **i.** thine hand this day;
1Ki 20:28 all this great multitude **i.** thine hand,
1Ki 20:30 the rest fled to Aphek, **i.** the city; 413
1Ki 20:30 Ben-hadad fled and came **i.** the city, 413
1Ki 20:30 fled, and came...**i.** an inner chamber. 413
1Ki 20:33 him to come up **i.** the chariot. 5921
1Ki 20:39 went out **i.** the midst of the battle;
1Ki 21:4 Ahab came **i.** his house heavy and 413
1Ki 22:6 shall deliver it **i.** the hand of the king.
1Ki 22:12 Lord shall deliver it **i.** the king's hand.
1Ki 22:15 shall deliver it **i.** the hand of the king.
1Ki 22:25 shalt go **i.** an inner chamber to hide
1Ki 22:30 thyself, and enter **i.** the battle;
1Ki 22:30 himself, and went **i.** the battle.
1Ki 22:35 wound **i.** the midst of the chariot. 413
2Ki 2:1 up Elijah **i.** heaven by a whirlwind,
2Ki 2:11 went up by a whirlwind **i.** heaven.
2Ki 2:16 upon some mountain, or **i.** some valley.
2Ki 3:10 to deliver them **i.** the hand of Moab!
2Ki 3:13 to deliver them **i.** the hand of Moab,
2Ki 3:18 deliver the Moabites also **i.** your hand.
2Ki 4:4 shalt pour out **i.** all those vessels, 5921
2Ki 4:11 and he turned **i.** the chamber, and 413
2Ki 4:32 when Elisha was come **i.** the house,
2Ki 4:39 went out **i.** the field to gather herbs, 413
2Ki 4:39 shred them **i.** the pot of pottage: 413
2Ki 4:41 bring meal. And he cast it **i.** the pot: 413
2Ki 5:18 master goeth **i.** the house of Rimmon
2Ki 6:5 the axe head fell **i.** the water: and 413
2Ki 6:20 when they were come **i.** Samaria, that
2Ki 6:23 came no more **i.** the land of Israel.
2Ki 7:4 If we say, We will enter **i.** the city,
2Ki 7:8 they went **i.** one tent, and did eat 413
2Ki 7:8 and entered **i.** another tent, and 413
2Ki 7:12 catch them alive, and get **i.** the city. 413
2Ki 8:21 and the people fled **i.** their tents.
2Ki 9:6 And he arose, and went **i.** the house;
2Ki 9:26 and cast him **i.** the plat of ground,
2Ki 10:15 took him up to him **i.** the chariot. 413
2Ki 10:21 And they came **i.** the house of Baal;
2Ki 10:23 son of Rechab, **i.** the house of Baal,
2Ki 10:24 I have brought **i.** your hands 5921
2Ki 11:4 them to him **i.** the house of the Lord,
2Ki 11:13 the people **i.** the temple of the Lord.
2Ki 11:16 the horses came **i.** the king's house:
2Ki 11:18 of the land went **i.** the house of Baal,
2Ki 12:4 is brought **i.** the house of the Lord,
2Ki 12:4 that cometh **i.** any man's heart 5921
2Ki 12:4 to bring **i.** the house of the Lord,
2Ki 12:9 one cometh **i.** the house of the Lord:
2Ki 12:9 brought **i.** the house of the Lord.
2Ki 12:11 **i.** the hands of them that did the 5921
2Ki 12:13 brought **i.** the house of the Lord:
2Ki 12:15 **i.** whose hand they delivered the 5921
2Ki 12:16 brought **i.** the house of the Lord:
2Ki 13:3 delivered them **i.** the hand of Hazael
2Ki 13:3 and **i.** the hand of Ben-hadad the son
2Ki 13:21 the man **i.** the sepulchre of Elisha:
2Ki 17:6 and carried Israel away **i.** Assyria,
2Ki 17:20 them **i.** the hand of spoilers,
2Ki 18:21 if a man lean, it will go **i.** his hand,
2Ki 18:30 be delivered **i.** the hand of the king
2Ki 19:1 and went **i.** the house of the Lord.
2Ki 19:10 be delivered **i.** the hand of the king
2Ki 19:14 went up **i.** the house of the Lord,
2Ki 19:18 And have cast their gods **i.** the fire:
2Ki 19:23 enter **i.** the lodgings of his borders,
2Ki 19:23 and **i.** the forest of his Carmel.
2Ki 19:25 waste fenced cities **i.** ruinous heaps.
2Ki 19:28 the tumult is come up **i.** mine ears,
2Ki 19:32 He shall not come **i.** this city, nor 413
2Ki 19:33 and shall not come **i.** this city, 413
2Ki 19:37 they escaped **i.** the land of Armenia.
2Ki 20:4 was gone out **i.** the middle court,
2Ki 20:8 I shall go up **i.** the house of the Lord
2Ki 20:17 shall be carried **i.** Babylon, 605
2Ki 20:20 conduit, and brought water **i.** the city,
2Ki 21:14 them **i.** the hand of their enemies;
2Ki 22:4 brought **i.** the house of the Lord,
2Ki 22:5 deliver it **i.** the hand of the doers 5921
2Ki 22:7 that was delivered **i.** their hand, 5921
2Ki 22:9 delivered it **i.** the hand of them that 5921
2Ki 22:20 be gathered **i.** thy grave in peace; 413
2Ki 23:2 went up **i.** the house of the Lord,
2Ki 23:12 dust of them **i.** the brook Kidron. 413
2Ki 24:15 carried he **i.** captivity from Jerusalem
1Ch 5:20 Hagarites were delivered **i.** their hand,
1Ch 6:15 And Jehozadak went **i.** captivity,
1Ch 10:9 and sent **i.** the land of the Philistines
1Ch 11:15 to David, **i.** the cave of Adullam; 413
1Ch 12:8 David **i.** the hold to the wilderness
1Ch 13:13 it aside **i.** the house of Obed-edom 413
1Ch 14:10 wilt thou deliver them **i.** mine hand?
1Ch 14:10 for I will deliver them **i.** thine hand
1Ch 14:17 fame of David went out **i.** all lands;
1Ch 16:7 **i.** the hand of Asaph and his brethren
1Ch 19:2 **i.** the land of the children of Ammon 413
1Ch 19:15 his brother, and entered **i.** the city.
1Ch 21:13 let me fall now **i.** the hand of the Lord;
1Ch 21:13 but let me not fall **i.** the hand of man.
1Ch 21:27 up his sword again **i.** the sheath 413
1Ch 22:18 inhabitants of the land **i.** mine hand;
1Ch 22:19 **i.** the house that is to be built to the
1Ch 23:6 David divided them **i.** courses among
1Ch 24:19 service to come **i.** the house of the Lord,
2Ch 5:7 the house, **i.** the most holy place, 413
2Ch 6:41 arise, O Lord God, **i.** thy resting place,
2Ch 7:2 not enter **i.** the house of the Lord, 413
2Ch 7:10 he sent the people away **i.** their tents,
2Ch 7:11 all that came **i.** Solomon's heart 5921
2Ch 9:4 he went up **i.** the house of the Lord;
2Ch 12:11 king entered **i.** the house of the Lord,
2Ch 12:11 them again **i.** the guard chamber. 413
2Ch 13:16 and God delivered them **i.** their hand.
2Ch 15:12 And they entered **i.** a covenant to seek
2Ch 15:18 And he brought **i.** the house of God
2Ch 16:8 Lord, he delivered them **i.** thine hand.
2Ch 18:5 for God will deliver it **i.** the king's hand.
2Ch 18:11 shall deliver it **i.** the hand of the king.
2Ch 18:14 they shall be delivered **i.** your hand.
2Ch 18:24 shalt go **i.** an inner chamber to hide
2Ch 20:20 went forth **i.** the wilderness of Tekoa:
2Ch 21:17 And they came up **i.** Judah,
2Ch 21:17 and brake **i.** it, and carried away
2Ch 23:1 the son of Zichri, **i.** covenant with him.
2Ch 23:6 none come **i.** the house of the Lord,
2Ch 23:7 whosoever else cometh **i.** the house,
2Ch 23:12 to the people **i.** the house of the Lord:
2Ch 23:20 the high gate **i.** the king's house,
2Ch 24:10 and cast **i.** the chest, until they had
2Ch 24:24 a very great host **i.** their hand, because
2Ch 25:20 them **i.** the hand of their enemies,
2Ch 26:16 and went **i.** the temple of the Lord 413
2Ch 27:2 not **i.** the temple of the Lord. And 413
2Ch 28:5 him **i.** the hand of the king of Syria;
2Ch 28:5 **i.** the hand of the king of Israel.
2Ch 28:9 he hath delivered them **i.** your hand,
2Ch 28:27 they brought him not **i.** the sepulchres
2Ch 29:4 them together **i.** the east street,
2Ch 29:16 **i.** the inner part of the house of the
2Ch 29:16 **i.** the court of the house of the Lord.
2Ch 29:16 it out abroad **i.** the brook Kidron.
2Ch 29:31 offerings **i.** the house of the Lord.
2Ch 30:8 enter **i.** his sanctuary, which he hath
2Ch 30:9 that they shall come again **i.** this land:
2Ch 30:14 and cast them **i.** the brook Kidron.
2Ch 30:15 offerings **i.** the house of the Lord.
2Ch 31:1 to his possession, **i.** their own cities.
2Ch 31:10 the offerings **i.** the house of the Lord,
2Ch 31:16 that entereth **i.** the house of the Lord,
2Ch 32:1 and entered **i.** Judah, and encamped
2Ch 32:21 he was come **i.** the house of his god,
2Ch 33:13 again to Jerusalem **i.** his kingdom.
2Ch 34:7 beaten the graven images **i.** powder,
2Ch 34:9 was brought **i.** the house of God,
2Ch 34:14 brought **i.** the house of the Lord,
2Ch 34:17 it **i.** the hand of the overseers, 5921
2Ch 34:30 king went up **i.** the house of the Lord,
2Ch 36:17 for age: he gave them all **i.** his hand.
Ezr 5:8 we went **i.** the province of Judea, to
Ezr 5:12 them **i.** the hand of Nebuchadnezzar
Ezr 5:12 carried the people away **i.** Babylon.
Ezr 5:14 brought them **i.** the temple of Babylon,
Ezr 5:15 carry them **i.** the temple that is in
Ezr 9:7 delivered **i.** the hand of the kings of
Ezr 10:6 went **i.** the chamber of Johanan 413
Ne 2:7 convey me over till I come **i.** Judah; 413
Ne 2:8 for the house that I shall enter **i.**. 5921
Ne 5:5 we bring **i.** bondage our sons and
Ne 6:11 go **i.** the temple to save his life? 413
Ne 7:5 my God put **i.** mine heart to gather 413
Ne 8:1 as one man **i.** the street that was 413
Ne 9:11 persecutors thou threwest **i.** the deeps,
Ne 9:11 as a stone **i.** the mighty waters
Ne 9:22 and didst divide them **i.** corners: so
Ne 9:23 and broughtest them **i.** the land, 413
Ne 9:24 and gavest them **i.** their hands, with
Ne 9:27 them **i.** the hands of their enemies,
Ne 9:30 **i.** the hand of the people of the lands.
Ne 10:29 their nobles, and entered **i.** a curse,

Ne 10:29 and **i.** an oath, to walk in God's law,
Ne 10:34 to bring it **i.** the house of our God,
Ne 10:38 the chambers, **i.** the treasure-house.
Ne 12:44 to gather **i.** them out of the fields of
Ne 13:1 not come **i.** the congregation of God
Ne 13:2 our God turned the curse **i.** a blessing.
Ne 13:15 **i.** Jerusalem on the sabbath day:
Es 1:22 letters **i.** all the king's provinces, 413
Es 1:22 **i.** every province according to the
Es 2:14 she returned **i.** the second house 413
Es 2:16 Ahasuerus **i.** his house royal in the 413
Es 3:9 to bring it **i.** the king's treasuries 413
Es 3:13 by posts **i.** all the king's provinces, 413
Es 4:1 out **i.** the midst of the city, and
Es 4:2 none might enter **i.** the king's gate 413
Es 4:11 unto the king **i.** the inner court, 413
Es 6:4 Haman was come **i.** the outward court
Es 7:7 wrath went **i.** the palace garden: 413
Es 7:8 the palace garden **i.** the place of the 413
Es 9:22 and from mourning **i.** a good day:
Job 3:6 come **i.** the number of the months
Job 9:24 is given **i.** the hand of the wicked:
Job 10:9 wilt thou bring me **i.** dust again? 413
Job 12:6 **i.** whose hand God bringeth
Job 14:3 bringest me **i.** judgment with thee?
Job 16:11 me over **i.** the hands of the wicked 413
Job 17:12 They change the night **i.** day: the
Job 18:8 For he is cast **i.** a net by his own feet,
Job 18:18 shall be driven from light **i.** darkness,
Job 22:4 will he enter with thee **i.** judgment?
Job 30:3 fleeing **i.** the wilderness in former
Job 30:19 He hath cast me **i.** the mire, and I am
Job 30:31 and my organ **i.** the voice of them that
Job 33:28 deliver his soul from going **i.** the pit,
Job 34:23 that he should enter **i.** judgment with 606
Job 36:16 thee out of the strait **i.** a broad place,
Job 37:8 Then the beasts go **i.** dens, and 1119
Job 38:16 Hast thou entered **i.** the springs of 5704
Job 38:22 Hast thou entered **i.** the treasures 413
Job 38:38 When the dust groweth **i.** hardness,
Job 39:12 thy seed, and gather it **i.** thy barn?
Job 40:23 can draw up Jordan **i.** his mouth. 413
Job 41:2 Canst thou put a hook **i.** his nose?
Job 41:22 sorrow is turned **i.** joy before him.
Job 41:28 are turned with him **i.** stubble
Ps 4:2 long will ye turn my glory **i.** shame?
Ps 5:7 I will come **i.** thy house in the
Ps 7:15 and is fallen **i.** the ditch which he
Ps 9:17 The wicked shall be turned **i.** hell,
Ps 10:9 poor, when he draweth him **i.** his net
Ps 16:4 take up their names **i.** my lips. 5921
Ps 18:6 cry came before him, even **i.** his ears.
Ps 18:19 brought me forth also **i.** a large place;
Ps 22:15 hast brought me **i.** the dust of death.
Ps 24:3 shall ascend **i.** the hill of the Lord?
Ps 28:1 like them that go down **i.** the pit.
Ps 30:11 for me my mourning **i.** dancing:
Ps 31:5 **I.** thine hand I commit my spirit:
Ps 31:8 not shut me up **i.** the hand of the
Ps 32:4 is turned **i.** the drought of summer.
Ps 35:8 **i.** that very destruction let him fall
Ps 35:13 my prayer returned **i.** mine own 5921
Ps 37:15 sword shall enter **i.** their own heart,
Ps 37:20 **i.** smoke shall they consume away.
Ps 45:2 grace is poured **i.** thy lips: therefore
Ps 45:15 they shall enter **i.** the King's palace.
Ps 46:2 be carried **i.** the midst of the sea;
Ps 55:15 and let them go down quick **i.** hell:
Ps 55:23 them down **i.** the pit of destruction:
Ps 56:8 put thou my tears **i.** thy bottle: are
Ps 57:6 **i.** the midst whereof they are fallen
Ps 60:9 Who will bring me **i.** the strong city?
Ps 60:9 who will lead me **i.** Edom? 5704
Ps 63:9 shall go **i.** the lower parts of the earth.
Ps 66:6 He turned the sea **i.** dry land: they
Ps 66:11 Thou broughtest us **i.** the net; thou
Ps 66:12 broughtest us out **i.** a wealthy place
Ps 66:13 go **i.** thy house with burnt offerings:
Ps 69:2 I am come **i.** deep waters, where the
Ps 69:27 them not come **i.** thy righteousness.
Ps 73:17 I went **i.** the sanctuary of God; 413
Ps 73:18 castedst them down **i.** destruction.
Ps 73:19 How are they brought **i.** desolation,
Ps 74:7 They have cast fire **i.** thy sanctuary,
Ps 76:6 and horse are cast **i.** a dead sleep.
Ps 78:44 And had turned their rivers **i.** blood;
Ps 78:61 And delivered his strength **i.** captivity,
Ps 78:61 his glory **i.** the enemy's hand
Ps 79:1 heathen are come **i.** thine inheritance:
Ps 79:12 neighbours sevenfold **i.** their bosom 413
Ps 88:4 with them that go down **i.** the pit:
Ps 88:18 and mine acquaintance **i.** darkness.
Ps 95:11 they should not enter **i.** my rest. 413
Ps 96:8 an offering, and come **i.** his courts.
Ps 100:4 Enter **i.** his gates with thanksgiving,
Ps 100:4 and **i.** his courts with praise: be
Ps 104:10 He sendeth the springs **i.** the valleys,
Ps 105:23 Israel also came **i.** Egypt; and Jacob
Ps 105:29 He turned their waters **i.** blood, and
Ps 106:15 but sent leanness **i.** their soul,
Ps 106:20 changed their glory **i.** the similitude
Ps 106:41 And he gave them **i.** the hand of the
Ps 106:42 they were brought **i.** subjection
Ps 107:33 He turneth rivers **i.** a wilderness, and
Ps 107:33 the watersprings **i.** dry ground;
Ps 107:34 A fruitful land **i.** barrenness, for the
Ps 107:35 the wilderness **i.** a standing water,
Ps 107:35 and dry ground **i.** watersprings.
Ps 108:10 Who will bring me **i.** the strong city?
Ps 108:10 who will lead me **i.** Edom? 5704
Ps 109:18 let it come **i.** his bowels like water,
Ps 109:18 and like oil **i.** his bones.
Ps 114:8 turned the rock **i.** a standing water,
Ps 114:8 the flint **i.** a fountain of waters.
Ps 115:17 neither any that go down **i.** silence.
Ps 118:19 I will go **i.** them, and I will praise the
Ps 118:20 **i.** which the righteous shall enter.
Ps 122:1 Let us go **i.** the house of the Lord.
Ps 132:3 I will not come **i.** the tabernacle of
Ps 132:3 of my house, nor go up **i.** my bed; 5921
Ps 132:7 We will go **i.** his tabernacles: we will
Ps 132:8 Arise, O Lord, **i.** thy rest; thou, and
Ps 135:9 and wonders **i.** the midst of thee,
Ps 136:13 which divided the Red sea **i.** parts:
Ps 139:8 If I ascend up **i.** heaven, thou art
Ps 140:10 them: let them be cast **i.** the fire;
Ps 140:10 **i.** deep pits, that they rise not up
Ps 141:10 Let the wicked fall **i.** their own nets,
Ps 143:2 not **i.** judgment with thy servant:
Ps 143:7 unto them that go down **i.** the pit.
Ps 143:10 lead me **i.** the land of uprightness.
Pr 1:12 as those that go down **i.** the pit:
Pr 2:10 wisdom entereth **i.** thine heart,
Pr 4:14 Enter not **i.** the path of the wicked,
Pr 6:3 art come **i.** the hand of thy friend;
Pr 13:17 wicked messenger falleth **i.** mischief:
Pr 16:29 him **i.** the way that is not good.
Pr 16:33 The lot is cast **i.** the lap; but the
Pr 17:10 reproof entereth more **i.** a wise man
Pr 17:10 than an hundred stripes **i.** a fool.
Pr 17:20 a perverse tongue falleth **i.** mischief.
Pr 18:6 A fool's lips enter **i.** contention, and
Pr 18:8 **i.** the innermost parts of the belly.
Pr 18:10 righteous runneth **i.** it, and is safe.
Pr 19:15 Slothfulness casteth **i.** a deep sleep;
Pr 23:10 enter not **i.** the fields of the fatherless:
Pr 24:16 but the wicked shall fall **i.** mischief.
Pr 26:9 goeth up **i.** the hand of a drunkard,
Pr 26:22 **i.** the innermost parts of the belly.
Pr 27:10 neither go **i.** thy brother's house in
Pr 28:10 he shall fall himself **i.** his own pit:
Pr 28:14 his heart shall fall **i.** mischief.
Pr 29:8 men bring a city **i.** a snare:
Pr 30:4 Who hath ascended up **i.** heaven,
Ec 1:7 All the rivers run **i.** the sea; yet 413
Ec 10:8 He that diggeth a pit shall fall **i.** it;
Ec 11:9 God will bring thee **i.** judgment.
Ec 12:14 shall bring every work **i.** judgment,
Ca 1:4 hath brought me **i.** his chambers:
Ca 3:4 brought him **i.** my mother's house, 413
Ca 3:4 **i.** the chamber of her that conceived 413
Ca 4:16 Let my beloved come **i.** his garden,
Ca 5:1 I am come **i.** my garden, my sister, my
Ca 6:2 beloved is gone down **i.** his garden,
Ca 6:11 I went down **i.** the garden of nuts 413
Ca 7:11 beloved, let us go forth **i.** the field;
Ca 8:2 bring thee **i.** my mother's house, 413
Isa 2:4 beat their swords **i.** plowshares,
Isa 2:4 and their spears **i.** pruninghooks:
Isa 2:10 Enter **i.** the rock, and hide thee in the
Isa 2:19 they shall go **i.** the holes of the rocks,
Isa 2:19 and **i.** the caves of the earth, for fear
Isa 2:21 To go **i.** the clefts of the rocks,
Isa 2:21 and **i.** the tops of the ragged rocks,
Isa 3:14 The Lord will enter **i.** judgment with
Isa 5:13 my people are gone **i.** captivity,
Isa 5:14 he that rejoiceth, shall descend **i.** it.
Isa 9:8 The Lord sent a word **i.** Jacob, and it
Isa 9:10 but we will change them **i.** cedars.
Isa 13:2 they may go **i.** the gates of the nobles.
Isa 13:14 and flee every one **i.** his own land. 413
Isa 14:7 quiet: they break forth **i.** singing.
Isa 14:13 I will ascend **i.** heaven, I will exalt my
Isa 19:1 swift cloud, and shall come **i.** Egypt:
Isa 19:4 I give over **i.** the hand of a cruel lord;
Isa 19:8 they that cast angle **i.** the brooks
Isa 19:23 the Assyrian shall come **i.** Egypt,
Isa 19:23 and the Egyptian **i.** to Assyria, and the
Isa 21:4 of my pleasure hath he turned **i.** fear
Isa 22:18 thee like a ball **i.** a large country: 413
Isa 22:21 commit thy government **i.** his hand:
Isa 23:9 **i.** contempt all the honourable
Isa 24:18 noise of the fear shall fall **i.** the pit; 413
Isa 26:20 my people, enter thou **i.** thy chambers,
Isa 29:17 shall be turned **i.** a fruitful field,
Isa 30:2 That walk to go down **i.** Egypt, and
Isa 30:6 **i.** the land of trouble and anguish,
Isa 30:20 be removed **i.** a corner any more,
Isa 30:29 to come **i.** the mountain of the Lord,
Isa 34:9 thereof shall be turned **i.** pitch,
Isa 34:9 and the dust thereof **i.** brimstone,
Isa 36:6 it will go **i.** his hand, and pierce it:
Isa 36:15 be delivered **i.** the hand of the king
Isa 37:1 and went **i.** the house of the Lord.
Isa 37:10 not be given **i.** the hand of the king
Isa 37:19 And have cast their gods **i.** the fire:
Isa 37:24 I will enter **i.** the height of his border,
Isa 37:26 waste defenced cities **i.** ruinous heaps.
Isa 37:29 thy tumult, is come up **i.** mine ears,
Isa 37:33 He shall not come **i.** this city, 413
Isa 37:34 shall not come **i.** this city, saith the 413
Isa 37:38 they escaped **i.** the land of Armenia:
Isa 38:18 go down **i.** the pit cannot hope for thy
Isa 40:9 get thee up **i.** the high mountain; 5921
Isa 44:23 break forth **i.** singing, ye mountains,
Isa 46:2 but themselves are gone **i.** captivity.
Isa 47:5 thou silent, and get thee **i.** darkness,
Isa 47:6 and given them **i.** thine hand:
Isa 49:13 break forth **i.** singing, O mountains:
Isa 51:23 put it **i.** the hand of them that afflict
Isa 52:1 there shall no more come **i.** thee the
Isa 52:4 people went down aforetime **i.** Egypt
Isa 52:9 Break forth **i.** joy, sing together,
Isa 54:1 break forth **i.** singing, and cry aloud,
Isa 55:12 shall break forth before you **i.** singing,
Isa 57:2 He shall enter **i.** peace: they shall
Isa 59:5 is crushed breaketh out **i.** a viper.
Isa 63:14 As a beast goeth down **i.** the valley,
Isa 65:6 even recompense **i.** their bosom, 5921
Isa 65:7 their former work **i.** their bosom. 5921
Isa 65:17 be remembered, nor come **i.** mind. 5921
Isa 66:20 offering in a clean vessel **i.** the house
Jer 2:7 brought you **i.** a plentiful country, 413
Jer 2:21 art thou turned **i.** the degenerate plant
Jer 4:5 and let us go **i.** the defenced cities. 413
Jer 4:29 they shall go **i.** thickets, and climb
Jer 6:9 as a grapegatherer **i.** the baskets. 5921
Jer 6:25 Go not forth **i.** the field, nor walk by
Jer 7:31 not, neither came it **i.** my heart. 5921
Jer 8:6 as the horse rusheth **i.** the battle.
Jer 8:14 let us enter **i.** the defenced cities, 413
Jer 9:21 For death is come up **i.** our windows,
Jer 9:21 and is entered **i.** our palaces, to cut off
Jer 10:9 Silver spread **i.** plates is brought
Jer 12:7 of my soul **i.** the hand of her enemies.
Jer 13:16 he turn it **i.** the shadow of death,
Jer 14:18 If I go forth **i.** the field, then behold
Jer 14:18 and if I enter **i.** the city, then behold
Jer 14:18 about **i.** a land that they know not. 413
Jer 15:4 removed **i.** all kingdoms of the earth,
Jer 15:14 **i.** a land which thou knowest not:
Jer 16:5 Enter not **i.** the house of mourning,
Jer 16:8 not also go **i.** the house of feasting,
Jer 16:13 land **i.** a land that ye know not, 5921
Jer 16:15 **i.** their land that I gave unto their 5921
Jer 17:25 there enter **i.** the gates of this city
Jer 19:5 neither came it **i.** my mind: 5921
Jer 20:4 all Judah **i.** the hand of the king
Jer 20:4 shall carry them captive **i.** Babylon,
Jer 20:5 I give **i.** the hand of their enemies,

Jer 20:6 in thine house, shall go **i.** captivity:
Jer 21:4 them **i.** the midst of this city. 413
Jer 21:7 **i.** the hand of Nebuchadrezzar king
Jer 21:7 and **i.** the hand of their enemies,
Jer 21:7 and **i.** the hand of those that seek
Jer 21:10 **i.** the hand of the king of Babylon,
Jer 21:13 or who shall enter **i.** our habitations?
Jer 22:7 cedars, and cast them **i.** the fire. 5921
Jer 22:22 and thy lovers shall go **i.** captivity:
Jer 22:25 **i.** the hand of them that seek thy life,
Jer 22:25 and **i.** the hand of them whose face
Jer 22:25 even **i.** the hand of Nebuchadrezzar
Jer 22:25 and **i.** the hand of the Chaldeans.
Jer 22:26 **i.** another country, where ye were 5921
Jer 22:28 cast **i.** a land which they know not? 5921
Jer 23:15 profaneness gone forth **i.** all the land
Jer 24:5 this place **i.** the land of the Chaldeans,
Jer 24:9 to be removed **i.** all the kingdoms of
Jer 26:21 was afraid, and fled, and went **i.** Egypt;
Jer 26:22 the king sent men **i.** Egypt, namely,
Jer 26:22 and certain men with him **i.** Egypt. 413
Jer 26:23 **i.** the graves of the common people. 413
Jer 26:24 not give him **i.** the hand of the people
Jer 27:6 lands **i.** the hand of Nebuchadnezzar 413
Jer 28:3 again **i.** this place all the vessels of
Jer 28:4 of Judah, that went **i.** Babylon, saith
Jer 28:6 captive, from Babylon **i.** this place. 413
Jer 29:14 bring you again **i.** the place whence 413
Jer 29:16 are not gone forth with you **i.** captivity;
Jer 29:21 them **i.** the hand of Nebuchadrezzar
Jer 30:6 and all faces are turned **i.** paleness?
Jer 30:16 every one of them, shall go **i.** captivity;
Jer 31:13 for I will turn their mourning **i.** joy,
Jer 32:3 give this city **i.** the hand of the king of
Jer 32:4 be delivered **i.** the hand of the king of
Jer 32:18 of the fathers **i.** the bosom of their 413
Jer 32:24 is given **i.** the hand of the Chaldeans,
Jer 32:25 is given **i.** the hand of the Chaldeans
Jer 32:28 this city **i.** the hand of the Chaldeans,
Jer 32:28 and **i.** the hand of Nebuchadrezzar
Jer 32:35 neither came it **i.** my mind, that 5921
Jer 32:36 be delivered **i.** the hand of the king of
Jer 32:43 it is given **i.** the hand of the Chaldeans
Jer 33:11 of praise **i.** the house of the Lord
Jer 34:2 give this city **i.** the hand of the king
Jer 34:3 be taken, and delivered **i.** his hand;
Jer 34:10 which had entered **i.** the covenant,
Jer 34:11 and brought them **i.** subjection for
Jer 34:16 and brought them **i.** subjection, to be
Jer 34:17 to be removed **i.** all the kingdoms of
Jer 34:20 give them **i.** the hand of their enemies,
Jer 34:20 and **i.** the hand of them that seek their
Jer 34:21 I give **i.** the hand of their enemies,
Jer 34:21 and **i.** the hand of them that seek their
Jer 34:21 and **i.** the hand of the king of Babylon's
Jer 35:2 bring them **i.** the house of the Lord,
Jer 35:2 **i.** one of the chambers, and give 413
Jer 35:4 brought them **i.** the house of the Lord,
Jer 35:4 i. the chamber of the sons of Hanan, 413
Jer 35:11 king of Babylon came up **i.** the land, 413
Jer 36:5 I cannot go **i.** the house of the Lord:
Jer 36:12 Then he went down **i.** the king's house,
Jer 36:12 **i.** the scribe's chamber: and, lo, 5921
Jer 36:20 they went in to the king **i.** the court,
Jer 36:23 **i.** the fire that was on the hearth, 413
Jer 37:4 for they had not put him **i.** prison
Jer 37:7 return to Egypt **i.** their own land
Jer 37:12 to go **i.** the land of Benjamin,
Jer 37:16 was entered **i.** the dungeon, and 413
Jer 37:16 and **i.** the cabins, and Jeremiah 413
Jer 37:17 be delivered **i.** the hand of the king
Jer 37:21 Jeremiah **i.** the court of the prison,
Jer 38:3 be given **i.** the hand of the king surely
Jer 38:6 him **i.** the dungeon of Malchiah 413
Jer 38:9 whom they have cast **i.** the dungeon; 413
Jer 38:11 and went **i.** the house of the king
Jer 38:11 down by cords **i.** the dungeon 413
Jer 38:14 prophet unto him **i.** the third entry 413
Jer 38:16 I give thee **i.** the hand of these men
Jer 38:18 be given **i.** the hand of the Chaldeans,
Jer 38:19 lest they deliver me **i.** their hand, and
Jer 39:9 carried away captive **i.** Babylon the
Jer 39:17 given **i.** the hand of the men of whom
Jer 40:4 good...to come with me **i.** Babylon,
Jer 40:4 ill...to come with me **i.** Babylon,
Jer 41:7 they came **i.** the midst of the city, 413
Jer 41:7 and cast them **i.** the midst of the pit, 413
Jer 41:17 Beth-lehem, to go to enter **i.** Egypt,
Jer 42:14 we will go **i.** the land of Egypt, where
Jer 42:15 set your faces to enter **i.** Egypt,
Jer 42:17 to go **i.** Egypt to sojourn there; 935
Jer 42:18 when ye shall enter **i.** Egypt: 935
Jer 42:19 Go ye not **i.** Egypt: know certainly
Jer 43:2 to say, Go not **i.** Egypt to sojourn there:...
Jer 43:3 carry us away captives **i.** Babylon. 607
Jer 43:3 to deliver us **i.** the hand of the
Jer 43:7 So they came **i.** the land of Egypt: for
Jer 44:12 faces to go **i.** the land of Egypt
Jer 44:14 gone **i.** the land of Egypt to sojourn
Jer 44:14 should return **i.** the land of Judah,
Jer 44:21 them, and came it not **i.** his mind? 5921
Jer 44:28 the land of Egypt **i.** the land of Judah,
Jer 44:28 gone **i.** the land of Egypt to sojourn
Jer 44:30 of Egypt **i.** the hand of his enemies,
Jer 44:30 **i.** the hand of them that seek his life;
Jer 44:30 Judah **i.** the hand of Nebuchadrezzar
Jer 46:11 Go up **i.** Gilead, and take balm, O
Jer 46:19 furnish thyself to go **i.** captivity: for
Jer 46:24 **i.** the hand of the people of the north
Jer 46:26 them **i.** the hand of those that seek
Jer 46:26 and **i.** the hand of Nebuchadrezzar
Jer 46:26 and **i.** the hand of his servants: and
Jer 47:6 put up thyself **i.** thy scabbard, 413
Jer 48:7 Chemosh shall go forth **i.** captivity
Jer 48:11 neither hath he gone **i.** captivity:
Jer 48:44 from the fear shall fall **i.** the pit; 413
Jer 49:3 for their king shall go **i.** captivity, and
Jer 49:32 I will scatter **i.** all winds them that
Jer 51:9 us go every one **i.** his own country:
Jer 51:50 let Jerusalem come **i.** your mind 5921
Jer 51:51 come **i.** the sanctuaries of the Lord's 5921
Jer 51:59 Zedekiah the king of Judah **i.** Babylon
Jer 51:63 cast it **i.** the midst of Euphrates: 413
Jer 52:12 the king of Babylon, **i.** Jerusalem,
La 1:3 Judah is gone **i.** captivity because 1473
La 1:5 her children are gone **i.** captivity
La 1:7 people fell **i.** the hand of the enemy,
La 1:10 the heathen entered **i.** her sanctuary,
La 1:10 should not enter **i.** thy congregation
La 1:13 above hath he sent fire **i.** my bones,
La 1:14 Lord hath delivered me **i.** their hands,
La 1:18 my young men are gone **i.** captivity.
La 2:7 given up **i.** the hand of the enemy the
La 2:9 Her gates are sunk **i.** the ground; he
La 2:12 poured out **i.** their mothers' bosom. 413
La 3:2 and brought me **i.** darkness, but not
La 3:13 of his quiver to enter **i.** my reins.
La 4:12 enter **i.** the gates of Jerusalem
La 4:22 more carry thee away **i.** captivity:
La 5:15 our dance is turned **i.** mourning.
Eze 2:2 the spirit entered **i.** me when he spake
Eze 3:22 Arise, go forth **i.** the plain, and I 413
Eze 3:23 I arose, and went forth **i.** the plain: 413
Eze 3:24 the spirit entered **i.** me, and set me
Eze 4:14 there abominable flesh **i.** my mouth.
Eze 5:4 cast them **i.** the midst of the fire, 413
Eze 5:4 come forth **i.** all the house of Israel 413
Eze 5:6 changed my judgments **i.** wickedness
Eze 5:10 of thee will I scatter **i.** all the winds
Eze 5:12 scatter a third part **i.** all the winds,
Eze 7:11 is risen up **i.** a rod of wickedness:
Eze 7:21 will give it **i.** the hands of the strangers
Eze 7:22 for the robbers shall enter **i.** it, and
Eze 8:16 he brought me **i.** the inner court 413
Eze 10:7 and put it **i.** the hands of him that 413
Eze 11:5 the things that come **i.** your mind,
Eze 11:9 deliver you **i.** the hands of strangers,
Eze 11:24 vision by the Spirit of God **i.** Chaldea,
Eze 12:4 as they that go forth **i.** captivity.
Eze 12:11 shall remove and go **i.** captivity 608
Eze 13:5 Ye have not gone up **i.** the gaps,
Eze 13:9 shall they enter **i.** the land of Israel;
Eze 14:19 Or if I send a pestilence **i.** that land, 413
Eze 15:4 Behold, it is cast **i.** the fire for fuel;
Eze 16:8 and entered **i.** a covenant with thee,
Eze 16:13 and thou didst prosper **i.** a kingdom.
Eze 16:39 And I will also give thee **i.** their hand,
Eze 17:4 and carried it **i.** a land of traffick; he
Eze 17:15 in sending his ambassadors **i.** Egypt,
Eze 19:9 they brought him **i.** holds, that his
Eze 20:6 **i.** a land that I had espied for them, 413
Eze 20:10 and brought them **i.** the wilderness. 413
Eze 20:15 not bring them **i.** the land which I 413
Eze 20:28 when I had brought them **i.** the land, 413
Eze 20:32 that which cometh **i.** your mind 5921
Eze 20:35 I will bring you **i.** the wilderness 413
Eze 20:37 bring you **i.** the bond of the covenant:
Eze 20:38 shall not enter **i.** the land of Israel: 413
Eze 20:42 shall bring you **i.** the land of Israel, 413
Eze 20:42 **i.** the country for the which I lifted 413
Eze 21:11 to give it **i.** the hand of the slayer.
Eze 21:14 which entereth **i.** their privy chambers.
Eze 21:30 I cause it to return **i.** his sheath?
Eze 21:31 thee **i.** the hand of brutish men,
Eze 22:19 you **i.** the midst of Jerusalem. 413
Eze 22:20 **i.** the midst of the furnace, to blow 413
Eze 23:9 delivered her **i.** the hand of her lovers,
Eze 23:9 **i.** the hand of the Assyrians, upon
Eze 23:16 messengers unto them **i.** Chaldea.
Eze 23:17 came to her **i.** the bed of love,
Eze 23:28 deliver thee **i.** the hand of them whom
Eze 23:28 **i.** the hand of them from whom thy
Eze 23:31 will I give her cup **i.** thine hand.
Eze 23:39 the same day **i.** my sanctuary 413
Eze 24:3 set it on, and also pour water **i.** it:
Eze 24:4 Gather the pieces thereof **i.** it, even
Eze 25:3 Judah, when they went **i.** captivity;
Eze 26:10 when he shall enter **i.** thy gates,
Eze 26:10 as men enter **i.** a city wherein is
Eze 26:20 with them that descend **i.** the pit,
Eze 27:26 have brought thee **i.** great waters:
Eze 27:27 shall fall **i.** the midst of the seas in
Eze 28:4 gold and silver **i.** thy treasures:
Eze 28:23 For I will send **i.** her pestilence, and
Eze 28:23 and blood **i.** her streets; and the
Eze 29:5 leave thee thrown **i.** the wilderness,
Eze 29:14 them to return **i.** the land of Pathros,
Eze 29:14 **i.** the land of their habitation, 5921
Eze 30:12 the land **i.** the hand of the wicked:
Eze 30:17 and these cities shall go **i.** captivity
Eze 30:18 her daughters shall go **i.** captivity.
Eze 30:25 put my sword **i.** the hand of the king
Eze 31:11 him **i.** the hand of the mighty one
Eze 31:16 hell with them that descend **i.** the pit:
Eze 31:17 They also went down **i.** hell with him
Eze 32:9 **i.** the countries which thou hast 5921
Eze 32:18 with them that go down **i.** the pit.
Eze 32:24 down uncircumcised **i.** the nether 413
Eze 36:5 my land **i.** their possession with the
Eze 36:24 will bring you **i.** your own land. 413
Eze 37:5 I will cause breath to enter **i.** you,
Eze 37:10 and the breath came **i.** them, and they
Eze 37:12 and bring you **i.** the land of Israel. 413
Eze 37:17 join them one to another **i.** one stick;
Eze 37:21 and bring them **i.** their own land: 413
Eze 37:22 be divided **i.** two kingdoms any more
Eze 38:4 and put hooks **i.** thy jaws, and I will
Eze 38:8 thou shalt come **i.** the land that is 413
Eze 38:10 shall things come **i.** thy mind, 5921
Eze 39:23 went **i.** captivity for their iniquity:
Eze 39:23 them **i.** the hand of their enemies:
Eze 39:28 them to be led **i.** captivity among
Eze 40:2 brought he me **i.** the land of Israel, 413
Eze 40:17 brought he me **i.** the outward court, 413
Eze 40:32 he brought me **i.** the inner court 413
Eze 41:6 they entered **i.** the wall which was of
Eze 42:1 brought me forth **i.** the utter court, 413
Eze 42:1 and he brought me **i.** the chamber 413
Eze 42:9 as one goeth **i.** them from the utter
Eze 42:12 the east, as one entereth **i.** them.
Eze 42:14 of the holy place **i.** the utter court, 413
Eze 43:4 Lord came **i.** the house by the way 413
Eze 43:5 brought me **i.** the inner court; and, 413
Eze 44:7 rought **i.** my sanctuary strangers
Eze 44:9 shall enter **i.** my sanctuary, of any 413
Eze 44:12 the house of Israel to fall **i.** iniquity;
Eze 44:16 they shall enter **i.** my sanctuary, 413
Eze 44:19 they go forth **i.** the utter court, even 413
Eze 44:19 even **i.** the utter court to the people, 413
Eze 44:21 when they enter **i.** the inner court. 413
Eze 44:27 day that he goeth **i.** the sanctuary, 413
Eze 46:19 **i.** the holy chambers of the priests, 413
Eze 46:20 they bear them not out **i.** the utter 413
Eze 46:21 brought me forth **i.** the utter court, 413
Eze 47:8 country, and go down **i.** the desert, 5921
Eze 47:8 the desert, and go down **i.** the sea:
Eze 47:8 which being brought forth **i.** the sea,
Da 1:2 Jehoiakim king of Judah **i.** his hand,
Da 1:2 **i.** the land of Shinar to the house of
Da 1:2 brought the vessels **i.** the treasure

Da 1:9 brought Daniel i. favour and tender
Da 2:29 came i. thy mind upon thy bed,
Da 2:38 heaven hath he given i. thine hand,
Da 3:6, 11,15 i. the midst of a burning fiery
Da 3:20 cast them i. the burning fiery furnace
Da 3:21 cast i. the midst of the burning fiery
Da 3:23 bound i. the midst of the burning fiery
Da 3:24 men bound i. the midst of the fire?
Da 5:10 his lords came i. the banquet house:
Da 6:7 he shall be cast i. the den of lions.
Da 6:10 was signed, he went i. his house; and his
Da 6:12 king, shall be cast i. the den of lions?
Da 6:16 and cast him i. the den of lions.
Da 6:24 they cast them i. the den of lions,
Da 7:25 they shall be given i. his hand until
Da 10:8 was turned in me i. corruption, and
Da 11:7 shall enter i. the fortress of the king
Da 11:8 also carry captives i. Egypt their gods,
Da 11:9 the south shall come i. his kingdom,
Da 11:9 and shall return i. his own land. 413
Da 11:11 multitude shall be given i. his hand.
Da 11:28 he return i. his land with great riches;
Da 11:40 and he shall enter i. the countries,
Da 11:41 He shall enter also i. the glorious land,
Ho 2:14 her, and bring her i. the wilderness,
Ho 4:7 will I change their glory i. shame.
Ho 9:4 not come i. the house of the Lord.
Ho 11:5 not return i. the land of Egypt, 413
Ho 11:9 thee: and I will not enter i. the city.
Ho 12:1 Assyrians, and oil is carried i. Egypt
Ho 12:12 And Jacob fled i. the country of Syria,
Joe 1:14 land i. the house of the Lord your God,
Joe 2:20 will drive him i. a land barren and 413
Joe 2:31 The sun shall be turned i. darkness,
Joe 2:31 and the moon i. blood, before the
Joe 3:2 bring them down i. the valley of 413
Joe 3:5 and have carried i. your temples my
Joe 3:8 daughters i. the hand of the children
Joe 3:10 Beat your plowshares i. swords,
Joe 3:10 and your pruninghooks i. spears;
Am 1:4 send a fire i. the house of Hazael,
Am 1:5 Syria shall go i. captivity unto Kir,
Am 1:15 their king shall go i. captivity, he and
Am 2:1 the bones of the king of Edom i. lime:
Am 4:3 ye shall cast them i. the palace, saith
Am 5:5 seek not Beth-el, nor enter i. Gilgal,
Am 5:5 Gilgal shall surely go i. captivity,
Am 5:8 the shadow of death i. the morning,
Am 5:19 or went i. the house, and leaned his
Am 5:27 will I cause you to go i. captivity
Am 6:12 ye have turned judgment i. gall, and
Am 6:12 the fruit of righteousness i. hemlock:
Am 7:12 flee thee away i. the land of Judah, 413
Am 7:17 Israel shall surely go i. captivity
Am 8:10 I will turn your feasts i. mourning,
Am 8:10 all your songs i. lamentation; and I
Am 9:2 Though they dig i. hell, thence shall
Am 9:4 though they go i. captivity before
Ob 11 and foreigners entered i. his gates,
Ob 13 shouldest not have entered i. the gate
Jon 1:3 and went down i. it, to go with them
Jon 1:4 sent out a great wind i. the sea, 413
Jon 1:5 that were in the ship i. the sea, to 413
Jon 1:5 gone down i. the sides of the ship; 413
Jon 1:12 me up, and cast me forth i. the sea; 413
Jon 1:15 Jonah, and cast him forth i. the sea: 413
Jon 2:3 For thou hadst cast me i. the deep,
Jon 2:7 in unto thee, i. thine holy temple. 413
Jon 3:4 to enter i. the city a day's journey,
Mic 1:6 down the stones thereof i. the valley,
Mic 1:16 for they are gone i. captivity from
Mic 3:5 that putteth not i. their mouths, 5921
Mic 4:3 shall beat their swords i. plowshares,
Mic 4:3 and their spears i. pruninghooks:
Mic 4:12 gather them as the sheaves i. the floor.
Mic 5:5 the Assyrian shall come i. our land:
Mic 5:6 when he cometh i. our land, and when
Mic 7:19 all their sins i. the depths of the sea.
Na 3:10 carried away, she went i. captivity:
Na 3:12 fall i. the mouth of the eater. 5921
Na 3:14 go i. clay, and tread the morter, make
Hab 3:16 rottenness entered i. my bones, and I
Hag 1:6 wages to put it i. a bag with holes. 413
Zec 5:4 shall enter i. the house of the thief, 413
Zec 5:4 i. the house of him that sweareth 413
Zec 5:8 he cast it i. the midst of the ephah; 413
Zec 6:6 go forth i. the north country; 413
Zec 6:10 and go i. the house of Josiah the son
Zec 10:10 bring them i. the land of Gilead 413
Zec 11:6 men every one i. his neighbour's hand,
Zec 11:6 and i. the hand of his king: and they
Zec 14:2 of the city shall go forth i. captivity,
Mal 3:10 all the tithes i. the storehouse, 413
Mt 1:17 until the carrying away i. Babylon. 3350
Mt 1:17 from the carrying away i. Babylon 3350
Mt 2:11 when they were come i. the house, 1519
Mt 2:12 departed i. their own country 1519
Mt 2:13 and his mother, and flee i. Egypt, 1519
Mt 2:14 by night, and departed i. Egypt: 1519
Mt 2:20 mother, and go i. the land of Israel: 1519
Mt 2:21 and came i. the land of Israel. 1519
Mt 2:22 turned aside i. the parts of Galilee: 1519
Mt 3:10 is hewn down, and cast i. the fire. 1519
Mt 3:12 gather his wheat i. the garner; 1519
Mt 4:1 i. the wilderness to be tempted of 1519
Mt 4:5 devil taketh him up i. the holy city, 1519
Mt 4:8 up i. an exceeding high mountain, 1519
Mt 4:12 that John was cast i. prison,
Mt 4:12 prison, he departed i. Galilee; 1519
Mt 4:18 casting a net i. the sea: for they 1519
Mt 5:1 he went up i. a mountain: and 1519
Mt 5:20 **in no case enter i. the kingdom** 1519
Mt 5:25 **officer, and thou be cast i. prison.** 1519
Mt 5:29, 30 **whole body should be cast i.** 1519
Mt 6:6 **thou prayest, enter i. thy closet,** 1519
Mt 6:13 **lead us not i. temptation, but** 1519
Mt 6:26 **do they reap, nor gather i. barns;** 1519
Mt 6:30 **and to morrow is cast i. the oven,** 1519
Mt 7:19 **is hewn down, and cast i. the fire.** 1519
Mt 7:21 **enter i. the kingdom of heaven;** 1519
Mt 8:5 Jesus was entered i. Capernaum, 1519
Mt 8:12 **shall be cast out i. outer darkness:** 1519
Mt 8:14 Jesus was come i. Peter's house, 1519
Mt 8:23 And when he was entered i. a ship, 1519
Mt 8:28 i. the country of the Gergesenes, 1519
Mt 8:31 us to go away i. the herd of swine. 1519
Mt 8:32 out, they went i. the herd of swine: 1519
Mt 8:32 down a steep place i. the sea, 1519
Mt 8:33 fled, and went their ways i. the city, 1519
Mt 9:1 And he entered i. a ship, and passed 1519
Mt 9:1 over, and came i. his own city, 1519
Mt 9:17 **do men put new wine i. old bottles:** 1519
Mt 9:17 **they put new wine i. new bottles,** 1519
Mt 9:23 Jesus came i. the ruler's house, and 1519
Mt 9:26 hereof went abroad i. all that land. 1519
Mt 9:28 when he was come i. the house, the 1519
Mt 9:38 **send forth labourers i. his harvest** 1519
Mt 10:5 **Go not i. the way of the Gentiles,** 1519
Mt 10:5 **i. any city of the Samaritans enter** 1519
Mt 10:11 **And i. whatsoever city or town ye** 1519
Mt 10:12 **when ye come i. an house, salute** 1519
Mt 10:23 **you in this city, flee ye i. another:** 1519
Mt 11:7 **went ye out i. the wilderness to** 1519
Mt 12:4 **How he entered i. the house of** 1519
Mt 12:9 thence, he went i. their synagogue: 1519
Mt 12:11 **fall i. a pit on the sabbath day,** 1519
Mt 12:29 **one enter i. a strong man's house,** 1519
Mt 12:44 **I will return i. my house from** 1519
Mt 13:2 so that he went i. a ship, and sat; 1519
Mt 13:8 **But other fell i. good ground, and** 1909
Mt 13:20 **received the seed i. stony places,** 1909
Mt 13:23 **received seed i. the good ground is** 1909
Mt 13:30 **but gather the wheat i. my barn.** 1519
Mt 13:36 away, and went i. the house: 1519
Mt 13:42 **shall cast them i. a furnace of fire:** 1519
Mt 13:47 **unto a net, that was cast i. the** 1519
Mt 13:48 **and gathered the good i. vessels,** 1519
Mt 13:50 **cast them i. the furnace of fire:** 1519
Mt 13:54 he was come i. his own country, he 1519
Mt 14:13 thence by ship i. a desert place 1519
Mt 14:15 that they may go i. the villages, 1519
Mt 14:22 his disciples to get i. a ship, and to 1519
Mt 14:23 up i. a mountain apart to pray: and 1519
Mt 14:32 when they were come i. the ship, 1519
Mt 14:34 came i. the land of Gennesaret. 1519
Mt 14:35 they sent out i. all that country 1519
Mt 15:11 **Not that which goeth i. the mouth** 1519
Mt 15:14 **blind, both shall fall i. the ditch.** 1519
Mt 15:17 **in at the mouth goeth i. the belly,** 1519
Mt 15:17 **and is cast out i. the draught?** 1519
Mt 15:21 i. the coasts of Tyre and Sidon. 1519
Mt 15:29 and went up i. a mountain, and sat 1519
Mt 15:39 and came i. the coasts of Magdala. 1519
Mt 16:13 When Jesus came i. the coasts of 1519
Mt 17:1 them up i. an high mountain apart, 1519
Mt 17:15 for ofttimes he falleth i. the fire, 1519
Mt 17:15 and oft i. the water. 1519
Mt 17:22 **be betrayed i. the hands of men:** 1519
Mt 17:25 when he was come i. the house, 1519
Mt 18:3 **shall not enter i. the kingdom of** 1519
Mt 18:8 **thee to enter i. life halt or** 1519
Mt 18:8 **two feet to be cast i. everlasting** 1519
Mt 18:9 **thee to enter i. life with one eye,** 1519
Mt 18:9 **two eyes to be cast i. hell fire.** 1519
Mt 18:12 **and goeth i. the mountains, and** 1909
Mt 18:30 **but went and cast him i. prison,** 1519
Mt 19:1 and came i. the coasts of Judaea 1519
Mt 19:17 **if thou wilt enter i. life, keep the** 1519
Mt 19:23 **enter i. the kingdom of heaven.** 1519
Mt 19:24 **man to enter i. the kingdom of** 1519
Mt 20:1 **to hire labourers i. his vineyard.** 1519
Mt 20:2 **a day, he sent them i. his vineyard.** 1519
Mt 20:4 **Go ye also i. the vineyard, and** 1519
Mt 20:7 **them, Go ye also i. the vineyard;** 1519
Mt 21:2 **Go i. the village over against you,** 1519
Mt 21:10 when he was come i. Jerusalem, 1519
Mt 21:12 Jesus went i. the temple of God, 1519
Mt 21:17 went out of the city i. Bethany; 1519
Mt 21:18 as he returned i. the city, he 1519
Mt 21:21 **removed, and be thou cast i. the** 1519
Mt 21:23 when he was come i. the temple, 1519
Mt 21:31 **harlots go i. the kingdom of God** 1519
Mt 21:33 **to husbandmen, and went i. a far** 1519
Mt 22:9 **Go ye therefore i. the highways,** 1909
Mt 22:10 **servants went out i. the highways,** 1519
Mt 22:13 **cast him i. outer darkness; there** 1519
Mt 24:16 **be in Judaea flee i. the mountains:** 1909
Mt 24:38 **day that Noe entered i. the ark.** 1519
Mt 25:14 **as a man traveling i. a far country,**
Mt 25:21, 23 **enter thou i. the joy of thy lord.** 1519
Mt 25:30 **ye the unprofitable servant i. outer** 1519
Mt 25:41 **me, ye cursed, i. everlasting fire,** 1519
Mt 25:46 **go away i. everlasting punishment:** 1519
Mt 25:46 **but the righteous i. life eternal.** 1519
Mt 26:18 **Go i. the city to such a man, and** 1519
Mt 26:30 they went out i. the mount of Olives. 1519
Mt 26:32 **I will go before you i. Galilee.** 1519
Mt 26:41 **that ye enter not i. temptation:** 1519
Mt 26:45 **is betrayed i. the hands of sinners.** 1519
Mt 26:52 **Put up again thy sword i. his** 1519
Mt 26:71 when he was gone out i. the porch, 1519
Mt 27:6 for to put them i. the treasury, 1519
Mt 27:27 took Jesus i. the common hall, 1519
Mt 27:53 and went i. the holy city, and 1519
Mt 28:7 he goeth before you i. Galilee; 1519
Mt 28:10 **my brethren that they go i.** 1519
Mt 28:11 some of the watch came i. the city, 1519
Mt 28:16 disciples went away i. Galilee. 1519
Mt 28:16 i. a mountain where Jesus had 1519
Mk 1:12 spirit driveth him i. the wilderness. 1519
Mk 1:14 Jesus came i. Galilee, preaching 1519
Mk 1:16 brother casting a net i. the sea: 1722
Mk 1:21 And they went i. Capernaum; and 1519
Mk 1:21 day he entered i. the synagogue, 1519
Mk 1:29 they entered i. the house of Simon 1519
Mk 1:35 and departed i. a solitary place, 1519
Mk 1:38 **Let us go i. the next towns, that I** 1519
Mk 1:45 no more openly enter i. the city, 1519
Mk 2:1 again he entered i. Capernaum after 1519
Mk 2:11 **and go thy way i. thine house** 1519
Mk 2:22 **putteth new wine i. old bottles:** 1519
Mk 2:22 **wine must be put i. new bottles** 1519
Mk 2:26 **he went i. the house of God in the** 1519
Mk 3:1 he entered again i. the synagogue; 1519
Mk 3:13 he goeth up i. a mountain, and 1519
Mk 3:19 him: and they went i. an house 1519
Mk 3:27 **can enter i. a strong man's house,** 1519
Mk 4:1 that he entered i. a ship, and sat 1519
Mk 4:26 **should cast seed i. the ground;** 1909
Mk 4:37 the waves beat i. the ship, so that 1519
Mk 5:1 i. the country of the Gadarenes. 1519
Mk 5:12 him, saying, Send us i. the swine, 1519
Mk 5:12 that we may enter i. them. 1519
Mk 5:13 went out, and entered i. the swine: 1519
Mk 5:13 down a steep place i. the sea, 1519
Mk 5:18 And when he was come i. the ship, 1519
Mk 6:1 and came i. his own country; and 1519
Mk 6:10 **place soever ye enter i. an house,** 1519
Mk 6:31 **yourselves apart i. a desert place,** 1519
Mk 6:32 i. a desert place by ship privately. 1519

Mk 6:36 may go i. the country round about, … 1519
Mk 6:36 and i. the villages, and buy … 1519
Mk 6:45 his disciples to get i. the ship, and … 1519
Mk 6:46 he departed i. a mountain to pray … 1519
Mk 6:51 went up unto them i. the ship; and … 1519
Mk 6:53 came i. the land of Gennesaret, … 1909
Mk 6:56 he entered, i. villages, or cities, or … 1519
Mk 7:15 **that entering i. him can defile him:** 1519
Mk 7:17 And when he was entered i. the … 1519
Mk 7:18 **from without entereth i. the man,** … 1519
Mk 7:19 **not i. his heart, but i. the belly** … 1519
Mk 7:19 **and goeth out i. the draught,** … 1519
Mk 7:24 i. the borders of Tyre and Sidon, … 1519
Mk 7:24 and entered i. a house, and would … 1519
Mk 7:33 and put his fingers i. his ears, and … 1519
Mk 8:10 entered i. a ship with his disciples, … 1519
Mk 8:10 came i. the parts of Dalmanutha … 1519
Mk 8:13 and entering i. the ship again … 1519
Mk 8:26 **Neither go i. the town, nor tell it** … 1519
Mk 8:27 i. the towns of Caesarea Philippi: … 1519
Mk 9:2 up i. a high mountain apart by … 1519
Mk 9:22 ofttimes it hath cast him i. the fire, … 1519
Mk 9:22 and i. the waters, to destroy him: … 1519
Mk 9:25 **of him, and enter no more i. him** … 1519
Mk 9:28 when he was come i. the house, his … 1519
Mk 9:31 **is delivered i. the hands of men,** … 1519
Mk 9:42 **neck, and he were cast i. the sea** … 1519
Mk 9:43 **for thee to enter i. life maimed,** … 1519
Mk 9:43 **having two hands to go i. hell,** … 1519
Mk 9:43 **i. the fire that never shall be** … 1519
Mk 9:45 **better for thee to enter halt i. life,** … 1519
Mk 9:45 **having two feet to be cast i. hell,** … 1519
Mk 9:45 **i. the fire that never shall be** … 1519
Mk 9:47 **to enter i. the kingdom of God** … 1519
Mk 9:47 **having two eyes to be cast i. hell** … 1519
Mk 10:1 i. the coast of Judaea by the farther … 1519
Mk 10:17 when he was gone forth i. the way, … 1519
Mk 10:23 **have riches enter i. the kingdom of** 1519
Mk 10:24 **to enter i. the kingdom of God!** … 1519
Mk 10:25 **man to enter i. the kingdom of** … 1519
Mk 11:2 **way i. the village over against you:** 1519
Mk 11:2 **as soon as ye be entered i. it, ye** … 1519
Mk 11:11 And Jesus entered i. Jerusalem, … 1519
Mk 11:11 and i. the temple: and when he … 1519
Mk 11:15 and Jesus went i. the temple, and … 1519
Mk 11:23 **be thou cast i. the sea: and shall** …
Mk 12:1 **husbandmen, and went i. a far** …
Mk 12:41 people cast money i. the treasury … 1519
Mk 12:43 **which have cast i. the treasury:** … 1519
Mk 13:15 **housetop not go down i. the house,** 1519
Mk 14:13 **Go ye i. the city, and there shall** … 1519
Mk 14:16 came i. the city, and found as he … 1519
Mk 14:26 they went out i. the mount of Olives. … 1519
Mk 14:28 **I will go before you i. Galilee.** … 1519
Mk 14:38 **pray, lest ye enter i. temptation,** … 1519
Mk 14:41 **is betrayed i. the hands of sinners** … 1519
Mk 14:54 i. the palace of the high priest: … 2080, 1519
Mk 14:68 he went out i. the porch: and the … 1519
Mk 15:16 soldiers led him away i. the hall, … 2080
Mk 16:5 And entering i. the sepulchre, they … 1519
Mk 16:7 that he goeth before you i. Galilee: … 1519
Mk 16:12 walked, and went i. the country … 1519
Mk 16:15 **Go ye i. all the world, and preach** . 1519
Mk 16:19 he was received up i. heaven, and … 1519
Lu 1:9 he went i. the temple of the Lord. … 1519
Lu 1:39 went i. the hill country with haste, … 1519
Lu 1:39 with haste, i. a city of Juda; … 1519
Lu 1:40 entered i. the house of Zacharias, … 1519
Lu 1:79 guide our feet i. the way of peace. … 1519
Lu 2:3 be taxed, every one i. his own city. … 1519
Lu 2:4 i. Judaea, unto the city of David … 1519
Lu 2:15 gone away from them i. heaven, … 1519
Lu 2:27 he came by the Spirit i. the temple: … 1519
Lu 2:39 they returned i. Galilee, to their … 1519
Lu 3:3 he came i. all the country about … 1519
Lu 3:9 is hewn down, and cast i. the fire. … 1519
Lu 3:17 will gather the wheat i. his garner; … 1519
Lu 4:1 led by the Spirit i. the wilderness, … 1519
Lu 4:5 taking him up i. a high mountain, … 1519
Lu 4:14 the power of the Spirit i. Galilee: … 1519
Lu 4:16 i. the synagogue on the sabbath … 1519
Lu 4:37 out i. every place of the country … 1519
Lu 4:38 and entered i. Simon's house. And … 1519
Lu 4:42 departed and went i. a desert place: … 1519
Lu 5:3 And he entered i. one of the ships, … 1519
Lu 5:4 **Launch out i. the deep, and let** … 1519

Lu 5:16 withdrew himself i. the wilderness, … 1722
Lu 5:19 couch i. the midst before Jesus. … 1519
Lu 5:24 **up thy couch, and go i. thine** … 1519
Lu 5:37 **putteth new wine i. old bottles;** … 1519
Lu 5:38 **wine must be put i. new bottles;** … 1519
Lu 6:4 **How he went i. the house of God,** … 1519
Lu 6:6 he entered i. the synagogue and … 1519
Lu 6:12 he went out i. a mountain to pray, … 1519
Lu 6:38 **over, shall men give i. your bosom.** 1519
Lu 6:39 **shall they not both fall i. the** … 1519
Lu 7:1 people, he entered i. Capernaum. … 1519
Lu 7:11 that he went i. a city called Nain; … 1519
Lu 7:24 **ye out i. the wilderness for to see?** . 1519
Lu 7:36 he went i. the Pharisee's house, … 1519
Lu 7:44 **I entered i. thine house, thou** … 1519
Lu 8:22 went i. a ship with his disciples: … 1519
Lu 8:29 driven of the devil i. the wilderness. … 1519
Lu 8:30 many devils were entered i. him. … 1519
Lu 8:31 command them to go out i. the deep. … 1519
Lu 8:32 would suffer them to enter i. them. … 1519
Lu 8:33 the man, and entered i. the swine: … 1519
Lu 8:33 down a steep place i. the lake, … 1519
Lu 8:37 and he went up i. the ship, and … 1519
Lu 8:41 that he would come i. his house: … 1519
Lu 8:51 And when he came i. the house, he … 1519
Lu 9:4 **whatsoever house ye enter i., there** 1519
Lu 9:10 aside privately i. a desert place … 1519
Lu 9:12 may go i. the towns and country … 1519
Lu 9:28 and went up i. a mountain to pray. … 1519
Lu 9:34 feared as they entered i. the cloud. … 1519
Lu 9:44 **sayings sink down i. your ears:** … 1519
Lu 9:44 **be delivered i. the hands of men.** … 1519
Lu 9:52 i. a village of the Samaritans, … 1519
Lu 10:1 two before his face i. every city … 1519
Lu 10:2 **send forth labourers i. his harvest** … 1519
Lu 10:5 **And i. whatsoever house ye enter,** . 1519
Lu 10:8 **And i. whatsoever city ye enter,** … 1519
Lu 10:10 **But i. whatsoever city ye enter,** … 1519
Lu 10:10 **ways out i. the streets of the same,** 1519
Lu 10:38 that he entered i. a certain village: … 1519
Lu 10:38 Martha received him i. her house. … 1519
Lu 11:4 **And lead us not i. temptation; but** . 1519
Lu 12:5 **killed hath power to cast i. hell;** … 1519
Lu 12:28 **and to morrow is cast i. the oven;** . 1519
Lu 12:58 **and the officer cast thee i. prison.** . 1519
Lu 13:19 **a man took, and cast i. his garden;** 1519
Lu 14:1 i. the house of one of the chief … 1519
Lu 14:5 **have an ass or an ox fallen i. a pit** . 1519
Lu 14:21 **out quickly i. the streets and lanes** . 1519
Lu 14:23 **Go out i. the highways and hedges,** 1519
Lu 15:13 **took his journey i. a far country,** … 1519
Lu 15:15 **sent him i. his fields to feed swine.** 1519
Lu 16:4 **they may receive me i. their** … 1519
Lu 16:9 **you i. everlasting habitations** … 1519
Lu 16:16 **and every man presseth i. it** … 1519
Lu 16:22 **by the angels i. Abraham's bosom:** . 1519
Lu 16:28 **also come i. this place of torment.** . 1519
Lu 17:2 **his neck, and he cast i. the sea,** … 1519
Lu 17:12 as he entered i. a certain village, … 1519
Lu 17:27 **day that Noe entered i. the ark,** … 1519
Lu 18:10 **men went up i. the temple to pray;** . 1519
Lu 18:24 **riches enter i. the kingdom of God!** 1519
Lu 18:25 **man to enter i. the kingdom of** … 1519
Lu 19:4 up i. a sycomore tree to see him: … 1909
Lu 19:12 **nobleman went i. a far country** … 1519
Lu 19:23 **not thou my money i. the bank,** … 1909
Lu 19:30 **ye i. the village over against you;** . 1519
Lu 19:45 And he went i. the temple, and … 1519
Lu 20:9 **went i. a far country for a long time** …
Lu 21:1 casting their gifts i. the treasury. … 1519
Lu 21:12 **up to the synagogues, and i. prisons,** …
Lu 21:24 **be led away captive i. all nations:** . 1519
Lu 22:3 Satan i. Judas surnamed Iscariot, … 1519
Lu 22:10 **when ye are entered i. the city,** … 1519
Lu 22:10 **him i. the house where he entereth** 1519
Lu 22:33 thee, both i. prison, and to death. … 1519
Lu 22:40 **that ye enter not i. temptation** … 1519
Lu 22:46 **pray, lest ye enter i. temptation.** … 1519
Lu 22:54 him i. the high priest's house. … 1519
Lu 22:66 and led him i. their council, saying, … 1519
Lu 23:19 and for murder, was cast i. prison. … 1519
Lu 23:25 and murder, was cast i. prison, … 1519
Lu 23:42 when thou comest i. thy kingdom. … 1722
Lu 23:46 **i. thy hands I commend my spirit:** . 1519
Lu 24:7 delivered i. the hands of sinful men, … 1519

Lu 24:26 **things, and to enter i. his glory?** … 1519
Lu 24:51 them, and carried up i. heaven. … 1519
Joh 1:9 every man that cometh i. the world. … 1519
Joh 1:43 Jesus would go forth i. Galilee, … 1519
Joh 3:4 second time i. his mother's womb, … 1519
Joh 3:5 **cannot enter i. the kingdom of** … 1519
Joh 3:17 **not his Son i. the world to** … 1519
Joh 3:19 **that light is come i. the world, and** 1519
Joh 3:22 his disciples i. the land of Judaea; … 1519
Joh 3:24 For John was not yet cast i. prison. … 1519
Joh 3:35 hath given all things i. his hand. … 1722
Joh 4:3 and departed again i. Galilee. … 1519
Joh 4:14 **springing up i. everlasting life** … 1519
Joh 4:28 went her way i. the city, and saith … 1519
Joh 4:38 **and ye are entered i. their labours.** 1519
Joh 4:43 thence, and went i. Galilee. … 1519
Joh 4:45 Then when he was come i. Galilee, … 1519
Joh 4:46 Jesus came again i. Cana of Galilee, … 1519
Joh 4:47 was come out of Judaea i. Galilee, … 1519
Joh 4:54 was come out of Judaea i. Galilee. … 1519
Joh 5:4 down at a certain season i. the pool, … 1722
Joh 5:7 is troubled, to put me i. the pool: … 1519
Joh 5:24 **shall not come i. condemnation;** … 1519
Joh 6:3 And Jesus went up i. a mountain, … 1519
Joh 6:14 that should come i. the world. … 1519
Joh 6:15 again i. a mountain himself alone. … 1519
Joh 6:17 And entered i. a ship, and went … 1519
Joh 6:21 willingly received him i. the ship: … 1519
Joh 6:22 not with his disciples i. the boat, … 1519
Joh 7:3 and go i. Judaea, that thy disciples … 1519
Joh 7:14 feast Jesus went up i. the temple, … 1519
Joh 8:2 he came again i. the temple, … 1519
Joh 9:39 **judgment I am come i. this world.** . 1519
Joh 10:1 **not by the door i. the sheepfold,** … 1519
Joh 10:36 **sanctified, and sent i. the world,** … 1519
Joh 10:40 Jordan i. the place where John … 1519
Joh 11:7 **disciples, Let us go i. Judaea again** . 1519
Joh 11:27 which should come i. the world. … 1519
Joh 11:30 Jesus was not yet come i. the town, … 1519
Joh 11:54 wilderness, i. a city called Ephraim, … 1519
Joh 12:24 **a corn of wheat fall i. the ground** . 1519
Joh 12:46 **I am come a light i. the world,** … 1519
Joh 13:2 having now put i. the heart of Judas … 1519
Joh 13:3 had given all things i. his hands, … 1519
Joh 13:5 that he poureth water i. a bason, … 1519
Joh 13:27 after the sop Satan entered i. him. … 1519
Joh 15:6 **them, and cast them i. the fire,** … 1519
Joh 16:13 **come, he will guide you i. all truth** 1519
Joh 16:20 **your sorrow shall be turned i. joy.** . 1519
Joh 16:21 **joy that a man is born i. the world.** 1519
Joh 16:28 **Father, and am come i. the world:** . 1519
Joh 17:18 **As thou hast sent me i. the world** … 1519
Joh 17:18 **have I also sent them i. the world** . 1519
Joh 18:1 a garden, i. the which he entered, … 1519
Joh 18:11 **Put up thy sword i. the sheath:** … 1519
Joh 18:15 i. the palace of the high priest. … 1519
Joh 18:28 went not i. the judgment hall, lest … 1519
Joh 18:33 entered i. the judgment hall again, … 1519
Joh 18:37 **for this cause came I i. the world,** … 1519
Joh 19:9 went again i. the judgment hall, … 1519
Joh 19:17 cross went forth i. a place called … 1519
Joh 20:6 and went i. the sepulchre, and seeth … 1519
Joh 20:11 down, and looked i. the sepulchre, … 1519
Joh 20:25 my finger i. the print of the nails, … 1519
Joh 20:25 and thrust my hand i. his side, I will … 1519
Joh 20:27 **thy hand, and thrust it i. my side:** … 1519
Joh 21:3 and entered i. a ship immediately; … 1519
Joh 21:7 and did cast himself i. the sea. … 1519
Ac 1:11 why stand ye gazing up i. heaven? … 1519
Ac 1:11 is taken up from you i. heaven, … 1519
Ac 1:11 as ye have seen him go i. heaven. … 1519
Ac 1:13 they went up i. an upper room, … 1519
Ac 2:20 The sun shall be turned i. darkness, … 1519
Ac 2:20 and the moon i. blood, before that … 1519
Ac 2:34 is not ascended i. the heavens: … 1519
Ac 3:1 i. the temple at the hour of prayer, … 1519
Ac 3:2 of them that entered i. the temple; … 1519
Ac 3:3 and John about to go i. the temple, … 1519
Ac 3:8 entered with them i. the temple, … 1519
Ac 5:15 brought forth the sick i. the streets, … 2596
Ac 5:21 i. the temple early in the morning, … 1519
Ac 7:3 i. the land which I shall shew thee. … 1519
Ac 7:4 removed him i. this land, wherein … 1519
Ac 7:6 they should bring them i. bondage, …
Ac 7:9 with envy, sold Joseph i. Egypt: … 1519
Ac 7:15 Jacob went down i. Egypt, and died, … 1519

Ac 7:16 were carried over **i.** Sychem, and....... *1519*
Ac 7:23 **i.** his heart to visit his brethren......... *1909*
Ac 7:34 come, I will send thee **i.** Egypt.......... *1519*
Ac 7:39 hearts turned back again **i.** Egypt,...... *1519*
Ac 7:45 **i.** the possession of the Gentiles, ... *1722*
Ac 7:55 looked up stedfastly **i.** heaven,.......... *1519*
Ac 8:3 entering **i.** every house, and haling..... *1531*
Ac 8:38 they went down both **i.** the water, ... *1519*
Ac 9:6 **Arise, and go i. the city, and it**..... *1519*
Ac 9:8 and brought him **i.** Damascus. *1519*
Ac 9:11 **i. the street...called Straight.**........ *1909*
Ac 9:17 his way, and entered **i.** the house; *1519*
Ac 9:39 brought him **i.** the upper chamber: *1519*
Ac 10:10 they made ready, he fell **i.** a trance, ... *1909*
Ac 10:16 was received up again **i.** heaven......... *1519*
Ac 10:22 angel to send for thee **i.** his house, ... *1519*
Ac 10:24 after they entered **i.** Caesarea. *1519*
Ac 11:8 at any time entered **i.** my mouth....... *1519*
Ac 11:10 all were drawn up again **i.** heaven. *1519*
Ac 11:12 and we entered **i.** the man's house: *1519*
Ac 12:17 departed, and went **i.** another place: ... *1519*
Ac 13:14 **i.** the synagogue on the sabbath......... *1519*
Ac 14:1 **i.** the synagogue of the Jews, ... *1519*
Ac 14:20 he rose up, and came **i.** the city: *1519*
Ac 14:22 enter **i.** the kingdom of God............. *1519*
Ac 14:25 Perga, they went down **i.** Attalia:....... *1519*
Ac 16:7 they assayed to go **i.** Bithynia: *2596*
Ac 16:9 Come over **i.** Macedonia, and help...... *1519*
Ac 16:10 endeavoured to go **i.** Macedonia,......... *1519*
Ac 16:15 Lord, come **i.** my house, and abide..... *1519*
Ac 16:19 **i.** the marketplace unto the rulers, ... *1519*
Ac 16:23 they cast them **i.** prison, charging *1519*
Ac 16:24 thrust them **i.** the inner prison,.......... *1519*
Ac 16:34 he had brought them **i.** his house, ... *1519*
Ac 16:37 Romans, and have cast us **i.** prison;.... *1519*
Ac 16:40 and entered **i.** the house of Lydia:...... *1519*
Ac 17:10 went **i.** the synagogue of the Jews...... *1519*
Ac 18:7 entered **i.** a certain man's house, ... *1519*
Ac 18:18 sailed thence **i.** Syria, and with him *1519*
Ac 18:19 he himself entered **i.** the synagogue,... *1519*
Ac 18:27 he was disposed to pass **i.** Achaia, ... *1519*
Ac 19:8 he went **i.** the synagogue, and spake .. *1519*
Ac 19:22 he sent **i.** Macedonia two of them *1519*
Ac 19:29 with one accord **i.** the theatre. *1519*
Ac 19:31 adventure himself **i.** the theatre. *1519*
Ac 20:1 departed for to go **i.** Macedonia. *1519*
Ac 20:2 exhortation, he came **i.** Greece,.......... *1519*
Ac 20:3 as he was about to sail **i.** Syria, ... *1519*
Ac 20:4 accompanied him **i.** Asia Sopater.......... *891*
Ac 20:9 Eutychus, being fallen **i.** a deep sleep:.......
Ac 20:18 the first day that I came **i.** Asia, ... *1519*
Ac 21:3 sailed **i.** Syria, and landed at Tyre: *1519*
Ac 21:8 entered **i.** the house of Philip the *1519*
Ac 21:11 him **i.** the hands of the Gentiles......... *1519*
Ac 21:26 with them entered **i.** the temple,........ *1519*
Ac 21:28 brought Greeks also **i.** the temple, ... *1519*
Ac 21:29 that Paul had brought **i.** the temple..... *1519*
Ac 21:34 him to be carried **i.** the castle. *1519*
Ac 21:37 as Paul was to be led **i.** the castle,..... *1519*
Ac 21:38 and leddest out **i.** the wilderness........ *1519*
Ac 22:4 **i.** prisons both men and women........... *1519*
Ac 22:10 **Arise, and go i. Damascus; and**...... *1519*
Ac 22:11 were with me, I came **i.** Damascus...... *1519*
Ac 22:23 clothes, and threw dust **i.** the air, ... *1519*
Ac 22:24 him to be brought **i.** the castle, ... *1519*
Ac 23:10 them, and to bring him **i.** the castle.... *1519*
Ac 23:16 he went and entered **i.** the castle,....... *1519*
Ac 23:20 down Paul to morrow **i.** the council, ... *1519*
Ac 23:28 brought him forth **i.** their council:....... *1519*
Ac 24:27 Porcius Festus came **i.** Felix' room:..........
Ac 25:1 when Festus was come **i.** the province,.....
Ac 25:23 was entered **i.** the place of hearing, ... *1519*
Ac 27:1 determined...we should sail **i.** Italy, ... *1519*
Ac 27:2 entering **i.** a ship of Adramyttium, ...
Ac 27:6 ship of Alexandria sailing **i.** Italy;........ *1519*
Ac 27:15 and could not bear up **i.** the wind, ...
Ac 27:17 they should fall **i.** the quicksands,....... *1519*
Ac 27:30 had let down the boat **i.** the sea, ... *1519*
Ac 27:38 and cast out the wheat **i.** the sea. *1519*
Ac 27:39 **i.** the which they were minded, ... *1519*
Ac 27:41 **i.** a place where two seas met,.......... *1519*
Ac 27:43 should cast themselves first **i.** the sea,.......
Ac 28:5 he shook off the beast **i.** the fire,....... *1519*
Ac 28:17 **i.** the hands of the Romans: *1519*
Ac 28:23 came many to him **i.** his lodging;........ *1519*
Ro 1:23 **i.** an image made like to corruptible.... *1722*
Ro 1:25 changed the truth of God **i.** a lie, ... *1722*
Ro 1:26 **i.** that which is against nature:........... *1519*
Ro 5:2 faith **i.** this grace wherein we stand, ... *1519*
Ro 5:12 one man sin entered **i.** the world, ... *1519*
Ro 6:3 us as were baptized **i.** Jesus Christ..... *1519*
Ro 6:3 were baptized **i.** his death? *1519*
Ro 6:4 with him by baptism **i.** death: *1519*
Ro 7:23 me **i.** captivity to the law of sin ....
Ro 8:21 **i.** the glorious liberty of the *1519*
Ro 10:6 Who shall ascend **i.** heaven? that is,.... *1519*
Ro 10:7 Or, Who shall descend **i.** the deep? *1519*
Ro 10:18 their sound went **i.** all the earth,........ *1519*
Ro 11:24 to nature **i.** a good olive tree:............ *1519*
Ro 11:24 be graffed **i.** their own olive tree? ....
Ro 15:24 I take my journey **i.** Spain, I will........ *1519*
Ro 15:28 fruit, I will come by you **i.** Spain......... *1519*
1Co 2:9 have entered **i.** the heart of man,....... *1909*
1Co 4:17 bring you **i.** remembrance of my ways.......
1Co 9:27 my body, and bring it **i.** subjection:...........
1Co 11:20 together therefore **i.** one place, ... *1909*
1Co 12:13 are we all baptized **i.** one body, ... *1519*
1Co 12:13 been all made to drink **i.** one Spirit..... *1519*
1Co 14:9 spoken? for ye shall speak **i.** the air.... *1519*
1Co 14:23 be come together **i.** one place, ... *1909*
2Co 1:16 And to pass by you **i.** Macedonia, ... *1519*
2Co 2:13 I went from thence **i.** Macedonia........ *1519*
2Co 3:18 **i.** the same image from glory to glory, ...
2Co 7:5 when we were come **i.** Macedonia,..... *1519*
2Co 8:16 earnest care **i.** the heart of Titus *1722*
2Co 10:5 bringing **i.** captivity every thought to.........
2Co 11:13 themselves **i.** the apostles of Christ.... *1519*
2Co 11:14 is transformed **i.** an angel of light. *1519*
2Co 11:20 if a man bring you **i.** bondage, ...
2Co 12:4 that he was caught up **i.** paradise, ... *1519*
Ga 1:6 called you **i.** the grace of Christ *1722*
Ga 1:17 but I went **i.** Arabia, and returned...... *1519*
Ga 1:21 **i.** the regions of Syria and Cilicia;....... *1519*
Ga 2:4 they might bring us **i.** bondage:................
Ga 3:27 baptized **i.** Christ have put on........... *1519*
Ga 4:6 the Spirit of his Son **i.** your hearts, ... *1519*
Eph 4:9 **i.** the lower parts of the earth?.......... *1519*
Eph 4:15 may grow up **i.** him in all things,........ *1519*
Col 1:13 translated us **i.** the kingdom of his...... *1519*
Col 2:18 intruding **i.** those things which ....
2Th 3:5 direct your heart **i.** the love of God, ... *1519*
2Th 3:5 and **i.** the patient waiting for Christ. ... *1519*
1Ti 1:3 when I went **i.** Macedonia, that *1519*
1Ti 1:12 faithful, putting me **i.** the ministry; *1519*
1Ti 1:15 came **i.** the world to save sinners;...... *1519*
1Ti 3:6 **i.** the condemnation of the devil. *1519*
1Ti 3:7 he fall **i.** reproach and the snare of..... *1519*
1Ti 3:16 in the world, received up **i.** glory. *1722*
1Ti 5:9 not a widow be taken **i.** the number ....
1Ti 6:7 we brought nothing **i.** this world, ... *1519*
1Ti 6:9 rich fall **i.** temptation and a snare, ... *1519*
1Ti 6:9 **i.** many foolish and heartful lusts, ... *1519*
2Ti 3:6 are they which creep **i.** houses, ... *1519*
Heb 1:6 in the firstbegotten **i.** the world, he.... *1519*
Heb 3:11 They shall not enter **i.** my rest......... *1519*
Heb 3:18 they should not enter **i.** his rest,........ *1519*
Heb 4:1 being left us of entering **i.** his rest, ... *1519*
Heb 4:3 which have believed do enter **i.** rest, .. *1519*
Heb 4:3 wrath, if they shall enter **i.** my rest: ... *1519*
Heb 4:5 again, If they shall enter **i.** my rest. ... *1519*
Heb 4:10 For he that is entered **i.** his rest, he .. *1519*
Heb 4:11 labour therefore to enter **i.** that rest,.. *1519*
Heb 4:14 priest, that is passed **i.** the heavens,.........
Heb 6:19 entereth **i.** that within the veil; *1519*
Heb 8:10 I will put my laws **i.** their mind,.......... *1519*
Heb 9:6 went always **i.** the first tabernacle, ... *1519*
Heb 9:7 **i.** the second went the high priest...... *1519*
Heb 9:8 the way **i.** the holiest of all was not yet.....
Heb 9:12 he entered in once **i.** the holy place,... *1519*
Heb 9:24 is not entered **i.** the holy places......... *1519*
Heb 9:24 but **i.** heaven itself, now to appear *1519*
Heb 9:25 entereth **i.** the holy place every......... *1519*
Heb 10:5 when he cometh **i.** the world, he *1519*
Heb 10:16 I will put my laws **i.** their hearts,....... *1909*
Heb 10:19 **i.** the holiest by the blood of Jesus, ...
Heb 10:31 fall **i.** the hands of the living God. *1519*
Heb 11:8 **i.** a place which he should after.......... *1519*
Heb 13:11 blood is brought **i.** the sanctuary by.... *1519*
Jas 1:2 joy when ye fall **i.** divers temptations; ....
Jas 1:25 looketh **i.** the perfect law of liberty,.... *1519*
Jas 4:13 to morrow we will go **i.** such a city,.... *1519*
Jas 5:4 **i.** the ears of the Lord of sabaoth....... *1519*
Jas 5:12 lest ye fall **i.** condemnation................ *5259*
1Pe 1:12 things the angels desire to look **i.**....... *1519*
1Pe 2:9 darkness **i.** his marvellous light: *1519*
1Pe 3:22 Who is gone **i.** heaven, and is on *1519*
2Pe 1:11 **i.** the everlasting kingdom of our........ *1519*
2Pe 2:4 delivered them **i.** chains of darkness, ...
2Pe 2:6 of Sodom and Gomorrha **i.** ashes..............
1Jo 4:1 prophets are gone out **i.** the world. *1519*
1Jo 4:9 his only begotten Son **i.** the world,..... *1519*
2Jo 7 deceivers are entered **i.** the world,..... *1519*
2Jo 10 receive him not **i.** your house,........... *1519*
Jude 4 grace of our God **i.** lasciviousness, ... *1519*
Re 2:10 **shall cast some of you i. prison,**.... *1519*
Re 2:22 **Behold, I will cast her i. a bed,**..... *1519*
Re 2:22 **with her i. great tribulation,**......... *1519*
Re 5:6 of God sent forth **i.** all the earth. *1519*
Re 8:5 the altar, and cast it **i.** the earth: *1519*
Re 8:8 with fire was cast **i.** the sea:.............. *1519*
Re 11:11 of life from God entered **i.** them, ... *1909*
Re 12:6 the woman fled **i.** the wilderness,....... *1519*
Re 12:9 he was cast out **i.** the earth, and *1519*
Re 12:14 she might fly **i.** the wilderness,.......... *1519*
Re 12:14 **i.** her place, where she is nourished ... *1519*
Re 13:10 He that leadeth **i.** captivity shall..............
Re 13:10 captivity shall go **i.** captivity:............. *1519*
Re 14:10 **i.** the cup of his indignation;.............. *1722*
Re 14:19 thrust in his sickle **i.** the earth,.......... *1519*
Re 14:19 **i.** the great winepress of the wrath..... *1519*
Re 15:8 man was able to enter **i.** the temple, .. *1519*
Re 16:16 gathered them together **i.** a place....... *1519*
Re 16:17 angel poured out his vial **i.** the air; *1519*
Re 16:19 great city was divided **i.** three parts,.... *1519*
Re 17:3 away in the spirit **i.** the wilderness: *1519*
Re 17:8 bottomless pit, and go **i.** perdition: *1519*
Re 17:11 of the seven, and goeth **i.** perdition. ... *1519*
Re 18:21 millstone, and cast it **i.** the sea,......... *1519*
Re 19:20 alive **i.** a lake of fire burning with...... *1519*
Re 20:3 And cast him **i.** the bottomless pit, ... *1519*
Re 20:10 was cast **i.** the lake of fire and.......... *1519*
Re 20:14 and hell were cast **i.** the lake of fire. .. *1519*
Re 20:15 of life was cast **i.** the lake of fire....... *1519*
Re 21:24 bring their glory and honour **i.** it......... *1519*
Re 21:26 and honour of the nations **i.** it. *1519*
Re 21:27 enter **i.** it any thing that defileth, ... *1519*
Re 22:14 in through the gates **i.** the city. *1519*

INTREAT See also ENTREAT; INTREATED.
Ge 23:8 **i.** for me to Ephron the son of.......... 6293
Ex 8:8 **I.** the Lord, that he may take............ 6279
Ex 8:9 when shall I **i.** for thee, and for thy.... 6279
Ex 8:28 not go very far away: **i.** for me. 6279
Ex 8:29 **i.** the Lord that the swarms of flies 6279
Ex 9:28 **I.** the Lord (for it is enough) that....... 6279
Ex 10:17 once, and **i.** the Lord your God, ... 6279
Ru 1:16 Ruth said, **I.** me not to leave thee,..... 6293
1Sa 2:25 the Lord, who shall **i.** for him? 6419
1Ki 13:6 **I.** now the face of the Lord thy 2470
Ps 45:12 the people shall **i.** thy favour............. 2470
Pr 19:6 will **i.** the favour of the prince: 2470
1Co 4:13 Being defamed, we **i.**: we are *3870*
Php 4:3 I **i.** thee also, true yokefellow,........... *2065*
1Ti 5:1 an elder, but **i.** him as a father; *3870*

INTREATED See also ENTREATED.
Ge 25:21 Isaac **i.** the Lord for his wife,........... 6279
Ge 25:21 and the Lord was **i.** of him, and......... 6279
Ex 8:30 out from Pharaoh, and **i.** the Lord...... 6279
Ex 10:18 out from Pharaoh, and **i.** the Lord...... 6279
Jg 13:8 Then Manoah **i.** the Lord, and said,.... 6279
2Sa 21:14 after that God was **i.** for the land....... 6279
2Sa 24:25 So the Lord was **i.** for the land, and... 6279
1Ch 5:20 in the battle, and he was **i.** of them;... 6279
2Ch 33:13 and he was **i.** of him, and heard......... 6279
2Ch 33:19 also, and how God was **i.** of him, ... 6279
Ezr 8:23 God for this: and he was **i.** of us. 6279
Job 19:16 answer; I **i.** him with my mouth......... 2603
Job 19:17 I **i.** for the children's sake of............ 2589
Ps 119:58 I **i.** thy favour with my whole............ 2470
Isa 19:22 Lord, and he shall be **i.** of them,........ 6279
Lu 15:28 **came his father out, and i. him**.... *3870*
Heb 12:19 **i.** that the word should not be *3868*
Jas 3:17 and easy to be **i.**, full of mercy and *2138*

INTREATETH See ENTREATETH.

INTREATIES
Pr 18:23 The poor useth **i.**; but the rich.......... 8469

INTREATY See also INTREATIES.
2Co 8:4 Praying us with much **i.** that we *3874*

INTRUDING
Col 2:18 i. into those things which he hath ... *1687*

INVADE See also INVADED.
2Ch 20:10 thou wouldest not let Israel i., ... 935
Hab 3:16 he will i. them with his troops. ... 1464

INVADED
1Sa 23:27 for the Philistines have i. the land. ... 6584
1Sa 27:8 went up, and i. the Geshurites, ... 6584
1Sa 30:1 the Amalekites had i. the south, ... 6584
2Ki 13:20 bands of the Moabites i. the land ... 935
2Ch 28:18 Philistines also had i. the cities ... 6584

INVASION
1Sa 30:14 We made an i. upon the south of ... 6584

INVENT See also INVENTED.
Am 6:5 i. to themselves instruments of ... 2803

INVENTED
2Ch 26:15 engines, i. by cunning men, ... 2803

INVENTIONS
Ps 99:8 thou tookest vengeance of their i.. ... 5949
Ps 106:29 provoked him to anger with their i.. ... 4611
Ps 106:39 went a whoring with their own i.. ... 4611
Pr 8:12 and find out knowledge of witty i.. ... 4209
Ec 7:29 but they have sought out many i.. ... 2810

INVENTORS
Ro 1:30 i. of evil things, disobedient to ... *2182*

INVISIBLE
Ro 1:20 For the i. things of him from the ... *517*
Col 1:15 Who is the image of the i. God, ... *517*
Col 1:16 and that are in earth, visible and i., ... *517*
1Ti 1:17 unto the King eternal, immortal, i., ... *517*
Heb 11:27 endured, as seeing him who is i.. ... *517*

INVITED
1Sa 9:24 since I said, I have i. the people. ... 7121
2Sa 13:23 and Absalom i. all the king's sons. ... 7121
Es 5:12 am I i. unto her also with the king, ... 7121

INWARD See also INWARDS.
Ex 28:26 is in the side of the ephod i.. ... 1004
Ex 39:19 was on the side of the ephod i.. ... 1004
Le 13:55 it is fret i., whether it be bare ...
2Sa 5:9 round about from Millo and i.. ... 1004
1Ki 7:25 and all their hinder parts were i.. ... 1004
2Ch 3:13 their feet, and their faces were i.. ... 1004
2Ch 4:4 and all their hinder parts were i.. ... 1004
Job 19:19 All my i. friends abhorred me: ... 5475
Job 38:36 hath put wisdom in the i. parts? ... 2910
Ps 5:9 their i. part is very wickedness; ... 7130
Ps 49:11 Their i. thought is, that their ... 7130
Ps 51:6 thou desirest truth in the i. parts: ... 2910
Ps 64:6 i. thought of every one of them, ... 7130
Pr 20:27 all the i. parts of the belly. ... 2315
Pr 20:30 do stripes the i. parts of the belly. ... 2315
Isa 16:11 and mine i. parts for Kir-haresh. ... 7130
Jer 31:33 I will put my law in their i. parts, ... 7130
Eze 40:9 and the porch of the gate was i.. ... 1004
Eze 40:16 and windows were round about i.. ... 6441
Eze 41:3 Then went he i., and measured the ... 6441
Eze 42:4 a walk of ten cubits breadth i., ... 6442
Lu 11:39 **your i. part is full of ravening** ... *2081*
Ro 7:22 the law of God after the i. man: ... *2080*
2Co 4:16 the i. man is renewed day by day. ... *2081*
2Co 7:15 his i. affection is more abundant ... *4698*

INWARDLY
Ps 62:4 their mouth, but they curse i.. ... 7130
Mt 7:15 **but i. they are ravening wolves.** ... *2081*
Ro 2:29 he is a Jew, which is one i.; ... *1722,2927*

INWARDS
Ex 29:13 all the fat that covereth the i., ... 7130
Ex 29:17 in pieces, and wash the i. of him, ... 7130
Ex 29:22 and the fat that covereth the i., and ... 7130
Le 1:9 his i. and his legs shall he wash in ... 7130
Le 1:13 he shall wash the i. and the legs ... 7130
Le 3:3 the fat that covereth the i., ... 7130
Le 3:3 and all the fat that is upon the i., ... 7130
Le 3:9 and the fat that covereth the i., ... 7130
Le 3:9 and all the fat that is upon the i., ... 7130
Le 3:14 the fat that covereth the i., ... 7130
Le 3:14 and all the fat that is upon the i., ... 7130
Le 4:8 the fat that covereth the i., ... 7130
Le 4:8 and all the fat that is upon the i., ... 7130
Le 4:11 and with his legs, and his i., and his ... 7130
Le 7:3 and the fat that covereth the i., ... 7130
Le 8:16 took all the fat that was upon the i., ... 7130
Le 8:21 And he washed the i. and the legs ... 7130
Le 8:25 and all the fat that was upon the i., ... 7130
Le 9:14 he did wash the i. and the legs, ... 7130
Le 9:19 and that which covereth the i., and ...

IPHEDEIAH (if-e-di'-ah)
1Ch 8:25 And I., and Penuel, the sons of ... 3301

IR (ur) See also IR-NAHASH; IR-SHEMESH.
1Ch 7:12 and Huppim, the children of I., ... 5893

IRA (i'-rah)
2Sa 20:26 I. also the Jairite was a chief ... 5896
2Sa 23:26 I. the son of Ikkesh the Tekoite, ... 5896
2Sa 23:38 I. an Ithrite, Gareb an Ithrite, ... 5896
1Ch 11:28 I. the son of Ikkesh the Tekoite, ... 5896
1Ch 11:40 I. the Ithrite, Gareb the Ithrite, ... 5896
1Ch 27:9 I. the son of Ikkesh the Tekoite: ... 5896

IRAD (i'-rad)
Ge 4:18 And unto Enoch was born I.. ... 5897
Ge 4:18 I. begat Mehujael: and Mehujael ... 5897

IRAM (i'-ram)
Ge 36:43 Duke Magdiel, duke I.: these be ... 5902
1Ch 1:54 Duke Magdiel, duke I.. These are ... 5902

IRI (i'-ri)
1Ch 7:7 and I., five; heads of the house ... 5901

IRIJAH (i-ri'-jah)
Jer 37:13 whose name was I., the son of ... 3376
Jer 37:14 I. took Jeremiah, and brought him ... 3376

IR-NAHASH (ur-na'-hash)
1Ch 4:12 and Tehinnah, the father of I.. ... 5904

IRON See also IRONS.
Ge 4:22 of every artificer in brass and i.. ... 1270
Le 26:19 I will make your heaven as i., and ... 1270
Nu 31:22 the silver, the brass, the i., the tin, ... 1270
Nu 35:16 smite him with an instrument of i., ... 1270
De 3:11 his bedstead was a bedstead of i.; ... 1270
De 4:20 you forth out of the i. furnace, even ... 1270
De 8:9 a land whose stones are i., and out ... 1270
De 27:5 thou shalt not lift up any i. tool ... 1270
De 28:23 earth that is under thee shall be i.. ... 1270
De 28:48 shall put a yoke of i. upon thy neck, ... 1270
De 33:25 Thy shoes shall be i. and brass; ... 1270
Jos 6:19 gold, and vessels of brass and i., ... 1270
Jos 6:24 and the vessels of brass and of i., ... 1270
Jos 8:31 which no man hath lift up any i.. ... 1270
Jos 17:16 of the valley have chariots of i., ... 1270
Jos 17:18 though they have i. chariots, and ... 1270
Jos 22:8 gold, and with brass, and with i.. ... 1270
Jg 1:19 because they had chariots of i.. ... 1270
Jg 4:3 he had nine hundred chariots of i.; ... 1270
Jg 4:13 even nine hundred chariots of i., ... 1270
1Sa 17:7 weighed six hundred shekels of i.. ... 1270
2Sa 12:31 saws, and under harrows of i., ... 1270
2Sa 12:31 and under axes of i., and made ... 1270
2Sa 23:7 be fenced with i. and the staff of a ... 1270
1Ki 6:7 any tool of i. heard in the house, ... 1270
1Ki 8:51 from the midst of the furnace of i.. ... 1270
1Ki 22:11 Chenaanah made him horns of i.: ... 1270
2Ki 6:6 it in thither; and the i. did swim. ... 1270
1Ch 20:3 with harrows of i., and with axes, ... 1270
1Ch 22:3 David prepared i. in abundance ... 1270
1Ch 22:14 and of brass and i. without weight; ... 1270
1Ch 22:16 the brass, and the i., there is no ... 1270
1Ch 29:2 of brass, the i. for things of i., ... 1270
1Ch 29:7 one hundred thousand talents of i.. ... 1270
2Ch 2:7 in brass, and in i., and in purple, ... 1270
2Ch 2:14 in silver, in brass, in i., in stone, ... 1270
2Ch 18:10 had made him horns of i., ... 1270
2Ch 24:12 also such as wrought i. and brass ... 1270
Job 19:24 they were graven with an i. pen ... 1270
Job 20:24 He shall flee from the i. weapon, ... 1270
Job 28:2 I. is taken out of the earth, and ... 1270
Job 40:18 brass; his bones are like bars of i.. ... 1270
Job 41:27 He esteemeth i. as straw, and brass ... 1270
Ps 2:9 shalt break them with a rod of i.; ... 1270
Ps 105:18 hurt with fetters: he was laid in i.. ... 1270
Ps 107:10 being bound in affliction and i.; ... 1270
Ps 107:16 and cut the bars of i. in sunder. ... 1270
Ps 149:8 and their nobles with fetters of i.; ... 1270
Pr 27:17 I. sharpeneth i.; so a man ... 1270
Ec 10:10 If the i. be blunt, and he do not ... 1270
Isa 10:34 the thickets of the forest with i., ... 1270
Isa 45:2 and cut in sunder the bars of i.. ... 1270
Isa 48:4 thy neck is as an i. sinew, and thy ... 1270
Isa 60:17 gold, and for i. I will bring silver, ... 1270
Isa 60:17 for wood brass, and for stones i.. ... 1270
Jer 1:18 and an i. pillar, and brasen walls ... 1270
Jer 6:28 they are brass and i.; they are all ... 1270
Jer 11:4 land of Egypt, from the i. furnace, ... 1270
Jer 15:12 Shall i. break the northern i. and ... 1270
Jer 17:1 of Judah is written with a pen of i., ... 1270
Jer 28:13 shalt make for them yokes of i.. ... 1270
Jer 28:14 have put a yoke of i. upon the neck ... 1270
Eze 4:3 take thou unto thee an i. pan, ... 1270
Eze 4:3 and set it for a wall of i. between ... 1270
Eze 22:18 are brass, and tin, and i., and lead, ... 1270
Eze 22:20 silver, and brass, and i., and lead, ... 1270
Eze 27:12 with silver, i., tin, and lead, they ... 1270
Eze 27:19 bright i., cassia, and calamus, were ... 1270
Da 2:33 His legs of i., his feet part of i. and ... 6523
Da 2:34 image upon his feet that were of i.. ... 6523
Da 2:35 Then was the i., the clay, the brass, ... 6523
Da 2:40 kingdom shall be strong as i.. ... 6523
Da 2:40 i. breaketh in pieces and subdueth ... 6523
Da 2:40 and as i. that breaketh all these, ... 6523
Da 2:41 part of potters' clay, and part of i., ... 6523
Da 2:41 be in it of the strength of the i., ... 6523
Da 2:41 sawest the i. mixed with miry clay. ... 6523
Da 2:42 the toes of the feet were part of i., ... 6523
Da 2:43 sawest i. mixed with miry clay, ... 6523
Da 2:43 even as i. is not mixed with clay. ... 6523
Da 2:45 it brake in pieces the i., the brass, ... 6523
Da 4:15, 23 even with a band of i. and brass, ... 6523
Da 5:4 of gold, and of silver, of brass, of i., ... 6523
Da 5:23 gods of silver, and gold, of brass, i., ... 6523
Da 7:7 it had great i. teeth: it devoured ... 6523
Da 7:19 whose teeth were of i., and his nails ... 6523
Am 1:3 with threshing instruments of i.. ... 1270
Mic 4:13 for I will make thine horn i., and I ... 1270
Ac 12:10 they came unto the i. gate that ... *4603*
1Ti 4:2 conscience seared with a hot i.; ...
Re 2:27 **shall rule them with a rod of i.** ... *4603*
Re 9:9 as it were breastplates of i.; ... *4603*
Re 12:5 to rule all nations with a rod of i.. ... *4603*
Re 18:12 and of brass, and i., and marble, ... *4604*
Re 19:15 he shall rule them with a rod of i.. ... *4603*

IRON (i'-ron)
Jos 19:38 And I., and Migdal-el, Horem, ... 3375

IRONS
Job 41:7 thou fill his skin with barbed i.? ... 7905

IRPEEL (ur'-pe-el)
Jos 18:27 Rekem, and I., and Taralah, ... 3416

IR-SHEMESH (ur-she'-mesh)
Jos 19:41 was Zorah, and Eshtaol, and I., ... 5905

IRU (i'-ru)
1Ch 4:15 Caleb the son of Jephunneh; I., ... 5902

IS See in the APPENDIX.

ISAAC (i'-za-ak) See also ISAAC'S.
Ge 17:19 and thou shalt call his name I.. ... 3327
Ge 17:21 covenant will I establish with I., ... 3327
Ge 21:3 him, whom Sarah bare to him, I.. ... 3327
Ge 21:4 Abraham circumcised his son I.. ... 3327
Ge 21:5 when his son I. was born unto him. ... 3327
Ge 21:8 the same day that I. was weaned. ... 3327
Ge 21:10 be heir with my son, even with I.. ... 3327
Ge 21:12 for in I. shall thy seed be called. ... 3327
Ge 22:2 Take now thy son, thine only son I.. ... 3327
Ge 22:3 men with him, and I. his son, ... 3327
Ge 22:6 offering, and laid it upon I. his son; ... 3327
Ge 22:7 and I. spake unto Abraham his ... 3327
Ge 22:9 and bound I. his son, and laid him ... 3327
Ge 24:4 and take a wife unto my son I.. ... 3327
Ge 24:14 hast appointed for thy servant I.; ... 3327
Ge 24:62 I. came from the way of the well ... 3327
Ge 24:63 I. went out to meditate in the field ... 3327
Ge 24:64 saw I., she lighted off the camel. ... 3327
Ge 24:66 told I. all things that he had done. ... 3327
Ge 24:67 I. brought her into his mother ... 3327
Ge 24:67 I. was comforted after his mother's ... 3327
Ge 25:5 gave all that he had unto I.. ... 3327
Ge 25:6 sent them away from I. his son. ... 3327
Ge 25:9 his sons I. and Ishmael buried him ... 3327
Ge 25:11 that God blessed his son I.; ... 3327
Ge 25:11 and I. dwelt by the well Lahai-roi. ... 3327

Ge 25:19 these are the generations of I., 3327
Ge 25:19 Abraham's son: Abraham begat I. 3327
Ge 25:20 I. was forty years old when he took 3327
Ge 25:21 I. entreated the Lord for his wife, 3327
Ge 25:26 I. was threescore years old when 3327
Ge 25:28 I. loved Esau, because he did eat 3327
Ge 26:1 I. went unto Abimelech king of 3327
Ge 26:6 And I. dwelt in Gerar: 3327
Ge 26:8 I. was sporting with Rebekah his 3327
Ge 26:9 Abimelech called I., and said, 3327
Ge 26:9 I. said unto him, Because I said, 3327
Ge 26:12 I. sowed in that land, and received 3327
Ge 26:16 Abimelech said unto I., Go from 3327
Ge 26:17 I. departed thence, and pitched 3327
Ge 26:18 I. digged again the wells of water, 3327
Ge 26:27 I. said unto them, Wherefore come 3327
Ge 26:31 I. sent them away, and they 3327
Ge 26:35 which were a grief of mind unto I. 3327
Ge 27:1 when I. was old, and his eyes were 3327
Ge 27:5 when I. spake to Esau his son 3327
Ge 27:20 I. said unto his son, How is it that 3327
Ge 27:21 I. said unto Jacob, Come near, I 3327
Ge 27:22 Jacob went near unto I. his father; 3327
Ge 27:26 his father I. said unto him, Come 3327
Ge 27:30 I. had made an end of blessing 3327
Ge 27:30 gone out from the presence of I. 3327
Ge 27:32 I. his father said unto him, Who 3327
Ge 27:33 I. trembled very exceedingly, and 3327
Ge 27:37 I. answered and said unto Esau, 3327
Ge 27:39 I. his father answered and said 3327
Ge 27:46 Rebekah said to I., I am weary of 3327
Ge 28:1 I. called Jacob, and blessed him, 3327
Ge 28:5 I. sent away Jacob: and he went 3327
Ge 28:6 saw that I. had blessed Jacob, 3327
Ge 28:8 daughters of Canaan pleased not I. 3327
Ge 28:13 thy father, and the God of I. 3327
Ge 31:18 for to go to I. his father in the land 3327
Ge 31:42 Abraham, and the fear of I., had 3327
Ge 31:53 sware by the fear of his father I. 3327
Ge 32:9 and God of my father I., the Lord 3327
Ge 35:12 land which I gave Abraham and I., 3327
Ge 35:27 Jacob came unto I. his father unto 3327
Ge 35:27 where Abraham and I. sojourned 3327
Ge 35:28 I. were a hundred and fourscore 3327
Ge 35:29 And I. gave up the ghost, and died, 3327
Ge 46:1 unto the God of his father I. 3327
Ge 48:15 fathers Abraham and I. did walk, 3327
Ge 48:16 of my fathers Abraham and I.; 3327
Ge 49:31 buried I. and Rebekah his wife; 3327
Ge 50:24 to Abraham, to I., and to Jacob. 3327
Ex 2:24 Abraham, with I., and with Jacob. 3327
Ex 3:6 Abraham, the God of I., and the 3327
Ex 3:15 the God of I., and the God of Jacob, 3327
Ex 3:16 God of Abraham, of I., and of 3327
Ex 4:5 the God of I., and the God of Jacob, 3327
Ex 6:3 I appeared unto Abraham, unto I., 3327
Ex 6:8 give it to Abraham, to I., and to 3327
Ex 32:13 Remember Abraham, I., and Israel, 3327
Ex 33:1 swear unto Abraham, to I., and to 3327
Le 26:42 and also my covenant with I., 3327
Nu 32:11 swear unto Abraham, unto I., and 3327
De 1:8 your fathers, Abraham, I., and 3327
De 6:10 to Abraham, to I., and to Jacob, 3327
De 9:5 fathers, Abraham, I., and Jacob. 3327
De 9:27 servants, Abraham, I., and Jacob; 3327
De 29:13 to Abraham, to I., and to Jacob, 3327
De 30:20 to Abraham, to I., and to Jacob, 3327
De 34:4 I sware unto Abraham, unto I., 3327
Jos 24:3 multiplied his seed, and gave him I. 3327
Jos 24:4 I gave unto I. Jacob and Esau: 3327
1Ki 18:36 God of Abraham, I., and of Israel, 3327
2Ki 13:23 his covenant with Abraham, I., and 3327
1Ch 1:28 sons of Abraham; I., and Ishmael. 3327
1Ch 1:34 And Abraham begat I. 3327
1Ch 1:34 The sons of I.; Esau and Israel. 3327
1Ch 16:16 Abraham, and of his oath unto I.; 3327
1Ch 29:18 God of Abraham, I., and of Israel, 3327
2Ch 30:6 God of Abraham, I., and Israel, 3327
Ps 105:9 Abraham, and his oath unto I.; 3446
Jer 33:26 seed of Abraham, I., and Jacob: 3446
Am 7:9 high places of I. shall be desolate, 3446
Am 7:16 thy word against the house of I. 3446
Mt 1:2 begat I.; and I. begat Jacob; *2664*
Mt 8:11 **sit down with Abraham, and I.,** *2664*
Mt 22:32 **God of I., and the God of Jacob?** *2664*
Mk 12:26 **of Abraham, and the God of I.,** *2664*
Lu 3:34 which was the son of I., which was *2664*
Lu 13:28 **see Abraham, and I., and Jacob,** *2664*
Lu 20:37 **and the God of I., and the God of.** *2664*
Ac 3:13 The God of Abraham, and of I., *2664*
Ac 7:8 Abraham begat I., and circumcised *2664*
Ac 7:8 and I. begat Jacob; and Jacob *2664*
Ac 7:32 God of Abraham, and the God of I., *2664*
Ro 9:7 but, In I. shall thy seed be called. *2664*
Ro 9:10 by one, even by our father I.; *2664*
Ga 4:28 Now we, brethren, as I. was, are *2664*
Heb 11:9 dwelling in tabernacles with I. and *2664*
Heb 11:17 when he was tried, offered up I. *2664*
Heb 11:18 That in I. shall thy seed be called: *2664*
Heb 11:20 By faith I. blessed Jacob and Esau *2664*
Jas 2:21 offered I. his son upon the altar? *2664*

ISAAC'S (i'-za-aks)
Ge 26:19 I. servants digged in the valley, 3327
Ge 26:20 Gerar did strive with I. herdmen, 3327
Ge 26:25 and there I. servants digged a well 3327
Ge 26:32 I. servants came, and told him 3327

ISAIAH (i-za'-yah) See also ESAIAS.
2Ki 19:2 to I. the prophet the son of Amoz 3470
2Ki 19:5 of king Hezekiah came to I. 3470
2Ki 19:6 And I. said unto them, Thus shall 3470
2Ki 19:20 Then I. the son of Amoz sent to 3470
2Ki 20:1 I. the son of Amoz came to him, 3470
2Ki 20:4 I. was gone out into the middle 3470
2Ki 20:7 And I. said, Take a lump of figs 3470
2Ki 20:8 Hezekiah said unto I., What shall 3470
2Ki 20:9 I. said, This sign shalt thou have of 3470
2Ki 20:11 I. the prophet cried unto the Lord: 3470
2Ki 20:14 I. the prophet unto king Hezekiah, 3470
2Ki 20:16 I. said unto Hezekiah, Hear the 3470
2Ki 20:19 said Hezekiah unto I., Good is the 3470
2Ch 26:22 did I. the prophet, the son of Amoz, 3470
2Ch 32:20 I. the son of Amoz, prayed and 3470
Isa *general title* The Book Of The Prophet I. 3470
2Ch 32:32 in the vision of I. the prophet, 3470
Isa 1:1 The vision of I. the son of Amoz, 3470
Isa 2:1 word that I. the son of Amoz saw 3470
Isa 7:3 Then said the Lord unto I., Go 3470
Isa 13:1 which I. the son of Amoz did see 3470
Isa 20:2 the same time spake the Lord by I. 3470
Isa 20:3 my servant I. hath walked naked 3470
Isa 37:2 unto I. the prophet the son of Amoz 3470
Isa 37:5 of king Hezekiah came to I. 3470
Isa 37:6 I. said unto them, Thus shall ye say 3470
Isa 37:21 Then I. the son of Amoz sent unto 3470
Isa 38:1 I. the prophet the son of Amoz 3470
Isa 38:4 came the word of the Lord to I., 3470
Isa 38:21 I. had said, Let them take a lump 3470
Isa 39:3 I. the prophet unto king Hezekiah, 3470
Isa 39:5 Then said I. to Hezekiah, Hear the 3470
Isa 39:8 Then said Hezekiah to I., Good is 3470

ISCAH (is'-cah) See also SARAH.
Ge 11:29 of Milcah, and the father of I. 3252

ISCARIOT (is-car'-e-ot) See also JUDAS.
Mt 10:4 Judas I., who also betrayed him. *2469*
Mt 26:14 one of the twelve, called Judas I., *2469*
Mk 3:19 Judas I., which also betrayed him: *2469*
Mk 14:10 And Judas I., one of the twelve *2469*
Lu 6:16 Judas I., which also was the traitor. *2469*
Lu 22:3 Satan into Judas surnamed I., *2469*
Joh 6:71 spake of Judas I. the son of Simon: *2469*
Joh 12:4 one of his disciples, Judas I., *2469*
Joh 13:2 now put it into the heart of Judas I., *2469*
Joh 13:26 the sop, he gave it to Judas I., the *2469*
Joh 14:22 Judas saith unto him, not I., Lord, *2469*

ISH See ISH-BOSHETH; ISH-TOB.

ISHBAH (ish'-bah)
1Ch 4:17 and I. the father of Eshtemoa 3431

ISHBAK (ish'-bak)
Ge 25:2 and Midian, and I., and Shuah. 3435
1Ch 1:32 and Midian, and I., and Shuah. 3435

ISHBI-BENOB (ish''-bi-be'-nob)
2Sa 21:16 And I., which was of the sons of 3430

ISH-BOSHETH (ish-bo'-sheth) See also ESH-BAAL.
2Sa 2:8 took I. the son of Saul, and 378
2Sa 2:10 I. Saul's son was forty years old 378
2Sa 2:12 the servants of I. the son of Saul, 378
2Sa 2:15 pertained to I. the son of Saul, 378
2Sa 3:7 I. said to Abner, Wherefore hast
2Sa 3:8 very wroth for the words of I., 378
2Sa 3:14 David sent messengers to I. Saul's 378
2Sa 3:15 I. sent, and took her from her 378
2Sa 4:5 heat of the day to the house of I., 378
2Sa 4:8 brought the head of I. unto David 378
2Sa 4:8 Behold the head of I. the son of 378
2Sa 4:12 they took the head of I., and buried 378

ISHI (i'-shi)
1Ch 2:31 of Appaim; I.. And the sons of I.; 3469
1Ch 4:20 the sons of I. were, Zoheth, and 3469
1Ch 4:42 and Uzziel, the sons of I. 3469
1Ch 5:24 of their fathers, even Epher, and I., 3469
Ho 2:16 Lord, that thou shalt call me I.; 376

ISHIAH (i-shi'-ah) See also ISHIJAH; ISSHIAH.
1Ch 7:3 and Obadiah, and Joel, I., five: 3449

ISHIJAH (i-shi'-jah) See also ISHIAH; JESIAH.
Ezr 10:31 the sons of Harim; Eliezer, I., 3449

ISHMA (ish'-mah)
1Ch 4:3 Jezreel, and I., and Idbash: and 3457

ISHMAEL (ish'-ma-el) See also ISHMAELITE; ISHMAEL'S.
Ge 16:11 a son, and shalt call his name I.; 3458
Ge 16:15 son's name, which Hagar bare, I. 3458
Ge 16:16 old, when Hagar bare I. to Abram 3458
Ge 17:18 O that I. might live before thee! 3458
Ge 17:20 And as for I., I have heard thee: 3458
Ge 17:23 And Abraham took I. his son, and 3458
Ge 17:25 I. his son was thirteen years old, 3458
Ge 17:26 circumcised, and I. his son 3458
Ge 25:9 his sons Isaac and I. buried him 3458
Ge 25:12 these are the generations of I., 3458
Ge 25:13 are the names of the sons of I., 3458
Ge 25:13 the firstborn of I., Nebajoth; and 3458
Ge 25:16 These are the sons of I., and these 3458
Ge 25:17 these are the years of the life of I., 3458
Ge 28:9 Then went Esau unto I., and took 3458
Ge 28:9 Mahalath the daughter of I., 3458
2Ki 25:23, 25 even I. the son of Nethaniah, 3458
1Ch 1:28 sons of Abraham; Isaac, and I. 3458
1Ch 1:29 The firstborn of I., Nebaioth; then 3458
1Ch 1:31 Kedemah. These are the sons of I. 3458
1Ch 8:38 I., and Sheariah, and Obadiah, and 3458
1Ch 9:44 I., and Sheariah, and Obadiah, and 3458
2Ch 19:11 Zebadiah the son of I., the ruler 3458
2Ch 23:1 I. the son of Jehohanan, and 3458
Ezr 10:22 Pashur; Elioenai, Maaseiah, I., 3458
Jer 40:8 even I. the son of Nethaniah, and 3458
Jer 40:14 hath sent I. the son of Nethaniah 3458
Jer 40:15 I will slay I. the son of Nethaniah, 3458
Jer 40:16 for thou speakest falsely of I. 3458
Jer 41:1 month, that I. the son of Nethaniah 3458
Jer 41:2 Then arose I. the son of Nethaniah, 3458
Jer 41:3 I. also slew all the Jews that were 3458
Jer 41:6 And I. the son of Nethaniah went 3458
Jer 41:7 I. the son of Nethaniah slew them, 3458
Jer 41:8 among them that said unto I., 3458
Jer 41:9 I. had cast all the dead bodies 3458
Jer 41:9 I. the son of Nethaniah filled it with 3458
Jer 41:10 I. carried away captive all the 3458
Jer 41:10 I. the son of Nethaniah carried 3458
Jer 41:11 I. the son of Nethaniah had done, 3458
Jer 41:12 fight with I. the son of Nethaniah, 3458
Jer 41:13 which were with I. saw Johanan 3458
Jer 41:14 people that I. had carried away 3458
Jer 41:15 But I. the son of Nethaniah escaped 3458
Jer 41:16 he had recovered from I. the son of 3458
Jer 41:18 I. the son of Nethaniah had slain 3458

ISHMAELITE (ish'-ma-el-ite) See also ISHMAELITES; ISHMEELITE.
1Ch 27:30 the camels also was Obil the I. 3459

ISHMAELITES (ish'-ma-el-ites) See also ISHMEELITES.
Jg 8:24 earrings, because they were I. 3459
Ps 83:6 tabernacles of Edom, and the I.; 3459

ISHMAEL'S (ish'-ma-els)
Ge 36:3 And Bashemath I. daughter, sister 3458

ISHMAIAH (ish-ma-i'-ah) See also ISMAIAH.
1Ch 27:19 Zebulun, I. the son of Obadiah: 3460

ISHMEELITE (ish'-me-el-ite) See also ISHMAELITE; ISHMEELITES.
1Ch 2:17 of Amasa was Jether the I. 3459

ISHMEELITES (ish'-me-el-ites) See also ISHMAELITES.
Ge 37:25 I. came from Gilead, with their 3459
Ge 37:27 Come, and let us sell him to the the I., 3459

Ge 37:28 sold Joseph to the **I.** for twenty......... 3459
Ge 39:1 bought him of the hands of the **I.**,....... 3459

ISHMERAI (ish'-me-rahee)
1Ch 8:18 **I.** also, and Jezliah, and Jobab,........... 3461

ISHOD (i'-shod)
1Ch 7:18 his sister Hammoleketh bare **I.**, ... 379

ISHPAN (ish'-pan)
1Ch 8:22 And **I.**, and Heber, and Eliel, ... 3473

ISH-TOB (ish'-tob)
2Sa 10:6 and of **I.** twelve thousand men. 382
2Sa 10:8 and of Zoba, and of Rehob, and **I.**, ... 382

ISHUAH (ish'-u-ah) See also ISUAH.
Ge 46:17 and **I.**, and Isui, and Beriah,............... 3438

ISHUAI (ish'-u-ahee) See also ISHUI.
1Ch 7:30 and Isuah, and **I.**, and Beriah, ... 3440

ISHUI (ish'-u-i) See also ISHUAI; JESUI.
1Sa 14:49 Saul were Jonathan, and **I.**, and 3440

ISLAND See also ISLANDS; ISLE.
Job 22:30 shall deliver the **i.** of the innocent,....... 336
Isa 34:14 meet with the wild beasts of the **i.**,....... 338
Ac 27:16 a certain **i.** which is called Clauda,...... *3519*
Ac 27:26 we must be cast upon a certain **i.**. *3520*
Ac 28:1 knew that the **i.** was called Melita. *3520*
Ac 28:7 the chief man of the **i.**, whose name... *3520*
Ac 28:9 which had diseases in the **i.**, came,..... *3520*
Re 6:14 every mountain and **i.** were moved...... *3520*
Re 16:20 And every **i.** fled away, and the.......... *3520*

ISLANDS See also ISLES.
Isa 11:11 Hamath, and from the **i.** of the sea. 339
Isa 13:22 the wild beasts of the **i.** shall cry in 338
Isa 41:1 Keep silence before me, O **i.**; and....... 339
Isa 42:12 and declare his praise in the **i.**. 339
Isa 42:15 I will make the rivers **i.**, and I will....... 339
Isa 59:18 to the **i.** he will repay recompence....... 339
Jer 50:39 beasts of the **i.** shall dwell there,......... 339

ISLE See also ISLAND; ISLES.
Isa 20:6 inhabitants of this **i.** shall say in.......... 339
Isa 23:2 Be still, ye inhabitants of the **i.**; 339
Isa 23:6 howl, ye inhabitants of the **i.**.............. 339
Ac 13:6 gone through the **i.** unto Paphos, ... *3520*
Ac 28:11 which had wintered in the **i.**, whose.... *3520*
Re 1:9 was in the **i.** that is called Patmos, ... *3520*

ISLES See also ISLANDS.
Ge 10:5 were the **i.** of the Gentiles divided....... 339
Es 10:1 the land, and upon the **i.** of the sea...... 339
Ps 72:10 and of the **i.** shall bring presents: 339
Ps 97:1 the multitude of **i.** be glad thereof........ 339
Isa 24:15 God of Israel in the **i.** of the sea. 339
Isa 40:15 taketh up the **i.** as a very little thing. ... 339
Isa 41:5 The **i.** saw it, and feared; the ends....... 339
Isa 42:4 and the **i.** shall wait for his law........... 339
Isa 42:10 the **i.**, and the inhabitants thereof. 339
Isa 49:1 Listen, O **i.**, unto me; and hearken, ... 339
Isa 51:5 the **i.** shall wait upon me, and on......... 339
Isa 60:9 Surely the **i.** shall wait for me, and 339
Isa 66:19 to Tubal, and Javan, to the **i.** afar off,... 339
Jer 2:10 pass over the **i.** of Chittim, and see;.... 339
Jer 25:22 the **i.** which are beyond the sea, ... 339
Jer 31:10 declare it in the **i.** afar off, and say, ... 339
Eze 26:15 the **i.** shake at the sound of thy fall,..... 339
Eze 26:18 the **i.** tremble in the day of thy fall; 339
Eze 26:18 the **i.** that are in the sea shall be......... 339
Eze 27:3 merchant of the people for many **i.**, ... 339
Eze 27:6 brought out of the **i.** of Chittim. 339
Eze 27:7 and purple from the **i.** of Elishah 339
Eze 27:15 many **i.** were the merchandise of......... 339
Eze 27:35 All the inhabitants of the **i.** shall be...... 339
Eze 39:6 them that dwell carelessly in the **i.**....... 339
Da 11:18 shall he turn his face unto the **i.**, ... 339
Zep 2:11 place, even all the **i.** of the heathen. 339

ISMACHIAH (is-ma-ki'-ah)
2Ch 31:13 and Jozabad, and Eliel, and **I.**, ... 3253

ISMAIAH (is-ma-i'-ah) See also ISHMAIAH.
1Ch 12:4 And **I.** the Gibeonite, a mighty 3460

ISPAH (is'-pah)
1Ch 8:16 And Michael, and **I.**, and Joha, ... 3472

ISRAEL (iz'-ra-el) See also EL-ELOHE-ISRAEL; ISRAELITE; ISRAEL'S; JACOB; JESHURUN.
Ge 32:28 be called no more Jacob, but **I.**.......... 3478
Ge 32:32 children of **I.** eat not of the sinew 3478
Ge 34:7 because he had wrought folly in **I.**....... 3478
Ge 35:10 Jacob, but **I.** shall be thy name; 3478
Ge 35:10 and he called his name **I.**.................. 3478
Ge 35:21 **I.** journeyed, and spread his tent........ 3478
Ge 35:22 when **I.** dwelt in that land, that........... 3478
Ge 35:22 father's concubine: and **I.** heard it. 3478
Ge 36:31 any king over the children of **I.**.......... 3478
Ge 37:3 **I.** loved Joseph more than all his........ 3478
Ge 37:13 **I.** said unto Joseph, Do not thy.......... 3478
Ge 42:5 the sons of **I.** came to buy corn......... 3478
Ge 43:6 **I.** said, Wherefore dealt ye so ill........ 3478
Ge 43:8 Judah said unto **I.** his father, ... 3478
Ge 43:11 **I.** said unto them, If it must be so 3478
Ge 45:21 And the children of **I.** did so: and....... 3478
Ge 45:28 **I.** said, It is enough; Joseph my......... 3478
Ge 46:1 **I.** took his journey with all that he...... 3478
Ge 46:2 God spake unto **I.** in the visions of..... 3478
Ge 46:5 the sons of **I.** carried Jacob their......... 3478
Ge 46:8 are the names of the children of **I.**, ... 3478
Ge 46:29 went up to meet **I.** his father, to 3478
Ge 46:30 **I.** said unto Joseph, Now let me die.... 3478
Ge 47:27 And **I.** dwelt in the land of Egypt, ... 3478
Ge 47:29 time drew nigh that **I.** must die: 3478
Ge 47:31 **I.** bowed himself upon the bed's......... 3478
Ge 48:2 **I.** strengthened himself, and sat......... 3478
Ge 48:8 **I.** beheld Joseph's sons, and said,....... 3478
Ge 48:10 the eyes of **I.** were dim for age, ... 3478
Ge 48:11 **I.** said unto Joseph, I had not........... 3478
Ge 48:14 And **I.** stretched out his right hand, ... 3478
Ge 48:20 In thee shall **I.** bless, saying, God...... 3478
Ge 48:21 **I.** said unto Joseph, Behold, I die:...... 3478
Ge 49:2 and hearken unto **I.** your father. 3478
Ge 49:7 in Jacob, and scatter them in **I.**......... 3478
Ge 49:16 people, as one of the tribes of **I.**........ 3478
Ge 49:24 is the shepherd, the stone of **I.**. 3478
Ge 49:28 these are the twelve tribes of **I.**. 3478
Ge 50:2 and the physicians embalmed **I.**........... 3478
Ge 50:25 took an oath of the children of **I.**,........ 3478
Ex 1:1 are the names of the children of **I.**, ... 3478
Ex 1:7 the children of **I.** were fruitful, and..... 3478
Ex 1:9 the children of **I.** are more and.......... 3478
Ex 1:12 because of the children of **I.**.............. 3478
Ex 1:13 children of **I.** to serve with rigour: 3478
Ex 2:23 of **I.** sighed by reason of bondage,....... 3478
Ex 2:25 God looked upon the children of **I.**, ... 3478
Ex 3:9 the cry of the children of **I.** is come ... 3478
Ex 3:10 forth my people the children of **I.**........ 3478
Ex 3:11 bring forth the children of **I.** out of..... 3478
Ex 3:13 when I come unto the children of **I.**,... 3478
Ex 3:14, 15 thou say unto the children of **I.**, ... 3478
Ex 3:16 gather the elders of **I.** together, ... 3478
Ex 3:18 come, thou and the elders of **I.**, ... 3478
Ex 4:22 Thus saith the Lord, **I.** is my son, ... 3478
Ex 4:29 all the elders of the children of **I.**. 3478
Ex 4:31 Lord had visited the children of **I.**, ... 3478
Ex 5:1 Thus saith the Lord God of **I.**, Let..... 3478
Ex 5:2 should obey his voice to let **I.** go?....... 3478
Ex 5:2 the Lord, neither will I let **I.** go.......... 3478
Ex 5:14 the officers of the children of **I.**, ... 3478
Ex 5:15 officers of the children of **I.** came........ 3478
Ex 5:19 officers of the children of **I.** did see.... 3478
Ex 6:5 the groaning of the children of **I.**,........ 3478
Ex 6:6 say unto the children of **I.**, I am 3478
Ex 6:9 spake so unto the children of **I.**. 3478
Ex 6:11 children of **I.** go out of his land.......... 3478
Ex 6:12 of **I.** have not hearkened unto me; 3478
Ex 6:13 a charge unto the children of **I.**,........... 3478
Ex 6:13 the children of **I.** out of the land of..... 3478
Ex 6:14 sons of Reuben the firstborn of **I.**; 3478
Ex 6:26 Bring out the children of **I.** from........ 3478
Ex 6:27 to bring out the children of **I.** from..... 3478
Ex 7:2 that he send the children of **I.** out...... 3478
Ex 7:4 and my people the children of **I.**, ... 3478
Ex 7:5 and bring out the children of **I.**.......... 3478
Ex 9:4 shall sever between the cattle of **I.**..... 3478
Ex 9:4 die of all that is the children's of **I.**..... 3478
Ex 9:6 cattle of the children of **I.** died not 3478
Ex 9:26 where the children of **I.** were, was...... 3478
Ex 9:35 would he let the children of **I.** go; 3478
Ex 10:20 would not let the children of **I.** go. 3478
Ex 10:23 of **I.** had light in their dwellings. 3478
Ex 11:7 children of **I.** shall not a dog move 3478
Ex 11:7 between the Egyptians and **I.** 3478
Ex 11:10 the children of **I.** go out of his land..... 3478
Ex 12:3 ye unto all the congregation of **I.**, ... 3478
Ex 12:6 assembly of the congregation of **I.**....... 3478
Ex 12:15 that soul shall be cut off from **I.**......... 3478
Ex 12:19 cut off from the congregation of **I.**,...... 3478
Ex 12:21 Moses called for all the elders of **I.**, ... 3478
Ex 12:27 the houses of the children of **I.** in 3478
Ex 12:28 And the children of **I.** went away, ... 3478
Ex 12:31 both ye and the children of **I.**. 3478
Ex 12:35 of **I.** did according to the word of....... 3478
Ex 12:37 And the children of **I.** journeyed.......... 3478
Ex 12:40 the sojourning of the children of **I.**,..... 3478
Ex 12:42 children of **I.** in their generations. 3478
Ex 12:47 the congregation of **I.** shall keep it. 3478
Ex 12:50 Thus did all the children of **I.**; as 3478
Ex 12:51 bring the children of **I.** out of the....... 3478
Ex 13:2 womb among the children of **I.**, ... 3478
Ex 13:18 children of **I.** went up harnessed.......... 3478
Ex 13:19 straitly sworn the children of **I.**,.......... 3478
Ex 14:2 Speak unto the children of **I.**, that...... 3478
Ex 14:3 will say of the children of **I.**, They 3478
Ex 14:5 we have let **I.** go from serving us?..... 3478
Ex 14:8 he pursued after the children of **I.**........ 3478
Ex 14:8 of **I.** went out with an high hand. 3478
Ex 14:10 children of **I.** lifted up their eyes........ 3478
Ex 14:10 of **I.** cried out unto the Lord. 3478
Ex 14:15 Speak unto the children of **I.**, that...... 3478
Ex 14:16 of **I.** shall go on dry ground 3478
Ex 14:19 which went before the camp of **I.**,....... 3478
Ex 14:20 the Egyptians and the camp of **I.**; 3478
Ex 14:22 of **I.** went into the midst of the sea 3478
Ex 14:25 Let us flee from the face of **I.**; for 3478
Ex 14:29 children of **I.** walked upon dry land...... 3478
Ex 14:30 the Lord saved **I.** that day out of....... 3478
Ex 14:30 **I.** saw the Egyptians dead upon......... 3478
Ex 14:31 **I.** saw that great work which the 3478
Ex 15:1 sang Moses and the children of **I.** 3478
Ex 15:19 the children of **I.** went on dry land 3478
Ex 15:22 Moses brought **I.** from the Red sea, ... 3478
Ex 16:1 congregation of the children of **I.**........ 3478
Ex 16:2 children of **I.** murmured against 3478
Ex 16:3 the children of **I.** said unto them, ... 3478
Ex 16:6 said unto all the children of **I.**,........... 3478
Ex 16:9 all the congregation of the...of **I.**,......... 3478
Ex 16:10 whole congregation of the...of **I.**, ... 3478
Ex 16:12 murmurings of the children of **I.**......... 3478
Ex 16:15 when the children of **I.** saw it, they..... 3478
Ex 16:17 And the children of **I.** did so, and........ 3478
Ex 16:31 **I.** called the name thereof Manna. 3478
Ex 16:35 children of **I.** did eat manna forty 3478
Ex 17:1 **I.** journeyed from the wilderness........ 3478
Ex 17:5 take with thee of the elders of **I.**; 3478
Ex 17:6 so in the sight of the elders of **I.**. 3478
Ex 17:7 the chiding of the children of **I.**,.......... 3478
Ex 17:8 and fought with **I.** in Rephidim........... 3478
Ex 17:11 held up his hand, that **I.** prevailed: 3478
Ex 18:1 for Moses, and for **I.** his people,......... 3478
Ex 18:1 Lord had brought **I.** out of Egypt;...... 3478
Ex 18:9 which the Lord had done to **I.**, ... 3478
Ex 18:12 Aaron came, and all the elders of **I.**,.... 3478
Ex 18:25 Moses chose able men out of all **I.**, ... 3478
Ex 19:1 children of **I.** were gone forth out 3478
Ex 19:2 there **I.** camped before the mount. 3478
Ex 19:3 Jacob, and tell the children of **I.**;......... 3478
Ex 19:6 shalt speak unto the children of **I.**. 3478
Ex 20:22 shalt say unto the children of **I.**, ... 3478
Ex 24:1 and seventy of the elders of **I.**; 3478
Ex 24:4 according to the twelve tribes of **I.**....... 3478
Ex 24:5 young men of the children of **I.**,.......... 3478
Ex 24:9 and seventy of the elders of **I.**; 3478
Ex 24:10 And they saw the God of **I.**: and......... 3478
Ex 24:11 the nobles of the children of **I.** he 3478
Ex 24:17 in the eyes of the children of **I.**. 3478
Ex 25:2 Speak unto the children of **I.**, that...... 3478
Ex 25:22 unto the children of **I.**....................... 3478
Ex 27:20 shalt command the children of **I.**, ... 3478
Ex 27:21 on the behalf of the children of **I.**. 3478
Ex 28:1 from among the children of **I.**, that...... 3478
Ex 28:9, 11 the names of the children of **I.** 3478
Ex 28:12 memorial unto the children of **I.**.......... 3478
Ex 28:21 the names of the children of **I.**, ... 3478
Ex 28:29 bear the names of the children of **I.**..... 3478
Ex 28:30 the judgment of the children of **I.**....... 3478
Ex 28:38 **I.** shall hallow in all their holy............ 3478
Ex 29:28 for ever from the children of **I.**.......... 3478
Ex 29:28 offering from the children of **I.**........... 3478
Ex 29:43 will meet with the children of **I.**,......... 3478
Ex 29:45 will dwell among the children of **I.**, ... 3478
Ex 30:12 takest the sum of the children of **I.** 3478
Ex 30:16 money of the children of **I.**, ... 3478

Ex 30:16 memorial unto the children of **I.** 3478
Ex 30:31 shalt speak unto the children of **I.**, 3478
Ex 31:13 thou also unto the children of **I.**, 3478
Ex 31:16 of **I.** shall keep the sabbath, 3478
Ex 31:17 between me and the children of **I.** 3478
Ex 32:4,8 these be thy gods, O **I.**, which 3478
Ex 32:13 Remember Abraham, Isaac, and **I.**, 3478
Ex 32:20 made the children of **I.** drink of it 3478
Ex 32:27 Thus saith the Lord God of **I.**, Put 3478
Ex 33:5 Say unto the children of **I.**, Ye are 3478
Ex 33:6 of **I.** stripped themselves of their 3478
Ex 34:23 before the Lord God, the God of **I.** 3478
Ex 34:27 covenant with thee and with **I.** 3478
Ex 34:30 all the children of **I.** saw Moses, 3478
Ex 34:32 all the children of **I.** came nigh: 3478
Ex 34:34 and spake unto the children of **I.** 3478
Ex 34:35 children of **I.** saw the face of Moses, 3478
Ex 35:1 congregation of the children of **I.** 3478
Ex 35:4 congregation of the children of **I.**, 3478
Ex 35:20 children of **I.** departed from 3478
Ex 35:29 of **I.** brought a willing offering unto 3478
Ex 35:30 Moses said unto the children of **I.**, 3478
Ex 36:3 of **I.** had brought for the service 3478
Ex 39:6 the names of the children of **I.** 3478
Ex 39:7 a memorial to the children of **I.**; 3478
Ex 39:14 to the names of the children of **I.**, 3478
Ex 39:32 children of **I.** did according to all 3478
Ex 39:42 children of **I.** made all the work. 3478
Ex 40:36 of **I.** went onward in all their 3478
Ex 40:38 in the sight of all the house of **I.**, 3478
Le 1:2 Speak unto the children of **I.**, and 3478
Le 4:2 Speak unto the children of **I.**, 3478
Le 4:13 congregation of **I.** sin through 3478
Le 7:23, 29 Speak unto the children of **I.**, 3478
Le 7:34 have I taken of the children of **I.** 3478
Le 7:34 ever from among the children of **I.** 3478
Le 7:36 be given them of the children of **I.** 3478
Le 7:38 the children of **I.** to offer their 3478
Le 9:1 and his sons, and the elders of **I.**; 3478
Le 9:3 the children of **I.** thou shalt speak, 3478
Le 10:6 brethren, the whole house of **I.**, 3478
Le 10:11 that ye may teach the children of **I.** 3478
Le 10:14 peace offerings of the children of **I.** 3478
Le 11:2 Speak unto the children of **I.**, 3478
Le 12:2 Speak unto the children of **I.**, 3478
Le 15:2 Speak unto the children of **I.**, and 3478
Le 15:31 shall ye separate the children of **I.** 3478
Le 16:5 of **I.** two kids of the goats for a sin 3478
Le 16:16 uncleanness of the children of **I.**, 3478
Le 16:17 and for all the congregation of **I.** 3478
Le 16:19 uncleanness of the children of **I.** 3478
Le 16:21 the iniquities of the children of **I.**, 3478
Le 16:34 the children of **I.** for all their sins 3478
Le 17:2 unto all the children of **I.**, and say 3478
Le 17:3 soever there be of the house of **I.**, 3478
Le 17:5 of **I.** may bring their sacrifices, 3478
Le 17:8, 10 man there be of the house of **I.** 3478
Le 17:12 I said unto the children of **I.**, No 3478
Le 17:13 man there be of the children of **I.**, 3478
Le 17:14 I said unto the children of **I.**, Ye 3478
Le 18:2 Speak unto the children of **I.**, and 3478
Le 19:2 congregation of the children of **I.**, 3478
Le 20:2 shalt say to the children of **I.**, 3478
Le 20:2 he be of the children of **I.**, or of the 3478
Le 20:2 strangers that sojourn in **I.**, that 3478
Le 21:24 and unto all the children of **I.** 3478
Le 22:2 holy things of the children of **I.**, 3478
Le 22:3 children of **I.** hallow unto the Lord, 3478
Le 22:15 holy things of the children of **I.**, 3478
Le 22:18 and unto all the children of **I.**, 3478
Le 22:18 Whatsoever he be of the house of **I.**, 3478
Le 22:18 the strangers in **I.**, that will offer 3478
Le 22:32 hallowed among the children of **I.** 3478
Le 23:2, 10 Speak unto the children of **I.**, and 3478
Le 23:24, 34 Speak unto the children of **I.**, 3478
Le 23:43 children of **I.** to dwell in booths, 3478
Le 23:44 unto the children of **I.** the feasts of 3478
Le 24:2 Command the children of **I.**, that 3478
Le 24:8 being taken from the children of **I.** 3478
Le 24:10 went out among the children of **I.** 3478
Le 24:10 of **I.** strove together in the camp; 3481
Le 24:15 speak unto the children of **I.**, 3478
Le 24:23 Moses spake to the children of **I.**, 3478
Le 24:23 of **I.** did as the Lord commanded 3478
Le 25:2 Speak unto the children of **I.**, and 3478
Le 25:33 possession among the children of **I.** 3478
Le 25:46 your brethren the children of **I.**, 3478
Le 25:55 me the children of **I.** are servants; 3478
Le 26:46 between him and the children of **I.** 3478
Le 27:2 Speak unto the children of **I.**, and 3478
Le 27:34 Moses for the children of **I.** in 3478
Nu 1:2 congregation of the children of **I.**, 3478
Nu 1:3 are able to go forth to war in **I.** 3478
Nu 1:16 fathers, heads of thousands in **I.** 3478
Nu 1:44 the princes of **I.**, being twelve men: 3478
Nu 1:45 numbered of the children of **I.**, 3478
Nu 1:45 were able to go forth to war in **I.**; 3478
Nu 1:49 of them among the children of **I.**: 3478
Nu 1:52 children of **I.** shall pitch their tents, 3478
Nu 1:53 congregation of the children of **I.** 3478
Nu 1:54 children of **I.** did according to all 3478
Nu 2:2 children of **I.** shall pitch by his own 3478
Nu 2:32 were numbered of the children of **I.** 3478
Nu 2:33 numbered among the children of **I.**; 3478
Nu 2:34 children of **I.** did according to all 3478
Nu 3:8 the charge of the children of **I.**, to 3478
Nu 3:9 unto him out of the children of **I.** 3478
Nu 3:12 from among the children of **I.** 3478
Nu 3:12 matrix among the children of **I.** 3478
Nu 3:13 unto me all the firstborn in **I.**, 3478
Nu 3:38 for the charge of the children of **I.**; 3478
Nu 3:40 of the males of the children of **I.** 3478
Nu 3:41 firstborn among the children of **I.**; 3478
Nu 3:41 the cattle of the children of **I.** 3478
Nu 3:42 firstborn among the children of **I.** 3478
Nu 3:45 firstborn among the children of **I.**, 3478
Nu 3:46 the firstborn of the children of **I.**, 3478
Nu 3:50 the firstborn of the children of **I.** 3478
Nu 4:46 Aaron and the chief of **I.** numbered, 3478
Nu 5:2 Command the children of **I.**, that 3478
Nu 5:4 the children of **I.** did so, and put 3478
Nu 5:4 unto Moses, so did the children of **I.** 3478
Nu 5:6 Speak unto the children of **I.**, When 3478
Nu 5:9 holy things of the children of **I.**, 3478
Nu 5:12 Speak unto the children of **I.**, and 3478
Nu 6:2 Speak unto the children of **I.**, and 3478
Nu 6:23 ye shall bless the children of **I.**, 3478
Nu 6:27 my name upon the children of **I.**; 3478
Nu 7:2 That the princes of **I.**, heads of the 3478
Nu 7:84 was anointed, by the princes of **I.** 3478
Nu 8:6 from among the children of **I.**, 3478
Nu 8:9 whole assembly of the children of **I.** 3478
Nu 8:10 children of **I.** shall put their hands 3478
Nu 8:11 for an offering of the children of **I.**, 3478
Nu 8:14 from among the children of **I.** 3478
Nu 8:16 me from among the children of **I.**; 3478
Nu 8:16 firstborn of all the children of **I.**, 3478
Nu 8:17 firstborn of the children of **I.** are 3478
Nu 8:18 the firstborn of the children of **I.** 3478
Nu 8:19 sons from among the children of **I.**, 3478
Nu 8:19 do the service of the children of **I.** 3478
Nu 8:19 atonement for the children of **I.** 3478
Nu 8:19 no plague among the children of **I.**, 3478
Nu 8:19 the children of **I.** come nigh unto 3478
Nu 8:20 congregation of the children of **I.**, 3478
Nu 8:20 so did the children of **I.** unto them. 3478
Nu 9:2 children of **I.** also keep the passover 3478
Nu 9:4 Moses spake unto the children of **I.**, 3478
Nu 9:5 Moses, so did the children of **I.** 3478
Nu 9:7 season among the children of **I.**? 3478
Nu 9:10 Speak unto the children of **I.**, 3478
Nu 9:17 that the children of **I.** journeyed: 3478
Nu 9:17 children of **I.** pitched their tents. 3478
Nu 9:18 Lord the children of **I.** journeyed, 3478
Nu 9:19 of **I.** kept the charge of the Lord, 3478
Nu 9:22 children of **I.** abode in their tents, 3478
Nu 10:4 are heads of the thousands of **I.**, 3478
Nu 10:12 children of **I.** took their journeys 3478
Nu 10:28 journeyings of the children of **I.**, 3478
Nu 10:29 hath spoken good concerning **I.**, 3478
Nu 10:36 unto the many thousands of **I.** 3478
Nu 11:4 the children of **I.** also wept again, 3478
Nu 11:16 me seventy men of the elders of **I.**, 3478
Nu 11:30 the camp, he and the elders of **I.** 3478
Nu 13:2 which I give unto the children of **I.** 3478
Nu 13:3 were heads of the children of **I.** 3478
Nu 13:24 which the children of **I.** cut down 3478
Nu 13:26 congregation of the children of **I.**, 3478
Nu 13:32 had searched unto the children of **I.**, 3478
Nu 14:2 of **I.** murmured against Moses and 3478
Nu 14:5 congregation of the children of **I.** 3478
Nu 14:7 the company of the children of **I.**, 3478
Nu 14:10 before all the children of **I.** 3478
Nu 14:27 murmurings of the children of **I.**, 3478
Nu 14:39 sayings unto all the children of **I.** 3478
Nu 15:2, 18 Speak unto the children of **I.**, 3478
Nu 15:25, 26 congregation of the children of **I.**, 3478
Nu 15:29 is born among the children of **I.**, 3478
Nu 15:32 of **I.** were in the wilderness, 3478
Nu 15:38 Speak unto the children of **I.**, and 3478
Nu 16:2 with certain of the children of **I.**, 3478
Nu 16:9 the God of **I.** hath separated you 3478
Nu 16:9 you from the congregation of **I.**, to 3478
Nu 16:25 and the elders of **I.** followed him. 3478
Nu 16:34 all **I.** that were round about them 3478
Nu 16:38 be a sign unto the children of **I.** 3478
Nu 16:40 memorial unto the children of **I.**, 3478
Nu 16:41 children of **I.** murmured against 3478
Nu 17:2 Speak unto the children of **I.**, and 3478
Nu 17:5 murmurings of the children of **I.**, 3478
Nu 17:6 Moses spake unto the children of **I.**, 3478
Nu 17:9 Lord unto all the children of **I.** 3478
Nu 17:12 the children of **I.** spake unto Moses, 3478
Nu 18:5 any more upon the children of **I.** 3478
Nu 18:6 from among the children of **I.** 3478
Nu 18:8 hallowed things of the children of **I.**; 3478
Nu 18:11 wave offerings of the children of **I.** 3478
Nu 18:14 Every thing devoted in **I.** shall be 3478
Nu 18:19 which the children of **I.** offer unto 3478
Nu 18:20 inheritance among the children of **I.** 3478
Nu 18:21 the tenth in **I.** for an inheritance, 3478
Nu 18:22 children of **I.** henceforth come nigh 3478
Nu 18:23 of **I.** they have no inheritance. 3478
Nu 18:24 But the tithes of the children of **I.**, 3478
Nu 18:24 of **I.** they shall have no inheritance. 3478
Nu 18:26 take of the children of **I.** the tithes 3478
Nu 18:28 ye receive of the children of **I.**; 3478
Nu 18:32 the holy things of the children of **I.**, 3478
Nu 19:2 Speak unto the children of **I.**, that 3478
Nu 19:9 congregation of the children of **I.** 3478
Nu 19:10 it shall be unto the children of **I.**, 3478
Nu 19:13 that soul shall be cut off from **I.** 3478
Nu 20:1 Then came the children of **I.**, even 3478
Nu 20:12 me in the eyes of the children of **I.**, 3478
Nu 20:13 children of **I.** strove with the Lord, 3478
Nu 20:14 Thus saith thy brother **I.**, Thou 3478
Nu 20:19 the children of **I.** said unto him, 3478
Nu 20:21 Edom refused to give **I.** passage 3478
Nu 20:21 wherefore **I.** turned away from him. 3478
Nu 20:22 the children of **I.**, even the whole 3478
Nu 20:24 I have given unto the children of **I.**, 3478
Nu 20:29 thirty days, even all the house of **I.** 3478
Nu 21:1 **I.** came by the way of the spies; 3478
Nu 21:1 he fought against **I.**, and took some 3478
Nu 21:2 And **I.** vowed a vow unto the Lord, 3478
Nu 21:3 Lord hearkened to the voice of **I.**, 3478
Nu 21:6 people; and much people of **I.** died. 3478
Nu 21:10 the children of **I.** set forward, and 3478
Nu 21:17 **I.** sang this song, Spring up, O 3478
Nu 21:21 **I.** sent messengers unto Sihon 3478
Nu 21:23 suffer **I.** to pass through his border: 3478
Nu 21:23 out against **I.** into the wilderness: 3478
Nu 21:23 to Jahaz, and fought against **I.** 3478
Nu 21:24 **I.** smote him with the edge of the 3478
Nu 21:25 And **I.** took all these cities: 3478
Nu 21:25 and **I.** dwelt in all the cities of the 3478
Nu 21:31 **I.** dwelt in the land of the Amorites. 3478
Nu 22:1 the children of **I.** set forward, and 3478
Nu 22:2 that **I.** had done to the Amorites. 3478
Nu 22:3 because of the children of **I.** 3478
Nu 23:7 curse me Jacob, and come, defy **I.** 3478
Nu 23:10 number of the fourth part of **I.**? 3478
Nu 23:21 hath he seen perverseness in **I.** 3478
Nu 23:23 is there any divination against **I.** 3478
Nu 23:23 it shall be said of Jacob and of **I.**, 3478
Nu 24:1 that it pleased the Lord to bless **I.**, 3478
Nu 24:2 and he saw **I.** abiding in his tents 3478
Nu 24:5 O Jacob, and thy tabernacles, O **I.**! 3478
Nu 24:17 a Sceptre shall rise out of **I.**, and 3478
Nu 24:18 enemies; and **I.** shall do valiantly. 3478
Nu 25:1 And **I.** abode in Shittim, and the 3478
Nu 25:3 **I.** joined himself unto Baal-peor: 3478
Nu 25:3 of the Lord was kindled against **I.** 3478
Nu 25:4 Lord may be turned away from **I.** 3478
Nu 25:5 Moses said unto the judges of **I.**, 3478
Nu 25:6 behold, one of the children of **I.** 3478
Nu 25:6 congregation of the children of **I.**, 3478
Nu 25:8 after the man of **I.** into the tent, 3478

Nu	25:8	the man of **I.**, and the woman	3478
Nu	25:8	was stayed from the children of **I.**.	3478
Nu	25:11	wrath away from the children of **I.**,	3478
Nu	25:11	the children of **I.** in my jealousy.	3478
Nu	25:13	an atonement for the children of **I.**.	3478
Nu	26:2	congregation of the children of **I.**,	3478
Nu	26:2	all that are able to go to war in **I.**.	3478
Nu	26:4	Moses and the children of **I.**,	3478
Nu	26:5	Reuben, the eldest son of **I.**: the	3478
Nu	26:51	the numbered of the children of **I.**,	3478
Nu	26:62	numbered among the children of **I.**,	3478
Nu	26:62	them among the children of **I.**.	3478
Nu	26:63	the children of **I.** in the plains of	3478
Nu	26:64	the children of **I.** in the wilderness	3478
Nu	27:8	shalt speak unto the children of **I.**,	3478
Nu	27:11	children of **I.** a statute of judgment,	3478
Nu	27:12	I have given unto the children of **I.**	3478
Nu	27:20	the children of **I.** may be obedient.	3478
Nu	27:21	and all the children of **I.** with him,	3478
Nu	28:2	Command the children of **I.**, and	3478
Nu	29:40	of **I.** according to all that the Lord	3478
Nu	30:1	tribes concerning the children of **I.**,	3478
Nu	31:2	children of **I.** of the Midianites:	3478
Nu	31:4	throughout all the tribes of **I.**, shall	3478
Nu	31:5	delivered out of the thousands of **I.**,	3478
Nu	31:9	children of **I.** took all the women	3478
Nu	31:12	congregation of the children of **I.**,	3478
Nu	31:16	these caused the children of **I.**,	3478
Nu	31:54	the children of **I.** before the Lord.	3478
Nu	32:4	smote before the congregation of **I.**,	3478
Nu	32:7	ye the heart of the children of **I.**	3478
Nu	32:9	the heart of the children of **I.**,	3478
Nu	32:13	Lord's anger was kindled against **I.**,	3478
Nu	32:14	fierce anger of the Lord toward **I.**	3478
Nu	32:17	armed before the children of **I.**,	3478
Nu	32:18	of **I.** have inherited every man his	3478
Nu	32:22	before the Lord, and before **I.**;	3478
Nu	32:28	of the tribes of the children of **I.**	3478
Nu	33:1	the journeys of the children of **I.**,	3478
Nu	33:3	after the passover the children of **I.**	3478
Nu	33:5	of **I.** removed from Rameses,	3478
Nu	33:38	of **I.** were come out of the land of	3478
Nu	33:40	of the coming of the children of **I.**.	3478
Nu	33:51	Speak unto the children of **I.**, and	3478
Nu	34:2	Command the children of **I.**, and,	3478
Nu	34:13	commanded the children of **I.**,	3478
Nu	34:29	children of **I.** in the land of Canaan.	3478
Nu	35:2	Command the children of **I.**, that	3478
Nu	35:8	the possession of the children of **I.**	3478
Nu	35:10	Speak unto the children of **I.**, and	3478
Nu	35:15	both for the children of **I.**, and for	3478
Nu	35:34	dwell among the children of **I.**.	3478
Nu	36:1	chief fathers of the children of **I.**	3478
Nu	36:2	by lot to the children of **I.**	3478
Nu	36:3	other tribes of the children of **I.**,	3478
Nu	36:4	jubile of the children of **I.** shall be,	3478
Nu	36:5	Moses commanded the children of **I.**	3478
Nu	36:7	of **I.** remove from tribe to tribe:	3478
Nu	36:7	Every one of the children of **I.** shall	3478
Nu	36:8	in any tribe of the children of **I.**,	3478
Nu	36:8	of **I.** may enjoy every man the	3478
Nu	36:9	of **I.** shall keep himself to his own	3478
Nu	36:13	children of **I.** in the plains of Moab	3478
De	1:1	words which Moses spake unto all **I.**	3478
De	1:3	Moses spake unto the children of **I.**,	3478
De	1:38	for he shall cause **I.** to inherit it.	3478
De	2:12	as **I.** did unto the land of his	3478
De	3:18	your brethren the children of **I.**,	3478
De	4:1	Now therefore hearken, O **I.**, unto	3478
De	4:44	Moses set before the children of **I.**	3478
De	4:45	Moses spake unto the children of **I.**,	3478
De	4:46	Moses and the children of **I.** smote,	3478
De	5:1	Moses called all **I.**, and said unto	3478
De	5:1	Hear, O **I.**, the statutes and	3478
De	6:3	Hear therefore, O **I.**, and observe	3478
De	6:4	Hear, O **I.**: The Lord our God is	3478
De	9:1	Hear, O **I.**: Thou art to pass over	3478
De	10:6	the children of **I.** took their journey	3478
De	10:12	**I.**, what doth the Lord thy God	3478
De	11:6	possession, in the midst of all **I.**	3478
De	13:11	And all **I.** shall hear, and fear, and	3478
De	17:4	such abomination is wrought in **I.**	3478
De	17:12	shalt put away the evil from **I.**	3478
De	17:20	and his children, in the midst of **I.**	3478
De	18:1	no part nor inheritance with **I.**	3478
De	18:6	from any of thy gates out of all **I.**,	3478
De	19:13	guilt of innocent blood from **I.**,	3478
De	20:3	Hear, O **I.**, ye approach this day	3478
De	21:8	merciful, O Lord, unto thy people **I.**,	3478
De	21:21	you; and all **I.** shall hear, and fear.	3478
De	22:19	an evil name upon a virgin of **I.**	3478
De	22:21	she hath wrought folly in **I.**, to play	3478
De	22:22	shalt thou put away evil from **I.**.	3478
De	23:17	be no whore of the daughters of **I.**,	3478
De	23:17	nor a sodomite of the sons of **I.**	3478
De	24:7	his brethren of the children of **I.**,	3478
De	25:6	that his name be not put out of **I.**.	3478
De	25:7	up unto his brother a name in **I.**,	3478
De	25:10	his name shall be called in **I.**, The	3478
De	26:15	and bless thy people **I.**, and the	3478
De	27:1	elders of **I.** commanded the people,	3478
De	27:9	the Levites spake unto all **I.**,	3478
De	27:9	Take heed, and hearken, O **I.**; this	3478
De	27:14	and say unto all the men of **I.** with	3478
De	29:1	children of **I.** in the land of Moab,	3478
De	29:2	And Moses called unto all **I.**, and	3478
De	29:10	officers, with all the men of **I.**,	3478
De	29:21	unto evil out of all the tribes of **I.**,	3478
De	31:1	and spake these words unto all **I.**	3478
De	31:7	said unto him in the sight of all **I.**,	3478
De	31:9	Lord, and unto all the elders of **I.**.	3478
De	31:11	**I.** is come to appear before the Lord	3478
De	31:11	law before all **I.** in their hearing.	3478
De	31:19	and teach it the children of **I.**: put	3478
De	31:19	for me against the children of **I.**	3478
De	31:22	and taught it the children of **I.**.	3478
De	31:23	bring the children of **I.** into the land	3478
De	31:30	ears of all the congregation of **I.**	3478
De	32:8	to the number of children of **I.**.	3478
De	32:45	speaking all these words to all **I.**	3478
De	32:49	the children of **I.** for a possession:	3478
De	32:51	against me among the children of **I.**	3478
De	32:51	in the midst of the children of **I.**.	3478
De	32:52	which I give the children of **I.**.	3478
De	33:1	of God blessed the children of **I.**	3478
De	33:5	of the people and the tribes of **I.**	3478
De	33:10	thy judgments, and **I.** thy law.	3478
De	33:21	Lord, and his judgments with **I.**.	3478
De	33:28	**I.** then shall dwell in safety alone:	3478
De	33:29	Happy art thou, O **I.**: who is like	3478
De	34:8	of **I.** wept for Moses in the plains	3478
De	34:9	children of **I.** hearkened unto him,	3478
De	34:10	prophet since in **I.** like unto Moses,	3478
De	34:12	Moses shewed in the sight of all **I.**,	3478
Jos	1:2	them, even to the children of **I.**	3478
Jos	2:2	of **I.** to search out the country.	3478
Jos	3:1	Jordan, he and all the children of **I.**,	3478
Jos	3:7	magnify thee in the sight of all **I.**,	3478
Jos	3:9	Joshua said unto the children of **I.**,	3478
Jos	3:12	twelve men out of the tribes of **I.**,	3478
Jos	4:4	had prepared of the children of **I.**,	3478
Jos	4:5	of the tribes of the children of **I.**	3478
Jos	4:7	a memorial unto the children of **I.**	3478
Jos	4:8	of **I.** did so as Joshua commanded,	3478
Jos	4:8	of the tribes of the children of **I.**,	3478
Jos	4:12	armed before the children of **I.**,	3478
Jos	4:14	Joshua in the sight of all **I.**;	3478
Jos	4:21	he spake unto the children of **I.**,	3478
Jos	4:22	**I.** came over this Jordan on dry	3478
Jos	5:1	from before the children of **I.**,	3478
Jos	5:1	more, because of the children of **I.**	3478
Jos	5:2	circumcise again the children of **I.**	3478
Jos	5:3	and circumcised the children of **I.**	3478
Jos	5:6	children of **I.** walked forty years	3478
Jos	5:10	children of **I.** encamped in Gilgal,	3478
Jos	5:12	children of **I.** manna any more;	3478
Jos	6:1	up because of the children of **I.**	3478
Jos	6:18	and make the camp of **I.** a curse,	3478
Jos	6:23	left them without the camp of **I.**.	3478
Jos	6:25	and she dwelleth in **I.** even unto	3478
Jos	7:1	children of **I.** committed a trespass	3478
Jos	7:1	kindled against the children of **I.**.	3478
Jos	7:6	he and the elders of **I.**, and put	3478
Jos	7:8	I say, when **I.** turneth their backs	3478
Jos	7:11	**I.** hath sinned, and they have also	3478
Jos	7:12	the children of **I.** could not stand	3478
Jos	7:13	for thus saith the Lord God of **I.**,	3478
Jos	7:13	thing in the midst of thee, O **I.**	3478
Jos	7:15	because he hath wrought folly in **I.**.	3478
Jos	7:16	and brought **I.** by their tribes;	3478
Jos	7:19	thee, glory to the Lord God of **I.**,	3478
Jos	7:20	sinned against the Lord God of **I.**,	3478
Jos	7:23	and unto all the children of **I.**,	3478
Jos	7:24	And Joshua, and all **I.** with him,	3478
Jos	7:25	And all **I.** stoned him with stones,	3478
Jos	8:10	and went up, he and the elders of **I.**,	3478
Jos	8:14	city went out against **I.** to battle,	3478
Jos	8:15	all **I.** made as if they were beaten	3478
Jos	8:17	Beth-el, that went not out after **I.**	3478
Jos	8:17	the city open, and pursued after **I.**.	3478
Jos	8:21	**I.** saw that the ambush had taken	3478
Jos	8:22	so they were in the midst of **I.**,	3478
Jos	8:24	when **I.** had made an end of slaying	3478
Jos	8:27	and the spoil of that city **I.** took	3478
Jos	8:30	an altar unto the Lord God of **I.**	3478
Jos	8:31	Lord commanded the children of **I.**,	3478
Jos	8:32	the presence of the children of **I.**.	3478
Jos	8:33	all **I.**, and their elders, and officers,	3478
Jos	8:33	they should bless the people of **I.**,	3478
Jos	8:35	before all the congregation of **I.**,	3478
Jos	9:2	to fight with Joshua, and with **I.**,	3478
Jos	9:6	said unto him, and to the men of **I.**,	3478
Jos	9:7	the men of **I.** said unto the Hivites,	3478
Jos	9:17	And the children of **I.** journeyed,	3478
Jos	9:18	the children of **I.** smote them not,	3478
Jos	9:18	unto them by the Lord God of **I.**.	3478
Jos	9:19	unto them by the Lord God of **I.**	3478
Jos	9:26	out of the hand of the children of **I.**,	3478
Jos	10:1	of Gibeon had made peace with **I.**,	3478
Jos	10:4	Joshua and with the children of **I.**.	3478
Jos	10:10	Lord discomfited them before **I.**,	3478
Jos	10:11	came to pass, as they fled before **I.**,	3478
Jos	10:11	children of **I.** slew with the sword.	3478
Jos	10:12	Amorites before the children of **I.**,	3478
Jos	10:12	he said in the sight of **I.**, Sun, stand	3478
Jos	10:14	a man: for the Lord fought for **I.**.	3478
Jos	10:15	returned, and all **I.** with him,	3478
Jos	10:20	of **I.** had made an end of slaying	3478
Jos	10:21	against any of the children of **I.**.	3478
Jos	10:24	Joshua called for all the men of **I.**,	3478
Jos	10:29	Makkedah, and all **I.** with him,	3478
Jos	10:30	king thereof, into the hand of **I.**;	3478
Jos	10:31	from Libnah, and all **I.** with him,	3478
Jos	10:32	Lachish into the hand of **I.**,	3478
Jos	10:34	unto Eglon, and all **I.** with him;	3478
Jos	10:36	up from Eglon, and all **I.** with him,	3478
Jos	10:38	returned, and all **I.** with him, to	3478
Jos	10:40	as the Lord God of **I.** commanded.	3478
Jos	10:42	the Lord God of **I.** fought for **I.**	3478
Jos	10:43	returned, and all **I.** with him, unto	3478
Jos	11:5	waters of Merom, to fight against **I.**.	3478
Jos	11:6	deliver them up all slain before **I.**	3478
Jos	11:8	delivered them into the hand of **I.**,	3478
Jos	11:13	**I.** burned none of them, save Hazor	3478
Jos	11:14	the children of **I.** took for a prey	3478
Jos	11:16	mountain of **I.**, and the valley	3478
Jos	11:19	made peace with the children of **I.**,	3478
Jos	11:20	should come against **I.** in battle,	3478
Jos	11:21	and from all the mountains of **I.**	3478
Jos	11:22	in the land of the children of **I.**	3478
Jos	11:23	gave it for an inheritance unto **I.**	3478
Jos	12:1	which the children of **I.** smote, and	3478
Jos	12:6	Lord and the children of **I.** smite:	3478
Jos	12:7	of **I.** smote on the side Jordan on	3478
Jos	12:7	unto the tribes of **I.** for a possession	3478
Jos	13:6	out from before the children of **I.**	3478
Jos	13:13	of **I.** expelled not the Geshurites,	3478
Jos	13:14	of the Lord God of **I.** made by fire	3478
Jos	13:22	the children of **I.** slay with sword	3478
Jos	13:33	God of **I.** was their inheritance,	3478
Jos	14:1	which the children of **I.** inherited	3478
Jos	14:1	of the tribes of the children of **I.**,	3478
Jos	14:5	Moses, so the children of **I.** did,	3478
Jos	14:10	of **I.** wandered in the wilderness:	3478
Jos	14:14	wholly followed the Lord God of **I.**.	3478
Jos	17:13	children of **I.** were waxen strong,	3478
Jos	18:1	of **I.** assembled together at Shiloh,	3478
Jos	18:2	the children of **I.** seven tribes,	3478
Jos	18:3	Joshua said unto the children of **I.**,	3478
Jos	18:10	the land unto the children of **I.**	3478
Jos	19:49	of **I.** gave an inheritance to Joshua	3478
Jos	19:51	of the tribes of the children of **I.**,	3478
Jos	20:2	Speak to the children of **I.**, saying,	3478
Jos	20:9	appointed for all the children of **I.**,	3478
Jos	21:1	of the tribes of the children of **I.**;	3478
Jos	21:3	children of **I.** gave unto the Levites	3478
Jos	21:8	of **I.** gave by lot unto the Levites	3478
Jos	21:41	the possession of the children of **I.**	3478
Jos	21:43	the Lord gave unto **I.** all the land	3478
Jos	21:45	had spoken unto the house of **I.**;	3478
Jos	22:9	departed from the children of **I.**	3478

Jos 22:11 children of **I.** heard say, Behold, ... 3478
Jos 22:11 at the passage of the children of **I.**. 3478
Jos 22:12 when the children of **I.** heard of it, ... 3478
Jos 22:12 of **I.** gathered themselves together 3478
Jos 22:13 **I.** sent unto the children of Reuben, ... 3478
Jos 22:14 throughout all the tribes of **I.**; 3478
Jos 22:14 fathers among the thousands of **I.**. 3478
Jos 22:16 committed against the God of **I.**, ... 3478
Jos 22:18 with the whole congregation of **I.**. 3478
Jos 22:20 fell on all the congregation of **I.**? 3478
Jos 22:21 the heads of the thousands of **I.**, ... 3478
Jos 22:22 he knoweth, and **I.** he shall know: 3478
Jos 22:24 ye to do with the Lord God of **I.**? 3478
Jos 22:30 and heads of the thousands of **I.** 3478
Jos 22:31 ye have delivered the children of **I.** 3478
Jos 22:32 land of Canaan, to the children of **I.**, ... 3478
Jos 22:33 thing pleased the children of **I.**; 3478
Jos 22:33 and the children of **I.** blessed God, ... 3478
Jos 23:1 that the Lord had given rest unto **I.** ... 3478
Jos 23:2 And Joshua called for all **I.**, and 3478
Jos 24:1 all the tribes of **I.** to Shechem, ... 3478
Jos 24:1 and called for the elders of **I.**, and...... 3478
Jos 24:2 Thus saith the Lord God of **I.**, ... 3478
Jos 24:9 Moab, arose and warred against **I.**, ... 3478
Jos 24:23 your heart unto the Lord God of **I.**..... 3478
Jos 24:31 **I.** served the Lord all the days of....... 3478
Jos 24:31 the Lord, that he had done for **I.**. 3478
Jos 24:32 of **I.** brought up out of Egypt, ... 3478
Jg 1:1 the children of **I.** asked the Lord,....... 3478
Jg 1:28 came to pass, when **I.** was strong, ... 3478
Jg 2:4 words unto all the children of **I.**, ... 3478
Jg 2:6 children of **I.** went every man unto..... 3478
Jg 2:7 of the Lord, that he did for **I.**............ 3478
Jg 2:10 works which he had done for **I.**. 3478
Jg 2:11 **I.** did evil in the sight of the Lord, ... 3478
Jg 2:14 of the Lord was hot against **I.**, ... 3478
Jg 2:20 of the Lord was hot against **I.**; 3478
Jg 2:22 That through them I may prove **I.**, ... 3478
Jg 3:1 the Lord left, to prove **I.** by them, ... 3478
Jg 3:1 as many of **I.** as had not known ....
Jg 3:2 of the children of **I.** might know, to 3478
Jg 3:4 And they were to prove **I.** by them, ... 3478
Jg 3:5 of **I.** dwelt among the Canaanites, ... 3478
Jg 3:7 **I.** did evil in the sight of the Lord, ... 3478
Jg 3:8 of the Lord was hot against **I.**, ... 3478
Jg 3:8 the children of **I.** served...eight 3478
Jg 3:9 children of **I.** cried unto the Lord, ... 3478
Jg 3:9 up a deliverer to the children of **I.**, ... 3478
Jg 3:10 came upon him, and he judged **I.**, ... 3478
Jg 3:12 **I.** did evil again in the sight of the...... 3478
Jg 3:12 Eglon the king of Moab against **I.**, ... 3478
Jg 3:13 Amalek, and went and smote **I.**, ... 3478
Jg 3:14 children of **I.** served Eglon the king.... 3478
Jg 3:15 children of **I.** cried unto the Lord, ... 3478
Jg 3:15 of **I.** sent a present unto Eglon the..... 3478
Jg 3:27 children of **I.** went down with him 3478
Jg 3:30 that day under the hand of **I.**............ 3478
Jg 3:31 ox goad: and he also delivered **I.**. 3478
Jg 4:1 **I.** again did evil in the sight of the...... 3478
Jg 4:3 children of **I.** cried unto the Lord: 3478
Jg 4:3 oppressed the children of **I.**. 3478
Jg 4:4 she judged **I.** at that time. 3478
Jg 4:5 of **I.** came up to her for judgment. 3478
Jg 4:6 not the Lord God of **I.** commanded, ... 3478
Jg 4:23 of Canaan before the children of **I.**. 3478
Jg 4:24 hand of the children of **I.** prospered, ... 3478
Jg 5:2 ye the Lord for the avenging of **I.**, ... 3478
Jg 5:3 sing praise to the Lord God of **I.**. 3478
Jg 5:5 from before the Lord God of **I.**.......... 3478
Jg 5:7 villages ceased, they ceased in **I.**, ... 3478
Jg 5:7 arose, that I arose a mother in **I.**....... 3478
Jg 5:8 seen among forty thousand in **I.**? 3478
Jg 5:9 heart is toward the governors of **I.**, ... 3478
Jg 5:11 the inhabitants of his villages in **I.** 3478
Jg 6:1 **I.** did evil in the sight of the Lord: 3478
Jg 6:2 of Midian prevailed against **I.**............ 3478
Jg 6:2 children of **I.** made them the dens 3478
Jg 6:3 **I.** had sown, that the Midianites......... 3478
Jg 6:4 left no sustenance for **I.**, neither........ 3478
Jg 6:6 And **I.** was greatly impoverished........ 3478
Jg 6:6 children of **I.** cried unto the Lord. 3478
Jg 6:7 children of **I.** cried unto the Lord....... 3478
Jg 6:8 a prophet unto the children of **I.**, ... 3478
Jg 6:8 Thus saith the Lord God of **I.**, I 3478
Jg 6:14 shalt save **I.** from the hand of the 3478
Jg 6:15 Lord, wherewith shall I save **I.**? 3478
Jg 6:36 said unto God. If thou wilt save **I.**....... 3478
Jg 6:37 shall I know that thou wilt save **I.**...... 3478
Jg 7:2 **I.** vaunt themselves against me,......... 3478
Jg 7:8 rest of **I.** every man unto his tent, ... 3478
Jg 7:14 the son of Joash, a man of **I.**............ 3478
Jg 7:15 and returned into the host of **I.**, ... 3478
Jg 7:23 **I.** gathered themselves together......... 3478
Jg 8:22 the men of **I.** said unto Gideon, ... 3478
Jg 8:27 **I.** went thither a whoring after it:......... 3478
Jg 8:28 subdued before the children of **I.**,........ 3478
Jg 8:33 the children of **I.** turned again, ... 3478
Jg 8:34 of **I.** remembered not the Lord.......... 3478
Jg 8:35 which he had shewed unto **I.**............. 3478
Jg 9:22 had reigned three years over **I.**, ... 3478
Jg 9:55 of **I.** saw that Abimelech was dead, ... 3478
Jg 10:1 there arose to defend **I.** Tola the....... 3478
Jg 10:2 And he judged **I.** twenty and three 3478
Jg 10:3 Jair, a Gileadite, and judged **I.**.......... 3478
Jg 10:6 **I.** did evil again in the sight of the...... 3478
Jg 10:7 of the Lord was hot against **I.**, ... 3478
Jg 10:8 and oppressed the children of **I.**.......... 3478
Jg 10:8 of **I.** that were on the other side........ 3478
Jg 10:9 so that **I.** was sore distressed. 3478
Jg 10:10 children of **I.** cried unto the Lord, ... 3478
Jg 10:11 Lord said unto the children of **I.**, ... 3478
Jg 10:15 children of **I.** said unto the Lord, ... 3478
Jg 10:16 was grieved for the misery of **I.**. 3478
Jg 10:17 **I.** assembled themselves together,...... 3478
Jg 11:4 of Ammon made war against **I.**. 3478
Jg 11:5 of Ammon made war against **I.**, ... 3478
Jg 11:13 Because **I.** took away my land, ... 3478
Jg 11:15 **I.** took not away the land of Moab,...... 3478
Jg 11:16 But when **I.** came up from Egypt, ... 3478
Jg 11:17 **I.** sent messengers unto the king 3478
Jg 11:17 consent: and **I.** abode in Radesh. 3478
Jg 11:19 **I.** sent messengers unto Sihon.......... 3478
Jg 11:19 **I.** said unto him, Let us pass, we........ 3478
Jg 11:20 But Sihon trusted not **I.** to pass......... 3478
Jg 11:20 in Jahaz, and fought against **I.**........... 3478
Jg 11:21 Lord God of **I.** delivered Sihon and..... 3478
Jg 11:21 all his people into the hand of **I.**, ... 3478
Jg 11:21 so **I.** possessed all the land of the 3478
Jg 11:23 God of **I.** hath dispossessed the......... 3478
Jg 11:23 from before his people **I.**, and 3478
Jg 11:25 did he ever strive against **I.**, or did 3478
Jg 11:26 While **I.** dwelt in Heshbon and her 3478
Jg 11:27 between the children of **I.** and the...... 3478
Jg 11:33 subdued before the children of **I.**....... 3478
Jg 11:39 no man. And it was a custom in **I.**, ... 3478
Jg 11:40 the daughters of **I.** went yearly to...... 3478
Jg 12:7 And Jephthah judged **I.** six years........ 3478
Jg 12:8 him Ibzan of Beth-lehem judged **I.**...... 3478
Jg 12:9 And he judged **I.** seven years............ 3478
Jg 12:11 him Elon, a Zebulonite, judged **I.**; 3478
Jg 12:11 and he judged **I.** ten years................ 3478
Jg 12:13 of Hillel, a Pirathonite, judged **I.**. 3478
Jg 12:14 colts: and he judged **I.** eight years...... 3478
Jg 13:1 **I.** did evil again in the sight of the...... 3478
Jg 13:5 **I.** out of the hand of the Philistines..... 3478
Jg 14:4 Philistines had dominion over **I.**. 3478
Jg 15:20 he judged **I.** in the days of the........... 3478
Jg 16:31 And he judged **I.** twenty years. 3478
Jg 17:6 those days there was no king in **I.**, ... 3478
Jg 18:1 those days there was no king in **I.** 3478
Jg 18:1 unto them among the tribes of **I.**. 3478
Jg 18:19 unto a tribe and a family in **I.**?......... 3478
Jg 18:29 their father, who was born unto **I.**....... 3478
Jg 19:1 days, when there was no king in **I.**,.... 3478
Jg 19:12 that is not of the children of **I.**; 3478
Jg 19:29 and sent her into all the coasts of **I.**. .. 3478
Jg 19:30 **I.** came up out of the land of Egypt 3478
Jg 20:1 Then all the children of **I.** went out, ... 3478
Jg 20:2 even of all the tribes of **I.**, presented.. 3478
Jg 20:3 heard that the children of **I.** were....... 3478
Jg 20:3 Then said the children of **I.**, Tell........ 3478
Jg 20:6 country of the inheritance of **I.** 3478
Jg 20:6 committed lewdness and folly in **I.**...... 3478
Jg 20:7 Behold, ye are all children of **I.**; 3478
Jg 20:10 throughout all the tribes of **I.**, ... 3478
Jg 20:10 folly that they have wrought in **I.**. 3478
Jg 20:11 all the men of **I.** were gathered 3478
Jg 20:12 tribes of **I.** sent men through all 3478
Jg 20:13 death, and put away evil from **I.**. 3478
Jg 20:13 of their brethren the children of **I.**...... 3478
Jg 20:14 to battle against the children of **I.**....... 3478
Jg 20:17 men of **I.**, beside Benjamin, were....... 3478
Jg 20:18 And the children of **I.** arose, and........ 3478
Jg 20:19 children of **I.** rose up in the morning, .. 3478
Jg 20:20 the men of **I.** went out to battle 3478
Jg 20:20 **I.** put themselves in array to fight 3478
Jg 20:22 men of **I.** encouraged themselves, ... 3478
Jg 20:23 children of **I.** went up and wept 3478
Jg 20:24 children of **I.** came near against 3478
Jg 20:25 **I.** again eighteen thousand men;......... 3478
Jg 20:26 Then all the children of **I.**, and all 3478
Jg 20:27 children of **I.** enquired of the Lord,..... 3478
Jg 20:29 **I.** set liers in wait round about 3478
Jg 20:30 **I.** went up against the children of....... 3478
Jg 20:31 in the field, about thirty men of **I.**. 3478
Jg 20:32 the children of **I.** said, Let us flee, ... 3478
Jg 20:33 men of **I.** rose up out of their place, ... 3478
Jg 20:33 liers in wait of **I.** came forth out of..... 3478
Jg 20:34 thousand chosen men out of all **I.**,...... 3478
Jg 20:35 Lord smote Benjamin before **I.**.......... 3478
Jg 20:35 of **I.** destroyed of the Benjamites 3478
Jg 20:36 of **I.** gave place to the Benjamites, ... 3478
Jg 20:38 sign between the men of **I.** and the 3478
Jg 20:39 the men of **I.** retired in the battle, ... 3478
Jg 20:39 the men of **I.** about thirty persons:..... 3478
Jg 20:41 when the men of **I.** turned again, ... 3478
Jg 20:42 their backs before the men of **I.** 3478
Jg 20:48 **I.** turned again upon the children........ 3478
Jg 21:1 men of **I.** had sworn in Mizpeh, ... 3478
Jg 21:3 And said, O Lord God of **I.**, why is 3478
Jg 21:3 why is this come to pass in **I.**, that 3478
Jg 21:3 be to day one tribe lacking in **I.**? 3478
Jg 21:5 And the children of **I.** said, Who is 3478
Jg 21:5 all the tribes of **I.** that came not up 3478
Jg 21:6 of **I.** repented them for Benjamin 3478
Jg 21:6 one tribe cut off from **I.** this day........ 3478
Jg 21:8 of **I.** that came not up to Mizpeh to.... 3478
Jg 21:15 made a breach in the tribes of **I.**........ 3478
Jg 21:17 a tribe be not destroyed out of **I.**....... 3478
Jg 21:18 for the children of **I.** had sworn, ... 3478
Jg 21:24 the children of **I.** departed thence....... 3478
Jg 21:25 those days there was no king in **I.** 3478
Ru 2:12 be given thee of the Lord God of **I.**,.... 3478
Ru 4:7 the manner in former time in **I.** 3478
Ru 4:7 and this was a testimony in **I.**. 3478
Ru 4:11 which two did build the house of **I.**..... 3478
Ru 4:14 that his name may be famous in **I.**....... 3478
1Sa 1:17 God of **I.** grant thee thy petition 3478
1Sa 2:22 all that his sons did unto all **I.**; 3478
1Sa 2:28 choose him out of all the tribes of **I.**.... 3478
1Sa 2:28 made by fire of the children of **I.**? 3478
1Sa 2:29 all the offerings of **I.** my people?......... 3478
1Sa 2:30 Wherefore the Lord God of **I.** saith, ... 3478
1Sa 2:32 the wealth which God shall give **I.**...... 3478
1Sa 3:11 Behold, I will do a thing in **I.**, at........ 3478
1Sa 3:20 all **I.** from Dan even to Beer-sheba..... 3478
1Sa 4:1 the word of Samuel came to all **I.**. 3478
1Sa 4:1 **I.** went out against the Philistines....... 3478
1Sa 4:2 put themselves in array against **I.**....... 3478
1Sa 4:2 **I.** was smitten before the 3478
1Sa 4:3 **I.** said, Wherefore hath the Lord........ 3478
1Sa 4:5 all **I.** shouted with a great shout, ... 3478
1Sa 4:10 fought, and **I.** was smitten, and they... 3478
1Sa 4:10 fell of **I.** thirty thousand footmen........ 3478
1Sa 4:17 **I.** is fled before the Philistines, ... 3478
1Sa 4:18 And he had judged **I.** forty years........ 3478
1Sa 4:21, 22 The glory is departed from **I.**:........ 3478
1Sa 5:7 ark of the God of **I.** shall not abide..... 3478
1Sa 5:8 do with the ark of the God of **I.**? 3478
1Sa 5:8 the ark of the God of **I.** be carried 3478
1Sa 5:8 they carried the ark of the God of **I.**.... 3478
1Sa 5:10 about the ark of the God of **I.** to us, .. 3478
1Sa 5:11 Send away the ark of the God of **I.**, ... 3478
1Sa 6:3 send away the ark of the God of **I.**,.... 3478
1Sa 6:5 shall give glory unto the God of **I.**....... 3478
1Sa 7:2 house of **I.** lamented after the Lord. ... 3478
1Sa 7:3 spake unto all the house of **I.**, ... 3478
1Sa 7:4 of **I.** did put away Baalim and........... 3478
1Sa 7:5 Gather all **I.** to Mizpeh, and I will 3478
1Sa 7:6 judged the children of **I.** in Mizpeh. 3478
1Sa 7:7 of **I.** were gathered together to 3478
1Sa 7:7 the Philistines went up against **I.**........ 3478
1Sa 7:7 when the children of **I.** heard it, ... 3478
1Sa 7:8 the children of **I.** said to Samuel, ... 3478
1Sa 7:9 Samuel cried unto the Lord for **I.**;...... 3478
1Sa 7:10 drew near to battle against **I.** 3478
1Sa 7:10 and they were smitten before **I.**......... 3478
1Sa 7:11 the men of **I.** went out of Mizpeh, ... 3478

1Sa 7:13 came no more into the coast of I. 3478
1Sa 7:14 taken from I. were restored to I., 3478
1Sa 7:14 I. deliver out of the hands of the 3478
1Sa 7:14 peace between I. and the Amorites. 3478
1Sa 7:15 judged I. all the days of his life. 3478
1Sa 7:16 and judged I. in all those places. 3478
1Sa 7:17 and there he judged I.; and there 3478
1Sa 8:1 he made his sons judges over I. 3478
1Sa 8:4 elders of I. gathered themselves 3478
1Sa 8:22 Samuel said unto the men of I., 3478
1Sa 9:2 of I. a goodlier person than he: 3478
1Sa 9:9 Beforetime in I., when a man went 3478
1Sa 9:16 to be captain over my people I., 3478
1Sa 9:20 on whom is all the desire of I.? Is 3478
1Sa 9:21 the smallest of the tribes of I.? 3478
1Sa 10:18 And said unto the children of I., 3478
1Sa 10:18 Thus saith the Lord God of I., 3478
1Sa 10:18 I brought up I. out of Egypt, and 3478
1Sa 10:20 all the tribes of I. to come near, 3478
1Sa 11:2 lay it for a reproach upon all I. 3478
1Sa 11:3 messengers unto all the coasts of I. 3478
1Sa 11:7 them throughout all the coasts of I. 3478
1Sa 11:8 of I. were three hundred thousand, 3478
1Sa 11:13 Lord hath wrought salvation in I. 3478
1Sa 11:15 all the men of I. rejoiced greatly. 3478
1Sa 12:1 And Samuel said unto all I., 3478
1Sa 13:1 he had reigned two years over I., 3478
1Sa 13:2 chose...three thousand men of I.; 3478
1Sa 13:4 I. heard say that Saul had smitten 3478
1Sa 13:4 that I. also was had in abomination 3478
1Sa 13:5 themselves together to fight with I., 3478
1Sa 13:6 of I. saw that they were in a strait, 3478
1Sa 13:13 thy kingdom upon I. for ever. 3478
1Sa 13:19 found throughout all the land of I. 3478
1Sa 14:12 delivered them into the hand of I. 3478
1Sa 14:18 at that time with the children of I. 3478
1Sa 14:22 men of I. which had hid themselves 3478
1Sa 14:23 So the Lord saved I. that day: and 3478
1Sa 14:24 men of I. were distressed that day: 3478
1Sa 14:37 deliver them into the hand of I.? 3478
1Sa 14:39 as the Lord liveth, which saveth I., 3478
1Sa 14:40 Then said he unto all I., Be ye on 3478
1Sa 14:41 Saul said unto the Lord God of I., 3478
1Sa 14:45 wrought this great salvation in I.? 3478
1Sa 14:47 So Saul took the kingdom over I., 3478
1Sa 14:48 and delivered I. out of the hands of 3478
1Sa 15:1 to be king over his people, over I. 3478
1Sa 15:2 that which Amalek did to I., how 3478
1Sa 15:6 kindness to all the children of I., 3478
1Sa 15:17 not made the head of the tribes of I., 3478
1Sa 15:17 the Lord anointed thee king over I.? 3478
1Sa 15:26 thee from being king over I. 3478
1Sa 15:28 rent the kingdom of I. from thee 3478
1Sa 15:29 Strength of I. will not lie nor repent: 3478
1Sa 15:30 elders of my people, and before I., 3478
1Sa 15:35 that he had made Saul king over I. 3478
1Sa 16:1 rejected him from reigning over I.? 3478
1Sa 17:2 men of I. were gathered together, 3478
1Sa 17:3 I. stood on a mountain on the other 3478
1Sa 17:8 and cried unto the armies of I., 3478
1Sa 17:10 I defy the armies of I. this day; 3478
1Sa 17:11 Saul and all I. heard those words 3478
1Sa 17:19 and they, and all the men of I., 3478
1Sa 17:21 I. and the Philistines had put the 3478
1Sa 17:24 all the men of I., when they saw 3478
1Sa 17:25 men of I. said, Have ye seen this 3478
1Sa 17:25 surely to defy I. is he come up: 3478
1Sa 17:25 make his father's house free in I. 3478
1Sa 17:26 taketh away the reproach from I.? 3478
1Sa 17:45 hosts, the God of the armies of I., 3478
1Sa 17:46 may know that there is a God in I. 3478
1Sa 17:52 the men of I. and of Judah arose, 3478
1Sa 17:53 of I. returned from chasing after 3478
1Sa 18:6 women came out of all cities of I., 3478
1Sa 18:16 But all I. and Judah loved David, 3478
1Sa 18:18 my life, or my father's family in I., 3478
1Sa 19:5 wrought a great salvation for all I. 3478
1Sa 20:12 said unto David, O Lord God of I., 3478
1Sa 23:10 Then said David, O Lord God of I., 3478
1Sa 23:11 O Lord God of I., I beseech thee, 3478
1Sa 23:17 and thou shalt be king over I., and 3478
1Sa 24:2 thousand chosen men out of all I., 3478
1Sa 24:14 whom is the king of I. come out? 3478
1Sa 24:20 kingdom of I. shall be established 3478
1Sa 25:30 have appointed thee ruler over I.; 3478
1Sa 25:32 Blessed be the Lord God of I., 3478
1Sa 25:34 deed, as the Lord God of I. liveth, 3478
1Sa 26:2 three thousand chosen men of I. 3478
1Sa 26:15 man? and who is like to thee in I.? 3478
1Sa 26:20 king of I. is come out to seek a flea, 3478
1Sa 27:1 me any more in any coast of I. 3478
1Sa 27:12 his people I. utterly to abhor him; 3478
1Sa 28:1 for warfare, to fight with I. 3478
1Sa 28:3 dead, and all I. had lamented him, 3478
1Sa 28:4 Saul gathered all I. together, and 3478
1Sa 28:19 the Lord will also deliver I. with 3478
1Sa 28:19 Lord also shall deliver the host of I. 3478
1Sa 29:3 the servant of Saul the king of I., 3478
1Sa 30:25 a statute and an ordinance for I. 3478
1Sa 31:1 the Philistines fought against I. 3478
1Sa 31:1 I. fled from before the Philistines, 3478
1Sa 31:7 of I. that were on the other side 3478
1Sa 31:7 Jordan, saw that the men of I. fled, 3478
2Sa 1:3 Out of the camp of I. am I escaped. 3478
2Sa 1:12 the Lord, and for the house of I.; 3478
2Sa 1:19 beauty of I. is slain upon thy high 3478
2Sa 1:24 Ye daughters of I., weep over Saul, 3478
2Sa 2:9 and over Benjamin, and over all I. 3478
2Sa 2:10 old when he began to reign over I. 3478
2Sa 2:17 Abner was beaten, and the men of I., 3478
2Sa 2:28 still, and pursued after I. no more, 3478
2Sa 3:10 set up the throne of David over I. 3478
2Sa 3:12 to bring about all I. unto thee. 3478
2Sa 3:17 communication with the elders of I., 3478
2Sa 3:18 I will save my people I. out of the 3478
2Sa 3:19 Hebron all that seemed good to I., 3478
2Sa 3:21 gather all I. unto my lord the king, 3478
2Sa 3:37 all the people and all I. understood 3478
2Sa 3:38 a great man fallen this day in I.? 3478
2Sa 5:1 came all the tribes of I. to David 3478
2Sa 5:2 leddest out and broughtest in I. 3478
2Sa 5:2 thee, Thou shalt feed my people I., 3478
2Sa 5:2 and thou shalt be a captain over I. 3478
2Sa 5:3 elders of I. came to the king to 3478
2Sa 5:3 they anointed David king over I. 3478
2Sa 5:5 thirty and three years over all I. 3478
2Sa 5:12 had established him king over I., 3478
2Sa 5:17 had anointed David king over I., 3478
2Sa 6:1 together all the chosen men of I., 3478
2Sa 6:5 house of I. played before the Lord 3478
2Sa 6:15 the house of I. brought up the ark 3478
2Sa 6:19 among the whole multitude of I., 3478
2Sa 6:20 glorious was the king of I. to day, 3478
2Sa 6:21 over the people of the Lord, over I. 3478
2Sa 7:6 up the children of I. out of Egypt, 3478
2Sa 7:7 walked with all the children of I. 3478
2Sa 7:7 a word with any of the tribes of I., 3478
2Sa 7:7 I commanded to feed my people I., 3478
2Sa 7:8 to be ruler over my people, over I. 3478
2Sa 7:10 appoint a place for my people I., 3478
2Sa 7:11 judges to be over my people I., 3478
2Sa 7:23 is like thy people, even like I., 3478
2Sa 7:24 confirmed to thyself thy people I. 3478
2Sa 7:26 Lord of hosts is the God over I. 3478
2Sa 7:27 For thou, O Lord of hosts, God of I., 3478
2Sa 8:15 And David reigned over all I.; and 3478
2Sa 10:9 he chose of all the choice men of I., 3478
2Sa 10:15 that they were smitten before I., 3478
2Sa 10:17 he gathered all I. together, and 3478
2Sa 10:18 And the Syrians fled before I.; and 3478
2Sa 10:19 that they were smitten before I., 3478
2Sa 10:19 they made peace with I., and served 3478
2Sa 11:1 his servants with him, and all I.; 3478
2Sa 11:11 The ark, and I., and Judah, abide 3478
2Sa 12:7 Thus saith the Lord God of I., 3478
2Sa 12:7 I anointed thee king over I., and 3478
2Sa 12:8 thee the house of I. and of Judah; 3478
2Sa 12:12 I will do this thing before all I., 3478
2Sa 13:12 such thing ought to be done in I. 3478
2Sa 13:13 shalt be as one of the fools in I. 3478
2Sa 14:25 in all I. there was none to be so 3478
2Sa 15:2 servant is of one of the tribes of I. 3478
2Sa 15:6 this manner did Absalom to all I. 3478
2Sa 15:6 stole the hearts of the men of I. 3478
2Sa 15:10 spies throughout all the tribes of I., 3478
2Sa 15:13 hearts of the men of I. are after 3478
2Sa 16:3 house of I. restore me the kingdom 3478
2Sa 16:15 and all the people the men of I., 3478
2Sa 16:18 this people, and all the men of I., 3478
2Sa 16:21 I. shall hear that thou art abhorred 3478
2Sa 16:22 concubines in the sight of all I. 3478
2Sa 17:4 well, and all the elders of I. 3478
2Sa 17:10 all I. knoweth that thy father is a 3478
2Sa 17:11 that all I. be generally gathered 3478
2Sa 17:13 shall all I. bring ropes to that city, 3478
2Sa 17:14 Absalom and all the men of I. said, 3478
2Sa 17:15 Absalom and the elders of I.; 3478
2Sa 17:24 he and all the men of I. with him. 3478
2Sa 17:26 I. and Absalom pitched in the land 3478
2Sa 18:6 went out into the field against I. 3478
2Sa 18:7 the people of I. were slain before 3478
2Sa 18:16 returned from pursuing after I. 3478
2Sa 18:17 all I. fled every one to his tent. 3478
2Sa 19:8 I. had fled every man to his tent. 3478
2Sa 19:9 strife throughout all the tribes of I., 3478
2Sa 19:11 speech of all I. is come to the king, 3478
2Sa 19:22 man be put to death this day in I.? 3478
2Sa 19:22 that I am this day king over I.? 3478
2Sa 19:40 king, and also half the people of I. 3478
2Sa 19:41 all the men of I. came to the king, 3478
2Sa 19:42 of Judah answered the men of I., 3478
2Sa 19:43 the men of I. answered the men of 3478
2Sa 19:43 than the words of the men of I. 3478
2Sa 20:1 Jesse: every man to his tents, O I. 3478
2Sa 20:2 man of I. went up from after David, 3478
2Sa 20:14 he went through all the tribes of I. 3478
2Sa 20:19 are peaceable and faithful in I. 3478
2Sa 20:19 destroy a city and a mother in I. 3478
2Sa 20:23 Joab was over all the host of I. 3478
2Sa 21:2 were not of the children of I., but 3478
2Sa 21:2 and the children of I. had sworn 3478
2Sa 21:2 zeal to the children of I. and Judah. 3478
2Sa 21:4 for us shalt thou kill any man in I. 3478
2Sa 21:5 remaining in any of the coasts of I., 3478
2Sa 21:15 had yet war again with I.; 3478
2Sa 21:17 that thou quench not the light of I. 3478
2Sa 21:21 when he defied I., Jonathan the 3478
2Sa 23:1 Jacob, and the sweet psalmist of I., 3478
2Sa 23:3 God of I. said, the Rock of I. spake 3478
2Sa 23:9 and the men of I. were gone away: 3478
2Sa 24:1 of the Lord was kindled against I., 3478
2Sa 24:1 to say, Go, number I. and Judah. 3478
2Sa 24:2 Go now through all the tribes of I., 3478
2Sa 24:4 king, to number the people of I. 3478
2Sa 24:9 were in I. eight hundred thousand 3478
2Sa 24:15 the Lord sent a pestilence upon I. 3478
2Sa 24:25 the plague was stayed from I. 3478
1Ki 1:3 throughout all the coast of I. 3478
1Ki 1:20 the eyes of all I. are upon the, 3478
1Ki 1:30 unto thee by the Lord God of I., 3478
1Ki 1:34 anoint him there king over I. 3478
1Ki 1:35 appointed him to be ruler over I. 3478
1Ki 1:48 Blessed be the Lord God of I., 3478
1Ki 2:4 (said he) a man on the throne of I. 3478
1Ki 2:5 the two captains of the hosts of I., 3478
1Ki 2:11 David reigned over I. were forty 3478
1Ki 2:15 that all I. set their faces on me, 3478
1Ki 2:32 son of Ner, captain of the host of I. 3478
1Ki 3:28 I. heard of the judgment which the 3478
1Ki 4:1 king Solomon was king over all I. 3478
1Ki 4:7 had twelve officers over all I. 3478
1Ki 4:20 Judah and I. were many, as the 3478
1Ki 4:25 Judah and I. dwelt safely, every 3478
1Ki 5:13 Solomon raised a levy out of all I.; 3478
1Ki 6:1 of I. were come out of the land of 3478
1Ki 6:1 year of Solomon's reign over I., 3478
1Ki 6:13 will dwell among the children of I., 3478
1Ki 6:13 and will not forsake my people I. 3478
1Ki 8:1 Solomon assembled the elders of I., 3478
1Ki 8:1 the fathers of the children of I., 3478
1Ki 8:2 men of I. assembled themselves 3478
1Ki 8:3 all the elders of I. came, and all the 3478
1Ki 8:5 and all the congregation of I., that 3478
1Ki 8:9 a covenant with the children of I., 3478
1Ki 8:14 blessed all the congregation of I. 3478
1Ki 8:14 all the congregation of I. stood; 3478
1Ki 8:15 Blessed be the Lord God of I., 3478
1Ki 8:16 forth my people I. out of Egypt 3478
1Ki 8:16 no city out of all the tribes of I. 3478
1Ki 8:16 chose David to be over my people I. 3478
1Ki 8:17 for the name of the Lord God of I. 3478
1Ki 8:20 father, and sit on the throne of I. 3478
1Ki 8:20 for the name of the Lord God of I. 3478
1Ki 8:22 of all the congregation of I. 3478
1Ki 8:23 Lord God of I., there is no God like 3478
1Ki 8:25 Lord God of I., Keep with thy 3478
1Ki 8:25 my sight to sit on the throne of I.; 3478
1Ki 8:26 O God of I., let thy word, I pray 3478
1Ki 8:30 of thy people I., when they shall 3478
1Ki 8:33 people I. be smitten down before 3478
1Ki 8:34 forgive the sin of thy people I., 3478

1Ki 8:36 thy servants, and of thy people **I.**, ... 3478
1Ki 8:38 any man, or by all thy people **I.**, ... 3478
1Ki 8:41 stranger, that is not of thy people **I.**, ... 3478
1Ki 8:43 to fear thee, as do thy people **I.**; ... 3478
1Ki 8:52 the supplication of thy people **I.**, ... 3478
1Ki 8:55 congregation of **I.** with a loud voice, ... 3478
1Ki 8:56 hath given rest unto his people **I.**, ... 3478
1Ki 8:59 cause of his people **I.** at all times, ... 3478
1Ki 8:62 And the king, and all **I.** with him, ... 3478
1Ki 8:63 **I.** dedicated the house of the Lord ... 3478
1Ki 8:65 held a feast, and all **I.** with him, ... 3478
1Ki 8:66 his servant, and for **I.** his people ... 3478
1Ki 9:5 the throne of thy kingdom upon **I.** ... 3478
1Ki 9:5 thee a man upon the throne of **I.** ... 3478
1Ki 9:7 I cut off **I.** out of the land which I ... 3478
1Ki 9:7 **I.** shall be a proverb and a byword ... 3478
1Ki 9:20 which were not of the children of **I.**, ... 3478
1Ki 9:21 of **I.** also were not able utterly to ... 3478
1Ki 9:22 **I.** did Solomon make no bondmen: ... 3478
1Ki 10:9 thee, to set thee on the throne of **I.** ... 3478
1Ki 10:9 the Lord loved **I.** forever, therefore ... 3478
1Ki 11:2 Lord said unto the children of **I.**, ... 3478
1Ki 11:9 turned from the Lord God of **I.**, ... 3478
1Ki 11:16 did Joab remain there with all **I.**, ... 3478
1Ki 11:25 And he was an adversary to **I.** all ... 3478
1Ki 11:25 and he abhorred **I.**, and reigned ... 3478
1Ki 11:31 thus saith the Lord, the God of **I.**, ... 3478
1Ki 11:32 chosen out of all the tribes of **I.** ... 3478
1Ki 11:37 desireth, and shall be a king over **I.** ... 3478
1Ki 11:38 David, an will give **I.** unto thee ... 3478
1Ki 11:42 reigned in Jerusalem over all **I.** ... 3478
1Ki 12:1 **I.** were come to Shechem to make ... 3478
1Ki 12:3 and all the congregation of **I.** came, ... 3478
1Ki 12:16 **I.** saw that the king hearkened not ... 3478
1Ki 12:16 to your tents, O **I.**: now see to ... 3478
1Ki 12:16 So **I.** departed unto their tents ... 3478
1Ki 12:17 children of **I.** which dwelt in the ... 3478
1Ki 12:18 all **I.** stoned him with stones, that ... 3478
1Ki 12:19 so **I.** rebelled against the house of ... 3478
1Ki 12:20 **I.** heard that Jeroboam was come ... 3478
1Ki 12:20 and made him king over all **I.** ... 3478
1Ki 12:21 to fight against the house of **I.**, ... 3478
1Ki 12:24 your brethren the children of **I.** ... 3478
1Ki 12:28 thy gods, O **I.**, which brought thee ... 3478
1Ki 12:33 a feast unto the children of **I.** ... 3478
1Ki 14:7 thus saith the Lord God of **I.**, ... 3478
1Ki 14:7 made thee prince over my people **I.**, ... 3478
1Ki 14:10 **I.** him that is shut up and left in **I.**, ... 3478
1Ki 14:13 **I.** shall mourn for him, and bury ... 3478
1Ki 14:13 God of **I.** in the house of Jeroboam ... 3478
1Ki 14:14 shall raise him up a king over **I.**, ... 3478
1Ki 14:15 the Lord shall smite **I.**, as a reed ... 3478
1Ki 14:15 he shall root up **I.** out of this good ... 3478
1Ki 14:16 give **I.** up because of the sin of ... 3478
1Ki 14:16 did sin, and who made **I.** to sin ... 3478
1Ki 14:18 him; and all **I.** mourned for him, ... 3478
1Ki 14:19 of the chronicles of the kings of **I.** ... 3478
1Ki 14:21 did choose out of all the tribes of **I.**, ... 3478
1Ki 14:24 cast out before the children of **I.** ... 3478
1Ki 15:9 year of Jeroboam king of **I.** reigned ... 3478
1Ki 15:16 between Asa and Baasha king of **I.** ... 3478
1Ki 15:17 king of **I.** went up against Judah, ... 3478
1Ki 15:19 thy league with Baasha king of **I.**, ... 3478
1Ki 15:20 which he had against the cities of **I.**, ... 3478
1Ki 15:25 Jeroboam began to reign over **I.** ... 3478
1Ki 15:25 and reigned over **I.** two years ... 3478
1Ki 15:26 sin wherewith he made **I.** to sin ... 3478
1Ki 15:27 and all **I.** laid siege to Gibbethon ... 3478
1Ki 15:30 and which he made **I.** sin, by his ... 3478
1Ki 15:30 provoked the Lord God of **I.** to ... 3478
1Ki 15:31 the chronicles of the kings of **I.**? ... 3478
1Ki 15:32 Baasha king of **I.** all their days. ... 3478
1Ki 15:33 to reign over all **I.** in Tirzah, ... 3478
1Ki 15:34 sin wherewith he made **I.** to sin ... 3478
1Ki 16:2 made thee prince over my people **I.**; ... 3478
1Ki 16:2 hast made my people **I.** to sin, to ... 3478
1Ki 16:5 of the chronicles of the kings of **I.**? ... 3478
1Ki 16:8 Baasha to reign over **I.** in Tirzah, ... 3478
1Ki 16:13 by which they made **I.** to sin, in ... 3478
1Ki 16:13 Lord God of **I.** to anger with their ... 3478
1Ki 16:14 of the chronicles of the kings of **I.**? ... 3478
1Ki 16:16 wherefore all **I.** made Omri, the ... 3478
1Ki 16:16 king over **I.** that day in the camp. ... 3478
1Ki 16:17 from Gibbethon, and all **I.** with him, ... 3478
1Ki 16:19 which he did, to made **I.** to sin ... 3478
1Ki 16:20 of the chronicles of the kings of **I.**? ... 3478
1Ki 16:21 people of **I.** divided into two parts: ... 3478
1Ki 16:23 began Omri to reign over **I.**, twelve ... 3478
1Ki 16:26 his sin wherewith he made **I.** to sin, ... 3478
1Ki 16:26 Lord God of **I.** to anger with their ... 3478
1Ki 16:27 of the chronicles of the kings of **I.**? ... 3478
1Ki 16:29 the son of Omri to reign over **I.** ... 3478
1Ki 16:29 Omri reigned over **I.** in Samaria ... 3478
1Ki 16:33 provoke the Lord God of **I.** to anger ... 3478
1Ki 16:33 kings of **I.** that were before him. ... 3478
1Ki 17:1 As the Lord God of **I.** liveth, before ... 3478
1Ki 17:14 thus saith the Lord God of **I.**, The ... 3478
1Ki 18:17 him, Art thou he that troubleth **I.**? ... 3478
1Ki 18:18 answered, I have not troubled **I.**; ... 3478
1Ki 18:19 to me all **I.** unto mount Carmel, ... 3478
1Ki 18:20 sent unto all the children of **I.**, ... 3478
1Ki 18:31 came, saying, **I.** shall be thy name: ... 3478
1Ki 18:36 God of Abraham, Isaac, and of **I.**, ... 3478
1Ki 18:36 this day that thou art God in **I.**, ... 3478
1Ki 19:10, 14 of **I.** have forsaken thy covenant, ... 3478
1Ki 19:16 thou anoint to be king over **I.** ... 3478
1Ki 19:18 have left me seven thousand in **I.**, ... 3478
1Ki 20:2 messengers to Ahab king of **I.** ... 3478
1Ki 20:4 the king of **I.** answered and said, ... 3478
1Ki 20:7 the king of **I.** called all the elders ... 3478
1Ki 20:11 the king of **I.** answered and said, ... 3478
1Ki 20:13 a prophet unto Ahab, king of **I.**, ... 3478
1Ki 20:15 even all the children of **I.**, being ... 3478
1Ki 20:20 Syrians fled; and **I.** pursued them: ... 3478
1Ki 20:21 the king of **I.** went out, and smote ... 3478
1Ki 20:22 the prophet came to the king of **I.**, ... 3478
1Ki 20:26 up to Aphek, to fight against **I.** ... 3478
1Ki 20:27 the children of **I.** were numbered, ... 3478
1Ki 20:27 of **I.** pitched before them like two ... 3478
1Ki 20:28 spake unto the king of **I.**, and ... 3478
1Ki 20:29 children of **I.** slew of the Syrians ... 3478
1Ki 20:31 that the kings of the house of **I.** ... 3478
1Ki 20:31 heads, and go out to the king of **I.** ... 3478
1Ki 20:32 came to the king of **I.**, and said, ... 3478
1Ki 20:40 the king of **I.** said unto him, So ... 3478
1Ki 20:41 king of **I.** discerned him that he ... 3478
1Ki 20:43 king of **I.** went to his house heavy ... 3478
1Ki 21:7 thou now govern the kingdom of **I.**? ... 3478
1Ki 21:18 go down to meet Ahab king of **I.**, ... 3478
1Ki 21:21 him that is shut up and left in **I.**, ... 3478
1Ki 21:22 me to anger, and made **I.** to sin. ... 3478
1Ki 21:26 cast out before the children of **I.** ... 3478
1Ki 22:1 without war between Syria and **I.** ... 3478
1Ki 22:2 Judah came down to the king of **I.** ... 3478
1Ki 22:3 king of **I.** said unto his servants, ... 3478
1Ki 22:4 Jehoshaphat said to the king of **I.**, ... 3478
1Ki 22:5 said unto the king of **I.**, Enquire, ... 3478
1Ki 22:6 king of **I.** gathered the prophets ... 3478
1Ki 22:8 king of **I.** said unto Jehoshaphat, ... 3478
1Ki 22:9 king of **I.** called an officer, and ... 3478
1Ki 22:10 king of **I.** and Jehoshaphat the ... 3478
1Ki 22:17 saw all **I.** scattered upon the hills, ... 3478
1Ki 22:18 king of **I.** said unto Jehoshaphat, ... 3478
1Ki 22:26 the king of **I.** said, Take Micaiah, ... 3478
1Ki 22:29 king of **I.** and Jehoshaphat the ... 3478
1Ki 22:30 king of **I.** said unto Jehoshaphat, ... 3478
1Ki 22:30 the king of **I.** disguised himself, ... 3478
1Ki 22:31 great, save only with the king of **I.** ... 3478
1Ki 22:32 they said, Surely it is the king of **I.** ... 3478
1Ki 22:33 that it was not the king of **I.**, ... 3478
1Ki 22:34 smote the king of **I.** between the ... 3478
1Ki 22:39 of the chronicles of the kings of **I.**? ... 3478
1Ki 22:41 the fourth year of Ahab king of **I.** ... 3478
1Ki 22:44 made peace with the king of **I.** ... 3478
1Ki 22:51 son of Ahab began to reign over **I.** ... 3478
1Ki 22:51 and reigned two years over **I.** ... 3478
1Ki 22:52 son of Nebat, who made **I.** to sin: ... 3478
1Ki 22:53 to anger the Lord God of **I.**, ... 3478
2Ki 1:1 Moab rebelled against **I.** after the ... 3478
2Ki 1:3, 6 because there is not a God in **I.**, ... 3478
2Ki 1:16 not because there is no God in **I.** to ... 3478
2Ki 1:18 of the chronicles of the kings of **I.**? ... 3478
2Ki 2:12 the chariot of **I.**, and the horsemen ... 3478
2Ki 3:1 son of Ahab began to reign over **I.** ... 3478
2Ki 3:3 son of Nebat, which made **I.** to sin; ... 3478
2Ki 3:4 of **I.** an hundred thousand lambs, ... 3478
2Ki 3:5 Moab rebelled against the king of **I.** ... 3478
2Ki 3:6 the same time, and numbered all **I.** ... 3478
2Ki 3:9 So the king of **I.** went, and the king ... 3478
2Ki 3:10 king of **I.** said, Alas! that the Lord ... 3478
2Ki 3:12 king of **I.** and Jehoshaphat and the ... 3478
2Ki 3:13 And Elisha said unto the king of **I.**, ... 3478
2Ki 3:13 the king of **I.** said unto him, Nay: ... 3478
2Ki 3:24 when they came to the camp of **I.**, ... 3478
2Ki 3:27 was great indignation against **I.** ... 3478
2Ki 5:2 out of the land of **I.** a little maid; ... 3478
2Ki 5:4 the maid that is of the land of **I.** ... 3478
2Ki 5:5 send a letter unto the king of **I.** ... 3478
2Ki 5:6 the letter unto the king of **I.**, ... 3478
2Ki 5:7 the king of **I.** had read the letter, ... 3478
2Ki 5:8 the king of **I.** had rent his clothes, ... 3478
2Ki 5:8 know that there is a prophet in **I.** ... 3478
2Ki 5:12 better than all the waters of **I.**? ... 3478
2Ki 5:15 no God in all the earth, but in **I.** ... 3478
2Ki 6:8 king of Syria warred against **I.**, ... 3478
2Ki 6:9 man of God sent unto the king of **I.**, ... 3478
2Ki 6:10 king of **I.** sent to the place which ... 3478
2Ki 6:11 which of us is for the king of **I.**? ... 3478
2Ki 6:12 Elisha, the prophet that is in **I.**, ... 3478
2Ki 6:12 telleth the king of **I.** the words that ... 3478
2Ki 6:21 king of **I.** said unto Elisha, when ... 3478
2Ki 6:23 came no more into the land of **I.** ... 3478
2Ki 6:26 king of **I.** was passing by upon the ... 3478
2Ki 7:6 king of **I.** hath hired against us ... 3478
2Ki 7:13 they are as all the multitude of **I.** ... 3478
2Ki 8:12 thou wilt do unto the children of **I.** ... 3478
2Ki 8:16 fifth year of Joram the...king of **I.**, ... 3478
2Ki 8:18 walked in the way of the kings of **I.**, ... 3478
2Ki 8:25 twelfth year of Joram...king of **I.** ... 3478
2Ki 8:26 the daughter of Omri king of **I.** ... 3478
2Ki 9:3 I have anointed thee king over **I.** ... 3478
2Ki 9:6 Thus saith the Lord God of **I.**, ... 3478
2Ki 9:6 the people of the Lord, even over **I.** ... 3478
2Ki 9:8 him that is shut up and left in **I.** ... 3478
2Ki 9:12 I have anointed thee king over **I.** ... 3478
2Ki 9:14 he and all **I.**, because of Hazael ... 3478
2Ki 9:21 Joram king of **I.** and Ahaziah king ... 3478
2Ki 10:21 And Jehu sent through all **I.**: and ... 3478
2Ki 10:28 Thus Jehu destroyed Baal out of **I.** ... 3478
2Ki 10:29 son of Nebat, who made **I.** to sin, ... 3478
2Ki 10:30 shall sit on the throne of **I.** ... 3478
2Ki 10:31 walk in the law of the Lord God of **I.** ... 3478
2Ki 10:31 of Jeroboam, which made **I.** to sin. ... 3478
2Ki 10:32 the Lord began to cut **I.** short: ... 3478
2Ki 10:32 smote them in all the coasts of **I.**; ... 3478
2Ki 10:34 of the chronicles of the kings of **I.**? ... 3478
2Ki 10:36 Jehu reigned over **I.** in Samaria ... 3478
2Ki 13:1 son of Jehu began to reign over **I.** ... 3478
2Ki 13:2 son of Nebat, which made **I.** to sin; ... 3478
2Ki 13:3 of the Lord was kindled against **I.**, ... 3478
2Ki 13:4 for he saw the oppression of **I.**, ... 3478
2Ki 13:5 And the Lord gave **I.** a saviour, so ... 3478
2Ki 13:5 children of **I.** dwelt in their tents, ... 3478
2Ki 13:6 of Jeroboam, who made **I.** sin, ... 3478
2Ki 13:8 of the chronicles of the kings of **I.**? ... 3478
2Ki 13:10 to reign over **I.** in Samaria, and ... 3478
2Ki 13:11 the son of Nebat, who made **I.** sin: ... 3478
2Ki 13:12 of the chronicles of the kings of **I.**? ... 3478
2Ki 13:13 in Samaria with the kings of **I.** ... 3478
2Ki 13:14 the king of **I.** came down unto him, ... 3478
2Ki 13:14 the chariot of **I.**, and the horsemen ... 3478
2Ki 13:16 And he said to the king of **I.**, Put ... 3478
2Ki 13:18 he said unto the king of **I.**, Smite ... 3478
2Ki 13:22 Hazael king of Syria oppressed **I.** ... 3478
2Ki 13:25 him, and recovered the cities of **I.** ... 3478
2Ki 14:1 second year of Joash...king of **I.** ... 3478
2Ki 14:8 messengers to Joash...king of **I.**, ... 3478
2Ki 14:9 the king of **I.** sent to Amaziah ... 3478
2Ki 14:11 Jehoash king of **I.** went up; ... 3478
2Ki 14:12 was put to the worse before **I.**; ... 3478
2Ki 14:13 Jehoash king of **I.** took Amaziah ... 3478
2Ki 14:15 of the chronicles of the kings of **I.**? ... 3478
2Ki 14:16 in Samaria with the kings of **I.**; ... 3478
2Ki 14:17 Jehoahaz king of **I.** fifteen years. ... 3478
2Ki 14:23 of Joash king of **I.** began to reign ... 3478
2Ki 14:24 son of Nebat, who made **I.** to sin. ... 3478
2Ki 14:25 He restored the coast of **I.** from ... 3478
2Ki 14:25 to the word of the Lord God of **I.**, ... 3478
2Ki 14:26 For the Lord saw the affliction of **I.**, ... 3478
2Ki 14:26 nor any left, nor any helper for **I.** ... 3478
2Ki 14:27 he would blot out the name of **I.** ... 3478
2Ki 14:28 which belonged to Judah, for **I.**, ... 3478
2Ki 14:28 of the chronicles of the kings of **I.**? ... 3478
2Ki 14:29 fathers, even with the kings of **I.**; ... 3478
2Ki 15:1 year of Jeroboam king of **I.** began ... 3478
2Ki 15:8 the son of Jeroboam reigned over **I.** ... 3478
2Ki 15:9 son of Nebat, who made **I.** to sin. ... 3478
2Ki 15:11 of the chronicles of the kings of **I.** ... 3478
2Ki 15:12 Thy sons shall sit on the throne of **I.** ... 3478
2Ki 15:15 of the chronicles of the kings of **I.** ... 3478
2Ki 15:17 the son of Gadi to reign over **I.**, ... 3478

2Ki 15:18 son of Nebat, who made I. to sin....... 3478
2Ki 15:20 Menahem exacted the money of I., ... 3478
2Ki 15:21 of the chronicles of the kings of I.? 3478
2Ki 15:23 of Menahem began to reign over I. 3478
2Ki 15:24 son of Nebat, who made I. to sin....... 3478
2Ki 15:26 of the chronicles of the kings of I....... 3478
2Ki 15:27 of Remaliah began to reign over I. 3478
2Ki 15:28 son of Nebat, who made I. to sin....... 3478
2Ki 15:29 In the days of Pekah king of I. 3478
2Ki 15:31 of the chronicles of the kings of I....... 3478
2Ki 15:32 Pekah the son of Remaliah king of I.... 3478
2Ki 16:3 walked in the way of the kings of I.,... 3478
2Ki 16:3 out from before the children of I........ 3478
2Ki 16:5 Pekah son of Remaliah king of I.......... 3478
2Ki 16:7 out of the hand of the king of I.,........ 3478
2Ki 17:1 of Elah to reign in Samaria over I. 3478
2Ki 17:2 kings of I. that were before him. 3478
2Ki 17:6 and carried I. away into Assyria,........ 3478
2Ki 17:7 of I. had sinned against the Lord........ 3478
2Ki 17:8 out from before the children of I.,...... 3478
2Ki 17:8 and of the kings of I., which they....... 3478
2Ki 17:9 children of I. did secretly those 3478
2Ki 17:13 Yet the Lord testified against I., ... 3478
2Ki 17:18 the Lord was very angry with I., ... 3478
2Ki 17:19 walked in the statutes of I. which........ 3478
2Ki 17:20 the Lord rejected all the seed of I.,.... 3478
2Ki 17:21 he rent I. from the house of David;.... 3478
2Ki 17:21 Jeroboam drave I. from following........ 3478
2Ki 17:22 I. walked in all the sins of Jeroboam... 3478
2Ki 17:23 Lord removed I. out of his sight, ... 3478
2Ki 17:23 was I. carried away out of their own... 3478
2Ki 17:24 instead of the children of I................ 3478
2Ki 17:34 of Jacob, whom he named I.; 3478
2Ki 18:1 of Hoshea son of Elah king of I., ... 3478
2Ki 18:4 of I. did burn incense to it:.............. 3478
2Ki 18:5 He trusted in the Lord God of I.; 3478
2Ki 18:9 of Hoshea son of Elah king of I., ... 3478
2Ki 18:10 ninth year of Hoshea king of I., ... 3478
2Ki 18:11 king of Assyria did carry away I......... 3478
2Ki 19:15 O Lord God of I., which dwellest....... 3478
2Ki 19:20 Thus saith the Lord God of I., ... 3478
2Ki 19:22 even against the Holy One of I.......... 3478
2Ki 21:2 cast out before the children of I......... 3478
2Ki 21:3 a grove, as did Ahab king of I.; 3478
2Ki 21:7 have chosen out of all tribes of I.,...... 3478
2Ki 21:8 make the feet of I. move any more 3478
2Ki 21:9 destroyed before the children of I.. 3478
2Ki 21:12 thus saith the Lord God of I., ... 3478
2Ki 22:15, 18 thus saith the Lord God of I., ... 3478
2Ki 23:13 Solomon the king of I. had builded...... 3478
2Ki 23:15 son of Nebat, who made I. to sin,...... 3478
2Ki 23:19 kings of I. had made to provoke the ... 3478
2Ki 23:22 days of the judges that judged I.,....... 3478
2Ki 23:22 nor in all the days of the kings of I.,... 3478
2Ki 23:27 of my sight, as I have removed I., ... 3478
2Ki 24:13 gold which Solomon king of I. had...... 3478
1Ch 1:34 The sons of Isaac; Esau and I........... 3478
1Ch 1:43 reigned over the children of I.; 3478
1Ch 2:1 These are the sons of I.; Reuben,....... 3478
1Ch 2:7 Achar, the troubler of I., who 3478
1Ch 4:10 Jabez called on the God of I., ... 3478
1Ch 5:1 sons of Reuben the firstborn of I., ... 3478
1Ch 5:1 the sons of Joseph the son of I......... 3478
1Ch 5:3 of Reuben the firstborn of I. were,..... 3478
1Ch 5:17 the days of Jeroboam king of I........... 3478
1Ch 5:26 the God of I. stirred up the spirit....... 3478
1Ch 6:38 the son of Levi, the son of I.. 3478
1Ch 6:49 and to make an atonement for I., ... 3478
1Ch 6:64 I. gave to the Levites these cities...... 3478
1Ch 7:29 the children of Joseph the son of I...... 3478
1Ch 9:1 I. were reckoned by genealogies; 3478
1Ch 9:1 book of the kings of I. and Judah, ... 3478
1Ch 10:1 the Philistines fought against I.; 3478
1Ch 10:1 men of I. fled from before the........... 3478
1Ch 10:7 men of I. that were in the valley........ 3478
1Ch 11:1 all I. gathered themselves to David..... 3478
1Ch 11:2 leddest out and broughtest in I. 3478
1Ch 11:2 Thou shalt feed my people I., and...... 3478
1Ch 11:2 shalt be ruler over my people I.. 3478
1Ch 11:3 came all the elders of I. to the king.... 3478
1Ch 11:3 they anointed David king over I., ... 3478
1Ch 11:4 David and all I. went to Jerusalem,..... 3478
1Ch 11:10 and with all I., to make him king,....... 3478
1Ch 11:10 the word of the Lord concerning I...... 3478
1Ch 12:32 to know what I. ought to do; 3478
1Ch 12:38 to make David king over all I. 3478
1Ch 12:38 all the rest of I. were of one heart..... 3478
1Ch 12:40 for there was joy in I.. 3478
1Ch 13:2 unto all the congregation of I.,........... 3478
1Ch 13:2 that are left in all the land of I.,.......... 3478
1Ch 13:5 So David gathered all I. together, ... 3478
1Ch 13:6 And David went up, and all I., to....... 3478
1Ch 13:8 David and all I. played before God...... 3478
1Ch 14:2 had confirmed him king over I., ... 3478
1Ch 14:2 on high, because of his people I......... 3478
1Ch 14:8 David was anointed king over all I.,.... 3478
1Ch 15:3 David gathered all I. together to........ 3478
1Ch 15:12 up the ark of the Lord God of I......... 3478
1Ch 15:14 up the ark of the Lord God of I......... 3478
1Ch 15:25 the elders of I., and the captains........ 3478
1Ch 15:28 Thus all I. brought up the ark of........ 3478
1Ch 16:3 And he dealt to every one of I., ... 3478
1Ch 16:4 thank and praise the Lord God of I..... 3478
1Ch 16:13 O ye seed of I. his servant, ye.......... 3478
1Ch 16:17 to I. for an everlasting covenant, ... 3478
1Ch 16:36 Blessed be the Lord God of I. for....... 3478
1Ch 16:40 the Lord, which he commanded I.; 3478
1Ch 17:5 since the day that I brought up I........ 3478
1Ch 17:6 I have walked with all I., spake I....... 3478
1Ch 17:6 a word to any of the judges of I., ... 3478
1Ch 17:7 be ruler over my people I................. 3478
1Ch 17:9 will ordain a place for my people I.,.... 3478
1Ch 17:10 judges to be over my people I........... 3478
1Ch 17:21 in the earth is like thy people I.,........ 3478
1Ch 17:22 thy people I. didst thou make thine 3478
1Ch 17:24 is the God of I., even a God to I........ 3478
1Ch 18:14 So David reigned over all I., and....... 3478
1Ch 19:10 he chose out of all the choice of I., ... 3478
1Ch 19:16 were put to the worse before I., ... 3478
1Ch 19:17 he gathered all I., and passed over..... 3478
1Ch 19:18 But the Syrians fled before I.; and 3478
1Ch 19:19 were put to the worse before I., ... 3478
1Ch 20:7 But when he defied I., Jonathan......... 3478
1Ch 21:1 And Satan stood up against I.,........... 3478
1Ch 21:1 and provoked David to number I......... 3478
1Ch 21:2 number I. from Beer-sheba even to.... 3478
1Ch 21:3 will he be a cause of trespass to I.? ... 3478
1Ch 21:4 and went throughout all I., and.......... 3478
1Ch 21:5 And all they of I. were a thousand 3478
1Ch 21:7 this thing; therefore he smote I.......... 3478
1Ch 21:12 throughout all the coasts of I............ 3478
1Ch 21:14 the Lord sent pestilence upon I. 3478
1Ch 21:14 fell of I. seventy thousand men........... 3478
1Ch 21:16 Then David and the elders of I., ...
1Ch 22:1 altar of the burnt offering for I.. 3478
1Ch 22:2 the strangers...in the land of I.;......... 3478
1Ch 22:6 an house for the Lord God of I.......... 3478
1Ch 22:9 give peace and quietness unto I. 3478
1Ch 22:10 the throne of his kingdom over I........ 3478
1Ch 22:12 give thee charge concerning I.,........... 3478
1Ch 22:13 charged Moses with concerning I. 3478
1Ch 22:17 commanded all the princes of I. to...... 3478
1Ch 23:1 made Solomon his son king over I...... 3478
1Ch 23:2 together all the princes of I., ... 3478
1Ch 23:25 Lord God of I. hath give rest unto 3478
1Ch 24:19 Lord God of I. had commanded 3478
1Ch 26:29 for the outward business over I., ... 3478
1Ch 26:30 were officers among them of I. on...... 3478
1Ch 27:1 children of I. after their number,......... 3478
1Ch 27:16 Furthermore over the tribes of I......... 3478
1Ch 27:22 were the princes of the tribes of I...... 3478
1Ch 27:23 would increase I. like to the stars 3478
1Ch 27:24 there fell wrath for it against I.;......... 3478
1Ch 28:1 assembled all the princes of I., ... 3478
1Ch 28:4 Lord God of I. chose me before all..... 3478
1Ch 28:4 of my father to be king over I........... 3478
1Ch 28:4 me to make me king over all I. 3478
1Ch 28:5 of the kingdom of the Lord over I...... 3478
1Ch 28:8 sight of all I. the congregation of........ 3478
1Ch 29:6 and princes of the tribes of I.,........... 3478
1Ch 29:10 thou, Lord God of I. our father, ... 3478
1Ch 29:18 God of Abraham, Isaac, and of I., ... 3478
1Ch 29:21 sacrifices in abundance for all I. 3478
1Ch 29:23 prospered; and all I. obeyed him......... 3478
1Ch 29:25 exceedingly in the sight of all I., ... 3478
1Ch 29:25 been on any king before him in I........ 3478
1Ch 29:26 the son of Jesse reigned over all I...... 3478
1Ch 29:27 the time that he reigned over I. was... 3478
1Ch 29:30 that went over him, and over I., ... 3478
2Ch 1:2 Then Solomon spake unto all I.,......... 3478
2Ch 1:2 and to every governor in all I.,........... 3478
2Ch 1:13 congregation, and reigned over I........ 3478
2Ch 2:4 This is an ordinance for ever to I....... 3478
2Ch 2:12 Blessed be the Lord God of I., that.... 3478
2Ch 2:17 all the strangers...in the land of I.,..... 3478
2Ch 5:2 Solomon assembled the elders of I., ... 3478
2Ch 5:2 of the fathers of the children of I., ... 3478
2Ch 5:3 men of I. assembled themselves 3478
2Ch 5:4 And all the elders of I. came; and 3478
2Ch 5:6 all the congregation of I. that were..... 3478
2Ch 5:10 a covenant with the children of I., ... 3478
2Ch 6:3 the whole congregation of I............... 3478
2Ch 6:3 all the congregation of I. stood. 3478
2Ch 6:4 Blessed be the Lord God of I.,........... 3478
2Ch 6:5 no city among all the tribes of I......... 3478
2Ch 6:5 man to be a ruler over my people I.... 3478
2Ch 6:6 David to be over my people I............. 3478
2Ch 6:7 for the name of the Lord God of I....... 3478
2Ch 6:10 and am set on the throne of I., as...... 3478
2Ch 6:10 for the name of the Lord God of I...... 3478
2Ch 6:11 he made with the children of I........... 3478
2Ch 6:12 of all the congregation of I.,.............. 3478
2Ch 6:13 before all the congregation of I., ... 3478
2Ch 6:14 God of I., there is no God like thee ... 3478
2Ch 6:16 God of I., keep with thy servant........ 3478
2Ch 6:16 sight to sit upon the throne of I.;....... 3478
2Ch 6:17 O Lord God of I., let thy word be 3478
2Ch 6:21 of thy servant, and of thy people I., ... 3478
2Ch 6:24 thy people I. be put to the worse 3478
2Ch 6:25 and forgive the sin of my people I., ... 3478
2Ch 6:27 thy servants, and of thy people I., ... 3478
2Ch 6:29 of any man, or of all thy people I., ... 3478
2Ch 6:32 which is not of thy people I., ... 3478
2Ch 6:33 fear thee, as doth thy people I., ... 3478
2Ch 7:3 of I. saw how the fire came down, ... 3478
2Ch 7:6 before them, and all I. stood............. 3478
2Ch 7:8 seven days, and all I. with him, ... 3478
2Ch 7:10 to Solomon, and to I. his people. 3478
2Ch 7:18 not fail thee a man to be ruler in I.. ... 3478
2Ch 8:2 the children of I. to dwell there. 3478
2Ch 8:7 the Jebusites, which were not of I., ... 3478
2Ch 8:8 whom the children of I. consumed...... 3478
2Ch 8:9 children of I. did Solomon make no..... 3478
2Ch 8:11 in the house of David king of I., ... 3478
2Ch 9:8 because thy God loved I., to.............. 3478
2Ch 9:30 in Jerusalem over all I. forty years. 3478
2Ch 10:1 for to Shechem were all I. come to 3478
2Ch 10:3 all I. came and spake to Rehoboam,.... 3478
2Ch 10:16 all I. saw that the king would not....... 3478
2Ch 10:16 every man to your tents, O I.: and 3478
2Ch 10:16 So all I. went to their tents. 3478
2Ch 10:17 I. that dwelt in the cities of Judah 3478
2Ch 10:18 of I. stoned him with stones, that 3478
2Ch 10:19 I. rebelled against the house of.......... 3478
2Ch 11:1 were warriors, to fight against I.,....... 3478
2Ch 11:3 to all I. in Judah and Benjamin, ... 3478
2Ch 11:13 and the Levites that were in all I....... 3478
2Ch 11:16 after them out of all the tribes of I..... 3478
2Ch 11:16 hearts to seek the Lord God of I........ 3478
2Ch 12:1 law of the Lord, and all I. with him. ... 3478
2Ch 12:6 princes of I. and the king humbled...... 3478
2Ch 12:13 chosen out of all the tribes of I.,........ 3478
2Ch 13:4 me, thou Jeroboam, and all I.; 3478
2Ch 13:5 know that the Lord God of I. gave..... 3478
2Ch 13:5 gave the kingdom over I. to David..... 3478
2Ch 13:12 children of I., fight ye not against....... 3478
2Ch 13:15 God smote Jeroboam and all I. 3478
2Ch 13:16 children of I. fled before Judah:.......... 3478
2Ch 13:17 slain of I. five hundred thousand 3478
2Ch 13:18 children of I. were brought under........ 3478
2Ch 15:3 I. hath been without the true God,..... 3478
2Ch 15:4 did turn unto the Lord God of I., ... 3478
2Ch 15:9 fell to him out of I. in abundance,....... 3478
2Ch 15:13 would not seek the Lord God of I. 3478
2Ch 15:17 were not taken away out of I. 3478
2Ch 16:1 king of I. came up against Judah, ... 3478
2Ch 16:3 thy league with Baasha king of I., ... 3478
2Ch 16:4 his armies against the cities of I.;....... 3478
2Ch 16:11 book of the kings of Judah and I.. 3478
2Ch 17:1 strengthened himself against I.. 3478
2Ch 17:4 and not after the doings of I............. 3478
2Ch 18:3 king of I. said unto Jehoshaphat 3478
2Ch 18:4 Jehoshaphat said unto the king of I., ... 3478
2Ch 18:5 of I. gathered together of prophets..... 3478
2Ch 18:7 king of I. said unto Jehoshaphat, ... 3478
2Ch 18:8 of I. called for one of his officers, ... 3478
2Ch 18:9 the king of I. and Jehoshaphat king..... 3478
2Ch 18:16 I. scattered upon the mountains, ... 3478

2Ch 18:17 the king of **I.** said to Jehoshaphat, 3478
2Ch 18:19 Who shall entice Ahab king of **I.**, 3478
2Ch 18:25 Then the king of **I.** said, Take ye 3478
2Ch 18:28 So the king of **I.** and Jehoshaphat 3478
2Ch 18:29 king of **I.** said unto Jehoshaphat, I 3478
2Ch 18:29 So the king of **I.** disguised himself; 3478
2Ch 18:30 great, save only with the king of **I.** 3478
2Ch 18:31 that they said, It is the king of **I.** 3478
2Ch 18:32 that it was not the king of **I.**, they 3478
2Ch 18:33 smote the king of **I.** between the 3478
2Ch 18:34 **I.** stayed himself up in his chariot 3478
2Ch 19:8 and of the chief of the fathers of **I.**, 3478
2Ch 20:7 of this land before thy people **I.**, 3478
2Ch 20:10 thou wouldest not let **I.** invade, 3478
2Ch 20:19 up to praise the Lord God of **I.** 3478
2Ch 20:29 fought against the enemies of **I.** 3478
2Ch 20:34 in the book of the kings of **I.** 3478
2Ch 20:35 himself with Ahaziah king of **I.**, 3478
2Ch 21:2 the sons of Jehoshaphat king of **I.** 3478
2Ch 21:4 and divers also of the princes of **I.** 3478
2Ch 21:6, 13 in the way of the kings of **I.**, 3478
2Ch 22:5 Ahab king of **I.** to war against 3478
2Ch 23:2 and the chief of the fathers of **I.**, 3478
2Ch 24:5 gather of all **I.** money to repair the 3478
2Ch 24:6 and of the congregation of **I.**, for 3478
2Ch 24:9 the servant of God laid upon **I.** 3478
2Ch 24:16 he had done good in **I.**, both toward 3478
2Ch 25:6 mighty men of valour out of **I.** 3478
2Ch 25:7 let not the army of **I.** go with thee; 3478
2Ch 25:7 for the Lord is not with **I.**, to wit, 3478
2Ch 25:9 which I have given to the army of **I.**? 3478
2Ch 25:17 the son of Jehu, king of **I.**, saying, 3478
2Ch 25:18 king of **I.** sent to Amaziah king of 3478
2Ch 25:21 So Joash the king of **I.** went up; 3478
2Ch 25:22 was put to the worse before **I.**, 3478
2Ch 25:23 king of **I.** took Amaziah king of 3478
2Ch 25:25 of Joash son of Jehoahaz king of **I.** 3478
2Ch 25:26 book of the kings of Judah and **I.**? 3478
2Ch 27:7 book of the kings of **I.** and Judah. 3478
2Ch 28:2 walked in the ways of the kings of **I.**, 3478
2Ch 28:3 cast out before the children of **I.** 3478
2Ch 28:5 into the hand of the king of **I.**, 3478
2Ch 28:8 of **I.** carried away captive of their 3478
2Ch 28:13 and there is fierce wrath against **I.** 3478
2Ch 28:19 low because of Ahaz king of **I.**; 3478
2Ch 28:23 were the ruin of him, and of all **I.** 3478
2Ch 28:26 book of the kings of Judah and **I.** 3478
2Ch 28:27 the sepulchres of the kings of **I.** 3478
2Ch 29:7 the holy place unto the God of **I.** 3478
2Ch 29:10 covenant with the Lord God of **I.**, 3478
2Ch 29:24 to make an atonement for all **I.** 3478
2Ch 29:24 offering should be made for all **I.** 3478
2Ch 29:27 ordained by David king of **I.** 3478
2Ch 30:1 Hezekiah sent to all **I.** and Judah, 3478
2Ch 30:1 passover unto the Lord God of **I.** 3478
2Ch 30:5 proclamation throughout all **I.**, 3478
2Ch 30:5 passover unto the Lord God of **I.** 3478
2Ch 30:6 and his princes throughout all **I.** 3478
2Ch 30:6 Ye children of **I.**, turn again unto 3478
2Ch 30:6 God of Abraham, Isaac, and **I.**, 3478
2Ch 30:21 **I.** that were present at Jerusalem 3478
2Ch 30:25 congregation that came out of **I.** 3478
2Ch 30:25 that came out of the land of **I.**, 3478
2Ch 30:26 Solomon the son of David king of **I.** 3478
2Ch 31:1 all **I.** that were present went out to 3478
2Ch 31:1 Then all the children of **I.** returned, 3478
2Ch 31:5 of **I.** brought in abundance the first 3478
2Ch 31:6 the children of **I.** and Judah, 3478
2Ch 31:8 blessed the Lord, and his people **I.** 3478
2Ch 32:17 letters to rail on the Lord God of **I.**, 3478
2Ch 32:32 book of the kings of Judah and **I.** 3478
2Ch 33:2 cast out before the children of **I.** 3478
2Ch 33:7 chosen before all the tribes of **I.**, 3478
2Ch 33:8 I any more remove the foot of **I.** 3478
2Ch 33:9 destroyed before the children of **I.** 3478
2Ch 33:16 Judah to serve the Lord God of **I.** 3478
2Ch 33:18 in the name of the Lord God of **I.**, 3478
2Ch 33:18 in the book of the kings of **I.** 3478
2Ch 34:7 idols throughout all the land of **I.**, 3478
2Ch 34:9 and of all the remnant of **I.**, 3478
2Ch 34:21 them that are left in **I.** and in Judah, 3478
2Ch 34:23 Thus saith the Lord God of **I.**, Tell 3478
2Ch 34:26 of **I.** concerning the words which 3478
2Ch 34:33 that pertained to the children of **I.**, 3478
2Ch 34:33 all that were present in **I.** to serve, 3478
2Ch 35:3 unto the Levites that taught all **I.**, 3478
2Ch 35:3 son of David king of **I.** did build; 3478
2Ch 35:3 Lord your God, and his people **I.**, 3478
2Ch 35:4 to the writing of David king of **I.**, 3478
2Ch 35:17 of **I.** that were present kept the 3478
2Ch 35:18 no passover like to that kept in **I.** 3478
2Ch 35:18 kings of **I.** keep such a passover as 3478
2Ch 35:18 all Judah and **I.** that were present, 3478
2Ch 35:25 and made them an ordinance in **I.** 3478
2Ch 35:27 in the book of the kings of **I.** 3478
2Ch 36:8 in the book of the kings of **I.** 3478
2Ch 36:13 turning unto the Lord God of **I.** 3478
Ezr 1:3 the house of the Lord God of **I.**, 3478
Ezr 2:2 of the men of the people of **I.** 3478
Ezr 2:59 their seed, whether they were of **I.** 3478
Ezr 2:70 their cities, and all **I.** in their cities. 3478
Ezr 3:1 the children of **I.** were in the cities, 3478
Ezr 3:2 builded the altar of the God of **I.**, 3478
Ezr 3:10 the ordinance of David king of **I.** 3478
Ezr 3:11 mercy endureth for ever toward **I.** 3478
Ezr 4:1 temple unto the Lord God of **I.**; 3478
Ezr 4:3 rest of the chief of the fathers of **I.**, 3478
Ezr 4:3 will build unto the Lord God of **I.**, 3478
Ezr 5:1 in the name of the God of **I.**, even 3479
Ezr 5:11 which a great king of **I.** builded 3478
Ezr 6:14 the commandment of the God of **I.**, 3479
Ezr 6:16 the children of **I.**, the priests, and 3479
Ezr 6:17 and for a sin offering for all **I.**, 3479
Ezr 6:17 to the number of the tribes of **I.** 3479
Ezr 6:21 **I.**, which were come again out of 3478
Ezr 6:21 land, to seek the Lord God of **I.**, 3478
Ezr 6:22 of the house of God, the God of **I.** 3478
Ezr 7:6 which the Lord God of **I.** had given: 3478
Ezr 7:7 went up some of the children of **I.**, 3478
Ezr 7:10 teach in **I.** statutes and judgments. 3478
Ezr 7:11 the Lord, and of his statutes to **I.** 3478
Ezr 7:13 that all they of the people of **I.** 3479
Ezr 7:15 freely offered unto the God of **I.**, 3479
Ezr 7:28 out of **I.** chief men to go up with 3478
Ezr 8:18 Mahli, the son of Levi, the son of **I.**; 3478
Ezr 8:25 his lords, and all **I.** there present, 3478
Ezr 8:29 and chief of the fathers of **I.**, 3478
Ezr 8:35 burnt offerings unto the God of **I.**, 3478
Ezr 8:35 twelve bullocks for all **I.**, ninety 3478
Ezr 9:1 The people of **I.**, and the priests, 3478
Ezr 9:4 at the words of the God of **I.**, 3478
Ezr 9:15 Lord God of **I.**, thou art righteous; 3478
Ezr 10:1 assembled unto him out of **I.** a 3478
Ezr 10:2 is hope in **I.** concerning this thing 3478
Ezr 10:5 all **I.**, to swear that they should do 3478
Ezr 10:10 wives, to increase the trespass of **I.** 3478
Ezr 10:25 Moreover of **I.**: of the sons of 3478
Ne 1:6 for the children of **I.** thy servants, 3478
Ne 1:6 confess the sins of the children of **I.**, 3478
Ne 2:10 the welfare of the children of **I.** 3478
Ne 7:7 say, of the men of the people of **I.** 3478
Ne 7:61 their seed, whether they were of **I.** 3478
Ne 7:73 and all **I.**, dwelt in their cities; 3478
Ne 7:73 children of **I.** were in their cities. 3478
Ne 8:1 the Lord had commanded to **I.** 3478
Ne 8:14 children of **I.** should dwell in booths 3478
Ne 8:17 had not the children of **I.** done so. 3478
Ne 9:1 of **I.** were assembled with fasting, 3478
Ne 9:2 **I.** separated themselves from all 3478
Ne 10:33 to make an atonement for **I.**, 3478
Ne 10:39 the children of **I.** and the children 3478
Ne 11:3 to wit, **I.**, the priests, and the 3478
Ne 11:20 And the residue of **I.**, of the priests, 3478
Ne 12:47 all **I.** in the days of Zerubbabel, 3478
Ne 13:2 of **I.** with bread and with water, 3478
Ne 13:3 separated from **I.** all the mixed 3478
Ne 13:18 wrath upon **I.** by profaning the 3478
Ne 13:26 king of **I.** sin by these things? 3478
Ne 13:26 and God made him king over all **I.** 3478
Ps 14:7 salvation of **I.** were come out of 3478
Ps 14:7 shall rejoice, and **I.** shall be glad. 3478
Ps 22:3 that inhabitest the praises of **I.** 3478
Ps 22:23 and fear him, all ye the seed of **I.** 3478
Ps 25:22 Redeem **I.**, O God, out of all his 3478
Ps 41:13 Blessed be the Lord God of **I.** from 3478
Ps 50:7 O **I.**, and I will testify against thee: 3478
Ps 53:6 salvation of **I.** were come out of 3478
Ps 53:6 shall rejoice, and **I.** shall be glad. 3478
Ps 59:5 Lord God of hosts, the God of **I.**, 3478
Ps 68:8 the presence of God, the God of **I.** 3478
Ps 68:26 the Lord, from the fountain of **I.** 3478
Ps 68:34 his excellency is over **I.**, and his 3478
Ps 68:35 God of **I.** is he that giveth strength 3478
Ps 69:6 confounded for my sake, O God of **I.** 3478
Ps 71:22 the harp, O thou Holy One of **I.** 3478
Ps 72:18 be the Lord God, the God of **I.**, 3478
Ps 73:1 God is good to **I.**, even to such as 3478
Ps 76:1 God known: his name is great in **I.** 3478
Ps 78:5 Jacob, and appointed a law in **I.**, 3478
Ps 78:21 and anger also came up against **I.**; 3478
Ps 78:31 smote down the chosen men of **I.** 3478
Ps 78:41 and limited the Holy One of **I.** 3478
Ps 78:55 tribes of **I.** to dwell in their tents. 3478
Ps 78:59 wroth, and greatly abhorred **I.** 3478
Ps 78:71 his people, and **I.** his inheritance. 3478
Ps 80:1 Give ear, O Shepherd of **I.**, thou 3478
Ps 81:4 For this was a statute for **I.**, and 3478
Ps 81:8 O **I.**, if thou wilt hearken unto me; 3478
Ps 81:11 voice; and **I.** would none of me. 3478
Ps 81:13 me, and **I.** had walked in my ways! 3478
Ps 83:4 name of **I.** may be no more in 3478
Ps 89:18 and the Holy One of **I.** is our king. 3478
Ps 98:3 his truth toward the house of **I.** 3478
Ps 103:7 his acts unto the children of **I.** 3478
Ps 105:10 to **I.** for an everlasting covenant: 3478
Ps 105:23 **I.** also came into Egypt; and Jacob 3478
Ps 106:48 Blessed be the Lord God of **I.** from 3478
Ps 114:1 When **I.** went out of Egypt, the 3478
Ps 114:2 his sanctuary, and **I.** his dominion. 3478
Ps 115:9 O **I.**, trust thou in the Lord: he is 3478
Ps 115:12 he will bless the house of **I.**; he 3478
Ps 118:2 **I.** now say, that his mercy endureth 3478
Ps 121:4 keepeth **I.** shall neither slumber 3478
Ps 122:4 unto the testimony of **I.**, to give 3478
Ps 124:1 was on our side, now may **I.** say; 3478
Ps 125:5 but peace shall be upon **I.** 3478
Ps 128:6 children, and peace upon **I.** 3478
Ps 129:1 from my youth, may **I.** now say: 3478
Ps 130:7 Let **I.** hope in the Lord: for with 3478
Ps 130:8 And he shall redeem **I.** from all 3478
Ps 131:3 Let **I.** hope in the Lord from 3478
Ps 135:4 and **I.** for his peculiar treasure. 3478
Ps 135:12 an heritage unto **I.** his people. 3478
Ps 135:19 Bless the Lord, O house of **I.** 3478
Ps 136:11 brought out **I.** from among them: 3478
Ps 136:14 made **I.** to pass through the midst 3478
Ps 136:22 an heritage unto **I.** his servant: 3478
Ps 147:2 together the outcasts of **I.** 3478
Ps 147:19 statutes and his judgments unto **I.** 3478
Ps 148:14 the children of **I.**, a people near 3478
Ps 149:2 Let **I.** rejoice in him that made 3478
Pr 1:1 the son of David, king of **I.**; 3478
Ec 1:12 was king over **I.** in Jerusalem. 3478
Ca 3:7 are about it, of the valiant of **I.** 3478
Isa 1:3 **I.** doth not know, my people doth 3478
Isa 1:4 provoked the Holy One of **I.** unto 3478
Isa 1:24 Lord of hosts, the Mighty One of **I.**, 3478
Isa 4:2 for them that are escaped of **I.** 3478
Isa 5:7 Lord of hosts is the house of **I.**, 3478
Isa 5:19 of the Holy One of **I.** draw nigh 3478
Isa 5:24 the word of the Holy One of **I.** 3478
Isa 7:1 the son of Remaliah, king of **I.**, 3478
Isa 8:14 of offence to both the houses of **I.**, 3478
Isa 8:18 for signs and for wonders in **I.** 3478
Isa 9:8 Jacob, and it hath lighted upon **I.** 3478
Isa 9:12 shall devour **I.** with open mouth. 3478
Isa 9:14 Lord will cut off from **I.** head and 3478
Isa 10:17 the light of **I.** shall be for a fire, 3478
Isa 10:20 that the remnant of **I.**, and such as 3478
Isa 10:20 upon the Lord, the Holy One of **I.**, 3478
Isa 10:22 people **I.** be as the sand of the sea, 3478
Isa 11:12 shall assemble the outcasts of **I.**, 3478
Isa 11:16 like as it was to **I.** in the day that 3478
Isa 12:6 great is the Holy One of **I.** in the 3478
Isa 14:1 will yet choose **I.**, and set them in 3478
Isa 14:2 the house of **I.** shall possess them 3478
Isa 17:3 be as the glory of the children of **I.**, 3478
Isa 17:6 thereof, saith the Lord God of **I.** 3478
Isa 17:7 have respect to the Holy One of **I.** 3478
Isa 17:9 left because of the children of **I.** 3478
Isa 19:24 In that day shall **I.** be the third 3478
Isa 19:25 my hands, and **I.** mine inheritance. 3478
Isa 21:10 of the Lord of hosts, the God of **I.**, 3478
Isa 21:17 the Lord God of **I.** hath spoken it, 3478
Isa 24:15 of the Lord God of **I.** in the isles of 3478
Isa 27:6 **I.** shall blossom and bud, and fill 3478
Isa 27:12 one by one, O ye children of **I.** 3478
Isa 29:19 shall rejoice in the Holy One of **I.** 3478

Isa 29:23 and shall fear the God of **I.**. 3478
Isa 30:11 cause the Holy One of **I.** to cease 3478
Isa 30:12 thus saith the Holy One of **I.**, 3478
Isa 30:15 the Lord God, the Holy One of **I.**; 3478
Isa 30:29 the Lord, to the mighty One of **I.**. 3478
Isa 31:1 look not unto the Holy One of **I.**, 3478
Isa 31:6 children of **I.** have deeply revolted 3478
Isa 37:16 O Lord of hosts, God of **I.**, that 3478
Isa 37:21 Thus saith the Lord God of **I.**, 3478
Isa 37:23 even against the Holy One of **I.**. 3478
Isa 40:27 thou, O Jacob, and speakest, O **I.**, 3478
Isa 41:8 But thou, **I.**, art my servant, Jacob 3478
Isa 41:14 thou worm Jacob, and ye men of **I.**; 3478
Isa 41:14 thy redeemer, the Holy One of **I.**. 3478
Isa 41:16 shalt glory in the Holy One of **I.**. 3478
Isa 41:17 the God of **I.** will not forsake them 3478
Isa 41:20 the Holy One of **I.** hath created it 3478
Isa 42:24 for a spoil, and **I.** to the robbers? 3478
Isa 43:1 and he that formed thee, O **I.**, Fear 3478
Isa 43:3 Lord thy God, the Holy One of **I.**, 3478
Isa 43:14 redeemer, the Holy One of **I.**; 3478
Isa 43:15 One, the Creator of **I.**, your King. 3478
Isa 43:22 thou hast been weary of me, O **I.**. 3478
Isa 43:28 the curse, and **I.** to reproaches. 3478
Isa 44:1 and **I.**, whom I have chosen: 3478
Isa 44:5 surname himself by the name of **I.**. 3478
Isa 44:6 Thus saith the Lord the King of **I.**, 3478
Isa 44:21 Remember these, O Jacob and **I.**; 3478
Isa 44:21 O **I.**, thou shalt not be forgotten of 3478
Isa 44:23 Jacob, and glorified himself in **I.**. 3478
Isa 45:3 thee by thy name, am the God of **I.**. 3478
Isa 45:4 servant's sake, and **I.** mine elect, 3478
Isa 45:11 saith the Lord, the Holy One of **I.**, 3478
Isa 45:15 God that hidest thyself, O God of **I.**. 3478
Isa 45:17 But **I.** shall be saved in the Lord 3478
Isa 45:25 shall all the seed of **I.** be justified, 3478
Isa 46:3 all the remnant of the house of **I.**, 3478
Isa 46:13 salvation in Zion for **I.** my glory. 3478
Isa 47:4 is his name, the Holy One of **I.**. 3478
Isa 48:1 which are called by the name of **I.**, 3478
Isa 48:1 and make mention of the God of **I.**, 3478
Isa 48:2 stay themselves upon the God of **I.**; 3478
Isa 48:12 Hearken unto me, O Jacob and **I.**, 3478
Isa 48:17 thy Redeemer, the Holy One of **I.**; 3478
Isa 49:3 Thou art my servant, O **I.**, in whom 3478
Isa 49:5 Though **I.** be not gathered, yet 3478
Isa 49:6 and to restore the preserved of **I.**: 3478
Isa 49:7 Redeemer of **I.**, and his Holy One, 3478
Isa 49:7 is faithful, and the Holy One of **I.**, 3478
Isa 52:12 the God of **I.** will be your rereward. 3478
Isa 54:5 thy Redeemer the Holy One of **I.**; 3478
Isa 55:5 thy God, and for the Holy One of **I.**; 3478
Isa 56:8 which gathereth the outcasts of **I.** 3478
Isa 60:9 thy God, and to the Holy One of **I.**, 3478
Isa 60:14 The Zion of the Holy One of **I.** 3478
Isa 63:7 goodness toward the house of **I.**, 3478
Isa 63:16 of us, and **I.** acknowledge us not: 3478
Isa 66:20 of **I.** bring an offering in a clean 3478
Jer 2:3 **I.** was holiness unto the Lord, and 3478
Jer 2:4 all the families of the house of **I.** 3478
Jer 2:14 Is **I.** a servant? is he a homeborn 3478
Jer 2:26 so is the house of **I.** ashamed, 3478
Jer 2:31 Have I been a wilderness unto **I.**? 3478
Jer 3:6 which backsliding **I.** hath done? 3478
Jer 3:8 backsliding **I.** committed adultery 3478
Jer 3:11 The backsliding **I.** hath justified 3478
Jer 3:12 Return, thou backsliding **I.**, saith 3478
Jer 3:18 shall walk with the house of **I.**, 3478
Jer 3:20 dealt treacherously...O house of **I.**, 3478
Jer 3:21 supplications of the children of **I.** 3478
Jer 3:23 Lord our God is the salvation of **I.**. 3478
Jer 4:1 wilt return, O **I.**, saith the Lord, 3478
Jer 5:11 house of **I.** and the house of Judah 3478
Jer 5:15 upon you from far, O house of **I.**, 3478
Jer 6:9 glean the remnant of **I.** as a vine: 3478
Jer 7:3 the Lord of hosts, the God of **I.**, 3478
Jer 7:12 the wickedness of my people **I.**. 3478
Jer 7:21 the Lord of hosts, the God of **I.**; 3478
Jer 9:15 the Lord of hosts, the God of **I.**; 3478
Jer 9:26 the house of **I.** are uncircumcised 3478
Jer 10:1 speaketh unto you, O house of **I.** 3478
Jer 10:16 and **I.** is the rod of his inheritance: 3478
Jer 11:3 Thus saith the Lord God of **I.**; 3478
Jer 11:10 house of **I.** and the house of Judah 3478
Jer 11:17 for the evil of the house of **I.** and of 3478
Jer 12:14 caused my people **I.** to inherit; 3478
Jer 13:11 cleave unto me...whole house of **I.** 3478
Jer 13:12 Thus saith the Lord God of **I.**, 3478
Jer 14:8 the hope of **I.**, the saviour thereof 3478
Jer 16:9 the Lord of hosts, the God of **I.**; 3478
Jer 16:14 of **I.** out of the land of Egypt; 3478
Jer 16:15 of **I.** from the land of the north, 3478
Jer 17:13 O Lord, the hope of **I.**, all that 3478
Jer 18:6 O house of **I.**, cannot I do with you 3478
Jer 18:6 are ye in mine hand, O house of **I.** 3478
Jer 18:13 virgin of **I.** hath done a...horrible 3478
Jer 19:3, 15 the Lord of hosts, the God of **I.**; 3478
Jer 21:4 Thus saith the Lord God of **I.**; 3478
Jer 23:2 Lord God of **I.** against the pastors 3478
Jer 23:6 be saved, and **I.** shall dwell safely: 3478
Jer 23:7 of **I.** out of the land of Egypt; 3478
Jer 23:8 which led the seed of the house of **I.** 3478
Jer 23:13 and caused my people **I.** to err. 3478
Jer 24:5 Thus saith the Lord, the God of **I.**; 3478
Jer 25:15 saith the Lord God of **I.** unto me; 3478
Jer 25:27 the Lord of hosts, the God of **I.**; 3478
Jer 27:4 the Lord of hosts, the God of **I.**; 3478
Jer 27:21 the Lord of hosts, the God of **I.**, 3478
Jer 28:2 the Lord of hosts, the God of **I.**, 3478
Jer 28:14 the Lord of hosts, the God of **I.**; 3478
Jer 29:4 the Lord of hosts, the God of **I.**, 3478
Jer 29:8 the Lord of hosts, the God of **I.**; 3478
Jer 29:21 the Lord of hosts, the God of **I.**, 3478
Jer 29:23 they have committed villainy in **I.**, 3478
Jer 29:25 the Lord of hosts, the God of **I.**, 3478
Jer 30:2 Thus speaketh the Lord God of **I.**, 3478
Jer 30:3 again the captivity of my people **I.** 3478
Jer 30:4 that the Lord spake concerning **I.** 3478
Jer 30:10 neither be dismayed, O **I.**: for, lo, 3478
Jer 31:1 be the God of all the families of **I.**, 3478
Jer 31:2 even **I.**, when I went to cause him 3478
Jer 31:4 thou shalt be built, O virgin of **I.** 3478
Jer 31:7 save thy people, the remnant of **I.** 3478
Jer 31:9 for I am a father to **I.**, and Ephraim 3478
Jer 31:10 He that scattered **I.** will gather 3478
Jer 31:21 O virgin of **I.**, turn again to these 3478
Jer 31:23 the Lord of hosts, the God of **I.**; 3478
Jer 31:27 I will sow the house of **I.** and the 3478
Jer 31:31 new covenant with the house of **I.**, 3478
Jer 31:33 I will make with the house of **I.**; 3478
Jer 31:36 the seed of **I.** also shall cease from 3478
Jer 31:37 I will also cast off all the seed of **I.** 3478
Jer 32:14, 15 the Lord of hosts, the God of **I.**; 3478
Jer 32:20 and in **I.**, and among other men; 3478
Jer 32:21 people **I.** out of the land of Egypt 3478
Jer 32:30 the children of **I.** and the children 3478
Jer 32:30 children of **I.** have only provoked 3478
Jer 32:32 of all the evil of the children of **I.** 3478
Jer 32:36 thus saith the Lord, the God of **I.**, 3478
Jer 33:4 thus saith the Lord, the God of **I.**, 3478
Jer 33:7 and the captivity of **I.** to return, 3478
Jer 33:14 have promised unto the house of **I.** 3478
Jer 33:17 upon the throne of the house of **I.**; 3478
Jer 34:2, 13 saith the Lord, the God of **I.**; 3478
Jer 35:13 the Lord of hosts, the God of **I.**; 3478
Jer 35:17 Lord God of hosts, the God of **I.**; 3478
Jer 35:18, 19 the Lord of hosts, the God of **I.**; 3478
Jer 36:2 I have spoken unto thee against **I.**, 3478
Jer 37:7 Thus saith the Lord, the God of **I.**; 3478
Jer 38:17 the God of hosts, the God of **I.**; 3478
Jer 39:16 the Lord of hosts, the God of **I.**; 3478
Jer 41:9 made for fear of Baasha king of **I.** 3478
Jer 42:9 Thus saith the Lord, the God of **I.**, 3478
Jer 42:15, 18 the Lord of hosts, the God of **I.**; 3478
Jer 43:10 the Lord of hosts, the God of **I.**; 3478
Jer 44:2 the Lord of hosts, the God of **I.**; 3478
Jer 44:7 the God of hosts, the God of **I.**; 3478
Jer 44:11 the Lord of hosts, the God of **I.**; 3478
Jer 44:25 the Lord of hosts, the God of **I.**, 3478
Jer 45:2 Thus saith the Lord, the God of **I.**, 3478
Jer 46:25 The Lord of hosts, the God of **I.**, 3478
Jer 46:27 Jacob, and be not dismayed, O **I.** 3478
Jer 48:1 the Lord of hosts, the God of **I.**; 3478
Jer 48:13 house of **I.** was ashamed of Beth-el 3478
Jer 48:27 For was not **I.** a derision to thee? 3478
Jer 49:1 Hath **I.** no sons? hath he no heir? 3478
Jer 49:2 shall **I.** be heir unto them that were 3478
Jer 50:4 the children of **I.** shall come, 3478
Jer 50:17 **I.** is a scattered sheep; the lions 3478
Jer 50:18 the Lord of hosts, the God of **I.**; 3478
Jer 50:19 will bring **I.** again to his habitation, 3478
Jer 50:20 iniquity of **I.** shall be sought for, 3478
Jer 50:29 Lord, against the Holy One of **I.** 3478
Jer 50:33 of **I.** and...Judah were oppressed 3478
Jer 51:5 For **I.** hath not been forsaken, nor 3478
Jer 51:5 with sin against the Holy One of **I.** 3478
Jer 51:19 and **I.** is the rod of his inheritance
Jer 51:33 the Lord of hosts, the God of **I.**; 3478
Jer 51:49 hath caused the slain of **I.** to fall, 3478
La 2:1 unto the earth the beauty of **I.**, 3478
La 2:3 his fierce anger all the horn of **I.** 3478
La 2:5 enemy: he hath swallowed up **I.**, 3478
Eze 2:3 I send thee to the children of **I.**, 3478
Eze 3:1 and go speak unto the house of **I.** 3478
Eze 3:4 go, get thee unto the house of **I.**, 3478
Eze 3:5 language, but to the house of **I.**; 3478
Eze 3:7 of **I.** will not hearken unto thee; 3478
Eze 3:7 **I.** are impudent and hardhearted. 3478
Eze 3:17 a watchman unto the house of **I.** 3478
Eze 4:3 shall be a sign to the house of **I.** 3478
Eze 4:4 iniquity of the house of **I.** upon it: 3478
Eze 4:5 bear the iniquity of the house of **I.**. 3478
Eze 4:13 children of **I.** eat their defiled bread 3478
Eze 5:4 come forth into all the house of **I.**. 3478
Eze 6:2 face toward the mountains of **I.**, 3478
Eze 6:3 Ye mountains of **I.**, hear the word 3478
Eze 6:5 dead carcases of the children of **I.** 3478
Eze 6:11 abominations of the house of **I.**! 3478
Eze 7:2 the Lord God unto the land of **I.**; 3478
Eze 8:4 glory of the God of **I.** was there, 3478
Eze 8:6 that the house of **I.** committeth 3478
Eze 8:10 and all the idols of the house of **I.**, 3478
Eze 8:11 of the ancients of the house of **I.**, 3478
Eze 8:12 the ancients of the house of **I.** do in 3478
Eze 9:3 glory of the Lord of **I.** was gone up 3478
Eze 9:8 thou destroy all the residue of **I.** 3478
Eze 9:9 The iniquity of the house of **I.** and 3478
Eze 10:19 glory of the God of **I.** was over them. 3478
Eze 10:20 that I saw under the God of **I.** 3478
Eze 11:5 Thus have ye said, O house of **I.** 3478
Eze 11:10 I will judge you in the border of **I.**; 3478
Eze 11:11 I will judge you in the border of **I.** 3478
Eze 11:13 a full end of the remnant of **I.**? 3478
Eze 11:15 and all the house of **I.** wholly, 3478
Eze 11:17 and I will give you the land of **I.**. 3478
Eze 11:22 glory of the God of **I.** was over them. 3478
Eze 12:6 thee for a sign unto the house of **I.**. 3478
Eze 12:9 of man, hath not the house of **I.**, 3478
Eze 12:10 house of **I.** that are among them. 3478
Eze 12:19 of Jerusalem, and of the land of **I.**; 3478
Eze 12:22 proverb...ye have in the land of **I.**, 3478
Eze 12:23 no more use it as a proverb in **I.**; 3478
Eze 12:24 divination within the house of **I.**. 3478
Eze 12:27 behold, they of the house of **I.** say, 3478
Eze 13:2 prophesy against the prophets of **I.** 3478
Eze 13:4 O **I.**, thy prophets are like the foxes 3478
Eze 13:5 up the hedge for the house of **I.** 3478
Eze 13:9 in the writing of the house of **I.**, 3478
Eze 13:9 shall they enter into the land of **I.**; 3478
Eze 13:16 the prophets of **I.** which prophesy 3478
Eze 14:1 certain of the elders of **I.** unto me, 3478
Eze 14:4 Every man of the house of **I.** that 3478
Eze 14:5 the house of **I.** in their own heart, 3478
Eze 14:6 Therefore say unto the house of **I.**, 3478
Eze 14:7 For every one of the house of **I.**, 3478
Eze 14:7 the stranger that sojourneth in **I.**, 3478
Eze 14:9 him from the midst of my people **I.**. 3478
Eze 14:11 house of **I.** may go no more astray 3478
Eze 17:2 a parable unto the house of **I.**; 3478
Eze 17:23 In the mountain of the height of **I.** 3478
Eze 18:2 proverb concerning the land of **I.**, 3478
Eze 18:3 any more to use this proverb in **I.** 3478
Eze 18:6, 15 to the idols of the house of **I.**, 3478
Eze 18:25 Hear now, O house of **I.**; Is not my 3478
Eze 18:29 Yet saith the house of **I.**, The way 3478
Eze 18:29 O house of **I.**, are not my ways 3478
Eze 18:30 I will judge you, O house of **I.**, 3478
Eze 18:31 for why will ye die, O house of **I.**? 3478
Eze 19:1 a lamentation for the princes of **I.**, 3478
Eze 19:9 be heard upon the mountains of **I.** 3478
Eze 20:1 of the elders of **I.** came to enquire 3478
Eze 20:3 of man, speak unto the elders of **I.**, 3478
Eze 20:5 In the day when I chose **I.**, and 3478
Eze 20:13 the house of **I.** rebelled against me 3478
Eze 20:27 of man, speak unto the house of **I.**, 3478
Eze 20:30 Wherefore say unto the house of **I.**, 3478
Eze 20:31 enquired of by you, O house of **I.**? 3478
Eze 20:38 shall not enter into the land of **I.** 3478
Eze 20:39 As for you, O house of **I.**, thus saith 3478

Eze 20:40 in the mountain of the height of I., 3478
Eze 20:40 there shall all the house of I., all 3478
Eze 20:42 shall bring you into the land of I., 3478
Eze 20:44 corrupt doings, O ye house of I., 3478
Eze 21:2 prophesy against the land of I., 3478
Eze 21:3 say to the land of I., Thus saith 3478
Eze 21:12 shall be upon all the princes of I. 3478
Eze 21:25 thou, profane wicked prince of I., 3478
Eze 22:6 Behold, the princes of I., every one 3478
Eze 22:18 house of I. is to me become dross: 3478
Eze 24:21 Speak unto the house of I., Thus 3478
Eze 25:3 against the land of I., when it was 3478
Eze 25:6 thy despite against the land of I.; 3478
Eze 25:14 Edom by the hand of my people I. 3478
Eze 27:17 land of I., they were thy merchants: 3478
Eze 28:24 pricking brier unto the house of I., 3478
Eze 28:25 shall have gathered the house of I. 3478
Eze 29:6 a staff of reed to the house of I. 3478
Eze 29:16 the confidence of the house of I., 3478
Eze 29:21 horn of the house of I. to bud forth, 3478
Eze 33:7 a watchman unto the house of I.; 3478
Eze 33:10 of man, speak unto the house of I.; 3478
Eze 33:11 for why will ye die, O house of I.? 3478
Eze 33:20 O ye house of I., I will judge you 3478
Eze 33:24 those wastes of the land of I. 3478
Eze 33:28 mountains of I. shall be desolate, 3478
Eze 34:2 against the shepherds of I., 3478
Eze 34:2 Woe be to the shepherds of I. that 3478
Eze 34:13 feed them upon the mountains of I. 3478
Eze 34:14 upon the high mountains of I. shall 3478
Eze 34:14 they feed upon the mountains of I. 3478
Eze 34:30 even the house of I., are my people, 3478
Eze 35:5 shed blood of the children of I. by 3478
Eze 35:12 spoken against the mountains of I., 3478
Eze 35:15 the inheritance of the house of I., 3478
Eze 36:1 prophesy unto the mountains of I., 3478
Eze 36:1 Ye mountains of I., hear the word 3478
Eze 36:4 ye mountains of I., hear the word 3478
Eze 36:6 therefore concerning the land of I., 3478
Eze 36:8 But ye, O ye mountains of I., ye 3478
Eze 36:8 yield your fruit to my people of I.; 3478
Eze 36:10 all the house of I., even all of it: 3478
Eze 36:12 walk upon you, even my people I.; 3478
Eze 36:17 house of I. dwelt in their own land, 3478
Eze 36:21 which the house of I. had profaned 3478
Eze 36:22 Therefore say unto the house of I., 3478
Eze 36:22 this for your sakes, O house of I., 3478
Eze 36:32 for your own ways, O house of I. 3478
Eze 36:37 be enquired of by the house of I., 3478
Eze 37:11 bones are the whole house of I. 3478
Eze 37:12 and bring you into the land of I. 3478
Eze 37:16 the children of I. his companions: 3478
Eze 37:16 all the house of I. his companions: 3478
Eze 37:19 the tribes of I. his fellows, and will 3478
Eze 37:21 I will take the children of I. from 3478
Eze 37:22 the land upon the mountains of I.; 3478
Eze 37:28 know that I the Lord do sanctify I., 3478
Eze 38:8 people, against the mountains of I., 3478
Eze 38:14 my people of I. dwelleth safely, 3478
Eze 38:16 come up against my people of I., 3478
Eze 38:17 by my servants the prophets of I., 3478
Eze 38:18 shall come against the land of I., 3478
Eze 38:19 a great shaking in the land of I.; 3478
Eze 39:2 thee upon the mountains of I. 3478
Eze 39:4 shalt fall upon the mountains of I., 3478
Eze 39:7 known in the midst of my people I.; 3478
Eze 39:7 I am the Lord, the Holy One in I. 3478
Eze 39:9 they that dwell in the cities of I. 3478
Eze 39:11 Gog a place there of graves in I., 3478
Eze 39:12 the house of I. be burying of them, 3478
Eze 39:17 sacrifice upon the mountains of I., 3478
Eze 39:22 house of I. shall know that I am 3478
Eze 39:23 house of I. went into captivity for 3478
Eze 39:25 mercy upon the whole house of I., 3478
Eze 39:29 out my spirit upon the house of I., 3478
Eze 40:2 brought he me into the land of I., 3478
Eze 40:4 that thou seest to the house of I. 3478
Eze 43:2 glory of the God of I. came from 3478
Eze 43:7 in the midst of the children of I. 3478
Eze 43:7 shall the house of I. no more defile, 3478
Eze 43:10 shew the house to the house of I., 3478
Eze 44:2 Lord, the God of I., hath entered in 3478
Eze 44:6 rebellious, even to the house of I., 3478
Eze 44:6 O ye house of I., let it suffice you 3478
Eze 44:9 that is among the children of I. 3478
Eze 44:10 far from me, when I. went astray, 3478
Eze 44:12 the house of I. to fall into iniquity; 3478
Eze 44:15 children of I. went astray from me, 3478
Eze 44:22 take maidens...of the house of I., 3478
Eze 44:28 shall give them no possession in I. 3478
Eze 44:29 dedicated thing in I. shall be theirs. 3478
Eze 45:6 shall be for the whole house of I. 3478
Eze 45:8 land shall be his possession in I. 3478
Eze 45:8 shall they give to the house of I. 3478
Eze 45:9 Let it suffice you, O princes of I. 3478
Eze 45:15 out of the fat pastures of I.; 3478
Eze 45:16 this oblation for the prince in I. 3478
Eze 45:17 all solemnities of the house of I. 3478
Eze 45:17 reconciliation for the house of I. 3478
Eze 47:13 according to the twelve tribes of I. 3478
Eze 47:18 and from the land of I. by Jordan, 3478
Eze 47:21 you according to the tribes of I. 3478
Eze 47:22 country among the children of I.; 3478
Eze 47:22 with you among the tribes of I. 3478
Eze 48:11 when the children of I. went astray, 3478
Eze 48:19 serve it out of all the tribes of I. 3478
Eze 48:29 unto the tribes of I. for inheritance, 3478
Eze 48:31 after the names of the tribes of I. 3478
Da 1:3 bring certain of the children of I., 3478
Da 9:7 of Jerusalem, and unto all I., 3478
Da 9:11 all I. have transgressed thy law, 3478
Da 9:20 my sin and the sin of my people I., 3478
Ho 1:1 the son of Joash, king of I. 3478
Ho 1:4 the kingdom of the house of I. 3478
Ho 1:5 break the bow of I. in the valley 3478
Ho 1:6 have mercy upon the house of I.; 3478
Ho 1:10 I. shall be as the sand of the sea, 3478
Ho 1:11 children of I. be gathered together, 3478
Ho 3:1 Lord toward the children of I., 3478
Ho 3:4 I. shall abide many days without a 3478
Ho 3:5 shall the children of I. return, and 3478
Ho 4:1 word of the Lord, ye children of I. 3478
Ho 4:15 Though thou, I., play the harlot, yet 3478
Ho 4:16 I. slideth back as a backsliding 3478
Ho 5:1 and hearken, ye house of I.; 3478
Ho 5:3 Ephraim, and I. is not hid from me: 3478
Ho 5:3 whoredom, and I. is defiled. 3478
Ho 5:5 pride of I. doth testify to his face: 3478
Ho 5:5 shall I. and Ephraim fall in their 3478
Ho 5:9 tribes of I. have I made known that 3478
Ho 6:10 horrible thing in the house of I. 3478
Ho 6:10 whoredom of Ephraim, I. is defiled. 3478
Ho 7:1 When I would have healed I., then 3478
Ho 7:10 the pride of I. testifieth to his face: 3478
Ho 8:2 I. shall cry unto me, My God, we 3478
Ho 8:3 I. hath cast off the thing that is 3478
Ho 8:6 from I. was it also: the workman 3478
Ho 8:8 I. is swallowed up: now shall they 3478
Ho 8:14 I. hath forgotten his Maker, and 3478
Ho 9:1 Rejoice not, O I., for joy, as other 3478
Ho 9:7 are come; I. shall know it: 3478
Ho 9:10 I. like grapes in the wilderness; 3478
Ho 10:1 I. is an empty vine, he bringeth 3478
Ho 10:6 I. shall be ashamed of his own 3478
Ho 10:8 the sin of I., shall be destroyed: 3478
Ho 10:9 I., thou hast sinned from the days 3478
Ho 10:15 shall the king of I. utterly be cut off. 3478
Ho 11:1 When I. was a child, then I loved 3478
Ho 11:8 how shall I deliver thee, I.? how 3478
Ho 11:12 and the house of I. with deceit: 3478
Ho 12:12 I. served for a wife, and for a wife 3478
Ho 12:13 the Lord brought I. out of Egypt, 3478
Ho 13:1 trembling he exalted himself in I.; 3478
Ho 13:9 O I., thou hast destroyed thyself; 3478
Ho 14:1 O I., return unto the Lord thy God; 3478
Ho 14:5 I will be as the dew unto I.: he 3478
Joe 2:27 know that I am in the midst of I., 3478
Joe 3:2 my people and for my heritage I., 3478
Joe 3:16 the strength of the children of I. 3478
Am 1:1 concerning I. in the days of Uzziah 3478
Am 1:1 the son of Joash king of I., 3478
Am 2:6 For three transgressions of I., and 3478
Am 2:11 not even thus, O ye children of I.? 3478
Am 3:1 spoken against you, O children of I., 3478
Am 3:12 shall the children of I. be taken out 3478
Am 3:14 I shall visit the transgressions of I. 3478
Am 4:5 this liketh you, O ye children of I., 3478
Am 4:12 thus will I do unto thee, O I. 3478
Am 4:12 prepare to meet thy God, O I. 3478
Am 5:1 even a lamentation, O house of I. 3478
Am 5:2 The virgin of I. is fallen; she shall 3478
Am 5:3 shall leave ten, to the house of I. 3478
Am 5:4 saith the Lord unto the house of I., 3478
Am 5:25 wilderness forty years, O house of I.? 3478
Am 6:1 to whom the house of I. came! 3478
Am 6:14 against you a nation, O house of I., 3478
Am 7:8 in the midst of my people I. 3478
Am 7:9 sanctuaries of I. shall be laid waste; 3478
Am 7:10 Beth-el sent to Jeroboam king of I., 3478
Am 7:10 thee in the midst of the house of I. 3478
Am 7:11 I. shall surely be led away captive 3478
Am 7:15 Go, prophesy unto my people I. 3478
Am 7:16 sayest, Prophesy not against I., 3478
Am 7:17 and I. shall surely go into captivity 3478
Am 8:2 end is come upon my people of I.; 3478
Am 9:7 unto me, O children of I.? 3478
Am 9:7 not I brought up I. out of the land 3478
Am 9:9 will sift the house of I. among all 3478
Am 9:14 the captivity of my people of I., 3478
Ob 20 of this host of the children of I. 3478
Mic 1:5 and for the sins of the house of I. 3478
Mic 1:13 transgressions of I. were found in 3478
Mic 1:14 shall be a lie to the kings of I. 3478
Mic 1:15 come unto Adullam the glory of I. 3478
Mic 2:12 surely gather the remnant of I.; 3478
Mic 3:1 and ye princes of the house of I.; 3478
Mic 3:8 his transgression, and to I. his sin. 3478
Mic 3:9 and princes of the house of I., 3478
Mic 5:1 smite the judge of I. with a rod 3478
Mic 5:2 unto me that is to be ruler in I.; 3478
Mic 5:3 shall return unto the children of I. 3478
Mic 6:2 people, and he will plead with I. 3478
Na 2:2 of Jacob, as the excellency of I. 3478
Zep 2:9 Lord of hosts, the God of I., 3478
Zep 3:13 remnant of I. shall not do iniquity, 3478
Zep 3:14 O daughter of Zion; shout, O I.; be 3478
Zep 3:15 the king of I., even the Lord, is in 3478
Zec 1:19 scattered Judah, I., and Jerusalem. 3478
Zec 8:13 O house of Judah, and house of I.; 3478
Zec 9:1 of man, as of all the tribes of I., 3478
Zec 11:14 brotherhood between Judah and I. 3478
Zec 12:1 of the word of the Lord for I., 3478
Mal 1:1 word of the Lord to I. by Malachi. 3478
Mal 1:5 be magnified from the border of I. 3478
Mal 2:11 an abomination is committed in I. 3478
Mal 2:16 the Lord, the God of I., saith that 3478
Mal 4:4 unto him in Horeb for all I., 3478
Mt 2:6 that shall rule my people I. *2474*
Mt 2:20 mother, and go into the land of I. *2474*
Mt 2:21 and came into the land of I. *2474*
Mt 8:10 **found so great faith, no, not in I.** *2474*
Mt 9:33 saying, It was never so seen in I. *2474*
Mt 10:6 **to the lost sheep of the house of I.** *2474*
Mt 10:23 **not have gone over the cities of I.,** *2474*
Mt 15:24 **the lost sheep of the house of I.** *2474*
Mt 15:31 and they glorified the God of I. *2474*
Mt 19:28 **judging the twelve tribes of I.** *2474*
Mt 27:9 they of the children of I. did value; *2474*
Mt 27:42 If he be the King of I., let him now *2474*
Mk 12:29 **the commandments is, Hear, O I.;** *2474*
Mk 15:32 Let Christ the King of I. descend *2474*
Lu 1:16 of the children of I. shall he turn *2474*
Lu 1:54 He hath holpen his servant I., *2474*
Lu 1:68 Blessed be the Lord God of I.; for *2474*
Lu 1:80 till the day of his shewing unto I. *2474*
Lu 2:25 waiting for the consolation of I. *2474*
Lu 2:32 and the glory of thy people I. *2474*
Lu 2:34 fall and rising again of many in I.; *2474*
Lu 4:25 **many widows were in I. in the** *2474*
Lu 4:27 **many lepers were in I. in the** *2474*
Lu 7:9 **found so great faith, no, not in I.** *2474*
Lu 22:30 **judging the twelve tribes of I.** *2474*
Lu 24:21 he which should have redeemed I. *2474*
Joh 1:31 he should be made manifest to I., *2474*
Joh 1:49 Son of God; thou art the King of I. *2474*
Joh 3:10 **Art thou a master of I., and** *2474*
Joh 12:13 King of I. that cometh in the name *2474*
Ac 1:6 restore again the kingdom to I.? *2474*
Ac 2:22 Ye men of I., hear these words; *2475*
Ac 2:36 all the house of I. know assuredly, *2474*
Ac 3:12 Ye men of I., why marvel ye at this? *2475*
Ac 4:8 of the people, and elders of I., *2474*
Ac 4:10 you all, and to all the people of I., *2474*
Ac 4:27 the Gentiles, and the people of I., *2474*
Ac 5:21 all the senate of the children of I., *2474*
Ac 5:31 for to give repentance to I., and *2474*
Ac 5:35 Ye men of I., take heed to *2475*
Ac 7:23 his brethren the children of I. *2474*
Ac 7:37 which said unto the children of I., *2474*
Ac 7:42 O ye house of I., have ye offered to *2474*
Ac 9:15 **and kings, and the children of I.** *2474*

Ac 10:36 God sent unto the children of **I.**, *2474*
Ac 13:16 Men of **I.**, and ye that fear God, *2475*
Ac 13:17 The God of this people of **I.** chose *2474*
Ac 13:23 promise raised unto **I.** a Saviour, *2474*
Ac 13:24 repentance to all the people of **I.**. *2474*
Ac 21:28 Crying out, Men of **I.**, help: This *2475*
Ac 28:20 that for the hope of **I.** I am bound *2474*
Ro 9:6 they are not all **I.**, which are of **I.** *2474*
Ro 9:27 Esaias also crieth concerning **I.**, *2474*
Ro 9:27 children of **I.** be as the sand of the *2474*
Ro 9:31 But **I.**, which followed after the law *2474*
Ro 10:1 desire and prayer to God for **I.** is, *2474*
Ro 10:19 But I say, Did not **I.** know? *2474*
Ro 10:21 But to **I.** he saith, All day long I *2474*
Ro 11:2 intercession to God against **I.**, *2474*
Ro 11:7 **I.** hath not obtained that which he *2474*
Ro 11:25 blindness in part is happened to **I.**, *2474*
Ro 11:26 And so all **I.** shall be saved: as it is *2474*
1Co 10:18 Behold **I.** after the flesh: are not *2474*
2Co 3:7 of **I.** could not stedfastly behold *2474*
2Co 3:13 of **I.** could not stedfastly look to *2474*
Ga 6:16 and mercy, and upon the **I.** of God *2474*
Eph 2:12 aliens from the commonwealth of **I.**, *2474*
Php 3:5 of the stock of **I.**, of the tribe of *2474*
Heb 8:8 a new covenant with the house of **I.** *2474*
Heb 8:10 that I will make with the house of **I.** *2474*
Heb 11:22 the departing of the children of **I.**; *2474*
Re 2:14 **a stumblingblock before...of I.**, *2474*
Re 7:4 of all the tribes of the children of **I.** *2474*
Re 21:12 twelve tribes of the children of **I.** *2474*

ISRAELITE (iz'-ra-el-ite) See also ISRAELITES; ISRAELITISH.
Nu 25:14 name of the **I.** that was slain, 1121,3478
2Sa 17:25 son, whose name was Ithra an **I.**, 3481
Joh 1:47 **Behold an I. indeed, in whom is** *2475*
Ro 11:1 For I also am an **I.**, of the seed of *2475*

ISRAELITES (iz'-ra-el-ites)
Ex 9:7 not one of the cattle of the **I.** dead 3478
Le 23:42 are **I.** born shall dwell in booths: 3478
Jos 3:17 the **I.** passed over on dry ground, 3478
Jos 8:24 all the **I.** returned unto Ai, and 3478
Jos 13:6 lot unto the **i.** for an inheritance, 3478
Jos 13:13 dwell among the **I.** until this day. 3478
Jg 20:21 to the ground of the **I.** that day 3478
1Sa 2:14 in Shiloh unto all the **I.** that came 3478
1Sa 13:20 the **I.** went down to the Philistines, 3478
1Sa 14:21 be with the **I.** that were with Saul 3478
1Sa 25:1 all the **I.** were gathered together, 3478
1Sa 29:1 **I.** pitched by a fountain which is 3478
2Sa 4:1 feeble, and all the **I.** were troubled 3478
2Ki 3:24 **I.** rose up and smote the Moabites, 3478
2Ki 7:13 even as all the multitude of the **I.** 3478
1Ch 9:2 the **I.**, the priests, Levites, and 3478
Ro 9:4 Who are **I.**; to whom pertaineth *2475*
2Co 11:22 Are they **I.**? so am I. Are they *2475*

ISRAELITISH (iz'-ra-el-i-tish)
Le 24:10 the son of an **I.** woman, whose 3482
Le 24:10 this son of the **I.** woman and a man 3482
Le 24:11 the **I.** woman's son blasphemed 3482

ISRAEL'S (iz'-ra-els)
Ge 48:13 his right hand toward **I.** left hand, 3478
Ge 48:13 his left hand toward **I.** right hand, 3478
Ex 18:8 and to the Egyptians for **I.** sake, 3478
Nu 1:20 children of Reuben, **I.** eldest son, 3478
Nu 31:30 the children of **I.** half, thou shalt 3478
Nu 31:42 the children of **I.** half, which Moses 3478
Nu 31:47 Even of the children of **I.** half, 3478
De 21:8 blood unto thy people of **I.** charge. 3478
2Sa 5:12 his kingdom for his people **I.** sake. 3478
2Ki 3:11 And one of the king of **I.** servants 3478

ISSACHAR (is'-sa-kar)
Ge 30:18 and she called his name **I.**. 3485
Ge 35:23 and Judah, and **I.**, and Zebulun: 3485
Ge 46:13 the sons of **I.**; Tola, and Phuvah, 3485
Ge 49:14 **I.** is a strong ass couching down 3485
Ex 1:3 **I.**, Zebulun, and Benjamin, 3485
Nu 1:8 Of **I.**; Nethaneel the son of Zuar. 3485
Nu 1:28 children of **I.**, by their generations, 3485
Nu 1:29 of the tribe of **I.**, were fifty and four 3485
Nu 2:5 unto him shall be the tribe of **I.** 3485
Nu 2:5 shall be captain of the children of **I.**. 3485
Nu 7:18 the son of Zuar, prince of **I.**, 3485
Nu 10:15 host of the tribe of the children of **I.** 3485
Nu 13:7 tribe of **I.**, Igal the son of Joseph. 3485
Nu 26:23 the sons of **I.** after their families: 3485
Nu 26:25 These are the families of **I.** 3485
Nu 34:26 of the tribe of the children of **I.**, 3485
De 27:12 Judah, and **I.**, and Joseph, and 3485
De 33:18 thy going out; and, **I.**, in thy tents. 3485
Jos 17:10 on the north, and in **I.** on the east. 3485
Jos 17:11 Manasseh had in **I.** and in Asher 3485
Jos 19:17 came out to **I.**, for the children of **I.** 3485
Jos 19:23 of the tribe of the children of **I.** 3485
Jos 21:6 out of the families of the tribe of **I.**, 3485
Jos 21:28 out of the tribe of **I.**, Kishon with 3485
Jg 5:15 of **I.** were with Deborah; even **I.**, 3485
Jg 10:1 Puah, the son of Dodo, a man of **I.**; 3485
1Ki 4:17 the son of Paruah, in **I.** 3485
1Ki 15:27 son of Ahijah, of the house of **I.**, 3485
1Ch 2:1 Simeon, Levi, and Judah, **I.**, and 3485
1Ch 6:62 their families out of the tribe of **I.**, 3485
1Ch 6:72 And out of the tribe of **I.**; Kedesh 3485
1Ch 7:1 sons of **I.** were, Tola, and Puah, 3485
1Ch 7:5 the families of **I.** were valiant men 3485
1Ch 12:32 the children of **I.**, which were men 3485
1Ch 12:40 that were nigh them, even unto **I.** 3485
1Ch 26:5 Ammiel the sixth, **I.** the seventh, 3485
1Ch 27:18 of **I.**, Omri the son of Michael: 3485
2Ch 30:18 many of Ephraim, and Manasseh, **I.**, 3485
Eze 48:25 unto the west side, **I.** a portion. 3485
Eze 48:26 And by the border of **I.**, from the 3485
Eze 48:33 one gate of **i.**, one gate of Zebulun. 3485
Re 7:7 Of the tribe of **I.** were sealed *2466*

ISSHIAH (is-shi'-ah) See also ISAIAH; JESIAH.
1Ch 24:21 sons of Rehabiah, the first was **I.** 3449
1Ch 24:25 The brother of Michah was **I.** 3449
1Ch 24:25 of the sons of **I.**; Zechariah

ISSUE See also ISSUED; ISSUES.
Ge 48:6 And thy **i.**, which thou begettest 4138
Le 12:7 cleansed from the **i.** of her blood 4726
Le 15:2 When any man hath a running **i.** 2100
Le 15:2 because of his **i.** he is unclean. 2101
Le 15:3 shall be his uncleanness in his **i.** 2101
Le 15:3 whether his flesh run with his **i.**, or 2101
Le 15:3 his flesh be stopped from his **i.**, 2101
Le 15:4 whereon he lieth that hath the **i.**, 2100
Le 15:6 whereon he sat that hath the **i.** 2100
Le 15:7 the flesh of him that hath the **i.** 2100
Le 15:8 if he that hath the **i.** spit upon him 2100
Le 15:9 he rideth upon that hath the **i.** shall 2100
Le 15:11, 12 he toucheth that hath the **i.**, 2100
Le 15:13 And when he that hath an **i.** 2100
Le 15:13 is cleansed of his **i.**, 2101
Le 15:15 for him before the Lord for his **i.** 2101
Le 15:19 And if a woman have an **i.**, 2100
Le 15:19 and her **i.** in her flesh be blood, 2101
Le 15:25 if a woman have an **i.** of her blood 2100
Le 15:25 days of the **i.** of her uncleanness 2101
Le 15:26 she lieth all the days of her **i.** 2101
Le 15:28 But if she be cleansed of her **i.**, 2101
Le 15:30 atonement before the Lord for the **i.** 2101
Le 15:32 is the law of him that hath an **i.**, 2100
Le 15:33 of him that hath an **i.**, of the man, 2100
Le 22:4 is a leper, or hath a running **i.**; 2100
Nu 5:2 leper, and every one that hath an **i.**, 2100
2Sa 3:29 house of Joab one that hath an **i.**, 2100
2Ki 20:18 of thy sons that shall **i.** from thee, 3318
Isa 22:24 house, the offspring and the **i.**, all 6849
Isa 39:7 thy sons that shall **i.** from thee, 3318
Eze 23:20 and whose **i.** is like the **i.** of horses 2231
Eze 47:8 waters **i.** out toward the east 3318
Mt 9:20 with an **i.** of blood twelve years, *131*
Mt 22:25 having no **i.**, left his wife unto his *4690*
Mk 5:25 had an **i.** of blood twelve years, *4511*
Lu 8:43 having an **i.** of blood twelve years, *4511*
Lu 8:44 and immediately her **i.** of blood *4511*

ISSUED
Jos 8:22 the other **i.** out of the city against 3318
Job 38:8 as if it had **i.** out of the womb? 3318
Eze 47:1 waters **i.** out from under the 3318
Eze 47:12 waters they **i.** out of the sanctuary: 3318
Da 7:10 A fiery stream **i.** and came forth 5047
Re 9:17 out of their mouths **i.** fire and *1607*
Re 9:18 which **i.** out of their mouths. *1607*

ISSUES
Ps 68:20 the Lord belong the **i.** from death. 8444
Pr 4:23 for out of it are the **i.** of life. 8444

ISUAH (is'-u-ah) See also ISHUAH.
1Ch 7:30 Imnah, and **I.**, and Ishuai, and 3440

ISUI (is'-u-i) See also ISHUI.
Ge 46:17 Jimnah, and Ishuah, and **I.**, and 3440

IT See in the APPENDIX; also ALBEIT; HOWBEITH; ITS; ITSELF.

ITALIAN (it-al'-yan)
Ac 10:1 of the band called the **I.** band, *2483*

ITALY (it'-a-lee)
Ac 18:2 in Pontus, lately come from **I.**, *2482*
Ac 27:1 that we should sail into **I.**, *2482*
Ac 27:6 ship of Alexandria sailing into **I.**; *2482*
Heb 13:24 the saints. They of **I.** salute you. *2482*
Heb *subsc.* Written to the Hebrews from **I.**

ITCH See also ITCHING.
De 28:27 and with the scab, and with the **i.**, 2775

ITCHING
2Ti 4:3 teachers, having **i.** ears; *2833*

ITHAI (ith'-a-i) See also ITTAI.
1Ch 11:31 **I.** the son of Ribai of Gibeah, that 2833

ITHAMAR (ith'-a-mar)
Ex 6:23 Nadab and Abihu, Eleazar, and **I.** 385
Ex 28:1 Abihu, Eleazar and **I.**, Aaron's sons 385
Ex 38:21 by the hand of **I.**, son to Aaron the 385
Le 10:6 unto Eleazar and unto **I.**, his sons, 385
Le 10:12 Aaron, unto Eleazar and unto **I.**, 385
Le 10:16 he was angry with Eleazar and **I.**, 385
Nu 3:2 firstborn, and Abihu, Eleazar, and **I.** 385
Nu 3:4 **I.** ministered in the priest's office 385
Nu 4:28 shall be under the hand of **I.** the 385
Nu 4:33 under the hand of **I.** the son of 385
Nu 7:8 under the hand of **I.** the son of 385
Nu 26:60 Nadab, and Abihu, Eleazar, and **I.** 385
1Ch 6:3 Nadab, and Abihu, Eleazar, and **I.** 385
1Ch 24:1 Nadab, and Abihu, Eleazar, and **I.** 385
1Ch 24:2 Eleazar and **I.** executed the priest's 385
1Ch 24:3 and Ahimelech of the sons of **I.**, 385
1Ch 24:4 of Eleazar than of the sons of **I.**; 385
1Ch 24:4 and eight among the sons of **I.** 385
1Ch 24:5 of Eleazar, and of the sons of **I.**. 385
1Ch 24:6 for Eleazar, and one taken for **I.**. 385
Ezr 8:2 Gershom: of the sons of **I.**; Daniel: 385

ITHIEL (ith'-e-el)
Ne 11:7 son of Maaseiah, the son of **I.**, the 384
Pr 30:1 man spake unto **I.**, even unto **I.** and 384

ITHMAH (ith'-mah)
1Ch 11:46 of Elnaam, and **I.** the Moabite, 3495

ITHNAN (ith'-nan)
Jos 15:23 And Kedesh, and Hazor, and **I.**, 3497

ITHRA (ith'-rah) See also JETHER.
2Sa 17:25 whose name was **I.** an Israelite, 3501

ITHRAN (ith'-ran)
Ge 36:26 Hemdan, and Eshban, and **I.**, 3506
1Ch 1:41 Amram, and Eshban, and **I.**, 3506
1Ch 7:37 and Shilshah, and **I.**, and Beera. 3506

ITHREAM (ith'-re-am)
2Sa 3:5 sixth, **I.**, by Eglah David's wife. 3507
1Ch 3:3 the sixth, **I.** by Eglah his wife. 3507

ITHRITE (ith'-rite) See also ITHRITES.
2Sa 23:38 Ira an **I.**, Gareb an **I.**, 3505
1Ch 11:40 Ira the **I.**, Gareb the **I.**, 3505

ITHRITES (ith'-rites)
1Ch 2:53 families of Kirjath-jearim; the **I.**, 3505

ITS
Le 25:5 That which groweth of **i.** own accord

ITSELF
Ge 1:11 whose seed is in **i.**, upon the earth:
Ge 1:12 yielding fruit, whose seed was in **i.**,
Le 7:24 fat of the beast that dieth of **i.**, and
Le 17:15 soul that eateth that which dieth of **i.**
Le 18:25 land **i.** vomiteth out her inhabitants.
Le 22:8 That which dieth of **i.**, or is torn
Le 25:11 neither reap that which groweth of **i.**
De 14:21 not eat of any thing that died of **i.**
1Ki 7:34 undersetters were of the very base **i.**
Job 10:22 A land of darkness, as darkness **i.**;
Ps 41:6 his heart gathereth iniquity to **i.**;
Ps 68:8 Sinai **i.** was moved at the presence 2088
Pr 18:2 but that his heart may discover **i.**
Pr 23:31 in the cup, when it moveth **i.** aright
Pr 27:16 of his right hand, which bewrayeth **i.**.

Pr 27:25 and the tender grass sheweth **i.**,
Isa 10:15 Shall the axe boast **i.** against him that
Isa 10:15 shall the saw magnify **i.** against him
Isa 10:15 rod should shake **i.** against them that
Isa 10:15 as if the staff should lift up **i.**, as if it
Isa 37:30 eat this year such as groweth of **i.**; and
Isa 55:2 and let your soul delight **i.** in fatness
Isa 60:20 neither shall thy moon withdraw **i.**
Jer 31:24 there shall dwell in Judah **i.**, and in
Eze 1:4 a great cloud, and a fire infolding **i.**,
Eze 4:14 not eaten of that which dieth of **i.**,
Eze 17:14 be base, that it might not lift **i.** up,
Eze 29:15 neither shall it exalt **i.** any more above
Eze 44:31 eat of any thing that is dead of **i.**,
Da 7:5 a bear, and it raised up **i.** on one side,
Mt 6:34 **take thought for the things of i.** *1438*
Mt 12:25 **Every kingdom divided against i.** *1438*
Mt 12:25 **city or house divided against i.** *1438*
Mk 3:24 **if a kingdom be divided against i.**, *1438*
Mk 3:25 **if a house be divided against i.**, *1438*
Lu 11:17 **Every kingdom divided against i. is** *1438*
Jo 15:4 **the branch cannot bear fruit of i.**, *1438*
Jo 20:7 wrapped together in a place by **i.** *5565*
Jo 21:25 even the world **i.** could not contain *846*
Ro 8:16 Spirit **i.** beareth witness with our *846*
Ro 8:21 creature **i.** also shall be delivered *846*
Ro 8:26 the Spirit **i.** maketh intercession for *846*
Ro 14:14 there is nothing unclean of **i.**: but *1438*
1Co 11:14 Doth not even nature **i.** teach you, *846*
1Co 13:4 charity vaunteth not **i.**, is not puffed
1Co 13:5 Doth not behave **i.** unseemly,
2Co 10:5 every high thing that exalteth **i.**
Eph 4:16 of the body unto the edifying of **i.** *1438*
Heb 9:24 into heaven **i.**, now to appear in the *846*
3Jo 12 of all men, and of the truth **i.** *846*

ITTAH-KAZIN (it''-tah-ka'-zin)
Jos 19:13 the east to Gittah-hepher, to **I.**, 6278

ITTAI (it'-ta-i) See also ITHAI.
2Sa 15:19 said the king to **I.** the Gittite, 863
2Sa 15:21 **I.** answered the king, and said, 863
2Sa 15:22 David said to **I.**, Go and pass over 863
2Sa 15:22 And **I.** the Gittite passed over, 863
2Sa 18:2 a third part...under the hand of **I.** 863
2Sa 18:5 commanded Joab and Abishai and **I.**, 863
2Sa 18:12 charged thee and Abishai and **I.**, 863
2Sa 23:29 **I.** the son of Ribai out of Gibeah 863

ITURAEA (i-tu-re'-ah)
Lu 3:1 his brother Philip tetrarch of **I.** *2484*

IVAH (i'-vah) See also AHAVA; AVA.
2Ki 18:34 of Sepharvaim, Hena, and **I.**? 5755
2Ki 19:13 of Sepharvaim, of Hena, and **I.**? 5755
Isa 37:13 city of Sepharvaim, Hena, and **I.**? 5755

IVORY
1Ki 10:18 the king made a great throne of **i.**, 8127
1Ki 10:22 silver, **i.**, and apes, and peacocks. 8143
1Ki 22:39 and the **i.** house which he made, 8127
2Ch 9:17 the king made a great throne of **i.**, 8127
2Ch 9:21 silver, **i.**, and apes, and peacocks. 8143
Ps 45:8 and cassia, out of the **i.** palaces, 8127
Ca 5:14 his belly is as bright **i.** overlaid 8127
Ca 7:4 Thy neck is as a tower of **i.**; thine 8127
Eze 27:6 have made thy benches of **i.**, 8127
Eze 27:15 for a present horns of **i.** and ebony 8127
Am 3:15 houses of **i.** shall perish, and the 8127
Am 6:4 That lie upon beds of **i.**, and stretch 8127
Re 18:12 wood, and all manner vessels of **i.**, *1661*

IZEHAR (iz'-e-har) See also IZEHARITES; IZHAR.
Nu 3:19 families; Amram, and **I.**, Hebron, 3324

IZEHARITES (iz'-e-har-ites) See also IZHARITE.
Nu 3:27 and the family of the **I.**, and the 3325

IZHAR (iz-har) See also IZEHAR; IZHARITES.
Ex 6:18 sons of Kohath; Amram, and **I.**, 3324
Ex 6:21 the sons of **I.**; Korah, and Nepheg, 3324
Nu 16:1 the son of **I.**, the son of Kohath, 3324
1Ch 6:2 the sons of Kohath; Amram, **I.**, 3324
1Ch 6:18 of Kohath were, Amram, and **I.**, 3324
1Ch 6:38 The son of **I.**, the son of Kohath, 3324
1Ch 23:12 of Kohath; Amram, **I.**, Hebron, 3324
1Ch 23:18 sons of **I.** Shelomith the chief: 3324

IZHARITES (iz'-har-ites) See also IZEHARITES.
1Ch 24:22 Of the **I.**; Shelomoth: of the sons 3325
1Ch 26:23 Of the Amramites, and the **I.**, 3325
1Ch 26:29 Of the **I.**, Chenaniah and his sons 3325

IZRAHIAH (iz-ra-hi'-ah) See also JEZRAHIAH.
1Ch 7:3 And the sons of Uzzi; **I.**: and the 3156
1Ch 7:3 sons of **I.**; Michael, and Obadiah, 3156

IZRAHITE (iz'-ra-hite) See also EZRAHITE.
1Ch 27:8 fifth month was Shamhuth the **I.** 3155

IZRI (iz'-ri) See also ZERI.
1Ch 25:11 fourth to **I.**, he, his sons, and his 3342

J.

JAAKAN (ja'-a-kan) See also AKAN; BENE-JAAKAN.
De 10:6 Beeroth of the children of **J.** to 3292

JAAKOBAH (ja-ak'-o-bah)
1Ch 4:36 Elioenai, and **J.**, and Jeshohaiah, 3291

JAALA (ja'-a-lah) See also JAALAH.
Ne 7:58 The children of **J.**, the children 3279

JAALAH (ja'-a-lah) See also JAALA.
Ezr 2:56 The children of **J.**, the children of 3279

JAALAM (ja'-a-lam)
Ge 36:5 Aholibamah bare Jeush, and **J.**, 3281
Ge 36:14 to Esau Jeush and **J.**, and Korah 3281
Ge 36:18 duke Jeush, duke **J.**, duke Korah: 3281
1Ch 1:35 and Jeush, and **J.**, and Korah. 3281

JAAN See DAN-JAAN.

JAANAI (ja'-a-nahee)
1Ch 5:12 and **J.**, and Shaphat in Bashan. 3285

JAARE-OREGIM (ja''-a-re-or'-eg-im) See also JAIR.
2Sa 21:19 where Elhanan the son of **J.**, 3296

JAASAU (ja-a'-saw)
Ezr 10:37 Mattaniah, Mattenai, and **J.**, 3299

JAASIEL (ja-a'-se-el)
1Ch 27:21 of Benjamin, **J.** the son of Abner: 3300

JAAZANIAH (ja-az-a-ni'-ah) See also JEZANIAH.
2Ki 25:23 and **J.** the son of a Maachathite, 2970
Jer 35:3 Then I took **J.** the son of Jeremiah, 2970
Eze 8:11 them stood **J.** the son of Shaphan, 2970
Eze 11:1 whom I saw **J.** the son of Azur, 2970

JAAZER (ja-a'-zer) See also JAZER.
Nu 21:32 And Moses sent to spy out **J.**, 3270
Nu 32:35 And Atroth, Shophan, and **J.**, 3270

JAAZIAH (ja-a-zi'-ah)
1Ch 24:26 and Mushi: the sons of **J.**; Beno 3269
1Ch 24:27 The sons of Merari by **J.**; Beno, and 3269

JAAZIEL (ja-a'-ze-el) See also AZIEL.
1Ch 15:18 degree, Zechariah, Ben, and **J.**, 3268

JABAL (ja'-bal)
Ge 4:20 Adah bare **J.**: he was the father 2989

JABBOK (jab'-bok)
Ge 32:22 and passed over the ford **J.** 2999
Nu 21:24 his land from Arnon unto **J.**, 2999
De 2:37 nor unto any place of the river **J.**, 2999
De 3:16 the border even unto the river **J.**, 2999
Jos 12:2 half Gilead, even unto the river **J.**, 2999
Jg 11:13 from Arnon even unto **J.**, and unto 2999
Jg 11:22 Amorites, from Arnon even unto **J.**, 2999

JABESH (ja'-besh) See also JABESH-GILEAD.
1Sa 11:1 the men of **J.** said unto Nahash, 3003
1Sa 11:3 And the elders of **J.** said unto him, 3003
1Sa 11:5 him the tidings of the men of **J.** 3003
1Sa 11:9 and shewed it to the men of **J.**; 3003
1Sa 11:10 the men of **J.** said, To morrow we 3003
1Sa 31:12 and came to **J.**, and burnt them 3003
1Sa 31:13 and buried them under a tree at **J.**, 3003
2Ki 15:10 the son of **J.** conspired against him, 3003
2Ki 15:13 the son of **J.** began to reign 3003
2Ki 15:14 and smote Shallum the son of **J.** 3003
1Ch 10:12 and brought them to **J.**, and buried 3003
1Ch 10:12 their bones under the oak in **J.**, 3003

JABESH-GILEAD (ja''-besh-ghil'-e-ad)
Jg 21:8 none to the camp from **J.** to 3003,1568
Jg 21:9 none of the inhabitants of **J.** 3003,1568
Jg 21:10 and smite the inhabitants of **J.** 3003,1568
Jg 21:12 among the inhabitants of **J.** 3003,1568
Jg 21:14 saved alive of the women of **J.** 3003,1568
1Sa 11:1 up, and encamped against **J.** 3003,1568
1Sa 11:9 shall ye say unto the men of **J.**, 3003,1568
1Sa 31:11 inhabitants of **J.** heard of that 3003,1568
2Sa 2:4 men of **J.** were they that buried 3003,1568
2Sa 2:5 messengers unto the men of **J.**, 3003,1568
2Sa 21:12 his son from the men of **J.**, 3003,1568
1Ch 10:11 **J.** heard all that the Philistines 3003,1568

JABEZ (ja'-bez)
1Ch 2:55 of the scribes which dwelt at **J.**; 3258
1Ch 4:9 **J.** was more honourable than his 3258
1Ch 4:9 and his mother called his name **J.**, 3258
1Ch 4:10 And **J.** called on the God of Israel, 3258

JABIN (ja'-bin) See also JABIN'S.
Jos 11:1 when **J.** king of Hazor had heard 2985
Jg 4:2 into the hand of **J.** king of Canaan, 2985
Jg 4:17 was peace between **J.** the king of 2985
Jg 4:23 God subdued on that day **J.** the 2985
Jg 4:24 prevailed against **J.** the king of 2985
Jg 4:24 until they had destroyed **J.** king of 2985
Ps 83:9 as to **J.** at the brook of Kison: 2985

JABIN'S (ja'-bins)
Jg 4:7 Sisera, the captain of **J.** army, 2985

JABNEEL (jab'-ne-el) See also JABNEH.
Jos 15:11 mount Baalah, and went unto **J.**; 2995
Jos 19:33 Adami, Nekeb, and **J.**, unto Lakum; 2995

JABNEH (jab'-neh) See also JABNEEL.
2Ch 26:6 wall of Gath, and the wall of **J.**, 2996

JACHAN (ja'-kan) See also AKAN.
1Ch 5:13 Jorai, and **J.**, and Zia, and Heber 3275

JACHIN (ja'-kin) See also JACHINITES; JARIB.
Ge 46:10 Jamin, and Ohad, and **J.**, and 3199
Ex 6:15 Jamin, and Ohad, and **J.**, and 3199
Nu 26:12 of **J.**, the family of the Jachinites: 3199
1Ki 7:21 and called the name thereof **J.** 3199
1Ch 9:10 Jedaiah, and Jehoiarib, and **J.**, 3199
1Ch 24:17 The one and twentieth to **J.**, the 3199
2Ch 3:17 name of that on the right hand **J.** 3199
Ne 11:10 Jedaiah the son of Joiarib, **J.** 3199

JACHINITES (ja'-kin-ites)
Nu 26:12 of Jachin, the family of the **J.** 3200

JACINTH
Re 9:17 breastplates of fire, and of **j.** *5191*
Re 21:20 the eleventh, a **j.**; the twelfth, an *5192*

JACOB (ja'-cub) See also ISRAEL; JACOB'S; JAMES.
Ge 25:26 heel; and his name was called **J.** 3290
Ge 25:27 **J.** was a plain man, dwelling in 3290
Ge 25:28 venison: but Rebekah loved **J.** 3290
Ge 25:29 And **J.** sod pottage: and Esau came 3290
Ge 25:30 Esau said to **J.**, Feed me, I pray 3290
Ge 25:31 and **J.** said, Sell me this day thy 3290
Ge 25:33 And **J.** said, Swear to me this day; 3290
Ge 25:33 and he sold his birthright unto **J.** 3290
Ge 25:34 **J.** gave Esau bread and pottage of 3290
Ge 27:6 Rebekah spake unto **J.** her son, 3290
Ge 27:11 **J.** said to Rebekah his mother, 3290
Ge 27:15 put them upon **J.** her younger son: 3290
Ge 27:17 into the hand of her son **J.** 3290
Ge 27:19 **J.** said unto his father, I am Esau 3290
Ge 27:21 Isaac said unto **J.**, Come near, I 3290
Ge 27:22 **J.** went near unto Isaac his father; 3290
Ge 27:30 had made an end of blessing **J.**, 3290

Ge	27:30	**J.** was yet scarce gone out from	3290
Ge	27:36	said, Is not he rightly named **J.**?	3290
Ge	27:41	Esau hated **J.** because of the	3290
Ge	27:41	then will I slay my brother **J.**.	3290
Ge	27:42	sent and called **J.** her younger son,	3290
Ge	27:46	if **J.** take a wife of the daughters of	3290
Ge	28:1	Isaac called **J.**, and blessed him,	3290
Ge	28:5	Isaac sent away **J.**: and he went	3290
Ge	28:6	Esau saw that Isaac had blessed **J.**,	3290
Ge	28:7	**J.** obeyed his father and his mother,	3290
Ge	28:10	**J.** went out from Beer-sheba, and	3290
Ge	28:16	**J.** awaked out of his sleep, and he	3290
Ge	28:18	**J.** rose up early in the morning,	3290
Ge	28:20	**J.** vowed a vow, saying, If God will	3290
Ge	29:1	Then **J.** went on his journey, and	3290
Ge	29:4	**J.** said unto them, My brethren,	3290
Ge	29:10	when **J.** saw Rachel the daughter	3290
Ge	29:10	**J.** went near, and rolled the stone	3290
Ge	29:11	and **J.** kissed Rachel, and lifted up	3290
Ge	29:12	**J.** told Rachel that he was her	3290
Ge	29:13	when Laban heard the tidings of **J.**	3290
Ge	29:15	Laban said unto **J.**, Because thou	3290
Ge	29:18	**J.** loved Rachel; and said, I will	3290
Ge	29:20	**J.** served seven years for Rachel;	3290
Ge	29:21	**J.** said unto Laban, Give me my	3290
Ge	29:28	**J.** did so, and fulfilled her week:	3290
Ge	30:1	saw that she bare **J.** no children,	3290
Ge	30:1	and said unto **J.**, Give me children,	3290
Ge	30:4	to wife: and **J.** went in unto her.	3290
Ge	30:5	Bilhah conceived, and bare **J.** a son.	3290
Ge	30:7	again, and bare **J.** a second son.	3290
Ge	30:9	her maid, and gave her **J.** to wife.	3290
Ge	30:10	Zilpah Leah's maid bare **J.** a son.	3290
Ge	30:12	Leah's maid bare **J.** a second son.	3290
Ge	30:16	And **J.** came out of the field in the	3290
Ge	30:17	conceived, and bare **J.** the fifth son.	3290
Ge	30:19	again, and bare **J.** the sixth son.	3290
Ge	30:25	**J.** said unto Laban, Send me away,	3290
Ge	30:31	**J.** said, Thou shalt not give me any	3290
Ge	30:36	journey betwixt himself and **J.**	3290
Ge	30:36	**J.** fed the rest of Laban's flocks.	3290
Ge	30:37	**J.** took him rods of green poplar,	3290
Ge	30:40	**J.** did separate the lambs, and set	3290
Ge	30:41	that **J.** laid the rods before the eyes	3290
Ge	31:1	**J.** hath taken away all that was our	3290
Ge	31:2	**J.** beheld the countenance of	3290
Ge	31:3	the Lord said unto **J.**, Return unto	3290
Ge	31:4	**J.** sent and called Rachel and Leah	3290
Ge	31:11	unto me in a dream, saying, **J.**	3290
Ge	31:17	**J.** rose up, and set his sons and his	3290
Ge	31:20	**J.** stole away unawares to Laban	3290
Ge	31:22	on the third day that **J.** was fled.	3290
Ge	31:24	speak not to **J.** either good or bad	3290
Ge	31:25	Then Laban overtook **J.**.	3290
Ge	31:25	Now **J.** had pitched his tent in the	3290
Ge	31:26	Laban said to **J.**, What hast thou	3290
Ge	31:29	speak not to **J.** either good or bad	3290
Ge	31:31	**J.** answered and said to Laban,	3290
Ge	31:32	**J.** knew not that Rachel had stolen	3290
Ge	31:36	And **J.** was wroth, and chode with	3290
Ge	31:36	and **J.** answered and said to Laban,	3290
Ge	31:43	Laban answered and said unto **J.**,	3290
Ge	31:45	**J.** took a stone, and set it up for a	3290
Ge	31:46	**J.** said unto his brethren, Gather	3290
Ge	31:47	but **J.** called it Galeed.	3290
Ge	31:51	Laban said to **J.**, Behold this heap,	3290
Ge	31:53	**J.** sware by the fear of his father	3290
Ge	31:54	**J.** offered sacrifice upon the mount,	3290
Ge	32:1	**J.** went on his way, and the angels	3290
Ge	32:2	when **J.** saw them, he said, This is	3290
Ge	32:3	**J.** sent messengers before him to	3290
Ge	32:4	Esau; Thy servant **J.** saith thus,	3290
Ge	32:6	the messengers returned to **J.**,	3290
Ge	32:7	Then **J.** was greatly afraid and	3290
Ge	32:9	And **J.** said, O God of my father	3290
Ge	32:20	Behold, thy servant **J.** is behind us.	3290
Ge	32:24	And **J.** was left alone: and there	3290
Ge	32:27	What is thy name? And he said, **J.**.	3290
Ge	32:28	name shall be called no more **J.**,	3290
Ge	32:29	**J.** asked him, and said, Tell me,	3290
Ge	32:30	And **J.** called the name of the place	3290
Ge	33:1	**J.** lifted up his eyes, and looked,	3290
Ge	33:10	And **J.** said, Nay, I pray thee, if	3290
Ge	33:17	**J.** journeyed to Succoth, and built	3290
Ge	33:18	And **J.** came to Shalem, a city of	3290
Ge	34:1	of Leah, which she bare unto **J.**,	3290
Ge	34:3	unto Dinah the daughter of **J.**,	3290
Ge	34:5	**J.** heard that he had defiled Dinah	3290
Ge	34:5	**J.** held his peace until they were	3290
Ge	34:6	out unto **J.** to commune with him.	3290
Ge	34:7	the sons of **J.** came out of the field	3290
Ge	34:13	the sons of **J.** answered Shechem	3290
Ge	34:25	two of the sons of **J.**, Simeon and	3290
Ge	34:27	The sons of **J.** came upon the slain,	3290
Ge	34:30	**J.** said to Simeon and Levi, Ye have	3290
Ge	35:1	God said unto **J.**, Arise, go up to	3290
Ge	35:2	**J.** said unto his household, and to	3290
Ge	35:4	gave unto **J.** all the strange gods	3290
Ge	35:4	**J.** hid them under the oak which	3290
Ge	35:5	did not pursue after the sons of **J.**	3290
Ge	35:6	**J.** came to Luz, which is in the land	3290
Ge	35:9	God appeared unto **J.** again, when	3290
Ge	35:10	said unto him, Thy name is **J.**	3290
Ge	35:10	shall not be called any more **J.**,	3290
Ge	35:14	**J.** set up a pillar in the place where	3290
Ge	35:15	And **J.** called the name of the place	3290
Ge	35:20	And **J.** set a pillar upon her grave:	3290
Ge	35:22	Now the sons of **J.** were twelve:	3290
Ge	35:26	these are the sons of **J.**, which were	3290
Ge	35:27	**J.** came unto Isaac his father unto	3290
Ge	35:29	his sons Esau and **J.** buried him.	3290
Ge	36:6	from the face of his brother **J.**	3290
Ge	37:1	**J.** dwelt in the land wherein his	3290
Ge	37:2	These are the generations of **J.**.	3290
Ge	37:34	And **J.** rent his clothes, and put	3290
Ge	42:1	when **J.** saw that there was corn in	3290
Ge	42:1	**J.** said unto his sons, Why do ye	3290
Ge	42:4	**J.** sent not with his brethren;	3290
Ge	42:29	they came unto **J.** their father unto	3290
Ge	42:36	And **J.** their father said unto them,	3290
Ge	45:25	into the land of Canaan unto **J.**	3290
Ge	45:27	the spirit of **J.** their father revived:	3290
Ge	46:2	of the night, and said, **J.**, **J.**	3290
Ge	46:5	And **J.** rose up from Beer-sheba:	3290
Ge	46:5	the sons of Israel carried **J.** their	3290
Ge	46:6	came into Egypt, **J.**, and all his	3290
Ge	46:8	came into Egypt, **J.** and his sons:	3290
Ge	46:15	of Leah, which she bare unto **J.** in	3290
Ge	46:18	and these she bare unto **J.**, even	3290
Ge	46:22	of Rachel, which were born to **J.**	3290
Ge	46:25	and she bare these unto **J.**: all the	3290
Ge	46:26	souls that came with **J.** into Egypt,	3290
Ge	46:27	all the souls of the house of **J.**,	3290
Ge	47:7	Joseph brought in **J.** his father,	3290
Ge	47:7	Pharaoh: and **J.** blessed Pharaoh.	3290
Ge	47:8	Pharaoh said unto **J.**, How old art	3290
Ge	47:9	**J.** said unto Pharaoh, The days of	3290
Ge	47:10	**J.** blessed Pharaoh, and went out	3290
Ge	47:28	And **J.** lived in the land of Egypt	3290
Ge	47:28	whole age of **J.** was an hundred	3290
Ge	48:2	one told **J.**, and said, Behold, thy	3290
Ge	48:3	**J.** said unto Joseph, God Almighty	3290
Ge	49:1	**J.** called unto his sons, and said,	3290
Ge	49:2	together, and hear, ye sons of **J.**;	3290
Ge	49:7	I will divide them in **J.**, and scatter	3290
Ge	49:24	the hands of the mighty God of **J.**;	3290
Ge	49:33	**J.** had made an end of commanding	3290
Ge	50:24	to Abraham, to Isaac, and to **J.**.	3290
Ex	1:1	and his household came with **J.**	3290
Ex	1:5	that came out of the loins of **J.**	3290
Ex	2:24	Abraham, with Isaac, and with **J.**,	3290
Ex	3:6,	15 God of Isaac, and the God of **J.**	3290
Ex	3:16	of Abraham, of Isaac, and of **J.**,	3290
Ex	4:5	the God of Isaac, and the God of **J.**,	3290
Ex	6:3	Abraham, unto Isaac, and unto **J.**,	3290
Ex	6:8	to Abraham, to Isaac, and to **J.**;	3290
Ex	19:3	shalt thou say to the house of **J.**,	3290
Ex	33:1	to Abraham, to Isaac, and to **J.**,	3290
Le	26:42	I remember my covenant with **J.**,	3290
Nu	23:7	Come, curse me **J.**, and come, defy	3290
Nu	23:10	Who can count the dust of **J.**, and	3290
Nu	23:21	He hath not beheld iniquity in **J.**,	3290
Nu	23:23	there is no enchantment against **J.**,	3290
Nu	23:23	this time it shall be said of **J.** and	3290
Nu	24:5	How goodly are thy tents, O **J.**,	3290
Nu	24:17	there shall come a Star out of **J.**,	3290
Nu	24:19	Out of **J.** shall come he that shall	3290
Nu	32:11	Abraham, unto Isaac, and unto **J.**;	3290
De	1:8	fathers, Abraham, Isaac, and **J.**,	3290
De	6:10	to Abraham, to Isaac, and to **J.**,	3290
De	9:5	fathers, Abraham, Isaac, and **J.**	3290
De	9:27	servants, Abraham, Isaac, and **J.**;	3290
De	29:13	to Abraham, to Isaac, and to **J.**.	3290
De	30:20	to Abraham, to Isaac, and to **J.**,	3290
De	32:9	**J.** is the lot of his inheritance.	3290
De	33:4	inheritance of...congregation of **J.**.	3290
De	33:10	They shall teach **J.** thy judgments,	3290
De	33:28	fountain of **J.** shall be upon a land	3290
De	34:4	Abraham, unto Isaac, and unto **J.**,	3290
Jos	24:4	And I gave unto Isaac **J.** and Esau:	3290
Jos	24:4	but **J.** and his children went down	3290
Jos	24:32	parcel of ground which **J.** bought	3290
1Sa	12:8	When **J.** was come into Egypt, and	3290
2Sa	23:1	the anointed of the God of **J.**, and	3290
1Ki	18:31	of the tribes of the sons of **J.**,	3290
2Ki	13:23	with Abraham, Isaac, and **J.**, and	3290
2Ki	17:34	Lord commanded the children of **J.**,	3290
1Ch	16:13	ye children of **J.**, his chosen ones.	3290
1Ch	16:17	confirmed the same to **J.** for a law,	3290
Ps	14:7	**J.** shall rejoice, and Israel shall be	3290
Ps	20:1	name of the God of **J.** defend thee;	3290
Ps	22:23	all ye the seed of **J.**, glorify him;	3290
Ps	24:6	seek him, that seek thy face, O **J.**.	3290
Ps	44:4	God: command deliverances for **J.**.	3290
Ps	46:7,	11 the God of **J.** is our refuge.	3290
Ps	47:4	the excellency of **J.** whom he loved.	3290
Ps	53:6	**J.** shall rejoice, and Israel shall be	3290
Ps	59:13	let them know that God ruleth in **J.**	3290
Ps	75:9	I will sing praises to the God of **J.**.	3290
Ps	76:6	At thy rebuke, O God of **J.**, both	3290
Ps	77:15	people, the sons of **J.** and Joseph.	3290
Ps	78:5	he established a testimony in **J.**,	3290
Ps	78:21	so a fire was kindled against **J.**,	3290
Ps	78:71	brought him to feed **J.** his people,	3290
Ps	79:7	For they have devoured **J.**, and	3290
Ps	81:1	a joyful noise unto the God of **J.**.	3290
Ps	81:4	Israel, and a law of the God of **J.**.	3290
Ps	84:8	my prayer: give ear, O God of **J.**	3290
Ps	85:1	brought back the captivity of **J.**	3290
Ps	87:2	more than all the dwellings of **J.**.	3290
Ps	94:7	neither shall the God of **J.** regard it.	3290
Ps	99:4	judgment and righteousness in **J.**	3290
Ps	105:6	ye children of **J.** his chosen.	3290
Ps	105:10	confirmed the same unto **J.** for a	3290
Ps	105:23	**J.** sojourned in the land of Ham.	3290
Ps	114:1	house of **J.** from a people of strange	3290
Ps	114:7	at the presence of the God of **J.**;	3290
Ps	132:2	vowed unto the mighty God of **J.**;	3290
Ps	132:5	habitation for the mighty God of **J.**	3290
Ps	135:4	Lord hath chosen **J.** unto himself,	3290
Ps	146:5	that hath the God of **J.** for his help,	3290
Ps	147:19	He sheweth his word unto **J.**, his	3290
Isa	2:3	Lord, to the house of the God of **J.**;	3290
Isa	2:5	O house of **J.**, come ye, and let us	3290
Isa	2:6	forsaken thy people the house of **J.**,	3290
Isa	8:17	his face from the house of **J.**,	3290
Isa	9:8	The Lord sent a word into **J.**, and	3290
Isa	10:20	as are escaped of the house of **J.**,	3290
Isa	10:21	return, even the remnant of **J.**,	3290
Isa	14:1	For the Lord will have mercy on **J.**,	3290
Isa	14:1	they shall cleave to the house of **J.**	3290
Isa	17:4	the glory of **J.** shall be made thin,	3290
Isa	27:6	them that come of **J.** to take root:	3290
Isa	27:9	shall the iniquity of **J.** be purged;	3290
Isa	29:22	concerning the house of **J.**,	3290
Isa	29:22	**J.** shall not now be ashamed,	3290
Isa	29:23	and sanctify the Holy One of **J.**,	3290
Isa	40:27	Why sayest thou, O **J.**, and	3290
Isa	41:8	**J.** whom I have chosen, the seed	3290
Isa	41:14	Fear not, thou worm **J.**, and ye	3290
Isa	41:21	strong reasons, saith the King of **J.**.	3290
Isa	42:24	Who gave **J.** for a spoil, and Israel	3290
Isa	43:1	the Lord that created thee, O **J.**,	3290
Isa	43:22	thou hast not called upon me, O **J.**;	3290
Isa	43:28	and have given **J.** to the curse, and	3290
Isa	44:1	Yet now hear, O **J.** my servant;	3290
Isa	44:2	Fear not, O **J.**, my servant; and	3290
Isa	44:5	shall call himself by the name of **J.**;	3290
Isa	44:21	Remember these, O **J.** and Israel;	3290
Isa	44:23	for the Lord hath redeemed **J.**,	3290
Isa	45:4	For **J.** my servant's sake, and	3290
Isa	45:19	I said not unto the seed of **J.**, Seek	3290
Isa	46:3	Hearken unto me, O house of **J.**,	3290
Isa	48:1	Hear ye this, O house of **J.**, which	3290
Isa	48:12	Hearken unto me, O **J.** and Israel,	3290
Isa	48:20	Lord hath redeemed his servant **J.**.	3290
Isa	49:5	servant, to bring **J.** again to him,	3290
Isa	49:6	servant to raise up the tribes of **J.**,	3290

Isa 49:26 thy Redeemer, the mighty One of **J.** 3290
Isa 58:1 and the house of **J.** their sins. 3290
Isa 58:14 feed thee with the heritage of **J.** 3290
Isa 59:20 that turn from transgression in **J.**, 3290
Isa 60:16 thy Redeemer, the mighty One of **J.**, 3290
Isa 65:9 I will bring forth a seed out of **J.**, 3290
Jer 2:4 word of the Lord, O house of **J.**, 3290
Jer 5:20 Declare this in the house of **J.**, and 3290
Jer 10:16 The portion of **J.** is not like them: 3290
Jer 10:25 for they have eaten up **J.**, and 3290
Jer 30:10 fear thou not, O my servant **J.**, 3290
Jer 30:10 and **J.** shall return, and shall be in 3290
Jer 31:7 Sing with gladness for **J.**, and 3290
Jer 31:11 For the Lord hath redeemed **J.**, 3290
Jer 33:26 Then will I cast away the seed of **J.**, 3290
Jer 33:26 the seed of Abraham, Isaac, and **J.** 3290
Jer 46:27 fear not thou, O my servant **J.**, 3290
Jer 46:27 **J.** shall return, and be in rest and 3290
Jer 46:28 Fear thou not, O **J.** my servant, 3290
Jer 51:19 The portion of **J.** is not like them; 3290
La 1:17 hath commanded concerning **J.**, 3290
La 2:2 swallowed...the habitations of **J.**, 3290
La 2:3 burned against **J.** like a flaming 3290
Eze 20:5 unto the seed of the house of **J.**, 3290
Eze 28:25 that I have given to my servant **J.** 3290
Eze 37:25 the land that I have given unto **J.** 3290
Eze 39:25 I bring again the captivity of **J.**, 3290
Ho 10:11 plow, and **J.** shall break his clods. 3290
Ho 12:2 punish **J.** according to his ways; 3290
Ho 12:12 **J.** fled into the country of Syria, 3290
Am 3:13 ye, and testify in the house of **J.**, 3290
Am 6:8 I abhor the excellency of **J.**, and 3290
Am 7:2,5 thee: by whom shall **J.** arise? 3290
Am 8:7 hath sworn by the excellency of **J.**, 3290
Am 9:8 not utterly destroy the house of **J.**, 3290
Ob 10 thy violence against thy brother **J.** 3290
Ob 17 **J.** shall possess their posessions. 3290
Ob 18 And the house of **J.** shall be a fire, 3290
Mic 1:5 the transgression of **J.** is all this, 3290
Mic 1:5 What is the transgression of **J.**? 3290
Mic 2:7 that art named the house of **J.**, 3290
Mic 2:12 surely assemble, O **J.**, all of thee; 3290
Mic 3:1 Hear, I pray you, O heads of **J.**, 3290
Mic 3:8 declare unto **J.** his transgression, 3290
Mic 3:9 you, ye heads of the house of **J.**, 3290
Mic 4:2 and to the house of the God of **J.**; 3290
Mic 5:7 remnant of **J.** shall be in the midst 3290
Mic 5:8 remnant of **J.** shall be among the 3290
Mic 7:20 Thou wilt perform the truth to **J.**, 3290
Na 2:2 turned away the excellency of **J.**, 3290
Mal 1:2 saith the Lord: yet I loved **J.**, 3290
Mal 2:12 out of the tabernacles of **J.**, 3290
Mal 3:6 ye sons of **J.** are not consumed. 3290
Mt 1:2 begat **J.**; and **J.** begat Judas *2384*
Mt 1:15 Matthan; and Matthan begat **J.**; *2384*
Mt 1:16 And **J.** begat Joseph the husband *2384*
Mt 8:11 **with Abraham, and Isaac, and J.,** *2384*
Mt 22:32 **God of Isaac, and the God of J.?** *2384*
Mk 12:26 **God of Isaac, and the God of J.?** *2384*
Lu 1:33 he shall reign over the house of **J.** *2384*
Lu 3:34 Which was the son of **J.**, which was *2384*
Lu 13:28 **see Abraham, and Isaac, and J.,** *2384*
Lu 20:37 **God of Isaac, and the God of J.** *2384*
Joh 4:5 that **J.** gave to his son Joseph. *2384*
Joh 4:12 Art thou greater than our father **J.**, *2384*
Ac 3:13 of Abraham, and of Isaac, and of **J.**, *2384*
Ac 7:8 begat **J.**; and **J.** begat the twelve *2384*
Ac 7:12 when **J.** heard that there was corn *2384*
Ac 7:14 and called his father **J.** to him, *2384*
Ac 7:15 **J.** went down into Egypt, and died, *2384*
Ac 7:32 the God of Isaac, and the God of **J.** *2384*
Ac 7:46 find a tabernacle for the God of **J.** *2384*
Ro 9:13 **J.** have I loved, but Esau have I *2384*
Ro 11:26 turn away ungodliness from **J.** *2384*
Heb 11:9 in tabernacles with Isaac and **J.**, *2384*
Heb 11:20 By faith, Isaac blessed **J.** and Esau *2384*
Heb 11:21 By faith **J.**, when he was a dying, *2384*

JACOB'S (ja'-cubs)
Ge 27:22 voice is **J.** voice, but the hands 3290
Ge 28:5 Rebekah, **J.** and Esau's mother. 3290
Ge 30:2 And **J.** anger was kindled against 3290
Ge 30:42 were Laban's, and the stronger **J.** 3290
Ge 31:33 And Laban went into **J.** tent, and 3290
Ge 32:18 shalt say, They be thy servant **J.**; 3290
Ge 32:25 hollow of **J.** thigh was out of joint, 3290
Ge 32:32 he touched the hollow of **J.** thigh 3290
Ge 34:7 in Israel in lying with **J.** daughter; 3290
Ge 34:19 he had delight in **J.** daughter: 3290
Ge 35:23 Reuben, **J.** firstborn, and Simeon, 3290
Ge 45:26 **J.** heart fainted, for he believed
Ge 46:8 and his sons: Reuben, **J.** firstborn. 3290
Ge 46:19 sons of Rachel **J.** wife; Joseph, and 3290
Ge 46:26 of his loins, besides **J.** son's wives, 3290
Jer 30:7 it is even the time of **J.** trouble; 3290
Jer 30:18 again the captivity of **J.** tents, 3290
Mal 1:2 Was not Esau **J.** brother? saith 3290
Joh 4:6 Now **J.** well was there. Jesus *2384*

JADA (ja'-dah)
1Ch 2:28 of Onam were, Shammai, and **J.** 3047
1Ch 2:32 And the sons of **J.** the brother of 3047

JADAU (ja'-daw)
Ezr 10:43 Zabad, Zebina, **J.**, and Joel, 3035

JADDUA (jad'-du-ah)
Ne 10:21 Meshezabeel, Zadok, **J.**, 3037
Ne 12:11 Jonathan, and Jonathan begat **J.** 3037
Ne 12:22 Joiada, and Johanan, and **J.**, 3037

JADON (ja'-don)
Ne 3:7 and **J.** the Meronothite, the men 3036

JAEL (ja'-el)
Jg 4:17 away on his feet to the tent of **J.** 3278
Jg 4:18 And **J.** went out to meet Sisera, and 3278
Jg 4:21 **J.** Heber's wife took a nail of the 3278
Jg 4:22 **J.** came out to meet him, and said 3278
Jg 5:6 in the days of **J.**, the highways were 3278
Jg 5:24 Blessed above women shall **J.** the 3278

JAGUR (ja'-gur)
Jos 15:21 were Kabzeel, and Eder, and **J.**, 3017

JAH (jah) See also JEHOVAH.
Ps 68:4 upon the heavens by his name **J.**, 3050

JAHATH (ja'-hath)
1Ch 4:2 Reaiah the son of Shobal begat **J.**; 3189
1Ch 4:2 and **J.** begat Ahumai, and Lahad 3189
1Ch 6:20 Libni his son, **J.** his son, Zimmah 3189
1Ch 6:43 The son of **J.**, the son of Gershom, 3189
1Ch 23:10 sons of Shimei were, **J.**, Zina, and 3189
1Ch 23:11 And **J.** was the chief, and Zirah the 3189
1Ch 24:22 of the sons of Shelomoth; **J.** 3189
2Ch 34:12 the overseers of them were **J.** and 3189

JAHAZ (ja'-haz) See also JAHAZA; JAHAZAH; JAHZAH.
Nu 21:23 he came to **J.**, and fought against 3096
De 2:32 he and all his people, to fight at **J.** 3096
Jg 11:20 pitched in **J.**, and fought against 3096
Isa 15:4 voice shall be heard even unto **J.** 3096
Jer 48:34 even unto **J.**, have they uttered 3096

JAHAZA (ja-ha'-zah) See also JAHAZ.
Jos 13:18 **J.**, and Kedemoth, and Mephaath, 3096

JAHAZAH (ja-ha'-zah) See also JAHAZ.
Jos 21:36 suburbs, and **J.** with her suburbs, 3096
Jer 48:21 and upon **J.**, and upon Mephaath, 3096

JAHAZIAH (ja-ha-zi'-ah)
Ezr 10:15 and **J.** the son of Tikvah were 3167

JAHAZIEL (ja-ha'-ze-el)
1Ch 12:4 Jeremiah, and **J.**, and Johanan, 3166
1Ch 16:6 Benaiah also and **J.** the priests 3166
1Ch 23:19 **J.** the third, and Jekameam the 3166
1Ch 24:23 **J.** the third, Jekameam the fourth. 3166
2Ch 20:14 Then upon **J.** the son of Zechariah, 3166
Ezr 8:5 the son of **J.**, and with him three 3166

JAHDAI (jah'-dahee)
1Ch 2:47 sons of **J.**; Regem, and Jotham, 3056

JAHDIEL (jah'-de-el)
1Ch 5:24 and **J.**, mighty men of valour, 3164

JAHDO (jah'-do)
1Ch 5:14 the son of **J.**, the son of Buz; 3163

JAHLEEL (jah'-le-el) See also JAHLEELITES.
Ge 46:14 Zebulun; Sered, and Elon, and **J.** 3177
Nu 26:26 of **J.**, the family of the Jahleelites. 3177

JAHLEELITES (jah'-le-el-ites)
Nu 26:26 of Jahleel, the family of the **J.** 3178

JAHMAI (jah'-mahee)
1Ch 7:2 and Jeriel, and **J.**, and Jibsam, 3181

JAHZAH (jah'-zah) See also JAHAZ.
1Ch 6:78 suburbs, and **J.** with her suburbs, 3096

JAHZEEL (jah'-ze-el) See also JAHZEELITES; JAHZIEL.
Ge 46:24 sons of Naphtali; **J.**, and Guni, 3183
Nu 26:48 **J.**, the family of the Jahzeelites: 3183

JAHZEELITES (jah'-ze-el-ites)
Nu 26:48 of Jahzeel, the family of the **J.**: of 3184

JAHZERAH (jah'-ze-rah) See also AHAZAI.
1Ch 9:12 Adiel, the son of **J.**, the son of 3170

JAHZIEL (jah'-ze-el) See also JAHZEEL.
1Ch 7:13 sons of Naphtali; **J.**, and Guni, 3185

JAILOR
Ac 16:23 charging the **j.** to keep them *1200*

JAIR (ja'-ur) See also HAVOTH-JAIR; JAARE-ORE-GIM; JAIRITE.
Nu 32:41 **J.** the son of Manasseh went and 2971
De 3:14 **J.** the son of Manasseh took all 2971
Jos 13:30 towns of **J.**, which are in Bashan, 2971
Jg 10:3 And after him arose **J.**, a Gileadite, 2971
Jg 10:5 **J.** died, and was buried in Camon. 2971
1Ki 4:13 to him pertained the towns of **J.** 2971
1Ch 2:22 Segub begat **J.**, who had three and 2971
1Ch 2:23 and Aram, with the towns of **J.**, 2971
1Ch 20:5 Elhanan the son of **J.** slew Lahmi 3265
Es 2:5 name was Mordecai, the son of **J.**, 2971

JAIRITE (ja'-ur-ite)
2Sa 20:26 Ira also the **J.** was a chief ruler 2972

JAIRUS (ja-i'-rus)
Mk 5:22 of the synagogue, **J.** by name; *2383*
Lu 8:41 there came a man named **J.**, and *2383*

JAKAN (ja'-kan) See also AKAN; JAAKAN.
1Ch 1:42 Ezer; Bilhan, and Zavan, and **J.** 3292

JAKEH (ja'-keh)
Pr 30:1 The words of Agur the son of **J.**, 3348

JAKIM (ja'-kim)
1Ch 8:19 And **J.**, and Zichri, and Zabdi, 3356
1Ch 24:12 to Eliashib, the twelfth to **J.**, 3356

JALON (ja'-lon)
1Ch 4:17 and Mered, and Epher, and **J.** 3210

JAMBRES (jam'-brees)
2Ti 3:8 Jannes and **J.** withstood Moses. *2387*

JAMES (james) See also JACOB.
Mt 4:21 **J.** the son of Zebedee, and John *2385*
Mt 10:2 **J.** the son of Zebedee, and John *2385*
Mt 10:3 **J.** the son of Alphaeus, and *2385*
Mt 13:55 brethren, **J.**, and Joses, and Simon, *2385*
Mt 17:1 Jesus taketh Peter, **J.**, and John his *2385*
Mt 27:56 Mary the mother of **J.** and Joses, *2385*
Mk 1:19 **J.** the son of Zebedee, and John *2385*
Mk 1:29 and Andrew, with **J.** and John. *2385*
Mk 3:17 **J.**...and John the brother of **J.**; *2385*
Mk 3:18 and **J.** the son of Alphaeus, and *2385*
Mk 5:37 and **J.**, and John the brother of **J.** *2385*
Mk 6:3 the brother of **J.**, and Joses, and of *2385*
Mk 9:2 with him Peter, and **J.**, and John, *2385*
Mk 10:35 **J.** and John, the sons of Zebedee, *2385*
Mk 10:41 much displeased with **J.** and John. *2385*
Mk 13:3 Peter and **J.** and John and Andrew *2385*
Mk 14:33 with him Peter and **J.** and John, *2385*
Mk 15:40 Mary the mother of **J.** the less and *2385*
Mk 16:1 Mary the mother of **J.**, and Salome, *2385*
Lu 5:10 **J.**, and John, the sons of Zebedee, *2385*
Lu 6:14 Andrew his brother, **J.** and John, *2385*
Lu 6:15 Thomas, **J.** the son of Alphaeus, *2385*
Lu 6:16 And Judas the brother of **J.**, and *2385*
Lu 8:51 go in, save Peter, and **J.**, and John, *2385*
Lu 9:28 he took Peter and John and **J.**, and *2385*
Lu 9:54 his disciples **J.** and John saw this, *2385*
Lu 24:10 and Mary the mother of **J.**, and *2385*
Ac 1:13 abode...Peter, and **J.**, and John, *2385*
Ac 1:13 Matthew, **J.** the son of Alphaeus, *2385*
Ac 1:13 and Judas the brother of **J.** *2385*
Ac 12:2 he killed **J.** the brother of John *2385*
Ac 12:17 Go shew these things unto **J.**, and *2385*
Ac 15:13 **J.** answered, saying, Men and *2385*
Ac 21:18 Paul went in with us unto **J.**; *2385*
1Co 15:7 After that, he was seen of **J.**; then *2385*
Ga 1:19 I none, save **J.** the Lord's brother. *2385*
Ga 2:9 **J.**, Cephas, and John, who seemed *2385*
Ga 2:12 before that certain came from **J.**, *2385*

Jas *general title* The General Epistle Of **J.**........... *2385*
Jas 1:1 **J.**, a servant of God and of the.......... *2385*
Jude 1 of Jesus Christ, and brother of **J.**, ... *2385*

JAMIN (ja'-min) See also JAMINITES.
Ge 46:10 Jemuel, and **J.**, and Ohab, and........... 3226
Ex 6:15 Jemuel, and **J.**, and Ohab, and........... 3226
Nu 26:12 of **J.**, the family of the Jaminites: 3226
1Ch 2:27 of Jerahmeel were, Maaz, and **J.**,........ 3226
1Ch 4:24 of Simeon were, Nemuel, and **J.**, ... 3226
Ne 8:7 Sherebiah, **J.**, Akkub, Shabbethai, ... 3226

JAMINITES (ja'-min-ites)
Nu 26:12 of Jamin, the family of the **J.**............. 3228

JAMLECH (jam'-lek)
1Ch 4:34 Meshobab, and **J.**, and Joshah 3230

JANGLING
1Ti 1:6 turned aside unto vain **j.**; have........... *3150*

JANNA (jan'-nah)
Lu 3:24 Melchi, which was the son of **J.**,........ *2388*

JANNES (jan'-nees)
2Ti 3:8 **J.** and Jambres withstood Moses, ... *2389*

JANOAH (ja-no'-ah) See also JANOHAH.
2Ki 15:29 **J.**, and Kedesh, and Hazor, and......... 3239

JANOHAH (ja-no'-hah) See also JANOAH.
Jos 16:6 and passed by it on the east to **J.**; 3239
Jos 16:7 it went down from **J.** to Ataroth, ... 3239

JANUM (ja'-num)
Jos 15:53 And **J.**, and Beth-tappuah, and........... 3241

JAPHETH (ja'-feth)
Ge 5:32 Noah begat Shem, Ham, and **J.**. 3315
Ge 6:10 three sons, Shem, Ham, and **J.**. 3315
Ge 7:13 Noah, and Shem, and Ham, and **J.**, ... 3315
Ge 9:18 ark, were Shem, and Ham, and **J.**....... 3315
Ge 9:23 And Shem and **J.** took a garment, ... 3315
Ge 9:27 shall enlarge **J.**, and he shall dwell...... 3315
Ge 10:1 sons of Noah, Shem, Ham, and **J.**....... 3315
Ge 10:2 The sons of **J.**; Gomer, and Magog, ... 3315
Ge 10:21 of Eber, brother of **J.** the elder, ... 3315
1Ch 1:4 Noah, Shem, Ham, and **J.**................. 3315
1Ch 1:5 The sons of **J.**; Gomer, and Magog, ... 3315

JAPHIA (ja-fi'-ah)
Jos 10:3 and unto **J.** king of Lachish, and......... 3309
Jos 19:12 out to Daberath, and goeth up to **J.**,... 3309
2Sa 5:15 and Elishua, and Nepheg, and **J.**, ... 3309
1Ch 3:7 And Nogah, and Nepheg, and **J.**,......... 3309
1Ch 14:6 And Nogah, and nepheg, and **J.**, ... 3309

JAPHLET (jaf'-let) See also JAPHLETI.
1Ch 7:32 Heber begat **J.**, and Shomer, and....... 3310
1Ch 7:33 And the sons of **J.**; Pasach, and......... 3310
1Ch 7:33 These are the children of **J.**.............. 3310

JAPHLETI (jaf'-let-i) See also JAPHLET.
Jos 16:3 down westward to the coast of **J.**,....... 3311

JAPHO (ja'-fo) See also JOPPA.
Jos 19:46 Rakkon, with the border before **J.**...... 3305

JARAH (ja'-rah) See also JEHOADAH.
1Ch 9:42 And Ahaz begat **J.**; and **J.** begat........ 3294

JAREB (ja'-reb)
Ho 5:13 the Assyrian, and sent to king **J.**........ 3377
Ho 10:6 Assyria for a present to king **J.** 3377

JARED (ja'-red) See also JERED.
Ge 5:15 sixty and five years, and begat **J.**........ 3382
Ge 5:16 Mahalaleel lived after he begat **J.** 3382
Ge 5:18 **J.** lived an hundred sixty and two........ 3382
Ge 5:19 And **J.** lived after he begat Enoch 3382
Ge 5:20 the days of **J.** were nine hundred 3382
Lu 3:37 Enoch, which was the son of **J.**, ... *2391*

JARESIAH (ja-re-si'-ah)
1Ch 8:27 **J.**, and Eliah, and Zichri, the sons 3298

JARHA (jar'-hah)
1Ch 2:34 an Egyptian, whose name was **J.**........ 3398
1Ch 2:35 Sheshan gave his daughter to **J.**......... 3398

JARIB (ja'-rib) see also JACHIN.
1Ch 4:24 and Jamin, **J.**, Zerah, and Shaul:......... 3402
Ezr 8:16 for Elnathan, and for **J.**, and for......... 3402
Ezr 10:18 and Eliezer, and **J.**, and Gedaliah. 3402

JARKON See ME-JARKON.

JARMUTH (jar'-muth) See also REMETH.
Jos 10:3 unto Piram king of **J.**, and unto.......... 3412
Jos 10:3, 5 king of **J.**, the king of Lachish,......... 3412
Jos 10:23 the king of Hebron, the king of **J.** ....
Jos 12:11 The king of **J.**, one; the king of......... 3412
Jos 15:35 **J.**, and Adullam, Socoh, and Azekah,... 3412
Jos 21:29 **J.** with her suburbs, En-gannim 3412
Ne 11:29 and at Zareah, and at **J.**, ... 3412

JAROAH (ja-ro'-ah)
1Ch 5:14 the son of Huri, the son of **J.**,........... 3386

JASHEN (ja'-shen) See also HASHEM.
2Sa 23:32 the Shaalbonite, of the sons of **J.**, ... 3464

JASHER (ja'-shur)
Jos 10:13 not this written in the book of **J.**? 3477
2Sa 1:18 it is written in the book of **J.**............. 3477

JASHOBEAM (jash-o'-be-am)
1Ch 11:11 **J.**, an Hachmonite, the chief of the..... 3434
1Ch 12:6 and Joezer, and **J.**, the Korhites, ... 3434
1Ch 27:2 month was **J.** the son of Zabdiel:........ 3434

JASHUB (ja'-shub) See also JASHUBI-LEHEM; JOB; JASHUBITES; SHEAR-JASHUB.
Nu 26:24 **J.**, the family of the Jashubites:.......... 3437
1Ch 7:1 Puah, **J.**, and Shimrom, four. 3437
Ezr 10:29 and Adaiah, **J.**, and Sheal, and........... 3437

JASHUBI-LEHEM (jash''-u-bi-le'-hem)
1Ch 4:22 had the dominion in Moab, and **J.**....... 3433

JASHUBITES (jash'-u-bites)
Nu 26:24 Of Jashub, the family of the **J.**........... 3432

JASIEL (ja'-se-el)
1Ch 11:47 and Obed, and **J.** the Mesobaite..............

JASON (ja'-sun)
Ac 17:5 and assaulted the house of **J.**, and...... *2394*
Ac 17:6 they drew **J.** and certain brethren *2394*
Ac 17:7 Whom **J.** hath received: and these...... *2394*
Ac 17:9 when they had taken security of **J.**, ... *2394*
Ro 16:21 Lucius, and **J.**, and Sosipater, my....... *2394*

JASPER
Ex 28:20 a beryl, and an onyx, and a **j.**............ 3471
Ex 39:13 row, a beryl, an onyx, and a **j.** 3471
Eze 28:13 the onyx, and the **j.**, the sapphire, ... 3471
Re 4:3 to look upon like a **j.** and a sardine..... *2393*
Re 21:11 even like a **j.** stone, clear as crystal;... *2393*
Re 21:18 building of the wall of it was of **j.**........ *2393*
Re 21:19 The first foundation was **j.**; the.......... *2393*

JATHNIEL (jath'-ne-el)
1Ch 26:2 Zebadiah the thrid, **J.** the fourth,........ 3496

JATTIR (jat'-tur)
Jos 15:48 in the mountains, Shamir, and **J.**, ... 3492
Jos 21:14 **J.** with her suburbs, and Eshtemoa..... 3492
1Sa 30:27 and to them which were in **J.**,............. 3492
1Ch 6:57 Libnah with her suburbs, and **J.**, ... 3492

JAVAN (ja'-van)
Ge 10:2 and **J.**, and Tubal, and Meshech,......... 3120
Ge 10:4 And the sons of **J.**; Elishah, and 3120
1Ch 1:5 and **J.**, and Tubal, and Meshech,......... 3120
1Ch 1:7 And the sons of **J.**; Elishah, and 3120
Isa 66:19 that draw the bow, to Tubal, and **J.**,... 3120
Eze 27:13 **J.**, Tubal, and Meshech, they were 3120
Eze 27:19 Dan also and **J.** going to and fro 3120

JAVELIN
Nu 25:7 and took a **j.** in his hand;.................. 7420
1Sa 18:10 and there was a **j.** in Saul's hand.......... 2595
1Sa 18:11 And Saul cast the **j.**; for he said, I 2595
1Sa 19:9 in his house with his **j.** in his hand:..... 2595
1Sa 19:10 David even to the wall with the **j.**; 2595
1Sa 19:10 and he smote the **j.** into the wall:....... 2595
1Sa 20:33 Saul cast a **j.** at him to smite him:...... 2595

JAW See also JAWBONE; JAWS.
Jg 15:16 with the **j.** of an ass have I slain a...... 3895
Jg 15:19 clave an hollow place that in the **j.**,..... 3895
Job 41:2 or bore his **j.** through with a thorn?.... 3895
Pr 30:14 their **j.** teeth as knives, to devour....... 4973

JAWBONE
Jg 15:15 he found a new **j.** of an ass, and 3895
Jg 15:16 With the **j.** of an ass, heaps upon........ 3895
Jg 15:17 he cast away the **j.** out of his hand,...... 3895

JAWS
Job 29:17 I brake the **j.** of the wicked, and........ 4973
Ps 22:15 and my tongue cleaveth to my **j.**; 4455
Isa 30:28 be a bridle in the **j.** of the people, ... 3895
Eze 29:4 I will put hooks in thy **j.**, and I will..... 3895
Eze 38:4 thee back, and put hooks into thy **j.**,... 3895
Ho 11:4 that take off the yoke on their **j.**, ... 3895

JAW-TEETH See JAW and TEETH.

JAZER (ja'-zur) See also JAAZER.
Nu 32:1 and when they saw the land of **J.**, ... 3270
Nu 32:3 Ataroth, and Dibon, and **J.**, and......... 3270
Jos 13:25 their coast was **J.**, and all the cities.... 3270
Jos 21:39 her suburbs, **J.** with her suburbs;....... 3270
2Sa 24:5 of the river of Gad, and toward **J.**........ 3270
1Ch 6:81 suburbs, and **J.** with her suburbs. 3270
1Ch 26:31 them men of valour at **J.** of Gilead. 3270
Isa 16:8 they are come even unto **J.**, they........ 3270
Isa 16:9 I will bewail with the weeping of **J.**..... 3270
Jer 48:32 weep for thee with the weeping of **J.**... 3270
Jer 48:32 they reach even to the sea of **J.** 3270

JAZIZ (ja'-ziz)
1Ch 27:31 over the flocks was **J.** the Hagerite 3151

JEALOUS
Ex 20:5 Lord thy God am a **j.** God, visiting..... 7067
Ex 34:14 Lord, whose name is **J.**, is a **j.** God: .. 7067
Nu 5:14 and he be **j.** of his wife, and she be.... 7065
Nu 5:14 he be **j.** of his wife, and she be not.... 7065
Nu 5:30 and he be **j.** over his wife, and shall ... 7065
De 4:24 is a consuming fire, even a **j.** God. 7067
De 5:9 for I the Lord thy God am a **j.** God. ... 7067
De 6:15 Lord thy God is a **j.** God among you).. 7067
Jos 24:19 he is an holy God; he is a **j.** God; 7072
1Ki 19:10, 14 I have been very **j.** for the Lord.... 7065
Eze 39:25 and will be **j.** for my holy name; 7065
Joe 2:18 Then will the Lord be **j.** for his land, .. 7065
Na 1:2 God is **j.**, and the Lord revengeth; 7072
Zec 1:14 I am **j.** for Jerusalem and for Zion 7065
Zec 8:2 I was **j.** for Zion with great jealousy,... 7065
Zec 8:2 and I was **j.** for her with great fury. ... 7065
2Co 11:2 am **j.** over you with godly jealousy: *2206*

JEALOUSIES
Nu 5:29 This is the law of **j.**, when a wife....... 7068

JEALOUSY See also JEALOUSIES.
Nu 5:14 And the spirit of **j.** come upon him, ... 7068
Nu 5:14 or if the spirit of **j.** come upon him, ... 7068
Nu 5:15 for it is an offering of **j.**, an offering.... 7068
Nu 5:18 her hands, which is the **j.** offering: 7068
Nu 5:25 the priest shall take the **j.** offering...... 7068
Nu 5:30 the spirit of **j.** cometh upon him, ... 7068
Nu 25:11 not the children of Israel in my **j.**........ 7068
De 29:20 his **j.** shall smoke against that man, ... 7068
De 32:16 provoked him to **j.** with strange 7065
De 32:21 They have moved me to **j.** with that... 7065
De 32:21 I will move them to **j.** with those 7065
1Ki 14:22 provoked him to **j.** with their sins....... 7065
Ps 78:58 moved him to **j.** with their graven 7065
Ps 79:5 for ever? shall thy **j.** burn like fire?..... 7068
Pr 6:3 For **j.** is the rage of a man: 7068
Ca 8:6 as death; **j.** is cruel as the grave:....... 7068
Isa 42:13 he shall stir up **j.** like a man of war: ... 7068
Eze 8:3 was the seat of the image of **j.**, ... 7068
Eze 8:3 which provoketh to **j.**........................ 7069
Eze 8:5 altar this image of **j.** in the entry........ 7068
Eze 16:38 I will give thee blood in fury and **j.**...... 7068
Eze 16:42 and my **j.** shall depart from thee, ... 7068
Eze 23:25 And I will set my **j.** against thee, ... 7068
Eze 36:5 in the fire of my **j.** have I spoken........ 7068
Eze 36:6 have spoken in my **j.** and in my fury,.. 7068
Eze 38:19 in my **j.** and in the fire of my wrath.... 7068
Zep 1:18 be devoured by the fire of his **j.** 7068
Zep 3:8 be devoured with the fire of my **j.**....... 7068
Zec 1:14 jealous...for Zion with a great **j.**.......... 7068
Zec 8:2 I was jealous for Zion with great **j.**, ... 7068
Ro 10:19 I will provoke you to **j.** by them...............
Ro 11:11 Gentiles, for to provoke them to **j.**..........
1Co 10:22 Do we provoke the Lord to **j.**? are we......
2Co 11:2 am jealous over you with godly **j.**........ *2205*

JEARIM (je'-a-rim) See also KIRJATH-JEARIM.
Jos 15:10 along unto the side of mount **J.**,.......... 3297

JEATERAI (je-at'-e-rahee)
1Ch 6:21 his son, Zerah his son, **J.** his son........ 2979

JEBERCHIAH (je-ber''-e-ki'-ah)
Isa 8:2 priest, and Zechariah the son of **J.**...... 3000

JEBUS (je'-bus) See also JEBUSI; JEBUSITE; JERUSALEM.
Jg 19:10 departed...came over against **J.**, ... 2982
Jg 19:11 And when they were by **J.**, the day..... 2982
1Ch 11:4 went to Jerusalem, which is **J.**;.......... 2982
1Ch 11:5 the inhabitants of **J.** said to David,...... 2982

JEBUSI (jeb'-u-si) See also JEBUSITE.
Jos 18:16 to the side of **J.** on the south, ... 2983
Jos 18:28 Eleph, and **J.**, which is Jerusalem, ... 2983

JEBUSITE (jeb'-u-site) See also JEBUSITES.
Ge 10:16 the **J.**, and the Amorite, and the........ 2983
Ex 33:2 the Perizzite, the Hivite, and the **J.**.... 2983
Ex 34:11 Perizzite, and the Hivite, and the **J.**.... 2983
Jos 9:1 Hivite, and the **J.**, heard thereof; 2983
Jos 11:3 and the **J.** in the mountains, ... 2983
Jos 15:8 unto the southside of the **J.**; 2983
2Sa 24:16 threshingplace of Araunah the **J.**. 2983
2Sa 24:18 threshingfloor of Araunah the **J.**. 2983
1Ch 1:14 The **J.** also, and the Amorite, and...... 2983
1Ch 21:15, 18 threshingfloor of Ornan the **J.**........ 2983
1Ch 21:28 the threshingfloor of Ornan the **J.**,...... 2983
2Ch 3:1 the threshingfloor of Ornan the **J.**....... 2983
Zec 9:7 in Judah, and Ekron as a **J.**.............. 2983

JEBUSITES (jeb'-u-sites)
Ge 15:21 and the Girgashites, and the **J.**. 2983
Ex 3:8 and the Hivites, and the **J.**................ 2983
Ex 3:17 and the Hivites, and the **J.**, unto a 2983
Ex 13:5 and the Hivites, and the **J.**, which...... 2983
Ex 23:23 Canaanites, the Hivites, and the **J.** 2983
Nu 13:29 the **J.**, and the Amorites, dwell in 2983
De 7:1 and the Hivites, and the **J.**, seven....... 2983
De 20:17 Perizzites, the Hivites, and the **J.**; 2983
Jos 3:10 and the Amorites, and the **J.**............ 2983
Jos 12:8 Perizzites, the Hivites, and the **J.** 2983
Jos 15:63 **J.** the inhabitants of Jerusalem, ... 2983
Jos 15:63 **J.** dwell with the children of Judah...... 2983
Jos 24:11 Girgashites, the Hivites, and the **J.**;.... 2983
Jg 1:21 out the **J.** that inhabited Jerusalem;..... 2983
Jg 1:21 the **J.** dwell with the children of......... 2983
Jg 3:5 and Perizzites, and Hivites, and **J.**....... 2983
Jg 19:11 let us turn in into this city of the **J.**,... 2983
2Sa 5:6 men went to Jerusalem unto the **J.**,.... 2983
2Sa 5:8 and smiteth the **J.**, and the lame........ 2983
1Ki 9:20 Hittites, Perizzites, Hivites, and **J.**,.... 2983
1Ch 11:4 where the **J.** were, the inhabitants 2983
1Ch 11:6 Whosoever smiteth the **J.** first shall.... 2983
2Ch 8:7 and the Hivites, and the **J.**, which...... 2983
Ezr 9:1 the Hittites, the Perizzites, the **J.**, ... 2983
Ne 9:8 and the **J.**, and the Girgashites, ... 2983

JECAMIAH (jek-a-mi'-ah) See also JEKAMIAH.
1Ch 3:18 and Shenazar, **J.**, Hoshama, and......... 3359

JECHOLIAH (jek-o-li'-ah) See also JECOLIAH.
2Ki 15:2 And his mother's name was **J.** of 3203

JECHONIAS (jek-o-ni'-as) See also JECONIAH.
Mt 1:11 Josias begat **J.** and his brethren, ... *2423*
Mt 1:12 to Babylon, **J.** begat Salathiel; *2423*

JECOLIAH (jek-o-li'-ah) See also JECHOLIAH.
2Ch 26:3 His mother's name also was **J.** of....... 3203

JECONIAH (jek-o-ni'-ah) See also CONIAH; JECHONIAS; JEHOIACHIN.
1Ch 3:16 **J.** his son, Zedekiah his son. 3204
1Ch 3:17 the sons of **J.**; Assir, Salathiel his 3204
Es 2:6 which had been carried away with **J.**.... 3204
Jer 24:1 had carried away captive **J.** the son 3204
Jer 27:20 when he carried away captive **J.** 3204
Jer 28:4 I will bring again to this place **J.** 3204
Jer 29:2 (After that **J.** the king, and the.......... 3204

JEDAIAH (jed-a-i'-ah)
1Ch 4:37 the son of Allon, the son of **J.**, the..... 3042
1Ch 9:10 of the priests; **J.**, and Jehoiarib, ... 3048
1Ch 24:7 forth to Jehoiarib, the second to **J.**, ... 3048
Ezr 2:36 the children of **J.**, of the house of 3048
Ne 3:10 repaired **J.** the son of Harumaph, ... 3042
Ne 7:39 the children of **J.**, of the house of 3048
Ne 11:10 Of the priests: **J.** the son of Joiarib,.... 3048
Ne 12:6 Shemaiah, and Joiarib, **J.**, ... 3048
Ne 12:7 Sallu, Amok, Hilkiah, **J.**................... 3048
Ne 12:19 of Joiarib, Mattenai; of **J.**, Uzzi;......... 3048
Ne 12:21 Hashabiah; of **J.**, Nethaneel............... 3048
Zec 6:10 of Heldai, of Tobijah, and of **J.**, ... 3048
Zec 6:14 Helem, and to Tobijah, and to **J.**,....... 3048

JEDIAEL (jed-e-a'-el)
1Ch 7:6 Bela, and Becher, and **J.**, three. 3043
1Ch 7:10 The sons also of **J.**; Bilhan: and......... 3043
1Ch 7:11 All these the sons of **J.**, by the 3043
1Ch 11:45 **J.** the son of Shimri, and Joha his....... 3043
1Ch 12:20 and Jozabad, and **J.**, and Michael,....... 3043
1Ch 26:2 the firstborn, **J.** the second,.............. 3043

JEDIDAH (je-di'-dah)
2Ki 22:1 his mother's name was **J.**, the.......... 3040

JEDIDIAH (jed-id-i'-ah) See also SOLOMON.
2Sa 12:25 called his name **J.**, because of the...... 3041

JEDUTHUN (jed'-u-thun)
1Ch 9:16 son of Galal, the son of **J.**, and.......... 3038
1Ch 16:38 Obed-edom also the son of **J.** and 3038
1Ch 16:41 And with them Heman and **J.**, and...... 3038
1Ch 16:42 And with them Heman and **J.** with...... 3038
1Ch 16:42 And the sons of **J.** were porters. 3038
1Ch 25:1 of Asaph, and of Heman, and of **J.**, ... 3038
1Ch 25:3 Of **J.**: the sons of **J.**; Gedaliah, and.... 3038
1Ch 25:3 under the hands of their father **J.**,...... 3038
1Ch 25:6 order to Asaph, **J.**, and Heman........... 3038
2Ch 5:12 of them of Asaph, of Heman, of **J.**, ... 3038
2Ch 29:14 and of the sons of **J.**; Shemaiah, ... 3038
2Ch 35:15 and Heman, and **J.** the king's seer;..... 3038
Ne 11:17 the son of Galal, the son **J.**............... 3038
Ps 39:*title* To the chief Musician, even to **J.**,....... 3038
Ps 62:*title* To the chief Musician, to **J.**, ... 3038
Ps 77:*title* To the chief Musician, to **J.**, ... 3038

JEEZER (je-e'-zur) See also ABIEZER; JEEZERITES.
Nu 26:30 of **J.**, the family of the Jeezerites:........ 372

JEEZERITES (je-e'-zur-ites)
Nu 26:30 of Jeezer, the family of the **J.** 373

JEGAR-SAHADUTHA (je''-gar-sa-ha-du'-thah) See also GALEED.
Ge 31:47 And Laban called it **J.**: but Jacob........ 3026

JEHALELEEL (je-hal-e'-le-el) See also JEHALELEL.
1Ch 4:16 the sons of **J.**: Ziph, and Ziphah, ... 3094

JEHALELEL (je-hal'-e-lel) See also JEHALELEEL.
2Ch 29:12 and Azariah the son of **J.**................... 3094

JEHDEIAH (jeh-di'-ah)
1Ch 24:20 of the sons of Shubael; **J.**. 3165
1Ch 27:30 the asses was **J.** the Meronothite:...... 3165

JEHEZEKEL (je-hez'-e-kel) See also EZEKIEL.
1Ch 24:16 to Pethahiah, the twentieth to **J.**,....... 3168

JEHIAH (je-hi'-ah) See also JEHIEL.
1Ch 15:24 **J.** were doorkeepers for the ark. 3174

JEHIEL (je-hi'-el) See also JEHIAH; JEIEL; JEHIELI.
1Ch 9:35 dwelt the father of Gibeon, **J.**,........... 3273
1Ch 11:44 Shama and **J.** the sons of Hothan 3273
1Ch 15:18, 20 Shemiramoth, and **J.**, and Unni, ... 3171
1Ch 16:5 and Shemiramoth, and **J.**, and........... 3171
1Ch 23:8 the chief was **J.**, and Zetham, and...... 3171
1Ch 27:32 **J.** the son of Hachmoni was with the .. 3171
1Ch 29:8 by the hand of **J.** the Gershonite........ 3171
2Ch 21:2 Azariah, and **J.**, and Zechariah, ... 3171
2Ch 29:14 sons of Heman; **J.**, and Shimei: 3171
2Ch 31:13 And **J.**, and Azaziah, and Nahath, ... 3171
2Ch 35:8 and Zechariah and **J.**, rulers of the 3171
Ezr 8:9 Obadiah the son of **J.**, and with him.... 3171
Ezr 10:2 Shechaniah the son of **J.**, one of the ... 3171
Ezr 10:21 and Elijah, and Shemaiah, and **J.**, ... 3171
Ezr 10:26 Zechariah, and **J.**, and Abdi, and........ 3171

JEHIELI (je-hi'-el-i) See also JEHIEL.
1Ch 26:21 Laadan the Gershonite, were **J.**. 3172
1Ch 26:22 The sons of **J.**; Zetham, and Joel 3172

JEHIZKIAH (je-hiz-ki'-ah) See also HEZEKIAH.
2Ch 28:12 **J.** the son of Shallum, and Amasa....... 3169

JEHOADAH (je-ho'-a-dah) See also JARAH.
1Ch 8:36 Ahaz begat **J.**; and **J.** begat 3085

JEHOADDAN (je-ho-ad'-dan)
2Ki 14:2 And his mother's name was **J.** of 3086
2Ch 25:1 And his mother's name was **J.** of 3086

JEHOAHAZ (je-ho'-a-haz) See also AHAZIAH; JOAHAZ; SHALLUM.
2Ki 10:35 **J.** his son reigned in his stead. 3059
2Ki 13:1 **J.** the son of Jehu began to reign 3059
2Ki 13:4 **J.** besought the Lord, and the Lord.... 3059
2Ki 13:7 leave of the people to **J.** but fifty 3059
2Ki 13:8 the rest of the acts of **J.**, and all........ 3059
2Ki 13:9 **J.** slept with his fathers; and they 3059
2Ki 13:10 began Jehoash the son of **J.** to reign... 3059
2Ki 13:22 oppressed Israel all the days of **J.**. 3059
2Ki 13:25 Jehoash the son of **J.** took again......... 3059
2Ki 13:25 he had taken out of the hand of **J.**....... 3059
2Ki 14:1 the second year of Joash son of **J.**....... 3099
2Ki 14:8 Jehoash, the son of **J.** son of Jehu, ... 3059
2Ki 14:17 after the death of Jehoash son of **J.** 3059
2Ki 23:30 the land took **J.** the son of Josiah, ... 3059
2Ki 23:31 **J.** was twenty and three years old...... 3059
2Ki 23:34 to Jehoiakim, and took **J.** away: 3059
2Ch 21:17 save **J.**, the youngest of his sons. 3059
2Ch 25:17 and sent to Joash, the son of **J.**, ... 3059
2Ch 25:23 the son of Joash, the son of **J.**, at 3059
2Ch 25:25 after the death of Joash son of **J.** 3059
2Ch 36:1 the land took **J.** the son of Josiah, ... 3059
2Ch 36:2 **J.** was twenty and three years old...... 3059
2Ch 36:4 Necho took **J.** his brother, and 3059

JEHOASH (je-ho'-ash) See also JOASH.
2Ki 11:21 Seven years old was **J.** when he 3060
2Ki 12:1 year of Jehu **J.** began to reign; 3060
2Ki 12:2 **J.** did that which was right in the 3060
2Ki 12:4 **J.** said to the priests, All the money ... 3060
2Ki 12:6 three and twentieth year of king **J.**...... 3060
2Ki 12:7 Then king **J.** called for Jehoiada the 3060
2Ki 12:18 And **J.** king of Judah took all the 3060
2Ki 13:10 began **J.** the son of Jehoahaz to 3060
2Ki 13:25 **J.** the son of Jehoahaz took again 3060
2Ki 14:8 Amaziah sent messengers to **J.**,......... 3060
2Ki 14:9 **J.** the king of Israel sent to Amaziah... 3060
2Ki 14:11 Therefore **J.** king of Israel went up; ... 3060
2Ki 14:13 And **J.** king of Israel took Amaziah 3060
2Ki 14:13 the son of **J.** the son of Ahaziah,........ 3060
2Ki 14:15 rest of the acts of **J.** which he did, ... 3060
2Ki 14:16 **J.** slept with his fathers, and was 3060
2Ki 14:17 the death of **J.** son of Jehoahaz 3060

JEHOHANAN (je-ho'-ha-nan) See also JOHANAN; JOHN.
1Ch 26:3 **J.** the sixth, Elioenai the seventh. 3076
2Ch 17:15 And next to him was **J.** the captain..... 3076
2Ch 23:1 Jeroham, and Ishmael the son of **J.**,.... 3076
Ezr 10:28 Of the sons also of Bebai; **J.**, ... 3076
Ne 12:13 Ezra, Meshullam; of Amariah, **J.**; 3076
Ne 12:42 Uzzi, and **J.**, and Malchijah, and......... 3076

JEHOIACHIN (je-hoy'-a-kin) See also CONIAH; JECONIAH; JECONIAS; JEHOIACHIN'S.
2Ki 24:6 **J.** his son reigned in his stead. 3078
2Ki 24:8 **J.** was eighteen years old when he 3078
2Ki 24:12 **J.** the king of Judah went out to......... 3078
2Ki 24:15 he carried away **J.** to Babylon, and..... 3078
2Ki 25:27 thirtieth year of the captivity of **J.** 3078
2Ki 25:27 lift up the head of **J.** king of Judah...... 3078
2Ch 36:8 **J.** his son reigned in his stead. 3078
2Ch 36:9 **J.** was eight years old when he.......... 3078
Jer 52:31 thirtieth year of the captivity of **J.** 3078
Jer 52:31 lifted up the head of **J.** king of........... 3078

JEHOIACHIN'S (je-hoy'-a-kins)
Eze 1:2 fifth year of king **J.** captivity,............ 3112

JEHOIADA (je-hoy'-a-dah) See also BERECHIAS; JOIADA.
2Sa 8:18 Benaiah the son of **J.** was over.......... 3111
2Sa 20:23 Benaiah the son of **J.** was over the..... 3111
2Sa 23:20 Benaiah the son of **J.**, the son of a..... 3111
2Sa 23:22 things did Benaiah the son of **J.**, ... 3111
1Ki 1:8 and Benaiah the son of **J.**, and........... 3111
1Ki 1:26 and Benaiah the son of **J.**, and thy 3111
1Ki 1:32 prophet, and Benaiah the son of **J.**. 3111
1Ki 1:36 Benaiah the son of **J.** answered 3111
1Ki 1:38, 44 and Benaiah the son of **J.**, and 3111
1Ki 2:25 the hand of Benaiah the son of **J.**; 3111
1Ki 2:29 Solomon sent Benaiah the son of **J.**, ... 3111
1Ki 2:34 So Benaiah the son of **J.** went up,...... 3111
1Ki 2:35 Benaiah the son of **J.** in his room....... 3111
1Ki 2:46 commanded Benaiah the son of **J.**;...... 3111
1Ki 4:4 Benaiah the son of **J.** was over the..... 3111
2Ki 11:4 **J.** sent and fetched the rulers over...... 3111
2Ki 11:9 that **J.** the priest commanded: 3111
2Ki 11:9 sabbath, and came to **J.** the priest...... 3111
2Ki 11:15 But **J.**...commanded the captains........ 3111
2Ki 11:17 **J.** made a covenant between the 3111
2Ki 12:2 **J.** the priest instructed him............. 3111
2Ki 12:7 Jehoash caled for **J.** the priest, ... 3111
2Ki 12:9 **J.** the priest took a chest, and bored .. 3111

1Ch 11:22 Benaiah the son of **J.**, the son of....... 3111
1Ch 11:24 things did Benaiah the son of **J.**,........ 3111
1Ch 12:27 **J.** was the leader of the Aaronites,..... 3111
1Ch 18:17 And Benaiah the son of **J.** was over.... 3111
1Ch 27:5 month was Benaiah the son of **J.**,....... 3111
1Ch 27:34 was **J.** the son of Benaiah, and.......... 3111
2Ch 22:11 But Jehoshabeath,...the wife of **J.**....... 3111
2Ch 23:1 year **J.** strengthened himself, ... 3111
2Ch 23:8 that **J.** the priest had commanded,...... 3111
2Ch 23:8 for **J.**...dismissed not the courses....... 3111
2Ch 23:9 **J.**...delivered to the captains 3111
2Ch 23:11 **J.** and his sons anointed him, and........ 3111
2Ch 23:14 Then **J.**...brought out the captains...... 3111
2Ch 23:16 **J.** made a covenant between him,....... 3111
2Ch 23:18 **J.** appointed the offices of the house... 3111
2Ch 24:2 sight of the Lord all the days of **J.** 3111
2Ch 24:3 **J.** took for him two wives; and he...... 3111
2Ch 24:6 the king called for **J.** the chief, and..... 3111
2Ch 24:12 **J.** gave it to such as did the work....... 3111
2Ch 24:14 the money before the king and **J.**,...... 3111
2Ch 24:14 Lord continually all the days of **J.**.. 3111
2Ch 24:15 **J.** waxed old, and was full of days...... 3111
2Ch 24:17 the death of **J.** came the princes........ 3111
2Ch 24:20 came upon Zechariah the son of **J.**...... 3111
2Ch 24:22 kindness which **J.** his father had......... 3111
2Ch 24:25 him for the blood of the sons of **J.** 3111
Ne 3:6 gate repaired **J.** the son of Paseah,..... 3111
Jer 29:26 made thee priest in the stead of **J.**...... 3111

JEHOIAKIM (je-hoy'-a-kim) See also ELIAKIM; JOIAKIM.
2Ki 23:34 father, and turned his name to **J.**, ... 3079
2Ki 23:35 **J.** gave the silver and the gold to....... 3079
2Ki 23:36 **J.** was twenty and five years old......... 3079
2Ki 24:1 **J.** became his servant three years:..... 3079
2Ki 24:5 Now the rest of the acts of **J.**, ... 3079
2Ki 24:6 So **J.** slept with his fathers: 3079
2Ki 24:19 according to all that **J.** had done......... 3079
1Ch 3:15 firstborn Johanan, the second **J.**, ... 3079
1Ch 3:16 the sons of **J.**: Jeconiah his son.......... 3079
2Ch 36:4 and turned his name to **J.**................. 3079
2Ch 36:5 **J.** was twenty and five years old........ 3079
2Ch 36:8 Now the rest of the acts of **J.**, ... 3079
Jer 1:3 It came also in the days of **J.**............. 3079
Jer 22:18 thus saith the Lord concerning **J.**......... 3079
Jer 22:24 Coniah the son of **J.** king of Judah...... 3079
Jer 24:1 away captive Jeconiah the son of **J.**...... 3079
Jer 25:1 fourth year of **J.** the son of Josiah...... 3079
Jer 26:1 In the beginning of the reign of **J.**...... 3079
Jer 26:21 **J.** the king, with all his mighty........... 3079
Jer 26:22 **J.** the king sent men into Egypt,........... 3079
Jer 26:23 and brought him unto **J.** the king;........ 3079
Jer 27:1 In the beginning of the reign of **J.**...... 3079
Jer 27:20 away captive Jeconiah the son of **J.**...... 3079
Jer 28:4 to this place Jeconiah the son of **J.**..... 3079
Jer 35:1 in the days of **J.** the son of Josiah....... 3079
Jer 36:1 came to pass in the fourth year of **J.**.. 3079
Jer 36:9 came to pass in the fifth year of **J.**..... 3079
Jer 36:28 **J.** the king of Judah hath burned. 3079
Jer 36:29 thou shalt say to **J.** king of Judah, ... 3079
Jer 36:30 saith the Lord of **J.** king of Judah; 3079
Jer 36:32 which **J.**...had burned in the fire: 3079
Jer 37:1 instead of Coniah the son of **J.**, ... 3079
Jer 45:1 fourth year of **J.** the son of Josiah...... 3079
Jer 46:2 smote in the fourth year of **J.**............ 3079
Jer 52:2 according to all that **J.** had done......... 3079
Da 1:1 In the third year of the reign of **J.**...... 3079
Da 1:2 the Lord gave **J.** king of Judah into..... 3079

JEHOIARIB (je-hoy'-a-rib) See also JOIARIB.
1Ch 9:10 Jedaiah, and **J.**, and Jachin, ... 3080
1Ch 24:7 Now the first lot came forth to **J.**,...... 3080

JEHONADAB (je-hon'-a-dab) See also JONADAB.
2Ki 10:15 he lighted on **J.** the son of Rechab 3082
2Ki 10:15 thy heart? And **J.** answered, It is....... 3082
2Ki 10:23 went, and **J.** the son of Rechab, ... 3082

JEHONATHAN (je-hon'-a-than) See also JONATHAN.
1Ch 27:25 castles, was **J.** the son of Uzziah: 3083
2Ch 17:8 and Shemiramoth, and **J.**, and........... 3083
Ne 12:18 Shammua: of Shemaiah, **J.**; 3083

JEHORAM (je-ho'-ram) See also HADORAM; JORAM.
1Ki 22:50 **J.** his son reigned in his stead. 3088
2Ki 1:17 And **J.** reigned in his stead 3088
2Ki 1:17 in the second year of **J.** the son of..... 3088
2Ki 3:1 **J.** the son of Ahab began to reign 3088
2Ki 3:6 And king **J.** went out of Samaria 3088
2Ki 8:16 **J.** the son of Jehoshaphat king of........ 3088
2Ki 8:25 Ahaziah the son of **J.** king of Judah..... 3088
2Ki 8:29 son of **J.** king of Judah went down....... 3088
2Ki 9:24 and smote **J.** between his arms,......... 3088
2Ki 12:18 **J.**, and Ahaziah, his fathers, kings...... 3088
2Ch 17:8 with them Elishama and **J.**, priests. 3088
2Ch 21:1 And **J.** his sons reigned in his stead.... 3088
2Ch 21:3 but the kingdom gave he to **J.**;........... 3088
2Ch 21:4 **J.** was risen up to the kingdom of...... 3088
2Ch 21:5 **J.** was thirty and two years old.......... 3088
2Ch 21:9 Then **J.** went forth with his princes. ... 3088
2Ch 21:16 Lord stirred up against **J.** the spirit 3088
2Ch 22:1 Ahaziah the son of **J.** king of Judah..... 3088
2Ch 22:5 **J.** the son of Ahab king of Israel......... 3088
2Ch 22:6 Azariah the son of **J.** king of Judah..... 3088
2Ch 22:6 went down to see **J.** the son of Ahab.. 3088
2Ch 22:7 he went out with **J.** against Jehu........ 3088
2Ch 22:11 the daughter of king **J.**, the wife of...... 3088

JEHOSHABEATH (je-ho-shab'-e-ath) See also JEHOSHEBA.
2Ch 22:11 But **J.**, the daughter of the king,........ 3090
2Ch 22:11 **J.**, the daughter of king Jehoram, ... 3090

JEHOSHAPHAT (je-hosh'-a-fat) See also JOSAPHAT; JOSHAPHAT.
2Sa 8:16 **J.** the son of Ahilud was recorder;...... 3092
2Sa 20:24 **J.** the son of Ahilud was recorder:...... 3092
1Ki 4:3 **J.** the son of Ahilud, the recorder. 3092
1Ki 4:17 **J.** the son of Paruah, in Issachar:....... 3092
1Ki 15:24 and **J.** his son reigned in his stead...... 3092
1Ki 22:2 **J.** the king of Judah came down 3092
1Ki 22:4 he said unto **J.**, Wilt thou go with 3092
1Ki 22:4 **J.** said to the king of Israel, I am....... 3092
1Ki 22:5 And **J.** said unto the king of Israel,...... 3092
1Ki 22:7 **J.** said, Is there not here a prophet.... 3092
1Ki 22:8 said unto **J.**, There is yet one man, ... 3092
1Ki 22:8 And **J.** said, Let not the king say so... 3092
1Ki 22:10 and **J.** the king of Judah sat each........ 3092
1Ki 22:18 king of Israel said unto **J.**, Did I 3092
1Ki 22:29 and **J.** the king of Judah went up........ 3092
1Ki 22:30 king of Israel said unto **J.**, I will.......... 3092
1Ki 22:32 captains of the chariots saw **J.**, that.... 3092
1Ki 22:32 fight against him: and **J.** cried out....... 3092
1Ki 22:41 **J.** the son of Asa began to reign......... 3092
1Ki 22:42 **J.** was thirty and five years old.......... 3092
1Ki 22:44 **J.** made peace with the king of........... 3092
1Ki 22:45 the rest of the acts of **J.**, and his....... 3092
1Ki 22:48 **J.** made ships of Tharshish to go........ 3092
1Ki 22:49 Ahaziah the son of Ahab unto **J.**,......... 3092
1Ki 22:49 in the ships. But **J.** would not. 3092
1Ki 22:50 **J.** slept with his fathers, and was....... 3092
1Ki 22:51 the seventeenth year of **J.** king of....... 3092
2Ki 1:17 year of Jehoram the son of **J.** king...... 3092
2Ki 3:1 the eighteenth year of **J.** king of........ 3092
2Ki 3:7 and sent to **J.** the king of Judah, ... 3092
2Ki 3:11 **J.** said, Is there not here a prophet.... 3092
2Ki 3:12 **J.** said, The word of the Lord is........ 3092
2Ki 3:12 **J.** and the king of Edom went down..... 3092
2Ki 3:14 not that I regard the presence of **J.**..... 3092
2Ki 8:16 Israel, **J.** being then king of Judah, ... 3092
2Ki 8:16 Jehoram the son of **J.** king of Judah 3092
2Ki 9:2 look out there Jehu the son of **J.**......... 3092
2Ki 9:14 Jehu the son of **J.**...conspired............ 3092
2Ki 12:18 took all the hallowed things that **J.**, ... 3092
1Ch 3:10 his son, Asa his son, **J.** his son, ... 3092
1Ch 15:24 Shebaniah, and **J.**, and Nethaneel, ... 3046
1Ch 18:15 and **J.** the son of Alihud, recorder. 3092
2Ch 17:1 And **J.** his son reigned in his stead,..... 3092
2Ch 17:3 the Lord was with **J.**, because he........ 3092
2Ch 17:5 all Judah brought to **J.** presents; 3092
2Ch 17:10 that they made no war against **J.** 3092
2Ch 17:11 the Philistines brought **J.** presents...... 3092
2Ch 17:12 And **J.** waxed great exceedingly;......... 3092
2Ch 18:1 Now **J.** had riches and honour in........ 3092
2Ch 18:3 Ahab king of Israel said unto **J.**.......... 3092
2Ch 18:4 And **J.** said unto the king of Israel,..... 3092
2Ch 18:6 **J.** said, Is there not here a prophet.... 3092
2Ch 18:7 And the king of Israel said unto **J.**,...... 3092
2Ch 18:7 And **J.** said, Let not the king say so... 3092
2Ch 18:9 and **J.** king of Judah sat either.......... 3092
2Ch 18:17 And the king of Israel said to **J.**,....... 3092
2Ch 18:28 and **J.** the king of Judah went up....... 3092
2Ch 18:29 And the king of Israel said unto **J.**,..... 3092
2Ch 18:31 the captains of the chariot saw **J.**,...... 3092
2Ch 18:31 **J.** cried out, and the Lord helped....... 3092
2Ch 19:1 **J.** the king of Judah returned to........ 3092
2Ch 19:2 to meet him, and said to king **J.**, ... 3092
2Ch 19:4 And **J.** dwelt at Jerusalem: and he...... 3092
2Ch 19:8 Jerusalem did **J.** set of the Levites, ... 3092
2Ch 20:1 came against **J.** to battle.................. 3092
2Ch 20:2 Then there came some that told **J.**,.... 3092
2Ch 20:3 **J.** feared, and set himself to seek....... 3092
2Ch 20:5 **J.** stood in the congregation of........... 3092
2Ch 20:15 of Jerusalem, and thou king **J.**, ... 3092
2Ch 20:18 **J.** bowed his head with his face to...... 3092
2Ch 20:20 **J.** stood and said, Hear me, O Judah,.. 3092
2Ch 20:25 **J.** and his people came to take away... 3092
2Ch 20:27 **J.** in the forefront of them, to go 3092
2Ch 20:30 So the realm of **J.** was quiet: for........ 3092
2Ch 20:31 And **J.** reigned over Judah: he was..... 3092
2Ch 20:34 Now the rest of the acts of **J.**, first.... 3092
2Ch 20:35 did **J.** king of Judah join himself......... 3092
2Ch 20:37 of Mareshah prophesied against **J.**, ... 3092
2Ch 21:1 **J.** slept with his fathers, and was....... 3092
2Ch 21:2 And he had brethren the sons of **J.**, ... 3092
2Ch 21:2 all these were the sons of **J.** king....... 3092
2Ch 21:12 hast not walked in the ways of **J.**....... 3092
2Ch 22:9 said they, he is the son of **J.**, who 3092
Joe 3:2 them down into the valley of **J.**,.......... 3092
Joe 3:12 and come up to the valley of **J.**........... 3092

JEHOSHEBA (je-hosh'-e-bah) See also JEHOSHA-BEATH.
2Ki 11:2 **J.**, the daughter of king Joram, ... 3089

JEHOSHUA (je-hosh'-u-ah) See also JEHOSHUAH; JOSHUA.
Nu 13:16 called Oshea the son of Nun **J.**.......... 3091

JEHOSHUAH (je-hosh'-u-ah) See also JEHOSHUA.
1Ch 7:27 Non his son, **J.** his son. 3091

JEHOVAH (je-ho'-vah) See also GOD; JAH; JEHOVAH-JIREH; JEHOVAH-NISSI; JEHOVAH-SHALOM; LORD.
Ex 6:3 name **J.** was I not known to them. 3068
Ps 83:18 thou, whose name alone is **J.**, art....... 3068
Isa 12:2 **J.** is my strength and my song; 3068
Isa 26:4 the Lord **J.** is everlasting strength...... 3068

JEHOVAH-JIREH (je-ho''-vah-ji'-reh)
Ge 22:14 called the name of that place **J.**.......... 3070

JEHOVAH-NISSI (je-ho''-vah-nis'-si)
Ex 17:15 altar, and called the name of it **J.**........ 3071

JEHOVAH-SHALOM (je-ho''-vah-sha'-lom)
Jg 6:24 unto the Lord, and called it **J.**........... 3073

JEHOZABAD (je-hoz'-a-bad) See also JOZABAD.
2Ki 12:21 **J.** the son of Shomer, his servants, ... 3075
1Ch 26:4 **J.** the second, Joah the third,............ 3075
2Ch 17:18 next him was **J.**, and with him an....... 3075
2Ch 24:26 **J.** the son of Shimrith a Moabitess. 3075

JEHOZADAK (je-hoz'-a-dak) See also JOZADAK.
1Ch 6:14 Seraiah, and Seraiah begat **J.**,............ 3087
1Ch 6:15 **J.** went into captivity, when the......... 3087

JEHU (je-hu)
1Ki 16:1 word of the Lord came to **J.** the........ 3058
1Ki 16:7 also by the hand of the prophet **J.**....... 3058
1Ki 16:12 he spake against Baasha by **J.** the...... 3058
1Ki 19:16 **J.**...shalt thou anoint to be king 3058
1Ki 19:17 the sword of Hazael shall **J.** slay: 3058
1Ki 19:17 that escapeth from the sword of **J.**...... 3058
2Ki 9:2 there **J.** the son of Jehoshaphat.......... 3058
2Ki 9:5 And **J.** said, Unto which of all us? 3058
2Ki 9:11 **J.** came forth to the servants of his.... 3058
2Ki 9:13 with trumpets, saying, **J.** is king. 3058
2Ki 9:14 **J.** the son of Jehoshaphat the son....... 3058
2Ki 9:15 And **J.** said, If it be your minds, ... 3058
2Ki 9:16 So **J.** rode in a chariot, and went to.... 3058
2Ki 9:17 spied the company of **J.** as he came,... 3058
2Ki 9:18 **J.** said, What hast thou to do with...... 3058
2Ki 9:19 **J.** answered, What hast thou to do..... 3058
2Ki 9:20 the driving is like the driving of **J.**...... 3058
2Ki 9:21 they went out against **J.**, and met 3058
2Ki 9:22 it came to pass, when Joram saw **J.**,... 3058
2Ki 9:22 that he said, Is it peace, **J.**?............. 3058
2Ki 9:24 And **J.** drew a bow with his full 3058
2Ki 9:25 Then said **J.** to Bidkar his captain,...........
2Ki 9:27 **J.** followed after him, and said, ... 3058
2Ki 9:30 And when **J.** was come to Jezreel, ... 3058
2Ki 9:31 as **J.** entered in at the gate, she 3058
2Ki 10:1 And **J.** wrote letters, and sent to 3058
2Ki 10:5 up of the children, sent to **J.**, saying,... 3058
2Ki 10:11 **J.** slew all that remained of the......... 3058
2Ki 10:13 **J.** met with the brethren of Ahaziah.... 3058
2Ki 10:18 **J.** gathered all the people together, ... 3058
2Ki 10:18 little; but **J.** shall serve him much....... 3058

2Ki 10:19 **J.** did it in subtility, to the intent........ 3058
2Ki 10:20 And **J.** said, Proclaim a solemn 3058
2Ki 10:21 And **J.** sent through all Israel: 3058
2Ki 10:23 **J.** went, and Jehonadab the son of.......... 3058
2Ki 10:24 **J.** appointed fourscore men without, ... 3058
2Ki 10:25 And **J.** said to the guard and to the 3058
2Ki 10:28 **J.** destroyed Baal out of Israel........... 3058
2Ki 10:29 **J.** departed not from after them, ... 3058
2Ki 10:30 the Lord said unto **J.**, Because thou ... 3058
2Ki 10:31 **J.** took no heed to walk in the law 3058
2Ki 10:34 the rest of the acts of **J.**, and all........ 3058
2Ki 10:35 And **J.** slept with his fathers: and....... 3058
2Ki 10:36 time that **J.** reigned over Israel.......... 3058
2Ki 12:1 seventh year of **J.** Jehoash began 3058
2Ki 13:1 Jehoahaz the son of **J.** began to 3058
2Ki 14:8 the son of Jehoahaz son of **J.**,............ 3058
2Ki 15:12 of the Lord which he spake unto **J.**, ... 3058
1Ch 2:38 And Obed begat **J.**, and **J.** begat........ 3058
1Ch 4:35 Joel, and **J.**, the son of Josibiah,......... 3058
1Ch 12:3 Berachah, and **J.** the Antothite, ... 3058
2Ch 19:2 **J.** the son of Hanani the seer went....... 3058
2Ch 20:34 they are written in the book of **J.**....... 3058
2Ch 22:7 went out with Jehoram against **J.** 3058
2Ch 22:8 **J.** was executing judgment upon......... 3058
2Ch 22:9 in Samaria,) and brought him to **J.**....... 3058
2Ch 25:17 the son of Jehoahaz, the son of **J.**, ... 3058
Ho 1:4 of Jezreel upon the house of **J.**, ... 3058

JEHUBBAH (je-hub'-bah)
1Ch 7:34 of Shamer; Ahi, and Rohgah, **J.**, ... 3160

JEHUCAL (je-hu'-kal) See also JUCAL.
Jer 37:3 king sent **J.** the son of Shelemiah 3081

JEHUD (je'-hud)
Jos 19:45 And **J.**, and Bene-berak, and............. 3055

JEHUDI (je-hu'-di)
Jer 36:14 Therefore all the princes sent **J.** 3065
Jer 36:21 So the king sent **J.** to fetch the roll: ... 3065
Jer 36:21 **J.** read it in the ears of the king, ... 3065
Jer 36:23 **J.** had read three or four leaves, he.... 3065

JEHUDIJAH (je-hu-di'-jah) See also HODIAH.
1Ch 4:18 And his wife **J.** bare Jered the.......... 3057

JEHUSH (je'-hush) See also JEUSH.
1Ch 8:39 **J.** the second, and Eliphelet the......... 3266

JEIEL (je-i'-el) See also JEHIEL; JEUEL.
1Ch 5:7 were the chief, **J.**, and Zecariah, ... 3273
1Ch 15:18 Obed-edom, and **J.**, the porters.......... 3273
1Ch 15:21 Obed-edom, and **J.**, and Azaziah, ... 3273
1Ch 16:5 and next to him Zechariah, **J.**, and...... 3273
1Ch 16:5 **J.** with psalteries and with harps; 3273
2Ch 20:14 of Benaiah, the son of **J.**, the son of... 3273
2Ch 26:11 account by the hand of **J.** the scribe ... 3273
2Ch 29:13 sons of Elizaphan; Shimri, and **J.**........ 3273
2Ch 35:9 Hashabiah and **J.** and Jozabad, ... 3273
Ezr 8:13 names are these, Eliphelet, **J.**, and..... 3273
Ezr 10:43 the sons of Nebo; **J.**, Mattithiah,......... 3273

JEKABZEEL (je-kab'-ze-el) See also KABZEEL.
Ne 11:25 at **J.**, and in the villages thereof,......... 3343

JEKAMEAM (je-kam'-e-am)
1Ch 23:19 the third, and **J.** the fourth. 3360
1Ch 24:23 Jahaziel the third, **J.** the fourth. 3360

JEKAMIAH (jek-a-mi'-ah) See also JECAMIAH.
1Ch 2:41 Shallum begat **J.**, and **J.** begat........... 3359

JEKUTHIEL (je-ku'-the-el)
1Ch 4:18 and **J.** the father of Zanoah. 3354

JEMIMA (je-mi'-mah)
Job 42:14 he called the name of the first, **J.**;...... 3224

JEMUEL (je-mu'-el) See also NEMUEL.
Ge 46:10 sons of Simeon; **J.**, and Jamin,........... 3223
Ex 6:15 the sons of Simeon; **J.**, and Jamin, ... 3223

JEOPARDED
Jg 5:18 a people that **j.** their lives unto the..... 2778

JEOPARDY
2Sa 23:17 the men that went in **j.** of their lives? ....
1Ch 11:19 that have put their lives in **j.**?...................
1Ch 11:19 for with the **j.** of their lives they brought...
1Ch 12:19 master Saul to the **j.** of our heads. ....
Lu 8:23 filled with water, and were in **j.**. *2793*
1Co 15:30 And why stand we in **j.** every hour? ... *2793*

JEPHTHAE (jef'-thah-e) See also JEPHTHAH.
Heb 11:32 Barak, and of Samson, and of **J.**; *2422*

JEPHTHAH (jef'-thah) See also JEPHTHAE; JIPHTHAH-EL.
Jg 11:1 Now **J.** the Gileadite was a mighty 3316
Jg 11:1 of an harlot: and Gilead begat **J.**. 3316
Jg 11:2 they thrust out **J.**, and said unto 3316
Jg 11:3 Then **J.** fled from his brethren, ... 3316
Jg 11:3 there were gathered vain men to **J.**,... 3316
Jg 11:5 the elders of Gilead went to fetch **J.**.... 3316
Jg 11:6 they said unto **J.**, Come, and be our... 3316
Jg 11:7 **J.** said unto the elders of Gilead,........ 3316
Jg 11:8 the elders of Gilead said unto **J.**,......... 3316
Jg 11:9 **J.** said unto the elders of Gilead,......... 3316
Jg 11:10 the elders of Gilead said unto **J.**,......... 3316
Jg 11:11 **J.** went with the elders of Gilead, ... 3316
Jg 11:11 **J.** uttered all his words before the........ 3316
Jg 11:12 **J.** sent messengers unto the king....... 3316
Jg 11:13 answered...the messengers of **J.**, ... 3316
Jg 11:14 **J.** sent messengers again unto the...... 3316
Jg 11:15 Thus saith **J.**, Israel took not away..... 3316
Jg 11:28 hearkened not unto the words of **J.** 3316
Jg 11:29 Spirit of the Lord came upon **J.**, ... 3316
Jg 11:30 **J.** vowed a vow unto the Lord, and.... 3316
Jg 11:32 **J.** passed over unto the children of..... 3316
Jg 11:34 **J.** came to Mizpeh unto his house, ... 3316
Jg 11:40 yearly to lament the daughter of **J.**...... 3316
Jg 12:1 went northward, and said unto **J.**, ... 3316
Jg 12:2 **J.** said unto them, I and my people..... 3316
Jg 12:4 **J.** gathered together all the men of..... 3316
Jg 12:7 And **J.** judged Israel six years. 3316
Jg 12:7 Then died **J.** the Gileadite, and was.... 3316
1Sa 12:11 sent Jerubbaal, and Bedan, and **J.**,....... 3316

JEPHUNNEH (je-fun'-neh)
Nu 13:6 tribe of Judah, Caleb the son of **J.**...... 3312
Nu 14:6 son of Nun, and Caleb the son of **J.**..... 3312
Nu 14:30 therein, save Caleb the son of **J.**,....... 3312
Nu 14:38 son of Nun, and Caleb the son of **J.**,... 3312
Nu 26:65 of them, save Caleb the son of **J.**,...... 3312
Nu 32:12 Save Caleb the son of **J.** the 3312
Nu 34:19 tribe of Judah, Caleb the son of **J.**...... 3312
De 1:36 Save Caleb the son of **J.**; he shall 3312
Jos 14:6 Caleb the son of **J.** the Kenezite said.. 3312
Jos 14:13 and gave unto Caleb the son of **J.** 3312
Jos 14:14 inheritance of Caleb the son of **J.** 3312
Jos 15:13 unto Caleb the son of **J.** he gave a..... 3312
Jos 21:12 gave they to Caleb the son of **J.** 3312
1Ch 4:15 the sons of Caleb the son of **J.**; Iru, ... 3312
1Ch 6:56 they gave to Caleb the son of **J.**. 3312
1Ch 7:38 the sons of Jether; **J.**, and Pispah,...... 3312

JERAH (je'-rah)
Ge 10:26 and Hazarmaveth, and **J.**, ... 3392
1Ch 1:20 and Hazarmaveth, and **J.**, ... 3392

JERAHMEEL (je-rah'-me-el) See also JERAHMEELITES.
1Ch 2:9 **J.**, and Ram, and Chelubai. 3396
1Ch 2:25 sons of **J.** the firstborn of Hezron....... 3396
1Ch 2:26 **J.** had also another wife, whose......... 3396
1Ch 2:27 the sons of Ram the firstborn of **J.**...... 3396
1Ch 2:33 These were the sons of **J.**. 3396
1Ch 2:42 sons of Caleb the brother of **J.** were,.. 3396
1Ch 24:29 Kish: the son of Kish was **J.**. 3396
Jer 36:26 **J.** the son of Hammelech, ... 3396

JERAHMEELITES (je-rah'-me-el-ites)
1Sa 27:10 and against the south of the **J.**,.......... 3397
1Sa 30:29 which were in the cities of the **J.**, ... 3397

JERED (je'-red) See also JARED.
1Ch 1:2 Kenan, Mahalaleel, **J.**, ... 3382
1Ch 4:18 wife Jehudijah bare **J.** the father of..... 3382

JEREMAI (jer'-e-mahee)
Ezr 10:33 Zabad, Eliphelet, **J.**, Manasseh, ... 3413

JEREMIAH (jer-e-mi'-ah) See also JEREMIAH'S; JEREMIAS; JEREMY.
2Ki 23:31 the daughter of **J.** of Libnah. 3414
2Ki 24:18 the daughter of **J.** of Libnah. 3414
1Ch 5:24 and Azriel, and **J.**, and Hodaviah, ... 3414
1Ch 12:4 and **J.**, and Jahaziel, and Johanan, ... 3414
1Ch 12:10 the fourth, **J.** the fifth, ... 3414
1Ch 12:13 **J.** the tenth, Machbanai the............... 3414
2Ch 35:25 And **J.** lamented for Josiah: 3414
2Ch 36:12 and humbled not himself before **J.** 3414
2Ch 36:21 word of the Lord by the mouth of **J.**,.. 3414
2Ch 36:22 the Lord spoken by the mouth of **J.**..... 3414
Ezr 1:1 word of the Lord by the mouth of **J.**.... 3414
Ne 10:2 Seraiah, Azariah, **J.**, ... 3414
Ne 12:1 and Jeshua: Seraiah, **J.**, Ezra,............ 3414
Ne 12:12 Seraiah, Meraiah; of **J.**, Hananiah; 3414
Ne 12:34 Benjamin, and Shemaiah, and **J.**, ... 3414
Jer *general* *title* The Book Of The Prophet **J.**........ 3414
Jer 1:1 The words of **J.** the son of Hilkiah, ... 3414
Jer 1:11 me, saying, **J.**, what seest thou?......... 3414
Jer 7:1 word that came to **J.** from the Lord,... 3414
Jer 11:1 word that came to **J.** from the Lord,... 3414
Jer 14:1 came to **J.** concerning the dearth. 3414
Jer 18:1 word which came to **J.** from the 3414
Jer 18:18 let us devise devices against **J.**; 3414
Jer 19:14 Then came **J.** from Tophet, ... 3414
Jer 20:1 heard that **J.** prophesied these........... 3414
Jer 20:2 Then Pashur smote **J.** the prophet, ... 3414
Jer 20:3 brought forth **J.** out of the stocks....... 3414
Jer 20:3 Then said **J.** unto him, The Lord 3414
Jer 21:1 which came unto **J.** from the Lord,..... 3414
Jer 21:3 Then said **J.** unto them, Thus shall..... 3414
Jer 24:3 Lord unto me, What seest thou, **J.**? ... 3414
Jer 25:1 word that came to **J.** concerning 3414
Jer 25:2 The which **J.** the prophet spake......... 3414
Jer 25:13 **J.** hath prophesied against all the........ 3414
Jer 26:7 the people heard **J.** speaking these..... 3414
Jer 26:8 **J.** had made an end of speaking all 3414
Jer 26:9 people were gathered against **J.** in...... 3414
Jer 26:12 spake **J.** unto all the princes and........ 3414
Jer 26:20 according to all the words of **J.**.......... 3414
Jer 26:24 the son of Shaphan was with **J.**,......... 3414
Jer 27:1 this word unto **J.** from the Lord,......... 3414
Jer 28:5 **J.** said unto the prophet Hananiah....... 3414
Jer 28:6 prophet **J.** said, Amen: the Lord do.... 3414
Jer 28:11 And the prophet **J.** went his way. 3414
Jer 28:12 word of the Lord came unto **J.** the..... 3414
Jer 28:12 from off the neck of the prophet **J.**,.... 3414
Jer 28:15 said the prophet **J.** unto Hananiah....... 3414
Jer 29:1 are the words of the letter that **J.**........ 3414
Jer 29:27 why hast thou not reproved **J.** of 3414
Jer 29:29 read this letter in the ears of **J.**.......... 3414
Jer 29:30 came the word of the Lord unto **J.**,..... 3414
Jer 30:1 word that came to **J.** from the Lord,... 3414
Jer 32:1 The word that came to **J.** from the..... 3414
Jer 32:2 **J.** the prophet was shut up in the....... 3414
Jer 32:6 **J.** said, The word of the Lord came.... 3414
Jer 32:26 came the word of the Lord unto **J.**, ... 3414
Jer 33:1 Lord came unto **J.** the second time,.... 3414
Jer 33:19 the word of the Lord came unto **J.**,.... 3414
Jer 33:23 the word of the Lord came to **J.**, ... 3414
Jer 34:1 which came unto **J.** from the Lord,..... 3414
Jer 34:6 Then **J.** the prophet spake all these..... 3414
Jer 34:8 that came unto **J.** from the Lord, ... 3414
Jer 34:12 the word of the Lord came to **J.**......... 3414
Jer 35:1 which came unto **J.** from the Lord,..... 3414
Jer 35:3 I took Jaazaniah the son of **J.**, ... 3414
Jer 35:12 came the word of the Lord unto **J.**,..... 3414
Jer 35:18 And **J.** said unto...the Rechabites, ... 3414
Jer 36:1 word came unto **J.** from the Lord,...... 3414
Jer 36:4 **J.** called Baruch the son of Neriah: 3414
Jer 36:4 Baruch wrote from the mouth of **J.**...... 3414
Jer 36:5 **J.** commanded Baruch, saying, I......... 3414
Jer 36:8 **J.** the prophet commanded him, ... 3414
Jer 36:10 Baruch in the book the words of **J.**...... 3414
Jer 36:19 Baruch, Go, hide thee, thou and **J.**;..... 3414
Jer 36:26 the scribe and **J.** the prophet: 3414
Jer 36:27 the word of the Lord came to **J.**, ... 3414
Jer 36:27 Baruch wrote at the mouth of **J.**, ... 3414
Jer 36:32 Then took **J.** another roll, and gave.... 3414
Jer 36:32 wrote therein from the mouth of **J.**...... 3414
Jer 37:2 which he spake by the prophet **J.**........ 3414
Jer 37:3 the priest to the prophet **J.**, saying,..... 3414
Jer 37:4 **J.** came in and went out among 3414
Jer 37:6 of the Lord unto the prophet **J.**, ... 3414
Jer 37:12 Then **J.** went forth out of Jerusalem ... 3414
Jer 37:13 and he took **J.** the prophet, saying, ... 3414
Jer 37:14 Then said **J.**, It is false; I fall not....... 3414
Jer 37:14 so Irijah took **J.**, and brought him....... 3414
Jer 37:15 the princes were wroth with **J.**,.......... 3414
Jer 37:16 **J.** was entered into the dungeon, ... 3414
Jer 37:16 **J.** had remained there many days; 3414
Jer 37:17 And **J.** said, There is: for, said he,..... 3414
Jer 37:18 **J.** said unto king Zedekiah, What........ 3414
Jer 37:21 should commit **J.** into the court of...... 3414
Jer 37:21 **J.** remained in the court of the 3414
Jer 38:1 heard the words that **J.** had spoken.... 3414
Jer 38:6 took they **J.**, and cast him into the..... 3414

Jer 38:6 and they let down **J.** with cords......... 3414
Jer 38:6 but mire: so **J.** sunk in the mire. 3414
Jer 38:7 they had put **J.** in the dungeon; 3414
Jer 38:9 evil in all that they have done to **J.**...... 3414
Jer 38:10 **J.** the prophet out of the dungeon, ... 3414
Jer 38:11 by cords into the dungeon to **J.**. 3414
Jer 38:12 the Ethiopian said unto **J.**, Put now 3414
Jer 38:12 under the cords. And **J.** did so. 3414
Jer 38:13 So they drew up **J.** with cords, and 3414
Jer 38:13 **J.** remained in the court of the 3414
Jer 38:14 and took **J.** the prophet unto him 3414
Jer 38:14 the king said unto **J.**, I will ask.......... 3414
Jer 38:15 **J.** said unto Zedekiah, If I declare 3414
Jer 38:16 the king sware secretly unto **J.**,......... 3414
Jer 38:17 said **J.** unto Zedekiah, Thus saith 3414
Jer 38:19 Zedekiah the king said unto **J.**, I........ 3414
Jer 38:20 **J.** said, They shall not deliver thee..... 3414
Jer 38:24 Then said Zedekiah unto **J.**, Let no 3414
Jer 38:27 Then came all the princes unto **J.**,......... 3414
Jer 38:28 **J.** abode in the court of the prison...... 3414
Jer 39:11 Babylon gave charge concerning **J.** 3414
Jer 39:14 sent, and took **J.** out of the court....... 3414
Jer 39:15 the word of the Lord came unto **J.**, ... 3414
Jer 40:1 that came to **J.** from the Lord, ... 3414
Jer 40:2 the captain of the guard took **J.**, ... 3414
Jer 40:6 Then went **J.** unto Gedaliah the......... 3414
Jer 42:2 And said unto **J.** the prophet, Let, ... 3414
Jer 42:4 **J.** the prophet said unto them, I 3414
Jer 42:5 they said to **J.**, The Lord be a true 3414
Jer 42:7 the word of the Lord came unto **J.**..... 3414
Jer 43:1 **J.** had made an end of speaking 3414
Jer 43:2 and all proud men, saying unto **J.**,....... 3414
Jer 43:6 **J.** the prophet and Baruch the son...... 3414
Jer 43:8 came the word of the Lord unto **J.**...... 3414
Jer 44:1 word that came to **J.** concerning 3414
Jer 44:15 in Pathros, answered **J.**, saying, ... 3414
Jer 44:20 Then **J.** said unto all the people, to 3414
Jer 44:24 **J.** said unto all the people, and to....... 3414
Jer 45:1 word that **J.** the prophet spake unto ... 3414
Jer 45:1 words in a book at the mouth of **J.**,..... 3414
Jer 46:1 word of the Lord which came to **J.**...... 3414
Jer 46:13 The word that the Lord spake to **J.**..... 3414
Jer 47:1 word of the Lord that came to **J.**......... 3414
Jer 49:34 word of the Lord that came to **J.** 3414
Jer 50:1 the land of the Chaldeans by **J.**.......... 3414
Jer 51:59 which **J.** the prophet commanded 3414
Jer 51:60 **J.** wrote in a book all the evil that...... 3414
Jer 51:61 **J.** said to Seraiah, When thou comest.. 3414
Jer 51:64 Thus far are the words of **J.**.............. 3414
Jer 52:1 the daughter of **J.** of Libnah. 3414
La *general* *title* The Lamentations Of **J.**....................
Da 9:2 the word of the Lord came to **J.** the... 3414

JEREMIAH'S (jer-e-mi'-ahz)
Jer 28:10 yoke from off the prophet **J.** neck, ... 3414

JEREMIAS (jer-e-mi'-as) See also JEREMIAH.
Mt 16:14 others, **J.**, or one of the prophets. *2408*

JEREMOTH (jer'-e-moth) See also JERIMOTH.
1Ch 8:14 And Ahio, Shashak, and **J.**, ... 3406
1Ch 23:23 Mahli, and Eder, and **J.**, three........... 3406
1Ch 25:22 The fifteenth to **J.**, he, his sons, and .. 3406
Ezr 10:26 and Jehiel, and Abdi, and **J.**, and......... 3406
Ezr 10:27 Mattaniah, and **J.**, and Zabad, and 3406

JEREMY (jer'-e-mee) See also JEREMIAH.
Mt 2:17 that which was spoken by **J.** the *2408*
Mt 27:9 that which was spoken by **J.** the *2408*

JERIAH (je-ri'-ah) See also JERIJAH.
1Ch 23:19 Of the sons of Hebron; **J.** the first, ... 3404
1Ch 24:23 **J.** the first, Amariah the second, ... 3404

JERIBAI (jer'-ib-ahee)
1Ch 11:46 Eliel the Mahavite, and **J.**, and 3403

JERICHO (jer'-ik-o)
Nu 22:1 of Moab on this Jordan by **J.**............. 3405
Nu 26:3 plains of Moab by Jordan near **J.**,........ 3405
Nu 26:63 plains of Moab by Jordan near **J.**........ 3405
Nu 31:12 Moab, which are by Jordan near **J.**. 3405
Nu 33:48 plains of Moab by Jordan near **J.**......... 3405
Nu 33:50 plains of Moab by Jordan near **J.**,........ 3405
Nu 34:15 this side Jordan near **J.** eastward,........ 3405
Nu 35:1 plains of Moab by Jordan near **J.**, ... 3405
Nu 36:13 plains of Moab by Jordan near **J.**........ 3405
De 32:49 of Moab, that is over against **J.**; 3405
De 34:1 of Pisgah, that is over against **J.**........ 3405
De 34:3 and the plain of the valley of **J.**, the.... 3405
Jos 2:1 saying, Go view the land, even **J.**. 3405
Jos 2:2 it was told the king of **J.**, saying, ... 3405
Jos 2:3 And the king of **J.** sent unto Rahab,.... 3405
Jos 3:16 people passed over right against **J.**..... 3405
Jos 4:13 Lord unto battle, to the plains of **J.**. ... 3405
Jos 4:19 in Gilgal, in the east border of **J.** 3405
Jos 5:10 month at even in the plains of **J.**. 3405
Jos 5:13 to pass, when Joshua was by **J.**, ... 3405
Jos 6:1 **J.** was straitly shut up because of....... 3405
Jos 6:2 I have given into thine hand **J.**,.......... 3405
Jos 6:25 which Joshua sent to spy out **J.**. 3405
Jos 6:26 riseth up and buildeth this city **J.** 3405
Jos 7:2 And Joshua sent men from **J.** to Ai,...... 3405
Jos 8:2 as thou didst unto **J.** and her king: 3405
Jos 9:3 what Joshua had done unto **J.**............ 3405
Jos 10:1 as he had done to **J.** and her king, ... 3405
Jos 10:28 as he did unto the king of **J.**. 3405
Jos 10:30 thereof as he did unto the king of **J.**. ... 3405
Jos 12:9 The king of **J.**, one; the king of Ai, ... 3405
Jos 13:32 Moab, on the other side Jordan, by **J.**,.3405
Jos 16:1 of Joseph fell from Jordan by **J.**,.......... 3405
Jos 16:1 unto the water of **J.** on the east, ... 3405
Jos 16:1 wilderness that goeth up from **J.**......... 3405
Jos 16:7 and to Naarath, and came to **J.**,.......... 3405
Jos 18:12 border went up to the side of **J.** on.... 3405
Jos 18:21 according to their families were **J.**, ... 3405
Jos 20:8 And on the other side Jordan by **J.**...... 3405
Jos 24:11 over Jordan, and came unto **J.**: 3405
Jos 24:11 the men of **J.** fought against you, ... 3405
2Sa 10:5 Tarry at **J.** until your beards be.......... 3405
1Ki 16:34 did Hiel the Beth-elite build **J.** 3405
2Ki 2:4 for the Lord hath sent me to **J.**. 3405
2Ki 2:4 not leave thee. So they came to **J.**..... 3405
2Ki 2:5 sons of the prophets that were at **J.**.... 3405
2Ki 2:15 prophets which were to view at **J.**....... 3405
2Ki 2:18 again to him, (for he tarried at **J.**,) 3405
2Ki 25:5 overtook him in the plains of **J.**.......... 3405
1Ch 6:78 And on the other side Jordan by **J.**, ... 3405
1Ch 19:5 Tarry at **J.** until your beards be.......... 3405
2Ch 28:15 upon asses, and brought them to **J.**, ... 3405
Ezr 2:34 The children of **J.**, three hundred....... 3405
Ne 3:2 unto him builded the men of **J.**. 3405
Ne 7:36 The children of **J.**, three hundred....... 3405
Jer 39:5 Zedekiah in the plains of **J.** 3405
Jer 52:8 Zedekiah in the plains of **J.**; 3405
Mt 20:29 And as they departed from **J.**, a *2410*
Mk 10:46 came to **J.**: and as he went out of **J.**.. *2410*
Lu 10:30 **went down from Jerusalem to J.**,... *2410*
Lu 18:35 that as he was come nigh unto **J.**, ... *2410*
Lu 19:1 entered and passed through **J.**. *2410*
Heb 11:30 By faith the walls of **J.** fell down, ... *2410*

JERIEL (je-ri'-el)
1Ch 7:2 Uzzi, and Rephaiah, and **J.**, and......... 3400

JERIJAH (je-ri'-jah) See also JERIAH.
1Ch 26:31 the Hebronites was **J.** the chief, ... 3404

JERIMOTH (jer'-im-oth) See also JEREMOTH.
1Ch 7:7 Uzzi, and Uzziel, and **J.**, and Iri, ... 3406
1Ch 7:8 and Elioenai, and Omri, and **J.**,........... 3406
1Ch 12:5 Eluzai, and **J.**, and Bealiah, and 3406
1Ch 24:30 of Mushi; Mahli, and Eder, and **J.**. 3406
1Ch 25:4 Mattaniah, Uzziel, Shebuel, and **J.**,..... 3406
1Ch 27:19 of Naphtali, **J.** the son of Azriel: 3406
2Ch 11:18 him Mahalath the daughter of **J.**.......... 3406
2Ch 31:13 and Nahath, and Asahel, and **J.**,.......... 3406

JERIOTH (je'-re-oth)
1Ch 2:18 of Azubah his wife, and of **J.**.............. 3408

JEROBOAM (jer-o-bo'-am) See also JEROBOAM'S.
1Ki 11:26 **J.** the son of Nebat, an Ephrathite...... 3379
1Ki 11:28 **J.** was a mighty man of valour: 3379
1Ki 11:29 when **J.** went out of Jerusalem, ... 3379
1Ki 11:31 And he said to **J.**, Take thee ten 3379
1Ki 11:40 Solomon sought therefore to kill **J.**. 3379
1Ki 11:40 And **J.** arose, and fled into Egypt, ... 3379
1Ki 12:2 to pass, when **J.** the son of Nebat,..... 3379
1Ki 12:2 Solomon, and **J.** dwelt in Egypt;) 3379
1Ki 12:3 And **J.** and all the congregation of 3379
1Ki 12:12 So **J.** and all the people came to 3379
1Ki 12:15 by Ahijah the Shilonite unto **J.**........... 3379
1Ki 12:20 all Israel heard that **J.** was come........ 3379
1Ki 12:25 Then **J.** built Shechem in mount......... 3379
1Ki 12:26 **J.** said in his heart, Now shall the 3379
1Ki 12:32 **J.** ordained a feast in the eighth......... 3379
1Ki 13:1 and **J.** stood by the altar to burn........ 3379
1Ki 13:4 **J.** heard the saying of the man of....... 3379
1Ki 13:33 **J.** returned not from his evil way, ... 3379
1Ki 13:34 became sin unto the house of **J.**, ... 3379
1Ki 14:1 time Abijah the son of **J.** fell sick. 3379
1Ki 14:2 **J.** said to his wife, Arise, I pray 3379
1Ki 14:2 be not known to be the wife of **J.**; 3379
1Ki 14:5 Behold, the wife of **J.** cometh to ask... 3379
1Ki 14:6 he said, Come in, thou wife of **J.**; 3379
1Ki 14:7 Go, tell **J.**, Thus saith the Lord God... 3379
1Ki 14:10 will bring evil upon the house of **J.**, ... 3379
1Ki 14:10 will cut off from **J.** him that pisseth 3379
1Ki 14:10 the remnant of the house of **J.**, ... 3379
1Ki 14:11 Him that dieth of **J.** in the city........... 3379
1Ki 14:13 only of **J.** shall come to the grave, ... 3379
1Ki 14:13 God of Israel in the house of **J.**. 3379
1Ki 14:14 cut off the house of **J.** that day: 3379
1Ki 14:16 Israel up because of the sins of **J.**, ... 3379
1Ki 14:19 the rest of the acts of **J.**, how he....... 3379
1Ki 14:20 **J.** reigned were two and twenty.......... 3379
1Ki 14:30 was war between Rehoboam and **J.** 3379
1Ki 15:1 in the eighteenth year of king **J.** 3379
1Ki 15:6 was war between Rehoboam and **J.** 3379
1Ki 15:7 was war between Abijam and **J.**.......... 3379
1Ki 15:9 twentieth year of **J.** king of Israel....... 3379
1Ki 15:25 Nadab the son of **J.** began to reign...... 3379
1Ki 15:29 that he smote all the house of **J.**;...... 3379
1Ki 15:29 he left not to **J.** any that breathed, ... 3379
1Ki 15:30 of the sins of **J.** which he sinned, ... 3379
1Ki 15:34 walked in the way of **J.**, and in his 3379
1Ki 16:2 thou hast walked in the way of **J.**, ... 3379
1Ki 16:3 make thy house like the house of **J.**.... 3379
1Ki 16:7 in being like the house of **J.**; 3379
1Ki 16:19 in walking in the way of **J.**, and in...... 3379
1Ki 16:26 For he walked in all the way of **J.** 3379
1Ki 16:31 for him to walk in the sins of **J.**......... 3379
1Ki 21:22 thine house like the house of **J.** 3379
1Ki 22:52 of his mother, and in the way of **J.**...... 3379
2Ki 3:3 he cleaved unto the sins of **J.** the...... 3379
2Ki 9:9 house of Ahab like the house of **J.**....... 3379
2Ki 10:29 from the sins of **J.** the son of Nebat, .. 3379
2Ki 10:31 he departed not from the sins of **J.**,..... 3379
2Ki 13:2 and followed the sins of **J.** the son 3379
2Ki 13:6 not from the sins of the house of **J.**,.... 3379
2Ki 13:11 departed not from all the sins of **J.**..... 3379
2Ki 13:13 and **J.** sat upon his throne: 3379
2Ki 14:16 and **J.** his son reigned in his stead...... 3379
2Ki 14:23 **J.** the son of Joash king of Israel........ 3379
2Ki 14:24 departed not from all the sins of **J.**...... 3379
2Ki 14:27 he saved them by the hand of **J.**......... 3379
2Ki 14:28 the rest of the acts of **J.**, and all......... 3379
2Ki 14:29 **J.** slept with his fathers, even with..... 3379
2Ki 15:1 twenty and seventh year of **J.** king..... 3379
2Ki 15:8 did Zachariah the son of **J.** reign 3379
2Ki 15:9 he departed not from the sins of **J.**...... 3379
2Ki 15:18 not all his days from the sins of **J.**...... 3379
2Ki 15:24, 28 departed not from the sins of **J.**...... 3379
2Ki 17:21 they made **J.** the son of Nebat king: ... 3379
2Ki 17:21 **J.** drave Israel from following the........ 3379
2Ki 17:22 of Israel walked in all the sins of **J.** 3379
2Ki 23:15 the high place which **J.** the son of........ 3379
1Ch 5:17 and in the days of **J.** king of Israel. 3379
2Ch 9:29 visions of Iddo the seer against **J.** 3379
2Ch 10:2 came to pass, when **J.**...heard it, ... 3379
2Ch 10:2 it, that **J.** returned out of Egypt......... 3379
2Ch 10:3 **J.** and all Israel came and spake to..... 3379
2Ch 10:12 So **J.** and all the people came to 3379
2Ch 10:15 hand of Ahijah the Shilonite to **J.**......... 3379
2Ch 11:4 returned from going against **J.**. 3379
2Ch 11:14 **J.** and his sons had cast them off 3379
2Ch 12:15 wars between Rehoboam and **J.**.......... 3379
2Ch 13:1 in the eighteenth year of king **J.** 3379
2Ch 13:2 was war between Abijah and **J.**........... 3379
2Ch 13:3 **J.** also set the battle in array............. 3379
2Ch 13:4 Hear me, thou **J.**, and all Israel; 3379
2Ch 13:6 **J.** the son of Nebat, the servant of...... 3379
2Ch 13:8 calves, which **J.** made you for gods. 3379
2Ch 13:13 **J.** caused an ambushment to come...... 3379
2Ch 13:15 God smote **J.** and all Israel before...... 3379
2Ch 13:19 Abijah pursued after **J.**, and took........ 3379
2Ch 13:20 Neither did **J.** recover strength.......... 3379
Ho 1:1 in the days of **J.** the son of Joash, ... 3379
Am 1:1 in the days of **J.** the son of Joash 3379
Am 7:9 I will rise against the house of **J.** 3379
Am 7:10 the priest of Beth-el sent to **J.** king.... 3379
Am 7:11 saith, **J.** shall die by the sword, ... 3379

JEROBOAM'S (jer-o-bo'-ams)
1Ki 14:4 And J. wife did so, and arose, and 3379
1Ki 14:17 J. wife arose, and departed, and 3379

JEROHAM (je-ro'-ham)
1Sa 1:1 name was Elkanah, the son of J.,....... 3395
1Ch 6:27 son, J. his son, Elkanah his son......... 3395
1Ch 6:34 The son of Elkanah, the son of J., ... 3395
1Ch 8:27 Eliah, and Zichri, the sons of J.. 3395
1Ch 9:8 Ibneiah the son of J., and Elah the..... 3395
1Ch 9:12 And Adaiah the son of J., the son of... 3395
1Ch 12:7 Zebadiah, the sons of J. of Gedor....... 3395
1Ch 27:22 Of Dan, Azareel the son of J............ 3395
2Ch 23:1 Azariah the son of J., and Ishmael...... 3395
Ne 11:12 and Adaiah the son of J., the son of ... 3395

JERUBBAAL (je-rub'-ba-al) See also GIDEON; JERUBBESHETH.
Jg 6:32 on that day he called him J., ... 3378
Jg 7:1 J., who is Gideon, and all the people .. 3378
Jg 8:29 J. the son of Joash went and dwelt..... 3378
Jg 8:35 they kindness to the house of J., ... 3378
Jg 9:1 Abimelech the son of J. went to 3378
Jg 9:2 that all the sons of J....reign over 3378
Jg 9:5 slew his brethren the sons of J.,........ 3378
Jg 9:5 the youngest son of J. was left;......... 3378
Jg 9:16 and if ye have dealt well with J.......... 3378
Jg 9:19 dealt truly and sincerely with J. 3378
Jg 9:24 and ten sons of J. might come,.......... 3378
Jg 9:28 serve him? is not he the son of J.?..... 3378
Jg 9:57 the curse of Jotham the son of J.. 3378
1Sa 12:11 And the Lord sent J., and Bedan, ... 3378

JERUBBESHETH (je-rub'-be-sheth) See also JERUB-BAAL.
2Sa 11:21 smote Abimelech the son of J.? 3380

JERUEL (je-ru'-el)
2Ch 20:16 brook, before the wilderness of J.. 3385

JERUSALEM (je-ru'-sa-lem) See also JERUSALEM'S; SALEM.
Jos 10:1 king of J. had heard how Joshua........ 3389
Jos 10:3 king of J. sent unto Hoham king of....... 3389
Jos 10:5, 23 king of J., the king of Hebron, ... 3389
Jos 12:10 The king of J., one; the king of.......... 3389
Jos 15:8 side of the Jebusite; the same is J.:..... 3389
Jos 15:63 the Jebusites the inhabitants of J., ... 3389
Jos 15:63 with the children of Judah at J.......... 3389
Jos 18:28 Eleph, and Jebusi, which is J.,........... 3389
Jg 1:7 they brought him to J., and there....... 3389
Jg 1:8 of Judah had fought against J., ... 3389
Jg 1:21 out the Jebusites that inhabited J.;...... 3389
Jg 1:21 of Benjamin in J. unto this day. 3389
Jg 19:10 over against Jebus, which is J.;.......... 3389
1Sa 17:54 the Philistine, and brought it to J.; 3389
2Sa 5:5 in J. he reigned thirty and three 3389
2Sa 5:6 the king and his men went to J.......... 3389
2Sa 5:13 concubines and wives out of J., ... 3389
2Sa 5:14 those that were born unto him in J.;... 3389
2Sa 8:7 Hadadezer, and brought them to J...... 3389
2Sa 9:13 So Mephibosheth dwelt in J.: for........ 3389
2Sa 10:14 children of Ammon, and came to J...... 3389
2Sa 11:1 But David tarried still at J.. 3389
2Sa 11:12 So Uriah abode in J. that day, and...... 3389
2Sa 12:31 and all the people returned unto J.. 3389
2Sa 14:23 Geshur, and brought Absalom to J...... 3389
2Sa 14:28 Absalom dwelt two full years in J.,..... 3389
2Sa 15:8 shall bring me again indeed to J., ... 3389
2Sa 15:11 went two hundred men out of J., ... 3389
2Sa 15:14 servants that were with him at J.,...... 3389
2Sa 15:29 carried the ark of God again to J.:...... 3389
2Sa 15:37 the city, and Absalom came into J.. 3389
2Sa 16:3 the king, Behold, he abideth at J.:...... 3389
2Sa 16:15 people the men of Israel, came to J.,.. 3389
2Sa 17:20 not find them, they returned to J.. 3389
2Sa 19:19 that my lord the king went out of J., .. 3389
2Sa 19:25 he was come to J. to meet the king, .. 3389
2Sa 19:33 and I will feed thee with me in J........ 3389
2Sa 19:34 should go up with the king unto J.? 3389
2Sa 20:2 their king, from Jordan even to J.. 3389
2Sa 20:3 And David came to his house at J.; 3389
2Sa 20:7 and they went out of J., to pursue 3389
2Sa 20:22 Joab returned to J. unto the king. 3389
2Sa 24:8 they came to J. at the end of nine....... 3389
2Sa 24:16 out his hand upon J. to destroy it,...... 3389
1Ki 2:11 and three years reigned he in J.. 3389
1Ki 2:36 unto him, Build thee an house in J., ... 3389
1Ki 2:38 And Shimei dwelt in J. many days...... 3389
1Ki 2:41 Shimei had gone from J. to Gath,........ 3389
1Ki 3:1 and the wall of J. round about. 3389
1Ki 3:15 he came to J., and stood before the ... 3389
1Ki 8:1 of Israel, unto king Solomon in J., ... 3389
1Ki 9:15 and the wall of J., and Hazor, and...... 3389
1Ki 9:19 Solomon desired to build in J.,........... 3389
1Ki 10:2 she came to J. with a very great 3389
1Ki 10:26 chariots, and with the king at J.......... 3389
1Ki 10:27 made silver to be in J. as stones,....... 3389
1Ki 11:7 in the hill that is before J., and for..... 3389
1Ki 11:29 when Jeroboam went out of J., ... 3389
1Ki 11:36 have a light alway before me in J.. 3389
1Ki 11:42 the time that Solomon reigned in J. 3389
1Ki 12:18 him up to his chariot, to flee to J.. 3389
1Ki 12:21 when Rehoboam was come to J., ... 3389
1Ki 12:27 in the house of the Lord at J.,........... 3389
1Ki 12:28 is too much for you to go up to J.:..... 3389
1Ki 14:21 he reigned seventeen years in J.,........ 3389
1Ki 14:25 king of Egypt came up against J.:....... 3389
1Ki 15:2 Three years reigned he in J.. 3389
1Ki 15:4 Lord his God give him a lamp in J.,.... 3389
1Ki 15:4 son after him, and to establish J.: 3389
1Ki 15:10 forty and one years reigned he in J.. .. 3389
1Ki 22:42 reigned twenty and five years in J...... 3389
2Ki 8:17 and he reigned eight years in J.. 3389
2Ki 8:26 and he reigned one year in J.. 3389
2Ki 9:28 carried him in a chariot to J., ... 3389
2Ki 12:1 and forty years reigned he in J.. 3389
2Ki 12:7 Hazael set his face to go up to J.. 3389
2Ki 12:18 of Syria: and he went away from J.. 3389
2Ki 14:2 reigned twenty and nine years in J.. ... 3389
2Ki 14:2 name was Jehoaddan of J.................. 3389
2Ki 14:13 at Beth-shemesh, and came to J., ... 3389
2Ki 14:13 and brake down the wall of J. from..... 3389
2Ki 14:19 a conspiracy against him in J.: 3389
2Ki 14:20 he was buried at J. with his fathers.... 3389
2Ki 15:2 reigned two and fifty years in J.......... 3389
2Ki 15:2 name was Jecholiah of J.. 3389
2Ki 15:33 and he reigned sixteen years in J.. 3389
2Ki 16:2 and reigned sixteen years in J., ... 3389
2Ki 16:5 king of Israel came up to J. to war:.... 3389
2Ki 18:2 reigned twenty and nine years in J.. ... 3389
2Ki 18:17 with a great host against J.:............. 3389
2Ki 18:17 And they went up and came to J.,...... 3389
2Ki 18:22 and hath said to Judah and J.,........... 3389
2Ki 18:22 worship before this altar in J.?.......... 3389
2Ki 18:35 should deliver J. out of mine hand?..... 3389
2Ki 19:10 J. shall not be delivered into the 3389
2Ki 19:21 daughter of J. hath shaken her head ... 3389
2Ki 19:31 out of J. shall go forth a remnant, ... 3389
2Ki 21:1 reigned fifty and five years in J.......... 3389
2Ki 21:4 Lord said, In J. will I put my name. ... 3389
2Ki 21:7 and in J., which I have chosen........... 3389
2Ki 21:12 I am bringing such evil upon J. and..... 3389
2Ki 21:13 stretch over J. the line of Samaria,..... 3389
2Ki 21:13 wipe J. as a man wipeth a dish, ... 3389
2Ki 21:16 filled J. from one end to another; 3389
2Ki 21:19 and he reigned two years in J.. 3389
2Ki 22:1 reigned thirty and one years in J....... 3389
2Ki 22:14 (now she dwelt in J. in the college;) 3389
2Ki 23:1 all the elders of Judah and of J.. 3389
2Ki 23:2 all the inhabitants of J. with him,....... 3389
2Ki 23:4 he burned them without J. in the 3389
2Ki 23:5 and in the places round about J.;........ 3389
2Ki 23:6 without J., unto the brook Kidron, ... 3389
2Ki 23:9 not up to the altar of the Lord in J.,... 3389
2Ki 23:13 the high places that were before J.,.... 3389
2Ki 23:20 upon them, and returned to J.. 3389
2Ki 23:23 was holden to the Lord in J.. 3389
2Ki 23:24 spied in the land of Judah and in J., ... 3389
2Ki 23:27 off this city J. which I have chosen,.... 3389
2Ki 23:30 brought him to J., and buried him 3389
2Ki 23:31 and he reigned three months in J.. 3389
2Ki 23:33 that he might not reign in J.;............ 3389
2Ki 23:36 and he reigned eleven years in J.. 3389
2Ki 24:4 for he filled J. with innocent blood;..... 3389
2Ki 24:8 and he reigned in J. three months. 3389
2Ki 24:8 the daughter of Elnathan of J.. 3389
2Ki 24:10 king of Babylon came up against J., ... 3389
2Ki 24:14 he carried away all J., and all the....... 3389
2Ki 24:15 carried he into captivity from J. to...... 3389
2Ki 24:18 and he reigned eleven years in J......... 3389
2Ki 24:20 it came to pass in J. and Judah, ... 3389
2Ki 25:1 he, and all his host, against J., ... 3389
2Ki 25:8 of the king of Babylon, unto J.: 3389
2Ki 25:9 house, and all the houses of J., ... 3389
2Ki 25:10 down the walls of J. round about........ 3389
1Ch 3:4 in J. he reigned thirty and three 3389
1Ch 3:5 these were born unto him in J.;......... 3389
1Ch 6:10 temple that Solomon built in J.:) 3389
1Ch 6:15 Lord carried away Judah and J........... 3389
1Ch 6:32 built the house of the Lord in J.: 3389
1Ch 8:28 chief men. These dwelt in J.............. 3389
1Ch 8:32 dwelt with their brethren in J., ... 3389
1Ch 9:3 in J. dwelt of the children of Judah, ... 3389
1Ch 9:34 their generations; these dwelt at J...... 3389
1Ch 9:38 dwelt with their brethren at J., ... 3389
1Ch 11:4 David and all Israel went to J., ... 3389
1Ch 14:3 And David took more wives at J.: 3389
1Ch 14:4 of his children which he had in J.; 3389
1Ch 15:3 gathered all Israel together to J., ... 3389
1Ch 18:7 Hadarezer, and brought them to J.. 3389
1Ch 19:15 into the city. Then Joab came to J...... 3389
1Ch 20:1 But David tarried at J.. And Joab 3389
1Ch 20:3 and all the people returned to J.. 3389
1Ch 21:4 throughout all Israel and came to J.. ... 3389
1Ch 21:15 And God sent an angel unto J. to....... 3389
1Ch 21:16 in his hand stretched out over J......... 3389
1Ch 23:25 that they may dwell in J. for ever: 3389
1Ch 28:1 with all the valiant men, unto J.......... 3389
1Ch 29:27 and three years reigned he in J.. 3389
2Ch 1:4 he had pitched a tent for it at J.. 3389
2Ch 1:13 high place that was at Gibeon to J.,.... 3389
2Ch 1:14 cities, and with the king at J.. 3389
2Ch 1:15 silver and gold at J. as plenteous 3389
2Ch 2:7 are with me in Judah and in J............ 3389
2Ch 2:16 and thou shalt carry it up to J.. 3389
2Ch 3:1 to build the house of the Lord at J. 3389
2Ch 5:2 unto J., to bring up the ark of........... 3389
2Ch 6:6 But I have chosen J., that my name ... 3389
2Ch 8:6 that Solomon desired to build in J.,...... 3389
2Ch 9:1 Solomon with hard questions at J., ... 3389
2Ch 9:25 cities,and with the king at J.. 3389
2Ch 9:27 king made silver in J. as stones, ... 3389
2Ch 9:30 And Solomon reigned in J. over all..... 3389
2Ch 10:18 him up to his chariot, to flee to J.. 3389
2Ch 11:1 when Rehoboam was come to J., ... 3389
2Ch 11:5 Rehoboam dwelt in J., and built......... 3389
2Ch 11:14 and came to Judah and J.:................. 3389
2Ch 11:16 the Lord God of Israel came to J., ... 3389
2Ch 12:2 king of Egypt came up against J.,....... 3389
2Ch 12:4 pertained to Judah, and came to J.. 3389
2Ch 12:5 that were gathered together to J......... 3389
2Ch 12:7 shall not be poured out upon J........... 3389
2Ch 12:9 king of Egypt came up against J.,....... 3389
2Ch 12:13 strengthened himself in J., and 3389
2Ch 12:13 he reigned seventeen years in J.,........ 3389
2Ch 13:2 He reigned three years in J.. His....... 3389
2Ch 14:15 in abundance, and returned to J.. 3389
2Ch 15:10 gathered themselves together at J...... 3389
2Ch 17:13 mighty men of valour, were in J.. 3389
2Ch 19:1 returned to his house in peace to J..... 3389
2Ch 19:4 Jehoshaphat dwelt at J.: and he 3389
2Ch 19:8 in J. did Jehoshaphat set of the.......... 3389
2Ch 19:8 when they returned to J.,................... 3389
2Ch 20:5 the congregation of Judah and J., ... 3389
2Ch 20:15 all Judah, and ye inhabitants of J., ... 3389
2Ch 20:17 the Lord with you, O Judah and J.: 3389
2Ch 20:18 the inhabitants of J. fell before the 3389
2Ch 20:20 O Judah, and ye inhabitants of J.;....... 3389
2Ch 20:27 every man of Judah and J., ... 3389
2Ch 20:27 of them, to go again to J. with joy; 3389
2Ch 20:28 they came to J. with psalteries and..... 3389
2Ch 20:31 reigned twenty and five years in J.. 3389
2Ch 21:5 and he reigned eight years in J.. 3389
2Ch 21:11 the inhabitants of J. to commit.......... 3389
2Ch 21:13 inhabitants of J. to go a whoring, ... 3389
2Ch 21:20 he reigned in J. eight years, and........ 3389
2Ch 22:1 inhabitants of J. made Ahaziah his 3389
2Ch 22:2 reign, and he reigned one year in J.. .. 3389
2Ch 23:2 of Israel, and they came to J............. 3389
2Ch 24:1 and he reigned forty years in J.. 3389
2Ch 24:6 Judah and out of J. the collection,....... 3389
2Ch 24:9 proclamation through Judah and J., ... 3389
2Ch 24:18 wrath came upon Judah and J. for 3389
2Ch 24:23 and they came to Judah and J., and 3389
2Ch 25:1 reigned twenty and nine years in J.. ... 3389
2Ch 25:1 mother's name...Jehoaddan of J.......... 3389
2Ch 25:23 and brought him to J., and brake 3389
2Ch 25:23 brake down the wall of J. from the..... 3389
2Ch 25:27 a conspiracy against him in J.; 3389
2Ch 26:3 he reigned fifty and two years in J.. ... 3389
2Ch 26:3 name also was Jecoliah of J.............. 3389

2Ch 26:9 Moreover Uzziah built towers in **J.** 3389
2Ch 26:15 he made in **J.** engines, invented 3389
2Ch 27:1 and he reigned sixteen years in **J.** 3389
2Ch 27:8 and reigned sixteen years in **J.** 3389
2Ch 28:1 and he reigned sixteen years in **J.**: 3389
2Ch 28:10 under the children of Judah and **J.** 3389
2Ch 28:24 him altars in every corner of **J.** 3389
2Ch 28:27 buried him in the city, even in **J.**: 3389
2Ch 29:1 reigned nine and twenty years in **J.** 3389
2Ch 29:8 of the Lord was upon Judah and **J.**, 3389
2Ch 30:1 come to the house of the Lord at **J.**, 3389
2Ch 30:2 and all the congregation in **J.**, 3389
2Ch 30:3 gathered themselves together to **J.** 3389
2Ch 30:5 unto the Lord God of Israel at **J.**: 3389
2Ch 30:11 themselves, and came to **J.** 3389
2Ch 30:13 there assembled at **J.** much people 3389
2Ch 30:14 took away the altars that were in **J.**, 3389
2Ch 30:21 of Israel that were present at **J.** 3389
2Ch 30:26 So there was great joy in **J.**: for 3389
2Ch 30:26 Israel there was not the like in **J.** 3389
2Ch 31:4 the people that dwelt in **J.** to give 3389
2Ch 32:2 he was purposed to fight against **J.**, 3389
2Ch 32:9 of Assyria send his servants to **J.**, 3389
2Ch 32:9 and unto all Judah that were at **J.**, 3389
2Ch 32:10 that ye abide in the siege in **J.**? 3389
2Ch 32:12 and commanded Judah and **J.**, 3389
2Ch 32:18 people of **J.** that were on the wall, 3389
2Ch 32:19 they spake against the God of **J.**, 3389
2Ch 32:22 Hezekiah and the inhabitants of **J.** 3389
2Ch 32:23 brought gifts unto the Lord to **J.**, 3389
2Ch 32:25 upon him, and upon Judah and **J.** 3389
2Ch 32:26 both he and the inhabitants of **J.**, 3389
2Ch 32:33 inhabitants of **J.** did him honour at 3389
2Ch 33:1 he reigned fifty and five years in **J.**: 3389
2Ch 33:4 In **J.** shall my name be for ever. 3389
2Ch 33:7 and in **J.**, which I have chosen 3389
2Ch 33:9 and the inhabitants of **J.** to err, 3389
2Ch 33:13 him again to **J.** into his kingdom, 3389
2Ch 33:15 in **J.**, and cast them out of the city. 3389
2Ch 33:21 reign, and reigned two years in **J.** 3389
2Ch 34:1 reigned in **J.** one and thirty years. 3389
2Ch 34:3 he began to purge Judah and **J.** 3389
2Ch 34:5 altars, and cleansed Judah and **J.** 3389
2Ch 34:7 land of Israel, he returned to **J.** 3389
2Ch 34:9 Benjamin; and they returned to **J.** 3389
2Ch 34:22 (now she dwelt in **J.** in the college:) 3389
2Ch 34:29 all the elders of Judah and **J.** 3389
2Ch 34:30 of Judah, and the inhabitants of **J.**, 3389
2Ch 34:32 he caused all that were present in **J.** 3389
2Ch 34:32 the inhabitants of **J.** did according 3389
2Ch 35:1 kept a passover unto the Lord in **J.**: 3389
2Ch 35:18 present, and the inhabitants of **J.** 3389
2Ch 35:24 they brought him to **J.**, and he died, 3389
2Ch 35:24 Judah and **J.** mourned for Josiah. 3389
2Ch 36:1 him king in his father's stead in **J.** 3389
2Ch 36:2 and he reigned three months in **J.** 3389
2Ch 36:3 king of Egypt put him down at **J.** 3389
2Ch 36:4 his brother king over Judah and **J.**, 3389
2Ch 36:5 and he reigned eleven years in **J.**: 3389
2Ch 36:9 three months and ten days in **J.**: 3389
2Ch 36:10 his brother king over Judah and **J.** 3389
2Ch 36:11 and reigned eleven years in **J.** 3389
2Ch 36:14 Lord which he had hallowed in **J.** 3389
2Ch 36:19 and brake down the wall of **J.**, 3389
2Ch 36:23 me to build him an house in **J.**, 3389
Ezr 1:2 me to build him an house at **J.**, 3389
Ezr 1:3 with him, and let him go up to **J.**, 3389
Ezr 1:3(he is the God,) which is in **J.** 3389
Ezr 1:4 for the house of God that is in **J.** 3389
Ezr 1:5 house of the Lord which is in **J.** 3389
Ezr 1:7 had brought forth out of **J.**, 3389
Ezr 1:11 brought up from Babylon unto **J.** 3389
Ezr 2:1 and came again unto **J.** and Judah, 3389
Ezr 2:68 house of the Lord which is at **J.**, 3389
Ezr 3:1 together as one man to **J.** 3389
Ezr 3:8 coming unto the house of God at **J.**, 3389
Ezr 3:8 come out of the captivity unto **J.**; 3389
Ezr 4:6 the inhabitants of Judah and **J.** 3389
Ezr 4:8 the scribe wrote a letter against **J.** 3390
Ezr 4:12 from thee to us are come unto **J.**, 3390
Ezr 4:20 have been mighty kings also over **J.**, 3390
Ezr 4:23 up in haste to **J.** unto the Jews, 3390
Ezr 4:24 of the house of God which is at **J.** 3390
Ezr 5:1 the Jews that were in Judah and **J.** 3390
Ezr 5:2 the house of God which is at **J.**: 3390
Ezr 5:14 out of the temple that was in **J.**, 3390
Ezr 5:15 them into the temple that is in **J.**, 3390
Ezr 5:16 of the house of God which is in **J.**: 3390
Ezr 5:17 to build this house of God at **J.**, 3390
Ezr 6:3 concerning the house of God at **J.**, 3390
Ezr 6:5 out of the temple which is a **J.**, 3390
Ezr 6:5 again unto the temple which is at **J.**, 3390
Ezr 6:9 of the priests which are at **J.**, 3390
Ezr 6:12 this house of God which is at **J.** 3390
Ezr 6:18 the service of God, which is at **J.**; 3390
Ezr 7:7 and the Nethinims, unto **J.**, 3389
Ezr 7:8 he came to **J.** in the fifth month, 3389
Ezr 7:9 of the fifth month came he to **J.**, 3389
Ezr 7:13 their own freewill to go up to **J.**, 3390
Ezr 7:14 enquire concerning Judah and **J.**, 3390
Ezr 7:15 of Israel, whose habitation is in **J.**, 3390
Ezr 7:16 house of their God which is in **J.**: 3390
Ezr 7:17 house of your God which is in **J.** 3390
Ezr 7:19 deliver thou before the God of **J.** 3390
Ezr 7:27 house of the Lord which is in **J.**: 3389
Ezr 8:29 at **J.**, in the chambers of the house 3389
Ezr 8:30 to bring them to **J.** unto the house 3389
Ezr 8:31 of the first month, to go unto **J.**: 3389
Ezr 8:32 And we came to **J.**, and abode there 3389
Ezr 9:9 give us a wall in Judah and in **J.** 3389
Ezr 10:7 made proclamation throughout...**J.** 3389
Ezr 10:7 gather themselves together unto **J.**; 3389
Ezr 10:9 together unto **J.** within three days. 3389
Ne 1:2 of the captivity, and concerning **J.** 3389
Ne 1:3 the wall of **J.** also is broken down, 3389
Ne 2:11 So I came to **J.**, and was there three 3389
Ne 2:12 God had put in my heart to do at **J.**: 3389
Ne 2:13 viewed the walls of **J.**, which were 3389
Ne 2:17 how **J.** lieth waste, and the gates 3389
Ne 2:17 let us build up the wall of **J.**, that 3389
Ne 2:20 nor right, nor memorial, in **J.** 3389
Ne 3:8 fortified **J.** unto the broad wall. 3389
Ne 3:9 Hur, the ruler of the half part of **J.** 3389
Ne 3:12 the ruler of the half part of **J.**, 3389
Ne 4:7 that the walls of **J.** were made up, 3389
Ne 4:8 to come and to fight against **J.**, 3389
Ne 4:22 with his servant lodge within **J.**, 3389
Ne 6:7 prophets to preach of thee at **J.**, 3389
Ne 7:2 ruler of the palace, charge over **J.**: 3389
Ne 7:3 Let not the gates of **J.** be opened 3389
Ne 7:3 watches of the inhabitants of **J.**, 3389
Ne 7:6 and came again to **J.** and to Judah, 3389
Ne 8:15 proclaim in...their cities, and in **J.**, 3389
Ne 11:1 the rulers of the people dwelt at **J.**: 3389
Ne 11:1 of ten to dwell in **J.** the holy city, 3389
Ne 11:2 offered themselves to dwell at **J.** 3389
Ne 11:3 of the province that dwelt in **J.**: 3389
Ne 11:4 at **J.** dwelt certain of the children 3389
Ne 11:6 the sons of Perez that dwelt at **J.** 3389
Ne 11:22 overseer also of the Levites at **J.** 3389
Ne 12:27 at the dedication of the wall of **J.** 3389
Ne 12:27 to bring them to **J.**, to keep the 3389
Ne 12:28 the plain country round about **J.**, 3389
Ne 12:29 them villages round about **J.** 3389
Ne 12:43 the joy of **J.** was heard even afar off 3389
Ne 13:6 But in all this time was not I at **J.**: 3389
Ne 13:7 I came to **J.**, and understood of the 3389
Ne 13:15 they brought into **J.** on the sabbath 3389
Ne 13:16 the children of Judah, and in **J.** 3389
Ne 13:19 the gates of **J.** began to be dark 3389
Ne 13:20 all kind of ware lodged without **J.** 3389
Es 2:6 Who had been carried away from **J.** 3389
Ps 51:18 Zion: build thou the walls of **J.** 3389
Ps 68:29 of thy temples at **J.** shall kings bring 3389
Ps 79:1 defiled; they have laid **J.** on heaps. 3389
Ps 79:3 shed like water round about **J.**; 3389
Ps 102:21 Lord in Zion, and his praise in **J.**; 3389
Ps 116:19 house, in the midst of thee, O **J.** 3389
Ps 122:2 shall stand within thy gates, O **J.** 3389
Ps 122:3 **J.** is builded as a city that is 3389
Ps 122:6 Pray for the peace of **J.**: they shall 3389
Ps 125:2 the mountains are round about **J.**, 3389
Ps 128:5 thou shalt see the good of **J.** all the 3389
Ps 135:21 out of Zion, which dwelleth at **J.** 3389
Ps 137:5 If I forget thee, O **J.**, let my right 3389
Ps 137:6 if I prefer not **J.** above my chief joy 3389
Ps 137:7 children of Edom in the day of **J.**; 3389
Ps 147:2 The Lord doth build up **J.**: he 3389
Ps 147:12 Praise the Lord, O **J.**; praise thy 3389
Ec 1:1 the son of David, king in **J.** 3389
Ec 1:12 Preacher was king over Israel in **J.** 3389
Ec 1:16 they that have been before me in **J.**: 3389
Ec 2:7 above all that were in **J.** before me: 3389
Ec 2:9 than all that were before me in **J.**: 3389
Ca 1:5 but comely. O ye daughters of **J.**, 3389
Ca 2:7 I charge you, O ye daughters of **J.**, 3389
Ca 3:5 I charge you, O ye daughters of **J.**, 3389
Ca 3:10 with love, for the daughters of **J.** 3389
Ca 5:8 I charge you, O daughters of **J.**, 3389
Ca 5:16 this is my friend, O daughters of **J.** 3389
Ca 6:4 O my love, as Tirzah, comely as **J.**, 3389
Ca 8:4 I charge you, O daughters of **J.**, 3389
Isa 1:1 he saw concerning Judah and **J.** 3389
Isa 2:1 Amoz saw concerning Judah and **J.** 3389
Isa 2:3 and the word of the Lord from **J.** 3389
Isa 3:1 take away from **J.** and from Judah 3389
Isa 3:8 **J.** is ruined, and Judah is fallen: 3389
Isa 4:3 and he that remaineth in **J.**, shall be 3389
Isa 4:3 is written among the living in **J.**: 3389
Isa 4:4 shall have purged the blood of **J.** 3389
Isa 5:3 now, O inhabitants of **J.**, and men of 3389
Isa 7:1 went up toward **J.** to war against 3389
Isa 8:14 for a snare to the inhabitants of **J.** 3389
Isa 10:10 graven images did excel them of **J.** 3389
Isa 10:11 her idols, so do to **J.** and her idols? 3389
Isa 10:12 work upon mount Zion and on **J.**, 3389
Isa 10:32 the daughter of Zion, the hill of **J.** 3389
Isa 22:10 ye have numbered the houses of **J.**, 3389
Isa 22:21 be a father to the inhabitants of **J.**, 3389
Isa 24:23 shall reign in mount Zion, and in **J.**, 3389
Isa 27:13 the Lord in the holy mount at **J.** 3389
Isa 28:14 that rule this people which is in **J.** 3389
Isa 30:19 the people shall dwell in Zion at **J.**: 3389
Isa 31:5 so will the Lord of hosts defend **J.**; 3389
Isa 31:9 fire is in Zion, and his furnace in **J.** 3389
Isa 33:20 eyes shall see **J.** a quiet habitation, 3389
Isa 36:2 sent Rabshakeh from Lachish to **J.** 3389
Isa 36:7 away, and said to Judah and to **J.**, 3389
Isa 36:20 Lord should deliver **J.** out of my 3389
Isa 37:10 **J.** shall not be given into the hand 3389
Isa 37:22 the daughter of **J.** hath shaken her 3389
Isa 37:32 out of **J.** shall go forth a remnant, 3389
Isa 40:2 Speak ye comfortably to **J.**, and cry 3389
Isa 40:9 O **J.**, that bringest good tidings, 3389
Isa 41:27 give to **J.** one that bringeth good 3389
Isa 44:26 saith to **J.**, Thou shalt be inhabited; 3389
Isa 44:28 saying to **J.**, Thou shalt be built; 3389
Isa 51:17 Awake, awake, stand up, O **J.**, 3389
Isa 52:1 put on thy beautiful garments, O **J.**, 3389
Isa 52:2 arise, and sit down, O **J.**: loose 3389
Isa 52:9 sing together, ye waste places of **J.**: 3389
Isa 52:9 his people, he hath redeemed **J.** 3389
Isa 62:6 set watchmen upon thy walls, O **J.**, 3389
Isa 62:7 till he make **J.** a praise in the earth. 3389
Isa 64:10 Zion is a wilderness, **J.** a desolation. 3389
Isa 65:18 I create **J.** a rejoicing, and her 3389
Isa 65:19 I will rejoice in **J.**, and joy in my 3389
Isa 66:10 Rejoice ye with **J.**, and be glad with 3389
Isa 66:13 and ye shall be comforted in **J.** 3389
Isa 66:20 beasts, to my holy mountain **J.**, 3389
Jer 1:3 unto the carrying away of **J.** captive 3389
Jer 1:15 at the entering of the gates of **J.**, 3389
Jer 2:2 Go and cry in the ears of **J.**, saying, 3389
Jer 3:17 shall call **J.** the throne of the Lord; 3389
Jer 3:17 it, to the name of the Lord, to **J.**: 3389
Jer 4:3 Lord to the men of Judah and **J.**, 3389
Jer 4:4 men of Judah and inhabitants of **J.**: 3389
Jer 4:5 ye in Judah, and publish in **J.**; 3389
Jer 4:10 greatly deceived this people and **J.**, 3389
Jer 4:11 it be said to this people and to **J.**, 3389
Jer 4:14 O **J.**, wash thine heart from 3389
Jer 4:16 publish against **J.**, that watchers 3389
Jer 5:1 to and fro through the streets of **J.**, 3389
Jer 6:1 to flee out of the midst of **J.**, 3389
Jer 6:6 trees, and cast a mount against **J.**: 3389
Jer 6:8 Be thou instructed, O **J.**, lest my 3389
Jer 7:17 of Judah and in the streets of **J.**? 3389
Jer 7:29 Cut off thine hair, O **J.**, and cast it
Jer 7:34 Judah, and from the streets of **J.**, 3389
Jer 8:1 the bones of the inhabitants of **J.**, 3389
Jer 8:5 is this people of **J.** slidden back 3389
Jer 9:11 I will make **J.** heaps, and a den of 3389
Jer 11:2 Judah, and to the inhabitants of **J.**; 3389
Jer 11:6 of Judah, and in the streets of **J.**, 3389
Jer 11:9 and among the inhabitants of **J.** 3389
Jer 11:12 of Judah and inhabitants of **J.** go, 3389
Jer 11:13 to the number of streets of **J.** 3389
Jer 13:9 of Judah, and the great pride of **J.** 3389

Jer	13:13	all the inhabitants of J., and	3389
Jer	13:27	Woe unto thee, O J.! wilt thou not	3389
Jer	14:2	and the cry of J. is gone up.	3389
Jer	14:16	shall be cast out in the streets of J.	3389
Jer	15:4	Judah, for that which he did in J..	3389
Jer	15:5	shall have pity upon thee, O J.?	3389
Jer	17:19	go out, and in all the gates of J.;	3389
Jer	17:20	all the inhabitants of J., that enter	3389
Jer	17:21	nor bring it in by the gates of J.;	3389
Jer	17:25	Judah, and the inhabitants of J.:	3389
Jer	17:26	Judah, and from the places about J.,	3389
Jer	17:27	even entering in at the gates of J.	3389
Jer	17:27	it shall devour the palaces of J.,	3389
Jer	18:11	Judah, and to the inhabitants of J.,	3389
Jer	19:3	of Judah, and inhabitants of J.;	3389
Jer	19:7	void the counsel of Judah and J.	3389
Jer	19:13	the houses of J., and the houses of	3389
Jer	22:19	cast forth beyond the gates of J..	3389
Jer	23:14	have seen also in the prophets of J.	3389
Jer	23:15	the prophets of J. is profaneness	3389
Jer	24:1	the carpenters and smiths, from J.,	3389
Jer	24:8	his princes, and the residue of J.,	3389
Jer	25:2	to all the inhabitants of J., saying,	3389
Jer	25:18	To wit, J., and the cities of Judah,	3389
Jer	26:18	a field, and J. shall become heaps,	3389
Jer	27:3	of the messengers which come to J.	3389
Jer	27:18	of the king of Judah, and at J., go	3389
Jer	27:20	king of Judah from J. to Babylon,	3389
Jer	27:20	and all the nobles of Judah and J.;	3389
Jer	27:21	of the king of Judah and of J.;	3389
Jer	29:1	Jeremiah the prophet sent from J.	3389
Jer	29:1	away captive from J. to Babylon;	3389
Jer	29:2	the princes of Judah and J., and	3389
Jer	29:2	the smiths, were departed from J.;)	3389
Jer	29:4	caused to be carried away from J.	3389
Jer	29:20	I have sent from J. to Babylon:	3389
Jer	29:25	unto all the people that are at J.,	3389
Jer	32:2	king of Babylon's army besieged J.	3389
Jer	32:32	of Judah, and the inhabitants of J.	3389
Jer	32:44	and in the places about J., and in	3389
Jer	33:10	the streets of J., that are desolate,	3389
Jer	33:13	and in the places about J., and in	3389
Jer	33:16	be saved, and J. shall dwell safely:	3389
Jer	34:1	all the people, fought against J.,	3389
Jer	34:6	unto Zedekiah king of Judah in J.,	3389
Jer	34:7	Babylon's army fought against J..	3389
Jer	34:8	with all the people which were at J.,	3389
Jer	34:19	of Judah, and the princes of J.,	3389
Jer	35:11	Come, and let us go to J. for fear	3389
Jer	35:11	of the Syrians: so we dwell at J.	3389
Jer	35:13	of Judah and the inhabitants of J.,	3389
Jer	35:17	upon all the inhabitants of J. all	3389
Jer	36:9	the Lord to all the people in J.,	3389
Jer	36:9	from the cities of Judah unto J.	3389
Jer	36:31	and upon the inhabitants of J.,	3389
Jer	37:5	Chaldeans that besieged J. heard	3389
Jer	37:5	of them, they departed from J..	3389
Jer	37:11	was broken up from J. for fear of	3389
Jer	37:12	Jeremiah went forth out of J. to go	3389
Jer	38:28	until the day that J. was taken:	3389
Jer	38:28	he was there when J. was taken.	3389
Jer	39:1	Babylon and all his army against J.,	3389
Jer	39:8	and brake down the walls of J..	3389
Jer	40:1	away captive of J. and Judah,	3389
Jer	42:18	forth upon the inhabitants of J.;	3389
Jer	44:2	evil that I have brought upon J.,	3389
Jer	44:6	of Judah and in the streets of J.;	3389
Jer	44:9	of Judah, and in the streets of J.?	3389
Jer	44:13	as I have punished J., by the sword,	3389
Jer	44:17	of Judah, and in the streets of J.	3389
Jer	44:21	of Judah, and in the streets of J.,	3389
Jer	51:35	inhabitants of Chaldea, shall J. say.	3389
Jer	51:50	and let J. come into your mind.	3389
Jer	52:1	and he reigned eleven years in J.	3389
Jer	52:3	it came to pass in J. and Judah,	3389
Jer	52:4	he and all his army, against J.,	3389
Jer	52:12	served the king of Babylon, into J.,	3389
Jer	52:13	and all the houses of J., and all the	3389
Jer	52:14	brake down all the walls of J. round	3389
Jer	52:29	he carried away captive from J.	3389
La	1:7	J. remembered in the days of her	3389
La	1:8	J. hath grievously sinned;	3389
La	1:17	J. is as a menstruous woman	3389
La	2:10	virgins of J. hand down their heads	3389
La	2:13	I liken to thee, O daughter of J.?	3389
La	2:15	their head at the daughter of J.,	3389
La	4:12	have entered into the gates of J..	3389
Eze	4:1	pourtray upon it the city, even J.	3389
Eze	4:7	set thy face toward the siege of J.,	3389
Eze	4:16	I will break the staff of bread in J.	3389
Eze	5:5	saith the Lord God; This is J.	3389
Eze	8:3	me in the visions of God to J.,	3389
Eze	9:4	of the city, through the midst of J.,	3389
Eze	9:8	pouring out of thy fury upon J.?	3389
Eze	11:15	the inhabitants of J. have said,	3389
Eze	12:10	burden concerneth the prince in J.,	3389
Eze	12:19	Lord God of the inhabitants of J.,	3389
Eze	13:16	which prophesy concening J.,	3389
Eze	14:21	my four sore judgments upon J.,	3389
Eze	14:22	evil that I have brought upon J.,	3389
Eze	15:6	so will I give the inhabitants of J..	3389
Eze	16:2	cause J. to know her abominations,	3389
Eze	16:3	Thus saith the Lord God unto J.;	3389
Eze	17:12	the king of Babylon is come to J.,	3389
Eze	21:2	Son of man, set thy face toward J.,	3389
Eze	21:20	and to Judah in J. the defenced.	3389
Eze	21:22	right hand was the divination for J.,	3389
Eze	22:19	will gather you into the midst of J..	3389
Eze	23:4	Samaria is Aholah, and J. Aholibah.	3389
Eze	24:2	of Babylon set himself against J.	3389
Eze	26:2	that Tyrus hath said against J.,	3389
Eze	33:21	one that had escaped out of J. came	3389
Eze	36:38	the flock of J. in her solemn feasts;	3389
Da	1:1	came Nebuchadnezzar...unto J.,	3389
Da	5:2	out of the temple which was in J.;	3390
Da	5:3	the house of God which was at J.;	3390
Da	6:10	open in his chamber toward J.,	3390
Da	9:2	years in the desolation of J..	3389
Da	9:7	Judah, and to the inhabitants of J.,	3389
Da	9:12	done as hath been done upon J.	3389
Da	9:16	be turned away from thy city J.,	3389
Da	9:16	J. and thy people are become a	3389
Da	9:25	to restore and to build J. unto the	3389
Joe	2:32	Zion and in J. shall be deliverance,	3389
Joe	3:1	again the captivity of Judah and J.,	3389
Joe	3:6	the children of J. have ye sold unto	3389
Joe	3:16	of Zion, and utter his voice from J.;	3389
Joe	3:17	mountain: then shall J. be holy,	3389
Joe	3:20	J. from generation to generation.	3389
Am	1:2	Zion, and utter his voice from J.;	3389
Am	2:5	it shall devour the palaces of J.	3389
Ob	11	his gates, and cast lots upon J.,	3389
Ob	20	Zarephath; and the captivity of J.,	3389
Mic	1:1	he saw concerning Samaria and J..	3389
Mic	1:5	places of Judah? are they not J.?	3389
Mic	1:9	the gate of my people, even to J..	3389
Mic	1:12	from the Lord unto the gate of J.	3389
Mic	3:10	with blood, and J. with iniquity.	3389
Mic	3:12	a field, and J. shall become heaps,	3389
Mic	4:2	and the word of the Lord from J..	3389
Mic	4:8	shall come to the daughter of J.	3389
Zep	1:4	and upon all the inhabitants of J.;	3389
Zep	1:12	that I will search J. with candles,	3389
Zep	3:14	with all the heart, O daughter of J.	3389
Zep	3:16	In that day it shall be said to J.,	3389
Zec	1:12	long wilt thou not have mercy on J.	3389
Zec	1:14	I am jealous for J. and for Zion	3389
Zec	1:16	I am returned to J. with mercies:	3389
Zec	1:16	shall be stretched forth upon J.	3389
Zec	1:17	Zion, and shall yet choose J..	3389
Zec	1:19	scattered Judah, Israel, and J..	3389
Zec	2:2	he said unto me, To measure J.,	3389
Zec	2:4	J. shall be inhabited as towns	3389
Zec	2:12	land, and shall choose J. again.	3389
Zec	3:2	Lord that hath chosen J. rebuke	3389
Zec	7:7	J. was inhabited and in prosperity,	3389
Zec	8:3	and will dwell in the midst of J.:	3389
Zec	8:3	J. shall be called a city of truth;	3389
Zec	8:4	women dwell in the streets of J.,	3389
Zec	8:8	they shall dwell in the midst of J.:	3389
Zec	8:15	to do well unto J. and to the house	3389
Zec	8:22	come to seek the Lord of hosts in J.,	3389
Zec	9:9	shout, O daughter of J.: behold,	3389
Zec	9:10	Ephraim, and the horse from J.,	3389
Zec	12:2	I will make J. a cup of trembling	3389
Zec	12:2	both against Judah and against J..	3389
Zec	12:3	make J. a burdensome stone for all	3389
Zec	12:5	The inhabitants of J. shall be my	3389
Zec	12:6	and J. shall be inhabited again	3389
Zec	12:6	in her own place, even in J..	3389
Zec	12:7	the glory of the inhabitants of J.	3389
Zec	12:8	Lord defend the inhabitants of J.;	3389
Zec	12:9	the nations that come against J..	3389
Zec	12:10	and upon the inhabitants of J., the	3389
Zec	12:11	there be a great mourning in J.,	3389
Zec	13:1	and to the inhabitants of J. for sin	3389
Zec	14:2	I will gather all nations against J.	3389
Zec	14:4	which is before J. on the east,	3389
Zec	14:8	living waters shall go out from J.;	3389
Zec	14:10	from Geba to Rimmon south of J.:	3389
Zec	14:11	but J. shall be safely inhabited.	3389
Zec	14:12	people that have fought against J.;	3389
Zec	14:14	And Judah also shall fight at J.;	3389
Zec	14:16	the nations which came against J.	3389
Zec	14:7	earth unto J. to worship the King,	3389
Zec	14:21	every pot in J. and in Judah shall	3389
Mal	2:11	is committed in Israel and in J.;	3389
Mal	3:4	offering of Judah and J. be pleasant	3389
Mt	2:1	wise men from the east to J.,	*2414*
Mt	2:3	was troubled, and all J. with him.	*2414*
Mt	3:5	went out to him J., and all Judaea,	*2414*
Mt	4:25	from J., and from Judaea, and from	*2414*
Mt	5:35	**neither by J.; for it is the city of**	*2414*
Mt	15:1	and Pharisees, which were of J.,	*2414*
Mt	16:21	how that he must go unto J., and	*2414*
Mt	20:17	And Jesus going up to J. took the	*2414*
Mt	20:18	**Behold, we go up to J.; and the**	*2414*
Mt	21:1	And when they drew nigh unto J.,	*2414*
Mt	21:10	when he was come into J., all the	*2414*
Mt	23:37	**O J., J., thou that killest the**	*2419*
Mk	1:5	the land of Judaea, and they of J.,	*2414*
Mk	3:8	And from J., and from Idumaea, and	*2414*
Mk	3:22	scribes which came down from J.	*2414*
Mk	7:1	of the scribes, which came from J..	*2414*
Mk	10:32	were in the way going up to J.;	*2414*
Mk	10:33	Saying, **Behold, we go up to J.;**	*2414*
Mk	11:1	when they came nigh to J., unto	*2419*
Mk	11:11	Jesus entered into J., and into the	*2414*
Mk	11:15	they come to J.: and Jesus went	*2414*
Mk	11:27	And they come again to J.: and as	*2414*
Mk	15:41	which came up with him unto J..	*2414*
Lu	2:22	they brought him to J., to present	*2414*
Lu	2:25	there was a man in J., whose	*2419*
Lu	2:38	that looked for redemption in J..	*2419*
Lu	2:41	his parents went to J. every year	*2419*
Lu	2:42	went up to J. after the custom	*2414*
Lu	2:43	child Jesus tarried behind in J.;	*2419*
Lu	2:45	not, they turned back again to J.,	*2419*
Lu	4:9	he brought him to J., and set him	*2419*
Lu	5:17	town of Galilee, and Judaea, and J.:	*2419*
Lu	6:17	of people out of all Judaea and J.,	*2419*
Lu	9:31	which he should accomplish at J..	*2419*
Lu	9:51	stedfastly set his face to go to J.,	*2419*
Lu	9:53	was as though he would go to J..	*2419*
Lu	10:30	**man went down from J. to Jericho,**	*2419*
Lu	13:4	**above all men that dwelt in J.?**	*2419*
Lu	13:22	teaching, and journeying toward J..	*2419*
Lu	13:33	**be that a prophet perish out of J.**	*2419*
Lu	13:34	**O J., J., which killest the prophets,**	*2419*
Lu	17:11	it came to pass, as he went to J.,	*2419*
Lu	18:31	unto them, **Behold, we go up to J.,**	*2414*
Lu	19:11	parable, because he was nigh to J.,	*2419*
Lu	19:28	he went before, ascending up to J.	*2414*
Lu	21:20	**see J. compassed with armies,**	*2419*
Lu	21:24	**and J. shall be trodden down of**	*2419*
Lu	23:7	himself also was at J. at that	*2414*
Lu	23:28	**Daughters of J., weep not for me,**	*2419*
Lu	24:13	from J. about threescore furlongs.	*2419*
Lu	24:18	him, Art thou only a stranger in J.,	*2419*
Lu	24:33	the same hour, and returned to J.,	*2419*
Lu	24:47	**among all nations, beginning at J.**	*2419*
Lu	24:49	**tarry ye in the city of J., until ye**	*2419*
Lu	24:52	and returned to J. with great joy:	*2419*
Joh	1:19	sent priests and Levites from J.	*2414*
Joh	2:13	at hand, and Jesus went up to J.,	*2414*
Joh	2:23	when he was in J. at the passover,	*2414*
Joh	4:20	in J. is the place where men ought	*2414*
Joh	4:21	**in this mountain, nor yet at J.,**	*2414*
Joh	4:45	things that he did at J. at the feast:	*2414*
Joh	5:1	the Jews; and Jesus went up to J..	*2414*
Joh	5:2	is at J. by the sheep market a pool,	*2414*
Joh	7:25	Then said some of them of J., Is	*2414*
Joh	10:22	was at J. the feast of the dedication,	*2414*
Joh	11:18	Now Bethany was nigh unto J.,	*2414*
Joh	11:55	went out of the country up to J.	*2414*
Joh	12:12	heard that Jesus was coming to J.,	*2414*
Ac	1:4	they should not depart from J.,	*2414*
Ac	1:8	**be witnesses unto me both in J.,**	*2419*

Ac 1:12 Then returned they unto J. from *2419*
Ac 1:12 is from J. a sabbath day's journey. *2419*
Ac 1:19 known unto all the dwellers at J.; *2419*
Ac 2:5 there were dwelling at J. Jews, *2419*
Ac 2:14 Judaea, and all ye that dwell at J., *2419*
Ac 4:6 were gathered together at J. *2419*
Ac 4:16 to all them that dwell in J.; *2419*
Ac 5:16 of the cities round about unto J., *2419*
Ac 5:28 ye have filled J. with your doctrine, *2419*
Ac 6:7 disciples multiplied in J. greatly; *2419*
Ac 8:1 the church which was at J.; *2414*
Ac 8:14 the apostles which were at J. heard *2414*
Ac 8:25 returned to J., and preached the *2419*
Ac 8:26 that goeth down from J. unto Gaza, *2419*
Ac 8:27 and had come to J. for to worship, *2419*
Ac 9:2 might bring them bound unto J. *2419*
Ac 9:13 evil he hath done to thy saints at J. *2419*
Ac 9:21 which called on this name in J., *2419*
Ac 9:26 And when Saul was come to J., *2419*
Ac 9:28 them coming in and going out at J. *2419*
Ac 10:39 in the land of the Jews, and in J.; *2419*
Ac 11:2 when Peter was come up to J., *2414*
Ac 11:22 ears of the church which was in J. *2419*
Ac 11:27 prophets from J. unto Antioch. *2414*
Ac 12:25 and Saul returned from J., *2419*
Ac 13:13 John departing...returned to J. *2414*
Ac 13:27 For they that dwell at J., and their *2419*
Ac 13:31 up with him from Galilee to J., *2419*
Ac 15:2 go up to J. unto the apostles and *2419*
Ac 15:4 And when they were come to J., *2419*
Ac 16:4 and elders which were at J. *2419*
Ac 18:21 keep this feast that cometh in J. *2414*
Ac 19:21 Macedonia and Achaia, to go to J., *2419*
Ac 20:16 to be at J. the day of Pentecost *2414*
Ac 20:22 I go bound in the spirit unto J., *2419*
Ac 21:4 that he should not go up to J. *2419*
Ac 21:11 So shall the Jews at J. bind the man *2419*
Ac 21:12 besought him not to go up to J. *2419*
Ac 21:13 to die at J. for the name of the Lord *2419*
Ac 21:15 up our carriages, and went up to J. *2419*
Ac 21:17 And when we were come to J., *2414*
Ac 21:31 band, that all J. was in an uproar. *2419*
Ac 22:5 which were there bound unto J., *2419*
Ac 22:17 that, when I was come again to J., *2419*
Ac 22:18 **and get thee quickly out of J.** *2419*
Ac 23:11 **as thou hast testified of me in J.,** *2419*
Ac 24:11 since I went up to J. for to worship *2419*
Ac 25:1 he ascended from Caesarea to J. *2414*
Ac 25:3 that he would send for him to J., *2419*
Ac 25:7 Jews which came down from J. *2414*
Ac 25:9 Wilt thou go up to J., and there be *2414*
Ac 25:15 About whom, when I was at J., the *2414*
Ac 25:20 him whether he would go to J., *2419*
Ac 25:24 dealt with me, both at J., and also *2414*
Ac 26:4 first among mine own nation at J., *2414*
Ac 26:10 Which thing I also did in J.: *2414*
Ac 26:20 unto them of Damascus, and at J. *2414*
Ac 28:17 yet was I delivered prisoner from J. *2414*
Ru 15:19 so that from J., and round about *2419*
Ru 15:25 But not I go unto J. to minister *2419*
Ru 15:26 for the poor saints which are at J. *2419*
Ru 15:31 that my service which I have for J. *2419*
1Co 16:3 to bring your liberality unto J. *2419*
Ga 1:17 Neither went I up to J. to them *2414*
Ga 1:18 I went up to J. to see Peter, *2414*
Ga 2:1 went up again to J. with Barnabas, *2414*
Ga 4:25 and answereth to J. which now is, *2419*
Ga 4:26 But J. which is above is free, which *2419*
Heb 12:22 of the living God, the heavenly J., *2419*
Re 3:12 **city of my God, which is new J.,** *2419*
Re 21:2 saw the holy city, new J., coming *2419*
Re 21:10 great city, the holy J., descending *2419*

JERUSALEM'S (je-ru'-sa-lems)
1Ki 11:13 for J. sake which I have chosen. 3389
1Ki 11:32 David's sake, and for J. sake, the 3389
Isa 62:1 and for J. sake I will not rest, until 3389

JERUSHA (je-ru'-shah) See also JERUSHAH.
2Ki 15:33 And his mother's name was J., the 3388

JERUSHAH (je-ru'-shah) See also JERUSHA.
2Ch 27:1 His mother's name also was J., 3388

JESAIAH (jes-a-i'-ah) See also ISAIAH; JESHAIAH.
1Ch 3:21 of Hananiah; Pelatiah, and J.: 3470
Ne 11:7 the son of Ithiel, the son of J. 3470

JESHAIAH (jesh-a-i'-ah) See also JESAIAH.
1Ch 25:3 and Zeri, and J., Hashabiah, and 3470
1Ch 25:15 The eighth to J., he, his sons, and 3470
1Ch 26:25 Rehabiah his son, and J. his son, 3470
Ezr 8:7 of Elam; J. the son of Athaliah, 3470
Ezr 8:19 with him J. of the sons of Merari. 3470

JESHANAH (je-sha'-nah)
2Ch 13:19 and J. with the towns thereof, and 3466

JESHARELAH (je-shar'-e-lah) See also ASARELAH.
1Ch 25:14 The seventh to J., he, his sons, 3480

JESHEBEAB (je-sheb'-e-ab)
1Ch 24:13 to Huppah, the fourteenth to J., 3434

JESHER (je'-shur)
1Ch 2:18 sons are these; J., and Shobab, 3475

JESHIMON (jesh'-im-on)
Nu 21:20 Pisgah, which looketh toward J. 3452
Nu 23:28 of Peor, that looketh toward J. 3452
1Sa 23:19 which is on the south of J.? 3452
1Sa 23:24 in the plain on the south of J. 3452
1Sa 26:1 of Hachilah, which is before J.? 3452
1Sa 26:3 hill of Hachilah, which is before J., 3452

JESHIMOTH See BETH-JESHIMOTH.

JESHISHAI (jesh'-i-shahee)
1Ch 5:14 the son of J., the son of Jahdo, 3454

JESHOHAIAH (je-sho-ha-i'-ah)
1Ch 4:36 Elioenai, and Jaakobah, and J., 3439

JESHUA (jesh'-u-ah) See also JESHUAH; JOSHUA.
2Ch 31:15 were Eden, and Miniamin, and J., 3442
Ezr 2:2 J., Nehemiah, Seraiah, Reelaiah, 3442
Ezr 2:6 of the children of J. and Joab, two 3442
Ezr 2:36 of Jedaiah, of the house of J., nine 3442
Ezr 2:40 the children of J. and Kadmiel, of 3442
Ezr 3:2 stood up J. the son of Jozadak, 3442
Ezr 3:8 and J. the son of Jozadak, and the 3442
Ezr 3:9 Then stood J. with his sons and his 3442
Ezr 4:3 But Zerubbabel, and J., and the rest 3442
Ezr 5:2 and J. the son of Jozadak, 3443
Ezr 8:33 them was Jozabad the son of J., 3443
Ezr 10:18 the sons of J. the son of Jozadak, 3442
Ne 3:19 to him repaired Ezer the son of J., 3442
Ne 7:7 with Zerubbabel, J., Nehemiah, 3442
Ne 7:11 of the children of J. and Joab, 3442
Ne 7:39 of Jedaiah, of the house of J., 3442
Ne 7:43 the children of J., of Kadmiel, and 3442
Ne 8:7 Also J., and Bani, and Sherebiah, 3442
Ne 8:17 since the days of J. the son of Nun 3442
Ne 9:4 stairs, of the Levites, J., and Bani, 3442
Ne 9:5 Then the Levites, J., and Kadmiel, 3442
Ne 10:9 both J. the son of Azaniah, Binnui 3442
Ne 11:26 And at J., and at Moladah, and at 3442
Ne 12:1 the son of Shealtiel, and J.: 3442
Ne 12:7 of their brethren in the days of J. 3442
Ne 12:8 the Levites: J., Binnnui, Kadmiel, 3442
Ne 12:10 And J. begat Joiakim, Joiakim also 3442
Ne 12:24 and J. the son of Kadmiel, 3442
Ne 12:26 the days of Joiakim the son of J., 3442

JESHUAH (jesh'-u-ah) See also JESHUA.
1Ch 24:11 The ninth to J., the tenth to 3442

JESHURUN (jesh'-u-run) See also ISRAEL; JESURUN.
De 32:15 But J. waxed fat, and kicked: 3484
De 33:5 he was king in J., when the heads 3484
De 33:26 is none like unto the God of J., 3484

JESIAH (je-si'-ah) See also ISHIAH.
1Ch 12:6 Elkanah, and J., and Azareel, 3449
1Ch 23:20 Micah the first, and J. the second 3449

JESIMIEL (Je-sim'-e-el)
1Ch 4:36 and Adiel, and J., and Benaiah, 3450

JESIMOTH See BETH-JESIMOTH.

JESSE (jes'-se)
Ru 4:17 he is the father of J., the father 3448
Ru 4:22 Obed begat J., and J. begat David. 3448
1Sa 16:1 send thee to J. the Beth-lehemite: 3448
1Sa 16:3 call J. to the sacrifice, and I will 3448
1Sa 16:5 And he sanctified J. and his sons, 3448
1Sa 16:8 J. called Abinadab, and made him 3448
1Sa 16:9 Then J. made Shammah to pass 3448
1Sa 16:10 J. made seven of his sons to pass 3448
1Sa 16:10 Samuel said unto J., The Lord hath 3448
1Sa 16:11 Samuel said unto J., Are here all 3448
1Sa 16:11 And Samuel said unto J., Send and 3448
1Sa 16:18 Behold, I have seen a son of J. 3448
1Sa 16:19 Saul sent messengers unto J., and 3448
1Sa 16:20 J. took an ass laden with bread, 3448
1Sa 16:22 Saul sent to J., saying, Let David, I 3448
1Sa 17:12 whose name was J.; and he had 3448
1Sa 17:13 three eldest sons of J. went and 3448
1Sa 17:17 J. said unto David his son, Take 3448
1Sa 17:20 and went, as J. had commanded 3448
1Sa 17:58 I am the son of thy servant J. the 3448
1Sa 20:27 cometh not the son of J. to meat, 3448
1Sa 20:30 chosen the son of J. to thine own 3448
1Sa 20:31 as long as the son of J. liveth upon 3448
1Sa 22:7 the son of J. give every one of you 3448
1Sa 22:8 made a league with the son of J., 3448
1Sa 22:9 I saw the son of J. coming to Nob, 3448
1Sa 22:13 against me, thou and the son of J., 3448
1Sa 25:10 David? and who is the son of J.? 3448
2Sa 20:1 we inheritance in the son of J. 3448
2Sa 23:1 David the son of J. said, and the 3448
1Ki 12:16 we inheritance in the son of J. 3448
1Ch 2:12 begat Obed, and Obed begat J., 3448
1Ch 2:13 And J. begat his firstborn Eliab, 3448
1Ch 10:14 kingdom unto David the son of J. 3448
1Ch 12:18 and on thy side, thou son of J. 3448
1Ch 29:26 David the son of J. reigned over all 3448
2Ch 10:16 none inheritance in the son of J. 3448
2Ch 11:18 daughter of Eliab the son of J.; 3448
Ps 72:20 The prayers of David the son of J. 3448
Isa 11:1 forth a rod out of the stem of J., 3448
Isa 11:10 that day there shall be a root of J., 3448
Mt 1:5 Obed of Ruth; and Obed begat J.; *2421*
Mt 1:6 And J. begat David the king; and *2421*
Lu 3:32 Which was the son of J., which was *2421*
Ac 13:22 I have found David the son of J., *2421*
Ro 15:12 saith, There shall be a root of J., *2421*

JESTING
Eph 5:4 nor foolish talking, nor j., which *2160*

JESUI (jes'-u-i) See also ISHUI; JESUITES.
Nu 26:44 of J., the family of the Jesuites: 3440

JESUITES (jes'-u-ites)
Nu 26:44 of Jesui, the family of the J.: of 3441

JESURUN (jes'-u-run) See also JESHURUN.
Isa 44:2 thou, J., whom I have chosen. 3484

JESUS (je'-zus) See also BAR-JESUS; CHRIST; JESUS'; JOSHUA; JUSTUS.
Mt 1:1 book of the generation of J. Christ, *2424*
Mt 1:16 of whom was born J., who is called *2424*
Mt 1:18 birth of J. Christ was on this wise: *2424*
Mt 1:21 son, and thou shalt call his name J.: *2424*
Mt 1:25 son: and he called his name J. *2424*
Mt 2:1 when J. was born in Bethlehem of *2424*
Mt 3:13 cometh J. from Galilee to Jordan *2424*
Mt 3:15 J. answering said unto him, **Suffer** *2424*
Mt 3:16 J., when he was baptized, went up *2424*
Mt 4:1 was J. led up of the spirit into the *2424*
Mt 4:7 J. said unto him, **It is written** *2424*
Mt 4:10 saith J. unto him, **Get thee hence,** *2424*
Mt 4:12 J. had heard that John was cast *2424*
Mt 4:17 From that time J. began to preach, *2424*
Mt 4:18 J., walking by the sea of Galilee, *2424*
Mt 4:23 J. went about all Galilee, teaching *2424*
Mt 7:28 when J. had ended these sayings, *2424*
Mt 8:3 J. put forth his hand, and touched *2424*
Mt 8:4 J. saith unto him, **See thou tell no** *2424*
Mt 8:5 J. was entered into Capernaum, *2424*
Mt 8:7 J. saith unto him, **I will come and** *2424*
Mt 8:10 When J. heard it, he marvelled, *2424*
Mt 8:13 J. said unto the centurion, **Go thy** *2424*
Mt 8:14 J. was come into Peter's house, *2424*
Mt 8:18 Now when J. saw great multitudes *2424*
Mt 8:20 J. saith unto him, **The foxes have** *2424*
Mt 8:22 But J. said unto him, **Follow me;** *2424*
Mt 8:29 do with thee, J., thou son of God? *2424*
Mt 8:34 the whole city came out to meet J.: *2424*
Mt 9:2 J. seeing their faith said unto the *2424*
Mt 9:4 And J. knowing their thoughts said, *2424*
Mt 9:9 And as J. passed forth from thence, *2424*
Mt 9:10 pass, as J. sat at meat in the house, *2424*
Mt 9:12 when J. heard that, he said unto *2424*
Mt 9:15 J. said unto them, **Can the children** *2424*
Mt 9:19 J. arose, and followed him, and so *2424*

Mt 9:22 J. turned him about, and when he 2424
Mt 9:23 when J. came into the ruler's house,.... 2424
Mt 9:27 when J. departed thence, two blind 2424
Mt 9:28 J. saith unto them, **Believe ye that**... 2424
Mt 9:30 and Jesus straitly charged them,......... 2424
Mt 9:35 And J. went about all the cities and 2424
Mt 10:5 These twelve J. sent forth, and......... 2424
Mt 11:1 J....made an end of commanding........ 2424
Mt 11:4 J. answered and said unto them,......... 2424
Mt 11:7 J. began to say unto the multitudes 2424
Mt 11:25 J. answered and said, **I thank thee,**.. 2424
Mt 12:1 J. went on the sabbath day through 2424
Mt 12:15 But when J. knew it, he withdrew...... 2424
Mt 12:25 J. knew their thoughts, and said 2424
Mt 13:1 same day went J. out of the house, ... 2424
Mt 13:34 things spake J. unto the multitudes...... 2424
Mt 13:36 Then J. sent the multitude away, ... 2424
Mt 13:51 J. saith... **Have ye understood all**..... 2424
Mt 13:53 when J. had finished these parables, ... 2424
Mt 13:57 But J. said unto them, **A prophet is**.. 2424
Mt 14:1 tetrarch heard of the fame of J., ... 2424
Mt 14:12 and buried it, and went and told J.. 2424
Mt 14:13 When J. heard of it, he departed......... 2424
Mt 14:14 J. went forth, and saw a great........... 2424
Mt 14:16 J. said unto them, **They need not**..... 2424
Mt 14:22 J. constrained his disciples to get........ 2424
Mt 14:25 fourth watch of the night J. went 2424
Mt 14:27 straightway J. spake unto them,.......... 2424
Mt 14:29 he walked on the water, to go to J..... 2424
Mt 14:31 immediately J. stretched forth his........ 2424
Mt 15:1 came to J. scribes and Pharisees,........ 2424
Mt 15:16 J. said, **Are ye also yet without**....... 2424
Mt 15:21 J. went thence, and departed into 2424
Mt 15:28 J. answered and said unto her, **O**....... 2424
Mt 15:29 J. departed from thence, and came..... 2424
Mt 15:32 J. called his disciples unto him, ... 2424
Mt 15:34 And J. saith unto them, **How many**... 2424
Mt 16:6 Then J. said unto them, **Take heed**... 2424
Mt 16:8 Which when J. perceived, he said....... 2424
Mt 16:13 When J. came into the coasts of 2424
Mt 16:17 J. answered and said unto him,........... 2424
Mt 16:20 should tell no man that he was J. 2424
Mt 16:21 that time forth began J. to shew 2424
Mt 16:24 said J. unto his disciples, **If any**........ 2424
Mt 17:1 And after six days J. taketh Peter, ... 2424
Mt 17:4 and said unto J., Lord, it is good 2424
Mt 17:7 J. came and touched them, and.......... 2424
Mt 17:8 they saw no man, save J. only. 2424
Mt 17:9 the mountain, J. charged them,.......... 2424
Mt 17:11 J. answered and said unto them, ... 2424
Mt 17:17 J. answered and said, **O faithless**..... 2424
Mt 17:18 and J. rebuked the devil; and he 2424
Mt 17:19 Then came the disciples to J. apart, ... 2424
Mt 17:20 J. said unto them, **Because of your**... 2424
Mt 17:22 abode in Galilee, J. said unto them, ... 2424
Mt 17:25 into the house, J. prevented him,........ 2424
Mt 17:26 J. saith unto him, **Then are the**........ 2424
Mt 18:1 time came the disciples unto J., ... 2424
Mt 18:2 J. called a little child unto him, ... 2424
Mt 18:22 J. saith unto him, **I say not unto**...... 2424
Mt 19:1 when J. had finished these sayings, ... 2424
Mt 19:14 J. said, **Suffer little children, and**... 2424
Mt 19:18 J. said, **Thou shalt do no murder,** .. 2424
Mt 19:21 J. said unto him, **If thou wilt be**....... 2424
Mt 19:23 said J. unto his disciples, **Verily I**..... 2424
Mt 19:26 J. beheld them, and said unto them, ... 2424
Mt 19:28 J. said unto them, **Verily I say unto**..2424
Mt 20:17 J. going up to Jerusalem took the....... 2424
Mt 20:22 J. answered and said, **Ye know not** .. 2424
Mt 20:25 J. called them unto him, and said, ... 2424
Mt 20:30 when they heard that J. passed by, ... 2424
Mt 20:32 J. stood still, and called them, and...... 2424
Mt 20:34 J. had compassion on them, and.......... 2424
Mt 21:1 Olives, then sent J. two disciples, ... 2424
Mt 21:6 and did as J. commanded them. 2424
Mt 21:11 This is J. the prophet of Nazareth...... 2424
Mt 21:12 J. went into the temple of God, and ... 2424
Mt 21:16 J. said unto them, **Yea; have ye**........ 2424
Mt 21:21 J. answered and said unto them, ... 2424
Mt 21:24 J. answered and said unto them, **I** 2424
Mt 21:27 they answered J., and said, We......... 2424
Mt 21:31 J. saith unto them, **Verily I say** 2424
Mt 21:42 J. saith unto them, **Did ye never** 2424
Mt 22:1 J. answered and spake unto them....... 2424
Mt 22:18 But J. perceived their wickedness, ... 2424
Mt 22:29 J. answered and said unto them, ... 2424
Mt 22:37 J. said unto him, **thou shalt love**........ 2424
Mt 22:41 gathered together, J. asked them,...... 2424
Mt 23:1 Then spake J. to the multitude, ... 2424
Mt 24:1 J. went out, and departed from the 2424
Mt 24:2 J. said unto them, **See ye not all**...... 2424
Mt 24:4 J. answered and said unto them, ... 2424
Mt 26:1 when J. had finished all these............ 2424
Mt 26:4 that they might take J. by subtility, ... 2424
Mt 26:6 J. was in Bethany, in the house of 2424
Mt 26:10 When J. understood it, he said 2424
Mt 26:17 bread the disciples came to J., ... 2424
Mt 26:19 disciples did as J. had appointed......... 2424
Mt 26:26 J. took bread, and blessed it, ... 2424
Mt 26:31 saith J. unto them, **All ye shall be**.... 2424
Mt 26:34 J. said unto him, **Verily I say unto** .. 2424
Mt 26:36 cometh J. with them unto a place....... 2424
Mt 26:49 forthwith he came to J., and said, ... 2424
Mt 26:50 J. said unto him, **Friend, wherefore**. 2424
Mt 26:50 came they, and laid hands on J., ... 2424
Mt 26:51 which were with J. stretched out 2424
Mt 26:52 said J. unto him, **Put up again thy**... 2424
Mt 26:55 In that same hour said J. to the......... 2424
Mt 26:57 they that had laid hold on J. led......... 2424
Mt 26:59 sought false witness against J., ... 2424
Mt 26:63 J. held his peace. And the high.......... 2424
Mt 26:64 J. saith unto him, **Thou hast said:**.... 2424
Mt 26:69 Thou also wast with J. of Galilee. 2424
Mt 26:71 was also with J. of Nazareth. 2424
Mt 26:75 Peter remembered the word of J., ... 2424
Mt 27:1 took counsel against J. to put him 2424
Mt 27:11 And J. stood before the governor:...... 2424
Mt 27:11 J. said unto him, **Thou sayest**. 2424
Mt 27:17 or J. which is called Christ? 2424
Mt 27:20 ask Barabbas, and destroy J.............. 2424
Mt 27:22 then with J. which is called Christ?..... 2424
Mt 27:26 he had scourged J., he delivered......... 2424
Mt 27:27 soldiers of the governor took J. 2424
Mt 27:37 This Is J. The King Of The Jews. 2424
Mt 27:46 ninth hour J. cried again with a.......... 2424
Mt 27:54 watching J., saw the earthquake, ... 2424
Mt 27:55 which followed J. from Galilee. 2424
Mt 27:58 Pilate, and begged the body of J......... 2424
Mt 28:5 I know that ye seek J., which was 2424
Mt 28:9 J. met them, saying, **All hail.** And.... 2424
Mt 28:10 said J. unto them, **Be not afraid:**..... 2424
Mt 28:16 into a mountain where J. had 2424
Mt 28:18 J. came and spake unto them,............ 2424
Mk 1:1 beginning of the gospel of J. Christ,.... 2424
Mk 1:9 J. came from Nazareth of Galille, ... 2424
Mk 1:14 J. came into Galilee, preaching the 2424
Mk 1:17 J. said unto them, **Come ye after**..... 2424
Mk 1:24 do with thee, thou J. of Nazareth? 2424
Mk 1:25 J. rebuked him, saying, **Hold thy**...... 2424
Mk 1:41 J., moved with compassion, put 2424
Mk 1:45 insomuch that J. could no more 2424
Mk 2:5 When J. saw their faith, he said......... 2424
Mk 2:8 when J. perceived in his spirit 2424
Mk 2:15 that, as J. sat at meat in his house,.... 2424
Mk 2:15 sat also together with J. and his 2424
Mk 2:17 When J. heard it, he saith unto.......... 2424
Mk 2:19 J. said unto them, **Can the children**..2424
Mk 3:7 J. withdrew himself with his............. 2424
Mk 5:6 when he saw J. afar off, he ran and.... 2424
Mk 5:7 What have I to do with thee, J., ... 2424
Mk 5:13 And forthwith J. gave them leave. 2424
Mk 5:15 they come to J., and see him that...... 2424
Mk 5:19 Howbeith J. suffered him not, but 2424
Mk 5:20 great things J. had done for him: 2424
Mk 5:21 when J. was passed over again by...... 2424
Mk 5:24 J. went with him; and much...................
Mk 5:27 When she had heard of J., came in..... 2424
Mk 5:30 J., immediately knowing in................ 2424
Mk 5:36 As soon as J. heard the word that...... 2424
Mk 6:4 J. said unto them, **A prophet is not**.. 2424
Mk 6:30 themselves together unto J., ... 2424
Mk 6:34 J., when he came out, saw much......... 2424
Mk 7:27 J. said unto her, **Let the children**.... 2424
Mk 8:1 J. called his disciples unto him, ... 2424
Mk 8:17 And when J. knew it, he saith unto 2424
Mk 8:27 And J. went out, and his disciples, ... 2424
Mk 9:2 six days J. taketh with him Peter, ... 2424
Mk 9:4 and they were talking with J.. 2424
Mk 9:5 Peter answered and said to J., ... 2424
Mk 9:8 more, save J. only with themselves. ... 2424
Mk 9:23 J. said unto him, **If thou canst**........ 2424
Mk 9:25 When J. saw that the people came 2424
Mk 9:27 J. took him by the hand, and lifted 2424
Mk 9:39 J. said, **Forbid him not: for there**... 2424
Mk 10:5 J. answered and said unto them, ... 2424
Mk 10:14 when J. saw it, he was much 2424
Mk 10:18 J. said unto him, **Why callest thou**... 2424
Mk 10:21 Then J. beholding him loved him, ... 2424
Mk 10:23 J. looked round about, and saith......... 2424
Mk 10:24 J. answereth again, and saith unto...... 2424
Mk 10:27 J. looking upon them saith, **With**....... 2424
Mk 10:29 J. answered and said, **Verily I say**.... 2424
Mk 10:32 J. went before them: and they were... 2424
Mk 10:38 J. said unto them, **Ye know not**........ 2424
Mk 10:39 J. said unto them, **Ye shall indeed**... 2424
Mk 10:42 J. called them to him, and saith 2424
Mk 10:47 he heard that it was J. of Nazareth,.... 2424
Mk 10:47 out, and say, J., thou son of David,.... 2424
Mk 10:49 J. stood still, and commanded him...... 2424
Mk 10:50 his garment, rose, and came to J.. 2424
Mk 10:51 J. answered and said unto him,.......... 2424
Mk 10:52 J. said unto him, **Go thy way;**.......... 2424
Mk 10:52 sight, and followed J. in the way. 2424
Mk 11:6 them even as J. had commanded:........ 2424
Mk 11:7 they brought the colt to J., and 2424
Mk 11:11 J. entered into Jerusalem, and into 2424
Mk 11:14 J. answered and said unto it, **No** 2424
Mk 11:15 J. went into the temple, and began..... 2424
Mr 11:22 J. answering saith unto them,............ 2424
Mr 11:29 J. answered and said unto them, ... 2424
Mk 11:33 they answered and said unto J., ... 2424
Mk 11:33 J. answering saith unto them,............ 2424
Mk 12:17 J. answering said unto them,............. 2424
Mk 12:24 J. answering said unto them, **Do**........ 2424
Mk 12:29 J. answered him, **The first of all**..... 2424
Mk 12:34 when J. saw that he answered........... 2424
Mk 12:35 J. answered and said, while he 2424
Mk 12:41 J. sat over against the treasury, ... 2424
Mk 13:2 J. answering said unto him, **Seest**...... 2424
Mk 13:5 J. answering them began to say, ... 2424
Mk 14:6 J. said, **Let her alone; why trouble**. 2424
Mk 14:18 eat, J. said, **Verily I say unto you,** ..2424
Mk 14:22 J. took bread, and blessed. and 2424
Mk 14:27 And J. saith unto them, **All ye shall**.. 2424
Mk 14:30 And J. saith unto him, **Verily I say**... 2424
Mk 14:48 J. answered and said unto them, ... 2424
Mk 14:53 they led J. away to the high priest: 2424
Mk 14:55 sought for witness against J. to put 2424
Mk 14:60 and asked J., saying, Answerest 2424
Mk 14:62 And J. said, **I am: and ye shall see** ..2424
Mk 14:67 thou also wast with J. of Nazareth...... 2424
Mk 14:72 called to mind the word that J. said.... 2424
Mk 15:1 bound J., and carried him away,......... 2424
Mk 15:5 J. yet answered nothing; so that 2424
Mk 15:15 delivered J., when he had scourged.... 2424
Mk 15:34 ninth hour J. cried with a loud 2424
Mk 15:37 and J. cried with a loud voice, and 2424
Mk 15:43 Pilate, and craved the body of J......... 2424
Mk 16:6 Ye seek J. of Nazareth, which was..... 2424
Mk 16:9 Now when J. was risen early the ....
Lu 1:31 son, and shalt call his name J.. 2424
Lu 2:21 his name was called J., which was...... 2424
Lu 2:27 the parents brought in the child J.,..... 2424
Lu 2:43 the child J. tarried behind in............. 2424
Lu 2:52 And J. increased in wisdom and.......... 2424
Lu 3:21 pass, that J. also being baptized,........ 2424
Lu 3:23 J. himself began to be about thirty 2424
Lu 4:1 And J. being full of the Holy Ghost..... 2424
Lu 4:4 And J. answered him, saying, **It is**..... 2424
Lu 4:8 J. answered and said unto him, ... 2424
Lu 4:12 J. answering said unto him, **It is** 2424
Lu 4:14 J. returned in the power of the.......... 2424
Lu 4:34 J. of Nazareth? art thou come to......... 2424
Lu 4:35 And J. rebuked him, saying, **Hold**...... 2424
Lu 5:10 And J. said unto Simon, **Fear not;** 2424
Lu 5:12 who seeing J. fell on his face,............ 2424
Lu 5:19 his couch into the midst before J........ 2424
Lu 5:22 But when J. perceived their............... 2424
Lu 5:31 And J. answering said unto them,........ 2424
Lu 6:3 J. answering them said, **Have ye**....... 2424
Lu 6:9 Then said J. unto them, **I will ask**.... 2424
Lu 6:11 another what they might do to J.. 2424
Lu 7:3 And when he heard of J., he sent 2424
Lu 7:4 when they came to J., they 2424
Lu 7:6 Then J. went with them. And............ 2424

Lu 7:9 When J. heard these things, he 2424
Lu 7:19 two of his disciples sent them to J., 2424
Lu 7:22 Then J. answering said unto them, 2424
Lu 7:37 when she knew that J. sat at meat
Lu 7:40 And J. answering said unto him, 2424
Lu 8:28 When he saw J., he cried out, and 2424
Lu 8:28 What have I to do with thee, J., 2424
Lu 8:30 J. asked him, saying, What is thy 2424
Lu 8:35 and came to J., and found the man, 2424
Lu 8:35 sitting at the feet of J., clothed, 2424
Lu 8:38 be with him: but J. sent him away, 2424
Lu 8:39 great things J. had done unto him. 2424
Lu 8:40 pass, that, when J. was returned, 2424
Lu 8:45 J. said, Who touched me? When all 2424
Lu 8:46 J. said, Somebody hath touched 2424
Lu 8:50 But when J. heard it, he answered 2424
Lu 9:33 Peter said unto J., Master, it is 2424
Lu 9:36 voice was past, J. was found alone. 2424
Lu 9:41 And J. answering said, O faithless 2424
Lu 9:42 And J. rebuked the unclean spirit, 2424
Lu 9:43 every one at all things which J. did, 2424
Lu 9:47 And J., perceiving the thought of 2424
Lu 9:50 And J. said unto him, Forbid him 2424
Lu 9:58 And J. said unto him, Foxes have 2424
Lu 9:60 J. said unto him, Let the dead bury 2424
Lu 9:62 And J. said unto him, No man, 2424
Lu 10:21 In that hour J. rejoiced in spirit, 2424
Lu 10:29 said unto J., And who is my 2424
Lu 10:30 And J. answering said, A certain 2424
Lu 10:37 Then said J. unto him, Go, and do 2424
Lu 10:41 And J. answered and said unto 2424
Lu 13:2 And J. answering said unto them, 2424
Lu 13:12 And when J. saw her, he called her 2424
Lu 13:14 J. had healed on the sabbath day, 2424
Lu 14:3 And J. answering spake unto the 2424
Lu 17:13 J., Master, have mercy on us. 2424
Lu 17:17 J. answering said, Were there not 2424
Lu 18:16 J. called them unto him, and said, 2424
Lu 18:19 J. said unto him, Why callest thou 2424
Lu 18:22 Now when J. heard these things, he 2424
Lu 18:24 when J. saw that he was very 2424
Lu 18:37 him, that J. of Nazareth passeth by. 2424
Lu 18:38 saying, J., thou son of David, have 2424
Lu 18:40 J. stood, and commanded him to be 2424
Lu 18:42 J. said unto him, Receive thy sight: 2424
Lu 19:1 J. entered and passed through
Lu 19:3 he sought to see J. who he was; 2424
Lu 19:5 And when J. came to the place, he 2424
Lu 19:9 And J. said unto him, This day is 2424
Lu 19:35 they brought him to J.: and they 2424
Lu 19:35 the colt, and they set J. thereon. 2424
Lu 20:8 J. said unto them, Neither tell I 2424
Lu 20:34 And J. answering said unto them, 2424
Lu 22:47 and drew near unto J. to kiss him. 2424
Lu 22:48 J. said unto him, Judas, betrayest 2424
Lu 22:51 J. answered and said, Suffer ye 2424
Lu 22:52 Then J. said unto the chief priests, 2424
Lu 22:63 the men that held J. mocked him, 2424
Lu 23:8 And when Herod saw J., he was 2424
Lu 23:20 willing to release J., spake again 2424
Lu 23:25 but he delivered J. to their will. 2424
Lu 23:26 cross, that he might bear it after J. 2424
Lu 23:28 But J. turning unto them said, 2424
Lu 23:34 Then said J., Father, forgive them; 2424
Lu 23:42 he said unto J., Lord, remember 2424
Lu 23:43 J. said unto him, Verily I say unto 2424
Lu 23:46 when J. had cried with a loud 2424
Lu 23:52 Pilate, and begged the body of J. 2424
Lu 24:3 found not the body of the Lord J. 2424
Lu 24:15 J. himself drew near, and went 2424
Lu 24:19 Concerning J. of Nazareth, which 2424
Lu 24:36 J. himself stood in the midst of 2424
Joh 1:17 grace and truth came by J. Christ. 2424
Joh 1:29 John seeth J. coming unto him, 2424
Joh 1:36 looking upon J. as he walked, he 2424
Joh 1:37 him speak, and they followed J. 2424
Joh 1:38 J. turned, and saw them following, 2424
Joh 1:42 And he brought him to J. 2424
Joh 1:42 when J. beheld him, he said, Thou 2424
Joh 1:43 The day following J. would go 2424
Joh 1:45 prophets, did write, J. of Nazareth, 2424
Joh 1:47 J. saw Nathanael coming to him, 2424
Joh 1:48, 50 J. answered and said unto him, 2424
Joh 2:1 and the mother of J. was there: 2424
Joh 2:2 J. was called, and his disciples, to 2424
Joh 2:3 the mother of J. saith unto him, 2424
Joh 2:4 J. saith unto her, Woman, what 2424
Joh 2:7 J. saith unto them, Fill the 2424
Joh 2:11 This beginning of miracles did J. 2424
Joh 2:13 hand, and J. went up to Jerusalem. 2424
Joh 2:19 J. answered and said unto them, 2424
Joh 2:22 and the word which J. had said. 2424
Joh 2:24 J. did not commit himself unto 2424
Joh 3:2 The same came to J. by night, and 2424
Joh 3:3 J. answered and said unto him, 2424
Joh 3:5 J. answered, Verily, verily, I say 2424
Joh 3:10 J. answered and said unto him, 2424
Joh 3:22 After these things came J. and his 2424
Joh 4:1 that J. made and baptized more 2424
Joh 4:2 Though J. himself baptized not, 2424
Joh 4:6 J. therefore, being wearied with 2424
Joh 4:7 J. saith unto her, Give me to drink. 2424
Joh 4:10, 13 J. answered and said unto her, 2424
Joh 4:16 J. saith unto her, Go, call thy 2424
Joh 4:17 J. said unto her, Thou hast well 2424
Joh 4:21 J. saith unto her, Woman, believe 2424
Joh 4:26 J. saith unto her, I that speak unto 2424
Joh 4:34 J. saith unto them, My meat is to 2424
Joh 4:44 J. himself testified, that a prophet 2424
Joh 4:46 J. came again into Cana of Galilee, 2424
Joh 4:47 he heard that J. was come out of 2424
Joh 4:48 Then said J. unto him, Except ye 2424
Joh 4:50 J. saith unto him, Go thy way; 2424
Joh 4:50 man believed the word that J. had 2424
Joh 4:53 J. said unto him, Thy son liveth: 2424
Joh 4:54 the second miracle that J. did, 2424
Joh 5:1 and J. went up to Jerusalem. 2424
Joh 5:6 When J. saw him lie, and knew 2424
Joh 5:8 J. saith unto him, Rise, take up 2424
Joh 5:13 for J. had conveyed himself away, 2424
Joh 5:14 Afterward J. findeth him in the 2424
Joh 5:15 told the Jews that it was J., which 2424
Joh 5:16 therefore did the Jews persecute J., 2424
Joh 5:17 J. answered the, My Father 2424
Joh 5:19 Then answered J. and said unto 2424
Joh 6:1 J. went over the sea of Galilee, 2424
Joh 6:3 J. went up into a mountain, and 2424
Joh 6:5 When J. then lifted up his eyes, 2424
Joh 6:10 J. said, Make the men sit down. 2424
Joh 6:11 J. took the loaves; and when he 2424
Joh 6:14 had seen the miracle that J. did, 2424
Joh 6:15 When J. therefore perceived that 2424
Joh 6:17 dark, and J. was not come to them. 2424
Joh 6:19 they see J. walking on the sea, and 2424
Joh 6:22 that J. went not with his disciples 2424
Joh 6:24 therefore saw that J. was not there, 2424
Joh 6:24 came to Capernaum, seeking for J. 2424
Joh 6:26 J. answered them and said, Verily, 2424
Joh 6:29 J. answered and said unto them, 2424
Joh 6:32 Then J. said unto them, Verily 2424
Joh 6:35 J. said unto them, I am the bread 2424
Joh 6:42 Is not this J., the son of Joseph, 2424
Joh 6:43 J. therefore answered and said 2424
Joh 6:53 Then J. said unto them, Verily, 2424
Joh 6:61 When J. knew in himself that his 2424
Joh 6:64 J. knew from the beginning who 2424
Joh 6:67 Then said J. unto the twelve, Will 2424
Joh 6:70 J. answered them, Have not I 2424
Joh 7:1 these things J. walked in Galilee: 2424
Joh 7:6 Then J. said unto them, My time 2424
Joh 7:14 feast J. went up into the temple, 2424
Joh 7:16 J. answered them, and said, My 2424
Joh 7:21 J. answered and said unto them, 2424
Joh 7:28 Then cried J. in the temple as he 2424
Joh 7:33 Then said J. unto them, Yet a little 2424
Joh 7:37 J. stood and cried, saying, If any 2424
Joh 7:39 that J. was not yet glorified. 2424
Joh 7:50 (he that came to J. by night, being 846
Joh 8:1 J. wnet unto the mount of Olives. 2424
Joh 8:6 But J. stooped down, and with his 2424
Joh 8:9 J. was left alone, and the woman 2424
Joh 8:10 When J. had lifted up himself, and 2424
Joh 8:11 And J. said unto her, Neither do I 2424
Joh 8:12 Then spake J. again unto them, 2424
Joh 8:14 J. answered and said unto them, 2424
Joh 8:19 J. answered, Ye neither know me 2424
Joh 8:20 These words spake J. in the 2424
Joh 8:21 Then said J. again unto them, I go 2424
Joh 8:25 J. saith unto them, Even the same 2424
Joh 8:28 Then said J. unto them, When ye 2424
Joh 8:31 Then said J. to those Jews which 2424
Joh 8:34 J. answered them, Verily, verily, I 2424
Joh 8:39 J. saith unto them, If ye were 2424
Joh 8:42 J. said unto them, If God were 2424
Joh 8:49 J. answered, I have not a devil; 2424
Joh 8:54 J. answered, If I honour myself, 2424
Joh 8:58 J. said unto them, Verily, verily, I 2424
Joh 8:59 J. hid himself, and went out of the 2424
Joh 9:1 And as J. passed by, he saw a man
Joh 9:3 J. answered Neither hath this 2424
Joh 9:11 A man that is called J. made clay, 2424
Joh 9:14 sabbath day when J. made the clay, 2424
Joh 9:35 J. heard that they had cast him 2424
Joh 9:37 J. said unto him, Thou hast both 2424
Joh 9:39 J. said, For judgment I am come 2424
Joh 9:41 J. said unto them, If ye were blind, 2424
Joh 10:6 This parable spake J. unto them: 2424
Joh 10:7 Then said J. unto them again, 2424
Joh 10:23 J. walked in the temple in 2424
Joh 10:25 J. answered them, I told you, and 2424
Joh 10:32 J. answered them, Many good 2424
Joh 10:34 J. answered them, Is it not written, 2424
Joh 11:4 When J. heard that, he said, This 2424
Joh 11:5 J. loved Martha, and her sister, 2424
Joh 11:9 J. answered, Are there not twelve 2424
Joh 11:13 Howbeit J. spake of his death: but 2424
Joh 11:14 Then said J. unto them plainly, 2424
Joh 11:17 when J. came, he found that he had 2424
Joh 11:20 as soon as she heard that J. was 2424
Joh 11:21 Then said Martha unto J., Lord, 2424
Joh 11:23 J. saith unto her, Thy brother 2424
Joh 11:25 J. saith..., I am the resurrection, 2424
Joh 11:30 Now J. was not yet come into the 2424
Joh 11:32 when Mary was come where J. was, 2424
Joh 11:33 When J. therefore saw her weeping, 2424
Joh 11:35 J. wept. 2424
Joh 11:38 J. therefore again groaning in 2424
Joh 11:39 J. said, Take ye away the stone. 2424
Joh 11:40 J. saith unto her, Said I not unto 2424
Joh 11:41 And J. lifted up his eyes, and said, 2424
Joh 11:44 J. saith unto them, Loose him, and 2424
Joh 11:45 had seen the things which J. did, 2424
Joh 11:46 told them what things J. had done. 2424
Joh 11:51 that J. should die for that nation; 2424
Joh 11:54 J. therefore walked no more openly 2424
Joh 11:56 Then sought they for J., and spake 2424
Joh 12:1 J. six days before the passover 2424
Joh 12:3 and anointed the feet of J., and 2424
Joh 12:7 Then said J., Let her alone: 2424
Joh 12:11 Jews went away, and believed on J. 2424
Joh 12:12 they heard that J. was coming to 2424
Joh 12:14 And J., when he had found a young 2424
Joh 12:16 but when J. was glorified, then 2424
Joh 12:21 him, saying, Sir, we would see J. 2424
Joh 12:22 again Andrew and Philip tell J. 2424
Joh 12:23 And J. answered them, saying, 2424
Joh 12:30 J. answered and said, This voice 2424
Joh 12:35 Then J. said unto them, Yet a little 2424
Joh 12:36 things spake J., and departed, and 2424
Joh 12:44 J. cried and said, He that believeth 2424
Joh 13:1 J. knew that his hour was come 2424
Joh 13:3 J. knowing that the Father had 2424
Joh 13:7 J. answered and said unto him, 2424
Joh 13:8 J. answered him, If I wash thee 2424
Joh 13:10 J. saith to him, He that is washed 2424
Joh 13:21 When J. had thus said, he was 2424
Joh 13:23 one of his disciples, whom J. loved. 2424
Joh 13:26 J. answered, He it is, to whom I 2424
Joh 13:27 Then said J. unto him, That thou 2424
Joh 13:29 J. had said unto him, Buy those 2424
Joh 13:31 J. said, Now is the Son of man 2424
Joh 13:36 J. answered him, Whither I go, 2424
Joh 13:38 J. answered him, Wilt thou lay 2424
Joh 14:6 J. saith unto him, I am the way, 2424
Joh 14:9 J. saith unto him, Have I been so 2424
Joh 14:23 J. answered and said unto him, If 2424
Joh 16:19 J. knew that they were desirous 2424
Joh 16:31 J. answered..., Do ye now believe? 2424
Joh 17:1 These words spake J., and lifted up 2424
Joh 17:3 J. Christ, whom thou hast sent. 2424
Joh 18:1 When J. had spoken these words, 2424
Joh 18:2 for J. ofttimes resorted thither 2424
Joh 18:4 J. therefore, knowing all things 2424
Joh 18:5 They answered him, J. of Nazareth. 2424
Joh 18:5 J. saith unto them, I am he. 2424
Joh 18:7 And they said, J. of Nazareth. 2424
Joh 18:8 J. answered, I have told you that 2424
Joh 18:11 Then said J. unto Peter, Put up thy 2424

Joh	18:12	and officers of the Jews took **J.**,	*2424*
Joh	18:15	Simon Peter followed **J.**, and so	*2424*
Joh	18:15	went in with **J.** into the palace of	*2424*
Joh	18:19	The high priest then asked **J.** of	*2424*
Joh	18:20	**J.** answered him, **I spake openly to**	*2424*
Joh	18:22	struck **J.** with the palm of his hand,	*2424*
Joh	18:23	**J.** answered him, **If I have spoken**	*2424*
Joh	18:28	Then led they **J.** from Caiaphas	*2424*
Joh	18:32	the saying of **J.** might be fulfilled,	*2424*
Joh	18:33	and called **J.**, and said unto him,	*2424*
Joh	18:34	**J.** answered him, **Sayest thou this**	*2424*
Joh	18:36	**J.** answered, **My kingdom is not of**	*2424*
Joh	18:37	**J.** answered, **Thou sayest that I**	*2424*
Joh	19:1	Then Pilate therefore took **J.**, and	*2424*
Joh	19:5	came **J.** forth, wearing the crown	*2424*
Joh	19:9	saith unto **J.**, Whence art thou?	*2424*
Joh	19:9	But **J.** gave him no answer.	*2424*
Joh	19:11	**J.** answered, **Thou couldest have**	*2424*
Joh	19:13	he brought **J.** forth, and sat down	*2424*
Joh	19:16	they took **J.**, and led him away.	*2424*
Joh	19:18	side one, and **J.** in the midst.	*2424*
Joh	19:19	**J.** of Nazareth the King of the	*2424*
Joh	19:20	the place where **J.** was crucified	*2424*
Joh	19:23	when they had crucified **J.**, took	*2424*
Joh	19:25	stood by the cross of **J.** his mother,	*2424*
Joh	19:26	When **J.** therefore saw his mother,	*2424*
Joh	19:28	**J.** knowing that all things were	*2424*
Joh	19:30	When **J.** therefore had received	*2424*
Joh	19:33	when they came to **J.**, and saw that	*2424*
Joh	19:38	Arimathaea, being a disciple of **J.**,	*2424*
Joh	19:38	he might take away the body of **J.**:	*2424*
Joh	19:38	therefore, and took the body of **J.**	*2424*
Joh	19:39	at the first came to **J.** by night,	*2424*
Joh	19:40	Then took they the body of **J.**,	*2424*
Joh	19:42	There laid they **J.** therefore	*2424*
Joh	20:2	the other disciple, whom **J.** loved,	*2424*
Joh	20:12	where the body of **J.** had lain.	*2424*
Joh	20:14	herself back, and saw **J.** standing,	*2424*
Joh	20:14	and knew not that it was **J.**	*2424*
Joh	20:15	**J.** saith unto her, **Woman, why**	*2424*
Joh	20:16	**J.** saith unto her, **Mary.** She	*2424*
Joh	20:17	**J.** saith unto her, **Touch me not;**	*2424*
Joh	20:19	came **J.** and stood in the midst,	*2424*
Joh	20:21	Then said **J.** to them again, **Peace**	*2424*
Joh	20:24	was not with them when **J.** came.	*2424*
Joh	20:26	then came **J.**, the doors being shut,	*2424*
Joh	20:29	**J.** saith unto him, **Thomas, because**	*2424*
Joh	20:30	many other signs truly did **J.** in	*2424*
Joh	20:31	might believe that **J.** is the Christ,	*2424*
Joh	21:1	**J.** shewed himself again to his	*2424*
Joh	21:4	now come, **J.** stood on the shore:	*2424*
Joh	21:4	disciples knew not that it was **J.**.	*2424*
Joh	21:5	**J.** saith unto them, **Children, have**	*2424*
Joh	21:7	that disciple whom **J.** loved saith	*2424*
Joh	21:10	**J.** saith unto them, **Bring of the fish**	*2424*
Joh	21:12	**J.** saith unto them, **Come and dine**	*2424*
Joh	21:13	**J.** then cometh, and taketh bread,	*2424*
Joh	21:14	third time that **J.** shewed himself	*2424*
Joh	21:15	**J.** saith to Simon Peter, **Simon,**	*2424*
Joh	21:17	**J.** saith unto him, **Feed my sheep.**	*2424*
Joh	21:20	disciple whom **J.** loved following;	*2424*
Joh	21:21	Peter seeing him saith to **J.**, Lord,	*2424*
Joh	21:22	**J.** saith unto him, **If I will that he**	*2424*
Joh	21:23	yet **J.** said not unto him, He shall	*2424*
Joh	21:25	many other things which **J.** did,	*2424*
Ac	1:1	that **J.** began both to do and teach,	*2424*
Ac	1:11	this same **J.**, which is taken up	*2424*
Ac	1:14	Mary the mother of **J.**, and with	*2424*
Ac	1:16	was guide to them that took **J.**.	*2424*
Ac	1:21	Lord **J.** went in and out among us,	*2424*
Ac	2:22	**J.** of Nazareth, a man approved of	*2424*
Ac	2:32	This **J.** hath God raised up,	*2424*
Ac	2:36	God hath made that same **J.**, whom	*2424*
Ac	2:38	one of you in the name of **J.** Christ	*2424*
Ac	3:6	In the name of **J.** Christ of	*2424*
Ac	3:13	fathers, hath glorified his Son **J.**;	*2424*
Ac	3:20	he shall send **J.** Christ, which	*2424*
Ac	3:26	God, having raised up his Son **J.**,	*2424*
Ac	4:2	preached through **J.** the	*2424*
Ac	4:10	the name of **J.** Christ of Nazareth,	*2424*
Ac	4:13	them, that they had been with **J.**.	*2424*
Ac	4:18	at all nor teach in the name of **J.**.	*2424*
Ac	4:27	a truth against thy holy child **J.**,	*2424*
Ac	4:30	by the name of thy holy child **J.**	*2424*
Ac	4:33	of the resurrection of the Lord **J.**:	*2424*
Ac	5:30	God of our fathers raised up **J.**,	*2424*
Ac	5:40	should not speak in the name of **J.**	*2424*
Ac	5:42	not to teach and preach **J.** Christ.	*2424*
Ac	6:14	**J.** of Nazareth shall destroy this	*2424*
Ac	7:45	with **J.** into the possession of the	*2424*
Ac	7:55	**J.** standing on the right hand of	*2424*
Ac	7:59	saying, Lord **J.**, receive my spirit.	*2424*
Ac	8:12	of God, and the name of **J.** Christ,	*2424*
Ac	8:16	baptized in the name of the Lord **J.**.)	*2424*
Ac	8:35	and preached unto him **J.**	*2424*
Ac	8:37	that **J.** Christ is the Son of God.	*2424*
Ac	9:5	**I am J. whom thou persecutest:**	*2424*
Ac	9:17	even **J.**, that appeared unto thee in	*2424*
Ac	9:27	at Damascus in the name of **J.**	*2424*
Ac	9:29	boldly in the name of the Lord **J.**,	*2424*
Ac	9:34	**J.** Christ maketh thee whole:	*2424*
Ac	10:36	preaching peace by **J.** Christ: (he is	*2424*
Ac	10:38	How God anointed **J.** of Nazareth	*2424*
Ac	11:17	who believed on the Lord **J.** Christ;	*2424*
Ac	11:20	Grecians, preaching the Lord **J.**.	*2424*
Ac	13:23	raised unto Israel a Saviour, **J.**:	*2424*
Ac	13:33	in that he hath raised up **J.** again;	*2424*
Ac	15:11	the grace of the Lord **J.** Christ we	*2424*
Ac	15:26	for the name of our Lord **J.** Christ.	*2424*
Ac	16:18	in the name of **J.** Christ to come out	*2424*
Ac	16:31	Believe on the Lord **J.** Christ, and	*2424*
Ac	17:3	this **J.**, whom I preach unto you,	*2424*
Ac	17:7	that there is another king, one **J.**.	*2424*
Ac	17:18	because he preached unto them **J.**,	*2424*
Ac	18:5	to the Jews that **J.** was Christ.	*2424*
Ac	18:28	by the scriptures that **J.** was Christ.	*2424*
Ac	19:4	come after him, that is, on Christ **J.**.	*2424*
Ac	19:5	baptized in the name of the Lord **J.**.	*2424*
Ac	19:10	Asia heard the word of the Lord **J.**,	*2424*
Ac	19:13	evil spirits the name of the Lord **J.**,	*2424*
Ac	19:13	We adjure you by **J.** whom Paul	*2424*
Ac	19:15	said, **J.** I know, and Paul I know;	*2424*
Ac	19:17	name of the Lord **J.** was magnified.	*2424*
Ac	20:21	and faith toward our Lord **J.** Christ.	*2424*
Ac	20:24	which I have received of the Lord **J.**,	*2424*
Ac	20:35	remember the words of the Lord **J.**,	*2424*
Ac	21:13	to die...for the name of the Lord **J.**	*2424*
Ac	22:8	said unto me, **I am J. of Nazareth,**	*2424*
Ac	25:19	and of one **J.**, which was dead,	*2424*
Ac	26:9	things contrary to the name of **J.** of	*2424*
Ac	26:15	**I am J. whom thou persecutest.**	*2424*
Ac	28:23	persuading them concerning **J.**,	*2424*
Ac	28:31	which concern the Lord **J.** Christ,	*2424*
Ro	1:1	Paul, a servant of **J.** Christ, called	*2424*
Ro	1:3	concerning his Son **J.** Christ our	*2424*
Ro	1:6	are ye also the called of **J.** Christ:	*2424*
Ro	1:7	our Father, and the Lord **J.** Christ.	*2424*
Ro	1:8	I thank my God through **J.** Christ	*2424*
Ro	2:16	the secrets of men by **J.** Christ.	*2424*
Ro	3:22	of God which is by faith of **J.** Christ	*2424*
Ro	3:24	the redemption that is in Christ **J.**:	*2424*
Ro	3:26	of him which believeth in **J.**	*2424*
Ro	4:24	believe on him that raised up **J.**	*2424*
Ro	5:1	God through our Lord **J.** Christ:	*2424*
Ro	5:11	in God through our Lord **J.** Christ,	*2424*
Ro	5:15	which is by one man, **J.** Christ,	*2424*
Ro	5:17	shall reign in life by one, **J.** Christ.)	*2424*
Ro	5:21	unto eternal life by **J.** Christ our	*2424*
Ro	6:3	us as were baptized into **J.** Christ	*2424*
Ro	6:11	unto God through **J.** Christ our	*2424*
Ro	6:23	God is eternal life through **J.** Christ	*2424*
Ro	7:25	I thank God through **J.** Christ our	*2424*
Ro	8:1	to them which are in Christ **J.**,	*2424*
Ro	8:2	law of the Spirit of life in Christ **J.**	*2424*
Ro	8:11	if the Spirit of him that raised up **J.**	*2424*
Ro	8:39	God, which is in Christ **J.** our Lord.	*2424*
Ro	10:9	confess with thy mouth the Lord **J.**,	*2424*
Ro	13:14	But put ye on the Lord **J.** Christ,	*2424*
Ro	14:14	and am persuaded by the Lord **J.**,	*2424*
Ro	15:5	another according to Christ **J.**:	*2424*
Ro	15:6	the Father of our Lord **J.** Christ.	*2424*
Ro	15:8	I say that **J.** Christ was a minister	*2424*
Ro	15:16	should be the minister of **J.** Christ	*2424*
Ro	15:17	I may glory through **J.** Christ in	*2424*
Ro	15:30	for the Lord **J.** Christ's sake,	*2424*
Ro	16:3	Aquilla my helpers in Christ **J.**:	*2424*
Ro	16:18	such serve not our Lord **J.** Christ,	*2424*
Ro	16:20	grace of our Lord **J.** Christ be with	*2424*
Ro	16:24	grace of our Lord **J.** Christ be with	*2424*
Ro	16:25	and the preaching of **J.** Christ,	*2424*
Ro	16:27	be glory through **J.** Christ for ever.	*2424*
1Co	1:1	called to be an apostle of **J.** Christ	*2424*
1Co	1:2	them that are sanctified in Christ **J.**,	*2424*
1Co	1:2	call upon the name of **J.** Christ our	*2424*
1Co	1:3	Father, and from the Lord **J.** Christ.	*2424*
1Co	1:4	which is given you by **J.** Christ;	*2424*
1Co	1:7	the coming of our Lord **J.** Christ:	*2424*
1Co	1:8	in the day of our Lord **J.** Christ.	*2424*
1Co	1:9	of his Son **J.** Christ our Lord.	*2424*
1Co	1:10	by the name of our Lord **J.** Christ,	*2424*
1Co	1:30	But of him are ye in Christ **J.**,	*2424*
1Co	2:2	save **J.** Christ, and him crucified.	*2424*
1Co	3:11	than that is laid, which is **J.** Christ.	*2424*
1Co	4:15	for in Christ **J.** I have begotten you	*2424*
1Co	5:4	In the name of our Lord **J.** Christ,	*2424*
1Co	5:4	the power of our Lord **J.** Christ,	*2424*
1Co	5:5	be saved in the day of the Lord **J.**.	*2424*
1Co	6:11	justified in the name of the Lord **J.**,	*2424*
1Co	8:6	and one Lord **J.** Christ, by whom are	*2424*
1Co	9:1	have I not seen **J.** Christ our Lord?	*2424*
1Co	11:23	he Lord **J.** the same night in which	*2424*
1Co	12:3	Spirit of God calleth **J.** accursed:	*2424*
1Co	12:3	no man can say that **J.** is the Lord,	*2424*
1Co	15:31	rejoicing which I have in Christ **J.**	*2424*
1Co	15:57	victory through our Lord **J.** Christ.	*2424*
1Co	16:22	man love not the Lord **J.** Christ,	*2424*
1Co	16:23	The grace of our Lord **J.** Christ be	*2424*
1Co	16:24	My love be with you all in Christ **J.**	*2424*
2Co	1:1	Paul, an apostle of **J.** Christ by the	*2424*
2Co	1:2	Father, and from the Lord **J.** Christ.	*2424*
2Co	1:3	the Father of our Lord **J.** Christ,	*2424*
2Co	1:14	are ours in the day of the Lord **J.**.	*2424*
2Co	1:19	For the Son of God, **J.** Christ, who	*2424*
2Co	4:5	ourselves, but Christ **J.** the Lord;	*2424*
2Co	4:6	glory of God in the face of **J.** Christ.	*2424*
2Co	4:10	the body the dying of the Lord **J.**,	*2424*
2Co	4:10,	11 the life also of **J.** might be made	*2424*
2Co	4:14	that he which raised up the Lord **J.**	*2424*
2Co	4:14	shall raise up us also by **J.**, and	*2424*
2Co	5:18	hath reconciled us...by **J.** Christ,	*2424*
2Co	8:9	the grace of our Lord **J.** Christ,	*2424*
2Co	11:4	that cometh preacheth another **J.**,	*2424*
2Co	11:31	and Father of our Lord **J.** Christ,	*2424*
2Co	13:5	how that **J.** Christ is in you, except	*2424*
2Co	13:14	The grace of the Lord **J.** Christ,	*2424*
Ga	1:1	neither by man, but by **J.** Christ,	*2424*
Ga	1:3	Father, and from our Lord **J.** Christ,	*2424*
Ga	1:12	but by the revelation of **J.** Christ.	*2424*
Ga	2:4	liberty which we have in Christ **J.**,	*2424*
Ga	2:16	law, but by the faith of **J.** Christ,	*2424*
Ga	2:16	even we have believed in **J.** Christ,	*2424*
Ga	3:1	**J.** Christ hath been evidently set	*2424*
Ga	3:14	on the Gentiles through **J.** Christ;	*2424*
Ga	3:22	that the promise by faith of **J.** Christ	*2424*
Ga	3:26	of God by faith in Christ **J.**.	*2424*
Ga	3:28	for ye are all one in Christ **J.**.	*2424*
Ga	4:14	an angel of God, even as Christ **J.**.	*2424*
Ga	5:6	in **J.** Christ neither circumcision	*2424*
Ga	6:14	in the cross of our Lord **J.** Christ,	*2424*
Ga	6:15	in Christ **J.** neither circumcision	*2424*
Ga	6:17	my body the marks of the Lord **J.**	*2424*
Ga	6:18	grace of our Lord **J.** Christ be with	*2424*
Eph	1:1	Paul, an apostle of **J.** Christ by the	*2424*
Eph	1:1	and to the faithful in Christ **J.**:	*2424*
Eph	1:2	Father, and from the Lord **J.** Christ.	*2424*
Eph	1:3	and Father of our Lord **J.** Christ,	*2424*
Eph	1:5	adoption of children by **J.** Christ	*2424*
Eph	1:15	I heard of your faith in the Lord **J.**,	*2424*
Eph	1:17	That the God of our Lord **J.** Christ,	*2424*
Eph	2:6	in heavenly places in Christ **J.**:	*2424*
Eph	2:7	toward us through Christ **J.**.	*2424*
Eph	2:10	created in Christ **J.** unto good works,	*2424*
Eph	2:13	in Christ **J.** ye who sometimes were	*2424*
Eph	2:20	**J.** Christ himself being the chief	*2424*
Eph	3:1	the prisoner of **J.** Christ for you	*2424*
Eph	3:9	who created all things by **J.** Christ:	*2424*
Eph	3:11	he purposed in Christ **J.** our Lord:	*2424*
Eph	3:14	the Father of our Lord **J.** Christ,	*2424*
Eph	3:21	be glory in the church by Christ **J.**	*2424*
Eph	4:21	taught by him, as the truth is in **J.**:	*2424*
Eph	5:20	in the name of our Lord **J.** Christ;	*2424*
Eph	6:23	the Father and the Lord **J.** Christ.	*2424*
Eph	6:24	love our Lord **J.** Christ in sincerity.	*2424*
Php	1:1	the servants of **J.** Christ,	*2424*
Php	1:1	to all the saints in Christ **J.** which	*2424*

Php 1:2 Father, and from the Lord **J.** Christ.... *2424*
Php 1:6 perform it until the day of **J.** Christ: ... *2424*
Php 1:8 you all in the bowels of **J.** Christ........ *2424*
Php 1:11 which are by **J.** Christ, unto the *2424*
Php 1:19 the supply of the Spirit of **J.** Christ,.... *2424*
Php 1:26 may be more abundant in **J.** Christ..... *2424*
Php 2:5 in you, which was also in Christ **J.**: *2424*
Php 2:10 That at the name of **J.** every knee *2424*
Php 2:11 confess that **J.** Christ is Lord, ... *2424*
Php 2:19 But I trust in the Lord **J.** to send *2424*
Php 2:21 not the things which are **J.** Christ's. ... *2424*
Php 3:3 the spirit, and rejoice in Christ **J.**, ... *2424*
Php 3:8 knowledge of Christ **J.** my Lord:........ *2424*
Php 3:12 also I am apprehended of Christ **J.** *2424*
Php 3:14 the high calling of God in Christ **J.**. *2424*
Php 3:20 for the Saviour, the Lord **J.** Christ: *2424*
Php 4:7 hearts and minds through Christ **J.**. *2424*
Php 4:19 to his riches in glory by Christ **J.**, ... *2424*
Php 4:21 Salute every saint in Christ **J.**. The *2424*
Php 4:23 grace of our Lord **J.** Christ be with *2424*
Col 1:1 Paul, an apostle of **J.** Christ by the..... *2424*
Col 1:2 our Father and the Lord **J.** Christ. *2424*
Col 1:3 the Father of our Lord **J.** Christ, ... *2424*
Col 1:4 we heard of your faith in Christ **J.**,..... *2424*
Col 1:28 every man perfect in Christ **J.**:.......... *2424*
Col 2:6 received Christ **J.** the Lord, so walk... *2424*
Col 3:17 do all in the name of the Lord **J.**,........ *2424*
Col 4:11 And **J.**, which is called Justus, who..... *2424*
1Th 1:1 Father and in the Lord **J.** Christ: *2424*
1Th 1:1 Father, and the Lord **J.** Christ,.......... *2424*
1Th 1:3 of hope in our Lord **J.** Christ,............ *2424*
1Th 1:10 he raised from the dead, even **J.**,........ *2424*
1Th 2:14 which in Judaea are in Christ **J.**: *2424*
1Th 2:15 Who both killed the Lord **J.**, and........ *2424*
1Th 2:19 the presence of our Lord **J.** Christ *2424*
1Th 3:11 Father, and our Lord **J.** Christ, ... *2424*
1Th 3:13 at the coming of our Lord **J.** Christ *2424*
1Th 4:1 and exhort you by the Lord **J.**, that.... *2424*
1Th 4:2 we gave you by the Lord **J.**.............. *2424*
1Th 4:14 if we believe that **J.** died and rose...... *2424*
1Th 4:14 which sleep in **J.** will God bring *2424*
1Th 5:9 salvation by our Lord **J.** Christ, ... *2424*
1Th 5:18 this is the will of God in Christ **J.** *2424*
1Th 5:23 the coming of our Lord **J.** Christ........ *2424*
1Th 5:28 grace of our Lord **J.** Christ be with *2424*
2Th 1:1 our Father and the Lord **J.** Christ: *2424*
2Th 1:2 our Father and the Lord **J.** Christ. *2424*
2Th 1:7 the Lord **J.** shall be revealed from...... *2424*
2Th 1:8 not the gospel of our Lord **J.** Christ: .. *2424*
2Th 1:12 name of our Lord **J.** Christ may be..... *2424*
2Th 1:12 of our God and the Lord **J.** Christ...... *2424*
2Th 2:1 the coming of our Lord **J.** Christ, ... *2424*
2Th 2:14 of the glory of our Lord **J.** Christ....... *2424*
2Th 2:16 Now our Lord **J.** Christ himself, ... *2424*
2Th 3:6 in the name of our Lord **J.** Christ,...... *2424*
2Th 3:12 and exhort by our Lord **J.** Christ, ... *2424*
2Th 3:18 grace of our Lord **J.** Christ be with *2424*
1Ti 1:1 Paul, an apostle of **J.** Christ by the..... *2424*
1Ti 1:1 our Saviour, and Lord **J.** Christ, ... *2424*
1Ti 1:2 our Father and **J.** Christ our Lord. *2424*
1Ti 1:12 And I thank Christ **J.** our Lord, ... *2424*
1Ti 1:14 faith and love which is in Christ **J.**...... *2424*
1Ti 1:15 Christ **J.** came into the world to save.. *2424*
1Ti 1:16 in me first **J.** Christ might shew....... *2424*
1Ti 2:5 God and men, the man Christ **J.**; *2424*
1Ti 3:13 in the faith which is in Christ **J.**. *2424*
1Ti 4:6 shalt be a good minister of **J.** Christ, .. *2424*
1Ti 5:21 before God, and the Lord **J.** Christ,.... *2424*
1Ti 6:3 the words of our Lord **J.** Christ, ... *2424*
1Ti 6:13 all things, and before Christ **J.**,......... *2424*
1Ti 6:14 appearing of our Lord **J.** Christ:.......... *2424*
2Ti 1:1 Paul, an apostle of **J.** Christ by the..... *2424*
2Ti 1:1 promise of life which is in Christ **J.**,.... *2424*
2Ti 1:2 the Father and Christ **J.** our Lord. *2424*
2Ti 1:9 was given us in Christ **J.** before the ... *2424*
2Ti 1:10 appearing of our Saviour **J.** Christ, ... *2424*
2Ti 1:13 faith and love which is in Christ **J.**...... *2424*
2Ti 2:1 in the grace that is in Christ **J.**. *2424*
2Ti 2:3 as a good soldier of **J.** Christ............ *2424*
2Ti 2:8 that **J.** Christ of the seed of David *2424*
2Ti 2:10 the salvation which is in Christ **J.**...... *2424*
2Ti 3:12 all that will live godly in Christ **J.**....... *2424*
2Ti 3:15 through faith which is in Christ **J.**....... *2424*
2Ti 4:1 before God, and the Lord **J.** Christ,.... *2424*
2Ti 4:22 Lord **J.** Christ be with thy spirit. *2424*
Tit 1:1 of God, and an apostle of **J.** Christ, ... *2424*
Tit 1:4 and the Lord **J.** Christ our Saviour. *2424*
Tit 2:13 God and our Saviour **J.** Christ; *2424*
Tit 3:6 through **J.** Christ our Saviour; *2424*
Phm 1 Paul, a prisoner of **J.** Christ, and *2424*
Phm 3 our Father and the Lord **J.** Christ. *2424*
Phm 5 which thou hast toward the Lord **J.**, ... *2424*
Phm 6 thing which is in you in Christ **J.**........ *2424*
Phm 9 now also a prisoner of **J.** Christ......... *2424*
Phm 23 my fellowprisoner in Christ **J.**;........... *2424*
Phm 25 grace of our Lord **J.** Christ be with *2424*
Heb 2:9 see **J.**, who was made a little lower.... *2424*
Heb 3:1 Priest of our profession, Christ **J.**; *2424*
Heb 4:8 For if **J.** had given them rest, then..... *2424*
Heb 4:14 the heavens **J.** the Son of God, ... *2424*
Heb 6:20 even **J.**, made an high priest for ever.. *2424*
Heb 7:22 was **J.** made a surety of a better *2424*
Heb 10:10 of the body of **J.** Christ once for all. ... *2424*
Heb 10:19 into the holiest by the blood of **J.**........ *2424*
Heb 12:2 Looking unto **J.** the author and......... *2424*
Heb 12:24 And to **J.** the mediator of the new...... *2424*
Heb 13:8 **J.** Christ the same yesterday, and...... *2424*
Heb 13:12 Wherefore **J.** also, that he might........ *2424*
Heb 13:20 again from the dead our Lord **J.**,........ *2424*
Heb 13:21 in his sight, through **J.** Christ;........... *2424*
Jas 1:1 of God and of the Lord **J.** Christ,....... *2424*
Jas 2:1 not the faith of our Lord **J.** Christ, ... *2424*
1Pe 1:1 Peter, an apostle of **J.** Christ, to the .. *2424*
1Pe 1:2 sprinkling of the blood of **J.** Christ:..... *2424*
1Pe 1:3 and Father of our Lord **J.** Christ, ... *2424*
1Pe 1:3 hope by the resurrection of **J.** Christ .. *2424*
1Pe 1:7 glory at the appearing of **J.** Christ: *2424*
1Pe 1:13 you at the revelation of **J.** Christ;....... *2424*
1Pe 2:5 acceptable to God by **J.** Christ........... *2424*
1Pe 3:21 by the resurrection of **J.** Christ:......... *2424*
1Pe 4:11 may be glorified through **J.** Christ, ... *2424*
1Pe 5:10 unto his eternal glory by Christ **J.**, ... *2424*
1Pe 5:14 be with you all that are in Christ **J.**. ... *2424*
2Pe 1:1 servant and an apostle of **J.** Christ, ... *2424*
2Pe 1:1 of God and our Saviour **J.** Christ:....... *2424*
2Pe 1:2 the knowledge...of **J.** our Lord, ... *2424*
2Pe 1:8 knowledge of our Lord **J.** Christ. *2424*
2Pe 1:11 of our Lord and Saviour **J.** Christ....... *2424*
2Pe 1:14 our Lord **J.** Christ hath shewed me. ... *2424*
2Pe 1:16 and coming of our Lord **J.** Christ, ... *2424*
2Pe 2:20 of the Lord and Saviour **J.** Christ, ... *2424*
2Pe 3:18 of our Lord and Saviour **J.** Christ....... *2424*
1Jo 1:3 Father, and with his Son **J.** Christ....... *2424*
1Jo 1:7 blood of **J.** Christ his Son cleanseth *2424*
1Jo 2:1 the Father, **J.** Christ the righteous: *2424*
1Jo 2:22 that denieth that **J.** is the Christ?....... *2424*
1Jo 3:23 on the name of his Son **J.** Christ,....... *2424*
1Jo 4:2,3 that **J.** Christ is come in the flesh *2424*
1Jo 4:15 shall confess that **J.** is the Son of....... *2424*
1Jo 5:1 believeth that **J.** is the Christ is......... *2424*
1Jo 5:5 believeth that **J.** is the Son of God? *2424*
1Jo 5:6 by water and blood, even **J.** Christ; *2424*
1Jo 5:20 is true, even in his Son **J.** Christ, ... *2424*
2Jo 3 from the Lord **J.** Christ, the Son of.... *2424*
2Jo 7 that **J.** Christ is come in the flesh. *2424*
Jude 1 Jude, the servant of **J.** Christ, and...... *2424*
Jude 1 preserved in **J.** Christ, and called: *2424*
Jude 4 Lord God, and our Lord **J.** Christ. *2424*
Jude 17 the apostles of our Lord **J.** Christ; *2424*
Jude 21 for the mercy of our Lord **J.** Christ *2424*
Re 1:1 The Revelation of **J.** Christ, which...... *2424*
Re 1:2 and of the testimony of **J.** Christ,....... *2424*
Re 1:5 from **J.** Christ, who is the faithful....... *2424*
Re 1:9 kingdom and patience of **J.** Christ,...... *2424*
Re 1:9 and for the testimony of **J.** Christ....... *2424*
Re 12:17 and have the testimony of **J.** Christ. ... *2424*
Re 14:12 of God, and the faith of **J.**. *2424*
Re 17:6 with the blood of the martyrs of **J.**: *2424*
Re 19:10 that have the testimony of **J.**:............ *2424*
Re 19:10 the testimony of **J.** is the spirit of *2424*
Re 20:4 were beheaded for the witness of **J.**, .. *2424*
Re 22:16 **I J. have sent mine angel to testify** *2424*
Re 22:20 Amen. Even so, come, Lord **J.**.......... *2424*
Re 22:21 grace of our Lord **J.** Christ be with *2424*

JESUS' (je'-zus)
Mt 15:30 and cast them down at **J.** feet; *2424*
Mt 27:57 who also himself was **J.** disciple: *2424*
Lu 5:8 saw it, he fell down at **J.** knees, ... *2424*
Lu 8:41 fell down at **J.** feet, and besought....... *2424*
Lu 10:39 Mary, which also sat at **J.** feet, ... *2424*
Joh 12:9 they came not for **J.** sake only, but *2424*
Joh 13:23 Now there was leaning on **J.** bosom.... *2424*
Joh 13:25 He then lying on **J.** breast saith......... *2424*
2Co 4:5 ourselves your servants for **J.** sake. ... *2424*
2Co 4:11 delivered unto death for **J.** sake, ... *2424*

JESUS CHRIST See JESUS and CHRIST.

JETHER (je'-thur) See also HOBAB; ITHRA; ITHRITES; JETHRO; RAGUEL.
Jg 8:20 he said unto **J.** his firstborn, Up,........ 3500
1Ki 2:5 Ner, and unto Amasa the son of **J.**, ... 3500
1Ki 2:32 and Amasa the son of **J.**, captain of.... 3500
1Ch 2:17 and the father of Amasa was **J.** the 3500
1Ch 2:32 of Shammai; **J.**, and Jonathan:............ 3500
1Ch 2:32 and **J.** died without children. 3500
1Ch 4:17 sons of Ezra were, **J.**, and Mered, ... 3500
1Ch 7:38 sons of **J.**; Jephunneh, and Pispah, ... 3500

JETHETH (je'-theth)
Ge 36:40 Timnah, duke Alvah, duke **J.**,............ 3509
1Ch 1:51 Timnah, duke Aliah, duke **J.**,............. 3509

JETHLAH (jeth'-lah)
Jos 19:42 Shaalabbin, and Ajalon, and **J.**,........... 3494

JETHRO (je'-thro) See also JETHER.
Ex 3:1 Now Moses kept the flock of **J.** his 3503
Ex 4:18 Moses went and returned to **J.** his..... 3503
Ex 4:18 And **J.** said to Moses, Go in peace..... 3503
Ex 18:1 When **J.**, the priest of Midian, ... 3503
Ex 18:2 Then **J.**, Moses' father in law, took.... 3503
Ex 18:5 **J.**, Moses' father in law, came with 3503
Ex 18:6 father in law **J.** am come unto thee,.... 3503
Ex 18:9 **J.** rejoiced for all the goodness 3503
Ex 18:10 **J.** said, Blessed be the Lord, who...... 3503
Ex 18:12 **J.**, Moses' father in law, took a 3503

JETUR (je'-tur)
Ge 25:15 Hadar, and Tema, **J.**, Naphish. 3195
1Ch 1:31 **J.**, Naphish, and Kedemah. These...... 3195
1Ch 5:19 Hagarites, with **J.**, and Nephish, ... 3195

JEUEL (je-u'-el) See also JEIEL.
1Ch 9:6 the sons of Zerah; **J.**, and their 3262

JEUSH (je'-ush) See also JEHUSH.
Ge 36:5 Aholibamah bare **J.**, and Jaalam,......... 3266
Ge 36:14 she bare to Esau **J.**, and Jaalam,........ 3266
Ge 36:18 duke **J.**, duke Jaalam, duke Korah: 3266
1Ch 1:35 Reuel, and **J.**, and Jaalam, and.......... 3266
1Ch 7:10 **J.**, and Benjamin, and Ehud, and........ 3266
1Ch 23:10 Jahath, Zina, and **J.**, and Beriah. 3266
1Ch 23:11 **J.** and Beriah had not many sons;....... 3266
2Ch 11:19 **J.**, and Shamariah, and Zaham. 3266

JEUZ (je'-uz)
1Ch 8:10 And **J.**, and Shachia, and Mirma......... 3263

JEW (jew) See also JEWESS; JEWISH; JEWS.
Es 2:5 the palace there was a certain **J.**,....... 3064
Es 3:4 he had told them that he was a **J.**. 3064
Es 5:13 Mordecai the **J.** sitting at the king's.... 3064
Es 6:10 do even so to Mordecai the **J.**, that.... 3064
Es 8:7 the queen and to Mordecai the **J.**,....... 3064
Es 9:29 of Abihail, and Mordecai the **J.**, ... 3064
Es 9:31 Mordecai the **J.** and Esther the 3064
Es 10:3 Mordecai the **J.** was next unto king.... 3064
Jer 34:9 them, to wit, of a **J.** his brother. 3064
Zec 8:23 hold of the skirt of him that is a **J.**, ... 3064
Joh 4:9 being a **J.**, askest drink of me, ... *2453*
Joh 18:35 Pilate answered, Am I a **J.**? Thine...... *2453*
Ac 10:28 man that is a **J.** to keep company,...... *2453*
Ac 13:6 a **J.**, whose name was Bar-jesus: *2453*
Ac 18:2 found a certain **J.** named Aquila, ... *2453*
Ac 18:24 certain **J.** named Apollos, born at....... *2453*
Ac 19:14 Sceva, a **J.**, and chief of the priests,... *2453*
Ac 19:34 when they knew that he was a **J.**,...... *2453*
Ac 21:39 a man which am a **J.** of Tarsus, ... *2453*
Ac 22:3 man which am a **J.** born in Tarsus,..... *2453*
Ro 1:16 the **J.** first, and also to the Greek. *2453*
Ro 2:9 the **J.** first, and also of the Gentile; *2453*
Ro 2:10 the **J.** first, and also to the Gentile: *2453*
Ro 2:17 Behold, thou art called a **J.**, and *2453*
Ro 2:28 is not a **J.**, which is one outwardly; *2453*
Ro 2:29 he is a **J.**, which is one inwardly; *2453*
Ro 3:1 What advantage then hath the **J.**?....... *2453*
Ro 10:12 between the **J.** and the Greek: *2453*
1Co 9:20 And to the Jews I became as a **J.**, ... *2453*
Ga 2:14 If thou, being a **J.**, livest after the...... *2453*

Ga 3:28 There is neither **J.** nor Greek, ... *2453*
Col 3:11 Where there is neither Greek nor **J.**,.. *2453*

JEWEL See also JEWELS.
Pr 11:22 As a **j.** of gold in a swine's snout, ... 5141
Pr 20:15 lips of knowledge are a precious **j.**...... 3627
Eze 16:12 I put a **j.** on thy forehead, and.......... 5141

JEWELS
Ge 24:53 servant brought forth **j.** of silver, ... 3627
Ge 24:53 and **j.** of gold, and raiment, and 3627
Ex 3:22 sojourneth in her house, **j.** of silver, ... 3627
Ex 3:22 and **j.** of gold, and raiment: and ye..... 3627
Ex 11:2 neighbor, **j.** of silver, and **j.** of gold. ... 3627
Ex 12:35 of the Egyptians **j.** of silver,............. 3627
Ex 12:35 and **j.** of gold, and raiment:............... 3627
Ex 35:22 rings, and tablets, all **j.** of gold: 3627
Nu 31:50 of **j.** of gold, chains, and bracelets, ... 3627
Nu 31:51 gold of them, even all wrought **j.**. 3627
1Sa 6:8 put the **j.** of gold, which ye return...... 3627
1Sa 6:15 with it, wherein the **j.** of gold were, ... 3627
2Ch 20:25 precious **j.**, which they stripped off..... 3627
2Ch 32:27 and for all manner of pleasant **j.**;........ 3627
Job 28:17 it shall not be for **j.** of fine gold. 3627
Ca 1:10 cheeks are comely with rows of **j.**, ... 3627
Ca 7:1 joints of thy thighs are like **j.**, the...... 2484
Isa 3:21 The rings, and nose **j.**, ... 5141
Isa 61:10 bride adorneth herself with her **j.**. 3627
Eze 16:17 Thou hast also taken thy fair **j.** of 3627
Eze 16:39 shall take thy fair **j.**, and leave thee..... 3627
Eze 23:26 clothes, and take away thy fair **j.**. 3627
Ho 2:13 with her earrings and her **j.**, ... 2484
Mal 3:17 that day when I make up my **j.**;.......... 5459

JEWESS (jew'-ess)
Ac 16:1 certain woman, which was a **J.**, ... *2453*
Ac 24:24 his wife Drusilla, which was a **J.**, ... *2453*

JEWISH (jew'-ish)
Tit 1:14 Not giving heed to **J.** fables,and......... *2451*

JEWRY (jew'-ree) See also JUDAEA.
Da 5:13 king my father brought out of **J.**? 3061
Lu 23:5 people, teaching throughout all **J.**, ... *2449*
Joh 7:1 he would not walk in **J.**, because......... *2449*

JEWS (jews) See also JEWS'.
2Ki 16:6 Syria, and drave the **J.** from Elath:..... 3064
2Ki 25:25 the **J.** and the Chaldees that were...... 3064
Ezr 4:12 the **J.** which came up from thee to...... 3062
Ezr 4:23 in haste to Jerusalem unto the **J.**,....... 3062
Ezr 5:1 son of Iddo, prophesied unto the **J.** 3062
Ezr 5:5 God was upon the elders of the **J.**,..... 3062
Ezr 6:7 alone; let the governors of the **J.** 3062
Ezr 6:7 and the elders of the **J.** build this....... 3062
Ezr 6:8 shall do to the elders of these **J.**......... 3062
Ezr 6:14 the elders of the **J.** builded, and......... 3062
Ne 1:2 concerning the **J.** that had escaped, ... 3064
Ne 2:16 neither had I as yet told it to the **J.**,... 3064
Ne 4:1 indignation, and mocked the **J.**........... 3064
Ne 4:2 and said, What do these feeble **J.**? 3064
Ne 4:12 the **J.** which dwelt by them came, ... 3064
Ne 5:1 wives against their brethren the **J.**. 3064
Ne 5:8 have redeemed our brethren the **J.**,..... 3064
Ne 5:17 were at my table...**J.** and rulers,......... 3064
Ne 6:6 that thou and the **J.** think to rebel: 3064
Ne 13:23 In those days also saw I **J.** that 3064
Es 3:6 Haman sought to destroy all the **J.**..... 3064
Es 3:13 kill, and to cause to perish, all **J.**, ... 3064
Es 4:3 was great mourning among the **J.**,...... 3064
Es 4:7 to the king's treasuries for the **J.**, ... 3064
Es 4:13 king's house, more than all the **J.**........ 3064
Es 4:14 and deliverance arise to the **J.**........... 3064
Es 4:16 gather together all the **J.** that are....... 3064
Es 6:13 Mordecai be of the seed of the **J.**, ... 3064
Es 8:3 that he had devised against the **J.**. 3064
Es 8:5 which he wrote to destroy the **J.**........ 3064
Es 8:7 he laid his hand upon the **J.**. 3064
Es 8:8 Write ye also for the **J.**, as it liketh.... 3064
Es 8:9 Mordecai commanded unto the **J.**, ... 3064
Es 8:9 the **J.** according to their writing, ... 3064
Es 8:11 Wherein the king granted the **J.**......... 3064
Es 8:13 **J.** should be ready against that day..... 3064
Es 8:16 The **J.** had light, and gladness, and..... 3064
Es 8:17 the **J.** had joy and gladness, a feast 3064
Es 8:17 the people of the land became **J.**........ 3054
Es 8:17 the fear of the **J.** fell upon them. 3064
Es 9:1 **J.** hoped to have power over them, ... 3064
Es 9:1 the **J.** had rule over them that.......... 3064
Es 9:2 **J.** gathered themselves together 3064
Es 9:3 officers of the king, helped the **J.**;...... 3064
Es 9:5 the **J.** smote all their enemies with..... 3064
Es 9:6 Shushan the palace the **J.** slew and..... 3064
Es 9:10 the enemy of the **J.**, slew they;......... 3064
Es 9:12 The **J.** have slain and destroyed......... 3064
Es 9:13 king, let it be granted to the **J.**.......... 3064
Es 9:15 For the **J.** that were in Shushan......... 3064
Es 9:16 **J.** that were in the king's provinces 3064
Es 9:18 **J.** that were in Shushan assembled 3064
Es 9:19 Therefore the **J.** of the villages,......... 3064
Es 9:20 sent letters unto all the **J.** that 3064
Es 9:22 the **J.** rested from their enemies,....... 3064
Es 9:23 the **J.** undertook to do as they had..... 3064
Es 9:24 Agagite, the enemy of all the **J.**, ... 3064
Es 9:24 devised against the **J.** to destroy........ 3064
Es 9:25 which he devised against the **J.**,......... 3064
Es 9:27 **J.** ordained, and took upon them, ... 3064
Es 9:28 should not fail from among the **J.**, ... 3064
Es 9:30 he sent the letter unto all the **J.**, ... 3064
Es 10:3 Ahasuerus, great among the **J.**, ... 3064
Jer 32:12 **J.** that sat in the court of the prison. .. 3064
Jer 38:19 afraid of the **J.** that are fallen to......... 3064
Jer 40:11 when all the **J.** that were in Moab, ... 3064
Jer 40:12 all the **J.** returned out of all places 3064
Jer 40:15 all the **J.** which are gathered unto 3064
Jer 41:3 Ishmael also slew all the **J.** that 3064
Jer 44:1 concerning all the **J.** which dwell........ 3064
Jer 52:28 the seventh year three thousand **J.**...... 3064
Da 3:8 came near, and accused the **J.**........... 3064
Da 3:12 certain **J.** whom thou hast set 3064
Mt 2:2 is he that is born King of the **J.**? *2453*
Mt 27:11 saying, Art thou the King of the **J.**?.... *2453*
Mt 27:29 him, saying, Hail, King of the **J.**! *2453*
Mt 27:37 This Is Jesus The King Of The **J.**. *2453*
Mt 28:15 is commonly reported among the **J.** *2453*
Mk 7:3 For the Pharisees, and all the **J.**, ... *2453*
Mk 15:2 him, Art thou the King of the **J.**?....... *2453*
Mk 15:9 release unto you the King of the **J.**? ... *2453*
Mk 15:12 whom ye call the King of the **J.**?........ *2453*
Mk 15:18 to salute him, Hail, King of the **J.**! *2453*
Mk 15:26 written over, The King Of The **J.**. *2453*
Lu 7:3 sent unto him the elders of the **J.** *2453*
Lu 23:3 saying, Art thou the King of the **J.**?.... *2453*
Lu 23:37 If thou be the king of the **J.**, save...... *2453*
Lu 23:38 This Is The King Of The **J.**. *2453*
Lu 23:51 was of Arimathaea, a city of the **J.**..... *2453*
Joh 1:19 when the **J.** sent priests and Levites... *2453*
Joh 2:6 manner of the purifying of the **J.**, ... *2453*
Joh 2:18 Then answered the **J.** and said unto.... *2453*
Joh 2:20 Then said the **J.**, Forty and six........... *2453*
Joh 3:1 named Nicodemus, a ruler of the **J.**: ... *2453*
Joh 3:25 of John's disciples and the **J.** *2453*
Joh 4:9 the **J.** have no dealings with the......... *2453*
Joh 4:22 **worship: for salvation is of the J.**.. *2453*
Joh 5:1 this there was a feast of the **J.**; *2453*
Joh 5:10 **J.** therefore said unto him that was..... *2453*
Joh 5:15 and told the **J.** that it was Jesus,........ *2453*
Joh 5:16 therefore did the **J.** persecute Jesus,... *2453*
Joh 5:18 the **J.** sought the more to kill him, ... *2453*
Joh 6:4 passover, a feast of the **J.**, was nigh... *2453*
Joh 6:41 The **J.** then murmured at him,........... *2453*
Joh 6:52 The **J.** therefore strove among *2453*
Joh 7:1 because the **J.** sought to kill him. *2453*
Joh 7:11 Then the **J.** sought him at the feast,... *2453*
Joh 7:13 openly of him for fear of the **J.**. *2453*
Joh 7:15 And the **J.** marvelled, saying, How..... *2453*
Joh 7:35 said the **J.** among themselves, ... *2453*
Joh 8:22 said the **J.**, Will he kill himself?......... *2453*
Joh 8:31 Jesus to those **J.** which believed *2453*
Joh 8:48 Then answered the **J.**, and said *2453*
Joh 8:52 Then said the **J.** unto him, Now we.... *2453*
Joh 8:57 Then said the **J.** unto him, Thou........ *2453*
Joh 9:18 the **J.** did not believe concerning........ *2453*
Joh 9:22 parents, because they feared the **J.**: ... *2453*
Joh 9:22 for the **J.** had agreed already, that...... *2453*
Joh 10:19 was a division...again among the **J.**..... *2453*
Joh 10:24 Then came the **J.** round about him, ... *2453*
Joh 10:31 Then the **J.** took up stones again *2453*
Joh 10:33 The **J.** answered him, saying, For....... *2453*
Joh 11:8 the **J.** of late sought to stone thee;..... *2453*
Joh 11:19 many of the **J.** came to Martha.......... *2453*
Joh 11:31 The **J.** then which were with her *2453*
Joh 11:33 weeping, and the **J.** also weeping....... *2453*
Joh 11:36 Then said the **J.**, Behold how he........ *2453*
Joh 11:45 many of the **J.** which came to Mary,... *2453*
Joh 11:54 no more openly among the **J.**; *2453*
Joh 12:9 people of the **J.** therefore knew *2453*
Joh 12:11 of him many of the **J.** went away. *2453*
Joh 13:33 **as I said unto the J., Whither I go,** *2453*
Joh 18:12 and officers of the **J.** took Jesus,........ *2453*
Joh 18:14 he, which gave counsel to the **J.**, ... *2453*
Joh 18:20 **whither the J. always resort;**......... *2453*
Joh 18:31 The **J.** therefore said unto him, It *2453*
Joh 18:33 him, Art thou the King of the **J.**?....... *2453*
Joh 18:36 **I should not be delivered to the J.**. *2453*
Joh 18:38 he went out again unto the **J.**, and *2453*
Joh 18:39 release unto you the King of the **J.**? ... *2453*
Joh 19:3 And said, Hail, King of the **J.**! and *2453*
Joh 19:7 **J.** answered him, We have a law,....... *2453*
Joh 19:12 but the **J.** cried out, saying, If thou *2453*
Joh 19:14 he saith unto the **J.**, Behold your *2453*
Joh 19:19 Of Nazareth The King Of The **J.**.......... *2453*
Joh 19:20 This title then read many of the **J.**; *2453*
Joh 19:21 Then said the chief priests of the **J.**.... *2453*
Joh 19:21 Write not, The King of the **J.**; but *2453*
Joh 19:21 that he said, I am King of the **J.**. *2453*
Joh 19:31 The **J.** therefore,...besought Pilate *2453*
Joh 19:38 but secretly for fear of the **J.**, ... *2453*
Joh 19:40 as the manner of the **J.** is to bury. *2453*
Joh 20:19 were assembled for fear of the **J.**,...... *2453*
Ac 2:5 were dwelling at Jerusalem **J.**,........... *2453*
Ac 2:10 of Rome, **J.** and proselytes, ... *2453*
Ac 9:22 the **J.** which dwelt at Damascus,......... *2453*
Ac 9:23 the **J.** took counsel to kill him: *2453*
Ac 10:22 among all the nation of the **J.**, ... *2453*
Ac 10:39 he did both in the land of the **J.**,........ *2453*
Ac 11:19 word to none but unto the **J.** only. *2453*
Ac 12:3 because he saw it please the **J.**, ... *2453*
Ac 12:11 expectation of the people of the **J.**....... *2453*
Ac 13:5 of God in the synagogues of the **J.**..... *2453*
Ac 13:42 **J.** were gone out of the synagogue, ... *2453*
Ac 13:43 many of the **J.** and religious *2453*
Ac 13:45 when the **J.** saw the multitudes, ... *2453*
Ac 13:50 the **J.** stirred up the devout and.......... *2453*
Ac 14:1 into the synagogue of the **J.**,............. *2453*
Ac 14:1 great multitude both of the **J.** and *2453*
Ac 14:2 the unbelieving **J.** stirred up the......... *2453*
Ac 14:4 and part held with the **J.**, and part *2453*
Ac 14:5 and also of the **J.** with their rulers,..... *2453*
Ac 14:19 thither certain **J.** from Antioch........... *2453*
Ac 16:3 circumcised him because of the **J.** *2453*
Ac 16:20 being **J.**, do exceedingly trouble......... *2453*
Ac 17:1 where was a synagogue of the **J.** *2453*
Ac 17:5 But the **J.** which believed not,........... *2453*
Ac 17:10 went into the synagogue of the **J.**. *2453*
Ac 17:13 But when the **J.** of Thessalonica *2453*
Ac 17:17 he in the synagogue of the **J.**, ... *2453*
Ac 18:2 all **J.** to depart from Rome:)............. *2453*
Ac 18:4 persuaded the **J.** and the Greeks........ *2453*
Ac 18:5 testified to the **J.** that Jesus was....... *2453*
Ac 18:12 the **J.** made insurrection with one....... *2453*
Ac 18:14 Gallio said unto the **J.**, If it were *2453*
Ac 18:14 O ye **J.**, reason would that I should.... *2453*
Ac 18:19 and reasoned with the **J.**. *2453*
Ac 18:28 For he mightily convinced the **J.**, ... *2453*
Ac 19:10 Lord Jesus, both **J.** and Greeks. *2453*
Ac 19:13 Then certain of the vagabond **J.**,......... *2453*
Ac 19:17 And this was known to all the **J.**......... *2453*
Ac 19:33 the **J.** putting him forward. *2453*
Ac 20:3 And when the **J.** laid wait for him,...... *2453*
Ac 20:19 me by the lying in wait of the **J.**: *2453*
Ac 20:21 Testifying both to the **J.**, and also....... *2453*
Ac 21:11 So shall the **J.** at Jerusalem bind *2453*
Ac 21:20 how many thousands of **J.** there are ... *2453*
Ac 21:21 thou teacheth all the **J.** which are....... *2453*
Ac 21:27 the **J.** which were of Asia, when........ *2453*
Ac 22:12 a good report of all the **J.** which *2453*
Ac 22:30 wherefore he was accused of the **J.**,... *2453*
Ac 23:12 certain of the **J.** banded together,....... *2453*
Ac 23:20 The **J.** have agreed to desire thee...... *2453*
Ac 23:27 This man was taken of the **J.**, ... *2453*
Ac 23:30 that the **J.** laid wait for the man,........ *2453*
Ac 24:5 mover of sedition among all the **J.**....... *2453*
Ac 24:9 the **J.** also assented, saying that *2453*
Ac 24:18 certain **J.** from Asia found me........... *2453*
Ac 24:27 willing to shew the **J.** a pleasure, ... *2453*
Ac 25:2 the chief of the **J.** informed him *2453*
Ac 25:7 the **J.** which came down from............ *2453*
Ac 25:8 Neither against the law of the **J.**, ... *2453*

Ac 25:9 willing to do the **J.** a pleasure, *2453*
Ac 25:10 to the **J.** have I done no wrong, as *2453*
Ac 25:15 the elders of the **J.** informed me, *2453*
Ac 25:24 the multitude of the **J.** have dealt *2453*
Ac 26:2 whereof I am accused of the **J.**: *2453*
Ac 26:2 questions which are among the **J.**: *2453*
Ac 26:4 at Jerusalem, know all the **J.**; *2453*
Ac 26:7 Agrippa, I am accused of the **J.**. *2453*
Ac 26:21 the **J.** caught me in the temple, *2453*
Ac 28:17 days Paul called the chief of the **J.** *2453*
Ac 28:19 But when the **J.** spake against it, *2453*
Ac 28:29 said these words, the **J.** departed, *2453*
Ro 3:9 before proved both **J.** and Gentiles, *2453*
Ro 3:29 Is he the God of the **J.** only? *2453*
Ro 9:24 called, not of the **J.** only, but also *2453*
1Co 1:22 For the **J.** require a sign, and the *2453*
1Co 1:23 unto the **J.** a stumblingblock, and *2453*
1Co 1:24 are called, both **J.** and Greeks, *2453*
1Co 9:20 And unto the **J.** I became as a Jew, *2453*
1Co 9:20 that I might gain the **J.**; to them *2453*
1Co 10:32 none offence, neither to the **J.**, nor *2453*
1Co 12:13 whether we be **J.** of Gentiles, *2453*
2Co 11:24 Of the **J.** five times received I forty *2453*
Ga 2:13 the other **J.** dissembled likewise *2453*
Ga 2:14 of Gentiles, and not as do the **J.**, *2452*
Ga 2:14 the Gentiles to live as do the **J.**? *2450*
Ga 2:15 We who are **J.** by nature, and not *2453*
1Th 2:14 even as they have of the **J.**: *2453*
Re 2:9 **which say they are J., and are not,** *2453*
Re 3:9 **which say they are J., and are not,** *2453*

JEWS' (jews)
2Ki 18:26 talk not with us in the **J.** language 3066
2Ki 18:28 a loud voice in the **J.** language, 3066
2Ch 32:18 with a loud voice in the **J.** speech 3066
Ne 13:24 not speak in the **J.** language, but 3066
Es 3:10 the Agagite, the **J.** enemy. 3064
Es 8:1 the house of Haman the **J.** enemy 3064
Isa 36:11 speak not to us in the **J.** language, 3064
Isa 36:13 a loud voice in the **J.** language, 3064
Joh 2:13 the **J.** passover was at hand, and *2453*
Joh 7:2 the **J.** feast of tabernacles was at *2453*
Joh 11:55 the **J.** passover was nigh at hand: *2453*
Joh 19:42 because of the **J.** preparation day; *2453*
Ga 1:13 in time past in the **J.** religion, *2454*
Ga 1:14 profited in the **J.** religion above *2454*

JEZANIAH (jez-a-ni'-ah) See also JAAZANIAH.
Jer 40:8 and **J.** the son of a Maachathite, 3153
Jer 42:1 Kareah, and **J.** the son of Hoshaiah, 3153

JEZEBEL (jez'-e-bel) See also JEZEBEL'S.
1Ki 16:31 he took to wife **J.** the daughter of 348
1Ki 18:4 when **J.** cut off the prophets of the 348
1Ki 18:13 what I did when **J.** slew the prophets 348
1Ki 19:1 And Ahab told **J.** all that Elijah had 348
1Ki 19:2 **J.** sent a messenger unto Elijah, 348
1Ki 21:5 **J.** his wife came to him, and said 348
1Ki 21:7 **J.** his wife said unto him, Dost thou 348
1Ki 21:11 did as **J.** had sent unto them, and 348
1Ki 21:14 sent to **J.**, saying, Naboth is stoned, 348
1Ki 21:15 **J.** heard that Naboth was stoned, 348
1Ki 21:15 that **J.** said to Ahab, Arise, take 348
1Ki 21:23 And of **J.** also spake the Lord, 348
1Ki 21:23 The dogs shall eat **J.** by the wall of 348
1Ki 21:25 Lord, whom **J.** his wife stirred up 348
2Ki 9:7 of the Lord, at the hand of **J.**. 348
2Ki 9:10 the dogs shall eat **J.** in the portion 348
2Ki 9:22 as the whoredoms of thy mother **J.** 348
2Ki 9:30 was come to Jezreel, **J.** heard of it; 348
2Ki 9:36 Jezreel shall dogs eat the flesh of **J.**: 348
2Ki 9:37 the carcase of **J.** shall be as dung 348
2Ki 9:37 so that they shall not say, This is **J.** 348
Re 2:20 **thou sufferest that woman J.,** *2403*

JEZEBEL'S (jez'-e-bels)
1Ki 18:19 four hundred which eat at **J.** table 348

JEZER (je'-zur) See also JEZERITES.
Ge 46:24 and Guni, and **J.**, and Shillem, 3337
Nu 26:49 Of **J.**, the family of the Jezerites: 3337
1Ch 7:13 and Guni, and **J.**, and Shallum, 3337

JEZERITES (je'-zur-ites)
Nu 26:49 of Jezer, the family of the **J.** 3339

JEZIAH (je-zi'-ah)
Ezr 10:25 Ramiah, and **J.**, and Malchiah, 3150

JEZIEL (je'-ze-el)
1Ch 12:3 and **J.**, and Pelet, the sons of 3149

JEZLIAH (jez-li'-ah)
1Ch 8:18 **J.**, and Jobab, the sons of Elpaal; 3152

JEZOAR (je-zo'-ar) See also ZOAR.
1Ch 4:7 of Helah were, Zereth, and **J.**, 3328

JEZRAHIAH (jez-ra-hi'-ah) See also IZRAHIAH.
Ne 12:42 sang loud, with **J.** their overseer 3156

JEZREEL (jez'-re-el) See also JEZREELITE.
Jos 15:56 **J.**, and Jokdeam, and Zanoah, 3157
Jos 17:16 they who are of the valley of **J.**. 3157
Jos 19:18 And their border was toward **J.** 3157
Jg 6:33 and pitched in the valley of **J.**. 3157
1Sa 25:43 David also took Ahinoam of **J.**; 3157
1Sa 29:1 pitched by a fountain which is in **J.**. 3157
1Sa 29:11 And the Philistines went up to **J.**. 3157
2Sa 2:9 and over **J.**, and over Ephraim, and 3157
2Sa 4:4 of Saul and Jonathan out of **J.**, 3157
1Ki 4:12 which is by Zartanah beneath **J.**, 3157
1Ki 18:45 And Ahab rode, and went to **J.**. 3157
1Ki 18:46 before Ahab to the entrance to **J.** 3157
1Ki 21:1 had a vineyard, which was in **J.**, 3157
1Ki 21:23 shall eat Jezebel by the wall of **J.**. 3157
2Ki 8:29 Joram went back to be healed in **J.** 3157
2Ki 8:29 to see Joram the son of Ahab in **J.**, 3157
2Ki 9:10 eat Jezebel in the portion of **J.**, 3157
2Ki 9:15 was returned to be healed in **J.** 3157
2Ki 9:15 out of the city to go to tell it in **J.** 3157
2Ki 9:16 rode in a chariot, and went to **J.**; 3157
2Ki 9:17 a watchman on the tower of **J.**, 3157
2Ki 9:30 And when Jehu was come to **J.**, 3157
2Ki 9:36 In the portion of **J.** shall dogs eat 3157
2Ki 9:37 of the field in the portion of **J.**; 3157
2Ki 10:1 to Samaria, unto the rulers of **J.**, 3157
2Ki 10:6 and come to me to **J.** by to morrow 3157
2Ki 10:7 baskets, and sent him them to **J.**. 3157
2Ki 10:11 remained of the house of Ahab in **J.**, 3157
1Ch 4:3 Etam; **J.**, and Ishma, and Idbash: 3157
2Ch 22:6 he returned to be healed in **J.** 3157
2Ch 22:6 Jehoram the son of Ahab at **J.**, 3157
Ho 1:4 said unto him, Call his name **J.**; 3157
Ho 1:4 I will avenge the blood of **J.** upon 3157
Ho 1:5 bow of Israel in the valley of **J.**. 3157
Ho 1:11 for great shall be the day of **J.**. 3157
Ho 2:22 the oil; and they shall hear **J.** 3157

JEZREELITE (jez'-re-el-ite) See also JEZREELITESS.
1Ki 21:1 that Naboth the **J.** had a vineyard, 3158
1Ki 21:4 Naboth the **J.** had spoken to him: 3158
1Ki 21:6 Because I spake unto Naboth the **J.**, 3158
1Ki 21:7 thee the vineyard of Naboth the **J.**. 3158
1Ki 21:15 of the vineyard of Naboth the **J.**, 3158
1Ki 21:16 to the vineyard of Naboth the **J.**, 3158
2Ki 9:21 him in the portion of Naboth the **J.** 3158
2Ki 9:25 of the field of Naboth the **J.**: 3158

JEZREELITESS (jez'-re-el-i-tess)
1Sa 27:3 his two wives, Ahinoam the **J.**, 3159
1Sa 30:5 taken captives, Ahinoam the **J.**, 3159
2Sa 2:2 two wives also, Ahinoam the **J.**, 3159
2Sa 3:2 was Amnon, of Ahinoam the **J.**; 3159
1Ch 3:1 Amnon, of Ahinoam the **J.**; 3159

JIBSAM (jib'-sam)
1Ch 7:2 and Jahmai, and **J.**, and Shemuel, 3005

JIDLAPH (jid'-laf)
Ge 22:22 and Pildash, and **J.**, and Bethuel. 3044

JIMNA (jim'-nah) See also IMNA; JIMNAH; JIMNITES.
Nu 26:44 of **J.**, the family of the Jimnites: 3232

JIMNAH (jim'-nah) See also JIMNA.
Ge 46:17 sons of Asher; **J.**, and Ishuah, 3232

JIMNITES (jim'-nites)
Nu 26:44 of Jimna, the family of the **J.** 3232

JIPHTAH (jif'-tah) See also JEPHTHAH; JIPHTHAH-EL.
Jos 15:43 And **J.**, and Ashnah, and Nezib, 3316

JIPHTHAH-EL (jif'-thah-el)
Jos 19:14 thereof are in the valley of **J.** 3317
Jos 19:27 to the valley of **J.** toward the north 3317

JOAB (jo'-ab) See also ATAROTH; HOUSE; JOAB'S.
1Sa 26:6 the son of Zeruiah, brother to **J.** 3097
2Sa 2:13 **J.** the son of Zeruiah, and the 3097
2Sa 2:14 Abner said to **J.**, Let the young 3097
2Sa 2:14 And **J.** said, Let them arise 3097
2Sa 2:18 three sons of Zeruiah there, **J.**, and 3097
2Sa 2:22 should I hold up my face to **J.** 3097
2Sa 2:24 **J.** also and Abishai pursued after 3097
2Sa 2:26 Abner called to **J.**, and said, Shall 3097
2Sa 2:27 **J.** said, As God liveth, unless thou 3097
2Sa 2:28 So **J.** blew a trumpet, and all the 3097
2Sa 2:30 **J.** returned from following Abner: 3097
2Sa 2:32 **J.** and his men went all night, and 3097
2Sa 3:22 servants of David and **J.** came 3097
2Sa 3:23 When **J.** and all the host that was 3097
2Sa 3:23 they told **J.**, saying, Abner the son 3097
2Sa 3:24 Then **J.** came to the king, and 3097
2Sa 3:26 when **J.** was come out from David, 3097
2Sa 3:27 **J.** took him aside in the gate to 3097
2Sa 3:29 Let it rest on the head of **J.**, and on 3097
2Sa 3:29 not fail from the house of **J.** one 3097
2Sa 3:30 So **J.** and Abishai his brother slew 3097
2Sa 3:31 David said to **J.**, and to all the 3097
2Sa 8:16 **J.** the son of Zeruiah was over the 3097
2Sa 10:7 when David heard of it, he sent **J.**, 3097
2Sa 10:9 When **J.** saw that the front of the 3097
2Sa 10:13 **J.** drew nigh, and the people that 3097
2Sa 10:14 So **J.** returned from the children 3097
2Sa 11:1 that David sent **J.**, and his servants 3097
2Sa 11:6 David sent to **J.**, saying, Send me 3097
2Sa 11:6 and **J.** sent Uriah to David. 3097
2Sa 11:7 David demanded of him how **J.** did, 3097
2Sa 11:11 and my lord **J.**, and the servants 3097
2Sa 11:14 David wrote a letter to **J.**, and sent 3097
2Sa 11:16 to pass, when **J.** observed the city, 3097
2Sa 11:17 city went out, and fought with **J.** 3097
2Sa 11:18 **J.** sent and told David all the 3097
2Sa 11:22 David all that **J.** had sent him for. 3097
2Sa 11:25 Thus shalt thou say unto **J.**, Let 3097
2Sa 12:26 **J.** fought against Rabbah of the 3097
2Sa 12:27 **J.** sent messengers to David, and 3097
2Sa 14:1 **J.** the son of Zeruiah perceived 3097
2Sa 14:2 **J.** sent to Tekoah, and fetched 3097
2Sa 14:3 So **J.** put the words in her mouth 3097
2Sa 14:19 Is not the hand of **J.** with thee in 3097
2Sa 14:19 for thy servant **J.**, he bade me, 3097
2Sa 14:20 hath thy servant **J.** done this thing: 3097
2Sa 14:21 the king said unto **J.**, Behold now, 3097
2Sa 14:22 **J.** fell to the ground on his face, 3097
2Sa 14:22 **J.** said, To day thy servant knoweth 3097
2Sa 14:23 **J.** arose and went to Geshur, and 3097
2Sa 14:29 Absalom sent for **J.**, to have sent 3097
2Sa 14:31 **J.** arose, and came to Absalom 3097
2Sa 14:32 Absalom answered **J.**, Behold, I 3097
2Sa 14:33 **J.** came to the king, and told him: 3097
2Sa 17:25 captain of the host instead of **J.**: 3097
2Sa 18:2 of the people under the hand of **J.**, 3097
2Sa 18:5 the king commanded **J.** and 3097
2Sa 18:10 a certain man saw it, and told **J.**, 3097
2Sa 18:11 **J.** said unto the man that told him, 3097
2Sa 18:12 the man said unto **J.**, Though I 3097
2Sa 18:14 Then said **J.**, I may not tarry thus 3097
2Sa 18:16 **J.** blew the trumpet, and the people 3097
2Sa 18:16 for **J.** held back the people 3097
2Sa 18:20 **J.** said unto them, Thou shalt not 3097
2Sa 18:21 Then said **J.** to Cushi, Go tell the 3097
2Sa 18:21 Cushi bowed himself unto **J.**, and 3097
2Sa 18:22 the son of Zadok yet again to **J.**, 3097
2Sa 18:22 **J.** said, Wherefore wilt thou run, 3097
2Sa 18:29 When **J.** sent the king's servant, 3097
2Sa 19:1 it was told **J.**, Behold, the king 3097
2Sa 19:5 **J.** came into the house to the king, 3097
2Sa 19:13 me continually in the room of **J.** 3097
2Sa 20:9 **J.** said to Amasa, Art thou in 3097
2Sa 20:9 **J.** took Amasa by the beard with 3097
2Sa 20:10 So **J.** and Abishai his brother 3097
2Sa 20:11 and said, He that favoureth **J.**, 3097
2Sa 20:11 is for David, let him go after **J.**. 3097
2Sa 20:13 all the people went on after **J.**, to 3097
2Sa 20:15 people that were with **J.** battered 3097
2Sa 20:16 say, I pray you, unto **J.**, come near 3097
2Sa 20:17 her, the woman said, Art thou **J.**? 3097
2Sa 20:20 **J.** answered and said, Far be it, 3097
2Sa 20:21 the woman said unto **J.**, Behold, 3097
2Sa 20:22 son of Bichri, and cast it out to **J.**. 3097
2Sa 20:22 **J.** returned to Jerusalem unto the 3097
2Sa 20:23 **J.** was over all the host of Israel: 3097
2Sa 23:18 Abishai, the brother of **J.**, the son 3097

2Sa 23:24 brother of J. was one of the thirty; 3097
2Sa 23:37 armourbearer to J. the son of 3097
2Sa 24:2 the king said to J. the captain of 3097
2Sa 24:3 J. said unto the king, Now the 3097
2Sa 24:4 king's word prevailed against J., 3097
2Sa 24:4 J. and the captains of the host 3097
2Sa 24:9 J. gave up the sum of the number 3097
1Ki 1:7 he conferred with J. the son of 3097
1Ki 1:19 and J. the captain of the host: 3097
1Ki 1:41 J. heard the sound of the trumpet, 3097
1Ki 2:5 J. the son of Zeruiah did to me, 3097
1Ki 2:22 and for J. the son of Zeruiah. 3097
1Ki 2:28 Then tidings came to J.: 3097
1Ki 2:28 for J. had turned after Adonijah, 3097
1Ki 2:28 J. fled into the tabernacle of the 3097
1Ki 2:29 that J. was fled unto the tabernacle 3097
1Ki 2:30 Thus said J., and thus he answered 3097
1Ki 2:31 the innocent blood, which J. shed, 3097
1Ki 2:33 therefore return upon the head of J., 3097
1Ki 11:15 J. the captain of the host was gone 3097
1Ki 11:16 For six months did J. remain there 3097
1Ki 11:21 J. the captain of the host was dead, 3097
1Ch 2:16 sons of Zeruiah; Abishai and J., 3097
1Ch 2:54 Ataroth, the house of J., and half 5854
1Ch 4:14 Seraiah begat J., the father of 3097
1Ch 11:6 So J. the son of Zeruiah went first 3097
1Ch 11:8 J. repaired the rest of the city 3097
1Ch 11:20 the brother of J., he was chief of 3097
1Ch 11:26 were, Asahel the brother of J., 3097
1Ch 11:39 the armourbearer of J. the son of 3097
1Ch 18:15 J. the son of Zeruiah was over the 3097
1Ch 19:8 when David heard of it, he sent J., 3097
1Ch 19:10 when J. saw that the battle was 3097
1Ch 19:14 So J. and the people that were 3097
1Ch 19:15 city. then J. came to Jerusalem 3097
1Ch 20:1 J. led forth the power of the army, 3097
1Ch 20:1 J. smote Rabbah, and destroyed it 3097
1Ch 21:2 David said to J. and to the rulers 3097
1Ch 21:3 And J. answered, The Lord make 3097
1Ch 21:4 king's word prevailed against J. 3097
1Ch 21:4 Wherefore J. departed, and went 3097
1Ch 21:5 J. gave the sum of the number of 3097
1Ch 21:6 king's word was abominable to J. 3097
1Ch 26:28 and J. the son of Zeruiah, had 3097
1Ch 27:7 month was Asahel the brother of J., 3097
1Ch 27:24 J. the son of Zeruiah began to 3097
1Ch 27:34 general of the king's army was J. 3097
Ezr 2:6 of the children of Jeshua and J., 3097
Ezr 8:9 Of the sons of J.; Obadiah the son 3097
Ne 7:11 of the children of Jeshua and J., 3097
Ps 60:*title* when J. returned, and smote of 3097

JOAB'S (jo'-abs)
2Sa 14:30 J. field is near mine, and he hath 3097
2Sa 17:25 Nahash, sister to Zeruiah J. mother, 3097
2Sa 18:2 the son of Zeruiah, J. brother, 3097
2Sa 18:15 young men that bare J. armour 3097
2Sa 20:7 there went out after him J. men, 3097
2Sa 20:8 J. garment that he had put on was 3097
2Sa 20:10 to the sword that was in J. hand: 3097
2Sa 20:11 one of J. men stood by him, and 3097

JOAH (jo'-ah) See also ETHAN.
2Ki 18:18 J. the son of Asaph the recorder 3098
2Ki 18:26 Shebna, and J., unto Rab-shakeh, 3098
2Ki 18:37 J. the son of Asaph the recorder, 3098
1Ch 6:21 J. his son, Iddo his son, Zerah his 3098
1Ch 26:4 J. the third, and Sacar the fourth, 3098
2Ch 29:12 Gershonites; J. the son of Zimmah, 3098
2Ch 29:12 and Eden the son of J.: 3098
2Ch 34:8 J. the son of Joahaz the recorder, 3098
Isa 36:3 and J., Asaph's son, the recorder 3098
Isa 36:11 Shebna and J. unto Rabshakeh, 3098
Isa 36:22 J., the son of Asaph, the recorder, 3098

JOAHAZ (jo'-a-haz) See also JEHOAHAZ.
2Ch 34:8 Joah the son of J. the recorder, 3098

JOANNA (jo-an'-nah)
Lu 3:27 Which was the son of J., which *2489*
Lu 8:3 And J. the wife of Chuza Herod's *2489*
Lu 24:10 It was Mary Magdalene, and J., *2489*

JOASH (jo'-ash) See also JEHOASH.
Jg 6:11 pertained unto J. the Abi-ezrite: 3101
Jg 6:29 the son of J. hath done this thing 3101
Jg 6:30 men of the city said unto J., Bring 3101
Jg 6:31 J. said unto all that stood against 3101
Jg 7:14 the sword of Gideon the son of J., 3101
Jg 8:13 the son of J. returned from battle 3101
Jg 8:29 the son of J. went and dwelt in his 3101
Jg 8:32 Gideon the son of J. died in a good 3101
Jg 8:32 in the sepulchre of J. his father, 3101
1Ki 22:26 the city, and to J. the king's son; 3101
2Ki 11:2 took J. the son of Ahaziah, and 3101
2Ki 12:19 the rest of the acts of J., and all 3101
2Ki 12:20 slew J. in the house of Millo, which 3101
2Ki 13:1 the three and twentieth year of J. 3101
2Ki 13:9 and J. his son reigned in his stead 3101
2Ki 13:10 the thirty and seventh year of J. 3101
2Ki 13:12 the rest of the acts of J., and all 3101
2Ki 13:13 And J. slept with his fathers; and 3101
2Ki 13:13 J. was buried in Samaria with the 3101
2Ki 13:14 J. the king of Israel came down 3101
2Ki 13:25 Three times did J. beat him, and 3101
2Ki 14:1 second year of J. son of Jehoahaz 3101
2Ki 14:1 the son of J. king of Judah 3101
2Ki 14:3 to all things as J. his father did 3101
2Ki 14:17 the son of J. king of Judah 3101
2Ki 14:23 year of Amaziah the son of J. 3101
2Ki 14:23 Jeroboam the son of J. king of 3101
2Ki 14:27 the hand of Jeroboam the son of J. 3101
1Ch 3:11 son, Ahaziah his son, J. his son, 3101
1Ch 4:22 J., and Saraph, who had the 3101
1Ch 7:8 Zemira, and J., and Eliezer, and 3135
1Ch 12:3 The chief was Ahiezer, then J., 3101
1Ch 27:28 and over the cellars of oil was J.: 3135
2Ch 18:25 the city, and to J. the king's son; 3101
2Ch 22:11 took J. the son of Ahaziah, and 3101
2Ch 24:1 J. was seven years old when he 3101
2Ch 24:2 J. did that which was right in the 3101
2Ch 24:4 J. was minded to repair the house 3101
2Ch 24:22 Thus J. the king remembered not 3101
2Ch 24:24 they executed judgment against J. 3101
2Ch 25:17 Judah took advice, and sent to J., 3101
2Ch 25:18 J. king of Israel sent to Amaziah 3101
2Ch 25:21 so J. the king of Israel went up; 3101
2Ch 25:23 J. the king of Israel took Amaziah 3101
2Ch 25:23 king of Judah, the son of J., the 3101
2Ch 25:25 Amaziah the son of J. king of Judah 3101
2Ch 25:25 death of J. son of Jehoahaz king of 3101
Ho 1:1 days of Jeroboam the son of J., 3101
Am 1:1 days of Jeroboam the son of J. 3101

JOATHAM (jo'-a-tham) See also JOTHAM.
Mt 1:9 And Ozias begat J.; and J. begat *2488*

JOB (jobe) See also JASHUB; JOB'S.
Ge 46:13 Tola, and Phuvah, and J., and 3102
Job *general* *title* The Book of J. 347
Job 1:1 land of Uz, whose name was J.; 347
Job 1:5 that J. sent and sanctified them, 347
Job 1:5 J. said, It may be that my sons have 347
Job 1:5 hearts. Thus did J. continually 347
Job 1:8 Hast thou considered my servant J., 347
Job 1:9 said, Doth J. fear God for nought? 347
Job 1:14 there came a messenger unto J., 347
Job 1:20 Then J. arose, and rent his mantle, 347
Job 1:22 In all this J. sinned not, nor charged 347
Job 2:3 Hast thou considered my servant J., 347
Job 2:7 smote J. with sore boils from the 347
Job 2:10 In all this did not J. sin with his 347
Job 3:1 After this opened J. his mouth, and 347
Job 3:2 And J. spake, and said, 347
Job 6:1 But J. answered, and said, 347
Job 9:1 Then J. answered and said, 347
Job 12:1 And J. answered and said, 347
Job 16:1 Then J. answered and said, 347
Job 19:1 Then J. answered and said, 347
Job 21:1 But J. answered and said, 347
Job 23:1 Then J. answered and said, 347
Job 26:1 But J. answered and said, 347
Job 27:1 Moreover J. continued his parable, 347
Job 29:1 Moreover J. continued his parable, 347
Job 31:40 barley. The words of J. are ended. 347
Job 32:1 three men ceased to answer J., 347
Job 32:2 against J. was his wrath kindled, 347
Job 32:3 and yet had condemned J. 347
Job 32:4 Elihu had waited till J. had spoken, 347
Job 32:12 was none of you that convinced J., 347
Job 33:1 J., I pray thee, hear my speeches, 347
Job 33:31 Mark well, O J., hearken unto me: 347
Job 34:5 For J. hath said, I am righteous: 347
Job 34:7 What man is like J., who drinketh 347
Job 34:35 J. hath spoken without knowledge, 347
Job 34:36 My desire is that J. may be tried 347
Job 35:16 doth J. open his mouth in vain; 347
Job 37:14 Hearken unto this, O J.: stand still, 347
Job 38:1 the Lord answered J. out of the 347
Job 40:1 the Lord answered J., and said, 347
Job 40:3 J. answered the Lord, and said, 347
Job 40:6 answered the Lord unto J. out of 347
Job 42:1 J. answered the Lord, and said, 347
Job 42:7 had spoken these words unto J., 347
Job 42:7 that is right, as my servant J. hath. 347
Job 42:8 go to my servant J., and offer up 347
Job 42:8 my servant J. shall pray for you: 347
Job 42:8 which is right, like my servant J. 347
Job 42:9 them: the Lord also accepted J. 347
Job 42:10 the Lord turned the captivity of J., 347
Job 42:10 gave J. twice as much as he had 347
Job 42:12 Lord blessed the latter end of J. 347
Job 42:15 found so fair as the daughter of J. 347
Job 42:16 lived J. a hundred and forty years, 347
Job 42:17 So J. died, being old and full of 347
Eze 14:14 three men, Noah, Daniel, and J., 347
Eze 14:20 Noah, Daniel, and J., were in it, as 347
Jas 5:11 have heard of the patience of J., *2492*

JOB'S (jobes)
Job 2:11 when J. three friends heard of all 347

JOBAB (jo'-bab)
Ge 10:29 And Ophir, and Havilah, and J. 3103
Ge 36:33 and J. the son of Zerah of Bozrah 3103
Ge 36:34 and J. died, and Husham of the 3103
Jos 11:1 he sent to J. king Madon, and 3103
1Ch 1:23 And Ophir, and Havilah, and J. 3103
1Ch 1:44 J. the son of Zerah of Bozrah 3103
1Ch 1:45 And when J. was dead, Husham 3103
1Ch 8:9 he begat of Hodesh his wife, J. 3103
1Ch 8:18 Ishmerai also, and Jezliah, and J., 3103

JOCHEBED (jok'-e-bed)
Ex 6:20 Amram took him j. his father's 3115
Nu 26:59 the name of Amram's wife was J., 3115

JOD (yode)
Ps 119:73 *title* [ʼ] J.

JOED (jo'-ed)
Ne 11:7 the son of J., the son of Pedaiah, 3133

JOEL (jo'-el)
1Sa 8:2 the name of his firstborn was J.; 3100
1Ch 4:35 J., and Jehu the son of Josibiah, 3100
1Ch 5:4 The sons of J.; Shemaiah his son, 3100
1Ch 5:8 the son of J., who dwelt in Aroer, 3100
1Ch 5:12 J. the chief, and Shapham the next, 3100
1Ch 6:33 Heman a singer, the son of J., the 3100
1Ch 6:36 Elkanah, the son of J., the son of 3100
1Ch 7:3 and Obadiah, and J.; Ishiah, five: 3100
1Ch 11:38 J. the brother of Nathan, Mibhar 3100
1Ch 15:7 the sons of Gershom; J. the chief, 3100
1Ch 15:11 Levites, for Uriel, Asaiah, and J., 3100
1Ch 15:17 appointed Heman the son of J.; 3100
1Ch 23:8 Jehiel, and Zatham, and J., three 3100
1Ch 26:22 Zetham, and J. his brother, which 3100
1Ch 27:20 Manasseh, J. the son of Pedaiah: 3100
2Ch 29:12 Amasai, and J. the son of Azariah, 3100
Ezr 10:43 Zabad, Zebina, Jadau, and J., 3100
Ne 11:9 And J. the son of Zichri was their 3100
Joe *general* *title* J. 3100
Joe 1:1 word of the Lord that came to J. 3100
Ac 2:16 was spoken by the prophet J.; *2493*

JOELAH (jo-e'-lah)
1Ch 12:7 J., and Zebadiah, the sons of 3132

JOEZER (jo-e'-zer)
1Ch 12:6 and Jesiah, and Azareel, and J., 3134

JOGBEHAH (jog'-be-hah)
Nu 32:35 Shophan, and Jaazer, and J., 3011
Jg 8:11 tents on the east of Nobah and J. 3011

JOGLI (jog'-li)
Nu 34:22 of Dan, Bukki the son of J. 3020

JOHA (jo'-hah)
1Ch 8:16 And Michael, and Ispah, and J., 3109
1Ch 11:45 son of Shimri, and J. his brother, 3109

JOHANAN (jo-ha'-nan) See also JEHOHANAN, JOHN.
2Ki 25:23 and J. the son of Careah, 3110
1Ch 3:15 sons of Josiah were, the firstborn J., 3110
1Ch 3:24 and J., and Dalaiah, and Anani, 3110

1Ch 6:9 Azariah, and Azariah begat **J.**, ... 3110
1Ch 6:10 **J.** begat Azariah, (he it is that 3110
1Ch 12:4 Jahaziel, and **J.**, and Josabad the 3110
1Ch 12:12 **J.** the eighth, Elzabad the ninth, ... 3110
2Ch 28:12 Ephraim, Azariah the son of **J.**, ... 3076
Ezr 8:12 **J.** the son of Hakkatan, and with 3110
Ezr 10:6 and went into the chamber of **J.**, ... 3076
Ne 6:18 his son **J.** had taken the daughter 3076
Ne 12:22 **J.**, and Jaddua, were recorded 3110
Ne 12:23 even until the days of **J.** the son of 3110
Jer 40:8 and **J.** and Jonathan the sons of 3110
Jer 40:13 Moreover **J.** the son of Kareah, and ... 3110
Jer 40:15 Then **J.** the son of Kareah spake to 3110
Jer 40:16 the son of Ahikam said unto **J.** the 3110
Jer 41:11 But when **J.** the son of Kareah, ... 3110
Jer 41:13 which were with Ishmael saw **J.** 3110
Jer 41:14 and went unto **J.** the son of Kareah. ... 3110
Jer 41:15 escaped from **J.** with eight men, ... 3110
Jer 41:16 Then took **J.** the son of Kareah, ... 3110
Jer 42:1 the captains of the forces, and **J.** 3110
Jer 42:8 Then called he **J.** the son of Kareah, .. 3110
Jer 43:2 **J.** the son of Kareah, and all the 3110
Jer 43:4 So **J.** the son of Kareah, and all 3110
Jer 43:5 But **J.** the son of Kareah, and all 3110

JOHN (jon) See also BAPTIST; JEHOHANAN; JOHN'S; MARK.
Mt 3:1 In these days came **J.** the Baptist, ... *2491*
Mt 3:4 same **J.** had his raiment of camel's *2491*
Mt 3:13 from Galilee to Jordan unto **J.**, ... *2491*
Mt 3:14 **J.** forbade him, saying, I have need *2491*
Mt 4:12 heard that **J.** was cast into prison, ... *2491*
Mt 4:21 son of Zebedee, and **J.** his brother, ... *2491*
Mt 9:14 came to him the disciples of **J.**, ... *2491*
Mt 10:2 son of Zebedee, and **J.** his brother; *2491*
Mt 11:2 when **J.** had heard in the prison *2491*
Mt 11:4 **Go and shew J. again those things** . *2491*
Mt 11:7 unto the multitudes concerning **J.**, ... *2491*
Mt 11:11 **risen a greater than J. the Baptist:** *2491*
Mt 11:12 **from the days of J. the Baptist** *2491*
Mt 11:13 **and the law prophesied until J.** *2491*
Mt 11:18 **J. came neither eating nor** *2491*
Mt 14:2 his servants, This is **J.** the Baptist; *2491*
Mt 14:3 For Herod had laid hold on **J.**, ... *2491*
Mt 14:4 **J.** said unto him, It is not lawful *2491*
Mt 14:8 **J.** the Baptist's head in a charger. *2491*
Mt 14:10 sent, and beheaded **J.** in the prison. ... *2491*
Mt 16:14 say that thou art **J.** the Baptist; *2491*
Mt 17:1 Peter, James, and **J.** his brother, ... *2491*
Mt 17:13 spake unto them of **J.** the Baptist. *2491*
Mt 21:25 **The baptism of J., whence was it?** . *2491*
Mt 21:26 people; for all hold **J.** as a prophet. *2491*
Mt 21:32 **J. came unto you in the way of** *2491*
Mk 1:4 **J.** did baptize in the wilderness, ... *2491*
Mk 1:6 **J.** was clothed with camel's hair, ... *2491*
Mk 1:9 and was baptized of **J.** in Jordan. *2491*
Mk 1:14 Now after that **J.** was put in prison, ... *2491*
Mk 1:19 son of Zebedee, and **J.** his brother, ... *2491*
Mk 1:29 and Andrew, with James and **J.** *2491*
Mk 2:18 the disciples of **J.** and of the *2491*
Mk 2:18 Why do the disciples of **J.** and of *2491*
Mk 3:17 and **J.** the brother of James; *2491*
Mk 5:37 James, and **J.** the brother of James. *2491*
Mk 6:14 **J.** the Baptist was risen from the *2491*
Mk 6:16 he said, It is **J.**, whom I beheaded: *2491*
Mk 6:17 laid hold upon **J.**, and bound him *2491*
Mk 6:18 **J.** had said unto Herod, It is not *2491*
Mk 6:20 Herod feared **J.**, knowing that he *2491*
Mk 6:24 said, The head of **J.** the Baptist. *2491*
Mk 6:25 charger the head of **J.** the Baptist. *2491*
Mk 8:28 they answered, **J.** the Baptist: *2491*
Mk 9:2 with him Peter and James, and **J.**, ... *2491*
Mk 9:38 **J.** answered him, saying, Master, ... *2491*
Mk 10:35 James and **J.**, the sons of Zebedee, ... *2491*
Mk 10:41 much displeased with James and **J.** *2491*
Mk 11:30 **baptism of J., was it from heaven,** . *2491*
Mk 11:32 all men counted **J.**, that he was a *2491*
Mk 13:3 Peter, and James, and **J.**, and *2491*
Mk 14:33 with him Peter and James and **J.**, ... *2491*
Lu 1:13 and thou shalt call his name **J.** *2491*
Lu 1:60 Not so; but he shall be called **J.** *2491*
Lu 1:63 and wrote, saying, His name is **J.** *2491*
Lu 3:2 the word of God came unto **J.** the *2491*
Lu 3:15 all men mused in their hearts of **J.**, ... *2491*
Lu 3:16 **J.** answered, saying unto them all, ... *2491*
Lu 3:20 all, that he shut up **J.** in prison. *2491*
Lu 5:10 James, and **J.**, the sons of Zebedee, ... *2491*
Lu 5:33 Why do the disciples of **J.** fast often, .. *2491*
Lu 6:14 and **J.**, Philip and Bartholomew, ... *2491*
Lu 7:18 disciples of **J.** shewed him of all *2491*
Lu 7:19 **J.** calling unto him two of his *2491*
Lu 7:20 **J.** the Baptist hath sent us...thee, ... *2491*
Lu 7:22 **tell J. what things ye have seen** *2491*
Lu 7:24 messengers of **J.** were departed, ... *2491*
Lu 7:24 unto the people concerning **J.**, ... *2491*
Lu 7:28 **prophet than J. the Baptist:** *2491*
Lu 7:29 baptized with the baptism of **J.** *2491*
Lu 7:33 **J. the Baptist came neither eating**. *2491*
Lu 8:51 save Peter, and James, and **J.**, ... *2491*
Lu 9:7 that **J.** was risen from the dead; *2491*
Lu 9:9 Herod said, **J.** have I beheaded: *2491*
Lu 9:19 answering said, **J.** the Baptist; *2491*
Lu 9:28 he took Peter and **J.** and James. *2491*
Lu 9:49 And **J.** answered and said, Master, ... *2491*
Lu 9:54 his disciples James and **J.** saw this, ... *2491*
Lu 11:1 as **J.** also taught his disciples. *2491*
Lu 16:16 **law and the prophets were until J.** . *2491*
Lu 20:4 **baptism of J., was it from heaven,** . *2491*
Lu 20:6 be persuaded that **J.** was a prophet. ... *2491*
Lu 22:8 he sent Peter and **J.**, saying, **Go and** . *2491*
Joh *general* *title* Gospel According To S. [St.] **J.** ... *2491*
Joh 1:6 sent from God, whose name was **J.** *2491*
Joh 1:15 **J.** bare witness of him, and cried, ... *2491*
Joh 1:19 And this is the record of **J.**, when *2491*
Joh 1:26 **J.** answered them, saying, I baptize *2491*
Joh 1:28 Jordan, where **J.** was baptizing. *2491*
Joh 1:29 The next day **J.** seeth Jesus coming *2491*
Joh 1:32 And **J.** bare record, saying, I saw *2491*
Joh 1:35 **J.** stood, and two of his disciples; *2491*
Joh 1:40 of the two which heard **J.** speak, ... *2491*
Joh 3:23 And **J.** also was baptizing in AEnon *2491*
Joh 3:24 For **J.** was not yet cast into prison. *2491*
Joh 3:26 And they came unto **J.**, and said *2491*
Joh 3:27 **J.** answered and said, A man can *2491*
Joh 4:1 baptized more disciples than **J.**, ... *2491*
Joh 5:33 **sent unto J., and he bare witness** .. *2491*
Joh 5:36 **greater witness than that of J.:** *2491*
Joh 10:40 the place where **J.** at first baptized; *2491*
Joh 10:41 him, and said, **J.** did no miracle: *2491*
Joh 10:41 that **J.** spake of this man were true. ... *2491*
Ac 1:5 **For J. truly baptized with water;** ... *2491*
Ac 1:13 abode both Peter, and James, and **J.**, .. *2491*
Ac 1:22 Beginning from the baptism of **J.**, ... *2491*
Ac 3:1 Peter and **J.** went up together into *2491*
Ac 3:3 seeing Peter and **J.** about to go into *2491*
Ac 3:4 fastening his eyes upon him with **J.**, ... *2491*
Ac 3:11 which was healed held Peter and **J.**, ... *2491*
Ac 4:6 Caiaphas, and **J.**, and Alexander, ... *2491*
Ac 4:13 saw the boldness of Peter and **J.**, ... *2491*
Ac 4:19 But Peter and **J.** answered and said *2491*
Ac 8:14 they sent unto them Peter and **J.** *2491*
Ac 10:37 the baptism which **J.** preached; *2491*
Ac 11:16 **J. indeed baptized with water;** *2491*
Ac 12:2 killed James the brother of **J.** with *2491*
Ac 12:12 of **J.**, whose surname was Mark; *2491*
Ac 12:25 them **J.**, whose surname was Mark. *2491*
Ac 13:5 they had also **J.** to their minister. *2491*
Ac 13:13 **J.** departing from them returned *2491*
Ac 13:24 When **J.** had first preached before *2491*
Ac 13:25 And as **J.** fulfilled his course, he *2491*
Ac 15:37 them **J.**, whose surname was Mark. ... *2491*
Ac 18:25 knowing only the baptism of **J.** *2491*
Ac 19:4 **J.** verily baptized with the baptism *2491*
Gal 2:9 Cephas, and **J.**, who seemed to be *2491*
1Jo *general* *title* The First Epistle General Of **J.** *2491*
2Jo *general* *title* The Second Epistle Of **J.** *2491*
3Jo *general* *title* The Third Epistle Of **J.** *2491*
Re *general* *title* The Revelation Of S. [St.] **J.** *2491*
Re 1:1 it by his angel unto his servant **J.**: *2491*
Re 1:4 **J.** to the seven churches which are *2491*
Re 1:9 I **J.**, who also am your brother, ... *2491*
Re 21:2 And I **J.** saw the holy city, new *2491*
Re 22:8 And I **J.** saw these things, and *2491*

JOHN'S (jonz)
Joh 3:25 between some of **J.** disciples and *2491*
Ac 19:3 And they said, Unto **J.** baptism. *2491*

JOIADA (joy'-a-dah) See also JEHOIADA.
Ne 12:10 Eliashib, and Eliashib begat **J.**, ... 3111
Ne 12:11 **J.** begat Jonathan, and Jonathan 3111
Ne 12:22 Levites in the days of Eliashib, **J.**, ... 3111
Ne 13:38 one of the sons of **J.**, the son of 3111

JOIAKIM (joy'-a-kim) See also JEHOIAKIM.
Ne 12:10 Jeshua begat **J.**, **J.** also begat 3113
Ne 12:12 in the days of **J.** were priests, the 3113
Ne 12:26 in the days of **J.** the son of Jeshua, ... 3113

JOIARIB (joy'-a-rib) See also JEHOIARIB.
Ezr 8:16 for **J.**, and for Elnathan, men of 3114
Ne 11:5 the son of Adaiah, the son of **J.**, ... 3114
Ne 11:10 the priests: Jedaiah the son of **J.**, ... 3114
Ne 12:6 Shemaiah, and **J.**, Jedaiah, ... 3114
Ne 12:19 of **J.**, Mattenai; of Jedaiah, Uzzi; 3114

JOIN See also JOINED; JOINING.
Ex 1:10 they **j.** also unto our enemies, and 3254
2Ch 20:35 king of Judah **j.** himself with 2266
Ezr 9:14 and **j.** in affinity with the people of 2859
Pr 11:21 Though hand **j.** in hand, the wicked ....
Pr 16:5 though hand **j.** in hand, he shall not be ......
Isa 5:8 unto them that **j.** house to house, ... 5060
Isa 9:11 him, and **j.** his enemies together; 5526
Isa 56:6 that **j.** themselves to the Lord, to 3867
Jer 50:5 let us **j.** ourselves to the Lord in a 3867
Eze 37:17 **j.** them one to another into one 7126
Da 11:6 they shall **j.** themselves together; 2266
Ac 5:13 durst no man **j.** himself to them; *2853*
Ac 8:29 near, and **j.** thyself to this chariot *2853*
Ac 9:26 assayed to **j.** himself to the disciples: .. *2853*

JOINED See also ENJOINED.
Ge 14:3 these were **j.** together in the vale 2266
Ge 14:8 they **j.** battle with them in the vale 6186
Ge 29:34 will my husband be **j.** unto me, ... 3867
Ex 28:7 shoulderpieces thereof **j.** at the two 2266
Ex 28:7 and so it shall be **j.** together. 2266
Nu 18:2 that they may be **j.** unto thee, and 3867
Nu 18:4 they shall be **j.** unto thee, and keep 3867
Nu 25:3 Israel **j.** himself unto Baal-peor: 6775
Nu 25:5 men that were **j.** unto Baal-peor. 6775
1Sa 4:2 they **j.** battle, Israel was smitten 5203
1Ki 7:32 of the wheels were **j.** to the base: ....
1Ki 20:29 the seventh day the battle was **j.**: 7126
2Ch 18:1 and **j.** affinity with Ahab. 2859
2Ch 20:36 **j.** himself with him to make ships 2266
2Ch 20:37 thou hast **j.** thyself with Ahaziah, ... 2266
Ezr 4:12 thereof, and **j.** the foundations. 2338
Ne 4:6 all the wall was **j.** together unto 7194
Es 9:27 such as **j.** themselves unto them, ... 3867
Job 3:6 not be **j.** unto the days of the year, ... 2302
Job 41:17 They are **j.** one to another, they 1692
Job 41:23 flakes of his flesh are **j.** together: 1692
Ps 83:8 Assur also is **j.** with them: they 3867
Ps 106:28 **j.** themselves also unto Baal-peor, ... 6775
Ec 9:4 to him that is **j.** to all the living 977
Isa 13:15 every one that is **j.** unto them 5595
Isa 14:1 strangers shall be **j.** with them, ... 3867
Isa 14:20 shalt not be **j.** with them in burial, ... 3161
Isa 56:3 that hath **j.** himself to the Lord, ... 3867
Eze 1:9 wings were **j.** one to another; 2266
Eze 1:11 two wings of every one were **j.** one ... 2266
Eze 46:22 there were courts **j.** of forty cubits 7000
Ho 4:17 Ephraim is **j.** to idols: let him 2266
Zec 2:11 nations shall be **j.** to the Lord 3867
Mt 19:6 **therefore God hath j. together,** *4801*
Mk 10:9 **therefore God hath j. together,** *4801*
Lu 15:15 **and j. himself to a citizen of that** .. *2853*
Ac 5:36 about four hundred, **j.** themselves: *4347*
Ac 18:7 house **j.** hard to the synagogue. *4927*
1Co 1:10 that ye be perfectly **j.** together *2675*
1Co 6:16 not that he which is **j.** to an harlot *2853*
1Co 6:17 he that is **j.** unto the Lord is one *2853*
Eph 4:16 the whole body fitly **j.** together *4883*
Eph 5:31 shall be **j.** unto his wife, and they *4347*

JOINING See also JOININGS.
2Ch 3:12 **j.** to the wing of the other cherub. 1692

JOININGS
1Ch 22:3 doors of the gates, and for the **j.**; 4226

JOINT See also JOINT-HEIRS; JOINTS.
Ge 32:25 of Jacob's thigh was out of **j.**, ... 3363
Ps 22:14 and all my bones are out of **j.** 6504
Pr 25:19 broken tooth, and a foot out of **j.** 4154
Eph 4:16 by that which every **j.** supplieth, ... *860*

JOINT-HEIRS
Ro 8:17 heirs of God, and **j.** with Christ; *4789*

JOINTS
1Ki 22:34 between the **j.** of the harness: 1694

2Ch 18:33 between the **j.** of the harness: 1694
Ca 7:1 the **j.** of thy thighs are like jewels, 2542
Da 5:6 that the **j.** of his loins were loosed, 7001
Col 2:19 all the body by **j.** and bands having *860*
Heb 4:12 spirit, and of the **j.** and marrow, *719*

JOKDEAM (jok'-de-am)
Jos 15:56 And Jezreel, and **J.**, and Zanoah, 3347

JOKIM (jo'-kim)
1Ch 4:22 **J.**, and the men of Chozeba, and 3137

JOKMEAM (jok'-me-am) See also JOKNEAM.
1Ch 6:68 and **J.** with her suburbs, and 3361

JOKNEAM (jok'-ne-am) See also JOKMEAM; KIBZAIM.
Jos 12:22 the king of **J.** of Carmel, one; 3362
Jos 19:11 to the river that is before **J.**; 3362
Jos 21:34 **J.** with her suburbs, and Kartah 3362
1Ki 4:12 unto the place that is beyond **J.**: 3362

JOKSHAN (jok'-shan)
Ge 25:2 she bare him Zimran, and **J.**, and 3370
Ge 25:3 And **J.** begat Sheba, and Dedan. 3370
1Ch 1:32 she bare Zimran, and **J.**, and 3370
1Ch 1:32 the sons of **J.**; Sheba, and Dedan. 3370

JOKTAN (jok'-tan)
Ge 10:25 and his brother's name was **J.**. 3355
Ge 10:26 **J.** begat Almodad, and Sheleph, 3355
Ge 10:29 Jobab: all these were the sons of **J.** 3355
1Ch 1:19 and his brother's name was **J.** 3355
1Ch 1:20 **J.** begat Almodad, and Sheleph, 3355
1Ch 1:23 Joab. All these were the sons of **J.** 3355

JOKTHEEL (jok'-the-el) See also SELAH.
Jos 15:38 and Dilean, and Mizpeh, and **J.**, 3371
2Ki 14:7 and called the name of it **J.** unto 3371

JONA (jo'-nah) See also BAR-JONA; JONAH; JONAS.
Joh 1:42 **Thou art Simon the son of J.** *2495*

JONADAB (jon'-a-dab) See also JEHONADAB.
2Sa 13:3 had a friend, whose name was **J.**, 3122
2Sa 13:3 and **J.** was a very subtle man. 3122
2Sa 13:5 **J.** said unto him, Lay thee down 3122
2Sa 13:32 and **J.**, the son of Shimeah David's 3122
2Sa 13:35 And **J.** said unto the king, Behold, 3122
Jer 35:6 for **J.** the son of Rechab our father 3122
Jer 35:8 have we obeyed the voice of **J.** 3082
Jer 35:10 that **J.** our father commanded us. 3122
Jer 35:14 the words of **J.** the son of Rechab 3082
Jer 35:16 the sons of **J.** the son of Rechab 3082
Jer 35:18 obeyed the commandment of **J.** 3082
Jer 35:19 **J.** the son of Rechab shall not 3122

JONAH (jo'-nah) See also JONA; JONAS.
2Ki 14:25 by the hand of his servant **J.**, 3124
Jon *general* *title* The Book of **J.** 3124
Jon 1:1 the word of the Lord came unto **J.** 3124
Jon 1:3 **J.** rose up to flee unto Tarshish 3124
Jon 1:5 **J.** was gone down into the sides of 3124
Jon 1:7 cast lots, and the lot fell upon **J.** 3124
Jon 1:15 took up **J.**, and cast him forth into 3124
Jon 1:17 a great fish to swallow up **J.**. 3124
Jon 1:17 **J.** was in the belly of the fish three 3124
Jon 2:1 **J.** prayed unto the Lord his God 3124
Jon 2:10 it vomited out **J.** upon the dry land. 3124
Jon 3:1 word of the Lord came unto **J.** the 3124
Jon 3:3 So **J.** arose, and went unto Nineveh, 3124
Jon 3:4 **J.** began to enter into the city a 3124
Jon 4:1 But it displeased **J.** exceedingly, 3124
Jon 4:5 **J.** went out of the city, and sat on 3124
Jon 4:6 and made it to come up over **J.**, 3124
Jon 4:6 **J.** was exceeding glad of the gourd. 3124
Jon 4:8 the sun beat upon the head of **J.**, 3124
Jon 4:9 God said unto **J.**, Doest thou well 3124

JONAN (jo'-nan)
Lu 3:30 Joseph, which was the son of **J.**, *2492*

JONAS (jo'-nas) See also JONA; JONAH.
Mt 12:39 **it, but the sign of the prophet J.** *2495*
Mt 12:40 **For as J. was three days and three** *2495*
Mt 12:41 **repented at the preaching of J.;** *2495*
Mt 12:41 **behold, a greater than J. is here** *2495*
Mt 16:4 **it, but the sign of the prophet J.** *2495*
Lu 11:29 **it, but the sign of J. the prophet.** *2495*
Lu 11:30 **J. was a sign unto the Ninevites,** *2495*
Lu 11:32 **repented at the preaching of J.;** *2495*
Lu 11:32 **behold, a greater than J. is here** *2495*
Joh 21:15, 16,17 **Simon, son of J., lovest thou** *2495*

JONATHAN (jon'-a-than) See also JEHONATHAN; JONATHAN'S.
Jg 18:30 **J.**, the son of Gershom, the son of 3129
1Sa 13:2 a thousand were with **J.** in Gibeah 3129
1Sa 13:3 **J.** smote the garrison of the 3129
1Sa 13:16 Saul, and **J.** his son, and the people 3129
1Sa 13:22 people that were with Saul and **J.** 3129
1Sa 13:22 with **J.** his son was there found. 3129
1Sa 14:1 **J.** the son of Saul said unto the 3129
1Sa 14:3 people knew not that **J.** was gone. 3129
1Sa 14:4 which **J.** sought to go over unto 3129
1Sa 14:6 **J.** said to the young man that 3083
1Sa 14:8 said **J.**, Behold, we will pass over 3083
1Sa 14:12 **J.** and his armourbearer, 3129
1Sa 14:12 **J.** said unto his armourbearer, 3129
1Sa 14:13 **J.** climbed up upon his hands and 3129
1Sa 14:13 and they fell before **J.**; and his 3129
1Sa 14:14 which **J.** and his armourbearer 3129
1Sa 14:17 behold, **J.** and his armourbearer 3129
1Sa 14:21 that were with Saul and **J.** 3129
1Sa 14:27 But **J.** heard not when his father 3129
1Sa 14:29 said **J.**, My father hath troubled 3129
1Sa 14:39 it be in **J.** my son, he shall surely 3129
1Sa 14:40 I and **J.** my son will be on the 3129
1Sa 14:41 Saul and **J.** were taken: but the 3129
1Sa 14:42 lots between me and **J.** my son. 3129
1Sa 14:42 And **J.** was taken. 3129
1Sa 14:43 Then Saul said to **J.**, tell me what 3129
1Sa 14:43 And **J.** told him, and said, I did but 3129
1Sa 14:44 also: for thou shalt surely die, **J.** 3129
1Sa 14:45 people said unto Saul, Shall **J.** die, 3129
1Sa 14:45 So the people rescued **J.**, that he 3129
1Sa 14:49 the sons of Saul were **J.**, and Ishui, 3129
1Sa 18:1 soul of **J.** was knit with the soul of 3083
1Sa 18:1 and **J.** loved him as his own soul. 3083
1Sa 18:3 **J.** and David made a covenant, 3083
1Sa 18:4 **J.** stripped himself of the robe that 3083
1Sa 19:1 Saul spake to **J.** his son, and to all 3129
1Sa 19:2 **J.** Saul's son delighted much in 3083
1Sa 19:2 **J.** told David, saying, Saul my 3083
1Sa 19:4 **J.** spake good of David unto Saul 3083
1Sa 19:6 hearkened unto the voice of **J.** 3083
1Sa 19:7 **J.** called David, and **J.** shewed him 3083
1Sa 19:7 **J.** brought David to Saul, and he 3083
1Sa 20:1 said before **J.**, What have I done? 3083
1Sa 20:3 Let not **J.** know this, lest he be 3083
1Sa 20:4 Then said **J.** unto David, 3083
1Sa 20:5 And David said to **J.**, Behold 3083
1Sa 20:9 And **J.** said, Far be it from thee: 3083
1Sa 20:10 Then said David to **J.**, Who shall 3083
1Sa 20:11 **J.** said unto David, Come, and let 3083
1Sa 20:12 **J.** said unto David, O Lord God of 3083
1Sa 20:13 Lord do so and much more to **J.** 3083
1Sa 20:16 **J.** made a covenant with the house 3083
1Sa 20:17 **J.** caused David to swear again, 3083
1Sa 20:18 **J.** said to David, To-morrow is the 3083
1Sa 20:25 **J.** arose, and Abner sat by Saul's 3083
1Sa 20:27 Saul said unto **J.** his son, Wherefore 3083
1Sa 20:28 **J.** answered Saul, David earnestly 3083
1Sa 20:30 Saul's anger was kindled against **J.**, 3083
1Sa 20:32 **J.** answered Saul his father, and 3083
1Sa 20:33 **J.** knew that it was determined 3083
1Sa 20:34 So **J.** arose from the table in fierce 3083
1Sa 20:35 **J.** went out into the field at the time 3083
1Sa 20:37 of the arrow which **J.** had shot, 3083
1Sa 20:37 **J.** cried after the lad, and said, Is 3083
1Sa 20:38 **J.** cried after the lad, Make speed, 3083
1Sa 20:39 only **J.** and David knew the matter. 3083
1Sa 20:40 **J.** gave his artillery unto his lad, 3083
1Sa 20:42 And **J.** said to David, Go in peace, 3083
1Sa 20:42 departed: and **J.** went into the city. 3083
1Sa 23:16 **J.** Saul's son arose, and went to 3083
1Sa 23:18 the wood, and **J.** went to his house. 3083
1Sa 31:2 Philistines slew **J.**, and Abinadab, 3083
2Sa 1:4 Saul and **J.** his son are dead also. 3083
2Sa 1:5 that Saul and **J.** his son be dead? 3083
2Sa 1:12 even, for Saul, and for **J.** his son, 3083
2Sa 1:17 lamentation over Saul and over **J.** 3083
2Sa 1:22 the bow of **J.** turned not back, and 3083
2Sa 1:23 Saul and **J.** were lovely and 3083
2Sa 1:25 O **J.**, thou wast slain in thine high 3083
2Sa 1:26 distressed for thee, my brother **J.** 3083
2Sa 4:4 **J.**, Saul's son, had a son that was 3083
2Sa 4:4 the tidings came of Saul and **J.** 3083
2Sa 9:3 **J.** hath yet a son, which is lame 3083
2Sa 9:6 when Mephibosheth, the son of **J.**, 3083
2Sa 9:7 kindness for **J.** thy father's sake, 3083
2Sa 15:27 thy son, and **J.** the son of Abiathar. 3083
2Sa 15:36 Zadok's son, and **J.** Abiathar's son; 3083
2Sa 17:17 Now **J.** and Ahimaaz stayed by 3083
2Sa 17:20 said, Where is Ahimaaz and **J.**? 3083
2Sa 21:7 spared Mephibosheth, the son of **J.** 3083
2Sa 21:7 between David and **J.** the son of 3083
2Sa 21:12 bones of Saul and the bones of **J.** 3083
2Sa 21:13 Saul and the bones of **J.** his son; 3083
2Sa 21:14 the bones of Saul and **J.** his son 3083
2Sa 21:21 **J.** the son of Shimeah the brother 3083
2Sa 23:32 of the sons of Jashen, **J.**, 3083
1Ki 1:42 **J.** the son of Abiathar the priest 3129
1Ki 1:43 **J.** answered and said to Adonijah, 3129
1Ch 2:32 of Shammai; Jether, and **J.** 3129
1Ch 2:33 And the sons of **J.**; Peleth, and 3129
1Ch 8:33 Saul begat **J.**, and Malchi-shua, 3083
1Ch 8:34 And the son of **J.** was Merib-baal; 3083
1Ch 9:39 Saul begat **J.**, and Malchi-shua, 3083
1Ch 9:40 And the son of **J.** was Merib-baal: 3083
1Ch 10:2 and the Philistines slew **J.**, and 3129
1Ch 11:34 **J.** the son of Shage the Hararite, 3129
1Ch 20:7 **J.** the son of Shimea David's 3083
1Ch 27:32 **J.** David's uncle was a counsellor, 3083
Ezr 8:6 Ebed the son of **J.**, and with him 3083
Ezr 10:15 Only **J.** the son of Asahel and 3083
Ne 12:11 And Joiada begat **J.**, and **J.** begat 3083
Ne 12:14 Of Melicu, **J.**; of Shebaniah, 3083
Ne 12:35 Zechariah the son of **J.**, the son of 3083
Jer 37:15 prison in the house of **J.** the scribe: 3083
Jer 37:20 return to the house of **J.** the scribe, 3083
Jer 40:8 Johanan and **J.** the sons of Kareah, 3129

JONATHAN'S (jon'-a-thans)
1Sa 20:38 **J.** lad gathered up the arrows, 3129
2Sa 9:1 shew him kindness for **J.** sake? 3129
Jer 38:26 to return to **J.** house, to die there 3129

JONATH-ELEM-RECHOKIM (jo'''-nath-e''-lem-re-ko'-kim)
Ps 56:*title* the chief Musician upon **J.**, 3128

JOPPA (jop'-pah) See also JAPHO.
2Ch 2:16 it to thee in floats by sea to **J.**, 3305
Ezr 3:7 trees from Lebanon to the sea of **J.** 3305
Jon 1:3 of the Lord, and went down to **J.**; 3305
Ac 9:36 there was at **J.** a certain disciple *2445*
Ac 9:38 as Lydda was nigh to **J.**, and the *2445*
Ac 9:42 it was known throughout all **J.**; *2445*
Ac 9:43 he tarried many days in **J.** with one *2445*
Ac 10:5 now send men to **J.**, and call for one *2445*
Ac 10:8 unto them, he sent them to **J.** *2445*
Ac 10:23 and certain brethren from **J.** *2445*
Ac 10:32 Send therefore to **J.**, and call *2445*
Ac 11:5 I was in the city of **J.** praying: and *2445*
Ac 11:13 Send men to **J.**, and call for Simon, *2445*

JORAH (jo'-rah) See also HARIPH.
Ezr 2:18 the children of **J.**, an hundred and 3139

JORAI (jo'-rahee)
1Ch 5:13 Sheba, and **J.**, and Jachan, and 3140

JORAM (jo'-ram) See also JEHORAM.
2Sa 8:10 Toi sent **J.** his son unto king David, 3141
2Sa 8:10 **J.** brought with him vessels of silver,
2Ki 8:16 the fifth year of **J.** the son of Ahab 3141
2Ki 8:21 So **J.** went over to Zair, and all the 3141
2Ki 8:23 And the rest of the acts of **J.**, and all 3141
2Ki 8:24 **J.** slept with his fathers, and was 3141
2Ki 8:25 twelfth year of **J.** the son of Ahab 3141
2Ki 8:28 he went with **J.** the son of Ahab to 3141
2Ki 8:28 and the Syrians wounded **J.** 3141
2Ki 8:29 And king **J.** went back to be healed 3141
2Ki 8:29 went down to see **J.** the son of Ahab 3141
2Ki 9:14 son of Nimshi conspired against **J.** 3141
2Ki 9:14 (Now **J.** had kept Ramoth-gilead, he 3141
2Ki 9:15 king **J.** was returned to be healed 3188
2Ki 9:16 went to Jezreel; for **J.** lay there 3141
2Ki 9:16 of Judah was come down to see **J.** 3141
2Ki 9:17 And **J.** said, Take an horseman, 3188
2Ki 9:21 And **J.** said, Make ready. And his 3188
2Ki 9:21 **J.** king of Israel and Ahaziah king 3188
2Ki 9:22 it came to pass, when **J.** saw Jehu, 3188
2Ki 9:23 And **J.** turned his hands, and fled, 3188
2Ki 9:29 eleventh year of **J.** the son of Ahab 3188
2Ki 11:2 Jehosheba, the daughter of king **J.**, 3141

1Ch 3:11 **J.** his son, Ahaziah his son, Joash....... 3141
1Ch 26:25 **J.** his son, and Zichri his son, and 3141
2Ch 22:5 and the Syrians smote **J.**................. 3141
2Ch 22:7 was of God by coming to **J.**: 3141
Mt 1:8 Josaphat begat **J.**; and **J.** begat.......... *2496*

JORDAN (jor'-dan)
Ge 13:10 and beheld all the plain of **J.**,............ 3383
Ge 13:11 Lot chose him all the plain of **J.**;........ 3383
Ge 32:10 with my staff I passed over this **J.**; 3383
Ge 50:10 of Atad, which is beyond **J.**, and........ 3383
Ge 50:11 Abel-mizraim, which is beyond **J.**. 3383
Nu 13:29 of the sea, and by the coast of **J.**........ 3383
Nu 22:1 in the plains of Moab on this side **J.** ... 3383
Nu 26:3 them in the plains of Moab by **J.**......... 3383
Nu 26:63 Israel in the plains of Moab by **J.**........ 3383
Nu 31:12 the plains of Moab, which are by **J.** 3383
Nu 32:5 possession, and bring us not over **J.**... 3383
Nu 32:19 inherit with them on yonder side **J.**, ... 3383
Nu 32:19 fallen to us on this side **J.** eastward.... 3383
Nu 32:21 And will go all of you armed over **J.** ... 3383
Nu 32:29 Reuben will pass with you over **J.**, ... 3383
Nu 32:32 on this side **J.** may be ours................ 3383
Nu 33:48 pitched in the plains of Moab by **J.**. 3383
Nu 33:49 pitched by **J.**, from Beth-jesimoth....... 3383
Nu 33:50 Moses in the plains of Moab by **J.**....... 3383
Nu 33:51 over **J.** into the land of Canaan; 3383
Nu 34:12 the border shall go down to **J.**, and 3383
Nu 34:15 their inheritance this side **J.** near 3383
Nu 35:1 Moses in the plains of Moab by **J.**....... 3383
Nu 35:10 ye be come over **J.** into the land of.... 3383
Nu 35:14 give three cities on this side **J.**, ... 3383
Nu 36:13 Israel in the plains of Moab by **J.** 3383
De 1:1 on this side **J.** in the wilderness,...... 3383
De 1:5 On this side **J.**, in the land of Moab,... 3383
De 2:29 until I shall pass over **J.** into the........ 3383
De 3:8 the land that was on this side **J.**, ... 3383
De 3:17 plain also, and **J.**, and the coast, ... 3383
De 3:20 God hath given them beyond **J.**: 3383
De 3:25 see the good land that is beyond **J.**, ... 3383
De 3:27 for thou shalt not go over this **J.**........ 3383
De 4:21 sware that I should not go over **J.**,...... 3383
De 4:22 in this land, I must not go over **J.**...... 3383
De 4:26 whereunto ye go over **J.** to possess ... 3383
De 4:41 severed three cities on this side **J.**...... 3383
De 4:46 On this side **J.**, in the valley over 3383
De 4:47 this side **J.** toward the sunrising;........ 3383
De 4:49 And all the plain on this side **J.**.......... 3383
De 9:1 Thou art to pass over **J.** this day, ... 3383
De 11:30 Are they not on the other side **J.**,....... 3383
De 11:31 For ye shall pass over **J.** to go in to... 3383
De 12:10 But when ye go over **J.**, and dwell..... 3383
De 27:2 when ye shall pass over **J.** unto the..... 3383
De 27:4 shall be when ye be gone over **J.**,....... 3383
De 27:12 people, when ye are come over **J.**;...... 3383
De 30:18 passest over **J.** to go to possess it. 3383
De 31:2 Thou shalt not go over this **J.**. 3383
De 31:13 in the land whither ye go over **J.** 3383
De 32:47 whither ye go over **J.** to possess it. ... 3383
Jos 1:2 go over this **J.**, thou, and all this 3383
Jos 1:11 days ye shall pass over this **J.**,.......... 3383
Jos 1:14 Moses gave you on this side **J.**;........... 3383
Jos 1:15 this side **J.** toward the sunrising......... 3383
Jos 2:7 them the way to **J.** unto the fords:...... 3383
Jos 2:10 were on the other side **J.**, Sihon........ 3383
Jos 3:1 from Shittim, and came to **J.**, ... 3383
Jos 3:8 to the brink of the water of **J.**, ... 3383
Jos 3:8 ye shall stand still in **J.**. 3383
Jos 3:11 passeth over before you into **J.**........... 3383
Jos 3:13 earth, shall rest in the waters of **J.**,.... 3383
Jos 3:13 the waters of **J.** shall be cut off 3383
Jos 3:14 from their tents, to pass over **J.**, ... 3383
Jos 3:15 bare the ark were come unto **J.**,.......... 3383
Jos 3:15 **J.** overfloweth all his banks all the...... 3383
Jos 3:17 on dry ground in the midst of **J.**, ... 3383
Jos 3:17 people were passed clean over **J.**....... 3383
Jos 4:1 people were clean passed over **J.**, ... 3383
Jos 4:3 you hence out of the midst of **J.**, ... 3383
Jos 4:5 Lord your God into the midst of **J.**,.... 3383
Jos 4:7 the waters of **J.** were cut off before ... 3383
Jos 4:7 the Lord; when it passed over **J.**. 3383
Jos 4:7 the waters of **J.** were cut off: and....... 3383
Jos 4:8 twelve stones out of the midst of **J.**,.... 3383
Jos 4:9 up twelve stones in the midst of **J.**,.... 3383
Jos 4:10 the ark stood in the midst of **J.**, ... 3383
Jos 4:16 that they come up out of **J.**............... 3383
Jos 4:17 saying, Come ye up out of **J.**. 3383
Jos 4:18 come up out of the midst of **J.**, ... 3383
Jos 4:18 waters of **J.** returned unto their........ 3383
Jos 4:19 came up out of **J.** on the tenth day..... 3383
Jos 4:20 stones, which they took out of **J.**, ... 3383
Jos 4:22 Israel came over this **J.** on dry.......... 3383
Jos 4:23 God dried up the waters of **J.** from 3383
Jos 5:1 were on the side of **J.** westward,....... 3383
Jos 5:1 Lord had dried up the waters of **J.** 3383
Jos 7:7 at all brought this people over **J.**,....... 3383
Jos 7:7 and dwelt on the other side **J.**! 3383
Jos 9:1 kings which were on this side **J.**, ... 3383
Jos 9:10 the Amorites, that were beyond **J.**, ... 3383
Jos 12:1 their land on the other side **J.** 3383
Jos 12:7 smote on this side **J.** on the west, ... 3383
Jos 13:8 gave them, beyond **J.** eastward,......... 3383
Jos 13:23 And the border...of Reuben was **J.**, ... 3383
Jos 13:27 of Heshbon, **J.** and his border, ... 3383
Jos 13:27 on the other side **J.** eastward............ 3383
Jos 13:32 plains of Moab, on the other side **J.**,... 3383
Jos 14:3 an half tribe on the other side **J.**: 3383
Jos 15:5 salt sea, even unto the end of **J.**. 3383
Jos 15:5 the sea at the uttermost part of **J.**: 3383
Jos 16:1 of Joseph fell from **J.** by Jericho, ... 3383
Jos 16:7 to Jericho, and went out at **J.**............ 3383
Jos 17:5 which were on the other side **J.**;......... 3383
Jos 18:7 received their inheritance beyond **J.**.... 3383
Jos 18:12 on the north side was from **J.**; 3383
Jos 18:19 the salt sea at the south end of **J.**: 3383
Jos 18:20 **J.** was the border of it on the east..... 3383
Jos 19:22 outgoings of their border were at **J.**:... 3383
Jos 19:33 the outgoings thereof were at **J.**: 3383
Jos 19:34 to Judah upon **J.** toward the............. 3383
Jos 20:8 other side **J.** by Jericho eastward, ... 3383
Jos 22:4 Lord gave you on the other side **J.**..... 3383
Jos 22:7 brethren on this side **J.** westward. 3383
Jos 22:10 they came unto the borders of **J.**, ... 3383
Jos 22:10 Manasseh built there an altar by **J.**,.... 3383
Jos 22:11 in the borders of **J.**, at the passage 3383
Jos 22:25 the Lord hath made **J.** a border......... 3383
Jos 23:4 inheritance for your tribes, from **J.**, ... 3383
Jos 24:8 which dwelt on the other side **J.**; 3383
Jos 24:11 ye went over **J.**, and came unto........ 3383
Jg 3:28 took the fords of **J.** toward Moab, ... 3383
Jg 5:17 Gilead abode beyond **J.**: and why 3383
Jg 7:24, 24 waters unto Beth-barah and **J.**....... 3383
Jg 7:25 Zeeb to Gideon on the other side **J.**. .. 3383
Jg 8:4 Gideon came to **J.**, and passed over, .. 3383
Jg 10:8 that were on the other side **J.** in........ 3383
Jg 10:9 children of Ammon passed over **J.**...... 3383
Jg 11:13 even unto Jabbok, and unto **J.**: 3383
Jg 11:22 from the wilderness even unto **J.**. 3383
Jg 12:5 Gileadites took the passages of **J.**....... 3383
Jg 12:6 slew him at the passages of **J.**:........... 3383
1Sa 13:7 some of the Hebrews went over **J.**...... 3383
1Sa 31:7 they that were on the other side **J.**, ... 3383
2Sa 2:29 passed over **J.**, and went through........ 3383
2Sa 10:17 Israel together, and passed over **J.**,..... 3383
2Sa 17:22 with him, and they passed over **J.**:...... 3383
2Sa 17:22 of them that was not gone over **J.**...... 3383
2Sa 17:24 Absalom passed over **J.**, he and all..... 3383
2Sa 19:15 the king returned, and came to **J.**. 3383
2Sa 19:15 king, to conduct the king over **J.**......... 3383
2Sa 19:17 they went over **J.** before the king. 3383
2Sa 19:18 the king, as he was come over **J.**;......... 3383
2Sa 19:31 from Rogelim, and went over **J.**........... 3383
2Sa 19:31 the king, to conduct him over **J.**. 3383
2Sa 19:36 servant will go a little way over **J.**...... 3383
2Sa 19:39 And all the people went over **J.**. 3383
2Sa 19:41 David's men with him, over **J.**?.......... 3383
2Sa 20:2 king, from **J.** even to Jerusalem. 3383
2Sa 24:5 they passed over **J.**, and pitched........ 3383
1Ki 2:8 he came down to meet me at **J.**, ... 3383
1Ki 7:46 In the plain of **J.** did the king cast...... 3383
1Ki 17:3,5 brook Cherith, that is before **J.**.......... 3383
2Ki 2:6 for the Lord hath sent me to **J.**. 3383
2Ki 2:7 afar off: and they two stood by **J.**. 3383
2Ki 2:13 back, and stood by the bank of **J.**;...... 3383
2Ki 5:10 Go and wash in **J.** seven times, ... 3383
2Ki 5:14 dipped himself seven times in **J.**,........ 3383
2Ki 6:2 Let us go, we pray thee, unto **J.**, ... 3383
2Ki 6:4 when they came to **J.**, they cut 3383
2Ki 7:15 they went after them unto **J.**: and, ... 3383
2Ki 10:33 From **J.** eastward, all...Gilead,.......... 3383
1Ch 6:78 on the other side **J.** by Jericho, ... 3383
1Ch 6:78 on the east side of **J.**, were given...... 3383
1Ch 12:15 they that went over **J.** in the first...... 3383
1Ch 12:37 on the other side of **J.**, of the 3383
1Ch 19:17 all Israel, and passed over **J.**,............ 3383
1Ch 26:30 among them of Israel on this side **J.** ... 3383
2Ch 4:17 In the plain of **J.** did the king cast...... 3383
Job 40:23 he can draw up **J.** into his mouth. 3383
Ps 42:6 remember thee from the land of **J.**,.... 3383
Ps 114:3 and fled: **J.** was driven back............. 3383
Ps 114:5 thou **J.**, that thou wast driven back? ... 3383
Isa 9:1 by the way of the sea, beyond **J.**,...... 3383
Jer 12:5 wilt thou do in the swelling of **J.**? 3383
Jer 49:19 like a lion from the swelling of **J.** 3383
Jer 50:44 like a lion from the swelling of **J.** 3383
Eze 47:18 and from the land of Israel by **J.**, ... 3383
Zec 11:3 lions; for the pride of **J.** is spoiled...... 3383
Mt 3:5 and all the region round about **J.**,....... *2446*
Mt 3:6 baptized of him in **J.**, confessing.......... *2446*
Mt 3:13 cometh Jesus from Galilee to **J.**.......... *2446*
Mt 4:15 by the way of the sea, beyond **J.**,...... *2446*
Mt 4:25 from Judaea, and from beyond **J.**........ *2446*
Mt 19:1 into the coasts of Judaea beyond **J.**;..... *2446*
Mk 1:5 baptized of him in the river of **J.**,........ *2446*
Mk 1:9 and was baptized of John in **J.**........... *2446*
Mk 3:8 Idumaea, and from beyond **J.**; *2446*
Mk 10:1 of Judaea by the farther side of **J.**: *2446*
Lu 3:3 came into all the country about **J.**,....... *2446*
Lu 4:1 the Holy Ghost returned from **J.**,........ *2446*
Joh 1:28 were done in Bethabara beyond **J.**,...... *2446*
Joh 3:26 he that was with thee beyond **J.**, ... *2446*
Joh 10:40 went away again beyond **J.** into *2446*

JORIM (jo'-rim)
Lu 3:29 Eliezer, which was the son of **J.**, ... *2497*

JORKOAM (jor'-ko-am)
1Ch 2:44 begat Raham, the father of **J.**: 3421

JOSABAD (jos'-a-bad) See also JOZABAD.
1Ch 12:4 Johanan, and **J.** the Gederathite, ... 3107

JOSAPHAT (jos'-a-fat) See also JEHOSHAPHAT.
Mt 1:8 Asa begat **J.**; and **J.** begat Joram, ... *2498*

JOSE (jo'-ze) See also JOSES.
Lu 3:29 Which was the son of **J.**, which *2499*

JOSEDECH (jos'-e-dek) See also JOZADAK.
Hag 1:1 to Joshua the son of **J.**, the high......... 3087
Hag 1:12 and Joshua the son of **J.**, the high....... 3087
Hag 1:14 spirit of Joshua the son of **J.**, the....... 3087
Hag 2:2 to Joshua the son of **J.**, the high......... 3087
Hag 2:4 Joshua, son of **J.**, the high priest;....... 3087
Zec 6:11 the head of Joshua the son of **J.**,......... 3087

JOSEPH (jo'-zef)
Ge 30:24 And she called his name **J.**; and.......... 3130
Ge 30:25 to pass, when Rachel had borne **J.**, ... 3130
Ge 33:2 and Rachel and **J.** hindermost............ 3130
Ge 33:7 and after came **J.** near and Rachel, ... 3130
Ge 35:24 sons of Rachel; **J.**, and Benjamin:........ 3130
Ge 37:2 **J.**, being seventeen years old, was..... 3130
Ge 37:2 **J.** brought unto his father...report...... 3130
Ge 37:3 Israel loved **J.** more than all his 3130
Ge 37:5 **J.** dreamed a dream, and he told........ 3130
Ge 37:13 Israel said unto **J.**, Do not thy........... 3130
Ge 37:17 **J.** went after his brethren, and 3130
Ge 37:23 when **J.** was come unto his brethren,.. 3130
Ge 37:23 that they stript **J.** out of his coat,....... 3130
Ge 37:28 drew and lifted up **J.** out of the pit, ... 3130
Ge 37:28 and sold **J.** to the Ishmeelites for 3130
Ge 37:28 and they brought **J.** into Egypt. 3130
Ge 37:29 behold, **J.** was not in the pit; and....... 3130
Ge 37:33 **J.** is without doubt rent in pieces. 3130
Ge 39:1 **J.** was brought down to Egypt;............ 3130
Ge 39:2 And the Lord was with **J.**, and he 3130
Ge 39:4 **J.** found grace in his sight, and 3130
Ge 39:6 **J.** was a goodly person, and well......... 3130
Ge 39:7 master's wife cast her eyes upon **J.**; ... 3130
Ge 39:10 as she spake to **J.** day by day, ... 3130
Ge 39:11 that **J.** went into the house to do ....
Ge 39:21 But the Lord was with **J.**, and........... 3130
Ge 40:3 the place where **J.** was bound. 3130
Ge 40:4 of the guard charged **J.** with them, ... 3130
Ge 40:6 And **J.** came in unto them in the......... 3130
Ge 40:8 And **J.** said unto them, Do not 3130
Ge 40:9 chief butler told his dream to **J.**, ... 3130
Ge 40:12 And **J.** said unto him, This is the 3130
Ge 40:16 he said unto **J.**, I also was in my 3130
Ge 40:18 **J.** answered and said, This is the 3130

Ge 40:22 as **J.** had interpreted to them........... 3130
Ge 40:23 not the chief butler remember **J.**,....... 3130
Ge 41:14 Pharaoh sent and called **J.**, and......... 3130
Ge 41:15 And Pharaoh said unto **J.**, I have 3130
Ge 41:16 **J.** answered Pharaoh, saying, It is...... 3130
Ge 41:17 Pharaoh said unto **J.**, In my dream, ... 3130
Ge 41:25 **J.** said unto Pharaoh, The dream........ 3130
Ge 41:39 Pharaoh said unto **J.**, Forasmuch........ 3130
Ge 41:41 Pharaoh said unto **J.**, See, I have....... 3130
Ge 41:44 Pharaoh said unto **J.**, I am............... 3130
Ge 41:45 And **J.** went out over all the land of.... 3130
Ge 41:46 **J.** was thirty years old when he......... 3130
Ge 41:46 **J.** went out from the presence of....... 3130
Ge 41:49 **J.** gathered corn as the sand of the 3130
Ge 41:50 unto **J.** were born two sons before...... 3130
Ge 41:51 **J.** called the name of the firstborn...... 3130
Ge 41:54 to come, according as **J.** had said:...... 3130
Ge 41:55 unto all the Egyptians, Go unto **J.**;..... 3130
Ge 41:56 **J.** opened all the storehouses, and...... 3130
Ge 41:57 came into Egypt to **J.** for to buy......... 3130
Ge 42:6 **J.** was the governor over the land,..... 3130
Ge 42:7 **J.** saw his brethren, and he knew....... 3130
Ge 42:8 **J.** knew his brethren, but they knew... 3130
Ge 42:9 **J.** remembered the dreams which....... 3130
Ge 42:14 **J.** said unto them, That is it that I 3130
Ge 42:18 **J.** said unto them the third day,......... 3130
Ge 42:23 knew not that **J.** understood them;..... 3130
Ge 42:25 **J.** commanded to fill their sacks......... 3130
Ge 42:36 **J.** is not, and Simeon is not, and ye.... 3130
Ge 43:15 down to Egypt, and stood before **J.**.... 3130
Ge 43:16 when **J.** saw Benjamin with them, ... 3130
Ge 43:17 And the man did as **J.** bade; and........ 3130
Ge 43:25 present against **J.** came at noon:........ 3130
Ge 43:26 when **J.** came home, they brought...... 3130
Ge 43:30 **J.** made haste; for his bowels did....... 3130
Ge 44:2 to the word that **J.** had spoken.......... 3130
Ge 44:4 **J.** said unto his steward, Up, follow.... 3130
Ge 44:15 **J.** said unto them, What deed is......... 3130
Ge 45:1 Then **J.** could not refrain himself........ 3130
Ge 45:1 while **J.** made himself known unto 3130
Ge 45:3 **J.** said unto his brethren, I am **J.**;...... 3130
Ge 45:4 **J.** said unto his brethren, Come......... 3130
Ge 45:4 I am **J.** your brother, whom ye sold ... 3130
Ge 45:9 Thus saith thy son **J.**, God hath......... 3130
Ge 45:17 Pharaoh said unto **J.**, Say unto thy..... 3130
Ge 45:21 **J.** gave them wagons, according to..... 3130
Ge 45:26 told him, saying, **J.** is yet alive, ... 3130
Ge 45:27 they told him all the words of **J.**, ... 3130
Ge 45:27 saw the wagons which **J.** had sent....... 3130
Ge 45:28 It is enough; **J.** my son is yet alive:.... 3130
Ge 46:4 **J.** shall put his hand upon thine.......... 3130
Ge 46:19 sons of Rachel Jacob's wife; **J.**, and 3130
Ge 46:20 unto **J.** in the land of Egypt were....... 3130
Ge 46:27 sons of **J.**, which were born him in....... 3130
Ge 46:28 he sent Judah before him unto **J.**,........ 3130
Ge 46:29 **J.** made ready his chariot, and went.... 3130
Ge 46:30 Israel said unto **J.**, Now let me die,.... 3130
Ge 46:31 **J.** said unto his brethren, and unto 3130
Ge 47:1 Then **J.** came and told Pharaoh, and.... 3130
Ge 47:5 And Pharoah spake unto **J.**, saying, ... 3130
Ge 47:7 And **J.** brought in Jacob his father, ... 3130
Ge 47:11 And **J.** placed his father and his 3130
Ge 47:12 **J.** nourished his father, and his 3130
Ge 47:14 **J.** gathered up all the money that........ 3130
Ge 47:14 **J.** brought the money into Pharaoh's... 3130
Ge 47:15 the Egyptians came unto **J.**, and 3130
Ge 47:16 **J.** said, Give your cattle; and I will..... 3130
Ge 47:17 they brought their cattle unto **J.**:........ 3130
Ge 47:17 **J.** gave them bread in exchange for 3130
Ge 47:20 **J.** brought all the land of Egypt for..... 3130
Ge 47:23 **J.** said unto the people, Behold, I........ 3130
Ge 47:26 **J.** made it a law over the land of........ 3130
Ge 47:29 and he called his son **J.**, and said 3130
Ge 48:1 told **J.**, Behold, thy father is sick: 3130
Ge 48:2 thy son **J.** cometh unto thee: 3130
Ge 48:3 Jacob said unto **J.**, God Almighty......... 3130
Ge 48:9 **J.** said unto his father, They are 3130
Ge 48:11 And Israel said unto **J.**, I had not....... 3130
Ge 48:12 **J.** brought them out from between 3130
Ge 48:13 **J.** took them both, Ephraim in his 3130
Ge 48:15 he blessed **J.**, and said, God, before.... 3130
Ge 48:17 when **J.** saw that his father laid his..... 3130
Ge 48:18 **J.** said unto his father, Not so, my..... 3130
Ge 48:21 Israel said unto **J.**, Behold, I die: 3130
Ge 49:22 **J.** is a fruitful bough, even a fruitful.... 3130
Ge 49:26 shall be on the head of **J.**, and on 3130
Ge 50:1 **J.** fell upon his father's face, and........ 3130
Ge 50:2 **J.** commanded...the physicians to 3130
Ge 50:4 **J.** spake unto the house of Pharaoh, ... 3130
Ge 50:7 **J.** went up to bury his father: and...... 3130
Ge 50:8 And all the house of **J.**, and his 3130
Ge 50:14 **J.** returned into Egypt, he, and his..... 3130
Ge 50:15 said, **J.** will peradventure hate us, ... 3130
Ge 50:16 And they sent a messenger unto **J.**, ... 3130
Ge 50:17 So shall ye say unto **J.**, Forgive, I....... 3130
Ge 50:17 **J.** wept when they spake unto him. 3130
Ge 50:19 **J.** said unto them, Fear not: for am.... 3130
Ge 50:22 And **J.** dwelt in Egypt, he, and his 3130
Ge 50:22 **J.** lived an hundred and ten years....... 3130
Ge 50:23 **J.** saw Ephraim's children of the 3130
Ge 50:24 **J.** said unto his brethren, I die: 3130
Ge 50:25 **J.** took an oath of the children of 3130
Ge 50:26 **J.** died, being an hundred and ten....... 3130
Ex 1:5 souls: for **J.** was in Egypt already. 3130
Ex 1:6 **J.** died, and all his brethren, and........ 3130
Ex 1:8 king over Egypt, which knew not **J.**...... 3130
Ex 13:19 Moses took the bones of **J.** with........ 3130
Nu 1:10 Of the children of **J.**: of Ephraim;....... 3130
Nu 1:32 Of the children of **J.**, namely, of 3130
Nu 13:7 tribe of Issachar, Igal the son of **J.**..... 3130
Nu 13:11 Of the tribe of **J.**, namely, of the 3130
Nu 26:28 The sons of **J.** after their families......... 3130
Nu 26:37 the sons of **J.** after their families........ 3130
Nu 27:1 families of Manasseh the son of **J.**:...... 3130
Nu 32:33 tribe of Manasseh the son of **J.**, ... 3130
Nu 34:23 prince of the children of **J.**, for the..... 3130
Nu 36:1 of the families of the sons of **J.**,......... 3130
Nu 36:5 The tribe of the sons of **J.** hath said.... 3130
Nu 36:12 the sons of Manasseh the son of **J.**, ... 3130
De 27:12 Issachar, and **J.**, and Benjamin:.......... 3130
De 33:13 And of **J.** he said, Blessed of the 3130
De 33:16 blessing come upon the head of **J.**,..... 3130
Jos 14:4 the children of **J.** were two tribes, ... 3130
Jos 16:1 the children of **J.** fell from Jordan 3130
Jos 16:4 So the children of **J.**, Manasseh and.... 3130
Jos 17:1 for he was the firstborn of **J.**;............ 3130
Jos 17:2 children of Manasseh the son of **J.** 3130
Jos 17:14 children of **J.** spake unto Joshua, ... 3130
Jos 17:16 And the children of **J.** said, The hill 3130
Jos 17:17 Joshua spake unto the house of **J.**, ... 3130
Jos 18:5 the house of **J.** shall abide in their...... 3130
Jos 18:11 of Judah and the children of **J.** 3130
Jos 24:32 And the bones of **J.**, which the........... 3130
Jos 24:32 the inheritance of the children of **J.**...... 3130
Jg 1:22 the house of **J.**, they also went up 3130
Jg 1:23 house of **J.** sent to descry Beth-el...... 3130
Jg 1:35 hand of the house of **J.** prevailed,........ 3130
2Sa 19:20 first this day of all the house of **J.**....... 3130
1Ki 11:28 all the charge of the house of **J.**.......... 3130
1Ch 2:2 Dan, **J.**, and Benjamin, Naphtali, ... 3130
1Ch 5:1 was given unto the sons of **J.**............ 3130
1Ch 7:29 In these dwelt the children of **J.** 3130
1Ch 25:2 the sons of Asaph; Zaccur, and **J.**, ... 3130
1Ch 25:9 first lot came forth for Asaph to **J.**: 3130
Ezr 10:42 Shallum, Amariah, and **J.**.................. 3130
Ne 12:14 Melicu, Jonathan; of Shebaniah, **J.**; 3130
Ps 77:15 thy people, the sons of Jacob and **J.**. .. 3130
Ps 78:67 he refused the tabernacle of **J.**, ... 3130
Ps 80:1 thou that leadest **J.** like a flock; 3130
Ps 81:5 he ordained in **J.** for a testimony,....... 3084
Ps 105:17 sent a man before them, even **J.**,........ 3130
Eze 37:16 For **J.**, the stick of Ephraim, and 3130
Eze 37:19 I will take the stick of **J.**, which is...... 3130
Eze 47:13 Israel: **J.** shall have two portions........ 3130
Eze 48:32 and one gate of **J.**, one gate of.......... 3130
Am 5:6 out like fire in the house of **J.**, and..... 3130
Am 5:15 be gracious unto the remnant of **J.**... 3130
Am 6:6 not grieved for the affliction of **J.**. 3130
Ob 18 a fire, and the house of **J.** a flame, ... 3130
Zec 10:6 and I will save the house of **J.**, and 3130
Mt 1:16 begat **J.** the husband of Mary, ... *2501*
Mt 1:18 mother Mary was espoused to **J.**, ... *2501*
Mt 1:19 Then **J.** her husband, being a just *2501*
Mt 1:20 **J.**, thou son of David, fear not to....... *2501*
Mt 1:24 **J.** being raised from sleep did as....... *2501*
Mt 2:13 Lord appeareth to **J.** in a dream,......... *2501*
Mt 2:19 Lord appeareth in a dream to **J.**......... *2501*
Mt 27:57 rich man of Arimathaea, named **J.**, ... *2501*
Mt 27:59 And when **J.** had taken the body, he... *2501*
Mk 15:43 **J.** of Arimathaea, an honourable *2501*
Mk 15:45 centurion, he gave the body to **J.**....... *2501*
Lu 1:27 to a man whose name was **J.**, ... *2501*
Lu 2:4 And **J.** also went up from Galilee, ... *2501*
Lu 2:16 found Mary, and **J.**, and the babe....... *2501*
Lu 2:33 **J.** and his mother marvelled at.......... *2501*
Lu 2:43 **J.** and his mother knew not of it. *2501*
Lu 3:23 (as was supposed) the son of **J.**,......... *2501*
Lu 3:24 of Janna, which was the son of **J.**,...... *2501*
Lu 3:26 of Semei, which was the son of **J.**,..... *2501*
Lu 3:30 of Juda, which was the son of **J.**, ... *2501*
Lu 23:50 was a man named **J.**, a counsellor; *2501*
Joh 1:45 Jesus of Nazareth, the son of **J.**......... *2501*
Joh 4:5 that Jacob gave to his son **J.**............ *2501*
Joh 6:42 Is not this Jesus, the son of **J.**, ... *2501*
Joh 19:38 after this **J.** of Arimathaea, being a..... *2501*
Ac 1:23 **J.** called Barsabas, who was............ *2501*
Ac 7:9 with envy, sold **J.** into Egypt: *2501*
Ac 7:13 **J.** was made known to his brethren; ... *2501*
Ac 7:14 Then sent **J.**, and called his father...... *2501*
Ac 7:18 king arose, which knew not **J.**. *2501*
Heb 11:21 dying, blessed both the sons of **J.**; *2501*
Heb 11:22 By faith **J.**, when he died, made *2501*
Re 7:8 Of the tribe of **J.** were sealed........... *2501*

JOSEPH'S (jo'-zefs)

Ge 37:31 they took **J.** coat, and killed a kid....... 3130
Ge 39:5 the Egyptian's house for **J.** sake; 3130
Ge 39:6 he left all that he had in **J.** hand;........ 3130
Ge 39:20 **J.** master took him, and put him 3130
Ge 39:22 prison committed to **J.** hand all the..... 3130
Ge 41:42 his hand, and put it upon **J.** hand, ... 3130
Ge 41:45 called **J.** name Zaphnath-paaneah; 3130
Ge 42:3 **J.** ten brethren went down to buy 3130
Ge 42:4 Benjamin, **J.** brother, Jacob sent 3130
Ge 42:6 **J.** brethren came, and bowed down 3130
Ge 43:17 man brought the men into **J.** house..... 3130
Ge 43:18 they were brought into **J.** house; 3130
Ge 43:19 near to the steward of **J.** house, ... 3130
Ge 43:24 man brought the men into **J.** house,.... 3130
Ge 44:14 and his brethren came to **J.** house;..... 3130
Ge 45:16 house, saying, **J.** brethren are come: .. 3130
Ge 48:8 Israel beheld **J.** sons, and said, Who... 3130
Ge 50:15 **J.** brethren saw that their father 3130
Ge 50:23 were brought up upon **J.** knees.......... 3130
1Ch 5:2 ruler; but the birthright was **J.**:) 3130
Lu 4:22 And they said, is not this **J.** son? *2501*
Ac 7:13 **J.** kindred was made known unto *2501*

JOSES (jo'-zez) See also JOSE.

Mt 13:55 James, and **J.**, and Simon, and........... *2500*
Mt 27:56 Mary the mother of James and **J.**,....... *2500*
Mk 6:3 the brother of James, and **J.**, and....... *2500*
Mk 15:40 mother of James the less and of **J.**, ... *2500*
Mk 15:47 Mary the mother of **J.** beheld where... *2500*
Ac 4:36 **J.**, who...was surnamed Barnabas,....... *2500*

JOSHAH (jo'-shah)

1Ch 4:34 and **J.** the son of Amaziah,................ 3144

JOSHAPHAT (josh'-a-fat) See also JEHOSHAPHAT; JOSAPHAT.

1Ch 11:43 Maachah, and **J.** the Mithnite, ... 3146

JOSHAVIAH (josh-a-vi'-ah)

1Ch 11:46 Jeribai, and **J.**, the sons of Elnaam, ... 3145

JOSHBEKASHAH (josh-bek'-a-shah)

1Ch 25:4 **J.**, Mallothi, Hothir, and.................. 3436
1Ch 25:24 The seventeenth to **J.**, he, his sons,.... 3436

JOSHUA (josh'-u-ah) See also HOSEA; HOSHEA; JEHOSHUAH; JESHUA; JESHUAH; JESUS; OSEA; OSHEA.

Ex 17:9 Moses said unto **J.**, Choose us out..... 3091
Ex 17:10 So **J.** did as Moses had said to him, ... 3091
Ex 17:13 And **J.** discomfited Amalek and his...... 3091
Ex 17:14 and rehearse it in the ears of **J.**:........ 3091
Ex 24:13 Moses rose up, and his minister **J.**:.... 3091
Ex 32:17 And when **J.** heard the noise of the 3091
Ex 33:11 but his servant **J.**, the son of Nun, ... 3091
Nu 11:28 **J.** the son of Nun, the servant of....... 3091
Nu 14:6 **J.** the son of Nun, and Caleb the 3091
Nu 14:30 Jephunneh, and **J.** the son of Nun....... 3091
Nu 14:38 But **J.** the son of Nun, and Caleb....... 3091
Nu 26:65 Jephunneh, and **J.** the son of Nun....... 3091
Nu 27:18 Take thee **J.** the son of Nun, a man ... 3091
Nu 27:22 and he took **J.**, and set him before 3091
Nu 32:12 the Kenezite, and **J.** the son of Nun: .. 3091
Nu 32:28 **J.** the son of Nun, and the chief......... 3091
Nu 34:17 the priest, and **J.** the son of Nun. 3091
De 1:38 **J.** the son of Nun, which standeth 3091
De 3:21 And I commanded **J.** at that time, ... 3091

De 3:28 But charge **J.**, and encourage him, ... 3091
De 31:3 and **J.**, he shall go over before thee,... 3091
De 31:7 Moses called unto **J.**, and said unto 3091
De 31:14 call **J.**, and present yourselves in 3091
De 31:14 Moses and **J.** went, and presented 3091
De 31:23 he gave **J.** the son of Nun a charge, ... 3091
De 34:9 **J.** the son of Nun was full of the........ 3091
Jos *general title* The Book Of **J.** 3091
Jos 1:1 Lord spake unto **J.** the son of Nun, ... 3091
Jos 1:10 Then **J.** commanded the officers of..... 3091
Jos 1:12 half the tribe of Manasseh, spake **J.**,.... 3091
Jos 1:16 they answered **J.**, saying, All that 3091
Jos 2:1 And **J.** the son of Nun sent out of...... 3091
Jos 2:23 came to **J.** the son of Nun, and told.... 3091
Jos 2:24 said unto **J.**, Truly the Lord hath 3091
Jos 3:1 **J.** rose early in the morning; and 3091
Jos 3:5 **J.** said unto the people, Sanctify......... 3091
Jos 3:6 **J.** spake unto the priests, saying, ... 3091
Jos 3:7 the Lord said unto **J.**, this day will 3091
Jos 3:9 **J.** said unto the children of Israel, ... 3091
Jos 3:10 **J.** said, Hereby ye shall know that...... 3091
Jos 4:1 that the Lord spake unto **J.**, saying, ... 3091
Jos 4:4 Then **J.** called the twelve men,.......... 3091
Jos 4:5 **J.** said unto them, Pass over before.... 3091
Jos 4:8 of Israel did so as **J.** commanded, ... 3091
Jos 4:8 Jordan, as the Lord spake unto **J.**, ... 3091
Jos 4:9 **J.** set up twelve stones in the midst ... 3091
Jos 4:10 Lord commanded **J.** to speak unto...... 3091
Jos 4:10 to all that Moses commanded **J.**:......... 3091
Jos 4:14 On that day the Lord magnified **J.**....... 3091
Jos 4:15 And the Lord spake unto **J.**, saying, ... 3091
Jos 4:17 **J.** therefore commanded the priests, ... 3091
Jos 4:20 out of Jordan, did **J.** pitch in Gilgal. 3091
Jos 5:2 At that time the Lord said unto **J.**,..... 3091
Jos 5:3 And **J.** made him sharp knives, and 3091
Jos 5:4 the cause why **J.** did circumcise:........ 3091
Jos 5:7 their stead, them **J.** circumcised:........ 3091
Jos 5:9 Lord said unto **J.**, This day have I...... 3091
Jos 5:13 to pass, when **J.** was by Jericho,........ 3091
Jos 5:13 **J.** went unto him, and said unto......... 3091
Jos 5:14 **J.** fell on his face to the earth, and..... 3091
Jos 5:15 the Lord's host said unto **J.**, Loose 3091
Jos 5:15 standest is holy. And **J.** did so.......... 3091
Jos 6:2 Lord said unto **J.**, See, I have given ... 3091
Jos 6:6 **J.** the son of Nun called the priests, ... 3091
Jos 6:8 when **J.** had spoken unto the people, .. 3091
Jos 6:10 **J.** had commanded the people,........... 3091
Jos 6:12 **J.** rose early in the morning, and 3091
Jos 6:16 **J.** said unto the people, Shout; for...... 3091
Jos 6:22 **J.** had said unto the two men that...... 3091
Jos 6:25 **J.** saved Rahab the harlot alive, ... 3091
Jos 6:25 which **J.** sent to spy out Jericho......... 3091
Jos 6:26 And **J.** adjured them at that time,....... 3091
Jos 6:27 So the Lord was with **J.**; and his 3091
Jos 7:2 **J.** sent men from Jericho to Ai, ... 3091
Jos 7:3 they returned to **J.**, and said unto 3091
Jos 7:6 **J.** rent his clothes, and fell to the........ 3091
Jos 7:7 **J.** said, Alas, O Lord God, wherefore . 3091
Jos 7:10 the Lord said unto **J.**, Get thee up; 3091
Jos 7:16 So **J.** rose up early in the morning, ... 3091
Jos 7:19 **J.** said unto Achan, My son, give, I.... 3091
Jos 7:20 Achan answered **J.**, and said, indeed... 3091
Jos 7:22 So **J.** sent messengers, and they........ 3091
Jos 7:23 brought them unto **J.**, and unto all...... 3091
Jos 7:24 **J.**, and all Israel with him, took 3091
Jos 7:25 **J.** said, Why hast thou troubled us? 3091
Jos 8:1 Lord said unto **J.**, Fear not, neither.... 3091
Jos 8:3 **J.** arose, and all the people of war,..... 3091
Jos 8:3 **J.** chose out thirty thousand...men...... 3091
Jos 8:9 **J.** therefore sent them forth; and 3091
Jos 8:9 **J.** lodged that night among the.......... 3091
Jos 8:10 **J.** rose up early in the morning,......... 3091
Jos 8:13 **J.** went that night into the midst of..... 3091
Jos 8:15 **J.** and all Israel made as if they 3091
Jos 8:16 they pursued after **J.**, and were......... 3091
Jos 8:18 Lord said unto **J.**, Stretch out the 3091
Jos 8:18 **J.** stretched out the spear that he 3091
Jos 8:21 when **J.** and all Israel saw that 3091
Jos 8:23 took alive, and brought him to **J.**........ 3091
Jos 8:26 for **J.** drew not his hand back, ... 3091
Jos 8:27 the Lord which he commanded **J.**......... 3091
Jos 8:28 **J.** burnt Ai, and made it an heap for ... 3091
Jos 8:29 **J.** commanded that they should.......... 3091
Jos 8:30 **J.** built an altar unto the Lord............ 3091
Jos 8:35 which **J.** read not before all the 3091
Jos 9:2 to fight with **J.** and with Israel,.......... 3091
Jos 9:3 Gibeon heard what **J.** had done.......... 3091
Jos 9:6 went to **J.** unto the camp at Gilgal,...... 3091
Jos 9:8 And they said unto **J.**, We are thy...... 3091
Jos 9:8 And **J.** said unto them, Who are ye?... 3091
Jos 9:15 **J.** made peace with them, and........... 3091
Jos 9:22 **J.** called for them, and he spake 3091
Jos 9:24 they answered **J.**, and said, Because... 3091
Jos 9:27 **J.** made them that day hewers of....... 3091
Jos 10:1 had heard how **J.** had taken Ai, ... 3091
Jos 10:4 it hath made peace with **J.** and 3091
Jos 10:6 men of Gibeon sent unto **J.** to the...... 3091
Jos 10:7 So **J.** ascended from Gilgal, he, and.... 3091
Jos 10:8 Lord said unto **J.**, Fear them not: 3091
Jos 10:9 **J.** therefore came unto them 3091
Jos 10:12 Then spake **J.** to the Lord in the 3091
Jos 10:15 **J.** returned, and all Israel with him, ... 3091
Jos 10:17 it was told **J.**, saying, the five kings.... 3091
Jos 10:18 **J.** said, Roll great stones upon the 3091
Jos 10:20 when **J.** and the children of Israel....... 3091
Jos 10:21 people returned to the camp to **J.** 3091
Jos 10:22 said **J.**, Open the mouth of the cave, .. 3091
Jos 10:24 brought out those kings unto **J.**, ... 3091
Jos 10:24 **J.** called for all the men of Israel, ... 3091
Jos 10:25 **J.** said unto them, Fear not, nor be.... 3091
Jos 10:26 afterward **J.** smote them, and slew..... 3091
Jos 10:27 that **J.** commanded, and they took....... 3091
Jos 10:28 that day **J.** took Makkedah, and......... 3091
Jos 10:29 **J.** passed from Makkedah, and all....... 3091
Jos 10:31 **J.** passed from Libnah, and all........... 3091
Jos 10:33 **J.** smote him and his people, until 3091
Jos 10:34 from Lachish **J.** passed unto Eglon, ... 3091
Jos 10:36 **J.** went up from Eglon, and all........... 3091
Jos 10:38 **J.** returned, and all Israel with him, ... 3091
Jos 10:40 So **J.** smote all the country of the 3091
Jos 10:41 **J.** smote them from Kadesh-barnea..... 3091
Jos 10:42 their land did **J.** take at one time, ... 3091
Jos 10:43 **J.** returned, and all Israel with him, ... 3091
Jos 11:6 Lord said unto **J.**, Be not afraid 3091
Jos 11:7 **J.** came, and all the people of war...... 3091
Jos 11:9 **J.** did unto them as the Lord bade...... 3091
Jos 11:10 **J.** at that time turned back, and......... 3091
Jos 11:12 all the kings of them, did **J.** take,....... 3091
Jos 11:13 save Hazor only; that did **J.** burn. 3091
Jos 11:15 Moses command **J.**, and so did **J.**; 3091
Jos 11:16 So **J.** took all that land, the hills,........ 3091
Jos 11:18 **J.** made war a long time with all 3091
Jos 11:21 at that time came **J.**, and cut off........ 3091
Jos 11:21 **J.** destroyed them utterly with........... 3091
Jos 11:23 So **J.** took the whole land, according... 3091
Jos 11:23 **J.** gave it for an inheritance unto........ 3091
Jos 12:7 the kings of the country which **J.** 3091
Jos 12:7 **J.** gave unto the tribes of Israel......... 3091
Jos 13:1 **J.** was old and stricken in years;........ 3091
Jos 14:1 the priest, and **J.** the son of Nun, ... 3091
Jos 14:6 children of Judah came unto **J.**........... 3091
Jos 14:13 **J.** blessed him, and gave unto Caleb ... 3091
Jos 15:13 commandment of the Lord to **J.**,......... 3091
Jos 17:4 priest, and before **J.** the son of Nun, .. 3091
Jos 17:14 children of Joseph spake unto **J.**,........ 3091
Jos 17:15 **J.** answered them, If thou be a.......... 3091
Jos 17:17 **J.** spake unto the house of Joseph, ... 3091
Jos 18:3 **J.** said unto the children of Israel, ... 3091
Jos 18:8 **J.** charged them that went to 3091
Jos 18:9 again to **J.** to the host at Shiloh. 3091
Jos 18:10 **J.** cast lots for them in Shiloh............ 3091
Jos 18:10 there **J.** divided the land unto the....... 3091
Jos 19:49 of Israel gave an inheritance to **J.**....... 3091
Jos 19:51 **J.** the son of Nun, and the heads of..... 3091
Jos 20:1 The Lord also spake unto **J.**, saying, .. 3091
Jos 21:1 unto **J.** the son of Nun, and unto 3091
Jos 22:1 Then **J.** called the Reubenites, and..... 3091
Jos 22:6 So **J.** blessed them, and sent them..... 3091
Jos 22:7 unto the other half thereof gave **J.** 3091
Jos 22:7 when **J.** sent them away also unto...... 3091
Jos 23:1 **J.** waxed old and stricken in age. 3091
Jos 23:2 **J.** called for all Israel, and for their..... 3091
Jos 24:1 **J.** gathered all the tribes of Israel....... 3091
Jos 24:2 **J.** said unto all the people, Thus 3091
Jos 24:19 **J.** said unto the people, Ye cannot...... 3091
Jos 24:21 And the people said unto **J.**, Nay; 3091
Jos 24:22 **J.** said unto the people, Ye are......... 3091
Jos 24:24 the people said unto **J.**, The Lord 3091
Jos 24:25 **J.** made a covenant with the people 3091
Jos 24:26 **J.** wrote these words in the book of ... 3091
Jos 24:27 **J.** said unto all the people, Behold, ... 3091
Jos 24:28 So **J.** let the people depart, every...... 3091
Jos 24:29 **J.** the son of Nun, the servant of....... 3091
Jos 24:31 served the Lord all the days of **J.**, ... 3091
Jos 24:31 days of the elders that overlived **J.**,..... 3091
Jg 1:1 after the death of **J.** it came to pass, .. 3091
Jg 2:6 when **J.** had let the people go, the 3091
Jg 2:7 served the Lord all the days of **J.**, ... 3091
Jg 2:7 days of the elders that outlived **J.**, ... 3091
Jg 2:8 **J.** the son of Nun, the servant of....... 3091
Jg 2:21 nations which **J.** left when he died:..... 3091
Jg 2:23 he them into the hand of **J.**............... 3091
1Sa 6:14 the cart came into the field of **J.**, ... 3091
1Sa 6:18 unto this day in the field of **J.**, the 3091
1Ki 16:34 he spake by **J.** the son of Nun........... 3091
2Ki 23:8 in the entering in of the gate of **J.**....... 3091
Hag 1:1 and to **J.** the son of Josedech, the...... 3091
Hag 1:12 **J.** the son of Josedech, the high......... 3091
Hag 1:14 the spirit of **J.** the son of Josedech, ... 3091
Hag 2:2 and to **J.** the son of Josedech, the...... 3091
Hag 2:4 be strong, O **J.**, son of Josedech,....... 3091
Zec 3:1 he shewed me **J.** the high priest 3091
Zec 3:3 Now **J.** was clothed with filthy........... 3091
Zec 3:6 angel of the Lord protested unto **J.**, ... 3091
Zec 3:8 Hear now, O **J.** the high priest, ... 3091
Zec 3:9 stone that I have laid before **J.**; 3091
Zec 6:11 and set them upon the head of **J.**........ 3091

JOSIAH (jo-si'-ah) See also JOSIAS.
1Ki 13:2 the house of David, **J.** by name; 2977
2Ki 21:24 of the land made **J.** his son king......... 2977
2Ki 21:26 and **J.** his son reigned in his stead...... 2977
2Ki 22:1 **J.** was eight years old when he.......... 2977
2Ki 22:3 in the eighteenth year of king **J.**, ... 2977
2Ki 23:16 as **J.** turned himself, he spied the....... 2977
2Ki 23:19 **J.** took away, and did to them 2977
2Ki 23:23 in the eighteenth year of king **J.**, ... 2977
2Ki 23:24 **J.** put away, that he might perform..... 2977
2Ki 23:28 the rest of the acts of **J.**, and all........ 2977
2Ki 23:29 king **J.** went against him; and he........ 2977
2Ki 23:30 land took Jehoahaz the son of **J.**,........ 2977
2Ki 23:34 the son of **J.** king in the room of **J.**.... 2977
1Ch 3:14 Amon his son, **J.** his son.................. 2977
1Ch 3:15 the sons of **J.** were, the firstborn......... 2977
2Ch 33:25 of the land made **J.** his son king......... 2977
2Ch 34:1 **J.** was eight years old when he.......... 2977
2Ch 34:33 **J.** took away all the abominations 2977
2Ch 35:1 **J.** kept a passover unto the Lord in.... 2977
2Ch 35:7 **J.** gave to the people, of the flock,..... 2977
2Ch 35:16 to the commandment of king **J.**.......... 2977
2Ch 35:18 keep such a passover as **J.** kept, ... 2977
2Ch 35:19 reign of **J.** was this passover kept. 2977
2Ch 35:20 when **J.** had prepared the temple, ... 2977
2Ch 35:20 and **J.** went out against him. 2977
2Ch 35:22 **J.** would not turn his face from him, ... 2977
2Ch 35:23 the archers shot at king **J.**; and 2977
2Ch 35:24 and Jerusalem mourned for **J.**............ 2977
2Ch 35:25 Jeremiah lamented for **J.**: and all........ 2977
2Ch 35:25 spake of **J.** in their lamentations......... 2977
2Ch 35:26 the rest of the acts of **J.**, and his........ 2977
2Ch 36:1 land took Jehoahaz the son of **J.**,........ 2977
Jer 1:2 days of **J.** the son of Amon king of..... 2977
Jer 1:3 days of Jehoiakim the son of **J.** king.... 2977
Jer 1:3 year of Zedekiah the son of **J.** king..... 2977
Jer 3:6 said also unto me in the days of **J.** 2977
Jer 22:11 Lord touching Shallum the son of **J.**..... 2977
Jer 22:11 reigned instead of **J.** his father,.......... 2977
Jer 22:18 concerning Jehoiakim the son of **J.**....... 2977
Jer 25:1 year of Jehoiakim the son of **J.** king.... 2977
Jer 25:3 year of **J.** the son of Amon king of....... 2977
Jer 26:1 the reign of Jehoiakim the son of **J.** 2977
Jer 27:1 the reign of Jehoiakim the son of **J.** 2977
Jer 35:1 the days of Jehoiakim the son of **J.**...... 2977
Jer 36:1 year of Jehoiakim the son of **J.** 2977
Jer 36:2 from the days of **J.**, even unto this..... 2977
Jer 36:9 year of Jehoiakim the son of **J.** king..... 2977
Jer 37:1 Zedekiah the son of **J.** reigned........... 2977
Jer 45:1 year of Jehoiakim the son of **J.** king.... 2977
Jer 46:2 year of Jehoiakim the son of **J.** king.... 2977
Zep 1:1 days of **J.** the son of Amon, king of.... 2977
Zec 6:10 house of **J.** the son of Zephaniah; 2977

JOSIAS (jo-si'-as) See also JOSIAH.
Mt 1:10 begat Amon; and Amon begat **J.**; *2502*
Mt 1:11 And **J.** begat Jechonias and his........... *2502*

JOSIBIAH (jos-ib-i'-ah)
1Ch 4:35 And Joel, and Jehu the son of **J.**, ... 3143

JOSIPHIAH (jos-if-i'-ah)
Ezr 8:10 sons of Shelomith; the son of J.,........ 3131

JOSTLE See JUSTLE.

JOT
Mt 5:18 one j. or one tittle shall in no wise.2503

JOTBAH (jot'-bah)
2Ki 21:19 the daughter of Haruz of J.............. 3192

JOTBATH (jot'-bath) See also JOTBATHAH.
De 10:7 from Gudgodah to J., a land of.......... 3193

JOTBATHAH (jot'-ba-thah) See also JOTBATH.
Nu 33:33 Hor-hagidgad, and pitched in J.......... 3193
Nu 33:34 removed from J., and encamped........ 3193

JOTHAM (jo'-tham) See also JOATHAM.
Jg 9:5 J. the youngest son of Jerubbaal........ 3147
Jg 9:7 And when they told it to J., he went.. 3147
Jg 9:21 J. ran away, and fled, and went to..... 3147
Jg 9:57 upon them came the curse of J........... 3147
2Ki 15:5 And J. the king's son was over the..... 3147
2Ki 15:7 and J. his son reigned in his stead...... 3147
2Ki 15:30 year of J. the son of Uzziah............. 3147
2Ki 15:32 J. the son of Uzziah king of Judah...... 3147
2Ki 15:36 the rest of the acts of J., and all........ 3147
2Ki 15:38 J. slept with his fathers, and was....... 3147
2Ki 16:1 Ahaz the son of J. king of Judah........ 3147
1Ch 2:47 the sons of Jahdai; Regem, and J.,..... 3147
1Ch 3:12 his son, Azariah his son, J. his son,.... 3147
1Ch 5:17 by genealogies in the days of J.......... 3147
2Ch 26:21 and J. his son was over the king's...... 3147
2Ch 26:23 and J. his son reigned in his stead...... 3147
2Ch 27:1 J. was twenty and five years old......... 3147
2Ch 27:6 So J. became mighty, because he........ 3147
2Ch 27:7 the rest of the acts of J., and all........ 3147
2Ch 27:9 J. slept with his fathers, and they...... 3147
Isa 1:1 in the days of Uzziah, J., Ahaz, and.... 3147
Isa 7:1 in the days of Ahaz the son of J.,..... 3147
Ho 1:1 in the days of Uzziah, J., Ahaz, and.... 3147
Mic 1:1 the days of J., Ahaz, and Hezekiah,.... 3147

JOURNEY See also JOURNEYED; JOURNEYING; JOURNEYS.
Ge 24:21 had made his j. prosperous or not...... 1870
Ge 29:1 Jacob went on his j., and........... 5575,7272
Ge 30:36 set three days' j. betwixt himself....... 1870
Ge 31:23 pursued after him seven days' j.;....... 1870
Ge 33:12 Let us take our j., and let us go,........ 5265
Ge 46:1 Israel took his j. with all that he........ 5265
Ex 3:18 three days' j. into the wilderness,...... 1870
Ex 5:3 thee, three days' j. into the desert,.... 1870
Ex 8:27 three days' j. into the wilderness,...... 1870
Ex 13:20 they took their j. from Succoth,........ 5265
Ex 16:1 And they took their j. from Elim......... 5265
Nu 9:10 or be in a j. afar off, yet he shall....... 1870
Nu 9:13 man that is clean, and is not in a j.,..... 1870
Nu 10:6 the south side shall take their j.:........ 5265
Nu 10:13 they first took their j. according to...... 5265
Nu 10:33 mount of the Lord three days' j.:........ 1870
Nu 10:33 before them in the three days' j.,........ 1870
Nu 11:31 as it were a day's j. on this side,....... 1870
Nu 11:31 it were a day's j. on the other side,.... 1870
Nu 33:8 went three days' j. in the wilderness... 1870
Nu 33:12 took their j. out of the wilderness...... 5265
De 1:2 eleven days' j. from Horeb by the way......
De 1:7 Turn you, and take your j., and......... 5265
De 1:40 take your j. into the wilderness by..... 5265
De 2:1 took our j. into the wilderness by........ 5265
De 2:24 take your j., and pass over the river.... 5265
De 10:6 of Israel took their j. from Beeroth...... 5265
De 10:11 Arise, take thy j. before the people,.... 4550
Jos 9:11 Take victuals with you for the j.,....... 1870
Jos 9:13 old by reason of the very long j........ 1870
Jg 4:9 the j. that thou takest shall not be...... 1870
1Sa 15:18 the Lord sent thee on a j., and said,... 1870
2Sa 11:10 Uriah, Camest thou not from thy j.?... 1870
1Ki 18:27 or he is pursuing, or he is in a j.,...... 1870
1Ki 19:4 went a day's j. into the wilderness,.... 1870
1Ki 19:7 because the j. is too great for thee...... 1870
2Ki 3:9 fetched a compass of seven days' j.:... 1870
2Ch 1:13 Solomon came from his j. to the high........
Ne 2:6 For how long shall thy j. be? and....... 4109
Pr 7:19 not at home, he is gone a long j.:...... 1870
Jon 3:3 great city of three days' j................ 4109
Jon 3:4 to enter into the city a day's j.,......... 4109
Mt 10:10 nor scrip for your j., neither two... *3598*
Mt 25:15 ability; and straightway took his j.. *589*
Mk 6:8 should take nothing for their j.,.......... *3598*
Mk 13:34 of man is as a man taking a far j.,..*590*
Lu 2:44 in the company, went a day's j.;........ *3598*
Lu 9:3 Take nothing for your j., neither... *3598*
Lu 11:6 a friend of mine in his j. is come.. *3598*
Lu 15:13 and took his j. into a far country,.. *589*
Joh 4:6 therefore, being wearied with his j.,... *3597*
Ac 1:12 from Jerusalem a sabbath day's j........ *3598*
Ac 10:9 as they went on their j., and drew..... *3596*
Ac 22:6 as I made my j., and was come......... *4198*
Ro 1:10 I might have a prosperous j. by......... *2137*
Ro 15:24 I take my j. into Spain, I will............ *4198*
Ro 15:24 I trust to see you in my j., and to...... *1279*
1Co 16:6 may bring me on my j. whithersoever.......
Tit 3:13 and Apollos on their j. diligently,.............
3Jo 6 if thou bring forward on their j.................

JOURNEYED
Ge 11:2 to pass, as they j. from the east,....... 5265
Ge 12:9 Abram j., going on still toward the..... 5265
Ge 13:11 and Lot j. east: and they separated.... 5265
Ge 20:1 Abraham j. from thence toward the.... 5265
Ge 33:17 Jacob j. to Succoth, and built him....... 5265
Ge 35:5 And they j.: and the terror of God...... 5265
Ge 35:16 they j. from Beth-el; and there was.... 5265
Ge 35:21 And Israel j., and spread his tent....... 5265
Ex 12:37 children of Israel j. from Rameses...... 5265
Ex 17:1 Israel j. from the wilderness of Sin,.... 5265
Ex 40:37 they j. not till the day that it was....... 5265
Nu 9:17 after that the children of Israel j.:...... 5265
Nu 9:18 of the Lord the children of Israel j.,..... 5265
Nu 9:19 the charge of the Lord, and j. not...... 5265
Nu 9:20 commandment of the Lord they j........ 5265
Nu 9:21 up in the morning, then they j.:......... 5265
Nu 9:21 that the cloud was taken up, they j..... 5265
Nu 9:22 abode in their tents, and j. not:......... 5265
Nu 9:22 but when it was taken up, they j........ 5265
Nu 9:23 commandment of the Lord they j.:...... 5265
Nu 11:35 people j. from Kibroth-hattaavah........ 5265
Nu 12:15 j. not till Miriam was brought in......... 5265
Nu 20:22 whole congregation, j. from Kadesh,... 5265
Nu 21:4 And they j. from mount Hor by the.... 5265
Nu 21:11 And they j. from Oboth, and pitched... 5265
Nu 33:22 they j. from Rissah, and pitched in..... 5265
De 10:7 From thence they j. unto Gudgodah;... 5265
Jos 9:17 children of Israel j., and came unto....... 5265
Jg 17:8 the house of Micah, as he j....... 6213,1870
Lu 10:33 But a certain Samaritan, as he j.,..*3593*
Ac 9:3 as he j., he came near Damascus:...... *4198*
Ac 9:7 the men which j. with him stood........ *4922*
Ac 26:13 me and them which j. with me.......... *4198*

JOURNEYING See also JOURNEYINGS.
Nu 10:2 and for the j. of the camps............... 4550
Nu 10:29 We are j. into the place of which....... 5265
Lu 13:22 and j. toward Jerusalem............ *4197,4160*

JOURNEYINGS
Nu 10:28 the j. of the children of Israel............ 4550
2Co 11:26 in j. often, in perils of waters,........... *3597*

JOURNEYS
Ge 13:3 he went on his j. from the south........ 4550
Ex 17:1 after their j., according to the........... 4550
Ex 40:36 Israel went onward in all their j......... 4550
Ex 40:38 of Israel, throughout all their j........... 4550
Nu 10:6 they shall blow an alarm for their j..... 4550
Nu 10:12 the children of Israel took their j........ 4550
Nu 33:1 are in the j. of the children of Israel,.. 4550
Nu 33:2 goings out according to their j.......... 4550
Nu 33:2 j. according to their goings out.......... 4550

JOY See also ENJOY; JOYED; JOYFUL; JOYING.
1Sa 18:6 king Saul, with tabrets, with j.,.......... 8057
1Ki 1:40 rejoiced with great j., so that the........ 8057
1Ch 12:40 abundantly: for there was j. in Israel... 8057
1Ch 15:16 by lifting up the voice with j............. 8057
1Ch 15:25 of the house of Obed-edom with j...... 8057
1Ch 29:9 the king also rejoiced with great j....... 8057
1Ch 29:17 now have I seen with j. thy people,...... 8057
2Ch 20:27 to go again to Jerusalem with j.;........ 8057
2Ch 30:26 there was great j. in Jerusalem: for.... 8057
Ezr 3:12 and many shouted aloud for j.:............ 8057
Ezr 3:13 discern the noise of the shout of j...... 8057
Ezr 6:16 of this house of God with j................ 2305
Ezr 6:22 kept...bread seven days with j.:......... 8057
Ne 8:10 the j. of the Lord is your strength...... 2304
Ne 12:43 made them rejoice with great j.:........ 8057
Ne 12:43 that the j. of Jerusalem was heard...... 8057
Es 8:16 had light, and gladness, and j.,.......... 8342
Es 8:17 the Jews had j. and gladness, a.......... 8057
Es 9:22 turned unto them from sorrow to j.,... 8057
Es 9:22 make them days of feasting and j.,..... 8057
Job 8:19 Behold, this is the j. of his way,......... 4885
Job 20:5 and the j. of the hypocrite but for...... 8057
Job 29:13 the widow's heart to sing for j........... 7442
Job 33:26 he shall see his face with j.: for he..... 8643
Job 38:7 all the sons of God shouted for j.?............
Job 41:22 sorrow is turned into j. before him..........
Ps 5:11 let them ever shout for j., because...........
Ps 16:11 in thy presence is fulness of j.;.......... 8057
Ps 21:1 The king shall j. in thy strength,........ 8055
Ps 27:6 in his tabernacle sacrifices of j.;......... 8643
Ps 30:5 but j. cometh in the morning............. 7440
Ps 32:11 shout for j., all ye that are upright............
Ps 35:27 Let them shout for j., and be glad,...........
Ps 42:4 with the voice of j. and praise,........... 7440
Ps 43:4 God, unto God my exceeding j.:.......... 1524
Ps 48:2 the j. of the whole earth, is mount..... 4885
Ps 51:8 Make me to hear j. and gladness;...... 8342
Ps 51:12 unto me the j. of thy salvation;.......... 8342
Ps 65:13 corn; they shout for j., they also sing.......
Ps 67:4 let the nations be glad and sing for j.:.......
Ps 105:43 brought forth his people with j.,......... 8342
Ps 126:5 that sow in tears shall reap in j.......... 7440
Ps 132:9 and let thy saints shout for j............ 7442
Ps 132:16 her saints shall shout aloud for j......... 7442
Ps 137:6 not Jerusalem above my chief j.......... 8057
Pr 12:20 but to the counsellors of peace is j..... 8057
Pr 14:10 doth not intermeddle with his j.......... 8057
Pr 15:21 Folly is j. to him that is destitute of.... 8057
Pr 15:23 man hath j. by the answer of his........ 8057
Pr 17:21 and the father of a fool hath no j....... 8056
Pr 21:15 It is j. to the just to do judgment:...... 8057
Pr 23:24 begetteth a wise child shall have j....... 8056
Ec 2:10 withheld not my heart from any j.;..... 8057
Ec 2:26 wisdom, and knowledge, and j.:........... 8057
Ec 5:20 answereth him in the j. of his heart.... 8057
Ec 9:7 eat thy bread with j., and drink thy.... 8057
Isa 9:3 the nation, and not increased the j.:.... 8057
Isa 9:3 they j. before thee according to.......... 8055
Isa 9:3 according to the j. in harvest,............ 8055
Isa 9:17 shall have no j. in their young men,.... 8055
Isa 12:3 with j. shall ye draw water out of....... 8342
Isa 16:10 and j. out of the plentiful field;........... 1524
Isa 22:13 j. and gladness, slaying oxen, and....... 8342
Isa 24:8 endeth, the j. of the harp ceaseth....... 4885
Isa 24:11 all j. is darkened, the mirth of the...... 8057
Isa 29:19 meek also shall increase their j.......... 8057
Isa 32:13 yea, upon all the houses of j. in the.... 4885
Isa 32:14 a j. of wild asses, a pasture of........... 4885
Isa 35:2 rejoice even with j. and singing:.......... 1525
Isa 35:10 with songs and everlasting j. upon...... 8057
Isa 35:10 they shall obtain j. and gladness,........ 8057
Isa 51:3 j. and gladness shall be found........... 8342
Isa 51:11 everlasting j. shall be upon their........ 8057
Isa 51:11 they shall obtain gladness and j.;........ 8057
Isa 52:9 Break forth into j., sing together,.............
Isa 55:12 For ye shall go out with j., and be..... 8057
Isa 60:15 a j. of many generations.................... 4885
Isa 61:3 the oil of j. for mourning, the.............. 8342
Isa 61:7 everlasting j. shall be unto them........ 8057
Isa 65:14 servants shall sing for j. of heart,....... 2898
Isa 65:18 a rejoicing, and her people a j.......... 4885
Isa 65:19 Jerusalem, and j. in my people:.......... 7796
Isa 66:5 he shall appear to your j., and........... 8057
Isa 66:10 love her: rejoice for j. with her,......... 4885
Jer 15:16 the j. and rejoicing of mine heart:....... 8342
Jer 31:13 I will turn their mourning into j.,........ 8342
Jer 33:9 And it shall be to me a name of j.,...... 8342
Jer 33:11 The voice of j., and the voice of........ 8342
Jer 48:27 spakest of him, thou skippedst for j.... 8342
Jer 48:33 j. and gladness is taken from the........ 8057
Jer 49:25 of praise not left, the city of my j.!.... 4885
La 2:15 beauty, The j. of the whole earth?..... 4885
La 5:15 The j. of our heart is ceased; our...... 4885
Eze 24:25 the j. of their glory, the desire of....... 4885
Eze 36:5 with the j. of all their heart,............ 8057
Ho 9:1 Rejoice not, O Israel, for j., as.......... 1524
Joe 1:12 j. is withered away from the sons...... 8342
Joe 1:16 j. and gladness from the house of....... 8057
Hab 3:18 I will j. in the God of my salvation..... 1523
Zep 3:17 he will rejoice over thee with j.;........ 8057

Zep 3:17 he will j. over thee with singing......... 1523
Zec 8:19 house of Judah j. and gladness,.......... 8342
Mt 2:10 rejoiced with exceeding great j.. .... *5479*
Mt 13:20 **word, and anon with j. receiveth**... *5479*
Mt 13:44 **for j. thereof goeth and selleth all**. *5479*
Mt 25:21, 23 **enter thou into the j. of thy**...... *5479*
Mt 28:8 sepulchre with fear and great j.; *5479*
Lu 1:14 thou shalt have j. and gladness; *5479*
Lu 1:44 the babe leaped in my womb for j.. .... *20*
Lu 2:10 bring you good tidings of great j., ... *5479*
Lu 6:23 **ye in that day, and leap for j.:** ....
Lu 8:13 **hear, receive the word with j.;** *5479*
Lu 10:17 the seventy returned again with j., ... *5479*
Lu 15:7 **j. shall be in heaven over one**........ *5479*
Lu 15:10 **is j. in the presence of the angels**.. *5479*
Lu 24:41 while they yet believed not for j., ... *5479*
Lu 24:52 returned to Jerusalem with great j.:...... *5479*
Joh 3:29 this my j. therefore is fulfilled............ *5479*
Joh 15:11 **you, that my j. might remain in**.... *5479*
Joh 15:11 **and that your j. might be full**....... *5479*
Joh 16:20 **your sorrow shall be turned into j.**.. *5479*
Joh 16:21 **for j. that a man is born into the**.. *5479*
Joh 16:22 **your j. no man taketh from you**.... *5479*
Joh 16:24 **receive, that your j. may be full**.... *5479*
Joh 17:13 **have my j. fulfilled in themselves**...*5479*
Ac 2:28 thou shalt make me full of j. with....... *2167*
Ac 8:8 And there was great j. in that city...... *5479*
Ac 13:52 the disciples were filled with j., and.... *5479*
Ac 15:3 caused great j. unto all the brethren. .. *5479*
Ac 20:24 I might finish my course with j., ... *5479*
Ro 5:11 j. in God through our Lord Jesus *2744*
Ro 14:17 peace, and j. in the Holy Ghost. *5479*
Ro 15:13 fill you with all j. and peace in.......... *5479*
Ro 15:32 That I may come unto you with j........ *5479*
2Co 1:24 faith, but are helpers of your j.:......... *5479*
2Co 2:3 in you all, that my j. is...of you all. *5479*
2Co 2:3 in you all, that...is the j. of you all. ....
2Co 7:13 more joyed we for the j. of Titus, ... *5479*
2Co 8:2 abundance of their j. and their deep.... *5479*
Ga 5:22 fruit of the Spirit is love, j., peace,..... *5479*
Php 1:4 for you all making request with j.,...... *5479*
Php 1:25 for your furtherance and j. of faith;...... *5479*
Php 2:2 Fulfill ye my j., that ye be............... *5479*
Php 2:17 faith, I j., and rejoice with you all....... *5463*
Php 2:18 For the same cause also do ye j., ... *5463*
Php 4:1 and longed for, my j. and crown, ... *5479*
1Th 1:6 affliction, with j. of the Holy Ghost:.... *5479*
1Th 2:19 what is our hope, or j., or crown of ... *5479*
1Th 2:20 For ye are our glory and j.............. *5479*
1Th 3:9 for all the j....for your sakes before.... *5479*
1Th 3:9 wherewith we j. for your sakes *5463*
2Ti 1:4 tears, that I may be filled with j.;....... *5479*
Phm 7 we have great j. and consolation *5485*
Phm 20 let me have j. of thee in the Lord: *3685*
Heb 12:2 who for the j. that was set before...... *5479*
Heb 13:17 that they may do it with j., and not.... *5479*
Jas 1:2 count it all j. when ye fall into.......... *5479*
Jas 4:9 mourning, and your j. to heaviness. *5479*
1Pe 1:8 rejoice with j. unspeakable and full...... *5479*
1Pe 4:13 may be glad also with exceeding j.. .... *21*
1Jo 1:4 unto you, that your j. may be full....... *5479*
2Jo 12 face to face, that our j. may be full..... *5479*
3Jo 4 I have no greater j. than to hear......... *5479*
Jude 24 of his glory with exceeding j................ *20*

JOYED
2Co 7:13 the more j. we for the joy of Titus, ... *5463*

JOYFUL
1Ki 8:66 went unto their tents j. and glad of..... 8056
Ezr 6:22 for the Lord had made them j., ... 8055
Es 5:9 Haman went forth that day j. and....... 8056
Job 3:7 let no j. voice come therein. 7445
Ps 5:11 them also that love thy name be j. 5970
Ps 35:9 my soul shall be j. in the Lord:......... 1523
Ps 63:5 mouth shall praise thee with j. lips: 7445
Ps 66:1 Make a j. noise unto God, all ye.............
Ps 81:1 make a j. noise unto the God of..............
Ps 89:15 the people that know the j. sound: 8643
Ps 95:1 let us make a j. noise to the rock..........
Ps 95:2 make a j. noise unto him with psalms.......
Ps 96:12 Let the field be j., and all that is........ 5937
Ps 98:4 Make a j. noise unto the Lord, all...........
Ps 98:6 make a j. noise before the Lord, the.........
Ps 98:8 hands: let the hills be j. together 7442
Ps 100:1 Make a j. noise unto the Lord, all...........
Ps 113:9 and to be a j. mother of children........ 8056
Ps 149:2 children of Zion be j. in their King...... 1523
Ps 149:5 Let the saints be j. in glory: let.......... 5937
Ec 7:14 In the day of prosperity be j., but...... 2896
Isa 49:13 Sing, O heavens; and be j., O earth; .. 1523
Isa 56:7 them j. in my house of prayer: 8055
Isa 61:10 my soul shall be j. in my God;........... 1523
2Co 7:4 I am exceeding j. in all our............... *5479*

JOYFULLY
Ec 9:9 Live j. with the wife whom thou 2416
Lu 19:6 came down, and received him j.......... *5463*
Heb 10:34 took j. the spoiling of your......... *3326,5479*

JOYFULNESS
De 28:47 not the Lord thy God with j.,............ 8057
Col 1:11 and longsuffering with j.; *5479*

JOYING
Col 2:5 spirit, j. and beholding your order, ... *5463*

JOYOUS
Isa 22:2 stirs, a tumultuous city, a j. city: 5947
Isa 23:7 Is this your j. city, whose antiquity..... 5947
Isa 32:13 all the houses of joy in the j. city: 5947
Heb 12:11 for the present seemeth to be j., ... *5479*

JOZABAD (joz'-a-bad) See also JEHOZABAD; JOSABAD.
1Ch 12:20 J., and Jediael, and Michael, and........ 3107
1Ch 12:20 J., and Elihu, and Zilthai, captians 3107
2Ch 31:13 and Jerimoth, and J., and Eliel,.......... 3107
2Ch 35:9 Jeiel and J., chief of the Levites.......... 3107
Ezr 8:33 with them was J. the son of Jeshua, ... 3107
Ezr 10:22 Ishmael, Nethaneel, J., and Elasah. 3107
Ezr 10:23 Also of the Levites; J., and Shimei, ... 3107
Ne 8:7 Azariah, J., Hanan, Pelaiah, and......... 3107
Ne 11:16 Shabbathai and J., of the chief of......... 3107

JOZACHAR (joz'-a-kar) See also ZABAD.
2Ki 12:21 For J. the son of Shimeath, and.......... 3108

JOZADAK (joz'-a-dak) See also JEHOZADAK; JOSEDECH.
Ezr 3:2 stood up Jeshua the son of J.............. 3136
Ezr 3:8 and Jeshua the son of J., and the......... 3136
Ezr 5:2 and Jeshua the son of J., and began...... 3136
Ezr 10:18 of the sons of Jeshua the son of J., ... 3136
Ne 12:26 the son of Jeshua, the son of J., ... 3136

JUBAL (ju'-bal)
Ge 4:21 And his brother's name was J.: he 3106

JUBILE (ju'-bi-lee)
Le 25:9 the trumpet of the j. to sound on....... 8643
Le 25:10 it shall be a j. unto you; and ye 3104
Le 25:11 A j. shall that fiftieth year be unto...... 3104
Le 25:12 For it is the j.; it shall be holy unto..... 3104
Le 25:13 In the year of this j. ye shall return.... 3104
Le 25:15 after the j. thou shalt buy of thy......... 3104
Le 25:28 hath bought it until the year of j. 3104
Le 25:28 in the j. it shall go out, and he shall.... 3104
Le 25:30 it shall not go out in the j................. 3104
Le 25:31 and they shall go out in the j.............. 3104
Le 25:33 shall go out in the year of j................ 3104
Le 25:40 shall serve thee unto the year of j........ 3104
Le 25:50 was sold to him unto the year of j........ 3104
Le 25:52 but few years unto the year of j., ... 3104
Le 25:54 then he shall go out in the year of j.,.. 3104
Le 27:17 sanctify his field from the year of j., ... 3104
Le 27:18 if he sanctify his field after the j.,......... 3104
Le 27:18 remain, even unto the year of the j., .. 3104
Le 27:21 field, when it goeth out in the j., ... 3104
Le 27:23 even unto the year of the j.:.............. 3104
Le 27:24 year of the j. the field shall return...... 3104
Nu 36:4 when the j. of the children of Israel.... 3104

JUBILEE See JUBILE.

JUCAL (ju'-kal) See also JEHUCAL.
Jer 38:1 and J. the son of Shelemiah, and......... 3116

JUDA (ju'-dah) See also JUDAH.
Mt 2:6 thou Bethlehem, in the land of J., ... *2455*
Mt 2:6 the least among the princes of J.: *2455*
Mk 6:3 of James, and Joses, and of J., ... *2455*
Lu 1:39 with haste, into a city of J.;............. *2448*
Lu 3:26 of Joseph, which was the son of J., ... *2455*
Lu 3:30 of Simeon, which was the son of J., ... *2455*
Lu 3:33 Phares, which was the son of J., ... *2455*
Heb 7:14 that our Lord sprang out of J.; *2455*
Re 5:5 behold, the Lion of the tribe of J., ... *2455*
Re 7:5 Of the tribe of J. were sealed.............. *2455*

JUDAEA (ju-de'-ah) See also JEWRY; JUDAH; JUDEA.
Mt 2:1 Jesus was born in Bethlehem of J........ *2449*
Mt 2:5 said unto him, In Bethlehem of J........ *2449*
Mt 2:22 heard that Archelaus did reign in J. *2449*
Mt 3:1 preaching in the wilderness of J.,......... *2449*
Mt 3:5 out to him Jerusalem, and all J., ... *2449*
Mt 4:25 and from Jerusalem, and from J., ... *2449*
Mt 19:1 the coasts of J. beyond Jordan;.......... *2449*
Mt 24:16 **be in J. flee into the mountains**: ... *2449*
Mk 1:5 out unto him all the land of J.,.......... *2449*
Mk 3:7 Galilee followed him, and from J., ... *2449*
Mk 10:1 and cometh into the coasts of J. *2449*
Mk 13:14 **that be in J. flee to the mountains**: *2449*
Lu 1:5 the days of Herod, the king of J., ... *2449*
Lu 1:65 all the hill country of J.. .... *2449*
Lu 2:4 out of the city of Nazareth, into J., ... *2449*
Lu 3:1 Pontius Pilate being governor of J., ... *2449*
Lu 5:17 out of every town of Galilee, and J.,... *2449*
Lu 6:17 multitude of people out of all J........... *2449*
Lu 7:17 him went forth throughout all J.,......... *2449*
Lu 21:21 **are in J. flee to the mountains;**..... *2449*
Joh 3:22 his disciples into the land of J.;........... *2449*
Joh 4:3 He left J., and departed again into........ *2449*
Joh 4:47 that Jesus was come out of J. into...... *2449*
Joh 4:54 he was come out of J. into Galilee....... *2449*
Joh 7:3 Depart hence, and go into J., that....... *2449*
Joh 11:7 disciples, **Let us go into J. again.** ... *2449*
Ac 1:8 **and in all J., and in Samaria, and.** *2449*
Ac 2:9 dwellers in Mesopotamia, and in J., ... *2449*
Ac 2:14 Ye men of J., and all ye that dwell..... *2453*
Ac 8:1 the regions of J. and Samaria, ... *2449*
Ac 9:31 rest throughout all J. and Galilee........ *2449*
Ac 10:37 was published throughout all J., ... *2449*
Ac 11:1 and brethren that were in J. heard *2449*
Ac 11:29 unto the brethren which dwelt in J.: ... *2449*
Ac 12:19 he went down from J. to Caesarea, ... *2449*
Ac 15:1 men which came down from J. *2449*
Ac 21:10 there came down from J. a certain *2449*
Ac 26:20 and throughout all the coasts of J.,...... *2449*
Ac 28:21 neither received letters out of J.......... *2449*
Ro 15:31 from them that do not believe in J.;.... *2449*
2Co 1:16 be brought on my way toward J.......... *2449*
Ga 1:22 by face unto the churches of J............ *2449*
1Th 2:14 which in J. are in Christ Jesus: *2449*

JUDAH (ju'-dah) See also BETHLEHEM-JUDAH; JUDA; JUDAH'S; JUDAS; JUDAEA; JUDE.
Ge 29:35 therefore she called his name J.;........ 3063
Ge 35:23 and Levi, and J., and Issachar, and...... 3063
Ge 37:26 And J. said unto his brethren, What.... 3063
Ge 38:1 J. went down from his brethren, ... 3063
Ge 38:2 And J. saw there a daughter of a....... 3063
Ge 38:6 J. took a wife for Er his firstborn,....... 3063
Ge 38:8 J. said unto Onan, Go in unto thy 3063
Ge 38:11 said J. to Tamar his daughter in........... 3063
Ge 38:12 J. was comforted, and went up unto ... 3063
Ge 38:15 When J. saw her, he thought her to ... 3063
Ge 38:20 J. sent the kid by the hand of his........ 3063
Ge 38:22 And he returned to J., and said, I....... 3063
Ge 38:23 J. said, let her take it to her, lest...... 3063
Ge 38:24 that it was told J., saying, Tamar....... 3063
Ge 38:24 J. said, Bring her forth, and let her.... 3063
Ge 38:26 J. acknowledged them, and said, ... 3063
Ge 43:3 J. spake unto him, saying, The man.... 3063
Ge 43:8 J. said unto Israel his father, Send 3063
Ge 44:14 And J. and his brethren came to........ 3063
Ge 44:16 J. said, What shall we say unto my..... 3063
Ge 44:18 J. came near unto him, and said,........ 3063
Ge 46:12 the sons of J.; Er, and Onan, and........ 3063
Ge 46:28 he sent J. before him unto Joseph, ... 3063
Ge 49:8 J., thou art he whom thy brethren 3063
Ge 49:9 J. is a lion's whelp: from the prey, ... 3063
Ge 49:10 sceptre shall not depart from J., ... 3063
Ex 1:2 Reuben, Simeon, Levi, and J.,........... 3063
Ex 31:2 the son of Hur, of the tribe of J.: 3063
Ex 35:30 the son of Hur, of the tribe of J.; 3063
Ex 38:22 the son of Hur, of the tribe of J., ... 3063
Nu 1:7 J.; Nahshon the son of Amminadab. ... 3063
Nu 1:26 children of J., by their generations, ... 3063
Nu 1:27 of them, even of the tribe of J., ... 3063
Nu 2:3 of the standard of the camp of J. 3063
Nu 2:3 be captain of the children of J............ 3063
Nu 2:9 numbered in the camp of J. were an.... 3063
Nu 7:12 of Amminadab, of the tribe of J.: 3063
Nu 10:14 of the camp of the children of J. 3063
Nu 13:6 Of the tribe of J., Caleb the son of..... 3063

Nu 26:19 the sons of **J.** were Er and Onan: 3063
Nu 26:20 sons of **J.** after their families were: 3063
Nu 26:22 are the families of **J.** according to....... 3063
Nu 34:19 Of the tribe of **J.**, Caleb the son of...... 3063
De 27:12 and Levi, and **J.**, and Issachar, and...... 3063
De 33:7 this is the blessing of **J.**: and he 3063
De 33:7 said, Hear, Lord, the voice of **J.**, ... 3063
De 34:2 all the land of **J.**, unto the utmost 3063
Jos 7:1 son of Zerah, of the tribe of **J.**, took... 3063
Jos 7:16 and the tribe of **J.** was taken:............ 3063
Jos 7:17 he brought the family of **J.**; and he...... 3063
Jos 7:18 Zerah, of the tribe of **J.**, was taken. ... 3063
Jos 11:21 and from all the mountains of **J.**,........ 3063
Jos 14:6 of **J.** came unto Joshua in Gilgal: 3063
Jos 15:1 lots of the tribe of the children of **J.** ... 3063
Jos 15:12 is the coast of the children of **J.**.......... 3063
Jos 15:13 a part among the children of **J.**, ... 3063
Jos 15:20, 21 of the tribe of the children of **J.**...... 3063
Jos 15:63 children of **J.** could not drive them 3063
Jos 15:63 dwell with the children of **J.** unto 3063
Jos 18:5 **J.** shall abide in their coast on the 3063
Jos 18:11 forth between the children of **J.**.......... 3063
Jos 18:14 a city of the children of **J.**.................. 3063
Jos 19:1 inheritance of the children of **J.**.......... 3063
Jos 19:9 of the portion of the children of **J.**...... 3063
Jos 19:9 part of the children of **J.** was too 3063
Jos 19:34 and to **J.** upon Jordan toward the 3063
Jos 20:7 is Hebron, in the mountain of **J.**.......... 3063
Jos 21:4 had by lot out of the tribe of **J.**,......... 3063
Jos 21:9 out of the tribe of the children of **J.**,... 3063
Jos 21:11 is Hebron, in the hill country of **J.**,..... 3063
Jg 1:2 And the Lord said, **J.** shall go up: 3063
Jg 1:3 **J.** said unto Simeon his brother,........ 3063
Jg 1:4 **J.** went up; and the Lord delivered...... 3063
Jg 1:8 **J.** had fought against Jerusalem, ... 3063
Jg 1:9 children of **J.** went down to fight......... 3063
Jg 1:10 And **J.** went against the Canaanites...... 3063
Jg 1:16 of **J.** into the wilderness of **J.**,........... 3063
Jg 1:17 **J.** went with Simeon his brother, ... 3063
Jg 1:18 **J.** took Gaza with the coast thereof, ... 3063
Jg 1:19 Lord was with **J.**; and he drave out 3063
Jg 10:9 over Jordan to fight also against **J.**,...... 3063
Jg 15:9 Philistines went...and pitched in **J.**,...... 3063
Jg 15:10 men of **J.** said, Why are ye come up... 3063
Jg 15:11 thousand men of **J.** went to the top 3063
Jg 17:7 Bethlehem-judah to the family of **J.**,.... 3063
Jg 18:12 pitched in Kirjath-jearim, in **J.**:.......... 3063
Jg 20:18 the Lord said, **J.** shall go up first. 3063
Ru 1:7 way to return unto the land of **J.**. 3063
Ru 4:12 Pharez, whom Tamar bare unto **J.**,...... 3063
1Sa 11:8 and the men of **J.** thirty thousand....... 3063
1Sa 15:4 and ten thousand men of **J.**.............. 3063
1Sa 17:1 at Shochoh, which belongeth to **J.**, ... 3063
1Sa 17:52 the men of Israel and of **J.** arose, ... 3063
1Sa 18:16 But all Israel and **J.** loved David, ... 3063
1Sa 22:5 and get thee into the land of **J.**.......... 3063
1Sa 23:3 Behold, we be afraid here in **J.**........... 3063
1Sa 23:23 throughout all the thousands of **J.**....... 3063
1Sa 27:6 pertaineth unto the kings of **J.**........... 3063
1Sa 27:10 David said, Against the south of **J.**, ... 3063
1Sa 30:14 the coast which belongeth to **J.**,.......... 3063
1Sa 30:16 Philistines, and out of the land of **J.**. ... 3063
1Sa 30:26 of the spoil unto the elders of **J.**, ... 3063
2Sa 1:18 children of **J.** the use of the bow:....... 3063
2Sa 2:1 I go up into any of the cities of **J.**?...... 3063
2Sa 2:4 the men of **J.** came, and there they.... 3063
2Sa 2:4 David king over the house of **J.**. 3063
2Sa 2:7 house of **J.** have anointed me king...... 3063
2Sa 2:10 But the house of **J.** followed David. 3063
2Sa 2:11 king of Hebron over the house of **J.** ... 3063
2Sa 3:8 which against **J.** do shew kindness...... 3063
2Sa 3:10 of David over Israel and over **J.**,........ 3063
2Sa 5:5 he reigned over **J.** seven years and 3063
2Sa 5:5 three years over all Israel and **J.**......... 3063
2Sa 6:2 were with him from Baale of **J.**,........ 3063
2Sa 11:11 and Israel, and **J.**, abide in tents; 3063
2Sa 12:8 thee in the house of Israel and of **J.**; .. 3063
2Sa 19:11 Speak unto the elders of **J.**, saying, ... 3063
2Sa 19:14 bowed the heart of all the men of **J.**, .. 3063
2Sa 19:15 **J.** came to Gilgal, to go to meet the... 3063
2Sa 19:16 the men of **J.** to meet king David....... 3063
2Sa 19:40 the people of **J.** conducted the king, ... 3063
2Sa 19:41 the men of **J.** stolen thee away,......... 3063
2Sa 19:42 all the men of **J.** answered the men.... 3063
2Sa 19:43 of Israel answered the men of **J.**,....... 3063
2Sa 19:43 words of the men of **J.** were fiercer ... 3063
2Sa 20:2 the men of **J.** clave unto their king, ... 3063
2Sa 20:4 Assemble me the men of **J.** within...... 3063
2Sa 20:5 went to assemble the men of **J.**:......... 3063
2Sa 21:2 zeal to the children of Israel and **J.**:.... 3063
2Sa 24:1 to say, Go, number Israel and **J.**......... 3063
2Sa 24:7 they went out to the south of **J.**, ... 3063
2Sa 24:9 of **J.** were five hundred thousand 3063
1Ki 1:9 the men of **J.** the king's servants: 3063
1Ki 1:35 to be ruler over Israel and over **J.**. 3063
1Ki 2:32 of Jether, captain of the host of **J.**...... 3063
1Ki 4:20 **J.** and Israel were many, as the......... 3063
1Ki 4:25 **J.** and Israel dwelt safely, every 3063
1Ki 12:17 which dwelt in the cities of **J.**, ... 3063
1Ki 12:20 of David, but the tribe of **J.** only......... 3063
1Ki 12:21 he assembled all the house of **J.**, ... 3063
1Ki 12:23 the son of Solomon, king of **J.**, ... 3063
1Ki 12:23 all the house of **J.** and Benjamin,........ 3063
1Ki 12:27 even unto Rehoboam king of **J.**,.......... 3063
1Ki 12:27 go again to Rehoboam king of **J.**. 3063
1Ki 12:32 like unto the feast that is in **J.**,.......... 3063
1Ki 13:1 there came a man of God out of **J.**...... 3063
1Ki 13:12 of God went, which came from **J.**........ 3063
1Ki 13:14 man of God that camest from **J.**? 3063
1Ki 13:21 the man of God that came from **J.**,...... 3063
1Ki 14:21 the son of Solomon reigned in **J.**........ 3063
1Ki 14:22 **J.** did evil in the sight of the Lord, ... 3063
1Ki 14:29 of the chronicles of the kings of **J.**? 3063
1Ki 15:1 of Nebat reigned Abijam over **J.**.......... 3063
1Ki 15:7 of the chronicles of the kings of **J.**? 3063
1Ki 15:9 king of Israel reigned Asa over **J.**........ 3063
1Ki 15:17 king of Israel went up against **J.**, ... 3063
1Ki 15:17 go out or come in to Asa king of **J.**. ... 3063
1Ki 15:22 a proclamation throughout all **J.**;......... 3063
1Ki 15:23 of the chronicles of the kings of **J.**? 3063
1Ki 15:25 the second year of Asa king of **J.**....... 3063
1Ki 15:28, 33 the third year of Asa king of **J.**...... 3063
1Ki 16:8 and sixth year of Asa king of **J.** 3063
1Ki 16:10 and seventh year of Asa king of **J.**, ... 3063
1Ki 16:15 and seventh year of Asa king of **J.** 3063
1Ki 16:23 and first year of Asa king of **J.** 3063
1Ki 16:29 and eighth year of Asa king of **J.**......... 3063
1Ki 19:3 Beer-sheba, which belongeth to **J.**,...... 3063
1Ki 22:2 king of **J.** came down to the king 3063
1Ki 22:10 and Jehoshaphat the king of **J.** 3063
1Ki 22:29 Jehoshaphat the king of **J.** went up..... 3063
1Ki 22:41 son of Asa began to reign over **J.** 3063
1Ki 22:45 of the chronicles of the kings of **J.**? 3063
1Ki 22:51 year of Jehoshaphat king of **J.**,.......... 3063
2Ki 1:17 the son of Jehoshaphat king of **J.**;........ 3063
2Ki 3:1 year of Jehoshaphat king of **J.**,............ 3063
2Ki 3:7 sent to Jehoshaphat the king of **J.**, ... 3063
2Ki 3:9 of Israel went, and the king of **J.**, ... 3063
2Ki 3:14 of Jehoshaphat the king of **J.**, ... 3063
2Ki 8:16 Jehoshaphat being then king of **J.**, ... 3063
2Ki 8:16 son of Jehoshaphat king of **J.** began.... 3063
2Ki 8:19 Lord would not destroy **J.** for David ... 3063
2Ki 8:20 revolted from under the hand of **J.**, ... 3063
2Ki 8:22 revolted from under the hand of **J.** 3063
2Ki 8:23 of the chronicles of the kings of **J.**? 3063
2Ki 8:25 Jehoram king of **J.** begin to reign. 3063
2Ki 8:29 king of **J.** went down to see Joram..... 3063
2Ki 9:16 of **J.** was come down to see Joram. 3063
2Ki 9:21 and Ahaziah king of **J.** went out......... 3063
2Ki 9:27 Ahaziah the king of **J.** saw this, he 3063
2Ki 9:29 began Ahaziah to reign over **J.**. 3063
2Ki 10:13 the brethren of Ahaziah king of **J.**, ... 3063
2Ki 12:18 Jehoash king of **J.** took all the............ 3063
2Ki 12:18 fathers, kings of **J.**, had dedicated, ... 3063
2Ki 12:19 of the chronicles of the kings of **J.**? 3063
2Ki 13:1 Joash the son of Ahaziah king of **J.**...... 3063
2Ki 13:10 seventh year of Joash king of **J.**.......... 3063
2Ki 13:12 fought against Amaziah king of **J.**, ... 3063
2Ki 14:1 Amaziah the son of Joash king of **J.**. ... 3063
2Ki 14:9 Israel sent to Amaziah king of **J.**, ... 3063
2Ki 14:10 fall, even thou, and **J.** with thee? 3063
2Ki 14:11 he and Amaziah king of **J.** looked 3063
2Ki 14:11 which belongeth to **J.**........................ 3063
2Ki 14:12 And **J.** was put to the worse before.... 3063
2Ki 14:13 of Israel took Amaziah king of **J.**, ... 3063
2Ki 14:15 he fought with Amaziah king of **J.**,....... 3063
2Ki 14:17 the son of Joash king of **J.** lived......... 3063
2Ki 14:18 of the chronicles of the kings of **J.**? 3063
2Ki 14:21 all the people of **J.** took Azariah,........ 3063
2Ki 14:22 built Elath, and restored it to **J.**,........ 3063
2Ki 14:23 Amaziah the son of Joash king of **J.** 3063
2Ki 14:28 and Hamath, which belonged to **J.**,...... 3063
2Ki 15:1 son of Amaziah king of **J.** to reign. 3063
2Ki 15:6 of the chronicles of the kings of **J.**? 3063
2Ki 15:8 eighth year of Azariah king of **J.** 3063
2Ki 15:13 thirtieth year of Uzziah king of **J.**; 3063
2Ki 15:17 thirtieth year of Azariah king of **J.**....... 3063
2Ki 15:23 fiftieth year of Azariah king of **J.** 3063
2Ki 15:27 fiftieth year of Azariah king of **J.**......... 3063
2Ki 15:32 son of Uzziah king of **J.** to reign. 3063
2Ki 15:36 of the chronicles of the kings of **J.**? 3063
2Ki 15:37 the Lord began to send against **J.** 3063
2Ki 16:1 Jotham king of **J.** began to reign. 3063
2Ki 16:19 of the chronicles of the kings of **J.**? 3063
2Ki 17:1 the twelfth year of Ahaz king of **J.** 3063
2Ki 17:13 against Israel, and against **J.**, ... 3063
2Ki 17:18 none left but the tribe of **J.** only. 3063
2Ki 17:19 Also **J.** kept not the commandments ... 3063
2Ki 18:1 of Ahaz king of **J.** began to reign. 3063
2Ki 18:5 like him among all the kings of **J.**, ... 3063
2Ki 18:13 against all the fenced cities of **J.**, ... 3063
2Ki 18:14 Hezekiah king of **J.** sent to the king.... 3063
2Ki 18:14 appointed unto Hezekiah king of **J.** 3063
2Ki 18:16 Hezekiah king of **J.** had overlaid,........ 3063
2Ki 18:22 and hath said to **J.** and Jerusalem, ... 3063
2Ki 19:10 ye speak to Hezekiah king of **J.**,.......... 3063
2Ki 19:30 that is escaped of the house of **J.**........ 3063
2Ki 20:20 of the chronicles of the kings of **J.**? 3063
2Ki 21:11 Manasseh king of **J.** hath done these... 3063
2Ki 21:11 made **J.** also to sin with his idols:....... 3063
2Ki 21:12 such evil upon Jerusalem and **J.**, ... 3063
2Ki 21:16 sin wherewith he made **J.** to sin, ... 3063
2Ki 21:17, 25 the chronicles of the kings of **J.**?..... 3063
2Ki 22:13 for all **J.**, concerning the words of...... 3063
2Ki 22:16 book which the king of **J.** had read: 3063
2Ki 22:18 king of **J.** which sent you to inquire ... 3063
2Ki 23:1 the elders of **J.** and of Jerusalem........ 3063
2Ki 23:2 and all the men of **J.** and all the......... 3063
2Ki 23:5 kings of **J.** had ordained to burn......... 3063
2Ki 23:5 in the high places in the cities of **J.**, ... 3063
2Ki 23:8 the priests out of the cities of **J.**, ... 3063
2Ki 23:11 the horses that the kings of **J.** had 3063
2Ki 23:12 which the kings of **J.** had made,.......... 3063
2Ki 23:17 man of God, which came from **J.**,........ 3063
2Ki 23:22 of Israel, nor of the kings of **J.**; 3063
2Ki 23:24 that were spied in the land of **J.** 3063
2Ki 23:26 his anger was kindled against **J.**, ... 3063
2Ki 23:27 will remove **J.** also out of my sight, ... 3063
2Ki 23:28 of the chronicles of the kings of **J.**? 3063
2Ki 24:2 sent them against **J.** to destroy it,...... 3063
2Ki 24:3 of the Lord came this upon **J.**, ... 3063
2Ki 24:5 of the chronicles of the kings of **J.**? 3063
2Ki 24:12 Jehoiachin the king of **J.** went out....... 3063
2Ki 24:20 came to pass in Jerusalem and **J.**, ... 3063
2Ki 25:21 **J.** was carried away out of their......... 3063
2Ki 25:22 that remained in the land of **J.**, ... 3063
2Ki 25:27 captivity of Jehoiachin king of **J.**, ... 3063
2Ki 25:27 up the head of Jehoiachin king of **J.**, ... 3063
1Ch 2:1 Simeon, Levi, and **J.**, Isaachar,........... 3063
1Ch 2:3 the sons of **J.**; Er, and Onan, and 3063
1Ch 2:3 Er, the firstborn of **J.**, was evil in...... 3063
1Ch 2:4 Zerah. All the sons of **J.** were five. 3063
1Ch 2:10 prince of the children of **J.**;.............. 3063
1Ch 4:1 The sons of **J.**; Pharez, Hezron, ... 3063
1Ch 4:21 sons of Shelah the son of **J.** were, ... 3063
1Ch 4:27 multiply, like to the children of **J.**........ 3063
1Ch 4:41 the days of Hezekiah king of **J.**,.......... 3063
1Ch 5:2 **J.** prevailed above his brethren, ... 3063
1Ch 5:17 in the days of Jotham king of **J.**, ... 3063
1Ch 6:15 Lord carried away **J.** and Jerusalem.... 3063
1Ch 6:55 gave them Hebron in the land of **J.**,.... 3063
1Ch 6:57 Aaron then gave the cities of **J.**, ... 3063
1Ch 6:65 of the tribe of the children of **J.**, ... 3063
1Ch 9:1 book of the kings of Israel and **J.**, ... 3063
1Ch 9:3 dwelt of the children of **J.**, and of....... 3063
1Ch 9:4 children of Pharez the son of **J.**......... 3063
1Ch 12:16 of the children of Benjamin and **J.** 3063
1Ch 12:24 children of **J.** that bare shield and....... 3063
1Ch 13:6 which belonged to **J.**, to bring up 3063
1Ch 21:5 **J.** was four hundred threescore.......... 3063
1Ch 27:18 Of **J.**, Elihu, one of the brethren of 3063
1Ch 28:4 he hath chosen **J.** to be the ruler; 3063
1Ch 28:4 of the house of **J.**, the house of my.... 3063
2Ch 2:7 cunning men that are with me in **J.**...... 3063
2Ch 9:11 such seen before in the land of **J.**........ 3063

2Ch	10:17	Israel that dwelt in the cities of **J.**,	3063
2Ch	11:1	of the house of **J.** and Benjamin	3063
2Ch	11:3	the son of Solomon, king of **J.**,	3063
2Ch	11:3	to all Israel in **J.** and Benjamin,	3063
2Ch	11:5	and built cities for defence in **J.**.	3063
2Ch	11:10	Aijalon, and Hebron, which are in **J.**	3063
2Ch	11:12	having **J.** and Benjamin on his side.	3063
2Ch	11:14	their possession, and came to **J.**	3063
2Ch	11:17	strengthened the kingdom of **J.**,	3063
2Ch	11:23	the countries of **J.** and Benjamin,	3063
2Ch	12:4	fenced cities which pertained to **J.**,	3063
2Ch	12:5	Rehoboam, and to the princes of **J.**.	3063
2Ch	12:12	and also in **J.** things went well.	3063
2Ch	13:1	began Abijah to reign over **J.**.	3063
2Ch	13:13	so they were before **J.**, and the	3063
2Ch	13:14	when **J.** looked back, behold, the	3063
2Ch	13:15	Then the men of **J.** gave a shout:	3063
2Ch	13:15	as the men of **J.** shouted, it came	3063
2Ch	13:15	and all Israel before Abijah and **J.**	3063
2Ch	13:16	the children of Israel fled before **J.**	3063
2Ch	13:18	children of **J.** prevailed, because	3063
2Ch	14:4	commanded **J.** to seek the Lord God	3063
2Ch	14:5	all the cities of **J.** the high places,	3063
2Ch	14:6	And he build fenced cities in **J.**:	3063
2Ch	14:7	therefore he said unto **J.**, Let us	3063
2Ch	14:8	out of **J.** three hundred thousand;	3063
2Ch	14:12	before Asa, and before **J.**; and the	3063
2Ch	15:2	me, Asa, and all **J.** and Benjamin;	3063
2Ch	15:8	idols out of all the land of **J.** and	3063
2Ch	15:9	he gathered all **J.** and Benjamin,	3063
2Ch	15:15	And all **J.** rejoiced at the oath:	3063
2Ch	16:1	king of Israel came up against **J.**,	3063
2Ch	16:1	go out or come in to Asa king of **J.**.	3063
2Ch	16:6	Asa the king took all **J.**; and they	3063
2Ch	16:7	the seer came to Asa king of **J.**.	3063
2Ch	16:11	book of the kings of **J.** and Israel.	3063
2Ch	17:2	forces in all the fenced cities of **J.**,	3063
2Ch	17:2	set garrisons in the land of **J.**, and	3063
2Ch	17:5	**J.** brought to Jehoshaphat presents;	3063
2Ch	17:6	high places and groves out of **J.**,	3063
2Ch	17:7	to teach in the cities of **J.**,	3063
2Ch	17:9	they taught in **J.**, and had the book	3063
2Ch	17:9	throughout all the cities of **J.**,	3063
2Ch	17:10	the lands that were round about **J.**,	3063
2Ch	17:12	he built in **J.** castles, and cities of	3063
2Ch	17:13	much business in the cities of **J.**;	3063
2Ch	17:14	Of **J.**, the captains of thousands;	3063
2Ch	17:19	the fenced cities throughout all **J.**.	3063
2Ch	18:3	said unto Jehoshaphat king of **J.**,	3063
2Ch	18:9	Israel and Jehoshaphat king of **J.**	3063
2Ch	18:28	Jehoshaphat the king of **J.** went up	3063
2Ch	19:1	Jehoshaphat king of **J.** returned to	3063
2Ch	19:5	all the fenced cities of **J.**, city by	3063
2Ch	19:11	the ruler of the house of **J.**, for all	3063
2Ch	20:3	proclaimed a fast throughout all **J.**.	3063
2Ch	20:4	**J.** gathered themselves together, to	3063
2Ch	20:4	out of the cities of **J.** they came to	3063
2Ch	20:5	stood in the congregation of **J.** and	3063
2Ch	20:13	all **J.** stood before the Lord, with	3063
2Ch	20:15	he said, Hearken ye, all **J.**, and ye	3063
2Ch	20:17	Lord with you, O **J.** and Jerusalem:	3063
2Ch	20:18	all **J.** and the inhabitants of	3063
2Ch	20:20	stood and said, Hear me, O **J.**,	3063
2Ch	20:22	Seir, which were come against **J.**;	3063
2Ch	20:24	when **J.** came toward the watch	3063
2Ch	20:27	every man of **J.** and Jerusalem,	3063
2Ch	20:31	Jehoshaphat reigned over **J.**: he	3063
2Ch	20:35	Jehoshaphat king of **J.** join himself	3063
2Ch	21:3	things, with fenced cities in **J.**:	3063
2Ch	21:8	from under the dominion of **J.**,	3063
2Ch	21:10	revolted from under the hand of **J.**	3063
2Ch	21:11	high places in the mountains of **J.**,	3063
2Ch	21:11	and compelled **J.** thereto.	3063
2Ch	21:12	nor in the ways of Asa king of **J.**,	3063
2Ch	21:13	hast made **J.** and the inhabitants	3063
2Ch	21:17	they came up into **J.**, and brake	3063
2Ch	22:1	son of Jehoram king of **J.** reigned.	3063
2Ch	22:6	Jehoram king of **J.** went down to	3063
2Ch	22:8	found the princes of **J.**, and the	3063
2Ch	22:10	all the seed royal of the house of **J.**	3063
2Ch	23:2	they went about in **J.**, and gathered	3063
2Ch	23:2	the Levites out of all the cities of **J.**,	3063
2Ch	23:8	Levites and all **J.** did according to	3063
2Ch	24:5	Go out unto the cities of **J.**, and	3063
2Ch	24:6	the Levites to bring in out of **J.**	3063
2Ch	24:9	made a proclamation through **J.**	3063
2Ch	24:17	Jehoiada came the princes of **J.**,	3063
2Ch	24:18	wrath came upon **J.** and Jerusalem	3063
2Ch	24:23	they came to **J.** and Jerusalem,	3063
2Ch	25:5	Amaziah gathered **J.** together, and	3063
2Ch	25:5	of their fathers, throughout all **J.**	3063
2Ch	25:10	was greatly kindled against **J.**,	3063
2Ch	25:12	children of **J.** carry away captive,	3063
2Ch	25:13	fell upon the cities of **J.**, from	3063
2Ch	25:17	Amaziah king of **J.** took advice,	3063
2Ch	25:18	Israel sent to Amaziah king of **J.**,	3063
2Ch	25:19	fall, even thou, and **J.** with thee?	3063
2Ch	25:21	both he and Amaziah king of **J.**,	3063
2Ch	25:21	which belongeth to **J.**	3063
2Ch	25:22	**J.** was put to the worse before	3063
2Ch	25:23	of Israel took Amaziah king of **J.**,	3063
2Ch	25:25	son of Joash king of **J.** lived after	3063
2Ch	25:26	book of the kings of **J.** and Israel?	3063
2Ch	25:28	with his fathers in the city of **J.**.	3063
2Ch	26:1	all the people of **J.** took Uzziah,	3063
2Ch	26:2	built Eloth, and restored it to **J.**,	3063
2Ch	27:4	built cities in the mountains of **J.**,	3063
2Ch	27:7	book of the kings of Israel and **J.**.	3063
2Ch	28:6	slew in **J.** a hundred and twenty	3063
2Ch	28:9	of your fathers was wroth with **J.**,	3063
2Ch	28:10	to keep under the children of **J.**	3063
2Ch	28:17	Edomites had come and smitten **J.**,	3063
2Ch	28:18	low country, and of the south of **J.**,	3063
2Ch	28:19	brought **J.** low because of Ahaz	3063
2Ch	28:19	he made **J.** naked, and transgressed	3063
2Ch	28:25	city of **J.** he made high places to	3063
2Ch	28:26	book of the kings of **J.** and Israel.	3063
2Ch	29:8	the wrath of the Lord was upon **J.**	3063
2Ch	29:21	and for the sanctuary, and for **J.**.	3063
2Ch	30:1	Hezekiah sent to all Israel and **J.**.	3063
2Ch	30:6	throughout all Israel and **J.**,	3063
2Ch	30:12	in **J.** the hand of God was to give	3063
2Ch	30:24	Hezekiah king of **J.** did give to the	3063
2Ch	30:25	the congregation of **J.**, with the	3063
2Ch	30:25	and that dwelt in **J.**, rejoiced.	3063
2Ch	31:1	present went out to the cities of **J.**,	3063
2Ch	31:1	places and the altars out of all **J.**	3063
2Ch	31:6	the children of Israel and **J.**, that	3063
2Ch	31:6	dwelt in the cities of **J.**, they also	3063
2Ch	31:20	did Hezekiah throughout all **J.**,	3063
2Ch	32:1	entered into **J.**, and encamped	3063
2Ch	32:8	the words of Hezekiah king of **J.**	3063
2Ch	32:9	unto Hezekiah king of **J.**, and unto	3063
2Ch	32:9	unto all **J.** that were at Jerusalem,	3063
2Ch	32:12	commanded **J.** and Jerusalem,	3063
2Ch	32:23	presents to Hezekiah king of **J.**:	3063
2Ch	32:25	was wrath upon him, and upon **J.**	3063
2Ch	32:32	book of the kings of **J.** and Israel.	3063
2Ch	32:33	all **J.** and the inhabitants of	3063
2Ch	33:9	Manasseh made **J.** and the	3063
2Ch	33:14	war in all the fenced cities of **J.**.	3063
2Ch	33:16	commanded **J.** to serve the Lord	3063
2Ch	34:3	twelfth year he began to purge **J.**	3063
2Ch	34:5	and cleansed **J.** and Jerusalem.	3063
2Ch	34:9	the remnant of Israel, and of all **J.**	3063
2Ch	34:11	which the kings of **J.** had destroyed.	3063
2Ch	34:21	that are left in Israel and in **J.**,	3063
2Ch	34:24	have read before the king of **J.**:	3063
2Ch	34:26	as for the king of **J.**, who sent you	3063
2Ch	34:29	all the elders of **J.** and Jerusalem.	3063
2Ch	34:30	the Lord, and all the men of **J.**,	3063
2Ch	35:18	all **J.** and Israel that was present,	3063
2Ch	35:21	to do with thee, thou king of **J.**?	3063
2Ch	35:24	all **J.** and Jerusalem mourned for	3063
2Ch	35:27	book of the kings of Israel and **J.**.	3063
2Ch	36:4	Eliakim his brother king over **J.**	3063
2Ch	36:8	book of the kings of Israel and **J.**:	3063
2Ch	36:10	Zedekiah his brother king over **J.**	3063
2Ch	36:23	house in Jerusalem, which is in **J.**	3063
Ezr	1:2	house at Jerusalem, which is in **J.**.	3063
Ezr	1:3	go up to Jerusalem, which is in **J.**,	3063
Ezr	1:5	rose up the chief of the fathers of **J.**	3063
Ezr	1:8	unto Sheshbazzar, the prince of **J.**.	3063
Ezr	2:1	again unto Jerusalem and **J.**,	3063
Ezr	3:9	his sons, the sons of **J.**, together,	3063
Ezr	4:1	the adversaries of **J.** and Benjamin	3063
Ezr	4:4	the hands of the people of **J.**,	3063
Ezr	4:6	against the inhabitants of **J.** and	3063
Ezr	5:1	unto the Jews that were in **J.**	3061
Ezr	7:14	to enquire concerning **J.** and	3061
Ezr	9:9	to give us a wall in **J.** and in	3063
Ezr	10:7	made proclamation throughout **J.**	3063
Ezr	10:9	men of **J.** and Benjamin gathered	3063
Ezr	10:23	Kelita,) Pethahiah, **J.**, and Eliezer.	3063
Ne	1:2	came, he and certain men of **J.**;	3063
Ne	2:5	thou wouldest send me unto **J.**,	3063
Ne	2:7	convey me over till I come into **J.**;	3063
Ne	4:10	**J.** said, The strength of the bearers	3063
Ne	4:16	were behind all the house of **J.**.	3063
Ne	5:14	be their governor in the land of **J.**,	3063
Ne	6:7	saying, There is a king in **J.**:	3063
Ne	6:17	nobles of **J.** sent many letters unto	3063
Ne	6:18	were many in **J.** sworn unto him,	3063
Ne	7:6	came again to Jerusalem and to **J.**,	3063
Ne	11:3	in the cities of **J.** dwelt every one	3063
Ne	11:4	dwelt certain of the children of **J.**,	3063
Ne	11:4	the children of **J.**; Athaiah the son	3063
Ne	11:9	**J.** the son of Senuah was second	3063
Ne	11:20	Levites, were in all the cities of **J.**,	3063
Ne	11:24	the children of Zerah the son of **J.**,	3063
Ne	11:25	some of the children of **J.** dwelt at	3063
Ne	11:36	the Levites were divisions in **J.**,	3063
Ne	12:8	Sherebiah, **J.**, and Mattaniah,	3063
Ne	12:31	up the princes of **J.** upon the wall,	3063
Ne	12:32	and half of the princes of **J.**,	3063
Ne	12:34	**J.**, and Benjamin, and Shemaiah,	3063
Ne	12:36	Nethaneel, and **J.**, Hanani, with	3063
Ne	12:44	**J.** rejoiced for the priests and for	3063
Ne	13:12	brought all **J.** the tithe of the corn	3063
Ne	13:15	days saw I in **J.** some treading	3063
Ne	13:16	the sabbath day unto the children of **J.**,	3063
Ne	13:17	contended with the nobles of **J.**,	3063
Es	2:6	away with Jeconiah king of **J.**,	3063
Ps	48:11	let the daughters of **J.** be glad,	3063
Ps	60:7	of mine head; **J.** is my lawgiver;	3063
Ps	63:*title*	he was in the wilderness of **J.**.	3063
Ps	68:27	the princes of **J.** and their council,	3063
Ps	69:35	Zion, and will build the cities of **J.**:	3063
Ps	76:1	In **J.** is God known: his name is	3063
Ps	78:68	But chose the tribe of **J.**, the	3063
Ps	97:8	the daughters of **J.** rejoiced.	3063
Ps	108:8	of mine head; **J.** is my lawgiver:	3063
Ps	114:2	**J.** was his sanctuary, and Israel	3063
Pr	25:1	men of Hezekiah king of **J.** copied	3063
Isa	1:1	which he saw concerning **J.** and	3063
Isa	1:1	Ahaz and Hezekiah, kings of **J.**.	3063
Isa	2:1	the son of Amoz saw concerning **J.**	3063
Isa	3:1	and from **J.** the stay and the staff,	3063
Isa	3:8	Jerusalem is ruined, and **J.** is falled:	3063
Isa	5:3	men of **J.**, judge, I pray you,	3063
Isa	5:7	the men of **J.** his pleasant plant:	3063
Isa	7:1	the son of Uzziah, king of **J.**,	3063
Isa	7:6	Let us go up against **J.**, and vex it,	3063
Isa	7:17	that Ephraim departed from **J.**;	3063
Isa	8:8	he shall pass through **J.**; he shall	3063
Isa	9:21	they together shall be against **J.**	3063
Isa	11:12	gather together the dispersed of **J.**	3063
Isa	11:13	adversaries of **J.** shall be cut off:	3063
Isa	11:13	Ephraim shall not envy **J.**,	3063
Isa	11:13	and **J.** shall not vex Ephraim.	3063
Isa	19:17	the land of **J.** shall be a terror unto	3063
Isa	22:8	he discovered the covering of **J.**,	3063
Isa	22:21	Jerusalem, and to the house of **J.**.	3063
Isa	26:1	this song be sung in the land of **J.**;	3063
Isa	36:1	against all the defenced cities of **J.**,	3063
Isa	36:7	said to **J.** and to Jerusalem, Ye	3063
Isa	37:10	ye speak to Hezekiah king of **J.**,	3063
Isa	37:31	that is escaped of the house of **J.**	3063
Isa	38:9	The writing of Hezekiah king of **J.**,	3063
Isa	40:9	say unto the cities of **J.**, Behold	3063
Isa	44:26	to the cities of **J.**, Ye shall be built,	3063
Isa	48:1	come forth out of the waters of **J.**,	3063
Isa	65:9	**J.** an inheritor of my mountains:	3063
Jer	1:2	Josiah the son of Amon king of **J.**,	3063
Jer	1:3	Jehoiakim...of Josiah king of **J.**,	3063
Jer	1:3	Zedekiah...of Josiah king of **J.**,	3063
Jer	1:15	and against all the cities of **J.**.	3063
Jer	1:18	whole land, against the kings of **J.**,	3063
Jer	2:28	of thy cities are thy gods, O **J.**.	3063
Jer	3:7	her treacherous sister **J.** saw it.	3063
Jer	3:8	treacherous sister **J.** feared not,	3063
Jer	3:10	her treacherous sister **J.** hath not	3063
Jer	3:11	herself more than treacherous **J.**	3063
Jer	3:18	the house of **J.** shall walk with the	3063
Jer	4:3	saith the Lord to the men of **J.**	3063
Jer	4:4	Ye men of **J.** and inhabitants of	3063

Jer 4:5 Declare ye in **J.**, and publish in.......... 3063
Jer 4:16 their voice against the cities of **J.**....... 3063
Jer 5:11 the house of **J.** have dealt very........... 3063
Jer 5:20 of Jacob, and publish it in **J.**,............ 3063
Jer 7:2 the word of the Lord, all ye of **J.**,....... 3063
Jer 7:17 not what they do in the cities of **J.**...... 3063
Jer 7:30 children of **J.** have done evil in my..... 3063
Jer 7:34 cause to cease from the cities of **J.**, ... 3063
Jer 8:1 out the bones of the kings of **J.**, ... 3063
Jer 9:11 will make the cities of **J.** desolate,...... 3063
Jer 9:26 **J.**, and Edom, and the children of....... 3063
Jer 10:22 make the cities of **J.** desolate, and...... 3063
Jer 11:2 speak unto the men of **J.**, and to 3063
Jer 11:6 all these words in the cities of **J.**, ... 3063
Jer 11:9 is found among the men of **J.**, ... 3063
Jer 11:10 house of **J.** have broken...covenant..... 3063
Jer 11:12 the cities of **J.** and inhabitants the 3063
Jer 11:13 of thy cities were thy gods, O **J.**; 3063
Jer 11:17 of Israel and of the house of **J.**,......... 3063
Jer 12:14 pluck out the house of **J.** from........... 3063
Jer 13:9 manner will I mar the pride of **J.**,........ 3063
Jer 13:11 of Israel and the whole house of **J.**,.... 3063
Jer 13:19 **J.** shall be carried away captive all...... 3063
Jer 14:2 **J.** mourneth, and the gates thereof..... 3063
Jer 14:19 Hast thou utterly rejected **J.**? hath 3063
Jer 15:4 the son of Hezekiah king of **J.**,.......... 3063
Jer 17:1 sin of **J.** is written with a pen of........ 3063
Jer 17:19 the kings of **J.** come in, and by the 3063
Jer 17:20 the Lord, ye kings of **J.**, and all **J.**, ... 3063
Jer 17:25 their princes the men of **J.**, and......... 3063
Jer 17:26 shall come from the cities of **J.**,......... 3063
Jer 18:11 go to, speak to the men of **J.**,........... 3063
Jer 19:3 word of the Lord, O kings of **J.**,........ 3063
Jer 19:4 have known, nor the kings of **J.**,......... 3063
Jer 19:7 I will make void the counsel of **J.**........ 3063
Jer 19:13 houses of the kings of **J.**, shall be 3063
Jer 20:4 give all **J.** unto the hand of the king..... 3063
Jer 20:5 all the treasures of the kings of **J.**..... 3063
Jer 21:7 I will deliver Zedekiah king of **J.**, ... 3063
Jer 21:11 touching the house of the king of **J.**,... 3063
Jer 22:1 down to the house of the king of **J.**, ... 3063
Jer 22:2 O king of **J.**, that sitteth upon the...... 3063
Jer 22:6 Lord unto the king's house of **J.**; 3063
Jer 22:11 Shallum...of Josiah king of **J.**, ... 3063
Jer 22:18 Jehoiakim...of Josiah king of **J.**;.......... 3063
Jer 22:24 the son of Jehoiakim king of **J.**........... 3063
Jer 22:30 David, and ruling any more in **J.** 3063
Jer 23:6 In his days **J.** shall be saved, and....... 3063
Jer 24:1 the son of Jehoiakim king of **J.**,.......... 3063
Jer 24:1 and the princes of **J.**, with the........... 3063
Jer 24:5 that are carried away captive of **J.**,..... 3063
Jer 24:8 will I give Zedekiah the king of **J.**,...... 3063
Jer 25:1 concerning all the people of **J.**, ... 3063
Jer 25:1 Jehoiakim...of Josiah king of **J.**, ... 3063
Jer 25:2 spake unto all the people of **J.**........... 3063
Jer 25:3 Josiah the son of Amon king of **J.**,...... 3063
Jer 25:18 cities of **J.**, and the kings thereof, ... 3063
Jer 26:1 Jehoiakim...of Josiah king of **J.**.......... 3063
Jer 26:2 and speak unto all the cities of **J.**, ... 3063
Jer 26:10 princes of **J.** heard these things, ... 3063
Jer 26:18 in the days of Hezekiah king of **J.**, ... 3063
Jer 26:18 spake to all the people of **J.**, saying,... 3063
Jer 26:19 Did Hezekiah king of **J.** and all 3063
Jer 26:19 and all **J.** put him at all to death? 3063
Jer 27:1 Jehoiakim...of Josiah king of **J.**........... 3063
Jer 27:3 come...unto Zedekiah king of **J.**; 3063
Jer 27:12 I spake also to Zedekiah king of **J.** 3063
Jer 27:18 in the house of the king of **J.**, and...... 3063
Jer 27:20 the son of Jehoiakim king of **J.**........... 3063
Jer 27:20 all the nobles of **J.** and Jerusalem; 3063
Jer 27:21 in the house of the king of **J.** and....... 3063
Jer 28:1 of the reign of Zedekiah king of **J.**...... 3063
Jer 28:4 the son of Jehoiakim king of **J.**,.......... 3063
Jer 28:4 with all the captives of **J.**, that went... 3063
Jer 29:2 the princes of **J.** and Jerusalem,......... 3063
Jer 29:3 (whom Zedekiah king of **J.** sent 3063
Jer 29:22 up a curse by all the captivity of **J.**...... 3063
Jer 30:3 the captivity of my people...**J.**, ... 3063
Jer 30:4 spake concerning Israel and...**J.**.......... 3063
Jer 31:23 use this speech in the land of **J.**......... 3063
Jer 31:24 there shall dwell in **J.** itself, and in 3063
Jer 31:27 house of **J.** with the seed of man, ... 3063
Jer 31:31 of Israel, and with the house of **J.**:...... 3063
Jer 32:1 tenth year of Zedekiah king of **J.**,....... 3063
Jer 32:3 king of **J.** had shut him up, saying, ... 3063
Jer 32:4 king of **J.** shall not escape out of........ 3063
Jer 32:30 children of **J.** have only done evil....... 3063
Jer 32:32 of Israel and of the children of **J.**, ... 3063
Jer 32:32 their prophets, and the men of **J.**, ... 3063
Jer 32:35 this abomination, to cause **J.** to sin..... 3063
Jer 32:44 Jerusalem, and in the cities of **J.**, ... 3063
Jer 33:4 the houses of the kings of **J.**,............ 3063
Jer 33:7 And I will cause the captivity of **J.**....... 3063
Jer 33:10 beast, even in the cities of **J.**, ... 3063
Jer 33:13 in the cities of **J.**, shall the flocks....... 3063
Jer 33:14 of Israel and to the house of **J.**.......... 3063
Jer 33:16 In those days shall **J.** be saved, and.... 3063
Jer 34:2 speak to Zedekiah king of **J.**, and....... 3063
Jer 34:4 of the Lord, O Zedekiah king of **J.**; 3063
Jer 34:6 words unto Zedekiah king of **J.** in....... 3063
Jer 34:7 against all the cities of **J.** that were.... 3063
Jer 34:7 cities remained of the cities of **J.**......... 3063
Jer 34:19 princes of **J.**, and the princes of......... 3063
Jer 34:21 Zedekiah king of **J.** and his princes..... 3063
Jer 34:22 make the cities of **J.** a desolation 3063
Jer 35:1 Jehoiakim...of Josiah king of **J.**,.......... 3063
Jer 35:13 Go and tell the men of **J.** and the....... 3063
Jer 35:17 I will bring upon **J.** and upon all......... 3063
Jer 36:1 Jehoiakim...of Josiah king of **J.**,.......... 3063
Jer 36:2 thee against Israel, and against **J.**,...... 3063
Jer 36:3 be that the house of **J.** will hear all..... 3063
Jer 36:6 shalt read them in the ears of all **J.**..... 3063
Jer 36:9 Jehoiakim...of Josiah king of **J.**,.......... 3063
Jer 36:9 that came from the cities of **J.** unto.... 3063
Jer 36:28 which...the king of **J.** hath burned. 3063
Jer 36:29 shalt say to Jehoiakim king of **J.**, ... 3063
Jer 36:30 the Lord of Jehoiakim king of **J.**;........ 3063
Jer 36:31 and upon the men of **J.**, all the evil 3063
Jer 36:32 Jehoiakim king of **J.** had burned 3063
Jer 37:1 Babylon made king in the land of **J.**. ... 3063
Jer 37:7 Thus shall ye say to the king of **J.**, ... 3063
Jer 39:1 ninth year of Zedekiah king of **J.**, ... 3063
Jer 39:4 Zedekiah the king of **J.** saw them, ... 3063
Jer 39:6 of Babylon slew all the nobles of **J.**...... 3063
Jer 39:10 which had nothing, in the land of **J.**, ... 3063
Jer 40:1 away captive of Jerusalem and **J.**,....... 3063
Jer 40:5 made governor over the cities of **J.**, ... 3063
Jer 40:11 Babylon had left a remnant of **J.**, ... 3063
Jer 40:12 driven, and came to the land of **J.**, ... 3063
Jer 40:15 and the remnant in **J.** perish? 3063
Jer 42:15 word of the Lord, ye remnant of **J.**; ... 3063
Jer 42:19 concerning you, O ye remnant of **J.**;... 3063
Jer 43:4 the Lord, to dwell in the land of **J.**..... 3063
Jer 43:5 forces, took all the remnant of **J.**. 3063
Jer 43:5 driven, to dwell in the land of **J.**: 3063
Jer 43:9 in the sight of the men of **J.**;............. 3064
Jer 44:2 and upon all the cities of **J.**;.............. 3063
Jer 44:6 and was kindled in the cities of **J.**....... 3063
Jer 44:7 child and suckling, out of **J.**,............. 3063
Jer 44:9 the wickedness of the kings of **J.**, ... 3063
Jer 44:9 have committed in the land of **J.**, ... 3063
Jer 44:11 you for evil, and to cut off all **J.**........ 3063
Jer 44:12 And I will take the remnant of **J.**, ... 3063
Jer 44:14 So that none of the remnant of **J.**,...... 3063
Jer 44:14 should return into the land of **J.**,........ 3063
Jer 44:17 and our princes, in the cities of **J.**, ... 3063
Jer 44:21 that ye burned in the cities of **J.**,....... 3063
Jer 44:24 all **J.** that are in the land of Egypt:..... 3063
Jer 44:26 all **J.** that dwell in the land of Egypt; .. 3063
Jer 44:26 in the mouth of any man of **J.** in all 3063
Jer 44:27 all men of **J.** that are in the land of..... 3063
Jer 44:28 land of Egypt into the land of **J.**,........ 3063
Jer 44:28 all the remnant of **J.**, that are gone 3063
Jer 44:30 I gave Zedekiah king of **J.** into the 3063
Jer 45:1 Jehoiakim...of Josiah king of **J.**,.......... 3063
Jer 46:2 Jehoiakim...of Josiah king of **J.**........... 3063
Jer 49:34 of the reign of Zedekiah king of **J.**,..... 3063
Jer 50:4 they and the children of **J.** together, ... 3063
Jer 50:20 the sins of **J.**, and they shall not be.... 3063
Jer 50:33 the children of **J.** were oppressed....... 3063
Jer 51:5 been forsaken, nor **J.** of his God, ... 3063
Jer 51:59 went with Zedekiah the king of **J.**....... 3063
Jer 52:3 came to pass in Jerusalem and **J.**. 3063
Jer 52:10 he slew also all the princes of **J.** in..... 3063
Jer 52:27 **J.** was carried away captive out of...... 3063
Jer 52:31 captivity of Jehoiachin king of **J.**,........ 3063
Jer 52:31 the head of Jehoiachin king of **J.**,....... 3063
La 1:3 **J.** is gone into captivity because of..... 3063
La 1:15 the virgin, the daughter of **J.** as in 3063
La 2:2 strong holds of the daughter of **J.**;...... 3063
La 2:5 increased in the daughter of **J.**........... 3063
La 5:11 and the maids in the cities of **J.**. 3063
Eze 4:6 bear the iniquity of the house of **J.**..... 3063
Eze 8:1 and the elders of **J.** sat before me,...... 3063
Eze 8:17 Is it a light thing to the house of **J.** 3063
Eze 9:9 of Israel and **J.** is exceeding great, ... 3063
Eze 21:20 to **J.** in Jerusalem the defenced.......... 3063
Eze 25:3 and against the house of **J.**, when 3063
Eze 25:8 of **J.** is like unto all the heathen;........ 3063
Eze 25:12 hath dealt against the house of **J.**........ 3063
Eze 27:17 **J.**, and the land of Israel, they were... 3063
Eze 37:16 For **J.**, and for the children of Israel... 3063
Eze 37:19 with him, even with the stick of **J.**, ... 3063
Eze 48:7 unto the west side, a portion for **J.**. ... 3063
Eze 48:8 And by the border of **J.**, from the...... 3063
Eze 48:22 between the border of **J.** and the....... 3063
Eze 48:31 one gate of **J.**, one gate of Levi......... 3063
Da 1:1 of the reign of Jehoiakim king of **J.**..... 3063
Da 1:2 gave Jehoiakim king of **J.** into his 3063
Da 1:6 these were of the children of **J.**, ... 3063
Da 2:25 found a man of the captives of **J.**, ... 3061
Da 5:13 the children of the captivity of **J.**,....... 3061
Da 6:13 the children of the captivity of **J.**,....... 3061
Da 9:7 to the men of **J.**, and to the............. 3063
Ho 1:1 Ahaz, and Hezekiah, kings of **J.**, ... 3063
Ho 1:7 have mercy upon the house of **J.**, ... 3063
Ho 1:11 Then shall the children of **J.** and 3063
Ho 4:15 the harlot, yet let not **J.** offend;......... 3063
Ho 5:5 **J.** also shall fall with them................ 3063
Ho 5:10 princes of **J.** were like them that......... 3063
Ho 5:12 to the house of **J.** as rottenness......... 3063
Ho 5:13 his sicknesss, and **J.** saw his wound,... 3063
Ho 5:14 as a young lion to the house of **J.**: 3063
Ho 6:4 O **J.**, what shall I do unto thee?......... 3063
Ho 6:11 O **J.**, he hath set an harvest for thee,..3063
Ho 8:14 **J.** hath multiplied fenced cities: 3063
Ho 10:11 **J.** shall plow, and Jacob shall break..... 3063
Ho 11:12 but **J.** yet ruleth with God, and is 3063
Ho 12:2 hath also a controversy with **J.**, ... 3063
Joe 3:1 shall bring again the captivity of **J.**...... 3063
Joe 3:6 children also of **J.** and the children...... 3063
Joe 3:8 into the land of the children of **J.**, ... 3063
Joe 3:18 rivers of **J.** shall flow with waters,...... 3063
Joe 3:19 violence against the children of **J.**, ... 3063
Joe 3:20 But **J.** shall dwell forever, and........... 3063
Am 1:1 in the days of Uzziah king of **J.**,........ 3063
Am 2:4 For three transgressions of **J.**, and..... 3063
Am 2:5 I will send a fire upon **J.**, and it......... 3063
Am 7:12 flee thee away into the land of **J.**, ... 3063
Ob 12 rejoiced over the children of **J.** in....... 3063
Mic 1:1 Ahaz, and Hezekiah, kings of **J.**, ... 3063
Mic 1:5 and what are the high places of **J.**?..... 3063
Mic 1:9 is incurable; for it is come unto **J.**; 3063
Mic 5:2 be little among the thousands of **J.**, ... 3063
Na 1:15 O **J.**, keep thy solemn feasts,............ 3063
Zep 1:1 Josiah the son of Amon, king of **J.**...... 3063
Zep 1:4 also stretch out mine hand upon **J.**, ... 3063
Zep 2:7 for the remnant of the house of **J.**;.... 3063
Hag 1:1, 14 son of Shealtiel, governor of **J.**,..... 3063
Hag 2:2 the son of Shealtiel, governor of **J.**,.... 3063
Hag 2:21 speak to Zerubbabel, governor of **J.**,... 3063
Zec 1:12 on Jerusalem and on the cities of **J.**,... 3063
Zec 1:19, 21 horns which have scattered **J.**, ... 3063
Zec 1:21 horn over the land of **J.** to scatter...... 3063
Zec 2:12 the Lord shall inherit **J.** his portion..... 3063
Zec 8:13 among the heathen, O house of **J.**,..... 3063
Zec 8:15 Jerusalem and to the house of **J.**:........ 3063
Zec 8:19 to the house of **J.** joy and gladness,.... 3063
Zec 9:7 God, and he be as a governor in **J.**, ... 3063
Zec 9:13 have bent **J.** for me, filled the bow..... 3063
Zec 10:3 visited his flock the house of **J.**,......... 3063
Zec 10:6 I will strengthen the house of **J.**, ... 3063
Zec 11:14 brotherhood between **J.** and Israel...... 3063
Zec 12:2 be in the siege both against **J.** and 3063
Zec 12:4 mine eyes upon the house of **J.**, ... 3063
Zec 12:5 governors of **J.** shall say in their........ 3063
Zec 12:6 will I make the governors of **J.** like 3063
Zec 12:7 also shall save the tents of **J.** first, ... 3063
Zec 12:7 not magnify themselves against **J.**........ 3063
Zec 14:5 in the days of Uzziah king of **J.**:......... 3063
Zec 14:14 **J.** also shall fight at Jerusalem; 3063
Zec 14:21 every pot in Jerusalem and in **J.**.......... 3063
Mal 2:11 **J.** hath dealt treacherously, and 3063
Mal 2:11 for **J.** hath profaned the holiness 3063
Mal 3:4 shall the offering of **J.**...be pleasant 3063
Heb 8:8 of Israel and with the house of **J.**:...... *2455*

JUDAH'S (ju'-dahs)
Ge 38:7 And Er, **J.** firstborn, was wicked........ 3063
Ge 38:12 daughter of Shuah **J.** wife died;.......... 3063
Jer 32:2 which was in the king of **J.** house....... 3063
Jer 38:22 that are left in the king of **J.** house..... 3063

JUDAS (ju'-das) See also BARSABAS; ISCARIOT; JUDAH; JUDE; LEBBAEUS; THADDAEUS.
Mt 1:2 Jacob begat **J.** and his brethren;......... *2455*
Mt 1:3 And **J.** begat Phares and Zara of........ *2455*
Mt 10:4 **J.** Iscariot, who also betrayed him...... *2455*
Mt 13:55 and Joses, and Simon, and **J.**? *2455*
Mt 26:14 twelve, called **J.** Iscariot, went *2455*
Mt 26:25 **J.**, which betrayed him, answered *2455*
Mt 26:47 lo, **J.**, one of the twelve, came, ... *2455*
Mt 27:3 **J.**, which had betrayed him, when *2455*
Mk 3:19 **J.** Iscariot, which also betrayed.......... *2455*
Mk 14:10 **J.** Iscariot, one of the twelve, went *2455*
Mk 14:43 cometh **J.**, one of the twelve, and...... *2455*
Lu 6:16 And **J.** the brother of James, and *2455*
Lu 6:16 **J.** Iscariot, which...was the traitor...... *2455*
Lu 22:3 Satan into **J.** surnamed Iscariot, ... *2455*
Lu 22:47 and he that was called **J.**, one of......... *2455*
Lu 22:48 **J., betrayest thou the Son of man** . *2455*
Joh 6:71 He spake of **J.** Iscariot the son of *2455*
Joh 12:4 disciples, **J.** Iscariot, Simon's son, ... *2455*
Joh 13:2 put into the heart of **J.** Iscariot, ... *2455*
Joh 13:26 the sop, he gave it to **J.** Iscariot,....... *2455*
Joh 13:29 thought, because **J.** had the bag,........ *2455*
Joh 14:22 **J.** saith to him, not Iscariot, Lord,...... *2455*
Joh 18:2 **J.** also, which betrayeth him, knew..... *2455*
Joh 18:3 **J.** then having received a band of....... *2455*
Joh 18:5 **J.** also, which betrayed him, stood...... *2455*
Ac 1:13 and **J.** the brother of James............... *2455*
Ac 1:16 David spake before concerning **J.**, ... *2455*
Ac 1:25 from which **J.** by transgression fell, ... *2455*
Ac 5:37 After this man rose up **J.** of Galilee *2455*
Ac 9:11 **the house of J. for one called Saul,** *2455*
Ac 15:22 **J.** surnamed Barsabas, and Silas,........ *2455*
Ac 15:27 have sent therefore **J.** and Silas, ... *2455*
Ac 15:32 **J.** and Silas, being prophets also *2455*

JUDAS-ISCARIOT See JUDAS and ISCARIOT.

JUDE (jood) See also JUDAS.
Jude *general title* The General Epistle Of **J.**........... *2455*
Jude 1 **J.**, the servant of Jesus Christ, ... *2455*

JUDEA (ju-de'-ah) See also JUDAEA.
Ezr 5:8 we went into the province of **J.**. 3061

JUDGE See also JUDGED; JUDGES; JUDGEST; JUDGETH; JUDGING.
Ge 15:14 whom they shall serve, will I **j.**:......... 1777
Ge 16:5 the Lord **j.** between me and thee....... 8199
Ge 18:25 not the **j.** of all the earth do right? 8199
Ge 19:9 sojourn, and he will needs be a **j.**:...... 8199
Ge 31:37 that they may **j.** betwixt us both. 3198
Ge 31:53 God of their father, **j.** betwixt us. 8199
Ge 49:16 Dan shall **j.** his people, as one of 1777
Ex 2:14 thee a prince and a **j.** over us? 8199
Ex 5:21 The Lord look upon you, and **j.**; 8199
Ex 18:13 that Moses sat to **j.** the people:......... 8199
Ex 18:16 and I **j.** between one and another,...... 8199
Ex 18:22 let them **j.** the people at all seasons:... 8199
Ex 18:22 every small matter they shall **j.**:......... 8199
Le 19:15 shalt thou **j.** thy neighbour................ 8199
Nu 35:24 the congregation shall **j.** between 8199
De 1:16 **j.** righteously between every man....... 8199
De 16:18 and they shall **j.** the people with just... 8199
De 17:9 the **j.** that shall be in those days, ... 8199
De 17:12 the Lord thy God, or unto the **j.**,....... 8199
De 25:1 that the judges may **j.** them;............. 8199
De 25:2 the **j.** shall cause him to lie down, ... 8199
De 32:36 For the Lord shall **j.** his people,......... 1777
Jg 2:18 Lord was with the **j.**, and delivered 8199
Jg 2:18 their enemies all the days of the **j.**: 8199
Jg 2:19 the **j.** was dead, that they returned, ... 8199
Jg 11:27 Lord the **J.** be **j.** this day between..... 8199
1Sa 2:10 Lord shall **j.** the ends of the earth;..... 1777
1Sa 2:25 against another, the **j.** shall...him:........ 430
1Sa 2:25 against another, the...shall **j.** him: 6419
1Sa 3:13 that I will **j.** his house for ever for 8199
1Sa 8:5 make us a king to **j.** us like all the 8199
1Sa 8:6 they said, Give us a king to **j.** us. 8199
1Sa 8:20 that our king may **j.** us, and go out 8199
1Sa 24:12 The Lord **j.** between me and thee,..... 8199
1Sa 24:15 The Lord therefore be **j.**, and 1784
1Sa 24:15 and **j.** between me and thee, and 8199
2Sa 15:4 Oh that I were made **j.** in the land, ... 8199
1Ki 3:9 understanding heart to **j.** thy people,... 8199
1Ki 3:9 for who is able to **j.** this thy so great.. 8199
1Ki 7:7 for the throne where he might **j.**,........ 8199
1Ki 8:32 heaven, and do, and **j.** thy servants, ... 8199
1Ch 16:33 because he cometh to **j.** the earth...... 8199
2Ch 1:10 who can **j.** this thy people, that is 8199
2Ch 1:11 that thou mayest **j.** my people, ... 8199
2Ch 6:23 heaven, and do, and **j.** thy servants, ... 8199
2Ch 19:6 ye **j.** not for man, but for the Lord,.... 8199
2Ch 20:12 O our God, wilt thou not **j.** them?...... 8199
Ezr 7:25 which may **j.** all the people that .. 1934,1778
Job 9:15 would make supplication to my **j.**......... 8199
Job 22:13 can he **j.** through the dark cloud? 8199
Job 23:7 I be delivered for ever from my **j.**....... 8199
Job 31:28 iniquity to be punished by the **j.**:........ 6416
Ps 7:8 The Lord shall **j.** the people:............. 1777
Ps 7:8 **j.** me, O Lord, according to my 8199
Ps 9:8 shall **j.** the world in righteousness, ... 8199
Ps 10:18 **j.** the fatherless and the oppressed, ... 8199
Ps 26:1 **J.** me, O Lord; for I have walked....... 8199
Ps 35:24 **J.** me, O Lord my God, according...... 8199
Ps 43:1 **J.** me, O God, and plead my cause..... 8199
Ps 50:4 earth, that he may **j.** his people. 1777
Ps 50:6 for God is **j.** himself. 8199
Ps 54:1 name, and **j.** me by thy strength. 1777
Ps 58:1 do ye **j.** uprightly, O ye sons of......... 8199
Ps 67:4 thou shalt **j.** the people righteously, ... 8199
Ps 68:5 a **j.** of the widows, is God in his 1781
Ps 72:2 **j.** thy people with righteousness,....... 1777
Ps 72:4 He shall **j.** the poor of the people,...... 8199
Ps 75:2 congregation I will **j.** uprightly. 8199
Ps 75:7 God is the **j.**: he putteth down one,.... 8199
Ps 82:2 How long will ye **j.** unjustly, and 8199
Ps 82:8 Arise, O God, **j.** the earth: for thou.... 8199
Ps 94:2 Lift up thyself, thou **j.** of the earth: ... 8199
Ps 96:10 he shall **j.** the people righteously. 1777
Ps 96:13 for he cometh to **j.** the earth:........... 8199
Ps 96:13 **j.** the world with righteousness, ... 8199
Ps 98:9 for he cometh to **j.** the earth:........... 8199
Ps 98:9 righteousness shall he **j.** the world,...... 8199
Ps 110:6 He shall **j.** among the heathen, he 1777
Ps 135:14 Lord will **j.** his people, and he will...... 1777
Pr 31:9 Open thy mouth, **j.** righteously, ... 8199
Ec 3:17 God shall **j.** the righteous and the....... 8199
Isa 1:17 **j.** the fatherless, plead for the 8199
Isa 1:23 they **j.** not the fatherless, neither...... 8199
Isa 2:4 he shall **j.** among the nations, and 8199
Isa 3:2 man of war, the **j.**, and the prophet, ... 8199
Isa 3:13 and standeth to **j.** the people............ 1777
Isa 5:3 **j.**, I pray you, betwixt me and.......... 8199
Isa 11:3 not **j.** after the sight of his eyes,........ 8199
Isa 11:4 righteousness shall he **j.** the poor, ... 8199
Isa 33:22 the Lord is our **j.**, the Lord is our...... 8199
Isa 51:5 and mine arms shall **j.** the people; 8199
Jer 5:28 they **j.** not the cause, the cause of..... 1777
Jer 5:28 right of the needy do they not **j.**. 8199
La 3:59 seen my wrong: **j.** thou my cause. 8199
Eze 7:3, 8 will **j.** thee according to thy ways, ... 8199
Eze 7:27 to their deserts will I **j.** them; 8199
Eze 11:10 I will **j.** you in the border of Israel; 8199
Eze 11:11 I will **j.** you in the border of Israel: 8199
Eze 16:38 I will **j.** thee, as women that break..... 8199
Eze 18:30 Therefore I will **j.** you, O house of..... 8199
Eze 20:4 Wilt thou **j.** them, son of man,........... 8199
Eze 20:4 wilt thou **j.** them? cause them to........ 8199
Eze 21:30 I will **j.** thee in the place where thou .. 8199
Eze 22:2 Now, thou son of man, wilt thou **j.**,.... 8199
Eze 22:2 wilt thou **j.** the bloody city? yea,....... 8199
Eze 23:24 they shall **j.** thee according to their..... 8199
Eze 23:36 Son of man, wilt thou **j.** Aholah and.... 8199
Eze 23:45 they shall **j.** them after the manner..... 8199
Eze 24:14 to thy doings, shall they **j.** thee, ... 8199
Eze 33:20 I will **j.** every one after his ways........ 8199
Eze 34:17 I **j.** between cattle and cattle,........... 8199
Eze 34:20 even I, will **j.** between the fat cattle ... 8199
Eze 34:22 I will **j.** between cattle and cattle. 8199
Eze 44:24 **j.** it according to my judgments:......... 8199
Joe 3:12 there will I sit to **j.** all the heathen 8199
Am 2:3 cut off the **j.** from the midst thereof, .. 8199
Ob 21 Zion to **j.** the mount of Esau; 8199
Mic 3:11 heads thereof **j.** for rewards, and the.. 8199
Mic 4:3 And he shall **j.** among many people,.... 8199
Mic 5:1 shall smite the **j.** of Israel with a rod .. 8199
Mic 7:3 and the **j.** asketh for a reward; 8199
Zec 3:7 then thou shalt also **j.** my house, ... 1777
Mt 5:25 **adversary deliver thee to the j.,** *2923*
Mt 5:25 **the j. deliver thee to the officer,**.... *2923*
Mt 7:1 **J. not, that ye be not judged.**........ *2919*
Mt 7:2 **with what judgment ye j., ye shall** .*2919*
Lu 6:37 **J. not, and ye shall not be judged:**..*2919*
Lu 12:14 **made me a j. or a divider over you?***1348*
Lu 12:57 **yourselves j. ye not what is right?**..*2919*
Lu 12:58 **him; lest he hale thee to the j.,**...... *2923*
Lu 12:58 **and the j. deliver thee to the**........ *2923*
Lu 18:2 **There was in a city a j., which**...... *2923*
Lu 18:6 said, **Hear what the unjust j. saith.**.*2923*
Lu 19:22 **of thine own mouth will I j. thee,**..*2919*
Joh 5:30 **as I hear, I j.: and my judgment** ... *2919*
Joh 7:24 **J. not according to the appearance,***2919*
Joh 7:24 **but j. righteous judgment.**........... *2919*
Joh 7:51 Doth our law **j.** any man, before it *2919*
Joh 8:15 **Ye j. after the flesh; I j. no man**... *2919*
Joh 8:16 **And yet if I j., my judgment is**...... *2919*
Joh 8:26 **many things to say and to j. of**..... *2919*
Joh 12:47 **words, and believe not, I j. him**..... *2919*
Joh 12:47 **for I came not to j. the world,** *2919*
Joh 12:48 **the same shall j. him in the last**.... *2919*
Joh 18:31 and **j.** him according to your law. *2919*
Ac 4:19 you more than unto God, **j.** ye. *2919*
Ac 7:7 they shall be in bondage will I **j.**, ... *2919*
Ac 7:27 made thee a ruler and **j.** over us? *1348*
Ac 7:35 Who made thee a ruler and a **j.**?........ *1348*
Ac 10:42 to be the **J.** of quick and dead. *2923*
Ac 13:46 **j.** yourselves unworthy of...life, ... *2919*
Ac 17:31 will **j.** the world in righteousness........ *2919*
Ac 18:15 for I will be no **j.** of such matters....... *2923*
Ac 23:3 sittest thou to **j.** me after the law, ... *2919*
Ac 24:10 thou hast been of many years a **j.** *2923*
Ro 2:16 God shall **j.** the secrets of men.......... *2919*
Ro 2:27 if it fulfil the law, **j.** thee, who by...... *2919*
Ro 3:6 then how shall God **j.** the world?........ *2919*
Ro 14:3 which eateth not **j.** him that eateth: *2919*
Ro 14:10 But why dost thou **j.** thy brother? *2919*
Ro 14:13 Let us not therefore **j.** one another *2919*
Ro 14:13 but **j.** this rather, that no man put...... *2919*
1Co 4:3 yea, I **j.** not mine own self. *350*
1Co 4:5 **j.** nothing before the time, until *2919*
1Co 5:12 to **j.** them also that are without? *2919*
1Co 5:12 do not ye **j.** them that are within? *2919*
1Co 6:2 that the saints shall **j.** the world? *2919*
1Co 6:2 are ye unworthy to **j.** the smallest...... *2922*
1Co 6:3 ye not that we shall **j.** angels? *2919*
1Co 6:4 them to **j.** who are least esteemed ....
1Co 6:5 be able to **j.** between his brethren? *1252*
1Co 10:15 as to wise men; **j.** ye what I say........ *2919*
1Co 11:13 **J.** in yourselves: is it comely that....... *2919*
1Co 11:31 we would **j.** ourselves, we should....... *1252*
1Co 14:29 two or three, and let the others **j.**....... *1252*
2Co 5:14 because we thus **j.**, that if one *2919*
Col 2:16 Let no man therefore **j.** you in *2919*
2Ti 4:1 who shall **j.** the quick and the dead..... *2919*
2Ti 4:8 which the Lord, the righteous **j.**,......... *2923*
Heb 10:30 again, The Lord shall **j.** his people...... *2919*
Heb 12:23 to God the **J.** of all, and to the.......... *2923*
Heb 13:4 and adulterers God will **j.**. *2919*
Jas 4:11 the law: but if thou **j.** the law,........... *2919*
Jas 4:11 art not a doer of the law, but a **j.**. *2923*
Jas 5:9 the **j.** standeth before the door. *2923*
1Pe 4:5 ready to **j.** the quick and the dead. *2919*
Re 6:10 thou not **j.** and avenge our blood......... *2919*
Re 19:11 he doth **j.** and make war. *2919*

JUDGED
Ge 30:6 And Rachel said, God hath **j.** me,....... 1777
Ex 18:26 they **j.** the people at all seasons:........ 8199
Ex 18:26 small matter they **j.** themselves. 8199
Jg 3:10 he **j.** Israel, and went out to war: 8199
Jg 4:4 Lapidoth, she **j.** Israel at that time. 8199
Jg 10:2 he **j.** Israel twenty and three years,.... 8199
Jg 10:3 and **j.** Israel twenty and two years. 8199
Jg 12:7 And Jephthah **j.** Israel six years. 8199
Jg 12:8 him Ibzan of Beth-lehem **j.** Israel. 8199
Jg 12:9 sons. And he **j.** Israel seven years. 8199
Jg 12:11 him Elon, a Zebulonite, **j.** Israel; 8199
Jg 12:11 and he **j.** Israel ten years. 8199
Jg 12:13 of Hillel, a Pirathonite, **j.** Israel.......... 8199
Jg 12:14 colts: and he **j.** Israel eight years. 8199
Jg 15:20 And he **j.** Israel in the days of the...... 8199
Jg 16:31 And he **j.** Israel twenty years. 8199

1Sa 4:18 heavy. And he j. Israel forty years. 8199
1Sa 7:6 Samuel j. the children of Israel in 8199
1Sa 7:15 Samuel j. Israel all the days of his 8199
1Sa 7:16 and j. Israel in all those places 8199
1Sa 7:17 there he j. Israel; and there he 8199
1Ki 3:28 judgment which the king had j.; 8199
2Ki 23:22 days of the judges that j. Israel, 8199
Ps 9:19 let the heathen be j. in thy sight. 8199
Ps 37:33 nor condemn him when he is j. 8199
Ps 109:7 he shall be j., let him be condemned: 8199
Jer 22:16 He j. the cause of the poor and 1777
Eze 16:38 wedlock and shed blood are j.; 4941
Eze 16:52 also, which hast j. thy sisters, 6419
Eze 28:23 the wounded shall be j. in the 5307
Eze 35:11 among them, when I have j. thee. 8199
Eze 36:19 according to their doings I j. them. 8199
Da 9:12 and against our judges that j. us, 8199
Mt 7:1 **Judge not, that ye be not j.** 2919
Mt 7:2 **judgment ye judge, ye shall be j.** 2919
Lu 6:37 **Judge not, and ye shall not be j.** 2919
Lu 7:43 said unto him, **Thou hast rightly j.** 2919
Joh 16:11 **the prince of this world is j.** 2919
Ac 16:15 If ye have j. me to be faithful to 2919
Ac 24:6 would have j. according to our law. 2919
Ac 25:9 be j. of these things before me? 2919
Ac 25:10 seat, where I ought to be j.: to the 2919
Ac 25:20 and there be j. of these matters. 2919
Ac 26:6 now I stand and am j. for the hope 2919
Ro 2:12 in the law shall be j. by the law; 2919
Ro 3:4 mightest overcome when thou art j. 2919
Ro 3:7 why yet am I also j. as a sinner? 2919
1Co 2:15 things, yet he himself is j. of no man. 350
1Co 4:3 thing that I should be j. of you, 350
1Co 5:3 present in spirit, have j. already, 2919
1Co 6:2 if the world shall be j. by you, are 2919
1Co 10:29 why is my liberty j. of another 2919
1Co 11:31 ourselves, we should not be j. 2919
1Co 11:32 when we are j., we are chastened 2919
1Co 14:24 he is convinced of all, he is j. of all: 350
Heb 11:11 she j. him faithful who had 2233
Jas 2:12 as they that shall be j. by the law 2919
1Pe 4:6 they might be j. according to men 2919
Re 11:18 of the dead, that they should be j., 2919
Re 16:5 shalt be, because thou hast j. thus. 2919
Re 19:2 for he hath j. the great whore, 2919
Re 20:12 the dead were j. out of those things 2919
Re 20:13 they were j. every man according to 2919

JUDGES

Ex 21:6 master shall bring him unto the j.; 430
Ex 21:22 he shall pay as the j. determine. 6414
Ex 22:8 house shall be brought unto the j., 430
Ex 22:9 parties shall come before the j.; 430
Ex 22:9 whom the j. shall condemn, he shall 430
Nu 25:5 Moses said unto the j. of Israel, 8199
De 1:16 And I charged your j. at that time, 8199
De 16:18 J. and officers shalt thou make 8199
De 19:17 before the priests and j., which 8199
De 19:18 j. shall make diligent inquisition: 8199
De 21:2 elders and thy j. shall come forth, 8199
De 25:1 that the j. may judge them; then 8199
De 32:31 our enemies themselves being j.. 6414
Jos 8:33 their j., stood on this side the ark 8199
Jos 23:2 for their j., and for their officers, 8199
Jos 24:1 for their j., and for their officers; 8199
Jg *general* *title* The General Epistle Of J.. 2455
Jg 2:16 Nevertheless the Lord raised up j., 8199
Jg 2:17 would not hearken unto their j., 8199
Jg 2:18 when the Lord raised them up j., 8199
Ru 1:1 pass in the days when the j. ruled, 8199
1Sa 8:1 that he made his sons j. over Israel. 8199
1Sa 8:2 Abiah: they were j. in Beer-sheba. 8199
2Sa 7:11 since the time that I commanded j. 8199
2Ki 23:22 the days of the j. that judged Israel, 8199
1Ch 17:6 I a word to any of the j. of Israel, 8199
1Ch 17:10 since the time that I commanded j. 8199
1Ch 23:4 six thousand were officers and j.: 8199
1Ch 26:29 over Israel, for officers and j. 8199
2Ch 1:2 to the j., and to every governor in 8199
2Ch 19:5 he set j. in the land throughout all 8199
2Ch 19:6 said to the j., Take heed what ye do: 8199
Ezr 7:25 thine hand, set magistrates and j., 1782
Ezr 10:14 of every city, and the j. thereof, 8199
Job 9:24 covereth the faces of the j. thereof; 8199
Job 12:17 spoiled, and maketh the j. fools. 8199
Job 31:11 iniquity to be punished by the j. 6414
Ps 2:10 be instructed, ye j. of the earth. 8199
Ps 141:6 their j. are overthrown in...places, 8199
Ps 148:11 princes, and all j. of the earth: 8199
Pr 8:16 nobles, even all the j. of the earth. 8199
Isa 1:26 I will restore thy j. as at the first, 8199
Isa 40:23 maketh the j. of the earth as vanity. 8199
Da 3:2 governors, and the captains, the j., 148
Da 3:3 the governors, and captains, the j., 148
Da 9:12 against our j. that judged us, by 8199
Ho 7:7 oven, and have devoured their j.; 8199
Ho 13:10 thy j. of whom thou saidst, Give me 8199
Zep 3:3 her j. are evening wolves; they 8199
Mt 12:27 **therefore they shall be your j.** 2923
Lu 11:19 **therefore shall they be your j.** 2923
Ac 13:20 And after that he gave unto them j. 2923
Jas 2:4 And are become j. of evil thoughts? 2923

JUDGEST

Ps 51:4 and be clear when thou j.. 8199
Jer 11:20 O Lord of hosts, that j. righteously, 8199
Ro 2:1 O man, whosoever thou art that j.; 2919
Ro 2:1 for wherein thou j. another, thou 2919
Ro 2:1 thou that j. doest the same things. 2919
Ro 2:3 that j. them which do such things, 2919
Ro 14:4 Who art thou that j. another man's 2919
Jas 4:12 who art thou that j. another? 2919

JUDGETH

Job 21:22 seeing he j. those that are high. 8199
Job 36:31 by them j. he the people; he giveth 1777
Ps 7:11 God j. the righteous, and God is 8199
Ps 58:11 he is a God that j. in the earth. 8199
Ps 82:1 the mighty; he j. among the gods. 8199
Pr 29:14 The king that faithfully j. the poor, 8199
Joh 5:22 **the Father j. no man, but hath** 2919
Joh 8:50 **there is one that seeketh and j.** 2919
Joh 12:48 **not my words, hath one that j.** 2919
1Co 2:15 But he that is spiritual j. all things, 350
1Co 4:4 but he that j. me is the Lord. 350
1Co 5:13 But them that are without God j.. 2919
Jas 4:11 evil...brother, and j. his brother, 2919
Jas 4:11 evil of the law, and j. the law: 2919
1Pe 1:17 j. according to every man's work, 2919
1Pe 2:23 himself to him that j. righteously: 2919
Re 18:8 strong is the Lord God who j. her. 2919

JUDGING

2Ki 15:5 house, j. the people of the land. 8199
2Ch 26:21 house, j. the people of the land. 8199
Ps 9:4 thou satest in the throne j. right. 8199
Isa 16:5 of David, j., and seeking judgment, 8199
Mt 19:28 **j. the twelve tribes of Israel.** 2919
Lu 22:30 **thrones j. the twelve tribes of** 2919

JUDGMENT See also JUDGMENTS.

Ge 18:19 of the Lord, to do justice and j.; 4941
Ex 12:12 gods of Egypt I will execute j.: 8201
Ex 21:31 according to this j. shall it be done 4941
Ex 23:2 to decline after many to wrest j.:
Ex 23:6 shalt not wrest the j. of thy poor 4941
Ex 28:15 make the breastplate of j. with 4941
Ex 28:29 the breastplate of j. upon his heart, 4941
Ex 28:30 thou shalt put in the breastplate of j. 4941
Ex 28:30 Aaron shall bear the j. of the 4941
Le 19:15 shall do no unrighteousness in j.: 4941
Le 19:35 shall do no unrighteousness in j., 4941
Nu 27:11 the children of Israel a statute of j., 4941
Nu 27:21 after the j. of Urim before the Lord: 4941
Nu 35:12 stand before the congregation in j. 4941
Nu 35:29 shall be for a statute of j. unto you. 4941
De 1:17 ye shall not respect persons in j.; 4941
De 1:17 for the j. is God's: and the cause 4941
De 10:18 He doth execute the j. of the 4941
De 16:18 shall judge the people with just j. 4941
De 16:19 Thou shalt not wrest j.; thou shalt 4941
De 17:8 a matter too hard for thee in j., 4941
De 17:9 shall shew thee the sentence of j.: 4941
De 17:11 according to the j. which they shall 4941
De 24:17 not pervert the j. of the stranger, 4941
De 25:1 they come unto j., that the judges 4941
De 27:19 perverteth the j. of the stranger, 4941
De 30:16 And his statutes and his j., that 4941
De 32:4 all his ways are j.: a God of truth 4941
De 32:41 and mine hand take hold on j.; 4941
Jos 20:6 stand before the congregation for j., 4941
Jg 4:5 of Israel came up to her for j., 4941
Jg 5:10 ye that sit in j., and walk by the 4055
1Sa 8:3 and took bribes, and perverted j.. 4941
2Sa 8:15 David executed j. and justice unto 4941
2Sa 15:2 controversy came to the king for j., 4941
2Sa 15:6 Israel that came to the king for j.: 4941
1Ki 3:11 thyself understanding to discern j.; 4941
1Ki 3:28 Israel heard of the j. which the king 4941
1Ki 3:28 wisdom of God was in him, to do j. 4941
1Ki 7:7 might judge, even the porch of j.: 4941
1Ki 10:9 he thee king, to do j. and justice. 4941
1Ki 20:40 said unto him, So shall thy j. be; 4941
2Ki 25:6 Riblah; and they gave j. upon him. 4941
1Ch 18:14 executed j. and justice among all 4941
2Ch 9:8 king over them, to do j. and justice. 4941
2Ch 19:6 who is with you in the j. 1697,4941
2Ch 19:8 for the j. of the Lord, and for 4941
2Ch 20:9 j., or pestilence, or famine, we 8196
2Ch 22:8 when Jehu was executing j. upon 8199
2Ch 24:24 So they executed j. against Joash. 8201
Ezr 7:26 let j. be executed speedily upon 1780
Es 1:13 toward all that knew law and j.: 1779
Job 8:3 Doth God pervert j.? or doth the 4941
Job 9:19 and if of j., who shall set me a time 4941
Job 9:32 and we should come together in j. 4941
Job 14:3 and bringest me into j. with thee? 4941
Job 19:7 I cry aloud, but there is no j. 4941
Job 19:29 that ye may know there is a j.. 1779
Job 22:4 will he enter with thee into j.? 4941
Job 27:2 liveth, who hath taken away my j.; 4941
Job 29:14 my j. was as a robe and a diadem. 4941
Job 32:9 neither do the aged understand j. 4941
Job 34:4 Let us choose to us j.: let us know 4941
Job 34:5 and God hath taken away my j.. 4941
Job 34:12 neither will the Almighty pervert j. 4941
Job 34:23 he should enter into j. with God. 4941
Job 35:14 not see him, yet j. is before him; 1779
Job 36:17 hast fulfilled the j. of the wicked: 1779
Job 36:17 j. and justice take hold on thee. 1779
Job 37:23 he is excellent in power, and in j., 4941
Job 40:8 Wilt thou also disannul my j.? wilt 4941
Ps 1:5 ungodly shall not stand in the j., 4941
Ps 7:6 to the j. that thou hast commanded. 4941
Ps 9:7 he hath prepared his throne for j. 4941
Ps 9:8 he shall minister j. to the people 1777
Ps 9:16 by the j. which he executeth: 4941
Ps 25:9 The meek will he guide in j.: and 4941
Ps 33:5 He loveth righteousness and j.: the 4941
Ps 35:23 awake to my j., even with my cause, 4941
Ps 37:6 the light, and thy j. as the noonday. 4941
Ps 37:28 Lord loveth j., and forsaketh not 4941
Ps 37:30 wisdom, and his tongue talketh of j. 4941
Ps 72:2 righteousness, and...poor with j.. 4941
Ps 76:8 didst cause j. to be heard from 1779
Ps 76:9 God arose to j., to save all the 4941
Ps 89:14 Justice and j. are the habitation 4941
Ps 94:15 j. shall return unto righteousness: 4941
Ps 97:2 righteousness and j. are the 4941
Ps 99:4 The king's strength also loveth j.; 4941
Ps 99:4 executest j. and righteousness in 4941
Ps 101:1 I will sing of mercy and j.: unto 4941
Ps 103:6 and j. for all that are oppressed. 4941
Ps 106:3 Blessed are they that keep j., and 4941
Ps 106:30 up Phinehas, and executed j.: 6419
Ps 111:7 of his hands are verity and j.; 4941
Ps 119:66 Teach me good j. and knowledge: 2940
Ps 119:84 when wilt thou execute j. on them 4941
Ps 119:121 I have done j. and justice: leave 4941
Ps 119:149 quicken me according to thy j. 4941
Ps 122:5 For there are set thrones of j., the 4941
Ps 143:2 enter not into j. with thy servant: 4941
Ps 146:7 executeth j. for the oppressed: 4941
Ps 149:9 execute upon them the j. written: 4941
Pr 1:3 wisdom, justice, and j., and equity; 4941
Pr 2:8 He keepeth the paths of j., and 4941
Pr 2:9 understand righteousness, and j., 4941
Pr 8:20 in the midst of the paths of j.: 4941
Pr 13:23 is that is destroyed for want of j. 4941
Pr 16:10 his mouth transgresseth not in j. 4941
Pr 17:23 the bosom to pervert the ways of j.. 4941
Pr 18:5 to overthrow the righteous in j.. 4941
Pr 19:28 An ungodly witness scorneth j.: 4941
Pr 20:8 that sitteth in the throne of j. 1779
Pr 21:3 To do justice and j. is more 4941
Pr 21:7 them; because they refuse to do j.. 4941
Pr 21:15 It is joy to the just to do j.: but 4941
Pr 24:23 to have respect of persons in j.. 4941

Pr 28:5 Evil men understand not **j.**: but 4941
Pr 29:4 king by **j.** establisheth the land: 4941
Pr 29:26 every man's **j.** cometh from the 4941
Pr 31:5 pervert the **j.** of any of the afflicted.... 1779
Ec 3:16 I saw under the sun the place of **j.**, ... 4941
Ec 5:8 violent perverting of **j.** and justice 4941
Ec 8:5 heart discerneth both time and **j.**........ 4941
Ec 8:6 every purpose there is time and **j.**,...... 4941
Ec 11:9 things God will bring thee into **j.**........ 4941
Ec 12:14 God shall bring every work into **j.**, ... 4941
Isa 1:17 well; seek **j.**, relieve the oppressed, ... 4941
Isa 1:21 it was full of **j.**; righteousness........... 4941
Isa 1:27 Zion shall be redeemed with **j.**, and 4941
Isa 3:14 The Lord will enter into **j.** with the 4941
Isa 4:4 the midst thereof by the spirit of **j.**,..... 4941
Isa 5:7 and he looked for **j.**, but behold 4941
Isa 5:16 Lord of hosts shall be exalted in **j.**, ... 4941
Isa 9:7 to establish it with **j.** and with 4941
Isa 10:2 To turn aside the needy from **j.**, ... 1779
Isa 16:3 Take counsel, execute **j.**; make 6415
Isa 16:5 and seeking **j.**, and hasting............... 4941
Isa 28:6 a spirit of **j.** to him that sitteth in **j.**,... 4941
Isa 28:7 err in vision, they stumble in **j.**......... 6417
Isa 28:17 **J.** also will I lay to the line, and......... 4941
Isa 30:18 you: for the Lord is a God of **j.**: 4941
Isa 32:1 and princes shall rule in **j.**................ 4941
Isa 32:16 **j.** shall dwell in the wilderness, ... 4941
Isa 33:5 filled Zion with **j.** and righteousness. ... 4941
Isa 34:5 upon the people of my curse, to **j.**. 4941
Isa 40:14 and taught him in the path of **j.**,......... 4941
Isa 40:27 my **j.** is passed over from my God?.... 4941
Isa 41:1 let us come near together to **j.**. 4941
Isa 42:1 shall bring forth **j.** to the Gentiles....... 4941
Isa 42:3 he shall bring forth **j.** unto truth......... 4941
Isa 42:4 till he have set **j.** in the earth: 4941
Isa 49:4 yet surely my **j.** is with the Lord. 4941
Isa 51:4 make my **j.** to rest for a light of the ... 4941
Isa 53:8 was taken from prison and from **j.**:...... 4941
Isa 54:17 that shall rise against thee in **j.**.......... 4941
Isa 56:1 Keep ye **j.**, and do justice: for my...... 4941
Isa 59:8 there is no **j.** in their goings: they...... 4941
Isa 59:9 Therefore is **j.** far from us, neither..... 4941
Isa 59:11 we look for **j.**, but there is none; 4941
Isa 59:14 **j.** is turned away backward, and......... 4941
Isa 59:15 displeased him that there was no **j.**..... 4941
Isa 61:8 I the Lord love **j.**, I hate robbery....... 4941
Jer 4:2 in truth, in **j.**, and in righteousness; 4941
Jer 5:1 if there be any that executeth **j.**,........ 4941
Jer 5:4 of the Lord, nor the **j.** of their God. ... 4941
Jer 5:5 of the Lord, and the **j.** of their God: ... 4941
Jer 7:5 if ye thoroughly execute **j.** between 4941
Jer 8:7 people know not the **j.** of the Lord..... 4941
Jer 9:24 **j.**, and righteousness, in the earth: 4941
Jer 10:24 O Lord, correct me, but with **j.**; 4941
Jer 21:12 Execute **j.** in the morning, and 4941
Jer 22:3 Execute ye **j.** and righteousness,........ 4941
Jer 22:15 eat and drink, and do **j.** and justice, ... 4941
Jer 23:5 execute **j.** and justice in the earth. 4941
Jer 33:15 shall execute **j.** and righteousness....... 4941
Jer 39:5 where he gave **j.** upon him. 4941
Jer 48:21 **j.** is come upon the plain country; 4941
Jer 48:47 Lord: Thus far is the **j.** of Moab. 4941
Jer 49:12 whose **j.** was not to drink of the cup.... 4941
Jer 51:9 her **j.** reacheth unto heaven, and is..... 4941
Jer 51:47 will do **j.** upon the graven images....... 6485
Jer 51:52 will do **j.** upon her graven images:...... 6485
Jer 52:9 where he gave **j.** upon him. 4941
Eze 18:8 executed true **j.** between man and...... 4941
Eze 23:10 for they had executed **j.** upon her. 8196
Eze 23:24 I will set **j.** before them, and they 4941
Eze 34:16 the strong; I will feed them with **j.**..... 4941
Eze 39:21 heathen shall see my **j.** that I have..... 4941
Eze 44:24 they shall stand in **j.**;...................... 8199
Eze 45:9 spoil, and execute **j.** and justice, ... 4941
Da 4:37 works are truth, and his ways **j.**: 1780
Da 7:10 the **j.** was set, and the books were 1780
Da 7:22 **j.** was given to the saints of the most . 1780
Da 7:26 But the **j.** shall sit, and they shall....... 1780
Ho 2:19 and in **j.**, and in lovingkindness, ... 4941
Ho 5:1 **j.** is toward you, because ye have 4941
Ho 5:11 is oppressed and broken in **j.**, ... 4941
Ho 10:4 thus **j.** springeth up as hemlock in...... 4941
Ho 12:6 keep mercy and **j.**, and wait on thy 4941
Am 5:7 Ye who turn **j.** to wormwood, and...... 4941
Am 5:15 good, and establish **j.** in the gate:....... 4941
Am 5:24 But let **j.** run down as waters, and..... 4941
Am 6:12 ye have turned **j.** into gall, and the..... 4941
Mic 3:1 Israel; Is it not for you to know **j.**? 4941
Mic 3:8 and of **j.**, and of might, to declare 4941
Mic 3:9 that abhor **j.**, and pervert all equity. ... 4941
Mic 7:9 my cause, and execute **j.** for me:....... 4941
Hab 1:4 slacked, and **j.** doth never go forth: 4941
Hab 1:4 therefore wrong **j.** proceedeth. 4941
Hab 1:7 **j.** and their dignity shall proceed 4941
Hab 1:12 thou hast ordained them for **j.**; 4941
Zep 2:3 earth, which have wrought his **j.**; 4941
Zep 3:5 morning doth he bring his **j.** to light,... 4941
Zec 7:9 Execute true **j.**, and shew mercy 4941
Zec 8:16 execute the **j.** of truth and peace in.... 4941
Mal 2:17 them; or, Where is the God of **j.**? 4941
Mal 3:5 And I will come near to you to **j.**; 4941
Mt 5:21 **kill shall be in danger of the j.: ....** *2920*
Mt 5:22 **a cause shall be in danger of the j.:** *2920*
Mt 7:2 **with what j. ye judge, ye shall be..** *2917*
Mt 10:15 **and Gomorrha in the day of j., ...** *2920*
Mt 11:22 **for Tyre and Sidon at the day of j.,** *2920*
Mt 11:24 **the land of Sodom in the day of j.,** *2920*
Mt 12:18 and he shall shew **j.** to the Gentiles.... *2920*
Mt 12:20 till he send forth **j.** unto victory. *2920*
Mt 12:36 **account thereof in the day of j......** *2920*
Mt 12:41 **The men of Nineveh shall rise in j..** *2920*
Mt 12:42 **of the south shall rise up in the j...** *2920*
Mt 23:23 **of the law, j., mercy, and faith: ....** *2920*
Mt 27:19 he was set down on the **j.** seat, ... *968*
Mk 6:11 **and Gomorrah in the day of j., ...** *2920*
Lu 10:14 **for Tyre and Sidon at the j., than ..** *2920*
Lu 11:31 **of the south shall rise up in the j...** *2920*
Lu 11:32 **of Nineve shall rise up in the j......** *2920*
Lu 11:42 **pass over j. and the love of God: ...** *2920*
Joh 5:22 **hath committed all j. unto the Son:** *2920*
Joh 5:27 **him authority to execute j. also, ...** *2920*
Joh 5:30 **as I hear, I judge: and my j. is .....** *2920*
Joh 7:24 **appearance, but judge righteous j...** *2920*
Joh 8:16 **And yet if I judge, my j. is true: ...** *2920*
Joh 9:39 **For j. I am come into this world,..** *2917*
Joh 12:31 **Now is the j. of this world: now....** *2920*
Joh 16:8 **sin, and of righteousness, and of j.:** *2920*
Joh 16:11 **Of j., because the prince of this ....** *2920*
Joh 18:28 from Caiaphas unto the hall of **j.**: *4232*
Joh 18:28 went not into the **j.** hall, lest they *4232*
Joh 18:33 Pilate entered into the **j.** hall............ *4232*
Joh 19:9 And went again into the **j.** hall, ... *4232*
Joh 19:13 and sat down in the **j.** seat in a *968*
Ac 8:33 humiliation his **j.** was taken away:....... *2920*
Ac 18:12 Paul, and brought him to the **j.** seat, ... *968*
Ac 18:16 And he drave them from the **j.** seat. *968*
Ac 18:17 and beat him before the **j.** seat. *968*
Ac 23:35 him to be kept in Herod's **j.** hall. *4232*
Ac 24:25 temperance, and **j.** to come, ... *2917*
Ac 25:6 the next day sitting on the **j.** seat........ *968*
Ac 25:10 said Paul, I stand at Caesar's **j.** seat,.... *968*
Ac 25:15 desiring to have **j.** against him. *1349*
Ac 25:17 on the morrow I sat on the **j.** seat, ... *968*
Ro 1:32 Who knowing the **j.** of God, that *1345*
Ro 2:2 the **j.** of God is according to truth *2917*
Ro 2:3 that thou shalt escape the **j.** of God?... *2917*
Ro 2:5 of the righteous **j.** of God; *1341*
Ro 5:16 the **j.** was by one to condemnation, ... *2917*
Ro 5:18 by the offence of one **j.** came upon all.......
Ro 14:10 all stand before the **j.** seat of Christ. *968*
1Co 1:10 the same mind and in the same **j.**........ *1106*
1Co 4:3 be judged of you, or of man's **j.**: *2250*
1Co 7:25 yet I give my **j.**, as one that hath....... *1106*
1Co 7:40 happier if she so abide, after my **j.**: *1106*
2Co 5:10 appear before the **j.** seat of Christ; *968*
Ga 5:10 that troubleth you shall bear his **j.**, ... *2917*
Php 1:9 more in knowledge and in all **j.**;........... *144*
2Th 1:5 token of the righteous **j.** of God,........ *2920*
1Ti 5:24 open beforehand, going before to **j.**; ... *2920*
Heb 6:2 of the dead, and of eternal **j.**............ *2917*
Heb 9:27 once to die, but after this the **j.**:........ *2920*
Heb 10:27 certain fearful looking for of **j.** and...... *2920*
Jas 2:6 and draw you before the **j.** seats? *2922*
Jas 2:13 For he shall have **j.** without mercy, ... *2920*
Jas 2:13 and mercy rejoiceth against **j.**........... *2920*
1Pe 4:17 time is come that **j.** must begin *2917*
2Pe 2:3 **j.** now of a long time lingereth........... *2917*
2Pe 2:4 darkness, to be reserved unto **j.**; *2920*
2Pe 2:9 reserve the unjust unto the day of **j.**.... *2920*
2Pe 3:7 against the day of **j.** and perdition....... *2920*
1Jo 4:17 may have boldness in the day of **j.**: *2920*
Jude 6 unto the **j.** of the great day.............. *2920*
Jude 15 To execute **j.** upon all, and to............ *2920*
Re 14:7 him; for the hour of his **j.** is come:..... *2920*
Re 17:1 thee the **j.** of the great whore *2917*
Re 18:10 for in one hour is thy **j.** come............ *2920*
Re 20:4 them, and **j.** was given unto them: *2917*

JUDGMENT-HALL See JUDGMENT and HALL.

JUDGMENTS

Ex 6:6 out arm, and with great **j.**.................. 8201
Ex 7:4 out of the land of Egypt by great **j.**. ... 8201
Ex 21:1 are the **j.** which thou shalt set........... 4941
Ex 24:3 the words of the Lord, and all the **j.**.... 4941
Le 18:4 Ye shall do my **j.**, and keep mine 4941
Le 18:5 keep my statutes, and my **j.**............... 4941
Le 18:26 keep my statutes and my **j.**,.............. 4941
Le 19:37 statutes, and all my **j.**, and do them:... 4941
Le 20:22 keep all my statutes, and all my **j.**, ... 4941
Le 25:18 shall do my statutes, and keep my **j.**,.. 4941
Le 26:15 statutes, or if your soul abhor my **j.**, .. 4941
Le 26:43 because they despised my **j.**, and....... 4941
Le 26:46 the statutes and **j.** and laws, which..... 4941
Nu 33:4 gods also the Lord executed **j.**. 8201
Nu 35:24 of blood according to these **j.**: 4941
Nu 36:13 are the commandments and the **j.**,....... 4941
De 4:1 unto the statutes, and unto the **j.**, ... 4941
De 4:5 I have taught you statutes and **j.**,....... 4941
De 4:8 hath statutes and **j.** so righteous 4941
De 4:14 time to teach you statutes and **j.**,....... 4941
De 4:45 the statutes, and the **j.**, which Moses . 4941
De 5:1 the statutes and **j.** which I speak in 4941
De 5:31 and the **j.**, which thou shalt teach....... 4941
De 6:1 and the **j.**, which the Lord your God... 4941
De 6:20 and the **j.**, which the Lord our God 4941
De 7:11 and the **j.**, which I command thee 4941
De 7:12 if ye hearken to these **j.**, and keep, ... 4941
De 8:11 and his **j.**, and his statutes, which I.... 4941
De 11:1 charge, and his statutes, and his **j.**, ... 4941
De 11:32 observe to do all the statutes and **j.**.... 4941
De 12:1 These are the statues and **j.**, which..... 4941
De 26:16 thee to do these statutes and **j.**: 4941
De 26:17 and his commandments, and his **j.**, ... 4941
De 33:10 shall teach Jacob thy **j.**, and Israel...... 4941
De 33:21 of the Lord and his **j.** with Israel........ 4941
2Sa 22:23 For all his **j.** were before me: and as.. 4941
1Ki 2:3 and his **j.**, and his testimonies, ... 4941
1Ki 6:12 and execute my **j.**, and keep all my 4941
1Ki 8:58 and his **j.**, which he commanded......... 4941
1Ki 9:4 wilt keep my statutes and my **j.**: 4941
1Ki 11:33 my statutes and my **j.**, as did David.... 4941
1Ch 16:12 wonders, and the **j.** of his mouth;....... 4941
1Ch 16:14 our God; his **j.** are in all the earth...... 4941
1Ch 22:13 to fulfill the statutes and **j.** which 4941
1Ch 28:7 do my commandments and my **j.**, ... 4941
2Ch 7:17 observe my statutes and my **j.**; 4941
2Ch 19:10 and commandment, statutes and **j.**,...... 4941
Ezr 7:10 to teach in Israel statutes and **j.**.......... 4941
Ne 1:7 nor the statutes, nor the **j.**, which...... 4941
Ne 9:13 gavest them right **j.**, and true laws, ... 4941
Ne 9:29 but sinned against thy **j.**, (which if a ... 4941
Ne 10:29 Lord, and his **j.** and his statutes;....... 4941
Ps 10:5 thy **j.** are far above out of his sight: ... 4941
Ps 18:22 For all his **j.** were before me, and I.... 4941
Ps 19:9 the **j.** of the Lord are true and 4941
Ps 36:6 thy **j.** are a great deep: O Lord, ... 4941
Ps 48:1 Judah be glad, because of thy **j.**......... 4941
Ps 72:1 Give the king thy **j.**, O God, and thy .. 4941
Ps 89:30 my law, and walk not in my **j.**; 4941
Ps 97:8 of Judah rejoiced because of thy **j.**, ... 4941
Ps 105:5 wonders, and the **j.** of his mouth;....... 4941
Ps 105:7 our God: his **j.** are all in the earth...... 4941
Ps 119:7 shall have learned thy righteous **j.**. 4941
Ps 119:13 I declared all the **j.** of thy mouth. 4941
Ps 119:20 that it hath unto thy **j.** at all times...... 4941
Ps 119:30 truth: thy **j.** have I laid before me. 4941
Ps 119:39 which I fear: for thy **j.** are good......... 4941
Ps 119:43 mouth; for I have hoped in thy **j.**. 4941
Ps 119:52 I remembered thy **j.** of old, O Lord;... 4941
Ps 119:62 thee because of thy righteous **j.**. 4941
Ps 119:75 know, O Lord, that thy **j.** are right,.... 4941
Ps 119:102 I have not departed from thy **j.**.......... 4941
Ps 119:106 that I will keep thy righteous **j.**.......... 4941
Ps 119:108 mouth, O Lord, and teach me thy **j.**. .. 4941
Ps 119:120 of thee; and I am afraid of thy **j.**. 4941
Ps 119:137 O Lord, and upright are thy **j.**. 4941

Ps 119:156 quicken me according to thy **j.** 4941
Ps 119:160 every one of thy righteous **j.** 4941
Ps 119:164 thee because of thy righteous **j.** 4941
Ps 119:175 praise thee; and let thy **j.** help me 4941
Ps 147:19 his statutes and his **j.** unto Israel. 4941
Ps 147:20 as for his **j.**, they have not known 4941
Pr 19:29 **J.** are prepared for scorners, and 8201
Isa 26:8 Yea, in the way of thy **j.**, O Lord, 4941
Isa 26:9 for when thy **j.** are in the earth, 4941
Jer 1:16 And I will utter my **j.** against them 4941
Jer 12:1 yet let me talk with thee of thy **j.** 4941
Eze 5:6 she hath changed my **j.** into 4941
Eze 5:6 for they have refused my **j.** and my 4941
Eze 5:7 statutes, neither have kept my **j.**, 4941
Eze 5:7 have done according to the **j.** of 4941
Eze 5:8 will execute **j.** in the midst of thee 4941
Eze 5:10 and I will execute **j.** in thee, 8201
Eze 5:15 when I shall execute **j.** in thee in 8201
Eze 11:9 and will execute **j.** among you. 8201
Eze 11:12 statutes, neither executed my **j.**, 4941
Eze 14:21 my four sore **j.** upon Jerusalem, 8201
Eze 16:41 execute **j.** upon thee in the sight of 8201
Eze 18:9 my statutes, and hath kept my **j.**, 4941
Eze 18:17 hath executed my **j.**, hath walked in 4941
Eze 20:11 my statutes, and shewed them my **j.**, 4941
Eze 20:13 statutes, and they despised my **j.**, 4941
Eze 20:16 they despised my **j.**, and walked not 4941
Eze 20:18 neither observe their **j.**, nor defile 4941
Eze 20:19 walk in my statutes, and keep my **j.**, 4941
Eze 20:21 neither kept my **j.** to do them, 4941
Eze 20:24 they had not executed my **j.**, 4941
Eze 20:25 and **j.** whereby they should not live; 4941
Eze 23:24 judge thee according to their **j.** 4941
Eze 25:11 And I will execute **j.** upon Moab; 8201
Eze 28:22 when I shall have executed **j.** in her, 8201
Eze 28:26 when I have executed **j.** upon all 8201
Eze 30:14 in Zoan, and will execute **j.** in No. 8201
Eze 30:19 Thus will I execute **j.** in Egypt: 8201
Eze 36:27 ye shall keep my **j.**, and do them. 4941
Eze 37:24 also walk in my **j.**, and observe my 4941
Eze 44:24 shall judge it according to my **j.**: 4941
Da 9:5 from thy precepts and from thy **j.**: 4941
Ho 6:5 thy **j.** are as the light that goeth 4941
Zep 3:15 the Lord hath taken away thy **j.**, 4941
Mal 4:4 all Israel, with the statutes and **j.** 4941
Ro 11:33 how unsearchable are his **j.**, and *2917*
1Co 6:4 ye have **j.** of things pertaining to *2922*
Re 15:4 thee; for thy **j.** are made manifest. *1345*
Re 16:7 true and righteous are thy **j.** *2920*
Re 19:2 For true and righteous are his **j.**: *2920*

JUDGMENT-SEAT See JUDGMENT and SEAT.

JUDITH (ju'-dith)
Ge 26:34 Esau...when he took to wife **J.** 3067

JUICE
Ca 8:2 wine of the **j.** of my pomegranate. 6071

JULIA (ju'-le-ah)
Ro 16:15 Salute Philologus, and **J.**, Nereus, *2456*

JULIUS (ju'-le-us)
Ac 27:1 unto one named **J.**, a centurion of *2457*
Ac 27:3 And **J.** courteously entreated Paul, *2457*

JUMPING
Na 3:2 horses, and of the **j.** chariots. 7540

JUNIA (ju'-ne-ah)
Ro 16:7 Salute Andronicus and **J.**, my *2458*

JUNIAS See JUNIA.

JUNIPER
1Ki 19:4 and sat down under a **j.** tree: 7574
1Ki 19:5 as he lay and slept under a **j.** tree, 7574
Job 30:4 bushes, and **j.** roots for their meat. 7574
Ps 120:4 of the mighty, with coals of **j.** 7574

JUPITER (ju'-pit-ur)
Ac 14:12 And they called Barnabas, **J.**; *2203*
Ac 14:13 Then the priest of **J.**, which was *2203*
Ac 19:35 image which fell down from **J.**? *1356*

JURISDICTION
Lu 23:7 that he belonged unto Herod's **j.**, *1849*

JUSHAB-HESED (ju''-shab-he'-sed)
1Ch 3:20 and Berechiah, and Hasadiah, **J.**, 3142

JUST See also UNJUST.
Ge 6:9 Noah was a **j.** man and perfect in 6662
Le 19:36 **J.** balances, **j.** weights, a **j.** ephah, 6664
Le 19:36 and a **j.** hin, shall ye have; I am 6664
De 16:18 judge the people with **j.** judgment. 6664
De 16:20 is altogether **j.** shalt thou follow, 6664
De 25:15 shalt have a perfect and **j.** weight, 6664
De 25:15 a perfect and **j.** measure shalt thou 6664
De 32:4 without iniquity, **j.** and right is he. 6662
2Sa 23:3 He that ruleth over men must be **j.**, 6662
Ne 9:33 thou art **j.** in all that is brought 6662
Job 4:17 mortal man be more **j.** than God? 6663
Job 9:2 how should man be **j.** with God? 6663
Job 12:4 the **j.** upright man is laughed to 6662
Job 27:17 prepare it, but the **j.** shall put it on, 6662
Job 33:12 in this thou art not **j.**: I will 6663
Job 34:17 thou condemn him that is most **j.**? 6662
Ps 7:9 establish the **j.**: for the righteous 6662
Ps 37:12 The wicked plotteth against the **j.**, 6662
Pr 3:33 he blesseth the habitation of the **j.** 6662
Pr 4:18 path of the **j.** is as the shining light, 6662
Pr 9:9 teach a **j.** man, and he will increase 6662
Pr 10:6 Blessings...upon the head of the **j.**: 6662
Pr 10:7 The memory of the **j.** is blessed: 6662
Pr 10:20 tongue of the **j.** is as choice silver: 6662
Pr 10:31 The mouth of the **j.** bringeth forth 6662
Pr 11:1 but a **j.** weight is his delight. 8003
Pr 11:9 shall the **j.** be delivered. 6662
Pr 12:13 But the **j.** shall come out of trouble. 6662
Pr 12:21 There shall no evil happen to the **j.**: 6662
Pr 13:22 of the sinner is laid up for the **j.** 6662
Pr 16:11 A **j.** weight and balance are the 4941
Pr 17:15 and he that condemneth the **j.**, 6662
Pr 17:26 Also to punish the **j.** is not good, 6662
Pr 18:17 is first in his own cause seemeth **j.**; 6662
Pr 20:7 The **j.** man walketh in his integrity: 6662
Pr 21:15 It is joy to the **j.** to do judgment: 6662
Pr 24:16 For a **j.** man falleth seven times, 6662
Pr 29:10 upright: but the **j.** seek his soul. 3477
Pr 29:27 man is an abomination to the **j.**: 6662
Ec 7:15 there is a **j.** man that perisheth in 6662
Ec 7:20 there is not a **j.** man upon earth, 6662
Ec 8:14 that there be **j.** men, unto whom it 6662
Isa 26:7 the way of the **j.** is uprightness: 6662
Isa 26:7 dost weigh the path of the **j.** 6662
Isa 29:21 aside the **j.** for a thing of nought. 6662
Isa 45:21 a **j.** God and a Saviour; there is none. 6662
La 4:13 have shed the blood of the **j.** in the 6662
Eze 18:5 if a man be **j.**, and do that which is 6662
Eze 18:9 he is **j.**, he shall surely live, saith 6662
Eze 45:10 Ye shall have **j.** balances, 6664
Eze 45:10 and a **j.** ephah, and a **j.** bath. 6664
Ho 14:9 right, and the **j.** shall walk in them: 6662
Am 5:12 they afflict the **j.**, they take a bribe, 6662
Hab 2:4 but the **j.** shall live by his faith. 6662
Zep 3:5 The **j.** Lord is in the midst thereof; 6662
Zec 9:9 he is **j.**, and having salvation; 6662
Mt 1:19 her husband, being a **j.** man, and *1342*
Mt 5:45 **rain on the j. and on the unjust.** *1342*
Mt 13:49 **the wicked from among the j.**, *1342*
Mt 27:19 nothing to do with that **j.** man: *1342*
Mt 27:24 of the blood of this **j.** person: *1342*
Mk 6:20 that he was a **j.** man and an holy, *1342*
Lu 1:17 disobedient to the wisdom of the **j.**; *1342*
Lu 2:25 the same man was **j.** and devout, *1342*
Lu 14:14 **at the resurrection of the j.** *1342*
Lu 15:7 **over ninety and nine j. persons,** *1342*
Lu 20:20 should feign themselves **j.** men, *1342*
Lu 23:50 and he was a good man, and a **j.**: *1342*
Joh 5:20 **I judge: and my judgment is j.**; *1342*
Ac 3:14 ye denied the Holy One and the **J.**, *1342*
Ac 7:52 before of the coming of the **J.** One; *1342*
Ac 10:22 Cornelius the centurion, a **j.** man, *1342*
Ac 22:14 know his will, and see that **J.** One, *1342*
Ac 24:15 the dead, both of the **j.** and unjust. *1342*
Ro 1:17 written, The **j.** shall live by faith. *1342*
Ro 2:13 of the law are **j.** before God, *1342*
Ro 3:8 may come? whose damnation is **j.** *1738*
Ro 3:26 that he might be **j.**, and the justifier *1342*
Ro 7:12 commandment holy, and **j.**, and *1342*
Ga 3:11 for, The **j.** shall live by faith. *1342*
Php 4:8 honest, whatsoever things are **j.**, *1342*
Col 4:1 servants that which is **j.** and equal; *1342*
Tit 1:8 a lover of good men, sober, **j.**, holy, *1342*
Heb 2:2 a **j.** recompence of reward: *1738*
Heb 10:38 Now the **j.** shall live by faith: but *1342*
Heb 12:23 the spirits of **j.** men made perfect, *1342*
Jas 5:6 have condemned and killed the **j.**; *1342*
1Pe 3:18 for sins, the **j.** for the unjust, that *1342*
2Pe 2:7 And delivered **j.** Lot, vexed with *1342*
1Jo 1:9 and **j.** to forgive us our sins, and to *1342*
Re 15:3 **j.** and true are thy ways, thou King *1342*

JUSTICE See also INJUSTICE.
Ge 18:19 the Lord, to do **j.** and judgment; 6666
De 33:21 he executed the **j.** of the Lord, 6666
2Sa 8:15 David executed judgment and **j.** 6666
2Sa 15:4 unto me, and I would do him **j.**! 6663
1Ki 10:9 thee king, to do judgment and **j.** 6666
1Ch 18:14 executed judgment and **j.** among 6666
2Ch 9:8 over them, to do judgment and **j.** 6666
Job 8:3 or doth the Almighty pervert **j.**? 6664
Job 36:17 judgment and **j.** take hold on thee. 4941
Job 37:23 in judgment, and in plenty of **j.**: 6666
Ps 82:3 do **j.** to the afflicted and needy. 6663
Ps 89:14 **J.** and judgment are the 6664
Ps 119:121 I have done judgment and **j.**: 6664
Pr 1:3 of wisdom, **j.**, and judgment, and 6664
Pr 8:15 kings reign, and princes decree **j.** 6664
Pr 21:3 To do **j.** and judgment is more 6666
Ec 5:8 perverting of judgment and **j.** in 6664
Isa 9:7 it with judgment and with **j.** from 6666
Isa 56:1 Lord, Keep ye judgment, and do **j.**: 6666
Isa 58:2 ask of me the ordinances of **j.**; 6664
Isa 59:4 None calleth for **j.**, nor any pleadeth 6664
Isa 59:9 us, neither doth **j.** overtake us: 6666
Isa 59:14 backward, and **j.** standeth afar off: 6666
Jer 22:15 and drink, and do judgment and **j.**, 6666
Jer 23:5 shall execute judgment and **j.** in the 6666
Jer 31:23 O habitation of **j.**, and mountain 6664
Jer 50:7 the habitation of **j.**, even the Lord, 6664
Eze 45:9 and execute judgment and **j.**, take 6666

JUSTIFICATION
Ro 4:25 and was raised again for our **j.** *1347*
Ro 5:16 gift is of many offences unto **j.** *1345*
Ro 5:18 came upon all men unto **j.** of life. *1347*

JUSTIFIED
Job 11:2 should a man full of talk be **j.**? 6663
Job 13:18 cause; I know that I shall be **j.** 6663
Job 25:4 How then can man be **j.** with God? 6663
Job 32:2 he **j.** himself rather than God. 6663
Ps 51:4 mightest be **j.** when thou speakest, 6663
Ps 143:2 thy sight shall no man living be **j.** 6663
Isa 43:9 their witnesses, that they may be **j.** 6663
Isa 43:26 declare thou, that thou mayest be **j.** 6663
Isa 45:25 shall all the seed of Israel be **j.**, 6663
Jer 3:11 backsliding Israel hath **j.** herself 6663
Eze 16:51 and hast **j.** thy sisters in all thine 6663
Eze 16:52 in that thou hast **j.** thy sisters. 6663
Mt 11:19 **But wisdom is j. of her children.** *1344*
Mt 12:37 **For by thy words thou shalt be j.**, *1344*
Lu 7:29 and the publicans, **j.** God, being *1344*
Lu 7:35 **wisdom is j. of all her children.** *1344*
Lu 18:14 **this man went down to his house j.** *1344*
Ac 13:39 that believe are **j.** from all things, *1344*
Ac 13:39 could not be **j.** by the law of Moses. *1344*
Ro 2:13 but the doers of the law shall be **j.** *1344*
Ro 3:4 thou mightest be **j.** in thy sayings, *1344*
Ro 3:20 shall no flesh be **j.** in his sight: *1344*
Ro 3:24 Being **j.** freely by his grace through *1344*
Ro 3:28 that a man is **j.** by faith without the *1344*
Ro 4:2 For if Abraham were **j.** by works, *1344*
Ro 5:1 being **j.** by faith, we have peace *1344*
Ro 5:9 then, being now **j.** by his blood, *1344*
Ro 8:30 whom he called, them he also **j.**: *1344*
Ro 8:30 whom he **j.**, them he also glorified. *1344*
1Co 4:4 yet am I not hereby **j.**: but he that *1344*
1Co 6:11 **j.** in the name of the Lord Jesus, *1344*
Ga 2:16 is not **j.** by the works of the law, *1344*
Ga 2:16 might be **j.** by the faith of Christ, *1344*
Ga 2:16 works of the law shall no flesh be **j.** *1344*
Ga 2:17 if, while we seek to be **j.** by Christ, *1344*
Ga 3:11 no man is **j.** by the law in the sight *1344*
Ga 3:24 Christ, that we might be **j.** by faith. *1344*
Ga 5:4 whosoever of you are **j.** by the law; *1344*
1Ti 3:16 manifest in the flesh, **j.** in the Spirit, *1344*
Tit 3:7 being **j.** by his grace, we should be *1344*
Jas 2:21 not Abraham our father **j.** by works *1344*
Jas 2:24 then how that by works a man is **j.**, *1344*
Jas 2:25 not Rahab the harlot **j.** by works, *1344*

JUSTIFIER
Ro 3:26 **j.** of him which believeth in Jesus. *1344*

JUSTIFIETH
Pr 17:15 He that **h.** the wicked, and he that..... 6663
Isa 50:8 He is near that **j.** me; who will......... 6663
Ro 4:5 on him that **j.** the ungodly,............... *1344*
Ro 8:33 of God's elect? It is God that **j.**. *1344*

JUSTIFY See also JUSTIFIED; JUSTIFIETH; JUSTIFYING.
Ex 23:7 not: for I will not **j.** the wicked.......... 6663
De 25:1 then they shal **j.** the righteous, ... 6663
Job 9:20 I **j.** myself, mine own mouth shall....... 6663
Job 27:5 God forbid that I should **j.** you: till 6663
Job 33:32 me: speak, for I desire to **j.** thee....... 6663
Isa 5:23 Which **j.** the wicked for reward,.......... 6663
Isa 53:11 shall my righteous servant **j.** many; 6663
Lu 10:29 he, willing to **j.** himself, said unto....... *1344*
Lu 16:15 **which j. yourselves before men,**..... *1344*
Ro 3:30 shall **j.** the circumcision by faith, ... *1344*
Ga 3:8 would **j.** the heathen through faith, ... *1344*

JUSTIFYING
1Ki 8:32 and **j.** the righteous, to give him........ 6663
2Ch 6:23 by **j.** the righteous, by giving him........ 6663

JUSTLE
Na 2:4 they shall **j.** one against another......... 8264

JUSTLY See also UNJUSTLY.
Mic 6:8 but to do **j.**, and love mercy,............ 4941
Lu 23:41 And we indeed **j.**; for we receive....... *1346*
1Th 2:10 how holily and **j.** and unblameably....... *1346*

JUSTUS (jus'-tus) See also BARSABAS; JESUS.
Ac 1:23 Barsabas, who was surnamed **J.**,......... *2459*
Ac 18:7 **J.**, one that worshipped God, ... *2459*
Col 4:11 And Jesus, which is called **J.**, who...... *2459*

JUTTAH (jut'-tah)
Jos 15:55 Maon, Carmel, and Ziph, and **J.**, ... 3194
Jos 21:16 and **J.** with her suburbs, and............ 3194

K.

KABZEEL (kab'-ze-el) See also JEKABZEEL.
Jos 15:21 coast of Edom southward were **K.**,..... 6909
2Sa 23:20 the son of a valiant man, of **K.**, ... 6909
1Ch 11:22 the son of a valiant man of **K.**, ... 6909

KADESH (ka'-desh) See also EN-MISHPAT; KADESH-BARNEA; KEDESH.
Ge 14:7 came to En-mishpat, which is **K.**,......... 6946
Ge 16:14 behold, it is between **K.** and Bered. ... 6946
Ge 20:1 dwelled between **K.** and Shur, and 6946
Nu 13:26 the wilderness of Paran, to **K.**;.......... 6946
Nu 20:1 the people abode in **K.**; and Miriam.... 6946
Nu 20:14 Moses sent messengers from **K.**........ 6946
Nu 20:16 behold, we are in **K.**, a city in the...... 6946
Nu 20:22 congregation, journeyed from **K.**, ... 6946
Nu 27:14 that is the water of Meribah in **K.**....... 6946
Nu 33:36 the wilderness of Zin, which is **K.**. 6946
Nu 33:37 they removed from **K.**, and pitched 6946
De 1:46 abode in **K.** many days, according 6946
Jg 11:16 unto the Red sea, and came to **K.**;..... 6946
Jg 11:17 consent: and Israel abode in **K.**......... 6946
Ps 29:8 Lord shaketh the wilderness of **K.**...... 6946
Eze 47:19 even to the waters of strife in **K.**,...... 6946
Eze 48:28 unto the waters of strife in **K.**,.......... 6946

KADESH-BARNEA (ka"-desh-bar'-ne-ah) See also KADESH.
Nu 32:8 sent them from **K.** to see the land. 6947
Nu 34:4 shall be from the south to **K.**,............ 6947
De 1:2 by the way of mount Seir unto **K.**,).... 6947
De 1:19 commanded us; and we came to **K.**. ... 6947
De 2:14 space in which we came from **K.**,........ 6947
De 9:23 when the Lord sent you from **K.**,........ 6947
Jos 10:41 Joshua smote them from **K.** even....... 6947
Jos 14:6 God concerning me and thee in **K.**. 6947
Jos 14:7 servant of the Lord sent me from **K.**... 6947
Jos 15:3 up on the south side unto **K.**,............ 6947

KADMIEL (kad'-me-el)
Ezr 2:40 the children of Jeshua and **K.**, ... 6934
Ezr 3:9 **K.** and his sons, the sons of Judah, ... 6934
Neh 7:43 the children of Jeshua, of **K.**, and....... 6934
Neh 9:4 the Levites, Jeshua, and Bani, **K.**,....... 6934
Neh 9:5 the Levites, Jeshua, and **K.**, Bani,....... 6934
Neh 10:9 Binnui of the sons of Henadad, **K.**;..... 6934
Neh 12:8 Binnui, **K.**, Sherebiah, Judah, ... 6934
Neh 12:24 and Jeshua the son of **K.**, with their ... 6934

KADMONITES (kad'-mo-nites)
Ge 15:19 and the Kennizzites, and the **K.**,........ 6935

KALLAI (kal'-la-i)
Neh 12:20 Of Sallai, **K.**; of Amok, Eber;............ 7040

KANAH (ka'-nah)
Jos 16:8 westward into the river **K.**;............... 7071
Jos 17:9 coast descended unto the river **K.**,..... 7071
Jos 19:28 and **K.**, even unto great Zidon;.......... 7071

KAREAH (ka'-re-ah) See also CAREAH.
Jer 40:8 and Jonathan the sons of **K.**, ... 7143
Jer 40:13 Johanan the son of **K.**, and all the 7143
Jer 40:15 the son of **K.** spake to Gedaliah in...... 7143
Jer 40:16 said unto Johanan the son of **K.**, ... 7143
Jer 41:11 when Johanan the son of **K.**, and........ 7143
Jer 41:13 Johanan the son of **K.**, and all the 7143
Jer 41:14 went unto Johanan the son of **K.**........ 7143
Jer 41:16 took Johanan the son of **K.**, and all..... 7143
Jer 42:1 and Johanan the son of **K.**, and.......... 7143
Jer 42:8 called he Johanan the son of **K.**,......... 7143
Jer 43:2 Johanan the son of **K.**, and all the 7143
Jer 43:4 So Johanan the son of **K.**, and all 7143
Jer 43:5 But Johanan the son of **K.**, and all....... 7143

KARKAA (kar'-ka-ah)
Jos 15:3 and fetched a compass to **K.** 7173

KARKOR (kar'-kor)
Jg 8:10 Zebah and Zalmunna were in **K.**,........ 7174
Ge 14:5 the Rephaims in Ashteroth **K.**, ... 6255

KARTAH (kar'-tah) See also KATTATH.
Jos 21:34 suburbs, and **K.** with her suburbs,...... 7177

KARTAN (kar'-tan) See also KIRJATHAIM.
Jos 21:32 **K.** with her suburbs; three cities........ 7178

KATTATH (kat'-tath) See also KARTAH; KITRON.
Jos 19:15 And **K.**, and Nahallal, and................. 7005

KEDAR (ke'-dar)
Ge 25:13 of Ishamel, Nebajoth; and **K.**,............. 6938
1Ch 1:29 of Ishamel, Nebaioth; then **K.**,............ 6938
Ps 120:5 that I dwell in the tents of **K.**!........... 6938
Ca 1:5 of Jerusalem, the tents of **K.**,............. 6938
Isa 21:16 and all the glory of **K.** shall fail: 6938
Isa 21:17 mighty men of the children of **K.**,........ 6938
Isa 42:11 the villages that **K.** doth inhabit: 6938
Isa 60:7 the flocks of **K.** shall be gathered........ 6938
Jer 2:10 and send unto **K.**, and consider............ 6938
Jer 49:28 Concerning **K.**, and concerning the 6938
Jer 49:28 go up to **K.**, and spoil the men of 6938
Eze 27:21 Arabia, and all the princes of **K.**,......... 6938

KEDEMAH (ked'-e-mah)
Ge 25:15 Tema, Jetur, Naphish, and **K.**:........... 6929
1Ch 1:31 Jetur, Naphish, **K.**. These are the...... 6929

KEDEMOTH (ked'-e-moth)
De 2:26 out of the wilderness of **K.** unto 6932
Jos 13:18 Jahaza, and **K.**, and Mephaath, ... 6932
Jos 21:37 **K.** with her suburbs, and Mephaath.... 6932
1Ch 6:79 **K.** also with her suburbs, and............ 6932

KEDESH (ke'-desh) See also KADESH; KEDESH-NAPHTALI; KISHION.
Jos 12:22 The king of **K.**, one; the king of 6943
Jos 15:23 And **K.**, and Hazor, and Ithnan, ... 6943
Jos 19:37 And **K.**, and Edrei, and En-hazor, ... 6943
Jos 20:7 And they appointed **K.** in Galilee........ 6943
Jos 21:32 **K.** in Galilee with her suburbs, ... 6943
Jg 4:9 arose, and went with Barak to **K.**. 6943
Jg 4:10 Zebulun and Naphtali to **K.**;............... 6943
Jg 4:11 plain of Zaanaim, which is by **K.**.......... 6943
2Ki 15:29 and **K.**, and Hazor, and Gilead, and 6943
1Ch 6:72 **K.** with her suburbs, Daberath 6943
1Ch 6:76 **K.** in Galilee with her suburbs, and..... 6943

KEDESH-NAPHTALI (ke"-desh-naf'-ta-li)
Jg 4:6 the son of Abinoam out of **K.**, ... 6943,5321

KEEP See also KEEPEST; KEEPETH; KEEPING; KEPT.
Ge 2:15 of Eden to dress it and to **k.** it.......... 8104
Ge 3:24 way, to **k.** the way of the tree of life...8104
Ge 6:19 the ark, to **k.** them alive with thee;.... 8104
Ge 6:20 come unto thee, to **k.** them alive. 8104
Ge 7:3 to **k.** seed alive upon the face of..............
Ge 17:9 shalt **k.** my covenant therefore, ... 8104
Ge 17:10 is my covenant, which ye shall **k.**,...... 8104
Ge 18:19 they shall **k.** the way of the Lord, ... 8104
Ge 28:15 will **k.** thee in all places whither......... 8104
Ge 28:20 and will **k.** me in this way that I go, ... 8104
Ge 30:31 I will again feed and **k.** thy flock. 8104
Ge 33:9 **k.** that thou hast unto thyself. 1961
Ge 41:35 and let them **k.** food in the cities. 8104
Ex 6:5 whom the Egyptians **k.** in bondage; ....
Ex 12:6 shall **k.** it up until the fourteenth........ 4931
Ex 12:14 ye shall **k.** it a feast to the Lord......... 2287
Ex 12:14 shall **k.** it a feast by an ordinance....... 2287
Ex 12:25 that ye shall **k.** this service............... 8104
Ex 12:47 congregation of Israel shall **k.** it. 6213
Ex 12:48 and will **k.** the passover to the Lord, .. 6213
Ex 12:48 then let him come near and **k.** it;....... 6213
Ex 13:5 thou shalt **k.** this service in this......... 5647
Ex 13:10 shalt therefore **k.** this ordinance......... 8104
Ex 15:26 and **k.** all his statutes, I will put.......... 8104
Ex 16:28 refuse ye to **k.** my commandments..... 8104
Ex 19:5 voice indeed, and **k.** my covenant,...... 8104
Ex 20:6 love me, and **k.** my commandments.... 8104
Ex 20:8 the sabbath day, to **k.** it holy. 6942
Ex 22:7 neighbour money or stuff to **k.**,......... 8104
Ex 22:10 ox, or a sheep, or any beast, to **k.**;..... 8104
Ex 23:7 **K.** thee far from a false matter;.......... 7368
Ex 23:14 Three times thou shalt **k.** a feast 2287
Ex 23:15 Thou shalt **k.** the feast of...bread:...... 8104
Ex 23:20 before thee, to **k.** thee in the way,..... 8104
Ex 31:13 Verily my sabbaths ye shall **k.**: 8104
Ex 31:14 Ye shall **k.** the sabbath therefore;....... 8104
Ex 31:16 of Israel shall **k.** the sabbath, ... 8104
Ex 34:18 of unleavened bread shalt thou **k.**. 8104
Le 6:2 which was delivered him to **k.**, ...
Le 6:4 which was delivered him to **k.**, ... 6485
Le 8:35 **k.** the charge of the Lord, that ye....... 8104
Le 18:4 **k.** mine ordinances, to walk therein: ... 8104
Le 18:5 Ye shall therefore **k.** my statutes, ... 8104
Le 18:26 Ye shall therefore **k.** my statutes 8104
Le 18:30 shall ye **k.** mine ordinance, that 8104
Le 19:3 and his father, and **k.** my sabbaths: 8104
Le 19:19 ye shall **k.** my statutes. Thou shalt..... 8104
Le 19:30 Ye shall **k.** my sabbaths, and............ 8104
Le 20:8 ye shall **k.** my statutes, and do.......... 8104
Le 20:22 shall therefore **k.** all my statutes,....... 8104
Le 22:9 shall therefore **k.** mine ordinance,....... 8104
Le 22:31 shall ye **k.** my commandments, ... 8104
Le 23:39 ye shall **k.** a feast unto the Lord........ 2287
Le 23:41 ye shall **k.** it a feast unto the Lord..... 2287
Le 25:2 the land **k.** a sabbath unto the Lord. ....
Le 25:18 **k.** my judgments, and do them; 8104
Le 26:2 Ye shall **k.** my sabbaths, and............. 8104
Le 26:3 and **k.** my commandments, and do...... 8104
Nu 1:53 **k.** the charge of the tabernacle of....... 8104
Nu 3:7 And they shall **k.** his charge, and 8104
Nu 3:8 they shall **k.** all the instruments of...... 8104
Nu 3:32 that **k.** the charge of the sanctuary..... 8104
Nu 6:24 The Lord bless thee, and **k.** thee:....... 8104
Nu 8:26 to **k.** the charge, and shall do no......... 8104
Nu 9:2 of Israel also **k.** the passover at.......... 6213
Nu 9:3 shall **k.** it in his appointed season....... 6213
Nu 9:3 ceremonies thereof, shall ye **k.** it....... 6213

Nu	9:4	that they should **k.** the passover.	6213
Nu	9:6	not **k.** the passover on that day:	6213
Nu	9:10	yet he shall **k.** the passover unto	6213
Nu	9:11	month at even they shall **k.** it,	6213
Nu	9:12	of the passover they shall **k.** it.	6213
Nu	9:13	and forbeareth to **k.** the passover,	6213
Nu	9:14	will **k.** the passover unto the Lord;	6213
Nu	18:3	they shall **k.** thy charge, and the	8104
Nu	18:4	**k.** the charge of the tabernacle of	8104
Nu	18:5	shall **k.** the charge of the sanctuary,	8104
Nu	18:7	with thee shall **k.** your priest's	8104
Nu	29:12	ye shall **k.** a feast unto the Lord	2287
Nu	31:18	with him, **k.** alive for yourselves.	
Nu	31:30	**k.** the charge of the tabernacle	8104
Nu	36:7	**k.** himself to the inheritance	1692
Nu	36:9	**k.** himself to his own inheritance.	1692
De	4:2	ye may **k.** the commandments of	8104
De	4:6	**K.** therefore and do them; for this	8104
De	4:9	and **k.** thy soul diligently, lest thou	8104
De	4:40	shalt **k.** therefore his statutes, and	8104
De	5:1	learn them, and **k.**, and do them.	8104
De	5:10	love me and **k.** my commandments.	8104
De	5:12	**K.** the sabbath day to sanctify it,	8104
De	5:15	commanded thee to **k.** the sabbath	6213
De	5:29	**k.** all my commandments always,	8104
De	6:2	God, to **k.** all his statutes and his	8104
De	6:17	diligently **k.** the commandments of	8104
De	7:8	and because he would **k.** the oath	8104
De	7:9	**k.** his commandments to a thousand	8104
De	7:11	therefore **k.** the commandments,	8104
De	7:12	judgments, and **k.**, and do them,	8104
De	7:12	shall **k.** unto thee the covenant	8104
De	8:2	wouldest **k.** his commandments, or	8104
De	8:6	thou shalt **k.** the commandments	8104
De	10:13	to **k.** the commandments of the	8104
De	11:1	and **k.** his charge, and his statutes,	8104
De	11:8	shall ye **k.** all the commandments	8104
De	11:22	For if ye shall diligently **k.** all these	8104
De	13:4	**k.** his commandments, and obey	8104
De	13:18	to **k.** all his commandments which	8104
De	16:1	**k.** the passover unto the Lord	6213
De	16:10	**k.** the feast of weeks unto the Lord	6213
De	16:15	days shalt thou **k.** a solemn feast	2287
De	17:19	to **k.** all the words of this law and	8104
De	19:9	shalt **k.** all these commandments	8104
De	23:9	**k.** thee from every wicked thing.	8104
De	23:23	out of thy lips thou shalt **k.** and	8104
De	26:16	**k.** and do them with all thine heart,	8104
De	26:17	ways, and to **k.** his statutes, and his	8104
De	26:18	shouldest **k.** all his commandments;	8104
De	27:1	**K.** all the commandments which I	8104
De	28:9	**k.** the commandments of the Lord	8104
De	28:45	to **k.** his commandments and his	8104
De	29:9	**K.**...the words of this covenant,	8104
De	30:10,	16 to **k.** his commandments and his	8104
Jos	6:18	**k.** yourselves from the accursed	8104
Jos	10:18	and set men by it for to **k.** them:	8104
Jos	22:5	to **k.** his commandments, and to	8104
Jos	23:6	to **k.** and to do all that is written in	8104
Jg	2:22	will **k.** the way of the Lord to walk	8104
Jg	2:22	as their fathers did **k.** it, or not.	8104
Jg	3:19	thee, O king: who said, **K.** silence.	
Ru	2:21	shalt **k.** fast by my young men,	1692
1Sa	2:9	will **k.** the feet of his saints, and	8104
1Sa	7:1	his son to **k.** the ark of the Lord.	8104
2Sa	8:2	death, and with one full line to **k.** alive.	
2Sa	15:16	were concubines, to **k.** the house	8104
2Sa	16:21	which he hath left to **k.** the house;	8104
2Sa	18:18	I have no son to **k.** my name in	
2Sa	20:3	whom he had left to **k.** the house,	8104
1Ki	2:3	**k.** the charge of the Lord thy God,	8104
1Ki	2:3	walk in his ways, to **k.** his statutes,	8104
1Ki	3:14	walk in my ways, to **k.** my statutes	8104
1Ki	6:12	**k.** all my commandments to walk	8104
1Ki	8:25	**k.** with thy servant David my father	8104
1Ki	8:58	ways, and to **k.** his commandments,	8104
1Ki	8:61	and to **k.** his commandments, as at	8104
1Ki	9:4	**k.** my statutes and my judgments:	8104
1Ki	9:6	and will not **k.** my commandments	8104
1Ki	11:33	to **k.** my statutes and my judgments,	
1Ki	11:38	in my sight, to **k.** my statutes and	8104
1Ki	20:39	unto me, and said, **K.** this man:	8104
2Ki	11:6	shall ye **k.** the watch of the house,	8104
2Ki	11:7	they shall **k.** the watch of the house	8104
2Ki	17:13	and **k.** my commandments and my	8104
2Ki	23:3	to **k.** his commandments and his	8104
2Ki	23:21	**K.** the passover unto the Lord	6213
1Ch	4:10	that thou wouldest **k.** me from evil,	6213
1Ch	12:33	thousand, which could **k.** rank:	5737
1Ch	12:38	men of war, that could **k.** rank,	5737
1Ch	22:12	mayest **k.** the law of the Lord thy	8104
1Ch	23:32	**k.** the charge of the tabernacle	8104
1Ch	28:8	**k.** and seek for...the commandments	8104
1Ch	29:18	**k.** this for ever in the imagination	8104
1Ch	29:19	heart, to **k.** thy commandments,	8104
2Ch	6:16	**k.** thy servant David my father	8104
2Ch	13:11	we **k.** the charge of the Lord our	8104
2Ch	22:9	no power to **k.** still the kingdom.	6113
2Ch	23:6	shall **k.** the watch of the Lord.	8104
2Ch	28:10	to **k.** under the children of Judah	3533
2Ch	30:1	to **k.** the passover unto the Lord	6213
2Ch	30:2	to **k.** the passover in the second	6213
2Ch	30:3	they could not **k.** it at that time,	6213
2Ch	30:5	to **k.** the passover unto the Lord	6213
2Ch	30:13	to **k.** the feast of unleavened bread	6213
2Ch	30:23	took counsel to **k.** other seven days:	6213
2Ch	34:31	Lord, and to **k.** his commandments,	8104
2Ch	35:16	the same day, to **k.** the passover,	6213
2Ch	35:18	kings of Israel **k.** such a passover	6213
Ezr	8:29	and **k.** them, until ye weigh them	8104
Ne	1:9	and **k.** my commandments, and do	8104
Ne	12:27	to **k.** the dedication with gladness,	6213
Ne	13:22	they should come and **k.** the gates,	8104
Es	3:8	neither **k.** they the king's laws:	6213
Es	9:21	**k.** the fourteenth day of the month	6213
Es	9:27	would **k.** these two days according	6213
Job	14:13	**k.** me secret, until thy wrath be	
Job	20:13	but **k.** it still within his mouth:	4513
Ps	12:7	Thou shalt **k.** them, O Lord, thou	8104
Ps	17:8	**K.** me as the apple of the eye,	8104
Ps	19:13	**K.** back thy servant also from	2820
Ps	22:29	and none can **k.** alive his own soul.	
Ps	25:10	such as **k.** his covenant and his	5341
Ps	25:20	O **k.** my soul, and deliver me; let	8104
Ps	31:20	shalt **k.** them secretly in a pavilion.	
Ps	33:10	and to **k.** them in famine.	
Ps	34:13	**K.** thy tongue from evil, and thy	5341
Ps	35:22	hast seen, O Lord: **k.** not silence:	
Ps	37:34	Wait on the Lord, and **k.** his way,	8104
Ps	39:1	I will **k.** my mouth with a bridle,	8104
Ps	41:2	preserve him, and **k.** him alive;	
Ps	50:3	come, and shall not **k.** silence:	
Ps	78:7	God, but **k.** his commandments:	5341
Ps	83:1	**K.** not thou silence, O God: hold not	
Ps	89:28	My mercy will I **k.** for him for	8104
Ps	89:31	and **k.** not my commandments;	8104
Ps	91:11	over thee, to **k.** thee in all thy ways.	8104
Ps	103:9	neither will he **k.** his anger for	5201
Ps	103:18	to such as **k.** his covenant, and to	8104
Ps	105:45	his statutes, and **k.** his laws.	5341
Ps	106:3	are they that **k.** judgment, and he	8104
Ps	113:9	the barren woman to **k.** house,	
Ps	119:2	are they that **k.** his testimonies,	5341
Ps	119:4	us to **k.** thy precepts diligently.	8104
Ps	119:5	were directed to **k.** thy statutes!	8104
Ps	119:8	I will **k.** thy statutes: O forsake	8104
Ps	119:17	that I may live, and **k.** thy word.	8104
Ps	119:33	and I shall **k.** it unto the end.	5341
Ps	119:34	and I shall **k.** thy law;	5341
Ps	119:44	So shall I **k.** thy law continually	8104
Ps	119:57	said that I would **k.** thy words.	8104
Ps	119:60	not to **k.** thy commandments.	8104
Ps	119:63	and of them that **k.** thy precepts.	8104
Ps	119:69	will **k.** thy precepts with my whole	5341
Ps	119:88	I **k.** the testimony of thy mouth.	8104
Ps	119:100	because I **k.** thy precepts.	5341
Ps	119:101	way, that I might **k.** thy word.	8104
Ps	119:106	I will **k.** thy righteous judgments.	8104
Ps	119:115	I will **k.** the commandments of my	5341
Ps	119:129	therefore doth my soul **k.** them.	5341
Ps	119:134	of man: so will I **k.** thy precepts.	8104
Ps	119:136	eyes, because they **k.** not thy law.	8104
Ps	119:145	me, O Lord: I will **k.** thy statutes.	5341
Ps	119:146	me, and I shall **k.** thy testimonies.	8104
Ps	127:1	except the Lord **k.** the city, the	8104
Ps	132:12	If thy children will **k.** my covenant	8104
Ps	140:4	**K.** me, O Lord, from the hands of	8104
Ps	141:3	my mouth; **k.** the door of my lips.	5341
Ps	141:9	**K.** me from the snares which they	8104
Pr	2:11	thee, understanding shall **k.** thee:	5341
Pr	2:20	and **k.** the paths of the righteous.	8104
Pr	3:1	thine heart **k.** my commandments	5341
Pr	3:21	**k.** sound wisdom and discretion:	5341
Pr	3:26	shall **k.** thy foot from being taken.	8104
Pr	4:4	**k.** my commandments, and live.	8104
Pr	4:6	love her, and she shall **k.** thee.	5341
Pr	4:13	instruction; let her not go: **k.** her;	5341
Pr	4:21	**k.** them in the midst of thine heart.	8104
Pr	4:23	**K.** thy heart with all diligence;	5341
Pr	5:2	that thy lips may **k.** knowledge.	5341
Pr	6:20	son, **k.** thy father's commandment,	5341
Pr	6:22	thou sleepest, it shall **k.** thee;	8104
Pr	6:24	To **k.** thee from the evil woman,	8104
Pr	7:1	My son, **k.** my words, and lay up	8104
Pr	7:2	**K.** my commandments, and live;	8104
Pr	7:5	**k.** thee from the strange woman,	8104
Pr	8:32	blessed are they that **k.** my ways.	8104
Pr	22:5	he that doth **k.** his soul shall be far	8104
Pr	22:18	thing if thou **k.** them within thee;	8104
Pr	28:4	as **k.** the law contend with them.	8104
Ec	3:6	time to **k.**, and a time to cast away;	8104
Ec	3:7	time to **k.** silence, and a time to speak;	
Ec	5:1	**K.** thy foot when thou goest to the	8104
Ec	8:2	to **k.** the king's commandment,	8104
Ec	12:13	God, and **k.** his commandments:	8104
Ca	8:12	those that **k.** the fruit thereof two	5201
Isa	26:3	Thou wilt **k.** him in perfect peace,	5341
Isa	27:3	I the Lord do **k.** it; I will water it	5341
Isa	27:3	hurt it, I will **k.** it night and day.	5341
Isa	41:1	**K.** silence before me, O islands;	
Isa	42:6	hold thine hand, and will **k.** thee,	5341
Isa	43:6	and to the south, **K.** not back;	3607
Isa	56:1	saith the Lord, **K.** ye judgment,	8104
Isa	56:4	the eunuchs that **k.** my sabbaths,	8104
Isa	62:6	mention of the Lord, **k.** not silence,	
Isa	65:6	I will not **k.** silence, but will	
Jer	3:5	ever? will he **k.** it to the end?	8104
Jer	3:12	and I will not **k.** anger for ever,	5201
Jer	31:10	**k.** him, as a shepherd doth his	8104
Jer	42:4	I will **k.** nothing back from you.	4513
La	2:10	sit upon the ground, and **k.** silence:	
Eze	11:20	**k.** mine ordinances, and do them:	8104
Eze	18:21	**k.** all my statutes, and do that which	8104
Eze	20:19	**k.** my judgments, and do them;	8104
Eze	36:27	ye shall **k.** my judgments, and do	8104
Eze	43:11	that they may **k.** the whole form	8104
Eze	44:16	me, and they shall **k.** my charge.	8104
Eze	44:24	and they shall **k.** my laws and my	8104
Da	9:4	them that **k.** his commandments;	8104
Ho	12:6	**k.** mercy and judgment, and wait	8104
Am	5:13	the prudent shall **k.** silence in that	
Mic	7:5	**k.** the doors of thy mouth from	8104
Na	1:15	O Judah, **k.** thy solemn feasts,	2287
Na	2:1	**k.** the munition, watch the way,	5341
Hab	2:20	let all the earth **k.** silence before him.	
Zec	3:7	if thou wilt **k.** my charge, then	8104
Zec	3:7	and shalt also **k.** my courts,	8104
Zec	13:5	man taught me to **k.** cattle from	7069
Zec	14:16	to **k.** the feast of tabernacles.	2287
Zec	14:18,	19 up to **k.** the feast of tabernacles.	2287
Mal	2:7	priest's lips should **k.** knowledge,	2287
Mt	19:17	**into life, k. the commandments.**	*5083*
Mt	26:18	**I will k. the passover at thy house**	*4160*
Mk	7:9	**that ye may k. your own tradition.**	*5083*
Lu	4:10	charge over thee, to **k.** thee:	*1314*
Lu	8:15	**having heard the word, k. it.**	*2722*
Lu	11:28	**hear the word of God, and k. it.**	*5442*
Lu	19:43	**and k. thee in on every side,**	*4912*
Joh	8:51	**If a man k. my saying, he shall**	*5083*
Joh	8:52	If a man **k.** my saying	
Joh	8:55	**but I know him, and k. his saying.**	*5083*
Joh	12:25	**world shall k. it unto life eternal.**	*5442*
Joh	14:15	**ye love me, k. my commandments.**	*5083*
Joh	14:23	**a man love me, he will k. my**	*5083*
Joh	15:10	**If ye k. my commandments, ye.**	*5083*
Joh	15:20	**my saying, they will k. yours also.**	*5083*
Joh	17:11	**Holy Father, k. through thine own**	*5083*
Joh	17:15	**shouldest k. them from the evil.**	*5083*
Ac	5:3	to **k.** back part of the price of the	*3557*
Ac	10:28	man that is a Jew to **k.** company,	*2853*
Ac	12:4	quaternions of soldiers to **k.** him;	*5442*
Ac	15:5	them to **k.** the law of Moses.	*5083*
Ac	15:24	be circumcised, and **k.** the law:	*5083*
Ac	15:29	from which if ye **k.** yourselves, ye	*1301*
Ac	16:4	deliver them the decrees for to **k.**,	*5442*
Ac	16:23	the jailor to **k.** them safely:	*5083*

Ac 18:21 I must by all means **k.** this feast........ *4160*
Ac 21:25 only that they **k.** themselves from...... *5442*
Ac 24:23 a centurion to **k.** Paul, and............... *5083*
Ro 2:25 verily profiteth, if thou **k.** the law:...... *4238*
Ro 2:26 **k.** the righteousness of the law,......... *5442*
1Co 5:8 Therefore let us **k.** the feast, not....... *1858*
1Co 5:11 unto you not to **k.** company, ... *4874*
1Co 7:37 heart that he will **k.** his virgin, ... *5083*
1Co 9:27 I **k.** under my body, and bring it........ *5299*
1Co 11:2 **k.** the ordinances, as I delivered........ *2722*
1Co 14:28 let him **k.** silence in the church;......... *4601*
1Co 14:34 women **k.** silence in the churches:...... *4601*
1Co 15:2 ye **k.** in memory what I preached....... *2722*
2Co 11:9 unto you, and so will I **k.** myself........ *5083*
Ga 6:13 who are circumcised **k.** the law;......... *5442*
Eph 4:3 to **k.** the unity of the Spirit in the *5083*
Php 4:7 shall **k.** your hearts and minds........... *5432*
2Th 3:3 stablish you, and **k.** you from evil...... *5442*
1Ti 5:22 other men's sins: **k.** thyself pure........ *5083*
1Ti 6:14 **k.** this commandment without........... *5083*
1Ti 6:20 **k.** that which is committed to thy....... *5442*
2Ti 1:12 **k.** that which I have committed.......... *5442*
2Ti 1:14 unto thee **k.** by the Holy Ghost......... *5442*
Jas 1:27 to **k.** himself unspotted from the *5083*
Jas 2:10 whosoever shall **k.** the whole law,....... *5083*
1Jo 2:3 him, if we **k.** his commandments........ *5083*
1Jo 3:22 because we **k.** his commandments, ... *5083*
1Jo 5:2 God, and **k.** his commandments. *5083*
1Jo 5:3 that we **k.** his commandments: *5083*
1Jo 5:21 children, **k.** yourselves from idols....... *5442*
Jude 21 **K.** yourselves in the love of God,........ *5083*
Jude 24 that is able to **k.** you from falling, ... *5442*
Re 1:3 **k.** those things which are written....... *5083*
Re 3:10 **also will k. thee from the hour of** ..*5083*
Re 12:17 which **k.** the commandments of.......... *5083*
Re 14:12 that **k.** the commandments of God,..... *5083*
Re 22:9 which **k.** the sayings of this book: *5083*

KEEPER See also DOORKEEPER; KEEPERS.
Ge 4:2 Abel was a **k.** of the sheep, but......... 7462
Ge 4:9 know not: Am I my brother's **k.**?....... 8104
Ge 39:21 the sight of the **k.** of the prison.......... 8269
Ge 39:22 the **k.** of the prison committed to....... 8269
Ge 39:23 The **k.** of the prison looked not to...... 8269
1Sa 17:20 and left the sheep with a **k.**, ... 8104
1Sa 17:22 carriage in the hand of the **k.** of......... 8104
1Sa 28:2 make thee **k.** of mine head for ever.... 8104
2Ki 22:14 son of Harhas, **k.** of the wardrobe;..... 8104
2Ch 34:22 son of Hasrah, **k.** of the wardrobe;..... 8104
Ne 2:8 Asaph the **k.** of the king's forest,....... 8104
Ne 3:29 Shemaiah...the **k.** of the east gate...... 8104
Es 2:3 chamberlain, **k.** of the women;........... 8104
Es 2:8 custody of Hegai, **k.** of the women..... 8104
Es 2:15 chamberlain, the **k.** of the women, ... 8104
Job 27:18 and as a booth that the **k.** maketh...... 5341
Ps 121:5 the Lord is thy **k.**: the Lord is thy..... 8104
Ca 1:6 made me **k.** of the vineyards; but........ 5201
Jer 35:4 Maaseiah...the **k.** of the door: 8104
Ac 16:27 the **k.** of the prison awaking out *1200*
Ac 16:36 the **k.** of the prison told this *1200*

KEEPERS See also DOORKEEPERS.
2Ki 11:5 even be **k.** of the watch of the 8104
2Ki 22:4 which the **k.** of the door have............ 8104
2Ki 23:4 the **k.** of the door, to bring forth 8104
2Ki 25:18 priest, and the three **k.** of the door: ... 8104
1Ch 9:19 **k.** of the gates of the tabernacle: 8104
1Ch 9:19 of the Lord, were **k.** of the entry........ 8104
Es 6:2 chamberlains, the **k.** of the door, ... 8104
Ec 12:3 day when the **k.** of the house shall..... 8104
Ca 5:7 **k.** of the walls took away any veil 8104
Ca 8:11 he let out the vineyard unto **k.**; 5201
Jer 4:17 As **k.** of a field, are they against........ 8104
Jer 52:24 and the three **k.** of the door:............ 8104
Eze 40:45 the **k.** of the charge of the house....... 8104
Eze 40:46 the **k.** of the charge of the altar:........ 8104
Eze 44:8 ye have set **k.** of my charge in my..... 8104
Eze 44:14 them **k.** of the charge of the house,.... 8104
Mt 28:4 for fear of him the **k.** did shake, ... *5083*
Ac 5:23 **k.** standing without before the *5441*
Ac 12:6 **k.** before the door kept the prison...... *5441*
Ac 12:19 him not, he examined the **k.**, and........ *5441*
Tit 2:5 discreet, chaste, **k.** at home, good, ... *3626*

KEEPEST
1Ki 8:23 who **k.** covenant and mercy with........ 8104
2Ch 6:14 which **k.** covenant, and shewest......... 8104
Ne 9:32 who **k.** covenant and mercy, let not.... 8104
Ac 21:24 walkest orderly, and **k.** the law.......... *5442*

KEEPETH
Ex 21:18 and he die not, but **k.** his bed: 5307
De 7:9 **k.** covenant and mercy with them....... 8104
1Sa 16:11 and, behold, he **k.** the sheep............ 7462
Ne 1:5 that **k.** covenant and mercy for.......... 8104
Job 33:18 He **k.** back his soul from the pit, ... 2820
Ps 34:20 He **k.** all his bones: not one of.......... 8104
Ps 121:3 he that **k.** thee will not slumber......... 8104
Ps 121:4 he that **k.** Israel shall neither 8104
Ps 146:6 therein is: which **k.** truth for ever: 8104
Pr 2:8 He **k.** the paths of judgment, and....... 5341
Pr 10:17 the way of life that **k.** instruction: 8104
Pr 13:3 He that **k.** his mouth...his life:........... 5341
Pr 13:3 He that...his mouth **k.** his life:........... 8104
Pr 13:6 **k.** him that is upright in the way; 5341
Pr 16:17 he that **k.** his way preserveth his....... 5341
Pr 19:8 he that **k.** understanding shall............ 8104
Pr 19:16 **k.** the commandment **k.** his own........ 8104
Pr 21:23 Whoso **k.** his mouth and his............. 8104
Pr 21:23 tongue **k.** his soul from troubles......... 8104
Pr 24:12 he that **k.** thy soul, doth not he......... 5341
Pr 27:18 Whoso **k.** the fig tree shall eat the 5341
Pr 28:7 Whoso **k.** the law is a wise son: but... 5341
Pr 29:3 he that **k.** company with harlots..............
Pr 29:11 a wise man **k.** it in till afterwards....... 7623
Pr 29:18 he that **k.** the law, happy is he......... 8104
Ec 8:5 Whoso **k.** the commandment shall....... 8104
Isa 26:2 nation which **k.** the truth may enter.... 8104
Isa 56:2 that **k.** the sabbath from polluting....... 8104
Isa 56:2 **k.** his hand from doing any evil.......... 8104
Isa 56:6 that **k.** the sabbath from polluting....... 8104
Jer 48:10 that **k.** back his sword from blood. 4513
La 3:28 He sitteth alone and **k.** silence,................
Hab 2:5 he is a proud man, neither **k.** at home, ...
Lu 11:21 **a strong man armed k. his palace,** .*5442*
Joh 7:19 **and yet none of you k. the law?**.... *4160*
Joh 9:16 because he **k.** not the sabbath day...... *5083*
Joh 14:21 **my commandments, and k. them**... *5083*
Joh 14:24 **loveth me not k. not my sayings:**.. *5083*
1Jo 2:4 and **k.** not his commandments, ... *5083*
1Jo 2:5 whoso **k.** his word, in him verily is...... *5083*
1Jo 3:24 And he that **k.** his commandments....... *5083*
1Jo 5:18 that is begotten of God **k.** himself, ... *5083*
Re 2:26 **and k. my works unto the end,** *5083*
Re 16:15 that watcheth, and **k.** his garments,.... *5083*
Re 22:7 blessed is he that **k.** the sayings of..... *5083*

KEEPING
Ex 34:7 **K.** mercy for thousands, forgiving....... 5341
Nu 3:28 **k.** the charge of the sanctuary........... 8104
Nu 3:38 **k.** the charge of the sanctuary for...... 8104
De 8:11 God, in not **k.** his commandments, ... 8104
1Sa 25:16 we were with them **k.** the sheep. 7462
Ne 12:25 were porters **k.** the ward at the 8104
Ps 19:11 in **k.** of them there is great reward. ... 8104
Eze 17:14 by **k.** of his covenant it might stand.... 8104
Da 9:4 **k.** the covenant and mercy to them.... 8104
Lu 2:8 **k.** watch over their flock by night....... *5442*
1Co 7:19 **k.** of the commandments of God. *5084*
1Pe 4:19 commit the **k.** of their souls to him in ....

KEHELATHAH (ke-hel'-a-thah)
Nu 33:22 from Rissah, and pitched in **K.**........... 6954
Nu 33:23 they went from **K.**, and pitched in...... 6954

KEILAH (ki'-lah)
Jos 15:44 **K.**, and Achzib, and Mareshah;.......... 7084
1Sa 23:1 the Philistines fight against **K.**,.......... 7084
1Sa 23:2 smite the Philistines, and save **K.**........ 7084
1Sa 23:3 much more then if we come to **K.**....... 7084
1Sa 23:4 and said, Arise, go down to **K.**; 7084
1Sa 23:5 So David and his men went to **K.**,....... 7084
1Sa 23:5 David saved the inhabitants of **K.**. 7084
1Sa 23:6 of Ahimelech fled to David to **K.**, ... 7084
1Sa 23:7 Saul that David was come to **K.**......... 7084
1Sa 23:8 to go down to **K.**, to besiege David.... 7084
1Sa 23:10 that Saul seeketh to come to **K.**, ... 7084
1Sa 23:11 men of **K.** deliver me up into his......... 7084
1Sa 23:12 men of **K.** deliver me and my men 7084
1Sa 23:13 arose and departed out of **K.**,............ 7084
1Sa 23:13 that David was escaped from **K.**; 7084
1Ch 4:19 the father of **K.** the Garmite, ... 7084
Ne 3:17 the ruler of the half part of **K.**, in 7084
Ne 3:18 the ruler of the half part of **K.**........... 7084

KELAIAH (kel-ah'-yah) See also KELITA.
Ezr 10:23 Jozabad, and Shimei, and **K.**,............. 7041

KELITA (kel'-i-tah) See also KELAIAH.
Ezr 10:23 and Kelaiah, (the same is **K.**,)........... 7042
Ne 8:7 Maaseiah, **K.**, Azariah, Jozabad,.......... 7042
Ne 10:10 Hodijah, **K.**, Pelaiah, Hanan, ... 7042

KEMUEL (kem-u'-el)
Ge 22:21 and **K.** the father of Aram, ... 7055
Nu 34:24 Ephraim, **K.** the son of Shiphtan. 7055
1Ch 27:17 Levites, Hashabiah the son of **K.**: 7055

KENAN (ke'-nan) See also CAINAN.
1Ch 1:2 **K.**, Mahalaleel, Jered,....................... 7018

KENATH (ke'-nath) See also NOBAH.
Nu 32:42 And Nobah went and took **K.**, ... 7079
1Ch 2:23 with **K.**, and the towns thereof,.......... 7079

KENAZ (ke'-naz) See also KENEZITE.
Ge 36:11 Omar, Zepho, and Gatam, and **K.**....... 7073
Ge 36:15 duke Omar, duke Zepho, duke **K.**, ... 7073
Ge 36:42 Duke **K.**, duke Teman, duke............ 7073
Jos 15:17 Othniel the son of **K.**, the brother...... 7073
Jg 1:13 And Othniel the son of **K.**, Caleb's 7073
Jg 3:9 even Othniel the son of **K.**, Caleb's 7073
Jg 3:11 And Othniel the son of **K.** died. 7073
1Ch 1:36 Zephi, and Gatam, **K.**, and Timna,...... 7073
1Ch 1:53 Duke **K.**, duke Teman, duke............. 7073
1Ch 4:13 And the sons of **K.**; Othniel, and......... 7073
1Ch 4:15 and the sons of Elah, even **K.**. 7073

KENEZITE (ken'-e-zite) See also KENIZZITES.
Nu 32:12 the son of Jephunneh the **K.**, ... 7074
Jos 14:6,14 the son of Jephunneh the **K.**............ 7074

KENITE (ken'-ite) See also KENITES.
Nu 24:22 the **K.** shall be wasted, until............. 7014
Jg 1:16 children of the **K.**, Moses' father........ 7017
Jg 4:11 Now Heber the **K.**, which was of....... 7014
Jg 4:17 of Jael the wife of Heber the **K.**:........ 7017
Jg 4:17 and the house of Heber the **K.**. 7017
Jg 5:24 Jael the wife of Heber the **K.** be, ... 7017

KENITES (ken'-ites) See also MIDIANITES.
Ge 15:19 The **K.**, and the Kenizzites, and 7017
Nu 24:21 he looked on the **K.**, and took up....... 7017
Jg 4:11 had severed himelf from the **K.**, ... 7017
1Sa 15:6 Saul said unto the **K.**, Go, depart,...... 7017
1Sa 15:6 So the **K.** departed from among......... 7017
1Sa 27:10 and against the south of the **K.**.......... 7017
1Sa 30:29 which were in the cities of the **K.**, ... 7017
1Ch 2:55 These are the **K.** that came of 7017

KENIZZITES (ken'-iz-zites) See also KENEZITE.
Ge 15:19 The Kenites, and the **K.**, and the....... 7074

KEPT
Ge 26:5 **k.** my charge, my commandments, ... 8104
Ge 29:9 father's sheep: for she **k.** them......... 7462
Ge 39:9 neither hath he **k.** back any thing........ 2820
Ge 42:16 and ye shall be **k.** in prison, that 631
Ex 3:1 Moses **k.** the flock of Jethro his......... 7462
Ex 16:23 for you to be **k.** until the morning. 4931
Ex 16:32 of it to be **k.** for your generations; 4931
Ex 16:33 Lord, to be **k.** for your generations. ... 4931
Ex 16:34 up before the Testimony, to be **k.**....... 4931
Ex 21:29 owner, and he hath not **k.** him in, ... 8104
Ex 21:36 and his owner hath not **k.** him in;........ 8104
Nu 5:13 of her husband, and be **k.** close, ... 5641
Nu 9:5 **k.** the passover on the fourteenth 6213
Nu 9:7 wherefore are we **k.** back, that we..... 1639
Nu 9:19 of Israel **k.** the charge of the Lord, ... 8104
Nu 9:23 they **k.** the charge of the Lord, at........ 8104
Nu 17:10 **k.** for a token against the rebels; 4931
Nu 19:9 it shall be **k.** for the congregation....... 4931
Nu 24:11 hath **k.** thee back from honour........... 4513
Nu 31:47 **k.** the charge of the tabernacle 8104
De 32:10 he **k.** him as the apple of his eye. 5341
De 33:9 thy word, and **k.** thy covenant........... 5341
Jos 5:10 **k.** the passover on the fourteenth 6213
Jos 14:10 behold, the Lord hath **k.** me alive,............
Jos 22:2 have **k.** all that Moses the servant 8104
Jos 22:3 **k.** the charge of the commandment..... 8104
Ru 2:23 she **k.** fast by the maidens of Boaz..... 1692
1Sa 9:24 this time hath it been **k.** for thee 8104
1Sa 13:13 hast not **k.** the commandment of......... 8104
1Sa 13:14 hast not **k.** that which the Lord 8104
1Sa 17:34 Thy servant **k.** his father's sheep, ... 7462
1Sa 21:4 have **k.** themselves...from women. 8104

1Sa 21:5 women have been **k.** from us 6113
1Sa 25:21 vain have I **k.** all that this fellow 8104
1Sa 25:33 hast **k.** me this day from coming 3607
1Sa 25:34 **k.** me back from hurting thee, 4513
1Sa 25:39 and hath **k.** his servant from evil: 2820
1Sa 26:15 thou not **k.** thy lord the king? 8104
1Sa 26:16 because ye have not **k.** your master, .. 8104
2Sa 13:34 And the young man that **k.** the watch
2Sa 22:22 I have **k.** the ways of the Lord, and ... 8104
2Sa 22:24 have **k.** myself from mine iniquity, 8104
2Sa 22:44 **k.** me to be head of the heathen: 8104
1Ki 2:43 Why then hast thou not **k.** the oath 8104
1Ki 3:6 hast **k.** for him this great kindness, 8104
1Ki 8:24 Who hast **k.** with thy servant David 8104
1Ki 11:10 but he **k.** not that which the Lord 8104
1Ki 11:11 thou hast not **k.** my covenant and 8104
1Ki 11:34 because he **k.** my commandments 8104
1Ki 13:21 and hast not **k.** the commandment 8104
1Ki 14:8 who **k.** my commandments, and 8104
1Ki 14:27 **k.** the door of the king's house 8104
2Ki 9:14 (Now Joram had **k.** Ramoth-gilead, 8104
2Ki 12:9 and the priests that **k.** the door put 8104
2Ki 17:19 Judah **k.** not the commandments of 8104
2Ki 18:6 but **k.** his commandments, which 8104
1Ch 10:13 word of the Lord, which he **k.** not, 8104
1Ch 12:1 **k.** himself close because of Saul 6113
1Ch 12:29 part of them had **k.** the ward of 8104
2Ch 6:15 hast **k.** with thy servant David 8104
2Ch 7:8 Solomon **k.** the feast seven days, 6213
2Ch 7:9 they **k.** the dedication of the altar 6213
2Ch 12:10 **k.** the entrance of the king's house 8104
2Ch 30:21 present at Jerusalem **k.** the feast 6213
2Ch 30:23 **k.** other seven days with gladness 6213
2Ch 34:9 the Levites that **k.** the doors had 8104
2Ch 34:21 our fathers have not **k.** the word of 8104
2Ch 35:1 Moreover Josiah **k.** a passover 6213
2Ch 35:17 **k.** the passover at that time, 6213
2Ch 35:18 no passover like to that **k.** in Israel 6213
2Ch 35:18 keep such a passover as Josiah **k.**, 6213
2Ch 35:19 reign of Josiah was this passover **k.**. 6213
2Ch 36:21 as she lay desolate she **k.** sabbath, 7673
Ezr 3:4 **k.** also the feast of tabernacles, 6213
Ezr 6:16 **k.** the dedication of this house of 5648
Ezr 6:19 of the captivity **k.** the passover 6213
Ezr 6:22 **k.** the feast of unleavened bread 6213
Ne 1:7 have not **k.** the commandments, 8104
Ne 8:18 they **k.** the feast seven days; and 6213
Ne 9:34 priests, nor our fathers, **k.** thy law, 6213
Ne 11:19 brethren that **k.** the gates, were 8104
Ne 12:45 singers and the porters **k.** the ward 8104
Es 2:14 which **k.** the concubines: 8104
Es 2:21 of those which **k.** the door, were 8104
Es 9:28 days should be remembered and **k.** 6213
Job 23:11 his way have I **k.**, and not 8104
Job 28:21 **k.** close from the fowls of the air. 5641
Job 29:21 waited, and **k.** silence at my counsel.
Job 31:34 I **k.** silence, and went not out of the
Ps 17:4 I have **k.** me from the paths of the 8104
Ps 18:21 For I have **k.** the ways of the Lord, 8104
Ps 18:23 and I **k.** myself from mine iniquity. 8104
Ps 30:3 hast **k.** me alive, that I should not
Ps 32:3 When I **k.** silence, my bones 2790
Ps 42:4 with a multitude that **k.** holyday 2287
Ps 50:21 hast thou done, and I **k.** silence; 2790
Ps 78:10 they **k.** not the covenant of God, 8104
Ps 78:56 God, and **k.** not his testimonies: 8104
Ps 99:7 they **k.** his testimonies, and the 8104
Ps 119:22 for I have **k.** thy testimonies. 5341
Ps 119:55 in the night, and have **k.** thy law 8104
Ps 119:56 I had, because I **k.** thy precepts. 5341
Ps 119:67 but now have I **k.** thy word. 8104
Ps 119:158 because they **k.** not thy word 8104
Ps 119:167 My soul hath **k.** thy testimonies; 8104
Ps 119:168 I have **k.** thy precepts and thy 8104
Ec 2:10 eyes desired I **k.** not from them, 680
Ec 5:13 riches **k.** for the owners thereof to 8104
Ca 1:6 mine own vineyard have I not **k.** 5201
Isa 30:29 night when a holy solemnity is **k.**; 6942
Jer 16:11 me, and have not **k.** my law; 8104
Jer 35:18 your father, and **k.** all his precepts, 8104
Eze 5:7 neither have **k.** my judgments, 6213
Eze 18:9 and hath **k.** my judgments, to deal 8104
Eze 18:19 hath **k.** all my statutes, and hath 8104
Eze 20:21 neither **k.** my judgments to do them, .. 8104
Eze 44:8 ye have not **k.** the charge of mine 8104
Eze 44:15 that **k.** the charge of my sanctuary 8104
Eze 48:11 which have **k.** my charge, which 8104
Da 5:19 whom he would he **k.** alive; and
Da 7:28 but I **k.** the matter in my heart. 5202
Ho 12:12 a wife, and for a wife he **k.** sheep. 8104
Am 1:11 and he **k.** his wrath for ever: 8104
Am 2:4 have not **k.** his commandments, 8104
Mic 6:16 For the statutes of Omri are **k.**, and 8104
Mal 2:9 as ye have not **k.** my ways, but 8104
Mal 3:7 ordinances, and have not **k.** them. 8104
Mal 3:14 is it that we have **k.** his ordinance, 8104
Mt 8:33 they that **k.** them fled, and went *1006*
Mt 13:35 things which have been **k.** secret
Mt 14:6 But when Herod's birthday was **k.**, *71*
Mt 19:20 things have I **k.** from my youth up: *5442*
Mk 4:22 **neither was any thing k. secret,** *1096*
Mk 9:10 **k.** that saying with themselves, *2902*
Lu 2:19 But Mary **k.** all these things, and *4933*
Lu 2:51 his mother **k.** all these sayings in *1301*
Lu 8:29 he was **k.** bound with chains and *5442*
Lu 9:36 they **k.** it close, and told no man *4601*
Lu 18:21 these have I **k.** from my youth up. *5442*
Lu 19:20 **I have k. laid up in a napkin:** *2192*
Joh 2:10 hast **k.** the good wine until now. *5083*
Joh 12:7 **of my burying hath she k. this.** *5083*
Joh 15:10 **even as I have k. my Father's** *5083*
Joh 15:20 **if they have k. my saying, they** *5083*
Joh 17:6 **me; and they have k. thy word.** *5083*
Joh 17:12 **the world, I k. them in thy name:** *5083*
Joh 17:12 **that thou gavest me I have k.,** *5442*
Joh 18:16 and spake unto her that **k.** the door, *2377*
Joh 18:17 saith the damsel that **k.** the door *2377*
Ac 5:2 **k.** back part of the price, his wife *3557*
Ac 7:53 of angels, and have not **k.** it. *5442*
Ac 9:33 which had **k.** his bed eight years, *2621*
Ac 12:5 Peter therefore was **k.** in prison: *5083*
Ac 12:6 before the door **k.** the prison. *5083*
Ac 15:12 Then all the multitude **k.** silence, *4601*
Ac 20:20 how I **k.** back nothing that was *5288*
Ac 22:2 them, they **k.** the more silence: *3930*
Ac 22:20 **k.** the raiment of them that slew *5442*
Ac 23:35 to be **k.** in Herod's judgment hall. *5442*
Ac 25:4 Paul should be **k.** at Caesarea, and *5083*
Ac 25:21 him to be **k.** till I might send him to *5083*
Ac 27:43 Paul, **k.** them from their purpose; *2967*
Ac 28:16 himself with a soldier that **k.** him. *5442*
Ro 16:25 **k.** secret since the world began,
2Co 11:9 **k.** myself from being burdensome *5083*
2Co 11:32 **k.** the city of the Damascenes *5432*
Ga 3:23 we were **k.** under the law, shut up *5432*
2Ti 4:7 my course, I have **k.** the faith: *5083*
Heb 11:28 Through faith he **k.** the passover, *4160*
Jas 5:4 which is of you **k.** back by fraud, *650*
1Pe 1:5 **k.** by the power of God through *5432*
2Pe 3:7 by the same word are **k.** in store, *2343*
Jude 6 which **k.** not their first estate, *5083*
Re 3:8 **strength, and hast k. my word,** *5083*
Re 3:10 **hast k. the word of my patience,** *5083*

KERCHIEFS See also HANDKERCHIEFS.
Eze 13:18 make **k.** upon the head of every 4556
Eze 13:21 Your **k.** also will I tear, and deliver 4556

KEREN-HAPUCH (ke''-ren-hap'-puk)
Job 42:14 and the name of the third, **K.** 7163

KERIOTH (ke'-re-oth) See also ISCARIOT; KIRIOTH.
Jos 15:25 Hadattah, and **K.**, and Hezron, 7152
Jer 48:24 And upon **K.**, and upon Bozrah, 7152
Jer 48:41 **K.** is taken, and the strong holds 7152

KERNELS
Nu 6:4 from the **k.** even to the husk. 2785

KEROS (ke'-ros)
Ezr 2:44 The children of **K.**, the children 7026
Ne 7:47 The children of **K.**, the children of 7026

KETTLE
1Sa 2:14 he struck it into the pan, or **k.**, or 1731

KETURAH (ket-u'-rah)
Ge 25:1 took a wife, and her name was **K.** 6989
Ge 25:4 All these were the children of **K.** 6989
1Ch 1:32 Now the sons of **K.**, Abraham's 6989
1Ch 1:33 All these are the sons of **K.** 6989

KEY See also KEYS.
Jg 3:25 they took a **k.**, and opened them: 4668
Isa 22:22 the **k.** of the house of David will I 4668
Lu 11:52 **taken away the k. of knowledge:** *2807*
Re 3:7 **true, he that hath the k. of David,** *2807*
Re 9:1 given the **k.** of the bottomless pit *2807*
Re 20:1 having the **k.** of the bottomless pit *2807*

KEYS
Mt 16:19 **the k. of the kingdom of heaven:** *2807*
Re 1:18 **have the k. of hell and of death.** *2807*

KEZIA (ke-zi'-ah)
Job 42:14 and the name of the second, **K.**; 7103

KEZIZ (ke'-ziz)
Jos 18:21 Beth-hoglah, and the valley of **K.**, 7104

KIBROTH-HATTAAVAH (kib''-roth-hat-ta'-a-vah)
Nu 11:34 called the name of that place **K.**: 6914
Nu 11:35 journeyed from **K.** unto Hazeroth; 6914
Nu 33:16 desert of Sinai, and pitched at **K.** 6914
Nu 33:17 And they departed from **K.**, and 6914
De 9:22 and at **K.**, ye provoked the Lord to 6914

KIBZAIM (kib-za'-im) See also JOKMEAM.
Jos 21:22 And **K.** with her suburbs, and 6911

KICK See also KICKED.
1Sa 2:29 Wherefore **k.** ye at my sacrifice 1163
Ac 9:5 **for thee to k. against the pricks.** *2979*
Ac 26:14 **for thee to kick against the pricks.** *2979*

KICKED
De 32:15 Jeshurun waxed fat, and **k.**: thou 1163

KID See also KIDS.
Ge 37:31 killed a **k.** of the goats, and dipped 8163
Ge 38:17 will send thee a **k.** from the flock 1423
Ge 38:20 Judah sent the **k.** by the hand 1423
Ge 38:23 I sent this **k.**, and thou hast not 1423
Ex 23:19 seethe a **k.** in his mother's milk 1423
Ex 34:26 seethe a **k.** in his mother's milk 1423
Le 4:23 a **k.** of the goats, a male without 8163
Le 4:28 his offering, a **k.** of the goats, 8166
Le 5:6 a **k.** of the goats, for a sin offering; 8166
Le 9:3 a **k.** of the goats for a sin offering; 8163
Le 23:19 shall sacrifice one **k.** of the goats 8163
Nu 7:16, 22,28,34,40,46,52,58,64,70,76,82
One **k.** of the goats for a sin offering .. 8163
Nu 15:11 for one ram, or for a lamb, or a **k.** 5795
Nu 15:24 one **k.** of the goats for a sin 8163
Nu 28:15 one **k.** of the goats for a sin 8163
Nu 28:30 one **k.** of the goats to make an 8163
Nu 29:5 one **k.** of the goats for a sin 8163
Nu 29:11 One **k.** of the goats for a sin 8163
Nu 29:16, 19,25 one **k.** of the goats for a sin 8163
De 14:21 seethe a **k.** in his mother's milk 1423
Jg 6:19 went in, and made ready a **k.**, 1423,5795
Jg 13:15 have made ready a **k.** for thee 1423,5795
Jg 13:19 took a **k.** with a meat offering, 1423,5795
Jg 14:6 him as he would have rent a **k.**, 1423
Jg 15:1 visited his wife with a **k.**; 1423,5795
1Sa 16:20 and a bottle of wine, and a **k.**, 1423,5795
Isa 11:6 leopard shall lie down with the **k.**; 1423
Eze 43:22 offer a **k.** of the goats without 8163
Eze 45:23 a **k.** of the goats daily for a sin 8163
Lu 15:29 **thou never gavest me a k., that I** *2056*

KIDNEYS
Ex 29:13, 22 the two **k.**, and the fat that is 3629
Le 3:4 the two **k.**, and the fat that is on 3629
Le 3:4 caul above the liver, with the **k.**, 3629
Le 3:10 the two **k.**, and the fat that is upon 3629
Le 3:10 caul above the liver, with the **k.**, 3629
Le 3:15 the two **k.**, and the fat that is upon 3629
Le 3:15 caul above the liver, with the **k.**, 3629
Le 4:9 the two **k.**, and the fat that is upon 3629
Le 4:9 caul above the liver, with the **k.**, 3629
Le 7:4 the two **k.**, and the fat that is on 3629
Le 7:4 that is above the liver, with the **k.** 3629
Le 8:16, 25 above the liver, and the two **k.** 3629
Le 9:10 the fat, and the **k.**, and the caul 3629
Le 9:19 the **k.**, and the caul above the liver: 3629
De 32:14 goats, with the fat of **k.** of wheat; 3629
Isa 34:6 goats, with the fat of the **k.** of rams: 3629

KIDRON (kid'-ron) See also CEDRON.
2Sa 15:23 himself passed over the brook **K.**, 6939
1Ki 2:37 and passest over the brook **K.**, 6939
1Ki 15:13 idol, and burnt it by the brook **K.** 6939
2Ki 23:4 Jerusalem in the fields of **K.**, 6939
2Ki 23:6 Jerusalem, unto the brook **K.**, 6939
2Ki 23:6 and burned it at the brook **K.**, and 6939
2Ki 23:12 dust of them into the brook **K.** 6939
2Ch 15:16 it, and burnt it at the brook **K.** 6939
2Ch 29:16 it out abroad into the brook **K.** 6939

2Ch 30:14 and cast them into the brook **K.**....... 6939
Jer 31:40 all the fields unto the brook of **K.**,....... 6939

KIDS
Ge 27:9 thence two good **k.** of the goats; 1423
Ge 27:16 put the skins of the **k.** of the goats 1423
Le 16:5 two kids of the goats for a sin........... 8163
Nu 7:87 the **k.** of the goats for sin offering...... 8163
1Sa 10:3 Beth-el, one carrying three **k.**, ... 1423
1Ki 20:27 them like two little flocks of **k.**; 5795
2Ch 35:7 of the flock, lambs and **k.**, all..... 1121,5795
Ca 1:8 feed thy **k.** beside the shepherds'....... 1423

KILL See also KILLED; KILLEST; KILLETH; KILLING.
Ge 4:15 any finding him should **k.** him. 5221
Ge 12:12 they will **k.** me, but they will save 2026
Ge 26:7 place should **k.** me for Rebekah; 2026
Ge 27:24 himself, purposing to **k.** thee............. 2026
Ge 37:21 and said, Let us not **k.** him.............. 5221
Ex 1:16 it be a son, then ye shall **k.** him: 4191
Ex 2:14 intendest thou to **k.** me, as thou........ 2026
Ex 4:24 met him, and sought to **k.** him. 4191
Ex 12:6 Israel shall **k.** it in the evening. 7819
Ex 12:21 your families, and **k.** the passover...... 7819
Ex 16:3 to **k.** this whole assembly with 4191
Ex 17:3 to **k.** us and our children and our........ 4191
Ex 20:13 Thou shalt not **k.**.......................... 7523
Ex 22:1 ox, or a sheep, and **k.** it, or sell it; 2873
Ex 22:24 and I will **k.** you with the sword; 2026
Ex 29:11 thou shalt **k.** the bullock before........... 7819
Ex 29:20 Then shalt thou **k.** the ram, and 7819
Le 1:5 shall **k.** the bullock before the Lord: ... 7819
Le 1:11 he shall **k.** it on the side of the altar... 7819
Le 3:2 **k.** it at the door of the tabernacle 7819
Le 3:8, 13 **k.** it before the tabernacle of the ... 7819
Le 4:4 and **k.** the bullock before the Lord. 7819
Le 4:24 and **k.** it in the place where they 7819
Le 4:24 **k.** the burnt offering before the Lord: ..7819
Le 4:33 where they **k.** the burnt offering. 7819
Le 7:2 where they **k.** the burnt offering 7819
Le 7:2 shall they **k.** the trespass offering:...... 7819
Le 14:13 where he shall **k.** the sin offering....... 7819
Le 14:19 he shall **k.** the burnt offering: 7819
Le 14:25 **k.** the lamb of the trespass offering, ... 7819
Le 14:50 he shall **k.** the one of the birds in 7819
Le 16:11 **k.** the bullock of the sin offering 7819
Le 16:15 he **k.** the goat of the sin offering,....... 7819
Le 20:4 seed unto Molech, and **k.** him not: 4191
Le 20:16 thou shalt **k.** the woman, and the....... 2026
Le 22:28 ye shall not **k.** it and her young 7819
Nu 11:15 thus with me, **k.** me, I pray thee, ... 2026
Nu 14:15 thou shalt **k.** all this people as one 4191
Nu 16:13 to **k.** us in the wilderness, except 4191
Nu 22:29 hand, for now would I **k.** thee. 2026
Nu 31:17 **k.** every male among the little ones, ... 2026
Nu 31:17 **k.** every woman that hath known 2026
Nu 35:27 revenger of blood **k.** the slayer;......... 7523
De 4:42 should **k.** his neighbour unawares, ... 7523
De 5:17 Thou shalt not **k.** 7523
De 12:15 **k.** and eat flesh in all thy gates,.......... 2076
De 12:21 shalt **k.** of thy herd and of thy........... 2076
De 13:9 thou shalt surely **k.** him; thine.......... 2026
De 32:39 I **k.**, and I make alive; I would, ... 4191
Jg 13:23 If the Lord were pleased to **k.** us, ... 4191
Jg 15:13 but surely we will not **k.** thee. 4191
Jg 16:2 when it is day, we shall **k.** him. 2026
Jg 20:31 to smite of the people, and **k.**, ... 2491
Jg 20:39 smite and **k.** of the men of Israel....... 2491
1Sa 16:2 if Saul hear it, he will **k.** me. And 2026
1Sa 17:9 fight with me, and to **k.** me, then 5221
1Sa 17:9 prevail against him, and **k.** him, ... 5221
1Sa 19:1 that they should **k.** David. 4191
1Sa 19:2 Saul my father seeketh to **k.** thee: 4191
1Sa 19:17 Let me go; why should I **k.** thee? 4191
1Sa 24:10 some bade me **k.** thee: but mine........ 2026
1Sa 30:15 God, that thou wilt neither **k.** me,....... 4191
2Sa 13:28 Amnon; then **k.** him, fear not: 4191
2Sa 14:7 that we may **k.** him, for the life of 4191
2Sa 14:32 any iniquity in me, let him **k.** me. 4191
2Sa 21:4 shalt thou **k.** any man in Israel. 4191
1Ki 11:40 sought therefore to **k.** Jeroboam. 4191
1Ki 12:27 they shall **k.** me, and go again to 2026
2Ki 5:7 Am I God, to **k.** and make alive,......... 4191
2Ki 7:4 and if they **k.** us, we shall but die. 4191
2Ki 11:15 followeth her **k.** with the sword. 4191
2Ch 35:6 So **k.** the passover, and sanctify 7819
Es 3:13 to **k.**, and to cause to perish, all......... 2026
Ps 59:*title* watched the house to **k.** him............. 4191
Ec 3:3 A time to **k.**, and a time to heal; 2026
Isa 14:30 I will **k.** thy root with famine,............ 4191
Isa 29:1 to year; let them **k.** sacrifices............ 5362
Eze 34:3 the wool, ye **k.** them that are fed: 2076
Mt 5:21 **of old time, Thou shalt not k.;**...... *5407*
Mt 5:21 **shall k. shall be in danger of the**... *5407*
Mt 10:28 **fear not them which k. the body,**..... *615*
Mt 10:28 **but are not able to k. the soul:**........ *615*
Mt 17:23 **they shall k. him, and the third day.***615*
Mt 21:38 **let us k. him, and let us seize on**.... *615*
Mt 23:34 **some of them ye shall k. and**.......... *615*
Mt 24:9 **up to be afflicted, and shall k. you:** .*615*
Mt 26:4 take Jesus by subtilty, and **k.** him......... *615*
Mk 3:4 **or to do evil? to save life, or to k.?** ..*615*
Mk 9:31 **hands of men, and they shall k.**...... *615*
Mk 10:19 **Do not k., Do not steal, Do not**..... *5407*
Mk 10:34 **spit upon him, and shall k. him:**..... *615*
Mk 12:7 **let us k. him, and the inheritance**... *615*
Lu 12:4 **not afraid of them that k. the body,**.*615*
Lu 13:31 depart thence: for Herod will **k.** thee.... *615*
Lu 15:23 **hither the fatted calf, and k. it;** *2380*
Lu 18:20 **not commit adultery, Do not k.,**.... *5407*
Lu 20:14 **is the heir: come, let us k. him,**...... *615*
Lu 22:2 sought how they might **k.** him;........... *337*
Joh 5:18 the Jews sought the more to **k.** him, ... *615*
Joh 7:1 because the Jews sought to **k.** him........ *615*
Joh 7:19 **the law? Why go ye about to k. me?** *615*
Joh 7:20 devil: who goeth about to **k.** thee?....... *615*
Joh 7:25 Is not this he, whom they seek to **k.**? .. *615*
Joh 8:22 said the Jews, Will he **k.** himself? *615*
Joh 8:37 **ye seek to k. me, because my word** . *615*
Joh 8:40 **now ye seek to k. me, a man that**... *615*
Joh 10:10 **not, but for to steal, and to k.,** *2380*
Ac 7:28 Wilt thou **k.** me, as thou didst the *337*
Ac 9:23 the Jews took counsel to **k.** him: *337*
Ac 9:24 the gates day and night to **k.** him. *337*
Ac 10:13 to him, Rise, Peter; **k.**, and eat........ *2380*
Ac 21:31 And as they went about to **k.** him,....... *615*
Ac 23:15 he come near, are ready to **k.** him......... *337*
Ac 25:3 laying wait in the way to **k.** him. *337*
Ac 26:21 temple, and went about to **k.** me. *1315*
Ac 27:42 counsel was to **k.** the prisoners,........... *615*
Ro 13:9 Thou shalt not **k.**, Thou shalt not....... *5407*
Jas 2:11 adultery, said also, Do not **k.**. *5407*
Jas 2:11 yet if thou **k.**, thou art become a *5407*
Jas 4:2 ye **k.**, and desire to have, and............. *5407*
Re 2:23 **I will k. her children with death;**.... *615*
Re 6:4 that they should **k.** one another: *4969*
Re 6:8 to **k.** with sword, and with hunger, ... *615*
Re 9:5 given that they should not **k.** them,...... *615*
Re 11:7 shall overcome them, and **k.** them. *615*

KILLED See also KILLEDST.
Ge 37:31 **k.** a kid of the goats, and dipped......... 7819
Ex 21:29 him in, but that he hath **k.** a man....... 4191
Le 4:15 the bullock shall be **k.** before the 7819
Le 6:25 place where the burnt offering is **k.** 7819
Le 6:25 sin offering be **k.** before the Lord: 7819
Le 8:19 And he **k.** it; and Moses sprinkled....... 7819
Le 14:5 one of the birds be **k.** in an earthen.... 7819
Le 14:6 in the blood of the bird that was **k.** 7819
Nu 16:41 Ye have **k.** the people of the Lord...... 4191
Nu 31:19 whosoever hath **k.** any person,.......... 2026
1Sa 24:11 skirt of thy robe, and **k.** thee not,...... 2026
1Sa 25:11 that I have **k.** for my shearers,.......... 2873
1Sa 28:24 hasted, and **k.** it, and took flour,........ 2076
2Sa 12:9 hast **k.** Uriah the Hittite with the 5221
2Sa 21:17 smote the Philistine, and **k.** him........ 4191
1Ki 16:7 Jeroboam; and because he **k.** him........ 5221
1Ki 16:10 in and smote him, and **k.** him,........... 4191
1Ki 21:19 Hast thou **k.**, and also taken 7523
2Ki 15:25 **k.** him, and reigned in his room. 4191
1Ch 19:18 **k.** Shophach the captain of the host. ... 4191
2Ch 18:2 Ahab **k.** sheep and oxen for him 3076
2Ch 25:3 servants that had **k.** the king his........ 5221
2Ch 29:22 So they **k.** the bullocks, and the 7819
2Ch 29:22 when they had **k.** the rams, they 7819
2Ch 29:22 they **k.** also the lambs, and they......... 7819
2Ch 29:24 And the priests **k.** them, and they...... 7819
2Ch 30:15 **k.** the passover on the fourteenth 7819
2Ch 35:1 **k.** the passover on the fourteenth 7819
2Ch 35:11 they **k.** the passover, and the........... 7819
Ezr 6:20 **k.** the passover for all the children 7819
Ps 44:22 for thy sake are we **k.** all the day 2026
Pr 9:2 She hath **k.** her breasts; she hath 2873
La 2:21 anger; thou hast **k.**, and not pitied...... 2873
Mt 16:21 be **k.**, and be raised again the third...... *615*
Mt 21:35 **beat one, and k. another, and**......... *615*
Mt 22:4 **my fatlings are k., and all things** .. *2380*
Mt 23:31 **of them which k. the prophets.** *5407*
Mk 6:19 him, and would have **k.** him;.............. *615*
Mk 8:31 and be **k.**, and after three days rise *615*
Mk 9:31 **after that he is k., he shall rise the** .*615*
Mk 12:5 **and him they k., and many others;** ..*615*
Mk 12:8 **they took him, and k. him, and cast** *615*
Mk 14:12 when they **k.** the passover,................ *2380*
Lu 11:47 **prophets, and your fathers k. them.** .*615*
Lu 11:48 **for they indeed k. them, and ye**...... *615*
Lu 12:5 **after he hath k. hath power to cast.** *615*
Lu 15:27 **thy father hath k. the fatted calf,** . *2380*
Lu 15:30 **thou hast k. for him the fatted** *2380*
Lu 20:15 **out of the vineyard, and k. him.**..... *615*
Lu 22:7 when the passover must be **k.**.............. *2380*
Ac 3:15 And **k.** the Prince of life, whom God.... *615*
Ac 12:2 he **k.** James the brother of John *337*
Ac 16:27 sword, and would have **k.** himself, ... *337*
Ac 23:12 eat nor drink till they had **k.** Paul. *615*
Ac 23:21 eat nor drink till they have **k.** him:....... *337*
Ac 23:27 and should have been **k.** of them: *615*
Ro 8:36 For thy sake we are **k.** all the day *2289*
Ro 11:3 Lord, they have **k.** thy prophets,.......... *615*
2Co 6:9 we live; as chastened, and not **k.**;...... *2289*
1Th 2:15 Who both **k.** the Lord Jesus, and......... *615*
Jas 5:6 have condemned and **k.** the just;........ *5407*
Re 6:11 should be **k.** as they were, should *615*
Re 9:18 three was the third part of men **k.**,....... *615*
Re 9:20 which were not **k.** by these plagues *615*
Re 11:5 them, he must in this manner be **k.**. *615*
Re 13:10 sword must be **k.** with the sword. *615*
Re 13:15 the image of the beast should be **k.**. *615*

KILLEDST
Ex 2:14 kill me, as thou **k.** the Egyptian?........ 2026
1Sa 24:18 me into thine hand, thou **k.** me not. ... 2026

KILLEST
Mt 23:37 **Jerusalem,...that k. the prophets,** ... *615*
Lu 13:34 **Jerusalem, which k. the prophets,**... *615*

KILLETH
Le 17:3 of Israel, that **k.** an ox, or lamb, ... 7819
Le 17:3 camp, or that **k.** it out of the camp,..... 7819
Le 24:17 he that **k.** any man shall surely.......... 5221
Le 24:18 that **k.** a beast shall make it good;....... 5221
Le 24:21 he that **k.** a beast, he shall restore..... 5221
Le 24:21 he that **k.** a man, he shall be put to..... 5221
Nu 35:11 which **k.** any person at unawares. 5221
Nu 35:15 one that **k.** any person unawares........ 5221
Nu 35:30 Whoso **k.** any person, the murderer ... 5221
De 19:4 Whoso **k.** his neighbour ignorantly, ... 5221
Jos 20:3 slayer that **k.** any person unawares..... 5221
Jos 20:9 whosoever **k.** any...at unawares......... 5221
1Sa 2:6 The Lord **k.**, and maketh alive: 4191
1Sa 17:25 who **k.** him, the king will enrich......... 5221
1Sa 17:26 to the man that **k.** this Philistine, ... 5221
1Sa 17:27 it be done to the man that **k.** him. 5221
Job 5:2 For wrath **k.** the foolish man, and...... 2026
Job 24:14 the light **k.** the poor and needy,......... 6991
Pr 21:25 The desire of the slothful **k.** him; 4191
Isa 66:3 He that **k.** an ox is as if he slew........ 7819
Joh 16:2 **whosoever k. you will think that he**.*615*
2Co 3:6 letter **k.**, but the spirit giveth life. *615*
Re 13:10 he that **k.** with the sword must be....... *615*

KILLING
Jg 9:24 him in the **k.** of his brethren. 2026
2Ch 30:17 charge of the **k.** of the passovers 7821
Isa 22:13 slaying oxen, and **k.** sheep, eating...... 7819
Ho 4:2 By swearing, and lying, and **k.**, ... 7523
Mk 12:5 **others; beating some, and k. some.** ..*615*

KIN See also KINSFOLK; KINSMAN; KINSWOMAN.
Le 18:6 any that is near of **k.** to him, ... 1320
Le 20:19 for he uncovereth his near **k.**: 7607
Le 21:2 for his **k.**, that is near unto him, ... 7607
Le 25:25 if any of his **k.** come to redeem it, ... 7138
Le 25:49 any that is nigh of **k.** unto him of....... 1320
Ru 2:20 man is near of **k.** unto us, one of our........
2Sa 19:42 Because the king is near of **k.** to us: ....
Mk 6:4 **country, and among his own k.,**.... *4773*

KINAH (ki'-nah)
Jos 15:22 **K.**, and Dimonah, and Adadah, ... 7016

KIND See also KINDS; MANKIND; WOMANKIND.
Ge 1:11 tree yielding fruit after his **k.**, ... 4327
Ge 1:12 and herb yielding seed after his **k.**,..... 4327

Ge 1:12 seed was in itself, after his **k.**: 4327
Ge 1:21 forth abundantly, after their **k.**, 4327
Ge 1:21 every winged fowl after his **k.**: 4327
Ge 1:24 the living creature after his **k.**, 4327
Ge 1:24 beast of the earth after his **k.**: and 4327
Ge 1:25 the beast of the earth after his **k.**, 4327
Ge 1:25 and cattle after their **k.**, and every 4327
Ge 1:25 creepeth upon the earth after his **k.**: 4327
Ge 6:20 Of fowls after their **k.**, 4327
Ge 6:20 and of cattle after their **k.**, 4327
Ge 6:20 thing of the earth after his **k.**, 4327
Ge 7:14 They, and every beast after his **k.**, 4327
Ge 7:14 all the cattle after their **k.**, and 4327
Ge 7:14 creepeth upon the earth after his **k.**, 4327
Ge 7:14 and every fowl after his **k.**, every 4327
Le 11:14 vulture, and the kite after his **k.**; 4327
Le 11:15 Every raven after his **k.**; 4327
Le 11:16 cuckow, and the hawk after his **k.**, 4327
Le 11:19 the stork, the heron after her **k.**, 4327
Le 11:22 ye may eat; the locust after his **k.**, 4327
Le 11:22 and the bald locust after his **k.**, 4327
Le 11:22 and the beetle after his **k.**, 4327
Le 11:22 and the grasshopper after his **k.** 4327
Le 11:29 mouse, and the tortoise after his **k.**, 4327
Le 19:19 thy cattle gender with a diverse **k.**:
De 14:13 kite, and the vulture after his **k.**, 4327
De 14:14 And every raven after his **k.**, 4327
De 14:15 cuckow, and the hawk after his **k.**, 4327
De 14:18 the stork, and the heron after her **k.**, 4327
1Ch 28:14 instruments of every **k.** of service:
2Ch 10:7 If thou be **k.** to this people, and 2896
Ne 13:20 merchants and sellers of all **k.** of ware
Ec 2:5 trees in them of all **k.** of fruits:
Eze 27:12 of the multitude of all **k.** of riches;
Mt 13:47 **the sea, and gathered of every k.:** *1085*
Mt 17:21 **this k. goeth not out but by prayer.** *1085*
Mk 9:29 **This k. can come forth by nothing,** *1085*
Lu 6:35 **he is k. unto the unthankful and** *5543*
1Co 13:4 Charity suffereth long, and is **k.**; *5541*
1Co 15:39 but there is one **k.** of flesh of men,
Eph 4:32 And be ye **k.** one to another, *5543*
Jas 1:18 a **k.** of firstfruits of his creatures *5100*
Jas 3:7 For every **k.** of beasts, and of *5449*

KINDLE See also KINDLED; KINDLETH.
Ex 35:3 shall **k.** no fire throughout your 1197
Pr 26:21 is a contentious man to **k.** strife 2787
Isa 9:18 **k.** in the thickets of the forest, 3341
Isa 10:16 **k.** a burning like the burning of a 3344
Isa 30:33 a stream of brimstone, doth **k.** it. 1197
Isa 43:2 shall the flame **k.** upon thee. 1197
Isa 50:11 all ye that **k.** a fire, that compass 6919
Jer 7:18 wood, and the fathers **k.** the fire, 1197
Jer 17:27 then will I **k.** a fire in the gates 3341
Jer 21:14 I will **k.** a fire in the forest thereof, 3341
Jer 33:18 and to **k.** meat offerings, and to do 6999
Jer 43:12 **k.** a fire in the houses of the gods 3341
Jer 49:27 **k.** a fire in the wall of Damascus, 3341
Jer 50:32 and I will **k.** a fire in his cities, 3341
Eze 20:47 God; Behold, I will **k.** a fire in thee, 3341
Eze 24:10 **k.** the fire, consume the flesh, 1814
Am 1:14 **k.** a fire in the wall of Rabbah, 3341
Ob 18 they shall **k.** in them, and devour 1814
Mal 1:10 neither do ye **k.** fire on mine altar 215

KINDLED
Ge 30:2 And Jacob's anger was **k.** against 2734
Ge 39:19 to me; that his wrath was **k.** 2734
Ex 4:14 of the Lord was **k.** against Moses, 2734
Ex 22:6 he that **k.** the fire shall surely 1197
Le 10:6 burning which the Lord hath **k.** 8313
Nu 11:1 heard it; and his anger was **k.**; 2734
Nu 11:10 anger of the Lord was **k.** greatly; 2734
Nu 11:33 wrath of the Lord was **k.** against 2734
Nu 12:9 and the anger of the Lord was **k.** 2734
Nu 22:22 And God's anger was **k.** because he 2734
Nu 22:27 Balaam's anger was **k.**, and he 2734
Nu 24:10 Balak's anger was **k.** against 2734
Nu 25:3 anger of the Lord was **k.** against 2734
Nu 32:10 Lord's anger was **k.** the same time, 2734
Nu 32:13 Lord's anger was **k.** against Israel,
De 6:15 anger of the Lord thy God be **k.** 2734
De 7:4 the anger of the Lord be **k.** against 2734
De 11:17 Lord's wrath be **k.** against you, 2734
De 29:27 anger of the Lord was **k.** against 2734
De 31:17 my anger shall be **k.** against them 2734
De 32:22 For a fire is **k.** in mine anger, and 6919
Jos 7:1 anger of the Lord was **k.** against 2734
Jos 23:16 shall the anger of the Lord be **k.** 2734
Jg 9:30 the son of Ebed, his anger was **k.** 2734
Jg 14:19 And his anger was **k.**, and he went 2734
1Sa 11:6 and his anger was **k.** greatly. 2734
1Sa 17:28 Eliab's anger was **k.** against David, 2734
1Sa 20:30 Saul's anger was **k.** against 2734
2Sa 6:7 anger of the Lord was **k.** against 2734
2Sa 12:5 And David's anger was greatly **k.** 2734
2Sa 22:9 devoured: coals were **k.** by it. 1197
2Sa 22:13 before him were coals of fire **k.** 1197
2Sa 24:1 anger of the Lord was **k.** against 2734
2Ki 13:3 anger of the Lord was **k.** against 2734
2Ki 22:13 wrath of the Lord that is **k.** against 3341
2Ki 22:17 my wrath shall be **k.** against this 3341
2Ki 23:26 his anger was **k.** against Judah, 2734
1Ch 13:10 And the anger of the Lord was **k.** 2734
2Ch 25:10 wherefore their anger was greatly **k.** 2734
2Ch 25:15 anger of the Lord was **k.** against 2734
Job 19:11 hath also **k.** his wrath against me, 2734
Job 32:2 Then was **k.** the wrath of Elihu the 2734
Job 32:2 against Job was his wrath **k.**, 2734
Job 32:3 his three friends was his wrath **k.**, 2734
Job 32:5 three men, then his wrath was **k.** 2734
Job 42:7 My wrath is **k.** against thee, and 2734
Ps 2:12 when his wrath is **k.** but a little. 1197
Ps 18:8 devoured: coals were **k.** by it. 1197
Ps 78:21 so a fire was **k.** against Jacob, and 5400
Ps 106:18 a fire was **k.** in their company; 1197
Ps 106:40 was the wrath of the Lord **k.** 2734
Ps 124:3 their wrath was **k.** against us: 2734
Isa 5:25 is the anger of the Lord **k.** against 2734
Isa 50:11 and in the sparks that ye have **k.** 1197
Jer 11:16 tumult he hath **k.** fire upon it, 3341
Jer 15:14 a fire is **k.** in mine anger, which 6919
Jer 17:4 ye have **k.** a fire in mine anger, 6919
Jer 44:6 was **k.** in the cities of Judah and 1197
La 4:11 hath **k.** a fire in Zion, and it hath 3341
Eze 20:48 see that I the Lord have **k.** it: 1197
Ho 8:4 mine anger is **k.** against them: 2734
Ho 11:8 me, my repentings are **k.** together. 3648
Zec 10:3 was **k.** against the shepherds, 2734
Lu 12:49 **what will I, if it be already k.?** *381*
Lu 22:55 they had **k.** a fire in the midst of *681*
Ac 28:2 for they **k.** a fire, and received us *381*

KINDLETH
Job 41:21 His breath **k.** coals, and a flame 3857
Isa 44:15 yea, he **k.** it; and baketh bread; 5400
Jas 3:5 how great a matter a little fire **k.**! *381*

KINDLY
Ge 24:49 if ye will deal **k.** and truly with 2617
Ge 34:3 and spake **k.** unto the damsel. 5921,3820
Ge 47:29 and deal **k.** and truly with me; 2617
Ge 50:21 and spake **k.** unto them. 5921,3820
Jos 2:14 will deal **k.** and truly with thee. 2617
Ru 1:8 Lord deal **k.** with you, as ye have 2617
1Sa 20:8 shalt deal **k.** with thy servant; 2617
2Ki 25:28 he spake **k.** to him, and set his 2896
Jer 52:32 spake **k.** unto him, and set his 2896
Ro 12:10 Be **k.** affectioned one to another *5387*

KINDLY-AFFECTIONED See KINDLY and AFFECTIONED.

KINDNESS See also LOVINGKINDNESS.
Ge 20:13 is thy **k.** which thou shalt shew 2617
Ge 21:23 to the **k.** that I have done unto thee, 2617
Ge 24:12 shew **k.** unto my master Abraham. 2617
Ge 24:14 hast shewed **k.** unto my master. 2617
Ge 40:14 be well with thee, and shew **k.**, 2617
Jos 2:12 Lord, since I have shewed you **k.**, 2617
Jos 2:12 shew **k.** unto my father's house, 2617
Jg 8:35 shewed they **k.** to the house of 2617
Ru 2:20 not left off his **k.** to the living and 2617
Ru 3:10 shewed more **k.** in the latter end 2617
1Sa 15:6 ye shewed **k.** to all the children of 2617
1Sa 20:14 I live shew me the **k.** of the Lord, 2617
1Sa 20:15 not cut off thy kindness from my 2617
2Sa 2:5 have shewed this **k.** unto your lord, 2617
2Sa 2:6 the Lord shew **k.** and truth unto 2617
2Sa 2:6 will requite you this **k.**, because 2896
2Sa 3:8 Judah do shew **k.** this day unto 2617
2Sa 9:1 shew him **k.** for Jonathan's sake? 2617
2Sa 9:3 may shew the **k.** of God unto him? 2617
2Sa 9:7 shew thee **k.** for Jonathan thy 2617
2Sa 10:2 will shew **k.** unto Hanun the son of 2617
2Sa 10:2 as his father shewed **k.** unto me. 2617
2Sa 16:17 Hushai, Is this thy **k.** to thy friend? 2617
1Ki 2:7 shew **k.** unto the sons of Barzillai 2617
1Ki 3:6 hast kept for him this great **k.**, 2617
1Ch 19:2 shew **k.** unto Hanun the son of 2617
1Ch 19:2 because his father shewed **k.** to me. 2617
2Ch 24:22 king remembered not the **k.** which 2617
Ne 9:17 slow to anger, and of great **k.**, and 2617
Es 2:9 him, and she obtained **k.** of him; 2617
Ps 31:21 hath shewed me his marvellous **k.** 2617
Ps 117:2 For his merciful **k.** is great toward 2617
Ps 119:76 thy merciful **k.** be for my comfort, 2617
Ps 141:5 smite me; it shall be a **k.**: 2617
Pr 19:22 The desire of a man is his **k.**: and 2617
Pr 31:26 and in her tongue is the law of **k.** 2617
Isa 54:8 with everlasting **k.** will I have 2617
Isa 54:10 my **k.** shall not depart from thee, 2617
Jer 2:2 remember thee, the **k.** of thy youth, 2617
Joe 2:13 slow to anger, and of great **k.**, and 2617
Jon 4:2 slow to anger, and of great **k.**, and 2617
Ac 28:2 people shewed us no little **k.**: *5368*
2Co 6:6 by **k.**, by the Holy Ghost, by love *5544*
Eph 2:7 in his **k.** toward us through Christ *5544*
Col 3:12 **k.**, humbleness of mind, meekness, *5544*
Tit 3:4 after that the **k.** and love of God *5544*
2Pe 1:7 to godliness brotherly **k.**; and to *5360*
2Pe 1:7 and to brotherly **k.** charity. *5360*

KINDRED See also KINDREDS.
Ge 12:1 of thy country, and from thy **k.**, 4138
Ge 24:4 go unto my country, and to my **k.**, 4138
Ge 24:7 from the land of my **k.**, and which 4138
Ge 24:38 my father's house, and to my **k.**; 4940
Ge 24:40 take a wife for my son of my **k.**, 4940
Ge 24:41 oath, when thou comest to my **k.**; 4940
Ge 31:3 land of thy fathers, and to thy **k.**; 4138
Ge 31:13 return unto the land of thy **k.** 4138
Ge 32:9 unto thy country, and to thy **k.**, 4138
Ge 43:7 straitly of our state, and of our **k.**, 4138
Nu 10:30 to mine own land, and to my **k.** 4138
Jos 6:23 and they brought out all her **k.**, 4940
Ru 2:3 who was of the **k.** of Elimelech. 4940
Ru 3:2 And now is not Boaz of our **k.**, 4130
1Ch 12:29 of Benjamin, the **k.** of Saul, 250
Es 2:10 not shewed her people nor her **k.**: 4138
Es 2:20 Esther had not yet shewed her **k.** 4138
Es 8:6 to see the destruction of my **k.**? 4138
Job 32:2 the Buzite, of the **k.** of Ram: 4940
Eze 11:15 thy brethren, the men of thy **k.**, 1353
Lu 1:61 thy **k.** that is called by this name. *4772*
Ac 4:6 were of the **k.** of the high priest, *1085*
Ac 7:3 of thy country, and from thy **k.**, *4772*
Ac 7:13 Joseph's **k.** was made known unto *1085*
Ac 7:14 all his **k.**, threescore and fifteen *4772*
Ac 7:19 same dealt subtilly with our **k.**, *1085*
Re 5:9 blood out of every **k.**, and tongue, *5443*
Re 14:6 every nation, and **k.**, and tongue, *5443*

KINDREDS
1Ch 16:28 unto the Lord, ye **k.** of the people, 4940
Ps 22:27 all the **k.** of the nations shall 4940
Ps 96:7 O ye **k.** of the people, give unto the 4940
Ac 3:25 all the **k.** of the earth be blessed. *3965*
Re 1:7 all **k.** of the earth shall wail. *5443*
Re 7:9 of all nations, and **k.**, and people, *5443*
Re 11:9 and **k.** and tongues and nations *5443*
Re 13:7 power was given him over all **k.**, *5443*

KINDS
Ge 8:19 upon the earth, after their **k.**, 4940
2Ch 16:14 odours and divers **k.** of spices 2177
Jer 15:3 I will appoint over them four **k.**, 4940
Eze 47:10 fish shall be according to their **k.**, 4327
Da 3:5 dulcimer, and all **k.** of musick, ye 2177
Da 3:7 all **k.** of musick, all the people, the 2177
Da 3:10 and all **k.** of musick, shall fall down 2177
Da 3:15 all **k.** of musick, ye fall down and 2177
1Co 12:10 another divers **k.** of tongues; to *1085*
1Co 14:10 so many **k.** of voices in the world, *1085*

KINE See also COW.
Ge 32:15 forty **k.**, and ten bulls, twenty she 6510
Ge 41:2 river seven well favoured **k.** and 6510
Ge 41:3 seven other **k.** came up after them 6510
Ge 41:3 the other **k.** upon the brink of the 6510
Ge 41:4 ill favoured and leanfleshed **k.** 6510
Ge 41:4 the seven well favoured and fat **k.** 6510
Ge 41:18 came up out of the river seven **k.**, 6510
Ge 41:19 seven other **k.** came up after them, 6510
Ge 41:20 the lean and ill favoured **k.** did eat 6510

Ge 41:20 did eat up the first seven fat **k.** 6510
Ge 41:26 The seven good **k.** are seven years; ... 6510
Ge 41:27 the seven thin and ill favoured **k.** 6510
De 7:13 increase of thy **k.**, and the flocks......... 504
De 28:4, 18 increase of thy **k.**, and the flocks..... 504
De 28:51 increase of thy **k.**, or flocks of thy....... 504
De 32:14 Butter of **k.**, and milk of sheep,.......... 1241
1Sa 6:7 new cart, and take two milch **k.**,......... 6510
1Sa 6:7 no yoke, and tie the **k.** to the cart, ... 6510
1Sa 6:10 and took two milch **k.**, and tied 6510
1Sa 6:12 the **k.** took the straight way to the..... 6510
1Sa 6:14 and offered the **k.** a burnt offering...... 6510
2Sa 17:29 sheep, and cheese of **k.**, for David, ... 1241
Am 4:1 Hear this word, ye **k.** of Bashan, ... 6510

KING See also KING'S; KINGS.
Ge 14:1 **k.** of Shinar, Arioch **k.** of Ellasar, ... 4428
Ge 14:1 **k.** of Elam, and Tidal **k.** of nations; 4428
Ge 14:2 made war with Bera **k.** of Sodom, ... 4428
Ge 14:2 and with Birsha **k.** of Gomorrah, ... 4428
Ge 14:2 Shinab **k.** of Admah, and Shemeber 4428
Ge 14:2 **k.** of Zeboiim, and the **k.** of Bela, ... 4428
Ge 14:8 **k.** of Sodom, and the **k.** of Gomorrah, .4428
Ge 14:8 **k.** of Admah, and the **k.** of Zeboiim, ... 4428
Ge 14:8 and the **k.** of Bela (the same is Zora;)..4428
Ge 14:9 With Chedorlaomer the **k.** of Elam, ... 4428
Ge 14:9 and with Tidal **k.** of nations,............. 4428
Ge 14:9 **k.** of Shinar, and Arioch **k.** of............ 4428
Ge 14:17 **k.** of Sodom went out to meet him..... 4428
Ge 14:18 **k.** of Salem brought forth bread......... 4428
Ge 14:21 the **k.** of Sodom said unto Abram,...... 4428
Ge 14:22 Abram said to the **k.** of Sodom, ... 4428
Ge 20:2 **k.** of Gerar sent, and took Sarah........ 4428
Ge 26:1 **k.** of the Philistines unto Gerar.......... 4428
Ge 26:8 **k.** of the Philistines looked out of....... 4428
Ge 36:31 reigned any **k.** over the children 4428
Ge 40:1 butler of the **k.** of Egypt and his........ 4428
Ge 40:1 offended their lord the **k.** of Egypt. 4428
Ge 40:5 and the baker of the **k.** of Egypt,........ 4428
Ge 41:46 stood before Pharaoh **k.** of Egypt....... 4428
Ex 1:8 there arose up a new **k.** over Egypt, .. 4428
Ex 1:15 **k.** of Egypt spake to the Hebrew....... 4428
Ex 1:17 the **k.** of Egypt commanded them,...... 4428
Ex 1:18 **k.** of Egypt called for the midwives, ... 4428
Ex 2:23 of time that the **k.** of Egypt died:....... 4428
Ex 3:18 of Israel, unto the **k.** of Egypt,.......... 4428
Ex 3:19 the **k.** of Egypt will not let you go, ... 4428
Ex 5:4 And the **k.** of Egypt said unto them,... 4428
Ex 6:11 speak unto Pharaoh **k.** of Egypt, ... 4428
Ex 6:13 and unto Pharaoh **k.** of Egypt, to 4428
Ex 6:27 which spake to Pharaoh **k.** of Egypt,... 4428
Ex 6:29 thou unto Pharaoh **k.** of Egypt........... 4428
Ex 14:5 it was told the **k.** of Egypt that the 4428
Ex 14:8 the heart of Pharaoh **k.** of Egypt,....... 4428
Nu 20:14 from Kadesh unto the **k.** of Edom, ... 4428
Nu 21:1 And when **k.** Arad the Canaanite,....... 4428
Nu 21:21 unto Sihon **k.** of the Amorites, ... 4428
Nu 21:26 city of Sihon the **k.** of the Amorites,... 4428
Nu 21:26 against the former **k.** of Moab, ... 4428
Nu 21:29 unto Sihon **k.** of the Amorites. 4428
Nu 21:33 and Og the **k.** of Bashan went out...... 4428
Nu 21:34 didst unto Sihon **k.** of the Amorites, ... 4428
Nu 22:4 of Zippor was **k.** of the Moabites 4428
Nu 22:10 **k.** of Moab, hath sent unto me, ... 4428
Nu 23:7 the **k.** of Moab hath brought me 4428
Nu 23:21 the shout of a **k.** is among them. 4428
Nu 24:7 his **k.** shall be higher than Agag, ... 4428
Nu 32:33 kingdom of Sihon **k.** of the Amorites,.. 4428
Nu 32:33 the kingdom of Og **k.** of Bashan,........ 4428
Nu 33:40 **k.** Arad the Canaanite, which dwelt 4428
De 1:4 slain Sihon the **k.** of the Amorites, ... 4428
De 1:4 Og the **k.** of Bashan, which dwelt at... 4428
De 2:24 Sihon the Amorite, **k.** of Heshbon, ... 4428
De 2:26 Sihon **k.** of Heshbon with words of..... 4428
De 2:30 Sihon **k.** of Heshbon would not let..... 4428
De 3:1 and Og the **k.** of Bashan came out 4428
De 3:2 didst unto Sihon **k.** of the Amorites, ... 4428
De 3:3 hands Og also, the **k.** of Bashan, ... 4428
De 3:6 we did unto Sihon **k.** of Heshbon, ... 4428
De 3:11 only Og **k.** of Bashan remained of 4428
De 4:46 land of Sihon **k.** of the Amorites, ... 4428
De 4:47 and the land of Og **k.** of Bashan,........ 4428
De 7:8 the hand of Pharaoh **k.** of Egypt. 4428
De 11:3 unto Pharaoh the **k.** of Egypt, ... 4428
De 17:14 I will set a **k.** over me, like as all 4428
De 17:15 set him **k.** over thee, whom the Lord ..4428
De 17:15 brethren shalt thou set **k.** over thee: .. 4428
De 28:36 **k.** which thou shalt set over thee,...... 4428
De 29:7 Sihon the **k.** of Heshbon, and Og....... 4428
De 29:7 and Og the **k.** of Bashan, came out 4428
De 33:5 he was **k.** in Jeshurun, when the........ 4428
Jos 2:2 was told the **k.** of Jericho, saying, ... 4428
Jos 2:3 the **k.** of Jericho sent unto Rahab,...... 4428
Jos 6:2 hand Jericho, and the **k.** thereof,........ 4428
Jos 8:1 into thy hand the **k.** of Ai, and his....... 4428
Jos 8:2 thou shalt do to Ai and her **k.** as 4428
Jos 8:2 thou didst unto Jericho and her **k.**: 4428
Jos 8:14 when the **k.** of Ai saw it, that they..... 4428
Jos 8:23 **k.** of Ai they took alive, and brought... 4428
Jos 8:29 **k.** of Ai he hanged on a tree until 4428
Jos 9:10 Jordan, to Sihon **k.** of Heshbon,......... 4428
Jos 9:10 and to Og **k.** of Bashan, which was 4428
Jos 10:1 **k.** of Jerusalem had heard how 4428
Jos 10:1 he had done to Jericho and her **k.**, ... 4428
Jos 10:1 so he had done to Ai and her **k.**; 4428
Jos 10:3 Adoni-zedec **k.** of Jerusalem............. 4428
Jos 10:3 sent unto Hoham **k.** of Hebron, ... 4428
Jos 10:3 and unto Piram **k.** of Jarmuth, ... 4428
Jos 10:3 and unto Japhia **k.** of Lachish,............ 4428
Jos 10:3 and unto Debir **k.** of Eglon, saying, ... 4428
Jos 10:5 **k.** of Jerusalem, the **k.** of Hebron, ... 4428
Jos 10:5 **k.** of Jarmuth, the **k.** of Lachish,........ 4428
Jos 10:5 **k.** of Eglon, gathered themselves....... 4428
Jos 10:23 of the cave, the **k.** of Jerusalem,........ 4428
Jos 10:23 **k.** of Hebron, the **k.** of Jarmuth,........ 4428
Jos 10:23 **k.** of Lachish, and the **k.** of Eglon....... 4428
Jos 10:28 the **k.** thereof he utterly destroyed,.... 4428
Jos 10:28 and he did to the **k.** of Makkedah....... 4428
Jos 10:28 as he did unto the **k.** of Jericho. 4428
Jos 10:30 delivered it also, and the **k.** thereof, ... 4428
Jos 10:30 but did unto the **k.** thereof............... 4428
Jos 10:30 as he did unto the **k.** of Jericho. 4428
Jos 10:33 Horam **k.** of Gezer came up to help.... 4428
Jos 10:37 and the **k.** thereof, and all the cities ... 4428
Jos 10:39 And he took it, and the **k.** thereof,...... 4428
Jos 10:39 did to Debir, and to the **k.** thereof; 4428
Jos 10:39 done also to Libnah, and to her **k.**....... 4428
Jos 11:1 **k.** of Hazor had heard those things, ... 4428
Jos 11:1 that he sent to Jobab **k.** of Madon, ... 4428
Jos 11:1 Madon, and to the **k.** of Shimron, ... 4428
Jos 11:1 and to the **k.** of Achshaph,................ 4428
Jos 11:10 Hazor, and smote the **k.** thereof........ 4428
Jos 12:2 Sihon **k.** of the Amorites, who........... 4428
Jos 12:4 And the coast of Og **k.** of Bashan, ... 4428
Jos 12:5 the border of Sihon **k.** of Heshbon...... 4428
Jos 12:9 The **k.** of Jericho, one; 4428
Jos 12:9 the **k.** of Ai, which is beside Beth-el, .. 4428
Jos 12:10 The **k.** of Jerusalem, one;................. 4428
Jos 12:10 the **k.** of Hebron, one;...................... 4428
Jos 12:11 The **k.** of Jarmuth, one; 4428
Jos 12:11 the **k.** of Lachish, one;...................... 4428
Jos 12:12 The **k.** of Eglon, one; 4428
Jos 12:12 the **k.** of Gezer, one; 4428
Jos 12:13 The **k.** of Debir, one; 4428
Jos 12:13 the **k.** of Geder, one; 4428
Jos 12:14 The **k.** of Hormah, one; 4428
Jos 12:14 the **k.** of Arad, one; 4428
Jos 12:15 The **k.** of Libnah, one;...................... 4428
Jos 12:15 the **k.** of Adullam, one;.................... 4428
Jos 12:16 The **k.** of Makkedah, one; 4428
Jos 12:16 the **k.** of Beth-el, one; 4428
Jos 12:17 The **k.** of Tappuah, one; 4428
Jos 12:17 the **k.** of Hepher, one;...................... 4428
Jos 12:18 The **k.** of Aphek, one; 4428
Jos 12:18 the **k.** of Lasharon, one;.................... 4428
Jos 12:19 The **k.** of Madon, one;...................... 4428
Jos 12:19 the **k.** of Hazor, one;....................... 4428
Jos 12:20 The **k.** of Shimron-meron, one;.......... 4428
Jos 12:20 the **k.** of Achshaph, one; 4428
Jos 12:21 The **k.** of Taanach, one;................... 4428
Jos 12:21 the **k.** of Megiddo, one; 4428
Jos 12:22 The **k.** of Kedesh, one;..................... 4428
Jos 12:22 the **k.** of Jokneam of Carmel, one;...... 4428
Jos 12:23 The **k.** of Dor in the coast of Dor, ... 4428
Jos 12:23 the **k.** of the nations of Gilgal, one; 4428
Jos 12:24 The **k.** of Tirzah, one: all the kings 4428
Jos 13:10 cities of Sihon **k.** of the Amorites, ... 4428
Jos 13:21 kingdom of Sihon **k.** of the Amorites, .. 4428
Jos 13:27 the kingdom of Sihon **k.** of Heshbon, .. 4428
Jos 13:30 all the kingdom of Og **k.** of Bashan,..... 4428
Jos 24:9 Balak the son of Zippor, **k.** of Moab, .. 4428
Jg 3:8 the hand of...**k.** of Mesopotamia:........ 4428
Jg 3:10 **k.** of Mesopotamia into his hand;........ 4428
Jg 3:12 strengthened Eglon the **k.** of Moab..... 4428
Jg 3:14 of Israel served the **k.** of Moab 4428
Jg 3:15 present unto Eglon the **k.** of Moab..... 4428
Jg 3:17 the present unto Eglon **k.** of Moab:.... 4428
Jg 3:19 a secret errand unto thee, O **k.**: 4428
Jg 4:2 into the hand of Jabin **k.** of Canaan, ... 4428
Jg 4:17 between Jabin the **k.** of Hazor and...... 4428
Jg 4:23 on that day Jabin the **k.** of Canaan...... 4428
Jg 4:24 against Jabin the **k.** of Canaan,........... 4428
Jg 4:24 had destroyed Jabin **k.** of Canaan. 4428
Jg 8:18 one resembled the children of a **k.**. 4428
Jg 9:6 and made Abimelech **k.**,.................... 4428
Jg 9:8 on a time to anoint a **k.** unto them; 4428
Jg 9:15 If in truth ye anoint me **k.** over you, .. 4428
Jg 9:16 that ye have made Abimelech **k.**,........ 4427
Jg 9:18 made...**k.** over the men of Shechem, .. 4427
Jg 11:12 sent messengers unto the **k.** of the 4428
Jg 11:13 the **k.** of the children of Ammon 4428
Jg 11:14 sent messengers again unto the **k.** 4428
Jg 11:17 messengers unto the **k.** of Edom, ... 4428
Jg 11:17 the **k.** of Edom would not hearken 4428
Jg 11:17 they sent unto the **k.** of Moab:.......... 4428
Jg 11:19 Sihon **k.** of the Amorites, the **k.** of 4428
Jg 11:25 Balak the son of Zippor, **k.** of Moab? .. 4428
Jg 11:28 the **k.** of the children of Ammon, ... 4428
Jg 17:6 days there was no **k.** in Israel, ... 4428
Jg 18:1 days there was no **k.** in Israel: 4428
Jg 19:1 when there was no **k.** in Israel, ... 4428
Jg 21:25 days there was no **k.** in Israel: 4428
1Sa 2:10 he shall give strength unto his **k.**, ... 4428
1Sa 8:5 make us a **k.** to judge us like all 4428
1Sa 8:6 they said, Give us a **k.** to judge us..... 4428
1Sa 8:9 manner of the **k.** that shall reign........ 4428
1Sa 8:10 the people that asked of him a **k.**. 4428
1Sa 8:11 manner of the **k.** that shall reign........ 4428
1Sa 8:18 your **k.** which ye shall have chosen..... 4428
1Sa 8:19 Nay; but we will have a **k.** over us;.... 4428
1Sa 8:20 that our **k.** may judge us, and go 4428
1Sa 8:22 voice, and make them a **k.**................ 4428
1Sa 10:19 unto him, Nay, but set a **k.** over us. .. 4428
1Sa 10:24 shouted, and said, God save the **k.**..... 4428
1Sa 11:15 they made Saul **k.** before the Lord..... 4427
1Sa 12:1 and have made a **k.** over you. 4428
1Sa 12:2 behold, the **k.** walketh before you: 4428
1Sa 12:9 into the hand of the **k.** of Moab, ... 4428
1Sa 12:12 the **k.** of the children of Ammon 4428
1Sa 12:12 Nay; but a **k.** shall reign over us:....... 4428
1Sa 12:12 the Lord your God was your **k.**. 4428
1Sa 12:13 behold the **k.** whom ye have chosen, .. 4428
1Sa 12:13 the Lord hath set a **k.** over you......... 4428
1Sa 12:14 also the **k.** that reigneth over you 4428
1Sa 12:17 sight of the Lord, in asking you a **k.**... 4428
1Sa 12:19 all our sins this evil, to ask us a **k.**..... 4428
1Sa 12:25 be consumed, both ye and your **k.**. 4428
1Sa 15:1 anoint thee to be **k.** over his people, .. 4428
1Sa 15:8 took Agag the **k.** of the Amalekites 4428
1Sa 15:11 that I have set up Saul to be **k.**: 4428
1Sa 15:17 Lord anointed thee **k.** over Israel?...... 4428
1Sa 15:20 brought Agag the **k.** of Amalek, ... 4428
1Sa 15:23 also rejected thee from being **k.**.......... 4428
1Sa 15:26 thee from being **k.** over Israel. 4428
1Sa 15:32 me Agag the **k.** of the Amalekites. 4428
1Sa 15:35 he had made Saul **k.** over Israel........ 4427
1Sa 16:1 provided me a **k.** among his sons. 4428
1Sa 17:25 **k.** will enrich him with great riches,.... 4428
1Sa 17:55 thy soul liveth, O **k.**, I cannot tell. 4428
1Sa 17:56 the **k.** said, Enquire thou whose son... 4428
1Sa 18:6 and dancing, to meet **k.** Saul, ... 4428
1Sa 18:18 I should be son in law to the **k.**?........ 4428
1Sa 18:22 Behold, the **k.** hath delight in thee, ... 4428
1Sa 18:25 The **k.** desireth not any dowry, ... 4428
1Sa 18:27 they gave them in full tale to the **k.**,.... 4428
1Sa 19:4 not the **k.** sin against his servant, ... 4428
1Sa 20:5 not fail to sit with the **k.** at meat: 4428
1Sa 20:24 the **k.** sat him down to eat meat. 4428
1Sa 20:25 the **k.** sat upon his seat, as at other... 4428
1Sa 21:2 **k.** hath commanded me a business,..... 4428
1Sa 21:10 and went to Achish the **k.** of Gath...... 4428
1Sa 21:11 Is not this David the **k.** of the land? ... 4428
1Sa 21:12 sore afraid of Achish the **k.** of Gath. ... 4428
1Sa 22:3 and he said unto the **k.** of Moab, ... 4428
1Sa 22:4 brought them before the **k.** of Moab: .. 4428
1Sa 22:11 **k.** sent to call Ahimelech the priest, ... 4428
1Sa 22:11 and they came all of them to the **k.**... 4428
1Sa 22:14 Then Ahimelech answered the **k.**, ... 4428
1Sa 22:15 let not the **k.** impute any thing unto.... 4428
1Sa 22:16 the **k.** said, Thou shalt surely die, ... 4428
1Sa 22:17 **k.** said unto the footmen that stood 4428

1Sa 22:17 the servants of the **k.** would not put… 4428
1Sa 22:18 **k.** said to Doeg, Turn thou, and fall… 4428
1Sa 23:17 and thou shalt be **k.** over Israel, 4427
1Sa 23:20 therefore, O **k.**, come down 4428
1Sa 24:8 after Saul, saying, My lord the **k.** 4428
1Sa 24:14 After whom is the **k.** of Israel come… 4428
1Sa 24:20 well that thou shalt surely be **k.**, 4428
1Sa 25:36 in his house, like the feast of a **k.**; 4428
1Sa 26:14 Who art thou that criest to the **k.**? 4428
1Sa 26:15 hast thou not kept thy lord the **k.**? 4428
1Sa 26:15 people in to destroy the **k.** thy lord. 4428
1Sa 26:17 said, It is my voice, my lord, O **k.**. 4428
1Sa 26:19 let my lord the **k.** hear the words of… 4428
1Sa 26:20 the **k.** of Israel is come out to seek 4428
1Sa 27:2 Achish, the son of Maoch, **k.** of Gath…4428
1Sa 28:13 the **k.** said unto her, Be not afraid: 4428
1Sa 29:3 the servant of Saul the **k.** of Israel, 4428
1Sa 29:8 the enemies of my lord the **k.**? 4428
2Sa 2:4 David **k.** over the house of Judah. 4428
2Sa 2:7 of Judah have anointed me **k.** over 4428
2Sa 2:9 And made him **k.** over Gilead, 4427
2Sa 2:11 time that David was **k.** in Hebron 4428
2Sa 3:3 daughter of Talmai **k.** of Geshur; 4428
2Sa 3:17 for David in times past to be **k.** over 4428
2Sa 3:21 gather all Israel unto my lord the **k.**, 4428
2Sa 3:23 Abner the son of Ner came to the **k.**, 4428
2Sa 3:24 Then Joab came to the **k.**, and said, 4428
2Sa 3:31 **k.** David himself followed the bier. 4428
2Sa 3:32 the **k.** lifted up his voice, and wept 4428
2Sa 3:33 the **k.** lamented over Abner, and 4428
2Sa 3:36 whatsoever the **k.** did pleased all 4428
2Sa 3:37 it was not of the **k.** to slay Abner 4428
2Sa 3:38 And the **k.** said unto his servants, 4428
2Sa 3:39 this day weak, though anointed **k.**, 4428
2Sa 4:8 and said to the **k.**, Behold the head 4428
2Sa 4:8 Lord hath avenged my lord the **k.** 4428
2Sa 5:2 when Saul was **k.** over us, thou wast 4428
2Sa 5:3 the elders of Israel came to the **k.** 4428
2Sa 5:3 **k.** David made a league with them 4428
2Sa 5:3 they anointed David **k.** over Israel 4428
2Sa 5:6 **k.** and his men went to Jerusalem 4428
2Sa 5:11 Hiram **k.** of Tyre sent messengers 4428
2Sa 5:12 had established him **k.** over Israel, 4428
2Sa 5:17 had anointed David **k.** over Israel, 4428
2Sa 6:12 And it was told **k.** David, saying, 4428
2Sa 6:16 saw **k.** David leaping and dancing 4428
2Sa 6:20 How glorious was the **k.** of Israel 4428
2Sa 7:1 pass, when the **k.** sat in his house, 4428
2Sa 7:2 the **k.** said unto Nathan the prophet, 4428
2Sa 7:3 And Nathan said to the **k.**, Go, do all 4428
2Sa 7:18 Then went **k.** David in, and sat 4428
2Sa 8:3 the son of Rehob, **k.** of Zobah, 4428
2Sa 8:5 to succour Hadadezer **k.** of Zobah, 4428
2Sa 8:8 **k.** David took…much brass 4428
2Sa 8:9 When Toi **k.** of Hamath heard that 4428
2Sa 8:10 sent Joram his son unto **k.** David, 4428
2Sa 8:11 **k.** David did dedicate unto the Lord, 4428
2Sa 8:12 son of Rehob, **k.** of Zobah. 4428
2Sa 9:2 the **k.** said unto him, Art thou Ziba? 4428
2Sa 9:3 And the **k.** said, Is there not yet any 4428
2Sa 9:3 Ziba said unto the **k.**, Jonathan hath 4428
2Sa 9:4 the **k.** said unto him, Where is he? 4428
2Sa 9:4 Ziba said unto the **k.**, Behold, he is 4428
2Sa 9:5 Then **k.** David sent, and fetched 4428
2Sa 9:9 Then the **k.** called to Ziba, Saul's 4428
2Sa 9:11 said Ziba unto the **k.**, According 4428
2Sa 9:11 my lord the **k.** hath commanded his 4428
2Sa 9:11 As for Mephibosheth, said the **k.**, 4428
2Sa 10:1 **k.** of the children of Ammon died, 4428
2Sa 10:5 **k.** said, Tarry at Jericho until your 4428
2Sa 10:6 and of **k.** Maacah a thousand men, 4428
2Sa 11:8 him a mess of meat from the **k.** 4428
2Sa 11:19 the matters of the war unto the **k.**, 4428
2Sa 12:7 I anointed thee **k.** over Israel, and I 4428
2Sa 13:6 when the **k.** was come to see him, 4428
2Sa 13:6 unto the **k.**, I pray thee, let Tamar 4428
2Sa 13:13 I pray thee, speak unto the **k.**; 4428
2Sa 13:21 when **k.** David heard of all these 4428
2Sa 13:24 Absalom came to the **k.**, and said, 4428
2Sa 13:24 let the **k.**, I beseech thee, and his 4428
2Sa 13:25 the **k.** said to Absalom, Nay, my son, 4428
2Sa 13:26 the **k.** said unto him, Why should 4428
2Sa 13:31 the **k.** arose, and tare his garments, 4428
2Sa 13:33 let not my lord the **k.** take the thing 4428
2Sa 13:35 Jonadab said unto the **k.**, Behold, 4428
2Sa 13:36 the **k.** also and all his servants wept 4428
2Sa 13:37 the son of Ammihud, **k.** of Geshur. 4428
2Sa 13:39 soul of **k.** David longed to go forth 4428
2Sa 14:3 come to the **k.**, and speak on this 4428
2Sa 14:4 woman of Tekoah spake to the **k.**, 4428
2Sa 14:4 did obeisance, and said, Help, O **k.**. 4428
2Sa 14:5 the **k.** said unto her, What aileth 4428
2Sa 14:8 the **k.** said unto the woman, Go to 4428
2Sa 14:9 woman of Tekoah said unto the **k.**, 4428
2Sa 14:9 My lord, O **k.**, the iniquity be on me, 4428
2Sa 14:9 the **k.** and his throne be guiltless. 4428
2Sa 14:10 the **k.** said, Whosoever saith ought 4428
2Sa 14:11 the **k.** remember the Lord thy God, 4428
2Sa 14:12 speak one word unto my lord the **k.**. 4428
2Sa 14:13 the **k.** doth speak this thing as one 4428
2Sa 14:13 **k.** doth not fetch home again his 4428
2Sa 14:15 of this thing unto my lord the **k.**, 4428
2Sa 14:15 said, I will now speak unto the **k.**; 4428
2Sa 14:16 For the **k.** will hear, to deliver his 4428
2Sa 14:17 The word of my lord the **k.** shall 4428
2Sa 14:17 so is my lord the **k.** to discern good 4428
2Sa 14:18 the **k.** answered and said unto the 4428
2Sa 14:18 said, Let my lord the **k.** now speak. 4428
2Sa 14:19 the **k.** said, Is not the hand of Joab 4428
2Sa 14:19 As thy soul liveth, my lord the **k.**, 4428
2Sa 14:19 that my lord the **k.** hath spoken: 4428
2Sa 14:21 the **k.** said unto Joab, Behold now, 4428
2Sa 14:22 bowed himself, and thanked the **k.**: 4428
2Sa 14:22 grace in thy sight, my lord, O **k.**, 4428
2Sa 14:22 **k.** hath fulfilled the request of his 4428
2Sa 14:24 the **k.** said, Let him turn to his own 4428
2Sa 14:29 Joab, to have sent him to the **k.**; 4428
2Sa 14:32 that I may sent thee to the **k.**, to 4428
2Sa 14:33 Joab came to the **k.**, and told him: 4428
2Sa 14:33 came to the **k.**, and bowed himself 4428
2Sa 14:33 face to the ground before the **k.**: 4428
2Sa 14:33 and the **k.** kissed Absalom. 4428
2Sa 15:2 came to the **k.** for judgment, 4428
2Sa 15:3 man deputed of the **k.** to hear thee. 4428
2Sa 15:6 that came to the **k.** for judgment: 4428
2Sa 15:7 Absalom said unto the **k.**, I pray 4428
2Sa 15:9 the **k.** said unto him, Go in peace. 4428
2Sa 15:15 the king's servants said unto the **k.**, 4428
2Sa 15:15 my lord the **k.** shall appoint 4428
2Sa 15:16 And the **k.** went forth, and all his 4428
2Sa 15:16 the **k.** left ten women, which were 4428
2Sa 15:17 the **k.** went forth, and all the people 4428
2Sa 15:18 from Gath, passed on before the **k.** 4428
2Sa 15:19 Then said the **k.** to Ittai the Gittite, 4428
2Sa 15:19 thy place, and abide with the **k.**: 4428
2Sa 15:21 And Ittai answered the **k.**, and said 4428
2Sa 15:21 liveth, and as my lord the **k.** liveth, 4428
2Sa 15:21 what place my lord the **k.** shall be, 4428
2Sa 15:23 the **k.** also himself passed over the 4428
2Sa 15:25 the **k.** said unto Zadok, Carry back 4428
2Sa 15:27 **k.** said also unto Zadok the priest, 4428
2Sa 15:34 Absalom, I will be thy servant, O **k.**; 4428
2Sa 16:2 **k.** said unto Ziba, What meanest 4428
2Sa 16:3 And the **k.** said, And where is thy 4428
2Sa 16:3 And Ziba said unto the **k.**, Behold, he 4428
2Sa 16:4 Then said the **k.** to Ziba, Behold, 4428
2Sa 16:4 grace in thy sight, my lord, O **k.**. 4428
2Sa 16:5 when **k.** David came to Bahurim, 4428
2Sa 16:6 and at all the servants of **k.** David: 4428
2Sa 16:9 of Zeruiah unto the **k.**, Why should 4428
2Sa 16:9 this dead dog curse my lord the **k.**? 4428
2Sa 16:10 And the **k.** said, What have I to do 4428
2Sa 16:14 And the **k.**, and all the people that 4428
2Sa 16:16 God save the **k.**, God save the **k.** 4428
2Sa 17:2 flee; and I will smite the **k.** only: 4428
2Sa 17:16 lest the **k.** be swallowed up, and all 4428
2Sa 17:17 and they went and told **k.** David. 4428
2Sa 17:21 well, and went and told **k.** David, 4428
2Sa 18:2 the **k.** said unto the people, I will 4428
2Sa 18:4 **k.** said unto them, What seemeth 4428
2Sa 18:4 the **k.** stood by the gate side, and 4428
2Sa 18:5 And the **k.** commanded Joab and 4428
2Sa 18:5 the **k.** gave all the captains charge 4428
2Sa 18:12 in our hearing the **k.** charged thee 4428
2Sa 18:13 there is no matter hid from the **k.**, 4428
2Sa 18:19 now run, and bear the **k.** tidings, 4428
2Sa 18:21 Go tell the **k.** what thou hast seen. 4428
2Sa 18:25 watchman cried, and told the **k.** 4428
2Sa 18:26 **k.** said, He also bringeth tidings 4428
2Sa 18:27 the **k.** said, He is a good man, and 4428
2Sa 18:28 and said unto the **k.**, All is well. 4428
2Sa 18:28 earth upon his face before the **k.**, 4428
2Sa 18:28 their hand against my lord the **k.** 4428
2Sa 18:29 And the **k.** said, Is the young man 4428
2Sa 18:30 the **k.** said unto him, Turn aside, 4428
2Sa 18:31 Cushi said, Tidings, my lord the **k.**: 4428
2Sa 18:32 the **k.** said unto Cushi, Is the young 4428
2Sa 18:32 enemies of my lord the **k.**, and all 4428
2Sa 18:33 the **k.** was much moved, and went 4428
2Sa 19:1 the **k.** weepeth and mourneth for 4428
2Sa 19:2 how the **k.** was grieved for his son 4428
2Sa 19:4 But the **k.** covered his face, 4428
2Sa 19:4 and the **k.** cried with a loud voice, 4428
2Sa 19:5 Joab came into the house to the **k.**, 4428
2Sa 19:8 the **k.** arose, and sat in the gate 4428
2Sa 19:8 Behold, the **k.** doth sit in the gate 4428
2Sa 19:8 all the people came before the **k.**: 4428
2Sa 19:9 The **k.** saved us out of the hand of 4428
2Sa 19:10 not a word of bringing the **k.** back? 4428
2Sa 19:11 And **k.** David sent to Zadok and to 4428
2Sa 19:11 to bring the **k.** back to his house? 4428
2Sa 19:11 speech of…Israel is come to the **k.**, 4428
2Sa 19:12 are ye the last to bring back the **k.**? 4428
2Sa 19:14 they sent this word unto the **k.**, 4428
2Sa 19:15 So the **k.** returned, and came to 4428
2Sa 19:15 go to meet the **k.**, to conduct the **k.** 4428
2Sa 19:16 the men of Judah to meet **k.** David 4428
2Sa 19:17 they went over Jordan before the **k.** 4428
2Sa 19:18 son of Gera fell down before the **k.**, 4428
2Sa 19:19 said unto the **k.**, Let not my lord 4428
2Sa 19:19 lord the **k.** went out of Jerusalem, 4428
2Sa 19:19 the **k.** should take it to his heart 4428
2Sa 19:20 to go down to meet my lord the **k.**. 4428
2Sa 19:22 that I am this day **k.** over Israel? 4428
2Sa 19:23 **k.** said unto Shimei, Thou shalt not 4428
2Sa 19:23 die. And the **k.** sware unto him. 4428
2Sa 19:24 of Saul came down to meet the **k.**, 4428
2Sa 19:24 from the day the **k.** departed until 4428
2Sa 19:25 come to Jerusalem to meet the **k.**, 4428
2Sa 19:25 the **k.** said unto him, Wherefore 4428
2Sa 19:26 lord, O **k.**, my servant deceived me: 4428
2Sa 19:26 may ride thereon, and go to the **k.**; 4428
2Sa 19:27 thy servant unto my lord the **k.**: 4428
2Sa 19:27 my lord the **k.** is as an angel of God: 4428
2Sa 19:28 dead men before my lord the **k.**: 4428
2Sa 19:28 I yet to cry any more unto the **k.**? 4428
2Sa 19:29 the **k.** said unto him, Why speakest 4428
2Sa 19:30 And Mephibosheth said unto the **k.**, 4428
2Sa 19:30 lord the **k.** is come again in peace 4428
2Sa 19:31 and went over Jordan with the **k.**, 4428
2Sa 19:32 had provided the **k.** of sustenance 4428
2Sa 19:33 the **k.** said unto Barzillai, Come 4428
2Sa 19:34 Barzillai said unto the **k.**, How long 4428
2Sa 19:34 go up with the **k.** unto Jerusalem? 4428
2Sa 19:35 yet a burden unto my lord the **k.**? 4428
2Sa 19:36 little way over Jordan with the **k.**: 4428
2Sa 19:36 why should the **k.** recompense it me 4428
2Sa 19:37 let him go over with my lord the **k.**; 4428
2Sa 19:38 the **k.** answered, Chimham shall go 4428
2Sa 19:39 And when the **k.** was come over, 4428
2Sa 19:39 the **k.** kissed Barzillai, and blessed 4428
2Sa 19:40 Then the **k.** went on to Gilgal, and 4428
2Sa 19:40 people of Judah conducted the **k.**, 4428
2Sa 19:41 all the men of Israel came to the **k.**, 4428
2Sa 19:41 and said unto the **k.**, Why have our 4428
2Sa 19:41 brought the **k.**, and his household, 4428
2Sa 19:42 Because the **k.** is near of kin to us: 4428
2Sa 19:43 said, We have ten parts in the **k.**, 4428
2Sa 19:43 first had in bringing back our **k.**? 4428
2Sa 20:2 men of Judah clave unto their **k.**, 4428
2Sa 20:3 and the **k.** took the ten women his 4428
2Sa 20:4 said the **k.** to Amasa, Assemble me 4428
2Sa 20:21 lifted up his hand against the **k.**, 4428
2Sa 20:22 returned to Jerusalem unto the **k.**. 4428
2Sa 21:2 the **k.** called the Gibeonites, and 4428
2Sa 21:5 they answered the **k.**, The man that 4428
2Sa 21:6 And the **k.** said, I will give them 4428
2Sa 21:7 the **k.** spared Mephibosheth, the son 4428
2Sa 21:8 the **k.** took the two sons of Rizpah 4428
2Sa 21:14 all that the **k.** commanded 4428
2Sa 22:51 is the tower of salvation for his **k.**: 4428
2Sa 24:2 the **k.** said to Joab the captain of 4428
2Sa 24:3 Joab said unto the **k.**, Now the Lord 4428
2Sa 24:3 eyes of my lord the **k.** may see it: 4428
2Sa 24:3 doth my lord the **k.** delight in this 4428
2Sa 24:4 out from the presence of the **k.**, 4428
2Sa 24:9 number of the people unto the **k.**: 4428
2Sa 24:20 Araunah looked, and saw the **k.** and 4428
2Sa 24:20 bowed himself before the **k.** on his 4428
2Sa 24:21 lord the **k.** come to his servant? 4428
2Sa 24:22 Let my lord the **k.** take and offer up 4428

2Sa 24:23 Araunah, as a **k.**, give unto the **k.** 4428
2Sa 24:23 Araunah said unto the **k.**, The Lord 4428
2Sa 24:24 And the **k.** said unto Araunah, Nay; 4428
1Ki 1:1 Now **k.** David was old and stricken 4428
1Ki 1:2 for my lord the **k.** a young virgin: 4428
1Ki 1:2 let her stand before the **k.**, and let 4428
1Ki 1:2 that my lord the **k.** may get heat. 4428
1Ki 1:3 and brought her to the **k.** 4428
1Ki 1:4 was very fair, and cherished the **k.**, 4428
1Ki 1:4 to him: but the **k.** knew her not. 4428
1Ki 1:5 himself, saying, I will be **k.**: 4427
1Ki 1:13 get thee in unto **k.** David, and say 4428
1Ki 1:13 Didst not thou, my lord, O **k.**, swear 4428
1Ki 1:14 thou yet talkest there with the **k.**, 4428
1Ki 1:15 in unto the **k.** into the chamber: 4428
1Ki 1:15 and the **k.** was very old; and 4428
1Ki 1:15 Shunammite ministered unto the **k.** 4428
1Ki 1:16 and did obeisance unto the **k.** 4428
1Ki 1:16 the **k.** said, What wouldest thou? 4428
1Ki 1:18 my lord the **k.**, thou knowest it not: 4428
1Ki 1:19 hath called all the sons of the **k.**, 4428
1Ki 1:20 O **k.**, the eyes of Israel are upon 4428
1Ki 1:20 on the throne of my lord the **k.** after 4428
1Ki 1:21 the **k.** shall sleep with his fathers, 4428
1Ki 1:22 while she yet talked with the **k.**, 4428
1Ki 1:23 told the **k.**, saying, Behold Nathan 4428
1Ki 1:23 when he was come in before the **k.**, 4428
1Ki 1:23 he bowed himself before the **k.** with 4428
1Ki 1:24 said, My lord, O **k.**, hast thou said, 4428
1Ki 1:25 him, and say, God save **k.** Adonijah 4428
1Ki 1:27 Is this thing done by my lord the **k.**, 4428
1Ki 1:27 throne of my lord the **k.** after him? 4428
1Ki 1:28 **k.** David answered and said, Call 4428
1Ki 1:28 presence, and stood before the **k.** 4428
1Ki 1:29 And the **k.** sware, and said, As the 4428
1Ki 1:31 earth, and did reverence to the **k.**, 4428
1Ki 1:31 Let my lord **k.** David live for ever 4428
1Ki 1:32 **k.** David said, Call me Zadok the 4428
1Ki 1:32 And they came before the **k.** 4428
1Ki 1:33 The **k.** also said unto them, Take 4428
1Ki 1:34 anoint him there **k.** over Israel: 4428
1Ki 1:34 and say, God save **k.** Solomon 4428
1Ki 1:35 he shall be **k.** in my stead: for I 4427
1Ki 1:36 son of Jehoiada answered the **k.**, 4428
1Ki 1:36 Lord God of my lord the **k.** say so 4428
1Ki 1:37 Lord hath been with my lord the **k.**, 4428
1Ki 1:37 than the throne of my lord **k.** David 4428
1Ki 1:38 to ride upon **k.** David's mule, 4428
1Ki 1:39 people said, God save **k.** Solomon. 4428
1Ki 1:43 lord **k.** David hath made Solomon 4428
1Ki 1:43 David hath made Solomon **k.** 4427
1Ki 1:44 the **k.** hath sent with him Zadok 4428
1Ki 1:45 have anointed him **k.** in Gihon: 4428
1Ki 1:47 came to bless our lord **k.** David, 4428
1Ki 1:47 the **k.** bowed himself upon the bed 4428
1Ki 1:48 And also thus said the **k.**, Blessed 4428
1Ki 1:51 Adonijah feareth **k.** Solomon: 4428
1Ki 1:51 **k.** Solomon swear unto me to day 4428
1Ki 1:53 **k.** Solomon sent, and they brought 4428
1Ki 1:53 and bowed himself to **k.** Solomon: 4428
1Ki 2:17 I pray thee, unto Solomon the **k.**, 4428
1Ki 2:18 I will speak for thee unto the **k.** 4428
1Ki 2:19 therefore went unto **k.** Solomon, 4428
1Ki 2:19 And the **k.** rose up to meet her, and 4428
1Ki 2:20 the **k.** said unto her, Ask on, my 4428
1Ki 2:22 And **k.** Solomon answered and said 4428
1Ki 2:23 Then **k.** Solomon sware by the Lord, 4428
1Ki 2:25 And **k.** Solomon sent by the hand of 4428
1Ki 2:26 unto Abiathar the priest said the **k.**, 4428
1Ki 2:29 it was told **k.** Solomon that Joab 4428
1Ki 2:30 him, Thus saith the **k.**, Come forth. 4428
1Ki 2:30 Benaiah brought the **k.** word again, 4428
1Ki 2:31 the **k.** said unto him, Do as he hath 4428
1Ki 2:35 **k.** put Benaiah the son of Jehoiada 4428
1Ki 2:35 the **k.** put in the room of Abiathar 4428
1Ki 2:36 the **k.** sent and called for Shimei, 4428
1Ki 2:38 Shimei said unto the **k.**, The saying 4428
1Ki 2:38 as my lord the **k.** hath said, so will 4428
1Ki 2:39 Achish son of Maachah **k.** of Gath. 4428
1Ki 2:42 the **k.** sent and called for Shimei, 4428
1Ki 2:44 The **k.** said moreover to Shimei, 4428
1Ki 2:45 **k.** Solomon shall be blessed, and 4428
1Ki 2:46 the **k.** commanded Benaiah the son 4428
1Ki 3:1 affinity with Pharaoh **k.** of Egypt, 4428
1Ki 3:4 the **k.** went to Gibeon to sacrifice 4428
1Ki 3:7 hast made thy servant **k.** instead of 4427
1Ki 3:16 that were harlots, unto the **k.**, 4428
1Ki 3:22 son. Thus they spake before the **k.** 4428
1Ki 3:23 Then said the **k.**, The one saith, 4428
1Ki 3:24 And the **k.** said, Bring me a sword 4428
1Ki 3:24 they brought a sword before the **k.** 4428
1Ki 3:25 the **k.** said, Divide the living child 4428
1Ki 3:26 the living child was unto the **k.**, 4428
1Ki 3:27 the **k.** answered and said, Give her 4428
1Ki 3:28 judgment which the **k.** had judged; 4428
1Ki 3:28 and they feared the **k.**: for they saw 4428
1Ki 4:1 **k.** Solomon was **k.** over all Israel 4428
1Ki 4:7 provided victuals for the **k.** and his 4428
1Ki 4:19 in the country of Sihon **k.** of the 4428
1Ki 4:19 Amorites, and of Og **k.** of Bashan; 4428
1Ki 4:27 provided victual for **k.** Solomon, 4428
1Ki 4:27 that came unto **k.** Solomon's table, 4428
1Ki 5:1 Hiram **k.** of Tyre sent his servants 4428
1Ki 5:1 anointed him **k.** in the room of his 4428
1Ki 5:13 **k.** Solomon raised a levy out of all 4428
1Ki 5:17 **k.** commanded, and they brought 4428
1Ki 6:2 house which **k.** Solomon built for 4428
1Ki 7:13 **k.** Solomon sent and fetched Hiram 4428
1Ki 7:14 he came to **k.** Solomon, and wrought 4428
1Ki 7:40 work that he made **k.** Solomon for 4428
1Ki 7:45 which Hiram made to **k.** Solomon 4428
1Ki 7:46 plain of Jordan did the **k.** cast them, 4428
1Ki 7:51 work that **k.** Solomon made for the 4428
1Ki 8:1 unto **k.** Solomon in Jerusalem, 4428
1Ki 8:2 themselves unto **k.** Solomon at the 4428
1Ki 8:5 And **k.** Solomon, and all the 4428
1Ki 8:14 the **k.** turned his face about, and 4428
1Ki 8:62 And the **k.**, and all Israel with him, 4428
1Ki 8:63 the **k.** and all the children of Israel 4428
1Ki 8:64 did the **k.** hallow the middle of the 4428
1Ki 8:66 they blessed the **k.**, and went unto 4428
1Ki 9:11 Hiram the **k.** of Tyre had furnished 4428
1Ki 9:11 **k.** Solomon gave Hiram twenty 4428
1Ki 9:14 sent to the **k.** sixscore talents of 4428
1Ki 9:15 the levy which **k.** Solomon raised; 4428
1Ki 9:16 Pharaoh **k.** of Egypt had gone up, 4428
1Ki 9:26 **k.** Solomon made a navy of ships 4428
1Ki 9:28 and brought it to **k.** Solomon. 4428
1Ki 10:3 was not any thing hid from the **k.**, 4428
1Ki 10:6 And she said to the **k.**, It was a true 4428
1Ki 10:9 for ever, therefore made he thee **k.**, 4428
1Ki 10:10 And she gave the **k.** an hundred and 4428
1Ki 10:10 queen of Sheba gave to **k.** Solomon. 4428
1Ki 10:12 **k.** made of the almug trees pillars 4428
1Ki 10:13 **k.** Solomon gave unto the queen of 4428
1Ki 10:16 And **k.** Solomon made two hundred 4428
1Ki 10:17 the **k.** put them in the house of the 4428
1Ki 10:18 the **k.** made a great throne of ivory, 4428
1Ki 10:21 all **k.** Solomon's drinking vessels 4428
1Ki 10:22 **k.** had at sea a navy of Tharshish 4428
1Ki 10:23 **k.** Solomon exceeded all the kings 4428
1Ki 10:26 and with the **k.** at Jerusalem. 4428
1Ki 10:27 **k.** made silver to be in Jerusalem as 4428
1Ki 11:1 But **k.** Solomon loved many strange 4428
1Ki 11:18 Egypt, unto Pharaoh **k.** of Egypt; 4428
1Ki 11:23 his lord Hadadezer **k.** of Zobah: 4428
1Ki 11:26 he lifted up his hand against the **k.** 4428
1Ki 11:27 he lifted up his hand against the **k.**: 4428
1Ki 11:37 and shalt be **k.** over Israel. 4428
1Ki 11:40 Egypt, unto Shishak **k.** of Egypt, 4428
1Ki 12:1 come to Shechem to make him **k.** 4427
1Ki 12:2 from the presence of **k.** Solomon, 4428
1Ki 12:6 **k.** Rehoboam consulted with the old 4428
1Ki 12:12 third day, as the **k.** had appointed, 4428
1Ki 12:13 the **k.** answered the people roughly, 4428
1Ki 12:15 **k.** hearkened not unto the people; 4428
1Ki 12:16 the **k.** hearkened not unto them, 4428
1Ki 12:16 the people answered the **k.**, saying, 4428
1Ki 12:18 **k.** Rehoboam sent Adoram, who 4428
1Ki 12:18 **k.** Rehoboam made speed to get him 4428
1Ki 12:20 and made him **k.** over all Israel: 4427
1Ki 12:23 the son of Solomon, **k.** of Judah, 4428
1Ki 12:27 even unto Rehoboam **k.** of Judah, 4428
1Ki 12:27 go again to Rehoboam **k.** of Judah. 4428
1Ki 12:28 Whereupon the **k.** took counsel, 4428
1Ki 13:4 when **k.** Jeroboam heard the saying 4428
1Ki 13:6 **k.** answered and said unto the man 4428
1Ki 13:7 the **k.** said unto the man of God, 4428
1Ki 13:8 the man of God said unto the **k.**, If 4428
1Ki 13:11 which he had spoken unto the **k.**, 4428
1Ki 14:2 I should be **k.** over this people. 4428
1Ki 14:14 Lord shall raise him up a **k.** over 4428
1Ki 14:25 in the fifth year of **k.** Rehoboam, kings 4428
1Ki 14:25 that Shishak **k.** of Egypt came up 4428
1Ki 14:27 **k.** Rehoboam made in their stead 4428
1Ki 14:28 **k.** went into the house of the Lord, 4428
1Ki 15:1 eighteenth year of **k.** Jeroboam 4428
1Ki 15:9 year of Jeroboam **k.** of Israel 4428
1Ki 15:16 between Asa and Baasha **k.** of Israel 4428
1Ki 15:17 And Baasha **k.** of Israel went up 4428
1Ki 15:17 out or come in to Asa **k.** of Judah. 4428
1Ki 15:18 **k.** Asa sent them to Ben-hadad, 4428
1Ki 15:18 the son of Hezion, **k.** of Syria, 4428
1Ki 15:19 thy league with Baasha **k.** of Israel, 4428
1Ki 15:20 Ben-hadad hearkened unto **k.** Asa, 4428
1Ki 15:22 Then **k.** Asa made a proclamation 4428
1Ki 15:22 **k.** Asa built with them Geba of 4428
1Ki 15:25 the second year of Asa **k.** of Judah, 4428
1Ki 15:28 the third year of Asa **k.** of Judah 4428
1Ki 15:32 between Asa and Baasha **k.** of Israel 4428
1Ki 15:33 the third year of Asa **k.** of Judah 4428
1Ki 16:8 and sixth year of Asa **k.** of Judah 4428
1Ki 16:10 seventh year of Asa **k.** of Judah, 4428
1Ki 16:15 seventh year of Asa **k.** of Judah 4428
1Ki 16:16 and hath also slain the **k.**: 4428
1Ki 16:16 Israel made Omri...**k.** over Israel 4427
1Ki 16:21 the son of Ginath, to make him **k.**; 4427
1Ki 16:23 and first year of Asa **k.** of Judah 4428
1Ki 16:29 and eighth year of Asa **k.** of Judah 4428
1Ki 16:31 of Ethbaal **k.** of the Zidonians, 4428
1Ki 19:15 anoint Hazael to be **k.** over Syria: 4428
1Ki 19:16 thou anoint to be **k.** over Israel: 4428
1Ki 20:1 the **k.** of Syria gathered all his hosts 4428
1Ki 20:2 to Ahab **k.** of Israel into the city, 4428
1Ki 20:4 the **k.** of Israel answered and said, 4428
1Ki 20:4 My lord, O **k.**, according to thy 4428
1Ki 20:7 the **k.** of Israel called all the elders 4428
1Ki 20:9 Tell my lord the **k.**, All that thou 4428
1Ki 20:11 the **k.** of Israel answered and said, 4428
1Ki 20:13 a prophet unto Ahab **k.** of Israel, 4428
1Ki 20:20 the **k.** of Syria escaped on an horse 4428
1Ki 20:21 the **k.** of Israel went out, and smote 4428
1Ki 20:22 the prophet came to the **k.** of Israel, 4428
1Ki 20:22 year the **k.** of Syria will come up 4428
1Ki 20:23 servants of the **k.** of Syria said unto 4428
1Ki 20:28 and spake unto the **k.** of Israel, 4428
1Ki 20:31 and go out to the **k.** of Israel: 4428
1Ki 20:32 heads, and came to the **k.** of Israel, 4428
1Ki 20:38 and waited for the **k.** by the way, 4428
1Ki 20:39 And as the **k.** passed by, he cried 4428
1Ki 20:39 he cried unto the **k.**: and he said, 4428
1Ki 20:40 **k.** of Israel said unto him, So shall 4428
1Ki 20:41 **k.** of Israel discerned him that he 4428
1Ki 20:43 the **k.** of Israel went to his house 4428
1Ki 21:1 the palace of Ahab **k.** of Samaria. 4428
1Ki 21:10 didst blaspheme God and the **k.** 4428
1Ki 21:13 did blaspheme God and the **k.** 4428
1Ki 21:18 go down to meet Ahab **k.** of Israel, 4428
1Ki 22:2 **k.** of Judah came down to the **k.** of 4428
1Ki 22:3 **k.** of Israel said unto his servants, 4428
1Ki 22:3 out of the hand of the **k.** of Syria? 4428
1Ki 22:4 Jehoshaphat said to the **k.** of Israel, 4428
1Ki 22:5 said unto the **k.** of Israel, I enquire, 4428
1Ki 22:6 **k.** of Israel gathered the prophets 4428
1Ki 22:6 deliver it into the hand of the **k.** 4428
1Ki 22:8 **k.** of Israel said unto Jehoshaphat, 4428
1Ki 22:8 said, Let not the **k.** say so. 4428
1Ki 22:9 the **k.** of Israel called an officer, 4428
1Ki 22:10 And the **k.** of Israel and 4428
1Ki 22:10 Jehoshaphat the **k.** of Judah sat 4428
1Ki 22:13 prophets declare good unto the **k.** 4428
1Ki 22:15 came to the **k.**. And the **k.** said 4428
1Ki 22:15 deliver it into the hand of the **k.** 4428
1Ki 22:16 the **k.** said unto him, How many 4428
1Ki 22:18 **k.** of Israel said unto Jehoshaphat, 4428
1Ki 22:26 And the **k.** of Israel said, Take 4428
1Ki 22:27 Thus saith the **k.**, Put this fellow 4428
1Ki 22:29 So the **k.** of Israel and 4428
1Ki 22:29 Jehoshaphat the **k.** of Judah went 4428
1Ki 22:30 **k.** of Israel said unto Jehoshaphat, 4428
1Ki 22:30 **k.** of Israel disguised himself, and 4428
1Ki 22:31 **k.** of Syria commanded his thirty 4428
1Ki 22:31 save only with the **k.** of Israel. 4428
1Ki 22:32 said, Surely it is the **k.** of Israel. 4428
1Ki 22:33 that it was not the **k.** of Israel, that 4428
1Ki 22:34 smote the **k.** of Israel between the 4428
1Ki 22:35 the **k.** was stayed up in his chariot 4428
1Ki 22:37 the **k.** died, and was brought to 4428

1Ki 22:37 and they buried the **k.** in Samaria....... 4428
1Ki 22:41 the fourth year of Ahab **k.** of Israel.... 4428
1Ki 22:44 made peace with the **k.** of Israel........ 4428
1Ki 22:47 no **k.** in Edom: a deputy was **k.**.......... 4428
1Ki 22:51 year of Jehoshaphat **k.** of Judah,......... 4428
2Ki 1:3 messengers of the **k.** of Samaria,....... 4428
2Ki 1:6 again unto the **k.** that sent you,......... 4428
2Ki 1:9 Then the **k.** sent unto him a captain... 4428
2Ki 1:9 Thou man of God, the **k.** hath said,.... 4428
2Ki 1:11 the **k.** said, Come down quickly......... 4428
2Ki 1:15 went down with him unto the **k.**.......... 4428
2Ki 1:17 the son of Jehoshaphat **k.** of Judah;..... 4428
2Ki 3:1 year of Jehoshaphat **k.** of Judah,......... 4428
2Ki 3:4 **k.** of Moab was a sheepmaster,......... 4428
2Ki 3:4 rendered unto the **k.** of Israel an....... 4428
2Ki 3:5 Ahab was dead, that the **k.** of Moab... 4428
2Ki 3:5 rebelled against the **k.** of Israel......... 4428
2Ki 3:6 **k.** Jehoram went out of Samaria......... 4428
2Ki 3:7 to Jehoshaphat the **k.** of Judah,......... 4428
2Ki 3:7 **k.** of Moab hath rebelled against........ 4428
2Ki 3:9 the **k.** of Israel went, and the **k.** of.... 4428
2Ki 3:9 the **k.** of Edom: and they fetched....... 4428
2Ki 3:10 **k.** of Israel said, Alas! that the.......... 4428
2Ki 3:11 one of the **k.** of Israel's servants........ 4428
2Ki 3:12 the **k.** of Israel and Jehoshaphat......... 4428
2Ki 3:12 the **k.** of Edom went down to him...... 4428
2Ki 3:13 Elisha said unto the **k.** of Israel,........ 4428
2Ki 3:13 And the **k.** of Israel said unto him,...... 4428
2Ki 3:14 of Jehoshaphat the **k.** of Judah,.......... 4428
2Ki 3:26 the **k.** of Moab saw that the battle..... 4428
2Ki 3:26 through even unto the **k.** of Edom:..... 4428
2Ki 4:13 thou be spoken for to the **k.**,............ 4428
2Ki 5:1 of the host of the **k.** of Syria,........... 4428
2Ki 5:5 And the **k.** of Syria said, Go to, go,... 4428
2Ki 5:5 send a letter unto the **k.** of Israel...... 4428
2Ki 5:6 the letter to the **k.** of Israel, saying,... 4428
2Ki 5:7 when the **k.** of Israel had read the..... 4428
2Ki 5:8 the **k.** of Israel had rent his clothes,... 4428
2Ki 5:8 that he sent to the **k.**, saying,........... 4428
2Ki 6:8 **k.** of Syria warred against Israel,....... 4428
2Ki 6:9 of God sent unto the **k.** of Israel,........ 4428
2Ki 6:10 the **k.** of Israel sent to the place........ 4428
2Ki 6:11 the heart of the **k.** of Syria was sore.. 4428
2Ki 6:11 which of us is for the **k.** of Israel?...... 4428
2Ki 6:12 servants said, None, my lord, O **k.**:... 4428
2Ki 6:12 telleth the **k.** of Israel the words........ 4428
2Ki 6:21 the **k.** of Israel said unto Elisha,........ 4428
2Ki 6:24 **k.** of Syria gathered all his host,........ 4428
2Ki 6:26 as the **k.** of Israel was passing by...... 4428
2Ki 6:26 him, saying, Help, my lord, O **k.**....... 4428
2Ki 6:28 the **k.** said unto her, What aileth........ 4428
2Ki 6:30 when the **k.** heard the words of the.... 4428
2Ki 6:32 the **k.** sent a man from before him:..........
2Ki 7:2 lord on whose hand the **k.** leaned........ 4428
2Ki 7:6 the **k.** of Israel hath hired against....... 4428
2Ki 7:12 the **k.** arose in the night, and said...... 4428
2Ki 7:14 the **k.** sent after the host of the........ 4428
2Ki 7:15 returned, and told the **k.**................. 4428
2Ki 7:17 the **k.** appointed the lord on whose.... 4428
2Ki 7:17 when the **k.** came down to him.......... 4428
2Ki 7:18 man of God had spoken to the **k.**,...... 4428
2Ki 8:3 to cry unto the **k.** for her house........ 4428
2Ki 8:4 And the **k.** talked with Gehazi the...... 4428
2Ki 8:5 telling the **k.** how he had restored...... 4428
2Ki 8:5 cried to the **k.** for her house and for... 4428
2Ki 8:5 My lord, O **k.**, this is the woman,...... 4428
2Ki 8:6 And when the **k.** asked the woman,.... 4428
2Ki 8:6 the **k.** appointed unto her a certain..... 4428
2Ki 8:7 Beh-hadad the **k.** of Syria was sick;.... 4428
2Ki 8:8 the **k.** said unto Hazael, Take a......... 4428
2Ki 8:9 **k.** of Syria hath sent me to thee,....... 4428
2Ki 8:13 that thou shalt be **k.** over Syria......... 4428
2Ki 8:16 Joram the son of Ahab **k.** of Israel,..... 4428
2Ki 8:16 Jehoshaphat being...**k.** of Judah,........ 4428
2Ki 8:16 Jehoram **k.** of Judah began to reign..... 4428
2Ki 8:20 and made a **k.** over themselves......... 4428
2Ki 8:25 Joram the son of Ahab **k.** of Israel,..... 4428
2Ki 8:25 the son of Jehoram **k.** of Judah......... 4428
2Ki 8:26 the daughter of Omri **k.** of Israel........ 4428
2Ki 8:26 the son of Jehoshaphat **k.** of Judah...... 4428
2Ki 8:28 **k.** of Syria in Ramoth-gilead;............ 4428
2Ki 8:29 **k.** Joram went back to be healed in.... 4428
2Ki 8:29 fought against Hazael **k.** of Syria........ 4428
2Ki 9:3 I have anointed thee **k.** over Israel...... 4428
2Ki 9:6 I have anointed thee **k.** over the........ 4428
2Ki 9:12 I have anointed thee **k.** over Israel..... 4428
2Ki 9:13 with trumpets, saying, Jehu is **k.**........ 4427

2Ki 9:14 because of Hazael **k.** of Syria........... 4428
2Ki 9:15 **k.** Joram was returned to be healed.... 4428
2Ki 9:15 he fought with Hazael **k.** of Syria.)...... 4428
2Ki 9:16 **k.** of Judah was come down to see..... 4428
2Ki 9:18, 19 Thus saith the **k.**, Is it peace?....... 4428
2Ki 9:21 **k.** of Israel and Ahaziah **k.** of Judah.... 4428
2Ki 9:27 Ahaziah the **k.** of Judah saw this,....... 4428
2Ki 10:5 we will not make any **k.**: do thou....... 4427
2Ki 10:13 brethren of Ahaziah **k.** of Judah,......... 4428
2Ki 10:13 children of the **k.** and the children...... 4428
2Ki 11:2 the daughter of **k.** Joram, sister of..... 4428
2Ki 11:7 the house of the Lord about the **k.**...... 4428
2Ki 11:8 shall compass the **k.** round about,....... 4428
2Ki 11:8 be ye with the **k.** as he goeth out...... 4428
2Ki 11:10 give **k.** David's spears and shields,..... 4428
2Ki 11:11 in his hand, round about the **k.**,......... 4428
2Ki 11:12 and they made him **k.**, and anointed.... 4427
2Ki 11:12 hands, and said, God save the **k.**....... 4428
2Ki 11:14 the **k.** stood by a pillar, as the.......... 4428
2Ki 11:14 and the trumpeters by the **k.**, and...... 4428
2Ki 11:17 between the Lord and the **k.** and....... 4428
2Ki 11:17 between the **k.** also and the people..... 4428
2Ki 11:19 they brought down the **k.** from the..... 4428
2Ki 12:6 twentieth year of **k.** Jehoash the........ 4428
2Ki 12:7 **k.** Jehoash called for Jehoiada the....... 4428
2Ki 12:17 Hazael **k.** of Syria went up, and......... 4428
2Ki 12:18 Jehoash **k.** of Judah took all the......... 4428
2Ki 12:18 and sent it to Hazael **k.** of Syria:....... 4428
2Ki 13:1 the son of Ahaziah **k.** of Judah........... 4428
2Ki 13:3 into the hand of Hazael **k.** of Syria,.... 4428
2Ki 13:4 the **k.** of Syria oppressed them.......... 4428
2Ki 13:7 the **k.** of Syria had destroyed them,.... 4428
2Ki 13:10 seventh year of Joash **k.** of Judah....... 4428
2Ki 13:12 against Amaziah **k.** of Judah,............ 4428
2Ki 13:14 Joash the **k.** of Israel came down....... 4428
2Ki 13:16 said to the **k.** of Israel, Put thine....... 4428
2Ki 13:18 he said unto the **k.** of Israel, Smite.... 4428
2Ki 13:22 Hazael **k.** of Syria oppressed Israel..... 4428
2Ki 13:24 So Hazael **k.** of Syria died; and.......... 4428
2Ki 14:1 son of Jehoahaz **k.** of Israel reigned.... 4428
2Ki 14:1 the son of Joash **k.** of Judah............. 4428
2Ki 14:5 which had slain the **k.** his father......... 4428
2Ki 14:8 Jehoahaz son of Jehu, **k.** of Israel,...... 4428
2Ki 14:9 And Jehoash the **k.** of Israel sent....... 4428
2Ki 14:9 sent to Amaziah **k.** of Judah, saying,... 4428
2Ki 14:11 Jehoash **k.** of Israel went up;........... 4428
2Ki 14:11 Amaziah **k.** of Judah looked one......... 4428
2Ki 14:13 And Jehoash **k.** of Israel took........... 4428
2Ki 14:13 Amaziah **k.** of Judah, the son of......... 4428
2Ki 14:15 fought with Amaziah **k.** of Judah,........ 4428
2Ki 14:17 the son of Joash **k.** of Judah lived....... 4428
2Ki 14:17 son of Jehoahaz **k.** of Israel.............. 4428
2Ki 14:21 made him **k.** instead of his father...... 4427
2Ki 14:22 that the **k.** slept with his fathers........ 4428
2Ki 14:23 the son of Joash **k.** of Judah............. 4428
2Ki 14:23 the son of Joash **k.** of Israel began..... 4428
2Ki 15:1 year of Jeroboam **k.** of Israel began..... 4428
2Ki 15:1 Azariah son of Amaziah **k.** of Judah..... 4428
2Ki 15:5 the Lord smote the **k.**, so that he...... 4428
2Ki 15:8 eighth year of Azariah **k.** of Judah...... 4428
2Ki 15:13 nine...year of Uzziah **k.** of Judah;....... 4428
2Ki 15:17 year of Azariah **k.** of Judah began....... 4428
2Ki 15:19 **k.** of Assyria came against the land:.... 4428
2Ki 15:20 of silver, to give to the **k.** of Assyria.. 4428
2Ki 15:20 the **k.** of Assyria turned back, and...... 4428
2Ki 15:23 the fiftieth...of Azariah **k.** of Judah...... 4428
2Ki 15:27 and fiftieth...of Azariah **k.** of Judah..... 4428
2Ki 15:29 In the days of Pekah **k.** of Israel......... 4428
2Ki 15:29 Tiglath-pileser **k.** of Assyria, and........ 4428
2Ki 15:32 the son of Remaliah **k.** of Israel......... 4428
2Ki 15:32 son of Uzziah **k.** of Judah to reign...... 4428
2Ki 15:37 against Judah Rezin the **k.** of Syria,.... 4428
2Ki 16:1 Ahaz son of Jotham **k.** of Judah.......... 4428
2Ki 16:5 Then Rezin **k.** of Syria and Pekah...... 4428
2Ki 16:5 son of Remaliah **k.** of Israel came........ 4428
2Ki 16:6 Rezin **k.** of Syria recovered Elath to... 4428
2Ki 16:7 to Tiglath-pileser **k.** of Assyria,......... 4428
2Ki 16:7 me out of the hand of the **k.** of Syria,..4428
2Ki 16:7 out of the hand of the **k.** of Israel,..... 4428
2Ki 16:8 it for a present to the **k.** of Assyria.... 4428
2Ki 16:9 **k.** of Assyria hearkened unto him:...... 4428
2Ki 16:9 the **k.** of Assyria went up against........ 4428
2Ki 16:10 And **k.** Ahaz went to Damascus to..... 4428
2Ki 16:10 meet Tiglath-pileser **k.** of Assyria,...... 4428
2Ki 16:10 **k.** Ahaz sent to Urijah the priest the... 4428
2Ki 16:11 **k.** Ahaz had sent from Damascus:...... 4428
2Ki 16:11 **k.** Ahaz came from Damascus............ 4428

2Ki 16:12 the **k.** was come from Damascus,....... 4428
2Ki 16:12 the **k.** saw the altar:...................... 4428
2Ki 16:12 and the **k.** approached to the altar,..... 4428
2Ki 16:15 And **k.** Ahaz commanded Urijah the.... 4428
2Ki 16:16 to all that **k.** Ahaz commanded........... 4428
2Ki 16:17 **k.** Ahaz cut off the borders of the...... 4428
2Ki 16:18 of the Lord for the **k.** of Assyria........ 4428
2Ki 17:1 the twelfth year of Ahaz **k.** of Judah... 4428
2Ki 17:3 came up Shalmaneser **k.** of Assyria;..... 4428
2Ki 17:4 the **k.** of Assyria found conspiracy...... 4428
2Ki 17:4 sent messengers to So **k.** of Egypt,.... 4428
2Ki 17:4 no present to the **k.** of Assyria,......... 4428
2Ki 17:4 the **k.** of Assyria shut him up,........... 4428
2Ki 17:5 **k.** of Assyria came up throughout....... 4428
2Ki 17:6 the **k.** of Assyria took Samaria, and.... 4428
2Ki 17:7 the hand of Pharaoh **k.** of Egypt,....... 4428
2Ki 17:21 made Jeroboam the son of Nebat **k.**:... 4427
2Ki 17:24 the **k.** of Assyria brought men from.... 4428
2Ki 17:26 they spake to the **k.** of Assyria,......... 4428
2Ki 17:27 Then the **k.** of Assyria commanded,.... 4428
2Ki 18:1 of Hoshea son of Elah **k.** of Israel,..... 4428
2Ki 18:1 the son of Ahaz **k.** of Judah began...... 4428
2Ki 18:7 rebelled against the **k.** of Assyria,...... 4428
2Ki 18:9 in the fourth year of **k.** Hezekiah,...... 4428
2Ki 18:9 of Hoshea son of Elah **k.** of Israel,..... 4428
2Ki 18:9 Shalmaneser **k.** of Assyria came up..... 4428
2Ki 18:10 the ninth year of Hoshea **k.** of Israel,.. 4428
2Ki 18:11 **k.** of Assyria did carry away Israel.... 4428
2Ki 18:13 the fourteenth year of **k.** Hezekiah..... 4428
2Ki 18:13 Sennacherib **k.** of Assyria come up..... 4428
2Ki 18:14 **k.** of Judah sent to the **k.** of Assyria... 4428
2Ki 18:14 the **k.** of Assyria appointed unto........ 4428
2Ki 18:14 Hezekiah **k.** of Judah three hundred.... 4428
2Ki 18:16 Hezekiah **k.** of Judah had overlaid,...... 4428
2Ki 18:16 and gave it to the **k.** of Assyria......... 4428
2Ki 18:17 the **k.** of Assyria sent Tartan and....... 4428
2Ki 18:17 from Lachish to **k.** Hezekiah with....... 4428
2Ki 18:18 when they had called to the **k.**, there.. 4428
2Ki 18:19 saith the great **k.**, the **k.** of Assyria,.. 4428
2Ki 18:21 so is Pharaoh **k.** of Egypt unto all...... 4428
2Ki 18:23 pledges to my lord the **k.** of Assyria,.. 4428
2Ki 18:28 of the great **k.**, the **k.** of Assyria:...... 4428
2Ki 18:29 Thus saith the **k.**, Let not Hezekiah... 4428
2Ki 18:30 into the hand of the **k.** of Assyria....... 4428
2Ki 18:31 thus saith the **k.** of Assyria, Make an.. 4428
2Ki 18:33 out of the hand of the **k.** of Assyria?... 4428
2Ki 19:1 when **k.** Hezekiah heard it, that he..... 4428
2Ki 19:4 **k.** of Assyria his master hath sent..... 4428
2Ki 19:5 servants of **k.** Hezekiah came to........ 4428
2Ki 19:6 servants of the **k.** of Assyria have...... 4428
2Ki 19:8 the **k.** of Assyria warring against........ 4428
2Ki 19:9 heard say of Tirhakah **k.** of Ethiopia,.. 4428
2Ki 19:10 ye speak to Hezekiah **k.** of Judah,...... 4428
2Ki 19:10 into the hand of the **k.** of Assyria....... 4428
2Ki 19:13 **k.** of Hamath, and the **k.** of Arpad,.... 4428
2Ki 19:13 and the **k.** of the city of Sepharvaim,.. 4428
2Ki 19:20 against Sennacherib **k.** of Assyria...... 4428
2Ki 19:32 Lord concerning the **k.** of Assyria,..... 4428
2Ki 19:36 Sennacherib **k.** of Assyria departed,.... 4428
2Ki 20:6 out of the hand of the **k.** of Assyria;... 4428
2Ki 20:12 **k.** of Babylon, sent letters and a........ 4428
2Ki 20:14 Isaiah the prophet unto **k.** Hezekiah,... 4428
2Ki 20:18 in the palace of the **k.** of Babylon....... 4428
2Ki 21:3 a grove, as did Ahab **k.** of Israel;........ 4428
2Ki 21:11 Manasseh **k.** of Judah hath done......... 4428
2Ki 21:23 and slew the **k.** in his own house....... 4428
2Ki 21:24 had conspired against **k.** Amon;......... 4428
2Ki 21:24 made Josiah his son **k.** in his stead..... 4427
2Ki 22:3 the eighteenth year of **k.** Josiah,........ 4428
2Ki 22:3 that the **k.** sent Shaphan the son of.... 4428
2Ki 22:9 Shaphan the scribe came to the **k.**,...... 4428
2Ki 22:9 brought the **k.** word again, and said,... 4428
2Ki 22:10 Shaphan the scribe shewed the **k.**,..... 4428
2Ki 22:10 And Shaphan read it before the **k.**...... 4428
2Ki 22:11 **k.** had heard the words of the book.... 4428
2Ki 22:12 **k.** commanded Hilkiah the priest,....... 4428
2Ki 22:16 which the **k.** of Judah hath read:........ 4428
2Ki 22:18 to the **k.** of Judah which sent you to... 4428
2Ki 22:20 they brought the **k.** word again.......... 4428
2Ki 23:1 the **k.** sent, and they gathered unto.... 4428
2Ki 23:2 the **k.** went up into the house of the... 4428
2Ki 23:3 the **k.** stood by a pillar, and made a.... 4428
2Ki 23:4 the **k.** commanded Hilkiah the high..... 4428
2Ki 23:12 **k.** beat down, and brake them down... 4428
2Ki 23:13 the **k.** of Israel had builded for.......... 4428
2Ki 23:13 children of Ammon, did the **k.** defile... 4428
2Ki 23:21 the **k.** commanded all the people,....... 4428

2Ki	23:23	in the eighteenth year of **k.** Josiah,	4428
2Ki	23:25	unto him was there no **k.** before him,	4428
2Ki	23:29	Pharaoh-nechoh **k.** of Egypt went up	4428
2Ki	23:29	against the **k.** of Assyria to the river	4428
2Ki	23:29	**k.** Josiah went against him; and he	4428
2Ki	23:30	made him **k.** in his father's stead	4427
2Ki	23:34	made Eliakim the son of Josiah **k.**	4427
2Ki	24:1	**k.** of Babylon came up,	4428
2Ki	24:7	the **k.** of Egypt came not again any	4428
2Ki	24:7	the **k.** of Babylon had taken from	4428
2Ki	24:7	that pertained to the **k.** of Egypt	4428
2Ki	24:10	of Nebuchadnezzar **k.** of Babylon	4428
2Ki	24:11	**k.** of Babylon came against the city,	4428
2Ki	24:12	Jehoiachin the **k.** of Judah went	4428
2Ki	24:12	went out to the **k.** of Babylon, he	4428
2Ki	24:12	the **k.** of Babylon took him in the	4428
2Ki	24:13	which Solomon **k.** of Israel had made	4428
2Ki	24:16	the **k.** of Babylon brought captive	4428
2Ki	24:17	the **k.** of Babylon made Mattaniah	4428
2Ki	24:17	made...his father's brother **k.** in	4427
2Ki	24:20	rebelled against the **k.** of Babylon	4428
2Ki	25:1	Nebuchadnezzar **k.** of Babylon came,	4428
2Ki	25:2	the eleventh year of **k.** Zedekiah	4428
2Ki	25:4	**k.** went the way toward the plain.	
2Ki	25:5	the Chaldees pursued after the **k.**,	4428
2Ki	25:6	they took the **k.**, and brought him	4428
2Ki	25:6	up to the **k.** of Babylon to Riblah;	4428
2Ki	25:8	**k.** Nebuchadnezzar **k.** of Babylon,	4428
2Ki	25:8	a servant of the **k.** of Babylon, unto	4428
2Ki	25:11	that fell away to the **k.** of Babylon,	4428
2Ki	25:20	them to the **k.** of Babylon to Riblah:	4428
2Ki	25:21	And the **k.** of Babylon smote them,	4428
2Ki	25:22	Nebuchadnezzar **k.** of Babylon had	4428
2Ki	25:23	heard the **k.** of Babylon had made	4428
2Ki	25:24	the land, and serve the **k.** of Babylon;	4428
2Ki	25:27	captivity of Jehoiachin **k.** of Judah,	4428
2Ki	25:27	Evil-merodach **k.** of Babylon in the	4428
2Ki	25:27	the head of Jehoiachin **k.** of Judah	4428
2Ki	25:30	allowance given him of the **k.**,	4428
1Ch	1:43	before any **k.** reigned over the	4428
1Ch	3:2	daughter of Talmai **k.** of Geshur:	4428
1Ch	4:23	they dwelt with the **k.** for his work.	4428
1Ch	4:41	the days of Hezekiah **k.** of Judah,	4428
1Ch	5:6	**k.** of Assyria carried away captive:	4428
1Ch	5:17	in the days of Jotham **k.** of Judah,	4428
1Ch	5:17	in the days of Jeroboam **k.** of Israel.	4428
1Ch	5:26	up the spirit of Pul **k.** of Assyria,	4428
1Ch	5:26	of Tilgath-pilneser **k.** of Assyria,	4428
1Ch	11:2	when Saul was **k.**, thou wast he that	4428
1Ch	11:3	came all the elders of Israel to the **k.**	4428
1Ch	11:3	they anointed David **k.** over Israel,	4428
1Ch	11:10	with all Israel, to make him **k.**,	4427
1Ch	12:31	name, to come and make David **k.**	4427
1Ch	12:38	to make David **k.** over all Israel:	4427
1Ch	12:38	were of one heart to make David **k.**	4427
1Ch	14:1	Hiram **k.** of Tyre sent messengers	4428
1Ch	14:2	had confirmed him **k.** over Israel,	4428
1Ch	14:8	was anointed **k.** over all Israel,	4428
1Ch	15:29	saw **k.** David dancing and playing:	4428
1Ch	17:16	David the **k.** came and sat before	4428
1Ch	18:3	David smote Hadarezer **k.** of Zobah	4428
1Ch	18:5	came to help Hadarezer **k.** of Zobah,	4428
1Ch	18:9	when Tou **k.** of Hamath heard how	4428
1Ch	18:9	the host of Hadarezer **k.** of Zobah;	4428
1Ch	18:10	sent Hadoram his son to **k.** David,	4428
1Ch	18:11	**k.** David dedicated unto the Lord,	4428
1Ch	18:17	of David were chief about the **k.**	4428
1Ch	19:1	the **k.** of the children of Ammon	4428
1Ch	19:5	the **k.** said, Tarry at Jericho until	4428
1Ch	19:7	the **k.** of Maachah and his people;	4428
1Ch	20:2	David took the crown of their **k.**	4428
1Ch	21:3	my lord the **k.**, are they not all my	4428
1Ch	21:23	let my lord the **k.** do that which is	4428
1Ch	21:24	**k.** David said to Ornan, Nay; but I	4428
1Ch	23:1	made Solomon...**k.** over Israel.	4427
1Ch	24:6	Levites, wrote them before the **k.**,	4428
1Ch	24:31	in the presence of David the **k.**,	4428
1Ch	25:2	according to the order of the **k.**	4428
1Ch	26:26	David the **k.**, and the chief fathers,	4428
1Ch	26:30	Lord, and in the service of the **k.**	4428
1Ch	26:32	whom **k.** David made rulers over	4428
1Ch	26:32	to God, and affairs of the **k.**	4428
1Ch	27:1	and their officers that served the **k.**	4428
1Ch	27:24	account of the chronicles of **k.** David	4428
1Ch	27:31	the substance which was **k.** David's.	4428
1Ch	28:1	that ministered to the **k.** by course,	4428
1Ch	28:1	substance and possession of the **k.**,	4428
1Ch	28:2	David the **k.** stood up upon his feet,	4428
1Ch	28:4	father to be **k.** over Israel for ever:	4428
1Ch	28:4	me to make me **k.** over all Israel:	4427
1Ch	29:1	David the **k.** said unto all the	4428
1Ch	29:9	David the **k.** also rejoiced with great	4428
1Ch	29:20	and worshipped the Lord, and the **k.**	4428
1Ch	29:22	made Solomon the son of David **k.**	4428
1Ch	29:23	sat on the throne of the Lord as **k.**	4428
1Ch	29:24	all the sons likewise of **k.** David,	4428
1Ch	29:24	themselves unto Solomon the **k.**	4428
1Ch	29:25	been on any **k.** before him in Israel.	4428
1Ch	29:29	the acts of David the **k.**, first and	4428
2Ch	1:9	hast made me **k.** over a people	4427
2Ch	1:11	over whom I have made thee **k.**:	4427
2Ch	1:14	and with the **k.** at Jerusalem.	4428
2Ch	1:15	And the **k.** made silver and gold at	4428
2Ch	2:3	sent to Huram the **k.** of Tyre,	4428
2Ch	2:11	Huram the **k.** of Tyre answered	4428
2Ch	2:11	he hath made thee **k.** over them.	4427
2Ch	2:12	given to David the **k.** a wise son,	4428
2Ch	4:11	that he was to make for **k.** Solomon	4428
2Ch	4:16	make to **k.** Solomon for the house	4428
2Ch	4:17	plain of Jordan did the **k.** cast them,	4428
2Ch	5:3	themselves unto the **k.** in the feast	4428
2Ch	5:6	**k.** Solomon, and all the congregation	4428
2Ch	6:3	the **k.** turned his face, and blessed	4428
2Ch	7:4	the **k.** and all the people offered	4428
2Ch	7:5	And **k.** Solomon offered a sacrifice	4428
2Ch	7:5	**k.** and all the people dedicated the	4428
2Ch	7:6	the **k.** had made to praise the Lord,	4428
2Ch	8:10	the chief of **k.** Solomon's officers,	4428
2Ch	8:11	in the house of David **k.** of Israel,	4428
2Ch	8:15	the commandment of the **k.** unto	4428
2Ch	8:18	and brought them to **k.** Solomon.	4428
2Ch	9:5	And she said to the **k.**, It was a true	4428
2Ch	9:8	throne, to be **k.** for the Lord thy God:	4428
2Ch	9:8	therefore made he thee **k.** over them,	4428
2Ch	9:9	she gave the **k.** an hundred and	4428
2Ch	9:9	queen of Sheba gave **k.** Solomon.	4428
2Ch	9:11	the **k.** made of the algum trees	4428
2Ch	9:12	**k.** Solomon gave to the queen of	4428
2Ch	9:12	which she had brought unto the **k.**	4428
2Ch	9:15	**k.** Solomon made two hundred	4428
2Ch	9:16	**k.** put them in the house of the forest.	4428
2Ch	9:17	the **k.** made a great throne of ivory,	4428
2Ch	9:20	the drinking vessels of **k.** Solomon	4428
2Ch	9:22	**k.** Solomon passed all the kings of	4428
2Ch	9:25	cities, and with the **k.** at Jerusalem	4428
2Ch	9:27	**k.** made silver in Jerusalem as	4428
2Ch	10:1	all Israel come to make him **k.**	4427
2Ch	10:2	the presence of Solomon the **k.**,	4428
2Ch	10:6	**k.** Rehoboam took counsel with the	4428
2Ch	10:12	on the third day, as the **k.** bade,	4428
2Ch	10:13	And the **k.** answered them roughly;	4428
2Ch	10:13	**k.** Rehoboam forsook the counsel of	4428
2Ch	10:15	**k.** hearkened not unto the people:	4428
2Ch	10:16	the **k.** would not hearken unto them,	4428
2Ch	10:16	the people answered the **k.**, saying,	4428
2Ch	10:18	Then **k.** Rehoboam sent Hadoram	4428
2Ch	10:18	**k.** Rehoboam made speed to get him	4428
2Ch	11:3	the son of Solomon, **k.** of Judah,	4428
2Ch	11:22	for he thought to make him **k.**	4427
2Ch	12:2	in the fifth year of **k.** Rehoboam	4428
2Ch	12:2	Shishak **k.** of Egypt came up against	4428
2Ch	12:6	and the **k.** humbled themselves;	4428
2Ch	12:9	Shishak **k.** of Egypt came up against	4428
2Ch	12:10	**k.** Rehoboam made shields of brass,	4428
2Ch	12:11	**k.** entered into the house of the Lord,	4428
2Ch	12:13	**k.** Rehoboam strengthened himself	4428
2Ch	13:1	the eighteenth year of **k.** Jeroboam	4428
2Ch	15:16	Maachah the mother of Asa the **k.**,	4428
2Ch	16:1	Baasha **k.** of Israel came up against	4428
2Ch	16:1	out or come in to Asa **k.** of Judah.	4428
2Ch	16:2	and sent to Ben-hadad **k.** of Syria,	4428
2Ch	16:3	thy league with Baasha **k.** of Israel,	4428
2Ch	16:4	Ben-hadad hearkened unto **k.** Asa,	4428
2Ch	16:6	Then Asa the **k.** took all Judah;	4428
2Ch	16:7	the seer came to Asa **k.** of Judah;	4428
2Ch	16:7	thou hast relied on the **k.** of Syria,	4428
2Ch	16:7	the host of the **k.** of Syria escaped	4428
2Ch	17:19	These waited on the **k.**, beside	4428
2Ch	17:19	whom the **k.** put in the fenced cities?	4428
2Ch	18:3	**k.** of Israel said unto Jehoshaphat	4428
2Ch	18:3	said unto Jehoshaphat **k.** of Judah,	4428
2Ch	18:4	said unto the **k.** of Israel, Enquire,	4428
2Ch	18:5	the **k.** of Israel gathered together	4428
2Ch	18:7	**k.** of Israel said unto Jehoshaphat,	4428
2Ch	18:7	said, Let not the **k.** say so.	4428
2Ch	18:8	**k.** of Israel called for one of his	4428
2Ch	18:9	the **k.** of Israel and Jehoshaphat	4428
2Ch	18:9	the **k.** of Judah sat either of them	4428
2Ch	18:11	deliver it into the hand of the **k.**	4428
2Ch	18:12	the prophets declare good to the **k.**	4428
2Ch	18:14	come to the **k.**, the **k.** said unto him,	4428
2Ch	18:15	the **k.** said to him, how many times	4428
2Ch	18:17	the **k.** of Israel said to Jehoshaphat,	4428
2Ch	18:19	Who shall entice Ahab **k.** of Israel,	4428
2Ch	18:25	**k.** of Israel said, Take ye Micaiah,	4428
2Ch	18:26	Thus saith the **k.**, Put this fellow in	4428
2Ch	18:28	the **k.** of Israel and Jehoshaphat	4428
2Ch	18:28	the **k.** of Judah went up to	4428
2Ch	18:29	**k.** of Israel said unto Jehoshaphat,	4428
2Ch	18:29	the **k.** of Israel disguised himself;	4428
2Ch	18:30	the **k.** of Syria had commanded the	4428
2Ch	18:30	save only with the **k.** of Israel.	4428
2Ch	18:31	that they said, It is the **k.** of Israel	4428
2Ch	18:32	that it was not the **k.** of Israel,	4428
2Ch	18:33	smote the **k.** of Israel between the	4428
2Ch	18:34	the **k.** of Israel stayed himself up in	4428
2Ch	19:1	Jehoshaphat the **k.** of Judah	4428
2Ch	19:2	him, and said to **k.** Jehoshaphat,	4428
2Ch	20:15	and thou **k.** Jehoshaphat, Thus	4428
2Ch	20:35	this did Jehoshaphat **k.** of Judah	4428
2Ch	20:35	himself with Ahaziah **k.** of Israel,	4428
2Ch	21:2	sons of Jehoshaphat **k.** of Israel.	4428
2Ch	21:8	and made themselves a **k.**	4428
2Ch	21:12	in the ways of Asa **k.** of Judah,	4428
2Ch	22:1	made Ahaziah his...son **k.** in his	4427
2Ch	22:1	of Jehoram **k.** of Judah reigned.	4428
2Ch	22:5	the son of Ahab **k.** of Israel	4428
2Ch	22:5	to war against Hazael **k.** of Syria at	4428
2Ch	22:6	he fought with Hazael **k.** of Syria.	4428
2Ch	22:6	the son of Jehoram **k.** of Judah	4428
2Ch	22:11	the daughter of the **k.**, took Joash	4428
2Ch	22:11	the daughter of **k.** Jehoram, the	4428
2Ch	23:3	made a covenant with the **k.** in the	4428
2Ch	23:7	shall compass the **k.** round about,	4428
2Ch	23:7	be ye with the **k.** when he cometh	4428
2Ch	23:9	shields, that had been **k.** David's,	4428
2Ch	23:10	the temple, by the **k.** round about.	4428
2Ch	23:11	the testimony, and made him **k.**	4427
2Ch	23:11	him, and said, God save the **k.**	4428
2Ch	23:12	people running and praising the **k.**,	4428
2Ch	23:13	**k.** stood at his pillar at the entering	4428
2Ch	23:13	princes and the trumpets by the **k.**:	4428
2Ch	23:16	all the people, and between the **k.**,	4428
2Ch	23:20	the **k.** from the house of the Lord:	4428
2Ch	23:20	**k.** upon the throne of the kingdom.	4428
2Ch	24:6	the **k.** called for Jehoiada the chief,	4428
2Ch	24:12	the **k.** and Jehoiada gave it to such	4428
2Ch	24:14	the rest of the money before the **k.**	4428
2Ch	24:17	and made obeisance to the **k.**	4428
2Ch	24:17	Then the **k.** hearkened unto them.	4428
2Ch	24:21	at the commandment of the **k.** in	4428
2Ch	24:22	**k.** remembered not the kindness	4428
2Ch	24:23	of them unto the **k.** of Damascus.	4428
2Ch	25:3	that had killed the **k.** his father.	4428
2Ch	25:7	a man of God to him, saying, O **k.**,	4428
2Ch	25:16	with him, that the **k.** said unto him,	
2Ch	25:17	Amaziah **k.** of Judah took advice,	4428
2Ch	25:17	the son of Jehu, **k.** of Israel,	4428
2Ch	25:18	Joash **k.** of Israel sent to Amaziah	4428
2Ch	25:18	to Amaziah **k.** of Judah, saying,	4428
2Ch	25:21	So Joash the **k.** of Israel went up;	4428
2Ch	25:21	both he and Amaziah **k.** of Judah,	4428
2Ch	25:23	And Joash the **k.** of Israel took	4428
2Ch	25:23	Amaziah **k.** of Judah, the son of	4428
2Ch	25:25	the son of Joash **k.** of Judah lived	4428
2Ch	25:25	Joash son of Jehoahaz **k.** of Israel	4428
2Ch	26:1	sixteen years old, and made him **k.**	4427
2Ch	26:2	that the **k.** slept with his fathers.	4428
2Ch	26:13	to help the **k.** against the enemy.	4428
2Ch	26:18	And they withstood Uzziah the **k.**,	4428
2Ch	26:21	Uzziah the **k.** was a leper unto the	4428
2Ch	27:5	He fought also with the **k.** of the	4428
2Ch	28:5	him into the hand of the **k.** of Syria;	4428
2Ch	28:5	into the hand of the **k.** of Israel,	4428
2Ch	28:7	Elkanah that was next to the **k.**	4428
2Ch	28:16	**k.** Ahaz send unto the kings of	4428
2Ch	28:19	low because of Ahaz **k.** of Israel;	4428
2Ch	28:20	Tilgath-pilneser **k.** of Assyria came	4428

2Ch	28:21	out of the house of the **k.**, and of	4428
2Ch	28:21	and gave it unto the **k.** of Assyria:	4428
2Ch	28:22	the Lord: this is that **k.** Ahaz.	4428
2Ch	29:15	to the commandment of the **k.**,	4428
2Ch	29:18	they went in to Hezekiah the **k.**,	4428
2Ch	29:19	which **k.** Ahaz in his reign did cast	4428
2Ch	29:20	Then Hezekiah the **k.** rose early,	4428
2Ch	29:23	before the **k.** and the congregation;	4428
2Ch	29:24	the **k.** commanded that the burnt	4428
2Ch	29:27	ordained by David **k.** of Israel.	4428
2Ch	29:29	the **k.** and all that were present	4428
2Ch	29:30	Hezekiah the **k.** and the princes	4428
2Ch	30:2	For the **k.** had taken counsel, and	4428
2Ch	30:4	the thing pleased the **k.** and all the	4428
2Ch	30:6	went with the letters from the **k.**,	4428
2Ch	30:6	to the commandment of the **k.**,	4428
2Ch	30:12	the commandment of the **k.** and of	4428
2Ch	30:24	Hezekiah **k.** of Judah did give to	4428
2Ch	30:26	the son of David **k.** of Israel their	4428
2Ch	31:13	commandment of Hezekiah the **k.**,	4428
2Ch	32:1	Sennacherib **k.** of Assyria came,	4428
2Ch	32:7	nor dismayed for the **k.** of Assyria,	4428
2Ch	32:8	the words of Hezekiah **k.** of Judah.	4428
2Ch	32:9	**k.** of Assyria send his servants to	4428
2Ch	32:9	unto Hezekiah **k.** of Judah, and	4428
2Ch	32:10	saith Sennacherib, **k.** of Assyria,	4428
2Ch	32:11	of the hand of the **k.** of Assyria?	4428
2Ch	32:20	for this cause Hezekiah the **k.**, and	4428
2Ch	32:21	in the camp of the **k.** of Assyria.	4428
2Ch	32:22	of Sennacherib the **k.** of Assyria,	4428
2Ch	32:23	presents to Hezekiah **k.** of Judah	4428
2Ch	33:11	of the host of the **k.** of Assyria,	4428
2Ch	33:25	had conspired against **k.** Amon;	4428
2Ch	33:25	made Josiah his son **k.** in his stead.	4427
2Ch	34:16	Shaphan carried the book to the **k.**	4428
2Ch	34:16	brought the **k.** word back again,	4428
2Ch	34:18	Shaphan the scribe told the **k.**,	4428
2Ch	34:18	And Shaphan read it before the **k.**	4428
2Ch	34:19	when the **k.** had heard the words of	4428
2Ch	34:20	the **k.** commanded Hilkiah, and	4428
2Ch	34:22	they that the **k.** had appointed,	4428
2Ch	34:24	have read before the **k.** of Judah:	4428
2Ch	34:26	as for the **k.** of Judah, who sent you	4428
2Ch	34:28	So they brought the **k.** word again.	4428
2Ch	34:29	the **k.** sent and gathered together	4428
2Ch	34:30	the **k.** went up into the house of the	4428
2Ch	34:31	the **k.** stood in his place, and made	4428
2Ch	35:3	son of David **k.** of Israel did build;	4428
2Ch	35:4	to the writing of David **k.** of Israel,	4428
2Ch	35:16	to the commandment of **k.** Josiah.	4428
2Ch	35:20	Necho **k.** of Egypt came up to fight	4428
2Ch	35:21	I to do with thee, thou **k.** of Judah?	4428
2Ch	35:23	the archers shot at **k.** Josiah;	4428
2Ch	35:23	**k.** said to his servants, Have me	4428
2Ch	36:1	made him **k.** in his father's stead	4427
2Ch	36:3	the **k.** of Egypt put him down at	4428
2Ch	36:4	the **k.** of Egypt made Eliakim his	4428
2Ch	36:4	made Eliakim...**k.** over Judah	4427
2Ch	36:6	came up Nebuchadnezzar **k.** of	4428
2Ch	36:10	**k.** Nebuchadnezzar sent, and	4428
2Ch	36:10	made Zedekiah...**k.** over Judah	4427
2Ch	36:13	against **k.** Nebuchadnezzar,	4428
2Ch	36:17	upon them the **k.** of the Chaldees,	4428
2Ch	36:18	the treasures of the **k.**, and of his	4428
2Ch	36:22	the first year of Cyrus **k.** of Persia,	4428
2Ch	36:22	up the spirit of Cyrus **k.** of Persia,	4428
2Ch	36:23	Thus saith Cyrus **k.** of Persia, All	4428
Ezr	1:1	the first year of Cyrus **k.** of Persia,	4428
Ezr	1:1	up the spirit of Cyrus **k.** of Persia,	4428
Ezr	1:2	Thus saith Cyrus **k.** of Persia, The	4428
Ezr	1:7	the **k.** brought forth the vessels	4428
Ezr	1:8	did Cyrus **k.** of Persia bring forth	4428
Ezr	2:1	the **k.** of Babylon had carried away	4428
Ezr	3:7	they had of Cyrus **k.** of Persia	4428
Ezr	3:10	the ordinance of David **k.** of Israel	4428
Ezr	4:2	days of Esar-haddon **k.** of Assur,	4428
Ezr	4:3	as **k.** Cyrus the **k.** of Persia hath	4428
Ezr	4:5	all the days of Cyrus **k.** of Persia,	4428
Ezr	4:5	the reign of Darius **k.** of Persia.	4428
Ezr	4:7	unto Artaxerxes **k.** in this sort:	4430
Ezr	4:8	to Artaxerxes the **k.** in this sort:	4430
Ezr	4:11	him, even unto Artaxerxes the **k.**;	4430
Ezr	4:12	Be it known unto the **k.**, that the	4430
Ezr	4:13	Be it known now unto the **k.**, that,	4430
Ezr	4:14	have we sent and certified the **k.**;	4430
Ezr	4:16	We certify the **k.** that, if this city be	4430
Ezr	4:17	sent the **k.** an answer unto Rehum	4430
Ezr	4:23	of **k.** Artaxerxes' letter was read	4430
Ezr	4:24	of the reign of Darius **k.** of Persia.	4430
Ezr	5:6	the river, sent unto Darius the **k.**:	4430
Ezr	5:7	thus; Unto Darius the **k.**, all peace.	4430
Ezr	5:8	known unto the **k.**, that we went	4430
Ezr	5:11	which a great **k.** of Israel builded	4430
Ezr	5:12	Nebuchadnezzar the **k.** of Babylon,	4430
Ezr	5:13	first year of Cyrus the **k.** of Babylon	4430
Ezr	5:13	**k.** Cyrus made a decree to build	4430
Ezr	5:14	the **k.** take out of the temple of	4430
Ezr	5:17	therefore, if it seem good to the **k.**,	4430
Ezr	5:17	decree was made of Cyrus the **k.** to	4430
Ezr	5:17	let the **k.** send his pleasure to us	4430
Ezr	6:1	Darius the **k.** made a decree, and	4430
Ezr	6:3	In the first year of Cyrus the **k.** the	4430
Ezr	6:3	same Cyrus the **k.** made a decree	4430
Ezr	6:10	pray for the life of the **k.**, and of his	4430
Ezr	6:13	that which Darius the **k.** had sent,	4430
Ezr	6:14	Darius, and Artaxerxes **k.** of Persia.	4430
Ezr	6:15	year of the reign of Darius the **k.**	4430
Ezr	6:22	heart of the **k.** of Assyria unto	4428
Ezr	7:1	reign of Artaxerxes **k.** of Persia,	4428
Ezr	7:6	the **k.** granted him all his request,	4428
Ezr	7:7	seventh year of Artaxerxes the **k.**	4428
Ezr	7:8	was in the seventh year of the **k.**	4428
Ezr	7:11	the **k.** Artaxerxes gave unto Ezra	4428
Ezr	7:12	Artaxerxes, **k.** of kings, unto Ezra	4430
Ezr	7:14	as thou art sent of the **k.**, and of his	4430
Ezr	7:15	**k.** and his counsellors have freely	4430
Ezr	7:21	And I, even I Artaxerxes the **k.**, do	4430
Ezr	7:23	wrath against the realm of the **k.**	4430
Ezr	7:26	of thy God, and the law of the **k.**,	4430
Ezr	7:28	mercy unto me before the **k.**,	4428
Ezr	8:1	in the reign of Artaxerxes the **k.**	4428
Ezr	8:22	require of the **k.** a band of soldiers	4428
Ezr	8:22	we had spoken unto the **k.**, saying,	4428
Ezr	8:25	which the **k.**, and his counsellors,	4428
Ne	2:1	twentieth year of Artaxerxes the **k.**,	4428
Ne	2:1	the wine, and gave it unto the **k.**	4428
Ne	2:2	the **k.** said unto me, Why is thy	4428
Ne	2:3	unto the **k.**, Let the **k.** live for ever:	4428
Ne	2:4	**k.** said unto me, For what dost thou	4428
Ne	2:5	said unto the **k.**, If it please the **k.**,	4428
Ne	2:6	the **k.** said unto me, (the queen also	4428
Ne	2:6	it pleased the **k.** to send me; and I	4428
Ne	2:7	said unto the **k.**, If it please the **k.**,	4428
Ne	2:8	And the **k.** granted me, according	4428
Ne	2:9	**k.** had sent captains of the army	4428
Ne	2:19	ye do? will ye rebel against the **k.**?	4428
Ne	5:14	thirtieth year of Artaxerxes the **k.**	4428
Ne	6:6	thou mayest be their **k.**, according	4428
Ne	6:7	There is a **k.** in Judah: and now	4428
Ne	6:7	reported to the **k.** according to	4428
Ne	7:6	the **k.** of Babylon had carried away,	4428
Ne	9:22	and the land of the **k.** of Heshbon,	4428
Ne	9:22	and the land of Og **k.** of Bashan.	4428
Ne	13:6	and thirtieth year of Artaxerxes **k.**	4428
Ne	13:6	of Babylon came I unto the **k.**, and	4428
Ne	13:6	days obtained I leave of the **k.**:	4428
Ne	13:26	**k.** of Israel sin by these things?	4428
Ne	13:26	many nations were there no **k.** like	4428
Ne	13:26	God made him **k.** over all Israel:	4428
Es	1:2	the **k.** Ahasuerus sat on the throne	4428
Es	1:5	the **k.** made a feast unto all the	4428
Es	1:7	according to the state of the **k.**	4428
Es	1:8	for so the **k.** had appointed to all	4428
Es	1:9	which belonged to **k.** Ahasuerus.	4428
Es	1:10	the heart of the **k.** was merry with	4428
Es	1:10	the presence of Ahasuerus the **k.**,	4428
Es	1:11	Vashti the queen before the **k.**	4428
Es	1:12	therefore was the **k.** very wroth, and	4428
Es	1:13	the **k.** said to the wise men, which	4428
Es	1:15	the commandment of the **k.**	4428
Es	1:16	Memucan answered before the **k.**	4428
Es	1:16	hath not done wrong to the **k.** only,	4428
Es	1:16	the provinces of the **k.** Ahasuerus.	4428
Es	1:17	The **k.** Ahasuerus commanded	4428
Es	1:19	If it please the **k.**, let there go a	4428
Es	1:19	come no more before **k.** Ahasuerus;	4428
Es	1:19	let the **k.** give her royal estate unto	4428
Es	1:21	pleased the **k.** and the princes;	4428
Es	1:21	the **k.** did according to the word of	4428
Es	2:1	the wrath of **k.** Ahasuerus was	4428
Es	2:2	young virgins sought for the **k.**:	4428
Es	2:3	let the **k.** appoint officers in all the	4428
Es	2:4	maiden which pleaseth the **k.** be	4428
Es	2:4	the thing pleased the **k.**; and he	4428
Es	2:6	away with Jeconiah **k.** of Judah,	4428
Es	2:6	**k.** of Babylon had carried away.	4428
Es	2:12	was come to go in to **k.** Ahasuerus,	4428
Es	2:13	came every maiden unto the **k.**;	4428
Es	2:14	she came in unto the **k.** no more,	4428
Es	2:14	except the **k.** delighted in her, and	4428
Es	2:15	was come to go in unto the **k.**, she	4428
Es	2:16	was taken unto **k.** Ahasuerus into	4428
Es	2:17	the **k.** loved Esther above all the	4428
Es	2:18	the **k.** made a great feast unto all	4428
Es	2:18	according to the state of the **k.**	4428
Es	2:21	to lay hand on the **k.** Ahasuerus.	4428
Es	2:22	Esther certified the **k.** thereof in	4428
Es	2:23	book of the chronicles before the **k.**	4428
Es	3:1	did **k.** Ahasuerus promote Haman	4428
Es	3:2	for the **k.** had so commanded	4428
Es	3:7	in the twelfth year of **k.** Ahasuerus,	4428
Es	3:8	And Haman said unto **k.** Ahasuerus,	4428
Es	3:9	If it please the **k.**, let it be written	4428
Es	3:10	the **k.** took his ring from his hand,	4428
Es	3:11	**k.** said unto Haman, The silver is	4428
Es	3:12	in the name of **k.** Ahasuerus was it	4428
Es	3:15	**k.** and Haman sat down to drink;	4428
Es	4:8	that she should go in unto the **k.**,	4428
Es	4:11	unto the **k.** into the inner court,	4428
Es	4:11	**k.** shall hold out the golden sceptre,	4428
Es	4:11	been called to come in unto the **k.**	4428
Es	4:16	and so will I go in unto the **k.**,	4428
Es	5:1	the **k.** sat upon his royal throne in	4428
Es	5:2	**k.** saw Esther the queen standing	4428
Es	5:2	the **k.** held out to Esther the golden	4428
Es	5:3	said the **k.** unto her, What wilt thou,	4428
Es	5:4	If it seem good unto the **k.**, let	4428
Es	5:4	the **k.** and Haman come this day	4428
Es	5:5	the **k.** said, Cause Haman to make	4428
Es	5:5	**k.** and Haman came to the banquet	4428
Es	5:6	**k.** said unto Esther at the banquet	4428
Es	5:8	found favour in the sight of the **k.**,	4428
Es	5:8	please the **k.** to grant my petition,	4428
Es	5:8	**k.** and Haman come to the banquet	4428
Es	5:8	do to morrow as the king hath said.	4428
Es	5:11	wherein the **k.** had promoted him,	4428
Es	5:11	the princes and servants of the **k.**	4428
Es	5:12	did let no man come in with the **k.**	4428
Es	5:12	I invited unto her also with the **k.**	4428
Es	5:14	to morrow speak thou unto the **k.**	4428
Es	5:14	then go thou in merrily with the **k.**	4428
Es	6:1	On that night could not the **k.** sleep,	4428
Es	6:1	and they were read before the **k.**	4428
Es	6:2	to lay hand on the **k.** Ahasuerus.	4428
Es	6:3	**k.** said, What honour and dignity	4428
Es	6:4	And the **k.** said, Who is in the court?	4428
Es	6:4	speak unto the **k.** to hang Mordecai	4428
Es	6:5	And the **k.** said, Let him come in.	4428
Es	6:6	the **k.** said unto him, What shall be	4428
Es	6:6	whom the **k.** delighteth to honour?	4428
Es	6:6	would the **k.** delight to do honour	4428
Es	6:7	Haman answered the **k.**, For the	4428
Es	6:7	whom the **k.** delighteth to honour,	4428
Es	6:8	brought which the **k.** useth to wear,	4428
Es	6:8	the horse that the **k.** rideth upon,	4428
Es	6:9	whom the **k.** delighteth to honour,	4428
Es	6:9	whom the **k.** delighteth to honour.	4428
Es	6:10	the **k.** said to Haman, Make haste,	4428
Es	6:11	whom the **k.** delighteth to honour.	4428
Es	7:1	the **k.** and Haman came to banquet.	4428
Es	7:2	the **k.** said again unto Esther on	4428
Es	7:3	have found favour in thy sight, O **k.**,	4428
Es	7:3	and if it please the **k.**, let my life be	4428
Es	7:5	the **k.** Ahasuerus answered and said	4428
Es	7:6	Haman was afraid before the **k.** and	4428
Es	7:7	**k.** arising from the banquet of wine	4428
Es	7:7	determined against him by the **k.**	4428
Es	7:8	the **k.** returned out of the palace	4428
Es	7:8	said the **k.**, Will he force the queen	4428
Es	7:9	chamberlains, said before the **k.**,	4428
Es	7:9	who had spoken good for the **k.**,	4428
Es	7:9	Then the **k.** said, Hang him thereon.	4428
Es	8:1	did the **k.** Ahasuerus give the house	4428
Es	8:1	And Mordecai came before the **k.**;	4428
Es	8:2	the **k.** took off his ring, which he	4428
Es	8:3	spake yet again before the **k.**,	4428
Es	8:4	the **k.** held out the golden sceptre	4428
Es	8:4	arose, and stood before the **k.**,	4428
Es	8:5	If it please the **k.**, and if I have	4428
Es	8:5	the thing seem right before the **k.**,	4428
Es	8:7	the **k.** Ahasuerus said unto Esther	4428

Es	8:10	he wrote in the **k.** Ahasuerus' name,	4428
Es	8:11	Wherein the **k.** granted the Jews	4428
Es	8:12	the provinces of the **k.** Ahasuerus,	4428
Es	8:15	went out from the presence of the **k.**	4428
Es	9:2	the provinces of the **k.** Ahasuerus,	4428
Es	9:3	officers of the **k.**, helped the Jews;	4428
Es	9:11	palace was brought before the **k.**	4428
Es	9:12	the **k.** said unto Esther the queen,	4428
Es	9:13	If it please the **k.**, let it be granted	4428
Es	9:14	the **k.** commanded it so to be done:	4428
Es	9:20	the provinces of the **k.** Ahasuerus,	4428
Es	9:25	when Esther came before the **k.**, he	4428
Es	10:1	And the **k.** Ahasuerus laid a tribute	4428
Es	10:2	whereunto the **k.** advanced him,	4428
Es	10:3	Jew was next unto **k.** Ahasuerus,	4428
Job	15:24	him, as a **k.** ready to the battle.	4428
Job	18:14	shall bring him to the **k.** of terrors.	4428
Job	29:25	chief, and dwelt as a **k.** in the army,	4428
Job	34:18	fit to say to a **k.**, Thou art wicked?	4428
Job	41:34	a **k.** over all the children of pride.	4428
Ps	2:6	Yet have I set my **k.** upon my holy	4428
Ps	5:2	voice of my cry, my **K.**, and my God:	4428
Ps	10:16	The Lord is **K.** for ever and ever:	4428
Ps	18:50	deliverance giveth he to his **k.**;	4428
Ps	20:9	let the **k.** hear us when we call.	4428
Ps	21:1	The **k.** shall joy in thy strength, O	4428
Ps	21:7	For the **k.** trusteth in the Lord,	4428
Ps	24:7	and the **K.** of glory shall come in.	4428
Ps	24:8	Who is this **K.** of glory? The Lord	4428
Ps	24:9	and the **K.** of glory shall come in.	4428
Ps	24:10	Who is this **K.** of glory? The Lord	4428
Ps	24:10	Lord of hosts, he is the **K.** of glory.	4428
Ps	29:10	yea, the Lord sitteth **K.** for ever.	4428
Ps	33:16	no **k.** saved by the multitude of an	4428
Ps	44:4	Thou art my **K.**, O God: command	4428
Ps	45:1	which I have made touching the **k.**:	4428
Ps	45:11	the **k.** greatly desire thy beauty:	4428
Ps	45:14	be brought unto the **k.** in raiment	4428
Ps	47:2	he is a great **K.** over all the earth.	4428
Ps	47:6	praises unto our **K.**, sing praises.	4428
Ps	47:7	For God is the **K.** of all the earth:	4428
Ps	48:2	the north, the city of the great **K.**	4428
Ps	63:11	But the **k.** shall rejoice in God;	4428
Ps	68:24	the goings of my God, my **K.**, in the	4428
Ps	72:1	Give the **k.** thy judgments, O God,	4428
Ps	74:12	For God is my **K.** of old, working	4428
Ps	84:3	O Lord of hosts, my **K.**, and my God.	4428
Ps	89:18	and the Holy One of Israel is our **k.**	4428
Ps	95:3	God, and a great **K.** above all gods.	4428
Ps	98:6	joyful noise before the Lord, the **K.**	4428
Ps	105:20	The **k.** sent and loosed him; even	4428
Ps	135:11	Sihon **k.** of the Amorites, and Og **k.**	4428
Ps	136:19	Sihon **k.** of the Amorites: for his	4428
Ps	136:20	And Og the **k.** of Bashan: for his	4428
Ps	145:1	I will extol thee, my God, O **k.**; and	4428
Ps	149:2	children of Zion be joyful in their **K.**	4428
Pr	1:1	the son of David, **k.** of Israel;	4428
Pr	16:10	sentence is in the lips of the **k.**:	4428
Pr	16:14	The wrath of a **k.** is as messengers	4428
Pr	20:2	The fear of a **k.** is as the roaring of	4428
Pr	20:8	A **k.** that sitteth in the throne of	4428
Pr	20:26	A wise **k.** scattereth the wicked,	4428
Pr	20:28	Mercy and truth preserve the **k.**:	4428
Pr	22:11	of his lips the **k.** shall be his friend.	4428
Pr	24:21	son, fear thou the Lord and the **k.**:	4428
Pr	25:1	of Hezekiah **k.** of Judah copied out.	4428
Pr	25:5	away the wicked from before the **k.**,	4428
Pr	25:6	thyself in the presence of the **k.**,	4428
Pr	29:4	The **k.** by judgment establisheth	4428
Pr	29:14	**k.** that faithfully judgeth the poor,	4428
Pr	30:27	The locusts have no **k.**, yet go they	4428
Pr	30:31	**k.** against whom there is no rising	4428
Pr	31:1	words of **k.** Lemuel, the prophecy	4428
Ec	1:1	the son of David, **k.** in Jerusalem.	4428
Ec	1:12	I the Preacher was **k.** over Israel in	4428
Ec	2:12	man do that cometh after the **k.**?	4428
Ec	4:13	wise child than an old and foolish **k.**,	4428
Ec	5:9	the **k.** himself is served by the field.	4428
Ec	8:4	Where the word of a **k.** is, there is	4428
Ec	9:14	there came a great **k.** against it,	4428
Ec	10:16	thee, O land, when thy **k.** is a child,	4428
Ec	10:17	when thy **k.** is the son of nobles,	4428
Ec	10:20	Curse not the **k.**, no not in thy	4428
Ca	1:4	the **k.** hath brought me into his	4428
Ca	1:12	While the **k.** sitteth at his table,	4428
Ca	3:9	**K.** Solomon made himself a chariot	4428
Ca	3:11	behold **k.** Solomon with the crown	4428
Ca	7:5	the **k.** is held in the galleries.	4428
Isa	6:1	In the year that **k.** Uzziah died I saw	4428
Isa	6:5	eyes have seen the **K.**, the Lord of	4428
Isa	7:1	the son of Uzziah, **k.** of Judah,	4428
Isa	7:1	Rezin the **k.** of Syria, and Pekah	4428
Isa	7:1	the son of Remaliah, **k.** of Israel,	4428
Isa	7:6	and set a **k.** in the midst of it, even	4428
Isa	7:17	Judah; even the **k.** of Assyria.	4428
Isa	7:20	the river, by the **k.** of Assyria,	4428
Isa	8:4	taken away before the **k.** of Assyria	4428
Isa	8:7	**k.** of Assyria, and all his glory:	4428
Isa	8:21	and curse their **k.** and their God,	4428
Isa	10:12	the stout heart of the **k.** of Assyria,	4428
Isa	14:4	proverb against the **k.** of Babylon,	4428
Isa	14:28	In the year that **k.** Ahaz died was	4428
Isa	19:4	and a fierce **k.** shall rule over them,	4428
Isa	20:1	Sargon the **k.** of Assyria sent him,)	4428
Isa	20:4	So shall the **k.** of Assyria lead away	4428
Isa	20:6	be delivered from the **k.** of Assyria:	4428
Isa	23:15	according to the days of one **k.**:	4428
Isa	30:33	old; yea, for the **k.** it is prepared;	4428
Isa	32:1	a **k.** shall reign in righteousness,	4428
Isa	33:17	eyes shall see the **k.** in his beauty:	4428
Isa	33:22	is our lawgiver, the Lord is our **k.**;	4428
Isa	36:1	the fourteenth year of **k.** Hezekiah,	4428
Isa	36:1	Sennacherib **k.** of Assyria came up	4428
Isa	36:2	the **k.** of Assyria sent Rabshakeh	4428
Isa	36:2	unto **k.** Hezekiah with a great army.	4428
Isa	36:4	saith the great **k.**, the **k.** of Assyria,	4428
Isa	36:6	so is Pharaoh **k.** of Egypt to all that	4428
Isa	36:8	to my master the **k.** of Assyria, and	4428
Isa	36:13	of the great **k.**, the **k.** of Assyria.	4428
Isa	36:14	Thus saith the **k.**, Let not Hezekiah	4428
Isa	36:15	into the hand of the **k.** of Assyria.	4428
Isa	36:16	thus saith the **k.** of Assyria, Make	4428
Isa	36:18	out of the hand of the **k.** of Assyria?	4428
Isa	37:1	when **k.** Hezekiah heard it, that he	4428
Isa	37:4	**k.** of Assyria his master hath sent	4428
Isa	37:5	the servants of **k.** Hezekiah came	4428
Isa	37:6	servants of the **k.** of Assyria have	4428
Isa	37:8	the **k.** of Assyria warring against	4428
Isa	37:9	concerning Tirhakah **k.** of Ethiopia,	4428
Isa	37:10	ye speak to Hezekiah **k.** of Judah,	4428
Isa	37:10	into the hand of the **k.** of Assyria.	4428
Isa	37:13	**k.** of Hamath, and the **k.** of Arphad,	4428
Isa	37:13	and the **k.** of the city of Sepharvaim,	4428
Isa	37:21	against Sennacherib **k.** of Assyria:	4428
Isa	37:33	Lord concerning the **k.** of Assyria,	4428
Isa	37:37	Sennacherib **k.** of Assyria departed,	4428
Isa	38:6	out of the hand of the **k.** of Assyria:	4428
Isa	38:9	writing of Hezekiah **k.** of Judah,	4428
Isa	39:1	Baladan, **k.** of Babylon, sent letters	4428
Isa	39:3	the prophet unto **k.** Hezekiah,	4428
Isa	39:7	in the palace of the **k.** of Babylon.	4428
Isa	41:21	reasons, saith the **K.** of Jacob.	4428
Isa	43:15	One, the creator of Israel, your **K.**	4428
Isa	44:6	saith the Lord the **K.** of Israel,	4428
Isa	57:9	wentest to the **k.** with ointment,	4428
Jer	1:2	Josiah the son of Amon **k.** of Judah,	4428
Jer	1:3,	3 the son of Josiah **k.** of Judah,	4428
Jer	3:6	unto me in the days of Josiah the **k.**,	4428
Jer	4:9	that the heart of the **k.** shall perish,	4428
Jer	8:19	Lord in Zion? is not her **k.** in her?	4428
Jer	10:7	not fear thee, O **K.** of nations?	4428
Jer	10:10	living God, and an everlasting **k.**:	4428
Jer	13:18	Say unto the **k.** and to the queen,	4428
Jer	15:4	the son of Hezekiah **k.** of Judah,	4428
Jer	20:4	into the hand of the **k.** of Babylon,	4428
Jer	21:1	when **k.** Zedekiah sent unto him	4428
Jer	21:2	**k.** of Babylon maketh war against	4428
Jer	21:4	ye fight against the **k.** of Babylon,	4428
Jer	21:7	I will deliver Zedekiah **k.** of Judah,	4428
Jer	21:7	of Nebuchadrezzar **k.** of Babylon,	4428
Jer	21:10	into the hand of the **k.** of Babylon,	4428
Jer	21:11	the house of the **k.** of Judah, say,	4428
Jer	22:1	to the house of the **k.** of Judah,	4428
Jer	22:2	the word of the Lord, O **k.** of Judah,	4428
Jer	22:11	the son of Josiah **k.** of Judah,	4428
Jer	22:18	the son of Josiah **k.** of Judah;	4428
Jer	22:24	the son of Jehoiakim **k.** of Judah	4428
Jer	22:25	of Nebuchadrezzar **k.** of Babylon,	4428
Jer	23:5	and a **K.** shall reign and prosper,	4428
Jer	24:1	**k.** of Babylon had carried away	4428
Jer	24:1	the son of Jehoiakim **k.** of Judah,	4428
Jer	24:8	I give Zedekiah the **k.** of Judah,	4428
Jer	25:1	the son of Josiah **k.** of Judah,	4428
Jer	25:1	of Nebuchadrezzar **k.** of Babylon;	4428
Jer	25:3	Josiah the son of Amon **k.** of Judah,	4428
Jer	25:9	the **k.** of Babylon, my servant, and	4428
Jer	25:11	shall serve the **k.** of Babylon seventy	4428
Jer	25:12	I will punish the **k.** of Babylon, and	4428
Jer	25:19	Pharaoh **k.** of Egypt, and his	4428
Jer	25:26	the **k.** of Shesach shall drink after	4428
Jer	26:1	son of Josiah **k.** of Judah came this	4428
Jer	26:18	the days of Hezekiah **k.** of Judah,	4428
Jer	26:19	Did Hezekiah **k.** of Judah and all	4428
Jer	26:21	when Jehoiakim the **k.**, with all his	4428
Jer	26:21	the **k.** sought to put him to death:	4428
Jer	26:22	the **k.** sent men into Egypt namely,	4428
Jer	26:23	brought him unto Jehoiakim the **k.**;	4428
Jer	27:1	the son of Josiah **k.** of Judah came	4428
Jer	27:3	send them to the **k.** of Edom, and to	4428
Jer	27:3	and to the **k.** of Moab, and to the	4428
Jer	27:3	and to the **k.** of the Ammonites,	4428
Jer	27:3	Ammonites, and to the **k.** of Tyrus,	4428
Jer	27:3	and to the **k.** of Zidon, by the hand	4428
Jer	27:3	unto Zedekiah **k.** of Judah;	4428
Jer	27:6,	8 Nebuchadnezzar...**k.** of Babylon,	4428
Jer	27:8	under the yoke of the **k.** of Babylon,	4428
Jer	27:9	shall not serve the **k.** of Babylon:	4428
Jer	27:11	under the yoke of the **k.** of Babylon,	4428
Jer	27:12	spake also to Zedekiah **k.** of Judah	4428
Jer	27:12	under the yoke of the **k.** of Babylon,	4428
Jer	27:13	will not serve the **k.** of Babylon?	4428
Jer	27:14	shall not serve the **k.** of Babylon:	4428
Jer	27:17	serve the **k.** of Babylon, and live:	4428
Jer	27:18	and in the house of the **k.** of Judah,	4428
Jer	27:20	**k.** of Babylon took not, when he	4428
Jer	27:20	**k.** of Judah from Jerusalem to	4428
Jer	27:21	in the house of the **k.** of Judah and	4428
Jer	28:1	the reign of Zedekiah **k.** of Judah,	4428
Jer	28:2	the yoke of the **k.** of Babylon.	4428
Jer	28:3	**k.** of Babylon took away from this	4428
Jer	28:4	**k.** of Judah, with all the captives of	4428
Jer	28:4	break the yoke of the **k.** of Babylon.	4428
Jer	28:11	of Nebuchadnezzar **k.** of Babylon.	4428
Jer	28:14	Nebuchadnezzar **k.** of Babylon;	4428
Jer	29:2	Jeconiah the **k.**, and the queen, and	4428
Jer	29:3	(whom Zedekiah **k.** of Judah sent	4428
Jer	29:3	to Nebuchadnezzar **k.** of Babylon)	4428
Jer	29:16	**k.** that sitteth upon the throne of	4428
Jer	29:21	of Nebuchadrezzar **k.** of Babylon;	4428
Jer	29:22	whom the **k.** of Babylon roasted in	4428
Jer	30:9	Lord their God, and David their **k.**,	4428
Jer	32:1	tenth year of Zedekiah **k.** of Judah,	4428
Jer	32:2	**k.** of Babylon's army besieged	4428
Jer	32:2	was in the **k.** of Judah's house.	4428
Jer	32:3	Zedekiah **k.** of Judah had shut him	4428
Jer	32:3	into the hand of the **k.** of Babylon,	4428
Jer	32:4	**k.** of Judah shall not escape out of	4428
Jer	32:4	into the hand of the **k.** of Babylon.	4428
Jer	32:28	of Nebuchadrezzar **k.** of Babylon,	4428
Jer	32:36	into the hand of the **k.** of Babylon	4428
Jer	34:1	**k.** of Babylon, and all his army,	4428
Jer	34:2	and speak to Zedekiah **k.** of Judah,	4428
Jer	34:2	into the hand of the **k.** of Babylon,	4428
Jer	34:3	behold the eyes of the **k.** of Babylon,	4428
Jer	34:4	the Lord, O Zedekiah **k.** of Judah;	4428
Jer	34:6	words unto Zedekiah **k.** of Judah in	4428
Jer	34:7	the **k.** of Babylon's army fought	4428
Jer	34:8	**k.** Zedekiah had made a covenant	4428
Jer	34:21	And Zedekiah **k.** of Judah and his	4428
Jer	34:21	hand of the **k.** of Babylon's army,	4428
Jer	35:1	the son of Josiah **k.** of Judah,	4428
Jer	35:11	**k.** of Babylon came up into the land,	4428
Jer	36:1,9	the son of Josiah **k.** of Judah,	4428
Jer	36:16	We will surely tell the **k.** of all these	4428
Jer	36:20	they went in to the **k.** into the court,	4428
Jer	36:20	all the words in the ears of the **k.**	4428
Jer	36:21	the **k.** sent Jehudi to fetch the roll:	4428
Jer	36:21	Jehudi read it in the ears of the **k.**,	4428
Jer	36:21	princes which stood beside the **k.**	4428
Jer	36:22	Now the **k.** sat in the winterhouse	4428
Jer	36:24	the **k.**, nor any of his servants that	4428
Jer	36:25	intercession to the **k.** that he would	4428
Jer	36:26	the **k.** commanded Jerahmeel the	4428
Jer	36:27	that the **k.** had burned the roll,	4428
Jer	36:28	the **k.** of Judah hath burned	4428
Jer	36:29	shalt say to Jehoiakim **k.** of Judah,	4428
Jer	36:29	The **k.** of Babylon shall certainly	4428
Jer	36:30	the Lord of Jehoiakim **k.** of Judah;	4428

Jer 36:32 **k.** of Judah had burned in the fire:...... 4428
Jer 37:1 And **k.** Zedekiah the son of Josiah...... 4428
Jer 37:1 Nebuchadrezzar **k.** of Babylon............ 4428
Jer 37:1 made **k.** in the land of Judah............ 4428
Jer 37:3 Zedekiah the **k.** sent Jehucal the........ 4428
Jer 37:7 Thus shall ye say to the **k.** of Judah, .. 4428
Jer 37:17 Zedekiah the **k.** sent, and took him..... 4428
Jer 37:17 and the **k.** asked him secretly in his..... 4428
Jer 37:17 into the hand of the **k.** of Babylon. 4428
Jer 37:18 Jeremiah said unto **k.** Zedekiah, ... 4428
Jer 37:19 The **k.** of Babylon shall not come....... 4428
Jer 37:20 now, I pray thee, O my lord the **k.**: ... 4428
Jer 37:21 Zedekiah the **k.** commanded that........ 4428
Jer 38:3 hand of the **k.** of Babylon's army,....... 4428
Jer 38:4 the princes said unto the **k.**, We........ 4428
Jer 38:5 Zedekiah the **k.** said, Behold, he is in .. 4428
Jer 38:5 for the **k.** is not he that can do any.... 4428
Jer 38:7 the **k.** then sitting in the gate of........ 4428
Jer 38:8 house, and spake to the **k.**, saying, ... 4428
Jer 38:9 My lord the **k.**, these men have done .. 4428
Jer 38:10 the **k.** commanded Ebed-melech......... 4428
Jer 38:11 went into the house of the **k.** under.... 4428
Jer 38:14 Then Zedekiah the **k.** sent, and took.... 4428
Jer 38:14 the **k.** said unto Jeremiah, I will ask.... 4428
Jer 38:16 Zedekiah the **k.** sware secretly unto ... 4428
Jer 38:17 unto the **k.** of Babylon's princes,........ 4428
Jer 38:18 forth to the **k.** of Babylon's princes,.... 4428
Jer 38:19 Zedekiah the **k.** said unto Jeremiah,..... 4428
Jer 38:22 are left in the **k.** of Judah's house....... 4428
Jer 38:22 forth to the **k.** of Babylon's princes,.... 4428
Jer 38:23 by the hand of the **k.** of Babylon:........ 4428
Jer 38:25 what thou hast said unto the **k.**, ... 4428
Jer 38:25 also what the **k.** said unto thee:......... 4428
Jer 38:26 my supplication before the **k.**, ... 4428
Jer 38:27 words that the **k.** had commanded...... 4428
Jer 39:1 ninth year of Zedekiah **k.** of Judah, ... 4428
Jer 39:1 Nebuchadrezzar **k.** of Babylon........... 4428
Jer 39:3 princes of the **k.** of Babylon came 4428
Jer 39:3 of the princes of the **k.** of Babylon. 4428
Jer 39:4 Zedekiah the **k.** of Judah saw them, ... 4428
Jer 39:5 to Nebuchadnezzar **k.** of Babylon 4428
Jer 39:6 the **k.** of Babylon slew the sons of..... 4428
Jer 39:6 the **k.** of Babylon slew all the nobles... 4428
Jer 39:11 Nebuchadrezzar **k.** of Babylon gave 4428
Jer 39:13 and all the **k.** of Babylon's princes; 4428
Jer 40:5 **k.** of Babylon hath made governor...... 4428
Jer 40:7 **k.** of Babylon had made Gedaliah....... 4428
Jer 40:9 land, and serve the **k.** of Babylon,...... 4428
Jer 40:11 **k.** of Babylon had left a remnant of..... 4428
Jer 40:14 Baalis the **k.** of the Ammonites.......... 4428
Jer 41:1 the princes of the **k.**, even ten men.... 4428
Jer 41:2 **k.** of Babylon had made governor........ 4428
Jer 41:9 which Asa the **k.** had made for fear.... 4428
Jer 41:9 for fear of Baasha **k.** of Israel........... 4428
Jer 41:18 the **k.** of Babylon made governor....... 4428
Jer 42:11 Be not afraid of the **k.** of Babylon, ... 4428
Jer 43:10 Nebuchadrezzar the **k.** of Babylon, ... 4428
Jer 44:30 give Pharaoh-hophra **k.** of Egypt........ 4428
Jer 44:30 Zedekiah **k.** of Judah into the hand...... 4428
Jer 44:30 of Nebuchadrezzar **k.** of Babylon,....... 4428
Jer 45:1 the son of Josiah **k.** of Judah, ... 4428
Jer 46:2 army of Pharaoh-necho **k.** of Egypt,.... 4428
Jer 46:2 Nebuchadrezzar **k.** of Babylon........... 4428
Jer 46:2 the son of Josiah **k.** of Judah. 4428
Jer 46:13 **k.** of Babylon should come and.......... 4428
Jer 46:17 Pharaoh **k.** of Egypt is but a noise; 4428
Jer 46:18 As I live, saith the **K.**, whose name.... 4428
Jer 46:26 of Nebuchadrezzar **k.** of Babylon,....... 4428
Jer 48:15 the **K.**, whose name is the Lord of..... 4428
Jer 49:1 why then doth their **k.** inherit Gad, ... 4428
Jer 49:3 their **k.** shall go into captivity, and...... 4428
Jer 49:28 **k.** of Babylon shall smite, ... 4428
Jer 49:30 **k.** of Babylon hath taken counsel........ 4428
Jer 49:34 the reign of Zedekiah **k.** of Judah, ... 4428
Jer 49:38 thence the **k.** and the princes............ 4428
Jer 50:17 **k.** of Assyria hath devoured him; 4428
Jer 50:17 **k.** of Babylon hath broken his bones. .. 4428
Jer 50:18 I will punish the **k.** of Babylon and 4428
Jer 50:18 I have punished the **k.** of Assyria....... 4428
Jer 50:43 The **k.** of Babylon hath heard the....... 4428
Jer 51:31 shew the **k.** of Babylon that his city.... 4428
Jer 51:34 the **k.** of Babylon hath devoured me, .. 4428
Jer 51:57 the **K.**, whose name is the Lord of..... 4428
Jer 51:59 went with Zedekiah the **k.** of Judah.... 4428
Jer 52:3 rebelled against the **k.** of Babylon....... 4428
Jer 52:4 **k.** of Babylon came, he and all his...... 4428
Jer 52:5 the eleventh year of **k.** Zedekiah. 4428
Jer 52:8 the Chaldeans pursued after the **k.**, ... 4428
Jer 52:9 they took the **k.**, and carried him up... 4428
Jer 52:9 unto the **k.** of Babylon to Riblah in..... 4428
Jer 52:10 the **k.** of Babylon slew the sons of..... 4428
Jer 52:11 **k.** of Babylon bound him in chains, ... 4428
Jer 52:12 of Nebuchadrezzar **k.** of Babylon,....... 4428
Jer 52:12 which served the **k.** of Babylon,.......... 4428
Jer 52:15 that fell to the **k.** of Babylon, and....... 4428
Jer 52:20 **k.** Solomon had made in the house..... 4428
Jer 52:26 brought them to the **k.** of Babylon...... 4428
Jer 52:27 the **k.** of Babylon smote them, and..... 4428
Jer 52:31 captivity of Jehoiachin **k.** of Judah,...... 4428
Jer 52:31 Evil-merodach **k.** of Babylon, in the.... 4428
Jer 52:31 the head of Jehoiachin **k.** of Judah,.... 4428
Jer 52:34 diet given him of the **k.** of Babylon,.... 4428
La 2:6 of his anger the **k.** and the priest. 4428
La 2:9 her **k.** and her princes are among....... 4428
Eze 1:2 year of **k.** Jehoiachin's captivity,......... 4428
Eze 7:27 The **k.** shall mourn, and the prince..... 4428
Eze 17:12 **k.** of Babylon is come to Jerusalem,.... 4428
Eze 17:12 and hath taken the **k.** thereof, and...... 4428
Eze 17:16 surely in the place where the **k.** 4428
Eze 17:16 dwelleth that made him **k.** whose....... 4427
Eze 19:9 brought him to the **k.** of Babylon: 4428
Eze 21:19 the sword of the **k.** of Babylon may.... 4428
Eze 21:21 **k.** of Babylon stood at the parting...... 4428
Eze 24:2 **k.** of Babylon set himself against........ 4428
Eze 26:7 **k.** of Babylon, a **k.** of kings, ... 4428
Eze 28:12 a lamentation upon the **k.** of Tyrus, ... 4428
Eze 29:2 face against Pharaoh **k.** of Egypt, ... 4428
Eze 29:3 against thee, Pharaoh **k.** of Egypt, ... 4428
Eze 29:18 **k.** of Babylon caused his army to....... 4428
Eze 29:19 Nebuchadrezzar **k.** of Babylon; 4428
Eze 30:10 of Nebuchadrezzar **k.** of Babylon......... 4428
Eze 30:21 the arm of Pharaoh **k.** of Egypt; 4428
Eze 30:22 I am against Pharaoh **k.** of Egypt, ... 4428
Eze 30:24, 25 the arms of the **k.** of Babylon, ... 4428
Eze 30:25 into the hand of the **k.** of Babylon, ... 4428
Eze 31:2 speak unto Pharaoh **k.** of Egypt, ... 4428
Eze 32:2 lamentation for Pharaoh **k.** of Egypt,... 4428
Eze 32:11 The sword of the **k.** of Babylon shall .. 4428
Eze 37:22 and one **k.** shall be **k.** to them all: 4428
Eze 37:24 David my servant shall be **k.** over...... 4428
Da 1:1 the reign of Jehoiakim **k.** of Judah....... 4428
Da 1:1 Nebuchadnezzar **k.** of Babylon........... 4428
Da 1:2 Lord gave Jehoiakim **k.** of Judah......... 4428
Da 1:3 **k.** spake unto Ashpenaz the master.... 4428
Da 1:5 **k.** appointed them a daily provision..... 4428
Da 1:5 they might stand before the **k.**. 4428
Da 1:10 unto Daniel, I fear my lord the **k.**, ... 4428
Da 1:10 me endanger my head to the **k.**. 4428
Da 1:18 **k.** had said he should bring them in, ... 4428
Da 1:19 the **k.** communed with them; and........ 4428
Da 1:19 therefore stood they before the **k.**...... 4428
Da 1:20 the **k.** enquired of them, he found...... 4428
Da 1:21 even unto the first year of **k.** Cyrus. .. 4428
Da 2:2 Then the **k.** commanded to call the..... 4428
Da 2:2 for to shew the **k.** his dreams. 4428
Da 2:2 they came and stood before the **k.**. 4428
Da 2:3 **k.** said unto them, I have dreamed..... 4428
Da 2:4 Then spake the Chaldeans to the **k.**.... 4428
Da 2:4 O **k.**, live for ever: tell thy servants... 4430
Da 2:5 The **k.** answered and said to the....... 4430
Da 2:7 **k.** tell his servants the dream, and..... 4430
Da 2:8 The **k.** answered and said, I know of.. 4430
Da 2:10 Chaldeans answered before the **k.**, ... 4430
Da 2:10 there is no **k.**, lord, nor ruler, ... 4430
Da 2:11 is a rare thing that the **k.** requireth, ... 4430
Da 2:11 other that can shew it before the **k.**, .. 4430
Da 2:12 For this cause the **k.** was angry and... 4430
Da 2:15 is the decree so hasty from the **k.**? 4430
Da 2:16 desired of the **k.** that he would give ... 4430
Da 2:16 shew the **k.** the interpretation. 4430
Da 2:24 **k.** had ordained to destroy the wise.... 4430
Da 2:24 bring me in before the **k.**, and I will... 4430
Da 2:24 shew unto the **k.** the interpretation..... 4430
Da 2:25 brought in Daniel before the **k.** in....... 4430
Da 2:25 will make known unto the **k.** the......... 4430
Da 2:26 The **k.** answered and said to Daniel, ... 4430
Da 2:27 answered in the presence of the **k.**,.... 4430
Da 2:27 secret which the **k.** hath demanded..... 4430
Da 2:27 the soothsayers, shew unto the **k.**;..... 4430
Da 2:28 known to the **k.** Nebuchadnezzar....... 4430
Da 2:29 As for thee, O **k.**, thy thoughts......... 4430
Da 2:30 known the interpretation to the **k.**, ... 4430
Da 2:31 Thou, O **k.**, sawest, and behold a 4430
Da 2:36 interpretation thereof before the **k.**.... 4430
Da 2:37 Thou, O **k.**, art a **k.** of kings: for 4430
Da 2:45 known to the **k.** what shall come........ 4430
Da 2:46 the **k.** Nebuchadnezzar fell upon his.... 4430
Da 2:47 The **k.** answered unto Daniel, and...... 4430
Da 2:48 the **k.** made Daniel a great man, ... 4430
Da 2:49 Then Daniel requested of the **k.**, ... 4430
Da 2:49 but Daniel sat in the gate of the **k.**...... 4430
Da 3:1 the **k.** made an image of gold, ... 4430
Da 3:2 Then Nebuchadnezzar the **k.** sent to... 4430
Da 3:2 Nebuchadnezzar the **k.** had set up...... 4430
Da 3:3 Nebuchadnezzar the **k.** had set up;..... 4430
Da 3:5 Nebuchadnezzar the **k.** hath set up: 4430
Da 3:7 Nebuchadnezzar the **k.** had set up...... 4430
Da 3:9 They spake and said to the **k.**........... 4430
Da 3:9 Nebuchadnezzar, O **k.**, live for ever. .. 4430
Da 3:10 Thou, O **k.**, hast made a decree, that. 4430
Da 3:12 men, O **k.**, have not regarded thee: ... 4430
Da 3:13 brought these men before the **k.**......... 4430
Da 3:16 said to the **k.**, O Nebuchadnezzar,...... 4430
Da 3:17 deliver us out of thine hand, O **k.**. 4430
Da 3:18 if not, be it known unto thee, O **k.**,.... 4430
Da 3:24 the **k.** was astonied, and rose up 4430
Da 3:24 and said unto the **k.**, True, O **k.**. 4430
Da 3:30 **k.** promoted Shadrach, Meshach, ... 4430
Da 4:1 Nebuchadnezzar the **k.**, unto all......... 4430
Da 4:18 This dream I **k.** Nebuchadnezzar........ 4430
Da 4:19 **k.** spake, and said, Belteshazzar, ... 4430
Da 4:22 It is thou, O **k.**, that art grown and.... 4430
Da 4:23 And whereas the **k.** saw a watcher..... 4430
Da 4:24 This is the interpretation, O **k.**,......... 4430
Da 4:24 which is come upon my lord the **k.**:.... 4430
Da 4:27 Wherefore, O **k.**, let my counsel be.... 4430
Da 4:28 came upon the **k.** Nebuchadnezzar..... 4430
Da 4:30 The **k.** spake, and said, Is not this..... 4430
Da 4:31 O **k.** Nebuchadnezzar, to thee it is..... 4430
Da 4:37 extol and honour the **K.** of heaven,..... 4430
Da 5:1 Belshazzar the **k.** made a great......... 4430
Da 5:2 that the **k.**, and his princes, his 4430
Da 5:3 and the **k.**, and his princes, and......... 4430
Da 5:5 the **k.** saw the part of the hand that ... 4430
Da 5:7 The **k.** cried aloud to bring in the....... 4430
Da 5:7 the **k.** spake, and said to the wise...... 4430
Da 5:8 known to the **k.** the interpretation...... 4430
Da 5:9 was **k.** Belshazzar greatly troubled, ... 4430
Da 5:10 by reason of the words of the **k.**........ 4430
Da 5:10 and the queen spake and said, O **k.**,.... 4430
Da 5:11 the **k.** Nebuchadnezzar thy father, ... 4430
Da 5:11 **k.**, I say, thy father, made master...... 4430
Da 5:12 whom the **k.** named Belteshazzar: 4430
Da 5:13 Daniel brought in before the **k.**.......... 4430
Da 5:13 the **k.** spake and said unto Daniel, ... 4430
Da 5:13 **k.** my father brought out of Jewry?..... 4430
Da 5:17 answered and said before the **k.**, ... 4430
Da 5:17 I will read the writing unto the **k.**, ... 4430
Da 5:18 O thou **k.**, the most high God gave 4430
Da 5:30 was...the **k.** of the Chaldeans slain. 4430
Da 6:2 and the **k.** should have no damage....... 4430
Da 6:3 the **k.** thought to set him over the 4430
Da 6:6 assembled together to the **k.**,............ 4430
Da 6:6 unto him, **K.** Darius, live for ever. 4430
Da 6:7 save of thee, O **k.**, he shall be cast.... 4430
Da 6:8 Now, O **k.**, establish the decree, and.. 4430
Da 6:9 **k.** Darius signed the writing and 4430
Da 6:12 spake before the **k.** concerning the..... 4430
Da 6:12 save of thee, O **k.**, shall be cast into .. 4430
Da 6:12 **k.** answered and said, The thing is..... 4430
Da 6:13 and said before the **k.**, That Daniel,.... 4430
Da 6:13 regardeth not thee, O **k.**, nor the 4430
Da 6:14 Then the **k.**, when he heard these 4430
Da 6:15 these men assembled unto the **k.**,...... 4430
Da 6:15 and said unto the **k.**, Know, O **k.**, ... 4430
Da 6:15 statute which the **k.** establisheth........ 4430
Da 6:16 **k.** commanded, and they brought 4430
Da 6:16 the **k.** spake and said unto Daniel,...... 4430
Da 6:17 the **k.** sealed it with his own signet, ... 4430
Da 6:18 Then the **k.** went to his palace, and.... 4430
Da 6:19 Then the **k.** arose very early in the.... 4430
Da 6:20 the **k.** spake and said to Daniel, O 4430
Da 6:21 unto the **k.**, O **k.**, live for ever. 4430
Da 6:22 before thee, O **k.**, have I done no...... 4430
Da 6:23 was the **k.** exceeding glad for him...... 4430
Da 6:24 **k.** commanded, and they brought........ 4430
Da 6:25 **k.** Darius wrote unto all people,......... 4430
Da 7:1 year of Belshazzar **k.** of Babylon......... 4430
Da 8:1 year of the reign of **k.** Belshazzar 4428
Da 8:21 the rough goat is the **k.** of Grecia: 4428
Da 8:21 is between his eyes is the first **k.**. 4428

Da 8:23 the full, a **k.** of fierce countenance,..... 4428
Da 9:1 was made **k.** over the realm of the..... 4427
Da 10:1 third year of Cyrus **k.** of Persia......... 4428
Da 11:3 And a mighty **k.** shall stand up, that... 4428
Da 11:5 the **k.** of the south shall be strong,..... 4428
Da 11:6 shall come to the **k.** of the north........ 4428
Da 11:7 the fortress of the **k.** of the north,..... 4428
Da 11:8 more years than the **k.** of the north.... 4428
Da 11:9 **k.** of the south shall come into his...... 4428
Da 11:11 the **k.** of the south shall be moved..... 4428
Da 11:11 him, even with the **k.** of the north:.... 4428
Da 11:13 For the **k.** of the north shall return,... 4428
Da 11:14 up against the **k.** of the south:........... 4428
Da 11:15 **k.** of the north shall come, and cast.... 4428
Da 11:25 against the **k.** of the south with a....... 4428
Da 11:25 **k.** of the south shall be stirred up...... 4428
Da 11:36 **k.** shall do according to his will;......... 4428
Da 11:40 the **k.** of the south push at him:........ 4428
Da 11:40 **k.** of the north shall come against....... 4428
Ho 1:1 the son of Joash, **k.** of Israel............ 4428
Ho 3:4 shall abide many days without a **k.**,.... 4428
Ho 3:5 Lord their God, and David their **k.**;..... 4428
Ho 5:1 and give ye ear, O house of the **k.**;..... 4428
Ho 5:13 the Assyrian, and sent to **k.** Jareb:..... 4428
Ho 7:3 the **k.** glad with their wickedness,...... 4428
Ho 7:5 In the day of our **k.** the princes......... 4428
Ho 8:10 for the burden of the **k.** of princes..... 4428
Ho 10:3 We have no **k.**, because we feared..... 4428
Ho 10:3 what then should a **k.** do to us?......... 4428
Ho 10:6 Assyria for a present to **k.** Jareb:........ 4428
Ho 10:7 her **k.** is cut off as the foam upon...... 4428
Ho 10:15 shall the **k.** of Israel utterly be cut..... 4428
Ho 11:5 Assyrian shall be his **k.**, because....... 4428
Ho 13:10 I will be thy **k.**: where is any other..... 4428
Ho 13:10 saidst, Give me a **k.** and princes?...... 4428
Ho 13:11 I gave thee a **k.** in mine anger, and.... 4428
Am 1:1 In the days of Uzziah **k.** of Judah,...... 4428
Am 1:1 the son of Joash **k.** of Israel,............ 4428
Am 1:15 their **k.** shall go into captivity, he...... 4428
Am 2:1 burned the bones of the **k.** of Edom... 4428
Am 7:10 sent to Jeroboam **k.** of Israel,............ 4428
Jon 3:6 word came unto the **k.** of Nineveh,.... 4428
Jon 3:7 the decree of the **k.** and his nobles,.... 4428
Mic 2:13 and their **k.** shall pass before them,.... 4428
Mic 4:9 no **k.** in thee? is thy counsellor.......... 4428
Mic 6:5 what Balak **k.** of Moab consulted,....... 4428
Na 3:18 shepherds slumber, O **k.** of Assyria:... 4428
Zep 1:1 the son of Amon, **k.** of Judah............ 4428
Zep 3:15 the **k.** of Israel, even the Lord, is in... 4428
Hag 1:1 in the second year of Darius the **k.**,... 4428
Hag 1:15 in the second year of Darius the **k.**.... 4428
Zec 7:1 pass in the fourth year of **k.** Darius,... 4428
Zec 9:5 the **k.** shall perish from Gaza, and...... 4428
Zec 9:9 behold, thy **K.** cometh unto thee:........ 4428
Zec 11:6 hand, and into the hand of his **k.**:....... 4428
Zec 14:5 the days of Uzziah **k.** of Judah:.......... 4428
Zec 14:9 Lord shall be **k.** over all the earth:..... 4428
Zec 14:16 to worship the **K.**, the Lord of hosts,.. 4428
Zec 14:17 unto Jerusalem to worship the **K.**,...... 4428
Mal 1:14 I am a great **K.**, saith the Lord of...... 4428
Mt 1:6 And Jesse begat David the **k.**;............ 935
Mt 1:6 and David the **k.** begat Solomon.......... 935
Mt 2:1 Judaea in the days of Herod the **k.**,...... 935
Mt 2:2 is he that is born **K.** of the Jews?........ 935
Mt 2:3 When Herod the **k.** had heard these..... 935
Mt 2:9 When they had heard the **k.**, they....... 935
Mt 5:35 **for it is the city of the great K.**....... 935
Mt 14:9 the **k.** was sorry: nevertheless for....... 935
Mt 18:23 **of heaven likened unto a certain k.**,.. 935
Mt 21:5 Behold, thy **K.** cometh unto thee,........ 935
Mt 22:2 **of heaven is like unto a certain k.**,.. 935
Mt 22:7 **when the k. heard thereof, he was**.. 935
Mt 22:11 **the k. came in to see the guests**,...... 935
Mt 22:13 **Then said the k. to the servants**,...... 935
Mt 25:34 **Then shall the K. say unto them**..... 935
Mt 25:40 **the K. shall answer and say unto**.... 935
Mt 27:11 Art thou the **K.** of the Jews?............ 935
Mt 27:29 him, saying, Hail, **K.** of the Jews!........ 935
Mt 27:37 This Is Jesus The **K.** Of The Jews....... 935
Mt 27:42 If he be the **K.** of Israel, let him......... 935
Mk 6:14 And **k.** Herod heard of him; (for his..... 935
Mk 6:22 him, the **k.** said unto the damsel,........ 935
Mk 6:25 straightway with haste unto the **k.**,...... 935
Mk 6:26 the **k.** was exceeding sorry; yet for..... 935
Mk 6:27 the **k.** sent an executioner,................ 935
Mk 15:2 him, Art thou the **K.** of the Jews?....... 935
Mk 15:9 release unto you the **K.** of the Jews?.... 935
Mk 15:12 whom ye call the **K.** of the Jews?........ 935
Mk 15:18 salute him, Hail, **K.** of the Jews!........ 935
Mk 15:26 written over, The **K.** Of The Jews...... 935
Mk 15:32 Let Christ the **K.** of Israel descend...... 935
Lu 1:5 the days of Herod, the **k.** of Judaea,.... 935
Lu 14:31 **Or what k., going to make war**....... 935
Lu 14:31 **against another k., sitteth not down** 935
Lu 19:38 Blessed be the **K.** that cometh in........ 935
Lu 23:2 that he himself is Christ a **K.**............. 935
Lu 23:3 Art thou the **K.** of the Jews?............. 935
Lu 23:37 If thou be the **K.** of the Jews, save...... 935
Lu 23:38 This Is The **K.** Of The Jews.............. 935
Joh 1:49 of God; thou art the **K.** of Israel......... 935
Joh 6:15 take him by force, to make him a **k.**,... 935
Joh 12:13 Blessed is the **K.** of Israel that............ 935
Joh 12:15 thy **K.** cometh, sitting on an ass's......... 935
Joh 18:33 him, Art thou the **K.** of the Jews?....... 935
Joh 18:37 said unto him, Art thou a **k.** then?....... 935
Joh 18:37 **Thou sayest that I am a k.. To this** .935
Joh 18:39 unto you the **K.** of the Jews?............. 935
Joh 19:3 said, Hail, **K.** of the Jews! and they..... 935
Joh 19:12 maketh himself a **k.** speaketh............. 935
Joh 19:14 unto the Jews, Behold your **K.**!.......... 935
Joh 19:15 unto them, Shall I crucify your **K.**?...... 935
Joh 19:15 answered, We have no **k.** but Caesar... 935
Joh 19:19 Jesus Of Nazareth The **K.** Of The....... 935
Joh 19:21 Write not, The **K.** of the Jews;........... 935
Joh 19:21 that he said, I am **K.** of the Jews........ 935
Ac 7:10 the sight of Pharaoh **k.** of Egypt;.......... 935
Ac 7:18 Till another **k.** arose, which knew........ 935
Ac 12:1 Herod the **k.** stretched forth his.......... 935
Ac 13:21 And afterward they desired a **k.**:......... 935
Ac 13:22 unto them David to be their **k.**;........... 935
Ac 17:7 that there is another **k.**, one Jesus....... 935
Ac 25:13 days **k.** Agrippa and Bernice came....... 935
Ac 25:14 declared Paul's cause unto the **k.**,........ 935
Ac 25:24 Festus said, **K.** Agrippa, and all.......... 935
Ac 25:26 specially before thee, O **k.** Agrippa,..... 935
Ac 26:2 I think myself happy, **k.** Agrippa,......... 935
Ac 26:7 For which hope's sake, **k.** Agrippa,...... 935
Ac 26:13 At midday, O **k.**, I saw in the way a.... 935
Ac 26:19 O **k.** Agrippa, I was not disobedient..... 935
Ac 26:26 For the **k.** knoweth of these things,..... 935
Ac 26:27 **K.** Agrippa, believest thou the............ 935
Ac 26:30 the **k.** rose up, and the governor,........ 935
2Co 11:32 governor under Aretas the **k.** kept....... 935
1Ti 1:17 Now unto the **K.** eternal, immortal,...... 935
1Ti 6:15 **K.** of kings, and Lord of lords;............ 935
Heb 7:1 Melchisedec, **k.** of Salem, priest.......... 935
Heb 7:2 interpretation **K.** of righteousness,....... 935
Heb 7:2 **K.** of Salem, which is, **K.** of peace;..... 935
Heb 11:27 not fearing the wrath of the **k.**: for...... 935
1Pe 2:13 whether it be to the **k.**, as supreme;.... 935
1Pe 2:17 Fear God. Honour the **k.**.................. 935
Re 9:11 they had a **k.** over them, which is........ 935
Re 15:3 are thy ways, thou **K.** of saints........... 935
Re 17:14 is Lord of lords, and **K.** of kings:.......... 935
Re 19:16 **K.** of Kings, And Lord Of Lords.......... 935

KINGDOM See also KINGDOMS.

Ge 10:10 the beginning of his **k.** was Babel,...... 4467
Ge 20:9 on me and on my **k.** a great sin?....... 4467
Ex 19:6 ye shall be unto me a **k.** of priests,.... 4467
Nu 24:7 Agag, and his **k.** shall be exalted........ 4438
Nu 32:33 **k.** of Sihon king of the Amorites,....... 4467
Nu 32:33 and the **k.** of Og king of Bashan,....... 4467
De 3:4 of Argob, the **k.** of Og in Bashan....... 4467
De 3:10 cities of the **k.** of Og in Bashan......... 4467
De 3:13 being the **k.** of Og, gave I unto the.... 4467
De 17:18 sitteth upon the throne of his **k.**,....... 4467
De 17:20 he may prolong his days in his **k.**,...... 4467
Jos 13:12 All the **k.** of Og in Bashan, which........ 4468
Jos 13:21 **k.** of Sihon king of the Amorites,....... 4468
Jos 13:27 the **k.** of Sihon king of Heshbon,........ 4468
Jos 13:30 all the **k.** of Og king of Bashan,......... 4468
Jos 13:31 cities of the **k.** of Og in Bashan,........ 4468
1Sa 10:16 But of the matter of the **k.**, whereof... 4410
1Sa 10:25 the people the manner of the **k.**,........ 4410
1Sa 11:14 to Gilgal, and renew the **k.** there........ 4410
1Sa 13:13 Lord have established thy **k.** upon...... 4467
1Sa 13:14 But now thy **k.** shall not continue:...... 4467
1Sa 14:47 So Saul took the **k.** over Israel,......... 4410
1Sa 15:28 The Lord hath rent the **k.** of Israel.... 4468
1Sa 18:8 can he have more but the **k.**?............ 4410
1Sa 20:31 not be established, nor thy **k.**............ 4438
1Sa 24:20 **k.** of Israel shall be established.......... 4467
1Sa 28:17 hath rent the **k.** out of thine hand,..... 4467
2Sa 3:10 the **k.** from the house of Saul............ 4467
2Sa 3:28 I and my **k.** are guiltless before the.... 4467
2Sa 5:12 he had exalted his **k.** for his people.... 4467
2Sa 7:12 bowels, and I will establish his **k.**....... 4467
2Sa 7:13 I will stablish the throne of his **k.**....... 4467
2Sa 7:16 and thy **k.** shall be established for...... 4467
2Sa 16:3 restore me the **k.** of my father.......... 4468
2Sa 16:8 the **k.** into the hand of Absalom.......... 4410
1Ki 1:46 sitteth on the throne of the **k.**............ 4410
1Ki 2:12 and his **k.** was established greatly...... 4438
1Ki 2:15 Thou knowest that the **k.** was mine,... 4410
1Ki 2:15 howbeit the **k.** is turned about,.......... 4410
1Ki 2:22 ask for him the **k.** also; for he is........ 4410
1Ki 2:46 **k.** was established in the hand of....... 4467
1Ki 9:5 the throne of thy **k.** upon Israel......... 4467
1Ki 10:20 was not the like made in any **k.**......... 4467
1Ki 11:11 I will surely rend the **k.** from thee,.... 4467
1Ki 11:13 I will not rend away all the **k.**; but..... 4467
1Ki 11:31 I will rend the **k.** out of the hand....... 4467
1Ki 11:34 will not take the whole **k.** out of his... 4467
1Ki 11:35 I will take the **k.** out of his son's...... 4410
1Ki 12:21 bring the **k.** again to Rehoboam......... 4410
1Ki 12:26 the **k.** return to the house of David.... 4467
1Ki 14:8 rent the **k.** away from the house........ 4467
1Ki 18:10 God liveth, there is no nation or **k.**,... 4467
1Ki 18:10 he took an oath of the **k.** and........... 4467
1Ki 21:7 thou now govern the **k.** of Israel?...... 4410
2Ki 14:5 the **k.** was confirmed in his hand,....... 4467
2Ki 15:19 him to confirm the **k.** in his hand....... 4467
1Ch 10:14 turned the **k.** unto David the son....... 4410
1Ch 11:10 themselves with him in his **k.**,........... 4438
1Ch 12:23 to turn the **k.** of Saul to him,............ 4438
1Ch 14:2 for his **k.** was lifted up on high,......... 4438
1Ch 16:20 from one **k.** to another people;.......... 4467
1Ch 17:11 sons; and I will establish his **k.**.......... 4438
1Ch 17:14 mine house and in my **k.** for ever:..... 4438
1Ch 22:10 I will establish the throne of his **k.**..... 4438
1Ch 28:5 the throne of the **k.** of the Lord........ 4438
1Ch 28:7 I will establish his **k.** for ever, if........ 4438
1Ch 29:11 thine is the **k.**, O Lord, and thou....... 4467
2Ch 1:1 David was strengthened in his **k.**,...... 4438
2Ch 2:1 the Lord, and an house for his **k.**....... 4438
2Ch 2:12 for the Lord, and an house for his **k.**.. 4438
2Ch 7:18 will I stablish the throne of thy **k.**,..... 4438
2Ch 9:19 was not the like made in any **k.**......... 4467
2Ch 11:1 bring the **k.** again to Rehoboam......... 4467
2Ch 11:17 strengthened the **k.** of Judah,............ 4438
2Ch 12:1 Rehoboam had established the **k.**,...... 4438
2Ch 13:5 gave the **k.** over Israel to David......... 4467
2Ch 13:8 withstand the **k.** of the Lord in the..... 4467
2Ch 14:5 and the **k.** was quiet before him......... 4467
2Ch 17:5 the Lord stablished the **k.** in his........ 4467
2Ch 21:3 the **k.** gave he to Jehoram; because.... 4467
2Ch 21:4 Jehoram was risen up to the **k.** of..... 4467
2Ch 22:9 had no power to keep still the **k.**...... 4467
2Ch 23:20 the king upon the throne of the **k.**...... 4467
2Ch 25:3 when the **k.** was established to him,... 4467
2Ch 29:21 goats, for a sin offering for the **k.**,..... 4467
2Ch 32:15 no god of any nation or **k.** was able.... 4467
2Ch 33:13 again to Jerusalem into his **k.**.......... 4438
2Ch 36:20 until the reign of the **k.** of Persia:...... 4438
2Ch 36:22 proclamation throughout all his **k.**,...... 4438
Ezr 1:1 proclamation throughout all his **k.**,...... 4438
Ne 9:35 have not served thee in their **k.**,........ 4438
Es 1:2 sat on the throne of his **k.**, which...... 4438
Es 1:4 shewed the riches of his glorious **k.**.... 4438
Es 1:14 and which sat the first in the **k.**;)....... 4438
Es 2:3 in all the provinces of his **k.**, that....... 4438
Es 3:6 the whole **k.** of Ahasuerus,................ 4438
Es 3:8 people in all the provinces of thy **k.**;... 4438
Es 4:14 art come to the **k.** for such a time..... 4438
Es 5:3 even given thee to the half of the **k.**.... 4438
Es 5:6 even to the half of the **k.** it shall be.... 4438
Es 7:2 performed, even to the half of the **k.**.. 4438
Es 9:30 twenty and seven provinces of the **k.**... 4438
Ps 22:28 For the **k.** is the Lord's; and he........ 4410
Ps 45:6 sceptre of thy **k.** is a right sceptre..... 4438
Ps 103:19 heavens; and his **k.** ruleth over all...... 4438
Ps 105:13 from one **k.** to another people;.......... 4467
Ps 145:11 shall speak of the glory of thy **k.**,........ 4438
Ps 145:12 and the glorious majesty of his **k.**....... 4438
Ps 145:13 Thy **k.** is an everlasting **k.**, and......... 4438
Ec 4:14 is born in his **k.** becometh poor.......... 4438
Isa 9:7 upon his **k.**, to order it, and to.......... 4467
Isa 17:3 the **k.** from Damascus, and the.......... 4467
Isa 19:2 city against city, and **k.** against **k.**...... 4467
Isa 34:12 call the nobles thereof to the **k.**,......... 4410

Isa 60:12 k. that will not serve thee shall 4467
Jer 18:7 concerning a k., to pluck up, and 4467
Jer 18:9 concerning a k., to build and to 4467
Jer 27:8 nation and k. which will not serve 4467
La 2:2 hath polluted the princes and the k. 4467
Eze 16:13 and thou didst prosper into a k. 4410
Eze 17:14 That the k. might be base, that it 4467
Eze 29:14 and they shall be there a base k. 4467
Da 2:37 of heaven hath given thee a k., 4437
Da 2:39 shall arise another k. inferior to 4437
Da 2:39 and another third k. of brass, which 4437
Da 2:40 fourth k. shall be strong as iron: 4437
Da 2:41 part of iron, the k. shall be divided; 4437
Da 2:42 so the k. shall be partly strong, 4437
Da 2:44 shall the God of heaven set up a k., 4437
Da 2:44 the k. shall not be left to other 4437
Da 4:3 his k. is an everlasting k., and his 4437
Da 4:17 most High ruleth in the k. of men, 4437
Da 4:18 the wise men of my k. are not able 4437
Da 4:25 most High ruleth in the k. of men, 4437
Da 4:26 thy k. shall be sure unto thee, after 4437
Da 4:29 in the palace of the k. of Babylon 4437
Da 4:30 I have built for the house of the k. 4437
Da 4:31 The k. is departed from thee. 4437
Da 4:32 most High ruleth in the k. of men, 4437
Da 4:34 his k. is from generation to 4437
Da 4:36 for the glory of my k., mine honour 4437
Da 4:36 and I was established in my k., 4437
Da 5:7 shall be the third ruler in the k. 4437
Da 5:11 There is a man in thy k., in whom 4437
Da 5:16 shalt be the third ruler in the k. 4437
Da 5:18 Nebuchadnezzar thy father a k., 4437
Da 5:21 high God ruled in the k. of men, 4437
Da 5:26 Mene; God hath numbered thy k., 4437
Da 5:28 Peres; Thy k. is divided, and given 4437
Da 5:29 should be the third ruler in the k. 4437
Da 5:31 And Darius the Median took the k., 4437
Da 6:1 pleased Darius to set over the k. 4437
Da 6:1 which should be over the whole k.; 4437
Da 6:4 against Daniel concerning the k.; 4437
Da 6:7 All the presidents of the k., the 4437
Da 6:26 That in every dominion of my k. 4437
Da 6:26 his k. that which shall not be 4437
Da 7:14 him dominion, and glory, and a k., 4437
Da 7:14 his k. that which shall not be 4437
Da 7:18 of the most High shall take the k., 4437
Da 7:18 possess the k. for ever, even for ever 4437
Da 7:22 that the saints possessed the k. 4437
Da 7:23 shall be the fourth k. upon earth, 4437
Da 7:24 out of this k. are ten kings that shall 4437
Da 7:27 And the k. and dominion, and the 4437
Da 7:27 greatness of the k. under the whole 4437
Da 7:27 High, whose k. is an everlasting k., 4437
Da 8:23 And in the latter time of their k., 4438
Da 10:13 But the prince of the k. of Persia 4438
Da 11:4 stand up, his k. shall be broken, 4438
Da 11:4 for his k. shall be plucked up, even 4438
Da 11:9 of the south shall come into his k., 4438
Da 11:17 with the strength of his whole k., 4438
Da 11:20 of taxes in the glory of the k.: 4438
Da 11:21 shall not give the honour of the k.: 4438
Da 11:21 and obtain the k. by flatteries. 4438
Ho 1:4 cease the k. of the house of Israel. 4468
Am 9:8 Lord God are upon the sinful k., 4467
Ob 21 and the k. shall be the Lord's 4410
Mic 4:8 the k. shall come to the daughter 4467
Mt 3:2 ye: for the k. of heaven is at hand. 932
Mt 4:17 for the k. of heaven is at hand. 932
Mt 4:23 and preaching the gospel of the k., 932
Mt 5:3 spirit: for theirs is the k. of heaven. 932
Mt 5:10 sake: for theirs is the k. of heaven. 932
Mt 5:19 called the least in the k. of heaven: 932
Mt 5:19 be called great in the k. of heaven. 932
Mt 5:20 no case enter into the k. of heaven. 932
Mt 6:10 Thy k. come. Thy will be done in 932
Mt 6:13 For thine is the k., and the power, 932
Mt 6:33 seek ye first the k. of God, and his 932
Mt 7:21 shall enter into the k. of heaven, 932
Mt 8:11 Isaac, and Jacob, in the k. of 932
Mt 8:12 children of the k. shall be cast out 932
Mt 9:35 and preaching the gospel of the k., 932
Mt 10:7 saying, The k. of heaven is at hand. 932
Mt 11:11 least in the k. of heaven is greater 932
Mt 11:12 the k. of heaven suffereth violence, 932
Mt 12:25 k. divided against itself is brought 932
Mt 12:26 how shall then his k. stand? 932
Mt 12:28 then the k. of God is come unto 932
Mt 13:11 the mysteries of the k. of heaven, 932
Mt 13:19 any one heareth the word of the k., 932
Mt 13:24 k. of heaven is likened unto a man 932
Mt 13:31 k. of heaven is like to a grain of 932
Mt 13:33 k. of heaven is like unto leaven, 932
Mt 13:38 good seed are the children of the k.; 932
Mt 13:41 shall gather out of his k. all things. 932
Mt 13:43 as the sun in the k. of their Father. 932
Mt 13:44 the k. of heaven is like unto 932
Mt 13:45 k. of heaven is like unto a merchant 932
Mt 13:47 the k. of heaven is like unto a net, 932
Mt 13:52 is instructed unto the k. of heaven, 932
Mt 16:19 thee the keys of the k. of heaven: 932
Mt 16:28 the Son of man coming in his k. 932
Mt 18:1 is the greatest in the k. of heaven? 932
Mt 18:3 shall not enter into the k. of 932
Mt 18:4 same is greatest in the k. of heaven. 932
Mt 18:23 k. of heaven likened unto a certain 932
Mt 19:12 eunuchs for the k. of heaven's sake. 932
Mt 19:14 me; for of such is the k. of heaven. 932
Mt 19:23 hardly enter into the k. of heaven. 932
Mt 19:24 for a rich man to enter into the k. 932
Mt 20:1 k. of heaven is like unto a man that 932
Mt 20:21 and the other on the left, in thy k. 932
Mt 21:31 harlots go into the k. of God before 932
Mt 21:43 k. of God shall be taken from you, 932
Mt 22:2 The k. of heaven is like unto a 932
Mt 23:13 ye shut up the k. of heaven against 932
Mt 24:7 against nation, and k. against k.: 932
Mt 24:14 gospel of the k. shall be preached 932
Mt 25:1 k. of heaven be likened unto ten 932
Mt 25:14 k. of heaven is as a man travelling 932
Mt 25:34 inherit the k. prepared for you from 932
Mt 26:29 it new with you in my Father's k. 932
Mk 1:14 preaching the gospel of the k. of God, 932
Mk 1:15 fulfilled, and the k. of God is at 932
Mk 3:24 if a k. be divided against itself, 932
Mk 3:24 that k. cannot stand. 932
Mk 4:11 know the mystery of the k. of God: 932
Mk 4:26 So is the k. of God, as if a man 932
Mk 4:30 Whereunto shall we liken the k. of 932
Mk 6:23 give it thee, unto the half of my k. 932
Mk 9:1 have seen the k. of God come with 932
Mk 9:47 enter into the k. of God with one 932
Mk 10:14 not: for of such is the k. of God. 932
Mk 10:15 shall not receive the k. of God as a 932
Mk 10:23 have riches enter into the k. of God! 932
Mk 10:24 in riches to enter into the k. of 932
Mk 10:25 rich man to enter into the k. of 932
Mk 11:10 Blessed be the k. of our father David, 932
Mk 12:34 Thou art not far from the k. of 932
Mk 13:8 against nation, and k. against k.: 932
Mk 14:25 that I drink it new in the k. of God 932
Mk 15:43 which also waited for the k. of God, 932
Lu 1:33 of his k. there shall be no end. 932
Lu 4:43 preach the k. of God to other cities 932
Lu 6:20 ye poor: for yours is the k. of God. 932
Lu 7:28 he that is least in the k. of God is 932
Lu 8:1 the glad tidings of the k. of God: 932
Lu 8:10 know the mysteries of the k. of 932
Lu 9:2 sent them to preach the k. of God, 932
Lu 9:11 spake unto them of the k. of God, 932
Lu 9:27 of death, till they see the k. of God. 932
Lu 9:60 go thou and preach the k. of God. 932
Lu 9:62 looking back, is fit for the k. of 932
Lu 10:9 The k. of God is come nigh unto 932
Lu 10:11 the k. of God is come nigh unto 932
Lu 11:2 Thy k. come. Thy will be done, as 932
Lu 11:17 Every k. divided against itself is 932
Lu 11:18 himself, how shall his k. stand? 932
Lu 11:20 no doubt the k. of God is come 932
Lu 12:31 But rather seek ye the k. of God; 932
Lu 12:32 good pleasure to give you the k. 932
Lu 13:18 he, unto what is the k. of God like? 932
Lu 13:20 whereunto shall I liken the k. 932
Lu 13:28 all the prophets, in the k. of God, 932
Lu 13:29 and shall sit down in the k. of God. 932
Lu 14:15 that shall eat bread in the k. 932
Lu 16:16 that time the k. of God is preached, 932
Lu 17:20 when the k. of God should come, he 932
Lu 17:20 The k. of God cometh not with 932
Lu 17:21 behold, the k. of God is within you. 932
Lu 18:16 not: for of such is the k. of God. 932
Lu 18:17 shall not receive the k. of God as a 932
Lu 18:24 have riches enter into the k. of God! 932
Lu 18:25 rich man to enter into the k. 932
Lu 18:29 or children, for the k. of God's 932
Lu 19:11 they thought that the k. of God 932
Lu 19:12 to receive for himself a k., and to 932
Lu 19:15 returned, having received the k., 932
Lu 21:10 against nation, and k. against k.: 932
Lu 21:31 ye that the k. of God is nigh at 932
Lu 22:16 until it be fulfilled in the k. of God. 932
Lu 22:18 vine, until the k. of God shall come. 932
Lu 22:29 I appoint unto you a k., as my 932
Lu 22:30 eat and drink at my table in my k., 932
Lu 23:42 me when thou comest into thy k. 932
Lu 23:51 himself waited for the k. of God. 932
Joh 3:3 again, he cannot see the k. of God. 932
Joh 3:5 he cannot enter into the k. of God. 932
Joh 18:36 answered, My k. is not of this world: 932
Joh 18:36 if my k. were of this world, then 932
Joh 18:36 but now is my k. not from hence 932
Ac 1:3 things pertaining to the k. of God: 932
Ac 1:6 time restore again the k. to Israel? 932
Ac 8:12 things concerning the k. of God, 932
Ac 14:22 tribulation enter into the k. of God. 932
Ac 19:8 things concerning the k. of God. 932
Ac 20:25 have gone, preaching the k. of God, 932
Ac 28:23 and testified the k. of God, 932
Ac 28:31 Preaching the k. of God, and 932
Ro 14:17 For the k. of God is not meat and 932
1Co 4:20 the k. of God is not in word, but in 932
1Co 6:9 shall not inherit the k. of God? 932
1Co 6:10 nor..., shall inherit the k. of God. 932
1Co 15:24 have delivered up the k. to God, 932
1Co 15:50 blood cannot inherit the k. of God; 932
Ga 5:21 shall not inherit the k. of God. 932
Eph 5:5 any inheritance in the k. of Christ 932
Col 1:13 us into the k. of his dear Son: 932
Col 4:11 fellow-workers unto the k. of God, 932
1Th 2:12 called you unto his k. and glory. 932
2Th 1:5 be counted worthy of the k. of God, 932
2Ti 4:1 dead at his appearing and his k.; 932
2Ti 4:18 preserve me unto his heavenly k.: 932
Heb 1:8 righteousness is the sceptre of thy k. 932
Heb 12:28 we receiving a k. which cannot be 932
Jas 2:5 heirs of the k. which he hath 932
2Pe 1:11 into the everlasting k. of our Lord 932
Re 1:9 in the k. and patience of Jesus 932
Re 12:10 strength, and the k. of our God, 932
Re 16:10 his k. was full of darkness; and 932
Re 17:12 which have received no k. as yet; 932
Re 17:17 give their k. unto the beast, until 932

KINGDOMS

De 3:21 all the k. whither thou passest 4467
De 28:25 removed into all the k. of the earth. 4467
Jos 11:10 was the head of all those k. 4467
1Sa 10:18 and out of the hand of all k., 4467
1Ki 4:21 And Solomon reigned over all k. 4467
2Ki 19:15 thou alone, of all the k. of the earth; 4467
2Ki 19:19 all the k. of the earth may know 4467
1Ch 29:30 over all the k. of the countries. 4467
2Ch 12:8 service of the k. of the countries. 4467
2Ch 17:10 fell upon all the k. of the lands 4467
2Ch 20:6 over all the k. of the heathen? 4467
2Ch 20:29 the fear of God was on all the k. 4467
2Ch 36:23 All the k. of the earth hath the Lord 4467
Ezr 1:2 given me all the k. of the earth; 4467
Ne 9:22 thou gavest them k. and nations, 4467
Ps 46:6 heathen raged, the k. were moved: 4467
Ps 68:32 Sing unto God, ye k. of the earth; 4467
Ps 79:6 and upon the k. that have not called 4467
Ps 102:22 and the k., to serve the Lord. 4467
Ps 135:11 Bashan, and all the k. of Canaan: 4467
Isa 10:10 hand hath found the k. of the idols, 4467
Isa 13:4 tumultuous noise of the k. of nations 4467
Isa 13:19 And Babylon, the glory of k., 4467
Isa 14:16 earth to tremble, that did shake k.; 4467
Isa 23:11 over the sea, he shook the k.: 4467
Isa 23:17 commit fornication with all the k. 4467
Isa 37:16 alone, of all the k. of the earth: 4467
Isa 37:20 that all the k. of the earth may know 4467
Isa 47:5 no more be called, The lady of k. 4467
Jer 1:10 over the nations and over the k., 4467
Jer 1:15 the families of the k. of the north, 4467
Jer 10:7 of the nations, and in all their k., 4467
Jer 15:4 be removed into all k. of the earth, 4467
Jer 24:9 be removed into the k. of the earth 4467
Jer 25:26 another, and all the k. of the world, 4467
Jer 28:8 countries, and against great k., 4467

Jer 29:18 be removed to all the **k.** of the earth, 4467
Jer 34:1 and all the **k.** of the earth of his 4467
Jer 34:17 removed into all the **k.** of the earth. 4467
Jer 49:28 and concerning the **k.** of Hazor. 4467
Jer 51:20 and with thee will I destroy **k.**; 4467
Jer 51:27 against her the **k.** of Ararat, 4467
Eze 29:15 It shall be the basest of the **k.**; 4467
Eze 37:22 divided into two **k.** any more at all: 4467
Da 2:44 in pieces and consume all these **k.**, 4437
Da 7:23 which shall be diverse from all **k.**, 4437
Da 8:22 four **k.** shall stand up out of the 4438
Am 6:2 be they better than these **k.**? 4467
Na 3:5 nakedness, and the **k.** thy shame. 4467
Zep 3:8 nations, that I may assemble the **k.**, 4467
Hag 2:22 I will overthrow the throne of **k.**, 4467
Hag 2:22 I will destroy the strength of the **k.** 4467
Mt 4:8 sheweth him all the **k.** of the world, *932*
Lu 4:5 unto him all the **k.** of the world in *932*
Heb 11:33 Who through faith subdued **k.**, *932*
Re 11:15 The **k.** of this world are become *932*
Re 11:15 the **k.** of our Lord, and of his Christ; *932*

KINGLY

Da 5:20 was deposed from his **k.** throne, 4437

KING'S

Ge 14:17 Shaveh, which is in the **k.** dale. 4428
Ge 39:20 where the **k.** prisoners were bound: 4428
Nu 20:17 we will go by the **k.** high way, we 4428
Nu 21:22 we will go along by the **k.** high way, 4428
1Sa 18:22 now therefore be the **k.** son in law. 4428
1Sa 18:23 a light thing to be a **k.** son in law, 4428
1Sa 18:25 to be avenged of the **k.** enemies. 4428
1Sa 18:26 David well to be the **k.** son in law: 4428
1Sa 18:27 that he might be the **k.** son in law. 4428
1Sa 20:29 he cometh not unto the **k.** table. 4428
1Sa 21:8 the **k.** business required haste. 4428
1Sa 22:14 David, which is the **k.** son in law, 4428
1Sa 23:20 be to deliver him into the **k.** hand. 4428
1Sa 26:16 And now see where the **k.** spear is, 4428
1Sa 26:22 and said, Behold the **k.** spear! 4428
2Sa 9:11 at my table, as one of the **k.** sons. 4428
2Sa 9:13 did eat continually at the **k.** table; 4428
2Sa 11:2 upon the roof of the **k.** house: 4428
2Sa 11:8 Uriah departed out of the **k.** house, 4428
2Sa 11:9 slept at the door of the **k.** house 4428
2Sa 11:20 And if so be that the **k.** wrath arise, 4428
2Sa 11:24 some of the **k.** servants be dead, 4428
2Sa 12:30 he took their **k.** crown from off his 4428
2Sa 13:4 Why art thou, being the **k.** son, 4428
2Sa 13:18 such robes were the **k.** daughters 4428
2Sa 13:23 Absalom invited all the **k.** sons. 4428
2Sa 13:27 and all the **k.** sons go with him. 4428
2Sa 13:29 Then all the **k.** sons arose, and 4428
2Sa 13:30 Absalom hath slain all the **k.** sons, 4428
2Sa 13:32 slain all the young men the **k.** sons; 4428
2Sa 13:33 think that all the **k.** sons are dead: 4428
2Sa 13:35 Behold, the **k.** sons come: as thy 4428
2Sa 13:36 the **k.** sons came, and lifted up 4428
2Sa 14:1 the **k.** heart was toward Absalom. 4428
2Sa 14:24 house, and saw not the **k.** face. 4428
2Sa 14:26 hundred shekels after the **k.** weight. 4428
2Sa 14:28 Jerusalem, and saw not the **k.** face. 4428
2Sa 14:32 therefore let me see the **k.** face; 4428
2Sa 15:15 the **k.** servant said unto the king, 4428
2Sa 15:35 thou shalt hear out of the **k.** house, 4428
2Sa 16:2 The asses be for the **k.** household. 4428
2Sa 18:12 mine hand against the **k.** son: 4428
2Sa 18:18 pillar, which is in the **k.** dale: 4428
2Sa 18:20 because the **k.** son is dead. 4428
2Sa 18:29 When Joab sent the **k.** servant, 4428
2Sa 19:18 boat to carry over the **k.** household, 4428
2Sa 19:42 have we eaten at all of the **k.** cost? 4428
2Sa 24:4 the **k.** word prevailed against Joab, 4428
1Ki 1:9 called all his brethren the **k.** sons, 4428
1Ki 1:9 the men of Judah the **k.** servants: 4428
1Ki 1:25 and hath called all the **k.** sons, 4428
1Ki 1:28 she came into the **k.** presence, and 4428
1Ki 1:44 him to ride upon the **k.** mule: 4428
1Ki 1:47 **k.** servants came to bless our lord 4428
1Ki 2:19 a seat to be set for the **k.** mother; 4428
1Ki 4:5 principal officer, and the **k.** friend: 4428
1Ki 9:1, 10 of the Lord, and the **k.** house, 4428
1Ki 10:12 of the Lord, and for the **k.** house, 4428
1Ki 10:28 the **k.** merchants received the linen 4428
1Ki 11:14 he was of the **k.** seed in Edom. 4428
1Ki 13:6 **k.** hand was restored him again, 4428
1Ki 14:26 and the treasures of the **k.** house; 4428
1Ki 14:27 which kept the door of the **k.** house. 4428
1Ki 15:18 and the treasures of the **k.** house, 4428
1Ki 16:18 went into the palace of the **k.** house, 4428
1Ki 16:18 and burnt the **k.** house over him 4428
1Ki 22:12 shall deliver it into the **k.** hand. 4428
1Ki 22:26 of the city, and to Joash the **k.** son; 4428
2Ki 7:9 may go and tell the **k.** household 4428
2Ki 7:11 they told it to the **k.** house within. 4428
2Ki 9:34 bury her: for she is a **k.** daughter. 4428
2Ki 10:6 the **k.** sons, being seventy persons, 4428
2Ki 10:7 that they took the **k.** sons, and slew 4428
2Ki 10:8 brought the heads of the **k.** sons. 4428
2Ki 11:2 stole him from among the **k.** sons 4428
2Ki 11:4 Lord, and shewed them the **k.** son. 4428
2Ki 11:5 of the watch of the **k.** house; 4428
2Ki 11:12 he brought forth the **k.** son, and put 4428
2Ki 11:16 the horses came into the **k.** house: 4428
2Ki 11:19 gate of the guard to the **k.** house. 4428
2Ki 11:20 with the sword beside the **k.** house. 4428
2Ki 12:10 the **k.** scribe and the high priest 4428
2Ki 12:18 of the Lord, and in the **k.** house, 4428
2Ki 13:16 put his hands upon the **k.** hands. 4428
2Ki 14:14 and in the treasures of the **k.** house, 4428
2Ki 15:5 And Jotham the **k.** son was over the 4428
2Ki 15:25 in the palace of the **k.** house, 4428
2Ki 16:8 and in the treasures of the **k.** house, 4428
2Ki 16:15 the **k.** burnt sacrifice, and his meat 4428
2Ki 16:18 the house, and the **k.** entry without, 4428
2Ki 18:15 and in the treasures of the **k.** house. 4428
2Ki 18:36 for the **k.** commandment was, 4428
2Ki 22:12 and Asahiah a servant of the **k.**, 4428
2Ki 24:13 and the treasures of the **k.** house, 4428
2Ki 24:15 the **k.** mother, and the **k.** wives, and 4428
2Ki 25:4 walls, which is by the **k.** garden: 4428
2Ki 25:9 house of the Lord, and the **k.** house, 4428
2Ki 25:19 them that were in the **k.** presence. 4428
1Ch 9:18 Who hitherto waited in the **k.** gate 4428
1Ch 21:4 Nevertheless the **k.** word prevailed 4428
1Ch 21:6 **k.** word was abominable to Joab. 4428
1Ch 25:5 Heman the **k.** seer in the words of 4428
1Ch 25:6 according to the **k.** order to Asaph, 4428
1Ch 27:25 over the **k.** treasures was Azmaveth 4428
1Ch 27:32 of Hachmoni was with the **k.** sons: 4428
1Ch 27:33 Ahithophel was the **k.** counsellor: 4428
1Ch 27:33 the Archite was the **k.** companion: 4428
1Ch 27:34 the general of the **k.** army was Joab. 4428
1Ch 29:6 the rulers of the **k.** work, offered 4428
2Ch 1:16 the **k.** merchants received the linen 4428
2Ch 7:11 house of the Lord, and the **k.** house: 4428
2Ch 9:11 of the Lord, and to the **k.** palace, 4428
2Ch 9:21 the **k.** ships went to Tarshish with 4428
2Ch 12:9 and the treasures of the **k.** house; 4428
2Ch 12:10 kept the entrance of the **k.** house. 4428
2Ch 16:2 of the Lord and of the **k.** house, 4428
2Ch 18:5 God will deliver it into the **k.** hand. 4428
2Ch 18:25 the city, and to Joash the **k.** son; 4428
2Ch 19:11 of Judah, for all the **k.** matters: 4428
2Ch 21:17 that was found in the **k.** house, 4428
2Ch 22:11 stole him from among the **k.** sons 4428
2Ch 23:3 Behold, the **k.** son shall reign, as 4428
2Ch 23:5 third part shall be at the **k.** house; 4428
2Ch 23:11 Then they brought out the **k.** son, 4428
2Ch 23:15 of the horse gate by the **k.** house, 4428
2Ch 23:20 the high gate into the **k.** house, 4428
2Ch 24:8 at the **k.** commandment they made 4428
2Ch 24:11 chest was brought unto the **k.** office 4428
2Ch 24:11 the **k.** scribe and the high priest's 4428
2Ch 25:16 Arth thou made of the **k.** counsel? 4428
2Ch 25:24 and the treasures of the **k.** house, 4428
2Ch 26:11 of Hananiah, one of the **k.** captains. 4428
2Ch 26:21 his son was over the **k.** house, 4428
2Ch 28:7 Ephraim, slew Maaseiah the **k.** son, 4428
2Ch 29:25 of God the **k.** seer, and Nathan the 4428
2Ch 31:3 He appointed also the **k.** portion of 4428
2Ch 34:20 Asaiah a servant of the **k.**, saying, 4428
2Ch 35:7 these were of the **k.** substance. 4428
2Ch 35:10 according to the **k.** commandment. 4428
2Ch 35:15 Heman, and Jeduthun the **k.** seer; 4428
Ezr 4:14 maintenance from the **k.** palace, 4430
Ezr 4:14 meet for us to see the **k.** dishonour, 4430
Ezr 5:17 made in the **k.** treasure house, 4430
Ezr 6:4 expences be given out of the **k.** house. 4430
Ezr 6:8 of the **k.** goods, even of the tribute 4430
Ezr 7:20 bestow it out of the **k.** treasure 4430
Ezr 7:27 such a thing as this in the **k.** heart, 4428
Ezr 7:28 before all the **k.** mighty princes. 4428
Ezr 8:36 they delivered the **k.** commissions 4428
Ezr 8:36 commissions unto the **k.** lieutenants, 4428
Ne 1:11 man. For I was the **k.** cupbearer. 4428
Ne 2:8 Asaph the keeper of the **k.** forest, 4428
Ne 2:9 river, and gave them the **k.** letters. 4428
Ne 2:14 of the fountain, and to the **k.** pool: 4428
Ne 2:18 the **k.** words that he had spoken 4428
Ne 3:15 the pool of Siloah by the **k.** garden, 4428
Ne 3:25 lieth out from the **k.** high house, 4428
Ne 5:4 borrowed money for the **k.** tribute, 4428
Ne 11:23 **k.** commandment concerning them, 4428
Ne 11:24 was at the **k.** hand in all matters 4428
Es 1:5 of the garden of the **k.** palace; 4428
Es 1:12 to come at the **k.** commandment 4428
Es 1:13 so was the **k.** manner toward all 4428
Es 1:14 which saw the **k.** face, and which 4428
Es 1:18 say this day unto all the **k.** princes, 4428
Es 1:20 the **k.** decree, which he shall make 4428
Es 1:22 sent letters into all the **k.** provinces, 4428
Es 2:2 said the **k.** servants that ministered 4428
Es 2:3 Hege the **k.** chamberlain, keeper of 4428
Es 2:8 when the **k.** commandment and his 4428
Es 2:8 was brought also unto the **k.** house, 4428
Es 2:9 to be given her, out of the **k.** house: 4428
Es 2:13 of the women unto the **k.** house. 4428
Es 2:14 the **k.** chamberlain, which kept the 4428
Es 2:15 but what Hegai the **k.** chamberlain, 4428
Es 2:19 then Mordecai sat in the **k.** gate. 4428
Es 2:21 while Mordecai sat in the **k.** gate, 4428
Es 2:21 two of the **k.** chamberlains, Bigthan 4428
Es 3:2 **k.** servants, that were in the **k.** gate, 4428
Es 3:3 **k.** servants, which were in the **k.** gate, 4428
Es 3:3 thou the **k.** commandment? 4428
Es 3:8 neither keep they the **k.** laws: 4428
Es 3:8 not for the **k.** profit to suffer them. 4428
Es 3:9 to bring it into the **k.** treasuries. 4428
Es 3:12 Then were the **k.** scribes called on 4428
Es 3:12 commanded unto the **k.** lieutenants, 4428
Es 3:12 written, and sealed with the **k.** ring. 4428
Es 3:13 by posts into all the **k.** provinces, 4428
Es 3:15 hastened by the **k.** commandment, 4428
Es 4:2 And came even before the **k.** gate: 4428
Es 4:2 none might enter into the **k.** gate 4428
Es 4:3 whithersoever the **k.** commandmennt 4428
Es 4:5 one of the **k.** chamberlains, whom 4428
Es 4:6 city, which was before the **k.** gate. 4428
Es 4:7 promised to pay to the **k.** treasuries 4428
Es 4:11 All the **k.** servants, and the people 4428
Es 4:11 and the people of the **k.** provinces, 4428
Es 4:13 thou shalt escape in the **k.** house, 4428
Es 5:1 in the inner court of the **k.** house, 4428
Es 5:1 house, over against the **k.** house: 4428
Es 5:9 Haman saw Mordecai in the **k.** gate, 4428
Es 5:13 Mordecai...sitting at the **k.** gate. 4428
Es 6:2 Teresh, two of the **k.** chamberlains, 4428
Es 6:3 the **k.** servants that ministered unto 4428
Es 6:4 the outward court of the **k.** house, 4428
Es 6:5 **k.** servants said unto him, Behold, 4428
Es 6:9 of one of the**k.** most noble princes, 4428
Es 6:10 the Jew, that sitteth at the **k.** gate: 4428
Es 6:12 Mordecai came again to the **k.** gate. 4428
Es 6:14 with him, came the **k.** chamberlains, 4428
Es 7:4 not countervail the **k.** damage. 4428
Es 7:8 the word went out of the **k.** mouth. 4428
Es 7:10 Then was the **k.** wrath pacified. 4428
Es 8:5 which are in all the **k.** provinces; 4428
Es 8:8 as it liketh you, in the **k.** name, 4428
Es 8:8 name, and seal it with the **k.** ring: 4428
Es 8:8 which is written in the **k.** name, 4428
Es 8:8 name, and sealed with the **k.** ring, 4428
Es 8:9 the **k.** scribes called at that time 4428
Es 8:10 sealed it with the **k.** ring, and sent 4428
Es 8:14 pressed on by the **k.** commandment. 4428
Es 8:17 whithersoever the **k.** commandment 4428
Es 9:1 **k.** commandment and his decree 4428
Es 9:4 Mordecai was great in the **k.** house, 4428
Es 9:12 done in the rest of the **k.** provinces? 4428
Es 9:16 Jews that were in the **k.** provinces 4428
Ps 45:5 sharp in the heart of the **k.** enemies; 4428
Ps 45:13 **k.** daughter is all glorious within 4428
Ps 45:15 they shall enter into the **k.** palace. 4428
Ps 61:6 Thou wilt prolong the **k.** life: and 4428
Ps 72:1 thy righteousness unto the **k.** son. 4428
Ps 99:4 **k.** strength also loveth judgment; 4428
Pr 14:28 multitude of people is the **k.** honour: 4428

Pr 14:35 **k.** favour is toward a wise servant:..... 4428
Pr 16:15 In the light of the **k.** countenance....... 4428
Pr 19:12 The **k.** wrath is as the roaring of a..... 4428
Pr 21:1 The **k.** heart is in the hand of the 4428
Ec 8:2 thee to keep the **k.** commandment, ... 4428
Isa 36:21 for the **k.** commandment was, ... 4428
Jer 22:6 Lord unto the **k.** house of Judah; 4428
Jer 26:10 came up from the **k.** house unto the... 4428
Jer 36:12 he went down into the **k.** house,........ 4428
Jer 38:7 eunuchs which was in the **k.** house,.... 4428
Jer 38:8 went forth out of the **k.** house, and.... 4428
Jer 39:4 by the way of the **k.** garden, by the ... 4428
Jer 39:8 the Chaldeans burned the **k.** house,.... 4428
Jer 41:10 even the **k.** daughters, and all the...... 4428
Jer 43:6 and children, and the **k.** daughters,...... 4428
Jer 52:7 walls, which was by the **k.** garden;..... 4428
Jer 52:13 house of the Lord, and the **k.** house;.. 4428
Jer 52:25 them that were near the **k.** person..... 4428
Eze 17:13 hath taken of the **k.** seed, and........... 4410
Da 1:3 and of the **k.** seed, and of the 4410
Da 1:4 in them to stand in the **k.** palace,....... 4428
Da 1:5 a daily provision of the **k.** meat,........ 4428
Da 1:8 with the portion of the **k.** meat,......... 4428
Da 1:13 eat of the portion of the **k.** meat:....... 4428
Da 1:15 did eat the portion of the **k.** meat. 4428
Da 2:10 earth that can shew the **k.** matter: 4430
Da 2:14 Arioch the captain of the **k.** guard, ... 4430
Da 2:15 and said to Arioch the **k.** captain, ... 4430
Da 2:23 made known unto us the **k.** matter...... 4430
Da 3:22 the **k.** commandment was urgent,....... 4430
Da 3:27 captains, and the **k.** counsellors, ... 4430
Da 3:28 him, and have changed the **k.** word, ... 4430
Da 4:31 the word was in the **k.** mouth, ... 4430
Da 5:5 plaister of the wall of the **k.** palace:.... 4430
Da 5:6 the **k.** countenance was changed, ... 4430
Da 5:8 Then came in all the **k.** wise men: 4430
Da 6:12 the king concerning the **k.** decree; 4430
Da 8:27 rose up, and did the **k.** business; 4428
Da 11:6 the **k.** daughter of the south shall....... 4428
Am 7:1 latter growth after the **k.** mowings. 4428
Am 7:13 Beth-el: for it is the **k.** chapel, ... 4428
Am 7:13 chapel, and it is the **k.** court. 4467
Zep 1:8 the princes, and the **k.** children, ... 4428
Zec 14:10 Hananeel unto the **k.** winepresses. 4428
Ac 12:20 Blastus the **k.** chamberlain their *935*
Ac 12:20 was nourished by the **k.** country.......... *937*
Heb 11:23 afraid of the **k.** commandment............. *935*

KINGS See also KINGS'.

Ge 14:5 and the **k.** that were with him, and..... 4428
Ge 14:9 king of Ellasar; four **k.** with five......... 4428
Ge 14:10 the **k.** of Sodom and Gomorrah fled, ... 4428
Ge 14:17 of the **k.** that were with him, at the ... 4428
Ge 17:6 thee, and **k.** shall come out of thee. ... 4428
Ge 17:16 nations; **k.** of people shall be of her.... 4428
Ge 35:11 and **k.** shall come out of thy loins;...... 4428
Ge 36:31 the **k.** that reigned in the land of........ 4428
Nu 31:8 they slew the **k.** of Midian, beside....... 4428
Nu 31:8 Hur, and Reba, five **k.** of Midian:....... 4428
De 3:8 hand of the two **k.** of the Amorites..... 4428
De 3:21 God hath done unto these two **k.**:...... 4428
De 4:47 of Bashan, two **k.** of the Amorites,..... 4428
De 7:24 deliver their **k.** into thine hand,......... 4428
De 31:4 Sihon and to Og, **k.** of the Amorites,.. 4428
Jos 2:10 unto the two **k.** of the Amorites, ... 4428
Jos 5:1 all the **k.** of the Amorites, which........ 4428
Jos 5:1 and all the **k.** of the Canaanites,......... 4428
Jos 9:1 all the **k.** which were on this side....... 4428
Jos 9:10 did to the two **k.** of the Amorites,....... 4428
Jos 10:5 the five **k.** of the Amorites, the 4428
Jos 10:6 all the **k.** of the Amorites that dwell ... 4428
Jos 10:16 these five **k.** fled, and hid themselves . 4428
Jos 10:17 the five **k.** are found hid in a cave...... 4428
Jos 10:22 bring out those five **k.** unto me out 4428
Jos 10:23 brought forth those five **k.** unto him ... 4428
Jos 10:24 brought out those **k.** unto Joshua, ... 4428
Jos 10:24 your feet upon the necks of these **k.**.. 4428
Jos 10:40 and of the springs, and all their **k.**:..... 4428
Jos 10:42 all these **k.** and their land did........... 4428
Jos 11:2 the **k.** that were on the north of the... 4428
Jos 11:5 all these **k.** were met together, ... 4428
Jos 11:12 And all the cities of those **k.**, ... 4428
Jos 11:12 all the **k.** of them, did Joshua take,..... 4428
Jos 11:17 their **k.** he took, and smote them,...... 4428
Jos 11:18 war a long time with all those **k.**........ 4428
Jos 12:1 these are the **k.** of the land, which..... 4428
Jos 12:7 **k.** of the country which Joshua and..... 4428
Jos 12:24 one: all the **k.** thirty and one............ 4428
Jos 24:12 even the two **k.** of the Amorites;....... 4428
Jg 1:7 Threescore and ten **k.**, having their.... 4428
Jg 5:3 Hear, O ye **k.**; give ear, O ye.......... 4428
Jg 5:19 The **k.** came and fought, then 4428
Jg 5:19 fought the **k.** of Canaan in Taanach..... 4428
Jg 8:5 Zebah and Zalmunna, **k.** of Midian. 4428
Jg 8:12 took the two **k.** of Midian, Zebah 4428
Jg 8:26 purple raiment that was on the **k.** 4428
1Sa *general* *title* Called, The First Book Of The **K.**.....
1Sa 14:47 Edom, and against the **k.** of Zobah, ... 4428
1Sa 27:6 pertaineth unto the **k.** of Judah 4428
2Sa *general* *title* The Second Book Of The **K.**.........
2Sa 10:19 **k.** that were servants to Hadarezer 4428
2Sa 11:1 the time when **k.** go forth to battle,.... 4428
1Ki *general* *title* The First Book Of The **K.**.......... 4428
1Ki *general* *title* Called, The Third Book Of The **K.**, ...
1Ki 3:13 there shall not be any among the **k.**.... 4428
1Ki 4:24 all the **k.** on this side the river: 4428
1Ki 4:34 from all **k.** of the earth, which had 4428
1Ki 10:15 and of all the **k.** of Arabia, and of....... 4428
1Ki 10:23 king Solomon exceeded all the **k.** 4428
1Ki 10:29 and so for all the **k.** of the Hittites, ... 4428
1Ki 10:29 and for the **k.** of Syria, did they......... 4428
1Ki 14:19 of the chronicles of the **k.** of Israel..... 4428
1Ki 14:29 of the chronicles of the **k.** of Judah?.... 4428
1Ki 15:7, 23 chronicles of the **k.** of Judah? 4428
1Ki 15:31 of the chronicles of the **k.** of Israel? ... 4428
1Ki 16:5, 14,20,27 chronicles of...**k.** of Israel? ... 4428
1Ki 16:33 all the **k.** of Israel that were before 4428
1Ki 20:1 were thirty and two **k.** with him, ... 4428
1Ki 20:12 he and the **k.** in the pavilions, that..... 4428
1Ki 20:16 in the pavilions, he and the **k.**, ... 4428
1Ki 20:16 thirty and two **k.** that helped him. 4428
1Ki 20:24 Take the **k.** away, every man out of... 4428
1Ki 20:31 have heard that the **k.** of the house.... 4428
1Ki 20:31 house of Israel are merciful **k.**: 4428
1Ki 22:39 the chronicles of the **k.** of Israel? 4428
1Ki 22:45 the chronicles of the **k.** of Judah? 4428
2Ki *general* *title* The Second Book Of The **K.**, ... 4428
2Ki *general* *title* The Fourth Book Of The **K.**..............
2Ki 1:18 the chronicles of the **k.** of Israel?......... 4428
2Ki 3:10, 13 called these three **k.** together, ... 4428
2Ki 3:21 that the **k.** were come up to fight 4428
2Ki 3:23 **k.** are surely slain, and they have....... 4428
2Ki 7:6 against us the **k.** of the Hittites, ... 4428
2Ki 7:6 the **k.** of the Egyptians, to come......... 4428
2Ki 8:18 walked in the way of the **k.** of Israel,.. 4428
2Ki 8:23 the chronicles of the **k.** of Judah? 4428
2Ki 10:4 two **k.** stood not before him: how 4428
2Ki 10:34 the chronicles of the **k.** of Israel?....... 4428
2Ki 11:19 And he sat on the throne of the **k.**...... 4428
2Ki 12:18 **k.** of Judah, had dedicated, and his 4428
2Ki 12:19 the chronicles of the **k.** of Judah? 4428
2Ki 13:8, 12 chronicles of the **k.** of Israel? 4428
2Ki 13:13 in Samaria with the **k.** of Israel.......... 4428
2Ki 14:15 the chronicles of the **k.** of Israel?....... 4428
2Ki 14:16 in Samaria with the **k.** of Israel;......... 4428
2Ki 14:18 the chronicles of the **k.** of Judah? 4428
2Ki 14:28 the chronicles of the **k.** of Israel? 4428
2Ki 14:29 fathers, even with the **k.** of Israel; 4428
2Ki 15:6 the chronicles of the **k.** of Judah? 4428
2Ki 15:11, 15 chronicles of the **k.** of Israel. 4428
2Ki 15:21 the chronicles of the **k.** of Israel?....... 4428
2Ki 15:26, 31 the chronicles of the **k.** of Israel. ... 4428
2Ki 15:36 the chronicles of the **k.** of Judah? 4428
2Ki 16:3 walked in the way of the **k.** of Israel,.. 4428
2Ki 16:19 the chronicles of the **k.** of Judah? 4428
2Ki 17:2 not as the **k.** of Israel that were 4428
2Ki 17:8 of Israel, and of the **k.** of Israel, ... 4428
2Ki 18:5 him among all the **k.** of Judah, ... 4428
2Ki 19:11 **k.** of Assyria have done to all lands, ... 4428
2Ki 19:17 **k.** of Assyria have destroyed the........ 4428
2Ki 20:20 the chronicles of the **k.** of Judah? 4428
2Ki 21:17, 25 chronicles of the **k.** of Judah? 4428
2Ki 23:5 **k.** of Judah had ordained to burn........ 4428
2Ki 23:11 **k.** of Judah had given to the sun, ... 4428
2Ki 23:12 which the **k.** of Judah had made, ... 4428
2Ki 23:19 **k.** of Israel had made to provoke 4428
2Ki 23:22 in all the days of the **k.** of Israel, ... 4428
2Ki 23:22 nor of the **k.** of Judah; 4428
2Ki 23:28 the chronicles of the **k.** of Judah? 4428
2Ki 24:5 of the chronicles of the **k.** of Judah?.... 4428
2Ki 25:28 **k.** that were with him in Babylon; 4428
1Ch 1:43 **k.** that reigned in the land of Edom 4428
1Ch 9:1 book of the **k.** of Israel and Judah, ... 4428
1Ch 16:21 yea, he reproved **k.** for their sakes, ... 4428
1Ch 19:9 and the **k.** that were come were by.... 4428
1Ch 20:1 at the time that **k.** go out to battle, ... 4428
2Ch 1:12 such as none of the **k.** have had that .. 4428
2Ch 1:17 horses for all the **k.** of the Hittites, ... 4428
2Ch 1:17 and for the **k.** of Syria, by their......... 4428
2Ch 9:14 all the **k.** of Arabia and governors of... 4428
2Ch 9:22 passed all the **k.** of the earth in 4428
2Ch 9:23 **k.** of the earth sought the presence... 4428
2Ch 9:26 And he reigned over all the **k.** from.... 4428
2Ch 16:11 book of the **k.** of Judah and Israel. 4428
2Ch 20:34 in the book of the **k.** of Israel........... 4428
2Ch 21:6, 13 in the way of the **k.** of Israel, ... 4428
2Ch 21:20 but not in the sepulchres of the **k.**. 4428
2Ch 24:16 in the city of David among the **k.**,...... 4428
2Ch 24:25 him not in the sepulchres of the **k.**. 4428
2Ch 24:27 in the story of the book of the **k.**....... 4428
2Ch 25:26 book of the **k.** of Judah and Israel? 4428
2Ch 26:23 the burial which belonged to the **k.**;..... 4428
2Ch 27:7 book of the **k.** of Israel and Judah. 4428
2Ch 28:2 in the ways of the **k.** of Israel,.......... 4428
2Ch 28:16 Ahaz send unto the **k.** of Assyria 4428
2Ch 28:23 gods of the **k.** of Syria help them,....... 4428
2Ch 28:26 book of the **k.** of Judah and Israel. 4428
2Ch 28:27 the sepulchres of the **k.** of Israel: 4428
2Ch 30:6 out of the hand of the **k.** of Assyria.... 4428
2Ch 32:4 Why should the **k.** of Assyria come, ... 4428
2Ch 32:32 book of the **k.** of Judah and Israel. 4428
2Ch 33:18 in the book of the **k.** of Israel........... 4428
2Ch 34:11 which the **k.** of Judah had destroyed. .. 4428
2Ch 35:18 the **k.** of Israel keep such a passover.. 4428
2Ch 35:27 book of the **k.** of Israel and Judah. 4428
2Ch 36:8 book of the **k.** of Israel and Judah: 4428
Ezr 4:13 endamage the revenue of the **k.**......... 4430
Ezr 4:15 and hurtful unto **k.** and provinces, ... 4430
Ezr 4:19 hath made insurrection against **k.**, ... 4430
Ezr 4:20 been mighty **k.** also over Jerusalem, ... 4430
Ezr 4:22 damage grow to the hurt of the **k.**? 4430
Ezr 6:12 there destroy all **k.** and people, ... 4430
Ezr 7:12 Artaxerxes, king of **k.**, unto Ezra........ 4428
Ezr 9:7 have we, our **k.**, and our priests,......... 4428
Ezr 9:7 into the hand of the **k.** of the lands,.... 4428
Ezr 9:9 us in the sight of the **k.** of Persia,...... 4428
Ne 9:24 with their **k.**, and the people of the 4428
Ne 9:32 upon us, on our **k.**, on our princes, ... 4428
Ne 9:32 since the time of the **k.** of Assyria 4428
Ne 9:34 Neither have our **k.**, our princes,....... 4428
Ne 9:37 the **k.** whom thou hast set over us...... 4428
Es 10:2 of the chronicles of the **k.** of Media 4428
Job 3:14 With **k.** and counsellors of the earth, .. 4428
Job 12:18 He looseth the bond of **k.**, and.......... 4428
Job 36:7 but with **k.** are they on the throne; 4428
Ps 2:2 **k.** of the earth set themselves, and 4428
Ps 2:10 Be wise now therefore, O ye **k.**: be ... 4428
Ps 48:4 For, lo, the **k.** were assembled, they.. 4428
Ps 68:12 **K.** of armies did flee apace: and she ... 4428
Ps 68:14 Almighty scattered **k.** in it, it was 4428
Ps 68:29 shall **k.** bring presents unto thee......... 4428
Ps 72:10 **k.** of Tarshish and of the isles shall 4428
Ps 72:10 **k.** of Sheba and Seba shall offer gifts. ..4428
Ps 72:11 all **k.** shall fall down before him:......... 4428
Ps 76:12 he is terrible to the **k.** of the earth..... 4428
Ps 89:27 higher than the **k.** of the earth. 4428
Ps 102:15 and all the **k.** of the earth thy glory.... 4428
Ps 105:14 Yea, he reproved **k.** for their sakes; ... 4428
Ps 105:30 in the chambers of their **k.**. 4428
Ps 110:5 shall strike through **k.** in the day of.... 4428
Ps 119:46 of thy testimonies also before **k.**, ... 4428
Ps 135:10 great nations and slew mighty **k.**;....... 4428
Ps 136:17 To him which smote great **k.**: for....... 4428
Ps 136:18 And slew famour **k.**: for his mercy 4428
Ps 138:4 the **k.** of the earth shall praise thee, ... 4428
Ps 144:10 is he that giveth salvation unto **k.**:...... 4428
Ps 148:11 **K.** of the earth, and all people; 4428
Ps 149:8 To bind their **k.** with chains, and........ 4428
Pr 8:15 By me **k.** reign, and princes decree.... 4428
Pr 16:12 It is an abomination to **k.** to commit ... 4428
Pr 16:13 Righteous lips are the delight of **k.**; 4428
Pr 22:29 business? he shall stand before **k.**; 4428
Pr 25:2 but the honour of **k.** is to search out .. 4428
Pr 25:3 and the heart of **k.** is unsearchable. 4428
Pr 31:3 ways to that which destroyeth **k.**. 4428
Pr 31:4 It is not for **k.**, Lemuel, it is not....... 4428
Pr 31:4 it is not for **k.** to drink wine; nor for .. 4428
Ec 2:8 the peculiar treasure of **k.** and of 4428
Isa 1:1 Ahaz, and Hezekiah, **k.** of Judah. 4428
Isa 7:16 shall be forsaken of both her **k.**. 4428
Isa 10:8 Are not my princes altogether **k.**? 4428

Isa 14:9 thrones all the **k.** of the nations. 4428
Isa 14:18 All the **k.** of the nations, even all of 4428
Isa 19:11 of the wise, the son of ancient **k.**? 4428
Isa 24:21 the **k.** of the earth upon the earth. 4428
Isa 37:11 heard what the **k.** of Assyria have 4428
Isa 37:18 the **k.** of Assyria have laid waste all 4428
Isa 41:2 him, and made him ruler over **k.**? 4428
Isa 45:1 I will loose the loins of **k.**, to open 4428
Isa 49:7 **K.** shall see and arise, princes also 4428
Isa 49:23 And **k.** shall be thy nursing fathers, 4428
Isa 52:15 **k.** shall shut their mouths at him: 4428
Isa 60:3 **k.** to the brightness of thy rising 4428
Isa 60:10 their **k.** shall minister unto thee: 4428
Isa 60:11 and that their **k.** may be brought 4428
Isa 60:16 and shalt suck the breast of **k.**: 4428
Isa 62:2 righteousness, and all **k.** thy glory: 4428
Jer 1:18 whole land, against the **k.** of Judah, 4428
Jer 2:26 they, their **k.**, their princes, and 4428
Jer 8:1 out the bones of the **k.** of Judah, 4428
Jer 13:13 the **k.** that sit upon David's throne, 4428
Jer 17:19 whereby the **k.** of Judah come in, 4428
Jer 17:20 word of the Lord, ye **k.** of Judah, 4428
Jer 17:25 city **k.** and princes sitting upon the 4428
Jer 19:3 the word of the Lord, O **k.** of Judah, 4428
Jer 19:4 have known, nor the **k.** of Judah, 4428
Jer 19:13 and the houses of the **k.** of Judah, 4428
Jer 20:5 all the treasures of the **k.** of Judah 4428
Jer 22:4 **k.** sitting upon the throne of David, 4428
Jer 25:14 great **k.** shall serve themselves of 4428
Jer 25:18 cities of Judah, and the **k.** thereof, 4428
Jer 25:20 and all the **k.** of the land of Uz, 4428
Jer 25:20 the **k.** of the land of the Philistines, 4428
Jer 25:22 **k.** of Tyrus, and all the **k.** of Zidon, 4428
Jer 25:22 the **k.** of the isles which are beyond 4428
Jer 25:24 And all the **k.** of Arabia, 4428
Jer 25:24 and all the **k.** of the mingled people 4428
Jer 25:25 **k.** of Zimri, and all the **k.** of Elam, 4428
Jer 25:25 and all the **k.** of the Medes, 4428
Jer 25:26 all the **k.** of the north, far and near, 4428
Jer 27:7 great **k.** shall serve themselves of 4428
Jer 32:32 they, their **k.**, their princes, their 4428
Jer 33:4 the houses of the **k.** of Judah, 4428
Jer 34:5 former **k.** which were before thee, 4428
Jer 44:9 the wickedness of the **k.** of Judah, 4428
Jer 44:17 fathers, our **k.**, and our princes, 4428
Jer 44:21 fathers, your **k.**, and your princes, 4428
Jer 46:25 Egypt, with their gods, and their **k.**; 4428
Jer 50:41 and many **k.** shall be raised up from 4428
Jer 51:11 up the spirit of the **k.** of the Medes: 4428
Jer 51:28 nations with the **k.** of the Medes, 4428
Jer 52:32 **k.** that were with him in Babylon, 4428
La 4:12 The **k.** of the earth, and all the 4428
Eze 26:7 king of Babylon, a king of **k.**, 4428
Eze 27:33 thou didst enrich the **k.** of the earth 4428
Eze 27:35 and their **k.** shall be sore afraid, 4428
Eze 28:17 I will lay thee before **k.**, that they 4428
Eze 32:10 **k.** shall be horribly afraid for thee, 4428
Eze 32:29 Edom, her **k.**, and all her princes, 4428
Eze 43:7 defile, neither they, nor their **k.**, 4428
Eze 43:7 carcases of their **k.** in their high 4428
Eze 43:9 the carcases of their **k.**, far from me, 4428
Da 2:21 he removeth **k.**, and setteth up **k.**: 4430
Da 2:37 Thou, O king, art a king of **k.**: for 4430
Da 2:44 in the days of these **k.** shall the God 4430
Da 2:47 is a God of gods, and a Lord of **k.**, 4430
Da 7:17 beasts, which are four, are four **k.**, 4430
Da 7:24 kingdom are ten **k.** that shall arise: 4430
Da 7:24 first, and he shall subdue three **k.** 4430
Da 8:20 are the **k.** of Media and Persia. 4428
Da 9:6 which spake in thy name to our **k.**, 4428
Da 9:8 to our **k.**, to our princes, and to our 4428
Da 10:13 remained there with the **k.** of Persia 4428
Da 11:2 stand up yet three **k.** in Persia; 4428
Ho 1:1 Ahaz, and Hezekiah, **k.** of Judah, 4428
Ho 7:7 all their **k.** are fallen: there is 4428
Ho 8:4 They have set up **k.**, but not by me: 4428
Mic 1:1 Ahaz, and Hezekiah, **k.** of Judah, 4428
Mic 1:14 shall be a lie to the **k.** of Israel. 4428
Hab 1:10 they shall scoff at the **k.**, and the 4428
Mt 10:18 **governors and k. for my sake,** *935*
Mt 17:25 **of whom do the k. of the earth take** *935*
Mk 13:9 **before rulers and k. for my sake,** *935*
Lu 10:24 **prophets and k. have desired to see** *935*
Lu 21:12 **k. and rulers for my name's sake** *935*
Lu 22:25 **The k. of the Gentiles exercise** *935*
Ac 4:26 The **k.** of the earth stood up, and *935*
Ac 9:15 **name before the Gentiles, and k.,** *935*
1Co 4:8 ye have reigned as **k.** without us:
1Ti 2:2 For **k.**, and for all that are in *935*
1Ti 6:15 the King of **k.**, and Lord of lords; *936*
Heb 7:1 returning from the slaughter of **k.**, *935*
Re 1:5 the prince of the **k.** of the earth. *935*
Re 1:6 hath made us **k.** and priests unto *935*
Re 5:10 us unto our God **k.** and priests: *935*
Re 6:15 the **k.** of the earth, and the great *935*
Re 10:11 and nations, and tongues, and **k.**. *935*
Re 16:12 the way of the **k.** of the east might *935*
Re 16:14 go forth unto the **k.** of the earth *935*
Re 17:2 With whom the **k.** of the earth have *935*
Re 17:10 there are seven **k.**: five are fallen, *935*
Re 17:12 horns which thou sawest are ten **k.**, *935*
Re 17:12 receive power as **k.** one hour with *935*
Re 17:14 he is Lord of lords, and King of **k.**: *935*
Re 17:18 reigneth over the **k.** of the earth. *935*
Re 18:3 the **k.** of the earth have committed *935*
Re 18:9 the **k.** of the earth, who have *935*
Re 19:16 King of **K.**, And Lord Of Lords. *935*
Re 19:18 That ye may eat the flesh of **k.**, *935*
Re 19:19 the beast, and the **k.** of the earth, *935*
Re 21:24 the **k.** of the earth do bring their *935*

KINGS'
Ps 45:9 **k.** daughters were among thy 4428
Pr 30:28 her hands, and is in **k.** palaces. 4428
Da 11:27 both these **k.** hearts shall be to do 4428
Mt 11:8 **wear soft clothing are in k. houses.** *935*
Lu 7:25 **and live delicately, are in k. courts,** *933*

KING'S-DALE See KING'S and DALE.

KING'S-POOL See KING'S and POOL.

KINSFOLK See also KINSFOLKS.
Job 19:14 My **k.** have failed, and my familiar 7138
Lu 2:44 they sought him among their **k.** *4773*

KINSFOLKS
1Ki 16:11 neither of his **k.**, nor of his 1350
2Ki 10:11 his great men, and his **k.**, and his 3045
Lu 21:16 **and brethren, and k., and friends** *4773*

KINSMAN See also KINSMAN'S; KINSMEN.
Nu 5:8 the man have no **k.** to recompence 1350
Nu 27:11 give his inheritance unto his **k.** 7607
Ru 2:1 Naomi had a **k.** of her of husband's, 3045
Ru 3:9 handmaid; for thous art a near **k.** 1350
Ru 3:12 it is true that I am thy near **k.**: 1350
Ru 3:12 howbeit there is a **k.** nearer than I. 1350
Ru 3:13 perform unto thee the part of a **k.**, 1350
Ru 3:13 will not do the part of a **k.** to thee, 1350
Ru 3:13 will I do the part of a **k.** to thee, 1350
Ru 4:1 the **k.** of whom Boaz spake came 1350
Ru 4:3 he said unto the **k.**, Naomi, that is 1350
Ru 4:6 the **k.** said, I cannot redeem it for 1350
Ru 4:8 the **k.** said unto Boaz, Buy it for 1350
Ru 4:14 not left thee this day without a **k.**,
Joh 18:26 being his **k.** whose ear Peter cut *4773*
Ro 16:11 Salute Herodion my **k.**. Greet them *4773*

KINSMAN'S
Ru 3:13 let him do the **k.** part: but if he 1350

KINSMEN
Ru 2:20 of kin unto us, one of our next **k.** 1350
Ps 38:11 sore; and my **k.** stand afar off. 7138
Lu 14:12 **neither thy k., nor thy rich** *4773*
Ac 10:24 together his **k.** and near friends. *4773*
Ro 9:3 my **k.** according to the flesh: *4773*
Ro 16:7 Andronicus and Junia, my **k.**, and *4773*
Ro 16:21 and Jason, and Sosipater, my **k.**, *4773*

KINSWOMAN See also KINSWOMEN.
Le 18:12 sister: she is thy father's near **k.** 7607
Le 18:13 for she is thy mother's near **k.** 7607
Pr 7:4 and call understanding thy **k.**: 4129

KINSWOMEN
Le 18:17 for they are her near **k.**: it is 7608

KIR (kur) See also KIR-HARESH.
2Ki 16:9 the people of it captive to **K.**, 7024
Isa 15:1 **K.** of Moab is laid waste, 7024
Isa 22:6 and **K.** uncovered the shield. 7024
Am 1:5 shall go into captivity unto **K.**, 7024
Am 9:7 Caphtor, and the Syrians from **K.**? 7024

KIR-HARASETH (kur-har'-a-seth) See also KIR-HARESETH.
2Ki 3:25 in **K.** left they the stones thereof; 7025

KIR-HARESETH (kur-har'-e-seth) See alo KIRHARESH.
Isa 16:7 foundations of **K.** shall ye mourn; 7025

KIR-HARESH (kur-ha'-resh) See also KIR-HARASETH; KIR-HARESEH; KIR-HERES.
Isa 16:11 and mine inward parts of **K.**. 7025

KIR-HERES (kur-he'-res) See also KIR-HARESH.
Jer 48:31 shall mourn for the men of **K.**. 7025
Jer 48:36 sound like pipes for the men of **K.**; 7025

KIRIATHAIM (kir-e-a-thay'-im) See also KIRTAN; KIRJATH-AIM.
Ge 14:5 and the Emims in Shaveh **K.**, 7741
Jer 48:1 **K.** is confounded and taken: 7156
Jer 48:23 upon **K.**, and upon Beth-gamul, 7156
Eze 25:9 Baal-meon, and **K.**, 7156

KIRIOTH (kir'-e-oth) See also KERIOTH.
Am 2:2 it shall devour the palaces of **K.** 7152

KIRJATH (kur'-jath) See also KIRJATH-ARBA; KIRJATH- ARIM; KIRJATH-BAAL; KIRJATH-HUZOTH; KIRJATH-JEARIM KIRJATH-SAN-NAH; KIRJATH-SEPHER.
Jos 18:28 Jerusalem, Gibeath, and **K.**; 7157

KIRJATHAIM (kur''-jath-a'-im) See also KIRIATHAIM.
Nu 32:37 Heshbon, and Elealeh, and **K.**, 7156
Jos 13:19 And **K.**, and Sibmah, and 7156
1Ch 6:76 suburbs, and **K.** with her suburbs 7156

KIRJATH-ARBA (kur''-jath-ar'-bah) See also HEBRON.
Ge 23:2 And Sarah died in **K.**; the same 7153
Jos 14:15 the name of Hebron before was **K.**; 7153
Jos 15:54 and **K.**, which is Hebron, and Zior; 7153
Jos 20:7 and **K.**, which is Hebron, in the 7153
Jg 1:10 name of Hebron before was **K.**:) 7153
Ne 11:25 the children of Judah dwelt at **K.**, 7153

KIRJATH-ARIM (kur''-jath-a'-rim) See also KIRJATH-JEARIM.
Ezr 2:25 The children of **K.**, Chephirah, 7157

KIRJATH-BAAL (kur''-jath-ba'-al) See also BAALAH; KIR-JATH-JEARIM.
Jos 15:60 **K.**, which is Kirjath-jearim, and 7154
Jos 18:14 the goings out thereof were at **K.**, 7154

KIRJATH-HUZOTH (kur''-jath-hu'-zoth)
Nu 22:39 Balak, and they came unto **K.**. 7155

KIRJATH-JEARIM (kur''-jath-je'-a-rim) See also KIRJATH; KIRJATH-ARIM; KIRJATH-BAAL.
Jos 9:17 Chephirah, and Beeroth, and **K.** 7157
Jos 15:9 was drawn to Baalah, which is **K.** 7155
Jos 15:60 Kirjath-baal, which is **K.**, and 7155
Jos 18:14 **K.**, a city of the children of Judah: 7155
Jos 18:15 quarter was from the end of **K.**, 7155
Jg 18:12 they went up, and pitched in **K.**, 7155
Jg 18:12 this day: behold, it is behind **K.** 7155
1Sa 6:21 sent...to the inhabitants of **K.**, 7155
1Sa 7:1 the men of **K.** came, and fetched 7155
1Sa 7:2 to pass, while the ark abode in **K.**, 7155
1Ch 2:50 Ephratah; Shobal the father of **K.**, 7155
1Ch 2:52 Shobal the father of **K.** had sons; 7155
1Ch 2:53 the families of **K.**; the Ithrites, 7155
1Ch 13:5 to bring the ark of God from **K.** 7155
1Ch 13:6 all Israel, to Baalah, that is, to **K.**, 7155
2Ch 1:4 had David brought up from **K.** to 7155
Ne 7:29 The men of **K.**, Chephirah, and 7155
Jer 26:20 Urijah the son of Shemaiah of **K.**, 7155

KIRJATH-SANNAH (kur''-jath-san'-nah) See also KIR-JATH-SEPHER; SANSANNAH.
Jos 15:49 Dannah, and **K.**, which is Debir, 7158

KIRJATH-SEPHER (kur''-jath-se'-fer) See also DEBIR; KIR-JATH-SANNAH.
Jos 15:15 the name of Debir before was **K.**. 7158
Jos 15:16 He that smiteth **K.**, and taketh it, 7158
Jg 1:11 the name of Debir before was **K.** 7158
Jg 1:12 He that smiteth **K.**, and taketh it, 7158

KISH (kish) See also CIS.
1Sa 9:1 of Benjamin, whose name was **K.**, 7027
1Sa 9:3 asses of **K.** Saul's father were lost. 7027
1Sa 9:3 **K.** said to Saul his son, Take now 7027
1Sa 10:11 that is come unto the son of **K.**? 7027
1Sa 10:21 and Saul the son of **K.** was taken: 7027
1Sa 14:51 **K.** was the father of Saul; and Ner 7027
2Sa 21:14 in the sepulchre of **K.** his father: 7027
1Ch 8:30 son Abdon, and Zur, and **K.**, and 7027
1Ch 8:33 Ner begat **K.**, and **K.** begat Saul, 7027

1Ch 9:36 son Abdon, then Zur, and **K.**, and...... 7027
1Ch 9:39 Ner begat **K.**; and **K.** begat Saul;....... 7027
1Ch 12:1 because of Saul the son of **K.**........... 7027
1Ch 23:21 the sons of Mahli; Eleazar, and **K.**. 7027
1Ch 23:22 brethren the sons of **K.** took them. 7027
1Ch 24:29 Concerning **K.**; the son of **K.** was...... 7027
1Ch 26:28 Saul the son of **K.**, and Abner the...... 7027
2Ch 29:12 sons of Merari, **K.** the son of Abdi, ... 7027
Es 2:5 Shimei, the son of **K.**, a Benjamite; 7027

KISHI (kish'-i) See also KUSHAIAH.
1Ch 6:44 Ethan the son of **K.**, the son of......... 7029

KISHION (kish'-e-on) See also KEDESH; KISHON.
Jos 19:20 And Rabbith, and **K.**, and Abez,......... 7191

KISHON (ki'-shon) See also KISHION; KISON.
Jos 21:28 of Issachar, **K.** with her suburbs,....... 7191
Jg 4:7 draw unto thee to the river **K.** 7028
Jg 4:13 of the Gentiles unto the river of **K.**. ... 7028
Jg 5:21 The river of **K.** swept them away, ... 7028
Jg 5:21 that ancient river, the river **K.**. 7028
1Ki 18:40 brought them down to the brook **K.**,.... 7028

KISON (ki'-son) See also KISHON.
Ps 83:9 as to Jabin, at the brook of **K.**........... 7028

KISS See also KISSED; KISSES.
Ge 27:26 near now, and **k.** me, my son. 5401
Ge 31:28 to **k.** my sons and my daughters?......... 5401
2Sa 20:9 beard with the right hand to **k.** him. ... 5401
1Ki 19:20 thee, **k.** my father and my mother,..... 5401
Ps 2:12 **K.** the Son, lest he be angry, and...... 5401
Pr 24:26 shall **k.** his lips that giveth a right 5401
Ca 1:2 Let him **k.** me with the kisses of his... 5401
Ca 8:1 find thee without, I would **k.** thee; 5401
Ho 13:2 the men that sacrifice **k.** the calves. ... 5401
Mt 26:48 Whomsoever I shall **k.**, that same *5368*
Mk 14:44 Whomsoever I shall **k.**, that same *5368*
Lu 7:45 **Thou gavest me no k.; but this**..... *5370*
Lu 7:45 **in hath not ceased to k. my feet**.... *2705*
Lu 22:47 drew near unto Jesus to **k.** him. *5368*
Lu 22:48 **thou the Son of man with a k.?**...... *5370*
Ro 16:16 Salute one another with an holy **k.**. *5370*
1Co 16:20 ye one another with an holy **k.**......... *5370*
2Co 13:12 Greet one another with an holy **k.**...... *5370*
1Th 5:26 all the brethren with an holy **k.**......... *5370*
1Pe 5:14 ye one another with a **k.** of charity..... *5370*

KISSED
Ge 27:27 And he came near, and **k.** him:.......... 5401
Ge 29:11 Jacob **k.** Rachel, and lifted up his 5401
Ge 29:13 him, and embraced him, and **k.** him, ... 5401
Ge 31:55 and **k.** his sons and his daughters,...... 5401
Ge 33:4 and fell on his neck, and **k.** him: 5401
Ge 45:15 Moreover he **k.** all his brethren, ... 5401
Ge 48:10 he **k.** them, and embraced them. 5401
Ge 50:1 and wept upon him, and **k.** him.......... 5401
Ex 4:27 in the mount of God, and **k.** him. 5401
Ex 18:7 law, and did obeisance, and **k.** him; 5401
Ru 1:9 Then she **k.** them; and they lifted up.. 5401
Ru 1:14 and Orpah **k.** her mother in law;........ 5401
1Sa 10:1 poured it upon his head, and **k.** him,... 5401
1Sa 20:41 they **k.** one another, and wept one..... 5401
2Sa 14:33 the king: and the king **k.** Absalom. 5401
2Sa 15:5 his hand, and took him, and **k.** him..... 5401
2Sa 19:39 the king **k.** Barzillai, and blessed........ 5401
1Ki 19:18 every mouth which hath not **k.** him. 5401
Job 31:27 or my mouth hath **k.** my hand: 5401
Ps 85:10 righteousness and peace have **k.**......... 5401
Pr 7:13 So she caught him, and **k.** him, and.... 5401
Mt 26:49 said, Hail, master; and **k.** him. *2705*
Mk 14:45 saith, Master, master; and **k.** him. *2705*
Lu 7:38 and **k.** his feet, and anointed them...... *2705*
Lu 15:20 **and fell on his neck, and k. him**. .. *2705*
Ac 20:37 and fell on Paul's neck, and **k.** him, ... *2705*

KISSES
Pr 27:6 the **k.** of an enemy are deceitful. 5390
Ca 1:2 kiss me with the **k.** of his mouth:....... 5390

KITE
Le 11:14 vulture, and the **k.** after his kind; 344
De 14:13 the **k.**, and the vulture after his kind, ... 344

KITHLISH (kith'-lish)
Jos 15:40 Cabbon, and Lahmam, and **K.**,........... 3798

KITRON (ki'-tron) See also KATTAH.
Jg 1:30 drive out the inhabitants of **K.**, ... 7003

KITTIM (kit'-tim) See also CHITTIM.
Ge 10:4 and Tarshish, **K.**, and Dodanim.......... 3794
1Ch 1:7 and Tarshish, **K.**, and Dodanim.......... 3794

KNEAD See also KNEADED; KNEADINGTROUGHS.
Ge 18:6 of fine meal, **k.** it, and make cakes..... 3888
Jer 7:18 and the women **k.** their dough, to 3888

KNEADED
1Sa 28:24 took flour, and **k.** it, and did bake 3888
2Sa 13:8 she took flour, and **k.** it, and made..... 3888
Ho 7:4 raising after he hath **k.** the dough,...... 3888

KNEADINGTROUGHS
Ex 8:3 into thine ovens, and into thy **k.**: 4863
Ex 12:34 **k.** being bound up in their clothes 4863

KNEE See also KNEES.
Ge 41:43 they cried before him, Bow the **k.**...........
Isa 45:23 That unto me every **k.** shall bow, ... 1290
Mt 27:29 they bowed the **k.** before him, and..........
Ro 11:4 have not bowed the **k.** to the image ... *1119*
Ro 14:11 the Lord, every **k.** shall bow to me, ... *1119*
Php 2:10 name of Jesus every **k.** should bow, ... *1119*

KNEEL See also KNEELED; KNEELING.
Ge 24:11 he made his camels to **k.** down.......... 1288
Ps 95:6 let us **k.** before the Lord our maker. .. 1288

KNEELED
2Ch 6:13 **k.** down upon his knees before 1288
Da 6:10 he **k.** upon his knees three times......... 1289
Mk 10:17 came one running, and **k.** to him,....... *1120*
Lu 22:41 case, and **k.** down, and prayed, .. *5087,1119*
Ac 7:60 he **k.** down, and cried with a...... *5087,1119*
Ac 9:40 forth, and **k.** down, and prayed;.. *5087,1119*
Ac 20:36 he **k.** down, and prayed with...... *5087,1119*
Ac 21:5 we **k.** down on the shore, and.... *5087,1119*

KNEELING
1Ki 8:54 from **k.** on his knees with his........... 3766
Mt 17:14 a certain man, **k.** down to him,.......... *1120*
Mk 1:40 beseeching him, and **k.** down to him, .. *1120*

KNEES
Ge 30:3 she shall bear upon my **k.**, that I 1290
Ge 48:12 them out from between his **k.**, ... 1290
Ge 50:23 were brought up upon Joseph's **k.**. 1290
De 28:35 The Lord shall smite thee in the **k.**, ... 1290
Jg 7:5 boweth down upon his **k.** to drink. 1290
Jg 7:6 down upon their **k.** to drink water. 1290
Jg 16:19 made him sleep upon her **k.**; and 1290
1Ki 8:54 kneeling on his **k.** with hands 1290
1Ki 18:42 and put his face between his **k.**, ... 1290
1Ki 19:18 **k.** which have not bowed unto Baal, ... 1290
2Ki 1:13 and fell on his **k.** before Elijah, ... 1290
2Ki 4:20 he sat on her **k.** till noon, and then 1290
2Ch 6:13 kneeled down upon his **k.** before all.... 1290
Ezr 9:5 I fell upon my **k.**, and spread out 1290
Job 3:12 Why did the **k.** prevent me? or why ... 1290
Job 4:4 hast strengthened the feeble **k.**.......... 1290
Ps 109:24 My **k.** are weak through fasting; 1290
Isa 35:3 hands, and confirm the feeble **k.**. 1290
Isa 66:12 sides, and be dandled upon her **k.**. 1290
Eze 7:17 and all **k.** shall be weak as water. 1290
Eze 21:7 and all **k.** shall be weak as water: 1290
Eze 47:4 waters; the waters were to the **k.**...... 1290
Da 5:6 and his **k.** smote one against............... 755
Da 6:10 kneeled upon his **k.** three times a 1291
Da 10:10 which set me upon my **k.** and upon 1290
Na 2:10 and the **k.** smite together, and 1290
Mr 15:19 bowing their **k.** worshipped him. *1119*
Lu 5:8 he fell down at Jesus' **k.**, saying,......... *1119*
Eph 3:14 I bow my **k.** unto the Father of our.... *1119*
Heb 12:12 hand down, and the feeble **k.**; *1119*

KNEW See also FOREKNEW; KNEWEST.
Ge 3:7 and they **k.** that they were naked;...... 3045
Ge 4:1 Adam **k.** Eve his wife; and she.......... 3045
Ge 4:17 Cain **k.** his wife; and she conceived, ... 3045
Ge 4:25 Adam **k.** his wife again; and she.......... 3045
Ge 8:11 Noah **k.** that the waters were abated.. 3045
Ge 9:24 **k.** what his younger son had done...... 3045
Ge 28:16 Lord is in this place; and I **k.** it not.... 3045
Ge 31:32 **k.** not that Rachel had stolen them. 3045
Ge 37:33 he **k.** it, and said, It is my son's 5234
Ge 38:9 Onan **k.** that the seed should not 3045
Ge 38:16 he **k.** not that she was his daughter.... 3045
Ge 38:26 son. And he **k.** her again no more..... 3045
Ge 39:6 he **k.** not ought he had, save the 3045
Ge 42:7 saw his brethren, and he **k.** them,...... 5234
Ge 42:8 Joseph **k.** his brethren, but they **k.** 5234
Ge 42:23 they **k.** not that Joseph understood..... 3045
Ex 1:8 over Egypt, which **k.** not Joseph......... 3045
Nu 22:34 I **k.** not that thou stoodest in the 3045
Nu 24:16 and **k.** the knowledge of the most 3045
De 8:16 manna, which thy fathers **k.** not,........ 3045
De 9:24 Lord from the day that I **k.** you......... 3045
De 29:26 gods whom they **k.** not, and whom...... 3045
De 32:17 to gods whom they **k.** not, to new 3045
De 33:9 brethren, nor **k.** his own children: 3045
De 34:10 whom the Lord **k.** face to face, ... 3045
Jg 2:10 which **k.** not the Lord, nor yet the..... 3045
Jg 3:2 least such as before **k.** nothing 3045
Jg 11:39 had vowed: and she **k.** no man. 3045
Jg 13:16 Manoah **k.** not that he was an angel ... 3045
Jg 13:21 **k.** that he was an angel of the Lord.... 3045
Jg 14:4 mother **k.** not that it was of the......... 3045
Jg 18:3 they **k.** the voice of the young man 5234
Jg 19:25 they **k.** her, and abused her all the 3045
Jg 20:34 they **k.** not that evil was near them. ... 3045
1Sa 1:19 Elkanah **k.** Hannah his wife; and 3045
1Sa 2:12 of Belial; they **k.** not the Lord. 3045
1Sa 3:20 **k.** that Samuel was established to....... 3045
1Sa 10:11 all that **k.** him beforetime saw that 3045
1Sa 14:3 **k.** not that Jonathan was gone. 3045
1Sa 18:28 **k.** that the Lord was with David, ... 3045
1Sa 20:9 If I **k.** certainly that evil were........... 3045
1Sa 20:33 Jonathan **k.** that it was determined 3045
1Sa 20:39 the lad **k.** not any thing: only 3045
1Sa 20:39 Jonathan and David **k.** the matter. 3045
1Sa 22:15 thy servant **k.** nothing of all this, ... 3045
1Sa 22:17 because they **k.** when he fled, and 3045
1Sa 22:22 I **k.** it that day, when Doeg the 3045
1Sa 23:9 David **k.** that Saul secretly practised... 3045
1Sa 26:12 and no man saw it, nor **k.** it, neither .. 3045
1Sa 26:17 Saul **k.** David's voice, and said,......... 5234
2Sa 3:26 well of Sirah; but David **k.** it not......... 3045
2Sa 11:16 where he **k.** that valiant men were. 3045
2Sa 11:20 **k.** ye not that they would shoot the.... 3045
2Sa 15:11 simplicity, and they **k.** not any thing. .. 3045
2Sa 18:29 tumult, but I **k.** not what it was......... 3045
2Sa 22:44 which I **k.** not shall serve me. 3045
1Ki 1:4 to him: but the king **k.** her not. 3045
1Ki 18:7 and he **k.** him, and fell on his face,..... 5234
2Ki 4:39 of pottage: for they **k.** them not. 3045
2Ch 33:13 **k.** that the Lord he was God............ 3045
Ne 2:16 the rulers **k.** not whither I went, ... 3045
Es 1:13 the wise men, which **k.** the times, ... 5234
Es 1:13 all that **k.** law and judgment: 5234
Job 2:12 and **k.** him not, they lifted up their..... 5234
Job 23:3 I knew where I might find him!.......... 3045
Job 29:16 cause which I **k.** not I searched out.... 3045
Job 42:3 wonderful for me, which I **k.** not........ 3045
Ps 35:11 my charge things that I **k.** not. 3045
Ps 35:15 together against me, and I **k.** it not;... 3045
Pr 24:12 Behold, we **k.** it not; doth not he....... 3045
Isa 42:16 blind by a way that they **k.** not;......... 3045
Isa 42:25 on fire round about, yet he **k.** not; 3045
Isa 48:4 I **k.** that thou art obstinate, and......... 1847
Isa 48:7 shouldest say, Behold, I **k.** them......... 3045
Isa 48:8 I **k.** that thou wouldest deal very 3045
Isa 55:5 nations that **k.** not thee shall run........ 3045
Jer 1:5 formed thee in the belly I **k.** thee; 3045
Jer 2:8 they that handle the law **k.** me not: ... 3045
Jer 11:19 I **k.** not that they had devised 3045
Jer 32:8 Then I **k.** that this was the word 3045
Jer 41:4 slain Gedaliah, and no man **k.** it, ... 3045
Jer 44:3 serve other gods, whom they **k.** not,.. 3045
Jer 44:15 the men which **k.** that their wives 3045
Eze 10:20 I **k.** that they were the cherubims. 3045
Eze 19:7 And he **k.** their desolate palaces, ... 3045
Da 5:21 he **k.** that the most high God ruled...... 3046
Da 6:10 when Daniel **k.** that the writing.......... 3046
Da 11:38 his fathers **k.** not shall he honour 3045
Ho 8:4 have made princes, and I **k.** it not:..... 3045
Ho 11:3 but they **k.** not that I healed them..... 3045
Jon 1:10 the men **k.** that he fled from the........ 3045
Jon 4:2 I **k.** that thou art a gracious God,....... 3045
Zec 7:14 all the nations whom they **k.** not. 3045
Zec 11:11 **k.** that it was the word of the Lord. ... 3045
Mt 1:25 **k.** her not till she had brought *1097*
Mt 7:23 **profess unto them, I never k. you:** .*1097*
Mt 12:15 But when Jesus **k.** it, he withdrew *1097*
Mt 12:25 Jesus **k.** their thoughts, and said *1492*
Mt 17:12 **already, and they k. him not,**........ *1912*
Mt 24:39 **k. not until the flood came, and**.... *1097*

Mt 25:24 **I k. thee that thou art an...man,** *1097*
Mt 27:18 For he **k.** that for envy they had *1492*
Mk 1:34 to speak, because they **k.** him *1492*
Mk 6:33 them departing, and many **k.** him, *1921*
Mk 6:38 when they **k.**, they say, Five, and *1097*
Mk 6:54 of the ship, straight way they **k.** him, *1921*
Mk 8:17 when Jesus **k.** it, he saith unto *1097*
Mk 12:12 **k.** that he had spoken the parable *1097*
Mk 15:10 he **k.** that the chief priests had *1097*
Mk 15:45 when he **k.** it of the centurion, he *1097*
Lu 2:43 Joseph and his mother **k.** not of it *1097*
Lu 4:41 for they **k.** that he was Christ.
Lu 6:8 But he **k.** their thoughts, and said *1492*
Lu 7:37 when she **k.** that Jesus sat at meat *1921*
Lu 9:11 when they **k.** it, followed him: *1097*
Lu 12:47 **servant, which k. his lord's will,** *1097*
Lu 12:48 **he that k. not, and did commit** *1097*
Lu 18:34 neither **k.** they the things which *1097*
Lu 23:7 as soon as he **k.** that he belonged *1921*
Lu 24:31 were opened, and they **k.** him; *1921*
Joh 1:10 by him, and the world **k.** him not *1097*
Joh 1:31 I **k.** him not: but that he should *1492*
Joh 1:33 I **k.** him not: but he that sent me *1492*
Joh 2:9 wine, and **k.** not whence it was: *1492*
Joh 2:9 servants which drew the water **k.**;) *1492*
Joh 2:24 unto them, because he **k.** all men, *1097*
Joh 2:25 of man: for he **k.** what was in man *1097*
Joh 4:1 the Lord **k.** how the Pharisees had *1097*
Joh 4:53 father **k.** that it was at the same *1097*
Joh 5:6 **k.** that he had been now a long *1097*
Joh 6:6 he himself **k.** what he would do *1492*
Joh 6:61 When Jesus **k.** in himself that his *1492*
Joh 6:64 For Jesus **k.** from the beginning *1492*
Joh 11:42 **I k. that thou hearest me always:** *1492*
Joh 11:57 that, if any man **k.** where he were, *1097*
Joh 12:9 the Jews therefore **k.** that he was *1097*
Joh 13:1 Jesus **k.** that his hour was come *1492*
Joh 13:11 For he **k.** who should betray him; *1492*
Joh 13:28 **k.** for what intent he spake this *1097*
Joh 16:19 **k.** that they were desirous to ask *1097*
Joh 18:2 which betrayed him, **k.** the place: *1492*
Joh 20:9 For as yet they **k.** not the scripture, *1492*
Joh 20:14 and **k.** not that it was Jesus *1492*
Joh 21:4 disciples **k.** not that it was Jesus *1492*
Ac 3:10 **k.**...it was he which sat for alms *1921*
Ac 7:18 king arose, which **k.** not Joseph *1492*
Ac 9:30 Which when the brethren **k.**, they *1921*
Ac 12:14 And when she **k.** Peter's voice, she *1921*
Ac 13:27 because they **k.** him not, nor yet the *50*
Ac 16:3 **k.** all that his father was a Greek *1492*
Ac 19:32 **k.** not wherefore they were come *1492*
Ac 19:34 when they **k.** that he was a Jew, *1921*
Ac 22:29 after he **k.** that he was a Roman, *1921*
Ac 26:5 Which **k.** me from the beginning, *4267*
Ac 27:39 it was day, they **k.** not the land: *1921*
Ac 28:1 **k.** that the island was called Melita *1921*
Ro 1:21 when they **k.** God, they glorified *1097*
1Co 1:21 the world by wisdom **k.** not God, *1097*
1Co 2:8 of the princes of this world **k.**: *1097*
2Co 5:21 him to be sin for us, who **k.** no sin; *1097*
2Co 12:2 **k.** a man in Christ above fourteen *1492*
2Co 12:3 I **k.** such a man, (whether in the *1492*
Ga 4:8 when ye **k.** not God, ye did service *1492*
Col 1:6 and **k.** the grace of God in truth: *1921*
Col 2:1 that ye **k.** what great conflict I *1492*
1Jo 3:1 us not, because it **k.** him not *1097*
Jude 5 though ye once **k.** this, how that *1492*
Re 19:12 a name written, that no man **k.**, *1492*

KNEWEST

De 8:3 with manna, which thou **k.** not, 3045
Ru 2:11 people which thou **k.** not heretofore 3045
Ne 9:10 for thou **k.** that they dealt proudly 3045
Ps 142:3 within me, then thou **k.** my path 3045
Isa 48:8 thou heardest not; yea, thou **k.** not; 3045
Da 5:22 heart, though thou **k.** all this; 3046
Mt 25:26 **thou k. that I reap where I sowed** *1492*
Lu 19:22 **Thou k. that I was an austere** *1492*
Lu 19:44 **k. not the time of thy visitation** *1097*
Joh 4:10 **If thou k. the gift of God, and who** *1492*

KNIFE See KNIVES; PENKNIFE.

Ge 22:6 took the fire in his hand, and a **k.**; 3979
Ge 22:10 hand, and took the **k.** to slay his son 3979
Jg 19:29 he took a **k.**, and laid hold on his 3979
Pr 23:2 put a **k.** to thy throat, if thou be a 7915
Eze 5:1 take thee a sharp **k.**, take thee a 2719
Eze 5:2 part, and smite about it with a **k.**: 2719

KNIT

Jg 20:11 the city, **k.** together as one man 2270
1Sa 18:1 Jonathan was **k.** with the soul of 7194
1Ch 12:17 mine heart shall be **k.** unto you: 3162
Ac 10:11 great sheet **k.** at the four corners, *1210*
Col 2:2 being **k.** together in love, and unto *4822*
Col 2:19 and **k.** together, increaseth with the *4822*

KNIVES

Jos 5:2 thee sharp **k.**, and circumcise 2719
Jos 5:3 him sharp **k.**, and circumcised the 2719
1Ki 18:28 their manner with **k.** and lancets, 2719
Ezr 1:9 of silver, nine and twenty **k.**, 4252
Pr 30:14 swords, and their jaw teeth as **k.**, 3979

KNOCK See also KNOCKED; KNOCKETH; KNOCKING.

Mt 7:7 **k., and it shall be opened unto** *2925*
Lu 11:9 **k., and it shall be opened unto** *2925*
Lu 13:25 **stand without, and to k. at the** *2925*
Re 3:20 **I stand at the door, and k.** *2925*

KNOCKED

Ac 12:13 And as Peter **k.** at the door of the *2925*

KNOCKETH

Ca 5:2 is the voice of my beloved that **k.**, 1849
Mt 7:8 **to him that k. it shall be opened** *2925*
Lu 11:10 **to him that k. it shall be opened** *2925*
Lu 12:36 **that when he cometh and k., they** *2925*

KNOCKING

Ac 12:16 But Peter continued **k.**: and when *2925*

KNOP See also KNOPS.

Ex 25:33 a **k.** and a flower in one branch; 3730
Ex 25:33 branch, with a **k.** and a flower: 3730
Ex 25:35, 35,35 **k.** under two branches of the 3730
Ex 37:19 in one branch, a **k.** and a flower; 3730
Ex 37:19 in another branch, a **k.** and a flower: 3730
Ex 37:21, 21,21 **k.** under two branches of the 3730

KNOPS

Ex 25:31 his **k.**, and his flowers, shall be of 3730
Ex 25:34 with their **k.** and their flowers 3730
Ex 25:36 **k.** and their branches shall be of 3730
Ex 37:17 his **k.**, and his flowers were of the 3730
Ex 37:20 almonds, his **k.**, and his flowers: 3730
Ex 37:22 **k.** and their branches were of the 3730
1Ki 6:18 carved with **k.** and open flowers: 6497
1Ki 7:24 about there were **k.** compassing it, 6497
1Ki 7:24 the **k.** were cast in two rows, when 6497

KNOW See also FOREKNOW; KNEW; KNOWEST; KNOWETH; KNOWING; KNOWN.

Ge 3:5 God doth **k.** that in the day ye eat 3045
Ge 3:22 as one of us, to **k.** good and evil: 3045
Ge 4:9 I **k.** not: Am I my brother's keeper? 3045
Ge 12:11 I **k.** that thou art a fair woman to 3045
Ge 15:8 shall I **k.** that I shall inherit it? 3045
Ge 15:13 **K.** of a surety that thy seed shall 3045
Ge 18:19 For I **k.** him, that he will command 3045
Ge 18:21 come unto me; and if not, I will **k.** 3045
Ge 19:5 out unto us, that we may **k.** them 3045
Ge 20:6 Yea, I **k.** that thou didst this in the 3045
Ge 20:7 **k.** thou that thou shalt surely die, 3045
Ge 22:12 for now I **k.** that thou fearest God, 3045
Ge 24:14 I **k.** that thou hast shewed kindness 3045
Ge 27:2 old, I **k.** not the day of my death: 3045
Ge 29:5 **K.** ye Laban the son of Nahor? 3045
Ge 29:5 And they said, We **k.** him 3045
Ge 31:6 And ye **k.** that with all my power I 3045
Ge 37:32 **k.** now whether it be thy son's coat 5234
Ge 42:33 shall I **k.** that ye are true men; 3045
Ge 42:34 then shall I **k.** that ye are not spies, 3045
Ge 43:7 we certainly **k.** that he would say, 3045
Ge 44:27 **k.** that my wife bare me two sons: 3045
Ge 48:19 and said, I **k.** it, my son, I **k.** it: 3045
Ex 3:7 taskmasters; for I **k.** their sorrows; 3045
Ex 4:14 I **k.** that he can speak well 3045
Ex 5:2 I **k.** not the Lord, neither will I let 3045
Ex 6:7 ye shall **k.** that I am the Lord your 3045
Ex 7:5 shall **k.** that I am the Lord, when I 3045
Ex 7:17 thou shalt **k.** that I am the Lord: 3045
Ex 8:10 **k.** that there is none like unto the 3045
Ex 8:22 end mayest **k.** that I am the Lord 3045
Ex 9:14 **k.** that there is none like me in all 3045
Ex 9:29 **k.** how that the earth is the Lord's 3045
Ex 9:30 **k.** that ye will not yet fear the Lord 3045
Ex 10:2 ye may **k.** how that I am the Lord 3045
Ex 10:26 we **k.** not with what we must serve 3045
Ex 11:7 may **k.** how that the Lord doth put 3045
Ex 14:4 may **k.** that I am the Lord 3045
Ex 14:18 shall **k.** that I am the Lord, when I 3045
Ex 16:6 shall **k.** that the Lord hath brought 3045
Ex 16:12 ye shall **k.** that I am the Lord your 3045
Ex 18:11 I **k.** that the Lord is greater than all 3045
Ex 18:16 make them **k.** the statutes of God, 3045
Ex 23:9 for ye **k.** the heart of a stranger, 3045
Ex 29:46 they shall **k.** that I am the Lord 3045
Ex 31:13 that ye may **k.** that I am the Lord 3045
Ex 33:5 that I may **k.** what to do unto thee 3045
Ex 33:12 not let me **k.** whom thou wilt send 3045
Ex 33:12 I **k.** thee by name, and thou hast 3045
Ex 33:13 that I may **k.** thee, that I may find 3045
Ex 33:17 in my sight, and I **k.** thee by name 3045
Ex 36:1 **k.** how to work all manner of work 3045
Le 23:43 That your generations may **k.** that 3045
Nu 14:31 **k.** the land which ye have despised 3045
Nu 14:34 ye shall **k.** my breach of promise 3045
Nu 16:28 ye shall **k.** that the Lord hath sent 3045
Nu 22:19 that I may **k.** what the Lord will say 3045
De 3:19 (for I **k.** that ye have much cattle,) 3045
De 4:35 mightest **k.** that the Lord he is God; 3045
De 4:39 **K.** therefore this day, and consider 3045
De 7:9 **K.** therefore that the Lord thy God, 3045
De 8:2 to **k.** what was in thine heart, 3045
De 8:3 not, neither did thy fathers **k.**; 3045
De 8:3 thee **k.** that man doth not live by 3045
De 11:2 And **k.** ye this day: for I speak not 3045
De 13:3 to **k.** whether ye love the Lord your 3045
De 18:21 How shall we **k.** the word which the 3045
De 22:2 if thou **k.** him not, then thou shalt 3045
De 29:6 that ye might **k.** that I am the Lord 3045
De 29:16 ye **k.** how we have dwelt in the land 3045
De 31:21 I **k.** their imagination which they 3045
De 31:27 I **k.** thy rebellion, and thy stiff neck: 3045
De 31:29 For I **k.** that after my death ye will 3045
Jos 2:9 **k.** that the Lord hath given you the 3045
Jos 3:4 **k.** the way by which ye must go: 3045
Jos 3:7 may **k.** that, as I was with Moses, 3045
Jos 3:10 **k.** that the living God is among you 3045
Jos 4:22 Then ye shall let your children **k.**, 3045
Jos 4:24 earth might **k.** the hand of the Lord, 3045
Jos 22:22 he knoweth, and Israel he shall **k.**; 3045
Jos 23:13 **K.** for a certainty that the Lord 3045
Jos 23:14 **k.** in all your hearts and in all your 3045
Jg 3:2 Israel might **k.**, to teach them war, 3045
Jg 3:4 to **k.** whether they would hearken 3045
Jg 6:37 shall I **k.** that thou wilt save Israel 3045
Jg 17:13 **k.** I that the Lord will do me good, 3045
Jg 18:5 **k.** whether our way which we go 3045
Jg 18:14 **k.** that there is in these houses an 3045
Jg 19:22 thine house, that we may **k.** him 3045
Ru 3:11 **k.** that thou art a virtuous woman 3045
Ru 3:14 up before one could **k.** another 5234
Ru 3:18 thou **k.** how the matter will fall: 3045
Ru 4:4 it, then tell me, that I may **k.**: 3045
1Sa 3:7 Samuel did not yet **k.** the Lord, 3045
1Sa 6:9 **k.** that it is not his hand that smote 3045
1Sa 14:38 **k.** and see wherein this sin hath 3045
1Sa 17:28 I **k.** thy pride, and the naughtiness 3045
1Sa 17:46 may **k.** that there is a God in Israel 3045
1Sa 17:47 **k.**...the Lord saveth not with sword 3045
1Sa 20:3 Let not Jonathan **k.** this, lest he be 3045
1Sa 20:30 I **k.** that thou hast chosen the son 3045
1Sa 21:2 no man **k.** any thing of the business 3045
1Sa 22:3 till I **k.** what God will do for me 3045
1Sa 23:22 **k.** and see his place where his haunt 3045
1Sa 24:11 **k.** thou and see that there is neither 3045
1Sa 24:20 I **k.**...that thou shalt surely be king, 3045
1Sa 25:11 whom I **k.** not whence they be? 3045
1Sa 25:17 **k.** and consider what thou wilt do; 3045
1Sa 28:1 **K.** thou assuredly, that thou shalt 3045
1Sa 28:2 shalt **k.** what thy servant can do 3045
1Sa 29:9 I **k.** that thou art good in my sight, 3045
2Sa 3:25 to **k.** thy going out and thy coming 3045
2Sa 3:25 in, and to **k.** all that thou doest 3045
2Sa 3:38 **K.** ye not that there is a prince and 3045
2Sa 7:21 things, to make thy servant **k.** them 3045
2Sa 14:20 **k.** all things that are in the earth 3045
2Sa 19:20 servant doth **k.** that I have sinned: 3045
2Sa 19:22 do not I **k.** that I am this day king 3045
2Sa 24:2 I may **k.** the number of the people 3045
1Ki 2:37 **k.** for certain that thou shalt surely 3045
1Ki 2:42 **K.** for a certain, on the day thou 3045
1Ki 3:7 I **k.** not how to go out or come in 3045
1Ki 8:38 which shall **k.** every man the plague 3045

1Ki 8:43 people of the earth may **k.** thy name, 3045
1Ki 8:43 that they may **k.** that this house, 3045
1Ki 8:60 earth may **k.** that the Lord is God, 3045
1Ki 17:24 I **k.** that thou art a man of God, 3045
1Ki 18:12 shall carry thee whither I **k.** not; 3045
1Ki 18:37 may **k.** that thou art the Lord God, 3045
1Ki 20:13 thou shalt **k.** that I am the Lord. 3045
1Ki 20:28 and ye shall **k.** that I am the Lord. 3045
1Ki 22:3 **K.** ye that Ramoth in Gilead is ours, 3045
2Ki 2:3,5 Yea, I **k.** it; hold ye your peace. 3045
2Ki 5:8 he shall **k.** that there is a prophet 3045
2Ki 5:15 I **k.** that there is no God in all the 3045
2Ki 7:12 They **k.** that we be hungry; 3045
2Ki 8:12 I **k.** the evil that thou wilt do unto 3045
2Ki 9:11 he said unto them, Ye **k.** the man, 3045
2Ki 10:10 **K.** now that there shall fall unto 3045
2Ki 17:26 **k.** not the manner of the God of the 3045
2Ki 17:26 they **k.** not the manner of the God 3045
2Ki 19:19 may **k.** that thou art the Lord God, 3045
2Ki 19:27 I **k.** thy abode, and thy going out, 3045
1Ch 12:32 to **k.** what Israel ought to do; 3045
1Ch 21:2 of them to me, that I may **k.** it. 3045
1Ch 28:9 son, **k.** thou the God of thy father, 3045
1Ch 29:17 I **k.** also, my God, that thou triest 3045
2Ch 2:8 I **k.** that thy servants can skill to 3045
2Ch 6:29 every one shall **k.** his own sore and 3045
2Ch 6:33 of the earth may **k.** thy name, 3045
2Ch 6:33 **k.** that this house which I have 3045
2Ch 12:8 that they may **k.** my service, and 3045
2Ch 13:5 Ought ye not to **k.** that the Lord 3045
2Ch 20:12 neither **k.** we what to do: but our 3045
2Ch 25:16 I **k.** that God hath determined to 3045
2Ch 32:13 **K.** ye not what I and my fathers 3045
2Ch 32:31 might **k.** all that was in his heart. 3045
Ezr 4:15 and **k.** that this city is a rebellious 3046
Ezr 7:25 all such as **k.** the laws of thy God; 3046
Ezr 7:25 teach ye them that **k.** them not. 3046
Ne 4:11 They shall not **k.**, neither see, till 3045
Es 2:11 to **k.** how Esther did, and what 3045
Es 4:5 to **k.** what it was, and why it was. 3045
Es 4:11 people of the king's provinces, do **k.**, 3045
Job 5:24 thou shalt **k.** that thy tabernacle 3045
Job 5:25 shalt **k.** also that thy seed shall be 3045
Job 5:27 hear it, and **k.** thou it for thy good. 3045
Job 7:10 shall his place **k.** him any more. 5234
Job 8:9 but of yesterday, and **k.** nothing, 3045
Job 9:2 I **k.** it is so of a truth: but how 3045
Job 9:5 the mountains, and they **k.** not: 3045
Job 9:21 perfect, yet would I not **k.** my soul: 3045
Job 9:28 I **k.** that thou wilt not hold me 3045
Job 10:13 heart: I **k.** that this is with thee. 3045
Job 11:6 **K.** therefore that God exacteth of 3045
Job 11:8 than hell; what canst thou **k.**? 3045
Job 13:2 What ye **k.**, the same do I...also: 1847
Job 13:2 What ye...the same do I **k.** also: 3045
Job 13:18 cause; I **k.** that I shall be justified. 3045
Job 13:23 make me to **k.** my transgression 3045
Job 15:9 What knowest thou, that we **k.** not? 3045
Job 19:6 **K.** now that God hath overthrown 3045
Job 19:25 For I **k.** that my redeemer liveth, 3045
Job 19:29 that ye may **k.** there is a judgment. 3045
Job 21:19 rewardeth him, and he shall **k.** it. 3045
Job 21:27 Behold, I **k.** your thoughts, and 3045
Job 21:29 and do ye not **k.** their tokens, 5234
Job 22:13 thou sayest, How doth God **k.**? 3045
Job 23:5 I would **k.** the words which he 3045
Job 24:1 they that **k.** him not see his days? 5234
Job 24:13 they **k.** not the ways thereof, nor 5234
Job 24:16 daytime: they **k.** not the light. 3045
Job 24:17 if one **k.** them, they are in the 5234
Job 30:23 I **k.** that thou wilt bring...death, 3045
Job 31:6 that God may **k.** mine integrity. 3045
Job 32:22 I **k.** not to give flattering titles; 3045
Job 34:4 **k.** among ourselves what is good. 3045
Job 36:26 God is great, and we **k.** him not, 3045
Job 37:7 man; that all men may **k.** his work. 3045
Job 37:15 Dost thou **k.** when God disposed 3045
Job 37:16 **k.** the balancings of the clouds, 3045
Job 38:12 the dayspring to **k.** his place; 3045
Job 38:20 that thou shouldest **k.** the paths 995
Job 42:2 I **k.** that thou canst do every thing, 3045
Ps 4:3 But **k.** that the Lord hath set apart 3045
Ps 9:10 they that **k.** thy name will put their 3045
Ps 9:20 nations may **k.** themselves...men. 3045
Ps 20:6 Now **k.** I that the Lord saveth his 3045
Ps 36:10 lovingkindness...them that **k.** thee; 3045

Ps 39:4 Lord, make me to **k.** mine end, 3045
Ps 39:4 it is; that I may **k.** how frail I am. 3045
Ps 41:11 this I **k.** that thou favourest me, 3045
Ps 46:10 Be still, and **k.** that I am God: 3045
Ps 50:11 I **k.** all the fowls of the mountains: 3045
Ps 51:6 thou shalt make me to **k.** wisdom. 3045
Ps 56:9 back: this I **k.**; for God is for me. 3045
Ps 59:13 them **k.** that God ruleth in Jacob 3045
Ps 71:15 day; I **k.** not the numbers thereof. 3045
Ps 73:11 And they say, How doth God **k.**? 3045
Ps 73:16 When I thought to **k.** this, it was 3045
Ps 78:6 generation to come might **k.** them, 3045
Ps 82:5 They **k.** not, neither will they 3045
Ps 83:18 That men may **k.** that thou, whose 3045
Ps 87:4 and Babylon to them that **k.** me: 3045
Ps 89:15 the people that **k.** the joyful sound: 3045
Ps 94:10 man knowledge, shall not he **k.**?
Ps 100:3 **K.** ye that the Lord he is God: it 3045
Ps 101:4 me: I will not **k.** a wicked person. 3045
Ps 103:16 place thereof shall **k.** it no more. 5234
Ps 109:27 they may **k.** that this is thy hand; 3045
Ps 119:75 I **k.**...that thy judgments are right, 3045
Ps 119:125 that I may **k.** thy testimonies. 3045
Ps 135:5 For I **k.** that the Lord is great, 3045
Ps 139:23 me, O God, and **k.** my heart: 3045
Ps 139:23 heart: try me, and **k.** my thoughts: 3045
Ps 140:12 **k.** that the Lord will maintain the 3045
Ps 142:4 was no man that would **k.** me: 5234
Ps 143:8 cause me to **k.** the way wherein I 3045
Pr 1:2 To **k.** wisdom and instruction; to 3045
Pr 4:1 and attend to **k.** understanding. 3045
Pr 4:19 they **k.** not at what they stumble. 3045
Pr 5:6 that thou canst not **k.** them. 3045
Pr 10:32 righteous **k.** what is acceptable: 3045
Pr 22:21 That I might make thee **k.** the 3045
Pr 24:12 keepeth thy soul, doth not he **k.** it? 3045
Pr 25:8 less thou **k.** not what to do in the end
Pr 27:23 diligent to **k.** the state of...flocks, 3045
Pr 29:7 the wicked regardeth not to **k.** it. 1847
Pr 30:18 for me, yea, four which I **k.** not: 3045
Ec 1:17 I gave my heart to **k.** wisdom, 3045
Ec 1:17 and to **k.** madness and folly: 3045
Ec 3:12 I **k.** that there is no good in them, 3045
Ec 3:14 I **k.** that, whatsoever God doeth, it 3045
Ec 7:25 I applied mine heart to **k.**, and to 3045
Ec 7:25 to **k.** the wickedness of folly, even 3045
Ec 8:12 yet surely I **k.** that it shall be well 3045
Ec 8:16 I applied mine heart to **k.** wisdom, 3045
Ec 8:17 though a wise man think to **k.** it, 3045
Ec 9:5 the living **k.** that they shall die: but 3045
Ec 9:5 the dead **k.** not any thing, neither 3045
Ec 11:9 but **k.** thou, that for all these things 3045
Ca 1:8 If thou **k.** not, O thou fairest 3045
Isa 1:3 Israel doth not **k.**, my people doth 3045
Isa 5:19 nigh and come, that we may **k.** it! 3045
Isa 7:15 that he may **k.** to refuse the evil, 3045
Isa 7:16 the child shall **k.** to refuse the evil, 3045
Isa 9:9 And all the people shall **k.**, even 3045
Isa 19:12 and let them **k.** what the Lord of 3045
Isa 19:21 and the Egyptians shall **k.** the Lord 3045
Isa 37:20 all the kingdoms of the earth may **k.** 3045
Isa 37:28 But I **k.** thy abode, and thy going 3045
Isa 41:20 That they may see, and **k.**, and 3045
Isa 41:22 them, and **k.** the latter end of them; 3045
Isa 41:23 that we may **k.** that ye are gods: 3045
Isa 41:26 the beginning, that we may **k.**? 3045
Isa 43:10 that ye may **k.** and believe me, 3045
Isa 43:19 spring forth; shall ye not **k.** it? 3045
Isa 44:8 yea, there is no God; I **k.** not any. 3045
Isa 44:9 own witnesses; they see not, nor **k.**; 3045
Isa 45:3 that thou mayest **k.** that I, the 3045
Isa 45:6 may **k.** from the rising of the sun, 3045
Isa 47:8 shall I **k.** the loss of children: 3045
Isa 47:11 shalt not **k.** from whence it riseth: 3045
Isa 47:11 suddenly, which thou shalt not **k.**. 3045
Isa 48:6 things, and thou didst not **k.** them. 3045
Isa 49:23 thou shalt **k.** that I am the Lord: 3045
Isa 49:26 all flesh shall **k.** that I the Lord 3045
Isa 50:4 that I should **k.** how to speak a 3045
Isa 50:7 I **k.** that I shall not be ashamed. 3045
Isa 51:7 unto me, ye that **k.** righteousness, 3045
Isa 52:6 my people shall **k.** my name: 3045
Isa 52:6 they shall **k.** in that day that I am
Isa 58:2 daily, and delight to **k.** my ways, 1847
Isa 59:8 The way of peace they **k.** not; 3045
Isa 59:8 goeth therein shall not **k.** peace. 3045

Isa 59:12 as for our iniquities, we **k.** them; 3045
Isa 60:16 and thou shalt **k.** that I the Lord 3045
Isa 66:18 I **k.** their works and their thoughts:
Jer 2:19 **k.** therefore and see that it is an 3045
Jer 2:23 valley, **k.** what thou hast done: 3045
Jer 5:1 of Jerusalem, and see now, and **k.**, 3045
Jer 5:4 for they **k.** not the way of the Lord, 3045
Jer 6:18 Therefore hear, ye nations, and **k.**, 3045
Jer 6:27 thou mayest **k.** and try their way. 3045
Jer 7:9 after other gods whom ye **k.** not; 3045
Jer 8:7 people **k.** not the judgment of the 3045
Jer 9:3 and they **k.** not me, saith the Lord. 3045
Jer 9:6 through deceit they refuse to **k.** me, 3045
Jer 10:23 I **k.** that the way of man is not in 3045
Jer 10:25 upon the heathen that **k.** thee not, 3045
Jer 11:18 me knowledge of it, and I **k.** it: 3045
Jer 13:12 **k.** that every bottle shall be filled 3045
Jer 14:18 about into a land that they **k.** not. 3045
Jer 15:15 **k.** that for thy sake I have suffered 3045
Jer 16:13 land into a land that ye **k.** not, 3045
Jer 16:21 I will this once cause them to **k.**, 3045
Jer 16:21 shall **k.** that my name is The Lord. 3045
Jer 17:9 desperately wicked: who can **k.** it? 3045
Jer 22:16 was not this to **k.** me? saith the 1847
Jer 22:28 into a land which they **k.** not? 3045
Jer 24:7 I will give them an heart to **k.** me, 3045
Jer 26:15 **k.** ye for certain, that if ye put me 3045
Jer 29:11 For I **k.** the thoughts that I think 3045
Jer 29:16 **k.** that thus saith the Lord of the
Jer 29:23 even I **k.**, and am a witness, saith 3045
Jer 31:34 for they shall all **k.** me,
Jer 31:34 his brother, saying, **K.** the Lord: 3045
Jer 36:19 and let no man **k.** where ye be. 3045
Jer 38:24 Let no man **k.** of these words, and 3045
Jer 40:14 Dost thou certainly **k.** that Baalis 3045
Jer 40:15 Nethaniah, and no man shall **k.** it: 3045
Jer 42:19 **k.** certainly that I have admonished 3045
Jer 42:22 **k.** certainly that ye shall die by the 3045
Jer 44:28 shall **k.** whose words shall stand, 3045
Jer 44:29 **k.** that my words shall surely stand 3045
Jer 48:17 all ye that **k.** his name, say, How is 3045
Jer 48:30 I **k.** his wrath, saith the Lord; but 3045
Eze 2:5 **k.** that there hath been a prophet 3045
Eze 5:13 **k.** that I the Lord have spoken it 3045
Eze 6:7 and ye shall **k.** that I am the Lord. 3045
Eze 6:10 they shall **k.** that I am the Lord, 3045
Eze 6:13 Shall ye **k.** that I am the Lord, 3045
Eze 6:14 they shall **k.** that I am the Lord. 3045
Eze 7:4 and ye shall **k.** that I am the Lord. 3045
Eze 7:9 shall **k.** I am the Lord that smiteth. 3045
Eze 7:27 they shall **k.** that I am the Lord. 3045
Eze 11:5 I **k.** the things that come into your 3045
Eze 11:10 and ye shall **k.**that I am the Lord. 3045
Eze 11:12 And ye shall **k.** that I am the Lord: 3045
Eze 12:15 they shall **k.** that I am the Lord. 3045
Eze 12:16 they shall **k.** that I am the Lord. 3045
Eze 12:20 and ye shall **k.** that I am the Lord. 3045
Eze 13:9 ye shall **k.** that I am the Lord God. 3045
Eze 13:14, 21,23 shall **k.** that I am the Lord. 3045
Eze 14:8 and ye shall **k.** that I am the Lord. 3045
Eze 14:23 **k.**...I have not done without cause 3045
Eze 15:7 and ye shall **k.** that I am the Lord, 3045
Eze 16:2 Jerusalem to **k.** her abominations, 3045
Eze 16:62 thou shalt **k.** that I am the Lord: 3045
Eze 17:12 **K.** ye not what these things mean? 3045
Eze 17:21 **k.** that I the Lord have spoken it. 3045
Eze 17:24 of the field shall **k.** that I the Lord 3045
Eze 20:4 to **k.** the abominations of their 3045
Eze 20:12 **k.** that I am the Lord that sanctify 3045
Eze 20:20 **k.** that I am the Lord your God. 3045
Eze 20:26 they might **k.** that I am the Lord. 3045
Eze 20:38 and ye shall **k.** that I am the Lord. 3045
Eze 20:42, 44 ye shall **k.** that I am the Lord, 3045
Eze 21:5 all flesh may **k.** that I the Lord have 3045
Eze 22:16 thou shalt **k.** that I am the Lord. 3045
Eze 22:22 **k.** that I the Lord have poured out 3045
Eze 23:49 ye shall **k.** that I am the Lord God. 3045
Eze 24:24 ye shall **k.** that I am the Lord God. 3045
Eze 24:27 they shall **k.** that I am the Lord. 3045
Eze 25:5 and ye shall **k.** that I am the Lord. 3045
Eze 25:7 thou shalt **k.** that I am the Lord. 3045
Eze 25:11 they shall **k.** that I am the Lord. 3045
Eze 25:14 and they shall **k.** my vengeance, 3045
Eze 25:17 they shall **k.** that I am the Lord, 3045
Eze 26:6 they shall **k.** that I am the Lord. 3045
Eze 28:19 they that **k.** thee among the people 3045

Eze 28:22 they shall k. that I am the Lord, 3045
Eze 28:23 they shall k. that I am the Lord. 3045
Eze 28:24 they shall k. that I am the Lord God. 3045
Eze 28:26 they shall k. that I am the Lord 3045
Eze 29:6 all the inhabitants of Egypt shall k. 3045
Eze 29:9 they shall k. that I am the Lord: 3045
Eze 29:16 they shall k. that I am the Lord God. 3045
Eze 29:21 they shall k. that I am the Lord. 3045
Eze 30:8 they shall k. that I am the Lord, 3045
Eze 30:19 they shall k. that I am the Lord. 3045
Eze 30:25 they shall k. that I am the Lord, 3045
Eze 30:26 they shall k. that I am the Lord. 3045
Eze 32:15 shall they k. that I am the Lord. 3045
Eze 33:29 shall they k. that I am the Lord, 3045
Eze 33:33 they k. that a prophet hath been 3045
Eze 34:27 and shall k. that I am the Lord, 3045
Eze 34:30 Thus shall they k. that I the Lord 3045
Eze 35:4 thou shalt k. that I am the Lord. 3045
Eze 35:9 and ye shall k. that I am the Lord. 3045
Eze 35:12 thou shalt k. that I am the Lord, 3045
Eze 35:15 they shall k. that I am the Lord. 3045
Eze 36:11 and ye shall k. that I am the Lord. 3045
Eze 36:23 heathen shall k. that I am the Lord, 3045
Eze 36:36 k. that I the Lord build the ruined 3045
Eze 36:38 they shall k. that I am the Lord. 3045
Eze 37:6 and ye shall k. that I am the Lord. 3045
Eze 37:13 And ye shall k. that I am the Lord, 3045
Eze 37:14 ye k. that I the Lord have spoken 3045
Eze 37:28 heathen shall k. that I the Lord do 3045
Eze 38:14 dwelleth safely, shalt thou not k. it? 3045
Eze 38:16 that the heathen may k. me, when 3045
Eze 38:23 they shall k. that I am the Lord. 3045
Eze 39:6 they shall k. that I am the Lord. 3045
Eze 39:7 heathen shall k. that I am the Lord, 3045
Eze 39:22 Israel shall k. that I am the Lord 3045
Eze 39:23 heathen shall k. that the house of 3045
Eze 39:28 shall they k. that I am the Lord 3045
Da 2:3 spirit was troubled to k. the dream. 3045
Da 2:8 k. of certainty that ye would gain 3046
Da 2:9 I shall k. that ye can shew me the 3046
Da 2:21 to them that k. understanding: 3046
Da 2:30 k. the thoughts of thy heart. 3046
Da 4:9 I k. that the spirit of the holy gods 3046
Da 4:17 intent that the living may k. that 3046
Da 4:25 till thou k. that the most High 3046
Da 4:32 until thou k. that the most High 3046
Da 5:23 which see not, nor hear, nor k.: 3046
Da 6:15 K.,...that the law of the Medes and 3046
Da 7:16 and made me k. the interpretation 3046
Da 7:19 I would k. the truth of the fourth 3046
Da 8:19 k. what shall be in the last end 3045
Da 9:25 K. therefore and understand, that 3045
Da 11:32 the people that do k. their God shall 3045
Ho 2:8 she did not k. that I gave her corn, 3045
Ho 2:20 and thou shalt k. the Lord. 3045
Ho 5:3 I k. Ephraim, and Israel is not hid 3045
Ho 6:3 Then shall we k., if we follow on to 3045
Ho 6:3 if we follow on to k. the Lord: 3045
Ho 8:2 cry unto me, My God, we k. thee. 3045
Ho 9:7 are come; Israel shall k. it: 3045
Ho 13:4 and thou shalt k. no god but me: 3045
Ho 13:5 I did k. thee in the wilderness, in 3045
Ho 14:9 prudent, and he shall k. them? 3045
Joe 2:27 ye shall k. that I am in the midst 3045
Joe 3:17 So shall ye k. that I am the Lord 3045
Am 3:10 they k. not to do right, saith the 3045
Am 5:12 I k. your manifold transgressions 3045
Jon 1:7 may k. for whose cause this evil is 3045
Jon 1:12 k....for my sake this great tempest 3045
Mic 3:1 Is it not for you to k. judgment? 3045
Mic 4:12 k. not the thoughts of the Lord, 3045
Mic 6:5 k. the righteousness of the Lord. 3045
Zec 2:9,11 k....the Lord of hosts hath sent 3045
Zec 4:9 k. that the Lord of hosts hath sent 3045
Zec 6:15 k. that the Lord of hosts hath sent 3045
Mal 2:4 k....I have sent this commandment 3045
Mt 6:3 left hand k. what thy right hand 1097
Mt 7:11 k. how to give good gifts unto your 1492
Mt 7:16 Ye shall k. them by their fruits 1921
Mt 7:20 by their fruits ye shall k. them. 1921
Mt 9:6 k. that the Son of man hath power 1492
Mt 9:30 saying, See that no man k. it. 1097
Mt 13:11 k. the mysteries of the kingdom of 1097
Mt 20:22 and said, Ye k. not what ye ask 1492
Mt 20:25 k. that the princes of the Gentiles 1492
Mt 22:16 Master, we k. that thou art true, 1492
Mt 24:32 leaves, ye k. that summer is nigh: 1097
Mt 24:33 all these things, k. that it is near, 1097
Mt 24:42 for ye k. not what hour your Lord 1492
Mt 24:43 But k. this, that if the goodman 1097
Mt 25:12 I say unto you, I k. you not 1492
Mt 25:13 ye k. neither the day nor the hour 1492
Mt 26:2 k. that after two days is the feast 1492
Mt 26:70 saying, I k. not what thou sayest. 1492
Mt 26:72 with an oath, I do not k. the man. 1492
Mt 26:74 to swear, saying, I k. not the man. 1492
Mt 28:5 I k. that ye seek Jesus, which was 1492
Mk 1:24 k. thee who thou art, the Holy One 1492
Mk 2:10 k. that the Son of man hath power 1492
Mk 4:11 to k. the mystery of the kingdom 1097
Mk 4:13 K. ye not this parable? and how 1492
Mk 4:13 how then will ye k. all parables? 1097
Mk 5:43 straitly that no man should k. it; 1097
Mk 7:24 house, and would have no man k. it: 1097
Mk 9:30 would not that any man should k. it. 1097
Mk 10:38 unto them, Ye k. not what ye ask: 1492
Mk 10:42 k. that they which are accounted 1492
Mk 12:14 Master, we k. that thou art true, 1492
Mk 12:24 because ye k. not the scriptures, 1492
Mk 13:28 leaves, ye k. that summer is near: 1097
Mk 13:29 come to pass, k. that it is nigh, 1097
Mk 13:33 for ye k. not when the time is 1492
Mk 13:35 k. not when the master of the 1492
Mk 14:68 he denied, saying, I k. not, neither 1492
Mk 14:71 I k. not this man of whom ye speak. 1492
Lu 1:4 mightest k. the certainty of those 1921
Lu 1:18 the angel, Whereby shall I k. this? 1097
Lu 1:34 shall this be, seeing I k. not a man? 1097
Lu 4:34 I k. thee who thou art; the Holy 1492
Lu 5:24 k. that the Son of man hath power 1492
Lu 8:10 k. the mysteries of the kingdom of 1097
Lu 9:55 Ye k. not what manner of spirit 1492
Lu 11:13 k. how to give good gifts unto your 1492
Lu 12:39 And this k., that if the goodman of 1097
Lu 13:25 you, I k. you not whence ye are: 1492
Lu 13:27 you, I k. you not whence ye are; 1492
Lu 19:15 he might k. how much every man 1097
Lu 20:21 k. that thou sayest and teachest 1492
Lu 21:20 k. that the desolation thereof is 1097
Lu 21:30 ye see and k. of your own selves 1097
Lu 21:31 k. ye that the kingdom of God is 1097
Lu 22:57 him, saying, Woman, I k. him not. 1492
Lu 22:60 Man, I k. not what thou sayest. 1492
Lu 23:34 them; for they k. not what they 1492
Lu 24:16 that they should not k. him. 1921
Joh 1:26 one among you, whom ye k. not; 1492
Joh 3:2 we k. that thou art a teacher come 1492
Joh 3:11 We speak that we do k., 1492
Joh 4:22 Ye worship ye k. not what: 1492
Joh 4:22 we k. what we worship: for 1492
Joh 4:25 unto him, I k. that Messias cometh, 1492
Joh 4:32 have meat to eat that ye k. not of. 1492
Joh 4:42 k. that this is indeed the Christ, 1492
Joh 5:32 and I k. that the witness which he 1492
Joh 5:42 I k. you, that ye have not the love 1097
Joh 6:42 whose father and mother we k.? 1492
Joh 7:17 he shall k. of the doctrine 1097
Joh 7:26 k. indeed...this is the very Christ? 1097
Joh 7:27 we k. this man whence he is: 1492
Joh 7:28 k. me, and ye k. whence I am 1492
Joh 7:28 sent me is true, whom ye k. not, 1492
Joh 7:29 But I k. him: for I am from him, 1492
Joh 7:51 hear him, and k. what he doeth? 1097
Joh 8:14 I k. whence I came, and whither I 1492
Joh 8:19 Ye neither k. me, nor my Father: 1492
Joh 8:28 man, then shall ye k. that I am he, 1097
Joh 8:32 ye shall k. the truth, and the truth 1097
Joh 8:37 I k. that ye are Abraham's seed; 1097
Joh 8:52 Now we k. that thou hast a devil. 1097
Joh 8:55 have not known him; but I k. him: 1492
Joh 8:55 if I should say, I k. him not, 1492
Joh 8:55 but I k. him, and keep his saying 1492
Joh 9:12 Where is he? He said, I k. not. 1492
Joh 9:20 We k. that this is our son, and that 1492
Joh 9:21 means he now seeth, we k. not; 1492
Joh 9:21 hath opened his eyes, we k. not: 1492
Joh 9:24 we k. that this man is a sinner. 1492
Joh 9:25 he be a sinner or no, I k. not: 1492
Joh 9:25 one thing I k., that, whereas I was 1492
Joh 9:29 We k. that God spake unto Moses: 1492
Joh 9:29 fellow, we k. not from whence he is 1492
Joh 9:30 that ye k. not from whence he is, 1492
Joh 9:31 we k. that God heareth not sinners: 1492
Joh 10:4 follow him: for they k. his voice. 1492
Joh 10:5 they k. not the voice of strangers. 1492
Joh 10:14 good shepherd, and k. my sheep, 1097
Joh 10:15 me, even so k. I the Father: 1097
Joh 10:27 sheep hear my voice, and I k. 1097
Joh 10:38 that ye may k., and believe, that 1097
Joh 11:22 I k., that even now, whatsoever 1492
Joh 11:24 I k. that he shall rise again in the 1492
Joh 11:49 said unto them, Ye k. nothing at all, 1492
Joh 12:50 I k. that his commandment is life 1492
Joh 13:7 now; but thou shalt k. hereafter 1097
Joh 13:12 K. ye what I have done to you? 1097
Joh 13:17 If ye k. these things, happy are ye 1492
Joh 13:18 you all: I k. whom I have chosen: 1492
Joh 13:35 all men k. that ye are my disciples, 1097
Joh 14:4 And whither I go ye k., and the 1492
Joh 14:4 whither I go...,and the way ye k. 1492
Joh 14:5 Lord, we k. not whither thou goest; 1492
Joh 14:5 goest; and how can we k. the way?
Joh 14:7 and from henceforth ye k. him, 1097
Joh 14:17 but ye k. him; for he dwelleth 1492
Joh 14:20 ye shall k. that I am in my Father, 1097
Joh 14:31 world may k. that I love the 1097
Joh 15:18 k. that it hated me before it hated 1097
Joh 15:21 they k. not him that sent me. 1492
Joh 17:3 might k. thee the only true God, 1097
Joh 17:23 may k. that thou hast sent me, 1097
Joh 18:21 behold, they k. what I said. 1492
Joh 19:4 may k. that I find no fault in him. 1097
Joh 20:2 k. not where they have laid him. 1492
Joh 20:13 I k. not where they have laid him. 1492
Joh 21:24 we k. that his testimony is true. 1492
Ac 1:7 not for you to k. the times or the 1097
Ac 2:22 you, as ye yourselves also know: 1492
Ac 2:36 the house of Israel k. assuredly, 1097
Ac 3:16 man strong, whom ye see and k.: 1492
Ac 10:28 Ye k. how that it is an unlawful 1987
Ac 10:37 That word, I say, ye k., which was 1492
Ac 12:11 Now I k. of a surety, that the Lord 1492
Ac 15:7 ye k. how that a good while ago 1987
Ac 17:19 May we k. what this new doctrine, 1097
Ac 17:20 k. therefore what these things mean 1097
Ac 19:15 and said, Jesus I k., and Paul 1097
Ac 19:15 and Paul I k.; but who are ye? 1987
Ac 19:25 ye k. that by this craft we have our 1987
Ac 20:18 Ye k., from the first day that I came 1987
Ac 20:25 I k. that ye all, among whom I 1492
Ac 20:29 I k. this, that after my departing 1492
Ac 20:34 ye yourselves k., that these hands 1097
Ac 21:24 all may know that those things, 1097
Ac 21:34 he could not k. the certainty for the 1097
Ac 22:14 that thou shouldest k. his will, and 1097
Ac 22:19 they k. that I imprisoned and beat 1987
Ac 22:24 k. wherefore they cried so against 1921
Ac 24:10 as I k. that thou hast been of many 1987
Ac 24:22 k. the uttermost of your matter. 1231
Ac 26:3 I k. thee to be expert in all customs
Ac 26:4 at Jerusalem, k. all the Jews; 2467
Ac 26:27 prophets? I k. that thou believest. 1492
Ac 28:22 we k. that every where it is spoken 1110
Ro 3:19 k. that what things soever the law 1492
Ro 6:3 K. ye not, that so many of us as 50
Ro 6:16 K. ye not, that to whom ye yield 1492
Ro 7:1 K. ye not, brethren, (for I speak to 50
Ro 7:1 speak to them that k. the law,) 1097
Ro 7:14 For we k. that the law is spiritual: 1492
Ro 7:18 For I k. that in me (that is, in my 1492
Ro 8:22 For we k. that the whole creation 1492
Ro 8:26 we k. not what we should pray for 1492
Ro 8:28 we k. that all things work together 1492
Ro 10:19 But I say, Did not Israel k.? First 1097
Ro 14:14 k., and am persuaded by the Lord 1492
1Co 1:16 k. not whether I baptized any other 1492
1Co 2:2 not to k. any thing among you, save 1492
1Co 2:12 might k. the things that are freely 1492
1Co 2:14 neither can he k. them, because 1097
1Co 3:16 K. ye not that ye are the temple 1492
1Co 4:4 For I k. nothing by myself; yet am 4892
1Co 4:19 and will k., not the speech of them 1097
1Co 5:6 K. ye not that a little leaven 1492
1Co 6:2 ye not k. that the saints shall judge 1492
1Co 6:3 K. ye not...we shall judge angels? 1492
1Co 6:9 K. ye not that the unrighteous 1492
1Co 6:15 K. ye not that your bodies are the 1492
1Co 6:16 k. ye not that he which is joined to 1492
1Co 6:19 k. ye not...your body is the temple 1492

1Co	8:1	we **k.** that we all have knowledge.	*1492*
1Co	8:2	nothing yet as he ought to **k.**.	*1097*
1Co	8:4	we **k.** that an idol is nothing in the	*1492*
1Co	9:13	ye not **k.** that they which minister	*1492*
1Co	9:24	**K.** ye not that they which run in a	*1492*
1Co	11:3	I would have you **k.**, that the head	*1492*
1Co	12:2	Ye **k.** that ye were Gentiles, carried	*1492*
1Co	13:9	we **k.** in part, and we prophesy in	*1097*
1Co	13:12	now I **k.** in part; but then shall I	*1097*
1Co	13:12	shall I **k.** even as also I am known.	*1921*
1Co	14:11	I **k.** not the meaning of the voice,	*1492*
1Co	15:58	ye **k.** that your labour is not in vain	*1492*
1Co	16:15	(ye **k.** the house of Stephanas, that	*1492*
2Co	2:4	ye might **k.** the love which I have	*1097*
2Co	2:9	I might **k.** the proof of you, whether	*1097*
2Co	5:1	we **k.** that if our earthly house of	*1492*
2Co	5:16	**k.** we no man after the flesh:	*1492*
2Co	5:16	now henceforth **k.** we him no more.	*1097*
2Co	8:9	ye **k.** the grace of our Lord Jesus	*1097*
2Co	9:2	I **k.** the forwardness of your mind,	*1492*
2Co	13:5	**K.** ye not your own selves, how	*1921*
2Co	13:6	**k.** that we are not reprobates	*1097*
Ga	3:7	**K.** ye therefore that they which are	*1097*
Ga	4:13	Ye **k.** how through infirmity of the	*1492*
Eph	1:18	**k.** what is the hope of his calling,	*1492*
Eph	3:19	And to **k.** the love of Christ, which	*1097*
Eph	5:5	this ye **k.**, that no whoremonger,	*1097*
Eph	6:21	But that ye also may **k.** my affairs,	*1492*
Eph	6:22	that ye might **k.** our affairs,	*1097*
Php	1:19	For I **k.** that this shall turn to my	*1492*
Php	1:25	I **k.** that I shall abide and continue	*1492*
Php	2:19	good comfort, when I **k.** your state.	*1097*
Php	2:22	But ye **k.** the proof of him, that, as	*1097*
Php	3:10	That I may **k.** him, and the power	*1097*
Php	4:12	I **k.** both how to be abased, and	*1492*
Php	4:12	abased, and I **k.** how to abound:	*1492*
Php	4:15	Now ye Phillippians **k.** also, that in	*1492*
Col	4:6	ye may **k.** how ye ought to answer	*1492*
Col	4:8	that he might **k.** your estate, and	*1097*
1Th	1:5	ye **k.** what manner of men we were	*1492*
1Th	2:1	**k.** our entrance in unto you, that it	*1492*
1Th	2:2	were shamefully entreated, as ye **k.**,	*1492*
1Th	2:5	used we flattering words, as ye **k.**,	*1492*
1Th	2:11	**k.** how we exhorted and comforted	*1492*
1Th	3:3	yourselves **k.** that we are appointed	*1492*
1Th	3:4	even as it came to pass, and ye **k.**.	*1492*
1Th	3:5	forbear, I sent to **k.** your faith,	*1097*
1Th	4:2	**k.** what commandments we gave	*1492*
1Th	4:4	should **k.** how to possess his vessel	*1492*
1Th	4:5	as the Gentiles which **k.** not God:	*1492*
1Th	5:2	yourselves **k.** perfectly that the day	*1492*
1Th	5:12	**k.** them which labour among you,	*1492*
2Th	1:8	vengeance on them that **k.** not God,	*1492*
2Th	2:6	now ye **k.** what withholdeth that he	*1492*
2Th	3:7	**k.** how ye ought to follow us:	*1492*
1Ti	1:8	But we **k.** that the law is good,	*1492*
1Ti	3:5	a man **k.** not how to rule his own	*1492*
1Ti	3:15	**k.** how thou oughtest to behave	*1492*
1Ti	4:3	which believe and **k.** the truth.	*1921*
2Ti	1:12	for I **k.** whom I have believed,	*1492*
2Ti	3:1	This **k.** also, that in the last days	*1097*
Tit	1:16	They profess that they **k.** God;	*1492*
Heb	8:11	his brother, saying, **K.** the Lord:	*1097*
Heb	8:11	for all shall **k.** me, from the least	*1492*
Heb	10:30	**k.** him that hath said, Vengeance	*1492*
Heb	12:17	For ye **k.** how that afterward,	*2467*
Heb	13:23	**K.** ye that our brother Timothy is	*1097*
Jas	2:20	wilt thou **k.**, O vain man, that faith	*1097*
Jas	4:4	**k.** ye not that the friendship of the	*1492*
Jas	4:14	**k.** not what shall be on the morrow.	*1987*
Jas	5:20	him **k.**, that he which converteth	*1097*
1Pe	1:18	ye **k.** that ye were not redeemed	*1492*
2Pe	1:12	of these things, though ye **k.** them,	*1492*
2Pe	3:17	seeing ye **k.** these things before,	*4267*
1Jo	2:3	hereby we do **k.** that we **k.** him,	*1097*
1Jo	2:4	He that saith, I **k.** him, and keepeth	*1097*
1Jo	2:5	hereby **k.** we that we are in him.	*1097*
1Jo	2:18	whereby we **k.** that it is the last time.	*1097*
1Jo	2:20	the Holy One, and ye **k.** all things.	*1492*
1Jo	2:21	you because ye **k.** not the truth,	*1492*
1Jo	2:21	but because ye **k.** it, and that no lie	*1492*
1Jo	2:29	If ye **k.** that he is righteous,	*1492*
1Jo	2:29	ye **k.** that every one that doeth	*1097*
1Jo	3:2	we **k.** that, when he shall appear,	*1492*
1Jo	3:5	**k.** that he was manifested to take	*1492*
1Jo	3:14	We **k.** that we have passed from	*1492*
1Jo	3:15	ye **k.** that no murderer hath eternal	*1492*
1Jo	3:19	we **k.** that we are of the truth,	*1097*
1Jo	3:24	hereby we **k.** that he abideth in us,	*1097*
1Jo	4:2	Hereby **k.** ye the Spirit of God:	*1097*
1Jo	4:6	Hereby **k.** we the spirit of truth,	*1097*
1Jo	4:13	Hereby **k.** we that we dwell in him,	*1097*
1Jo	5:2	we **k.** that we love the children of	*1097*
1Jo	5:13	may **k.** that ye have eternal life,	*1492*
1Jo	5:15	if we **k.** that he hear us, whatsoever	*1492*
1Jo	5:15	we **k.** that we have the petitions	*1492*
1Jo	5:18	We **k.** that whosoever is born of God	*1492*
1Jo	5:19	we **k.** that we are of God, and the	*1492*
1Jo	5:20	we **k.** that the Son of God is come,	*1492*
1Jo	5:20	that we may **k.** him that is true,	*1097*
3Jo	12	and ye **k.** that our record is true.	*1492*
Jude	10	of those things which they **k.** not:	*1492*
Jude	10	but what they **k.** naturally, as	*1987*
Re	2:2	**I k. thy works, and thy labour,**	*1492*
Re	2:2	**I k. thy works, and tribulation,**	*1492*
Re	2:2	**I k. the blasphemy of them which say**	
Re	2:13	**I k. thy works, and where thou**	*1492*
Re	2:19	**I k. thy works, and charity, and**	*1492*
Re	2:23	**k. that I am he which searcheth**	*1097*
Re	3:1	**I k. thy works, that thou hast a**	*1492*
Re	3:3	**shalt not k. what hour I will come**	*1097*
Re	3:8	**I k. thy works; behold, I have set**	*1492*
Re	3:9	**and to k. that I have loved thee.**	*1097*
Re	3:15	**I k. thy works, that thou art**	*1492*

KNOWEST

Ge	30:26	thou **k.** my service which I have	3045
Ge	30:29	Thou **k.** how I have served thee,	3045
Ge	47:6	and if thou **k.** any men of activity	3045
Ex	10:7	**k.** thou not...Egypt is destroyed?	3045
Ex	32:22	thou **k.** the people, that they are set	3045
Nu	10:31	as thou **k.** how we are to encamp	3045
Nu	11:16	whom thou **k.** to be the elders of the	3045
Nu	20:14	**k.** all the travel that hath befallen	3045
De	7:15	diseases of Egypt, which thou **k.**,	3045
De	9:2	of the Anakims, whom thou **k.**, and	3045
De	20:20	Only the trees which thou **k.** that	3045
De	28:33	a nation which thou **k.** not eat up;	3045
Jos	14:6	Thou **k.** the thing that the Lord	3045
Jg	15:11	**K.** thou not that the Philistines	3045
1Sa	28:9	thou **k.** what Saul hath done, how	3045
2Sa	1:5	How **k.** thou that Saul and Jonathan	3045
2Sa	2:26	**k.** thou not that it will be bitterness	3045
2Sa	3:25	Thou **k.** Abner the son of Ner, that	3045
2Sa	7:20	for thou, Lord God, **k.** thy servant.	3045
2Sa	17:8	thou **k.** thy father and his men,	3045
1Ki	1:18	my lord the king, thou **k.** it not:	3045
1Ki	2:5	thou **k.** also what Joab the son of	3045
1Ki	2:9	**k.** what thou oughtest to do unto	3045
1Ki	2:15	Thou **k.** that the kingdom was mine,	3045
1Ki	2:44	Thou **k.** all the wickedness which	3045
1Ki	5:3	Thou **k.** how that David my father	3045
1Ki	5:6	thou **k.** that there is not among us	3045
1Ki	8:39	to his ways, whose heart thou **k.**;	3045
1Ki	8:39	**k.** the hearts of all the children of	3045
2Ki	2:3,	5 **k.** thou that the Lord will take	3045
2Ki	4:1	thou **k.** that thy servant did fear	3045
1Ch	17:18	servant? for thou **k.** thy servant.	3045
2Ch	6:30	only **k.** the hearts of the children	3045
Job	10:7	Thou **k.** that I am not wicked;	1847
Job	15:9	What **k.** thou, that we know not?	3045
Job	20:4	**K.** thou not this of old, since man	3045
Job	34:33	therefore speak what thou **k.**.	3045
Job	38:5	the measures thereof, if thou **k.**?	3045
Job	38:18	the earth? declare if thou **k.** it all.	3045
Job	38:21	**K.** thou it, because thou wast then	3045
Job	38:33	**K.** thou the ordinances of heaven?	3045
Job	39:1	**K.** thou the time when the wild	3045
Job	39:2	**k.** thou the time when they bring	3045
Ps	40:9	refrained my lips, O Lord, thou **k.**	3045
Ps	69:5	O God, thou **k.** my foolishness;	3045
Ps	139:2	Thou **k.** my downsitting and mine	3045
Ps	139:4	lo, O Lord, thou **k.** it altogether.	3045
Pr	27:1	thou **k.** not what a day may bring	3045
Ec	11:2	thou **k.** not what evil shall be upon	3045
Ec	11:5	thou **k.** not what is the way of the	3045
Ec	11:5	so thou **k.** not the works of God	3045
Ec	11:6	thou **k.** not whether shall prosper,	3045
Isa	55:5	shalt call a nation that thou **k.** not,	3045
Jer	5:15	nation whose language thou **k.** not,	3045
Jer	12:3	But thou, O Lord, **k.** me: thou hast	3045
Jer	15:4	into a land which thou **k.** not:	3045
Jer	15:15	O Lord, thou **k.**: remember me,	3045
Jer	17:4	in the land which thou **k.** not:	3045
Jer	17:16	thou **k.**: that which came out of	3045
Jer	18:23	thou **k.** all their counsel against me	3045
Jer	33:3	mighty things, which thou **k.** not.	3045
Eze	37:3	I answered, O Lord God, thou **k.**.	3045
Da	10:20	**K.**...wherefore I come unto thee?	3045
Zec	4:5	me, **K.** thou not what these be?	3045
Zec	4:13	said, **K.** thou not what these be?	3045
Mt	15:12	**K.** thou that the Pharisees were	*1492*
Mk	10:19	**Thou k. the commandments, Do**	*1492*
Lu	18:20	**Thou k. the commandments, Do**	*1492*
Lu	22:34	**shalt thrice deny that thou k. me**	*1492*
Joh	1:48	unto him, Whence **k.** thou me?	*1097*
Joh	3:10	**of Israel, and k. not these things?**	*1097*
Joh	13:7	**him, What I do thou k. not now;**	*1492*
Joh	16:30	are we sure that thou **k.** all things,	*1492*
Joh	19:10	**k.** thou not that I have power to	*1492*
Joh	21:15,	16 Lord; thou **k.** that I love thee.	*1492*
Joh	21:17	unto him, Lord, thou **k.** all things;	*1492*
Joh	21:17	thou **k.** that I love thee.	*1097*
Ac	1:24	which **k.** the hearts of all men,	*2589*
Ac	25:10	no wrong, as thou very well **k.**	*1921*
Ro	2:18	**k.** his will, and approvest the	*1097*
1Co	7:16	For what **k.** thou, O wife, whether	*1492*
1Co	7:16	or how **k.** thou, O man, whether	*1492*
2Ti	1:15	This thou **k.**, that all they which	*1492*
2Ti	1:18	me at Ephesus, thou **k.** very well.	*1097*
Re	3:17	**and k. not that thou art wretched?**	*1492*
Re	7:14	And I said unto him, Sir, thou **k.**.	*1492*

KNOWETH

Ge	33:13	**k.** that the children are tender,	3045
Le	5:3,4	when he **k.** of it, then he shall be	3045
De	2:7	he **k.** thy walking through this	3045
De	34:6	no man **k.** of his sepulchre unto	3045
Jos	22:22	gods, the Lord God of gods, he **k.**,	3045
1Sa	3:13	ever for the iniquity which he **k.**;	3045
1Sa	20:3	Thy father certainly **k.** that I have	3045
1Sa	23:17	and that also Saul my father **k.**.	3045
2Sa	14:22	thy servant **k.**...I have found grace	3045
2Sa	17:10	Israel **k.** that thy father is a mighty	3045
1Ki	1:11	reign, and David our lord **k.** it not?	3045
Es	4:14	who **k.** whether thou art come to	3045
Job	11:11	he **k.** vain men: he seeth wickedness	3045
Job	12:3	who **k.** not such things as these:	854
Job	12:9	Who **k.** not in all these that the	3045
Job	14:21	come to honour, and he **k.** it not;	3045
Job	15:23	he **k.** that the day of darkness is	3045
Job	18:21	is the place of him that **k.** not God.	3045
Job	23:10	he **k.** the way that I take: when he	3045
Job	28:7	There is a path which no fowl **k.**,	3045
Job	28:13	Man **k.** not the price thereof;	3045
Job	28:23	thereof, and he **k.** the place thereof.	3045
Job	34:25	Therefore he **k.** their works, and	5234
Job	35:15	yet he **k.** it not in great extremity:	3045
Ps	1:6	Lord **k.** the way of the righteous:	3045
Ps	37:18	The Lord **k.** the days of the upright:	3045
Ps	39:6	and **k.** not who shall gather them.	3045
Ps	44:21	for he **k.** the secrets of the heart.	3045
Ps	74:9	among us any that **k.** how long.	3045
Ps	90:11	Who **k.** the power of thine anger?	3045
Ps	92:6	A brutish man **k.** not; neither doth	3045
Ps	94:11	The Lord **k.** the thoughts of man,	3045
Ps	103:14	he **k.** our frame; he remembereth	3045
Ps	104:19	seasons: the sun **k.** his going down.	3045
Ps	138:6	lowly: but the proud he **k.** afar off.	3045
Ps	139:14	and that my soul **k.** right well.	3045
Pr	7:23	and **k.** not that it is for his life.	3045
Pr	9:13	she is simple, and **k.** nothing.	3045
Pr	9:18	he **k.** not that the dead are there;	3045
Pr	14:10	The heart **k.** his own bitterness;	3045
Pr	24:22	and who **k.** the ruin of them both?	3045
Ec	2:19	who **k.** whether he shall be a wise	3045
Ec	3:21	Who **k.** the spirit of man that	3045
Ec	6:8	that **k.** to walk before the living?	3045
Ec	6:12	who **k.** what is good for man in this	3045
Ec	7:22	also thine own heart **k.** that thou	3045
Ec	8:1	who **k.** the interpretation of a	3045
Ec	8:7	For he **k.** not that which shall be:	3045
Ec	9:1	no man **k.** either love or hatred by	3045
Ec	9:12	For man also **k.** not his time: as the	3045
Ec	10:15	he **k.** not how to go to the city.	3045
Isa	1:3	The ox **k.** his owner, and the ass	3045
Isa	29:15	Who seeth us: and who **k.** us?	3045
Jer	8:7	the heaven **k.** her appointed times;	3045
Jer	9:24	that he understandeth and **k.** me,	3045
Da	2:22	he **k.** what is in the darkness, and	3046
Ho	7:9	his strength, and he **k.** it not:	3045

Ho	7:9	and there upon him, yet he **k.** not	3045
Joe	2:14	Who **k.** if he will return and repent,	3045
Na	1:7	and he **k.** them that trust in him.	3045
Zep	3:5	not; but the unjust **k.** no shame.	3045
Mt	6:8	**k. what things ye have need of,**	*1492*
Mt	6:32	**k. that ye have need of all these**	*1492*
Mt	11:27	**no man k. the Son, but the Father;**	*1921*
Mt	11:27	**neither k. any man the Father,**	*1921*
Mt	24:36	**of that day and hour k. no man,**	*1492*
Mk	4:27	**spring and grow up, he k. not how.**	*1492*
Mk	13:32	**that day and that hour k. no man,**	*1492*
Lu	10:22	**and no man k. who the Son is,**	*1097*
Lu	12:30	**k. that ye have need of all these**	*1492*
Lu	16:15	**men; but God k. your hearts:**	*1097*
Joh	7:15	saying, How **k.** this man letters,	*1492*
Joh	7:27	cometh, no man **k.** whence he is.	*1097*
Joh	7:49	who **k.** not the law are cursed.	*1097*
Joh	10:15	**As the Father k. me, even so know**	*1097*
Joh	12:35	**darkness k. not whither he goeth.**	*1492*
Joh	14:17	**it seeth him not, neither k. him:**	*1097*
Joh	15:15	**servant k. not what his lord doeth:**	*1492*
Joh	19:35	**he k. that he saith true, that ye**	*1492*
Ac	15:8	And God, which **k.** the hearts, bare	*2589*
Ac	19:35	there that **k.** not how that the city	*1097*
Ac	26:26	the king **k.** of these things, before	*1987*
Ro	8:27	**k.** what is the mind of the Spirit,	*1492*
1Co	2:11	what man **k.** the things of a man,	*1492*
1Co	2:11	the things of God **k.** no man, but	*1492*
1Co	3:20	Lord **k.** the thoughts of the wise,	*1097*
1Co	8:2	man think that he **k.** any thing,	*1492*
1Co	8:2	he **k.** nothing yet as he ought to	*1097*
1Co	11:11	because I love you not? God **k.**	*1492*
1Co	11:31	for evermore, **k.** that I lie not.	*1492*
1Co	12:2,3	of the body, I cannot tell: God **k.**;)	*1492*
2Ti	2:19	seal, The Lord **k.** them that are his	*1097*
Jas	4:17	to him that **k.** to do good, and	*1492*
2Pe	2:9	Lord **k.** how to deliver the godly	*1492*
1Jo	2:11	**k.** not whither he goeth, because	*1492*
1Jo	3:1	the world **k.** us not, because it	*1097*
1Jo	3:20	than our heart, and **k.** all things.	*1097*
1Jo	4:6	he that **k.** God heareth us; he that	*1097*
1Jo	4:7	loveth is born of God, and **k.** God.	*1097*
1Jo	4:8	He that loveth not, **k.** not God; for	*1097*
Re	2:17	**no man k. saving he that receiveth.**	*1097*
Re	12:12	he **k.**...he hath but a short time.	*1492*

KNOWING

Ge	3:5	shall be as gods, **k.** good and evil.	3045
1Ki	2:32	my father David not **k.** thereof,	3045
Mt	9:4	And Jesus **k.** their thoughts said,	*1492*
Mt	22:29	**Ye do err, not k. the scriptures,**	*1492*
Mk	5:30	**k.** in himself that virtue had gone	*1921*
Mk	5:33	**k.** what was done in her, came	*1492*
Mk	6:20	**k.** that he was a just man and an	*1492*
Mk	12:15	**k.** their hypocrisy, said unto them.	*1492*
Lu	8:53	him to scorn, **k.** that she was dead.	*1492*
Lu	9:33	one for Elias: not **k.** what he said.	*1492*
Lu	11:17	**k.** their thoughts, said unto them,	*1492*
Joh	13:3	Jesus **k.** that the Father had given	*1492*
Joh	18:4	**k.** all things that should come upon	*1492*
Joh	19:28	Jesus **k.** that all things were now	*1492*
Joh	21:12	art thou? **k.** that it was the Lord.	*1492*
Ac	2:30	**k.** that God had sworn with an oath	*1492*
Ac	5:7	not **k.** what was done, came in.	*1492*
Ac	18:25	Lord, **k.** only the baptism of John.	*1987*
Ac	20:22	not **k.** the things that shall befall	*1492*
Ro	1:32	Who **k.** the judgment of God, that	*1921*
Ro	2:4	not **k.** that the goodness of God	*50*
Ro	5:3	**k.** that tribulation worketh	*1492*
Ro	6:6	**K.** this, that our old man is	*1097*
Ro	6:9	**K.** that Christ being raised from	*1492*
Ro	13:11	**k.** the time, that now it is high time	*1492*
2Co	1:7	**k.**, that as ye are partakers of the	*1492*
2Co	4:14	**K.** that he which raised up the Lord	*1492*
2Co	5:6	**k.** that, whilst we are at home in	*1492*
2Co	5:11	**K.** therefore the terror of the Lord,	*1492*
Ga	2:16	**K.** that a man is not justified by	*1492*
Eph	6:8	**K.** that whatsoever good thing any	*1492*
Eph	6:9	**k.** that your Master...is in heaven;	*1492*
Php	1:17	**k.** that I am set for the defence of	*1492*
Col	3:24	**K.** that of the Lord ye shall receive	*1492*
Col	4:1	**k.** that ye...have a Master in heaven.	*1492*
1Th	1:4	**K.**, brethren beloved, your election	*1492*
1Ti	1:9	**K.** this, that the law is not made	*1492*
1Ti	6:4	**k.** nothing, but doting about	*1987*
2Ti	2:23	**k.** that they do gender strifes.	*1492*
2Ti	3:14	**k.** of whom thou hast learned them;	*1492*
Tit	3:11	**K.** that he that is such is subverted,	*1492*
Phm	21	**k.** that thou wilt also do more than	*1492*
Heb	10:34	**k.** in yourselves that ye have in	*1097*
Heb	11:8	went out, not **k.** whither he went.	*1987*
Jas	1:3	**K.** this, that the trying of your	*1097*
Jas	3:1	**k.** that we shall receive the greater	*1492*
1Pe	3:9	**k.** that ye are thereunto called,	*1492*
1Pe	5:9	**k.** that the same afflictions are	*1492*
2Pe	1:14	**K.** that shortly I must put off this	*1492*
2Pe	1:20	**K.** this first, that no prophecy of	*1097*
2Pe	3:3	**K.** this first, that there shall come	*1097*

KNOWLEDGE See also ACKNOWLEDGE; FOREKNOWLEDGE.

Ge	2:9	the tree of **k.** of good and evil.	1847
Ge	2:17	the tree of the **k.** of good and evil,	1847
Ex	31:3	and in understanding, and in **k.**,	1847
Ex	35:31	in understanding, and in **k.**,	1847
Le	4:23,28	he hath sinned, come to his **k.**;	3045
Nu	15:24	without the **k.** of the congregation,	5869
Nu	24:16	and knew the **k.** of the most High,	1847
De	1:39	had no **k.** between good and evil,	3045
Ru	2:10	that thou shouldest take **k.** of me,	5234
Ru	2:19	be he that did take **k.** of thee.	5234
1Sa	2:3	the Lord is a God of **k.**, and by	1844
1Sa	23:23	take **k.** of all the lurking places	3045
1Ki	9:27	shipmen that had **k.** of the sea,	3045
2Ch	1:10	Give me now wisdom and **k.**, that	4093
2Ch	1:11	asked wisdom and **k.** for thyself,	4093
2Ch	1:12	Wisdom and **k.** is granted unto	4093
2Ch	8:18	servants that had **k.** of the sea;	3045
2Ch	30:22	taught the good **k.** of the Lord:	7922
Ne	10:28	every one having **k.**, and having	3045
Job	15:2	Should a wise man utter vain **k.**,	1847
Job	21:14	for we desire not the **k.** of thy ways.	1847
Job	21:22	Shall any teach God **k.**? seeing he	1847
Job	33:3	and my lips shall utter **k.** clearly.	1847
Job	34:2	give ear unto me, ye that have **k.**	3045
Job	34:35	Job hath spoken without **k.**, and	1847
Job	35:16	he multiplieth words without **k.**	1847
Job	36:3	I will fetch my **k.** from afar,	1843
Job	36:4	that is perfect in **k.** is with thee.	1844
Job	36:12	and they shall die without **k.**	1847
Job	37:16	of him which is perfect in **k.**?	1843
Job	38:2	counsel by words without **k.**?	1847
Job	42:3	he that hideth counsel without **k.**?	1847
Ps	14:4	all the workers of iniquity no **k.**?	3045
Ps	19:2	and night unto night sheweth **k.**	1847
Ps	53:4	the workers of iniquity no **k.**?	3045
Ps	73:11	and is there **k.** in the Most High?	1844
Ps	94:10	he that teacheth man **k.**, shall not	1847
Ps	119:66	Teach me good judgment and **k.**:	1847
Ps	139:6	Such **k.** is too wonderful for me;	1847
Ps	144:3	man, that thou takest **k.** of him!	3045
Pr	1:4	the young man **k.** and discretion.	1847
Pr	1:7	the Lord is the beginning of **k.**:	1847
Pr	1:22	their scorning, and fools hate **k.**?	1847
Pr	1:29	For that they hated **k.**, and did not	1847
Pr	2:3	Yea, if thou criest after **k.**, and	998
Pr	2:5	the Lord, and find the **k.** of God.	1847
Pr	2:6	out of his mouth cometh **k.** and	1847
Pr	2:10	and **k.** is pleasant unto thy soul;	1847
Pr	3:20	By his **k.** the depths are broken up,	1847
Pr	5:2	and that thy lips may keep **k.**	1847
Pr	8:9	and right to them that find **k.**	1847
Pr	8:10	and **k.** rather than choice gold.	1847
Pr	8:12	and find out **k.** of witty inventions.	1847
Pr	9:10	the **k.** of the holy is understanding.	1847
Pr	10:14	Wise men lay up **k.**; but the mouth	1847
Pr	11:9	but through **k.** shall the just be	1847
Pr	12:1	Whoso loveth instruction loveth **k.**	1847
Pr	12:23	A prudent man concealeth **k.**:	1847
Pr	13:16	Every prudent man dealeth with **k.**:	1847
Pr	14:6	but **k.** is easy unto him that	1847
Pr	14:7	perceivest not in him the lips of **k.**	1847
Pr	14:18	the prudent are crowned with **k.**	1847
Pr	15:2	tongue of the wise useth **k.** aright:	1847
Pr	15:7	The lips of the wise disperse **k.**:	1847
Pr	15:14	hath understanding seeketh **k.**:	1847
Pr	17:27	He that hath **k.** spareth his words:	1847
Pr	18:15	heart of the prudent getteth **k.**;	1847
Pr	18:15	and the ear of the wise seeketh **k.**	1847
Pr	19:2	Also, that the soul be without **k.**,	1847
Pr	19:25	and he will understand **k.**	1847
Pr	19:27	causeth to err from the words of **k.**	1847
Pr	20:15	the lips of **k.** are a precious jewel.	1847
Pr	21:11	wise is instructed, he receiveth **k.**	1847
Pr	22:12	The eyes of the Lord preserve **k.**,	1847
Pr	22:17	and apply thine heart unto my **k.**	1847
Pr	22:20	excellent things in counsels and **k.**,	1847
Pr	23:12	and thine ears to the words of **k.**	1847
Pr	24:4	by **k.** shall the chambers be filled	1847
Pr	24:5	a man of **k.** increaseth strength.	1847
Pr	24:14	So shall the **k.** of wisdom be unto	3045
Pr	28:2	a man of understannding and **k.**	3045
Pr	30:3	nor have the **k.** of the holy.	1847
Ec	1:16	great experience of wisdom and **k.**	1847
Ec	1:18	increaseth **k.** increaseth sorrow.	1847
Ec	2:21	labour is in wisdom, and in **k.**,	1847
Ec	2:26	good in his sight wisdom, and **k.**,	1847
Ec	7:12	the excellency of **k.** is, that wisdom	1847
Ec	9:10	there is no work, nor device, nor **k.**,	1847
Ec	12:9	wise, he still taught the people **k.**;	1847
Isa	5:13	captivity, because they have no **k.**:	1847
Isa	8:4	the child shall have **k.** to cry,	3045
Isa	11:2	the spirit of **k.** and of the fear of	1847
Isa	11:9	shall be full of the **k.** of the Lord,	1844
Isa	28:9	Whom shall he teach **k.**? and whom	1844
Isa	32:4	of the rash shall understand **k.**,	1847
Isa	33:6	wisdom and **k.** shall be the stability	1847
Isa	40:14	taught him **k.**, and shewed to him	1847
Isa	44:19	there **k.** nor understanding to say,	1847
Isa	44:25	and maketh their **k.** foolish;	1847
Isa	45:20	have no **k.** that set up the wood	3045
Isa	47:10	thy **k.**, it hath perverted thee;	1847
Isa	53:11	by his **k.** shall my righteous servant	1847
Isa	58:3	soul, and thou takest no **k.**?	3045
Jer	3:15	which shall feed you with **k.** and	1844
Jer	4:22	but to do good they have no **k.**	3045
Jer	10:14	Every man is brutish in his **k.**:	1847
Jer	11:18	the Lord hath given me **k.** of it,	3045
Jer	51:17	Every man is brutish by his **k.**;	1847
Da	1:4	in all wisdom, and cunning in **k.**,	1847
Da	1:17	God gave them **k.** and skill in all	4093
Da	2:21	wise, and **k.** to them that know	998
Da	5:12	as an excellent spirit, and **k.**, and	998
Da	12:4	and fro, and **k.** shall be increased.	1847
Ho	4:1	nor mercy, nor **k.** of God in the land.	1847
Ho	4:6	people are destroyed for lack of **k.**:	1847
Ho	4:6	because thou hast rejected **k.**, I will	1847
Ho	6:6	**k.** of God more than burnt offerings.	1847
Hab	2:14	be filled with the **k.** of the glory of	3045
Mal	2:7	the priest's lips should keep **k.**,	1847
Mt	14:35	men of that place had **k.** of him,	*1921*
Lu	1:77	give **k.** of salvation unto his people	*1108*
Lu	11:52	**ye have taken away the key of k.**	*1108*
Ac	4:13	and they took **k.** of them, that they	*1921*
Ac	17:13	the Jews of Thessalonica had **k.**	*1097*
Ac	24:8	mayest take **k.** of all these things,	*1921*
Ac	24:22	having more perfect **k.** of that way,	*1492*
Ro	1:28	not like to retain God in their **k.**,	*1922*
Ro	2:20	hast the form of **k.** and of the truth	*1108*
Ro	3:20	for by the law is the **k.** of sin.	*1922*
Ro	10:2	zeal of God, but not according to **k.**	*1922*
Ro	11:33	both of the wisdom and **k.** of God!	*1108*
Ro	15:14	full of goodness, filled with all **k.**,	*1108*
1Co	1:5	him, in all utterance, and in all **k.**;	*1108*
1Co	8:1	idols, we know that we all have **k.**	*1108*
1Co	8:1	**K.** puffeth up, but charity edifieth.	*1108*
1Co	8:7	there is not in every man that **k.**:	*1108*
1Co	8:10	see thee which hast **k.** sit at meat	*1108*
1Co	8:11	And through thy **k.** shall the weak	*1108*
1Co	12:8	the word of **k.** by the same Spirit;	*1108*
1Co	13:2	understand all mysteries, and all **k.**;	*1108*
1Co	13:8	whether there be **k.**, it shall vanish	*1108*
1Co	14:6	to you either by revelation, or by **k.**,	*1108*
1Co	15:34	for some have not the **k.** of God:	*56*
2Co	2:14	manifest the savour of his **k.** by us	*1108*
2Co	4:6	light of the **k.** of the glory of God	*1108*
2Co	6:6	pureness, by **k.**, by longsuffering,	*1108*
2Co	8:7	in faith, and utterance, and **k.**, and	*1108*
2Co	10:5	exalteth itself against the **k.** of God,	*1108*
2Co	11:6	I be rude in speech, yet not in **k.**;	*1108*
Eph	1:17	and revelation in the **k.** of him:	*1922*
Eph	3:4	my **k.** in the mystery of Christ)	*4907*
Eph	3:19	love of Christ, which passeth **k.**,	*1108*
Eph	4:13	and of the **k.** of the Son of God,	*1922*
Php	1:9	abound yet more and more in **k.**	*1922*
Php	3:8	excellency of the **k.** of Christ Jesus	*1108*
Col	1:9	be filled with the **k.** of his will in	*1922*
Col	1:10	and increasing in the **k.** of God;	*1922*
Col	2:3	all the treasures of wisdom and **k.**	*1108*
Col	3:10	is renewed in **k.** after the image of	*1922*
1Ti	2:4	and to come unto the **k.** of the truth	*1922*

2Ti 3:7 able to come to the **k.** of the truth *1922*
Heb 10:26 have received the **k.** of the truth, *1922*
Jas 3:13 and endued with **k.** among you? *1990*
1Pe 3:7 dwell with them according to **k.**, *1108*
2Pe 1:2 unto you through the **k.** of God, *1922*
2Pe 1:3 the **k.** of him that hath called us *1922*
2Pe 1:5 your faith virtue; and to virtue **k.**; *1108*
2Pe 1:6 And to **k.**, temperance; and to *1108*
2Pe 1:8 in the **k.** of our Lord Jesus Christ. *1922*
2Pe 2:20 in the **k.** of the Lord and Saviour *1922*
2Pe 3:18 in the **k.** of our Lord and Saviour *1108*

KNOWN See also UNKNOWN.
Ge 19:8 daughters which have not **k.** man; 3045
Ge 24:16 virgin, neither had any man **k.** her: 3045
Ge 41:21 could not be **k.** that they had eaten 3045
Ge 41:31 plenty shall not be **k.** in the land by 3045
Ge 45:1 Joseph made himself **k.** unto his 3045
Ex 2:14 and said, Surely this thing is **k.** 3045
Ex 6:3 name Jehovah was I not **k.** to them. 3045
Ex 21:36 be **k.** that the ox hath used to push 3045
Ex 33:16 it be **k.** here that I and thy people 3045
Le 4:14 they have sinned against it, is **k.**, 3045
Le 5:1 whether he hath seen or **k.** of it; 3045
Nu 12:6 Lord will make myself **k.** unto him 3045
Nu 31:17 kill every woman that hath **k.** man 3045
Nu 31:18 children, that have not **k.** a man by 3045
Nu 31:35 of women that had not **k.** man by 3045
De 1:13 and **k.** among your tribes, and I will 3045
De 1:15 wise men, and **k.**, and made them 3045
De 11:2 your children which have not **k.**, 3045
De 11:28 other gods, which ye have not **k.**. 3045
De 13:2,6 other gods, which thou hast not **k.**, 3045
De 13:13 other gods, which ye have not **k.**; 3045
De 21:1 and it be not **k.** who hath slain him: 3045
De 28:36 neither thou nor thy fathers have **k.**; 3045
De 28:64 neither thou nor thy fathers have **k.**, 3045
De 31:13 children, which have not **k.** any 3045
Jos 24:31 had **k.** all the works of the Lord, 3045
Jg 3:1 had not **k.** all the wars of Canaan; 3045
Jg 16:9 the fire. So his strength was not **k.**. 3045
Jg 21:12 young virgins, that had **k.** no man by 3045
Ru 3:3 make not thyself **k.** unto the man, 3045
Ru 3:14 Let it not be **k.** that a woman came 3045
1Sa 6:3 it shall be **k.** to you why his hand is 3045
1Sa 28:15 make **k.** unto me what I shall do 3045
2Sa 17:19 thereon; and the thing was not **k.**. 3045
1Ki 14:2 be not **k.** to be the wife of Jeroboam; 3045
1Ki 18:36 it be **k.** this day that thou art God 3045
1Ch 16:8 make **k.** his deeds among the 3045
1Ch 17:19 in making **k.** all these great things 3045
Ezr 4:12 it **k.** unto the king, that the Jews 3046
Ezr 4:13 Be it **k.** now unto the king, that, if 3046
Ezr 5:8 it **k.** unto the king, that we went 3046
Ne 4:15 our enemies heard that it was **k.** 3045
Ne 9:14 And madest **k.** unto them thy holy 3045
Es 2:22 And the thing was **k.** to Mordecai, 3045
Ps 9:16 The Lord is **k.** by the judgment 3045
Ps 18:43 a people whom I have not **k.** shall 3045
Ps 31:7 thou hast **k.** my soul in adversities; 3045
Ps 48:3 God is **k.** in her palaces for a refuge 3045
Ps 67:2 That thy way may be **k.** upon earth, 3045
Ps 69:19 Thou hast **k.** my reproach, and my 3045
Ps 76:1 in Judah is God **k.**: his name is 3045
Ps 77:19 waters, and thy footsteps are not **k.**. 3045
Ps 78:3 Which we have heard and **k.**, and 3045
Ps 78:5 make them **k.** to their children: 3045
Ps 79:6 the heathen that have not **k.** thee, 3045
Ps 79:10 let him be **k.** among the heathen in 3045
Ps 88:12 Shall thy wonders be **k.** in the dark? 3045
Ps 89:1 will I make **k.** thy faithfulness to 3045
Ps 91:14 high, because he hath **k.** my name. 3045
Ps 95:10 and they have not **k.** my ways: 3045
Ps 98:2 Lord hath made **k.** his salvation: 3045
Ps 103:7 He made **k.** his ways unto Moses, 3045
Ps 105:1 make **k.** his deeds among the people 3045
Ps 106:8 make his mighty power to be **k.**. 3045
Ps 119:79 those that have **k.** thy testimonies 3045
Ps 119:152 **k.** of old that thou hast founded 3045
Ps 139:1 thou hast searched me, and **k.** me 3045
Ps 145:12 To make **k.** to the sons of men his 3045
Ps 147:20 judgments, they have not **k.** them. 3045
Pr 1:23 I will make **k.** my words unto you. 3045
Pr 10:9 that perverteth his ways shall be **k.**. 3045
Pr 12:16 A fool's wrath is presently **k.**: but 3045
Pr 14:33 is in the midst of fools is made **k.**. 3045
Pr 20:11 Even a child is **k.** by his doings, 5234
Pr 22:19 I have made **k.** to thee this day, 3045
Pr 31:23 Her husband is **k.** in the gates, 3045
Ec 5:3 a fool's voice is **k.** by multitude of
Ec 6:5 not seen the sun, nor **k.** any thing: 3045
Ec 6:10 already, and it is **k.** that it is man: 3045
Isa 12:5 things: this is **k.** in all the earth. 3045
Isa 19:21 the Lord shall be **k.** to Egypt, and 3045
Isa 38:19 children shall make **k.** thy truth. 3045
Isa 40:21 Have ye not **k.**? have ye not heard? 3045
Isa 40:28 Hast thou not **k.**? hast thou not 3045
Isa 42:16 them in paths that they have not **k.**: 3045
Isa 44:18 They have not **k.** nor understood: 3045
Isa 45:4 thee, though thou hast not **k.** me. 3045
Isa 45:5 thee, though thou hast not **k.** me: 3045
Isa 61:9 seed shall be **k.** among the Gentiles, 3045
Isa 64:2 thy name **k.** to thine adversaries, 3045
Isa 66:14 hand of the Lord shall be **k.** toward 3045
Jer 4:22 is foolish, they have not **k.** me; 3045
Jer 5:5 they have **k.** the way of the Lord, 3045
Jer 9:16 they nor their fathers have **k.**: 3045
Jer 19:4 they nor their fathers have **k.**, 3045
Jer 28:9 pass, then shall the prophet be **k.**, 3045
La 4:8 they are not **k.** in the streets: 5234
Eze 20:5 and made myself **k.** unto them in 3045
Eze 20:9 whose sight I made myself **k.** unto 3045
Eze 32:9 countries which thou hast not **k.**. 3045
Eze 35:11 I will make myself **k.** among them, 3045
Eze 36:32 the Lord God, be it **k.** unto you: 3045
Eze 38:23 be **k.** in the eyes of many nations 3045
Eze 39:7 So will I make my holy name **k.** in 3045
Da 2:5, 9 not make **k.** unto me the dream, 3046
Da 2:15 Arioch made the thing **k.** to Daniel. 3046
Da 2:17 and made the thing **k.** to Hananiah, 3046
Da 2:23 hast made **k.** unto me now what 3046
Da 2:23 thou hast now made **k.** unto us the 3046
Da 2:25 that will make **k.** unto the king the 3046
Da 2:26 able to make **k.** unto me the dream 3046
Da 2:28 **k.** to the king Nebuchadnezzar 3046
Da 2:29 **k.** to thee what shall come to pass. 3046
Da 2:30 **k.** the interpretation to the king, 3046
Da 2:45 God hath made **k.** to the king what 3046
Da 3:18 be it **k.** unto thee, O king, that we 3046
Da 4:6,7 **k.** unto me the interpretation 3046
Da 4:18 make **k.** unto me the interpretation: 3046
Da 4:26 have **k.** that the heavens do rule. 3046
Da 5:8 nor make **k.** to the king the 3046
Da 5:15 make **k.** unto me the interpretation. 3046
Da 5:16 make **k.** to me the interpretation 3046
Da 5:17 make **k.** to him the interpretation. 3046
Ho 5:4 and they have not **k.** the Lord. 3045
Ho 5:9 made **k.** that which shall surely be 3045
Am 3:2 You only have I **k.** of all the 3045
Na 3:17 their place is not **k.** where they are. 3045
Hab 3:2 in the midst of the years make **k.**; 3045
Zec 14:7 day which shall be **k.** to the Lord, 3045
Mt 10:26 **and hid, that shall not be k..** *1097*
Mt 12:7 **if ye had k. what this meaneth,** *1097*
Mt 12:16 that they should not make him **k.**: *5318*
Mt 12:33 **for the tree is k. by his fruit** *1097*
Mt 24:43 **had k. in what watch the thief** *1492*
Mk 3:12 that they should not make him **k.**. *5318*
Lu 2:15 the Lord hath made **k.** unto us. *1107*
Lu 2:17 they made **k.** abroad the saying *1232*
Lu 6:44 **every tree is k. by his own fruit.** *1097*
Lu 7:39 **k.** who and what manner of woman *1097*
Lu 8:17 **shall not be k. and come abroad.** *1097*
Lu 12:2 **neither hid, that shall not be k..** *1097*
Lu 12:39 **had k. what hour the thief would** *1492*
Lu 19:42 Saying, **If thou hadst k., even thou,** *1097*
Lu 24:18 hast not **k.** the things which are *1097*
Lu 24:35 **k.** of them in breaking of bread. *1097*
Joh 7:4 he himself seeketh to be **k.** openly.
Joh 8:19 **nor my Father: if ye had k. me,** *1492*
Joh 8:19 **ye should have k. my Father also:** *1492*
Joh 8:55 **Yet ye have not k. him; but I** *1097*
Joh 10:14 **know my sheep, and am k. of** *1097*
Joh 14:7 **k. me, ye should have k. my** *1097*
Joh 14:9 **yet hast thou not k. me, Philip?** *1097*
Joh 15:15 **Father I have made k. unto you.** *1107*
Joh 16:3 **they have not k. the Father, nor** *1097*
Joh 17:7 **Now they have k. that all things** *1097*
Joh 17:8 **have k. surely that I came out** *1097*
Joh 17:25 **Father, the world hath not k. thee:** *1097*
Joh 17:25 **but I have k. thee, and these** *1097*
Joh 17:25 **have k. that thou hast sent me** *1097*
Joh 18:15 that disciple was **k.** unto the high *1110*
Joh 18:16 which was **k.** unto the high priest, *1110*
Ac 1:19 it was **k.** unto all the dwellers at *1110*
Ac 2:14 be this **k.** unto you, and hearken to *1110*
Ac 2:28 Thou hast made **k.** to me the ways *1107*
Ac 4:10 Be it **k.** unto you all, and to all *1110*
Ac 7:13 Joseph was made **k.** to his brethren; *319*
Ac 7:13 Joseph's kindred was made **k.** *5318*
Ac 9:24 their laying await was **k.** of Saul *1097*
Ac 9:42 it was **k.** throughout all Joppa; *1110*
Ac 13:38 Be it **k.** unto you therefore, men *1110*
Ac 15:18 **K.** unto God are all his works from *1110*
Ac 19:17 And this was **k.** to all the Jews *1110*
Ac 22:30 he would have **k.** the certainty *1097*
Ac 23:28 when I would have **k.** the cause *1097*
Ac 28:28 Be it **k.** therefore unto you, that *1110*
Ro 1:19 that which may be **k.** of God is *1110*
Ro 3:17 way of peace have they not **k.**: *1097*
Ro 7:7 I had not **k.** sin, but by the law: *1097*
Ro 7:7 I had not **k.** lust, except the law *1492*
Ro 9:22 wrath, and to make his power **k.**, *1107*
Ro 9:23 that he might make **k.** the riches *1107*
Ro 11:34 who hath **k.** the mind of the Lord? *1097*
Ro 16:26 made **k.** to all nations for the *1107*
1Co 2:8 for had they **k.** it, they would not *1097*
1Co 2:16 who hath **k.** the mind of the Lord, *1097*
1Co 8:3 love God, the same is **k.** of him *1097*
1Co 13:12 shall I know even as also I am **k.**. *1921*
1Co 14:7 it be **k.** what is piped or harped? *1097*
1Co 14:9 how shall it be **k.** what is spoken? *1097*
2Co 3:2 our hearts, **k.** and read of all men: *1097*
2Co 5:16 we have **k.** Christ after the flesh, *1097*
2Co 6:9 As unknown, and yet well **k.**; *1921*
Ga 4:9 But now, after ye have **k.** God *1097*
Ga 4:9 rather are **k.** of God, how turn ye *1097*
Eph 1:9 made **k.** unto us the mystery of his *1107*
Eph 3:3 he made **k.** unto me the mystery; *1107*
Eph 3:5 not made **k.** unto the sons of men, *1107*
Eph 3:10 be **k.** by the church the manifold *1107*
Eph 6:19 make **k.** the mystery of the gospel, *1107*
Eph 6:21 shall make **k.** to you all things: *1107*
Php 4:5 moderation be **k.** unto all men *1097*
Php 4:6 requests be made **k.** unto God. *1107*
Col 1:27 would make **k.** what is the riches *1107*
Col 4:9 shall make **k.** unto you all things *1107*
2Ti 3:10 thou hast fully **k.** my doctrine, *3877*
2Ti 3:15 thou hast **k.** the holy scriptures, *1492*
2Ti 4:17 the preaching might be fully **k.**, *4135*
Heb 3:10 and they have not **k.** my ways. *1097*
2Pe 1:16 we made **k.** unto you the power *1107*
2Pe 2:21 for them not to have **k.** the way *1921*
2Pe 2:21 than, after they have **k.** it, to turn *1921*
1Jo 2:13 **k.** him that is from the beginning. *1097*
1Jo 2:13 because ye have **k.** the Father. *1097*
1Jo 2:14 **k.** him that is from the beginning. *1097*
1Jo 3:6 hath not seen him, neither **k.** him. *1097*
1Jo 4:16 have **k.** and believed the love that *1097*
2Jo 1 also all they that have **k.** the truth; *1097*
Re 2:24 **have not k. the depths of Satan,** *1097*

KOA (ko'-ah)
Eze 23:23 and Shoa, and **K.**, and all the 6970

KOHATH (ko'-hath) See also KOHATHITES.
Ge 46:11 the sons of Levi; Gershon, **K.**, 6955
Ex 6:16 Gershon, **K.**, and Merari; 6955
Ex 6:18 And the sons of **K.**; Amram, and 6955
Ex 6:18 and the years of the life of **K.** were 6955
Nu 3:17 by their names; Gershon, and **K.**, 6955
Nu 3:19 the sons of **K.** by their families; 6955
Nu 3:27 of **K.** was the family of the 6955
Nu 3:29 The families of the sons of **K.** shall 6955
Nu 4:2 sum of the sons of **K.** from among 6955
Nu 4:4 be the service of the sons of **K.** 6955
Nu 4:15 sons of **K.** shall come to bear it: 6955
Nu 4:15 are the burden of the sons of **K.** 6955
Nu 7:9 unto the sons of **K.** he gave none: 6955
Nu 16:1 Izhar, the son of **K.**, the son of 6955
Nu 26:57 of **K.**, the family of the Kohathites: 6955
Nu 26:58 Kohathites. And **K.** begat Amram 6955
Jos 21:5 the rest of the children of **K.** had 6955
Jos 21:20 the families of the children of **K.**, 6955
Jos 21:20 remained of the children of **K.**, 6955
Jos 21:26 the children of **K.** that remained 6955
1Ch 6:1 sons of Levi; Gershon, **K.**, and 6955
1Ch 6:2 sons of **K.**; Amram, Izhar, and 6955
1Ch 6:16 sons of Levi; Gershon, **K.**, and 6955
1Ch 6:18 the sons of **K.** were, Amram, and 6955
1Ch 6:22 sons of **K.**; Amminadab his son, 6955
1Ch 6:38 The son of Izhar, the son of **K.**, 6955

1Ch 6:61 unto the sons of **K.**, which were........ 6955
1Ch 6:66 of the families of the sons of **K.**.......... 6955
1Ch 6:70 of the remnant of the sons of **K.**......... 6955
1Ch 15:5 of the sons of **K.**; Uriel the chief, ... 6955
1Ch 23:6 sons of Levi, namely, Gershon, **K.**, ... 6955
1Ch 23:12 The sons of **K.**; Amram, Izhar,.......... 6955

KOHATHITES (ko'-hath-ites)
Nu 3:27 these are the families of the **K.**. 6956
Nu 3:30 father of the families of the **K.**........... 6956
Nu 4:18 the tribe of the families of the **K.**........ 6956
Nu 4:34 numbered the sons of the **K.** after...... 6956
Nu 4:37 numbered of the families of the **K.**, ... 6956
Nu 10:21 **K.** set forward, bearing the.............. 6956
Nu 26:57 of Kohath, the family of the **K.**:.......... 6956
Jos 21:4 came out for the families of the **K.**: 6956
Jos 21:10 being of the families of the **K.**, ... 6956
1Ch 6:33 Of the sons of the **K.**: Heman a......... 6956
1Ch 6:54 Aaron, of the families of the **K.**: 6956
1Ch 9:32 brethren, of the sons of the **K.**,.......... 6956
2Ch 20:19 Levites, of the children of the **K.**, ... 6956
2Ch 29:12 Azariah, of the sons of the **K.**: 6956
2Ch 34:12 Meshullam, of the sons of the **K.**, ... 6956

KOLAIAH (ko-la-i'-ah)
Ne 11:7 the son of Pedaiah, the son of **K.**,...... 6964
Jer 29:21 of Israel, of Ahab the son of **K.**, ... 6964

HOPH (kofe)
Ps 119:145 *title* [ק] **K.**..

KORAH (ko'-rah) See also CORE; KORAHITE; KORE.
Ge 36:5 bare Jeush, and Jaalam, and **K.**.......... 7141
Ge 36:14 Esau Jeush, and Jaalam, and **K.**. 7141
Ge 36:16 Duke **K.**, duke Gatam, and duke........ 7141
Ge 36:18 duke Jeush, duke Jaalam, duke **K.**: 7141
Ex 6:21 And the sons of Izhar; **K.**, and.......... 7141
Ex 6:24 And the sons of **K.**: Assir, and.......... 7141
Nu 16:1 Now **K.**, the son of Izhar, the son of.. 7141
Nu 16:5 And he spake unto **K.** and unto all...... 7141
Nu 16:6 censers, **K.**, and all his company;....... 7141
Nu 16:8 Moses said unto **K.**, Hear, I pray...... 7141
Nu 16:16 And Moses said unto **K.**, Be thou 7141
Nu 16:19 **K.** gathered all the congregation......... 7141
Nu 16:24 from about the tabernacle of **K.**, ... 7141
Nu 16:27 gat up from the tabernacle of **K.**, ... 7141
Nu 16:32 the men that appertained unto **K.**,...... 7141
Nu 16:40 he be not as **K.**, and as his.............. 7141
Nu 16:49 that died about the matter of **K.**. 7141
Nu 26:9 Aaron in the company of **K.**, ... 7141
Nu 26:10 them up together with **K.**, when........ 7141
Nu 26:11 the children of **K.** died not................ 7141
Nu 27:3 the Lord in the company of **K.**; 7141
1Ch 1:35 and Jeush, and Jaalam, and **K.**. 7141
1Ch 2:43 the sons of Hebron; **K.**, and............. 7141
1Ch 6:22 Amminadab his son, **K.** his son, ... 7141
1Ch 6:37 son of Ebiasaph, the son of **K.**, ... 7141
1Ch 9:19 son of Ebiasaph, the son of **K.**, ... 7141
Ps 42:*title* Maschil, for the sons of **K.**. 7141
Ps 44:*title* Musician for the sons of **K.**............. 7141
Ps 45:*title* Shoshannim, for the sons of **K.**,........ 7141
Ps 46:*title* Musician for the sons of **K.**,............ 7141
Ps 47:*title* A Psalm for the sons of **K.**............... 7141
Ps 48:*title* and Psalm for the sons of **K.**............. 7141
Ps 49:*title* A Psalm for the sons of **K.**................ 7141
Ps 84:*title* A Psalm for the sons of **K.**. 7141
Ps 85:*title* A Psalm for the sons of **K.**. 7141
Ps 87:*title* Psalm or Song for the sons of **K.**....... 7141
Ps 88:*title* Song or Psalm for the sons of **K.**....... 7141

KORAHITE (ko'-ra-hite) See also KORAHITES; KORE.
1Ch 9:31 the firstborn of Shallum the **K.**, ... 7145

KORAHITES (ko'-ra-hites) See also KORATHITES; KORHITES.
1Ch 9:19 the **K.**, were over the work of the..... 7145

KORATHITES (ko'-ra-thites) See also KORAHITES.
Nu 26:58 Mushites, the family of the **K.**. 7145

KORE (ko'-re) See also KORAH; KORAHITE.
1Ch 9:19 And Shallum the son of **K.**,............... 6981
1Ch 26:1 was Meshelemiah the son of **K.**, ... 6981
1Ch 26:19 the porters among the sons of **K.**,....... 7145
2Ch 31:14 **K.** the son of Imnah the Levite,.......... 6981

KORHITES (kor'-hites) See also KORAHITES.
Ex 6:24 these are the families of the **K.**. 7145
1Ch 12:6 Joezer, and Jashobeam, the **K.**,.......... 7145
1Ch 26:1 **K.** was Meshelemiah the son of......... 7145
2Ch 20:19 and of the children of the **K.**, stood.... 7145

KOZ (coz) See also HAKKOZ.
Ezr 2:61 the children of **K.**, the children.......... 6976
Ne 3:4 the son of Urijah, the son of **K.**. 6976
Ne 3:21 the son of **K.** another piece, from 6976
Ne 7:63 of Habaiah, the children of **K.**, ... 6976

KUSHAIAH (cu-shah'-yah) See also KISHI.
1Ch 15:17 brethren, Ethan the son of **K.**; 6984

L.

LAADAH (la'-a-dah)
1Ch 4:21 **L.** the father of Mareshah, and.......... 3935

LAADAN (la'-a-dan) See also LIBNI.
1Ch 7:26 **L.** his son, Ammihud his son,............ 3936
1Ch 23:7 Of the Gershonites were, **L.**, and 3936
1Ch 23:8 The sons of **L.**; the chief was Jehiel, .. 3936
1Ch 23:9 were the chief of the fathers of **L.**. 3936
1Ch 26:21 As concerning the sons of **L.**; the 3936
1Ch 26:21 sons of the Gershonite **L.**, chief......... 3936
1Ch 26:21 even of **L.** the Gershonite, were........ 3936

LABAN (la'-ban) See also LABAN'S; LIBNAH.
Ge 24:29 a brother, and his name was **L.**: 3837
Ge 24:29 and **L.** ran out unto the man, unto 3837
Ge 24:50 **L.** and Bethuel answered and said, ... 3837
Ge 25:20 the sister to **L.** the Syrian. 3837
Ge 27:43 flee thou to **L.** my brother to Haran; .. 3837
Ge 28:2 from thence of the daughters of **L.**...... 3837
Ge 28:5 and he went to Padan-aram unto **L.**,... 3837
Ge 29:5 them, Know ye **L.** the son of Nahor?.. 3837
Ge 29:10 Jacob saw Rachel the daughter of **L.**.... 3837
Ge 29:10 sheep of **L.** his mother's brother,........ 3837
Ge 29:10 watered the flock of **L.** his mother's 3837
Ge 29:13 when **L.** heard the tidings of Jacob 3837
Ge 29:13 And he told **L.** all these things. 3837
Ge 29:14 **L.** said to him, Surely thou art my 3837
Ge 29:15 **L.** said unto Jacob, Because thou 3837
Ge 29:16 **L.** had two daughters: the name of...... 3837
Ge 29:19 **L.** said, It is better that I give her 3837
Ge 29:21 And Jacob said unto **L.**, Give me my .. 3837
Ge 29:22 **L.** gathered together all the men of.... 3837
Ge 29:24 **L.** gave unto his daughter Leah 3837
Ge 29:25 he said to **L.**, What is this thou hast... 3837
Ge 29:26 And **L.** said, It must not be so done.... 3837
Ge 29:29 And **L.** gave to Rachel his daughter.... 3837
Ge 30:25 Jacob said unto **L.**, Send me away,..... 3837
Ge 30:27 And **L.** said unto him, I pray thee, ... 3837
Ge 30:34 **L.** said, Behold, I would it might be ... 3837
Ge 30:40 and all the brown in the flock of **L.**;.... 3837
Ge 31:2 beheld the countenance of **L.**, and,..... 3837
Ge 31:12 seen all that **L.** doeth unto thee......... 3837
Ge 31:19 And **L.** went to shear his sheep:........ 3837
Ge 31:20 Jacob stole away unawares to **L.** the... 3837
Ge 31:22 told **L.** on the third day that Jacob...... 3837
Ge 31:24 came to **L.** the Syrian in a dream....... 3837
Ge 31:25 Then **L.** overtook Jacob. Now Jacob ... 3837
Ge 31:25 **L.** with his brethren pitched in the 3837
Ge 31:26 **L.** said to Jacob, What hast thou........ 3837
Ge 31:31 Jacob answered and said to **L.**, ... 3837
Ge 31:33 **L.** went into Jacob's tent, and into...... 3837
Ge 31:34 **L.** searched all the tent, but found 3837
Ge 31:36 was wroth, and chode with **L.**: 3837
Ge 31:36 Jacob answered and said unto **L.**, ... 3837
Ge 31:43 **L.** answered and said unto Jacob, ... 3837
Ge 31:47 And **L.** called it Jegar-sahadutha: 3837
Ge 31:48 And **L.** said, This heap is a witness..... 3837
Ge 31:51 **L.** said to Jacob, Behold this heap, ... 3837
Ge 31:55 **L.** rose up, and kissed his sons and.... 3837
Ge 31:55 **L.** departed, and returned unto his..... 3837
Ge 32:4 have sojourned with **L.**, and stayed 3837
Ge 46:18 whom **L.** gave to Leah his daughter;... 3837
Ge 46:25 which **L.** gave unto Rachel his.......... 3837
De 1:1 Tophel, and **L.**, and Hazeroth, and...... 3837

LABAN'S (la'-bans)
Ge 30:36 and Jacob fed the rest of **L.** flocks...... 3837
Ge 30:40 and put them not unto **L.** cattle. 3837
Ge 30:42 feebler were **L.**, and the stronger 3837
Ge 31:1 heard the words of **L.** sons, saying,.... 3837

LABOUR See also LABOURED; LABOURETH; LABOURING; LABOURS.
Ge 31:42 affliction and the **l.** of my hands, ... 3018
Ge 35:16 travailed, and she had hard **l.**. 3205
Ge 35:17 when she was in hard **l.**, that the....... 3205
Ex 5:9 the men, that they may **l.** therein;...... 6213
Ex 20:9 Six days shalt thou **l.**, and do all 5647
De 5:13 Six days thou shalt **l.**, and do all 5647
De 26:7 and our **l.**, and our oppression: 5999
Jos 7:3 not all the people to **l.** thither;........... 3021
Jos 24:13 you a land for which ye did not **l.**,....... 3021
Ne 4:22 be a guard to us, and **l.** on the day. ... 4399
Ne 5:13 from his house, and from his **l.**,.......... 3018
Job 9:29 be wicked, why then **l.** I in vain? 3021
Job 39:11 or wilt thou leave thy **l.** to him?......... 3018
Job 39:16 hers: her **l.** is in vain without fear; 3018
Ps 78:46 gave also...their **l.** unto the locust. 3018
Ps 90:10 yet is their strength **l.** and sorrow;..... 5999
Ps 104:23 forth unto his work and to his **l.** 5656
Ps 105:44 they inherited the **l.** of the people; 5999
Ps 107:12 he brought down their heart with **l.**; ... 5999
Ps 109:11 and let the strangers spoil his **l.**.......... 3018
Ps 127:1 house, they **l.** in vain that build it:...... 5998
Ps 128:2 shalt eat the **l.** of thine hands: 3018
Ps 144:14 our oxen may be strong to **l.**;............ 5445
Pr 10:16 **l.** of the righteous tendeth to life:....... 6468
Pr 13:11 that gathereth by **l.** shall increase....... 3027
Pr 14:23 In all **l.** there is profit: but the.......... 6089
Pr 21:25 him; for his hands refuse to **l.**. 6213
Pr 23:4 **L.** not to be rich: cease from thine..... 3021
Ec 1:3 What profit hath a man of all his **l.** 5999
Ec 1:8 All things are full of **l.**; man 3023
Ec 2:10 for my heart rejoiced in all my **l.**:........ 5999
Ec 2:10 and this was my portion of all my **l.**..... 5999
Ec 2:11 the **l.** that I had laboured to.............. 5999
Ec 2:18 I hated all my **l.** which I had taken 5999
Ec 2:19 he have rule over all my **l.**................. 5999
Ec 2:20 the **l.** which I took under the sun. 5999
Ec 2:21 is a man whose **l.** is in wisdom, and ... 5999
Ec 2:22 For what hath man of all his **l.**, and.... 5999
Ec 2:24 make his soul enjoy good in his **l.**....... 5999
Ec 3:13 and enjoy the good of all his **l.**, it is.... 5999
Ec 4:8 yet is there no end of all his **l.**; 5999
Ec 4:8 For whom do I **l.**, and bereave my..... 6001
Ec 4:9 have a good reward for their **l.**. 5999
Ec 5:15 shall take nothing of his **l.**, which....... 5999
Ec 5:18 enjoy the good of all his **l.** that he...... 5999
Ec 5:19 his portion, and to rejoice in his **l.**;...... 5999
Ec 6:7 All the **l.** of man is for his mouth, ... 5999
Ec 8:15 that shall abide with him of his **l.**........ 5999
Ec 8:17 though a man **l.** to seek it out, yet...... 5998
Ec 9:9 and in thy **l.** which thou takest 5999
Ec 10:15 **l.** of the foolish wearieth every one 5999
Isa 22:4 **l.** not to comfort me, because of the.... 213
Isa 45:14 The **l.** of Egypt, and merchandise....... 3018
Isa 55:2 your **l.** for that which satisfieth not?.... 3018
Isa 65:23 They shall not **l.** in vain, nor bring 3021
Jer 3:24 shame hath devoured the **l.** of our....... 3018
Jer 20:18 forth out of the womb to see **l.** and.... 5999
Jer 51:58 and the people shall **l.** in vain, and...... 3021
La 5:5 we **l.**, and have no rest.................... 3021
Eze 23:29 and shall take away all thy **l.**, and....... 3018
Eze 29:20 his **l.** wherewith he served against....... 6468
Mic 4:10 and **l.** to bring forth, O daughter........ 1518
Hab 2:13 the people shall **l.** in the very fire, ... 3021
Hab 3:17 the **l.** of the olive shall fail, and.......... 4639
Hag 1:11 and upon all the **l.** of the hands.......... 3018
Mt 11:28 **come unto me, all ye that l. and** ... *2872*
Joh 4:38 **that whereon ye bestowed no l.:**.... *2872*
Joh 6:27 **L. not for...meat which perisheth,**..*2038*
Ro 16:6 who bestowed much **l.** on us............. *2872*
Ro 16:12 and Tryphosa, who **l.** in the Lord....... *2872*
1Co 3:8 reward according to his own **l.**........... *2873*
1Co 4:12 **l.**, working with our own hands:......... *2872*
1Co 15:58 your **l.** is not in vain in the Lord. *2873*
2Co 5:9 Wherefore we **l.**, that, whether *5389*
Ga 4:11 have bestowed upon you **l.** in vain...... *2872*
Eph 4:28 rather let him **l.**, working with his *2872*

Php 1:22 the flesh, this is the fruit of my **l.**: *2041*
Php 2:25 my brother, and companion in **l.**,........ *4904*
Col 1:29 Whereunto I also **l.**, striving............ *2872*
1Th 1:3 your work of faith, and **l.** of love,....... *2873*
1Th 2:9 brethren, our **l.** and travail:............. *2873*
1Th 3:5 tempted you, and our **l.** be in vain...... *2873*
1Th 5:12 to know them which **l.** among you,..... *2872*
2Th 3:8 wrought with **l.** and travail night......... *2873*
1Ti 4:10 we both **l.** and suffer reproach,.......... *2872*
1Ti 5:17 who **l.** in the word and doctrine.......... *2872*
Heb 4:11 **l.** therefore to enter into that rest,..... *4704*
Heb 6:10 to forget your work and **l.** of love,..... *2873*
Re 2:2 **I know thy works, and thy l., and** *2873*

LABOURED
Ne 4:21 So we **l.** in the work: and half of........ 6213
Job 20:18 which he **l.** for shall he restore,......... 3022
Ec 2:11 on the labour that I had **l.** to do:......... 5998
Ec 2:19 all my labour wherein I have **l.**,......... 5998
Ec 2:21 to a man that hath not **l.** therein........ 5998
Ec 2:22 wherein he hath **l.** under the sun?...... 6001
Ec 5:16 hath he that hath **l.** for the wind?....... 5998
Isa 47:12 thou hast **l.** from thy youth;............. 3021
Isa 47:15 with whom thou hast **l.**, even thy......... 3021
Isa 49:4 Then I said, I have **l.** in vain, I have... 3021
Isa 62:8 thy wine, for the which thou hast **l.**:... 3021
Da 6:14 he **l.** till the going down of the sun..... 7712
Jon 4:10 for the which thou hast not **l.**,........... 5998
Joh 4:38 **other men l., and ye are entered**... *2872*
Ro 16:12 Persis, which **l.** much in the Lord....... *2872*
1Co 15:10 I **l.** more abundantly than they all:...... *2872*
Php 2:16 not run in vain, neither **l.** in vain........ *2872*
Php 4:3 which **l.** with me in the gospel,.......... *4866*
Re 2:3 **and for my name's sake hast l.,**.... *2872*

LABOURER See also FELLOWLABOURER; LABOURERS.
Lu 10:7 **for the l. is worthy of his hire**..... *2040*
1Ti 5:18 And, The **l.** is worthy of his reward.... *2040*

LABOURERS See also FELLOWLABOURERS.
Mt 9:37 **is plenteous, but the l. are few;**..... *2040*
Mt 9:38 **will end forth l. into his harvest**.... *2040*
Mt 20:1 **morning to hire l. into his**............ *2040*
Mt 20:2 **agreed with the l. for a penny a**.... *2040*
Mt 20:8 **Call the l., and give them their**..... *2040*
Lu 10:2 **truly is great, but the l. are few:**... *2040*
Lu 10:2 **that he would send forth l. into his** *2040*
1Co 3:9 For we are **l.** together with God:....... *4904*
Jas 5:4 the hire of the **l.** who have reaped..... *2040*

LABOURETH
Pr 16:26 He that **l.**...for himself; for.............. 6001
Pr 16:26 **l.** for himself; for his mouth.............. 5998
Ec 3:9 that worketh wherein he **l.**?.......... 6001
1Co 16:16 one that helpeth with us, and **l.**........ *2872*
2Ti 2:6 husbandman that **l.** must be first........ *2872*

LABOURING
Ec 5:12 The sleep of a **l.** man is sweet,......... 5647
Ac 20:35 so **l.** ye ought to support the weak,.... *2872*
Col 4:12 **l.** fervently for you in prayers,.............. *75*
1Th 2:9 for **l.** night and day, because we........ *2873*

LABOURS
Ex 23:16 of harvest, the firstfruits of thy **l.**,....... 4639
Ex 23:16 gathered in thy **l.** out of the field....... 4639
De 28:33 The fruit of thy land, and all thy **l.**,..... 3018
Pr 5:10 **l.** be in the house of a stranger;........ 6089
Isa 58:3 pleasure, and exact all your **l.**............ 6092
Jer 20:5 of this city, and all the **l.** thereof,....... 3018
Ho 12:8 my **l.** they shall find none iniquity......... 3018
Hag 2:17 hail in all the **l.** of your hands;........... 4639
Joh 4:38 **and ye are entered into their l.**..... *2873*
2Co 6:5 in imprisonments, in tumults, in **l.**,..... *2873*
2Co 10:15 measure, that is, of other men's **l.**;.... *2873*
2Co 11:23 in **l.** more abundant, in stripes........... *2873*
Re 14:13 that they may rest from their **l.**;........ *2873*

LACE
Ex 28:28 rings of the ephod with a **l.** of blue,.... 6616
Ex 28:37 And thou shalt put it on a blue **l.**,...... 6616
Ex 39:21 rings of the ephod with a **l.** of blue,.... 6616
Ex 39:31 And they tied unto it a **l.** of blue, to... 6616

LACHISH (la'-kish)
Jos 10:3 and unto Japhia king of **L.**, and......... 3923
Jos 10:5, 23 king of Jarmuth, the king of **L.**,...... 3923
Jos 10:31 and all Israel with him, unto **L.**,......... 3923
Jos 10:32 delivered **L.** into the hand of Israel,.... 3923
Jos 10:33 king of Gezer came up to help **L.**:....... 3923
Jos 10:34 from **L.** Joshua passed unto Eglon,..... 3923
Jos 10:35 to all that he had done to **L.**............ 3923
Jos 12:11 Jarmuth, one; the king of **L.**, one;...... 3923
Jos 15:39 **L.**, and Bozkath, and Eglon,............. 3923
2Ki 14:19 in Jerusalem: and he fled to **L.**;......... 3923
2Ki 14:19 they sent after him to **L.**, and slew.... 3923
2Ki 18:14 sent to the king of Assyria to **L.**,........ 3923
2Ki 18:17 sent...from **L.** to king Hezekiah......... 3923
2Ki 19:8 heard that he was departed from **L.**..... 3923
2Ch 11:9 And Adoraim, and **L.**, and Azekah,..... 3923
2Ch 25:27 in Jerusalem; and he fled to **L.**:......... 3923
2Ch 25:27 they sent to **L.** after him, and slew.... 3923
2Ch 32:9 he himself laid siege against **L.**,......... 3923
Ne 11:30 at **L.**, and the fields thereof, at.......... 3923
Isa 36:2 sent...from **L.** to Jerusalem unto........ 3923
Isa 37:8 heard that he was departed from **L.**..... 3923
Jer 34:7 of Judah that were left, against **L.**,..... 3923
Mic 1:13 O thou inhabitant of **L.**, bind the....... 3923

LACK See also LACKED; LACKEST; LACKETH; LACKING.
Ge 18:28 there shall **l.** five of the fifty............. 2637
Ge 18:28 destroy all the city for **l.** of five?.............
Ex 16:18 he that gathered little had no **l.**;......... 2637
De 8:9 thou shalt not **l.** any thing in it;......... 2637
Job 4:11 old lion perisheth for **l.** of prey,......... 1097
Job 38:41 God, they wander for **l.** of meat........ 1097
Ps 34:10 The young lions do **l.**, and suffer........ 7326
Pr 28:27 giveth unto the poor shall not **l.**:........ 4270
Ec 9:8 and let thy head **l.** no ointment.......... 2637
Ho 4:6 are destroyed for **l.** of knowledge:...... 1097
Mt 19:20 from my youth up: what **l.** I yet?....... *5302*
2Co 8:15 that had gathered little had no **l.**....... *1641*
Php 2:30 to supply your **l.** of service toward..... *5303*
1Th 4:12 that ye may have **l.** of nothing........... *5332*
Jas 1:5 If any of you **l.** wisdom, let him......... *3007*

LACKED
De 2:7 with thee: thou hast **l.** nothing........... 2637
2Sa 2:30 **l.** of David's servants nineteen........... 6485
2Sa 17:22 the morning light thee **l.** not one........ 5737
1Ki 4:27 man in his month: they **l.** nothing....... 5737
1Ki 11:22 But what hast thou **l.** with me,.......... 2638
Ne 9:21 wilderness, so that they **l.** nothing;..... 2637
Lu 8:6 **away, because it l. moisture**.. *3361,2192*
Lu 22:35 **scrip, and shoes, l. ye any thing?**.. *5302*
Ac 4:34 was there any among them that **l.**:..... *1729*
1Co 12:24 honour to that part which **l.**:............ *5302*
Php 4:10 also careful, but ye **l.** opportunity....... *170*

LACKEST
Mk 10:21 said unto him, **One thing thou l.**...... *5302*
Lu 18:22 unto him, **Yet l. thou one thing:**..... *3007*

LACKETH
Nu 31:49 and there **l.** not one man of us.......... 6485
2Sa 3:29 on the sword, or that **l.** bread........... 2638
Pr 6:32 with a woman **l.** understanding:.......... 2638
Pr 12:9 honoureth himself, and **l.** bread.......... 2638
2Pe 1:9 that **l.** these things is blind,....... *3361,3918*

LACKING
Le 2:13 to be **l.** from thy meat offering:......... 7673
Le 22:23 thing superfluous or **l.** in his parts,..... 7038
Jg 21:3 be to day one tribe **l.** in Israel?......... 6485
1Sa 30:19 And there was nothing **l.** to them,....... 5737
Jer 23:4 neither shall they be **l.**, saith the........ 6485
1Co 16:17 that which was **l.** on your part they..... *5303*
2Co 11:9 that which was **l.** to me the brethren... *5303*
1Th 3:10 that which is **l.** in your faith?............ *5303*

LAD See also LAD'S; LADS.
Ge 21:12 in thy sight because of the **l.**, and...... 5288
Ge 21:17 And God heard the voice of the **l.**:..... 5288
Ge 21:17 God hath heard the voice of the **l.**....... 5288
Ge 21:18 Arise, lift up the **l.**, and hold him in.... 5288
Ge 21:19 with water, and gave the **l.** drink........ 5288
Ge 21:20 God was with the **l.**; and he grew,..... 5288
Ge 22:5 and I and the **l.** will go yonder and..... 5288
Ge 22:12 Lay not thy hand upon the **l.**,........... 5288
Ge 37:2 the **l.** was with the sons of Bilhah,...... 5288
Ge 43:8 Send the **l.** with me, and we will........ 5288
Ge 44:22 The **l.** cannot leave his father: for...... 5288
Ge 44:30 father, and the **l.** be not with us;....... 5288
Ge 44:31 he seeth that the **l.** is not with us,...... 5288
Ge 44:32 thy servant became surety for the **l.**.... 5288
Ge 44:33 thy servant abide instead of the **l.**...... 5288
Ge 44:33 let the **l.** go up with his brethren........ 5288
Ge 44:34 father, and the **l.** be not with me?...... 5288
Jg 16:26 Samson said unto the **l.** that held....... 5288
1Sa 20:21 behold, I will send a **l.**, saying, Go,.... 5288
1Sa 20:21 If I expressly say unto the **l.**,............ 5288
1Sa 20:35 with David, and a little **l.** with him...... 5288
1Sa 20:36 he said unto his **l.**, Run, find out........ 5288
1Sa 20:36 And as the **l.** ran, he shot an arrow.... 5288
1Sa 20:37 when the **l.** was come to the place..... 5288
1Sa 20:37 Jonathan after the **l.**, and said,.......... 5288
1Sa 20:38 Jonathan cried after the **l.**, Make........ 5288
1Sa 20:38 And Jonathan's **l.** gathered up the....... 5288
1Sa 20:39 But the **l.** knew not any thing: only.... 5288
1Sa 20:40 gave his artillery unto his **l.**, and........ 5288
1Sa 20:41 as soon as the **l.** was gone, David........ 5288
2Sa 17:18 Nevertheless a **l.** saw them, and told.. 5288
2Ki 4:19 And he said to a **l.**, Carry him to his.. 5288
Joh 6:9 There is a **l.** here, which hath five..... *3808*

LADDER
Ge 28:12 behold a **l.** set up on the earth,......... 5551

LADE See also LADED; LADEN; LADETH; LADING; UNLADE.
Ge 45:17 **l.** your beasts, and go, get you.......... 2943
1Ki 12:11 did **l.** you with a heavy yoke,............ 6006
Lu 11:46 **l. men with burdens grievous to**.... *5412*

LADED
Ge 42:26 they **l.** their asses with the corn,....... 5375
Ge 44:13 and **l.** every man his ass, and........... 6006
Ne 4:17 bare burdens, with those that **l.**,........ 6006
Ac 28:10 **l.** us with such things as were........... *2007*

LADEN See also LOADEN.
Ge 45:23 ten asses **l.** with the good things........ 5375
Ge 45:23 ten she asses **l.** with corn and........... 5375
1Sa 16:20 And Jesse took an ass **l.** with bread,... 5375
Isa 1:4 people **l.** with iniquity, a seed of........ 3515
Mt 11:28 **all ye that labour and are heavy l.,** *5412*
2Ti 3:6 captive silly women **l.** with sins,.......... *4987*

LADETH See also LOADETH.
Hab 2:6 that **l.** himself with thick clay!........... 3515

LADIES
Jg 5:29 Her wise **l.** answered her, yea, she.... 8282
Es 1:18 **l.** of Persia and Media say this day..... 8282

LADING
Ne 13:15 bringing in sheaves, and **l.** asses;....... 6006
Ac 27:10 not only of the **l.** and ship, but.......... *5414*

LAD'S
Ge 44:30 his life is bound up in the **l.** life;......... 5288

LADS
Ge 48:16 me from all evil, bless the **l.**;............ 5288

LADY See also LADIES.
Isa 47:5 be called, The **l.** of kingdoms............ 1404
Isa 47:7 thou saidst, I shall be a **l.** for ever:.... 1404
2Jo 1 unto the elect **l.** and her children,...... *2959*
2Jo 5 I beseech thee, **l.**, not as though I..... *2959*

LAEL (la'-el)
Nu 3:24 shall be Eliasaph the son of **L.**........... 3815

LAHAD (la'-had)
1Ch 4:2 Jahath begat Ahumai, and **L.**............ 3854

LAHAI-ROI (la-hah'-ee-roy) See also BEER-LAHAIROI.
Ge 24:62 came from the way of the well **L.**;....... 883
Ge 25:11 and Isaac dwelt by the well **L.**........... 883

LAHMAM (lah'-mam)
Jos 15:40 And Cabbon, and **L.**, and Kithlish,)..... 3903

LAHMI (lah'-mi) See also BETHLEHEMITE.
1Ch 20:5 the son of Jair slew **L.** the............... 3902

LAID See also LAIDST; OVERLAID.
Ge 9:23 **l.** it upon both their shoulders,.......... 7760
Ge 15:10 **l.** each piece one against another:........ 5414
Ge 19:16 the men **l.** hold upon his hand,.................
Ge 22:6 and **l.** it upon Isaac his son;.............. 7760
Ge 22:9 there, and **l.** the wood in order,...............
Ge 22:9 **l.** him on the altar upon the wood........ 7760
Ge 30:41 Jacob **l.** the rods before the eyes....... 7760
Ge 38:19 **l.** by her vail from her, and put on..... 5493
Ge 39:16 she **l.** up his garment by her, until..... 3241
Ge 41:48 and **l.** up the food in the cities:.......... 5414
Ge 41:48 every city, **l.** he up in the same.......... 5414
Ge 48:14 and **l.** it upon Ephraim's head,............ 7896
Ge 48:17 **l.** his right hand upon the head of....... 7896
Ex 2:3 she **l.** it in the flags by the river's...... 7760
Ex 5:9 more work be **l.** upon the men,......... 3515
Ex 16:24 **l.** up till the morning, as Moses......... 3241

Ex 16:34 Aaron l. it up before the Testimony,... 3241
Ex 19:7 l. before their faces all these............ 7760
Ex 21:30 If...be l. on him a sum of money,........ 7896
Ex 21:30 his life whatsoever is l. upon him. 7896
Ex 24:11 of Israel he l. not his hand: also........ 7971
Le 8:14, 18,22 his sons l. their hands upon...... 5564
Nu 16:18 l. incense thereon, and stood in......... 7760
Nu 17:7 Moses l. up the rods before the 3241
Nu 21:30 l. them waste even unto Nophah, ...
Nu 27:23 he l. his hands upon him, and........... 5564
De 26:6 us, and l. upon us hard bondage: 5414
De 29:22 which the Lord hath l. upon it; 2470
De 32:34 Is not this l. up in store with me, ... 3647
De 34:9 Moses had l. his hands upon him: 5564
Jos 2:6 she had l. in order upon the roof.............
Jos 2:8 before they were l. down, she came... 7901
Jos 4:8 lodged, and l. them down there. 3241
Jos 7:23 and l. them out before the Lord.......... 3332
Jos 10:27 l. great stones in the cave's mouth,.... 7760
Jg 9:24 blood be l. upon Abimelech their........ 7760
Jg 9:34 l. wait against Shechem in four................
Jg 9:43 and l. wait in the field, and looked,..........
Jg 9:48 took it, and l. it on his shoulder,......... 7760
Jg 16:2 l. wait for him all night in the gate...........
Jg 19:29 l. hold on his concubine, and divided.........
Ru 3:7 uncovered his feet,...l. her down. 7901
Ru 3:15 of barley, and l. it on her: 7896
Ru 4:16 the child, and l. it in her bosom, ... 7896
1Sa 3:2 when Eli was l. down in his place,...... 7901
1Sa 3:3 and Samuel was l. down to sleep; 7901
1Sa 6:11 l. the ark of the Lord upon the.......... 7760
1Sa 10:25 book, and l. it up before the Lord. 3241
1Sa 15:2 how he l. wait for him in the way, ... 7760
1Sa 15:5 Amalek, and l. wait in the valley. ....
1Sa 15:27 l. hold upon the skirt of his mantel, ...
1Sa 19:13 took an image, and l. it in the bed,..... 7760
1Sa 21:12 David l. up these words in his........... 7760
1Sa 25:18 cakes of figs, and l. them on asses..... 7760
2Sa 13:8 Ammon's house;...he was l. down. 7901
2Sa 13:19 her, and l. her hand on her head,....... 7760
2Sa 18:17 and l. a very great heap of stones...... 5324
1Ki 3:20 slept, and l. it in her bosom, ... 7901
1Ki 3:20 l. her dead child in my bosom. 7901
1Ki 6:37 foundation of the house of the Lord l., .7901
1Ki 8:31 be l. upon him to cause him to.......... 5375
1Ki 13:29 man of God, and l. it upon the ass, ... 3241
1Ki 13:30 he l. his carcase in his own grave; 3241
1Ki 15:27 and all Israel l. siege to Gibbethon. ....
1Ki 16:34 he l. the foundation thereof in.................
1Ki 17:19 and l. him upon his own bed. 7901
1Ki 18:33 in pieces, and l. him on the wood,...... 7760
1Ki 19:6 drink, and l. him down again. 7901
1Ki 21:4 he l. him down upon his bed, and....... 7901
2Ki 4:21 l. him on the bed of the man of......... 7901
2Ki 4:31 and l. the staff upon the face of......... 7760
2Ki 4:32 was dead, and l. upon his bed. 7901
2Ki 5:23 l. them upon two of his servants;....... 5414
2Ki 9:25 the Lord l. this burden upon him;....... 5375
2Ki 11:16 they l. hands on her; and she........... 7760
2Ki 12:11 they l. it out to the carpenters 3318
2Ki 12:12 l. out for the house to repair it.......... 3318
2Ki 20:7 took and l. it on the boil, and he........ 7760
2Ki 20:17 thy fathers have l. up in store ....
2Ch 6:22 an oath be l. upon him to make 5375
2Ch 7:22 of Egypt, and l. hold on other gods, ...
2Ch 16:14 l. him in the bed which was filled....... 7901
2Ch 23:15 So they l. hands on her; and............ 7760
2Ch 24:9 the servant of God l. upon Israel.............
2Ch 24:27 greatness of the burdens l. upon him, ...
2Ch 29:23 they l. their hands upon them:.......... 5564
2Ch 31:6 their God, and l. them by heaps. 5414
2Ch 32:9 he himself l. siege against Lachish, ...
Ezr 3:6 foundation of the temple...was not yet l.....
Ezr 3:10 l. the foundation of the temple of ....
Ezr 3:11 foundation of...house of Lord was l..........
Ezr 3:12 foundation of this house was l.................
Ezr 5:8 and timber is l. in the walls,............. 7760
Ezr 5:16 l. the foundation of the house of 3052
Ezr 6:1 treasures were l. up in Babylon. 5182
Ezr 6:3 foundations thereof be strongly l.; 5446
Ne 3:3 build, who also l. the beams thereof, ...
Ne 3:6 they l. the beams thereof, and set..........
Ne 13:5 they l. the meat offerings, ... 5414
Es 8:7 he l. his hand upon the Jews............. 7971
Es 9:10 on the spoil l. they not their hand. 7971
Es 9:15 on the prey they l. not their hand. 7971
Es 9:16 they l. not their hands on the prey,..... 7971
Es 10:1 Ahasuerus l. a tribute upon the......... 7760
Job 6:2 and my calamity l. in the balances 5375
Job 18:10 snare is l. for him in the ground,.............
Job 29:9 and l. their hand on their mouth......... 7760
Job 31:9 l. wait at my neighbour's door; ....
Job 38:4 I l. the foundations of the earth? ....
Job 38:5 Who hath l. the measures thereof, ... 7760
Job 38:6 or who l. the corner stone thereof; 3384
Ps 3:5 I l. me down and slept; I awaked;...... 7901
Ps 21:5 majesty hast thou l. upon him........... 7737
Ps 31:4 net that they have l. privily for.......... 2934
Ps 31:19 hast l. up for them that fear thee;...... 6845
Ps 35:11 l. to my charge things that I knew...........
Ps 49:14 Like shee they are l. in the grave; 8371
Ps 62:9 to be l. in the balance, they are......... 5927
Ps 79:1 they have l. Jerusalem on heaps......... 7760
Ps 79:7 Jacob, and l. waste his dwelling place..........
Ps 88:6 Thou hast l. me in the lowest pit, ... 7896
Ps 89:19 l. help upon one that is mighty; 7737
Ps 102:25 thou l. the foundation of the earth: ....
Ps 104:5 Who l. the foundations of the earth,..........
Ps 105:18 with fetters: he was l. in iron: 935
Ps 119:30 judgments have I l. before me.......... 7737
Ps 119:110 wicked have l. a snare for me: 5414
Ps 139:5 before, and l. thine hand upon me. 7896
Ps 141:9 snares which they have l. for me, ... 3369
Ps 142:3 they privily l. a snare for me........... 2934
Pr 13:22 of the sinner is l. up for the just......... 6845
Ca 7:13 and old, which I have l. up for thee, ... 6845
Isa 6:7 he l. it upon my mouth, and said,....... 5060
Isa 10:28 he hath l. up his carriages: 6485
Isa 14:8 Since thou art l. down, no feller is 7901
Isa 15:1 the night Ar of Moab is l. waste, ... 7901
Isa 15:1 in the night Kir of Moab is l. waste, ...
Isa 15:7 that which they have l. up, shall 6486
Isa 23:1 for it is l. waste, so that there is ....
Isa 23:14 for your strength is l. waste...................
Isa 23:18 it shall not be treasured nor l. up;...... 2630
Isa 37:18 Assyria have l. waste all the nations, ...
Isa 39:6 thy fathers have l. up in store until...........
Isa 42:25 him, yet he l. it not to heart. 7760
Isa 44:28 temple, Thy foundation shall be l..............
Isa 47:6 hast thou very heavily l. thy yoke. ....
Isa 48:13 hath l. the foundation of the earth, ...
Isa 51:13 and l. the foundations of the earth;..........
Isa 51:23 hast l. thy body as the ground,.......... 7760
Isa 53:6 Lord hath l. on him the iniquity 6293
Isa 57:11 me, nor laid it to thy heart? 7760
Isa 64:11 all our pleasant things are l. waste. ....
Jer 4:7 and thy cities shall be l. waste,...............
Jer 27:17 should this city be l. waste?....................
Jer 36:20 they l. up the roll in the chamber of... 6485
Jer 50:24 I have l. a snare for thee, and thou ....
La 4:19 they l. wait for us in the wilderness..........
Eze 4:5 I have l. upon thee the years of......... 5414
Eze 6:6 the cities shall be l. waste, and the..........
Eze 6:6 your altars may be l. waste and made ....
Eze 11:7 Your slain whom ye have l. in the 7760
Eze 12:20 that are inhabited shall be l. waste, ...
Eze 19:7 palaces, and he l. waste their cities; ....
Eze 26:2 be replenished, now she is l. waste: ....
Eze 29:12 the cities that are l. waste shall be ....
Eze 32:19 be thou l. with the uncircumcised....... 7901
Eze 32:27 have l. their swords under heads, ... 5414
Eze 32:29 are l. by them that were slain 5414
Eze 32:32 he shall be l. in the midst of the 7901
Eze 33:29 I have l. the land most desolate 5414
Eze 35:12 They are l. desolate, they are given us .....
Eze 39:21 my hand that I have l. upon them. 7760
Eze 40:42 also they l. the instruments.............. 3240
Da 6:17 and l. upon the mouth of the den; 7760
Ho 11:4 jaws, and I l. meat unto them. 5186
Joe 1:7 He hath l. my vine waste, and........... 7760
Joe 1:17 clods, the garners are l. desolate, ...
Am 2:8 clothes l. to pledge by every altar, ...
Am 7:9 sanctuaries of Israel shall be l. waste; ....
Ob 7 eat thy bread have l. a wound 7760
Ob 13 have l. hands on their substance 7971
Jon 3:6 and he l. his robe from him,............. 5674
Mic 5:1 he hath l. siege against us: they 7760
Na 3:7 thee, and say, Nineveh is l. waste:..........
Hab 2:19 it is l. over with gold and silver, ... 8610
Hag 2:15 before a stone was l. upon a stone...... 7760
Hag 2:18 foundation of the Lord's temple was l.,......
Zec 3:9 behold the stone that I have l............ 5414
Zec 4:9 l. the foundation of this house;.................
Zec 7:14 they l. the pleasant land desolate. 7760
Zec 8:9 foundation of the house of...was l.,..... 7760
Mal 1:3 l. his mountains and his heritage 7760
Mt 3:10 axe is l. unto the root of the trees: *2749*
Mt 8:14 he saw his wife's mother l., and.......... *906*
Mt 14:3 Herod had l. hold on John, and bound ......
Mt 18:28 **he l. hands on him, and took him by...**
Mt 19:15 he l. his hands on them, and............ *2007*
Mt 26:50 came they, and l. hands on Jesus, ... *1911*
Mt 26:55 **the temple, and ye l. no hold on me. ...**
Mt 26:57 they that had l. hold on Jesus led him ....
Mt 27:60 l. it in his own new tomb, which........ *5087*
Mk 6:5 he l. his hands upon a few sick.......... *2007*
Mk 6:17 had sent forth and l. hold upon John, ...
Mk 6:29 up his corpse, and l. it in a tomb. *5087*
Mk 6:56 they l. the sick in the streets, and *5087*
Mk 7:30 and her daughter l. upon the bed......... *906*
Mk 14:46 they l. their hands on him, and.......... *1911*
Mk 14:51 the young men l. hold on him: and ....
Mk 15:46 l. him in a sepulchre which was *2698*
Mk 15:47 of Joses beheld where he was l.. .... *5087*
Mk 16:6 behold the place where they l. him..... *5087*
Lu 1:66 them l. them up in their hearts,......... *5087*
Lu 2:7 clothes, and l. him in a manger; *347*
Lu 3:9 axe is l. unto the root of the trees: *2749*
Lu 4:40 l. his hands on every one of them, ... *2007*
Lu 6:48 **and l. the foundation on a rock:....** *5087*
Lu 12:19 **much goods l. up for many years;** . *2749*
Lu 13:13 he l. his hands on her: and *2007*
Lu 14:19 **he hath l. the foundation, and** *5087*
Lu 16:20 **Lazarus, which was l. at his gate,** .. *906*
Lu 19:20 **which I have kept l. up in a napkin:** *606*
Lu 19:22 **taking up that I l. not down, and** .. *5087*
Lu 23:26 they l. hold upon one Simon, a ....
Lu 23:26 on him they l. the cross, that he........ *2007*
Lu 23:53 l. it in a sepulchre that was hewn....... *5087*
Lu 23:53 wherein never man before was l.. ...... *2749*
Lu 23:55 and how his body was l.................. *5087*
Lu 24:12 the linen clothes l. by themselves,...... *2749*
Joh 7:30 no man l. hands on him, because *1911*
Joh 7:44 him; but no man l. hands on him........ *1911*
Joh 8:20 temple; and no man l. hands on him; ....
Joh 11:34 **Where have ye l. him?** They said *5087*
Joh 11:41 the place where the dead was l.. .... *2749*
Joh 13:4 supper, and l. aside his garments: *5087*
Joh 19:41 wherein was never man yet l.. .... *5087*
Joh 19:42 There l. they Jesus therefore *5087*
Joh 20:2 know not where they have l. him. *5087*
Joh 20:13 I know not where they have l. him..... *5087*
Joh 20:15 tell me where thou hast l. him, and.... *5087*
Joh 21:9 and fish l. thereon, and bread........... *1945*
Ac 3:2 l. daily at the gate of the temple........ *5087*
Ac 4:3 they l. hands on them, and put.......... *1911*
Ac 4:35 l. them down at the apostles' feet: *5087*
Ac 4:37 and l. it at the apostles' feet. *5087*
Ac 5:2 part, and l. it at the apostles' feet. *5087*
Ac 5:15 and l. them on beds and couches, ... *5087*
Ac 5:18 l. their hands on the apostles, and...... *1911*
Ac 6:6 they l. their hands on them.............. *2007*
Ac 7:16 l. in the sepulchre that Abraham *5087*
Ac 7:58 witnesses l. down their clothes at........ *659*
Ac 8:17 Then l. they their hands on them, ... *2007*
Ac 9:37 they l. her in an upper chamber......... *5087*
Ac 13:3 and l. their hands on them, they *2007*
Ac 13:29 tree, and l. him in a sepulchre........... *5087*
Ac 13:36 was l. unto his fathers, and saw......... *4369*
Ac 16:23 had l. many stripes upon them,........... *2007*
Ac 19:6 Paul had l. his hands upon them,......... *2007*
Ac 20:3 And when the Jews l. wait for him, ... *1096*
Ac 21:27 all the people, and l. hands on him, ... *1911*
Ac 23:29 nothing l. to his charge worthy of....... *1462*
Ac 23:30 that the Jews l. wait for the man, ... *2071*
Ac 25:7 l. many and grievous complaints......... *5342*
Ac 25:16 the crime l. against him.................. *1462*
Ac 25:27 signify the crimes l. against him. ....
Ac 28:3 of sticks, and l. them on the fire, ... *2007*
Ac 28:8 l. his hands on him, and healed......... *2007*
Ro 16:4 my life l. down their own necks: *5294*
1Co 3:10 I have l. the foundation, and............. *5087*
1Co 3:11 can no man lay than that is l., ... *5087*
1Co 9:16 for necessity is l. upon me; yea, ... *1945*
Col 1:5 hope which is l. up for you in *606*
2Ti 4:8 there is l. up for me a crown of.......... *606*
2Ti 4:16 it may not be l. to their charge.......... *3049*
Heb 1:10 hast l. the foundation of the earth;...........
1Jo 3:16 becuase he l. down his life for us:........ *5087*
Re 1:17 he l. his right hand upon me, ... *2007*
Re 20:2 he l. hold on the dragon, that old ....

LAIDST See also LAYEDST.
Ps 66:11 thou l. affliction upon our loins.......... 7760

LAIN See also LIEN.
Nu 5:19 If no man have l. with thee, and........ 7901
Nu 5:20 some man have l. with thee....... 5414,7903
Jg 21:11 woman that hath l. by man. 3045,4904
Job 3:13 I have l. still and been quiet,............ 7901
Joh 11:17 had l. in the grave four days already. ....
Joh 20:12 where the body of Jesus had l.. .... *2749*

LAISH (la'-ish) See also DAN; LESHEM.
Jg 18:7 men departed, and came to L.,.......... 3919
Jg 18:14 went to spy out the country of L.,..... 3919
Jg 18:27 which he had, and came unto L.,...... 3919
Jg 18:29 the name of the city was L. at the..... 3919
1Sa 25:44 David's wife, to Phalti the son of L., .. 3919
2Sa 3:15 even from Phaltiel the son of L.. 3919
Isa 10:30 cause it to be heard unto L.,............ 3919

LAKE
Lu 5:1 God, stood by the l. of Gennesaret, ... *3041*
Lu 5:2 saw two ships standing by the l.: *3041*
Lu 8:22 **over unto the other side of the l.** ... *3041*
Lu 8:23 down a storm of wind on the l.;......... *3041*
Lu 8:33 down a steep place into the l., ... *3041*
Re 19:20 both were cast alive into a l. of fire *3041*
Re 20:10 them was cast into the l. of fire......... *3041*
Re 20:14 and hell were cast into the l. of fire.... *3041*
Re 20:15 of life was cast into the l. of fire. *3041*
Re 21:8 their part in the l. which burneth *3041*

LAKUM (la'-kum)
Jos 19:33 Nekeb, and Jabneel, unto L.; 3946

LAMA (la'-mah)
Mt 27:46 saying, **Eli, Eli, l. sabachthani?**..... *2982*
Mk 15:34 saying, **Eloi, Eloi, l. sabachthani?** .. *2982*

LAMB See also LAMBS; LAMB'S.
Ge 22:7 where is the l. for a burnt offering?.... 7716
Ge 22:8 God will provide himself a l. for a 7716
Ex 12:3 shall take to them every man a l.,...... 7716
Ex 12:3 of their fathers, a l. for an house: 7716
Ex 12:4 the household be too little for the l.,... 7716
Ex 12:4 shall make your count for the l.. 7716
Ex 12:5 Your l. shall be without blemish, a...... 7716
Ex 12:21 them, Draw out and take you a l. 6629
Ex 13:13 an ass thou shalt redeem with a l.;..... 7716
Ex 29:39 The one l. thou shalt offer in the 3532
Ex 29:39 the other l. thou shalt offer at even: ... 3532
Ex 29:40 with the one l. a tenth deal of flour 3532
Ex 29:41 the other l. thou shalt offer at even, ... 3532
Ex 34:20 an ass thou shalt redeem with a l.:..... 7716
Le 3:7 If he offer a l. for his offering, then.... 3775
Le 4:32 if he bring a l. for a sin offering, ... 3532
Le 4:35 fat of the l. is taken away from.......... 3775
Le 5:6 a l. or a kid of the goats, for a sin 3776
Le 5:7 he be not able to bring a l., then he.... 7716
Le 9:3 a calf and a l., both of the first........... 3532
Le 12:6 she shall bring a l. of the first year..... 3532
Le 12:8 she be not able to bring a l., then...... 7716
Le 14:10 one ewe l. of the first year without 3535
Le 14:12 priest shall take one he l., and 3532
Le 14:13 shall slay the l. in the place where 3532
Le 14:21 take one l. for a trespass offering....... 3532
Le 14:24 take the l. of the trespass offering,..... 3532
Le 14:25 kill the l. of the trespass offering, ... 3532
Le 17:3 that killeth an ox, or l., or goat, ... 3775
Le 22:23 l. that hath any thing superfluous 7716
Le 23:12 he l. without blemish of the first 3532
Nu 6:12 shall bring a l. of the first year for 3532
Nu 6:14 one he l. of the first year without 3532
Nu 6:14 one ewe l. of the first year without 3535
Nu 7:15, 21,27,33,39,45,51,57,63,69,75,81 one
l. of the first year, for a burnt.................
Nu 15:5 offering or sacrifice, for one l.. 3532
Nu 15:11 for one ram, or for a l., or a kid. 7716
Nu 28:4 The one l. shalt thou offer in the 3532
Nu 28:4 the other l. shalt thou offer at even;... 3532
Nu 28:7 fourth part of an hin for the one l.:..... 3532
Nu 28:8 the other l. shalt thou offer at even: ... 3532
Nu 28:13 oil for a meat offering unto one l.;...... 3532
Nu 28:14 and a fourth part of an hin unto a l.: ... 3532
Nu 28:21 deal shalt thou offer for every l., ... 3532
Nu 28:29 A several tenth deal unto one l.,......... 3532
Nu 29:4 one tenth deal for one l., throughout... 3532
Nu 29:10 A several tenth deal for one l.,.......... 3532
Nu 29:15 tenth deal to each l. of the fourteen.... 3532
1Sa 7:9 And Samuel took a sucking l., and...... 2924
1Sa 17:34 bear, and took a l. out of the flock: 7716
2Sa 12:3 had nothing, save one little ewe l.,..... 3535
2Sa 12:4 took the poor man's l., and dressed.... 3535
2Sa 12:6 And he shall restore the l. fourfold, ... 3535
Isa 11:6 wolf also shall dwell with the l.,......... 3532
Isa 16:1 Send ye the l. to the ruler of the....... 3733
Isa 53:7 is brought as a l. to the slaughter,...... 7716
Isa 65:25 wolf and the l. shall feed together, ... 2924
Isa 66:3 he that sacrificeth a l., as if he 7716
Jer 11:19 But I was like a l. or an ox that is 3532
Eze 45:15 one l. out of the flock, out of two...... 7716
Eze 46:13 of a l. of the first year without 3532
Eze 46:15 Thus shall they prepare the l., and..... 3532
Ho 4:16 feed them as a l. in a large place. 3532
Joh 1:29 and saith, Behold the L. of God, ... *286*
Joh 1:36 he saith, Behold the L. of God!........... *286*
Ac 8:32 like a l. dumb before his shearer, so *286*
1Pe 1:19 of Christ, as of a l. without blemish *286*
Re 5:6 stood a L. as it had been slain, ... *721*
Re 5:8 elders fell down before the L.,............. *721*
Re 5:12 Worthy is the L. that was slain to *721*
Re 5:13 the throne, and unto the L. for ever *721*
Re 6:1 when the L. opened one of the seals,... *721*
Re 6:16 and from the wrath of the L.:............. *721*
Re 7:9 before the throne, and before the L., ... *721*
Re 7:10 upon the throne, and unto the L.......... *721*
Re 7:14 them white in the blood of the L.......... *721*
Re 7:17 L. which is in the midst of the throne... *721*
Re 12:11 overcame him by the blood of the L.,... *721*
Re 13:8 written in the book of life of the L......... *721*
Re 13:11 and he had two horns like a l., and...... *721*
Re 14:1 lo, a L. stood on the mount Sion, and .. *721*
Re 14:4 These are they which follow the L....... *721*
Re 14:4 firstfruits unto God and to the L.......... *721*
Re 14:10 angels, and in the presence of the L.: .. *721*
Re 15:3 of God, and the song of the L.,........... *721*
Re 17:14 These shall make war with the L.,........ *721*
Re 17:14 and the L. shall overcome them: *721*
Re 19:7 for the marriage of the L. is come,...... *721*
Re 19:9 unto the marriage supper of the L.. ..... *721*
Re 21:14 of the twelve apostles of the L.. .... *721*
Re 21:22 Lord God Almighty and the L. are....... *721*
Re 21:23 it, and the L. is the light thereof. *721*
Re 22:1 of the throne of God and of the L......... *721*
Re 22:3 throne of God and of the L. shall be *721*

LAMB'S
Re 21:9 shew thee the bride, the L. wife. *721*
Re 21:27 are written in the L. book of life. *721*

LAMBS
Ge 21:28 Abraham set seven ewe l. of the 3535
Ge 21:29 What mean these seven ewe l. which.. 3535
Ge 21:30 these seven ewe l. shalt thou take 3535
Ge 30:40 And Jacob did separate the l., and...... 3775
Ex 29:38 two l. of the first year day by day....... 3532
Le 14:10 shall take two he l. without blemish,.. 3532
Le 23:18 the bread seven l. without blemish 3532
Le 23:19 two l. of the first year for a sacrifice .. 3532
Le 23:20 before the Lord, with the two l.: 3532
Nu 7:17, 23,29,35,41,47,53,59,65,71,77,83
five he goats, five l. of the first year.........
Nu 7:87 the l. of the first year twelve, ... 3532
Nu 7:88 sixty, the l. of the first year sixty. 3532
Nu 28:3 two l. of the first year without spot..... 3532
Nu 28:9 two l. of the first year without spot, ... 3532
Nu 28:11 seven l. of the first year without......... 3532
Nu 28:19 ram, and seven l. of the first year:..... 3532
Nu 28:21 every lamb, throughout the seven l.: .. 3532
Nu 28:27 one ram, seven l. of the first year;...... 3532
Nu 28:29 one lamb, throughout the seven l.;..... 3532
Nu 29:2 seven l. of the first year without........ 3532
Nu 29:4 one lamb, throughout the seven l.: 3532
Nu 29:8 ram, and seven l. of the first year;..... 3532
Nu 29:10 one lamb, throughout the seven l.: 3532
Nu 29:13 and fourteen l. of the first year;.......... 3532
Nu 29:15 deal to each lamb of the fourteen l.: ... 3532
Nu 29:17 fourteen l. of the first year without..... 3532
Nu 29:18 bullocks, for the rams, and for the l.,.. 3532
Nu 29:20 fourteen l. of the first year without..... 3532
Nu 29:21 bullocks, for the rams, and for the l.,.. 3532
Nu 29:23 fourteen l. of the first year without..... 3532
Nu 29:24 bullocks, for the rams, and for the l.,.. 3532
Nu 29:26 fourteen l. of the first year without..... 3532
Nu 29:27 bullocks, for the rams, and for the l.,.. 3532
Nu 29:29 fourteen l. of the first year without..... 3532
Nu 29:30 bullocks, for the rams, and for the l.,.. 3532
Nu 29:32 fourteen l. of the first year without..... 3532
Nu 29:33 bullocks, for the rams, and for the l.,.. 3532
Nu 29:36 seven l. of the first year without........ 3532
Nu 29:37 bullock, for the ram, and for the l., ... 3532
De 32:14 with fat of l., and rams of the breed... 3733
1Sa 15:9 and the l., and all that was good, ... 3733
2Ki 3:4 of Israel an hundred thousand l.,........ 3733
1Ch 29:21 thousand rams, and a thousand l., ... 3532
2Ch 29:21 seven l., and seven he goats, for a..... 3532
2Ch 29:22 they killed also the l., and they.......... 3532
2Ch 29:32 hundred rams, and two hundred l.: 3532
2Ch 35:7 the people, of the flock, l. and kids, ... 3532
Ezr 6:9 young bullocks, and rams, and l.,......... 563
Ezr 6:17 two hundred rams, four hundred l.;...... 563
Ezr 7:17 with this money bullocks, rams, l.,....... 563
Ezr 8:35 and six rams, seventy and seven l.,..... 3532
Ps 37:20 the Lord shall be as the fat of l.: 3733
Ps 114:4 and the little hills like l.. 1121,6629
Ps 114:6 rams; and ye little hills, like l.?... 1121,6629
Pr 27:26 The l. are for thy clothing, and.......... 3532
Isa 1:11 blood of bullocks, or of l., or of he..... 3532
Isa 5:17 the lambs feed after their manner,...... 3532
Isa 34:6 and with the blood of l. and goats, ... 3733
Isa 40:11 shall gather the l. with his arm, ... 2922
Jer 51:40 them down like l. to the slaughter, ... 3733
Eze 27:21 they occupied with thee in l., and....... 3733
Eze 39:18 princes of the earth, of rams, of l., ... 3733
Eze 46:4 six l. without blemish, and a ram 3532
Eze 46:5 and the meat offering for the l. as he.. 3532
Eze 46:6 blemish, and six l., and a ram: 3532
Eze 46:7 and for the l. according as his hand 3532
Eze 46:11 and to the l. as he is able to give,...... 3532
Am 6:4 eat the l. out of the flock, and the...... 3733
Lu 10:3 **send you forth as l. among wolves**. ..*704*
Joh 21:15 He saith unto him, **Feed my l.**. *721*

LAME
Le 21:18 a blind man, or a l., or he that hath.... 6455
De 15:21 as if it be l., or blind, or have any ill .. 6455
2Sa 4:4 had a son that was l. of his feet.......... 5223
2Sa 4:4 to flee, that he fell, and became l.. 6452
2Sa 5:6 take away the blind and the l., ... 6455
2Sa 5:8 Jebusites, and the l. and the blind, ... 6455
2Sa 5:8 the l. shall not come into the house.... 6455
2Sa 9:3 yet a son, which is l. on his feet.......... 5223
2Sa 9:13 table; and was l. on both his feet. 6455
2Sa 19:26 the king; because thy servant is l....... 6455
Job 29:15 the blind, and feet was I to the l.......... 6455
Pr 26:7 The legs of the l. are not equal: so 6455
Isa 33:23 spoil divide; the l. take the prey. 6455
Isa 35:6 shall the l. man leap as an hart, ... 6455
Jer 31:8 and with them the blind and the l.,..... 6455
Mal 1:8 offer the l. and sick, is it not evil?...... 6455
Mal 1:13 was torn, and the l., and the sick;...... 6455
Mt 11:5 **l. walk, the lepers are cleansed**, ... *5560*
Mt 15:30 with them those that were l., blind,.... *5560*
Mt 15:31 the l. to walk, and the blind to see:.... *5560*
Mt 21:14 the l. came to him in the temple; *5560*
Lu 7:22 **l. walk, the lepers are cleansed**, ... *5560*
Lu 14:13 **poor, the maimed, the l., the blind**: *5560*
Ac 3:2 man l. from his mother's womb *5560*
Ac 3:11 the l. man which was healed held....... *5560*
Ac 8:7 and that were l., were healed........... *5560*
Heb 12:13 which is l. be turned out of the way; .. *5560*

LAMECH (la'-mek)
Ge 4:18 and Methusael begat L..................... 3929
Ge 4:19 And L. took unto him two wives:....... 3929
Ge 4:23 And L. said unto his wives, Adah....... 3929
Ge 4:23 ye wives of L., harken unto my........... 3929
Ge 4:24 truly L. seventy and sevenfold........... 3929
Ge 5:25 and seven years, and begat L.:.......... 3929
Ge 5:26 Methuselah lived after he begat L. 3929
Ge 5:28 L. lived an hundred eighty and two..... 3929
Ge 5:30 L. lived after he begat Noah five........ 3929
Ge 5:31 the days of L. were seven hundred 3929
1Ch 1:3 Henoch, Methuselah, L.,.................. 3929
Lu 3:36 Noe, which was the son of L., ... *2984*

LAMED (law'-med)
Ps 119:89 *title* [ל] L...

LAMENT See also LAMENTABLE; LAMENTED.
Jg 11:40 to l. the daughter of Jephthah the....... 8567
Isa 3:26 And her gates shall l. and mourn; 578
Isa 19:8 cast angle into the brooks shall l., ... 56
Isa 32:12 They shall l. for the teats, for the...... 5594
Jer 4:8 you with sackcloth, l. and howl: 5594

Jer 16:5 neither go to l. nor bemoan them: 5594
Jer 16:6 neither shall men l. for them, nor 5594
Jer 22:18 They shall not l. for him, saying, 5594
Jer 22:18 they shall not l. for him, saying, 5594
Jer 34:5 they will l. thee, saying, Ah lord! 5594
Jer 49:3 l., and run to and fro by the hedges; 5594
La 2:8 the rampart and the wall to l.; 56
Eze 27:32 for thee, and l. over thee, saying, 6969
Eze 32:16 wherewith they shall l. her: 6969
Eze 32:16 daughters of the nations shall l. her: 6969
Eze 32:16 shall l. for her, even for Egypt, 6969
Joe 1:8 L. like a virgin girded with 421
Joe 1:13 Gird yourselves, and l., ye priests: 5594
Mic 2:4 and l. with a doleful lamentation, 5091
Joh 16:20 **That ye shall weep and l., but the.** *2354*
Re 18:9 shall bewail her, and l. for her, *2875*

LAMENTABLE

Da 6:20 cried with a l. voice unto Daniel: 6088

LAMENTATION See also LAMENTATIONS.

Ge 50:10 with a great and very sore l.: 4553
2Sa 1:17 with this l. over Saul and over 7015
Ps 78:64 and their widows made no l. 1058
Jer 6:26 as for an only son, most bitter l.: 4553
Jer 7:29 and take up a l. on high places; 7015
Jer 9:10 habitations of the wilderness a l., 7015
Jer 9:20 and every one her neighbour l. 7015
Jer 31:15 in Ramah, l., and bitter weeping; 5092
Jer 48:38 There shall be l. generally upon 4553
La 2:5 daughter of Judah mourning and l. 592
Eze 19:1 up a l. for the princes of Israel, 7015
Eze 19:14 This is a l., and shall be for a l. 7015
Eze 26:17 they shall take up a l. for thee, and 7015
Eze 27:2 son of man, take up a l. for Tyrus; 7015
Eze 27:32 they shall take up a l. for thee, and 7015
Eze 28:12 take up a l. upon the king of Tyrus, 7015
Eze 32:2 up a l. for Pharaoh king of Egypt, 7015
Eze 32:16 l. wherewith they shall lament her: 7015
Am 5:1 you, even a l., O house of Israel. 7015
Am 5:16 such as are skilful of l. to wailing. 5092
Am 8:10 and all your songs into l.; 7015
Mic 2:4 and lament with a doleful l., and 5092
Mt 2:18 a voice heard, l., and weeping, *2355*
Ac 8:2 burial, and made great l. over him. *2870*

LAMENTATIONS

2Ch 35:25 women spake of Josiah in their l. 7015
2Ch 35:25 behold, they are written in the l. 7015
La *general title* The L. Of Jeremiah 349
Eze 2:10 there was written therein l., and 7015

LAMENTED

1Sa 6:19 the people l., because the Lord had 56
1Sa 7:2 house of Israel l. after the Lord 5091
1Sa 25:1 and l. him, and buried him in his 5594
1Sa 28:3 Israel had l. him, and buried him 5594
2Sa 1:17 And David l. with this lamentation 6969
2Sa 3:33 the king l. over Abner, and said, 6969
2Ch 35:25 And Jeremiah l. for Josiah: and all 6969
Jer 16:4 they shall not be l.; neither shall 5594
Jer 25:33 they shall not be l., neither gathered, 5594
Mt 11:17 **unto you, and ye have not l.** *2875*
Lu 23:27 which also bewailed and l. him. *2354*

LAMP See also LAMPS.

Ge 15:17 burning l. that passed between 3940
Ex 27:20 to cause the l. to burn always. 5216
1Sa 3:3 l. of God went out in the temple the 5216
2Sa 22:29 For thou art my l., O Lord: and the 5216
1Ki 15:4 his God give him a l. in Jerusalem, 5216
Job 12:5 as a l. despised in the thought of 3940
Ps 119:105 Thy word is a l. unto my feet, 5216
Ps 132:17 ordained a l. for mine anointed. 5216
Pr 6:23 For the commandment is a l.; and 5216
Pr 13:9 the l. of the wicked shall be put out. 5216
Pr 20:20 his l. shall be put out in obscure 5216
Isa 62:1 the salvation thereof as a l. that 3940
Re 8:10 heaven, burning as it were a l., *2985*

LAMPS

Ex 25:37 shalt make the seven l. thereof: 5216
Ex 25:37 they shall light the l. thereof, that 5216
Ex 30:7 when he dresseth the l., he shall 5216
Ex 30:8 when Aaron lighteth the l. at even, 5216
Ex 35:14 and his l., with the oil for the light, 5216
Ex 37:23 And he made his seven l., and his 5216
Ex 39:37 candlestick, with the l. thereof, 5216
Ex 39:37 even with the l. to be set in order, 5216
Ex 40:4 candlestick, and light the l. thereof, 5216
Ex 40:25 he lighted the l. before the Lord; 5216
Le 24:2 to cause the l. to burn continually. 5216
Le 24:4 the l. upon the pure candlestick 5216
Nu 4:9 the light, and his l., and his tongs, 5216
Nu 8:2 unto him, When thou lightest the l., 5216
Nu 8:2 the seven l. shall give light over 5216
Nu 8:3 lighted the l. thereof over against 5216
Jg 7:16 and l. within the pitchers. 3940
Jg 7:20 and held the l. in their left hands, 3940
1Ki 7:49 and the l., and the tongs of gold, 5216
1Ch 28:15 and for their l. of gold, by weight 5216
1Ch 28:15 candlestick, and for the l. thereof: 5216
1Ch 28:15 and also for the l. thereof, 5216
2Ch 4:20 the candlesticks with their l., that 5216
2Ch 4:21 flowers, and the l., and the tongs, 5216
2Ch 13:11 of gold with the l. thereof, to burn 5216
2Ch 29:7 put out the l., and have not burned 5216
Job 41:19 Out of his mouth go burning l., 3940
Eze 1:13 fire, and like the appearance of l.: 3940
Da 10:6 lightning, and his eyes as l. of fire, 3940
Zec 4:2 top of it, and his seven l. thereon, 5216
Zec 4:2 and seven pipes to the seven l., 5216
Mt 25:1 **ten virgins, which took their l.,** *2985*
Mt 25:3 **foolish took their l., and took** *2985*
Mt 25:4 **oil in their vessels with their l.** *2985*
Mt 25:7 **virgins arose, and trimmed their l.** *2985*
Mt 25:8 **of your oil; for our l. are gone out.** *2985*
Re 4:5 seven l. of fire burning before the *2985*

LANCE

Jer 50:42 shall hold the bow and the l.: 3591

LANCETS

1Ki 18:28 their manner with knives and l., 7420

LAND See also ISLAND; LANDED; LANDING; LANDMARK; LANDS; OUTLANDISH.

Ge 1:9 place, and let the dry l. appear:
Ge 1:10 and God called the dry l. Earth; and
Ge 2:11 compasseth the whole l. of Havilah, 776
Ge 2:12 the gold of that l. is good: there is 776
Ge 2:13 compasseth the whole l. of Ethiopia. 776
Ge 4:16 dwelt in the l. of Nod, on the east 776
Ge 7:22 of all that was in the dry l., died.
Ge 10:10 and Calneh, in the l. of Shinar. 776
Ge 10:11 Out of that l. went forth Asshur, 776
Ge 11:2 found a plain in the l. of Shinar; 776
Ge 11:28 Terah in the l. of his nativity, 776
Ge 11:31 Chaldees, to go into the l. of Canaan; 776
Ge 12:1 unto a l. that I will shew thee: 776
Ge 12:5 forth to go into the l. of Canaan; 776
Ge 12:5 into the l. of Canaan they came. 776
Ge 12:6 Abram passed through the l. unto 776
Ge 12:6 the Canaanite was then in the l. 776
Ge 12:7 said, Unto thy seed will I give this l.: 776
Ge 12:10 was a famine in the l.: and Abram 776
Ge 12:10 the famine was grievous in the l. 776
Ge 13:6 the l. was not able to bear them, 776
Ge 13:7 Perizzite dwelled then in the l. 776
Ge 13:9 Is not the whole l. before thee? 776
Ge 13:10 like the l. of Egypt, as thou comest 776
Ge 13:12 Abram dwelled in the l. of Canaan, 776
Ge 13:15 For all the l. which thou seest, to 776
Ge 13:17 walk through the l. in the length of 776
Ge 15:7 to give thee this l. to inherit it. 776
Ge 15:13 a stranger in a l. that is not theirs, 776
Ge 15:18 Unto thy seed have I given this l., 776
Ge 16:3 dwelt ten years in the l. of Canaan, 776
Ge 17:8 the l. wherein thou art a stranger, 776
Ge 17:8 all the l. of Canaan, for...possession; 776
Ge 19:28 toward all the l. of the plain, and 776
Ge 20:15 my l. is before thee: dwell where it 776
Ge 21:21 him a wife out of the l. of Egypt. 776
Ge 21:23 l. wherein thou hast sojourned. 776
Ge 21:32 into the l. of the Philistines. 776
Ge 21:34 in the Philistines' l. many days. 776
Ge 22:2 and get thee into the l. of Moriah; 776
Ge 23:2 same is Hebron in the l. of Canaan: 776
Ge 23:7 bowed himself to the people of the l., 776
Ge 23:12 himself before the people of the l. 776
Ge 23:13 the audience of the people of the l., 776
Ge 23:15 the l. is worth four hundred 776
Ge 23:19 same is Hebron in the l. of Canaan. 776
Ge 24:5 be willing to follow me unto this l.: 776
Ge 24:5 the l. from whence thou camest? 776
Ge 24:7 from the l. of my kindred, and 776
Ge 24:7 Unto thy seed will I give this l.; 776
Ge 24:37 the Canaanites, in whose l. I dwell: 776
Ge 26:1 there was a famine in the l., beside 776
Ge 26:2 dwell in the l. which I shall tell thee 776
Ge 26:3 Sojourn in this l., and I will be with 776
Ge 26:12 Then Isaac sowed in that l., and 776
Ge 26:22 and we shall be fruitful in the l. 776
Ge 27:46 which are of the daughters of the l., 776
Ge 28:4 inherit the l. wherein thou art a 776
Ge 28:13 l. whereon thou liest, to thee will I 776
Ge 28:15 will bring thee again into this l.; 127
Ge 29:1 into the l. of the people of the east. 776
Ge 31:3 Return unto the l. of thy fathers, 776
Ge 31:13 now arise, get thee out from this l., 776
Ge 31:13 return unto the land of thy kindred. 776
Ge 31:18 Isaac his father in the l. of Canaan. 776
Ge 32:3 Esau his brother unto the l. of Seir, 776
Ge 33:18 which is in the l. of Canaan, 776
Ge 34:1 out to see the daughters of the l. 776
Ge 34:10 us: and the l. shall be before you; 776
Ge 34:21 let them dwell in the l., and trade 776
Ge 34:21 for the l., behold, it is large enough 776
Ge 34:30 among the inhabitants of the l. 776
Ge 35:6 Luz, which is in the l. of Canaan, 776
Ge 35:12 l. which I gave Abraham and Isaac, 776
Ge 35:12 seed after thee will I give the l. 776
Ge 35:22 to pass, when Israel dwelt in the l., 776
Ge 36:5 born unto him in the l. of Canaan. 776
Ge 36:6 which he had got in the l. of Canaan; 776
Ge 36:7 the l. wherein they were strangers 776
Ge 36:16 came of Eliphaz in the l. of Edom; 776
Ge 36:17 came of Reuel in the l. of Edom; 776
Ge 36:20 the Horite, who inhabited the l.; 776
Ge 36:21 children of Seir in the l. of Edom. 776
Ge 36:30 among their dukes in the l. of Seir. 776
Ge 36:31 kings that reigned in the l. of Edom, 776
Ge 36:34 Husham of the l. of Temani reigned 776
Ge 36:43 in the l. of their possession: 776
Ge 37:1 Jacob dwelt in the l. wherein his 776
Ge 37:1 was a stranger, in the l. of Canaan. 776
Ge 40:15 I was stolen away out of the l. of 776
Ge 41:19 I never saw in all the l. of Egypt 776
Ge 41:29 plenty throughout all the l. of Egypt: 776
Ge 41:30 be forgotten in the l. of Egypt; 776
Ge 41:30 and the famine shall consume the l.; 776
Ge 41:31 plenty shall not be known in the l. 776
Ge 41:33 and set him over the l. of Egypt. 776
Ge 41:34 let him appoint officers over the l., 776
Ge 41:34 fifth part of the l. of Egypt in the 776
Ge 41:36 that food shall be for store to the l. 776
Ge 41:36 that the l. perish not. 776
Ge 41:36 which shall be in the l. of Egypt; 776
Ge 41:41 have set thee over all the l. of Egypt. 776
Ge 41:43 him ruler over all the l. of Egypt. 776
Ge 41:44 hand or foot in all the l. of Egypt. 776
Ge 41:45 Joseph went out over all the l. of 776
Ge 41:46 went throughout all the l. of Egypt. 776
Ge 41:48 years, which were in the l. of Egypt, 776
Ge 41:52 be fruitful in the l. of my affliction. 776
Ge 41:53 that was in the l. of Egypt, were 776
Ge 41:54 in all the l. of Egypt...was bread. 776
Ge 41:55 all the l. of Egypt was famished, 776
Ge 41:56 famine waxed sore in the l. of Egypt. 776
Ge 42:5 the famine was in the l. of Canaan. 776
Ge 42:6 Joseph was the governor over the l., 776
Ge 42:6 that sold to all the people of the l. 776
Ge 42:7 From the l. of Canaan to buy food. 776
Ge 42:9, 12 nakedness of the l. ye are come 776
Ge 42:13 sons of one man in the l. of Canaan; 776
Ge 42:29 their father unto the l. of Canaan, 776
Ge 42:30 man, who is the lord of the l., spake 776
Ge 42:32 with our father in the l. of Canaan. 776
Ge 42:34 and ye shall traffick in the l. 776
Ge 43:1 And the famine was sore in the l. 776
Ge 43:11 take of the best fruits in the l. in 776
Ge 44:8 unto thee out of the l. of Canaan: 776
Ge 45:6 hath the famine been in the l. 776
Ge 45:8 ruler throughout all the l. of Egypt. 776
Ge 45:10 thou shalt dwell in the l. of Goshen, 776
Ge 45:17 go, get you unto the l. of Canaan; 776
Ge 45:18 give you the good of the l. of Egypt, 776
Ge 45:18 and ye shall eat the fat of the l. 776
Ge 45:19 you wagons out of the l. of Egypt. 776
Ge 45:20 good of all the l. of Egypt is yours. 776
Ge 45:25 into the l. of Canaan unto Jacob. 776
Ge 45:26 governor over all the l. of Egypt. 776
Ge 46:6 they had gotten in the l. of Canaan, 776
Ge 46:12 and Onan died in the l. of Canaan. 776
Ge 46:20 unto Joseph in the l. of Egypt were 776

Ge 46:28 and they came into the l. of Goshen..... 776
Ge 46:31 which were in the l. of Canaan, are...... 776
Ge 46:34 ye may dwell in the l. of Goshen;........ 776
Ge 47:1 are come out of the l. of Canaan;........ 776
Ge 47:1 behold, they are in the l. of Goshen..... 776
Ge 47:4 For to sojourn in the l. are we come;... 776
Ge 47:4 famine is sore in the l. of Canaan:....... 776
Ge 47:4 servants dwell in the l. of Goshen........ 776
Ge 47:6 l. of Egypt is before thee; in the........ 776
Ge 47:6 the best of the l. make thy father........ 776
Ge 47:6 in the l. of Goshen let them dwell:....... 776
Ge 47:11 them a possession in the l. of Egypt,... 776
Ge 47:11 best of the l., in the l. of Rameses,..... 776
Ge 47:13 there was no bread in all the l.;.......... 776
Ge 47:13 very sore, so that the l. of Egypt........ 776
Ge 47:13 and all the l. of Canaan fainted by........ 776
Ge 47:14 that was found in the l. of Egypt,........ 776
Ge 47:14 and in the l. of Canaan, for the corn..... 776
Ge 47:15 when money failed in the l. of Egypt,... 776
Ge 47:15 and in the l. of Canaan, all the............ 776
Ge 47:19 thine eyes, both we and our l.?........... 127
Ge 47:19 buy us and our l. for bread, and we..... 127
Ge 47:19 and we and our l. will be servants........ 127
Ge 47:19 not die, that the l. be not desolate....... 127
Ge 47:20 Joseph bought all the l. of Egypt......... 127
Ge 47:20 them: so the l. became Pharaoh's......... 776
Ge 47:22 Only the l. of the priests bought he...... 127
Ge 47:23 bought you this day and your l. for...... 127
Ge 47:23 seed for you, and ye shall sow the l..... 127
Ge 47:26 made it a law over the l. of Egypt....... 127
Ge 47:26 except the l. of the priests only,......... 127
Ge 47:27 And Israel dwelt in the l. of Egypt,...... 776
Ge 47:28 Jacob lived in the l. of Egypt............. 776
Ge 48:3 unto me at Luz in the l. of Canaan,........ 776
Ge 48:4 will give this l. to thy seed after.......... 776
Ge 48:5 born unto thee in the l. of Egypt.......... 776
Ge 48:7 Rachel died by me in the l. of Canaan... 776
Ge 48:21 again unto the l. of your fathers.......... 776
Ge 49:15 and the l. that it was pleasant;............ 776
Ge 49:30 before Mamre, in the l. of Canaan,....... 776
Ge 50:5 which I have digged for me in the l...... 776
Ge 50:7 all the elders of the l. of Egypt,........... 776
Ge 50:8 herds, they left in the l. of Goshen...... 776
Ge 50:11 And when the inhabitants of the l.,...... 776
Ge 50:13 carried him into the l. of Canaan,......... 776
Ge 50:24 you, and bring you out of this l.......... 776
Ge 50:24 the l. which he sware to Abraham,...... 776
Ex 1:7 and the l. was filled with them............ 776
Ex 1:10 and so get them up out of the l........... 776
Ex 2:15 and dwelt in the l. of Midian:............. 776
Ex 2:22 have been a stranger in a strange l...... 776
Ex 3:8 them up out of that l. unto a good l..... 776
Ex 3:8 a l. flowing with milk and honey;......... 776
Ex 3:17 Egypt unto the l. of the Canaanites,..... 776
Ex 3:17 a l. flowing with milk and honey.......... 776
Ex 4:9 river, and pour it upon the dry l............
Ex 4:9 shall become blood upon the dry l...........
Ex 4:20 and he returned to the l. of Egypt:...... 776
Ex 5:5 the people of the l. now are many,....... 776
Ex 5:12 throughout all the l. of Egypt............. 776
Ex 6:1 shall he drive them out of his l........... 776
Ex 6:4 them, to give them the l. of Canaan,.... 776
Ex 6:4 the l. of their pilgrimage, wherein........ 776
Ex 6:8 And I will bring you in unto the l.,........ 776
Ex 6:11 children of Israel go out of his l........... 776
Ex 6:13 of Israel out of the l. of Egypt............ 776
Ex 6:26 of Israel from the l. of Egypt............. 776
Ex 6:28 spake unto Moses in the l. of Egypt,.... 776
Ex 7:2 the children of Israel out of his l.......... 776
Ex 7:3 and my wonders in the l. of Egypt....... 776
Ex 7:4 out of the l. of Egypt by great............. 776
Ex 7:19 blood throughout all the l. of Egypt,..... 776
Ex 7:21 throughout all the l. of Egypt............. 776
Ex 8:5 to come up upon the l. of Egypt.......... 776
Ex 8:6 frogs came up, and covered the l......... 776
Ex 8:7 up frogs upon the l. of Egypt.............. 776
Ex 8:14 upon heaps: and the l. stank.............. 776
Ex 8:16 rod, and smite the dust of the l.,......... 776
Ex 8:16 lice throughout all the l. of Egypt........ 776
Ex 8:17 all the dust of the l. became lice.......... 776
Ex 8:17 lice throughout all the l. of Egypt........ 776
Ex 8:22 sever in that day the l. of Goshen,...... 776
Ex 8:24 houses, and into all the l. of Egypt:..... 776
Ex 8:24 l. was corrupted by reason of...flies..... 776
Ex 8:25 ye, sacrifice to your God in the l......... 776
Ex 9:5 Lord shall do this thing in the l........... 776
Ex 9:9 small dust in all the l. of Egypt,.......... 776
Ex 9:9 beast, throughout all the l. of Egypt..... 776
Ex 9:22 may be hail in all the l. of Egypt,....... 776
Ex 9:22 field, throughout the l. of Egypt.......... 776
Ex 9:23 rained hail upon the l. of Egypt........... 776
Ex 9:24 none like it in all the l. of Egypt.......... 776
Ex 9:25 hail smote throughout all the l. of........ 776
Ex 9:26 Only in the l. of Goshen, where the..... 776
Ex 10:12 over the l. of Egypt for the locusts,..... 776
Ex 10:12 may come upon the l. of Egypt,........... 776
Ex 10:12 and eat every herb of the l., even....... 776
Ex 10:13 forth his rod over the l. of Egypt,....... 776
Ex 10:13 east wind upon the l. all that day,........ 776
Ex 10:14 And locusts went up over all the l....... 776
Ex 10:15 earth, so that the l. was darkened;...... 776
Ex 10:15 and they did eat every herb of the l.,... 776
Ex 10:15 field, through all the l. of Egypt.......... 776
Ex 10:21 be darkness over the l. of Egypt,........ 776
Ex 10:22 thick darkness in all the l. of Egypt...... 776
Ex 11:3 Moses was...great in the l. of Egypt,... 776
Ex 11:5 firstborn in the l. of Egypt shall die,..... 776
Ex 11:6 be a great cry throughout all the l....... 776
Ex 11:9 be multiplied in the l. of Egypt........... 776
Ex 11:10 children of Israel go out of his l.......... 776
Ex 12:1 Moses and Aaron in the l. of Egypt,.... 776
Ex 12:12 pass through the l. of Egypt this......... 776
Ex 12:12 will smite all the firstborn in the l........ 776
Ex 12:13 you, when I smite the l. of Egypt........ 776
Ex 12:17 your armies out of the l. of Egypt:...... 776
Ex 12:19 he be a stranger, or born in the l........ 776
Ex 12:25 the l. which the Lord will give you,...... 776
Ex 12:29 smote all the firstborn in the l. of........ 776
Ex 12:33 send them out of the l. in haste;........ 776
Ex 12:41 Lord went out from the l. of Egypt...... 776
Ex 12:42 for bringing them out from the l. of...... 776
Ex 12:48 shall be as one that is born in the l...... 776
Ex 12:51 of Israel out of the l. of Egypt by........ 776
Ex 13:5 thee into the l. of the Canaanites,........ 776
Ex 13:5 a l. flowing with milk and honey,.......... 776
Ex 13:11 thee into the l. of the Canaanites,........ 776
Ex 13:15 all the firstborn in the l. of Egypt,....... 776
Ex 13:17 the way of the l. of the Philistines,...... 776
Ex 13:18 went up harnessed out of the l. of....... 776
Ex 14:3 Israel, They are entangled in the l.,..... 776
Ex 14:21 made the sea dry l., and the waters.........
Ex 14:29 Israel walked upon dry l. in the midst.......
Ex 15:19 children of Israel went on dry l. in...........
Ex 16:1 after their departing out of the l. of...... 776
Ex 16:3 hand of the Lord in the l. of Egypt,..... 776
Ex 16:6 brought you out from the l. of Egypt:... 776
Ex 16:32 you forth from the l. of Egypt............ 776
Ex 16:35 until they came to a l. inhabited;......... 776
Ex 16:35 unto the borders of the l. of Canaan..... 776
Ex 18:3 have been an alien in a strange l......... 776
Ex 18:27 he went his way into his own l............ 776
Ex 19:1 gone forth out of the l. of Egypt,........ 776
Ex 20:2 brought thee out of the l. of Egypt,..... 776
Ex 20:12 thy days may be long upon the l.......... 127
Ex 22:21 were strangers in the l. of Egypt......... 776
Ex 23:9 were strangers in the l. of Egypt......... 776
Ex 23:10 six years thou shalt sow thy l., and....... 776
Ex 23:19 The first of the firstfruits of thy l........ 127
Ex 23:26 young, nor be barren, in thy l............. 776
Ex 23:29 lest the l. become desolate, and the..... 776
Ex 23:30 thou be increased, and inherit the l...... 776
Ex 23:31 will deliver the inhabitants of the l....... 776
Ex 23:33 They shall not dwell in thy l., lest....... 776
Ex 29:46 them forth out of the l. of Egypt,......... 776
Ex 32:1 brought us up out of the l. of Egypt,.... 776
Ex 32:4 brought thee up out of the l. of Egypt...776
Ex 32:7 broughtest out of the l. of Egypt,......... 776
Ex 32:8 brought thee up out of the l. of Egypt...776
Ex 32:11 brought forth out of the l. of Egypt...... 776
Ex 32:13 all this l. that I have spoken of will...... 776
Ex 32:23 brought us up out of the l. of Egypt,.... 776
Ex 33:1 brought up out of the l. of Egypt,........ 776
Ex 33:1 the l. which I sware unto Abraham,...... 776
Ex 33:3 a l. flowing with milk and honey:......... 776
Ex 34:12 with the inhabitants of the l................ 776
Ex 34:15 with the inhabitants of the l.,.............. 776
Ex 34:24 neither shall any man desire thy l.,...... 776
Ex 34:26 The first of the firstfruits of thy l........ 127
Le 11:45 you up out of the l. of Egypt,............. 776
Le 14:34 ye be come into the l. of Canaan,......... 776
Le 14:34 a house of the l. of your possession;.... 776
Le 16:22 iniquities unto a l. not inhabited:.......... 776
Le 18:3 After the doings of the l. of Egypt,...... 776
Le 18:3 after the doings of the l. of Canaan,..... 776
Le 18:25 And the l. is defiled: therefore I do...... 776
Le 18:25 l. itself vomiteth out her inhabitants..... 776
Le 18:27 have the men of the l. done, which...... 776
Le 18:27 before you, and the l. is defiled;)......... 776
Le 18:28 That the l. spue not you out also,........ 776
Le 19:9 when ye reap the harvest of your l.,.... 776
Le 19:23 when ye shall come into the l., and...... 776
Le 19:29 whore; lest the l. fall to whoredom,..... 776
Le 19:29 and the l. become full of wickedness.... 776
Le 19:33 stranger sojourn with thee in your l.,... 776
Le 19:34 ye were strangers in the l. of Egypt:... 776
Le 19:36 brought you out of the l. of Egypt....... 776
Le 20:2 the people of the l. shall stone him...... 776
Le 20:4 if the people of the l. do any ways....... 776
Le 20:22 that the l., whither I bring you to........ 776
Le 20:24 unto you, Ye shall inherit their l.,........ 127
Le 20:24 l. that floweth with milk and honey:..... 776
Le 22:24 make any offering thereof in your l...... 776
Le 22:33 brought out of the l. of Egypt, to........ 776
Le 23:10 When ye be come into the l. which...... 776
Le 23:22 when ye reap the harvest of your l.,..... 776
Le 23:39 have gathered in the fruit of the l.,...... 776
Le 23:43 brought them out of the l. of Egypt:..... 776
Le 24:16 as he that is born in the l., when......... 249
Le 25:2 ye come into the l. which I give.......... 776
Le 25:2 shall the l. keep a sabbath unto the..... 776
Le 25:4 shall be a sabbath of rest unto the l.,... 776
Le 25:5 for it is a year of rest unto the l......... 776
Le 25:6 sabbath of the l. shall be meat for........ 776
Le 25:7 and for the beast that are in thy l........ 776
Le 25:9 sound throughout all your l................ 776
Le 25:10 liberty throughout all the l. unto......... 776
Le 25:18 ye shall dwell in the l. in safety........... 776
Le 25:19 And the l. shall yield her fruit, and....... 776
Le 25:23 The l. shall not be sold for ever:......... 776
Le 25:23 for the l. is mine; for ye are............... 776
Le 25:24 And in all the l. of your possession...... 776
Le 25:24 shall grant a redemption for the l......... 776
Le 25:38 you forth out of the l. of Egypt,........... 776
Le 25:38 to give you the l. of Canaan, and to..... 776
Le 25:42 brought forth out of the l. of Egypt:..... 776
Le 25:45 you, which they begat in your l........... 776
Le 25:55 brought forth out of the l. of Egypt:..... 776
Le 26:1 up any image of stone in your l.,......... 776
Le 26:4 and the l. shall yield her increase,........ 776
Le 26:5 the full, and dwell in your l. safely....... 776
Le 26:6 And I will give peace in the l., and...... 776
Le 26:6 I will rid evil beasts out of the l.,........ 776
Le 26:6 shall the sword go through your l......... 776
Le 26:13 you forth out of the l. of Egypt,.......... 776
Le 26:20 your l. shall not yield her increase,...... 776
Le 26:20 neither shall the trees of the l............ 776
Le 26:32 I will bring the l. into desolation:......... 776
Le 26:33 and your l. shall be desolate, and......... 776
Le 26:34 Then shall the l. enjoy her sabbaths,.... 776
Le 26:34 and ye be in your enemies' l.; even..... 776
Le 26:34 even then shall the l. rest, and........... 776
Le 26:38 l. of your enemies shall eat you up...... 776
Le 26:41 them into the l. of their enemies;........ 776
Le 26:42 and I will remember the l.................. 776
Le 26:43 The l. also shall be left of them,........ 776
Le 26:44 they be in the l. of their enemies,........ 776
Le 26:45 Brought forth out of the l. of Egypt..... 776
Le 27:24 the possession of the l. did belong....... 776
Le 27:30 And all the tithe of the l., whether....... 776
Le 27:30 whether of the seed of the l., or of...... 776
Nu 1:1 were come out of the l. of Egypt,........ 776
Nu 3:13 I smote all the firstborn in the l.......... 776
Nu 8:17 every firstborn in the l. of Egypt......... 776
Nu 9:1 were come out of the l. of Egypt,........ 776
Nu 9:14 and for him that was born in the l....... 776
Nu 10:9 if ye go to war in your l. against......... 776
Nu 10:30 but I will depart to mine own l.,.......... 776
Nu 11:12 l. which thou swearest unto their......... 127
Nu 13:2 they may search the l. of Canaan,......... 776
Nu 13:16 which Moses sent to spy out the l....... 776
Nu 13:17 them to spy out the l. of Canaan,........ 776
Nu 13:18 see the l., what it is; and the people.... 776
Nu 13:19 what the l. is that they dwell in,.......... 776
Nu 13:20 what the l. is, whether it be fat or........ 776
Nu 13:20 and bring of the fruit of the l............. 776
Nu 13:21 they went up, and searched the l.......... 776
Nu 13:25 returned from searching of the l.......... 776
Nu 13:26 and shewed them the fruit of the l....... 776
Nu 13:27 unto the l. whither thou sentest us,..... 776
Nu 13:28 people be strong that dwell in the l.,.... 776
Nu 13:29 The Amalekites dwell in the l. of the.... 776

Nu 13:32 brought up an evil report of the l. 776
Nu 13:32 The l., through which we have gone 776
Nu 13:32 is a l. that eateth up the inhabitants 776
Nu 14:2 that we had died in the l. of Egypt! 776
Nu 14:3 the Lord brought us unto this l., 776
Nu 14:6 were of them that searched the l., 776
Nu 14:7 The l., which we passed through to 776
Nu 14:7 to search it, is an exceeding good l. 776
Nu 14:8 then he will bring us into this l., and 776
Nu 14:8 a l. which floweth with milk and 776
Nu 14:9 neither fear ye the people of the l.; 776
Nu 14:14 tell it to the inhabitants of this l.. 776
Nu 14:16 able to bring this people into the l. 776
Nu 14:23 shall not see the l. which I sware 776
Nu 14:24 him will I bring into the l. whereinto 776
Nu 14:30 ye shall not come into the l., 776
Nu 14:31 they shall know the l. which ye have 776
Nu 14:34 the days in which ye searched the l., 776
Nu 14:36 which Moses sent to search the l., 776
Nu 14:36 by bringing up a slander upon the l., 776
Nu 14:37 bring up the evil report upon the l., 776
Nu 14:38 of the men that went to search the l., 776
Nu 15:2 When ye be come into the l. of your 776
Nu 15:18 When ye come into the l. whither I 776
Nu 15:19 when ye eat of the bread of the l., 776
Nu 15:30 whether he be born in the l., or a 249
Nu 15:41 brought you out of the l. of Egypt, 776
Nu 16:13 brought us up out of a l. that floweth 776
Nu 16:14 not brought us into a l. that floweth 776
Nu 18:13 whatsoever is first ripe in the l., 776
Nu 18:20 shalt have no inheritance in their l. 776
Nu 20:12 bring this congregation into the l. 776
Nu 20:23 Hor, by the coast of the l. of Edom, 776
Nu 20:24 he shall not enter into the l. which 776
Nu 21:4 Red sea, to compass the l. of Edom: 776
Nu 21:22 Let me pass through thy l.: we will 776
Nu 21:24 and possessed his l. from Arnon unto 776
Nu 21:26 taken all his l. out of his hand, even 776
Nu 21:31 Israel dwelt in the l. of the Amorites 776
Nu 21:34 hand, and all his people, and his l.; 776
Nu 21:35 him alive: and they possessed his l.. 776
Nu 22:5 river of the l. of the children of his 776
Nu 22:6 that I may drive them out of the l.. 776
Nu 22:13 Get you into your l.: for the Lord 776
Nu 26:4 went forth out of the l. of Egypt. 776
Nu 26:19 Er and Onan died in the l. of Canaan 776
Nu 26:53 Unto these the l. shall be divided 776
Nu 26:55 the l. shall be divided by lot: 776
Nu 27:12 see the l. which I have given unto 776
Nu 32:1 and when they saw the l. of Jazer, 776
Nu 32:1 and the l. of Gilead, that, behold, the 776
Nu 32:4 is a l. for cattle, and thy servants 776
Nu 32:5 let this l. be given unto thy servants 776
Nu 32:7 of Israel from going over into the l. 776
Nu 32:8 from Kadesh-barnea to see the l. 776
Nu 32:9 and saw the l., they discouraged the 776
Nu 32:9 that they should not go into the l. 776
Nu 32:11 l. which I sware unto Abraham, 127
Nu 32:17 because of the inhabitants of the l. 776
Nu 32:22 the l. be subdued before the Lord: 776
Nu 32:22 and this l. shall be your possession 776
Nu 32:29 the l. shall be subdued before you; 776
Nu 32:29 ye shall give them the l. of Gilead 776
Nu 32:30 among you in the l. of Canaan. 776
Nu 32:32 before the Lord into the l. of Canaan, 776
Nu 32:33 the l., with the cities thereof in the 776
Nu 33:1 went forth out of the l. of Egypt with 776
Nu 33:37 Hor, in the edge of the l. of Edom. 776
Nu 33:38 were come out of the l. of Egypt, 776
Nu 33:40 in the south in the l. of Canaan, 776
Nu 33:51 over Jordan into the l. of Canaan; 776
Nu 33:52 inhabitants of the l. from before you, 776
Nu 33:53 dispossess the inhabitants of the l., 776
Nu 33:53 I have given you the l. to possess it. 776
Nu 33:54 ye shall divide the l. by lot for an 776
Nu 33:55 not drive out the inhabitants of the l. 776
Nu 33:55 shall vex you in the l. wherein ye 776
Nu 34:2 When ye come into the l. of Canaan; 776
Nu 34:2 (this is the l. that shall fall unto you 776
Nu 34:2 even the l. of Canaan with the coasts 776
Nu 34:12 this shall be your l. with the coasts 776
Nu 34:13 This is the l. which ye shall inherit 776
Nu 34:17 which shall divide the l. unto you: 776
Nu 34:18 to divide the l. by inheritance. 776
Nu 34:29 children of Israel in the l. of Canaan. 776
Nu 35:10 over Jordan into the l. of Canaan; 776
Nu 35:14 shall ye give in the l. of Canaan, 776
Nu 35:28 slayer shall return into the l. of his 776
Nu 35:32 should come again to dwell in the l., 776
Nu 35:33 not pollute the l. wherein ye are: 776
Nu 35:33 ye are: for blood it defileth the l. 776
Nu 35:33 l. cannot be cleansed of the blood 776
Nu 35:34 Defile not therefore the l. which ye 776
Nu 36:2 to give the l. for an inheritance by 776
De 1:5 this side Jordan, in the l. of Moab, 776
De 1:7 to the l. of the Canaanites, and unto 776
De 1:8 Behold, I have set the l. before you: 776
De 1:8 go in and possess the l. which the 776
De 1:21 thy God hath set the l. before thee: 776
De 1:22 they shall search us out the l., and 776
De 1:25 they took of the fruit of the l. in their 776
De 1:25 is a good l. which the Lord our God 776
De 1:27 out of the l. of Egypt, to deliver us 776
De 1:35 this evil generation see that good l., 776
De 1:36 to him will I give the l. that he hath 776
De 2:5 I will not give you of their l., no, not 776
De 2:9 I will not give thee of their l. for a 776
De 2:12 as Israel did unto the l. of his 776
De 2:19 not give thee of the l. of the children 776
De 2:20 also was accounted a l. of giants: 776
De 2:24 Sihon...king of Heshbon, and his l. 776
De 2:27 Let me pass through thy l.: I will go 776
De 2:29 Jordan into the l. which the Lord 776
De 2:31 to give Sihon and his l. before thee: 776
De 2:31 that thou mayest inherit his l.. 776
De 2:37 unto the l. of the children of Ammon 776
De 3:2 his people, and his l., into thy hand; 776
De 3:8 the l. that was on this side Jordan, 776
De 3:12 this l., which we possessed at that 776
De 3:13 which was called the l. of giants. 776
De 3:18 hath given you this l. to possess it: 776
De 3:20 also possess the l. which the Lord 776
De 3:25 the good l. that is beyond Jordan, 776
De 3:28 cause them to inherit the l. which 776
De 4:1 in and possess the l. which the Lord 776
De 4:5 should do so in the l. whither ye go 776
De 4:21 I should not go in unto that good l., 776
De 4:22 But I must die in this l., I must not 776
De 4:22 go over, and possess that good l. 776
De 4:25 shall have remained long in the l., 776
De 4:26 soon utterly perish from off the l. 776
De 4:38 give thee their l. for an inheritance, 776
De 4:46 the l. of Sihon king of the Amorites, 776
De 4:47 they possessed his l., and the l. of Og 776
De 5:6 brought thee out of the l. of Egypt, 776
De 5:15 wast a servant in the l. of Egypt, 776
De 5:16 l. which the Lord thy God giveth 127
De 5:31 may do them in the l. which I give 776
De 5:33 ye may prolong your days in the l. 776
De 6:1 in the l. whither ye go to possess it: 776
De 6:3 l. that floweth with milk and honey. 776
De 6:10 thee into the l. which he sware unto 776
De 6:12 thee forth out of the l. of Egypt, 776
De 6:18 mayest go in and possess the good l. 776
De 6:23 give us the l. which he sware unto 776
De 7:1 thy God shall bring thee into the l. 776
De 7:13 thy womb, and the fruit of thy l., 127
De 7:13 l. which he sware unto thy fathers 127
De 8:1 go in and possess the l. which the 776
De 8:7 into a good l., a l. of brooks of water, 776
De 8:8 a l. of wheat, and barley, and vines, 776
De 8:8 a l. of oil olive, and honey; 776
De 8:9 A l. wherein thou shalt eat bread 776
De 8:9 a l. whose stones are iron, and out 776
De 8:10 the good l. which he hath given thee. 776
De 8:14 thee forth out of the l. of Egypt, 776
De 9:4 brought me in to possess this l.. 776
De 9:5 dost thou go to possess their l. 776
De 9:6 thy God giveth thee not this good l. 776
De 9:7 didst depart out of the l. of Egypt, 776
De 9:23 Go up and possess the l. which I 776
De 9:28 Lest the l. whence thou broughtest 776
De 9:28 into the l. which he promised them, 776
De 10:7 to Jotbath, a l. of rivers of waters. 776
De 10:11 they may go in and possess the l., 776
De 10:19 ye were strangers in the l. of Egypt. 776
De 11:3 king of Egypt, and unto all his l.; 776
De 11:8 strong, and go in and possess the l., 776
De 11:9 ye may prolong your days in the l., 127
De 11:9 l. that floweth with milk and honey. 776
De 11:10 For the l., whither thou goest in to 776
De 11:10 is not as the l. of Egypt, from whence 776
De 11:11 the l., whither ye go to possess it, 776
De 11:11 is a l. of hills and valleys, and 776
De 11:12 A l. which the Lord thy God careth 776
De 11:14 the rain of your l. in his due season, 776
De 11:17 and that the l. yield not her fruit; 127
De 11:17 perish quickly from off the good l. 776
De 11:21 the l. which the Lord sware unto 127
De 11:25 all the l. that ye shall tread upon, 776
De 11:29 unto the l. whither thou goest to 776
De 11:30 down, in the l. of the Canaanites, 776
De 11:31 to go in to possess the l. which the 776
De 12:1 ye shall observe to do in the l., 776
De 12:10 dwell in the l. which the Lord your 776
De 12:29 them, and dwellest in their l.; 776
De 13:5 brought you out of the l. of Egypt, 776
De 13:10 brought thee out of the l. of Egypt, 776
De 15:4 Lord shall greatly bless thee in the l. 776
De 15:7 within any of thy gates in thy l. 776
De 15:11 poor shall never cease out of the l.. 776
De 15:11 thy poor, and to thy needy, in thy l.. 776
De 15:15 wast a bondman in the l. of Egypt. 776
De 16:3 forth out of the l. of Egypt in haste: 776
De 16:3 camest forth out of the l. of Egypt 776
De 16:20 inherit the l. which the Lord thy God 776
De 17:14 When thou art come unto the l. 776
De 18:9 when thou art come into the l. 776
De 19:1 whose l. the Lord thy God giveth 776
De 19:2 cities for thee in the midst of thy l., 776
De 19:3 divide the coasts of thy l., which 776
De 19:8 give thee all the l. which he promised 776
De 19:10 innocent blood be not shed in thy l., 776
De 19:14 which thou shalt inherit in the l. 776
De 20:1 thee up out of the l. of Egypt. 776
De 21:1 If one be found slain in the l. which 127
De 21:23 that thy l. be not defiled, which the 127
De 23:7 thou wast a stranger in his l.. 776
De 23:20 in the l. whither thou goest to 776
De 24:4 thou shalt not cause the l. to sin. 776
De 24:14 strangers that are in thy l. within 776
De 24:22 wast a bondman in the l. of Egypt: 776
De 25:15 days may be lengthened in the l. 127
De 25:19 in the l. which the Lord thy God 776
De 26:1 when thou art come in unto the l. 776
De 26:2 shalt bring of thy l. that the Lord 776
De 26:9 place, and hath given us this l., 776
De 26:9 l. that floweth with milk and honey. 776
De 26:10 brought the firstfruits of the l., 127
De 26:15 and the l. which thou hast given us, 127
De 26:15 l. that floweth with milk and honey. 776
De 27:2 ye shall pass over Jordan unto the l. 776
De 27:3 that thou mayest go in unto the l. 776
De 27:3 l. that floweth with milk and honey; 776
De 28:8 bless thee in the l. which the Lord 776
De 28:11 l. which the Lord sware unto thy 127
De 28:12 the rain unto thy l. in his season, 776
De 28:18 of thy body, and the fruit of thy l., 127
De 28:21 have consumed thee from off the l., 127
De 28:24 the rain of thy l. powder and dust: 776
De 28:33 fruit of thy l., and all thy labours, 127
De 28:42 and fruit of thy l. shall the locust 127
De 28:51 of thy cattle, and the fruit of thy l., 127
De 28:52 trustedst, throughout all thy l.. 776
De 28:52 all thy gates throughout all thy l., 776
De 28:63 ye shall be plucked from off the l. 127
De 29:1 children of Israel in the l. of Moab, 776
De 29:2 before your eyes in the l. of Egypt 776
De 29:2 all his servants, and unto all his l.; 776
De 29:8 we took their l., and gave it for an 776
De 29:16 how we have dwelt in the l. of Egypt; 776
De 29:22 that shall come from a far l., 776
De 29:22 when they see the plagues of that l., 776
De 29:23 the whole l. thereof is brimstone, 776
De 29:24 the Lord done thus unto this l.? 776
De 29:25 them forth out of the l. of Egypt: 776
De 29:27 the Lord was kindled against this l., 776
De 29:28 rooted them out of their l. in anger, 127
De 29:28 and cast them into another l., 776
De 30:5 thy God will bring thee into the l. 776
De 30:9 thy cattle, and in the fruit of thy l., 127
De 30:16 thy God shall bless thee in the l. 776
De 30:18 not prolong your days upon the l., 127
De 30:20 thou mayest dwell in the l. which 127
De 31:4 Amorites, and unto the l. of them, 776
De 31:7 must go with this people unto the l. 776
De 31:13 as long as ye live in the l. whither 127
De 31:16 the gods of the strangers of the l., 776
De 31:20 into the l. which I sware unto their 127

De 31:21 them into the **l.** which I sware. 776
De 31:23 into the **l.** which I sware unto them: 776
De 32:10 He found him in a desert **l.**, and in 776
De 32:43 will be merciful unto his **l.**, and to 127
De 32:47 ye shall prolong your days in the **l.**, 127
De 32:49 Nebo, which is in the **l.** of Moab, 776
De 32:49 behold the **l.** of Canaan, which I 776
De 32:52 thou shalt see the **l.** before thee; 776
De 32:52 thither unto the **l.** which I give the 776
De 33:13 Blessed of the Lord be his **l.**, for 776
De 33:28 shall be upon a **l.** of corn and wine; 776
De 34:1 shewed him all the **l.** of Gilead, 776
De 34:2 the **l.** of Ephraim, and Manasseh, 776
De 34:2 all the **l.** of Judah, unto the utmost 776
De 34:4 the **l.** which I sware unto Abraham, 776
De 34:5 Lord died there in the **l.** of Moab, 776
De 34:6 him in a valley in the **l.** of Moab, 776
De 34:11 sent him to do in the **l.** of Egypt 776
De 34:11 to all his servants, and to all his **l.**, 776
Jos 1:2 unto the **l.** which I do give to them, 776
Jos 1:4 all the **l.** of the Hittites, and unto 776
Jos 1:6 thou divide for an inheritance the **l.**, 776
Jos 1:11 to go in to possess the **l.**, which the 776
Jos 1:13 you rest, and hath given you this **l.** 776
Jos 1:14 shall remain in the **l.** which Moses 776
Jos 1:15 they also have possessed the **l.** 776
Jos 1:15 return unto the **l.** of your possession, 776
Jos 2:1 saying, Go view the **l.**, even Jericho. 776
Jos 2:9 that the Lord hath given you the **l.**, 776
Jos 2:9 inhabitants of the **l.** faint because of 776
Jos 2:14 when the Lord hath given us the **l.**, 776
Jos 2:18 we come into the **l.**, thou shalt bind 776
Jos 2:24 delivered into our hands all the **l.** 776
Jos 4:18 feet were lifted up unto the dry **l.**,
Jos 4:22 Israel came over this Jordan on dry **l.**
Jos 5:6 that he would not shew them the **l.**, 776
Jos 5:6 **l.** that floweth with milk and honey. 776
Jos 5:11 eat of the old corn of the **l.** on the 776
Jos 5:12 had eaten of the old corn of the **l.**; 776
Jos 5:12 they did eat of the fruit of the **l.** of 776
Jos 7:9 the inhabitants of the **l.** shall hear 776
Jos 8:1 his people, and his city, and his **l.** 776
Jos 9:24 servant Moses to give you all the **l.**, 776
Jos 9:24 destroy all the inhabitants of the **l.** 776
Jos 10:42 these kings and their **l.** did Joshua 776
Jos 11:3 under Hermon in the **l.** of Mizpeh. 776
Jos 11:16 So Joshua took all that **l.**, the hills, 776
Jos 11:16 all the **l.** of Goshen, and the valley, 776
Jos 11:22 none of the Anakims left in the **l.** of 776
Jos 11:23 Joshua took the whole **l.**, according 776
Jos 11:23 tribes. And the **l.** rested from war. 776
Jos 12:1 these are the kings of the **l.**, which 776
Jos 12:1 possessed their **l.** on the other side 776
Jos 13:1 yet very much **l.** to be possessed. 776
Jos 13:2 This is the **l.** that yet remaineth: all 776
Jos 13:4 all the **l.** of the Canaanites, and 776
Jos 13:5 And the **l.** of the Giblites, and all 776
Jos 13:7 divide this **l.** for an inheritance 776
Jos 13:25 half the **l.** of the children of Ammon, 776
Jos 14:1 Israel inherited in the **l.** of Canaan, 776
Jos 14:4 no part unto the Levites in the **l.**, 776
Jos 14:5 Israel did, and they divided the **l.** 776
Jos 14:7 Kadesh-barnea to espy out the **l.**; 776
Jos 14:9 **l.** whereon thy feet have trodden 776
Jos 14:15 And the **l.** had rest from war. 776
Jos 15:19 for thou hast given me a south **l.**: 776
Jos 17:5 beside the **l.** of Gilead and Bashan, 776
Jos 17:6 Manasseh's sons had the **l.** of Gilead. 776
Jos 17:8 Manasseh had the **l.** of Tappuah: 776
Jos 17:12 Canaanites would dwell in that **l.** 776
Jos 17:15 **l.** of the Perizzites and of the giants, 776
Jos 17:16 that dwell in the **l.** of the valley 776
Jos 18:1 and the **l.** was subdued before them. 776
Jos 18:3 are ye slack to go to possess the **l.**, 776
Jos 18:4 they shall rise, and go through the **l.**, 776
Jos 18:6 describe the **l.** into seven parts, 776
Jos 18:8 them that went to describe the **l.** 776
Jos 18:8 saying, Go and walk through the **l.**, 776
Jos 18:9 men went and passed through the **l.**, 776
Jos 18:10 there Joshua divided the **l.** unto the 776
Jos 19:49 dividing the **l.** for inheritance by 776
Jos 21:2 them at Shiloh in the **l.** of Canaan, 776
Jos 21:43 the Lord gave unto Israel all the **l.** 776
Jos 22:4 and unto the **l.** of your possession, 776
Jos 22:9 Shiloh, which is in the **l.** of Canaan, 776
Jos 22:9 **l.** of their possession, whereof they 776
Jos 22:10 that are in the **l.** of Canaan, the 776
Jos 22:11 altar over against the **l.** of Canaan, 776
Jos 22:13 of Manasseh, into the **l.** of Gilead, 776
Jos 22:15 of Manasseh, unto the **l.** of Gilead, 776
Jos 22:19 the **l.** of your possession be unclean, 776
Jos 22:19 then pass ye over unto the **l.** of the 776
Jos 22:32 of Gad, out of the **l.** of Gilead, 776
Jos 22:32 unto the **l.** of Canaan, to the children 776
Jos 22:33 destroy the **l.** wherein the children 776
Jos 23:5 ye shall possess their **l.**, as the Lord 776
Jos 23:13 until ye perish from off the good **l.** 127
Jos 23:15 destroyed you from off this good **l.** 127
Jos 23:16 perish quickly from off the good **l.** 776
Jos 24:3 him throughout all the **l.** of Canaan, 776
Jos 24:8 you into the **l.** of the Amorites, 776
Jos 24:8 hand, that ye might possess their **l.**; 776
Jos 24:13 you a **l.** for which ye did not labour, 776
Jos 24:15 the Amorites, in whose **l.** ye dwell: 776
Jos 24:17 our fathers out of the **l.** of Egypt, 776
Jos 24:18 the Amorites which dwelt in the **l.** 776
Jg 1:2 have delivered the **l.** into his hand. 776
Jg 1:15 for thou hast given me a south **l.**; 776
Jg 1:26 men went into the **l.** of the Hittites, 776
Jg 1:27 Canaanites would dwell in that **l.** 776
Jg 1:32, 33 Canaanites,...inhabitants of the **l.**: 776
Jg 2:1 have brought you unto the **l.** which 776
Jg 2:2 with the inhabitants of this **l.**; 776
Jg 2:6 his inheritance to possess the **l.** 776
Jg 2:12 brought them out of the **l.** of Egypt, 776
Jg 3:11 And the **l.** had rest forty years. 776
Jg 3:30 And the **l.** had rest fourscore years. 776
Jg 5:31 And the **l.** had rest forty years. 776
Jg 6:5 they entered into the **l.** to destroy it. 776
Jg 6:9 before you, and gave you their **l.**; 776
Jg 6:10 the Amorites, in whose **l.** ye dwell: 776
Jg 9:37 people down by the middle of the **l.**, 776
Jg 10:4 day, which are in the **l.** of Gilead. 776
Jg 10:8 Jordan in the **l.** of the Amorites, 776
Jg 11:3 brethren, and dwelt in the **l.** of Tob: 776
Jg 11:5 fetch Jephthah out of the **l.** of Tob: 776
Jg 11:12 come against me to fight in my **l.**? 776
Jg 11:13 Because Israel took away my **l.**, 776
Jg 11:15 Israel took not away the **l.** of Moab, 776
Jg 11:15 nor the **l.** of the children of Ammon: 776
Jg 11:17 me, I pray thee, pass through thy **l.**: 776
Jg 11:18 the **l.** of Edom, and the **l.** of Moab, 776
Jg 11:18 by the east side of the **l.** of Moab, 776
Jg 11:19 thee, through thy **l.** into my place. 776
Jg 11:21 possessed all the **l.** of the Amorites, 776
Jg 12:15 in Pirathon in the **l.** of Ephraim, 776
Jg 18:2 to spy out the **l.**, and to search it; 776
Jg 18:2 said unto them, Go, search the **l.** 776
Jg 18:7 there was no magistrate in the **l.**, 776
Jg 18:9 for we have seen the **l.**, and, behold, 776
Jg 18:9 to go, and to enter to possess the **l.** 776
Jg 18:10 a people secure, and to a large **l.** 776
Jg 18:17 five men that went to spy out the **l.** 776
Jg 18:30 the day of the captivity of the **l.** 776
Jg 19:30 Israel came up out of the **l.** of Egypt 776
Jg 20:1 to Beer-sheba, with the **l.** of Gilead, 776
Jg 21:12 Shiloh, which is in the **l.** of Canaan. 776
Jg 21:21 Shiloh, and go to the **l.** of Benjamin. 776
Ru 1:1 that there was a famine in the **l.** 776
Ru 1:7 way to return unto the **l.** of Judah. 776
Ru 2:11 mother, and the **l.** of thy nativity, 776
Ru 4:3 of Moab, selleth a parcel of **l.**, 7704
1Sa 6:5 of your mice that mar the **l.**; 776
1Sa 6:5 off your gods, and from off your **l.** 776
1Sa 9:4 passed through the **l.** of Shalisha, 776
1Sa 9:4 passed through the **l.** of Shalim, 776
1Sa 9:4 through the **l.** of the Benjamites, 776
1Sa 9:5 they were come to the **l.** of Zuph, 776
1Sa 9:16 thee a man out of the **l.** of Benjamin, 776
1Sa 12:6 your fathers up out of the **l.** of Egypt. 776
1Sa 13:3 the trumpet throughout all the **l.**, 776
1Sa 13:7 went over Jordan to the **l.** of Gad 776
1Sa 13:17 to Ophrah, unto the **l.** of Shual. 776
1Sa 13:19 throughout all the **l.** of Israel: 776
1Sa 14:14 as it were an half acre of **l.**, which 7704
1Sa 14:25 all they of the **l.** came to a wood; 776
1Sa 14:29 My father hath troubled the **l.** 776
1Sa 21:11 not this David the king of the **l.**? 776
1Sa 22:5 and get thee into the **l.** of Judah. 776
1Sa 23:23 if he be in the **l.**, that I will search 776
1Sa 23:27 the Philistines have invaded the **l.** 776
1Sa 27:1 escape into the **l.** of the Philistines; 776
1Sa 27:8 were of old the inhabitants of the **l.**, 776
1Sa 27:8 to Shur, even unto the **l.** of Egypt. 776
1Sa 27:9 David smote the **l.**, and left neither 776
1Sa 28:3 and the wizards, out of the **l.** 776
1Sa 28:9 and the wizards, out of the **l.** 776
1Sa 29:11 return into the **l.** of the Philistines. 776
1Sa 30:16 out of the **l.** of the Philistines, 776
1Sa 30:16 and out of the **l.** of Judah. 776
1Sa 31:9 sent into the **l.** of the Philistines 776
2Sa 3:12 his behalf, saying, Whose is the **l.**? 776
2Sa 5:6 Jebusites, the inhabitants of the **l.** 776
2Sa 7:23 great things and terrible, for thy **l.**, 776
2Sa 9:7 thee all the **l.** of Saul thy father; 7704
2Sa 9:10 thy servants, shall till the **l.** for him, 127
2Sa 10:2 into the **l.** of the children of Ammon. 776
2Sa 15:4 Oh that I were made judge in the **l.**, 776
2Sa 17:26 Absalom pitched in the **l.** of Gilead. 776
2Sa 19:9 he is fled out of the **l.** for Absalom. 776
2Sa 19:29 said, Thou and Ziba divide the **l.** 7704
2Sa 21:14 that God was intreated for the **l.** 776
2Sa 24:6 and to the **l.** of Tahtim-hodshi; 776
2Sa 24:8 they had gone through all the **l.**, 776
2Sa 24:13 of famine come unto thee in thy **l.**? 776
2Sa 24:13 be three days' pestilence in thy **l.**? 776
2Sa 24:25 So the Lord was intreated for the **l.**, 776
1Ki 4:10 Sochoh, and all the **l.** of Hepher: 776
1Ki 4:19 the only officer which was in the **l.** 776
1Ki 4:21 river unto the **l.** of the Philistines, 776
1Ki 6:1 were come out of the **l.** of Egypt, 776
1Ki 8:9 they came out of the **l.** of Egypt. 776
1Ki 8:21 brought them out of the **l.** of Egypt. 776
1Ki 8:34 unto the **l.** which thou gavest unto 127
1Ki 8:36 give rain upon thy **l.**, which thou 776
1Ki 8:37 If there be in the **l.** famine, if there 776
1Ki 8:37 besiege them in the **l.** of their cities; 776
1Ki 8:40 all the days that they live in the **l.** 127
1Ki 8:46 captives unto the **l.** of the enemy, 776
1Ki 8:47 **l.** whither they were carried captives, 776
1Ki 8:47 make supplication unto thee in the **l.** 776
1Ki 8:48 in the **l.** of their enemies, which led 776
1Ki 8:48 and pray unto thee toward their **l.**, 776
1Ki 9:7 Then will I cut off Israel out of the **l.** 127
1Ki 9:8 hath the Lord done thus unto this **l.**, 776
1Ki 9:9 their fathers out of the **l.** of Egypt, 776
1Ki 9:11 twenty cities in the **l.** of Galilee. 776
1Ki 9:13 And he called them the **l.** of Cabul 776
1Ki 9:18 Tadmor in the wilderness, in the **l.**, 776
1Ki 9:19 and in all the **l.** of his dominion. 776
1Ki 9:21 that were left after them in the **l.**, 776
1Ki 9:26 of the Red sea, in the **l.** of Edom. 776
1Ki 10:6 report that I heard in mine own **l.** of 776
1Ki 11:18 him victuals, and gave him **l.** 776
1Ki 12:28 brought thee up out of the **l.** of Egypt. 776
1Ki 14:15 root up Israel out of this good **l.**, 127
1Ki 14:24 there were also sodomites in the **l.**: 776
1Ki 15:12 took away the sodomites out of the **l.**, 776
1Ki 15:20 Cinneroth, with all the **l.** of Naphtali. 776
1Ki 17:7 there had been no rain in the **l.** 776
1Ki 18:5 said unto Obadiah, Go into the **l.**, 776
1Ki 18:6 divided the **l.** between them to pass 776
1Ki 20:7 Israel called all the elders of the **l.**, 776
1Ki 22:46 his father Asa, he took out of the **l.** 776
2Ki 2:21 thence any more death or barren **l.**
2Ki 3:19 mar every good piece of **l.** with stones.
2Ki 3:25 on every good piece of **l.** cast every
2Ki 3:27 him, and returned to their own **l.** 776
2Ki 4:38 and there was a dearth in the **l.**; and 776
2Ki 5:2 out of the **l.** of Israel a little maid; 776
2Ki 5:4 the maid that is of the **l.** of Israel. 776
2Ki 6:23 came no more into the **l.** of Israel 776
2Ki 8:1 also come upon the **l.** seven years. 776
2Ki 8:2 the **l.** of the Philistines seven years. 776
2Ki 8:3 out of the **l.** of the Philistines: and 776
2Ki 8:3, 5 king for her house and for her **l.** 7704
2Ki 8:6 since the day that she left the **l.**, 776
2Ki 10:33 Jordan eastward, all the **l.** of Gilead, 776
2Ki 11:3 And Athaliah did reign over the **l.** 776
2Ki 11:14 all the people of the **l.** rejoiced, and 776
2Ki 11:18 people of the **l.** went into the house 776
2Ki 11:19 guard, and all the people of the **l.**; 776
2Ki 11:20 all the people of the **l.** rejoiced, and 776
2Ki 13:20 bands of the Moabites invaded the **l.** 776
2Ki 15:5 house, judging the people of the **l.** 776
2Ki 15:19 king of Assyria came against the **l.**: 776
2Ki 15:20 back, and stayed not there in the **l.** 776
2Ki 15:29 all the **l.** of Naphtali, and carried 776
2Ki 16:15 offering of all the people of the **l.**, 776
2Ki 17:5 came up throughout all the **l.**, and 776
2Ki 17:7 them up out of the **l.** of Egypt, from 776

2Ki	17:23	carried away out of their own l. to	127
2Ki	17:26	not the manner of the God of the l..	776
2Ki	17:26	not the manner of the God of the l..	776
2Ki	17:27	them the manner of the God of the l..	776
2Ki	17:36	brought you up out of the l. of Egypt	776
2Ki	18:25	said to me, Go up against this l., and	776
2Ki	18:32	you away to a l. like your own l.,	776
2Ki	18:32	a l. of corn and wine,	776
2Ki	18:32	a l. of bread and vineyards,	776
2Ki	18:32	a l. of oil olive and of honey,	776
2Ki	18:33	of the nations delivered at all his l.	776
2Ki	19:7	and shall return to his own l.; and	776
2Ki	19:7	him to fall by the sword in his own l..	776
2Ki	19:37	they escaped into the l. of Armenia.	776
2Ki	21:8	Israel move any more out of the l.	127
2Ki	21:24	people of the l. slew all them that	776
2Ki	21:24	people of the l. made Josiah his son	776
2Ki	23:24	that were spied in the l. of Judah	776
2Ki	23:30	people of the l. took Jehoahaz the	776
2Ki	23:33	bands at Riblah in the l. of Hamath,	776
2Ki	23:33	put the l. to a tribute of an hundred	776
2Ki	23:35	but he taxed the l. to give the money	776
2Ki	23:35	and the gold of the people of the l.,	776
2Ki	24:7	not again any more out of his l.	776
2Ki	24:14	poorest sort of the people of the l..	776
2Ki	24:15	his officers, and the mighty of the l.,	776
2Ki	25:3	was no bread for the people of the l.	776
2Ki	25:12	poor of the l. to be vinedressers and	776
2Ki	25:19	which mustered the people of the l.,	776
2Ki	25:19	threescore men of the people of the l.	776
2Ki	25:21	them at Riblah in the l. of Hamath.	776
2Ki	25:21	was carried away out of their l.	127
2Ki	25:22	that remained in the l. of Judah,	776
2Ki	25:24	dwell in the l., and serve the king of	776
1Ch	1:43	kings that reigned in the l. of Edom	776
1Ch	1:45	Husham of the l. of the Temanites	776
1Ch	2:22	and twenty cities in the l. of Gilead	776
1Ch	4:40	and the l. was wide, and quiet, and	776
1Ch	5:9	were multiplied in the l. of Gilead.	776
1Ch	5:10	throughout all the east l. of Gilead.	
1Ch	5:11	in the l. of Bashan unto Salcah:	776
1Ch	5:23	tribe of Manasseh dwelt in the l..	776
1Ch	5:25	after the gods of the people of the l.,	776
1Ch	6:55	gave them Hebron in the l. of Judah,	776
1Ch	7:21	Gath that were born in that l. slew,	776
1Ch	10:9	and sent into the l. of the Philistines	776
1Ch	11:4	Jebusites...the inhabitants of the l.	776
1Ch	13:2	that are left in all the l. of Israel,	776
1Ch	16:18	Unto thee will I give the l. of Canaan,	776
1Ch	19:2	into the l. of the children of Ammon	776
1Ch	19:3	to overthrow, and to spy out the l.?	776
1Ch	21:12	even the pestilence, in the l., and the	776
1Ch	22:2	the strangers...in the l. of Israel;	776
1Ch	22:18	given the inhabitants of the l. into	776
1Ch	22:18	the l. is subdued before the Lord,	776
1Ch	28:8	that ye may possess this good l.,	776
2Ch	2:17	the strangers...in the l. of Israel,	776
2Ch	6:5	forth my people out of the l. of Egypt	776
2Ch	6:25	bring them again unto the l. which	127
2Ch	6:27	and send rain upon thy l., which	776
2Ch	6:28	If there be dearth in the l., if there	776
2Ch	6:28	besiege them in the cities of their l.;	776
2Ch	6:31	long as they live in the l. which	127
2Ch	6:36	captives unto a l. far off or near;	776
2Ch	6:37	in the l. whither they are carried	776
2Ch	6:37	unto thee in the l. of their captivity,	776
2Ch	6:38	their soul in the l. of their captivity,	776
2Ch	6:38	captives, and pray toward their l.,	776
2Ch	7:13	command the locusts to devour the l.,	776
2Ch	7:14	their sin, and will heal their l..	776
2Ch	7:20	them up by the roots out of my l.	127
2Ch	7:21	hath the Lord done thus unto this l.,	776
2Ch	7:22	them forth out of the l. of Egypt,	776
2Ch	8:6	throughout all the l. of his dominion.	776
2Ch	8:8	who were left after them in the l.,	776
2Ch	8:17	at the sea side in the l. of Edom.	776
2Ch	9:5	report which I heard in mine own l.	776
2Ch	9:11	such seen before in the l. of Judah.	776
2Ch	9:12	turned, and went away to her own l.,	776
2Ch	9:26	even unto the l. of the Philistines,	776
2Ch	14:1	his days the l. was quiet ten years.	776
2Ch	14:6	for the l. had rest, and he had no war	776
2Ch	14:7	bars, while the l. is yet before us;	776
2Ch	15:8	idols out of all the l. of Judah and	776
2Ch	17:2	and set garrisons in the l. of Judah,	776
2Ch	19:3	taken away the groves out of the l.,	776
2Ch	19:5	he set judges in the l. throughout	776
2Ch	20:7	drive out the inhabitants of this l.	776
2Ch	20:10	they came out of the l. of Egypt,	776
2Ch	22:12	and Athaliah reigned over the l.	776
2Ch	23:13	all the people of the l. rejoiced, and	776
2Ch	23:20	people, and all the people of the l.,	776
2Ch	23:21	And all the people of the l. rejoiced:	776
2Ch	26:21	house, judging the people of the l..	776
2Ch	30:9	they shall come again into this l.	776
2Ch	30:25	that came out of the l. of Israel, and	776
2Ch	32:4	that ran through the midst of the l.,	776
2Ch	32:21	with shame of face to his own l.	776
2Ch	32:31	of the wonder that was done in the l.,	776
2Ch	33:8	the foot of Israel from out of the l.	127
2Ch	33:25	people of the l. slew all them that	776
2Ch	33:25	people of the l. made Josiah his son	776
2Ch	34:7	idols throughout all the l. of Israel,	776
2Ch	34:8	when he had purged the l., and the	776
2Ch	36:1	people of the l. took Jehoahaz the	776
2Ch	36:3	and condemned the l. in an hundred	776
2Ch	36:21	the l. had enjoyed her sabbaths:	776
Ezr	4:4	people of the l. weakened the hands	776
Ezr	6:21	the filthiness of the heathen of the l.,	776
Ezr	9:11	The l., unto which ye go to possess	776
Ezr	9:11	is an unclean l. with the filthiness of	776
Ezr	9:12	be strong, and eat the good of the l.,	776
Ezr	10:2	strange wives of the people of the l..	776
Ezr	10:11	yourselves from the people of the l.,	776
Ne	4:4	them for a prey in the l. of captivity:	776
Ne	5:14	be their governor in the l. of Judah,	776
Ne	5:16	this wall, neither bought we any l.	7704
Ne	9:8	to give the l. of the Canaanites, the	776
Ne	9:10	and on all the people of his l.	776
Ne	9:11	the midst of the sea on the dry l.;	
Ne	9:15	they should go in to possess the l.	776
Ne	9:22	so they possessed the l. of Sihon,	776
Ne	9:22	and the l. of the king of Heshbon,	776
Ne	9:22	and the l. of Og king of Bashan.	776
Ne	9:23	and broughtest them into the l.,	776
Ne	9:24	children went in and possessed the l.,	776
Ne	9:24	before them the inhabitants of the l.,	776
Ne	9:24	their kings, and the people of the l.,	776
Ne	9:25	they took strong cities, and a fat l.,	127
Ne	9:35	large and fat l. which thou gavest	776
Ne	9:36	for the l. that thou gavest unto our	776
Ne	10:30	daughters unto the people of the l.,	776
Ne	10:31	people of the l. bring ware or any	776
Es	8:17	of the people of the l. became Jews;	776
Es	10:1	Ahasuerus laid a tribute upon the l.,	776
Job	1:1	a man in the l. of Uz, whose name	776
Job	1:10	his substance is increased in the l.	776
Job	10:21	to the l. of darkness and the shadow	776
Job	10:22	A l. of darkness, as darkness itself;	776
Job	28:13	is it found in the l. of the living.	776
Job	31:38	If my l. cry against me, or that the	127
Job	37:13	correction, or for his l., or for mercy.	776
Job	39:6	and the barren l. his dwellings.	
Job	42:15	the l. were no women found so fair	776
Ps	10:16	heathen are perished out of his l..	776
Ps	27:13	of the Lord in the l. of the living.	776
Ps	35:20	against them that are quiet in the l..	776
Ps	37:3	shalt thou dwell in the l., and verily	776
Ps	37:29	The righteous shall inherit the l.,	776
Ps	37:34	he shall exalt thee to inherit the l..	776
Ps	42:6	remember thee from the l. of Jordan,	776
Ps	44:3	they got not the l. in possession by	776
Ps	52:5	root thee out of the l. of the living	776
Ps	63:1	for thee in a dry and thirsty l., where	776
Ps	66:6	He turned the sea into dry l.: they	776
Ps	68:6	but the rebellious dwell in a dry l..	
Ps	74:8	all the synagogues of God in the l.	776
Ps	78:12	of their fathers, in the l. of Egypt, in	776
Ps	80:9	to take deep root, and it filled the l.	776
Ps	81:5	he went out through the l. of Egypt:	776
Ps	81:10	brought thee out of the l. of Egypt:	776
Ps	85:1	hast been favourable unto thy l.:	776
Ps	85:9	him; that glory may dwell in our l..	776
Ps	85:12	and our l. shall yield her increase.	776
Ps	88:12	in the l. of forgetfulness?	776
Ps	95:5	it: and his hands formed the dry l.	
Ps	101:6	shall be upon the faithful of the l.,	776
Ps	101:8	early destroy all the wicked of the l.;	776
Ps	105:11	thee will I give the l. of Canaan,	776
Ps	105:16	he called for a famine upon the l.	776
Ps	105:23	Jacob sojourned in the l. of Ham.	776
Ps	105:27	them, and wonders in the l. of Ham.	776
Ps	105:30	Their l. brought forth frogs in	776
Ps	105:32	for rain, and flaming fire in their l..	776
Ps	105:35	did eat up all the herbs in their l.,	776
Ps	105:36	smote also all the firstborn in their l.,	776
Ps	106:22	Wondrous works in the l. of Ham,	776
Ps	106:24	they despised the pleasant l., they	776
Ps	106:38	and the l. was polluted with blood.	776
Ps	107:34	A fruitful l. into barrenness, for the	776
Ps	116:9	before the Lord in the l. of the living.	776
Ps	135:12	And gave their l. for an heritage, an	776
Ps	136:21	And gave their l. for an heritage: for	776
Ps	137:4	sing the Lord's song in a strange l.?	127
Ps	142:5	my portion in the l. of the living.	776
Ps	143:6	thirsteth after thee, as a thirsty l.	776
Ps	143:10	lead me into the l. of uprightness.	776
Pr	2:21	For the upright shall dwell in the l.,	776
Pr	12:11	that tilleth his l. shall be satisfied	127
Pr	28:2	For the transgression of a l. many	776
Pr	28:19	that tilleth his l. shall have plenty	127
Pr	29:4	by judgment establisheth the l.	776
Pr	31:23	he sitteth among the elders of the l..	776
Ec	10:16	Woe to thee, O l., when thy king is	776
Ec	10:17	Blessed art thou, O l., when thy king	776
Ca	2:12	voice of the turtle is heard in our l.;	776
Isa	1:7	your l., strangers devour it in your	127
Isa	1:19	ye shall eat the good of the l..	776
Isa	2:7	Their l. also is full of silver and gold,	776
Isa	2:7	their l. is also full of horses, neither	776
Isa	2:8	Their l. also is full of idols; they	776
Isa	5:30	look unto the l., behold darkness	776
Isa	6:11	man, and the l. be utterly desolate,	127
Isa	6:12	forsaking in the midst of the l..	776
Isa	7:16	the l. that thou abhorrest shall be	127
Isa	7:18	the bee that is in the l. of Assyria.	776
Isa	7:22	every one eat that is left in the l.	776
Isa	7:24	l. shall become briers and thorns.	776
Isa	8:8	wings shall fill the breadth of thy l.,	776
Isa	9:1	he lightly afflicted the l. of Zebulun,	776
Isa	9:1	of Zebulun and the l. of Naphtali,	776
Isa	9:2	in the l. of the shadow of death,	776
Isa	9:19	the Lord of hosts is the l. darkened,	776
Isa	10:23	in the midst of all the l..	776
Isa	11:16	he came up out of the l. of Egypt.	776
Isa	13:5	indignation, to destroy the whole l..	776
Isa	13:9	fierce anger, to lay the l. desolate:	776
Isa	13:14	and flee every one into his own l.	776
Isa	14:1	Israel, and set them in their own l.	127
Isa	14:2	possess them in the l. of the Lord	127
Isa	14:20	because thou hast destroyed thy l.,	776
Isa	14:21	they do not rise, nor possess the l.,	776
Isa	14:25	I will break the Assyrian in my l.,	776
Isa	15:9	and upon the remnant of the l.	127
Isa	16:1	ye the lamb to the ruler of the l.	776
Isa	16:4	oppressors...consumed out of the l..	776
Isa	18:1	Woe to the l. shadowing with wings,	776
Isa	18:2	whose l. the rivers have spoiled!	776
Isa	18:7	foot, whose l. the rivers have spoiled,	776
Isa	19:17	And the l. of Judah shall be a terror	127
Isa	19:18	five cities in the l. of Egypt speak	776
Isa	19:19	Lord in the midst of the l. of Egypt,	776
Isa	19:20	the Lord of hosts in the l. of Egypt:	776
Isa	19:24	even a blessing in the midst of the l.	776
Isa	21:1	from the desert, from a terrible l.	776
Isa	21:14	The inhabitants of the l. of Tema	776
Isa	23:1	from the l. of Chittim it is revealed	776
Isa	23:10	Pass through thy l. as a river, O	776
Isa	23:13	Behold the l. of the Chaldeans; this	776
Isa	24:3	The l. shall be utterly emptied, and	776
Isa	24:11	darkened, the mirth of the l. is gone.	776
Isa	24:13	shall be in the midst of the l. among	776
Isa	26:1	this song be sung in the l. of Judah;	776
Isa	26:10	in the l. of uprightness will he deal	776
Isa	27:13	ready to perish in the l. of Assyria,	776
Isa	27:13	and the outcasts in the l. of Egypt,	776
Isa	30:6	into the l. of trouble and anguish,	776
Isa	32:2	shadow of a great rock in a weary l..	776
Isa	32:13	Upon the l. of my people shall come	127
Isa	33:17	shall behold the l. that is very far off.	776
Isa	34:6	great slaughter in the l. of Idumea.	776
Isa	34:7	their l. shall be soaked with blood,	776
Isa	34:9	l. thereof...become burning pitch.	776
Isa	35:7	and the thirsty l. springs of water:	
Isa	36:10	Lord against this l., to destroy it?	776
Isa	36:10	Go up against this l., and destroy it.	776
Isa	36:17	a l. like your own l., a l. of corn and	776
Isa	36:17	wine, a l. of bread and vineyards.	776

Isa 36:18 delivered his l. out of the hand of the... 776
Isa 36:20 delivered their l. out of my hand, ... 776
Isa 37:7 a rumour, and return to his own l......... 776
Isa 37:7 to fall by the sword in his own l.. 776
Isa 37:38 they escaped into the l. of Armenia:..... 776
Isa 38:11 even the Lord, in the l. of the living: ... 776
Isa 41:18 and the dry l. springs of water........... 776
Isa 49:12 west: and these from the l. of Sinim. ... 776
Isa 49:19 places, and the l. of thy destruction, ... 776
Isa 53:8 was cut off out of the l. of the living: ... 776
Isa 57:13 his trust in me shall possess the l.,...... 776
Isa 60:18 shall no more be heard in thy l., ... 776
Isa 60:21 they shall inherit the l. for ever, the 776
Isa 61:7 in their l. they shall possess the.......... 776
Isa 62:4 thy l. any more be termed Desolate:.... 776
Isa 62:4 Hephzi-bah, and thy l. Beulah: for........ 776
Isa 62:4 in thee, and thy l. shall be married. 776
Jer 1:1 in Anathoth in the l. of Benjamin: 776
Jer 1:14 upon all the inhabitants of the l.. 776
Jer 1:18 brasen walls against the whole l., ... 776
Jer 1:18 and against the people of the l.. 776
Jer 2:2 wilderness, in a l. that was not sown.... 776
Jer 2:6 brought us up out of the l. of Egypt, ... 776
Jer 2:6 through a l. of deserts and of pits,....... 776
Jer 2:6 through a l. of drought, and of the....... 776
Jer 2:6 a l. that no man passed through, ... 776
Jer 2:7 when ye entered, ye defiled my l., ... 776
Jer 2:15 yelled, and they made his l. waste: 776
Jer 2:31 a l. of darkness? wherefore say my...... 776
Jer 3:1 shall not that l. be greatly polluted?...... 776
Jer 3:2 polluted the l. with thy whoredoms 776
Jer 3:9 she defiled the l., and committed......... 776
Jer 3:16 be multiplied and increased in the l., ... 776
Jer 3:18 together out of the l. of the north to.... 776
Jer 3:18 to the l. that I have given for an 776
Jer 3:19 and give thee a pleasant l., a goodly..... 776
Jer 4:5 say, Blow ye the trumpet in the l.. 776
Jer 4:7 his place to make thy l. desolate; 776
Jer 4:20 the whole l. is spoiled: suddenly are..... 776
Jer 4:27 said, The whole l. shall be desolate;..... 776
Jer 5:19 and served strange gods in your l.,...... 776
Jer 5:19 ye serve strangers in a l. that is not 776
Jer 5:30 horrible thing is committed in the l.;..... 776
Jer 6:8 thee desolate, a l. not inhabited........... 776
Jer 6:12 hand upon the inhabitants of the l., ... 776
Jer 7:7 in the l. that I gave to your fathers,..... 776
Jer 7:22 brought them out of the l. of Egypt, ... 776
Jer 7:25 came forth out of the l. of Egypt.......... 776
Jer 7:34 the bride: for the l. shall be desolate.... 776
Jer 8:16 whole l. trembled at the sound of........ 776
Jer 8:16 have devoured the l., and all that is 776
Jer 9:12 l. perisheth and is burned up like a 776
Jer 9:19 because we have forsaken the l.,.......... 776
Jer 10:17 Gather up thy wares out of the l., O.... 776
Jer 10:18 sling out the inhabitants of the l. at...... 776
Jer 11:4 them forth out of the l. of Egypt. 776
Jer 11:5 a l. flowing with milk and honey, ... 776
Jer 11:7 them up out of the l. of Egypt, ... 776
Jer 11:19 cut him off from the l. of the living, ... 776
Jer 12:4 How long shall the l. mourn, and the.... 776
Jer 12:5 and if in the l. of peace, wherein 776
Jer 12:11 the whole l. is made desolate,............. 776
Jer 12:12 devour from the one end of the l......... 776
Jer 12:12 even to the other end of the l............. 776
Jer 12:14 I will pluck them out of their l.,........... 127
Jer 12:15 heritage, and every man to his l.......... 776
Jer 13:13 will fill all the inhabitants of this l.,........ 776
Jer 14:8 thou be as a stranger in the l., and...... 776
Jer 14:15 and famine shall not be in this l.; 776
Jer 14:18 go about into a l. that they know not.... 776
Jer 15:7 with a fan in the gates of the l.; 776
Jer 15:14 into a l. which thou knowest not:......... 776
Jer 16:3 fathers that begat them in this l.; 776
Jer 16:6 and the small shall die in this l............ 776
Jer 16:13 will I cast you out of this l., into a....... 776
Jer 16:13 into a l. that ye know not, neither 776
Jer 16:14 of Israel out of the l. of Egypt; 776
Jer 16:15 of Israel from the l. of the north, ... 776
Jer 16:15 I will bring them again into their l........ 127
Jer 16:18 because they have defiled my l.,.......... 776
Jer 17:4 enemies in the l. which thou knowest... 776
Jer 17:6 in a salt l. and not inhabited............... 776
Jer 17:26 and from the l. of Benjamin, and 776
Jer 18:16 To make their l. desolate, and a.......... 776
Jer 22:12 and shall see this l. no more.............. 776
Jer 22:27 But to the l. whereunto they desire 776
Jer 22:28 cast into a l. which they know not?...... 776
Jer 23:7 of Israel out of the l. of Egypt; 776
Jer 23:8 and they shall dwell in their own l........ 127
Jer 23:10 For the l. is full of adulterers;............ 776
Jer 23:10 of swearing the l. mourneth;............... 776
Jer 23:15 profaneness gone forth into all the l.. ... 776
Jer 24:5 place into the l. of the Chaldeans for.... 776
Jer 24:6 I will bring them again to this l.: 776
Jer 24:8 of Jerusalem, that remain in this l., ... 776
Jer 24:8 them that dwell in the l. of Egypt: 776
Jer 24:10 they be consumed from off the l.......... 127
Jer 25:5 dwell in the l. that the Lord hath......... 127
Jer 25:9 and will bring them against this l., ... 776
Jer 25:11 this whole l. shall be a desolation,........ 776
Jer 25:12 and the l. of the Chaldeans, and will..... 776
Jer 25:13 will bring upon that l. all my words...... 776
Jer 25:20 and all the kings of the l. of Uz, and 776
Jer 25:20 the kings of the l. of the Philistines,..... 776
Jer 25:38 for their l. is desolate because of the.... 776
Jer 26:17 rose up certain of the elders of the l., .. 776
Jer 26:20 against this city and against this l......... 776
Jer 27:7 until the very time of his l. come:........ 776
Jer 27:10 you, to remove you far from your l.:.... 127
Jer 27:11 will I let remain still in their own l., ... 127
Jer 30:3 to return to the l. that I gave to.......... 776
Jer 30:10 seed from the l. of their captivity; 776
Jer 31:16 come again from the l. of the enemy. ... 776
Jer 31:23 use this speech in the l. of Judah......... 776
Jer 31:32 to bring them out of the l. of Egypt; 776
Jer 32:15 shall be possessed again in this l.. 776
Jer 32:20 signs and wonders in the l. of Egypt, ... 776
Jer 32:21 people Israel out of the l. of Egypt 776
Jer 32:22 hast given them this l., which thou 776
Jer 32:22 a l. flowing with milk and honey; 776
Jer 32:41 I will plant them in this l. assuredly...... 776
Jer 32:43 And fields shall be bought in this l., ... 776
Jer 32:44 take witnesses in the l. of Benjamin, ... 776
Jer 33:11 cause to return the captivity of the l., .. 776
Jer 33:13 and in the l. of Benjamin, and in the..... 776
Jer 33:15 judgment and righteousness in the l...... 776
Jer 34:13 them forth out of the l. of Egypt, ... 776
Jer 34:19 all the people of the l., which passed.... 776
Jer 35:7 live many days in the l. where ye......... 127
Jer 35:11 king of Babylon came up into the l., ... 776
Jer 35:15 dwell in the l. which I have given 127
Jer 36:29 certainly come and destroy this l., ... 776
Jer 37:1 made king in the l. of Judah............... 776
Jer 37:2 nor the people of the l., did hearken 776
Jer 37:7 return to Egypt into their own l.. 776
Jer 37:12 to go into the l. of Benjamin,.............. 776
Jer 37:19 come against you, nor against this l.? ... 776
Jer 39:5 to Riblah in the l. of Hamath, where 776
Jer 39:10 which had nothing, in the l. of Judah,.... 776
Jer 40:4 behold, all the l. is before thee: 776
Jer 40:6 the people that were left in the l.. 776
Jer 40:7 the son of Ahikam governor in the l. 776
Jer 40:7 children, and of the poor of the l., ... 776
Jer 40:9 dwell in the l., and serve the king of..... 776
Jer 40:12 driven, and came to the l. of Judah, ... 776
Jer 41:2 had made governor over the l.. 776
Jer 41:18 of Babylon made governor in the l.. 776
Jer 42:10 If ye will still abide in this l., then 776
Jer 42:12 cause you to return to your own l.. 127
Jer 42:13 ye say, We will not dwell in this l.,...... 776
Jer 42:14 but we will go into the l. of Egypt, ... 776
Jer 42:16 overtake you there in the l. of Egypt, .. 776
Jer 43:4 the Lord, to dwell in the l. of Judah. 776
Jer 43:5 driven, to dwell in the l. of Judah; 776
Jer 43:7 they came into the l. of Egypt: for....... 776
Jer 43:11 he shall smite the l. of Egypt, and....... 776
Jer 43:12 array himself with the l. of Egypt, ... 776
Jer 43:13 that is in the l. of Egypt, ... 776
Jer 44:1 Jews which dwell in the l. of Egypt, ... 776
Jer 44:8 unto other gods in the l. of Egypt,....... 776
Jer 44:9 have committed in the l. of Judah, ... 776
Jer 44:12 their faces to go into the l. of Egypt 776
Jer 44:12 consumed and fall in the l. of Egypt; 776
Jer 44:13 them that dwell in the l. of Egypt, ... 776
Jer 44:14 gone into the l. of Egypt to sojourn 776
Jer 44:14 should return into the l. of Judah, ... 776
Jer 44:15 people that dwelt in the l. of Egypt, ... 776
Jer 44:21 princes, and the people of the l., ... 776
Jer 44:22 therefore is your l. a desolation,........... 776
Jer 44:24 all Judah that are in the l. of Egypt: 776
Jer 44:26 Judah that dwell in the l. of Egypt; 776
Jer 44:26 man of Judah in all the l. of Egypt, ... 776
Jer 44:27 of Judah that are in the l. of Egypt 776
Jer 44:28 of the l. of Egypt into the l. of Judah, .. 776
Jer 44:28 gone into the l. of Egypt to sojourn 776
Jer 45:4 I will pluck up, even this whole l.. 776
Jer 46:12 shame, and thy cry hath filled the l.: 776
Jer 46:13 come and smite the l. of Egypt. 776
Jer 46:16 people, and to the l. of our nativity, ... 776
Jer 46:27 seed from the l. of their captivity; 776
Jer 47:2 flood, and shall overflow the l., and...... 776
Jer 47:2 the inhabitants of the l. shall howl. 776
Jer 48:24 upon all the cities of the l. of Moab,..... 776
Jer 48:33 field, and from the l. of Moab; 776
Jer 50:1 against the l. of the Chaldeans by........ 776
Jer 50:3 which shall make her l. desolate, ... 776
Jer 50:8 forth out of the l. of the Chaldeans, ... 776
Jer 50:12 a wilderness, a dry l., and a desert. ....
Jer 50:16 shall flee every one to his own l.......... 776
Jer 50:18 punish the king of Babylon and his l., ... 776
Jer 50:21 Go up against the l. of Merathaim,........ 776
Jer 50:22 A sound of battle is in the l., and of..... 776
Jer 50:25 of hosts in the l. of the Chaldeans. 776
Jer 50:28 and escape out of the l. of Babylon, ... 776
Jer 50:34 that he may give rest to the l., ... 776
Jer 50:38 up: for it is the l. of graven images,..... 776
Jer 50:45 against the l. of the Chaldeans: 776
Jer 51:2 shall fan her, and shall empty her l.. 776
Jer 51:4 shall fall in the l. of the Chaldeans, ... 776
Jer 51:5 their l. was filled with sin against......... 776
Jer 51:27 Set ye up a standard in the l., blow 776
Jer 51:28 and all the l. of his dominion.............. 776
Jer 51:29 And the l. shall tremble and sorrow: 776
Jer 51:29 make the l. of Babylon a desolation...... 776
Jer 51:43 Her cities are a desolation, a dry l.. 776
Jer 51:43 a l. wherein no man dwelleth, ... 776
Jer 51:46 rumour that shall be heard in the l.; 776
Jer 51:46 come a rumour, and violence in the l.... 776
Jer 51:47 her whole l. shall be confounded,......... 776
Jer 51:52 through all her l. the wounded shall...... 776
Jer 51:54 from the l. of the Chaldeans: 776
Jer 52:6 was no bread for the people of the l..... 776
Jer 52:9 to Riblah in the l. of Hamath; where 776
Jer 52:16 left certain of the poor of the l. for...... 776
Jer 52:25 who mustered the people of the l.; 776
Jer 52:25 threescore men of the people of the l., ..776
Jer 52:27 death in Riblah in the l. of Hamath....... 127
Jer 52:27 carried away captive out of his own l.... 127
La 4:21 Edom, that dwellest in the l. of Uz; 776
Eze 1:3 the l. of the Chaldeans by the river...... 776
Eze 6:14 them, and make the l. desolate, yea,..... 776
Eze 7:2 the Lord God unto the l. of Israel;....... 127
Eze 7:2 come upon the four corners of the l.. ... 776
Eze 7:7 thee, O thou that dwellest in the l.. 776
Eze 7:27 for the l. is full of bloody crimes,......... 776
Eze 7:28 people of the l. shall be troubled: 776
Eze 8:17 they have filled the l. with violence, ... 776
Eze 9:9 great, and the l. is full of blood, and..... 776
Eze 11:15 unto us is this l. given in possession. ... 776
Eze 11:17 and I will give you the l. of Israel. 127
Eze 12:13 Babylon to the l. of the Chaldeans; 776
Eze 12:19 say unto the people of the l., Thus 127
Eze 12:19 Jerusalem, and of the l. of Israel; 776
Eze 12:19 that her l. may be desolate from all...... 776
Eze 12:20 waste, and the l. shall be desolate; 776
Eze 12:22 that ye have in the l. of Israel,............ 127
Eze 13:9 shall they enter into the l. of Israel; 127
Eze 14:13 when the l. sinneth against me by........ 776
Eze 14:15 beasts to pass through the l., ... 776
Eze 14:16 delivered, but the l. shall be desolate. .. 776
Eze 14:17 Or if I bring a sword upon that l., ... 776
Eze 14:17 and say, Sword, go through the l.;....... 776
Eze 14:19 Or if I send a pestilence into that l., ... 776
Eze 15:8 I will make the l. desolate, because...... 776
Eze 16:3 thy nativity is of the l. of Canaan;......... 776
Eze 16:29 thy fornication in the l. of Canaan 776
Eze 17:4 and carried it into a l. of traffick; 776
Eze 17:5 He took also of the seed of the l., ... 776
Eze 17:13 hath also taken the mighty of the l....... 776
Eze 18:2 proverb concerning the l. of Israel, ... 127
Eze 19:4 with chains unto the l. of Egypt. 776
Eze 19:7 the l. was desolate, and the fulness...... 776
Eze 20:5 known unto them in the l. of Egypt,..... 776
Eze 20:6 forth of the l. of Egypt into a l. that I.. 776
Eze 20:8 them in the midst of the l. of Egypt. 776
Eze 20:9 them forth out of the l. of Egypt. 776
Eze 20:10 to go forth out of the l. of Egypt, ... 776
Eze 20:15 I would not bring them into the l., ... 776
Eze 20:28 when I had brought them into the l., ... 776
Eze 20:36 in the wilderness of the l. of Egypt, ... 776
Eze 20:38 shall not enter into the l. of Israel: 127

Eze 20:40 all of them in the l. serve me: 776
Eze 20:42 shall bring you into the l. of Israel, ... 127
Eze 21:2 prophesy against the l. of Israel. 127
Eze 21:3 say to the l. of Israel, Thus saith 127
Eze 21:19 twain shall come forth out of one l.. 776
Eze 21:30 wast created, in the l. of thy nativity.... 776
Eze 21:32 blood shall be in the midst of the l.; 776
Eze 22:24 thou art the l. that is not cleansed, ... 776
Eze 22:29 of the l. have used oppression, ... 776
Eze 22:30 stand in the gap before me for the l.. ... 776
Eze 23:15 of Chaldea, the l. of their nativity: 776
Eze 23:19 played the harlot in the l. of Egypt. 776
Eze 23:27 brought from the l. of Egypt:............. 776
Eze 23:48 cause lewdness to cease out of the l., .. 776
Eze 25:3 against the l. of Israel, when it was 127
Eze 25:6 thy despite against the l. of Israel; 127
Eze 26:20 shall set glory in the l. of the living; 776
Eze 27:17 and the l. of Israel, they were thy 776
Eze 27:29 ships, they shall stand upon the l.; 776
Eze 28:25 then shall they dwell in their l. that...... 127
Eze 29:9 l. of Egypt shall be desolate and......... 776
Eze 29:10 make the l. of Egypt utterly waste......... 776
Eze 29:12 and I will make the l. of Egypt desolate .776
Eze 29:14 them to return into the l. of Pathros, ... 776
Eze 29:14 into the l. of their habitation; and......... 776
Eze 29:19 I will give the l. of Egypt unto............ 776
Eze 29:20 I have given him the l. of Egypt for 776
Eze 30:5 the men of the l. that is in league, ... 776
Eze 30:11 shall be brought to destroy the l......... 776
Eze 30:11 Egypt, and fill the l. with the slain. 776
Eze 30:12 sell the l. into the hand of the wicked: .. 776
Eze 30:12 I will make the l. waste, and all that 776
Eze 30:13 no more a prince of the l. of Egypt: 776
Eze 30:13 I will put a fear in the l. of Egypt. 776
Eze 30:25 stretch it out upon the l. of Egypt. 776
Eze 31:12 are broken by all the rivers of the l.; ... 776
Eze 32:4 Then will I leave thee upon the l., I...... 776
Eze 32:6 will also water with thy blood the l. 776
Eze 32:8 thee, and set darkness upon thy l., ... 776
Eze 32:15 I shall make the l. of Egypt desolate, ... 776
Eze 32:23 caused terror in the l. of the living....... 776
Eze 32:24 their terror in the l. of the living; 776
Eze 32:25 terror was caused in the l. of the 776
Eze 32:26 their terror in the l. of the living. 776
Eze 32:27 of the mighty in the l. of the living....... 776
Eze 32:32 my terror in the l. of the living: 776
Eze 33:2 When I bring the sword upon a l., ... 776
Eze 33:2 if the people of the l. take a man of...... 776
Eze 33:3 he seeth the sword come upon the l., .. 776
Eze 33:24 those wastes of the l. of Israel............ 127
Eze 33:24 was one, and he inherited the l.. 776
Eze 33:24 the l. is given us for inheritance. 776
Eze 33:25 blood: and shall ye possess the l.? 776
Eze 33:26 wife: and shall ye possess the l.?......... 776
Eze 33:28 For I will lay the l. most desolate, ... 776
Eze 33:29 I have laid the l. most desolate, ... 776
Eze 34:13 and will bring them to their own l., ... 127
Eze 34:25 the evil beasts to cease out of the l.. ... 776
Eze 34:27 and they shall be safe in their l., ... 127
Eze 34:28 shall the beast of the l. devour............ 776
Eze 34:29 consumed with hunger in the l., ... 776
Eze 36:5 my l. into their possession with........... 776
Eze 36:6 therefore concerning the l. of Israel, ... 127
Eze 36:13 unto you. Thou l. devourest up men, ...
Eze 36:17 house of Israel dwelt in their own l., ... 127
Eze 36:18 blood that they had shed upon the l., ... 776
Eze 36:20 and are gone forth out of his l.,........... 776
Eze 36:24 and will bring you into your own l......... 127
Eze 36:28 ye shall dwell in the l. that I gave to.... 776
Eze 36:34 And the desolate l. shall be tilled, ... 776
Eze 36:35 This l. that was desolate is become...... 776
Eze 37:12 and bring you into the l. of Israel. 127
Eze 37:14 and I shall place you in your own l....... 127
Eze 37:21 and bring them into their own l.. 127
Eze 37:22 in the l. upon the mountains of............ 776
Eze 37:25 they shall dwell in the l. that I have..... 776
Eze 38:2 thy face against Gog, the l. of Magog,.. 776
Eze 38:8 thou shalt come into the l. that is........ 776
Eze 38:9 shalt be like a cloud to cover the l., ... 776
Eze 38:11 go up to the l. of unwalled villages; 776
Eze 38:12 that dwell in the midst of the l.. 776
Eze 38:16 of Israel, as a cloud to cover the l.; 776
Eze 38:16 and I will bring thee against my l., ... 776
Eze 38:18 shall come against the l. of Israel, ... 127
Eze 38:19 a great shaking in the l. of Israel; 127
Eze 39:12 them, that they may cleanse the l., ... 776
Eze 39:13 Yea, all the people of the l. shall 776
Eze 39:14 passing through the l. to bury with 776
Eze 39:15 passengers that pass through the l., ... 776
Eze 39:16 Thus shall they cleanse the l.. 776
Eze 39:26 when they dwelt safely in their l.,......... 127
Eze 39:28 gathered them unto their own l., ... 127
Eze 40:2 brought he me into the l. of Israel, ... 776
Eze 45:1 divide by lot the l. for inheritance, ... 776
Eze 45:1 the Lord, an holy portion of the l.. 776
Eze 45:4 The holy portion of the l. shall be........ 776
Eze 45:8 In the l. shall be his possession in 776
Eze 45:8 the l. shall they give to the house of 776
Eze 45:16 the people of the l. shall give this 776
Eze 45:22 all the people of the l. a bullock for....... 776
Eze 46:3 the people of the l. shall worship at 776
Eze 46:9 when the people of the l. shall come 776
Eze 47:13 ye shall inherit the l. according to........ 776
Eze 47:14 and this l. shall fall unto you for 776
Eze 47:15 this shall be the border of the l........... 776
Eze 47:18 and from the l. of Israel by Jordan, ... 776
Eze 47:21 So shall ye divide this l. unto you 776
Eze 48:12 this oblation of the l. that is offered 776
Eze 48:14 nor alienate the firstfruits of the l.. 776
Eze 48:29 This is the l. which ye shall divide by... 776
Da 1:2 he carried into the l. of Shinar to......... 776
Da 8:9 the east, and toward the pleasant l.. ....
Da 9:6 and to all the people of the l.............. 776
Da 9:15 people forth out of the l. of Egypt 776
Da 11:9 and shall return into his own l............. 127
Da 11:16 he shall stand in the glorious l............ 776
Da 11:19 face toward the fort of his own l.. 776
Da 11:28 return into his l. with great riches; 776
Da 11:28 do exploits, and return to his own l...... 776
Da 11:39 and shall divide the l. for gain. 127
Da 11:41 shall enter also into the glorious l., ... 776
Da 11:42 and the l. of Egypt shall not escape. 776
Ho 1:2 l. had committed great whoredom, ... 776
Ho 1:11 they shall come up out of the l............ 776
Ho 2:3 set her like a dry l., and slay her 776
Ho 2:15 she came up out of the l. of Egypt. 776
Ho 4:1 with the inhabitants of the l., ... 776
Ho 4:1 nor knowledge of God in the l............. 776
Ho 4:3 Therefore shall the l. mourn, and 776
Ho 7:16 their derision in the l. of Egypt. 776
Ho 9:3 shall not dwell in the Lord's l.;............ 776
Ho 10:1 according to the goodness of his l........ 776
Ho 11:5 shall not return into the l. of Egypt,..... 776
Ho 11:11 as a dove out of the l. of Assyria: 776
Ho 12:9 Lord thy God from the l. of Egypt....... 776
Ho 13:4 Lord thy God from the l. of Egypt,...... 776
Ho 13:5 wilderness, in the l. of great drought.... 776
Joe 1:2 give ear, all ye inhabitants of the l.. 776
Joe 1:6 a nation is come up upon my l., ... 776
Joe 1:10 The field is wasted, the l. mourneth; 127
Joe 1:14 and all the inhabitants of the l. 776
Joe 2:1 all the inhabitants of the l. tremble: 776
Joe 2:3 the l. is as the garden of Eden........... 776
Joe 2:18 will the Lord be jealous for his l., ... 776
Joe 2:20 him into a l. barren and desolate, ... 776
Joe 2:21 Fear not, O l.; be glad and rejoice: 127
Joe 3:2 among the nations, and parted my l...... 776
Joe 3:19 have shed innocent blood in their l...... 776
Am 2:10 brought you up from the l. of Egypt,.... 776
Am 2:10 to possess the l. of the Amorite. 776
Am 3:1 I brought up from the l. of Egypt, ... 776
Am 3:9 in the palaces in the l. of Egypt, and.... 776
Am 3:11 shall be even round about the l.; 776
Am 5:2 she is forsaken upon her l.; there........ 127
Am 7:2 an end of eating the grass of the l., ... 776
Am 7:10 l. is not able to bear all his words........ 776
Am 7:11 led away captive out of their own l., ... 127
Am 7:12 flee thee away into the l. of Judah, ... 776
Am 7:17 and thy l. shall be divided by line;........ 127
Am 7:17 and thou shalt die in a polluted l. 127
Am 7:17 go into captivity forth of his l............ 127
Am 8:4 to make the poor of the l. to fail, ... 776
Am 8:8 Shall not the l. tremble for this, and..... 776
Am 8:11 that I will send a famine in the l., ... 776
Am 9:5 of hosts is he that toucheth the l., ... 776
Am 9:7 up Israel out of the l. of Egypt? 776
Am 9:15 I will plant them upon their l., and....... 127
Am 9:15 no more be pulled out of their l.......... 127
Jon 1:9 which hath made the sea and dry l....... 127
Jon 1:13 men rowed hard to bring it to the l.; ... 3004
Jon 2:10 it vomited out Jonah upon the dry l.. .. 3004
Mic 5:5 the Assyrian shall come into our l.: 776
Mic 5:6 waste the l. of Assyria with the 776
Mic 5:6 l. of Nimrod in the entrances thereof:.... 776
Mic 5:6 when he cometh into our l., ... 776
Mic 5:11 And I will cut off the cities of thy l., ... 776
Mic 6:4 thee up out of the l. of Egypt, ... 776
Mic 7:13 the l. shall be desolate because of........ 776
Mic 7:15 of thy coming out of the l. of Egypt. 776
Na 3:13 gates of thy l. shall be set wide open ... 776
Hab 1:6 march through the breadth of the l...... 776
Hab 2:8, 17 and for the violence of the l., ... 776
Hab 3:7 curtains of the l. of Midian did 776
Hab 3:12 march through the l. in indignation, ... 776
Zep 1:2 consume all things from off the l.,......... 127
Zep 1:3 I will cut off man from off the l., ... 127
Zep 1:18 whole l. shall be devoured by fire 776
Zep 1:18 all them that dwell in the l.. 776
Zep 2:5 O Canaan, the l. of the Philistines, ... 776
Zep 3:19 get them praise and fame in every l..... 776
Hag 1:11 I called for a drought upon the l., ... 776
Hag 2:4 and be strong, all ye people of the l., ... 776
Hag 2:6 the earth, and the sea, and the dry l.; ......
Zec 1:21 their horn over the l. of Judah to......... 776
Zec 2:6 and flee from the l. of the north, ... 776
Zec 2:12 Judah his portion in the holy l., ... 127
Zec 3:9 I will remove the iniquity of that l........ 776
Zec 5:11 build it an house in the l. of Shinar: 776
Zec 7:5 Speak unto all the people of the l., ... 776
Zec 7:14 Thus the l. was desolate after them, ... 776
Zec 7:14 they laid the pleasant l. desolate.......... 776
Zec 9:1 of the Lord in the l. of Hadrach, ... 776
Zec 9:16 lifted up as an ensign upon his l.. 127
Zec 10:10 bring them again also out of the l. 776
Zec 10:10 will bring them into the l. of Gilead 776
Zec 11:6 more pity the inhabitants of the l., ... 776
Zec 11:6 his king: and they shall smite the l., ... 776
Zec 11:16 I will raise up a shepherd in the l., ... 776
Zec 12:12 the l. shall mourn, every family........... 776
Zec 13:2 off the names of the idols out of the l.,. 776
Zec 13:2 unclean spirit to pass out of the l.,....... 776
Zec 13:8 shall come to pass, that in all the l.,...... 776
Zec 14:10 all the l. shall be turned as a plain 776
Mal 3:12 for ye shall be a delightsome l., ... 776
Mt 2:6 thou Bethlehem in the l. of Juda, ... *1093*
Mt 2:20 mother, and go into the l. of Israel:.... *1093*
Mt 2:21 and came into the l. of Israel............. *1093*
Mt 4:15 The l. of Zabulon, and the *1093*
Mt 4:15 Zabulon, and the l. of Nephthalim, ... *1093*
Mt 9:26 hereof went abroad into all that l........ *1093*
Mt 10:15 **for the l. of Sodom and Gomorrha** .*1093*
Mt 11:24 **more tolerable for the l. of Sodom** .*1093*
Mt 14:34 they came into the l. of Gennesaret.... *1093*
Mt 23:15 **ye compass sea and l. to make one** .*3584*
Mt 27:45 there was darkness over all the l. *1093*
Mk 1:5 out unto him all the l. of Judaea......... *5561*
Mk 4:1 multitude was by the sea on the l.. .... *1095*
Mk 6:47 of the sea, and he alone on the l........ *1095*
Mk 6:53 they came into the l. of Gennesaret,... *1095*
Mk 15:33 there was darkness over the whole..... *1095*
Lu 4:25 **famine was throughout all the l.;** .. *1095*
Lu 5:3 would thrust out a little from the l....... *1095*
Lu 5:11 they had brought their ships to l., ... *1095*
Lu 8:27 when he went forth to l., there met ... *1095*
Lu 14:35 **It is neither fit for the l., nor yet**.. *1095*
Lu 15:14 **arose a mighty famine in that l.;**... *5561*
Lu 21:23 **shall be great distress in the l.,** *1093*
Joh 3:22 his disciples into the l. of Judaea; *1093*
Joh 6:21 the ship was at the l. whither they..... *1093*
Joh 21:8 were not far from l., but as it were.... *1093*
Joh 21:9 soon then as they were come to l., ... *1093*
Joh 21:11 drew the net to l. full of great fishes, ..*1093*
Ac 4:37 Having l., sold it, and brought the......... *68*
Ac 5:3 back part of the price of the l.? *5564*
Ac 5:8 whether ye sold the l. for so much? ... *5564*
Ac 7:3 come into the l. which I shall shew..... *1093*
Ac 7:4 he out of the l. of the Chaldeans,......... *1093*
Ac 7:4 he removed him into this l., wherein... *1093*
Ac 7:6 seed should sojourn in a strange l.; *1093*
Ac 7:11 dearth over all the l. of Egypt and...... *1093*
Ac 7:29 was a stranger in the l. of Madian, ... *1093*
Ac 7:36 and signs in the l. of Egypt, and in..... *1093*
Ac 7:40 brought us out of the l. of Egypt, ... *1093*
Ac 10:39 did both in the l. of the Jews, and...... *5561*
Ac 13:17 as strangers in the l. of Egypt,.......... *1093*
Ac 13:19 seven nations in the l. of Chanaan, ... *1093*
Ac 13:19 he divided their l. to them by lot. *1093*
Ac 27:39 it was day, they knew not the l.. .... *1093*
Ac 27:43 first into the sea, and get to l.. .... *1093*
Ac 27:44 pass, that they escaped all safe to l.. . *1093*

Heb 8:9 to lead them out of the l. of Egypt; *1093*
Heb 11:9 he sojourned in the l. of promise, *1093*
Heb 11:29 through the Red sea as by dry l.:
Jude 5 the people out of the l. of Egypt. *1093*

LANDED
Ac 18:22 when he had l. at Caesarea, and *2718*
Ac 21:3 sailed into Syria, and l. at Tyre: *2609*

LANDING
Ac 28:12 l. at Syracuse, we tarried there *2609*

LANDMARK See also LANDMARKS.
De 19:14 not remove thy neighbour's l., 1366
De 27:17 he that removeth his neighbour's l. 1366
Pr 22:28 Remove not the ancient l., which 1366
Pr 23:10 Remove not the old l.; and enter 1366

LANDMARKS
Job 24:2 Some remove the l.; they violently 1367

LANDS
Ge 10:5 of the Gentiles divided in their l.; 776
Ge 10:31 after their tongues, in their l., after 776
Ge 41:54 said: and the dearth was in all l.; 776
Ge 41:57 that the famine was so sore in all l.. 776
Ge 47:18 my lord, but our bodies, and our l.. 127
Ge 47:22 wherefore they sold not their l. 127
Le 26:36 hearts in the l. of their enemies; 776
Le 26:39 in their iniquity in your enemies' l.; 776
Jg 11:13 restore those l. again peaceably.
2Ki 19:11 kings of Assyria have done to all l., 776
2Ki 19:17 destroyed the nations and their l., 776
1Ch 14:17 fame of David went out into all l.; 776
2Ch 9:28 horses out of Egypt, and out of all l. 776
2Ch 13:9 manner of the nations of other l.? 776
2Ch 17:10 fell upon all the kingdoms of the l. 776
2Ch 32:13 done unto all the people of other l.? 776
2Ch 32:13 the gods of the nations of those l. 776
2Ch 32:13 any ways able to deliver their l. out 776
2Ch 32:17 As the gods of the nations of other l. 776
Ezr 9:1 themselves from the people of the l., 776
Ezr 9:2 mingled...with the people of those l. 776
Ezr 9:7 into the hand of the kings of the l., 776
Ezr 9:11 the filthiness of the people of the l., 776
Ne 5:3 said, We have mortgaged our l., 7704
Ne 5:4 and that upon our l. and vineyards. 7704
Ne 5:5 men have our l. and vineyards. 7704
Ne 5:11 Restore...their l., their vineyards, 7704
Ne 9:30 into the hand of the people of the l. 776
Ne 10:28 themselves from the people of the l. 776
Ps 49:11 call their l. after their own names. 127
Ps 66:1 a joyful noise unto God,all ye l. 776
Ps 100:1 joyful noise unto the Lord, all ye l. 776
Ps 105:44 And gave them the l. of the heathen: 776
Ps 106:27 nations, and to scatter them in the l. 776
Ps 107:3 gathered them out of the l., from 776
Isa 36:20 they among all the gods of these l., 776
Isa 37:11 have done to all l. by destroying 776
Jer 16:15 the l. whither he had driven them: 776
Jer 27:6 I given all these l. into the hand of 776
Eze 20:6, 15 honey, which is the glory of all l.. 776
Eze 39:27 them out of their enemies' l., 776
Mt 19:29 **children, or l., for my name's sake,** *68*
Mk 10:29 **wife, or children, or l., for my sake,** *68*
Mk 10:30 **and mothers, and children, and l.,** *68*
Ac 4:34 as were possessors of l. or houses *5564*

LANES
Lu 14:21 **into the streets and l. of the city** *4505*

LANGUAGE See also LANGUAGES.
Ge 11:1 And the whole earth was of one l., 8193
Ge 11:6 is one, and they have all one l.; 8193
Ge 11:7 down, and there confound their l., 8193
Ge 11:9 confound the l. of all the earth: 8193
2Ki 18:26 to thy servants in the Syrian l.;
2Ki 18:26 and talk not with us in the Jews' l.
2Ki 18:28 cried with a loud voice in the Jews' l.,
Ne 13:24 and could not speak in the Jews' l.,
Ne 13:24 according to the l. of each people. 3956
Es 1:22 and to every people after their l., 3956
Es 1:22 according to the l. of every people. 3956
Es 3:12 and to every people after their l.; 3956
Es 8:9 and unto every people after their l., 3956
Es 8:9 writing, and according to their l. 3956
Ps 19:3 There is no speech nor l., where 1697
Ps 81:5 heard a l. that I understood not. 8193
Ps 114:1 Jacob from a people of strange l.; 3937
Isa 19:18 of Egypt speak the l. of Canaan, 8193
Isa 36:11 unto thy servants in the Syrian l.;
Isa 36:11 and speak not to us in the Jews' l.,
Isa 36:13 cried with a loud voice in the Jews' l.,
Jer 5:15 nation whose l. thou knowest not, 3956
Eze 3:5, 6 strange speech and of an hard l., 3956
Da 3:29 That every people, nation, and l., 3961
Zep 3:9 will I turn to the people a pure l., 8193
Ac 2:6 heard them speak in his own l. *1258*

LANGUAGES
Da 3:4 O people, nations, and l., 3961
Da 3:7 the people, the nations, and the l., 3961
Da 4:1 unto all people, nations, and l., that 3961
Da 5:19 people, nations, and l., trembled 3961
Da 6:25 unto all people, nations, and l., that 3961
Da 7:14 that all people, nations, and l., 3961
Zec 8:23 hold out of all l. of the nations, 3956

LANGUISH See also LANGUISHED; LANGUISHETH; LANGUISHING.
Isa 16:8 For the fields of Heshbon l., and 535
Isa 19:8 spread nets upon the waters shall l.. 535
Isa 24:4 the haughty people of the earth do l. 535
Jer 14:2 mourneth, and the gates thereof l. 535
Hos 4:3 one that dwelleth therein shall l., 535

LANGUISHED
La 2:8 wall to lament; they l. together. 535

LANGUISHETH
Isa 24:4 the world l. and fadeth away, the 535
Isa 24:7 The new wine mourneth, the vine l., 535
Isa 33:9 earth mourneth and l.: Lebanon is 535
Jer 15:9 She that hath borne seven l.: she 535
Joe 1:10 the new wine is dried up, the oil l.. 535
Joe 1:12 vine is dried up, and the fig tree l.; 535
Na 1:4 rivers: Bashan l., and Carmel, 535
Na 1:4 and the flower of Lebanon l. 535

LANGUISHING
Ps 41:3 strengthen him upon the bed of l.. 1741

LANTERNS
Joh 18:3 cometh thither with l. and torches *5322*

LAODICEA (la-od-i-se'-ah) See also LAODICEANS.
Col 2:1 have for you, and for them at L., *2993*
Col 4:13 for you, and them that are in L., *2993*
Col 4:15 Salute the brethren which are in L., *2993*
Col 4:16 ye likewise read the epistle from L. *2993*
1Ti *subscr.* first to Timothy was written from L.
Re 1:11 **unto Philadelphia, and unto L.** *2993*

LAODICEANS (la-od-i-se'-uns)
Col 4:16 read also in the church of the L. *2994*
Rev 3:14 **angel of the church of the L.** *2994*

LAP See also LAPPED; LAPPETH; LAPPING.
2Ki 4:39 thereof wild gourds his l. full, and 899
Ne 5:13 Also I shook my l., and said, So 2684
Pr 16:33 The lot is cast into the l.: but the 2436

LAPIDOTH (lap'-i-doth)
Jg 4:4 the wife of L., she judged Israel 3941

LAPPED
Jg 7:6 And the number of them that l., 3952
Jg 7:7 By the three hundred men that l. 3952

LAPPETH
Jg 7:5 Every one that l. of the water with 3952
Jg 7:5 water with his tongue, as a dog l., 3952

LAPWING
Le 11:19 heron after her kind, and the l., 1744
De 14:18 heron after her kind, and the l., 1744

LARGE See also ENLARGE.
Ge 34:21 behold, it is l. enough for them; 7342
Ex 3:8 that land unto a good land and a l., 7342
Jg 18:10 people secure, and to a l. land: 7342,3027
2Sa 22:20 me forth also into a l. place. 4800
Ne 4:19 The work is great and l., and we 7342
Ne 7:4 the city was l. and great: but 7342,3027
Ne 9:35 in the l. and fat land which thou 7342
Ps 18:19 me forth also into a l. place; 4800
Ps 31:8 thou hast set my feet in a l. room. 4800
Ps 118:5 me, and set me in a l. place. 4800
Isa 22:18 like a ball into a l. country: 7342,3027
Isa 30:23 shall thy cattle feed in l. pastures. 7337
Isa 30:33 he hath made it deep and l. 7337
Jer 22:14 me a wide house and l. chambers, 7304
Eze 23:32 of thy sister's cup deep and l. 7342
Ho 4:16 feed them as a lamb in a l. place. 4800
Mt 28:12 gave l. money unto the soldiers, *2425*
Mk 14:15 **he will shew you a l. upper room** *3173*
Lu 22:12 **he shall shew you a l. upper room.** *3173*
Ga 6:11 see how l. a letter I have written. *4080*
Re 21:16 the length is as l. as the breadth: *5118*

LARGENESS
1Ki 4:29 exceeding much, and l. of heart, 7341

LASAEA See LASEA.

LASCIVIOUSNESS
Mk 7:22 **wickedness, deceit, l., an evil eye,** *766*
2Co 12:21 and l. which they have committed. *766*
Ga 5:19 fornication, uncleanness, l., *766*
Eph 4:19 have given themselves over unto l., *766*
1Pe 4:3 when we walked in l., lusts, excess *766*
Jude 4 turning the grace of our God into l., *766*

LASEA (la-se'-ah)
Ac 27:8 nigh whereunto was the city of L. *2996*

LASHA (la'-shah)
Ge 10:19 Admah, and Zeboim, even unto L. 3962

LASHARON (lash'-ar-on)
Jos 12:18 Aphek, one; the king of L., one; 8289

LAST See also LASTED; LASTING.
Ge 49:1 shall befall you in the l. days. 319
Ge 49:19 but he shall overcome at the l. 6119
Nu 23:10 and let my l. end be like his! 319
2Sa 19:11 ye the l. to bring the king back 314
2Sa 19:12 are ye the l. to bring back the king? 314
2Sa 23:1 Now these be the l. words of David. 314
1Ch 23:27 For by the l. words of David the 314
1Ch 29:29 acts of David the king, first and l., 314
2Ch 9:29 of the acts of Solomon, first and l., 314
2Ch 12:15 the acts of Rehoboam, first and l., 314
2Ch 16:11 behold, the acts of Asa, first and l., 314
2Ch 20:34 acts of Jehoshaphat, first and l., 314
2Ch 25:26 of the acts of Amaziah, first and l., 314
2Ch 26:22 of the acts of Uzziah, first and l., 314
2Ch 28:26 acts and of all his ways, first and l., 314
2Ch 35:27 And his deeds, first and l., behold, 314
Ezr 8:13 And of the l. sons of Adonikam, 314
Ne 8:18 from the first day unto the l. day, 314
Pr 5:11 And thou mourn at the l., when 319
Pr 23:32 At the l. it biteth like a serpent, 319
Isa 2:2 it shall come to pass in the l. days, 319
Isa 41:4 Lord, the first, and with the l.: 314
Isa 44:6 I am the first, and I am the l.; and 314
Isa 48:12 he; I am the first, I also am the l. 314
Jer 12:4 said, He shall not see our l. end. 319
Jer 50:17 and l. this Nebuchadrezzar king of 314
La 1:9 she remembereth not her l. end; 319
Da 4:8 at the l. Daniel came in before me, 318
Da 8:3 other, and the higher came up l.. 314
Da 8:19 thee know what shall be in the l. 319
Am 9:1 slay the l. of them with the sword: 319
Mic 4:1 in the l. days it shall come to pass, 319
Mt 12:45 **l. state of that man is worse than** *2078*
Mt 19:30 **many that are first shall be l.** *2078*
Mt 19:30 **and the l. shall be first.** *2078*
Mt 20:8 **beginning from the l. unto the** *2078*
Mt 20:12 **These l. have wrought but one** *2078*
Mt 20:14 **I will give unto this l., even as** *2078*
Mt 20:16 **l. shall be first, and the first l.** *2078*
Mt 21:37 **But l. of all he sent unto them his** *5305*
Mt 22:27 And l. of all the woman died also. *5305*
Mt 26:60 At the l. came two false witnesses, *5305*
Mt 27:64 the l. error shall be worse than *2078*
Mk 9:35 **be first, the same shall be l. of all,** *2078*
Mk 10:31 **are first shall be l.; and the l. first.** *2078*
Mk 12:6 **he sent him also l. unto them,** *2078*
Mk 12:22 seed: l. of all the woman died also. *2078*
Lu 11:26 **l. state of that man is worse than** *2078*
Lu 12:59 **till thou hast paid the very l. mite.** *2078*
Lu 13:30 **there are l. which shall be first,** *2078*
Lu 13:30 **there are first which shall be l.,** *2078*
Lu 20:32 L. of all the woman died also. *5305*
Joh 6:39 **raise it up again at the l. day.** *2078*
Joh 6:40, 44, 54 **raise him up at the l. day.** *2078*
Joh 7:37 In the l. day, that great day of the *2078*
Joh 8:9 at the eldest, even unto the l.: *2078*
Joh 11:24 in the resurrection at the l. day. *2078*
Joh 12:48 **same shall judge him in the l. day.** *2078*
Ac 2:17 it shall come to pass in the l. days, *2078*
1Co 4:9 hath set forth us the apostles l. *2078*
1Co 15:8 And l. of all he was seen of me also, *2078*

1Co 15:26 l. enemy that shall be destroyed is..... *2078*
1Co 15:45 the l. Adam was made a quickening.... *2078*
1Co 15:52 twinkling of an eye, at the l. trump: ... *2078*
Php 4:10 at the l. your care of me hath........... *4218*
2Ti 3:1 in the l. days perilous times shall....... *2078*
Heb 1:2 Hath in the l. days spoken unto us..... *2078*
Jas 5:3 treasure together for the l. days......... *2078*
1Pe 1:5 ready to be revealed in the l. time. *2078*
1Pe 1:20 manifest in these l. times for you,...... *2078*
2Pe 3:3 shall come in the l. days scoffers, ... *2078*
1Jo 2:18 Little children, it is the l. time: and.... *2078*
1Jo 2:18 we know that it is the l. time........... *2078*
Jude 18 should be mockers in the l. time,......... *2078*
Re 1:11 **and Omega, the first and the l.:**.... *2078*
Re 1:17 **Fear not; I am the first and the l.,**.. *2078*
Re 2:8 **things saith the first and the l.,**.... *2078*
Re 2:19 **and the l. to be more than the**...... *2078*
Re 15:1 angels having the seven l. plagues;...... *2078*
Re 21:9 vials full of the seven l. plagues,........ *2078*
Re 22:13 **and the end, the first and the l.**... *2078*

LASTED
Jg 14:17 the seven days, while their feast l..... 1961

LASTING See also EVERLASTING.
De 33:15 the precious things of the l. hills,....... 5769

LATCHET See also SHOELACHET.
Isa 5:27 nor the l. of their shoes be broken:.... 8288
Mk 1:7 l. of whose shoes I am not worthy..... *2438*
Lu 3:16 l. of whose shoes I am not worthy..... *2438*
Joh 1:27 shoe's l. I am not worthy to unloose... *2438*

LATE See also LAST; LATELY; LATTER.
Ps 127:2 you to rise up early, to sit up l.,......... 309
Mic 2:8 of l. my people is risen up as an.......... 865
Joh 11:8 Jews of l. sought to stone thee;......... *3568*

LATELY
Ac 18:2 l. come from Italy, with his wife........ *4373*

LATIN (lat'-in)
Lu 23:38 in letters of Greek, and L., and......... *4513*
Joh 19:20 in Hebrew, and Greek, and L............ *4513*

LATTER
Ex 4:8 will believe the voice of the l. sign....... 314
Nu 24:14 do to thy people in the l. days............ 319
Nu 24:20 but his l. end shall be that he perish 319
De 4:30 even in the l. days, if thou turn to....... 319
De 8:16 thee, to do thee good at thy l. end;..... 319
De 11:14 the first rain and the l. rain,.............. 4456
De 24:3 if the l. husband hate her, and........... 314
De 24:3 or if the l. husband die, which took...... 314
De 31:29 evil will befall you in the l. days;......... 319
De 32:29 they would consider their l. end!.......... 319
Ru 3:10 shewed more kindness in the l. end..... 314
2Sa 2:26 it will be bitterness in the l. end?......... 314
Job 8:7 thy l. end should greatly increase........ 319
Job 19:25 stand at the l. day upon the earth:....... 314
Job 29:23 their mouth wide as for the l. rain...... 4456
Job 42:12 the Lord blessed the l. end of Job....... 319
Pr 16:15 favour is as a cloud of the l. rain....... 4456
Pr 19:20 thou mayest be wise in thy l. end........ 319
Isa 41:22 and know the l. end of them; or........... 319
Isa 47:7 didst remember the l. end of it............ 319
Jer 3:3 and there hath been no l. rain;.......... 4456
Jer 5:24 rain, both the former and the l.,......... 4456
Jer 23:20 in the l. days ye shall consider it......... 319
Jer 30:24 in the l. days ye shall consider it.......... 319
Jer 48:47 the captivity of Moab in the l. days,..... 319
Jer 49:39 it shall come to pass in the l. days,...... 319
Eze 38:8 in the l. years thou shalt come into...... 319
Eze 38:16 the land; it shall be in the l. days,........ 319
Da 2:28 what shall be in the l. days................ 320
Da 8:23 And in the l. time of their kingdom,..... 319
Da 10:14 befall thy people in the l. days:........... 319
Da 11:29 not be as the former, or as the l.......... 314
Ho 3:5 and his goodness in the l. days............ 319
Ho 6:3 as the l. and former rain unto the...... 4456
Joe 2:23 and the l. rain in the first month......... 4456
Am 7:1 the shooting up of the l. growth;......... 3954
Am 7:1 l. growth after the king's mowings...... 3954
Hag 2:9 The glory of this l. house shall be........ 314
Zec 10:1 rain in the time of the l. rain;............ 4456
1Ti 4:1 l. times some shall depart from.......... *5305*
Jas 5:7 he receive the early and l. rain.......... *3797*
2Pe 2:20 l. end is worse with them than the..... *2078*

LATTICE
Jg 5:28 window, and cried through the l.,......... 822
2Ki 1:2 Ahaziah fell down through a l. in........ 7639
Ca 2:9 shewing himself through the l............ 2762

LAUD
Ro 15:11 Gentiles; and l. him, all ye people...... *1867*

LAUGH See also LAUGHED; LAUGHETH; LAUGHING.
Ge 18:13 Wherefore did Sarah l., saying,.......... 6711
Ge 18:15 And he said, Nay; but thou didst l...... 6711
Ge 21:6 said, God hath made me to l.............. 6712
Ge 21:6 that all that hear will l. with me.......... 6711
Job 5:22 and famine thou shalt l.: neither......... 7832
Job 9:23 will l. at the trial of the innocent......... 3932
Job 22:19 and the innocent l. them to scorn....... 3932
Ps 2:4 sitteth in the heavens shall l............... 7832
Ps 22:7 they that see me l. me to scorn:........ 3932
Ps 37:13 The Lord shall l. at him: for he.......... 7832
Ps 52:6 see, and fear, and shall l. at him:........ 7832
Ps 59:8 But thou, O Lord, shalt l. at them...... 7832
Ps 80:6 our enemies l. among themselves........ 3932
Pr 1:26 I also will l. at your calamity; I.......... 7832
Pr 29:9 he rage or l., there is no rest............ 7832
Ec 3:4 A time to weep, and a time to l.;......... 7832
Lu 6:21 **ye that weep now: for ye shall l.**... *1070*
Lu 6:25 **Woe unto you that l. now! for ye**.. *1070*

LAUGHED
Ge 17:17 Abraham fell upon his face, and l.,...... 6711
Ge 18:12 Sarah l. within herself, saying,........... 6711
Ge 18:15 Sarah denied, saying, I l. not; for....... 6711
2Ki 19:21 despised thee, and l. thee to scorn;.... 3932
2Ch 30:10 they l. them to scorn, and mocked..... 7832
Ne 2:19 heard it, they l. us to scorn, and........ 3932
Job 12:4 the just upright man is l. to scorn...... 7832
Job 29:24 If I l. on them, they believed it not;... 7832
Isa 37:22 despised thee, and l. thee to scorn;... 3932
Eze 23:32 be l. to scorn and had in derision;...... 6712
Mt 9:24 And they l. him to scorn.................. *2606*
Mk 5:40 they l. him to scorn. But when he...... *2606*
Lu 8:53 they l. him to scorn, knowing that...... *2606*

LAUGHETH
Job 41:29 he l. at the shaking of a spear........... 7832

LAUGHING
Job 8:21 Till he fill thy mouth with l., and....... 7814

LAUGHTER
Ps 126:2 Then was our mouth filled with l.,...... 7814
Pr 14:13 Even in l. the heart is sorrowful;....... 7814
Ec 2:2 I said of l., It is mad: and of mirth,.... 7814
Ec 7:3 Sorrow is better than l.: for by the.... 7814
Ec 7:6 under a pot, so is the l. of the fool:.... 7814
Ec 10:19 A feast is made for l., and wine......... 7814
Jas 4:9 let your l. be turned to mourning,...... *1071*

LAUNCH See also LAUNCHED.
Lu 5:4 **L. out into the deep, and let down** .*1877*

LAUNCHED
Lu 8:22 **of the lake.** And they l. forth........... *321*
Ac 21:1 were gotten from them, and had l.,...... *321*
Ac 27:2 we l., meaning to sail by the............. *321*
Ac 27:4 And when we l. from thence, we......... *321*

LAVER See also LAVERS; LAVISH.
Ex 30:18 Thou shalt also make a l. of brass,..... 3595
Ex 30:28 his vessels, and the l. and his foot...... 3595
Ex 31:9 furniture, and the l. and his foot,....... 3595
Ex 35:16 all his vessels, the l. and his foot,...... 3595
Ex 38:8 made the l. of brass, and the foot...... 3595
Ex 39:39 all his vessels, the l. and his foot,...... 3595
Ex 40:7 shalt set the l. between the tent......... 3595
Ex 40:11 shalt anoint the l. and his foot,.......... 3595
Ex 40:30 he set the l. between the tent of....... 3595
Le 8:11 the l. and his foot, to sanctify them.... 3595
1Ki 7:30 under the l. were undersetters.......... 3595
1Ki 7:38 one l. contained forty baths:.............. 3595
1Ki 7:38 every l. was four cubits: and............. 3595
1Ki 7:38 every one of the ten bases one l......... 3595
2Ki 16:17 and removed the l. from off them;....... 3595

LAVERS
1Ki 7:38 Then made he ten l. of brass: one..... 3595
1Ki 7:40 Hiram made the l., and the shovels,... 3595
1Ki 7:43 ten bases, and ten l. on the bases;..... 3595
2Ch 4:6 He made also ten l., and put five....... 3595
2Ch 4:14 and l. made he upon the bases;.......... 3595

LAVISH
Isa 46:6 They l. gold out of the bag, and........ 2107

LAW See also LAWFUL; LAWGIVER; LAWLESS; LAWS.
Ge 11:31 son, and Sarai his daughter in l.,........ 3618
Ge 19:12 son in l., and thy sons, and thy......... 2859
Ge 19:14 out, and spake unto his sons in l.,...... 2859
Ge 19:14 that mocked unto his sons in l............ 2859
Ge 38:11 Judah to Tamar his daughter in l.,...... 3618
Ge 38:13 father in l. goeth up to Timnath......... 2524
Ge 38:16 that she was his daughter in l..)......... 3618
Ge 38:24 thy daughter in l. hath played the....... 3618
Ge 38:25 forth, she sent to her father in l.,...... 2524
Ge 47:26 Joseph made it a l. over the land....... 2706
Ex 3:1 flock of Jethro his father in l.,............ 2859
Ex 4:18 returned to Jethro his father in l.,...... 2859
Ex 12:49 One l. shall be to him that is............ 8451
Ex 13:9 the Lord's l. may be in thy mouth:..... 8451
Ex 16:4 they will walk in my l., or no............ 8451
Ex 18:1 of Midian, Moses' father in l.,............ 2859
Ex 18:2 Moses' father in l., took Zipporah,...... 2859
Ex 18:5 Moses' father in l., came with his....... 2859
Ex 18:6 I thy father in l. Jethro am come........ 2859
Ex 18:7 went out to meet his father in l.,........ 2859
Ex 18:8 Moses told his father in l. all that........ 2859
Ex 18:12 Moses' father in l., took a burnt........ 2859
Ex 18:12 eat bread with Moses' father in l........ 2859
Ex 18:14 Moses' father in l. saw all that he...... 2859
Ex 18:15 Moses said unto his father in l.,......... 2859
Ex 18:17 Moses' father in l. said unto him,....... 2859
Ex 18:24 to the voice of his father in l.,........... 2859
Ex 18:27 Moses let his father in l. depart:......... 2859
Ex 24:12 give thee tables of stone, and a l.,...... 8451
Le 6:9 This is the l. of the burnt offering:..... 8451
Le 6:14 this is the l. of the meat offering:....... 8451
Le 6:25 This is the l. of the sin offering:........ 8451
Le 7:1 is the l. of the trespass offering:........ 8451
Le 7:7 offering: there is one l. for them:....... 8451
Le 7:11 is the l. of the sacrifice of peace........ 8451
Le 7:37 This is the l. of the burnt offering,..... 8451
Le 11:46 the l. of the beasts, and of the fowl,... 8451
Le 12:7 This is the l. for her that hath born.... 8451
Le 13:59 is the l. of the plague of leprosy........ 8451
Le 14:2 shall be the l. of the leper in the........ 8451
Le 14:32 the l. of him in whom is the plague.... 8451
Le 14:54 This is the l. for all manner of........... 8451
Le 14:57 is clean: this is the l. of leprosy.......... 8451
Le 15:32 the l. of him that hath an issue,......... 8451
Le 18:15 nakedness of thy daughter in l........... 3618
Le 20:12 a man lie with his daughter in l.,........ 3618
Le 24:22 Ye shall have one manner of l.,.......... 4941
Nu 5:29 This is the l. of jealousies, when......... 8451
Nu 5:30 shall execute upon her all this l.......... 8451
Nu 6:13 And this is the l. of the Nazarite,........ 8451
Nu 6:21 This is the l. of the Nazarite who........ 8451
Nu 6:21 do after the l. of his separation.......... 8451
Nu 10:29 the Midianite, Moses' father in l......... 2859
Nu 15:16 One l. and one manner shall be for..... 8451
Nu 15:29 have one l. for him that sinneth......... 8451
Nu 19:2 is the ordinance of the l. which the..... 8451
Nu 19:14 This is the l., when a man dieth in..... 8451
Nu 31:21 the ordinance of the l. which the........ 8451
De 1:5 Moses to declare this l., saying,......... 8451
De 4:8 so righteous as all this l., which.......... 8451
De 4:44 And this is the l. which Moses set...... 8451
De 17:11 to the sentence of the l. which they... 8451
De 17:18 write him a copy of this l. in a book... 8451
De 17:19 keep all the words of this l. and......... 8451
De 27:3 upon them all the words of this l.,....... 8451
De 27:8 all the words of this l. very plainly..... 8451
De 27:23 he that lieth with his mother in l.,...... 2859
De 27:26 all the words of this l. to do them...... 8451
De 28:58 do all the words of this l. that are...... 8451
De 28:61 is not written in the book of this l.,.... 8451
De 29:21 are written in this book of the l.......... 8451
De 29:29 we may do all the words of this l......... 8451
De 30:10 are written in this book of the l.,........ 8451
De 31:9 Moses wrote this l., and delivered..... 8451
De 31:11 shalt read this l. before all Israel........ 8451
De 31:12 to do all the words of this l............... 8451
De 31:24 the words of this l. in a book,............ 8451
De 31:26 Take this book of the l., and put it..... 8451
De 32:46 to do, all the words of this l.............. 8451
De 33:2 right hand went a fiery l. for them...... 1881
De 33:4 Moses commanded us a l., even........ 8451
De 33:10 thy judgments, and Israel thy l........... 8451
Jos 1:7 observe to do according to all the l.,... 8451
Jos 1:8 This book of the l. shall not depart..... 8451
Jos 8:31 in the book of the l. of Moses,.......... 8451
Jos 8:32 the stones a copy of the l. of Moses,.. 8451

Jos 8:34 he read all the words of the l., 8451
Jos 8:34 that is written in the book of the l. 8451
Jos 22:5 do the commandment and the l., 8451
Jos 23:6 in the book of the l. of Moses, 8451
Jos 24:26 words in the book of the l. of God, 8451
Jg 1:16 Moses' father in l., went up out of 2859
Jg 4:11 of Hobab the father in l. of Moses, 2859
Jg 15:6 Samson, the son in l. of the Timnite, 2859
Jg 19:4 his father in l., the damsel's father, 2859
Jg 19:5 father said unto his son in l., 2859
Jg 19:7 depart, his father in l. urged him: 2859
Jg 19:9 his servant, his father in l., the 2859
Ru 1:6 she arose with her daughters in l., 3618
Ru 1:7 her two daughters in l. with her; 3618
Ru 1:8 said unto her two daughters in l., 3618
Ru 1:14 Orpah kissed her mother in l.; 2545
Ru 1:15 thy sister in l. is gone back unto her 2994
Ru 1:15 return thou after thy sister in l. 2994
Ru 1:22 the Moabitess, her daughter in l., 3618
Ru 2:11 hast done unto thy mother in l. 2545
Ru 2:18 her mother in l. saw what she had 2545
Ru 2:19 her mother in l. said unto her, 2545
Ru 2:19 shewed her mother in l. with whom 2545
Ru 2:20 said unto her daughter in l., 3618
Ru 2:22 said unto Ruth her daughter in l., 3618
Ru 2:23 and dwelt with her mother in l. 2545
Ru 3:1 her mother in l. said unto her, 2545
Ru 3:6 all that her mother in l. bade her. 2545
Ru 3:16 when she came to her mother in l., 2545
Ru 3:17 Go not empty unto thy mother in l. 2545
Ru 4:15 thy daughter in l., which loveth 3618
1Sa 4:19 his daughter in l., Phinehas' wife, 3618
1Sa 4:19 her father in l. and her husband 2524
1Sa 4:21 because of her father in l. and her 2524
1Sa 18:18 I should be son in l. to the king? 2859
1Sa 18:21 Thou shalt this day be my son in l. 2860
1Sa 18:22 therefore be the king's son in l. 2860
1Sa 18:23 a light thing to be a king's son in l., 2860
1Sa 18:26 David well to be the king's son in l. 2860
1Sa 18:27 he might be the king's son in l. 2860
1Sa 22:14 which is the king's son in l., and 2859
1Ki 2:3 as it is written in the l. of Moses, 8451
2Ki 8:27 the son in l. of the house of Ahab. 2859
2Ki 10:31 to walk in the l. of the Lord God 8451
2Ki 14:6 in the book of the l. of Moses, 8451
2Ki 17:13 according to all the l. which I 8451
2Ki 17:34 or after the l. and commandment 8451
2Ki 17:37 and the l., and the commandment, 8451
2Ki 21:8 to all the l. that my servant Moses 8451
2Ki 22:8 I have found the book of the l. in 8451
2Ki 22:11 the words of the book of the l., 8451
2Ki 23:24 might perform the words of the l. 8451
2Ki 23:25 according to all the l. of Moses; 8451
1Ch 2:4 his daughter in l. bare him Pharez 3618
1Ch 16:17 the same to Jacob for a l., and 2706
1Ch 16:40 is written in the l. of the Lord, 8451
1Ch 22:12 thou mayest keep the l. of the Lord 8451
2Ch 6:16 heed to their way to walk in my l., 8451
2Ch 12:1 forsook the l. of the Lord, and all 8451
2Ch 14:4 to do the l. and the commandment. 8451
2Ch 15:3 a teaching priest, and without l. 8451
2Ch 17:9 had the book of the l. of the Lord 8451
2Ch 19:10 between l. and commandment, 8451
2Ch 23:18 as it is written in the l. of Moses, 8451
2Ch 25:4 as it is written in the l. of the book 8451
2Ch 30:16 according to the l. of Moses the 8451
2Ch 31:3 as it is written in the l. of the Lord. 8451
2Ch 31:4 encouraged in the l. of the Lord. 8451
2Ch 31:21 in the l., and in the commandments, 8451
2Ch 33:8 to the whole l. and the statutes 8451
2Ch 34:14 priest found a book of the l. of the 8451
2Ch 34:15 have found the book of the l. in the 8451
2Ch 34:19 king had heard the words of the l., 8451
2Ch 35:26 was written in the l. of the Lord, 8451
Ezr 3:2 as it is written in the l. of Moses 8451
Ezr 7:6 a ready scribe in the l. of Moses, 8451
Ezr 7:10 his heart to seek the l. of the Lord, 8451
Ezr 7:12 a scribe of the l. of the God of 1882
Ezr 7:14 according to the l. of thy God which 1882
Ezr 7:21 the scribe of the l. of the God of 1882
Ezr 7:26 will not do the l. of thy God, and 1882
Ezr 7:26 the l. of the king, let judgment be 1882
Ezr 10:3 let it be done according to the l. 8451
Ne 6:18 the son in l. of Shechaniah the son 2859
Ne 8:1 bring the book of the l. of Moses, 8451
Ne 8:2 And Ezra the priest brought the l. 8451
Ne 8:3 attentive unto the book of the l. 8451
Ne 8:7 the people to understand the l. 8451
Ne 8:8 read in the book in the l. of God 8451
Ne 8:9 when they heard the words of the l. 8451
Ne 8:13 to understand the words of the l. 8451
Ne 8:14 found written in the l. which the 8451
Ne 8:18 read in the book of the l. of God. 8451
Ne 9:3 read in the book of the l. of the 8451
Ne 9:26 cast thy l. behind their backs, and 8451
Ne 9:29 bring them again unto thy l. 8451
Ne 9:34 kept thy l., nor hearkened unto thy 8451
Ne 10:28 of the lands unto the l. of God, 8451
Ne 10:29 into an oath, to walk in God's l., 8451
Ne 10:34 our God, as it is written in the l. 8451
Ne 10:36 as it is written in the l., and the 8451
Ne 12:44 the portions of the l. for the priests 8451
Ne 13:3 to pass, when they had heard the l., 8451
Ne 13:28 was son in l. to Sanballat the 2859
Es 1:8 drinking was according to the l.; 1881
Es 1:13 all that knew l. and judgment: 1881
Es 1:15 the queen Vashti according to l., 1881
Es 4:11 is one l. of his to put him to death, 1881
Es 4:16 which is not according to the l. 1881
Job 22:22 I pray thee, the l. from his mouth, 8451
Ps 1:2 his delight is in the l. of the Lord; 8451
Ps 1:2 in his l. doth he meditate day and 8451
Ps 19:7 The l. of the Lord is perfect, 8451
Ps 37:31 The l. of his God is in his heart; 8451
Ps 40:8 God: yea, thy l. is within my heart. 8451
Ps 78:1 Give ear, O my people, to my l. 8451
Ps 78:5 Jacob, and appointed a l. in Israel, 8451
Ps 78:10 God, and refused to walk in his l.; 8451
Ps 81:4 and a l. of the God of Jacob. 4941
Ps 89:30 If his children forsake my l., and 8451
Ps 94:12 and teachest him out of thy l.; 8451
Ps 94:20 which frameth mischief by a l.? 2706
Ps 105:10 the same unto Jacob for a l., and 2706
Ps 119:1 who walk in the l. of the Lord. 8451
Ps 119:18 wondrous things out of thy l. 8451
Ps 119:29 and grant me thy l. graciously. 8451
Ps 119:34 and I shall keep thy l.; yea, I shall 8451
Ps 119:44 So shall I keep thy l. continually 8451
Ps 119:51 yet have I not declined from thy l. 8451
Ps 119:53 of the wicked that forsake thy l. 8451
Ps 119:55 in the night, and have kept thy l. 8451
Ps 119:61 but I have not forgotten thy l. 8451
Ps 119:70 as grease; but I delight in thy l. 8451
Ps 119:72 The l. of thy mouth is better unto 8451
Ps 119:77 may live: for thy l. is my delight. 8451
Ps 119:85 for me, which are not after thy l. 8451
Ps 119:92 Unless thy l. had been my delights, 8451
Ps 119:97 O how love I thy l.! it is my 8451
Ps 119:109 hand: yet do I not forget thy l. 8451
Ps 119:113 vain thoughts: but thy l. do I love. 8451
Ps 119:126 for they have made void thy l. 8451
Ps 119:136 eyes, because they keep not thy l. 8451
Ps 119:142 and thy l. is the truth. 8451
Ps 119:150 mischief: they are far from thy l. 8451
Ps 119:153 me: for I do not forget thy l. 8451
Ps 119:163 abhor lying: but thy l. do I love. 8451
Ps 119:165 peace have they which love thy l. 8451
Ps 119:174 O Lord; and thy l. is my delight. 8451
Pr 1:8 forsake not the l. of thy mother: 8451
Pr 3:1 My son, forget not my l.; but let 8451
Pr 4:2 doctrine, forsake ye not my l. 8451
Pr 6:20 forsake not the l. of thy mother: 8451
Pr 6:23 is a lamp; and the l. is light; 8451
Pr 7:2 my l. as the apple of thine eye. 8451
Pr 13:14 l. of the wise is a fountain of life, 8451
Pr 28:4 They that forsake the l. praise the 8451
Pr 28:4 as keep the l. contend with them. 8451
Pr 28:7 Whoso keepeth the l. is a wise son: 8451
Pr 28:9 away his ear from hearing the l., 8451
Pr 29:18 he that keepeth the l., happy is he. 8451
Pr 31:5 Lest they drink, and forget the l., 2710
Pr 31:26 in her tongue is the l. of kindness. 8451
Isa 1:10 give ear unto the l. of our God, ye 8451
Isa 2:3 for out of Zion shall go forth the l., 8451
Isa 5:24 have cast away the l. of the Lord 8451
Isa 8:16 seal the l. among my disciples. 8451
Isa 8:20 To the l. and to the testimony: 8451
Isa 30:9 will not hear the l. of the Lord: 8451
Isa 42:4 and the isles shall wait for his l. 8451
Isa 42:21 he will magnify the l., and make it 8451
Isa 42:24 were they obedient unto his l. 8451
Isa 51:4 for a l. shall proceed from me, and 8451
Isa 51:7 the people in whose heart is my l.; 8451
Jer 2:8 that handle the l. knew me not: 8451
Jer 6:19 unto my words, nor to my l., 8451
Jer 8:8 and the l. of the Lord is with us? 8451
Jer 9:13 they have forsaken my l. which I 8451
Jer 16:11 me, and have not kept my l.; 8451
Jer 18:18 for the l. shall not perish from the 8451
Jer 26:4 not hearken to me, to walk in my l., 8451
Jer 31:33 will put my l. in their inward parts, 8451
Jer 32:11 according to the l. and custom, 4687
Jer 32:23 thy voice, neither walked in thy l.; 8451
Jer 44:10 they feared, nor walked in my l., 8451
Jer 44:23 of the Lord, nor walked in his l., 8451
La 2:9 the l. is no more; her prophets also 8451
Eze 7:26 the l. shall perish from the priest, 8451
Eze 22:11 lewdly defiled his daughter in l.; 3618
Eze 22:26 Her priests have violated my l., 8451
Eze 43:12 This is the l. of the house; upon 8451
Eze 43:12 Behold, this is the l. of the house. 8451
Da 6:5 him concerning the l. of his God. 1882
Da 6:8, 12 l. of the Medes and Persians, 1882
Da 6:15 the l. of the Medes and Persians is, 1882
Da 9:11 Israel have transgressed thy l., 8451
Da 9:11 that is writtenin the l. of Moses the 8451
Da 9:13 As it is written in the l. of Moses, 8451
Ho 4:6 hast forgotten the l. of thy God, 8451
Ho 8:1 and trespassed against my l. 8451
Ho 8:12 to him the great things of my l., 8451
Am 2:4 have despised the l. of the Lord, 8451
Mic 4:2 for the l. shall go forth of Zion, and 8451
Mic 7:6 daughter in l. against her mother 3618
Mic 7:6 daughter...against her mother in l.; 2545
Hab 1:4 Therefore the l. is slacked, and 8451
Zep 3:4 they have done violence to the l. 8451
Hag 2:11 now the priests concerning the l., 8451
Zec 7:12 stone, lest they should hear the l., 8451
Mal 2:6 The l. of truth was in his mouth, 8451
Mal 2:7 should seek the l. at his mouth: 8451
Mal 2:8 caused many to stumble at the l.; 8451
Mal 2:9 but have been partial in the l. 8451
Mal 4:4 Remember ye the l. of Moses my 8451
Mt 5:17 **that I am come to destroy the l.,** 3551
Mt 5:18 **shall in no wise pass from the l.,** 3551
Mt 5:40 **if any man will sue thee at the l.,**
Mt 7:12 **for this is the l. and the prophets.** 3551
Mt 10:35 **daughter in l. against her mother** 3565
Mt 10:35 **daughter...against her mother in l.** 3994
Mt 11:13 **and the l. prophesied until John** 3551
Mt 12:5 **have ye not read in the l., how** 3551
Mt 22:36 the great commandment in the l.? 3551
Mt 22:40 **commandments hang all the l. and** 3551
Mt 23:23 **the weightier matters of the l.,** 3551
Lu 2:22 according to the l. of Moses were 3551
Lu 2:23 it is written in the l. of the Lord, 3551
Lu 2:24 which is said in the l. of the Lord, 3551
Lu 2:27 for him after the custom of the l., 3551
Lu 2:39 according to the l. of the Lord, 3551
Lu 5:17 and doctors of the l. sitting by, 3547
Lu 10:26 him, **What is written in the l.?** 3551
Lu 12:53 **mother in l. against her daughter.** 3994
Lu 12:53 **mother...against her daughter in l.** 3565
Lu 12:53 **daughter in l. against her mother.** 3565
Lu 12:53 **daughter...against her mother in l.** 3994
Lu 16:16 **The l. and the prophets were until** 3551
Lu 16:17 **pass, than one tittle of the l. to** 3551
Lu 24:44 **were written in the l. of Moses,** 3551
Joh 1:17 For the l. was given by Moses, but 3551
Joh 1:45 found him, of whom Moses in the l., 3551
Joh 7:19 **Did not Moses give you the l., and** 3551
Joh 7:19 **and yet none of you keepeth the l.?** 3551
Joh 7:23 **l. of Moses should not be broken;** 3551
Joh 7:49 who knoweth not the l. are cursed. 3551
Joh 7:51 Doth our l. judge any man, before 3551
Joh 8:5 Now Moses in the l. commanded us, 3551
Joh 8:17 **It is also written in your l., that** 3551
Joh 10:34 them, **Is it not written in your l.,** 3551
Joh 12:34 have heard out of the l. that Christ 3551
Joh 15:25 **fulfilled that is written in their l.,** 3551
Joh 18:13 for he was father in l. to Caiaphas, 3995
Joh 18:31 judge him according to your l. 3551
Joh 19:7 a l., and by our l. he ought to die. 3551
Ac 5:34 named Gamaliel, a doctor of the l., 3547
Ac 6:13 against this holy place, and the l.: 3551
Ac 7:53 received the l. by the disposition 3551
Ac 13:15 after the reading of the l. and the 3551
Ac 13:39 not be justified by the l. of Moses. 3551

Ac 15:5 them to keep the l. of Moses........... *3551*
Ac 15:24 be circumcised, and keep the l.; *3551*
Ac 18:13 to worship God contrary to the l........ *3551*
Ac 18:15 of words and names, and of your l., ... *3551*
Ac 19:38 l. is open, and there are deputies:......... *60*
Ac 21:20 and they are all zealous of the l.: *3551*
Ac 21:24 walkest orderly, and keepest the l...... *3551*
Ac 21:28 against the people, and the l., and...... *3551*
Ac 22:3 to the perfect manner of the l. of....... *3551*
Ac 22:12 a devout man according to the l., ... *3551*
Ac 23:3 sittest thou to judge me after the l., ... *3551*
Ac 23:3 to be smitten contrary to the l.? *3891*
Ac 23:29 be accused of questions of their l., ... *3551*
Ac 24:6 have judged according to our l.......... *3551*
Ac 24:14 all things which are written in the l..... *3551*
Ac 25:8 Neither against the l. of the Jews,...... *3551*
Ac 28:23 Jesus, both out of the l. of Moses,...... *3551*
Ro 2:12 as many as have sinned without l......... *460*
Ro 2:12 shall also perish without l.:................. *460*
Ro 2:12 as many as have sinned in the l. *3551*
Ro 2:12 shall be judged by the l.;.................. *3551*
Ro 2:13 not the hearers of the l. are just.......... *3551*
Ro 2:13 the doers of the l. shall be justified..... *3551*
Ro 2:14 the Gentiles, which have not the l., ... *3551*
Ro 2:14 do...the things contained in the l., ... *3551*
Ro 2:14 having not the l., are a l. unto *3551*
Ro 2:15 of the l. written in their hearts, ... *3551*
Ro 2:17 called a Jew, and restest in the l., ... *3551*
Ro 2:18 being instructed out of the l.: *3551*
Ro 2:20 knowledge and of the truth in the l..... *3551*
Ro 2:23 that makest thy boast of the l., ... *3551*
Ro 2:23 through breaking the l. dishonorest..... *3551*
Ro 2:25 verily profiteth, if thou keep the l.:..... *3551*
Ro 2:25 but if thou be a breaker of the l.,........ *3551*
Ro 2:26 keep the righteousness of the l.,........ *3551*
Ro 2:27 which is by nature, if it fulfill the l.,.... *3551*
Ro 2:27 thee, who...dost transgress the l.? *3551*
Ro 3:19 that what things soever the l. saith,.... *3551*
Ro 3:19 saith to them who are under the l.: *3551*
Ro 3:20 by the deeds of the l. there shall no ... *3551*
Ro 3:20 for by the l. is the knowledge of sin. .. *3551*
Ro 3:21 of God without the l. is manifested, ... *3551*
Ro 3:21 being witnessed by the l. and the....... *3551*
Ro 3:27 By what l.? of works? Nay: but by..... *3551*
Ro 3:27 Nay: but by the l. of faith............... *3551*
Ro 3:28 by faith without the deeds of the l...... *3551*
Ro 3:31 make void the l. through faith? *3551*
Ro 3:31 God forbid: yea, we establish the l. ... *3551*
Ro 4:13 or to his seed, through the l., but...... *3551*
Ro 4:14 if they which are of the l. be heirs, ... *3551*
Ro 4:15 Because the l. worketh wrath;........... *3551*
Ro 4:15 no l. is, there is no transgression....... *3551*
Ro 4:16 not to that only which is of the l.,...... *3551*
Ro 5:13 until the l. sin was in the world: *3551*
Ro 5:13 is not imputed where there is no l........ *3551*
Ro 5:20 Moreover the l. entered, that the *3551*
Ro 6:14 ye are not under the l., but under...... *3551*
Ro 6:15 we are not under the l., but under..... *3551*
Ro 7:1 I speak to them that know the l.,)...... *3551*
Ro 7:1 the l. hath dominion over a man as...... *3551*
Ro 7:2 is bound by the l. to her husband so... *3551*
Ro 7:2 is loosed from the l. of her husband.... *3551*
Ro 7:3 be dead she is free from that l.; *3551*
Ro 7:4 become dead to the l. by the body..... *3551*
Ro 7:5 sins, which were by the l., did work... *3551*
Ro 7:6 now we are delivered from the l., ... *3551*
Ro 7:7 say then, Is the l. sin? God forbid. *3551*
Ro 7:7 I had not known sin, but by the l.:...... *3551*
Ro 7:7 known lust, except the l. had said, ... *3551*
Ro 7:8 For without the l. sin was dead. *3551*
Ro 7:9 For I was alive without the l. once: *3551*
Ro 7:12 Wherefore the l. is holy, and the *3551*
Ro 7:14 For we know that the l. is spiritual:.... *3551*
Ro 7:16 I consent unto the l. that it is good. ... *3551*
Ro 7:21 I find then a l., that, when I would..... *3551*
Ro 7:22 I delight in the l. of God after the...... *3551*
Ro 7:23 I see another l. in my members,........ *3551*
Ro 7:23 warring against the l. of my mind, ... *3551*
Ro 7:23 me into captivity to the l. of sin......... *3551*
Ro 7:25 mind I myself serve the l. of God *3551*
Ro 7:25 but with the flesh the l. of sin. *3551*
Ro 8:2 the l. of the Spirit of life in Christ...... *3551*
Ro 8:2 me free from the l. of sin and death. .. *3551*
Ro 8:3 what the l. could not do, in that it...... *3551*
Ro 8:4 the righteousness of the l. might be.... *3551*
Ro 8:7 not subject to the l. of God, neither ... *3551*
Ro 9:4 and the giving of the l., and the........ *3548*
Ro 9:31 after the l. of righteousness, ... *3551*
Ro 9:31 attained to the l. of righteousness. *3551*
Ro 9:32 as it were by the works of the l.. ...... *3551*
Ro 10:4 For Christ is the end of the l. for *3551*
Ro 10:5 the righteousness which is of the l., ... *3551*
Ro 13:8 loveth another hath fulfilled the l.. ..... *3551*
Ro 13:10 love is the fulfilling of the l.. .... *3551*
1Co 6:1 go to l. before the unjust, and not...... *2919*
1Co 6:6 brother goeth to l. with brother, ... *2919*
1Co 6:7 ye go to l. one with another............. *2917*
1Co 7:39 wife is bound by the l. as long as....... *3551*
1Co 9:8 or saith not the l. the same also? *3551*
1Co 9:9 For it is written in the l. of Moses,.... *3551*
1Co 9:20 are under the l., as under the l., ... *3551*
1Co 9:20 gain them that are under the l.; *3551*
1Co 9:21 that are without l., as without l.,......... *459*
1Co 9:21 (being not without l. to God, ... *459*
1Co 9:21 but under the l. to Christ,) *1772*
1Co 9:21 might gain them that are without l.. ..... *459*
1Co 14:21 In the l. it is written, With men of..... *3551*
1Co 14:34 under obedience, as also saith the l.. .. *3551*
1Co 15:56 sin; and the strength of sin is the l..... *3551*
Ga 2:16 not justified by the works of the l., ... *3551*
Ga 2:16 and not by the works of the l.: for..... *3551*
Ga 2:16 by the works of the l. shall no flesh.... *3551*
Ga 2:19 I through the l. am dead to the l., ... *3551*
Ga 2:21 for if righteousness come by the l., ... *3551*
Ga 3:2 ye the Spirit by the works of the l., ... *3551*
Ga 3:5 doeth he it by the works of the l., ... *3551*
Ga 3:10 many as are of the works of the l. *3551*
Ga 3:10 are written in the book of the l. to..... *3551*
Ga 3:11 no man is justified by the l. in the...... *3551*
Ga 3:12 And the l. is not of faith: but, The *3551*
Ga 3:13 redeemed us from the curse of the l.,..*3551*
Ga 3:17 the l., which was four hundred and..... *3551*
Ga 3:18 For if the inheritance be of the l., ... *3551*
Ga 3:19 Wherefore then serveth the l.?.......... *3551*
Ga 3:21 Is the l. then against the promises *3551*
Ga 3:21 if there had been a l. given which *3551*
Ga 3:21 righteousness...have been by the l.. ... *3551*
Ga 3:23 came, we were kept under the l., ... *3551*
Ga 3:24 the l. was our schoolmaster to bring... *3551*
Ga 4:4 of a woman, made under the l., ... *3551*
Ga 4:5 redeem them that were under the l., .. *3551*
Ga 4:21 be under the l., do ye not hear the l.?.*3551*
Ga 5:3 he is a debtor to do the whole l.......... *3551*
Ga 5:4 of you are justified by the l.; *3551*
Ga 5:14 all the l. is fulfilled in one word,......... *3551*
Ga 5:18 the Spirit, ye are not under the l.. ..... *3551*
Ga 5:23 against such there is no l................. *3551*
Ga 6:2 and so fulfil the l. of Christ. *3551*
Ga 6:13 who are circumcised keep the l.; *3551*
Eph 2:15 l. of commandments contained.......... *3551*
Php 3:5 as touching the l., a Pharisee; *3551*
Php 3:6 the righteousness which is in the l., ... *3551*
Php 3:9 righteousness, which is of the l., ... *3551*
1Ti 1:7 Desiring to be teachers of the l.: *3547*
1Ti 1:8 But we know that the l. is good, ... *3551*
1Ti 1:9 l. is not made for a righteous man,..... *3551*
Tit 3:9 and strivings about the l.; *3544*
Heb 7:5 of the people according to the l., ... *3551*
Heb 7:11 under it the people received the l.,).... *3549*
Heb 7:12 necessity a change also of the l.. .,..... *3551*
Heb 7:16 the l. of a carnal commandment, ... *3551*
Heb 7:19 the l. made nothing perfect, but the.... *3551*
Heb 7:28 For the l. maketh men high priests..... *3551*
Heb 7:28 of the oath, which was since the l., ... *3551*
Heb 8:4 that offer gifts according to the l.: *3551*
Heb 9:19 to all the people according to the l., ... *3551*
Heb 9:22 are by the l. purged with blood; *3551*
Heb 10:1 l. having a shadow of good things....... *3551*
Heb 10:8 therein; which are offered by the l.; ... *3551*
Heb 10:28 He that despised Moses' l. died......... *3551*
Jas 1:25 into the perfect l. of liberty, ... *3551*
Jas 2:8 If ye fulfil the royal l. according to...... *3551*
Jas 2:9 sin, and are convinced of the l. as...... *3551*
Jas 2:10 whosoever shall keep the whole l., ... *3551*
Jas 2:11 art become a transgressor of the l. *3551*
Jas 2:12 shall be judged by the l. of liberty. *3551*
Jas 4:11 evil of the l., and judgeth the l.: *3551*
Jas 4:11 but if thou judge the l., thou art *3551*
Jas 4:11 not a doer of the l., but a judge......... *3551*
1Jo 3:4 sin transgresseth also the l.:........ *4160,458*
1Jo 3:4 sin is the transgression of the l.. .. *4160,458*

LAWFUL See also UNLAWFUL.
Ezr 7:24 it shall not be l. to impose toll,.......... 7990
Isa 49:24 mighty, or the l. captive delivered?..... 6662
Eze 18:5 and do that which is l. and right,........ 4941
Eze 18:19 have done that which is l. and right, ... 4941
Eze 18:21 and do that which is l. and right, he ... 4941
Eze 18:27 doeth that which is l. and right, he..... 4941
Eze 33:14 and do that which is l. and right;........ 4941
Eze 33:16 hath done that which is l. and right;..... 4941
Eze 33:19 and do that which is l. and right, he ... 4941
Mt 12:2 is not l. to do upon the sabbath day.... *1832*
Mt 12:4 **which was not l. for him to eat,** *1832*
Mt 12:10 Is it l. to heal on the sabbath days?.... *1832*
Mt 12:12 **l. to do well on the sabbath days**... *1832*
Mt 14:4 It is not l. for thee to have her......... *1832*
Mt 19:3 Is it l. for a man to put away his........ *1832*
Mt 20:15 **Is it not l. for me to do what I** *1833*
Mt 22:17 Is it l. to give tribute unto Caesar, ... *1833*
Mt 27:6 It is not l. for to put them into the...... *1833*
Mk 2:24 sabbath day that which is not l.? *1833*
Mk 2:26 **is not l. to eat but for the priests,** . *1833*
Mk 3:4 **Is it l. to do good on the sabbath** .. *1833*
Mk 6:18 It is not l....to have thy brother's....... *1833*
Mk 10:2 l. for a man to put away his wife? *1833*
Mk 12:14 Is it l. to give tribute to Caesar, or.... *1833*
Lu 6:2 which is not l. to do on the sabbath.... *1833*
Lu 6:4 **is not l. to eat but for the priests** .. *1833*
Lu 6:9 **it l. on the sabbath days to do** *1833*
Lu 14:3 **Is it l. to heal on the sabbath day?** .*1833*
Lu 20:22 l. for us to give tribute unto Caesar.... *1833*
Joh 5:10 it is not l. for thee to carry thy bed.... *1833*
Joh 18:31 l. for us to put any man to death: *1833*
Ac 16:21 which are not l. for us to receive, ... *1833*
Ac 19:39 be determined in a l. assembly. *1772*
Ac 22:25 l. for you to scourge a man that is *1832*
1Co 6:12 All things are l. unto me, but all *1832*
1Co 6:12 all things are l. for me, but I will *1832*
1Co 10:23 all things are l. for me, but all........... *1832*
1Co 10:23 all things are l. for me, but all........... *1832*
2Co 12:4 which it is not l. for a man to utter. ... *1832*

LAWFULLY
1Ti 1:8 the law is good, if a man use it l.;...... *3545*
2Ti 2:5 he not crowned, except he strive l...... *3545*

LAWGIVER
Ge 49:10 nor a l. from between his feet, ... 2710
Nu 21:18 digged it, by the direction of the l., ... 2710
De 33:21 a portion of the l., was he seated; 2710
Ps 60:7 of mine head; Judah is my l.; 2710
Ps 108:8 of mine head; Judah is my l.; 2710
Isa 33:22 the Lord is our l., the Lord is our...... 2710
Jas 4:12 There is one l., who is able to save ... *3550*

LAWLESS
1Ti 1:9 man, but for the l. and disobedient,...... *459*

LAWS
Ge 26:5 my statutes, and my l....................... 8451
Ex 16:28 keep my commandments and my l.?.... 8451
Ex 18:16 know the statutes of God, and his l... 8451
Ex 18:20 shalt teach them ordinances and l., ... 8451
Le 26:46 the statutes and judgments and l., ... 8451
Ezr 7:25 such as know the l. of thy God; 1882
Ne 9:13 them right judgments, and true l., ... 8451
Ne 9:14 them precepts, statutes, and l., ... 8451
Es 1:19 l. of the Persians and the Medes, ... 1881
Es 3:8 their l. are diverse from all people;..... 1881
Es 3:8 neither keep they the king's l.: 1881
Ps 105:45 observe his statutes,...keep his l........ 8541
Isa 24:5 they have transgressed the l., ... 8451
Eze 43:11 forms thereof, and all the l. thereof: ... 8451
Eze 44:5 of the Lord, and all the l. thereof; 8451
Eze 44:24 they shall keep my l. and my 8451
Da 7:25 and think to change times and l.: 1882
Da 9:10 to walk in his l., which he set 8451
Heb 8:10 I will put my l. into their mind,.......... *3551*
Heb 10:16 I will put my l. into their hearts, ... *3551*

LAWYER See also LAWYERS.
Mt 22:35 was a l., asked him a question, ... *3544*
Lu 10:25 a certain l. stood up, and tempted...... *3544*
Tit 3:13 Bring Zenas the l. and Apollos on....... *3544*

LAWYERS
Lu 7:30 and l. rejected the counsel of God...... *3544*
Lu 11:45 answered one of the l., and said *3544*
Lu 11:46 he said, **Woe unto you also, ye l.!**... *3544*
Lu 11:52 **Woe unto you, l.! for ye have** *3544*
Lu 14:3 spake unto the l. and Pharisees. *3544*

LAY See also LAID; LAIN; LAYEDST; LAYEST; LAYETH; LAYING; LIE; OVERLAY.

Ge 19:4 before they l. down, the men of........ 7901
Ge 19:33 went in, and l. with her father;......... 7901
Ge 19:33 he perceived not when she l. down, ... 7901
Ge 19:34 I l. yesternight with my father:......... 7901
Ge 19:35 the younger arose, and l. with him;.... 7901
Ge 19:35 he perceived not when she l. down, ... 7901
Ge 22:12 L. not thnie hand upon the lad,........... 7971
Ge 28:11 and l. down in thaat place to sleep. 7901
Ge 30:16 And he l. with her that night............ 7901
Ge 34:2 he took her, and l. with her, and....... 7901
Ge 35:22 Reuben went and l. with Bilhah his..... 7901
Ge 37:22 l. no hand upon him; that he............ 7971
Ge 41:35 and l. up corn under the hand of........ 6651
Ex 5:8 heretofore, ye shall l. upon them; 7760
Ex 7:4 I may l. my hand upon Egypt, ...5414
Ex 16:13 the dew l. round about the host......... 7902
Ex 16:14 when the dew that l. was gone up,...... 7902
Ex 16:14 the wilderness there l. a small round ....
Ex 16:23 remaineth over l. up for you to.......... 3241
Ex 16:33 l. it up before the Lord, to be kept 3241
Ex 21:22 woman's husband will l. upon him;...... 7896
Ex 22:25 shalt thou l. upon him usury............ 7760
Le 1:7 l. the wood in order upon the fire: ....
Le 1:8 shall l. the parts,..in order upon...........
Le 1:12 the priest shall l. them in order on...........
Le 2:15 it, and l. frankincense thereon: 7760
Le 3:2, 8,13 he shall l. his hand upon the....... 5564
Le 4:4 shall l. his hand upon the bullock's...... 5564
Le 4:15 shall l. their hands upon the head....... 5564
Le 4:24, 29,33 he shall l. his hand upon the 5564
Le 6:12 l. the burnt offering in order upon............
Le 16:21 Aaron shall l. both his hands upon...... 5564
Le 24:14 him l. their hands upon his head, ... 5564
Nu 8:12 Levites shall l. their hands upon......... 5564
Nu 12:11 thee, l. not the sin upon us,............. 7896
Nu 17:4 shalt l. them up in the tabernacle....... 3241
Nu 19:9 l. them up without the camp in a 3241
Nu 24:9 He couched, he l. down as a lion, ... 7901
Nu 27:18 and l. thine hand upon him;.............. 5564
De 7:15 will l. them upon all them that.......... 5414
De 11:18 shall ye l. up these my words in........ 7760
De 11:25 your God shall l. the fear of you........ 5414
De 14:28 shalt l. it up within thy gates:........... 3241
De 21:8 l. not innocent blood unto thy............ 5414
De 21:19 his father and his mother l. hold............
De 22:22 the man that l. with the woman, ... 7901
De 22:25 man only that l. with her shall die: 7901
De 22:28 and l. hold on her, and lie with her,..........
De 22:29 man that l. with her shall give........... 7901
Jos 6:26 he shall l. the foundation thereof.............
Jos 8:2 l. thee an ambush for the city............ 7760
Jos 15:46 unto the sea, all that l. near Ashdod, ...
Jg 4:22 Sisera l. dead, and the nail was 5307
Jg 5:27 feet he bowed, he fell, he l. down:...... 7901
Jg 6:20 cakes, and l. them upon this rock,...... 3241
Jg 7:12 children of the east l. along in the 5307
Jg 7:13 overturned it, that the tent l. along. ... 5307
Jg 14:17 her, because she l. sore upon him:...........
Jg 16:3 Samson l. till midnight, and arose......... 7901
Jg 18:19 l. thine hand upon thy mouth,............ 7760
Ru 3:4 uncover his feet, and l. thee down; 7901
Ru 3:8 and, behold, a woman l. at his feet..... 7901
Ru 3:14 she l. at his feet until the morning:...... 7901
1Sa 2:22 how they l. with the women that 7901
1Sa 3:5 again. And he went and l. down.......... 7901
1Sa 3:9 Samuel went and l. down in his 7901
1Sa 3:15 And Samuel l. until the morning,........ 7901
1Sa 6:8 the Lord, and l. it upon the cart; 5414
1Sa 11:2 l. it for a reproach upon all Israel....... 7760
1Sa 19:24 l. down naked all that day and all 5307
1Sa 26:5 beheld the place where Saul l.,.......... 7901
1Sa 26:5 Saul l. in the trench, and the people. .. 7901
1Sa 26:7 Saul l. sleeping within the trench,........ 7901
1Sa 26:7 and the people l. round about him. 7901
2Sa 2:21 and l. thee hold on one of the young.........
2Sa 4:5 who l. on a bed at noon.................... 7901
2Sa 4:7 l. on his bed in his bedchamber, ... 7901
2Sa 11:4 in unto him, and he l. with her; 7901
2Sa 12:3 his own cup, and l. in his bosom, ... 7901
2Sa 12:16 and l. all night upon the earth............ 7901
2Sa 12:24 went in unto her, and l. with her: 7901
2Sa 13:5 L. thee down on thy bed, and make ... 7901
2Sa 13:6 Amnon l. down, and made himself...... 7901
2Sa 13:14 than she, forced her, and l. with her... 7901
2Sa 13:31 his garments, and l. on the earth; 7901
2Sa 19:32 while he l. at Mahanaim; for he 7871
1Ki 5:17 to l. the foundation of the house..............
1Ki 7:3 l. on forty-five pillars, fifteen in a row. ......
1Ki 13:4 the altar, saying, L. hold on him. ....
1Ki 13:31 l. my bones beside his bones: 3241
1Ki 18:23 cut it in pieces, and l. it on wood,...... 7760
1Ki 18:23 other bullock, and l. it on wood, ... 7760
1Ki 19:5 l. and slept under a juniper tree,........ 7901
1Ki 21:27 fasted, and l. in sackcloth, and........... 7901
2Ki 4:11 into the chamber, and l. there. 7901
2Ki 4:29 l. my staff upon the face of the.......... 7760
2Ki 4:34 he went up, and l. upon the child,....... 7901
2Ki 9:16 went to Jezreel; for Joram l. there. 7901
2Ki 10:8 L. ye them in two heaps at the 7760
2Ki 19:25 l. waste fenced cities into ruinous............
2Ch 31:7 l. the foundation of the heaps, ...
2Ch 36:21 as long as she l. desolate she kept...........
Ezr 8:31 of such as l. in wait by the way. ....
Ne 13:21 do so again, I will l. hands on you...... 7971
Es 2:21 sought to l. hand on the king............ 7971
Es 3:6 scorn to l. hands on Mordecai alone;... 7971
Es 4:3 many l. in sackcloth and ashes.......... 3331
Es 6:2 who sought to l. hand on the king........ 7971
Es 9:2 to l. hand on such as sought their 7971
Job 9:33 might l. his hand upon us both........... 7896
Job 17:3 L. down now, put me in a surety....... 7760
Job 21:5 l. your hand upon your mouth. 7760
Job 22:22 and l. up his words in thine heart...... 7760
Job 22:24 Then shalt thou l. up gold as dust, ... 7896
Job 29:19 dew l. all night upon my branch. 3885
Job 34:23 he will not l. upon man more than...... 7760
Job 40:4 I will l. mine hand upon my mouth. 7760
Job 41:8 L. thine hand upon him, remember..... 7760
Ps 4:8 I will both l. me down in peace,......... 7901
Ps 7:5 and l. mine honour in the dust........... 7931
Ps 38:12 that seek after my life l. snares...............
Ps 71:10 they that l. wait for my soul take............
Ps 84:3 where she may l. her young, ... 7896
Ps 104:22 and l. them down in their dens. 7257
Pr 1:11 with us, let us l. wait for blood,..............
Pr 1:18 they l. wait for their own blood;..............
Pr 3:18 life to them that l. hold upon her:.............
Pr 7:1 l. up my commandments with thee. 6845
Pr 10:14 Wise men l. up knowledge: but the 6845
Pr 24:15 L. not wait, O wicked man, against ....
Pr 30:32 evil, l. thine hand upon thy mouth. ....
Ec 2:3 and to l. hold on folly, till I might see ......
Ec 7:2 the living will l. it to his heart. 5414
Isa 5:6 And I will l. it waste: it shall not be..........
Isa 5:8 that l. field to field, till there be no..... 7126
Isa 5:29 shall roar, and l. hold of the prey, ...
Isa 11:14 they shall l. their hand upon Edom..... 7971
Isa 13:9 anger, to l. the land desolate:..................
Isa 13:11 will l. low the haughtiness of the...........
Isa 22:22 key...will I l. upon his shoulder;......... 5414
Isa 25:12 walls shall he bring down, l. low, ...
Isa 28:16 l. in Zion for a foundation a stone,...........
Isa 28:17 Judgment also will I l. to the line, ... 7760
Isa 29:3 l. siege against thee with a mount, ...
Isa 29:21 l. a snare for him that reproveth in...........
Isa 30:32 which the Lord shall l. upon him, ... 5117
Isa 34:15 great owl make her nest, and l.,........ 4422
Isa 35:7 where each l., shall be grass with...... 7258
Isa 37:26 l. waste defenced cities into ruinous..........
Isa 38:21 and l. it for a plaister upon the boil,..........
Isa 47:7 didst not l....things to thy heart, ... 7760
Isa 51:16 and l. the foundations of the earth, ...
Isa 54:11 will l. thy stones with fair colours,...... 7257
Isa 54:11 and l. thy foundations with sapphires.........
Jer 5:26 l. wait, as he that setteth snares;..............
Jer 6:21 will l. stumblingblocks before............ 5414
Jer 6:23 shall l. hold on bow and spear: ....
Eze 3:20 I l. a stumblingblock before him, ... 5414
Eze 4:1 thee a tile, and l. it before thee,........ 5414
Eze 4:2 l. siege against it, and build a fort 5414
Eze 4:3 and thou shalt l. siege against it..............
Eze 4:4 l. the iniquity of the house of........... 7760
Eze 4:8 behold, I will l. bands upon thee, ...
Eze 6:5 I will l. the dead carcases of the........ 5414
Eze 19:2 lioness: she l. down among lions, ... 7257
Eze 23:8 for in her youth they l. with her, ... 7901
Eze 25:14 will l. my vengeance upon Edom........ 5414
Eze 25:17 when I shall l. my vengeance upon..... 5414
Eze 26:12 they shall l. thy stones and thy.......... 7760
Eze 26:16 l. away their robes, and put off.......... 5493
Eze 28:17 I will l. thee before kings, that.......... 5414
Eze 32:5 will l. thy flesh upon the mountains,.... 5414
Eze 33:28 I will l. the land most desolate,.......... 5414
Eze 35:4 I will l. thy cities waste, and thou 7760
Eze 36:29 it, and l. no famine upon you............ 5414
Eze 36:34 whereas it l. desolate in the sight of.........
Eze 37:6 I will l. sinews upon you, and will 5414
Eze 42:13 shall they l. the most holy things, ... 3241
Eze 42:14 there they shall l. their garments 3241
Eze 44:19 l. them in the holy chambers,and 3241
Am 2:8 they l. themselves down upon 5186
Jon 1:5 and he l., and was fast asleep. 7901
Jon 1:14 and l. not upon us innocent blood: 5414
Mic 1:7 the idols thereof will I l. desolate: 7760
Mic 7:16 l. their hand upon their mouth, ... 7760
Zec 14:13 they shall l. hold every one on.................
Mal 2:2 and if ye will not l. it to heart, ... 7760
Mal 2:2 because ye do not l. it to heart. 7760
Mt 6:19 **L. not up for yourselves treasures**.......
Mt 6:20 **l. up for yourselves treasures in**..........
Mt 8:20 **man hath not where to l. his head**..*2827*
Mt 9:18 come and l. thy hand upon her, ... *2007*
Mt 12:11 **will he not l. hold on it, and lift it**.....
Mt 21:46 they sought to l. hands on him, ...
Mt 23:4 **and l. them on men's shoulders;**.... *2007*
Mt 28:6 see the place where the Lord l.......... *2749*
Mk 1:30 Simon's wife's mother l. sick of a....... *2621*
Mk 2:4 bed wherein the sick of the palsy l.... *2621*
Mk 3:21 it, they went out to l. hold on him:.........
Mk 5:23 come and l. thy hands on her, that......... *2007*
Mk 12:12 And they sought to l. hold on him, ...
Mk 15:7 one named Barabbas, which l. bound.........
Mk 16:18 **they shall l. hands on the sick,**..... *2007*
Lu 5:18 him in, and to l. him before him.......... *5087*
Lu 5:25 and took up that whereon he l.,......... *2621*
Lu 8:42 years of age, and she l. a dying..............
Lu 9:58 **man hath not where to l. his head**..*2827*
Lu 19:44 **shall l. thee even with the ground,**.. *1474*
Lu 20:19 hour sought to l. hands on him;......... *1911*
Lu 21:12 **they shall l. their hands on you,**... *1911*
Joh 5:3 l. a great multitude of impotent.......... *2621*
Joh 10:15 **and I l. down my life for the**.......... *5087*
Joh 10:17 **love me, because I l. down my life,** *5087*
Joh 10:18 **from me, but I l. it down of**.......... *5087*
Joh 10:18 **I have power to l. it down, and I**... *5087*
Joh 11:38 was a cave, and a stone l. upon it...... *1945*
Joh 13:37 I will l. down my life for thy sake. *5087*
Joh 13:38 **Wilt thou l. down thy life for my**.. *5087*
Joh 15:13 **man l. down his life for his**.......... *5087*
Ac 7:60 l. not this sin to their charge............. *2476*
Ac 8:19 that on whomsoever I l. hands, ... *2007*
Ac 15:28 to l. upon you no greater burden *2007*
Ac 27:20 and no small tempest l. on us, all....... *1945*
Ac 28:8 father of Publius l. sick of a fever *2621*
Ro 8:33 Who shall l. any thing to the charge.... *1458*
Ro 9:33 I l. in Sion a stumblingstone and *5087*
1Co 3:11 other foundation can no man l............ *5087*
1Co 16:2 every one of you l. by him in store, ... *5087*
2Co 12:14 ought not to l. up for the parents,...... *2343*
1Ti 5:22 L. hands suddenly on no man,........... *2007*
1Ti 6:12 of faith, l. hold on eternal life, ... *1949*
1Ti 6:19 they may l. hold on eternal life........... *1949*
Heb 6:18 to l. hold upon the hope set before us:.......
Heb 12:1 let us l. aside every weight, and the *659*
Jas 1:21 Wherefore l. apart all filthiness........... *659*
1Pe 2:6 I l. in Sion a chief corner stone, ... *5087*
1Jo 3:16 we ought to l. down our lives for....... *5087*

LAYEDST See also LAIDST.

Lu 19:21 **takest up that thou l. not down,** .. *5087*

LAYEST

Nu 11:11 l. the burden of all this people........... 7760
1Sa 28:9 then l. thou a snare for my life, to ....

LAYETH

Job 21:19 God l. up his iniquity for his............ 6845
Job 24:12 out: yet God l. not folly to them. 7760
Job 41:26 sword of him that l. at him cannot...... 5381
Ps 33:7 he l. up the depth in storehouses. 5414
Ps 104:3 Who l. the beams of his chambers...... 7760
Pr 2:7 He l. up sound wisdom for the 6845
Pr 13:16 but a fool l. open his folly.......................
Pr 26:24 lips, and l. up deceit within him; 7896
Pr 31:19 She l. her hands to the spindle, ... 7971
Isa 26:5 high; the lofty city, he l. it low; ....
Isa 26:5 he l. it low, even to the ground;..............
Isa 56:2 the son of man that l. hold on it;.............

- Isa 57:1 and no man l. it to heart: and 7760
- Jer 9:8 mouth, but in heart he l. his wait 7760
- Jer 12:11 because no man l. it to heart 7760
- Zec 12:1 l. the foundation of the earth, and
- Lu 12:21 **he that l. up treasure for himself,**
- Lu 15:5 **found it, he l. it on his shoulders,** *2007*

LAYING See also OVERLAYING.
- Nu 35:20 or hurl at him by l. of wait, that
- Nu 35:22 him any thing without l. of wait,
- Ps 64:5 they commune of l. snares privily; 2934
- Mr 7:8 **l. aside the commandment of God,** *863*
- Lu 11:54 L. wait for him, and seeking to *1748*
- Ac 8:18 through l. on of the apostles' hands *1936*
- Ac 9:24 their l. await was known of Saul. *1917*
- Ac 25:3 l. wait in the way to kill him. *4160*
- 1Ti 4:14 with the l. on of the hands of the *1936*
- 1Ti 6:19 L. up in store for themselves a good *597*
- Heb 6:1 not l. again the foundation of *2598*
- Heb 6:2 baptisms, and of l. on of hands, *1936*
- 1Pe 2:1 l. aside all malice, and all guile, *659*

LAZARUS (laz'-a-rus)
- Lu 16:20 **was a certain beggar named L.,** *2976*
- Lu 16:23 **afar off, and L. in his bosom.** *2976*
- Lu 16:24 **have mercy on me, and send L.,** *2976*
- Lu 16:25 **things, and likewise L. evil things:** *2976*
- Joh 11:1 a certain man was sick, named L., *2976*
- Joh 11:2 her hair, whose brother L. was sick.) *2976*
- Joh 11:5 Martha, and her sister, and L. *2976*
- Joh 11:11 unto them, **Our friend L. sleepeth;** *2976*
- Joh 11:14 unto them plainly, **L. is dead.** *2976*
- Joh 11:43 with a loud voice, **L., come forth.** *2976*
- Joh 12:1 where L. was which had been dead, *2976*
- Joh 12:2 L. was one of them that sat at the *2976*
- Joh 12:9 might see L. also, whom he had *2976*
- Joh 12:10 they might put L. also to death; *2976*
- Joh 12:17 when he called L. out of his grave, *2976*

LEACH See HORSELEACH.

LEAD See also LEADEST; LEADETH; LED.
- Ge 33:14 I will l. on softly, according as the 5095
- Ex 13:21 of a cloud, to l. them the way; 5148
- Ex 15:10 sank as l. in the mighty waters 5777
- Ex 32:34 l. the people unto the place of 5148
- Nu 27:17 which may l. them out, and which 3318
- Nu 31:22 brass, the iron, the tin, and the l., 5777
- De 4:27 whither the Lord shall l. you. 5090
- De 20:9 of the armies to l. the people 7218
- De 28:37 whither the Lord shall l. thee. 5090
- De 32:12 the Lord alone did l. him, and 5148
- Jg 5:12 and l. thy captivity captive, thou
- 1Sa 30:22 that they may l. them away, and 5090
- 2Ch 30:9 before them that l. them captive,
- Ne 9:19 by day, to l. them in the way; 5148
- Job 19:24 graven with an iron pen and l. 5777
- Ps 5:8 L. me, O Lord, in thy righteousness 5148
- Ps 25:5 L. me in thy truth, and teach me: 1869
- Ps 27:11 l. me in a plain path, because of 5148
- Ps 31:3 name's sake l. me, and guide me. 5148
- Ps 43:3 let them l. me; let them bring me 5148
- Ps 60:9 city? who will l. me into Edom? 5148
- Ps 61:2 l. me to the rock that is higher 5148
- Ps 108:10 city? who will l. me into Edom? 5148
- Ps 125:5 Lord shall l. them forth with the 3212
- Ps 139:10 Even there shall thy hand l. me, 5148
- Ps 139:24 and l. me in the way everlasting. 5148
- Ps 143:10 l. me into the land of uprightness. 5148
- Pr 6:22 When thou goest, it shall l. thee; 5148
- Pr 8:20 I l. in the way of righteousness, 1980
- Ca 8:2 I would l. thee, and bring thee 5090
- Isa 3:12 they which l. thee cause thee to err, 833
- Isa 11:6 and a little child shall l. them. 5090
- Isa 20:4 of Assyria l. away the Egyptians 5090
- Isa 40:11 shall gently l. those that are with 5095
- Isa 42:16 l. them in paths that they have not 1869
- Isa 49:10 hath mercy on them shall l. them, 5090
- Isa 57:18 I will l. him also, and restore 5148
- Isa 63:14 so didst thou l. thy people, to make 5090
- Jer 6:29 the l. is consumed of the fire; 5777
- Jer 31:9 with supplications will I l. them: 2986
- Jer 32:5 he shall l. Zedekiah to Babylon, 3212
- Eze 22:18 brass, and tin, and iron, and l., 5777
- Eze 22:20 silver, and brass, and iron, and l., 5777
- Eze 27:12 silver, iron, tin, and l., they 5777
- Na 2:7 maids shall l. her as with the voice 5090
- Zec 5:7 there was lifted up a talent of l.: 5777
- Zec 5:8 the weight of l. upon the mouth 5777
- Mt 6:13 **And l. us not into temptation, but** *1533*
- Mt 15:14 **if the blind l. the blind, both shall** *3594*
- Mk 13:11 **when they shall l. you, and deliver** *71*
- Mk 14:44 take him, and l. him away safely *520*
- Lu 6:39 them, **Can the blind l. the blind?** *3594*
- Lu 11:4 **And l. us not into temptation; but** *1533*
- Lu 13:15 **stall, and l. him away to watering?** *520*
- Ac 13:11 seeking some to l. him by the hand. *5497*
- 1Co 9:5 we not power to l. about a sister, *4013*
- 1Ti 2:2 may l. a quiet and peaceable life *1236*
- 2Ti 3:6 l. captive silly women laden with *162*
- Heb 8:9 to l. them out of the land of Egypt; *1806*
- Re 7:17 shall l. them unto living fountains *3594*

LEADER See also LEADERS; RINGLEADER.
- 1Ch 12:27 was the l. of the Aaronites, and 5057
- 1Ch 13:1 and hundreds, and with every l. 5057
- Isa 55:4 a l. and commander to the people. 5057

LEADERS
- 2Ch 32:21 the l. and captains in the camp of 5057
- Isa 9:16 the l. of this people cause them to 833
- Mt 15:14 **alone: they be blind l. of the blind.** *3595*

LEADEST
- Ps 80:1 thou that l. Joseph like a flock; 5090

LEADETH
- 1Sa 13:17 turned unto the way that l. to Ophrah,
- Job 12:17 He l. counsellors away spoiled, 3212
- Job 12:19 He l. princes away spoiled, and 3212
- Ps 23:2 he l. me beside the still waters 5095
- Pr 16:29 l....into the way that is not good. 3212
- Isa 48:17 which l. thee by the way that thou 1869
- Mt 7:13 **is the way, that l. to destruction,** *520*
- Mt 7:14 **narrow is the way, which l. unto** *520*
- Mk 9:2 l. them up into an high mountain *399*
- Joh 10:3 **sheep by name, and l. them out.** *1806*
- Ac 12:10 the iron gate that l. unto the city; *5342*
- Ro 2:4 of God l. thee to repentance? *71*
- Re 13:10 He that l. into captivity shall go *4863*

LEAF See also LEAVED; LEAVES.
- Ge 8:11 lo, in her mouth was an olive l. 5929
- Le 26:36 the sound of a shaken l. shall chase 5929
- Job 13:25 thou break a l. driven to and fro? 5929
- Ps 1:3 his l. also shall not wither; and 5929
- Isa 1:30 shall be as an oak whose l. fadeth, 5929
- Isa 34:4 as the l. falleth off from the vine, 5929
- Isa 64:6 rags; and we all do fade as a l.: 5929
- Jer 8:13 on the fig tree, and the l. shall fade; 5929
- Jer 17:8 cometh, but her l. shall be green; 5929
- Eze 47:12 whose l. shall not fade, neither shall 5929
- Eze 47:12 and the l. thereof for medicine 5929

LEAGUE
- Jos 9:6 therefore make ye a l. with us. 1285
- Jos 9:7 how shall we make a l. with you? 1285
- Jos 9:11 therefore now make ye a l. with us. 1285
- Jos 9:15 them, and made a l. with them, 1285
- Jos 9:16 after they had made a l. with them, 1285
- Jg 2:2 make no l. with the inhabitants of 1285
- 1Sa 22:8 made a l. with the son of Jesse, 3772
- 2Sa 3:12 Make thy l. with me, and, behold, 1285
- 2Sa 3:13 Well; I will make a l. with thee: 1285
- 2Sa 3:21 that they may make a l. with thee, 1285
- 2Sa 5:3 king David made a l. with them in 1285
- 1Ki 5:12 and they two made a l. together. 1285
- 1Ki 15:19 There is a l. between me and thee, 1285
- 1Ki 15:19 break thy l. with Baasha king of 1285
- 2Ch 16:3 There is a l. between me and thee, 1285
- 2Ch 16:3 break thy l. with Baasha king of 1285
- Job 5:23 thou shalt be in l. with the stones 1285
- Eze 30:5 and the men of the land that is in l., 1285
- Da 11:23 after the l. made with him he shall 2266

LEAH (le'-ah) See also LEAH'S.
- Ge 29:16 the name of the elder was L., and 3812
- Ge 29:17 L. was tender eyed; but Rachel 3812
- Ge 29:23 that he took L. his daughter, and 3812
- Ge 29:24 gave unto his daughter L. Zilpah 3812
- Ge 29:25 in the morning, behold, it was L.: 3812
- Ge 29:30 he loved also Rachel more than L., 3812
- Ge 29:31 the Lord saw that L. was hated, he 3812
- Ge 29:32 And L. conceived, and bare a son, 3812
- Ge 30:9 L. saw that she had left bearing, 3812
- Ge 30:11 L. said, A troop cometh: and she 3812
- Ge 30:13 And L. said, Happy am I, for the 3812
- Ge 30:14 brought them unto his mother L. 3812
- Ge 30:14 Rachel said to L., Give me, I pray 3812
- Ge 30:16 and l. went out to meet him, and 3812
- Ge 30:17 God hearkened unto L., and she 3812
- Ge 30:18 L. said, God hath given me my 3812
- Ge 30:19 L. conceived again, and bare Jacob 3812
- Ge 30:20 L. said, God hath endued me with 3812
- Ge 31:4 Jacob sent and called Rachel and L. 3812
- Ge 31:14 Rachel and L. answered and said 3812
- Ge 33:1 he divided the children unto L., 3812
- Ge 33:2 and L. and her children after, and 3812
- Ge 33:7 And L. also with her children came 3812
- Ge 34:1 Dinah the daughter of L., which 3812
- Ge 35:23 The sons of L.; Reuben, Jacob's 3812
- Ge 46:15 These be the sons of L., which she 3812
- Ge 46:18 Laban gave to L. his daughter, 3812
- Ge 49:31 his wife; and there I buried L. 3812
- Ru 4:11 house like Rachel and like L., 3812

LEAH'S (le'-ahs)
- Ge 30:10 Zilpah L. maid bare Jacob a son. 3812
- Ge 30:12 Zilpah L. maid bare Jacob a second 3812
- Ge 31:33 into Jacob's tent, and into L. tent, 3812
- Ge 31:33 went he out of L. tent, and entered 3812
- Ge 35:26 the sons of Zilpah, L. handmaid; 3812

LEAN See also LEANED; LEANETH; LEANFLESHED; LEANING.
- Ge 41:20 l. and the ill favoured kine did eat 7534
- Nu 13:20 the land is, whether it be fat or l., 7330
- Jg 16:26 standeth, that I may l. upon them. 8172
- 2Sa 13:4 the king's son, l. from day to day? 1800
- 2Ki 18:21 on which if a man l., it will go into 5564
- Job 8:15 He shall l. upon his house, but it 8172
- Pro 3:5 l. not unto thine...understanding 8172
- Isa 17:4 fatness of his flesh shall wax l. 7329
- Isa 36:6 whereon if a man l., it will go into 5564
- Eze 34:20 fat cattle and between the l. cattle. 7330
- Mic 3:11 yet will they l. upon the Lord, and 8172

LEANED
- 2Sa 1:6 behold Saul l. upon his spear; 8172
- 2Ki 7:2 a lord on whose hand the king l. 8172
- 2Ki 7:17 the lord on whose hand he l. to have 8172
- Eze 29:7 and when they l. upon thee, thou 8172
- Am 5:19 house, and l. his hand on the wall, 5564
- Joh 21:20 also l. on his breast at supper, *377*

LEANETH
- 2Sa 3:29 or that l. on a staff, or that falleth 2388
- 2Ki 5:18 and he l. on my hand, and I bow 8127

LEANFLESHED
- Ge 41:3 the river, ill favoured and l.; 1851,1320
- Ge 41:4 ill favoured and l. kine did eat 1851,1320
- Ge 41:19 poor and very ill favoured and l., 7534

LEANING
- Ca 8:5 wilderness, l. upon her beloved? 7514
- Joh 13:23 therewas l. on Jesus' bosom one *345*
- Heb 11:21 worshipped, l. upon the top of his staff

LEANNESS
- Job 16:8 and my l. rising up in me beareth 3585
- Ps 106:15 request but sent l. into their soul. 7332
- Isa 10:16 hosts, send among his fat ones l.; 7332
- Isa 24:16 I said, My l., my l., woe unto me! 7334

LEANNOTH (le-an'-noth)
- Ps 88:*title* Musician upon Mahalath L., 6030

LEAP See also LEAPED; LEAPING.
- Ge 31:12 the rams which l. upon the cattle 5927
- Le 11:21 feet, to l. withal upon the earth; 5425
- De 33:22 whelp: he shall l. from Bashan. 2178
- Job 41:19 lamps, and sparks of fire l. out. 4422
- Ps 68:16 Why l. ye, ye high hills? this is 7520
- Isa 35:6 Then shall the lamp man l. as an 1801
- Joe 2:5 the tops of mountains shall they l., 7540
- Zep 1:9 all those that l. on the threshold, 1801
- Lu 6:23 **ye in that day, and l. for joy:** *4640*

LEAPED
- Ge 31:10 the rams which l. upon the cattle 5927
- 2Sa 22:30 by my God have I l. over a wall. 1801
- 1Ki 18:26 they l. upon the altar which was 6452
- Ps 18:29 by my God have I l. over a wall. 1801
- Lu 1:41 of Mary, the babe l. in her womb; *4640*
- Lu 1:44 the babe l. in my womb for joy. *4640*
- Ac 14:10 on thy feet. And he l. and walked. *242*
- Ac 19:16 the evil spirit was l. on them, and *2177*

LEAPING
- 2Sa 6:16 David l. and dancing before the 6339
- Ca 2:8 he cometh l. upon the mountains, 1801

Ac 3:8 And he l. up stood, and walked, ... *1814*
Ac 3:8 walking, and l., and praising God. *242*

LEARN See also LEARNED; LEARNING.
De 4:10 that they may l. to fear me all the...... 3925
De 5:1 that ye may l. them, and keep, and..... 3925
De 14:23 mayest l. to fear the Lord thy God..... 3925
De 17:19 he may l. to fear the Lord his God,.... 3925
De 18:9 not l. to do after the abominations...... 3925
De 31:12 that they may l., and fear the Lord 3925
De 31:13 and l. to fear the Lord your God, as... 3925
Ps 119:71 that I might l. thy statutes................ 3925
Ps 119:73 that I may l. thy commandments......... 3925
Pr 22:25 Lest thou l. his ways, and get a.......... 502
Isa 1:17 L. to do well; seek judgment, ... 3925
Isa 2:4 neither shall they l. war any more...... 3925
Isa 26:9 of the world will l. righteousness........ 3925
Isa 26:10 yet will he not l. righteousness:......... 3925
Isa 29:24 that murmured shall l. doctrine.......... 3925
Jer 10:2 Lord, L. not the way of the heathen,.. 3925
Jer 12:16 diligently l. the ways of my people, ... 3925
Mic 4:3 neither shall they l. war any more....... 3925
Mt 9:13 **go ye and l. what that meaneth,**.... *3129*
Mt 11:29 **my yoke upon you, and l. of me;**... *3129*
Mt 24:32 **Now l. a parable of the fig tree;**.... *3129*
Mk 13:28 **Now l. a parable of the fig tree;**.... *3129*
1Co 4:6 might l. in us not to think of men....... *3129*
1Co 14:31 one by one, that all may l., and all...... *3129*
1Co 14:35 And if they will l. any thing, let *3129*
Ga 3:2 This only would I l. of you,............... *3129*
1Ti 1:20 they may l. not to blaspheme............ *3811*
1Ti 2:11 Let the woman l. in silence with *3129*
1Ti 5:4 them l. first to shew piety at home, ... *3129*
1Ti 5:13 withal they l. to be idle, wandering..... *3129*
Tit 3:14 also l. to maintain good works for *3129*
Re 14:3 no man could l. that song but the....... *3129*

LEARNED See also UNLEARNED.
Ge 30:27 I have l. by exerience that the 5172
Ps 106:35 the heathen, and l. their works.......... 3925
Ps 119:7 have l. thy righteous judgments.......... 3925
Pr 30:3 I neither l. wisdom, nor have the....... 3925
Isa 29:11 men deliver to one that is l.,....... 3045,5612
Isa 29:12 delivered to him that is not l.,..... 3045,5612
Isa 29:12 thee: and he saith, I am not l...... 3045,5612
Isa 50:4 given me the tongue of the l.,........... 3928
Isa 50:4 mine ear to hear as the l.................. 3928
Eze 19:3 lion and it l. to catch the prey;........... 3925
Eze 19:6 young lion, and l. to catch the prey, ... 3925
Joh 6:45 **heard, and hath l. of the Father,**... *3129*
Joh 7:15 this man letters,having never l.? *3129*
Ac 7:22 Moses was l. in all the wisdom.......... *3811*
Ro 16:17 to the doctrine which ye have l.;......... *3129*
Eph 4:20 But ye have not so l. Christ;.............. *3129*
Php 4:9 things, which ye have both l., and....... *3129*
Php 4:11 for I have l., in whatsoever state I...... *3129*
Col 1:7 As ye also l. of Epaphras our dear *3129*
2Ti 3:14 in the things which thou hast l. and *3129*
2Ti 3:14 knowing of whom thou hast l. them;... *3129*
Heb 5:8 yet l. he obedience by the things *3129*

LEARNING
Pr 1:5 will hear, and will increase l.;............ 3948
Pr 9:9 just man, and he will increase in l.. 3948
Pr 16:21 sweetness of the lips increaseth l........ 3948
Pr 16:23 his mouth, and addeth l. to his lips..... 3948
Da 1:4 whom they might teach the l. and 5612
Da 1:17 them knowledge and skill in all l......... 5612
Ac 26:24 much l. doth make thee mad.......... *1121*
Ro 15:4 aforetime were written for our l.,........ *1319*
2Ti 3:7 Ever l., and never able to come to..... *3129*

LEASING See also LYING.
Ps 4:2 ye love vanity, and seek after l.? 3577
Ps 5:6 shalt destroy them that speak l.:......... 3577

LEAST
Ge 24:55 with us a few days, at the l. ten;......... 176
Ge 32:10 worthy of the l. of all the mercies, ... 6994
Nu 11:32 gathered l. gathered ten homers:....... 4591
Jg 3:2 at the l. such as before knew........... 7535
Jg 6:15 I am the l. in my father's house......... 6810
1Sa 9:21 my family the l. of all the families....... 6810
1Sa 21:4 kept themselves at l. from women........ 389
2Ki 18:24 of the l. of my master's servants, ... 6996
1Ch 12:14 one of the l. was over an hundred,..... 6996
Isa 36:9 of the l. of my master's servants, ... 6996
Jer 6:13 l. of them even unto the greatest....... 6996
Jer 8:10 from the l. even unto the greatest...... 6996
Jer 31:34 the l. of them unto the greatest......... 6996
Jer 42:1 from the l. even unto the greatest,..... 6996
Jer 42:8 from the l. even to the greatest,........ 6996
Jer 44:12 from the l. even unto the greatest,..... 6996
Jer 49:20 the l. of the flock shall draw them...... 6810
Jer 50:45 the l. of the flock shall draw them...... 6810
Am 9:9 not the l. grain fall upon the earth. ....
Jon 3:5 of them even to the l. of them. 6996
Mt 2:6 the l. among the princes of Juda: *1646*
Mt 5:19 **one of these l. commandments,** *1646*
Mt 5:19 **the l. in the kingdom of heaven:** ... *1646*
Mt 11:11 **is l. in the kingdom of heaven is** ... *3398*
Mt 13:32 **Which indeed is the l. of all seeds:** .*3398*
Mt 25:40 **one of the l. of these my brethren,** .*1646*
Mt 25:45 **did it not to one of the l. of these,** .*1646*
Lu 7:28 **that is l. in the kingdom of God**.... *3398*
Lu 9:48 **for he that is l. among you all, the** *3398*
Lu 12:26 **able to do that thing which is l.,**... *1646*
Lu 16:10 **that is faithful in that which is l.**.. *1646*
Lu 16:10 **he that is unjust in the l. is unjust**.*1646*
Lu 19:42 **even thou, at l. in this thy day,**..... *2534*
Ac 5:15 that at the l. the shadow of Peter *2579*
Ac 8:10 heed, from the l. to the greatest,....... *3398*
1Co 6:4 to judge who are l. esteemed............ *1848*
1Co 15:9 I am the l. of the apostles, that am *1646*
Eph 3:8 who am less than the l. of all saints,... *1647*
Heb 8:11 me, from the l. to the greatest.......... *3398*

LEATHER
2Ki 1:8 with a girdle of l. about his loins. 5785

LEATHERN
Mt 3:4 and a l. girdle about his loins;............ *1193*

LEAVE See also LEAVETH; LEAVING; LEFT.
Ge 2:24 man l. his father and his mother, ... 5800
Ge 28:15 I will not l. thee, until I have done..... 5800
Ge 33:15 now l. with thee some of the folk...... 3322
Ge 42:33 l. one of your brethren here with....... 3241
Ge 44:22 The lad cannot l. his father: 5800
Ge 44:22 for if he should l. his father, his......... 5800
Ex 16:19 Let no man l. of it till the morning. 3498
Ex 23:11 what they l. the beasts...shall eat....... 3499
Le 7:15 not l. any of it until the morning. 3241
Le 16:23 holy place, and shall l. them there:..... 3241
Le 19:10 l. them for the poor and stranger:...... 5800
Le 22:30 l. none of it until the morrow: 3498
Le 23:22 thou shalt l. them unto the poor, ... 5800
Nu 9:12 l. none of it unto the morning,.......... 7604
Nu 10:31 he said, L. us not, I pray thee; 5800
Nu 22:13 Lord refuseth to give me l. to go....... 5414
Nu 32:15 again l. them in the wilderness; 3241
De 28:51 shall not l. thee either corn, wine,....... 7604
De 28:54 of his children which he shall l.: 3498
Jos 4:3 and l. them in the lodging place, ... 3241
Jg 9:9 unto them, Should I l. my fatness, ... 2308
Jg 9:13 unto them, Should I l. my wine, ... 2308
Ru 1:16 said, Intreat me not to l. thee, or 5800
Ru 2:16 l. them, that she may glean them,...... 5800
1Sa 9:5 my father l. caring for the asses, ... 2308
1Sa 14:36 and let us not l. a man of them.......... 7604
1Sa 20:6 asked l. of me that he might run..........
1Sa 20:28 asked l. of me to go to Beth-lehem: ....
1Sa 25:22 if I l. of all that pertain to him........... 7604
2Sa 14:7 not l. to my husband neither name 7604
1Ki 8:57 let him not l. us, nor forsake us: 5800
2Ki 2:2,4,6 soul liveth, I will not l. thee............ 5800
2Ki 4:30 as thy soul liveth, I will not l. thee..... 5800
2Ki 4:43 They shall eat, and shall l. thereof...... 3498
2Ki 13:7 he l. of the people to Jehoahaz 7604
1Ch 28:8 l. it for an inheritance for your 5157
Ezr 9:8 l. us a remnant to escape, and to....... 7604
Ezr 9:12 l. it for an inheritance to your..................
Ne 5:10 I pray you, let us l. off this usury. 5800
Ne 6:3 the work cease, whilst I l. it,............ 7503
Ne 10:31 we would l. the seventh year, ... 5203
Ne 13:6 days obtained I l. of the king:........... 7592
Job 9:27 I will l. off my heaviness, and............ 5800
Job 10:1 l. my complaint upon myself;............. 5800
Job 39:11 or wilt thou l. thy labour to him? 5800
Ps 16:10 thou wilt not l. my soul in hell;........... 5800
Ps 17:14 l. the rest of their substance to 3241
Ps 27:9 l. me not, neither forsake me, O 5203
Ps 37:33 Lord will not l. him in his hand,......... 5800
Ps 49:10 perish, and l. their wealth to others.... 5800
Ps 119:121 l. me not to mine oppressors. 3241
Ps 141:8 trust; l. not my soul destitute........... 6168
Pr 2:13 Who l. the paths of uprightness, ... 5800
Pr 17:14 therefore l. off contention, before....... 5203
Ec 2:18 l. it unto the man that shall be........... 3241
Ec 2:21 shall he l. it for his portion. 5414
Ec 10:4 up against thee, l. not thy place;........ 3241
Isa 10:3 and where will ye l. your glory?......... 5800
Isa 65:15 l. your name for a curse unto my....... 3241
Jer 9:2 that I might l. my people, and go....... 5800
Jer 14:9 are called by thy name; l. us not........ 3241
Jer 17:11 shall l. them in the midst of his 5800
Jer 18:14 a man l. the snow of Lebanon........... 5800
Jer 30:11 not l. thee altogether unpunished. ....
Jer 44:7 Judah, to l. you none to remain; 3498
Jer 46:28 I not l. thee wholly unpunished. ....
Jer 48:28 in Moab, l. the cities, and dwell......... 5800
Jer 49:9 they not l. some gleaning grapes? 7604
Jer 49:11 L. thy fatherless children, I will......... 5800
Eze 6:8 Yet will I l. a remnant, that ye may.... 3498
Eze 12:16 I will l. a few men of them from 3498
Eze 16:39 and l. thee naked and bare................ 3241
Eze 22:20 I will l. you there, and melt you. 3241
Eze 23:29 and shall l. thee naked and bare:........ 5800
Eze 29:5 l. thee thrown into the wilderness, ... 5203
Eze 32:4 Then will I l. thee upon the land, I...... 5203
Eze 39:2 and l. but the sixth part of thee, ... 8338
Da 4:15 l. the stump of his roots in the.......... 7662
Da 4:23 l. the stump of the roots thereof in 7662
Da 4:26 to l. the stump of the tree roots; 7662
Ho 12:14 shall he l. his blood upon him, ... 5203
Joe 2:14 and l. a blessing behind him; 7604
Am 5:3 by a thousand shall l. an hundred, ... 7604
Am 5:3 forth by an hundred shall l. ten,......... 7604
Am 5:7 l. off righteousness in the earth, ... 3241
Ob 5 would they not l. some grapes? 7604
Zep 3:12 l. in the midst of thee an afflicted....... 7604
Mal 4:1 l. them neither root nor branch.......... 5800
Mt 5:24 **L. there thy gift before the altar,** ... *863*
Mt 18:12 **doth he not l. the ninety and nine,** ..*863*
Mt 19:5 **shall a man l. father and mother,**.. *2641*
Mt 23:23 **and not to l. the other undone**........ *863*
Mk 5:13 And forthwith Jesus gave them l.. ..... *2010*
Mk 10:7 **a man l. his father and mother,** *2641*
Mk 12:19 die, and l. his wife behind him,.......... *2641*
Mk 12:19 and l. no children, that his brother........ *863*
Lu 11:42 **and not to l. the other undone**........ *863*
Lu 15:4 **doth not l. the ninety and nine in** ..*2641*
Lu 19:44 **shall not l. in thee one stone upon**.. *863*
Joh 14:18 **I will not l. you comfortless: I will** . *863*
Joh 14:27 **Peace I l. with you, my peace I give** *863*
Joh 16:28 **I l. the world, and go to the Father.** *863*
Joh 16:32 **to his own, and shall l. me alone:**... *863*
Joh 19:38 of Jesus: and Pilate gave him l........... *2010*
Ac 2:27 thou wilt not l. my soul in hell.......... *1459*
Ac 6:2 that we should l. the word of God,..... *2641*
Ac 18:18 then took his l. of the brethren, ... *657*
Ac 21:6 had taken our l. one of another, ... *782*
1Co 7:13 dwell with her, let her not l. him.......... *863*
2Co 2:13 taking my l. of them, I went from........ *657*
Eph 5:31 a man l. his father and mother,.......... *2641*
Heb 13:5 I will never l. thee, nor forsake........... *447*
Re 11:2 which is without the temple l. out, ... *1544*

LEAVED
Isa 45:1 open before him the two l. gates; 1817

LEAVEN See also LEAVENED.
Ex 12:15 put away l. out of your houses: 7603
Ex 12:19 be no l. found in your houses: 7603
Ex 13:7 shall there be l. seen with thee in...... 7603
Ex 34:25 the blood of my sacrifice with l.;........ 2557
Le 2:11 No...offering...shall be made with l.:... 2557
Le 2:11 for ye shall burn no l.,...................... 7603
Le 6:17 It shall not be baked with l. I............ 2557
Le 10:12 eat it without l. beside the altar: 4682
Le 23:17 they shall be baken with l.; they 2557
Am 4:5 sacrifice of thanksgiving with l.,.......... 2557
Mt 13:33 **kingdom of heaven is like unto l.,** ...*2219*
Mt 16:6,11 **beware of the l. of the Pharisees** ... *2219*
Mt 16:12 not beware of the l. of bread,............ *2219*
Mk 8:15 **beware of the l. of the Pharisees,** .. *2219*
Mk 8:15 **and of the l. of Herod**.................. *2219*
Lu 12:1 **Beware ye of the l. of the**.............. *2219*
Lu 13:21 **It is like l., which a woman took** .. *2219*
1Co 5:6 little l. leaveneth the whole lump? *2219*
1Co 5:7 Purge out therefore the old l., that..... *2219*
1Co 5:8 us keep the feast, not with old l., ... *2219*
1Co 5:8 neither with the l. of malice and......... *2219*
Ga 5:9 little l. leaveneth the whole lump......... *2219*

LEAVENED See also UNLEAVENED; LEAVENETH.
Ex 12:15 whosoever eateth l. bread from......... 2557
Ex 12:19 whosoever eateth that which is l.,...... 2557
Ex 12:20 Ye shall eat nothing l.; in all your....... 2557
Ex 12:34 took their dough before it was l.,....... 2557
Ex 12:39 forth out of Egypt, for it was not l.;... 2557
Ex 13:3 there shall no l. bread be eaten. 2557
Ex 13:7 shall no l. bread be seen with thee,.... 2557
Ex 23:18 blood of my sacrifice with l. bread;..... 2557
Le 7:13 shall offer for his offering l. bread...... 2557
De 16:3 Thou shalt eat no l. bread with it;...... 2557
De 16:4 shall be no l. bread seen with thee..... 7603
Ho 7:4 kneaded the dough, until it be l.. 2557
Mt 13:33 **of meal, till the whole was l.**......... *2220*
Lu 13:21 **of meal, till the whole was l.**......... *2220*

LEAVENETH
1Co 5:6 a little leaven l. the whole lump?........ *2220*
Ga 5:9 A little leaven l. the whole lump. *2220*

LEAVES
Ge 3:7 they sewed fig l. together, and.......... 5929
1Ki 6:34 the two l. of the one door were.......... 6763
1Ki 6:34 the two l. of the other door were 7050
Isa 6:13 is in them, when they cast their l............
Jer 36:23 Jehudi had read three or four l., ... 1817
Eze 17:9 wither in all the l. of her spring, ... 2964
Eze 41:24 had two l. apiece, two turning l.;....... 1817
Eze 41:24 two l. for the one door ....
Eze 41:24 and two l. for the other door............. 1817
Da 4:12 The l. thereof were fair, and the......... 6074
Da 4:14 off his branches, shake off his l.,......... 6074
Da 4:21 Whose l. were fair, and the fruit.......... 6074
Mt 21:19 found nothing thereon, but l. only,....... *5444*
Mt 24:32 **yet tender, and putteth forth l.,**.... *5444*
Mk 11:13 seeing a fig tree afar off having l......... *5444*
Mk 11:13 came to it, he found nothing but l.; *5444*
Mk 13:28 **yet tender, and putteth forth l.,**.... *5444*
Re 22:2 l. of the trees were for the healing..... *5444*

LEAVETH
Job 39:14 Which l. her eggs in the earth, ... 5800
Pr 13:22 A good man l. an inheritance to his..........
Pr 28:3 like a sweeping rain which l. no food..........
Zec 11:17 the idol shepherd that l. the flock!...... 5800
Mt 4:11 Then the devil l. him, and, behold, ... *863*
Joh 10:12 **coming, and l. the sheep, and**......... *863*

LEAVING
Mt 4:13 l. Nazareth, he came and dwelt *2641*
Lu 10:30 **and departed, l. him half dead**........ *863*
Ro 1:27 l. the natural use of the woman,.......... *863*
Heb 6:1 l. the principles of the doctrine of........ *863*
1Pe 2:21 suffered for us, l. us an example,....... *5277*

LEBANA (leb'-a-nah) See also LEBANAH.
Ne 7:48 The children of L., the children 3848

LEBANAH (leb'-a-nah) See also LEBANA.
Ezr 2:45 The children of L., the children 3848

LEBANON (leb'-a-non)
De 1:7 unto L., unto the great river, the....... 3844
De 3:25 that goodly mountain, and L................ 3844
De 11:24 from the wilderness and L., from........ 3844
Jos 1:4 From the wilderness and this L. 3844
Jos 9:1 of the great sea over against L.,.......... 3844
Jos 11:17 unto Baal-gad in the valley of L. 3844
Jos 12:7 in the valley of L. even unto the........ 3844
Jos 13:5 the land of the Giblites, and all L.,..... 3844
Jos 13:6 of the hill country from L. unto 3844
Jg 3:3 the Hivites that dwelt in mount L.,...... 3844
Jg 9:15 and devour the cedars of L................. 3844
1Ki 4:33 from the cedar tree that in in L............ 3844
1Ki 5:6 they hew me cedar trees out of L.;...... 3844
1Ki 5:9 shall bring them down from L.............. 3844
1Ki 5:14 he sent them to L., ten thousand....... 3844
1Ki 5:14 a month they were in L., and two...... 3844
1Ki 7:2 also the house of the forest of L.;....... 3844
1Ki 9:19 to build in Jerusalem, and in L.,......... 3844
1Ki 10:17 in the house of the forest of L. 3844
1Ki 10:21 of the house of the forest of L. were.. 3844
2Ki 14:9 The thistle that was in L. sent to....... 3844
2Ki 14:9 to the cedar that was in L., saying,.... 3844
2Ki 14:9 by a wild beast that was in L., and..... 3844
2Ki 19:23 of the mountains, to the sides of L.,... 3844
2Ch 2:8 trees, and algum trees, out of L.: 3844
2Ch 2:8 can skill to cut timber in L.;............... 3844
2Ch 2:16 we will cut wood out of L., as much.... 3844
2Ch 8:6 to build in Jerusalem, and in L.,......... 3844
2Ch 9:16 them in the house of the forest of L....3844
2Ch 9:20 of the house of the forest of L. were.. 3844
2Ch 25:18 The thistle that was in L. sent to....... 3844
2Ch 25:18 to the cedar that was in L., saying,.... 3844
2Ch 25:18 and by a wild beast that was in L.,..... 3844
Ezr 3:7 cedar trees from L. to the sea of........ 3844
Ps 29:5 the Lord breaketh the cedars of L......... 3844
Ps 29:6 L. and Sirion like a young unicorn. 3844
Ps 72:16 the fruit thereof shall shake like L.:..... 3844
Ps 92:12 he shall grow like a cedar in L.. 3844
Ps 104:16 cedars of L., which he hath planted;... 3844
Ca 3:9 himself a chariot of the wood of L...... 3844
Ca 4:8 Come with me from L., my spouse,... 3844
Ca 4:8 with me from L.: look from the top.... 3844
Ca 4:11 thy garments is like the smell of L.... 3844
Ca 4:15 living waters, and streams from L.. 3844
Ca 5:15 his countenance is as L., excellent..... 3844
Ca 7:4 thy nose is as the tower of L. which .. 3844
Isa 2:13 upon all the cedars of L., that are...... 3844
Isa 10:34 and L. shall fall by a mighty one. 3844
Isa 14:8 at thee, and the cedars of L., saying, ..3844
Isa 29:17 L. shall be turned into a fruitful 3844
Isa 33:9 L. is ashamed and hewn down:.......... 3844
Isa 35:2 the glory of L. shall be given unto...... 3844
Isa 37:24 the mountains, to the sides of L.;....... 3844
Isa 40:16 L. is not sufficient to burn, nor the 3844
Isa 60:13 The glory of L. shall come unto......... 3844
Jer 18:14 leave the snow of L. which cometh 3844
Jer 22:6 Gilead unto me, and the head of L.: ... 3844
Jer 22:20 Go up to L., and cry; and lift up......... 3844
Jer 22:23 O inhabitant of L., that makest thy..... 3844
Eze 17:3 came unto L., and took the highest 3844
Eze 27:5 cedars from L. to make masts........... 3844
Eze 31:8 the Assyrian was a cedar in L. with.... 3844
Eze 31:15 and I caused L. to mourn for him,....... 3844
Eze 31:16 of Eden, the choice and best of L.,..... 3844
Ho 14:5 lily, and cast forth his roots as L.. 3844
Ho 14:6 as the olive tree, and his smell as L.. . 3844
Ho 14:7 thereof shall be as the wine of L......... 3844
Na 1:4 and the flower of L. languisheth.......... 3844
Hab 2:17 the violence of L. shall cover thee,...... 3844
Zec 10:10 them into the land of Gilead and L.; ... 3844
Zec 11:1 Open thy doors, O L., that the fire.... 3844

LEBAOTH (leb'-a-oth) See also BETH-LEBAOTH.
Jos 15:32 And L., and Shilhim, and Ain, and...... 3822

LEBBAEUS (leb-be'-us) See also JUDAS; THAD-DAEUS.
Mt 10:3 James the son of Alphaeus, and L., ... *3002*

LEBONAH (le-bo'-nah)
Jg 21:19 Shechem, and on the south of L.. 3829

LECAH (le'-cah)
1Ch 4:21 Er the father of L., and Laadah......... 3922

LED See also LEDDEST.
Ge 24:27 l. me to the house of my master's...... 5148
Ge 24:48 which had l. me in the right way......... 5148
Ex 3:1 l. the flock to the backside of the....... 5090
Ex 13:17 l. them not through the way of the..... 5148
Ex 13:18 God l. the people about, through........ 5437
Ex 15:13 thy mercy hast l. forth the people 5148
De 8:2 God l. thee these forty years in the.... 3212
De 8:15 Who l. thee through that great and..... 3212
De 29:5 l. you forty years in the wilderness: ... 3212
De 32:10 he l. him about, he instructed him,..... 5437
Jos 24:3 l. him throughout all the land of......... 3212
1Ki 8:48 which l. them away captive, ...
2ki 6:19 seek. But he l. them to Samaria. 3212
1Ch 20:1 l. forth the power of the army, and 5090
2Ch 25:11 himself, and l. forth his people,.......... 5090
Ps 68:18 high, thou hast l. captivity captive: ....
Ps 78:14 also he l. them with a cloud, ... 5148
Ps 78:53 And he l. them on safely so that.......... 5148
Ps 106:9 so he l. them through the depths, ... 3212
Ps 107:7 he l. them forth by the right way,....... 1869
Ps 136:16 which l. his people through the.......... 3212
Pr 4:11 I have l. thee in right paths. 1869
Isa 9:16 that are l. of them are destroyed......... 833
Isa 48:21 he l. them through the deserts: 3212
Isa 55:12 joy, and be l. forth with peace:.......... 2986
Isa 63:12 l. them by the right hand of Moses 3212
Isa 63:13 That l. them through the deep, as....... 3212
Jer 2:6 that l. us through the wilderness,........ 3212
Jer 2:17 God, when he l. thee by the way? 3212
Jer 22:12 whither they have l. him captive, ...
Jer 23:8 l. the seed of the house of Israel......... 935
La 3:2 He hath l. me, and brought me.......... 5090
Eze 17:12 and l. them with him to Babylon;......... 935
Eze 39:28 caused them to be l. into captivity............
Eze 47:2 and l. me about the way without......... 5437
Am 2:10 and l. you forty years through the...... 3212
Am 7:11 Israel shall surely be l. away captive.........
Na 2:7 Huzzab shall be l. away captive,...............
Mt 4:1 Then was Jesus l. up of the spirit........ *321*
Mt 26:57 had laid hold on Jesus l. him away *520*
Mt 27:2 had bound him, they l. him away, ... *520*
Mt 27:31 him, and l. him away to crucify him...... *520*
Mk 8:23 hand, and l. him out of the town;........ *1806*
Mk 14:53 And they l. Jesus away to the high *520*
Mk 15:16 the soldiers l. him away into the hall, ... *520*
Mk 15:20 him, and l. him out to crucify him. *1806*
Lu 4:1 l. by the spirit into the wilderness,......... *71*
Lu 4:29 and l. him unto the brow of the hill *71*
Lu 21:24 **be l. away captive into all nations:** ..*163*
Lu 22:54 Then they took him, and l. him, and....... *71*
Lu 22:66 and l. him into their council, ... *321*
Lu 23:1 of them arose, and l. him unto Pilate. *71*
Lu 23:26 as they l. him away, they laid hold *520*
Lu 23:32 l. with him to be put to death. *71*
Lu 24:50 he l. them out as far as to Bethany,... *1806*
Joh 18:13 And l. him away to Annas first; for...... *520*
Joh 18:28 Then l. they Jesus from Caiaphas.......... *71*
Joh 19:16 they took Jesus, and l. him away......... *520*
Ac 8:32 was l. as a sheep to the slaughter;......... *71*
Ac 9:8 l. him by the hand, and brought......... *5496*
Ac 21:37 Paul was to be l. into the castle.......... *1521*
Ac 22:11 being l. by the hand of them that......... *5496*
Ro 8:14 many as are l. by the Spirit of God, ... *71*
1Co 12:2 these dumb idols, even as ye were l...... *71*
Ga 5:18 But if ye be l. of the Spirit, ye are not... *71*
Eph 4:8 up on high, he l. captivity captive, ... *162*
2Ti 3:6 with sins, l. away with divers lusts,........ *71*
2Pe 3:17 being l. away with the error of........... *4879*

LEDDEST
2Sa 5:2 wast he that l. out and broughtest...... 3318
1Ch 11:2 wast he that l. out and broughtest...... 3318
Ne 9:12 l. them in the day by a cloudy........... 5148
Ps 77:20 Thou l. thy people like a flock by....... 5148
Ac 21:38 and l. out into the wilderness four...... *1806*

LEDGES
1Ki 7:28 the borders were between the l.:......... 7948
1Ki 7:29 the borders that were between the l... 7948
1Ki 7:29 upon the l. there was a base above: ... 7948
1Ki 7:35 the top of the base the l. thereof....... 3027
1Ki 7:36 on the plates of the l. thereof, and...... 3027

LEEKS
Nu 11:5 and the l., and the onions, and the..... 2682

LEES
Isa 25:6 things, a feast of wines on the l.,........ 8105
Isa 25:6 of wines on the l. well refined. 8105
Jer 48:11 hath settled on his l., and hath not..... 8105
Zep 1:12 the men that are settled on their l.:..... 8105

LEFT See also LEFTEST; LEFTHANDED.
Ge 11:8 and they l. off to build the city. 2308
Ge 13:9 if thou wilt take the l. hand, then......... 8040
Ge 13:9 right hand, then I will go to the l.. 8041
Ge 14:15 is on the l. hand of Damascus. 8040
Ge 17:22 And he l. off talking with him, ... 3615
Ge 18:33 had l. communing with Abraham:........ 3615
Ge 24:27 hath not l. destitute my master of........ 5800
Ge 24:49 turn to the right hand, or to the l.. 8040
Ge 29:35 his name Judah; and l. bearing............ 5975
Ge 30:9 Leah saw that she had l. bearing,........ 5975
Ge 32:8 company which is l. shall escape. 7604
Ge 32:24 And Jacob was l. alone; and there 3498
Ge 39:6 l. all that he had in Joseph's hand;...... 5800
Ge 39:12 he l. his garment in her hand, and........ 5800
Ge 39:13 she saw that he had l. his garment..... 5800
Ge 39:15 that he l. his garment with me, and.... 5800
Ge 39:18 l. his garment with me, and fled 5800
Ge 41:49 very much, until he l. numbering;......... 2308
Ge 42:38 brother is dead, and he is l. alone: 7604
Ge 44:12 the eldest, and l. at the youngest:...... 3615
Ge 44:20 brother is dead, and he alone is l. 3498
Ge 47:18 is not ought l. in the sight of my.......... 7604
Ge 48:13 right hand toward Israel's l. hand, ... 8040
Ge 48:13 Manasseh in his l. hand toward.......... 8040
Ge 48:14 his l. hand upon Manasseh's head,...... 8040
Ge 50:8 they l. in the land of Goshen.............. 5800
Ex 2:20 why is it that ye have l. the man?...... 5800
Ex 9:21 l. his servants and his cattle in the..... 5800

Ex 10:12 land, even all that the hail hath l.. 7604
Ex 10:15 of the trees which the hail had l.: 3498
Ex 10:26 shall not an hoof be l. behind; 7604
Ex 14:22, 29 right hand, and on their l. 8040
Ex 16:20 of them l. of it until the morning, 3498
Ex 34:25 passover be l. until the morning. 3885
Le 2:10 which is l. of the meat offering 3498
Le 10:12 unto Ithamar, his sons that were l., 3498
Le 10:16 sons of Aaron which were l. alive, 3498
Le 14:15 into the palm of his own l. hand: 8042
Le 14:16 in the oil that is in his l. hand, 8042
Le 14:26 into the palm of his own l. hand: 8042
Le 14:27 some of the oil that is in his l. hand. 8042
Le 26:36 upon them that are l. alive of you 7604
Le 26:39 they that are l. of you shall pine 7604
Le 26:43 The land also shall be l. of them, 5800
Nu 20:17 to the right hand nor to the l., 8040
Nu 21:35 until there was none l. him alive: 7604
Nu 22:26 to the right hand or to the l. 8040
Nu 26:25 there was not l. a man of them, 3498
De 2:27 unto the right hand nor to the l.. 8040
De 2:34 every city, we l. none to remain: 7604
De 3:3 until none was l. to him remaining. 7604
De 4:27 shall be l. few in number among 7604
De 5:32 aside to the right hand or to the l.. 8040
De 7:20 among them, until they that are l., 7604
De 17:11 to the right hand, nor to the l.. 8040
De 17:20 to the right hand, or to the l.: 8040
De 28:14 day, to the right hand, or to the l., 8040
De 28:55 hath nothing l. him in the siege, 7604
De 28:62 And ye shall be l. few in number, 7604
De 32:36 and there is none shut up, or l.. 5800
Jos 1:7 it to the right hand or to the l., 8040
Jos 6:23 l. them without the camp of 3241
Jos 8:17 there was not a man l. in Ai or 7604
Jos 8:17 l. the city open, and pursued after 5800
Jos 10:33 until he had l. him none remaining. 7604
Jos 10:37 he l. none remaining, according to 7604
Jos 10:39 therein; he l. none remaining: 7604
Jos 10:40 he l. none remaining, but utterly 7604
Jos 11:8 until they l. them none remaining. 7604
Jos 11:11 there was not any l. to breathe: 3498
Jos 11:14 neither l. they any to breathe. 7604
Jos 11:15 l. nothing undone of all that the 5493
Jos 11:22 There was none of the Anakims l. 3498
Jos 19:27 goeth out to Cabul on the l. hand, 8040
Jos 22:3 not l. your brethren these many 5800
Jos 23:6 to the right hand or to the l.; 8040
Jg 2:21 of the nations which Joshua l. 5800
Jg 2:23 the Lord l. those nations, without 3241
Jg 3:1 are the nations which the Lord l., 3241
Jg 3:21 And Ehud put forth his l. hand, 8040
Jg 4:16 sword; and there was not a man l. 7604
Jg 6:4 and l. no sustenance for Israel, 7604
Jg 7:20 held the lamps in their l. hands, 8040
Jg 8:10 l. of all the hosts of the children 3498
Jg 9:5 youngest son of Jerubbaal was l.; 3498
Jg 16:29 hand, and of the other with his l.. 8040
Ru 1:3 and she was l., and her two sons. 7604
Ru 1:5 woman was l. of her two sons and 7604
Ru 1:18 then she l. speaking unto her. 2308
Ru 2:11 hast l. thy father and thy mother, 5800
Ru 2:14 did eat, and was sufficed, and l.. 3498
Ru 2:20 not l. off his kindness to the living 5800
Ru 4:14 hath not l. thee this day without a 7673
1Sa 2:36 every one that is l. in thine house 3498
1Sa 5:4 the stump of Dagon was l. to him. 7604
1Sa 6:12 aside to the right hand or to the l.; 8040
1Sa 9:24 said, Behold that which is l.! 7604
1Sa 10:2 father hath l. the care of the asses, 5203
1Sa 11:11 two of them were not l. together. 7604
1Sa 17:20 and l. the sheep with a keeper, 5203
1Sa 17:22 David l. his carriage in the hand of 5203
1Sa 17:28 whom hast thou l. those few sheep 5203
1Sa 25:34 had not been l. unto Nabal by the 3498
1Sa 27:9 l. neither man nor woman alive.
1Sa 30:9 those that were l. behind stayed. 3498
1Sa 30:13 my master l. me, because three 5800
2Sa 2:19 nor to the l. from following Abner. 8040
2Sa 2:21 aside to thy right hand or to thy l., 8040
2Sa 5:21 And there they l. their images, 5800
2Sa 9:1 any that is l. of the house of Saul, 3498
2Sa 13:30 and there is not one of them l. 3498
2Sa 14:7 shall quench my coal which is l., 7604
2Sa 14:19 turn to the right hand or to the l. 8041
2Sa 15:16 the king l. ten women, which were 5800
2Sa 16:6 on his right hand and on his l.. 8040
2Sa 16:21 he hath l. to keep the house; 3241
2Sa 17:12 shall not be l. so much as one. 3498
2Sa 20:3 whom he had l. to keep the house, 3241
1Ki 7:21 he set up the l. pillar, and called 8042
1Ki 7:39 five on the l. side of the house: 8040
1Ki 7:47 And Solomon l. all the vessels 3241
1Ki 7:49 the right side, and five on the l., 8040
1Ki 9:20 all the people that were l. of the 3498
1Ki 9:21 that were l. after them in the land, 3498
1Ki 14:10 him that is shut up and l. in Israel, 5800
1Ki 15:18 gold that were l. in the treasures 3498
1Ki 15:21 that he l. off building of Ramah, 2308
1Ki 15:29 he l. not to Jeroboam any that 7604
1Ki 16:11 he l. him not one that pisseth 7604
1Ki 17:17 that there was no breath l. in him. 3498
1Ki 19:3 Judah, and l. his servant there. 3241
1Ki 19:10, 14 and I, even I only, am l.; and 3498
1Ki 19:18 Yet I have l. me seven thousand 7604
1Ki 19:20 And he l. the oxen, and ran after 5800
1Ki 20:30 thousand of the men that were l.. 3498
1Ki 21:21 him that is shut up and l. in Israel, 5800
1Ki 22:19 on his right hand and on his l.. 8040
2Ki 3:25 in Kir-haraseth l. they the stones 7604
2Ki 4:44 and l. thereof, according to the 3498
2Ki 7:7 in the twilight, and l. their tents, 5800
2Ki 7:13 remain, which are l. in the city, 7604
2Ki 7:13 multitude of Israel that are l. in it: 7604
2Ki 8:6 since the day that she l. the land, 5800
2Ki 9:8 him that is shut up and l. in Israel:
2Ki 10:11 until he l. him none remaining. 7604
2Ki 10:14 men; neither l. he any of them. 7604
2Ki 10:21 was not a man l. that came not. 7604
2Ki 11:11 to the l. corner of the temple, 8042
2Ki 14:26 was not any shut up, nor any l., 5800
2Ki 17:16 l. all the commandments of the 5800
2Ki 17:18 none l. but the tribe of Judah only. 7604
2Ki 19:4 prayer for the remnant that are l.. 4672
2Ki 20:17 into Babylon: nothing shall be l., 3498
2Ki 22:2 aside to the right hand or to the l.. 8040
2Ki 23:8 were on a man's l. hand at the gate. 8040
2Ki 25:11 the people that were l. in the city, 7604
2Ki 25:12 captain of the guard l. of the poor 7604
2Ki 25:22 king of Babylon had l., even over 7604
1Ch 6:44 sons of Merari stood on the l. hand: 8040
1Ch 6:61 were l. of the family of that tribe, 3498
1Ch 12:2 hand and the l. in hurling stones 8041
1Ch 13:2 that are l. in all the land of Israel, 7604
1Ch 14:12 when they had l. their gods there, 5800
1Ch 16:37 he l. there before the ark of the 5800
2Ch 3:17 hand, and the other on the l.; 8040
2Ch 3:17 the name of that on the l. Boaz. 8042
2Ch 4:6 the right hand, and five on the l., 8040
2Ch 4:7 the right hand, and five on the l. 8040
2Ch 4:8 on the right side, and five on the l.. 8040
2Ch 8:7 people that were l. of the Hittites, 3498
2Ch 8:8 who were l. after them in the land, 3498
2Ch 11:14 the Levites l. their suburbs and 5800
2Ch 12:5 also l. you in the hand of Shishak. 5800
2Ch 16:5 that he l. off building of Ramah, 2308
2Ch 18:18 on his right hand and on his l.. 8040
2Ch 21:17 that there was never a son l. him, 7604
2Ch 23:10 temple to the l. side of the temple, 8042
2Ch 24:18 they l. the house of the Lord God 5800
2Ch 24:25 for they l. him in great diseases,) 5800
2Ch 25:12 And other ten thousand l. alive did the
2Ch 28:14 armed men l. the captives and the 5800
2Ch 31:10 enough to eat, and have l. plenty: 3498
2Ch 31:10 that which is l. is this great store. 3498
2Ch 32:31 God l. him, to try him, that he 5800
2Ch 34:2 to the right hand, nor to the l.. 8040
2Ch 34:21 that are l. in Israel and in Judah, 7604
Ne 1:2 which were l. of the captivity, 7604
Ne 1:3 remnant that are l. of the captivity 7604
Ne 6:1 there was no breach l. therein; 3498
Ne 8:4 his l. hand, Pedaiah and Mishael, 8040
Job 20:21 There shall none of his meat be l.; 8300
Job 20:26 it shall go ill with him that is l. in 8300
Job 23:9 On the l. hand, where he doth 8040
Job 32:15 no more; they l. off speaking. 6275
Ps 36:3 he hath l. off to be wise, and to do 2308
Ps 106:11 there was not one of them l. 3498
Pr 3:16 in her l. hand riches and honour. 8040
Pr 4:27 not to the right hand nor to the l.: 8040
Pr 29:15 a child l. to himself bringeth his 7971
Ec 10:2 hand; but a fool's heart at his l.. 8040
Ca 2:6 His l. hand is under my head, and 8040
Ca 8:3 His l. hand should be under my 8040
Isa 1:8 daughter of Zion is l. as a cottage 3498
Isa 1:9 the Lord of hosts had l. unto us 3498
Isa 4:3 to pass, that he that is l. in Zion, 7604
Isa 7:22 every one eat that is l. in the land. 3498
Isa 9:20 and he shall eat on the l. hand, 8040
Isa 10:14 as one gathereth eggs that are l., 5800
Isa 11:11, 16, his people, which shall be l., 7604
Isa 17:6 Yet gleaning grapes shall be l. in it, 7604
Isa 17:9 they l. because of the children of 5800
Isa 18:6 They shall be l. together unto the 5800
Isa 24:6 earth are burned, and few men l.. 7604
Isa 24:12 In the city is l. desolation, and the 7604
Isa 27:10 forsaken, and l. like a wilderness: 5800
Isa 30:17 be l. as a beacon upon the top of a 3498
Isa 30:21 hand, and when ye turn to the l. 8041
Isa 32:14 multitude of the city shall be l.; 5800
Isa 37:4 prayer for the remnant that is l. 4672
Isa 39:6 to Babylon: nothing shall be l.. 3498
Isa 49:21 I was l. alone; these, where had 7604
Isa 54:3 on the right hand and on the l.; 8040
Jer 12:7 house, I have l. mine heritage; 5203
Jer 21:7 are l. this city from the pestilence, 7604
Jer 27:18 vessels which are l. in the house 3498
Jer 31:2 people which were l. of the sword 8300
Jer 34:7 all the cities of Judah that were l., 3498
Jer 38:22 women that are l. in the king of 7604
Jer 38:27 they l. off speaking with him; for 2790
Jer 39:10 captain of the guard l. of the poor 7604
Jer 40:6 the people that were l. in the land 7604
Jer 40:11 had l. a remnant of Judah, and 5414
Jer 42:2 (for we are l. but a few of many, as 7604
Jer 43:6 captain of the guard had l. with 3240
Jer 44:18 l. off to burn incense to the queen 2308
Jer 49:25 How is the city of praise not l., the 5800
Jer 50:26 utterly: let nothing of her be l.. 7611
Jer 52:16 captain of the guard l. certain of 7604
Eze 1:10 the face of an ox on the l. side; 8040
Eze 4:4 Lie thou also upon thy l. side, and 8042
Eze 9:8 were slaying them, and I was l., 7604
Eze 14:22 therein shall be l. a remnant that 3498
Eze 16:46 daughters that dwell at thy l. hand: 8040
Eze 21:16 on the right hand or on the l., 8041
Eze 23:8 Neither l. she her whoredoms 5800
Eze 24:21 your daughters whom ye have l. 5800
Eze 31:12 have cut him off, and have l. him: 5203
Eze 31:12 from his shadow, and have l. him. 5203
Eze 36:36 heathen that are l. round about 7604
Eze 39:3 smite thy bow out of thy l. hand, 8040
Eze 39:28 l. none of them any more there. 3498
Eze 41:9 that which was l. was the place of 3240
Eze 41:11 were toward the place that was l., 3240
Eze 41:11 place that was l. was five cubits 3240
Eze 48:15 that are l. in the breadth over 3498
Da 2:44 kingdom shall not be l. to other 7662
Da 10:8 I was l. alone, and saw this great 7604
Da 10:17 me, neither is there breath l. in me. 7604
Da 12:7 hand and his l. hand unto heaven, 8040
Ho 4:10 l. off to take heed to the Lord. 5800
Ho 9:12 them, that there shall not be a man l.:
Joe 1:4 which the palmerworm hath l. 3499
Joe 1:4 that which the locust hath l. hath 3499
Joe 1:4 that which the cankerworm hath l. 3499
Jon 4:11 their right hand and their l. hand; 8040
Hag 2:3 Who is l. among you that saw this 7604
Zec 4:3 the other upon the l. side thereof. 8040
Zec 4:11 and upon the l. side thereof? 8040
Zec 12:6 on the right hand and on the l.: 8040
Zec 13:8 but the third shall be l. therein. 3498
Zec 14:16 one that is l. of all the nations 3498
Mt 4:20 they straightway l. their nets, and *863*
Mt 4:22 they immediately l. the ship and *863*
Mt 6:3 **let not thy l. hand know what thy** *710*
Mt 8:15 her hand, and the fever l. her: *863*
Mt 15:37 broken meat that was l. seven *4052*
Mt 16:4 And he l. them, and departed. *2641*
Mt 20:21 the other on the l., in thy kingdom. *2176*
Mt 20:23 **sit on my right hand, and on my l.,** *2176*
Mt 21:17 he l. them, and went out of the *2641*
Mt 22:22 and l. him, and went their way. *863*
Mt 22:25 issue, l. his wife unto his brother: *863*
Mt 23:38 **your house is l. unto you desolate** *863*
Mt 24:2 **shall not be l. here one stone upon.** *863*
Mt 24:40, 41 **shall be taken, and the other l.** *863*
Mt 25:33 **right hand, but the goats on the l.** *2176*
Mt 25:41 **say also unto them on the l. hand,** *2176*
Mt 26:44 he l. them, and went away again, *863*
Mt 27:38 right hand, and another on the l. *2176*

Mk 1:20 and they l. their father Zebedee in....... *863*
Mk 1:31 and immediately the fever l. her,......... *863*
Mk 8:8 meat that was l. seven baskets.......... *4051*
Mk 8:13 he l. them, and entering into the......... *863*
Mk 10:28 we have l. all, and have followed......... *863*
Mk 10:29 **There is no man that hath l. house,** .*863*
Mk 10:37 the other on thy l. hand, in thy *2176*
Mk 10:40 **on my l. hand is not mine to give;**. *2176*
Mk 12:12 they l. him, and went their way. *863*
Mk 12:20 took a wife, and dying l. no seed.......... *863*
Mk 12:21 her, and died, neither l. he any seed:... *863*
Mk 12:22 the seven had her, and l. no seed:....... *863*
Mk 13:2 **there shall not be l. one stone upon** .*863*
Mk 13:34 **a far journey, who l. his house,** *863*
Mk 14:52 he l. the linen cloth, and fled from...... *2641*
Mk 15:27 right hand, and the other on his l.. ..... *2176*
Lu 4:39 rebuked the fever; and it l. her:.......... *863*
Lu 5:4 when he had l. speaking, he said........ *3973*
Lu 5:28 And he l. all, rose up, and followed *2641*
Lu 10:40 my sister hath l. me to serve alone?... *2641*
Lu 13:35 **your house is l. unto you desolate:** .*863*
Lu 17:34 **be taken, and the other shall be l..** . *863*
Lu 17:35 **shall be taken, and the other l.**....... *863*
Lu 17:36 **shall be taken, and the other l.**....... *863*
Lu 18:28 Peter said, Lo, we have l. all, and....... *863*
Lu 18:29 **There is no man that hath l. house,** .*863*
Lu 20:31 seven also: and they l. no children, ... *2641*
Lu 21:6 **not be l. one stone upon another**. ... *863*
Lu 23:33 right hand, and the other on the l.. ...... *710*
Joh 4:3 He l. Judaea, and departed again *863*
Joh 4:28 woman then l. her waterpot, and......... *863*
Joh 4:52 at the seventh hour the fever l. him..... *863*
Joh 8:9 Jesus was l. alone, and the woman..... *2641*
Joh 8:29 **the Father hath not l. me alone;**..... *863*
Ac 2:31 his soul was not l. in hell, neither *2641*
Ac 14:17 he l. not himself without witness, ... *863*
Ac 18:19 to Ephesus, and l. them there:.......... *2641*
Ac 21:3 we had discovered Cyprus, we l. it *2641*
Ac 21:3 it on the l. hand, and sailed into......... *2176*
Ac 21:32 soldiers, they l. beating of Paul........... *3973*
Ac 23:32 l. the horsemen to go with him,......... *1439*
Ac 24:27 Jews a pleasure, l. Paul bound.......... *2641*
Ac 25:14 certain man l. in bonds by Felix:........ *2641*
Ro 9:29 Lord of Sabaoth had l. us a seed,....... *1459*
Ro 11:3 and I am l. alone, and they seek....... *5275*
2Co 6:7 on the right hand and on the l.,........... *710*
1Th 3:1 thought it good to be l. at Athens *2641*
2Ti 4:13 cloke that I l. at Troas with Carpus, ... *620*
2Ti 4:20 Trophimus have I l. at Miletum sick.... *620*
Tit 1:5 For this cause l. I thee in Crete, ... *2641*
Heb 2:8 l. nothing that is not put under him...... *863*
Heb 4:1 a promise being l. us of entering........ *2641*
Jude 6 estate, but l. their own habitation, ... *620*
Re 2:4 **because thou hast l. thy first love**... *863*
Re 10:2 sea, and his l. foot on the earth,........ *2176*

LEFTEST
Ne 9:28 therefore l. thou them in the hand...... 5800

LEFT-FOOT See LEFT and FOOT.

LEFT-HAND See LEFT and HAND; also LEFTHANDED.

LEFTHANDED
Jg 3:15 a Benjamite, a man l.:......... 334,3027,3225
Jg 20:16 hundred chosen men l.; 334,3027,3225

LEFT-SIDE See LEFT and SIDE.

LEG See also LEGS.
Isa 47:2 make bare the l., uncover the 7640

LEGION See also LEGIONS.
Mk 5:9 My name is L.: for we are many. *3003*
Mk 5:15 with the devil, and had the l.,........... *3003*
Lu 8:30 **What is thy name? And he said, L.:** .*3003*

LEGIONS
Mt 26:53 **me more than twelve l. of angels?** ..*3003*

LEGS
Ex 12:9 his head with his l., and with the 3767
Ex 29:17 wash the inwards of him, and his l., ... 3767
Le 1:9 inwards and his l. shall he wash in...... 3767
Le 1:13 he shall wash the inwards and the l. ... 3767
Le 4:11 flesh, with his head, and with his l., ... 3767
Le 8:21 he washed the inwards and the l......... 3767
Le 9:14 he did wash the inwards and the l., ... 3767
Le 11:21 which have l. above their feet, to....... 3767
De 28:35 thee in the knees, and in the l.,......... 7785
1Sa 17:6 had greaves of brass upon his l.,........ 7272
Ps 147:10 not pleasure in the l. of a man.......... 7785
Pr 26:7 The l. of the lame are not equal: so ... 7785
Ca 5:15 His l. are as pillars of marble, set 7785
Isa 3:20 the ornaments of the l., and the 6807
Da 2:33 His l. of iron, his feet part of iron 8243
Am 3:12 out of the mouth of the lion two l., ... 3767
Joh 19:31 that their l. might be broken, and....... *4628*
Joh 19:32 and brake the l. of the first, and of..... *4628*
Joh 19:33 dead already, they brake not his l.: *4628*

LEHABIM (le'-ha-bim)
Ge 10:13 Ludim, and Anamim, and L., and 3853
1Ch 1:11 begat Ludim, and Anamim, and L.,..... 3853

LEHEM See BETH-LEHEM; JESHUBI-LEHEM.

LEHI (le'-hi) See also RAMATH-LEHI.
Jg 15:9 and spread themselves in L.. 3896
Jg 15:14 And when he came unto L., the 3896
Jg 15:19 which is n L. unto this day. 3896

LEISURE
Mk 6:31 they had no l. so much as to eat........ *2119*

LEMUEL (lem'-u-el)
Pr 31:1 words of king L., the prophecy.......... 3927
Pr 31:4 O L., it is not for kings to drink 3927

LEND See also LENDETH; LENT.
Ex 22:25 thou l. money to any of my people..... 3867
Le 25:37 l. him thy victuals for increase........... 5414
De 15:6 thou shalt l. unto many nations, ... 5670
De 15:8 shalt surely l. him sufficient for his..... 5670
De 23:19 Thou shalt not l. upon usury to 5391
De 23:20 thou mayest l. upon usury; 5391
De 23:20 thou shalt not l. upon usury: 5391
De 24:10 When thou dost l. thy brother any........ 5383
De 24:11 the man to whom thou dost l. shall..... 5383
De 28:12 thou shalt l. unto many nations, ... 3867
De 28:44 l. to thee, and thou shalt not l. to...... 3867
Lu 6:34 **if ye l. to them of whom ye hope** .. *1155*
Lu 6:34 **sinners also l. to sinners, to receive** *1155*
Lu 6:35 **and l., hoping for nothing again;**.... *1155*
Lu 11:5 **him, Friend, l. me three loaves;** *5531*

LENDER
Pr 22:7 the borrower is servant to the l......... 3867
Isa 24:2 as with the l., so with the borrower; .. 3867

LENDETH
De 15:2 Every creditor that l. ought unto........ 5383
Ps 37:26 He is ever merciful, and l.; and 3867
Ps 112:5 good man sheweth favour, and l.:...... 3867
Pr 19:17 pity upon the poor l. unto the Lord; ... 3867

LENGTH
Ge 6:15 l. of the ark shall be three hundred...... 753
Ge 13:17 walk through the land in the l. of it...... 753
Ex 25:10, 17 cubits and a half shall be the l......... 753
Ex 25:23 two cubits shall be the l. thereof. 753
Ex 26:2 The l. of one curtain shall be eight....... 753
Ex 26:8 The l. of one curtain shall be thirty...... 753
Ex 26:13 remaineth in the l. of the curtains 753
Ex 26:16 Ten cubits shall be the l. of a board, ... 753
Ex 27:11 side in l. there shall be hangings.......... 753
Ex 27:18 l. of the court shall be an hundred 753
Ex 28:16 a span shall be the l. thereof, and a 753
Ex 30:2 A cubit shall be the l. thereof, and a 753
Ex 36:9 The l. of one curtain was twenty......... 753
Ex 36:15 The l. of one curtain was thirty.......... 753
Ex 36:21 The l. of a board was ten cubits, and ... 753
Ex 37:1 two cubits and a half was the l. of it, ... 753
Ex 37:6 cubits and a half was the l. thereof, ... 753
Ex 37:10 two cubits was the l. thereof, and a 753
Ex 37:25 the l. of it was a cubit, and the........... 753
Ex 38:1 five cubits was the l. thereof, and......... 753
Ex 38:18 and twenty cubits was the l., and the ... 753
Ex 39:9 a span was the l. thereof, and a span ... 753
De 3:11 nine cubits was the l. thereof, and....... 753
De 30:20 he is thy life, and the l. of thy days: 753
Jg 3:16 which had two edges, of a cubit l.; 753
1Ki 6:2 the l. thereof was threescore cubits, ... 753
1Ki 6:3 twenty cubits was the l. thereof, ... 753
1Ki 6:20 the forepart was twenty cubits in l.,..... 753
1Ki 7:2 the l. thereof was an hundred cubits,.... 753
1Ki 7:6 the l. thereof was fifty cubits, and 753
1Ki 7:27 four cubits was the l. of one base, ... 753
2Ch 3:3 l. by cubits after the first measure 753
2Ch 3:4 l. of it was according to the breadth..... 753
2Ch 3:8 the l. thereof was according to the....... 753
2Ch 4:1 of brass, twenty cubits the l. thereof,... 753
Job 12:12 and in l. of days understanding. 753
Ps 21:4 even l. of days for ever and ever. 753
Pr 3:2 For l. of days, and long life, and.......... 753
Pr 3:16 L. of days is in her right hand; and...... 753
Pr 29:21 have him become his son at the l.. 319
Eze 31:7 greatness,in the l. of his branches:........ 753
Eze 40:11 the l. of the gate, thirteen cubits.......... 753
Eze 40:18 over against the l. of the gates was 753
Eze 40:20 he measured the l. thereof, and the 753
Eze 40:21 the l. thereof was fifty cubits, and 753
Eze 40:25 windows: the l. was fifty cubits, ... 753
Eze 40:36 the l. was fifty cubits, and the............. 753
Eze 40:49 l. of the porch was twenty cubits,........•753
Eze 41:2 measured the l. thereof, forty cubits: ... 753
Eze 41:4 So he measured the l. thereof,............ 753
Eze 41:12 and the l. thereof ninety cubits............ 753
Eze 41:15 he measured the l. of the building........ 753
Eze 41:22 high, and the l. thereof two cubits; 753
Eze 41:22 the l. thereof, and the walls thereof, ... 753
Eze 42:2 the l. of an hundred cubits was the...... 753
Eze 42:7 the l. thereof was fifty cubits. 753
Eze 42:8 the l. of the chambers that were in...... 753
Eze 45:1 the l. shall be the l. of five and.......... 753
Eze 45:2 for the sanctuary five hundred in l., ...
Eze 45:3 measure shalt thou measure the l. 753
Eze 45:5 the five and twenty thousand of l.,....... 753
Eze 45:7 the l. shall be over against one of........ 753
Eze 43:8 and in l. as one of the other parts, ... 753
Eze 43:9 be of five and twenty thousand in l., ... 753
Eze 43:10 north five and twenty thousand in l., ... 753
Eze 43:10 south five and twenty thousand in l.: 753
Eze 43:13 have five and twenty thousand in l.,..... 753
Eze 43:13 l. shall be five and twenty thousand,..... 753
Eze 43:18 the residue in l. over against the 753
Zec 2:2 thereof, and what is the l. thereof. 753
Zec 5:2 the l. thereof is twenty cubits, and 753
Ro 1:10 at l. I might have a prosperous.......... *4218*
Eph 3:18 what is the breadth, and l., and......... *3372*
Re 21:16 the l. is as large as the breadth: *3372*
Re 21:16 l. and the breadth and the height *3372*

LENGTHEN See also LENGTHENED; LENGTHENING.
1Ki 3:14 did walk then will I l. thy days. 748
Isa 54:2 l. thy cords, and strengthen thy 748

LENGTHENED
De 25:15 that thy days may be l. in the land....... 748

LENGTHENING
Da 4:27 if it may be a l. of thy tranquillity. 754

LENT
Ex 12:36 l. unto them such things as they........ 7592
De 23:19 of any thing that is l. upon usury: 5391
1Sa 1:28 also I have l. him to the Lord;........... 7592
1Sa 1:28 he liveth he shall be l. to the Lord. 7592
1Sa 2:20 the loan which is l. to the Lord. 7592
Jer 15:10 I have neither l. on usury, nor 5383
Jer 15:10 nor men have l. to me on usury; 5383

LENTILES
Ge 25:34 gave Esau bread and pottage of l.; 5742
2Sa 17:28 parched corn, and beans, and l., ... 5742
2Sa 23:11 was a piece of ground full of l.: 5742
Eze 4:9 and beans, and l., and millet, and....... 5742

LEOPARD See also LEOPARDS.
Isa 11:6 the l. shall lie down with the kid; 5246
Jer 5:6 a l. shall watch over their cities: 5246
Jer 13:23 change his skin, or the l. his spots?.... 5246
Da 7:6 I beheld, and lo another, like a l., ... 5245
Ho 13:7 as a l. by the way will I observe........ 5246
Re 13:2 which I saw was like unto a l., ... *3917*

LEOPARDS
Ca 4:8 from the mountains of the l.............. 5246
Hab 1:8 horses also are swifter than the l., ... 5246

LEPER See also LEPERS.
Le 13:45 And the l. in whom the plague is, ... 6879
Le 14:2 this shall be the law of the l. in 6879
Le 14:3 plague of leprosy be healed in the l.; .. 6879
Le 22:4 soever of the seed of Aaron is a l.. 6879
Nu 5:2 they put out of the camp every l........ 6879
2Sa 3:29 that hath an issue, or that is a l.,........ 6879
2Ki 5:1 man in valour, but he was a l.. 6879
2Ki 5:11 over the place, and recover the l.. 6879
2Ki 5:27 he went out from his presence a l...... 6879
2Ki 15:5 was a l. unto the day of his death, ... 6879
2Ch 26:21 Uzziah the king was a l. unto the....... 6879
2Ch 26:21 dwelt in a several house, being a l.: ... 6879

2Ch 26:23 the kings; for they said, He is a **l.**...... 6879
Mt 8:2 there came a **l.** and worshipped........ *3015*
Mt 26:6 in the house of Simon the **l.**,............ *3015*
Mk 1:40 there came a **l.** to him, beseeching..... *3015*
Mk 14:3 in the house of Simon the **l.**, as he..... *3015*

LEPERS

2Ki 7:8 **l.** came to the uttermost part of........ 6879
Mt 10:8 **sick, cleanse the l., raise the dead,**. *3015*
Mt 11:5 **the l. are cleansed, and the deaf**.... *3015*
Lu 4:27 **And many l. were in Israel in the**.. *3015*
Lu 7:22 **the l. are cleansed, the deaf hear,** . *3015*
Lu 17:12 there met him ten men that were **l.**,.... *3015*

LEPROSY

Le 13:2 of his flesh like the plague of **l.**;........ 6883
Le 13:3 skin of his flesh, it is a plague of **l.**:.... 6883
Le 13:8 pronounce him unclean: it is a **l.**.. 6883
Le 13:9 when the plague of **l.** is in a man, ... 6883
Le 13:11 is an old **l.** in the skin of his flesh, ... 6883
Le 13:12 if a **l.** break out abroad in the skin,..... 6883
Le 13:12 and the **l.** cover all the skin of him..... 6883
Le 13:13 if the **l.** have covered all his flesh,...... 6883
Le 13:15 the raw flesh is unclean: it is a **l.**....... 6883
Le 13:20 plague of **l.** broken out of the boil. 6883
Le 13:25 it is a **l.** broken out of the burning:..... 6883
Le 13:25, 27 unclean: it is the plague of **l.**......... 6883
Le 13:30 even a **l.** upon the head or beard. 6883
Le 13:42 it is a **l.** sprung up in his bald head,..... 6883
Le 13:43 as the **l.** appeareth in the skin of the .. 6883
Le 13:47 garment...that the plague of **l.** is in,.... 6883
Le 13:49 a plague of **l.**, and shall be shewed..... 6883
Le 13:51 plague is a fretting **l.**; it is unclean...... 6883
Le 13:52 for it is a fretting **l.**; it shall be burnt .. 6883
Le 13:59 This is the law of the plague of **l.**....... 6883
Le 14:3 plague of **l** be healed in the leper; 6883
Le 14:7 him that is to be cleansed from **l.**........ 6883
Le 14:32 of him in whom is the plague of **l.**, ... 6883
Le 14:34 I put the plague of **l.** in a house of 6883
Le 14:44 it is a fretting **l.** in the house: it is 6883
Le 14:54 law for all manner of plague of **l.**,........ 6883
Le 14:55 And for the **l.** of a garment, and of..... 6883
Le 14:57 when it is clean: this is the law of **l.**.. 6883
De 24:8 Take heed in the plague of **l.**, that 6883
2Ki 5:3 for he would recover him of his **l.**.. 6883
2Ki 5:6 thou mayest recover him of his **l.**........ 6883
2Ki 5:7 unto me to recover a man of his **l.**?.... 6883
2Ki 5:27 The **l.** therefore of Naaman shall........ 6883
2Ch 26:19 the **l.** even rose up in his forehead...... 6883
Mt 8:3 immediately his **l.** was cleansed........... *3014*
Mr 1:42 immediately the **l.** departed from........ *3014*
Lu 5:12 certain city, behold a man full of **l.**: *3014*
Lu 5:13 immediately the **l.** departed from........ *3014*

LEPROUS

Ex 4:6 behold, his hand was **l.** as snow......... 6879
Le 13:44 He is a **l.** man, he is unclean:............ 6879
Nu 12:10 Miriam became **l.**, white as snow: 6879
Nu 12:10 Miriam, and, behold, she was **l.**......... 6879
2Ki 7:3 were four **l.** men at the entering in...... 6879
2Ch 26:20 behold, he was **l.** in his forehead,....... 6879

LESHEM (le'-shem) See also LAISH.

Jos 19:47 Dan went up to fight against **L.**, ... 3959
Jos 19:47 dwelt therein, and called **L.**, Dan, ... 3959

LESS See also BLAMELESS; BOTTOMLESS; CAUSELESS; CHILDLESS; COMFORTLESS; DOUBTLESS; ENDLESS; FAITHLESS; FATHERLESS; FAULTLESS; HARMLESS; LAWLESS; LESSER; NEVERTHELESS; SHAMELESSLY; SPEECHLESS; UNLESS.

Ex 16:17 and gathered, some more, some **l.**. 4591
Ex 30:15 the poor shall not give **l.** than half...... 4591
Nu 22:18 the Lord my God, to do **l.** or more. ... 6996
Nu 26:54 thou shalt give the **l.** inheritance; 4591
Nu 33:54 ye shall give the **l.** inheritance: 4591
1Sa 22:15 nothing of all this, **l.** or more............ 6996
1Sa 25:36 she told him nothing, **l.** or more, ... 6996
1Ki 8:27 how much **l.** this house that I have..........
2Ch 6:18 how much **l.** this house which I have ....
2Ch 32:15 how much **l.** shall your God deliver...........
Ezr 9:13 punished us **l.** than our iniquities........ 4295
Job 4:19 How much **l.** in them that dwell in...........
Job 9:14 How much **l.** shall I answer him, and........
Job 11:6 exacteth of thee **l.** than thine iniquity.........
Job 25:6 How much **l.** man, that is a worm?..........
Job 34:19 How much **l.** to him that accepteth..........
Pr 17:7 a fool: much **l.** do lying lips a prince.........
Pr 19:10 much **l.** for a servant to have rule over.....
Isa 40:17 are counted to him **l.** than nothing, ... 657
Eze 15:5 how much **l.** shall it be meet yet for lest ...
Mk 4:31 **l. than all the seeds that be in the.** *3398*
Mk 15:40 Mary the mother of James the **l.**......... *3398*
1Co 12:23 which we think to be **l.** honourable,....... *820*
2Co 12:15 I love you, the **l.** I be loved............. *2276*
Eph 3:8 am **l.** than the least of all saints, ... *1647*
Php 2:28 and that I may be the **l.** sorrowful. *253*
Heb 7:7 the **l.** is blessed of the better. *1640*

LESSER

Ge 1:16 and the **l.** light to rule the night:........ 6996
Isa 7:25 and for the treading of **l.** cattle. 7716
Eze 43:14 and from the **l.** settle even to the 6996

LEST

Ge 3:3 neither shall ye touch it, **l.** ye die....... 6435
Ge 3:22 **l.** he put forth his hand, and take....... 6435
Ge 4:15 **l.** any finding him should kill him. 1115
Ge 11:4 **l.** we be scattered abroad upon the..... 6435
Ge 14:23 **l.** thou shouldest say, I have made 3808
Ge 19:15 **l.** thou be consumed in the 6435
Ge 19:17 mountain, **l.** thou be consumed. 6435
Ge 19:19 **l.** some evil take me, and I die. 6435
Ge 26:7 **l.**, said he, the men of the place 6435
Ge 26:9 Because I said, **L.** I die for her. 6435
Ge 32:11 him, **l.** he will come and smite me,..... 6435
Ge 38:9 **l.** that he should give seed to his 1115
Ge 38:11 **L.** peradventure he die also, as his..... 6435
Ge 38:23 her take it to her, **l.** we be shamed:... 6435
Ge 42:4 **L.** peradventure mischief befall 6435
Ge 44:34 **l.** peradventure I see the evil that...... 6435
Ge 45:11 **l.** thou, and thy household, and all...... 6435
Ex 1:10 **l.** they multiply, and it come to pass, .. 6435
Ex 5:3 **l.** he fall upon us with pestilence, ... 6435
Ex 13:17 **L.** peradventure the people repent 6435
Ex 19:21 **l.** they break through unto the Lord.... 6435
Ex 19:22 **l.** the Lord break forth upon them...... 6435
Ex 19:24 Lord, **l.** he break forth upon them...... 6435
Ex 20:19 let not God speak with us, **l.** we die... 6435
Ex 23:29 **l.** the land become desolate, and the... 6435
Ex 23:33 **l.** they make thee sin against me:....... 6435
Ex 33:3 **l.** I consume thee in the way............ 6435
Ex 34:12 **l.** thou make a covenant with the 6435
Ex 34:12 **l.** it be for a snare in the midst of...... 6435
Ex 34:15 **L.** thou make a covenant with the...... 6435
Le 10:6 neither rend your clothes; **l.** ye 3808
Le 10:6 **l.** wrath come upon all the people............
Le 10:7 of the congregation, **l.** ye die: 6435
Le 10:9 of the congregation, **l.** ye die: 3808
Le 19:29 **l.** the land fall to whoredom, and........ 3808
Le 22:9 **l.** they bear sin for it, and die........... 3808
Nu 4:15 not touch any holy thing, **l.** they die. ....
Nu 4:20 the holy things are covered, **l.** they die. ....
Nu 16:26 **l.** ye be consumed in all their sins. 6435
Nu 16:34 **L.** the earth swallow us up also. 6435
Nu 18:22 congregation, **l.** they bear sin, and die.......
Nu 18:32 of the children of Israel, **l.** ye die. 3808
Nu 20:18 **l.** I come out against thee with the sword. .
De 1:42 you; **l.** ye be smitten before your....... 3808
De 4:9 **l.** thou forget the things which........... 6435
De 4:9 **l.** they depart from thy heart all the.... 6435
De 4:16 **L.** ye corrupt yourselves, and make.... 6435
De 4:19 And **l.** thou lift up thine eyes unto...... 6435
De 4:23 **l.** ye forget the covenant of the Lord.. 6435
De 6:12 Then beware **l.** thou forget the Lord,.. 6435
De 6:15 **l.** the anger of the Lord thy God be ... 6435
De 7:22 **l.** the beasts of the field increase 6435
De 7:25 unto thee, **l.** thou be snared therein:... 6435
De 7:26 **l.** thou be a cursed thing like it:..............
De 8:12 **L.** when thou hast eaten and art 6435
De 9:28 **L.** the land whence thou broughtest.... 6435
De 11:17 **l.** ye perish quickly from off the good........
De 19:6 **L.** the avenger of the blood pursue..... 6435
De 20:5, 6,7 **l.** he die in the battle, and........... 6435
De 20:8 **l.** his brethren's heart faint as well 6435
De 22:9 **l.** the fruit of thy seed which thou....... 6435
De 24:15 **l.** he cry against thee unto the Lord, .. 3808
De 25:3 **l.**, if he should exceed, and beat, ... 6435
De 29:18 **L.** there should be among you man,.... 6435
De 29:18 **l.** there should be among you a root ... 6435
De 32:27 **l.** their adversaries should behave....... 6435
De 32:27 and **l.** they should say, Our hand is 6435
Jos 2:16 **l.** the pursuers meet you;................. 6435
Jos 6:18 **l.** ye make yourselves accursed, ... 6435
Jos 9:20 let them live, **l.** wrath be upon us, ... 3808
Jos 24:27 unto you, **l.** ye deny your God. 6435
Jg 7:2 **l.** Israel vaunt themselves against...... 6435
Jg 14:15 **l.** we burn thee and thy father's......... 6435
Jg 18:25 **l.** angry fellows run upon thee, and..... 6435
Ru 4:6 **l.** I mar mine own inheritance:........... 6435
1Sa 9:5 **l.** my father leave caring for the......... 6435
1Sa 13:19 **L.** the Hebrews make them swords.... 6435
1Sa 15:6 **l.** I destroy you with them: for ye...... 6435
1Sa 20:3 know this, **l.** he be grieved: 6435
1Sa 27:11 **L.** they should tell on us, saying, ... 6435
1Sa 29:4 **l.** in the battle he be an adversary...... 3808
1Sa 31:4 **l.** these uncircumcised come and 6435
2Sa 1:20 **l.** the daughters of the Philistines 6435
2Sa 1:20 rejoice, **l.** the daughters of the 6435
2Sa 12:28 **l.** I take the city, and it be called 6435
2Sa 13:25 go, **l.** we be chargeable unto thee. 3808
2Sa 14:11 any more, **l.** they destroy my son. ....
2Sa 15:14 depart, **l.** he overtake us suddenly,..... 6435
2Sa 17:16 **l.** the king be swallowed up, and all.... 6435
2Sa 20:6 **l.** he get him fenced cities, and.......... 6435
2Ki 2:16 **l.** peradventure the Spirit of the......... 6435
1Ch 10:4 **l.** these uncircumcised come and........ 6435
Job 32:13 **L.** ye should say, We have found. 6435
Job 34:30 reign not,**l.** the people be ensnared...........
Job 36:18 beware **l.** he take thee away with......... 6435
Job 42:8 **l.** I deal with you after your folly,........ 1115
Ps 2:12 Kiss the Son, **l.** he be angry, and....... 6435
Ps 7:2 **L.** he tear my soul like a lion, ... 6435
Ps 13:3 eyes, **l.** I sleep the sleep of death; 6435
Ps 13:4 **L.** mine enemy say, I have prevailed .. 6435
Ps 28:1 **l.**, if thou be silent to me, I become ... 6435
Ps 32:9 **l.** they come near unto thee.............. 1077
Ps 38:16 **l.** otherwise they should rejoice 6435
Ps 50:22 **l.** I tear you in pieces, and there be ... 6435
Ps 59:11 Slay them not, **l.** my people forget: 6435
Ps 91:12 **l.** thou dash thy foot against a 6435
Ps 106:23 his wrath, **l.** he should destroy them.........
Ps 125:3 **l.** the righteous put forth........... 4616,3808
Ps 140:8 device; **l.** they exalt themselves...............
Ps 143:7 **l.** I be like unto them that go down ....
Pr 5:6 **L.** thou shouldest ponder the 6435
Pr 5:9 **L.** thou give thine honour unto 6435
Pr 5:10 **L.** strangers be filled with thy 6435
Pr 9:8 not a scorner, **l.** he hate thee:........... 6435
Pr 20:13 not sleep, **l.** thou come to poverty; 6435
Pr 22:25 **L.** thou learn his ways, and get a........ 6435
Pr 24:18 **L.** the Lord see it, and it displease...... 6435
Pr 25:8 **l.** thou know not what to do in the..... 6435
Pr 25:10 **L.** he that heareth it put thee to........ 6435
Pr 25:16 **l.** thou be filled therewith, and........... 6435
Pr 25:17 **l.** he be weary of thee, and so hate...... 6435
Pr 26:4 folly, **l.** thou also be like unto him. 6435
Pr 26:5 **l.** he be wise in his own conceit......... 6435
Pr 30:6 **l.** he reprove thee, and thou be.......... 6435
Pr 30:9 **L.** I be full, and deny thee, and say,... 6435
Pr 30:9 or **l.** I be poor, and steal, and take..... 6435
Pr 30:10 **l.** he curse thee, and thou be found..... 6435
Pr 31:5 **L.** they drink, and forget the law, ... 6435
Ec 7:21 **l.** thou hear thy servant curse...... 634,3808
Isa 6:10 **l.** they see with their eyes, and......... 6435
Isa 27:3 **l.** any hurt it, I will keep it night........ 6435
Isa 28:22 **l.** your bands be made strong: for 6435
Isa 36:18 Beware **l.** Hezekiah persuade you,....... 6435
Isa 48:5 **l.** thou shouldest say, Mine idol 6435
Isa 48:7 **l.** thou shouldest say, Behold, I 6435
Jer 1:17 **l.** I confound thee before them. 6435
Jer 4:4 **l.** my fury come forth like fire, and..... 6435
Jer 6:8 **l.** my soul depart from thee; 6435
Jer 6:8 **l.** I make thee desolate, a land not 6435
Jer 10:24 anger, **l.** thou bring me to nothing...... 6435
Jer 21:12 **l.** my fury go out like fire, and burn.... 6435
Jer 37:20 Jonathan the scribe, **l.** I die there........ 3808
Jer 38:19 **l.** they deliver me into their hand, ... 6435
Jer 51:46 And **l.** your heart faint, and ye fear 6435
Ho 2:3 **L.** I strip her naked, and set her as.... 6435
Am 5:6 **l.** he break out like fire in the house... 6435
Zec 7:12 **l.** they should hear the law, and the.... 6435
Mal 4:6 **l.** I come and smite the earth with 6435
Mt 4:6 **l.** at any time thou dash thy foot......... *3379*
Mt 5:25 **l. at any time the adversary deliver** *3379*
Mt 7:6 **l. they trample them under their**... *3379*
Mt 13:15 **l. at any time they should see with.** *3379*
Mt 13:29 **l. while ye gather up the tares, ye.** *3379*
Mt 15:32 **fasting, l. they faint in the way.** ... *3379*
Mt 17:27 **l. we should offend them, go**.. *2443,3361*
Mt 25:9 **l. there be not enough for us and**.. *3379*
Mt 26:5 **l.** there be an uproar among....... *2443,3361*
Mt 27:64 **l.** his disciples come by night, and...... *3379*

Mk 3:9 l. they should throng him. 2443,3361
Mk 4:12 l....time they should be converted, 3379
Mk 13:5 Take heed l. any man deceive you: 3361
Mk 13:36 L. coming suddenly he find you 3361
Mk 14:2 l. there be an uproar of the people. 3379
Mk 14:38 l. ye enter into temptation. 2443,3361
Lu 4:11 l. at any time thou dash thy foot 3379
Lu 8:12 l. they should believe and be 2443,3361
Lu 12:58 him; l. he hale thee to the judge, 3379
Lu 14:8 l. a more honourable man than 3379
Lu 14:12 l. they also bid thee again, and a 3379
Lu 14:29 L. haply, after he hath 2443,3361
Lu 16:28 l. they also come into this 2443,3361
Lu 18:5 l. by her continual coming she 2443,3361
Lu 21:34 l. at any time your hearts be 3379
Lu 22:46 l. ye enter into temptation. 2443,3361
Joh 3:20 l. his deeds should be reproved. 2443,3361
Joh 5:14 l. a worse thing come unto 2443,3361
Joh 12:35 l. darkness come upon you: 2443,3361
Joh 12:42 l. they should be put out of the 2443,3361
Joh 18:28 hall, l. they should be defiled; 2443,3361
Ac 5:26 l. they should have been stoned 2443,3361
Ac 5:39 l. haply ye be found even to fight 3379
Ac 13:40 therefore, l. that come upon you, 3361
Ac 23:10 fearing l. Paul should have been 3361
Ac 27:17 fearing l. they should fall into the 3361
Ac 27:29 fearing l. we should have fallen 3381
Ac 27:42 l. any of them should swim out, 3361
Ac 28:27 l. they should see with their eyes, 3379
Ro 11:21 take heed l. he also spare not thee. 3381
Ro 11:25 l. ye should be wise in your 2443,3361
Ro 15:20 l. I should build upon another 2443,3361
1Co 1:15 L. any should say that I had 2443,3361
1Co 1:17 l. the cross of Christ should be 2443,3361
1Co 8:9 heed l. by any means this liberty 3381
1Co 8:13 l. I make my brother to offend. 2443,3361
1Co 9:12 l. we should hinder the gospel 2443,3361
1Co 9:27 l. that by any means, when I have 3381
1Co 10:12 he standeth take heed l. he fall. 3361
2Co 2:3 l., when I came, I should have 2443,3361
2Co 2:7 l. perhaps such a one should be 3381
2Co 2:11 L. Satan should get an 2443,3361
2Co 4:4 l. the light of the glorious 1519,3588,3361
2Co 9:3 l. our boasting of you should 3588,3361
2Co 9:4 L. haply if they of Macedonia 3381
2Co 11:3 l. by any means, as the serpent 3381
2Co 12:6 l. any man should think of me 3361
2Co 12:7 l. I should be...above measure, 2443,3361
2Co 12:7 l. I should be...above measure. 2443,3361
2Co 12:20 For I fear, l., when I come, I shall 3381
2Co 12:20 l. there be debates, envyings, 3381
2Co 12:21 l., when I come again, my God 3361
2Co 13:10 l. being present I should use 2443,3361
Ga 2:2 l. by any means I should run, or 3381
Ga 4:11 l. I have bestowed upon you labour 3381
Ga 6:1 thyself, l. thou also be tempted. 3361
Ga 6:12 only l. they should suffer 2443,3361
Eph 2:9 l. any man should boast. 2443,3361
Php 2:27 l. I should have sorrow upon 2443,3361
Col 2:4 l. any man should beguile 2443,3361
Col 2:8 Beware l. any man spoil you 3361
Col 3:21 l. they be discouraged. 2443,3361
1Th 3:5 l. by some means the tempter have 3381
1Ti 3:6 l. being lifted up with pride 2443,3361
1Ti 3:7 l. he fall into reproach and the 2443,3361
Heb 2:1 l. at any time we should let them 3379
Heb 3:12 l. there be in any of you an evil 3379
Heb 3:13 l. any of you be hardened 2443,3361
Heb 4:1 fear, l., a promise being left us of 3379
Heb 4:11 l. any man fall after the same 2443,3361
Heb 11:28 l. he that destroyed the 2443,3361
Heb 12:3 l. ye be wearied and faint in 2443,3361
Heb 12:13 l. that which is lame be 2443,3361
Heb 12:15 l. any man fail of the grace of God; 3361
Heb 12:15 l. any root of bitterness springing 3361
Heb 12:16 L. there be any fornicator, or
Jas 5:9 l. ye be condemned: behold, 2443,3361
Jas 5:12 l. ye fall into condemnation. 2443,3361
2Pe 3:17 beware l. ye also, being led 2443,3361
Re 16:15 l. he walk naked, and they see 2443,3361

LET See also LETTEST; LETTETH; LETTING.

Ge 1:3 And God said, L. there be light: and
Ge 1:6 l. it divide the waters from the waters.
Ge 1:6 L. there be a firmament in the midst
Ge 1:9 place, and l. the dry land appear:
Ge 1:9 L. the waters...the heaven be gathered
Ge 1:11 L. the earth bring forth grass, the
Ge 1:14 L. there be lights in the firmament of
Ge 1:14 l. them be for signs, and for seasons,
Ge 1:15 l. them be for lights in the firmament
Ge 1:20 L. the waters bring forth abundantly
Ge 1:22 seas, and l. fowl multiply in the earth.
Ge 1:24 L. the earth bring forth the living
Ge 1:26 L. us make man in our image, after
Ge 1:26 l. them have dominion over the fish
Ge 11:3 to, l. us make brick, and burn them
Ge 11:4 Go to, l. us build us a city and a tower,
Ge 11:4 and l. us make us a name, lest we be
Ge 11:7 Go to, l. us go down, and there
Ge 13:8 L. there be no strife, I pray thee,
Ge 14:24 Mamre; l. them take their portion.
Ge 18:4 L. a little water, I pray you, be fetched,
Ge 18:30, 32 Oh l. not the Lord be angry, and I
Ge 19:8 l. me, I pray you, bring them out unto
Ge 19:20 a little one: Oh, l. me escape thither,
Ge 19:32 l. us make our father drink wine,
Ge 19:34 l. us make him drink wine this night
Ge 21:12 L. it not be grievous in thy sight.
Ge 21:16 L. me not see the death of the child.
Ge 24:14 And l. it come to pass, that the damsel
Ge 24:14 L. down thy pitcher, I pray thee, 5186
Ge 24:14 l. the same be she that thou hast
Ge 24:17 L. me, I pray thee, drink a little
Ge 24:18 she hasted, and l. down her pitcher 3381
Ge 24:44 l. the same be the woman whom the
Ge 24:45 unto her, L. me drink, I pray thee.
Ge 24:46 haste, and l. down her pitcher 3381
Ge 24:51 and l. her be thy master's son's wife,
Ge 24:55 L. the damsel abide with us a few
Ge 24:60 l. thy seed possess the gate of those
Ge 26:28 L. there be now an oath betwixt us,
Ge 26:28 and l. us make a covenant with thee;
Ge 27:29 L. people serve thee, and nations bow
Ge 27:29 l. thy mother's sons bow down to thee:
Ge 27:31 L. my father arise, and eat of his son's
Ge 30:26 whom I have served thee, and l. me go:
Ge 31:32 thou findest thy gods, l. him not live:
Ge 31:35 L. it not displease my lord that I
Ge 31:44 l. us make a covenant, I and thou;
Ge 31:44 l. it be for a witness between me and
Ge 32:26 L. me go, for the day breaketh.
Ge 32:26 I will not l. thee go, except thou
Ge 33:12 L. us take our journey, and l. us go,
Ge 33:14 L. my lord, I pray thee, pass over
Ge 33:15 L. me now leave with thee some of
Ge 33:15 l. me find grace in the sight of my
Ge 34:11 L. me find grace in your eyes, and
Ge 34:21 therefore l. them dwell in the land,
Ge 34:21 l. us take their daughters to us for
Ge 34:21 and l. us give them our daughters.
Ge 34:23 only l. us consent unto them, and they
Ge 35:3 And l. us arise, and go up to Bethel;
Ge 37:17 heard them say, L. us go to Dothan.
Ge 37:20 l. us slay him, and cast him into some
Ge 37:21 hands; and said, L. us not kill him.
Ge 37:27 and l. us sell him to the Ishmeelites,
Ge 37:27 and l. not our hand be upon him; for
Ge 38:16 I pray thee, l. me come in unto thee;
Ge 38:23 L. her take it to her, lest we be
Ge 38:24 Bring her forth, and l. her be burnt.
Ge 41:33 therefore l. Pharaoh look out a man
Ge 41:34 L. Pharaoh do this, and l. him appoint
Ge 41:35 l. them gather all the food of those
Ge 41:35 and l. them keep food in the cities
Ge 42:16 l. him fetch your brother, and ye shall
Ge 42:19 l. one of your brethren be bound in
Ge 43:9 then l. me bear the blame forever.
Ge 44:9 both l. him die, and we also will be
Ge 44:10 Now also l. it be according unto your
Ge 44:18 lord, l. thy servant, I pray thee, speak
Ge 44:18 l. not thine anger burn against thy
Ge 44:33 l. thy servant abide instead of the lad
Ge 44:33 and l. the lad go up with his brethren.
Ge 46:30 Now l. me die, since I have seen thy
Ge 47:4 l. thy servants dwell in the land of
Ge 47:6 in the land of Goshen l. them dwell:
Ge 47:25 l. us find grace in the sight of my
Ge 48:16 l. my name be named on them, and the
Ge 48:16 l. them grow into a multitude in the
Ge 49:21 Naphtali is a hind l. loose: he giveth
Ge 50:5 Now therefore l. me go up, I pray thee,
Ex 1:10 l. us deal wisely with them; lest they
Ex 3:18 now l. us go, we beseech thee, three
Ex 3:19 king of Egypt will not l. you go, 5414
Ex 3:20 and after that he will l. you go.
Ex 4:18 L. me go, I pray thee, and return unto
Ex 4:21 that he shall not l. the people go.
Ex 4:23 L. my son go, that he may serve
Ex 4:23 and if thou refuse to l. him go,
Ex 4:26 So he l. him go: then she said: A
Ex 5:1 L. my people go, that they may
Ex 5:2 obey his voice to l. Israel go?
Ex 5:2 Lord, neither will I l. Israel go.
Ex 5:3 l. us go, we pray thee, three days'
Ex 5:4 l. the people from their works 6544
Ex 5:7 l. them go and gather straw for
Ex 5:8 L. us go and sacrifice to our God.
Ex 5:9 L. there more work be laid upon the
Ex 5:9 and l. them not regard vain words.
Ex 5:17 L. us go and do sacrifice to the Lord.
Ex 6:1 with a strong hand shall he l. them go,
Ex 6:11 he l. the children of Israel go out
Ex 7:14 he refuseth to l. the people go.
Ex 7:16 L. my people go, that they may
Ex 8:1 L. my people go, that they may
Ex 8:2 And if thou refuse to l. them go,
Ex 8:8 I will l. the people go, that they may
Ex 8:20 L. my people go, that they may
Ex 8:21 if thou wilt not l. my people go,
Ex 8:28 said, I will l. you go, that ye may
Ex 8:29 l. not Pharaoh deal deceitfully any
Ex 8:32 neither would he l. the people go.
Ex 9:1 L. my people go, that they may
Ex 9:2 For if thou refuse to l. them go,
Ex 9:7 and he did not l. the people go.
Ex 9:8 l. Moses sprinkle it toward the heaven
Ex 9:13 L. my people go, that they may
Ex 9:17 that thou wilt not l. them go?
Ex 9:28 I will l. you go, and ye shall stay as
Ex 9:35 he l. the children of Israel go;
Ex 10:3 l. my people go, that they may
Ex 10:4 if thou refuse to l. my people go.
Ex 10:7 l. the men go, that they may serve
Ex 10:10 them, L. the Lord be so with you,
Ex 10:10 I will l. you go, and your little ones:
Ex 10:20 not l. the children of Israel go.
Ex 10:24 only l. your flocks and your herds be
Ex 10:24 l. your little ones also go with you.
Ex 10:27 and he would not l. them go.
Ex 11:1 afterwards he will l. you go hence:
Ex 11:1 when he shall l. you go, he shall
Ex 11:2 l. every man borrow of his neighbour,
Ex 11:10 would not l. the children of Israel go
Ex 12:4 l. him and his neighbour next...take it
Ex 12:10 shall l. nothing of it remain until the
Ex 12:48 Lord, l. all his males be circumcised,
Ex 12:48 then l. him come near and keep it;
Ex 13:15 Pharaoh would hardly l. us go,
Ex 13:17 when Pharaoh had l. the people go,
Ex 14:5 have l. Israel go from serving us?
Ex 14:12 L. us flee from the face of Israel;
Ex 14:25 L. us flee from the face of Israel;
Ex 16:19 L. no man leave of it till the morning.
Ex 16:29 l. no man go out of his place on the
Ex 17:11 when he l. down his hand, Amalek 5117
Ex 18:22 l. them judge the people at all seasons:
Ex 18:27 Moses l. his father in law depart;
Ex 19:10 morrow, and l. them wash their clothes,
Ex 19:22 And l. the priests also...sanctify
Ex 19:24 but l. not the priests and people break
Ex 20:19 l. not God speak with us, lest we die.
Ex 21:8 then shall he l. her be redeemed:
Ex 21:26 l. him go free for his eye's sake.
Ex 21:27 l. him go free for his tooth's sake.
Ex 22:7 the thief be found, l. him pay double.
Ex 22:13 pieces, then l. him bring it for witness,
Ex 23:11 thou shalt l. it rest and lie still;
Ex 23:13 neither l. it be heard out of thy mouth
Ex 24:14 matters to do, l. him come unto them.
Ex 25:8 And l. them make me a sanctuary;
Ex 32:10 Now therefore l. me alone, that
Ex 32:22 L. not the anger of my lord wax hot:
Ex 32:24 hath any gold, l. them break it off.
Ex 32:26 the Lord's side? l. him come unto me.
Ex 33:12 l. me know whom thou wilt send
Ex 34:3 neither l. any man be seen throughout
Ex 34:3 neither l. the flocks nor herds feed
Ex 34:9 Lord, l. my Lord, I pray thee, go among
Ex 35:5 l. him bring it, an offering of the Lord:

1Ki 2:21 **L.** Abishag the Shunammite be given
1Ki 3:26 **L.** it be neither mine nor thine, but
1Ki 8:26 **l.** thy word, I pray thee, be verified,
1Ki 8:57 **l.** him not leave us, nor forsake us:
1Ki 8:59 And **l.** these my words...be nigh unto
1Ki 8:61 **L.** your heart therefore be perfect
1Ki 11:21 **l.** me depart, that I may go to
1Ki 11:22 howbeit **l.** me go in any wise
1Ki 17:21 **l.** this child's soul come into him
1Ki 18:23 **L.** them...give us two bullocks;
1Ki 18:23 **l.** them choose one bullock for
1Ki 18:24 that answereth by fire, **l.** him be God.
1Ki 18:36 **l.** it be known this day that thou art
1Ki 18:40 of Baal; **l.** not one of them escape.
1Ki 19:2 So **l.** the gods do to me, and more
1Ki 19:20 **L.** me, I pray thee, kiss my father and
1Ki 20:11 **L.** not him that girdeth on his harness
1Ki 20:23 **l.** us fight against them in the plain,
1Ki 20:31 **l.** us, I pray thee, put sackcloth on
1Ki 20:32 saith, I pray thee, **l.** me live.
1Ki 20:42 hast **l.** go out of thy hand a man
1Ki 21:7 bread, and **l.** thine heart be merry:
1Ki 22:8 said, **L.** not the king say so.
1Ki 22:13 **l.** thy word, I pray thee, be like the
1Ki 22:17 **l.** them return every man to his
1Ki 22:49 **L.** my servants go with thy
2Ki 1:10, 12 **l.** fire come down from heaven,
2Ki 1:13 **l.** my life, and the life...be precious in
2Ki 1:14 **l.** my life now be precious in thy sight.
2Ki 2:9 **l.** a double portion of thy spirit be
2Ki 2:16 **l.** them go, we pray thee, and seek
2Ki 4:10 **L.** us make a little chamber, I pray
2Ki 4:10 **l.** us set for him there a bed, and a
2Ki 4:27 man of God said, **L.** her alone;
2Ki 5:8 **l.** him come now to me, and he shall
2Ki 5:24 and he **l.** the men go, and they
2Ki 6:2 **L.** us go, we pray thee, unto
2Ki 6:2 **l.** us make us a place there, where we
2Ki 7:4 **l.** us fall unto the hose of the Syrians:
2Ki 7:13 **L.** some take, I pray thee, five of the
2Ki 7:13 consumed:) and **l.** us send and see.
2Ki 9:15 **l.** none go forth nor escape out of the
2Ki 9:17 meet them, and **l.** him say, Is it peace?
2Ki 10:19 all his priests; **l.** none be wanting:
2Ki 10:25 and slay them; **l.** none come forth.
2Ki 11:8 within the ranges, **l.** him be slain:
2Ki 11:15 **L.** her not be slain in the house of the
2Ki 12:5 **L.** the priests take it to them, every
2Ki 12:5 **l.** them repair the breaches of the
2Ki 13:21 when the man was **l.** down, and 3212
2Ki 14:8 **l.** us look one another in the face.
2Ki 17:27 and **l.** them go and dwell there,
2Ki 17:27 **l.** him teach them the manner of the
2Ki 18:29 the king, **L.** not Hezekiah deceive you:
2Ki 18:30 Neither **l.** Hezekiah make you trust in
2Ki 19:10 **L.** not thy God in whom thou trustest
2Ki 20:10 but **l.** the shadow return backward
2Ki 22:5 **l.** them deliver it into the hand of
2Ki 22:5 **l.** them give it to the doers of the
2Ki 23:18 **L.** him alone; **l.** no man move his 3240
2Ki 23:18 So they **l.** his bones alone, with the
1Ch 13:2 **l.** us send abroad unto our
1Ch 13:3 **l.** us bring again the ark of our God to
1Ch 16:10 **l.** the heart of them rejoice that seek
1Ch 16:31 **L.** the heavens be glad, and **l.** the
1Ch 16:31 and **l.** men say among the nations, the
1Ch 16:32 **L.** the sea roar, and the fulness
1Ch 16:32 **l.** the fields rejoice, and all that is
1Ch 17:23 **l.** the thing that thou...be established
1Ch 17:24 **L.** it even be established, that thy
1Ch 17:24 **l.** the house of David...be established
1Ch 17:27 **l.** it please thee to bless the house of
1Ch 19:13 and **l.** us behave ourselves valiantly
1Ch 19:13 and **l.** the Lord do that which is good
1Ch 21:13 **l.** me fall now into the hand of the
1Ch 21:13 but **l.** me not fall into the hand of man.
1Ch 21:17 **l.** thine hand...O Lord my God, be on me..
1Ch 21:23 **l.** my lord the king do that which is
2Ch 1:9 **l.** thy promise unto David my father
2Ch 2:15 of, **l.** him send unto his servants:
2Ch 6:17 God of Israel, **l.** thy word be verified,
2Ch 6:40 **l.**, I beseech thee, thine eyes be open,
2Ch 6:40 **l.** thine ears be attent unto the prayer
2Ch 6:41 **l.** thy priests, O Lord God, be clothed
2Ch 6:41 and **l.** thy saints rejoice in goodness
2Ch 14:7 unto Judah, **L.** us build these cities,
2Ch 14:11 God; **l.** not man prevail against thee.
2Ch 15:7 and **l.** not your hands be weak:
2Ch 16:1 that he might **l.** none go out or 5414
2Ch 16:5 of Ramah, and **l.** his work cease.
2Ch 18:7 said, **L.** not the king say so.
2Ch 18:12 **l.** thy word therefore, I pray thee, be like..
2Ch 18:16 **l.** them return therefore every man
2Ch 19:7 now **l.** the fear of the Lord be upon
2Ch 20:10 thou wouldest not **l.** Israel invade,
2Ch 23:6 But **l.** none come into the house of the
2Ch 23:14 her, **l.** him be slain with the sword.
2Ch 25:7 **l.** not the army of Israel go with thee;
2Ch 25:17 **l.** us see one another in the face.
2Ch 32:15 therefore **l.** not Hezekiah deceive you,
2Ch 36:23 his God be with him, and **l.** him go up.
Ezr 1:3 **l.** him go up to Jerusalem, which is in
Ezr 1:4 **l.** the men of his place help him with
Ezr 4:2 **L.** us build with you: for we seek
Ezr 5:15 **l.** the house of God be builded in his
Ezr 5:17 **l.** there be search made in the king's
Ezr 5:17 **l.** the king send his pleasure to us
Ezr 6:3 **L.** the house be builded, the place
Ezr 6:3 **l.** the foundations thereof be strongly
Ezr 6:4 **l.** the expences be given out of the
Ezr 6:5 **l.** the golden and...vessels...be restored
Ezr 6:7 **L.** the work of this house of God alone;
Ezr 6:7 **l.** the governor of the Jews...build
Ezr 6:9 **l.** it be given them day by day without
Ezr 6:11 **l.** timber be pulled down from his
Ezr 6:11 set up, **l.** him be hanged thereon;
Ezr 6:11 and **l.** his house be made a dunghill for
Ezr 6:12 a decree; **l.** it be done with speed.
Ezr 7:23 **l.** it be diligently done for the house of
Ezr 7:26 **l.** judgment be executed speedily
Ezr 10:3 **l.** us make a covenant with our God
Ezr 10:3 and **l.** it be done according to the law.
Ezr 10:14 **L.** now our rulers of all the...stand,
Ezr 10:14 **l.** all them which have taken...come
Ne 1:6 **L.** thine ear now be attentive, and
Ne 1:11 **l.** now thine ear be attentive to the
Ne 2:3 the king, **L.** the king live for ever:
Ne 2:7 **l.** letters be given me to the,
Ne 2:17 **l.** us build up the wall of Jerusalem.
Ne 2:18 And they said, **L.** us rise up and build.
Ne 4:5 **l.** not their sin be blotted out from
Ne 4:22 **L.** every one with his servant lodge
Ne 5:10 I pray you, **l.** us leave off this usury.
Ne 6:2 Come, **l.** us meet together in some one
Ne 6:7 and **l.** us take counsel together.
Ne 6:10 **L.** us meet together in the house of
Ne 6:10 and **l.** us shut the doors of the temple:
Ne 7:3 **L.** not the gates of Jerusalem be
Ne 7:3 **l.** them shut the doors, and bar them:
Ne 9:32 **l.** not all the trouble seem little before
Es 1:19 **l.** there go a royal commandment
Es 1:19 **l.** it be written among the laws of the
Es 1:19 **l.** the king give her royal estate
Es 2:2 **L.** there be fair young virgins sought
Es 2:3 And **l.** the king appoint officers in all
Es 2:3 **l.** their things for purification be given
Es 2:4 **l.** the maiden which pleaseth...be queen.
Es 3:9 **l.** it be written that they may be
Es 5:4 **l.** the king and Haman come this day
Es 5:8 **l.** the king and Haman come to the
Es 5:12 the queen did **l.** no man come in with
Es 5:14 **L.** a gallows be made of fifty cubits
Es 6:5 And the king said, **L.** him come in.
Es 6:8 **L.** the royal apparel be brought which
Es 6:9 **l.** this apparel and horse be delivered
Es 6:10 **l.** nothing fail of all that thou hast
Es 7:3 **l.** my life be given me at my
Es 8:5 **l.** it be written to reverse the letters
Es 9:13 **l.** it be granted to the Jews which
Es 9:13 **l.** Haman's ten sons be hanged upon
Job 3:3 **L.** the day perish wherein I was born,
Job 3:4 **L.** that day be darkness;
Job 3:4 **l.** not God regard it from above,
Job 3:4 neither **l.** the light shine upon it.
Job 3:5 **L.** darkness and the shadow of death
Job 3:5 stain it; **l.** a cloud dwell upon it;
Job 3:5 **l.** the blackness of the day terrify it.
Job 3:6 that night, **l.** darkness seize upon it;
Job 3:6 **l.** it not be joined unto the days of the
Job 3:6 **l.** it not come into the number of the
Job 3:7 Lo, **l.** that night be solitary,
Job 3:7 **l.** no joyful voice come therein.
Job 3:8 **L.** them curse it that curse the day
Job 3:9 **L.** the stars of the twilight thereof be
Job 3:9 **l.** it look for light, but have none;
Job 3:9 neither **l.** it see the dawning of the
Job 6:9 he would **l.** loose his hand, and cut me
Job 6:10 **l.** him not spare; for I have not
Job 6:29 **l.** it not be iniquity; yea, return again,
Job 7:16 not live alway: **l.** me alone; for
Job 7:19 nor **l.** me alone till I swallow down
Job 9:34 **L.** him take his rod away from me,
Job 9:34 and **l.** not his fear terrify me:
Job 10:20 and **l.** me alone, that I may take
Job 11:14 and **l.** not wickedness dwell in thy
Job 13:13 Hold your peace, **l.** me alone, that I
Job 13:13 speak, and **l.** come on me what will.
Job 13:21 and **l.** not thy dread make me afraid.
Job 13:22 or **l.** me speak, and answer thou me.
Job 15:31 **L.** not him that is deceived trust in
Job 16:18 my blood, and **l.** my cry have no place.
Job 21:2 and **l.** this be your consolations.
Job 27:6 I hold fast, and will not **l.** it go:
Job 27:7 **L.** my enemy be as the wicked, and he
Job 30:11 have also **l.** loose the bridle before me.
Job 31:6 **L.** me be weighed in an even balance,
Job 31:8 Then **l.** me sow, and **l.** another eat;
Job 31:8 Yea, **l.** my offspring be rooted out.
Job 31:10 Then **l.** my wife grind unto another,
Job 31:10 and **l.** others bow down upon her.
Job 31:22 **l.** mine arm fall from my shoulder
Job 31:40 **L.** thistles grow instead of wheat, and
Job 32:21 **L.** me not, I pray you, accept any
Job 32:21 neither **l.** me give flattering titles unto
Job 34:4 **L.** us choose to us judgment:
Job 34:4 **l.** us know among ourselves what is
Job 34:34 **L.** men of understanding tell me,
Job 34:34 and **l.** a wise man hearken unto me.
Job 40:2 reproveth God, **l.** him answer it.
Ps 2:3 **L.** us break their bands asunder, and
Ps 5:10 **l.** them fall by their own counsels;
Ps 5:11 **l.** all those that put their trust...rejoice:
Ps 5:11 **l.** them ever shout for joy, because
Ps 5:11 **l.** them...that love thy name be joyful
Ps 6:10 **L.** all mine enemies be ashamed and
Ps 6:10 **l.** them return and be ashamed
Ps 7:5 **L.** the enemy persecute my soul, and
Ps 7:5 **l.** him tread down my life upon the
Ps 7:9 **l.** the wickedness of the wicked come
Ps 9:19 Arise, O Lord; **l.** not man prevail:
Ps 9:19 **l.** the heathen be judged in thy sight.
Ps 10:2 **l.** them be taken in the devices that
Ps 17:2 **L.** my sentence come forth from thy
Ps 17:2 **l.** thine eyes behold the things that are
Ps 18:46 **l.** the God of my salvation be exalted.
Ps 19:13 **l.** them not have dominion over me;
Ps 19:14 **L.** the words of my...be acceptable
Ps 20:9 **l.** the king hear us when we call.
Ps 22:8 **l.** him deliver him, seeing he delighted
Ps 25:2 trust in thee: **l.** me not be ashamed,
Ps 25:2 **l.** not mine enemies triumph over me.
Ps 25:3 **l.** none that wait on thee be ashamed:
Ps 25:3 **l.** them be ashamed which transgress
Ps 25:20 **l.** me not be ashamed; for I put my
Ps 25:21 **L.** integrity and uprightness preserve
Ps 31:1 put my trust; **l.** me never be ashamed:
Ps 31:17 **L.** me not be ashamed, O Lord; for I
Ps 31:17 upon thee: **l.** the wicked be ashamed,
Ps 31:17 and **l.** them be silent in the grave.
Ps 31:18 **L.** the lying lips be put to silence;
Ps 33:8 **L.** all the earth fear the Lord:
Ps 33:8 **l.** all the inhabitants...stand in awe
Ps 33:22 **L.** thy mercy, O Lord, be upon us,
Ps 34:3 me, and **l.** us exalt his name together.
Ps 35:4 **L.** them be confounded and put to
Ps 35:4 **l.** them be turned back and brought
Ps 35:5 **L.** them be as chaff before the wind:
Ps 35:5 **l.** the angel of the Lord chase them.
Ps 35:6 **L.** their way be dark and slippery:
Ps 35:6 **l.** the angel of the Lord persecute
Ps 35:8 **L.** destruction come upon him at
Ps 35:8 **l.** his net that he hath hid catch
Ps 35:8 into that very destruction **l.** him fall.
Ps 35:19 **L.** not them...mine enemies rejoice
Ps 35:19 neither **l.** them wink with the eye that
Ps 35:24 and **l.** them not rejoice over me.
Ps 35:25 **L.** them not say in their hearts, Ah, so
Ps 35:25 **l.** them not say, We have swallowed
Ps 35:26 **L.** them be ashamed and brought to

Ps 35:26 l. them be clothed with shame and
Ps 35:27 L. them shout for joy, and be glad,
Ps 35:27 cause: yea, l. them say continually,
Ps 35:27 L. the Lord be magnified, which hath
Ps 36:11 L. not the foot of pride come against
Ps 36:11 l. not the hand of the wicked remove
Ps 40:11 l. thy lovingkindness and...preserve me,
Ps 40:14 L. them be ashamed and confounded
Ps 40:14 l. them be driven backward and put to
Ps 40:15 L. them be desolate for a reward of
Ps 40:16 L. all those that seek thee rejoice
Ps 40:16 l. such as love thy salvation say
Ps 43:3 light and thy truth: l. them lead me;
Ps 43:3 l. them bring me unto thy holy hill,
Ps 48:11 L. mount Zion rejoice,
Ps 48:11 l. the daughters of Judah be glad,
Ps 55:15 L. death seize upon them,
Ps 55:15 and l. them go down quick into hell:
Ps 57:5, 11 l. thy glory be above all the earth.
Ps 58:7 L. them melt away as waters which
Ps 58:7 his arrows, l. them be as cut in pieces.
Ps 58:8 l. every one of them pass away:
Ps 59:10 God shall l. me see my desire upon
Ps 59:12 l. them even be taken in their pride:
Ps 59:13 l. them know that God ruleth in Jacob
Ps 59:14 And at evening l. them return;
Ps 59:14 l. them make a noise like a dog, and
Ps 59:15 L. them wander up and down for
Ps 66:7 l. not the rebellious exalt themselves.
Ps 67:3 L. the people praise thee, O God;
Ps 67:3 l. all the people praise thee.
Ps 67:4 O l. the nations be glad and sing for
Ps 67:5 L. the people praise thee, O God;
Ps 67:5 l. all the people praise thee.
Ps 68:1 L. God arise, l. his enemies be
Ps 68:1 l. them also that hate him flee before
Ps 68:2 so l. the wicked perish at the presence
Ps 68:3 But l. the righteous be glad;
Ps 68:3 l. them rejoice before God:
Ps 68:3 yea, l. them exceedingly rejoice.
Ps 69:6 L. not them that wait on...be ashamed
Ps 69:6 l. not those that seek...be confounded
Ps 69:14 out of the mire, and l. me not sink:
Ps 69:14 l. me be delivered from them that hate
Ps 69:15 L. not the waterflood overflow me,
Ps 69:15 neither l. the deep swallow me up,
Ps 69:15 l. not the pit shut her mouth upon me.
Ps 69:22 L. their table become a snare before
Ps 69:22 for their welfare, l. it become a trap,
Ps 69:23 L. their eyes be darkened, that they
Ps 69:24 l. thy wrathful anger take hold of
Ps 69:25 L. their habitation be desolate;
Ps 69:25 and l. none dwell in their tents.
Ps 69:27 and l. them not come into thy
Ps 69:28 L. them be blotted out of the book of
Ps 69:29 l. thy salvation, O God, set me up on
Ps 69:34 L. the heaven and earth praise him,
Ps 70:2 L. them be ashamed and confounded
Ps 70:2 l. them be turned backward, and put
Ps 70:3 L. them be turned back for a reward
Ps 70:4 L. all those that seek thee rejoice and
Ps 70:4 and l. such as love thy salvation say
Ps 70:4 say continually, L. God be magnified.
Ps 71:1 trust; l. me never be put to confusion.
Ps 71:8 L. my mouth be filled with thy praise
Ps 71:13 L. them be confounded and consumed
Ps 71:13 l. them be covered with reproach and
Ps 72:19 l. the whole earth be filled with his
Ps 74:8 hearts, L. us destroy them together:
Ps 74:21 O l. not the oppressed return ashamed:
Ps 74:21 l. the poor and needy praise thy name.
Ps 76:11 l. all that be round about him bring
Ps 78:28 he l. it fall in the midst of their camp,
Ps 79:8 l. thy tender mercies speedily prevent
Ps 79:10 l. him be known among the heathen in
Ps 79:11 L. the sighing of the prisoner come
Ps 80:17 L. thy hand be upon the man of thy
Ps 83:4 l. us cut them off from being a nation;
Ps 83:12 L. us take to ourselves the houses of
Ps 83:17 L. them be confounded and troubled
Ps 83:17 l. them be put to shame, and perish:
Ps 85:8 l. them not turn again to folly.
Ps 88:2 L. my prayer come before thee:
Ps 90:13 l. it repent thee concerning thy
Ps 90:16 L. thy work appear unto thy servants,
Ps 90:17 l. the beauty of the Lord our God be
Ps 95:1 O come, l. us sing unto the Lord:
Ps 95:1 l. us make a joyful noise to the rock
Ps 95:2 L. us come before his presence with
Ps 95:6 O come, l. us worship and bow down:
Ps 95:6 l. us kneel before the Lord our maker
Ps 96:11 L. the heavens rejoice, and l. the earth
Ps 96:11 l. the sea roar, and the fulness thereof.
Ps 96:12 L. the field be joyful, and all that is
Ps 97:1 l. the earth rejoice; l. the multitude
Ps 98:7 L. the sea roar, and the fulness
Ps 98:8 L. the floods clap their hands:
Ps 98:8 l. the hills be joyful together.
Ps 99:1 Lord reigneth; l. the people tremble:
Ps 99:1 cherubims; l. the earth be moved.
Ps 99:3 L. them praise thy great and terrible
Ps 102:1 O Lord, and l. my cry come unto thee.
Ps 104:35 L. the sinners be consumed out of the
Ps 104:35 and l. the wicked be no more. Bless
Ps 105:3 l. the heart of them rejoice that seek
Ps 105:20 ruler of the people, and l. him go free.
Ps 106:48 and l. all the people say, Amen.
Ps 107:2 L. the redeemed of the Lord say so,
Ps 107:22 And l. them sacrifice the sacrifices of
Ps 107:32 L. them exalt him also in the
Ps 109:6 and l. Satan stand at his right hand.
Ps 109:7 be judged, l. him be condemned:
Ps 109:7 and l. his prayer become sin.
Ps 109:8 L. his days be few; and l. another
Ps 109:9 L. his children be fatherless, and his
Ps 109:10 L. his children be continually
Ps 109:10 l. them seek their bread also out of
Ps 109:11 L. the extortioner catch all that he
Ps 109:11 and l. the strangers spoil his labour.
Ps 109:12 L. there be none to extend mercy unto
Ps 109:12 neither l. there be any to favour his
Ps 109:13 L. his posterity be cut off; and in the
Ps 109:13 following l. their name be blotted out.
Ps 109:14 L. the iniquity of his fathers be
Ps 109:14 and l. not the sin of his mother be
Ps 109:15 L. them be before the Lord
Ps 109:17 loved cursing, so l. it come unto him:
Ps 109:17 not in blessing, so l. it be far from him.
Ps 109:18 so l. it come into his bowels like water,
Ps 109:19 L. it be unto him as the garment
Ps 109:20 L. this be the reward of mine
Ps 109:28 L. them curse, but bless thou: when
Ps 109:28 they arise, l. them be ashamed;
Ps 109:28 but l. thy servant rejoice.
Ps 109:29 L. mine adversaries be clothed with
Ps 109:29 l. them cover themselves with their
Ps 118:2 L. Israel now say, that his mercy
Ps 118:3 L. the house of Aaron now say, that
Ps 118:4 L. them now that fear the Lord say,
Ps 119:10 O l. me not wander from thy
Ps 119:41 L. thy mercies come also unto me, O
Ps 119:76 L., I pray thee, thy merciful kindness
Ps 119:77 L. thy tender mercies come unto me,
Ps 119:78 L. the proud be ashamed; for they
Ps 119:79 L. those that fear thee turn unto me,
Ps 119:80 L. my heart be sound in thy statutes;
Ps 119:116 and l. me not be ashamed of my hope.
Ps 119:122 good: l. not the proud oppress me.
Ps 119:133 l. not any iniquity have dominion over
Ps 119:169 L. my cry come near before thee, O
Ps 119:170 L. my supplication come before thee:
Ps 119:173 L. thine hand help me; for I have
Ps 119:175 L. my soul live, and it shall praise
Ps 119:175 thee; and l. thy judgments help me.
Ps 122:1 L. us go into the house of the Lord,
Ps 129:5 L. them all be confounded and turned
Ps 129:6 L. them be as the grass upon the
Ps 130:2 l. thine ears be attentive to the voice
Ps 130:7 L. Israel hope in the Lord: for with
Ps 131:3 L. Israel hope in the Lord from
Ps 132:9 L. thy priests be clothed with
Ps 132:9 and l. thy saints shout for joy.
Ps 137:5 l. my right hand forget her cunning.
Ps 137:6 l. my tongue cleave to the roof of my
Ps 140:9 l. the mischief of their own lips cover
Ps 140:10 L. burning coals fall upon them:
Ps 140:10 l. them be cast into the fire; into deep
Ps 140:11 L. not an evil speaker be established
Ps 141:2 L. my prayer be set forth before thee.
Ps 141:4 and l. me not eat of their dainties.
Ps 141:5 L. the righteous smite me; it shall be
Ps 141:5 l. him reprove me; it shall be an
Ps 141:10 L. the wicked fall into their own nets,
Ps 145:21 l. all flesh bless his holy name for ever.
Ps 148:5, 13 L. them praise the name of the Lord:
Ps 149:2 L. Israel rejoice in him that made
Ps 149:2 l. the children of Zion be joyful in their
Ps 149:3 L. them praise his name in the dance:
Ps 149:3 l. them sing praises unto him with the
Ps 149:5 L. the saints be joyful in glory:
Ps 149:5 l. them sing aloud upon their beds.
Ps 149:6 L. the high praises of God be in their
Ps 150:6 L. every thing that hath breath praise
Pr 1:11 Come with us, l. us lay wait for blood,
Pr 1:11 l. us lurk privily for the innocent
Pr 1:12 L. us swallow them up alive as the
Pr 1:14 among us; l. us have one purse:
Pr 3:1 l. thine heart keep my commandments:
Pr 3:3 L. not mercy and truth forsake thee:
Pr 3:21 l. not them depart from thine eyes:
Pr 4:4 me, L. thine heart retain my words:
Pr 4:13 l. her not go: keep her; for she is
Pr 4:21 L. them not depart from thine eyes;
Pr 4:25 L. thine eyes look right on, and
Pr 4:25 L. thine eyelids look straight before
Pr 4:26 and l. all thy ways be established.
Pr 5:16 L. thy fountains be dispersed abroad,
Pr 5:17 L. them be only thine own, and not
Pr 5:18 L. thy fountain be blessed: and
Pr 5:19 L. her be as the loving hind and
Pr 5:19 l. her breasts satisfy thee at all times;
Pr 6:25 neither l. her take thee with her
Pr 7:18 l. us take our fill of love until the
Pr 7:18 l. us solace ourselves with loves.
Pr 7:25 L. not thine heart decline to her ways,
Pr 9:4,16 is simple, l. him turn in hither:
Pr 17:12 L. a bear robbed of her whelps meet a
Pr 19:18 l. not thy soul spare for his crying.
Pr 23:17 L. not thine heart envy sinners: but
Pr 23:26 and l. thine eyes observe my ways.
Pr 24:17 l. not thine heart be glad when he
Pr 27:2 L. another man praise thee, and not
Pr 28:17 flee to the pit; l. no man stay him.
Pr 31:7 L. him drink, and forget his poverty,
Pr 31:31 l. her own works praise her in the
Ec 5:2 l. not thine heart be hasty to utter any
Ec 5:2 earth: therefore l. thy words be few.
Ec 9:8 L. thy garments be always white;
Ec 9:8 and l. thy head lack no ointment.
Ec 11:8 l. him remember the days of darkness;
Ec 11:9 l. thy heart cheer thee in the days of
Ec 12:13 L. us hear the conclusion of the whole
Ca 1:2 L. him kiss me with the kisses of his
Ca 2:14 l. me see thy countenance, l. me hear
Ca 3:4 held him, and would not l. him go,
Ca 4:16 L. my beloved come into his garden,
Ca 7:11 beloved, l. us go forth into the field;
Ca 7:11 l. us lodge in the villages.
Ca 7:12 L. us get up early to the vineyards;
Ca 7:12 l. us see if the vine flourish, whether
Ca 8:11 l. out the vineyards unto keepers; 5414
Isa 1:18 Come now, and l. us reason together,
Isa 2:3 l. us go up to the mountain of the
Isa 2:5 l. us walk in the light of the Lord.
Isa 3:6 and l. this ruin be under thy hand:
Isa 4:1 only l. us be called by thy name, to
Isa 5:19 L. him make speed and hasten his
Isa 5:19 l. the counsel of the Holy...draw nigh
Isa 7:6 L. us go up against Judah, and vex it,
Isa 7:6 l. us make a breach therein for us,
Isa 8:13 hosts himself; and l. him be your fear.
Isa 8:13 and l. him be your dread.
Isa 16:4 L. mine outcasts dwell with thee,
Isa 19:12 wise men? and l. them tell thee now,
Isa 19:12 l. them know what the Lord of hosts
Isa 21:6 l. him declare what he seeth.
Isa 22:13 l. us eat and drink; for to-morrow we
Isa 26:10 L. favour be shewed to the wicked, yet
Isa 27:5 Or l. him take hold of my strength,
Isa 29:1 ye year to year; l. them kill sacrifices.
Isa 34:1 l. the earth hear, and all that is
Isa 36:14 king, L. not Hezekiah deceive you:
Isa 36:15 Neither l. Hezekiah make you trust in
Isa 37:10 L. not thy God, in whom...deceive thee,
Isa 38:21 had said, L. them take a lump of figs,
Isa 41:1 l. the people renew their strength:
Isa 41:1 l. them come near; then l. them speak:
Isa 41:1 l. us come near together to judgment.
Isa 41:22 L. them bring them forth, and shew us
Isa 41:22 l. them shew the former things, what

Isa	42:11	L. the wilderness and the cities thereof	
Isa	42:11	l. the inhabitants of the rock sing,	
Isa	42:11	l. them shout from the top of the	
Isa	42:12	L. them give glory unto the Lord,	
Isa	43:9	L. all the nations be gathered together,	
Isa	43:9	and l. the people be assembled:	
Isa	43:9	l. them bring forth their witnesses,	
Isa	43:9	or l. them hear, and say, It is truth.	
Isa	43:13	I will work, and who shall l. it?	7725
Isa	43:26	in remembrance: l. us plead together:	
Isa	44:7	shall come, l. them shew unto them.	
Isa	44:11	l. them all be gathered together.	
Isa	44:11	l. them stand up; yet they shall fear,	
Isa	45:8	l. the skies pour down righteousness:	
Isa	45:8	l. the earth open, and l. them bring	
Isa	45:8	l. righteousness spring up together;	
Isa	45:9	L. the potsherd strive with the	
Isa	45:13	he shall l. go my captives, not for	
Isa	45:21	l. them take counsel together: who	
Isa	47:13	L. now the astrologers,...stand up,	
Isa	50:8	contend with me? l. us stand together:	
Isa	50:8	adversary? l. him come near to me.	
Isa	50:10	l. him trust in the name of the Lord,	
Isa	54:2	l. them stretch forth the curtains of	
Isa	55:2	l. your soul delight itself in fatness.	
Isa	55:7	L. the wicked forsake his way, and	
Isa	55:7	l. him return unto the Lord, and	
Isa	56:3	Neither l. the son of the...speak,	
Isa	56:3	neither l. the eunuch say, Behold, I	
Isa	57:13	criest, l. thy companies deliver thee;	
Isa	58:6	to the l. the oppressed go free, and	
Isa	66:5	L. the Lord be glorified: but he shall	
Jer	2:28	l. them arise, if they can save thee in	
Jer	4:5	and l. us go into the defenced cities.	
Jer	5:24	L. us now fear the Lord our God, that	
Jer	6:4	her; arise, and l. us go up at noon.	
Jer	6:5	Arise, and l. us go by night,	
Jer	6:5	and l. us destroy her palaces.	
Jer	8:14	l. us enter into the defenced cities,	
Jer	8:14	and l. us be silent there: for the Lord	
Jer	9:18	And l. them make haste, and take up	
Jer	9:20	and l. your ear receive the word of his	
Jer	9:23	L. not the wise man glory in his	
Jer	9:23	neither l. the mighty man glory in his	
Jer	9:23	l. not the rich man glory in his riches:	
Jer	9:24	But l. him that glorieth glory in this,	
Jer	11:19	L. us destroy the tree with the fruit	
Jer	11:19	l. us cut him off from the land of the	
Jer	11:20	l. me see thy vengeance on them:	
Jer	12:1	l. me talk with thee of thy judgments:	
Jer	14:17	L. mine eyes run down with tears	
Jer	14:17	night and day, and l. them not cease:	
Jer	15:1	out of my sight, and l. them go forth.	
Jer	15:19	l. them return unto thee; but	
Jer	17:15	the word of the Lord? l. it come now.	
Jer	17:18	L. them be confounded that persecute	
Jer	17:18	but l. not me be confounded:	
Jer	17:18	l. them be dismayed,	
Jer	17:18	but l. not me be dismayed:	
Jer	18:18	l. us devise devices against Jeremiah;	
Jer	18:18	and l. us smite him with the tongue,	
Jer	18:18	l. us not give heed to any of his words.	
Jer	18:21	l. their wives be bereaved of their	
Jer	18:21	and l. their men be put to death;	
Jer	18:21	l. their young men be slain by the	
Jer	18:22	L. a cry be heard from their houses,	
Jer	18:23	but l. them be overthrown before thee;	
Jer	20:12	l. me see thy vengeance on them:	
Jer	20:14	l. not the day wherein my mother bare	
Jer	20:16	And l. that man be as the cities which	
Jer	20:16	l. him hear the cry in the morning,	
Jer	23:28	that hath a dream, l. him tell a dream;	
Jer	23:28	word, l. him speak my word faithfully.	
Jer	27:11	those will I l. remain still in their	
Jer	27:18	l. them now make intercession to the	
Jer	29:8	L. not your prophets and your	
Jer	31:6	l. us go up to Zion unto the Lord our	
Jer	34:9	man should l. his manservant...go free;	
Jer	34:10	one should l. his manservant...go free,	
Jer	34:10	then they obeyed, and l. them go.	
Jer	34:11	whom they had l. go free, to return,	
Jer	34:14	l. ye go every man his brother an	
Jer	34:14	thou shalt l. him go free from thee:	
Jer	35:11	and l. us go to Jerusalem for fear of	
Jer	36:19	and l. no man know where ye be.	
Jer	37:20	l. my supplication,...be accepted	
Jer	38:4	thee, l. this man be put to death:	
Jer	38:6	they l. down Jeremiah with cords.	7971
Jer	38:11	and l. them down by cords into the	7971
Jer	38:24	L. no man know of these words, and	
Jer	40:1	captain of the guard had l. him go	
Jer	40:5	victuals and a reward, and l. him go.	
Jer	40:15	Mizpah secretly, saying, L. me go,	
Jer	42:2	L....our supplication be accepted	
Jer	46:6	L. not the swift flee away, nor the	
Jer	46:9	and l. the mighty men come forth;	
Jer	46:16	l. us go again to our own people,	
Jer	48:2	l. us cut it off from being a nation.	
Jer	49:11	alive; and l. thy widows trust in me.	
Jer	50:5	and l. us join ourselves to the Lord	
Jer	50:26	her utterly: l. nothing of her be left.	
Jer	50:27	l. them go down to the slaughter:	
Jer	50:29	about; l. none therefore escape:	
Jer	50:33	them fast; they refused to l. them go.	
Jer	51:3	bendeth l. the archer bend his bow,	
Jer	51:9	l. us go every one into his own	
Jer	51:10	l. us declare in Zion the work of the	
Jer	51:50	l. Jerusalem come into your mind.	
La	1:22	L. all their wickedness come before	
La	2:18	l. tears run down like a river day	
La	2:18	l. not the apple of thine eye cease.	
La	3:40	L. us search and try our ways, and	
La	3:41	L. us lift up our heart with our hands	
Eze	1:24	stood, they l. down their wings.	7503
Eze	1:25	stood, and had l. down their wings.	7503
Eze	3:27	God; He that heareth, l. him hear;	
Eze	3:27	and he that forbeareth, l. him forbear:	
Eze	7:12	l. not the buyer rejoice, nor the seller	
Eze	9:5	l. not your eye spare, neither have ye	
Eze	11:3	l. us build houses: this city is the	
Eze	13:20	will l. the souls go, even the souls	
Eze	21:14	and l. the sword be doubled the third	
Eze	24:5	l. them seethe the bones of it therein.	
Eze	24:6	piece by piece; l. no lot fall upon it.	
Eze	24:10	spice it well...l. the bones be burned.	
Eze	39:7	I will not l. them pollute my holy	
Eze	43:9	now l. them put away their whoredom,	
Eze	43:10	and l. them measure the pattern.	
Eze	44:6	Israel, l. it suffice you of all your	
Eze	45:9	L. it suffice you, O prince of Israel:	
Da	1:12	l. them give us pulse to eat, and water	
Da	1:13	l. our countenances be looked upon	
Da	2:7	L. the king tell his servants the dream,	
Da	4:14	l. the beasts get away from under it,	
Da	4:15	l. it be wet with the dew of heaven,	
Da	4:15	l. his portion be with the beasts in the	
Da	4:16	L. his heart be changed from man's,	
Da	4:16	l. a beast's heart be given unto him;	
Da	4:16	and l. seven times pass over him.	
Da	4:19	l. not the dream, or the...trouble thee.	
Da	4:23	l. it be wet with the dew of heaven,	
Da	4:23	l. his portion be with the beasts of the	
Da	4:27	l. my counsel be acceptable unto thee,	
Da	5:10	ever: l. not thy thoughts trouble thee,	
Da	5:10	nor l. thy countenance be changed:	
Da	5:12	now l. Daniel be called, and he will	
Da	5:17	L. thy gifts be to thyself, and give thy	
Da	9:16	l. thine anger and thy fury be turned	
Da	10:19	said, L. my lord speak; for thou hast	
Ho	2:2	l. her therefore put away her	
Ho	4:4	Yet l. no man strive, nor reprove	
Ho	4:15	the harlot, yet l. not Judah offend;	
Ho	4:17	is joined to idols: l. him alone.	
Ho	6:1	and l. us return unto the Lord:	
Ho	13:2	L. the men that sacrifice kiss the	
Joe	1:3	l. your children tell their children, and	
Joe	2:1	l. all the inhabitants of the...tremble:	
Joe	2:16	l. the bridegroom go forth of his	
Joe	2:17	L. the priests...weep...l. them say.	
Joe	3:9	men, l. all the men of war draw near;	
Joe	3:9	l. them come up:	
Joe	3:10	spears: l. the weak say, I am strong.	
Joe	3:12	L. the heathen be wakened, and come	
Am	4:1	their masters, Bring, and l. us drink.	
Am	5:24	But l. judgment run down as waters,	
Ob	1	and l. us rise up against her in battle.	
Jon	1:7	Come, and l. us cast lots, that we may	
Jon	1:14	l. us not perish for this man's life, and	
Jon	3:7	L. neither man nor beast, herd...taste	
Jon	3:7	l. them not feed, nor drink water:	
Jon	3:8	But l. man and beast be covered with	
Jon	3:8	l. them turn every one from his	
Mic	1:2	l. the Lord God be witness against	
Mic	4:2	and l. us go up to the mountain of the	
Mic	4:11	L. her be defiled, and l. our eye look	
Mic	6:1	and l. the hills hear thy voice.	
Mic	7:14	l. them feed in Bashan and Gilead, as	
Hab	2:16	also, and l. thy foreskin be uncovered:	
Hab	2:20	l. all the earth keep silence before	
Zep	3:16	to Zion, L. not thine hands be slack.	
Zec	3:5	L. them set a fair mitre upon his head.	
Zec	7:10	l. none of you imagine evil against his	
Zec	8:9	L. your hands be strong, ye that hear	
Zec	8:13	fear not, but l. your hands be strong.	
Zec	8:17	l. none of you imagine evil in your	
Zec	8:21	L. us go speedily to pray before the	
Zec	11:9	not feed you: that that dieth, l. it die;	
Zec	11:9	that that is to be cut off, l. it be cut off;	
Zec	11:9	and l. the rest eat every one the flesh	
Mal	2:15	l. none deal treacherously against the	
Mt	5:16	L. your light so shine before men, that.	
Mt	5:31	his wife, l. him give her a writing of	
Mt	5:37	l. your communication be, Yea,	
Mt	5:40	thy coat, l. him have thy cloke also.	
Mt	6:3	l. not thy left hand know what thy	
Mt	7:4	L. me pull out the mote out of	863
Mt	8:22	me; and l. the dead bury their dead.	863
Mt	10:13	be worthy, l. your peace come	
Mt	10:13	worthy, l. your peace return to you.	
Mt	11:15	He that hath ears to hear, l. him	
Mt	13:9	Who hath ears to hear, l. him hear.	
Mt	13:30	L. both grow together until the	863
Mt	13:43	Who hath ears to hear, l. him hear.	
Mt	15:4	father or mother, l. him die the	
Mt	15:14	L. them alone: they be blind	
Mt	16:24	l. him deny himself, and take up his	
Mt	17:4	l. us make here three tabernacles;	
Mt	18:17	l. him be unto thee as an heathen	
Mt	19:6	together, l. not man put asunder.	
Mt	19:12	able to receive it, l. him receive it.	
Mt	20:26	you, l. him be your minister;	
Mt	20:27	among you, l. him be your servant:	
Mt	21:19	L. no fruit grow on thee henceforward.	
Mt	21:33	l. it out to husbandmen, and went.	1554
Mt	21:38	and l. us seize on his inheritance.	
Mt	21:38	This is the heir; come, l. us kill him,	
Mt	21:41	will l. out his vineyard unto other	1554
Mt	24:15	(whoso readeth, l. him understand:)	
Mt	24:16	l. them which be in Judaea flee	
Mt	24:17	L. him which is on the housetop not	
Mt	24:18	Neither l. him which is in the field	
Mt	26:39	be possible, l. this cup pass from me:	
Mt	26:46	l. us be going: behold, he is at hand	
Mt	27:22	all say unto him, L. him be crucified.	
Mt	27:23	the more, saying, L. him be crucified.	
Mt	27:42	l. him now come down from the cross,	
Mt	27:43	l. him deliver him now, if he will	
Mt	27:49	The rest said, L. be,	863
Mt	27:49	l. us see whether Elias will come	
Mk	1:24	L. us alone; what have we to do	1439
Mk	1:38	L. us go into the next town, that I	
Mk	2:4	l. down the bed wherein the sick	5465
Mk	4:9	He that hath ears to hear, l. him hear.	
Mk	4:23	man have ears to hear, l. him hear.	
Mk	4:35	L. us pass over unto the other side.	
Mk	7:10	father or mother, l. him die the death:	
Mk	7:16	man have ears to hear, l. him hear.	
Mk	7:27	her, L. the children first be filled:	863
Mk	8:34	l. him deny himself, and take up his	
Mk	9:5	and l. us make three tabernacles;	
Mk	10:9	together, l. not man put asunder.	
Mk	11:6	commanded: and they l. them go.	863
Mk	12:1	l. it out to husbandmen, and went.	1554
Mk	12:7	This is the heir; come, l. us kill him,	
Mk	13:14	not, (l. him that readeth understand,)	
Mk	13:14	l. them that be in Judaea flee to the	
Mk	13:15	l. him that is on the housetop not	
Mk	13:16	l. him that is in the field not turn	
Mk	14:6	And Jesus said, L. her alone; why	863
Mk	14:42	Rise up, l. us go; lo, he that betrayeth	
Mk	15:32	L. Christ the King of Israel descend	
Mk	15:36	to drink, saying, L. alone;	863
Mk	15:36	l. us see whether Elias will come	
Lu	2:15	L. us now go even unto Bethlehem,	
Lu	3:11	l. him impart to him that hath none;	
Lu	3:11	he that hath meat, l. him do likewise.	
Lu	4:34	Saying, L. us alone; what have	1439
Lu	5:4	l. your nets down for a draught.	5465

Lu 5:5 at thy word I will l. down the net. 5465
Lu 5:19 and l. him down through the tiling 2524
Lu 6:42 **l. me pull out the mote that is in** 863
Lu 8:8 **He that hath ears to hear, l. him hear**
Lu 8:22 **L. us go over unto the other side of**
Lu 9:23 **l. him deny himself, and take up his**
Lu 9:33 l. us make three tabernacles; one for
Lu 9:44 **L. these sayings sink down into your**
Lu 9:60 him, **L. the dead bury their dead:** 863
Lu 9:61 l. me first go bid them farewell, 2010
Lu 12:35 **L. your loins be girded about, and**
Lu 13:8 **Lord, l. it alone this year also, till I** 863
Lu 14:4 him, and healed him, and l. him go;
Lu 14:35 **He that hath ears to hear, l. him hear**
Lu 15:23 **kill it; and l. us eat, and be merry:**
Lu 16:29 **and the prophets; l. them hear them**
Lu 17:31 **l. him not come down to take it away:**
Lu 17:31 **field, l. him likewise not return back**
Lu 20:9 **and l. it forth to husbandmen,** 1554
Lu 20:14 **is the heir; come, l. us kill him,**
Lu 21:21 **l. them which are in Judaea flee to**
Lu 21:21 **l. them which are in the midst...depart.**
Lu 21:21 **l. not them...in the countries enter**
Lu 22:26 **among you, l. him be as the younger;**
Lu 22:36 **l. him take, it, and likewise his script:**
Lu 22:36 **l. him sell his garment, and buy one.**
Lu 22:68 **ye will not answer me, nor l. me go.** 630
Lu 23:22 therefore chastise him, and l. him go.
Lu 23:35 l. him save himself, if he be Christ, the
Joh 7:37 **thirst, l. him come unto me and drink**
Joh 8:7 **you, l. him first cast a stone at her**
Joh 11:7 disciples, **L. us go into Judaea again**
Joh 11:15 **nevertheless l. us go unto him**
Joh 11:16 L. us also go, that we may die with
Joh 11:44 them, **Loose him, and l. him go** 863
Joh 11:48 If we l. him thus alone, all men will 863
Joh 12:7 said Jesus, **L. her alone: against** 863
Joh 12:26 **any man serve me, l. him follow me;**
Joh 14:1 **L. not your heart be troubled: ye**
Joh 14:27 **L. not your heart be troubled,**
Joh 14:27 **neither l. it be afraid**
Joh 14:31 **even so I do. Arise, l. us go hence.**
Joh 18:8 **ye seek me, l. these go their way:** 863
Joh 19:12 If thou l. this man go, thou art not 630
Joh 19:24 L. us not rend it, but cast lots for it,
Ac 1:20 L. his habitation be desolate,
Ac 1:20 and l. no man dwell therein:
Ac 1:20 and his bishoprick l. another take.
Ac 2:29 l. me freely speak unto you of the 1832
Ac 2:36 l. all the house of Israel know
Ac 3:13 he was determined to l. him go. 630
Ac 4:17 l. us straitly threaten them, that they
Ac 4:21 threatened them, they l. them go,
Ac 4:23 And being l. go, they went to their own
Ac 5:38 these men, and l. them alone: 1439
Ac 5:40 in the name of Jesus, and l. them go. 630
Ac 9:25 l. him down by the wall in a 5465,2524
Ac 10:11 corners, and l. down to the earth: 2524
Ac 11:5 sheet, l. down from heaven by four 2524
Ac 15:33 they were l. go in peace from the 630
Ac 15:36 L. us go again and visit our brethren
Ac 16:35 serjeants, saying, L. those men go. 630
Ac 16:36 magistrates have sent to l. you go: 630
Ac 16:37 l. them come themselves and fetch us
Ac 17:9 and of the other, they l. them go. 630
Ac 19:38 deputies: l. them implead one another.
Ac 23:9 to him, l. us not fight against God.
Ac 23:22 then l. the young man depart, 630
Ac 24:20 Or else l. these same here say, if they
Ac 24:23 keep Paul, and to l. him have liberty,
Ac 25:5 L. them therefore,...go down with me,
Ac 27:15 up into the wind, we l. her drive. 1929
Ac 27:30 had l. down the boat into the sea, 5465
Ac 27:32 ropes of the boat, and l. her fall off. 1439
Ac 28:18 examined me, would have l. me go, 630
Ro 1:13 unto you, (but was l. hitherto,) 2967
Ro 3:4 yea, l. God be true, but every man a
Ro 3:8 L. us do evil, that good may come?
Ro 6:12 L. not sin therefore reign in your
Ro 11:9 L. their table be made a snare, and a
Ro 11:10 L. their eyes be darkened, that they
Ro 12:6 l. us prophesy according to the
Ro 12:7 ministry, l. us wait on our ministering:
Ro 12:8 giveth, l. him do it with simplicity;
Ro 12:9 L. love be without dissimulation.
Ro 13:1 L. every soul be subject unto the
Ro 13:12 l. us therefore cast off the works of
Ro 13:12 and l. us put on the armour of light.
Ro 13:13 L. us walk honestly, as in the day;
Ro 14:3 L. not him that eateth despise him
Ro 14:3 l. not him which eateth not judge him
Ro 14:5 L. every man be fully persuaded in
Ro 14:13 L. us not therefore judge one another
Ro 14:16 L. not then your good be evil spoken
Ro 14:19 L. us therefore follow after the things
Ro 15:2 L. every one...please his neighbour
1Co 1:31 that glorieth, l. him glory in the Lord.
1Co 3:10 l. every man take heed how he buildeth
1Co 3:18 L. no man deceive himself. If any
1Co 3:18 l. him become a fool, that he may be
1Co 3:21 Therefore l. no man glory in men.
1Co 4:1 L. a man so account of us, as of the
1Co 5:8 Therefore l. us keep the feast, not
1Co 7:2 l. every man have his own wife, and
1Co 7:2 l. every woman have her own husband.
1Co 7:3 L. the husband render unto the wife
1Co 7:9 if they cannot contain, l. them marry:
1Co 7:10 L. not the wife depart from her
1Co 7:11 she depart, l. her remain unmarried,
1Co 7:11 l. not the husband put away his wife.
1Co 7:12 with him, l. him not put her away.
1Co 7:13 to dwell with her, l. her not leave him.
1Co 7:15 the unbelieving depart, l. him depart.
1Co 7:17 hath called every one, so l. him walk.
1Co 7:18 l. him not become uncircumcised.
1Co 7:18 l. him not be circumcised.
1Co 7:20 L. every man abide in the same calling
1Co 7:24 l. every man, wherein he is...abide
1Co 7:36 need so require, l. him do what he will,
1Co 7:36 will he sinneth not: l. them marry.
1Co 10:8 Neither l. us commit fornication, as
1Co 10:9 Neither l. us tempt Christ, as some of
1Co 10:12 l. him that...he standeth take heed
1Co 10:24 L. no man seek his own, but every
1Co 11:6 be not covered, l. her also be shorn:
1Co 11:6 be shorn or shaven, l. her be covered.
1Co 11:28 But l. a man examine himself, and
1Co 11:28 so l. him eat of that bread, and drink
1Co 11:34 any man hunger, l. him eat at home;
1Co 14:13 l. him that speaketh in an...pray
1Co 14:26 L. all things be done unto edifying.
1Co 14:27 l. it be by two, or at most by three,
1Co 14:27 that by course; and l. one interpret.
1Co 14:28 l. him keep silence in the church;
1Co 14:28 l. him speak to himself, and to God.
1Co 14:29 L. the prophets speak two or three,
1Co 14:29 two or three, and l. the other judge.
1Co 14:30 sitteth by, l. the first hold his peace.
1Co 14:34 L. your women keep silence in the
1Co 14:35 l. them ask their husbands at home:
1Co 14:37 l. him acknowledge that the things
1Co 14:38 man be ignorant, l. him be ignorant.
1Co 14:40 L. all things be done decently and in
1Co 15:32 l. us eat and drink; for to morrow we
1Co 16:2 l. every one of you lay by him in store,
1Co 16:11 L. no man therefore despise him: but
1Co 16:14 L. all your things be done with charity.
1Co 16:22 l. him be Anathema Maran-atha
2Co 7:1 l. us cleanse ourselves from all
2Co 9:7 purposeth in his heart, so l. him give;
2Co 10:7 l. him of himself think this again, that,
2Co 10:11 L. such an one think this, that, such
2Co 10:17 that glorieth, l. him glory in the Lord.
2Co 11:16 say again, L. no man think me a fool;
2Co 11:33 basket was I l. down by the wall, 5465
Ga 1:8 unto you, l. him be accursed.
Ga 1:9 have received, l. him be accursed.
Ga 5:25 the Spirit, l. us also walk in the Spirit.
Ga 5:26 L. us not be desirous of vain glory,
Ga 6:4 But l. every man prove his own work,
Ga 6:6 L. him that is taught...communicate
Ga 6:9 l. us not be weary in well doing: for
Ga 6:10 l. us do good unto all men, especially
Ga 6:17 henceforth l. no man trouble me:
Eph 4:26 l. not the sun go down upon your
Eph 4:28 L. him that stole steal no more: but
Eph 4:28 but rather l. him labour, working with
Eph 4:29 L. no corrupt communication proceed
Eph 4:31 L. all bitterness, and...be put away
Eph 5:3 l. it not be once named among you, as
Eph 5:6 L. no man deceive you with vain
Eph 5:24 l. the wives be to their own husbands
Eph 5:33 l. every one of you in particular so love
Php 1:27 l. your conversation be as it becometh
Php 2:3 L. nothing be done through strife or
Php 2:3 mind l. each esteem other better than
Php 2:5 L. this mind be in you, which was also
Php 3:15 L. us therefore, as...be thus minded:
Php 3:16 attained, l. us walk by the same rule,
Php 3:16 l. us mind the same thing.
Php 4:5 L. your moderation be known unto all
Php 4:6 l. your requests be made known unto
Col 2:16 L. no man therefore judge you in
Col 2:18 L. no man beguile you of your reward
Col 3:15 l. the peace of God rule in your hearts,
Col 3:16 L. the word of Christ dwell in you
Col 4:6 L. your speech be alway with grace,
1Th 5:6 Therefore l. us not sleep, as do others;
1Th 5:6 but l. us watch and be sober.
1Th 5:8 But l. us, who are of the day, be sober,
2Th 2:3 L. no man deceive you by any means:
2Th 2:7 only he who now letteth will l., 2722
1Ti 2:11 L. the woman learn in silence with all
1Ti 3:10 And l. these also first be proved; then
1Ti 3:10 then l. them use the office of a deacon,
1Ti 3:12 L. the deacons be the husbands of
1Ti 4:12 L. no man despise thy youth; but be
1Ti 5:4 them learn first to show piety at
1Ti 5:9 L. not a widow be taken into the
1Ti 5:16 have widows, l. them relieve them.
1Ti 5:16 and l. not the church be charged; that
1Ti 5:17 L. the elders that rule well be counted
1Ti 6:1 L. as many servants as are...count
1Ti 6:2 masters, l. them not despise them.
1Ti 6:8 raiment l. us be therewith content.
2Ti 2:19 L. every one that nameth...depart
Tit 2:15 authority. L. no man despise thee.
Tit 3:14 l. ours also learn to maintain good
Phm 20 l. me have joy of thee in the Lord:
Heb 1:6 l. all the angels of God worship him.
Heb 2:1 at any time we should l. them slip.
Heb 4:1 L. us therefore fear, lest, a promise
Heb 4:11 L. us labor therefore to enter into
Heb 4:14 of God, l. us hold fast our profession.
Heb 4:16 L. us therefore come boldly unto the
Heb 6:1 of Christ, l. us go on unto perfection;
Heb 10:22 L. us draw near with a true heart in
Heb 10:23 L. us hold fast the profession of our
Heb 10:24 l. us consider one another to provoke
Heb 12:1 l. us lay aside every weight, and the
Heb 12:1 l. us run with patience the race that is
Heb 12:13 of the way; but l. it rather be healed.
Heb 12:28 l. us have grace, whereby we may
Heb 13:1 L. brotherly love continue.
Heb 13:5 L. your conversation be without
Heb 13:13 L. us go forth therefore unto him
Heb 13:15 l. us offer the sacrifice of praise to God
Jas 1:4 But l. patience have her perfect work,
Jas 1:5 you lack wisdom, l. him ask of God,
Jas 1:6 But l. him ask in faith, nothing
Jas 1:7 For l. not that man think that he shall
Jas 1:9 L. the brother of low degree rejoice
Jas 1:13 L. no man say when he is tempted, I
Jas 1:19 l. every man be swift to hear, slow to
Jas 3:13 l. him shew out of a good conversation
Jas 4:9 l. your laughter be turned to mourning,
Jas 5:12 l. your yea be yea; and your nay, nay;
Jas 5:13 any among you afflicted? l. him pray.
Jas 5:13 Is any merry? l. him sing psalms.
Jas 5:14 l. him call for the elders of the church;
Jas 5:14 l. them pray over him, anointing him
Jas 5:20 L. him know, that he which converteth
1Pe 3:3 l. it not be that outward adorning
1Pe 3:4 But l. it be the hidden man of the
1Pe 3:10 l. him refrain his tongue from evil,
1Pe 3:11 L. him eschew evil, and do good,
1Pe 3:11 l. him seek peace, and ensue it.
1Pe 4:11 l. him speak as the oracles of God;
1Pe 4:11 l. him do it as of the ability which
1Pe 4:15 l. none of you suffer as a murderer,
1Pe 4:16 as a Christian, l. him not be ashamed;
1Pe 4:16 but l. him glorify God on this behalf.
1Pe 4:19 l. them that suffer according to the
1Jo 2:24 L. that therefore abide in you, which
1Jo 3:7 Little children, l. no man deceive you:
1Jo 3:18 little children, l. us not love in word,
1Jo 4:7 l. us love one another: for love is of
Re 2:7, 11,17,29 **l. him hear what the Spirit**
Re 3:6, 13,22 **l. him hear what the Spirit saith**
Re 13:9 If any man have an ear, l. him hear.
Re 13:18 L. him that hath understanding count

Re 19:7 L. us be glad and rejoice, and give
Re 22:11 that is unjust, l. him be unjust still:
Re 22:11 he which is filthy, l. him be filthy still:
Re 22:11 is righteous, l. him be righteous still:
Re 22:11 and he that is holy, l. him be holy still.
Re 22:17 and l. him that heareth say, Come.
Re 22:17 And l. him that is athirst come.
Re 22:17 l. him take the water of life freely.

LETTER See also LETTERS.
2Sa 11:14 David wrote a l. to Joab, and sent 5612
2Sa 11:15 And he wrote in the l., saying, Set 5612
2Ki 5:5 and I will send a l. unto the king of 5612
2Ki 5:6 And he brought the l. to the king of 5612
2Ki 5:6 Now when this l. is come unto thee, 5612
2Ki 5:7 the king of Israel had read the l., 5612
2Ki 10:2 as soon as this l. cometh to you, 5612
2Ki 10:6 Then he wrote a l. the second time 5612
2Ki 10:7 to pass, when the l. came to them, 5612
2Ki 19:14 And Hezekiah received the l. of the 5612
Ezr 4:7 writing of the l. was written in the 5406
Ezr 4:8 and Shimshai the scribe wrote a l. 104
Ezr 4:11 the copy of the l. that they sent unto 104
Ezr 4:18 The l. which ye sent unto us hath 5407
Ezr 4:23 the copy of king Artaxerxes' l. was 5407
Ezr 5:5 returned answer by l. concerning 5407
Ezr 5:6 The copy of the l. that Tatnai, 104
Ezr 5:7 They sent a l. unto him, wherein 6600
Ezr 7:11 is the copy of the l. that the king 5406
Ne 2:8 And a l. unto Asaph the keeper of 107
Ne 6:5 time with an open l. in his hand; 107
Es 9:26 Therefore for all the words of this l., 107
Es 9:29 to confirm this second l. of Purim. 107
ISa 37:14 Hezekiah received the l. from the 5612
Jer 29:1 words of the l. that Jeremiah the 5612
Jer 29:29 the priest read this l. in the ears of 5612
Ac 23:25 he wrote a l. after this manner: *1992*
Ac 23:34 when the governor had read the l.,
Ro 2:27 who by the l. and circumcision *1121*
Ro 2:29 heart, in the spirit, and not in the l.; *1121*
Ro 7:6 and not in the oldness of the l. *1121*
2Co 3:6 not of the l., but of the spirit: *1121*
2Co 3:6 the l. killeth, but the spirit giveth *1121*
2Co 7:8 though I made you sorry with a l., *1992*
Ga 6:11 Ye see how large a l. I have *1121*
2Th 2:2 nor by word, nor by l. as from us, *1992*
Heb 13:22 I have written a l. unto you in few *1989*

LETTERS
1Ki 21:8 So she wrote l. in Ahab's name, 5612
1Ki 21:8 and sent the l. unto the elders and 5612
1Ki 21:9 And she wrote in the l., saying, 5612
1Ki 21:11 as it was written in the l. which she 5612
2Ki 10:1 And Jehu wrote l., and sent to 5612
2Ki 20:12 sent l. and a present unto Hezekiah: 5612
2Ch 30:1 and wrote l. also to Ephraim and 107
2Ch 30:6 the posts went with the l. from the 107
2Ch 32:17 He wrote also l. to rail on the Lord 5612
Ne 2:7 let l. be given me to the governors 107
Ne 2:9 river, and gave them the king's l. 107
Ne 6:17 Judah sent many l. unto Tobiah, 107
Ne 6:17 the l. of Tobiah came unto them.
Ne 6:19 And Tobiah sent l. to put me in fear. 107
Es 1:22 For he sent l. into all the king's 5612
Es 3:13 the l. were sent by posts into all 5612
Es 8:5 let it be written to reverse the l. 5612
Es 8:10 and sent l. by posts on horseback, 5612
Es 9:20 sent l. unto all the Jews that were 5612
Es 9:25 he commanded by l. that his wicked 5612
Es 9:30 And he sent the l. unto all the Jews, 5612
Isa 39:1 sent l. and a present to Hezekiah: 5612
Jer 29:25 thou hast sent l. in thy name unto 5612
Lu 23:38 written over him in l. of Greek, *1121*
Joh 7:15 How knoweth this man l., having *1121*
Ac 9:2 And desired of him l. to Damascus *1992*
Ac 15:23 And they wrote l. by them after this
Ac 22:5 I received l. unto the brethren, *1992*
Ac 28:21 We neither received l. out of Judaea *1121*
1Co 16:3 whomsoever...approve by your l., *1992*
2Co 3:1 you, or l. of commendation from you?
2Co 10:9 seem as if I would terrify you by l. *1992*
2Co 10:10 For his l., say they, are weighty *1992*
2Co 10:11 in word by l. when we are absent, *1992*

LETTEST
Job 15:13 l. such words go out of thy mouth?
Job 41:1 with a cord which thou l. down? 8257
Lu 2:29 now l. thou thy servant depart in *630*

LETTETH
2Ki 10:24 he that l. him go, his life shall be for
Pr 17:14 strife is as when one l. out water: 6362
2Th 2:7 only he who not l. will let, until *2722*

LETTING
Ex 8:29 in not l. the people go to sacrifice

LETUSHIM (le-tu'-shim)
Ge 25:3 of Dedan were Asshurim, and L., 3912

LEUMMIM (le-um'-mim)
Ge 25:3 Asshurim, and Letushim, and L. 3817

LEVI (le'-vi) See also LEVITE; LEVITICAL; MATTHEW.
Ge 29:34 therefore was his name called L. 3878
Ge 34:25 the sons of Jacob, Simeon and L., 3878
Ge 34:30 And Jacob said to Simeon and L., 3878
Ge 35:23 firstborn, Simeon, and L., and 3878
Ge 46:11 sons of L.; Gershon, Kohath, and 3878
Ge 49:5 Simeon and L. are brethren; 3878
Ex 1:2 Reuben, Simeon, L., and Judah, 3878
Ex 2:1 there went a man of the house of L., 3878
Ex 2:1 and took to wife a daughter of L. 3878
Ex 6:16 are the names of the sons of L. 3878
Ex 6:16 life of L. were an hundred thirty 3878
Ex 6:19 Mushi: these are the families of L. 3878
Ex 32:26 the sons of L. gathered themselves 3878
Ex 32:28 of L. did according to the word of 3878
Nu 1:49 shalt not number the tribe of L., 3878
Nu 3:6 Bring the tribe of L. near, and 3878
Nu 3:15 Number the children of L. after the 3878
Nu 3:17 were the sons of L. by their names; 3878
Nu 4:2 Kohath from among the sons of L., 3878
Nu 16:1 the son of L., and Dathan and 3878
Nu 16:7 too much upon you, ye sons of L. 3878
Nu 16:8 Hear, I pray you, ye sons of L.: 3878
Nu 16:10 brethren the sons of L. with thee: 3878
Nu 17:3 Aaron's name upon the rod of L. 3878
Nu 17:8 for the house of L. was budded, 3878
Nu 18:2 thy brethren also of the tribe of L., 3878
Nu 18:21 I have given the children of L. all 3878
Nu 26:59 was Jochebed, the daughter of L., 3878
Nu 26:59 her mother bare to L. in Egypt: 3878
De 10:8 the Lord separated the tribe of L., 3878
De 10:9 L. hath no part nor inheritance 3878
De 18:1 the Levites, and all the tribe of L., 3878
De 21:5 the sons of L. shall come near: 3878
De 27:12 Simeon, and L., and Judah, and 3878
De 31:9 it unto the priests the sons of L., 3878
De 33:8 of L. he said, Let thy Thummim 3878
Jos 13:14 of L. he gave none inheritance; 3878
Jos 13:33 L. Moses gave not any inheritance: 3878
Jos 21:10 who were of the children of L., had: 3878
1Ki 12:31 which were not of the sons of L. 3878
1Ch 2:1 Reuben, Simeon, L., and Judah, 3878
1Ch 6:1, 16 The sons of L.; Gershon, 3878
1Ch 6:38 the son of L., the son of Israel. 3878
1Ch 6:43 the son of Gershom, the son of L. 3878
1Ch 6:47 the son of Merari, the son of L. 3878
1Ch 9:18 the companies of the children of L. 3878
1Ch 12:26 Of the children of L. four thousand 3878
1Ch 21:6 L. and Benjamin counted he not 3878
1Ch 23:6 into courses among the sons of L., 3878
1Ch 23:14 sons were named of the tribe of L. 3878
1Ch 23:24 These were the sons of L. after the 3878
1Ch 24:20 rest of the sons of L. were these: 3878
Ezr 8:15 found there none of the sons of L. 3878
Ezr 8:18 the son of L., the son of Israel; 3878
Ne 10:39 the children of L. shall bring the 3878
Ne 12:23 sons of L., the chief of the fathers, 3878
Ps 135:20 Bless the Lord, O house of L.: ye 3878
Eze 40:46 sons of Zadok among the sons of L., 3878
Eze 48:31 one gate of Judah, one gate of L. 3878
Zec 12:13 The family of the house of L. apart, 3878
Mal 2:4 that my covenant might be with L., 3878
Mal 2:8 have corrupted the covenant of L., 3878
Mal 3:3 he shall purify the sons of L., and 3878
Mk 2:14 he saw L. the son of Alphaeus *3018*
Lu 3:24, 29 Matthat, which was the son of L., *3017*
Lu 5:27 saw a publican, named L., sitting *3018*
Lu 5:29 L. made him a great feast in his *3018*
Heb 7:5 they that are of the sons of L., *3017*
Heb 7:9 say, L. also, who receiveth tithes, *3017*
Re 7:7 Of the tribe of L. were sealed twelve *3017*

LEVIATHAN (le-vi'-ath-un)
Job 41:1 Canst thou draw out l. with an 3882
Ps 74:14 brakest the heads of l. in pieces, 3882
Ps 104:26 is that l., whom thou hast made 3882
Isa 27:1 shall punish l. the piercing serpent, 3882
Isa 27:1 even l. that crooked serpent; and he 3882

LEVITE (le'-vite) See also LEVITES; LEVITICAL.
Ex 4:14 Is not Aaron the L. thy brother? 3881
De 12:12 the L. that is within your gates; 3881
De 12:18 and the L. that is within thy gates: 3881
De 12:19 forsake not the L. as long as thou 3881
De 14:27 the L. that is within thy gates; 3881
De 14:29 the L., (because he hath no part 3881
De 16:11 and the L. that is within thy gates, 3881
De 16:14 and the L., the stranger, and the 3881
De 18:6 if a L. come from any of thy gates 3881
De 26:11 the L., and the stranger that is 3881
De 26:12 and hast given it unto the L., 3881
De 26:13 also have given them unto the L., 3881
Jg 17:7 the family of Judah, who was a L., 3881
Jg 17:9 I am a L. of Beth-lehem-judah, 3881
Jg 17:10 and thy victuals. So the L. went in. 3881
Jg 17:11 the L. was content to dwell with 3881
Jg 17:12 Micah consecrated the L.; and the 3881
Jg 17:13 seeing I have a L. to my priest. 3881
Jg 18:3 the voice of the young man the L. 3881
Jg 18:15 the house of the young man the L., 3881
Jg 19:1 there was a certain L. sojourning 3881
Jg 20:4 the L., the husband of the woman 3881
2Ch 20:14 a L. of the sons of Asaph, came the 3881
2Ch 31:12 which Cononiah the L. was ruler, 3881
2Ch 31:14 And Kore the son of Imnah the L., 3881
Ezr 10:15 Shabbethai the L. helped them. 3881
Lu 10:31 **likewise a L., when he was at the** *3019*
Ac 4:36 The son of consolation,) a L., and *3019*

LEVITES (le'-vites)
Ex 6:25 the heads of the fathers of the L. 3881
Ex 38:21 of Moses for the service of the L., 3881
Le 25:32 Notwithstanding the cities of the L., 3881
Le 25:32 may the L. redeem at any time. 3881
Le 25:33 And if a man purchase of the L., 3881
Le 25:33 for the houses of the cities of the L. 3881
Nu 1:47 L. after the tribe of their fathers 3881
Nu 1:50 appoint the L. over the tabernacle 3881
Nu 1:51 forward, the L. shall take it down: 3881
Nu 1:51 to be pitched, the L. shall set it up: 3881
Nu 1:53 the L. shall pitch round about the 3881
Nu 1:53 the L. shall keep the charge of the 3881
Nu 2:17 with the camp of the L. in the midst 3881
Nu 2:33 L. were not numbered among the 3881
Nu 3:9 shalt give the L. unto Aaron and to 3881
Nu 3:12 I have taken the L. from among the 3881
Nu 3:12 therefore the L. shall be mine; 3881
Nu 3:20 These are the families of the L. 3881
Nu 3:32 be chief over the chief of the L., 3881
Nu 3:39 All that were numbered of the L., 3881
Nu 3:41 And thou shalt take the L. for me 3881
Nu 3:41 the cattle of the L. instead of all the 3881
Nu 3:45 the L. instead of all the firstborn 3881
Nu 3:45 the cattle of the L. instead of their 3881
Nu 3:45 the L. shall be mine: I am the Lord 3881
Nu 3:46 Israel, which are more than the L.; 3881
Nu 3:49 them that were redeemed by the L.; 3881
Nu 4:18 the Kohathites from among the L. 3881
Nu 4:46 that were numbered of the L., 3881
Nu 7:5 thou shalt give them unto the L., 3881
Nu 7:6 oxen, and gave them unto the L. 3881
Nu 8:6 Take the L. from among the 3881
Nu 8:9 bring the L. before the tabernacle 3881
Nu 8:10 shalt bring the L. before the Lord: 3881
Nu 8:10 shall put their hands upon the L. 3881
Nu 8:11 shall offer the L. before the Lord 3881
Nu 8:12 the L. shall lay their hands upon 3881
Nu 8:12 to make an atonement for the L. 3881
Nu 8:13 thou shalt set the L. before Aaron, 3881
Nu 8:14 thou separate the L. from among 3881
Nu 8:14 of Israel: and the L. shall be mine. 3881
Nu 8:15 shall the L. go in to do the service 3881
Nu 8:18 taken the L. for all the firstborn 3881
Nu 8:19 have given the L. as a gift to Aaron 3881
Nu 8:20 did to the L. according unto all that 3881
Nu 8:20 Moses concerning the L., so did 3881
Nu 8:21 And the L. were purified, and they 3881
Nu 8:22 went the L. in to do their service 3881
Nu 8:22 Moses concerning the L., so did 3881
Nu 8:24 is it that belongeth unto the L. 3881
Nu 8:26 Thus shalt thou do unto the L. 3881
Nu 18:6 I have taken your brethren the L. 3881

Nu 18:23 the **L.** shall do the service of the....... 3881
Nu 18:24 I have given to the **L.** to inherit: 3881
Nu 18:26 Thus speak unto the **L.**, and say........ 3881
Nu 18:30 counted unto the **L.** as the increase.... 3881
Nu 26:57 they that were numbered of the **L.**..... 3881
Nu 26:58 These are the families of the **L.**........ 3881
Nu 31:30 and give them unto the **L.**, which....... 3881
Nu 31:47 and gave them unto the **L.**, which...... 3881
Nu 35:2 that they give unto the **L.** of the........ 3881
Nu 35:2 shall give also unto the **L.** suburbs..... 3881
Nu 35:4 which ye shall give unto the **L.**,........ 3881
Nu 35:6 which ye shall give unto the **L.**......... 3881
Nu 35:7 cities which ye shall give to the **L.**..... 3881
Nu 35:8 shall give of his cities unto the **L.** 3881
De 17:9 shalt come unto the priests the **L.**,..... 3881
De 17:18 which is before the priests the **L.**. 3881
De 18:1 The priests the **L.**, and all the tribe.... 3881
De 18:7 as all his brethren the **L.** do, which.... 3881
De 24:8 the priests the **L.** shall teach you....... 3881
De 27:9 priests the **L.** spake unto all Israel, ... 3881
De 27:14 the **L.** shall speak, and say unto all..... 3881
De 31:25 Moses commanded the **L.**, which....... 3881
Jos 3:3 the priests the **L.** bearing it, then...... 3881
Jos 8:33 that side before the priests the **L.**,..... 3881
Jos 14:3 the **L.** he gave none inheritance......... 3881
Jos 14:4 they gave no part unto the **L.** in........ 3881
Jos 18:7 the **L.** have no part among you;.......... 3881
Jos 21:1 the heads of the fathers of the **L.** 3881
Jos 21:3 children of Israel gave unto the **L.**...... 3881
Jos 21:4 the priest, which were of the **L.**, ... 3881
Jos 21:8 gave by lot unto the **L.** these cities.... 3881
Jos 21:20 **L.** which remained of the children 3881
Jos 21:27 of the families of the **L.**, out of the 3881
Jos 21:34 the rest of the **L.**, out of the tribe 3881
Jos 21:40 remaining of the families of the **L.**,..... 3881
Jos 21:41 All the cities of the **L.** within the 3881
1Sa 6:15 **L.** took down the ark of the Lord, ... 3881
2Sa 15:24 also, and all the **L.** were with him,..... 3881
1Ki 8:4 did the priests and the **L.** bring up..... 3881
1Ch 6:19 And these are the families of the **L.** ... 3881
1Ch 6:48 brethren also the **L.** were appointed... 3881
1Ch 6:64 of Israel gave to the **L.** these cities.... 3881
1Ch 9:2 the priests, **L.**, and the Nethinims...... 3881
1Ch 9:14 And of the **L.**; Shemaiah the son of.... 3881
1Ch 9:26 For these **L.**, the four chief porters,... 3881
1Ch 9:31 one of the **L.**, who was the firstborn .. 3881
1Ch 9:33 chief of the fathers of the **L.**, who...... 3881
1Ch 9:34 These chief fathers of the **L.** were..... 3881
1Ch 13:2 with them also to the priests and **L.**.... 3881
1Ch 15:2 carry the ark of God but the **L.**......... 3881
1Ch 15:4 the children of Aaron, and the **L.**........ 3881
1Ch 15:11 for the **L.**, for Uriel, Asaiah, and 3881
1Ch 15:12 the chief of the fathers of the **L.**........ 3881
1Ch 15:14 and the **L.** sanctified themselves........ 3881
1Ch 15:15 the children of the **L.** bare the ark..... 3881
1Ch 15:16 David spake to the chief of the **L.**........ 3881
1Ch 15:17 the **L.** appointed Heman the son of..... 3881
1Ch 15:22 chief of the **L.**, was for song: he........ 3881
1Ch 15:26 when God helped the **L.** that bare...... 3881
1Ch 15:27 and all the **L.** that bare the ark,......... 3881
1Ch 16:4 he appointed certain of the **L.** to........ 3881
1Ch 23:2 Israel, with the priests and the **L.**...... 3881
1Ch 23:3 Now the **L.** were numbered from....... 3881
1Ch 23:26 And also unto the **L.**; they shall no..... 3881
1Ch 23:27 **L.** were numbered from twenty........... 3881
1Ch 24:6 Nethaneel the scribe, one of the **L.**, ... 3878
1Ch 24:6 the fathers of the priests and **L.**. 3881
1Ch 24:30 These were the sons of the **L.** after... 3881
1Ch 24:31 the fathers of the priests and **L.**, ... 3881
1Ch 26:17 Eastward were six **L.**, northward....... 3881
1Ch 26:20 And of the **L.**, Ahijah was over the 3881
1Ch 27:17 Of the **L.**, Hashabiah the son of......... 3881
1Ch 28:13, 21 courses of the priests and the **L.**,.. 3881
2Ch 5:4 came; and the **L.** took up the ark....... 3881
2Ch 5:5 did the priests and the **L.** bring up..... 3881
2Ch 5:12 Also the **L.** which were the singers,... 3881
2Ch 7:6 the **L.** also with instruments of.......... 3881
2Ch 8:14 the **L.** to their charges, to praise....... 3881
2Ch 8:15 of the king unto the priests and **L.**..... 3881
2Ch 11:13 and the **L.** that were in all Israel........ 3881
2Ch 11:14 the **L.** left their suburbs and their...... 3881
2Ch 13:9 the sons of Aaron, and the **L.**, ... 3881
2Ch 13:10 the **L.** wait upon their business:......... 3881
2Ch 17:8 And with them he sent **L.**, even......... 3881
2Ch 17:8 Tobijah, and Tob-adonijah, **L.**;........... 3881
2Ch 19:8 did Jehoshaphat set of the **L.**, ... 3881
2Ch 19:11 the **L.** shall be officers before you...... 3881
2Ch 20:19 And the **L.**, of the children of the 3881
2Ch 23:2 gathered the **L.** out of all the cities 3881
2Ch 23:4 of the priests and of the **L.**, shall....... 3881
2Ch 23:6 and they that minister of the **L.**;........ 3881
2Ch 23:7 And the **L.** shall compass the king...... 3881
2Ch 23:8 the **L.** and all Judah did according....... 3881
2Ch 23:18 by the hand of the priests the **L.**, ... 3881
2Ch 24:5 together the priests and the **L.**,......... 3881
2Ch 24:5 Howbeit the **L.** hastened it not.......... 3881
2Ch 24:6 hast thou not required of the **L.** to..... 3881
2Ch 24:11 king's office by the hand of the **L.**,..... 3881
2Ch 29:4 brought in the priests and the **L.**, ... 3881
2Ch 29:5 And said unto them, hear me, ye **L.**,.. 3881
2Ch 29:12 Then the **L.** arose, Mahath the son.... 3881
2Ch 29:16 And the **L.** took it, to carry it out...... 3881
2Ch 29:25 he set the **L.** in the house of the....... 3881
2Ch 29:26 the **L.** stood with the instruments...... 3881
2Ch 29:30 commanded the **L.** to sing praise 3881
2Ch 29:34 their brethren the **L.** did help them, ... 3881
2Ch 29:34 the **L.** were more upright in heart...... 3881
2Ch 30:15 priests and the **L.** were ashamed, ... 3881
2Ch 30:16 they received of the hand of the **L.**. ... 3881
2Ch 30:17 the **L.** had the charge of the killing..... 3881
2Ch 30:21 the **L.** and the priests praised the 3881
2Ch 30:22 spake comfortably unto all the **L.** 3881
2Ch 30:25 Judah, with the priests and the **L.**, ... 3881
2Ch 30:27 **L.** arose and blessed the people:........ 3881
2Ch 31:2 and the **L.** after their courses,........... 3881
2Ch 31:2 **L.** for burnt offerings and for peace.... 3881
2Ch 31:4 portion of the priests and the **L.**, ... 3881
2Ch 31:9 with the priests and the **L.**.............. 3881
2Ch 31:17 the **L.** from twenty years old and......... 3881
2Ch 31:19 by genealogies among the **L.**............. 3881
2Ch 34:9 which the **L.** that kept the doors had.. 3881
2Ch 34:12 were Jahath and Obadiah, the **L.**........ 3881
2Ch 34:12 other of the **L.**, all that could skill...... 3881
2Ch 34:13 of the **L.** there were scribes, and....... 3881
2Ch 34:30 the priests, and the **L.**, and all the..... 3881
2Ch 35:3 unto the **L.** that taught all Israel, ... 3881
2Ch 35:5 division of the families of the **L.**........ 3881
2Ch 35:8 to the priests, and to the **L.**. 3881
2Ch 35:9 Jeiel and Jozabad, chief of the **L.**,......... 3881
2Ch 35:9 gave unto the **L.** for passover 3881
2Ch 35:10 place, and the **L.** in their courses,...... 3881
2Ch 35:11 their hands, and the **L.** flayed them.... 3881
2Ch 35:14 the **L.** prepared for themselves,......... 3881
2Ch 35:15 brethren the **L.** prepared for them. 3881
2Ch 35:18 and the priests, and the **L.**, and all...... 3881
Ezr 1:5 and the priests, and the **L.**, with all.... 3881
Ezr 2:40 The **L.**: the children of Jeshua........... 3881
Ezr 2:70 and the **L.**, and some of the people, ... 3881
Ezr 3:8 brethren the priests and the **L.**,......... 3881
Ezr 3:8 appointed the **L.**, from twenty years... 3881
Ezr 3:9 sons and their brethren the **L.**........... 3881
Ezr 3:10 **L.** the sons of Asaph with cymbals, ... 3881
Ezr 3:12 of the priests and **L.** and chief of 3881
Ezr 6:16 of Israel, the priests and the **L.**, ... 3879
Ezr 6:18 and the **L.** in their courses, for the 3879
Ezr 6:20 and the **L.** were purified together,...... 3881
Ezr 7:7 the **L.**, and the singers, and the 3881
Ezr 7:13 and of his priests and **L.**, in my......... 3879
Ezr 7:24 touching any of the priests and **L.**, ... 3879
Ezr 8:20 appointed for the service of the **L.**, ... 3881
Ezr 8:29 the chief of the priests of the **L.**, ... 3881
Ezr 8:30 So took the priests and the **L.** the 3881
Ezr 8:33 Noadiah the son of Binnui, **L.**;........... 3881
Ezr 9:1 the priests, and the **L.**, have not 3881
Ezr 10:5 chief priests, the **L.**, and all Israel,..... 3881
Ezr 10:23 of the **L.**; Jozabad, and Shimei,.......... 3881
Ne 3:17 After him repaired the **L.**, Rehum........ 3881
Ne 7:1 singers and the **L.** were appointed,..... 3881
Ne 7:43 The **L.**: the children of Jeshua, ... 3881
Ne 7:73 So the priests, and the **L.**, and the..... 3881
Ne 8:7 and the **L.**, caused the people to........ 3881
Ne 8:9 and the **L.** that taught the people,...... 3881
Ne 8:11 the **L.** stilled all the people, saying, ... 3881
Ne 8:13 and the **L.**, unto Ezra the scribe,....... 3881
Ne 9:4 upon the stairs, of the **L.**, Jeshua,...... 3881
Ne 9:5 Then the **L.**, Jeshua, and Kadmiel, ... 3881
Ne 9:38 princes, **L.**, and priests, seal unto it. .. 3881
Ne 10:9 And the **L.**: both Jeshua the son of..... 3881
Ne 10:28 the priests, the **L.**, the porters, the ... 3881
Ne 10:34 the lots among the priests, the **L.**,..... 3881
Ne 10:37 tithes of our ground unto the **L.**, ... 3881
Ne 10:37 **L.** might have the tithes in all the 3881
Ne 10:38 with the **L.**, when the **L.** take tithes: ..3881
Ne 10:38 **L.** shall bring up the tithe of the........ 3881
Ne 11:3 wit, Israel, the priests, and the **L.**, ... 3881
Ne 11:15 Also of the **L.**: Shemaiah the son....... 3881
Ne 11:16 Jozabad, of the chief of the **L.**, ... 3881
Ne 11:18 All the **L.** in the holy city were two.... 3881
Ne 11:20 Israel, of the priests, and the **L.**,....... 3881
Ne 11:22 overseer also of the **L.** at Jerusalem... 3881
Ne 11:36 of the **L.** were divisions in Judah,....... 3881
Ne 12:1 priests and the **L.** that went up......... 3881
Ne 12:8 Moreover the **L.**: Jeshua, Binnui,....... 3881
Ne 12:22 **L.** in the days of Eliashib, Joiada,....... 3881
Ne 12:24 And the chief of the **L.**: Hashabiah, ... 3881
Ne 12:27 sought the **L.** out of all their places, ... 3881
Ne 12:30 and the **L.** purified themselves,.......... 3881
Ne 12:44 of the law for the priests and **L.**. 3881
Ne 12:44 for the priests and for the **L.** that 3881
Ne 12:47 sanctified holy things unto the **L.**; 3881
Ne 12:47 the **L.** sanctified them unto the.......... 3881
Ne 13:5 commanded to be given to the **L.**,....... 3881
Ne 13:10 portions of the **L.** had not been given ..3881
Ne 13:10 the **L.** and the singers, that did the.... 3881
Ne 13:13 the scribe,and of the **L.**, Pedaiah: 3881
Ne 13:22 And I commanded the **L.** that they..... 3881
Ne 13:29 of the priesthood, and of the **L.**,........ 3881
Ne 13:30 the wards of the priests and the **L.**, ... 3881
Isa 66:21 take of them for priests and for **L.**, ... 3881
Jer 33:18 shall the priests the **L.** want a man 3881
Jer 33:21 and with the **L.**, the priests, my 3881
Jer 33:22 and the **L.** that minister unto me. 3881
Eze 43:19 thou shalt give to the priests the **L.** ... 3881
Eze 44:10 **L.** that are gone far away from me,.... 3881
Eze 44:15 priests the **L.**, the sons of Zadok, ... 3881
Eze 45:5 shall also the **L.**, the ministers of...... 3881
Eze 48:11 went astray, as the **L.** went astray..... 3881
Eze 48:12 most holy by the border of the **L.**. 3881
Eze 48:13 the **L.** shall have five and twenty 3881
Eze 48:22 from the possession of the **L.**, and..... 3881
Joh 1:19 when the Jews sent priests and **L.** *3019*

LEVITICAL

Heb 7:11 were by the **L.** priesthood,............... *3020*
Le *general title* Third Book of Moses, Called **L.**... 7121

LEVY

Nu 31:28 And **l.** a tribute unto the Lord of........ 7311
1Ki 5:13 king Solomon raised a **l.** out of all 4522
1Ki 5:13 and the **l.** was thirty thousand men..... 4522
1Ki 5:14 and Adoniram was over the **l.**............ 4522
1Ki 9:15 the **l.** which king Solomon raised;........ 4522
1Ki 9:21 upon those did Solomon **l.** a tribute 5927

LEWD

Eze 16:27 which are ashamed of thy **l.** way........ 2154
Eze 23:44 and unto Aholibah, the **l.** women......... 2154
Ac 17:5 certain **l.** fellows of the baser sort,..... *4190*

LEWDLY

Eze 22:11 hath **l.** defiled his daughter in law;...... 2154

LEWDNESS

Jg 20:6 committed **l.** and folly in Israel........... 2154
Jer 11:15 she hath wrought **l.** with many, ... 4209
Jer 13:27 neighings, the **l.** of thy whoredom, ... 2154
Eze 16:43 shalt not commit this **l.** above all......... 2154
Eze 16:58 Thou hast borne thy **l.** and thine........ 2154
Eze 22:9 in the midst of thee they commit **l.**...... 2154
Eze 23:21 to remembrance the **l.** of thy youth, ... 2154
Eze 23:27 Thus will I make thy **l.** to cease 2154
Eze 23:29 both thy **l.** and thy whoredoms.......... 2154
Eze 23:35 therefore bear thou also thy **l.** and 2154
Eze 23:48 Thus will I cause **l.** to cease out of..... 2154
Eze 23:48 be taught not to do after your **l.**. 2154
Eze 23:49 shall recompense your **l.** upon you,..... 2154
Eze 24:13 In thy filthiness is **l.**: because I.......... 2154
Ho 2:10 And now will I discover her **l.** in........ 5040
Ho 6:9 by consent: for they commit **l.**........... 2154
Ac 18:14 a matter of wrong or wicked **l.**, ... *4467*

LIAR See also LIARS.

Job 24:25 not so now, who will make me a **l.**,.... 3576
Pr 17:4 **l.** giveth ear to a naughty tongue. 8267
Pr 19:22 a poor man is better than a **l.**. 376,3576
Pr 30:6 thee, and thou be found a **l.**. 376,3576
Jer 15:18 thou be altogether unto me as a **l.**, ... 391
Joh 8:44 **for he is a l., and the father of it**...*5583*
Joh 8:55 **him not, I shall be a l. like unto**... *5583*
Ro 3:4 let God be true, but every man a **l.**;..... *5583*
1Jo 1:10 have not sinned, we make him a **l.**, ... *5583*
1Jo 2:4 not his commandments, is a **l.**, and..... *5583*
1Jo 2:22 Who is a **l.** but he that denieth that.... *5583*

1Jo 4:20 and hateth his brother, he is a l........ *5583*
1Jo 5:10 not God hath made him a l.; *5583*

LIARS
De 33:29 shall be found l. unto thee; 3584
Ps 116:11 I said in my haste, All men are l......... 3576
Isa 44:25 frustrateth the tokens of the l., and 907
Jer 50:36 A sword is upon the l.; and they 907
1Ti 1:10 for l., for perjured persons, and if....... *5583*
Tit 1:12 said, The Cretians are alway l., ... *5583*
Re 2:2 **are not, and hast found them l.**...... *5571*
Re 21:8 sorcerers, and idolaters, and all l., ... *5571*

LIBERAL
Pr 11:25 The l. soul shall be made fat: and 1293
Isa 32:5 person shall be no more called l.,....... 5081
Isa 32:8 But the l. deviseth l. things; and 5081
Isa 32:8 and by l. things shall he stand. 5081
2Co 9:13 for your l. distribution unto them,........ *572*

LIBERALITY
1Co 16:3 to bring your l. unto Jerusalem. *5485*
2Co 8:2 abounded unto the riches of their l...... *572*

LIBERALLY
De 15:14 furnish him l. out of thy flock, ... 6059
Jas 1:5 ask of God, that giveth to all men l.,.... *574*

LIBERTINES (lib'-ur-tins)
Ac 6:9 is called the synagogue of the L.,........ *3032*

LIBERTY
Le 25:10 proclaim l. throughout all the land....... 1865
Ps 119:45 And I will walk at l.: for I seek thy 7342
Isa 61:1 to proclaim l. to the captive, and........ 1865
Jer 34:8 to proclaim l. unto them;.................. 1865
Jer 34:15 in proclaiming l. every man to his....... 1865
Jer 34:16 he had set at l. at their pleasure,....... 2670
Jer 34:17 in proclaiming l., every one to his 1865
Jer 34:17 behold, I proclaim a l. for you, saith ... 1865
Eze 46:17 then it shall be his to the year of l.; ... 1865
Lu 4:18 **to set at l. them that are bruised,**... *859*
Ac 24:23 to keep Paul, and to let him have l., ... *425*
Ac 26:32 This man might have been set at l.,..... *630*
Ac 27:3 gave him l. to go unto his friends....... *2010*
Ro 8:21 glorious l. of the children of God......... *1657*
1Co 7:39 she is at l. to be married to whom...... *1658*
1Co 8:9 any means this l. of yours become *1849*
1Co 10:29 for why is my l. judged of another...... *1657*
2Co 3:17 the Spirit of the Lord is, there is l.: ... *1657*
Ga 2:4 to spy out our l. which we have in..... *1657*
Ga 5:1 the l. wherewith Christ hath made...... *1657*
Ga 5:13 For...ye have been called unto l.;...... *1657*
Ga 5:13 only use not l. for an occasion to *1657*
Heb 13:23 our brother Timothy is set at l.;.......... *630*
Jas 1:25 looketh into the perfect law of l., ... *1657*
Jas 2:12 that shall be judged by the law of l..... *1657*
1Pe 2:16 and not using your l. for a cloke of..... *1657*
2Pe 2:19 While they promise them l., they....... *1657*

LIBNAH (lib'-nah) See also LABAN.
Nu 33:20 Rimmon-parez, and pitched in L......... 3841
Nu 33:21 they removed from L., and pitched..... 3841
Jos 10:29 unto L., and fought against L............ 3841
Jos 10:31 And Joshua passed from L., and all..... 3841
Jos 10:32 to all that he had done to L.. 3841
Jos 10:39 as he had done also to L., and to........ 3841
Jos 12:15 The king of L., one; the king of 3841
Jos 15:42 L., and Ether, and Ashan, ... 3841
Jos 21:13 slayer; and L. with her suburbs, ... 3841
2Ki 8:22 Then L. revolted at the same time. 3841
2Ki 19:8 king of Assyria warring against L.. 3841
2Ki 23:31 the daughter of Jeremiah of L............ 3841
2Ki 24:18 the daughter of Jeremiah of L............ 3841
1Ch 6:57 of refuge, and L. with her suburbs, ... 3841
2Ch 21:10 did L. revolt from under his hand;...... 3841
Isa 37:8 king of Assyria warring against L.. 3841
Jer 52:1 the daughter of Jeremiah of L............ 3841

LIBNATH See SHIHOR-LIBNATH.

LIBNI (lib'-ni) See also LAADAN; LIBNITES.
Ex 6:17 sons of Gershon; L., and Shimi, ... 3845
Nu 3:18 Gershon by their families; L., and....... 3845
1Ch 6:17 sons of Gershom; L., and Shimei. 3845
1Ch 6:20 Of Gershom; L. his son, Jahath his..... 3845
1Ch 6:29 L. his son, Shimei his son, Uzza his ... 3845

LIBNITES (lib'-nites)
Nu 3:21 Gershon was the family of the L.,...... 3864
Nu 26:58 the family of the L., the family of...... 3864

LIBYA (lib'-e-ah) See also LIBYANS.
Eze 30:5 Ethiopia, and L., and Lydia, and 6316
Eze 38:5 Ethiopia, and L. with them; 6316
Ac 2:10 and in the parts of L. about Cyrene,... *3033*

LIBYANS (lib'-e-uns) See also LEHABIM.
Jer 46:9 the Ethiopians and the L., that.......... 6316
Da 11:43 the L. and the Ethiopians shall be 3864

LICE
Ex 8:16 may become l. throughout all the 3654
Ex 8:17 it became l. in man, and in beast; 3654
Ex 8:17 all the dust of the land became l. 3654
Ex 8:18 enchantments to bring forth l., ... 3654
Ex 8:18 so there were l. upon man, and upon.. 3654
Ps 105:31 of flies, and l. in all their coasts, ... 3654

LICENCE
Ac 21:40 when he had given him l., Paul.......... *2010*
Ac 25:16 and have l. to answer for himself........ *5117*

LICK See also LICKED; LICKETH.
Nu 22:4 Now shall this company l. up all......... 3897
1Ki 21:19 of Naboth shall dogs l. thy blood,....... 3952
Ps 72:9 and his enemies shall l. the dust. 3897
Isa 49:23 and l. up the dust of thy feet; 3897
Mic 7:17 They shall l. the dust like a serpent,... 3897

LICKED
1Ki 18:38 l. up the water that was in the 3897
1Ki 21:19 where dogs l. the blood of Naboth...... 3952
1Ki 22:38 and the dogs l. up his blood;............. 3952
Lu 16:21 **the dogs came and l. his sores.**....... *621*

LICKETH
Nu 22:4 as the ox l. up the grass of the 3897

LID See also EYELIDS.
2Ki 12:9 and bored a hole in the l. of it,......... 1817

LIE See also LAIN; LAY; LIED; LIEN; LIES; LIEST; LIETH; LYING.
Ge 19:32 we will l. with him, that we may........ 7901
Ge 19:34 go thou in, and l. with him, that 7901
Ge 30:15 he shall l. with thee to night for......... 7901
Ge 39:7 Joseph; and she said, L. with me. 7901
Ge 39:10 her, to l. by her, or to be with her. ... 7901
Ge 39:12 by his garment, saying, L. with me: ... 7901
Ge 39:14 he came in unto me to l. with me, ... 7901
Ge 47:30 I will l. with my fathers, and thou 7901
Ex 21:13 if a man l. not in wait, but God.......... 6658
Ex 22:16 is not betrothed, and l. with her, ... 7901
Ex 23:11 thou shall let it rest and l. still;.......... 5203
Le 6:2 and l. unto his neighbour in that......... 3584
Le 15:18 also with whom man shall l. with........ 7901
Le 15:24 And if any man l. with her at all, ... 7901
Le 18:20 thou shall not l. carnally with...... 5414,7903
Le 18:22 Thou shalt not l. with mankind, ... 7901
Le 18:23 Neither shalt thou l. with any,.... 5414,7903
Le 18:23 before a beast to l. down thereto:...... 7250
Le 19:11 falsely, neither l. one to another. 8266
Le 20:12 if a man l. with his daughter in law,.... 7901
Le 20:13 If a man also l. with mankind, as......... 7901
Le 20:15 if a man l. with a beast, he........ 5414,7903
Le 20:16 any beast, and l. down thereto, ... 7250
Le 20:18 if a man shall l. with a woman........... 7901
Le 20:20 man shall l. with his uncle's wife, ... 7901
Le 26:6 ye shall l. down, and none shall 7901
Nu 5:13 And a man l. with her carnally,........... 7901
Nu 10:5 camps that l. on the east parts 2583
Nu 10:6 camps that l. on the south side.......... 2583
Nu 23:19 is not a man, that he should l.;.......... 3576
Nu 23:24 l. down until he eat of the prey, ... 7901
De 19:11 neighbour, and l. in wait for him,......... 693
De 22:23 her in the city, and l. with her; 7901
De 22:25 the man force her, and l. with her:..... 7901
De 22:28 lay hold on her, and l. with her, ... 7901
De 25:2 judge shall cause him to l. down, ... 5307
De 28:30 and another man shall l. with her: 7693
De 29:20 written in this book shall l. upon 7257
Jos 8:4 ye shall l. in wait against the city,........ 693
Jos 8:9 they went ot l. in ambush, and abode........
Jos 8:12 l. in ambush between Beth-el and............
Jg 9:32 with thee, and l. in wait in the field: ....
Jg 19:20 let all thy wants l. upon me; only............
Jg 21:20 Go and l. in wait in the vineyards;............
Ru 3:4 mark the place where he shall l., ... 7901
Ru 3:7 he went to l. down at the end of the .. 7901
Ru 3:13 liveth: l. down until the morning. 7901
1Sa 3:5 said, I called not; l. down again. 7901
1Sa 3:6 called not, my son; l. down again. 7901
1Sa 3:9 Eli said unto Samuel, Go, l. down: 7901
1Sa 15:29 of Israel will not l. nor repent: 8266
1Sa 22:8, 13 me, to l. in wait, as at this day? ....
2Sa 11:11 to drink, and to l. with my wife? 7901
2Sa 11:13 at even he went out to l. on his bed... 7901
2Sa 12:11 he shall l. with thy wives in the......... 7901
2Sa 13:11 her, Come l. with me, my sister........ 7901
1Ki 1:2 him, and let her l. in thy bosom,........ 7901
2Ki 4:16 do not l. unto thine handmaid. 3576
Job 6:28 for it is evident unto you if I l.. 3576
Job 7:4 When I l. down, I say, When shall 7901
Job 11:19 Also thou shalt l. down, and none 7257
Job 20:11 shall l. down with him in the dust....... 7901
Job 21:26 They shall l. down alike in the dust, ... 7901
Job 27:19 The rich man shall l. down, but he 7901
Job 34:6 Should I l. against my right? my 3576
Job 38:40 abide in the covert to l. in wait? ....
Ps 23:2 me to l. down in green pastures: 7257
Ps 57:4 I l. even among them that are set...... 7901
Ps 59:3 For, lo, they l. in wait for my soul: ....
Ps 62:9 and men of high degree are a l.:........ 3576
Ps 88:5 like the slain that l. in the grave, ... 7901
Ps 89:35 that I will not l. unto David.............. 3576
Ps 119:69 The proud have forged a l. against 3576
Pr 3:24 yea, thou shalt l. down, and thy......... 7901
Pr 12:6 wicked are to l. in wait for blood:............
Pr 14:5 A faithful witness will not l.: but 3576
Ec 4:11 if two l. together, then they have....... 7901
Ca 1:13 l. all night betwixt my breasts. 3885
Isa 11:6 leopard shall l. down with the kid;...... 7257
Isa 11:7 their young ones shall l. down........... 7257
Isa 13:21 wild beasts of the desert shall l. 7257
Isa 14:18 all of them, l. in glory, every one....... 7901
Isa 14:30 the needy shall l. down in safety:....... 7257
Isa 17:2 be for flocks, which shall l. down, ... 7257
Isa 27:10 and there shall he l. down, and.......... 7257
Isa 33:8 The highways l. waste, the wayfaring........
Isa 34:10 to generation it shall l. waste; none..........
Isa 43:17 they shall l. down together, they......... 7901
Isa 44:20 Is there not a l. in my right hand?....... 3576
Isa 50:11 hand; ye shall l. down in sorrow. 7901
Isa 51:20 they l. at the head of all the streets, .. 7901
Isa 63:8 people, children that will not l.. 8266
Isa 65:10 a place for the herds to l. down in, ... 7258
Jer 3:25 We l. down in our shame, and our 7901
Jer 27:10 prophesy a l. unto you, to remove 8267
Jer 27:14 for they prophesy a l. unto you, ... 8267
Jer 27:15 they prophesy a l. in my name; 8267
Jer 27:16 for they prophesy a l. unto you, ... 8267
Jer 28:15 makest this people to trust in a l.. 8267
Jer 29:21 prophesy a l. unto you in my name;.... 8267
Jer 29:31 and he caused you to trust in a l.:........ 8267
Jer 33:12 causing their flocks to l. down. 7257
La 2:21 young and the old l. on the ground..... 7901
Eze 4:4 L. thou also upon thy left side,.......... 7901
Eze 4:4 the days that thou shalt l. upon it....... 7901
Eze 4:6 l. again on thy right side, and thou..... 7901
Eze 4:9 days that thou shalt l. upon thy 7901
Eze 21:29 Whiles they divine a l. unto thee,....... 3576
Eze 31:18 l. in the midst of...uncircumcised........ 7901
Eze 32:21 they l. uncircumcised, slain by the...... 7901
Eze 32:27 they shall not l. with the mighty 7901
Eze 32:28 shalt l. with them that are slain 7901
Eze 32:29 shall l. with the uncircumcised, ... 7901
Eze 32:30 they l. uncircumcised with them.......... 7901
Eze 34:14 there shall they l. in a good fold, ... 7257
Eze 34:15 I will cause them to l. down, saith...... 7257
Ho 2:18 will make them to l. down safely......... 7901
Ho 7:6 like an oven, whiles they l. in wait: ....
Joe 1:13 l. all night in sackcloth,...ministers...... 3885
Am 6:4 That l. upon beds of ivory, and.......... 7901
Mic 1:14 shall be a l. to the kings of Israel. 391
Mic 2:11 in the spirit and falsehood do l.,......... 3576
Mic 7:2 men: they all l. in wait for blood;.............
Hab 2:3 the end it shall speak, and not l.......... 3576
Zep 2:7 shall they l. down in the evening:....... 7527
Zep 2:14 flocks shall l. down in the midst of 7527
Zep 2:15 a place for beasts to l. down in!......... 4769
Zep 3:13 for they shall feed and l. down, ... 7257
Hag 1:4 houses, and this house l. waste? ....
Zec 10:2 and the diviners have seen a l., ... 8267
Joh 5:6 When Jesus saw him l., and knew *2621*
Joh 8:44 **When he speaketh a l., he** *5579*
Joh 20:6 and seeth the linen clothes l.,............ *2749*
Ac 5:3 hath Satan filled thine heart to l. *5574*
Ac 23:21 there l. in wait for him of them more........

Ro 1:25 changed the truth of God into a l., ... *5579*
Ro 3:7 through my l. unto his glory;............ *5582*
Ro 9:1 I say the truth in Christ, I l. not,....... *5574*
2Co 11:31 evermore, knoweth that I l. not......... *5574*
Ga 1:20 you, behold, before God, I l. not.......... *5574*
Eph 4:14 whereby they l. in wait to deceive;..... *3180*
Col 3:9 **L.** not one to another, seeing that....... *5574*
2Th 2:11 that they should believe a l.............. *5579*
1Ti 2:7 the truth in Christ, and l. not;)......... *5574*
Tit 1:2 life, which God, that cannot l.,............ *893*
Heb 6:18 it was impossible for God to l.,.......... *5574*
Jas 3:14 not, and l. not against the truth......... *5574*
1Jo 1:6 darkness, we l., and do not the truth:..*5574*
1Jo 2:21 it, and that no l. is of the truth......... *5579*
1Jo 2:27 and is truth, and is no l., and even...... *5579*
Re 3:9 **are Jews, and are not, but do l.;**.... *5574*
Re 11:8 dead bodies shall l. in the street of..........
Re 21:27 abomination, or maketh a l.:.............. *5579*
Re 22:15 whosoever loveth and maketh a l.. ..... *5579*

LIED See also BELIED.

1Ki 13:18 drink water. But he l. unto him. 3584
Ps 78:36 l. unto him with their tongues. 3576
Isa 57:11 or feared, that thou hast l., and......... 3576
Ac 5:4 thou hast not l. unto men, but unto.... *5574*

LIEN See also LAIN.

Ge 26:10 lightly have l. with thy wife,............. 7901
Ps 68:13 Though ye have l. among the pots, ... 7901
Jer 3:2 where thou hast not been l. with. 7693

LIERS

Jos 8:13 l. in wait on the west of the city,............
Jos 8:14 were l. in ambush against him.................
Jg 9:25 of Shechem set l. in wait for him in..........
Jg 16:12 l. in wait abiding in the chamber...............
Jg 20:29 set l. in wait round about Gibeah.............
Jg 20:33 the l. in wait of Israel came forth............
Jg 20:36 they trusted unto the l. in wait which........
Jg 20:37 the l. in wait hasted, and rushed...............
Jg 20:37 the l. in wait drew themselves along,........
Jg 20:38 the men of Israel and the l. in wait,..........

LIES

Jg 16:10, 13 hast mocked me, and told me l...... 3576
Job 11:3 thy l. make men hold their peace?....... 907
Job 13:4 But ye are forgers of l., ye are all 8267
Ps 40:4 proud, nor such as turn aside to l.. 3576
Ps 58:3 soon as they be born, speaking l......... 3576
Ps 62:4 they delight in l.: they bless with........ 3576
Ps 63:11 mouth of them that speak l. shall be.... 8267
Ps 101:7 telleth l. shall not tarry in my sight.... 8267
Pr 6:19 A false witness that speaketh l., ... 3576
Pr 14:5 lie: but a false witness will utter l.. 3576
Pr 14:25 but a deceitful witness speaketh l......... 3576
Pr 19:5 he that speaketh l. shall not escape. ... 3576
Pr 19:9 and he that speaketh l. shall perish...... 3576
Pr 29:12 If a ruler hearken to l., all his 1697,8267
Pr 30:8 far from me vanity and l.:.................. 3576
Isa 9:15 the prophet that teacheth l., he is....... 8267
Isa 16:6 wrath: but his l. shall not be so.......... 907
Isa 28:15 we have made l. our refuge, and.......... 3576
Isa 28:17 shall sweep away the refuge of l., ... 3576
Isa 59:3 your lips have spoken l., your........... 8267
Isa 59:4 they trust in vanity, and speak l.;....... 7723
Jer 9:3 their tongue like their bow for l. 8267
Jer 9:5 taught their tongue to speak l.,........... 8267
Jer 14:14 prophets prophesy l. in my name: 8267
Jer 16:19 Surely our fathers have inherited l.,.... 8267
Jer 20:6 to whom thou hast prophesied l. 8267
Jer 23:14 commit adultery, and walk in l. 8267
Jer 23:25 said,that prophesy l. in my name,......... 8267
Jer 23:26 of the prophets that prophesy l.? 8267
Jer 23:32 cause my people to err by their l., ... 8267
Jer 48:30 be so; his l. shall not so effect it. 907
Eze 13:8 ye have spoken vanity, and seen l.,.... 3576
Eze 13:9 that see vanity, and that divine l. 3576
Eze 13:19 to my people that hear your l.? 3576
Eze 13:22 with l. ye have made the heart of 3576
Eze 22:28 vanity, and divining l. unto them, ... 3576
Eze 24:12 She hath wearied herself with l., ... 8383
Da 11:27 they shall speak l. at one table; 3576
Ho 7:3 and the princes with their l.............. 3585
Ho 7:13 they have spoken l. against me.......... 3576
Ho 10:13 ye have eaten the fruit of l. 3585
Ho 11:12 compasseth me about with l., and 3585
Ho 12:1 daily increaseth l. and desolation; 3576
Am 2:4 and their l. caused them to err, ... 3576
Mic 6:12 inhabitants thereof have spoken l.,....... 8267
Na 3:1 city! it is all full of l. and robbery; 3585
Hab 2:18 molten image, and a teacher of l., ... 8267
Zep 3:13 shall not do iniquity, nor speak l.; 3576
Zec 13:3 speakest l. in the name of the Lord:... 8267
1Ti 4:2 Speaking l. in hypocrisy; having *5573*

LIEST

Ge 28:13 land whereon thou l., to thee will....... 7901
De 6:7 when thou l. down, and when thou..... 7901
De 11:19 when thou l. down, and when thou...... 7901
Jos 7:10 l. thou thus upon thy face? 5307
Pr 3:24 When thou l. down, thou shalt not....... 7901

LIETH

Ge 4:7 doest not well, sin l. at the door........ 7257
Ge 49:25 blessings of the deep that l. under,..... 7257
Ex 22:19 Whosoever l. with a beast shall 7901
Le 6:3 was lost, and l. concerning it,............ 3584
Le 14:47 he that l. in the house shall wash....... 7901
Le 15:4 whereon he l. that hath the issue, ... 7901
Le 15:20 every thing that she l. upon in her 7901
Le 15:24 bed whereon he l. shall be unclean. 7901
Le 15:26 Every bed whereon she l. all the 7901
Le 15:33 him that l. with her is unclean. 7901
Le 19:20 whosoever l. carnally with a woman,... 7901
Le 20:11 man that l. with his father's wife........ 7901
Le 20:13 mankind, as he l. with a woman,......... 4904
Le 26:34 her sabbaths, as long as it l. desolate,.......
Le 26:35 As long as it l. desolate it shall rest;..........
Le 26:43 while she l. desolate without them:...........
Nu 21:15 and l. upon the border of Moab. 8172
De 27:20 be he that l. with his father's wife; 7901
De 27:21 that l. with any manner of beast. 7901
De 27:22 Cursed be he that l. with his sister, ... 7901
De 27:23 he that l. with his mother in law. 7901
Jos 15:8 mountain that l. before the valley of..........
Jos 17:7 Michmethah, that l. before Shechem; ....
Jos 18:13 the hill that l. on the south side of the ......
Jos 18:14 the hill that l. before Beth-horon.............
Jos 18:16 the mountain that l. before the valley........
Jg 1:16 Judah, which l. in the south of Arad;.........
Jg 16:5 and see wherein his great strength l.,.......
Jg 16:6 thee, wherein thy great strength l.,..........
Jg 16:15 tole me wherein thy great strength l.........
Jg 18:28 in the valley that l. by Beth-rehob............
Ru 3:4 when he l. down, that thou shalt........ 7901
2Sa 2:24 that l. before Giah by the way of the........
2Sa 24:5 city that l. in the midst of the river of.......
Ne 2:3 of my fathers' sepulchres, l. waste, ...
Ne 2:17 Jerusalem l. waste, and the gates............
Ne 3:25 tower which l. out from the king's...... 3318
Ne 3:26 the east, and the tower that l. out. 3318
Ne 3:27 against the great tower that l. out, ... 3318
Job 14:12 So man l. down, and riseth not;.......... 7901
Job 40:21 He l. under the shady trees, in the 7901
Ps 10:9 l. in wait secretly as a lion in his............
Ps 10:9 he l. in wait to catch the poor; he...........
Ps 41:8 now that he l. he shall rise up no......... 7901
Ps 88:7 Thy wrath l. hard upon me, and 5564
Pr 7:12 and l. in wait at every corner.)...............
Pr 23:28 She also l. in wait as for a prey, ...
Pr 23:34 thou shall be as he that l. down in...... 7901
Pr 23:34 as he that l. upon the top of a mast.... 7901
Eze 9:2 gate, which l. toward the north,..............
Eze 29:3 great dragon that l. in the midst 6437
Mic 7:5 from her that l. in thy bosom. 7901
Mt 8:6 my servant l. at home sick of the........ *906*
Mk 5:23 daughter l. at the point of death:......... *2192*
Ac 14:6 unto the region that l. round about: *2192*
Ac 27:12 l. toward the south west and north *991*
Ro 12:18 as much as l. in you, live peaceably..........
1Jo 5:19 the whole world l. in wickedness........ *2749*
Re 21:16 And the city l. foursquare, and the..... *2749*

LIEUTENANTS

Ezr 8:36 commissions unto the king's l., and...... 323
Es 3:12 had commanded unto the king's l., ... 323
Es 8:9 unto the Jews, and to the l., and.......... 323
Es 9:3 rulers of the provinces, and the l.,........ 323

LIFE See also LIFETIME; LIVES.

Ge 1:20 moving creature that hath l.,............. 2416
Ge 1:30 the earth, wherein there is l., ... 2416
Ge 2:7 into his nostrils the breath of l.;......... 2416
Ge 2:9 the tree of l. also in the midst of....... 2416
Ge 3:14 shalt thou eat all the days of thy l....... 2416
Ge 3:17 thou eat of it all the days of thy l.; 2416
Ge 3:22 take also of the tree of l., and eat...... 2416
Ge 3:24 to keep the way of the tree of l......... 2416
Ge 6:17 flesh, wherein is the breath of l., ... 2416
Ge 7:11 the six hundredth year of Noah's l.,..... 2416
Ge 7:15 flesh, wherein is the breath of l. 2416
Ge 7:22 whose nostrils was the breath of l.,..... 2416
Ge 9:4 But flesh with the l. thereof, which 5315
Ge 9:5 brother will I require the l. of man. 5315
Ge 18:10 thee according to the time of l.;......... 2416
Ge 18:14 thee, according to the time of l.,......... 2416
Ge 19:17 Escape for thy l.; look not behind 5315
Ge 19:19 shewed unto me in saving my l.;......... 5315
Ge 23:1 were the years of the l. of Sarah. 2416
Ge 25:7 the years of Abraham's l. which he..... 2416
Ge 25:17 are the years of the l. of Ishmael,........ 2416
Ge 27:46 I am weary of my l. because of the.... 2416
Ge 27:46 land, what good shall my l. do me?..... 2416
Ge 32:30 to face, and my l. is preserved. 5315
Ge 42:15 By the l. of Pharaoh ye shall not........ 2416
Ge 42:16 by the l. of Pharaoh surely ye are....... 2416
Ge 44:30 his l. is bound up in the lad's l.; 5315
Ge 45:5 did send me before you to preserve l.........
Ge 47:9 days of the years of my l. been, ... 2416
Ge 47:9 of the years of the l. of my fathers..... 2416
Ge 48:15 the God which fed me all my l. long ....
Ex 4:19 men are dead which sought thy l.......... 5315
Ex 6:16 the years of the l. of Levi were an..... 2416
Ex 6:18 years of the l. of Kohath were an 2416
Ex 6:20 the years of the l. of Amram were 2416
Ex 21:23 then thou shalt give l. for l.,............... 5315
Ex 21:30 for the ransom of his l. whatsoever 5315
Le 17:11 the l. of the flesh is in the blood: 5315
Le 17:14 For it is the l. of all flesh: 5315
Le 17:14 the blood of it is for the l. thereof:..... 5315
Le 17:14 l. of all flesh is the blood thereof:........ 5315
Le 18:18 beside the other in her l. time........... 2416
Nu 35:31 for the l. of a murderer, which is........ 5315
De 4:9 thy heart all the days of thy l. 2416
De 6:2 thy son's son, all the days of thy l.;.... 2416
De 12:23 the blood: for the blood is the l.; 5315
De 12:23 mayest not eat the l. with the flesh. ... 5315
De 16:3 land of Egypt all the days of thy l.. 2416
De 17:19 read therein all the days of his l......... 2416
De 19:21 l. shall go for l., eye for eye, tooth.... 5315
De 20:19 (for the tree of the field is man's l.)..........
De 24:6 for he taketh a man's l. to pledge........ 5315
De 28:66 And thy l. shall hang in doubt............ 2416
De 28:66 shalt have none assurance of thy l. 2416
De 30:15 set before thee this day l. and good,.... 2416
De 30:19 I have set before you l. and death,..... 2416
De 30:19 therefore choose l., that both thou 2416
De 30:20 for he is thy l., and the length of....... 2416
De 32:47 thing for you; because it is your l. 2416
Jos 1:5 before thee all the days of thy l. 2416
Jos 2:14 Our l. for yours, if ye utter not 5315
Jos 4:14 feared Moses, all the days of his l...... 2416
Jg 9:17 for you, and adventured his l. far, ... 5315
Jg 12:3 I put my l. in my hands, and passed... 5315
Jg 16:30 than they which he slew in his l......... 2416
Jg 18:25 run upon thee, and thou lose thy l.,..... 5315
Ru 4:15 be unto thee a restorer of thy l., ... 5315
1Sa 1:11 unto the Lord all the days of his l., ... 2416
1Sa 7:15 judged Israel all the days of his l......... 2416
1Sa 18:18 and what is my l., or my father's 2416
1Sa 19:5 For he did put his l. in his hand,........ 5315
1Sa 19:11 If thou save not thy l. to night, ... 5315
1Sa 20:1 thy father, that he seeketh my l.? 5315
1Sa 22:23 he that seeketh my l. seeketh thy l.... 5315
1Sa 23:15 Saul was come out to seek his l......... 5315
1Sa 25:29 shall be bound in the bundle of l. 2416
1Sa 26:24 as thy l. was much set by this day..... 5315
1Sa 26:24 my l. be much set by in the eyes of... 5315
1Sa 28:9 then layest thou a snare for my l., ... 5315
1Sa 28:21 and I have put my l. in my hand, ... 5315
2Sa 1:9 because my l. is yet whole in me. 5315
2Sa 4:8 thine enemy, which sought thy l.; 5315
2Sa 14:7 the l. of his brother whom he slew;.... 5315
2Sa 15:21 shall be, whether in death or l., ... 2416
2Sa 16:11 forth of my bowels, seeketh my l......... 5315
2Sa 18:13 falsehood against mine own l.: for 5315
2Sa 19:5 which this day have saved thy l., ... 5315
1Ki 1:12 that thou mayest save thine own l., ... 5315
1Ki 1:12 and the l. of thy son Solomon............ 5315
1Ki 2:23 spoken this word against his own l. 5315
1Ki 3:11 hast not asked for thyself long l.;....... 3117
1Ki 3:11 hast asked the l. of thine enemies; 5315
1Ki 4:21 Solomon all the days of his l............. 2416
1Ki 11:34 him prince all the days of his l. for..... 2416

1Ki	15:5	commanded...all the days of his l.,	2416
1Ki	15:6	and Jeroboam all the days of his l..	2416
1Ki	19:2	if I make not thy l. as the l. of one	5315
1Ki	19:3	that, he arose, and went for his l.,	5315
1Ki	19:4	now, O Lord, take away my l.; for	5315
1Ki	19:10,	14 they seek my l., to take it away.	5315
1Ki	20:31	peradventure he will save thy l..	5315
1Ki	20:39	then shall thy l. be for his l., or else	5315
1Ki	20:42	therefore thy l. shall go for his l.,	5315
2Ki	1:13	let my l., and the l. of these fifty	5315
2Ki	1:14	my l. now be precious in thy sight.	5315
2Ki	4:16	season, according to the time of l.,	2416
2Ki	4:17	unto her, according to the time of l..	2416
2Ki	7:7	camp as it was, and fled for their l..	5315
2Ki	8:1	whose son he had restored to l.,	2421
2Ki	8:5	he had restored a dead body to l.,	2421
2Ki	8:5	whose son he had restored to l.,	2421
2Ki	8:5	her son, whom Elisha restored to l.	2421
2Ki	10:24	go, his l. shall be for the l. of him.	5315
2Ki	25:29	before him all the days of his l..	2416
2Ki	25:30	for every day, all the days of his l..	2416
2Ch	1:11	nor the l. of thine enemies,	5315
2Ch	1:11	neither yet hast asked long l.; but	3117
Ezr	6:10	and pray for the l. of the king, and	2417
Ne	6:11	go into the temple to save his l.?	2425
Es	7:3	king, let my l. be given me at my	5315
Es	7:7	stood up to make request for his l.	5315
Es	8:11	and to stand for their l., to destroy,	5315
Job	2:4	a man hath will he give for his l..	5315
Job	2:6	he is in thine hand; but save his l..	5315
Job	3:20	and l. unto the bitter in soul;	2416
Job	6:11	end, that I should prolong my l.?	5315
Job	7:7	O remember that my l. is wind:	2416
Job	7:15	and death rather than my l..	6106
Job	9:21	my soul: I would despise my l..	2416
Job	10:1	My soul is weary of my l.; I will	2416
Job	10:12	hast granted me l. and favour,	2416
Job	13:14	teeth, and put my l. in mine hand?	5315
Job	24:22	riseth up, and no man is sure of l..	2416
Job	31:39	the owners thereof to lose their l..	5315
Job	33:4	of the Almighty hath given me l..	2421
Job	33:18	his l. from perishing by the sword.	2416
Job	33:20	So that his l. abhorreth bread, and	2416
Job	33:22	grave, and his l. to the destroyers.	2416
Job	33:28	the pit, and his l. shall see the light.	2416
Job	36:6	preserveth not the l. of the wicked:	2421
Job	36:14	and their l. is among the unclean.	2416
Ps	7:5	tread down my l. upon the earth,	2416
Ps	16:11	Thou wilt shew me the path of l..	2416
Ps	17:14	which have their portion in this l.,	2416
Ps	21:4	He asked l. of thee, and thou gavest	2416
Ps	23:6	follow me all the days of my l..	2416
Ps	26:9	sinners, nor my l. with bloody men:	2416
Ps	27:1	the Lord is the strength of my l.;	2416
Ps	27:4	of the Lord all the days of my l.,	2416
Ps	30:5	but a moment; in his favour is l..	2416
Ps	31:10	For my l. is spent with grief, and	2416
Ps	31:13	they devised to take away my l..	5315
Ps	34:12	What man is he that desireth l.,	2416
Ps	36:9	For with thee is the fountain of l..	2416
Ps	38:12	They also that seek after my l..	5315
Ps	42:8	my prayer unto the God of my l..	2416
Ps	61:6	wilt prolong the king's l..	3117,5921
Ps	63:3	lovingkindness is better than l.,	2416
Ps	64:1	preserve my l. from fear of the	2416
Ps	66:9	which holdeth our soul in l., and	2416
Ps	78:50	gave their l. over to the pestilence;	2416
Ps	88:3	my l. draweth nigh unto the grave.	2416
Ps	91:16	With long l. will I satisfy him, and	3117
Ps	103:4	redeemeth thy l. from destruction;	2416
Ps	128:5	of Jerusalem all the days of thy l..	2416
Ps	133:3	the blessing, even l. for evermore.	2416
Ps	143:3	he hath smitten my l. down to the	2416
Pr	1:19	taketh away the l. of the owners.	5315
Pr	2:19	take they hold of the paths of l..	2416
Pr	3:2	For length of days, and long l.,	2416
Pr	3:18	She is a tree of l. to them that lay	2416
Pr	3:22	So shall they be l. unto thy soul,	2416
Pr	4:10	the years of thy l. shall be many.	2416
Pr	4:13	not go: keep her; for she is thy l..	2416
Pr	4:22	are l. unto those that find them,	2416
Pr	4:23	for out of it are the issues of l..	2416
Pr	5:6	shouldest ponder the path of l.,	2416
Pr	6:23	of instruction are the way of l..	2416
Pr	6:26	will hunt for the precious l..	5315
Pr	7:23	and knoweth not that it is for his l..	5315
Pr	8:35	For whoso findeth me findeth l.,	2416
Pr	9:11	years of thy l. shall be increased.	2416
Pr	10:11	of a righteous man is a well of l..	2416
Pr	10:16	of the righteous tendeth to l.:	2416
Pr	10:17	He is in the way of l. that keepeth	2416
Pr	11:19	As righteousness tendeth to l.: so	2416
Pr	11:30	fruit of the righteous is a tree of l.;	2416
Pr	12:10	man regardeth the l. of his beast:	5315
Pr	12:28	In the way of righteousness is l.;	2416
Pr	13:3	keepeth his mouth keepeth his l.:	5315
Pr	13:8	ransom of a man's l. are his riches:	5315
Pr	13:12	desire cometh, it is a tree of l..	2416
Pr	13:14	law of the wise is a fountain of l.,	2416
Pr	14:27	fear of the Lord is a fountain of l.,	2416
Pr	14:30	A sound heart is the l. of the flesh:	2416
Pr	15:4	A wholesome tongue is a tree of l..	2416
Pr	15:24	The way of l. is above to the wise,	2416
Pr	15:31	ear that heareth the reproof of l.	2416
Pr	16:15	light of the king's countenance is l.;	2416
Pr	16:22	is a wellspring of l. unto him that	2416
Pr	18:21	Death and l. are in the power of the	2416
Pr	19:23	The fear of the Lord tendeth to l..	2416
Pr	21:21	righteousness and mercy findeth l.,	2416
Pr	22:4	Lord are riches, and honour, and l..	2416
Pr	31:12	and not evil all the days of her l..	2416
Ec	2:3	the heaven all the days of their l..	2416
Ec	2:17	Therefore I hated l.; because the	2416
Ec	3:12	to rejoice, and to do good in his l..	2416
Ec	5:18	under the sun all the days of his l.,	2416
Ec	5:20	much remember the days of his l.;	2416
Ec	6:12	what is good for man in this l., all	2416
Ec	6:12	days of his vain l. which he spendeth	2416
Ec	7:12	giveth l. to them that have it.	2421
Ec	7:15	prolongeth his l. in his wickedness.	
Ec	8:15	him of his labour the days of his l.,	2416
Ec	9:9	lovest all the days of the l. of thy	2416
Ec	9:9	for that is thy portion in this l.,	2416
Isa	15:4	his l. shall be grievous unto him.	5315
Isa	38:12	I have cut off like a weaver my l..	2416
Isa	38:16	these things is the l. of my spirit:	2416
Isa	38:20	all the days of our l. in the house.	2416
Isa	43:4	men for thee, and people for thy l..	5315
Isa	57:10	hast found the l. of thine hand;	2416
Jer	4:30	despise thee, they will seek thy l..	5315
Jer	8:3	shall be chosen rather than l. by	2416
Jer	11:21	men of Anathoth, that seek thy l.,	5315
Jer	21:7	hand of those that seek their l..	5315
Jer	21:8	I set before you the way of l., and	2416
Jer	21:9	his l. shall be unto him for a prey.	5315
Jer	22:25	the hand of them that seek thy l.,	5315
Jer	34:20	the hand of them that seek their l..	5315
Jer	34:21	the hand of them that seek their l.,	5315
Jer	38:2	he shall have his l. for a prey, and	5315
Jer	38:16	hand of these men that seek thy l..	5315
Jer	39:18	thy l. shall be for a prey unto thee:	5315
Jer	44:30	the hand of them that seek his l.,	5315
Jer	44:30	his enemy, and that sought his l..	5315
Jer	45:5	thy l. will I give unto thee for a prey	5315
Jer	49:37	and before them that seek their l..	5315
Jer	52:33	before him all the days of his l..	2416
Jer	52:34	of his death, all the days of his l..	2416
La	2:19	for the l. of thy young children,	5315
La	3:53	have cut off my l. in the dungeon,	2416
La	3:58	soul; thou hast redeemed my l..	
Eze	3:18	from his wicked way, to save his l.;	2421
Eze	7:13	himself in the iniquity of his l..	2416
Eze	13:22	wicked way, by promising him l.:	2421
Eze	32:10	every man for his own l., in the	5315
Eze	33:15	robbed, walk in the statutes of l.,	2416
Da	12:2	awake, some to everlasting l.,	2416
Jon	1:14	let us not perish for this man's l.,	5315
Jon	2:6	hast thou brought up my l. from	2416
Jon	4:3	take, I beseech thee, my l. from me;	5315
Mal	2:5	My covenant was with him l.	2416
Mt	2:20	which sought the young child's l..	5590
Mt	6:25	Take no thought for your l., what	5590
Mt	6:25	Is not the l. more than meat, and	5590
Mt	7:14	is the way, which leadeth unto l.,	2222
Mt	10:39	He that findeth his l. shall lose it:	5590
Mt	10:39	he that loseth his l. for my sake	5590
Mt	16:25	will save his l. shall lose it:	5590
Mt	16:25	will lose his l. for my sake shall	5590
Mt	18:8	better for thee to enter into l. halt	2222
Mt	18:9	thee to enter into l. with one eye.	2222
Mt	19:16	I do, that I may have eternal l.?	2222
Mt	19:17	but if thou wilt enter into l., keep	2222
Mt	19:29	and shall inherit everlasting l..	2222
Mt	20:28	to give his l. a ransom for many.	5590
Mt	25:46	but the righteous into l. eternal.	2222
Mk	3:4	or to do evil? to save l., or to kill?	5590
Mk	8:35	will save his l. shall lose it;	5590
Mk	8:35	shall lose his l. for my sake and	5590
Mk	9:43	for thee to enter into l. maimed,	2222
Mk	9:45	better for thee to enter halt into l.,	2222
Mk	10:17	I do that I may inherit eternal l.?	2222
Mk	10:30	in the world to come eternal l..	2222
Mk	10:45	to give his l. a ransom for many.	5590
Lu	1:75	before him, all the days of our l..	2222
Lu	6:9	evil? to save l., or to destroy it?	5590
Lu	8:14	and riches and pleasures of this l.,	979
Lu	9:24	will save his l. shall lose it:	5590
Lu	9:24	will lose his l. for my sake, the	5590
Lu	10:25	shall I do to inherit eternal l.?	2222
Lu	12:15	for a man's l. consisteth not in the	2222
Lu	12:22	Take no thought for your l., what	5590
Lu	12:23	The l. is more than meat, and the	5590
Lu	14:26	sisters, yea, and his own l. also,	5590
Lu	17:33	seek to save his l. shall lose it;	5590
Lu	17:33	shall lose his l. shall preserve it.	5590
Lu	18:18	shall I do to inherit eternal l.?	2222
Lu	18:30	in the world to come l. everlasting.	2222
Lu	21:34	drunkenness, and cares of this l.,	982
Joh	1:4	In him was l.; and the l. was the	2222
Joh	3:15	not perish, but have eternal l..	2222
Joh	3:16	not perish, but have everlasting l..	2222
Joh	3:36	on the Son hath everlasting l..	2222
Joh	3:36	believeth not the Son shall not see l.;	2222
Joh	4:14	springing up into everlasting l..	2222
Joh	4:36	gathereth fruit unto l. eternal:	2222
Joh	5:24	that sent me, hath everlasting l.,	2222
Joh	5:24	but is passed from death unto l..	2222
Joh	5:26	For as the Father hath l. in	2222
Joh	5:26	to the Son to have l. in himself:	2222
Joh	5:29	good, unto the resurrection of l.;	2222
Joh	5:39	them ye think ye have eternal l.:	2222
Joh	5:40	come to me, that ye might have l..	2222
Joh	6:27	which endureth unto everlasting l.,	2222
Joh	6:33	and giveth l. unto the world.	2222
Joh	6:35	unto them, I am the bread of l..	2222
Joh	6:40	on him, may have everlasting l..	2222
Joh	6:47	believeth on me hath everlasting l..	2222
Joh	6:48	I am that bread of l..	2222
Joh	6:51	I will give for the l. of the world.	2222
Joh	6:53	his blood, ye have no l. in you.	2222
Joh	6:54	drinketh my blood, hath eternal l.;	2222
Joh	6:63	they are spirit, and they are l..	2222
Joh	6:68	thou hast the words of eternal l..	2222
Joh	8:12	but shall have the light of l..	2222
Joh	10:10	I am come that they might have l.,	2222
Joh	10:11	giveth his l. for the sheep.	5590
Joh	10:15	and I lay down my l. for the sheep.	5590
Joh	10:17	because I lay down my l., that I	5590
Joh	10:28	I give unto them eternal l.; and	2222
Joh	11:25	I am the resurrection, and the l..	2222
Joh	12:25	He that loveth his l. shall lose it;	5590
Joh	12:25	hateth his l. in this world shall	5590
Joh	12:25	shall keep it unto l. eternal.	2222
Joh	12:50	his commandment is l. everlasting:	2222
Joh	13:37	I will lay down my l. for thy sake.	5590
Joh	13:38	thou lay down thy l. for my sake?	5590
Joh	14:6	am the way, the truth, and the l..	2222
Joh	15:13	man lay down his l. for his friends.	5590
Joh	17:2	should give eternal l. to as many	2222
Joh	17:3	this is l. eternal, that they might	2222
Joh	20:31	ye might have l. through his name.	2222
Ac	2:28	made known to me the ways of l.;	2222
Ac	3:15	And killed the Prince of l., whom	2222
Ac	5:20	the people all the words of this l..	2222
Ac	8:33	for his l. is taken from the earth.	2222
Ac	11:18	Gentiles granted repentance unto l..	2222
Ac	13:46	unworthy of everlasting l., lo, we	2222
Ac	13:48	many as were ordained to eternal l..	2222
Ac	17:25	seeing he giveth to all l., and breath,	2222
Ac	20:10	not yourselves; for his l. is in him.	5590
Ac	20:24	count I my l. dear unto myself,	5590
Ac	26:4	My manner of l. from my youth,	981
Ac	27:22	shall be no loss of any man's l..	5590
Ro	2:7	honour and immortality, eternal l..	2222
Ro	5:10	we shall be saved by his l..	2222
Ro	5:17	reign in l. by one, Jesus Christ.)	2222
Ro	5:18	upon all men unto justification of l..	2222
Ro	5:21	righteousness unto eternal l. by	2222

Ro 6:4 also should walk in newness of l.. *2222*
Ro 6:22 holiness, and the end everlasting l.. *2222*
Ro 6:23 but the gift of God is eternal l.. *2222*
Ro 7:10 which was ordained to l., I found *2222*
Ro 8:2 the law of the Spirit of l. in Christ *2222*
Ro 8:6 to be spiritually minded is l. and *2222*
Ro 8:10 Spirit is l. because of righteousness. *2222*
Ro 8:38 neither death, nor l., nor angels, *2222*
Ro 11:3 am left alone, and they seek my l.. *5590*
Ro 11:15 of them be, but l. from the dead? *2222*
Ro 16:4 have for my l. laid down their own *5590*
1Co 3:22 or l., or death, or things present, *2222*
1Co 6:3 more things that pertain to this l.? *982*
1Co 6:4 of things pertaining to this l., set *982*
1Co 14:7 even things without l. giving sound, *895*
1Co 15:19 If in this l. only we have hope in *2222*
2Co 1:8 that we despaired even of l.; *2198*
2Co 2:16 the other the savour of l. unto l.. *2222*
2Co 3:6 killeth, but the spirit giveth l.. *2227*
2Co 4:10, 11 the l. also of Jesus might be *2222*
2Co 4:12 death worketh in us, but l. in you. *2222*
2Co 5:4 might be swallowed up of l.. *2222*
Ga 2:20 and the l. which I now live in the flesh
Ga 3:21 given which could have given l., *2227*
Ga 6:8 of the Spirit reap l. everlasting. *2222*
Eph 4:18 being alienated from the l. of God *2222*
Php 1:20 in my body, whether it be by l., or *2222*
Php 2:16 Holding forth the word of l.; that *2222*
Php 2:30 unto death, not regarding his l., to *5590*
Php 4:3 whose names are in the book of l.. *2222*
Col 3:3 your l. is hid with Christ in God. *2222*
Col 3:4 When Christ, who is our l., shall *2222*
1Ti 1:16 believe on him to l. everlasting. *2222*
1Ti 2:2 lead a quiet and peaceable l. in all *979*
1Ti 4:8 promise of the l. that now is, and *2222*
1Ti 6:12 lay hold on eternal l., whereunto *2222*
1Ti 6:19 that they may lay hold on eternal l.. *2222*
2Ti 1:1 promise of l. which is in Christ *2222*
2Ti 1:10 hath brought l. and immortality to *2222*
2Ti 2:4 himself with the affairs of this l.; *979*
2Ti 3:10 known my doctrine, manner of l., *72*
Tit 1:2 In hope of eternal l., which God *2222*
Tit 3:7 according to the hope of eternal l.. *2222*
Heb 7:3 beginning of days, nor end of l.; *2222*
Heb 7:16 but after the power of an endless l.. *2222*
Heb 11:35 received their dead raised to l. again:
Jas 1:12 he shall receive the crown of l.. *2222*
Jas 4:14 For what is your l.? It is even a *2222*
1Pe 3:7 heirs together of the grace of l.; *2222*
1Pe 3:10 For he that will love l., and see good.. *2222*
1Pe 4:3 time past of our l. may suffice us *979*
2Pe 1:3 that pertain unto l. and godliness, *2222*
1Jo 1:1 have handled, of the Word of l.; *2222*
1Jo 1:2 the l. was manifested, and we have *2222*
1Jo 1:2 and shew unto you that eternal l., *2222*
1Jo 2:16 the pride of l., is not of the Father, *979*
1Jo 2:25 hath promised us, even eternal l.. *2222*
1Jo 3:14 we have passed from death unto l., *2222*
1Jo 3:15 hath eternal l. abiding in him. *2222*
1Jo 3:16 he laid down his l. for us: and we *5590*
1Jo 5:11 God hath given to us eternal l., *2222*
1Jo 5:11 and this l. is in his Son. *2222*
1Jo 5:12 He that the Son hath l.; *2222*
1Jo 5:12 hath not the Son of God hath not l.. *2222*
1Jo 5:13 may know that ye have eternal l., *2222*
1Jo 5:16 shall give him l. for them that sin *2222*
1Jo 5:20 This is the true God, and eternal l.. *2222*
Jude 21 Lord Jesus Christ unto eternal l.. *2222*
Re 2:7 **will I give to eat of the tree of l.** *2222*
Re 2:10 **and I will give thee a crown of l..** *2222*
Re 3:5 **out his name out of the book of l.,** *2222*
Re 8:9 were in the sea, and had l., died; *5590*
Re 11:11 Spirit of l. from God entered into *2222*
Re 13:8 are not written in the book of l.. *2222*
Re 13:15 power to give l. unto the image of *4151*
Re 17:8 were not written in the book of l.. *2222*
Re 20:12 was opened, which is the book of l.. *2222*
Re 20:15 not found written in the book of l.. *2222*
Re 21:6 fountain of the water of l. freely. *2222*
Re 21:27 written in the Lamb's book of l.. *2222*
Re 22:1 me a pure river of water of l., *2222*
Re 22:2 was there the tree of l., which bare *2222*
Re 22:14 may have right to the tree of l., *2222*
Re 22:17 let him take the water of l. freely. *2222*
Re 22:19 away his part out of the book of l., *2222*

LIFETIME
2Sa 18:18 Absalom in his l. had taken and 2416
Lu 16:25 **thou in thy l. receivedst thy good..** *2222*
Heb 2:15 all their l. subject to bondage. *2198*

LIFT See also LIFTED; LIFTEST; LIFTETH; LIFTING.
Ge 7:17 and it was l. up above the earth. 7311
Ge 13:14 L. up now thine eyes, and look 5375
Ge 14:22 I have l. up mine hand unto the 7311
Ge 18:2 And he l. up his eyes and looked, 5375
Ge 21:16 him, and l. up her voice, and wept. 5375
Ge 21:18 Arise, l. up the lad, and hold him in 5375
Ge 31:12 L. up now thine eyes, and see, all 5375
Ge 40:13 shall Pharaoh l. up thine head, 5375
Ge 40:19 three days shall Pharaoh l. up thy 5375
Ge 41:44 shall no man l. up his hand or foot 7311
Ex 14:16 l. thou up thy rod, and stretch out 7311
Ex 20:25 if thou l. up thy tool upon it, thou 5130
Nu 6:26 The Lord l. up his countenance 5375
Nu 16:3 then l. ye up yourselves above the 5375
Nu 23:24 and l. up himself as a young lion: 5375
De 3:27 and l. up thine eyes westward, and 5375
De 4:19 And lest thou l. up thine eyes unto 5375
De 22:4 help him to l. them up again. 6965
De 27:5 not l. up any iron tool upon them. 5130
De 32:40 For I l. up my hand to heaven, and 5375
Jos 8:31 which no man hath l. up any iron: 5130
2Sa 23:8 l. up his spear against eight hundred,
2Ki 19:4 l. up thy prayer for the remnant 5375
2Ki 25:27 did l. up the head of Jehoiachin 5375
1Ch 25:5 the words of God, to l. up the horn. 7311
Ezr 9:6 and blush to l. up my face to thee, 7311
Job 10:15 yet will I not l. up my head. 5375
Job 11:15 thou l. up thy face without spot; 5375
Job 22:26 and shalt l. up thy face unto God. 5375
Job 38:34 Canst thou l. up thy voice to the 7311
Ps 4:6 Lord, l. thou up the light of thy 5375
Ps 7:6 l. up thyself because of the rage of 5375
Ps 10:12 O Lord; O God, l. up thine hand: 5375
Ps 24:7 L. up your heads, O ye gates; 5375
Ps 24:7 be ye l. up, ye everlasting doors; 5375
Ps 24:9 L. up your heads, O ye gates; even 5375
Ps 24:9 l. them up, ye everlasting doors; 5375
Ps 25:1 thee, O Lord, do I l. up my soul. 5375
Ps 28:2 I l. up my hands toward thy holy 5375
Ps 28:9 them also, and l. them up for ever. 5375
Ps 63:4 I will l. up my hands in thy name. 5375
Ps 74:3 L. up thy feet unto the perpetual 7311
Ps 75:4 to the wicked, L. not up the horn: 7311
Ps 75:5 L. not up your horn on high: speak 7311
Ps 86:4 thee, O Lord, do I l. up my soul. 5375
Ps 93:3 voice; the floods l. up their waves. 5375
Ps 94:2 L. up thyself, thou judge of the 5375
Ps 110:7 therefore shall he l. up the head. 7311
Ps 119:48 My hands also will I l. up unto thy 5375
Ps 121:1 I will l. up mine eyes unto the hills, 5375
Ps 123:1 Unto thee l. I up mine eyes, O thou 5375
Ps 134:2 L. up your hands in the sanctuary, 5375
Ps 143:8 walk; for I l. up my soul unto thee. 5375
Ec 4:10 fall, the one will l. up his fellow: 6965
Isa 2:4 nation shall not l. up sword against 5375
Isa 5:26 he will l. up an ensign to the nations 5375
Isa 10:15 itself against them that l. it up. 7311
Isa 10:15 if the staff should l. up itself, as if it 7311
Isa 10:24 shall l. up his staff against thee, 5375
Isa 10:26 so shall he l. it up after the manner 5375
Isa 10:30 L. up thy voice, O daughter of 6670
Isa 13:2 L. ye up a banner upon the high 5375
Isa 24:14 They shall l. up their voice, they 5375
Isa 33:10 exalted; now will I l. up myself. 5375
Isa 37:4 wherefore l. up thy prayer for the 5375
Isa 40:9 l. up thy voice with strength; 7311
Isa 40:9 l. it up, be not afraid; say unto the 7311
Isa 40:26 L. up your eyes on high, and 5375
Isa 42:2 He shall not cry, nor l. up, nor 5375
Isa 42:11 the cities thereof l. up their voice, 5375
Isa 49:18 L. up thine eyes round about, and 5375
Isa 49:22 will l. up mine hand to the Gentiles, 5375
Isa 51:6 L. up your eyes to the heavens, and 5375
Isa 52:8 watchmen shall l. up the voice; 5375
Isa 58:1 not, l. up thy voice like a trumpet, 7311
Isa 59:19 the Lord shall l. up a standard 5127
Isa 60:4 L. up thine eyes round about, and 5375
Isa 62:10 l. up a standard for the people. 7311
Jer 3:2 L. up thine eyes unto the high 5375
Jer 7:16 neither l. up cry nor prayer for 5375
Jer 11:14 neither l. up a cry or prayer for 5375
Jer 13:20 L. up your eyes, and behold them 5375
Jer 22:20 l. up thy voice in Bashan, and cry 5414
Jer 51:14 they shall l. up a shout against 6030
La 2:19 l. up thy hands toward him for the 5375
La 3:41 Let us l. up our heart with our hands 5375
Eze 8:5 man, l. up thine eyes now the way 5375
Eze 11:22 did the cherubims l. up their wings, 5375
Eze 17:14 be base, that it might not l. itself up, 5375
Eze 21:22 to l. up the voice with shouting, to 7311
Eze 23:27 thou shalt not l. up thine eyes unto 5375
Eze 26:8 and l. up the buckler against thee. 6965
Eze 33:25 l. up your eyes toward your idols, 5375
Mic 4:3 nation shall not l. up a sword 5375
Zec 1:21 so that no man did l. up his head: 5375
Zec 5:5 L. up now thine eyes, and see what 5375
Mt 12:11 **he not lay hold on it, and l. it out?** *1458*
Lu 13:11 and could in no wise l. up herself. *352*
Lu 16:23 **in hell he l. up his eyes, and in** *1869*
Lu 18:13 would not l. up so much as his *1869*
Lu 21:28 **then look up, and l. up your heads;** *1869*
Joh 4:35 **L. up your eyes, and look on the..** *1869*
Heb 12:12 l. up the hands which hang down, *461*
Jas 4:10 of the Lord, and he shall l. you up. *5312*

LIFTED See also LIFT.
Ge 13:10 Lot l. up his eyes, and beheld all 5375
Ge 22:4 third day Abraham l. up his eyes, 5375
Ge 22:13 Abraham l. up his eyes, and looked, 5375
Ge 24:63 and he l. up his eyes, and saw, and 5375
Ge 24:64 Rebekah l. up her eyes, and when 5375
Ge 27:38 And Esau l. up his voice, and wept. 5375
Ge 29:11 Rachel, and l. up his voice, and wept.. 5375
Ge 31:10 that I l. up mine eyes, and saw in a 5375
Ge 33:1 Jacob l. up his eyes, and looked, 5375
Ge 33:5 And he l. up his eyes, and saw the 5375
Ge 37:25 they l. up their eyes and looked, 5375
Ge 37:28 and l. up Joseph out of the pit, 5927
Ge 39:15 that I l. up my voice and cried, 7311
Ge 39:18 pass, as I l. up my voice and cried, 7311
Ge 40:20 he l. up the head of the chief butler 5375
Ge 43:29 And he l. up his eyes, and saw his 5375
Ex 7:20 l. up the rod, and smote the waters 7311
Ex 14:10 children of Israel l. up their eyes, 5375
Le 9:22 Aaron l. up his hand toward the 5375
Nu 14:1 the congregation l. up their voice, 5375
Nu 20:11 Moses l. up his hand, and with his 7311
Nu 24:2 Balaam l. up his eyes and he saw 5375
De 8:14 Then thine heart be l. up, and thou 7311
De 17:20 That his heart be not l. up above 7311
Jos 4:18 soles of the priests' feet were l. up 5423
Jos 5:13 that he l. up his eyes and looked, 5375
Jg 2:4 people l. up their voice, and wept. 5375
Jg 8:28 that they l. up their heads no more. 5375
Jg 9:7 and l. up his voice, and cried, and 5375
Jg 19:17 when he had l. up his eyes, he saw 5375
Jg 21:2 l. up their voices, and wept sore; 5375
Ru 1:9 and they l. up their voice, and wept. 5375
Ru 1:14 And they l. up their voice, and wept 5375
1Sa 6:13 l. up their eyes, and saw the ark, 5375
1Sa 11:4 people l. up their voices, and wept. 5375
1Sa 24:16 And Saul l. up his voice, and wept. 5375
1Sa 30:4 with him l. up their voice and wept, 5375
2Sa 3:32 the king l. up his voice, and wept at 5375
2Sa 13:34 that kept the watch l. up his eyes, 5375
2Sa 13:36 came, and l. up their voice and wept: 5375
2Sa 18:24 and l. up his eyes, and looked, and 5375
2Sa 18:28 men that l. up their hand against 5375
2Sa 20:21 l. up his hand against the king, 5375
2Sa 22:49 thou also hast l. me up on high 7311
2Sa 23:18 he l. up his spear against three 5782
1Ki 11:26 he l. up his hand against the king. 7311
1Ki 11:27 he l. up his hand against the king: 7311
2Ki 9:32 he l. up his face to the window, 5375
2Ki 14:10 and thine heart hath l. thee up: 5375
2Ki 19:22 and l. up thine eyes on high? even 5375
1Ch 11:11 he l. up his spear against three 5782
1Ch 14:2 for his kingdom was l. up on high, 5375
1Ch 21:16 David l. up his eyes, and saw the 5375
2Ch 5:13 when they l. up their voice with the 7311
2Ch 17:6 heart was l. up in the ways of the 1361
2Ch 26:16 heart was l. up to his destruction: 1361
2Ch 32:25 unto him; for his heart was l. up: 1361
Job 2:12 when they l. up their eyes afar off, 5375
Job 2:12 they l. up their voice, and wept; 5375
Job 31:21 I have l. up my hand against the 5130
Job 31:29 l. up myself when evil found him: 5782
Ps 24:4 hath not l. up his soul unto vanity, 5375

Ps 27:6 head be l. up above mine enemies...... 7311
Ps 30:1 for thou hast l. me up, and hast......... 1802
Ps 41:9 hath l. up his heel against me........... 1431
Ps 74:5 had l. up axes upon the thick trees...... 935
Ps 83:2 that hate thee have l. up the head....... 5375
Ps 93:3 The floods have l. up, O Lord,.......... 5375
Ps 93:3 the floods have l. up their voice,........ 5375
Ps 102:10 for thou hast l. me up, and cast me.... 5375
Ps 106:26 he l. up his hand against them,.......... 5375
Pr 30:13 eyes! and their eyelids are l. up......... 5375
Isa 2:12 and upon every one that is l. up: 5375
Isa 2:13 of Lebanon, that are high and l. up,.... 5375
Isa 2:14 and upon all the hills that are l. up, ... 5375
Isa 6:1 upon a throne, high and l. up, and...... 5375
Isa 26:11 when thy hand is l. up, they will........ 7311
Isa 37:23 voice, and l. up thine eyes on high?.... 5375
Jer 51:9 heaven, and is l. up even to the skies. .5375
Jer 52:31 l. up the head of Jehoiachin king of...... 5375
Eze 1:19 when the living creatures were l. up... 5375
Eze 1:19 the earth, the wheels were l. up......... 5375
Eze 1:20 the wheels were l. up over against....... 5375
Eze 1:21 those were l. up from the earth,......... 5375
Eze 1:21 the wheels were l. up over against...... 5375
Eze 3:14 So the spirit l. me up, and took me.... 5375
Eze 8:3 spirit l. me up between the earth....... 5375
Eze 8:5 I l. up mine eyes the way toward....... 5375
Eze 10:15 And the cherubims were l. up. 7426
Eze 10:16 the cherubims l. up their wings.......... 5375
Eze 10:17 stood; and when they were l. up,....... 7311
Eze 10:17 these l. up themselves also: for......... 7426
Eze 10:19 the cherubims l. up their wings,.......... 5375
Eze 11:1 the spirit l. me up, and brought me.... 5375
Eze 18:6 neither hath l. up his eyes to the....... 5375
Eze 18:12 and hath l. up his eyes to the idols,.... 5375
Eze 18:15 neither hath l. up his eyes to the....... 5375
Eze 20:5 and l. up mine hand unto the seed....... 5375
Eze 20:5 when I l. up mine hand unto them,...... 5375
Eze 20:6 that I l. up mine hand unto them,........ 5375
Eze 20:15 Yet also I l. up my hand unto them..... 5375
Eze 20:23 I l. up mine hand unto them also......... 5375
Eze 20:28 I l. up mine hand to give it to them,... 5375
Eze 20:42 I l. up mine hand to give it to your 5375
Eze 28:2 Because thine heart is l. up, and........ 1361
Eze 28:5 heart is l. up because of thy riches:.... 1361
Eze 28:17 was l. up because of thy beauty,......... 1361
Eze 31:10 thou hast l. up thyself in height, ... 1361
Eze 31:10 and his heart is l. up in his height; 7311
Eze 36:7 I have l. up mine hand, Surely the 5375
Eze 44:12 have I l. up mine hand against them, .. 5375
Eze 47:14 the which I l. up mine hand to give 5375
Da 4:34 I Nebuchadnezzar l. up mine eyes....... 5191
Da 5:20 when his heart was l. up, and his....... 7313
Da 5:23 hast l. up thyself against the Lord...... 7313
Da 7:4 it was l. up from the earth, and......... 5191
Da 8:3 Then I l. up mine eyes, and saw,....... 5375
Da 10:5 Then I l. up mine eyes, and looked, ... 5375
Da 11:12 multitude, his heart shall be l. up;...... 7311
Mic 5:9 Thine hand shall be l. up upon thine ... 7311
Hab 2:4 soul which is l. up is not upright........ 6075
Hab 3:10 voice, and l. up his hands on high....... 5375
Zec 1:18 Then l. I up mine eyes, and saw,........ 5375
Zec 1:21 which l. up their horn over the land.... 5375
Zec 2:1 I l. up mine eyes again, and looked, ... 5375
Zec 5:1 Then I turned, and l. up mine eyes, ... 5375
Zec 5:7 there was l. up a talent of lead: and..........
Zec 5:9 Then l. I up mine eyes, and looked, ... 5375
Zec 5:9 l. up the ephah between the earth....... 5375
Zec 6:1 And I turned, and l. up mine eyes,..... 5375
Zec 9:16 l. up as an ensign upon his land......... 5264
Zec 14:10 and it shall be l. up, and inhabited....... 7213
Mt 17:8 when they had l. up their eyes, ... *1869*
Mk 1:31 her by the hand, and l. her up;.......... *1453*
Mk 9:27 him by the hand, and l. him up; *1453*
Lu 6:20 he l. up his eyes on his disciples,........ *1869*
Lu 11:27 of the company l. up her voice, ... *1869*
Lu 17:13 they l. up their voices, and said, ... *142*
Lu 24:50 and he l. up his hands, and blessed *1869*
Joh 3:14 **as Moses l. up the serpent in the**... *5312*
Joh 3:14 **so must the Son of man be l. up:** .. *5312*
Joh 6:5 When Jesus then l. up his eyes,.......... *1869*
Joh 8:7 l. up himself, and said unto them,........ *352*
Joh 8:10 When Jesus had l. up himself, and *352*
Joh 8:28 **When ye have l. up the Son of**...... *5312*
Joh 11:41 And Jesus l. up his eyes, and said, ... *142*
Joh 12:32 **And I, if I be l. up from the earth,** *5312*
Joh 12:34 thou, The Son of man must be l. up?.. *5312*
Joh 13:18 **me hath l. up his heel against me.** *1869*
Joh 17:1 Jesus, and l. up his eyes to heaven, ... *1869*
Ac 2:14 But Peter,...l. up his voice, and......... *1869*
Ac 3:7 by the right hand, and l. him up:........ *1453*
Ac 4:24 l. up their voice to God with one......... *142*
Ac 9:41 gave her his hand, and l. her up,......... *450*
Ac 14:11 they l. up their voices, saying in......... *1869*
Ac 22:22 and then l. up their voices, and said, .. *1869*
1Ti 3:6 lest being l. up with pride he fall........ *5188*
Re 10:5 the earth l. up his hand to heaven, ... *142*

LIFTER

Ps 3:3 glory, and the l. up of mine head. 7311

LIFTEST

Job 30:22 Thou l. me up to the wind; thou........ 5375
Ps 9:13 thou that l. me up from the gates 7311
Ps 18:48 thou l. me up above those that rise..... 7311
Pr 2:3 l. up they voice for understanding; 5414

LIFTETH

1Sa 2:7 rich: he bringeth low, and l. up......... 7311
1Sa 2:8 l. up the beggar from the dunghill, ... 7311
2Ch 25:19 thine heart l. thee up to boast........... 5375
Job 39:18 time she l. up herself on high, she 4754
Ps 107:25 which l. up the waves thereof. 7311
Ps 113:7 l. the needy out of the dunghill;......... 7311
Ps 147:6 The Lord l. up the meek: he............ 5749
Isa 18:3 when he l. up an ensign on the.......... 5375
Jer 51:3 l. himself up in his brigandine:........... 5927
Na 3:3 horseman l. up both the bright 5927

LIFTING

1Ch 11:20 for l. up his spear against three 5782
1Ch 15:16 by l. up the voice with joy................ 7311
Ne 8:6 Amen, with l. up their hands:............ 4607
Job 22:29 thou shalt say, There is l. up; 1466
Ps 141:2 l. up of my hands as the evening 4864
Pr 30:32 hast done foolishly in l. up thyself, ... 5375
Isa 9:18 mount up like the l. up of smoke. 1348
Isa 33:3 at the l. up of thyself the nations 7427
1Ti 2:8 l. up holy hands, without wrath.......... *1869*

LIGHT See also ALIGHT; DELIGHT; ENLIGHTEN; LIGHTED; LIGHTER; LIGHTEST; LIGHTETH; LIGHTING; LIGHTS; TWILIGHT.

Ge 1:3 Let there be l.: and there was l......... 216
Ge 1:4 God saw the l., that it was good: 216
Ge 1:4 divided the l. from the darkness. 216
Ge 1:5 And God called the l. Day, and the 216
Ge 1:15 heaven to give l. upon the earth:......... 216
Ge 1:16 the greater l. to rule the day,............ 3974
Ge 1:16 and the lesser l. to rule the night:...... 3974
Ge 1:17 heaven to give l. upon the earth,......... 216
Ge 1:18 to divide the l. from the darkness:....... 216
Ge 44:3 As soon as the morning was l., the...... 216
Ex 10:23 of Israel had l. in their dwellings......... 216
Ex 13:21 in a pillar of fire, to give them l.;......... 216
Ex 14:20 but it gave l. by night to these:........... 216
Ex 25:6 Oil for the l., spices for anointing....... 3974
Ex 25:37 they shall l. the lamps thereof, ... 5927
Ex 25:37 they may give l. over against it.......... 216
Ex 27:20 thee pure oil olive beaten for the l., ... 3974
Ex 35:8 oil for the l.,...spices for anointing...... 3974
Ex 35:14 The candlestick also for the l., and..... 3974
Ex 35:14 and his lamps, with the oil for the l., .. 3974
Ex 35:28 oil for the l., and for the anointing...... 3974
Ex 39:37 vessels thereof, and the oil for l., ... 3974
Ex 40:4 in the candlestick, and l. the lamps...... 5927
Le 24:2 thee pure oil olive beaten for he l., ... 3974
Nu 4:9 cover the candlestick of the l., and..... 3974
Nu 4:16 priest pertaineth the oil for the l., ... 3974
Nu 8:2 the seven lamps shall give l. over........ 216
Nu 21:5 our soul loatheth this l. bread............ 7052
De 27:16 be he that setteth l. by his father....... 7034
Jg 9:4 hired vain and l. persons, which......... 6348
Jg 19:26 where her lord was, till it was l.. 216
Ru 2:3 hap was to l. on a part of the field 7136
1Sa 14:36 spoil them until the morning l.,.......... 216
1Sa 18:23 Seemeth it to you a l. thing to be 7043
1Sa 25:22 pertain to him by the morning l........... 216
1Sa 25:34 left unto Nabal by the morning l.......... 216
1Sa 25:36 less or more, until the morning l......... 216
1Sa 29:10 early in the morning, and have l., ... 216
2Sa 2:18 Asahel was as l. of foot as a wild....... 7031
2Sa 17:12 l. upon him as the dew falleth on 5117
2Sa 17:22 by the morning l. there lacked not 216
2Sa 21:17 thou quench not the l. of Israel......... 5216
2Sa 23:4 shall be as the l. of the morning, ... 216
1Ki 7:4,5 l. was against l. in three ranks.......... 4237
1Ki 11:36 l. alway before me in Jerusalem, ... 5216
1Ki 16:31 had been a l. thing for him to walk...... 7043
2Ki 3:18 is but a l. thing in the sight of the...... 7043
2Ki 7:9 we tarry till the morning l., some 216
2Ki 8:19 him to give him alway a l., and to 5216
2Ki 20:10 It is a l. thing for the shadow to 7043
2Ch 21:7 promised to give a l. to him and 5216
Ne 9:12 l. in the way wherein they should 216
Ne 9:19 of fire by night, to shew them l.,.......... 216
Es 8:16 The Jews had l., and gladness, and...... 219
Job 3:4 neither let the l. shine upon it. 5105
Job 3:9 let it look for l., but have none; 216
Job 3:16 been; as infants which never saw l....... 216
Job 3:20 is l. given to him that is in misery, ... 216
Job 3:23 why is l. given to a man whose way is......
Job 10:22 and where the l. is as darkness. 3313
Job 12:22 out to l. the shadow of death............. 216
Job 12:25 They grope in the dark without l., ... 216
Job 17:12 the l. is short because of darkness....... 216
Job 18:5 the l. of the wicked shall be put out,.... 216
Job 18:6 The l. shall be dark in his tabernacle, ... 216
Job 18:18 shall be driven from l. into darkness,.... 216
Job 22:28 the l. shall shine upon thy ways. 216
Job 24:13 of those that rebel against the l.;......... 216
Job 24:14 murderer rising with the l. killeth 216
Job 24:16 the daytime: they know not the l......... 216
Job 25:3 upon whom doth not his l. arise? 216
Job 28:11 that is hid bringeth he forth to l.. 216
Job 29:3 by his l. I walked through darkness;..... 216
Job 29:24 the l. of my countenance they cast........ 216
Job 30:26 and when I waited for l., there came.... 216
Job 33:28 the pit, and his life shall see the l.. 216
Job 33:30 enlightened with the l. of the living. 216
Job 36:30 Behold, he spreadeth his l. upon it,...... 216
Job 36:32 With clouds he covereth the l.;........... 216
Job 37:15 caused the l. of his cloud to shine? 216
Job 37:21 men see not the bright l. which is in.... 216
Job 38:15 the wicked their l. is withholden, ... 216
Job 38:19 Where is the way where l. dwelleth?.... 216
Job 38:24 By what way is the l. parted, which..... 216
Job 41:18 By his neesings a l. doth shine, and..... 216
Ps 4:6 the l. of thy countenance upon us 216
Ps 18:28 For thou wilt l. my candle: the Lord 215
Ps 27:1 The Lord is my l. and my salvation;..... 216
Ps 36:9 of life: in thy l. shall we see l............ 216
Ps 37:6 forth thy righteousness as the l.,......... 216
Ps 38:10 as for the l. of mine eyes, it also is 216
Ps 43:3 O send out thy l. and thy truth: let...... 216
Ps 44:3 arm, and the l. of thy countenance,....... 216
Ps 49:19 his fathers; they shall never see l......... 216
Ps 56:13 before God in the l. of the living? 216
Ps 74:16 hast prepared the l. and the sun. 3974
Ps 78:14 and all the night with a l. of fire. 216
Ps 89:15 Lord, in the l. of thy countenance........ 216
Ps 90:8 sins in the l. of thy countenance. 3974
Ps 97:11 L. is sown for the righteous, and......... 216
Ps 104:2 coverest thyself with l. as with a......... 216
Ps 105:39 and fire to give l. in the night. 216
Ps 112:4 Unto the upright there ariseth l. in 216
Ps 118:27 the Lord, which hath shewed us l......... 216
Ps 119:105 my feet, and a l. unto my path............ 216
Ps 119:130 entrance of thy words giveth l.; it......... 216
Ps 139:11 even the night shall be l. about me. 216
Ps 139:12 darkness and the l. are both alike 219
Ps 148:3 moon: praise him, all ye stars of l......... 216
Pr 4:18 path of the just is as the shining l.,...... 216
Pr 6:23 is a lamp; and the law is l.; and.......... 216
Pr 13:9 The l. of the righteous rejoiceth: 216
Pr 15:30 l. of the eyes rejoiceth the heart:....... 3974
Pr 16:15 In the l. of the king's countenance 216
Ec 2:13 folly, as far as l. excelleth darkness...... 216
Ec 11:7 Truly the l. is sweet, and a pleasant 216
Ec 12:2 While the sun, or the l., or the moon,.. 216
Isa 2:5 let us walk in the l. of the Lord. 216
Isa 5:20 darkness for l., and l. for darkness; 216
Isa 5:30 the l. is darkened in the heavens.......... 216
Isa 8:20 is because there is no l. in them. 7837
Isa 9:2 in darkness have seen a great l.. 216
Isa 9:2 death, upon them hath the l. shined. 216
Isa 10:17 the l. of Israel shall be for a fire,.......... 216
Isa 13:10 thereof shall not give their l................ 216
Isa 13:10 moon shall not cause her l. to shine. 216
Isa 30:26 Moreover the l. of the moon shall........ 216
Isa 30:26 moon shall be as the l. of the sun,....... 216
Isa 30:26 the l. of the sun shall be sevenfold,....... 216
Isa 30:26 as the l. of seven days, in the day....... 216

Isa 42:6 the people, for a l. of the Gentiles;...... 216
Isa 42:16 will make darkness l. before them,....... 216
Isa 45:7 I form the l., and create darkness:....... 216
Isa 49:6 It is a l. thing that thou shouldest...... 7043
Isa 49:6 give thee for a l. to the Gentiles,........ 216
Isa 50:10 in darkness, and hath no l.? let.......... 5051
Isa 50:11 walk in the l. of your fire, and in........ 217
Isa 51:4 to rest for a l. of the people.............. 216
Isa 58:8 Then shall thy l. break forth as the...... 216
Isa 58:10 shall thy l. rise in obscurity, and thy.... 216
Isa 59:9 we wait for l., but behold obscurity;..... 216
Isa 60:1 Arise, shine; for thy l. is come, and..... 216
Isa 60:3 Gentiles shall come to thy l., and........ 216
Isa 60:19 sun shall be no more thy l. by day;...... 216
Isa 60:19 shall the moon give l. unto thee:......... 216
Isa 60:19 shall be unto thee an everlasting l.,...... 216
Isa 60:20 Lord shall be thine everlasting l.,......... 216
Jer 4:23 and the heavens, and they had no l....... 216
Jer 13:16 while ye look for l., he turn it into....... 216
Jer 25:10 millstones, and the l. of the candle....... 216
Jer 31:35 which giveth the sun for a l. by day,.... 216
Jer 31:35 and of the stars for a l. by night,......... 216
La 3:2 me into darkness, but not into l.......... 216
Eze 8:17 Is it a l. thing to the house of Judah... 7043
Eze 22:7 In thee have they set l. by father....... 7043
Eze 32:7 and the moon shall not give her l......... 216
Da 2:22 and the l. dwelleth with him............. 5094
Da 5:11 of thy father l. and understanding....... 5094
Da 5:14 and that l. and understanding and........ 5094
Ho 6:5 thy judgments are as the l. that.......... 216
Am 5:18 the Lord is darkness, and not l........... 216
Am 5:20 the Lord be darkness, and not l.?........ 216
Mic 2:1 when the morning is l., they practise..... 216
Mic 7:8 the Lord shall be a l. unto me............ 216
Mic 7:9 he will bring me forth to the l., and..... 216
Hab 3:4 his brightness was as the l.; he had..... 216
Hab 3:11 at the l. of thine arrows they went,..... 216
Zep 3:4 prophets are l. and treacherous......... 6348
Zep 3:5 doth he bring his judgment to l.,......... 216
Zec 14:6 the l. shall not be clear, nor dark:....... 216
Zec 14:7 that at evening time it shall be l.......... 216
Mt 4:16 which sat in darkness saw great l.;..... *5457*
Mt 4:16 shadow of death l. is sprung up.......... *5457*
Mt 5:14 **Ye are the l. of the world. A city**.. *5457*
Mt 5:15 **Neither do men l. a candle, and**.... *2545*
Mt 5:15 **giveth l. unto all that are in the**.... *2989*
Mt 5:16 **Let your l. so shine before men,**..... *5457*
Mt 6:22 **The l. of the body is the eye: if**..... *5460*
Mt 6:22 **thy whole body shall be full of l**.... *3088*
Mt 6:23 **the l. that is in thee be darkness,**.. *5457*
Mt 10:27 **in darkness, that speak ye in l**...... *5457*
Mt 11:30 **yoke is easy, and my burden is l**.... *1645*
Mt 17:2 his raiment was white as the l........... *5457*
Mt 22:5 **they made l. of it, and went their**... *272*
Mt 24:29 **and the moon shall not give her l.,**.*5338*
Mk 13:24 **and the moon shall not give her l.,**.*5338*
Lu 1:79 give l. to them that sit in darkness..... *2014*
Lu 2:32 A l. to lighten the Gentiles, and....... *5457*
Lu 8:16 **they which enter in may see the l**.. *5457*
Lu 11:33 **they which come in may see the l**.. *5338*
Lu 11:34 **The l. of the body is the eye:**....... *3088*
Lu 11:34 **thy whole body also is full of l.;**.... *5460*
Lu 11:35 **that the l. which is in thee be not**. *5457*
Lu 11:36 **whole body therefore be full of l.,**..*5460*
Lu 11:36 **dark, the whole shall be full of l.,**. *5460*
Lu 11:36 **of a candle doth give thee l**........ *5461*
Lu 12:3 **darkness shall be heard in the l.;**.. *5457*
Lu 15:8 **doth not l. a candle, and sweep the**..*681*
Lu 16:8 **wiser than the children of l**......... *5457*
Joh 1:4 and the life was the l. of men............ *5457*
Joh 1:5 And the l. shineth in darkness; and..... *5457*
Joh 1:7 witness, to bear witness of the L.,....... *5457*
Joh 1:8 He was not that L., but was sent....... *5457*
Joh 1:8 was sent to bear witness of that L...... *5457*
Joh 1:9 That was the true L., which............. *5457*
Joh 3:19 **that l. is come into the world, and**.*5457*
Joh 3:19 **men loved darkness rather than l.,**..*5457*
Joh 3:20 **one that doeth evil hateth the l.,**.... *5457*
Joh 3:20 **neither cometh to the l., lest his**... *5457*
Joh 3:21 **that doeth truth cometh to the l.,**. *5457*
Joh 5:35 **was a burning and a shining l**....... *3088*
Joh 5:35 **for a season to rejoice in his l**....... *5457*
Joh 8:12 saying, **I am the l. of the world:**..... *5457*
Joh 8:12 **but shall have the l. of life**.......... *5457*
Joh 9:5 **the world, I am the l. of the world**.*5457*
Joh 11:9 **because he seeth the l. of this**....... *5457*
Joh 11:10 **because there is no l. in him**......... *5457*
Joh 12:35 **Yet a little while is the l. with**...... *5457*
Joh 12:35 **Walk while ye have the l., lest**...... *5457*
Joh 12:36 **ye have the l., believe in the l.,**..... *5457*
Joh 12:36 **that ye may be the children of l**.... *5457*
Joh 12:46 **I am come a l. into the world, that** *5457*
Ac 9:3 round about him a l. from heaven:....... *5457*
Ac 12:7 him, and a l. shined in the prison:....... *5457*
Ac 13:47 set thee to be a l. of the Gentiles,..... *5457*
Ac 16:29 he called for a l., and sprang in,........ *5457*
Ac 22:6 shone from heaven a great l. round.... *5457*
Ac 22:9 that were with me saw indeed the l.,... *5457*
Ac 22:11 could not see for the glory of that l.,.. *5457*
Ac 26:13 I saw in the way a l. from heaven,...... *5457*
Ac 26:18 **to turn them from darkness to l.,**.. *5457*
Ac 26:23 and should shew l. unto the people,.... *5457*
Ro 2:19 a l. of them which are in darkness,...... *5457*
Ro 13:12 and let us put on the armour of l........ *5457*
1Co 4:5 will bring to l. the hidden things......... *5461*
2Co 4:4 l. of the glorious gospel of Christ,....... *5462*
2Co 4:6 commanded the l. to shine out of........ *5457*
2Co 4:6 to give the l. of the knowledge of...... *5462*
2Co 4:17 our l. affliction, which is but for a....... *1645*
2Co 6:14 communion hath l. with darkness?...... *5457*
2Co 11:14 is transformed into an angel of l......... *5457*
Eph 5:8 but now are ye l. in the Lord:........... *5457*
Eph 5:8 walk as children of l.......................... *5457*
Eph 5:13 are made manifest by the l.: for......... *5457*
Eph 5:13 whatsoever doth make manifest is l... *5457*
Eph 5:14 and Christ shall give thee l............. *2017*
Col 1:12 the inheritance of the saints in l......... *5457*
1Th 5:5 Ye are the children of l., and............ *5457*
1Ti 6:16 dwelling in the l. which no man.......... *5457*
2Ti 1:10 brought life and immortality to l......... *5461*
1Pe 2:9 of darkness into his marvelous l......... *5457*
2Pe 1:19 as unto a l. that shineth in a dark...... *3088*
1Jo 1:5 declare unto you, that God is l.,......... *5457*
1Jo 1:7 if we walk in the l., as he is in the l.,...*5457*
1Jo 2:8 past, and the true l. now shineth........ *5457*
1Jo 2:9 He that saith he is in the l., and........ *5457*
1Jo 2:10 loveth his brother abideth in the l.,...... *5457*
Re 7:16 neither shall the sun l. on them,......... *4098*
Re 18:23 l. of a candle shall shine no more....... *5457*
Re 21:11 her l. was like unto a stone most........ *5458*
Re 21:23 it, and the Lamb is the l. thereof....... *3088*
Re 21:24 saved shall walk in the l. of it:.......... *5457*
Re 22:5 no candle, neither l. of the sun;.......... *5457*
Re 22:5 for the Lord God giveth them l.......... *5461*

LIGHTED See also DELIGHTED.
Ge 24:64 she saw Isaac, she l. off the camel..... 5307
Ge 28:11 And he l. upon a certain place, and..... 6293
Ex 40:25 he l. the lamps before the Lord; as.... 5927
Nu 8:3 he l. the lamps thereof over against.... 5927
Jos 15:18 a field: and she l. off her ass; and...... 6795
Jg 1:14 a field: and she l. from off her ass;..... 6795
Jg 4:15 that Sisera l. down off his chariot,...... 3381
1Sa 25:23 l. off the ass, and fell before David..... 3381
2Ki 5:21 he l. down from the chariot to........... 5307
2Ki 10:15 l. on Jehonadab the son of Rechab...... 4672
Isa 9:8 Jacob, and it hath l. upon Israel......... 5307
Lu 8:16 **No man, when he hath l. a candle,**. *681*
Lu 11:33 **No man, when he hath l. a candle,**. *681*

LIGHTEN See also ENLIGHTEN; LIGHTENED; LIGHTENETH; LIGHTNING.
1Sa 6:5 he will l. his hand from off you,......... 7043
2Sa 22:29 and the Lord will l. my darkness........ 5050
Ezr 9:8 that our God may l. our eyes, and........ 215
Ps 13:3 l. mine eyes, lest I sleep the sleep...... 215
Jon 1:5 ship into the sea, to l. it of them....... 7043
Lu 2:32 A light to l. the Gentiles, and the........ *602*
Re 21:23 the glory of God did l. it, and the...... *5461*

LIGHTENED See also ENLIGHTENED.
Ps 34:5 looked unto him, and were l............. 5102
Ps 77:18 the lightnings l. the world: the........... 215
Ac 27:18 the next day they l. the ship;..... *1546,4160*
Ac 27:38 they l. the ship, and cast out the....... *2893*
Re 18:1 the earth was l. with his glory........... *5461*

LIGHTENETH
Pr 29:13 the Lord l. both their eyes................ 215
Lu 17:24 **that l. out of the one part under**..... *797*

LIGHTER
1Ki 12:4 make...which he put upon us, l.,........ 7043
1Ki 12:9 Make...father did put upon us l.?....... 7043
1Ki 12:10 heavy, but make thou it l. unto us;..... 7043
2Ch 10:10 make thou it somewhat l. for us;....... 7043
Ps 62:9 they are altogether l. than vanity........ 7043

LIGHTEST
Nu 8:2 unto him, When thou l. the lamps,..... 5927

LIGHTETH
Ex 30:8 when Aaron l. the lamps at even,....... 5927
De 19:5 and l. upon his neighbour, that.......... 4672
Joh 1:9 which l. every man that cometh........... *5461*

LIGHTING
Isa 30:30 shall shew the l. down of his arm,...... 5183
Mt 3:16 like a dove, and l. upon him:............ *2064*

LIGHTLY
Ge 26:10 might l. have lien with thy wife,......... 4592
De 32:15 and l. esteemed the Rock of his......... 5034
1Sa 2:30 despise me shall be l. esteemed......... 7043
1Sa 18:23 I am a poor man, and l. esteemed?.... 7034
Isa 9:1 he l. afflicted the land of Zebulun....... 7043
Jer 4:24 trembled, and all the hills moved l....... 7043
Mk 9:39 **that can l. speak evil of me**........... *5035*

LIGHTNESS
Jer 3:9 through the l. of her whoredom,........ 6963
Jer 23:32 err by their lies, and by their l.;........ 6350
2Co 1:17 was thus minded, did I use l.?........... *1644*

LIGHTNING See also LIGHTNINGS.
2Sa 22:15 them; l., and discomfited them.......... 1300
Job 28:26 a way for the l. of the thunder:......... 2385
Job 37:3 his l. unto the ends of the earth.......... 216
Job 38:25 or a way for the l. of thunder;........... 2385
Ps 144:6 Cast forth l., and scatter them:.......... 1300
Eze 1:13 and out of the fire went forth l.......... 1300
Eze 1:14 as the appearance of a flash of l......... 965
Da 10:6 his face as the appearance of l.,......... 1300
Zec 9:14 his arrow shall go forth as the l.:....... 1300
Mt 24:27 **For as the l. cometh out of the east,** *796*
Mt 28:3 His countenance was like l., and......... *796*
Lu 10:18 **I beheld Satan as l. fall from**.......... *796*
Lu 17:24 **For as the l., that lighteneth out of**. *796*

LIGHTNINGS
Ex 19:16 that there were thunders and l.,......... 1300
Ex 20:18 saw the thunderings, and the l.,......... 3940
Job 38:35 Canst thou sent l., that they may....... 1300
Ps 18:14 and he shot out l., and discomfited..... 1300
Ps 77:18 the l. lightened the world: the earth... 1300
Ps 97:4 His l. enlightened the world: the........ 1300
Ps 135:7 he maketh l. for the rain; he............. 1300
Jer 10:13 he maketh l. with rain, and bringeth... 1300
Jer 51:16 he maketh l. with rain, and bringeth... 1300
Na 2:4 torches, they shall run like the l........ 1300
Re 4:5 out of the throne proceeded l. and....... *796*
Re 8:5 were voices, and thunderings, and l.,... *796*
Re 11:19 and there were l., and voices, and....... *796*
Re 16:18 were voices, and thunders, and l.;....... *796*

LIGHTS See also DELIGHTS.
Ge 1:14 Let there be l. in the firmament of..... 3974
Ge 1:15 let them be for l. in the firmament..... 3974
Ge 1:16 God made two great l.; the greater.... 3974
1Ki 6:4 he made windows of narrow l............ 8261
Ps 136:7 To him that made great l.: for his........ 216
Eze 32:8 bright l. of heaven will I make.......... 3974
Lu 12:35 **about, and your l. burning;**........... *3088*
Ac 20:8 there were many l. in the upper........ *2985*
Php 2:15 whom ye shine as l. in the world;...... *5458*
Jas 1:17 cometh down from the Father of l.,.... *5457*

LIGN
Nu 24:6 as the trees of l. aloes which the Lord......

LIGN-ALOES See LIGN and ALOES.

LIGURE (li'-gure)
Ex 28:19 And the third row a l., an agate,........ 3958
Ex 39:12 the third row, a l., an agate, and....... 3958

LIKE See also ALIKE; LIKED; LIKETH; LIKING; LIKEMINDED; LIKEWISE; LIONLIKE.
Ge 13:10 l. the land of Egypt, as thou comest........
Ge 25:25 out red, all over l. an hairy garment;.......
Ex 7:11 also did in l. manner with her............ 3651
Ex 8:10 that there is none l. unto the Lord...........
Ex 9:14 there is none l. me in all the earth..... 3644
Ex 9:24 none l. it in all the land of Egypt........ 3644
Ex 11:6 none l. it, nor shall be l. it any more... 3644
Ex 15:11 Who is l. unto thee, O Lord, among... 3644
Ex 15:11 who is l. thee, glorious in holiness,..... 3644

Ex 16:31	and it was l. coriander seed, white;	
Ex 16:31	the taste of it was l. wafers made with	
Ex 23:11	l. manner thou shalt deal with thy	3651
Ex 24:17	glory of the Lord was l. devouring fire	
Ex 25:33	Three bowls made l. unto almonds,	
Ex 25:33	three bowls made l. almonds in the	
Ex 25:34	be four bowls made l. unto almonds,	
Ex 28:11	l. the engravings of a signet, shalt	
Ex 28:21	l. the engravings of a signet; every	
Ex 28:36	upon it, l. the engravings of a signet,	
Ex 30:32	shall ye make any other l. it, after	3644
Ex 30:33	Whosoever compoundeth any l. it, or	3644
Ex 30:34	of each shall there be a l. weight:	
Ex 30:38	shall make l. unto that, to smell	3644
Ex 34:1	two tables of stone l. unto the first:	
Ex 34:4	two tables of stone l. unto the first;	
Ex 37:19	and three bowls made l. almonds in	
Ex 37:20	were four bowls made l. almonds,	
Ex 39:8	work, l. the work of the ephod;	
Ex 39:14	l. the engravings of a signet, every one	
Ex 39:30	l. to the engravings of a signet,	
Le 13:2	his flesh l. the plague of leprosy;	
Nu 23:10	and let my last end be l. his!	3644
De 4:32	thing is, or hath been heard l. it?	3644
De 7:26	lest thou be a cursed thing l. it:	3644
De 10:1,3	two tables of stone l. unto the first,	
De 17:14	l. as all the nations that are about me;	
De 18:8	They shall have l. portions to eat,	
De 18:15	thee, of thy brethren, l. unto me;	3644
De 18:18	among their brethren, l. unto thee,	3644
De 22:3	In l. manner shalt thou do with	3651
De 25:7	l. not to take his brother's wife,	2654
De 25:8	to it, and say, I l. not to take her;	2654
De 29:23	l. the overthrow of Sodom, and	
De 33:17	glory is l. the firstling of his bullock,	
De 33:17	his horns are l. the horns of unicorns:	
De 33:26	is none l. unto the God of Jeshurun,	
De 33:29	who is l. unto thee, O people saved	3644
De 34:10	prophet since in Israel l. unto Moses,	
Jos 10:14	no day l. that before it or after it,	
Jg 7:12	lay along in the valley l. grasshoppers	
Jg 11:17	in l. manner they sent unto the	1571
Jg 13:6	l. the countenance of an angel of God,	
Jg 16:12	them from off his arms l. a thread.	
Jg 16:17	become weak, and be l. any other man.	
Ru 2:13	not l. unto one of thine handmaidens.	
Ru 4:11	into thine house l. Rachel and l. Leah.	
Ru 4:12	let thy house be l. the house of Pharez,	
1Sa 2:2	neither is there any rock l. our God.	
1Sa 4:9	Be strong, and quit yourselves l. men,	
1Sa 4:9	quit yourselves l. men, and fight.	
1Sa 8:5	us a king to judge us l. all the nations.	
1Sa 8:20	That we also may be l. all the nations;	
1Sa 10:24	none l. him among all the people?	3644
1Sa 17:7	his spear was l. a weaver's beam;	
1Sa 19:24	before Samuel in l. manner,	1571
1Sa 21:9	David said, There is none l. that;	
1Sa 25:36	in his house, l. the feast of a king;	
1Sa 26:15	and who is l. to thee in Israel?	3644
2Sa 7:9	l. unto the name of the great men that	
2Sa 7:22	Lord God: for there is none l. thee,	3644
2Sa 7:23	earth is l. thy people, even l. Israel,	
2Sa 18:27	foremost is l. the running of Ahimaaz	
2Sa 21:19	whose spear was l. a weaver's beam.	
2Sa 22:34	He maketh my feet l. hinds' feet:	7737
1Ki 3:12	there was none l. thee before thee,	3644
1Ki 3:12	after thee shall any arise l. unto thee.	3644
1Ki 3:13	be any among the kings l. unto thee	3644
1Ki 5:6	to hew timber l. unto the Sidonians.	
1Ki 7:8	the porch, which was of the l. work.	
1Ki 7:8	had taken to wife, l. unto this porch.	
1Ki 7:26	was wrought l. the brim of a cup,	
1Ki 7:33	was l. the work of a chariot wheel:	
1Ki 8:23	of Israel, there is no God l. thee,	3644
1Ki 10:20	not the l. made in any kingdom.	3651
1Ki 12:32	l. unto the feast that is in Judah, and	
1Ki 16:3	thy house l. the house of Jeroboam	
1Ki 16:7	in being l. the house of Jeroboam;	
1Ki 18:44	cloud out of the sea, l. a man's hand.	
1Ki 20:25	army, l. the army that thou hast lost,	
1Ki 20:27	pitched before them l. two little flocks.	
1Ki 21:22	thine house l. the house of Jeroboam	
1Ki 21:22	l. the house of Baasha the son of	
1Ki 21:25	But there was none l. unto Ahab,	
1Ki 22:13	thee, be l. the word of one of them,	
2Ki 3:2	not l. his father, and l. his mother:	
2Ki 5:14	again l. unto the flesh of a little child,	
2Ki 9:9	of Ahab l. the house of Jeroboam	
2Ki 9:9	l. the house of Baasha the son of	
2Ki 9:20	the driving is l. the driving of Jehu	
2Ki 13:7	made them l. the dust by threshing.	
2Ki 14:3	the Lord, yet not l. David his father:	
2Ki 16:2	the Lord his God, l. David his father.	
2Ki 17:14	necks, l. to the neck of their fathers,	
2Ki 17:15	that they should not do l. them.	
2Ki 18:5	none l. him among all the kings	3644
2Ki 18:32	you away to a land l. your own land,	
2Ki 23:25	And l. unto him was there no king	3644
2Ki 23:25	after him arose there any l. him.	3644
2Ki 25:17	l. unto these had the second pillar	
1Ch 4:27	multiply, l. to the children of Judah.	
1Ch 11:23	hand was a spear l. a weaver's beam;	
1Ch 12:8	whose faces were l. the faces of lions,	
1Ch 12:22	it was a great host, l. the host of God.	
1Ch 14:11	hand l. the breaking forth of waters:	
1Ch 17:8	a name l. the name of the great men	
1Ch 17:20	O Lord, there is none l. thee,	3644
1Ch 17:21	in the earth is l. thy people Israel,	
1Ch 20:5	spear staff was l. a weaver's beam.	
1Ch 27:23	would increase Israel l. to the stars of	
2Ch 1:9	a people l. the dust of the earth in	
2Ch 1:12	there any after thee have the l.	3651
2Ch 4:5	of it l. the work of the brim of a cup,	
2Ch 6:14	no God l. thee in the heavens, nor	3644
2Ch 9:19	not the l. made in any kingdom.	3651
2Ch 18:12	l. one of theirs, and speak thou good.	
2Ch 21:6	of Israel, l. as did the house of Ahab:	
2Ch 21:13	l. to the whoredoms of the house of	
2Ch 21:19	for him, l. the burning of his fathers.	
2Ch 22:4	sight of the Lord l. the house of Ahab:	
2Ch 28:1	sight of the Lord, l. David his father:	
2Ch 30:7	l. your fathers, and l. your brethren,	
2Ch 30:26	there was not the l. in Jerusalem.	2063
2Ch 33:2	l. unto the abominations of the	
2Ch 35:18	no passover l. to that kept in Israel	3644
Ne 6:5	his servant unto me in l. manner	2088
Ne 13:26	nations was there no king l. him,	3644
Es 2:20	l. as when she was brought up with	
Job 1:8	there is none l. him in the earth,	3644
Job 2:3	there is none l. him in the earth,	3644
Job 3:24	roarings are poured out l. the waters.	
Job 5:26	l. as a shock of corn cometh in in his	
Job 7:1	days also l. the days of an hireling?	
Job 8:2	of thy mouth be l. a strong wind?	
Job 10:10	out as milk, and curdled me l. cheese?	
Job 11:12	man be born l. a wild ass's colt.	
Job 12:25	them to stagger l. a drunken man.	
Job 13:12	remembrances are l. unto ashes,	4911
Job 14:2	forth l. a flower, and is cut down:	
Job 14:9	and bring forth boughs l. a plant.	3644
Job 15:16	man, which drinketh iniquity l. water?	
Job 16:14	beach, he runneth upon me l. a giant.	
Job 19:10	mine hope hath he removed l. a tree.	
Job 20:7	shall perish for ever l. his own dung:	
Job 21:11	send forth their little ones l. a flock,	
Job 30:19	I am become l. dust and ashes.	4911
Job 32:19	it is ready to burst l. new bottles?	
Job 34:7	l. Job, who drinketh up scorning l.	
Job 36:22	his power: who teacheth l. him?	3644
Job 38:3	Gird up now thy loins l. a man;	
Job 40:7	Gird up thy loins now l. a man: I will	
Job 40:9	Hast thou an arm l. God?	
Job 40:9	thou thunder with a voice l. him?	3644
Job 40:17	He moveth his tail l. a cedar: the	3644
Job 40:18	of brass; his bones are l. bars of iron.	
Job 41:18	eyes are l. the eyelids of the morning.	
Job 41:31	He maketh the deep to boil l. a pot:	
Job 41:31	he maketh the sea l. a pot of ointment.	
Job 41:33	Upon earth there is not his l., who	4915
Job 42:8	thing which is right, l. my servant Job.	
Ps 1:3	And he shall be l. a tree planted by the	
Ps 1:4	are l. the chaff which the wind driveth	
Ps 2:9	dash them in pieces l. a potter's vessel.	
Ps 7:2	Lest he tear my soul l. a lion, rending	
Ps 17:12	L. as a lion that is greedy of his	1825
Ps 18:33	He maketh my feet l. hinds' feet and	
Ps 22:14	I am poured out l. water, and all my	
Ps 22:14	my heart is l. wax; it is melted in the	
Ps 22:15	my strength is dried up l. a potsherd;	
Ps 28:1	I become l. them that go down	5973
Ps 29:6	Lebanon and Sirion l. a young unicorn.	
Ps 29:6	maketh them also to skip l. a calf;	3644
Ps 31:12	out of mind: I am l. a broken vessel.	
Ps 35:10	who is l. unto thee, which deliverest	3644
Ps 36:6	Thy righteousness is l. the great	
Ps 37:2	shall soon be cut down l. the grass,	
Ps 37:35	spreading himself l. a green bay tree.	
Ps 39:11	his beauty to consume away l. a moth:	
Ps 44:11	Thou hast given us l. sheep appointed	
Ps 49:12	he is l. the beasts that perish.	4911
Ps 49:14	L. sheep they are laid in the grave;	
Ps 49:20	not, is l. the beasts that perish.	4711
Ps 52:2	l. a sharp razor, working deceitfully.	
Ps 52:8	I am l. a green olive tree in the house	
Ps 55:6	said, Oh that I had wings l. a dove!	
Ps 58:4	Their poison is l. the poison of a	1823
Ps 58:4	they are l. the deaf adder that	3644
Ps 58:8	l. the untimely birth of a woman, that	
Ps 59:6	they make a noise l. a dog, and go	
Ps 59:14	let them make a noise l. a dog, and go	
Ps 64:3	Who whet their tongue l. a sword,	
Ps 71:19	O God, who is l. unto thee!	3644
Ps 72:6	down l. rain upon the mown grass:	
Ps 72:16	city shall flourish l. grass of the earth.	
Ps 72:16	fruit thereof shall shake l. Lebanon:	
Ps 73:5	are they plagued l. other men.	5973
Ps 77:20	Thou leddest thy people l. a flock by	
Ps 78:16	and caused waters to run down l. rivers.	
Ps 78:27	feathered fowls l. as the sand of the	
Ps 78:52	his own people to go forth l. sheep,	
Ps 78:52	them in the wilderness l. a flock.	
Ps 78:57	and dealt unfaithfully l. their fathers:	
Ps 78:57	were turned aside l. a deceitful bow.	
Ps 78:65	and l. a mighty man that shouteth by	
Ps 78:69	he built his sanctuary l. high palaces,	
Ps 78:69	l. the earth which he hath established	
Ps 79:3	Their blood have they shed l. water	
Ps 79:5	ever? shall thy jealousy burn l. fire?	
Ps 80:1	thou that leadest Joseph l. a flock;	
Ps 80:10	thereof were l. the goodly cedars.	
Ps 82:7	But ye shall die l. men,	
Ps 82:7	and fall l. one of the princes.	
Ps 83:11	Make their nobles l. Oreb, and	
Ps 83:11	Make their nobles...l. Zeeb:	
Ps 83:13	O my God, make them l. a wheel; as	
Ps 86:8	the gods there is none l. unto thee, O	
Ps 86:8	are there any works l. unto thy works.	
Ps 88:5	l. the slain that lie in the grave,	3644
Ps 88:17	came round about me daily l. water;	
Ps 89:8	who is a strong Lord l. unto thee?	3644
Ps 89:46	for ever? shall thy wrath burn l. fire?	
Ps 90:5	they are l. grass which groweth up.	
Ps 92:10	thou exalt l. the horn of an unicorn:	
Ps 92:12	shall flourish l. the palm tree:	
Ps 92:12	he shall grow l. a cedar in Lebanon.	
Ps 97:5	hills melted l. wax at the presence of	
Ps 102:3	For my days are consumed l. smoke,	
Ps 102:4	heart is smitten, and withered l. grass;	
Ps 102:6	I am l. a pelican of the wilderness:	1819
Ps 102:6	I am l. an owl of the desert.	
Ps 102:9	For I have eaten ashes l. bread, and	
Ps 102:11	days are l. a shadow that declineth;	
Ps 102:11	and I am withered l. grass.	
Ps 102:26	them shall wax old l. a garment;	1819
Ps 103:5	thy youth is renewed l. the eagle's.	
Ps 103:13	L. as a father pitieth his children, so	
Ps 104:2	stretchest out the heavens l. a curtain:	
Ps 105:41	they ran in the dry places l. a river.	
Ps 107:27	fro, and stagger l. a drunken man,	
Ps 107:41	and maketh him families l. a flock.	
Ps 109:18	with cursing l. as with his garment,	
Ps 109:18	so let it come into his bowels l. water,	
Ps 109:18	water, and l. oil into his bones.	
Ps 109:23	gone l. the shadow when it declineth:	
Ps 113:5	Who is l. unto the Lord our God, who	
Ps 114:4	The mountains skipped l. rams,	
Ps 114:4	rams, and the little hills l. lambs.	
Ps 114:6	mountains, that ye skipped l. rams;	
Ps 114:6	rams; and ye little hills, l. lambs?	
Ps 115:8	make them are l. unto them;	3644
Ps 118:12	They compassed me about l. bees;	
Ps 119:83	I am become l. a bottle in the smoke;	
Ps 119:119	all the wicked of the earth l. dross.	
Ps 119:176	I have gone astray l. a lost sheep:	
Ps 126:1	of Zion, we were l. them that dream.	
Ps 128:3	children l. olive plants round about	
Ps 133:2	It is l. the precious ointment upon the	
Ps 135:18	that make them are l. unto them:	3644
Ps 140:3	their tongues l. a serpent;	
Ps 143:7	lest I be l. unto them that go down	4911
Ps 144:4	Man is l. to vanity: his days are as	1819

Ps 147:16 He giveth snow l. wool:
Ps 147:16 he scattereth the hoarfrost l. ashes.
Ps 147:17 He casteth forth his ice l. morsels:
Pr 12:18 speaketh l. the piercings of a sword:
Pr 17:22 merry heart doeth good l. a medicine:
Pr 18:19 contentions are l. the bars of a castle.
Pr 20:5 in the heart of man is l. deep water;
Pr 23:32 l. a serpent, and stingeth l. an adder.
Pr 25:11 A word fitly spoken is l. apples of gold
Pr 25:14 of a false gift is l. clouds and wind
Pr 25:19 in time of trouble is l. a broken tooth,
Pr 25:28 spirit is l. a city that is broken down,
Pr 26:4 lest thou also be l. unto him. 7737
Pr 26:17 is l. one that taketh a dog by the ears.
Pr 26:23 and a wicked heart are l. a potsherd
Pr 28:3 is l. a sweeping rain which leaveth no
Pr 31:14 She is l. the merchants' ships; she
Ca 2:9 My beloved is l. a roe or a young 1819
Ca 2:17 and be thou l. a roe or a young hart 1819
Ca 3:6 of the wilderness l. pillars of smoke,
Ca 4:2 Thy teeth are l. a flock of sheep that
Ca 4:3 Thy lips are l. a thread of scarlet, and
Ca 4:3 are l. a piece of a pomegranate
Ca 4:4 Thy neck is l. the tower of David
Ca 4:5 Thy two breasts are l. two young roes
Ca 4:11 garments is l. the smell of Lebanon.
Ca 5:13 his lips l. lilies, dropping sweet
Ca 6:12 me l. the chariots of Ammi-nadib.
Ca 7:1 joints of thy thighs are l. jewels, 3644
Ca 7:2 Thy navel is l. a round goblet, which
Ca 7:2 thy belly is l. an heap of wheat set
Ca 7:3 Thy two breasts are l. two young roes
Ca 7:4 thine eyes l. the fishpools in Heshbon,
Ca 7:5 Thine head upon thee is l. Carmel,
Ca 7:5 and the hair of thine head l. purple;
Ca 7:7 thy statute is l. to a palm tree, 1819
Ca 7:8 and the smell of thy nose l. apples;
Ca 7:9 the roof of thy mouth l. the best wine
Ca 8:10 I am a wall, and my breasts l. towers:
Ca 8:14 be thou l. to a roe or to a young 1819
Isa 1:9 have been l. unto Gomorrah. 1819
Isa 1:18 though they be red l. crimson, 1819
Isa 2:6 and are soothsayers l. the Philistines,
Isa 3:18 and their round tires l. the moon,
Isa 5:28 horses' hoofs shall be counted l. flint,
Isa 5:28 and their wheels like a whirlwind:
Isa 5:29 Their roaring shall be l. a lion,
Isa 5:29 they shall roar l. young lions: yea,
Isa 5:30 against them l. the roaring of the sea:
Isa 9:18 mount up l. the lifting up of smoke.
Isa 10:6 to tread them down l. the mire of the
Isa 10:13 the inhabitants l. a valiant man:
Isa 10:16 a burning l. the burning of a fire.
Isa 11:7 and the lion shall eat straw l. the ox.
Isa 11:16 l. as it was to Israel in the day that he
Isa 13:4 mountains, l. as of a great people; 1823
Isa 14:10 as we? art thou become l. unto us? 4911
Isa 14:14 clouds; I will be l. the most High. 1819
Isa 14:19 of thy grave l. an abominable branch,
Isa 16:11 shall sound l. an harp for Moab,
Isa 17:12 make a noise l. the noise of the seas;
Isa 17:12 l. the rushing of mighty waters!
Isa 17:13 rush l. the rushing of many waters:
Isa 17:13 l. a rolling thing before the whirlwind.
Isa 18:4 l. a clear heat upon herbs, and
Isa 18:4 l. a cloud of dew in the heat of harvest.
Isa 19:16 day shall Egypt be l. unto women:
Isa 20:3 L. as my servant Isaiah hath walked
Isa 22:18 toss thee l. a ball into a large country:
Isa 24:20 shall reel to and fro l. a drunkard,
Isa 24:20 and shall be removed l. a cottage; for
Isa 26:17 L. as a woman with child, that 3644
Isa 27:10 forsaken, and left l. a wilderness:
Isa 29:5 thy strangers shall be l. small dust,
Isa 30:33 of the Lord, l. a stream of brimstone,
Isa 31:4 L. as the lion and the young lion
Isa 33:4 l. the gathering of the caterpiller:
Isa 33:9 Sharon is l. a wilderness; and Bashan
Isa 36:17 you away to a land l. your own land,
Isa 38:12 I have cut off l. a weaver my life: he
Isa 38:14 L. a crane or a swallow, so did I
Isa 40:11 He shall feed his flock l. a shepherd:
Isa 42:13 shall stir up jealousy l. a man of war:
Isa 42:14 now will I cry l. a travailing woman;
Isa 46:5 compare me, that we may be l.? 1819
Isa 46:9 I am God, and there is none l. me, 3644
Isa 48:19 of thy bowels l. the gravel thereof;
Isa 49:2 made my mouth l. a sharp sword;
Isa 50:7 therefore have I set my face l. a flint,
Isa 51:3 will make her wilderness l. Eden,
Isa 51:3 her desert l. the garden of the Lord;
Isa 51:6 heavens shall vanish away l. smoke,
Isa 51:6 the earth shall wax old l. a garment,
Isa 51:6 therein shall die in l. manner: 3644
Isa 51:8 moth shall eat them up l. a garment,
Isa 51:8 and the worm shall eat them l. wool:
Isa 53:6 All we l. sheep have gone astray;
Isa 57:20 the wicked are l. the troubled sea,
Isa 58:1 lift up thy voice l. a trumpet, and
Isa 58:11 thou shalt be l. a watered garden,
Isa 58:11 l. a spring of water, whose waters
Isa 59:10 We grope for the wall l. the blind,
Isa 59:11 We roar all l. bears, and mourn sore
Isa 59:11 bears, and mourn sore l. doves:
Isa 59:19 the enemy shall come in l. a flood,
Isa 63:2 thy garments l. him that treadeth in
Isa 64:6 our iniquities, l. the wind, have taken
Isa 65:25 the lion shall eat straw l. the bullock:
Isa 66:12 I will extend peace to her l. a river,
Isa 66:12 of the Gentiles l. a flowing stream:
Isa 66:14 your bones shall flourish l. an herb:
Isa 66:15 and with his chariots l. a whirlwind,
Jer 2:30 your prophets, l. a destroying lion.
Jer 4:4 lest my fury come forth l. fire, and
Jer 5:19 L. as ye have forsaken me, and served
Jer 6:23 their voice roareth l. the sea; and
Jer 9:3 they bend their tongues l. their bow
Jer 9:12 and is burned up l. a wilderness.
Jer 10:6 as there is none l. unto thee, O 3644
Jer 10:7 there is none l. unto thee. 3644
Jer 10:16 The portion of Jacob is not l. them:
Jer 11:19 But I was l. a lamb or an ox that is
Jer 12:3 them out l. sheep for the slaughter,
Jer 14:6 they snuffed up the wind l. dragons;
Jer 17:6 he shall be l. the heath in the desert,
Jer 21:12 lest my fury go out l. fire, and burn
Jer 23:9 bones shake; I am l. a drunken man,
Jer 23:9 l. a man whom wine hath overcome,
Jer 23:29 Is not my word l. as a fire? saith 3541
Jer 23:29 l. a hammer that breaketh the rock in
Jer 24:2 even l. the figs that are first ripe:
Jer 24:5 L. these good figs, so will I
Jer 25:34 and ye shall fall l. a pleasant vessel.
Jer 26:6 Then will I make this house l. Shiloh,
Jer 26:9 This house shall be l. Shiloh, and this
Jer 26:18 Zion shall be plowed l. a field, and
Jer 29:17 will make them l. vile figs, that cannot
Jer 29:22 make thee l. Zedekiah and l. Ahab,
Jer 30:7 day is great, so that none is l. it: 3644
Jer 31:28 that l. as I have watched over them,
Jer 32:42 L. as I have brought all this great evil
Jer 36:32 besides unto them many l. words. 1922
Jer 38:9 he is l. to die for hunger in the place
Jer 46:8 Egypt riseth up l. a flood, and
Jer 46:8 his waters are moved l. the rivers;
Jer 46:20 Egypt is l. a very fair heifer, but
Jer 46:21 in the midst of her l. fatted bullocks;
Jer 46:22 The voice thereof shall go l. a serpent;
Jer 48:6 be l. the heath in the wilderness. 2421
Jer 48:28 be l. the dove that maketh her nest in
Jer 48:36 heart shall sound for Moab l. pipes,
Jer 48:36 heart shall sound l. pipes for the men
Jer 48:38 for I have broken Moab l. a vessel
Jer 49:19 Behold, he shall come up l. a lion from
Jer 49:19 appoint over her? for who is l. me? 3644
Jer 50:42 their voice shall roar l. the sea, and
Jer 50:42 put in array, l. a man to the battle,
Jer 50:44 Behold, he shall come up l. a lion from
Jer 50:44 appoint over her? for who is l. me? 3644
Jer 51:19 The portion of Jacob is not l. them;
Jer 51:33 of Babylon is l. a threshingfloor,
Jer 51:34 he hath swallowed me up l. a dragon,
Jer 51:38 They shall roar together l. lions:
Jer 51:40 I will bring them down l. lambs to the
Jer 51:40 slaughter, l. rams with he goats.
Jer 51:55 her waves do roar l. great waters,
Jer 52:22 the pomegranates were l. unto these.
La 1:6 princes are become l. harts that find
La 1:12 be any sorrow l. unto my sorrow,
La 1:21 and they shall be l. unto me. 3644
La 2:3 burned against Jacob l. a flaming fire,
La 2:4 He hath bent his bow l. an enemy;
La 2:4 of Zion: he poured out his fury l. fire.
La 2:13 for thy breach is great l. the sea:
La 2:18 let tears run down l. a river day and
La 2:19 pour out thine heart l. water before
La 3:52 enemies chased me sore, l. a bird,
La 4:3 l. the ostriches in the wilderness.
La 4:8 it is withered, it is become l. a stick.
La 5:10 Our skin was black l. an oven because
Eze 1:7 feet was l. the sole of a calf's foot:
Eze 1:7 l. the colour of burnished brass.
Eze 1:13 appearance was l. burning coals of fire,
Eze 1:13 and l. the appearance of lamps:
Eze 1:16 work was l. unto the colour of a beryl:
Eze 1:24 wings, l. the noise of great waters,
Eze 2:8 rebellious l. that rebellious house:
Eze 5:9 I will not do any more the l., 3644
Eze 7:16 and shall be on the mountains l. doves
Eze 12:11 l. as I have done, so shall it be done
Eze 13:4 thy prophets are l. the foxes in the
Eze 16:16 the l. things shall not come, neither
Eze 18:10 doeth the l. to any one of these 251
Eze 18:14 considereth, and doeth not such l.,
Eze 19:10 Thy mother is l. a vine in thy blood,
Eze 20:36 L. as I pleaded with your fathers in
Eze 22:25 l. a roaring lion ravening the prey;
Eze 22:27 thereof are l. wolves ravening the prey,
Eze 23:18 l. as my mind was alienated from her
Eze 23:20 whose issue is l. the issue of horses.
Eze 25:8 of Judah is l. unto all the heathen;
Eze 26:4 her, and make her l. the top of a rock.
Eze 26:14 I will make thee l. the top of a rock:
Eze 26:19 l. the cities that are not inhabited;
Eze 27:32 over thee, saying, What city is l. Tyrus,
Eze 27:32 l. the destroyed in the midst of the
Eze 31:2 Whom art thou l. in thy greatness? 1819
Eze 31:8 chesnut trees were not l. his branches;
Eze 31:8 the fir trees were not l. his boughs, 1819
Eze 31:8 God was l. unto him in his beauty. 1819
Eze 31:18 To whom art thou thus l. in glory 1819
Eze 32:2 art l. a young lion of the nations, 1819
Eze 32:14 cause their rivers to run l. oil, saith
Eze 36:35 is become l. the garden of Eden;
Eze 36:37 increase them with men l. a flock.
Eze 38:9 shalt ascend and come l. a storm,
Eze 38:9 thou shalt be l. a cloud to cover the
Eze 40:3 was l. the appearance of brass,
Eze 40:25 round about, l. those windows:
Eze 41:25 trees, l. as were made upon the walls;
Eze 42:11 was l. the appearance of the chambers
Eze 43:2 voice was l. a noise of many waters:
Eze 43:3 visions were l. the vision that I saw
Eze 45:25 he do the l. in the feast of the seven
Da 1:19 them all was found none l. Daniel,
Da 2:35 became l. the chaff of the summer
Da 3:25 of the fourth is l. the Son of God. 1821
Da 4:33 hairs were grown l. eagles' feathers,
Da 4:33 and his nails l. birds' claws.
Da 5:11 wisdom, l. the wisdom of the gods,
Da 5:21 his heart was made l. the beasts, 5974
Da 5:21 they fed him with grass l. oxen, and
Da 7:4 The first was l. a lion, and had eagles'
Da 7:5 beast, a second, l. to a bear, and it 1821
Da 7:6 and lo another, l. a leopard, which had
Da 7:8 horn were eyes l. the eyes of man,
Da 7:9 the hair of his head l. the pure wool:
Da 7:9 his throne was l. the fiery flame, and
Da 7:13 one l. the Son of man came with the
Da 10:6 His body also was l. the beryl, and his
Da 10:6 his feet l. in colour to polished brass,
Da 10:6 his words l. the voice of a multitude.
Da 10:16 one l. the similitude of the sons of lo
Da 10:18 me one l. the appearance of a man,
Da 11:40 shall come against him l. a whirlwind,
Ho 2:3 set her l. a dry land, and slay her with
Ho 4:9 And there shall be, l. people, l. priest:
Ho 5:10 were l. them that remove the bound:
Ho 5:10 out my wrath upon them l. water.
Ho 6:7 l. men have transgressed the covenant.
Ho 7:6 made ready their heart l. an oven,
Ho 7:11 Ephraim also is l. a silly dove without
Ho 7:16 they are l. a deceitful bow: their
Ho 9:10 Israel l. grapes in the wilderness;
Ho 9:11 their glory shall fly away l. a bird,
Ho 11:10 he shall roar l. a lion: when he shall
Ho 13:8 there will I devour them l. a lion:
Ho 14:8 I am l. a green fir tree. From me is

Joe 1:8 Lament l. a virgin girded with
Joe 2:2 there hath not been ever the l., 3644
Joe 2:5 L. the noise of chariots on the tops of
Joe 2:5 l. the noise of a flame of fire that
Joe 2:7 They shall run l. mighty men; they
Joe 2:7 they shall climb the wall l. men of war;
Joe 2:9 shall enter in at the windows l. a thief
Am 2:9 height was l. the height of the cedars,
Am 5:6 lest he break out l. fire in the house of
Am 6:5 instruments of musick, l. David;
Am 9:5 and it shall rise up wholly l. a flood;
Am 9:9 nations, l. as corn is sifted in a sieve,
Jon 1:4 that the ship was l. to be broken. 2803
Mic 1:8 I will make a wailing l. the dragons,
Mic 4:10 of Zion, l. a woman in travail:
Mic 7:17 They shall lick the dust l. a serpent,
Mic 7:17 of their holes l. worms of the earth:
Mic 7:18 Who is a God l. unto thee, that 3644
Na 1:6 his fury is poured out l. fire, and the
Na 2:4 ways: they shall seem l. torches,
Na 2:4 they shall run l. the lightnings
Na 2:8 Nineveh is of old l. a pool of water:
Na 3:12 thy strong holds shall be l. fig trees
Na 3:15 it shall eat thee up l. the cankerworm:
Hab 3:19 and he will make my feet l. hind's feet,
Zep 1:17 men, that they shall walk l. blind men,
Zep 2:13 a desolation, and dry l. a wilderness.
Zec 1:6 L. as the Lord of hosts thought to do
Zec 5:9 had wings l. the wings of a stork:
Zec 9:15 and they shall be filled l. bowls, and as
Zec 10:7 of Ephraim shall be l. a mighty man,
Zec 12:6 governors of Judah l. a hearth of fire
Zec 12:6 wood, and l. a torch of fire in a sheaf;
Zec 14:5 l. as ye fled from before the earthquake
Zec 14:20 shall be l. the bowls before the altar.
Mal 3:2 l. a refiner's fire, and l. a fullers' sope:
Mt 3:16 Spirit of God descending l. a dove, 5616
Mt 6:8 **Be not ye therefore l. unto them:** 3666
Mt 6:29 **was not arrayed l. one of these.** 5613
Mt 11:16 **It is l. unto children sitting in the** 3664
Mt 12:13 was restored whole, l. as the other. 5613
Mt 13:31 **is l. to a grain of mustard seed,** 3664
Mt 13:33 **kingdom of heaven is l. unto** 3664
Mt 13:44 **is l. unto treasure hid in a field;** 3664
Mt 13:45 **heaven is l. unto a merchant man,** 3664
Mt 13:47 **kingdom of heaven is l. unto a net,** 3664
Mt 13:52 **l. unto a man that is an** 3664
Mt 20:1 **l. unto a man that is an** 3664
Mt 21:24 **I in l. wise will tell you by what** 2504
Mt 22:2 **of heaven is l. unto a certain king,** 3666
Mt 22:39 **And the second is l. unto it, Thou.** 3664
Mt 23:27 **ye are l. unto whited sepulchres,** 3945
Mt 28:3 His countenance was l. lightning, 5613
Mk 1:10 and the Spirit l. a dove descending 5616
Mk 4:31 **It is l. a grain of mustard seed,** 5613
Mk 7:8 **many other such l. things ye do.** 3946
Mk 7:13 **and many such l. things do ye.** 3946
Mk 12:31 **And the second is l., namely this,** 3664
Mk 13:29 **So ye in l. manner, when ye shall** 2532
Lu 3:22 descended...bodily shape l. a dove 5616
Lu 6:23 **in the l. manner did their fathers** 5024
Lu 6:47 **I will shew you to whom he is l.:** 3664
Lu 6:48 **He is l. a man which built an** 3664
Lu 6:49 **l. a man that without a foundation** 3664
Lu 7:31 **and to what are they l.?** 3664
Lu 7:32 **They are l. unto children sitting in** 3664
Lu 12:27 **was not arrayed l. one of these.** 5613
Lu 12:36 **yourselves l. unto men that wait** 3664
Lu 13:18 **what is the kingdom of God l.?** 3664
Lu 13:19 **It is l. a grain of mustard seed,** 3664
Lu 13:21 **It is l. leaven, which a woman** 3664
Lu 20:31 and in l. manner the seven also: 5615
Joh 1:32 descending from heaven l. a dove, 5616
Joh 7:46 Never man spake l. this man 3779
Joh 8:55 **I shall be a liar l. unto you: but I** 3664
Joh 9:9 is he: others said, He is l. him: 3664
Ac 1:11 shall so come in l. manner as ye 3779
Ac 2:3 them cloven tongues l. as of fire, 5616
Ac 3:22 you of your brethren, l. unto me; 3945
Ac 7:37 you of your brethren, l. unto me; 5613
Ac 8:32 l. a lamb dumb before his shearer, 5613
Ac 11:17 God gave them the l. gift as he did 2470
Ac 14:15 also are men of l. passions with you, 3663
Ac 17:29 that the Godhead is l. unto gold, 3664
Ac 19:25 with the workmen of l. occupation, 5108
Ro 1:23 image made l. to corruptible man, 3667
Ro 1:28 as they did not l. to retain God 1381
Ro 6:4 l. as Christ was raised up from 5618
Ro 9:29 and been made l. unto Gomorrha. 3666
1Co 16:13 the faith, quit you l. men, be strong. 407
Ga 5:21 revellings, and such l.: 3664
Php 3:21 be fashioned l. unto his glorious 4832
1Th 2:14 have suffered l. things of your own 5024
1Ti 2:9 In l. manner also, that women 5615
Heb 2:17 to be made l. unto his brethren, 3666
Heb 4:15 all points tempted l. as we are, 2596,3665
Heb 7:3 but made l. unto the Son of God; 871
Jas 1:6 wavereth is l. a wave of the sea 1503
Jas 1:23 he is l. unto a man beholding his 1503
Jas 5:17 a man subject to l. passions as we 3663
1Pe 3:21 The l. figure whereunto even 499
2Pe 1:1 that have obtained l. precious faith 2472
1Jo 3:2 shall appear, we shall be l. him; 3664
Jude 7 cities about them in l. manner, 3664
Re 1:13 candlesticks one l. unto the Son of 3664
Re 1:14 and his hairs were white l. wool, 5616
Re 1:15 his feet l. unto fine brass, as if 3664
Re 2:18 **his eyes l. unto a flame of fire,** 5613
Re 2:18 **and his feet are l. fine brass;** 3664
Re 4:3 that sat was to look upon l. a jasper 3664
Re 4:3 throne, in sight l. unto an emerald 3664
Re 4:6 was a sea of glass l. unto crystal: 3664
Re 4:7 And the first beast was l. a lion, 3664
Re 4:7 and the second beast l. a calf, and 3664
Re 4:7 the fourth beast was l. a flying eagle 3664
Re 9:7 of the locusts were l. unto horses 3664
Re 9:7 were as it were crowns l. gold, 3664
Re 9:10 they had tails l. unto scorpions, and 3664
Re 9:19 their tails were l. unto serpents, 3664
Re 11:1 was given me a reed l. unto a rod: 3664
Re 13:2 which I saw was l. unto a leopard, 3664
Re 13:4 Who is l. unto the beast? who is 3664
Re 13:11 he had two horns l. a lamb, and he 3664
Re 14:14 cloud one sat l. unto the Son of man, 3664
Re 16:13 I saw three unclean spirits l. frogs 3664
Re 18:18 What city is l. unto this great city! 3664
Re 18:21 up a stone l. a great millstone, 5613
Re 21:11 her light was l. unto a stone most 3664
Re 21:11 even l. a jasper stone, clear as 5613
Re 21:18 was pure gold, l. unto clear glass 3664

LIKED

1Ch 28:4 he l. me to make me king over all 7521

LIKEMINDED

Ro 15:5 to be l. one toward another 3588,846,5426
Php 2:2 ye my joy, that ye be l., 3588,846,5426
Php 2:20 For I have no man l., who will 2473

LIKEN See also LIKENED.

Isa 40:18 To whom then will ye l. God? or 1819
Isa 40:25 To whom then will ye l. me, or 1819
Isa 46:5 To whom will ye l. me, and make 1819
La 2:13 what thing shall I l. to thee, O 1819
Mt 7:24 **I will l. him unto a wise man,** 3666
Mt 11:16 **shall I l. this generation?** 3666
Mk 4:30 **shall we l. the kingdom of God?** 3666
Lu 7:31 **then shall I l. the men of this** 3666
Lu 13:20 **shall I l. the kingdom of God?** 3666

LIKENED

Ps 89:6 mighty can be l. unto the Lord? 1819
Jer 6:2 have l. the daughter of Zion to a 1819
Mt 7:26 **shall be l. unto a foolish man,** 3666
Mt 13:24 **of heaven is l. unto a man which** 3666
Mt 18:23 **of heaven l. unto a certain king,** 3666
Mt 25:1 **of heaven be l. unto ten virgins,** 3666

LIKENESS

Ge 1:26 man in our image, after our l.: 1823
Ge 5:1 man, in the l. of God made he him; 1823
Ge 5:3 begat a son in his own l., after his 1823
Ex 20:4 or any l. of any thing that is in 8544
De 4:16 figure, the l. of male or female, 8403
De 4:17 The l. of any beast that is on the 8403
De 4:17 the l. of any winged fowl that flieth 8403
De 4:18 The l. of any thing that creepeth on 8403
De 4:18 the l. of any fish that is in the 8403
De 4:23 image, or the l. of any thing, 8544
De 4:25 graven image, or the l. of any thing, 8544
De 5:8 any l. of any thing that is in heaven 8544
Ps 17:15 satisfied, when I awake, with thy l. 8544
Isa 40:18 what l. will ye compare unto him? 1823
Eze 1:5 came the l. of four living creatures. 1823
Eze 1:5 they had the l. of a man 1823
Eze 1:10 As for the l. of their faces, they four 1823
Eze 1:13 As for the l. of the living creatures, 1823
Eze 1:16 a beryl: and they four had one l.: 1823
Eze 1:22 the l. of the firmament upon their 1823
Eze 1:26 their heads was the l. of a throne, 1823
Eze 1:26 and upon the l. of the throne was the 1823
Eze 1:26 l. as the appearance of a man above 1823
Eze 1:28 of the l. of the glory of the Lord 1823
Eze 8:2 and lo a l. as the appearance of fire: 1823
Eze 10:1 the appearance of the l. of a throne 1823
Eze 10:10 appearances, they four had one l., 1823
Eze 10:21 and the l. of the hands of a man 1823
Eze 10:22 the l. of their faces was the same 1823
Ac 14:11 come down to us in the l. of men. 3666
Ro 6:5 together in the l. of his death, 3667
Ro 6:5 be also in the l. of his resurrection:
Ro 8:3 his own Son in the l. of sinful flesh, 3667
Php 2:7 and was made in the l. of men: 3667

LIKETH

De 23:16 thy gates, where it l. him best: 2896
Es 8:8 ye also for the Jews, as it l. you, 2896
Am 4:5 for this l. you, O ye children of 157

LIKEWISE

Ex 22:30 L. shalt thou do with thine oxen, 3651
Ex 26:4 l. shalt thou make in the uttermost 3651
Ex 27:11 l. for the north side in length there 3651
Ex 36:11 l. he made in the uttermost side of 3651
Le 7:1 L. this is the law of the trespass 2063
De 9:23 L. when the Lord sent you from
De 12:30 their gods? even so will I do l. 3651
De 15:17 thy maidservant thou shalt do l. 3651
De 22:3 thou hast found, shalt thou do l. 3651
Jg 1:3 I l. will go with thee into thy lot. 1571
Jg 7:5 l. every one that boweth down upon
Jg 7:17 unto them, Look on me, and do l. 3651
Jg 8:8 Penuel, and spake unto them l. 2063
Jg 9:49 people l. cut down every man his 1571
1Sa 14:22 L. all the men of Israel which had hid
1Sa 19:21 and they prophesied l. 1571
1Sa 31:5 was dead, he fell l. upon his sword, 1571
2Sa 1:11 l. all the men that were with him: 1571
2Sa 17:5 and let us hear l. what he saith. 1571
1Ki 11:8 l. did for all his strange wives, 3651
1Ch 10:5 was dead, he fell l. on the sword, 1571
1Ch 18:8 L. from Tibhath, and from Chun,
1Ch 19:15 l. fled before Abishai his brother, 1571
1Ch 23:30 praise the Lord, and l. at even; 3651
1Ch 24:31 These l. cast lots over against 1571
1Ch 27:4 in his course l. were twenty and four
1Ch 28:16 and l. silver for the tables of silver:
1Ch 28:17 l. silver by weight for every bason of
1Ch 29:24 and all the sons l. of king David, 1571
2Ch 3:11 and the other wing was l. five cubits,
2Ch 29:22 l., when they had killed the rams,
Ne 4:22 L. at the same time said I unto 1571
Ne 5:10 I, l., and my brethren, and my 1571
Es 1:18 L. shall the ladies of Persia and
Es 4:16 I also and my maidens will fast l.; 3651
Job 31:38 the furrows l. thereof complain; 3162
Job 37:6 l. to the small rain, and to the great
Ps 49:10 l. the fool and the brutish person
Ps 52:5 God shall l. destroy thee for ever, 1571
Ec 7:22 thou thyself l. hast cursed others. 1571
Isa 30:24 The oxen l. and the young asses that
Jer 40:11 L. when all the Jews that were in 1571
Eze 13:17 L., thou son of man, set thy face
Eze 40:16 round about, and l. to the arches: 3651
Eze 46:3 L. the people of the land shall worship
Na 1:12 they be quiet, and l. many, yet 3651
Mt 17:12 **L. shall also the Son of man** 3779
Mt 18:35 **So l. shall my heavenly Father do** 2532
Mt 20:5 **sixth and ninth hour, and did l.** 5615
Mt 20:10 **they l. received every man a penny.** 2532
Mt 21:30 **he came to the second, and said l.** 5615
Mt 21:36 **first: and they did unto them l.** 5615
Mt 22:26 **L. the second also, and the third,** 3668
Mt 24:33 **So l. ye, when ye shall see all** 2532
Mt 25:17 l. he that had received two, he also 5615
Mt 26:35 thee. L. also said all the disciples. 3668
Mt 27:41 L. also the chief priests mocking 3668
Mk 4:16 **these are they l. which are sown** 3668
Mk 12:21 left he any seed: and the third l. 5615
Mk 14:31 in any wise. L. also said they all. 5615
Mk 15:31 L. also the chief priests mocking 3668
Lu 2:38 gave thanks l. unto the Lord, and 437
Lu 3:11 he that hath meat, let him do l. 3668
Lu 3:14 the soldiers l. demanded of him, 2532

Lu 5:33 l. the disciples of the Pharisees; *3668*
Lu 6:31 do to you, do ye also to them l.. ... *3668*
Lu 10:32 And l. a Levite, when he was at.... *3668*
Lu 10:37 Jesus unto him, Go, and do thou l.. .*3668*
Lu 13:3 ye repent, ye shall all l. perish...... *5615*
Lu 13:5 ye repent, ye shall all l. perish...... *3668*
Lu 14:33 So l., whosoever he be of you that..*3779*
Lu 15:7 that l. joy shall be in heaven over..*3779*
Lu 15:10 L., I say unto you, there is joy in. *3779*
Lu 16:25 things, and l. Lazarus evil things:..*3668*
Lu 17:10 So l. ye, when ye shall have done.. *2532*
Lu 17:28 L. also as it was in the days of...... *3668*
Lu 17:31 the field, let him l. not return....... *3668*
Lu 19:19 And he said l. to him, Be thou...... *2532*
Lu 21:31 So l. ye, when ye see these things..*2532*
Lu 22:20 L. also the cup after supper,............. *5615*
Lu 22:36 let him take it, and l. his scrip:..... *3668*
Joh 5:19 doeth, these also doeth the Son l... *3668*
Joh 6:11 l. of the fishes as much as they......... *3668*
Joh 21:13 bread and giveth them, and fish l.. ..... *3668*
Ac 3:24 have l. foretold of these days............ *2532*
Ro 1:27 And l. also the men, leaving the *3668*
Ro 6:11 L. reckon ye also yourselves to be..... *3779*
Ro 8:26 L. the Spirit also helpeth our *5615*
Ro 16:5 L. greet the church that is in their..... *2532*
1Co 7:3 l. also the wife unto the husband........ *3668*
1Co 7:4 l. also the husband hath not power of.. *3668*
1Co 7:22 l. also he that is called, being free, is.. *3668*
1Co 14:9 So l. ye, except ye utter by the *2532*
Ga 2:13 other Jews dissembled l. with him; *2532*
Col 4:16 that ye l. read the epistle from........... *2532*
1Ti 3:8 L. must the deacons be grave, not...... *5615*
1Ti 5:25 L. also the good works of some are ... *5615*
Tit 2:3 The aged woman l., that they be in.... *5615*
Tit 2:6 Young men l. exhort to be sober *5615*
Heb 2:14 himself l. took part of the same; *3898*
Heb 9:21 sprinkled l. with blood both the.......... *3668*
Jas 2:25 L. also was not Rahab the harlot......... *3668*
1Pe 3:1 L. ye wives, be in subjection to.......... *3668*
1Pe 3:7 L., ye husbands, dwell with them........ *3664*
1Pe 4:1 arm yourselves l. with the same *2532*
1Pe 5:5 L., ye younger, submit yourselves *3668*
Jude 8 L. also these filthy dreamers defile..... *3668*
Re 8:12 third part of it, and the night l............ *3668*

LIKHI (lik'-hi)
1Ch 7:19 Ahian, and Shechem, and L., and....... 3949

LIKING
Job 39:4 Their young ones are in good l.,......... 2492
Da 1:10 should he see your faces worse l. than......

LILIES
1Ki 7:26 brim of a cup, with flowers of l.:........ 7799
2Ch 4:5 brim of a cup, with flowers of l.;......... 7799
Ca 2:16 I am his: he feedeth among the l.. 7799
Ca 4:5 are twins, which feed among the l...... 7799
Ca 5:13 his lips like l., dropping sweet........... 7799
Ca 6:2 in the gardens, and to gather l.. 7799
Ca 6:3 is mine: he feedeth among the l.......... 7799
Ca 7:2 an heap of wheat set about with l....... 7799
Mt 6:28 Consider the l. of the field, how.... *2918*
Lu 12:27 Consider the l. how they grow:..... *2918*

LILY See LILIES.
1Ki 7:19 pillars were of l. work in the porch,..... 7799
1Ki 7:22 the top of the pillars was l. work: 7799
Ca 2:1 of Sharon, and the l. of the valleys. 7799
Ca 2:2 As the l. among thorns, so is my....... 7799
Ho 14:5 he shall grow as the l., and cast 7799

LILY-WORK See LILY and WORK.

LIME
Isa 33:12 shall be as the burnings of l.: 7875
Am 2:1 bones of the king of Edom into l.:...... 7875

LIMIT See also LIMITED; LIMITETH.
Eze 43:12 the whole l. thereof round about........ 1366

LIMITED
Ps 78:41 and l. the Holy One of Israel............. 8428

LIMITETH
Heb 4:7 he l. a certain day, saying to David, ... *3724*

LINE See also LINES; PLUMBLINE.
Jos 2:18 shalt bind this l. of scarlet thread....... 8615
Jos 2:21 bound the scarlet l. in the window...... 8615
2Sa 8:2 and measured them with a l.,............ 2256
2Sa 8:2 and with one full l. to keep alive. 2256
1Ki 7:15 a l. of twelve cubits did compass........ 2339
1Ki 7:23 a l. of thirty cubits did compass......... 6957
2Ki 21:13 over Jerusalem the l. of Samaria, ... 6957
2Ch 4:2 a l. of thirty cubits did compass it 6957
Job 38:5 who hath stretched the l. upon it?...... 6957
Ps 19:4 Their l. is gone out through all the..... 6957
Ps 78:55 divided them an inheritance by l.,....... 2256
Isa 28:10, 13 l. upon l., l. upon l.; here a......... 6957
Isa 28:17 Judgment also will I lay to the l., ... 6957
Isa 34:11 out upon it the l. of confusion,........... 6957
Isa 34:17 hand hath divided it unto them by l.:... 6957
Isa 44:13 he marketh it out with a l.; he........... 8279
Jer 31:39 the measuring l. shall yet go forth...... 6957
La 2:8 he hath stretched out a l., he hath..... 6957
Eze 40:3 with a l. of flax in his hand, and......... 6616
Eze 47:3 man that had the l. in his hand 6957
Am 7:17 thy land shall be divided by l.;........... 2256
Zec 1:16 a l. shall be stretched forth upon........ 6957
Zec 2:1 with a measuring l. in his hand. 2256
2Co 10:16 not to boast in another man's l.......... *2583*

LINEAGE
Lu 2:4 was of the house and l. of David:)...... *3965*

LINEN
Ge 41:42 arrayed him in vestures of fine l., ... 8336
Ex 25:4 purple, and scarlet, and fine l.,.......... 8336
Ex 26:1 with ten curtains of fine twined l.,...... 8336
Ex 26:31 and fine twined l. of cunning work:..... 8336
Ex 26:36 and scarlet, and fine twined l.,........... 8336
Ex 27:9 for the court of fine twined l. of an..... 8336
Ex 27:16 and scarlet, and fine twined l.,........... 8336
Ex 27:18 height five cubits of fine twined l.,....... 8336
Ex 28:5 and purple, and scarlet, and fine l......... 8336
Ex 28:6 purple, of scarlet, and fine twined l.,... 8336
Ex 28:8 and scarlet, and fine twined l............ 8336
Ex 28:15 and of scarlet, and of fine twined l.,.... 8336
Ex 28:39 shalt embroider the coat of fine l.,....... 8336
Ex 28:39 thou shalt make the mitre of fine l.,...... 8336
Ex 28:42 make them l. breeches to cover.......... 906
Ex 35:6,23 purple, and scarlet, and fine l.,.......... 8336
Ex 35:25 purple, and of scarlet, and of fine l.. ... 8336
Ex 35:35 in purple, in scarlet, and in fine l.,...... 8336
Ex 36:8 made ten curtains of fine twined l.,...... 8336
Ex 36:35 and scarlet, and fine twined l.:........... 8336
Ex 36:37 and scarlet, and fine twined l.,........... 8336
Ex 38:9 of the court were of fine twined l.,...... 8336
Ex 38:16 round about were of fine twined l........ 8336
Ex 38:18 and scarlet, and fine twined l.:............ 8336
Ex 38:23 purple, and in scarlet, and fine l.. 8336
Ex 39:2 and scarlet, and fine twined l............ 8336
Ex 39:3 and in the scarlet, and in the fine l., ... 8336
Ex 39:5 and scarlet, and fine twined l.;.......... 8336
Ex 39:8 and scarlet, and fine twined l............ 8336
Ex 39:24 and purple, and scarlet, and twined l.........
Ex 39:27 made coats of fine l. of woven work ... 8336
Ex 39:28 fine l., and goodly bonnets of fine l., .. 8336
Ex 39:28 and l. breeches of fine twined............ 906
Ex 39:28 and breeches of fine twined l.,........... 8336
Ex 39:29 And a girdle of fine twined l., and....... 8336
Le 6:10 priest shall put on his l. garment, ... 906
Le 6:10 l. breeches shall be put upon his 906
Le 13:47 woollen garment, or a l. garment; 6593
Le 13:48 warp, or woof; of l., or of woollen; 6593
Le 13:52 warp or woof, in woolen or in l., ... 6593
Le 13:59 leprosy in a garment of woollen or l.,.. 6593
Le 16:4 He shall put on the holy l. coat, ... 906
Le 16:4 have the l. breeches upon his flesh, ... 906
Le 16:4 and shall be girded with a l. girdle, ... 906
Le 16:4 with the l. mitre shall he be attired:..... 906
Le 16:23 shall put off the l. garments, which...... 906
Le 16:32 and shall put on the l. clothes, even..... 906
Le 19:19 garment mingled of l. and woollen...... 8162
De 22:11 divers sorts, as of woollen and l. 6593
1Sa 2:18 a child, girded with a l. ephod. 906
1Sa 22:18 persons that did wear a l. ephod. 906
2Sa 6:14 David was girded with a l. ephod......... 906
1Ki 10:28 brought out of Egypt, and l. yarn:...... 4723
1Ki 10:28 received the l. yard at a price. 4723
1Ch 4:21 house of them that wrought fine l., ... 948
1Ch 15:27 was clothed with a robe of fine l.,........ 948
1Ch 15:27 also had upon him an ephod of l.......... 906
2Ch 1:16 brought out of Egypt, and l. yarn:...... 4723
2Ch 1:16 received the l. yard at a price. 4723
2Ch 2:14 blue, and in fine l., and in crimson: 948
2Ch 3:14 and purple, and crimson, and fine l....... 948
2Ch 5:12 brethren, being arrayed in white l., ... 948
Es 1:6 hangings, fastened...cords of fine l...... 948
Es 8:15 with a garment of fine l. and purple:..... 948
Pr 7:16 carved works, with fine l. of Egypt. 948
Pr 31:24 She maketh fine l., and selleth it;........ 5466
Isa 3:23 The glasses, and the fine l., and.......... 5466
Jer 13:1 Go and get thee a l. girdle, and......... 6593
Eze 9:2 among them was clothed with l., ... 906
Eze 9:3 called to the man clothed with l.,......... 906
Eze 9:11 behold, the man clothed with l., ... 906
Eze 10:2 spake unto the man clothed with l.,...... 906
Eze 10:6 commanded the man clothed with l.,..... 906
Eze 10:7 of him that was clothed with l.:............ 906
Eze 16:10 I girded thee about with fine l., ... 8336
Eze 16:13 thy raiment was of fine l., and silk, ... 8336
Eze 27:7 Fine l. with broidered work from 8336
Eze 27:16 broidered work,...fine l., and coral,...... 948
Eze 44:17 shall be clothed with l. garments;........ 6593
Eze 44:18 have l. bonnets upon their heads,........ 6593
Eze 44:18 have l. breeches upon their loins;........ 6593
Da 10:5 behold a certain man clothed in l., ... 906
Da 12:6 one said to the man clothed in l., ... 906
Da 12:7 And I heard the man clothed in l., ... 906
Mt 27:59 he wrapped it in a clean l. cloth, ... *4616*
Mk 14:51 l. cloth cast about his naked body;...... *4616*
Mk 14:52 And he left the l. cloth, and fled *4616*
Mk 15:46 And he bought fine l., and took him..... *4616*
Mk 15:46 wrapped him in the l., and laid him..... *4616*
Lu 16:19 was clothed in purple and fine l.,.. *1040*
Lu 23:53 took it down, and wrapped it in l., ... *4616*
Lu 24:12 the l. clothes laid by themselves. *3608*
Joh 19:40 of Jesus, and wound it in l. clothes..... *3608*
Joh 20:5 looking in, saw the l. clothes lying;..... *3608*
Joh 20:6 and seeth the l. clothes lie,............... *3608*
Joh 20:7 not lying with the l. clothes, but *3608*
Re 15:6 clothed in pure and white l., and......... *3043*
Re 18:12 pearls, and fine l., and purple,........... *1040*
Re 18:16 city, that was clothed in fine l., ... *1039*
Re 19:8 that she should be arrayed in fine l.,... *1039*
Re 19:8 for the fine l. is the righteousness...... *1039*
Re 19:14 clothed in fine l., white and clean. *1039*

LINES
2Sa 8:2 even with two l. measured he to......... 2256
Ps 16:6 The l. are fallen unto me in pleasant ... 2256

LINGERED See also LINGERETH.
Ge 19:16 And while he l., the men laid hold...... 4102
Ge 43:10 For except we had l., surely now......... 4102

LINGERETH See also LINGERED.
2Pe 2:3 judgment now of a long time l. not,...... *691*

LINTEL See also LINTELS.
Ex 12:22 strike the l. and the two side posts 4947
Ex 12:23 when he seeth the blood upon the l.,.. 4947
1Ki 6:31 the l. and side posts were a fifth......... 352
Am 9:1 he said, Smite the l. of the door, ... 3730

LINTELS
Zep 2:14 shall lodge in the upper l. of it:.......... 3730

LINUS (li'-nus)
2Ti 4:21 and L., and Claudia, and all the *3044*

LION See also LIONESS; LIONLIKE; LION'S; LIONS.
Ge 49:9 stooped down, he couched as a l.,....... 738
Ge 49:9 and as an old l.; who shall rouse........ 3833
Nu 23:24 people shall rise up as a great l., ... 3833
Nu 23:24 and lift up himself as a young l.:.......... 738
Nu 24:9 He couched, he lay down as a l.,......... 738
Nu 24:9 and as a great l.: who shall stir 3833
De 33:20 he dwelleth as a l., and teareth 3833
Jg 14:5 a young l. roared against him............ 738
Jg 14:8 aside to see the carcase of the l.:......... 738
Jg 14:8 and honey in the carcase of the l.......... 738
Jg 14:9 honey out of the carcase of the l.......... 738
Jg 14:18 and what is stronger than a l.?............ 738
1Sa 17:34 and there came a l., and a bear,.......... 738
1Sa 17:36 slew both the l. and the bear:............ 738
1Sa 17:37 delivered me out of the paw of the l., . 738
2Sa 17:10 whose heart is as the heart of a l.,....... 738
2Sa 23:20 slew a l. in the midst of a pit in time.... 738
1Ki 13:24 l. met him by the way, and slew him:.... 738
1Ki 13:24 the l. also stood by the carcase........... 738
1Ki 13:25 and the l. standing by the carcase:........ 738
1Ki 13:26 Lord hath delivered him unto the l.,...... 738
1Ki 13:28 and the l. standing by the carcase:........ 738
1Ki 13:28 the l. had not eaten the carcase, nor.... 738
1Ki 20:36 from me, a l. shall slay thee.............. 738
1Ki 20:36 him, a l. found him, and slew him......... 738

1Ch 11:22 and slew a l. in a pit in a snowy day. 738
Job 4:10 The roaring of the l., and the voice 738
Job 4:10 the voice of the fierce l., and the 7826
Job 4:11 old l. perisheth for lack of prey, 3918
Job 10:16 Thou huntest me as a fierce l.: 7826
Job 28:8 it, nor the fierce l. passed by it. 7826
Job 38:39 Wilt thou hunt the prey for the l.? 3833
Ps 7:2 Lest he tear my soul like a l., 738
Ps 10:9 in wait secretly as a l. in his den: 738
Ps 17:12 Like as a l. that is greedy of his prey, 738
Ps 17:12 as it were a young l. lurking in 3715
Ps 22:13 as a ravening and a roaring l. 738
Ps 91:13 shalt tread upon the l. and adder: 7826
Ps 91:13 the young l. and the dragon shalt 3715
Pr 19:12 king's wrath is as the roaring of a l.; 3715
Pr 20:2 of a king is as the roaring of a l.: 3715
Pr 22:13 There is a l. without, I shall be 738
Pr 26:13 man saith, There is a l. in the way; 738
Pr 26:13 a l. is in the streets. 738
Pr 28:1 but the righteous are bold as a l. 3715
Pr 28:15 As a roaring l., and a ranging bear; 739
Pr 30:30 A l. which is strongest among 3918
Ec 9:4 living dog is better than a dead l. 738
Isa 5:29 Their roaring shall be like a l., 3833
Isa 11:6 young l. and the fatling together; 3715
Isa 11:7 the l. shall eat straw like the ox. 738
Isa 21:8 And he cried, A l.: My lord, I stand 738
Isa 30:6 whence come the young and old l., 3918
Isa 31:4 Like as the l. and the young 738
Isa 31:4 the young l. roaring on his prey, 3715
Isa 35:9 No l. shall be there, nor any 738
Isa 38:13 as a l., so will he break all my bones: 738
Isa 65:25 l. shall eat straw like the bullock: 738
Jer 2:30 your prophets, like a destroying l. 738
Jer 4:7 The l. is come up from his thicket, 738
Jer 5:6 a l. out of the forest shall slay them, 738
Jer 12:8 Mine heritage is unto me as a l. in 738
Jer 25:38 hath forsaken his covert, as the l.: 3715
Jer 49:19 Behold, he shall come up like a l. 738
Jer 50:44 Behold, he shall come up like a l. 738
La 3:10 in wait, and as a l. in secret places. 738
Eze 1:10 the face of a l., on the right side: 738
Eze 10:14 man, and the third the face of a l., 738
Eze 19:3 it become a young l., and it 3715
Eze 19:5 whelps, and made him a young l. 3715
Eze 19:6 he became a young l., and learned 3715
Eze 22:25 like a roaring l. ravening the prey; 738
Eze 32:2 art like a young l. of the nations, 3715
Eze 41:19 face of a young l. toward the palm 3715
Da 7:4 first was like a l., and had eagle's 738
Ho 5:14 For I will be unto Ephraim as a l., 7826
Ho 5:14 a young l. to the house of Judah: 3715
Ho 11:10 the Lord: he shall roar like a l.; 738
Ho 13:7 I will be unto them as a l.: 7826
Ho 13:8 there will I devour them like a l.: 3833
Joe 1:6 whose teeth are the teeth of a l., 738
Joe 1:6 hath the cheek teeth of a great l. 3833
Am 3:4 Will a l. roar in the forest, when he 738
Am 3:4 will a young l. cry out of his den, 3715
Am 3:8 The l. hath roared, who will not 738
Am 3:12 taketh out of the mouth of the l. 738
Am 5:19 As if a man did flee from a l., and a 738
Mic 5:8 as a l. among the beasts of the forest, 738
Mic 5:8 as a young l. among the flocks of 3715
Na 2:11 of the young lions, where the l., 739
Na 2:11 even the old l., walked, and the 3833
Na 2:12 The l. did tear in pieces enough 738
2Ti 4:17 delivered out of the mouth of the l. *3023*
1Pe 5:8 adversary the devil, as a roaring l., *3023*
Re 4:7 And the first beast was like a l., *3023*
Re 5:5 behold, the L. of the tribe of Juda, *3023*
Re 10:3 loud voice, as when a l. roareth: *3023*
Re 13:2 and his mouth as the mouth of a l.: *3023*

LIONESS See also LIONESSES.
Eze 19:2 What is thy mother? A l.: she lay 3833

LIONESSES
Na 2:12 and strangled for his l., and filled 3833

LIONLIKE
2Sa 23:20 acts, he slew two l. men of Moab: 739
1Ch 11:22 acts; he slew two l. men of Moab: 739

LION'S
Ge 49:9 Judah is a l. whelp: from the prey, 738
De 33:22 of Dan he said, Dan is a l. whelp: 738
Job 4:11 the stout l. whelps are scattered 3833
Job 28:8 The l. whelps have not trodden it 7830
Ps 22:21 Save me from the l. mouth: for 738
Na 2:11 old lion, walked, and the l. whelp, 738

LIONS See also LIONS'.
2Sa 1:23 eagles, they were stronger than l. 738
1Ki 7:29 between the ledges were l., oxen, and 738
1Ki 7:29 beneath the l. and oxen were certain 738
1Ki 7:36 he graved cherubims, l., and palm 738
1Ki 10:19 and two l. stood beside the stays. 738
1Ki 10:20 twelve l. stood there on the one side 738
2Ki 17:25 the Lord sent l. among them, which 738
2Ki 17:26 he hath sent l. among them, and 738
1Ch 12:8 whose faces were like the faces of l., 738
2Ch 9:18 and two l. standing by the stays: 738
2Ch 9:19 twelve l. stood there on the one side 738
Job 4:10 teeth of the young l., are broken. 3715
Job 38:39 or fill the appetite of the young l., 3715
Ps 34:10 The young l. do lack, and suffer 3715
Ps 35:17 destructions, my darling from the l. 3715
Ps 57:4 My soul is among l.: and I lie even 3833
Ps 58:6 out the great teeth of the young l., 3715
Ps 104:21 The young l. roar after their prey, 3715
Isa 5:29 lion, they shall roar like young l.: 3715
Isa 15:9 l. upon him that escapeth of Moab, 738
Jer 2:15 The young l. roared upon him, and 3715
Jer 50:17 the l. have driven him away: first 738
Jer 51:38 They shall roar together like l.: 3715
Eze 19:2 A lioness: she lay down among l., 738
Eze 19:2 her whelps among young l. 3715
Eze 19:6 he went up and down among the l., 738
Eze 38:13 with all the young l. thereof, shall 3715
Da 6:7 he shall be cast into the den of l. 744
Da 6:12 king, shall be cast into the den of l.? 744
Da 6:16 and cast him into the den of l. 744
Da 6:19 and went in haste unto the den of l. 744
Da 6:20 able to deliver thee from the l.? 744
Da 6:24 they cast them into the den of l., 744
Da 6:24 and the l. had the mastery of them, 744
Da 6:27 Daniel from the power of the l. 744
Na 2:11 Where is the dwelling of the l., and 738
Na 2:11 the feedingplace of the young l., 3715
Na 2:13 the sword shall devour thy young l.: 3715
Zep 3:3 princes within her are roaring l.; 738
Zec 11:3 a voice of the roaring of young l.; 3715
Heb 11:33 promises, stopped the mouths of l., *3023*
Re 9:8 their teeth were as the teeth of l. *3023*
Re 9:17 the horses were as the heads of l.; *3023*

LIONS'
Ca 4:8 and Hermon, from the l. dens, from 738
Jer 51:38 lions: they shall yell as l. whelps. 738
Da 6:22 angel, and hath shut the l. mouths, 744

LIP See also LIPS.
Le 13:45 put a covering upon his upper l., 822
Ps 22:7 they shoot out the l., they shake 8193
Pr 12:19 The l. of truth shall be established 8193

LIPS
Ex 6:12 me, who am of uncircumcised l.? 8193
Ex 6:30 Behold, I am of uncircumcised l., 8193
Le 5:4 pronouncing with his l. to do evil 8193
Nu 30:6 vowed, or uttered ought out of her l., 8193
Nu 30:8 that which she uttered with her l., 8193
Nu 30:12 whatsoever proceeded out of her l. 8193
De 23:23 That which is gone out of thy l. 8193
1Sa 1:13 only her l. moved, but her voice 8193
2Ki 19:28 in thy nose, and my bridle in thy l., 8193
Job 2:10 all this did not Job sin with his l. 8193
Job 8:21 laughing, and thy l. with rejoicing. 8193
Job 11:5 speak, and open his l. against thee; 8193
Job 13:6 hearken to the pleadings of my l. 8193
Job 15:6 thine own l. testify against thee. 8193
Job 16:5 the moving of my l. should asswage. 8193
Job 23:12 from the commandment of his l.; 8193
Job 27:4 My l. shall not speak wickedness, 8193
Job 32:20 I will open my l. and answer. 8193
Job 33:3 my l. shall utter knowledge clearly. 8193
Ps 12:2 with flattering l. and with a double 8193
Ps 12:3 Lord shall cut off all flattering l., 8193
Ps 12:4 our l. are our own: who is lord over 8193
Ps 16:4 nor take up their names into my l. 8193
Ps 17:1 that goeth not out of feigned l. 8193
Ps 17:4 by the word of thy l. I have kept me 8193
Ps 21:2 not withholden the request of his l. 8193
Ps 31:18 Let the lying l. be put to silence; 8193
Ps 34:13 evil, and thy l. from speaking guile. 8193
Ps 40:9 I have not refrained my l., O Lord, 8193
Ps 45:2 of men: grace is poured into thy l.: 8193
Ps 51:15 O Lord, open thou my l.; and my 8193
Ps 59:7 their mouth: swords are in their l.: 8193
Ps 59:12 the words of their l. let them even 8193
Ps 63:3 than life, my l. shall praise thee. 8193
Ps 63:5 shall praise thee with joyful l.: 8193
Ps 66:14 Which my l. have uttered, and my 8193
Ps 71:23 My l. shall greatly rejoice when I 8193
Ps 89:34 the thing that is gone out of my l. 8193
Ps 106:33 he spake unadvisedly with his l. 8193
Ps 119:13 With my l. have I declared all the 8193
Ps 119:171 My l. shall utter praise, when thou 8193
Ps 120:2 my soul, O Lord, from lying l., 8193
Ps 140:3 adders' poison is under their l. 8193
Ps 140:9 mischief of their own l. cover them. 8193
Ps 141:3 my mouth; keep the door of my l. 8193
Pr 4:24 and perverse l. put far from thee. 8193
Pr 5:2 that thy l. may keep knowledge. 8193
Pr 5:3 For the l. of a strange woman drop 8193
Pr 7:21 with the flattering of her l. she 8193
Pr 8:6 the opening of my l. shall be right 8193
Pr 8:7 is an abomination to my l. 8193
Pr 10:13 l. of him that hath understanding 8193
Pr 10:18 He that hideth hatred with lying l., 8193
Pr 10:19 but he that refraineth his l. is wise. 8193
Pr 10:21 The l. of the righteous feed many: 8193
Pr 10:32 The l. of the righteous know what 8193
Pr 12:13 snared by the transgression of his l.: 8193
Pr 12:22 Lying l. are abomination to the 8193
Pr 13:3 he that openeth wide his l. shall 8193
Pr 14:3 but the l. of the wise shall preserve 8193
Pr 14:7 not in him the l. of knowledge. 8193
Pr 14:23 talk of the l. tendeth only to penury. 8193
Pr 15:7 l. of the wise disperse knowledge: 8193
Pr 16:10 A divine sentence is in the l. of the 8193
Pr 16:13 Righteous l. are the delight of kings; 8193
Pr 16:21 the sweetness of the l. increaseth 8193
Pr 16:23 mouth, and addeth learning to his l. 8193
Pr 16:27 in his l. there is as a burning fire. 8193
Pr 16:30 moving his l. he bringeth evil to 8193
Pr 17:4 wicked doer giveth heed to false l.; 8193
Pr 17:7 fool: much less do lying l. a prince. 8193
Pr 17:28 he that shutteth his l. is esteemed 8193
Pr 18:6 A fool's l. enter into contention. 8193
Pr 18:7 and his l. are the snare of his soul. 8193
Pr 18:20 increase of his l. shall he be filled. 8193
Pr 19:1 he that is perverse in his l., and is a 8193
Pr 20:15 the l. of knowledge are a precious 8193
Pr 20:19 with him that flattereth with his l. 8193
Pr 22:11 the grace of his l. the king shall be 8193
Pr 22:18 they shall withal be fitted in thy l. 8193
Pr 23:16 when thy l. speak right things. 8193
Pr 24:2 and their l. talk of mischief. 8193
Pr 24:26 Every man shall kiss his l. that 8193
Pr 24:28 cause; and deceive not with thy l. 8193
Pr 26:23 Burning l. and a wicked heart are 8193
Pr 26:24 that hateth dissembleth with his l., 8193
Pr 27:2 a stranger, and not thine own l. 8193
Ec 10:12 but the l. of a fool shall swallow up 8193
Ca 4:3 Thy l. are like a thread of scarlet, 8193
Ca 4:11 Thy l., O my spouse, drop as the 8193
Ca 5:13 his l. like lilies, dropping sweet 8193
Ca 7:9 the l. of those that are asleep to 8193
Isa 6:5 because I am a man of unclean l., 8193
Isa 6:5 the midst of a people of unclean l.: 8193
Isa 6:7 said, Lo, this hath touched thy l.; 8193
Isa 11:4 with the breath of his l. shall he 8193
Isa 28:11 with stammering l. and another 8193
Isa 29:13 and with their l. do honour me, 8193
Isa 30:27 his l. are full of indignation, and 8193
Isa 37:29 thy nose, and my bridle in thy l., 8193
Isa 57:19 I create the fruit of the l.; Peace, 8193
Isa 59:3 your l. have spoken lies, your 8193
Jer 17:16 which came out of my l. was right 8193
La 3:62 The l. of those that rose up against 8193
Eze 24:17 cover not thy l., and eat not the 8222
Eze 24:22 ye shall not cover your l., nor eat 8222
Eze 36:3 are taken up in the l. of talkers, 8193
Da 10:16 of the sons of men touched my l.: 8193
Ho 14:2 will we render the calves of our l. 8193
Mic 3:7 yea, they shall all cover their l.; 8222
Hab 3:16 my l. quivered at the voice: 8193
Mal 2:6 and iniquity was not found in his l.: 8193
Mal 2:7 priest's l. should keep knowledge, 8193
Mt 15:8 **and honoureth me with their l.;** *5491*
Mk 7:6 **people honoureth me with their l.,** *5491*

Ro 3:13 the poison of asps is under their l. *5491*
1Co 14:21 men of other tongues and other l. *5491*
Heb 13:15 the fruit of our l. giving thanks to *5491*
1Pe 3:10 and his l. that they speak no guile: *5491*

LIQUOR See also LIQUORS.
Nu 6:3 shall he drink any l. of grapes, ... 4952
Ca 7:2 round goblet, which wanteth not l.: 4197

LIQUORS
Ex 22:29 of thy ripe fruits, and of thy l.: 1831

LISTED
Mt 17:12 **done unto him whatsoever they l.** .. *2309*
Mk 9:13 **done unto him whatsoever they l.,** . *2309*

LISTEN
Isa 49:1 L., O isles, unto me; and hearken, ... 8085

LISTETH
Joh 3:8 **the wind bloweth where it l., and** .. *2309*
Jas 3:4 whithersoever...governor l. *3730,1014*

LITTERS
Isa 66:20 horses, and in chariots, and in l., ... 6632

LITTLE See also LEAST; LESS.
Ge 18:4 a l. water, I pray you, be fetched, ... 4592
Ge 19:20 near to flee unto, and it is a l. one: 4705
Ge 19:20 escape thither, (is it not a l. one?) 4705
Ge 24:17 drink a l. water of thy pitcher. 4592
Ge 24:43 a l. water of thy pitcher to drink; 4592
Ge 30:30 l. which thou hadst before I came, ... 4592
Ge 34:29 all their l. ones, and their wives 2945
Ge 34:16 but a l. way to come to Ephrath: 3530
Ge 43:2 them, Go again, buy us a l. food. 4592
Ge 43:8 we, and thou, and also our l. ones. 2945
Ge 43:11 a present, a l. balm, and a l. honey, ... 4592
Ge 44:20 and a child of his old age, a l. one; 6996
Ge 44:25 Go again, and buy us a l. food. 4592
Ge 45:19 the land of Egypt for your l. ones, ... 2945
Ge 46:5 and their l. ones, and their wives, ... 2945
Ge 47:24 and for food for your l. ones. 2945
Ge 48:7 a l. way to come unto Ephrath: 3530
Ge 50:8 only their l. ones, and their flocks, ... 2945
Ge 50:21 will nourish you, and your l. ones 2945
Ex 10:10 I will let you go, and your l. ones: 2945
Ex 10:24 let your l. ones also go with you. 2945
Ex 12:4 household be too l. for the lamb, ... 4591
Ex 16:18 he that gathered l. had no lack; 4591
Ex 23:30 By l. and l. I will drive them out 4592
Le 11:17 And the l. owl, and the cormorant, ... 3563
Nu 14:31 But your l. ones, which ye said 2945
Nu 16:27 their sons, and their l. children. 2945
Nu 31:9 Midian captives, and their l. ones, ... 2945
Nu 31:17 kill every male among the l. ones, ... 2945
Nu 32:16 our cattle, and cities for our l. ones: ... 2945
Nu 32:17 our l. ones shall dwell in the fenced 2945
Nu 32:24 Build you cities for your l. ones, ... 2945
Nu 32:26 Our l. ones, our wives, our flocks, ... 2945
De 1:39 your l. ones, which ye said should 2945
De 2:34 the women, and the l. ones, of every .. 2945
De 3:19 your wives, and your l. ones, and 2945
De 7:22 nations before thee by l. and l.: 4592
De 14:16 The l. owl, and the great owl, and 3563
De 20:14 the women, and the l. ones, and 2945
De 28:38 field, and shalt gather but l. in; 4592
De 29:11 Your l. ones, your wives, and thy 2945
Jos 1:14 Your wives, your l. ones, and your 2945
Jos 8:35 the women, and the l. ones, and the ... 2945
Jos 19:47 of Dan went out too l. for them: ....
Jos 22:17 Is the iniquity of Peor too l. for us, ... 4592
Jg 4:19 I pray thee, a l. water to drink; 4592
Jg 18:21 put the l. ones and the cattle and 2945
Ru 2:7 that she tarried a l. in the house. 4592
1Sa 2:19 his mother made him a l. coat, ... 6996
1Sa 14:29 because I tasted a l. of this honey 4592
1Sa 14:43 I did but taste a l. honey with the 4592
1Sa 15:17 thou wast l. in thine own sight, ... 6996
1Sa 20:35 with David, and a l. lad with him. 6996
2Sa 12:3 had nothing, save one l. ewe lamb, ... 6996
2Sa 12:8 and if that had been too l., I would 4592
2Sa 15:22 all the l. ones that were with him. 2945
2Sa 16:1 was a l. past the top of the hill, ... 4592
2Sa 19:36 servant will go a l. way over Jordan 4592
1Ki 3:7 I am but a l. child: I know not how 6996
1Ki 8:64 too l. to receive the burnt offerings, ... 6996
1Ki 11:17 Egypt; Hadad being yet a l. child. 6996
1Ki 12:10 My l. finger shall be thicker than 6996
1Ki 17:10 Fetch me, I pray thee, a l. water. 4592
1Ki 17:12 in a barrel, and a l. oil in a cruse: 4592
1Ki 17:13 but make me thereof a l. cake first, ... 6996
1Ki 18:44 ariseth a l. cloud out of the sea, ... 6996
1Ki 20:27 them like two l. flocks of kids; 2835
2Ki 2:23 forth l. children out of the city, ... 6996
2Ki 4:10 Let us make a l. chamber, I pray 6996
2Ki 5:2 out of the land of Israel a l. maid; 6996
2Ki 5:14 like unto the flesh of a l. child, and 6995
2Ki 5:19 So he departed from him a l. way. 3530
2Ki 10:18 unto them, Ahab served Baal a l.; 4592
2Ch 10:10 My l. finger shall be thicker than 6996
2Ch 20:13 before the Lord, with their l. ones, ... 2945
2Ch 31:18 the genealogy of all their l. ones, ... 2945
Ezr 8:21 way for us, and for our l. ones, and ... 2945
Ezr 9:8 now for a l. space grace hath been 4592
Ezr 9:8 give us a l. reviving in our bondage. ... 4592
Ne 9:32 all the trouble seem l. before thee, ... 4591
Es 3:13 l. children and women, in one day, ... 2945
Es 8:11 them, both l. ones and women, ... 2945
Job 4:12 and mine ear received a l. thereof. 8102
Job 10:20 alone, that I may take comfort a l., ... 4592
Job 21:11 forth their l. ones like a flock, ... 5759
Job 24:24 They are exalted for a l. while, ... 4592
Job 26:14 how l. a portion is heard of him? 8102
Job 36:2 Suffer me a l., and I will shew 2191
Ps 2:12 when his wrath is kindled but a l. 4592
Ps 8:5 made him a l. lower than the angels, .. 4592
Ps 37:10 For yet a l. while, and the wicked 4592
Ps 37:16 A l. that a righteous man hath is 4592
Ps 65:12 the l. hills rejoice on every side. ....
Ps 68:27 There is l. Benjamin with their 6810
Ps 72:3 and the l. hills, by righteousness. ....
Ps 114:4 like rams, and the l. hills like lambs. ....
Ps 114:6 rams; and ye l. hills, like lambs? ....
Ps 137:9 dasheth thy l. ones against the 5768
Pr 6:10 Yet a l. sleep, a l. slumber, ... 4592
Pr 6:10 a l. folding of the hands to sleep: 4592
Pr 10:20 the heart of the wicked is l. worth. 4592
Pr 15:16 is l. with the fear of the Lord, than 4592
Pr 16:8 Better is a l. with righteousness, ... 4592
Pr 24:33 Yet a l. sleep, a l. slumber, ... 4592
Pr 24:33 a l. folding of the hands to sleep: 4592
Pr 30:24 four things which are l. upon the 6996
Ec 5:12 sweet, whether he eat l. or much: 4592
Ec 9:14 There was a l. city, and few men 6996
Ec 10:1 so doth a l. folly him that is in 4592
Ca 2:15 Take us the foxes, the l. foxes, ... 6996
Ca 3:4 but a l. that I passed from them, ... 4592
Ca 8:8 We have a l. sister, and she hath 6996
Isa 10:25 For yet a very l. while, and the 4592
Isa 11:6 and a l. child shall lead them. 6995
Isa 26:20 thyself as it were for a l. moment, ... 4592
Isa 28:10 line; here a l., and there a l.: 2191
Isa 28:13 upon line; here a l., and there a l.; 2191
Isa 29:17 Is it not yet a very l. while, and 4592
Isa 40:15 up the isles as a very l. thing. 1851
Isa 54:8 In a l. wrath I hid my face from 8241
Isa 60:22 A l. one shall become a thousand, ... 6996
Isa 63:18 have possessed it but a l. while: 4705
Jer 14:3 sent their l. ones to the waters: 6810
Jer 48:4 her l. ones have caused a cry to be 6810
Jer 51:33 yet a l. while, and the time of her 4592
Eze 9:6 maids, and l. children, and women: 2945
Eze 11:16 I be to them as a l. sanctuary in 4592
Eze 16:47 if that were a very l. thing, thou 4592
Eze 31:4 out her l. rivers unto all the trees 8585
Eze 40:7 every l. chamber was one reed ....
Eze 40:7 between the l. chambers were five ....
Eze 40:10 And the l. chambers of the gate ....
Eze 40:12 space also before the l. chambers ....
Eze 40:12 the l. chambers were six cubits on ....
Eze 40:13 from the roof of one l. chamber to ....
Eze 40:16 narrow windows to the l. chambers, ...
Eze 40:21 the l. chambers thereof were three ....
Eze 40:29, 33 the l. chambers thereof, and ....
Eze 40:36 The l. chambers thereof, the posts ....
Da 7:8 up among them another l. horn, ... 2192
Da 8:9 one of them came forth a l. horn, ... 4704
Da 11:34 they shall be holpen with a l. help: 4592
Ho 1:4 for yet a l. while, and I will avenge 4592
Ho 8:10 shall sorrow a l. for the burden of 4592
Am 6:11 and the l. house with clefts. 6996
Mic 5:2 thou be l. among the thousands of 6810
Hag 1:6 have sown much, and bring in l.; 4592
Hag 1:9 for much, and, lo, it came to l.; 4592
Hag 2:6 Yet once, it is a l. while, and I will 4592
Zec 1:15 I was but a l. displeased, and they 4592
Zec 13:7 turn mine hand upon the l. ones. 6819
Mt 6:30 **more clothe you, O ye of l. faith?** .. *3640*
Mt 8:26 **are ye fearful, O ye of l. faith** *3640*
Mt 10:42 **to drink unto one of these l. ones.** . *3398*
Mt 14:31 **O thou of l. faith, wherefore didst** . *3640*
Mt 15:34 they said, Seven, and a few l. fishes ... *2485*
Mt 16:8 **O ye of l. faith, why reason ye** *3640*
Mt 18:2 Jesus called a l. child unto him, ... *3813*
Mt 18:3 **and become as l. children** *3813*
Mt 18:4 **humble himself as this l. child,** *3813*
Mt 18:5 **receive one such l. child in my** *3813*
Mt 18:6 **shall offend one of these l. ones** *3398*
Mt 18:10 **ye despise not one of these l. ones;** . *3398*
Mt 18:14 **one of these l. ones should perish.** .. *3398*
Mt 19:13 brought unto him l. children, that *3813*
Mt 19:14 Jesus said, **Suffer l. children, and** ... *3813*
Mt 26:39 went a l. farther, and fell on his *3397*
Mk 1:19 he had gone a l. farther thence, ... *3641*
Mk 4:36 were also with him other l. ships. *4142*
Mk 5:23 My l. daughter lieth at the point *2365*
Mk 9:42 **shall offend one of these l. ones** *3398*
Mk 10:14 **Suffer the l. children to come unto** *3813*
Mk 10:15 **the kingdom of God as a l. child,** .. *3813*
Mk 14:35 And he went forward a l., and fell *3397*
Mk 14:70 And a l. after, they that stood by *3397*
Lu 5:3 would thrust out a l. from the land. *3641*
Lu 7:47 **l. is forgiven, the same loveth l.** *3641*
Lu 12:28 **will he clothe you, O ye of l. faith?** *3640*
Lu 12:32 **Fear not, l. flock; for it is your** *3398*
Lu 17:2 **should offend one of these l. ones** . *3398*
Lu 18:16 **Suffer l. children to come unto me.** 3813
Lu 18:17 **the kingdom of God as a l. child** ... 3813
Lu 19:3 press, because he was l. of stature. ... *3398*
Lu 19:17 **thou hast been faithful in a very l.** *1646*
Lu 22:58 after a l. while another saw him, ... *1024*
Joh 6:7 every one of them may take a l. *1024*
Joh 7:33 **Yet a l. while am I with you, and.** *3398*
Joh 12:35 **Yet a l. while is the light with you** *3398*
Joh 13:33 **L. children, yet a...while I am** *5040*
Joh 13:33 **children, yet a l. while I am with** .. *3397*
Joh 14:19 **Yet a l. while, and the world seeth** *3397*
Joh 16:16 **A l. while, and ye shall not see me:** *3397*
Joh 16:16 **a l. while, and ye shall see me:** *3397*
Joh 16:17 A l. while, and ye shall not see me: ... *3397*
Joh 16:17 a l. while, and ye shall see me: *3397*
Joh 16:18 What is this that he saith, A l. while? .. *3397*
Joh 16:19 **A l. while, and ye shall not see me.** *3397*
Joh 16:19 **a l. while, and ye shall see me?** *3397*
Joh 21:8 other disciples came in a l. ship; *4142*
Ac 5:34 to put the apostles forth a l. space; *1024*
Ac 20:12 alive, and were not a l. comforted. *3357*
Ac 27:28 when they had gone a l. further, ... *1024*
Ac 28:2 people shewed us no l. kindness: *5177*
1Co 5:6 not that a l. leaven leaveneth the *3398*
2Co 8:15 that had gathered l. had no lack. *3641*
2Co 11:1 could bear with me a l. in my folly: *3397*
2Co 11:16 me, that I may boast myself a l. *3397*
Ga 4:19 My l. children, of whom I travail in *5040*
Ga 5:9 A l. leaven leaveneth the whole *3398*
1Ti 4:8 For bodily exercise profiteth l.: *3641*
1Ti 5:23 a l. wine for thy stomach's sake *3641*
Heb 2:7 him a l. lower than the angels; *1024*
Heb 2:9 made a l. lower than the angels for *1024*
Heb 10:37 For yet a l. while, and he that shall ... *3397*
Jas 3:5 Even so the tongue is a l. member, ... *3398*
Jas 3:5 great a matter a l. fire kindleth! *3641*
Jas 4:14 vapour, that appeareth for a l. time, ... *3641*
1Jo 2:1 My l. children, these things write *5040*
1Jo 2:12 I write unto you, l. children, ... *5040*
1Jo 2:13 I write unto you, l. children, ... *3813*
1Jo 2:18 L. children, it is the last time: and *3813*
1Jo 2:28 And now, l. children, abide in him; *5040*
1Jo 3:7 L. children, let no man deceive you: ... *5040*
1Jo 3:18 My l. children, let us not love in *5040*
1Jo 4:4 Ye are of God, l. children, and have ... *5040*
1Jo 5:21 L. children, keep yourselves from *5040*
Re 3:8 **for thou hast a l. strength, and** *3398*
Re 6:11 they should rest yet for a l. season, ... *3398*
Re 10:2 he had in his hand a l. book open: *974*
Re 10:8 take the l. book which is open in *974*
Re 10:9 said unto him, Give me the l. book. *974*
Re 10:10 the l. book out of the angel's hand, ... *974*
Re 20:3 that he must be loosed a l. season. *3398*

LITTLE-OWL See LITTLE and OWL.

LIVE See also ALIVE; LIVED; LIVES; LIVEST; LIVETH; LIVING.
Ge 3:22 tree of life, and eat, and l. for ever: ... 2425

Ge 12:13 my soul shall l. because of thee. 2421
Ge 17:18 unto God, O that Ishmael might l. 2421
Ge 19:20 not a little one?) and my soul shall l. 2421
Ge 20:7 pray for thee, and thou shalt l.: 2421
Ge 27:40 by thy sword shalt thou l., and shalt 2421
Ge 31:32 thou findest thy gods, let him not l.: 2421
Ge 42:2 for us from thence; that we may l.; 2421
Ge 42:18 them the third day, This do, and l.; 2421
Ge 43:8 that we may l., and not die, both we, 2421
Ge 45:3 am Joseph; doth my father yet l.? 2416
Ge 47:19 and give us seed, that we may l., 2421
Ex 1:16 if it be a daughter, then she shall l. 2425
Ex 19:13 it be beast or man, it shall not l.: 2421
Ex 21:35 they shall sell the l. ox, and divide 2416
Ex 22:18 Thou shalt not suffer a witch to l. 2421
Ex 33:20 there shall no man see me, and l. 2425
Le 16:20 altar, he shall bring the l. goat: 2416
Le 16:21 hands upon the head of the l. goat, 2416
Le 18:5 if a man do, he shall l. in them: 2425
Le 25:35 that he may l. with thee. 2416
Le 25:36 that thy brother may l. with thee. 2416
Nu 4:19 do unto them, that they may l., 2421
Nu 14:21 But as truly as I l., all the earth 2416
Nu 14:28 As truly as I l., saith the Lord, 2416
Nu 21:8 when he looketh upon it, shall l. 2425
Nu 24:23 who shall l. when God doeth this! 2421
De 4:1 ye may l., and go in and possess 2421
De 4:10 all the days that they shall l. upon 2416
De 4:33 the fire, as thou hast heard, and l.? 2421
De 4:42 one of these cities he might l. 2425
De 5:33 that ye may l., and that it may be 2421
De 8:1 to do, that ye may l., and multiply, 2421
De 8:3 that man doth not l. by bread only, 2421
De 8:3 the mouth of the Lord doth man l. 2421
De 12:1 the days that ye l. upon the earth. 2416
De 16:20 that thou mayest l., and inherit 2421
De 19:4 shall flee thither, that he may l. 2425
De 19:5 flee unto one of those cities, and l. 2425
De 30:6 all thy soul, that thou mayest l. 2416
De 30:16 that thou mayest l. and multiply; 2421
De 30:19 that both thou and thy seed may l. 2421
De 31:13 as long as ye l. in the land whither 2416
De 32:40 to heaven, and say, I l. for ever. 2416
De 33:6 Let Reuben l., and not die; and let 2421
Jos 6:17 only Rahab the harlot shall l., she 2421
Jos 9:15 a league with them, to let them l. 2421
Jos 9:20 we will even let them l., lest wrath 2421
Jos 9:21 princes said unto them, Let them l.; 2421
1Sa 20:14 not only while yet I l. shew me the 2416
2Sa 1:10 not l. after that he was fallen: 2421
2Sa 12:22 to me, that the child may l.? 2416
2Sa 19:34 How long have I to l., that I should 2416
1Ki 1:31 Let my lord king David l. for ever. 2421
1Ki 8:40 all the days that they l. in the land 2416
1Ki 20:32 saith, I pray thee, let me l.. And 2421
2Ki 4:7 l. thou and thy children of the rest. 2421
2Ki 7:4 if they save us alive, we shall l.; 2421
2Ki 10:19 shall be wanting, he shall not l. 2421
2Ki 18:32 honey, that ye may l., and not die: 2421
2Ki 20:1 order; for thou shalt die, and not l. 2421
2Ch 6:31 so long as they l. in the land which 2416
Ne 2:3 the king, Let the king l. for ever: 2421
Ne 5:2 for them, that we may eat, and l. 2421
Ne 9:29 if a man do, he shall l. in them;) 2421
Es 4:11 the golden sceptre, that he may l. 2421
Job 7:16 I loathe it; I would not l. alway: 2421
Job 14:14 If a man die, shall he l. again? 2421
Job 21:7 Wherefore do the wicked l., become 2421
Job 27:6 not reproach me so long as I l. 3117
Ps 22:26 him: your heart shall l. for ever. 2421
Ps 49:9 That he should still l. for ever, 2421
Ps 55:23 men shall not l. out half their days;
Ps 63:4 I bless thee while I l.: I will lift 2416
Ps 69:32 your heart shall l. that seek God. 2421
Ps 72:15 And he shall l., and to him shall 2421
Ps 104:33 sing unto the Lord as long as I l. 2416
Ps 116:2 will I call upon him as long as I l. 3117
Ps 118:17 I shall not die, but l., and declare 2421
Ps 119:17 that I may l., and keep thy word. 2421
Ps 119:77 mercies come unto me, that I may l. 2421
Ps 119:116 unto thy word, that I may l.: and 2421
Ps 119:144 me understanding, and I shall l. 2421
Ps 119:175 Let my soul l., and it shall praise 2421
Ps 146:2 While I l. will I praise the Lord: 2416
Pr 4:4 keep my commandments, and l. 2421
Pr 7:2 Keep my commandments, and l.; 2421
Pr 9:6 Forsake the foolish, and l.; and go 2421
Pr 15:27 but he that hateth gifts shall l. 2421
Ec 6:3 children, and l. many years, so that 2421
Ec 6:6 Yea, though he l. a thousand years 2421
Ec 9:3 is in their heart while they l., and 2416
Ec 9:9 L. joyfully with the wife whom 2416
Ec 11:8 But if a man l. many years, and 2421
Isa 6:6 me, having a l. coal in his hand, 7531
Isa 26:14 They are dead, they shall not l.; 2421
Isa 26:19 Thy dead men shall l., together 2421
Isa 38:1 for thou shalt die, and not l. 2421
Isa 38:16 O Lord, by these things men l., 2421
Isa 38:16 thou recover me, and make me to l. 2421
Isa 49:18 As I l., saith the Lord, thou shalt 2416
Isa 55:3 hear, and your soul shall l.; and I 2421
Jer 21:9 that besiege you, he shall l., and 2421
Jer 22:24 As I l., saith the Lord, though 2416
Jer 27:12 serve him and his people, and l. 2421
Jer 27:17 serve the king of Babylon, and l.: 2421
Jer 35:7 that ye may l. many days in the 2421
Jer 38:2 forth to the Chaldeans shall l.; 2421
Jer 38:2 his life for a prey, and shall l. 2425
Jer 38:17 princes, then thy soul shall l., 2421
Jer 38:17 and thou shalt l., and thine house: 2421
Jer 38:20 unto thee, and thy soul shall l.. 2421
Jer 46:18 As I l., saith the King, whose name 2416
La 4:20 said, Under his shadow we shall l. 2421
Eze 3:21 he doth not sin, he shalt surely l., 2421
Eze 5:11 as I l., saith the Lord God; Surely, 2416
Eze 13:19 the souls alive that should not l., 2421
Eze 14:16 as I l., saith the Lord God, they 2416
Eze 14:18, 20 as I l., saith the Lord God, 2416
Eze 16:6 when thou wast in thy blood, L.; 2421
Eze 16:6 when thou wast in thy blood, L.. 2421
Eze 16:48 As I l., saith the Lord God, Sodom 2416
Eze 17:16 As I l., saith the Lord God, surely 2416
Eze 17:19 As I l., surely mine oath that he 2416
Eze 18:3 As I l., saith the Lord God, ye shall 2416
Eze 18:9 he is just, he shall surely l., saith 2421
Eze 18:13 taken increase: shall he be then l.? 2425
Eze 18:13 shall he then...he shall not l.: 2421
Eze 18:17 of his father, he shall surely l. 2421
Eze 18:19 hath done them, he shall surely l.. 2421
Eze 18:21 he shall surely l., he shall not die. 2421
Eze 18:22 that he hath done he shall l. 2421
Eze 18:23 should return from his ways, and l.? 2421
Eze 18:24 the wicked man doeth, shall he l.? 2425
Eze 18:28 he shall surely l., he shall not die. 2421
Eze 18:32 wherefore turn yourselves, and l. ye. 2421
Eze 20:3 As I l., saith the Lord God, I will 2416
Eze 20:11 man do, he shall even l. in them; 2425
Eze 20:13, 21 do, he shall even l. in them; 2425
Eze 20:25 whereby they should not l.; 2421
Eze 20:31 As I l., saith the Lord God, I will 2416
Eze 20:33 As I l., saith the Lord God, surely
Eze 33:10 in them, how should we then l.? 2421
Eze 33:11 As I l., saith the Lord God, I have 2416
Eze 33:11 wicked turn from his way and l.: 2421
Eze 33:12 shall the righteous be able to l. for 2421
Eze 33:13 righteous, that he shall surely l.; 2421
Eze 33:15 he shall surely l., he shall not die. 2421
Eze 33:16 lawful and right; he shall surely l. 2421
Eze 33:19 and right, he shall l. thereby. 2421
Eze 33:27 As I l., surely they that are in the 2416
Eze 34:8 As I l., saith the Lord God, surely 2416
Eze 35:6, 11 as I l., saith the Lord God, I will 2416
Eze 37:3 Son of man, can these bones l.? 2421
Eze 37:5 to enter into you, and ye shall l.: 2421
Eze 37:6 put breath in you, and ye shall l.; 2421
Eze 37:9 upon these slain, that they may l. 2421
Eze 37:14 put my spirit in you, and ye shall l., 2421
Eze 47:9 the rivers shall come, shall l.: 2421
Eze 47:9 thing shall l. whither the river 2425
Da 2:4 in Syriack, O king, l. for ever: 2418
Da 3:9 Nebuchadnezzar, O king, l. for ever. 2418
Da 5:10 spake and said, O king, l. for ever: 2414
Da 6:6 unto him, King Darius, l. for ever. 2414
Da 6:21 unto the king, O king, l. for ever. 2414
Ho 6:2 us up, and we shall l. in his sight. 2421
Am 5:4 Israel, Seek ye me, and ye shall l.: 2421
Am 5:6 Seek the Lord, and ye shall l.; lest 2421
Am 5:14 good, and not evil, that ye may l.: 2421
Jon 4:3 is better for me to die than to l. 2416
Jon 4:8 It is better for me to die than to l. 2416
Hab 2:4 but the just shall l. by his faith. 2421
Zep 2:9 as I l., saith the Lord of hosts, 2416
Zec 1:5 the prophets, do they l. for ever? 2421
Zec 10:9 they shall l. with their children, 2421
Zec 13:3 say unto him, Thou shalt not l.; 2421
Mt 4:4 Man shall not l. by bread alone, 2198
Mt 9:18 thy hand upon her, and she shall l. 2198
Mk 5:23 she may be healed; and she shall l. 2198
Lu 4:4 man shall not l. by bread alone, 2198
Lu 7:25 apparelled, and l. delicately, are 5225
Lu 10:28 right: this do, and thou shalt l. 2198
Lu 20:38 of the living: for all l. unto him. 2198
Joh 5:25 of God: and they that hear shall l. 2198
Joh 6:51 of this bread, he shall l. for ever: 2198
Joh 6:57 hath sent me, and I l. by the 2198
Joh 6:57 eateth me, even he shall l. by me. 2198
Joh 6:58 eateth of this bread shall l. for 2198
Joh 11:25 he were dead, yet shall he l.: 2198
Joh 14:19 because I l., ye shall l. also 2198
Ac 7:19 to the end they might not l. 2225
Ac 17:28 For in him we l., and move, and 2198
Ac 22:22 for it is not fit that he should l. 2198
Ac 25:24 that he ought not to l. any longer. 2198
Ac 28:4 yet vengeance suffereth not to l. 2198
Ro 1:17 written, The just shall l. by faith. 2198
Ro 6:2 dead to sin, l. any longer therein? 2198
Ro 6:8 that we shall also l. with him: 4800
Ro 8:12 not to the flesh, to l. after the flesh. 2198
Ro 8:13 For if ye l. after the flesh, ye shall 2198
Ro 8:13 the deeds of the body, ye shall l. 2198
Ro 10:5 doeth those things shall l. by them. 2198
Ro 12:18 in you, l. peaceably with all men. 1514
Ro 14:8 whether we l., we l. unto the Lord; 2198
Ro 14:8 whether we l. therefore, or die, we 2198
Ro 14:11 As I l., saith the Lord, every knee 2198
1Co 9:13 holy things l. of the things of the 2068
1Co 9:14 the gospel should l. of the gospel. 2198
2Co 4:11 For we which l. are alway delivered 2198
2Co 5:15 he died for all, that they which l. 2198
2Co 5:15 not henceforth l. unto themselves, 2198
2Co 6:9 as dying, and, behold, we l.; as 2198
2Co 7:3 our hearts to die and l. with you. 4800
2Co 13:4 we shall l. with him by the power 2198
2Co 13:11 be of one mind, and l. in peace; 1514
Ga 2:14 the Gentiles to l. as do the Jews? 2198
Ga 2:19 the law, that I might l. unto God. 2198
Ga 2:20 with Christ: nevertheless I l.; 2198
Ga 2:20 the life which I now l. in the flesh 2198
Ga 2:20 I l. by the faith of the Son of God, 2198
Ga 3:11 for, The just shall l. by faith. 2198
Ga 3:12 that doeth them shall l. in them. 2198
Ga 5:25 If we l. in the Spirit, let us also walk 2198
Eph 6:3 mayest l. long on the earth. 2071,3118
Php 1:21 For to me to l. is Christ, and to 2198
Php 1:22 But if I l. in the flesh, this is the 2198
1Th 3:8 For now we l., if ye stand fast in the 2198
1Th 5:10 we should l. together with him. 2198
2Ti 2:11 with him, we shall also l. with him: 4800
2Ti 3:12 and all that will l. godly in Christ 2198
Tit 2:12 we should l. soberly, righteously. 2198
Heb 10:38 Now the just shall l. by faith: but 2198
Heb 12:9 unto the Father of spirits, and l.? 2198
Heb 13:18 in all things willing to l. honestly. 390
Jas 4:15 If the Lord will, we shall l., and 2198
1Pe 2:24 sins, should l. unto righteousness: 2198
1Pe 4:2 longer should l. the rest of his time 980
1Pe 4:6 l. according to God in the spirit. 2198
2Pe 2:6 those that after should l. ungodly;
2Pe 2:18 escaped from them who l. in error. 390
1Jo 4:9 that we might l. through him. 2198
Re 13:14 the wound by a sword, and did l. 2198

LIVED See also OUTLIVED; OVERLIVED.

Ge 5:3 Adam l. an hundred and thirty 2421
Ge 5:5 And all the days that Adam l. were 2425
Ge 5:6 Seth l. an hundred and five years, 2421
Ge 5:7 Seth l. after he begat Enos eight 2421
Ge 5:9 Enos l. ninety years, and begat 2421
Ge 5:10 Enos l. after he begat Cainan eight 2421
Ge 5:12 Cainan l. seventy years, and begat 2421
Ge 5:13 Cainan l. after he begat Mahalaleel 2421
Ge 5:15 Mahalaleel l. sixty and five years, 2421
Ge 5:16 Mahalaleel l. after he begat Jared 2421
Ge 5:18 Jared l. an hundred sixty and two 2421
Ge 5:19 Jared l. after he begat Enoch eight 2421
Ge 5:21 Enoch l. sixty and five years, and 2421
Ge 5:25 Methuselah l. an hundred eighty 2421
Ge 5:26 And Methuselah l. after he begat 2421
Ge 5:28 Lamech l. an hundred eighty and 2421
Ge 5:30 Lamech l. after he begat Noah five 2421
Ge 9:28 And Noah l. after the flood three 2421

Ge 11:11 Shem l. after he begat Arphaxad.......... 2421
Ge 11:12 Arphaxad l. five and thirty years,........ 2425
Ge 11:13 Arphaxad l. after he begat Salah......... 2421
Ge 11:14 Salah l. thirty years, and begat.......... 2425
Ge 11:15 Salah l. after he begat Eber four......... 2421
Ge 11:16 Eber l. four and thirty years, and....... 2421
Ge 11:17 Eber l. after he begat Peleg four........ 2421
Ge 11:18 Peleg l. thirty years, and begat.......... 2421
Ge 11:19 Peleg l. after he begat Reu two.......... 2421
Ge 11:20 Reu l. two and thirty years, and......... 2421
Ge 11:21 Reu l. after he begat Serug two.......... 2421
Ge 11:22 Serug l. thirty years, and begat......... 2421
Ge 11:23 Serug l. after he begat Nahor two....... 2421
Ge 11:24 Nahor l. nine and twenty years, and... 2421
Ge 11:25 Nahor l. after he begat Terah an......... 2421
Ge 11:26 Terah l. seventy years, and begat........ 2421
Ge 25:6 Isaac his son, while he yet l.............. 2416
Ge 25:7 of Abraham's life which he l................ 2425
Ge 47:28 And Jacob l. in the land of Egypt........ 2421
Ge 50:22 Joseph l. an hundred and ten years..... 2421
Nu 14:38 went to search the land, l. still.......... 2421
Nu 21:9 beheld the serpent of brass, he l......... 2425
De 5:26 of the fire, as we have, and l.?........... 2421
2Sa 19:6 I perceive, that if Absalom had l.,....... 2416
1Ki 12:6 Solomon his father while he yet l.,...... 2416
2Ki 14:17 the son of Joash king of Judah l.......... 2421
2Ch 10:6 Solomon his father while he yet l.,...... 2416
2Ch 25:25 the son of Joash king of Judah l.......... 2421
Job 42:16 After this l. Job an hundred and.......... 2421
Ps 49:18 while he l. he blessed his soul:.......... 2416
Eze 37:10 breath came into them, and they l.,..... 2421
Lu 2:36 and had l. with an husband seven......... *2198*
Ac 23:1 I have l. in all good conscience........... *4176*
Ac 26:5 sect of our religion I l. a Pharisee....... *2198*
Col 3:7 some time, when ye l. in them............. *2198*
Jas 5:5 have l. in pleasure on the earth,.......... *5171*
Re 18:7 glorified herself, and l. deliciously,............
Re 18:9 and l. deliciously with her, shall...............
Re 20:4 they l. and reigned with Christ a........ *2198*
Re 20:5 rest of the dead l. not again until.......... *326*

LIVELY
Ex 1:19 for they are l., and are delivered........ 2422
Ps 38:19 But mine enemies are l., and they........ 2416
Ac 7:38 the l. oracles to give unto us:............. *2198*
1Pe 1:3 begotten us again unto a l. hope......... *2198*
1Pe 2:5 as l. stones, are built up a spiritual...... *2198*

LIVER
Ex 29:13 the caul that is above the l., and......... 3516
Ex 29:22 the caul above the l., and the two....... 3516
Le 3:4, 10,15 the caul above the l., with......... 3516
Le 4:9 and the caul above the l., with the...... 3516
Le 7:4 the caul that is above the l., with........ 3516
Le 8:16, 25 the caul above the l., and the......... 3516
Le 9:10 caul above the l. of the sin offering,..... 3516
Le 9:19 kidneys, and the caul above the l.......... 3516
Pr 7:23 Till a dart strike through his l.:.......... 3516
La 2:11 my l. is poured upon the earth,........... 3516
Eze 21:21 with images, he looked in the l........... 3516

LIVES
Ge 9:5 your blood of your l. will I require;...... 5315
Ge 45:7 save your l. by a great deliverance...... 2421
Ge 47:25 they said, Thou hast saved our l......... 2421
Ex 1:14 their l. bitter with hard bondage,......... 2416
Jos 2:13 and deliver our l. from death............. 5315
Jos 9:24 were sore afraid of our l. because....... 5315
Jg 5:18 a people that jeoparded their l............ 5315
Jg 18:25 life, with the l. of thy household.......... 5315
2Sa 1:23 lovely and pleasant in their l.,............. 2416
2Sa 19:5 and the l. of thy sons and of thy........ 5315
2Sa 19:5 l. of thy wives, and the l. of thy......... 5315
2Sa 23:17 that went in jeopardy of their l.?......... 5315
1Ch 11:19 that have put their l. in jeopardy?........ 5315
1Ch 11:19 jeopardy of their l. they brought it....... 5315
Es 9:16 together, and stood for their l.,........... 5315
Pr 1:18 they lurk privily for their own l........... 5315
Jer 19:7 hands of them that seek their l........... 5315
Jer 19:9 they that seek their l., shall straiten.... 5315
Jer 46:26 hand of those that seek their l.,.......... 5315
Jer 48:6 Flee, save your l., and be like the....... 5315
La 5:9 our bread with the peril of our l........... 5315
Da 7:12 yet their l. were prolonged for a......... 2417
Lu 9:56 **is not come to destroy men's l.,**...... *5590*
Ac 15:26 Men that have hazarded their l........... *5590*
Ac 27:10 lading and ship, but also of our l......... *5590*
1Jo 3:16 to lay down our l. for the brethren...... *5590*
Re 12:11 loved not their l. unto the death.......... *5590*

LIVEST
De 12:19 as long as thou l. upon the earth......... 3117
2Sa 11:11 as thou l., and as thy soul liveth,....... 2416
Ga 2:14 l. after the manner of Gentiles,........... *2198*
Re 3:1 **name that thou l., and art dead.** ... *2198*

LIVETH
Ge 9:3 Every moving thing that l. shall.......... 2416
De 5:24 God doth talk with man, and he l........ 2425
Jg 8:19 as the Lord l., if ye had saved............ 2416
Ru 3:13 a kinsman to thee, as I the Lord l....... 2416
1Sa 1:26 she said, Oh my Lord, as thy soul l.,... 2416
1Sa 1:28 as long as he l. he shall be lent to...... 3117
1Sa 14:39 For, as the Lord l., which saveth.......... 2416
1Sa 14:45 as the Lord l., there shall not one....... 2416
1Sa 17:55 Abner said, As thy soul l., O king,...... 2416
1Sa 19:6 Saul sware, As the Lord l., he shall..... 2416
1Sa 20:3 as the Lord l., and as thy soul l.,....... 2416
1Sa 20:21 thee, and no hurt; as the Lord l........... 2416
1Sa 20:31 long as the son of Jesse l. upon the..... 2425
1Sa 25:6 ye say to him that l. in prosperity,...... 2416
1Sa 25:26 as the Lord l., and as thy soul l........... 2416
1Sa 25:34 as the Lord God of Israel l., which...... 2416
1Sa 26:10 As the Lord l., the Lord shall smite...... 2416
1Sa 26:16 As the Lord l., ye are worthy to die,.... 2416
1Sa 28:10 saying, As the Lord l., there shall no.. 2416
1Sa 29:6 unto him, Surely, as the Lord l.,......... 2416
2Sa 2:27 Joab said, As God l., unless thou......... 2416
2Sa 4:9 and said unto them, As the Lord l.,....... 2416
2Sa 11:11 thy soul l., I will not do this thing....... 2416
2Sa 12:5 said to Nathan, As the Lord l., the...... 2416
2Sa 14:11 As the Lord l., there shall not one....... 2416
2Sa 14:19 answered and said, As thy soul l.,........ 2416
2Sa 15:21 the king, and said, As the Lord l.,....... 2416
2Sa 15:21 and as my lord the king l., surely........ 2416
2Sa 22:47 The Lord l.; and blessed be my........... 2416
1Ki 1:29 king sware, and said, As the Lord l.,.. 2416
1Ki 2:24 Now therefore, as the Lord l., which.. 2416
1Ki 3:23 This is my son that l., and thy son...... 2416
1Ki 17:1 Ahab, As the Lord God of Israel l.,..... 2416
1Ki 17:12 she said, As the Lord thy God l.,........ 2416
1Ki 17:23 and Elijah said, See, thy son l............ 2416
1Ki 18:10 As the Lord thy God l., there is no..... 2416
1Ki 18:15 Elijah said, As the Lord of hosts l.,..... 2416
1Ki 22:14 Micaiah said, As the Lord l., what...... 2416
2Ki 2:2, 4, 6 the Lord l., and as thy soul l.,..... 2416
2Ki 3:14 Elisha said, As the Lord of hosts l.,... 2416
2Ki 4:30 As the Lord l., and as thy soul l., I.... 2416
2Ki 5:16 But he said, As the Lord l., before...... 2416
2Ki 5:20 As the Lord l., I will run after him,.... 2416
2Ch 18:13 Micaiah said, As the Lord l., even....... 2416
Job 19:25 For I know that my redeemer l.,.......... 2416
Job 27:2 As God l., who hath taken away my..... 2416
Ps 18:46 The Lord l.; and blessed be my.......... 2416
Ps 89:48 What man is he that l., and shall........ 2421
Jer 4:2 The Lord l., in truth, in judgment,....... 2416
Jer 5:2 And though they say, The Lord l.;........ 2416
Jer 12:16 to swear by my name, The Lord l.;...... 2416
Jer 16:14 shall no more be said, The Lord l.,...... 2416
Jer 16:15 The Lord l., that brought up the.......... 2416
Jer 23:7 they shall no more say, The Lord l.,.... 2416
Jer 23:8 But, The Lord l., which brought up...... 2416
Jer 38:16 As the Lord l., that made us this......... 2416
Jer 44:26 of Egypt, saying, The Lord God l.......... 2416
Eze 47:9 pass, that every thing that l., which..... 2416
Da 4:34 and honoured him that l. for ever,....... 2416
Da 12:7 sware by him that l. for ever that it.... 2416
Ho 4:15 Beth-aven, nor swear, The Lord l.......... 2416
Am 8:14 and say, Thy god, O Dan, l.; and.......... 2416
Am 8:14 The manner of Beer-sheba l.; even....... 2416
Joh 4:50 unto him, **Go thy way; thy son l.**..... *2198*
Joh 4:51 and told him, saying, Thy son l............ *2198*
Joh 4:53 Jesus said unto him, Thy son l.:.......... *2198*
Joh 11:26 **whosoever l. and believeth in me,**.. *2198*
Ro 6:10 but in that he l., he l. unto God........... *2198*
Ro 7:1 over a man as long as he l.?.............. *2198*
Ro 7:2 law to her husband so long as he l.;.... *2198*
Ro 7:3 So then if, while her husband l., she.... *2198*
Ro 14:7 For none of us l. to himself, and no..... *2198*
1Co 7:39 the law as long as her husband l.;....... *2198*
2Co 13:4 yet he l. by the power of God. For...... *2198*
Ga 2:20 live; yet not I, but Christ l. in me:...... *2198*
1Ti 5:6 l. in pleasure is dead while she l.......... *2198*
Heb 7:8 of whom it is witnessed that he l......... *2198*
Heb 7:25 he ever l. to make intercession............ *2198*
Heb 9:17 strength at all while the testator l....... *2198*
1Pe 1:23 by the word of God, which l. and......... *2198*
Re 1:18 **I am he that l., and was dead;**...... *2198*
Re 4:9 the throne, who l. for ever and ever,.. *2198*
Re 4:10 him that l. for ever and ever,............. *2198*
Re 5:14 him that l. for ever and ever.............. *2198*
Re 10:6 by him that l. for ever and ever,......... *2198*
Re 15:7 wrath of God, who l. for ever and........ *2198*

LIVING See also QUICK.
Ge 1:21 and every l. creature that moveth,...... 2416
Ge 1:24 bring forth the l. creature after his...... 2416
Ge 1:28 over every l. thing that moveth.......... 2416
Ge 2:7 of life; and man became a l. soul......... 2416
Ge 2:19 Adam called every l. creature,............ 2416
Ge 3:20 because she was the mother of all l..... 2416
Ge 6:19 of every l. thing of all flesh, two of..... 2416
Ge 7:4 and every l. substance that I have.............
Ge 7:23 And every l. substance was destroyed........
Ge 8:1 Noah, and every l. thing, and all......... 2416
Ge 8:17 every l. thing that is with thee,.......... 2416
Ge 8:21 again smite any more every thing l.,.... 2416
Ge 9:10 with every l. creature that is with....... 2416
Ge 9:12 and every l. creature that is with you, .2416
Ge 9:15 and every l. creature of all flesh;........ 2416
Ge 9:16 and every l. creature of all flesh......... 2416
Le 11:10 any l. thing which is in the waters,...... 2416
Le 11:46 every l. creature that moveth in the...... 2416
Le 14:6 As for the l. bird, he shall take it,....... 2416
Le 14:6 the l. bird in the blood of the bird....... 2416
Le 14:7 the l. bird loose into the open field...... 2416
Le 14:51 and the l. bird, and dip them in the..... 2416
Le 14:52 running water, and with the l. bird,..... 2416
Le 14:53 shall let go the l. bird out of the city.. 2416
Le 20:25 any manner of l. thing that creepeth..........
Nu 16:48 stood between the dead and the l.;...... 2416
De 5:26 hath heard the voice of the l. God....... 2416
Jos 3:10 know that the l. God is among you,..... 2416
Ru 2:20 not left off his kindness to the l.......... 2416
1Sa 17:26 defy the armies of the l. God?........... 2416
1Sa 17:36 defied the armies of the l. God........... 2416
2Sa 20:3 of their death, l. in widowhood........... 2424
1Ki 3:22 said, Nay; but the l. is my son,........... 2416
1Ki 3:22 is thy son, and the l. is my son........... 2416
1Ki 3:23 is the dead, and my son is the l.......... 2416
1Ki 3:25 king said, Divide the l. child in two,.... 2416
1Ki 3:26 the woman whose the l. child was........ 2416
1Ki 3:26 said, O my lord, give her the l. child, . 2416
1Ki 3:27 and said, Give her the l. child,........... 2416
2Ki 19:4 hath sent to reproach the l. God;........ 2416
2Ki 19:16 sent him to reproach the l. God.......... 2416
Job 12:10 hand is the soul of every l. thing,........ 2416
Job 28:13 is it found in the land of the l............ 2416
Job 28:21 it is hid from the eyes of all l., and..... 2416
Job 30:23 to the house appointed for all l........... 2416
Job 33:30 enlightened with the light of the l........ 2416
Ps 27:13 of the Lord in the land of the l........... 2416
Ps 42:2 thirsteth for God, for the l. God:........ 2416
Ps 52:5 root thee out of the land of the l......... 2416
Ps 56:13 walk before God in the light of the l.?...2416
Ps 58:9 both l., and in his wrath.................... 2416
Ps 69:28 be blotted out of the book of the l.,..... 2416
Ps 84:2 my flesh crieth out for the l. God......... 2416
Ps 116:9 before the Lord in the land of the l...... 2416
Ps 142:5 and my portion in the land of the l...... 2416
Ps 143:2 sight shall no man l. be justified,......... 2416
Ps 145:16 satisfiest the desire of every l. thing... 2416
Ec 4:2 than the l. which are yet alive........... 2416
Ec 4:15 I considered all the l. which walk......... 2416
Ec 6:8 that knoweth to walk before the l.?..... 2416
Ec 7:2 and the l. will lay it to his heart......... 2416
Ec 9:4 For to him that is joined to all the l..... 2416
Ec 9:4 a l. dog is better than a dead lion......... 2416
Ec 9:5 For the l. know that they shall die:..... 2416
Ca 4:15 of gardens, a well of l. waters,........... 2416
Isa 4:3 written among the l. in Jerusalem:....... 2416
Isa 8:19 their God? for the l. to the dead?........ 2416
Isa 37:4 hath sent to reproach the l. God,......... 2416
Isa 37:17 hath sent to reproach the l. God.......... 2416
Isa 38:11 even the Lord, in the land of the l....... 2416
Isa 38:19 The l., the l., he shall praise thee,...... 2416
Isa 53:8 was cut off out of the land of the l...... 2416
Jer 2:13 me the fountain of l. waters,............... 2416
Jer 10:10 is the true God, he is the l. God,......... 2416
Jer 11:19 cut him off from the land of the l.,...... 2416
Jer 17:13 the Lord, the fountain of l. waters...... 2416

Jer 23:36 perverted the words of the **l.** God,..... 2416
La 3:39 Wherefore doth a **l.** man complain, ... 2416
Eze 1:5 the likeness of four **l.** creatures. 2416
Eze 1:13 for the likeness of the **l.** creatures,...... 2416
Eze 1:13 and down among the **l.** creatures; 2416
Eze 1:14 the **l.** creatures ran and returned 2416
Eze 1:15 as I beheld the **l.** creatures, behold 2416
Eze 1:15 upon the earth by the **l.** creatures,..... 2416
Eze 1:19 And when the **l.** creatures went, the... 2416
Eze 1:19 when the **l.** creatures were lifted up ... 2416
Eze 1:20, 21 spirit of the **l.** creature was in....... 2416
Eze 1:22 upon the heads of the **l.** creature 2416
Eze 3:13 of the wings of the **l.** creatures that.... 2416
Eze 10:15 This is the **l.** creature that I saw by ... 2416
Eze 10:17 the spirit of the **l.** creature was in...... 2416
Eze 10:20 This is the **l.** creature that I saw 2416
Eze 26:20 shall set glory in the land of the **l.**;..... 2416
Eze 32:23 caused terror in the land of the **l.**....... 2416
Eze 32:24 their terror in the land of the **l.**; 2416
Eze 32:25 was caused in the land of the **l.**, ... 2416
Eze 32:26 their terror in the land of the **l.** 2416
Eze 32:27 of the mighty in the land of the **l.**....... 2416
Eze 32:32 my terror in the land of the **l.**: 2416
Da 2:30 that I have more than any **l.**,............. 2417
Da 4:17 **l.** may know that the most High......... 2417
Da 6:20 Daniel, servant of the **l.** God, is thy ... 2417
Da 6:26 God of Daniel: for he is the **l.** God, ... 2417
Ho 1:10 them, Ye are the sons of the **l.** God. .. 2416
Zec 14:8 that **l.** waters shall go out from.......... 2416
Mt 16:16 the Christ, the Son of the **l.** God. *2198*
Mt 22:32 **the God of the dead, but of the l.**.. *2198*
Mt 26:63 him, I adjure thee by the **l.** God, ... *2198*
Mk 12:27 **of the dead, but the God of the l.**:..*2198*
Mk 12:44 **in all that she had, even all her l.**... *979*
Lu 8:43 had spent all her **l.** upon physicians, ... *979*
Lu 15:12 **And he divided unto them his l.**....... *979*
Lu 15:13 **his substance with riotous l.** *2198*
Lu 15:30 **hath devoured thy l. with harlots**,... *979*
Lu 20:38 **God of the dead, but of the l.**......... *2198*
Lu 21:4 **hath cast in all the l. that she had**.. *979*
Lu 24:5 seek ye the **l.** among the dead? *2198*
Joh 4:10 **he would have given thee l. water** . *2198*
Joh 4:11 then hast thou that **l.** water? *2198*
Joh 6:51 **I am the l. bread which came** *2198*
Joh 6:57 **As the l. Father hath sent me, and**.*2198*
Joh 6:69 that Christ, the Son of the **l.** God. *2198*
Joh 7:38 **belly shall flow rivers of l. water**... *2198*
Ac 14:15 from these vanities unto the **l.** God, ... *2198*
Ro 9:26 be called the children of the **l.** God..... *2198*
Ro 12:1 present your bodies a **l.** sacrifice,....... *2198*
Ro 14:9 be Lord both of the dead and **l.**.......... *2198*
1Co 15:45 first man Adam was made a **l.** soul;.... *2198*
2Co 3:3 but with the Spirit of the **l.** God;........ *2198*
2Co 6:16 for ye are the temple of the **l.** God; ... *2198*
Col 2:20 why, as though **l.** in the world, are...... *2198*
1Th 1:9 idols to serve the **l.** and true God; *2198*
1Ti 3:15 which is the church of the **l.** God, ... *2198*
1Ti 4:10 because we trust in the **l.** God, who... *2198*
1Ti 6:17 uncertain riches, but in the **l.** God, ... *2198*
Tit 3:3 pleasures, **l.** in malice and envy, ... *1236*
Heb 3:12 in departing from the **l.** God............. *2198*
Heb 9:14 dead works to serve the **l.** God?........ *2198*
Heb 10:20 By a new and **l.** way, which he hath... *2198*
Heb 10:31 to fall into the hands of the **l.** God...... *2198*
Heb 12:22 and unto the city of the **l.** God, ... *2198*
1Pe 2:4 whom coming, as unto a **l.** stone,....... *2198*
Re 7:2 east, having the seal of the **l.** God:..... *2198*
Re 7:17 them unto **l.** fountains of waters:........ *2198*
Re 16:3 and every **l.** soul died in the sea. *2198*

LIZARD

Le 11:30 and the chameleon, and the **l.**,........... 3911

LO

Ge 8:11 **l.**, in her mouth was an olive leaf....... 2009
Ge 15:3 **l.**, one born in my house is mine........ 2009
Ge 15:12 **l.**, an horror of great darkness fell...... 2009
Ge 18:2 **l.**, three men stood by him: and......... 2009
Ge 18:10 **l.**, Sarah thy wife shall have a son. 2009
Ge 19:28 **l.**, the smoke of the country went 2009
Ge 29:2 **l.**, there were three flocks of sheep.... 2009
Ge 29:7 And he said, **L.**, it is yet high day,...... 2005
Ge 37:7 **l.**, my sheaf arose, and also stood...... 2009
Ge 42:28 **l.**, it is even in my sack: and their...... 2009
Ge 47:23 **l.**, here is seed for you, and ye 1883
Ge 48:11 **l.**, God hath shewed me also thy........ 2009
Ge 50:5 made me swear, saying, **L.**, I die:...... 2009
Ex 7:15 **l.**, he goeth out unto the water;......... 2009
Ex 8:20 **l.**, he cometh forth to the water; 2009
Ex 8:26 **l.**,...we sacrifice the abomination........ 2005
Ex 19:9 **L.**, I come unto thee in a thick.......... 2009
Nu 14:40 **L.**, we be here, and will go up unto ... 2009
Nu 22:38 Balak, **L.**, I am come unto thee: 2009
Nu 23:6 **l.**, he stood by his burnt sacrifice, ... 2009
Nu 23:9 **l.**, the people shall dwell alone,.......... 2005
Nu 24:11 **l.**, the Lord hath kept thee back 2009
De 22:17 **l.**, he hath given occasions of speech .. 2009
Jos 14:10 **l.**, I am this day fourscore and five...... 2009
Jg 7:13 **l.**, a cake of barley bread tumbled...... 2009
Jg 13:5 **l.**, thou shalt conceive, and bear a...... 2009
1Sa 4:13 **l.**, Eli sat upon a seat by the wayside ..2009
1Sa 10:2 **l.**, thy father hath left the care of....... 2009
1Sa 14:43 in mind hand, and, **l.**, I must die. 2114
1Sa 21:14 **L.**, ye see the man is mad:.............. 2009
2Sa 1:6 and, **l.**, the chariots and horsemen...... 2009
2Sa 15:24 **l.** Zadok also, and all the Levites........ 2009
2Sa 24:17 said, **L.**, I have sinned, and done. 2009
1Ki 1:22 **l.**, while she yet talked with the......... 2009
1Ki 1:51 **l.**, he hath caught hold on the horns ... 2009
1Ki 3:12 **l.**, I have given thee a wise and an..... 2009
2Ki 7:6 **L.**, the king of Israel hath hired......... 2009
2Ki 7:15 **l.**, all the way was full of garments..... 2009
1Ch 17:1 **L.**, I dwell in an house of cedars........ 2009
1Ch 21:23 **l.**, I give thee the oxen also for 7200
2Ch 16:11 **l.**, they are written in the book of...... 2009
2Ch 25:19 **L.**, thou hast smitten the Edomites; ... 2009
2Ch 27:7 **l.**, they are written in the book of...... 2005
2Ch 29:9 **l.**, our fathers have fallen by the 2009
Ne 5:5 **l.**, we bring into bondage our sons 2009
Ne 6:12 **l.**, I perceived that God had not......... 2009
Job 3:7 **L.**, let that night be solitary, let no 2009
Job 5:27 **L.** this, we have searched it, so it...... 2009
Job 9:11 **L.**, he goeth by me, and I see him...... 2005
Job 9:19 speak of strength, **l.**, he is strong: 2009
Job 13:1 **L.**, mine eye hath seen all this, ... 2005
Job 21:16 **L.**, their good is not in their hand: 2005
Job 26:14 **L.**, these are parts of his ways: but.... 2005
Job 33:29 **L.**, all these things worketh God........ 2005
Job 40:16 **L.** now, his strength is in his loins, ... 2009
Ps 11:2 For, **l.**, the wicked bend their bow, ... 2009
Ps 37:36 passed away, and **l.**, he was not: 2009
Ps 40:7 Then said I, **L.**, I come: in the.......... 2009
Ps 40:9 **l.**, I have not refrained my lips, O...... 2009
Ps 48:4 For, **l.**, the kings were assembled, ... 2009
Ps 52:7 **L.**, this is the man that made not........ 2009
Ps 55:7 **L.**, then would I wander far off,........ 2009
Ps 59:3 For, **l.**, they lie in wait for my soul: ... 2009
Ps 68:33 **l.**, he doth send out his voice, and 2005
Ps 73:27 **l.**, they that are far from thee shall..... 2005
Ps 83:2 **l.**, thine enemies make a tumult: 2009
Ps 92:9 For, **l.**, thine enemies, O Lord, ... 2009
Ps 92:9 for, **l.**, thine enemies shall perish; 2009
Ps 127:3 **L.**, children are an heritage of the...... 2009
Ps 132:6 **L.**, we heard of it at Ephratah: we...... 2009
Ps 139:4 but, **l.**, O Lord, thou knowest it 2005
Pr 24:31 And, **l.**, it was all grown over with...... 2009
Ec 1:16 **L.**, I am come to great estate, and..... 2009
Ec 7:29 **L.**, this only have I found, that.......... 7200
Ca 2:11 **l.**, the winter is past, the rain is 2009
Isa 6:7 said, **L.**, this hath touched thy lips; 2009
Isa 25:9 said in that day, **L.**, this is our God;... 2009
Isa 36:6 **L.**, thou trustest in the staff of this 2009
Isa 49:12 **l.**, these from the north and from....... 2009
Isa 50:9 **l.**, they all shall wax old as a............ 2005
Jer 1:15 **l.**, I will call all the families of the 2009
Jer 4:23 earth, and **l.**, it was without form,...... 2009
Jer 4:24 mountains, and, **l.**, they trembled....... 2009
Jer 4:25 I beheld, and, **l.**, there was no man, ... 2009
Jer 4:26 I beheld, and, **l.**, the fruitful place 2009
Jer 5:15 **L.**, I will bring a nation upon you 2009
Jer 8:8 **L.**, certainly in vain made he it;......... 2009
Jer 8:9 **l.**, they have rejected the word of 2009
Jer 25:29 **l.**, I begin to bring evil on the city...... 2009
Jer 30:3 **l.**, the days come, saith the Lord, ... 2009
Jer 30:10 **l.**, I will save thee from afar, and....... 2009
Jer 36:12 **l.**, all the princes sat there, even 2009
Jer 49:15 **l.**, I will make thee small among 2009
Jer 50:9 **l.**, I will raise and cause to come up ... 2009
Eze 2:9 and, **l.**, a roll of a book was therein;... 2009
Eze 4:15 **L.**, I have given thee cow's dung....... 7200
Eze 8:2 **l.** a likeness as the appearance of....... 2009
Eze 8:17 **l.**, they put the branch to their nose... 2009
Eze 13:10 **l.**, others daubed it with...morter: 2009
Eze 13:12 **L.**, when the wall is fallen, shall it...... 2009
Eze 17:18 when, **l.**, he had given his hand, ... 2009
Eze 18:14 **l.**, if he beget a son, that seeth all 2009
Eze 18:18 **l.**, even he shall die in his iniquity. 2009
Eze 23:39 **l.**, thus have they done in the midst ... 2009
Eze 23:40 was sent; and, **l.**, they came: 2009
Eze 30:9 the day of Egypt: for, **l.**, it cometh..... 2009
Eze 30:21 **l.**, it shall not be bound up to be........ 2009
Eze 33:32 **l.**, thou art unto them as a very......... 2009
Eze 33:33 cometh to pass, (**l.**, it will come,)....... 2009
Eze 37:2 valley; and **l.**, they were very dry. 2009
Eze 37:8 **l.**, the sinews and the flesh came 2009
Eze 40:17 and, **l.**, there were chambers, and a ... 2009
Eze 42:8 and, **l.**, before the temple were an 2009
Da 3:25 **L.**, I see four men loose, walking....... 1888
Da 7:6 and **l.** another, like a leopard, ... 718
Da 10:13 but, **l.**, Michael, one of the chief........ 2009
Da 10:20 **l.**, the prince of Grecia shall come. 2009
Ho 9:6 For, **l.**, they are gone because of....... 2009
Am 4:2 **l.**, the days shall come upon you, ... 2009
Am 4:13 **l.**, he that formeth the mountains, ... 2009
Am 7:1 **l.**, it was the latter growth after the ... 2009
Am 9:9 **l.**, I will command, and I will sift........ 2009
Hab 1:6 **l.**, I raise up the Chaldeans, that........ 2009
Hag 1:9 for much, and, **l.**, it came to little; 2009
Zec 2:10 **l.**, I come, and I will dwell in the ....
Zec 11:6 **l.**, I will deliver the men every one...........
Zec 11:16 **l.**, I will raise up a shepherd in the...........
Mt 2:9 **l.**, the star, which they saw in the...... *2400*
Mt 3:16 **l.**, the heavens were opened unto *2400*
Mt 3:17 And **l.** a voice from heaven, saying, ... *2400*
Mt 24:23 **L., here is Christ, or there; believe.***2400*
Mt 25:25 **l., there thou hast that is thine**..... *2396*
Mt 26:47 **l.**, Judas, one of the twelve, came,..... *2400*
Mt 28:7 ye see him: **l.**, I have told you. *2400*
Mt 28:20 **l., I am with you alway, even unto**.*2400*
Mk 10:28 say unto him, **L.**, we have left all,...... *2400*
Mk 13:21 **L., here is Christ; or, l., he is**....... *2400*
Mk 14:42 **l., he that betrayeth me is at hand.***2400*
Lu 1:44 For, **l.**, as soon as the voice of thy *2400*
Lu 2:9 **l.**, the angel of the Lord came upon.... *2400*
Lu 9:39 And, **l.**, a spirit taketh him, and he..... *2400*
Lu 13:16 **l., these eighteen years, be loosed**... *2400*
Lu 15:29 **L., these many years do I serve**...... *2400*
Lu 17:21 **shall they say, L., here! or,...there!***2400*
Lu 17:21 **here! or, l. there! for, behold,** *2400*
Lu 18:28 Peter said, **L.**, we have left all, and.... *2400*
Lu 23:15 **l.**, nothing worthy of death is done *2400*
Joh 7:26 But, **l.**, he speaketh boldly, and......... *2396*
Joh 16:29 him, **L.**, now speakest thou plainly, ... *2396*
Ac 13:46 life, **l.**, we turn to the Gentiles. *2400*
Ac 27:24 **l.**, God hath given thee all them......... *2400*
Heb 10:7 **L.**, I come (in the volume of the........ *2400*
Heb 10:9 **L.**, I come to do thy will, O God. *2400*
Re 5:6 **l.**, in the midst of the throne and *2400*
Re 6:5 And I beheld, and **l.** a black horse;..... *2400*
Re 6:12 **l.**, there was a great earthquake; *2400*
Re 7:9 **l.**, a great multitude, which no man *2400*
Re 14:1 **l.**, a Lamb stood on the mount Sion.... *2400*

LO See LO-AMMI; LO-DEBAR; LO-RUHAMAH.

LOADEN See also LADEN.

Isa 46:1 your carriages were heavy **l.**;............ 6006

LOADETH See also LADETH.

Ps 68:19 who daily **l.** us with benefits;............. 6006

LOAF See also LOAVES.

Ex 29:23 And one **l.** of bread, and one cake...... 3603
1Ch 16:3 to every one a **l.** of bread, and a 3603
Mk 8:14 ship with them more than one **l.**.......... *740*

LO-AMMI (lo-am'-mi)

Ho 1:9 Then said God, Call his name **L.**:....... 3818

LOAN

1Sa 2:20 the **l.** which is lent to the Lord.......... 7596

LOATHE See also LOATHETH; LOATHSOME; LOTHE.

Job 7:16 I **l.** it; I would not live alway: let 3988

LOATHETH See also LOTHETH.

Nu 21:5 and our soul **l.** this light bread........... 6973
Pr 27:7 The full soul **l.** an honeycomb; but 947

LOATHSOME

Nu 11:20 nostrils, and it be **l.** unto you: 2214
Job 7:5 my skin is broken, and become **l.**........ 3988

Ps 38:7 loins are filled with a l. disease:......... 7033
Pr 13:5 a wicked man is l., and cometh to 887

LOAVES
Le 23:17 two wave l. of two tenth deals: 3899
Jg 8:5 l. of bread unto the people that 3603
1Sa 10:3 another carrying three l. of bread,...... 3603
1Sa 10:4 thee, and give thee two l. of bread;..........
1Sa 17:17 this parched corn, and these ten l., ... 3899
1Sa 21:3 give me five l. of bread in mine hand, ...
1Sa 25:18 haste, and took two hundred l., ... 3899
2Sa 16:1 upon them two hundred l. of bread,..........
1Ki 14:3 take with thee ten l., and cracknels, ... 3899
2Ki 4:42 the firstfruits, twenty l. of barley, ... 3899
Mt 14:17 We have here but five l., and two *740*
Mt 14:19 took the five l., and the two fishes, ... *740*
Mt 14:19 and gave the l. to his disciples, and....... *740*
Mt 15:34 unto them, **How many l. have ye?**..... *740*
Mt 15:36 he took the seven l. and the fishes, ... *740*
Mt 16:9 **remember the five l. of the five**...... *740*
Mt 16:10 **Neither the seven l. of the four**....... *740*
Mk 6:38 unto them, **How many l. have ye?**..... *740*
Mk 6:41 when he had taken the five l. and........ *740*
Mk 6:41 and blessed, and brake the l., and *740*
Mk 6:44 they that did eat of the l. were about ... *740*
Mk 6:52 not the miracle of the l.: considered..... *740*
Mk 8:5 asked them, **How many l. have ye?**... *740*
Mk 8:6 took the seven l., and gave thanks,...... *740*
Mk 8:19 **When I brake the five l. among five** *740*
Lu 9:13 We have no more but five l. and two ... *740*
Lu 9:16 Then he took the five l. and the two.... *740*
Lu 11:5 **unto him, Friend, lend me three l.**:..*740*
Joh 6:9 lad here, which hath five barley l., ... *740*
Joh 6:11 Jesus took the l.; and when he had...... *740*
Joh 6:13 the fragments of the five barley l., ... *740*
Joh 6:26 **but because ye did eat of the l., and** *740*

LOCK See also LOCKED; LOCKS; WEDLOCK.
Ca 5:5 myrrh, upon the handles of the l.. 4514
Eze 8:3 and took me by a l. of mine head; 6734

LOCKED
Jg 3:23 the parlour upon him, and l. them. 5274
Jg 3:24 the doors of the parlour were l., ... 5274

LOCKS
Nu 6:5 the l. of the hair of his head grow...... 6545
Jg 16:13 weavest the seven l. of my head........ 4253
Jg 16:19 to shave off the seven l. of his head; .. 4253
Ne 3:3, 6,13,14,15 thereof, the l. thereof, ... 4514
Ca 4:1 thou hast doves' eyes within thy l.: 6777
Ca 4:3 of a pomegranate within thy l.. 6777
Ca 5:2 my l. with the drops of the night. 6977
Ca 5:11 his l. are bushy, and black as a.......... 6977
Ca 6:7 are thy temples within thy l.. 6777
Isa 47:2 uncover thy l., make bare the leg, ... 6777
Eze 44:20 nor suffer their l. to grow long; 6545

LOCUST See also LOCUSTS.
Ex 10:19 not one l. in all the coasts of Egypt, ... 697
Le 11:22 ye may eat; the l. after his kind, ... 697
Le 11:22 and the bald l. after his kind, and....... 5556
De 28:38 little in; for the l. shall consume it. 697
De 28:42 of thy land shall the l. consume. 6767
1Ki 8:37 pestilence, blasting, mildew, l., ... 697
Ps 78:46 and their labour unto the l.................. 697
Ps 109:23 I am tossed up and down as the l........ 697
Joe 1:4 hath left hath the l. eaten; and............ 697
Joe 1:4 that which the l. hath left hath the....... 697
Joe 2:25 you the years that the l. hath eaten, ... 697

LOCUSTS
Ex 10:4 will I bring the l. into thy coast: 697
Ex 10:12 over the land of Egypt for the l.,......... 697
Ex 10:13 the east wind brought the l.. 697
Ex 10:14 the l. went up over all the land of........ 697
Ex 10:14 them there were no such l. as they, ... 697
Ex 10:19 westwind, which took away the l., ... 697
2Ch 6:28 there be blasting, or mildew, l., or 697
2Ch 7:13 command the l. to devour the land, ... 2284
Ps 105:34 He spake, and the l. came, and........... 697
Pr 30:27 The l. have no king, yet go they 697
Isa 33:4 as the running to and fro of l. shall..... 1357
Na 3:15 make thyself many as the l................ 697
Na 3:17 Thy crowned are as the l., and thy...... 697
Mt 3:4 his meat was l. and wild honey. *200*
Mk 1:6 and he did eat l. and wild honey; *200*
Re 9:3 there came out of the smoke l. upon.... *200*
Re 9:7 of the l. were like unto horses............ *200*

LOD (lod) See also LYDDA.
1Ch 8:12 Shamed, who built Ono, and L., ... 3850
Ezr 2:33 The children of L., Hadid, and Ono, ... 3850
Ne 7:37 The children of L., Hadid, and Ono, ... 3850
Ne 11:35 L., and Ono, the valley of craftsmen... 3850

LO-DEBAR (lo-de'-bar)
2Sa 9:4,5 Machir, the son of Ammiel, in L.. 3810
2Sa 17:27 Machir the son of Ammiel of L., ... 3810

LODGE See also LODGED; LODGEST; LODGETH; LODGING.
Ge 24:23 thy father's house for us to l. in? 3885
Ge 24:25 and provender...and room to l. in....... 3885
Nu 22:8 L. here this night, and I will bring...... 3885
Jos 4:3 place, where ye shall l. this night....... 3885
Jg 19:9 the day groweth to an end, l. here..... 3885
Jg 19:11 city of the Jebusites, and l. in it......... 3885
Jg 19:13 one of these places to l. all night, ... 3885
Jg 19:15 to go in and to l. in Gibeah: 3885
Jg 19:20 upon me; only l. not in the street. 3885
Jg 20:4 Benjamin, I and my concubine, to l.... 3885
Ru 1:16 and where thou lodgest, I will l.: 3885
2Sa 17:8 war, and will not l. with the people. ... 3885
2Sa 17:16 L. not this night in the plains of......... 3885
Ne 4:22 Let every one with his servant l. 3885
Ne 13:21 unto them, Why l. ye about the wall?.. 3885
Job 24:7 the naked to l. without clothing,......... 3885
Job 31:32 stranger did not l. in the street: 3885
Ca 7:11 the field; let us l. in the villages......... 3885
Isa 1:8 as a l. in a garden of cucumbers, ... 4412
Isa 21:13 In the forest in Arabia shall ye l.,........ 3885
Isa 65:4 graves, and l. in the monuments, ... 3885
Jer 4:14 How long shall thy vain thoughts l....... 3885
Zep 2:14 bittern shall l. in the upper lintels....... 3885
Mt 13:32 **and l. in the branches thereof**....... *2681*
Mk 4:32 **of the air may l. under the shadow***2681*
Lu 9:12 and country round about, and l., ... *2647*
Ac 21:16 disciple, with whom we should l., ... *3579*

LODGED
Ge 32:13 And he l. there that same night; 3885
Ge 32:21 himself l. that night in the company. ... 3885
Jos 2:1 house, named Rahab, and l. there. 7901
Jos 3:1 l. there before they passed over. 3885
Jos 4:8 them unto the place where they l.,...... 4411
Jos 6:11 into the camp, and l. in the camp. 3885
Jos 8:9 Joshua l. that night among the........... 3885
Jg 18:2 the house of Micah, they l. there....... 3885
Jg 19:4 they did eat and drink, and l. there. ... 3885
Jg 19:7 him: therefore he l. there again. 3885
1Ki 19:9 thither unto a cave, and l. there; 3885
1Ch 9:27 l. round about the house of God, ... 3885
Ne 13:20 sellers of all kind of ware l. without.... 3885
Isa 1:21 Judgment; rightousness l. in it; 3885
Mt 21:17 city into Bethany; and he l. there. *835*
Lu 13:19 **fowls of the air l. in the branches**..*2681*
Ac 10:18 was surnamed Peter, were l. there. ... *3579*
Ac 10:23 Then called he them in, and l. them. .. *3579*
Ac 10:32 he is l. in the house of one Simon...... *3579*
Ac 28:7 and l. us three days courteously. *3579*
1Ti 5:10 children, if she have l. strangers, ... *3580*

LODGEST
Ru 1:16 and where thou l., I will lodge: 3885

LODGETH
Ac 10:6 He l. with one Simon a tanner, ... *3579*

LODGING See also LODGINGS.
Jos 4:3 and leave them in the l. place,........... 4411
Jg 19:15 that took them into his house to l.. 3885
Isa 10:29 have taken up there l. at Geba; 4411
Jer 9:2 I had in the wilderness a l. place.......... 4411
Ac 28:23 there came many to him into his l.; *3578*
Phm 22 But withal prepare me also a l.: *3578*

LODGINGS
2Ki 19:23 enter into the l. of his borders, ... 4411

LOFT
1Ki 17:19 carried him up into a l., where he...... 5944
Ac 20:9 and fell down from the third l.,........... 5152

LOFTILY
Ps 73:8 oppression: they speak l.................... 4791

LOFTINESS
Isa 2:17 the l. of man shall be bowed down, ... 1365
Jer 48:29 his l., and his arrogancy, and his........ 1363

LOFTY
Ps 131:1 is not haughty, nor mine eyes l.: 7311
Pr 30:13 generation, O how l. are their eyes! ... 7311
Isa 2:11 l. looks of man shall be humbled, ... 1365
Isa 2:12 every one that is proud and l., ... 7311
Isa 5:15 eyes of the l. shall be humbled: 1364
Isa 26:5 high; the l. city, he layeth it low; 7682
Isa 57:7 Upon a l. and high mountain hast 1364
Isa 57:15 l. One that inhabiteth eternity,........... 5375

LOG
Le 14:10 mingled with oil, and one l. of oil. 3849
Le 14:12 trespass offering, and the l. of oil,...... 3849
Le 14:15 priest shall take some of the l. of oil,.. 3849
Le 14:21 for a meat offering, and a l. of oil;...... 3849
Le 14:24 trespass offering, and the l. of oil,...... 3849

LOINS
Ge 35:11 and kings shall come out of thy l.;...... 2504
Ge 37:34 and put sackcloth upon his l., ... 4975
Ge 46:26 which came out of his l., besides 3409
Ex 1:5 souls that came out of the l. of Jacob.. 3409
Ex 12:11 with your l. girded, your shoes on...... 4975
Ex 28:42 from the l. even unto the thighs 4975
De 33:11 smite through the l. of them that 4975
2Sa 20:8 with a sword fastened upon his l....... 4975
1Ki 2:5 his girdle that was about his l., ... 4975
1Ki 8:19 that shall come forth out of thy l., ... 2504
1Ki 12:10 be thicker than my father's l.. 4975
1Ki 18:46 and he girded up his l., and ran......... 4975
1Ki 20:31 put sackcloth on our l., and ropes 4975
1Ki 20:32 So they girded sackcloth on their l., ... 4975
2Ki 1:8 with a girdle of leather about his l....... 4975
2Ki 4:29 Gird up thy l., and take my staff in 4975
2Ki 9:1 Gird up thy l., and take this box of 4975
2Ch 6:9 shall come forth out of thy l.,............ 2504
2Ch 10:10 be thicker than my father's l.. 4975
Job 12:18 and girdeth their l. with a girdle........ 4975
Job 31:20 If his l. have not blessed me, and 2504
Job 38:3 Gird up now thy l. like a man; for...... 2504
Job 40:7 Gird up thy l. now like a man: I......... 2504
Job 40:16 his strength is in his l., and his.......... 4975
Ps 38:7 my l. are filled with a loathsome 3689
Ps 66:11 thou laidst affliction upon our l.......... 4975
Ps 69:23 make their l. continually to shake. 4975
Pr 31:17 She girdeth her l. with strength, ... 4975
Isa 5:27 the girdle of their l. be loosed, ... 2504
Isa 11:5 righteousness...the girdle of his l., ... 4975
Isa 20:2 loose the sackcloth from off thy l., ... 4975
Isa 21:3 Therefore are my l. filled with pain:.... 4975
Isa 32:11 and gird sackcloth upon your l.. 2504
Isa 45:1 I will loose the l. of kings, to open...... 4975
Jer 1:17 Thou therefore gird up thy l., and...... 4975
Jer 13:1 linen girdle, and put it upon thy l., ... 4975
Jer 13:2 of the Lord, and put it on my l........... 4975
Jer 13:4 thou hast got, which is upon thy l., ... 4975
Jer 13:11 as the girdle cleaveth to the l. of a..... 4975
Jer 30:6 every man with his hands on his l., ... 2504
Jer 48:37 cuttings, and upon the l. sackcloth...... 4975
Eze 1:27 appearance of his l. even upward, ... 4975
Eze 1:27 appearance of his l. even downward,... 4975
Eze 8:2 apearance of his l. even upward, ... 4975
Eze 8:2 and from his l. even upward, as the.... 4975
Eze 21:6 of man, with the breaking of thy l.; 4975
Eze 23:15 Girded with girdles upon their l., ... 4975
Eze 29:7 madest all their l. to be at a stand...... 4975
Eze 44:18 have linen breeches upon their l.;........ 4975
Eze 47:4 through; the waters were to the l.. 4975
Da 5:6 the joints of his l. were loosed, ... 2783
Da 10:5 l. were girded with fine gold of.......... 4975
Am 8:10 will bring up sackcloth upon all l.,........ 4975
Na 2:1 watch the way, make thy l. strong, ... 4975
Na 2:10 together, and much pain is in all l.,...... 4975
Mt 3:4 and a leathern girdle about his l.; *3751*
Mk 1:6 with a girdle of a skin about his l.; *3751*
Lu 12:35 **Let your l. be girded about, and**.... *3751*
Ac 2:30 to him, that of the fruit of his l., ... *3751*
Eph 6:14 having your l. girt about with truth, ... *3751*
Heb 7:5 they come out of the l. of Abraham: ... *3751*
Heb 7:10 For he was yet in the l. of his father, ..*3751*
1Pe 1:13 gird up the l. of your mind, be sober, . *3751*

LOIS (lo'-is)
2Ti 1:5 dwelt first in thy grandmother L., ... *3090*

LONG See also HEADLONG; LONGED; LONGER; LONGETH; LONGING; LONGSUFFERING; LONGWINGED; PROLONG.
Ge 26:8 when he had been there a l. time, ... 748

Ge 48:15 the God which fed me all my life l...... 5750
Ex 10:3 How l. wilt thou refuse to humble...... 4970
Ex 10:7 How l. shall this man be a snare........ 5704
Ex 16:28 How l. refuse ye to keep my........... 5704
Ex 19:13 when the trumpet soundeth l.,.......... 4900
Ex 19:19 the voice of the trumpet sounded l., ...
Ex 20:12 days may be l. upon the land which...... 748
Ex 27:1 altar of shittim wood, five cubits l.,...... 753
Ex 27:9 of an hundred cubits l. for one side:..... 753
Ex 27:11 be hangings of an hundred cubits l.,..... 753
Le 18:19 as l. as she is put apart for her ....
Le 26:34 sabbaths, as l. as it lieth desolate,...... 3117
Le 26:35 As l. as it lieth desolate it shall rest; .. 3117
Nu 9:18 as l. as the cloud abode upon the....... 3117
Nu 9:19 And when the cloud tarried l. upon..........
Nu 14:11 How l. will this people provoke me? ... 5704
Nu 14:11 how l. will it be ere they believe me,.. 5704
Nu 14:27 How l. shall I bear with this evil........ 5704
Nu 20:15 we have dwelt in Egypt a l. time; 7227
De 1:6 have dwelt l. enough in this mount:.... 7227
De 2:3 this mountain l. enough: turn you........ 7227
De 4:25 shall have remained l. in the land, ...
De 12:19 as l. as thou livest upon the earth...... 3117
De 14:24 if the way be too l. for thee, so that... 7235
De 19:6 overtake him, because the way is l.,... 7235
De 20:19 thou shalt besiege a city a l. time,........ 7227
De 28:32 longing for them all the day l.:.................
De 28:59 great plagues, and of l. continuance, ...
De 28:59 sicknesses, and of l. continuance..............
De 31:13 as l. as ye live in the land whither...... 3117
De 33:12 shall cover him all the day l., and he.........
Jos 6:5 make a l. last with the ram's horn,..... 4900
Jos 9:13 by reason of the very l. journey......... 7230
Jos 11:18 made war a l. time with all those....... 7227
Jos 18:3 How l. are ye slack to go to possess.. 5704
Jos 23:1 a l. time after that the Lord had......... 7227
Jos 24:7 dwelt in the wilderness a l. season..... 7227
Jg 5:28 Why is his chariot so l. in coming?....... 954
1Sa 1:14 How l. wilt thou be drunken? put....... 5704
1Sa 1:28 as l. as he liveth he shall be lent to.... 3117
1Sa 7:2 Kirjath-jearim, that...time was l.; 7235
1Sa 16:1 How l. wilt thou mourn for Saul,........ 5704
1Sa 20:31 as l. as the son of Jesse liveth upon ... 3117
1Sa 25:15 l. as were conversant with them,....... 3117
1Sa 29:8 so l. as I have been with thee unto.... 3117
2Sa 2:26 how l. shall it be then, ere thou bid.... 5704
2Sa 3:1 Now there was l. war between the...... 752
2Sa 14:2 be as a woman that had a l. time....... 7227
2Sa 19:34 the king, How l. have I to live,.......... 3117
1Ki 3:11 hast not asked for thyself l. life; 7227
1Ki 6:17 temple before it, was forty cubits l...........
1Ki 18:21 How l. halt ye between two.............. 5704
2Ki 9:22 so l. as the whoredoms of thy........... 5704
2Ki 19:25 Hast thou not heard l. ago how I........ 7350
2Ch 1:11 neither yet hast asked l. life; but 7227
2Ch 3:11 cherubims were twenty cubits l.:......... 753
2Ch 6:13 a brasen scaffold, of five cubits l.,........ 753
2Ch 6:31 so l. as they live in the land which..... 3117
2Ch 15:3 for a l. season Israel hath been.......... 7227
2Ch 26:5 as l. as he sought the Lord, God......... 3117
2Ch 30:5 they had not done it of a l. time 7230
2Ch 36:21 as l. as she lay desolate she kept....... 3117
Ne 2:6 For how l. shall thy journey be? and.... 5704
Es 5:13 so l. as I see Mordecai the Jew......... 6256
Job 3:21 Which l. for death, but it cometh 2442
Job 6:8 grant me the thing that I l. for! 8615
Job 7:19 How l. wilt thou not depart from........ 4101
Job 8:2 How l. wilt thou speak these............. 5704
Job 8:2 how l. shall the words of thy mouth..........
Job 18:2 How l. will it be ere ye make............ 5704
Job 19:2 How l. will ye vex my soul, and 5704
Job 27:6 not reproach me so l. as I live. 3117
Ps 4:2 how l. will ye turn my glory into........ 5704
Ps 4:2 how l. will ye love vanity, and seek..........
Ps 6:3 vexed: but thou, O Lord, how l.?......... 5704
Ps 13:1 How l. wilt thou forget me, O Lord? .. 5704
Ps 13:1 how l. wilt thou hide thy face from..... 5704
Ps 13:2 How l. shall I take counsel in my soul,.5704
Ps 13:2 how l. shall mine enemy be exalted.... 5704
Ps 32:3 old through my roaring all the day l.........
Ps 35:17 Lord, how l. wilt thou look on?.......... 5704
Ps 35:28 and of thy praise all the day l...............
Ps 38:6 greatly; I go mourning all the day l...........
Ps 38:12 and imagine deceits all the day l..............
Ps 44:8 In God we boast all the day l., and..........
Ps 44:22 for thy sake are we killed all the day l.; ....
Ps 62:3 How l. will ye imagine mischief.......... 5704
Ps 71:24 of thy righteousness all the day l.:............
Ps 72:5 as l. as the sun and moon endure,...... 5973
Ps 72:7 peace so l. as the moon endureth....... 5704
Ps 72:17 be continued as l. as the sun:............ 6440
Ps 73:14 the day l. have I been plagued,................
Ps 74:9 among us any that knoweth how l.. 5704
Ps 74:10 how l. shall the adversary reproach? ... 5704
Ps 79:5 How l., Lord? wilt thou be angry....... 5704
Ps 80:4 how l. wilt thou be angry against the .. 5704
Ps 82:2 How l. will ye judge unjustly, and....... 5704
Ps 89:46 How l., Lord? wilt thou hide thyself.... 5704
Ps 90:13 Return, O Lord, how l.? and let it....... 5704
Ps 91:16 With l. life will I satisfy him, and......... 753
Ps 94:3 Lord, how l. shall the wicked, ... 5704
Ps 94:3 how l. shall the wicked triumph?........ 5704
Ps 94:4 How l. shall they utter and speak....... 5704
Ps 95:10 Forty years l. was I grieved with this ....
Ps 104:33 sing unto the Lord as l. as I live:....... 5704
Ps 116:2 will I call upon him as l. as I live. 3117
Ps 120:6 My soul hath l. dwelt with him......... 7227
Ps 129:3 back: they made l. their furrows......... 748
Ps 143:3 as those that have been l. dead. 5769
Pr 1:22 How l., ye simple ones, will ye love... 5704
Pr 3:2 l. life, and peace, shall they add.......... 753
Pr 6:9 How l. wilt thou sleep, O sluggard?.... 5704
Pr 7:19 at home, he is gone a l. journey: 7350
Pr 21:26 He coveteth greedily all the day l.: but......
Pr 23:17 in the fear of the Lord all the day l...........
Pr 23:30 They that tarry l. at the wine; they..........
Pr 25:15 By l. forbearing is a prince................. 753
Ec 12:5 because man goeth to his l. home, ... 5769
Isa 6:11 Then said I, Lord, how l.? And he..... 5704
Isa 22:11 unto him that fashioned it l. ago......... 7350
Isa 37:26 Hast thou not heard l. ago, how I...... 7350
Isa 42:14 I have l. time holden my peace; I........ 5769
Isa 65:22 elect shall l. enjoy the work of their ....
Jer 4:14 How l. shall...vain thoughts lodge....... 5704
Jer 4:21 How l. shall I see the standard, and ... 5704
Jer 12:4 How l. shall the land mourn, and........ 5704
Jer 23:26 How l. shall this be in the heart of..... 5704
Jer 29:28 This captivity is l.: build ye houses, ... 752
Jer 31:22 How l. wilt thou go about, O thou...... 5704
Jer 47:5 valley: how l. wilt thou cut thyself? 5704
Jer 47:6 how l. will it be ere thou be quiet?...... 5704
La 2:20 their fruit, and children of a span l.? ....
La 5:20 for ever, and forsake us so l. time? 753
Eze 31:5 his branches became l. because of....... 748
Eze 40:5 a measuring reed of six cubits l. by..........
Eze 40:7 little chamber was one reed l.,............ 753
Eze 40:29 it was fifty cubits l., and five and......... 753
Eze 40:30 about were five and twenty cubits l.,.... 753
Eze 40:33 it was fifty cubits l., and five and......... 753
Eze 40:42 of a cubit and an half l., and a cubit 753
Eze 40:47 the court, an hundred cubits l., and...... 753
Eze 41:13 the house, a hundred cubits l.; and...... 753
Eze 41:13 walls thereof, an hundred cubits l.; 753
Eze 42:11 as l. as they, and as broad as they: 753
Eze 42:20 round about, five hundred reeds l., ... 753
Eze 43:16 the altar shall be twelve cubits l.,........ 753
Eze 43:17 the settle shall be fourteen cubits l. 753
Eze 44:20 nor suffer their locks to grow l.; ....
Eze 45:6 and five and twenty thousand l.,.......... 753
Eze 46:22 courts joined of forty cubits l. and........ 753
Da 8:13 l. shall be the vision concerning 5704
Da 10:1 but the time appointed was l.: 1419
Da 12:6 How l. shall it be to the end of these.. 5704
Ho 8:5 how l. will it be ere they attain to...... 5704
Ho 13:13 should not stay l. in the place of..............
Hab 1:2 O Lord, how l. shall I cry, and thou ... 5704
Hab 2:6 that which is not his! how l.? 5704
Zec 1:12 how l. wilt thou not have mercy on 5704
Mt 9:15 **mourn, as l. as the bridegroom is** .. *1909*
Mt 11:21 **repented l. ago in sackcloth and**.... *3819*
Mt 17:17 **how l. shall I be with you?** *2193*
Mt 17:17 **how l. shall I suffer you? bring**..... *2193*
Mt 23:14 **for a pretence make l. prayer:**....... *3117*
Mt 25:19 **After a l. time the lord of those** *4183*
Mk 2:19 **l. as they have the bridegroom** *5550*
Mk 9:19 **how l. shall I be with you?** *2193*
Mk 9:19 **how l. shall I suffer you? bring** *2193*
Mk 9:21 **How l. is it ago since this came** *4214*
Mk 12:38 **which love to go in l. clothing, and** .....
Mk 12:40 **for a pretence make l. prayers:** *3117*
Mk 16:5 side, clothed in a l. white garment;...........
Lu 1:21 that he tarried so l. in the temple............
Lu 8:27 man, which had devils l. time. *2425*
Lu 9:41 **how l. shall I be with you, and** *2193*
Lu 18:7 **him, though he bear l. with them?** *3114*
Lu 20:9 **into a far country for a l. time.** *2425*
Lu 20:46 **which desire to walk in l. robes,** ....
Lu 20:47 **and for a shew make l. prayers:** *3117*
Lu 23:8 to see him of a l. season,................ *2425*
Joh 5:6 been now a l. time in that case,......... *4183*
Joh 9:5 **As l. as I am in the world, I am**.... *3752*
Joh 10:24 How l. dost thou make us to............ *2193*
Joh 14:9 **Have I been so l. time with you**. ... *5118*
Ac 8:11 of l. time he had betwitched them...... *2425*
Ac 14:3 L. time therefore abode they *2425*
Ac 14:28 they abode l. time with the........ *3756,3641*
Ac 20:9 as Paul was l. preaching, he....... *1909,4119*
Ac 20:11 and talked a l. while, even till........... *2425*
Ac 27:14 not l. after there arose against it........ *4183*
Ac 27:21 after l. abstinence Paul stood forth *4183*
Ro 1:11 I l. to see you, that I may impart....... *1971*
Ro 7:1 over a man as l. as he liveth?............ *5550*
Ro 7:2 law to her husband so l. as he liveth;........
Ro 8:36 thy sake we are killed all the day l.; ....
Ro 10:21 All day l. I have stretched forth my..........
1Co 7:39 as l. as her husband liveth;............... *5550*
1Co 11:14 if a man have l. hair, it is a shame *2863*
1Co 11:15 But if a woman have l. hair, it is a *2863*
1Co 13:4 Charity suffereth l., and is kind;......... *3114*
2Co 9:14 l. after you for the exceeding grace *1971*
Ga 4:1 the heir, as l. as he is a child,........... *5550*
Eph 6:3 thou mayest live l. on the earth. *2118*
Php 1:8 how greatly I l. after you all in.......... *1971*
1Ti 3:15 But if I tarry l., that thou mayest............
Heb 4:7 in David, To day, after so l. a time; ... *5118*
Jas 5:7 earth, and hath l. patience for it,........ *3114*
1Pe 3:6 daughters ye are, as l. as ye do well, ...
2Pe 1:13 as l. as I am in this tabernacle, to stir.......
2Pe 2:3 now of a l. time lingereth not, ...
Re 6:10 How l., O Lord, holy and true,........... *2193*

LONGED See also LONGEDST; PROLONGED.

2Sa 13:39 David l. to go forth unto Absalom: 3615
2Sa 23:15 And David l., and said, Oh that one 183
1Ch 11:17 And David l., and said, Oh that one 183
Ps 119:40 I have l. after thy precepts: 8373
Ps 119:131 for I l. for thy commandments. 2968
Ps 119:174 I have l. for thy salvation, O Lord;..... 8373
Php 2:26 For he l. after you all, and was *1971*
Php 4:1 brethren dearly beloved and l. for, ... *1973*

LONGEDST

Ge 31:30 sore l. after thy father's house, ... 3700

LONGER

Ex 2:3 when she could not l. hide him, ... 5750
Ex 9:28 let you go, and ye shall stay no l. 3254
Jg 2:14 and l. stand before their enemies. 5750
2Sa 20:5 he tarried l. than the set time which.........
2Ki 6:33 should I wait for the Lord any l.?....... 5750
Job 11:9 measure thereof is l. than the earth, ... 752
Jer 44:22 So that the Lord could no l. bear, ... 5750
Lu 16:2 **for thou mayest be no l. steward** ... *2089*
Ac 18:20 desired him to tarry l. time with........ *4119*
Ac 25:24 that he ought not to live any l.......... *3370*
Ro 6:2 dead to sin, live any l. therein?.......... *2089*
Ga 3:25 we are no l. under a schoolmaster....... *2089*
1Th 3:1 we could no l. forbear, we thought *3371*
1Th 3:5 this cause, when I could no l. forbear,. *3371*
1Ti 5:23 Drink no l. water, but use a little *3371*
1Pe 4:2 he no l. should live the rest of his...... *3371*
Re 10:6 that there should be time no l.; *2089*

LONGETH See also PROLONGETH.

Ge 34:8 soul of my son Shechem l. for your.... 2836
De 12:20 because thy soul l. to eat flesh;.......... 183
Ps 63:1 my flesh l. for thee in a dry and 3642
Ps 84:2 My soul l., yea, even fainteth for....... 3700

LONGING

De 28:32 fail with l. for them all the day long: ....
Ps 107:9 he satisfieth the l. soul,and filleth....... 8264
Ps 119:20 My soul breaketh for the l. that it...... 8375

LONGSUFFERING

Ex 34:6 merciful and gracious, l., and......... 750,639
Nu 14:18 Lord is l., and of great mercy, ... 750,639
Ps 86:15 l., and plenteous in mercy and....... 750,639
Jer 15:15 take me not away in thy l.:........... 750,639
Ro 2:4 goodness and forbearance and l.;........ *3115*
Ro 9:22 endured with much l. the vessels....... *3115*
2Co 6:6 by l., by kindness, by the Holy........... *3115*
Ga 5:22 of the Spirit is love, joy, peace, l., ... *3115*

Eph 4:2 with **l.**, forbearing one another in ... *3115*
Col 1:11 all patience and **l.** with joyfulness; ... *3115*
Col 3:12 humbleness of mind, meekness, **l.**; ... *3115*
1Ti 1:16 Christ might shew forth all **l.**, ... *3115*
2Ti 3:10 of life, purpose, faith, **l.**, charity, ... *3115*
2Ti 4:2 exhort with all **l.** and doctrine ... *3115*
1Pe 3:20 the **l.** of God waited in the days of ... *3115*
2Pe 3:9 but is **l.** to us-ward, not willing ... *3114*
2Pe 3:15 the **l.** of our Lord is salvation; ... *3115*

LONGWINGED
Eze 17:3 great eagle with great wings, **l.**, ... 750,83

LOOK See also LOOKED; LOOKEST; LOOKETH; LOOKING; LOOKS.
Ge 9:16 and I will **l.** upon it, that I may ... 7200
Ge 12:11 thou art a fair woman to **l.** upon: ... 4758
Ge 13:14 **l.** from the place where thou art ... 7200
Ge 15:5 **L.** now toward heaven, and tell the ... 5027
Ge 19:17 **l.** not behind thee, neither stay thou ... 5027
Ge 24:16 damsel was very fair to **l.** upon, ... 4758
Ge 26:7 because she was fair to **l.** upon ... 4758
Ge 40:7 Wherefore **l.** ye so sadly to day? ... 6440
Ge 41:33 **l.** out a man discreet and wise, ... 7200
Ge 42:1 Why do ye **l.** one upon another? ... 7200
Ex 3:6 for he was afraid to **l.** upon God. ... 5027
Ex 5:21 The Lord **l.** upon you, and judge; ... 7200
Ex 10:10 **l.** to it; for evil is before you ... 7200
Ex 25:20 their faces shall **l.** one to another; ...
Ex 25:40 **l.** that thou make them after their ... 7200
Ex 39:43 And Moses did **l.** upon all the work, ... 7200
Le 13:3 the priest shall **l.** on the plague in ... 7200
Le 13:3 and the priest shall **l.** on him, and ... 7200
Le 13:5 And the priest shall **l.** on him the ... 7200
Le 13:6 the priest shall **l.** on him again the ... 7200
Le 13:21 But if the priest shall **l.** on it, and, ... 7200
Le 13:25 Then the priest shall **l.** upon it: and, ... 7200
Le 13:26 But if the priest **l.** on it, and, behold, ... 7200
Le 13:27 And the priest shall **l.** upon him the ... 7200
Le 13:31 priest **l.** on the plague of the scall, ... 7200
Le 13:32 the priest shall **l.** on the plague: ... 7200
Le 13:34 day the priest shall **l.** on the scall: ... 7200
Le 13:36 Then the priest shall **l.** on him: and, ... 7200
Le 13:39 Then the priest shall **l.**: and, ... 7200
Le 13:43 Then the priest shall **l.** upon it: ... 7200
Le 13:50 the priest shall **l.** upon the plague, ... 7200
Le 13:51 And he shall **l.** on the plague on the ... 7200
Le 13:53 if the priest shall **l.**, and, behold, ... 7200
Le 13:55 And the priest shall **l.** on the plague, .. 7200
Le 13:56 And if the priest **l.**, and, behold, ... 7200
Le 14:3 the priest shall **l.**, and, behold, if ... 7200
Le 14:37 And he shall **l.** on the plague, and, ... 7200
Le 14:39 shall **l.**: and, behold, if the plague ... 7200
Le 14:44 Then the priest shall come and **l.**, ... 7200
Le 14:48 priest shall come in, and **l.** upon it, ... 7200
Nu 15:39 for a fringe, that ye may **l.** upon it, ... 7200
De 9:27 **l.** not unto the stubbornness of ... 6437
De 26:15 **L.** down from thy holy habitation, ... 8259
De 28:32 thine eyes shall **l.**, and fail with ... 7200
Jg 7:17 them, **L.** on me, and do likewise: ... 7200
1Sa 1:11 **l.** on the affliction of thine handmaid, ... 7200
1Sa 16:7 **L.** not on his countenance, or on ... 5027
1Sa 16:12 countenance, and goodly to **l.** to. ... 7210
1Sa 17:18 and **l.** how thy brethren fare, and ... 6485
2Sa 9:8 **l.** upon such a dead dog as I am? ... 6437
2Sa 11:2 was very beautiful to **l.** upon. ... 4758
2Sa 16:12 the Lord will **l.** on mine affliction, ... 7200
1Ki 18:43 Go up now, **l.** toward the sea ... 5027
2Ki 3:14 I would not **l.** toward thee, nor see ... 5027
2Ki 6:32 **l.**, when the messenger cometh, ... 7200
2Ki 9:2 thither, **l.** out there Jehu the son of ... 7200
2Ki 10:3 **L.** even out the best and meetest of ... 7200
2Ki 10:23 **l.** that there be here with you none ... 7200
2Ki 14:8 let us **l.** one another in the face ... 7200
1Ch 12:17 the God of our fathers **l.** thereon, ... 7200
2Ch 24:22 The Lord **l.** upon it, and require ... 7200
Es 1:11 for she was fair to **l.** on. ... 4758
Job 3:9 let it **l.** for light, but have none; ... 6960
Job 6:28 therefore be content, **l.** upon me; ... 6437
Job 20:21 shall no man **l.** for his goods. ... 2342
Job 35:5 **L.** unto the heavens, and see; and ... 5027
Job 40:12 **L.** on every one that is proud, and ... 7200
Ps 5:3 prayer unto thee, and will **l.** up ... 6822
Ps 22:17 bones: they **l.** and stare upon me ... 5027
Ps 25:18 **L.** upon mine affliction and my ... 7200
Ps 35:17 Lord, how long wilt thou **l.** on? ... 7200
Ps 40:12 me, so that I am not able to **l.** up; ... 7200
Ps 80:14 **l.** down from heaven, and behold, ... 5027
Ps 84:9 **l.** upon the face of thine anointed. ... 5027
Ps 85:11 righteousness shall **l.** down from ... 8259
Ps 101:5 hath an high **l.** and a proud heart ... 5869
Ps 119:132 **L.**...upon me, and be merciful ... 6437
Ps 123:2 eyes of servants **l.** unto the hand of ...
Pr 4:25 Let thine eyes **l.** right on, and let ... 5027
Pr 4:25 thine eyelids **l.** straight before thee ...
Pr 6:17 A proud **l.**, a lying tongue, and ... 5869
Pr 21:4 An high **l.**, and a proud heart, and ... 5869
Pr 23:31 **L.** not thou upon the wine when it ... 7200
Pr 27:23 flocks, and **l.** well to thy herds. ... 7896
Ec 12:3 those that **l.** out of the windows ... 7200
Ca 1:6 **L.** not upon me, because I am black, .. 7200
Ca 4:8 **l.** from the top of Amana, from the ... 7789
Ca 6:13 return, that we may **l.** upon thee. ... 2372
Isa 5:30 and if one **l.** unto the land, behold ... 5027
Isa 8:17 of Jacob, and I will **l.** for him ... 6960
Isa 8:21 and their God, and **l.** upward ... 6437
Isa 8:22 And they shall **l.** unto the earth; ... 5027
Isa 14:16 thee shall narrowly **l.** upon thee, ... 7688
Isa 17:7 day shall a man **l.** to his Maker, ... 8159
Isa 17:8 And he shall not **l.** to the altars, ... 8159
Isa 22:4 **L.** away from me; I will weep ... 8159
Isa 22:8 didst **l.** in that day to the armour ... 5027
Isa 31:1 they **l.** not unto the Holy One of ... 8159
Isa 33:20 **L.** upon Zion, the city of our ... 2372
Isa 42:18 and **l.**, ye blind, that ye may see ... 5027
Isa 45:22 **L.** unto me, and be ye saved, all ... 6437
Isa 51:1 **l.** unto the rock whence ye are ... 5027
Isa 51:2 **L.** unto Abraham your father, and ... 5027
Isa 51:6 and **l.** upon the earth beneath: ... 5027
Isa 56:11 they all **l.** to their own way, every ... 6437
Isa 59:11 **l.** for judgment, but there is none; ... 6960
Isa 63:15 **L.** down from heaven, and behold ... 5027
Isa 66:2 but to this man will I **l.**, even to him .. 5027
Isa 66:24 **l.** upon the carcases of the men ... 7200
Jer 13:16 while ye **l.** for light, he turn it into ... 6960
Jer 39:12 Take him, and **l.** well to him, ... 7760
Jer 40:4 and I will **l.** well unto thee: ... 7760
Jer 46:5 are fled apace, and **l.** not back: ... 6437
Jer 47:3 the fathers shall not **l.** back to their ... 6437
La 3:50 Till the Lord **l.** down, and behold ... 8259
Eze 23:15 heads, all of them princes to **l.** to, ... 4758
Eze 29:16 when they shall **l.** after them: ... 6437
Eze 43:17 his stairs shall **l.** toward the east ... 6437
Da 7:20 whose **l.** was more stout than his ... 2376
Ho 3:1 of Israel, who **l.** to other gods, ... 6437
Jon 2:4 **l.** again toward thy holy temple ... 5027
Mic 4:11 and let our eye **l.** upon Zion ... 2372
Mic 7:7 Therefore I will **l.** unto the Lord; ... 6822
Na 2:8 they cry; but none shall **l.** back ... 6437
Na 3:7 all they that **l.** upon thee shall flee ... 7200
Hab 1:13 evil, and canst not **l.** on iniquity: ... 5027
Hab 2:15 thou mayest **l.** on their nakedness! ... 5027
Zec 12:10 shall **l.** upon me whom they have ... 5027
Mt 11:3 come, or do we **l.** for another? ... *4328*
Mk 8:25 upon his eyes, and made him **l.** up; ... *308*
Lu 7:19, 20 come? or **l.** we for another? ... *4328*
Lu 9:38 I beseech thee, **l.** upon my son: ... *1914*
Lu 21:28 **then l. up, and lift up your heads:** .. *352*
Joh 4:35 **up your eyes, and l. on the fields;** .. *2300*
Joh 7:52 Search, and **l.**: for out of ... *1492*
Joh 19:37 shall **l.** on him whom they pierced. ... *3700*
Ac 3:4 upon him with John, said, **L.** on us. ... *991*
Ac 3:12 or why **l.** ye so earnestly on us, as ... *816*
Ac 6:3 **l.** ye out among you seven men of ... *1980*
Ac 18:15 names, and of your law, **l.** ye to it; ... *3700*
1Co 16:11 for I **l.** for him with the brethren. ... *1551*
2Co 3:13 could not stedfastly **l.** to the end of ... *816*
2Co 4:18 **l.** not at the things which are seen, ... *4648*
2Co 10:7 Do ye **l.** on things after the outward ... *991*
Php 2:4 **L.** not every man on his own ... *4648*
Php 3:20 whence also we **l.** for the Saviour, ... *553*
Heb 9:28 unto them that **l.** for him shall he ... *553*
1Pe 1:12 things the angels desire to **l.** into. ... *3879*
2Pe 3:13 **l.** for new heavens and a new ... *4328*
2Pe 3:14 seeing that ye **l.** for such things, ... *4328*
2Jo 8 **L.** to yourselves, that we lose not ... *991*
Re 4:3 was to **l.** upon like a jasper and ... *3706*
Re 5:3 open the book, neither to **l.** thereon. ... *991*
Re 5:4 read the book, neither to **l.** thereon. ... *991*

LOOKED
Ge 6:12 And God **l.** upon the earth, and, ... 7200
Ge 8:13 the covering of the ark, and **l.**, and, ... 7200
Ge 16:13 here **l.** after him that seeth me? ... 7200
Ge 18:2 he lift up his eyes and **l.**, and, lo, ... 7200
Ge 18:16 from thence, and **l.** toward Sodom: ... 8259
Ge 19:26 But his wife **l.** back from behind ... 5027
Ge 19:28 he **l.** toward Sodom and Gomorrah, ... 8259
Ge 22:13 Abraham lifted up his eyes, and **l.**, ... 7200
Ge 26:8 the Philistines **l.** out at a window, ... 8259
Ge 29:2 he **l.**, and behold a well in the field, ... 7200
Ge 29:32 Lord hath **l.** upon my affliction; ... 7200
Ge 33:1 Jacob lifted up his eyes, and **l.**, and, ... 7200
Ge 37:25 they lifted up the eyes and **l.**, and, ... 7200
Ge 39:23 The keeper of the prison **l.** not to ... 7200
Ge 40:6 in the morning, and **l.** upon them, ... 7200
Ex 2:11 brethren, and **l.** on their burdens: ... 7200
Ex 2:12 he **l.** this way and that way, and ... 6437
Ex 2:25 God **l.** upon the children of Israel, ... 7200
Ex 3:2 he **l.**, and, behold, the bush burned ... 7200
Ex 4:31 he had **l.** upon their affliction, ... 7200
Ex 14:24 in the morning watch the Lord **l.** ... 8259
Ex 16:10 that they **l.** toward the wilderness, ... 6437
Ex 33:8 **l.** after Moses, until he was gone ... 5027
Nu 12:10 and Aaron **l.** upon Miriam, and, ... 6437
Nu 16:42 **l.** toward the tabernacle of the ... 6437
Nu 17:9 they **l.**, and took every man his ... 7200
Nu 24:20 when he **l.** on Amalek, he took up ... 7200
Nu 24:21 he **l.** on the Kenites, and took up ... 7200
De 9:16 And I **l.**, and, behold, ye had sinned ... 7200
De 26:7 **l.** on our affliction, and our labour, ... 7200
Jos 5:13 that he lifted up his eyes and **l.**, ... 7200
Jos 8:20 And when the men of Ai **l.** behind ... 6437
Jg 5:28 of Sisera **l.** out at a window, ... 8259
Jg 6:14 the Lord **l.** upon him, and said, ... 6437
Jg 9:43 and laid wait in the field, and **l.**, ... 7200
Jg 13:19 and Manoah and his wife **l.** on. ... 7200
Jg 13:20 and Manoah and his wife **l.** on it, ... 7200
Jg 20:40 the Benjamites **l.** behind them, ... 6437
1Sa 6:19 had **l.** into the ark of the Lord, ... 7200
1Sa 9:16 I have **l.** upon my people, because ... 7200
1Sa 14:16 of Saul in Gibeah of Benjamin **l.**; ... 7200
1Sa 16:6 they were come, that he **l.** on Eliab, ... 7200
1Sa 17:42 And when the Philistine **l.** about, ... 5027
1Sa 24:8 And when Saul **l.** behind him, David ... 5027
2Sa 1:7 when he **l.** behind him, he saw me, ... 6437
2Sa 2:20 Then Abner **l.** behind him, and ... 6437
2Sa 6:16 daughter **l.** through a window, ... 8259
2Sa 13:34 watch lifted up his eyes, and **l.**, ... 7200
2Sa 18:24 wall, and lifted up his eyes, and **l.**, ... 7200
2Sa 22:42 They **l.**, but there was none to ... 8159
2Sa 24:20 And Araunah **l.**, and saw the king ... 8259
1Ki 18:43 And he went up, and **l.**, and said, ... 5027
1Ki 19:6 And he **l.**, and, behold, there was a ... 5027
2Ki 2:24 he turned back, and **l.** on them, ... 7200
2Ki 6:30 by upon the wall, and the people **l.**, ... 7200
2Ki 9:30 her head, and **l.** out at a window ... 8259
2Ki 9:32 **l.** out to him two or three eunuchs ... 8259
2Ki 11:14 And when she **l.**, behold, the king ... 7200
2Ki 14:11 of Judah **l.** one another in the face ... 7200
1Ch 21:21 Ornan, Ornan **l.** and saw David, ... 5027
2Ch 13:14 when Judah **l.** back, behold, the ... 6437
2Ch 20:24 they **l.** unto the multitude, and, ... 6437
2Ch 23:13 she **l.**, and, behold, the king stood ... 7200
2Ch 26:20 and all the priests, **l.** upon him, ... 6437
Ne 4:14 I **l.**, and rose up, and said unto the ... 7200
Es 2:15 sight of all them that **l.** upon her ... 6437
Job 6:19 troops of Tema **l.**, the companies ... 5027
Job 30:26 When I **l.** for good, then evil came ... 6960
Ps 14:2 Lord **l.** down from heaven upon ... 8259
Ps 34:5 They **l.** unto him, and were ... 5027
Ps 53:2 God **l.** down from heaven upon ... 8259
Ps 69:20 I **l.** for some to take pity, but there ... 6960
Ps 102:19 he hath **l.** down from the height of ... 8259
Ps 109:25 when they **l.** upon me, they shaked ... 7200
Ps 142:4 I **l.** on my right hand, and beheld, ... 5027
Pr 7:6 house I **l.** through my casement, ... 8259
Pr 24:32 it well: I **l.** upon it, and received ... 7200
Ec 2:11 Then I **l.** on all the works that my ... 6437
Ca 1:6 because the sun hath **l.** upon me: ... 7805
Isa 5:2 he **l.** that it should bring forth ... 6960
Isa 5:4 I **l.** that it should bring forth ... 6960
Isa 5:7 and he **l.** for judgment, but behold ... 6960
Isa 22:11 but ye have not **l.** unto the maker ... 5027
Isa 63:5 I **l.**, and there was none to help; ... 5027
Isa 64:3 terrible things which we **l.** not for, ... 6960
Jer 8:15 We **l.** for peace, but no good came; ... 6960
Jer 14:19 we **l.** for peace, and there is no ... 6960
La 2:16 this is the day that we **l.** for; we ... 6960
Eze 1:4 And I **l.**, and, behold, a whirlwind ... 7200
Eze 2:9 and when I **l.**, behold, an hand was ... 7200
Eze 8:7 when I **l.**, behold a hole in the wall ... 7200
Eze 10:1 I **l.**, and, behold, in the firmament ... 7200

Eze 10:9 when I **l.**, behold the four wheels by... 7200
Eze 10:11 the head **l.** they followed it; they 6437
Eze 16:8 I passed by thee, and **l.** upon thee, ... 7200
Eze 21:21 with images, he **l.** in the liver........... 7200
Eze 40:20 court that **l.** toward the north,........... 6440
Eze 44:4 I **l.**, and, behold, the glory of the....... 7200
Eze 46:19 priests, which **l.** toward the north: 6437
Da 1:13 let our countenances be **l.** upon 7200
Da 10:5 Then I lifted up mine eyes, and **l.**, ... 7200
Da 12:5 I Daniel **l.**, and, behold, there stood 7200
Ob 12 shouldest not have **l.** on the day 7200
Ob 13 not have **l.** on their affliction in 7200
Hag 1:9 Ye **l.** for much, and, lo, it came to 6437
Zec 2:1 lifted up mine eyes again, and **l.**,......... 7200
Zec 4:2 I have **l.**, and behold a candlestick...... 7200
Zec 5:1 and lifted up mine eyes, and **l.**,........... 7200
Zec 5:9 Then lifted I up mine eyes, and **l.**, ... 7200
Zec 6:1 and lifted up mine eyes, and **l.**,......... 7200
Mk 3:5 when he had **l.** round about on *4017*
Mk 3:34 he **l.** round about on them which........ *4017*
Mk 5:32 he **l.** round about to see her that *4017*
Mk 6:41 he **l.** up to heaven, and blessed, and *308*
Mk 8:24 he **l.** up, and said, I see men as trees, ..*308*
Mk 8:33 about and **l.** on his disciples, ... *1492*
Mk 9:8 when they had **l.** round about, they *4017*
Mk 10:23 And Jesus **l.** round about, and saith *4017*
Mk 11:11 when he had **l.** round about upon *4017*
Mk 14:67 warming himself, she **l.** upon him, ... *1689*
Mk 16:4 And when they **l.**, they saw that the *308*
Lu 1:25 in the days wherein he **l.** on me, ... *1896*
Lu 2:38 to all them that **l.** for redemption *4327*
Lu 10:32 **came and l. on him, and passed** *1492*
Lu 19:5 to the place, he **l.** up, and saw him, ... *308*
Lu 21:1 he **l.** up, and saw the rich men............ *308*
Lu 22:56 the fire, and earnestly **l.** upon him, ... *816*
Lu 22:61 Lord turned, and **l.** upon Peter. *1689*
Joh 13:22 the disciples **l.** one on another, ... *991*
Joh 20:11 down, and **l.** into the sepulchre...............
Ac 1:10 they **l.** stedfastly toward heaven *816*
Ac 7:55 **l.** up stedfastly into heaven, and *816*
Ac 10:4 when he **l.** on him, he was afraid, ... *816*
Ac 22:13 the same hour I **l.** up upon him. *308*
Ac 28:6 they **l.** when he should have.............. *4328*
Ac 28:6 but after they had **l.** a great while, ... *4328*
Heb 11:10 **l.** for a city which hath foundations, ... *1551*
1Jo 1:1 which we have **l.** upon, and our *2300*
Re 4:1 After this I **l.**, and, behold, door *1492*
Re 6:8 And I **l.**, and behold a pale horse: *1492*
Re 14:1 I **l.**, and, lo, a Lamb stood on the *1492*
Re 14:14 I **l.**, and behold a white cloud, and...... *1492*
Re 15:5 And after that I **l.**, and, behold, the.... *1492*

LOOKEST
Job 13:27 and **l.** narrowly unto all my paths; 8104
Hab 1:13 wherefore **l.** thou upon them that....... 5027

LOOKETH
Le 13:12 wheresoever the priest **l.**; 4758,5869
Nu 21:8 when he **l.** upon it, shall live. 7200
Nu 21:20 Pisgah, which **l.** toward Jeshimon. 8259
Nu 23:28 of Peor, that **l.** toward Jeshimon. 8259
Jos 15:2 from the bay that **l.** southward: 6437
1Sa 13:18 the border that **l.** to the valley of....... 8259
1Sa 16:7 man **l.** on the outward appearance, ... 7200
1Sa 16:7 but the Lord **l.** on the heart............. 7200
Job 7:2 an hireling **l.** for the reward of his...... 6960
Job 28:24 For he **l.** to the ends of the earth, ... 5027
Job 33:27 He **l.** upon men, and if any say,......... 7789
Ps 33:13 The Lord **l.** from heaven; he............ 5027
Ps 33:14 he **l.** upon all the inhabitants of.......... 7688
Ps 104:32 He **l.** on the earth, and it trembleth:... 5027
Pr 14:15 prudent man **l.** well to his going. 995
Pr 31:27 She **l.** well to the ways of her 6822
Ca 2:9 wall, he **l.** forth at the windows, ... 7688
Ca 6:10 is she that **l.** forth as the morning, ... 8259
Ca 7:4 which **l.** toward Damascus. 6822
Isa 28:4 when he that **l.** upon it seeth, ... 7200
Eze 8:3 gate that **l.** toward the north; 6437
Eze 11:1 Lord's house, which **l.** eastward:........ 6437
Eze 40:6 the gate which **l.** toward the east,....... 6440
Eze 40:22 of the gate that **l.** toward the east;...... 6440
Eze 43:1 the gate that **l.** toward the east: 6437
Eze 44:1 sanctuary which **l.** toward the east; 6437
Eze 46:1 inner court that **l.** toward the east...... 6437
Eze 46:12 the gate that **l.** toward the east, ... 6437
Eze 47:2 gate by the way that **l.** eastward;....... 6437
Mt 5:28 **l. on a woman to lust after her**....... *991*
Mt 24:50 **in a day when he l. not for him,** ... *4328*
Lu 12:46 **in a day when he l. not for him,** ... *4328*
Jas 1:25 **l.** into the perfect law of liberty, ... *3879*

LOOKING See also LOOKINGGLASSES.
Jos 15:7 so northward, **l.** toward Gilgal, ... 6437
1Ki 7:25 oxen, three **l.** toward the north, ... 6437
1Ki 7:25 and three **l.** toward the west,............ 6437
1Ki 7:25 and three **l.** toward the south,........... 6437
1Ki 7:25 and three **l.** toward the east:............. 6437
1Ch 15:29 **l.** out at a window saw king David...... 8259
2Ch 4:4 oxen three **l.** toward the north, ... 6437
2Ch 4:4 and three **l.** toward the west............. 6437
2Ch 4:4 and three **l.** toward the south,........... 6437
2Ch 4:4 and three **l.** toward the east:............. 6437
Job 37:18 strong, and as a molten **l.** glass? 7209
Isa 38:14 dove: mine eyes fail with **l.** upward: ....
Mt 14:19 and **l.** up to heaven, he blessed, and *308*
Mk 7:34 And **l.** up to heaven, he sighed, and..... *308*
Mk 10:27 Jesus **l.** upon them saith, **With men** .. *1689*
Mk 15:40 were also women **l.** on afar off: *2334*
Lu 6:10 **l.** round about upon them all, he *4017*
Lu 9:16 **l.** up to heaven, he blessed them,......... *308*
Lu 9:62 **his hand to the plough, and l. back,** .*991*
Lu 21:26 **and for l. after those things which**.*4329*
Joh 1:36 **l.** upon Jesus as he walked, he *1689*
Joh 20:5 And he stooping down, and **l.** in, saw.........
Ac 6:15 **l.** stedfastly on him, saw his face as *816*
Ac 23:21 ready, **l.** for a promise from thee. *4327*
Tit 2:13 **L.** for that blessed hope, and the *4327*
Heb 10:27 a certain fearful **l.** for of judgment *1561*
Heb 12:2 **L.** unto Jesus the author and *872*
Heb 12:15 **L.** diligently lest any man fail of......... *1983*
2Pe 3:12 **L.** for and hasting unto the coming..... *4328*
Jude 21 **l.** for the mercy of our Lord Jesus...... *4327*

LOOKING-GLASS See LOOKING and GLASS; also LOOKING GLASSES.

LOOKINGGLASSES
Ex 38:8 the **l.** of the women assembling, ... 4759

LOOKS
Ps 18:27 but wilt bring down high **l.**................ 5869
Isa 2:11 lofty **l.** of man shall be humbled, ... 5869
Isa 10:12 Assyria, and the glory of his high **l.**.. ... 5869
Eze 2:6 words, nor be dismayed at their **l.**,..... 6440
Eze 3:9 not, neither be dismayed at their **l.**,..... 6440

LOOPS
Ex 26:4 make **l.** of blue upon the edge of........ 3924
Ex 26:5 Fifty **l.** shalt thou make in the one...... 3924
Ex 26:5 fifty **l.** shalt thou make in the edge 3924
Ex 26:5 the **l.** may take hold one of another. 3924
Ex 26:10 make fifty **l.** on the edge of the one.... 3924
Ex 26:10 and fifty **l.** in the edge of the curtain... 3924
Ex 26:11 and put the taches into the **l.**, and...... 3924
Ex 36:11 made **l.** of blue on the edge of one..... 3924
Ex 36:12 Fifty **l.** made he in one curtain, and..... 3924
Ex 36:12 fifty **l.** made he in the edge of the...... 3924
Ex 36:12 the **l.** held one curtain to another. 3924
Ex 36:17 fifty **l.** upon the uttermost edge of...... 3924
Ex 36:17 fifty **l.** made he upon the edge of the .. 3924

LOOSE See also LOOSED; LOOSETH; LOOSING; UNLOOSE.
Ge 49:21 Naphtali is a hind let **l.**: he giveth....... 7971
Le 14:7 the living bird **l.** into the open field. 7971
De 25:9 and **l.** his shoe from off his foot, ... 2502
Jos 5:15 **L.** thy shoe from off thy foot; for........ 5394
Job 6:9 that he would let **l.** his hand, and 5425
Job 30:11 also let **l.** the bridle before me. 7971
Job 38:31 Pleiades, or **l.** the bands of Orion? 6605
Ps 102:20 **l.** those that are appointed to death; ... 6605
Isa 20:2 **l.** the sackcloth from off thy loins, ... 6605
Isa 45:1 I will **l.** the loins of kings, to open...... 6605
Isa 52:2 **l.** thyself from the bands of thy neck,.. 6605
Isa 58:6 to **l.** the bands of wickedness, to 6605
Jer 40:4 I **l.** thee this day from the chains 6605
Da 3:25 Lo, I see four men **l.**, walking in......... 8271
Mt 16:19 **whatsoever thou shalt l. on earth** .. *3089*
Mt 18:18 **whatsoever ye shall l. on earth**...... *3089*
Mt 21:2 **l. them, and bring them unto me**.... *3089*
Mk 11:2 **man sat; l. him, and bring him**. *3089*
Mk 11:4 two ways met; and they **l.** him. *3089*
Lu 13:15 **on the sabbath l. his ox or his ass**..*3089*
Lu 19:30 **sat: l. him, and bring him thither**. .*3089*
Lu 19:31 **man ask you, Why do ye l. him** *3089*
Lu 19:33 said unto them, Why **l.** ye the colt?.... *3089*
Joh 11:44 unto them, **L. him, and let him go**.. *3089*
Ac 13:25 of his feet I am not worthy to **l.** *3089*
Ac 24:26 him of Paul, that he might **l.** him:....... *3089*
Re 5:2,5 and to **l.** the seven seals thereof. *3089*
Re 9:14 **L.** the four angels which are bound..... *3089*

LOOSED
Ex 28:28 the breastplate be not **l.** from the....... 2118
Ex 39:21 the breastplate might not be **l.** from.... 2118
De 25:10 house of him that hath his shoe **l.** 2502
Jg 15:14 his bands **l.** from off his hands. 4549
Job 30:11 Because he hath **l.** my cord, and........ 6605
Job 39:5 hath **l.** the bands of the wild ass? 6605
Ps 105:20 The king sent and **l.** him; even.......... 5425
Ps 116:16 handmaid: thou hast **l.** my bonds. 6605
Ec 12:6 Or ever the silver cord be **l.**, or the... 7368
Isa 5:27 shall the girdle of their loins be **l.**,...... 6605
Isa 33:23 Thy tacklings are **l.**; they could.......... 5203
Isa 51:14 exile hasteneth that he may be **l.**, ... 6605
Da 5:6 that the joints of his loins were **l.**,...... 8271
Mt 16:19 **loose on earth shall be l. in**............ *3089*
Mt 18:18 **on earth shall be l. in heaven** *3089*
Mt 18:27 **with compassion, and l. him, and**.. *630*
Mk 7:35 and the string of his tongue was **l.**, ... *3089*
Lu 1:64 and his tongue **l.**, and he spake, and.........
Lu 13:12 **thou art l. from thine infirmity**..... *630*
Lu 13:16 **l. from this bond on the sabbath**.. *3089*
Ac 2:24 up, having **l.** the pains of death:........ *3089*
Ac 13:13 and his company **l.** from Paphos, ... *321*
Ac 16:26 and every one's bands were **l.** *447*
Ac 22:30 Jews, he **l.** him from his bands, ... *3089*
Ac 27:21 me, and not have **l.** from Crete, ... *321*
Ac 27:40 **l.** the rudder bands, and hoisted up..... *447*
Ro 7:2 is **l.** from the law of her husband. *2673*
1Co 7:27 unto a wife? seek not to be **l.** *3089*
1Co 7:27 Art thou **l.** from a wife? seek not..... *3080*
Re 9:15 And the four angels were **l.**, which.... *3089*
Re 20:3 that he must be **l.** a little season........ 3089
Re 20:7 Satan shall be **l.** out of his prison, ... 3089

LOOSETH
Job 12:18 He **l.** the bond of kings, and............. 6605
Ps 146:7 hungry. The Lord **l.** the prisoners: 5425

LOOSING
Mk 11:5 unto them, What do ye, **l.** the colt?.... *3089*
Lu 19:33 And as they were **l.** the colt, the....... *3089*
Ac 16:11 Therefore **l.** from Troas, we came....... *321*
Ac 27:13 **l.** thence, they sailed close by............ *142*

LOP
Isa 10:33 shall **l.** the bough with terror:........... 5586

LORD See also LORD'S; LORDS.
Ge 2:4 that the **L.** God made the earth......... 3068
Ge 2:5 **L.** God had not caused it to rain........ 3068
Ge 2:7 **L.** God formed man of the dust 3068
Ge 2:8 And the **L.** God planted a garden....... 3068
Ge 2:9 made the **L.** God to grow every 3068
Ge 2:15 the **L.** God took the man, and put...... 3068
Ge 2:16 the **L.** God commanded the man, ... 3068
Ge 2:18 **L.** God said, It is not good that 3068
Ge 2:19 the **L.** God formed every beast 3068
Ge 2:21 **L.** God caused a deep sleep to fall 3068
Ge 2:22 rib, which the **L.** God had taken 3068
Ge 3:1 field which the **L.** God had made......... 3068
Ge 3:8 heard the voice of the **L.** God 3068
Ge 3:8 presence of the **L.** God amongst 3068
Ge 3:9 **L.** God called unto Adam, and 3068
Ge 3:13 the **L.** God said unto the woman,........ 3068
Ge 3:14 the **L.** God said unto the serpent, ... 3068
Ge 3:21 the **L.** God made coats of skins, ... 3068
Ge 3:22 the **L.** God said, Behold, the man 3068
Ge 3:23 **L.** God sent him forth from the 3068
Ge 4:1 I have gotten a man from the **L.**......... 3068
Ge 4:3 ground an offering unto the **L.**........... 3068
Ge 4:4 **L.** had respect unto Abel and to 3068
Ge 4:6 **L.** said unto Cain, Why art thou......... 3068
Ge 4:9 **L.** said unto Cain, Where is Abel?...... 3068
Ge 4:13 And Cain said unto the **L.**, My 3068
Ge 4:15 the **L.** said unto him, Therefore......... 3068
Ge 4:15 **L.** set a mark upon Cain, lest any 3068
Ge 4:16 out from the presence of the **L.**......... 3068
Ge 4:26 to call upon the name of the **L.** 3068
Ge 5:29 ground which the **L.** hath cursed......... 3068
Ge 6:3 the **L.** said, My Spirit shall not.......... 3068
Ge 6:6 the **L.** that he had made man on......... 3068
Ge 6:7 the **L.** said, I will destroy man 3068
Ge 6:8 found grace in the eyes of the **L.**....... 3068
Ge 7:1 And the **L.** said unto Noah, Come........ 3068
Ge 7:5 all that the **L.** commanded him. 3068
Ge 7:16 him: and the **L.** shut him in. 3068

Ge 8:20 builded an altar unto the **L.**;............ 3068
Ge 8:21 the **L.** smelled a sweet savour;......... 3068
Ge 8:21 the **L.** said in his heart, I will not....... 3068
Ge 9:26 Blessed be the **L.** God of Shem;........ 3068
Ge 10:9 a mighty hunter before the **L.**.......... 3068
Ge 10:9 the mighty hunter before the **L.**.......... 3068
Ge 11:5 **L.** came down to see the city and...... 3068
Ge 11:6 the **L.** said, Behold, the people.......... 3068
Ge 11:8 **L.** scattered them abroad from.......... 3068
Ge 11:9 the **L.** did there confound the........... 3068
Ge 11:9 did the **L.** scatter them abroad.......... 3068
Ge 12:1 Now the **L.** had said unto Abram,...... 3068
Ge 12:4 as the **L.** had spoken unto him;......... 3068
Ge 12:7 the **L.** appeared unto Abram, and........ 3068
Ge 12:7 builded he an altar unto the **L.**,......... 3068
Ge 12:8 he builded an altar unto the **L.**,......... 3068
Ge 12:8 called upon the name of the **L.**.......... 3068
Ge 12:17 the **L.** plagued Pharaoh and his.......... 3068
Ge 13:4 called on the name of the **L.**............ 3068
Ge 13:10 before the **L.** destroyed Sodom......... 3068
Ge 13:10 even as the garden of the **L.**, like...... 3068
Ge 13:13 sinners before the **L.** exceedingly........ 3068
Ge 13:14 the **L.** said unto Abram, after that...... 3068
Ge 13:18 built there an altar unto the **L.**......... 3068
Ge 14:22 lift up mine hand unto the **L.**,........... 3068
Ge 15:1 word of the **L.** came unto Abram....... 3068
Ge 15:2 said, **L.** God, what wilt thou give........ 136
Ge 15:4 the word of the **L.** came unto him,...... 3068
Ge 15:6 And he believed in the **L.**; and he...... 3068
Ge 15:7 **L.** that brought thee out of Ur of....... 3068
Ge 15:8 **L.** God, whereby shall I know that....... 136
Ge 15:18 **L.** made a covenant with Abram,....... 3068
Ge 16:2 the **L.** hath restrained me from.......... 3068
Ge 16:5 **L.** judge between me and thee.......... 3068
Ge 16:7 the angel of the **L.** found her by........ 3068
Ge 16:9, 10,11 angel of the **L.** said unto.......... 3068
Ge 16:11 because the **L.** hath heard thy........... 3068
Ge 16:13 And she called the name of the **L.**....... 3068
Ge 17:1 **L.** appeared to Abram, and said......... 3068
Ge 18:1 the **L.** appeared unto him in the......... 3068
Ge 18:3 My **L.**, if now I have found favour....... 136
Ge 18:12 have pleasure, my **l.** being old also?..... 113
Ge 18:13 And the **L.** said unto Abraham,........... 3068
Ge 18:14 Is any thing too hard for the **L.**?........ 3068
Ge 18:17 And the **L.** said, Shall I hide from...... 3068
Ge 18:19 they shall keep the way of the **L.**,...... 3068
Ge 18:19 the **L.** may bring upon Abraham......... 3068
Ge 18:20 the **L.** said, Because the cry of......... 3068
Ge 18:22 Abraham stood yet before the **L.**....... 3068
Ge 18:26 the **L.** said, If I find in Sodom.......... 3068
Ge 18:27 upon me to speak unto the **L.**,............ 136
Ge 18:30 Oh let not the **L.** be angry, and I........ 136
Ge 18:31 upon me to speak unto the **L.**:............ 136
Ge 18:32 Oh let not the **L.** be angry, and I........ 136
Ge 18:33 the **L.** went his way, as soon as he..... 3068
Ge 19:13 great before the face of the **L.**;......... 3068
Ge 19:13 the **L.** hath sent us to destroy it........ 3068
Ge 19:14 for the **L.** will destroy this city.......... 3068
Ge 19:16 the **L.** being merciful unto him:.......... 3068
Ge 19:18 unto them, Oh, not so, my **L.**............ 113
Ge 19:24 **L.** rained upon Sodom and upon......... 3068
Ge 19:24 brimstone and fire from the **L.**.......... 3068
Ge 19:27 where he stood before the **L.**............ 3068
Ge 20:4 **L.**, wilt thou slay also a righteous........ 136
Ge 20:18 the **L.** had fast closed up all the.......... 3068
Ge 21:1 **L.** visited Sarah as he had said,......... 3068
Ge 21:1 the **L.** did unto Sarah as he had......... 3068
Ge 21:33 there on the name of the **L.**, the....... 3068
Ge 22:11 angel of the **L.** called unto him......... 3068
Ge 22:14 mount of the **L.** it shall be seen......... 3068
Ge 22:15 the angel of the **L.** called unto.......... 3068
Ge 22:16 myself have I sworn, saith the **L.**,...... 3068
Ge 23:6 Hear us, my **l.**: thou art a mighty........ 113
Ge 23:11 Nay, my **l.**, hear me: the field give....... 113
Ge 23:15 My **l.**, hearken unto me: the land is..... 113
Ge 24:1 **L.** had blessed Abraham in all........... 3068
Ge 24:3 I will make thee swear by the **L.**,...... 3068
Ge 24:7 The **L.** God of heaven, which took..... 3068
Ge 24:12 O **L.** God of my master Abraham,...... 3068
Ge 24:18 And she said, Drink, my **l.**: and......... 113
Ge 24:21 wit whether the **L.** had made his....... 3068
Ge 24:26 his head, and worshipped the **L.**........ 3068
Ge 24:27 **L.** God of my master Abraham,.......... 3068
Ge 24:27 the **L.** led me to the house of my...... 3068
Ge 24:31 Come in, thou blessed of the **L.**;....... 3068
Ge 24:35 the **L.** hath blessed my master......... 3068
Ge 24:40 The **L.**, before whom I walk, will....... 3068
Ge 24:42 O **L.** God of my master Abraham,...... 3068
Ge 24:44 be the woman whom the **L.** hath....... 3068
Ge 24:48 my head, and worshipped the **L.**,....... 3068
Ge 24:48 **L.** God of my master Abraham,......... 3068
Ge 24:50 thing proceedeth from the **L.**:.......... 3068
Ge 24:51 son's wife, as the **L.** hath spoken....... 3068
Ge 24:52 he worshipped the **L.**, bowing.......... 3068
Ge 24:56 the **L.** hath prospered my way;......... 3068
Ge 25:21 And Isaac intreated the **L.** for his....... 3068
Ge 25:21 the **L.** was intreated of him, and........ 3068
Ge 25:22 And she went to enquire of the **L.**..... 3068
Ge 25:23 the **L.** said unto her, Two nations...... 3068
Ge 26:2 the **L.** appeared unto him, and.......... 3068
Ge 26:12 and the **L.** blessed him................... 3068
Ge 26:22 the **L.** hath made room for us,.......... 3068
Ge 26:24 And the **L.** appeared unto him the...... 3068
Ge 26:25 called upon the name of the **L.**,......... 3068
Ge 26:28 certainly that the **L.** was with........... 3068
Ge 26:29 art now the blessed of the **L.**........... 3068
Ge 27:7 bless thee before the **L.** before........ 3068
Ge 27:20 the **L.** thy God brought it to me........ 3068
Ge 27:27 a field which the **L.** hath blessed:....... 3068
Ge 27:29 be **l.** over thy brethren, and let......... 1376
Ge 27:37 I have made him thy **l.**, and all his..... 1376
Ge 28:13 behold, the **L.** stood above it, and...... 3068
Ge 28:13 I am the **L.** God of Abraham thy........ 3068
Ge 28:16 Surely the **L.** is in this place; and....... 3068
Ge 28:21 then shall the **L.** be my God:........... 3068
Ge 29:31 the **L.** saw that Leah was hated,......... 3068
Ge 29:32 the **L.** hath looked upon my............. 3068
Ge 29:33 **L.** hath heard that I was hated,......... 3068
Ge 29:35 she said, Now will I praise the **L.**...... 3068
Ge 30:24 **L.** shall add to me another son.......... 3068
Ge 30:27 **L.** hath blessed me for thy sake......... 3068
Ge 30:30 the **L.** hath blessed thee since my...... 3068
Ge 31:3 the **L.** said unto Jacob, Return.......... 3068
Ge 31:35 Let it not displease my **l.** that I.......... 113
Ge 31:49 The **L.** watch between me and.......... 3068
Ge 32:4 shall ye speak unto my **l.** Esau;........... 113
Ge 32:5 I have sent to tell my **l.**, that I may..... 113
Ge 32:9 the **L.** which saidst unto me,............ 3068
Ge 32:18 is a present sent unto my **l.** Esau:....... 113
Ge 33:8 to find grace in the sight of my **l.**........ 113
Ge 33:13 My **l.** knoweth that the children are..... 113
Ge 33:14 Let my **l.**, I pray thee, pass over........ 113
Ge 33:14 until I come unto my **l.** unto Seir......... 113
Ge 33:15 me find grace in the sight of my **l.**....... 113
Ge 38:7 was wicked in the sight of the **L.**;...... 3068
Ge 38:7 and the **L.** slew him....................... 3068
Ge 38:10 which he did displeased the **L.**:.......... 3068
Ge 39:2 the **L.** was with Joseph, and he......... 3068
Ge 39:3 saw that the **L.** was with him,.......... 3068
Ge 39:3 that the **L.** made all that he did to...... 3068
Ge 39:5 that the **L.** blessed the Egyptian's...... 3068
Ge 39:5 blessing of the **L.** was upon all.......... 3068
Ge 39:16 by her, until his **l.** came home............ 113
Ge 39:21 But the **L.** was with Joseph, and......... 3068
Ge 39:23 because the **L.** was with him, and...... 3068
Ge 39:23 he did, the **L.** made it to prosper....... 3068
Ge 40:1 offended their **l.** the king of Egypt....... 113
Ge 42:10 And they said unto him, Nay, my **l.**,.... 113
Ge 42:30 The man, who is the **l.** of the land,...... 113
Ge 42:33 the **l.** of the country, said unto us,....... 113
Ge 44:5 not this it in which my **l.** drinketh,....... 113
Ge 44:7 Wherefore saith my **l.** these words?..... 113
Ge 44:16 What shall we say unto my **l.**?............ 113
Ge 44:18 Oh my **l.**, let thy servant, I pray......... 113
Ge 44:19 My **l.** asked his servants, saying,........ 113
Ge 44:20 And we said unto my **l.**, We have a..... 113
Ge 44:22 we said unto my **l.**, The lad cannot...... 113
Ge 44:24 we told him the words of my **l.**.......... 113
Ge 44:33 of the lad a bondman to my **l.**;........... 113
Ge 45:8 and **l.** of all his house, and a ruler....... 113
Ge 45:9 God hath made me **l.** of all Egypt:....... 113
Ge 47:18 We will not hide it from my **l.**, how..... 113
Ge 47:18 my **l.** also hath our herds of cattle;...... 113
Ge 47:18 not ought left in the sight of my **l.**,...... 113
Ge 47:25 us find grace in the sight of my **l.**,....... 113
Ge 49:18 waited for thy salvation, O **L.**........... 3068
Ex 3:2 the angel of the **L.** appeared unto...... 3068
Ex 3:4 **L.** saw that he turned aside to see,.... 3068
Ex 3:7 the **L.** said, I have surely seen.......... 3068
Ex 3:15, 16 The **L.** God of your fathers,.......... 3068
Ex 3:18 The **L.** God of the Hebrews hath....... 3068
Ex 3:18 may sacrifice to the **L.** our God......... 3068
Ex 4:1 **L.** hath not appeared unto thee.......... 3068
Ex 4:2 And the **L.** said unto him, What is...... 3068
Ex 4:4 the **L.** said unto Moses, Put forth....... 3068
Ex 4:5 they may believe in the **L.** God of...... 3068
Ex 4:6 **L.** said furthermore unto him,........... 3068
Ex 4:10 And Moses said unto the **L.**,............. 3068
Ex 4:10 O my **L.**, I am not eloquent,............. 136
Ex 4:11 the **L.** said unto him, Who hath......... 3068
Ex 4:11 or the blind? have not I the **L.**?......... 3068
Ex 4:13 And he said, O my **L.**, send, I pray..... 136
Ex 4:14 the anger of the **L.** was kindled......... 3068
Ex 4:19 the **L.** said unto Moses in Midian,...... 3068
Ex 4:21 **L.** said unto Moses, When thou......... 3068
Ex 4:22 Thus saith the **L.**, Israel is my.......... 3068
Ex 4:24 the **L.** met him, and sought to.......... 3068
Ex 4:27 the **L.** said to Aaron, Go into the....... 3068
Ex 4:28 told Aaron all the words of the **L.**...... 3068
Ex 4:30 the **L.** had spoken unto Moses,......... 3068
Ex 4:31 heard that the **L.** had visited the........ 3068
Ex 5:1 Thus saith the **L.** God of Israel,........ 3068
Ex 5:2 Pharaoh said, Who is the **L.**, that....... 3068
Ex 5:2 I know not the **L.**, neither will I........ 3068
Ex 5:3 and sacrifice unto the **L.** our God;...... 3068
Ex 5:17 us go and do sacrifice to the **L.**......... 3068
Ex 5:21 The **L.** look upon you, and judge;...... 3068
Ex 5:22 And Moses returned unto the **L.**,........ 3068
Ex 5:22 **L.**, wherefore hast thou so evil........... 136
Ex 6:1 Then the **L.** said unto Moses, Now.... 3068
Ex 6:2 and said unto him, I am the **L.**:......... 3068
Ex 6:6 I am the **L.**, and I will bring you........ 3068
Ex 6:7 know that I am the **L.** your God,........ 3068
Ex 6:8 you for an heritage: I am the **L.**........ 3068
Ex 6:10 the **L.** spake unto Moses, saying,...... 3068
Ex 6:12 Moses spake before the **L.**, saying,.... 3068
Ex 6:13 **L.** spake unto Moses and Aaron,....... 3068
Ex 6:26 and Moses, to whom the **L.** said,....... 3068
Ex 6:28 **L.** spake unto Moses in the land........ 3068
Ex 6:29 the **L.** spake unto Moses, saying,...... 3068
Ex 6:29 I am the **L.**: speak thou unto............ 3068
Ex 6:30 Moses said before the **L.**, Behold,..... 3068
Ex 7:1 And the **L.** said unto Moses, See, I.... 3068
Ex 7:5 shall know that I am the **L.**, when...... 3068
Ex 7:6 did as the **L.** commanded them,......... 3068
Ex 7:8 the **L.** spake unto Moses and unto..... 3068
Ex 7:10 did so as the **L.** had commanded:....... 3068
Ex 7:13 not unto them; as the **L.** had said...... 3068
Ex 7:14 the **L.** said unto Moses, Pharaoh's..... 3068
Ex 7:16 The **L.** God of the Hebrews hath....... 3068
Ex 7:17 Thus saith the **L.**, In this thou.......... 3068
Ex 7:17 thou shalt know that I am the **L.**........ 3068
Ex 7:19 And the **L.** spake unto Moses, Say..... 3068
Ex 7:20 did so, as the **L.** commanded;........... 3068
Ex 7:22 unto them; as the **L.** had said........... 3068
Ex 7:25 that the **L.** had smitten the river........ 3068
Ex 8:1 the **L.** spake unto Moses, Go unto..... 3068
Ex 8:1 Thus saith the **L.**, Let my people....... 3068
Ex 8:5 And the **L.** spake unto Moses, Say..... 3068
Ex 8:8 Intreat the **L.**, that he may take........ 3068
Ex 8:8 they may do sacrifice unto the **L.**........ 3068
Ex 8:10 is none like unto the **L.** our God........ 3068
Ex 8:12 Moses cried unto the **L.** because....... 3068
Ex 8:13 **L.** did according to the word of......... 3068
Ex 8:15 not unto them; as the **L.** had said...... 3068
Ex 8:16 the **L.** said unto Moses, Say unto...... 3068
Ex 8:19 not unto them; as the **L.** had said...... 3068
Ex 8:20 the **L.** said unto Moses, Rise up........ 3068
Ex 8:20 Thus saith the **L.**, Let my people....... 3068
Ex 8:22 I am the **L.** in the midst of the......... 3068
Ex 8:24 the **L.** did so; and there came a......... 3068
Ex 8:26 the Egyptians to the **L.** our God:....... 3068
Ex 8:27 and sacrifice to the **L.** our God,......... 3068
Ex 8:28 may sacrifice to the **L.** your God........ 3068
Ex 8:29 intreat the **L.** that the swarms of....... 3068
Ex 8:29 people go to sacrifice to the **L.**.......... 3068
Ex 8:30 Pharaoh, and intreated the **L.**............ 3068
Ex 8:31 **L.** did according to the word of......... 3068
Ex 9:1 the **L.** said unto Moses, Go in........... 3068
Ex 9:1 saith the **L.** God of the Hebrews,....... 3068
Ex 9:3 hand of the **L.** is upon thy cattle........ 3068
Ex 9:4 **L.** shall sever between the cattle....... 3068
Ex 9:5 And the **L.** appointed a set time,....... 3068
Ex 9:5 To morrow the **L.** shall do this.......... 3068
Ex 9:6 And the **L.** did that thing on the........ 3068
Ex 9:8 the **L.** said unto Moses and unto........ 3068
Ex 9:12 **L.** hardened the heart of Pharaoh,...... 3068
Ex 9:12 as the **L.** had spoken unto Moses....... 3068

Ex 9:13 the **L.** said unto Moses, Rise up ... 3068
Ex 9:13 saith the **L.** God of the Hebrews, ... 3068
Ex 9:20 He that feared the word of the **L.** ... 3068
Ex 9:21 regarded not the word of the **L.** ... 3068
Ex 9:22 the **L.** said unto Moses, Stretch ... 3068
Ex 9:23 and the **L.** sent thunder and hail, ... 3068
Ex 9:23 the **L.** rained hail upon the land ... 3068
Ex 9:27 the **L.** is righteous, and I and my ... 3068
Ex 9:28 Intreat the **L.** (for it is enough) ... 3068
Ex 9:29 abroad my hands unto the **L.**; ... 3068
Ex 9:30 ye will not yet fear the **L.** God ... 3068
Ex 9:33 abroad his hands unto the **L.**: ... 3068
Ex 9:35 as the **L.** had spoken by Moses. ... 3068
Ex 10:1 And the **L.** said unto Moses, Go in ... 3068
Ex 10:2 may know how that I am the **L.** ... 3068
Ex 10:3 saith the **L.** God of the Hebrews, ... 3068
Ex 10:7 they may serve the **L.** their God: ... 3068
Ex 10:8 them, Go, serve the **L.** your God: ... 3068
Ex 10:9 we must hold a feast unto the **L.** ... 3068
Ex 10:10 Let the **L.** be so with you, as I ... 3068
Ex 10:11 that are men, and serve the **L.**; ... 3068
Ex 10:12 the **L.** said unto Moses, Stretch ... 3068
Ex 10:13 the **L.** brought an east wind upon ... 3068
Ex 10:16 sinned against the **L.** your God, ... 3068
Ex 10:17 and intreat the **L.** your God, that ... 3068
Ex 10:18 Pharaoh, and intreated the **L.** ... 3068
Ex 10:19 **L.** turned a mighty strong west ... 3068
Ex 10:20 the **L.** hardened Pharaoh's heart, ... 3068
Ex 10:21 the **L.** said unto Moses, Stretch ... 3068
Ex 10:24 and said, Go ye, serve the **L.**; ... 3068
Ex 10:25 may sacrifice unto the **L.** our God. ... 3068
Ex 10:26 we take to serve the **L.** our God; ... 3068
Ex 10:26 with what we must serve the **L.**, ... 3068
Ex 10:27 the **L.** hardened Pharaoh's heart, ... 3068
Ex 11:1 the **L.** said unto Moses, Yet will I ... 3068
Ex 11:3 the **L.** gave the people favour in ... 3068
Ex 11:4 saith the **L.**, About midnight will ... 3068
Ex 11:7 **L.** doth put a difference between ... 3068
Ex 11:9 the **L.** said unto Moses, Pharaoh ... 3068
Ex 11:10 the **L.** hardened Pharaoh's heart, ... 3068
Ex 12:1 **L.** spake unto Moses and Aaron ... 3068
Ex 12:12 execute judgment: I am the **L.** ... 3068
Ex 12:14 ye shall keep it a feast to the **L.** ... 3068
Ex 12:23 the **L.** will pass through to smite ... 3068
Ex 12:23 the **L.** will pass over the door, ... 3068
Ex 12:25 land which the **L.** will give you, ... 3068
Ex 12:28 did as the **L.** had commanded ... 3068
Ex 12:29 the **L.** smote all the firstborn in ... 3068
Ex 12:31 go, serve the **L.**, as ye have said ... 3068
Ex 12:36 the **L.** gave the people favour in ... 3068
Ex 12:41 all the hosts of the **L.** went out ... 3068
Ex 12:42 to be much observed unto the **L.** ... 3068
Ex 12:42 this is that night of the **L.** to be ... 3068
Ex 12:43 **L.** said unto Moses and Aaron, ... 3068
Ex 12:48 will keep the passover to the **L.**, ... 3068
Ex 12:50 as the **L.** commanded Moses and ... 3068
Ex 12:51 the **L.** did bring the children of ... 3068
Ex 13:1 the **L.** spake unto Moses, saying, ... 3068
Ex 13:3 **L.** brought you out from this ... 3068
Ex 13:5 when the **L.** shall bring thee into ... 3068
Ex 13:6 day shall be a feast to the **L.** ... 3068
Ex 13:8 because of that which the **L.** did ... 3068
Ex 13:9 hath the **L.** brought thee out of ... 3068
Ex 13:11 **L.** shall bring thee into the land ... 3068
Ex 13:12 thou shalt set apart unto the **L.** ... 3068
Ex 13:14 **L.** brought us out from Egypt, ... 3068
Ex 13:15 the **L.** slew all the firstborn in the ... 3068
Ex 13:15 I sacrifice to the **L.** all that ... 3068
Ex 13:16 **L.** brought us forth out of Egypt. ... 3068
Ex 13:21 **L.** went before them by day in a ... 3068
Ex 14:1 And the **L.** spake unto Moses, ... 3068
Ex 14:4 may know that I am the **L.** And ... 3068
Ex 14:8 **L.** hardened the heart of Pharaoh ... 3068
Ex 14:10 of Israel cried out unto the **L.** ... 3068
Ex 14:13 and see the salvation of the **L.**, ... 3068
Ex 14:14 The **L.** shall fight for you, and ye ... 3068
Ex 14:15 the **L.** said unto Moses, Wherefore ... 3068
Ex 14:18 shall know that I am the **L.**, when ... 3068
Ex 14:21 **L.** caused the sea to go back by a ... 3068
Ex 14:24 the **L.** looked unto the host of the ... 3068
Ex 14:25 **L.** fighteth for them against the ... 3068
Ex 14:26 the **L.** said unto Moses, Stretch ... 3068
Ex 14:27 **L.** overthrew the Egyptians in the ... 3068
Ex 14:30 **L.** saved Israel that day out of ... 3068
Ex 14:31 great work which the **L.** did upon ... 3068
Ex 14:31 feared the **L.**, and believed the **L.**, ... 3068
Ex 15:1 of Israel this song unto the **L.**, ... 3068
Ex 15:1 I will sing unto the **L.**, for he ... 3068
Ex 15:2 The **L.** is my strength and song, ... 3068
Ex 15:3 **L.** is a man of war; the **L.** is his ... 3068
Ex 15:6 Thy right hand, O **L.**, is become ... 3068
Ex 15:6 thy right hand, O **L.**, hath dashed ... 3068
Ex 15:11 Who is like unto thee, O **L.**, ... 3068
Ex 15:16 till thy people pass over, O **L.**, ... 3068
Ex 15:17 in the place, O **L.**, which thou ... 3068
Ex 15:17 Sanctuary, O **L.**, which thy hands ... 3068
Ex 15:18 The **L.** shall reign for ever and ... 3068
Ex 15:19 **L.** brought again the waters of ... 3068
Ex 15:21 answered them, Sing ye to the **L.**, ... 3068
Ex 15:25 And he cried unto the **L.**; ... 3068
Ex 15:25 and the **L.** shewed him a tree, ... 3068
Ex 15:26 hearken to the voice of the **L.** thy ... 3068
Ex 15:26 for I am the **L.** that healeth thee. ... 3068
Ex 16:3 We had died by the hand of the **L.** ... 3068
Ex 16:4 Then said the **L.** unto Moses, ... 3068
Ex 16:6 ye shall know that the **L.** hath ... 3068
Ex 16:7 ye shall see the glory of the **L.**; ... 3068
Ex 16:7 your murmurings against the **L.** ... 3068
Ex 16:8 when the **L.** shall give you in the ... 3068
Ex 16:8 the **L.** heareth your murmurings ... 3068
Ex 16:8 against us, but against the **L.** ... 3068
Ex 16:9 Israel, Come near before the **L.** ... 3068
Ex 16:10 of the **L.** appeared in the cloud. ... 3068
Ex 16:11 And the **L.** spake unto Moses, ... 3068
Ex 16:12 ye shall know that I am the **L.** ... 3068
Ex 16:15 bread which the **L.** hath given ... 3068
Ex 16:16 which the **L.** hath commanded, ... 3068
Ex 16:23 is that which the **L.** hath said. ... 3068
Ex 16:23 of the holy sabbath unto the **L.** ... 3068
Ex 16:25 to day is a sabbath unto the **L.** ... 3068
Ex 16:28 the **L.** said unto Moses, How long ... 3068
Ex 16:29 the **L.** hath given you the sabbath, ... 3068
Ex 16:32 thing which the **L.** commandeth, ... 3068
Ex 16:33 and lay it up before the **L.**, to be ... 3068
Ex 16:34 As the **L.** commanded Moses, so ... 3068
Ex 17:1 to the commandment of the **L.**, ... 3068
Ex 17:2 Wherefore do ye tempt the **L.**? ... 3068
Ex 17:4 Moses cried unto the **L.**, saying, ... 3068
Ex 17:5 And the **L.** said unto Moses, Go on ... 3068
Ex 17:7 and because they tempted the **L.**, ... 3068
Ex 17:7 Is the **L.** among us, or not? ... 3068
Ex 17:14 the **L.** said unto Moses, Write ... 3068
Ex 17:16 Because the **L.** hath sworn that ... 3068
Ex 17:16 the **L.** will have war with Amalek ... 3068
Ex 18:1 the **L.** hath brought Israel out of ... 3068
Ex 18:8 law all that the **L.** had done unto ... 3068
Ex 18:8 and how the **L.** delivered them. ... 3068
Ex 18:9 goodness which the **L.** had done ... 3068
Ex 18:10 Jethro said, Blessed be the **L.**, ... 3068
Ex 18:11 the **L.** is greater than all gods: ... 3068
Ex 19:3 the **L.** called unto him out of the ... 3068
Ex 19:7 words which the **L.** commanded ... 3068
Ex 19:8 the **L.** hath spoken we will do. ... 3068
Ex 19:8 words of the people unto the **L.** ... 3068
Ex 19:9 And the **L.** said unto Moses, Lo, I ... 3068
Ex 19:9 words of the people unto the **L.** ... 3068
Ex 19:10 the **L.** said unto Moses, Go unto ... 3068
Ex 19:11 third day the **L.** will come down ... 3068
Ex 19:18 the **L.** descended upon it in fire: ... 3068
Ex 19:20 **L.** came down upon mount Sinai, ... 3068
Ex 19:20 **L.** called Moses up to the top of ... 3068
Ex 19:21 the **L.** said unto Moses, Go down, ... 3068
Ex 19:21 they break through unto the **L.** ... 3068
Ex 19:22 also, which come near to the **L.**, ... 3068
Ex 19:22 the **L.** break forth upon them. ... 3068
Ex 19:23 And Moses said unto the **L.**, The ... 3068
Ex 19:24 the **L.** said unto him, Away, get ... 3068
Ex 19:24 through to come up unto the **L.**, ... 3068
Ex 20:2 I am the **L.** thy God, which have ... 3068
Ex 20:5 the **L.** thy God am a jealous God, ... 3068
Ex 20:7 name of the **L.** thy God in vain; ... 3068
Ex 20:7 the **L.** will not hold him guiltless ... 3068
Ex 20:10 day is the sabbath of the **L.** thy ... 3068
Ex 20:11 the **L.** made heaven and earth, ... 3068
Ex 20:11 the **L.** blessed the sabbath day, ... 3068
Ex 20:12 the land which the **L.** thy God ... 3068
Ex 20:22 the **L.** said unto Moses, Thus ... 3068
Ex 22:11 an oath of the **L.** be between ... 3068
Ex 22:20 any god, save unto the **L.** only, ... 3068
Ex 23:17 males shall appear before the **L.** ... 3068
Ex 23:19 bring into the house of the **L.** ... 3068
Ex 23:25 ye shall serve the **L.** your God, ... 3068
Ex 24:1 Come up unto the **L.**, thou, and ... 3068
Ex 24:2 alone shall come near the **L.** ... 3068
Ex 24:3 the people all the words of the **L.**, ... 3068
Ex 24:3 All the words which the **L.** hath ... 3068
Ex 24:4 wrote all the words of the **L.**, ... 3068
Ex 24:5 offerings of oxen unto the **L.** ... 3068
Ex 24:7 All that the **L.** hath said will we ... 3068
Ex 24:8 which the **L.** hath made with you ... 3068
Ex 24:12 the **L.** said unto Moses, Come up ... 3068
Ex 24:16 glory of the **L.** abode upon mount ... 3068
Ex 24:17 glory of the **L.** was like devouring ... 3068
Ex 25:1 And the **L.** spake unto Moses, ... 3068
Ex 27:21 evening to morning before the **L.** ... 3068
Ex 28:12 bear their names before the **L.** ... 3068
Ex 28:29 before the **L.** continually ... 3068
Ex 28:30 when he goeth in before the **L.** ... 3068
Ex 28:30 heart before the **L.** continually. ... 3068
Ex 28:35 unto the holy place before the **L.**, ... 3068
Ex 28:36 of a signet, Holiness To The **L.** ... 3068
Ex 28:38 may be accepted before the **L.** ... 3068
Ex 29:11 kill the bullock before the **L.**, ... 3068
Ex 29:18 it is a burnt offering unto the **L.** ... 3068
Ex 29:18 offering made by fire unto the **L.** ... 3068
Ex 29:23 bread that is before the **L.**: ... 3068
Ex 29:24 for a wave offering before the **L.** ... 3068
Ex 29:25 for a sweet savour before the **L.** ... 3068
Ex 29:25 offering made by fire unto the **L.** ... 3068
Ex 29:26 for a wave offering before the **L.** ... 3068
Ex 29:28 their heave offering unto the **L.** ... 3068
Ex 29:41 offering made by fire unto the **L.** ... 3068
Ex 29:42 of the congregation before the **L.** ... 3068
Ex 29:46 know that I am the **L.** their God, ... 3068
Ex 29:46 them: I am the **L.** their God. ... 3068
Ex 30:8 a perpetual incense before the **L.** ... 3068
Ex 30:10 it is most holy unto the **L.** ... 3068
Ex 30:11 And the **L.** spake unto Moses, ... 3068
Ex 30:12 ransom for his soul unto the **L.**, ... 3068
Ex 30:13 shall be the offering of the **L.** ... 3068
Ex 30:14 shall give an offering unto the **L.** ... 3068
Ex 30:15 they give an offering unto the **L.**, ... 3068
Ex 30:16 children of Israel before the **L.**, ... 3068
Ex 30:17 And the **L.** spake unto Moses, ... 3068
Ex 30:20 offering made by fire unto the **L.** ... 3068
Ex 30:22 the **L.** spake unto Moses, saying, ... 3068
Ex 30:34 And the **L.** said unto Moses, Take ... 3068
Ex 30:37 shall be unto thee holy for the **L.** ... 3068
Ex 31:1, 12 And the **L.** spake unto Moses, ... 3068
Ex 31:13 am the **L.** that doth sanctify you. ... 3068
Ex 31:15 the sabbath of rest, holy to the **L.** ... 3068
Ex 31:17 the **L.** made heaven and earth, ... 3068
Ex 32:5 To morrow is a feast to the **L.** ... 3068
Ex 32:7 the **L.** said unto Moses, Go, get ... 3068
Ex 32:9 the **L.** said unto Moses, I have ... 3068
Ex 32:11 Moses besought the **L.** his God, ... 3068
Ex 32:11 **L.**, Why doth thy wrath wax hot ... 3068
Ex 32:14 **L.** repented of the evil which he ... 3068
Ex 32:22 Let not the anger of my **l.** wax hot: ... 113
Ex 32:27 Thus saith the **L.** God of Israel, ... 3068
Ex 32:29 yourselves to day to the **L.**, even ... 3068
Ex 32:30 and now I will go up unto the **L.**; ... 3068
Ex 32:31 Moses returned unto the **L.**, and ... 3068
Ex 32:33 And the **L.** said unto Moses, ... 3068
Ex 32:35 And the **L.** plagued the people, ... 3068
Ex 33:1 the **L.** said unto Moses, Depart, ... 3068
Ex 33:5 the **L.** had said unto Moses, Say ... 3068
Ex 33:7 every one which sought the **L.** ... 3068
Ex 33:9 and the **L.** talked with Moses. ...
Ex 33:11 **L.** spake unto Moses face to face, ... 3068
Ex 33:12 Moses said unto the **L.**, See, thou ... 3068
Ex 33:17 the **L.** said unto Moses, I will do ... 3068
Ex 33:19 will proclaim the name of the **L.** ... 3068
Ex 33:21 And the **L.** said, Behold, there is a ... 3068
Ex 34:1 the **L.** said unto Moses, Hew thee ... 3068
Ex 34:4 Sinai, as the **L.** had commanded ... 3068
Ex 34:5 the **L.** descended in the cloud, ... 3068
Ex 34:5 proclaimed the name of the **L.** ... 3068
Ex 34:6 the **L.** passed by before him, and ... 3068
Ex 34:6 The **L.**, The **L.** God, merciful and ... 3068
Ex 34:9 O **L.**, let my **L.**, I pray thee, go ... 136
Ex 34:10 art shall see the work of the **L.** ... 3068
Ex 34:14 for the **L.**, whose name is Jealous, ... 3068
Ex 34:23 appear before the **L.** God, ... 3068
Ex 34:24 the **L.** thy God thrice in the year. ... 3068
Ex 34:26 bring unto the house of the **L.** thy ... 3068
Ex 34:27 And the **L.** said unto Moses, Write ... 3068
Ex 34:28 there with the **L.** forty days and ... 3068
Ex 34:32 that the **L.** hath spoken with him ... 3068
Ex 34:34 before the **L.** to speak with him, ... 3068
Ex 35:1 These are words which the **L.** hath ... 3068

Ex 35:2 day, a sabbath of rest to the **L.**: 3068
Ex 35:4 thing which the **L.** commanded, 3068
Ex 35:5 you an offering unto the **L.**: 3068
Ex 35:5 bring it, an offering of the **L.**; 3068
Ex 35:10 all that the **L.** hath commanded; 3068
Ex 35:22 an offering of gold unto the **L.**. 3068
Ex 35:29 a willing offering unto the **L.**, 3068
Ex 35:29 which the **L.** had commanded to 3068
Ex 35:30 See, the **L.** hath called by name 3068
Ex 36:1 in whom the **L.** put wisdom and 3068
Ex 36:1 all that the **L.** had commanded. 3068
Ex 36:2 heart the **L.** had put wisdom, 3068
Ex 36:5 which the **L.** commanded to make. 3068
Ex 38:22 all that the **L.** commanded Moses. 3068
Ex 39:1, 5,7,21,26,29 **L.** commanded Moses. 3068
Ex 39:30 of a signet, Holiness To The **L.**. 3068
Ex 39:31 as the **L.** commanded Moses. 3068
Ex 39:32, 42 that the **L.** commanded Moses, 3068
Ex 39:43 done it as the **L.** had commanded, 3068
Ex 40:1 And the **L.** spake unto Moses, 3068
Ex 40:16 to all that the **L.** commanded him, 3068
Ex 40:19, 21 as the **L.** commanded Moses. 3068
Ex 40:23 in order upon it before the **L.**; 3068
Ex 40:23 as the **L.** had commanded Moses. 3068
Ex 40:25 he lighted the lamps before the **L.**; 3068
Ex 40:25, 27,29,32 **L.** commanded Moses. 3068
Ex 40:34, 35 the glory of the **L.** filled the 3068
Ex 40:38 the cloud of the **L.** was upon the 3068
Le 1:1 And the **L.** called unto Moses, 3068
Le 1:2 you bring an offering unto the **L.**, 3068
Le 1:3 of the congregation before the **L.**. 3068
Le 1:5 shall kill the bullock before the **L.**: 3068
Le 1:9 of a sweet savour unto the **L.**. 3068
Le 1:11 the altar northward before the **L.**: 3068
Le 1:13 of a sweet savour unto the **L.**. 3068
Le 1:14 his offering to the **L.** be of fowls, 3068
Le 1:17 of a sweet savour unto the **L.**. 3068
Le 2:1 offer a meat offering unto the **L.**, 3068
Le 2:2 of a sweet savour unto the **L.**: 3068
Le 2:3 offerings of the **L.** made by fire. 3068
Le 2:8 made of these things unto the **L.**: 3068
Le 2:9 of a sweet savour unto the **L.**. 3068
Le 2:10 offerings of the **L.** made by fire. 3068
Le 2:11 which ye shall bring unto the **L.**, 3068
Le 2:11 any offering of the **L.** made by fire. 3068
Le 2:12 ye shall offer them unto the **L.**: 3068
Le 2:14 of thy firstfruits unto the **L.**, 3068
Le 2:16 offering made by fire unto the **L.**. 3068
Le 3:1 it without blemish before the **L.**. 3068
Le 3:3 offering made by fire unto the **L.**; 3068
Le 3:5 of a sweet savour unto the **L.**. 3068
Le 3:6 offering unto the **L.** be of the flock; 3068
Le 3:7 then shall he offer it before the **L.**. 3068
Le 3:9 offering made by fire unto the **L.**; 3068
Le 3:11 offering made by fire unto the **L.**. 3068
Le 3:12 he shall offer it before the **L.**. 3068
Le 3:14 offering made by fire unto the **L.**; 3068
Le 4:1 And the **L.** spake unto Moses, 3068
Le 4:2 of the commandments of the **L.** 3068
Le 4:3 bullock without blemish unto the **L.** 3068
Le 4:4 of the congregation before the **L.**; 3068
Le 4:4 and kill the bullock before the **L.**. 3068
Le 4:6 blood seven times before the **L.**, 3068
Le 4:7 of sweet incense before the **L.**, 3068
Le 4:13 of the commandments of the **L.** 3068
Le 4:15 head of the bullock before the **L.**: 3068
Le 4:15 bullock shall be killed before the **L.**. 3068
Le 4:17 it seven times before the **L.**, 3068
Le 4:18 of the altar which is before the **L.**, 3068
Le 4:22 of the commandments of the **L.** 3068
Le 4:24 the burnt offering before the **L.**: 3068
Le 4:27 of the commandments of the **L.** 3068
Le 4:31 for a sweet savour unto the **L.**; 3068
Le 4:35 offerings made by fire unto the **L.**: 3068
Le 5:6 his trespass offering unto the **L.** 3068
Le 5:7 or two young pigeons, unto the **L.**; 3068
Le 5:12 offerings made by fire unto the **L.**: 3068
Le 5:14 And the **L.** spake unto Moses, 3068
Le 5:15 in the holy things of the **L.**; 3068
Le 5:15 bring for his trespass unto the **L.** 3068
Le 5:17 by the commandments of the **L.**; 3068
Le 5:19 certainly trespassed against the **L.** 3068
Le 6:1 And the **L.** spake unto Moses, 3068
Le 6:2 commit a trespass against the **L.**, 3068
Le 6:6 his trespass offering unto the **L.**, 3068
Le 6:7 atonement for him before the **L.**: 3068
Le 6:8 And the **L.** spake unto Moses, 3068
Le 6:14 of Aaron shall offer it before the **L.**, 3068
Le 6:15 the memorial of it, unto the **L.**. 3068
Le 6:18 offerings of the **L.** made by fire: 3068
Le 6:19 And the **L.** spake unto Moses, 3068
Le 6:20 offer unto the **L.** in the day when 3068
Le 6:21 for a sweet savour unto the **L.**. 3068
Le 6:22 it is a statute for ever unto the **L.**; 3068
Le 6:24 And the **L.** spake unto Moses, 3068
Le 6:25 sin offering be killed before the **L.**: 3068
Le 7:5 offering made by fire unto the **L.**: 3068
Le 7:11 which he shall offer unto the **L.**. 3068
Le 7:14 for an heave offering unto the **L.**, 3068
Le 7:20 offerings that pertain unto the **L.**, 3068
Le 7:21 which pertain unto the **L.**, 3068
Le 7:22 And the **L.** spake unto Moses, 3068
Le 7:25 offering made by fire unto the **L.**, 3068
Le 7:28 And the **L.** spake unto Moses, 3068
Le 7:29 of his peace offerings unto the **L.** 3068
Le 7:29 shall bring his oblation unto the **L.** 3068
Le 7:30 offerings of the **L.** made by fire, 3068
Le 7:30 for a wave offering before the **L.** 3068
Le 7:35 offerings of the **L.** made by fire, 3068
Le 7:35 minister unto the **L.** in the priest's 3068
Le 7:36 the **L.** commanded to be given 3068
Le 7:38 **L.** commanded Moses in mount 3068
Le 7:38 offer their oblations unto the **L.**, 3068
Le 8:1 And the **L.** spake unto Moses, 3068
Le 8:4 Moses did as the **L.** commanded 3068
Le 8:5 the **L.** commanded to be done. 3068
Le 8:9, 13,17 the **L.** commanded Moses. 3068
Le 8:21 offering made by fire unto the **L.**; 3068
Le 8:21 as the **L.** commanded Moses. 3068
Le 8:26 bread, that was before the **L.**, 3068
Le 8:27 for a wave offering before the **L.**. 3068
Le 8:28 offering made by fire unto the **L.**. 3068
Le 8:29 for a wave offering before the **L.**: 3068
Le 8:29 as the **L.** commanded Moses. 3068
Le 8:34 so the **L.** hath commanded to do, 3068
Le 8:35 keep the charge of the **L.**, that ye 3068
Le 8:36 the **L.** commanded by the hand of 3068
Le 9:2 and offer them before the **L.**. 3068
Le 9:4 to sacrifice before the **L.**; 3068
Le 9:4 to day the **L.** will appear unto you. 3068
Le 9:5 drew near and stood before the **L.**. 3068
Le 9:6 **L.** commanded that ye should do: 3068
Le 9:6 glory of the **L.** shall appear unto 3068
Le 9:7 for them; as the **L.** commanded. 3068
Le 9:10 as the **L.** commanded Moses. 3068
Le 9:21 for a wave offering before the **L.**; 3068
Le 9:23 glory of the **L.** appeared unto all 3068
Le 9:24 came a fire out from before the **L.**, 3068
Le 10:1 offered strange fire before the **L.**, 3068
Le 10:2 there went out fire from the **L.**, 3068
Le 10:2 and they died before the **L.**. 3068
Le 10:3 This is it that the **L.** spake, 3068
Le 10:6 burning...the **L.** hath kindled. 3068
Le 10:7 anointing oil of the **L.** is upon 3068
Le 10:8 the **L.** spake unto Aaron, saying, 3068
Le 10:11 statutes which the **L.** hath spoken 3068
Le 10:12 offerings of the **L.** made by fire, 3068
Le 10:13 sacrifices of the **L.** made by fire: 3068
Le 10:15 for a wave offering before the **L.**; 3068
Le 10:15 ever; as the **L.** hath commanded. 3068
Le 10:17 atonement for them before the **L.**? 3068
Le 10:19 their burnt offering before the **L.**; 3068
Le 10:19 accepted in the sight of the **L.**? 3068
Le 11:1 **L.** spake unto Moses and to Aaron, 3068
Le 11:44 I am the **L.** your God: ye shall 3068
Le 11:45 I am the **L.** that bringeth you up 3068
Le 12:1 And the **L.** spake unto Moses, 3068
Le 12:7 Who shall offer it before the **L.**, 3068
Le 13:1 **L.** spake unto Moses and Aaron, 3068
Le 14:1 And the **L.** spake unto Moses, 3068
Le 14:11 before the **L.**, at the door of the 3068
Le 14:12 for a wave offering before the **L.**: 3068
Le 14:16 finger seven times before the **L.**: 3068
Le 14:18 atonement for him before the **L.**. 3068
Le 14:23 of the congregation, before the **L.**. 3068
Le 14:24 for a wave offering before the **L.**: 3068
Le 14:27 hand seven times before the **L.**: 3068
Le 14:29 atonement for him before the **L.**. 3068
Le 14:31 that is to be cleansed before the **L.** 3068
Le 14:33 the **L.** spake unto Moses and unto 3068
Le 15:1 **L.** spake unto Moses and to Aaron, 3068
Le 15:14 come before the **L.** unto the door 3068
Le 15:15 atonement for him before the **L.** 3068
Le 15:30 atonement for her before the **L.** 3068
Le 16:1 And the **L.** spake unto Moses 3068
Le 16:1 when they offered before the **L.**, 3068
Le 16:2 the **L.** said unto Moses, Speak 3068
Le 16:7 and present them before the **L.** 3068
Le 16:8 one lot for the **L.**, and the other 3068
Le 16:10 be presented alive before the **L.**, 3068
Le 16:12 from off the altar before the **L.**, 3068
Le 16:13 upon the fire before the **L.**, incense 3068
Le 16:18 the altar that is before the **L.**, 3068
Le 16:30 from all your sins before the **L.**. 3068
Le 16:34 did as the **L.** commanded Moses. 3068
Le 17:1 the **L.** spake unto Moses, saying, 3068
Le 17:2 which the **L.** hath commanded, 3068
Le 17:4 to offer an offering unto the **L.** 3068
Le 17:4 before the tabernacle of the **L.**; 3068
Le 17:5 they may bring them unto the **L.**, 3068
Le 17:5 for peace offerings unto the **L.**. 3068
Le 17:6 the blood upon the altar of the **L.** 3068
Le 17:6 for a sweet savour unto the **L.**. 3068
Le 17:9 to offer it unto the **L.**; even 3068
Le 18:1 the **L.** spake unto Moses, saying, 3068
Le 18:2 unto them, I am the **L.** your God. 3068
Le 18:4 therein: I am the **L.** your God. 3068
Le 18:5 he shall live in them: I am the **L.** 3068
Le 18:6 their nakedness: I am the **L.**. 3068
Le 18:21 the name of thy God: I am the **L.** 3068
Le 18:30 therein: I am the **L.** your God. 3068
Le 19:1 the **L.** spake unto Moses, saying, 3068
Le 19:2 for I the **L.** your God am holy. 3068
Le 19:3 sabbaths: I am the **L.** your God. 3068
Le 19:4 gods: I am the **L.** your God. 3068
Le 19:5 of peace offerings unto the **L.**, 3068
Le 19:8 the hallowed thing of the **L.**; 3068
Le 19:10 stranger: I am the **L.** your God. 3068
Le 19:12 the name of thy God: I am the **L.** 3068
Le 19:14 shalt fear thy God: I am the **L.**. 3068
Le 19:16 of thy neighbour: I am the **L.** 3068
Le 19:18 neighbour as thyself: I am the **L.** 3068
Le 19:21 his trespass offering unto the **L.**, 3068
Le 19:22 the trespass offering before the **L.** 3068
Le 19:24 be holy to praise the **L.** withal. 3068
Le 19:25 thereof: I am the **L.** your God. 3068
Le 19:28 any marks upon you: I am the **L.** 3068
Le 19:30 my sanctuary: I am the **L.** 3068
Le 19:31 by them: I am the **L.** your God. 3068
Le 19:32 and fear thy God: I am the **L.** 3068
Le 19:34 of Egypt: I am the **L.** your God. 3068
Le 19:36 I am the **L.** your God, which 3068
Le 19:37 and do them: I am the **L.** 3068
Le 20:1 the **L.** spake unto Moses, saying, 3068
Le 20:7 ye holy: for I am the **L.** your God. 3068
Le 20:8 I am the **L.** which sanctify you. 3068
Le 20:24 I am the **L.** your God, which have 3068
Le 20:26 holy unto me: for I the **L.** am holy, 3068
Le 21:1 the **L.** said unto Moses, Speak 3068
Le 21:6 offerings of the **L.** made by fire, 3068
Le 21:8 for I the **L.**, which sanctify you, 3068
Le 21:12 his God is upon him: I am the **L.** 3068
Le 21:15 for I the **L.** do sanctify him. 3068
Le 21:16 the **L.** spake unto Moses, saying, 3068
Le 21:21 offerings of the **L.** made by fire: 3068
Le 21:23 for I the **L.** do sanctify them. 3068
Le 22:1 the **L.** spake unto Moses, saying, 3068
Le 22:2 they hallow unto me: I am the **L.** 3068
Le 22:3 of Israel hallow unto the **L.**, 3068
Le 22:3 from my presence: I am the **L.**. 3068
Le 22:8 himself therewith: I am the **L.** 3068
Le 22:9 it: I the **L.** do sanctify them. 3068
Le 22:15 which they offer unto the **L.**; 3068
Le 22:16 for I the **L.** do sanctify them. 3068
Le 22:17 the **L.** spake unto Moses, saying, 3068
Le 22:18 they will offer unto the **L.** for a 3068
Le 22:21 unto the **L.** to accomplish his vow, 3068
Le 22:22 shall not offer these unto the **L.**, 3068
Le 22:22 them upon the altar unto the **L.** 3068
Le 22:24 unto the **L.** that which is bruised, 3068
Le 22:26 the **L.** spake unto Moses, saying, 3068
Le 22:27 offering made by fire unto the **L.**. 3068
Le 22:29 of thanksgiving unto the **L.**, offer 3068
Le 22:30 it until the morrow: I am the **L.**. 3068
Le 22:31 and do them: I am the **L.** 3068
Le 22:32 I am the **L.** which hallow you, 3068
Le 22:33 to be your God: I am the **L.** 3068
Le 23:1 the **L.** spake unto Moses, saying, 3068
Le 23:2 Concerning the feasts of the **L.**, 3068

Le	23:3	the sabbath of the **L.** in all your	3068
Le	23:4	These are the feasts of the **L.**,	3068
Le	23:6	of unleavened bread unto the **L.**	3068
Le	23:8	offering made by fire unto the **L.**	3068
Le	23:9	the **L.** spake unto Moses, saying,	3068
Le	23:11	wave the sheaf before the **L.**,	3068
Le	23:12	for a burnt offering unto the **L.**	3068
Le	23:13	offering made by fire unto the **L.**	3068
Le	23:16	a new meat offering unto the **L.**.	3068
Le	23:17	they are the firstfruits unto the **L.**	3068
Le	23:18	for a burnt offering unto the **L.**,	3068
Le	23:18	fire, of sweet savour unto the **L.**.	3068
Le	23:20	for a wave offering before the **L.**,	3068
Le	23:20	be holy to the **L.** for the priest	3068
Le	23:22	stranger: I am the **L.** your God.	3068
Le	23:23	the **L.** spake unto Moses, saying,	3068
Le	23:25	offering made by fire unto the **L.**.	3068
Le	23:26	the **L.** spake unto Moses, saying,	3068
Le	23:27	offering made by fire unto the **L.**.	3068
Le	23:28	atonement for you before the **L.**	3068
Le	23:33	the **L.** spake unto Moses, saying,	3068
Le	23:34	for seven days unto the **L.**.	3068
Le	23:36,	offering...by fire unto the **L.**	3068
Le	23:37	These are the feasts of the **L.**,	3068
Le	23:37	offering made by fire unto the **L.**,	3068
Le	23:38	Beside the sabbaths of the **L.**,	3068
Le	23:38	offerings, which ye give unto the **L.**.	3068
Le	23:39	keep a feast unto the **L.** seven	3068
Le	23:40	rejoice before the **L.** your God	3068
Le	23:41	keep it a feast unto the **L.** seven	3068
Le	23:43	of Egypt: I am the **L.** your God.	3068
Le	23:44	of Israel the feasts of the **L.**.	3068
Le	24:1	the **L.** spake unto Moses, saying,	3068
Le	24:3	before the **L.** continually: morning	3068
Le	24:4	the pure candlestick before the **L.**	3068
Le	24:6	upon the pure table before the **L.**.	3068
Le	24:7	offering made by fire unto the **L.**.	3068
Le	24:8	shall set it in order before the **L.**	3068
Le	24:9	offerings of the **L.** made by fire	3068
Le	24:11	blasphemed the name of the **L.**,	
Le	24:12	mind of the **L.** might be shewed	3068
Le	24:13	the **L.** spake unto Moses, saying,	3068
Le	24:16	blasphemeth the name of the **L.**,	3068
Le	24:22	for I am the **L.** your God.	3068
Le	24:23	did as the **L.** commanded Moses.	3068
Le	25:1	**L.** spake unto Moses in mount	3068
Le	25:2	land keep a sabbath unto the **L.**	3068
Le	25:4	the land, a sabbath for the **L.**	3068
Le	25:17	God: for I am the **L.** your God.	3068
Le	25:38	I am the **L.** your God, which	3068
Le	25:55	of Egypt: I am the **L.** your God.	3068
Le	26:1	unto it: for I am the **L.** your God.	3068
Le	26:2	my sanctuary: I am the **L.**.	3068
Le	26:13	I am the **L.** your God, which	3068
Le	26:44	them: for I am the **L.** their God.	3068
Le	26:45	might be their God: I am the **L.**.	3068
Le	26:46	laws, which the **L.** made between	3068
Le	27:1	the **L.** spake unto Moses, saying,	3068
Le	27:2	be for the **L.** by thy estimation.	3068
Le	27:9	men bring an offering unto the **L.**,	3068
Le	27:9	man giveth of such unto the **L.**	3068
Le	27:11	not offer a sacrifice unto the **L.**,	3068
Le	27:14	his house to be holy unto the **L.**,	3068
Le	27:16	a man shall sanctify unto the **L.**	3068
Le	27:21	jubile, shall be holy unto the **L.**,	3068
Le	27:22	man sanctify unto the **L.** a field	3068
Le	27:23	day, as a holy thing unto the **L.**	3068
Le	27:28	devote unto the **L.** of all that he	3068
Le	27:28	thing is most holy unto the **L.**.	3068
Le	27:30	is the Lord's: it is holy unto the **L.**.	3068
Le	27:32	tenth shall be holy unto the **L.**.	3068
Le	27:34	which the **L.** commanded Moses	3068
Nu	1:1	the **L.** spake unto Moses in the	3068
Nu	1:19	As the **L.** commanded Moses, so	3068
Nu	1:48	**L.** had spoken unto Moses, saying,	3068
Nu	1:54	all that the **L.** commanded Moses,	3068
Nu	2:1	the **L.** spake unto Moses and unto	3068
Nu	2:33	as the **L.** commanded Moses.	3068
Nu	2:34	all that the **L.** commanded Moses:	3068
Nu	3:1	**L.** spake with Moses in mount	3068
Nu	3:4	and Abihu died before the **L.**,	3068
Nu	3:4	offered strange fire before the **L.**,	3068
Nu	3:5,	11 **L.** spake unto Moses, saying,	3068
Nu	3:13	mine shall they be: I am the **L.**.	3068
Nu	3:14	the **L.** spake unto Moses in the	3068
Nu	3:16	according to the word of the **L.**,	3068
Nu	3:39	at the commandment of the **L.**,	3068
Nu	3:40	the **L.** said unto Moses, Number	3068
Nu	3:41	the Levites for me (I am the **L.**)	3068
Nu	3:42	as the **L.** commanded him, all	3068
Nu	3:44	the **L.** spake unto Moses, saying,	3068
Nu	3:45	shall be mine: I am the **L.**.	3068
Nu	3:51	according to the word of the **L.**,	3068
Nu	3:51	as the **L.** commanded Moses.	3068
Nu	4:1,	17 **L.** spake unto Moses and unto	3068
Nu	4:21	the **L.** spake unto Moses, saying,	3068
Nu	4:37	to the commandment of the **L.**	3068
Nu	4:41	to the commandment of the **L.**	3068
Nu	4:45	according to the word of the **L.**	3068
Nu	4:49	to the commandment of the **L.**	3068
Nu	4:49	as the **L.** commanded Moses.	3068
Nu	5:1	the **L.** spake unto Moses, saying,	3068
Nu	5:4	as the **L.** spake unto Moses, so	3068
Nu	5:5	the **L.** spake unto Moses, saying,	3068
Nu	5:6	to do a trespass against the **L.**,	3068
Nu	5:8	be recompensed unto the **L.**, even	3068
Nu	5:11	the **L.** spake unto Moses, saying,	3068
Nu	5:16	near, and set her before the **L.**	3068
Nu	5:18	shall set the woman before the **L.**,	3068
Nu	5:21	**L.** make thee a curse and an oath	3068
Nu	5:21	**L.** doth make thy thigh to rot,	3068
Nu	5:25	wave the offering before the **L.**,	3068
Nu	5:30	shall set the woman before the **L.**,	3068
Nu	6:1	the **L.** spake unto Moses, saying,	3068
Nu	6:2	separate themselves unto the **L.**	3068
Nu	6:5	separateth himself unto the **L.**,	3068
Nu	6:6	separateth himself unto the **L.**	3068
Nu	6:8	separation he is holy unto the **L.**	3068
Nu	6:12	consecrate unto the **L.** the days	3068
Nu	6:14	shall offer his offering unto the **L.**,	3068
Nu	6:16	shall bring them before the **L.**.	3068
Nu	6:17	of peace offerings unto the **L.**,	3068
Nu	6:20	for a wave offering before the **L.**	3068
Nu	6:21	of his offering unto the **L.** for his	3068
Nu	6:22	the **L.** spake unto Moses, saying,	3068
Nu	6:24	The **L.** bless thee, and keep thee:	3068
Nu	6:25	**L.** make his face shine upon thee,	3068
Nu	6:26	**L.** lift up his countenance upon	3068
Nu	7:3	their offering before the **L.**,	3068
Nu	7:4	the **L.** spake unto Moses, saying,	3068
Nu	7:11	And the **L.** said unto Moses, They	3068
Nu	8:1	the **L.** spake unto Moses, saying,	3068
Nu	8:3	as the **L.** commanded Moses.	3068
Nu	8:4	pattern which the **L.** had shewed	3068
Nu	8:5	the **L.** spake unto Moses, saying,	3068
Nu	8:10	bring the Levites before the **L.**	3068
Nu	8:11	offer the Levites before the **L.**	3068
Nu	8:11	may execute the service of the **L.**	3068
Nu	8:12	for a burnt offering, unto the **L.**,	3068
Nu	8:13	them for an offering unto the **L.**.	3068
Nu	8:20	all that the **L.** commanded Moses	3068
Nu	8:21	them as an offering before the **L.**;	3068
Nu	8:22	as the **L.** had commanded Moses	3068
Nu	8:23	the **L.** spake unto Moses, saying,	3068
Nu	9:1	the **L.** spake unto Moses in the	3068
Nu	9:5	all that the **L.** commanded Moses,	3068
Nu	9:7	of the **L.** in his appointed season	3068
Nu	9:8	hear what the **L.** will command	3068
Nu	9:9	the **L.** spake unto Moses, saying,	3068
Nu	9:10	keep the passover unto the **L.**	3068
Nu	9:13	of the **L.** in his appointed season,	3068
Nu	9:14	keep the passover unto the **L.**;	3068
Nu	9:18	At the commandment of the **L.**	3068
Nu	9:18	at the commandment of the **L.**	3068
Nu	9:19	Israel kept the charge of the **L.**,	3068
Nu	9:20,	20 to the commandment of the **L.**	3068
Nu	9:23	At the commandment of the **L.**	3068
Nu	9:23	at the commandment of the **L.**	3068
Nu	9:23	they kept the charge of the **L.**,	3068
Nu	9:23	at the commandment of the **L.**	3068
Nu	10:1	the **L.** spake unto Moses, saying,	3068
Nu	10:9	be remembered before the **L.**	3068
Nu	10:10	your God: I am the **L.** your God.	3068
Nu	10:13	to the commandment of the **L.** by	3068
Nu	10:29	the place of which the **L.** said,	3068
Nu	10:29	**L.** hath spoken good concerning	3068
Nu	10:32	goodness the **L.** shall do unto us,	3068
Nu	10:33	departed from the mount of the **L.**	3068
Nu	10:33	the ark of the covenant of the **L.**	3068
Nu	10:34	cloud of the **L.** was upon them	3068
Nu	10:35	Rise up, **L.**, and let thine enemies	3068
Nu	10:36	Return, O **L.**, unto the many	3068
Nu	11:1	complained, it displeased the **L.**	3068
Nu	11:1	the **L.** heard it; and his anger	3068
Nu	11:1	fire of the **L.** burnt among them,	3068
Nu	11:2	when Moses prayed unto the **L.**,	3068
Nu	11:3	fire of the **L.** burnt among them.	3068
Nu	11:10	the anger of the **L.** was kindled	3068
Nu	11:11	Moses said unto the **L.**, Wherefore	3068
Nu	11:16	the **L.** said unto Moses, Gather	3068
Nu	11:18	have wept in the ears of the **L.**,	3068
Nu	11:18	the **L.** will give you flesh, and ye	3068
Nu	11:20	that ye have despised the **L.**	3068
Nu	11:23	the **L.** said unto Moses, Is the	3068
Nu	11:24	the people the words of the **L.**,	3068
Nu	11:25	And the **L.** came down in a cloud,	3068
Nu	11:28	and said, My **l.** Moses, forbid them	113
Nu	11:29	the **L.** would put his spirit upon	3068
Nu	11:31	went forth a wind from the **L.**,	3068
Nu	11:33	the wrath of the **L.** was kindled	3068
Nu	11:33	**L.** smote the people with a very	3068
Nu	12:2	Hath the **L.** indeed spoken only	3068
Nu	12:2	also by us? And the **L.** heard it.	3068
Nu	12:4	**L.** spake suddenly unto Moses,	3068
Nu	12:5	**L.** came down in the pillar of the	3068
Nu	12:6	I the **L.** will make myself known	3068
Nu	12:8	the similitude of the **L.** shall he	3068
Nu	12:9	the anger of the **L.** was kindled	3068
Nu	12:11	Aaron said unto Moses, Alas, my **l.**,	113
Nu	12:13	Moses cried unto the **L.**, saying,	3068
Nu	12:14	the **L.** said unto Moses, If her	3068
Nu	13:1	the **L.** spake unto Moses, saying,	3068
Nu	13:3	by the commandment of the **L.**	3068
Nu	14:3	wherefore hath the **L.** brought us	3068
Nu	14:8	If the **L.** delight in us, then he	3068
Nu	14:9	Only rebel not ye against the **L.**,	3068
Nu	14:9	from them, and the **L.** is with us:	3068
Nu	14:10	the glory of the **L.** appeared in	3068
Nu	14:11	the **L.** said unto Moses, How long	3068
Nu	14:13	Moses said unto the **L.**, Then the	3068
Nu	14:14	thou **L.** art among this people,	3068
Nu	14:14	that thou **L.** art seen face to face,	3068
Nu	14:16	the **L.** was not able to bring this	3068
Nu	14:17	let the power of my **L.** be great,	136
Nu	14:18	The **L.** is longsuffering, and of	3068
Nu	14:20	And the **L.** said, I have pardoned	3068
Nu	14:21	be filled with the glory of the **L.**	3068
Nu	14:26	The **L.** spake unto Moses and	3068
Nu	14:28	As truly as I live, saith the **L.**, as	3068
Nu	14:35	I the **L.** have said, I will surely	3068
Nu	14:37	died by the plague before the **L.**	3068
Nu	14:40	place which the **L.** hath promised:	3068
Nu	14:41	the commandment of the **L.**?	3068
Nu	14:42	for the **L.** is not among you;	3068
Nu	14:43	ye are turned away from the **L.**,	3068
Nu	14:43	the **L.** will not be with you.	3068
Nu	14:44	the ark of the covenant of the **L.**,	3068
Nu	15:1	the **L.** spake unto Moses, saying,	3068
Nu	15:3	offering by fire unto the **L.**,	3068
Nu	15:3	a sweet savour unto the **L.**,	3068
Nu	15:4	offereth his offering unto the **L.**	3068
Nu	15:7	for a sweet savour unto the **L.**.	3068
Nu	15:8	or peace offerings unto the **L.**	3068
Nu	15:10,	13 of a sweet savour unto the **L.**.	3068
Nu	15:14	of a sweet savour unto the **L.**;	3068
Nu	15:15	the stranger be before the **L.**	3068
Nu	15:17	the **L.** spake unto Moses, saying,	3068
Nu	15:19	for an heave offering unto the **L.**.	3068
Nu	15:21	give unto the **L.** a heave offering	3068
Nu	15:22	the **L.** hath spoken unto Moses,	3068
Nu	15:23	that the **L.** hath commanded you	3068
Nu	15:23	that the **L.** commanded Moses,	3068
Nu	15:24	for a sweet savour unto the **L.**.	3068
Nu	15:25	sacrifice made by fire unto the **L.**,	3068
Nu	15:25	their sin offering before the **L.**,	3068
Nu	15:28	by ignorance before the **L.**, to	3068
Nu	15:30	the same reproacheth the **L.**;	3068
Nu	15:31	hath despised the word of the **L.**,	3068
Nu	15:35	the **L.** said unto Moses, The man	3068
Nu	15:36	as the **L.** commanded Moses.	3068
Nu	15:37	the **L.** spake unto Moses, saying,	3068
Nu	15:39	all the commandments of the **L.**,	3068
Nu	15:41	I am the **L.** your God, which	3068
Nu	15:41	your God: I am the **L.** your God.	3068
Nu	16:3	them, and the **L.** is among them:	3068
Nu	16:3	above the congregation of the **L.**?	3068
Nu	16:5	the **L.** will shew who are his,	3068
Nu	16:7	incense in them before the **L.**	3068
Nu	16:7	man whom the **L.** doth choose,	3068
Nu	16:9	service of the tabernacle of the **L.**,	3068
Nu	16:11	gathered together against the **L.**	3068

Nu 16:15 very wroth, and said unto the **L.**, ... 3068
Nu 16:16 all thy company before the **L.**,........... 3068
Nu 16:17 bring ye before the **L.** every man 3068
Nu 16:19 the glory of the **L.** appeared unto....... 3068
Nu 16:20 the **L.** spake unto Moses and unto 3068
Nu 16:23 the **L.** spake unto Moses, saying, ... 3068
Nu 16:28 shall know that the **L.** hath sent 3068
Nu 16:29 then the **L.** hath not sent me. 3068
Nu 16:30 if the **L.** make a new thing, and......... 3068
Nu 16:30 these men have provoked the **L.**......... 3068
Nu 16:35 there came out a fire from the **L.**, ... 3068
Nu 16:36 the **L.** spake to Moses, saying, ... 3068
Nu 16:38 they offered them before the **L.**,......... 3068
Nu 16:40 to offer incense before the **L.**;........... 3068
Nu 16:40 **L.** said to him by the hand of........... 3068
Nu 16:41 have killed the people of the **L.** 3068
Nu 16:42 And the glory of the **L.** appeared. 3068
Nu 16:44 the **L.** spake unto Moses, saying, ... 3068
Nu 16:46 is wrath gone out from the **L.**; 3068
Nu 17:1 the **L.** spake unto Moses, saying, ... 3068
Nu 17:7 laid up the rods before the **L.** in........ 3068
Nu 17:9 all the rods from before the **L.** 3068
Nu 17:10 And the **L.** said unto Moses, Bring..... 3068
Nu 17:11 as the **L.** commanded him, so did....... 3068
Nu 17:13 the tabernacle of the **L.** shall die:....... 3068
Nu 18:1 the **L.** said unto Aaron, Thou and 3068
Nu 18:6 they are given as a gift for the **L.**, ... 3068
Nu 18:8 the **L.** spake unto Aaron, Behold, ... 3068
Nu 18:12 which they shall offer unto the **L.**,...... 3068
Nu 18:13 which they shall bring unto the **L.**, ... 3068
Nu 18:15 which they bring unto the **L.**............ 3068
Nu 18:17 for a sweet savour unto the **L.**........... 3068
Nu 18:19 children of Israel offer unto the **L.**,..... 3068
Nu 18:19 of salt for ever before the **L.** unto...... 3068
Nu 18:20 the **L.** spake unto Aaron, Thou.......... 3068
Nu 18:24 as an heave offering unto the **L.**, ... 3068
Nu 18:25 the **L.** spake unto Moses, saying, ... 3068
Nu 18:26 an heave offering of it for the **L.**,....... 3068
Nu 18:28 an heave offering unto the **L.** of......... 3068
Nu 18:29 every heave offering of the **L.**, of 3068
Nu 19:1 the **L.** spake unto Moses and unto 3068
Nu 19:2 which the **L.** hath commanded, ... 3068
Nu 19:13 defileth the tabernacle of the **L.**; 3068
Nu 19:20 defiled the sanctuary of the **L.**........... 3068
Nu 20:3 our brethren died before the **L.**! 3068
Nu 20:4 up the congregation of the **L.** into 3068
Nu 20:6 the glory of the **L.** appeared unto....... 3068
Nu 20:7 the **L.** spake unto Moses, saying, ... 3068
Nu 20:9 took the rod from before the **L.**,......... 3068
Nu 20:12 **L.** spake unto Moses and Aaron, ... 3068
Nu 20:13 of Israel strove with the **L.**, and........ 3068
Nu 20:16 And when we cried unto the **L.**, he.... 3068
Nu 20:23 **L.** spake unto Moses and Aaron 3068
Nu 20:27 Moses did as the **L.** commanded:........ 3068
Nu 21:2 Israel vowed a vow unto the **L.**,........ 3068
Nu 21:3 the **L.** hearkened to the voice of......... 3068
Nu 21:6 **L.** sent fiery serpents among the 3068
Nu 21:7 we have spoken against the **L.** 3068
Nu 21:7 pray unto the **L.**, that he take............ 3068
Nu 21:8 And the **L.** said unto Moses, Make 3068
Nu 21:14 in the book of the wars of the **L.**,....... 3068
Nu 21:16 whereof the **L.** spake unto Moses, ... 3068
Nu 21:34 the **L.** said unto Moses, Fear him...... 3068
Nu 22:8 as the **L.** shall speak unto me: 3068
Nu 22:13 **L.** refuseth to give me leave to go..... 3068
Nu 22:18 the word of the **L.** my God, to.......... 3068
Nu 22:19 I may know what the **L.** will say........ 3068
Nu 22:22 angel of the **L.** stood in the way........ 3068
Nu 22:23 saw the angel of the **L.** standing........ 3068
Nu 22:24 angel of the **L.** stood in a path of....... 3068
Nu 22:25 the ass saw the angel of the **L.**, ... 3068
Nu 22:26 angel of the **L.** went further, and........ 3068
Nu 22:27 the ass saw the angel of the **L.**, ... 3068
Nu 22:28 **L.** opened the mouth of the ass, ... 3068
Nu 22:31 **L.** opened the eyes of Balaam, ... 3068
Nu 22:31 saw the angel of the **L.** standing........ 3068
Nu 22:32 the angel of the **L.** said unto him. 3068
Nu 22:34 said unto the angel of the **L.**, ... 3068
Nu 22:35 angel of the **L.** said unto Balaam, ... 3068
Nu 23:3 the **L.** will come to meet me;........... 3068
Nu 23:5 **L.** put a word in Balaam's mouth, ... 3068
Nu 23:8 whom the **L.** hath not defied?............ 3068
Nu 23:12 the **L.** hath put in my mouth?........... 3068
Nu 23:15 while I meet the **L.** yonder.....................
Nu 23:16 And the **L.** met Balaam, and put........ 3068
Nu 23:17 him, What hath the **L.** spoken?.......... 3068
Nu 23:21 the **L.** his God is with him, and 3068

Nu 23:26 All that the **L.** speaketh, that I.......... 3068
Nu 24:1 saw that it pleased the **L.** to bless 3068
Nu 24:6 aloes which the **L.** hath planted, ... 3068
Nu 24:11 the **L.** hath kept thee back from 3068
Nu 24:13 the commandment of the **L.**, ... 3068
Nu 24:13 but what the **L.** saith, that will I 3068
Nu 25:3 the anger of the **L.** was kindled 3068
Nu 25:4 the **L.** said unto Moses, Take all 3068
Nu 25:4 and hang them up before the **L.**......... 3068
Nu 25:4 and fierce anger of the **L.** may be...... 3068
Nu 25:10, 16 And the **L.** spake unto Moses, ... 3068
Nu 26:1 the **L.** spake unto Moses and unto 3068
Nu 26:4 as the **L.** commanded Moses and....... 3068
Nu 26:9 when they strove against the **L.** 3068
Nu 26:52 the **L.** spake unto Moses, saying, ... 3068
Nu 26:61 offered strange fire before the **L.**....... 3068
Nu 26:65 For the **L.** had said of them, They 3068
Nu 27:3 against the **L.** in the company of........ 3068
Nu 27:5 brought their cause before the **L.**,...... 3068
Nu 27:6 the **L.** spake unto Moses, saying, ... 3068
Nu 27:11 as the **L.** commanded Moses............. 3068
Nu 27:12 the **L.** said unto Moses, Get thee 3068
Nu 27:15 Moses spake unto the **L.**, saying, ... 3068
Nu 27:16 Let the **L.**, the God of the spirits 3068
Nu 27:17 congregation of the **L.** be not as 3068
Nu 27:18 the **L.** said unto Moses, Take thee...... 3068
Nu 27:21 judgment of Urim before the **L.**......... 3068
Nu 27:22 Moses did as the **L.** commanded........ 3068
Nu 27:23 **L.** commanded by the hand of........... 3068
Nu 28:1 the **L.** spake unto Moses, saying, ... 3068
Nu 28:3 which ye shall offer unto the **L.**; 3068
Nu 28:6 sacrifice made by fire unto the **L.**........ 3068
Nu 28:7 wine to be poured unto the **L.** for...... 3068
Nu 28:8 of a sweet savour unto the **L.** 3068
Nu 28:11 offer a burnt offering unto the **L.**; 3068
Nu 28:13 sacrifice made by fire unto the **L.**........ 3068
Nu 28:15 goats for a sin offering unto the **L.**..... 3068
Nu 28:16 month is the passover of the **L.**.......... 3068
Nu 28:19 for a burnt offering unto the **L.**;.......... 3068
Nu 28:24 of a sweet savour unto the **L.**: 3068
Nu 28:26 a new meat offering unto the **L.**, ... 3068
Nu 28:27 for a sweet savour unto the **L.**; 3068
Nu 29:2 for a sweet savour unto the **L.**; 3068
Nu 29:6 sacrifice made by fire unto the **L.**........ 3068
Nu 29:8 offer a burnt offering unto the **L.** 3068
Nu 29:12 a feast unto the **L.** seven days: 3068
Nu 29:13 of a sweet savour unto the **L.** 3068
Nu 29:36 of a sweet savour unto the **L.** 3068
Nu 29:39 things ye shall do unto the **L.** in 3068
Nu 29:40 all that the **L.** commanded Moses......... 3068
Nu 30:1 which the **L.** hath commanded. 3068
Nu 30:2 If a man vow a vow unto the **L.**, or ... 3068
Nu 30:3 also vow a vow unto the **L.**, ... 3068
Nu 30:5 the **L.** shall forgive her, because........ 3068
Nu 30:8 and the **L.** shall forgive her.............. 3068
Nu 30:12 void; and the **L.** shall forgive her. 3068
Nu 30:16 which the **L.** commanded Moses, ... 3068
Nu 31:1 the **L.** spake unto Moses, saying, ... 3068
Nu 31:3 and avenge the **L.** of Midian. 3068
Nu 31:7 as the **L.** commanded Moses;............ 3068
Nu 31:16 commit trespass against the **L.**.......... 3068
Nu 31:16 among the congregation of the **L.**........ 3068
Nu 31:21 the law which the **L.** commanded 3068
Nu 31:25 the **L.** spake unto Moses, saying, ... 3068
Nu 31:28 levy a tribute unto the **L.** of the 3068
Nu 31:29 for an heave offering of the **L.**........... 3068
Nu 31:30 charge of the tabernacle of the **L.** 3068
Nu 31:31 priest did as the **L.** commanded......... 3068
Nu 31:41 as the **L.** commanded Moses............. 3068
Nu 31:47 charge of the tabernacle of the **L.**; 3068
Nu 31:47 as the **L.** commanded Moses............. 3068
Nu 31:50 brought an oblation for the **L.**,........... 3068
Nu 31:50 for our souls before the **L.** 3068
Nu 31:52 that they offered up to the **L.**, ... 3068
Nu 31:54 children of Israel before the **L.** 3068
Nu 32:4 the country which the **L.** smote......... 3068
Nu 32:7 the land which the **L.** hath given........ 3068
Nu 32:9 the land which the **L.** had given......... 3068
Nu 32:12 they have wholly followed the **L.**......... 3068
Nu 32:13 done evil in the sight of the **L.**, ... 3068
Nu 32:14 anger of the **L.** toward Israel. 3068
Nu 32:20 go armed before the **L.** to war, ... 3068
Nu 32:21 armed over Jordan before the **L.**,....... 3068
Nu 32:22 land be subdued before the **L.**........... 3068
Nu 32:22 and be guiltless before the **L.**,........... 3068
Nu 32:22 be your possession before the **L.** 3068
Nu 32:23 ye have sinned against the **L.**............ 3068

Nu 32:25 will do as my **l.** commandeth.............. 113
Nu 32:27 for war, before the **L.** to battle, ... 3068
Nu 32:27 to battle, as my **l.** saith. 113
Nu 32:29 armed to battle, before the **L.**,........... 3068
Nu 32:31 the **L.** hath said unto thy servants,...... 3068
Nu 32:32 will pass over armed before the **L.**...... 3068
Nu 33:2 by the commandment of the **L.**:.......... 3068
Nu 33:4 the **L.** had smitten among them: 3068
Nu 33:4 also the **L.** executed judgments. 3068
Nu 33:38 at the commandment of the **L.**, ... 3068
Nu 33:50 **L.** spake unto Moses in the plains...... 3068
Nu 34:1 And the **L.** spake unto Moses, ... 3068
Nu 34:13 which the **L.** commanded to give........ 3068
Nu 34:16 And the **L.** spake unto Moses, ... 3068
Nu 34:29 the **L.** commanded to divide the......... 3068
Nu 35:1 **L.** spake unto Moses in the plains...... 3068
Nu 35:9 And the **L.** spake unto Moses, ... 3068
Nu 35:34 I the **L.** dwell among the children....... 3068
Nu 36:2 **L.** commanded...to give the land........ 3068
Nu 36:2 commanded my **l.** to give the land 113
Nu 36:2 my **l.** was commanded...to give the...... 113
Nu 36:2 was commanded by the **L.** to give...... 3068
Nu 36:5 according to the word of the **L.**, ... 3068
Nu 36:6 thing which the **L.** doth command....... 3068
Nu 36:10 the **L.** commanded Moses, so did....... 3068
Nu 36:13 the **L.** commanded by the hand of....... 3068
De 1:3 **L.** had given him in commandment 3068
De 1:6 **L.** our God spake unto us in Horeb, ... 3068
De 1:8 land which the **L.** sware unto your..... 3068
De 1:10 **L.** your God hath multiplied you,........ 3068
De 1:11 **L.** God of your fathers make you........ 3068
De 1:19 as the **L.** our God commanded us; 3068
De 1:20 which the **L.** our God doth give......... 3068
De 1:21 the **L.** thy God hath set the land........ 3068
De 1:21 **L.** God of thy fathers hath said.......... 3068
De 1:25 which the **L.** our God doth give......... 3068
De 1:26 commandment of the **L.** your God. 3068
De 1:27 Because the **L.** hated us, he hath....... 3068
De 1:30 **L.** your God which goeth before 3068
De 1:31 how that the **L.** thy God bare thee,.... 3068
De 1:32 ye did not believe the **L.** your God,.... 3068
De 1:34 **L.** heard the voice of your words, ... 3068
De 1:36 he hath wholly followed the **L.**........... 3068
De 1:37 the **L.** was angry with me for your..... 3068
De 1:41 We have sinned against the **L.**,.......... 3068
De 1:41 that the **L.** our God commanded 3068
De 1:42 **L.** said unto me, Say unto them,........ 3068
De 1:43 the commandment of the **L.**, ... 3068
De 1:45 returned and wept before the **L.**;....... 3068
De 1:45 the **L.** would not hearken to your...... 3068
De 2:1 Red sea, as the **L.** spake unto me:..... 3068
De 2:2 the **L.** spake unto me, saying,........... 3068
De 2:7 **L.** thy God hath blessed thee in all.... 3068
De 2:7 **L.** thy God hath been with thee;........ 3068
De 2:9 the **L.** said unto me, Distress not 3068
De 2:12 which the **L.** gave unto them. 3068
De 2:14 host, as the **L.** sware unto them........ 3068
De 2:15 hand of the **L.** was against them, ... 3068
De 2:17 the **L.** spake unto me, saying,........... 3068
De 2:21 **L.** destroyed them before them; 3068
De 2:29 land which the **L.** our God giveth....... 3068
De 2:30 **L.** thy God hardened his spirit,.......... 3068
De 2:31 the **L.** said unto me, Behold, I 3068
De 2:33 **L.** our God delivered him before......... 3068
De 2:36 **L.** our God delivered all unto us: 3068
De 2:37 the **L.** our God forbad us. 3068
De 3:2 **L.** said unto me, Fear him not:.......... 3068
De 3:3 the **L.** our God delivered into our 3068
De 3:18 **L.** your God hath given you this 3068
De 3:20 the **L.** hath given rest unto your........ 3068
De 3:20 which the **L.** your God hath given...... 3068
De 3:21 all that the **L.** your God hath done 3068
De 3:21 the **L.** do unto all the kingdoms......... 3068
De 3:22 **L.** your God he shall fight for you. 3068
De 3:23 I besought the **L.** at that time, ... 3068
De 3:24 O **L.** God, thou hast begun to shew..... 136
De 3:26 **L.** was wroth with me for your.......... 3068
De 3:26 the **L.** said unto me, Let it suffice...... 3068
De 4:1 **L.** God of your fathers giveth........... 3068
De 4:2 commandments of the **L.** your........... 3068
De 4:3 eyes have seen what the **L.** did......... 3068
De 4:3 **L.** thy God hath destroyed them........ 3068
De 4:4 did cleave unto the **L.** your God 3068
De 4:5 as the **L.** my God commanded me,..... 3068
De 4:7 as the **L.** our God is in all things 3068
De 4:10 stoodest before the **L.** thy God in...... 3068
De 4:10 when the **L.** said unto me, Gather...... 3068

De 4:12 the **L.** spake unto you out of the 3068
De 4:14 **L.** commanded me at that time to 3068
De 4:15 the **L.** spake unto you in Horeb......... 3068
De 4:19 **L.** thy God hath divided unto all......... 3068
De 4:20 **L.** hath taken you, and brought.......... 3068
De 4:21 the **L.** was angry with me for your..... 3068
De 4:21 which the **L.** thy God giveth thee....... 3068
De 4:23 forget the covenant of the **L.** your 3068
De 4:23 **L.** thy God hath forbidden thee.......... 3068
De 4:24 **L.** thy God is a consuming fire, ... 3068
De 4:25 evil in the sight of the **L.** thy God,...... 3068
De 4:27 **L.** shall scatter you among the 3068
De 4:27 whither the **L.** shall lead you............. 3068
De 4:29 thou shalt seek the **L.** thy God,......... 3068
De 4:30 if thou turn to the **L.** thy God, ... 3068
De 4:31 the **L.** thy God is a merciful God;) 3068
De 4:34 **L.** your God did for you in Egypt....... 3068
De 4:35 know that the **L.** he is God;.............. 3068
De 4:39 that the **L.** he is God in heaven......... 3068
De 4:40 which the **L.** thy God giveth thee,...... 3068
De 5:2 **L.** our God made a covenant with 3068
De 5:3 **L.** made not this covenant with.......... 3068
De 5:4 **L.** talked with you face to face in....... 3068
De 5:5 (I stood between the **L.** and you........ 3068
De 5:5 to shew you the word of the **L.**;......... 3068
De 5:6 am the **L.** thy God, which brought 3068
De 5:9 the **L.** thy God am a jealous God, ... 3068
De 5:11 name of the **L.** thy God in vain:......... 3068
De 5:11 the **L.** will not hold him guiltless 3068
De 5:12 **L.** thy God hath commanded thee. 3068
De 5:14 is the sabbath of the **L.** thy God:....... 3068
De 5:15 the **L.** thy God brought thee out........ 3068
De 5:15 **L.** thy God commanded...to keep....... 3068
De 5:16 the **L.** thy God hath commanded........ 3068
De 5:16 land which the **L.** thy God giveth........ 3068
De 5:22 **L.** spake unto all your assembly........ 3068
De 5:24 **L.** our God hath shewed us his.......... 3068
De 5:25 hear the voice of the **L.** our God 3068
De 5:27 all that the **L.** our God shall say: 3068
De 5:27 all that the **L.** our God shall speak 3068
De 5:28 **L.** heard the voice of your words, ... 3068
De 5:28 the **L.** said unto me, I have heard...... 3068
De 5:32, 33 **L.** your God hath commanded 3068
De 6:1 **L.** your God commanded to teach...... 3068
De 6:2 thou mightest fear the **L.** thy God,..... 3068
De 6:3 **L.** God of thy fathers...promised........ 3068
De 6:4 Israel: The **L.** our God is one **L.**:...... 3068
De 6:5 love the **L.** thy God with all thine 3068
De 6:10 the **L.** thy God shall have brought...... 3068
De 6:12 beware lest thou forget the **L.**,........... 3068
De 6:13 Thou shalt fear the **L.** thy God,......... 3068
De 6:15 the **L.** thy God is a jealous God......... 3068
De 6:15 anger of the **L.** thy God be kindled..... 3068
De 6:16 shall not tempt the **L.** your God, ... 3068
De 6:17 keep the commandments of the **L.** 3068
De 6:18 and good in the sight of the **L.**: 3068
De 6:18 the good land which the **L.** sware 3068
De 6:19 before thee, as the **L.** hath spoken..... 3068
De 6:20 **L.** our God hath commanded you?...... 3068
De 6:21 **L.** brought us out of Egypt with 3068
De 6:22 **L.** shewed signs and wonders,........... 3068
De 6:24 **L.** commanded us to do all these 3068
De 6:24 statutes, to fear the **L.** our God, ... 3068
De 6:25 commandments before the **L.** our........ 3068
De 7:1 **L.** thy God shall bring thee into........ 3068
De 7:2 the **L.** thy God shall deliver them....... 3068
De 7:4 the anger of the **L.** be kindled........... 3068
De 7:6 holy people unto the **L.** thy God: 3068
De 7:6 **L.** thy God hath chosen thee to be..... 3068
De 7:7 **L.** did not set his love upon you, ... 3068
De 7:8 But because the **L.** loved you,........... 3068
De 7:8 **L.** brought you out with a mighty....... 3068
De 7:9 that the **L.** thy God, he is God,......... 3068
De 7:12 **L.** thy God shall keep unto thee 3068
De 7:15 **L.** will take away from thee all 3068
De 7:16 which the **L.** thy God shall deliver...... 3068
De 7:18 the **L.** thy God did unto Pharaoh,....... 3068
De 7:19 the **L.** thy God brought thee out:....... 3068
De 7:19 so shall the **L.** thy God do unto all..... 3068
De 7:20 **L.** thy God will send the hornet 3068
De 7:21 for the **L.** thy God is among you,....... 3068
De 7:22 the **L.** thy God will put out those....... 3068
De 7:23 **L.** thy God shall deliver them unto..... 3068
De 7:25 an abomination to the **L.** thy God....... 3068
De 8:1 land which the **L.** sware unto your 3068
De 8:2 way which the **L.** thy God led thee 3068
De 8:3 word...out of the mouth of the **L.** 3068
De 8:5 son, so the **L.** thy God chasteneth 3068
De 8:6 keep the commandments of the **L.** 3068
De 8:7 **L.** thy God bringeth thee into a 3068
De 8:10 shalt bless the **L.** thy God for the...... 3068
De 8:11 thou forget not the **L.** thy God,......... 3068
De 8:14 and thou forget the **L.** thy God,......... 3068
De 8:18 shalt remember the **L.** thy God: 3068
De 8:19 do at all forget the **L.** thy God, ... 3068
De 8:20 nations which the **L.** destroyeth......... 3068
De 8:20 unto the voice of the **L.** your God....... 3068
De 9:3 **L.** thy God is he which goeth over..... 3068
De 9:3 as the **L.** hath said unto thee. 3068
De 9:4 the **L.** thy God hath cast them out..... 3068
De 9:4 **L.** hath brought me in to possess....... 3068
De 9:4 the **L.** doth drive them out from......... 3068
De 9:5 **L.** thy God doth drive them out......... 3068
De 9:5 the word which the **L.** sware unto...... 3068
De 9:6 **L.** thy God giveth thee not this 3068
De 9:7 provokedst the **L.** thy God to wrath... 3068
De 9:7 been rebellious against the **L.**........... 3068
De 9:8 ye provoked the **L.** to wrath, so........ 3068
De 9:8 so that the **L.** was angry with you...... 3068
De 9:9 covenant which the **L.** made with....... 3068
De 9:10 **L.** delivered unto me two tables of..... 3068
De 9:10 **L.** spake with you in the mount 3068
De 9:11 **L.** gave me the two tables of stone, ... 3068
De 9:12 **L.** said unto me, Arise, get thee........ 3068
De 9:13 the **L.** spake unto me, saying, I......... 3068
De 9:16 sinned against the **L.** your God,......... 3068
De 9:16 out of the way which the **L.** had......... 3068
De 9:18 I fell down before the **L.**, as at the 3068
De 9:18 wickedly in the sight of the **L.**, to...... 3068
De 9:19 the **L.** was wroth against you to 3068
De 9:19 the **L.** hearkened unto me at that....... 3068
De 9:20 **L.** was very angry with Aaron to 3068
De 9:22 ye provoked the **L.** to wrath. 3068
De 9:23 **L.** sent you from Kadesh-barnea, ... 3068
De 9:23 commandment of the **L.** your God, ... 3068
De 9:24 been rebellious against the **L.**........... 3068
De 9:25 fell down before the **L.** forty days...... 3068
De 9:25 **L.** had said he would destroy you....... 3068
De 9:26 I prayed therefore unto the **L.**,.......... 3068
De 9:26 O **L.** God, destroy not thy people........ 136
De 9:28 the **l.** was not able to bring them....... 3068
De 10:1 that time the **L.** said unto me,........... 3068
De 10:4 **L.** spake unto you in the mount......... 3068
De 10:4 and the **L.** gave them unto me. 3068
De 10:5 they be, as the **L.** commanded me. 3068
De 10:8 the **L.** separated the tribe of Levi, ... 3068
De 10:8 the ark of the covenant of the **L.**, ... 3068
De 10:8 before the **L.** to minister unto him, ... 3068
De 10:9 the **L.** is his inheritance, ... 3068
De 10:9 as the **L.** thy God promised him. 3068
De 10:10 the **L.** hearkened unto me at that....... 3068
De 10:10 and the **L.** would not destroy thee. 3068
De 10:11 **L.** said unto me, Arise, take thy........ 3068
De 10:12 what doth the **L.** thy God require 3068
De 10:12 but to fear the **L.** thy God, to walk.... 3068
De 10:12 to serve the **L.** thy God with all 3068
De 10:13 the commandments of the **L.**,............ 3068
De 10:15 **L.** had a delight in thy fathers 3068
De 10:17 the **L.** your God is God of gods,........ 3068
De 10:17 **L.** of lords, a great God, a mighty, ... 113
De 10:20 Thou shalt fear the **L.** thy God;.......... 3068
De 10:22 **L.** thy God hath made thee as the...... 3068
De 11:1 love the **L.** thy God, and keep his...... 3068
De 11:2 chastisement of the **L.** your God,........ 3068
De 11:4 **L.** hath destroyed them unto this........ 3068
De 11:7 great acts of the **L.** which he did. 3068
De 11:9 the **L.** sware unto your fathers........... 3068
De 11:12 land which the **L.** thy God careth....... 3068
De 11:12 eyes of the **L.** thy God are always 3068
De 11:13 to love the **L.** your God, and to.......... 3068
De 11:17 good land which the **L.** giveth you...... 3068
De 11:21 the **L.** sware unto your fathers........... 3068
De 11:22 to love the **L.** your God, to walk 3068
De 11:23 the **L.** drive out all these nations 3068
De 11:25 **L.** your God shall lay the fear of........ 3068
De 11:27, 28 obey...commandments of the **L.**..... 3068
De 11:29 **L.** thy God hath brought thee in 3068
De 11:31 the land which the **L.** your God 3068
De 12:1 **L.** God of thy fathers giveth thee....... 3068
De 12:4 not do so unto the **L.** your God......... 3068
De 12:5 the **L.** your God shall choose out 3068
De 12:7 shall eat before the **L.** your God,....... 3068
De 12:7 the **L.** thy God hath blessed thee....... 3068
De 12:9 which the **L.** your God giveth you...... 3068
De 12:10 the land which the **L.** your God......... 3068
De 12:11 the **L.** your God shall choose to.......... 3068
De 12:11 vows which ye vow unto the **L.**:........ 3068
De 12:12 rejoice before the **L.** your God, ... 3068
De 12:14 place which the **L.** shall choose........... 3068
De 12:15 to the blessing of the **L.** thy God 3068
De 12:18 thou must eat them before the **L.** 3068
De 12:18 which the **L.** thy God shall choose,..... 3068
De 12:18 rejoice before the **L.** thy God in 3068
De 12:20 the **L.** thy God shall enlarge thy 3068
De 12:21 which the **L.** thy God hath chosen...... 3068
De 12:21 which the **L.** hath given thee,............ 3068
De 12:25 is right in the sight of the **L.**............. 3068
De 12:26 place which the **L.** shall choose:......... 3068
De 12:27 upon the altar of the **L.** thy God:....... 3068
De 12:27 upon the altar of the **L.** thy God, ... 3068
De 12:28 and right in the sight of the **L.** 3068
De 12:29 the **L.** thy God shall cut off the 3068
De 12:31 not do so unto the **L.** thy God: 3068
De 12:31 for every abomination to the **L.**, ... 3068
De 13:3 for the **L.** your God proveth you,....... 3068
De 13:3 ye love the **L.** your God with all........ 3068
De 13:4 shall walk after the **L.** your God, ... 3068
De 13:5 to turn you away from the **L.**............ 3068
De 13:5 the **L.** thy God commanded thee........ 3068
De 13:10 to thrust thee away from the **L.** 3068
De 13:12 the **L.** thy God hath given thee to...... 3068
De 13:16 every whit, for the **L.** thy God: 3068
De 13:17 **L.** may turn from the fierceness 3068
De 13:18 hearken to the voice of the **L.** thy...... 3068
De 13:18 is right in the eyes of the **L.** which 3068
De 14:1 the children of the **L.** your God: 3068
De 14:2 holy people unto the **L.** thy God, ... 3068
De 14:2 the **L.** hath chosen thee to be a......... 3068
De 14:21 holy people unto the **L.** thy God. 3068
De 14:23 shalt eat before the **L.** thy God, ... 3068
De 14:23 to fear the **L.** thy God always. 3068
De 14:24 **L.** thy God shall choose to set his...... 3068
De 14:24 the **L.** thy God hath blessed thee:...... 3068
De 14:25 which the **L.** thy God shall choose:..... 3068
De 14:26 eat there before the **L.** thy God, ... 3068
De 14:29 **L.** thy God may bless thee in all........ 3068
De 15:4 **L.** shall greatly bless thee in the........ 3068
De 15:4 land which the **L.** thy God giveth....... 3068
De 15:5 unto the voice of the **L.** thy God, ... 3068
De 15:6 For the **L.** thy God blesseth thee,...... 3068
De 15:7 land which the **L.** thy God giveth....... 3068
De 15:9 cry unto the **L.** against thee, and....... 3068
De 15:10 **L.** thy God shall bless thee in all........ 3068
De 15:14 the **L.** thy God hath blessed thee........ 3068
De 15:15 the **L.** thy God redeemed thee: 3068
De 15:18 **L.** thy God shall bless thee in all........ 3068
De 15:19 shalt sanctify unto the **L.** thy God: 3068
De 15:20 shalt eat it before the **L.** thy God 3068
De 15:20 place which the **L.** shall choose,......... 3068
De 15:21 not sacrifice unto the **L.** thy God. 3068
De 16:1 the passover unto the **L.** thy God: 3068
De 16:1 **L.** thy God brought thee forth out...... 3068
De 16:2 the passover unto the **L.** thy God, ... 3068
De 16:2 place which the **L.** shall choose.......... 3068
De 16:5 which the **L.** thy God giveth thee:...... 3068
De 16:6 which the **L.** thy God shall choose...... 3068
De 16:7 which the **L.** thy God shall choose:..... 3068
De 16:8 a solemn assembly to the **L.** thy....... 3068
De 16:10 feast of weeks unto the **L.** thy God.... 3068
De 16:10 shalt give unto the **L.** thy God,...............
De 16:10 the **L.** thy God hath blessed thee:...... 3068
De 16:11 shalt rejoice before the **L.** thy God,.... 3068
De 16:11 which the **L.** thy God hath chosen...... 3068
De 16:15 solemn feast unto the **L.** thy God....... 3068
De 16:15 place which the **L.** shall choose:......... 3068
De 16:15 the **L.** thy God shall bless thee in 3068
De 16:16 all thy males appear before the **L.**....... 3068
De 16:16 not appear before the **L.** empty: 3068
De 16:17 to the blessing of the **L.** thy God 3068
De 16:18 which the **L.** thy God giveth thee,...... 3068
De 16:20 land which the **L.** thy God giveth....... 3068
De 16:21 unto the altar of the **L.** thy God, ... 3068
De 16:22 which the **L.** thy God hateth. 3068
De 17:1 not sacrifice unto the **L.** thy God 3068
De 17:1 abomination unto the **L.** thy God....... 3068
De 17:2 gates which the **L.** thy God giveth 3068
De 17:2 wickedness in the sight of the **L.** 3068
De 17:8 which the **L.** thy God shall choose;..... 3068
De 17:10 place which the **L.** shall choose.......... 3068
De 17:12 to minister there before the **L.** thy..... 3068
De 17:14 land which the **L.** thy God giveth....... 3068

De 17:15 whom the **L.** thy God shall choose: 3068
De 17:16 forasmuch as the **L.** hath said 3068
De 17:19 may learn to fear the **L.** his God, 3068
De 18:1 offerings of the **L.** made by fire, 3068
De 18:2 the **L.** is their inheritance, as he 3068
De 18:5 **L.** thy God hath chosen him out 3068
De 18:5 to minister in the name of the **L.**, 3068
De 18:6 place which the **L.** shall choose; 3068
De 18:7 minister in the name of the **L.** his 3068
De 18:7 which stand there before the **L.** 3068
De 18:9 land which the **L.** thy God giveth 3068
De 18:12 are an abomination unto the **L.**: 3068
De 18:12 **L.** thy God doth drive them out 3068
De 18:13 be perfect with the **L.** thy God. 3068
De 18:14 **L.** thy God hath not suffered thee 3068
De 18:15 **L.** thy God will raise up into thee 3068
De 18:16 thou desiredst of the **L.** thy God 3068
De 18:16 again the voice of the **L.** my God, 3068
De 18:17 **L.** said unto me, They have well 3068
De 18:21 which the **L.** hath not spoken? 3068
De 18:22 speaketh in the name of the **L.**, 3068
De 18:22 which the **L.** hath not spoken, 3068
De 19:1 **L.** thy God hath cut off the nations 3068
De 19:1 whose land the **L.** thy God giveth 3068
De 19:2 **L.** thy God giveth thee to possess 3068
De 19:3 **L.** thy God giveth thee to inherit, 3068
De 19:8 the **L.** thy God enlarge thy coast, 3068
De 19:9 this day, to love the **L.** thy God, 3068
De 19:10 land, which the **L.** thy God giveth 3068
De 19:14 **L.** thy God giveth thee to possess 3068
De 19:17 shall stand before the **L.**, before 3068
De 20:1 for the **L.** thy God is with thee, 3068
De 20:4 **L.** your God is he that goeth with 3068
De 20:13 **L.** thy God hath delivered it into 3068
De 20:14 the **L.** thy God hath given thee. 3068
De 20:16 the **L.** thy God doth give thee for 3068
De 20:17 **L.** thy God hath commanded thee: 3068
De 20:18 so should ye sin against the **L.** 3068
De 21:1 land which the **L.** thy God giveth 3068
De 21:5 them the **L.** thy God hath chosen 3068
De 21:5 to bless in the name of the **L.**; 3068
De 21:8 Be merciful, O **L.**, unto thy people 3068
De 21:9 is right in the sight of the **L.** 3068
De 21:10 **L.** thy God hath delivered them 3068
De 21:23 the **L.** thy God giveth thee for an 3068
De 22:5 do so are abominations unto the **L.** 3068
De 23:1 into the congregation of the **L.** 3068
De 23:2 into the congregation of the **L.**; 3068
De 23:2 into the congregation of the **L.** 3068
De 23:3 into the congregation of the **L.**; 3068
De 23:3 into the congregation of the **L.** 3068
De 23:5 **L.** thy God would not hearken 3068
De 23:5 **L.** thy God turned the curse into 3068
De 23:5 because the **L.** thy God loved thee 3068
De 23:8 into the congregation of the **L.** 3068
De 23:14 **L.** thy God walketh in the midst 3068
De 23:18 into the house of the **L.** thy God 3068
De 23:18 are abomination unto the **L.** thy 3068
De 23:20 **L.** thy God may bless thee in all 3068
De 23:21 vow a vow unto the **L.** thy God, 3068
De 23:21 **L.** thy God will surely require it 3068
De 23:23 hast vowed unto the **L.** thy God, 3068
De 24:4 is abomination before the **L.**: 3068
De 24:4 the **L.** thy God giveth thee for an 3068
De 24:9 the **L.** thy God did unto Miriam 3068
De 24:13 unto thee before the **L.** thy God. 3068
De 24:15 he cry against thee unto the **L.**, 3068
De 24:18 **L.** thy God redeemed thee thence: 3068
De 24:19 **L.** thy God may bless thee in all 3068
De 25:15 land which the **L.** thy God giveth 3068
De 25:16 abomination unto the **L.** thy God. 3068
De 25:19 **L.** thy God hath given thee rest 3068
De 25:19 land which the **L.** thy God giveth 3068
De 26:1 land which the **L.** thy God giveth 3068
De 26:2 land that the **L.** thy God giveth 3068
De 26:2 which the **L.** thy God shall choose 3068
De 26:3 I profess this day unto the **L.** thy 3068
De 26:3 country which the **L.** swear unto 3068
De 26:4 before the altar of the **L.** thy God. 3068
De 26:5 and say before the **L.** thy God, 3068
De 26:7 we cried unto the **L.** God of our 3068
De 26:7 **L.** heard our voice, and looked 3068
De 26:8 **L.** brought us forth out of Egypt 3068
De 26:10 which thou, O **L.**, hast given me 3068
De 26:10 shalt set it before the **L.** thy God, 3068
De 26:10 worship before the **L.** thy God: 3068
De 26:11 which the **L.** thy God hath given 3068
De 26:13 shalt say before the **L.** thy God, 3068
De 26:14 to the voice of the **L.** my God, 3068
De 26:16 the **L.** thy God hath commanded 3068
De 26:17 avouched the **L.** this day to be thy 3068
De 26:18 **L.** hath avouched thee this day to 3068
De 26:19 holy people unto the **L.** thy God, 3068
De 27:2,3 land which the **L.** thy God giveth 3068
De 27:3 **L.** God of thy fathers...promised 3068
De 27:5 build an altar unto the **L.** thy God, 3068
De 27:6 build the altar of the **L.** thy God 3068
De 27:6 offerings thereon unto the **L.** thy 3068
De 27:7 and rejoice before the **L.** thy God. 3068
De 27:9 the people of the **L.** thy God. 3068
De 27:10 obey the voice of the **L.** thy God, 3068
De 27:15 an abomination unto the **L.**, 3068
De 28:1 unto the voice of the **L.** thy God, 3068
De 28:1 **L.** thy God will set thee on high 3068
De 28:2 unto the voice of the **L.** thy God. 3068
De 28:7 **L.** shall cause thine enemies that 3068
De 28:8 **L.** shall command the blessing 3068
De 28:8 land which the **L.** thy God giveth 3068
De 28:9 **L.** shall establish thee an holy 3068
De 28:9 keep the commandments of the **L.** 3068
De 28:10 art called by the name of the **L.**; 3068
De 28:11 **L.** shall make thee plenteous in 3068
De 28:11 land which the **L.** sware unto thy 3068
De 28:12 **L.** shall open unto thee his good 3068
De 28:13 the **L.** shall make thee the head, 3068
De 28:13 unto commandments of the **L.** thy 3068
De 28:15 unto the voice of the **L.** thy God, 3068
De 28:20 **L.** shall send upon thee cursing, 3068
De 28:21 The **L.** shall make the pestilence 3068
De 28:22 The **L.** shall smite thee with a 3068
De 28:24 **L.** shall make the rain of thy land 3068
De 28:25 **L.** shall cause thee to be smitten 3068
De 28:27 **L.** will smite thee with the botch 3068
De 28:28 **L.** shall smite thee with madness, 3068
De 28:35 **L.** shall smite thee in the knees, 3068
De 28:36 **L.** shall bring thee, and thy king 3068
De 28:37 whither the **L.** shall lead thee. 3068
De 28:45 not unto the voice of the **L.** thy 3068
De 28:47 thou servedst not the **L.** thy God 3068
De 28:48 enemies which the **L.** shall send 3068
De 28:49 **L.** shall bring a nation against 3068
De 28:52 the **L.** thy God hath given thee. 3068
De 28:53 the **L.** thy God hath given thee, 3068
De 28:58 fearful name, The Lord Thy God; 3068
De 28:59 Then the **L.** will make thy plagues 3068
De 28:61 will the **L.** bring upon thee, until 3068
De 28:62 not obey the voice of the **L.** thy 3068
De 28:63 **L.** rejoiced over you to do you good, 3068
De 28:63 **L.** will rejoice over you to destroy 3068
De 28:64 **L.** shall scatter thee among all 3068
De 28:65 **L.** shall give thee...a trembling 3068
De 28:68 the **L.** shall bring thee into Egypt 3068
De 29:1 the **L.** commanded Moses to make 3068
De 29:2 seen all that the **L.** did before your 3068
De 29:4 **L.** hath not given you an heart to 3068
De 29:6 know that I am the **L.** your God. 3068
De 29:10 of you before the **L.** your God; 3068
De 29:12 covenant with the **L.** thy God, 3068
De 29:12 the **L.** thy God maketh with thee 3068
De 29:15, 18 this day before the **L.** our God, 3068
De 29:20 The **L.** will not spare him, but 3068
De 29:20 anger of the **L.** and his jealousy 3068
De 29:20 **L.** shall blot out his name from 3068
De 29:21 **L.** shall separate him unto evil 3068
De 29:22 sicknesses which the **L.** hath laid 3068
De 29:23 the **L.** overthrew in his anger, 3068
De 29:24 the **L.** done thus unto the land? 3068
De 29:25 forsaken the covenant of the **L.** 3068
De 29:27 the anger of the **L.** was kindled 3068
De 29:28 **L.** rooted them out of their land 3068
De 29:29 belong unto the **L.** our God: 3068
De 30:1 the **L.** thy God hath driven thee, 3068
De 30:2 shalt return unto the **L.** thy God, 3068
De 30:3 **L.** thy God will turn thy captivity, 3068
De 30:3 **L.** thy God hath scattered thee 3068
De 30:4 will the **L.** thy God gather thee, 3068
De 30:5 **L.** thy God will bring thee into 3068
De 30:6 **L.** thy God will circumcise thine 3068
De 30:6 to love the **L.** thy God with all 3068
De 30:7 the **L.** thy God will put all these 3068
De 30:8 and obey the voice of the **L.**, 3068
De 30:9 the **L.** thy God will make thee 3068
De 30:9 **L.** will again rejoice over thee 3068
De 30:10 unto the voice of the **L.** thy God, 3068
De 30:10 turn unto the **L.** thy God with all 3068
De 30:16 this day to love the **L.** thy God, 3068
De 30:16 **L.** thy God shall bless thee in the 3068
De 30:20 thou mayest love the **L.** thy God, 3068
De 30:20 in the land which the **L.** sware 3068
De 31:2 the **L.** hath said unto me, Thou 3068
De 31:3 The **L.** thy God, he will go over 3068
De 31:3 before thee, as the **L.** hath said, 3068
De 31:4 **L.** shall do unto them as he did 3068
De 31:5 **L.** shall give them up before your 3068
De 31:6 the **L.** thy God, he it is that doth 3068
De 31:7 land which the **L.** hath sworn 3068
De 31:8 And the **L.**, he it is that doth go 3068
De 31:9 the ark of the covenant of the **L.**, 3068
De 31:11 is come to appear before the **L.** 3068
De 31:12 learn, and fear the **L.** your God, 3068
De 31:13 learn to fear the **L.** your God, as 3068
De 31:14 the **L.** said unto Moses, Behold, 3068
De 31:15 the **L.** appeared in the tabernacle 3068
De 31:16 the **L.** said unto Moses, Behold, 3068
De 31:25 the ark of the covenant of the **L.**, 3068
De 31:26 the ark of the covenant of the **L.** 3068
De 31:27 been rebellious against the **L.**; 3068
De 31:29 will do evil in the sight of the **L.**, 3068
De 32:3 will publish the name of the **L.**: 3068
De 32:6 Do ye thus requite the **L.**, O 3068
De 32:12 So the **L.** alone did lead him, and 3068
De 32:19 when the **L.** saw it, he abhorred 3068
De 32:27 and the **L.** hath not done all this. 3068
De 32:30 and the **L.** hath shut them up? 3068
De 32:36 For the **L.** shall judge his people, 3068
De 32:48 And the **L.** spake unto Moses that 3068
De 33:2 he said, The **L.** came from Sinai, 3068
De 33:7 Hear, **L.**, the voice of Judah, and 3068
De 33:11 Bless, **L.**, his substance, and 3068
De 33:12 The beloved of the **L.** shall dwell 3068
De 33:12 the **L.** shall cover him all the day
De 33:13 Blessed of the **L.** be his land, for 3068
De 33:21 he executed the justice of the **L.**, 3068
De 33:23 full with the blessing of the **L.**, 3068
De 33:29 O people saved by the **L.**, the 3068
De 34:1 the **L.** shewed him all the land of 3068
De 34:4 And the **L.** said unto him, This is 3068
De 34:5 the servant of the **L.** died there 3068
De 34:5 according to the word of the **L.** 3068
De 34:9 did as the **l.** commanded Moses. 3068
De 34:10 whom the **L.** knew face to face, 3068
De 34:11 which the **L.** sent him to do in 3068
Jos 1:1 death of Moses...servant of the **L.**, 3068
Jos 1:1 **L.** spake unto Joshua the son of 3068
Jos 1:9 for the **L.** thy God is with thee 3068
Jos 1:11 **L.** your God giveth you to possess 3068
Jos 1:13 servant of the **L.** commanded you, 3068
Jos 1:13 **L.** your God hath given you rest, 3068
Jos 1:15 **L.** have given your brethren rest, 3068
Jos 1:15 the land which the **L.** your God 3068
Jos 1:17 only the **L.** thy God be with thee, 3068
Jos 2:9 the **L.** hath given you the land, 3068
Jos 2:10 how the **L.** dried up the water of 3068
Jos 2:11 for the **L.** your God, he is God in 3068
Jos 2:12 you, swear unto me by the **L.**, 3068
Jos 2:14 the **L.** hath given us the land, 3068
Jos 2:24 **L.** hath delivered into our hands 3068
Jos 3:3 the ark of the covenant of the **L.** 3068
Jos 3:5 **L.** will do wonders among you. 3068
Jos 3:7 And the **L.** said unto Joshua, 3068
Jos 3:9 hear the words of the **L.** your 3068
Jos 3:11 the ark of the covenant of the **L.** 113
Jos 3:13 priests that bear the ark of the **L.**, 3068
Jos 3:13 the **L.** of all the earth, shall rest 113
Jos 3:17 the ark of the covenant of the **L.** 3068
Jos 4:1 that the **L.** spake unto Joshua, 3068
Jos 4:5 Pass over before the ark of the **L.** 3068
Jos 4:7 the ark of the covenant of the **L.**; 3068
Jos 4:8 as the **L.** spake unto Joshua, 3068
Jos 4:10 finished that the **L.** commanded 3068
Jos 4:11 the ark of the **L.** passed over, 3068
Jos 4:13 for war passed over before the **L.** 3068
Jos 4:14 that day the **L.** magnified Joshua 3068
Jos 4:15 the **L.** spake unto Joshua, saying, 3068
Jos 4:18 the ark of the covenant of the **L.** 3068
Jos 4:23 **L.** your God dried up the waters 3068
Jos 4:23 **L.** your God did to the Red sea, 3068
Jos 4:24 might know the hand of the **L.** 3068

Jos	4:24	fear the **L.** your God for ever.	3068
Jos	5:1	the **L.** had dried up the waters of	3068
Jos	5:2	time the **L.** said unto Joshua,	3068
Jos	5:6	obeyed not the voice of the **L.**:	3068
Jos	5:6	**L.** sware that he would not shew	3068
Jos	5:6	the **L.** sware unto their fathers	3068
Jos	5:9	the **L.** said unto Joshua, This	3068
Jos	5:14	as captain of the host of the **L.**	3068
Jos	5:14	What saith my **l.** unto his servant?	113
Jos	6:2	the **L.** said unto Joshua, See, I	3068
Jos	6:6	horns before the ark of the **L.**	3068
Jos	6:7	pass on before the ark of the **L.**.	3068
Jos	6:8	horns passed on before the **L.**,	3068
Jos	6:8	the ark of the covenant of the **L.**	3068
Jos	6:11	So the ark of the **L.** compassed	3068
Jos	6:12	priests took up the ark of the **L.**	3068
Jos	6:13	before the ark of the **L.** went on	3068
Jos	6:13	came after the ark of the **L.**,	3068
Jos	6:16	the **L.** hath given you the city.	3068
Jos	6:17	and all that are therein, to the **L.**:	3068
Jos	6:19	iron, are consecrated unto the **L.**:	3068
Jos	6:19	come into the treasury of the **L.**.	3068
Jos	6:24	treasury of the house of the **L.**	3068
Jos	6:26	Cursed be the man before the **L.**,	3068
Jos	6:27	So the **L.** was with Joshua; and	3068
Jos	7:1	the anger of the **L.** was kindled	3068
Jos	7:6	face before the ark of the **L.** until	3068
Jos	7:7	And Joshua said, Alas, O **L.** God,	136
Jos	7:8	O **L.**, what shall I say, when Israel	136
Jos	7:10	the **L.** said unto Joshua, Get thee	3068
Jos	7:13	thus saith the **L.** God of Israel,	3068
Jos	7:14	that the tribe which the **L.** taketh	3068
Jos	7:14	the family which the **L.** shall take	3068
Jos	7:14	household which the **L.** shall take	3068
Jos	7:15	transgressed the covenant of the **L.**,	3068
Jos	7:19	glory to the **L.** God of Israel,	3068
Jos	7:20	have sinned against the **L.** God	3068
Jos	7:23	and laid them out before the **L.**.	3068
Jos	7:25	the **L.** shall trouble thee this day.	3068
Jos	7:26	**L.** turned from the fierceness of	3068
Jos	8:1	the **L.** said unto Joshua, Fear not,	3068
Jos	8:7	**L.** your God will deliver it into	3068
Jos	8:8	to the commandment of the **L.**	3068
Jos	8:18	the **L.** said unto Joshua, Stretch	3068
Jos	8:27	unto the word of the **L.** which he	3068
Jos	8:30	built an altar unto the **L.** God	3068
Jos	8:31	the servant of the **L.** commanded	3068
Jos	8:31	burnt offerings unto the **L.**,	3068
Jos	8:33	the ark of the covenant of the **L.**,	3068
Jos	8:33	servant of the **L.** had commanded	3068
Jos	9:9	of the name of the **L.** thy God:	3068
Jos	9:14	counsel at the mouth of the **L.**.	3068
Jos	9:18,	19 sworn unto them by the **L.** God	3068
Jos	9:24	that the **L.** thy God commanded	3068
Jos	9:27	and for the altar of the **L.**, even	3068
Jos	10:8	And the **L.** said unto Joshua, Fear	3068
Jos	10:10	**L.** discomfited them before Israel,	3068
Jos	10:11	**L.** cast down great stones from	3068
Jos	10:12	Then spake Joshua to the **L.** in	3068
Jos	10:12	the **L.** delivered up the Amorites	3068
Jos	10:14	**L.** hearkened unto the voice of a	3068
Jos	10:14	man: for the **L.** fought for Israel.	3068
Jos	10:19	**L.** your God hath delivered them	3068
Jos	10:25	shall the **L.** do to all your enemies	3068
Jos	10:30	the **L.** delivered it also, and the	3068
Jos	10:32	**L.** delivered Lachish into the hand	3068
Jos	10:40	the **L.** God of Israel commanded.	3068
Jos	10:42	**L.** God of Israel fought for Israel.	3068
Jos	11:6	the **L.** said unto Joshua, Be not	3068
Jos	11:8	**L.** delivered them into the hand	3068
Jos	11:9	did unto them as the **L.** bade him:	3068
Jos	11:12	the servant of the **L.** commanded.	3068
Jos	11:15	As the **L.** commanded Moses his	3068
Jos	11:15	all that the **L.** commanded Moses.	3068
Jos	11:20	of the **L.** to harden their hearts,	3068
Jos	11:20	as the **L.** commanded Moses.	3068
Jos	11:23	all that the **L.** said unto Moses;	3068
Jos	12:6	Moses the servant of the **L.** and	3068
Jos	12:6	the servant of the **L.** gave it for a	3068
Jos	13:1	the **L.** said unto him, Thou art old	3068
Jos	13:8	the servant of the **L.** gave them;	3068
Jos	13:14	sacrifices of the **L.** God of Israel	3068
Jos	13:33	the **L.** God of Israel was their	3068
Jos	14:2	the **L.** commanded by the hand of	3068
Jos	14:5	As the **L.** commanded Moses, so	3068
Jos	14:6	thing that the **L.** said unto Moses	3068
Jos	14:7	servant of the **L.** sent me from	3068
Jos	14:8	I wholly followed the **L.** my God.	3068
Jos	14:9	wholly followed the **L.** my God.	3068
Jos	14:10	behold, the **L.** hath kept me alive,	3068
Jos	14:10	**L.** spake this word unto Moses,	3068
Jos	14:12	whereof the **L.** spake in that day;	3068
Jos	14:12	if so be the **L.** will be with me,	3068
Jos	14:12	to drive them out, as the **L.** said.	3068
Jos	14:14	followed the **L.** God of Israel.	3068
Jos	15:13	to the commandment of the **L.** to	3068
Jos	17:4	**L.** commanded Moses to give us	3068
Jos	17:4	to the commandment of the **L.**	3068
Jos	17:14	the **L.** hath blessed me hitherto?	3068
Jos	18:3	**L.** God of your fathers hath given	3068
Jos	18:6	cast lots for you here before the **L.**	3068
Jos	18:7	the priesthood of the **L.** is their	3068
Jos	18:7	Moses the servant of the **L.** gave	3068
Jos	18:8	cast lots for you before the **L.** in	3068
Jos	18:10	for them in Shiloh before the **L.**:	3068
Jos	19:50	According to the word of the **L.**	3068
Jos	19:51	by lot in Shiloh before the **L.**,	3068
Jos	20:1	The **L.** also spake unto Joshua,	3068
Jos	21:2	**L.** commanded by the hand of	3068
Jos	21:3	at the commandment of the **L.**,	3068
Jos	21:8	**L.** commanded by the hand of	3068
Jos	21:43	**L.** gave unto Israel all the land	3068
Jos	21:44	**L.** gave them rest round about,	3068
Jos	21:44	the **L.** delivered all their enemies	3068
Jos	21:45	**L.** had spoken unto the house of	3068
Jos	22:2	servant of the **L.** commanded you,	3068
Jos	22:3	of the commandment of the **L.**	3068
Jos	22:4	**L.** your God hath given rest unto	3068
Jos	22:4	the servant of the **L.** gave you on	3068
Jos	22:5	the servant of the **L.** charged you,	3068
Jos	22:5	to love the **L.** your God, and to	3068
Jos	22:9	the word of the **L.** by the hand of	3068
Jos	22:16	the whole congregation of the **L.**,	3068
Jos	22:16	this day from following the **L.**,	3068
Jos	22:16	rebel this day against the **L.**?	3068
Jos	22:17	in the congregation of the **L.**,	3068
Jos	22:18	this day from following the **L.**?	3068
Jos	22:18	ye rebel to day against the **L.**,	3068
Jos	22:19	land of the possession of the **L.**,	3068
Jos	22:19	but rebel not against the **L.**, nor	3068
Jos	22:19	beside the altar of the **L.** our God.	3068
Jos	22:22	The **L.** God of gods, the **L.** God	3068
Jos	22:22	in transgression against the **L.**,	3068
Jos	22:23	to turn from following the **L.**, or	3068
Jos	22:23	let the **L.** himself require it;	3068
Jos	22:24	What have ye to do with the **L.**	3068
Jos	22:25	**L.** hath made Jordan a border	3068
Jos	22:25	of Gad; ye have no part in the **L.**:	3068
Jos	22:25	children cease from fearing the **L.**.	3068
Jos	22:27	do the service of the **L.** before	3068
Jos	22:27	come, Ye have no part in the **L.**.	3068
Jos	22:28	the pattern of the altar of the **L.**,	3068
Jos	22:29	we should rebel against the **L.**,	3068
Jos	22:29	this day from following the **L.**,	3068
Jos	22:29	beside the altar of the **L.** our God.	3068
Jos	22:31	perceive that the **L.** is among us,	3068
Jos	22:31	this trespass against the **L.**:	3068
Jos	22:31	of Israel out of the hand of the **L.**.	3068
Jos	22:34	between us that the **L.** is God.	3068
Jos	23:1	the **L.** had given rest unto Israel	3068
Jos	23:3	all that the **L.** your God hath done	3068
Jos	23:3	the **L.** your God is he that hath	3068
Jos	23:5	And the **L.** your God, he shall	3068
Jos	23:5	**L.** your God hath promised unto	3068
Jos	23:8	But cleave unto the **L.** your God,	3068
Jos	23:9	**L.** hath driven out from before	3068
Jos	23:10	for the **L.** your God, he it is that	3068
Jos	23:11	that ye love the **L.** your God.	3068
Jos	23:13	**L.** your God will no more drive	3068
Jos	23:13	land which the **L.** your God hath	3068
Jos	23:14	things which the **L.** your God	3068
Jos	23:15	which the **L.** your God promised	3068
Jos	23:15	**L.** bring upon you all evil things,	3068
Jos	23:15	land which the **L.** your God hath	3068
Jos	23:16	the covenant of the **L.** your God,	3068
Jos	23:16	the anger of the **L.** be kindled	3068
Jos	24:2	Thus saith the **L.** God of Israel,	3068
Jos	24:7	And when they cried unto the **L.**,	3068
Jos	24:14	Now therefore fear the **L.**, and	3068
Jos	24:14	in Egypt; and serve ye the **L.**.	3068
Jos	24:15	evil unto you to serve the **L.**,	3068
Jos	24:15	my house, we will serve the **L.**.	3068
Jos	24:16	that we should forsake the **L.**, to	3068
Jos	24:17	For the **L.** our God, he it is that	3068
Jos	24:18	**L.** drave out from before us all	3068
Jos	24:18	will we also serve the **L.**; for he	3068
Jos	24:19	people, Ye cannot serve the **L.**:	3068
Jos	24:20	If ye forsake the **L.**, and serve	3068
Jos	24:21	Nay; but we will serve the **L.**.	3068
Jos	24:22	that ye have chosen you the **L.**,	3068
Jos	24:23	incline your heart unto the **L.** God	3068
Jos	24:24	The **L.** our God will we serve,	3068
Jos	24:26	was by the sanctuary of the **L.**.	3068
Jos	24:27	hath heard all the words of the **L.**	3068
Jos	24:29	son of Nun, the servant of the **L.**,	3068
Jos	24:31	Israel served the **L.** all the days	3068
Jos	24:31	had known all the works of the **L.**,	3068
Jg	1:1	children of Israel asked the **L.**,	3068
Jg	1:2	the **L.** said, Judah shall go up:	3068
Jg	1:4	the **L.** delivered the Canaanites	3068
Jg	1:19	And the **L.** was with Judah; and	3068
Jg	1:22	and the **L.** was with them.	3068
Jg	2:1	an angel of the **L.** came up from	3068
Jg	2:4	the angel of the **L.** spake these	3068
Jg	2:5	they sacrificed there unto the **L.**.	3068
Jg	2:7	And the people served the **L.** all	3068
Jg	2:7	seen all the great works of the **L.**,	3068
Jg	2:8	son of Nun, the servant of the **L.**,	3068
Jg	2:10	them, which knew not the **L.**, nor	3068
Jg	2:11	did evil in the sight of the **L.**,	3068
Jg	2:12	they forsook the **L.** God of their	3068
Jg	2:12	and provoked the **L.** to anger.	3068
Jg	2:13	forsook the **L.**, and served Baal	3068
Jg	2:14	anger of the **L.** was hot against	3068
Jg	2:15	hand of the **L.** was against them	3068
Jg	2:15	**L.** had said,...as the **L.** had sworn	3068
Jg	2:16	the **L.** raised up judges, which	3068
Jg	2:17	the commandments of the **L.**;	3068
Jg	2:18	the **L.** raised them up judges,	3068
Jg	2:18	then the **L.** was with the judge,	3068
Jg	2:18	repented the **L.** because of their	3068
Jg	2:20	anger of the **L.** was hot against	3068
Jg	2:22	will keep the way of the **L.** to	3068
Jg	2:23	Therefore the **L.** left those nations,	3068
Jg	3:1	are the nations which the **L.** left,	3068
Jg	3:4	the commandments of the **L.**,	3068
Jg	3:7	did evil in the sight of the **L.**,	3068
Jg	3:7	and forgat the **L.** their God, and	3068
Jg	3:8	anger of the **L.** was hot against	3068
Jg	3:9	children of Israel cried unto the **L.**,	3068
Jg	3:9	**L.** raised up a deliverer to the	3068
Jg	3:10	Spirit of the **L.** came upon him,	3068
Jg	3:10	**L.** delivered Chushan-rishathaim	3068
Jg	3:12	evil again in the sight of the **L.**:	3068
Jg	3:12	**L.** strengthened Eglon the king	3068
Jg	3:12	done evil in the sight of the **L.**.	3068
Jg	3:15	children of Israel cried unto the **L.**,	3068
Jg	3:15	the **L.** raised them up a deliverer,	3068
Jg	3:25	their **l.** was fallen down dead on	113
Jg	3:28	**L.** hath delivered your enemies	3068
Jg	4:1	did evil in the sight of the **L.**,	3068
Jg	4:2	the **L.** sold them into the hand of	3068
Jg	4:3	children of Israel cried unto the **L.**:	3068
Jg	4:6	the **L.** God of Israel commanded,	3068
Jg	4:9	**L.** shall sell Sisera into the hand	3068
Jg	4:14	the **L.** hath delivered Sisera into	3068
Jg	4:14	is not the **L.** gone out before thee?	3068
Jg	4:15	the **L.** discomfited Sisera, and all	3068
Jg	4:18	him, Turn in, my **l.**, turn in to me;	113
Jg	5:2	Praise ye the **L.** for the avenging	3068
Jg	5:3	I, even I, will sing unto the **L.**;	3068
Jg	5:3	I will sing praise to the **L.** God of	3068
Jg	5:4	**L.**, when thou wentest out of Seir,	3068
Jg	5:5	mountains melted...before the **L.**,	3068
Jg	5:5	from before the **L.** God of Israel.	3068
Jg	5:9	among the people. Bless ye the **L.**.	3068
Jg	5:11	the righteous acts of the **L.**,	3068
Jg	5:11	people of the **L.** go down to the	3068
Jg	5:13	**L.** made me have dominion over	3068
Jg	5:23	Meroz, said the angel of the **L.**,	3068
Jg	5:23	came not to the help of the **L.**,	3068
Jg	5:23	help of the **L.** against the mighty.	3068
Jg	5:31	all thine enemies perish, O **L.**:	3068
Jg	6:1	did evil in the sight of the **L.**:	3068
Jg	6:1	**L.** delivered them into the hand	3068
Jg	6:6	children of Israel cried unto the **L.**.	3068
Jg	6:7	children of Israel cried unto the **L.**	3068
Jg	6:8	**L.** sent a prophet unto the children	3068
Jg	6:8	Thus saith the **L.** God of Israel,	3068
Jg	6:10	unto you, I am the **L.** your God;	3068
Jg	6:11	there came an angel of the **L.**,	3068

Book	Ref	Context	Strong's
Jg	6:12	the angel of the **L.** appeared unto	3068
Jg	6:12	The **L.** is with thee, thou mighty	3068
Jg	6:13	Gideon said unto him, Oh my **L.**,	113
Jg	6:13	if the **L.** be with us, why then is	3068
Jg	6:13	the **L.** bring us up from Egypt?	3068
Jg	6:13	now the **L.** hath forsaken us, and	3068
Jg	6:14	the **L.** looked upon him, and said,	3068
Jg	6:15	Oh my **L.**, wherewith shall I save	136
Jg	6:16	And the **L.** said unto him, Surely	3068
Jg	6:21	the angel of the **L.** put forth the	3068
Jg	6:21	Then the angel of the **L.** departed	3068
Jg	6:22	that he was an angel of the **L.**,	136
Jg	6:22	Gideon said, Alas, O **L.** God! for	3068
Jg	6:22	seen an angel of the **L.** face to	3068
Jg	6:23	the **L.** said unto him, Peace be	3068
Jg	6:24	build an altar there unto the **L.**,	3068
Jg	6:25	that the **L.** said unto him, Take	3068
Jg	6:26	build an altar unto the **L.** thy God	3068
Jg	6:27	did as the **L.** had said unto him:	3068
Jg	6:34	Spirit of the **L.** came upon Gideon,	3068
Jg	7:2,4	the **L.** said unto Gideon, The	3068
Jg	7:5	the **L.** said unto Gideon, Every	3068
Jg	7:7	the **L.** said unto Gideon, By the	3068
Jg	7:9	the **L.** said unto him, Arise, get	3068
Jg	7:15	**L.** hath delivered into your hand	3068
Jg	7:18	and say, The sword of the **L.**, and	3068
Jg	7:20	they cried, The sword of the **L.**,	3068
Jg	7:22	**L.** set every man's sword against	3068
Jg	8:7	when the **L.** hath delivered Zebah	3068
Jg	8:19	as the **L.** liveth, if ye had saved	3068
Jg	8:23	you: the **L.** shall rule over you.	3068
Jg	8:34	of Israel remembered not the **L.**	3068
Jg	10:6	evil again in the sight of the **L.**,	3068
Jg	10:6	Philistines, and forsook the **L.**,	3068
Jg	10:7	anger of the **L.** was hot against	3068
Jg	10:10	children of Israel cried unto the **L.**,	3068
Jg	10:11	the **L.** said unto the children of	3068
Jg	10:15	children of Israel said unto the **L.**,	3068
Jg	10:16	among them, and served the **L.**:	3068
Jg	11:9	the **L.** deliver them before me,	3068
Jg	11:10	The **L.** be witness between us,	3068
Jg	11:11	uttered all his words before the **L.**	3068
Jg	11:21	**L.** God of Israel delivered Sihon	3068
Jg	11:23	**L.** God of Israel hath dispossessed	3068
Jg	11:24	the **L.** our God shall drive out	3068
Jg	11:27	the **L.** the Judge be judge this day	3068
Jg	11:29	the Spirit of the **L.** came upon	3068
Jg	11:30	Jephthah vowed a vow unto the **L.**,	3068
Jg	11:32	**L.** delivered them into his hands.	3068
Jg	11:35	opened my mouth unto the **L.**,	3068
Jg	11:36	opened thy mouth unto the **L.**,	3068
Jg	11:36	as the **L.** hath taken vengeance	3068
Jg	12:3	**L.** delivered them into my hand:	3068
Jg	13:1	evil again in the sight of the **L.**;	3068
Jg	13:1	**L.** delivered them into the hand	3068
Jg	13:3	angel of the **L.** appeared unto	3068
Jg	13:8	Then Manoah entreated the **L.**,	3068
Jg	13:8	O my **L.**, let the man of God which	3068
Jg	13:13	angel of the **L.** said unto Manoah,	3068
Jg	13:15	said unto the angel of the **L.**,	3068
Jg	13:16	angel of the **L.** said unto Manoah,	3068
Jg	13:16	thou must offer it unto the **L.**.	3068
Jg	13:16	that he was an angel of the **L.**.	3068
Jg	13:17	said unto the angel of the **L.**,	3068
Jg	13:18	the angel of the **L.** said unto him,	3068
Jg	13:19	offered it upon a rock unto the **L.**:	3068
Jg	13:20	the angel of the **L.** ascended in	3068
Jg	13:21	the angel of the **L.** did no more	3068
Jg	13:21	that he was an angel of the **L.**	3068
Jg	13:23	If the **L.** were pleased to kill us,	3068
Jg	13:24	grew, and the **L.** blessed him.	3068
Jg	13:25	the Spirit of the **L.** began to move	3068
Jg	14:4	knew not that it was of the **L.**,	3068
Jg	14:6	the Spirit of the **L.** came mightily	3068
Jg	14:19	Spirit of the **L.** came upon him	3068
Jg	15:14	the Spirit of the **L.** came mightily	3068
Jg	15:18	sore athirst, and called on the **L.**,	3068
Jg	16:20	wist not that the **L.** was departed	3068
Jg	16:28	Samson called unto the **L.**,and	3068
Jg	16:28	O **L.** God, remember me, I pray	136
Jg	17:2	said, Blessed be thou of the **L.**,	3068
Jg	17:3	dedicated the silver unto the **L.**	3068
Jg	17:13	I that the **L.** will do me good,	3068
Jg	18:6	peace: before the **L.** is your way	3068
Jg	19:18	now going to the house of the **L.**;	3068
Jg	19:26	the man's house where her **l.** was,	113
Jg	19:27	And her **l.** rose up in the morning,	113
Jg	20:1	Gilead, unto the **L.** in Mizpeh.	3068
Jg	20:18	And the **L.** said, Judah shall go	3068
Jg	20:23	went up and wept before the **L.**	3068
Jg	20:23	even, and asked counsel of the **L.**,	3068
Jg	20:23	the **L.** said, Go up against him.)	3068
Jg	20:26	and sat there before the **L.**, and	3068
Jg	20:26	and peace offerings before the **L.**	3068
Jg	20:27	of Israel enquired of the **L.**,	3068
Jg	20:28	And the **L.** said, Go up; for to	3068
Jg	20:35	**L.** smote Benjamin before Israel:	3068
Jg	21:3	O **L.** God of Israel, Why is this	3068
Jg	21:5	the congregation unto the **L.**?	3068
Jg	21:5	came not up to the **L.** to Mizpeh,	3068
Jg	21:7	seeing we have sworn by the **L.**	3068
Jg	21:8	came not up to Mizpeh to the **L.**?	3068
Jg	21:15	the **L.** had made a breach in the	3068
Jg	21:19	there is a feast of the L. in Shiloh	3068
Ru	1:6	**L.** had visited his people in giving	3068
Ru	1:8	the **L.** deal kindly with you, as ye	3068
Ru	1:9	**L.** grant you that ye may find rest,	3068
Ru	1:13	the hand of the **L.** is gone out	3068
Ru	1:17	the **L.** do so to me, and more also,	3068
Ru	1:21	**L.** hath brought me home again	3068
Ru	1:21	seeing the **L.**...testified against	3068
Ru	2:4	the reapers, The **L.** be with you.	3068
Ru	2:4	answered him, The **L.** bless thee.	3068
Ru	2:12	The **L.** recompense thy work,	3068
Ru	2:12	reward be given thee of the **L.**	3068
Ru	2:13	me find favour in thy sight, my **l.**;	113
Ru	2:20	Blessed be he of the **L.**, who hath	3068
Ru	3:10	Blessed be thou of the **L.** my	3068
Ru	3:13	kinsman to thee, as the **L.** liveth:	3068
Ru	4:11	**L.** make the woman that is come	3068
Ru	4:12	seed which the **L.** shall give thee	3068
Ru	4:13	the **L.** gave her conception, and	3068
Ru	4:14	Blessed be the **L.**, which hath not	3068
1Sa	1:3	to sacrifice unto the **L.** of hosts	3068
1Sa	1:3	Phinehas, the priests of the **L.**,	3068
1Sa	1:5,	6 the **L.** had shut up her womb.	3068
1Sa	1:7	went up to the house of the **L.**,	3068
1Sa	1:9	by a post of the temple of the **L.**	3068
1Sa	1:10	and prayed unto the **L.**, and wept	3068
1Sa	1:11	O **L.** of hosts, if thou wilt indeed	3068
1Sa	1:11	give him unto the **L.** all the days	3068
1Sa	1:12	continued praying before the **L.**,	3068
1Sa	1:15	answered and said, No, my **l.**, I am	113
1Sa	1:15	poured out my soul before the **L.**	3068
1Sa	1:19	and worshipped before the **L.**,	3068
1Sa	1:19	wife; and the **L.** remembered her	3068
1Sa	1:20	I have asked him of the **L.**.	3068
1Sa	1:21	up to offer unto the **L.** the yearly	3068
1Sa	1:22	that he may appear before the **L.**,	3068
1Sa	1:23	only the **L.** establish his word.	3068
1Sa	1:24	the house of the **L.** in Shiloh:	3068
1Sa	1:26	said, Oh my **l.**, as thy soul liveth,	113
1Sa	1:26	my **l.**, I am the woman that stood	113
1Sa	1:26	thee here, praying unto the **L.**.	3068
1Sa	1:27	the **L.** hath given me my petition	3068
1Sa	1:28	also I have lent him to the **L.**;	3068
1Sa	1:28	liveth he shall be lent to the **L.**.	3068
1Sa	1:28	And he worshipped the **L.** there.	3068
1Sa	2:1	said, My heart rejoiceth in the **L.**,	3068
1Sa	2:1	mine horn is exalted in the **L.**:	3068
1Sa	2:2	There is none holy as the **L.**;	3068
1Sa	2:3	for the **L.** is a God of knowledge,	3068
1Sa	2:6	The **L.** killeth, and maketh alive:	3068
1Sa	2:7	The **L.** maketh poor, and maketh	3068
1Sa	2:10	adversaries of the **L.** shall be	3068
1Sa	2:10	the **L.** shall judge the ends of the	3068
1Sa	2:11	the child did minister unto the **L.**	3068
1Sa	2:12	of Belial; they knew not the **L.**.	3068
1Sa	2:17	men was very great before the **L.**:	3068
1Sa	2:17	abhorred the offering of the **L.**.	3068
1Sa	2:18	Samuel ministered before the **L.**,	3068
1Sa	2:20	**L.** give thee seed of this woman	3068
1Sa	2:20	the loan which is lent to the **L.**	3068
1Sa	2:21	the **L.** visited Hannah, so that	3068
1Sa	2:21	child Samuel grew before the **L.**.	3068
1Sa	2:25	but if a man sin against the **L.**,	3068
1Sa	2:25	because the **L.** would slay them.	3068
1Sa	2:26	was in favour both with the **L.**,	3068
1Sa	2:27	Thus saith the **L.**, Did I plainly	3068
1Sa	2:30	the **L.** God of Israel saith, I said	3068
1Sa	2:30	but now the **L.** saith, Be it far	3068
1Sa	3:1	Samuel ministered unto the **L.**	3068
1Sa	3:1	the word of the **L.** was precious	3068
1Sa	3:3	went out in the temple of the **L.**,	3068
1Sa	3:4	the **L.** called Samuel: and he	3068
1Sa	3:6	the **L.** called yet again, Samuel.	3068
1Sa	3:7	Samuel did not yet know the **L.**,	3068
1Sa	3:7	the word of the **L.** yet revealed	3068
1Sa	3:8	**L.** called Samuel again the third	3068
1Sa	3:8	perceived that the **L.** had called	3068
1Sa	3:9	that thou shalt say, Speak, **L.**;	3068
1Sa	3:10	And the **L.** came, and stood, and	3068
1Sa	3:11	the **L.** said to Samuel, Behold,	3068
1Sa	3:15	the doors of the house of the **L.**.	3068
1Sa	3:17	is the thing that the **L.** hath said	
1Sa	3:18	It is the **L.**: let him do what	3068
1Sa	3:19	grew, and the **L.** was with him,	3068
1Sa	3:20	to be a prophet of the **L.**.	3068
1Sa	3:21	the **L.** appeared again in Shiloh:	3068
1Sa	3:21	**L.** revealed himself to Samuel	3068
1Sa	3:21	in Shiloh by the word of the **L.**	3068
1Sa	4:3	hath the **L.** smitten us to day	3068
1Sa	4:3,	4,5 ark of the covenant of the **L.**	3068
1Sa	4:6	that the ark of the **L.** was come	3068
1Sa	5:3	the earth before the ark of the **L.**.	3068
1Sa	5:4	ground before the ark of the **L.**;	3068
1Sa	5:6	hand of the **L.** was heavy upon	3068
1Sa	5:9	hand of the **L.** was against the city	3068
1Sa	6:1	ark of the **L.** was in the country	3068
1Sa	6:2	shall we do to the ark of the **L.**?	3068
1Sa	6:8	take the ark of the **L.**, and lay it	3068
1Sa	6:11	laid the ark of the **L.** upon the cart,	3068
1Sa	6:14	kine a burnt offering unto the **L.**.	3068
1Sa	6:15	Levites took...the ark of the **L.**,	3068
1Sa	6:15	offered...the same day unto the **L.**.	3068
1Sa	6:17	a trespass offering unto the **L.**;	3068
1Sa	6:18	they set down the ark of the **L.**:	3068
1Sa	6:19	had looked into the ark of the **L.**,	3068
1Sa	6:19	**L.** had smitten many of the people	3068
1Sa	6:20	to stand before this holy **L.** God?	3068
1Sa	6:21	brought again the ark of the **L.**;	3068
1Sa	7:1	and fetched up the ark of the **L.**,	3068
1Sa	7:1	his son to keep the ark of the **L.**.	3068
1Sa	7:2	of Israel lamented after the **L.**	3068
1Sa	7:3	return unto the **L.** with all your	3068
1Sa	7:3	prepare your hearts unto the **L.**,	3068
1Sa	7:4	Ashtaroth, and served the **L.** only.	3068
1Sa	7:5	I will pray for you unto the **L.**	3068
1Sa	7:6	and poured it out before the **L.**,	3068
1Sa	7:6	We have sinned against the **L.**	3068
1Sa	7:8	Cease not to cry unto the **L.** our	3068
1Sa	7:9	burnt offering wholly unto the **L.**:	3068
1Sa	7:9	and Samuel cried unto the **L.**	3068
1Sa	7:9	for Israel; and the **L.** heard him.	3068
1Sa	7:10	**L.** thundered with a great thunder	3068
1Sa	7:12	Hitherto hath the **L.** helped us.	3068
1Sa	7:13	hand of the **L.** was against the	3068
1Sa	7:17	there he built an altar unto the **L.**.	3068
1Sa	8:6	And Samuel prayed unto the **L.**.	3068
1Sa	8:7	the **L.** said unto Samuel, Hearken	3068
1Sa	8:10	Samuel told all the words of the **L.**	3068
1Sa	8:18	**L.** will not hear you in that day.	3068
1Sa	8:21	rehearsed...in the ears of the **L.**.	3068
1Sa	8:22	the **L.** said to Samuel, Hearken	3068
1Sa	9:15	**L.** had told Samuel in his ear a	3068
1Sa	9:17	**L.** said unto him, Behold the man	3068
1Sa	10:1	because the **L.** hath anointed thee	3068
1Sa	10:6	Spirit of the **L.** will come upon	3068
1Sa	10:17	together unto the **L.** to Mizpeh;	3068
1Sa	10:18	Thus saith the **L.** God of Israel, I	3068
1Sa	10:19	present yourselves before the **L.**	3068
1Sa	10:22	they enquired of the **L.** further,	3068
1Sa	10:22	**L.** answered, Behold, he hath hid	3068
1Sa	10:24	him whom the **L.** hath chosen,	3068
1Sa	10:25	book, and laid it up before the **L.**	3068
1Sa	11:7	fear of the **L.** fell on the people,	3068
1Sa	11:13	the **L.** hath wrought salvation in	3068
1Sa	11:15	made Saul king before the **L.** in	3068
1Sa	11:15	of peace offerings before the **L.**;	3068
1Sa	12:3	witness against me before the **L.**,	3068
1Sa	12:5	The **L.** is witness against you,	3068
1Sa	12:6	It is the **L.** that advanced Moses	3068
1Sa	12:7	may reason with you before the **L.**	3068
1Sa	12:7	of all the righteous acts of the **L.**,	3068
1Sa	12:8	your fathers cried unto the **L.**,	3068
1Sa	12:8	then the **L.** sent Moses and Aaron,	3068
1Sa	12:9	when they forgat the **L.** their God,	3068
1Sa	12:10	they cried unto the **L.**, and said,	3068
1Sa	12:10	because we have forsaken the **L.**,	3068
1Sa	12:11	the **L.** sent Jerubbaal, and Bedan,	3068
1Sa	12:12	the **L.** your God was your king	3068

1Sa 12:13 the **L.** hath set a king over you. 3068
1Sa 12:14 If ye will fear the **L.**, and serve......... 3068
1Sa 12:14 the commandment of the **L.**, ... 3068
1Sa 12:14 continue following the **L.** your 3068
1Sa 12:15 will not obey the voice of the **L.**, ... 3068
1Sa 12:15 the commandment of the **L.**, ... 3068
1Sa 12:15 the hand of the **L.** be against you,...... 3068
1Sa 12:16 the **L.** will do before your eyes. 3068
1Sa 12:17 I will call unto the **L.**, and he shall 3068
1Sa 12:17 have done in the sight of the **L.**,......... 3068
1Sa 12:18 So Samuel called unto the **L.**;........... 3068
1Sa 12:18 and the **L.** sent thunder and rain......... 3068
1Sa 12:18 greatly feared the **L.** and Samuel. 3068
1Sa 12:19 Pray for thy servants unto the **L.**....... 3068
1Sa 12:20 not aside from following the **L.**, ... 3068
1Sa 12:20 serve the **L.** with all your heart;........ 3068
1Sa 12:22 **L.** will not forsake his people for......... 3068
1Sa 12:22 pleased the **L.** to make you his.......... 3068
1Sa 12:23 that I should sin against the **L.** 3068
1Sa 12:24 Only fear the **L.**, and serve him in 3068
1Sa 13:12 made supplication unto the **L.**:........... 3068
1Sa 13:13 kept the commandment of the **L.** 3068
1Sa 13:13 **L.** have established thy kingdom 3068
1Sa 13:14 **L.** hath sought him a man after........... 3068
1Sa 13:14 **L.**...commanded him to be captain...... 3068
1Sa 13:14 which the **L.** commaned thee. 3068
1Sa 14:6 be that the **L.** will work for us: 3068
1Sa 14:6 is no restraint to the **L.** to save......... 3068
1Sa 14:10 **L.** hath delivered them into our 3068
1Sa 14:12 **L.** hath delivered them into the 3068
1Sa 14:23 So the **L.** saved Israel that day:......... 3068
1Sa 14:33 people sin against the **L.**, in that........ 3068
1Sa 14:34 sin not against the **L.** in eating 3068
1Sa 14:35 Saul built an altar unto the **L.**:........... 3068
1Sa 14:35 first altar that he built unto the **L.**...... 3068
1Sa 14:39 For, as the **L.** liveth, which saveth..... 3068
1Sa 14:41 Saul said unto the **L.** God of Israel,.... 3068
1Sa 14:45 as the **L.** liveth, there shall not 3068
1Sa 15:1 **L.** sent me to anoint thee to be......... 3068
1Sa 15:1 the voice of the words of the **L.**. 3068
1Sa 15:2 saith the **L.** of hosts, I remember 3068
1Sa 15:10 the word of the **L.** unto Samuel, ... 3068
1Sa 15:11 and he cried unto the **L.** all night. 3068
1Sa 15:13 him, Blessed be thou of the **L.**: 3068
1Sa 15:13 the commandment of the **L.**. 3068
1Sa 15:15 to sacrifice unto the **L.** thy God;........ 3068
1Sa 15:16 what the **L.** hath said to me this........ 3068
1Sa 15:17 **L.** anointed thee king over Israel?...... 3068
1Sa 15:18 the **L.** sent thee on a journey, and..... 3068
1Sa 15:19 thou not obey the voice of the **L.**,....... 3068
1Sa 15:19 didst evil in the sight of the **L.**?......... 3068
1Sa 15:20 I have obeyed the voice of the **L.**, ... 3068
1Sa 15:20 gone the way which the **L.** sent me,... 3068
1Sa 15:21 to sacrifice unto the **L.** thy God in 3068
1Sa 15:22 the **L.** as great delight in burnt.......... 3068
1Sa 15:22 as in obeying the voice of the **L.**? 3068
1Sa 15:23 hast rejected the word of the **L.**, ... 3068
1Sa 15:24 the commandment of the **L.**, ... 3068
1Sa 15:25 with me, that I may worship the **L.**. ... 3068
1Sa 15:26 hast rejected the word of the **L.**, ... 3068
1Sa 15:26 **L.** hath rejected thee from being......... 3068
1Sa 15:28 **L.** hath rent the kingdom of Israel....... 3068
1Sa 15:30 that I may worship the **L.** thy God..... 3068
1Sa 15:31 Saul; and Saul worshipped the **L.**. 3068
1Sa 15:33 hewed Agag in pieces before the **L.**.... 3068
1Sa 15:35 **L.** repented that he had made Saul..... 3068
1Sa 16:1 the **L.** said unto Samuel, How long..... 3068
1Sa 16:2 And the **L.** said, Take an heifer, ... 3068
1Sa 16:2 I am come to sacrifice to the **L.**. 3068
1Sa 16:4 did that which the **L.** spake,............. 3068
1Sa 16:5 am come to sacrifice unto the **L.**:........ 3068
1Sa 16:7 **L.** said unto Samuel, Look not on 3068
1Sa 16:7 **L.** seeth not as man seeth; for 3068
1Sa 16:7 but the **L.** looketh on the heart. 3068
1Sa 16:8, 9 Neither hath the **L.** chosen this....... 3068
1Sa 16:10 The **L.** hath not chosen these. 3068
1Sa 16:12 the **L.** said, Arise, anoint him:........... 3068
1Sa 16:13 Spirit of the **L.** came upon David 3068
1Sa 16:14 Spirit of the **L.** departed from Saul, ... 3068
1Sa 16:14 an evil spirit from the **L.** troubled 3068
1Sa 16:16 our **l.** now command thy servants, ... 113
1Sa 16:18 person, and the **L.** is with him. 3068
1Sa 17:37 **L.** that delivered me out of the paw ... 3068
1Sa 17:37 Go, and the **L.** be with thee. 3068
1Sa 17:45 in the name of the **L.** of hosts,.......... 3068
1Sa 17:46 This day will the **L.** deliver thee 3068
1Sa 17:47 the **L.** saveth not with sword and....... 3068
1Sa 18:12 because the **L.** was with him, and...... 3068
1Sa 18:14 ways; and the **L.** was with him. 3068
1Sa 18:28 knew that the **L.** was with David, ... 3068
1Sa 19:5 **L.** wrought a great salvation for......... 3068
1Sa 19:6 As the **L.** liveth, he shall not be 3068
1Sa 19:9 evil spirit from the **L.** was upon......... 3068
1Sa 20:3 as the **L.** liveth, and as thy soul 3068
1Sa 20:8 into a covenant of the **L.** with thee..... 3068
1Sa 20:12 unto David, O **L.** God of Israel,......... 3068
1Sa 20:13 The **L.** do so and much more to 3068
1Sa 20:13 **L.** be with thee, as he hath been 3068
1Sa 20:14 shew me the kindness of the **L.**,........ 3068
1Sa 20:15 **L.** hath cut off...enemies of David...... 3068
1Sa 20:16 Let the **L.** even require it at the........ 3068
1Sa 20:21 and no hurt; as the **L.** liveth. 3068
1Sa 20:22 for the **L.** hath sent thee away. 3068
1Sa 20:23 **L.** be between thee and me for 3068
1Sa 20:42 both of us in the name of the **L.**, ... 3068
1Sa 20:42 The **L.** be between me and thee,....... 3068
1Sa 21:6 that was taken from before the **L.**,...... 3068
1Sa 21:7 that day, detained before the **L.**;....... 3068
1Sa 22:10 he enquired of the **L.** for him, ... 3068
1Sa 22:12 And he answered, Here I am, my **l.**..... 113
1Sa 22:17 and slay the priests of the **L.**; 3068
1Sa 22:17 to fall upon the priests of the **L.**. 3068
1Sa 23:2 David enquired of the **L.**, saying, ... 3068
1Sa 23:2 the **L.** said unto David, Go, and......... 3068
1Sa 23:4 David enquired of the **L.** yet............. 3068
1Sa 23:4 the **L.** answered him and said,............ 3068
1Sa 23:10 O **L.** God of Israel, thy servant 3068
1Sa 23:11 O **L.** God of Israel, I beseech thee,.... 3068
1Sa 23:11 the **L.** said, He will come down. 3068
1Sa 23:12 And the **L.** said, They will deliver...... 3068
1Sa 23:18 made a covenant before the **L.**: 3068
1Sa 23:21 Saul said, Blessed be ye of the **L.**;...... 3068
1Sa 24:4 the day of which the **L.** said unto....... 3068
1Sa 24:6 **L.** forbid that I should do this........... 3068
1Sa 24:6 he is the anointed of the **L.**. 3068
1Sa 24:8 after Saul, saying, My **l.** the king......... 113
1Sa 24:10 the **L.** had delivered thee to day......... 3068
1Sa 24:10 put forth mine hand against my **l.**; 113
1Sa 24:12 **L.** judge between me and thee, ... 3068
1Sa 24:12 and the **L.** avenge me of thee: but 3068
1Sa 24:15 The **L.** therefore be judge, and.......... 3068
1Sa 24:18 **L.** had delivered me into thine........... 3068
1Sa 24:19 **L.** reward thee good for that thou...... 3068
1Sa 24:21 now therefore unto me by the **L.**,....... 3068
1Sa 25:24 Upon me, my **l.**, upon me let this........ 113
1Sa 25:25 Let not my **l.**, I pray thee, regard 113
1Sa 25:25 saw not the young men of my **l.**, ... 113
1Sa 25:26 Now therefore, my **l.**, as the............. 113
1Sa 25:26 as the **L.** liveth, and as thy soul 3068
1Sa 25:26 the **L.** hath withholden thee from 3068
1Sa 25:26 they that seek evil to my **l.**, be as....... 113
1Sa 25:27 handmaid hath brought unto my **l.**, ... 113
1Sa 25:27 the young men that follow my **l.**. 113
1Sa 25:28 handmaid: for the **L.** will 3068
1Sa 25:28 certainly make my **l.** a sure house; 113
1Sa 25:28 because my **l.** fighteth the battles 113
1Sa 25:28 fighteth the battles of the **L.**, and....... 3068
1Sa 25:29 but the soul of my **l.** shall be bound 113
1Sa 25:29 bundle of life with the **L.** thy God; 3068
1Sa 25:30 pass, when the **L.** shall have done...... 3068
1Sa 25:30 done to my **l.** according to all the 113
1Sa 25:31 thee, nor offence of heart unto my **l.**,.... 136
1Sa 25:31 or that my **l.** hath avenged himself: 136
1Sa 25:31 when the **L.** shall have dealt well 3068
1Sa 25:31 have dealt well with my **l.**, then 113
1Sa 25:32 Blessed be the **L.** God of Israel,........ 3068
1Sa 25:34 deed, as the **L.** God of Israel liveth, ... 3068
1Sa 25:38 that the **L.** smote Nabal, that he......... 3068
1Sa 25:39 said, Blessed be the **L.**, that hath 3068
1Sa 25:39 **L.** hath returned the wickedness........ 3068
1Sa 25:41 the feet of the servants of my **l.**.......... 113
1Sa 26:10 said furthermore, As the **L.** liveth, ... 3068
1Sa 26:10 the **L.** shall smite him; or his day....... 3068
1Sa 26:11 **L.** forbid that I should stretch 3068
1Sa 26:12 deep sleep from the **L.** was fallen 3068
1Sa 26:15 hast thou not kept thy **l.** the king? 113
1Sa 26:15 people in to destroy the king thy **l.**. 113
1Sa 26:16 As the **L.** liveth, ye are worthy to 3068
1Sa 26:17 David said, It is my voice, my **l.**, O 113
1Sa 26:18 doth my **l.** thus pursue after his 113
1Sa 26:19 my **l.** the king hear the words of his 113
1Sa 26:19 **L.** have stirred thee up against.......... 3068
1Sa 26:19 men, cursed be they before the **L.**;.... 3068
1Sa 26:19 abiding in...inheritance of the **L.**,........ 3068
1Sa 26:20 earth before the face of the **L.**: 3068
1Sa 26:23 The **L.** render to every man his 3068
1Sa 26:23 **L.** delivered thee into my hand.......... 3068
1Sa 26:24 much set by in the eyes of the **L.**, ... 3068
1Sa 28:6 And when Saul enquired of the **L.**, ... 3068
1Sa 28:6 the **L.** answered him not, neither....... 3068
1Sa 28:10 And Saul sware to her by the **L.**,....... 3068
1Sa 28:10 As the **L.** liveth, there shall no.......... 3068
1Sa 28:16 the **L.** is departed from thee, and 3068
1Sa 28:17 **L.** hath done to him, as he spake....... 3068
1Sa 28:17 **L.** hath rent the kingdom out of......... 3068
1Sa 28:18 obeyedst not the voice of the **L.**, ... 3068
1Sa 28:18 the **L.** done this thing unto thee 3068
1Sa 28:19 the **L.** will also deliver Israel with 3068
1Sa 28:19 **L.** also shall deliver the host of......... 3068
1Sa 29:6 Surely, as the **L.** liveth, thou hast...... 3068
1Sa 29:8 the enemies of my **l.** the king?............ 113
1Sa 30:6 encouraged himself in the **L.** his 3068
1Sa 30:8 And David enquired at the **L.**, ... 3068
1Sa 30:23 that which the **L.** hath given us, ... 3068
1Sa 30:26 the spoil of the enemies of the **L.**; 3068
2Sa 1:10 brought them hither unto my **l.** 113
2Sa 1:12 and for the people of the **L.**; and 3068
2Sa 2:1 that David enquired of the **L.**, ... 3068
2Sa 2:1 And the **L.** said unto him, Go up. 3068
2Sa 2:5 them, Blessed be ye of the **L.**,.......... 3068
2Sa 2:5 shewed this kindness unto your **l.**, ... 113
2Sa 2:6 **L.** shew kindness and truth unto.......... 3068
2Sa 3:9 as the **L.** hath sworn to David,.......... 3068
2Sa 3:18 for the **L.** hath spoken of David, ... 3068
2Sa 3:21 will gather all Israel unto my **l.**........... 113
2Sa 3:28 guiltless before the **L.** for ever.......... 3068
2Sa 3:39 **L.** shall reward the doer of evil 3068
2Sa 4:8 thy life; and the **L.** hath avenged 3068
2Sa 4:8 avenged my **l.** the king this day of....... 113
2Sa 4:9 them, As the **L.** liveth, who hath....... 3068
2Sa 5:2 **L.** said to thee, Thou shalt feed....... 3068
2Sa 5:3 them in Hebron before the **L.**: 3068
2Sa 5:10 the **L.** God of hosts was with him. 3068
2Sa 5:12 **L.** had established him king over........ 3068
2Sa 5:19 David enquired of the **L.**, saying, ... 3068
2Sa 5:19 the **L.** said unto David, Go up: 3068
2Sa 5:20 **L.** hath broken forth upon mine 3068
2Sa 5:23 David enquired of the **L.**, he said, ... 3068
2Sa 5:24 then shall the **L.** go out before 3068
2Sa 5:25 as the **L.** had commanded him;........... 3068
2Sa 6:2 **L.** of hosts that dwelleth between 3068
2Sa 6:5 house of Israel played before the **L.** ... 3068
2Sa 6:7 anger of the **L.** was kindled against 3068
2Sa 6:8 **L.**...made a breach upon Uzzah: 3068
2Sa 6:9 David was afraid of the **L.** that 3068
2Sa 6:9 the ark of the **L.** come to me? 3068
2Sa 6:10 not remove the ark of the **L.** unto...... 3068
2Sa 6:11 the ark of the **L.** continued in the 3068
2Sa 6:11 **L.** blessed Obed-edom, and all his...... 3068
2Sa 6:12 The **L.** hath blessed the house of....... 3068
2Sa 6:13 they that bare the ark of the **L.**......... 3068
2Sa 6:14 David danced before the **L.** with........ 3068
2Sa 6:15 brought up the ark of the **L.** with....... 3068
2Sa 6:16 ark of the **L.** came into the city of 3068
2Sa 6:16 leaping and dancing before the **L.**;....... 3068
2Sa 6:17 they brought in the ark of the **L.**, ... 3068
2Sa 6:17 and peace offerings before the **L.**. 3068
2Sa 6:18 in the name of the **L.** of hosts........... 3068
2Sa 6:21 unto Michal, It was before the **L.**,....... 3068
2Sa 6:21 me ruler over the people of the **L.**,.... 3068
2Sa 6:21 therefore will I play before the **L.**. 3068
2Sa 7:1 **L.** had given him rest round about...... 3068
2Sa 7:3 heart; for the **L.** is with thee. 3068
2Sa 7:4 word of the **L.** came unto Nathan,...... 3068
2Sa 7:5 Thus saith the **L.**, Shalt thou 3068
2Sa 7:8 Thus saith the **L.** of hosts, I took 3068
2Sa 7:11 **L.** telleth thee that he will make 3068
2Sa 7:18 David in, and sat before the **L.**,.......... 3068
2Sa 7:18 Who am I, O **L.** God? and what is....... 136
2Sa 7:19 a small thing in thy sight, O **L.** God;..... 136
2Sa 7:19 this the manner of man, O **L.** God? 136
2Sa 7:20 thou, **L.** God, knowest thy servant. 136
2Sa 7:22 thou art great, O **L.** God: for............ 3068
2Sa 7:24 thou, **L.**, art become their God............ 3068
2Sa 7:25 O **L.** God, the word that thou hast..... 3068
2Sa 7:26 **L.** of hosts is the God over Israel: 3068
2Sa 7:27 thou, O **L.** of hosts, God of Israel,..... 3068
2Sa 7:28 now, O **L.** God, thou art that God,...... 136
2Sa 7:29 for thou, O **L.** God, hast spoken it: 136

2Sa 8:6 **L.** preserved David whithersoever...... 3068
2Sa 8:11 David did dedicate unto the **L.**,.......... 3068
2Sa 8:14 **L.** preserved David whithersoever...... 3068
2Sa 9:11 to all that my **l.** the king hath............ 113
2Sa 10:3 Ammon said unto Hanun their **l.**,......... 113
2Sa 10:12 the **L.** do that which seemeth him...... 3068
2Sa 11:9 house with all the servants of his **l.**,..... 113
2Sa 11:11 and my **l.** Joab, and the servants of...... 113
2Sa 11:11 servants of my **l.**, are encamped in...... 113
2Sa 11:13 on his bed with the servants of his **l.**,.... 113
2Sa 11:27 David had done displeased the **L.**....... 3068
2Sa 12:1 the **L.** sent Nathan unto David. 3068
2Sa 12:5 As the **L.** liveth, the man that hath 3068
2Sa 12:7 Thus saith the **L.** God of Israel, I...... 3068
2Sa 12:9 the commandment of the **L.**,............. 3068
2Sa 12:11 Thus saith the **L.**, Behold, I will........ 3068
2Sa 12:13 I have sinned against the **L.**............. 3068
2Sa 12:13 **L.** also hath put away thy sin; 3068
2Sa 12:14 occasion to the enemies of the **L.** 3068
2Sa 12:15 **L.** struck the child that Uriah's.......... 3068
2Sa 12:20 and came into the house of the **L.**,...... 3068
2Sa 12:24 Solomon: and the **L.** loved him. 3068
2Sa 12:25 name Jedidiah, because of the **L.**........ 3068
2Sa 13:32 Let not my **l.** suppose that they.......... 113
2Sa 13:33 let not my **l.** the king take the thing..... 113
2Sa 14:9 My **l.**, O king, the iniquity be on me, ... 113
2Sa 14:11 let the king remember the **L.** thy....... 3068
2Sa 14:11 As the **L.** liveth, there shall not one ... 3068
2Sa 14:12 speak one word unto my **l.** the king. 113
2Sa 14:15 to speak of this thing unto my **l.** the 113
2Sa 14:17 The word of my **l.** the king shall now ... 113
2Sa 14:17 so is my **l.** the king to discern good..... 113
2Sa 14:17 the **L.** thy God will be with thee........ 3068
2Sa 14:18 said, Let my **l.** the king now speak. 113
2Sa 14:19 As thy soul liveth, my **l.** the king, ... 113
2Sa 14:19 that my **l.** the king hath spoken:.......... 113
2Sa 14:20 and my **l.** is wise, according to the 113
2Sa 14:22 grace in thy sight, my **l.**, O king, ... 113
2Sa 15:7 which I have vowed unto the **L.**, ... 3068
2Sa 15:8 **L.** shall bring me again indeed to 3068
2Sa 15:8 Jerusalem, then I will serve the **L.**..... 3068
2Sa 15:15 my **l.** the king shall appoint................ 113
2Sa 15:21 king, and said, As the **L.** liveth,......... 3068
2Sa 15:21 and as my **l.** the king liveth, surely...... 113
2Sa 15:21 in what place my **l.** the king shall be, ... 113
2Sa 15:25 find favour in the eyes of the **L.**, ... 3068
2Sa 15:31 And David said, O **L.**, I pray thee,...... 3068
2Sa 16:4 grace in thy sight, my **l.**, O king. 113
2Sa 16:8 **L.** hath returned upon thee all........... 3068
2Sa 16:8 **L.** hath delivered the kingdom into..... 3068
2Sa 16:9 this dead dog curse my **l.** the king?...... 113
2Sa 16:10 the **L.** hath said unto him, Curse 3068
2Sa 16:11 for the **L.** hath bidden him............... 3068
2Sa 16:12 the **L.** will look on mine affliction, ... 3068
2Sa 16:12 the **L.** will requite me good for his..... 3068
2Sa 16:18 but whom the **L.**, and this people,........ 3068
2Sa 17:14 **L.**...appointed to defeat the good....... 3068
2Sa 17:14 **L.** might bring evil upon Absalom....... 3068
2Sa 18:19 **L.** hath avenged him of his enemies.... 3068
2Sa 18:28 Blessed be the **L.** thy God, which...... 3068
2Sa 18:28 their hand against my **l.** the king. 113
2Sa 18:31 Cushi said, Tidings, my **l.** the king:....... 113
2Sa 18:31 **L.** hath avenged thee this day of........ 3068
2Sa 18:32 The enemies of my **l.** the king, and...... 113
2Sa 19:7 I swear by the **L.**, if thou go not 3068
2Sa 19:19 Let not my **l.** impute iniquity unto........ 113
2Sa 19:19 my **l.** the king went out of Jerusalem,... 113
2Sa 19:20 to go down to meet my **l.** the king. 113
2Sa 19:26 My **l.**, O king, my servant deceived..... 113
2Sa 19:27 slandered thy servant unto my **l.** the.... 113
2Sa 19:27 my **l.** the king is as an angel of God:.... 113
2Sa 19:28 but dead men before my **l.** the king: 113
2Sa 19:30 my **l.** the king is come again in peace ... 113
2Sa 19:35 be yet a burden unto my **l.** the king?.... 113
2Sa 19:37 let him go over with my **l.** the king;..... 113
2Sa 20:19 up the inheritance of the **L.**?............ 3068
2Sa 21:1 and David enquired of the **L.**:............ 3068
2Sa 21:1 the **L.** answered, It is for Saul, ... 3068
2Sa 21:3 bless the inheritance of the **L.**?......... 3068
2Sa 21:6 we will hang them up unto the **L.** 3068
2Sa 21:6 of Saul, whom the **L.** did choose........ 3068
2Sa 21:9 them in the hill before the **L.**: 3068
2Sa 22:1 And David spake unto the **L.** the 3068
2Sa 22:1 day that the **L.** had delivered him....... 3068
2Sa 22:2 **L.** is my rock, and my fortress,......... 3068
2Sa 22:4 will call on the **L.**, who is worthy....... 3068
2Sa 22:7 my distress I called upon the **L.**, ... 3068
2Sa 22:14 The **L.** thundered from heaven, ... 3068
2Sa 22:16 at the rebuking of the **L.**,................ 3068
2Sa 22:19 but the **L.** was my stay.................... 3068
2Sa 22:21 **L.** rewarded me according to my 3068
2Sa 22:22 I have kept the ways of the **L.**, ... 3068
2Sa 22:25 **L.** hath recompensed me according..... 3068
2Sa 22:29 For thou art my lamp, O **L.**:.............. 3068
2Sa 22:29 the **L.** will lighten my darkness.......... 3068
2Sa 22:31 the word of the **L.** is tried: he is....... 3068
2Sa 22:32 For who is God, save the **L.**? and...... 3068
2Sa 22:42 even unto the **L.**, but he answered..... 3068
2Sa 22:47 The **L.** liveth; and blessed be my........ 3068
2Sa 22:50 I will give thanks unto thee, O **L.**, ... 3068
2Sa 23:2 The Spirit of the **L.** spake by me, ... 3068
2Sa 23:10 **L.** wrought a great victory that.......... 3068
2Sa 23:12 the **L.** wrought a great victory. 3068
2Sa 23:16 but poured it out unto the **L.** 3068
2Sa 23:17 Be it far from me, O **L.**, that I.......... 3068
2Sa 24:1 the anger of the **L.** was kindled......... 3068
2Sa 24:3 **L.** thy God add unto the people, ... 3068
2Sa 24:3 eyes of my **l.** the king may see it: 113
2Sa 24:3 doth my **l.** the king delight in this........ 113
2Sa 24:10 David said unto the **L.**, I have.......... 3068
2Sa 24:10 O **L.**, take away the iniquity of.......... 3068
2Sa 24:11 word of the **L.** came unto...Gad,........ 3068
2Sa 24:12 Thus saith the **L.**, I offer thee........... 3068
2Sa 24:14 us fall now into the hand of the **L.** 3068
2Sa 24:15 **L.** sent a pestilence upon Israel......... 3068
2Sa 24:16 the **L.** repented him of the evil,.......... 3068
2Sa 24:16 the angel of the **L.** was by the 3068
2Sa 24:17 David spake unto the **L.** when he....... 3068
2Sa 24:18 Go up, rear an altar unto the **L.** 3068
2Sa 24:19 went up as the **L.** commanded........... 3068
2Sa 24:21 my **l.** the king come to his servant? 113
2Sa 24:21 to build an altar unto the **L.**,............ 3068
2Sa 24:22 Let my **l.** the king take and offer up..... 113
2Sa 24:23 king, The **L.** thy God accept thee. 3068
2Sa 24:24 offer burnt offerings unto the **L.** 3068
2Sa 24:25 built there an altar unto the **L.**, ... 3068
2Sa 24:25 the **L.** was intreated for the land,....... 3068
1Ki 1:2 for my **l.** the king a young virgin: 113
1Ki 1:2 that my **l.** the king may get heat. 113
1Ki 1:11 and David our **l.** knoweth it not? 113
1Ki 1:13 Didst not thou, my **l.**, O king, swear..... 113
1Ki 1:17 said unto him, My **l.**, thou swarest 113
1Ki 1:17 thou swarest by the **L.** thy God......... 3068
1Ki 1:18 my **l.** the king, thou knowest it not:..... 113
1Ki 1:20 my **l.**, O king, the eyes of all Israel 113
1Ki 1:20 on the throne of my **l.** the king after..... 113
1Ki 1:21 when my **l.** the king shall sleep with..... 113
1Ki 1:24 Nathan said, My **l.**, O king, hast thou... 113
1Ki 1:27 Is this thing done by my **l.** the king, ... 113
1Ki 1:27 on the throne of my **l.** the king after.... 113
1Ki 1:29 sware, and said, As the **L.** liveth, ... 3068
1Ki 1:30 I sware unto thee by the **L.** God of.... 3068
1Ki 1:31 Let my **l.** king David live for ever........ 113
1Ki 1:33 Take with you the servants of your **l.**,.. 113
1Ki 1:36 **L.** God of...the king say so too. 3068
1Ki 1:36 God of my **l.** the king say so too. 113
1Ki 1:37 As the **L.** hath been with my 3068
1Ki 1:37 hath been with my **l.** the king, ... 113
1Ki 1:37 than the throne of my **l.** king David...... 113
1Ki 1:43 **l.** king David hath made Solomon......... 113
1Ki 1:47 came to bless our **l.** king David,.......... 113
1Ki 1:48 Blessed be the **L.** God of Israel,........ 3068
1Ki 2:3 keep the charge of the **L.** thy God, ... 3068
1Ki 2:4 **L.** may continue his word which......... 3068
1Ki 2:8 and I sware to him by the **L.**, ... 3068
1Ki 2:15 brother's: for it was his from the **L.** .. 3068
1Ki 2:23 Solomon sware by the **L.**, saying, ... 3068
1Ki 2:24 Now therefore, as the **L.** liveth, ... 3068
1Ki 2:26 thou barest the ark of the **L.** God........ 136
1Ki 2:27 from being priest unto the **L.**; 3068
1Ki 2:27 he might fulfil the word of the **L.**, ... 3068
1Ki 2:28 fled unto the tabernacle of the **L.**,...... 3068
1Ki 2:29 fled unto the tabernacle of the **L.**; 3068
1Ki 2:30 came to the tabernacle of the **L.**, ... 3068
1Ki 2:32 **L.** shall return his blood upon his....... 3068
1Ki 2:33 there be peace for ever from the **L.** .. 3068
1Ki 2:38 as my **l.** the king hath said, so will........ 113
1Ki 2:42 not make thee to swear by the **L.**;..... 3068
1Ki 2:43 thou not kept the oath of the **L.**, ... 3068
1Ki 2:44 **L.** shall return thy wickedness........... 3068
1Ki 2:45 established before the **L.** for ever. 3068
1Ki 3:1 house, and the house of the **L.**,......... 3068
1Ki 3:2 house built unto the name of the **L.**,... 3068
1Ki 3:3 Solomon loved the **L.**, walking in 3068
1Ki 3:5 the **L.** appeared to Solomon in a........ 3068
1Ki 3:7 O **L.** my God, thou hast made thy 3068
1Ki 3:10 And the speech pleased the **L.**, that..... 136
1Ki 3:15 the ark of the covenant of the **L.**, ... 3068
1Ki 3:17 O my **l.**, I and this woman dwell 113
1Ki 3:26 O my **l.**, give her the living child, ... 113
1Ki 5:3 unto the name of the **L.** his God........ 3068
1Ki 5:3 the **L.** put them under the soles 3068
1Ki 5:4 **L.** my God hath given me rest on...... 3068
1Ki 5:5 unto the name of the **L.** my God, ... 3068
1Ki 5:5 as the **L.** spake unto David my.......... 3068
1Ki 5:7 Blessed be the **L.** this day, which 3068
1Ki 5:12 the **L.** gave Solomon wisdom, as........ 3068
1Ki 6:1 began to build the house of the **L.**...... 3068
1Ki 6:2 king Solomon built for the **L.**,............ 3068
1Ki 6:11 word of the **L.** came to Solomon,......... 3068
1Ki 6:19 the ark of the covenant of the **L.** 3068
1Ki 6:37 foundation of the house of the **L.** 3068
1Ki 7:12 inner court of the house of the **L.**, ... 3068
1Ki 7:40 Solomon for the house of the **L.**: 3068
1Ki 7:45 Solomon for the house of the **L.**, ... 3068
1Ki 7:48 unto the house of the **L.**: 3068
1Ki 7:51 made for the house of the **L.** 3068
1Ki 7:51 treasures of the house of the **L.** 3068
1Ki 8:1 the ark of the covenant of the **L.** 3068
1Ki 8:4 they brought up the ark of the **L.**, ... 3068
1Ki 8:6 the ark of the covenant of the **L.** 3068
1Ki 8:9 when the **L.** made a covenant 3068
1Ki 8:10 cloud filled the house of the **L.**, ... 3068
1Ki 8:11 glory of the **L.** had filled the 3068
1Ki 8:11 had filled the house of the **L.** 3068
1Ki 8:12 The **L.** said that he would dwell......... 3068
1Ki 8:15 Blessed be the **L.** God of Israel,........ 3068
1Ki 8:17 the name of the **L.** God of Israel. 3068
1Ki 8:18 **L.** said unto David my father,............ 3068
1Ki 8:20 **L.** hath performed his word that 3068
1Ki 8:20 of Israel, as the **L.** promised,............ 3068
1Ki 8:20 the name of the **L.** God of Israel. 3068
1Ki 8:21 wherein is the covenant of the **L.**,...... 3068
1Ki 8:22 stood before the altar of the **L.** 3068
1Ki 8:23 **L.** God of Israel, there is no God....... 3068
1Ki 8:25 **L.** God of Israel, keep with thy 3068
1Ki 8:28 O **L.** my God, to hearken unto........... 3068
1Ki 8:44 pray unto the **L.** toward the city......... 3068
1Ki 8:53 our fathers out of Egypt, O **L.** God. 136
1Ki 8:54 and supplication unto the **L.**, ... 3068
1Ki 8:54 from before the altar of the **L.**, ... 3068
1Ki 8:56 Blessed be the **L.**, that hath given 3068
1Ki 8:57 The **L.** our God be with us, as he...... 3068
1Ki 8:59 made supplication before the **L.**, ... 3068
1Ki 8:59 be nigh unto the **L.** our God day........ 3068
1Ki 8:60 may know that the **L.** is God, ... 3068
1Ki 8:61 be perfect with the **L.** our God,......... 3068
1Ki 8:62 offered sacrifice before the **L.** 3068
1Ki 8:63 which he offered unto the **L.**,............ 3068
1Ki 8:63 dedicated the house of the **L.**............ 3068
1Ki 8:64 was before the house of the **L.**:.......... 3068
1Ki 8:64 altar that was before the **L.** was........ 3068
1Ki 8:65 before the **L.** our God, seven days....... 3068
1Ki 8:66 the goodness that the **L.** had done 3068
1Ki 9:1 building of the house of the **L.**,.......... 3068
1Ki 9:2 the **L.** appeared to Solomon the......... 3068
1Ki 9:3 And the **L.** said unto him, I have 3068
1Ki 9:8 Why hath the **L.** done this unto 3068
1Ki 9:9 they forsook the **L.** their God, ... 3068
1Ki 9:9 **L.** brought upon them all this............ 3068
1Ki 9:10 the house of the **L.**, and the king's..... 3068
1Ki 9:15 for to build the house of the **L.**, ... 3068
1Ki 9:25 altar which he built unto the **L.**,........ 3068
1Ki 9:25 the altar that was before the **L.** 3068
1Ki 10:1 concerning the name of the **L.**,.......... 3068
1Ki 10:5 went up unto the house of the **L.**;...... 3068
1Ki 10:9 Blessed be the **L.** thy God, which...... 3068
1Ki 10:9 the **L.** loved Israel for ever,.............. 3068
1Ki 10:12 pillars for the house of the **L.**,........... 3068
1Ki 11:2 concerning which the **L.** said............. 3068
1Ki 11:4 not perfect with the **L.** his God, ... 3068
1Ki 11:6 did evil in the sight of the **L.**,............ 3068
1Ki 11:6 went not fully after the **L.**, as did 3068
1Ki 11:9 the **L.** was angry with Solomon, ... 3068
1Ki 11:9 heart was turned from the **L.** God...... 3068
1Ki 11:10 not that which the **L.** commanded. 3068
1Ki 11:11 the **L.** said unto Solomon,................. 3068
1Ki 11:14 **L.** stirred up an adversary unto 3068

1Ki 11:23 which fled from his l. Hadadezer.......... 113
1Ki 11:31 for thus saith the L., the God of........ 3068
1Ki 12:15 for the cause was from the L.,......... 3068
1Ki 12:15 which the L. spake by Ahijah the....... 3068
1Ki 12:24 Thus saith the L., Ye shall not go...... 3068
1Ki 12:24 therefore to the word of the L., ... 3068
1Ki 12:24 according to the word of the L.. 3068
1Ki 12:27 sacrifice in the house of the L. at....... 3068
1Ki 12:27 people turn again unto their l.,........... 113
1Ki 13:1 Judah by the word of the L. unto....... 3068
1Ki 13:2 the altar in the word of the L.,.......... 3068
1Ki 13:2 O altar, altar, thus saith the L.;......... 3068
1Ki 13:3 sign which the L. hath spoken;.......... 3068
1Ki 13:5 had given by the word of the L.. 3068
1Ki 13:6 now the face of the L. thy God, ... 3068
1Ki 13:6 the man of God besought the L., ... 3068
1Ki 13:9 charged me by the word of the L.,...... 3068
1Ki 13:17 said to me by the word of the L.,...... 3068
1Ki 13:18 unto me by the word of the L.,.......... 3068
1Ki 13:20 the word of the L. came unto the...... 3068
1Ki 13:21 Judah, saying, Thus saith the L., ... 3068
1Ki 13:21 disobeyed the mouth of the L.,.......... 3068
1Ki 13:21 which the L. thy God commanded....... 3068
1Ki 13:22 the which the L. did say unto thee,..........
1Ki 13:26 unto the word of the L.: 3068
1Ki 13:26 L. hath delivered him unto the 3068
1Ki 13:26 according to the word of the L., ... 3068
1Ki 13:32 he cried by the word of the L. 3068
1Ki 14:5 the L. said unto Ahijah, Behold,......... 3068
1Ki 14:7 Thus saith the L. God of Israel, ... 3068
1Ki 14:11 eat: for the L. hath spoken it. 3068
1Ki 14:13 some good thing toward the L........... 3068
1Ki 14:14 L. shall raise him up a king over........ 3068
1Ki 14:15 L. shall smite Israel, as a reed.......... 3068
1Ki 14:15 groves, provoking the L. to anger...... 3068
1Ki 14:18 according to the word of the L., ... 3068
1Ki 14:21 the city which the L. did choose........ 3068
1Ki 14:22 did evil in the sight of the L.,.......... 3068
1Ki 14:24 the nations which the L. cast out....... 3068
1Ki 14:26 treasures of the house of the L., ... 3068
1Ki 14:28 went into the house of the L.,............ 3068
1Ki 15:3 not perfect with the L. his God, ... 3068
1Ki 15:4 the L. his God give him a lamp 3068
1Ki 15:5, 11 was right in the eyes of the L.,..... 3068
1Ki 15:14 heart was perfect with the L. all........ 3068
1Ki 15:15 into the house of the L., silver, ... 3068
1Ki 15:18 treasures of the house of the L., ... 3068
1Ki 15:26 he did evil in the sight of the L., ... 3068
1Ki 15:29 unto the saying of the L., which 3068
1Ki 15:30 provoked the L. God of Israel to 3068
1Ki 15:34 he did evil in the sight of the L., ... 3068
1Ki 16:1 the word of the L. came to Jehu........ 3068
1Ki 16:7 word of the L. against Baasha, ... 3068
1Ki 16:7 that he did in the sight of the L.,........ 3068
1Ki 16:12 according to the word of the L., ... 3068
1Ki 16:13 provoking the L. God of Israel to....... 3068
1Ki 16:19 doing evil in the sight of the L., ... 3068
1Ki 16:25 wrought evil in the eyes of the L.,...... 3068
1Ki 16:26 to provoke the L. God of Israel......... 3068
1Ki 16:30 Omri did evil in the sight of the L...... 3068
1Ki 16:33 provoke the L. God of Israel to......... 3068
1Ki 16:34 according to the word of the L., ... 3068
1Ki 17:1 As the L. God of Israel liveth, ... 3068
1Ki 17:2 the word of the L. came unto him,..... 3068
1Ki 17:5 according unto the word of the L.: 3068
1Ki 17:8 the word of the L. came unto him,..... 3068
1Ki 17:12 As the L. thy God liveth, I have........ 3068
1Ki 17:14 thus saith the L. God of Israel, ... 3068
1Ki 17:14 the day that the L. sendeth rain 3068
1Ki 17:16 according to the word of the L., ... 3068
1Ki 17:20 he cried unto the L., and said, ... 3068
1Ki 17:20 O L. my God, hast thou also............. 3068
1Ki 17:21 and cried unto the L., and said,.......... 3068
1Ki 17:21 O L. my God, I pray thee, let........... 3068
1Ki 17:22 the L. heard the voice of Elijah; 3068
1Ki 17:24 the word of the L. in thy mouth 3068
1Ki 18:1 the word of the L. came to Elijah 3068
1Ki 18:3 Obadiah feared the L. greatly: 3068
1Ki 18:4 cut off the prophets of the L.,............ 3068
1Ki 18:7 said, Art thou that my l. Elijah? 113
1Ki 18:8 go, tell thy l., Behold, Elijah is............ 113
1Ki 18:10 As the L. thy God liveth, there.......... 3068
1Ki 18:10 whither my l. hath not sent to 113
1Ki 18:11 Go, tell thy l., Behold, Elijah is........... 113
1Ki 18:12 Spirit of the L. shall carry thee.......... 3068
1Ki 18:12 but I thy servant fear the L. from...... 3068
1Ki 18:13 Was it not told my l. what I did 113
1Ki 18:13 slew the prophets of the L., ... 3068
1Ki 18:14 Go, tell thy l., Behold, Elijah is........... 113
1Ki 18:15 said, As the L. of hosts liveth, ... 3068
1Ki 18:18 the commandments of the L.,............ 3068
1Ki 18:21 if the L. be God, follow him: but 3068
1Ki 18:22 only, remain a prophet of the L.; 3068
1Ki 18:24 I will call on the name of the L.:........ 3068
1Ki 18:30 repaired the altar of the L. that......... 3068
1Ki 18:31 unto whom the word of the L. 3068
1Ki 18:32 an altar in the name of the L.:........... 3068
1Ki 18:36 and said, L. God of Abraham, ... 3068
1Ki 18:37 Hear me, O L., hear me, that this..... 3068
1Ki 18:37 know that thou art the L. God, ... 3068
1Ki 18:38 Then the fire of the L. fell, and......... 3068
1Ki 18:39 L., he is the God; the L., he is the ... 3068
1Ki 18:46 the hand of the L. was on Elijah; 3068
1Ki 19:4 now, O L., take away my life; for...... 3068
1Ki 19:7 the angel of the L. came again 3068
1Ki 19:9 the word of the L. came to him,......... 3068
1Ki 19:10 jealous for the L. God of hosts: 3068
1Ki 19:11 upon the mount before the L.. 3068
1Ki 19:11 the L. passed by, and a great and...... 3068
1Ki 19:11 in pieces the rocks before the L.; 3068
1Ki 19:11 but the L. was not in the wind: 3068
1Ki 19:11 L. was not in the earthquake: 3068
1Ki 19:12 but the L. was not in the fire:........... 3068
1Ki 19:14 jealous for the L. God of hosts: 3068
1Ki 19:15 the L. said unto him, Go, return........ 3068
1Ki 20:4 Israel answered and said, My l.,........... 113
1Ki 20:9 Tell my l. the king, All that thou 113
1Ki 20:13 Thus saith the L., Hast thou seen...... 3068
1Ki 20:13 thou shalt know that I am the L.. 3068
1Ki 20:14 Thus saith the L., Even by the 3068
1Ki 20:28 Thus saith the L., Because the.......... 3068
1Ki 20:28 said, The L. is God of the hills,......... 3068
1Ki 20:28 ye shall know that I am the L.. 3068
1Ki 20:35 neighbour in the word of the L., ... 3068
1Ki 20:36 not obeyed the voice of the L., ... 3068
1Ki 20:42 Thus saith the L., Because thou 3068
1Ki 21:3 said to Ahab, The L. forbid it me,....... 3068
1Ki 21:17 the word of the L. came to Elijah 3068
1Ki 21:19 Thus saith the L., Hast thou............. 3068
1Ki 21:19 Thus saith the L., In the place 3068
1Ki 21:20 to work evil in the sight of the L.. 3068
1Ki 21:23 And of Jezebel also spake the L.,....... 3068
1Ki 21:25 wickedness in the sight of the L., ... 3068
1Ki 21:26 Amorites, whom the L. cast out 3068
1Ki 21:28 the word of the L. came to Elijah 3068
1Ki 22:5 thee, at the word of the L. to day. 3068
1Ki 22:6 L. shall deliver it into the hand of........ 136
1Ki 22:7 there not here a prophet of the L. 3068
1Ki 22:8 whom we may enquire of the L.: 3068
1Ki 22:11 Thus saith the L., With these 3068
1Ki 22:12 L. shall deliver it into the king's......... 3068
1Ki 22:14 Micaiah said, As the L. liveth,........... 3068
1Ki 22:14 what the L. saith unto me, that......... 3068
1Ki 22:15 L. shall deliver it into the hand of 3068
1Ki 22:16 is true in the name of the L.? 3068
1Ki 22:17 L. said, These have no master: 3068
1Ki 22:19 thou therefore the word of the L.: 3068
1Ki 22:19 I saw the L. sitting on his throne,...... 3068
1Ki 22:20 the L. said, Who shall persuade......... 3068
1Ki 22:21 a spirit, and stood before the L., ... 3068
1Ki 22:22 L. said unto him, Wherewith?............ 3068
1Ki 22:23 L. hath put a lying spirit in the.......... 3068
1Ki 22:23 L. hath spoken evil concerning 3068
1Ki 22:24 went the Spirit of the L. from me...... 3068
1Ki 22:28 the L. hath not spoken by me. 3068
1Ki 22:38 according unto the word of the L. 3068
1Ki 22:43 was right in the eyes of the L.: 3068
1Ki 22:52 he did evil in the sight of the L., ... 3068
1Ki 22:53 and provoked to anger the L. God 3068
2Ki 1:3 angel of the L. said to Elijah the........ 3068
2Ki 1:4 thus saith the L., Thou shalt not.......... 3068
2Ki 1:6 saith the L., Is it not because 3068
2Ki 1:15 angel of the L. said unto Elijah, ... 3068
2Ki 1:16 Thus saith the L., Forasmuch as......... 3068
2Ki 1:17 according to the word of the L. 3068
2Ki 2:1 the L. would take up Elijah into.......... 3068
2Ki 2:2 for the L. hath sent me to Beth-el. 3068
2Ki 2:2 said unto him, As the L. liveth, ... 3068
2Ki 2:3 the L. will take away thy master........ 3068
2Ki 2:4 for the L. hath sent me to Jericho...... 3068
2Ki 2:4 said, As the L. liveth, and as thy........ 3068
2Ki 2:5 the L. will take away thy master........ 3068
2Ki 2:6 for the L. hath sent me to Jordan. 3068
2Ki 2:6 said, As the L. liveth, and as thy....... 3068
2Ki 2:14 Where is the L. God of Elijah? 3068
2Ki 2:16 Spirit of the L. hath taken him 3068
2Ki 2:19 this city is pleasant, as my l. seeth: 113
2Ki 2:21 Thus saith the L., I have healed........ 3068
2Ki 2:24 cursed them in the name of the L.. 3068
2Ki 3:2 wrought evil in the sight of the L.;..... 3068
2Ki 3:10 L. hath called these three kings......... 3068
2Ki 3:11 there not here a prophet of the L., ... 3068
2Ki 3:11 we may enquire of the L. by him?...... 3068
2Ki 3:12 The word of the L. is with him. 3068
2Ki 3:13 L. hath called these three kings......... 3068
2Ki 3:14 As the L. of hosts liveth, before........ 3068
2Ki 3:15 hand of the L. came upon him. 3068
2Ki 3:16 saith the L., Make this valley............ 3068
2Ki 3:17 For thus saith the L., Ye shall not 3068
2Ki 3:18 light thing in the sight of the L.: 3068
2Ki 4:1 that thy servant did fear the L.: 3068
2Ki 4:16 said, Nay, my l., thou man of God,...... 113
2Ki 4:27 the L. hath hid it from me, and 3068
2Ki 4:28 said, Did I desire a son of my l.?......... 113
2Ki 4:30 the child said, As the L. liveth, ... 3068
2Ki 4:33 twain, and prayed unto the L.. 3068
2Ki 4:43 thus saith the L., They shall eat, ... 3068
2Ki 4:44 according to the word of the L.. 3068
2Ki 5:1 the L. had given deliverance unto....... 3068
2Ki 5:3 God my l. were with the prophet 113
2Ki 5:4 one went in, and told his l., saying, ... 113
2Ki 5:11 and call on the name of the L............ 3068
2Ki 5:16 As the L. liveth, before whom I 3068
2Ki 5:17 unto other gods, but unto the L......... 3068
2Ki 5:18 thing the L. pardon thy servant, ... 3068
2Ki 5:18 the L. pardon thy servant in this........ 3068
2Ki 5:20 as the L. liveth, I will run after 3068
2Ki 6:12 servants said, None, my l., O king: 113
2Ki 6:17 L., I pray thee, open his eyes,.......... 3068
2Ki 6:17 L. opened the eyes of the young 3068
2Ki 6:18 Elisha prayed unto the L., and 3068
2Ki 6:20 L., open the eyes of these men,......... 3068
2Ki 6:20 And the L. opened their eyes, and..... 3068
2Ki 6:26 him, saying, Help, my l., O king. 113
2Ki 6:27 said, If the L. do not help thee,......... 3068
2Ki 6:33 said, Behold, this evil is of the L.; 3068
2Ki 6:33 I wait for the L. any longer?............. 3068
2Ki 7:1 said, Hear ye the word of the L.; 3068
2Ki 7:1 Thus saith the L., To morrow........... 3068
2Ki 7:2 l. on whose hand the king leaned....... 7991
2Ki 7:2 if the L. would make windows in........ 3068
2Ki 7:6 L. had made the host of Syrians.......... 136
2Ki 7:16 according to the word of the L.. 3068
2Ki 7:17 king appointed the l. on whose 7991
2Ki 7:19 that l. answered the man of God,....... 7991
2Ki 7:19 if the L. should make windows in....... 3068
2Ki 8:1 the L. hath called for a famine;.......... 3068
2Ki 8:5 Gehazi said, My l., O king, this is 113
2Ki 8:8 enquire of the L. by him, saying, ... 3068
2Ki 8:10 L. hath shewed me that he shall....... 3068
2Ki 8:12 Hazael said, Why weepeth my l.? 113
2Ki 8:13 The L. hath shewed me that thou...... 3068
2Ki 8:18 he did evil in the sight of the L.. 3068
2Ki 8:19 L. would not destroy Judah for.......... 3068
2Ki 8:27 and did evil in the sight of the L., ... 3068
2Ki 9:3 saith the L., I have anointed............. 3068
2Ki 9:6 Thus saith the L. God of Israel, ... 3068
2Ki 9:6 king over the people of the L.,........... 3068
2Ki 9:7 blood of all the servants of the L., ... 3068
2Ki 9:11 came forth to the servants of his l.: 113
2Ki 9:12 Thus said the L., I have anointed....... 3068
2Ki 9:25 the L. laid this burden upon him; 3068
2Ki 9:26 the blood of his sons, saith the L.; 3068
2Ki 9:26 thee in this plat, saith the L............. 3068
2Ki 9:26 according to the word of the L.. 3068
2Ki 9:36 This is the word of the L., which....... 3068
2Ki 10:10 nothing of the word of the L.. 3068
2Ki 10:10 L. spake concerning the house of....... 3068
2Ki 10:10 L. hath done that which he spake....... 3068
2Ki 10:16 me, and see my zeal for the L.. 3068
2Ki 10:17 according to the saying of the L.,....... 3068
2Ki 10:23 none of the servants of the L.,.......... 3068
2Ki 10:30 the L. said unto Jehu, Because.......... 3068
2Ki 10:31 to walk in the law of the L. God........ 3068
2Ki 10:32 the L. began to cut Israel short: 3068
2Ki 11:3 hid in the house of the L. six years.... 3068
2Ki 11:4 to him into the house of the L.,......... 3068
2Ki 11:4 of them in the house of the L., ... 3068
2Ki 11:7 the watch of the house of the L. 3068
2Ki 11:10 that were in the temple of the L......... 3068
2Ki 11:13 people into the temple of the L.. 3068

2Ki	11:15	not be slain in the house of the **L.**.	3068
2Ki	11:17	covenant between the **L.** and the	3068
2Ki	11:18	officers over the house of the **L.**	3068
2Ki	11:19	the king from the house of the **L.**,	3068
2Ki	12:2	was right in the sight of the **L.** all	3068
2Ki	12:4	brought into the house of the **L.**,	3068
2Ki	12:4	to bring into the house of the **L.**,	3068
2Ki	12:9	cometh into the house of the **L.**,	3068
2Ki	12:9	brought into the house of the **L.**.	3068
2Ki	12:10	was found in the house of the **L.**.	3068
2Ki	12:11	oversight of the house of the **L.**.	3068
2Ki	12:11	wrought upon the house of the **L.**,	3068
2Ki	12:12	breaches of the house of the **L.**,	3068
2Ki	12:13	not made for the house of the **L.**	3068
2Ki	12:13	brought into the house of the **L.**.	3068
2Ki	12:14	therewith the house of the **L.**	3068
2Ki	12:16	brought into the house of the **L.**.	3068
2Ki	12:18	treasures of the house of the **L.**,	3068
2Ki	13:2	was evil in the sight of the **L.**,	3068
2Ki	13:3	anger of the **L.** was kindled	3068
2Ki	13:4	And Jehoahaz besought the **L.**,	3068
2Ki	13:4	and the **L.** hearkened unto him:	3068
2Ki	13:5	(And the **L.** gave Israel a saviour,	3068
2Ki	13:11	was evil in the sight of the **L.**;	3068
2Ki	13:23	the **L.** was gracious unto them,	3068
2Ki	14:3	was right in the sight of the **L.**,	3068
2Ki	14:6	wherein the **L.** commanded,	3068
2Ki	14:14	were found in the house of the **L.**,	3068
2Ki	14:24	was evil in the sight of the **L.**.	3068
2Ki	14:25	according to the word of the **L.** God	3068
2Ki	14:26	the **L.** saw the affliction of Israel,	3068
2Ki	14:27	**L.** said not that he would blot out	3068
2Ki	15:3	was right in the sight of the **L.**,	3068
2Ki	15:5	the **L.** smote the king, so that he	3068
2Ki	15:9	was evil in the sight of the **L.**,	3068
2Ki	15:12	the word of the **L.** which he spake	3068
2Ki	15:18,	24,28 evil in the sight of the **L.**.	3068
2Ki	15:34	was right in the sight of the **L.**	3068
2Ki	15:35	higher gate of the house of the **L.**	3068
2Ki	15:37	**L.** began to send against Judah	3068
2Ki	16:2	was right in the sight of the **L.**	3068
2Ki	16:3	whom the **L.** cast out from before	3068
2Ki	16:8	was found in the house of the **L.**,	3068
2Ki	16:14	altar, which was before the **L.**,	3068
2Ki	16:14	the altar and the house of the **L.**,	3068
2Ki	16:18	he from the house of the **L.** for	3068
2Ki	17:2	was evil in the sight of the **L.**,	3068
2Ki	17:7	sinned against the **L.** their God,	3068
2Ki	17:8	heathen, whom the **L.** cast out	3068
2Ki	17:9	that were not right against the **L.**	3068
2Ki	17:11	whom the **L.** carried away before	3068
2Ki	17:11	things to provoke the **L.** to anger:	3068
2Ki	17:12	the **L.** had said unto them, Ye	3068
2Ki	17:13	the **L.** testified against Israel,	3068
2Ki	17:14	that did not believe in the **L.** their	3068
2Ki	17:15	concerning whom the **L.** had	3068
2Ki	17:16	all the commandments of the **L.**	3068
2Ki	17:17	to do evil in the sight of the **L.**,	3068
2Ki	17:18	the **L.** was very angry with Israel,	3068
2Ki	17:19	not the commandments of the **L.**	3068
2Ki	17:20	**L.** rejected all the seed of Israel,	3068
2Ki	17:21	Israel from following the **L.**,	3068
2Ki	17:23	**L.** removed Israel out of his sight,	3068
2Ki	17:25	there, that they feared not the **L.**.	3068
2Ki	17:25	the **L.** sent lions among them,	3068
2Ki	17:28	how they should fear the **L.**	3068
2Ki	17:32	So they feared the **L.**, and made	3068
2Ki	17:33	They feared the **L.**, and served	3068
2Ki	17:34	they fear not the **L.**, neither do	3068
2Ki	17:34	and commandment which the **L.**	3068
2Ki	17:35	the **L.** had made a covenant,	3068
2Ki	17:36	the **L.**, who brought you up out	3068
2Ki	17:39	the **L.** your God ye shall fear;	3068
2Ki	17:41	So these nations feared the **L.**,	3068
2Ki	18:3	was right in the sight of the **L.**,	3068
2Ki	18:5	trusted in the **L.** God of Israel;	3068
2Ki	18:6	he clave to the **L.**, and departed	3068
2Ki	18:6	which the **L.** commanded Moses.	3068
2Ki	18:7	And the **L.** was with him; and he	3068
2Ki	18:12	obeyed not the voice of the **L.**	3068
2Ki	18:12	the servant of the **L.** commanded,	3068
2Ki	18:15	was found in the house of the **L.**,	3068
2Ki	18:16	the doors of the temple of the **L.**,	3068
2Ki	18:22	me, We trust in the **L.** our God:	3068
2Ki	18:23	give pledges to my **l.** the king of	113
2Ki	18:25	Am I now come up without the **L.**	3068
2Ki	18:25	The **L.** said to me, Go up against	3068
2Ki	18:30	Hezekiah make you trust in the **L.**,	3068
2Ki	18:30	The **L.** will surely deliver us, and	3068
2Ki	18:32	saying, The **L.** will deliver us.	3068
2Ki	18:35	**L.** should deliver Jerusalem out	3068
2Ki	19:1	and went into the house of the **L.**.	3068
2Ki	19:4	**L.** thy God will hear all the words	3068
2Ki	19:4	which the **L.** thy God hath heard:	3068
2Ki	19:6	Thus saith the **L.**, Be not afraid	3068
2Ki	19:14	went up into the house of the **L.**,	3068
2Ki	19:14	and spread it before the **L.**.	3068
2Ki	19:15	Hezekiah prayed before the **L.**,	3068
2Ki	19:15	O **L.** God of Israel, which dwellest	3068
2Ki	19:16	**L.**, bow down thine ear, and hear:	3068
2Ki	19:16	open, **L.**, thine eyes, and see:	3068
2Ki	19:17	Of a truth, **L.**, the kings of Assyria	3068
2Ki	19:19	O **L.** our God, I beseech thee, save	3068
2Ki	19:19	know that thou art the **L.** God,	3068
2Ki	19:20	Thus saith the **L.** God of Israel,	3068
2Ki	19:21	the word that the **L.** hath spoken	3068
2Ki	19:23	thou hast reproached the **L.**,	3068
2Ki	19:31	zeal of the **L.** of hosts shall do	3068
2Ki	19:32	thus saith the **L.** concerning the	3068
2Ki	19:33	come into this city, saith the **L.**.	3068
2Ki	19:35	that the angel of the **L.** went out,	3068
2Ki	20:1	Thus saith the **L.**, Set thine house	3068
2Ki	20:2	the wall, and prayed unto the **L.**,	3068
2Ki	20:3	I beseech thee, O **L.**, remember	3068
2Ki	20:4	the word of the **L.** came to him,	3068
2Ki	20:5	Thus saith the **L.**, the God of	3068
2Ki	20:5	go up unto the house of the **L.**	3068
2Ki	20:8	be the sign that the **L.** will heal	3068
2Ki	20:8	go up into the house of the **L.**	3068
2Ki	20:9	sign shalt thou have of the **L.**,	3068
2Ki	20:9	**L.** will do the thing that he hath	3068
2Ki	20:11	the prophet cried unto the **L.**:	3068
2Ki	20:16	Hear the word of the **L.**	3068
2Ki	20:17	nothing shall be left, saith the **L.**	3068
2Ki	20:19	Good is the word of the **L.** which	3068
2Ki	21:2	was evil in the sight of the **L.**,	3068
2Ki	21:2	**L.** cast out before the children of	3068
2Ki	21:4	built altars in the house of the **L.**,	3068
2Ki	21:4	**L.** said, In Jerusalem will I put my	3068
2Ki	21:5	two courts of the house of the **L.**.	3068
2Ki	21:6	wickedness in the sight of the **L.**,	3068
2Ki	21:7	of which the **L.** said to David,	3068
2Ki	21:9	nations whom the **L.** destroyed	3068
2Ki	21:10	the **L.** spake by his servants the	3068
2Ki	21:12	thus saith the **L.** God of Israel,	3068
2Ki	21:16	was evil in the sight of the **L.**.	3068
2Ki	21:20	was evil in the sight of the **L.**,	3068
2Ki	21:22	forsook the **L.** God of his fathers,	3068
2Ki	21:22	walked not in the way of the **L.**	3068
2Ki	22:2	was right in the sight of the **L.**,	3068
2Ki	22:3	the scribe, to the house of the **L.**,	3068
2Ki	22:4	brought into the house of the **L.**,	3068
2Ki	22:5	oversight of the house of the **L.**:	3068
2Ki	22:5	which is in the house of the **L.**,	3068
2Ki	22:8	of the law in the house of the **L.**.	3068
2Ki	22:9	oversight of the house of the **L.**.	3068
2Ki	22:13	enquire of the **L.** for me, and for	3068
2Ki	22:13	great is the wrath of the **L.** that	3068
2Ki	22:15	Thus saith the **L.** God of Israel,	3068
2Ki	22:16	Thus saith the **L.**, Behold, I will	3068
2Ki	22:18	sent you to enquire of the **L.**,	3068
2Ki	22:18	Thus saith the **L.** God of Israel,	3068
2Ki	22:19	humbled thyself before the **L.**,	3068
2Ki	22:19	have heard thee, saith the **L.**	3068
2Ki	23:2	went up into the house of the **L.**,	3068
2Ki	23:2	was found in the house of the **L.**.	3068
2Ki	23:3	made a covenant before the **L.**,	3068
2Ki	23:3	to walk after the **L.**, and to keep	3068
2Ki	23:4	forth out of the temple of the **L.**	3068
2Ki	23:6	grove from the house of the **L.**,	3068
2Ki	23:7	that were by the house of the **L.**,	3068
2Ki	23:9	came not up to the altar of the **L.**	3068
2Ki	23:11	entering in of the house of the **L.**,	3068
2Ki	23:12	two courts of the house of the **L.**,	3068
2Ki	23:16	according to the word of the **L.**	3068
2Ki	23:19	made to provoke the **L.** to anger,	
2Ki	23:21	Keep the passover unto the **L.**	3068
2Ki	23:23	passover was holden to the **L.** in	3068
2Ki	23:24	found in the house of the **L.**	3068
2Ki	23:25	that turned to the **L.** with all his	3068
2Ki	23:26	**L.** turned not from the fierceness	3068
2Ki	23:27	the **L.** said, I will remove Judah	3068
2Ki	23:32,	37 was evil in the sight of the **L.**,	3068
2Ki	24:2	the **L.** sent against him bands of	3068
2Ki	24:2	according to the word of the **L.**,	3068
2Ki	24:3	at the commandment of the **L.**	3068
2Ki	24:4	which the **L.** would not pardon.	3068
2Ki	24:9	was evil in the sight of the **L.**,	3068
2Ki	24:13	treasures of the house of the **L.**,	3068
2Ki	24:13	had made in the temple of the **L.**,	3068
2Ki	24:13	as the **L.** had said.	3068
2Ki	24:19	was evil in the sight of the **L.**,	3068
2Ki	24:20	For through the anger of the **L.**	3068
2Ki	25:9	he burnt the house of the **L.**, and	3068
2Ki	25:13	that were in the house of the **L.**,	3068
2Ki	25:13	that was in the house of the **L.**,	3068
2Ki	25:16	made for the house of the **L.**;	3068
1Ch	2:3	was evil in the sight of the **L.**;	3068
1Ch	6:15	when the **L.** carried away Judah	3068
1Ch	6:31	of song in the house of the **L.**,	3068
1Ch	6:32	had built the house of the **L.** in	3068
1Ch	9:19	being over the host of the **L.**,	3068
1Ch	9:20	past, and the **L.** was with him.	3068
1Ch	9:23	the gates of the house of the **L.**,	3068
1Ch	10:13	he committed against the **L.**,	3068
1Ch	10:13	even against the word of the **L.**,	3068
1Ch	10:14	enquired not of the **L.**: therefore	3068
1Ch	11:2	the **L.** thy God said unto thee,	3068
1Ch	11:3	them in Hebron before the **L.**;	3068
1Ch	11:3	the word of the **L.** by Samuel.	3068
1Ch	11:9	for the **L.** of hosts was with him.	3068
1Ch	11:10	word of the **L.** concerning Israel.	3068
1Ch	11:14	and the **L.** saved them by a great	3068
1Ch	11:18	of it, but poured it out to the **L.**,	3068
1Ch	12:23	according to the word of the **L.**.	3068
1Ch	13:2	and that it be of the **L.** our God,	3068
1Ch	13:6	up thence the ark of God the **L.**,	3068
1Ch	13:10	the anger of the **L.** was kindled	3068
1Ch	13:11	**L.** had made a breach upon Uzza:	3068
1Ch	13:14	And the **L.** blessed the house of	3068
1Ch	14:2	**L.** had confirmed him king over	3068
1Ch	14:10	the **L.** said unto him, Go up; for	3068
1Ch	14:17	**L.** brought the fear of him upon	3068
1Ch	15:2	them hath the **L.** chosen to carry	3068
1Ch	15:3	bring up the ark of the **L.** unto	3068
1Ch	15:12	up the ark of the **L.** God of Israel	3068
1Ch	15:13	**L.** our God made a breach upon	3068
1Ch	15:14	up the ark of the **L.** God of Israel.	3068
1Ch	15:15	according to the word of the **L.**.	3068
1Ch	15:25	the ark of the covenant of the **L.**	3068
1Ch	15:26	the ark of the covenant of the **L.**,	3068
1Ch	15:28,	29 ark of the covenant of the **L.**	3068
1Ch	16:2	the people in the name of the **L.**	3068
1Ch	16:4	minister before the ark of the **L.**,	3068
1Ch	16:4	thank and praise the **L.** God of	3068
1Ch	16:7	first this psalm to thank the **L.**	3068
1Ch	16:8	Give thanks unto the **L.**, call upon	3068
1Ch	16:10	of them rejoice that seek the **L.**.	3068
1Ch	16:11	Seek the **L.** and his strength,	3068
1Ch	16:14	He is the **L.** our God; his	3068
1Ch	16:23	Sing unto the **L.**, all the earth;	3068
1Ch	16:25	For great is the **L.**, and greatly	3068
1Ch	16:26	but the **L.** made the heavens.	3068
1Ch	16:28	Give unto the **L.**, ye kindreds of	3068
1Ch	16:28	unto the **L.** glory and strength.	3068
1Ch	16:29	Give unto the **L.** the glory due	3068
1Ch	16:29	worship the **L.** in the beauty of	3068
1Ch	16:31	the nations, The **L.** reigneth.	3068
1Ch	16:33	sing out at the presence of the **L.**,	3068
1Ch	16:34	O give thanks unto the **L.**; for	3068
1Ch	16:36	Blessed be the **L.** God of Israel	3068
1Ch	16:36	said, Amen, and praised the **L.**	3068
1Ch	16:37	the ark of the covenant of the **L.**	3068
1Ch	16:39	before the tabernacle of the **L.**	3068
1Ch	16:40	offer burnt offerings unto the **L.**	3068
1Ch	16:40	that is written in the law of the **L.**,	3068
1Ch	16:41	by name, to give thanks to the **L.**,	3068
1Ch	17:1	the ark of the covenant of the **L.**	3068
1Ch	17:4	Thus saith the **L.**, Thou shalt not	3068
1Ch	17:7	Thus saith the **L.** of hosts, I took	3068
1Ch	17:10	the **L.** will build thee an house.	3068
1Ch	17:16	king came and sat before the **L.**,	3068
1Ch	17:16	Who am I, O **L.** God, and what	3068
1Ch	17:17	a man of high degree, O **L.** God.	3068
1Ch	17:19	O **L.**, for thy servant's sake, and	3068
1Ch	17:20	O **L.**, there is none like thee,	3068
1Ch	17:22	and thou, **L.**, becamest their God	3068
1Ch	17:23	Therefore now, **L.**, let the thing	3068
1Ch	17:24	the **L.** of hosts is the God of Israel,	3068
1Ch	17:26	And now, **L.**, thou art God, and	3068

1Ch 17:27 for thou blessest, O **L.**, and it shall 3068
1Ch 18:6 Thus the **L.** preserved David 3068
1Ch 18:11 king David dedicated unto the **L.**, 3068
1Ch 18:13 Thus the **L.** preserved David 3068
1Ch 19:13 let the **L.** do that which is good in 3068
1Ch 21:3 **L.** make his people an hundred 3068
1Ch 21:3 my **l.** the king, are they not all my 113
1Ch 21:3 why then doth my **l.** require this 113
1Ch 21:9 **L.** spake unto Gad, David's seer, 3068
1Ch 21:10 Thus saith the **L.**, I offer thee three 3068
1Ch 21:11 Thus saith the **L.**, Choose thee 3068
1Ch 21:12 three days the sword of the **L.**, 3068
1Ch 21:12 and the angel of the **L.** destroying 3068
1Ch 21:13 fall now into the hand of the **L.**; 3068
1Ch 21:14 **L.** sent pestilence upon Israel: 3068
1Ch 21:15 the **L.** beheld, and he repented 3068
1Ch 21:15 the angel of the **L.** stood by the 3068
1Ch 21:16 and saw the angel of the **L.** stand 3068
1Ch 21:17 hand, I pray thee, O **L.** my God, 3068
1Ch 21:18 angel of the **L.** commanded Gad 3068
1Ch 21:18 set up an altar unto the **L.** in the 3068
1Ch 21:19 he spake in the name of the **L.** 3068
1Ch 21:22 build an altar therein unto the **L.**: 3068
1Ch 21:23 my **l.** the king do that which is good 113
1Ch 21:24 take that which is thine for the **L.**, 3068
1Ch 21:26 built there an altar unto the **L.**, 3068
1Ch 21:26 offerings, and called upon the **L.**; 3068
1Ch 21:27 And the **L.** commanded the angel; 3068
1Ch 21:28 saw that the **L.** had answered him 3068
1Ch 21:29 tabernacle of the **L.**, which Moses 3068
1Ch 21:30 the sword of the angel of the **L.** 3068
1Ch 22:1 This is the house of the **L.** God, 3068
1Ch 22:5 **L.** must be exceeding magnifical, 3068
1Ch 22:6 to build an house for the **L.** God 3068
1Ch 22:7 unto the name of the **L.** my God: 3068
1Ch 22:8 the word of the **L.** came to me, 3068
1Ch 22:11 Now, my son, the **L.** be with thee; 3068
1Ch 22:11 build the house of the **L.** thy God, 3068
1Ch 22:12 Only the **L.** give thee wisdom and 3068
1Ch 22:12 keep the law of the **L.** thy God. 3068
1Ch 22:13 which the **L.** charged Moses with 3068
1Ch 22:14 prepared for the house of the **L.** 3068
1Ch 22:16 be doing, and the **L.** be with thee. 3068
1Ch 22:18 Is not the **L.** your God with you? 3068
1Ch 22:18 the land is subdued before the **L.**, 3068
1Ch 22:19 your soul to seek the **L.** your God; 3068
1Ch 22:19 ye the sanctuary of the **L.** God, 3068
1Ch 22:19 the ark of the covenant of the **L.**, 3068
1Ch 22:19 to be built in the name of the **L.** 3068
1Ch 23:4 the work of the house of the **L.**; 3068
1Ch 23:5 four thousand praised the **L.** with 3068
1Ch 23:13 to burn incense before the **L.**, 3068
1Ch 23:24 the service of the house of the **L.**, 3068
1Ch 23:25 **L.** God of Israel hath given rest 3068
1Ch 23:28 the service of the house of the **L.**, 3068
1Ch 23:30 to thank and praise the **L.**, and 3068
1Ch 23:31 all burnt sacrifices unto the **L.** in 3068
1Ch 23:31 them, continually before the **L.**: 3068
1Ch 23:32 the service of the house of the **L.** 3068
1Ch 24:19 to come into the house of the **L.**, 3068
1Ch 24:19 **L.** God of Israel had commanded 3068
1Ch 25:3 give thanks and to praise the **L.** 3068
1Ch 25:6 for song in the house of the **L.**, 3068
1Ch 25:7 instructed in the songs of the **L.**, 3068
1Ch 26:12 to minister in the house of the **L.** 3068
1Ch 26:22 treasures of the house of the **L.** 3068
1Ch 26:27 to maintain the house of the **L.** 3068
1Ch 26:30 in all the business of the **L.**, and 3068
1Ch 27:23 the **L.** had said he would increase 3068
1Ch 28:2 the ark of the covenant of the **L.**, 3068
1Ch 28:4 **L.** God of Israel chose me before 3068
1Ch 28:5 the **L.** hath given me many sons,) 3068
1Ch 28:5 throne of the kingdom of the **L.** 3068
1Ch 28:8 Israel the congregation of the **L.**, 3068
1Ch 28:8 all the commandments of the **L.** 3068
1Ch 28:9 the **L.** searcheth all hearts, and 3068
1Ch 28:10 **L.** hath chosen thee to build an 3068
1Ch 28:12 the courts of the house of the **L.**, 3068
1Ch 28:13 the service of the house of the **L.**, 3068
1Ch 28:13 of service in the house of the **L.** 3068
1Ch 28:18 the ark of the covenant of the **L.** 3068
1Ch 28:19 **L.** made me understand in writing 3068
1Ch 28:20 for the **L.** God, even my God, will 3068
1Ch 28:20 the service of the house of the **L.** 3068
1Ch 29:1 is not for man, but for the **L.** God. 3068
1Ch 29:5 his service this day unto the **L.**? 3068
1Ch 29:8 treasure of the house of the **L.**, 3068

1Ch 29:9 they offered willingly to the **L.**: 3068
1Ch 29:10 David blessed the **L.** before all 3068
1Ch 29:10 be thou, **L.** God of Israel our father, 3068
1Ch 29:11 Thine, O **L.**, is the greatness, and 3068
1Ch 29:11 thine is the kingdom, O **L.**, and 3068
1Ch 29:16 O **L.** our God, all this store that 3068
1Ch 29:18 O **L.** God of Abraham, Isaac, and 3068
1Ch 29:20 Now bless the **L.** your God. 3068
1Ch 29:20 congregation blessed the **L.** God 3068
1Ch 29:20 worshipped the **L.**, and the king. 3068
1Ch 29:21 sacrificed sacrifices unto the **L.**, 3068
1Ch 29:21 offered burnt offerings unto the **L.**, 3068
1Ch 29:22 did eat and drink before the **L.** 3068
1Ch 29:22 anointed him unto the **L.** to be 3068
1Ch 29:23 sat on the throne of the **L.** as king 3068
1Ch 29:25 And the **L.** magnified Solomon 3068
2Ch 1:1 the **L.** his God was with him, and 3068
2Ch 1:3 Moses the servant of the **L.** had 3068
2Ch 1:5 before the tabernacle of the **L.**: 3068
2Ch 1:6 to the brasen altar before the **L.**, 3068
2Ch 1:9 Now, O **L.** God, let thy promise 3068
2Ch 2:1 an house for the name of the **L.**, 3068
2Ch 2:4 to the name of the **L.** my God, 3068
2Ch 2:4 solemn feasts of the **L.** our God. 3068
2Ch 2:11 the **L.** hath loved his people, 3068
2Ch 2:12 Blessed be the **L.** God of Israel, 3068
2Ch 2:12 might build an house for the **L.**, 3068
2Ch 2:14 the cunning men of my **l.** David thy 113
2Ch 2:15 wine, which my **l.** hath spoken of, 113
2Ch 3:1 began to build the house of the **L.** 3068
2Ch 3:1 where the **L.** appeared unto David
2Ch 4:16 Solomon for the house of the **L.** 3068
2Ch 5:1 the house of the **L.** was finished: 3068
2Ch 5:2, 7 the ark of the covenant of the **L.** 3068
2Ch 5:10 the **L.** made a covenant with the 3068
2Ch 5:13 in praising and thanking the **L.**; 3068
2Ch 5:13 musick, and praised the **L.**, saying, 3068
2Ch 5:13 cloud, even the house of the **L.**; 3068
2Ch 5:14 glory of the **L.** had filled the house 3068
2Ch 6:1 **L.** hath said that he would dwell 3068
2Ch 6:4 Blessed be the **L.** God of Israel, 3068
2Ch 6:7 house for the name of the **L.** God 3068
2Ch 6:8 the **L.** said to David my father, 3068
2Ch 6:10 The **L.** therefore hath performed 3068
2Ch 6:10 of Israel, as the **L.** promised, 3068
2Ch 6:10 house for the name of the **L.** God 3068
2Ch 6:11 wherein is the covenant of the **L.**, 3068
2Ch 6:12 he stood before the altar of the **L.** 3068
2Ch 6:14 O **L.** God of Israel, there is no God 3068
2Ch 6:16 O **L.** God of Israel, keep with thy 3068
2Ch 6:17 O **L.** God of Israel, let thy word 3068
2Ch 6:19 O **L.** my God, to hearken unto the 3068
2Ch 6:41 arise, O **L.** God, into thy resting 3068
2Ch 6:41 thy priests, O **L.** God, be clothed 3068
2Ch 6:42 O **L.** God, turn not away the face 3068
2Ch 7:1 glory of the **L.** filled the house. 3068
2Ch 7:2 not enter into the house of the **L.**, 3068
2Ch 7:2 glory of the **L.** had filled the Lord's 3068
2Ch 7:3 glory of the **L.** upon the house, 3068
2Ch 7:3 and praised the **L.**, saying, For he 3068
2Ch 7:4 offered sacrifices before the **L.** 3068
2Ch 7:6 instruments of musick of the **L.**, 3068
2Ch 7:6 king had made to praise the **L.**, 3068
2Ch 7:7 was before the house of the **L.**: 3068
2Ch 7:10 goodness that the **L.** had shewed 3068
2Ch 7:11 finished the house of the **L.**, and 3068
2Ch 7:11 to make in the house of the **L.**, 3068
2Ch 7:12 **L.** appeared to Solomon by night, 3068
2Ch 7:21 Why hath the **L.** done thus unto 3068
2Ch 7:22 they forsook the **L.** God of their 3068
2Ch 8:1 had built the house of the **L.**, and 3068
2Ch 8:11 the ark of the **L.** hath come. 3068
2Ch 8:12 unto the **L.** on the altar of the **L.**, 3068
2Ch 8:16 foundation of the house of the **L.**, 3068
2Ch 8:16 the house of the **L.** was perfected. 3068
2Ch 9:4 went up into the house of the **L.**; 3068
2Ch 9:8 Blessed be the **L.** thy God, which 3068
2Ch 9:8 to be king for the **L.** thy God: 3068
2Ch 9:11 terraces to the house of the **L.**, 3068
2Ch 10:15 the **L.** might perform his word, 3068
2Ch 11:2 word of the **L.** came to Shemaiah 3068
2Ch 11:4 Thus saith the **L.**, Ye shall not 3068
2Ch 11:4 they obeyed the words of the **L.**, 3068
2Ch 11:14 the priest's office unto the **L.**: 3068
2Ch 11:16 set their hearts to seek the **L.** God 3068
2Ch 11:16 sacrifice unto the **L.** God of their 3068
2Ch 12:1 he forsook the law of the **L.**, and 3068

2Ch 12:2 had transgressed against the **L.**, 3068
2Ch 12:5 saith the **L.**, Ye have forsaken 3068
2Ch 12:6 and they said, the **L.** is righteous. 3068
2Ch 12:7 the **L.** saw that they humbled 3068
2Ch 12:7 word of the **L.** came to Shemaiah, 3068
2Ch 12:9 treasures of the house of the **L.**, 3068
2Ch 12:11 entered into the house of the **L.**, 3068
2Ch 12:12 wrath of the **L.** turned from him, 3068
2Ch 12:13 city which the **L.** had chosen out 3068
2Ch 12:14 not his heart to seek the **L.** 3068
2Ch 13:5 **L.** God of Israel gave the kingdom 3068
2Ch 13:6 and hath rebelled against his **l.** 113
2Ch 13:8 withstand the kingdom of the **L.** 3068
2Ch 13:9 not cast out the priests of the **L.**, 3068
2Ch 13:10 as for us, the **L.** is our God, and 3068
2Ch 13:10 which minister unto the **L.**, 3068
2Ch 13:11 burn unto the **L.** every morning 3068
2Ch 13:11 the charge of the **L.** our God; 3068
2Ch 13:12 fight ye not against the **L.** God of 3068
2Ch 13:14 they cried unto the **L.**, and the 3068
2Ch 13:18 they relied upon the **L.** God of 3068
2Ch 13:20 the **L.** struck him, and he died. 3068
2Ch 14:2 right in the eyes of the **L.** his God: 3068
2Ch 14:4 Judah to seek the **L.** God of their 3068
2Ch 14:6 because the **L.** had given him rest 3068
2Ch 14:7 we have sought the **L.** our God, 3068
2Ch 14:11 And Asa cried unto the **L.** his God, 3068
2Ch 14:11 **L.**, it is nothing with thee to help, 3068
2Ch 14:11 help us, O **L.** our God; for we 3068
2Ch 14:11 O **L.** thou art our God; let not 3068
2Ch 14:12 **L.** smote the Ethiopians before 3068
2Ch 14:13 they were destroyed before the **L.**, 3068
2Ch 14:14 fear of the **L.** came upon them: 3068
2Ch 15:2 The **L.** is with you, while ye be 3068
2Ch 15:4 trouble did turn unto the **L.** God 3068
2Ch 15:8 and renewed the altar of the **L.**, 3068
2Ch 15:8 was before the porch of the **L.** 3068
2Ch 15:9 that the **L.** his God was with him. 3068
2Ch 15:11 they offered unto the **L.** the same 3068
2Ch 15:12 seek the **L.** God of their fathers 3068
2Ch 15:13 not seek the **L.** God of Israel 3068
2Ch 15:14 sware unto the **L.** with a loud 3068
2Ch 15:15 **L.** gave them rest round about. 3068
2Ch 16:2 treasures of the house of the **L.** 3068
2Ch 16:7 and not relied on the **L.** thy God, 3068
2Ch 16:8 because thou didst rely on the **L.**, 3068
2Ch 16:9 the eyes of the **L.** run to and fro 3068
2Ch 16:12 his disease he sought not the **L.**, 3068
2Ch 17:3 And the **L.** was with Jehoshaphat, 3068
2Ch 17:4 But sought to the **L.** God of his father,
2Ch 17:5 the **L.** stablished the kingdom in 3068
2Ch 17:6 lifted up in the ways of the **L.**: 3068
2Ch 17:9 had the book of the law of the **L.** 3068
2Ch 17:10 the fear of the **L.** fell upon all the 3068
2Ch 17:16 offered himself unto the **L.**; 3068
2Ch 18:4 I pray thee, at the word of the **L.** 3068
2Ch 18:6 there not here a prophet of the **L.** 3068
2Ch 18:7 whom we may enquire of the **L.**: 3068
2Ch 18:10 Thus saith the **L.**, With these 3068
2Ch 18:11 **L.** shall deliver it into the hand of 3068
2Ch 18:13 Micaiah said, As the **L.** liveth, 3068
2Ch 18:15 truth to me in the name of the **L.**? 3068
2Ch 18:16 and the **L.** said, These have no 3068
2Ch 18:18 Therefore hear the word of the **L.**; 3068
2Ch 18:18 saw the **L.** sitting upon his throne, 3068
2Ch 18:19 And the **L.** said, Who shall entice 3068
2Ch 18:20 a spirit, and stood before the **L.**, 3068
2Ch 18:20 the **L.** said unto him, Wherewith? 3068
2Ch 18:21 And the **L.** said, Thou shalt entice
2Ch 18:22 the **L.** hath put a lying spirit in 3068
2Ch 18:22 **L.** hath spoken evil against thee 3068
2Ch 18:23 went the spirit of the **L.** from me 3068
2Ch 18:27 hath not the **L.** spoken by me. 3068
2Ch 18:31 cried out, and the **L.** helped him; 3068
2Ch 19:2 and love them that hate the **L.**? 3068
2Ch 19:2 upon thee from before the **L.** 3068
2Ch 19:4 back unto the **L.** God of their 3068
2Ch 19:6 but for the **L.**, who is with you in 3068
2Ch 19:7 the fear of the **L.** be upon you; 3068
2Ch 19:7 no iniquity with the **L.** our God, 3068
2Ch 19:8 for the judgment of the **L.**, and 3068
2Ch 19:9 do in the fear of the **L.**, faithfully, 3068
2Ch 19:10 they trespass not against the **L.**, 3068
2Ch 19:11 over you in all matters of the **L.**; 3068
2Ch 19:11 and the **L.** shall be with the good. 3068
2Ch 20:3 and set himself to seek the **L.**, 3068
2Ch 20:4 together, to ask help of the **L.** 3068

2Ch	20:4	Judah, they came to seek the **L.**.	3068
2Ch	20:5	in the house of the **L.**, before the	3068
2Ch	20:6	O **L.** God of our fathers, art not	3068
2Ch	20:13	all Judah stood before the **L.**,	3068
2Ch	20:14	Spirit of the **L.** in the midst of the	3068
2Ch	20:15	Thus saith the **L.** unto you, Be not	3068
2Ch	20:17	the salvation of the **L.** with you,	3068
2Ch	20:17	them: for the **L.** will be with you.	3068
2Ch	20:18	before the **L.**, worshipping the **L.**.	3068
2Ch	20:19	up to praise the **L.** God of Israel.	3068
2Ch	20:20	Believe in the **L.** your God, so	3068
2Ch	20:21	he appointed singers unto the **L.**,	3068
2Ch	20:21	say, Praise the **L.**; for his mercy	3068
2Ch	20:22	**L.** set ambushments against the	3068
2Ch	20:26	for there they blessed the **L.**:	3068
2Ch	20:27	**L.** had made them to rejoice over	3068
2Ch	20:28	trumpets unto the house of the **L.**	3068
2Ch	20:29	heard that the **L.** fought against	3068
2Ch	20:32	was right in the sight of the **L.**	3068
2Ch	20:37	the **L.** hath broken thy works.	3068
2Ch	21:6	was evil in the eyes of the **L.**	3068
2Ch	21:7	**L.** would not destroy the house of	3068
2Ch	21:10	he had forsaken the **L.** God of his	3068
2Ch	21:12	Thus saith the **L.** God of David	3068
2Ch	21:14	will the **L.** smite thy people, and	3068
2Ch	21:16	**L.** stirred up against Jehoram	3068
2Ch	21:18	**L.** smote him in his bowels with	3068
2Ch	22:4	evil in the sight of the **L.** like the	3068
2Ch	22:7	the **L.** had anointed to cut off the	3068
2Ch	22:9	sought the **L.** with all his heart.	3068
2Ch	23:3	**L.** hath said of the sons of David.	3068
2Ch	23:5	the courts of the house of the **L.**.	3068
2Ch	23:6	come into the house of the **L.**,	3068
2Ch	23:6	shall keep the watch of the **L.**.	3068
2Ch	23:12	people into the house of the **L.**:	3068
2Ch	23:14	her not in the house of the **L.**.	3068
2Ch	23:18	the offices of the house of the **L.**	3068
2Ch	23:18	distributed in the house of the **L.**,	3068
2Ch	23:18	offer the burnt offerings of the **L.**,	3068
2Ch	23:19	at the gates of the house of the **L.**,	3068
2Ch	23:20	the king from the house of the **L.**:	3068
2Ch	24:2	was right in the sight of the **L.**	3068
2Ch	24:4	to repair the house of the **L.**	3068
2Ch	24:6	of Moses the servant of the **L.**,	3068
2Ch	24:7	things of the house of the **L.** did	3068
2Ch	24:8	at the gate of the house of the **L.**.	3068
2Ch	24:9	bring in to the **L.** the collection	3068
2Ch	24:12	the service of the house of the **L.**,	3068
2Ch	24:12	to repair the house of the **L.**, and	3068
2Ch	24:12	brass to mend the house of the **L.**.	3068
2Ch	24:14	vessels for the house of the **L.**,	3068
2Ch	24:14	offerings in the house of the **L.**	3068
2Ch	24:18	left the house of the **L.** God of	3068
2Ch	24:19	to bring them again unto the **L.**;	3068
2Ch	24:20	ye the commandments of the **L.**,	3068
2Ch	24:20	because ye have forsaken the **L.**,	3068
2Ch	24:21	in the court of the house of the **L.**.	3068
2Ch	24:22	The **L.** look upon it, and require	3068
2Ch	24:24	the **L.** delivered a very great host	3068
2Ch	24:24	had forsaken the **L.** God of their	3068
2Ch	25:2	was right in the sight of the **L.**,	3068
2Ch	25:4	Moses, where the **L.** commanded,	3068
2Ch	25:7	for the **L.** is not with Israel, to wit,	3068
2Ch	25:9	**L.** is able to give thee much more	3068
2Ch	25:15	the anger of the **L.** was kindled	3068
2Ch	25:27	turn away from following the **L.**	3068
2Ch	26:4	was right in the sight of the **L.**,	3068
2Ch	26:5	as long as he sought the **L.**, God	3068
2Ch	26:16	for he transgressed against the **L.**	3068
2Ch	26:16	into the temple of the **L.** to burn	3068
2Ch	26:17	him fourscore priests of the **L.**,	3068
2Ch	26:18	to burn incense unto the **L.**,	3068
2Ch	26:18	for thine honour from the **L.** God.	3068
2Ch	26:19	the priests in the house of the **L.**,	3068
2Ch	26:20	because the **L.** had smitten him.	3068
2Ch	26:21	cut off from the house of the **L.**:	3068
2Ch	27:2	was right in the sight of the **L.**,	3068
2Ch	27:2	not into the temple of the **L.**	3068
2Ch	27:3	high gate of the house of the **L.**,	3068
2Ch	27:6	prepared his ways before the **L.**	3068
2Ch	28:1	was right in the sight of the **L.**,	3068
2Ch	28:3	heathen whom the **L.** had cast out	3068
2Ch	28:5	**L.** his God delivered him into the	3068
2Ch	28:6	had forsaken the **L.** God of their	3068
2Ch	28:9	a prophet of the **L.** was there,	3068
2Ch	28:9	**L.** God of your fathers was wroth	3068
2Ch	28:10	sins against the **L.** your God?	3068
2Ch	28:11	fierce wrath of the **L.** is upon you.	3068
2Ch	28:13	offended against the **L.** already,	3068
2Ch	28:19	**L.** brought Judah low because of	3068
2Ch	28:19	transgressed sore against the **L.**.	3068
2Ch	28:21	portion out of the house of the **L.**,	3068
2Ch	28:22	trespass yet more against the **L.**:	3068
2Ch	28:24	the doors of the house of the **L.**,	3068
2Ch	28:25	provoked to anger the **L.** God of	3068
2Ch	29:2	was right in the sight of the **L.**,	3068
2Ch	29:3	the doors of the house of the **L.**,	3068
2Ch	29:5	sanctify the house of the **L.** God	3068
2Ch	29:6	evil in the eyes of the **L.** our God,	3068
2Ch	29:6	from the habitation of the **L.**,	3068
2Ch	29:8	wrath of the **L.** was upon Judah	3068
2Ch	29:10	a covenant with the **L.** God of	3068
2Ch	29:11	the **L.** hath chosen you to stand	3068
2Ch	29:15	the king, by the words of the **L.**,	3068
2Ch	29:15	to cleanse the house of the **L.**	3068
2Ch	29:16	inner part of the house of the **L.**,	3068
2Ch	29:16	they found in the temple of the **L.**	3068
2Ch	29:16	the court of the house of the **L.**.	3068
2Ch	29:17	came they to the porch of the **L.**:	3068
2Ch	29:17	sanctified the house of the **L.** in	3068
2Ch	29:18	cleansed all the house of the **L.**,	3068
2Ch	29:19	they are before the altar of the **L.**	3068
2Ch	29:20	went up to the house of the **L.**	3068
2Ch	29:21	offer them on the altar of the **L.**.	3068
2Ch	29:25	the Levites in the house of the **L.**	3068
2Ch	29:25	was the commandment of the **L.**	3068
2Ch	29:27	the song of the **L.** began also with	3068
2Ch	29:30	Levites to sing praise unto the **L.**,	3068
2Ch	29:31	consecrated unto the **L.** their God,	3068
2Ch	29:31	offerings into the house of the **L.**.	3068
2Ch	29:32	for a burnt offering to the **L.**	3068
2Ch	29:35	house of the **L.** was set in order.	3068
2Ch	30:1	come to the house of the **L.** at	3068
2Ch	30:1,	5 to keep the passover unto the **L.**	3068
2Ch	30:6	turn again unto the **L.** God of	3068
2Ch	30:7	trespassed against the **L.** God of	3068
2Ch	30:8	but yield yourselves unto the **L.**,	3068
2Ch	30:8	and serve the **L.** your God, that	3068
2Ch	30:9	For if ye turn again unto the **L.**,	3068
2Ch	30:9	for the **L.** your God is gracious	3068
2Ch	30:12	princes, by the word of the **L.**.	3068
2Ch	30:15	offerings into the house of the **L.**.	3068
2Ch	30:17	to sanctify them unto the **L.**.	3068
2Ch	30:18	The good **L.** pardon every one	3068
2Ch	30:19	God, the **L.** God of his fathers,	3068
2Ch	30:20	the **L.** hearkened to Hezekiah,	3068
2Ch	30:21	priests praised the **L.** day by day,	3068
2Ch	30:21	loud instruments unto the **L.**.	3068
2Ch	30:22	the good knowledge of the **L.**:	3068
2Ch	30:22	making confession to the **L.** God	3068
2Ch	31:2	in the gates of the tents of the **L.**	3068
2Ch	31:3	it is written in the law of the **L.**.	3068
2Ch	31:4	encouraged in the law of the **L.**.	3068
2Ch	31:6	consecrated unto the **L.** their God,	3068
2Ch	31:8	blessed the **L.**, and his people	3068
2Ch	31:10	offerings into the house of the **L.**,	3068
2Ch	31:10	for the **L.** hath blessed his people;	3068
2Ch	31:11	chambers in the house of the **L.**;	3068
2Ch	31:14	distribute the oblations of the **L.**,	3068
2Ch	31:16	entereth into the house of the **L.**,	3068
2Ch	31:20	and truth before the **L.** his God.	3068
2Ch	32:8	with us is the **L.** our God to help	3068
2Ch	32:11	The **L.** our God shall deliver us	3068
2Ch	32:16	yet more against the **L.** God,	3068
2Ch	32:17	also letters to rail on the **L.** God	3068
2Ch	32:21	the **L.** sent an angel, which cut off	3068
2Ch	32:22	Thus the **L.** saved Hezekiah and	3068
2Ch	32:23	many brought gifts unto the **L.** to	3068
2Ch	32:24	death, and prayed unto the **L.**:	3068
2Ch	32:26	the wrath of the **L.** came not upon	3068
2Ch	33:2	was evil in the sight of the **L.**,	3068
2Ch	33:2	heathen, whom the **L.** had cast out	3068
2Ch	33:4	built altars in the house of the **L.**,	3068
2Ch	33:4	the **L.** had said, In Jerusalem	3068
2Ch	33:5	two courts of the house of the **L.**.	3068
2Ch	33:6	much evil in the sight of the **L.**,	3068
2Ch	33:9	whom the **L.** had destroyed before	3068
2Ch	33:10	the **L.** spake to Manasseh, and to	3068
2Ch	33:11	the **L.** brought upon them the	3068
2Ch	33:12	in affliction, he besought the **L.**,	3068
2Ch	33:13	knew that the **L.** he was God.	3068
2Ch	33:15	the idol out of the house of the **L.**,	3068
2Ch	33:15	the mount of the house of the **L.**,	3068
2Ch	33:16	he repaired the altar of the **L.**,	3068
2Ch	33:16	to serve the **L.** God of Israel.	3068
2Ch	33:17	yet unto the **L.** their God only.	3068
2Ch	33:18	the name of the **L.** God of Israel.	3068
2Ch	33:22	was evil in the sight of the **L.**,	3068
2Ch	33:23	humbled not himself before the **L.**,	3068
2Ch	34:2	was right in the sight of the **L.**,	3068
2Ch	34:8	repair the house of the **L.** his God.	3068
2Ch	34:10	oversight of the house of the **L.**,	3068
2Ch	34:10	wrought in the house of the **L.**,	3068
2Ch	34:14	brought into the house of the **L.**,	3068
2Ch	34:14	found a book of the law of the **L.**	3068
2Ch	34:15	of the law in the house of the **L.**.	3068
2Ch	34:17	was found in the house of the **L.**,	3068
2Ch	34:21	Go, enquire of the **L.** for me, and	3068
2Ch	34:21	great is the wrath of the **L.** that	3068
2Ch	34:21	have not kept the word of the **L.**,	3068
2Ch	34:23	Thus saith the **L.** God of Israel,	3068
2Ch	34:24	Thus saith the **L.**, Behold, I will	3068
2Ch	34:26	who sent you to enquire of the **L.**,	3068
2Ch	34:26	Thus saith the **L.** God of Israel	3068
2Ch	34:27	even heard thee also, saith the **L.**.	3068
2Ch	34:30	went up into the house of the **L.**,	3068
2Ch	34:30	was found in the house of the **L.**.	3068
2Ch	34:31	made a covenant before the **L.**,	3068
2Ch	34:31	to walk after the **L.**, and to keep	3068
2Ch	34:33	even to serve the **L.** their God.	3068
2Ch	34:33	departed not from following the **L.**,	3068
2Ch	35:1	Josiah kept a passover unto the **L.**	3068
2Ch	35:2	the service of the house of the **L.**,	3068
2Ch	35:3	which were holy unto the **L.**,	3068
2Ch	35:3	serve now the **L.** your God, and	3068
2Ch	35:6	according to the word of the **L.**	3068
2Ch	35:12	the people, to offer unto the **L.**,	3068
2Ch	35:16	service of the **L.** was prepared the	3068
2Ch	35:16	offerings upon the altar of the **L.**,	3068
2Ch	35:26	was written in the law of the **L.**,	3068
2Ch	36:5	evil in the sight of the **L.** his God.	3068
2Ch	36:7	the vessels of the house of the **L.**	3068
2Ch	36:9	was evil in the sight of the **L.**.	3068
2Ch	36:10	vessels of the house of the **L.**,	3068
2Ch	36:12	evil in the sight of the **L.** his God,	3068
2Ch	36:12	speaking from the mouth of the **L.**.	3068
2Ch	36:13	his heart from turning unto the **L.**	3068
2Ch	36:14	and polluted the house of the **L.**	3068
2Ch	36:15	the **L.** God of their fathers sent to	3068
2Ch	36:16	wrath of the **L.** arose against his	3068
2Ch	36:18	treasures of the house of the **L.**,	3068
2Ch	36:21	To fulfill the word of the **L.** by the	3068
2Ch	36:22	the word of the **L.** spoken by the	3068
2Ch	36:22	**L.** stirred up the spirit of Cyrus	3068
2Ch	36:23	the **L.** God of heaven given me;	3068
2Ch	36:23	The **L.** his God be with him, and	3068
Ezr	1:1	word of the **L.** by the mouth of	3068
Ezr	1:1	**L.** stirred up the spirit of Cyrus	3068
Ezr	1:2	**L.** God of heaven hath given me	3068
Ezr	1:3	build the house of the **L.** God of	3068
Ezr	1:5	build the house of the **L.** which is	3068
Ezr	1:7	the vessels of the house of the **L.**,	3068
Ezr	2:68	they came to the house of the **L.**	3068
Ezr	3:3	offerings thereon unto the **L.**,	3068
Ezr	3:5	of all the set feasts of the **L.** that	3068
Ezr	3:5	a freewill offering unto the **L.**	3068
Ezr	3:6	offer burnt offerings unto the **L.**.	3068
Ezr	3:6	foundation of the temple of the **L.**	3068
Ezr	3:8	the work of the house of the **L.**	3068
Ezr	3:10	foundation of the temple of the **L.**,	3068
Ezr	3:10	with cymbals, to praise the **L.**.	3068
Ezr	3:11	and giving thanks unto the **L.**;	3068
Ezr	3:11	shout, when they praised the **L.**,	3068
Ezr	3:11	foundation of the house of the **L.**	3068
Ezr	4:1	builded the temple unto the **L.**	3068
Ezr	4:3	build unto the **L.** God of Israel,	3068
Ezr	6:21	to seek the **L.** God of Israel, did	3068
Ezr	6:22	the **L.** had made them joyful, and	3068
Ezr	7:6	the **L.** God of Israel had given:	3068
Ezr	7:6	hand of the **L.** his God upon him.	3068
Ezr	7:10	heart to seek the law of the **L.**,	3068
Ezr	7:11	of the commandments of the **L.**,	3068
Ezr	7:27	Blessed be the **L.** God of our	3068
Ezr	7:27	to beautify the house of the **L.**	3068
Ezr	7:28	hand of the **L.** my God was upon	3068
Ezr	8:28	them, Ye are holy unto the **L.**;	3068
Ezr	8:28	freewill offering unto the **L.** God	3068
Ezr	8:29	chambers of the house of the **L.**.	3068

Ezr 8:35 was a burnt offering unto the **L.**. 3068
Ezr 9:5 spread out my hands unto the **L.** 3068
Ezr 9:8 grace...been shewed from the **L.** 3068
Ezr 9:15 O **L.** God of Israel, thou art 3068
Ezr 10:3 according to the counsel of my **l.**, 136
Ezr 10:11 make confession unto the **L.** God 3068
Ne 1:5 O **L.** God of heaven, the great and 3068
Ne 1:11 O **L.**, I beseech thee, let now thine 136
Ne 3:5 their necks to the work of their **L.** 113
Ne 4:14 remember the **L.**, which is great 136
Ne 5:13 said, Amen, and praised the **L.** 3068
Ne 8:1 which the **L.** had commanded to 3068
Ne 8:6 Ezra blessed the **L.**, the great God. 3068
Ne 8:6 and worshipped the **L.** with their 3068
Ne 8:9 This day is holy unto the **L.** your 3068
Ne 8:10 for this day is holy unto our **L.**: 113
Ne 8:10 the joy of the **L.** is your strength. 3068
Ne 8:14 law which the **L.** had commanded 3068
Ne 9:3 book of the law of the **L.** their 3068
Ne 9:3 and worshipped the **L.** their God 3068
Ne 9:4 with a loud voice unto the **L.** 3068
Ne 9:5 Stand up and bless the **L.** your 3068
Ne 9:6 Thou, even thou, art **L.** alone; 3068
Ne 9:7 Thou art the **L.** the God, who 3068
Ne 10:29 all the commandments of the **L.** 3068
Ne 10:29 all the commandments of...our **L.**, 113
Ne 10:34 to burn upon the altar of the **L.** 3068
Ne 10:35 by year, unto the house of the **L.**: 3068
Job 1:6 present themselves before the **L.**, 3068
Job 1:7 the **L.** said unto Satan, Whence 3068
Job 1:7 Satan answered the **L.**, and said, 3068
Job 1:8 the **L.** said unto Satan, Hast thou 3068
Job 1:9 Satan answered the **L.**, and said, 3068
Job 1:12 the **L.** said unto Satan, Behold, all 3068
Job 1:12 forth from the presence of the **L.** 3068
Job 1:21 **L.** gave, and the **L.** hath taken 3068
Job 1:21 blessed be the name of the **L.** 3068
Job 2:1 present themselves before the **L.**, 3068
Job 2:1 to present himself before the **L.**. 3068
Job 2:2 And the **L.** said unto Satan, From 3068
Job 2:2 Satan answered the **L.**, and said, 3068
Job 2:3 And the **L.** said unto Satan, Hast 3068
Job 2:4 Satan answered the **L.**, and said, 3068
Job 2:6 the **L.** said unto Satan, Behold, 3068
Job 2:7 forth from the presence of the **L.**, 3068
Job 12:9 hand of the **L.** hath wrought this? 3068
Job 28:28 the fear of the **L.**, that is wisdom; 136
Job 38:1 the **L.** answered Job out of the 3068
Job 40:1 the **L.** answered Job, and said, 3068
Job 40:3 Job answered the **L.**, and said, 3068
Job 40:6 Then answered the **L.** unto Job 3068
Job 42:1 Job answered the **L.**, and said, 3068
Job 42:7 **L.** had spoken these words unto 3068
Job 42:7 **L.** said to Eliphaz the Temanite, 3068
Job 42:9 according as the **L.** commanded 3068
Job 42:9 them: the **L.** also accepted Job. 3068
Job 42:10 **L.** turned the captivity of Job, 3068
Job 42:10 **L.** gave Job twice as much as he 3068
Job 42:11 evil that the **L.** had brought upon 3068
Job 42:12 **L.** blessed the latter end of Job 3068
Ps 1:2 his delight is in the law of the **L.**; 3068
Ps 1:6 the **L.** knoweth the way of the 3068
Ps 2:2 against the **L.**, and against his 3068
Ps 2:4 **L.** shall have them in derision. 136
Ps 2:7 **L.** hath said unto me, Thou art 3068
Ps 2:11 Serve the **L.** with fear, and rejoice 3068
Ps 3:1 **L.**, how are they increased that 3068
Ps 3:3 But thou, O **L.**, art a shield for 3068
Ps 3:4 I cried unto the **L.** with my voice, 3068
Ps 3:5 awaked; for the **L.** sustained me. 3068
Ps 3:7 Arise, O **L.**; save me, O my God: 3068
Ps 3:8 Salvation belongeth unto the **L.**: 3068
Ps 4:3 the **L.** hath set apart him that is 3068
Ps 4:3 the **L.** will hear when I call unto 3068
Ps 4:5 and put your trust in the **L.** 3068
Ps 4:6 **L.**, lift thou up the light of thy 3068
Ps 4:8 for thou, **L.**, only makest me 3068
Ps 5:1 Give ear to my words, O **L.**, 3068
Ps 5:3 thou hear in the morning, O **L.**; 3068
Ps 5:6 the **L.** will abhor the bloody and 3068
Ps 5:8 Lead me, O **L.**, in...righteousness 3068
Ps 5:12 thou, **L.**, wilt bless the righteous; 3068
Ps 6:1 O **L.**, rebuke me not in thine 3068
Ps 6:2 Have mercy upon me, O **L.**; for 3068
Ps 6:2 O **L.**, heal me; for my bones are 3068
Ps 6:3 vexed: but thou, O **L.**, how long? 3068
Ps 6:4 Return, O **L.**, deliver my soul: oh 3068
Ps 6:8 the **L.** hath heard the voice of my 3068
Ps 6:9 **L.** hath heard my supplication; 3068
Ps 6:9 the **L.** will receive my prayer. 3068
Ps 7:*title* David, which he sang unto the **L.**, 3068
Ps 7:1 O **L.** my God, in thee do I put my 3068
Ps 7:3 O **L.** my God, if I have done this; 3068
Ps 7:6 Arise, O **L.**, in thine anger, lift up 3068
Ps 7:8 The **L.** shall judge the people: 3068
Ps 7:8 **L.**, according to my righteousness, 3068
Ps 7:17 will praise the **L.** according to his 3068
Ps 7:17 sing praise to the name of the **L.** 3068
Ps 8:1 O **L.**...how excellent is thy name 3068
Ps 8:1 our **L.**, how excellent is thy name 113
Ps 8:9 O **L.**...how excellent is thy name 3068
Ps 8:9 our **L.**, how excellent is thy name 113
Ps 9:1 I will praise thee, O **L.**, with my 3068
Ps 9:7 But the **L.** shall endure for ever: 3068
Ps 9:9 **L.** also will be a refuge for the 3068
Ps 9:10 thou, **L.**, hast not forsaken them. 3068
Ps 9:11 Sing praises to the **L.**, which 3068
Ps 9:13 Have mercy upon me, O **L.**; 3068
Ps 9:16 The **L.** is known by the judgment 3068
Ps 9:19 Arise, O **L.**; let not man prevail: 3068
Ps 9:20 Put them in fear, O **L.**: that the 3068
Ps 10:1 Why standest thou afar off, O **L.**? 3068
Ps 10:3 covetous, whom the **L.** abhorreth. 3068
Ps 10:12 Arise, O **L.**; O God, lift up thine 3068
Ps 10:16 The **L.** is King for ever and ever: 3068
Ps 10:17 **L.**, thou hast heard the desire of 3068
Ps 11:1 In the **L.** put I my trust: how say 3068
Ps 11:4 The **L.** is in his holy temple, the 3068
Ps 11:5 The **L.** trieth the righteous: but 3068
Ps 11:7 righteous **L.** loveth righteousness; 3068
Ps 12:1 Help, **L.**; for the godly man 3068
Ps 12:3 **L.** shall cut off all flattering lips, 3068
Ps 12:4 lips are our own: who is **l.** over us? 113
Ps 12:5 now will I arise, saith the **L.**; 3068
Ps 12:6 words of the **L.** are pure words: 3068
Ps 12:7 Thou shalt keep them, O **L.**, thou 3068
Ps 13:1 long wilt thou forget me, O **L.**? 3068
Ps 13:3 and hear me, O **L.** my God: 3068
Ps 13:6 I will sing unto the **L.**, because 3068
Ps 14:2 The **L.** looked down from heaven 3068
Ps 14:4 bread, and call not upon the **L.** 3068
Ps 14:6 poor, because the **L.** is his refuge. 3068
Ps 14:7 **L.** bringeth back the captivity of 3068
Ps 15:1 **L.**, who shall abide in thy 3068
Ps 15:4 honoureth them that fear the **L.** 3068
Ps 16:2 soul, thou hast said unto the **L.**, 3068
Ps 16:2 Thou art my **L.**: my goodness 136
Ps 16:5 The **L.** is the portion of mine 3068
Ps 16:7 I will bless the **L.**. who hath given 3068
Ps 16:8 have set the **L.** always before me: 3068
Ps 17:1 Hear the right, O **L.**, attend unto 3068
Ps 17:13 Arise, O **L.**, disappoint him, cast 3068
Ps 17:14 men which are thy hand, O **L.**, 3068
Ps 18:*title* of David, the servant of the **L.**, 3068
Ps 18:*title* who spake unto the **L.** the words 3068
Ps 18:*title* the day that the **L.** delivered him 3068
Ps 18:1 I will love thee, O **L.**, my strength. 3068
Ps 18:2 **L.** is my rock, and my fortress, 3068
Ps 18:3 I will call upon the **L.**, who is 3068
Ps 18:6 my distress I called upon the **L.**, 3068
Ps 18:13 **L.** also thundered in the heavens, 3068
Ps 18:15 discovered at thy rebuke, O **L.**, 3068
Ps 18:18 calamity: but the **L.** was my stay. 3068
Ps 18:20 **L.** rewarded me according to my 3068
Ps 18:21 I have kept the ways of the **L.**, 3068
Ps 18:24 hath the **L.** recompensed me 3068
Ps 18:28 the **L.** my God will enlighten my 3068
Ps 18:30 the word of the **L.** is tried: 3068
Ps 18:31 For who is God save the **L.**? or 3068
Ps 18:41 even unto the **L.**, but he answered 3068
Ps 18:46 The **L.** liveth; and blessed be my 3068
Ps 18:49 will I give thanks unto thee, O **L.**, 3068
Ps 19:7 The law of the **L.** is perfect, 3068
Ps 19:7 the testimony of the **L.** is sure, 3068
Ps 19:8 The statutes of the **L.** are right, 3068
Ps 19:8 commandment of the **L.** is pure, 3068
Ps 19:9 The fear of the **L.** is clean, 3068
Ps 19:9 the judgments of the **L.** are true 3068
Ps 19:14 be acceptable in thy sight, O **L.**, 3068
Ps 20:1 **L.** hear thee in the day of trouble; 3068
Ps 20:5 the **L.** fulfill all thy petitions. 3068
Ps 20:6 I that the **L.** saveth his anointed; 3068
Ps 20:7 will remember the name of the **L.** 3068
Ps 20:9 Save, **L.**: let the king hear us 3068
Ps 21:1 shall joy in thy strength, O **L.**; 3068
Ps 21:7 For the king trusteth in the **L.**, 3068
Ps 21:9 **L.** shall swallow them up in his 3068
Ps 21:13 Be thou exalted, **L.**, in thine own 3068
Ps 22:8 trusted on the **L.** that he would 3068
Ps 22:19 But be not thou far from me, O **L.**: 3068
Ps 22:23 Ye that fear the **L.**, praise him; 3068
Ps 22:26 shall praise the **L.** that seek him: 3068
Ps 22:27 remember and turn unto the **L.**: 3068
Ps 22:30 it shall be accounted to the **L.** for a 136
Ps 23:1 The **L.** is my shepherd; I shall 3068
Ps 23:6 in the house of the **L.** for ever. 3068
Ps 24:3 shall ascend into the hill of the **L.**? 3068
Ps 24:5 receive the blessing from the **L.**, 3068
Ps 24:8 The **L.** strong and mighty, 3068
Ps 24:8 the **L.** mighty in battle. 3068
Ps 24:10 The **L.** of hosts, he is the King of 3068
Ps 25:1 Unto thee, O **L.**, do I lift up my 3068
Ps 25:4 Shew me thy ways, O **L.**; teach 3068
Ps 25:6 Remember, O **L.**, thy tender 3068
Ps 25:7 me for thy goodness' sake, O **L.** 3068
Ps 25:8 Good and upright is the **L.**: 3068
Ps 25:10 the paths of the **L.** are mercy and 3068
Ps 25:11 For thy name's sake, O **L.**, pardon 3068
Ps 25:12 man is he that feareth the **L.**? 3068
Ps 25:14 secret of the **L.** is with them that 3068
Ps 25:15 Mine eyes are ever toward the **L.**; 3068
Ps 26:1 Judge me, O **L.**; for I have walked 3068
Ps 26:1 I have trusted also in the **L.**; 3068
Ps 26:2 Examine me, O **L.**, and prove me; 3068
Ps 26:6 will I compass thine altar, O **L.**: 3068
Ps 26:8 **L.**, I have loved the habitation of 3068
Ps 26:12 congregations will I bless the **L.**. 3068
Ps 27:1 **L.** is my light and my salvation; 3068
Ps 27:1 the **L.** is the strength of my life; 3068
Ps 27:4 One thing have I desired of the **L.**, 3068
Ps 27:4 may dwell in the house of the **L.** 3068
Ps 27:4 to behold the beauty of the **L.**, 3068
Ps 27:6 I will sing praises unto the **L.** 3068
Ps 27:7 Hear, O **L.**, when I cry with my 3068
Ps 27:8 thee, Thy face, **L.**, will I seek 3068
Ps 27:10 me, then the **L.** will take me up. 3068
Ps 27:11 Teach me thy way, O **L.**, and lead 3068
Ps 27:13 goodness of the **L.** in the land of 3068
Ps 27:14 Wait on the **L.**: be of good 3068
Ps 27:14 thine heart: wait, I say, on the **L.** 3068
Ps 28:1 thee will I cry, O **L.** my rock; 3068
Ps 28:5 regard not the works of the **L.**, 3068
Ps 28:6 Blessed be the **L.**, because he 3068
Ps 28:7 The **L.** is my strength and my 3068
Ps 28:8 the **L.** is their strength, and he 3068
Ps 29:1 Give unto the **L.**, O ye mighty, 3068
Ps 29:1 give unto the **L.** glory and 3068
Ps 29:2 Give unto the **L.** the glory due 3068
Ps 29:2 worship the **L.** in the beauty of 3068
Ps 29:3 voice of the **L.** is upon the waters: 3068
Ps 29:3 the **L.** is upon many waters. 3068
Ps 29:4 The voice of the **L.** is powerful; 3068
Ps 29:4 voice of the **L.** is full of majesty. 3068
Ps 29:5 voice of the **L.** breaketh the cedars; 3068
Ps 29:5 **L.** breaketh the cedars of Lebanon. 3068
Ps 29:7 voice of the **L.** divideth the flames 3068
Ps 29:8 The voice of the **L.** shaketh the 3068
Ps 29:8 the **L.** shaketh the wilderness of 3068
Ps 29:9 voice of the **L.** maketh the hinds 3068
Ps 29:10 The **L.** sitteth upon the flood; 3068
Ps 29:10 yea, the **L.** sitteth King for ever. 3068
Ps 29:11 The **L.** will give strength unto his 3068
Ps 29:11 **L.** will bless his people with peace. 3068
Ps 30:1 I will extol thee, O **L.**; for thou 3068
Ps 30:2 O **L.** my God, I cried unto thee, 3068
Ps 30:3 O **L.**, thou hast brought up my soul 3068
Ps 30:4 Sing unto the **L.**, O ye saints of his, 3068
Ps 30:7 **L.**, by thy favour thou hast made 3068
Ps 30:8 I cried to thee, O **L.**; and unto 3068
Ps 30:8 unto the **L.** I made supplication. 3068
Ps 30:10 Hear, O **L.**, and have mercy upon 3068
Ps 30:10 upon me: **L.**, be thou my helper. 3068
Ps 30:12 O **L.** my God, I will give thanks 3068
Ps 31:1 In thee, O **L.**, do I put my trust; 3068
Ps 31:5 redeemed me, O **L.** God of truth. 3068
Ps 31:6 vanities: but I trust in the **L.** 3068
Ps 31:9 Have mercy upon me, O **L.**; for I 3068
Ps 31:14 But I trusted in thee, O **L.**: I said, 3068
Ps 31:17 Let me not be ashamed, O **L.**; for 3068
Ps 31:21 Blessed be the **L.**: for he hath 3068
Ps 31:23 O love the **L.**, all ye his saints: 3068

Ps 31:23 for the **L.** preserveth the faithful, 3068
Ps 31:24 heart, all ye that hope in the **L.** 3068
Ps 32:2 the **L.** imputeth not iniquity, 3068
Ps 32:5 my transgressions unto the **L.**; 3068
Ps 32:10 but he that trusteth in the **L.** 3068
Ps 32:11 Be glad in the **L.**, and rejoice, ye 3068
Ps 33:1 Rejoice in the **L.**, O ye righteous: 3068
Ps 33:2 Praise the **L.** with harp: sing unto 3068
Ps 33:4 For the word of the **L.** is right; 3068
Ps 33:5 is full of the goodness of the **L.** 3068
Ps 33:6 word of the **L.** were the heavens 3068
Ps 33:8 Let all the earth fear the **L.**: let 3068
Ps 33:10 The **L.** bringeth the counsel of the 3068
Ps 33:11 counsel of the **L.** standeth for ever, 3068
Ps 33:12 is the nation whose God is the **L.**; 3068
Ps 33:13 The **L.** looketh from heaven; he 3068
Ps 33:18 eye of the **L.** is upon them that fear 3068
Ps 33:20 Our soul waiteth for the **L.**: he is 3068
Ps 33:22 Let thy mercy, O **L.**, be upon us, 3068
Ps 34:1 I will bless the **L.** at all times: 3068
Ps 34:2 shall make her boast in the **L.**: 3068
Ps 34:3 O magnify the **L.** with me, and 3068
Ps 34:4 I sought the **L.**, and he heard me, 3068
Ps 34:6 man cried, and the **L.** heard him, 3068
Ps 34:7 angel of the **L.** encampeth round 3068
Ps 34:8 taste and see that the **L.** is good: 3068
Ps 34:9 O fear the **L.**, ye his saints: for 3068
Ps 34:10 that seek the **L.** shall not want any 3068
Ps 34:11 I will teach you the fear of the **L.** 3068
Ps 34:15 The eyes of the **L.** are upon the 3068
Ps 34:16 face of the **L.** is against them that 3068
Ps 34:17 the **L.** heareth, and delivereth 3068
Ps 34:18 **L.** is nigh unto them that are of 3068
Ps 34:19 **L.** delivereth him out of them all. 3068
Ps 34:22 The **L.** redeemeth the soul of his 3068
Ps 35:1 Plead my cause, O **L.**, with them 3068
Ps 35:5 the angel of the **L.** chase them. 3068
Ps 35:6 angel of the **L.** persecute them. 3068
Ps 35:9 my soul shall be joyful in the **L.**: 3068
Ps 35:10 All my bones shall say, **L.**, who is 3068
Ps 35:17 **L.**, how long wilt thou look on? 136
Ps 35:22 This thou hast seen, O **L.**: keep 3068
Ps 35:22 silence: O **L.**, be not far from me. 3068
Ps 35:23 unto my cause, my God and my **L.** 136
Ps 35:24 Judge me, O **L.** my God, 3068
Ps 35:27 Let the **L.** be magnified, which 3068
Ps 36:*title* of David the servant of the **L.** 3068
Ps 36:5 mercy, O **L.**, is in the heavens; 3068
Ps 36:6 O **L.**, thou preservest man and 3068
Ps 37:3 Trust in the **L.**, and do good; so 3068
Ps 37:4 Delight thyself also in the **L.**; 3068
Ps 37:5 Commit thy way unto the **L.**; 3068
Ps 37:7 Rest in the **L.**, and wait patiently 3068
Ps 37:9 but those that wait upon the **L.**, 3068
Ps 37:13 the **L.** shall laugh at him; for he 136
Ps 37:17 the **L.** upholdeth the righteous. 3068
Ps 37:18 The **L.** knoweth the days of the 3068
Ps 37:20 enemies of the **L.** shall be as the 3068
Ps 37:23 good man are ordered by the **L.**: 3068
Ps 37:24 **L.** upholdeth him with his hand. 3068
Ps 37:28 For the **L.** loveth judgment, and 3068
Ps 37:33 **L.** will not leave him in his hand, 3068
Ps 37:34 Wait on the **L.**, and keep his way, 3068
Ps 37:39 of the righteous is of the **L.**: 3068
Ps 37:40 **L.** shall help them, and deliver 3068
Ps 38:1 O **L.**, rebuke me not in thy wrath: 3068
Ps 38:9 **L.**, all my desire is before thee; 136
Ps 38:15 For in thee, O **L.**, do I hope: 3068
Ps 38:15 thou wilt hear, O **L.** my God. 136
Ps 38:21 Forsake me not, O **L.**: O my God, 3068
Ps 38:22 to help me, O **L.** my salvation. 136
Ps 39:4 **L.**, make me to know mine end, 3068
Ps 39:7 **L.**, what wait I for? my hope is in 136
Ps 39:12 Hear my prayer, O **L.**, and give 3068
Ps 40:1 I waited patiently for the **L.**; and 3068
Ps 40:3 and fear, and shall trust in the **L.** 3068
Ps 40:4 man that maketh the **L.** his trust, 3068
Ps 40:5 Many, O **L.** my God, are thy 3068
Ps 40:9 have not refrained my lips, O **L.**, 3068
Ps 40:11 tender mercies from me, O **L.**: 3068
Ps 40:13 Be pleased, O **L.**, to deliver me: 3068
Ps 40:13 O **L.**, make haste to help me. 3068
Ps 40:16 continually, The **L.** be magnified. 3068
Ps 40:17 yet the **L.** thinketh upon me: thou 136
Ps 41:1 the **L.** will deliver him in time of 3068
Ps 41:2 The **L.** will preserve him, and 3068
Ps 41:3 **L.** will strengthen him upon the 3068
Ps 41:4 I said, **L.**, be merciful unto me: 3068
Ps 41:10 But thou, O **L.**, be merciful unto 3068
Ps 41:13 Blessed be the **L.** God of Israel 3068
Ps 42:8 **L.** will command...lovingkindness 3068
Ps 44:23 Awake, why sleepest thou, O **L.**? 136
Ps 45:11 for he is thy **L.**; and worship thou 113
Ps 46:7 The **L.** of hosts is with us; the 3068
Ps 46:8 Come, behold the works of the **L.**, 3068
Ps 46:11 The **L.** of hosts is with us; the 3068
Ps 47:2 For the **L.** most high is terrible; 3068
Ps 47:5 **L.** with the sound of a trumpet. 3068
Ps 48:1 Great is the **L.**, and greatly to be 3068
Ps 48:8 seen in the city of the **L.** of hosts, 3068
Ps 50:1 The mighty God, even the **L.**, 3068
Ps 51:15 O **L.**, open thou my lips; and my 136
Ps 54:4 **L.** is with them that uphold my 136
Ps 54:6 I will praise thy name, O **L.**; for 3068
Ps 55:9 Destroy, O **L.**, and divide their 136
Ps 55:16 God; and the **L.** shall save me. 3068
Ps 55:22 Cast thy burden upon the **L.**, and 3068
Ps 56:10 in the **L.** will I praise his word. 3068
Ps 57:9 I will praise thee, O **L.**, among the 136
Ps 58:6 teeth of the young lions, O **L.** 3068
Ps 59:3 transgression, nor for my sin, O **L.** 3068
Ps 59:5 O **L.** God of hosts, the God of 3068
Ps 59:8 But thou, O **L.**, shalt laugh at 3068
Ps 59:11 bring them down, O **L.** our shield. 136
Ps 62:12 unto thee, O **L.**, belongeth mercy: 136
Ps 64:10 righteous shall be glad in the **L.**, 3068
Ps 66:18 my heart, the **L.** will not hear me: 136
Ps 68:11 The **L.** gave the word: great was 136
Ps 68:16 the **L.** will dwell in it for ever. 3068
Ps 68:17 the **L.** is among them, as in Sinai, 136
Ps 68:18 that the **L.** God might dwell among 3050
Ps 68:19 Blessed be the **L.**, who daily loadeth 136
Ps 68:20 unto God the **L.** belong the issues 136
Ps 68:22 The **L.** said, I will bring again from 136
Ps 68:26 even the **L.**, from the fountain of 136
Ps 68:32 earth; O sing praises unto the **L.**; 136
Ps 69:6 wait on thee, O **L.** God of hosts, 136
Ps 69:13 my prayer is unto thee, O **L.**, 3068
Ps 69:16 Hear me, O **L.**; for thy 3068
Ps 69:31 please the **L.** better than an ox 3068
Ps 69:33 For the **L.** heareth the poor, and 3068
Ps 70:1 me; make haste to help me, O **L.** 3068
Ps 70:5 O **L.**, make no tarrying. 3068
Ps 71:1 In thee, O **L.**, do I put my trust: 3068
Ps 71:5 thou art my hope, O **L.** God: thou 136
Ps 71:16 go in the strength of the **L.** God: 136
Ps 72:18 Blessed be the **L.** God, the God 3068
Ps 73:20 so, O **L.**, when thou awakest, thou 136
Ps 73:28 I have put my trust in the **L.** God, 136
Ps 74:18 the enemy hath reproached, O **L.**, 3068
Ps 75:8 the hand of the **L.** there is a cup, 3068
Ps 76:11 and pay unto the **L.** your God: 3068
Ps 77:2 day of my trouble I sought the **L.**: 136
Ps 77:7 Will the **L.** cast off for ever? and 136
Ps 77:11 remember the works of the **L.**: 3050
Ps 78:4 to come the praises of the **L.**, 3068
Ps 78:21 the **L.** heard this, and was wroth: 3068
Ps 78:65 **L.** awaked as one out of a sleep, 136
Ps 79:5 How long, **L.**? wilt thou be angry 3068
Ps 79:12 they have reproached thee, O **L.** 136
Ps 80:4 O **L.** God of hosts, how long wilt 3068
Ps 80:19 Turn us again, O **L.** God of hosts, 3068
Ps 81:10 I am the **L.** thy God, which brought 3068
Ps 81:15 The haters of the **L.** should have 3068
Ps 83:16 they may seek thy name, O **L.** 3068
Ps 84:1 thy tabernacles, O **L.** of hosts! 3068
Ps 84:2 fainteth for the courts of the **L.**: 3068
Ps 84:3 even thine altars, O **L.** of hosts, 3068
Ps 84:8 O **L.** God of hosts, hear my prayer: 3068
Ps 84:11 the **L.** God is a sun and shield: 3068
Ps 84:11 the **L.** will give grace and glory: 3068
Ps 84:12 O **L.** of hosts, blessed is the man 3068
Ps 85:1 **L.**, thou hast been favourable 3068
Ps 85:7 Shew us thy mercy, O **L.**, and 3068
Ps 85:8 hear what God the **L.** will speak: 3068
Ps 85:12 **L.** shall give that which is good; 3068
Ps 86:1 Bow down thine ear, O **L.**, hear 3068
Ps 86:3 Be merciful unto me, O **L.**: for I 136
Ps 86:4 unto thee, O **L.**, do I lift up my 136
Ps 86:5 For thou, **L.**, art good, and ready 136
Ps 86:6 Give ear, O **L.**, unto my prayer; 3068
Ps 86:8 there is none like unto thee, O **L.**; 136
Ps 86:9 and worship before thee, O **L.**; 136
Ps 86:11 Teach me thy way, O **L.**; I will 3068
Ps 86:12 I will praise thee, O **L.** my God, 136
Ps 86:15 But thou, O **L.**, art a God full of 136
Ps 86:17 because thou, **L.**, hast holpen me, 3068
Ps 87:2 **L.** loveth the gates of Zion more 3068
Ps 87:6 The **L.** shall count, when he 3068
Ps 88:1 O **L.** God of my salvation, I have 3068
Ps 88:9 **L.**, I have called daily upon thee, 3068
Ps 88:13 But unto thee have I cried, O **L.**; 3068
Ps 88:14 **L.**, why castest thou off my soul? 3068
Ps 89:1 I will sing of the mercies of the **L.** 3068
Ps 89:5 shall praise thy wonders, O **L.**: 3068
Ps 89:6 can be compared unto the **L.**? 3068
Ps 89:6 can be likened unto the **L.**? 3068
Ps 89:8 O **L.** God of hosts, who is a strong 3068
Ps 89:8 who is a strong **L.** like unto thee? 3050
Ps 89:15 shall walk, O **L.**, in the light of thy 3068
Ps 89:18 For the **L.** is our defence; and the 3068
Ps 89:46 How long, **L.**? wilt thou hide 3068
Ps 89:49 **L.**, where are thy former 136
Ps 89:50 Remember, **L.**, the reproach of thy 136
Ps 89:51 enemies have reproached, O **L.**; 3068
Ps 89:52 Blessed be the **L.** for evermore. 3068
Ps 90:1 **L.**, thou hast been our dwelling 136
Ps 90:13 Return, O **L.**, how long? and let it 3068
Ps 90:17 let the beauty of the **L.** our God be 3068
Ps 91:2 will say of the **L.**, He is my refuge 3068
Ps 91:9 Because thou hast made the **L.**, 3068
Ps 92:1 thing to give thanks unto the **L.**, 3068
Ps 92:4 For thou, **L.**, hast made me glad 3068
Ps 92:5 O **L.**, how great are thy works! 3068
Ps 92:8 But thou, **L.**, art most high for 3068
Ps 92:9 O **L.**, for, lo, thine enemies shall 3068
Ps 92:13 be planted in the house of the **L.** 3068
Ps 92:15 To shew that the **L.** is upright: 3068
Ps 93:1 The **L.** reigneth, he is clothed 3068
Ps 93:1 the **L.** is clothed with strength, 3068
Ps 93:3 The floods have lifted up, O **L.**, 3068
Ps 93:4 **L.** on high is mightier than the 3068
Ps 93:5 becometh thine house, O **L.**, 3068
Ps 94:1 O **L.** God, to whom vengeance 3068
Ps 94:3 **L.**, how long shall the wicked, 3068
Ps 94:5 break in pieces thy people, O **L.**, 3068
Ps 94:7 they say, The **L.** shall not see, 3050
Ps 94:11 **L.** knoweth the thoughts of man, 3068
Ps 94:12 man whom thou chastenest, O **L.**, 3050
Ps 94:14 the **L.** will not cast off his people, 3068
Ps 94:17 Unless the **L.** had been my help, 3068
Ps 94:18 thy mercy, O **L.**, held me up. 3068
Ps 94:22 But the **L.** is my defence; and my 3068
Ps 94:23 the **L.** our God shall cut them off. 3068
Ps 95:1 O come, let us sing unto the **L.**: 3068
Ps 95:3 For the **L.** is a great God, and a 3068
Ps 95:6 us kneel before the **L.** our maker. 3068
Ps 96:1 O sing unto the **L.** a new song: 3068
Ps 96:1 sing unto the **L.**, all the earth. 3068
Ps 96:2 Sing unto the **L.**, bless his name; 3068
Ps 96:4 For the **L.** is great, and greatly to 3068
Ps 96:5 but the **L.** made the heavens. 3068
Ps 96:7 Give unto the **L.**, O ye kindreds 3068
Ps 96:7 give unto the **L.** glory and 3068
Ps 96:8 Give unto the **L.** the glory due 3068
Ps 96:9 O worship the **L.** in the beauty of 3068
Ps 96:10 the heathen that the **L.** reigneth: 3068
Ps 96:13 Before the **L.**: for he cometh, for 3068
Ps 97:1 The **L.** reigneth; let the earth 3068
Ps 97:5 like wax at the presence of the **L.**, 3068
Ps 97:5 the presence of the **L.** of the whole 113
Ps 97:8 because of thy judgments, O **L.** 3068
Ps 97:9 For thou, **L.**, art high above all the 3068
Ps 97:10 Ye that love the **L.**, hate evil: he 3068
Ps 97:12 Rejoice in the **L.**, ye righteous; 3068
Ps 98:1 O sing unto the **L.** a new song; 3068
Ps 98:2 **L.** hath made known his salvation: 3068
Ps 98:4 Make a joyful noise unto the **L.**, 3068
Ps 98:5 Sing unto the **L.** with the harp; 3068
Ps 98:6 make a joyful noise before the **L.**, 3068
Ps 98:9 Before the **L.**; for he cometh to 3068
Ps 99:1 The **L.** reigneth; let the people 3068
Ps 99:2 The **L.** is great in Zion; and he is 3068
Ps 99:5 Exalt ye the **L.** our God, and 3068
Ps 99:6 they called upon the **L.**, and he 3068
Ps 99:8 answeredst them, O **L.** our God: 3068
Ps 99:9 Exalt the **L.** our God, and worship 3068
Ps 99:9 hill; for the **L.** our God is holy. 3068
Ps 100:1 Make a joyful noise unto the **L.**, 3068
Ps 100:2 Serve the **L.** with gladness: come 3068
Ps 100:3 Know ye that the **L.** he is God: 3068

Ps 100:5 For the **L.** is good; his mercy is 3068
Ps 101:1 unto thee, O **L.**, will I sing. 3068
Ps 101:8 doers from the city of the **L.** 3068
Ps 102:*title* out his complaint before the **L.** 3068
Ps 102:1 Hear my prayer, O **L.**, and let my 3068
Ps 102:12 thou, O **L.**, shalt endure for ever; 3068
Ps 102:15 shall fear the name of the **L.**, and 3068
Ps 102:16 When the **L.** shall build up Zion, 3068
Ps 102:18 be created shall praise the **L.** 3050
Ps 102:19 from heaven did the **L.** behold 3068
Ps 102:21 declare the name of the **L.** in Zion, 3068
Ps 102:22 and the kingdoms, to serve the **L.** 3068
Ps 103:1 Bless the **L.**, O my soul: and all 3068
Ps 103:2 Bless the **L.**, O my soul, and forget 3068
Ps 103:6 The **L.** executeth righteousness 3068
Ps 103:8 The **L.** is merciful and gracious, 3068
Ps 103:13 the **L.** pitieth them that fear him. 3068
Ps 103:17 mercy of the **L.** is from everlasting 3068
Ps 103:19 **L.** hath prepared his throne in the 3068
Ps 103:20 Bless the **L.**, ye his angels, that 3068
Ps 103:21 Bless ye the **L.**, all ye his hosts; 3068
Ps 103:22 Bless the **L.**, all his works in all 3068
Ps 103:22 bless the **L.**, O my soul. 3068
Ps 104:1 Bless the **L.**, O my soul. 3068
Ps 104:1 O **L.** my God, thou art very great; 3068
Ps 104:16 The trees of the **L.** are full of sap; 3068
Ps 104:24 O **L.**, how manifold are thy works! 3068
Ps 104:31 The glory of the **L.** shall endure 3068
Ps 104:31 the **L.** shall rejoice in his works. 3068
Ps 104:33 I will sing unto the **L.** as long as 3068
Ps 104:34 be sweet: I will be glad in the **L.** 3068
Ps 104:35 Bless thou the **L.**, O my soul. 3068
Ps 104:35 Praise ye the **L.** 3050
Ps 105:1 O give thanks unto the **L.**; call 3050
Ps 105:3 of them rejoice that seek the **L.** 3050
Ps 105:4 Seek the **L.**, and his strength: 3050
Ps 105:7 He is the **L.** our God: his 3050
Ps 105:19 came: the word of the **L.** tried him. 3050
Ps 105:21 He made him **l.** of his house, and 113
Ps 105:45 keep his laws. Praise ye the **L.** 3050
Ps 106:1 Praise ye the **L.** O give thanks 3050
Ps 106:1 O give thanks unto the **L.**; for he 3068
Ps 106:2 utter the mighty acts of the **L.**? 3068
Ps 106:4 Remember me, O **L.**, with the 3068
Ps 106:16 and Aaron the saint of the **L.** 3068
Ps 106:25 not unto the voice of the **L.** 3068
Ps 106:34 whom the **L.** commanded them: 3068
Ps 106:40 was the wrath of the **L.** kindled 3068
Ps 106:47 Save us, O **L.** our God, and gather 3068
Ps 106:48 Blessed be the **L.** God of Israel 3068
Ps 106:48 say, Amen. Praise ye the **L.** 3050
Ps 107:1 O give thanks unto the **L.**, for he 3068
Ps 107:2 Let the redeemed of the **L.** say so, 3068
Ps 107:6 cried unto the **L.** in their trouble, 3068
Ps 107:8 praise the **L.** for his goodness, 3068
Ps 107:13 cried unto the **L.** in their trouble, 3068
Ps 107:15 praise the **L.** for his goodness, 3068
Ps 107:19 cry unto the **L.** in their trouble, 3068
Ps 107:21 praise the **L.** for his goodness, 3068
Ps 107:24 These see the works of the **L.**, 3068
Ps 107:28 cry unto the **L.** in their trouble, 3068
Ps 107:31 praise the **L.** for his goodness, 3068
Ps 107:43 the lovingkindness of the **L.** 3068
Ps 108:3 I will praise thee, O **L.**, among the 3068
Ps 109:14 be remembered with the **L.**; 3068
Ps 109:15 them be before the **L.** continually, 3068
Ps 109:20 of mine adversaries from the **L.**, 3068
Ps 109:21 But do thou for me, O God the **L.**, for. 136
Ps 109:26 Help me, O **L.** my God: O save 3068
Ps 109:27 hand; that thou, **L.**, hast done it. 3068
Ps 109:30 praise the **L.** with my mouth; 3068
Ps 110:1 The **L.** said...Sit thou at my right 3068
Ps 110:1 said unto my **L.**, Sit thou at my 113
Ps 110:2 The **L.** shall send the rod of thy 3068
Ps 110:4 The **L.** hath sworn, and will not 3068
Ps 110:5 **L.** at thy right hand shall strike 136
Ps 111:1 Praise ye the **L.** I will praise 3050
Ps 111:1 will praise the **L.** with my whole 3068
Ps 111:2 The works of the **L.** are great, 3068
Ps 111:4 the **L.** is gracious and full of 3068
Ps 111:10 The fear of the **L.** is the beginning 3068
Ps 112:1 Praise ye the **L.** Blessed is the 3050
Ps 112:1 is the man that feareth the **L.**, 3068
Ps 112:7 heart is fixed, trusting in the **L.** 3068
Ps 113:1 Praise ye the **L.** Praise, O ye 3050
Ps 113:1 Praise, O ye servants of the **L.**, 3068
Ps 113:1 praise the name of the **L.** 3068
Ps 113:2 Blessed be the name of the **L.** 3068
Ps 113:4 The **L.** is high above all nations, 3068
Ps 113:5 Who is like unto the **L.** our God, 3068
Ps 113:9 of children. Praise ye the **L.** 3050
Ps 114:7 thou earth, at the presence of the **L.**, 113
Ps 115:1 Not unto us, O **L.**, not unto us, 3068
Ps 115:9 O Israel, trust thou in the **L.**: he 3068
Ps 115:10 O house of Aaron, trust in the **L.**: 3068
Ps 115:11 Ye that fear the **L.**, trust in the **L.**: 3068
Ps 115:12 The **L.** hath been mindful of us: 3068
Ps 115:13 He will bless them that fear the **L.**, 3068
Ps 115:14 **L.** shall increase you more and 3068
Ps 115:15 are blessed of the **L.** which made 3068
Ps 115:17 The dead praise not the **L.**, 3050
Ps 115:18 we will bless the **L.** from this time 3050
Ps 115:18 and for evermore. Praise the **L.** 3050
Ps 116:1 I love the **L.**, because he hath 3068
Ps 116:4 called I upon the name of the **L.**; 3068
Ps 116:4 O **L.**, I beseech thee, deliver my 3068
Ps 116:5 Gracious is the **L.**, and righteous; 3068
Ps 116:6 The **L.** preserveth the simple: 3068
Ps 116:7 the **L.** hath dealt bountifully with 3068
Ps 116:9 will walk before the **L.** in the land 3068
Ps 116:12 What shall I render unto the **L.** 3068
Ps 116:13 and call upon the name of the **L.** 3068
Ps 116:14 I will pay my vows unto the **L.** 3068
Ps 116:15 Precious in the sight of the **L.** is 3068
Ps 116:16 O **L.**, truly I am thy servant; I am 3068
Ps 116:17 will call upon the name of the **L.** 3068
Ps 116:18 I will pay my vows unto the **L.** 3068
Ps 116:19 O Jerusalem. Praise ye the **L.** 3068
Ps 117:1 O praise the **L.**, all ye nations: 3068
Ps 117:2 truth of the **L.** endureth for ever. 3068
Ps 117:2 for ever. Praise ye the **L.** 3050
Ps 118:1 O give thanks unto the **L.**; for he 3068
Ps 118:4 Let them now that fear the **L.** say, 3068
Ps 118:5 I called upon the **L.** in distress: 3050
Ps 118:5 the **L.** answered me, and set me in 3050
Ps 118:6 The **L.** is on my side: I will not 3068
Ps 118:7 **L.** taketh my part with them that 3068
Ps 118:8, 9 It is better to trust in the **L.** than 3068
Ps 118:10, name of the **L.** will I destroy them. 3068
Ps 118:11, 12 name of the **L.** I will destroy 3068
Ps 118:13 might fall: but the **L.** helped me. 3068
Ps 118:14 The **L.** is my strength and song, 3050
Ps 118:15 hand of the **L.** doeth valiantly. 3068
Ps 118:16 right hand of the **L.** is exalted: 3068
Ps 118:16 hand of the **L.** doeth valiantly. 3068
Ps 118:17 and declare the works of the **L.** 3050
Ps 118:18 The **L.** hath chastened me sore: 3050
Ps 118:19 into them, and I will praise the **L.** 3050
Ps 118:20 This gate of the **L.**, into which 3068
Ps 118:24 the day which the **L.** hath made; 3068
Ps 118:25 Save now, I beseech thee, O **L.** 3068
Ps 118:25 O **L.**, I beseech thee, send now 3068
Ps 118:26 that cometh in the name of the **L.** 3068
Ps 118:26 you out of the house of the **L.** 3068
Ps 118:27 God is the **L.**, which hath shewed 3068
Ps 118:29 O give thanks unto the **L.**; for he 3068
Ps 119:1 who walk in the law of the **L.** 3068
Ps 119:12 Blessed art thou, O **L.**: teach me 3068
Ps 119:31 O **L.**, put me not to shame. 3068
Ps 119:33 Teach me, O **L.**, the way of thy 3068
Ps 119:41 mercies come also unto me, O **L.**, 3068
Ps 119:52 thy judgments of old, O **L.**; 3068
Ps 119:55 remembered thy name, O **L.**, in 3068
Ps 119:57 Thou art my portion, O **L.**: I 3068
Ps 119:64 The earth, O **L.**, is full of thy 3068
Ps 119:65 dealt well with thy servant, O **L.**, 3068
Ps 119:75 O **L.**, that thy judgments are 3068
Ps 119:89 For ever, O **L.**, thy word is settled. 3068
Ps 119:107 quicken me, O **L.**, according unto 3068
Ps 119:108 offerings of my mouth, O **L.**, 3068
Ps 119:126 It is time for thee, **L.**, to work: 3068
Ps 119:137 Righteous art thou, O **L.**, and 3068
Ps 119:145 hear me, O **L.**: I will keep thy 3068
Ps 119:149 O **L.**, quicken me according to 3068
Ps 119:151 Thou art near, O **L.**; and all thy 3068
Ps 119:156 are thy tender mercies, O **L.**: 3068
Ps 119:159 quicken me, O **L.**, according to 3068
Ps 119:166 **L.**, I have hoped for thy salvation, 3068
Ps 119:169 cry come near before thee, O **L.**: 3068
Ps 119:174 longed for thy salvation, O **L.**; 3068
Ps 120:1 my distress I cried unto the **L.**, 3068
Ps 120:2 Deliver my soul, O **L.**, from lying 3068
Ps 121:2 My help cometh from the **L.**, 3068
Ps 121:5 The **L.** is thy keeper: the 3068
Ps 121:5 **L.** is thy shade upon thy right 3068
Ps 121:7 **L.** shall preserve thee from all 3068
Ps 121:8 **L.** shall preserve thy going out 3068
Ps 122:1 us go into the house of the **L.** 3068
Ps 122:4 tribes go up, the tribes of the **L.**, 3050
Ps 122:4 thanks unto the name of the **L.** 3068
Ps 122:9 of the house of the **L.** our God 3068
Ps 123:2 so our eyes wait upon the **L.** our 3068
Ps 123:3 Have mercy upon us, O **L.**, have 3068
Ps 124:1, 2 the **L.** who was on our side, 3068
Ps 124:6 Blessed be the **L.**, who hath not 3068
Ps 124:8 Our help is in the name of the **L.**, 3068
Ps 125:1 trust in the **L.** shall be as mount 3068
Ps 125:2 **L.** is round about his people from 3068
Ps 125:4 Do good, O **L.**, unto those that be 3068
Ps 125:5 **L.** shall lead them forth with the 3068
Ps 126:1 **L.** turned again the captivity of 3068
Ps 126:2 **L.** hath done great things for 3068
Ps 126:3 **L.** hath done great things for us; 3068
Ps 126:4 Turn again our captivity, O **L.**, 3068
Ps 127:1 Except the **L.** build the house, 3068
Ps 127:1 except the **L.** keep the city, the 3068
Ps 127:3 children are an heritage of the **L.**: 3068
Ps 128:1 is every one that feareth the **L.**; 3068
Ps 128:4 be blessed that feareth the **L.** 3068
Ps 128:5 **L.** shall bless thee out of Zion: 3068
Ps 129:4 The **L.** is righteous: he hath cut 3068
Ps 129:8 blessing of the **L.** be upon you: 3068
Ps 129:8 bless you in the name of the **L.** 3068
Ps 130:1 have I cried unto thee, O **L.** 3068
Ps 130:2 **L.**, hear my voice: let thine ears 136
Ps 130:3 **L.**, shouldest mark iniquities, 3050
Ps 130:3 O **L.**, who shall stand? 136
Ps 130:5 I wait for the **L.**, my soul doth 3068
Ps 130:6 My soul waiteth for the **L.** more 136
Ps 130:7 Let Israel hope in the **L.**: for 3068
Ps 130:7 with the **L.** there is mercy, and 3068
Ps 131:1 **L.**, my heart is not haughty, nor 3068
Ps 131:3 Let Israel hope in the **L.** from 3068
Ps 132:1 **L.**, remember David, and all his 3068
Ps 132:2 How he sware unto the **L.**, and 3068
Ps 132:5 Until I find out a place for the **L.**, 3068
Ps 132:8 Arise, O **L.**, into thy rest; thou 3068
Ps 132:11 The **L.** hath sworn in truth unto 3068
Ps 132:13 For the **L.** hath chosen Zion; he 3068
Ps 133:3 the **L.** commanded the blessing, 3068
Ps 134:1 Behold, bless ye the **L.**, 3068
Ps 134:1 all ye servants of the **L.**, which 3068
Ps 134:1 night stand in the house of the **L.** 3068
Ps 134:2 the sanctuary, and bless the **L.** 3068
Ps 134:3 **L.** that made heaven and earth 3068
Ps 135:1 Praise ye the **L.** Praise ye the 3050
Ps 135:1 Praise ye the name of the **L.**; 3068
Ps 135:1 him, O ye servants of the **L.** 3068
Ps 135:2 that stand in the house of the **L.**, 3068
Ps 135:3 Praise the **L.**; for...is good: 3050
Ps 135:3 for the **L.** is good: sing praises 3068
Ps 135:4 the **L.** hath chosen Jacob unto 3050
Ps 135:5 For I know that the **L.** is great, 3068
Ps 135:5 and that our **L.** is above all gods. 113
Ps 135:6 Whatsoever the **L.** pleased, that 3068
Ps 135:13 Thy name, O **L.**, endureth for 3068
Ps 135:13 they memorial, O **L.**, throughout 3068
Ps 135:14 For the **L.** will judge his people, 3068
Ps 135:19 Bless the **L.**, O house of Israel: 3068
Ps 135:19 bless the **L.**, O house of Aaron: 3068
Ps 135:20 Bless the **L.**, O house of Levi: 3068
Ps 135:20 ye that fear the **L.**, bless the **L.** 3068
Ps 135:21 Blessed be the **L.** out of Zion, 3068
Ps 135:21 at Jerusalem. Praise ye the **L.** 3050
Ps 136:1 O give thanks unto the **L.**; for 3068
Ps 136:3 O give thanks to the **L.** of lords: 113
Ps 137:7 Remember, O **L.**, the children of 3068
Ps 138:4 the earth shall praise thee, O **L.**, 3068
Ps 138:5 shall sing in the ways of the **L.**: 3068
Ps 138:5 for great is the glory of the **L.** 3068
Ps 138:6 Though the **L.** be high, yet hath 3068
Ps 138:8 The **L.** will perfect that which 3068
Ps 138:8 thy mercy, O **L.**, endureth for 3068
Ps 139:1 O **L.**, thou hast searched me, 3068
Ps 139:4 O **L.**, thou knowest it altogether. 3068
Ps 139:21 hate them, O **L.**, that hate thee? 3068
Ps 140:1 Deliver me, O **L.**, from the evil 3068
Ps 140:4 Keep me, O **L.**, from the hands of 3068

Ps 140:6 I said unto the **L.**, Thou art my......... 3068
Ps 140:6 voice of my supplications, O **L.**.......... 3068
Ps 140:7 O God the **L.**, the strength of my....... 136
Ps 140:8 Grant not, O **L.**, the desires of......... 3068
Ps 140:12 **L.** will maintain the cause of the........ 3068
Ps 141:1 **L.**, I cry unto thee: make haste......... 3068
Ps 141:3 watch, O **L.**, before my mouth;......... 3068
Ps 141:8 eyes are unto thee, O God the **L.**:...... 136
Ps 142:1 cried unto the **L.** with my voice;......... 3068
Ps 142:1 my voice unto the **L.** did I make........ 3068
Ps 142:5 I cried unto thee, O **L.**: I said,.......... 3068
Ps 143:1 Hear my prayer, O **L.**, give ear to..... 3068
Ps 143:7 Hear me speedily, O **L.**: my spirit...... 3068
Ps 143:9 Deliver me, O **L.**, from mine........... 3068
Ps 143:11 Quicken me, O **L.**, for thy name's....... 3068
Ps 144:1 Blessed be the **L.** my strength,......... 3068
Ps 144:3 **L.**, what is man, that thou takest....... 3068
Ps 144:5 Bow thy heavens, O **L.**, and come..... 3068
Ps 144:15 that people, whose God is the **L.**...... 3068
Ps 145:3 Great is the **L.**, and greatly to be...... 3068
Ps 145:8 The **L.** is gracious, and full of........... 3068
Ps 145:9 The **L.** is good to all: and his........... 3068
Ps 145:10 thy works shall praise thee, O **L.**;...... 3068
Ps 145:14 The **L.** upholdeth all that fall,........... 3068
Ps 145:17 The **L.** is righteous in all his ways,..... 3068
Ps 145:18 **L.** is nigh unto all them that call........ 3068
Ps 145:20 **L.** preserveth all them that love......... 3068
Ps 145:21 shall speak the praise of the **L.**:......... 3068
Ps 146:1 Praise ye the **L.**. Praise the............. 3050
Ps 146:1 Praise the **L.**, O my soul................ 3068
Ps 146:2 While I live will I praise the **L.**: I...... 3068
Ps 146:5 whose hope is in the **L.** his God:....... 3068
Ps 146:7 The **L.** looseth the prisoners:........... 3068
Ps 146:8 **L.** openeth the eyes of the blind:....... 3068
Ps 146:8 **L.** raiseth them that are bowed......... 3068
Ps 146:8 the **L.** loveth the righteous:............. 3068
Ps 146:9 the **L.** preserveth the strangers;........ 3068
Ps 146:10 The **L.** shall reign for ever, even....... 3068
Ps 146:10 generations. Praise ye the **L.**........... 3050
Ps 147:1 Praise ye the **L.**: for it is good.......... 3050
Ps 147:2 **L.** doth build up Jerusalem: he.......... 3068
Ps 147:5 Great is our **L.**, and of great.............. 113
Ps 147:6 The **L.** lifteth up the meek: he.......... 3068
Ps 147:7 unto the **L.** with thanksgiving;........... 3068
Ps 147:11 **L.** taketh pleasure in them that......... 3068
Ps 147:12 Praise the **L.**, O Jerusalem;.............. 3068
Ps 147:20 known them. Praise ye the **L.**........... 3050
Ps 148:1 Praise ye the **L.**. Praise ye the........... 3050
Ps 148:1 Praise ye the **L.** from the................ 3068
Ps 148:5 them praise the name of the **L.**:........ 3068
Ps 148:7 Praise the **L.** from the earth, ye........ 3068
Ps 148:13 them praise the name of the **L.**:........ 3068
Ps 148:14 near unto him. Praise ye the **L.**......... 3050
Ps 149:1 Praise ye the **L.**. Sing unto the......... 3050
Ps 149:1 Sing unto the **L.** a new song,............ 3068
Ps 149:4 **L.** taketh pleasure in his people:........ 3068
Ps 149:9 all his saints. Praise ye the **L.**........... 3050
Ps 150:1 Praise ye the **L.**. Praise God in.......... 3050
Ps 150:6 that hath breath praise the **L.**............ 3050
Ps 150:6 Praise ye the **L.**............................ 3050
Pr 1:7 fear of the **L.** is the beginning of......... 3068
Pr 1:29 did not choose the fear of the **L.**:....... 3068
Pr 2:5 understand the fear of the **L.**,........... 3068
Pr 2:6 For the **L.** giveth wisdom: out of....... 3068
Pr 3:5 Trust in the **L.** with all thine............ 3068
Pr 3:7 fear the **L.**, and depart from evil......... 3068
Pr 3:9 Honour the **L.** with thy substance....... 3068
Pr 3:11 not the chastening of the **L.**;............. 3068
Pr 3:12 whom the **L.** loveth he correcteth;...... 3068
Pr 3:19 **L.** by wisdom hath founded the........... 3068
Pr 3:26 For the **L.** shall be thy confidence,..... 3068
Pr 3:32 froward is abomination to the **L.**:....... 3068
Pr 3:33 curse of the **L.** is in the house of....... 3068
Pr 5:21 man are before the eyes of the **L.**,...... 3068
Pr 6:16 These six things doth the **L.** hate:..... 3068
Pr 8:13 The fear of the **L.** is to hate evil:...... 3068
Pr 8:22 **L.** possessed me in the beginning....... 3068
Pr 8:35 and shall obtain favour of the **L.**......... 3068
Pr 9:10 fear of the **L.** is the beginning of........ 3068
Pr 10:3 **L.** will not suffer the soul of the........ 3068
Pr 10:22 The blessing of the **L.**, it maketh....... 3068
Pr 10:27 fear of the **L.** prolongeth days:.......... 3068
Pr 10:29 The way of the **L.** is strength to......... 3068
Pr 11:1 balance is abomination to the **L.**:........ 3068
Pr 11:20 heart are abomination to the **L.**:........ 3068
Pr 12:2 man obtaineth favour of the **L.**:......... 3068
Pr 12:22 lips are abomination to the **L.**:........... 3068
Pr 14:2 his uprightness feareth the **L.**:........... 3068
Pr 14:26 fear of the **L.** is strong confidence:...... 3068
Pr 14:27 fear of the **L.** is a fountain of life,...... 3068
Pr 15:3 eyes of the **L.** are in every place,...... 3068
Pr 15:8 is an abomination to the **L.**:............. 3068
Pr 15:9 is an abomination unto the **L.**:........... 3068
Pr 15:11 and destruction are before the **L.**:...... 3068
Pr 15:16 little with the fear of the **L.** than........ 3068
Pr 15:25 **L.** will destroy the house of the......... 3068
Pr 15:26 are an abomination to the **L.**:............ 3068
Pr 15:29 The **L.** is far from the wicked:.......... 3068
Pr 15:33 fear of the **L.** is the instruction.......... 3068
Pr 16:1 of the tongue, is from the **L.**............. 3068
Pr 16:2 but the **L.** weigheth the spirits.......... 3068
Pr 16:3 Commit thy works unto the **L.**,........... 3068
Pr 16:4 The **L.** hath made all things for......... 3068
Pr 16:5 is an abomination to the **L.**:.............. 3068
Pr 16:6 fear of the **L.** men depart from.......... 3068
Pr 16:7 When a man's ways please the **L.**,..... 3068
Pr 16:9 but the **L.** directeth his steps........... 3068
Pr 16:20 and whoso trusteth in the **L.**,............ 3068
Pr 16:33 disposing thereof is of the **L.**............ 3068
Pr 17:3 gold: but the **L.** trieth the hearts....... 3068
Pr 17:15 both are abomination to the **L.**........... 3068
Pr 18:10 name of the **L.** is a strong tower:...... 3068
Pr 18:22 and obtaineth favour of the **L.**........... 3068
Pr 19:3 his heart fretteth against the **L.**......... 3068
Pr 19:14 and a prudent wife is from the **L.**........ 3068
Pr 19:17 upon the poor lendeth unto the **L.**;..... 3068
Pr 19:21 the counsel of the **L.**, that shall......... 3068
Pr 19:23 The fear of the **L.** tendeth to life:...... 3068
Pr 20:10 are alike abomination to the **L.**.......... 3068
Pr 20:12 **L.** hath made even both of them......... 3068
Pr 20:22 wait on the **L.**, and he shall save....... 3068
Pr 20:23 are an abomination unto the **L.**;......... 3068
Pr 20:24 Man's goings are of the **L.**; how........ 3068
Pr 20:27 of man is the candle of the **L.**,.......... 3068
Pr 21:1 heart is in the hand of the **L.**,........... 3068
Pr 21:2 but the **L.** pondereth the hearts......... 3068
Pr 21:3 is more acceptable to the **L.** than....... 3068
Pr 21:30 nor counsel against the **L.**............... 3068
Pr 21:31 of battle: but safety is of the **L.**......... 3068
Pr 22:2 the **L.** is the maker of them all.......... 3068
Pr 22:4 and the fear of the **L.** are riches,........ 3068
Pr 22:12 eyes of the **L.** preserve knowledge,.... 3068
Pr 22:14 is abhorred of the **L.** shall fall............ 3068
Pr 22:19 That thy trust may be in the **L.**, I...... 3068
Pr 22:23 For the **L.** will plead their cause,....... 3068
Pr 23:17 fear of the **L.** all the day long........... 3068
Pr 24:18 Lest the **L.** see it, and it displease..... 3068
Pr 24:21 fear thou the **L.** and the king:........... 3068
Pr 25:22 and the **L.** shall reward thee............ 3068
Pr 28:5 seek the **L.** understand all things....... 3068
Pr 28:25 he that putteth his trust in the **L.**....... 3068
Pr 29:13 the **L.** lighteneth both their eyes......... 3068
Pr 29:25 whoso putteth his trust in the **L.**....... 3068
Pr 29:26 judgment cometh from the **L.**............ 3068
Pr 30:9 deny thee, and say, Who is the **L.**?.... 3068
Pr 31:30 a woman that feareth the **L.**, she....... 3068
Isa 1:2 for the **L.** hath spoken, I have.......... 3068
Isa 1:4 have forsaken the **L.**, they have........ 3068
Isa 1:9 the **L.** of hosts had left unto us a....... 3068
Isa 1:10 Hear the word of the **L.**, ye............. 3068
Isa 1:11 sacrifices unto me? saith the **L.**:........ 3068
Isa 1:18 us reason together, saith the **L.**:........ 3068
Isa 1:20 mouth of the **L.** hath spoken it.......... 3068
Isa 1:24 Therefore saith the **L.**,...the.............. 113
Isa 1:24 the **L.** of hosts, the mighty One........ 3068
Isa 1:28 they that forsake the **L.** shall be........ 3068
Isa 2:3 go up to the mountain of the **L.**,......... 3068
Isa 2:3 word of the **L.** from Jerusalem.......... 3068
Isa 2:5 let us walk in the light of the **L.**........ 3068
Isa 2:10 in the dust, for fear of the **L.**,........... 3068
Isa 2:11 **L.** alone shall be exalted in that......... 3068
Isa 2:12 **L.** of hosts shall be upon every......... 3068
Isa 2:17 **L.** alone shall be exalted in that......... 3068
Isa 2:19 of the earth, for fear of the **L.**........... 3068
Isa 2:21 ragged rocks, for fear of the **L.**,......... 3068
Isa 3:1 For, behold, the **L.**,...doth take.......... 113
Isa 3:1 the **L.** of hosts, doth take away.......... 3068
Isa 3:8 their doings are against the **L.**,.......... 3068
Isa 3:13 The **L.** standeth up to plead, and........ 3068
Isa 3:14 **L.** will enter into judgment with......... 3068
Isa 3:15 poor? saith the **L.** God of hosts........... 136
Isa 3:16 Moreover the **L.** saith, Because.......... 3068
Isa 3:17 the **L.** will smite with a scab the.......... 136
Isa 3:17 **L.** will discover their secret parts....... 3068
Isa 3:18 the **L.** will take away the bravery........ 136
Isa 4:2 branch of the **L.** be beautiful and......... 3068
Isa 4:4 **L.** shall have washed away the............ 136
Isa 4:5 And the **L.** will create upon every...... 3068
Isa 5:7 vineyard of the **L.** of hosts is the....... 3068
Isa 5:9 In mine ears said the **L.** of hosts,...... 3068
Isa 5:12 regard not the work of the **L.**,........... 3068
Isa 5:16 the **L.** of hosts shall be exalted in...... 3068
Isa 5:24 cast away the law of the **L.** of........... 3068
Isa 5:25 anger of the **L.** kindled against.......... 3068
Isa 6:1 also the **L.** sitting upon a throne,......... 136
Isa 6:3 Holy, holy, holy, is the **L.** of............. 3068
Isa 6:5 seen the king, the **L.** of hosts........... 3068
Isa 6:8 I heard the voice of the **L.**, saying,...... 136
Isa 6:11 Then said I, **L.**, how long? And he...... 136
Isa 6:12 **L.** have removed men far away,......... 3068
Isa 7:3 Then said the **L.** unto Isaiah, Go....... 3068
Isa 7:7 Thus saith the **L.** God, It shall not....... 136
Isa 7:10 the **L.** spake again unto Ahaz,........... 3068
Isa 7:11 Ask thee a sign of the **L.** thy God;..... 3068
Isa 7:12 ask, neither will I tempt the **L.**........... 3068
Isa 7:14 **L.** himself shall give you a sign;.......... 136
Isa 7:17 The **L.** shall bring upon thee, and....... 3068
Isa 7:18 the **L.** shall hiss for the fly that is...... 3068
Isa 7:20 day shall the **L.** shave with a rasor...... 136
Isa 8:1 the **L.** said unto me, Take thee a........ 3068
Isa 8:3 Then said the **L.** to me, Call his......... 3068
Isa 8:5 The **L.** spake also unto me again,....... 3068
Isa 8:7 the **L.** bringeth up upon them the........ 136
Isa 8:11 the **L.** spake thus to me with a.......... 3068
Isa 8:13 Sanctify the **L.** of hosts himself;......... 3068
Isa 8:17 I will wait upon the **L.**, that hideth..... 3068
Isa 8:18 children whom the **L.** hath given......... 3068
Isa 8:18 wonders in Israel from the **L.** of......... 3068
Isa 9:7 zeal of the **L.** of hosts will perform..... 3068
Isa 9:8 The **L.** sent a word into Jacob, and.... 3068
Isa 9:11 **L.** shall set up the adversaries of....... 3068
Isa 9:13 neither do they seek the **L.** of............ 3068
Isa 9:14 **L.** will cut off from Israel head and..... 3068
Isa 9:17 **L.** shall have no joy in their young....... 136
Isa 9:19 the wrath of the **L.** of hosts is the..... 3068
Isa 10:12 **L.** hath performed his whole work....... 136
Isa 10:16 shall the **L.**,...send among his fat......... 113
Isa 10:16 the **L.** of hosts, send among his fat...... 136
Isa 10:20 stay upon the **L.**, the Holy One of..... 3068
Isa 10:23 the **L.** God of hosts shall make a.......... 136
Isa 10:24 thus saith the **L.** God of hosts,........... 136
Isa 10:26 **L.** of hosts shall stir up a scourge...... 3068
Isa 10:33 the **L.**,...shall lop the bough with......... 113
Isa 10:33 the **L.** of hosts, shall lop the............. 3068
Isa 11:2 the spirit of the **L.** shall rest upon...... 3068
Isa 11:2 and of the fear of the **L.**;................ 3068
Isa 11:3 quick...in the fear of the **L.**:............. 3068
Isa 11:9 full of the knowledge of the **L.**,......... 3068
Isa 11:11 the **L.** shall set his hand again the....... 136
Isa 11:15 the **L.** shall utterly destroy the.......... 3068
Isa 12:1 shalt say, O **L.**, I will praise thee:...... 3068
Isa 12:2 **L.** Jehovah is my strength and........... 3050
Isa 12:4 day shall ye say, Praise the **L.**,.......... 3068
Isa 12:5 Sing unto the **L.**; for he hath............ 3068
Isa 13:4 **L.** of hosts mustereth the host of........ 3068
Isa 13:5 even the **L.**, and the weapons of......... 3068
Isa 13:6 for the day of the **L.** is at hand;......... 3068
Isa 13:9 Behold, the day of the **L.** cometh,...... 3068
Isa 13:13 in the wrath of the **L.** of hosts,......... 3068
Isa 14:1 the **L.** will have mercy on Jacob,........ 3068
Isa 14:2 them in the land of the **L.** for............ 3068
Isa 14:3 **L.** shall give thee rest from thy......... 3068
Isa 14:5 **L.** hath broken the staff of the.......... 3068
Isa 14:22 against them, saith the **L.** of hosts,.... 3068
Isa 14:22 and son, and nephew, saith the **L.**....... 3068
Isa 14:23 destruction, saith the **L.** of hosts....... 3068
Isa 14:24 The **L.** of hosts hath sworn,............. 3068
Isa 14:27 the **L.** of hosts hath purposed,.......... 3068
Isa 14:32 That the **L.** hath founded Zion,.......... 3068
Isa 16:13 **L.** hath spoken concerning Moab......... 3068
Isa 16:14 But now the **L.** hath spoken,............. 3068
Isa 17:3 of Israel, saith the **L.** of hosts........... 3068
Isa 17:6 saith the **L.** God of Israel................. 3068
Isa 18:4 For so the **L.** said unto me, I will...... 3068
Isa 18:7 be brought unto the **L.** of hosts......... 3068
Isa 18:7 of the name of the **L.** of hosts,.......... 3068
Isa 19:1 the **L.** rideth upon a swift cloud,........ 3068
Isa 19:4 over into the hand of a cruel **l.**;........... 113
Isa 19:4 shall rule over them, saith the **L.**,........ 113
Isa 19:4 over them, saith...the **L.** of hosts........ 3068
Isa 19:12 **L.** of hosts hath purposed upon......... 3068

Isa 19:14 **L.** hath mingled a perverse spirit 3068
Isa 19:16 of the hand of the **L.** of hosts,............ 3068
Isa 19:17 of the counsel of the **L.** of hosts, ... 3068
Isa 19:18 and swear to the **L.** of hosts;............ 3068
Isa 19:19 shall there be an altar to the **L.**......... 3068
Isa 19:19 at the border thereof to the **L.**......... 3068
Isa 19:20 for a witness unto the **L.** of hosts...... 3068
Isa 19:20 for they shall cry unto the **L.**............ 3068
Isa 19:21 the **L.** shall be known to Egypt, ... 3068
Isa 19:21 the Egyptians shall know the **L.**......... 3068
Isa 19:21 they shall vow a vow unto the **L.**,...... 3068
Isa 19:22 And the **L.** shall smite Egypt: he 3068
Isa 19:22 they shall return even to the **L.**,........ 3068
Isa 19:25 Whom the **L.** of hosts shall bless, ... 3068
Isa 20:2 same time spake the **L.** by Isaiah....... 3068
Isa 20:3 **L.** said, Like as my servant Isaiah...... 3068
Isa 21:6 For thus hath the **L.** said unto me, ... 136
Isa 21:8 My **l.**, I stand continually upon the....... 136
Isa 21:10 I have heard of the **L.** of hosts,......... 3068
Isa 21:16 For thus hath the **L.** said unto me, ... 136
Isa 21:17 the **L.** God of Israel hath spoken 3068
Isa 22:5 perplexity by the **L.** God of hosts........ 136
Isa 22:12 the **L.** God of hosts call to weeping, ... 136
Isa 22:14 in mine ears by the **L.** of hosts, ... 3068
Isa 22:14 ye die, saith the **L.** God of hosts......... 136
Isa 22:15 Thus saith the **L.** God of hosts, Go, ... 136
Isa 22:17 the **L.** will carry thee away with a...... 3068
Isa 22:25 In that day, saith the **L.** of hosts, ... 3068
Isa 22:25 cut off: for the **L.** hath spoken it........ 3068
Isa 23:9 The **L.** of hosts hath purposed it,........ 3068
Isa 23:11 **L.** hath given a commandment........... 3068
Isa 23:17 years, that the **L.** will visit Tyre, ... 3068
Isa 23:18 hire shall be holiness to the **L.**: 3068
Isa 23:18 for them that dwell before the **L.**,...... 3068
Isa 24:1 the **L.** maketh the earth empty,......... 3068
Isa 24:3 for the **L.** hath spoken this word........ 3068
Isa 24:14 sing for the majesty of the **L.**............ 3068
Isa 24:15 glorify ye the **L.** in the fires, even 3068
Isa 24:15 the name of the **L.** God of Israel 3068
Isa 24:21 **L.** shall punish the host of the.......... 3068
Isa 24:23 **L.** of hosts shall reign in mount 3068
Isa 25:1 O **L.**, thou art my God; I will exalt 3068
Isa 25:6 **L.** of hosts make unto all people 3068
Isa 25:8 **L.** God will wipe away tears from........ 136
Isa 25:8 earth: for the **L.** hath spoken it.......... 3068
Isa 25:9 this is the **L.**; we have waited for 3068
Isa 25:10 shall the hand of the **L.** rest,............. 3068
Isa 26:4 Trust ye in the **L.** forever: for 3068
Isa 26:4 in the **L.** Jehovah is everlasting........... 3050
Isa 26:8 in the way of thy judgments, O **L.**, ... 3068
Isa 26:10 not behold the majesty of the **L.**........ 3068
Isa 26:11 **L.**, when thy hand is lifted up, they.... 3068
Isa 26:12 **L.**, thou wilt ordain peace for us:....... 3068
Isa 26:13 O **L.** our God, other lords beside....... 3068
Isa 26:15 hast increased the nation, O **L.**,.......... 3068
Isa 26:16 **L.**, in trouble have they visited.......... 3068
Isa 26:17 so have we been in thy sight, O **L.**.... 3068
Isa 26:21 the **L.** cometh out of his place to........ 3068
Isa 27:1 the **L.** with his sore and great and 3068
Isa 27:3 I the **L.** do keep it; I will water it...... 3068
Isa 27:12 **L.** shall beat off from the channel....... 3068
Isa 27:13 worship the **L.** in the holy mount....... 3068
Isa 28:2 **L.** hath a mighty and strong one,......... 136
Isa 28:5 **L.** of hosts be for a crown of glory,..... 3068
Isa 28:13 the word of the **L.** was unto them...... 3068
Isa 28:14 hear the word of the **L.**, ye scornful... 3068
Isa 28:16 Therefore thus saith the **L.** God,......... 136
Isa 28:21 the **L.** shall rise up as in mount......... 3068
Isa 28:22 have heard from the **L.** God of hosts.... 136
Isa 28:29 cometh forth from the **L.** of hosts, ... 3068
Isa 29:6 shalt be visited of the **L.** of hosts....... 3068
Isa 29:10 **L.** hath poured out upon you the........ 3068
Isa 29:13 Wherefore the **L.** said, Forasmuch....... 136
Isa 29:15 to hide their counsel from the **L.**, ... 3068
Isa 29:19 shall increase their joy in the **L.**,........ 3068
Isa 29:22 thus saith the **L.**, who redeemed 3068
Isa 30:1 rebellious children, saith the **L.**,......... 3068
Isa 30:9 will not hear the law of the **L.**:.......... 3068
Isa 30:15 thus saith the **L.** God, the Holy One.... 136
Isa 30:18 And therefore will the **L.** wait, ... 3068
Isa 30:18 for the **L.** is a God of judgment: 3068
Isa 30:20 **L.** give you the bread of adversity, ... 136
Isa 30:26 **L.** bindeth up the breach of his.......... 3068
Isa 30:27 name of the **L.** cometh from far,......... 3068
Isa 30:29 come into the mountain of the **L.**, ... 3068
Isa 30:30 **L.** shall cause his glorious voice......... 3068
Isa 30:31 through the voice of the **L.** shall........ 3068
Isa 30:32 which the **L.** shall lay upon him, ... 3068
Isa 30:33 the breath of the **L.**, like a stream 3068
Isa 31:1 One of Israel, neither seek the **L.**!..... 3068
Isa 31:3 the **L.** shall stretch out his hand, ... 3068
Isa 31:4 thus hath the **L.** spoken unto me, ... 3068
Isa 31:4 the **L.** of hosts come down to fight..... 3068
Isa 31:5 the **L.** of hosts defend Jerusalem;....... 3068
Isa 31:9 afraid of the ensign, saith the **L.**, ... 3068
Isa 32:6 and to utter error against the **L.**,....... 3068
Isa 33:2 O **L.**, be gracious unto us; we............ 3068
Isa 33:5 The **L.** is exalted; for he dwelleth...... 3068
Isa 33:6 the fear of the **L.** is his treasure........ 3068
Isa 33:10 Now will I rise, saith the **L.**; now 3068
Isa 33:21 glorious **L.** will be unto us a place...... 3068
Isa 33:22 For the **L.** is our judge,.................. 3068
Isa 33:22 the **L.** is our lawgiver,..................... 3068
Isa 33:22 the **L.** is our king; he will save us...... 3068
Isa 34:2 indignation of the **L.** is upon all.......... 3068
Isa 34:6 sword of the **L.** is filled with blood, ... 3068
Isa 34:6 the **L.** hath a sacrifice in Bozrah, ... 3068
Isa 34:16 Seek ye out of the book of the **L.**,..... 3068
Isa 35:2 they shall see the glory of the **L.**,...... 3068
Isa 35:10 ransomed of the **L.** shall return, ... 3068
Isa 36:7 to me, We trust in the **L.** our God:.... 3068
Isa 36:10 am I now come up without the **L.**....... 3068
Isa 36:10 **L.** said unto me, Go up against.......... 3068
Isa 36:15 make you trust in the **L.**, saying,....... 3068
Isa 36:15 The **L.** will surely deliver us: 3068
Isa 36:18 saying, The **L.** will deliver us............ 3068
Isa 36:20 the **L.** should deliver Jerusalem.......... 3068
Isa 37:1 and went into the house of the **L.**...... 3068
Isa 37:4 **L.** thy God will hear the words of...... 3068
Isa 37:4 which the **L.** thy God hath heard: 3068
Isa 37:6 Thus saith the **L.**, Be not afraid......... 3068
Isa 37:14 went up unto the house of the **L.**,...... 3068
Isa 37:14 and spread it before the **L.**............. 3068
Isa 37:15 And Hezekiah prayed unto the **L.**,...... 3068
Isa 37:16 O **L.** of hosts, God of Israel, that 3068
Isa 37:17 Incline thine ear, O **L.**, and hear;....... 3068
Isa 37:17 open thine eyes, O **L.**, and see: 3068
Isa 37:18 **L.**, the kings of Assyria have laid........ 3068
Isa 37:20 O **L.** our God, save us from his......... 3068
Isa 37:20 may know that thou art the **L.**, ... 3068
Isa 37:21 Thus saith the **L.** God of Israel, ... 3068
Isa 37:22 word which the **L.** hath spoken.......... 3068
Isa 37:24 hast thou reproached the **L.**, and......... 136
Isa 37:32 zeal of the **L.** of hosts shall do 3068
Isa 37:33 thus saith the **L.** concerning the......... 3068
Isa 37:34 come into this city, saith the **L.**......... 3068
Isa 37:36 the angel of the **L.** went forth, ... 3068
Isa 38:1 Thus saith the **L.**, Set thine house 3068
Isa 38:2 the wall, and prayed unto the **L.**, ... 3068
Isa 38:3 Remember now, O **L.**, I beseech.......... 3068
Isa 38:4 came the word of the **L.** to Isaiah, ... 3068
Isa 38:5 saith the **L.**, the God of David.......... 3068
Isa 38:7 be a sign unto thee from the **L.**,......... 3068
Isa 38:7 that the **L.** will do this thing that 3068
Isa 38:11 shall not see the **L.**, even the **L.**,...... 3050
Isa 38:14 O **L.**, I am oppressed; undertake 3068
Isa 38:16 O **L.**, by these things men live, and..... 136
Isa 38:20 The **L.** was ready to save me: 3068
Isa 38:20 of our life in the house of the **L.**........ 3068
Isa 38:22 I shall go up to the house of the **L.**?... 3068
Isa 39:5 Hear the word of the **L.** of hosts:...... 3068
Isa 39:6 nothing shall be left, saith the **L.**....... 3068
Isa 39:8 Good is the word of the **L.** which 3068
Isa 40:3 Prepare ye the way of the **L.**........... 3068
Isa 40:5 glory of the **L.** shall be revealed, ... 3068
Isa 40:5 mouth of the **L.** hath spoken it.......... 3068
Isa 40:7 spirit of the **L.** bloweth upon it:......... 3068
Isa 40:10 **L.** God will come with strong hand, ... 136
Isa 40:13 hath directed the Spirit of the **L.**,........ 3068
Isa 40:27 My way is hid from the **L.**, and......... 3068
Isa 40:28 the **L.**, the Creator of the ends of...... 3068
Isa 40:31 that wait upon the **L.** shall renew....... 3068
Isa 41:4 I the **L.**, the first, and with the 3068
Isa 41:13 I the **L.** thy God will hold thy right 3068
Isa 41:14 I will help thee, saith the **L.**, and....... 3068
Isa 41:16 and thou shalt rejoice in the **L.**,........ 3068
Isa 41:17 I the **L.** will hear them, I the God....... 3068
Isa 41:20 the hand of the **L.** hath done this, ... 3068
Isa 41:21 Produce your cause, saith the **L.**; 3068
Isa 42:5 saith God the **L.**, he that created........ 3068
Isa 42:6 I the **L.** have called thee in............... 3068
Isa 42:8 I am the **L.**: that is my name:............ 3068
Isa 42:10 Sing unto the **L.** a new song, and 3068
Isa 42:12 Let them give glory unto the **L.**, ... 3068
Isa 42:13 **L.** shall go forth as a mighty man,...... 3068
Isa 42:21 The **L.** is well pleased for his........... 3068
Isa 42:24 did not the **L.**, he against whom 3068
Isa 43:1 thus saith the **L.** that created thee, ... 3068
Isa 43:3 I am the **L.** thy God, the Holy One.... 3068
Isa 43:10 Ye are my witnesses, saith the **L.**,..... 3068
Isa 43:11 I, even I, am the **L.**; and beside........ 3068
Isa 43:12 ye are my witnesses, saith the **L.**, ... 3068
Isa 43:14 Thus saith the **L.**, your redeemer, ... 3068
Isa 43:15 I am the **L.**, your Holy One, the........ 3068
Isa 43:16 Thus saith the **L.**, which maketh........ 3068
Isa 44:2 Thus saith the **L.** that made thee, ... 3068
Isa 44:5 with his hand unto the **L.**, ... 3068
Isa 44:6 saith the **L.** the King of Israel, ... 3068
Isa 44:6 and his redeemer the **L.** of hosts; 3068
Isa 44:23 heavens; for the **L.** hath done it: 3068
Isa 44:23 for the **L.** hath redeemed Jacob, ... 3068
Isa 44:24 saith the **L.**, thy redeemer, and......... 3068
Isa 44:24 am the **L.** that maketh all things; 3068
Isa 45:1 Thus saith the **L.** to his anointed, ... 3068
Isa 45:3 know that I, the **L.**, which call 3068
Isa 45:5 I am the **L.**, and there is none else, ... 3068
Isa 45:6 I am the **L.**, and there is none else. ... 3068
Isa 45:7 evil: I the **L.** do all these things......... 3068
Isa 45:8 together, I the **L.** have created it....... 3068
Isa 45:11 Thus saith the **L.**, the Holy One......... 3068
Isa 45:13 nor reward, saith the **L.** of hosts. 3068
Isa 45:14 saith the **L.**, The labour of Egypt,...... 3068
Isa 45:17 But Israel shall be saved in the **L.**...... 3068
Isa 45:18 the **L.** that created the heavens;........ 3068
Isa 45:18 I am the **L.**; and there is none else. ... 3068
Isa 45:19 I the **L.** speak righteousness,............ 3068
Isa 45:21 from that time? have not I the **L.**? 3068
Isa 45:24 in the **L.** have I righteousness and 3068
Isa 45:25 In the **L.** shall all the seed of Israel.... 3068
Isa 47:4 the **L.** of hosts is his name, the....... 3068
Isa 48:1 swear by the name of the **L.**, and...... 3068
Isa 48:2 The **L.** of hosts is his name............. 3068
Isa 48:14 The **L.** hath loved him: he will 3068
Isa 48:16 the **L.** God, and his Spirit, hath.......... 136
Isa 48:17 Thus saith the **L.**, thy Redeemer, ... 3068
Isa 48:17 **L.** thy God which teacheth thee........ 3068
Isa 48:20 The **L.** hath redeemed his servant...... 3068
Isa 48:22 There is no peace, saith the **L.**, ... 3068
Isa 49:1 **L.** hath called me from the womb;...... 3068
Isa 49:4 my judgment is with the **L.**, and........ 3068
Isa 49:5 saith the **L.** that formed me from........ 3068
Isa 49:5 be glorious in the eyes of the **L.**,....... 3068
Isa 49:7 Thus saith the **L.**, the Redeemer......... 3068
Isa 49:7 because of the **L.** that is faithful,........ 3068
Isa 49:8 Thus saith the **L.**, In an acceptable...... 3068
Isa 49:13 the **L.** hath comforted his people,....... 3068
Isa 49:14 said, The **L.** hath forsaken me,.......... 3068
Isa 49:14 and my **L.** hath forgotten me. 136
Isa 49:18 saith the **L.**, thou shalt surely 3068
Isa 49:22 Thus saith the **L.** God, Behold, I......... 136
Isa 49:23 thou shalt know that I am the **L.**: 3068
Isa 49:25 But thus saith the **L.**, Even the......... 3068
Isa 49:26 I the **L.** am thy Saviour and thy......... 3068
Isa 50:1 saith the **L.**, Where is the bill of........ 3068
Isa 50:4 **L.** God hath given me the tongue........ 136
Isa 50:5 **L.** God hath opened mine ear, and....... 136
Isa 50:7 For the **L.** God will help me;.............. 136
Isa 50:9 the **L.** God will help me; who is.......... 136
Isa 50:10 is among you that feareth the **L.**,....... 3068
Isa 50:10 trust in the name of the **L.**, and 3068
Isa 51:1 righteousness, ye that seek the **L.**: 3068
Isa 51:3 For the **L.** shall comfort Zion: 3068
Isa 51:3 desert like the garden of the **L.**;........ 3068
Isa 51:9 put on strength, O arm of the **L.**; 3068
Isa 51:11 redeemed of the **L.** shall return, ... 3068
Isa 51:13 forgettest the **L.** thy maker, that 3068
Isa 51:15 I am the **L.** thy God, that divided 3068
Isa 51:15 The **L.** of hosts is his name............. 3068
Isa 51:17 drunk at the hand of the **L.** the cup.... 3068
Isa 51:20 they are full of the fury of the **L.**, ... 3068
Isa 51:22 Thus saith thy **L.**...and thy God.......... 113
Isa 51:22 Thus saith...the **L.**, and thy God........ 3068
Isa 52:3 thus saith the **L.**, Ye have sold.......... 3068
Isa 52:4 thus saith the **L.** God, My people........ 136
Isa 52:5 what have I here, saith the **L.**,.......... 3068
Isa 52:5 make them to howl, saith the **L.**;....... 3068
Isa 52:8 when the **L.** shall bring again Zion...... 3068
Isa 52:9 the **L.** hath comforted his people,....... 3068
Isa 52:10 **L.** hath made bare his holy arm.......... 3068
Isa 52:11 that bear the vessels of the **L.**.......... 3068
Isa 52:12 for the **L.** will go before you; and 3068

Isa 53:1 is the arm of the **L.** revealed? 3068
Isa 53:6 **L.** hath laid on him the iniquity 3068
Isa 53:10 it pleased the **L.** to bruise him; 3068
Isa 53:10 pleasure of the **L.** shall prosper in 3068
Isa 54:1 of the married wife, saith the **L.**. 3068
Isa 54:5 the **L.** of hosts is his name; and 3068
Isa 54:6 **L.** hath called thee as a woman 3068
Isa 54:8 thee, saith the **L.** thy Redeemer. 3068
Isa 54:10 the **L.** that hath mercy on thee 3068
Isa 54:13 children shall be taught of the **L.**; 3068
Isa 54:17 heritage of the servants of the **L.**, 3068
Isa 54:17 righteousness is of me, saith the **L.**. 3068
Isa 55:5 thee because of the **L.** thy God, 3068
Isa 55:6 Seek ye the **L.** while he may be 3068
Isa 55:7 and let him return unto the **L.**, 3068
Isa 55:8 your ways my ways, saith the **L.**. 3068
Isa 55:13 it shall be to the **L.** for a name, 3068
Isa 56:1 saith the **L.**, Keep ye judgment, 3068
Isa 56:3 that hath joined himself to the **L.**, 3068
Isa 56:3 **L.** hath utterly separated me from 3068
Isa 56:4 saith the **L.** unto the eunuchs 3068
Isa 56:6 that join themselves to the **L.**, to 3068
Isa 56:6 love the name of the **L.**, to be his 3068
Isa 56:8 The **L.** God which gathereth the 136
Isa 57:19 to him that is near, saith the **L.**; 3068
Isa 58:5 and an acceptable day to the **L.**? 3068
Isa 58:8 the glory of the **L.** shall be thy 3068
Isa 58:9 thou call, and the **L.** shall answer; 3068
Isa 58:11 the **L.** shall guide thee continually, 3068
Isa 58:13 the holy of the **L.**, honourable; 3068
Isa 58:14 thou delight thyself in the **L.**; 3068
Isa 58:14 mouth of the **L.** hath spoken it. 3068
Isa 59:13 and lying against the **L.**, and 3068
Isa 59:15 the **L.** saw it, and it displeased 3068
Isa 59:19 fear the name of the **L.** from the 3068
Isa 59:19 the Spirit of the **L.** shall lift up a 3068
Isa 59:20 transgression in Jacob, saith the **L.**. 3068
Isa 59:21 covenant with them, saith the **L.**; 3068
Isa 59:21 of thy seed's seed, saith the **L.**, 3068
Isa 60:1 glory of the **L.** is risen upon thee 3068
Isa 60:2 the **L.** shall arise upon thee, and 3068
Isa 60:6 shew forth the praises of the **L.**. 3068
Isa 60:9 unto the name of the **L.** thy God, 3068
Isa 60:14 shall call thee, The city of the **L.**, 3068
Isa 60:16 I the **L.** am thy Saviour and thy 3068
Isa 60:19 but the **L.** shall be unto thee an 3068
Isa 60:20 the **L.** shall be thine everlasting 3068
Isa 60:22 I the **L.** will hasten it in his time 3068
Isa 61:1 Spirit of the **L.** God is upon me; 136
Isa 61:1 the **L.** hath anointed me to preach 3068
Isa 61:2 the acceptable year of the **L.**, and 3068
Isa 61:3 planting of the **L.**, that he might 3068
Isa 61:6 be named the Priests of the **L.**: 3068
Isa 61:8 I the **L.** love judgment, I hate 3068
Isa 61:9 seed which the **L.** hath blessed 3068
Isa 61:10 I will greatly rejoice in the **L.**, 3068
Isa 61:11 **L.** God will cause righteousness 136
Isa 62:2 the mouth of the **L.** shall name 3068
Isa 62:3 of glory in the hand of the **L.**, 3068
Isa 62:4 for the **L.** delighteth in thee, and 3068
Isa 62:6 ye that make mention of the **L.**, 3068
Isa 62:8 **L.** hath sworn by his right hand, 3068
Isa 62:9 it shall eat it, and praise the **L.**; 3068
Isa 62:11 **L.** hath proclaimed unto the end 3068
Isa 62:12 people, The redeemed of the **L.**: 3068
Isa 63:7 the lovingkindnesses of the **L.**, 3068
Isa 63:7 and the praises of the **L.**, 3068
Isa 63:7 that the **L.** hath bestowed on us, 3068
Isa 63:14 Spirit of the **L.** caused him to rest: 3068
Isa 63:16 thou, O **L.**, art our father, our 3068
Isa 63:17 O **L.**, why hast thou made us to err 3068
Isa 64:8 now, O **L.**, thou art our father; 3068
Isa 64:9 Be not wroth very sore, O **L.**, 3068
Isa 64:12 thyself for these things, O **L.**? 3068
Isa 65:7 your fathers together, saith the **L.**, 3068
Isa 65:8 saith the **L.**, As the new wine is 3068
Isa 65:11 ye are they that forsake the **L.**, 3068
Isa 65:13 thus saith the **L.** God, Behold, my 136
Isa 65:15 the **L.** God shall slay thee, and 136
Isa 65:23 the seed of the blessed of the **L.**, 3068
Isa 65:25 my holy mountain, saith the **L.**. 3068
Isa 66:1 saith the **L.**, The heaven is my 3068
Isa 66:2 things have been, saith the **L.**: 3068
Isa 66:5 Hear the word of the **L.**, ye that 3068
Isa 66:5 sake, said, Let the **L.** be glorified: 3068
Isa 66:6 a voice of the **L.** that rendereth 3068
Isa 66:9 to bring forth? saith the **L.**: 3068
Isa 66:12 thus saith the **L.**, Behold, I will 3068
Isa 66:14 the hand of the **L.** shall be known 3068
Isa 66:15 behold, the **L.** will come with fire, 3068
Isa 66:16 will the **L.** plead with all flesh: 3068
Isa 66:16 the slain of the **L.** shall be many. 3068
Isa 66:17 consumed together, saith the **L.**. 3068
Isa 66:20 for an offering unto the **L.** out of 3068
Isa 66:20 mountain Jerusalem, saith the **L.**, 3068
Isa 66:20 vessel into the house of the **L.**. 3068
Isa 66:21 and for Levites, saith the **L.**. 3068
Isa 66:22 remain before me, saith the **L.**, 3068
Isa 66:23 worship before me, saith the **L.**. 3068
Jer 1:2 To whom the word of the **L.** came 3068
Jer 1:4 the word of the **L.** came unto me, 3068
Jer 1:6 Ah, **L.** God! behold, I cannot speak: 136
Jer 1:7 But the **L.** said unto me, Say not, 3068
Jer 1:8 thee to deliver thee, saith the **L.**. 3068
Jer 1:9 the **L.** put forth his hand, and 3068
Jer 1:9 And the **L.** said unto me, Behold 3068
Jer 1:11 the word of the **L.** came unto me, 3068
Jer 1:12 Then said the **L.** unto me, Thou 3068
Jer 1:13 word of the **L.** came unto me the 3068
Jer 1:14 Then the **L.** said unto me, Out of 3068
Jer 1:15 kingdoms of the north, saith the **L.**; 3068
Jer 1:19 for I am with thee, saith the **L.**, 3068
Jer 2:1 the word of the **L.** came to me, 3068
Jer 2:2 Thus saith the **L.**; I remember 3068
Jer 2:3 Israel was holiness unto the **L.**, 3068
Jer 2:3 come upon them, saith the **L.**. 3068
Jer 2:4 Hear ye the word of the **L.**, O 3068
Jer 2:5 Thus saith the **L.**, What iniquity 3068
Jer 2:6 Where is the **L.** that brought us 3068
Jer 2:8 priests said not, Where is the **L.**? 3068
Jer 2:9 yet plead with you, saith the **L.**, 3068
Jer 2:12 be ye very desolate, saith the **L.**. 3068
Jer 2:17, 19 hast forsaken the **L.** thy God, 3068
Jer 2:19 not in thee, saith the **L.** God of hosts. 136
Jer 2:22 marked before me, saith the **L.** God. 136
Jer 2:29 against me, saith the **L.**. 3068
Jer 2:31 see ye the word of the **L.**. Have I 3068
Jer 2:37 **L.** hath rejected thy confidences, 3068
Jer 3:1 return again to me, saith the **L.**. 3068
Jer 3:6 **L.** said also unto me in the days 3068
Jer 3:10 heart, but feignedly, saith the **L.**. 3068
Jer 3:11 **L.** said unto me, The backsliding 3068
Jer 3:12 backsliding Israel, saith the **L.**; 3068
Jer 3:12 I am merciful, saith the **L.**, and 3068
Jer 3:13 transgressed against the **L.** thy 3068
Jer 3:13 not obeyed my voice, saith the **L.**. 3068
Jer 3:14 backsliding children, saith the **L.**; 3068
Jer 3:16 saith the **L.**, they shall say no more, 3068
Jer 3:16 The ark of the covenant of the **L.**: 3068
Jer 3:17 call Jerusalem the throne of the **L.**; 3068
Jer 3:17 unto it, to the name of the **L.**, to 3068
Jer 3:20 me, O house of Israel, saith the **L.**. 3068
Jer 3:21 have forgotten the **L.** their God. 3068
Jer 3:22 thee; for thou art the **L.** our God. 3068
Jer 3:23 in the **L.** our God is the salvation 3068
Jer 3:25 we have sinned against the **L.** our 3068
Jer 3:25 not obeyed the voice of the **L.** our 3068
Jer 4:1 wilt return, O Israel, saith the **L.**, 3068
Jer 4:2 **L.** liveth, in truth, in judgment, 3068
Jer 4:3 thus saith the **L.** to the men of 3068
Jer 4:4 Circumcise yourselves to the **L.**, 3068
Jer 4:8 anger of the **L.** is not turned back 3068
Jer 4:9 to pass at that day, saith the **L.**, 3068
Jer 4:10 **L.** God! surely thou hast greatly 136
Jer 4:17 rebellious against me, saith the **L.**. 3068
Jer 4:26 down at the presence of the **L.**, 3068
Jer 4:27 thus hath the **L.** said, The whole 3068
Jer 5:2 though they say, The **L.** liveth; 3068
Jer 5:3 O **L.**, are not thine eyes upon the 3068
Jer 5:4 they know not the way of the **L.**, 3068
Jer 5:5 they have known the way of the **L.**, 3068
Jer 5:9 for these things? saith the **L.**: 3068
Jer 5:11 very treacherously...saith the **L.**. 3068
Jer 5:12 They have belied the **L.**, and said, 3068
Jer 5:14 thus saith the **L.** God of hosts, 3068
Jer 5:15 O house of Israel, saith the **L.**: 3068
Jer 5:18 saith the **L.**, I will not make a full 3068
Jer 5:19 Wherefore doeth the **L.** our God 3068
Jer 5:22 Fear ye not me? saith the **L.**: will 3068
Jer 5:24 Let us now fear the **L.** our God, 3068
Jer 5:29 for these things? saith the **L.**: 3068
Jer 6:6 For thus hath the **L.** of hosts said, 3068
Jer 6:9 Thus saith the **L.** of hosts, They 3068
Jer 6:10 the word of the **L.** is unto them a 3068
Jer 6:11 I am full of the fury of the **L.**; 3068
Jer 6:12 inhabitants of...land, saith the **L.**. 3068
Jer 6:15 shall be cast down, saith the **L.**. 3068
Jer 6:16 Thus saith the **L.**, Stand ye in the 3068
Jer 6:21 thus saith the **L.**, Behold, I will lay 3068
Jer 6:22 Thus saith the **L.**, Behold, a people 3068
Jer 6:30 because the **L.** hath rejected them. 3068
Jer 7:1 came to Jeremiah from the **L.**, 3068
Jer 7:2 Hear the word of the **L.**, all ye of 3068
Jer 7:2 at these gates to worship the **L.**. 3068
Jer 7:3 saith the **L.** of hosts, the God of 3068
Jer 7:4 The temple of the **L.**, The temple 3068
Jer 7:4 of the **L.**, The temple of the **L.**, 3068
Jer 7:11 even I have seen it, saith the **L.**. 3068
Jer 7:13 done all these works, saith the **L.**, 3068
Jer 7:19 provoke me to anger? saith the **L.**: 3068
Jer 7:20 thus saith the **L.** God; Behold, mine 136
Jer 7:21 the **L.** of hosts, the God of Israel; 3068
Jer 7:28 that obeyeth not the voice of the **L.** 3068
Jer 7:29 **L.** hath rejected and forsaken the 3068
Jer 7:30 done evil in my sight, saith the **L.**: 3068
Jer 7:32 saith the **L.**, that it shall no more 3068
Jer 8:1 saith the **L.**, they shall bring out 3068
Jer 8:3 driven them, saith the **L.** of hosts. 3068
Jer 8:4 Thus saith the **L.**; Shall they fall, 3068
Jer 8:7 know not the judgment of the **L.**. 3068
Jer 8:8 and the law of the **L.** is with us? 3068
Jer 8:9 have rejected the word of the **L.**; 3068
Jer 8:12 shall be cast down, saith the **L.**. 3068
Jer 8:13 surely consume them, saith the **L.**: 3068
Jer 8:14 **L.** our God hath put us to silence, 3068
Jer 8:14 we have sinned against the **L.**. 3068
Jer 8:17 they shall bite you, saith the **L.**: 3068
Jer 8:19 Is not the **L.** in Zion? is not her 3068
Jer 9:3 they know not me, saith the **L.**. 3068
Jer 9:6 refuse to know me, saith the **L.**. 3068
Jer 9:7 thus saith the **L.** of hosts, Behold, 3068
Jer 9:9 for these things? saith the **L.**: 3068
Jer 9:12 the mouth of the **L.** hath spoken, 3068
Jer 9:13 the **L.** saith, Because they have 3068
Jer 9:15 the **L.** of hosts, the God of Israel; 3068
Jer 9:17 saith the **L.** of hosts, Consider 3068
Jer 9:20 Yet hear the word of the **L.**, O ye 3068
Jer 9:22 Speak, Thus saith the **L.**, Even 3068
Jer 9:23 Thus saith the **L.**, Let not the wise 3068
Jer 9:24 **L.** which exercise lovingkindness 3068
Jer 9:24 these things I delight, saith the **L.**. 3068
Jer 9:25 the days come, saith the **L.**, that 3068
Jer 10:1 the word which the **L.** speaketh 3068
Jer 10:2 Thus saith the **L.**, Learn not the 3068
Jer 10:6 there is none like unto thee, O **L.**; 3068
Jer 10:10 the **L.** is the true God, he is the 3068
Jer 10:16 The **L.** of hosts is his name. 3068
Jer 10:18 For thus saith the **L.**, Behold, I 3068
Jer 10:21 and have not sought the **L.**: 3068
Jer 10:23 O **L.**, I know that the way of man 3068
Jer 10:24 **L.**, correct me, but with judgment; 3068
Jer 11:1 that came to Jeremiah from the **L.**, 3068
Jer 11:3 Thus saith the **L.** God of Israel; 3068
Jer 11:5 answered I, and said, So be it, O **L.** 3068
Jer 11:6 the **L.** said unto me, Proclaim 3068
Jer 11:9 **L.** said unto me, A conspiracy 3068
Jer 11:11 thus saith the **L.**, Behold, I will 3068
Jer 11:16 The **L.** called thy name, A green 3068
Jer 11:17 For the **L.** of hosts, that planted 3068
Jer 11:18 **L.** hath given me knowledge of it, 3068
Jer 11:20 But, O **L.** of hosts, that judgest 3068
Jer 11:21 thus saith the **L.** of the men of 3068
Jer 11:21 prophesy not in the name of the **L.**, 3068
Jer 11:22 thus saith the **L.** of hosts, Behold, 3068
Jer 12:1 Righteous art thou, O **L.**, when I 3068
Jer 12:3 But thou, O **L.**, knowest me: thou 3068
Jer 12:12 sword of the **L.** shall devour from 3068
Jer 12:13 because of the fierce anger of the **L.** 3068
Jer 12:14 saith the **L.** against all mine evil 3068
Jer 12:16 swear by my name, The **L.** liveth; 3068
Jer 12:17 destroy that nation, saith the **L.**. 3068
Jer 13:1 saith the **L.** unto me, Go and get 3068
Jer 13:2 according to the word of the **L.**, 3068
Jer 13:3 the word of the **L.** came unto me 3068
Jer 13:5 Euphrates, as the **L.** commanded 3068
Jer 13:6 the **L.** said unto me, Arise, go to 3068
Jer 13:8 the word of the **L.** came unto me, 3068
Jer 13:9 saith the **L.**, After this manner 3068
Jer 13:11 whole house of Judah, saith the **L.**; 3068
Jer 13:12 Thus saith the **L.** God of Israel, 3068
Jer 13:13 Thus saith the **L.**, Behold, I will 3068

Jer 13:14 the sons together, saith the **L.**: 3068
Jer 13:15 not proud: for the **L.** hath spoken. 3068
Jer 13:16 Give glory to the **L.** your God, 3068
Jer 13:25 measures from me, saith the **L.**; 3068
Jer 14:1 The word of the **L.** that came to 3068
Jer 14:7 O **L.**, though our iniquities testify 3068
Jer 14:9 thou, O **L.**, art in the midst of us, 3068
Jer 14:10 Thus saith the **L.** unto this people, 3068
Jer 14:10 the **L.** doth not accept them; 3068
Jer 14:11 Then said the **L.** unto me, Pray 3068
Jer 14:13 Ah, **L.** God! behold, the prophets 136
Jer 14:14 **L.** said unto me, The prophets 3068
Jer 14:15 thus saith the **L.** concerning the 3068
Jer 14:20 We acknowledge, O **L.**, our 3068
Jer 14:22 art not thou he, O **L.** our God? 3068
Jer 15:1 Then said the **L.** unto me, Though 3068
Jer 15:2 Thus saith the **L.**; Such as are for 3068
Jer 15:3 over them four kinds, saith the **L.**: 3068
Jer 15:6 hast forsaken me, saith the **L.**, 3068
Jer 15:9 before their enemies, saith the **L.**. 3068
Jer 15:11 The **L.** said, Verily it shall be well 3068
Jer 15:15 O **L.**, thou knowest: remember 3068
Jer 15:16 by thy name, O **L.** God of hosts. 3068
Jer 15:19 thus saith the **L.**, If thou return, 3068
Jer 15:20 and to deliver thee, saith the **L.**. 3068
Jer 16:1 The word of the **L.** came also unto 3068
Jer 16:3 saith the **L.** concerning the sons 3068
Jer 16:5 thus saith the **L.**, Enter not into 3068
Jer 16:5 from this people, saith the **L.**, 3068
Jer 16:9 the **L.** of hosts, the God of Israel; 3068
Jer 16:10 **L.** pronounced all this great evil 3068
Jer 16:10 have committed against the **L.** our 3068
Jer 16:11 have forsaken me, saith the **L.**, 3068
Jer 16:14 the days come, saith the **L.**, that 3068
Jer 16:14, 15 The **L.** liveth, that brought up 3068
Jer 16:16 send for many fishers, saith the **L.**, 3068
Jer 16:19 **L.**, my strength, and my fortress, 3068
Jer 16:21 shall know that my name is The **L.**. 3068
Jer 17:5 Thus saith the **L.**; Cursed be the 3068
Jer 17:5 whose heart departeth from the **L.**. 3068
Jer 17:7 the man that trusteth in the **L.**, 3068
Jer 17:7 and whose hope the **L.** is. 3068
Jer 17:10 I the **L.** search the heart, I try the 3068
Jer 17:13 O **L.**, the hope of Israel, all that 3068
Jer 17:13 forsaken the **L.**, the fountain of 3068
Jer 17:14 Heal me, O **L.**, and I shall be 3068
Jer 17:15 Where is the word of the **L.**? let it 3068
Jer 17:19 said the **L.** unto me; Go and stand 3068
Jer 17:20 Hear ye the word of the **L.**, ye 3068
Jer 17:21 Thus saith the **L.**; Take heed to 3068
Jer 17:24 hearken unto me, saith the **L.**, 3068
Jer 17:26 praise, unto the house of the **L.**. 3068
Jer 18:1 came to Jeremiah from the **L.**, 3068
Jer 18:5 the word of the **L.** came to me, 3068
Jer 18:6 you as this potter? saith the **L.** 3068
Jer 18:11 saith the **L.**; Behold, I frame 3068
Jer 18:13 thus saith the **L.**; Ask ye now 3068
Jer 18:19 Give heed to me, O **L.**, and hearken 3068
Jer 18:23 **L.**, thou knowest all their counsel 3068
Jer 19:1 Thus saith the **L.**, Go and get a 3068
Jer 19:3 say, Hear ye the word of the **L.**, O 3068
Jer 19:3 Thus saith the **L.** of hosts, the 3068
Jer 19:6 the days come, saith the **L.**, that 3068
Jer 19:11 them, Thus saith the **L.** of hosts; 3068
Jer 19:12 I do unto this place, saith the **L.**, 3068
Jer 19:14 the **L.** had sent him to prophesy; 3068
Jer 19:15 Thus saith the **L.** of hosts, the 3068
Jer 20:1 governor in the house of the **L.**, 3068
Jer 20:2 which was by the house of the **L.**. 3068
Jer 20:3 The **L.** hath not called thy name 3068
Jer 20:4 thus saith the **L.**, Behold, I will 3068
Jer 20:7 O **L.**, thou hast deceived me, and 3068
Jer 20:8 word of the **L.** was made a reproach 3068
Jer 20:11 **L.** is with me as a mighty terrible 3068
Jer 20:12 But, O **L.** of hosts, that triest the 3068
Jer 20:13 Sing unto the **L.**, praise ye the **L.**: 3068
Jer 20:16 the cities which the **L.** overthrew, 3068
Jer 21:1 came unto Jeremiah from the **L.**, 3068
Jer 21:2 Enquire, I pray thee, of the **L.** for 3068
Jer 21:2 **L.** will deal with us according to 3068
Jer 21:4 Thus saith the **L.** God of Israel; 3068
Jer 21:7 And afterward, saith the **L.**, I will 3068
Jer 21:8 Thus saith the **L.**; Behold, I set 3068
Jer 21:10 and not for good, saith the **L.**: 3068
Jer 21:11 say, Hear ye the word of the **L.**; 3068
Jer 21:12 saith the **L.**; Execute judgment 3068
Jer 21:13 and rock of the plain, saith the **L.**; 3068
Jer 21:14 fruit of your doings, saith the **L.**: 3068
Jer 22:1 Thus saith the **L.**; Go down to 3068
Jer 22:2 Hear the word of the **L.**, O king 3068
Jer 22:3 Thus saith the **L.**; Execute ye 3068
Jer 22:5 I swear by myself, saith the **L.**, 3068
Jer 22:6 thus saith the **L.** unto the king's 3068
Jer 22:8 **L.** done thus unto this great city? 3068
Jer 22:9 forsaken the covenant of the **L.** 3068
Jer 22:11 saith the **L.** touching Shallum the 3068
Jer 22:16 not this to know me? saith the **L.**. 3068
Jer 22:18 saith the **L.** concerning Jehoiakim 3068
Jer 22:18 saying, Ah l.! or, Ah his glory! 113
Jer 22:24 As I live, saith the **L.**, though 3068
Jer 22:29 earth, hear the word of the **L.**. 3068
Jer 22:30 Thus saith the **L.**, Write ye this 3068
Jer 23:1 sheep of my pasture! saith the **L.**. 3068
Jer 23:2 thus saith the **L.** God of Israel 3068
Jer 23:2 evil of your doings, saith the **L.**. 3068
Jer 23:4 shall they be lacking, saith the **L.** 3068
Jer 23:5 the days come, saith the **L.**, that 3068
Jer 23:6 called, The **L.** Our Righteousness. 3068
Jer 23:7 the days come, saith the **L.**, that 3068
Jer 23:7, 8 The **L.** liveth, which brought up 3068
Jer 23:9 hath overcome, because of the **L.**, 3068
Jer 23:11 their wickedness, saith the **L.**. 3068
Jer 23:12 of their visitation, saith the **L.**. 3068
Jer 23:15 saith the **L.** of hosts concerning 3068
Jer 23:16 saith the **L.** of hosts, Hearken 3068
Jer 23:16 and not out of the mouth of the **L.**. 3068
Jer 23:17 The **L.** hath said, Ye shall have 3068
Jer 23:18 hath stood in the counsel of the **L.**, 3068
Jer 23:19 whirlwind of the **L.** is gone forth 3068
Jer 23:20 anger of the **L.** shall not return, 3068
Jer 23:23 Am I a God at hand, saith the **L.**, 3068
Jer 23:24 I shall not see him? saith the **L.**. 3068
Jer 23:24 heaven and earth? saith the **L.**. 3068
Jer 23:28 chaff to the wheat? saith the **L.**. 3068
Jer 23:29 word like as a fire? saith the **L.**; 3068
Jer 23:30, 31 the prophets, saith the **L.**, 3068
Jer 23:32 prophesy false dreams, saith the **L.**. 3068
Jer 23:32 this people at all, saith the **L.** 3068
Jer 23:33 What is the burden of the **L.**? 3068
Jer 23:33 will even forsake you, saith the **L.**. 3068
Jer 23:34 The burden of the **L.**, I will even 3068
Jer 23:35 What hath the **L.** answered? 3068
Jer 23:35 and, What hath the **L.** spoken? 3068
Jer 23:36 burden of the **L.** shall ye mention 3068
Jer 23:36 God, of the **L.** of hosts our God. 3068
Jer 23:37 What hath the **L.** answered thee? 3068
Jer 23:37 and, What hath the **L.** spoken? 3068
Jer 23:38 ye say, The burden of the **L.**; 3068
Jer 23:38 therefore thus saith the **L.**; 3068
Jer 23:38 this word, The burden of the **L.**, 3068
Jer 23:38 not say, The burden of the **L.**; 3068
Jer 24:1 The **L.** shewed me, and, behold, 3068
Jer 24:1 set before the temple of the **L.**, 3068
Jer 24:3 said the **L.** unto me, What seest 3068
Jer 24:4 the word of the **L.** came unto me, 3068
Jer 24:5 saith the **L.**, the God of Israel; 3068
Jer 24:7 to know me, that I am the **L.**: 3068
Jer 24:8 surely thus saith the **L.**, So will I 3068
Jer 25:3 word of the **L.** hath come unto me, 3068
Jer 25:4 the **L.** hath sent unto you all his 3068
Jer 25:5 in the land that the **L.** hath given 3068
Jer 25:7 hearkened unto me, saith the **L.**; 3068
Jer 25:8 thus saith the **L.** of hosts; Because 3068
Jer 25:9 of the north, saith the **L.**, and 3068
Jer 25:12 and that nation, saith the **L.**, for 3068
Jer 25:15 For thus saith the **L.** God of Israel 3068
Jer 25:17 unto whom the **L.** had sent me: 3068
Jer 25:27 Thus saith the **L.** of hosts, the God 3068
Jer 25:28 Thus saith the **L.** of hosts; Ye shall 3068
Jer 25:29 of the earth, saith the **L.** of hosts. 3068
Jer 25:30 The **L.** shall roar from on high, 3068
Jer 25:31 the **L.** hath a controversy with the 3068
Jer 25:31 wicked to the sword, saith the **L.**. 3068
Jer 25:32 Thus saith the **L.** of hosts, Behold, 3068
Jer 25:33 slain of the **L.** shall be at that day 3068
Jer 25:36 the **L.** hath spoiled their pasture. 3068
Jer 25:37 because of the fierce anger of the **L.**. 3068
Jer 26:1 Judah came this word from the **L.**, 3068
Jer 26:2 saith the **L.**; Stand in the court 3068
Jer 26:4 Thus saith the **L.**; If ye will not 3068
Jer 26:7 these words in the house of the **L.** 3068
Jer 26:8 all that the **L.** had commanded 3068
Jer 26:9 prophesied in the name of the **L.**, 3068
Jer 26:9 Jeremiah in the house of the **L.**. 3068
Jer 26:10 house unto the house of the **L.**, 3068
Jer 26:12 **L.** sent me to prophesy against 3068
Jer 26:13 obey the voice of the **L.** your God; 3068
Jer 26:13 **L.** will repent him of the evil that 3068
Jer 26:15 for of a truth the **L.** hath sent me 3068
Jer 26:16 us in the name of the **L.** our God. 3068
Jer 26:18 saith the **L.** of hosts; Zion shall 3068
Jer 26:19 fear the **L.**, and besought the **L.**, 3068
Jer 26:19 **L.** repented him of the evil which 3068
Jer 26:20 prophesied in the name of the **L.**, 3068
Jer 27:1 word unto Jeremiah from the **L.**, 3068
Jer 27:2 saith the **L.** to me; Make thee 3068
Jer 27:4 saith the **L.** of hosts, the God of 3068
Jer 27:8 nation will I punish, saith the **L.**, 3068
Jer 27:11 in their own land, saith the **L.**; 3068
Jer 27:13 as the **L.** hath spoken against the 3068
Jer 27:15 I have not sent them, saith the **L.**, 3068
Jer 27:16 Thus saith the **L.**; Hearken not to 3068
Jer 27:18 the word of the **L.** be with them, 3068
Jer 27:18 intercession to the **L.** of hosts, 3068
Jer 27:18 are left in the house of the **L.**, 3068
Jer 27:19 saith the **L.** of hosts concerning 3068
Jer 27:21 saith the **L.** of hosts, the God of 3068
Jer 27:21 remain in the house of the **L.**, 3068
Jer 27:22 day that I visit them, saith the **L.**; 3068
Jer 28:1 unto me in the house of the **L.**, 3068
Jer 28:2 speaketh the **L.** of hosts, the God 3068
Jer 28:4 went into Babylon, saith the **L.**: 3068
Jer 28:5 that stood in the house of the **L.**, 3068
Jer 28:6 the **L.** do so: the **L.** perform thy 3068
Jer 28:9 that the **L.** hath truly sent him. 3068
Jer 28:11 Thus saith the **L.**; Even so will I 3068
Jer 28:12 word of the **L.** came unto Jeremiah 3068
Jer 28:13 saith the **L.**; Thou hast broken 3068
Jer 28:14 saith the **L.** of hosts, the God of 3068
Jer 28:15 The **L.** hath not sent thee; but 3068
Jer 28:16 saith the **L.**; Behold, I will cast 3068
Jer 28:16 taught rebellion against the **L.**. 3068
Jer 29:4 saith the **L.** of hosts, the God of 3068
Jer 29:7 and pray unto the **L.** for it: for in 3068
Jer 29:8 saith the **L.** of hosts, the God of 3068
Jer 29:9 have not sent them, saith the **L.** 3068
Jer 29:10 saith the **L.**, That after seventy 3068
Jer 29:11 I think toward you, saith the **L.**, 3068
Jer 29:14 will be found of you, saith the **L.**: 3068
Jer 29:14 I have driven you, saith the **L.**; 3068
Jer 29:15 The **L.** hath raised us up prophets 3068
Jer 29:16 that thus saith the **L.** of the king 3068
Jer 29:17 saith the **L.** of hosts; Behold, I 3068
Jer 29:19 hearkened to my words...the **L.**, 3068
Jer 29:19 ye would not hear,saith the **L.** 3068
Jer 29:20 Hear ye...the word of the **L.**, all 3068
Jer 29:21 saith the **L.** of hosts, the God of 3068
Jer 29:22 **L.** make thee like Zedekiah and 3068
Jer 29:23 and am a witness, saith the **L.**. 3068
Jer 29:25 Thus speaketh the **L.** of hosts, the 3068
Jer 29:26 **L.** hath made thee priest in the 3068
Jer 29:26 be officers in the house of the **L.**, 3068
Jer 29:30 the word of the **L.** unto Jeremiah, 3068
Jer 29:31 saith the **L.** concerning Shemaiah 3068
Jer 29:32 thus saith the **L.**; Behold, I will 3068
Jer 29:32 will do for my people, saith the **L.**; 3068
Jer 29:32 taught rebellion against the **L.**. 3068
Jer 30:1 that came to Jeremiah from the **L.**, 3068
Jer 30:2 speaketh the **L.** God of Israel, 3068
Jer 30:3 the days come, saith the **L.**, that 3068
Jer 30:3 Israel and Judah, saith the **L.**: 3068
Jer 30:4 are the words that the **L.** spake 3068
Jer 30:5 thus saith the **L.**; We have heard 3068
Jer 30:8 saith the **L.** of hosts, that I will 3068
Jer 30:9 shall serve the **L.** their God, and 3068
Jer 30:10 O my servant Jacob, saith the **L.**; 3068
Jer 30:11 For I am with thee, saith the **L.**, 3068
Jer 30:12 thus saith the **L.**, Thy bruise is 3068
Jer 30:17 thee of thy wounds, saith the **L.**; 3068
Jer 30:18 Thus saith the **L.**; Behold, I will 3068
Jer 30:21 approach unto me? saith the **L.** 3068
Jer 30:23 whirlwind of the **L.** goeth forth 3068
Jer 30:24 anger of the **L.** shall not return, 3068
Jer 31:1 saith the **L.**, will I be the God of 3068
Jer 31:2 saith the **L.**, The people which 3068
Jer 31:3 **L.** hath appeared of old unto me, 3068
Jer 31:6 us go up to Zion unto the **L.** our 3068
Jer 31:7 saith the **L.**; Sing with gladness 3068

Jer	31:7	and say, O **L.**, save thy people,	3068
Jer	31:10	Hear the word of the **L.**, O ye	3068
Jer	31:11	For the **L.** hath redeemed Jacob,	3068
Jer	31:12	to the goodness of the **L.**, for	3068
Jer	31:14	with my goodness, saith the **L.**	3068
Jer	31:15	saith the **L.**; A voice was heard	3068
Jer	31:16	saith the **L.**; Refrain thy voice	3068
Jer	31:16	shall be rewarded, saith the **L.**;	3068
Jer	31:17	is hope in thine end, saith the **L.**,	3068
Jer	31:18	for thou art the **L.** my God	3068
Jer	31:20	mercy upon him, saith the **L.**.	3068
Jer	31:22	**L.** hath created a new thing in the	3068
Jer	31:23	saith the **L.** of hosts, the God of	3068
Jer	31:23	The **L.** bless thee, O habitation	3068
Jer	31:27	the days come, saith the **L.**, that	3068
Jer	31:28	build, and to plant, saith the **L.**	3068
Jer	31:31	the days come, saith the **L.**, that	3068
Jer	31:32	husband unto them, saith the **L.**:	3068
Jer	31:33	After those days, saith the **L.**, I	3068
Jer	31:34	Know the **L.**: for they shall all	3068
Jer	31:34	the greatest of them, saith the **L.**:	3068
Jer	31:35	Thus saith the **L.**, which giveth	3068
Jer	31:35	The **L.** of hosts is his name:	3068
Jer	31:36	from before me, saith the **L.**,	3068
Jer	31:37	saith the **L.**; If heaven above can	3068
Jer	31:37	that they have done, saith the **L.**.	3068
Jer	31:38	the days come, saith the **L.**, that	3068
Jer	31:38	city shall be built to the **L.** from	3068
Jer	31:40	east, shall be holy unto the **L.**;	3068
Jer	32:1	came to Jeremiah from the **L.** in	3068
Jer	32:3	Thus saith the **L.**, Behold, I will	3068
Jer	32:5	until I visit him, saith the **L.**:	3068
Jer	32:6	The word of the **L.** came unto me,	3068
Jer	32:8	according to the word of the **L.**,	3068
Jer	32:8	that this was the word of the **L.**.	3068
Jer	32:14	saith the **L.** of hosts, the God of	3068
Jer	32:15	For thus saith the **L.** of hosts,	3068
Jer	32:16	I prayed unto the **L.**, saying,	3068
Jer	32:17	Ah **L.** God! behold, thou hast made	136
Jer	32:18	God, The **L.** of hosts, is his name,	3068
Jer	32:25	thou hast said unto me, O **L.** God,	136
Jer	32:26	the word of the **L.** unto Jeremiah,	3068
Jer	32:27	Behold, I am the **L.**, the God of	3068
Jer	32:28	Therefore thus saith the **L.**;	3068
Jer	32:30	work of their hands, saith the **L.**	3068
Jer	32:36	therefore thus saith the **L.**, the	3068
Jer	32:42	For thus saith the **L.**; Like as I	3068
Jer	32:44	captivity to return, saith the **L.**	3068
Jer	33:1	the word of the **L.** came unto	3068
Jer	33:2	saith the **L.** the maker thereof,	3068
Jer	33:2	the **L.** that formed it, to establish	3068
Jer	33:2	establish it; The **L.** is his name;	3068
Jer	33:4	For thus saith the **L.**, the God of	3068
Jer	33:10	Thus saith the **L.**; again there	3068
Jer	33:11	shall say, Praise the **L.** of hosts:	3068
Jer	33:11	for the **L.** is good; for his mercy	3068
Jer	33:11	of praise into the house of the **L.**	3068
Jer	33:11	land, as at the first, saith the **L.**.	3068
Jer	33:12	Thus saith the **L.** of hosts; Again	3068
Jer	33:13	that telleth them, saith the **L.**.	3068
Jer	33:14	saith the **L.**, that I will perform	3068
Jer	33:16	called, The **L.** our righteousness.	3068
Jer	33:17	For thus saith the **L.**; David shall	3068
Jer	33:19	And the word of the **L.** came unto	3068
Jer	33:20	Thus saith the **L.**; If ye can break	3068
Jer	33:23	word of the **L.** came to Jeremiah,	3068
Jer	33:24	two families which the **L.** hath	3068
Jer	33:25	Thus saith the **L.**; If my covenant	3068
Jer	34:1	came unto Jeremiah from the **L.**,	3068
Jer	34:2	Thus saith the **L.**, the God of	3068
Jer	34:2	and tell him, Thus saith the **L.**;	3068
Jer	34:4	Yet hear the word of the **L.**, O	3068
Jer	34:4	Thus saith the **L.** of thee, Thou	3068
Jer	34:5	will lament thee, saying, Ah **l.**!	113
Jer	34:5	pronounced the word, saith the **L.**	3068
Jer	34:8	came unto Jeremiah from the **L.**,	3068
Jer	34:12	word of the **L.** came to Jeremiah	3068
Jer	34:12	came to Jeremiah from the **L.**,	3068
Jer	34:13	Thus saith the **L.**, the God of	3068
Jer	34:17	thus saith the **L.**; Ye have not	3068
Jer	34:17	a liberty for you, saith the **L.**,	3068
Jer	34:22	I will command, saith the **L.**, and	3068
Jer	35:1	came unto Jeremiah from the **L.**,	3068
Jer	35:2,	4 them into the house of the **L.**,	3068
Jer	35:12	the word of the **L.** unto Jeremiah,	3068
Jer	35:13	Thus saith the **L.** of hosts, the	3068
Jer	35:13	to my words? saith the **L.**.	3068
Jer	35:17	thus saith the **L.** God of hosts,	3068
Jer	35:18	Thus saith the **L.** of hosts, the	3068
Jer	35:19	thus saith the **L.** of hosts, the	3068
Jer	36:1	came unto Jeremiah from the **L.**,	3068
Jer	36:4	Jeremiah all the words of the **L.**,	3068
Jer	36:5	go into the house of the **L.**:	3068
Jer	36:6	words of the **L.** in the ears of the	3068
Jer	36:7	their supplication before the **L.**,	3068
Jer	36:7	fury that the **L.** hath pronounced	3068
Jer	36:8	in the book the words of the **L.** in	3068
Jer	36:9	proclaimed a fast before the **L.**	3068
Jer	36:10	Jeremiah in the house of the **L.**,	3068
Jer	36:11	the book all the words of the **L.**,	3068
Jer	36:26	the prophet: but the **L.** hid them.	3068
Jer	36:27	word of the **L.** came to Jeremiah,	3068
Jer	36:29	Thus saith the **L.**; Thou hast	3068
Jer	36:30	saith the **L.** of Jehoiakim king of	3068
Jer	37:2	hearken unto the words of the **L.**,	3068
Jer	37:3	Pray now unto the **L.** our God	3068
Jer	37:6	word of the **L.** unto the prophet	3068
Jer	37:7	Thus saith the **L.**, the God of	3068
Jer	37:9	Thus saith the **L.**; Deceive not	3068
Jer	37:17	Is there any word from the **L.**?	3068
Jer	37:20	I pray thee, O my **l.** the king;	113
Jer	38:2	Thus saith the **L.**, He that	3068
Jer	38:3	Thus saith the L., This city shall	3068
Jer	38:9	My **l.** the king, these men have	113
Jer	38:14	that is in the house of the **L.**:	3068
Jer	38:16	As the **L.** liveth, that made us this	3068
Jer	38:17	unto Zedekiah, Thus saith the **L.**,	3068
Jer	38:20	I beseech thee, the voice of the **L.**,	3068
Jer	38:21	the word that the **L.** hath shewed	3068
Jer	39:15	the word of the **L.** came unto	3068
Jer	39:16	saith the **L.** of hosts, the God of	3068
Jer	39:17	thee in that day, saith the **L.**:	3068
Jer	39:18	put thy trust in me, saith the **L.**.	3068
Jer	40:1	came to Jeremiah from the **L.**,	3068
Jer	40:2	**L.** thy God hath pronounced this	3068
Jer	40:3	Now the **L.** hath brought it, and	3068
Jer	40:3	ye have sinned against the **L.**,	3068
Jer	41:5	bring them to the house of the **L.**.	3068
Jer	42:2	pray for us unto the **L.** thy God,	3068
Jer	42:3	**L.** thy God may shew us the way	3068
Jer	42:4	I will pray unto the **L.** your God	3068
Jer	42:4	thing the **L.** shall answer you, I	3068
Jer	42:5	**L.** be a true and faithful witness	3068
Jer	42:5	**L.** thy God shall send thee to us.	3068
Jer	42:6	will obey the voice of the **L.** our	3068
Jer	42:6	we obey the voice of the **L.** our	3068
Jer	42:7	the word of the **L.** came unto	3068
Jer	42:9	saith the **L.**, the God of Israel,	3068
Jer	42:11	not afraid of him, saith the **L.**:	3068
Jer	42:13	neither obey the voice of the **L.**	3068
Jer	42:15	therefore hear the word of the **L.**,	3068
Jer	42:15,	18 saith the **L.** of hosts, the God	3068
Jer	42:19	The **L.** hath said concerning you,	3068
Jer	42:20	ye sent me unto the **L.** your God,	3068
Jer	42:20	Pray for us unto the **L.** our God;	3068
Jer	42:20	all that the **L.** our God shall say,	3068
Jer	42:21	not obeyed the voice of the **L.**	3068
Jer	43:1	all the words of the **L.** their God,	3068
Jer	43:1	the **L.** their God had sent him	3068
Jer	43:2	**L.** our God hath not sent thee to	3068
Jer	43:4	obeyed not the voice of the **L.**,	3068
Jer	43:7	obeyed not the voice of the **L.**:	3068
Jer	43:8	the word of the **L.** unto Jeremiah	3068
Jer	43:10	saith the **L.** of hosts, the God of	3068
Jer	44:2	saith the **L.** of hosts, the God of	3068
Jer	44:7	thus saith the **L.**, the God of hosts,	3068
Jer	44:11	saith the **L.** of hosts, the God of	3068
Jer	44:16	unto us in the name of the **L.**,	3068
Jer	44:21	did not the **L.** remember them,	3068
Jer	44:22	that the **L.** could no longer bear,	3068
Jer	44:23	ye have sinned against the **L.**,	3068
Jer	44:23	not obeyed the voice of the **L.**,	3068
Jer	44:24	Hear the word of the **L.**, all Judah	3068
Jer	44:25	saith the **L.** of hosts, the God of	3068
Jer	44:26	hear ye the word of the **L.**, all	3068
Jer	44:26	by my great name, saith the **L.**,	3068
Jer	44:26	Egypt, saying, The **L.** God liveth.	136
Jer	44:29	be a sign unto you, saith the **L.**,	3068
Jer	44:30	Thus saith the **L.**; Behold, I will	3068
Jer	45:2	saith the **L.**, the God of Israel,	3068
Jer	45:3	**L.** hath added grief to my sorrow;	3068
Jer	45:4	The **L.** saith thus; Behold, that	3068
Jer	45:5	evil upon all flesh, saith the **L.**:	3068
Jer	46:1	The word of the **L.** which came to	3068
Jer	46:5	was round about, saith the **L.**	3068
Jer	46:10	is the day of the **L.** God of hosts,	136
Jer	46:10	**L.** God of hosts hath a sacrifice in	136
Jer	46:13	The word that the **L.** spake to	3068
Jer	46:15	because the **L.** did drive them.	3068
Jer	46:18	whose name is the **L.** of hosts,	3068
Jer	46:23	cut down her forest, saith the **L.**,	3068
Jer	46:25	The **L.** of hosts, the God of Israel,	3068
Jer	46:26	in the days of old, saith the **L.**.	3068
Jer	46:28	O Jacob my servant, saith the **L.**:	3068
Jer	47:1	The word of the **L.** that came to	3068
Jer	47:2	Thus saith the **L.**; Behold, waters	3068
Jer	47:4	the **L.** will spoil the Philistines,	3068
Jer	47:6	O thou sword of the **L.**, how long	3068
Jer	47:7	seeing the **L.** hath given it a	3068
Jer	48:1	Against Moab thus saith the **L.**	3068
Jer	48:8	destroyed, as the **L.** hath spoken.	3068
Jer	48:10	he that doeth the work of the **L.**	3068
Jer	48:12	the days come, saith the **L.**, that	3068
Jer	48:15	whose name is the **L.** of hosts.	3068
Jer	48:25	his arm is broken, saith the **L.**.	3068
Jer	48:26	magnified himself against the **L.**:	3068
Jer	48:30	I know his wrath, saith the **L.**;	3068
Jer	48:35	to cease in Moab, saith the **L.**,	3068
Jer	48:38	is no pleasure, saith the **L.**.	3068
Jer	48:40	thus saith the **L.**; Behold, he shall	3068
Jer	48:42	magnified himself against the **L.**.	3068
Jer	48:43	inhabitant of Moab, saith the **L.**.	3068
Jer	48:44	of their visitation, saith the **L.**.	3068
Jer	48:47	in the latter days, saith the **L.**	3068
Jer	49:1	the Ammonites, thus saith the **L.**;	3068
Jer	49:2	saith the **L.**, that I will cause an	3068
Jer	49:2	that were his heirs, saith the **L.**.	3068
Jer	49:5	a fear upon thee, saith the **L.**	136
Jer	49:6	children of Ammon, saith the **L.**	3068
Jer	49:7	concerning Edom, thus saith the **L.**	3068
Jer	49:12	For thus saith the **L.**; Behold,	3068
Jer	49:13	sworn by myself, saith the **L.**,	3068
Jer	49:14	have heard a rumour from the **L.**,	3068
Jer	49:16	down from thence, saith the **L.**	3068
Jer	49:18	saith the **L.**, no man shall abide	3068
Jer	49:20	hear the counsel of the **L.**, that he	3068
Jer	49:26	cut off in that day, saith the **L.** of	3068
Jer	49:28	shall smite, thus saith the **L.**;	3068
Jer	49:30	inhabitants of Hazor, saith the **L.**;	3068
Jer	49:31	without care, saith the **L.**, which	3068
Jer	49:32	all sides thereof, saith the **L.**.	3068
Jer	49:34	The word of the **L.** that came to	3068
Jer	49:35	Thus saith the **L.** of hosts, Behold,	3068
Jer	49:37	even my fierce anger, saith the **L.**;	3068
Jer	49:38	and the princes, saith the **L.**.	3068
Jer	49:39	captivity of Elam, saith the **L.**.	3068
Jer	50:1	word that the **L.** spake against	3068
Jer	50:4	saith the **L.**, the children of Israel	3068
Jer	50:4	go, and seek the **L.** their God.	3068
Jer	50:5	and let us join ourselves to the **L.**	3068
Jer	50:7	they have sinned against the **L.**,	3068
Jer	50:7	even the **L.**, the hope of their	3068
Jer	50:10	her shall be satisfied, saith the **L.**.	3068
Jer	50:13	Because of the wrath of the **L.** it	3068
Jer	50:14	she hath sinned against the **L.**.	3068
Jer	50:15	for it is the vengeance of the **L.**:	3068
Jer	50:18	saith the **L.** of hosts, the God of	3068
Jer	50:20	saith the **L.**, the iniquity of Israel	3068
Jer	50:21	destroy after them, saith the **L.**,	3068
Jer	50:24	thou hast striven against the **L.**.	3068
Jer	50:25	The **L.** hath opened his armoury,	3068
Jer	50:25	for this is the work of the **L.** God	136
Jer	50:28	the vengeance of the **L.** our God,	3068
Jer	50:29	hath been proud against the **L.**,	3068
Jer	50:30	cut off in that day, saith the **L.**	3068
Jer	50:31	most proud, saith the **L.** God of	136
Jer	50:33	Thus saith the **L.** of hosts; The	3068
Jer	50:34	The **L.** of hosts is his name: he	3068
Jer	50:35	upon the Chaldeans, saith the **L.**,	3068
Jer	50:40	cities thereof, saith the **L.**;	3068
Jer	50:45	hear ye the counsel of the **L.**, that	3068
Jer	51:1	Thus saith the **L.**; Behold, I will	3068
Jer	51:5	of his God, of the **L.** of hosts;	3068
Jer	51:10	The **L.** hath brought forth our	3068
Jer	51:10	declare in Zion the work of the **L.**	3068
Jer	51:11	the **L.** hath raised up the spirit	3068
Jer	51:11	it is the vengeance of the **L.**,	3068
Jer	51:12	**L.** hath both devised and done	3068
Jer	51:14	**L.** of hosts hath sworn by himself,	3068
Jer	51:19	The **L.** of hosts is his name.	3068
Jer	51:24	Zion in your sight, saith the **L.**	3068

Jer	51:25	destroying mountain, saith the **L.**,	3068
Jer	51:26	be desolate for ever, saith the **L.**.	3068
Jer	51:29	every purpose of the **L.** shall be	3068
Jer	51:33	saith the **L.** of hosts, the God of	3068
Jer	51:36	thus saith the **L.**; Behold, I will	3068
Jer	51:39	and not awake, saith the **L.**.	3068
Jer	51:45	from the fierce anger of the **L.**.	3068
Jer	51:48	her from the north, saith the **L.**.	3068
Jer	51:50	remember the **L.** afar off, and let	3068
Jer	51:52	the days come, saith the **L.**, that	3068
Jer	51:53	come unto her, saith the **L.**.	3068
Jer	51:55	the **L.** hath spoiled Babylon, and	3068
Jer	51:56	the **L.** God of recompenses shall	3068
Jer	51:57	whose name is the **L.** of hosts.	3068
Jer	51:58	Thus said the **L.** of hosts; The	3068
Jer	51:62	O **L.**, thou hast spoken against	3068
Jer	52:2	was evil in the eyes of the **L.**,	3068
Jer	52:3	through the anger of the **L.** it	3068
Jer	52:13	burned the house of the **L.**, and	3068
Jer	52:17	that were in the house of the **L.**.	3068
Jer	52:17	that was in the house of the **L.**,	3068
Jer	52:20	had made in the house of the **L.**:	3068
La	1:5	the **L.** hath afflicted her for the	3068
La	1:9	O **L.**, behold my affliction: for	3068
La	1:11	see, O **L.**, and consider: for I am	3068
La	1:12	wherewith the **L.** hath afflicted	3068
La	1:14	the **L.** hath delivered me into their	136
La	1:15	**L.** hath trodden under foot all my	136
La	1:15	the **L.** hath trodden the virgin, the	136
La	1:17	the **L.** hath commanded...Jacob,	3068
La	1:18	The **L.** is righteous; for I have	3068
La	1:20	Behold, O **L.**; for I am in distress:	3068
La	2:1	hath the **L.** covered the daughter	136
La	2:2	The **L.** hath swallowed up all the	136
La	2:5	The **L.** was as an enemy: he hath	136
La	2:6	**L.** hath caused the solemn feasts	3068
La	2:7	the **L.** hath cast off his altar, he	136
La	2:7	a noise in the house of the **L.**,	3068
La	2:8	the **L.** hath purposed to destroy	3068
La	2:9	also find no vision from the **L.**.	3068
La	2:17	**L.** hath done that which he had	3068
La	2:18	Their heart cried unto the **L.**, O	136
La	2:19	water before the face of the **L.**:	136
La	2:20	Behold, O **L.**, and consider to	3068
La	2:20	be slain in the sanctuary of the **L.**?	136
La	3:18	my hope is perished from the **L.**:	3068
La	3:24	The **L.** is my portion, saith my	3068
La	3:25	**L.** is good unto them that wait	3068
La	3:26	wait for the salvation of the **L.**.	3068
La	3:31	For the **L.** will not cast off for ever:	136
La	3:36	in his cause, the **L.** approveth not.	136
La	3:37	when the **L.** commandeth it not?	136
La	3:40	ways, and turn again to the **L.**.	3068
La	3:50	Till the **L.** look down, and behold	3068
La	3:55	I called upon thy name, O **L.**, out	3068
La	3:58	O **L.**, thou hast pleaded the causes	136
La	3:59	O **L.**, thou hast seen my wrong:	3068
La	3:61	hast heard their reproach, O **L.**,	3068
La	3:64	unto them a recompense, O **L.**,	3068
La	3:66	from under the heavens of the **L.**	3068
La	4:11	**L.** hath accomplished his fury;	3068
La	4:16	The anger of the **L.** hath divided	3068
La	4:20	nostrils, the anointed of the **L.**,	3068
La	5:1	Remember, O **L.**, what is come	3068
La	5:19	Thou, O **L.**, remainest for ever;	3068
La	5:21	Turn thou us unto thee, O **L.**,	3068
Eze	1:3	The word of the **L.** came expressly	3068
Eze	1:3	the hand of the **L.** was there upon	3068
Eze	1:28	likeness of the glory of the **L.**.	3068
Eze	2:4	unto them, Thus saith the **L.** God.	136
Eze	3:11	tell them, Thus saith the **L.** God;	136
Eze	3:12	Blessed be the glory of the **L.**	3068
Eze	3:14	hand of the **L.** was strong upon	3068
Eze	3:16	the word of the **L.** came unto me,	3068
Eze	3:22	hand of the **L.** was there upon me;	3068
Eze	3:23	the glory of the **L.** stood there,	3068
Eze	3:27	Thus saith the **L.** God; He that	136
Eze	4:13	And the **L.** said, Even thus shall	3068
Eze	4:14	said I, Ah **L.** God! behold, my soul	136
Eze	5:5	Thus saith the **L.** God; This is	136
Eze	5:7,	8 Therefore thus saith the **L.** God;	136
Eze	5:11	as I live, saith the **L.** God; Surely,	136
Eze	5:13	the **L.** have spoken it in my zeal,	3068
Eze	5:15	rebukes. I the **L.** have spoken it.	3068
Eze	5:17	thee. I the **L.** have spoken it.	3068
Eze	6:1	the word of the **L.** came unto me,	3068
Eze	6:3	hear the word of the **L.** God; Thus	136
Eze	6:3	Thus saith the **L.** God to the	136
Eze	6:7	ye shall know that I am the **L.**.	3068
Eze	6:10	they shall know that I am the **L.**,	3068
Eze	6:11	Thus saith the **L.** God; Smite with	136
Eze	6:13	shall ye know that I am the **L.**,	3068
Eze	6:14	they shall know that I am the **L.**.	3068
Eze	7:1	the word of the **L.** came unto me,	3068
Eze	7:2	saith the **L.** God unto the land of	136
Eze	7:4	ye shall know that I am the **L.**.	3068
Eze	7:5	Thus saith the **L.** God; An evil,	136
Eze	7:9	that I am the **L.** that smiteth	3068
Eze	7:19	in the day of the wrath of the **L.**:	3068
Eze	7:27	they shall know that I am the **L.**.	3068
Eze	8:1	hand of the **L.** God fell there upon	136
Eze	8:12	they say, The **L.** seeth us not;	3068
Eze	8:12	the **L.** hath forsaken the earth.	3068
Eze	8:16	at the door of the temple of the **L.**,	3068
Eze	8:16	backs toward the temple of the **L.**,	3068
Eze	9:4	the **L.** said unto him, Go through	3068
Eze	9:8	Ah **L.** God! wilt thou destroy all	136
Eze	9:9	The **L.** hath forsaken the earth,	3068
Eze	9:9	the earth, and the **L.** seeth not.	3068
Eze	10:4	the glory of the **L.** went up from	3068
Eze	10:18	the glory of the **L.** departed from	3068
Eze	11:5	the Spirit of the **L.** fell upon me,	3068
Eze	11:5	Thus saith the **L.**; Thus have ye	3068
Eze	11:7	thus saith the **L.** God; Your slain	136
Eze	11:8	sword upon you, saith the **L.** God.	136
Eze	11:10	ye shall know that I am the **L.**.	3068
Eze	11:12	ye shall know that I am the **L.**:	3068
Eze	11:13	Ah **L.** God! wilt thou make a full	136
Eze	11:14	the word of the **L.** came unto me,	3068
Eze	11:15	have said, Get you far from the **L.**:	3068
Eze	11:16,	17 say, Thus saith the **L.** God;	136
Eze	11:21	their own heads, saith the **L.** God.	136
Eze	11:23	the glory of the **L.** went up from	3068
Eze	11:25	things that the **L.** had shewed me.	3068
Eze	12:1	word of the **L.** also came unto me,	3068
Eze	12:8	came the word of the **L.** unto me,	3068
Eze	12:10	unto them, Thus saith the **L.** God;	136
Eze	12:15	they shall know that I am the **L.**,	3068
Eze	12:16	they shall know that I am the **L.**.	3068
Eze	12:17	the word of the **L.** came to me,	3068
Eze	12:19	saith the **L.** God of the inhabitants	136
Eze	12:20	ye shall know that I am the **L.**.	3068
Eze	12:21	the word of the **L.** came unto me,	3068
Eze	12:23	Thus saith the **L.** God; I will make	136
Eze	12:25	I am the **L.**: I will speak, and the	3068
Eze	12:25	will perform it, saith the **L.** God.	136
Eze	12:26	the word of the **L.** came to me,	3068
Eze	12:28	saith the **L.** God; There shall	136
Eze	12:28	shall be done, saith the **L.** God.	136
Eze	13:1	the word of the **L.** came unto me,	3068
Eze	13:2	Hear ye the word of the **L.**;	3068
Eze	13:3	Thus saith the **L.** God; Woe unto	136
Eze	13:5	in the battle in the day of the **L.**.	3068
Eze	13:6	The **L.** saith: and the **L.** hath not	3068
Eze	13:7	whereas ye say, The **L.** saith it;	3068
Eze	13:8	thus saith the **L.** God; Because	136
Eze	13:8	I am against you, saith the **L.** God.	136
Eze	13:9	ye shall know that I am the **L.** God.	136
Eze	13:13	saith the **L.** God; I will even rend	136
Eze	13:14	ye shall know that I am the **L.**.	3068
Eze	13:16	there is no peace, saith the **L.** God.	136
Eze	13:18	Thus saith the **L.** God; Woe to the	136
Eze	13:20	Thus saith the **L.** God; Behold, I	136
Eze	13:21,	23 ye shall know that I am the **L.**.	3068
Eze	14:2	the word of the **L.** came unto me,	3068
Eze	14:4	Thus saith the **L.** God: Every man	136
Eze	14:4	**L.** will answer him that cometh	3068
Eze	14:6	of Israel, Thus saith the **L.** God;	136
Eze	14:7	**L.** will answer him by myself:	3068
Eze	14:8	ye shall know that I am the **L.**.	3068
Eze	14:9	**L.** have deceived that prophet,	3068
Eze	14:11	may be their God, saith the **L.** God.	136
Eze	14:12	word of the **L.** came again to me,	3068
Eze	14:14	righteousness, saith the **L.** God.	136
Eze	14:16,	18, 20 as I live, saith the **L.** God, they.	136
Eze	14:21	thus saith the **L.** God; How much	136
Eze	14:23	I have done in it, saith the **L.** God.	136
Eze	15:1	the word of the **L.** came unto me,	3068
Eze	15:6	thus saith the **L.** God; As the vine	136
Eze	15:7	ye shall know that I am the **L.**,	3068
Eze	15:8	a trespass, saith the **L.** God.	136
Eze	16:1	the word of the **L.** came unto me,	3068
Eze	16:3	saith the **L.** God unto Jerusalem;	136
Eze	16:8	covenant with thee, saith the **L.** God,	136
Eze	16:14	had put upon thee, saith the **L.** God.	136
Eze	16:19	and thus it was, saith the **L.** God.	136
Eze	16:23	woe unto thee! saith the **L.** God,)	136
Eze	16:30	weak is thine heart, saith the **L.** God,	136
Eze	16:35	O harlot, hear the word of the **L.**:	3068
Eze	16:36	Thus saith the **L.** God; Because	136
Eze	16:43	upon thine head, saith the **L.** God:	136
Eze	16:48	saith the **L.** God, Sodom thy sister	136
Eze	16:58	thine abominations, saith the **L.**.	3068
Eze	16:59	thus saith the **L.** God; I will even	136
Eze	16:62	thou shalt know that I am the **L.**:	3068
Eze	16:63	thou hast done, saith the **L.** God.	136
Eze	17:1	the word of the **L.** came unto me,	3068
Eze	17:3	saith the **L.** God; A great eagle	136
Eze	17:9	saith the **L.** God; Shall it prosper?	136
Eze	17:11	the word of the **L.** came unto me,	3068
Eze	17:16	As I live, saith the **L.** God, surely	136
Eze	17:19	Therefore thus saith the **L.** God; As	136
Eze	17:21	know that I the **L.** have spoken it.	3068
Eze	17:22	Thus saith the **L.** God; I will also	136
Eze	17:24	I the **L.** have brought down the	3068
Eze	17:24	**L.** have spoken and have done it.	3068
Eze	18:1	The word of the **L.** came unto me	3068
Eze	18:3	As I live, saith the **L.** God, ye shall	136
Eze	18:9	shall surely live, saith the **L.** God.	136
Eze	18:23	wicked should die? saith the **L.** God:	136
Eze	18:25	ye say, The way of the **L.** is not equal.	136
Eze	18:29	Israel, The way of the **L.** is not equal.	136
Eze	18:30	to his ways, saith the **L.** God.	136
Eze	18:32	of him that dieth, saith the **L.** God:	136
Eze	20:1	Israel came to enquire of the **L.**,	3068
Eze	20:2	came the word of the **L.** unto me,	3068
Eze	20:3	saith the **L.** God; Are ye come to	136
Eze	20:3	As I live, saith the **L.** God, I will not	136
Eze	20:5	Thus saith the **L.** God; In the day	136
Eze	20:5	saying, I am the **L.** your God;	3068
Eze	20:7	of Egypt: I am the **L.** your God.	3068
Eze	20:12	I am the **L.** that sanctify them.	3068
Eze	20:19	I am the **L.** your God; walk in my	3068
Eze	20:20	know that I am the **L.** your God.	3068
Eze	20:26	they might know that I am the **L.**.	3068
Eze	20:27	saith the **L.** God; Yet in this your	136
Eze	20:30	saith the **L.** God; Are ye polluted	136
Eze	20:31	As I live, saith the **L.** God, I will not	136
Eze	20:33	As I live, saith the **L.** God, surely	136
Eze	20:36	I plead with you, saith the **L.** God.	136
Eze	20:38	ye shall know that I am the **L.**.	3068
Eze	20:39	saith the **L.** God; Go ye, serve ye	136
Eze	20:40	the height of Israel, saith the **L.** God,	136
Eze	20:42,	44 shall know that I am the **L.**,	3068
Eze	20:44	ye house of Israel, saith the **L.** God.	136
Eze	20:45	the word of the **L.** came unto me,	3068
Eze	20:47	the south, Hear the word of the **L.**;	3068
Eze	20:47	Thus saith the **L.** God; Behold, I	136
Eze	20:48	see that I the **L.** have kindled it:	3068
Eze	20:49	Ah **L.** God! they say of me, Doth he	136
Eze	21:1	the word of the **L.** came unto me,	3068
Eze	21:3	Thus saith the **L.**; Behold, I am	3068
Eze	21:5	I the **L.** have drawn forth my sword	3068
Eze	21:7	brought to pass, saith the **L.** God.	136
Eze	21:8	the word of the **L.** came unto me,	3068
Eze	21:9	Thus saith the **L.**; Say, A sword,	3068
Eze	21:13	shall be no more, saith the **L.** God.	136
Eze	21:17	fury to rest: I the **L.** have said it.	3068
Eze	21:18	word of the **L.** came unto me again,	3068
Eze	21:24	thus saith the **L.** God; Because ye	136
Eze	21:26	thus saith the **L.** God; Remove the	136
Eze	21:28	thus saith the **L.** God concerning the	136
Eze	21:32	for I the **L.** have spoken it.	3068
Eze	22:1	the word of the **L.** came unto me,	3068
Eze	22:3	Thus saith the **L.** God; The city	136
Eze	22:12	hast forgotten me, saith the **L.** God.	136
Eze	22:14	I the **L.** have spoken it, and will	3068
Eze	22:16	thou shalt know that I am the **L.**.	3068
Eze	22:17	the word of the **L.** came unto me,	3068
Eze	22:19	Therefore thus saith the **L.** God;	136
Eze	22:22	I the **L.** have poured out my fury	3068
Eze	22:23	the word of the **L.** came unto me,	3068
Eze	22:28	saying, Thus saith the **L.** God,	136
Eze	22:28	when the **L.** hath not spoken.	3068
Eze	22:31	upon their heads, saith the **L.** God	136
Eze	23:1	word of the **L.** came again unto	3068
Eze	23:22	O Aholibah, thus saith the **L.** God;	136
Eze	23:28	For thus saith the **L.** God; Behold, I	136
Eze	23:32	Thus saith the **L.** God; Thou shalt	136
Eze	23:34	I have spoken it, saith the **L.** God.	136
Eze	23:35	Therefore thus saith the **L.** God;	136

Eze 23:36 **L.** said moreover unto me; Son of...... 3068
Eze 23:46 thus saith the **L.** God; I will bring........ 136
Eze 23:49 ye shall know that I am the **L.** God. 136
Eze 24:1 the word of the **L.** came unto me, ... 3068
Eze 24:3 Thus saith the **L.** God; Set on a pot, ... 136
Eze 24:6, 9 saith the **L.** God; Woe to the bloody . 136
Eze 24:14 I the **L.** have spoken it: it shall 3068
Eze 24:14 they judge thee, saith the **L.** God........ 136
Eze 24:15 the word of the **L.** came unto me, ... 3068
Eze 24:20 The word of the **L.** came unto me, ... 3068
Eze 24:21 Thus saith the **L.** God; Behold, I......... 136
Eze 24:24 ye shall know that I am the **L.** God. 136
Eze 24:27 they shall know that I am the **L.**........ 3068
Eze 25:1 word of the **L.** came again unto......... 3068
Eze 25:3 Hear the word of the L. God;............ 136
Eze 25:3 Thus saith the **L.** God; Because.......... 136
Eze 25:5 ye shall know that I am the **L.**. 3068
Eze 25:6 For thus saith the **L.** God; Because..... 136
Eze 25:7 thou shalt know that I am the **L.**. 3068
Eze 25:8 Thus saith the **L.** God; Because.......... 136
Eze 25:11 they shall know that I am the **L.**........ 3068
Eze 25:12 Thus saith the **L.** God; Because.......... 136
Eze 25:13 Therefore thus saith the **L.** God;......... 136
Eze 25:14 my vengeance, saith the **L.** God.......... 136
Eze 25:15 Thus saith the **L.** God; Because.......... 136
Eze 25:16 Therefore thus saith the **L.** God;......... 136
Eze 25:17 they shall know that I am the **L.**,....... 3068
Eze 26:1 the word of the **L.** came unto me, ... 3068
Eze 26:3 Therefore thus saith the **L.** God;......... 136
Eze 26:5 I have spoken it, saith the **L.** God: 136
Eze 26:6 they shall know that I am the **L.**......... 3068
Eze 26:7 For thus saith the **L.** God; Behold, ... 136
Eze 26:14 for I the **L.** have spoken it, saith 3068
Eze 26:14 I...have spoken it, saith the **L.** God. 136
Eze 26:15 Thus saith the **L.** God to Tyrus; 136
Eze 26:19 thus saith the **L.** God; When I shall 136
Eze 26:21 be found again, saith the **L.** God. 136
Eze 27:1 word of the **L.** came again unto......... 3068
Eze 27:3 Thus saith the **L.** God; O Tyrus,......... 136
Eze 28:1 word of the **L.** came again unto......... 3068
Eze 28:2 Thus saith the **L.** God; Because......... 136
Eze 28:6 thus saith the **L.** God; Because thou 136
Eze 28:10 I have spoken it, saith the **L.** God. 136
Eze 28:11 the word of the **L.** came unto me, ... 3068
Eze 28:12 Thus saith the **L.** God; Thou sealest 136
Eze 28:20 the word of the **L.** came unto me, ... 3068
Eze 28:22 Thus saith the **L.** God; Behold, I......... 136
Eze 28:22 they shall know that I am the **L.**,........ 3068
Eze 28:23 they shall know that I am the **L.**........ 3068
Eze 28:24 shall know that I am the **L.** God.......... 136
Eze 28:25 Thus saith the **L.** God; When I shall 136
Eze 28:26 know that I am the **L.** their God........ 3068
Eze 29:1 the word of the **L.** came unto me, ... 3068
Eze 29:3 Thus saith the **L.** God; Behold, I......... 136
Eze 29:6 Egypt shall know that I am the **L.**,..... 3068
Eze 29:8 Therefore thus saith the **L.** God;......... 136
Eze 29:9 they shall know that I am the **L.**:........ 3068
Eze 29:13 thus saith the **L.** God; At the end........ 136
Eze 29:16 they shall know that I am the **L.** God.. 136
Eze 29:17 the word of the **L.** came unto me, ... 3068
Eze 29:19 Therefore thus saith the **L.** God;......... 136
Eze 29:20 wrought for me, saith the **L.** God. 136
Eze 29:21 they shall know that I am the **L.**........ 3068
Eze 30:1 word of the **L.** came again unto......... 3068
Eze 30:2 Thus saith the **L.** God; Behold, I......... 136
Eze 30:3 even the day of the **L.** is near,........... 3068
Eze 30:6 Thus saith the **L.**; They also that....... 3068
Eze 30:6 in it by the sword, saith the **L.** God..... 136
Eze 30:8 they shall know that I am the **L.**,....... 3068
Eze 30:10 Thus saith the **L.** God; I will also........ 136
Eze 30:12 strangers: I the **L.** have spoken it...... 3068
Eze 30:13 Thus saith the **L.** God; I will also........ 136
Eze 30:19 they shall know that I am the **L.**........ 3068
Eze 30:20 the word of the **L.** came unto me, ... 3068
Eze 30:22 Therefore thus saith the **L.** God;......... 136
Eze 30:25 they shall know that I am the **L.**,....... 3068
Eze 30:26 they shall know that I am the **L.**........ 3068
Eze 31:1 the word of the **L.** came unto me, ... 3068
Eze 31:10 Therefore thus saith the **L.** God;......... 136
Eze 31:15 Thus saith the **L.** God; In the day 136
Eze 31:18 all his multitude, saith the **L.** God........ 136
Eze 32:1 the word of the **L.** came unto me, ... 3068
Eze 32:3 saith the **L.** God; I will therefore......... 136
Eze 32:8 upon thy land, saith the **L.** God.......... 136
Eze 32:11 thus saith the **L.** God; The sword........ 136
Eze 32:14 to run like oil, saith the **L.** God.......... 136
Eze 32:15 shall they know that I am the **L.**........ 3068
Eze 32:16 all her multitude, saith the **L.** God. 136
Eze 32:17 the word of the **L.** came unto me, ... 3068
Eze 32:31 by the sword, saith the **L.** God. 136
Eze 32:32 all his multitude, saith the **L.** God....... 136
Eze 33:1 the word of the **L.** came unto me, ... 3068
Eze 33:11 As I live, saith the **L.** God, I have....... 136
Eze 33:17 say, the way of the **L.** is not equal: 136
Eze 33:20 say, The way of the **L.** is not equal. 136
Eze 33:22 the hand of the **L.** was upon me 3068
Eze 33:23 the word of the **L.** came unto me, ... 3068
Eze 33:25 Thus saith the **L.** God; Ye eat with...... 136
Eze 33:27 saith the **L.** God; As I live, surely 136
Eze 33:29 shall they know that I am the **L.**,....... 3068
Eze 33:30 the word that cometh from the **L.**...... 3068
Eze 34:1 the word of the **L.** came unto me, ... 3068
Eze 34:2 Thus saith the **L.** God unto the........... 136
Eze 34:7 hear the word of the **L.**; 3068
Eze 34:8 As I live, saith the **L.** God, surely 136
Eze 34:9 hear the word of the **L.**; 3068
Eze 34:10 Thus saith the **L.** God; Behold, I......... 136
Eze 34:11 For thus saith the **L.** God; Behold, ... 136
Eze 34:15 them to lie down, saith the **L.** God. 136
Eze 34:17 O my flock, thus saith the **L.** God; 136
Eze 34:20 thus saith the **L.** God unto them; 136
Eze 34:24 And I the **L.** will be their God,.......... 3068
Eze 34:24 them; I the **L.** have spoken it. 3068
Eze 34:27 and shall know that I am the **L.**,........ 3068
Eze 34:30 I the **L.** their God am with them,....... 3068
Eze 34:30 are my people, saith the **L.** God.......... 136
Eze 34:31 and I am your God, saith the **L.** God. .. 136
Eze 35:1 the word of the **L.** came unto me, ... 3068
Eze 35:3 say unto it, Thus saith the **L.** God;...... 136
Eze 35:4 thou shalt know that I am the **L.**. 3068
Eze 35:6 live, saith the **L.** God, I will prepare 136
Eze 35:9 ye shall know that I am the **L.**. 3068
Eze 35:10 it; whereas the **L.** was there:........... 3068
Eze 35:11 I live, saith the **L.** God, I will even...... 136
Eze 35:12 thou shalt know that I am the **L.**, ... 3068
Eze 35:14 Thus saith the **L.** God; When the 136
Eze 35:15 they shall know that I am the **L.**........ 3068
Eze 36:1 of Israel, hear the word of the **L.**: 3068
Eze 36:2 Thus saith the **L.** God; Because the..... 136
Eze 36:3 Thus saith the **L.** God; Because they ... 136
Eze 36:4 Israel, hear the word of the **L.** God; 136
Eze 36:4 saith the **L.** God to the mountains, ... 136
Eze 36:5 saith the **L.** God; Surely in the fire 136
Eze 36:6 Thus saith the **L.** God; Behold, I......... 136
Eze 36:7 thus saith the **L.** God; I have lifted 136
Eze 36:11 ye shall know that I am the **L.**. 3068
Eze 36:13 Thus saith the **L.** God; Because.......... 136
Eze 36:14 nations any more, saith the **L.** God. 136
Eze 36:15 to fall any more, saith the **L.** God........ 136
Eze 36:16 the word of the **L.** came unto me, ... 3068
Eze 36:20 These are the people of the **L.**, and... 3068
Eze 36:22 Thus saith the **L.** God; I do not this 136
Eze 36:23 heathen shall know...I am the **L.**,........ 3068
Eze 36:23 saith the **L.** God, when I shall be 136
Eze 36:32 your sakes do I this, saith the **L.**, ... 136
Eze 36:33 Thus saith the **L.** God; In the day 136
Eze 36:36 I the **L.** build the ruined places,......... 3068
Eze 36:36 I the **L.** have spoken it, and I will...... 3068
Eze 36:37 saith the **L.** God; I will yet for this 136
Eze 36:38 they shall know that I am the **L.**........ 3068
Eze 37:1 The hand of the **L.** was upon me,...... 3068
Eze 37:1 me out in the spirit of the **L.**, and...... 3068
Eze 37:3 answered, O **L.** God, thou knowest. 136
Eze 37:4 bones, hear the word of the **L.**.......... 3068
Eze 37:5 saith the **L.** God unto these bones;...... 136
Eze 37:6 ye shall know that I am the **L.**. 3068
Eze 37:9 Thus saith the **L.** God; Come from...... 136
Eze 37:12 Thus saith the **L.** God; Behold, O my .. 136
Eze 37:13 ye shall know that I am the **L.**, ... 3068
Eze 37:14 know that I the **L.** have spoken it, ... 3068
Eze 37:14 it, and performed it, saith the **L.**. 136
Eze 37:15 word of the **L.** came again unto......... 3068
Eze 37:19, 21 Thus saith the **L.** God; Behold, I 136
Eze 37:28 that I the **L.** do sanctify Israel,.......... 3068
Eze 38:1 the word of the **L.** came unto me, ... 3068
Eze 38:3 Thus saith the **L.** God; Behold, I......... 136
Eze 38:10 Thus saith the **L.** God; It shall also..... 136
Eze 38:14 Thus saith the **L.** God; In that day 136
Eze 38:17 Thus saith the **L.** God; Art thou he 136
Eze 38:18 saith the **L.** God, that my fury shall 136
Eze 38:21 all my mountains, saith the **L.** God: 136
Eze 38:23 they shall know that I am the **L.**........ 3068
Eze 39:1 Thus saith the **L.** God; Behold, I......... 136
Eze 39:5 for I have spoken it, saith the **L.** God. . 136
Eze 39:6 they shall know that I am the **L.**........ 3068
Eze 39:7 heathen shall know...I am the **L.**,........ 3068
Eze 39:8 and it is done, saith the **L.** God; 136
Eze 39:10 that robbed them, saith the **L.** God..... 136
Eze 39:13 shall be glorified, saith the **L.** God. 136
Eze 39:17 son of man, thus saith the **L.** God; 136
Eze 39:20 all men of war, saith the **L.** God. 136
Eze 39:22 Israel shall know that I am the **L.** 3068
Eze 39:25 Therefore thus saith the **L.** God;.......... 136
Eze 39:28 know that I am the **L.** their God,........ 3068
Eze 39:29 house of Israel, saith the **L.** God. 136
Eze 40:1 the hand of the **L.** was upon me, ... 3068
Eze 40:46 come near to the **L.** to minister......... 3068
Eze 41:22 is the table that is before the **L.**. 3068
Eze 42:13 priests that approach unto the **L.** 3068
Eze 43:4 glory of the **L.** came into the house.... 3068
Eze 43:5 the glory of the **L.** filled the house. 3068
Eze 43:18 Son of man, thus saith the **L.** God;...... 136
Eze 43:19 minister unto me, saith the **L.** God, ... 136
Eze 43:24 shalt offer them before the **L.**, ... 3068
Eze 43:24 up for a burnt offering unto the **L.**. 3068
Eze 43:27 I will accept you, saith the **L.** God....... 136
Eze 44:2 Then said the **L.** unto me; This......... 3068
Eze 44:2 because the **L.**, the God of Israel,...... 3068
Eze 44:3 sit in it to eat bread before the **L.**;..... 3068
Eze 44:4 of the **L.** filled the house of the **L.**:.... 3068
Eze 44:5 the **L.** said unto me, Son of man,........ 3068
Eze 44:5 ordinances of the house of the **L.**,...... 3068
Eze 44:6 Thus saith the **L.** God; O ye house...... 136
Eze 44:9 Thus saith the **L.** God; No stranger, ... 136
Eze 44:12 hand against them, saith the **L.** God,.... 136
Eze 44:15 fat and blood, saith the **L.** God: 136
Eze 44:27 his sin offering, saith the **L.** God. 136
Eze 45:1 shall offer an oblation unto the **L.**,...... 3068
Eze 45:4 come near to minister unto the **L.**:..... 3068
Eze 45:9 saith the **L.** God; Let it suffice you,..... 136
Eze 45:9 from my people, saith the **L.** God........ 136
Eze 45:15 reconciliation...saith the **L.** God......... 136
Eze 45:18 Thus saith the **L.** God; In the first....... 136
Eze 45:23 prepare a burnt offering to the **L.**, ... 3068
Eze 46:1 Thus saith the **L.** God; The gate of 136
Eze 46:3 door of this gate before the **L.** 3068
Eze 46:4 the prince shall offer unto the **L.**........ 3068
Eze 46:9 of the land shall come before the **L.** ... 3068
Eze 46:12 offerings voluntarily unto the **L.**, ... 3068
Eze 46:13 a burnt offering unto the **L.** of a 3068
Eze 46:14 a perpetual ordinance unto the **L.**........ 3068
Eze 46:16 Thus saith the **L.** God; If the prince..... 136
Eze 47:13 Thus saith the **L.** God; This shall be 136
Eze 47:23 his inheritance, saith the **L.** God.......... 136
Eze 48:9 that ye shall offer unto the **L.**........... 3068
Eze 48:10 sanctuary of the **L.** shall be in........... 3068
Eze 48:14 the land: for it is holy unto the **L.**....... 3068
Eze 48:29 are their portions, saith the **L.** God...... 136
Eze 48:35 that day shall be, The **L.** is there....... 3068
Da 1:2 **L.** gave Jehoiakim king of Judah........... 136
Da 1:10 I fear my **l.** the king, who hath 113
Da 2:10 there is no king, **l.**, nor ruler, that 7229
Da 2:47 a God of gods, and a **L.** of kings,....... 4756
Da 4:19 My **l.**, the dream be to them that 4756
Da 4:24 which is come upon my **l.** the king: 4756
Da 5:23 thyself against the **L.** of heaven; 4756
Da 9:2 word of the **L.** came to Jeremiah 3068
Da 9:3 And I set my face unto the **L.** God,..... 136
Da 9:4 I prayed unto the **L.** my God, ... 3068
Da 9:4 O **L.**, the great and dreadful God, ... 136
Da 9:7 O **L.**, righteousness belongeth unto...... 136
Da 9:8 O **L.**, to us belongeth confusion of....... 136
Da 9:9 To the **L.** our God belong mercies....... 136
Da 9:10 we obeyed the voice of the **L.** our 3068
Da 9:13 not our prayer before the **L.** our........ 3068
Da 9:14 hath the **L.** watched upon the evil, ... 3068
Da 9:14 **L.** our God is righteous in all his......... 3068
Da 9:15 O **L.** our God, thou hast brought......... 136
Da 9:16 O **L.**, according to all thy.................. 136
Da 9:19 O **L.**, hear; O **L.**, forgive; 136
Da 9:19 O **L.**, hearken and do; defer not,.......... 136
Da 9:20 my supplication before the **L.** my....... 3068
Da 10:16 O my **l.**, by the vision my sorrows 113
Da 10:17 of this my **l.** talk with this my **l.**? 113
Da 10:19 Let my **l.** speak; for thou hast 113
Da 12:8 O my **L.**, what shall be the end of....... 113
Ho 1:1 The word of the **L.** that came 3068
Ho 1:2 of the word of the **L.** by Hosea. 3068

Ho	1:2	the **L.** said to Hosea, Go, take	3068
Ho	1:2	whoredom, departing from the **L.**.	3068
Ho	1:4	**L.** said unto him, Call his name	3068
Ho	1:7	will save them by the **L.** their	3068
Ho	2:13	and forgat me, saith the **L.**.	3068
Ho	2:16	saith the **L.**, that thou shalt call	3068
Ho	2:20	and thou shalt know the **L.**.	3068
Ho	2:21	that day, I will hear, saith the **L.**,	3068
Ho	3:1	Then said the **L.** unto me, Go yet,	3068
Ho	3:1	according to the love of the **L.**	3068
Ho	3:5	return, and seek the **L.** their God,	3068
Ho	3:5	shall fear the **L.** and his goodness	3068
Ho	4:1	Hear the word of the **L.**, ye	3068
Ho	4:1	the **L.** hath a controversy with	3068
Ho	4:10	left off to take heed to the **L.**	3068
Ho	4:15	nor swear, The **L.** liveth.	3068
Ho	4:16	the **L.** will feed them as a lamb	3068
Ho	5:4	and they have not known the **L.**.	3068
Ho	5:6	with their herds to seek the **L.**;	3068
Ho	5:7	treacherously against the **L.**:	3068
Ho	6:1	and let us return unto the **L.**:	3068
Ho	6:3	if we follow on to know the **L.**:	3068
Ho	7:10	not return to the **L.** their God,	3068
Ho	8:1	eagle against the house of the **L.**,	3068
Ho	8:13	but the **L.** accepteth them not;	3068
Ho	9:4	not offer wine offerings to the **L.**,	3068
Ho	9:4	not come into the house of the **L.**.	3068
Ho	9:5	in the day of the feast of the **L.**?	3068
Ho	9:14	Give them, O **L.**: what wilt thou	3068
Ho	10:3	because we feared not the **L.**;	3068
Ho	10:12	for it is time to seek the **L.**, till	3068
Ho	11:10	They shall walk after the **L.**: he	3068
Ho	11:11	them in their houses, saith the **L.**.	3068
Ho	12:2	**L.** hath also a controversy with	3068
Ho	12:5	Even the **L.** God of hosts;	3068
Ho	12:5	the **L.** is his memorial.	3068
Ho	12:9	I that am the **L.** thy God from the	3068
Ho	12:13	**L.** brought Israel out of Egypt,	3068
Ho	12:14	reproach shall his **L.** return unto	113
Ho	13:4	yet I am the **L.** thy God from the	3068
Ho	13:15	the wind of the **L.** shall come up	3068
Ho	14:1	return unto the **L.** thy God; for	3068
Ho	14:2	you words, and turn to the **L.**:	3068
Ho	14:9	for the ways of the **L.** are right,	3068
Joe	1:1	word of the **L.** that came to Joel	3068
Joe	1:9	cut off from the house of the **L.**;	3068
Joe	1:14	into the house of the **L.** your God,	3068
Joe	1:14	your God, and cry unto the **L.**,	3068
Joe	1:15	for the day of the **L.** is at hand,	3068
Joe	1:19	O **L.**, to thee will I cry: for the	3068
Joe	2:1	for the day of the **L.** cometh, for	3068
Joe	2:11	**L.** shall utter his voice before his	3068
Joe	2:11	for the day of the **L.** is great and	3068
Joe	2:12	also now, saith the **L.**, turn ye	3068
Joe	2:13	and turn unto the **L.** your God:	3068
Joe	2:14	drink offering unto the **L.** your	3068
Joe	2:17	the ministers of the **L.**, weep	3068
Joe	2:17	Spare thy people, O **L.**, and give	3068
Joe	2:18	the **L.** be jealous for his land,	3068
Joe	2:19	**L.** will answer and say unto his	3068
Joe	2:21	for the **L.** will do great things.	3068
Joe	2:23	and rejoice in the **L.** your God:	3068
Joe	2:26	and praise the name of the **L.**	3068
Joe	2:27	and that I am the **L.** your God,	3068
Joe	2:31	the terrible day of the **L.** come	3068
Joe	2:32	shall call on the name of the **L.**	3068
Joe	2:32	deliverance, as the **L.** hath said,	3068
Joe	2:32	remnant whom the **L.** shall call.	3068
Joe	3:8	far off: for the **L.** hath spoken it.	3068
Joe	3:11	mighty ones to come down, O **L.**.	3068
Joe	3:14	day of the **L.** is near in the valley	3068
Joe	3:16	The **L.** also shall roar out of Zion,	3068
Joe	3:16	**L.** will be the hope of his people,	3068
Joe	3:17	know that I am the **L.** your God	3068
Joe	3:18	come forth of the house of the **L.**,	3068
Joe	3:21	for the **L.** dwelleth in Zion.	3068
Am	1:2	the **L.** will roar from Zion, and	3068
Am	1:3	Thus saith the **L.**; For three	3068
Am	1:5	captivity unto Kir, saith the **L.**.	3068
Am	1:6	Thus saith the **L.**; For three	3068
Am	1:8	shall perish, saith the **L.** God.	136
Am	1:9,	11,13 Thus saith the **L.**; For three	3068
Am	1:15	his princes together, saith the **L.**.	3068
Am	2:1	Thus saith the **L.**; For three	3068
Am	2:3	thereof with him, saith the **L.**	3068
Am	2:4	Thus saith the **L.**; For three	3068
Am	2:4	have despised the law of the **L.**,	3068
Am	2:6	Thus saith the **L.**; For three	3068
Am	2:11	children of Israel? saith the **L.**.	3068
Am	2:16	naked in that day, saith the **L.**.	3068
Am	3:1	this word that the **L.** hath spoken	3068
Am	3:6	city, and the **L.** hath not done it?	3068
Am	3:7	Surely the **L.** God will do nothing,	136
Am	3:8	the **L.** God hath spoken, who can	136
Am	3:10	know not to do right, saith the **L.**,	3068
Am	3:11	Therefore thus saith the **L.** God;	136
Am	3:12	Thus saith the **L.**; As the	3068
Am	3:13	house of Jacob, saith the **L.** God,	136
Am	3:15	shall have an end, saith the **L.**	3068
Am	4:2	**L.** God hath sworn by his holiness,	136
Am	4:3	then into the palace, saith the **L.**.	3068
Am	4:5	of Israel, saith the **L.** God.	136
Am	4:6,	8,9,10,11 unto me, saith the **L.**.	3068
Am	4:13	The **L.**, The God of hosts, is his	3068
Am	5:3	For thus saith the **L.** God; The	136
Am	5:4	the **L.** unto the house of Israel,	3068
Am	5:6	Seek the **L.**, and ye shall live;	3068
Am	5:8	of the earth: The **L.** is his name:	3068
Am	5:14	so the **L.**, the God of hosts, shall	3068
Am	5:15	that the **L.** God of hosts will be	3068
Am	5:16	Therefore the **L.**, the God of hosts,	3068
Am	5:16	the **L.**, saith thus; Wailing shall	136
Am	5:17	pass through thee, saith the **L.**.	3068
Am	5:18	you that desire the day of the **L.**!	3068
Am	5:18	the day of the **L.** is darkness, and	3068
Am	5:20	not the day of the **L.** be darkness,	3068
Am	5:27	saith the **L.**, whose name is The	3068
Am	6:8	The **L.** God hath sworn by himself,	136
Am	6:8	saith the **L.** the God of hosts, I	3068
Am	6:10	mention of the name of the **L.**	3068
Am	6:11	the **L.** commandeth, and he will	3068
Am	6:14	saith the **L.** the God of hosts;	3068
Am	7:1	hath the **L.** God shewed unto me:	136
Am	7:2	O **L.** God, forgive, I beseech thee:	136
Am	7:3	The **L.** repented for this: It shall	3068
Am	7:3	this: It shall not be, saith the **L.**.	3068
Am	7:4	hath the **L.** God shewed unto me:	136
Am	7:4	the **L.** God called to contend by fire,	136
Am	7:5	I, O **L.** God, cease, I beseech thee;	136
Am	7:6	The **L.** repented for this: This	3068
Am	7:6	also shall not be, saith the **L.** God.	136
Am	7:7	the **L.** stood upon a wall made by a	136
Am	7:8	the **L.** said unto me, Amos, what	3068
Am	7:8	Then said the **L.**, Behold, I will set	136
Am	7:15	**L.** took me as I followed the flock,	3068
Am	7:15	the **L.** said unto me, Go, prophesy	3068
Am	7:16	hear thou the word of the **L.**:	3068
Am	7:17	thus saith the **L.**; Thy wife shall	3068
Am	8:1	hath the **L.** God shewed unto me:	136
Am	8:2	Then said the **L.** unto me, The	3068
Am	8:3	howlings in that day, saith the **L.**	136
Am	8:7	**L.** hath sworn by the excellency	3068
Am	8:9	pass in that day, saith the **L.** God,	136
Am	8:11	the days come, saith the **L.** God,	136
Am	8:11	of hearing the words of the **L.**:	3068
Am	8:12	and fro to seek the word of the **L.**,	3068
Am	9:1	saw the **L.** standing upon the altar:	136
Am	9:5	**L.** God of hosts is he that toucheth	136
Am	9:6	of the earth: The **L.** is his name.	3068
Am	9:7	O children of Israel? saith the **L.**	3068
Am	9:8	the eyes of the **L.** God are upon the	136
Am	9:8	the house of Jacob, saith the **L.**.	3068
Am	9:12	called by my name, saith the **L.**	3068
Am	9:13	the days come, saith the **L.**, that	3068
Am	9:15	given them, saith the **L.** thy God.	3068
Ob	1	Thus saith the **L.** God concerning	136
Ob	1	have heard a rumour from the **L.**,	3068
Ob	4	I bring thee down, saith the **L.**	3068
Ob	8	I not in that day, saith the **L.**,	3068
Ob	15	the day of the **L.** is near upon all	3068
Ob	18	Esau; for the **L.** hath spoken it.	3068
Jon	1:1	word of the **L.** came unto Jonah	3068
Jon	1:3	from the presence of the **L.**, and	3068
Jon	1:3	from the presence of the **L.**	3068
Jon	1:4	**L.** sent out a great wind into the	3068
Jon	1:9	I am an Hebrew; and I fear the **L.**,	3068
Jon	1:10	fled from the presence of the **L.**,	3068
Jon	1:14	they cried unto the **L.**, and said,	3068
Jon	1:14	O **L.**, we beseech thee, let us not	3068
Jon	1:14	thou, O **L.**, hast done as it pleased	3068
Jon	1:16	the men feared the **L.** exceedingly,	3068
Jon	1:16	and offered a sacrifice unto the **L.**,	3068
Jon	1:17	the **L.** had prepared a great fish to	3068
Jon	2:1	Jonah prayed unto the **L.** his God	3068
Jon	2:2	of mine affliction unto the **L.**,	3068
Jon	2:6	my life from corruption, O **L.** my	3068
Jon	2:7	within me I remembered the **L.**:	3068
Jon	2:9	have vowed. Salvation is of the **L.**	3068
Jon	2:10	the **L.** spake unto the fish, and it	3068
Jon	3:1	word of the **L.** came unto Jonah	3068
Jon	3:3	according to the word of the **L.**.	3068
Jon	4:2	he prayed unto the **L.**, and said, I	3068
Jon	4:2	I pray thee, O **L.**, was not this my	3068
Jon	4:3	O **L.**, take, I beseech thee, my life	3068
Jon	4:4	said the **L.**, Doest thou well to be	3068
Jon	4:6	the **L.** God prepared a gourd, and	3068
Jon	4:10	Then said the **L.**, Thou hast had	3068
Mic	1:1	The word of the **L.** that came to	3068
Mic	1:2	the **L.** God be witness against you,	136
Mic	1:2	the **L.** from his holy temple.	136
Mic	1:3	**L.** cometh forth out of his place,	3068
Mic	1:12	evil came down from the **L.** unto	3068
Mic	2:3	Therefore thus saith the **L.**;	3068
Mic	2:5	lot in the congregation of the **L.**.	3068
Mic	2:7	is the spirit of the **L.** straitened?	3068
Mic	2:13	and the **L.** on the head of them.	3068
Mic	3:4	Then shall they cry unto the **L.**,	3068
Mic	3:5	Thus saith the **L.** concerning the	3068
Mic	3:8	of power by the spirit of the **L.**,	3068
Mic	3:11	yet will they lean upon the **L.**,	3068
Mic	3:11	Is not the **L.** among us? none evil	3068
Mic	4:1	house of the **L.** shall be established	3068
Mic	4:2	us go up to the mountain of the **L.**,	3068
Mic	4:2	word of the **L.** from Jerusalem.	3068
Mic	4:4	of the **L.** of hosts hath spoken it.	3068
Mic	4:5	walk in the name of the **L.** our God	3068
Mic	4:6	In that day, saith the **L.**, will I	3068
Mic	4:7	the **L.** shall reign over them in	3068
Mic	4:10	the **L.** shall redeem thee from the	3068
Mic	4:12	know not the thoughts of the **L.**,	3068
Mic	4:13	consecrate their gain unto the **L.**,	3068
Mic	4:13	unto the **L.** of the whole earth.	113
Mic	5:4	and feed in the strength of the **L.**,	3068
Mic	5:4	the majesty of the name of the **L.**	3068
Mic	5:7	many people as a dew from the **L.**,	3068
Mic	5:10	to pass in that day, saith the **L.**,	3068
Mic	6:1	Hear ye now what the **L.** saith ;	3068
Mic	6:2	the **L.** hath a controversy with his	3068
Mic	6:5	know the righteousness of the **L.**	3068
Mic	6:6	shall I come before the **L.**, and	3068
Mic	6:7	the **L.** be pleased with thousands	3068
Mic	6:8	what doth the **L.** require of thee,	3068
Mic	7:7	Therefore I will look unto the **L.**;	3068
Mic	7:8	the **L.** shall be a light unto me.	3068
Mic	7:9	will bear the indignation of the **L.**,	3068
Mic	7:10	unto me, Where is the **L.** thy God?	3068
Mic	7:17	shall be afraid of the **L.** our God,	3068
Na	1:2	is jealous, and the **L.** revengeth;	3068
Na	1:2	The **L.** revengeth, and is furious;	3068
Na	1:2	The **L.** will take vengeance on his	3068
Na	1:3	The **L.** is slow to anger, and great	3068
Na	1:3	**L.** hath his way in the whirlwind	3068
Na	1:7	The **L.** is good, a strong hold in	3068
Na	1:9	do ye imagine against the **L.**?	3068
Na	1:11	that imagineth evil against the **L.**,	3068
Na	1:12	Thus saith the **L.**; Though they	3068
Na	1:14	the **L.** hath given a commandment	3068
Na	2:2	For the **L.** hath turned away the	3068
Na	2:13	against thee, saith the **L.** of hosts,	3068
Na	3:5	against thee, saith the **L.** of hosts;	3068
Hab	1:2	O **L.**, how long shall I cry, and	3068
Hab	1:12	not from everlasting, O **L.** my God,	3068
Hab	1:12	O **L.**, thou hast ordained them for	3068
Hab	2:2	And the **L.** answered me, and said,	3068
Hab	2:13	is it not of the **L.** of hosts that the	3068
Hab	2:14	knowledge of the glory of the **L.**,	3068
Hab	2:20	But the **L.** is in his holy temple:	3068
Hab	3:2	O **L.**, I have heard thy speech, and	3068
Hab	3:2	O **L.**, revive thy work in the midst	3068
Hab	3:8	Was the **L.** displeased against the	3068
Hab	3:18	Yet I will rejoice in the **L.**, I will	3068
Hab	3:19	The **L.** God is my strength, and he	3068
Zep	1:1	word of the **L.** which came unto	3068
Zep	1:2,	3 from the land, saith the **L.**	3068
Zep	1:5	worship and that swear by the **L.**,	3068
Zep	1:6	that are turned back from the **L.**;	3068
Zep	1:6	those that have not sought the **L.**,	3068
Zep	1:7	at the presence of the **L.** God:	136
Zep	1:7	for the day of the **L.** is at hand:	3068
Zep	1:7	the **L.** hath prepared a sacrifice,	3068
Zep	1:10	to pass in that day, saith the **L.**,	3068

Zep 1:12 The L. will not do good, neither 3068
Zep 1:14 The great day of the L. is near, it 3068
Zep 1:14 even the voice of the day of the L.: 3068
Zep 1:17 they have sinned against the L.: 3068
Zep 2:2 fierce anger of the L. come upon 3068
Zep 2:3 Seek ye the L., all ye meek of the 3068
Zep 2:5 the word of the L. is against you; 3068
Zep 2:7 the L. their God shall visit them, 3068
Zep 2:9 saith the L. of hosts, the God of 3068
Zep 2:10 the people of the L. of hosts 3068
Zep 2:11 The L. will be terrible unto them: 3068
Zep 3:2 she trusted not in the L.; she 3068
Zep 3:5 The just L. is in the midst thereof; 3068
Zep 3:8 wait ye upon me, saith the L., 3068
Zep 3:9 all call upon the name of the L., 3068
Zep 3:12 shall trust in the name of the L. 3068
Zep 3:15 L. hath taken away thy judgments, 3068
Zep 3:15 even the L., is in the midst of thee: 3068
Zep 3:17 L. thy God in the midst of thee is 3068
Zep 3:20 before your eyes, saith the L. 3068
Hag 1:1 the word of the L. by Haggai the 3068
Hag 1:2 speaketh the L. of hosts, saying, 3068
Hag 1:3 the word of the L. by Haggai the 3068
Hag 1:5, 7 saith the L. of hosts; Consider 3068
Hag 1:8 and I will be glorified, saith the L. 3068
Hag 1:9 it. Why? saith the L. of hosts 3068
Hag 1:12 obeyed the voice of the L. their 3068
Hag 1:12 as the L. their God had sent him, 3068
Hag 1:12 the people did fear before the L. 3068
Hag 1:13 saying, I am with you, saith the L. 3068
Hag 1:14 And the L. stirred up the spirit of 3068
Hag 1:14 did work in the house of the L. of 3068
Hag 2:1 the word of the L. by the prophet 3068
Hag 2:4 strong, O Zerubbabel, saith the L.; 3068
Hag 2:4 ye people of the land, saith the L., 3068
Hag 2:4 am with you, saith the L. of hosts: 3068
Hag 2:6 For thus saith the L. of hosts; 3068
Hag 2:7 with glory, saith the L. of hosts 3068
Hag 2:8 gold is mine, saith the L. of hosts. 3068
Hag 2:9 the former, saith the L. of hosts: 3068
Hag 2:9 I give peace, saith the L. of hosts 3068
Hag 2:10 the word of the L. by Haggai the 3068
Hag 2:11 Thus saith the L. of hosts; Ask 3068
Hag 2:14 nation before me, saith the L.; 3068
Hag 2:15 a stone in the temple of the L.: 3068
Hag 2:17 ye turned not to me, saith the L. 3068
Hag 2:20 word of the L. came unto Haggai 3068
Hag 2:23 In that day, saith the L. of hosts, 3068
Hag 2:23 will I take thee,...saith the L., and 3068
Hag 2:23 chosen thee, saith the L. of hosts. 3068
Zec 1:1 the word of the L. unto Zechariah, 3068
Zec 1:2 L. hath been sore displeased with 3068
Zec 1:3 them, Thus saith the L. of hosts; 3068
Zec 1:3 ye unto me, saith the L. of hosts, 3068
Zec 1:3 unto you, saith the L. of hosts. 3068
Zec 1:4 Thus saith the L. of hosts; Turn 3068
Zec 1:4 hearken unto me, saith the L. 3068
Zec 1:6 Like as the L. of hosts thought 3068
Zec 1:7 the word of the L. unto Zechariah, 3068
Zec 1:9 said I, O my l., what are these? 113
Zec 1:10 are they whom the L. hath sent 3068
Zec 1:11 they answered the angel of the L. 3068
Zec 1:12 the angel of the L. answered and 3068
Zec 1:12 O L. of hosts, how long wilt thou 3068
Zec 1:13 L. answered the angel that talked 3068
Zec 1:14 Thus saith the L. of hosts; I am 3068
Zec 1:16 thus saith the L.; I am returned 3068
Zec 1:16 be built in it, saith the L. of hosts, 3068
Zec 1:17 Thus saith the L. of hosts; My 3068
Zec 1:17 the L. shall yet comfort Zion, and 3068
Zec 1:20 L. shewed me four carpenters 3068
Zec 2:5 For I, saith the L., will be unto 3068
Zec 2:6 land of the north, saith the L. 3068
Zec 2:6 winds of the heaven, saith the L. 3068
Zec 2:8 thus saith the L. of hosts; After 3068
Zec 2:9 that the L. of hosts hath sent me 3068
Zec 2:10 in the midst of thee, saith the L. 3068
Zec 2:11 nations shall be joined to the L. 3068
Zec 2:11 that the L. of hosts hath sent me 3068
Zec 2:12 L. shall inherit Judah his portion 3068
Zec 2:13 silent, O all flesh, before the L.: 3068
Zec 3:1 priest...before the angel of the L., 3068
Zec 3:2 And the L. said unto Satan, 3068
Zec 3:2 The L. rebuke thee, O Satan; 3068
Zec 3:2 L. that hath chosen Jerusalem 3068
Zec 3:5 And the angel of the L. stood by. 3068
Zec 3:6 the angel of the L. protested unto 3068
Zec 3:7 Thus saith the L. of hosts; If thou 3068
Zec 3:9 the graving thereof, saith the L. 3068
Zec 3:10 In that day, saith the L. of hosts, 3068
Zec 4:4 me, saying, What are these, my l.? 113
Zec 4:5 these be? And I said, No, my l. 113
Zec 4:6 word of the L. unto Zerubbabel, 3068
Zec 4:6 by my Spirit, saith the L. of hosts 3068
Zec 4:8 the word of the L. came unto me, 3068
Zec 4:9 that the L. of hosts hath sent me 3068
Zec 4:10 they are the eyes of the L., which 3068
Zec 4:13 these be? And I said, No, my l. 113
Zec 4:14 stand by the L. of the whole earth 113
Zec 5:4 it forth, saith the L. of hosts, 3068
Zec 6:4 with me, What are these, my l.? 113
Zec 6:5 before the L. of all the earth. 113
Zec 6:9 the word of the L. came unto me, 3068
Zec 6:12 Thus speaketh the L. of hosts, 3068
Zec 6:12 shall build the temple of the L.: 3068
Zec 6:13 shall build the temple of the L.; 3068
Zec 6:14 memorial in the temple of the L. 3068
Zec 6:15 and build in the temple of the L., 3068
Zec 6:15 that the L. of hosts hath sent me 3068
Zec 6:15 diligently obey the voice of the L. 3068
Zec 7:1 word of...L. came unto Zechariah 3068
Zec 7:2 their men, to pray before the L., 3068
Zec 7:3 were in the house of the L. of 3068
Zec 7:4 word of the L. of hosts unto me, 3068
Zec 7:7 the words which the L. hath cried 3068
Zec 7:8 word of...L. came unto Zechariah, 3068
Zec 7:9 Thus speaketh the L. of hosts, 3068
Zec 7:12 words which the L. of hosts hath 3068
Zec 7:12 came a great wrath from the L. 3068
Zec 7:13 not hear, saith the L. of hosts: 3068
Zec 8:1 word of the L. of hosts came to me, 3068
Zec 8:2 Thus saith the L. of hosts; I was 3068
Zec 8:3 Thus saith the L.; I am returned 3068
Zec 8:3 the mountain of the L. of hosts 3068
Zec 8:4 Thus saith the L. of hosts; There 3068
Zec 8:6 Thus saith the L. of hosts; If it be 3068
Zec 8:6 mine eyes? saith the L. of hosts. 3068
Zec 8:7 Thus saith the L. of hosts; 3068
Zec 8:9 Thus saith the L. of hosts; Let 3068
Zec 8:9 foundation of the house of the L. 3068
Zec 8:11 former days, saith the L. of hosts. 3068
Zec 8:14 thus saith the L. of hosts; As I 3068
Zec 8:14 me to wrath, saith the L. of hosts, 3068
Zec 8:17 things that I hate, saith the L. 3068
Zec 8:18 the word of the L. of hosts came 3068
Zec 8:19 Thus saith the L. of hosts; The 3068
Zec 8:20 saith the L. of hosts; It shall yet 3068
Zec 8:21 go speedily to pray before the L., 3068
Zec 8:21 and to seek the L. of hosts: I will 3068
Zec 8:22 shall come to seek the L. of hosts 3068
Zec 8:22 and to pray before the L. 3068
Zec 8:23 saith the L. of hosts; In those 3068
Zec 9:1 The burden of the word of the L. 3068
Zec 9:1 of Israel, shall be toward the L. 3068
Zec 9:4 Behold, the L. will cast her out, 136
Zec 9:14 the L. shall be seen over them, 3068
Zec 9:14 the L. God shall blow the trumpet, 136
Zec 9:15 the L. of hosts shall defend them; 3068
Zec 9:16 L. their God shall save them in 3068
Zec 10:1 Ask ye of the L. rain in the time 3068
Zec 10:1 the L. shall make bright clouds, 3068
Zec 10:3 L. of hosts hath visited his flock 3068
Zec 10:5 because the L. is with them, and 3068
Zec 10:6 I am the L. their God, and will 3068
Zec 10:7 their heart shall rejoice in the L. 3068
Zec 10:12 will strengthen them in the L.; 3068
Zec 10:12 down in his name, saith the L. 3068
Zec 11:4 Thus saith the L. my God; Feed 3068
Zec 11:5 sell them say, Blessed be the L.; 3068
Zec 11:6 inhabitants of...land, saith the L.: 3068
Zec 11:11 that it was the word of the L. 3068
Zec 11:13 the L. said unto me, Cast it unto 3068
Zec 11:13 the potter in the house of the L. 3068
Zec 11:15 the L. said unto me, Take unto 3068
Zec 12:1 burden of the word of the L. for 3068
Zec 12:1 saith the L., which stretcheth 3068
Zec 12:4 In that day, saith the L., I will 3068
Zec 12:5 be my strength in the L. of hosts 3068
Zec 12:7 The L. also shall save the tents of 3068
Zec 12:8 the L. defend the inhabitants of 3068
Zec 12:8 the angel of the L. before them. 3068
Zec 13:2 in that day, saith the L. of hosts, 3068
Zec 13:3 lies in the name of the L.: 3068
Zec 13:7 is my fellow, saith the L. of hosts: 3068
Zec 13:8 that in all the land, saith the L., 3068
Zec 13:9 they shall say, The L. is my God. 3068
Zec 14:1 Behold, the day of the L. cometh, 3068
Zec 14:3 Then shall the L. go forth, and 3068
Zec 14:5 and the L. my God shall come, 3068
Zec 14:7 which shall be known to the L., 3068
Zec 14:9 L. shall be king over all the earth: 3068
Zec 14:9 in that day shall there be one L., 3068
Zec 14:12 the L. shall smite all the people 3068
Zec 14:13 a great tumult from the L. shall 3068
Zec 14:16, 17 to worship the King, the L. of 3068
Zec 14:18 the L. will smite the heathen 3068
Zec 14:20 horses, Holiness Unto The L.; 3068
Zec 14:21 be holiness unto the L. of hosts: 3068
Zec 14:21 in the house of the L. of hosts. 3068
Mal 1:1 The burden of the word of the L. 3068
Mal 1:2 I have loved you, saith the L. 3068
Mal 1:2 Jacob's brother? saith the L.: 3068
Mal 1:4 thus saith the L. of hosts, They 3068
Mal 1:4 people against whom the L. hath 3068
Mal 1:5 The L. will be magnified from 3068
Mal 1:6 saith the L. of hosts unto you, 3068
Mal 1:7 The table of the L. is contemptible. 3068
Mal 1:8 thy person? saith the L. of hosts. 3068
Mal 1:9 persons? saith the L. of hosts. 3068
Mal 1:10 in you, saith the L. of hosts, 3068
Mal 1:11 the heathen, saith the L. of hosts. 3068
Mal 1:12 The table of the L. is polluted; 3068
Mal 1:13 snuffed at it, saith the L. of hosts; 3068
Mal 1:13 this of your hand? saith the L. 3068
Mal 1:14 unto the L. a corrupt thing: 136
Mal 1:14 great King, saith the L. of hosts, 3068
Mal 2:2 my name, saith the L. of hosts, 3068
Mal 2:4 with Levi, saith the L. of hosts. 3068
Mal 2:7 the messenger of the L. of hosts. 3068
Mal 2:8 of Levi, saith the L. of hosts. 3068
Mal 2:11 profaned the holiness of the L. 3068
Mal 2:12 The L. will cut off the man that 3068
Mal 2:12 offereth an offering unto the L. 3068
Mal 2:13 the altar of the L. with tears, 3068
Mal 2:14 the L. hath been witness between 3068
Mal 2:16 For the L., the God of Israel, saith 3068
Mal 2:16 garment, saith the L. of hosts: 3068
Mal 2:17 wearied the L. with your words. 3068
Mal 2:17 evil is good in the sight of the L., 3068
Mal 3:1 and the L., whom ye seek, shall 113
Mal 3:1 shall come, saith the L. of hosts. 3068
Mal 3:3 may offer unto the L. an offering 3068
Mal 3:4 Jerusalem be pleasant unto the L., 3068
Mal 3:5 fear not me, saith the L. of hosts. 3068
Mal 3:6 For I am the L., I change not; 3068
Mal 3:7 unto you, saith the L. of hosts. 3068
Mal 3:10 herewith, saith the L. of hosts, 3068
Mal 3:11 in the field, saith the L. of hosts. 3068
Mal 3:12 land, saith the L. of hosts. 3068
Mal 3:13 stout against me, saith the L. 3068
Mal 3:14 walked mournfully before the L. 3068
Mal 3:16 that feared the L. spake often one 3068
Mal 3:16 and the L. hearkened, and heard 3068
Mal 3:16 him for them that feared the L., 3068
Mal 3:17 they shall be mine, saith the L. 3068
Mal 4:1 shall burn them up, saith the L. 3068
Mal 4:3 that I shall do this, saith the L. 3068
Mal 4:5 great and dreadful day of the L.: 3068
Mt 1:20 angel of the L. appeared unto him *2962*
Mt 1:22 spoken of the L. by the prophet, *2962*
Mt 1:24 angel of the L. had bidden him, *2962*
Mt 2:13 angel of the L. appeareth to Joseph *2962*
Mt 2:15 spoken of the L. by the prophet, *2962*
Mt 2:19 an angel of the L. appeareth in a *2962*
Mt 3:3 Prepare ye the way of the L., make *2962*
Mt 4:7 **shalt not tempt the L. thy God.** *2962*
Mt 4:10 **Thou shalt worship the L. thy God,** *2962*
Mt 5:33 **perform unto the L. thine oaths:** *2962*
Mt 7:21 **one that saith unto me, L., L.,** *2962*
Mt 7:22 **L., L., have we not prophesied in** *2962*
Mt 8:2 L., if thou wilt, thou canst make *2962*
Mt 8:6 L., my servant lieth at home sick *2962*
Mt 8:8 said, L., I am not worthy that thou *2962*
Mt 8:21 L., suffer me first to go and bury *2962*
Mt 8:25 awoke him, saying, L., save us: *2962*
Mt 9:28 **this?** They said unto him, Yea, L. *2962*
Mt 9:38 **ye therefore the L. of the harvest,** *2962*
Mt 10:24 **nor the servant above his l.** *2962*
Mt 10:25 **master, and the servant as his l.** *2962*
Mt 11:25 **O Father, L. of heaven and earth,** *2962*
Mt 12:8 **man is L. even of the sabbath day.** *2962*

Mt	13:51	**things?** They say unto him, Yea, **L.**	*2962*
Mt	14:28	**L.**, if it be thou, bid me come unto	*2962*
Mt	14:30	sink, he cried, saying, **L.**, save me	*2962*
Mt	15:22	Have mercy on me, O **L.**, thou son	*2962*
Mt	15:25	worshipped him, saying, **L.**, help me.	*2962*
Mt	15:27	Truth, **L.**: yet the dogs eat of the	*2962*
Mt	16:22	him, saying, Be it far from thee, **L.**;	*2962*
Mt	17:4	**L.**, it is good for us to be here: if	*2962*
Mt	17:15	**L.**, have mercy on my son: for he	*2962*
Mt	18:21	**L.**, how oft shall my brother sin	*2962*
Mt	18:25	**his l. commanded him to be sold,**	*2962*
Mt	18:26	**L., have patience with me, and I**	*2962*
Mt	18:27	**l. of that servant was moved with**	*2962*
Mt	18:31	**told unto their l. all that was done**	*2962*
Mt	18:32	**Then his l., after that he had**	*2962*
Mt	18:34	**And his l. was wroth, and delivered**	*2962*
Mt	20:8	**the l. of the vineyard saith unto**	*2962*
Mt	20:30,	31 Have mercy on us, O **L.**, thou	*2962*
Mt	20:33	**L.**, that our eyes may be opened.	*2962*
Mt	21:3	**say, The L. hath need of them;**	*2962*
Mt	21:9	that cometh in the name of the **L.**;	*2962*
Mt	21:40	**l. therefore of the vineyard**	*2962*
Mt	22:37	**love the L. thy God with all thy**	*2962*
Mt	22:43	**doth David in spirit call him L.,**	*2962*
Mt	22:44	**The L. said...Sit thou on my right**	*2962*
Mt	22:44	**unto my L., Sit thou on my right**	*2962*
Mt	22:45	**If David then call him L., how is**	*2962*
Mt	23:39	**that cometh in the name of the L.**	*2962*
Mt	24:42	**not what hour your L. doth come**	*2962*
Mt	24:45	**whom his l. hath made ruler over**	*2962*
Mt	24:46	**his l. when he cometh shall find so**	*2962*
Mt	24:48	**heart, My l. delayeth his coming;**	*2962*
Mt	24:50	**l. of that servant shall come in a**	*2962*
Mt	25:11	**virgins, saying, L., L., open to us**	*2962*
Mt	25:19	**time the l. of those servants**	*2962*
Mt	25:20	**L., thou deliveredst unto me five**	*2962*
Mt	25:21	**His l. said unto him, Well done,**	*2962*
Mt	25:21	**enter thou into the joy of thy l.**	*2962*
Mt	25:22	**L., thou deliveredst unto me two**	*2962*
Mt	25:23	**His l. said unto him, Well done,**	*2962*
Mt	25:23	**enter thou into the joy of thy l.**	*2962*
Mt	25:24	**L., I knew thee that thou art an**	*2962*
Mt	25:26	**His l. answered and said unto him,**	*2962*
Mt	25:37,	44 **L., when saw we thee an**	*2962*
Mt	26:22	of them to say unto him, **L.**, is it I?	*2962*
Mt	27:10	potter's field, as the **L.** appointed	*2962*
Mt	28:2	the angel of the **L.** descended from	*2962*
Mt	28:6	Come, see the place where the **L.** lay.	*2962*
Mk	1:3	Prepare ye the way of the **L.**, make	*2962*
Mk	2:28	**Son of man is L. also of the**	*2962*
Mk	5:19	**how great things the L. hath done**	*2962*
Mk	7:28	and said unto him, Yes, **L.**: yet the	*2962*
Mk	9:24	**L.**, I believe; help thou mine	*2962*
Mk	10:51	**L.**, that I might receive my sight.	*4462*
Mk	11:3	**ye that the L. hath need of him;**	*2962*
Mk	11:9	that cometh in the name of the **L.**	*2962*
Mk	11:10	that cometh in the name of the **L.**	*2962*
Mk	12:9	**therefore the l. of the vineyard do?**	*2962*
Mk	12:29	**Israel; The L. our God is one L.:**	*2962*
Mk	12:30	**love the L. thy God with all thy**	*2962*
Mk	12:36	**The L. said...Sit thou on my right**	*2962*
Mk	12:36	**to my L., Sit thou on my right**	*2962*
Mk	12:37	**therefore himself calleth him L.;**	*2962*
Mk	13:20	**the L. had shortened those days,**	*2962*
Mk	16:19	after the **L.** had spoken unto them,	*2962*
Mk	16:20	the **L.** working with them, and	*2962*
Lu	1:6	and ordinances of the **L.** blameless.	*2962*
Lu	1:9	he went into the temple of the **L.**	*2962*
Lu	1:11	appeared unto him an angel of the **L.**	*2962*
Lu	1:15	shall be great in the sight of the **L.**,	*2962*
Lu	1:16	shall he turn to the **L.** their God	*2962*
Lu	1:17	ready a people prepared for the **L.**	*2962*
Lu	1:25	Thus hath the **L.** dealt with me in	*2962*
Lu	1:28	highly favoured, the **L.** is with thee:	*2962*
Lu	1:32	the **L.** God shall give unto him the	*2962*
Lu	1:38	Behold the handmaid of the **L.**; be	*2962*
Lu	1:43	mother of my **L.** should come to me?	*2962*
Lu	1:45	which were told her from the **L.**	*2962*
Lu	1:46	said, My soul doth magnify the **L.**,	*2962*
Lu	1:58	how the **L.** had shewed great mercy	*2962*
Lu	1:66	the hand of the **L.** was with him.	*2962*
Lu	1:68	Blessed be the **L.** God of Israel; for	*2962*
Lu	1:76	shalt go before the face of the **L.** to	*2962*
Lu	2:9	the angel of the **L.** came upon them,	*2962*
Lu	2:9	glory of the **L.** shone round about	*2962*
Lu	2:11	a Saviour, which is Christ the **L.**	*2962*
Lu	2:15	which the **L.** hath made known unto	*2962*
Lu	2:22	Jerusalem, to present him to the **L.**;	*2962*
Lu	2:23	(As it is written in the law of the **L.**,	*2962*
Lu	2:23	womb shall be called holy to the **L.**;)	*2962*
Lu	2:24	which is said in the law of the **L.**,	*2962*
Lu	2:29	**L.**, now lettest thou thy servant	*1203*
Lu	2:38	gave thanks likewise unto the **L.**,	*2962*
Lu	2:39	according to the law of the **L.**, they	*2962*
Lu	3:4	Prepare ye the way of the **L.**, make	*2962*
Lu	4:8	**Thou shalt worship the L. thy God,**	*2962*
Lu	4:12	**shalt not tempt the L. thy God**	*2962*
Lu	4:18	**Spirit of the L. is upon me,**	*2962*
Lu	4:19	**the acceptable year of the L.**	*2962*
Lu	5:8	me; for I am a sinful man, O **L.**	*2962*
Lu	5:12	**L.**, if thou wilt, thou canst make me	*2962*
Lu	5:17	power of the **L.** was present to heal	*2962*
Lu	6:5	**Son of man is L. also of the**	*2962*
Lu	6:46	**why call ye me, L., L., and do not**	*2962*
Lu	7:6	unto him, **L.**, trouble not thyself:	*2962*
Lu	7:13	And when the **L.** saw her, he had	*2962*
Lu	7:31	the **L.** said, **Whereunto then shall**	*2962*
Lu	9:54	**L.**, wilt thou that we command fire	*2962*
Lu	9:57	**L.**, I will follow thee whithersoever	*2962*
Lu	9:59	**L.**, suffer me first to go and bury my	*2962*
Lu	9:61	also said, **L.**, I will follow thee; but	*2962*
Lu	10:1	the **L.** appointed other seventy also,	*2962*
Lu	10:2	**ye therefore the L. of the harvest,**	*2962*
Lu	10:17	**L.**, even the devils are subject unto	*2962*
Lu	10:21	**O Father, L. of heaven and earth,**	*2962*
Lu	10:27	love the **L.** thy God with all thy	*2962*
Lu	10:40	said, **L.**, dost thou not care that my	*2962*
Lu	11:1	**L.**, teach us to pray, as John also	*2962*
Lu	11:39	the **L.** said unto him, **Now do ye**	*2962*
Lu	12:36	**unto men that wait for their l.,**	*2962*
Lu	12:37	**the l. when he cometh shall find**	*2962*
Lu	12:41	**L.**, speakest thou this parable unto	*2962*
Lu	12:42	**L.** said, **Who then is that faithful**	*2962*
Lu	12:42	**whom his l. shall make ruler over**	*2962*
Lu	12:43	**his l. when he cometh shall find**	*2962*
Lu	12:45	**heart, My l. delayeth his coming;**	*2962*
Lu	12:46	**l. of that servant will come in a**	*2962*
Lu	13:8	**L., let it alone this year also, till**	*2962*
Lu	13:15	**L.** then answered him, and said,	*2962*
Lu	13:23	**L.**, are there few that be saved?	*2962*
Lu	13:25	**L.,...open unto us; and he shall**	*2962*
Lu	13:25	**L., open unto us; and he shall**	*2962*
Lu	13:35	**that cometh in the name of the L.**	*2962*
Lu	14:21	**and shewed his l. these things**	*2962*
Lu	14:22	**said, L., it is done as thou hast**	*2962*
Lu	14:23	**l. said unto the servant, Go out**	*2962*
Lu	16:3	**for my l. taketh away from me the**	*2962*
Lu	16:5	**How much owest thou unto my l.?**	*2962*
Lu	16:8	**l. commended the unjust steward,**	*2962*
Lu	17:5	apostles said unto the **L.**, Increase	*2962*
Lu	17:6	**L.** said, **If ye had faith as a grain**	*2962*
Lu	17:37	Where, **L.**? And he said unto them,	*2962*
Lu	18:6	**L.** said, **Hear what the unjust**	*2962*
Lu	18:41	**L.**, that I may receive my sight.	*2962*
Lu	19:8	Zacchaeus...and said unto the **L.**;	*2962*
Lu	19:8	**L.**, the half of my goods I give to	*2962*
Lu	19:16	**L., thy pound hath gained ten**	*2962*
Lu	19:18	**L., thy pound hath gained five**	*2962*
Lu	19:20	**L., behold, here is thy pound,**	*2962*
Lu	19:25	**unto him, L., he hath ten pounds.)**	*2962*
Lu	19:31	**Because the L. hath need of him**	*2962*
Lu	19:34	they said, The **L.** hath need of him.	*2962*
Lu	19:38	that cometh in the name of the **L.**	*2962*
Lu	20:13	**said the l. of the vineyard, What**	*2962*
Lu	20:15	**l. of the vineyard do unto them?**	*2962*
Lu	20:37	**calleth the L. the God of Abraham,**	*2962*
Lu	20:42	**The L. said...Sit thou on my right**	*2962*
Lu	20:42	**unto my L., Sit thou on my right**	*2962*
Lu	20:44	**David therefore calleth him L.,**	*2962*
Lu	22:31	the **L.** said, **Simon, Simon, behold,**	*2962*
Lu	22:33	**L.**, I am ready to go with thee.	*2962*
Lu	22:38	**L.**, behold, here are two swords.	*2962*
Lu	22:49	**L.**, shall we smite with the sword?	*2962*
Lu	22:61	**L.** turned, and looked upon Peter	*2962*
Lu	22:61	remembered the word of the **L.**,	*2962*
Lu	23:42	**L.**, remember me when thou comest	*2962*
Lu	24:3	found not the body of the **L.** Jesus.	*2962*
Lu	24:34	The **L.** is risen indeed, and hath	*2962*
Joh	1:23	Make straight the way of the **L.**, as	*2962*
Joh	4:1	the **L.** knew how the Pharisees had	*2962*
Joh	6:23	after that the **L.** had given thanks:)	*2962*
Joh	6:34	**L.**, evermore give us this bread	*2962*
Joh	6:68	him, **L.**, to whom shall we go?	*2962*
Joh	8:11	She said, no man, **L.**. And Jesus	*2962*
Joh	9:36	Who is he, **L.**, that I might believe	*2962*
Joh	9:38	**L.**, I believe. And he worshipped	*2962*
Joh	11:2	anointed the **L.** with ointment,	*2962*
Joh	11:3	**L.**, behold, he whom thou lovest is	*2962*
Joh	11:12	**L.**, if he sleep, he shall do well.	*2962*
Joh	11:21	Jesus, **L.**, if thou hadst been here,	*2962*
Joh	11:27	Yea, **L.**: I believe that thou art the	*2962*
Joh	11:32	**L.**, it thou hadst been here, my	*2962*
Joh	11:34	said unto him, **L.**, come and see.	*2962*
Joh	11:39	**L.**, by this time he stinketh: for he	*2962*
Joh	12:13	that cometh in the name of the **L.**	*2962*
Joh	12:38	**L.**, who hath believed our report?	*2962*
Joh	12:38	the arm of the **L.** been revealed?	*2962*
Joh	13:6	him, **L.**, dost thou wash my feet?	*2962*
Joh	13:9	**L.**, not my feet only, but also my	*2962*
Joh	13:13	**Ye call me Master and L.: and ye**	*2962*
Joh	13:14	**If I then, your L. and Master,**	*2962*
Joh	13:16	**servant is not greater than his l.;**	*2962*
Joh	13:25	saith unto him, **L.**, who is it?	*2962*
Joh	13:36	unto him, **L.**, whither goest thou?	*2962*
Joh	13:37	**L.**, why cannot I follow thee now?	*2962*
Joh	14:5	**L.**, we know not whither thou goest;	*2962*
Joh	14:8	him, **L.**, shew us the Father, and it	*2962*
Joh	14:22	**L.**, how is it that thou wilt manifest	*2962*
Joh	15:15	**knowest not what his l. doeth:**	*2962*
Joh	15:20	**servant is not greater than his l.**	*2962*
Joh	20:2	away the **L.** out of the sepulchre,	*2962*
Joh	20:13	they have taken away my **L.**, and I	*2962*
Joh	20:18	disciples that she had seen the **L.**,	*2962*
Joh	20:20	disciples glad, when they saw the **L.**	*2962*
Joh	20:25	said unto him, We have seen the **L.**	*2962*
Joh	20:28	said unto him, My **L.** and my God.	*2962*
Joh	21:7	loved saith unto Peter, It is the **L.**	*2962*
Joh	21:7	Peter heard that it was the **L.**, he	*2962*
Joh	21:12	thou? knowing that it was the **L.**	*2962*
Joh	21:15,	16 **L.**; thou knowest that I love	*2962*
Joh	21:17	**L.**, thou knowest all things; thou	*2962*
Joh	21:20	**L.**, which is he that betrayeth thee?	*2962*
Joh	21:21	**L.**, and what shall this man do?	*2962*
Ac	1:6	**L.**, wilt thou at this time restore	*2962*
Ac	1:21	time that the **L.** Jesus went in and	*2962*
Ac	1:24	Thou, **L.**, which knowest the hearts	*2962*
Ac	2:20	and notable day of the **L.** come:	*2962*
Ac	2:21	the name of the **L.** shall be saved.	*2962*
Ac	2:25	the **L.** always before my face; for	*2962*
Ac	2:34	The **L.** said... Sit thou on my right	*2962*
Ac	2:34	unto my **L.**, Sit thou on my right	*2962*
Ac	2:36	have crucified, both **L.** and Christ.	*2962*
Ac	2:39	many as the **L.** our God shall call.	*2962*
Ac	2:47	**L.** added to the church daily such	*2962*
Ac	3:19	come from the presence of the **L.**;	*2962*
Ac	3:22	prophet shall the **L.** your God raise	*2962*
Ac	4:24	**L.**, thou art God, which hast made	*1203*
Ac	4:26	gathered together against the **L.**,	*2962*
Ac	4:29	now, **L.**, behold their threatenings:	*2962*
Ac	4:33	of the resurrection of the **L.** Jesus:	*2962*
Ac	5:9	to tempt the Spirit of the **L.**?	*2962*
Ac	5:14	believers were...added to the **L.**,	*2962*
Ac	5:19	the angel of the **L.** by night opened	*2962*
Ac	7:30	angel of the **L.** in a flame of fire in	*2962*
Ac	7:31	the voice of the **L.** came unto him,	*2962*
Ac	7:33	Then said the **L.** to him, Put off thy	*2962*
Ac	7:37	prophet shall the **L.** your God raise	*2962*
Ac	7:49	will ye build me? saith the **L.**: or	*2962*
Ac	7:59	saying, **L.** Jesus, receive my spirit.	*2962*
Ac	7:60	**L.**, lay not this sin to their charge.	*2962*
Ac	8:16	in the name of the **L.** Jesus.)	*2962*
Ac	8:24	Pray ye to the **L.** for me, that none	*2962*
Ac	8:25	and preached the word of the **L.**,	*2962*
Ac	8:26	angel of the **L.** spake unto Philip,	*2962*
Ac	8:39	Spirit of the **L.** caught away Philip,	*2962*
Ac	9:1	against the disciples of the **L.**,	*2962*
Ac	9:5	And he said, Who art thou, **L.**?	*2962*
Ac	9:5	And the **L.** said, **I am Jesus whom**	*2962*
Ac	9:6	**L.**, what wilt thou have me to do?	*2962*
Ac	9:6	**L.** said unto him, **Arise, and go**	*2962*
Ac	9:10	said the **L.** in a vision, **Ananias**	*2962*
Ac	9:10	And he said, Behold, I am here, **L.**	*2962*
Ac	9:11	the **L.** said unto him, **Arise, and go**	*2962*
Ac	9:13	**L.**, I have heard by many of this	*2962*
Ac	9:15	the **L.** said unto him, **Go thy way:**	*2962*
Ac	9:17	the **L.**, even Jesus, that appeared	*2962*
Ac	9:27	how he had seen the **L.** in the way,	*2962*
Ac	9:29	boldly in the name of the **L.** Jesus,	*2962*
Ac	9:31	walking in the fear of the **L.**, and in	*2962*
Ac	9:35	saw him and turned to the **L.**	*2962*
Ac	9:42	and many believed in the **L.**	*2962*

Ac 10:4 was afraid, and said, What is it, **L.**? *2962*
Ac 10:14 Not so, **L.**; for I have never eaten *2962*
Ac 10:36 by Jesus Christ: (he is **L.** of all:) *2962*
Ac 10:48 be baptized in the name of the **L.** *2962*
Ac 11:8 not so, **L.**: for nothing common or *2962*
Ac 11:16 remembered I the word of the **L.**, *2962*
Ac 11:17 who believed on the **L.** Jesus Christ; *2962*
Ac 11:20 Grecians, preaching the **L.** Jesus. *2962*
Ac 11:21 the hand of the **L.** was with them: *2962*
Ac 11:21 believed, and turned unto the **L.** *2962*
Ac 11:23 they would cleave unto the **L.** *2962*
Ac 11:24 much people was added unto the **L.** *2962*
Ac 12:7 the angel of the **L.** came upon him, *2962*
Ac 12:11 that the **L.** hath sent his angel, and *2962*
Ac 12:17 how the **L.** had brought him out of *2962*
Ac 12:23 the angel of the **L.** smote him, *2962*
Ac 13:2 As they ministered to the **L.**, and *2962*
Ac 13:10 to pervert the right ways of the **L.**? *2962*
Ac 13:11 the hand of the **L.** is upon thee, and *2962*
Ac 13:12 astonished at the doctrine of the **L.** *2962*
Ac 13:47 For so hath the **L.** commanded us, *2962*
Ac 13:48 and glorified the word of the **L.**: *2962*
Ac 13:49 the word of the **L.** was published *2962*
Ac 14:3 they speaking boldly in the **L.**, *2962*
Ac 14:23 they commended them to the **L.**, *2962*
Ac 15:11 the grace of the **L.** Jesus Christ *2962*
Ac 15:17 of men might seek after the **L.**, *2962*
Ac 15:17 saith the **L.**, who doeth all these *2962*
Ac 15:26 for the name of our **L.** Jesus Christ. *2962*
Ac 15:35 and preaching the word of the **L.**, *2962*
Ac 15:36 have preached the word of the **L.**, *2962*
Ac 16:10 the **L.** had called us for to preach *2962*
Ac 16:14 whose heart the **L.** opened, that she *2962*
Ac 16:15 judged me to be faithful to the **L.**, *2962*
Ac 16:31 Believe on the **L.** Jesus Christ, and *2962*
Ac 16:32 spake unto him the word of the **L.**, *2962*
Ac 17:24 that he is **L.** of heaven and earth, *2962*
Ac 17:27 That they should seek the **L.**, if *2962*
Ac 18:8 believed on the **L.** with all his house; *2962*
Ac 18:9 spake the **L.** to Paul in the night by *2962*
Ac 18:25 was instructed in the way of the **L.**; *2962*
Ac 18:25 diligently the things of the **L.**, *2962*
Ac 19:5 baptized in the name of the **L.** Jesus. *2962*
Ac 19:10 Asia heard the word of the **L.** Jesus, *2962*
Ac 19:13 spirits the name of the **L.** Jesus, *2962*
Ac 19:17 name of the **L.** Jesus was magnified. *2962*
Ac 20:19 Serving the **L.** with all humility of *2962*
Ac 20:21 faith toward our **L.** Jesus Christ. *2962*
Ac 20:24 I have received of the **L.** Jesus, to *2962*
Ac 20:35 remember the words of the **L.** Jesus, *2962*
Ac 21:13 for the name of the **L.** Jesus. *2962*
Ac 21:14 saying, The will of the **L.** be done. *2962*
Ac 21:20 they heard it, they glorified the **L.**, *2962*
Ac 22:8 And I answered, Who art thou, **L.**? *2962*
Ac 22:10 And I said, What shall I do, **L.**? *2962*
Ac 22:10 And the **L.** said unto me, **Arise, and** *2962*
Ac 22:16 sins, calling on the name of the **L.** *2962*
Ac 22:19 **L.**, they know that I imprisoned and *2962*
Ac 23:11 night following the **L.** stood by him, *2962*
Ac 25:26 no certain thing to write unto my **l.** *2962*
Ac 26:15 And I said, Who art thou, **L.**? And *2962*
Ac 28:31 which concern the **L.** Jesus Christ, *2962*
Ro 1:3 his Son Jesus Christ our **L.**, which *2962*
Ro 1:7 our Father, and the **L.** Jesus Christ. *2962*
Ro 4:8 to whom the **L.** will not impute sin. *2962*
Ro 4:24 that raised up Jesus our **L.** from the *2962*
Ro 5:1 God through our **L.** Jesus Christ: *2962*
Ro 5:11 in God through our **L.** Jesus Christ, *2962*
Ro 5:21 eternal life by Jesus Christ our **L.** *2962*
Ro 6:11 God through Jesus Christ our **L.** *2962*
Ro 6:23 life through Jesus Christ our **L.** *2962*
Ro 7:25 God through Jesus Christ our **L.** *2962*
Ro 8:39 God, which is in Christ Jesus our **L.** *2962*
Ro 9:28 a short work will the **L.** make upon *2962*
Ro 9:29 the **L.** of Sabaoth had left us a seed, *2962*
Ro 10:9 confess with thy mouth the **L.** Jesus, *2962*
Ro 10:12 the same **L.** over all is rich unto all *2962*
Ro 10:13 shall call upon the name of the **L.** *2962*
Ro 10:16 **L.**, who hath believed our report? *2962*
Ro 11:3 **L.**, they have killed thy prophets, *2962*
Ro 11:34 who hath known the mind of the **L.**? *2962*
Ro 12:11 fervent in spirit; serving the **L.**; *2962*
Ro 12:19 is mine; I will repay, saith the **L.** *2962*
Ro 13:14 But put ye on the **L.** Jesus Christ, *2962*
Ro 14:6 the day, regardeth it unto the **L.**; *2962*
Ro 14:6 day, to the **L.** he doth not regard it. *2962*
Ro 14:6 He that eateth, eateth to the **L.**, for *2962*
Ro 14:6 eateth not, to the **L.** he eateth not, *2962*
Ro 14:8 whether we live, we live unto the **L.**; *2962*
Ro 14:8 whether we die, we die unto the **L.**: *2962*
Ro 14:9 be **L.** both of the dead and living. *2961*
Ro 14:11 As I live, saith the **L.**, every knee *2962*
Ro 14:14 and am persuaded by the **L.** Jesus, *2962*
Ro 15:6 the Father of our **L.** Jesus Christ. *2962*
Ro 15:11 again, Praise the **L.**, all ye Gentiles; *2962*
Ro 15:30 for the **L.** Jesus Christ's sake, and *2962*
Ro 16:2 That ye receive her in the **L.**, as *2962*
Ro 16:8 Greet Amplias my beloved in the **L.** *2962*
Ro 16:11 of Narcissus, which are in the **L.** *2962*
Ro 16:12 and Tryphosa, who labour in the **L.** *2962*
Ro 16:12 which laboured much in the **L.** *2962*
Ro 16:13 Salute Rufus chosen in the **L.**, and *2962*
Ro 16:18 such serve not our **L.** Jesus Christ, *2962*
Ro 16:20 grace of our **L.** Jesus Christ be with *2962*
Ro 16:22 this epistle, salute you in the **L.** *2962*
Ro 16:24 grace of our **L.** Jesus Christ be with *2962*
1Co 1:2 the name of Jesus Christ our **L.**, *2962*
1Co 1:3 and from the **L.** Jesus Christ. *2962*
1Co 1:7 the coming of our **L.** Jesus Christ: *2962*
1Co 1:8 in the day of our **L.** Jesus Christ. *2962*
1Co 1:9 of his Son Jesus Christ our **L.** *2962*
1Co 1:10 by the name of our **L.** Jesus Christ, *2962*
1Co 1:31 that glorieth, let him glory in the **L.** *2962*
1Co 2:8 not have crucified the **L.** of glory. *2962*
1Co 2:16 who hath known the mind of the **L.**, *2962*
1Co 3:5 even as the **L.** gave to every man? *2962*
1Co 3:20 **L.** knoweth the thoughts of the wise, *2962*
1Co 4:4 but he that judgeth me is the **L.** *2962*
1Co 4:5 before the time, until the **L.** come, *2962*
1Co 4:17 beloved son, and faithful in the **L.**, *2962*
1Co 4:19 come to you shortly, if the **L.** will, *2962*
1Co 5:4 In the name of our **L.** Jesus Christ, *2962*
1Co 5:4 the power of our **L.** Jesus Christ. *2962*
1Co 5:5 be saved in the day of the **L.** Jesus. *2962*
1Co 6:11 justified in the name of the **L.** Jesus, *2962*
1Co 6:13 not for fornication, but for the **L.**; *2962*
1Co 6:13 and the **L.** for the body. *2962*
1Co 6:14 God hath both raised up the **L.**, and *2962*
1Co 6:17 is joined unto the **L.** is one spirit. *2962*
1Co 7:10 I command, yet not I, but the **L.**, *2962*
1Co 7:12 But to the rest speak I, not the **L.**: *2962*
1Co 7:17 as the **L.** hath called every one, as *2962*
1Co 7:22 For he that is called in the **L.**, being *2962*
1Co 7:25 I have no commandment of the **L.**: *2962*
1Co 7:25 that hath obtained mercy of the **L.** *2962*
1Co 7:32 for the things that belong to the **L.**, *2962*
1Co 7:32 how he may please the **L.**: *2962*
1Co 7:34 careth for the things of the **L.**, that *2962*
1Co 7:35 ye may attend upon the **L.** without *2962*
1Co 7:39 to whom she will; only in the **L.** *2962*
1Co 8:6 and one **L.** Jesus Christ, by whom *2962*
1Co 9:1 have I not seen Jesus Christ our **L.**? *2962*
1Co 9:1 are not ye my work in the **L.**? *2962*
1Co 9:2 of mine apostleship are ye in the **L.** *2962*
1Co 9:5 and as the brethren of the **L.**, and *2962*
1Co 9:14 Even so hath the **L.** ordained that *2962*
1Co 10:21 Ye cannot drink the cup of the **L.**, *2962*
1Co 10:22 Do we provoke the **L.** to jealousy? *2962*
1Co 11:11 woman without the man, in the **L.** *2962*
1Co 11:23 I have received of the **L.** that which *2962*
1Co 11:23 That the **L.** Jesus the same night *2962*
1Co 11:27 bread, and drink this cup of the **L.**, *2962*
1Co 11:27 of the body and blood of the **L.** *2962*
1Co 11:32 judged, we are chastened of the **L.**, *2962*
1Co 12:3 no man can say that Jesus is the **L.**, *2962*
1Co 12:5 administrations, but the same **L.** *2962*
1Co 14:21 will they not hear me, saith the **L.** *2962*
1Co 14:37 are the commandments of the **L.** *2962*
1Co 15:31 which I have in Christ Jesus our **L.**, *2962*
1Co 15:47 second man is the **L.** from heaven. *2962*
1Co 15:57 victory through our **L.** Jesus Christ. *2962*
1Co 15:58 abounding in the work of the **L.**, *2962*
1Co 15:58 your labour is not in vain in the **L.** *2962*
1Co 16:7 a while with you, if the **L.** permit. *2962*
1Co 16:10 for he worketh the work of the **L.**, *2962*
1Co 16:19 Priscilla salute you much in the **L.**, *2962*
1Co 16:22 man love not the **L.** Jesus Christ, *2962*
1Co 16:23 grace of our **L.** Jesus Christ be with *2962*
2Co 1:2 and from the **L.** Jesus Christ. *2962*
2Co 1:3 the Father of our **L.** Jesus Christ, *2962*
2Co 1:14 are ours in the day of the **L.** Jesus. *2962*
2Co 2:12 door was opened unto me of the **L.**, *2962*
2Co 3:16 when it shall turn to the **L.**, the vail *2962*
2Co 3:17 Now the **L.** is that Spirit: and where *2962*
2Co 3:17 where the Spirit of the **L.** is, there *2962*
2Co 3:18 as in a glass the glory of the **L.**, *2962*
2Co 3:18 glory even as by the Spirit of the **L.** *2962*
2Co 4:5 ourselves, but Christ Jesus the **L.**; *2962*
2Co 4:10 the body the dying of the **L.** Jesus, *2962*
2Co 4:14 he which raised up the **L.** Jesus *2962*
2Co 5:6 body, we are absent from the **L.**: *2962*
2Co 5:8 body, and to be present with the **L.** *2962*
2Co 5:11 Knowing...the terror of the **L.**, we *2962*
2Co 6:17 and be ye separate, saith the **L.**, *2962*
2Co 6:18 daughters, saith the **L.** Almighty. *2962*
2Co 8:5 gave their own selves to the **L.**, and *2962*
2Co 8:9 ye know the grace of our **L.** Jesus *2962*
2Co 8:19 by us to the glory of the same **L.**, *2962*
2Co 8:21 not only in the sight of the **L.**, but *2962*
2Co 10:8 the **L.** hath given us for edification, *2962*
2Co 10:17 glorieth, let him glory in the **L.** *2962*
2Co 10:18 but whom the **L.** commendeth. *2962*
2Co 11:17 I speak, I speak it not after the **L.**, *2962*
2Co 11:31 and Father of our **L.** Jesus Christ, *2962*
2Co 12:1 visions and revelations of the **L.** *2962*
2Co 12:8 this thing I besought the **L.** thrice, *2962*
2Co 13:10 power which the **L.** hath given me *2962*
2Co 13:14 The grace of the **L.** Jesus Christ, *2962*
Ga 1:3 and from our **L.** Jesus Christ, *2962*
Ga 4:1 a servant, though he be **l.** of all; *2962*
Ga 5:10 confidence in you through the **L.**, *2962*
Ga 6:14 in the cross of our **L.** Jesus Christ, *2962*
Ga 6:17 my body the marks of the **L.** Jesus. *2962*
Ga 6:18 grace of our **L.** Jesus Christ be with *2962*
Eph 1:2 and from the **L.** Jesus Christ. *2962*
Eph 1:3 and Father of our **L.** Jesus Christ, *2962*
Eph 1:15 heard of your faith in the **L.** Jesus, *2962*
Eph 1:17 That the God of our **L.** Jesus Christ, *2962*
Eph 2:21 unto an holy temple in the **L.**: *2962*
Eph 3:11 he purposed in Christ Jesus our **L.**: *2962*
Eph 3:14 the Father of our **L.** Jesus Christ, *2962*
Eph 4:1 I therefore, the prisoner of the **L.**, *2962*
Eph 4:5 One **L.**, one faith, one baptism, *2962*
Eph 4:17 I say therefore, and testify in the **L.**, *2962*
Eph 5:8 but now are ye light in the **L.**: walk *2962*
Eph 5:10 what is acceptable unto the **L.** *2962*
Eph 5:17 what the will of the **L.** is. *2962*
Eph 5:19 melody in your heart to the **L.**; *2962*
Eph 5:20 in the name of our **L.** Jesus Christ; *2962*
Eph 5:22 your own husbands, as unto the **L.** *2962*
Eph 5:29 it, even as the **L.** the church: *2962*
Eph 6:1 obey your parents in the **L.**: for *2962*
Eph 6:4 nurture and admonition of the **L.** *2962*
Eph 6:7 good will doing service, as to the **L.**, *2962*
Eph 6:8 the same shall he receive of the **L.**, *2962*
Eph 6:10 my brethren, be strong in the **L.**, *2962*
Eph 6:21 and faithful minister in the **L.**, *2962*
Eph 6:23 the Father and the **L.** Jesus Christ. *2962*
Eph 6:24 them that love our **L.** Jesus Christ *2962*
Php 1:2 and from the **L.** Jesus Christ. *2962*
Php 1:14 And many of the brethren in the **L.**, *2962*
Php 2:11 confess that Jesus Christ is **L.**, to *2962*
Php 2:19 But I trust in the **L.** Jesus to send *2962*
Php 2:24 I trust in the **L.** that I also myself *2962*
Php 2:29 Receive him therefore in the **L.** with *2962*
Php 3:1 my brethren, rejoice in the **L.** *2962*
Php 3:8 knowledge of Christ Jesus my **L.**: *2962*
Php 3:20 for the Saviour, the **L.** Jesus Christ: *2962*
Php 4:1 and crown, so stand fast in the **L.**, *2962*
Php 4:2 they be of the same mind in the **L.** *2962*
Php 4:4 Rejoice in the **L.** alway: and again *2962*
Php 4:5 unto all men. The **L.** is at hand. *2962*
Php 4:10 But I rejoiced in the **L.** greatly, that *2962*
Php 4:23 grace of our **L.** Jesus Christ be with *2962*
Col 1:2 our Father and the **L.** Jesus Christ. *2962*
Col 1:3 the Father of our **L.** Jesus Christ, *2962*
Col 1:10 That ye might walk worthy of the **L.** *2962*
Col 2:6 received Christ Jesus the **L.**, so *2962*
Col 3:16 with grace in your hearts to the **L.** *2962*
Col 3:17 do all in the name of the **L.** Jesus, *2962*
Col 3:18 own husbands, as it is fit in the **L.** *2962*
Col 3:20 for this is well pleasing unto the **L.** *2962*
Col 3:23 ye do, do it heartily, as to the **L.**, *2962*
Col 3:24 of the **L.** ye shall receive the reward *2962*
Col 3:24 for ye serve the **L.** Christ. *2962*
Col 4:7 and fellowservant in the **L.**: *2962*
Col 4:17 which thou hast received in the **L.**, *2962*
1Th 1:1 Father and in the **L.** Jesus Christ: *2962*

1Th 1:1 Father, and the **L.** Jesus Christ. *2962*
1Th 1:3 of hope in our **L.** Jesus Christ, ... *2962*
1Th 1:6 followers of us, and of the **L.**, ... *2962*
1Th 1:8 you sounded out the word of the **L.** ... *2962*
1Th 2:15 Who both killed the **L.** Jesus, and *2962*
1Th 2:19 the presence of our **L.** Jesus Christ.... *2962*
1Th 3:8 we live, if ye stand fast in the **L.**. *2962*
1Th 3:11 our Father, and our **L.** Jesus Christ,... *2962*
1Th 3:12 **L.** make you to increase and abound... *2962*
1Th 3:13 the coming of our **L.** Jesus Christ *2962*
1Th 4:1 and exhort you by the **L.** Jesus, ... *2962*
1Th 4:2 we gave you by the **L.** Jesus............ *2962*
1Th 4:6 the **L.** is the avenger of all such, ... *2962*
1Th 4:15 say unto you by the word of the **L.**,... *2962*
1Th 4:15 remain unto the coming of the **L.**....... *2962*
1Th 4:16 the **L.** himself shall descend from....... *2962*
1Th 4:17 the clouds, to meet the **L.** in the air:.. *2962*
1Th 4:17 and so shall we ever be with the **L.**. .. *2962*
1Th 5:2 day of the **L.** so cometh as a thief...... *2962*
1Th 5:9 salvation by our **L.** Jesus Christ,......... *2962*
1Th 5:12 you, and are over you in the **L.**, and .. *2962*
1Th 5:23 the coming of our **L.** Jesus Christ. *2962*
1Th 5:27 I charge you by the **L.** that this......... *2962*
1Th 5:28 grace of our **L.** Jesus Christ be with... *2962*
2Th 1:1 our Father and the **L.** Jesus Christ:.... *2962*
2Th 1:2 our Father and the **L.** Jesus Christ..... *2962*
2Th 1:7 the **L.** Jesus shall be revealed from *2962*
2Th 1:8 the gospel of our **L.** Jesus Christ: *2962*
2Th 1:9 from the presence of the **L.**, and *2962*
2Th 1:12 name of our **L.** Jesus Christ may be ... *2962*
2Th 1:12 of our God and the **L.** Jesus Christ..... *2962*
2Th 2:1 the coming of our **L.** Jesus Christ, ... *2962*
2Th 2:8 whom the **L.** shall consume with the... *2962*
2Th 2:13 for you, brethren beloved of the **L.**, ... *2962*
2Th 2:14 of the glory of our **L.** Jesus Christ. *2962*
2Th 2:16 Now our **L.** Jesus Christ himself, ... *2962*
2Th 3:1 the word of the **L.** may have free *2962*
2Th 3:3 **L.** is faithful, who shall stablish.......... *2962*
2Th 3:4 confidence in the **L.** touching you, ... *2962*
2Th 3:5 **L.** direct your hearts into the love...... *2962*
2Th 3:6 in the name of our **L.** Jesus Christ, ... *2962*
2Th 3:12 and exhort by our **L.** Jesus Christ, ... *2962*
2Th 3:16 **L.** of peace himself give you peace..... *2962*
2Th 3:16 all means. The **L.** be with you all....... *2962*
2Th 3:18 grace of our **L.** Jesus Christ be with... *2962*
1Ti 1:1 our Saviour, and **L.** Jesus Christ, ... *2962*
1Ti 1:2 our Father, and Jesus Christ our **L.**.... *2962*
1Ti 1:12 And I thank Christ Jesus our **L.**,........ *2962*
1Ti 1:14 the grace of our **L.** was exceeding *2962*
1Ti 5:21 before God, and the **L.** Jesus Christ, .. *2962*
1Ti 6:3 even the words of our **L.** Jesus, ... *2962*
1Ti 6:14 appearing of our **L.** Jesus Christ: *2962*
1Ti 6:15 the King of kings, and **L.** of lords; *2962*
2Ti 1:2 the Father and Christ Jesus our **L.**:.... *2962*
2Ti 1:8 ashamed of the testimony of our **L.**, ... *2962*
2Ti 1:16 The **L.** give mercy unto the house of.. *2962*
2Ti 1:18 **L.** grant unto him that he may find..... *2962*
2Ti 1:18 find mercy of the **L.** in that day: *2962*
2Ti 2:7 **L.** give thee understanding in all *2962*
2Ti 2:14 charging them before the **L.** that........ *2962*
2Ti 2:19 The **L.** knoweth them that are his...... *2962*
2Ti 2:22 call on the **L.** out of a pure heart....... *2962*
2Ti 2:24 servant of the **L.** must not strive; *2962*
2Ti 3:11 out of them all the **L.** delivered me. ... *2962*
2Ti 4:1 before God, and the **L.** Jesus Christ, .. *2962*
2Ti 4:8 which the **L.**, the righteous judge,...... *2962*
2Ti 4:14 the **L.** reward him according to his..... *2962*
2Ti 4:17 **L.** stood with me, and strengthened ... *2962*
2Ti 4:18 **L.** shall deliver me from every evil..... *2962*
2Ti 4:22 **L.** Jesus Christ be with thy spirit. *2962*
Tit 1:4 the **L.** Jesus Christ our Saviour. *2962*
Phm 3 our Father and the **L.** Jesus Christ..... *2962*
Phm 5 which thou hast toward the **L.** Jesus,.. *2962*
Phm 16 both in the flesh, and in the **L.**?......... *2962*
Phm 20 let me have joy of thee in the **L.**: *2962*
Phm 20 refresh my bowels in the **L.**............. *2962*
Phm 25 grace of our **L.** Jesus Christ be with... *2962*
Heb 1:10 Thou, **L.**, in the beginning hast.......... *2962*
Heb 2:3 first began to be spoken by the **L.**, ... *2962*
Heb 7:14 that our **L.** sprang out of Juda; *2962*
Heb 7:21 The **L.** sware and will not repent, ... *2962*
Heb 8:2 tabernacle, which the **L.** pitched, ... *2962*
Heb 8:8 the days come, saith the **L.**, when *2962*
Heb 8:9 I regarded them not, saith the **L.**........ *2962*
Heb 8:10 Israel after those days, saith the **L.**;... *2962*
Heb 8:11 his brother, saying, Know the **L.**: *2962*
Heb 10:16 them after those days, saith the **L.**;.... *2962*
Heb 10:30 me, I will recompense, saith the **L.**.... *2962*
Heb 10:30 The **L.** shall judge his people. *2962*
Heb 12:5 not thou the chastening of the **L.**, ... *2962*
Heb 12:6 whom the **L.** loveth he chasteneth,..... *2962*
Heb 12:14 which no man shall see the **L.**: *2962*
Heb 13:6 boldly say, The **L.** is my helper, ... *2962*
Heb 13:20 again from the dead our **L.** Jesus, ... *2962*
Jas 1:1 of God and of the **L.** Jesus Christ, ... *2962*
Jas 1:7 shall receive any thing of the **L.**......... *2962*
Jas 1:12 which the **L.** hath promised to them ... *2962*
Jas 2:1 not the faith of our **L.** Jesus Christ,.... *2962*
Jas 2:1 **L.** of glory, with respect of persons..........
Jas 4:10 yourselves in the sight of the **L.**, ... *2962*
Jas 4:15 that ye ought to say, If the **L.** will, ... *2962*
Jas 5:4 into the ears of the **L.** of Sabaoth. *2962*
Jas 5:7 brethren unto the coming of the **L.**..... *2962*
Jas 5:8 the coming of the **L.** draweth nigh...... *2962*
Jas 5:10 have spoken in the name of the **L.**, ... *2962*
Jas 5:11 and have seen the end of the **L.**; *2962*
Jas 5:11 that the **L.** is very pitiful, and of......... *2962*
Jas 5:14 him with oil in the name of the **L.**:..... *2962*
Jas 5:15 sick, and the **L.** shall raise him up;..... *2962*
1Pe 1:3 and Father of our **L.** Jesus Christ,...... *2962*
1Pe 1:25 word of the **L.** endureth for ever. *2962*
1Pe 2:3 have tasted that the **L.** is gracious. *2962*
1Pe 3:6 obeyed Abraham, calling him **l.**: *2962*
1Pe 3:12 For the eyes of the **L.** are over the ... *2962*
1Pe 3:12 the face of the **L.** is against them....... *2962*
1Pe 3:15 sanctify the **L.** God in your hearts:..... *2962*
2Pe 1:2 of God, and of Jesus our **L.**, ... *2962*
2Pe 1:8 knowledge of our **L.** Jesus Christ. *2962*
2Pe 1:11 kingdom of our **L.** and Saviour.......... *2962*
2Pe 1:14 **L.** Jesus Christ hath shewed me. *2962*
2Pe 1:16 and coming of our **L.** Jesus Christ, ... *2962*
2Pe 2:1 denying the **L.** that brought them,...... *1203*
2Pe 2:9 The **L.** knoweth how to deliver the *2962*
2Pe 2:11 against them before the **L.**............... *2962*
2Pe 2:20 knowledge of the **L.** and Saviour........ *2962*
2Pe 3:2 the apostles of the **L.** and Saviour:..... *2962*
2Pe 3:8 one day is with the **L.** as a thousand .. *2962*
2Pe 3:9 The **L.** is not slack concerning his...... *2962*
2Pe 3:10 day of the **L.** will come as a thief....... *2962*
2Pe 3:15 that the longsuffering of our **L.** is...... *2962*
2Pe 3:18 knowledge of our **L.** and Saviour........ *2962*
2Jo 3 and from the **L.** Jesus Christ, the....... *2962*
Jude 4 and denying the only **L.** God, ... *2962*
Jude 4 God, and our **L.** Jesus Christ. *2962*
Jude 5 how that the **L.**, having saved the...... *2962*
Jude 9 but said, The **L.** rebuke thee. *2962*
Jude 14 the **L.** cometh with ten thousands *2962*
Jude 17 of the apostles of our **L.** Jesus *2962*
Jude 21 for the mercy of our **L.** Jesus Christ... *2962*
Re 1:8 and the ending, saith the **L.**, which..... *2962*
Re 4:8 Holy, holy, holy, **L.** God Almighty,..... *2962*
Re 4:11 Thou art worthy, O **L.**, to receive *2962*
Re 6:10 How long, O **L.**, holy and true, dost... *1203*
Re 11:8 where also our **L.** was crucified. *2962*
Re 11:15 are become the kingdoms of our **L.**, ... *2962*
Re 11:17 thee thanks, O **L.** God Almighty, ... *2962*
Re 14:13 are the dead which die in the **L.**. *2962*
Re 15:3 are thy works, **L.** God Almighty; *2962*
Re 15:4 Who shall not fear thee, O **L.**, and..... *2962*
Re 16:5 Thou art righteous, O **L.**, which *2962*
Re 16:7 Even so, **L.** God Almighty, true and... *2962*
Re 17:14 for he is **L.** of lords, and King of *2962*
Re 18:8 strong is the **L.** God which judgeth..... *2962*
Re 19:1 and power, unto the **L.** our God: *2962*
Re 19:6 the **L.** God omnipotent reigneth.......... *2962*
Re 19:16 King Of Kings, And **L.** of Lords. *2962*
Re 21:22 for the **L.** God Almighty and the........ *2962*
Re 22:5 the **L.** God giveth them light: and *2962*
Re 22:6 the **L.** God of the holy prophets *2962*
Re 22:20 Amen. Even so, come, **L.** Jesus. *2962*
Re 22:21 grace of our **L.** Jesus Christ be with... *2962*

LORDLY

Jg 5:25 brought forth butter in a **l.** dish. 117

LORD'S

Ge 40:7 him in the ward of his **l.** house............ 113
Ge 44:8 we steal out of thy **l.** house silver........ 113
Ge 44:9 and we also will be my **l.** bondmen. 113
Ge 44:16 behold, we are my **l.** servants, both...... 113
Ge 44:18 speak a word in my **l.** ears, and let...... 113
Ex 9:29 know how that the earth is the **L.**...... 3068
Ex 12:11 it in haste: it is the **L.** passover......... 3068
Ex 12:27 is the sacrifice of the **L.** passover, ... 3068
Ex 13:9 the **L.** law may be in thy mouth:........ 3068
Ex 13:12 hast: the male shall be the **L.**............ 3068
Ex 32:26 Who is on the **L.** side? let him 3068
Ex 35:21 they brought the **L.** offering to 3068
Ex 35:24 and brass brought the **L.** offering: 3068
Le 3:16 sweet savour: all the fat is the **L.**. 3068
Le 16:9 goat upon which the **L.** lot fell,.......... 3068
Le 23:5 month at even is the **L.** passover....... 3068
Le 27:26 which should be the **L.** firstling,......... 3068
Le 27:26 it be ox, or sheep; it is the **L.**........... 3068
Le 27:30 of the fruit of the tree, is the **L.**......... 3068
Nu 11:23 Is the **L.** hand waxed short? 3068
Nu 11:29 all the **L.** people were prophets, ... 3068
Nu 18:28 the **L.** heave offering to Aaron 3068
Nu 31:37 the **L.** tribute of the sheep was 3068
Nu 31:38, 39 the **L.** tribute was three score 3068
Nu 31:40 the **L.** tribute was thirty and two....... 3068
Nu 31:41 which was the **L.** heave offering, ... 3068
Nu 32:10 **L.** anger was kindled the same.......... 3068
Nu 32:13 the **L.** anger was kindled against........ 3068
De 10:14 of heavens is the **L.** thy God,............ 3068
De 11:17 **L.** wrath be kindled against you, ... 3068
De 15:2 because it is called the **L.** release. 3068
De 32:9 For the **L.** portion is his people; 3068
Jos 1:15 Moses the **L.** servant gave you 3068
Jos 5:15 captain of the **L.** host said unto 3068
Jos 22:19 wherein the **L.** tabernacle................. 3068
Jg 11:31 Ammon, shall surely be the **L.**, ... 3068
1Sa 2:8 the pillars of the earth are the **L.**,...... 3068
1Sa 2:24 make the **L.** people to transgress....... 3068
1Sa 14:3 son of Eli, the **L.** priest in Shiloh, ... 3068
1Sa 16:6 the **L.** anointed is before him. 3068
1Sa 17:47 for the battle is the **L.**, and he will..... 3068
1Sa 18:17 for me, and fight the **L.** battles.......... 3068
1Sa 22:21 that Saul had slain the **L.** priests........ 3068
1Sa 24:6 unto my master, the **L.** anointed,....... 3068
1Sa 24:20 lord; for he is the **L.** anointed. 3068
1Sa 26:9 his hand against the **L.** anointed,........ 3068
1Sa 26:11 hand against the **L.** anointed: 3068
1Sa 26:16 your master, the **L.** anointed............. 3068
1Sa 26:23 hand against the **L.** anointed. 3068
2Sa 1:14 hand to destroy the **L.** anointed?......... 3068
2Sa 1:16 I have slain the **L.** anointed. 3068
2Sa 19:21 because he cursed the **L.** anointed? 3068
2Sa 20:6 take thou thy **l.** servants, and............ 113
2Sa 21:7 **L.** oath that was between them, ... 3068
1Ki 18:13 an hundred men of the **L.** prophets 3068
2Ki 11:17 that they should be the **L.** people;...... 3068
2Ki 13:17 The arrow of the **L.** deliverance, ... 3068
1Ch 21:3 are they not all my **l.** servants?........... 113
2Ch 7:2 glory...had filled the **L.** house............ 3068
2Ch 23:16 that they should be the **L.** people....... 3068
Ps 11:4 the **L.** throne is in heaven: his 3068
Ps 22:28 For the kingdom is the **L.**: and.......... 3068
Ps 24:1 earth is the **L.**, and the fulness.......... 3068
Ps 113:3 the **L.** name is to be praised............. 3068
Ps 115:16 even the heavens, are the **L.**............ 3068
Ps 116:19 In the courts of the **L.** house, in........ 3068
Ps 118:23 This is the **L.** doing; it is 3068
Ps 137:4 How shall we sing the **L.** song in....... 3068
Pr 16:11 weight and balance are the **L.** 3068
Isa 2:2 that the mountains of the **L.** house..... 3068
Isa 22:18 shall be the shame of thy **l.** house. 113
Isa 34:8 is the day of the **L.** vengeance, ... 3068
Isa 40:2 received of the **L.** hand double 3068
Isa 42:19 and blind as the **L.** servant?.............. 3068
Isa 44:5 One shall say, I am the **L.**; and 3068
Isa 59:1 the **L.** hand is not shortened, that...... 3068
Jer 5:10 for they are not the **L.**. 3068
Jer 7:2 Stand in the gate of the **L.** house,...... 3068
Jer 13:17 **L.** flock is carried away captive.......... 3068
Jer 19:14 stood in the court of the **L.** house;..... 3068
Jer 25:17 took I the cup at the **L.** hand,........... 3068
Jer 26:2 Stand in the court of the **L.** house,..... 3068
Jer 26:2 come to worship in the **L.** house,....... 3068
Jer 26:10 of the new gate of the **L.** house. 3068
Jer 27:16 the vessels of the **L.** house shall......... 3068
Jer 28:3 all the vessels of the **L.** house,.......... 3068
Jer 28:6 again the vessels of the **L.** house, ... 3068
Jer 36:6 ears of the people in the **L.** house...... 3068
Jer 36:8 words of the Lord in the **L.** house. 3068
Jer 36:10 of the new gate of the **L.** house, ... 3068
Jer 51:6 is the time of the **L.** vengeance; 3068
Jer 51:7 been a golden cup in the **L.** hand, ... 3068
Jer 51:51 the sanctuaries of the **L.** house.......... 3068

La 2:22 day of the L. anger none escaped...... 3068
La 3:22 of the L. mercies that we are not...... 3068
Eze 8:14 door of the gate of the L. house........ 3068
Eze 8:16 the inner court of the L. house,......... 3068
Eze 10:4 of the brightness of the L. glory. 3068
Eze 10:19 of the east gate of the L. house; 3068
Eze 11:1 unto the east gate of the L. house, ... 3068
Da 9:17 that is desolate, for the L. sake. 136
Ho 9:3 shall not dwell in the L. land;........... 3068
Joe 1:9 priests, the L. ministers, mourn. 3068
Ob 21 and the kindgom shall be the L.......... 3068
Mic 6:2 O mountains, the L. controversy,....... 3068
Mic 6:9 The L. voice crieth unto the city, ... 3068
Hab 2:16 the cup of the L. right hand shall....... 3068
Zep 1:8 pass in the day of the L. sacrifice, ... 3068
Zep 1:18 them in the day of the L. wrath;......... 3068
Zep 2:2 before the day of the L. anger 3068
Zep 2:3 be hid in the day of the L. anger. 3068
Hag 1:2 that the L. house should be built........ 3068
Hag 1:13 spake Haggai the L. messenger 3068
Hag 1:13 in the L. message unto the people, ... 3068
Hag 2:18 the foundation of the L. temple.......... 3068
Zec 14:20 pots in the L. house shall be like 3068
Mt 21:42 **this is the L. doing, and it is** *2962*
Mt 25:18 **in the earth, and his his l. money.** .*2962*
Mk 12:11 **This was the L. doing, and it is** *2962*
Lu 2:26 before he had seen the L. Christ. *2962*
Lu 12:47 **servant, which knew his l. will,**..... *2962*
Lu 16:5 **he called every one of his l.**.......... *2962*
Ro 14:8 live therefore, or die, we are the L.... *2962*
1Co 7:22 being a servant, is the L. freeman:....... *2962*
1Co 10:21 cannot be partakers of the L. table,..... *2962*
1Co 10:26 the earth is the L., and the fullness.... *2962*
1Co 10:28 earth is the L., and the fullness......... *2962*
1Co 11:20 this is not to eat the L. supper.......... *2960*
1Co 11:26 do shew the L. death till he come...... *2962*
1Co 11:29 himself, not discerning the L. body..... *2962*
Ga 1:19 none, save James the L. brother........ *2962*
1Pe 2:13 ordinance of man for the L. sake: *2962*
Re 1:10 I was in the Spirit on the L. day,....... *2960*

LORDS
Ge 19:2 he said, Behold now, my l., turn in,..... 113
Nu 21:28 the l. of the high places of Arnon....... 1167
De 10:17 God is God of gods, and Lord of l., ... 113
Jos 13:3 five l. of the Philistines; the.............. 5633
Jg 3:3 five l. of the Philistines, and all the..... 5633
Jg 16:5 l. of the Philistines came up unto 5633
Jg 16:8 l. of the Philistines brought up to 5633
Jg 16:18 called for the l. of the Philistines,....... 5633
Jg 16:18 l. of the Philistines came up unto 5633
Jg 16:23 the l. of the Philistines gathered 5633
Jg 16:27 l. of the Philistines were there; 5633
Jg 16:30 the house fell upon the l., and upon.... 5633
1Sa 5:8 gathered all the l. of the Philistines..... 5633
1Sa 5:11 together all the l. of the Philistines,.... 5633
1Sa 6:4 number of the l. of the Philistines: 5633
1Sa 6:4 was on you all, and on your l. 5633
1Sa 6:12 l. of the Philistines went after them.... 5633
1Sa 6:16 five l. of the Philistines had seen it,.... 5633
1Sa 6:18 Philistines belonging to the five l.,...... 5633
1Sa 7:7 l. of the Philistines went up against 5633
1Sa 29:2 the l. of the Philistines passed on........ 5633
1Sa 29:6 nevertheless the l. favour thee not. 5633
1Sa 29:7 displease not the l. of the Philistines... 5633
1Ch 12:19 for the l. of the Philistines upon.......... 5633
Ezr 8:25 his l., and all Israel there present,....... 8269
Ps 136:3 O give thanks to the Lord of l.: 113
Isa 16:8 l. of the heathen have broken down.... 1167
Isa 26:13 other l. beside thee have had............. 113
Jer 2:31 say my people, We are l.; 7300
Eze 23:23 and rulers, great l. and renowned,....... 7991
Da 4:36 and my l. sought unto me; and.......... 7261
Da 5:1 a great feast to a thousand of his l., ... 7261
Da 5:9 in him, and his l. were astonied. 7261
Da 5:10 of the words of the king and his l....... 7261
Da 5:23 thou, and thy l., thy wives, and thy.... 7261
Da 6:17 and with the signet of his l.; 7261
Mk 6:21 birthday made a supper to his l.,......... *3175*
1Co 8:5 there be gods many, and l. many,) *2962*
1Ti 6:15 the King of kings, and Lord of l.;........ *2961*
1Pe 5:3 as being l. over God's heritage *2634*
Re 17:14 is Lord of l., and King of kings; *2634*
Re 19:16 King of Kings, and Lord of L. *2634*

LORDSHIP
Mk 10:42 **Gentiles exercise l. over them;** *2634*
Lu 22:25 **Gentiles exercise l. over them;** *2961*

LO-RUHAMAH (lo-ru-ha'-mah)
Ho 1:6 said unto him, Call her name L.......... 3819
Ho 1:8 Now when she had weaned L., she..... 3819

LOSE See also LOSETH; LOST.
Jg 18:25 and thou l. thy life, with the lives........ 622
1Ki 18:5 alive, that we l. not all the beasts. 3772
Job 31:39 the owners thereof to l. their life: 5307
Pr 23:8 vomit up, and l. thy sweet words....... 7843
Ec 3:6 A time to get, and a time to l.; a 6
Mt 10:39 **He that findeth his life shall l. it:**... *622*
Mt 10:42 **he shall in no wise l. his reward**.... *622*
Mt 16:25 **will save his life shall l. it**........... *622*
Mt 16:25 **will l. his life for my sake shall**...... *622*
Mt 16:26 **whole world, and l. his own soul?**.. *2210*
Mk 8:35 **will save his life shall l. it;**............ *622*
Mk 8:35 **shall l. his life for my sake and**........ *622*
Mk 8:36 **whole world, and l. his own soul?**.. *2210*
Mk 9:41 **unto you, he shall not l. his reward**.*622*
Lu 9:24 **will save his life shall l. it:**............ *622*
Lu 9:24 **will l. his life for my sake, the**....... *622*
Lu 9:25 **gain the whole world, and l.**........... *622*
Lu 15:4 **hundred sheep, if he l. one of them,**.*622*
Lu 15:8 **if she l. one piece, doth not light a**..*622*
Lu 17:33 **shall seek to save his life shall l. it;**.*622*
Lu 17:33 **shall l. his life shall preserve it.** *622*
Joh 6:39 **hath given me I should l. nothing,**.. *622*
Joh 12:25 **He that loveth his life shall l. it;**.... *622*
2Jo 8 l. not those things which we have......... *622*

LOSETH
Mt 10:39 **l. his life for my sake shall find it**...*622*

LOSS
Ge 31:39 not unto thee; I bare the l. of it; 2398
Ex 21:19 he shall pay for the l. of his time, ... 7674
Isa 47:8 shall I know the l. of children: 7921
Isa 47:9 in one day, the l. of children, and....... 7921
Ac 27:21 to have gained this harm and l........... *2209*
Ac 27:22 be no l. of any man's life among.......... *580*
1Co 3:15 shall be burned, he shall suffer l.: *2210*
Php 3:7 me, those I counted l. for Christ........ *2209*
Php 3:8 I count all things but l. for the.......... *2209*
Php 3:8 I have suffered the l. of all things,...... *2210*

LOST
Ex 22:9 or for any manner of l. thing, which........ 9
Le 6:3 Or have found that which was l., and 9
Le 6:4 keep, or the l. thing which he found,....... 9
Nu 6:12 days that were before shall be l.,........ 5307
De 22:3 with all l. thing of thy brother's, ... 9
De 22:3 which he hath l., and thou hast 6
1Sa 9:3 the asses of Kish Saul's father were l...... 6
1Sa 9:20 as for thine asses that were l. three........ 6
1Ki 20:25 like the army that thou hast l., ... 5307
Ps 119:176 I have gone astray like a l. sheep; 6
Isa 49:20 have, after thou hast l. the other, ... 7923
Isa 49:21 seeing I have l. my children, and 7908
Jer 50:6 My people hath been l. sheep: their........ 6
Eze 19:5 she had waited, and her hope was l., ... 6
Eze 34:4 have ye sought that which was l.; 6
Eze 34:16 I will seek that which was l., and............ 6
Eze 37:11 bones are dried, and our hope is l. 6
Mt 5:13 **but if the salt have l. his savour,**... *3471*
Mt 10:6 **the l. sheep of the house of Israel**... *622*
Mt 15:24 **the l. sheep of the house of Israel**... *622*
Mt 18:11 **is come to save that which was l.** ... *622*
Mk 9:50 **if the salt have l. his saltness,** ..*358,1096*
Lu 14:34 **but if the salt have l. his savour,**... *3471*
Lu 15:4 **and go after that which is l., until**.. *622*
Lu 15:6 **I found my sheep which was l.** *622*
Lu 15:9 **I found the piece which I had l.** *622*
Lu 15:24 **alive again; he was l., and is found**..*622*
Lu 15:32 **alive again; and was l., and is** *622*
Lu 19:10 **and to save that which was l.**.......... *622*
Joh 6:12 **that remain, that nothing be l.**........ *622*
Joh 17:12 **and none of them is l., but the son**..*622*
Joh 18:9 which thou gavest me have I l. none..... *622*
2Co 4:3 be hid, it is hid to them that are l.:...... *622*

LOT See also LOTS.
Le 16:8 the two goats; one l. for the Lord,..... 1486
Le 16:8 and the other l. for the scapegoat. 1486
Le 16:9 goat upon which the Lord's l. fell, ... 1486
Le 16:10 which the l. fell to be the scapegoat, .. 1486
Nu 26:55 the land shall be divided by l.:............ 1486
Nu 26:56 According to the l. shall the.............. 1486
Nu 33:54 ye shall divide the land by l. for an..... 1486
Nu 33:54 be in the place where his l. falleth;..... 1486
Nu 34:13 the land which ye shall inherit by l., ... 1486
Nu 36:2 give the land for an inheritance by l.... 1486
Nu 36:3 taken from the l. of our inheritance. ... 1486
De 32:9 Jacob is the l. of his inheritance. 2256
Jos 13:6 divide thou it by l. unto the Israelites........
Jos 14:2 By l. was their inheritance, as the...... 1486
Jos 15:1 was the l. of the tribe of...Judah........ 1486
Jos 16:1 the l. of the children of Joseph fell...... 1486
Jos 17:1 also a l. for the tribe of Manasseh;..... 1486
Jos 17:2 also a l. for the rest of the children..........
Jos 17:14 Why hast thou given me but one l...... 1486
Jos 17:17 thou shalt not have one l. only: 1486
Jos 18:11 the l. of the tribe of the children of.... 1486
Jos 18:11 coast of their l. came forth between ... 1486
Jos 19:1 the second l. came forth to Simeon, ... 1486
Jos 19:10 third l. came up for the children of..... 1486
Jos 19:17 the fourth l. came out to Issachar, ... 1486
Jos 19:24 the fifth l. came out for the tribe of.... 1486
Jos 19:32 sixth l. came out to the children of..... 1486
Jos 19:40 seventh l. came out for the tribe........ 1486
Jos 19:51 for an inheritance by l. in Shiloh......... 1486
Jos 21:4 the l. came out for the families of 1486
Jos 21:4 had by l. out of the tribe of Judah, ... 1486
Jos 21:5, 6 had by l. out of the families of the.... 1486
Jos 21:8 Israel gave by l. unto the Levites....... 1486
Jos 21:10 Levi, had: for theirs was the first l..... 1486
Jos 21:20 they had cities of their l. out of the.... 1486
Jos 21:40 were by their l. twelve cities. 1486
Jos 23:4 divided unto you by l. these nations..........
Jg 1:3 Come up with me into my l., that 1486
Jg 1:3 and I...will go with thee into thy l...... 1486
Jg 20:9 we will go up by l. against it;............ 1486
1Sa 14:41 Lord God of Israel, Give a perfect l..........
1Ch 6:54 Kohathites: for theirs was the l. 1486
1Ch 6:61 tribe of Manasseh, by l., ten cities........ 1486
1Ch 6:63 the sons of Merari were given by l.,.... 1486
1Ch 6:65 And they gave by l. out of the tribe ... 1486
1Ch 16:18 Canaan, the l. of your inheritance;...... 2256
1Ch 24:5 Thus were they divided by l., one........ 1486
1Ch 24:7 the first l. came forth to Jehoiarib, ... 1486
1Ch 25:9 the first l. came forth for Asaph to..... 1486
1Ch 26:14 the l. eastward fell to Shelemiah. 1486
1Ch 26:14 and his l. came out northward. 1486
1Ch 26:16 Hosah the l. came forth westward, ...
Es 3:7 they cast Pur, that is, the l.,............ 1486
Es 9:24 and had cast Pur, that is, the l., to 1486
Ps 16:5 of my cup: thou maintainest my l. 1486
Ps 105:11 Canaan, the l. of your inheritance:...... 2256
Ps 125:3 rest upon the l. of the righteous; 1486
Pr 1:14 Cast in thy l. among us; let us all 1486
Pr 16:33 The l. is cast into the lap; but the...... 1486
Pr 18:18 The l. causeth contentions to cease, ... 1486
Isa 17:14 and the l. of them that rob us. 1486
Isa 34:17 And he hath cast the l. for them, ... 1486
Isa 57:6 thy portion; they, they are thy l.: 1486
Jer 13:25 This is thy l., the portion of thy 1486
Eze 24:6 piece by piece; let no l. fall upon it..... 1486
Eze 45:1 when ye shall divide by l. the land for.......
Eze 47:22 shall divide it by l. for an inheritance.........
Eze 48:29 ye shall divide by l. unto the tribes.........
Da 12:13 and stand in thy l. at the end of......... 1486
Jon 1:7 cast lots, and the l. fell upon Jonah...... 1486
Mic 2:5 none that shall cast a cord by l. in...... 1486
Lu 1:9 his l. was to burn incense when.......... *2975*
Ac 1:26 and the l. fell upon Matthias;............ *2819*
Ac 8:21 neither part nor l. in this matter: *2819*
Ac 13:19 he divided their land to them by l....... *2624*

LOT (lot) See also LOT'S.
Ge 11:27 and Haran; and Haran begat L.......... 3876
Ge 11:31 L. the son of Haran his son's son,...... 3876
Ge 12:4 and L. went with him: and Abram...... 3876
Ge 12:5 his wife, and L. his brother's son,....... 3876
Ge 13:1 and L. with him, into the south, ... 3876
Ge 13:5 L. also, which went with Abram, ... 3876
Ge 13:8 Abram said unto L., Let there be no .. 3876
Ge 13:10 L. lifted up his eyes, and beheld all 3876
Ge 13:11 Then L. chose him all the plain of...... 3876
Ge 13:11 of Jordan; and L. journeyed east: 3876
Ge 13:12 L. dwelled in the cities of the plain,.... 3876
Ge 13:14 after...L. was separated from him, ... 3876
Ge 14:12 they took L., Abram's brother's son, ... 3876
Ge 14:16 also brought again his brother L.,....... 3876
Ge 19:1 and L. sat in the gate of Sodom:........ 3876
Ge 19:1 and L. seeing them rose up to meet... 3876
Ge 19:5 they called unto L., and said unto 3876

Ge 19:6 **L.** went out at the door unto them,.... 3876
Ge 19:9 pressed sore upon the man, even **L.**,.. 3876
Ge 19:10 pulled **L.** into the house to them,....... 3876
Ge 19:12 men said unto **L.**, Hast thou here 3876
Ge 19:14 **L.** went...and spake unto his sons...... 3876
Ge 19:15 then the angels hastened **L.**, saying,... 3876
Ge 19:18 And **L.** said unto them, Oh, not so,.... 3876
Ge 19:23 earth when **L.** entered into Zoar......... 3876
Ge 19:29 and sent **L.** out of the midst of the..... 3876
Ge 19:29 the cities in the which **L.** dwelt. 3876
Ge 19:30 **L.** went up out of Zoar, and dwelt in.. 3876
Ge 19:36 both the daughters of **L.** with child..... 3876
De 2:9 given Ar unto the children of **L.** for.... 3876
De 2:19 given it unto the children of **L.** for 3876
Ps 83:8 they have holpen the children of **L.** 3876
Lu 17:28 **also as it was in the days of L.**;.... *3091*
Lu 17:28 **same day that L. went out of**........ *3091*
2Pe 2:7 And delivered just **L.**, vexed with *3091*

LOTAN (lo'-tan) See also LOTAN'S.
Ge 36:20 **L.**, and Shobal, and Zibeon, and......... 3877
Ge 36:22 the children of **L.** were Hori and........ 3877
Ge 36:29 that came of the Horites; duke **L.**, ... 3877
1Ch 1:38 **L.**, and Shobal, and Zibeon, and......... 3877
1Ch 1:39 the sons of **L.**: Hori, and Homan: 3877

LOTAN'S (lo'-tans)
Ge 36:22 Hemam; and **L.** sister was Timna....... 3877
1Ch 1:39 Homam: and Timna was **L.** sister....... 3877

LOTHE See also LOATHE; LOTHED; LOTHETH; LOTHING.
Ex 7:18 Egyptians shall **l.** to drink of the 3811
Eze 6:9 shall **l.** themselves for the evils.......... 6962
Eze 20:43 **l.** yourselves in your own sight for..... 6962
Eze 36:31 **l.** yourselves in your own sight for..... 6962

LOTHED See also LOATHED.
Jer 14:19 hath thy soul **l.** Zion? why hast.......... 1602
Eze 16:45 which **l.** their husbands and their........ 1602
Zec 11:8 my soul **l.** them, and their soul.......... 7114

LOTHETH See also LOATHETH.
Eze 16:45 **l.** her husband and her children;......... 1602

LOTHING
Eze 16:5 open field, to the **l.** of thy person,...... 1604

LOT'S (lots)
Ge 13:7 and the herdman of **L.** cattle:............ 3876
Lu 17:32 **Remember L. wife**............................

LOTS
Le 16:8 shall cast **l.** upon the two goats; 1486
Jos 18:6 cast **l.** for you here before the Lord ... 1486
Jos 18:8 here cast **l.** for you before the Lord ... 1486
Jos 18:10 Joshua cast **l.** for them in Shiloh......... 1486
1Sa 14:42 Cast **l.** between me and Jonathan my ....
1Ch 24:31 cast **l.** over against their brethren 1486
1Ch 25:8 they cast **l.**, ward against ward, as..... 1486
1Ch 26:13 they cast **l.**, as well the small as the.... 1486
1Ch 26:14 son, a wise counsellor, they cast **l.**;.... 1486
Ne 10:34 we cast the **l.** among the priests, the.. 1486
Ne 11:1 the rest of the people also cast **l.**, to.. 1486
Ps 22:18 them, and cast **l.** upon my vesture. 1486
Joe 3:3 they have cast **l.** for my people; and... 1486
Ob 11 gates, and cast **l.** upon Jerusalem, ... 1486
Jon 1:7 Come, and let us cast **l.**, that we....... 1486
Jon 1:7 So they cast **l.**, and the lot fell upon... 1486
Na 3:10 they cast **l.** for her honourable men,... 1486
Mt 27:35 parted his garments, casting **l.**:......... *2819*
Mt 27:35 upon my vesture did they cast **l.**......... *2819*
Mk 15:24 garments, casting **l.** upon them,......... *2819*
Lu 23:34 they parted his raiment, and cast **l.** *2819*
Joh 19:24 Let us not rend it, but cast **l.** for it, ... *2819*
Joh 19:24 and for my vesture they did cast **l.**..... *2975*
Ac 1:26 they gave forth their **l.**; and the lot *2819*

LOUD See also LOUDER.
Ge 39:14 me, and I cried with a **l.** voice:.......... 1419
Ex 19:16 voice of the trumpet exceeding **l.**;...... 2389
De 27:14 the men of Israel with a **l.** voice, ... 7311
1Sa 28:12 Samuel, she cried with a **l.** voice:........ 1419
2Sa 15:23 all the country wept with a **l.** voice,.... 1419
2Sa 19:4 and the king cried with a **l.** voice, ... 1419
1Ki 8:55 congregation of Israel with a **l.** voice,.. 1419
2Ki 18:28 cried with a **l.** voice in the Jews'....... 1419
2Ch 15:14 sware unto the Lord with a **l.** voice,.... 1419
2Ch 20:19 Lord God of Israel with a **l.** voice 1419
2Ch 30:21 singing with **l.** instruments unto......... 5797
2Ch 32:18 cried with a **l.** voice in the Jews'......... 1419
Ezr 3:12 their eyes, wept with a **l.** voice; 1419
Ezr 3:13 the people shouted with a **l.** shout,..... 1419
Ezr 10:12 answered and said with a **l.** voice,...... 1419
Ne 9:4 cried with a **l.** voice unto the Lord...... 1419
Ne 12:42 the singers sang **l.**, with Jezrahiah...... 8085
Es 4:1 cried with a **l.** and a bitter cry;.......... 1419
Ps 33:3 song: play skilfully with a **l.** noise............
Ps 98:4 make a **l.** noise, and rejoice, and sing........
Ps 150:5 Praise him upon the **l.** cymbals:......... 8085
Pr 7:11 (She is **l.** and stubborn; her feet......... 1993
Pr 27:14 blesseth his friend with a **l.** voice, ... 1419
Isa 36:13 cried with a **l.** voice in the Jews'........ 1419
Eze 8:18 they cry in mine ears with a **l.** voice,.. 1419
Eze 9:1 also in mine ears with a **l.** voice,........ 1419
Eze 11:13 my face, and cried with a **l.** voice,...... 1419
Mt 27:46 Jesus cried with a **l.** voice, saying, ... *3173*
Mt 27:50 he had cried again with a **l.** voice, ... *3173*
Mk 1:26 torn him, and cried with a **l.** voice,..... *3173*
Mk 5:7 And cried with a **l.** voice, and said,..... *3173*
Mk 15:34 Jesus cried with a **l.** voice, saying, ... *3173*
Mk 15:37 And Jesus cried with a **l.** voice, and.... *3173*
Lu 1:42 she spake out with a **l.** voice, and....... *3173*
Lu 4:33 devil, and cried out with a **l.** voice,..... *3173*
Lu 8:28 and with a **l.** voice said, What have *3173*
Lu 17:15 and with a **l.** voice glorified God,........ *3173*
Lu 19:37 and praise God with a **l.** voice for *3173*
Lu 23:23 they were instant with **l.** voices, ... *3173*
Lu 23:46 Jesus had cried with a **l.** voice,.......... *3173*
Joh 11:43 he cried with a **l.** voice, **Lazarus**,..... *3173*
Ac 7:57 Then they cried out with a **l.** voice,.... *3173*
Ac 7:60 and cried with a **l.** voice, Lord, lay..... *3173*
Ac 8:7 unclean spirits, crying with **l.** voice,.... *3173*
Ac 14:10 Said with a **l.** voice, Stand upright...... *3173*
Ac 16:28 Paul cried with a **l.** voice, saying,...... *3173*
Ac 26:24 Festus said with a **l.** voice, Paul, ... *3173*
Re 5:2 angel proclaiming with a **l.** voice,........ *3173*
Re 5:12 Saying with a **l.** voice, Worthy is........ *3173*
Re 6:10 they cried with a **l.** voice, saying,....... *3173*
Re 7:2 with a **l.** voice to the four angels,....... *3173*
Re 7:10 and cried with a **l.** voice, saying,........ *3173*
Re 8:13 saying with a **l.** voice, Woe, woe, ... *3173*
Re 10:3 cried with a **l.** voice, as when a lion.... *3173*
Re 12:10 I heard a **l.** voice saying in heaven, ... *3173*
Re 14:7 Saying with a **l.** voice, Fear God,....... *3173*
Re 14:9 saying with a **l.** voice, If any man....... *3173*
Re 14:15 crying with a **l.** voice to him that *3173*
Re 14:18 cried with a **l.** voice to him that had ... *3173*
Re 19:17 he cried with a **l.** voice, saying to all... *3173*

LOUDER
Ex 19:19 sounded long, and waxed **l.** and **l.**,..... 3966

LOVE See also LOVED; LOVE'S; LOVES; LOVEST; LOVETH; LOVING.
Ge 27:4 make me savoury meat, such as I **l.**,.... 157
Ge 29:20 few days, for the **l.** he had to her........ 160
Ge 29:32 therefore my husband will **l.** me.......... 157
Ex 20:6 unto thousands of them that **l.** me, ... 157
Ex 21:5 I **l.** my master, my wife, and my......... 157
Le 19:18 but thou shalt **l.** thy neighbour as 157
Le 19:34 and thou shalt **l.** him as thyself; for...... 157
De 5:10 unto thousands of them that **l.** me 157
De 6:5 thou shalt **l.** the Lord thy God with...... 157
De 7:7 Lord did not set his **l.** upon you,......... 2836
De 7:9 mercy with them that **l.** him and......... 157
De 7:13 he will **l.** thee, and bless thee, and 157
De 10:12 walk in all his ways, and to **l.** him,....... 157
De 10:15 a delight in thy fathers to **l.** them, ... 157
De 10:19 **L.** ye therefore the stranger: for ye..... 157
De 11:1 Therefore thou shalt **l.** the Lord thy..... 157
De 11:13 you this day, to **l.** the Lord your God,.. 157
De 11:22 to **l.** the Lord your God, to walk in...... 157
De 13:3 whether ye **l.** the Lord your God......... 157
De 19:9 to **l.** the Lord thy God, and to walk 157
De 30:6 to **l.** the Lord thy God with all thine..... 157
De 30:16 thee this day to **l.** the Lord thy God, ... 157
De 30:20 thou mayest **l.** the Lord thy God, ... 157
Jos 22:5 to **l.** the Lord your God, and to walk.... 157
Jos 23:11 selves, that ye **l.** the Lord your God.... 157
Jg 5:31 let them that **l.** him be as the sun........ 157
Jg 16:15 How canst thou say, I **l.** thee, when 157
1Sa 18:22 in thee, and all his servants **l.** thee: 157
2Sa 1:26 me: thy **l.** to me was wonderful. 160
2Sa 1:26 wonderful, passing the **l.** of women...... 160
2Sa 13:4 Amnon said unto him, I **l.** Tamar, ... 157
2Sa 13:15 greater than the **l.** wherewith he had.... 160
1Ki 11:2 Solomon clave unto these in **l.** 160
2Ch 19:2 and **l.** them that hate the Lord?........... 157
Ne 1:5 and mercy for them that **l.** him and...... 157
Ps 4:2 how long will ye **l.** vanity, and seek 157
Ps 5:11 let them also that **l.** thy name be......... 157
Ps 18:1 I will **l.** thee, O Lord, my strength..... 7355
Ps 31:23 O **l.** the Lord, all ye his saints: for 157
Ps 40:16 let such as **l.** thy salvation say 157
Ps 69:36 they that **l.** his name shall dwell 157
Ps 70:4 and let such as **l.** thy salvation say....... 157
Ps 91:14 Because he hath set his **l.** upon me, ... 2836
Ps 97:10 Ye that **l.** the Lord, hate evil: he........ 157
Ps 109:4 For my **l.** they are my adversaries:...... 160
Ps 109:5 evil for good, and hatred for my **l.**....... 160
Ps 116:1 I **l.** the Lord, because he hath heard 157
Ps 119:97 O how **l.** I thy law! it is my................ 157
Ps 119:113 vain thoughts: but thy law do I **l.**......... 157
Ps 119:119 dross: therefore I **l.** thy testimonies..... 157
Ps 119:127 Therefore I **l.** thy commandments........... 157
Ps 119:132 to do unto those that **l.** thy name. 157
Ps 119:159 Consider how I **l.** thy precepts:........... 157
Ps 119:163 and abhor lying: buy thy law do I **l.**....... 157
Ps 119:165 peace have they which **l.** thy law:........ 157
Ps 119:167 and I **l.** them exceedingly.................. 157
Ps 122:6 they shall prosper that **l.** thee............. 157
Ps 145:20 Lord preserveth all them that **l.** him:.... 157
Pr 1:22 ye simple ones, will ye **l.** simplicity?..... 157
Pr 4:6 thee: **l.** her, and she shall keep thee. ... 157
Pr 5:19 thou ravished always with her **l.** 160
Pr 7:18 let us take our fill of **l.** until the......... 1730
Pr 8:17 I **l.** them that **l.** me; and those that 157
Pr 8:21 cause those that **l.** me to inherit.......... 157
Pr 8:36 soul: all they that hate me **l.** death....... 157
Pr 9:8 a wise man, and he will **l.** thee............. 157
Pr 10:12 up strifes: but **l.** covereth all sins. 160
Pr 15:17 is a dinner of herbs where **l.** is, than.... 160
Pr 16:13 and they **l.** him that speaketh right....... 157
Pr 17:9 covereth a transgression seeketh **l.**;..... 160
Pr 18:21 and they that **l.** it shall eat the fruit...... 157
Pr 20:13 **L.** not sleep, lest thou come to........... 157
Pr 27:5 rebuke is better than secret **l.** 160
Ec 3:8 A time to **l.**, and a time to hate; a....... 157
Ec 9:1 man knoweth either **l.** or hatred by...... 160
Ec 9:6 Also their **l.**, and their hatred, and....... 160
Ca 1:2 for thy **l.** is better than wine............. 1730
Ca 1:3 therefore do the virgins **l.** thee. 157
Ca 1:4 remember thy **l.** more than wine:....... 1730
Ca 1:4 than wine: the upright **l.** thee. 157
Ca 1:9 I have compared thee, O my **l.**, to..... 7474
Ca 1:15 Behold, thou art fair, my **l.**; behold,.... 7474
Ca 2:2 so is my **l.** among the daughters. 7474
Ca 2:4 and his banner over me was **l.** 160
Ca 2:5 me with apples: for I am sick of **l.** 160
Ca 2:7 up, nor awake my **l.**, till he please....... 160
Ca 2:10 Rise up, my **l.**, my fair one, and........ 7474
Ca 2:13 Arise, my **l.**, my fair one, and come ... 7474
Ca 3:5 up, nor awake my **l.**, till he please...... 160
Ca 3:10 midst thereof being paved with **l.**,......... 160
Ca 4:1 Behold, thou art fair, my **l.**;............. 7474
Ca 4:7 Thou art all fair, my **l.**; there is no..... 7474
Ca 4:10 How fair is thy **l.**, my sister, my....... 1730
Ca 4:10 how much better is thy **l.** than wine! .. 1730
Ca 5:2 to me, that my sister, my **l.**, my dove, 7474
Ca 5:8 that ye tell him, I am sick of **l.**............ 160
Ca 6:4 Thou art beautiful, O my **l.**, as 7474
Ca 7:6 and how pleasant art thou, O **l.**, for..... 160
Ca 8:4 that ye stir not up, nor awake my **l.**,..... 160
Ca 8:6 for **l.** is strong as death; jealousy......... 160
Ca 8:7 Many waters cannot quench **l.**,............ 160
Ca 8:7 all the substance of his house for **l.**,..... 160
Isa 38:17 but thou hast in **l.** to my soul............ 2836
Isa 56:6 to **l.** the name of the Lord, to be.......... 157
Isa 61:8 For I the Lord **l.** judgment, I hate 157
Isa 63:9 in his **l.** and in his pity he redeemed..... 160
Isa 66:10 be glad with her, all ye that **l.** her: 157
Jer 2:2 the **l.** of thine espousals, when thou..... 160
Jer 2:33 trimmest thou thy way to seek **l.**? 160
Jer 5:31 and my people **l.** to have it so: and...... 157
Jer 31:3 loved thee with an everlasting **l.**:......... 160
Eze 16:8 behold, thy time was the time of **l.**;.... 1730
Eze 23:11 more corrupt in her inordinate **l.**......... 5691
Eze 23:17 came to her into the bed of **l.**, and..... 1730
Eze 33:31 their mouth they shew much **l.**, ... 5690
Da 1:9 Daniel into favour and tender **l.**................
Da 9:4 and mercy to them that **l.** him,............ 157
Ho 3:1 **l.** a woman beloved of her friend, ... 157
Ho 3:1 according to the **l.** of the Lord 160
Ho 3:1 other gods, and **l.** flagons of wine. 157
Ho 4:18 her rulers with shame do **l.**, Give 157

Ho 9:15 mine house, I will **l.** them no more: 160
Ho 11:4 cords of a man, with bands of **l.**: 160
Ho 14:4 backsliding, I will **l.** them freely: 157
Am 5:15 Hate the evil, and **l.** the good, and 157
Mic 3:2 Who hate the good, and **l.** the evil; 157
Mic 6:8 but to do justly, and to **l.** mercy, 160
Zep 3:17 he will rest in his **l.**, he will joy over 160
Zec 8:17 **l.** no false oath: for all these are 157
Zec 8:19 therefore **l.** the truth and peace 157
Mt 5:43 **Thou shalt l. thy neighbour, and** *25*
Mt 5:44 **But I say unto you, L. your enemies,** *25*
Mt 5:46 **For if ye l. them which l. you, what** *25*
Mt 6:5 **for they l. to pray standing in the** *5368*
Mt 6:24 **he will hate the one, and l. the** *25*
Mt 19:19 **shalt l. thy neighbour as thyself** *25*
Mt 22:37 **Thou shalt l. the Lord thy God with** *25*
Mt 22:39 **shalt l. thy neighbour as thyself** *25*
Mt 23:6 **l. the uppermost rooms at feasts,** *5368*
Mt 24:12 **the l. of many shall wax cold** *26*
Mk 12:30 **thou shalt l. the Lord thy God with** *25*
Mk 12:31 **shalt l. thy neighbour as thyself** *25*
Mk 12:33 to **l.** him with all the heart, and with *25*
Mk 12:33 and to **l.** his neighbour as himself, *25*
Mk 12:38 **the scribes, which l. to go in long** *2309*
Mk 12:38 **l. salutations in the marketplaces,**
Lu 6:27 **L. your enemies, do good to them** *25*
Lu 6:32 **For if ye l. them which l. you, what** *25*
Lu 6:32 **for sinners also l. those that l. them** *25*
Lu 6:35 **But l. ye your enemies, and do good,** *25*
Lu 7:42 **which of them will l. him most?** *25*
Lu 10:27 Thou shalt **l.** the Lord thy God with *25*
Lu 11:42 **pass over judgment and the l. of** *26*
Lu 11:42 **for ye l. the uppermost seats in the** *25*
Lu 16:13 **he will hate the one, and l. the** *25*
Lu 20:46 **and l. greetings in the markets,** *5368*
Joh 5:42 **that ye have not the l. of God in you** *26*
Joh 8:42 **were your Father, ye would l. me:** *25*
Joh 10:17 **Therefore doth my Father l. me,** *25*
Joh 13:34 **give unto you, That ye l. one** *25*
Joh 13:34 **loved you, that ye also l. one** *25*
Joh 13:35 **disciples, if ye have l. one to** *26*
Joh 14:15 **ye l. me, keep my commandments** *25*
Joh 14:21 **and I will l. him, and will manifest** *25*
Joh 14:23 **a man l. me, he will keep my words:** *25*
Joh 14:23 **my Father will l. him, and we will** *25*
Joh 14:31 **may know that I l. the Father; and** *25*
Joh 15:9 **I loved you: continue ye in my l.,** *26*
Joh 15:10 **ye shall abide in my l.; even as I** *26*
Joh 15:10 **commandments, and abide in his l.,** *26*
Joh 15:12 **That ye l. one another, as I have** *26*
Joh 15:13 **Greater l. hath no man than this,** *26*
Joh 15:17 **command you, that ye l. one** *25*
Joh 15:19 **world, the world would l. his own:** *5368*
Joh 17:26 **l. wherewith thou hast loved me** *26*
Joh 21:15, 16,17 thou knowest that I **l.** thee. *5368*
Ro 5:5 because the **l.** of God is shed abroad *26*
Ro 5:8 God commendeth his **l.** toward us, *26*
Ro 8:28 together for good to them that **l.** God, *25*
Ro 8:35 separate us from the **l.** of Christ? *26*
Ro 8:39 able to separate us from the **l.** of God, *26*
Ro 12:9 Let **l.** be without dissimulation. *26*
Ro 12:10 one to another with brotherly **l.**; *5360*
Ro 13:8 any thing, but to **l.** one another: *25*
Ro 13:9 Thou shalt **l.** thy neighbour as *25*
Ro 13:10 **L.** worketh no ill to his neighbour: *26*
Ro 13:10 therefore **l.** is the fulfilling of the law. *26*
Ro 15:30 sake, and for the **l.** of the Spirit, *26*
1Co 2:9 hath prepared for them that **l.** him. *25*
1Co 4:21 come unto you with a rod, or in **l.**; *26*
1Co 8:3 if any man **l.** God, the same is known *25*
1Co 16:22 If any man **l.** not the Lord Jesus *5368*
1Co 16:24 My **l.** be with you all in Christ Jesus. *26*
2Co 2:4 ye might know the **l.** which I have *26*
2Co 2:8 would confirm your **l.** toward him. *26*
2Co 5:14 For the **l.** of Christ constraineth us; *26*
2Co 6:6 by the Holy Ghost, by **l.** unfeigned, *26*
2Co 8:7 in all diligence, and in your **l.** to us. *26*
2Co 8:8 and to prove the sincerity of your **l.**, *26*
2Co 8:24 the churches, the proof of your **l.**, *26*
2Co 11:11 because I **l.** you not? God knoweth. *25*
2Co 12:14 though the more abundantly I **l.** you, *25*
2Co 13:11 God of **l.** and peace shall be with you. *26*
2Co 13:14 the **l.** of God, and the communion *26*
Ga 5:6 but faith which worketh by **l.** *26*
Ga 5:13 flesh, but by **l.** serve one another. *26*
Ga 5:14 shalt **l.** thy neighbour as thyself. *25*
Ga 5:22 the fruit of the Spirit is **l.**, joy, peace, *26*

Eph 1:4 and without blame before him in **l.**: *26*
Eph 1:15 Jesus, and **l.** unto all the saints. *26*
Eph 2:4 great **l.** wherewith he loved us. *26*
Eph 3:17 ye, being rooted and grounded in **l.**, *26*
Eph 3:19 And to know the **l.** of Christ, which *26*
Eph 4:2 forbearing one another in **l.**; *26*
Eph 4:15 speaking the truth in **l.**, may grow *26*
Eph 4:16 body unto the edifying of itself in **l.**, *26*
Eph 5:2 And walk in **l.**, as Christ also hath *26*
Eph 5:25 Husbands, **l.** your wives, even as *25*
Eph 5:28 So ought men to **l.** their wives as *25*
Eph 5:33 so **l.** his wife even as himself; and *25*
Eph 6:23 be to the brethren, and **l.** with faith, *26*
Eph 6:24 with all them that **l.** our Lord Jesus *25*
Php 1:9 your **l.** may abound yet more and *26*
Php 1:17 the other of **l.**, knowing that I am *26*
Php 2:1 in Christ, if any comfort of **l.**, if any *26*
Php 2:2 be likeminded, having the same **l.**, *26*
Col 1:4 and of the **l.** which ye have to all the *26*
Col 1:8 Who also declared unto us your **l.** in *26*
Col 2:2 comforted, being knit together in **l.**, *26*
Col 3:19 Husbands, **l.** your wives, and be not *25*
1Th 1:3 your work of faith, and labour of **l.**, *26*
1Th 3:12 abound in **l.** one toward another, *25*
1Th 4:9 as touching brotherly **l.** ye need *5360*
1Th 4:9 are taught of God to **l.** one another. *25*
1Th 5:8 on the breastplate of faith and **l.**; *26*
1Th 5:13 highly in **l.** for their work's sake. *26*
2Th 2:10 they received not the **l.** of the truth, *26*
2Th 3:5 direct your hearts into the **l.** of God, *26*
1Ti 1:14 faith and **l.** which is in Christ Jesus. *26*
1Ti 6:10 **l.** of money is the root of all evil: *5365*
1Ti 6:11 faith, **l.**, patience, meekness. *26*
2Ti 1:7 and of **l.**, and of a sound mind. *26*
2Ti 1:13 faith and **l.** which is in Christ Jesus. *26*
2Ti 4:8 all them also that **l.** his appearing. *25*
Tit 2:4 to be sober, to **l.** their husbands, *5362*
Tit 2:4 to be sober,...to **l.** their children, *5388*
Tit 3:4 that the kindness and **l.** of God *5363*
Tit 3:15 Greet them that **l.** us in the faith. *5368*
Phm 5 Hearing of thy **l.** and faith, which *26*
Phm 5:7 great joy and consolation in thy **l.**, *26*
Heb 6:10 to forget your work and labour of **l.**, *26*
Heb 10:24 to provoke unto **l.** and to good works: *26*
Heb 13:1 Let brotherly **l.** continue. *5360*
Jas 1:12 hath promised to them that **l.** him. *25*
Jas 2:5 hath promised to them that **l.** him? *25*
Jas 2:8 shalt **l.** thy neighbour as thyself, *25*
1Pe 1:8 Whom having not seen, ye **l.**; in *25*
1Pe 1:22 unto unfeigned **l.** of the brethren, *5360*
1Pe 1:22 ye **l.** one another with a pure heart *25*
1Pe 2:17 **L.** the brotherhood. Fear God. *25*
1Pe 3:8 one to another, **l.** as brethren, be *5361*
1Pe 3:10 For he that will **l.** life, and see good *25*
1Jo 2:5 him verily is the **l.** of God perfected: *26*
1Jo 2:15 **L.** not the world, neither the things *25*
1Jo 2:15 If any man **l.** the world, *25*
1Jo 2:15 the **l.** of the Father is not in him. *26*
1Jo 3:1 what matter of **l.** the Father hath *26*
1Jo 3:11 that we should **l.** one another. *25*
1Jo 3:14 unto life, because we **l.** the brethren. *25*
1Jo 3:16 Hereby preceive we the **l.** of God, *26*
1Jo 3:17 how dwelleth the **l.** of God in him? *26*
1Jo 3:18 little children, let us not **l.** in word, *25*
1Jo 3:23 Son Jesus Christ, and **l.** one another, *25*
1Jo 4:7 Beloved, let us **l.** one another: *25*
1Jo 4:7 for **l.** is of God; and every one that *26*
1Jo 4:8 not knoweth not God; for God is **l.** *26*
1Jo 4:9 manifested the **l.** of God toward us, *26*
1Jo 4:10 Herein is **l.**, not that we loved God, *26*
1Jo 4:11 us, we ought also to **l.** one another. *25*
1Jo 4:12 If we **l.** one another, God dwelleth in *25*
1Jo 4:12 in us, and his **l.** is perfected in us. *26*
1Jo 4:16 believed the **l.** that God hath to us. *26*
1Jo 4:16 God is **l.**; and he that dwelleth in *26*
1Jo 4:16 that dwelleth in **l.** dwelleth in God, *26*
1Jo 4:17 Herein is our **l.** made perfect, that *26*
1Jo 4:18 There is no fear in **l.**; but perfect *26*
1Jo 4:18 but perfect **l.** casteth out fear: *26*
1Jo 4:18 that feareth is not made perfect in **l.** *26*
1Jo 4:19 We **l.** him, because he first loved us. *25*
1Jo 4:20 If a man say, I **l.** God, and hateth *25*
1Jo 4:20 how can he **l.** God whom he hath not *25*
1Jo 4:21 who loveth God **l.** his brother also. *25*
1Jo 5:2 know that we **l.** the children of God, *25*
1Jo 5:2 when we **l.** God, and keep his *25*
1Jo 5:3 this is the **l.** of God, that we keep *26*

2Jo 1 her children, whom I **l.** in the truth; *25*
2Jo 3 the Son of the Father, in truth and **l.** *26*
2Jo 5 beginning, that we **l.** one another. *25*
2Jo 6 And this is **l.**, that we walk after his *26*
3Jo 1 unto...Gaius, whom I **l.** in the truth. *25*
Jude 2 Mercy unto you, and peace, and **l.**, *26*
Jude 21 Keep yourselves in the **l.** of God, *26*
Re 2:4 **because thou hast left thy first l.** *26*
Re 3:19 **As many as I l., I rebuke and** *5368*

LOVED See also BELOVED; LOVEDST.

Ge 24:67 she became his wife; and he **l.** her: 157
Ge 25:28 And Isaac **l.** Esau, because he did 157
Ge 25:28 his venison: but Rebekah **l.** Jacob. 157
Ge 27:14 savoury meat, such as his father **l.** 157
Ge 29:18 Jacob **l.** Rachel; and said, I will 157
Ge 29:30 he **l.** also Rachel more than Leah, 157
Ge 34:3 he **l.** the damsel, and spake kindly 157
Ge 37:3 Now Israel **l.** Joseph more than all 157
Ge 37:4 saw that their father **l.** him more 157
De 4:37 because he **l.** thy fathers, therefore 157
De 7:8 But because the Lord **l.** you, and 160
De 23:5 because the Lord thy God **l.** thee. 157
De 33:3 Yea, he **l.** the people; all his 2245
Jg 16:4 **l.** a woman in the valley of Sorek, 157
1Sa 1:5 he **l.** Hannah: but the Lord had 157
1Sa 16:21 before him: and he **l.** him greatly: 157
1Sa 18:1 and Jonathan **l.** him as his own soul. 157
1Sa 18:3 because he **l.** him as his own soul. 160
1Sa 18:16 But all Israel and Judah **l.** David, 157
1Sa 18:20 Michal Saul's daughter **l.** David: 157
1Sa 18:28 that Michal Saul's daughter **l.** him. 157
1Sa 20:17 to swear again, because he **l.** him: 160
1Sa 20:17 for he **l.** him as he...his own soul. 157
1Sa 20:17 for he...him as he **l.** his own soul. 160
2Sa 12:24 name Solomon: and the Lord **l.** him. 157
2Sa 13:1 and Amnon the son of David **l.** her. 157
2Sa 13:15 the love wherewith he had **l.** her. 157
1Ki 3:3 And Solomon **l.** the Lord, walking 157
1Ki 10:9 because the Lord **l.** Israel for ever, 160
1Ki 11:1 Solomon **l.** many strange women, 157
2Ch 2:11 Because the Lord hath **l.** his people, 160
2Ch 9:8 thy God: because thy God **l.** Israel, 160
2Ch 11:21 And Rehoboam **l.** Maachah the 157
2Ch 26:10 and in Carmel: for he **l.** husbandry. 157
Es 2:17 And the king **l.** Esther above all the 157
Job 19:19 they whom I **l.** are turned against 157
Ps 26:8 Lord, I have **l.** the habitation of thy 157
Ps 47:4 the excellency of Jacob whom he **l.** 157
Ps 78:68 Judah, the mount Zion which he **l.** 157
Ps 109:17 As he **l.** cursing, so let it come unto 157
Ps 119:47 thy commandments, which I have **l.** 157
Ps 119:48 thy commandments, which I have **l.**; 157
Isa 43:4 been honourable, and I have **l.** thee: 157
Isa 48:14 The Lord hath **l.** him: he will do his 157
Jer 2:25 I have **l.** strangers, and after them 157
Jer 8:2 host of heaven, whom they have **l.**, 157
Jer 14:10 Thus have they **l.** to wander, they 157
Jer 31:3 I have **l.** thee with an everlasting 157
Eze 16:37 all them that thou hast **l.**, with all 157
Ho 9:1 **l.** a reward upon every cornfloor. 157
Ho 9:10 were according as they **l.** 157
Ho 11:1 Israel was a child, then I **l.** him, and 157
Mal 1:2 I have **l.** you, saith the Lord. 157
Mal 1:2 Yet ye say, Wherein hast thou **l.** us? 157
Mal 1:2 saith the Lord: yet I **l.** Jacob, 157
Mal 2:11 the holiness of the Lord which he **l.**, 157
Mr 10:21 Jesus beholding him **l.** him, and said *25*
Lu 7:47 **many, are forgiven; for she l. much:** *25*
Joh 3:16 **For God so l. the world, that he** *25*
Joh 3:19 **men l. darkness rather than light,** *25*
Joh 11:5 Now Jesus **l.** Martha, and her sister, *25*
Joh 11:36 the Jews, Behold how he **l.** him! *5368*
Joh 12:43 they **l.** the praise of men more than *25*
Joh 13:1 having **l.** his own which were in the *25*
Joh 13:1 the world, he **l.** them unto the end. *25*
Joh 13:23 one of his disciples, whom Jesus **l.** *25*
Joh 13:34 **as I have l. you, that ye also love** *25*
Joh 14:21 **loveth me shall be l. of my Father,** *25*
Joh 14:28 **If ye l. me, ye would rejoice, because** *25*
Joh 15:9 **As the Father hath l. me, so have I** *25*
Joh 15:9 **me, so have I l. you: continue ye in** *25*
Joh 15:12 **ye love one another, as I have l. you** *25*
Joh 16:27 **because ye have l. me, and have** *5368*
Joh 17:23 **and hast l. them, as thou hast l. me** *25*
Joh 17:26 **the love wherewith thou hast l. me** *25*
Joh 19:26 the disciple standing by whom he **l.**, *25*

Joh 20:2 the other disciple, whom Jesus l., ... *5368*
Joh 21:7 that disciple whom Jesus l. saith *25*
Joh 21:20 the disciple whom Jesus l. following; *25*
Ro 8:37 conquerors through him that l. us.......... *25*
Ro 9:13 As it is written, Jacob have I l., but *25*
2Co 12:15 abundantly I love you, the less I be l. *25*
Ga 2:20 faith of the Son of God, who l. me, ... *25*
Eph 2:4 his great love wherewith he l. us, ... *25*
Eph 5:2 in love, as Christ also hath l. us,........... *26*
Eph 5:25 even as Christ also l. the church,........... *25*
2Th 2:16 even our Father, which hath l. us, ... *25*
2Ti 4:10 me, having l. this present world,........... *25*
Heb 1:9 hast l. righteousness, and hated............ *25*
2Pe 2:15 who l. the wages of unrighteousness;..... *25*
1Jo 4:10 Herein is love, not that we l. God,......... *25*
1Jo 4:10 but that he l. us, and sent his Son to..... *25*
1Jo 4:11 Beloved, if God so l. us, we ought......... *25*
1Jo 4:19 We love him, because he first l. us. *25*
Re 1:5 Unto him that l. us, and washed us *25*
Re 3:9 **feet, and to know that I have l. thee.** *25*
Re 12:11 they l. not their lives unto the death...... *25*

LOVEDST
Isa 57:8 l. their bed where thou sawest it:........ 157
Joh 17:24 **l. me before the foundation of the**.... *25*

LOVELY
2Sa 1:23 and Jonathan were l. and pleasant 157
Ca 5:16 sweet: yea, he is altogether l............. 4261
Eze 33:32 art unto them as a very l. song of...... 5690
Php 4:8 are pure, whatsoever things are l.,...... *4375*

LOVER See also LOVERS.
1Ki 5:1 for Hiram was ever a l. of David. 157
Ps 88:18 L. and friend hast thou put far from..... 157
Tit 1:8 But a l. of hospitality,...of good *5382*
Tit 1:8 a l. of good men, sober, just, holy, ... *5358*

LOVERS
Ps 38:11 My l. and my friends stand aloof 157
Jer 3:1 played the harlot with many l.; 7453
Jer 4:30 thy l. will despise thee, they will........ 5689
Jer 22:20 for all thy l. are destroyed. 157
Jer 22:22 and thy l. shall go into captivity:.......... 157
Jer 30:14 All thy l. have forgotten thee: they...... 157
La 1:2 among all her l. she hath none to 157
La 1:19 I called for my l., but they deceived..... 157
Eze 16:33 but thou givest thy gifts to all thy l.,.... 157
Eze 16:36 through thy whoredoms with thy l., ... 157
Eze 16:37 therefore I will gather all thy l., ... 157
Eze 23:5 doted on her l., on the Assyrians 157
Eze 23:9 delivered her into the hand of her l.,.... 157
Eze 23:22 I will raise up thy l. against thee, ... 157
Ho 2:5 I will go after my l., that give me my... 157
Ho 2:7 she shall follow after her l., but she..... 157
Ho 2:10 her lewdness in the sight of her l., ... 157
Ho 2:12 rewards that my l. have given me:........ 157
Ho 2:13 she went after her l., and forgat me,.... 157
Ho 8:9 by himself: Ephraim hath hired l.......... 158
2Ti 3:2 men shall be l. of their own selves, ... *5367*
2Ti 3:4 highminded, l. of pleasures more........ *5369*
2Ti 3:4 of pleasures more than l. of God;....... *5377*

LOVE'S
Phm 9 for l. sake I rather beseech thee,.......... *26*

LOVES
Ps 45: *title* of Korah, Maschil, A Song of l. 3039
Pr 7:18 let us solace ourselves with l.............. 159
Ca 7:12 forth: there will I give thee my l........ 1730

LOVEST
Ge 22:2 thine only son Isaac, whom thou l.,....... 157
Jg 14:16 dost but hate me, and l. me not: 157
2Sa 19:6 In that thou l. thine enemies, and......... 157
Ps 45:7 Thou l. righteousness, and hatest 157
Ps 52:3 Thou l. evil more than good; and.......... 157
Ps 52:4 Thou l. all devouring words, O thou..... 157
Ec 9:9 joyfully with the wife whom thou l. 157
Joh 11:3 behold, he whom thou l. is sick. *5368*
Joh 21:15 **Jonas, l. thou me more than these?** .. *25*
Joh 21:16 **Simon, son of Jonas, l. thou me?**...... *25*
Joh 21:17 **Simon, son of Jonas, l. thou me?**... *5368*
Joh 21:17 him the third time, L. thou me?......... *5368*

LOVETH
Ge 27:9 meat for thy father, such as he l.: 157
Ge 44:20 of his mother, and his father l. him. 157
De 10:18 l. the stranger, in giving him food......... 157
De 15:16 because he l. thee and thine house, ... 157
Ru 4:15 thy daughter in law, which l. thee,........ 157
Ps 11:5 him that l. violence his soul hateth........ 157
Ps 11:7 the righteous Lord l. righteousness; 157
Ps 33:5 He l. righteousness and judgment: 157
Ps 34:12 that desireth life, and l. many days, ... 157
Ps 37:28 the Lord l. judgment, and forsaketh 157
Ps 87:2 The Lord l. the gates of Zion more........ 157
Ps 99:4 king's strength also l. judgment; 157
Ps 119:140 pure: therefore thy servant l. it........... 157
Ps 146:8 down: the Lord l. the righteous:............ 157
Pr 3:12 for whom the Lord l. he correcteth;....... 157
Pr 12:1 Whoso l. instruction l. knowledge: 157
Pr 13:24 that l. him chasteneth him betimes......... 157
Pr 15:9 but he l. him that followeth after 157
Pr 15:12 A scorner l. not one that reproveth....... 157
Pr 17:17 friend l. at all times, and a brother....... 157
Pr 17:19 He l. transgression that l. strife: 157
Pr 19:8 that getteth wisdom l. his own soul:...... 157
Pr 21:17 that l. pleasure shall be a poor man:...... 157
Pr 21:17 that l. wine and oil shall not be rich. 157
Pr 22:11 He that l. pureness of heart, for the 157
Pr 29:3 Whoso l. wisdom rejoiceth his............. 157
Ec 5:10 that l. silver shall not be satisfied 157
Ec 5:10 he that l. abundance with increase: 157
Ca 1:7 Tell me, O thou whom my soul l.,........ 157
Ca 3:1 bed I sought him whom my soul l.:....... 157
Ca 3:2 I will seek him whom my soul l.:.......... 157
Ca 3:3 I said, Saw ye him whom my soul l.? ... 157
Ca 3:4 but I found him whom my soul l.: 157
Isa 1:23 every one l. gifts, and followeth 157
Ho 10:11 taught, and l. to tread out the corn;...... 157
Ho 12:7 are in his hand: he l. to oppress............ 157
Mt 10:37 **l. father or mother more than me**.. *5368*
Mt 10:37 **l. son or daughter more than me**... *5368*
Lu 7:5 he l. our nation, and he hath built *25*
Lu 7:47 **little is forgiven, the same l. little,**... *25*
Joh 3:35 Father l. the Son, and hath given.......... *25*
Joh 5:20 **Father l. the Son, and sheweth** *5368*
Joh 12:25 **He that l. his life shall lose it; and**.*5368*
Joh 14:21 **keepeth them, he it is that l. me:**..... *25*
Joh 14:21 **l. me shall be loved by my Father,** ... *25*
Joh 14:24 **l. me not keepeth not my sayings:**.... *25*
Joh 16:27 **the Father himself l. you, because** .*5368*
Ro 13:8 that l. another hath fulfilled the law......... *25*
2Co 9:7 necessity: for God l. a cheerful giver. *25*
Eph 5:28 bodies. He that l. his wife l. himself. *25*
Heb 12:6 For whom the Lord l. he chasteneth,..... *25*
1Jo 2:10 l. his brother abideth in the light,.......... *25*
1Jo 3:10 neither he that l. not his brother........... *25*
1Jo 3:14 l. not his brother abideth in death. *25*
1Jo 4:7 and every one that l. is born of God,.... *25*
1Jo 4:8 He that l. not knoweth not God; for *25*
1Jo 4:20 l. not his brother whom he hath seen,..... *25*
1Jo 4:21 he who l. God love his brother also........ *25*
1Jo 5:1 and every one that l. him that begat...... *25*
1Jo 5:1 l. him also that is begotten of him.......... *25*
3Jo 9 l. to have the preeminence among...... *5383*
Re 22:15 and whosoever l. and maketh a lie...... *5368*

LOVING See also LOVINGKINDNESS.
Pr 5:19 be as the l. hind and pleasant roe; 158
Pr 22:1 l. favour rather than silver and 2896
Isa 56:10 sleeping, lying down, l. to slumber....... 157

LOVINGKINDNESS See also LOVINGKINDNESSES.
Ps 17:7 Shew thy marvellous l., O thou 2617
Ps 26:3 For thy l. is before mine eyes: and 2617
Ps 36:7 How excellent is thy l., O God! 2617
Ps 36:10 continue thy l. unto them that know ... 2617
Ps 40:10 I have not concealed thy l. and thy..... 2617
Ps 40:11 let thy l. and thy truth continually 2617
Ps 42:8 Yet the Lord will command his l. 2617
Ps 48:9 We have thought of thy l., O God,...... 2617
Ps 51:1 upon me, O God, according to thy l.:.. 2617
Ps 63:3 Because thy l. is better than life, ... 2617
Ps 69:16 Hear me, O Lord; for thy l. is good: .. 2617
Ps 88:11 Shall thy l. be declared in the grave? .. 2617
Ps 89:33 my l. will I not utterly take from........ 2617
Ps 92:2 To shew forth thy l. in the morning,...... 2617
Ps 103:4 crowneth thee with l. and tender 2617
Ps 107:43 shall understand the l. of the Lord...... 2617
Ps 119:88 Quicken me after thy l.; so shall I...... 2617
Ps 119:149 my voice according unto thy l.:......... 2617
Ps 119:159 me, O Lord, according to thy l. 2617
Ps 138:2 name for thy l. and for thy truth: 2617
Ps 143:8 me to hear thy l. in the morning; 2617
Jer 9:24 I am the Lord which exercise l., ... 2617
Jer 16:5 saith the Lord, even l. and mercies. ... 2617
Jer 31:3 therefore with l. have I drawn thee. ... 2617
Jer 32:18 Thou shewest l. unto thousands, ... 2617
Ho 2:19 judgment, and in l., and in mercies. 2617

LOVINGKINDNESSES
Ps 25:6 thy tender mercies and thy l.; 2617
Ps 89:49 Lord, where are thy former l., ... 2617
Isa 63:7 I will mention the l. of the Lord,........ 2617
Isa 63:7 according to the multitude of his l. 2617

LOW See also LOWER; LOWEST LOWETH; LOWING.
De 28:43 and thou shalt come down very l........ 4295
Jg 11:35 thou hast brought me very l., and...... 3766
1Sa 2:7 rich: he bringeth l., and lifteth up...... 8213
1Ch 27:28 trees that were in the l. plains 8219
2Ch 9:27 trees that are in the l. plains in 8219
2Ch 26:10 much cattle, both in the l. country,..... 8219
2Ch 28:18 invaded the cities of the l. country, ... 8219
2Ch 28:19 the Lord brought Judah l. because...... 3665
Job 5:11 To set up on high those that be l.;...... 8217
Job 14:21 and they are brought l., but he.......... 6819
Job 24:24 but are gone and brought l.; they....... 4355
Job 40:12 that is proud, and bring him l.: 3665
Ps 49:2 Both l. and high, rich and poor,........... 120
Ps 62:9 Surely men of l. degree are vanity, ...
Ps 79:8 us: for we are brought very l. 1809
Ps 106:43 were brought l. for their iniquity. 4355
Ps 107:39 they are minished and brought l. 7817
Ps 116:6 I was brought l., and he helped me. ... 1809
Ps 136:23 remembered us in our l. estate:.......... 8213
Ps 142:6 my cry; for I am brought very l.: 1809
Pr 29:23 A man's pride shall bring him l.: 8213
Ec 10:6 dignity, and the rich sit in l. place. 8216
Ec 12:4 the sound of the grinding is l., and..... 8217
Ec 12:4 of musick shall be brought l.;............. 7817
Isa 2:12 up; and he shall be brought l.:............ 8213
Isa 2:17 haughtiness of men shall be made l.:.... 8213
Isa 13:11 will lay l. the haughtiness of the.......... 8213
Isa 25:5 terrible ones shall be brought l. 6030
Isa 25:12 lay l., and bring to the ground, ... 8213
Isa 26:5 high; the lofty city, he layeth it l.;...... 8213
Isa 26:5 he layeth it l., even to the ground;....... 8213
Isa 29:4 speech shall be l. out of the dust, ... 7817
Isa 32:19 the forest; and the city shall be l. 8213
Isa 32:19 and the city shall be...in a l. place....... 8219
Isa 40:4 mountain and hill shall be made l.:...... 8213
La 3:55 O Lord, out of the l. dungeon. 8482
Eze 17:6 a spreading vine of l. stature, ... 8217
Eze 17:24 have exalted the l. tree, have dried.... 8217
Eze 21:26 exalt him that is l., and abase him...... 8217
Eze 26:20 thee in the l. parts of the earth, ... 8482
Lu 1:48 hath regarded the l. estate of his *5014*
Lu 1:52 and exalted them of l. degree............ *5011*
Lu 3:5 and hill shall be brought l.;............... *5013*
Ro 12:16 but condescend to men of l. estate..... *5011*
Jas 1:9 brother of l. degree rejoice in that...... *5011*
Jas 1:10 the rich, in that he is made l.:............ *5014*

LOWER See also LOWRING.
Ge 6:16 with l., second, and third stories........ 8482
Le 13:20 it be in sight l. than the skin, and 8217
Le 13:21 if it be not l. than the skin, but be 8217
Le 13:26 and it be no l. than the other skin,...... 8217
Le 14:37 which in sight are l. than the wall;...... 8217
Ne 4:13 set I in the l. places behind the 8482
Ps 8:5 him a little l. than the angels,............ 2637
Ps 63:9 go into the l. parts of the earth. 8482
Pr 25:7 l. in the presence of the prince.......... 8213
Isa 22:9 together the waters of the l. pool........ 8481
Isa 44:23 shout, ye l. parts of the earth: 8482
Eze 40:18 of the gates was the l. pavement. 8481
Eze 40:19 from the forefront of the l. gate......... 8481
Eze 42:5 were higher than these, than the l.,.... 8481
Eze 43:14 the ground even to the l. settle 8481
Eph 4:9 descended first into the l. parts *2737*
Heb 2:7 madest him a little l. than...angels;..... *1642*
Heb 2:9 was made a little l. than the angels..... *1642*

LOWERING See LOWRING.

LOWEST
De 32:22 and shall burn unto the l. hell,........... 8482
1Ki 12:31 priests of the l. of the people,........... 7098
1Ki 13:33 again of the l. of the people priests 7098
2Ki 17:32 of the l. of them priests of the high 7098
Ps 86:13 delivered my soul from the l. hell....... 8482
Ps 88:6 Thou hast laid me in the l. pit, in....... 8482

Ps 139:15 wrought in the lowest parts of the...... 8482
Eze 41:7 increased from the l. chamber to........ 8481
Eze 42:6 was straitened more than the l. 8481
Lu 14:9 **with shame to take the l. room.**..... *2078*
Lu 14:10 **go and sit down in the l. room;**..... *2078*

LOWETH
Job 6:5 grass? or l. the ox over his fodder?.... 1600

LOWING
1Sa 6:12 l. as they went, and turned not 1600
1Sa 15:14 the l. of the oxen which I hear?......... 6963

LOWLINESS
Eph 4:2 With all l. and meekness, with........... *5012*
Php 2:3 in l. of mind let each esteem other..... *5012*

LOWLY
Ps 138:6 yet hath he respect unto the l.: 8217
Pr 3:34 but he giveth grace unto the l. 6041
Pr 11:2 shame: but with the l. is wisdom. 6800
Pr 16:19 be of an humble spirit with the l., ... 6041
Zec 9:9 l., and riding upon an ass, and upon.... 6041
Mt 11:29 **me; for I am meek and l. in heart:**. *5011*

LOWRING
Mt 16:3 **to-day: for the sky is red and l.**..... *4768*

LUBIM (lu'-bim) See also LUBIMS.
Na 3:9 Put and L. were thy helpers. 3864

LUBIMS (lu'-bims) See also LEHABIM; LUBIM.
2Ch 12:3 the L., the Sukkiims, and the............ 3864
2Ch 16:8 Ethiopians and the L. a huge host, ... 3864

LUCAS (lu'-cas) See also LUKE.
2Co *subscr.* of Macedonia, by Titus, and L............ *3065*
Phm 24 Demas, L., my fellowlabourers, ...

LUCIFER (lu'-sif-ur)
Isa 14:12 O L., son of the morning! how.......... 1966

LUCIUS (lu'-she-us)
Ac 13:1 and L. of Cyrene, and Manaen, ... *3066*
Ro 16:21 Timotheus my workfellow, and L., ... *3066*

LUCRE See also LUCRE'S.
1Sa 8:3 but turned aside after l., and took...... 1215
1Ti 3:3 no striker, not greedy of filthy l.; *866*
1Ti 3:8 much wine, not greedy of filthy l.; *146*
Tit 1:7 no striker, not given to filthy l.; *146*
1Pe 5:2 not for filthy l., but of a ready *147*

LUCRE'S
Tit 1:11 they ought not, for filthy l. sake. *2771*

LUD (lud) See also LUDIM; LYDIA.
Ge 10:22 Asshur, and Arphaxad, and L., ... 3865
1Ch 1:17 and L., and Aram, and Uz, and 3865
Isa 66:19 Pul, and L., that draw the bow, ... 3865
Eze 27:10 They of Persia and of L. and of......... 3865

LUDIM (lu'-dim) See also LUD.
Ge 10:13 Mizraim begat L., and Anamim, ... 3866
1Ch 1:11 Mizraim begat L., and Anamim, ... 3866

LUHITH (lu'-hith)
Isa 15:5 mounting up of L. with weeping......... 3872
Jer 48:5 going up of L. continual weeping......... 3872

LUKE (luke) See also LUCAS.
Lu *general title* Gospel According To S. [St.] L.... *3065*
Col 4:14 L., the beloved physician, and........... *3065*
2Ti 4:11 Only L. is with me. Take Mark, ... *3065*

LUKEWARM
Re 3:16 **So then because thou art l., and**.... *5513*

LUMP
2Ki 20:7 And Isaiah said, Take a l. of figs........ 1690
Isa 38:21 had said, Let them take a l. of figs,.... 1690
Ro 9:21 same l. to make one vessel unto......... *5445*
Ro 11:16 firstfruit be holy, the l. is also holy:.... *5445*
1Co 5:6 little leaven leaveneth the whole l.? *5445*
1Co 5:7 old leaven, that ye may be a new l.,.... *5445*
Ga 5:9 little leaven leaveneth the whole l....... *5445*

LUNATICK
Mt 4:24 and those which were l., and those *4583*
Mt 17:15 son: for he is l., and sore vexed: *4583*

LURE See ALLURE.

LURK See also LURKING.
Pr 1:11 let us l. privily for the innocent......... 6845
Pr 1:18 they l. privily for their own lives........ 6845

LURKING
1Sa 23:23 take knowledge of all the l. places...... 4224
Ps 10:8 in the l. places of the village: 3993
Ps 17:12 a young lion l. in secret places. 3427

LURKING-PLACES See LURKING and PLACES.

LUST See also LUSTED; LUSTETH; LUSTING; LUSTS.
Ex 15:9 my l. shall be satisfied upon them; 5315
Ps 78:18 heart by asking meat for their l. 5315
Ps 78:30 were not estranged from their l. 8378
Ps 81:12 them up unto their own hearts' l.: 8307
Pr 6:25 L. not after her beauty in thine 2530
Mt 5:28 **looketh on a woman to l. after her**. 2530
Ro 1:27 burned in their l. one toward............. *3715*
Ro 7:7 for I had not know l., except the *1939*
1Co 10:6 should not l. after evil things,...... *1511,1938*
Ga 5:16 shall not fulfill the l. of the flesh......... *1939*
1Th 4:5 Not in the l. of concupiscence, ... *3806*
Jas 1:14 he is drawn away of his own l., ... *1939*
Jas 1:15 Then when l. hath conceived, it......... *1939*
Jas 4:2 Ye l., and have not: ye kill, and........... *1937*
2Pe 1:4 that is in the world through l.............. *1939*
2Pe 2:10 the flesh in the l. of uncleanness,......... *1939*
1Jo 2:16 l. of the flesh, and the l. of the eyes, .. *1939*
1Jo 2:17 passeth away, and the l. thereof: *1939*

LUSTED
Nu 11:34 there they buried the people that l....... 183
Ps 106:14 But l. exceedingly in the wilderness, ... 183
1Co 10:6 after evil things, as they also l........... *1937*
Re 18:14 the fruits that thy soul l. after are...... *1937*

LUSTETH
De 12:15 eat...whatsoever thy soul l. after, ... 183
De 12:20 flesh, whatsoever thy soul l. after........ 183
De 12:21 gates whatsoever thy soul l. after. 183
De 14:26 for whatsoever thy soul l. after, ... 183
Ga 5:17 For the flesh l. against the Spirit,....... *1937*
Jas 4:5 that dwelleth in us l. to envy? *1971*

LUSTING
Nu 11:4 that was among them fell a l. 8378

LUSTS
Mk 4:19 **the l. of other things entering in,**.. *1939*
Joh 8:44 **and the l. of your father ye will**.... *1939*
Ro 1:24 through the l. of their own hearts, to.. *1939*
Ro 6:12 ye should obey it in the l. thereof. *1939*
Ro 13:14 for the flesh, to fulfil the l. thereof. *1939*
Ga 5:24 the flesh with the affections and l. *1939*
Eph 2:3 in times past in the l. of our flesh, ... *1939*
Eph 4:22 corrupt according to the deceitful l.; ... *1939*
1Ti 6:9 and into many foolish and hurtful l., ... *1939*
2Ti 2:22 Flee also youthful l.: but follow........... *1939*
2Ti 3:6 with wins, led away with divers l., ... *1939*
2Ti 4:3 after their own l. shall they heap........ *1939*
Tit 2:12 denying ungodliness and worldly l., ... *1939*
Tit 3:3 serving divers l. and pleasures,.......... *1939*
Jas 4:1 your l. that war in your members? *2237*
Jas 4:3 ye may consume it upon your l. *2237*
1Pe 1:14 to the former l. in your ignorance: *1939*
1Pe 2:11 abstain from fleshly l., which war *1939*
1Pe 4:2 time in the flesh to the l. of men, ... *1939*
1Pe 4:3 walked in lasciviousness, l., excess...... *1939*
2Pe 2:18 allure through the l. of the flesh,........ *1939*
2Pe 3:3 scoffers, walking after their own l., ... *1939*
Jude 16 walking after their own l.;................. *1939*
Jude 18 walk after their own ungodly l. *1939*

LUSTY
Jg 3:29 men, all l., and all men of valour;....... 8082

LUZ (luz) See also BETH-EL.
Ge 28:19 the name of that city was called L....... 3870
Ge 35:6 So Jacob came to L., which is in the.... 3870
Ge 48:3 Almighty appeared unto me at L. 3870
Jos 16:2 And goeth out from Beth-el to L.,........ 3870
Jos 18:13 thence toward L., to the side of L.,.... 3870
Jg 1:23 the name of the city before was L.)..... 3870
Jg 1:26 and called the name thereof L.: 3870

LYCAONIA (li-ca-o'-ne-ah)
Ac 14:6 Lystra and Derbe, cities of L., and..... *3071*
Ac 14:11 voices, saying in the speech of L., ... *3071*

LYCIA (lish'-e-ah)
Ac 27:5 we came to Myra, a city of L............. *3073*

LYDDA (lid'-dah) See also LOD.
Ac 9:32 to the saints which dwelt at L. *3069*
Ac 9:35 And all that dwelt at L. and Saron...... *3069*
Ac 9:38 forasmuch as L. was nigh to Joppa, ... *3069*

LYDIA (lid'-e-ah) See also LUDIM; LYDIANS.
Eze 30:5 Ethopia, and Libya, and L., and.......... *3865*
Ac 16:14 And a certain woman named L., ... *3070*
Ac 16:40 and entered into the house of L.:........ *3070*

LYDIANS (lid'-e-uns) See also LUDIMS.
Jer 46:9 L., that handle and bend the bow........ 3866

LYING See also LEASING.
Ge 29:2 were three flocks of sheep l. by it;..... 7257
Ge 34:7 Israel in l. with Jacob's daughter; 7901
Ex 23:5 hateth thee l. under his burden,.......... 7257
Nu 31:17 hath known man by l. with him.......... 4904
Nu 31:18 not known a man by l. with him,........ 4904
Nu 31:35 not known a man by l. with him.......... 4904
De 21:1 l. in the field, and it be not known 5307
De 22:22 a man be found l. with a woman 7901
Jg 9:35 were with him, from l. in wait. ....
Jg 16:9 Now there were men l. in wait, ...
Jg 21:12 known no man by l. with any male: 4904
1Ki 22:22 be a l. spirit in the mouth of all his.... 8267
1Ki 22:23 Lord hath put a l. spirit in the mouth.. 8267
2Ch 18:21 be a l. spirit in the mouth of all his... 8267
2Ch 18:22 Lord hath put a l. spirit in the mouth.. 8267
Ps 31:6 them that regard l. vanities: 7723
Ps 31:18 Let the l. lips be put to silence;......... 8267
Ps 52:3 and l. rather than...righteousness. 8267
Ps 59:12 and for cursing and l., which they 3585
Ps 109:2 against me with a l. tongue. 8267
Ps 119:29 Remove from me the way of l. 8267
Ps 119:163 I hate and abhor l.: but thy law 8267
Ps 120:2 Deliver my soul, O Lord, from l. lips, . 8267
Ps 139:3 Thou compassest...my l. down, ... 7252
Pr 6:17 proud look, a l. tongue, and hands...... 8367
Pr 10:18 He that hideth hatred with l. lips,....... 8367
Pr 12:19 but a l. tongue is but for a moment. ... 8367
Pr 12:22 L. lips are abomination to the Lord:.... 8367
Pr 13:5 A righteous man hateth l.: but.... 1697,8367
Pr 17:7 fool: much less do l. lips a prince. 8267
Pr 21:6 getting of treasures by a l. tongue...... 8267
Pr 26:28 A l. tongue hateth those that are 8267
Isa 30:9 is a rebellious people, l. children, ... 3586
Isa 32:7 to destroy the poor with l. words,........ 8267
Isa 56:10 l. down, loving to slumber. 7901
Isa 59:13 and l. against the lord, and 3584
Jer 7:4 Trust ye not in l. words, saying,......... 8267
Jer 7:8 ye trust in l. words, that cannot 8267
Jer 29:23 have spoken l. words in my name, ... 8267
La 3:10 He was unto me as a bear l. in wait, ...
Eze 13:6 have seen vanity and l. divination, ... 3577
Eze 13:7 have ye not spoken a l. divination, ... 3577
Eze 13:19 by your l. to my people that hear....... 3576
Da 2:9 prepared l. and corrupt words to......... 3538
Ho 4:2 By swearing, and l., and killing, ... 3584
Jon 2:8 that observe l. vanities forsake 7723
Mt 9:2 a man sick of the palsy, l. on a bed: *906*
Mk 5:40 entereth in where...damsel was l.......... *345*
Lu 2:12 swaddling clothes, l. in a manger......... *2749*
Lu 2:16 Joseph, and the babe l. in a manger.... *2749*
Joh 13:25 He then l. on Jesus' breast saith *1968*
Joh 20:5 looking in, saw the linen clothes l.;..... *2749*
Joh 20:7 not l. with the linen clothes, but *2749*
Ac 20:19 me by the l. in wait of the Jews:.............
Ac 23:16 sister's son heard of their l. in wait, ...
Eph 4:25 Wherefore putting away l., speak *5579*
2Th 2:9 all power and signs and l. wonders, ... *5579*

LYSANIAS (li-sa'-ne-as)
Lu 3:1 and L. the tetrarch of Abilene, ... *3078*

LYSIAS (lis'-e-as)
Ac 23:26 Claudius L. unto...Felix sendeth......... *3079*
Ac 24:7 the chief captain L. came upon us, ... *3079*
Ac 24:22 L. the chief captain shall come........... *3079*

LYSTRA (lis'-trah)
Ac 14:6 fled unto L. and Derbe, cities of......... *3082*
Ac 14:8 And there sat a certain man at L., ... *3082*
Ac 14:21 they returned again to L., and to *3082*
Ac 16:1 Then came he to Derbe and L. *3082*
Ac 16:2 by the brethren that were at L. and ... *3082*
2Ti 3:11 me at Antioch, at Iconium, at L.; *3082*

M.

MAACAH (ma'-a-kah) See also MAACHAH.
2Sa 3:3 son of **M.** the daughter of Talmai....... 4601
2Sa 10:6 and of king **M.** a thousand men,......... 4601
2Sa 10:8 and **M.**, were by themselves in.......... 4601

MAACHAH (ma'-a-kah) See also BETH-MAACHAH; MAACAH; MAACHATHITE; SYRIA-MAACHAH.
Ge 22:24 and Gaham, and Thahash, and **M.**. 4601
1Ki 2:39 Achish son of **M.** king of Gath........... 4601
1Ki 15:2, 10 his mother's name was **M.**, the 4601
1Ki 15:13 And also **M.** his mother, even her...... 4601
1Ch 2:48 **M.**, Caleb's concubine, bare.............. 4601
1Ch 3:2 son of **M.** the daughter of Talmai....... 4601
1Ch 7:15 whose sister's name was **M.**,)........... 4601
1Ch 7:16 **M.** the wife of Machir bare a son,...... 4601
1Ch 8:29 whose wife's name was **M.**:.............. 4601
1Ch 9:35 Jeheil, whose wife's name was **M.**:..... 4601
1Ch 11:43 Hanan the son of **M.**, and................ 4601
1Ch 19:7 and the king of **M.** and his people; 4601
1Ch 27:16 Shephatiah the son of **M.**:................ 4601
2Ch 11:20 took **M.** the daughter of Absalom;...... 4601
2Ch 11:21 Rehoboam loved **M.** the daughter....... 4601
2Ch 11:22 Abijah the son of **M.** the chief, ... 4601
2Ch 15:16 concerning **M.** the mother of Asa....... 4601

MAACHATHI (ma-ak'-a-thi) See also MAACHATHITE.
De 3:14 the coasts of Geshuri and **M.**; 4602

MAACHATHITE (ma-ak'-a-thite) See also MAACHATHI; MAACHATHITES.
2Sa 23:24 son of Ahasbai, the son of the **M.**, ... 4602
2Ki 25:23 Jaazaniah the son of a **M.**, they.......... 4602
1Ch 4:19 Garmite, and Eshtemoa the **M.**.......... 4602
Jer 40:8 and Jezaniah the son of a **M.**,........... 4602

MAACHATHITES (ma-ak'-a-thites)
Jos 12:5 of the Geshurites and the **M.**, ... 4602
Jos 13:11 border of the Geshurites and **M.**,....... 4602
Jos 13:13 not the Geshurites, nor the **M.**:......... 4602
Jos 13:13 **M.** dwell among the Israelites........... 4602

MAADAI (ma'-a-dahee)
Ezr 10:34 of Bani; **M.**, Amram, and Uel, ... 4572

MAADIAH (ma-a-di'-ah) See also MOADIAH.
Ne 12:5 Miamin, **M.**, Bilgah, ... 4573

MAAI (ma'-ahee)
Ne 12:36 Milalai, Gilalai, **M.**, Nethaneel,......... 4597

MAALEH-ACRABBIM (ma''-a-leh-ac-rab'-bim) See also AKRABBIM.
Jos 15:3 went out to the south side to **M.**, ... 4610

MAARATH (ma'-a-rath)
Jos 15:59 And **M.**, and Beth-anoth, and 4638

MAASEIAH (ma-a-si'-ah)
1Ch 15:18 Eliab, and Benaiah, and **M.**, and......... 4641
1Ch 15:20 **M.**, and Benaiah, with psalteries 4641
2Ch 23:1 Obed, the **M.** the son of Adaiah,......... 4641
2Ch 26:11 Jeiel the scribe and **M.** the ruler, ... 4641
2Ch 28:7 a mighty man of Ephraim, slew **M.**...... 4641
2Ch 34:8 and **M.** the governor of the city,......... 4641
Ezr 10:18 **M.**, and Eliezer, and Jarib, and.......... 4641
Ezr 10:21 And of the sons of Harim; **M.**, and..... 4641
Ezr 10:22 the sons of Pashur; Elioenai, **M.**, ... 4641
Ezr 10:30 Chelal, Benaiah, **M.**, Mattaniah, ... 4641
Ne 3:23 repaired Azariah the son of **M.** the..... 4641
Ne 8:4 and **M.**, on his right hand; and........... 4641
Ne 8:7 Hodijah, **M.**, Kelita, Azariah,............ 4641
Ne 10:25 Rehum, Hashabnah, **M.**,................... 4641
Ne 11:5 And **M.** the son of Baruch, the son 4641
Ne 11:7 the son of **M.**, the son of Ithiel, the ... 4641
Ne 12:41 the priests; Eliakim, **M.**, Miniamin,..... 4641
Ne 12:41 **M.**, and Shemaiah, and Eleazar,......... 4641
Jer 21:1 Zephaniah the son of **M.** the priest, ... 4641
Jer 29:21 Zedekiah the son of **M.**, which........... 4641
Jer 29:25 to Zephaniah the son of **M.** the.......... 4641
Jer 32:12 the son of **M.**, in the sight of............ 4271
Jer 35:4 was above the chamber of **M.** 4641
Jer 37:3 Zephaniah the son of **M.** the............. 4641
Jer 51:59 the son of **M.**, when he went with 4271

MAASIAI (ma-a'-see-ahee)
1Ch 9:12 and **M.** the son of Adiel, the son........ 4640

MAATH (ma'-ath)
Lu 3:26 Which was the son of **M.**, which was.. *3092*

MAAZ (ma'-az)
1Ch 2:27 firstborn of Jerahmeel were, **M.**,........ 4619

MAAZIAH (ma-a-zi'-ah)
1Ch 24:18 the four and twentieth to **M.**............ 4590
Ne 10:8 **M.**, Bilgai, Shemaiah: these were....... 4590

MACEDONIA (mas-e-do'-nee-ah) See also MACEDONIAN.
Ac 16:9 stood a man of **M.**, and prayed.......... *3110*
Ac 16:9 Come over into **M.**, and help us. *3109*
Ac 16:10 we endeavoured to go into **M.**,........... *3109*
Ac 16:12 is the chief city of that part of **M.**, ... *3109*
Ac 18:5 and Timotheus were come from **M.**, ... *3109*
Ac 19:21 when he had passed through **M.** and... *3109*
Ac 19:22 he sent into **M.** two of them that....... *3109*
Ac 19:29 men of **M.**, Paul's companions in......... *3110*
Ac 20:1 and departed for to go into **M.**. *3109*
Ac 20:3 he purposed to return through **M.**...... *3109*
Ro 15:26 it hath pleased them of **M.** and.......... *3109*
1Co 16:5 when I shall pass through **M.**: *3109*
1Co 16:5 for I do pass through **M.**.................. *3109*
2Co 1:16 to pass by you into **M.**, and to *3109*
2Co 1:16 come again out of **M.** unto you, ... *3109*
2Co 2:13 them, I went from thence into **M.**...... *3109*
2Co 7:5 when we were come into **M.**, our...... *3109*
2Co 8:1 bestowed on the churches of **M.**; *3109*
2Co 9:2 I boast of you to them of **M.**, that...... *3110*
2Co 9:4 Lest haply if they of **M.** come with..... *3110*
2Co 11:9 the brethren which came from **M.** *3109*
2Co *subscr.* from Philippi, a city of **M.**,................ *3109*
Php 4:15 when I departed from **M.**, no *3109*
1Th 1:7 ensamples to all that believe in **M.** *3109*
1Th 1:8 word of the Lord not only in **M.** *3109*
1Th 4:10 the brethren which are in all **M.**:........ *3109*
1Ti 1:3 at Ephesus, when I went into **M.**,...... *3109*
Tit *subscr.* from Nicopolis of **M.**......................... *3109*

MACEDONIAN (mas-e-do'-nee-an)
Ac 27:2 Aristarchus,...being with a **M.** of........ *3110*

MACHBANAI (mak'-ba-nahee)
1Ch 12:13 the tenth, **M.** the eleventh................ 4344

MACHBENAH (mak'-be-nah)
1Ch 2:49 Sheva the father of **M.**, and the......... 4343

MACHI (ma'-ki)
Nu 13:15 tribe of Gad, Geuel the son of **M.**. 4352

MACHIR (ma'-kur) See also MACHIRITE.
Ge 50:23 also of **M.** the son of Manasseh 4353
Nu 26:29 of **M.**, the family of the Machirites: 4353
Nu 26:29 **M.** begat Gilead: of Gilead come 4353
Nu 27:1 son of **M.**, the son of Manasseh,........ 4353
Nu 32:39 children of **M.** the son of Manasseh 4353
Nu 32:40 unto **M.** the son of Manasseh, ... 4353
Nu 36:1 children of Gilead, the son of **M.**,....... 4353
De 3:15 And I gave Gilead unto **M.**................ 4353
Jos 13:31 pertaining unto the children of **M.**...... 4353
Jos 13:31 to the one half of the children of **M.** ... 4353
Jos 17:1 for **M.** the firstborn of Manasseh,....... 4353
Jos 17:3 son of **M.**, the son of Manasseh,.......... 4353
Jg 5:14 out of **M.** came down governors, ... 4353
2Sa 9:4 he is in the house of **M.**, the son of ... 4353
2Sa 9:5 fetched him out of the house of **M.**,.. 4353
2Sa 17:27 **M.** the son of Ammiel of Lo-debar,..... 4353
1Ch 2:21 went in to the daughter of **M.** the...... 4353
1Ch 2:23 these belonged to the sons of **M.**........ 4353
1Ch 7:14 concubine the Aramitess bare **M.**........ 4353
1Ch 7:15 And **M.** took to wife the sister of........ 4353
1Ch 7:16 the wife of **M.** bare a son, and 4353
1Ch 7:17 son of **M.**, the son of Manasseh.......... 4353

MACHIRITES (ma'-kur-ites)
Nu 26:29 of Machir, the family of the **M.**........... 4354

MACHNADEBAI (mak-nad'-e-bahee)
Ezr 10:40 **M.**, Shashai, Sharai, ... 4367

MACHPELAH (mak-pe'-lah)
Ge 23:9 he may give me the cave of **M.**,......... 4375
Ge 23:17 field of Ephron, which was in **M.**,........ 4375
Ge 23:19 wife in the cave of the field of **M.** 4375
Ge 25:9 buried him in the cave of **M.**, in......... 4375
Ge 49:30 In the cave that is in the field of **M.**, .. 4375
Ge 50:13 him in the cave of the field of **M.**,...... 4375

MAD
De 28:34 be **m.** for the sight of thine eyes........ 7696
1Sa 21:13 feigned himself **m.** in their hands,....... 1984
1Sa 21:14 servants, Lo, ye see the man is **m.**:... 7696
1Sa 21:15 Have I need of **m.** men, that ye 7696
1Sa 21:15 to play the **m.** man in my presence? ... 7696
2Ki 9:11 came this **m.** fellow to thee? And........ 7696
Ps 102:8 **m.** against me are sworn against......... 1984
Pr 26:18 a **m.** man who casteth firebrands,........ 3856
Ec 2:2 I said of laughter, It is **m.**: and of 1984
Ec 7:7 oppression maketh a wise man **m.**;...... 1984
Isa 44:25 liars, and maketh diviners **m.**; 1984
Jer 25:16 drink, and be moved, and be **m.**, ... 1984
Jer 29:26 every man that is **m.**, and maketh...... 7696
Jer 50:38 and they are **m.** upon their idols. 1984
Jer 51:7 wine; therefore the nations are **m.**. 1984
Ho 9:7 is a fool, the spiritual man is **m.**,...... 7696
Joh 10:20 said, He hath a devil, and is **m.**; *3105*
Ac 12:15 they said unto her, Thou art **m.**.......... *3105*
Ac 26:11 exceedingly **m.** against them, ... *1693*
Ac 26:24 learning doth make thee **m.**. *1519,3130*
Ac 26:25 I am not **m.**, most noble Festus; *3105*
1Co 14:23 will they not say that ye are **m.**? *3105*

MADAI (ma'-dahee) See also MEDE; MEDIA.
Ge 10:2 Magog, and **M.**, and Javan, and 4074
1Ch 1:5 Magog, and **M.**, and Javan, and 4074

MADE See also MADEST.
Ge 1:7 And God **m.** the firmament, and......... 6213
Ge 1:16 God made two great lights; the.......... 6213
Ge 1:16 to rule the night: he **m.** the stars also.......
Ge 1:25 And God **m.** the beast of the earth...... 6213
Ge 1:31 God saw every thing that he had **m.**,.. 6213
Ge 2:2 ended his work which he had **m.**;....... 6213
Ge 2:2 from all his work which he had **m.**...... 6213
Ge 2:3 work which God created and **m.**. 6213
Ge 2:4 the Lord God **m.** the earth and the 6213
Ge 2:9 of the ground **m.** the Lord God to grow....
Ge 2:22 taken from man, **m.** he a woman,....... 1129
Ge 3:1 beast...which the Lord God had **m.**. ... 6213
Ge 3:7 together, and **m.** themselves aprons. .. 6213
Ge 5:1 in the likeness of God **m.** he him; 6213
Ge 6:6 the Lord that he had **m.** man on 6213
Ge 6:7 repenteth me that I have **m.** them...... 6213
Ge 7:4 living substance that I have **m.** will...... 6213
Ge 8:1 God **m.** a wind to pass over the earth,......
Ge 8:6 window of the ark which he...**m.**:....... 6213
Ge 9:6 for in the image of God **m.** he man..... 6213
Ge 13:4 which he had **m.** there at the first:..... 6213
Ge 14:2 **m.** war with Bera king of Sodom,........ 6213
Ge 14:23 shouldest say, I have **m.** Abram rich:........
Ge 15:18 Lord **m.** a covenant with Abram,......... 3772
Ge 17:5 of many nations have I **m.** thee. 5414
Ge 19:3 he **m.** them a feast, and did bake 6213
Ge 19:33, 35 they **m.** their father drink wine...........
Ge 21:6 God hath **m.** me to laugh, so that all..........
Ge 21:8 and Abraham **m.** a great feast the 6213
Ge 21:27 and both of them **m.** a covenant......... 3772
Ge 21:32 they **m.** a covenant at Beer-sheba: 3772
Ge 23:17 borders round about, were **m.** sure ....
Ge 23:20 cave that is therein, were **m.** sure...........
Ge 24:11 And he **m.** his camels to kneel down..........
Ge 24:21 had **m.** his journey prosperous........... 6743
Ge 24:37 And my master **m.** me swear, saying,.......
Ge 24:46 And she **m.** haste, and let down..............
Ge 24:46 and she **m.** the camels drink also. ....
Ge 26:22 now the Lord hath **m.** room for us, ...
Ge 26:30 And he **m.** them a feast, and they...... 6213
Ge 27:14 and his mother **m.** savoury meat, ... 6213
Ge 27:30 had **m.** an end of blessing Jacob, ...
Ge 27:31 And he also had **m.** savoury meat, ... 6213
Ge 27:37 I have **m.** him thy lord, and all his...... 7760
Ge 29:22 men of the place, and **m.** a feast........ 6213
Ge 30:37 **m.** the white appear which was in the.......
Ge 31:46 they took stones, and **m.** an heap: 6213
Ge 33:17 house, and **m.** booths for his cattle:..... 6213
Ge 37:3 he **m.** him a coat of many colours. 6213
Ge 37:7 and **m.** obeisance to my sheaf.................
Ge 37:9 and the eleven stars **m.** obeisance...........

Ge	39:3	the Lord **m.** all that he did to prosper	
Ge	39:4	he **m.** him overseer over his house,	
Ge	39:5	had **m.** him overseer in his house,	
Ge	39:23	he did, the Lord **m.** it to prosper.	
Ge	40:20	**m.** a feast unto all his servants:	6213
Ge	41:43	he **m.** him to ride in the second chariot	
Ge	41:43	he **m.** him ruler over all the land	5414
Ge	41:51	said he, hath **m.** me forget all my toil,	
Ge	42:7	but **m.** himself strange unto them,	
Ge	43:25	they **m.** ready the present against	
Ge	43:28	their heads, and **m.** obeisance	
Ge	43:30	Joseph **m.** haste; for his bowels	
Ge	45:1	Joseph **m.** himself known unto his	
Ge	45:8	hath **m.** me a father to Pharaoh,	7760
Ge	45:9	God hath **m.** me lord of all Egypt:	7760
Ge	46:29	And Joseph **m.** ready his chariot,	
Ge	47:26	Joseph **m.** it a law over the land	7760
Ge	49:24	arms of his hands were **m.** strong	
Ge	49:33	had **m.** an end of commanding his	
Ge	50:5	My father **m.** me swear, saying, Lo, I	
Ge	50:6	according as he **m.** thee swear.	
Ge	50:10	he **m.** a mourning for his father	6213
Ex	1:13	me the children of Israel to serve	
Ex	1:14	and they **m.** their lives bitter with	
Ex	1:14	service, wherein they **m.** them serve,	
Ex	1:21	God, that he **m.** them houses.	6213
Ex	2:14	Who **m.** thee a prince and a judge	7760
Ex	4:11	him, Who hath **m.** man's mouth?	7760
Ex	5:21	ye have **m.** our savour to be abhorred	
Ex	7:1	I have **m.** thee a god to Pharaoh:	5414
Ex	9:20	**m.** his servants and his cattle flee into	
Ex	14:6	he **m.** ready his chariot, and took	
Ex	14:21	and **m.** the sea dry land, and the	7760
Ex	15:17	thou hast **m.** for thee to dwell in;	6466
Ex	15:25	waters, the waters were **m.** sweet:	
Ex	15:25	he **m.** for them a statute and an	7760
Ex	16:31	of it was like wafers **m.** with honey.	
Ex	18:25	**m.** them heads over the people,	5414
Ex	20:11	the Lord **m.** heaven and earth,	6213
Ex	24:8	which the Lord hath **m.** with you	3772
Ex	25:31	work shall the candlestick be **m.**:	6213
Ex	25:33	Three bowls **m.** like unto almonds,	
Ex	25:33	and three bowls **m.** like almonds in	
Ex	25:34	be four bowls **m.** like unto almonds,	
Ex	26:31	with cherubims shall it be **m.**:	6213
Ex	29:18,	25 offering **m.** by fire unto the Lord.	
Ex	29:33	wherewith the atonement was **m.**,	
Ex	29:36	thou hast **m.** an atonement for it,	
Ex	29:41	an offering **m.** by fire unto the Lord.	
Ex	30:20	offering **m.** by fire unto the Lord:	
Ex	31:17	the Lord **m.** heaven and earth,	6213
Ex	31:18	had **m.** an end of communing with	
Ex	32:4	after he had **m.** it a molten calf:	6213
Ex	32:5	Aaron **m.** proclamation, and said,	
Ex	32:8	they have **m.** them a molten calf,	6213
Ex	32:20	he took the calf which they had **m.**,	6213
Ex	32:20	**m.** the children of Israel drink of it.	
Ex	32:25	Aaron had **m.** them naked unto	
Ex	32:31	and have **m.** them gods of gold.	6213
Ex	32:35	they **m.** the calf, which Aaron **m.**	6213
Ex	34:8	And Moses **m.** haste, and bowed his	
Ex	34:27	I have **m.** a covenant with thee and	3772
Ex	35:21	every one whom his spirit **m.** willing,	
Ex	35:29	whose heart **m.** them willing to bring	
Ex	35:29	to be **m.** by the hand of Moses.	6213
Ex	36:4	man from his work which they **m.**;	6213
Ex	36:8	**m.** ten curtains of fine twined linen,	6213
Ex	36:8	of cunning work **m.** he them.	6213
Ex	36:11	And he **m.** loops of blue on the edge	6213
Ex	36:11	he **m.** in the uttermost side of	6213
Ex	36:12	Fifty loops **m.** he in one curtain,	6213
Ex	36:12	fifty loops **m.** he in the edge of the	6213
Ex	36:13	And he **m.** fifty taches of gold, and	6213
Ex	36:14	And he **m.** curtains of goats' hair	6213
Ex	36:14	eleven curtains he **m.** them.	6213
Ex	36:17	he **m.** fifty loops upon the uttermost	6213
Ex	36:17	and fifty loops **m.** he upon the edge	6213
Ex	36:18	he **m.** fifty taches of brass to couple	6213
Ex	36:19	And he **m.** a covering for the tent of	6213
Ex	36:20	he **m.** boards for the tabernacle of	6213
Ex	36:23	he **m.** boards for the tabernacle;	6213
Ex	36:24	forty sockets of silver he **m.** under	6213
Ex	36:25	north corner, he **m.** twenty boards,	6213
Ex	36:27	westward he **m.** six boards.	6213
Ex	36:28	two boards **m.** he for the corners of	6213
Ex	36:31	And he **m.** bars of shittim wood;	6213
Ex	36:33	**m.** the middle bar to shoot through	6213
Ex	36:34	**m.** their rings of gold to be places	6213
Ex	36:35	he **m.** a vail of blue, and purple,	6213
Ex	36:35	cherubims **m.** he it of cunning work.	6213
Ex	36:36	**m.** thereunto four pillars of shittim	6213
Ex	36:37	**m.** an hanging for the tabernacle	6213
Ex	37:1	Bezaleel **m.** the ark of shittim	6213
Ex	37:2	and **m.** a crown of gold to it round	6213
Ex	37:4	And he **m.** staves of shittim wood,	6213
Ex	37:6	he **m.** the mercy seat of pure gold:	6213
Ex	37:7	And he **m.** two cherubims of gold,	6213
Ex	37:7	beaten out of one piece **m.** he them,	6213
Ex	37:8	mercy seat **m.** he the cherubims	6213
Ex	37:10	And he **m.** the table of shittim wood:	6213
Ex	37:11	and **m.** thereunto a crown of gold.	6213
Ex	37:12	Also he **m.** thereunto a border of an	6213
Ex	37:12	**m.** a crown of gold for the border	6213
Ex	37:15	he **m.** the staves of shittim wood,	6213
Ex	37:16	**m.** the vessels which were upon the	6213
Ex	37:17	he **m.** the candlestick of pure gold:	6213
Ex	37:17	beaten work **m.** he the candlestick;	6213
Ex	37:19	**m.** after the fashion of almonds in	
Ex	37:19	and three bowls **m.** like almonds in	
Ex	37:20	were four bowls **m.** like almonds,	
Ex	37:23	he **m.** his seven lamps, and his	6213
Ex	37:24	Of a talent of pure gold **m.** he it,	6213
Ex	37:25	he **m.** the incense altar of shittim	6213
Ex	37:26	he **m.** unto it a crown of gold round	6213
Ex	37:27	he **m.** two rings of gold for it under	6213
Ex	37:28	**m.** the staves of shittim wood, and	6213
Ex	37:29	he **m.** the holy anointing oil, and	6213
Ex	38:1	he **m.** the altar of burnt offering of	6213
Ex	38:2	he **m.** the horns thereof on the four	6213
Ex	38:3	**m.** all the vessels of the altar, the	6213
Ex	38:3	the vessels thereof **m.** he of brass.	6213
Ex	38:4	he **m.** for the altar a brasen grate of	6213
Ex	38:6	**m.** the staves of shittim wood, and	6213
Ex	38:7	he **m.** the altar hollow with boards.	6213
Ex	38:8	And he **m.** the laver of brass, and	6213
Ex	38:9	And he **m.** the court: on the south	6213
Ex	38:22	**m.** all that the Lord commanded	6213
Ex	38:28	shekels he **m.** hooks for the pillars,	6213
Ex	38:30	he **m.** the sockets to the door of the	6213
Ex	39:1	**m.** cloths of service, to do service	6213
Ex	39:1	**m.** the holy garments for Aaron;	6213
Ex	39:2	he **m.** the ephod of gold, blue, and	6213
Ex	39:4	They **m.** shoulderpieces for it, to	6213
Ex	39:8	**m.** the breastplate of cunning work,	6213
Ex	39:9	they **m.** the breastplate double: a	6213
Ex	39:15	**m.** upon the breastplate chains at	6213
Ex	39:16	they **m.** two ouches of gold, and	6213
Ex	39:19	And they **m.** two rings of gold, and	6213
Ex	39:20	And they **m.** two other golden rings,	6213
Ex	39:22	**m.** the robe of the ephod of woven	6213
Ex	39:24	they **m.** upon the hems of the robe	6213
Ex	39:25	And they **m.** bells of pure gold, and	6213
Ex	39:27	**m.** coats of fine linen of woven work	6213
Ex	39:30	**m.** the plate of the holy crown of	6213
Ex	39:42	children of Israel **m.** all the work.	6213
Le	1:9,	13,17 an offering **m.** by fire, of a sweet	
Le	2:2	to be an offering **m.** by fire, of a sweet	
Le	2:3	of the offerings of the Lord **m.** by fire	
Le	2:7	it shall be **m.** of fine flour with oil.	6213
Le	2:8	offering that is **m.** of these things	6213
Le	2:9	it is an offering **m.** by fire, of a sweet	
Le	2:10	of the offerings of the Lord **m.** by fire	
Le	2:11	the Lord, shall be **m.** with leaven:	6213
Le	2:11	in an offering of the Lord **m.** by fire.	
Le	2:16	is an offering **m.** by fire unto the Lord.	
Le	3:3	an offering **m.** by fire unto the Lord;	
Le	3:5	it is an offering **m.** by fire, of a sweet	
Le	3:9	an offering **m.** by fire unto the Lord;	
Le	3:11	it is the food of the offering **m.** by fire	
Le	3:14	an offering **m.** by fire unto the Lord;	
Le	3:16	it is the food of the offering **m.** by fire	
Le	4:35	the offerings **m.** by fire unto the Lord:	
Le	5:12	the offerings **m.** by fire unto the Lord:	
Le	6:17	portion of my offerings **m.** by fire;	
Le	6:18	the offerings of the Lord **m.** by fire:	
Le	6:21	In a pan it shall be **m.** with oil;	6213
Le	7:5	an offering **m.** by fire unto the Lord:	
Le	7:25	an offering **m.** by fire unto the Lord,	
Le	7:30,	35 offerings of the Lord **m.** by fire,	
Le	8:21	an offering **m.** by fire unto the Lord;	
Le	8:28	is an offering **m.** by fire unto the Lord.	
Le	10:12	of the offerings of the Lord **m.** by fire,	
Le	10:13	of the sacrifices of the Lord **m.** by fire:	
Le	10:15	with the offerings **m.** by fire of the fat,	
Le	13:48	a skin, or in any thing **m.** of skin;	4399
Le	13:51	or in any work that is **m.** of skin;	6213
Le	14:11	the man that is to be **m.** clean,	6213
Le	14:36	in the house be not **m.** unclean:	
Le	16:17	have **m.** an atonement for himself,	
Le	16:20	he hath **m.** an end of reconciling	
Le	21:6	the offerings of the Lord **m.** by fire,	
Le	21:21	the offerings of the Lord **m.** by fire:	
Le	22:5	whereby he may be **m.** unclean,	
Le	22:27	an offering **m.** by fire unto the Lord.	
Le	23:8,	13 offering **m.** by fire unto the Lord	
Le	23:18	even an offering **m.** by fire, of sweet	
Le	23:15,	27 offering **m.** by fire unto the Lord.	
Le	23:36,	36 offering **m.** by fire unto the Lord:	
Le	23:37	an offering **m.** by fire unto the Lord,	
Le	23:43	I **m.** the children of Israel to dwell	
Le	24:7	an offering **m.** by fire unto the Lord.	
Le	24:9	Lord **m.** by fire by a perpetual statute.	
Le	26:13	of your yoke, and **m.** you go upright	
Le	26:46	which the Lord **m.** between him	5414
Nu	4:15	have **m.** an end of covering the	
Nu	4:26	service, and all that is **m.** for them:	6213
Nu	5:8	an atonement shall be **m.** for him.	
Nu	5:27	he hath **m.** her to drink the water,	
Nu	6:4	nothing that is **m.** of the vine tree,	6213
Nu	8:4	Moses, so he **m.** the candlestick.	6213
Nu	8:21	Aaron **m.** an atonement for them.	
Nu	11:8	baked it in pans, and **m.** cakes of	6213
Nu	14:36	**m.** all the congregation to murmur	
Nu	15:10,	13,14 an offering **m.** by fire, of a	
Nu	15:25	a sacrifice **m.** by fire unto the Lord,	
Nu	16:31	as he has **m.** an end of speaking	
Nu	16:39	they were **m.** broad plates for a	
Nu	16:47	**m.** an stonement for the people.	
Nu	18:17	an offering **m.** by fire, for a sweet	
Nu	20:5	ye **m.** us to come up out of Egypt,	
Nu	21:9	Moses **m.** a serpent of brass, and	6213
Nu	25:13	**m.** an atonement for the children	
Nu	28:2	my bread for my sacrifices **m.** by fire,	
Nu	28:3	This is the offering **m.** by fire which	
Nu	28:6	a sacrifice **m.** by fire unto the Lord.	
Nu	28:8	a sacrifice **m.** by fire, of a sweet savour	
Nu	28:13	a sacrifice **m.** by fire unto the Lord.	
Nu	28:19	ye shall offer a sacrifice **m.** by fire for	
Nu	28:24	meat of the sacrifice **m.** by fire, of a	
Nu	29:6	a sacrifice **m.** by fire unto the Lord.	
Nu	29:13,	36 offering, a sacrifice **m.** by fire,	
Nu	30:12	hath utterly **m.** them void on the day	
Nu	30:12	her husband hath **m.** them void; and	
Nu	31:20	and all that is **m.** of skins, and all	3627
Nu	31:20	goats' hair, and all things **m.** of wood.	
Nu	32:13	**m.** them wander in the wilderness	
De	1:15	and **m.** them heads over you,	5414
De	2:30	and **m.** his heart obstinate, that he	
De	4:23	covenant...which he **m.** with you,	
De	4:36	heaven he **m.** thee to hear his voice,	
De	5:2	our God, **m.** a covenant with us in	3772
De	5:3	The Lord **m.** not this covenant with	3772
De	9:9	covenant which the Lord **m.** with	3772
De	9:12	have **m.** them a molten image.	6213
De	9:16	had **m.** you a molten calf: ye had	6213
De	9:21	the calf which ye had **m.**, and burnt	6213
De	10:3	I **m.** an ark of shittim wood, and	6213
De	10:5	tables in the ark which I had **m.**;	6213
De	10:22	thy God hath **m.** thee as the stars	7760
De	11:4	**m.** the water of the Red sea to overflow	
De	18:1	of the offerings of the Lord **m.** by fire,	
De	20:9	officers have **m.** an end of speaking	
De	26:12	**m.** an end of tithing all the tithes	
De	26:19	all nations which he hath **m.**,	6213
De	29:1	covenant which he **m.** with them.	3772
De	29:25	he **m.** with them when he brought	3772
De	31:16	my covenant which I have **m.** with	3772
De	31:24	Moses had **m.** an end of writing	
De	32:6	not **m.** thee, and established thee	6213
De	32:13	**m.** him ride on the high places of the	
De	32:13	**m.** him to suck honey out of the rock,	
De	32:15	he forsook God which **m.** him,	6213
De	32:45	Moses **m.** an end of speaking all	
Jos	2:17	oath which thou hast **m.** us swear.	
Jos	2:20	oath which thou hast **m.** us to swear.	
Jos	5:3	And Joshua **m.** him sharp knives,	6213
Jos	8:15	all Israel **m.** as if they were beaten	
Jos	8:24	Israel had **m.** an end of slaying	
Jos	8:28	Ai, and **m.** it an heap for ever,	7760
Jos	9:4	**m.** as if they had been ambassadors,	
Jos	9:15	And Joshua **m.** peace with them,	6213

Jos 9:15 and **m.** a league with them, to let 6213
Jos 9:16 they had **m.** a league with them,........ 3772
Jos 9:27 Joshua **m.** them that day hewers........ 5414
Jos 10:1 Gibeon had **m.** peace with Israel, ...
Jos 10:4 it hath **m.** peace with Joshua and..............
Jos 10:5 before Gibeon; and **m.** war against it. ....
Jos 10:20 Israel had **m.** an end of slaying ....
Jos 11:18 Joshua **m.** war a long time with 6213
Jos 11:19 not a city that **m.** peace with the ....
Jos 13:14 sacrifices...of Israel **m.** by fire ....
Jos 14:8 me **m.** the heart of the people melt: ....
Jos 19:49 had **m.** an end of dividing the land............
Jos 19:51 **m.** an end of dividing the country. ....
Jos 22:25 hath **m.** Jordan a border between....... 5414
Jos 22:28 of the Lord, which our fathers **m.**. 6213
Jos 24:25 **m.** a covenant with the people that..... 3772
Jg 2:1 **m.** you to go up out of Egypt, and have....
Jg 3:16 **m.** him a dagger which had two......... 6213
Jg 3:18 had **m.** an end to offer the present, ...
Jg 5:13 he **m.** him that remaineth have ....
Jg 5:13 Lord **m.** me have dominion over the ....
Jg 6:2 of Israel **m.** them the dens which....... 6213
Jg 6:19 went in, and **m.** ready a kid, and 6213
Jg 8:27 Gideon **m.** an ephod thereof, and 6213
Jg 8:33 and **m.** Baal-berith their god............. 7760
Jg 9:6 and went, and **m.** Abimelech king,...........
Jg 9:16 in that ye have **m.** Abimelech king,...........
Jg 9:18 and have **m.** Abimelech, the son...king.......
Jg 9:27 and **m.** merry, and went into the 6213
Jg 11:4 of Ammon **m.** war against Israel..............
Jg 11:5 of Ammon **m.** war against Israel,..............
Jg 11:11 people **m.** him head and captain 7760
Jg 13:10 the woman **m.** haste, and ran, and............
Jg 13:15 shall have **m.** ready a kid for thee. 6213
Jg 14:10 and Samson **m.** there a feast; for 6213
Jg 15:17 he had **m.** an end of speaking, ...
Jg 16:19 And she **m.** him sleep upon her knees:......
Jg 16:25 prison house; and he **m.** them sport: ....
Jg 16:27 that beheld while Samson **m.** sport. ....
Jg 17:4 who **m.** thereof a graven image 6213
Jg 17:5 and **m.** an ephod, and teraphim,......... 6213
Jg 18:24 taken away my gods which I **m.**,......... 6213
Jg 18:27 took the things which Micah had **m.**,... 6213
Jg 18:31 Micah's graven image, which he **m.**, ... 6213
Jg 21:5 had **m.** a great oath concerning him..........
Jg 21:15 Lord had **m.** a breach in the tribes..... 6213
1Sa 2:19 his mother **m.** him a little coat,.......... 6213
1Sa 2:28 father all the offerings **m.** by fire.............
1Sa 3:13 his sons **m.** themselves vile, and.............
1Sa 4:18 when he **m.** mention of the ark of God,.....
1Sa 8:1 he **m.** his sons judges over Israel. 7760
1Sa 9:22 **m.** them sit in the chiefest place 5414
1Sa 10:13 he had **m.** an end of prophesying,..............
1Sa 11:15 they **m.** Saul king before the Lord...........
1Sa 12:1 me, and have **m.** a king over you. ....
1Sa 12:8 Egypt, and **m.** them dwell in this place.....
1Sa 13:10 as he had **m.** an end of offering ....
1Sa 13:12 I have not **m.** supplication unto ....
1Sa 14:14 and his armourbearer **m.**, was 5221
1Sa 15:17 wast thou not **m.** the head of the ....
1Sa 15:33 sword hath **m.** woman childless,...............
1Sa 15:35 he had **m.** Saul king over Israel. ....
1Sa 16:8 and **m.** him pass before Samuel.................
1Sa 16:9 Then Jesse **m.** Shammah to pass by. ....
1Sa 16:10 Jesse **m.** seven of his sons to pass...........
1Sa 18:1 he had **m.** an end of speaking unto ....
1Sa 18:3 and David **m.** a covenant, because...... 3772
1Sa 18:13 and **m.** him his captain over a........... 7760
1Sa 20:16 So Jonathan **m.** a covenant with......... 3772
1Sa 22:8 **m.** a league with the son of Jesse, ... 3772
1Sa 23:18 two **m.** a covenant before the Lord: ... 3772
1Sa 23:26 David **m.** haste to get away for................
1Sa 24:16 David had **m.** an end of speaking.............
1Sa 25:18 Abigail **m.** haste, and took two ....
1Sa 27:10 said, Whither have ye **m.** a road to day?....
1Sa 27:12 **m.** his people Israel utterly to abhor.........
1Sa 30:11 eat; and they **m.** him drink water;............
1Sa 30:14 We **m.** an invasion upon the south............
1Sa 30:21 whom they had **m.** also to abide at the......
1Sa 30:25 he **m.** it a statute and an ordinance..... 7760
2Sa 2:9 **m.** him king over Gilead, and over............
2Sa 3:6 Abner **m.** himself strong for the ....
2Sa 3:20 David **m.** Abner and the men that 6213
2Sa 4:4 she **m.** haste to flee, that he fell, ...
2Sa 5:3 king David **m.** a league with them 3772
2Sa 6:5 manner of instruments **m.** of fir wood, ...
2Sa 6:8 Lord had **m.** a breach upon Uzzah:..... 6555
2Sa 6:18 David had **m.** an end of offering..............
2Sa 7:9 have **m.** thee a great name, like 6213
2Sa 10:19 they **m.** peace with Israel, and.................
2Sa 11:13 before him; and he **m.** him drunk: ....
2Sa 11:19 thou hast **m.** an end of telling..................
2Sa 12:31 **m.** them pass through the brickkiln:.........
2Sa 13:6 lay down, and **m.** himself sick:................
2Sa 13:8 and **m.** cakes in his sight, and did 3835
2Sa 13:10 took the cakes which she had **m.**, ... 6213
2Sa 13:36 as he had **m.** an end of speaking, ...
2Sa 14:15 the people have **m.** me afraid: ....
2Sa 15:4 that I were **m.** judge in the land, ... 7760
2Sa 17:25 Absalom **m.** Amasa captain of the....... 7760
2Sa 22:5 of ungodly men **m.** me afraid:........... 7760
2Sa 22:12 he **m.** darkness pavilions round.......... 7896
2Sa 22:36 thy gentleness hath **m.** me great. ....
2Sa 23:5 he hath **m.** with me an everlasting...... 7760
1Ki 1:41 as they had **m.** an end of eating. ....
1Ki 1:43 king David hath **m.** Solomon king. ....
1Ki 2:24 who hath **m.** me an house, as he 6213
1Ki 3:1 Solomon **m.** affinity with Pharaoh king.......
1Ki 3:1 had **m.** an end of building his own ....
1Ki 3:7 hast **m.** thy servant king instead of..........
1Ki 3:15 and **m.** a feast to all his servants. 6213
1Ki 4:7 his month in a year **m.** provision. 6213
1Ki 5:12 and they two **m.** a league together. 3772
1Ki 6:4 he **m.** windows of narrow lights. 6213
1Ki 6:5 and he **m.** chambers round about: 6213
1Ki 6:6 house he **m.** narrowed rests round 5414
1Ki 6:7 of stone **m.** ready before it was ....
1Ki 6:21 **m.** a partition by the chains of gold..........
1Ki 6:23 the oracle he **m.** two cherubims.......... 6213
1Ki 6:31 the oracle he **m.** doors of olive tree:... 6213
1Ki 6:33 **m.** he for the door of the temple 6213
1Ki 7:6 And he **m.** a porch of pillars; the 6213
1Ki 7:7 **m.** a porch for the throne where he.... 6213
1Ki 7:8 **m.** also an house for Pharaoh's.......... 6213
1Ki 7:16 **m.** two chapiters of molten brass, ... 6213
1Ki 7:18 And he **m.** the pillars, and two rows.... 6213
1Ki 7:23 he **m.** a molten sea, ten cubits from ... 6213
1Ki 7:27 **m.** ten bases of brass; four cubits 6213
1Ki 7:29 certain additions **m.** of thin work. 6213
1Ki 7:37 this manner he **m.** the ten bases: 6213
1Ki 7:38 **m.** he ten lavers of brass: one laver ... 6213
1Ki 7:40 And Hiram **m.** the lavers, and the 6213
1Ki 7:40 **m.** an end of doing all the work 6213
1Ki 7:40 **m.** king Solomon for the house 6213
1Ki 7:45 Hiram **m.** to king Solomon for the 6213
1Ki 7:48 And Solomon **m.** all the vessels that ... 6213
1Ki 7:51 work that king Solomon **m.** for the..... 6213
1Ki 8:9 the Lord **m.** a covenant with the......... 3772
1Ki 8:21 Lord, which he **m.** with our fathers, ... 3772
1Ki 8:38 supplication soever be **m.** by any man, ...
1Ki 8:54 Solomon had **m.** an end of praying...........
1Ki 8:59 have **m.** supplication before the Lord, ...
1Ki 9:3 supplication, that thou hast **m.** before........
1Ki 9:26 king Solomon **m.** a navy of ships......... 6213
1Ki 10:9 therefore **m.** he thee king, to do......... 7760
1Ki 10:12 king **m.** of the almug trees pillars....... 6213
1Ki 10:16 **m.** two hundred targets of beaten 6213
1Ki 10:17 he **m.** three hundred shields of beaten.......
1Ki 10:18 king **m.** a great throne of ivory,.......... 6213
1Ki 10:20 was not the like **m.** in any kingdom. ... 6213
1Ki 10:27 king **m.** silver to be in Jerusalem........ 5414
1Ki 10:27 cedars **m.** he to be as the sycomore... 5414
1Ki 11:28 **m.** him ruler over all the charge of..... 5414
1Ki 12:4 Thy father **m.** our yoke grievous: now ......
1Ki 12:10 Thy father **m.** our hoke heavy, but..........
1Ki 12:14 My father **m.** your yoke heavy, and I........
1Ki 12:18 **m.** speed to get him up to his chariot, ...
1Ki 12:20 and **m.** him king over all Israel: ....
1Ki 12:28 counsel, and **m.** two calves of gold, ... 6213
1Ki 12:31 And he **m.** an house of high places, ... 6213
1Ki 12:31 **m.** priests of the lowest of...people, ... 6213
1Ki 12:32 unto the calves that he had **m.**: 6213
1Ki 12:32 of the high places which he had **m.**..... 6213
1Ki 12:33 upon the altar which he had **m.** in...... 6213
1Ki 13:33 **m.** again of the lowest of the people ... 6213
1Ki 14:7 and **m.** thee prince over my people 5414
1Ki 14:9 hast gone and **m.** thee other gods, ... 6213
1Ki 14:15 because they have **m.** their groves, ... 6213
1Ki 14:16 who did sin, and who **m.** Israel to sin. ......
1Ki 14:26 shields...which Solomon had **m.**. 6213
1Ki 14:27 **m.** in their stead brasen shields, ... 6213
1Ki 15:12 all the idols that his fathers had **m.**..... 6213
1Ki 15:13 she had **m.** an idol in a grove; 6213
1Ki 15:22 Then king Asa **m.** a proclamation ....
1Ki 15:26 his sin wherewith he **m.** Israel to sin. ....
1Ki 15:30 sinned, and which he **m.** Israel to sin,.......
1Ki 15:34 his sin wherewith he **m.** Israel to sin, ...
1Ki 16:2 and **m.** thee prince over my people 5414
1Ki 16:2 hast **m.** my people Israel to sin, to..........
1Ki 16:13 and by which they **m.** Israel to sin,...........
1Ki 16:16 all Israel **m.** Omri...king.........................
1Ki 16:26 his sin wherewith he **m.** Israel to sin, ...
1Ki 16:33 Ahab **m.** a grove; and Ahab did 6213
1Ki 18:26 upon the altar which was **m.**. 6213
1Ki 18:32 he **m.** a trench about the altar, as...... 6213
1Ki 20:34 as my father **m.** in Samaria. Then 7760
1Ki 20:34 So he **m.** a covenant with him, and..... 3772
1Ki 21:22 me to anger, and **m.** Israel to sin. ....
1Ki 22:11 son of Chenaanah **m.** him horns of...... 6213
1Ki 22:39 the ivory house which he **m.**, and 1129
1Ki 22:44 Jehoshaphat **m.** peace with the.................
1Ki 22:48 **m.** ships of Tharshish to go to 6235
1Ki 22:52 the son of Nebat, who **m.** Israel to sin:.....
2Ki 3:2 of Baal that his father had **m.**. 6213
2Ki 3:3 son of Nebat, which **m.** Israel to sin; ....
2Ki 7:6 had **m.** the host of the Syrians to hear......
2Ki 8:20 and **m.** a king over themselves. ....
2Ki 9:21 And his chariot was **m.** ready. ....
2Ki 10:16 So they **m.** him ride in his chariot. ....
2Ki 10:25 as he had **m.** an end of offering the ....
2Ki 10:27 **m.** it a draught house unto this.......... 7760
2Ki 10:29 the son of Nebat, who **m.** Israel to sin,.....
2Ki 10:31 of Jeroboam, which **m.** Israel to sin. ....
2Ki 11:4 and **m.** a covenant with them, and...... 3772
2Ki 11:12 they **m.** him king, and anointed................
2Ki 11:17 Jehoiada **m.** a covenant between 3772
2Ki 12:13 not **m.** for the house of the Lord 6213
2Ki 12:20 servants arose, and **m.** a conspiracy, ...
2Ki 13:2 son of Nebat, which **m.** Israel to sin; ....
2Ki 13:6 house of Jeroboam, who **m.** Israel sin, ...
2Ki 13:7 and had **m.** them like the dust by....... 7760
2Ki 13:11 the son of Nebat, who **m.** Israel sin:.........
2Ki 14:19 they **m.** a conspiracy against him.............
2Ki 14:21 **m.** him king instead of his father..............
2Ki 14:24 the son of Nebat, who **m.** Israel to sin. .....
2Ki 15:9 the son of Nebat, who **m.** Israel to sin. .....
2Ki 15:15 and his conspiracy which he **m.**,.......... 7194
2Ki 15:18, 24,28 Nebat, who **m.** Israel to sin. ....
2Ki 15:30 the son of Elah **m.** a conspiracy ....
2Ki 16:3 **m.** his son to pass through the fire, ...
2Ki 16:11 the priest **m.** it against king Ahaz....... 6213
2Ki 17:8 kings of Israel, which they had **m.**....... 6213
2Ki 17:15 his covenant that he **m.** with their...... 3772
2Ki 17:16 **m.** them molten images, even two...... 6213
2Ki 17:16 and **m.** a grove, and worshipped all 6213
2Ki 17:19 statutes of Israel which they **m.**......... 6213
2Ki 17:21 and they **m.** Jeroboam...king: 6213
2Ki 17:21 the Lord, and **m.** them sin a great sin..6213
2Ki 17:29 every nation **m.** gods of their own,..... 6213
2Ki 17:29 which the Samaritans had **m.**,............ 6213
2Ki 17:30 men of Babylon **m.** Succoth-benoth,.... 6213
2Ki 17:30 and the men of Cuth **m.** Nergal, ... 6213
2Ki 17:30 and the men of Hamath **m.** Ashima,.... 6213
2Ki 17:31 the Avites **m.** Nibhaz and Tartak,........ 6213
2Ki 17:32 **m.** unto themselves of the lowest of... 6213
2Ki 17:35 whom the Lord had **m.** a covenant, ... 3772
2Ki 17:38 covenant that I have **m.** with you........ 3772
2Ki 18:4 brasen serpent that Moses had **m.**: 6213
2Ki 19:15 thou hast **m.** heaven and earth. 6213
2Ki 20:20 how he **m.** a pool, and a conduit, ... 6213
2Ki 21:3 up altars for Baal, and **m.** a grove, ... 6213
2Ki 21:6 he **m.** his son pass through the fire, ...
2Ki 21:7 grove that he had **m.** in the house,..... 6213
2Ki 21:11 **m.** Judah also to sin with his idols: ....
2Ki 21:16 his sin wherewith he **m.** Judah to sin, ...
2Ki 21:24 of the land **m.** Josiah his son king............
2Ki 22:7 no reckoning **m.** with them of the.............
2Ki 23:3 and **m.** a covenant before the Lord,.... 3772
2Ki 23:4 all the vessels that were m. for Baal, ...
2Ki 23:12 which the kings of Judah had **m.**, ... 6213
2Ki 23:12 altars which Manasseh had **m.** in........ 6213
2Ki 23:15 the son of Nebat, who **m.** Israel to sin, ...
2Ki 23:15 which Jeroboam the son...had **m.**, ... 6213
2Ki 23:19 Israel had **m.** to provoke the Lord...... 6213
2Ki 23:30 **m.** him king to his father's stead. ....
2Ki 23:34 **m.** Eliakim the son of Josiah king ....
2Ki 24:13 had **m.** in the temple of the Lord, ... 6213
2Ki 24:17 **m.** Mattaniah his father's brother king ......
2Ki 25:16 Solomon had **m.** for the house of 6213
2Ki 25:22 over them he **m.** Gedeliah...ruler, ...
2Ki 25:23 Babylon had **m.** Gedaliah governor,...........

1Ch 5:10, 19 they **m.** war with the Hagarites, 6213
1Ch 9:30 of the priests **m.** the ointment of 7543
1Ch 9:31 things that were **m.** in the pans. 4639
1Ch 11:3 David **m.** a covenant with them in 3772
1Ch 12:18 and **m.** them captains of the band. 5414
1Ch 13:11 Lord had **m.** a breach upon Uzza: 5414
1Ch 15:1 David **m.** him houses in the city of 6213
1Ch 15:13 Lord our God **m.** a breach upon us,
1Ch 16:2 David had **m.** an end of offering
1Ch 16:5 Asaph **m.** a sound with cymbals;
1Ch 16:16 which he **m.** with Abraham, and 3772
1Ch 16:26 but the Lord **m.** the heavens. 6213
1Ch 17:8 **m.** thee a name like the name of 6213
1Ch 18:8 Solomon **m.** the brasen sea, and 6213
1Ch 19:6 had **m.** themselves odious to David,
1Ch 19:19 they **m.** peace with David, and
1Ch 21:29 which Moses **m.** in the wilderness, 6213
1Ch 22:8 abundantly, and hast **m.** great wars: 6213
1Ch 23:1 he **m.** Solomon his son king over
1Ch 23:5 with the instruments which I **m.**, 6213
1Ch 26:10 yet his father **m.** him the chief;) 7760
1Ch 26:32 whom king David **m.** rulers over the
1Ch 28:2 and had **m.** ready for the building:
1Ch 28:19 the Lord **m.** me understand in writing
1Ch 29:2 the gold for things to be **m.** of gold,
1Ch 29:5 manner of work to be **m.** by the hands
1Ch 29:19 for the which I have **m.** provision.
1Ch 29:22 they **m.** Solomon the son of David king
2Ch 1:3 the servant of the Lord had **m.** in 6213
2Ch 1:5 brasen altar, that Bezaleel...had **m.**, 6213
2Ch 1:8 hast **m.** me to reign in his stead.
2Ch 1:9 thou hast **m.** me king over a people
2Ch 1:11 over whom I have **m.** thee king:
2Ch 1:15 And the king **m.** silver and gold at 5414
2Ch 1:15 cedar trees **m.** he as the sycomore 5414
2Ch 2:11 he hath **m.** thee king over them. 5414
2Ch 2:12 Israel, that **m.** heaven and earth, 6213
2Ch 3:8 And he **m.** the most holy house, the 6213
2Ch 3:10 he **m.** two cherubims of image work, 6213
2Ch 3:14 he **m.** the vail of blue, and purple, 6213
2Ch 3:15 he **m.** before the house two pillars 6213
2Ch 3:16 And he **m.** chains, as in the oracle, 6213
2Ch 3:16 and **m.** an hundred pomegranates, 6213
2Ch 4:1 Moreover he **m.** an altar of brass, 6213
2Ch 4:2 he **m.** a molten sea of ten cubits 6213
2Ch 4:6 He **m.** also ten lavers, and put five 6213
2Ch 4:7 And he **m.** ten candlesticks of gold 6213
2Ch 4:8 He **m.** also ten tables, and placed 6213
2Ch 4:8 he **m.** an hundred basons of gold 6213
2Ch 4:9 he **m.** the court of the priests, and 6213
2Ch 4:11 Huram **m.** the pots, and the shovels, 6213
2Ch 4:14 He **m.** also bases, and lavers **m.** he 6213
2Ch 4:18 Thus Solomon **m.** all these vessels 6213
2Ch 4:19 And Solomon **m.** all the vessels that 6213
2Ch 4:21 lamps, and the tongs, **m.** he of gold, 6213
2Ch 5:1 all the work that Solomon **m.** for 6213
2Ch 5:10 when the Lord **m.** a covenant with 3772
2Ch 6:11 that he **m.** with the children of 3772
2Ch 6:13 Solomon had **m.** a brasen scaffold, 6213
2Ch 6:29 supplication soever shall be **m.** of any
2Ch 6:40 the prayer that is **m.** in this place
2Ch 7:1 Solomon had **m.** an end of praying,
2Ch 7:6 the king had **m.** to praise the Lord, 6213
2Ch 7:7 brasen altar which Solomon had **m.** 6213
2Ch 7:9 day they **m.** a solemn assembly: 6213
2Ch 7:15 the prayer that is **m.** in this place. 6213
2Ch 9:8 therefore **m.** he thee king over 5414
2Ch 9:11 king **m.** of the algum trees terraces 6213
2Ch 9:15 Solomon **m.** two hundred targets 6213
2Ch 9:16 hundred shields **m.** he of beaten gold:
2Ch 9:17 king **m.** a great throne of ivory, 6213
2Ch 9:19 not the like **m.** in any kingdom. 6213
2Ch 9:27 the king **m.** silver in Jerusalem as 5414
2Ch 9:27 cedar trees **m.** he as the sycomore 5414
2Ch 10:4 Thy father **m.** our yoke grievous:
2Ch 10:10 Thy father **m.** our yoke heavy, but
2Ch 10:14 My father **m.** your yoke heavy, but
2Ch 10:18 Rehoboam **m.** speed to get him up to
2Ch 11:12 and **m.** them exceeding strong,
2Ch 11:15 for the calves which he had **m.** 6213
2Ch 11:17 **m.** Rehoboam...son of Solomon strong
2Ch 11:22 **m.** Abijah the son...to be ruler among
2Ch 12:9 of gold which Solomon had **m.** 6213
2Ch 12:10 king Rehoboam **m.** shields of brass, 6213
2Ch 13:8 which Jeroboam **m.** you for gods. 6213
2Ch 13:9 **m.** you priests after the manner of 6213
2Ch 15:16 she had **m.** an idol in a grove: and 6213
2Ch 16:14 **m.** for himself in the city of David, 3738
2Ch 16:14 **m.** a very great burning for him.
2Ch 17:10 they **m.** no war against Jehoshaphat.
2Ch 18:10 Chenaanah had **m.** him horns of 6213
2Ch 20:23 had **m.** an end of the inhabitants
2Ch 20:27 **m.** them to rejoice over their enemies.
2Ch 20:36 they **m.** the ships in Ezion-gaber. 6213
2Ch 21:7 covenant...he had **m.** with David, 3772
2Ch 21:8 Judah, and **m.** themselves a king.
2Ch 21:11 **m.** high places in the mountains of 6213
2Ch 21:13 hast **m.** Judah and the inhabitants of
2Ch 21:19 his people **m.** no burning for him, 6213
2Ch 22:1 **m.** Ahaziah his youngest son king
2Ch 23:3 congregation **m.** a covenant with 3772
2Ch 23:11 the testimony, and **m.** him king,
2Ch 23:16 Jehoiada **m.** a covenant between 3772
2Ch 24:8 commandment they **m.** a chest, 6213
2Ch 24:9 **m.** a proclamation through Judah 5414
2Ch 24:10 the chest, until they had **m.** an end.
2Ch 24:14 were **m.** vessels for the house of 6213
2Ch 24:17 and **m.** obeisance to the king.
2Ch 25:5 **m.** them captains over thousands,
2Ch 25:16 Art thou **m.** of the king's counsel? 5414
2Ch 25:27 they **m.** a conspiracy against him
2Ch 26:1 and **m.** him king in the room of his
2Ch 26:5 the Lord, God **m.** him to prosper.
2Ch 26:13 that **m.** war with mighty power, to 6213
2Ch 26:15 And he **m.** in Jerusalem engines, 6213
2Ch 28:2 **m.** also molten images for Baalim. 6213
2Ch 28:19 for he **m.** Judah naked, and 6213
2Ch 28:24 he **m.** him altars in every corner 6213
2Ch 28:25 he **m.** high places to burn incense 6213
2Ch 29:17 of the first month they **m.** an end.
2Ch 29:24 they **m.** reconciliation with their
2Ch 29:24 offering should be **m.** for all Israel.
2Ch 29:29 they had **m.** an end of offering,
2Ch 32:5 **m.** darts and shields in abundance. 6213
2Ch 32:27 he **m.** himself treasuries for silver, 6213
2Ch 33:3 up altars for Baalim, and **m.** groves, 6213
2Ch 33:7 the idol which he had **m.**, in the 6213
2Ch 33:9 Manasseh **m.** Judah and the...to err,
2Ch 33:22 which Manasseh his father had **m.**, 6213
2Ch 33:25 the land **m.** Josiah his son king
2Ch 34:4 brake in pieces, and **m.** dust of them,
2Ch 34:31 and **m.** a covenant before the Lord, 3772
2Ch 34:33 **m.** all that were...in Israel to serve,
2Ch 35:14 they **m.** ready for themselves, and
2Ch 35:25 **m.** them an ordinance in Israel: 5414
2Ch 36:1 **m.** him king in his father's stead
2Ch 36:4 Egypt **m.** Eliakim his brother king
2Ch 36:10 **m.** Zedekiah his brother king over
2Ch 36:13 who had **m.** him swear by God:
2Ch 36:22 **m.** a proclamation throughout all his
Ezr 1:1 **m.** a proclamation throughout all his
Ezr 4:15 search may be **m.** in the book of
Ezr 4:19 and search hath been **m.**, and it is
Ezr 4:19 hath **m.** insurrection against kings,
Ezr 4:19 and sedition have been **m.** therein. 5648
Ezr 4:23 and **m.** them to cease by force and
Ezr 5:13 Cyrus **m.** a decree to build this 7761
Ezr 5:14 whom he had **m.** governor; 7761
Ezr 5:17 be search **m.** in the king's treasure
Ezr 5:17 decree was **m.** of Cyrus the king to 7761
Ezr 6:1 Darius the king **m.** a decree, and 7761
Ezr 6:1 search was **m.** in the house of the
Ezr 6:3 same Cyrus the king **m.** a decree 7761
Ezr 6:11 have **m.** a decree, that whosoever 7761
Ezr 6:11 let his house be **m.** a dunghill for 5648
Ezr 6:12 I Darius have **m.** a decree; let it 7761
Ezr 6:22 for the Lord had **m.** them joyful,
Ezr 10:5 **m.** the chief priests, the Levites...swear
Ezr 10:7 **m.** proclamation throughout Judah
Ezr 10:17 **m.** an end with all the men that
Ne 3:16 to the pool that was **m.**, and unto 6213
Ne 4:7 walls of Jerusalem were **m.** up, 5927,752
Ne 4:9 Nevertheless we **m.** our prayer
Ne 6:9 For they all **m.** us afraid, saying,
Ne 8:4 pulpit of wood, which they had **m.** 6213
Ne 8:16 them, and **m.** themselves booths, 6213
Ne 8:17 **m.** booths, and sat under the booths: 6213
Ne 9:6 thou hast **m.** heaven, the heaven of 6213
Ne 9:18 they had **m.** them a molten calf, 6213
Ne 10:32 Also we **m.** ordinances for us, to 5975
Ne 12:43 God had **m.** them rejoice with great joy:
Ne 13:13 I **m.** treasurers over the treasuries,
Ne 13:25 their hair, and **m.** them swear by God,
Ne 13:26 God **m.** him king over all Israel: 5414
Es 1:3 he **m.** a feast unto all his princes 6213
Es 1:5 king **m.** a feast unto all the people 6213
Es 1:9 Vashti the queen **m.** a feast for the 6213
Es 2:17 **m.** her queen instead of Vashti.
Es 2:18 Then the king **m.** a great feast 6213
Es 2:18 he **m.** a release to the provinces, 6213
Es 2:23 inquisition was **m.** of the matter,
Es 5:14 Let a gallows be **m.** of fifty cubits 6213
Es 5:14 and he caused the gallows to be **m.** 6213
Es 7:9 which Haman had **m.** for Mordecai, 6213
Es 9:17, 18 and **m.** it a day of feasting and 6213
Es 9:19 **m.** the fourteenth day of the month 6213
Job 1:10 not thou **m.** an hedge about him,
Job 1:17 The Chaldeans **m.** out three bands, 7760
Job 2:11 had **m.** an appointment together
Job 4:14 which **m.** all my bones to shake.
Job 7:3 am I **m.** to possess months of vanity,
Job 10:8 Thine hands have **m.** me and 6087
Job 10:9 that thou hast **m.** as the clay; 6213
Job 15:7 or wast thou **m.** before the hills? 2342
Job 16:7 But now he hath **m.** me weary:
Job 16:7 hast **m.** desolate all my company.
Job 17:6 **m.** me also a byword of the people; 3322
Job 17:13 have **m.** my bed in the darkness. 7502
Job 28:18 No mention shall be **m.** of coral, or of
Job 28:26 When he **m.** a decree for the rain, 6213
Job 31:1 I **m.** a covenant with mine eyes; 3772
Job 31:15 **m.** me in the womb make him? 6213
Job 31:24 If I have **m.** gold my hope, or have 7760
Job 33:4 The Spirit of God hath **m.** me, and 6213
Job 38:9 **m.** the cloud the garment thereof, 7760
Job 39:6 house I have **m.** the wilderness, 7760
Job 40:15 behemoth, which I **m.** with thee; 6213
Job 40:19 **m.** him can make his sword to 6213
Job 41:33 not his like, who is **m.** without fear 6213
Ps 7:12 hath bent his bow, and **m.** it ready.
Ps 7:15 He **m.** a pit, and digged it, and 3738
Ps 7:15 fallen into the ditch which he **m.** 6466
Ps 8:5 thou hast **m.** him a little lower
Ps 9:15 sunk down in the pit that they **m.**: 6213
Ps 18:4 of ungodly men **m.** me afraid.
Ps 18:11 He **m.** darkness his secret place; 7896
Ps 18:35 thy gentleness hath **m.** me great.
Ps 18:43 **m.** me the head of the heathen: 7760
Ps 21:6 **m.** him most blessed for ever: 7896
Ps 21:6 thou hast **m.** him exceeding glad
Ps 30:1 hast not **m.** my foes to rejoice over me.
Ps 30:7 **m.** my mountain to stand strong:
Ps 30:8 unto the Lord I **m.** supplication and
Ps 33:6 of the Lord were the heavens **m.**; 6213
Ps 39:5 **m.** my days as an handbreadth; 5414
Ps 45:1 things which I have **m.** touching 4639
Ps 45:8 whereby they have **m.** thee glad.
Ps 46:8 he hath **m.** in the earth. 7760
Ps 49:16 thou afraid when one is **m.** rich,
Ps 50:5 that have **m.** a covenant with me 3772
Ps 52:7 man that **m.** not God his strength; 7760
Ps 60:2 Thou hast **m.** the earth to tremble;
Ps 60:3 hast **m.** us to drink the wine of
Ps 69:11 I **m.** sackcloth also my garment; 5414
Ps 72:15 prayer also shall be **m.** for him
Ps 74:17 thou hast **m.** summer and winter. 3335
Ps 77:6 and my spirit **m.** diligent search.
Ps 78:13 **m.** the waters to stand as an heap,
Ps 78:50 He **m.** a way to his anger; he
Ps 78:52 **m.** his own people to go forth like
Ps 78:55 **m.** the tribes of Israel to dwell in their
Ps 78:64 their widows **m.** no lamentation.
Ps 86:9 nations whom thou hast **m.** shall 6213
Ps 88:8 hast **m.** me an abomination unto 7896
Ps 89:3 **m.** a covenant with my chosen, 3772
Ps 89:39 Thou hast **m.** void the covenant of thy
Ps 89:42 thou hast **m.** all his enemies to rejoice.
Ps 89:43 hast not **m.** him to stand in the battle.
Ps 89:44 Thou hast **m.** his glory to cease, and
Ps 89:47 hast thou **m.** all men in vain?
Ps 91:9 **m.** the Lord, which is my refuge, 7760
Ps 92:4 **m.** me glad through thy work:
Ps 95:5 The sea is his, and he **m.** it: and 6213
Ps 96:5 idols: but the Lord **m.** the heavens. 6213
Ps 98:2 Lord hath **m.** known his salvation:
Ps 100:3 he is God: it is he that hath **m.** us, 6213
Ps 103:7 He **m.** known his ways unto Moses,
Ps 104:24 in wisdom hast thou **m.** them all: 6213
Ps 104:26 thou hast **m.** to play therein. 3335
Ps 105:9 covenant he **m.** with Abraham, 3772
Ps 105:21 He **m.** him lord of his house, and 7760

Ps 105:24 and **m.** them stronger than their ...
Ps 105:28 He sent darkness, and **m.** it dark; ...
Ps 106:19 They **m.** a calf in Horeb, and ... 6213
Ps 106:46 He **m.** them also to be pitied of all ... 5414
Ps 111:4 He hath **m.** his wonderful works ... 6213
Ps 115:15 Lord which **m.** heaven and earth ... 6213
Ps 118:24 the day which the Lord hath **m.**; ... 6213
Ps 119:60 I **m.** haste, and delayed not to ...
Ps 119:73 Thy hands have **m.** me and ... 6213
Ps 119:98 hast **m.** me wiser than mine enemies: ...
Ps 119:126 work; for they have **m.** void thy law ...
Ps 121:2 Lord, which **m.** heaven and earth ... 6213
Ps 124:8 Lord, who **m.** heaven and earth ... 6213
Ps 129:3 back: they **m.** long their furrows ...
Ps 134:3 Lord that **m.** heaven and earth ... 6213
Ps 136:5 that by wisdom **m.** the heavens: ... 6213
Ps 136:7 To him that **m.** great lights: for ... 6213
Ps 136:14 **m.** Israel to pass through the midst of ...
Ps 139:14 for I am fearfully and wonderfuly **m.**: ...
Ps 139:15 when I was **m.** in secret, and ... 6213
Ps 143:3 he hath **m.** me to dwell in darkness, ...
Ps 146:6 Which **m.** heaven, and earth, the ... 6213
Ps 148:6 **m.** a decree which shall not pass ... 5414
Ps 149:2 Israel rejoice in him that **m.** him: ... 6213
Pr 8:26 as yet he had not **m.** the earth, nor ... 6213
Pr 11:25 The liberal soul shall be **m.** fat: ...
Pr 13:4 soul of the diligent shall be **m.** fat ...
Pr 14:33 is in the midst of fools is **m.** known ...
Pr 15:19 way of the righteous is **m.** plain ...
Pr 16:4 hath **m.** all things for himself: ... 6466
Pr 20:9 can say, I have **m.** my heart clean, ...
Pr 20:12 Lord hath **m.** even both of them ... 6213
Pr 21:11 is punished, the simple is **m.** wise: ...
Pr 22:19 I have **m.** known to thee this day, even ...
Pr 28:25 trust in the Lord shall be **m.** fat ...
Ec 1:15 is crooked cannot be **m.** straight: ...
Ec 2:4 I **m.** me great works; I builded me ...
Ec 2:5 I **m.** me gardens and orchards, ... 6213
Ec 2:6 I **m.** me pools of water, to water ... 6213
Ec 3:11 He hath **m.** every thing beautiful in ... 6213
Ec 7:3 countenance the heart is **m.** better ...
Ec 7:13 which he hath **m.** crooked? ...
Ec 7:29 that God hath **m.** man upright; ... 6213
Ec 10:19 A feast is **m.** for laughter, and wine ... 6213
Ca 1:6 **m.** me the keeper of the vineyards; ... 7760
Ca 3:9 Solomon **m.** himself a chariot of ... 6213
Ca 3:10 He **m.** the pillars thereof of silver, ... 6213
Ca 6:12 my soul **m.** me like the chariots of ... 7760
Isa 2:8 which their own fingers have **m.**: ... 6213
Isa 2:17 haughtiness...shall be **m.** low: ... 6213
Isa 2:20 they **m.** each one for himself to ...
Isa 5:2 and also **m.** a winepress therein: ... 2672
Isa 14:3 wherein thou wast **m.** to serve, ...
Isa 14:16 man that **m.** the earth to tremble, ...
Isa 14:17 That **m.** the world as a wilderness, ... 7760
Isa 16:10 **m.** their vintage shouting to cease ...
Isa 17:4 the glory of Jacob shall be **m.** thin, ...
Isa 17:8 that which his fingers have **m.**, ... 6213
Isa 21:2 sighing thereof have I **m.** to cease ...
Isa 22:11 **m.** also a ditch between the two ... 6213
Isa 25:2 thou hast **m.** of a city an heap; ... 7760
Isa 26:14 and **m.** all their memory to perish ...
Isa 27:11 that **m.** them will not have mercy ... 6213
Isa 28:15 have **m.** a covenant with death, ... 3772
Isa 28:15 for we have **m.** lies our refuge, ... 7760
Isa 28:22 lest your bands be **m.** strong: ...
Isa 28:25 hath **m.** plain the face thereof, ...
Isa 29:16 of him that **m.** it, He **m.** me not? ... 6213
Isa 30:33 he hath **m.** it deep and large: ...
Isa 31:7 idols of God, own hands have **m.** ... 6213
Isa 34:6 it is **m.** fat with fatness, and with ...
Isa 34:7 and their dust **m.** fat with fatness ...
Isa 37:16 thou hast **m.** heaven and earth ... 6213
Isa 40:4 mountain and hill shall be **m.** low: ...
Isa 40:4 the crooked shall be **m.** straight, and ...
Isa 41:2 him, and **m.** him rule over kings? ...
Isa 43:7 formed him; yea, I have **m.** him ... 6213
Isa 43:24 hast **m.** me to serve with thy sins, ... 6213
Isa 44:2 Thus saith the Lord that **m.** thee, ... 6213
Isa 45:12 have **m.** the earth, and created man ... 6213
Isa 45:18 that formed the earth and **m.** it; he ... 6213
Isa 46:4 I have **m.**, and I will bear; even I ... 6213
Isa 49:1 hath he **m.** mention of my name ...
Isa 49:2 **m.** my mouth like a sharp sword; ... 7760
Isa 49:2 hid me, and **m.** me a polished shaft; ... 7760
Isa 49:17 that **m.** thee waste shall go forth of ...
Isa 51:10 hath **m.** the depths of the sea a way ... 7760
Isa 51:12 man which shall be **m.** as grass; ... 5414
Isa 52:10 Lord hath **m.** bare his holy arm ...
Isa 53:9 he **m.** his grave with the wicked, ... 5414
Isa 53:12 many, and **m.** intercession for the ...
Isa 57:8 and **m.** thee a covenant with them; ... 3772
Isa 57:16 me, and the souls which I have **m.** ... 6213
Isa 59:8 they have **m.** them crooked paths: ...
Isa 63:17 hast thou **m.** us to err from thy ways, ...
Isa 66:2 those things hath mine hand **m.**, ... 6213
Isa 66:8 the earth be **m.** to bring forth in one ... 6213
Jer 1:18 I have **m.** thee this day a defenced ... 5414
Jer 2:7 **m.** mine heritage an abomination ... 7760
Jer 2:15 yelled, and they **m.** his land waste: ... 7896
Jer 2:28 thy gods that thou hast **m.** thee? ... 6213
Jer 5:3 **m.** their faces harder than a rock; ...
Jer 8:8 Lo, certainly in vain **m.** he it; ... 6213
Jer 10:11 gods that have not **m.** the heavens ... 5648
Jer 10:12 He hath **m.** the earth by his power, ... 6213
Jer 10:25 have **m.** his habitation desolate ... 6213
Jer 11:10 broken my covenant which I **m.** ... 3772
Jer 12:10 they have **m.** my pleasant portion ... 5414
Jer 12:11 They have **m.** it desolate, and being ... 7760
Jer 12:11 the whole land is **m.** desolate, ...
Jer 13:22 discovered, and thy heels **m.** bare ...
Jer 13:27 Jerusalem! wilt thou not be **m.** clean? ...
Jer 14:22 for thou hast **m.** all these things ... 6213
Jer 17:23 but **m.** their neck stiff, that they might ...
Jer 18:4 the vessel that he **m.** of clay was ... 6213
Jer 18:4 so he **m.** it again another vessel, as ... 6213
Jer 19:11 that cannot be **m.** whole again: ... 7495
Jer 20:8 word of the Lord was **m.** a reproach ... 1961
Jer 25:17 and **m.** all the nations to drink, ...
Jer 26:8 Jeremiah had **m.** an end of speaking ...
Jer 27:5 I have **m.** the earth, the man and ... 6213
Jer 29:26 The Lord hath **m.** thee priest in ... 5414
Jer 31:32 according to the covenant that I **m.** ... 3772
Jer 32:17 hast **m.** the heaven and earth ... 6213
Jer 32:20 and hast **m.** thee a name, as at this ... 6213
Jer 34:8 king Zedekiah had **m.** a covenant ... 3772
Jer 34:13 I **m.** a covenant with your fathers ... 3772
Jer 34:15 ye had **m.** a covenant before me in ... 3772
Jer 34:18 covenant which they had **m.** before ... 3772
Jer 36:25 Gemariah had **m.** intercession to ...
Jer 37:1 **m.** king in the land of Judah ...
Jer 37:15 for they had **m.** that the prison ... 6213
Jer 38:16 the Lord liveth, that **m.** us this soul, ... 6213
Jer 40:5 king of Babylon hath **m.** governor ...
Jer 40:7 had **m.** Gedaliah...governor in ...
Jer 41:2 king of Babylon had **m.** governor ...
Jer 41:9 which Asa the king had **m.** for fear ... 6213
Jer 41:18 the king of Babylon **m.** governor ...
Jer 43:1 Jeremiah had **m.** an end of speaking ...
Jer 46:10 and **m.** drunk with their blood: ...
Jer 46:16 He **m.** many to fall, yea, one fell ...
Jer 49:10 But I have **m.** Esau bare, I have ...
Jer 51:7 that **m.** all the earth drunken: ...
Jer 51:15 He hath **m.** the earth by his power, ... 6213
Jer 51:34 he hath **m.** me an empty vessel, he ... 3322
Jer 51:63 thou hast **m.** an end of reading this ...
Jer 52:20 Solomon had **m.** in the house of ... 6213
La 1:13 he hath **m.** me desolate and faint ... 5414
La 1:14 he hath **m.** my strength to fall, the ...
La 2:7 **m.** a noise in the house of the Lord, ... 5414
La 2:8 **m.** the rampart and the wall to lament; ...
La 3:4 flesh and my skin hath he **m.** old; ...
La 3:7 out: he hath **m.** my chain heavy ...
La 3:9 he hath **m.** my paths crooked ...
La 3:11 in pieces: he hath **m.** me desolate ... 7760
La 3:15 **m.** me drunken with wormwood ... 7760
La 3:45 Thou hast **m.** us as the offscouring ... 7760
Eze 3:8 I have **m.** thy face strong against ... 5414
Eze 3:9 than flint have I my thy forehead: ... 5414
Eze 3:17 **m.** thee a watchman unto the house ... 5414
Eze 6:6 may be laid waste and **m.** desolate, ...
Eze 7:20 **m.**...images of their abominations ... 6213
Eze 13:5 **m.** up the hedge for the house ... 1443
Eze 13:6 have **m.** others to hope that they ...
Eze 13:22 **m.** the heart of the righteous sad, ...
Eze 13:22 sad, whom I have not **m.** sad; and ...
Eze 16:24 hast **m.** thee an high place in every ... 6213
Eze 16:25 hast **m.** thy beauty to be abhorred, and ...
Eze 17:13 and **m.** a covenant with him, and ... 3772
Eze 17:16 king dwelleth that **m.** him king, ...
Eze 17:24 and have **m.** the dry tree to flourish: ...
Eze 19:5 whelps, and **m.** him a young lion ... 7760
Eze 20:5 and **m.** myself known unto them in the ...
Eze 20:9 sight I **m.** myself known unto them, ...
Eze 20:28 also they **m.** their sweet savour, ... 7760
Eze 21:15 it is **m.** bright, it is wrapped up for the ...
Eze 21:21 **m.** his arrows bright, he consulted ...
Eze 21:24 **m.** your iniquity to be remembered, ...
Eze 22:4 thine idols which thou hast **m.**; ... 7213
Eze 22:4 have I **m.** thee a reproach unto the ... 5414
Eze 22:13 dishonest gain which thou hast **m.**, ... 6213
Eze 22:25 have **m.** her many widows in the midst ...
Eze 26:10 into a city wherein is **m.** a breach ...
Eze 26:15 slaughter is **m.** in the midst of thee? ...
Eze 27:5 **m.** all thy ship boards of fir trees ... 1129
Eze 27:6 Bashan have they **m.** thine oars; ... 6213
Eze 27:6 have **m.** thy benches of ivory, ... 6213
Eze 27:11 they have **m.** thy beauty perfect ... 6213
Eze 27:24 bound with cords, and **m.** of cedar, ...
Eze 27:25 replenished, and **m.** very glorious ...
Eze 29:3 own, and I have **m.** it for myself ... 6213
Eze 29:9 The river is mine, and I have **m.** it ... 6213
Eze 29:18 every head was **m.** bald, and every ...
Eze 31:4 The waters **m.** him great, the deep ...
Eze 31:6 heaven **m.** their nests in his boughs, ...
Eze 31:9 **m.** him fair by the multitude of his ...
Eze 31:16 I **m.** the nations to shake at the ...
Eze 36:3 they have **m.** you desolate, and ...
Eze 39:26 land, and none **m.** them afraid ...
Eze 40:14 **m.** also posts of threescore cubits, ... 6213
Eze 40:17 a pavement **m.** for the court round ... 6213
Eze 41:18 it was **m.** with cherubims and palm ... 6213
Eze 41:19 was **m.** through all the house round ... 6213
Eze 41:20 were cherubims and palm trees **m.**, ... 6213
Eze 41:25 there were **m.** on them, on the doors ... 6213
Eze 41:25 like as were **m.** upon the walls; ... 6213
Eze 42:15 he had **m.** an end of measuring ...
Eze 43:23 thou hast **m.** an end of cleansing it, ...
Eze 46:23 it was **m.** with boiling places under ... 6213
Da 2:5 houses shall be **m.** a dunghill ... 7761
Da 2:15 Arioch **m.** the thing known to Daniel ...
Da 2:17 **m.** the thing known to Hananiah, ...
Da 2:23 hast **m.** known unto me now what we ...
Da 2:23 hast now **m.** known unto us the king's ...
Da 2:38 and hath **m.** thee ruler over them all ...
Da 2:45 God hath **m.** known to the king what ...
Da 2:48 the king **m.** Daniel a great man, ... 7236
Da 2:48 **m.** him ruler over the whole province ...
Da 3:1 the king **m.** an image of gold, ... 5648
Da 3:10 Thou, O king, hast **m.** a decree, ... 7761
Da 3:15 the image which I have **m.**; ... 5648
Da 3:29 houses shall be **m.** a dunghill: ... 7739
Da 4:5 saw a dream which **m.** me afraid, ...
Da 4:6 Therefore **m.** I a decree to bring ... 7761
Da 5:1 the king **m.** a great feast to a ... 5648
Da 5:11 father, **m.** master of the magicians, ...
Da 5:21 his heart was **m.** like the beasts, ... 7737
Da 5:29 and **m.** a proclamation concerning ...
Da 7:4 **m.** stand upon the feet as a man, ...
Da 7:16 **m.** me know the interpretation of ...
Da 7:21 same horn **m.** war with the saints, ... 5648
Da 9:1 was **m.** king over the realm of the ...
Da 9:4 my God, and **m.** my confession, ...
Da 9:13 yet **m.** we not our prayer before ...
Da 11:23 after the league **m.** with him he shall ...
Da 12:10 shall be purified, and **m.** white, ...
Ho 5:9 **m.** known that which shall surely ...
Ho 7:5 the princes have **m.** him sick with ...
Ho 7:6 they have **m.** ready their heart like ...
Ho 8:4 they have **m.** princes, and I knew ...
Ho 8:4 gold have they **m.** them idols, ... 6213
Ho 8:6 the workman **m.** it; therefore it is ... 6213
Ho 8:11 Ephraim hath **m.** many altars to sin, ... 6213
Ho 10:1 land they have **m.** goodly images ...
Ho 12:4 and **m.** supplication unto him: ...
Ho 13:2 **m.** them molten images of their ... 6213
Joe 1:7 he hath **m.** it clean bare, and cast ...
Joe 1:7 the branches thereof are **m.** white ...
Joe 1:18 the flocks of sheep are **m.** desolate ...
Am 4:10 **m.** the stink of your camp to come ...
Am 5:26 god, which ye **m.** to yourselves ... 6213
Am 7:2 had **m.** an end of eating the grass ...
Am 7:7 stood upon a wall **m.** by a plumbline, ...
Ob 2 **m.** thee small among the heathen: ... 5414
Jon 1:9 hath **m.** the sea and the dry land ... 6213
Jon 1:16 unto the Lord, and **m.** vows ...
Jon 4:5 city, and there **m.** him a booth, ... 6213
Jon 4:6 and **m.** it to come up over Jonah, ...
Na 2:3 shield of his mighty men is **m.** red, ...
Na 2:11 whelp, and none **m.** them afraid? ...
Hab 2:17 of beasts, which **m.** them afraid, ...

Hab	3:9	Thy bow was **m.** quite naked,	
Zep	3:6	I **m.** their streets waste, that none	
Zec	7:12	**m.** their hearts as an adamant	7760
Zec	9:13	**m.** thee as the sword of a mighty	7760
Zec	10:3	**m.** them as his goodly horse in the	7760
Zec	11:10	covenant which I had **m.** with all	3772
Mal	2:9	have I also **m.** you contemptible	5414
Mt	4:3	that these stones be **m.** bread.	1096
Mt	9:16	garment, and the rent is **m.** worse	1096
Mt	9:22	thy faith hath **m.** thee whole.	4982
Mt	9:22	the woman was **m.** whole from that	4982
Mt	11:1	had **m.** an end of commanding his	5055
Mt	14:36	touched were **m.** perfectly whole.	1295
Mt	15:6	**m.** the commandment…none effect	208
Mt	15:28	her daughter was **m.** whole from	2390
Mt	18:25	that he had, and payment to be **m.**	591
Mt	19:4	read, that he which **m.** them at	4160
Mt	19:4	beginning **m.** them male and	4160
Mt	19:12	which were **m.** eunuchs of men:	2134
Mt	19:12	have **m.** themselves eunuchs for	2134
Mt	20:12	thou hast **m.** them equal unto us,	4160
Mt	21:13	but ye have **m.** it a den of thieves.	4160
Mt	22:2	which **m.** a marriage for his son,	4160
Mt	22:5	they **m.** light of it, and went their	272
Mt	23:15	when he is **m.**, ye make him	1096
Mt	24:45	his lord hath **m.** ruler over his	2525
Mt	25:6	at midnight there was a cry **m.**,	1096
Mt	25:16	and **m.** them other five talents	4160
Mt	26:19	and they **m.** ready the passover	2090
Mt	27:24	but that rather a tumult was **m.**,	1096
Mt	27:64	sepulchre be **m.** sure until the third	805
Mt	27:66	they went, and **m.** the supulchre sure,	805
Mk	2:21	the old, and the rent is **m.** worse	1096
Mk	2:27	The sabbath was **m.** for man, and	1096
Mk	5:34	thy faith hath **m.** thee whole; go	4982
Mk	6:21	birthday **m.** a supper to his lords,	4160
Mk	6:56	as touched him were **m.** shole.	4982
Mk	8:25	upon his eyes, and **m.** him look up:	4160
Mk	10:6	God **m.** them male and female.	4160
Mk	10:51	way; thy faith hath **m.** thee whole.	4982
Mk	11:17	but ye have **m.** it a den of thieves.	4160
Mk	14:4	was this waste of the ointment **m.**?	1096
Mk	14:16	and they **m.** ready the passover	2090
Mk	14:58	this temple that is **m.** with hands,	5499
Mk	14:58	build another **m.** without hands	886
Mk	15:7	that had **m.** insurrection with him,	4955
Lu	1:62	they **m.** signs to his father, how	1770
Lu	2:2	taxing was first **m.** when Cyrenius	1096
Lu	2:15	the Lord hath **m.** known unto us	1107
Lu	2:17	they **m.** known abroad the saying	1232
Lu	3:5	the crooked shall be **m.** straight,	1519
Lu	3:5	the rough ways shall be **m.** smooth;	1519
Lu	4:3	this stone that it be **m.** bread.	1096
Lu	5:29	Levi **m.** him a great feast in his	4160
Lu	8:17	that shall not be **m.** manifest;	1096
Lu	8:48	thy faith hath **m.** thee whole; go	4982
Lu	8:50	believe only, she shall be **m.** whole.	4982
Lu	9:15	did so, and **m.** them all sit down.	347
Lu	11:40	he that **m.** that which is without	4160
Lu	12:14	**m.** me a judge or a divider over	2525
Lu	13:13	immediately she was **m.** straight,	461
Lu	14:12	and a recompense be **m.** thee.	1096
Lu	14:16	A certain man **m.** a great supper,	4160
Lu	17:19	way: thy faith hath **m.** thee whole.	4982
Lu	19:6	and he **m.** haste, and came down,	4692
Lu	19:46	but ye have **m.** it a den of thieves.	4160
Lu	22:13	and they **m.** ready the passover	2090
Lu	23:12	Pilate and Herod were **m.** friends	1096
Lu	23:19	a certain sedition **m.** in the city,	1096
Lu	24:22	of our company **m.** us astonished,	1839
Lu	24:28	**m.** as though he would have gone	4364
Joh	1:3	All things were **m.** by him; and	1096
Joh	1:3	was not anything **m.** that was **m.**	1096
Joh	1:10	the world was **m.** by him, and the	1096
Joh	1:14	the Word was **m.** flesh, and dwelt	1096
Joh	1:31	he should be **m.** manifest to Israel,	5319
Joh	2:9	tasted the water that was **m.** wine,	1096
Joh	2:15	had **m.** a scourge of small cords,	4160
Joh	3:21	that his deeds may be **m.** manifest,	5319
Joh	4:1	that Jesus **m.** and baptized more	4160
Joh	4:46	Galilee, where he **m.** the water wine.	4160
Joh	5:4	water stepped in was **m.** whole of	1096
Joh	5:6	unto him, Wilt thou be **m.** whole?	1096
Joh	5:9	immediately the man was **m.** whole,	1096
Joh	5:11	He that **m.** me whole, the same	4160
Joh	5:14	him, Behold, thou art made whole:	1096
Joh	5:15	Jesus, which had **m.** him whole.	4160
Joh	7:23	I have **m.** a man every whit whole	4160
Joh	8:33	sayest thou, Ye shall be **m.** free?	1096
Joh	9:3	of God should be **m.** manifest in him	
Joh	9:6	and **m.** clay of the spittle, and he	4160
Joh	9:11	man that is called Jesus **m.** clay,	4160
Joh	9:14	sabbath day when Jesus **m.** the clay,	4160
Joh	9:39	they which see might be **m.** blind	1096
Joh	12:2	There they **m.** him a supper; and	4160
Joh	15:15	Father I have **m.** known unto you	1107
Joh	17:23	that they may be **m.** perfect in	5048
Joh	18:18	and **m.** a fire of coals, for it was	4160
Joh	19:7	he **m.** himself the Son of God	4160
Joh	19:23	his garments, and **m.** four parts,	4160
Ac	1:1	The former treatise have I **m.**, O	4160
Ac	2:28	**m.** known to me the ways of life;	1107
Ac	2:36	hath **m.** that same Jesus…Lord	4160
Ac	3:12	we had **m.** this man to walk?	4160
Ac	3:16	name hath **m.** this man strong,	4732
Ac	3:25	which God **m.** with our fathers,	1303
Ac	4:9	by what means he is **m.** whole;	4982
Ac	4:24	which hast **m.** heaven, and earth,	4160
Ac	4:35	distribution was **m.** unto every man	1239
Ac	7:10	he **m.** him governor over Egypt	2525
Ac	7:13	Joseph was **m.** known to his	319
Ac	7:13	Joseph's kindred was **m.** known	1096
Ac	7:27	Who **m.** thee a ruler and a judge	2525
Ac	7:35	Who **m.** thee a ruler and a judge?	2525
Ac	7:41	they **m.** a calf in those days, and	3447
Ac	7:43	which ye **m.** to worship them;	4160
Ac	7:48	not in temples **m.** with hands; as	5499
Ac	7:50	not my hand **m.** all these things?	4160
Ac	8:2	**m.** great lamentation over him.	4160
Ac	8:3	for Saul, he **m.** havock of the church,	
Ac	9:39	and garments which Dorcas **m.**,	4160
Ac	10:10	they **m.** ready, he fell into a trance,	3903
Ac	10:17	had **m.** enquiry for Simon's house,	1239
Ac	12:5	prayer was **m.** without ceasing of	1096
Ac	12:20	**m.** Blastus the king's…their friend,	3982
Ac	12:21	and **m.** an oration unto them.	1215
Ac	13:32	which was **m.** unto the fathers,	1096
Ac	14:2	and **m.** their minds evil affected	2559
Ac	14:5	an assault **m.** both of the Gentiles,	1096
Ac	14:15	God, which **m.** heaven, and earth,	4160
Ac	15:7	ago God **m.** choice among us,	1586
Ac	16:13	where prayer was wont to be **m.**;	1511
Ac	16:24	and **m.** their feet fast in the stocks.	805
Ac	17:24	**m.** the world and all things therein,	4160
Ac	17:24	not in temples **m.** with hands;	5499
Ac	17:26	**m.** of one blood all nations of men	4160
Ac	18:12	Jews **m.** insurrection with one	2721
Ac	19:24	which **m.** silver shrines for Diana,	4160
Ac	19:26	no gods, which are **m.** with hands:	1096
Ac	19:33	have **m.** his defence unto the people.	626
Ac	20:28	Holy Ghost hath **m.** you overseers,	5087
Ac	21:40	when there was **m.** a great silence,	1096
Ac	22:6	as I **m.** my journey, and was come	4198
Ac	23:13	forty which had **m.** this conspiracy	4160
Ac	26:6	the hope of the promise **m.** of God	1096
Ac	27:40	to the wind, and **m.** toward shore.	2722
Ro	1:3	which was **m.** of the seed of David	1096
Ro	1:20	by the things that are **m.**, even	4161
Ro	1:23	an image **m.** like to corruptible man,	1096
Ro	2:25	circumcision…**m.** uncircumcision.	1096
Ro	4:14	of the law be heirs, faith is **m.** void,	2758
Ro	4:14	and the promise **m.** of none effect.	2673
Ro	4:17	**m.** thee a father of many nations,)	5087
Ro	5:19	disobedience…were **m.** sinners,	2525
Ro	5:19	of one shall many be **m.** righteous.	2525
Ro	6:18	Being then **m.** free from sin, ye	1659
Ro	6:22	But now being **m.** free from sin,	1659
Ro	7:13	which is good **m.** death unto me?	1096
Ro	8:2	hath **m.** me free from the law of	1659
Ro	8:20	creature was **m.** subject to vanity,	5293
Ro	9:20	it, Why hast thou **m.** me thus?	4160
Ro	9:29	and been **m.** like unto Gomorrha.	3666
Ro	10:10	confession is **m.** unto salvation.	3670
Ro	10:20	I was **m.** manifest unto them that	1096
Ro	11:9	Let their table be **m.** a snare, and a	1096
Ro	14:21	or is offended, or is **m.** weak.	770
Ro	15:8	the promises **m.** unto the fathers:	
Ro	15:27	Gentiles have been **m.** partakers	2841
Ro	16:26	now is **m.** manifest, and by the	5319
Ro	16:26	**m.** known to all nations for the	1107
1Co	1:17	Christ should be **m.** of none effect.	2758
1Co	1:20	not God **m.** foolish the wisdom of	3471
1Co	1:30	who of God is **m.** unto us wisdom,	1096
1Co	3:13	man's work shall be **m.** manifest:	1096
1Co	4:9	are **m.** a spectacle unto the world,	1096
1Co	4:13	we are **m.** as the filth of the world,	1096
1Co	7:21	if thou mayest be **m.** free, use it	1096
1Co	9:19	have I **m.** myself servant unto all,	1402
1Co	9:22	I am **m.** all things to all men, that	1096
1Co	11:19	may be **m.** manifest among you.	1096
1Co	12:13	been all **m.** to drink into one Spirit.	4222
1Co	14:25	secrets of his heart **m.** manifest;	1096
1Co	15:22	so in Christ shall all be **m.** alive.	2227
1Co	15:45	man Adam was **m.** a living soul;	1096
1Co	15:45	Adam was **m.** a quickening spirit.	1096
2Co	2:2	the same which is **m.** sorry by me?	3076
2Co	3:6	Who also hath **m.** us able ministers	2427
2Co	3:10	was **m.** glorious had no glory in	1392
2Co	4:10	might be **m.** manifest in our body.	5319
2Co	4:11	be **m.** manifest in our mortal flesh.	5319
2Co	5:1	God, an house not **m.** with hands,	886
2Co	5:11	but we are **m.** manifest unto God;	5319
2Co	5:11	**m.** manifest in your consciences.	5319
2Co	5:21	For he hath **m.** him to be sin for us,	4160
2Co	5:21	be **m.** the righteousness of God in	1096
2Co	7:8	though I **m.** you sorry with a letter,	3076
2Co	7:8	the same epistle hath **m.** you sorry,	3076
2Co	7:9	I rejoice, not that ye were **m.** sorry,	3076
2Co	7:9	were **m.** sorry after a godly manner,	3076
2Co	7:14	boasting, which I **m.** before Titus, is	
2Co	10:16	of things **m.** ready to our hand.	2092
2Co	11:6	have been thoroughly **m.** manifest	5319
2Co	12:9	strength is **m.** perfect in weakness	5048
Ga	3:3	are ye now **m.** perfect by the flesh?	2005
Ga	3:13	the law, being **m.** a curse for us:	1096
Ga	3:16	his seed were the promises **m.**	4483
Ga	3:19	come to whom the promise was **m.**;	1861
Ga	4:4	**m.** of a woman, **m.** under the law,	1096
Ga	5:1	wherewith Christ hath **m.** us free,	1659
Eph	1:6	**m.** us accepted in the beloved:	5487
Eph	1:9	Having **m.** known unto us the	1107
Eph	2:6	and **m.** us sit together in heavenly	4776
Eph	2:11	Circumcision in…flesh **m.** by hands;	5499
Eph	2:13	are **m.** nigh by the blood of Christ.	1096
Eph	2:14	our peace, who hath **m.** both one,	4160
Eph	3:3	**m.** known unto me the mystery;	1107
Eph	3:5	was not **m.** known unto the sons of	1107
Eph	3:7	Whereof I was **m.** a minister,	1096
Eph	5:13	reproved are **m.** manifest by…light:	5319
Php	2:7	But **m.** himself of no reputation,	1096
Php	2:7	and was **m.** in the likeness of men:	1096
Php	3:10	**m.** conformable unto his death;	4832
Php	4:6	requests be **m.** known unto God.	1107
Col	1:12	hath **m.** us meet to be partakers of	2427
Col	1:20	having **m.** peace through the blood	1517
Col	1:23	whereof I Paul am **m.** a minister;	1096
Col	1:25	Whereof I am **m.** a minister,	1096
Col	1:26	now is **m.** manifest to his saints:	5319
Col	2:11	circumcision **m.** without hands,	1096
Col	2:15	he **m.** a shew of them openly,	1165
1Ti	1:9	law is not **m.** for a righteous man,	2749
1Ti	1:19	faith have **m.** shipwreck:	3489
1Ti	2:1	giving of thanks, be **m.** for all men;	4160
2Ti	1:10	now **m.** manifest by the appearing	5319
Tit	3:7	**m.** heirs according to the hope of	1096
Heb	1:2	by whom also he **m.** the worlds;	4160
Heb	1:4	Being **m.** so much better than the	1096
Heb	2:9	**m.** a little lower than the angels	1642
Heb	2:17	to be **m.** like unto his brethren,	3666
Heb	3:14	For we are **m.** partakers of Christ,	1096
Heb	5:5	not himself to be **m.** an high priest;	1096
Heb	5:9	And being **m.** perfect, he became	5048
Heb	6:4	and were **m.** partakers of the Holy	1096
Heb	6:13	when God **m.** promise to Abraham,	1861
Heb	6:20	Jesus, **m.** an high priest for ever	1096
Heb	7:3	but **m.** like unto the Son of God;	871
Heb	7:12	is me of necessity a change also of	1096
Heb	7:16	Who is **m.**, not after the law of a	1096
Heb	7:19	For the law **m.** nothing perfect, but	5048
Heb	7:20	not without an oath he was **m.** priest:	5048
Heb	7:21	priests were **m.** without an oath;	1096
Heb	7:22	was Jesus **m.** a surety of a better	1096
Heb	7:26	and **m.** higher than the heavens;	1096
Heb	8:9	the covenant that I **m.** with their	4160
Heb	8:13	covenant, he hath **m.** the first old.	3822
Heb	9:2	For there was a tabernacle **m.**;	2680
Heb	9:8	holiest…was not yet **m.** manifest,	5319
Heb	9:11	tabernacle, not **m.** with hands,	5499
Heb	9:24	into the holy places **m.** with hands,	5499
Heb	10:3	is a remembrance again **m.** of sins	
Heb	10:13	till his enemies be **m.** his footstool.	5087

Heb 10:33 whilst ye were **m.** a gazingstock *2301*
Heb 11:3 not **m.** of things which do appear. *1096*
Heb 11:22 **m.** mention of the departing of the *3421*
Heb 11:34 out of weakness were **m.** strong, ... *1743*
Heb 11:40 without us should not be **m.** perfect.... *5048*
Heb 12:23 to the spirits of just men **m.** perfect, .. *5048*
Heb 12:27 shaken, as of things that are **m.**, ... *4160*
Jas 1:10 But the rich, in that he is **m.** low: *5014*
Jas 2:22 and by works was faith **m.** perfect? *5048*
Jas 3:9 are **m.** after the similitude of God. *1096*
1Pe 2:7 same is **m.** the head of the corner, ... *1096*
1Pe 3:22 powers being **m.** subject unto him. *5293*
2Pe 1:16 we **m.** known unto you the power *1107*
2Pe 2:12 **m.** to be taken and destroyed, ... *1080*
1Jo 2:19 that they might be **m.** manifest that.... *5319*
1Jo 4:17 Herein is our love **m.** perfect, that *5048*
1Jo 4:18 that feareth is not **m.** perfect in love... *5048*
1Jo 5:10 not God hath **m.** him a liar; *4160*
Re 1:6 **m.** us kings and priests unto God *4160*
Re 5:10 hast **m.** us unto our God kings and...... *4160*
Re 7:14 and **m.** them white in the blood of....... *3021*
Re 8:11 because they were **m.** bitter. *4087*
Re 14:7 worship him that **m.** heaven, and *4160*
Re 14:8 she **m.** all nations drink of the wine *4222*
Re 15:4 for thy judgments are **m.** manifest. *5319*
Re 17:2 have been **m.** drunk with the wine *3182*
Re 18:15 things, which were **m.** rich by her, ... *4147*
Re 18:19 were **m.** rich all that had ships in *4147*
Re 18:19 for in one hour is she **m.** desolate. *2049*
Re 19:7 his wife hath **m.** herself ready. *2090*

MADEST
Ne 9:8 **m.** a covenant with him to give 3772
Ne 9:14 And **m.** known unto them thy holy 3045
Ps 8:6 Thou **m.** him to have dominion over ....
Ps 80:15 that thou **m.** strong for thyself. ....
Ps 80:17 whom thou **m.** strong for thyself. ....
Eze 16:17 **m.** to thyself images of men, and 6213
Eze 29:7 **m.** all their loins to be at a stand. ....
Jon 4:10 not laboured, neither **m.** it grow; ....
Ac 21:38 before these days **m.** an uproar, ... *387*
Heb 2:7 **m.** him a little lower than the *1642*

MADIAN (ma'-de-an) See also MIDIAN.
Ac 7:29 was a stranger in the land of **M.**, ... *3099*

MADMAN See MAD and MAN.

MADMANNAH (mad-man'-nah)
Jos 15:31 Ziklag, and **M.**, and Sansannah, ... 4089
1Ch 2:49 bare also Shaaph the father of **M.**, ... 4089

MADMEN (mad'-men) See also MADMENAH.
Jer 48:2 thou shalt be cut down,, O **M.**; 4086

MADMENAH (mad-me'-nah) See also MADMEN.
Isa 10:31 **M.** is removed; the inhabitants of 4088

MADNESS
De 28:28 The Lord shall smite thee with **m.**, ... 7697
Ec 1:17 wisdom, and to know **m.**, and folly: 1947
Ec 2:12 behold wisdom, and **m.**, and folly: 1947
Ec 7:25 of folly, even of foolishness and **m.**: 1947
Ec 9:3 **m.** is in their heart while they live, ... 1947
Ec 10:13 end of his talk is mischievous **m.** 1948
Zec 12:4 and his rider with **m.**: 7697
Lu 6:11 And they were filled with **m.**; and *454*
2Pe 2:16 voice forbad the **m.** of the prophet. *3913*

MADON (ma'-don)
Jos 11:1 that he sent to Jobab king of **M.**, ... 4068
Jos 12:19 The king of **M.**, one; the king of 4068

MAG See RAB-MAG.

MAGBISH (mag'-bish)
Ezr 2:30 The children of **M.**, an hundred 4019

MAGDALA (mag'-da-lah) See also MAGDALENE.
Mt 15:39 and came into the coasts of **M.** *3093*

MAGDALENE (mag'-da-leen)
Mt 27:56 Among which was Mary **M.**, and *3094*
Mt 27:61 there was Mary **M.**, and the other *3094*
Mt 28:1 came Mary **M.** and the other Mary *3094*
Mk 15:40 among whom was Mary **M.**, and *3094*
Mk 15:47 Mary **M.** and Mary the mother of *3094*
Mk 16:1 Mary **M.**, and Mary the mother of *3094*
Mk 16:9 week, he appeared first to Mary **M.**, .. *3094*
Lu 8:2 Mary called **M.**, out of whom went *3094*
Lu 24:10 It was Mary **M.**, and Joanna, and *3094*
Joh 19:25 the wife of Cleophas, and Mary **M.** *3094*
Joh 20:1 day of the week cometh Mary **M.** *3094*
Joh 20:18 Mary **M.** came and told...disciples *3094*

MAGDIEL (mag'-de-el)
Ge 36:43 Duke **M.**, duke Iram: these be 4025
1Ch 1:54 Duke **M.**, duke Iram. These are 4025

MAGICIAN See also MAGICIANS.
Da 2:10 that asked such things at any **m.** 2749

MAGICIANS
Ge 41:8 and called for all the **m.** of Egypt, ... 2748
Ge 41:24 I told this unto the **m.**; but there 2748
Ex 7:11 now the **m.** of Egypt, they also did 2748
Ex 7:22 the **m.** of Egypt did so with their 2748
Ex 8:7 **m.** did so with their enchantments, ... 2748
Ex 8:18 **m.** did so with their enchantments 2748
Ex 8:19 Then the **m.** said unto Pharaoh, ... 2748
Ex 9:11 **m.** could not stand before Moses 2748
Ex 9:11 the boil was upon the **m.**, and upon 2748
Da 1:20 ten times better than all the **m.** and 2748
Da 2:2 the king commanded to call the **m.**, ... 2748
Da 2:27 wise men, the astrologers, the **m.**, ... 2749
Da 4:7 came in the **m.**, the astrologers, ... 2749
Da 4:9 O Belteshazzar, master of the **m.**, ... 2749
Da 5:11 thy father, made master of the **m.**, ... 2749

MAGISTRATE See also MAGISTRATES.
Jg 18:7 there was no **m.** in the land, ... 3423,6114
Lu 12:58 **with thine adversary to the m.**, ... *758*

MAGISTRATES
Ezr 7:25 set **m.** and judges, which may 8200
Lu 12:11 **unto the synagogues, and unto m.**, . *746*
Ac 16:20 brought them to the **m.**, saying, ... *4755*
Ac 16:22 and the **m.** rent off their clothes, ... *4755*
Ac 16:35 the **m.** sent the serjeants, saying, ... *4755*
Ac 16:36 The **m.** have sent to let you go: *4755*
Ac 16:38 told these words unto the **m.**: *4755*
Tit 3:1 to obey **m.**, to be ready to every *3980*

MAGNIFICAL
1Ch 22:5 the Lord must be exceeding **m.**, ... 1431

MAGNIFICENCE
Ac 19:27 and her **m.** should be destroyed, ... *3168*

MAGNIFIED
Ge 19:19 and thou hast **m.** thy mercy, ... 1431
Jos 4:14 **m.** Joshua in the sight of all Israel; 1431
2Sa 7:26 And let thy name be **m.** for ever, ... 1431
1Ch 17:24 that thy name may be **m.** for ever, ... 1431
1Ch 29:25 the Lord **m.** Solomon exceedingly 1431
2Ch 1:1 with him, and **m.** him exceedingly. 1431
2Ch 32:23 was **m.** in the sight of all nations 5375
Ps 35:27 Let the Lord be **m.**, which hath 1431
Ps 40:16 say continually, The Lord be **m.**. 1431
Ps 70:4 say continually, Let God be **m.**. 1431
Ps 138:2 **m.** thy word above all thy name. 1431
Jer 48:26 for he **m.** himself against the Lord: 1431
Jer 48:42 hath **m.** himself against the Lord. 1431
La 1:9 for the enemy hath **m.** himself. 1431
Da 8:11 he **m.** himself even to the prince 1431
Zep 2:8 **m.** themselves against their border 1431
Zep 2:10 **m.** themselves against the people 1431
Mal 1:5 Lord will be **m.** from the border of 1431
Ac 5:13 to them: but the people **m.** them. *3170*
Ac 19:17 the name of the Lord Jesus was **m.** *3170*
Php 1:20 also Christ shall be **m.** in my body, ... *3170*

MAGNIFY See also MAGNIFIED.
Jos 3:7 begin to **m.** thee in the sight of all 1431
Job 7:17 man, that thou shouldest **m.** him? 1431
Job 19:5 ye will **m.** yourselves against me, ... 1431
Job 36:24 Remember that thou **m.** his work, ... 7679
Ps 34:3 O **m.** the Lord with me, and let us 1431
Ps 35:26 that **m.** themselves against me. 1431
Ps 38:16 they **m.** themselves against me. 1431
Ps 55:12 me that did **m.** himself against me; 1431
Ps 69:30 and will **m.** him with thanksgiving. 1431
Isa 10:15 the saw **m.** itself against him that 1431
Isa 42:21 he will **m.** the law, and make it 1431
Eze 38:23 Thus will I **m.** myself, and sanctify 1431
Da 8:25 he shall **m.** himself in his heart, ... 1431
Da 11:36 and **m.** himself above every god, ... 1431
Da 11:37 for he shall **m.** himself above all. 1431
Zec 12:7 not **m.** themselves against Judah. 1431
Lu 1:46 said, My soul doth **m.** the Lord, ... *3170*
Ac 10:46 speak with tongues, and **m.** God. *3170*
Ro 11:13 of the Gentiles, I **m.** mine office: *1392*

MAGOG (ma'-gog)
Ge 10:2 sons of Japheth; Gomer, and **M.**, ... 4031
1Ch 1:5 sons of Japheth; Gomer, and **M.**, ... 4031
Eze 38:2 face against Gog, the land of **M.**, ... 4031
Eze 39:6 I will send a fire on **M.**, and among 4031
Re 20:8 quarters of the earth, Gog and **M.**, ... 3098

MAGOR-MISSABIB (ma''-gor-mis'-sa-bib)
Jer 20:3 called thy name Pashur, but **M.** 4036

MAGPIASH (mag'-pe-ash)
Ne 10:20 **M.**, Meshullam, Hezir, ... 4047

MAHALAH (ma'-ha-lah) See also MAHLAH.
1Ch 7:18 bare Ishod, and Abiezer, and **M.** 4244

MAHALALEEL (ma-hal'-a-le-el) See also MALELEEL.
Ge 5:12 lived seventy years, and begat **M.**: 4111
Ge 5:13 Cainan lived after he begat **M.** 4111
Ge 5:15 And **M.** lived sixty and five years, ... 4111
Ge 5:16 **M.** lived after he begat Jared eight 4111
Ge 5:17 And all the days of **M.** were eight 4111
1Ch 1:2 Kenan, **M.**, Jered, ... 4111
Ne 11:4 son of **M.**, of the children of Perez; 4111

MAHALATH (ma'-ha-lath) See also BASHEMATH.
Ge 28:9 had **M.** the daughter of Ishmael 4258
2Ch 11:18 Rehoboam took him **M.** the 4258
Ps 53:*title* to the chief Musician upon **M.**, ... 4257
Ps 88:*title* to the chief Musician upon **M.** 4257

MAHALI (ma'-ha-li) See also MAHLI.
Ex 6:19 sons of Merari; **M.** and Mushi: 4249

MAHANAIM (ma-ha-na'-im)
Ge 32:2 called the name of that place **M.**. 4266
Jos 13:26 from **M.** unto the border of Debir; 4266
Jos 13:30 And their coast was from **M.**, all 4266
Jos 21:38 slayer; and **M.** with her suburbs, ... 4266
2Sa 2:8 Saul, and brought him over to **M.**; 4266
2Sa 2:12 Saul, went out from **M.** to Gibeon. 4266
2Sa 2:29 all Bithron, and they came to **M.** 4266
2Sa 17:24 Then David came to **M.**. And 4266
2Sa 17:27 pass, when David was come to **M.**, ... 4266
2Sa 19:32 of sustenance while he lay at **M.**; 4266
1Ki 2:8 in the day when I went to **M.**: 4266
1Ki 4:14 Ahinadab the son of Iddo had **M.**: 4266
1Ch 6:80 suburbs, and **M.** with her suburbs, ... 4266

MAHANEH-DAN ma'-ha-neh-dan)
Jg 18:12 they called that place **M.** unto 4265

MAHARAI (ma'-ha-rahee)
2Sa 23:28 the Ahohite, **M.** the Netophathite, ... 4121
1Ch 11:30 **M.** the Netophathite, Heled the son 4121
1Ch 27:13 captain for the tenth month was **M.** 4121

MAHATH (ma'-hath) See also AHIMOTH.
1Ch 6:35 the son of **M.**, the son of Amasai, ... 4287
2Ch 29:12 arose, **M.** the son of Amasai, ... 4287
2Ch 31:13 **M.**, and Benaiah, were overseers 4287

MAHAVITE (ma'-ha-vite)
1Ch 11:46 Eliel the **M.**, and Jeribai, and 4233

MAHAZIOTH (ma-ha'-ze-oth)
1Ch 25:4 Mallothi, Hothir, and **M.**: 4238
1Ch 25:30 three and twentieth to **M.**, he, his 4238

MAHER-SHALAL-HASH-BAZ (ma''-her-sha''-lal-hash'- baz)
Isa 8:1 with a man's pen concerning **M.** 4122
Isa 8:3 the Lord to me, Call his name **M.** 4122

MAHLAH (mah'-lah) See also MAHALAH.
Nu 26:33 daughters of Zelophehad were **M.**, ... 4244
Nu 27:1 **M.**, Noah, and Hoglah, and Milcah, ... 4244
Nu 36:11 For **M.**, Tirzah, and Hoglah, and 4244
Jos 17:3 the names of his daughters, **M.**, ... 4244

MAHLI (mah'-li) See also MAHALI; MAHLITES.
Nu 3:20 of Merari by their families; **M.** 4249
1Ch 6:19 sons of Merari; **M.**, and Mushi. 4249
1Ch 6:29 sons of Merari; **M.**, Libni his son, ... 4249
1Ch 6:47 The son of **M.**, the son of Mushi, ... 4249
1Ch 23:21 sons of Merari; **M.**, and Mushi. 4249
1Ch 23:21 The sons of **M.**; Eleazar, and 4249
1Ch 23:23 sons of Mushi; **M.**, and Eder, and 4249
1Ch 24:26 sons of Merari were **M.** and Mushi: 4249
1Ch 24:28 Of **M.** came Eleazar, who had no 4249
1Ch 24:30 sons also of Mushi; **M.**, and Eder, ... 4249
Ezr 8:18 understanding, of the sons of **M.**, ... 4249

MAHLITES (mah'-lites)
Nu 3:33 Merari was the family of the **M.**, ... 4250
Nu 26:58 the family of the **M.**, the family of 4250

MAHLON (mah'-lon) See also MAHLON'S.
Ru 1:2 of his two sons **M.** and Chilion, ... 4248
Ru 1:5 **M.** and Chilion died also both of 4248
Ru 4:10 Ruth the Moabitess, the wife of **M.**, ... 4248

MAHLON'S (mah'-lons)
Ru 4:9 all that was Chilion's and **M.**, ... 4248

MAHOL (ma'-hol)
1Ki 4:31 and Darda, the sons of **M.**: 4235

MAID See also BONDMAID; HANDMAID; MAIDEN; MAID'S; MAIDS; MAIDSERVANT.
Ge 16:2 I pray thee, go in unto my **m.**; it 8198
Ge 16:3 took Hagar her **m.** the Egyptian, ... 8198
Ge 16:5 I have given my **m.** into thy bosom, ... 8198
Ge 16:6 Behold, thy **m.** is in thy hand; do 8198
Ge 16:8 Sarai's **m.**, Whence camest thou? 8198
Ge 29:24 Zilpah his **m.** for an handmaid. 8198
Ge 29:29 Bilhah his handmaid to be her **m.**. 8198
Ge 30:3 Behold my **m.** Bilhah, go in unto 519
Ge 30:7 Rachel's **m.** conceived again, and 8198
Ge 30:9 she took Zilpah her **m.**, and gave 8198
Ge 30:10 Zilpah Leah's **m.** bare Jacob a son. 8198
Ge 30:12 Leah's **m.** bare Jacob a second son. 8198
Ex 2:5 flags, she sent her **m.** to fetch it. 519
Ex 2:8 the **m.** went and called the child's 5959
Ex 21:20 a man smite his servant, or his **m.**, ... 519
Ex 21:26 or the eye of his **m.**, that it perish; 519
Ex 22:16 if a man entice a **m.** that is not 1330
Le 12:5 if she bear a **m.** child, then she 5347
Le 25:6 and for thy servant, and for thy **m.**, ... 519
De 22:14 came to her, I found her not a **m.**: 1331
De 22:17 I found not thy daughter a **m.**; 1331
2Ki 5:2 of the land of Israel a little **m.**; 5291
2Ki 5:4 Thus and thus said the **m.** that is of ... 5291
Es 2:7 and the **m.** was fair and beautiful; 5291
Job 31:1 then should I think upon a **m.**? 1330
Pr 30:19 and the way of a man with a **m.**. 5959
Isa 24:2 master; as with the **m.**, so with her ... 8198
Jer 2:32 Can a **m.** forget her ornaments, or 1330
Jer 51:22 pieces the young man and the **m.**; 1330
Am 2:7 father will go in unto the same **m.**, ... 5291
Mt 9:24 **the m. is not dead, but sleepeth.** ... *2877*
Mt 9:25 her by the hand, and the **m.** arose. *2877*
Mt 26:71 into the porch, another **m.** saw him, ...
Mk 14:69 a **m.** saw him again, and began to *3814*
Lu 8:54 hand, and called, saying, **M., arise** *3816*
Lu 22:56 a certain **m.** beheld him as he sat *3814*

MAIDEN See also HANDMAIDEN; MAIDENS.
Ge 30:18 have given my **m.** to my husband: 8198
Jg 19:24 Behold, here is my daughter a **m.**, ... 1330
2Ch 36:17 compassion upon young man or **m.**, ... 1330
Es 2:4 let the **m.** which pleaseth the king 5291
Es 2:9 **m.** pleased him, and she obtained 5291
Es 2:13 thus came every **m.** unto the king; 5291
Ps 123:2 eyes of a **m.** unto the hand of her 8198
Lu 8:51 father and the mother of the **m.**, ... *3816*

MAIDENS See also HANDMAIDENS.
Ex 2:5 her **m.** walked along by the river's 5291
Ru 2:8 but abide here fast by my **m.**: 5291
Ru 2:22 that thou go out with his **m.**, that 5291
Ru 2:23 So she kept fast by the **m.** of Boaz 5291
Ru 3:2 kindred, with those **m.** thou wast? 5291
1Sa 9:11 found young **m.** going out to draw 5291
Es 2:8 many **m.** were gathered together 5291
Es 2:9 as belonged to her, and seven **m.**, ... 5291
Es 4:16 I also and my **m.** will fast likewise; 5291
Job 41:5 or wilt thou bind him for thy **m.**? 5291
Ps 78:63 **m.** were not given to marriage. 1330
Ps 148:12 Both young men, and **m.**; old men, ... 1330
Pr 9:3 She hath sent forth her **m.**: she 5291
Pr 27:27 and for the maintenance for thy **m.** 5291
Pr 31:15 household, and a portion to her **m.** 5291
Ec 2:7 I got me servants and **m.**, and had 8198
Eze 44:22 they shall take **m.** of the seed of 1330
Lu 12:45 **to beat the menservants and m.,** *3814*

MAID-CHILD See MAID and CHILD.

MAID'S
Es 2:12 when every **m.** turn was come to 5291

MAIDS See also BONDMAIDS.
Ezr 2:65 Beside their servants and their **m.**, ... 519
Es 2:9 he preferred her and her **m.** unto 5291
Es 4:4 So Esther's **m.** and...chamberlains 5291
Job 19:15 my **m.**, count me for a stranger: 519
La 5:11 and the **m.** in the cities of Judah. 1330
Eze 9:6 utterly old and young, both **m.**, and 1330
Na 2:7 her **m.** shall lead her as with the 519
Zec 9:17 cheerful, and new wine the **m.**. 1330
Mk 14:66 one of the **m.** of the high priest: *3814*

MAIDSERVANT See also MAIDSERVANT'S; MAIDSERVANTS.
Ex 11:5 unto the firstborn of the **m.** that is 8198
Ex 20:10 thy manservant, nor thy **m.**, nor thy 519
Ex 20:17 his manservant, nor his **m.**, nor his 519
Ex 21:7 a man sell his daughter to be a **m.**, ... 519
Ex 21:32 ox shall push a manservant or a **m.**; 519
De 5:14 nor thy manservant, nor thy **m.**, nor 519
De 5:14 and thy **m.** may rest as well as thou. ... 519
De 5:21 or his manservant, or his **m.**, his ox, ... 519
De 12:18 thy manservant, and thy **m.**, and the 519
De 15:17 unto thy **m.** thou shalt do likewise. 519
De 16:11, 14 thy manservant, and thy **m.**, and 519
Jg 9:18 made Abimelech, the son of his **m.**, ... 519
Job 31:13 cause of my manservant or of my **m.**, .. 519
Jer 34:9 manservant, and every man his **m.**, ... 8198
Jer 34:10 manservant, and every one his **m.**, ... 8198

MAIDSERVANT'S
Ex 21:27 manservant's tooth, or his **m.** tooth; 519

MAIDSERVANTS See also MAIDSERVANTS'.
Ge 12:16 asses, and menservants, and **m.**, ... 8198
Ge 20:17 Abimelech, and his wife, and his **m.**; 519
Ge 24:35 menservants, and **m.**, and camels, ... 8198
Ge 30:43 cattle, and **m.**, and menservants, ... 8198
De 12:12 menservants, and your **m.**, and the 519
1Sa 8:16 menservants, and your **m.**, and 8198
2Sa 6:22 of the **m.** which thou hast spoken 519
2Ki 5:26 oxen, and menservants, and **m.**? 8198
Ne 7:67 their manservants and their **m.**, of 519

MAIDSERVANTS'
Ge 31:33 tent, and into the two **m.** tents; 519

MAIL
1Sa 17:5 he was armed with a coat of **m.**; 7193
1Sa 17:38 also he armed him with a coat of **m.**. ....

MAIMED
Le 22:22 Blind, or broken, or **m.**, or having 2782
Mt 15:30 that were lame, blind, dumb, **m.**, ... *2948*
Mt 15:31 dumb to speak, the **m.** to be whole, ... *2948*
Mt 18:8 **thee to enter into life halt or m.,** .. *2948*
Mk 9:43 **for thee to enter into life m.,** *2948*
Lu 14:13 **a feast, call the poor, the m., the** ... *376*
Lu 14:21 **in hither the poor, and the m.,** *376*

MAINSAIL
Ac 27:40 and hoisted up the **m.** to the wind, ... *736*

MAINTAIN See also MAINTAINED; MAINTAINEST.
1Ki 8:45 supplication, and **m.** their cause. 6213
1Ki 8:49 dwelling place, and **m.** their cause, ... 6213
1Ki 8:59 that he **m.** the cause of his servant, ... 6213
1Ch 26:27 to **m.** the house of the Lord. 2388
2Ch 6:35 supplication, and **m.** their cause. 6213
2Ch 6:39 supplications, and **m.** their cause, ... 6213
Job 13:15 I will **m.** mine own ways before 3198
Ps 140:12 will **m.** the cause of the afflicted, ... 6213
Tit 3:8 might be careful to **m.** good works. *4291*
Tit 3:14 let ours also learn to **m.** good works ... *4291*

MAINTAINED
Ps 9:4 hast **m.** my right and my cause; 6213

MAINTAINEST
Ps 16:5 and of my cup: thou **m.** my lot. 8551

MAINTENANCE
Ezr 4:14 have **m.** from the king's palace, ... 4415
Pr 27:27 and for the **m.** for thy maidens. 2416

MAJESTY
2Ch 29:11 glory, and the victory, and the **m.**: 1935
2Ch 29:25 bestowed upon him such royal **m.** 1935
Es 1:4 and the honour of his excellent **m.** 1420
Job 37:22 the north: with God is terrible **m.**. 1935
Job 40:10 Deck thyself now with **m.** and 1347
Ps 21:5 honour and **m.** hast thou laid upon 1926
Ps 29:4 the voice of the Lord is full of **m.**. 1926
Ps 45:3 mighty, with thy glory and thy **m.**. 1926
Ps 45:4 And in thy **m.** ride prosperously 1926
Ps 93:1 reigneth, he is clothed with **m.**; 1348
Ps 96:6 Honour and **m.** are before him: 1926
Ps 104:1 thou art clothed with honour and **m.**. .. 1926
Ps 145:5 of the glorious honour of thy **m.**, ... 1935
Ps 145:12 the glorious **m.** of his kingdom. 1926
Isa 2:10 Lord, and for the glory of his **m.**. 1347
Isa 2:19, 21 Lord, and for the glory of his **m.**, .. 1347
Isa 24:14 shall sing for the **m.** of the Lord, ... 1347
Isa 26:10 will not behold the **m.** of the Lord. 1348
Eze 7:20 of his ornament, he set it in **m.**: 1347
Da 4:30 and for the honour of my **m.**? 1923
Da 4:36 excellent **m.** was added unto me. 7238
Da 5:18 and **m.**, and glory, and honour: 7238
Da 5:19 And for the **m.** that he gave him, ... 7238
Mic 5:4 in the **m.** of the name of the Lord 1347
Heb 1:3 the right hand of the **M.** on high; *3172*
Heb 8:1 throne of the **M.** in the heavens; *3172*
2Pe 1:16 but were eyewitnesses of his **m.** *3168*
Jude 25 be glory and **m.**, dominion and *3172*

MAKAZ (ma'-kaz)
1Ki 4:9 The son of Dekar, in **M.**, and in 4739

MAKE See also MADE; MAKEST; MAKETH; MAKING.
Ge 1:26 said, Let us **m.** man in our image, ... 6213
Ge 2:18 I will **m.** him an help meet for him. 6213
Ge 3:6 a tree to be desired to **m.** one wise, ...
Ge 3:21 did the Lord **m.** coats of skins, ... 6213
Ge 6:14 **M.** thee an ark of gopher wood; 6213
Ge 6:14 rooms shalt thou **m.** in the ark, and 6213
Ge 6:15 fashion which thou shalt **m.** it of: 6213
Ge 6:16 window shalt thou **m.** to the ark, ... 6213
Ge 6:16 and third stories shalt thou **m.** it. 6213
Ge 9:12 covenant which I **m.** between me 5414
Ge 11:3 let us **m.** brick, and burn them ....
Ge 11:4 and let us **m.** us a name, lest we be ... 6213
Ge 12:2 And I will **m.** of thee a great nation, ... 6213
Ge 12:2 bless thee, and **m.** thy name great; ....
Ge 13:16 I will **m.** thy seed as the dust of 7760
Ge 17:2 will **m.** my covenant between me 5414
Ge 17:6 I will **m.** thee exceeding fruitful, ...
Ge 17:6 and I will **m.** nations of thee, and 5414
Ge 17:20 him, and will **m.** him fruitful, and will ....
Ge 17:20 and I will **m.** him a great nation. 5414
Ge 18:6 **M.** ready quickly three measures of ....
Ge 18:6 it, and **m.** cakes upon the hearth. 6213
Ge 19:32 let us **m.** our father drink wine, ...
Ge 19:34 let us **m.** him drink wine this night ....
Ge 21:13 the bondwoman will I **m.** a nation, ... 7760
Ge 21:18 for I will **m.** him a great nation. 7760
Ge 24:3 And I will **m.** thee swear by the Lord, ...
Ge 26:4 I will **m.** thy seed to multiply as ....
Ge 26:28 let us **m.** a covenant with thee: 3772
Ge 27:4 **m.** me savoury meat, such as I 6213
Ge 27:7 venison, and **m.** me savoury meat, ... 6213
Ge 27:9 I will **m.** them savoury meat for thy ... 6213
Ge 28:3 bless thee, and **m.** thee fruitful, ...
Ge 31:44 come thou, let us **m.** a covenant, ... 3772
Ge 32:13 **m.** thy seed as the sand of the sea, ... 7760
Ge 34:9 **m.** ye marriages with us, and give ....
Ge 34:30 have troubled me to **m.** me to stink ....
Ge 35:1 and **m.** there an altar unto God, ... 6213
Ge 35:3 I will **m.** there an altar unto God, ... 6213
Ge 40:14 and **m.** mention of me unto Pharaoh, ...
Ge 43:16 men home, and slay, and **m.** ready; ....
Ge 46:3 there **m.** of thee a great nation: 6213
Ge 47:6 **m.** thy father and brethren to dwell; ....
Ge 47:6 **m.** them rulers over my cattle. 7760
Ge 48:4 me, Behold, I will **m.** thee fruitful, ...
Ge 48:4 **m.** of thee a multitude of people; 5414
Ge 48:20 God **m.** thee as Ephraim and as 6213
Ex 5:5 ye **m.** them rest from their burdens. ....
Ex 5:7 give the people straw to **m.** brick, ...
Ex 5:8 which they did **m.** heretofore, ... 6213
Ex 5:16 and they say to us, **M.** brick: and, ... 6213
Ex 12:4 shall **m.** your count for the lamb. ....
Ex 18:16 **m.** them know the statutes of God, ... 5414
Ex 20:4 **m.** unto thee any graven image, ... 6213
Ex 20:23 shall not **m.** with me gods of silver, ... 6213
Ex 20:23 shall ye **m.** unto you gods of gold. 6213
Ex 20:24 An altar of earth thou shalt **m.** 6213
Ex 20:25 thou wilt **m.** me an altar of stone, ... 6213
Ex 21:34 owner of the pit shall **m.** it good, ...
Ex 22:3 for he should **m.** full restitution; ....
Ex 22:5 vineyard, shall he **m.** restitution. ....
Ex 22:6 the fire shall surely **m.** restitution. ....
Ex 22:11 thereof, and he shall not **m.** it good. ....
Ex 22:12 shall **m.** restitution unto the owner ....
Ex 22:13 he shall not **m.** good that which ....
Ex 22:14 with it, he shall surely **m.** it good. ....
Ex 22:15 be with it, he shall not **m.** it good: ....
Ex 23:13 **m.** no mention of the name of other ....
Ex 23:27 I will **m.** all thine enemies turn 5414
Ex 23:32 Thou shalt **m.** no covenant with 3772

Ex 23:33 land, lest they **m.** thee sin against me:......
Ex 25:8 And let them **m.** me a sanctuary;....... 6213
Ex 25:9 thereof, even so shall ye **m.** it.......... 6213
Ex 25:10 shall **m.** an ark of shittim wood:........ 6213
Ex 25:11 and shalt **m.** upon it a crown of gold... 6213
Ex 25:13 shalt **m.** staves of shittim wood, ... 6213
Ex 25:17 shalt **m.** a mercy seat of pure gold:.... 6213
Ex 25:18 thou shalt **m.** two cherubims of gold, .. 6213
Ex 25:18 of beaten work shalt thou **m.** them,.... 6213
Ex 25:19 And **m.** one cherub on the one end, ... 6213
Ex 25:19 ye **m.** the cherubims on the two ends. 6213
Ex 25:23 also **m.** a table of shittim wood:........ 6213
Ex 25:24 **m.** thereto a crown of gold round........ 6213
Ex 25:25 thou shalt **m.** unto it a border of an.... 6213
Ex 25:25 thou shalt **m.** a golden crown to......... 6213
Ex 25:26 shalt **m.** for it four rings of gold,........ 6213
Ex 25:28 shalt **m.** the staves of shittim wood, ... 6213
Ex 25:29 thou shalt **m.** the dishes thereof,........ 6213
Ex 25:29 of pure gold shalt thou **m.** them.......... 6213
Ex 25:31 shalt **m.** a candlestick of pure gold:..... 6213
Ex 25:37 shalt **m.** the seven lamps thereof: 6213
Ex 25:39 a talent of pure gold shall he **m.** it,..... 6213
Ex 25:40 thou **m.** them after their pattern, ... 6213
Ex 26:1 thou shalt **m.** the tabernacle with 6213
Ex 26:1 of cunning work shalt thou **m.** them.... 6213
Ex 26:4 thou shalt **m.** loops of blue upon the... 6213
Ex 26:4 shalt thou **m.** in the uttermost edge..... 6213
Ex 26:5 Fifty loops shalt thou **m.** in the one.... 6213
Ex 26:5 and fifty loops shalt thou **m.** in the 6213
Ex 26:6 thou shalt **m.** fifty taches of gold, ... 6213
Ex 26:7 thou shalt **m.** curtains of goats' hair.... 6213
Ex 26:7 eleven curtains shalt thou **m.**............. 6213
Ex 26:10 thou shalt **m.** fifty loops on the edge... 6213
Ex 26:11 thou shalt **m.** fifty taches of brass, ... 6213
Ex 26:14 shalt **m.** a covering for the tent of...... 6213
Ex 26:15 shalt **m.** boards for the tabernacle, ... 6213
Ex 26:17 thou **m.** for all the boards of the 6213
Ex 26:18 **m.** the boards for the tabernacle, ... 6213
Ex 26:19 thou shalt **m.** forty sockets of silver.... 6213
Ex 26:22 westward thou shalt **m.** six boards. 6213
Ex 26:23 two boards shalt thou **m.** for the........ 6213
Ex 26:26 thou shalt **m.** bars of shittim wood; 6213
Ex 26:29 **m.** their rings of gold for places for 6213
Ex 26:31 And thou shalt **m.** a vail of blue, ... 6213
Ex 26:36 And thous shalt **m.** an hanging for...... 6213
Ex 26:37 **m.** for the hanging five pillars........... 6213
Ex 27:1 shalt **m.** an altar of shittim wood,........ 6213
Ex 27:2 thou shalt **m.** the horns of it upon...... 6213
Ex 27:3 **m.** his pans to receive his ashes, ... 6213
Ex 27:3 vessels...thou shalt **m.** of brass. 6213
Ex 27:4 shalt **m.** for it a grate of network of ... 6213
Ex 27:4 shalt thou **m.** four brasen rings in....... 6213
Ex 27:6 thou shalt **m.** staves for the altar, ... 6213
Ex 27:8 Hollow with boards shalt thou **m.** it: ... 6213
Ex 27:8 in the mount, so shall they **m.** it........ 6213
Ex 27:9 shalt **m.** the court of the tabernacle: ... 6213
Ex 28:2 shalt **m.** holy garments for Aaron....... 6213
Ex 28:3 they may **m.** Aaron's garments to 6213
Ex 28:4 the garments which they shall **m.**;...... 6213
Ex 28:4 shall **m.** holy garments for Aaron 6213
Ex 28:6 they shall **m.** the ephod of gold,.......... 6213
Ex 28:11 **m.** them to be set in ouches of gold. .. 6213
Ex 28:13 And thou shalt **m.** ouches of gold; 6213
Ex 28:14 wreathen work shalt thou **m.** them, ... 6213
Ex 28:15 **m.** the breastplate of judgment 6213
Ex 28:15 work of the ephod thou shalt **m.** it; 6213
Ex 28:15 fine twined linen, shalt thou **m.** it....... 6213
Ex 28:22 **m.** upon the breastplate chains at....... 6213
Ex 28:23 **m.** upon the breastplate two rings...... 6213
Ex 28:26 And thou shalt **m.** two rings of gold,... 6213
Ex 28:27 other rings of gold thou shalt **m.**,....... 6213
Ex 28:31 **m.** the robe of the ephod all of blue.... 6213
Ex 28:33 shalt **m.** pomegranates of blue, and.... 6213
Ex 28:36 thou shalt **m.** a plate of pure gold,....... 6213
Ex 28:39 shalt **m.** the mitre of fine linen, and.... 6213
Ex 28:39 shalt **m.** the girdle of needlework. 6213
Ex 28:40 Aaron's sons thou shalt **m.** coats,........ 6213
Ex 28:40 **m.** for them girdles, and bonnets 6213
Ex 28:40 and bonnets shalt thou **m.** for them, ... 6213
Ex 28:42 **m.** them linen breeches to cover........ 6213
Ex 29:2 wheaten flour shalt thou **m.** them....... 6213
Ex 29:37 **m.** an atonement for the altar, and..... 6213
Ex 30:1 **m.** an altar to burn incense upon:....... 6213
Ex 30:1 of shittim wood shalt thou **m.** it. 6213
Ex 30:3 **m.** unto it a crown of gold round........ 6213
Ex 30:4 two golden rings shalt thou **m.** to it.... 6213
Ex 30:4 the two sides of it shalt thou **m.** it; 6213
Ex 30:5 shalt **m.** the staves of shittim wood, ... 6213
Ex 30:10 Aaron shall **m.** an atonement upon...........
Ex 30:10 in the year shall he **m.** atonement ....
Ex 30:15, 16 to **m.** an atonement for your souls. ......
Ex 30:18 shalt also **m.** a laver of brass, and...... 6213
Ex 30:25 shalt **m.** it an oil of holy ointment,...... 6213
Ex 30:32 neither shall ye **m.** any other like it, ... 6213
Ex 30:35 And thou shalt **m.** it a perfume, a 6213
Ex 30:37 the perfume which thou shalt **m.**, ... 6213
Ex 30:37 not **m.** to yourselves according to 6213
Ex 30:38 Whosoever shall **m.** like unto that, ... 6213
Ex 31:6 **m.** all that I have commanded thee;.... 6213
Ex 32:1 **m.** us gods, which shall go before 6213
Ex 32:10 and I will **m.** of thee a great nation..... 6213
Ex 32:23 **M.** us gods, which shall go before 6213
Ex 32:30 shall **m.** an atonement for your sin. ....
Ex 33:19 **m.** all my goodness pass before thee, ...
Ex 34:10 Behold, I **m.** a covenant: before......... 3772
Ex 34:12, 15 **m.** a covenant with...inhabitants..... 3772
Ex 34:16 **m.** thy sons go a whoring after their.........
Ex 34:17 Thou shalt **m.** thee no molten gods. ... 6213
Ex 35:10 and **m.** all that the Lord hath............ 6213
Ex 35:33 to **m.** any manner of cunning work. 6213
Ex 36:3 of the sanctuary, to **m.** it withal......... 6213
Ex 36:5 which the Lord commanded to **m.**. 6213
Ex 36:6 man nor woman **m.** any more work.... 6213
Ex 36:7 sufficient for all the work to **m.** it,...... 6213
Ex 36:22 did he **m.** for all the boards of the...... 6213
Le 1:4 for him to **m.** atonement for him............
Le 4:20, 26,31,35 priest shall **m.** an atonement.......
Le 5:6,10, 13 priest shall **m.** an atonement ....
Le 5:16 he shall **m.** amends for the harm.............
Le 5:16, 18 priest shall **m.** an atonement for ....
Le 6:7 the priest shall **m.** an atonement for ....
Le 8:15 it, to **m.** reconcilation upon it. ....
Le 8:34 to do, to **m.** an atonement for you...........
Le 9:7 and **m.** an atonement for thyself,.............
Le 9:7 and **m.** an atonement for them; as............
Le 10:17 **m.** atonement for them before the............
Le 11:43 not **m.** yourselves abominable..................
Le 11:43 ye **m.** yourselves unclean with................
Le 11:47 **m.** a difference between the unclean.........
Le 12:7 and **m.** an atonement for her; and ....
Le 12:8 priest shall **m.** an atonement for..............
Le 14:18 priest shall **m.** an atonement for him.........
Le 14:19 **m.** an atonement for him that is to ....
Le 14:20 priest shall **m.** an atonement for him, ...
Le 14:21 waved, to **m.** an atonement for him, ...
Le 14:29 to **m.** an atonement for him before ....
Le 14:31 priest shall **m.** an atonement for..............
Le 14:53 and **m.** an atonement for the house: ....
Le 15:15, 30 priest shall **m.** an atonement for ....
Le 16:6 **m.** an atonement for himself, and for ....
Le 16:10 to **m.** an atonement with him, and...........
Le 16:11 shall **m.** an atonement for himself, ...
Le 16:16 shall **m.** an atonement for the holy............
Le 16:17 in to **m.** an atonement in the holy............
Le 16:18 Lord, and **m.** an atonement for it; ....
Le 16:24 **m.** an atonement for himself, and for ....
Le 16:27 to **m.** atonement in the holy place, ...
Le 16:30 the priest **m.** an atonement for you, ...
Le 16:32 shall **m.** the atonement, and shall ....
Le 16:33 shall **m.** an atonement for the holy.............
Le 16:33 he shall **m.** an atonement for the.............
Le 16:33 **m.** an atonement for the priests,..............
Le 16:34 **m.** an atonement for the children of..........
Le 17:11 to **m.** an atonement for your souls:.............
Le 19:4 nor **m.** to yourselves molten gods: 6213
Le 19:22 priest shall **m.** an atonement for him.........
Le 19:28 not **m.** any cuttings in your flesh........ 5414
Le 20:25 **m.** your souls abominable by beast, ...
Le 21:5 not **m.** baldness upon their head,..............
Le 21:5 nor **m.** any cuttings in their flesh.............
Le 22:22 nor **m.** an offering by the fire of them..5414
Le 22:24 shall ye **m.** any offering thereof in...... 6213
Le 23:22 shalt not **m.** clean riddance of the............
Le 23:28 to **m.** an atonement for you before ....
Le 24:18 killeth a beast shall **m.** it good; ....
Le 25:9 ye **m.** the trumpet sound throughout.........
Le 26:1 shall **m.** you no idols nor graven 6213
Le 26:6 and none shall **m.** you afraid:...................
Le 26:9 unto you, and **m.** you fruitful, and ....
Le 26:19 and I will **m.** your heaven as iron, ... 5414
Le 26:22 cattle, and **m.** you few in number;............
Le 26:31 And I will **m.** your cities waste, ... 5414
Le 27:2 When a man shall **m.** a singular vow, ...
Nu 5:21 The Lord **m.** thee a curse and an....... 5414
Nu 5:21 the Lord doth **m.** thy thigh to rot,...... 5414
Nu 5:22 thy bowels, to **m.** thy belly to swell,.........
Nu 6:7 shall not **m.** himself unclean for...............
Nu 6:11 and **m.** an atonement for him, for.............
Nu 6:25 the Lord **m.** his face shine upon thee, ...
Nu 8:7 and so **m.** themselves clean. ....
Nu 8:12 **m.** an atonement for the Levites. ....
Nu 8:19 to **m.** an atonement for the children..........
Nu 10:2 **M.** thee two trumpets of silver; of 6213
Nu 10:2 a whole piece shalt thou **m.** them:...... 6213
Nu 12:6 I the Lord willing **m.** myself known ....
Nu 14:4 Let us **m.** a captain, and let us.......... 5414
Nu 14:12 will **m.** of thee a greater nation............ 6213
Nu 14:30 which I sware to **m.** you dwell therein, ...
Nu 15:3 will **m.** an offering by fire unto the 6213
Nu 15:3 to **m.** a sweet savour unto the Lord, .. 6213
Nu 15:25, 28 priest shall **m.** an atonement for ....
Nu 15:28 Lord, to **m.** an atonement for him; ....
Nu 15:38 **m.** them fringes in the borders 6213
Nu 16:13 **m.** thyself altogether a prince over ....
Nu 16:30 But if the Lord **m.** a new thing,......... 1254
Nu 16:38 **m.** them broad plates for a covering ....
Nu 16:46 and **m.** an atonement for them:................
Nu 17:5 and I will **m.** to cease from me the ....
Nu 21:8 **M.** thee a fiery serpent, and set it 6213
Nu 23:19 spoken, and shall he not **m.** it good?.........
Nu 28:22, 30 to **m.** an atonement for you. ....
Nu 29:5 to **m.** an atonement for you: ....
Nu 30:8 shall **m.** her vow which she vowed, ...
Nu 30:13 it, or her husband may **m.** it void. ....
Nu 30:15 shall any ways **m.** them void after that......
Nu 31:23 ye shall **m.** it go through the fire, ... 5674
Nu 31:23 ye shall **m.** go through the water. 5674
Nu 31:50 to **m.** an atonement for our souls....... 5674
De 1:11 **m.** you a thousand times so many...... 5674
De 1:13 and I will **m.** them rulers over you. 7760
De 4:10 and I will **m.** them hear my words,..........
De 4:16, 23,25 and **m.** you a graven image,...... 6213
De 5:8 shalt not **m.** thee any graven image, ... 6213
De 7:2 shalt **m.** no covenant with them, ... 3772
De 7:3 thou **m.** marriages with them;.................
De 8:3 might **m.** thee know that man doth not.......
De 9:14 I will **m.** of thee a nation mightier...... 6213
De 10:1 mount, and **m.** thee an ark of wood.... 6213
De 13:14 enquire, and **m.** search, and ask...............
De 14:1 nor **m.** any baldness between your..... 7760
De 15:1 years thou shalt **m.** a release. 6213
De 16:18 and officers shalt thou **m.** thee in....... 5414
De 16:21 thy God, which thou shalt **m.** thee. 6213
De 19:18 shall **m.** diligent inquisition: and,...............
De 20:9 they shall **m.** captains of the armies..........
De 20:11 if it **m.** thee answer of peace, and open.....
De 20:12 if it will **m.** no peace with thee, but will.....
De 21:14 shalt not **m.** merchandise of her,........ 6014
De 21:16 **m.** the son of the beloved firstborn...........
De 22:8 shalt **m.** a battlement for thy roof,....... 6213
De 22:12 Thou shalt **m.** thee fringes upon the... 6213
De 26:19 to **m.** thee high above all nations........ 6213
De 28:11 the Lord shall **m.** thee plenteous..............
De 28:13 the Lord shall **m.** thee the head,........ 5414
De 28:21 **m.** the pestilence cleave unto thee, ...
De 28:24 The Lord shall **m.** the rain of thy.......... 5414
De 28:59 Then the Lord will **m.** thy plagues...... 6381
De 29:1 the Lord commanded Moses to **m.**...... 3772
De 29:14 I **m.** this covenant and this oath;........ 3772
De 30:9 thy God will **m.** thee plenteous in............
De 32:26 **m.** the remembrance of them to cease ......
De 32:35 that shall come upon them **m.** haste..........
De 32:39 I kill, and I **m.** alive; I wound, and ....
De 32:42 **m.** mine arrows drunk with blood, ...
Jos 1:8 thou shalt **m.** thy way prosperous, ...
Jos 5:2 Joshua, **M.** thee sharp knives, and...... 6213
Jos 6:5 when they **m.** a long blast with the...........
Jos 6:10 shall not shout, nor **m.** any noise ....
Jos 6:18 ye **m.** yourselves accursed, when.............
Jos 6:18 and **m.** the camp of Israel a curse, ... 7760
Jos 7:3 and **m.** not all the people to labour ....
Jos 7:19 and **m.** confession unto him; and........ 5414
Jos 9:6 therefore **m.** ye a league with us. 3772
Jos 9:7 how shall we **m.** a league with you?.... 3772
Jos 9:11 now **m.** ye a league with us. 3772
Jos 22:25 **m.** our children cease from fearing ....
Jos 23:7 neither **m.** mention of the name of their ....
Jos 23:12 and shall **m.** marriages with them. ....
Jg 2:2 **m.** no league with the inhabitants....... 3772
Jg 9:48 **m.** haste, and do as I have done. ....

Jg	16:25	for Samson, that he may **m.** us sport	
Jg	17:3	**m.** a graven image and a molten	6213
Jg	20:38	should **m.** a great flame with smoke	
Ru	3:3	but **m.** not thyself known unto the	
Ru	4:11	Lord **m.** the woman...like Rachel	5414
1Sa	1:6	her sore, for to **m.** her fret, because	
1Sa	2:8	to **m.** them inherit the throne of	
1Sa	2:24	**m.** the Lord's people to transgress.	
1Sa	2:29	**m.** yourselves fat with the chiefest	
1Sa	3:12	when I begin, I will also **m.** an end.	
1Sa	6:5	shall **m.** images of your emerods,	6213
1Sa	6:7	Now therefore **m.** a new cart, and	6213
1Sa	8:5	**m.** us a king to judge us like all	7760
1Sa	8:12	and to **m.** his instruments of war,	6213
1Sa	8:22	their voice, and **m.** them a king.	
1Sa	9:12	**m.** haste now, for he came to day	
1Sa	11:1	**M.** a covenant with us, and we	3772
1Sa	11:2	will I **m.** a covenant with you,	3772
1Sa	12:22	the Lord to **m.** you his people.	6213
1Sa	13:19	Lest the Hebrews **m.** them swords	6213
1Sa	17:25	**m.** his father's house free in Israel.	6213
1Sa	18:25	Saul thought to **m.** David fall by	
1Sa	20:38	cried after the lad, **M.** speed, haste,	
1Sa	22:7	**m.** you all captains of thousands,	7760
1Sa	25:28	certainly **m.** my lord a sure house;	6213
1Sa	28:2	I **m.** thee keeper of mine head for	7760
1Sa	28:15	the Philistines **m.** war against me,	
1Sa	28:15	**m.** known unto me what I shall do	
1Sa	29:4	**M.** this fellow return, that he may	
2Sa	3:12	also, **M.** thy league with me, and,	3772
2Sa	3:13	Well; I will **m.** a league with thee:	3772
2Sa	3:21	they may **m.** a league with thee,	3772
2Sa	7:11	thee that he will **m.** thee an house.	6213
2Sa	7:21	to **m.** thy servant know them.	
2Sa	7:23	to himself, and to **m.** him a name,	7760
2Sa	11:25	**m.** thy battle more strong against	
2Sa	13:5	on thy bed, and **m.** thyself sick:	
2Sa	13:6	and **m.** me a couple of cakes in my	3823
2Sa	15:14	**m.** speed to depart, lest he overtake us	
2Sa	15:20	**m.** thee go up and down with us?	
2Sa	17:2	handed, and will **m.** him afraid:	
2Sa	21:3	shall I **m.** the atonement, that	
2Sa	23:5	although he **m.** it not to grow.	
1Ki	1:37	**m.** his throne greater than the throne	
1Ki	1:47	**m.** the name of Solomon better than	
1Ki	1:47	**m.** his throne greater than thy throne.	
1Ki	2:42	I not **m.** thee to swear by the Lord,	
1Ki	8:29	prayer which thy servant shall **m.**	
1Ki	8:33,	47 and **m.** supplication unto thee	
1Ki	9:22	did Solomon **m.** no bondmen: but	5414
1Ki	11:34	I will **m.** him prince all the days	
1Ki	12:1	come to Shechem to **m.** him king.	
1Ki	12:4	**m.** thou the grievous service of	
1Ki	12:9	**M.** the yoke which thy father...lighten?	
1Ki	12:10	but **m.** thou it lighter unto us;	
1Ki	16:3	**m.** thy house like the house of	5414
1Ki	16:19	which he did, to **m.** Israel to sin.	
1Ki	16:21	the son of Ginath, to **m.** him king;	
1Ki	17:13	**m.** me thereof a little cake first,	6213
1Ki	17:13	after **m.** for thee and for thy son.	6213
1Ki	19:2	**m.** not thy life as the life of one of	7760
1Ki	20:34	**m.** streets for thee in Damascus,	7760
1Ki	21:22	**m.** thine house like the house of	5414
2Ki	3:16	**M.** this valley full of ditches.	6213
2Ki	4:10	Let us **m.** a little chamber, I pray	6213
2Ki	5:7	Am I God, to kill and to **m.** alive,	
2Ki	6:2	let us **m.** us a place there, where	6213
2Ki	7:2	Lord would **m.** windows in heaven,	6213
2Ki	7:19	Lord should **m.** windows in heaven,	6213
2Ki	9:2	and **m.** him arise up from among his	
2Ki	9:9	And I will **m.** the house of Ahab	5414
2Ki	9:21	And Joram said, **M.** ready. And his	
2Ki	10:5	bid us; we will not **m.** any king:	
2Ki	18:30	let Hezekiah **m.** you trust in the Lord,	
2Ki	18:31	**M.** an agreement with me by a	6213
2Ki	21:8	will I **m.** the feet of Israel move	
2Ki	23:10	might **m.** his son...pass through the	
1Ch	6:49	and to **m.** an atonement for Israel,	
1Ch	11:10	with all Israel, to **m.** him king,	
1Ch	12:31	name, to come and **m.** David king.	
1Ch	12:38	to **m.** David king over all Israel:	
1Ch	12:38	were of one heart to **m.** David king.	
1Ch	16:8	name, **m.** known his deeds among	
1Ch	16:42	for those that should **m.** a sound,	
1Ch	17:21	to **m.** thee a name of greatness	7760
1Ch	17:22	didst thou **m.** thine own people	5414
1Ch	21:3	Lord **m.** his people an hundred...more	
1Ch	22:5	will therefore now **m.** preparation	
1Ch	28:4	me to **m.** me king over all Israel:	
1Ch	29:12	and in thine hand it is to **m.** great,	
2Ch	4:11	work that he was to **m.** for king	6213
2Ch	4:16	his father **m.** to king Solomon for	6213
2Ch	5:13	to **m.** one sound to be heard in	
2Ch	6:21	supplication...they shall **m.** toward	
2Ch	6:22	be laid upon him to **m.** him swear,	
2Ch	6:24	pray and **m.** supplication before	
2Ch	7:11	came into Solomon's heart to **m.**	6213
2Ch	7:20	and will **m.** it to be a proverb and	5414
2Ch	8:8	did Solomon **m.** to pay tribute	
2Ch	8:9	**m.** no servants for his work; but	5414
2Ch	10:1	all Israel come to **m.** him king.	
2Ch	10:10	**m.** thou it somewhat lighter for us;	
2Ch	11:22	for he thought to **m.** him king.	
2Ch	14:7	**m.** about them walls, and towers,	
2Ch	20:36	joined himself with him to **m.** ships	6213
2Ch	25:8	shall **m.** thee fall before the enemy:	
2Ch	29:10	**m.** a covenant with the Lord God	3772
2Ch	29:24	to **m.** an atonement for all Israel:	
2Ch	30:5	**m.** proclamation throughout all Israel,	
2Ch	35:21	God commanded me to **m.** haste:	
Ezr	5:3	house, and to **m.** up this wall?	3635
Ezr	5:4	of the men that **m.** this building?	1124
Ezr	5:9	house, and to **m.** up these walls?	3635
Ezr	6:8	I **m.** a decree what ye shall do to	7761
Ezr	7:13	I **m.** a decree, that all they of the	7761
Ezr	7:21	do **m.** a decree to all the treasurers	7761
Ezr	10:3	let us **m.** a covenant with our God	3772
Ezr	10:11	**m.** confession unto the Lord God	5414
Ne	2:4	me, For what dost thou **m.** request?	
Ne	2:8	timber to **m.** beams for the gates	
Ne	4:2	will they **m.** an end in a day? will	
Ne	8:12	portions, and to **m.** great mirth,	6213
Ne	8:15	of thick trees, to **m.** booths, as it	6213
Ne	9:38	of all this we **m.** a sure covenant,	3772
Ne	10:33	to **m.** an atonement for Israel,	
Es	1:20	king's decree which he shall **m.**	6213
Es	4:8	to **m.** supplication unto him, and	
Es	4:8	to **m.** request before him for her	
Es	5:5	said, Cause Haman to **m.** haste,	
Es	6:10	**M.** haste, and take the apparel and	
Es	7:7	Haman stood up to **m.** request for his	
Es	9:22	should **m.** them days of feasting	6213
Job	5:18	and his hands **m.** whole.	
Job	8:5	and **m.** thy supplication to the	
Job	8:6	**m.** the habitation of thy...prosperous	
Job	9:15	I would **m.** supplication to my judge.	
Job	9:30	and **m.** my hands never so clean;	
Job	11:3	thy lies **m.** men hold their peace?	
Job	11:3	shall no man **m.** thee ashamed?	
Job	11:19	and none shall **m.** thee afraid;	
Job	11:19	yea, many shall **m.** suit unto thee.	
Job	13:11	not his excellency **m.** you afraid?	
Job	13:21	and let not thy dread **m.** me afraid.	
Job	13:23	**m.** me to know my transgression	
Job	15:24	and anguish shall **m.** him afraid;	
Job	18:2	it be ere ye **m.** an end of words?	7760
Job	18:11	Terrors shall **m.** him afraid on	
Job	19:3	ye **m.** yourselves strange to me.	
Job	20:2	to answer, and for this I **m.** haste.	
Job	22:27	shalt **m.** thy prayer unto him, and	
Job	24:11	Which **m.** oil within their walls,	
Job	24:25	not so now, who will **m.** me a liar,	7760
Job	24:25	and **m.** my speech nothing worth?	7760
Job	28:25	To **m.** the weight for the winds:	6213
Job	31:15	made me in the womb **m.** him?	6213
Job	33:7	my terror shall not **m.** thee afraid,	
Job	34:29	who then can **m.** trouble? and	
Job	35:9	they **m.** the oppressed to cry:	
Job	39:20	**m.** him afraid as a grasshopper?	
Job	39:27	and **m.** her nest on high?	
Job	40:19	can **m.** his sword to approach unto	
Job	41:3	Will he **m.** many supplications	
Job	41:4	Will he **m.** a covenant with thee?	3772
Job	41:6	the companions **m.** a banquet of him?	
Job	41:28	The arrow cannot **m.** him flee:	
Ps	5:8	**m.** thy way straight before my face.	
Ps	6:6	all the night **m.** I my bed to swim;	
Ps	11:2	they **m.** ready their arrow upon	
Ps	21:9	shalt **m.** them as a fiery oven in	7896
Ps	21:12	shalt thou **m.** them turn their back,	
Ps	21:12	thou shalt **m.** ready thine arrows	
Ps	22:9	didst **m.** me hope when I was upon	
Ps	31:16	**M.** thy face to shine upon thy	
Ps	34:2	shall **m.** her boast in the Lord:	
Ps	36:8	shalt **m.** them drink of the river of	
Ps	38:22	**M.** haste to help me, O Lord my	
Ps	39:4	Lord, **m.** me to know mine end,	
Ps	39:8	**m.** me not the reproach of the	7760
Ps	40:13	me: O Lord, **m.** haste to help me.	
Ps	40:17	deliverer; **m.** no tarrying, O my God.	
Ps	41:3	wilt **m.** all his bed in his sickness.	2015
Ps	45:16	mayest **m.** princes in all the earth.	
Ps	45:17	**m.** thy name to be remembered in all	
Ps	46:4	shall **m.** glad the city of God,	
Ps	51:6	thou shalt **m.** me to know wisdom.	
Ps	51:8	**M.** me to hear joy and gladness;	
Ps	55:2	in my complaint, and **m.** a noise;	
Ps	57:1	of thy wings will I **m.** my refuge,	
Ps	59:6	they **m.** a noise like a dog, and go	
Ps	59:14	them **m.** a noise like a dog, and go	
Ps	64:8	shall **m.** their own tongue to fall	
Ps	66:1	**M.** a joyful noise unto God, all ye	
Ps	66:2	his name: **m.** his praise glorious.	7760
Ps	66:8	**m.** the voice of his praise to be heard:	
Ps	69:23	**m.** their loins continually to shake.	
Ps	70:1	**M.** haste, O God, to deliver me;	
Ps	70:1	**m.** haste to help me, O Lord.	
Ps	70:5	needy: **m.** haste unto me, O God:	
Ps	70:5	my deliverer; O Lord, **m.** no tarrying.	
Ps	71:12	O my God, **m.** haste for my help.	
Ps	71:16	will **m.** mention of thy righteousness,	
Ps	78:5	**m.** them known to their children:	
Ps	81:1	**m.** a joyful noise unto the God of	
Ps	83:2	For, lo, thine enemies **m.** a tumult:	
Ps	83:11	**M.** their nobles like Oreb, and like	7896
Ps	83:13	O my God, **m.** them like a wheel; as	7896
Ps	83:15	and **m.** them afraid with thy storm.	
Ps	84:6	the valley of Baca **m.** it a well;	6213
Ps	87:4	will **m.** mention of Rahab and Babylon	
Ps	89:1	will I **m.** known thy faithfulness to all	
Ps	89:27	I will **m.** him my firstborn, higher	5414
Ps	89:29	His seed also will I **m.** to endure	7760
Ps	90:15	**M.** us glad according to the days	
Ps	95:1	us **m.** a joyful noise to the rock of	
Ps	95:2	and **m.** a joyful noise unto him with	
Ps	98:4	**M.** a joyful noise unto the Lord, all	
Ps	98:4	**m.** a loud noise, and rejoice, and	
Ps	98:6	**m.** a joyful noise before the Lord,	
Ps	100:1	**M.** a joyful noise unto the Lord, all	
Ps	104:15	oil to **m.** his face to shine, and bread	
Ps	104:17	Where the birds **m.** their nests: as	
Ps	105:1	**m.** known his deeds among the people.	
Ps	106:8	**m.** his mighty power to be known.	
Ps	110:1	I **m.** thine enemies thy footstool.	7896
Ps	115:8	that **m.** them are like unto them;	6213
Ps	119:27	**M.** me to understand the way of thy	
Ps	119:35	**M.** me to go in the path of thy	
Ps	119:135	**M.** thy face to shine upon thy servant;	
Ps	132:17	will I **m.** the horn of David to bud:	
Ps	135:18	They that **m.** them are like unto	6213
Ps	139:8	if I **m.** my bed in hell, behold, thou	3331
Ps	141:1	cry unto thee: **m.** haste unto me;	
Ps	142:1	the Lord did I **m.** my supplication.	
Ps	145:12	To **m.** known to the sons of men his	
Pr	1:16	evil, and **m.** haste to shed blood.	
Pr	1:23	I will **m.** known my words unto you.	
Pr	6:3	thyself, and **m.** sure thy friend.	
Pr	14:9	Fools **m.** a mock at sin: but	
Pr	20:18	and with good advice **m.** war.	6213
Pr	20:25	holy, and after vows to **m.** enquiry.	
Pr	22:21	might **m.** thee know the certainty	
Pr	22:24	**M.** no friendship with an angry	
Pr	23:5	certainly **m.** themselves wings;	6213
Pr	24:6	wise counsel thou shalt **m.** thy war:	
Pr	24:27	and **m.** it fit for thyself in the field;	
Pr	27:11	be wise, and **m.** my heart glad,	
Pr	30:26	**m.** they their houses in the rocks;	7760
Ec	2:24	and that he should **m.** his soul enjoy	
Ec	7:13	who can **m.** that straight, which	
Ec	7:16	much; neither **m.** thyself over wise:	
Ca	1:11	We will **m.** thee borders of gold	6213
Ca	8:14	**M.** haste, my beloved, and be thou	
Isa	1:15	when ye **m.** many prayers, I will not	
Isa	1:16	Wash you, **m.** you clean; put away	
Isa	3:7	**m.** me not a ruler of the people.	7760
Isa	5:19	Let him **m.** speed, and hasten his work,	
Isa	6:10	**M.** the heart of this people fat,	
Isa	6:10	**m.** their ears heavy, and shut their	

Isa 7:6 let us **m.** a breach therein for us,…
Isa 10:23 of hosts shall **m.** a consumption, … 6213
Isa 11:3 **m.** him of quick understanding in…
Isa 11:15 and **m.** men go over dryshod…
Isa 12:4 **m.** mention that his name is exalted…
Isa 13:12 **m.** a man more precious than fine …
Isa 13:20 the shepherds **m.** their fold there. …
Isa 14:23 **m.** it a possession for the bittern, … 7760
Isa 16:3 **m.** thy shadow as the night in the … 7896
Isa 17:2 and none shall **m.** them afraid…
Isa 17:11 day shalt thou **m.** thy plant to grow, …
Isa 17:11 shalt thou **m.** thy seed to flourish: …
Isa 17:12 **m.** a noise like the noise of the seas; …
Isa 17:12 **m.** a rushing like the rushing of …
Isa 19:10 that **m.** sluices and ponds for fish. … 6213
Isa 23:16 **m.** sweet melody, sing many songs, …
Isa 25:6 **m.** unto all people a feast of fat … 6213
Isa 26:13 only will we **m.** mention of thy name. …
Isa 27:5 that he may **m.** peace with me; … 6213
Isa 27:5 and he shall **m.** peace with me. … 6213
Isa 28:9 shall he **m.** to understand doctrine? …
Isa 28:16 that believeth shall not **m.** haste…
Isa 29:21 That **m.** a man an offender for a word,…
Isa 32:6 **m.** empty the soul of the hungry,…
Isa 32:11 strip you, and **m.** you bare, and…
Isa 33:1 **m.** an end to deal treacherously. …
Isa 34:15 shall the great owl **m.** her nest,…
Isa 36:15 let Hezekiah **m.** you trust in the Lord, …
Isa 36:16 **M.** an agreement with me by a… 6213
Isa 37:9 He is come forth to **m.** war with thee. …
Isa 38:12, 13 wilt thou **m.** an end of me. …
Isa 38:16 thou recover me, and **m.** me to live. …
Isa 38:19 the children shall **m.** known thy truth. …
Isa 40:3 **m.**…in the desert a highway for…
Isa 41:15 I will **m.**…a new sharp threshing… 7760
Isa 41:15 and shalt **m.** the hills as chaff. … 7760
Isa 41:18 **m.** the wilderness a pool of water, … 7760
Isa 42:15 I will **m.** waste mountains and hills, … 7760
Isa 42:15 and I will **m.** the rivers islands, and… 7760
Isa 42:16 will **m.** darkness light before them,… 7760
Isa 42:21 the law, and **m.** it honourable. …
Isa 43:19 even **m.** a way in the wilderness,… 7760
Isa 44:9 They that **m.** a graven image are… 3335
Isa 44:19 shall I **m.** the residue thereof an… 6213
Isa 45:2 **m.** the crooked places straight: …
Isa 45:7 I **m.** peace, and create evil: I the… 6213
Isa 45:14 they shall **m.** supplication unto thee, …
Isa 46:5 will ye liken me, and **m.** me equal, …
Isa 47:2 **m.** bare the leg, uncover the thigh, …
Isa 48:1 and **m.** mention of the God of Israel, …
Isa 48:15 he shall **m.** his way prosperous. …
Isa 49:11 I will **m.** all my mountains a way,… 7760
Isa 49:17 Thy children shall **m.** haste: thy…
Isa 50:2 sea, I **m.** the rivers a wilderness: … 7760
Isa 50:3 and I **m.** sackcloth their covering. … 7760
Isa 51:3 will **m.** her wilderness like Eden, … 7760
Isa 51:4 **m.** my judgment to rest for a light of…
Isa 52:5 rule over them **m.** them to howl, …
Isa 53:10 thou shalt **m.** his soul an offering … 7760
Isa 54:3 **m.** the desolate cities to be inhabited. …
Isa 54:12 I will **m.** thy windows of agates, … 7760
Isa 55:3 I will **m.** an everlasting covenant… 3772
Isa 56:7 **m.** them joyful in my house of…
Isa 57:4 against whom **m.** ye a wide mouth, …
Isa 58:4 **m.** your voice to be heard on high. …
Isa 58:11 in drought, and **m.** fat thy bones: …
Isa 59:7 **m.** haste to shed innocent blood: …
Isa 60:13 **m.** the place of my feet glorious. … 7760
Isa 60:15 will **m.** thee an eternal excellency,… 7760
Isa 60:17 I will also **m.** thy officers peace, … 7760
Isa 61:8 I will **m.** an everlasting covenant… 3772
Isa 62:6 ye that **m.** mention of the Lord, keep …
Isa 62:7 till he **m.** Jerusalem a praise in … 7760
Isa 63:6 and **m.** them drunk in my fury, and …
Isa 63:12 **m.** himself an everlasting name?… 6213
Isa 63:14 to **m.** thyself a glorious name. … 6213
Isa 64:2 to **m.** thy name known to thine…
Isa 66:22 and the new earth, which I will **m.**, … 6213
Jer 4:7 his place to **m.** thy land desolate; … 7760
Jer 4:16 **M.** ye mention to the nations; behold, …
Jer 4:27 yet will I not **m.** a full end. … 6213
Jer 4:30 in vain shalt thou **m.** thyself fair; …
Jer 5:10 and destroy; but **m.** not a full end: … 6213
Jer 5:14 **m.** my words in thy mouth fire, … 5414
Jer 5:18 I will not **m.** a full end with you. … 6213
Jer 6:8 lest I **m.** thee desolate, a land not… 7760
Jer 6:26 **m.** thee mourning, as for an only … 6213
Jer 7:16 neither **m.** intercession to me: for …
Jer 7:18 dough, to **m.** cakes to the queen… 6213
Jer 9:11 And I will **m.** Jerusalem heaps, … 5414
Jer 9:11 will **m.** the cities of Judah desolate, … 5414
Jer 9:18 let them **m.** haste, and take up a …
Jer 10:22 to **m.** the cities of Judah desolate, … 7760
Jer 13:16 of death, and **m.** it gross darkness. … 7896
Jer 15:14 I will **m.** thee to pass with thine …
Jer 15:20 And I will **m.** thee unto this people… 5414
Jer 16:6 nor **m.** themselves bald for them: …
Jer 16:20 Shall a man **m.** gods unto himself, … 6213
Jer 18:4 seemed good to the potter to **m.** it. … 6213
Jer 18:11 **m.** your ways and your doings good. …
Jer 18:16 To **m.** their land desolate, and a … 7760
Jer 19:7 I will **m.** void the counsel of Judah. …
Jer 19:8 And I will **m.** this city desolate, … 7760
Jer 19:12 and even **m.** this city as Tophet: … 5414
Jer 20:4 I will **m.** thee a terror to thyself, … 5414
Jer 20:9 I will not **m.** mention of him, nor …
Jer 22:6 surely I will **m.** thee a wilderness,… 7896
Jer 23:15 and **m.** them drink the water of gall: …
Jer 23:16 prophesy unto you; they **m.** you vain: …
Jer 25:9 and **m.** them an astonishment, and … 7760
Jer 25:12 and will **m.** it perpetual desolations. … 7760
Jer 25:18 thereof, to **m.** them a desolation, … 5414
Jer 26:6 will I **m.** this house like Shiloh, … 5414
Jer 26:6 and will **m.** this city a curse to all … 5414
Jer 27:2 **M.** thee bonds and yokes, and put… 6213
Jer 27:18 now **m.** intercession to the Lord of…
Jer 28:13 shalt **m.** for them yokes of iron. … 6213
Jer 29:17 and will **m.** them like vile figs, that… 5414
Jer 29:22 The Lord **m.** thee like Zedekiah… 7760
Jer 30:10 and none shall **m.** him afraid. …
Jer 30:11 I **m.** a full end of all nations … 6213
Jer 30:11 yet will I not **m.** a full end of thee:… 6213
Jer 30:19 the voice of them that **m.** merry: …
Jer 31:4 the dances of them that **m.** merry. …
Jer 31:13 **m.** them rejoice from their sorrow. …
Jer 31:21 waymarks, **m.** thee high heaps: … 7760
Jer 31:31 **m.** a new covenant with the house … 3772
Jer 31:33 the covenant that I will **m.** with the… 3772
Jer 32:40 I will **m.** an everlasting covenant… 3772
Jer 34:17 I will **m.** you to be removed into all… 5414
Jer 34:22 and I will **m.** the cities of Judah a… 5414
Jer 44:19 we **m.** her cakes to worship her, … 6213
Jer 46:27 ease, and none shall **m.** him afraid. …
Jer 46:28 will **m.** a full end of all the nations… 6213
Jer 46:28 I will not **m.** a full end of thee, but… 6213
Jer 48:26 **M.** ye him drunken; for he…
Jer 49:15 **m.** thee small among the heathen, … 5414
Jer 49:16 **m.** thy nest as high as the eagle, …
Jer 49:19 will…**m.** him run away from her: …
Jer 49:20 shall **m.** their habitations desolate …
Jer 50:3 which shall **m.** her land desolate,… 7896
Jer 50:44 will **m.** them…run away from her: …
Jer 50:45 shall **m.** their habitation desolate …
Jer 51:11 **M.** bright the arrows; gather the…
Jer 51:12 **m.** the watch strong, set up the…
Jer 51:25 will **m.** thee a burnt mountain. … 5414
Jer 51:29 **m.** the land of Babylon a desolation … 7760
Jer 51:36 her sea, and **m.** her springs dry. …
Jer 51:39 In their heat I will **m.** their feasts, … 7896
Jer 51:39 and I will **m.** them drunken, that…
Jer 51:57 And I will **m.** drunk her princes, …
La 4:21 and shalt **m.** thyself naked. …
Eze 3:26 **m.** thy tongue cleave to the roof…
Eze 4:9 vessel, and **m.** thee bread thereof, … 6213
Eze 5:14 Moreover I will **m.** thee waste, … 5414
Eze 6:14 them, and **m.** the land desolate, … 5414
Eze 7:14 the trumpet, even to **m.** all ready; …
Eze 7:23 **M.** a chain: for the land is full of… 6213
Eze 7:24 **m.** the pomp of the strong to cease; …
Eze 11:13 **m.** a full end of the remnant of… 6213
Eze 12:23 I will **m.** this proverb to cease, and…
Eze 13:18 and **m.** kerchiefs upon the head of… 6213
Eze 13:20 hunt the souls to **m.** them fly, …
Eze 13:20 souls that ye hunt to **m.** them fly. …
Eze 14:8 will **m.** him a sign and a proverb, … 8074
Eze 15:8 And I will **m.** the land desolate, … 5414
Eze 16:42 I **m.** my fury toward thee to rest, …
Eze 17:17 company **m.** for him in the war, … 6213
Eze 18:31 and **m.** you a new heart and a new… 6213
Eze 20:17 neither did I **m.** an end of them in… 6213
Eze 20:26 that I might **m.** them desolate, to…
Eze 20:31 ye **m.** your sons to pass through the …
Eze 21:10 sharpened to **m.** a sore slaughter; …
Eze 21:10 glitter: should we then **m.** mirth? …
Eze 22:30 them, that should **m.** up the hedge,… 1443
Eze 23:27 will I **m.** thy lewdness to cease…
Eze 24:5 bones under it, and **m.** it boil well, …
Eze 24:9 will even **m.** the pile for fire great. …
Eze 24:17 cry, **m.** no mourning for the dead,… 6213
Eze 25:4 and **m.** their dwellings in thee: … 5414
Eze 25:5 **m.** Rabbah a stable for camels, … 5414
Eze 25:13 I will **m.** it desolate from Teman; … 5414
Eze 26:4 and **m.** her like the top of a rock. … 5414
Eze 26:8 and he shall **m.** a fort against thee,… 5414
Eze 26:12 they shall **m.** a spoil of thy riches,… 5414
Eze 26:12 **m.** a prey of thy merchandise: and …
Eze 26:14 I will **m.** thee like the top of a rock: …
Eze 26:19 shall **m.** thee a desolate city, like… 5414
Eze 26:21 I will **m.** thee a terror, and thou … 5414
Eze 27:5 cedars from Lebanon to **m.** masts … 6213
Eze 27:31 shall **m.** themselves utterly bald …
Eze 29:10 **m.** the land of Egypt utterly waste … 5414
Eze 29:12 will **m.** the land of Egypt desolate … 5414
Eze 30:9 **m.** the careless Ethiopians afraid, …
Eze 30:10 **m.** the multitude of Egypt to cease…
Eze 30:12 And I will **m.** the rivers dry, and…
Eze 30:12 and I will **m.** the land waste, and all…
Eze 30:14 And I will **m.** Pathros desolate, …
Eze 30:21 to **m.** it strong to hold the sword. …
Eze 32:7 and **m.** the stars thereof dark; I…
Eze 32:8 heaven will I **m.** dark over thee, …
Eze 32:10 **m.** many people amazed at thee, …
Eze 32:14 Then will I **m.** their waters deep, …
Eze 32:15 shall **m.** the land of Egypt desolate,… 5414
Eze 34:25 **m.** with them a covenant of peace, … 3772
Eze 34:26 will **m.** them and the places round… 5414
Eze 34:28 and none shall **m.** them afraid. …
Eze 35:3 and I will me thee most desolate. … 5414
Eze 35:7 will I **m.** mount Seir most desolate, … 5414
Eze 35:9 will **m.** thee perpetual desolations,… 5414
Eze 35:11 I will **m.** myself known among them, …
Eze 35:14 rejoiceth, I will **m.** thee desolate. … 6213
Eze 37:19 of Judah, and **m.** them one stick, … 6213
Eze 37:22 will **m.** them one nation in the land… 6213
Eze 37:26 I will **m.** a covenant of peace with… 3772
Eze 39:7 So will I **m.** my holy name known …
Eze 42:20 to **m.** a separation between the…
Eze 43:18 in the day when they shall **m.** it,… 6213
Eze 43:27 the priests shall **m.** yur burnt… 6213
Eze 44:14 I will **m.** them keepers of the charge …
Eze 45:15 to **m.** reconciliation for them, …
Eze 45:17 to **m.** reconciliation for the house of…
Da 1:10 shall ye **m.** me endanger my head …
Da 2:5,9 **m.** known unto me the dream,…
Da 2:25 will **m.** known unto the king the…
Da 2:26 able to **m.** known unto me the dream…
Da 2:30 shall **m.** known the interpretation …
Da 3:29 Therefore I **m.** a decree, that … 7761
Da 4:6 might **m.** known…the interpretation…
Da 4:7 not **m.** known…the interpretation…
Da 4:18 **m.** known unto me the interpretation: …
Da 4:25, 32 shall **m.** thee to eat grass as oxen,…
Da 5:8 nor **m.** known to the king the…
Da 5:15 **m.** known unto me the interpretation …
Da 5:16 thou canst **m.** interpretations, and …
Da 5:16 **m.** known to me the interpretation …
Da 5:17 **m.** known to him the interpretation. …
Da 6:7 statute, and to **m.** a firm decree, …
Da 6:25 I **m.** a decree, That in every… 7761
Da 8:16 **m.** this man to understand the vision. …
Da 8:19 **m.** thee know what shall be in the last …
Da 9:24 and to **m.** an end of sins, and to …
Da 9:24 to **m.** reconciliation for iniquity,…
Da 9:27 he shall **m.** it desolate, even until…
Da 10:14 **m.** thee understand what shall befall …
Da 11:6 of the north to **m.** an agreement: … 6213
Da 11:35 to purge, and to **m.** them white, …
Da 11:44 and utterly to **m.** away many…
Ho 2:3 and **m.** her as a wilderness, and … 7760
Ho 2:6 and **m.** a wall, that she shall not … 1443
Ho 2:12 and I will **m.** them a forest, and… 7760
Ho 2:18 day will I **m.** a covenant for them… 3772
Ho 2:18 and will **m.** them to lie down safely. …
Ho 5:2 are profound to **m.** slaughter, …
Ho 7:3 They **m.** the king glad with their…
Ho 10:11 I will **m.** Ephraim to ride; Judah shall…
Ho 11:8 how shall I **m.** thee as Admah?… 5414
Ho 12:1 **m.** a covenant with the Assyrians,… 3772
Ho 12:9 yet **m.** thee to dwell in tabernacles, …
Joe 2:19 no more **m.** you a reproach among… 5414
Am 6:10 **m.** mention of the name of the Lord. …

Am 8:4 even to m. the poor of the land to fail,
Am 8:10 I will m. it as the mourning of an 7760
Am 9:14 they shall also m. gardens, and 6213
Mic 1:6 I will m. Samaria as an heap of 7760
Mic 1:8 will m. a wailing like the dragons, 6213
Mic 1:16 M. thee bald, and poll thee for thy
Mic 2:12 they shall m. great noise by reason
Mic 3:5 the prophets that m. my people err,
Mic 4:4 none shall m. them afraid: for the
Mic 4:7 will m. her that halted a remnant, 7760
Mic 4:13 Zion: for I will m. thine horn iron, 7760
Mic 4:13 I will m. thy hoofs brass: and thou 7760
Mic 6:13 also will I m. thee sick in smiting
Mic 6:16 that I should m. thee a desolation, 5414
Na 1:8 will m. an utter end of the place 6213
Na 1:9 he will m. an utter end: affliction 6213
Na 1:14 I will m. thy grave; for thou art 7760
Na 2:1 m. thy loins strong, fortify thy
Na 2:5 shall m. haste to the wall thereof,
Na 3:6 filth upon thee, and m. thee vile,
Na 3:14 morter, m. strong the brickkiln.
Na 3:15 m. thyself many as the cankerworm,
Na 3:15 m. thyself many as the locusts.
Hab 2:2 and m. it plain upon the tables,
Hab 2:18 trusteth therein, to m. dumb idols? 6213
Hab 3:2 in the midst of the years m. known;
Hab 3:19 he will m. my feet like hinds' feet, 7760
Hab 3:19 he will m. me to walk upon mine high
Zep 1:18 he shall m. even a speedy riddance 6213
Zep 2:13 will m. Nineveh a desolation, and 7760
Zep 3:13 and none shall m. them afraid.
Zep 3:20 I will m. you a name and a praise 5414
Hag 2:23 will m. thee as a signet: for I have 7760
Zec 6:11 silver and gold, and m. crowns, 6213
Zec 9:15 and m. a noise as through wine;
Zec 9:17 shall m. the young men cheerful,
Zec 10:1 Lord shall m. bright clouds, and 6213
Zec 12:2 m. Jerusalem a cup of trembling 7760
Zec 12:3 m. Jerusalem a burdensome stone 7760
Zec 12:6 m. the governors of Judah like an 7760
Mal 2:15 And did not he m. one? Yet had he 6213
Mal 3:17 that day when I m. up my jewels; 6213
Mt 1:19 to m. her a publick example, was *3856*
Mt 3:3 of the Lord, m. his paths straight *4160*
Mt 4:19 and I will m. you fishers of men *4160*
Mt 5:36 canst not m. one hair white or *4160*
Mt 8:2 thou wilt, thou canst m. me clean. *2511*
Mt 12:16 they should not m. him known: *4160*
Mt 12:33 Either m. the tree good, and his *4160*
Mt 12:33 or else m. the tree corrupt, and *4160*
Mt 17:4 let us m. here three tabernacles; *4160*
Mt 22:44 I m. thine enemies thy footstool? *5087*
Mt 23:5 they m. broad their phylacteries, *4115*
Mt 23:14 and for a pretence m. long prayer: *4336*
Mt 23:15 sea and land to m. one proselyte, *4160*
Mt 23:15 m. him twofold more the child of *4160*
Mt 23:25 m. clean the outside of the cup *2511*
Mt 24:47 m. him ruler over all his goods. *2525*
Mt 25:21, 23 m. thee ruler over many things: *2525*
Mt 27:65 your way, m. it as sure as ye can. *805*
Mk 1:3 of the Lord, m. his paths straight *4160*
Mk 1:17 m. you to become fishers of men *4160*
Mk 1:40 thou wilt, thou canst m. me clean. *2511*
Mk 3:12 they should not m. him known *4160*
Mk 5:39 Why m. ye this ado, and weep? *2350*
Mk 6:39 m. all sit down by companies upon *347*
Mk 9:5 let us m. three tabernacles; one *4160*
Mk 12:36 I m. thine enemies thy footstool *5087*
Mk 12:40 for a pretence m. long prayers: *4336*
Mk 12:42 in two mites, which m. a farthing. *1510*
Mk 14:15 prepared: there m. ready for us *2090*
Lu 1:17 m. ready a people prepared for the *2090*
Lu 3:4 of the Lord, m. his paths straight. *4160*
Lu 5:12 thou wilt, thou canst m. me clean. *2511*
Lu 5:33 of John fast ofter, and m. prayers, *4160*
Lu 5:34 m. the children of the *4160*
Lu 9:14 M. them sit down by fifties in a *2625*
Lu 9:33 let us m. three tabernacles; one *4160*
Lu 9:52 Samaritans, to m. ready for him *2090*
Lu 11:39 ye Pharisees m. clean the outside *2511*
Lu 11:40 m. that which is within also? *4160*
Lu 12:37 and m. them to sit down to meat, *347*
Lu 12:42 whom his lord shall m. ruler over *2525*
Lu 12:44 that he will m. him ruler over all *2525*
Lu 14:18 one consent began to m. excuse. *3868*
Lu 14:31 to m. war against another king, *4820*
Lu 15:19 m. me as one of thy hired servants *4160*
Lu 15:29 I might m. merry with my friends: *2165*
Lu 15:32 was meet that we should m. merry, *2165*
Lu 16:9 M. to yourself friends of the *4160*
Lu 17:8 M. ready wherewith I may sup, *2090*
Lu 19:5 Zacchaeus, m. haste, and come *4692*
Lu 20:43 I m. thine enemies thy footstool *5087*
Lu 20:47 and for a shew m. long prayers: *4336*
Lu 22:12 room furnished: there m. ready. *2090*
Joh 1:23 M. straight the way of the Lord, *2116*
Joh 2:16 m. not my Father's house an *4160*
Joh 6:10 Jesus said, M. the men sit down. *4160*
Joh 6:15 take him by force, to m. him a king, *4160*
Joh 8:32 and the truth shall m. you free, *1659*
Joh 8:36 the Son therefore shall m. you *1659*
Joh 10:24 long dost thou m. us to doubt? *142*
Joh 14:23 him, and m. our abode with him *4160*
Ac 2:28 shalt m. me full of joy with thy *4137*
Ac 2:35 Until I m. thy foes thy footstool *5087*
Ac 7:40 Aaron, M. us gods to go before us: *4160*
Ac 7:44 m. it according to the fashion *4160*
Ac 9:34 thee whole: arise and m. thy bed. *4766*
Ac 22:1 my defence which I m. now unto you.
Ac 22:18 M. haste, and get thee quickly out *4692*
Ac 23:23 M. ready two hundred soldiers to *2090*
Ac 26:16 m. thee a minister and a witness *4400*
Ac 26:24 much learning doth m. thee mad. *4062*
Ro 1:9 m. mention of you always in my *4160*
Ro 3:3 m. the faith of God without effect? *2673*
Ro 3:31 then m. void the law through faith? *2673*
Ro 9:21 to m. one vessel unto honour, *4160*
Ro 9:22 wrath, and to m. his power known, *1107*
Ro 9:23 m. known the riches of his glory *1107*
Ro 9:28 short work will the Lord m. upon *4160*
Ro 13:14 and m. not provision for the flesh, *4160*
Ro 14:4 for God is able to m. him stand. *2476*
Ro 14:19 the things which m. for peace, *3753*
Ro 15:18 m. the Gentiles obedient, by word *1519*
Ro 15:26 to m. a certain contribution for the *4160*
1Co 4:5 will m. manifest the counsels of the *5319*
1Co 6:15 m. them the members of an harlot? *4160*
1Co 8:13 if meat m. my brother to offend, *4621*
1Co 8:13 lest I m. my brother to offend. *4621*
1Co 9:15 man should m. my glorying void. *2758*
1Co 9:18 m. the gospel of Christ without *5087*
1Co 10:13 temptation...m. a way to escape, *4160*
2Co 2:2 For if I m. you sorry, who is he *3076*
2Co 9:5 m. up beforehand your bounty, *4294*
2Co 9:8 God is able to m. all grace abound *4052*
2Co 10:12 dare not m. ourselves of the number,
2Co 12:17 Did I m. a gain of you by any of *4122*
2Co 12:18 Did Titus m. a gain of you? walked *4122*
Ga 2:18 I m. myself a transgressor. *4921*
Ga 3:17 m. the promise of none effect. *2673*
Ga 6:12 to m. a fair shew in the flesh, *2146*
Eph 2:15 to m. in himself of twain one new *2936*
Eph 3:9 to m. all men see...the fellowship *5461*
Eph 5:13 for whatsoever doth m. manifest *5319*
Eph 6:19 to m. known the mystery of the *1107*
Eph 6:21 shall m. known to you all things: *1107*
Col 1:27 m. known what is the riches of the *1107*
Col 4:4 That I may m. it manifest, as I *5319*
Col 4:9 m. known unto you all things *1107*
1Th 3:12 m. you to increase and abound in *4121*
2Th 3:9 to m. ourselves an ensample unto *1325*
2Ti 3:15 able to m. thee wise unto salvation *4679*
2Ti 4:5 m. full proof of thy ministry. *4135*
Heb 1:13 I m. thine enemies thy footstool? *5087*
Heb 2:10 m. the captain of...salvation perfect *5055*
Heb 2:17 to m. reconciliation for the sins of *2433*
Heb 7:25 he ever liveth to m. intercession *1793*
Heb 8:5 he was about to m. the tabernacle: *2005*
Heb 8:5 thou m. all things according to the *4160*
Heb 8:8 m. a new covenant with the house *4931*
Heb 8:10 this is the covenant that I will m. *1303*
Heb 9:9 m. him that did the service perfect, *5055*
Heb 10:1 m. the comers thereunto perfect. *5055*
Heb 10:16 This is the covenant that I will m. *1303*
Heb 12:13 m. straight paths for your feet, *4160*
Heb 13:21 M. you perfect in every good work *2675*
Jas 3:18 in peace of them that m. peace. *4160*
1Pe 5:10 m....perfect, stablish, strengthen, *2675*
2Pe 1:8 they m. you that ye shall neither *2525*
2Pe 1:10 m. your calling and election sure: *4160*
2Pe 2:3 words m. merchandise of you: *1710*
1Jo 1:10 have not sinned, we m. him a liar, *4160*
Re 3:9 I will m. them of the synagogue *1325*
Re 3:9 will m. them to come and worship *4160*
Re 3:12 will I m. a pillar in the temple of *4160*
Re 10:9 and it shall m. thy belly bitter, *4087*
Re 11:7 pit shall m. war against them, *4160*
Re 11:10 rejoice over them, and m. merry, *2165*
Re 12:17 went to m. war with the remnant *4160*
Re 13:4 who is able to m. war with him? *4170*
Re 13:7 to m. war with the saints, and to *4160*
Re 13:14 should m. an image to the beast, *4160*
Re 17:14 These shall m. war with the Lamb, *4170*
Re 17:16 shall m. her desolate and naked, *4160*
Re 19:11 he doth judge and m. war. *4170*
Re 19:19 to m. war against him that sat on *4160*
Re 21:5 said, Behold, I m. all things new. *4160*

MAKER See also MAKERS.
Job 4:17 a man be more pure than his m.? 6213
Job 32:22 my m. would soon take me away. 6213
Job 35:10 Where is God my m., who giveth 6213
Job 36:3 ascribe righteousness to my M.. 6466
Ps 95:6 us kneel before the Lord our M., 6213
Pr 14:31 the poor reproacheth his M. 6213
Pr 17:5 the poor reproacheth his M. 6213
Pr 22:2 the Lord is the m. of them all. 6213
Isa 1:31 tow, and the m. of it as a spark, 6467
Isa 17:7 day shall a man look to his M., 6213
Isa 22:11 not looked unto the m. thereof, 6213
Isa 45:9 him that striveth with his M.! 3335
Isa 45:11 the Holy One of Israel, and his M., 3335
Isa 51:13 And forgettest the Lord thy m., 6213
Isa 54:5 For thy M. is thine husband; The 6213
Jer 33:2 Thus saith the Lord the m. thereof, 6213
Ho 8:14 For Israel hath forgotten his M., 6213
Hab 2:18 the m. thereof hath graven it; 3335
Hab 2:18 the m. of his work trusteth therein, 3335
Heb 11:10 whose builder and m. is God. *1217*

MAKERS See also PEACEMAKERS; TENTMAKERS.
Isa 45:16 together that are m. of idols. 2796

MAKEST
Jg 18:3 and what m. thou in this place? 6213
Job 13:26 m. me to possess the iniquities of
Job 22:3 him, that thou m. thy ways perfect?
Ps 4:8 Lord, only m. me dwell in safety.
Ps 39:11 m. his beauty to consume away
Ps 44:10 Thou m. us to turn back from the
Ps 44:13 Thou m. us a reproach to our 6213
Ps 44:14 Thou m. us a byword among the 6213
Ps 65:8 thou m. the outgoings of...to rejoice
Ps 65:10 thou m. it soft with showers:
Ps 80:6 Thou m. us a strife unto our 7760
Ps 104:20 Thou m. darkness, and it is night: 7896
Ps 144:3 man, that thou m. account of him!
Ca 1:7 thou m. thy flock to rest at noon:
Isa 45:9 that fashioned it, What m. thou? 6213
Jer 22:23 that m. thy nest in the cedars,
Jer 28:15 thou m. this people to trust in a lie.
Eze 16:31 and m. thine high place in every 6213
Hab 1:14 And m. men as the fishes of the sea, 6213
Hab 2:15 to him, and m. him drunken also,
Lu 14:12 When thou m. a dinner or a *4160*
Lu 14:13 when thou m. a feast, call the *4160*
Joh 8:53 are dead: whom m. thou thyself? *4160*
Joh 10:33 thou, being a man, m. thyself God. *4160*
Ro 2:17 the law, and m. thy boast of God, *2744*
Ro 2:23 Thou that m. thy boast of the law, *2744*

MAKETH
Ex 4:11 who m. the dumb, or deaf, or the 7760
Le 7:7 the priest that m. atonement
Le 14:11 the priest that m. him clean shall
Le 17:11 blood that m. an atonement for the
De 18:10 m. his son or his daughter to pass
De 20:20 the city that m. war with thee, 6213
De 21:16 m. his sons to inherit that which
De 24:7 and m. merchandise of him, or
De 27:15 man that m. any graven or 6213
De 27:18 be he that m. the blind to wander out
De 29:12 the Lord thy God m. with thee this 3772
1Sa 2:6 The Lord killeth, and m. alive:
1Sa 2:7 The Lord m. poor, and m. rich:
2Sa 22:33 power: and he m. my way perfect.
2Sa 22:34 He m. my feet like hinds' feet; and 7737
Job 5:18 For he m. sore, and bindeth up: he
Job 9:9 Which m. Arcturus, Orion, and 6213
Job 12:17 spoiled, and m. the judges fools.

Job 12:25 m. them to stagger like a drunken
Job 15:27 m. collops of fat on his flanks. 6213
Job 23:16 For God m. my heart soft, and the
Job 25:2 he m. peace in his high places. 6213
Job 27:18 and as a booth that the keeper m. 6213
Job 35:11 and m. us wiser than the fowls of
Job 36:27 he m. small the drops of water:
Job 41:31 He m. the deep to boil like a pot: he
Job 41:31 m. the sea like a pot of ointment. 7760
Job 41:32 He m. a path to shine after him; one
Ps 9:12 When he m. inquisition for blood,
Ps 18:32 strength, and m. my way perfect. 5414
Ps 18:33 He m. my feet like hinds' feet, and 7737
Ps 23:2 He m. me to lie down in green
Ps 29:6 He m. them also to skip like a calf;
Ps 29:9 voice of the Lord m. the hinds to calve,
Ps 33:10 m. the devices of the people of none
Ps 40:4 man that m. the Lord his trust, 7760
Ps 46:9 He m. wars to cease unto the end
Ps 104:3 who m. the clouds his chariot: 7760
Ps 104:4 Who m. his angels spirits; his 6213
Ps 104:15 wine that m. glad the heart of
Ps 107:29 He m. the storm a calm, so that
Ps 107:36 there he m. the hungry to dwell,
Ps 107:41 and m. him families like a flock. 7760
Ps 113:9 He m. the barren woman to keep
Ps 135:7 he m. lightnings for the rain; 6213
Ps 147:8 who m. grass to grow upon the
Ps 147:14 He m. peace in thy borders, and 7760
Pr 10:1 A wise son m. a glad father: but a
Pr 10:4 the hand of the diligent m. rich.
Pr 10:22 The blessing of the Lord, it m. rich,
Pr 12:4 she that m. ashamed is as rottenness
Pr 12:25 in the heart of man m. it stoop:
Pr 12:25 but a good word m. it glad.
Pr 13:7 There is that m. himself rich, yet
Pr 13:7 there is that m. himself poor, yet
Pr 13:12 Hope deferred m. the heart sick:
Pr 15:13 A merry heart m. a cheerful
Pr 15:20 A wise son m. a glad father: but a
Pr 15:30 a good report m. the bones fat.
Pr 16:7 he m. even his enemies to be at peace
Pr 18:16 A man's gift m. room for him, and
Pr 19:4 Wealth m. many friends; but the
Pr 28:20 he that m. haste to be rich shall not
Pr 31:22 She m. herself coverings of 6213
Pr 31:24 She m. fine linen, and selleth it; 6213
Ec 3:11 can find out the work that God m. 6213
Ec 7:7 oppression m. a wise man mad;
Ec 8:1 man's wisdom m. his face to shine,
Ec 10:19 made for laughter, and wine m. merry:
Ec 11:5 not the works of God who m. all. 6213
Isa 19:17 every one that m. mention thereof
Isa 24:1 the Lord m. the earth empty,
Isa 24:1 and m. it waste, and turneth it upside
Isa 27:9 he m. all the stones of the altar 7760
Isa 40:23 he m. the judges of the earth as 6213
Isa 43:16 Lord, which m. a way in the sea, 5414
Isa 44:13 m. it after the figure of a man, 6213
Isa 44:15 he m. a god, and worshippeth it; 6466
Isa 44:15 he m. it a graven image, and 6213
Isa 44:17 the residue thereof he m. a god, 6213
Isa 44:24 I am the Lord that m. all things; 6213
Isa 44:25 of the liars, and m. diviners mad;
Isa 44:25 and m. their knowledge foolish;
Isa 46:6 a goldsmith; and he m. it a god: 6213
Isa 55:10 m. it bring forth and bud, that it
Isa 59:15 departeth from evil m. himself a prey:
Jer 4:19 my heart m. a noise in me;
Jer 10:13 he m. lightnings with rain, and 6213
Jer 17:5 trusteth in man, and m. flesh his arm,
Jer 21:2 king of Babylon m. war against us;
Jer 29:26 that is mad, and m. himself a prophet,
Jer 29:27 which m. himself a prophet to you?
Jer 48:28 dove that m. her nest in the sides
Jer 51:16 he m. lightnings with rain, and 6213
Eze 22:3 m. idols against herself to defile 6213
Da 2:28 and m. known to the king
Da 2:29 m. known to thee what shall come
Da 6:13 m. his petition three times a day
Da 11:31 the abomination that m. desolate.
Da 12:11 the abomination that m. desolate set
Am 4:13 that m. the morning darkness, 6213
Am 5:8 that m. the seven stars and Orion, 6213
Am 5:8 and m. the day dark with night:
Na 1:4 He rebuketh the sea, and m. it dry,
Mt 5:45 **for he m. his sun to rise on the evil** *393*
Mk 7:37 he m. both the deaf to hear, and *4160*
Lu 5:36 **then both the new m. a rent, and** *4977*
Joh 19:12 whosoever m. himself a king *4160*
Ac 9:34 Jesus Christ m. thee whole: *2390*
Ro 5:5 hope m. not ashamed; because *2617*
Ro 8:26 Spirit itself m. intercession for us *5241*
Ro 8:27 he m. intercession for the saints *1793*
Ro 8:34 who also m. intercession for us. *1793*
Ro 11:2 he m. intercession to God against *1793*
1Co 4:7 For who m. thee to differ from *1252*
2Co 2:2 who is he then that m. me glad, *2165*
2Co 2:14 and m. manifest the savour of his *5319*
Ga 2:6 they were, it m. no matter to me: *1308*
Eph 4:16 m. increase of the body unto the *4160*
Heb 1:7 Who m. his angels spirits, and his *4160*
Heb 7:28 law m. men high priests which *2525*
Heb 7:28 m. the Son, who is consecrated for
Re 13:13 he m. fire come down from heaven *4160*
Re 21:27 worketh abomination, or m. a lie:
Re 22:15 and whosoever loveth and m. a lie. *4160*

MAKHELOTH (mak'-he-loth)
Nu 33:25 from Haradah, and pitched in M. 4721
Nu 33:26 And they removed from M., and 4721

MAKING
Ex 5:14 not fulfilled your task in m. brick
De 20:19 time, in m. war against it to take it,
Jg 19:22 they were m. their hearts merry,
1Ki 4:20 and drinking, and m. merry.
1Ch 15:28 m. a noise with psalteries and
1Ch 17:19 m. known all these great things.
2Ch 30:22 m. confession to the Lord God of
Ps 19:7 Lord is sure, m. wise the simple.
Ec 12:12 m. many books there is no end; 6213
Isa 3:16 and m. a tinkling with their feet:
Jer 20:15 born unto thee; m. him very glad.
Eze 27:16 multitude of the wares of thy m.: 4639
Eze 27:18 multitude of the wares of thy m., 4639
Da 6:11 and m. supplication before his God.
Ho 10:4 swearing falsely in m. a covenant: 3772
Am 8:5 m. the ephah small, and the shekel
Mic 6:13 in m. thee desolate because of thy
Mt 9:23 and the people m. a noise, *2350*
Mk 7:13 **M. the word of God of none effect** *208*
Joh 5:18 Father, m. himself equal with God *4160*
Ro 1:10 M. request, if by any means now *1189*
2Co 6:10 as poor, yet m. many rich; as *4148*
Eph 1:16 m. mention of you in my prayers; *4160*
Eph 2:15 twain one new man, so m. peace; *4160*
Eph 5:19 and m. melody in your heart to the *5567*
Php 1:4 for you all m. request with joy, *4160*
1Th 1:2 m. mention of you in our prayers; *4160*
Phm 4 m. mention of thee always in my *4160*
2Pe 2:6 m. them an ensample unto those *4160*
Jude 22 have compassion, m. a difference: *1252*

MAKKEDAH (mak'-ke-dah)
Jos 10:10 them to Azekah, and unto M. 4719
Jos 10:16 and hid themselves in a cave at M. 4719
Jos 10:17 kings are found hid in a cave at M. 4719
Jos 10:21 the camp to Joshua at M. in peace: 4719
Jos 10:28 And that day Joshua took M., and 4719
Jos 10:28 he did to the king of M. as he did 4719
Jos 10:29 Then Joshua passed from M., and 4719
Jos 12:16 The king of M., one; the king of 4719
Jos 15:41 Beth-dagon, and Naamah, and M.; 4719

MAKTESH (mak'-tesh)
Zep 1:11 Howl, ye inhabitants of M., for all 4389

MALACHI (mal'-a-ki)
Mal *general* *title* M. 4401
Mal 1:1 word of the Lord to Israel by M. 4401

MALCHAM (mal'-kam) See also MILCOM.
1Ch 8:9 and Zibia, and Mesha, and M., 4445
Zep 1:5 the Lord, and that swear by M.; 4445

MALCHIAH (mal-ki'-ah) See also MALCHIJAH; MELCHIAH.
1Ch 6:40 son of Baaseiah, the son of M., 4441
Ezr 10:25 and Jeziah, and M., and Miamin, 4441
Ezr 10:31 Eliezer, Ishijah, M., Shemaiah, 4441
Ne 3:14 the dung gate repaired M. the son 4441
Ne 3:31 him repaired M. the goldsmith's 4441
Ne 8:4 Pedaiah, and Mishael, and M., 4441
Ne 11:12 the son of Pashur, the son of M., 4441
Jer 38:1 and Pashur the son of M., heard 4441
Jer 38:6 and cast him into the dungeon of M. 4441

MALCHIEL mal'-ke-el) See also MALCHIELITES.
Ge 46:17 sons of Beriah; Heber, and M. 4439
Nu 26:45 M., the family of the Malchielites. 4439
1Ch 7:31 sons of Beriah; Heber, and M., 4439

MALCHIELITES (mal'-ke-el-ites)
Nu 26:45 Malchiel, the family of the M. 4440

MALCHIJAH (mal-ki'-jah) See also MALCHIAH.
1Ch 9:12 the son of Pashur, the son of M., 4441
1Ch 24:9 The fifth to M., the sixth to 4441
Ezr 10:25 and Eleazar, and M., and Benaiah. 4441
Ne 3:11 M. the son of Harim, and Hashub 4441
Ne 10:3 Pashur, Amariah, M., 4441
Ne 12:42 Jehohanan, and M., and Elam, and 4441

MALCHIRAM (mal'-ki-ram)
1Ch 3:18 M. also, and Pedaiah, and 4443

MALCHI-SHUA (mal''-ki-shu'-ah) See also MELCHISHUA.
1Ch 8:33 Saul begat Jonathan, and M., 4444
1Ch 9:39 Saul begat Jonathan, and M., 4444
1Ch 10:2 and Abinadab, and M., the sons of 4444

MALCHUS (mal'-kus)
Joh 18:10 ear. The servant's name was M. *3124*

MALE See also MALES.
Ge 1:27 m. and female created he them. 2145
Ge 5:2 M. and female created he them; 2145
Ge 6:19 thee; they shall be m. and female. 2145
Ge 7:2 by sevens, the m. and his female: 376
Ge 7:2 clean by two, the m. and his female. 376
Ge 7:3 by sevens, the m. and the female; 2145
Ge 7:9 into the ark, the m. and the female, 2145
Ge 7:16 went in m. and female of all flesh, 2145
Ge 17:23 every m. among the men of 2145
Ge 34:15 every m. of you be circumcised; 2145
Ge 34:22 every m. among us be circumcised, 2145
Ge 34:24 and every m. was circumcised, all 2145
Ex 12:5 blemish, a m. of the first year: 2145
Ex 34:19 whether ox or sheep, that is m. 2142
Le 1:3 him offer a m. without blemish: 2145
Le 1:10 shall bring it a m. without blemish. 2145
Le 3:1 whether it be a m. or a female, he 2145
Le 3:6 Lord be of the flock; m. or female, 2145
Le 4:23 the goats, a m. without blemish: 2145
Le 7:6 Every m. among the priests shall 2145
Le 12:7 her that hath born a m. or a female. 2145
Le 22:19 own will a m. without blemish, 2145
Le 27:3 of the m. from twenty years old 2145
Le 27:5 shall be of the m. twenty shekels, 2145
Le 27:6 be of the m. five shekels of silver, 2145
Le 27:7 if it be a m., then thy estimation 2145
Nu 1:2 names, every m. by their polls; 2145
Nu 1:20, 22 every m. from twenty years old 2145
Nu 3:15 every m. from a month old and 2145
Nu 5:3 Both m. and female shall be put 2145
Nu 18:10 every m. shall eat it: it shall be 2145
Nu 31:17 kill every m. among the little ones, 2145
De 4:16 figure, the likeness of m. or female, 2145
De 7:14 be m. or female barren among you,
De 20:13 shalt smite every m. thereof with 2138
Jos 17:2 m. children of Manasseh the son 2145
Jg 21:11 Ye shall utterly destroy every m., 2145
Jg 21:12 no man by lying with any m.: 2145
1Ki 11:15 he had smitten every m. in Edom; 2145
1Ki 11:16 he had cut off every m. in Edom:) 2145
Mal 1:14 which hath in his flock a m., and 2145
Mt 19:4 **made them m. and female,** *730*
Mk 10:6 **God made them m. and female.** *730*
Lu 2:23 Every m. that openeth the womb *730*
Ga 3:28 free, there is neither m. nor female: *730*

MALEFACTOR See also MALEFACTORS.
Joh 18:30 If he were not a m., we would not *2555*

MALEFACTORS
Lu 23:32 m., led with him to be put to death. *2557*
Lu 23:33 they crucified him, and the m., *2557*
Lu 23:39 one of the m. which were hanged *2557*

MALELEEL (mal'-e-le-el) See also MAHALALEEL.
Lu 3:37 which was the son of M., which *3121*

MALES
Ge 34:25 the city boldly, and slew all the m. 2145
Ex 12:48 let all his m. be circumcised, and 2145
Ex 13:12 hast; the m. shall be the Lord's. 2145
Ex 13:15 that openeth the matrix, being m.; 2145
Ex 23:17 all thy m. shall appear before the 2138

Le 6:18 All the **m.** among the children of........ 2145
Le 6:29 the **m.** among the priests shall eat...... 2145
Nu 3:22 to the number of all the **m.**, from a.... 2145
Nu 3:22 In the number of all the **m.**, from a.... 2145
Nu 3:34 to the number of all the **m.**, from a.... 2145
Nu 3:39 **m.** from a month old and upward, ... 2145
Nu 3:40 Number all the firstborn of the **m.**...... 2145
Nu 3:43 the firstborn **m.** by the number of...... 2145
Nu 26:62 **m.** from a month old and upward: 2145
Nu 31:7 Moses; and they slew all the **m.**........ 2145
De 15:19 firstling **m.** that come of thy herd....... 2145
De 16:16 all thy **m.** appear before the Lord....... 2138
Jos 5:4 came out of Egypt, that were **m.**, ... 2145
2Ch 31:16 Beside their genealogy of **m.**, from..... 2145
2Ch 31:19 to give portions to all the **m.** among... 2145
Ezr 8:3 reckoned by genealogy of the **m.** an.... 2145
Ezr 8:4 and with him two hundred **m.**.......... 2145
Ezr 8:5 and with him three hundred **m.**.......... 2145
Ezr 8:6 of Jonathan, and with him fifty **m.**........ 2145
Ezr 8:7 Athaliah, and with him seventy **m.**...... 2145
Ezr 8:8 Michael, and with him fourscore **m.**..... 2145
Ezr 8:9 him two hundred and eighteen **m.**....... 2145
Ezr 8:10 him an hundred and threescore **m.**...... 2145
Ezr 8:11 and with him twenty and eight **m.**...... 2145
Ezr 8:12 with him an hundred and ten **m.**........ 2145
Ezr 8:13 and with him threescore **m.**............. 2145
Ezr 8:14 Zabbud, and with him seventy **m.**........ 2145

MALICE
1Co 5:8 the leaven of **m.** and wickedness;....... *2549*
1Co 14:20 howbeit in **m.** be ye children, but in... *2549*
Eph 4:31 be put away from you, with all **m.**:...... *2549*
Col 3:8 anger, wrath, **m.**, blasphemy,............ *2549*
Tit 3:3 living in **m.** and envy, hateful, and...... *2549*
1Pe 2:1 laying aside all **m.**, and all guile,......... *2549*

MALICIOUS
3Jo 10 prating against us with **m.** words:....... *4190*

MALICIOUSNESS
Ro 1:29 wickedness, covetousness, **m.**;.......... *2549*
1Pe 2:16 using your liberty for a cloke of **m.**,..... *2549*

MALIGNITY
Ro 1:29 envy, murder, debate, deceit, **m.**;...... *2550*

MALLOTHI (mal'-lo-thi)
1Ch 25:4 Romamti-ezer, Joshbekashah, **M.**, ... 4413
1Ch 25:26 The nineteenth to **M.**, he, his sons,.... 4413

MALLOWS
Job 30:4 Who cut up **m.** by the bushes, ... 4408

MALLUCH (mal'-luk) See also MELICU.
1Ch 6:44 the so of Abdi, the son of **M.**,.......... 4409
Ezr 10:29 the sons of Bani; Meshullam, **M.**,....... 4409
Ezr 10:32 Benjamin, **M.**, and Shemariah, ... 4409
Ne 10:4 Hattush, Shebaniah, **M.**,.................. 4409
Ne 10:27 **M.**, Harim, Baanah........................ 4409
Ne 12:2 Amariah, **M.**, Hattush, ... 4409

MAMMON (mam'-mon)
Mt 6:24 **Ye cannot serve God and m.**......... *3126*
Lu 16:9 **of the m. of unrighteousness;**........ *3126*
Lu 16:11 **faithful in the unrighteous m.**,...... *3126*
Lu 16:13 **Ye cannot serve God and m.**......... *3126*

MAMRE (mam'-re)
Ge 13:18 came and dwelt in the plain of **M.**, ... 4471
Ge 14:13 in the plain of **M.** the Amorite, ... 4471
Ge 14:24 with me, Aner, Eshcol, and **M.**;.......... 4471
Ge 18:1 unto him in the plains of **M.**:............. 4471
Ge 23:17 Machpelah, which was before **M.**, ... 4471
Ge 23:19 of the field of Machpelah before **M.**:... 4471
Ge 25:9 the Hittite, which is before **M.**; 4471
Ge 35:27 came unto Isaac his father unto **M.**,.... 4471
Ge 49:30 Machpelah, which is before **M.**, ... 4471
Ge 50:13 of Ephron the Hittite, before **M.**........ 4471

MAN See also BONDMAN; CRAFTSMAN; DAYSMAN; FREEMAN; HARVESTMAN; HERDMAN; HORSEMAN; HUSBANDMAN; KINSMAN; MAN'S; MANSERVANT; MANSLAYER; MANKIND; MEN; NOBLEMAN; PLOWMAN; SPOKESMAN; WATCHMAN; WOMAN; WORKMAN.
Ge 1:26 said, Let us make **m.** in our image,...... 120
Ge 1:27 So God created **m.** in his own image,... 120
Ge 2:5 there was not a **m.** to till the ground.... 120
Ge 2:7 Lord God formed **m.** of the dust of...... 120
Ge 2:7 of life; and **m.** became a living soul. ... 120
Ge 2:8 he put the **m.** whom he had formed. 120
Ge 2:15 the Lord God took the **m.**, and put...... 120
Ge 2:16 the Lord God commanded the **m.**, ... 120
Ge 2:18 good that the **m.** should be alone;........ 120
Ge 2:22 the Lord God had taken from **m.**,........ 120
Ge 2:22 woman, and brought her unto the **m.**.... 120
Ge 2:23 because she was taken out of **M.**......... 376
Ge 2:24 shall a **m.** leave his father and his........ 376
Ge 2:25 both naked, the **m.** and his wife, ... 120
Ge 3:12 the **m.** said, The woman whom thou 120
Ge 3:22 **m.** is become as one of us, to know..... 120
Ge 3:24 So he drove out the **m.**; and he 120
Ge 4:1 I have gotten a **m.** from the Lord......... 376
Ge 4:23 I have slain a **m.** to my wounding, ... 376
Ge 4:23 and a young **m.** to my hurt. ....
Ge 5:1 In the day that God created **m.**, in....... 120
Ge 6:3 shall not always strive with **m.**,.......... 120
Ge 6:5 that the wickedness of **m.** was great, ... 120
Ge 6:6 repented the Lord...he had made **m.**.... 120
Ge 6:7 will destroy **m.** whom I have created.... 120
Ge 6:7 both **m.**, and beast, and the creeping.... 120
Ge 6:9 Noah was a just **m.** and perfect in 376
Ge 7:21 upon the earth, and every **m.**: 120
Ge 7:23 both **m.**, and cattle, and the creeping ... 120
Ge 9:5 I require it, and at the hand of **m.**; 120
Ge 9:5 brother will I require the life of **m.**. 120
Ge 9:6 blood, by **m.** shall his blood be shed:.... 120
Ge 9:6 for in the image of God made he **m.**..... 120
Ge 13:16 if a **m.** can number the dust of the....... 376
Ge 16:12 And he will be a wild **m.**; his hand...... 120
Ge 16:12 his hand will be against every **m.**, and.......
Ge 17:10 Every **m.** child among you shall 2145
Ge 17:12 every **m.** child in your generations,..... 2145
Ge 17:14 the uncircumcised **m.** child whose......... 2145
Ge 18:7 good, and gave it unto a young **m.**; ....
Ge 19:8 which have not known **m.**; 376
Ge 19:9 And they pressed sore upon the **m.**, ... 376
Ge 19:31 not a **m.** in the earth to come in unto... 376
Ge 20:3 thou art but a dead **m.**,...........................
Ge 20:7 therefore restore the **m.** his wife;......... 376
Ge 24:16 neither had any **m.** known her: 376
Ge 24:21 **m.** wondering at her held his peace,..... 376
Ge 24:22 the **m.** took a golden earring of half..... 376
Ge 24:26 And the **m.** bowed down his head,........ 376
Ge 24:29 and Laban ran out unto the **m.**, unto.... 376
Ge 24:30 saying, Thus spake the **m.** unto me; 376
Ge 24:30 that he came unto the **m.**; and,........... 376
Ge 24:32 And the **m.** came into the house:......... 376
Ge 24:58 unto her, Wilt thou go with this **m.**?..... 376
Ge 24:61 the camels, and followed the **m.**: 376
Ge 24:65 **m.** is this that walketh in the field....... 376
Ge 25:8 old age, an old **m.**, and full of years;.........
Ge 25:27 a cunning hunter, a **m.** of the field; 376
Ge 25:27 and Jacob was a plain **m.**, dwelling....... 376
Ge 26:11 He that toucheth this **m.** or his wife..... 376
Ge 26:13 **m.** waxed great, and went forward,....... 376
Ge 27:11 is a hairy **m.**, and I am a smooth **m.**:... 376
Ge 29:19 that I should give her to another **m.**:.... 376
Ge 30:43 And the **m.** increased exceedingly,........ 376
Ge 31:50 my daughters, no **m.** is with us;.......... 376
Ge 32:24 there wrestled a **m.** with him until........ 376
Ge 34:19 the young **m.** deferred not to do the.........
Ge 34:25 brethren, took each **m.** his sword, ... 376
Ge 37:15 And a certain **m.** found him, and,......... 376
Ge 37:15 and the **m.** asked him, saying, What..... 376
Ge 37:17 And the **m.** said, They are departed...... 376
Ge 38:25 By the **m.**, whose these are, am I....... 376
Ge 39:2 Joseph, and he was a prosperous **m.**; ... 376
Ge 40:5 them, each **m.** his dream in one night,.. 376
Ge 40:5 **m.** according to the interpretation........ 376
Ge 41:11 **m.** according to the interpretation........ 376
Ge 41:12 there was there with us a young **m.**,..... 376
Ge 41:12 each **m.** according to his dream he....... 376
Ge 41:33 look out a **m.** discreet and wise,.......... 376
Ge 41:38 a **m.** in whom the Spirit of God is? 376
Ge 41:44 shall no **m.** lift up his hand or foot in.... 376
Ge 42:13 twelve brethren, the sons of one **m.** 376
Ge 42:30 The **m.**, who is the lord of the land, ... 376
Ge 42:33 the **m.**, the lord of the country, said 376
Ge 43:3 The **m.** did solemnly protest unto us, ... 376
Ge 43:5 the **m.** said unto us, Ye shall not see 376
Ge 43:6 as to tell the **m.** whether ye had yet a.. 376
Ge 43:7 **m.** asked us straitly of our state,......... 376
Ge 43:11 carry down the **m.** a present, a little.... 376
Ge 43:13 and arise, go again unto the **m.**:.......... 376
Ge 43:14 God...give you mercy before the **m.**,.... 376
Ge 43:17 And the **m.** did as Joseph bade;........... 376
Ge 43:17, 24 **m.** brought the men into Joseph's.... 376
Ge 43:27 well, the old **m.** of whom ye spake? ....
Ge 44:11 took down every **m.** his sack to the..... 376
Ge 44:11 and opened every **m.** his sack............ 376
Ge 44:13 clothes, and laded every **m.** his ass,..... 376
Ge 44:15 such a **m.** as I can certainly divine?...... 376
Ge 44:17 but the **m.** in whose hand the cup is 376
Ge 44:20 We have a father, an old **m.**, and a...... 376
Ge 45:1 Cause every **m.** to go out from me...... 376
Ge 45:1 there stood no **m.** with him, while 376
Ge 45:22 he gave each **m.** changes of raiment;.... 376
Ge 47:20 Egyptians sold every **m.** his field, ... 376
Ge 49:6 for in their anger they slew a **m.**,........ 376
Ex 1:1 every **m.** and his household came........ 376
Ex 2:1 there went a **m.** of the house of Levi, .. 376
Ex 2:12 when he saw that there was no **m.**, ... 376
Ex 2:20 why is it that ye have left the **m.**? 376
Ex 2:21 was content to dwell with the **m.**:........ 376
Ex 7:12 For they cast down every **m.** his rod, .. 376
Ex 8:17 it became lice in **m.**, and in beast; 120
Ex 8:18 were lice upon **m.**, and upon beast....... 120
Ex 9:9, 10 forth with blains upon **m.**, and 120
Ex 9:19 for upon every **m.** and beast which...... 120
Ex 9:22 hail in all the land of Egypt, upon **m.**,... 120
Ex 9:25 was in the field, both **m.** and beast; 120
Ex 10:7 long shall this **m.** be a snare unto us? ....
Ex 11:2 every **m.** borrow of his neighbour,....... 376
Ex 11:3 **m.** Moses was very great in the land 376
Ex 11:7 a dog move his tongue, against **m.** or... 376
Ex 12:3 shall take to them every **m.** a lamb,..... 376
Ex 12:4 **m.** according to his eating shall 376
Ex 12:12 firstborn...both **m.** and beast; 120
Ex 12:16 save that which every **m.** must eat,.... 5315
Ex 13:2 both of **m.** and of beast: it is mine....... 120
Ex 13:13 firstborn of **m.** among thy children........ 120
Ex 13:15 of Egypt, both the firstborn of **m.**,......... 120
Ex 15:3 The Lord is a **m.** of war: the Lord 376
Ex 16:16 it every **m.** according to his eating,...... 376
Ex 16:16 an omer for every **m.**, according........ 1538
Ex 16:16 take ye every **m.** for them which are ... 376
Ex 16:18 every **m.** according to his eating.......... 376
Ex 16:19 no **m.** leave of it till the morning. 376
Ex 16:21 every **m.** according to his eating:......... 376
Ex 16:22 much bread, two omers for one **m.**: ....
Ex 16:29 **m.** in his place, let no **m.** go out of 376
Ex 19:13 whether it be beast or **m.**, it shall 376
Ex 21:7 And if a **m.** sell his daughter to be a.... 376
Ex 21:12 He that smiteth a **m.**, so that he die, ... 376
Ex 21:13 And if a **m.** lie not in wait, but God..........
Ex 21:14 a **m.** come presumptuously upon his..... 376
Ex 21:16 he that stealeth a **m.**, and selleth......... 376
Ex 21:20 And if a **m.** smite his servant, or his.... 376
Ex 21:26 if a **m.** smite the eye of his servant, ... 376
Ex 21:28 If an ox gore a **m.** or a woman, that 376
Ex 21:29 that he hath killed a **m.** or a woman; 376
Ex 21:33 And if a **m.** shall open a pit, or if......... 376
Ex 21:33 a **m.** shall dig a pit, and not cover it,.... 376
Ex 22:1 If a **m.** shall steal an ox, or a sheep, ... 376
Ex 22:5 If a **m.** shall cause a field or 376
Ex 22:7 If a **m.**...deliver unto his neighbour 376
Ex 22:10 If a **m.** deliver unto his neighbour........ 376
Ex 22:10 hurt, or driven away, no **m.** seeing it:.......
Ex 22:14 And if a **m.** borrow ought of his 376
Ex 22:16 And if a **m.** entice a maid that is not 376
Ex 23:3 shalt thou countenance a poor **m.** in..........
Ex 24:14 if any **m.** have any matters to do, ... 1167
Ex 25:2 of every **m.** that giveth it willingly 376
Ex 30:12 give every **m.** a ransom for his soul..... 376
Ex 32:1, 23 the **m.** that brought us up out of...... 376
Ex 32:27 Put every **m.** his sword by his side,..... 376
Ex 32:27 camp, and slay every **m.** his brother, ... 376
Ex 32:27 and every **m.** his companion, ... 376
Ex 32:27 and every **m.** his neighbour. 376
Ex 32:29 every **m.** upon his son, and upon his.... 376
Ex 33:4 no **m.** did put on him his ornaments..... 376
Ex 33:8 stood every **m.** at his tent door, and.... 376
Ex 33:10 worshipped, every **m.** in his tent door. ..376
Ex 33:11 as a **m.** speaketh unto his friend.......... 376
Ex 33:11 the son of Nun, a young **m.**, departed.......
Ex 33:20 face: for there shall no **m.** see me, ... 120
Ex 34:3 And no **m.** shall come up with thee,..... 376
Ex 34:3 neither let...**m.** be seen throughout...... 376
Ex 34:24 neither shall any **m.** desire thy land,..... 376
Ex 35:22 every **m.** that offered offered an.......... 376
Ex 35:23, 24 every **m.**, with whom was found 376
Ex 35:29 every **m.** and woman, whose heart 376
Ex 36:1 every wise hearted **m.**, in whom the.... 376

Ex 36:2 and every wise hearted **m.**, in whose ... 376
Ex 36:4 came every **m.** from his work which..... 376
Ex 36:6 Let neither **m.** nor woman make any.... 376
Ex 36:8 every wise hearted **m.** among them.........
Ex 38:26 A bekah for every **m.**, that is, half..... 1538
Le 1:2 **m.** of you bring an offering unto......... 120
Le 5:3 Or if he touch the uncleanness of **m.**,... 120
Le 5:3 be that a **m.** shall be defiled withal, ...
Le 5:4 a **m.** shall pronounce with an oath,....... 120
Le 6:3 of all these that a **m.** doeth, sinning..... 120
Le 7:21 as the uncleanness of **m.**, or any......... 120
Le 12:2 conceived seed...born a **m.** child: 2145
Le 13:2 a **m.** shall have in the skin of his......... 120
Le 13:9 the plague of leprosy is in a **m.**, then ... 120
Le 13:29 If a **m.** or woman have a plague......... 376
Le 13:38 If a **m.** also or a woman have in the..... 376
Le 13:40 **m.** whose hair is fallen off his head, ... 376
Le 13:44 He is a leprous **m.**, he is unclean: 376
Le 14:11 present the **m.** that is to be clean,....... 376
Le 15:2 When any **m.** hath a running issue 376
Le 15:18 The woman also with whom **m.** shall..... 376
Le 15:24 if any **m.** lie with her at all, and her..... 376
Le 15:33 of the **m.**, and of the woman, and 2145
Le 16:17 shall be no **m.** in the tabernacle of....... 120
Le 16:21 away by the hand of a fit **m.** in the...... 376
Le 17:3 What **m.** soever there be of the house.. 376
Le 17:4 shall be imputed unto that **m.**; he 376
Le 17:4 that **m.** shall be cut off from among...... 376
Le 17:8 Whatsoever **m.** there be of the house... 376
Le 17:9 even that **m.** shall be cut off from........ 376
Le 17:10 whatsoever **m.** there be of the house ... 376
Le 17:13 And whatsoever **m.** there be of the....... 376
Le 18:5 which if a **m.** do, he shall live in.......... 120
Le 19:3 Ye shall fear every **m.** his mother,....... 376
Le 19:32 honour the face of the old **m.**, and...........
Le 20:3 I will set my face against that **m.**,......... 376
Le 20:4 ways hide their eyes from the **m.**,......... 376
Le 20:5 I will set my face against that **m.**,......... 376
Le 20:10 **m.** that committeth adultery with......... 376
Le 20:11 **m.** that lieth with his father's wife........ 376
Le 20:12 if a **m.** lie with his daughter in law,...... 376
Le 20:13 If a **m.** also lie with mankind, as he....... 376
Le 20:14 if a **m.** take a wife and her mother,....... 376
Le 20:15 And if a **m.** lie with a beast, he shall.... 376
Le 20:17 And if a **m.** shall take his sister, his..... 376
Le 20:18 if a **m.** shall lie with a woman having..... 376
Le 20:20 if am **m.** shall lie with his uncle's wife,.. 376
Le 20:21 if a **m.** shall take his brother's wife, ... 376
Le 20:27 A **m.** also or woman that hath a.......... 376
Le 21:4 being a chief **m.** among his people,..... 1167
Le 21:18 **m.** he be that hath a blemish, he......... 376
Le 21:18 a blind **m.**, or a lame, or he that hath... 376
Le 21:19 Or a **m.** that is brokenfooted, or 376
Le 21:21 No **m.** that hath a blemish of the......... 376
Le 22:4 What **m.** soever of the seed of Aaron... 376
Le 22:4 or a **m.** whose seed goeth from him:.... 376
Le 22:5 or a **m.** of whom he may take............ 120
Le 22:14 And if a **m.** eat of the holy thing.......... 376
Le 24:10 a **m.** of Israel strove together in the 376
Le 24:7 And he that killeth any **m.** shall.... 5315,120
Le 24:19 **m.** cause a blemish in his................... 376
Le 24:20 he hath caused a blemish in a **m.**,......... 120
Le 24:21 he that killeth a **m.**, he shall be put...... 120
Le 25:10 return every **m.** unto his possession,..... 376
Le 25:10 return every **m.** unto his family:.......... 376
Le 25:13 return every **m.** unto his possession..... 376
Le 25:26 And if the **m.** have none to redeem it,.. 376
Le 25:27 restore the overplus unto the **m.** to..... 376
Le 25:29 And if a **m.** sell a dwelling house in a... 376
Le 25:33 And if a **m.** purchase of the Levites,.........
Le 27:2 a **m.** shall make a singular vow, the..... 376
Le 27:9 all that any **m.** giveth of such unto...........
Le 27:14 when a **m.** shall sanctify his house....... 376
Le 27:16 if a **m.** shall sanctify unto the Lord....... 376
Le 27:20 he have sold the field to another **m.**,.... 376
Le 27:22 And if a **m.** sanctify unto the Lord a..... 376
Le 27:26 firstling, no **m.** shall sanctify it; 376
Le 27:28 that **m.** shall devote unto the Lord....... 376
Le 27:28 that he hath, both of **m.** and beast,...... 120
Le 27:31 **m.** will at all redeem ought of his 376
Nu 1:4 there shall be a **m.** of every tribe; 376
Nu 1:52 tents, every **m.** by his own camp, ... 376
Nu 1:52 and every **m.** by his own standard, ... 376
Nu 2:2 Every **m.** of the children of Israel........ 376
Nu 2:17 **m.** in his place by their standards. 376
Nu 3:13 in Israel, both **m.** and beast:............... 120
Nu 5:6 **m.** or woman shall commit any sin...... 376
Nu 5:8 But if the **m.** have no kinsman to 376
Nu 5:10 whatsoever any **m.** giveth the priest,.... 376
Nu 5:13 a **m.** lie with her carnally, and it be...... 376
Nu 5:15 the **m.** bring his wife unto the priest,... 376
Nu 5:19 if no **m.** have lain with thee, and if....... 376
Nu 5:20 some **m.** have lain with thee beside...... 376
Nu 5:31 the **m.** be guiltless from iniquity, ... 376
Nu 6:2 either **m.** or woman shall separate 376
Nu 6:9 if any **m.** die very suddenly by him,..........
Nu 7:5 every **m.** according to his service. 376
Nu 8:17 Israel are mine, both **m.** and beast:...... 120
Nu 9:6 defiled by the dead body of a **m.**, ... 120
Nu 9:7 are defiled by the dead body of a **m.**:... 120
Nu 9:10 if any **m.** of you or of your posterity 376
Nu 9:13 But the **m.** that is clean, and is not...... 376
Nu 9:13 season, that **m.** shall bear his sin......... 376
Nu 11:10 every **m.** in the door of his tent: 376
Nu 11:27 there ran a young **m.**, and told Moses,......
Nu 12:3 the **m.** Moses was very meek, above ... 376
Nu 13:2 of their fathers shall ye send a **m.**, ... 376
Nu 14:15 shalt kill all this people as one **m.**,....... 376
Nu 15:32 a **m.** that gathered sticks upon the......... 376
Nu 15:35 The **m.** shall be surely put to death: 376
Nu 16:7 the **m.** whom the Lord doth choose, ... 376
Nu 16:17 take every **m.** his censer, and put 376
Nu 16:17 before the Lord every **m.** his censer, ... 376
Nu 16:18 they took every **m.** his censer, and....... 376
Nu 16:22 shall one **m.** sin, and wilt thou be........ 376
Nu 17:9 looked, and took every **m.** his rod. 376
Nu 18:15 firstborn of **m.** shalt thou surely 120
Nu 19:9 a **m.** that is clean shall gather up the.... 376
Nu 19:11 the dead body of any **m.** shall be......... 120
Nu 19:13 dead body of any **m.** that is dead,........ 120
Nu 19:14 the law, when a **m.** dieth in a tent:...... 120
Nu 19:16 or a dead body, or a bone of a **m.**,...... 120
Nu 19:20 But the **m.** that shall be unclean, ... 376
Nu 21:9 if a serpent had bitten any **m.**,............ 376
Nu 23:19 God is not a **m.**, that he should lie;...... 376
Nu 23:19 neither the son of **m.**, that he should.... 120
Nu 24:3, 15 the **m.** whose eyes are open hath.. 1397
Nu 25:8 he went after the **m.** of Israel into....... 376
Nu 25:8 the **m.** of Israel, and the woman.......... 376
Nu 26:64 there was not a **m.** of them whom....... 376
Nu 26:65 there was not left a **m.** of them, save... 376
Nu 27:8 If a **m.** die, and have no son, then ye... 376
Nu 27:16 flesh, set a **m.** over the congregation, .. 376
Nu 27:18 a **m.** in whom is the spirit, and lay....... 376
Nu 30:2 If a **m.** vow a vow unto the Lord, or.... 376
Nu 30:16 Moses, between a **m.** and his wife,....... 376
Nu 31:17 hath known **m.** by lying with........ 376,2145
Nu 31:18 not known a **m.** by lying with him,.376,2145
Nu 31:26 was taken, both of **m.** and of beast, ... 120
Nu 31:35 not known **m.** by lying with him......... 2145
Nu 31:47 both of **m.** and of beast, and gave........ 120
Nu 31:49 and there lacketh not one **m.** of us. 376
Nu 31:50 what every **m.** hath gotten, of jewels ... 376
Nu 31:53 taken spoil, every **m.** for himself.)....... 376
Nu 32:18 inherited every **m.** his inheritance........ 376
Nu 32:27 pass over, every **m.** armed for war, ...
Nu 32:29 every **m.** armed to battle, before the ....
Nu 35:23 any stone, wherewith a **m.** may die, ...
Nu 36:8 enjoy every **m.** the inheritance of his.... 376
De 1:16 between every **m.** and his brother, ... 376
De 1:17 shall not be afraid of the face of **m.**;..... 376
De 1:31 as a **m.** doth bear his son, in all the..... 376
De 1:41 had girded on every **m.** his weapons 376
De 3:11 breadth of it, after the cubit of a **m.**..... 376
De 3:20 return every **m.** unto his possession,.... 376
De 4:32 the day that God created **m.** upon 120
De 5:24 that God doth talk with **m.**, and he 120
De 7:24 shall no **m.** be able to stand before 375
De 8:3 **m.** doth not live by bread only, but...... 120
De 8:3 the mouth of the Lord doth **m.** live...... 120
De 8:5 as a **m.** chasteneth his son, so the....... 376
De 11:25 shall no **m.** be able to stand before 376
De 12:8 every **m.** whatsoever is right in his...... 376
De 15:7 If there be among you a poor **m.** ....
De 15:12 if thy brother, an Hebrew **m.**, or an ....
De 16:17 Every **m.** shall give as he is able, ... 376
De 17:2 **m.** or woman, that hath wrought 376
De 17:5 bring forth that **m.** or that woman,....... 376
De 17:5 even that **m.** or that woman, and......... 376
De 17:12 the **m.** that will do presumptuously, ... 376
De 17:12 the judge, even that **m.** shall die: 376
De 19:5 As when a **m.** goeth into the wood with ....
De 19:11 But if any **m.** hate his neighbour,......... 376
De 19:15 rise up against a **m.** for any iniquity, ... 376
De 19:16 false witness rise up against any **m.** 376
De 20:5 What **m.** is there that hath built a........ 376
De 20:5 battle, and another **m.** dedicate it. 376
De 20:6 what **m.** is he that hath planted a 376
De 20:6 the battle, and another **m.** eat of it. 376
De 20:7 what **m.** is there that hath betrothed.... 376
De 20:7 the battle, and another **m.** take her...... 376
De 20:8 What **m.** is there that is fearful and...... 376
De 21:3 city which is next unto the slain **m.**,...... 376
De 21:6 city, that are next unto the slain **m.**,.........
De 21:15 If a **m.** have two wives, one beloved,... 376
De 21:18 **m.** have a stubborn and rebellious........ 376
De 21:22 If a **m.** have committed a sin worthy.... 376
De 22:5 that which pertaineth unto a **m.**, ... 1397
De 22:5 a **m.** put on a woman's garment:........ 1397
De 22:8 house, if any **m.** fall from thence...........
De 22:13 If any **m.** take a wife, and go in unto.... 376
De 22:16 my daughter unto this **m.** to wife,........ 376
De 22:18 shall take that **m.** and chastise him;...... 376
De 22:22 If a **m.** be found lying with a woman 376
De 22:22 the **m.** that lay with the woman, and.... 376
De 22:23 **m.** find her in the city, and lie with..... 376
De 22:24 the **m.**, because he hath humbled his.... 376
De 22:25 a **m.** find a betrothed damsel in the...... 376
De 22:25 the **m.** force her, and lie with her:....... 376
De 22:25 **m.** only that lay with her shall die:....... 376
De 22:26 a **m.** riseth against his neighbour, ... 376
De 22:28 a **m.** find a damsel that is a virgin,...... 376
De 22:29 **m.** that lay with her shall give unto...... 376
De 22:30 A **m.** shall not take his father's wife, ... 376
De 23:10 among you any **m.**, that is not clean..... 376
De 24:1 a **m.** hath taken a wife, and married..... 376
De 24:5 When a **m.** hath taken a new wife,....... 376
De 24:6 No **m.** shall take the nether or the ....
De 24:7 If a **m.** be found stealing any of his...... 376
De 24:11 **m.** to whom thou dost lend shall.......... 376
De 24:12 And if the **m.** be poor, thou shalt not ... 376
De 24:16 every **m.** shall be put to death for his... 376
De 25:2 the wicked **m.** be worthy to be beaten, ...
De 25:7 **m.** like not to take his brother's wife,... 376
De 25:9 be done unto that **m.** that will not........ 376
De 27:15 Cursed be the **m.** that maketh any....... 376
De 28:26 earth, and no **m.** shall fray them away.......
De 28:29 evermore, and no **m.** shall save thee. ....
De 28:30 and another **m.** shall lie with her: 376
De 28:54 the **m.** that is tender among you, ... 376
De 28:68 bondwomen, and no **m.** shall buy you........
De 29:18 Lest there should be among you **m.**, ... 376
De 29:20 shall smoke against that **m.**, and.......... 376
De 32:25 destroy both the young **m.** and the...........
De 32:25 also with the **m.** of gray hairs. 376
De 33:1 **m.** of God blessed the children of........ 376
De 34:6 but no **m.** knoweth of his sepulchre...... 376
Jos 1:5 shall not any **m.** be able to stand......... 376
Jos 2:11 remain any more courage in any **m.**, ... 376
Jos 3:12 of Israel, out of every tribe a **m.**. 376
Jos 4:2 the people, out of every tribe a **m.**, ... 376
Jos 4:4 of Israel, out of every tribe a **m.**: 376
Jos 4:5 take ye up every **m.** of you a stone..... 376
Jos 5:13 stood a **m.** over against him with a...... 376
Jos 6:5 up every **m.** straight before him. 376
Jos 6:20 every **m.** straight before him, and........ 376
Jos 6:21 was in the city, both **m.** and woman,..... 376
Jos 6:26 Cursed be the **m.** before the Lord, ... 376
Jos 7:14 shall take shall come **m.** by **m.**.......... 1397
Jos 7:17 family of the Zarhites **m.** by **m.**; 1397
Jos 7:18 he brought his household **m.** by **m.**; ... 1397
Jos 8:17 And there was not a **m.** left in Ai or 376
Jos 8:31 which no **m.** hath lifted up any iron:.........
Jos 10:8 there shall not a **m.** of them stand 376
Jos 10:14 hearkened unto the voice of a **m.**: 376
Jos 11:14 every **m.** they smote with the edge..... 120
Jos 14:6 Lord said unto Moses the **m.** of God..... 376
Jos 14:15 was a great **m.** among the Anakims...... 120
Jos 17:1 he was a **m.** of war, therefore he 376
Jos 21:44 stood not a **m.** of all their enemies....... 376
Jos 22:20 annd that **m.** perished not alone in....... 376
Jos 23:9 no **m.** hath been able to stand before ... 376
Jos 23:10 One **m.** of you...chase a thousand:....... 376
Jos 24:28 every **m.** unto his inheritance............. 376
Jg 1:24 spies saw a **m.** come forth out of the ... 376
Jg 1:25 they let go the **m.** and all his family. 376
Jg 1:26 And the **m.** went into the land of the.... 376
Jg 2:6 went every **m.** unto his inheritance 376
Jg 3:15 Gera, a Benjamite, a **m.** lefthanded: 376

Jg 3:17 Moab: and Eglon was a very fat **m.**. 376
Jg 3:28 and suffered not a **m.** to pass over. 376
Jg 3:29 valour; and there escaped not a **m.**. 376
Jg 4:16 sword; and there was not a **m.** left..........
Jg 4:20 when any **m.** doth come and enquire 376
Jg 4:20 say, Is there any **m.** here? that thou 376
Jg 4:22 I will shew thee the **m.** whom thou...... 376
Jg 5:30 to every **m.** a damsel or two; to........ 1397
Jg 6:12 is with thee, thou mighty **m.** of valour.......
Jg 6:16 smite the Midianites as one **m.**. 376
Jg 7:7 people go every **m.** unto his place. 376
Jg 7:8 rest of Israel every **m.** unto his tent, ... 376
Jg 7:13 was a **m.** that told a dream unto his..... 376
Jg 7:14 the son of Joash, a **m.** of Israel: 376
Jg 7:21 stood every **m.** in his place round......... 376
Jg 8:14 a young **m.** of the men of Succoth,..........
Jg 8:21 for as the **m.** is, so is his strength....... 376
Jg 8:24 give me every **m.** the earrings of his.... 376
Jg 8:25 cast therein every **m.** the earrings....... 376
Jg 9:9 by me they honour God and **m.**,........... 376
Jg 9:13 my wine, which cheereth God and **m.**,.. 376
Jg 9:49 cut down every **m.** his bough, and....... 376
Jg 9:54 unto the young **m.** his armourbearer, ...
Jg 9:54 And his young **m.** thrust him through,.......
Jg 9:55 departed every **m.** unto his place......... 376
Jg 10:1 the son of Dodo, a **m.** of Issachar;........ 376
Jg 10:18 What **m.** is he that will begin to 376
Jg 11:1 Gileadite was a mighty **m.** of valour,.........
Jg 11:39 had vowed: and she knew no **m.**, ... 376
Jg 13:2 there was a certain **m.** of Zorah, of....... 376
Jg 13:6 saying, A **m.** of God came unto me,..... 376
Jg 13:8 the **m.** of God which thou didst send.... 376
Jg 13:10 the **m.** hath appeared unto me, that..... 376
Jg 13:11 came to the **m.**, and said unto him,...... 376
Jg 13:11 Art thou the **m.** that spakest unto......... 376
Jg 16:7, 11 be weak, and be as another **m.**. 120
Jg 16:17 weak, and be like any other **m.**. 120
Jg 16:19 she called for a **m.**, and she caused...... 376
Jg 17:1 there was a **m.** of mount Ephraim,....... 376
Jg 17:5 the **m.** Micah had an house of gods,..... 376
Jg 17:6 every **m.** did that which was right........ 376
Jg 17:7 a young **m.** out of Beth-lehem-judah..........
Jg 17:8 And the **m.** departed out of the city..... 376
Jg 17:11 was content to dwell with the **m.**;......... 376
Jg 17:11 the young **m.** was unto him as one of ....
Jg 17:12 and the young **m.** became his preist,.........
Jg 18:3 they knew the voice of the young **m.**........
Jg 18:7 and had no business with any **m.**. 120
Jg 18:15 came to the house of the young **m.** ....
Jg 18:19 a priest unto the house of one **m.**,......... 376
Jg 18:28 they had no business with any **m.**; 120
Jg 19:6 damsel's father...said unto the **m.**, ... 376
Jg 19:7, 9 when the **m.** rose up to depart,........ 376
Jg 19:10 the **m.** would not tarry that night,........ 376
Jg 19:15 no **m.** that took them into his house..... 376
Jg 19:16 there came an old **m.** from his work..... 376
Jg 19:17 saw a wayfaring **m.** in the street of...... 376
Jg 19:17 and the old **m.** said, Whither goest 376
Jg 19:18 is no **m.** that receiveth me to house..... 376
Jg 19:19 for the young **m.** which is with thy ....
Jg 19:20 And the old **m.** said, Peace be with...... 376
Jg 19:22 the master of the house, the old **m.**,.... 376
Jg 19:22 the **m.** that came into thine house,....... 376
Jg 19:23 And the **m.**, the master of the house,... 376
Jg 19:23 this **m.** is come into mine house, ... 376
Jg 19:24 unto this **m.** do not so vile a thing....... 376
Jg 19:25 so the **m.** took his concubine, and........ 376
Jg 19:28 the **m.** took her up upon an ass, ... 376
Jg 19:28 the **m.** rose up, and gat him unto his.... 376
Jg 20:1 was gathered together as one **m.**,......... 376
Jg 20:8 And all the people arose as one **m.**, ... 376
Jg 20:11 the city, knit together as one **m.**. 376
Jg 21:11 every woman that hath lain by **m.**. 2145
Jg 21:12 had known no **m.** by lying with any....... 376
Jg 21:21 catch you every **m.** his wife of the....... 376
Jg 21:22 not to each **m.** his wife in the war: 376
Jg 21:24 every **m.** to his tribe and to his........... 376
Jg 21:24 thence every **m.** to his inheritance....... 376
Jg 21:25 every **m.** did that which was right in 376
Ru 1:1 a certain **m.** of Beth-lehem-judah 376
Ru 1:2 the name of the **m.** was Elimelech, ... 376
Ru 2:1 husband's, a mighty **m.** of wealth,........ 376
Ru 2:20 The **m.** is near of kin unto us, one of... 376
Ru 3:3 make not thyself known unto the **m.**, ... 376
Ru 3:8 that the **m.** was afraid, and turned......... 376
Ru 3:16 told her all that the **m.** had done to...... 376
Ru 3:18 for the **m.** will not be in rest, until....... 376
Ru 4:7 a **m.** plucked off his shoe, and gave 376
1Sa 1:1 Now there was a certain **m.** of............ 376
1Sa 1:3 And this **m.** went up out of his city...... 376
1Sa 1:11 unto thine handmaid a **m.** child............ 582
1Sa 1:21 the **m.** Elkanah, and all his house, ... 376
1Sa 2:9 for by strength shall no **m.** prevail. 376
1Sa 2:13 when any **m.** offered sacrifice, the 376
1Sa 2:15 said to the **m.** that sacrificed, Give 376
1Sa 2:16 if any **m.** said unto him, Let them........ 376
1Sa 2:25 If one **m.** sin against another, the 376
1Sa 2:25 but if a **m.** sin against the Lord, who.... 376
1Sa 2:27 there came a **m.** of God unto Eli, ... 376
1Sa 2:31 shall not be an old **m.** in thine house.........
1Sa 2:32 not be an old **m.** in thine house for...........
1Sa 2:33 And the **m.** of thine, whom I shall 376
1Sa 4:10 and they fled every **m.** into his tent: 376
1Sa 4:12 ran a **m.** of Benjamin out of the army, .. 376
1Sa 4:13 when the **m.** came into the city, and 376
1Sa 4:14 And the**m.** came in hastily, and told 376
1Sa 4:16 the **m.** said unto Eli, I am he that........ 376
1Sa 4:18 for he was an old **m.**, and heavy. 376
1Sa 8:22 Israel, Go ye every **m.** unto his city..... 376
1Sa 9:1 Now there was a **m.** of Benjamin,........ 376
1Sa 9:1 a Benjamite, a mighty **m.** of power. 376
1Sa 9:2 was Saul, a choice young **m.**, and a ....
1Sa 9:6 there is in this city a **m.** of God, ... 376
1Sa 9:6 he is an honourable **m.**; all that he....... 376
1Sa 9:7 if we go, what shall we bring the **m.**?... 376
1Sa 9:7 a present to bring to the **m.** of God: 376
1Sa 9:8 that will I give to the **m.** of God, to..... 376
1Sa 9:9 when a **m.** went to enquire of God, ... 376
1Sa 9:10 the city where the **m.** of God was. 376
1Sa 9:16 I will send thee a **m.** out of the land 376
1Sa 9:17 the **m.** whom I spake to thee of! 376
1Sa 10:6 and shalt be turned into another **m.**...... 376
1Sa 10:22 if the **m.** should yet come thither......... 376
1Sa 10:25 people away, every **m.** to his house. 376
1Sa 10:27 said, How shall this **m.** save us? ....
1Sa 11:3 if there be no **m.** to save us, we will ....
1Sa 11:13 shall not be a **m.** put to death this 376
1Sa 13:2 people he sent every **m.** to his tent. 376
1Sa 13:14 sought him a **m.** after his own heart,.... 376
1Sa 13:20 to sharpen every **m.** his share, and...... 376
1Sa 14:1 the son of Saul said unto the young **m.**......
1Sa 14:6 Jonathan said to the young **m.** that ....
1Sa 14:24 Cursed be the **m.** that eateth any 376
1Sa 14:26 but no **m.** put his hand to his mouth: ....
1Sa 14:28 Cursed be the **m.** that eateth any 376
1Sa 14:34 **m.** his ox, and every **m.** his sheep, ... 376
1Sa 14:34 brought every **m.** his ox with him 376
1Sa 14:36 and let us not leave a **m.** of them. 376
1Sa 14:39 was not a **m.** among all the people ....
1Sa 14:52 and when Saul saw any strong **m.**,........ 376
1Sa 14:52 or any valiant **m.**, he took him........... 1121
1Sa 15:3 slay both **m.** and woman, infant and 376
1Sa 15:29 for he is not a **m.**, that he should 120
1Sa 16:7 for the Lord seeth not as **m.** seeth; 120
1Sa 16:7 for **m.** looketh on the outward 120
1Sa 16:16 to seek out a **m.**, who is a cunning 376
1Sa 16:17 Provide me now a **m.** that can play...... 376
1Sa 16:18 in playing, and a mighty valiant **m.**, ... 376
1Sa 16:18 and a **m.** of war, and prudent in 376
1Sa 17:8 choose you a **m.** for you, and let him ... 376
1Sa 17:10 give me a **m.**, that we may fight 376
1Sa 17:12 the **m.** went among men for an old 376
1Sa 17:12 went among men for an old **m.** in the ....
1Sa 17:24 when they saw the **m.**, fled from him, .. 376
1Sa 17:25 ye seen this **m.** that is come up?.......... 376
1Sa 17:25 the **m.** who killeth him, the king.......... 376
1Sa 17:26 be done to the **m.** that killeth this........ 376
1Sa 17:27 be done to the **m.** that killeth him........ 376
1Sa 17:33 and he a **m.** of war from his youth........ 376
1Sa 17:41 **m.** that bare the shield went before 376
1Sa 17:58 Whose son art thou, thou young **m.**? ....
1Sa 18:23 am a poor **m.**, and lightly esteemed? 376
1Sa 20:22 if I say thus unto the young **m.**, ... 5958
1Sa 21:1 thou alone, and no **m.** with thee?.......... 376
1Sa 21:2 Let no **m.** know any thing of the 376
1Sa 21:7 a certain **m.** of the servants of Saul...... 376
1Sa 21:14 Lo, ye see the **m.** is mad: wherefore ... 376
1Sa 21:15 this fellow to play the mad **m.** in my.........
1Sa 24:19 if a **m.** find his enemy, will he let 376
1Sa 25:2 And there was a **m.** in Maon, whose.... 376
1Sa 25:2 and the **m.** was very great, and he 376
1Sa 25:3 Now the name of the **m.** was Nabal; 376
1Sa 25:3 the **m.** was churlish and evil in his 376
1Sa 25:10 away every **m.** from his master.......... 376
1Sa 25:13 men, Gird ye on every **m.** his sword.... 376
1Sa 25:13 they girded on every **m.** his sword; 376
1Sa 25:17 Belial, that a **m.** cannot speak to him. ....
1Sa 25:25 pray thee, regard this **m.** of Belial, ... 376
1Sa 25:29 Yet a **m.** is risen to pursue thee,......... 120
1Sa 26:12 they gat them away, and no **m.** saw it, ...
1Sa 26:15 Abner, Art not thou a valiant **m.**? 376
1Sa 26:23 The Lord render to every **m.** his......... 376
1Sa 27:3 every **m.** with his household, even......... 376
1Sa 27:9 and left neither **m.** nor woman alive, ... 376
1Sa 27:11 saved neither **m.** nor woman alive,........ 376
1Sa 28:14 An old **m.** cometh up; and he is 376
1Sa 30:6 every **m.** for his sons and for his......... 376
1Sa 30:13 I am a young **m.** of Egypt, servant..........
1Sa 30:17 there escaped not a **m.** of them, ... 376
1Sa 30:22 save to every **m.** his wife and his 376
2Sa 1:2 a **m.** came out of the camp from Saul ... 376
2Sa 1:5 said unto the young **m.** that told him,........
2Sa 1:6 the young **m.** that told him said, As I........
2Sa 1:13 said unto the young **m.** that told him,........
2Sa 2:3 up, every **m.** with his household:......... 376
2Sa 3:34 as a **m.** falleth before wicked men, ... 1121
2Sa 3:38 a great **m.** fallen this day in Israel?..........
2Sa 7:19 is this the manner of **m.**, O Lord.......... 120
2Sa 12:2 rich **m.** had exceeding many flocks ....
2Sa 12:3 But the poor **m.** had nothing, save one......
2Sa 12:4 came a traveller unto the rich **m.**,........ 376
2Sa 12:4 to dress for the wayfaring **m.** that............
2Sa 12:4 dressed it for the **m.** that was come..... 376
2Sa 12:5 was greatly kindled against the **m.**; 376
2Sa 12:5 **m.** that hath done this thing shall......... 376
2Sa 12:7 said to David, Thou art the **m.**............ 376
2Sa 13:3 and Jonadab was a very subtil **m.**......... 376
2Sa 13:9 they went out every **m.** from him.......... 376
2Sa 13:29 every **m.** gat him up upon his mule, ... 376
2Sa 13:34 And the young **m.** that kept the watch ......
2Sa 14:16 out of the hand of the **m.** that would 376
2Sa 14:21 bring the young **m.** Absalom again............
2Sa 15:2 any **m.** that had a controversy came..... 376
2Sa 15:3 is no **m.** deputed of the king to hear.........
2Sa 15:4 every **m.** which hath any suit or.......... 376
2Sa 15:5 that when any **m.** came nigh to him 376
2Sa 15:30 with him covered every **m.** his head,.... 376
2Sa 16:5 thence came out a **m.** of the family...... 376
2Sa 16:7 thou bloody **m.**, and thou **m.** of Belial:.. 376
2Sa 16:8 because thou art a bloody **m.**.............. 376
2Sa 16:23 as if a **m.** had enquired at the oracle 376
2Sa 17:3 the **m.** whom thou seekest is as if all ... 376
2Sa 17:8 thy father is a **m.** of war, and will........ 376
2Sa 17:10 that thy father is a mighty **m.**, and..........
2Sa 18:5 gently for my sake with the young **m.**,......
2Sa 18:10 a certain **m.** saw it, and told Joab, ... 376
2Sa 18:11 Joab said unto the **m.** that told him, ... 376
2Sa 18:12 And the **m.** said unto Joab, Though I.... 376
2Sa 18:12 none touch the young **m.** Absalom............
2Sa 18:24 and behold a **m.** running alone............. 376
2Sa 18:26 watchman saw another **m.** running: 376
2Sa 18:26 Behold another **m.** running alone. 376
2Sa 18:27 He is a good **m.**, and cometh with 376
2Sa 18:29 said, Is the young **m.** Absalom safe?.........
2Sa 18:32 Cushi, Is the young **m.** Absalom safe?.......
2Sa 18:32 do thee hurt, be as that young **m.** is..........
2Sa 19:8 Israel had fled every **m.** to his tent...... 376
2Sa 19:14 Judah, even as the heart of one **m.**; 376
2Sa 19:22 any **m.** be put to death this day in....... 376
2Sa 19:32 Barzillai was a very aged **m.**, even ....
2Sa 19:32 for he was a very great **m.**. 376
2Sa 20:1 happened to be there a **m.** of Belial, ... 376
2Sa 20:1 every **m.** to his tents, O Israel. 376
2Sa 20:2 So every **m.** of Israel went up from 376
2Sa 20:12 when the **m.** saw that all the people..... 376
2Sa 20:21 a **m.** of mount Ephraim, Sheba the....... 376
2Sa 20:22 from the city, every **m.** to his tent. 376
2Sa 21:4 for us shalt thou kill any **m.** in Israel. ... 376
2Sa 21:5 The **m.** that consumed us, and that...... 376
2Sa 21:20 was a **m.** of great stature, that had...... 376
2Sa 22:26 upright **m.** thou wilt shew thyself............
2Sa 22:49 delivered me from the violent **m.**......... 376
2Sa 23:1 the **m.** who was raised up on high,...... 1397
2Sa 23:7 **m.** that shall touch them must be 376
2Sa 23:20 the son of a valiant **m.**, of Kabzeel,....... 376
2Sa 23:21 he slew an Egyptian, a goodly **m.**: 376
2Sa 24:14 let me not fall into the hand of **m.**. 120
1Ki 1:6 and he also was a very goodly **m.**; ....
1Ki 1:42 thou art a valiant **m.**, and bringest 376
1Ki 1:49 rose up, and went every **m.** his way. ... 376
1Ki 1:52 he will shew himself a worthy **m.**, ... 1121

1Ki 2:2 therefore, and shew thyself a **m.**; 376
1Ki 2:4 a **m.** on the throne of Israel. 376
1Ki 2:9 for thou art a wise **m.**, and knowest 376
1Ki 4:7 each **m.** his month in a year made
1Ki 4:25 every **m.** under his vine and under 376
1Ki 4:27 table, every **m.** in his month: 376
1Ki 4:28 every **m.** according to his charge. 376
1Ki 7:14 and his father was a **m.** of Tyre, a 376
1Ki 8:25 shall not fail thee a **m.** in my sight 376
1Ki 8:31 **m.** trespass against his neighbour, 376
1Ki 8:38 supplication...be made by any **m.**, 120
1Ki 8:38 shall know every **m.** the plague of 376
1Ki 8:39 give to every **m.** according to his 376
1Ki 8:46 (for there is no **m.** that sinneth not,) 120
1Ki 9:5 not fail thee a **m.** upon the throne 376
1Ki 10:25 they brought every **m.** his present, 376
1Ki 11:28 And the **m.** Jeroboam was a mighty 376
1Ki 11:28 Jeroboam was a mighty **m.** of valour.
1Ki 11:28 young **m.** that he was industrious,
1Ki 12:22 came unto Shemaiah the **m.** of God, 376
1Ki 12:24 return every **m.** to his house; for 376
1Ki 13:1 there came a **m.** of God out of Judah 376
1Ki 13:4 heard the saying of the **m.** of God, 376
1Ki 13:5 sign which the **m.** of God had given 376
1Ki 13:6 said unto the **m.** of God, Intreat 376
1Ki 13:6 the **m.** of God besought the Lord, 376
1Ki 13:7 the king said unto the **m.** of God, 376
1Ki 13:8 the **m.** of God said unto the king, 376
1Ki 13:11 works that the **m.** of God had done 376
1Ki 13:12 seen what way the **m.** of God went, 376
1Ki 13:14 went after the **m.** of God, and found 376
1Ki 13:14 Art thou the **m.** of God that camest 376
1Ki 13:21 cried unto the **m.** of God that came 376
1Ki 13:26 he said, It is the **m.** of God, who was 376
1Ki 13:29 took up the carcase of the **m.** of God, 376
1Ki 13:31 wherein the **m.** of God is buried; 376
1Ki 14:10 as a **m.** taketh away dung, till it be all
1Ki 17:18 to do with thee, O thou **m.** of God? 376
1Ki 17:24 I know that thou art a **m.** of God, 376
1Ki 20:7 and see how this **m.** seeketh mischief:
1Ki 20:20 And they slew every one his **m.**: 376
1Ki 20:24 every **m.** out of his place, and put 376
1Ki 20:28 there came a **m.** of God, and spake 376
1Ki 20:35 **m.** of the sons of the prophets said 376
1Ki 20:35 And the **m.** refused to smite him. 376
1Ki 20:37 Then he found another **m.**, and said, 376
1Ki 20:37 the **m.** smote him, so that in smiting 376
1Ki 20:39 and, behold, a **m.** turned aside, 376
1Ki 20:39 and brought a **m.** unto me, and said, 376
1Ki 20:39 Keep this **m.**: if by any means he be 376
1Ki 20:42 hand a **m.** whom I appointed to utter 376
1Ki 22:8 There is yet one **m.**, Micaiah the son 376
1Ki 22:17 them return every **m.** to his house in 376
1Ki 22:34 certain **m.** drew a bow at a venture, 376
1Ki 22:36 Every **m.** to his city, and every **m.** to 376
2Ki 1:6 came a **m.** up to meet us, and said 376
2Ki 1:7 What manner of **m.** was he which 376
2Ki 1:8 He was an hairy **m.**, and girt with 376
2Ki 1:9 Thou **m.** of God, the king hath said, 376
2Ki 1:10 If I be a **m.** of God, then let fire come 376
2Ki 1:11 O **m.** of God, thus hath the king said, 376
2Ki 1:12 I be a **m.** of God, let fire come down 376
2Ki 1:13 O **m.** of God, I pray thee, let my life, 376
2Ki 3:25 of land cast every **m.** his stone, 376
2Ki 4:7 she came and told the **m.** of God. 376
2Ki 4:9 that this is an holy **m.** of God, 376
2Ki 4:16 Nay, my lord, thou **m.** of God, do not 376
2Ki 4:21 laid him on the bed of the **m.** of God, 376
2Ki 4:22 that I may run to the **m.** of God, 376
2Ki 4:25 came unto the **m.** of God to mount 376
2Ki 4:25 when the **m.** of God saw her afar off, 376
2Ki 4:27 when she came to the **m.** of God to 376
2Ki 4:27 the **m.** of God said, Let her alone; 376
2Ki 4:29 if thou meet any **m.**, salute him not; 376
2Ki 4:40 O thou **m.** of God, there is death in 376
2Ki 4:42 came a **m.** from Baal-shalisha, 376
2Ki 4:42 and brought the **m.** of God bread of 376
2Ki 5:1 was a great **m.** with his master, 376
2Ki 5:1 he was also a mighty **m.** in valour, 376
2Ki 5:7 that this **m.** doth send unto me to
2Ki 5:7 me to recover a **m.** of his leprosy? 376
2Ki 5:8 Elisha the **m.** of God had heard that 376
2Ki 5:14 to the saying of the **m.** of God: 376
2Ki 5:15 he returned to the **m.** of God, he and 376
2Ki 5:20 the servant of Elisha the **m.** of God, 376
2Ki 5:26 **m.** turned again from his chariot 376
2Ki 6:2 take thence every **m.** a beam, and 376
2Ki 6:6 the **m.** of God said, Where fell it? 376
2Ki 6:9 the **m.** of God sent unto the king of 376
2Ki 6:10 which the **m.** of God told him and 376
2Ki 6:15 servant of the **m.** of God was risen 376
2Ki 6:17 opened the eyes of the young **m.**;
2Ki 6:19 bring you to the **m.** whom ye seek. 376
2Ki 6:32 the king sent a **m.** from before him: 376
2Ki 7:2 king leaned answered the **m.** of God, 376
2Ki 7:5 Syria, behold, there was no **m.** there. 376
2Ki 7:10 and, behold, there was no **m.** there, 376
2Ki 7:10 neither voice of **m.**, but horses tied, 120
2Ki 7:17 he died, as the **m.** of God had said, 376
2Ki 7:18 as the **m.** of God had spoken to the 376
2Ki 7:19 that lord answered the **m.** of God, 376
2Ki 8:2 after the saying of the **m.** of God: 376
2Ki 8:4 Gehazi the servant of the **m.** of God, 376
2Ki 8:7 saying, The **m.** of God is come hither 376
2Ki 8:8 meet the **m.** of God, and enquire of 376
2Ki 8:11 ashamed: and the **m.** of God wept. 376
2Ki 9:4 So the young **m.**, even the young **m.**
2Ki 9:11 said unto them, Ye know the **m.**, 376
2Ki 9:13 took every **m.** his garment, and put 376
2Ki 10:21 was not a **m.** left that came not. 376
2Ki 11:8 every **m.** with his weapons in his 376
2Ki 11:9 and they took every **m.** his men that 376
2Ki 11:11 every **m.** with his weapons in his 376
2Ki 12:4 the money that every **m.** is set at, 5315
2Ki 12:5 every **m.** of his acquaintance: 376
2Ki 13:19 the **m.** of God was wroth with him, 376
2Ki 13:21 to pass, as they were burying a **m.**, 376
2Ki 13:21 they cast the **m.** into the sepulchre of 376
2Ki 13:21 and when the **m.** was let down, and 376
2Ki 14:6 every **m.** shall be put to death for 376
2Ki 14:12 and they fled every **m.** to their tents 376
2Ki 15:20 of each **m.** fifty shekels of silver, 376
2Ki 18:21 on which if a **m.** lean, it will go into 376
2Ki 18:31 eat ye every **m.** of his own vine, and 376
2Ki 21:13 wipe Jerusalem as a **m.** wipeth a dish,
2Ki 22:15 Tell the **m.** that sent you to me, 376
2Ki 23:10 that no **m.** might make his son or 376
2Ki 23:16 which the **m.** of God proclaimed, 376
2Ki 23:17 It is the sepulchre of the **m.** of God, 376
2Ki 23:18 alone; let no **m.** move his bones. 376
1Ch 11:22 the son of a valiant **m.** of Habzeel, 376
1Ch 11:23 Egyptian, a **m.** of great stature, five 376
1Ch 12:4 a mighty **m.** among the thirty, and
1Ch 12:28 Zadok, a young **m.** mighty of valour,
1Ch 16:3 both **m.** and woman, to every one a 376
1Ch 16:21 He suffered no **m.** to do them wrong: 376
1Ch 16:43 departed every **m.** to his house: 376
1Ch 17:17 to the estate of a **m.** of high degree, 120
1Ch 20:6 where was a **m.** of great stature, 376
1Ch 21:13 let me not fall into the hand of **m.**. 120
1Ch 22:9 to thee, who shall be a **m.** of rest; 376
1Ch 23:3 number by their polls, **m.** by **m.**, 1397
1Ch 23:14 concerning Moses the **m.** of God, 376
1Ch 27:32 counsellor, a wise **m.**, and a scribe: 376
1Ch 28:3 because thou hast been a **m.** of war, 376
1Ch 28:21 workmanship every willing skilful **m.**.
1Ch 29:1 for the palace is not for **m.**, but for 120
2Ch 2:7 Send...a **m.** cunning to work in gold, 376
2Ch 2:13 And now I have sent a cunning **m.**, 376
2Ch 2:14 his father was a **m.** of Tyre, skilful 376
2Ch 6:5 chose I any **m.** to be ruler over my 376
2Ch 6:16 not fail thee a **m.** in my sight to sit 376
2Ch 6:22 If a **m.** sin against his neighbour, 376
2Ch 6:29 soever shall be made of any **m.** 120
2Ch 6:30 **m.** according unto all his ways, 120
2Ch 6:36 there is no **m.** which sinneth not,) 120
2Ch 7:18 shall not fail thee a **m.** to be ruler 376
2Ch 8:14 David the **m.** of God commanded. 376
2Ch 9:24 they brought every **m.** his present, 376
2Ch 10:16 every **m.** to your tents, O Israel: and 376
2Ch 11:2 came to Shemaiah the **m.** of God, 376
2Ch 11:4 return every **m.** to his house: for 376
2Ch 14:11 let not **m.** prevail against thee. 582
2Ch 15:13 or great, whether **m.** or woman. 376
2Ch 17:17 Eliada a mighty **m.** of valour, and
2Ch 18:7 There is yet one **m.**, by whom we 376
2Ch 18:16 every **m.** to his house in peace. 376
2Ch 18:33 certain **m.** drew a bow at a venture, 376
2Ch 18:33 therefore he said to his chariot **m.**,
2Ch 19:6 for ye judge not for **m.**, but for the 120
2Ch 20:27 every **m.** of Judah and Jerusalem, 376
2Ch 23:7 every **m.** with his weapons in his 376
2Ch 23:8 took every **m.** his men that were to 376
2Ch 23:10 every **m.** having his weapon in his 376
2Ch 25:4 every **m.** shall die for his own sin. 376
2Ch 25:7 But there came a **m.** of God to him, 376
2Ch 25:9 Amaziah said to the **m.** of God, But 376
2Ch 25:9 the **m.** of God answered, The Lord is 376
2Ch 25:22 and they fled every **m.** to his tent. 376
2Ch 28:7 And Zichri, a mighty **m.** of Ephraim,
2Ch 30:16 to the law of Moses the **m.** of God: 376
2Ch 31:1 returned, every **m.** to his possession, 376
2Ch 31:2 every **m.** according to his service, 376
2Ch 32:19 were the work of the hands of **m.**. 120
2Ch 34:23 Tell ye the **m.** that sent you to me, 376
2Ch 36:17 no compassion upon young **m.** or
2Ch 36:17 or maiden, old **m.**, or him that stooped
Ezr 3:1 together as one **m.** to Jerusalem. 376
Ezr 3:2 in the law of Moses the **m.** of God. 376
Ezr 8:18 brought us a **m.** of understanding, 376
Ne 1:11 him mercy in the sight of this **m.** 376
Ne 2:10 was come a **m.** to seek the welfare 120
Ne 2:12 told I any **m.** what my Lord had put 120
Ne 5:13 shake out every **m.** from his house, 376
Ne 6:11 I said, Should such a **m.** as I flee? 376
Ne 7:2 for he was a faithful **m.**, and feared 376
Ne 8:1 themselves together as one **m.** into 376
Ne 9:29 (which if a **m.** do, he shall live in 120
Ne 12:24 of David the **m.** of God, ward over 376
Ne 12:36 instruments of David the **m.** of God, 376
Es 1:22 every **m.** should bear rule in his own 376
Es 4:11 whether **m.** or woman, shall come 376
Es 5:12 did let no **m.** come in with the king
Es 6:6,7 the **m.** whom the king delighteth 376
Es 6:9 they may array the **m.** withal whom 376
Es 6:9 Thus shall it be done to the **m.** 376
Es 6:11 Thus shall it be done unto the **m.** 376
Es 8:8 the king's ring, may no **m.** reverse.
Es 9:2 no **m.** could withstand them; for 376
Es 9:4 this **m.** Mordecai waxed greater and 376
Job 1:1 was a **m.** in the land of Uz, whose 376
Job 1:1 and that **m.** was perfect and upright, 376
Job 1:3 this **m.** was the greatest of all the 376
Job 1:8 a perfect and an upright **m.**, one 376
Job 2:3 perfect and an upright **m.**, one that 376
Job 2:4 all that a **m.** hath will he give for his 376
Job 3:3 said, There is a **m.** child conceived. 1397
Job 3:23 given to a **m.** whose way is hid, 1397
Job 4:17 Shall mortal **m.** be more just than 582
Job 4:17 shall a **m.** be more pure than his 1396
Job 5:2 For wrath killeth the foolish **m.**, and
Job 5:7 Yet **m.** is born unto trouble, as the 120
Job 5:17 Behold, happy is the **m.** whom God 582
Job 7:1 appointed time to **m.** upon earth? 582
Job 7:17 What is **m.**, that thou shouldest 582
Job 8:20 God will not cast away a perfect **m.**,
Job 9:2 how should **m.** be just with God? 582
Job 9:32 For he is not a **m.**, as I am, that I 376
Job 10:4 of flesh? or seest thou as **m.** seeth? 582
Job 10:5 Are thy days as the days of **m.**? 582
Job 11:2 should a **m.** full of talk be justified? 376
Job 11:3 shall no **m.** make thee ashamed?
Job 11:12 For vain **m.** would be wise, though 376
Job 11:12 **m.** be born like a wild ass's colt. 120
Job 12:4 just upright **m.** is laughed to scorn.
Job 12:14 he shutteth up a **m.**, and there can 376
Job 12:25 them to stagger like a drunken **m.**
Job 13:9 or as one **m.** mocketh another, do 582
Job 14:1 **M.** that is born of a woman is of 120
Job 14:10 But **m.** dieth, and wasteth away: 1397
Job 14:10 **m.** giveth up the ghost, and where 120
Job 14:12 So **m.** lieth down, and riseth not: 376
Job 14:14 If a **m.** die, shall he live again? all 1397
Job 14:19 and thou destroyest the hope of **m.** 582
Job 15:2 a wise **m.** utter vain knowledge,
Job 15:7 thou the first **m.** that was born? or 120
Job 15:14 What is **m.**, that he should be 582
Job 15:16 more abominable and filthy is **m.**, 376
Job 15:20 The wicked **m.** travaileth with pain
Job 15:28 houses which no **m.** inhabiteth, which
Job 16:21 one might plead for a **m.** with God, 1397
Job 16:21 as a **m.** pleadeth for his neighbour! 120
Job 17:10 I cannot find one wise **m.** among you.
Job 20:4 old, since **m.** was placed upon earth, 120
Job 20:21 shall no **m.** look for his goods.
Job 20:29 the portion of a wicked **m.** from God, 120
Job 21:4 As for me, is my complaint to **m.**? 120
Job 21:33 every **m.** shall draw after him, as 120
Job 22:2 Can a **m.** be profitable unto God, 1397
Job 22:8 But as for the mighty **m.**, he had 376
Job 22:8 and the honourable **m.** dwelt in it.

Job 24:22 he riseth up, and no **m.** is sure of life.......
Job 25:4 then can **m.** be justified with God?....... 582
Job 25:6 How much less **m.**, that is a worm?..... 582
Job 25:6 the son of **m.**, which is a worm?...... 120
Job 27:13 the portion of a wicked **m.** with God, ... 120
Job 27:19 The rich **m.** shall lie down, but he..........
Job 28:13 **M.** knoweth not the price thereof; 582
Job 28:28 unto **m.** he said, Behold, the fear of..... 120
Job 32:8 But there is a spirit in **m.**: and the 582
Job 32:13 God thrusteth him down, not **m.**. 376
Job 32:21 let me give flattering titles unto **m.**. 120
Job 33:12 thee, that God is greater than **m.**. 582
Job 33:14 yea twice, yet **m.** perceiveth it not..........
Job 33:17 may withdraw **m.** from his purpose, ... 120
Job 33:17 purpose, and hide pride from **m.**....... 1397
Job 33:23 to shew unto **m.** his uprightness:........ 120
Job 33:26 render unto **m.** his righteousness......... 582
Job 33:29 worketh God oftentimes with **m.**,....... 1397
Job 34:7 What **m.** is like Job, who drinketh...... 1397
Job 34:9 It profiteth a **m.** nothing that he......... 1397
Job 34:11 work of a **m.** shall he render unto........ 120
Job 34:11 cause every **m.** to find according......... 376
Job 34:14 If he set his heart upon **m.**, if he............
Job 34:15 and **m.** shall turn again unto dust........ 120
Job 34:21 his eyes are upon the ways of **m.**,....... 376
Job 34:23 not lay upon **m.** more than right;......... 376
Job 34:29 a nation, or against a **m.** only:............ 120
Job 34:34 let a wise **m.** hearken unto me.......... 1397
Job 35:8 Thy wickedness may hurt a **m.** as 376
Job 35:8 may profit the son of **m.**.................... 120
Job 36:25 Every **m.** may see it;......................... 120
Job 36:25 **m.** may behold it afar off.................... 582
Job 36:28 clouds do drop and distil upon **m.** 120
Job 37:7 He sealeth up the hand of every **m.**; 120
Job 37:20 if a **m.** speak, surely he shall be.......... 376
Job 38:3 Gird up now thy loins like a **m.**; 1397
Job 38:26 rain on the earth, where no **m.** is;....... 376
Job 38:26 wilderness, wherein there is no **m.**; 120
Job 40:7 Gird up thy loins now like a **m.**: 1397
Job 42:11 every **m.** also gave him a piece of 376
Ps 1:1 Blessed is the **m.** that walketh not....... 376
Ps 5:6 abhor the bloody and deceitful **m.**. 376
Ps 8:4 What is **m.**, that thou art mindful......... 582
Ps 8:4 son of **m.**, that thou visitest him? 120
Ps 9:19 Arise, O Lord; let not **m.** prevail:........ 582
Ps 10:15 arm of the wicked and the evil **m.**: ....
Ps 10:18 **m.** of the earth...no more oppress.......... 582
Ps 12:1 Help, Lord; for the godly **m.** ceaseth; ....
Ps 18:25 with an upright **m.** thou wilt shew...... 1397
Ps 18:48 delivered me from the violent **m.**.......... 376
Ps 19:5 rejoiceth as a strong **m.** to run a race.......
Ps 22:6 But I am a worm, and no **m.**; a.............. 376
Ps 25:12 What **m.** is he that feareth the Lord? ... 376
Ps 31:12 forgotten as a dead **m.** out of mind:..........
Ps 31:20 thy presence from the pride of **m.**: 376
Ps 32:2 Blessed is the **m.** unto whom the 120
Ps 33:16 mighty **m.** is not delivered by much..........
Ps 34:6 poor **m.** cried, and the Lord heard............
Ps 34:8 blessed is the **m.** that trusteth in 1397
Ps 34:12 What **m.** is he that desireth life,.......... 376
Ps 36:6 Lord, thou preservest **m.** and beast. 120
Ps 37:7 **m.** who bringeth wicked devices to...... 376
Ps 37:16 little that a righteous **m.** hath is better......
Ps 37:23 steps of a good **m.** are ordered by..... 1397
Ps 37:37 Mark the perfect **m.**, and behold the.........
Ps 37:37 for the end of that **m.** is peace............ 376
Ps 38:13 But I, as a deaf **m.**, heard not; and I........
Ps 38:13 I was as a dumb **m.** that openeth not........
Ps 38:14 I was as a **m.** that heareth not, and 376
Ps 39:5 **m.** at his best state is altogether 120
Ps 39:6 every **m.** walketh in a vain shew: 376
Ps 39:11 rebukes dost correct **m.** for iniquity, ... 376
Ps 39:11 a moth: surely every **m.** is vanity. 120
Ps 40:4 Blessed is that **m.** that maketh the...... 1397
Ps 43:1 from the deceitful and unjust **m.**. 376
Ps 49:12 **m.** being in honour abideth not:........... 120
Ps 49:20 **M.** that is in honour, and 120
Ps 52:1 thyself in mischief, O mighty **m.**? ....
Ps 52:7 this is the **m.** that made not God 1397
Ps 55:13 But it was thou, a **m.** mine equal,........ 582
Ps 56:1 God: for **m.** would swallow me up; 582
Ps 56:11 I will not be afraid what **m.** can do....... 120
Ps 58:11 So that a **m.** shall say, Verily there...... 120
Ps 60:11 trouble: for vain is the help of **m.**. 120
Ps 62:3 ye imagine mischief against a **m.**? 376
Ps 62:12 to every **m.** according to his work. 376
Ps 65:4 Blessed is the **m.** whom thou choosest,.....
Ps 71:4 hand of the unrighteous and cruel **m.**. ....
Ps 74:5 A **m.** was famous according as he had.......
Ps 74:22 the foolish **m.** reproacheth thee daily.........
Ps 76:10 the wrath of **m.** shall praise thee: 120
Ps 78:25 **M.** did eat angels' food: he sent 376
Ps 78:65 and like a mighty **m.** that shouteth...........
Ps 80:17 be upon the **m.** of thy right hand,........ 376
Ps 80:17 the son of **m.** whom thou madest 120
Ps 84:5 Blessed is the **m.** whose strength is..... 120
Ps 84:12 blessed is the **m.** that trusteth in......... 120
Ps 87:4 Ethiopia; this **m.** was born there. ....
Ps 87:5 This and that **m.** was born in her: 376
Ps 87:6 people, that this **m.** was born there..........
Ps 88:4 am as a **m.** that hath no strength: 1397
Ps 89:48 What **m.** is he that liveth, and shall 1397
Ps 90:*title* A Prayer of Moses the **m.** of God. 376
Ps 90:3 Thou turnest **m.** to destruction; 582
Ps 92:6 A brutish **m.** knoweth not; neither....... 376
Ps 94:10 he that teacheth **m.** knowledge,........... 120
Ps 94:11 Lord knoweth the thoughts of **m.**, ... 120
Ps 94:12 is the **m.** whom thou chastenest, ... 1397
Ps 103:15 As for **m.**, his days are as grass:......... 582
Ps 104:14 and herb for the service of **m.**: 120
Ps 104:15 that maketh glad the heart of **m.**, ... 582
Ps 104:23 **M.** goeth forth unto his work and 120
Ps 105:14 He suffered no **m.** to do them wrong: .. 120
Ps 105:17 He sent a **m.** before them, even 376
Ps 107:27 fro, and stagger like a drunken **m.**,...........
Ps 108:12 trouble: for vain is the help of **m.**. 120
Ps 109:6 Set thou a wicked **m.** over him: and ....
Ps 109:16 persecuted the poor and needy **m.**,...... 376
Ps 112:1 Blessed is the **m.** that feareth the....... 376
Ps 112:5 A good **m.** sheweth favour, and........... 376
Ps 118:6 not fear: what can **m.** do unto me? 120
Ps 118:8 Lord than to put confidence in **m.**. 120
Ps 119:9 shall a young **m.** cleanse his way? ....
Ps 119:134 me from the oppression of **m.**:............ 120
Ps 127:4 are in the hand of a mighty **m.**; ....
Ps 127:5 Happy is the **m.** that hath his........... 1397
Ps 128:4 shall the **m.** be blessed that feareth.... 1397
Ps 135:8 of Egypt, both of **m.** and beast. 120
Ps 140:1 me, O Lord, from the evil **m.**:............ 120
Ps 140:1, 4 preserve me from the violent **m.**; 376
Ps 140:11 evil shall hunt the violent **m.** to........... 376
Ps 142:4 there was no **m.** that would know me: ......
Ps 142:4 failed me; no **m.** cared for my soul. ....
Ps 143:2 sight shall no **m.** living be justified. ....
Ps 144:3 is **m.**, that thou takest knowledge........ 120
Ps 144:3 or the son of **m.**, that thou makest 582
Ps 144:4 **M.** is like to vanity: his days are 120
Ps 146:3 son of **m.**, in whom there is no help..... 120
Ps 147:10 not pleasure in the legs of a **m.**........... 376
Pr 1:4 to the young **m.** knowledge and ....
Pr 1:5 wise **m.** will hear, and will increase ....
Pr 1:5 **m.** of understanding shall attain.................
Pr 1:24 out my hand, and no **m.** regarded;..............
Pr 2:12 thee from the way of the evil **m.**,.............
Pr 2:12 **m.** that speaketh froward things; 376
Pr 3:4 favour...in the sight of God and **m.**. 120
Pr 3:13 Happy is the **m.** that findeth wisdom, ... 120
Pr 3:13 the **m.** that getteth understanding. 120
Pr 3:30 Strive not with a **m.** without cause,...... 120
Pr 5:21 ways of **m.** are before the eyes of....... 376
Pr 6:11 and thy want as an armed **m.**................ 376
Pr 6:12 A naughty person, a wicked **m.**,........... 376
Pr 6:26 a **m.** is brought to a piece of bread:..........
Pr 6:27 Can a **m.** take fire in his bosom, ... 376
Pr 6:34 For jealousy is the rage of a **m.**:......... 1397
Pr 7:7 a young **m.** void of understanding, ...
Pr 8:4 and my voice is to the sons of **m.**........... 120
Pr 8:34 Blessed is the **m.** that heareth me, ... 120
Pr 9:7 he that rebuketh a wicked **m.** getteth........
Pr 9:8 rebuke a wise **m.**, and he will love ....
Pr 9:9 Give instruction to a wise **m.**, and he........
Pr 9:9 teach a just **m.**, and he will increase ....
Pr 10:11 mouth of a righteous **m.** is a well of..........
Pr 10:23 **m.** of understanding hath wisdom......... 376
Pr 11:7 When a wicked **m.** dieth, his............... 120
Pr 11:12 **m.** of understanding holdeth his........... 376
Pr 11:17 merciful **m.** doeth good to his own......... 376
Pr 12:2 A good **m.** obtaineth favour of the............
Pr 12:2 but a **m.** of wicked devices will he 376
Pr 12:3 A **m.** shall not be established by.......... 120
Pr 12:8 **m.** shall be commended according 376
Pr 12:10 A righteous **m.** regardeth the life of.........
Pr 12:14 A **m.** shall be satisfied with good 376
Pr 12:16 but a prudent **m.** covereth shame............
Pr 12:23 prudent **m.** concealeth knowledge: 120
Pr 12:25 Heaviness in the heart of **m.**................ 376
Pr 12:27 slothful **m.** roasteth not that which he ....
Pr 12:27 the substance of a diligent **m.** is 120
Pr 13:2 **m.** shall eat good by the fruit of.......... 376
Pr 13:5 A righteous **m.** hateth lying: but a...........
Pr 13:5 but a wicked **m.** is loathsome, and...........
Pr 13:16 prudent **m.** dealeth with knowledge:..........
Pr 13:22 A good **m.** leaveth an inheritance to.........
Pr 14:7 from the presence of a foolish **m.**, ... 376
Pr 14:12 way which seemeth right unto a **m.**,...... 376
Pr 14:14 a good **m.** shall be satisfied from 376
Pr 14:15 prudent **m.** looketh well to his going. ....
Pr 14:16 A wise **m.** feareth, and departeth.............
Pr 14:17 a **m.** of wicked devices is hated........... 376
Pr 15:18 A wrathful **m.** stirreth up strife: but 376
Pr 15:19 way of the slothful **m.** is as an hedge........
Pr 15:20 a foolish **m.** despiseth his mother......... 120
Pr 15:21 but a **m.** of understanding walketh 376
Pr 15:23 A **m.** hath joy by the answer of his...... 376
Pr 16:1 The preparations of the heart in **m.**,..... 120
Pr 16:2 ways of a **m.** are clean in his own........ 376
Pr 16:14 death: but a wise **m.** will pacify it. 376
Pr 16:25 way that seemeth right unto a **m.**, ... 376
Pr 16:27 An ungodly **m.** diggeth up evil: and...... 376
Pr 16:28 A froward **m.** soweth strife: and a 376
Pr 16:29 A violent **m.** enticeth his neighbour, ... 376
Pr 17:10 a wise **m.** than an hundred stripes............
Pr 17:11 An evil **m.** seeketh only rebellion: ....
Pr 17:12 robbed of her whelps meet a **m.**........... 376
Pr 17:18 A **m.** void of understanding striketh...... 120
Pr 17:23 A wicked **m.** taketh a gift out of the ....
Pr 17:27 and a **m.** of understanding is of an 376
Pr 17:28 shutteth his lips is esteemed a **m.** of........
Pr 18:1 Through desire a **m.**, having ....
Pr 18:12 the heart of **m.** is haughty, and........... 376
Pr 18:14 The spirit of a **m.** will sustain his......... 376
Pr 18:24 A **m.** that hath friends must shew........ 376
Pr 19:3 The foolishness of **m.** perverteth 120
Pr 19:6 and every **m.** is a friend to him that.........
Pr 19:11 The discretion of a **m.** deferreth his..... 120
Pr 19:19 A **m.** of great wrath shall suffer..............
Pr 19:22 The desire of a **m.** is his kindness: 120
Pr 19:22 and a poor **m.** is better than a liar...........
Pr 19:24 A slothful **m.** hideth his hand in his..........
Pr 20:3 honour for a **m.** to cease from strife:.... 376
Pr 20:5 in the heart of **m.** is like deep water; ... 376
Pr 20:5 a **m.** of understanding will draw it......... 376
Pr 20:6 but a faithful **m.** who can find? 376
Pr 20:7 The just **m.** walketh in his integrity: ....
Pr 20:17 Bread of deceit is sweet to a **m.**; 376
Pr 20:24 how can a **m.** then understand his......... 120
Pr 20:25 is a snare to the **m.** who devoureth 120
Pr 20:27 spirit of **m.** is the candle of the Lord,... 120
Pr 21:2 way of a **m.** is right in his own........... 376
Pr 21:8 way of **m.** is froward and strange: 376
Pr 21:12 The righteous **m.** wisely considereth.........
Pr 21:16 The **m.** that wandereth out of the........ 120
Pr 21:17 loveth pleasure shall be a poor **m.**: 376
Pr 21:20 but a foolish **m.** spendeth it up............ 120
Pr 21:22 A wise **m.** scaleth the city of the ....
Pr 21:28 but the **m.** that heareth speaketh......... 376
Pr 21:29 A wicked **m.** hardeneth his face:.......... 376
Pr 22:3 A prudent **m.** foreseeth the evil, and 376
Pr 22:13 The slothful **m.** saith, There is a lion ....
Pr 22:24 no friendship with an angry **m.**; 1167
Pr 22:24 with a furious **m.** thou shalt not go: 376
Pr 22:29 thou a **m.** diligent in his business?........ 376
Pr 23:2 if thou be a **m.** given to appetite......... 1167
Pr 23:21 drowsiness shall clothe a **m.** with rags.......
Pr 24:5 A wise **m.** is strong; yea,................. 1397
Pr 24:5 yea, a **m.** of knowledge increaseth....... 376
Pr 24:12 to every **m.** according to his works?..... 120
Pr 24:15 Lay not wait, O wicked **m.**, against ....
Pr 24:16 For a just **m.** falleth seven times, and.......
Pr 24:20 shall be no reward to the evil **m.**; ....
Pr 24:26 Every **m.** shall kiss his lips that...............
Pr 28:17 flee to the pit; let no **m.** stay him ....
Pr 24:29 to the **m.** according to his work. 376
Pr 24:30 of the **m.** void of understanding; 120
Pr 24:34 and thy want as an armed **m.**............... 376
Pr 25:18 A **m.** that beareth false witness............ 376
Pr 25:19 Confidence in an unfaithful **m.** in..............
Pr 25:26 A righteous **m.** falleth down before............
Pr 26:12 thou a **m.** wise in his own conceit? 376
Pr 26:13 The slothful **m.** saith, There is a lion ....
Pr 26:18 As a mad **m.** who casteth firebrands, ...

Pr 26:19 **m.** that deceiveth his neighbour,.......... 376
Pr 26:21 is a contentious **m.** to kindle strife....... 376
Pr 27:2 Let another **m.** praise thee, and not ....
Pr 27:8 **m.** that wandereth from his place......... 376
Pr 27:12 A prudent **m.** foreseeth the evil, and ....
Pr 27:17 so a **m.** sharpeneth the countenance..... 376
Pr 27:19 to face, so the heart of **m.** to **m.**. 120
Pr 27:20 the eyes of **m.** are never satisfied........ 120
Pr 27:21 for gold; so is a **m.** to his praise.......... 376
Pr 28:1 The wicked flee when no **m.** pursueth:......
Pr 28:2 but by a **m.** of understanding and......... 120
Pr 28:3 poor **m.** that oppresseth the poor....... 1397
Pr 28:11 rich **m.** is wise in his own conceit; 376
Pr 28:12 the wicked rise, a **m.** is hidden. 120
Pr 28:14 Happy is the **m.** that feareth alway: 120
Pr 28:17 **m.** that doeth violence to the blood...... 120
Pr 28:20 A faithful **m.** shall abound with 376
Pr 28:21 of bread that **m.** will transgress. 1397
Pr 28:23 He that rebuketh a **m.** afterwards........ 120
Pr 29:5 **m.** that flattereth his neighbour.......... 1397
Pr 29:6 transgression of an evil **m.** there 376
Pr 29:9 **m.** contendeth with a foolish **m.**, ... 376
Pr 29:11 wise **m.** keepeth it in till afterwards..........
Pr 29:13 The poor and the deceitful **m.** meet 376
Pr 29:20 a **m.** that is hasty in his words?........... 376
Pr 29:22 An angry **m.** stirreth up strife, and 376
Pr 29:22 and a furious **m.** aboundeth in............ 1167
Pr 29:25 fear of **m.** bringeth a snare: but 120
Pr 29:27 An unjust **m.** is an abomination to........ 376
Pr 30:1 the **m.** spake unto Ithiel, even........... 1397
Pr 30:2 I am more brutish than any **m.**,............ 376
Pr 30:2 have not the understanding of a **m.**. 120
Pr 30:19 and the way of a **m.** with a maid.......... 1397
Ec 1:3 What profit hath a **m.** of all his........... 120
Ec 1:8 full of labour; **m.** cannot utter it: 376
Ec 1:13 God given to the sons of **m.** to be 120
Ec 2:12 what can the **m.** do that cometh.......... 120
Ec 2:16 And how dieth the wise **m.**? as the...........
Ec 2:18 I should leave it unto the **m.** that 120
Ec 2:19 he shall be a wise **m.** or a fool? yet..........
Ec 2:21 is a **m.** whose labour is in wisdom, ... 120
Ec 2:21 yet to a **m.** that hath not laboured 120
Ec 2:22 For what hath **m.** of all his labour, ... 120
Ec 2:24 There is nothing better for a **m.**,.......... 120
Ec 2:26 to a **m.** that is good in his sight........... 120
Ec 3:11 no **m.** can find out the work that God... 120
Ec 3:12 but for a **m.** to rejoice, and to do good......
Ec 3:13 that every **m.** should eat and drink,....... 120
Ec 3:19 so that a **m.** hath no preeminence......... 120
Ec 3:21 Who knoweth the spirit of **m.** 1121,120
Ec 3:22 a **m.** should rejoice in his own............. 120
Ec 4:4 a **m.** is envied of his neighbour. 376
Ec 5:12 The sleep of a labouring **m.** is sweet, ...
Ec 5:19 **m.** also to whom God hath given 120
Ec 6:2 **m.** to whom God hath given riches, ... 376
Ec 6:3 If a **m.** beget an hundred children, ... 376
Ec 6:7 labour of **m.** is for his mouth, and........ 120
Ec 6:10 already, and it is known that it is **m.**:... 120
Ec 6:11 vanity, what is **m.** the better?............ 120
Ec 6:12 what is good for **m.** in this life, all 120
Ec 6:12 who can tell a **m.** what shall be after.... 120
Ec 7:5 for a **m.** to hear the song of fools. 376
Ec 7:7 oppression maketh a wise **m.** mad; ....
Ec 7:14 **m.** should find nothing after him. 120
Ec 7:15 there is a just **m.** that perisheth in ....
Ec 7:15 wicked **m.** that prolongeth his life in ....
Ec 7:20 there is not a just **m.** upon earth, ... 120
Ec 7:28 one **m.** among a thousand have I......... 120
Ec 7:29 that God hath made **m.** upright; but 120
Ec 8:1 Who is as the wise **m.**? and who..............
Ec 8:6 the misery of **m.** is great upon him. 120
Ec 8:8 is no **m.** that hath power over the 120
Ec 8:9 **m.** ruleth over another to his hurt. 120
Ec 8:15 a **m.** hath no better thing under the 120
Ec 8:17 a **m.** cannot find out the work that....... 120
Ec 8:17 though a **m.** labour to seek it out, ... 120
Ec 8:17 a wise **m.** think to know it, yet shall.........
Ec 9:1 **m.** knoweth either love or hatred 120
Ec 9:12 For **m.** also knoweth not his time: 120
Ec 9:15 was found in it a poor wise **m.**,............ 376
Ec 9:15 yet no **m.** remembered that same........ 120
Ec 9:15 remembered that same poor **m.**. 376
Ec 10:14 a **m.** cannot tell what shall be; 120
Ec 11:8 But if a **m.** live many years, and 120
Ec 11:9 Rejoice, O young **m.**, in thy youth; and.....
Ec 12:5 because **m.** goeth to his long home, ... 120
Ec 12:13 for this is the whole duty of **m.**. 120
Ca 3:8 every **m.** hath his sword upon his........ 376
Ca 8:7 if a **m.** would give all the substance...... 376
Isa 2:9 And the mean **m.** boweth down, ... 1201
Isa 2:9 and the great **m.** humbleth himself: 376
Isa 2:11 lofty looks of **m.** shall be humbled,....... 120
Isa 2:17 loftiness of **m.** shall be bowed down, ... 120
Isa 2:20 In that day a **m.** shall cast his idols 120
Isa 2:22 Cease ye from **m.**, whose breath is...... 120
Isa 3:2 The mighty **m.**, and the...of war, ...
Isa 3:2 The mighty...and the **m.** of war, ... 376
Isa 3:3 the honourable **m.**, and the counsellor, ...
Isa 3:6 a **m.** shall take hold of his brother 376
Isa 4:1 women shall take hold of one **m.**, ... 376
Isa 5:15 the mean **m.** shall be brought down,..... 120
Isa 5:15 the mighty **m.** shall be humbled,.......... 376
Isa 6:5 because I am a **m.** of unclean lips, ... 376
Isa 6:11 and the houses without **m.**, and the 120
Isa 7:21 a **m.** shall nourish a young cow, ... 376
Isa 9:19 fire: no **m.** shall spare his brother........ 376
Isa 9:20 eat every **m.** the flesh of his own 376
Isa 10:13 down the inhabitants like a valiant **m.**: ......
Isa 13:12 I will make a **m.** more precious 582
Isa 13:12 even a **m.** than the golden wedge of..... 120
Isa 13:14 and as a sheep that no **m.** taketh up: ....
Isa 13:14 every **m.** turn to his own people, ... 376
Isa 14:16 **m.** that made the earth to tremble,...... 376
Isa 17:7 day shall a **m.** look to his Maker, ... 120
Isa 19:14 drunken **m.** staggereth in his vomit...........
Isa 24:10 is shut up, that no **m.** may come in...... 935
Isa 28:20 is shorter than that a **m.** can stretch.........
Isa 29:8 be as when an hungry **m.** dreameth, ...
Isa 29:8 or as when a thirsty **m.** dreameth, and,.....
Isa 29:21 make a **m.** an offender for a word,....... 120
Isa 31:7 every **m.** shall cast away his idols 376
Isa 31:8 with the sword, not of a mighty **m.**;..... 376
Isa 31:8 the sword, not of a mean **m.**, shall 120
Isa 32:2 a **m.** shall be as an hiding place 376
Isa 33:8 lie waste, the wayfaring **m.** ceaseth: ....
Isa 33:8 the cities, he regardeth no **m.**............. 582
Isa 35:6 shall the lame **m.** leap as an hart, and ....
Isa 36:6 whereon if a **m.** lean, it will go into...... 376
Isa 38:11 I shall behold **m.** no more with the 120
Isa 41:2 Who raised up the righteous **m.** from.......
Isa 41:28 For I beheld, and there was no **m.**; 376
Isa 42:13 Lord shall go forth as a mighty **m.**,....... 376
Isa 42:13 stir up jealousy like a **m.** of war: 376
Isa 44:13 maketh it after the figure of a **m.**, ... 376
Isa 44:13 according to the beauty of a **m.**;.......... 120
Isa 44:15 Then shall it be for a **m.** to burn: for ... 120
Isa 45:12 the earth, and created **m.** upon it: 120
Isa 46:11 the **m.** that executeth my counsel........ 376
Isa 47:3 and I will not meet thee as a **m.**.......... 120
Isa 49:7 One, to him whom **m.** despiseth, ... 5315
Isa 50:2 when I came, was there no **m.**? 376
Isa 51:12 be afraid of a **m.** that shall die,............ 582
Isa 51:12 son of **m.** which shall be made as 120
Isa 52:14 was so marred more than any **m.**, ... 376
Isa 53:3 a **m.** of sorrows, and acquainted with ... 376
Isa 55:7 the unrighteous **m.** his thoughts: 376
Isa 56:2 Blessed is the **m.** that doeth this, ... 582
Isa 56:2 the son of **m.** that layeth hold on it; 120
Isa 57:1 and no **m.** layeth it to heart:.............. 376
Isa 58:5 a day for a **m.** to afflict his soul? 120
Isa 59:16 he saw that there was no **m.**, and 376
Isa 60:15 hated, so that no **m.** went through thee,....
Isa 62:5 For as a young **m.** marrieth a virgin, ...
Isa 65:20 an old **m.** that hath not filled his days:.......
Isa 66:2 but to this **m.** will I look, even to him.......
Isa 66:3 killeth an ox is as if he slew a **m.**; 376
Isa 66:7 she was delivered of a **m.** child.......... 2145
Jer 2:6 a land that no **m.** passed through,......... 376
Jer 2:6 through, and where no **m.** dwelt? 120
Jer 3:1 If a **m.** put away his wife, and she........ 376
Jer 4:25 I beheld, and, lo, there was no **m.**,....... 120
Jer 4:29 and not a **m.** dwell therein. 376
Jer 5:1 if ye can find a **m.**, if there be any....... 376
Jer 7:5 between a **m.** and his neighbour; 376
Jer 7:20 this place, upon **m.**, and upon beast, ... 120
Jer 8:6 no **m.** repented...of his wickedness, ... 376
Jer 9:12 is the wise **m.**, that may understand..... 376
Jer 9:23 not the wise **m.** glory in his wisdom, ...
Jer 9:23 let the mighty **m.** glory in his might,.........
Jer 9:23 let not the rich **m.** glory in his riches: ....
Jer 10:14 **m.** is brutish in his knowledge:............ 120
Jer 10:23 that the way of **m.** is not in himself:..... 120
Jer 10:23 it is not in **m.** that walketh to driect ....
Jer 11:3 Cursed be the **m.** that obeyeth not 376
Jer 12:11 because no **m.** layeth it to heart. 376
Jer 12:15 them again, every **m.** to his heritage, ... 376
Jer 12:15 heritage, and every **m.** to his land. 376
Jer 13:11 girdle cleaveth to the loins of a **m.**,...... 376
Jer 14:8 as a wayfaring **m.** that turneth aside ....
Jer 14:9 shouldest thou be as a **m.** astonied, ... 376
Jer 14:9 as a mighty **m.** that cannot save?......... 376
Jer 15:10 hast borne me a **m.** of strife and a....... 376
Jer 15:10 **m.** of contention to the whole earth! 376
Jer 16:20 Shall a **m.** make gods unto himself,...... 120
Jer 17:5 Cursed be the **m.** that trusteth in....... 1397
Jer 17:5 that trusteth in **m.**, and maketh........... 120
Jer 17:7 is the **m.** that trusteth in the Lord, ... 1397
Jer 17:10 to give every **m.** according to his 376
Jer 18:14 Will a **m.** leave the snow of Lebanon ....
Jer 20:15 the **m.** who brought tidings to my........ 376
Jer 20:15 A **m.** child is born unto thee; 2145
Jer 20:16 let that **m.** be as the cities which......... 376
Jer 21:6 of this city, both **m.** and beast: 120
Jer 22:8 shall say every **m.** to his neighbour, ... 376
Jer 22:28 Is this **m.** Coniah a despised broken..... 376
Jer 22:30 the Lord, Write ye this **m.** childless, ... 376
Jer 22:30 a **m.** that shall not prosper in his 1397
Jer 22:30 for no **m.** of his seed shall prosper,...... 376
Jer 23:9 I am like a drunken **m.**, and like.......... 376
Jer 23:9 a **m.** whom wine hath overcome, ... 1397
Jer 23:27 they tell every **m.** to his neighbour, ... 376
Jer 23:34 even punish that **m.** and his house. 376
Jer 26:3 turn every **m.** from his evil way, that... 376
Jer 26:11 This **m.** is worthy to die; for he hath ... 376
Jer 26:16 This **m.** is not worthy to die: for he...... 376
Jer 26:20 there was also a **m.** that prophesied..... 376
Jer 27:5 the earth, the **m.** and the beast that..... 120
Jer 29:26 every **m.** that is mad, and maketh 376
Jer 29:32 shall not have a **m.** to dwell among...... 376
Jer 30:6 see whether a **m.** doth travail with..... 2145
Jer 30:6 **m.** with his hands on his loins, ... 1397
Jer 30:17 is Zion, whom no **m.** seeketh after. ....
Jer 31:22 A woman shall compass a **m.**. 1397
Jer 31:27 with the seed of **m.**, and with the........ 120
Jer 31:30 every **m.** that eateth the sour grape,.... 120
Jer 31:34 shall teach no more every **m.** his......... 376
Jer 31:34 neighbour, and every **m.** his brother,.... 376
Jer 32:43 It is desolate without **m.** or beast; 120
Jer 33:10 be desolate without **m.** and without...... 120
Jer 33:10 desolate, without **m.**, and without........ 120
Jer 33:12 is desolate without **m.** and without....... 120
Jer 33:17 David shall never want a **m.** to sit 376
Jer 33:18 Levites want a **m.** before me to offer... 376
Jer 34:9 every **m.** should let his manservant,..... 376
Jer 34:9 and every **m.** his maidservant, being 376
Jer 34:14 years let ye go every **m.** his brother.... 376
Jer 34:15 liberty every **m.** to his neighbour;........ 376
Jer 34:16 and caused every **m.** his servant, ... 376
Jer 34:16 and every **m.** his handmaid, whom....... 376
Jer 34:17 and every **m.** to his neighbour: 376
Jer 35:4 son of Igdaliah, a **m.** of God, which...... 376
Jer 35:15 ye now every **m.** from his evil way. 376
Jer 35:19 not want a **m.** to stand before me........ 376
Jer 36:3 return every **m.** from his evil way; 376
Jer 36:19 and let no **m.** know where ye be. 376
Jer 36:29 to cease from thence **m.** and beast?..... 120
Jer 37:10 they rise up every **m.** in his tent, ... 376
Jer 38:4 thee, let this **m.** be put to death: 376
Jer 38:4 this **m.** seeketh not the welfare of....... 376
Jer 38:24 Let no **m.** know of these words, and.... 376
Jer 40:15 Nethaniah, and no **m.** shall know it: 376
Jer 41:4 slain Gedaliah, and no **m.** knew it, ... 376
Jer 44:2 and no **m.** dwelleth therein, ...
Jer 44:7 to cut off from you **m.** and woman,...... 376
Jer 44:26 be named in the mouth of any **m.** of..... 376
Jer 46:6 flee away, nor the mighty **m.** escape;........
Jer 46:12 the mighty **m.** hath stumbled against........
Jer 49:5 and ye shall be driven out every **m.**..... 376
Jer 49:18 the Lord, no **m.** shall abide there, ... 376
Jer 49:18 neither shall a son of **m.** dwell in it. 120
Jer 49:19 who is a chosen **m.**, that I may appoint.....
Jer 49:33 ever: there shall no **m.** abide there, ... 376
Jer 49:33 nor any son of **m.** dwell in it.............. 120
Jer 50:3 they shall depart, both **m.** and beast..... 120
Jer 50:9 shall be as of a mighty expert **m.**;............
Jer 50:40 Lord; so shall no **m.** abide there,........... 376
Jer 50:40 shall any son of **m.** dwell therein. 120
Jer 50:42 put in array, like a **m.** to the battle, ... 376

Jer 50:44 who is a chosen **m.**, that I may appoint .....
Jer 51:6 and deliver every **m.** his soul:............ 376
Jer 51:17 **m.** is brutish by his knowledge;.......... 120
Jer 51:22 I break in pieces **m.** and woman;.......... 376
Jer 51:22 in pieces the young **m.** and the maid;........
Jer 51:43 a land wherein no **m.** dwelleth, ... 376
Jer 51:43 doth any son of **m.** pass thereby. 120
Jer 51:45 deliver ye every **m.** his soul from........ 376
Jer 51:62 remain in it, neither **m.** nor beast,........ 120
La 3:1 am the **m.** that hath seen affliction...... 1397
La 3:26 It is good that a **m.** should both hope........
La 3:27 good for a **m.** that he bear the yoke ... 1397
La 3:35 turn aside the right of a **m.** before 1397
La 3:36 subvert a **m.** in his cause, the Lord 120
La 3:39 doth a living **m.** complain, a............ 120
La 3:39 **m.** for the punishment of his sins?...... 1397
La 4:4 and no **m.** breaketh it unto them. ....
Eze 1:5 they had the likeness of a **m.**............. 120
Eze 1:8 hands of a **m.** under their wings 120
Eze 1:10 faces, they four had the face of a **m.**, ... 120
Eze 1:26 appearance of a **m.** above upon it. 120
Eze 2:1 Son of **m.**, stand upon thy feet, and..... 120
Eze 2:3 Son of **m.**, I send thee to the children .. 120
Eze 2:6 son of **m.**, be not afraid of them,......... 120
Eze 2:8 son of **m.**, hear what I say unto thee; .. 120
Eze 3:1 Son of **m.**, eat that thou findest;.......... 120
Eze 3:3 Son of **m.**, cause thy belly to eat,........ 120
Eze 3:4 Son of **m.**, go, get thee unto the house .120
Eze 3:10 Son of **m.**, all my words that I shall 120
Eze 3:17 Son of **m.**, I have made thee a........... 120
Eze 3:18 wicked **m.** shall die in his iniquity; ....
Eze 3:20 When a righteous **m.** doth turn from.........
Eze 3:21 if thou warn the righteous **m.**, that the......
Eze 3:25 O son of **m.**, behold, they shall put....... 120
Eze 4:1 son of **m.**, take thee a tile, and lay it ... 120
Eze 4:12 it with dung that cometh out of **m.**,....... 120
Eze 4:16 Son of **m.**, behold, I will break the....... 120
Eze 5:1 son of **m.**, take thee a sharp knife, ... 120
Eze 6:2 Son of **m.**, set thy face toward the 120
Eze 7:2 thou son of **m.**, thus saith the Lord....... 120
Eze 8:5 Son of **m.**, lift up thine eyes now the ... 120
Eze 8:6 Son of **m.**, seest thou what they do?.... 120
Eze 8:8 Son of **m.**, dig now in the wall: and...... 120
Eze 8:11 every **m.** his censer in his hand;.......... 376
Eze 8:12 Son of **m.**, hast thou seen what the 120
Eze 8:12 every **m.** in the chambers of his.......... 376
Eze 8:15, 17 thou seen this, O son of **m.**? 120
Eze 9:1 **m.** with his destroying weapon in......... 376
Eze 9:2 every **m.** a slaughter weapon in his...... 376
Eze 9:2 and one **m.** among them was clothed..... 376
Eze 9:3 called to the **m.** clothed with linen, ... 376
Eze 9:6 come not near any **m.** upon whom 376
Eze 9:11 behold, the **m.** clothed with linen,........ 376
Eze 10:2 spake unto the **m.** clothed with linen, ... 376
Eze 10:3 of the house, when the **m.** went in; 376
Eze 10:6 had commanded the **m.** clothed with..... 376
Eze 10:14 second face was the face of a **m.**,........ 120
Eze 10:21 the likeness of the hands of a **m.**......... 120
Eze 11:2 Then said he unto me, Son of **m.**, ... 120
Eze 11:4 against them, prophesy, O son of **m.**..... 120
Eze 11:15 Son of **m.**, thy brethren, even thy 120
Eze 12:2 Son of **m.**, thou dwellest in the midst.... 120
Eze 12:3 thou son of **m.**, prepare thee stuff 120
Eze 12:9 Son of **m.**, hath not the house of......... 120
Eze 12:18 Son of **m.**, eat...bread with quaking,..... 120
Eze 12:22 Son of **m.**, what is that proverb that 120
Eze 12:27 Son of **m.**, behold, they of the house.... 120
Eze 13:2 Son of **m.**, prophesy against the 120
Eze 13:17 thou son of **m.**, set thy face against 120
Eze 14:3 Son of **m.**, these men have set up....... 120
Eze 14:4 Every **m.** of the house of Israel 376
Eze 14:8 I will set my face against that **m.**,........ 376
Eze 14:13 Son of **m.**, when the land sinneth 120
Eze 14:13 will cut off **m.** and beast from it: 120
Eze 14:15 no **m.** may pass through because of.........
Eze 14:17 that I cut off **m.** and beast from it: 120
Eze 14:19 to cut off from it **m.**, and beast: 120
Eze 14:21 to cut off from it **m.** and beast?.......... 120
Eze 15:2 Son of **m.**, What is the vine tree 120
Eze 16:2 Son of **m.**, cause Jerusalem to know..... 120
Eze 17:2 Son of **m.**, put forth a riddle, and 120
Eze 18:5 But if a **m.** be just, and do that........... 376
Eze 18:8 true judgment between **m.** and **m.**,...... 376
Eze 18:24 abominations that the wicked **m.** doeth, ...
Eze 18:26 a righteous **m.** turneth away from his.........
Eze 18:27 when the wicked **m.** turneth away from.....
Eze 20:3 Son of **m.**, speak unto the elders of 120
Eze 20:4 Wilt thou judge them, son of **m.**, ... 120
Eze 20:7 ye away every **m.** the abominations...... 376
Eze 20:8 did not every **m.** cast away the........... 376
Eze 20:11, 13,21 which if a **m.** do, he shall even ... 120
Eze 20:27 son of **m.**, speak unto the house of...... 120
Eze 20:46 Son of **m.**, set thy face toward the 120
Eze 21:2 Son of **m.**, set thy face toward............ 120
Eze 21:6 Sigh therefore, thou son of **m.**, with..... 120
Eze 21:9 Son of **m.**, prophesy, and say, Thus..... 120
Eze 21:12 Cry and howl, son of **m.**: for it shall..... 120
Eze 21:14 Thou therefore, son of **m.**, prophesy, ... 120
Eze 21:19 thou son of **m.**, appoint thee two......... 120
Eze 21:28 And thou, son of **m.**, prophesy and 120
Eze 22:2 Now, thou son of **m.**, wilt thou judge, .. 120
Eze 22:18 Son of **m.**, the house of Israel is to...... 120
Eze 22:24 Son of **m.**, say unto her, Thou art 120
Eze 22:30 I sought for a **m.** among them, that 376
Eze 23:2 Son of **m.**, there were two women, ... 120
Eze 23:36 Son of **m.**, wilt thou judge Aholah 120
Eze 24:2 Son of **m.**, write thee the name of........ 120
Eze 24:16 Son of **m.**, behold, I take away from 120
Eze 24:25 thou son of **m.**, shall it not be in the 120
Eze 25:2 Son of **m.**, set thy face against the 120
Eze 25:13 will cut off **m.** and beast from it; 120
Eze 26:2 Son of **m.**, because that Tyrus hath 120
Eze 27:2 son of **m.**, take up a lamentation 120
Eze 28:2 Son of **m.**, say unto the prince of 120
Eze 28:2 yet thou art a **m.**, and not God, ... 120
Eze 28:9 thou shalt be a **m.**, and no God, in 120
Eze 28:12 Son of **m.**, take up a lamentation 120
Eze 28:21 Son of **m.**, set thy face against............ 120
Eze 29:2 Son of **m.**, set thy face against............ 120
Eze 29:8 and cut off **m.** and beast out of thee...... 120
Eze 29:11 No foot of **m.** shall pass through it, ... 120
Eze 29:18 Son of **m.**, Nebuchadrezzar king of....... 120
Eze 30:2 Son of **m.**, prophesy and say, Thus...... 120
Eze 30:21 Son of **m.**, I have broken the arm of.... 120
Eze 30:24 groanings of a deadly wounded **m.**............
Eze 31:2 Son of **m.**, speak unto Pharaoh king..... 120
Eze 32:2 Son of **m.**, take up a lamentation 120
Eze 32:10 every **m.** for his own life, in the day 376
Eze 32:13 shall the foot of **m.** trouble them 120
Eze 32:18 Son of **m.**, wail for the multitude of...... 120
Eze 33:2 Son of **m.**, speak to the children of...... 120
Eze 33:2 the land take a **m.** of their coasts, ... 376
Eze 33:7 O Son of **m.**, I have set thee a 120
Eze 33:8 O wicked **m.**, thou shalt surely die; ....
Eze 33:8 wicked **m.** shall die in his iniquity; ....
Eze 33:10 O thou son of **m.**, speak unto the 120
Eze 33:12 thou son of **m.**, say unto the children ... 120
Eze 33:24 Son of **m.**, they that inhabit those........ 120
Eze 33:30 thou son of **m.**, the children of thy....... 120
Eze 34:2 Son of **m.**, prophesy against the 120
Eze 35:2 Son of **m.**, set thy face against............ 120
Eze 36:1 thou son of **m.**, prophesy unto the 120
Eze 36:11 multiply upon you **m.** and beast; 120
Eze 36:17 Son of **m.**, when the house of Israel..... 120
Eze 37:3 Son of **m.**, can these bones live? 120
Eze 37:9 prophesy, son of **m.**, and say to the....... 120
Eze 37:11 Son of **m.**, these bones are the whole .. 120
Eze 37:16 thou son of **m.**, take thee one stick,..... 120
Eze 38:2 Son of **m.**, set thy face against Gog, ... 120
Eze 38:14 son of **m.**, prophesy and say unto.......... 120
Eze 39:1 thou son of **m.**, prophesy against 120
Eze 39:17 thou son of **m.**, thus saith the Lord...... 120
Eze 40:3 there was a **m.**, whose appearance 376
Eze 40:4 And the **m.** said unto me, ... 376
Eze 40:4 Son of **m.**, behold with thine eyes,....... 120
Eze 41:19 the face of a **m.** was toward the palm... 120
Eze 43:6 the house; and the **m.** stood by me...... 376
Eze 43:7 Son of **m.**, the place of my throne, ... 120
Eze 43:10 Thou son of **m.**, shew the house to 120
Eze 43:18 Son of **m.**, thus saith the Lord God;..... 120
Eze 44:2 and no **m.** shall enter in by it;............ 376
Eze 44:5 Son of **m.**, mark well, and behold 120
Eze 46:18 every **m.** from his possession. 376
Eze 47:3 when the **m.** that had the line in his..... 376
Eze 47:6 me, Son of **m.**, hast thou seen this?..... 120
Eze 47:20 till a **m.** come over against Hamath..........
Da 2:10 There is not a **m.** upon the earth 606
Da 2:25 I have found a **m.** of the captives....... 1400
Da 2:48 the king made Daniel a great **m.**, ...
Da 3:10 every **m.** that shall hear the sound........ 606
Da 5:11 There is a **m.** in thy kingdom, in........ 1400
Da 6:7 ask a petition of any God or **m.** for...... 606
Da 6:12 every **m.** that shall ask a petition......... 606
Da 6:12 a petition of any God or **m.** within 606
Da 7:4 made stand upon the feet as a **m.**,....... 606
Da 7:8 horn were eyes like the eyes of **m.**....... 606
Da 7:13 one like the Son of **m.** came with the ... 606
Da 8:15 me as the appearance of a **m.** 1397
Da 8:16 make this **m.** to understand the vision........
Da 8:17 Understand, O Son of **m.**; for at the 120
Da 9:21 even the **m.** Gabriel, whom I had........ 376
Da 10:5 a certain **m.** clothed in linen, whose 376
Da 10:11 me, O Daniel, a **m.** greatly beloved,..... 376
Da 10:18 one like the appearance of a **m.**,.......... 120
Da 10:19 O **m.** greatly beloved, fear not: 376
Da 12:6 one said to the **m.** clothed in linen, ... 376
Da 12:7 And I heard the **m.** clothed in linen, ... 376
Ho 3:3 thou shalt not be for another **m.**: 376
Ho 4:4 Yet let no **m.** strive, nor reprove 376
Ho 6:9 as troops of robbers wait for a **m.**, ... 376
Ho 9:7 is a fool, the spiritual **m.** is mad, ... 376
Ho 9:12 that there shall not be a **m.** left:.......... 120
Ho 11:4 I drew them with cords of a **m.**, ... 120
Ho 11:9 for I am God, and not **m.**; the Holy 376
Am 2:7 and a **m.** and his father will go in......... 376
Am 4:13 unto **m.** what is his thought, that......... 120
Am 5:19 As if a **m.** did flee from a lion, and 376
Jon 1:5 and cried every **m.** unto his god, and........
Jon 3:7 Let neither **m.** nor beast, herd nor 120
Jon 3:8 But let **m.** and beast be covered 120
Mic 2:2 they oppress a **m.** and his house,....... 1397
Mic 2:2 house, even a **m.** and his heritage. 376
Mic 2:11 If a **m.** walking in the spirit and........... 376
Mic 4:4 shall sit every **m.** under his vine and.... 376
Mic 5:5 this **m.** shall be the peace, when the.........
Mic 5:7 the grass, that tarrieth not for **m.**,....... 376
Mic 6:8 shewed thee, O **m.**, what is good; 120
Mic 6:9 the **m.** of wisdom shall see thy name: ....
Mic 7:2 The good **m.** is perished out of the,..........
Mic 7:2 they hunt every **m.** his brother 376
Mic 7:3 and the great **m.** he uttereth his ....
Na 3:18 mountains, and no **m.** gathereth them. ......
Hab 1:13 the wicked devoureth the **m.** that is ....
Hab 2:5 he is a proud **m.**, neither keepeth 1397
Zep 1:3 I will consume **m.** and beast; I............ 120
Zep 1:3 I will cut off **m.** from off the land,........ 120
Zep 1:14 the mighty **m.** shall cry there bitterly........
Zep 3:6 destroyed, so that there is no **m.**, ... 376
Hag 1:9 ye run every **m.** unto his own house. ... 376
Zec 1:8 a **m.** riding upon a red horse, and........ 376
Zec 1:10 the **m.** that stood among the myrtle..... 376
Zec 1:21 so that no **m.** did lift up his head: 376
Zec 2:1 behold a **m.** with a measureing line 376
Zec 2:4 Run, speak to this young **m.**, saying, ...
Zec 3:10 shall ye call every **m.** his neighbour ....
Zec 4:1 as a **m.** that is wakened out of his 376
Zec 6:12 the **m.** whose name is The Branch;....... 376
Zec 7:9 compassions every **m.** to his brother: ... 376
Zec 7:14 no **m.** passed through nor returned:..........
Zec 8:4 every **m.** with his staff in his hand 376
Zec 8:10 days there was no hire for **m.**, nor 120
Zec 8:16 Speak ye every **m.** the truth to his 376
Zec 9:1 the eyes of **m.**, as of all the tribes....... 120
Zec 9:13 thee as the sword of a mighty **m.**.............
Zec 10:7 of Ephraim shall be like a mighty **m.**, ...
Zec 12:1 and formeth the spirit of **m.** within....... 120
Zec 13:5 for **m.** taught me to keep cattle........... 120
Zec 13:7 against the **m.** that is my fellow, ... 1397
Mal 2:10 deal treacherously every **m.** against...... 376
Mal 2:12 will cut off the **m.** that doeth this, ... 376
Mal 3:8 Will a **m.** rob God? Yet ye have 120
Mal 3:17 as a **m.** spareth his own son that.......... 376
Mt 1:19 her husband,being a just **m.**, and.............
Mt 4:4 **M. shall not live by bread alone,**..... ***444***
Mt 5:40 **And if any m. will sue thee at the law,**.
Mt 6:24 **No m. can serve two masters: for**.. ***3762***
Mt 7:9 **what m. is there of you, whom if**..... ***444***
Mt 7:24 **I will liken him unto a wise m.,**..... ***435***
Mt 7:26 **shall be likened unto a foolish m.,**... ***435***
Mt 8:4 **See thou tell no m.; but go thy** ***3367***
Mt 8:9 For I am a **m.** under authority, ... *444*
Mt 8:9 I say to this **m.**, Go, and he goeth; and.....
Mt 8:20 **the Son of m. hath not where to**..... ***444***
Mt 8:27 What manner of **m.** is this, that even........
Mt 8:28 that no **m.** might pass by that way. *5100*
Mt 9:2 brought to him a **m.** sick of the palsy, ...
Mt 9:3 themselves, This **m.** blasphemeth. ....
Mt 9:6 **know that the Son of m. hath** ***444***
Mt 9:9 he saw a **m.**, named Matthew, sitting... *444*
Mt 9:16 **No m. putteth a piece of new cloth**.***3762***
Mt 9:30 **saying, See that no m. know it**....... ***3367***

Mt 9:32 they brought to him a dumb **m.**........... *444*
Mt 10:23 Israel, till the Son of m. be come.. *444*
Mt 10:35 I am come to set a m. at variance.. *444*
Mt 10:41 he that receiveth a righteous m. in......
Mt 10:41 in the name of a righteous m. shall.....
Mt 11:8 see? A m. clothed in soft raiment?.. *444*
Mt 11:19 The Son of m. came eating and...... *444*
Mt 11:19 Behold a m. gluttonous, and a........ *444*
Mt 11:27 no m. knoweth the Son, but the.... *3762*
Mt 11:27 neither knoweth any m. the Father,....
Mt 12:8 the Son of m. is Lord even of the... *444*
Mt 12:10 there was a **m.** which had his hand...... *444*
Mt 12:11 What m. shall there be among you, *444*
Mt 12:12 then is a m. better than a sheep?.... *444*
Mt 12:13 to the m., Stretch forth thine hand... *444*
Mt 12:19 shall any **m.** hear his voice in the............
Mt 12:29 except he first bind the strong m.?......
Mt 12:32 a word against the Son of m.,........ *444*
Mt 12:35 A good m. out of the good treasure.. *444*
Mt 12:35 an evil m. out of the evil treasure... *444*
Mt 12:40 so shall the Son of m. be three days *444*
Mt 12:43 unclean spirit is gone out of a m.,.. *444*
Mt 12:45 last state of that m. is worse than.. *444*
Mt 13:24 heaven is likened unto a m. which.. *444*
Mt 13:31 of mustard seed, which a m. took,.. *444*
Mt 13:37 the good seed is the Son of m.;....... *444*
Mt 13:41 The Son of m. shall send forth his.. *444*
Mt 13:44 the which when a m. hath found,... *444*
Mt 13:45 heaven is like unto a merchant m.,. *444*
Mt 13:52 unto a m. that is an householder,... *444*
Mt 13:54 Whence hath this **m.** this wisdom,............
Mt 13:56 then hath this **m.** all these things?............
Mt 15:11 goeth into the mouth defileth a m.; *444*
Mt 15:11 out of the mouth, this defileth a m.. *444*
Mt 15:18 the heart; and they defile the m..... *444*
Mt 15:20 are the things which defile a m.:.... *444*
Mt 15:20 unwashen hands defileth not a m.. *444*
Mt 16:13 men say that I the Son of m. am?... *444*
Mt 16:20 tell no **m.** that he was Jesus the........ *3367*
Mt 16:24 If any m. will come after me, let........
Mt 16:26 what is a m. profited, if he shall.... *444*
Mt 16:26 a m. give in exchange for his soul?. *444*
Mt 16:27 Son of m. shall come in the glory... *444*
Mt 16:27 reward every m. according to his.........
Mt 16:28 till they see the Son of m. coming.. *444*
Mt 17:8 they saw no **m.**, save Jesus only........ *3762*
Mt 17:9 saying, Tell the vision to no m....... *3367*
Mt 17:9 until the Son of m. be risen again.. *444*
Mt 17:12 shall also the Son of m. suffer of.... *444*
Mt 17:14 came to him a certain **m.**, kneeling...... *444*
Mt 17:22 Son of m. shall be betrayed into..... *444*
Mt 18:7 woe to that m. by whom the offence *444*
Mt 18:11 For the Son of m. is come to save.. *444*
Mt 18:12 if a m. have an hundred sheep, and *444*
Mt 18:17 let him be unto thee as an heathen m..
Mt 19:3 lawful for a **m.** to put away his wife..... *444*
Mt 19:5 this cause shall a m. leave father.... *444*
Mt 19:6 together, let not m. put asunder...... *444*
Mt 19:10 case of the **m.** be so with his wife,....... *444*
Mt 19:20 The young **m.** saith unto him, All....... *3495*
Mt 19:22 the young **m.** heard that saying,......... *3495*
Mt 19:23 rich m. shall hardly enter into the *3495*
Mt 19:24 than for a rich m. to enter into..... *3495*
Mt 19:28 when the Son of m. shall sit in the.. *444*
Mt 20:1 unto a m. that is an householder,... *444*
Mt 20:7 him, Because no m. hath hired us.. *3762*
Mt 20:9 hour, they received every m. a penny. .
Mt 20:10 likewise recieved every m. a penny......
Mt 20:18 Son of m. shall be betrayed unto.... *444*
Mt 20:28 Even as the Son of m. came not to.. *444*
Mt 21:3 And if any m. say ought unto you,.......
Mt 21:28 A certain m. had two sons; and he.. *444*
Mt 22:11 a m. which had not on a wedding... *444*
Mt 22:16 neither carest thou for any **m.**: for..... *3762*
Mt 22:24 If a **m.** die, having no children, his..... *5100*
Mt 22:46 no **m.** was able to answer him a........ *3762*
Mt 22:46 neither durst any **m.** from that day..........
Mt 23:9 And call no m. your father upon the...
Mt 24:4 Take heed that no m. deceive you. *5100*
Mt 24:23 Then if any m. shall say unto you,.......
Mt 24:27 also the coming of the Son of m. be *444*
Mt 24:30 the sign of the Son of m. in heaven: *444*
Mt 24:30 the Son of m. coming in the clouds *444*
Mt 24:36 that day and hour knoweth no m.,. *3762*
Mt 24:37, 39 the coming of the Son of m. be.. *444*
Mt 24:44 ye think not the Son of m. cometh. *444*
Mt 25:13 hour wherein the Son of m. cometh *444*
Mt 25:14 a m. travelling into a far country,.. *444*
Mt 25:15 every m. according to his...ability;......
Mt 25:24 knew thee that thou art an hard m., *444*
Mt 25:31 Son of m. shall come in his glory,.. *444*
Mt 26:2 and the Son of m. is betrayed to be *444*
Mt 26:18 Go into the city to such a m., and say.
Mt 26:24 Son of m. goeth as it is written of.. *444*
Mt 26:24 but woe unto that m. by whom the. *444*
Mt 26:24 by whom the Son of m. is betrayed! *444*
Mt 26:24 been good for that m. if he had not *444*
Mt 26:45 Son of m. is betrayed into the........ *444*
Mt 26:64 ye see the Son of m. sitting on the. *444*
Mt 26:72 with an oath, I do not know the **m.**....... *444*
Mt 26:74 to swear, saying, I know not the **m.**..... *444*
Mt 27:19 thou nothing to do with that just **m.**:.........
Mt 27:32 they found a **m.** of Cyrene, Simon....... *444*
Mt 27:47 that, said, This **m.** calleth for Elias..........
Mt 27:57 there came a rich **m.** of Arimathaea,..... *444*
Mk 1:23 a **m.** with an unclean spirit; and......... *444*
Mk 1:44 See thou say nothing to any m..... *3367*
Mk 2:7 doth this **m.** thus speak blasphemies?........
Mk 2:10 know that the Son of m. hath........ *444*
Mk 2:21 No m. also seweth a piece of new.. *3762*
Mk 2:22 no m. putteth new wine into old... *3762*
Mk 2:27 The sabbath was made for m......... *444*
Mk 2:27 and not m. for the sabbath............ *444*
Mk 2:28 the Son of m. is Lord also of the.... *444*
Mk 3:1 was a **m.** there which had a withered... *444*
Mk 3:3 the **m.** which had the withered hand,.... *444*
Mk 3:5 the m., Stretch forth thine hand....... *444*
Mk 3:27 No m. can enter into a strong....... *3762*
Mk 3:27 he will first bind the strong m.;.... *2478*
Mk 4:23 If any m. have ears to hear, let him....
Mk 4:26 as if a m. should cast seed into the. *444*
Mk 4:41 What manner of **m.** is this, that even........
Mk 5:2 tombs a **m.** with an unclean spirit,....... *444*
Mk 5:3 no **m.** could bind him, no, not with....... *3762*
Mk 5:4 neither could any **m.** tame him................
Mk 5:8 Come out of the m., thou unclean.. *444*
Mk 5:37 he suffered no **m.** to follow him,........ *3762*
Mk 5:43 that no **m.** should know it; and.......... *3367*
Mk 6:2 whence hath this **m.** these things?............
Mk 6:20 knowing that he was a just **m.** and....... *435*
Mk 7:11 If a m. shall say to his father or.... *444*
Mk 7:15 There is nothing from without a m., *444*
Mk 7:15 those are they that defile the m....... *444*
Mk 7:16 If any m. have ears to hear, let him....
Mk 7:18 from without entereth into the m.,. *444*
Mk 7:20 out of the m., that defileth the m... *444*
Mk 7:23 from within, and defile the m......... *444*
Mk 7:24 and would have no **m.** know it:......... *3762*
Mk 7:36 them that they should tell no **m.**:........ *3367*
Mk 8:4 can a **m.** satisfy these men with......... *5100*
Mk 8:22 and they bring a blind **m.** unto him,..........
Mk 8:23 And he took the blind **m.** by the hand,......
Mk 8:25 restored, and saw every **m.** clearly..........
Mk 8:30 that they should tell no **m.** of him...... *3367*
Mk 8:31 Son of **m.** must suffer many things,...... *444*
Mk 8:36 For what shall it profit a m., if he. *444*
Mk 8:37 a m. give in exchange for his soul?. *444*
Mk 8:38 shall the Son of m. be ashamed,..... *444*
Mk 9:8 saw no **m.** any more, save Jesus.......... *3762*
Mk 9:9 them that they should tell no **m.**......... *3367*
Mk 9:9 till the Son of **m.** were risen from........ *444*
Mk 9:12 how it is written of the Son of m.,.. *444*
Mk 9:30 not that any **m.** should know it.............
Mk 9:31 The Son of m. is delivered into the. *444*
Mk 9:35 If any m. desire to be first, the same...
Mk 9:39 is no m. which shall do a miracle.. *3762*
Mk 10:2 lawful for a **m.** to put away his wife?.... *435*
Mk 10:7 cause shall a m. leave his father..... *444*
Mk 10:9 together, let not m. put asunder..... *444*
Mk 10:25 a rich m. to enter into the kingdom....
Mk 10:29 is no m. that hath left house, or... *3762*
Mk 10:33 Son of m. shall be delivered unto.... *444*
Mk 10:45 For even the Son of m. came not to. *444*
Mk 10:49 And they call the blind **m.**, saying............
Mk 10:51 The blind **m.** said unto him, Lord,............
Mk 11:2 a colt tied, whereon never m. sat;... *444*
Mk 11:3 if any m. say unto you, Why do ye......
Mk 11:14 No m. eat fruit of thee hereafter... *3367*
Mk 11:16 any **m.** should carry any vessel................
Mk 12:1 A certain m. planted a vineyard,..... *444*
Mk 12:14 thou art true, and carest for no **m.**:..... *444*
Mk 12:34 no **m.** after that durst ask him any..... *3762*
Mk 13:5 Take heed lest any m. deceive you;......
Mk 13:21 then if any m. shall say to you, Lo,....
Mk 13:26 they see the Son of m. coming........ *444*
Mk 13:32 day and that hour knoweth no m., *3762*
Mk 13:34 For the Son of m. is as a...taking a.....
Mk 13:34 is as a m. taking a far journey....... *444*
Mk 13:34 servants, and to every m. his work,.....
Mk 14:13 meet you a m. bearing a pitcher..... *444*
Mk 14:21 The Son of m. indeed goeth, as....... *444*
Mk 14:21 woe to that m. by whom the Son of *444*
Mk 14:21 whom the Son of m. is betrayed!.... *444*
Mk 14:21 were it for that m. if he had never.. *444*
Mk 14:41 Son of m. is betrayed into the........ *444*
Mk 14:51 followed him a certain young **m.**,........ *3495*
Mk 14:62 ye shall see the Son of m. sitting...... *444*
Mk 14:71 know not this **m.** of whom ye speak..... *444*
Mk 15:24 upon them, what every **m.** should take......
Mk 15:39 Truly this **m.** was the Son of God........ *444*
Mk 16:5 they saw a young **m.** sitting on the..... *3495*
Mk 16:8 said they any thing to any **m.**;............ *3762*
Lu 1:18 for I am an old **m.**, and my wife well........
Lu 1:27 to a **m.** whose name was Joseph,........ *435*
Lu 1:34 shall this be, seeing I know not a **m.**?.. *435*
Lu 2:25 there was a **m.** in Jerusalem, whose..... *444*
Lu 2:25 the same **m.** was just and devout,....... *444*
Lu 2:52 and in favour with God and **m.**........... *444*
Lu 3:14 Do violence to no **m.**, neither............ *3367*
Lu 4:4 m. shall not live by bread alone,...... *444*
Lu 4:33 in the synagogue there was a **m.**,........ *444*
Lu 5:8 me; for I am a sinful **m.**, O Lord......... *435*
Lu 5:12 city; behold a **m.** full of leprosy:........... *435*
Lu 5:14 And he charged him to tell no m... *3367*
Lu 5:18 brought in a bed a **m.** which was.......... *444*
Lu 5:20 him, M., thy sins are forgiven thee.. *444*
Lu 5:24 Son of m. hath power upon earth... *444*
Lu 5:36 No m. putteth a piece of a new..... *3762*
Lu 5:37 no m. putteth new wine into old.... *3762*
Lu 5:39 No m. also having drunk old wine. *3762*
Lu 6:5 the Son of m. is Lord also of the.... *444*
Lu 6:6 a **m.** whose right hand was withered.... *444*
Lu 6:8 the **m.** which had the withered hand,..... *444*
Lu 6:10 he said unto the m., Stretch forth..... *444*
Lu 6:30 Give to every m. that asketh of thee;...
Lu 6:45 good m. out of the good treasure...... *444*
Lu 6:45 an evil m. out of the evil treasure of *444*
Lu 6:48 is like a m. which built an house,... *444*
Lu 6:49 like a m. that without a foundation. *444*
Lu 7:8 I also am a **m.** set under authority,...... *444*
Lu 7:12 there was a dead **m.** carried out,............
Lu 7:14 Young m., I say unto thee, Arise.. *3495*
Lu 7:25 see? A m. clothed in soft raiment?.. *444*
Lu 7:34 The Son of m. is come eating and... *444*
Lu 7:34 Behold a gluttonous m., and a....... *444*
Lu 7:39 This **m.**, if he were a prophet, would........
Lu 8:16 No m., when he hath lighted a...... *3762*
Lu 8:25 What manner of **m.** is this! for he...........
Lu 8:27 a certain **m.**, which had devils long....... *435*
Lu 8:29 unclean spirit to come out of the **m.**...... *444*
Lu 8:33 Then went the devils out of the **m.**,...... *444*
Lu 8:35 found the **m.**, out of whom the devils... *444*
Lu 8:38 the **m.** out of whom the devils were..... *435*
Lu 8:41 there came a **m.** named Jairus,............ *435*
Lu 8:51 he suffered no **m.** to go in, save........ *3762*
Lu 8:56 should tell no **m.** what was done.......... *3367*
Lu 9:21 commanded them to tell no **m.** that.... *3367*
Lu 9:22 The Son of m. must suffer many.... *444*
Lu 9:23 If any m. will come after me, let........
Lu 9:25 For what is a m. advantaged, if he. *444*
Lu 9:26 shall the Son of m. be ashamed,...... *444*
Lu 9:36 and told no **m.** in those days any of.... *3762*
Lu 9:38 a **m.** of the company cried out,........... *435*
Lu 9:44 for the Son of m. shall be delivered. *444*
Lu 9:56 Son of m. is not come to destroy.... *444*
Lu 9:57 a certain **m.** said unto him, Lord,...........
Lu 9:58 Son of m. hath not where to lay.......... *444*
Lu 9:62 No m., having put his hand to the.. *3762*
Lu 10:4 and salute no m. by the way........... *3367*
Lu 10:22 no m. knoweth who the Son is,..... *3762*
Lu 10:30 m. went down from Jerusalem to.... *444*
Lu 11:21 a strong m. armed keepeth his...........
Lu 11:24 unclean spirit is gone out of a m.,.. *444*
Lu 11:26 last state of that m. is worse than.. *444*
Lu 11:30 Son of the m. be to this generation. *444*
Lu 11:33 No m., when he hath lighted a....... *3762*
Lu 12:8 shall the Son of m. also confess...... *444*
Lu 12:10 a word against the Son of m.,........ *444*

Lu 12:14 unto him, M., who made me a judge..444
Lu 12:16 ground of a certain rich m............ 444
Lu 12:40 Son of m. cometh at an hour when..444
Lu 13:6 A certain m. had a fig tree planted.....
Lu 13:19 of mustard seed, which a m. took, ..444
Lu 14:2 a certain m. before him which had....... 444
Lu 14:8 art bidden of any m. to a wedding,. 444
Lu 14:8 lest a more honourable m. than...... 444
Lu 14:9 and say to thee, Give this m. place;.444
Lu 14:16 certain m. made a great supper,..... 444
Lu 14:26 If any m. come to me, and hate..........
Lu 14:30 This m. began to build, and was..... 444
Lu 15:2 This m. receiveth sinners, and eateth ....
Lu 15:4 What m. of you, having an hundred444
Lu 15:11 he said, A certain m. had two sons:..444
Lu 15:16 did eat: and no m. gave unto him...3762
Lu 16:1 There was a certain rich m., which..444
Lu 16:16 preached, and every m. presseth..........
Lu 16:19 There was a certain rich m.,.......... 444
Lu 16:22 rich m. also died, and was buried;........
Lu 17:22 one of the days of the Son of m.,... 444
Lu 17:24 so shall also the Son of m. be in.... 444
Lu 17:26 also in the days of the Son of m..... 444
Lu 17:30 day when the Son of m. is revealed..444
Lu 18:2 not God, neither regarded m.......... 444
Lu 18:4 I fear not God, nor regard m.;........ 444
Lu 18:8 when the Son of m. cometh, shall... 444
Lu 18:14 this m. went down to his house...........
Lu 18:25 a rich m. to enter into the kingdom....
Lu 18:29 is no m. that hath left house, or... 3762
Lu 18:31 prophets concerning the Son of m... 444
Lu 18:35 blind m. sat by the wayside begging: ....
Lu 19:2 was a m. named Zacchaeus, which........ 435
Lu 19:7 be guest with a m. that is a sinner. 435
Lu 19:8 have taken any thing from any m. ....
Lu 19:10 the Son of m. is come to seek and.. 444
Lu 19:14 will not have this m. to reign over......
Lu 19:15 how much every m. had gained by.......
Lu 19:21 because thou art an austere m.:...... 444
Lu 19:22 knewest that I was an austere m.,.. 444
Lu 19:30 colt tied, whereon yet never m. sat:.444
Lu 19:31 any m. ask you, Why do ye loose.........
Lu 20:9 A certain m. planted a vineyard,..... 444
Lu 21:27 see the Son of m. coming in a cloud444
Lu 21:36 and to stand before the Son of m.... 444
Lu 22:10 a m. meet you, bearing a pitcher.... 444
Lu 22:22 And truly the Son of m. goeth,........ 444
Lu 22:22 that m. by whom he is betrayed!..... 444
Lu 22:48 betrayest thou the Son of m........... 444
Lu 22:56 and said, This m. was also with him. ....
Lu 22:58 And Peter said, M., I am not............. 444
Lu 22:60 M., I know not what thou sayest......... 444
Lu 22:69 Hereafter shall the Son of m. sit 444
Lu 23:4 the people, I find no fault in this m...... 444
Lu 23:6 whether the m. were a Galilaean. 444
Lu 23:14 Ye have brought this m. unto me, as.... 444
Lu 23:14 I,...have found no fault in this m. 444
Lu 23:18 Away with this m., and release unto.........
Lu 23:41 but this m. hath done nothing amiss..........
Lu 23:47 Certainly this was a righteous m.......... 444
Lu 23:50 there was a m. named Joseph, a 435
Lu 23:50 and he was a good m., and a just: 435
Lu 23:52 This m. went unto Pilate, and begged........
Lu 23:53 wherein never m. before was laid....... 3762
Lu 24:7 The Son of m. must be delivered 444
Joh 1:6 There was a m. sent from God, whose..444
Joh 1:9 lighteth every m. that cometh into........ 444
Joh 1:13 nor of the will of m., but of God. 435
Joh 1:18 No m. hath seen God at any time; 3762
Joh 1:30 me cometh a m. which is preferred...... 435
Joh 1:51 and descending upon the Son of m...444
Joh 2:10 Every m. at the beginning doth set...... 444
Joh 2:25 not that any should testify of m.:......... 444
Joh 2:25 for he knew what was in m................ 444
Joh 3:1 There was a m. of the Pharisees,........ 444
Joh 3:2 for no m. can do these miracles.......... 3762
Joh 3:3 Except a m. be born again, he...... 5100
Joh 3:4 How can a m. be born when he is........ 444
Joh 3:5 Except a m. be born of water and..5100
Joh 3:13 no m. hath ascended up to heaven,.3762
Joh 3:13 the son of m. which is in heaven. 444
Joh 3:14 so must the Son of m. be lifted up:..444
Joh 3:27 A m. can receive nothing, except it....... 444
Joh 3:32 and no m. receiveth his testimony...... 3762
Joh 4:27 no m. said, What seekest thou? or, ... 3762
Joh 4:29 Come, see a m., which told me all....... 444
Joh 4:33 any m. brought him ought to eat?............
Joh 4:50 the m. believed the word that Jesus..... 444
Joh 5:5 certain m. was there, which had an...... 444
Joh 5:7 The impotent m. answered him, Sir,.........
Joh 5:7 I have no m., when the water is 444
Joh 5:9 immediately the m. was made whole, ... 444
Joh 5:12 What m. is that which said unto 444
Joh 5:15 m. departed, and told the Jews that..... 444
Joh 5:22 Father judgeth no m., but hath..... 3762
Joh 5:27 also, because he is the Son of m..... 444
Joh 5:34 I receive not testimony from m....... 444
Joh 6:27 the Son of m. shall give unto you:.. 444
Joh 6:44 No m. can come to me, except the.3762
Joh 6:45 Every m. therefore that hath heard,....
Joh 6:46 that any m. hath seen the Father,.......
Joh 6:50 a m. may eat thereof, and not die. .5100
Joh 6:51 if any m. eat of this bread, he shall....
Joh 6:52 can this m. give us his flesh to eat?..........
Joh 6:53 ye eat the flesh of the Son of m.,... 444
Joh 6:62 if ye shall see the Son of m. ascend.444
Joh 6:65 no m. can come unto me, except... 3762
Joh 7:4 is no m. that doeth any thing in......... 3762
Joh 7:12 some said, He is a good m.: others..........
Joh 7:13 no m. spake openly of him for fear..... 3762
Joh 7:15 How knoweth this m. letters, having.........
Joh 7:17 If any m. will do his will, he shall......
Joh 7:22 on the sabbath day circumcise a m. .444
Joh 7:23 If a m. on the sabbath day receive.. 444
Joh 7:23 made a m. every whit whole on the. 444
Joh 7:27 we know this m. whence he is: but..........
Joh 7:27 no m. knoweth whence he is............ 3762
Joh 7:30 him: but no m. laid hands on him, ... 3762
Joh 7:31 than these which this m. hath done? ....
Joh 7:37 If any m. thirst, let him come unto.....
Joh 7:44 him; but no m. laid hands on him. 3762
Joh 7:46 answered, Never m. spake like this 444
Joh 7:46 Never...spake like this m.................. 444
Joh 7:51 Doth our law judge any m., before....... 444
Joh 7:53 And every m. went unto his own house.....
Joh 8:10 hath no m. condemned thee?......... 3762
Joh 8:11 She said, No m., Lord. And Jesus...... 3762
Joh 8:15 after the flesh; I judge no m.,........ 3762
Joh 8:20 and no m. laid hands on him; for........ 3762
Joh 8:28 ye have lifted up the Son of m.,..... 444
Joh 8:33 and were never in bondage to any m. ....
Joh 8:40 a m. that hath told you the truth,.. 444
Joh 8:51, 52 If a m. keep my saying, he shall5100
Joh 9:1 he saw a m. which was blind from....... 444
Joh 9:2 who did sin, this m., or his parents, ...
Joh 9:3 hath this m. sinned, nor his parents:...
Joh 9:4 cometh, when no m. can work. 3762
Joh 9:6 he anointed the eyes of the blind m.........
Joh 9:11 A m. that is called Jesus made clay, ... 444
Joh 9:16 This m. is not of God, because he....... 444
Joh 9:16 said, How can a m. that is a sinner...... 444
Joh 9:17 say unto the blind m. again, What ....
Joh 9:22 if any m. did confess that he was............
Joh 9:24 called they the m. that was blind, ... 444
Joh 9:24 we know that this m. is a sinner. 444
Joh 9:30 m. answered and said unto them, ... 444
Joh 9:31 but if any m. be a worshipper of God,.......
Joh 9:32 that any m. opened the eyes of one..........
Joh 9:33 If this m. were not of God, he could do ....
Joh 10:9 by me if any m. enter in, he shall be...
Joh 10:18 No m. taketh it from me, but I lay.3762
Joh 10:28 any m. pluck them out of my hand. ....
Joh 10:29 no m. is able to pluck them out of.3762
Joh 10:33 being a m., makest thyself God........... 444
Joh 10:41 that John spake of this m. were true.........
Joh 11:1 a certain m. was sick, named Lazarus, ...
Joh 11:9 If any m. walk in the day, he ....
Joh 11:10 But if a m. walk in the night, he.. 5100
Joh 11:37 Could not this m., which opened the.........
Joh 11:37 even this m. should not have died?...........
Joh 11:47 for this m. doeth many miracles. 444
Joh 11:50 one m. should die for the people, ... 444
Joh 11:57 if any m. knew where he were, he..........
Joh 12:23 the Son of m. should be glorified.... 444
Joh 12:26 If any m. serve me, let him follow ......
Joh 12:26 if any m. serve me, him will my..........
Joh 12:34 The Son of m. must be lifted up? 444
Joh 12:34 who is this Son of m.? 444
Joh 12:47 And if any m. hear my words, and......
Joh 13:28 no m. at the table knew for what....... 3762
Joh 13:31 said, Now is the Son of m. glorified,.444
Joh 14:6 no m. cometh unto the Father, but3762
Joh 14:23 If a m. love me, he will keep my... 5100
Joh 15:6 If a m. abide not in me, he is cast.5100
Joh 15:13 Greater love hath no m. than this,.3762
Joh 15:13 that a m. lay down his life for his.5100
Joh 15:24 the works which none other m. did,....
Joh 16:21 joy that a m. is born into the world.444
Joh 16:22 your joy no m. taketh from you... 3762
Joh 16:30 not that any m. should ask thee:..............
Joh 16:32 shall be scattered, every m. to his own.
Joh 18:14 one m. should die for the people. 444
Joh 18:29 accusation bring ye against the m.?...... 444
Joh 18:31 lawful for us to put any m. to death:... 3762
Joh 18:40 saying, Not this m., but Barabbas ....
Joh 18:40 saying, Not this m., but Barabbas ....
Joh 19:5 saith unto them, Behold the m.! 444
Joh 19:12 If thou let this m. go, thou art not ....
Joh 19:41 wherein was never m. yet laid........... 3762
Joh 21:21 Jesus, Lord, and what shall this m. do? .....
Ac 1:18 this m. purchased a field with the............
Ac 1:20 desolate, and let no m. dwell therein: ....
Ac 2:6 m. heard them speak in his own........ 1520
Ac 2:8 we every m. in our own tongue,......... 1520
Ac 2:22 a m. approved of God among you........ 435
Ac 2:45 to all men, as every m. had need.............
Ac 3:2 m. lame from his mother's womb......... 435
Ac 3:11 lame m. which was healed held Peter........
Ac 3:12 holiness we had made this m. to walk?......
Ac 3:16 his name hath made this m. strong,..........
Ac 4:9 good deed done to the impotent m.,...... 444
Ac 4:10 doth this m. stand here before you...........
Ac 4:14 the m. which was healed standing........ 444
Ac 4:17 henceforth to no m. in this name. 444
Ac 4:22 the m. was above forty years old, ... 444
Ac 4:35 every m. according as he had need...........
Ac 5:1 a certain m. named Ananias, with 435
Ac 5:13 durst no m. join himself to them: 3762
Ac 5:23 had opened, we found no m. within. ... 3762
Ac 5:37 After this m. rose up Judas of Galilee ....
Ac 6:5 a m. full of faith and of the Holy........... 435
Ac 6:13 said, This m. ceaseth not to speak....... 444
Ac 7:56 Son of m. standing on the right hand.... 444
Ac 8:9 was a certain m., called Simon,........... 435
Ac 8:10 This m. is the great power of God. ....
Ac 8:27 behold, a m. of Ethiopia, an eunuch 435
Ac 8:31 I, except some m. should guide me?.........
Ac 8:34 this? of himself, or of some other m.?.......
Ac 9:7 hearing a voice, but seeing no m........ 3367
Ac 9:8 eyes were opened, he saw no m........ 3762
Ac 9:12 in a vision a m. named Ananias...... 435
Ac 9:13 heard by many of this m., how much..... 435
Ac 9:33 he found a certain m. named AEneas,... 444
Ac 10:1 m. in Caesarea called Cornelius,.......... 435
Ac 10:2 A devout m., and one that feared God .....
Ac 10:22 just m., and one that feareth God,....... 435
Ac 10:26 Stand up; I myself also am a m........... 444
Ac 10:28 a m. that is a Jew to keep company, ... 435
Ac 10:28 should not call any m. common or......... 444
Ac 10:30 a m. stood before me in bright............ 435
Ac 10:47 Can any m. forbid water, that 5100
Ac 11:24 he was a good m., and full of the 435
Ac 11:29 every m. according to his ability, ... 1538
Ac 12:22 the voice of a god, and not of a m....... 444
Ac 13:7 Sergius Paulus, a prudent m.; who........ 435
Ac 13:21 of Cis, a m. of the tribe of Benjamin, ... 435
Ac 13:22 of Jesse, a m. after mine own heart, ... 435
Ac 13:38 through this m. is preached unto you........
Ac 13:41 though a m. declare it unto you. 5100
Ac 14:8 there sat a certain m. at Lystra, ... 435
Ac 16:9 There stood a m. of Macedonia, and..... 435
Ac 17:31 by that m. whom he hath ordained;...... 435
Ac 18:10 no m. shall set on thee to hurt...... 3762
Ac 18:24 an eloquent m., and mighty in the........ 435
Ac 18:25 This m. was instructed in the way of........
Ac 19:16 them. in whom the evil spirit was......... 444
Ac 19:24 For a certain m. named Demetrius, ...
Ac 19:35 what m. is there that knoweth not....... 444
Ac 19:38 have a matter against any m., the law.......
Ac 20:9 sat in a window a certain young m. 3494
Ac 20:12 And they brought the young m. alive, ...
Ac 21:9 And the same m. had four daughters, ...
Ac 21:11 bind the m. that owneth this girdle, ... 435
Ac 21:28 This is the m., that teacheth all men.... 444
Ac 21:39 I am a m. which am a Jew of Tarsus, ... 444
Ac 22:3 I am verily a m. which am a Jew, ... 435
Ac 22:12 a devout m. according to the law,........ 435

Ac 22:25 to scourge a **m.** that is a Roman, ... *444*
Ac 22:26 thou doest: for this **m.** is a Roman....... *444*
Ac 23:9 saying, We find no evil in this **m.**: *444*
Ac 23:17 Bring this young **m.** unto the chief *3494*
Ac 23:18 to bring this young **m.** unto thee, ... *3494*
Ac 23:22 captain...let the young **m.** depart, ... *3494*
Ac 23:22 tell no **m.** that thou hast shewed *3367*
Ac 23:27 This **m.** was taken of the Jews, and *435*
Ac 23:30 that the Jews laid wait for the **m.**, ... *435*
Ac 24:5 have found this **m.** a pestilent fellow, ... *435*
Ac 24:12 the temple disputing with any **m.**, ...
Ac 25:5 down with me, and accuse this **m.**, ... *435*
Ac 25:11 no **m.** may deliver me unto them. *3762*
Ac 25:14 a certain **m.** left in bonds by Felix: *435*
Ac 25:16 the Romans to deliver any **m.** to die, ... *444*
Ac 25:17 commanded the **m.** to be brought *435*
Ac 25:22 I would also hear the **m.** myself. *444*
Ac 25:24 ye see this **m.**, about whom all the..........
Ac 26:31 This **m.** doeth nothing worthy of *444*
Ac 26:32 This **m.** might have been set at......... *444*
Ac 28:4 No doubt this **m.** is a murderer, ... *444*
Ac 28:7 possessions of the chief **m.** of the island, ...
Ac 28:31 all confidence, no **m.** forbidding him. ....
Ro 1:23 image made like to corruptible **m.**, ... *444*
Ro 2:1 inexcusable, O **m.**, whosoever thou....... *444*
Ro 2:3 And thinkest thou this, O **m.**, that *444*
Ro 2:6 to every **m.** according to his deeds: ....
Ro 2:9 every soul of **m.** that doeth evil, ... *444*
Ro 2:10 to every **m.** that worketh good, ... *3956*
Ro 2:21 that preachest a **m.** should not steal, ...
Ro 2:22 that sayest a **m.** should not commit ....
Ro 3:4 let God be true, but every **m.** a liar; *444*
Ro 3:5 taketh vengeance? (I speak as a **m.**)....... *444*
Ro 3:28 a **m.** is justified by faith without the *444*
Ro 4:6 describeth the blessedness of the **m.**, ... *444*
Ro 4:8 Blessed is the **m.** to whom the Lord *435*
Ro 5:7 for a righteous **m.** will one die: ....
Ro 5:7 good **m.** some would even dare to die.......
Ro 5:12 as by one **m.** sin entered into the *444*
Ro 5:15 gift by grace, which is by one **m.**, ...
Ro 6:6 our old **m.** is crucified with him, ... *444*
Ro 7:1 law hath dominion over a **m.** as long *444*
Ro 7:3 liveth, she be married to another **m.**, ... *435*
Ro 7:3 though she be married to another **m.**..... *435*
Ro 7:22 the law of God after the inward **m.**: *444*
Ro 7:24 O wretched **m.** that I am! who shall *444*
Ro 8:9 if any **m.** have not the Spirit of Christ, ...
Ro 8:24 for what a **m.** seeth, why doth he *5100*
Ro 9:20 O **m.**, who art thou that repliest *444*
Ro 10:5 the **m.** which doeth those things.......... *444*
Ro 10:10 For with the heart **m.** believeth unto ....
Ro 12:3 to every **m.** that is among you, not to.......
Ro 12:3 dealt to every **m.** the measure of..............
Ro 12:17 Recompense to no **m.** evil for evil. *3367*
Ro 13:8 Owe no **m.** any thing, but to love *3367*
Ro 14:5 One **m.** esteemeth one day above ....
Ro 14:5 Let every **m.** be fully persuaded in...........
Ro 14:7 himself, and no **m.** dieth to himself..... *3762*
Ro 14:13 that no **m.** put a stumblingblock ....
Ro 14:20 for that **m.** who eateth with offence. *444*
1Co 2:9 have entered into the heart of **m.**, ... *444*
1Co 2:11 For what **m.** knoweth the things.......... *444*
1Co 2:11 knoweth the things of a **m.**, save......... *444*
1Co 2:11 the spirit of **m.** which is in him? *444*
1Co 2:11 the things of God knoweth no **m.**, ... *3762*
1Co 2:14 natural **m.** receiveth not the things....... *444*
1Co 2:15 yet he himself is judged of no **m.**. *3762*
1Co 3:5 as the Lord gave to every **m.**? ....
1Co 3:8 and every **m.** shall receive his own.............
1Co 3:10 every **m.** take heed how he buildeth.........
1Co 3:11 can no **m.** lay than that is laid,........... *3762*
1Co 3:12 if any **m.** build upon this foundation...........
1Co 3:17 If any **m.** defile the temple of God,...........
1Co 3:18 Let no **m.** deceive himself. *3367*
1Co 3:18 any **m.** among you seemeth to be wise......
1Co 3:21 Therefore let no **m.** glory in men. *3367*
1Co 4:1 Let a **m.** so account of us, as of the *444*
1Co 4:2 that a **m.** be found faithful................ *5100*
1Co 4:5 shall every **m.** have praise of God. ....
1Co 5:11 if any **m.** that is called a brother be..........
1Co 6:5 that there is not a wise **m.** among you?.....
1Co 6:18 Every sin that a **m.** doeth is without *444*
1Co 7:1 good for a **m.** not to touch a woman. ... *444*
1Co 7:2 let every **m.** have his own wife, and.........
1Co 7:7 But every **m.** hath his proper gift.............
1Co 7:16 how knowest thou, O **m.**, whether....... *435*
1Co 7:17 God hath distributed to every **m.**, ...

1Co 7:18 any **m.** called being circumcised? ....
1Co 7:20 every **m.** abide in the same calling............
1Co 7:24 let every **m.**, wherein he is called, ...
1Co 7:26 say, that it is good for a **m.** so to be.... *444*
1Co 7:36 But if any **m.** think that he behaveth.........
1Co 8:2 if any **m.** think that he knoweth any..........
1Co 8:3 But if any **m.** love God, the same is ....
1Co 8:7 not in every **m.** that knowledge: *3956*
1Co 8:10 For if any **m.** see thee which hast............
1Co 9:8 Say I these things as a **m.**? or saith *444*
1Co 9:15 any **m.** should make my glorying..............
1Co 9:25 And every **m.** that striveth for the...........
1Co 10:13 you but such as is common to **m.**: *442*
1Co 10:24 Let no **m.** seek his own, ... *3367*
1Co 10:24 but every **m.** another's wealth. ....
1Co 10:28 But if any **m.** say unto you, This............
1Co 11:3 that the head of every **m.** is Christ; *435*
1Co 11:3 the head of the woman is the **m.**; *435*
1Co 11:4 Every **m.** praying or prophesying, ... *435*
1Co 11:7 a **m.** indeed ought not to cover his *435*
1Co 11:7 the woman is the glory of the **m.**. *435*
1Co 11:8 For the **m.** is not of the woman; *435*
1Co 11:8 woman; but the woman of the **m.**. *435*
1Co 11:9 was the **m.** created for the woman;...... *435*
1Co 11:9 woman; but the woman for the **m.**....... *435*
1Co 11:11 neither is the **m.** without the woman, ... *435*
1Co 11:11 neither the woman without the **m.**, ... *435*
1Co 11:12 For as the woman is of the **m.**, even ... *435*
1Co 11:12 so is the **m.** also by the woman; *435*
1Co 11:14 if a **m.** have long hair, it is a shame *435*
1Co 11:16 if any **m.** seem to be contentious, we ....
1Co 11:28 But let a **m.** examine himself, and........ *444*
1Co 11:34 if any **m.** hunger, let him eat at home;.. *444*
1Co 12:3 no **m.** speaking by the Spirit of God ... *3762*
1Co 12:3 that no **m.** can say that Jesus is the.... *3762*
1Co 12:7 given to every **m.** to profit withal...... *1533*
1Co 12:11 dividing to every **m.** severally as he.... *1533*
1Co 13:11 when I became a **m.**, I put away *435*
1Co 14:2 for not **m.** understandeth him; *3762*
1Co 14:27 any **m.** speak in an unknown tongue, ...
1Co 14:37 any **m.** think himself to be a prophet, ...
1Co 14:38 But if any **m.** be ignorant, let him be ....
1Co 15:21 For since by **m.** came death, ... *444*
1Co 15:21 by **m.** came also the resurrection of..... *444*
1Co 15:23 But every **m.** in his own order: ....
1Co 15:35 some **m.** will say, How are the dead.........
1Co 15:45 first **m.** Adam was made a living.......... *444*
1Co 15:47 The first **m.** is of the earth, earthy: *444*
1Co 15:47 second **m.** is the Lord from heaven...... *444*
1Co 16:11 Let no **m.** therefore despise him: *5100*
1Co 16:22 If any **m.** love not the Lord Jesus.........
2Co 2:6 Sufficient to such a **m.** is this ....
2Co 4:16 but though our outward **m.** perish, ... *444*
2Co 4:16 the inward **m.** is renewed day by day.........
2Co 5:16 know we no **m.** after the flesh: *3762*
2Co 5:17 Therefore if any **m.** be in Christ, he is......
2Co 7:2 us; we have wronged no **m.**, ... *3762*
2Co 7:2 we have corrupted no **m.**, ... *3762*
2Co 7:2 we have defrauded no **m.**. *3762*
2Co 8:12 is...according to that a **m.** hath, ... *5100*
2Co 8:20 that no **m.** should blame us in this...... *5100*
2Co 9:7 Every **m.** according as he purposeth ....
2Co 10:7 If any **m.** trust to himself that he is..........
2Co 11:9 I was chargeable to no **m.**: for *3762*
2Co 11:10 no **m.** shall stop me of this boasting..........
2Co 11:16 again, let no **m.** think me a fool; if *5100*
2Co 11:20 if a **m.** bring you into bondage, ... *5100*
2Co 11:20 if a **m.** devour you, if a **m.** take of..... *5100*
2Co 11:20 a **m.** exalt himself, if a **m.** smite........ *5100*
2Co 12:2 I knew a **m.** in Christ above *444*
2Co 12:3 I knew such a **m.**, (whether in the....... *444*
2Co 12:4 it is not lawful for a **m.** to utter........... *444*
2Co 12:6 any **m.** should think of me above.............
Ga 1:1 men, neither by **m.**, but by Jesus *444*
Ga 1:9 any **m.** preach any other gospel unto ....
Ga 1:11 was preached of me is not after **m.**....... *444*
Ga 1:12 I neither received it of **m.**, neither....... *444*
Ga 2:16 knowing that a **m.** is not justified by..... *444*
Ga 3:11 no **m.** is justified by the law in the *3762*
Ga 3:12 **m.** that doeth them shall live in........... *444*
Ga 3:15 no **m.** disannulleth, or addeth *3762*
Ga 5:3 I testify again to every **m.** that is *444*
Ga 6:1 if a **m.** be overtaken in a fault, ye......... *444*
Ga 6:3 For if a **m.** think himself to be.......... *5100*
Ga 6:4 let every **m.** prove his own work. *5100*
Ga 6:5 every **m.** shall bear his own burden. *5100*
Ga 6:7 whatsoever a **m.** soweth, that shall...... *444*

Ga 6:17 henceforth let no **m.** trouble me:........ *3367*
Eph 2:9 works, lest any **m.** should boast..............
Eph 2:15 in himself of twain one new **m.**, ... *444*
Eph 3:16 might by his Spirit in the inner **m.**; *444*
Eph 4:13 the Son of God, unto a perfect **m.**, ... *435*
Eph 4:22 former conversation the old **m.**, ... *444*
Eph 4:24 that ye put on the new **m.**, which........ *444*
Eph 4:25 every **m.** truth with his neighbour: ....
Eph 5:5 nor unclean person, nor covetous **m.**, ...
Eph 5:6 Let no **m.** deceive you with vain........ *3367*
Eph 5:29 For no **m.** ever yet hated his own........ *3762*
Eph 5:31 cause shall a **m.** leave his father.......... *444*
Eph 6:8 whatsoever good thing any **m.** doeth, ...
Php 2:4 Look not every **m.** on his own.................
Php 2:4 but every **m.** also on the things of............
Php 2:8 being found in fashion as a man, ... *444*
Php 2:20 I have no **m.** likeminded, who will *3762*
Php 3:4 If any other **m.** thinketh that he hath ....
Col 1:28 we preach, warning every **m.**, and....... *444*
Col 1:28 teaching every **m.** in all wisdom; *444*
Col 1:28 we may present every **m.** perfect in..... *444*
Col 2:4 lest any **m.** should beguile you.................
Col 2:8 Beware lest any **m.** spoil you ....
Col 2:16 Let no **m.** therefore judge you in *5100*
Col 2:18 Let no **m.** beguile you of your........... *3367*
Col 3:9 put off the old **m.** with his deeds; *444*
Col 3:10 And have put on the new **m.**, which is ......
Col 3:13 any **m.** have a quarrel against any: ....
Col 4:6 how ye ought to answer every **m.**...... *1520*
1Th 3:3 no **m.** should be moved by these *3367*
1Th 4:6 That no **m.** go beyond and defraud his ......
1Th 4:8 despiseth not **m.**, but God, who.......... *444*
1Th 5:15 none render evil for evil unto any **m.**; ....
2Th 2:3 Let no **m.** deceive you by any........... *5100*
2Th 2:3 that **m.** of sin be revealed, the son *444*
2Th 3:14 if any **m.** obey not our word by this.........
2Th 3:14 note that **m.**, and have no company ....
1Ti 1:8 is good, if a **m.** use it lawfully; *5100*
1Ti 1:9 the law is not made for a righteous **m.**, ...
1Ti 2:5 God and men, the **m.** Christ Jesus; *444*
1Ti 2:12 nor to usurp authority over the **m.**,....... *435*
1Ti 3:1 a **m.** desire the office of a bishop, ... *5100*
1Ti 3:5 if a **m.** know not how to rule his........ *5100*
1Ti 4:12 no **m.** despise thy youth; but be *3367*
1Ti 5:9 having been the wife of one **m.**, ... *435*
1Ti 5:16 If any **m.** or woman that believeth............
1Ti 5:22 Lay hands suddenly on no **m.**, ... *3367*
1Ti 6:3 If any **m.** teach otherwise, and ....
1Ti 6:11 O **m.** of God, flee these things; and *444*
1Ti 6:16 the light which no **m.** can approach...........
1Ti 6:16 whom no **m.** hath seen, nor can see: *444*
2Ti 2:4 No **m.** that warreth entangleth........... *3762*
2Ti 2:5 if a **m.** also strive for masteries, ... *5100*
2Ti 2:21 If a **m.** therefore purge himself........... *5100*
2Ti 3:17 That the **m.** of God may be perfect,..... *444*
2Ti 4:16 first answer no **m.** stood with me,....... *3762*
Tit 2:15 Authority. Let no **m.** despise thee...... *3367*
Tit 3:2 To speak evil of no **m.**, to be no *3367*
Tit 3:4 God our Saviour toward **m.** appeared, ...
Tit 3:10 A **m.** that is an heretick, after the *444*
Heb 2:6 What is **m.**, that thou art mindful......... *444*
Heb 2:6 son of **m.**, that thou visitest him? *444*
Heb 2:9 God should taste death for every **m.**.........
Heb 3:3 this **m.** was counted worthy of more........
Heb 3:4 every house is builded by some **m.**; ....
Heb 4:11 lest any **m.** fall after the same example .....
Heb 5:4 And no **m.** taketh this honour unto..... *5100*
Heb 7:4 consider how great this **m.** was, ...
Heb 7:13 no **m.** gave attendance at the altar. *3762*
Heb 7:24 But this **m.**, because he continueth..........
Heb 8:2 which the Lord pitched, and not **m.**....... *444*
Heb 8:3 this **m.** have somewhat also to offer. ....
Heb 8:11 shall not teach every **m.** his neighbour, ...
Heb 8:11 and every **m.** his brother, saying,.............
Heb 10:12 this **m.**, after he had offered one.............
Heb 10:38 but if any **m.** draw back, my soul............
Heb 12:14 which no **m.** shall see the Lord:.......... *3762*
Heb 12:15 any **m.** fail of the grace of God; ....
Heb 13:6 not fear what **m.** shall do unto me. *444*
Jas 1:7 that **m.** think that he shall receive........ *444*
Jas 1:8 double minded **m.** is unstable in............ *435*
Jas 1:11 the rich **m.** fade away in his ways. ....
Jas 1:12 Blessed is the **m.** that endureth *435*
Jas 1:13 no **m.** say when he is tempted, ... *3367*
Jas 1:13 evil, neither tempteth he any **m.**:........ *3762*
Jas 1:14 every **m.** is tempted, when he is.............
Jas 1:19 let every **m.** be swift to hear, slow...... *444*

Jas 1:20 For the wrath of **m.** worketh not the.... *435*
Jas 1:23 unto a **m.** beholding his natural face *435*
Jas 1:24 forgetteth what manner of **m.** he was........
Jas 1:25 this **m.** shall be blessed in his deed.........
Jas 1:26 any **m.** among you seem to be religious,....
Jas 2:2 assembly a **m.** with a gold ring,........... *435*
Jas 2:2 come in also a poor **m.** in vile raiment;......
Jas 2:14 though a **m.** say he hath faith, and *5100*
Jas 2:18 a **m.** may say, Thou hast faith, and *5100*
Jas 2:20 O vain **m.**, that faith without works....... *444*
Jas 2:24 how that by works a **m.** is justified, ... *444*
Jas 3:2 any **m.** offend not in word, the same ....
Jas 3:2 the same is a perfect **m.**, and able....... *435*
Jas 3:8 the tongue can no **m.** tame; it is an *444*
Jas 3:13 Who is a wise **m.** and endued with...........
Jas 5:16 fervent prayer of a righteous **m.**.............
Jas 5:17 **m.** subject to like passions as we......... *444*
1Pe 1:24 glory of **m.** as the flower of grass........ *444*
1Pe 2:13 ordinance of **m.** for the Lord's sake:...... *442*
1Pe 2:19 if a **m.** for conscience toward God...... *5100*
1Pe 3:4 it be the hidden **m.** of the heart, ... *444*
1Pe 3:15 answer to every **m.** that asketh...............
1Pe 4:10 As every **m.** hath received the gift, ...
1Pe 4:11 If any **m.** speak, let him speak as the ....
1Pe 4:11 if any **m.** minister, let him do it as of........
1Pe 4:16 if any **m.** suffer as a Christian, let him ......
2Pe 1:21 not in old time by the will of **m.**:......... *444*
2Pe 2:8 that righteous **m.** dwelling among.............
2Pe 2:19 of whom a **m.** is overcome, of the...... *5100*
1Jo 2:1 if any **m.** sin, we have an advocate...........
1Jo 2:15 If any **m.** love the world, the love............
1Jo 2:27 ye need not that any **m.** teach you: ....
1Jo 3:3 And every **m.** that hath this hope.............
1Jo 3:7 children, let no **m.** deceive you:......... *3367*
1Jo 4:12 No **m.** hath seen God at any time. *3762*
1Jo 4:20 If any **m.** say, I love God, and................
1Jo 5:16 If any **m.** see his brother sin a sin............
Re 1:13 one like unto the Son of **m.**, clothed..... *444*
Re 2:17 **which no m. knoweth saying he**.... *3762*
Re 3:7 **that openeth, and no m. shutteth;**.. *3762*
Re 3:7 **and shutteth, and no m. openeth;**.. *3762*
Re 3:8 **open door, and no m. can shut it:**..*3762*
Re 3:11 **hast, that no m. take thy crown**.... *3367*
Re 3:20 **if any m. hear my voice, and open**......
Re 4:7 the third beast had a face as a **m.**,...... *444*
Re 5:3 And no **m.** in heaven, nor in earth,...... *3762*
Re 5:4 no **m.** was found worthy to open........ *3762*
Re 6:15 every bondman, and every free **m.**,..........
Re 7:9 multitude,...no **m.** could number, ... *3762*
Re 9:5 a scorpion, when he striketh a **m.**. *444*
Re 11:5 And if any **m.** will hurt them, fire............
Re 11:5 and if any **m.** will hurt them, he must ....
Re 12:5 And she brought forth a **m.** child, ... *730*
Re 12:13 which brought forth the **m.** child.......... *730*
Re 13:9 If any **m.** have an ear, let him hear. ....
Re 13:17 And that no **m.** might buy or sell, ... *5100*
Re 13:18 for it is the number of a **m.**; and *444*
Re 14:3 no **m.** could learn that song but *3762*
Re 14:9 If any **m.** worship the beast and his...........
Re 14:14 cloud one sat like unto the Son of **m.**, .. *444*
Re 15:8 no **m.** was able to enter into the........ *3762*
Re 16:3 it became as the blood of a dead **m.**: ....
Re 18:11 no **m.** buyeth their merchandise......... *3762*
Re 19:12 a name written, that no **m.** knew, ... *3762*
Re 20:13 every **m.** according to their works.............
Re 21:17 according to the measure of a **m.**, ... *444*
Re 22:12 **every m. according as his work**...........
Re 22:18 every **m.** that heareth the words........ *3956*
Re 22:18 If any **m.** shall add unto these ....
Re 22:19 if any **m.** shall take away from the...........

MANAEN (man'-a-en)
Ac 13:1 and Lucius of Cyrene, and **M.**, ... *3127*

MANAHATH (man'-a-hath)
Ge 36:23 Alvan, and **M.**, and Ebal, Shepho, ... 4506
1Ch 1:40 Alian, and **M.**, and Ebal, Shephi, ... 4506
1Ch 8:6 and they removed them to **M.**:.......... 4506

MANAHETHITES (man'-a-heth-ites)
1Ch 2:52 sons; Haroeh, and half of the **M.**........ 2679
1Ch 2:54 and half of the **M.**, the Zorites........... 2680

MANASSEH (ma-nas'-seh) See also MANASSEH'S; MANASSES; MANASSITES.
Ge 41:51 the name of the firstborn **M.**............. 4519
Ge 46:20 Egypt were born **M.** and Ephraim, ... 4519
Ge 48:1 him his two sons, **M.** and Ephraim. 4519
Ge 48:5 now thy two sons, Ephraim and **M.**, ... 4519
Ge 48:13 **M.** in his left hand toward Israel's 4519
Ge 48:14 wittingly; for **M.** was the firstborn...... 4519
Ge 48:20 make thee as Ephraim and as **M.**: 4519
Ge 48:20 and he set Ephraim before **M.**........... 4519
Ge 50:23 also of Machir the son of **M.** were 4519
Nu 1:10 the son of Ammihud: of **M.**;............. 4519
Nu 1:34 Of the children of **M.**, by their 4519
Nu 1:35 even of the tribe of **M.**, were thirty.... 4519
Nu 2:20 by him shall be the tribe of **M.**: 4519
Nu 2:20 the captain of the children of **M.** 4519
Nu 7:54 prince of the children of **M.**:............... 4519
Nu 10:23 of the tribe of the children of **M.**......... 4519
Nu 13:11 Joseph, namely, of the tribe of **M.**,...... 4519
Nu 26:28 after their families were **M.** and......... 4519
Nu 26:29 Of the sons of **M.**: of Machir, the 4519
Nu 26:34 These are the families of **M.**, and...... 4519
Nu 27:1 son of **M.**, of the families of **M.**.......... 4519
Nu 32:33 unto half the tribe of **M.** the son 4519
Nu 32:39 children of Machir the son of **M.**........ 4519
Nu 32:40 Gilead unto Machir the son of **M.**;...... 4519
Nu 32:41 Jair the son of **M.** went and took 4519
Nu 34:14 the tribe of **M.** have received their..... 4519
Nu 34:23 for the tribe of the children of **M.**, ... 4519
Nu 36:1 the son of **M.**, of the families of the ... 4519
Nu 36:12 into the families of the sons of **M.**...... 4519
De 3:13 gave I unto the half tribe of **M.**; 4519
De 3:14 Jair the son of **M.** took all the 4519
De 29:8 Gadites, and to the half tribe of **M.**. ... 4520
De 33:17 and they are the thousands of **M.**........ 4519
De 34:2 and the land of Ephraim, and **M.**,........ 4519
Jos 1:12 and to half the tribe of **M.**, spake........ 4519
Jos 4:12 half the tribe of **M.**, passed over........ 4519
Jos 12:6 Gadites, and the half tribe of **M.**......... 4519
Jos 13:7 tribes, and the half tribe of **M.**, ... 4519
Jos 13:29 unto the half tribe of **M.**: and this 4519
Jos 13:29 the half tribe of the children of **M.**...... 4519
Jos 13:31 children of Machir the son of **M.**, ... 4519
Jos 14:4 of Joseph were two tribes, **M.** and 4519
Jos 16:4 **M.** and Ephraim, took their............... 4519
Jos 16:9 inheritance of the children of **M.**, ... 4519
Jos 17:1 was also a lot for the tribe of **M.**; 4519
Jos 17:1 for Machir the firstborn of **M.**, the 4519
Jos 17:2 for the rest of the children of **M.** 4519
Jos 17:2 these were the male children of **M.** 4519
Jos 17:3 the son of **M.**, had no sons, but......... 4519
Jos 17:5 And there fell ten portions to **M.**, ... 4519
Jos 17:6 Because the daughters of **M.** had an.... 4519
Jos 17:7 the coast of **M.** was from Asher 4519
Jos 17:8 Now **M.** had the land of Tappuah: 4519
Jos 17:8 but Tappuah on the border of **M.**........ 4519
Jos 17:9 are among the cities of **M.**: the 4519
Jos 17:9 coast of **M.** also was on the north...... 4519
Jos 17:11 **M.** had in Issachar and in Asher......... 4519
Jos 17:12 children of **M.** could not drive out 4519
Jos 17:17 and to **M.**, saying, Thou art a great.... 4519
Jos 18:7 half the tribe of **M.**, have received 4519
Jos 20:8 in Bashan out of the tribe of **M.**.......... 4519
Jos 21:5 Dan, and out of the half tribe of **M.**,.... 4519
Jos 21:6 of the half tribe of **M.** in Bashan, ... 4519
Jos 21:25 And out of the half tribe of **M.**, ... 4519
Jos 21:27 out of the other half tribe of **M.**.......... 4519
Jos 22:1 Gadites, and the half tribe of **M.**, ... 4519
Jos 22:7 to the one half of the tribe of **M.** 4519
Jos 22:9, 10,11 Gad and the half tribe of **M.** 4519
Jos 22:13, 15 Gad, and to the half tribe of **M.**,.... 4519
Jos 22:21 of Gad and the half tribe of **M.**........... 4519
Jos 22:30 Gad and the children of **M.** spake,...... 4519
Jos 22:31 of Gad, and to the children of **M.**, ... 4519
Jg 1:27 did **M.** drive out the inhabitants 4519
Jg 6:15 my family is poor in **M.**, and I am...... 4519
Jg 6:35 messengers throughout all **M.**;............ 4519
Jg 7:23 out of Asher, and out of all **M.**, ... 4519
Jg 11:29 he passed over Gilead, and **M.**, and.... 4519
Jg 18:30 the son of Gershom, the son of **M.**, ... 4519
1Ki 4:13 the towns of Jair the son of **M.**,.......... 4519
2Ki 20:21 and **M.** his son reigned in his stead. ... 4519
2Ki 21:1 **M.** was twelve years old when he 4519
2Ki 21:9 **M.** seduced them to do more evil........ 4519
2Ki 21:11 **M.** king of Judah had done these........ 4519
2Ki 21:16 **M.** shed innocent blood very much, ... 4519
2Ki 21:17 the rest of the acts of **M.**, and all 4519
2Ki 21:18 **M.** slept with his fathers, and was...... 4519
2Ki 21:20 of the Lord, as his father **M.** did......... 4519
2Ki 23:12 the altars which **M.** had made in 4519
2Ki 23:26 provocations that **M.** had provoked..... 4519
2Ki 24:3 for the sins of **M.**, according to all....... 4519
1Ch 3:13 son, Hezekiah his son, **M.** his son,..... 4519
1Ch 5:18 Gadites, and half the tribe of **M.**, ... 4519
1Ch 5:23 the children of the half tribe of **M.**....... 4519
1Ch 5:26 Gadites, and the half tribe of **M.**, ... 4519
1Ch 6:61 out of the half tribe of **M.**, by lot, ... 4519
1Ch 6:62 out of the tribe of **m.** in Bashan, ... 4519
1Ch 6:70 And out of the half tribe of **M.**; 4519
1Ch 6:71 the family of the half tribe of **M.**, ... 4519
1Ch 7:14 The sons of **M.**; Ashriel, whom she.... 4519
1Ch 7:17 Gilead, son of Machir, the son of **M.**. ..4519
1Ch 7:29 the borders of the children of **M.**, ... 4519
1Ch 9:3 the children of Ephraim, and **M.**;........ 4519
1Ch 12:19 And there fell some of **M.** to David, ... 4519
1Ch 12:20 there fell to him of **M.**, Adnah, and 4519
1Ch 12:20 of the thousands that were of **M.**. 4519
1Ch 12:31 of the half tribe of **M.** eighteen.......... 4519
1Ch 12:37 and of the half tribe of **m.**, with all..... 4519
1Ch 26:32 and the half tribe of **M.**, for every...... 4520
1Ch 27:20 the half tribe of **m.**, Joel the son of 4519
1Ch 27:21 Of the half tribe of **M.** in Gilead......... 4519
2Ch 15:9 with them out of Ephraim and **M.**,...... 4519
2Ch 30:1 letters also to Ephraim and **M.**, ... 4519
2Ch 30:10 the country of Ephraim and **M.**.......... 4519
2Ch 30:11 and **M.**, and of Zebulun humbled 4519
2Ch 30:18 even many of Ephraim and **M.**,........... 4519
2Ch 31:1 in Ephraim also and **m.**,until they....... 4519
2Ch 32:33 **M.** his son reigned in his stead......... 4519
2Ch 33:1 **M.** was twelve years old when he 4519
2Ch 33:9 So **M.** made Judah and the................ 4519
2Ch 33:10 the Lord spake to **M.**, and to his 4519
2Ch 33:11 which took **M.** among the thorns,....... 4519
2Ch 33:13 **M.** knew that the Lord he was God..... 4519
2Ch 33:18 the rest of the acts of **m.**, and his....... 4519
2Ch 33:20 So **M.** slept with his fathers, and 4519
2Ch 33:22 of the Lord, as did **M.** his father:....... 4519
2Ch 33:22 images which **M.** his father had.......... 4519
2Ch 33:23 as **M.** his father had humbled 4519
2Ch 34:6 And so did he in the cities of **M.**,....... 4519
2Ch 34:9 had gathered of the hand of **M.** and.... 4519
Ezr 10:30 Bezaleel, and Binnui, and **M.**............ 4519
Ezr 10:33 Eliphelet, Jeremai, **M.**, and Shimei..... 4519
Ps 60:7 Gilead is mine, and **M.** is mine; 4519
Ps 80:2 and **M.** stir up thy strength, and........ 4519
Ps 108:8 Gilead is mine; **M.** is mine;............... 4519
Isa 9:21 **M.**, Ephraim; and Ephraim, **M.**:.......... 4519
Jer 15:4 of **M.** the son of Hezekiah king of...... 4519
Eze 48:4 unto the west side, a portion for **M.**. . 4519
Eze 48:5 by the border of **M.**, from the east...... 4519

MANASSEH'S (ma-nas'-sez)
Ge 48:14 and his left hand upon **M.** head, ... 4519
Ge 48:17 Ephraim's head unto **M.** head.......... 4519
Jos 17:6 the rest of **M.** sons had the lands....... 4519
Jos 17:10 northward it was **M.**, and the sea....... 4519

MANASSES (ma-nas'-seez) See also MANASSEH.
Mt 1:10 And Ezekias begat **M.**; and................ *3128*
Mt 1:10 **M.** begat Amon; and Amon begat....... *3128*
Re 7:6 the tribe of **M.** were sealed twelve..... *3128*

MANASSITES (ma-nas'-sites)
De 4:43 and Golan in Bashan, of the **M.**. 4520
Jg 12:4 Ephraimites, and among the **M.**. 4519
2Ki 10:33 and the Reubenites, and the **M.**, ... 4520

MANDRAKES
Ge 30:14 found **m.** in the field, and brought 1736
Ge 30:14 Give me, I pray thee, of thy son's **m.**..1736
Ge 30:15 thou take away my son's **m.** also? 1736
Ge 30:15 with thee to night for thy son's **m.**...... 1736
Ge 30:16 have hired thee with my son's **m.** 1736
Ca 7:13 The **m.** give a smell, and our gates 1736

MANEH (ma'-neh)
Eze 45:12 fifteen shekels, shall be your **m.**. 4488

MANGER
Lu 2:7 clothes, and laid him in a **m.**; *5336*
Lu 2:12 in swaddling clothes, lying in a **m.**. *5336*
Lu 2:16 and the babe lying in the **m.**............. *5336*

MANIFEST See also MANIFESTED.
Ec 3:18 that God might **m.** them, and that...... 1305
Lu 8:17 **secret, that shall not be made m.**;.*5318*
Joh 1:31 he should be made **m.** to Israel, ... *5319*
Joh 3:21 **that his deeds may be made m.**,....... *5319*
Joh 9:3 **works of God should be made m.**... *5319*
Joh 14:21 **him, and will m. myself to him**.... *1718*
Joh 14:22 that thou wilt **m.** thyself unto us, ... *1718*
Ac 4:16 is **m.** to all them that dwell in............ *5319*

Ro 1:19 be known of God is **m.** in them; *5319*
Ro 10:20 I was made **m.** unto them that *1717*
Ro 16:26 But now is made **m.**, and by the *5319*
1Co 3:13 man's work shall be made **m.**: for *5318*
1Co 4:5 make **m.** the counsels of the hearts: *5319*
1Co 11:19 may be made **m.** among you. *5318*
1Co 14:25 the secrets of his heart made **m.**; *5318*
1Co 15:27 him, it is **m.** that he is excepted, *1212*
2Co 2:14 and maketh **m.** the savour of his *5319*
2Co 4:10 of Jesus...be made **m.** in our body *5319*
2Co 4:11 of Jesus might be made **m.** in our *5319*
2Co 5:11 but we are made **m.** unto God; and *5319*
2Co 5:11 I trust also are made **m.** in your *5319*
2Co 11:6 we have been thoroughly made **m.** *5319*
Ga 5:19 Now the works of the flesh are **m.**, *5318*
Eph 5:13 reproved are made **m.** by the light: *5319*
Eph 5:13 whatsoever doth make **m.** is light *5319*
Php 1:13 my bonds in Christ are **m.** in all *5318*
Col 1:26 but now is made **m.** to his saints: *5319*
Col 4:4 I may make it **m.**, as I ought to *5319*
2Th 1:5 a **m.** token of the righteous judgement
1Ti 3:16 God was **m.** in the flesh, justified *5319*
1Ti 5:25 the good works of some are **m.** *4271*
2Ti 1:10 is now made **m.** by the appearing *5319*
2Ti 3:9 folly shall be **m.** unto all men, as *1552*
Heb 4:13 creature that is not **m.** in his sight: *852*
Heb 9:8 holiest of all was not yet made **m.**, *5319*
1Pe 1:20 was **m.** in these last times for you, *5319*
1Jo 2:19 they might be made **m.** that they *5319*
1Jo 3:10 In this the children of God are **m.**, *5318*
Re 15:4 for thy judgments are made **m.** *5319*

MANIFESTATION
Ro 8:19 for the **m.** of the sons of God. *602*
1Co 12:7 But the **m.** of the Spirit is given to *5321*
2Co 4:2 by **m.** of the truth commending *5321*

MANIFESTED
Mk 4:22 **nothing hid, which shall not be m.;** *5319*
Joh 2:11 **of Galilee, and m. forth his glory;** *5319*
Joh 17:6 **I have m. thy name unto the men** *5319*
Ro 3:21 of God without the law is **m.**, being *5319*
Tit 1:3 But hath in due times **m.** his word *5319*
1Jo 1:2 the life was **m.**, and we have seen *5319*
1Jo 1:2 the Father, and was **m.** unto us;) *5319*
1Jo 3:5 that he was **m.** to take away our *5319*
1Jo 3:8 purpose the Son of God was **m.**, *5319*
1Jo 4:9 In this was **m.** the love of God *5319*

MANIFESTLY
2Co 3:3 **m.** declared to be the epistle of *5319*

MANIFOLD
Ne 9:19 thou in thy **m.** mercies forsookest 7227
Ne 9:27 according to thy **m.** mercies thou 7227
Ps 104:24 O Lord, how **m.** are thy works! in 7231
Am 5:12 I know your **m.** transgressions 7227
Lu 18:30 **Who shall not receive m. more in** *4179*
Eph 3:10 the church the **m.** wisdom of God, *4182*
1Pe 1:6 through **m.** temptations: *4164*
1Pe 4:10 stewards of the **m.** grace of God *4164*

MANKIND See also WOMANKIND.
Le 18:22 Thou shalt not lie with **m.**, as with 2145
Le 20:13 If a man also lie with **m.**, as he 2145
Job 12:10 thing, and the breath of all **m.**, 1320,376
1Co 6:9 nor abusers of themselves with **m.**, *733*
1Ti 1:10 them that defile themselves with **m.**, *733*
Jas 3:7 and hath been tamed of **m.**: *5449,442*

MANNA (man'-nah)
Ex 16:15 it, said one to another, It is **m.**: 4478
Ex 16:31 Israel called the name thereof **M.**: 4478
Ex 16:33 and put an omer full of **m.** therein, 4478
Ex 16:35 children of Israel did eat **m.** forty 4478
Ex 16:35 they did eat **m.**, until they came 4478
Nu 11:6 is nothing at all, besides this **m.**, 4478
Nu 11:7 And the **m.** was as coriander seed, 4478
Nu 11:9 in the night, the **m.** fell upon it 4478
De 8:3 and fed thee with **m.**, which thou 4478
De 8:16 fed thee in the wilderness with **m.**, 4478
Jos 5:12 And the **m.** ceased on the morrow 4478
Jos 5:12 the children of Israel **m.** any more; 4478
Ne 9:20 withheldest not thy **m.** from their 4478
Ps 78:24 rained down **m.** upon them to eat, 4478
Joh 6:31 Our fathers did eat **m.** in the *3131*
Joh 6:49 **Your fathers did eat m. in the** *3131*
Joh 6:58 **not as your fathers did eat m., and** *3131*
Heb 9:4 was the golden pot that had **m.**, *3131*
Re 2:17 **will I give to eat of the hidden m.,** *3131*

MANNER See also MANNERS.
Ge 18:11 with Sarah after the **m.** of women 734
Ge 18:25 far from thee to do after this **m.**, 1697
Ge 19:31 us after the **m.** of all the earth: 1870
Ge 25:23 two **m.** of people shall be separated
Ge 32:19 this **m.** shall ye speak unto Esau, 1697
Ge 39:19 After this **m.** did thy servant to me; 1697
Ge 40:13 the former **m.** when thou wast his 4941
Ge 40:17 of all **m.** of bakemeats for Pharaoh;
Ge 45:23 to his father he sent after this **m.**;
Ex 1:14 and in all **m.** of service in the field:
Ex 7:11 like **m.** with their enchantments. 3651
Ex 12:16 no **m.** of work shall be done in them,
Ex 21:9 with her after the **m.** of daughters 4941
Ex 22:9 For all **m.** of trespass, whether it 1697
Ex 22:9 or for any **m.** of lost thing, which
Ex 23:11 In like **m.** thou shalt deal with thy 3651
Ex 31:3 and in all **m.** of workmanship,
Ex 31:5 to work in all **m.** of workmanship.
Ex 35:29 willing to bring for all **m.** of work,
Ex 35:31 in all **m.** of workmanship; and
Ex 35:33 to make any **m.** of cunning work.
Ex 35:35 all **m.** of work, of the engraver, 3605
Ex 36:1 all **m.** of work for the sevice of the
Le 5:10 offering, according to the **m.**: 4941
Le 7:23 Ye shall eat no **m.** of fat, of ox, or of
Le 7:26 Moreover ye shall eat no **m.** of blood,
Le 7:27 soul it be that eateth any **m.** of blood,
Le 9:16 and offered it according to the **m.**. 4941
Le 11:27 among all **m.** of beasts that go on all
Le 11:44 with any **m.** of creeping thing
Le 14:54 law for all **m.** of plague of leprosy,
Le 17:10 you, that eateth any **m.** of blood;
Le 17:14 shall eat the blood of no **m.** of flesh:
Le 19:23 have planted all **m.** of trees for food,
Le 20:25 any **m.** of living thing that creepeth
Le 23:31 Ye shall do no **m.** of work: it shall be
Le 24:22 Ye shall have one **m.** of law, as 4941
Nu 5:13 her, neither she be taken with the **m.**;
Nu 9:14 and according to the **m.** thereof, 4941
Nu 15:13 shall do these things after this **m.**, 3541
Nu 15:16 One law and one **m.** shall be for 4941
Nu 15:24 drink offering, according to the **m.**, 4941
Nu 28:18 ye shall do no **m.** of servile work
Nu 28:24 After this **m.** ye shall offer daily,
Nu 29:6 offerings, according unto their **m.**, 4941
Nu 29:18, 21,24,27,30,33,37 according to their number, after the **m.**: 4941
Nu 31:30 and of the flocks, of all **m.** of beasts,
De 4:15 ye saw no **m.** of similitude on the day
De 15:2 And this is the **m.** of the release: 1697
De 22:3 like **m.** shalt thou do with his ass; 3651
De 27:21 be he that lieth with any **m.** of beast.
Jos 6:15 after the same **m.** seven times: 4941
Jg 8:18 **m.** of men were they whom ye slew at
Jg 11:17 in like **m.** they sent unto the king of
Jg 18:7 after the **m.** of the Zidonians, 4941
Ru 4:7 this was the **m.** in former time in
1Sa 8:9,11 **m.** of the king that shall reign 4941
1Sa 10:25 the people the **m.** of the kingdom, 4941
1Sa 17:27 people answered him after this **m.**, 1697
1Sa 17:30 and spake after the same **m.**: and 1697
1Sa 17:30 him again after the former **m.** 1697
1Sa 18:24 saying, On this **m.** spake David. 1697
1Sa 19:24 before Samuel in like **m.**, and 1571
1Sa 21:5 the bread is in a **m.** common, yea, 1870
1Sa 27:11 so will be his **m.** all the while he 3541
2Sa 6:5 **m.** of instruments made of fir wood,
2Sa 7:19 And is this the **m.** of man, O Lord 8452
2Sa 14:3 and speak on this **m.** unto him 1697
2Sa 15:6 And on this **m.** did Absalom to all 1697
2Sa 17:6 hath spoken after this **m.**: shall 1697
1Ki 7:28 the work of the bases was on this **m.**:
1Ki 7:37 After this **m.** he made the ten bases:
1Ki 18:28 cut themselves after their **m.** with 4941
1Ki 22:20 And one said on this **m.**, and 3541
1Ki 22:20 and another said on that **m.**. 3541
2Ki 1:7 What **m.** of man was he which 4941
2Ki 11:14 stood by a pillar, as the **m.** was, 4941
2Ki 17:26 not the **m.** of the God of the land. 4941
2Ki 17:27 them the **m.** of the God of the land. 4941
2Ki 17:33 after the **m.** of the nations whom 4941
2Ki 17:40 but they did after their former **m.** 4941
1Ch 6:48 appointed unto all **m.** of service of
1Ch 12:37 with all **m.** of instruments of war for
1Ch 18:10 all **m.** of vessels of gold and silver and
1Ch 22:15 and timer, and all **m.** of cunning men
1Ch 22:15 cunning men for every **m.** of work.
1Ch 23:29 and for all **m.** of measure and size;
1Ch 24:19 of the Lord, according to their **m.**, 4941
1Ch 28:14 for all instruments of all **m.** of service;
1Ch 28:21 with thee for all **m.** of workmanship
1Ch 28:21 skilful man, for any **m.** of service:
1Ch 29:2 and all **m.** of precious stones, and
1Ch 29:5 **m.** of work to be made by the hands
2Ch 2:14 also to grave any **m.** of graving, and
2Ch 4:20 should burn after the **m.** before 4941
2Ch 13:9 priests after the **m.** of the nations of
2Ch 18:19 one spake saying after this **m.**, 3541
2Ch 18:19 and another saying after that **m.**
2Ch 30:16 stood in their place after their **m.**, 4941
2Ch 32:15 nor persuade you on this **m.**, neither
2Ch 32:27 and for all **m.** of pleasant jewels;
2Ch 32:28 stalls for all **m.** of beasts, and cotes
2Ch 34:13 wrought the work in any **m.** of service:
Ezr 5:4 Then said we unto them after this **m.**,
Ne 6:4 answered them after the same **m.**. 1697
Ne 6:5 unto me in like **m.** the fifth time 1697
Ne 8:18 assembly, according unto the **m.**, 4941
Ne 10:37 the fruit of all **m.** of trees, of wine and
Ne 13:15 grapes, and figs, and all **m.** of burdens,
Ne 13:16 brought fish, and all **m.** of ware, and
Es 1:13 king's **m.** toward all that knew law 1697
Es 2:12 according to the **m.** of the women, 1881
Ps 107:18 Their soul abhorreth all **m.** of meat;
Ps 144:13 be full, affording all **m.** of store: 2177
Ca 7:13 our gates are all **m.** of pleasant fruits,
Isa 5:17 the lambs feed after their **m.**, 1699
Isa 10:24 against thee, after the **m.** of Egypt. 1870
Isa 10:26 he lift it up after the **m.** of Egypt. 1870
Isa 51:6 dwell therein shall die in like **m.**: 3654
Jer 13:9 After this **m.** will I mar the pride 3541
Jer 22:21 hath been thy **m.** from thy youth, 1870
Jer 30:18 shall remain after the **m.** thereof. 4941
Eze 20:30 after the **m.** of your fathers? 1870
Eze 23:15 after the **m.** of the Babylonians of 1823
Eze 23:45 them after the **m.** of adulteresses, 4941
Eze 23:45 the **m.** of women that shed blood; 4941
Da 6:23 no **m.** of hurt was found upon him,
Am 4:10 pestilence after the **m.** of Egypt: 1870
Am 8:14 The **m.** of Beer-sheba liveth; even 1870
Mt 4:23 and healing all **m.** of sickness and
Mt 4:23 all **m.** of disease among the people.
Mt 5:11 **shall say all m. of evil against you**
Mt 6:9 **After this m. therefore pray ye:** *3779*
Mt 8:27 What **m.** of man is this, that even *4217*
Mt 10:1 and to heal all **m.** of sickness and
Mt 10:1 of sickness and all **m.** of disease.
Mt 12:31 **All m. of sin and blasphemy shall**
Mk 4:41 What **m.** of man is this, that *686*
Mk 13:1 Master, see what **m.** of stones and *4217*
Mk 13:29 **So ye in like m., when ye shall see** *3779*
Lu 1:29 what **m.** of salutation this should *4217*
Lu 1:66 What **m.** of child shall this be! *686*
Lu 6:23 **in the like m. did their fathers**
Lu 7:39 who and what **m.** of woman this is *4217*
Lu 8:25 What **m.** of man is this! for he *686*
Lu 9:55 **not what m. of spirit ye are of.** *3634*
Lu 11:42 **mint and rue and all m. of herbs,**
Lu 20:31 and in like **m.** the seven also: and *5615*
Lu 24:17 **What m. of communications are**
Joh 2:6 the **m.** of the purifying of the Jews,
Joh 7:36 What **m.** of saying is this that he said,
Joh 19:40 as the **m.** of the Jews is to bury. *1485*
Ac 1:11 like **m.** as ye have seen him go *5158*
Ac 10:12 were all **m.** of fourfooted beasts of *1485*
Ac 15:1 circumcised after the **m.** of Moses, *1485*
Ac 15:23 letters by them after this **m.**; *3592*
Ac 17:2 And Paul, as his **m.** was, went *1486*
Ac 20:18 after what **m.** I have been with you *4458*
Ac 22:3 to the perfect **m.** of the law of the *195*
Ac 23:25 And he wrote a letter after this **m.**: *5179*
Ac 25:16 It is not the **m.** of the Romans to *1485*
Ac 25:20 doubted of such **m.** of questions, *4012*
Ac 26:4 My **m.** of life from my youth, which *981*
Ro 6:19 I speak after the **m.** of men because *442*
Ro 7:8 in me all **m.** of concupiscence.
1Co 7:7 one after this **m.**, and another *3779*
1Co 11:25 the same **m.** also he took the cup, *5615*
1Co 15:32 If after the **m.** of men I have fought
2Co 7:9 ye were made sorry after a godly **m.**,
Ga 2:14 livest after the **m.** of Gentiles, *1483*
Ga 3:15 I speak after the **m.** of men;

1Th 1:5 ye know what **m.** of men we were *3634*
1Th 1:9 what **m.** of entering in we had *3697*
1Ti 2:9 In like **m.** also, that women adorn ....
2Ti 3:10 known my doctrine, **m.** of life, ... *72*
Heb 10:25 together, as the **m.** of some is; *1485*
Jas 1:24 forgetteth what **m.** of man he was, ... *3697*
1Pe 1:11 what **m.** of time the Spirit of *4169*
1Pe 1:15 ye holy in all **m.** of conversation; ....
1Pe 3:5 For after this **m.** in the old time *3779*
2Pe 3:11 what **m.** of persons ought ye to be *4217*
1Jo 3:1 what **m.** of love the Father hath *4217*
Jude 7 cities about them in like **m.**, ... *5158*
Re 11:5 them, he must in this **m.** be killed, ... *3779*
Re 18:12 wood, and all **m.** vessels of ivory, ...
Re 18:12 and all **m.** vessels of most precious ....
Re 21:19 with all **m.** of precious stones. ....
Re 22:2 of life, which bare twelve **m.** of fruits, ...

MANNERS
Le 20:23 not walk in the **m.** of the nation, ... 2708
2Ki 17:34 day they do after the former **m.**: 4941
Eze 11:12 done after the **m.** of the heathen 4941
Ac 13:18 he their **m.** in the wilderness. *5159*
1Co 15:33 communications corrupt good **m.** *2239*
Heb 1:1 and in divers **m.** spake in time past *4187*

MANOAH (ma-no'-ah)
Jg 13:2 the Danites, whose name was **M.**; 4495
Jg 13:8 Then **M.** intreated the Lord, and 4495
Jg 13:9 God hearkened to the voice of **M.**; 4495
Jg 13:9 **M.** her husband was not with her 4495
Jg 13:11 **M.** arose, and went after his wife, ... 4495
Jg 13:12 **M.** said, Now let thy words come to ... 4495
Jg 13:13 the angel of the Lord said unto **M.**, ... 4495
Jg 13:15 **M.** said unto the angel of the Lord, ... 4495
Jg 13:16 the angel of the Lord said unto **M.**, ... 4495
Jg 13:16 **M.** knew not that he was an angel 4495
Jg 13:17 **M.** said unto the angel of the Lord, ... 4495
Jg 13:19 **M.** took a kid with a meat offering, ... 4495
Jg 13:19 and **M.** and his wife looked on. 4495
Jg 13:20 **M.** and his wife looked on it, and 4495
Jg 13:21 the Lord did no more appear to **M.** 4495
Jg 13:21 Then **M.** knew that he was an angel ... 4495
Jg 13:22 And **M.** said unto his wife, We shall 4495
Jg 16:31 the buryingplace of **M.** his father. 4495

MAN'S See also WOMAN'S.
Ge 8:21 the ground any more for **m.** sake; 120
Ge 8:21 the imagination of **m.** heart is evil 120
Ge 9:5 at the hand of every **m.** brother will 120
Ge 9:6 Whoso sheddeth **m.** blood, by man 120
Ge 16:12 and every **m.** hand against him; ....
Ge 20:3 hast taken; for she is a **m.** wife. 1167
Ge 42:11 We are all one **m.** sons; we are true 376
Ge 42:25 to restore every **m.** money into his 376
Ge 42:35 every **m.** bundle of money was in his ... 376
Ge 43:21 every **m.** money was in the mouth of ... 376
Ge 44:1 every **m.** money in his sack's mouth 376
Ge 44:26 we may not see the **m.** face, except 376
Ex 4:11 him, Who hath made **m.** mouth? 120
Ex 12:44 But every **m.** servant that is bought 376
Ex 21:35 if one **m.** ox hurt another's, that he 376
Ex 22:5 and shall feed in another **m.** field; 312
Ex 22:7 and it be stolen out of the **m.** house; 376
Ex 30:32 Upon **m.** flesh shall it not be 120
Le 7:8 that offereth any **m.** burnt offering, ... 376
Le 15:16 if any **m.** seed of copulation go out 376
Le 20:10 adultery with another **m.** wife. 376
Nu 5:10 every **m.** hallowed things shall be 376
Nu 5:12 If any **m.** wife go aside, and commit 376
Nu 17:2 write...every **m.** name upon his rod. 376
Nu 17:5 the **m.** rod, whom I shall choose, ... 376
Nu 33:54 every **m.** inheritance shall be in the ....
De 20:19 (for the tree of the field is **m.** life) 120
De 24:2 she may go and be another **m.** wife 376
De 24:6 for he taketh a **m.** life to pledge ....
Jg 7:16 he put a trumpet in every **m.** hand, ...
Jg 7:22 every **m.** sword against his fellow, ... 376
Jg 19:26 down at the door of the **m.** house 376
Ru 2:19 The **m.** name with whom I wrought 376
1Sa 12:4 thou taken ought of any **m.** hand. 376
1Sa 14:20 every **m.** sword...against his fellow 376
1Sa 17:32 Let no **m.** heart fail because of him; 120
2Sa 12:4 took the poor **m.** lamb, and dressed 376
2Sa 17:18 came to a **m.** house in Bahurim, ... 376
2Sa 17:25 which Amasa was a **m.** son, whose 376
1Ki 18:44 cloud out of the sea, like a **m.** hand. 376
2Ki 12:4 money that cometh into any **m.** heart ... 376
2Ki 23:8 which were on a **m.** left hand at the 376
2Ki 25:9 great **m.** house burnt he with fire ....
Es 1:8 do according to every **m.** pleasure. 376
Job 10:5 of man? are thy years as **m.** days, ... 1397
Job 32:21 I pray you, accept any **m.** person, ... 376
Ps 104:15 which strengtheneth **m.** heart. 582
Pr 10:15 The rich **m.** wealth is his strong city: ....
Pr 12:14 recompence of a **m.** hands shall be 120
Pr 13:8 ransom of a **m.** life are his riches: 376
Pr 16:7 When a **m.** ways please the Lord, he ... 376
Pr 16:9 A **m.** heart deviseth his way: but 120
Pr 18:4 words of a **m.** mouth are as deep 376
Pr 18:11 The rich **m.** wealth is his strong city, ...
Pr 18:16 A **m.** gift maketh room for him, and 120
Pr 18:20 A **m.** belly shall be satisfied with 376
Pr 19:21 are many devices in a **m.** heart; 376
Pr 20:24 **M.** goings are of the Lord; how 1397
Pr 27:9 so doth the sweetness of a **m.** friend ....
Pr 29:23 A **m.** pride shall bring him low: but 120
Pr 29:26 **m.** judgment cometh from the Lord 376
Ec 2:14 The wise **m.** eyes are in his head; but ......
Ec 8:1 a **m.** wisdom maketh his face to 120
Ec 8:5 wise **m.** heart discerneth both time ....
Ec 9:16 the poor **m.** wisdom is despised, and ....
Ec 10:2 A wise **m.** heart is at his right hand; ....
Ec 10:12 The words of a wise **m.** mouth are ....
Isa 8:1 roll, and write in it with a **m.** pen 582
Isa 13:7 faint, and every **m.** heart shall melt: 582
Jer 3:1 from him, and become another **m.**, ... 376
Jer 23:36 every **m.** word shall be his burden; 376
Eze 4:15 given thee cow's dung for **m.** dung, ... 120
Eze 10:8 form of a **m.** hand under their wings. ... 120
Eze 38:21 every **m.** sword shall be against his 376
Eze 39:15 when any seeth a **m.** bone, then 120
Eze 40:5 in the **m.** hand a measuring reed of ....
Da 4:16 Let his heart be changed from **m.**, ... 606
Da 5:5 hour came forth fingers of a **m.** hand, ... 606
Da 7:4 man, and a **m.** heart was given to it. 606
Da 8:16 heard a **m.** voice between the banks 120
Am 6:10 And a **m.** uncle shall take him up, and ....
Jon 1:14 let us not perish for this **m.** life, ... 376
Mic 7:6 a **m.** enemies are the men of his own ... 376
Mt 10:36 **a m. foes shall be they of his own** .. *444*
Mt 10:41 **shall receive a righteous m. reward.** ....
Mt 12:29 **can one enter into a strong m. house,** ..
Mk 3:27 **man can enter into a strong m. house,** .
Mk 12:19 If a **m.** brother die, and leave his *5100*
Lu 6:22 **as evil, for the Son of m. sake** *444*
Lu 12:15 **for a m. life consisteth not in the** .. *5100*
Lu 16:12 **in that which is another m., who** *245*
Lu 16:21 **which fell from the rich m. table:** ....
Lu 20:28 If any **m.** brother die, having a *5100*
Joh 18:17 thou also one of this **m.** disciples? *444*
Ac 5:28 to bring this **m.** blood upon us. *444*
Ac 7:58 their clothes at a young **m.** feet, ... *3494*
Ac 11:12 and we entered into the **m.** house: *435*
Ac 13:23 Of this **m.** seed hath God according ....
Ac 17:29 stone, graven by art and **m.** device *444*
Ac 18:7 and entered into a certain **m.** house, ...
Ac 20:33 I have coveted no **m.** silver, or *3762*
Ac 27:22 be no loss of any **m.** life among you, ...
Ro 5:17 For if by one **m.** offence death reigned ......
Ro 5:19 by one **m.** disobedience many were *444*
Ro 14:4 that judgest another **m.** servant? *245*
Ro 15:20 build upon another **m.** foundation: *245*
1Co 2:4 with enticing words of **m.** wisdom, ... *442*
1Co 2:13 words which **m.** wisdom teacheth, ... *442*
1Co 3:13 Every **m.** work...be made manifest: ....
1Co 3:13 fire shall try every **m.** work of what ....
1Co 3:14 If any **m.** work abide which he hath ....
1Co 3:15 If any **m.** work shall be burned, he ....
1Co 4:3 judged of you, or of **m.** judgment: *442*
1Co 10:29 judged of another **m.** conscience? ....
2Co 4:2 every **m.** conscience in the sight of *444*
2Co 10:16 boast in another **m.** line of things *245*
Ga 2:6 me: God accepteth no **m.** person:) *444*
Ga 3:15 Though it be but a **m.** covenant, yet *444*
2Th 3:8 we eat any **m.** bread for nought; ....
Jas 1:26 his own heart, this **m.** religion is vain ....
1Pe 1:17 according to every **m.** work, ...
2Pe 2:16 dumb ass speaking with **m.** voice *444*

MANSERVANT See also MANSERVANT'S; MANSERVANTS.
Ex 20:10 thy son, nor thy daughter, thy **m.**, ... 5650
Ex 20:17 thy neighbour's wife, nor his **m.**, ... 5650
Ex 21:32 If the ox shall push a **m.** or a) 5650
De 5:14 son, nor thy daughter, nor thy **m.**, ... 5650
De 5:14 that thy **m.** and thy maidservant 5650
De 5:21 house, his field, or his **m.**, or his 5650
De 12:18 son, and thy daughter, and thy **m.**, ... 5650
De 16:11, 14 and thy daughter, and thy **m.**, ... 5650
Job 31:13 If I did despise the cause of my **m.** 5650
Jer 34:9 That every man should let his **m.**, ... 5650
Jer 34:10 that every one should let his **m.**, ... 5650

MANSERVANT'S
Ex 21:27 And if he smite out his **m.** tooth, ... 5650

MANSERVANTS
Ne 7:67 Besides their **m.** and their 5650

MANSIONS
Joh 14:2 **my Father's house are many m.** *3438*

MANSLAYER See also MANSLAYERS.
Nu 35:6 which ye shall appoint for the **m.**, ... 7523
Nu 35:12 that the **m.** die not, until he stand 7523

MANSLAYERS
1Ti 1:9 and murderers of mothers, for **m.**, ... *409*

MANTLE See also MANTLES.
Jg 4:18 tent, she covered him with a **m.** 8063
1Sa 15:27 hold upon the skirt of his **m.**, and 4598
1Sa 28:14 up; and he is covered with a **m.**. 4598
1Ki 19:13 that he wrapped his face in his **m.**, ... 155
1Ki 19:19 by him, and cast his **m.** upon him. 155
2Ki 2:8 Elijah took his **m.**, and wrapped it 155
2Ki 2:13 He took up also the **m.** of Elijah that 155
2Ki 2:14 took the **m.** of Elijah that fell from 155
Ezr 9:3 I rent my garment and my **m.**, ... 4598
Ezr 9:5 rent my garment and my **m.**, I 4598
Job 1:20 Then Job arose, and rent his **m.**, ... 4598
Job 2:12 they rent every one his **m.**, and 4598
Ps 109:29 their own confusion, as with a **m.** 4598

MANTLES
Isa 3:22 suits of apparel, and the **m.**, and 4595

MANY See also MANIFOLD.
Ge 17:4 shalt be a father of **m.** nations. 1995
Ge 17:5 father of **m.** nations have I made 1995
Ge 21:34 in the Philistines' land **m.** days. 7227
Ge 37:3 and he made him a coat of **m.** colours. ......
Ge 37:23 his coat of **m.** colours that was on him; .....
Ge 37:32 And they sent the coat of **m.** colours, ...
Ge 37:34 and mourned for his son **m.** days. 7227
Ex 5:5 the people of the land now are **m.**, ... 7227
Ex 19:21 to gaze, and **m.** of them perish. 7227
Ex 23:2 decline after **m.** to wrest judgment: 7227
Ex 35:22 as **m.** as were willing hearted, and ....
Le 15:25 issue of her blood **m.** days out of 7227
Le 25:51 If there be yet **m.** years behind, ... 7227
Nu 9:19 long upon the tabernacle **m.** days, ... 7227
Nu 10:36 unto the **m.** thousands of Israel. 7233
Nu 13:18 they be strong or weak, few or **m.**; 7227
Nu 22:3 the people, because they were **m.**: 7227
Nu 24:7 his seed shall be in **m.** waters, and 7227
Nu 26:54 To **m.** thou shalt give the more 7227
Nu 26:56 be divided between **m.** and few. 7227
Nu 35:8 that have **m.** ye shall give 7227
Nu 35:8 that have...ye shall give **m.**: 7235
De 1:11 thousand times as **m.** more as ye are, ...
De 1:46 So ye abode in Kadesh **m.** days, ... 7227
De 2:1 we compassed mount Seir **m.** days. 7227
De 2:10, 21 and **m.**, and tall, as the Anakims; ... 7227
De 3:5 beside unwalled towns a great **m.** 7227
De 7:1 cast out **m.** nations before thee, the ... 7227
De 15:6 thou shalt lend unto **m.** nations, ... 7227
De 15:6 thou shalt reign over **m.** nations, ... 7227
De 25:3 him above these with **m.** stripes, ... 7227
De 28:12 thou shalt lend unto **m.** nations, ... 7227
De 31:17 **m.** evils and troubles shall befall 7227
De 31:21 when **m.** evils and troubles are 7227
De 32:7 consider the years of **m.** generations: ....
Jos 11:4 with horses and chariots very **m.**. 7227
Jos 22:3 left your brethren these **m.** days 7227
Jg 3:1 even as **m.** of Israel as had not known ......
Jg 7:2 are with thee are too **m.** for me to 7227
Jg 7:4 The people are yet too **m.**; bring 7227
Jg 8:30 begotten: for he had **m.** wives 7227
Jg 9:40 **m.** were overthrown and wounded, ... 7227
Jg 16:24 our country, which slew **m.** of us. 7235
1Sa 2:5 hath **m.** children is waxed feeble. 7227
1Sa 6:19 Lord had smitten **m.** of the people ....

1Sa	14:6	the Lord to save by **m.** or by few	7227
1Sa	25:10	be **m.** servants now a days that	7231
2Sa	1:4	**m.** of the people also are fallen	7235
2Sa	2:23	as **m.** as came to the place where	
2Sa	12:2	exceeding **m.** flocks and herds:	7235
2Sa	22:17	me; he drew me out of **m.** waters;	7227
2Sa	23:20	who had done **m.** acts, he slew two	7227
2Sa	24:3	the people, how **m.** soever they be,	
1Ki	2:38	dwelt in Jerusalem **m.** days.	7227
1Ki	4:20	Judah and Israel were **m.**, as the	7227
1Ki	7:47	because they were exceeding **m.**:	7230
1Ki	11:1	Solomon loved **m.** strange women,	7227
1Ki	17:15	he, and her house, did eat **m.** days.	
1Ki	18:1	it came to pass after **m.** days, that	7227
1Ki	18:25	for ye are **m.**; and call on the name	7227
1Ki	22:16	How **m.** time shall I adjure thee that	
2Ki	9:22	Jezebel and...witchcrafts are so **m.**?	7227
1Ch	4:27	his brethren had not **m.** children,	7227
1Ch	5:22	there fell down **m.** slain, because	7227
1Ch	7:4	for they had **m.** wives and sons.	7235
1Ch	7:22	Ephraim...mourned **m.** days, and	7227
1Ch	8:40	had **m.** sons, and sons's sons, an	7235
1Ch	11:22	Kabzeel, who had done **m.** acts;	7227
1Ch	21:3	an hundred times so **m.** more as they	
1Ch	23:11	and Beriah had not **m.** sons;	7235
1Ch	23:17	the sons of Rehabiah were very **m.**	7235
1Ch	28:5	the Lord hath given me **m.** sons,)	7227
2Ch	11:23	And he desired **m.** wives.	1995
2Ch	14:11	whether with **m.**, or with them	7227
2Ch	16:8	very **m.** chariots and horsemen?	7235
2Ch	18:15	How **m.** times shall I adjure thee that	
2Ch	26:10	the desert, and digged **m.** wells:	7227
2Ch	29:31	and as **m.** as were of a free heart	
2Ch	30:17	**m.** in the congregation that were	7227
2Ch	30:18	**m.** of Ephraim, and Manasseh, and	7227
2Ch	32:23	**m.** brought gifts unto the Lord to	7227
Ezr	3:12	But **m.** of the priests and Levites	7227
Ezr	3:12	voice; and **m.** shouted aloud for joy:	7227
Ezr	5:11	was builded these **m.** years ago,	7690
Ezr	10:13	But the people are **m.**, and it is a	7227
Ezr	10:13	we are **m.** that have transgressed	7235
Ne	5:2	sons, and our daughters, are **m.**:	7227
Ne	6:17	the nobles of Judah sent **m.** letters	7235
Ne	6:18	there were **m.** in Judah sworn unto	7227
Ne	7:2	man, and feared God above **m.**	7227
Ne	9:28	**m.** times didst thou deliver them	7227
Ne	9:30	**m.** years didst thou forbear them,	7227
Ne	13:26	among **m.** nations was there no	7227
Es	1:4	of his excellent majesty **m.** days,	7227
Es	2:8	when **m.** maidens were gathered	7227
Es	4:3	and **m.** lay in sackcloth and ashes	7227
Es	8:17	**m.** of the people of the land became	7227
Job	4:3	Behold, thou hast instructed **m.**,	7227
Job	11:19	yea, **m.** shall make suit unto thee	7227
Job	13:23	How **m.** are mine iniquities and sins?	
Job	16:2	I have heard **m.** such things:	7227
Job	23:14	and **m.** such things are with him.	7227
Job	41:3	Will he make **m.** supplications	7235
Ps	3:1	**m.** are they that rise up against	7227
Ps	3:2	**M.** there be which say of my soul,	7227
Ps	4:6	**m.** that say, Who will show us any	7227
Ps	18:16	me, he drew me out of **m.** waters	7227
Ps	22:12	**M.** bulls have compassed me:	7227
Ps	25:19	mine enemies; for they are **m.**;	7231
Ps	29:3	the Lord is upon **m.** waters.	7227
Ps	31:13	I have heard the slander of **m.**:	7227
Ps	32:10	**M.** sorrows shall be to the wicked:	7227
Ps	34:12	loveth **m.** days, that he may see good?	
Ps	34:19	**M.** are the afflictions of the	7227
Ps	37:16	better than the riches of **m.** wicked	7227
Ps	40:3	**m.** shall see it, and fear, and shall	7227
Ps	40:5	**M.**, O Lord my God, are thy	7227
Ps	55:18	me: for there were **m.** with me.	7227
Ps	56:2	they be **m.** that fight against me,	7227
Ps	61:6	life: and his years as **m.** generations	7227
Ps	71:7	I am as a wonder unto **m.**; but	7227
Ps	78:38	yea, **m.** a time turned he his anger	7235
Ps	93:4	than the noise of **m.** waters, yea,	7227
Ps	106:43	**M.** times did he deliver them; but	7227
Ps	110:6	wound the heads over **m.** countries.	7227
Ps	119:84	How **m.** are the days of thy servant?	
Ps	119:157	**M.** are my persecutors and mine	7227
Ps	129:1,2	**M.** a time have they afflicted me	7227
Pr	4:10	the years of thy life shall be **m.**	7235
Pr	6:35	though thou givest **m.** gifts.	7235
Pr	7:26	she hath cast down **m.** wounded:	7227
Pr	7:26	**m.** strong men have been slain by	3605
Pr	10:21	The lips of the righteous feed **m.**:	7227
Pr	14:20	but the rich hath **m.** friends.	7227
Pr	19:4	Wealth maketh **m.** friends; but the	7227
Pr	19:6	**M.** will intreat the favour of the	7227
Pr	19:21	are **m.** devices in a man's heart;	7227
Pr	28:2	of a land **m.** are the princes thereof:	7227
Pr	28:27	his eyes shall have **m.** a curse	7227
Pr	29:26	**M.** seek the ruler's favour; but	7227
Pr	31:29	**M.** daughters have done virtuously.	7227
Ec	5:7	multitude of dreams and **m.** words	7230
Ec	6:3	and live **m.** years, so that the	7227
Ec	6:3	so that the days of his years be **m.**,	7227
Ec	6:11	be **m.** things that increase vanity,	7235
Ec	7:29	have sought out **m.** inventions.	7227
Ec	11:1	thou shalt find it after **m.** days	7230
Ec	11:8	But if a man live **m.** years, and	7235
Ec	11:8	of darkness; for they shall be **m.**	7235
Ec	12:9	out, and set in order **m.** proverbs.	7235
Ec	12:12	of makings **m.** books there is no end;	7235
Ca	8:7	**M.** waters cannot quench love,	7227
Isa	1:15	when ye make **m.** prayers, I will	7235
Isa	2:3	And **m.** people shall go and say,	7227
Isa	2:4	and shall rebuke **m.** people: and	7227
Isa	5:9	truth **m.** houses shall be desolate,	7227
Isa	8:7	waters of the river, strong and **m.**,	7227
Isa	8:15	And **m.** among them shall stumble,	7227
Isa	17:12	Woe to the multitude of **m.** people.	7227
Isa	17:13	rush like the rushing of **m.** waters:	7227
Isa	22:9	the city of David, that they are **m.**:	7231
Isa	23:16	sweet melody, sing **m.** songs,	7235
Isa	24:22	after **m.** days...they be visited	7230
Isa	31:1	in chariots, because they are **m.**;	7227
Isa	32:10	**M.** days and years shall ye be troubled,	
Isa	42:20	Seeing **m.** things, but thou	7227
Isa	52:14	As **m.** were astonied at thee; his	7227
Isa	52:15	So shall he sprinkle **m.** nations;	7227
Isa	53:11	my righteous servant justify **m.**;	7227
Isa	53:12	and he bare the sin of **m.**, and made	7227
Isa	58:12	up the foundations of **m.** generations;	
Isa	60:15	excellency, a joy of **m.** generations.	
Isa	61:4	the desolations of **m.** generations	
Isa	66:16	the slain of the Lord shall be **m.**	7231
Jer	3:1	played the harlot with **m.** lovers;	7227
Jer	5:6	their transgressions are **m.**, and	7231
Jer	11:15	hath wrought lewdness with **m.**,	7227
Jer	12:10	**M.** pastors have destroyed my	7227
Jer	13:6	And it came to pass after **m.** days,	7227
Jer	14:7	for our backslidings are **m.**; we	7231
Jer	16:16	I will send for **m.** fishers, saith	7227
Jer	16:16	after will I send for **m.** hunters,	7227
Jer	20:10	For I heard the defaming of **m.**,	7227
Jer	22:8	**m.** nations shall pass by this city,	7227
Jer	25:14	**m.** nations and great kings shall	7227
Jer	27:7	**m.** nations and great kings shall	7227
Jer	28:8	both against **m.** countries, and	7227
Jer	32:14	that they may continue **m.** days.	7227
Jer	35:7	that ye may live **m.** days in the land	7227
Jer	36:32	besides unto them **m.** like words	7227
Jer	37:16	had remained there **m.** days;	7227
Jer	42:2	(for we are left but a few of **m.**, as	7235
Jer	46:11	vain shalt thou use **m.** medicines;	7235
Jer	46:16	He made **m.** to fall, yea, one fell	7235
Jer	50:41	**m.** kings shall be raised up from	7227
Jer	51:13	thou that dwellest upon **m.** waters,	7227
La	1:22	for my sighs are **m.**, and my heart	7227
Eze	3:6	Not to **m.** people of a strange speech	7227
Eze	12:27	he seeth is for **m.** days to come,	7227
Eze	16:41	upon thee in the sight of **m.** women:	7227
Eze	17:7	with great wings and **m.** feathers:	7227
Eze	17:9	**m.** people to pluck it up by the roots	7227
Eze	17:17	building forts, to cut off **m.** persons:	7227
Eze	19:10	of branches by reason of **m.** waters	7227
Eze	22:25	they have made her **m.** widows	7235
Eze	26:3	**m.** nations to come up against	7227
Eze	27:3	merchant of the people for **m.** isles,	7227
Eze	27:15	**m.** isles were the merchandise of	7227
Eze	27:33	of the seas, thou filledst **m.** people;	7227
Eze	32:3	thee with a company of **m.** people;	7227
Eze	32:9	also vex the hearts of **m.** people,	7227
Eze	32:10	make **m.** people amazed at thee,	7227
Eze	33:24	but we are **m.**; the land is given us	7227
Eze	37:2	were very **m.** in the open valley;	7227
Eze	38:6	bands: and **m.** people with thee.	7227
Eze	38:8	After **m.** days thou shalt be visited:	7227
Eze	38:8	and is gathered out of **m.** people,	7227
Eze	38:9	thy bands,and **m.** people with thee.	7227
Eze	38:15	thou, and **m.** people with thee, all	7227
Eze	38:17	prophesied in those days **m.** years	
Eze	38:22	the **m.** people that are with him,	7227
Eze	38:23	be known in the eyes of **m.** nations,	7227
Eze	39:27	in them in the sight of **m.** nations;	7227
Eze	43:2	voice was like a noise of **m.** waters:	7227
Eze	47:7	very **m.** trees on the one side and	7227
Eze	47:10	fish of the great sea, exceeding **m.**	7227
Da	2:48	and gave him **m.** great gifts, and	7690
Da	8:25	and by peace shall destroy **m.**:	7227
Da	8:26	vision; for it shall be for **m.** days.	7227
Da	9:27	shall confirm the covenant with **m.**	7227
Da	10:14	days: for yet the vision is for **m.** days	
Da	11:12	he shall cast down **m.** ten thousands:	
Da	11:14	there shall **m.** stand up against	7227
Da	11:18	unto the isles, and shall take **m.**:	7227
Da	11:26	and **m.** shall fall down slain.	7227
Da	11:33	among the people shall instruct **m.**:	7227
Da	11:33	by captivity, and by spoil, **m.** days.	7227
Da	11:34	but **m.** shall cleave to them with	7227
Da	11:39	shall cause them to rule over **m.**,	7227
Da	11:40	with horsemen, and with **m.** ships;	7227
Da	11:41	**m.** countries shall be overthrown:	7227
Da	11:44	and utterly to make away **m.**	7227
Da	12:2	**m.** of them that sleep in the dust	7227
Da	12:3	they that turn **m.** to righteousness	7227
Da	12:4	of the end: **m.** shall run to and fro,	7227
Da	12:10	**M.** shall be purified, and made	7227
Ho	3:3	Thou shalt abide for me **m.** days;	7227
Ho	3:4	Israel shall abide **m.** days without	7227
Ho	8:11	Ephraim hath made **m.** altars to	7235
Joe	2:2	it, even to the years of **m.** generations	
Am	8:3	be **m.** dead bodies in every place;	7227
Mic	4:2	**m.** nations shall come, and say,	7227
Mic	4:3	he shall judge among **m.** people,	7227
Mic	4:11	Now also **m.** nations are gathered	7227
Mic	4:13	thou shalt beat in pieces **m.** people:	7227
Mic	5:7	shall be in the midst of **m.** people	7227
Mic	5:8	Gentiles in the midst of **m.** people	7227
Na	1:12	they be quiet, and likewise **m.**,	7227
Na	3:15	thyself **m.** as the cankerworm,	3513
Na	3:15	make thyself **m.** as the locusts.	3513
Hab	2:8	thou hast spoiled **m.** nations, all	7227
Hab	2:10	thy house by cutting off **m.** people,	7227
Zec	2:11	**m.** nations shall be joined to the	7227
Zec	7:3	as I have done these so **m.** years?	
Zec	8:20	and the inhabitants of **m.** cities:	7227
Zec	8:22	**m.** people and strong nations shall	7227
Mal	2:6	did turn **m.** away from iniquity	7227
Mal	2:8	caused **m.** to stumble at the law;	7227
Mt	3:7	when he saw **m.** of the Pharisees	*4183*
Mt	7:13	**m. there be which go in thereat:**	4183
Mt	7:22	**M. will say to me in that day,**	4183
Mt	7:22	**name done m. wonderful works?**	4183
Mt	8:11	**m. shall come from the east and**	4183
Mt	8:16	**m.** that were possessed with devils:	4183
Mt	8:30	them an herd of **m.** swine feeding.	4183
Mt	9:10	**m.** publicans and sinners came and	4183
Mt	10:31	**of more value than m. sparrows.**	4183
Mt	13:3	he spake **m.** things...in parables,	4183
Mt	13:17	**m. prophets and righteous men**	4183
Mt	13:58	he did not **m.** mighty works there	4183
Mt	14:36	**m.** as touched were made perfectly	*3745*
Mt	15:30	dumb, maimed, and **m.** others,	*4183*
Mt	15:34	them, **How m. loaves have ye?**	*4214*
Mt	16:9,	**10 and how m. baskets ye took up?**	*4214*
Mt	16:21	suffer **m.** things of the elders and	*4183*
Mt	19:30	**m. that are first shall be last; and**	*4183*
Mt	20:16	**for m. be called, but few chosen.**	*4183*
Mt	20:28	**to give his life a ransom for m.**	*4183*
Mt	22:9	**as m. as ye shall find, bid to the**	*3745*
Mt	22:10	**together all as m. as they found,**	*3745*
Mt	22:14	**m. are called, but few are chosen.**	*4183*
Mt	24:5	**m. shall come in my name, saying,**	*4183*
Mt	24:5	**I am Christ; and shall deceive m.**	*4183*
Mt	24:10	**then shall m. be offended, and**	*4183*
Mt	24:11	**And m. false prophets shall rise,**	*4183*
Mt	24:11	**shall rise, and shall deceive m.**	*4183*
Mt	24:12	**the love of m. shall wax cold.**	*4183*
Mt	25:21,	**23 make thee ruler over m. things:**	*4183*
Mt	26:28	**shed for m. for the remission of**	*4183*
Mt	26:60	though **m.** false witnesses came,	*4183*
Mt	27:13	not how **m.** things they witness	*4214*
Mt	27:19	I have suffered **m.** things this day	*4183*
Mt	27:52	**m.** bodies of the saints which slept	*4183*
Mt	27:53	holy city, and appeared unto **m.**	*4183*
Mt	27:55	**m.** women were there beholding	*4183*
Mk	1:34	healed **m.** that were sick of divers	*4183*

Mk 1:34 and cast out **m.** devils; and suffered.... 4183
Mk 2:2 **m.** were gathered together,............. 4183
Mk 2:15 **m.** publicans and sinners sat also........ 4183
Mk 2:15 for there were **m.**, and they followed.. 4183
Mk 3:10 For he had healed **m.**; insomuch........ 4183
Mk 3:10 to touch him, as **m.** as had plagues....... 3745
Mk 4:2 he taught...**m.** things by parables....... 4183
Mk 4:33 with **m.** such parables spake he the.... 4183
Mk 5:9 My name is Legion: for we are **m.**..... 4183
Mk 5:26 suffered **m.** things of **m.** physicians, ... 4183
Mk 6:2 **m.** hearing him were astonished,........ 4183
Mk 6:13 And they cast out **m.** devils, and........ 4183
Mk 6:13 anointed with oil **m.** that were sick,.... 4183
Mk 6:20 he did **m.** things, and heard him......... 4183
Mk 6:31 there were **m.** coming and going,........ 4183
Mk 6:33 **m.** knew him, and ran afoot thither...... 4183
Mk 6:34 he began to teach them **m.** things....... 4183
Mk 6:38 them, **How m. loaves have ye?**....... 4214
Mk 6:56 as **m.** as touched him were made....... 3745
Mk 7:4 **m.** other things there be, which......... 4183
Mk 7:8 **m. other such like things ye do**........ 4183
Mk 7:13 **and m. such like things do ye**........ 4183
Mk 8:5 them, **How m. loaves have ye?**....... 4214
Mk 8:19, 20 **how m. baskets full of**............ 4214
Mk 8:31 Son of man must suffer **m.** things,..... 4183
Mk 9:12 **that he must suffer m. things, and**.4183
Mk 9:26 insomuch that **m.** said, He is dead...... 4183
Mk 10:31 **But m. that are first shall be last;**..4183
Mk 10:45 **to give his life a ransom for m.**...... 4183
Mk 10:48 And **m.** charged him that he should 4183
Mk 11:8 **m.** spread their garments in the......... 4183
Mk 12:5 **and him they killed, and m. others;**4183
Mk 12:41 and **m.** that were rich cast in much. ... 4183
Mk 13:6 **m. shall come in my name, saying,** 4183
Mk 13:6 **I am Christ; and shall deceive m.**.. 4183
Mk 14:24 **testament, which is shed for m.**... 4183
Mk 14:56 **m.** bare false witness against him,...... 4183
Mk 15:3 priests accused him of **m.** things:....... 4183
Mk 15:4 **m.** things they witness against.......... 4214
Mk 15:41 **m.** other women which came up 4183
Lu 1:1 as **m.** have taken in hand to set......... 4183
Lu 1:14 and **m.** shall rejoice at his birth......... 4183
Lu 1:16 **m.** of the children of Israel shall he 4183
Lu 2:34 and rising again of **m.** in Israel;......... 4183
Lu 2:35 the thoughts of **m.** hearts may be 4183
Lu 3:18 **m.** other things in his exhortation 4183
Lu 4:25 **m. widows were in Israel in the**.... 4183
Lu 4:27 **And m. lepers were in Israel in the** 4183
Lu 4:41 devils also came out of **m.** crying 4183
Lu 7:11 **m.** of his disciples went with him,....... 2425
Lu 7:21 cured **m.** of their infirmities and......... 4183
Lu 7:21 **m.** that were blind he gave sight........ 4183
Lu 7:47 **thee, Her sins, which are m., are**.. 4183
Lu 8:3 **m.** others, which ministered unto....... 4183
Lu 8:30 **m.** devils were entered into him. 4183
Lu 8:32 there an herd of **m.** swine feeding........ 2425
Lu 9:22 **Son of man must suffer m. things,**.4183
Lu 10:24 **m. prophets and kings have**......... 4183
Lu 10:41 **and troubled about m. things:**........ 4183
Lu 11:8 **and give him as m. as he needeth**...3745
Lu 11:53 provoke him to speak of **m.** things: 4119
Lu 12:7 **of more value than m. sparrows.**... 4183
Lu 12:19 **much goods laid up for m. years;**.. 4183
Lu 12:47 **shall be beaten with m. stripes**...... 4183
Lu 13:24 **m., I say unto you, will seek to**.... 4183
Lu 14:16 **made a great supper, and bade m.:**.4183
Lu 15:13 **not m. days after the younger son**. 4183
Lu 15:17 **m. hired servantss of my father's**.. 4214
Lu 15:29 **Lo, these m. years do I serve thee,**.5118
Lu 17:25 **first must he suffer m. things,**...... 4183
Lu 21:8 **m. shall come in my name,**........... 4183
Lu 22:65 And **m.** other things blasphemously..... 4183
Lu 23:8 he had heard **m.** things of him;.......... 4183
Lu 23:9 questioned with him in **m.** words;........ 2425
Joh 1:12 But as **m.** as received him, to them.... 3745
Joh 2:12 they continued there not **m.** days........ 4183
Joh 2:23 **m.** believed in his name, when they.... 4183
Joh 4:39 **m.** of the Samaritans of that city........ 4183
Joh 4:41 **m.** more believed because of his......... 4183
Joh 6:9 but what are they among so **m.**?........ 5118
Joh 6:60 **M.** therefore of his disciples, when...... 4183
Joh 6:66 time **m.** of his disciples went back,..... 4183
Joh 7:31 **m.** of the people believed on him, ... 4183
Joh 7:40 **M.** of the people therefore, when......... 4183
Joh 8:26 **m. things to say and to judge of**.... 4183
Joh 8:30 these words, **m.** believed on him. 4183
Joh 10:20 **m.** of them said, He hath a devil,...... 4183
Joh 10:32 **M. good works have I shewed you**..4183
Joh 10:41 **m.** resorted unto him, and said,......... 4183
Joh 10:42 And **m.** believed on him there............ 4183
Joh 11:19 **m.** of the Jews came to Martha and.... 4183
Joh 11:45 **m.** of the Jews which came to Mary, .. 4183
Joh 11:47 for this man doeth **m.** miracles. 4183
Joh 11:55 **m.** went out of the country up to....... 4183
Joh 12:11 of him **m.** of the Jews went away,....... 4183
Joh 12:37 done so **m.** miracles before them, ... 5118
Joh 12:42 rulers also **m.** believed on him;.......... 4183
Joh 14:2 **Father's house are m. mansions:**... 4183
Joh 16:12 **I have yet m. things to say unto**... 4183
Joh 17:2 **give eternal life to as m. as thou**.........
Joh 19:20 This title then read **m.** of the Jews:.... 4183
Joh 20:30 **m.** other signs truly did Jesus in 4183
Joh 21:11 for all there were so **m.**, yet was........ 5118
Joh 21:25 And there are also **m.** other things..... 4183
Ac 1:3 his passion by **m.** infallible proofs, ... 4183
Ac 1:5 **the Holy Ghost not m. days**........ 4183
Ac 2:39 as **m.** as the Lord our God shall call.... 3745
Ac 2:40 with **m.** other words did he testify 4119
Ac 2:43 **m.** wonders and signs were done 4183
Ac 3:24 as **m.** as have spoken, have likewise... 3745
Ac 4:4 **m.** of them which heard the word 4183
Ac 4:6 as **m.** as were of the kindred of the.... 3745
Ac 4:34 for a **m.** as were possessors of lands.. 3745
Ac 5:11 upon as **m.** as heard these things............
Ac 5:12 **m.** signs and wonders wrought 4183
Ac 5:36 **m.** as obeyed him, were scattered,....... 3745
Ac 5:37 as **m.** as obeyed him, were dispersed. .3745
Ac 8:7 came out of **m.** that were possessed... 4183
Ac 8:7 and **m.** taken with palsies, and that..... 4183
Ac 8:25 in **m.** villages of the Samaratians. 4183
Ac 9:13 I have heard by **m.** of this man,.......... 4183
Ac 9:23 after that **m.** days were fulfilled,........ 2425
Ac 9:42 and **m.** believed in the Lord.............. 4183
Ac 9:43 tarried **m.** days in Joppa with one....... 2425
Ac 10:27 found **m.** that were come together. 4183
Ac 10:45 as **m.** as came with Peter,................ 3745
Ac 12:12 **m.** were gathered together praying....... 2425
Ac 13:31 And he was seen **m.** days of them 4119
Ac 13:43 **m.** of the Jews and religious............. 4183
Ac 13:48 as **m.** as were ordained to eternal...... 3745
Ac 14:21 to that city, and had taught **m.**,........ 2425
Ac 15:32 the brethren with **m.** words, and......... 4183
Ac 15:35 of the Lord, with **m.** others also. 4183
Ac 16:18 And this did she **m.** days. But Paul, ... 4183
Ac 16:23 they had laid **m.** stripes upon them,..... 4183
Ac 17:12 Therefore **m.** of them believed; 4183
Ac 18:8 and **m.** of the Corinthians hearing........ 4183
Ac 19:18 And **m.** that believed came, and......... 4183
Ac 19:19 **M.** of them...which used curious 2425
Ac 20:8 were **m.** lights in the upper chamber,... 2425
Ac 20:19 with **m.** tears, and temptations, ... 4183
Ac 21:10 as we tarried there **m.** days, there 4119
Ac 21:20 how **m.** thousands of Jews there 4214
Ac 24:10 thou hast been of **m.** years a judge..... 4183
Ac 24:17 after **m.** years I came to bring........... 4119
Ac 25:7 laid **m.** and grievous complaints.......... 4183
Ac 25:14 when they had been there **m.** days,.... 4119
Ac 26:9 do **m.** things contrary to the name 4183
Ac 26:10 and **m.** of the saints did I shut up 4183
Ac 27:7 when we had sailed slowly **m.** days, ... 2425
Ac 27:20 nor stars in **m.** days appeared, ... 4119
Ac 28:10 honoured us with **m.** honours: 4183
Ac 28:23 came **m.** to him into his lodging; 4119
Ro 2:12 as **m.** as have sinned without law....... 3745
Ro 2:12 as **m.** as have sinned in the law.......... 3745
Ro 4:17 made thee a father of **m.** nations,)...... 4183
Ro 4:18 become the father of **m.** nations,......... 4183
Ro 5:15 the offence of one **m.** be dead,.......... 4183
Ro 5:15 Christ, hath abounded unto **m.**........... 4183
Ro 5:16 is of **m.** offences unto justification....... 4183
Ro 5:19 disobedience **m.** were made sinners,... 4183
Ro 5:19 of one shall **m.** be made righteous....... 4183
Ro 6:3 as **m.** of us as were baptized into....... 3745
Ro 8:14 as **m.** as are led by the Spirit of God,..3745
Ro 8:29 the firstborn among **m.** brethren. 4183
Ro 12:4 we have **m.** members in one body,....... 4183
Ro 12:5 So we, being **m.**, are one body in 4183
Ro 15:23 these **m.** years to come unto you;...... 4183
Ro 16:2 for she hath been a succourer of **m.**,.. 4183
1Co 1:26 that not **m.** wise men after the flesh,.. 4183
1Co 1:26 not **m.** mighty, not **m.** noble, are......... 4183
1Co 4:15 Christ, yet have ye not **m.** fathers: 4183
1Co 8:5 (as there be gods **m.**, and lords **m.**,).. 4183
1Co 10:5 with **m.** of them God was not well 4119
1Co 10:17 we being **m.** are one bread, and 4183
1Co 10:33 own profit, but the profit of **m.**,.......... 4183
1Co 11:30 For this cause **m.** are weak and......... 4183
1Co 11:30 sickly among you, and **m.** sleep. 2425
1Co 12:12 body is one, and hath **m.** members,..... 4183
1Co 12:12 members of that one body, being **m.**,.. 4183
1Co 12:14 the body is not one member, but **m.**... 4183
1Co 12:20 But now are they **m.** members, yet..... 4183
1Co 14:10 so **m.** kinds of voices in the world,..... 5118
1Co 16:9 me, and there are **m.** adversaries....... 4183
2Co 1:11 upon us by the means of **m.** persons .. 4183
2Co 1:11 thanks may be given by **m.** on our 4183
2Co 2:4 I wrote unto you with **m.** tears;.......... 4183
2Co 2:6 which was inflicted of **m.**................ 4119
2Co 2:17 we are not as **m.**, which corrupt........ 4183
2Co 4:15 through the thanksgiving of **m.** 4119
2Co 6:10 as poor, yet making **m.** rich; as......... 4183
2Co 8:22 proved diligent in **m.** things, but 4183
2Co 9:2 your zeal hath provoked very **m.**......... 4119
2Co 9:12 by **m.** thanksgivings unto God: 4183
2Co 11:18 Seeing that **m.** glory after the flesh, ... 4183
2Co 12:21 shall bewail **m.** which have sinned 4183
Ga 1:14 Jews' religion above **m.** my equals...... 4183
Ga 3:4 ye suffered so **m.** things in vain?......... 5118
Ga 3:10 as **m.** as are of the works of the law .. 3745
Ga 3:16 saith not, And to seeds, as of **m.**; 4183
Ga 3:27 as **m.** of you as have been baptized.... 3745
Ga 4:27 desolate hath **m.** more children.......... 4183
Ga 6:12 As **m.** as desire to make a fair shew... 3745
Ga 6:16 as **m.** as walk according to this rule,... 3745
Php 1:14 **m.** of the brethren in the Lord, ... 4119
Php 3:15 us therefore, as **m.** as be perfect,...... 3745
Php 3:18 (For **m.** walk, of whom I have told..... 4183
Col 2:1 as **m.** as have not seen my face in 3745
1Ti 6:1 Let as **m.** servants as are under the... 3745
1Ti 6:9 into **m.** foolish and hurtful lusts,......... 4183
1Ti 6:10 pierced...through with **m.** sorrows...... 4183
1Ti 6:12 good profession before **m.** witnesses... 4183
2Ti 1:18 in how **m.** things he ministered.......... 3745
2Ti 2:2 heard of me among **m.** witnesses, ... 4183
Tit 1:10 there are **m.** unruly and vain talkers ... 4183
Heb 2:10 in bringing **m.** sons unto glory, to 4183
Heb 5:11 Of whom we have **m.** things to say, ... 4183
Heb 7:23 And they truly were **m.** priests,......... 4119
Heb 9:28 once offered to bear the sins of **m.**;.... 4183
Heb 11:12 so **m.** as the stars of the sky in..............
Heb 12:15 you, and thereby **m.** be defiled; 4183
Jas 3:1 My brethren, be not **m.** masters,......... 4183
Jas 3:2 For in **m.** things we offend all. If 4183
2Pe 2:2 And **m.** shall follow their pernicious 4183
1Jo 2:18 even now are there **m.** antichrists; 4183
1Jo 4:1 **m.** false prophets are gone out into.... 4183
2Jo 7 For **m.** deceivers are entered into....... 4183
2Jo 12 Having **m.** things to write unto you, ... 4183
3Jo 13 I had **m.** things to write, but I will..... 4183
Re 1:15 his voice as the sound of **m.** waters.... 4183
Re 2:24 **as m. as have not this doctrine,** 3745
Re 3:19 **m. as I love, I rebuke and chasten:** 3745
Re 5:11 and I heard the voice of **m.** angels 4183
Re 8:11 and **m.** men died of the waters, ... 4183
Re 9:9 of **m.** horses running to battle. 4183
Re 10:11 prophesy again before **m.** peoples,...... 4183
Re 13:15 as **m.** as would not worship the 3745
Re 14:2 heaven, as the voice of **m.** waters,...... 4183
Re 17:1 whore that sitteth upon **m.** waters:..... 4183
Re 18:17 sailors, and as **m.** as trade by sea, ... 3745
Re 19:6 and as the voice of **m.** waters, and..... 4183
Re 19:12 and on his head were **m.** crowns;....... 4183

MAOCH (ma'-ok)
1Sa 27:2 the son of **M.**, king of Gath. 4582

MAON (ma'-on) See also MAONITES.
Jos 15:55 **M.**, Carmel, and Ziph, and Juttah,...... 4584
1Sa 23:24 men were in the wilderness of **M.**,...... 4584
1Sa 23:25 and abode in the wilderness of **M.**...... 4584
1Sa 23:25 after David in the wilderness of **M.**..... 4584
1Sa 25:2 And there was a man in **M.**, whose.... 4584
1Ch 2:45 And the son of Shammai was **M.**:....... 4584
1Ch 2:45 and **M.** was the father of Beth-zur....... 4584

MAONITES (ma'-on-ites) See also MEHUNIM.
Jg 10:12 and the **M.**, did oppress you; 4584

MAR See also MARRED.
Le 19:27 thou **m.** the corners of thy beard. 7843
Ru 4:6 lest I **m.** mine own inheritance: 7843
1Sa 6:5 of your mice that **m.** the land; 7843
2Ki 3:19 and **m.** every good piece of land 3510

Job 30:13 They m. my path, they set forward.... 5420
Jer 13:9 will I m. the pride of Judah, and 7843

MARA (ma'-rah)
Ru 1:20 Call me not Naomi, call me M.: 4755

MARAH (ma'-rah)
Ex 15:23 when they came to M., they could 4785
Ex 15:23 could not drink of the waters of M., ... 4785
Ex 15:23 the name of it was called M.. 4785
Nu 33:8 of Etham, and pitched in M.. 4785
Nu 33:9 they removed from M., and came 4785

MARALAH (mar'-a-lah)
Jos 19:11 went up toward the sea, and M., ... 4831

MARAN-ATHA (mar-an-a'-thah)
1Co 16:22 Christ, let him be Anathema M.. .... *3134*

MARBLE
1Ch 29:2 and m. stones in abundance. 7893
Es 1:6 to silver rings and pillars of m.: 8338
Es 1:6 and blue, and white, and black, m.. 8336
Ca 5:15 His legs are as pillars of m., set 8336
Re 18:12 and of brass, and iron, and m., ... *3139*

MARCABOTH See BETH-MARCABOTH.

MARCH See also MARCHED; MARCHEDST.
Ps 68:7 didst m. through the wilderness; 6805
Jer 46:22 for they shall m. with an army, ... 3212
Joe 2:7 they shall m. every one on his ways, .. 3212
Hab 1:6 shall m. through the breadth of 1980
Hab 3:12 Thou didst m. through the land in 6805

MARCHED See also MARCHEDST.
Ex 14:10 the Egyptians m. after them; 5265

MARCHEDST
Jg 5:4 thou m. out of the field of Edom, ... 6805

MARCUS (mar'-cus) See also MARK.
Col 4:10 and M., sister's son to Barnabas, ... *3138*
Phm 24 M., Aristarchus, Demas, Lucas, ... *3138*
1Pe 5:13 you; and so doth M. my son. *3138*

MARESHAH (mar'-e-shah)
Jos 15:44 And Keilah, and Achzib, and M.. 4762
1Ch 2:42 sons of M. the father of Hebron. 4762
1Ch 4:21 and Laadah the father of M., and 4762
2Ch 11:8 And Gath, and M., and Ziph, ... 4762
2Ch 14:9 chariots; and came unto M.. 4762
2Ch 14:10 in the valley of Zephathah at M.. 4762
2Ch 20:37 Eliezer the son of Dodavah of M.. 4762
Mic 1:15 heir unto thee, O inhabitant of M.. 4762

MARINERS
Eze 27:8 of Zidon and Arvad were thy m. 7751
Eze 27:9 the ships of the sea with their m. 4419
Eze 27:27 they m., and thy pilots, thy calkers, ... 4419
Eze 27:29 the m., and all the pilots of the sea, ... 4419
Jon 1:5 Then the m. were afraid, and cried 4419

MARISHES
Eze 47:11 m. thereof shall not be healed; 1360

MARK See also LANDMARK; MARKED; MARKEST; MARKETH; MARKS.
Ge 4:15 the Lord set a m. upon Cain, lest 226
Ru 3:4 m. the place where he shall lie, ... 3045
1Sa 20:20 thereof, as though I shot at a m.. 4307
2Sa 13:28 M. ye now when Amnon's heart 7200
1Ki 20:7 M., I pray you, and see how this 3045
1Ki 20:22 and m., and see what thou doest: 3045
Job 7:20 thou set me as a m. against thee, ... 4645
Job 16:12 pieces, and set me up for his m.. 4307
Job 18:2 m., and afterwards we will speak. 995
Job 21:5 M. me, and be astonished, and lay 6437
Job 33:31 M. well, O Job, hearken unto me: 7181
Job 39:1 thou m. when the hinds do calve? 8104
Ps 37:37 M. the perfect man, and behold 8104
Ps 48:13 M. ye well her bulwarks, consider 7896
Ps 56:6 they m. my steps, when they wait 8104
Ps 130:3 thou, Lord, shouldest m. iniquities, ... 8104
La 3:12 and set me as a m. for the arrow. 4307
Eze 9:4 m. upon the foreheads of the men 8420
Eze 9:6 any man upon whom is the m.; 8420
Eze 44:5 Son of man, m. well, and behold 7760
Eze 44:5 m. well the entering in of the 7760
Ro 16:17 m. them which cause divisions and *4648*
Php 3:14 press toward the m. for the prize *4649*
Php 3:17 m. them which walk so as ye have *4648*
Re 13:16 to receive a m. in their right hand, ... *5480*
Re 13:17 save he that had the m. or the *5480*
Re 14:9 and receive his m. in his forehead, ... *5480*
Re 14:11 receiveth the m. of his name. *5480*
Re 15:2 over his image, and over his m., ... *5480*
Re 16:2 upon the men which had the m. of *5480*
Re 19:20 had received the m. of the beast, ... *5480*
Re 20:4 had received his m. upon their *5480*

MARK See also MARCUS.
Mk *general title* According To S. [St.] M.. .... *3138*
Ac 12:12 of John, whose surname was M.; *3138*
Ac 12:25 John, whose surname was M.. .... *3138*
Ac 15:37 John, whose surname was M.. .... *3138*
Ac 15:39 and so Barnabas took M., and *3138*
2Ti 4:11 Take M., and bring him with thee: *3138*

MARKED
1Sa 1:12 the Lord, and Eli m. her mouth. 8104
Job 22:15 Hast thou m. the old way which 8104
Job 24:16 m. for themselves in the daytime: 2856
Jer 2:22 yet thine iniquity is m. before me, ... 3799
Jer 23:18 who hath m. his word, and heard 7181
Lu 14:7 when he m. how they chose out *1907*

MARKEST
Job 10:14 If I sin, then thou m. me, and 8104

MARKET See also MARKETPLACE; MARKETS.
Eze 27:13 and vessels of brass in thy m.. 4627
Eze 27:17 they traded in thy m. wheat of 4627
Eze 27:19 and calamus, were in thy m.. 4627
Eze 27:25 Tarshish did sing of thee in thy m.: 4627
Mk 7:4 And when they come from the m., ... *58*
Joh 5:2 at Jerusalem by the sheep m. a pool, ...
Ac 17:17 in the m. daily with them that met *58*

MARKETH
Job 33:11 in the stocks, he m. all my paths. 8104
Isa 44:13 m. it out with a line; he fitteth it 8388
Isa 44:13 m. it out with the compass, and 8388

MARKETPLACE
Mt 20:3 **saw others standing idle in the m.,** ... *58*
Lu 7:32 **like unto children sitting in the m.,** . *58*
Ac 16:19 them into the m. unto the rulers, ... *58*

MARKETPLACES
Mk 12:38 **and love salutations in the m.,** *58*

MARKETS
Mt 11:16 **like unto children sitting in the m.,** . *58*
Mt 23:7 **greetings in the m., and to be called** *58*
Lu 11:43 **synagogues, and greetings in the m.** . *58*
Lu 20:46 **robes, and love greetings in the m.,** . *58*

MARKS See also WAYMARKS.
Le 19:28 dead, nor print any m. upon you: 7085
Ga 6:17 my body the m. of the Lord Jesus *4742*

MAROTH (ma'-roth)
Mic 1:12 inhabitant of M. waited carefully 4796

MARRED
Isa 52:14 his visage was so m. more than 4893
Jer 13:7 the girdle was m., it was profitable 7843
Jer 18:4 vessel that he made of clay was m. 7843
Na 2:2 out, and m. their vine branches. 7843
Mk 2:22 **spilled, and the bottles will be m.:** .. *622*

MARRIAGE See also MARRIAGES.
Ex 21:10 her raiment, and her duty of m., ... 5772
Ps 78:63 maidens were not given to m.. 1984
Mt 22:2 **king which made a m. for his son,** . *1062*
Mt 22:4 **are ready: come unto the m.** *1062*
Mt 22:9 **as ye shall find, bid to the m.** *1062*
Mt 22:30 **neither marry, nor are given in m.,** *1548*
Mt 24:38 **marrying and giving in m., until** ... *1547*
Mt 25:10 **ready went in with him to the m.:** . *1062*
Mk 12:25 **neither marry, nor are given in m.;** *1061*
Lu 17:27 **they were given in m., until the** *1548*
Lu 20:34 **world marry, and are given in m.:** . *1548*
Lu 20:35 **neither marry, nor are given in m.:** *1548*
Jo 2:1 there was a m. in Cana of Galilee; *1062*
Jo 2:2 called, and his disciples, to the m.. ...... *1062*
1Co 7:38 that giveth her in m. doeth well; *1547*
1Co 7:38 giveth her not in m. doeth better. *1547*
Heb 13:4 M. is honourable in all, and the *1062*
Re 19:7 for the m. of the Lamb is come, ... *1062*
Re 19:9 unto the m. supper of the Lamb. *1062*

MARRIAGES
Ge 34:9 make ye m. with us, and give your 2859
De 7:3 Neither shalt thou make m. with 2859
Jos 23:12 shall make m. with them, and go 2859

MARRIED See also UNMARRIED.
Ge 19:14 in law, which m. his daughters, ... 3947
Ex 21:3 if he were m., then his wife 1166,802
Le 22:12 If the priest's daughter also be m. ....
Nu 12:1 of the...woman whom he had m.: 3947
Nu 12:1 he had m. an Ethiopian woman. 3947
Nu 36:3 And if they be m. to any of the sons 802
Nu 36:11 m. unto their father's brother's sons: 802
Nu 36:12 were m. into the families of the sons 802
De 22:22 with a woman m. to an husband 1166
De 24:1 hath taken a wife, and m. her, ... 1166
1Ch 2:21 he m. when he was threescore 3947
2Ch 13:21 mighty, and m. fourteen wives, ... 5375
Ne 13:23 that had m. wives of Ashdod, ... 3427
Pr 30:23 odious woman when she is m.; 1166
Isa 54:1 than the children of the m. wife, ... 1166
Isa 62:4 in thee, and thy land shall be m.. 1166
Jer 3:14 the Lord; for I am m. unto you: 1166
Mal 2:11 m. the daughter of a strange god. 1166
Mt 22:25 the first, when he had m. a wife, ... *1060*
Mk 6:17 Philip's wife: for he had m. her. *1060*
Mk 10:12 **husband, and be m. to another,** *1060*
Lu 14:20 **another said, I have m. a wife,** *1060*
Lu 17:27 **did eat, they drank, they m. wives,** *1060*
Ro 7:3 liveth, she be m. to another man, ... *1096*
Ro 7:3 though she be m. to another man. *1096*
Ro 7:4 that ye should be m. to another, ... *1096*
1Co 7:10 unto the m. I command, yet not I, ... *1060*
1Co 7:33 he that is m. careth for the things *1060*
1Co 7:34 she that is m. careth for the things *1060*
1Co 7:39 liberty to be m. to whom she will; *1060*

MARRIETH
Isa 62:5 For as a young man m. a virgin, ... 1166
Mt 19:9 **whoso m. her which is put away** ... *1060*
Lu 16:18 **away his wife, and m. another,** *1060*
Lu 16:18 **whosoever m. her that is put away.** *1060*

MARROW
Job 21:24 his bones are moistened with m.. 4221
Ps 63:5 satisfied as with m. and fatness; 2459
Pr 3:8 to thy navel, and m. to thy bones. 8250
Isa 25:6 of fat things full of m., of wines 4229
Heb 4:12 spirit, and of the joints and m., ... *3452*

MARRY See also MARRIED; MARRIETH; MARRYING.
Ge 38:8 thy brother's wife, and m. her, ... 2992
Nu 36:6 them m. to whom they think best; 802
Nu 36:6 tribe of their father shall they m.. 802
De 25:5 not m. without unto a stranger: 1961,376
Isa 62:5 virgin, so shall thy sons m. thee: 1166
Mt 5:32 **shall m. her that is divorced** *1060*
Mt 19:9 **m. another, committeth adultery:** .. *1060*
Mt 19:10 with his wife, it is not good to m.. ..... *1060*
Mt 22:24 his brother shall m. his wife, and *1918*
Mt 22:30 **in the resurrection they neither m.** *1060*
Mk 10:11 **put away his wife, and m. another,** *1060*
Mk 12:25 **they neither m., nor are given in** .. *1060*
Lu 20:34 **The children of this world m., and** *1060*
Lu 20:35 **the dead, neither m., nor are given** *1060*
1Co 7:9 they cannot contain, let them m.: *1060*
1Co 7:9 for it is better to m. than to burn. *1060*
1Co 7:28 if thou m., thou hast not sinned; *1060*
1Co 7:28 if a virgin m., she hath not sinned. *1060*
1Co 7:36 will, he sinneth not: let them m.. .... *1060*
1Ti 4:3 Forbidding to m., and commanding *1060*
1Ti 5:11 wanton against Christ, they will m.; *1060*
1Ti 5:14 that the younger women m., bear *1060*

MARRYING
Ne 13:27 our God in m. strange wives? 3427
Mt 24:38 **m. and giving in marriage, until** ... *1060*

MARS' (marz)
Ac 17:22 Paul stood in the midst of M. hill, ... *697*

MARSENA (mar'-se-nah)
Es 1:14 M., and Memucan, the seven 4826

MARSHES See MARISHES.

MARS'-HILL See MARS' and HILL; also AREOPAGUS.

MART
Isa 23:3 and she is a m. of nations 5505

MARTHA (mar'-thah)
Lu 10:38 and a certain woman named M. *3136*
Lu 10:40 But M. was cumbered about much *3136*

Lu 10:41 **M., M., thou art careful and**......... *3136*
Joh 11:1 the town of Mary and her sister **M.**..... *3136*
Joh 11:5 Jesus loved **M.**, and her sister,.......... *3136*
Joh 11:19 the Jews came to **M.** and Mary, to..... *3136*
Joh 11:20 Then **M.**, as soon as she heard that ... *3136*
Joh 11:21 Then said **M.** unto Jesus, Lord, if *3136*
Joh 11:24 **M.** saith unto him, I know that he...... *3136*
Joh 11:30 in that place where **M.** met him.......... *3136*
Joh 11:39 **M.**, the sister of him that was dead,... *3136*
Joh 12:2 made him a supper; and **M.** served:.... *3136*

MARTYR See also MARTYRS.
Ac 22:20 blood of thy **m.** Stephen was shed,..... *3144*
Re 2:13 **Antipas was my faithful m., who**... *3144*

MARTYRS
Re 17:6 with the blood of the **m.** of Jesus: *3144*

MARVEL See also MARVELLED; MARVELS.
Ec 5:8 in a province, **m.** not at the matter:.... 8539
Mk 5:20 done for him: and all men did **m.**. *2296*
Joh 3:7 **M. not that I said unto thee, Ye**... *2296*
Joh 5:20 **works than these, that ye may m.**. *2296*
Joh 5:28 **M. not at this: for the hour is**........ *2296*
Joh 7:21 **have done one work, and ye all m.**. *2296*
Ac 3:12 men of Israel, why **m.** ye at this? *2296*
2Co 11:14 And no **m.**; for Satan himself is *2298*
Ga 1:6 I **m.** that ye are so soon removed...... *2296*
1Jo 3:13 **M.** not, my brethren, if the world *2296*
Re 17:7 unto me, Wherefore didst thou **m.**? *2296*

MARVELLED
Ge 43:33 and the men **m.** one at another.......... 8539
Ps 48:5 They saw it, and so they **m.**; they....... 8539
Mt 8:10 When Jesus heard it, he **m.**, and....... *2296*
Mt 8:27 the men **m.**, saying, What manner...... *2296*
Mt 9:8 when the multitudes saw it, they **m.**,.. *2296*
Mt 9:33 the multitudes **m.**, saying, It was....... *2296*
Mt 21:20 when the disciples saw it, they **m.**, ... *2296*
Mt 22:22 had heard these words, they **m.**, ... *2296*
Mt 27:14 that the governor **m.** greatly. *2296*
Mk 6:6 he **m.** because of their unbelief........... *2296*
Mk 12:17 **are God's.** And they **m.** at him......... *2296*
Mk 15:5 answered nothing; so that Pilate **m.**.... *2296*
Mk 15:44 Pilate **m.** if he were already dead:....... *2296*
Lu 1:21 and **m.** that he tarried so long in the... *2296*
Lu 1:63 name is John. And they **m.** all. *2296*
Lu 2:33 And Joseph and his mother **m.** at....... *2296*
Lu 7:9 heard these things, he **m.** at him, ... *2296*
Lu 11:38 he **m.** that he had not first washed...... *2296*
Lu 20:26 and they **m.** at his answer, and held.... *2296*
Joh 4:27 **m.** that he talked with the woman: *2296*
Joh 7:15 the Jews **m.**, saying, How knoweth *2296*
Ac 2:7 they were all amazed and **m.**,............ *2296*
Ac 4:13 and ignorant men, they **m.**; and......... *2296*

MARVELLOUS
1Ch 16:12 Remember his **m.** works that he........ 6381
1Ch 16:24 his **m.** works among all nations.......... 6381
Job 5:9 **m.** things without number:................ 6381
Job 10:16 thou shewest thyself **m.** upon me....... 6381
Ps 9:1 I will shew forth all thy **m.** works. 6381
Ps 17:7 Shew thy **m.** lovingkindness, O.......... 6395
Ps 31:21 hath shewed me his **m.** kindness........ 6381
Ps 78:12 **M.** things did he in the sight of.......... 6382
Ps 98:1 for he hath done **m.** things: his.......... 6381
Ps 105:5 Remember his **m.** works that he........ 6381
Ps 118:23 Lord's doing; it is **m.** in our eyes. 6381
Ps 139:14 **m.** are thy works; and that my soul.... 6381
Isa 29:14 I will proceed to do a **m.** work 6381
Isa 29:14 even a **m.** work and a wonder: 6381
Da 11:36 speak **m.** things against the God of..... 6381
Mic 7:15 will I shew unto him **m.** things. 6381
Zec 8:6 it be **m.** in the eyes of the remnant 6381
Zec 8:6 should it also be **m.** in mine eyes?....... 6381
Mt 21:42 **doing, and it is m. in our eyes?**..... *2298*
Mk 12:11 **doing, and it is m. in our eyes?**..... *2298*
Joh 9:30 Why herein is a **m.** thing, that ye....... *2298*
1Pe 2:9 out of darkness into his **m.** light:......... *2298*
Re 15:1 sign in heaven, great and **m.**, seven ... *2298*
Re 15:3 Great and **m.** are thy works, Lord *2298*

MARVELLOUSLY
2Ch 26:15 for he was **m.** helped, till he was 6381
Job 37:5 God thundereth **m.** with his voice;....... 6381
Hab 1:5 and regard, and wonder **m.**: 8539

MARVELS
Ex 34:10 before all thy people I will do **m.**, ... 6381

MARY (ma'-ry) See also MIRIAM.
Mt 1:16 begat Joseph the husband of **M.**, ... *3137*
Mt 1:18 mother **M.** was espoused to Joseph, ... *3137*
Mt 1:20 fear not to take unto thee **M.** thy....... *3137*
Mt 2:11 young child with **M.** his mother,......... *3137*
Mt 13:55 son? is not his mother called **M.**? *3137*
Mt 27:56 Among which was **M.** Magdalene, ... *3137*
Mt 27:56 **M.** the mother of James and Joses,..... *3137*
Mt 27:61 And there was **M.** Magdalene, and *3137*
Mt 27:61 the other **M.**, sitting over against....... *3137*
Mt 28:1 came **M.** Magdalene and the other...... *3137*
Mt 28:1 the other **M.** to see the sepulchre. *3137*
Mk 6:3 this the carpenter, the son of **M.**, ... *3137*
Mk 15:40 among whom was **M.** Magdalene,....... *3137*
Mk 15:40 **M.** the mother of James the less........ *3137*
Mk 15:47 **M.** Magdalene and...the mother of....... *3137*
Mk 15:47 and **M.** the mother of Joses beheld..... *3137*
Mk 16:1 sabbath was past, **M.** Magdalene,....... *3137*
Mk 16:1 and **M.** the mother of James, and....... *3137*
Mk 16:9 he appeared first to **M.** Magdalene, ... *3137*
Lu 1:27 and the virgin's name was **M.**............ *3137*
Lu 1:30 angel said unto her, Fear not, **M.**:........ *3137*
Lu 1:34 Then said **M.** unto the angel, How *3137*
Lu 1:38 And **M.** said, Behold the handmaid *3137*
Lu 1:39 **M.** arose in those days, and went *3137*
Lu 1:41 heard the salutation of **M.**, the *3137*
Lu 1:46 And **M.** said, My soul doth magnify *3137*
Lu 1:56 And **M.** abode with her about three *3137*
Lu 2:5 be taxed with **M.** his espoused wife, ... *3137*
Lu 2:16 haste, and found **M.**, and Joseph, ... *3137*
Lu 2:19 But **M.** kept all these things, and........ *3137*
Lu 2:34 said unto **M.** his mother, Behold, ... *3137*
Lu 8:2 **M.** called Magdalene, out of whom *3137*
Lu 10:39 And she had a sister called **M.**, ... *3137*
Lu 10:42 **and M. hath chosen that good part,** *3137*
Lu 24:10 It was **M.** Magdalene, and Joanna,...... *3137*
Lu 24:10 **M.** the mother of James, and other...... *3137*
Joh 11:1 town of **M.** and her sister Martha. *3137*
Joh 11:2 that **M.** which anointed the Lord *3137*
Joh 11:19 the Jews came to Martha and **M.**,....... *3137*
Joh 11:20 him: but **M.** sat still in the house. *3137*
Joh 11:28 and called **M.** her sister secretly, ... *3137*
Joh 11:31 when they saw **M.**, that she rose up... *3137*
Joh 11:32 **M.** was come where Jesus was,......... *3137*
Joh 11:45 of the Jews which came to **M.**, and *3137*
Joh 12:3 Then took **M.** a pound of ointment *3137*
Joh 19:25 **M.** the wife of Cleophas, and *3137*
Joh 19:25 wife of Cleophas, and **M.** Magdalene... *3137*
Joh 20:1 week cometh **M.** Magdalene early, ... *3137*
Joh 20:11 **M.** stood without at the sepulchre...... *3137*
Joh 20:16 Jesus saith unto her, **M.**. She............ *3137*
Joh 20:18 **M.** Magdalene came and told the........ *3137*
Ac 1:14 and **M.** the mother of Jesus, and......... *3137*
Ac 12:12 house of **M.** the mother of John, ... *3137*
Ro 16:6 Greet **M.**, who bestowed much........... *3137*

MASCHIL (mas'-kil)
Ps 32:*title* A Psalm of David, **M.**..................... 4905
Ps 42:*title* To the chief Musican, **M.**, for the 4905
Ps 44:*title* for the sons of Korah, **M.**................. 4905
Ps 45:*title* for the sons of Korah, **M.**, A Song..... 4905
Ps 52:*title* To the chief Musician, **M.**, A 4905
Ps 53:*title* Musician upon Mahalath, **M.**, A 4905
Ps 54:*title* chief Musician on Neginoth, **M.**,........ 4905
Ps 55:*title* chief Musician on Neginoth, **M.**,........ 4905
Ps 74:*title* **M.** of Asaph. 4905
Ps 78:*title* **M.** of Asaph. 4905
Ps 88:*title* **M.** of Heman the Ezrahite. 4905
Ps 89:*title* **M.** of Ethan the Ezrahite. 4905
Ps 142:*title* **M.** of David; A Prayer when he......... 4905

MASH (mash)
Ge 10:23 Uz, and Hul, and Gether, and **M.**........ 4851

MASHAL (ma'-shal)
1Ch 6:74 **M.** with her suburbs, and Abdon........ 4913

MASONS
2Sa 5:11 trees, and carpenters, and **m.**: 2796,68
2Ki 12:12 And to **m.**, and hewers of stone, ... 1443
2Ki 22:6 carpenters, and builders, and **m.**, ... 1443
1Ch 14:1 with **m.** and carpenters, to 2796,7023
1Ch 22:2 he set **m.** to hew wrought stones....... 2672
2Ch 24:12 hired **m.** and carpenters to repair....... 2672
Ezr 3:7 They gave money also unto the **m.**,...... 2672

MASREKAH (mas'-re-kah)
Ge 36:36 Samlah of **M.** reigned in his stead....... 4957
1Ch 1:47 Samlah of **M.** reigned in his stead....... 4957

MASSA (mas'-sah)
Ge 25:14 And Mishma, and Dumah, and **M.**, ... 4854
1Ch 1:30 Dumah, **M.**, Hadad, and Tema,.......... 4854

MASSAH (mas'-sah) See also MERIBAH.
Ex 17:7 called the name of the place **M.**, ... 4532
De 6:16 your God, as ye tempted him in **M.**.... 4532
De 9:22 at **M.**, and at Kibroth-hattaavah, ... 4532
De 33:8 whom thou didst prove at **M.**, and...... 4532

MAST See also MASTS.
Pr 23:34 he that lieth upon the top of a **m.**. 2260
Isa 33:23 not well strengthen their **m.**,............. 8650

MASTER See also MASTERBUILDER; MASTER'S; MASTERS; MISTRESS; SCHOOLMASTERS; SHEEPMASTER; SHIPMASTER; TASKMASTERS.
Ge 24:9 under the thigh of Abraham his **m.**,...... 113
Ge 24:10 ten camels of the camels of his **m.**,...... 113
Ge 24:10 goods of his **m.** were in his hand: 113
Ge 24:12 said, O Lord God of my **m.** Abraham, .. 113
Ge 24:12 shew kindness unto my **m.** Abraham. ... 113
Ge 24:14 hast shewed kindness unto my **m.**. 113
Ge 24:27 be the Lord God of my **m.** Abraham, ... 113
Ge 24:27 hath not left destitute my **m.** of his...... 113
Ge 24:35 Lord hath blessed my **m.** greatly; 113
Ge 24:36 bare a son to my **m.** when she was 113
Ge 24:37 my **m.** made me swear, saying, Thou... 113
Ge 24:39 I said unto my **m.**, Peradventure 113
Ge 24:42 O Lord God of my **m.** Abraham, if....... 113
Ge 24:48 the Lord God of my **m.** Abraham,......... 113
Ge 24:49 deal kindly and truly with my **m.**, ... 113
Ge 24:54 he said, Send me away unto my **m.**. 113
Ge 24:56 me away that I may go to my **m.**. 113
Ge 24:65 the servant had said, It is my **m.**: 113
Ge 39:2 in the house of his **m.** the Egyptian...... 113
Ge 39:3 And his **m.** saw that the Lord was....... 113
Ge 39:8 my **m.** wotteth not what is with me 113
Ge 39:19 his **m.** heard the words of his wife,...... 113
Ge 39:20 And Joseph's **m.** took him, and put 113
Ex 21:4 If his **m.** have given him a wife, and..... 113
Ex 21:5 say, I love my **m.**, my wife, and my 113
Ex 21:6 **m.** shall bring him unto the judges; 113
Ex 21:6 his **m.** shall bore his ear through 113
Ex 21:8 If she please not her **m.**, who hath 113
Ex 21:32 give unto their **m.** thirty shekels of...... 113
Ex 22:8 **m.** of the house shall be brought........ 1167
De 23:15 not deliver unto his **m.** the servant 113
De 23:15 is escaped from his **m.** unto thee:........ 113
Jg 19:11 the servant said unto his **m.**, Come,..... 113
Jg 19:12 And his **m.** said unto him, We will 113
Jg 19:22 and spake to the **m.** of the house,...... 1167
Jg 19:23 the **m.** of the house, went out unto.... 1167
1Sa 20:38 up the arrows, and came to his **m.**. 113
1Sa 24:6 I should do this thing unto my **m.**, ... 113
1Sa 25:10 break away every man from his **m.**. 113
1Sa 25:14 of the wilderness to salute our **m.**; 113
1Sa 25:17 evil is determined against our **m.**. 113
1Sa 26:16 ye have not kept your **m.**, the Lord's... 113
1Sa 29:4 he reconcile himself unto his **m.**? 113
1Sa 30:13 my **m.** left me, because three days 113
1Sa 30:15 deliver me into the hands of my **m.**,...... 113
2Sa 2:7 your **m.** Saul is dead, and also the 113
1Ki 22:17 the Lord said, These have no **m.**: 113
2Ki 2:3,5 that the Lord will take away thy **m.** 113
2Ki 2:16 go, we pray thee, and seek thy **m.**: 113
2Ki 5:1 was a great man with his **m.**, and........ 113
2Ki 5:18 when my **m.** goeth into the house of.... 113
2Ki 5:20 my **m.** hath spared Naaman this 113
2Ki 5:22 well. My **m.** hath sent me, saying,....... 113
2Ki 5:25 he went in, and stood before his **m.**. 113
2Ki 6:5 said, Alas, **m.**! for it was borrowed. 113
2Ki 6:15 him, Alas, my **m.**! how shall we do?..... 113
2Ki 6:22 eat and drink, and go to their **m.**. 113
2Ki 6:23 away, and they went to their **m.**. 113
2Ki 8:14 from Elisha, and came to his **m.**; 113
2Ki 9:7 smite the house of Ahab thy **m.**, ... 113
2Ki 9:31 Had Zimri peace, who slew his **m.**? 113
2Ki 10:9 I conspired against my **m.**, and slew..... 113
2Ki 18:27 Hath my **m.** sent me to thy **m.**, and 113
2Ki 19:4 the king of Assyria his **m.** hath sent..... 113
2Ki 19:6 them, Thus shall ye say to your **m.**, ... 113
1Ch 12:19 He will fall to his **m.** Saul to the.......... 113
1Ch 15:27 and Chenaniah the **m.** of the song 8269
2Ch 18:16 These have no **m.**; let them return 113
Job 3:19 and the servant is free from his **m.**. 113
Pr 27:18 he that waiteth on his **m.** shall be........ 113

Pr 30:10 Accuse not a servant unto his **m.**, 113
Isa 24:2 as with the servant, so with his **m.**; 113
Isa 36:8 thee, to my **m.** the king of Assyria. 113
Isa 36:12 Hath my **m.** sent me to thy **m.** and to 113
Isa 37:4 the king of Assyria his **m.** hath sent 113
Isa 37:6 Thus shall ye say unto your **m.**, 113
Da 1:3 Ashpenaz the **m.** of his eunuchs, 7227
Da 4:9 Belteshazzar, **m.** of the magicians, 729
Da 5:11 father, made **m.** of the magicians, 729
Mal 1:6 his father, and a servant his **m.**: 113
Mal 1:6 and if I be a **m.**, where is my fear? 113
Mal 2:12 doeth this, the **m.** and the scholar, 5782
Mt 8:19 unto him, **M.**, I will follow thee *1320*
Mt 9:11 Why eateth your **M.** with publicans *1320*
Mt 10:24 **The disciple is not above his m.,** *1320*
Mt 10:25 **the disciple that he be as his m.,** *1320*
Mt 10:25 **have called the m. of the house** *1320*
Mt 12:38 **M.**, we would see a sign from thee. *1320*
Mt 17:24 said, Doth not your **m.** pay tribute? *1320*
Mt 19:16 Good **M.**, what good thing shall I *1320*
Mt 22:16 **M.**, we know that thou art true, *1320*
Mt 22:24 **M.**, Moses said, If a man die, *1320*
Mt 22:36 **M.**, which is...great commandment *1320*
Mt 23:8 **for one is your M., even Christ;** *2519*
Mt 23:10 **for one is your M., even Christ,** *2519*
Mt 26:18 **The M. saith, My time is at hand;** *1320*
Mt 26:25 answered and said, **M.**, is it I? *4461*
Mt 26:49 and said, Hail, **m.**; and kissed him. *4461*
Mk 4:38 him, **M.**, carest thou not that we *1320*
Mk 5:35 troublest thou the **M.** any further? *1320*
Mk 9:5 **M.**, it is good for us to be here: *4461*
Mk 9:17 **M.**, I have brought unto thee my *1320*
Mk 9:38 **M.**, we saw one casting out devils *1320*
Mk 10:17 Good **M.**, what shall I do that I *1320*
Mk 10:20 **M.**, all these have I observed from *1320*
Mk 10:35 **M.**, we would that thou shouldest *1320*
Mk 11:21 **M.**, behold, the fig tree which thou *4461*
Mk 12:14 **M.**, we know that thou art true, *1320*
Mk 12:19 **M.**, Moses wrote unto us, If a man's *1320*
Mk 12:32 Well, **M.**, thou hast said the truth: *1320*
Mk 13:1 **M.**, see what manner of stones and *1320*
Mk 13:35 **when the m. of the house cometh,** *2962*
Mk 14:14 **to the goodman...The M. saith,** *1320*
Mk 14:45 saith, **M.**, **m.**; and kissed him. *4461*
Lu 3:12 unto him, **M.**, what shall we do? *1320*
Lu 5:5 **M.**, we have toiled all the night, *1988*
Lu 6:40 **The disciple is not above his m.:** *1320*
Lu 6:40 **that is perfect shall be as his m.** *1320*
Lu 7:40 **thee.** And he saith, **M.**, say on. *1320*
Lu 8:24 him, saying, **M.**, **m.**, we perish. *1988*
Lu 8:45 **M.**, the multitude throng thee and *1988*
Lu 8:49 is dead; trouble not the **M.** *1320*
Lu 9:33 **M.**, it is good for us to be here: *1988*
Lu 9:38 **M.**, I beseech thee, look upon my *1320*
Lu 9:49 **M.**, we saw one casting out devils *1988*
Lu 10:25 **M.**, what shall I do to inherit *1320*
Lu 11:45 **M.**, thus saying thou reproachest *1320*
Lu 12:13 **M.**, speak to my brother, that he *1320*
Lu 13:25 **When once the m. of the house is** *3617*
Lu 14:21 **m. of the house being angry said** *3617*
Lu 17:13 said, Jesus, **M.**, have mercy on us. *1988*
Lu 18:18 Good **M.**, what shall I do to inherit *1320*
Lu 19:39 unto him, **M.**, rebuke thy disciples. *1320*
Lu 20:21 **M.**, we know that thou sayest and *1320*
Lu 20:28 **M.**, Moses wrote unto us, If any *1320*
Lu 20:39 said, **M.**, thou hast well said. *1320*
Lu 21:7 **M.**, but when shall these things be? *1320*
Lu 22:11 **The M. saith unto thee, Where is** *1320*
Joh 1:38 is to say, being interpreted, **M.**,) *1320*
Joh 3:10 **Art thou a m. of Israel, and** *1320*
Joh 4:31 prayed him, saying **M.**, eat. *4461*
Joh 8:4 **M.**, this woman was taken in *1320*
Joh 9:2 **M.**, who did sin, this man, or his *4461*
Joh 11:8 **M.**, the Jews of late sought to stone *4461*
Joh 11:28 The **M.** is come, and calleth for *1320*
Joh 13:13 **Ye call me M. and Lord: and ye** *1320*
Joh 13:14 **If I then, your Lord and M., have** *1320*
Joh 20:16 him, Rabboni; which is to say, **M.** *1320*
Ac 27:11 the **m.** and the owner of the ship, *2942*
Ro 14:4 to his own **m.** he standeth or *2962*
Eph 6:9 that your **M.** also is in heaven; *2962*
Col 4:1 that ye also have a **M.** in heaven. *2962*

MASTERBUILDER
1Co 3:10 is given unto me, as a wise **m.**, *753*

MASTER'S
Ge 24:27 me to the house of my **m.** brethren. 113
Ge 24:36 And Sarah my **m.** wife bore a son to 113
Ge 24:44 hath appointed out for my **m.** son. 113
Ge 24:48 to take my **m.** brother's daughter 113
Ge 24:51 and let her be thy **m.** son's wife, as 113
Ge 39:7 **m.** wife cast her eyes upon Joseph; 113
Ge 39:8 said unto his **m.** wife, Behold, my 113
Ex 21:4 and her children shall be her **m.**, 113
1Sa 29:10 thy **m.** servants that are come with 113
2Sa 9:9 have given unto thy **m.** son all that 113
2Sa 9:10 that thy **m.** son may have food to 113
2Sa 9:10 thy **m.** son shall eat bread alway 113
2Sa 12:8 I gave thee thy **m.** house, and thy 113
2Sa 12:8 thy **m.** wives into thy bosom, and 113
2Sa 16:3 said, And where is thy **m.** son? 113
2Ki 6:32 the sound of his **m.** feet behind him? 113
2Ki 10:2 seeing your **m.** sons are with you, 113
2Ki 10:3 best and meetest of your **m.** sons, 113
2Ki 10:3 throne, and fight for your **m.** house 113
2Ki 10:6 the heads of the men your **m.** sons, 113
2Ki 18:24 of the least of my **m.** servants, 113
Isa 1:3 his owner, and the ass his **m.** crib: 1167
Isa 36:9 of the least of my **m.** servants, and 113
2Ti 2:21 and meet for the **m.** use, and *1203*

MASTERS See also MASTERS'; TASKMASTERS.
Ps 123:2 look unto the hand of their **m.**, 113
Pr 25:13 for he refresheth the soul of his **m.** 113
Ec 12:11 fastened by the **m.** of assemblies, 1167
Jer 27:4 command them to say unto their **m.**, 113
Jer 27:4 Thus shall ye say unto your **m.**; 113
Am 4:1 which say to their **m.**, Bring, and 113
Mt 6:24 **No man can serve two m.; for** *2962*
Mt 23:10 **Neither be ye called m.: for one is** *2519*
Lu 16:13 **No servant can serve two m.: for** *2962*
Ac 16:16 which brought her **m.** much gain *2962*
Ac 16:19 when her **m.** saw that the hope of *2962*
Eph 6:5 obedient to them that are your **m.** *2962*
Eph 6:9 ye **m.**, do the same things unto *2962*
Col 3:22 Servants, obey in all things your **m.** *2962*
Col 4:1 **M.**, give unto your servants that *2962*
1Ti 6:1 their own **m.** worthy of all honour, *1203*
1Ti 6:2 And they that have believing **m.** *1203*
Tit 2:9 to be obedient unto their own **m.**, *1203*
Jas 3:1 My brethren, be not many **m.**, *1320*
1Pe 2:18 subject to your **m.** with all fear; *1203*

MASTERS'
Zep 1:9 fill their **m.** houses with violence 113
Mt 15:27 which fall from their **m.** table. *2962*

MASTERIES
2Ti 2:5 And if a man also strive for **m.**, yet

MASTERY See also MASTERIES.
Ex 32:18 voice of them that shout for **m.**, 1369
Da 6:24 and the lions had the **m.** of them, 6981
1Co 9:25 every man that striveth for the **m.**

MASTS
Eze 27:5 cedars from Lebanon to make **m.** 8650

MATE
Isa 34:15 gathered, every one with her **m.** 7468
Isa 34:16 shall fail, none shall want her **m.**: 7468

MATHUSALA (ma-thu'-sa-lah) See also METHUSALAH.
Lu 3:37 Which was the son of **M.**, which *3103*

MATRED (ma'-tred)
Ge 36:39 Mehetabel, the daughter of **M.**, 4308
1Ch 1:50 Mehetabel, the daughter of **M.**, 4308

MATRI (ma'-tri)
1Sa 10:21 the family of **M.** was taken, and 4309

MATRIX
Ex 13:12 the Lord all that openeth the **m.**, 7358
Ex 13:15 to the Lord all that openeth the **m.**, 7358
Ex 34:19 All that openeth the **m.** is mine; 7358
Nu 3:12 the firstborn that openeth the **m.** 7358
Nu 18:15 that openeth the **m.** in all flesh, 7358

MATTAN (mat'-tan)
2Ki 11:18 slew **M.** the priest of Baal before 4977
2Ch 23:17 slew **M.** the priest of Baal before 4977
Jer 38:1 Then Sehphatiah the son of **M.**, 4977

MATTANAH (mat'-ta-nah)
Nu 21:18 the wilderness they went to **M.**: 4980
Nu 21:19 And from **M.** to Nahaliel: and from 4980

MATTANIAH (mat-ta-ni'-ah) See also ZEDEKIAH.
2Ki 24:17 made **M.** his father's brother king 4983
1Ch 9:15 and **M.** the son of Micah, the son of 4983
1Ch 25:4 the sons of Heman; Bukkiah, **M.**, 4983
1Ch 25:16 The ninth to **M.**, he, his sons, and 4983
2Ch 20:14 the son of **M.**, a Levite of the sons 4983
2Ch 29:13 sons of Asaph; Zechariah, and **M.**: 4983
Ezr 10:26 sons of Elam; **M.**, Zechariah, 4983
Ezr 10:27 of Zattu; Elioenai, Eliashib, **M.**, 4983
Ezr 10:30 **M.**, Bezaleel, and Binnui, and 4983
Ezr 10:37 **M.**, Mattenai, and Jaasau, 4983
Ne 11:17 **M.** the son of Micha, the son of 4983
Ne 11:22 son of Hashabiah, the son of **M.**, 4983
Ne 12:8 Judah, and **M.**, which was over the 4983
Ne 12:25 **M.**, and Bakbukiah, Obadiah, 4983
Ne 12:35 the son of **M.**, the son of Michaiah, 4983
Ne 13:13 the son of Zaccur, the son of **M.**: 4983

MATTATHA (mat'-ta-thah) See also MATTATHAH.
Lu 3:31 which was the son of **M.**, which *3160*

MATTATHAH (mat'-ta-thah) See also MATTATHA.
Ezr 10:33 Mattenai, **M.**, Zabad, Eliphelet, 4992

MATTATHIAS (mat-ta-thi'-as) See also MATTITHIAH.
Lu 3:25 Which was the son of **M.**, which *3161*
Lu 3:26 of Maath, which was the son of **M.**, *3161*

MATTENAI (mat'-te-nahee)
Ezr 10:33 sons of Hashum; **M.**, Mattathah, 4982
Ezr 10:37 Mattaniah, **M.**, and Jaasau, 4982
Ne 12:19 And of Joiarib, **M.**; of Jedaiah, 4982

MATTER See also MATTERS.
Ge 24:9 sware to him concerning that **m.** 1697
Ge 30:15 Is it a small **m.** that thou hast taken
Ex 18:16 When they have a **m.**, they come 1697
Ex 18:22 every great **m.** they shall bring 1697
Ex 18:22 but every small **m.** they shall judge: 1697
Ex 18:26 but every small **m.** they judged 1697
Ex 23:7 Keep thee far from a false **m.**; and 1697
Nu 16:49 that died about the **m.** of Korah 1697
Nu 25:18 in the **m.** of Peor, and in the **m.** of 1697
Nu 31:16 against the Lord in the **m.** of Peor, 1697
De 3:26 speak no more unto me of this **m.** 1697
De 17:8 If there arise a **m.** too hard for thee 1697
De 19:15 shall the **m.** be established 1697
De 22:26 and slayeth him, even so is this **m.**: 1697
Ru 3:18 thou know how the **m.** will fall: 1697
1Sa 10:16 But of the **m.** of the kingdom, 1697
1Sa 20:23 as touching the **m.** which thou and 1697
1Sa 20:39 Jonathan and David knew the **m.** 1697
1Sa 30:24 will hearken unto you in this **m.**? 1697
2Sa 1:4 said unto him. How went the **m.**? 1697
2Sa 18:13 there is no **m.** hid from the king, 1697
2Sa 19:42 then be ye angry for this **m.**? 1697
2Sa 20:18 at Abel: and so they ended the **m.**
2Sa 20:21 The **m.** is not so: but a man of 1697
1Ki 8:59 all times, as the **m.** shall require: 1697
1Ki 15:5 only in the **m.** of Uriah the Hittite 1697
1Ch 26:32 for every **m.** pertaining to God, and 1697
1Ch 27:1 the king in any **m.** of the courses, 1697
2Ch 8:15 and Levites concerning any **m.**, or 1697
2Ch 24:5 year, and see that ye hasten the **m.** 1697
Ezr 5:5 to cease, till the **m.** came to Darius: 2941
Ezr 5:5 answer by letter concerning this **m.**
Ezr 5:17 pleasure to us concerning this **m.** 1836
Ezr 10:4 for this **m.** belongeth unto thee: 1697
Ezr 10:9 trembling because of this **m.**, and 1697
Ezr 10:14 fierce wrath of our God for this **m.** 1697
Ezr 10:15 Tikvah were employed about this **m.**:
Ezr 10:16 tenth month to examine the **m.** 1697
Ne 6:13 they might have **m.** for an evil report,
Es 2:23 inquisition was made of the **m.**, 1697
Es 9:26 they had seen concerning this **m.**, 3602
Job 19:28 the root of the **m.** is found in me? 1697
Job 32:18 I am full of **m.**, the spirit within 4405
Ps 45:1 My heart is inditing a good **m.**: 1697
Ps 64:5 encourage themselves in an evil **m.**: 1697
Pr 11:13 a faithful spirit concealeth the **m.** 1697
Pr 16:20 He that handleth a **m.** wisely shall 1697
Pr 17:9 he that repeateth a **m.** separateth 1697
Pr 18:13 answereth a **m.** before he heareth 1697
Pr 25:2 of kings is to search out a **m.** 1697
Ec 5:8 a province, marvel not at the **m.**: 2659
Ec 10:20 hath wings shall tell the **m.** 1697
Ec 12:13 the conclusion of the whole **m.**: 1697
Jer 38:27 him: for the **m.** was not perceived 1697
Eze 9:11 by his side, reported the **m.**, saying, 1697
Eze 16:20 this of thy whoredoms a small **m.**,
Da 1:14 he consented to them in this **m.**, 1697

Da 2:10 earth that can shew the king's **m.**: 4406
Da 2:23 made known unto us the king's **m.**. 4406
Da 3:16 careful to answer thee in this **m.** 6600
Da 4:17 This **m.** is by the decree of the 6600
Da 7:28 Hitherto is the end of the **m.**. 4406
Da 7:28 me: but I kept the **m.** in my heart. 4406
Da 9:23 understand the **m.**, and consider 1697
Mk 1:45 much, and to blaze abroad the **m.**, ... *3056*
Mk 10:10 asked him again of the same **m.**. ....
Ac 8:21 neither part nor lot in this **m.**: *3056*
Ac 11:4 rehearsed the **m.** from the beginning, ...
Ac 15:6 together for to consider of this **m.** *3056*
Ac 17:32 We will hear thee again of this **m.**. ....
Ac 18:14 a **m.** of wrong or wicked lewdness, ...
Ac 19:38 him, have a **m.** against any man, ... *3056*
Ac 24:22 know the uttermost of your **m.** *2596*
1Co 6:1 you, having a **m.** against another, ... *4229*
2Co 7:11 yourselves to be clear in this **m.**. *4229*
2Co 9:5 might be ready, as a **m.** of bounty, ...
Gal 2:6 they were, it maketh no **m.** to me: *1308*
1Th 4:6 and defraud his brother in any **m.**: *4229*
Jas 3:5 great a **m.** a little fire kindleth! *5208*

MATTERS
Ex 24:14 if any man have any **m.** to do, let 1697
De 17:8 **m.** of controversy within thy gates: 1697
1Sa 16:18 a man of war, and prudent in **m.**, ... 1697
2Sa 11:19 an end of telling the **m.** of the war 1697
2Sa 15:3 See, thy **m.** are good and right; 1697
2Sa 19:29 speakest thou any more of thy **m.**? 1697
2Ch 19:11 is over you in all **m.** of the Lord; 1697
2Ch 19:11 house of Judah, for all the king's **m.**: ... 1697
Ne 11:24 in all **m.** concerning the people. 1697
Es 3:4 whether Mordecai's **m.** would stand: ... 1697
Es 9:31 the **m.** of the fastings and their cry. ... 1697
Es 9:32 confirmed these **m.** of Purim; 1697
Job 33:13 giveth not account of any of his **m.**. 1697
Ps 35:20 devise deceitful **m.** against them 1697
Ps 131:1 do I exercise myself in great **m.**, ... 1419
Da 1:20 **m.** of wisdom and understanding, ... 1697
Da 7:1 dream, and told the sum of the **m.**. 4406
Mt 23:23 **omitted the weightier m. of the law**, ...
Ac 18:15 to it; for I will be no judge of such **m.** ....
Ac 19:39 enquire any thing concerning other **m.**, ...
Ac 25:20 and there be judged of these **m.**. ....
1Co 6:2 ye unworthy to judge the smallest **m.**? ......
1Pe 4:15 or as a busybody in other men's **m.**. ....

MATTHAN (mat'-than)
Mt 1:15 Eleazar begat **M.**; and **M.** begat *3157*

MATTHAT (mat'-that)
Lu 3:24 Which was the son of **M.**, which *3158*
Lu 3:29 which was the son of **M.**, which *3158*

MATTHEW (math'-ew) See also LEVI.
Mt *general title* According To S. [St.] **M.** *3156*
Mt 9:9 he saw a man, named **M.**, sitting *3156*
Mt 10:3 Thomas, and **M.** the publican; *3156*
Mk 3:18 Bartholomew, and **M.**, and Thomas, ... *3156*
Lu 6:15 **M.** and Thomas, James the son of *3156*
Ac 1:13 Thomas, Bartholomew, and **M.**, ... *3156*

MATTHIAS (mat'-thias)
Ac 1:23 was surnamed Justus, and **M.** *3159*
Ac 1:26 their lots; and the lot fell upon **M.**: *3159*

MATTITHIAH (mat-tith-i'-ah) See also MATTATHIAS.
1Ch 9:31 **M.**, one of the Levites, who was 4993
1Ch 15:18 And **M.**, and Elipheleh, and 4993
1Ch 15:21 and **M.**, and Elipheleh, and Mikneiah, .. 4993
1Ch 16:5 Shemiramoth, and Jehiel, and **M.**, ... 4993
1Ch 25:3 Jeshaiah, Hashabiah, and **M.**, ... 4993
1Ch 25:21 fourteenth to **M.**, he, his sons, and 4993
Ezr 10:43 Jeiel, **M.**, Zabad, Zebina, Jadau, ... 4993
Ne 8:4 and beside him stood **M.**, and 4993

MATTOCK See also MATTOCKS.
1Sa 13:20 coulter, and his axe, and his **m.** 4281
Isa 7:25 that shall be digged with the **m.**, ... 4576

MATTOCKS
1Sa 13:21 they had a file for the **m.**, and for 4281
2Ch 34:6 with their **m.** round about. 2719

MAUL
Pr 25:18 against his neighbour is a **m.**, and 4650

MAW
De 18:3 and the two cheeks, and the **m.** 6896

MAY See also MAYEST; MIGHT.
Ge 1:20 fowl that **m.** fly above the earth in the ......
Ge 3:2 We **m.** eat of the fruit of the trees of ....
Ge 8:17 they **m.** breed abundantly in the earth, ...
Ge 9:16 that I **m.** remember the everlasting ....
Ge 11:4 whose top **m.** reach unto heaven; ....
Ge 11:7 that they **m.** not understand one ....
Ge 12:13 it **m.** be well with me for thy sake; ....
Ge 16:2 it **m.** be that I...obtain children by 194
Ge 16:2 be that I **m.** obtain children by her ....
Ge 18:19 the Lord **m.** bring upon Abraham ....
Ge 19:5 out unto us, that we **m.** know them. ....
Ge 19:32, 34 we **m.** preserve seed of our father. ......
Ge 21:30 that they **m.** be a witness unto me, ...
Ge 23:4 I **m.** bury my dead out of my sight. ....
Ge 23:9 That he **m.** give me the cave of ....
Ge 24:14 pitcher, I pray thee, that I **m.** drink; ....
Ge 24:49 that I **m.** turn to the right hand, or to ....
Ge 24:56 me away that I **m.** go to my master. ....
Ge 27:4 and bring it to me, that I **m.** eat; ....
Ge 27:4 my soul **m.** bless thee before I die. ....
Ge 27:7 make me savoury meat, that I **m.** eat, ...
Ge 27:10 bring it to thy father, that he **m.** eat, ...
Ge 27:10 that he **m.** bless thee before his death. .....
Ge 27:19 my venison, that thy soul **m.** bless me. .....
Ge 27:21 I pray thee, that I **m.** feel thee, my ....
Ge 27:25 venison, that my soul **m.** bless thee. ....
Ge 27:31 venison, that thy soul **m.** bless me. ....
Ge 29:21 are fulfilled, that I **m.** go in unto her. ....
Ge 30:3 that I **m.** also have children by her. ....
Ge 30:25 that I **m.** go unto mine own place, ...
Ge 31:37 that they **m.** judge betwixt us both. ....
Ge 32:5 that I **m.** find grace in thy sight. ....
Ge 42:2 thence; that we **m.** live, and not die. ....
Ge 42:16 that your words **m.** be proved, ...
Ge 43:8 that we **m.** live, and not die, both we, ...
Ge 43:14 he **m.** send away your other brother, ...
Ge 43:18 that he **m.** seek occasion against us, ...
Ge 44:21 that I **m.** set mine eyes upon him. ....
Ge 44:26 for we **m.** not see the man's face, ... 3201
Ge 46:34 that ye **m.** dwell in the land of Goshen; .....
Ge 47:19 us seed, that we **m.** live, and not die, ...
Ge 49:1 I **m.** tell you that which shall befall ....
Ex 2:7 that she **m.** nurse the child for thee? ....
Ex 2:20 man? call him, that he **m.** eat bread. ....
Ex 3:18 we **m.** sacrifice to the Lord our God. ....
Ex 4:5 they **m.** believe that the Lord God ....
Ex 4:23 Let my son go, that he **m.** serve me: ....
Ex 5:1 people go, that they **m.** hold a feast ....
Ex 5:9 men, that they **m.** labour therein; ....
Ex 7:4 that I **m.** lay my hand upon Egypt, ...
Ex 7:16 they **m.** serve me in the wilderness: ....
Ex 7:19 water that they **m.** become blood; ....
Ex 7:19 there **m.** be blood throughout all the ....
Ex 8:1 my people go, that they **m.** serve me. ....
Ex 8:8 that he **m.** take away the frogs from ....
Ex 8:8 they **m.** do sacrifice unto the Lord. ....
Ex 8:9 they **m.** remain in the river only? ....
Ex 8:16 that it **m.** become lice throughout all ....
Ex 8:20 my people go, that they **m.** serve me. ......
Ex 8:28 that ye **m.** sacrifice to the Lord your ....
Ex 8:29 the swarms of flies **m.** depart from ....
Ex 9:1, 13 people go, that they **m.** serve me. ....
Ex 9:15 that I **m.** smite thee and thy people ....
Ex 9:16 my name **m.** be declared throughout ....
Ex 9:22 **m.** be hail in all the land of Egypt, ...
Ex 10:2 ye **m.** know how that I am the Lord. ....
Ex 10:3 my people go, that they **m.** serve me. ....
Ex 10:7 men go, that they **m.** serve the Lord ....
Ex 10:12 **m.** come up upon the land of Egypt, ...
Ex 10:17 he **m.** take away from me this death. ....
Ex 10:21 **m.** be darkness over the land of Egypt, ...
Ex 10:21 Egypt, even darkness which **m.** be felt. .....
Ex 10:25 **m.** sacrifice unto the Lord our God. ....
Ex 11:7 ye **m.** know how that the Lord doth ....
Ex 11:9 my wonders **m.** be multiplied in the ....
Ex 12:16 must eat, that only **m.** be done of you. .....
Ex 13:9 the Lord's law **m.** be in thy mouth: ....
Ex 14:4 **m.** know that I am the Lord. ....
Ex 14:12 that we **m.** serve the Egyptians? ....
Ex 14:26 the waters **m.** come again upon the ....
Ex 16:4 that I may prove them, whether they ....
Ex 16:32 **m.** see the bread wherewith I have fed ......
Ex 17:2 said, Give us water that we **m.** drink. ....
Ex 17:6 out of it, that the people **m.** drink. ....
Ex 19:9 people **m.** hear when I speak with ....
Ex 20:12 thy days **m.** be long upon the land. ....
Ex 20:20 that his fear **m.** be before your faces, ...
Ex 21:14 him from mine altar, that he **m.** die. ....
Ex 23:11 that the poor of thy people **m.** eat: ....
Ex 23:12 that thine ox and thine ass **m.** rest, and ....
Ex 23:12 and thy stranger, **m.** be refreshed. ....
Ex 25:8 that I **m.** dwell among them. ....
Ex 25:14 that the ark **m.** be borne with them. ....
Ex 25:28 that the table **m.** be borne with them. ....
Ex 25:37 that they **m.** give light over against it, ...
Ex 26:5 loops **m.** take hold one of another. ....
Ex 26:11 the tent together, that it **m.** be one. ....
Ex 27:5 net **m.** be even to the midst of the ....
Ex 28:1 **m.** minister unto me in the priest's ....
Ex 28:3 they **m.** make Aaron's garments to ....
Ex 28:3, 4 **m.** minister unto me in the priest's ....
Ex 28:28 it **m.** be above the curious girdle of ....
Ex 28:37 blue lace, that it **m.** be upon the mitre; .....
Ex 28:38 Aaron **m.** bear the iniquity of the holy ....
Ex 28:38 they **m.** be accepted before the Lord. ....
Ex 28:41 **m.** minister unto me in the priest's ....
Ex 29:46 Egypt, that I **m.** dwell among them: ....
Ex 30:16 **m.** be a memorial unto the children ....
Ex 30:29 them, that they **m.** be most holy: ....
Ex 30:30 **m.** minister unto me in the priest's ....
Ex 31:6 that they **m.** make all that I have ....
Ex 31:13 **m.** know that I am the Lord that doth ......
Ex 31:15 Six days **m.** work be done; but in the ....
Ex 32:10 my wrath **m.** wax hot against them, ...
Ex 32:10 and that I **m.** consume them: and I ....
Ex 32:29 **m.** bestow upon you a blessing this ....
Ex 33:5 that I **m.** know what to do unto thee. ....
Ex 33:13 now thy way, that I **m.** know thee, ...
Ex 33:13 that I **m.** find grace in thy sight: ....
Ex 35:34 put in his heart that he **m.** teach, ...
Ex 40:13, 15 **m.** minister unto me in the ....
Le 7:24 beasts, **m.** be used in any other use: ....
Le 7:30 **m.** be waved for a wave offering ....
Le 10:10 **m.** put difference between holy and ....
Le 10:11 **m.** teach the children of Israel all the ....
Le 11:21 **m.** ye eat of every flying creeping ....
Le 11:22 Even these of them ye **m.** eat; the ....
Le 11:34 Of all meat which **m.** be eaten, that on ......
Le 11:34 all drink that **m.** be drunk in every ....
Le 11:39 if any beast of which ye **m.** eat, ...
Le 11:47 between the beast that **m.** be eaten. ....
Le 11:47 and the beast that **m.** not be eaten. ....
Le 14:8 himself in water, that he **m.** be clean: ....
Le 16:13 the incense **m.** cover the mercy seat ....
Le 16:30 **m.** be clean from all your sins before ....
Le 17:5 of Israel **m.** bring their sacrifices, ...
Le 17:5 they **m.** bring them unto the Lord, ...
Le 17:13 any beast or fowl that **m.** be eaten; ....
Le 19:25 **m.** yield unto you the increase thereof: .....
Le 21:3 no husband; for her **m.** he be defiled. ....
Le 22:5 whereby he **m.** be made unclean, ...
Le 22:5 man of whom he **m.** take uncleanness, ...
Le 22:12 **m.** not eat of an offering of the holy ....
Le 23:21 it **m.** be a holy convocation unto you: ....
Le 23:43 That your generations **m.** know that I ....
Le 24:7 it **m.** be on the bread for a memorial, ...
Le 25:27 that he **m.** return unto his possession. ......
Le 25:29 then he **m.** redeem it within a whole. ....
Le 25:29 within a full year m. he redeem it. ....
Le 25:31 they **m.** be redeemed, and they shall ....
Le 25:32 **m.** the Levites redeem at any time. ....
Le 25:34 suburbs of their cities **m.** not be sold; ....
Le 25:35 a sojourner; that he **m.** live with thee. ......
Le 25:36 that thy brother **m.** live with thee. ....
Le 25:48 that he is sold he **m.** be redeemed ....
Le 25:48 one of his brethren **m.** redeem him: ....
Le 25:49 or his uncle's son, **m.** redeem him, ...
Le 25:49 him of his family **m.** redeem him; ....
Le 25:49 if he be able, he **m.** redeem himself. ....
Nu 3:6 priest, that they **m.** minister unto him. ......
Nu 4:19 thus do unto them, that they **m.** live, ...
Nu 6:20 after that the Nazarite **m.** drink wine. ....
Nu 7:5 they **m.** be to do the service of the ....
Nu 8:11 that they **m.** execute the service of the .....
Nu 9:7 that we **m.** not offer an offering of the ......
Nu 10:10 **m.** be to you for a memorial before ....
Nu 11:13 saying, Give us flesh, that we **m.** eat. ....
Nu 11:16 that they **m.** stand there with thee. ....
Nu 11:21 flesh, that they **m.** eat a whole month. ......
Nu 13:2 they **m.** search the land of Canaan, ...
Nu 15:39 that ye **m.** look upon it, and remember .....

Nu 15:40 That ye **m.** remember, and do all my........
Nu 16:21, 45 I **m.** consume them in a moment. ....
Nu 18:2 thee, that they **m.** be joined unto thee, ...
Nu 19:3 he **m.** bring her forth without the............
Nu 22:6 shall prevail, that we **m.** smite them, ...
Nu 22:6 that I **m.** drive them out of the land:.........
Nu 22:19 I **m.** know what the Lord will say unto......
Nu 25:4 Lord **m.** be turned away from Israel. ....
Nu 27:17 Which **m.** go out before them, and ....
Nu 27:17 which **m.** go in before them, and............
Nu 27:17 and which **m.** lead them out, and.............
Nu 27:17 which **m.** bring them in; that the.............
Nu 27:20 of the children of Israel **m.** be obedient .....
Nu 30:13 the soul, her husband **m.** establish it,........
Nu 30:13 it, or her husband **m.** make it void. ....
Nu 31:23 Every thing that **m.** abide the fire, ye ....
Nu 32:32 on this side Jordan **m.** be ours..................
Nu 35:6 manslayer, that he **m.** flee thither: ....
Nu 35:11 that the slayer **m.** flee thither, which ....
Nu 35:15 killeth any person unawares **m.** flee ....
Nu 35:17 a stone, wherewith he **m.** die, and ....
Nu 35:18 weapon of wood, wherewith he **m.** die, ...
Nu 35:23 any stone, wherewith a man **m.** die, ...
Nu 36:8 **m.** enjoy every man the inheritance ....
De 2:6 of them for money, that ye **m.** eat; ....
De 2:6 of them for money, that ye **m.** drink.........
De 2:28 sell me meat for money, that I **m.** eat;.......
De 2:28 me water for money, that I **m.** drink: ....
De 4:1 you, for to do them, that ye **m.** live, ...
De 4:2 ye **m.** keep the commandments of the.......
De 4:10 they **m.** learn to fear me all the days ....
De 4:10 and that they **m.** teach their children.........
De 4:40 this day, that it **m.** go well with thee, ...
De 5:1 **m.** learn them, and keep, and do them. .....
De 5:14 maidservant **m.** rest as well as thou. ....
De 5:16 that thy days **m.** be prolonged, ...
De 5:16 and that it **m.** go well with thee, ...
De 5:31 shall teach them, that they **m.** do them .....
De 5:33 hath commanded you, that ye **m.** live, ...
De 5:33 that it **m.** be well with you, and that ....
De 5:33 ye **m.** prolong your days in the land..........
De 6:2 and that thy days **m.** be prolonged. ....
De 6:3 to do it; that it **m.** be well with thee, ...
De 6:3 that ye **m.** increase mightily, as the..........
De 6:18 that it **m.** be well with thee, and that........
De 7:4 me, that they **m.** serve other gods: ....
De 8:1 shall ye observe to do, that ye **m.** live, ...
De 8:18 **m.** establish his covenant which he ....
De 9:5 and that he **m.** perform the word ....
De 9:14 that I **m.** destroy them, and blot out.........
De 10:11 they **m.** go in and possess the land,..........
De 11:8 that ye **m.** be strong, and go in and..........
De 11:9 ye **m.** prolong your days in the land, ...
De 11:18 **m.** be as frontlets between your eyes. ......
De 11:21 That your days **m.** be multiplied,.............
De 12:15 unclean and the clean **m.** eat thereof, ...
De 12:25, 28 that it **m.** go well with thee, and..........
De 13:17 Lord **m.** turn from the fierceness of ....
De 14:10 hath not fins and scales ye **m.** not eat; ......
De 14:20 But of all clean fowls ye **m.** eat. ....
De 14:21 that is in thy gates, that he **m.** eat it; ....
De 14:29 that the Lord thy God **m.** bless thee.........
De 17:19 he **m.** learn to fear the Lord his God, ...
De 17:20 **m.** prolong his days in his kingdom,.........
De 19:3 parts, that every slayer **m.** flee thither. .....
De 19:4 shall flee thither, that he **m.** live: ....
De 19:12 of the avenger of blood, that he **m.** die. ....
De 19:13 Israel, that it **m.** go well with thee. ....
De 21:16 **m.** not make the son of the beloved ... 3201
De 22:7 that it **m.** be well with thee, and that........
De 22:19, 29 he **m.** not put her away all his....... 3201
De 23:20 that the Lord thy God **m.** bless thee.........
De 24:2 she **m.** go and be another man's wife.........
De 24:4 **m.** not take her again to be his.......... 3201
De 24:13 that he **m.** sleep in his own raiment, ...
De 24:19 that the Lord thy God **m.** bless thee in .....
De 25:1 that the judges **m.** judge them; ....
De 25:3 Forty stripes he **m.** give him, and not.......
De 25:15 thy days **m.** be lengthened in the land.......
De 26:12 they **m.** eat within thy gates, and be.........
De 29:9 that ye **m.** prosper in all that ye do. ....
De 29:13 he **m.** establish thee to day for a people ....
De 29:13 and that he **m.** be unto thee a God, as......
De 29:29 we **m.** do all the words of this law. ....
De 30:12, 13 us, that we **m.** hear it, and do it? ....
De 30:19 that both thou and thy seed **m.** live: ....
De 31:5 that ye **m.** do unto them according...........
De 31:12 within thy gates, that they **m.** hear,..........
De 31:12 and that they **m.** learn, and fear the ....
De 31:13 have not known any thing, **m.** hear,..........
De 31:14 that I **m.** give him a charge.....................
De 31:19 that this song **m.** be a witness for me ....
De 31:26 it **m.** be there for a witness against ....
De 31:28 **m.** speak these words in their ears,..........
Jos 2:16 and afterward **m.** ye go your way.............
Jos 3:4 that ye **m.** know the way by which ye.........
Jos 3:7 that they **m.** know that, as I was with.......
Jos 4:6 That this **m.** be a sign among you, ...
Jos 9:19 therefore we **m.** not touch them. 3201
Jos 10:4 and help me, that we **m.** smite Gibeon: .....
Jos 18:6 that I **m.** cast lots for you here before ......
Jos 18:8 that I **m.** here cast lots for you before ......
Jos 20:3 and unwittingly **m.** flee thither: ....
Jos 20:4 a place, that he **m.** dwell among them. ....
Jos 22:27 But that it **m.** be a witness between us, ...
Jos 22:27 children **m.** not say to our children ....
Jos 22:28 we **m.** say again, Behold the pattern..........
Jg 1:3 my lot, that we **m.** fight against the..........
Jg 2:22 That through them I **m.** prove Israel,........
Jg 6:30 Bring out thy son, that he **m.** die:............
Jg 9:7 that God **m.** hearken unto you. ....
Jg 11:6 **m.** fight with the children of Ammon. ....
Jg 11:37 that I **m.** go up and down upon the...........
Jg 13:14 **m.** not eat of any thing that cometh..........
Jg 13:17 come to pass we **m.** do thee honour?........
Jg 14:13 Put forth thy riddle, that we **m.** hear it. ....
Jg 14:15 that he **m.** declare unto us the riddle, ...
Jg 15:12 **m.** deliver thee into the hand of the..........
Jg 16:5 means we **m.** prevail against him,.............
Jg 16:5 that we **m.** bind him to afflict him:.............
Jg 16:25 for Samson, that he **m.** make us sport. .....
Jg 16:26 Suffer me that I **m.** feel the pillars...........
Jg 16:26 standeth, that I **m.** lean upon them...........
Jg 16:28 that I **m.** be at once avenged of the..........
Jg 17:9 go to sojourn where I **m.** find a place........
Jg 18:5 **m.** know whether our way which we...........
Jg 18:9 Arise, that we **m.** go up against them: ......
Jg 19:9 here, that thine heart **m.** be merry;..........
Jg 19:22 thine house, that we **m.** know him. ....
Jg 20:10 for the people, that they **m.** do,..............
Jg 20:13 that we **m.** put them to death, and put......
Jg 21:18 we **m.** not give them wives of our...... 3201
Ru 1:9 Lord grant you that ye **m.** find rest, ...
Ru 1:11 womb, that they **m.** be your husbands? .....
Ru 2:16 leave them, that she **m.** glean them,.........
Ru 3:1 for thee, that it **m.** be well with thee?.......
Ru 4:4 it, then tell me, that I **m.** know: ....
Ru 4:14 that his name **m.** be famous in Israel. ....
1Sa 1:22 that he **m.** appear before the Lord, ...
1Sa 2:36 offices, that I **m.** eat a piece of bread. ......
1Sa 4:3 it **m.** save us out of the hand of our ....
1Sa 6:8 and send it away, that it **m.** go................
1Sa 8:20 and that our king **m.** judge us, and...........
1Sa 8:20 we also **m.** be like all the nations; ....
1Sa 9:16 he **m.** save my people out of the hand ......
1Sa 9:26 saying, Up, that I **m.** send thee away. ......
1Sa 9:27 that I **m.** shew thee the word of God........
1Sa 11:2 that I **m.** thrust out all your right eyes, ...
1Sa 11:3 that we **m.** send messengers unto all........
1Sa 11:12 men, that we **m.** put them to death..........
1Sa 12:7 **m.** reason with you before the Lord ....
1Sa 12:17 that ye **m.** perceive and see that your.......
1Sa 14:6 it **m.** be that the Lord will work for us:.....
1Sa 14:24 that I **m.** be avenged on mine enemies.......
1Sa 15:25 with me, that I **m.** worship the Lord.........
1Sa 15:30 that I **m.** worship the Lord thy God..........
1Sa 17:10 me a man, that we **m.** fight together. ....
1Sa 17:46 earth **m.** know that there is a God in........
1Sa 18:21 him her, that she **m.** be a snare to him, ...
1Sa 18:21 of the Philistines **m.** be against him. ....
1Sa 19:15 to me in the bed, that I **m.** slay him..........
1Sa 20:5 that I **m.** hide myself in the field unto ....
1Sa 27:5 in the country, that I **m.** dwell there:........
1Sa 28:7 I **m.** go to her, and enquire of her............
1Sa 29:4 that he **m.** go again to his place which.......
1Sa 29:8 I **m.** not go fight against the enemies........
1Sa 30:22 **m.** lead them away, and depart...............
2Sa 3:21 that they **m.** make a league with thee, ...
2Sa 7:10 they **m.** dwell in a place of their own, ...
2Sa 7:29 it **m.** continue for ever before thee:..........
2Sa 9:1 that I **m.** shew him kindness for...............
2Sa 9:3 **m.** shew the kindness of God unto him? ....
2Sa 9:10 thy master's son **m.** have food to eat: ....
2Sa 11:15 him, that he **m.** be smitten, and die.........
2Sa 12:22 to me, that the children **m.** live? ....
2Sa 13:5 the meat in my sight, that I **m.** see it, ...
2Sa 13:6 in my sight, that I **m.** eat at her hand. ......
2Sa 13:10 chamber, that I **m.** eat of thine hand.........
2Sa 14:7 **m.** kill him, for the life of his brother........
2Sa 14:15 **m.** be that the king will perform the ....
2Sa 14:32 that I **m.** send thee to the king, to say,.....
2Sa 15:20 seeing I go whither I **m.**, return thou,.......
2Sa 16:2 as be faint in the wilderness **m.** drink........
2Sa 16:4 thee that I **m.** find grace in thy sight, ...
2Sa 16:11 more now **m.** this Benjamite do it? ....
2Sa 16:12 It **m.** be that the Lord will look on ....
2Sa 18:14 Joab, I **m.** not tarry thus with thee..........
2Sa 19:26 me an ass, that I **m.** ride thereon,............
2Sa 19:37 again, that I **m.** die in mine own city,.......
2Sa 20:16 near hither, that I **m.** speak with thee.......
2Sa 21:3 ye **m.** bless the inheritance of the ....
2Sa 24:2 **m.** know the number of the people. ....
2Sa 24:3 the eyes of my lord the king **m.** see it: .....
2Sa 24:12 one of them, that I **m.** do it unto thee. .....
2Sa 24:21 plague **m.** be stayed from the people. ....
1Ki 1:2 that my lord the king **m.** get heat.............
1Ki 1:35 that he **m.** come and sit upon my.............
1Ki 2:4 That the Lord **m.** continue his word ....
1Ki 3:9 I **m.** discern between good and bad: ....
1Ki 8:29 That thine eyes **m.** be open toward ....
1Ki 8:40 they **m.** fear thee all the days that............
1Ki 8:43 people of the earth **m.** know thy name, ...
1Ki 8:43 that they **m.** know that this house, ...
1Ki 8:50 they **m.** have compassion on them:............
1Ki 8:52 eyes **m.** be open unto the supplication.......
1Ki 8:58 he **m.** incline our hearts unto him,............
1Ki 8:60 earth **m.** know that the Lord is God, ...
1Ki 11:21 that I **m.** go to mine own country.............
1Ki 11:36 David my servant **m.** have a light.............
1Ki 12:6 advise that I **m.** answer this people? ....
1Ki 12:9 give ye that we **m.** answer this people, ...
1Ki 13:6 my hand **m.** be restored me again. ....
1Ki 13:16 I **m.** not return with thee, nor go....... 3201
1Ki 13:18 that he **m.** eat bread and drink water. ....
1Ki 15:19 of Israel, that he **m.** depart from me.........
1Ki 17:10 water in a vessel, that I **m.** drink.............
1Ki 17:12 that I **m.** go in and dress it for me ....
1Ki 17:12 and my son, that we **m.** eat it, and die.....
1Ki 18:5 we **m.** find grass to save the horses ....
1Ki 18:37 people **m.** know that thou art the Lord......
1Ki 20:9 will do: but this thing I **m.** not do. 3201
1Ki 21:2 that I **m.** have it for a garden of herbs, ...
1Ki 21:10 out, and stone him, that he **m.** die. ....
1Ki 22:8 by whom we **m.** enquire of the Lord:........
1Ki 22:20 **m.** go up and fall at Ramoth-gilead? ....
2Ki 3:11 we **m.** enquire of the Lord by him? ....
2Ki 3:17 ye **m.** drink, both ye, and your cattle,.......
2Ki 4:22 I **m.** run to the man of God, and come......
2Ki 4:41 out for the people, that they **m.** eat.........
2Ki 4:42 Give unto the people, that they **m.** eat......
2Ki 4:43 Give the people, that they **m.** eat:............
2Ki 5:12 **m.** I not wash in them, and be clean? ....
2Ki 6:2 us a place there, where we **m.** dwell, ...
2Ki 6:13 he is, that I **m.** send and fetch him..........
2Ki 6:17 thee, open his eyes, that he **m.** see. ....
2Ki 6:20 eyes of these men, that they **m.** see. ....
2Ki 6:22 they **m.** eat and drink, and go to their.......
2Ki 6:28 thy son, that we **m.** eat him to day, ...
2Ki 6:29 Give thy son, that we **m.** eat him: and......
2Ki 7:9 **m.** go and tell the king's household..........
2Ki 9:7 **m.** avenge the blood of my servants ....
2Ki 18:27 that they **m.** eat their own dung, and........
2Ki 18:32 of honey, that ye **m.** live, and not die: ......
2Ki 19:4 It **m.** be the Lord thy God will hear..... 194
2Ki 19:19 earth **m.** know that thou art the Lord ....
2Ki 22:4 that he **m.** sum the silver which is............
1Ch 4:10 from evil, that it **m.** not grieve me! ....
1Ch 13:2 they **m.** gather themselves unto us:..........
1Ch 15:12 ye **m.** bring up the ark of the Lord God ....
1Ch 16:35 we **m.** give thanks to thy holy name, ...
1Ch 17:24 thy name **m.** be magnified for ever, ...
1Ch 17:27 that it **m.** be before thee for ever: ....
1Ch 21:2 of them to me, that I **m.** know it. ....
1Ch 21:10 one of them, that I **m.** do it unto thee. .....
1Ch 21:22 that I **m.** build an altar therein unto ....
1Ch 21:22 plague **m.** be stayed from the people. ....
1Ch 23:25 they **m.** dwell in Jerusalem for ever:.........
1Ch 28:8 that ye **m.** possess this good land, and......
2Ch 1:10 I **m.** go out and come in before this.........
2Ch 6:20 That thine eyes **m.** be open upon this ....
2Ch 6:31 That they **m.** fear thee, to walk in thy ......

2Ch 6:33 people of the earth **m.** know thy name,
2Ch 6:33 **m.** know that this house which I have
2Ch 7:16 that my name **m.** be there for ever:
2Ch 10:9 we **m.** return answer to this people,
2Ch 12:8 that they **m.** know my service, and the
2Ch 13:9 the same **m.** be a priest of them that
2Ch 16:3 of Israel, that he **m.** depart from me.
2Ch 18:7 by whom we **m.** enquire of the Lord:
2Ch 18:19 **m.** go up and fall at Ramoth-gilead?
2Ch 28:23 to them, that they **m.** help me.
2Ch 29:10 fierce wrath **m.** turn away from us.
2Ch 30:8 of his wrath **m.** turn away from you.
2Ch 35:6 **m.** do according to the word of the
Ezr 4:15 search **m.** be made in the book of the
Ezr 6:10 **m.** offer sacrifices of sweet savours
Ezr 7:25 which **m.** judge all the people that are
Ezr 9:8 our God **m.** lighten our eyes, and give
Ezr 9:12 that ye **m.** be strong, and eat the good
Ne 2:5 fathers' sepulchres, that I **m.** build it,
Ne 2:7 they **m.** convey me over till I come
Ne 2:8 he **m.** give me timber to make beams
Ne 4:22 in the night they **m.** be a guard to us,
Ne 5:2 take up corn for them, that we **m.** eat,
Es 2:3 they **m.** gather together all the fair
Es 3:9 be written that they **m.** be destroyed:
Es 4:11 the golden sceptre, that he **m.** live:
Es 5:5 that he **m.** do as Esther hath said.
Es 5:14 that Mordecai **m.** be hanged thereon:
Es 6:9 they **m.** array the man withal whom
Es 8:8 the king's ring, **m.** no man reverse.
Job 1:5 It **m.** be that my sons have sinned, 194
Job 5:11 which mourn **m.** be exalted to safety.
Job 10:20 alone, that I **m.** take comfort a little,
Job 13:13 peace, let me alone, that I **m.** speak,
Job 14:6 Turn from him, that he **m.** rest, till he
Job 19:29 that ye **m.** know there is a judgment.
Job 21:3 Suffer me that I **m.** speak; and after
Job 22:2 he that is wise **m.** be profitable unto
Job 27:17 He **m.** prepare it, but the just shall
Job 31:6 that God **m.** know mine integrity.
Job 32:20 I will speak, that I **m.** be refreshed:
Job 33:17 **m.** withdraw man from his purpose,
Job 34:22 the workers of iniquity **m.** hide
Job 34:36 is that Job **m.** be tried unto the end
Job 35:8 wickedness **m.** hurt a man as thou
Job 35:8 righteousness **m.** profit the son of
Job 36:25 Every man **m.** see it;
Job 36:25 man **m.** behold it afar off.
Job 37:7 man; that all men **m.** know his work.
Job 37:12 **m.** do whatsoever he commandeth
Job 38:34 abundance of waters **m.** cover thee?
Job 38:35 that they **m.** go, and say unto thee,
Job 39:15 that the foot **m.** crush them, or
Job 39:15 that the wild beast **m.** break them.
Ps 9:14 That I **m.** shew forth all thy praise in
Ps 9:20 **m.** know themselves to be but men.
Ps 10:10 the poor **m.** fall by his strong ones.
Ps 10:18 man of the earth **m.** no more oppress.
Ps 11:2 they **m.** privily shoot at the upright in
Ps 22:17 I **m.** tell all my bones: they look and
Ps 26:7 That I **m.** publish with the voice of
Ps 27:4 I **m.** dwell in the house of the Lord
Ps 30:5 weeping **m.** endure for a night, but joy
Ps 30:12 that my glory **m.** sing praise to thee,
Ps 34:12 loveth many days, that he **m.** see good?
Ps 39:4 it is; that I **m.** know how frail I am.
Ps 39:13 that I **m.** recover strength, before I go
Ps 41:10 raise me up, that I **m.** requite them.
Ps 48:13 that ye **m.** tell it to the generation.
Ps 50:4 the earth, that he **m.** judge his people.
Ps 51:8 bones...thou hast broken **m.** rejoice.
Ps 56:13 I **m.** walk before God in the light of
Ps 58:8 woman, that they **m.** not see the sun.
Ps 59:13 consume them, that they **m.** not be:
Ps 60:4 **m.** be displayed because of the truth.
Ps 60:5 That thy beloved **m.** be delivered;
Ps 61:7 and truth, which **m.** preserve him.
Ps 61:8 that I **m.** daily perform my vows.
Ps 64:4 they **m.** shoot in secret at the perfect:
Ps 65:4 thee, that he **m.** dwell in thy courts:
Ps 67:2 That thy way **m.** be known upon earth,
Ps 68:23 thy foot **m.** be dipped in the blood
Ps 69:35 that they **m.** dwell there, and have it
Ps 71:3 whereunto I **m.** continually resort:
Ps 73:28 God, that I **m.** declare all thy works.
Ps 76:7 and who **m.** stand in thy sight when
Ps 83:4 the name of Israel **m.** be no more in
Ps 83:16 that they **m.** seek thy name, O Lord.
Ps 83:18 That men **m.** know that thou, whose
Ps 84:3 nest...where she **m.** lay her young,
Ps 85:6 that thy people **m.** rejoice in thee?
Ps 85:9 him; that glory **m.** dwell in our land.
Ps 86:17 that they which hate me **m.** see it, and
Ps 90:12 we **m.** apply our hearts unto wisdom.
Ps 90:14 we **m.** rejoice and be glad all our days.
Ps 101:6 the land, that they **m.** dwell with me:
Ps 101:8 I **m.** cut off all wicked doers from the
Ps 104:9 set a bound that they **m.** not pass over;
Ps 104:14 **m.** bring forth food out of the earth;
Ps 106:5 That I **m.** see the good of thy chosen.
Ps 106:5 that I **m.** rejoice in the gladness of thy
Ps 106:5 that I **m.** glory with thine inheritance.
Ps 107:36 they **m.** prepare a city for habitation;
Ps 107:37 which **m.** yield fruits of increase.
Ps 108:6 That thy beloved **m.** be delivered:
Ps 109:15 he **m.** cut off the memory of them from
Ps 109:27 they **m.** know that this is thy hand;
Ps 111:6 he **m.** give them the heritage of the
Ps 113:8 he **m.** set him with princes, even with
Ps 119:17 that I **m.** live, and keep thy word.
Ps 119:18 I **m.** behold wondrous things out of
Ps 119:73 that I **m.** learn thy commandments.
Ps 119:77 mercies come unto me, that I **m.** live:
Ps 119:116 according unto thy word, that I **m.** live:
Ps 119:125 that I **m.** know thy testimonies.
Ps 124:1 was on our side, now **m.** Israel say;
Ps 129:1 me from my youth, **m.** Israel now say:
Ps 142:7 of prison, that I **m.** praise thy name:
Ps 144:12 our sons **m.** be as plants grown up in
Ps 144:12 our daughters **m.** be as corner stones,
Ps 144:13 That our garners **m.** be full, affording
Ps 144:13 our sheep **m.** bring forth thousands
Ps 144:14 That our oxen **m.** be strong to labour;
Pr 5:2 and that thy lips **m.** keep knowledge.
Pr 7:5 **m.** keep thee from the strange woman,
Pr 8:11 all things that **m.** be desired are not to
Pr 8:21 I **m.** cause those that love me to inherit
Pr 15:24 that he **m.** depart from hell beneath.
Pr 18:2 but that his heart **m.** discover itself.
Pr 20:21 An inheritance **m.** be gotten hastily at
Pr 22:19 That thy trust **m.** be in the Lord, I
Pr 27:1 knowest not what a day **m.** bring forth.
Pr 27:11 I **m.** answer him that reproacheth me.
Ec 1:10 there any thing whereof it **m.** be said,
Ec 2:26 **m.** give to him that is good before God.
Ec 5:15 which he **m.** carry away in his hand.
Ec 6:10 neither **m.** he contend with him 3201
Ec 8:4 and who **m.** say unto him, What doest
Ca 4:16 that the spices thereof **m.** flow out.
Ca 6:1 aside? that we **m.** seek him with thee.
Ca 6:13 return, that we **m.** look upon thee.
Isa 5:8 **m.** be placed alone in the midst of the
Isa 5:11 that they **m.** follow strong drink;
Isa 5:19 hasten his work, that we **m.** see it:
Isa 5:19 nigh and come, that we **m.** know it!
Isa 7:15 he **m.** know to refuse the evil, and
Isa 10:2 people, that widows **m.** be their prey,
Isa 10:2 and that they **m.** rob the fatherless!
Isa 10:19 be few, that a child **m.** write them.
Isa 13:2 they **m.** go into the gates of the nobles.
Isa 19:15 the head or tail, branch or rush, **m.** do.
Isa 24:10 is shut up, that no man **m.** come in.
Isa 26:2 which keepeth the truth **m.** enter in.
Isa 27:5 that he **m.** make peace with me;
Isa 28:12 ye **m.** cause the weary to rest;
Isa 28:21 that he **m.** do his work, his strange
Isa 30:1 my spirit, that they **m.** add sin to sin:
Isa 30:8 it **m.** be for the time to come for ever
Isa 30:18 wait, that he **m.** be gracious unto you,
Isa 30:18 that he **m.** have mercy upon you:
Isa 36:12 wall, that they **m.** eat their own dung,
Isa 37:4 It **m.** be the Lord thy God will hear the
Isa 37:20 all the kingdoms of the earth **m.** know
Isa 41:20 they **m.** see, and know, and consider,
Isa 41:22 that we **m.** consider them, and know
Isa 41:23 that we **m.** know that ye are gods:
Isa 41:23 that we **m.** be dismayed, and behold it
Isa 41:26 from the beginning, that we **m.** know?
Isa 41:26 that we **m.** say, He is righteous?
Isa 42:18 and look, ye blind, that ye **m.** see.
Isa 43:9 witnesses, that they **m.** be justified:
Isa 43:10 that ye **m.** know and believe me, and
Isa 44:9 nor know; that they **m.** be ashamed.
Isa 44:13 a man; that I **m.** remain in the house.
Isa 45:6 **m.** know from the rising of the sun,
Isa 46:5 and compare me, that we **m.** be like?
Isa 49:15 yea, they **m.** forget, yet will I not forget
Isa 49:20 me: give place to me that I **m.** dwell.
Isa 51:14 exile hasteneth that he **m.** be loosed.
Isa 51:16 that I **m.** plant the heavens, and lay
Isa 51:23 soul, Bow down, that we **m.** go over:
Isa 55:6 Seek ye the Lord while he **m.** be found,
Isa 55:10 bud, that it **m.** give seed to the sower,
Isa 60:11 that men **m.** bring unto thee the forces
Isa 60:11 and that their kings **m.** be brought.
Isa 60:21 of my hands, that I **m.** be glorified.
Isa 64:2 nations **m.** tremble at thy presence!
Isa 65:8 sakes, that I **m.** not destroy them all.
Isa 66:11 That ye **m.** suck, and be satisfied with
Isa 66:11 that ye **m.** milk out, and be delighted
Jer 6:10 and give warning, that they **m.** hear?
Jer 7:18 that they **m.** provoke me to anger.
Jer 7:23 you, that it **m.** be well unto you.
Jer 9:12 wise man, that **m.** understand this?
Jer 9:12 hath spoken, that he **m.** declare it,
Jer 9:17 mourning women, that they **m.** come;
Jer 9:17 cunning women, that they **m.** come:
Jer 9:18 that our eyes **m.** run down with tears,
Jer 10:18 distress them, that they **m.** find it so.
Jer 11:5 I **m.** perform the oath which I have
Jer 11:19 his name **m.** be no more remembered.
Jer 13:23 then **m.** ye also do good, that are 3201
Jer 13:26 thy face, that thy shame **m.** appear.
Jer 16:12 that they **m.** not hearken unto me:
Jer 21:2 works, that he **m.** go up from us.
Jer 26:3 that I **m.** repent me of the evil, which
Jer 28:14 they **m.** serve Nebuchadnezzar king
Jer 29:6 that they **m.** bear sons and daughters;
Jer 29:6 that ye **m.** be increased there, and not
Jer 32:14 that they **m.** continue many days.
Jer 32:39 one way, that they **m.** fear me for ever,
Jer 33:21 Then **m.** also my covenant be broken
Jer 35:7 that ye **m.** live many days in the land
Jer 36:3 It **m.** be that the house of Judah will
Jer 36:3 they **m.** return every man from his evil
Jer 36:3 I **m.** forgive their iniquity and their
Jer 36:7 It **m.** be they will present their
Jer 42:3 the Lord thy God **m.** shew us the way
Jer 42:3 shew us the way wherein we **m.** walk,
Jer 42:3 walk, and the thing that we **m.** do.
Jer 42:6 that it **m.** be well with us, when we
Jer 42:12 that he **m.** have mercy upon you, and
Jer 44:29 ye **m.** know that my words shall surely
Jer 46:10 he **m.** avenge him of his adversaries:
Jer 48:9 Moab, that it **m.** flee and get away:
Jer 49:19 man, that I **m.** appoint over her?
Jer 50:34 that he **m.** give rest to the land, and
Jer 50:44 man that I **m.** appoint over her?
Jer 51:8 for her pain, if so be she **m.** be healed.
Jer 51:39 that they **m.** rejoice, and sleep a
La 2:13 that I **m.** comfort thee, O virgin
La 3:29 in the dust; if so be there **m.** be hope.
Eze 4:17 That they **m.** want bread and water,
Eze 6:6 that your altars **m.** be laid waste and
Eze 6:6 and your idols **m.** be broken and cease,
Eze 6:6 and your images **m.** be cut down,
Eze 6:6 and your works **m.** be abolished.
Eze 6:8 ye **m.** have some that shall escape the
Eze 11:20 That they **m.** walk in my statutes, and
Eze 12:3 it **m.** be they will consider, though
Eze 12:16 they **m.** declare all their abominations
Eze 12:19 that her land **m.** be desolate from all
Eze 14:5 I **m.** take the house of Israel in their
Eze 14:11 That the house of Israel **m.** go no more
Eze 14:11 but that they **m.** be my people, and I
Eze 14:11 I **m.** be their God, saith the Lord God.
Eze 14:15 no man **m.** pass through because of
Eze 16:33 they **m.** come unto thee on every side
Eze 16:37 that they **m.** see all thy nakedness.
Eze 20:20 **m.** know that I am the Lord your God.
Eze 21:5 all flesh **m.** know that I the Lord
Eze 21:10 it is furbished that it **m.** glitter:
Eze 21:11 to be furbished, that it **m.** be handled:
Eze 21:15 that their heart **m.** faint, and their
Eze 21:19 sword of the king of Babylon **m.** come:
Eze 21:20 that the sword **m.** come to Rabbath
Eze 21:23 the iniquity, that they **m.** be taken.
Eze 22:3 midst of it, that her time **m.** come,
Eze 23:48 all women **m.** be taught not to do after
Eze 24:11 the brass of it **m.** be hot, and **m.** burn,
Eze 24:11 the filthiness of it **m.** be molten in it,

Eze 24:11 it, that the scum of it **m.** be consumed
Eze 25:10 the Ammonites **m.** not be remembered
Eze 28:17 before kings, that they **m.** behold thee.
Eze 34:10 that they **m.** not be meat for them
Eze 37:9 upon these slain, that they **m.** live.
Eze 38:16 that the heathen **m.** know me, when I
Eze 39:12 of them, that they **m.** cleanse the land.
Eze 39:17 that ye **m.** eat flesh, and drink blood
Eze 43:10 they **m.** be ashamed of their iniquities:
Eze 43:11 they **m.** keep the whole form thereof,
Eze 44:25 no husband, they **m.** defile themselves.
Eze 44:30 **m.** cause the blessing to rest in thine
Eze 45:11 the bath **m.** contain the tenth part of
Da 4:17 the living **m.** know that the Most High
Da 4:27 **m.** be a lengthening of thy tranquillity.
Da 6:15 the king establisheth **m.** be changed
Ho 8:4 them idols, that they **m.** be cut off.
Ho 13:10 that **m.** save thee in all thy cities?
Am 5:14 good, and not evil, that ye **m.** live:
Am 5:15 it **m.** be that the Lord God of hosts
Am 6:10 we **m.** not make mention of the name
Am 8:5 moon be gone, that we **m.** sell corn?
Am 8:5 that we **m.** set forth wheat, making
Am 8:6 That we **m.** buy the poor for silver,
Am 9:1 of the door, that the posts **m.** shake:
Am 9:12 they **m.** possess the remnant of Edom,
Ob 9 of Esau **m.** be cut off by slaughter
Jon 1:7 **m.** know for whose cause this evil is
Jon 1:11 thee, that the sea **m.** be calm unto us?
Mic 6:5 ye **m.** know the righteousness of the
Mic 7:3 **m.** do evil with both hands earnestly,
Hab 2:2 tables, that he **m.** run that readeth it.
Hab 2:9 house, that he **m.** set his rest on high,
Hab 2:9 **m.** be delivered from the power of evil!
Zep 2:3 it **m.** be ye shall be hid in the day of.... 194
Zep 3:8 that I **m.** assemble the kingdoms, to
Zep 3:9 **m.** all call upon the name of the Lord,
Zec 11:1 that the fire **m.** devour thy cedars.
Mal 3:2 who **m.** abide the day of his coming?
Mal 3:3 **m.** offer unto the Lord an offering
Mal 3:10 that there **m.** be meat in mine house,
Mt 2:8 that I **m.** come and worship him also.
Mt 5:16 that they m. see your good works, and
Mt 5:45 ye m. be the children of your Father
Mt 6:2 that they m. have glory of men
Mt 6:4 That thine alms m. be in secret: and
Mt 6:5 streets, that they m. be seen of men
Mt 6:16 that they m. appear unto men to fast.
Mt 9:6 that ye m. know that the Son of man
Mt 9:21 If I **m.** but touch his garment, I shall
Mt 14:15 away, that they **m.** go into the villages,
Mt 18:16 witnesses every word m. be established.
Mt 19:16 shall I do, that I **m.** have eternal life?
Mt 20:21 Grant that these my two sons **m.** sit,
Mt 20:33 him, Lord, that our eyes **m.** be opened.
Mt 23:26 the outside of them m. be clean also.
Mt 23:35 you m. come all the righteous blood
Mt 26:42 if this cup m. not pass away from. *1410*
Mk 1:38 next towns, that I **m.** preach there also:
Mk 2:10 that ye m. know that the Son of man
Mk 4:12 That seeing they m. see, and not
Mk 4:12 and hearing they m. hear, and not
Mk 4:32 fowls of the air m. lodge under the *1410*
Mk 5:12 the swine, that we **m.** enter into them.
Mk 5:23 hands on her, that she **m.** be healed;
Mk 5:28 If I **m.** touch but his clothes, I shall
Mk 6:36 **m.** go into the country round about,
Mk 7:9 that ye m. keep your own tradition.
Mk 10:17 shall I do that I **m.** inherit eternal life?
Mk 10:37 Grant unto us that we **m.** sit, one on
Mk 11:25 also which is in heaven m. forgive you.
Mk 12:15 me? bring me a penny, that I m. see it.
Mk 14:7 ye will ye m. do them good: but.... *1410*
Mk 15:32 the cross, that we **m.** see and believe.
Lu 2:35 thoughts of many hearts **m.** be revealed.
Lu 5:24 that ye m. know that the Son of man
Lu 8:16 they which enter in m. see the light.
Lu 9:12 they **m.** go into the towns and country
Lu 11:33 they which come in m. see the light.
Lu 11:50 m. be required of this generation.
Lu 12:36 they m. open unto him immediately.
Lu 14:10 he m. say unto thee, Friend, go up
Lu 14:23 to come in, that my house m. be filled.
Lu 16:4 they m. receive me into their houses.
Lu 16:9 they m. receive you into everlasting
Lu 16:24 he m. dip the tip of his finger in water,
Lu 16:28 that he m. testify unto them, lest they.
Lu 17:8 Make ready wherewith I m. sup, and
Lu 18:41 said, Lord, that I **m.** receive my sight.
Lu 20:13 it m. be they will reverence him.... *2481*
Lu 20:14 that the inheritance m. be ours:
Lu 21:22 which are written m. be fulfilled
Lu 21:36 ye m. be accounted worthy to
Lu 22:8 us the passover, that we m. eat
Lu 22:30 ye m. eat and drink at my table
Lu 22:31 you, that he m. sift you as wheat:
Joh 1:22 that we **m.** give an answer to them
Joh 3:21 his deeds m. be made manifest,
Joh 4:36 that reapeth m. rejoice together.
Joh 5:20 than these, that ye m. marvel.
Joh 6:5 we buy bread, that these m. eat?
Joh 6:7 that every one of them **m.** take a little.
Joh 6:30 shewest thou then, that we **m.** see,
Joh 6:40 on him, m. have everlasting life:
Joh 6:50 a man m. eat thereof, and not die.
Joh 7:3 thy disciples also **m.** see the works
Joh 10:38 ye m. know, and believe, that the
Joh 11:11 I go, that I m. awake him out of
Joh 11:15 to the intent that ye m. believe;
Joh 11:16 us also go, that we **m.** die with him.
Joh 11:42 they m. believe that thou hast sent
Joh 12:36 that ye m. be the children of light
Joh 13:18 that the scripture m. be fulfilled.
Joh 13:19 to pass, ye m. believe that I am he.
Joh 14:3 where I am, there ye m. be also.
Joh 14:13 Father m. be glorified in the Son.
Joh 14:16 that he m. abide with you for ever;
Joh 14:31 world m. know that I love the
Joh 15:2 that it m. bring forth more fruit.
Joh 15:16 Father in my name, he m. give it
Joh 16:4 ye m. remember that I told you of
Joh 16:24 receive, that your joy m. be full.
Joh 17:1 that thy Son also m. glorify thee:
Joh 17:11 me, that they m. be one, as we are.
Joh 17:21 That they all m. be one; as thou,
Joh 17:21 that they also m. be one in us:
Joh 17:21 that the world m. believe that thou
Joh 17:22 they m. be one, even as we are
Joh 17:23 they m. be made perfect in one;
Joh 17:23 the world m. know that thou hast
Joh 17:24 they m. behold my glory, which
Joh 17:26 thou hast loved me m. be in them,
Joh 19:4 that ye **m.** know I find no fault in him.
Ac 1:25 That they **m.** take part of this ministry
Ac 3:19 that your sins **m.** be blotted out, when
Ac 4:29 all boldness they **m.** speak thy word.
Ac 4:30 signs and wonders **m.** be done by the
Ac 6:3 wisdom, whom we **m.** appoint over
Ac 8:19 hands, he **m.** receive the Holy Ghost.
Ac 8:20 the gift of God **m.** be purchased with
Ac 8:22 thought of thine heart **m.** be forgiven
Ac 17:19 **M.** we know what this new doctrine, .. *1410*
Ac 19:40 whereby we **m.** give an account of..... *1410*
Ac 21:24 them, that they **m.** shave their heads:
Ac 21:24 and all **m.** know that those things,
Ac 21:37 captain, **M.** I speak unto thee? *1832*
Ac 23:24 them beasts, that they **m.** set Paul on,
Ac 25:11 no man **m.** deliver me unto them. *1410*
Ac 26:18 that they m. receive forgiveness of
Ro 1:11 I **m.** impart to you some spiritual gift,
Ro 1:11 gift, to the end ye **m.** be established;
Ro 1:12 that I **m.** be comforted together with
Ro 1:19 that which **m.** be known of God is
Ro 3:8 Let us do evil, that good **m.** come?
Ro 3:19 that every mouth **m.** be stopped, and
Ro 3:19 world **m.** become guilty before God.
Ro 6:1 continue in sin, that grace **m.** abound?
Ro 8:17 that we **m.** be also glorified together.
Ro 11:10 be darkened, that they **m.** not see,
Ro 11:14 any means I **m.** provoke to emulation.
Ro 11:31 your mercy they also **m.** obtain mercy
Ro 12:2 that ye **m.** prove what is that good, and
Ro 14:2 believeth that he **m.** eat all things:
Ro 14:19 wherewith one **m.** edify another,
Ro 15:6 ye **m.** with one mind and one mouth
Ro 15:13 **m.** abound in hope, through the power
Ro 15:17 I **m.** glory through Jesus Christ in
Ro 15:31 That I **m.** be delivered from them that
Ro 15:31 I have for Jerusalem **m.** be accepted
Ro 15:32 That I **m.** come unto you with joy by
Ro 15:32 of God, and **m.** with you be refreshed.
1Co 1:8 **m.** be blameless in the day of our Lord
1Co 2:16 of the Lord, that he **m.** instruct him?
1Co 3:18 him become a fool, that he **m.** be wise.
1Co 5:5 the spirit **m.** be saved in the day of the
1Co 5:7 old leaven, that ye **m.** be a new lump,
1Co 7:5 that ye **m.** give yourselves to fasting
1Co 7:32 the Lord, how he **m.** please the Lord:
1Co 7:33 the world, how he **m.** please his wife.
1Co 7:34 that she **m.** be holy both in body and
1Co 7:34 world, how she **m.** please her husband.
1Co 7:35 not that I **m.** cast a snare upon you,
1Co 7:35 and that ye **m.** attend upon the Lord
1Co 9:18 I **m.** make the gospel of Christ without
1Co 9:24 the prize? So run, that ye **m.** obtain.
1Co 10:13 to escape, that ye **m.** be able to bear it.
1Co 10:33 profit of many, that they **m.** be saved.
1Co 11:19 **m.** be made manifest among you.
1Co 14:1 gifts, but rather that ye **m.** prophesy.
1Co 14:5 that the church **m.** receive edifying.
1Co 14:10 There are, it **m.** be, so many kinds of
1Co 14:12 seek that ye **m.** excel to the edifying
1Co 14:13 tongue pray that he **m.** interpret.
1Co 14:31 For ye **m.** all prophesy one by one,.... *1410*
1Co 14:31 all **m.** learn, and all **m.** be comforted.
1Co 15:28 under him, that God **m.** be all in all.
1Co 15:37 it **m.** chance of wheat, or of some
1Co 16:6 And it **m.** be that I will abide, yea, and
1Co 16:6 that ye **m.** bring me on my journey
1Co 16:10 that he **m.** be with you without fear:
1Co 16:11 in peace, that he **m.** come unto me:
2Co 1:4 that we **m.** be able to comfort them
2Co 1:11 thanks **m.** be given by many on our
2Co 2:5 part: that I **m.** not overcharge you all.
2Co 4:7 excellency of the power **m.** be of God,
2Co 5:9 or absent, we **m.** be accepted of him.
2Co 5:10 that every one **m.** receive the things
2Co 5:12 that ye **m.** have somewhat to answer
2Co 8:11 so there **m.** be a performance also out
2Co 8:14 your abundance **m.** be a supply for
2Co 8:14 their abundance also **m.** be a supply
2Co 8:14 want: that there **m.** be equality:
2Co 9:3 that, as I said, ye **m.** be ready:
2Co 9:8 things, **m.** abound to every good work:
2Co 10:2 I **m.** not be bold when I am present
2Co 10:9 I **m.** not seem as if I would terrify you
2Co 11:2 I **m.** present you as a chaste virgin to
2Co 11:12 I **m.** cut off occasion from them which
2Co 11:12 glory, they **m.** be found even as we.
2Co 11:16 me, that I **m.** boast myself a little.
2Co 12:9 the power of Christ **m.** rest upon me.
Ga 6:13 that they **m.** glory in your flesh.
Eph 1:17 **m.** give unto you the spirit of wisdom
Eph 1:18 **m.** know what is the hope of his calling,
Eph 3:4 ye **m.** understand my knowledge *1410*
Eph 3:17 Christ **m.** dwell in your hearts by faith;
Eph 3:18 **M.** be able to comprehend with all
Eph 4:15 **m.** grow up into him in all things,
Eph 4:28 that he **m.** have to give to him that
Eph 4:29 it **m.** minister grace unto the hearers.
Eph 6:3 That it **m.** be well with thee, and thou
Eph 6:11 **m.** be able to stand against the wiles
Eph 6:13 ye **m.** be able to withstand in the evil
Eph 6:19 that utterance **m.** be given unto me,
Eph 6:19 that I **m.** open my mouth boldly, to
Eph 6:20 that therein I **m.** speak boldly, as I
Eph 6:21 But that ye also **m.** know my affairs,
Php 1:9 love **m.** abound yet more and more
Php 1:10 **m.** approve things that are excellent;
Php 1:10 ye **m.** be sincere and without offence
Php 1:26 your rejoicing **m.** be more abundant in
Php 1:27 I **m.** hear of your affairs, that ye
Php 2:15 ye **m.** be blameless and harmless, the
Php 2:16 that I **m.** rejoice in the day of Christ,
Php 2:19 I also **m.** be of good comfort, when I
Php 2:28 when ye see him again, ye **m.** rejoice,
Php 2:28 and that I **m.** be the less sorrowful.
Php 3:8 them but dung, that I **m.** win Christ,
Php 3:10 that I **m.** know him, and the power of
Php 3:12 I **m.** apprehend that for which also I
Php 3:21 that it **m.** be fashioned like unto his
Php 4:17 fruit that **m.** abound to your account.
Col 1:28 we **m.** present every man perfect in
Col 4:4 I **m.** make it manifest, as I ought to
Col 4:6 ye **m.** know how ye ought to answer
Col 4:12 that ye **m.** stand perfect and complete
1Th 3:13 To the end he **m.** stablish your hearts
1Th 4:12 ye **m.** walk honestly toward them that
1Th 4:12 and that ye **m.** have lack of nothing.
2Th 1:5 that ye **m.** be counted worthy of the
2Th 1:12 our Lord Jesus Christ **m.** be glorified

2Th 3:1 word of the Lord **m.** have free course,
2Th 3:2 we **m.** be delivered from unreasonable
2Th 3:14 with him, that he **m.** be ashamed.
1Ti 1:20 that they **m.** learn not to blaspheme.
1Ti 2:2 we **m.** lead a quiet and peacable life
1Ti 4:15 that thy profiting **m.** appear to all.
1Ti 5:7 in charge, that they **m.** be blameless.
1Ti 5:16 it **m.** relieve them that are widows
1Ti 5:20 before all, that others also **m.** fear.
1Ti 6:19 that they **m.** lay hold on eternal life.
2Ti 1:4 thy tears, that I **m.** be filled with joy;
2Ti 1:18 grant unto him that he **m.** find mercy
2Ti 2:4 he **m.** please him who hath chosen
2Ti 2:10 **m.** also obtain the salvation which is
2Ti 2:26 And that they **m.** recover themselves
2Ti 3:17 That the man of God **m.** be perfect,
2Ti 4:16 that it **m.** not be laid to their charge.
Tit 1:9 that he **m.** be able by sound doctrine
Tit 1:13 that they **m.** be sound in the faith;
Tit 2:4 they **m.** teach the young women to be
Tit 2:8 is of the contrary part **m.** be ashamed,
Tit 2:10 they **m.** adorn the doctrine of God our
Phm 6 of thy faith **m.** become effectual by
Heb 4:16 we **m.** obtain mercy, and find grace
Heb 5:1 he **m.** offer both gifts and sacrifices for
Heb 7:9 And as I **m.** so say, Levi also, who
Heb 10:9 first, that he **m.** establish the second.
Heb 12:27 which cannot be shaken **m.** remain.
Heb 12:28 whereby we **m.** serve God acceptably
Heb 13:6 So that we **m.** boldly say, The Lord is
Heb 13:17 that they **m.** do it with joy, and not
Heb 13:19 I **m.** be restored to you the sooner.
Jas 1:4 ye **m.** be perfect and entire, wanting
Jas 2:18 Yea, a man **m.** say, thou hast faith,
Jas 3:3 horses' mouths, that they **m.** obey us;
Jas 4:3 ye **m.** consume it upon your lusts
Jas 5:16 one for another that ye **m.** be healed.
1Pe 2:2 of the word, that ye **m.** grow thereby:
1Pe 2:12 they **m.** by your good works, which
1Pe 2:15 with well doing ye **m.** put to silence
1Pe 3:1 they also **m.** without the word be won
1Pe 3:16 **m.** be ashamed that falsely accuse
1Pe 4:3 **m.** suffice us to have wrought the will
1Pe 4:11 that God in all things **m.** be glorified
1Pe 4:13 ye **m.** be glad also with exceeding
1Pe 5:6 God, that he **m.** exalt you in due time:
1Pe 5:8 about, seeking whom he **m.** devour:
2Pe 1:15 that ye **m.** be able after my decease
2Pe 3:2 That ye **m.** be mindful of the words
2Pe 3:14 be diligent that ye **m.** be found of him
1Jo 1:3 ye also **m.** have fellowship with us:
1Jo 1:4 we unto you, that your joy **m.** be full.
1Jo 2:28 we **m.** have confidence, and not be
1Jo 4:17 that we **m.** have boldness in the day of
1Jo 5:13 ye **m.** know that ye have eternal life,
1Jo 5:13 ye **m.** believe on the name of the Son
1Jo 5:20 that we **m.** know him that is true;
2Jo 1:12 face to face, that our joy **m.** be full.
Re 2:10 **into prison, that ye m. be tried;**
Re 14:13 that they **m.** rest from their labours;
Re 19:18 That ye **m.** eat the flesh of kings, and
Re 22:14 they **m.** have right to the tree of life,
Re 22:14 **m.** enter in through the gates into the

MAYEST
Ge 2:16 tree of the garden thou **m.** freely eat:
Ge 23:6 but that thou **m.** bury thy dead.
Ge 28:3 that thou **m.** be a multitude of people;
Ge 28:4 thou **m.** inherit the land wherein thou
Ge 38:16 me, that thou **m.** come in unto me?
Ex 3:10 that thou **m.** bring forth my people
Ex 8:10 **m.** know that there is none like unto
Ex 8:22 thou **m.** know that I am the Lord in
Ex 9:14 **m.** know that there is none like me
Ex 9:29 **m.** know...that the earth is the Lord's
Ex 10:2 thou **m.** tell in the ears of thy son, and
Ex 18:19 thou **m.** bring the causes unto God:
Ex 24:12 written; that thou **m.** teach them.
Ex 26:33 **m.** bring in thither within the vail
Le 22:23 **m.** thou offer for a free will offering;
Nu 10:2 thou **m.** use them for the calling of
Nu 10:31 and thou **m.** be to us instead of eyes.
Nu 23:13 place, from whence thou **m.** see them:
Nu 23:27 thou **m.** curse me them from thence.
De 2:31 possess, that thou **m.** inherit his land.
De 4:40 that thou **m.** prolong thy days upon
De 6:18 **m.** go in and possess the good land
De 7:22 thou **m.** not consume them at once..... 3201
De 8:9 out of whose hills thou **m.** dig brass.
De 11:14 thou **m.** gather in thy corn, and thy
De 11:15 cattle, that thou **m.** eat and be full
De 12:15 thou **m.** kill and eat flesh in all thy
De 12:17 Thou **m.** not eat within thy gates 3201
De 12:20 thou **m.** eat flesh, whatsoever thy soul
De 12:23 thou **m.** not eat the life with the flesh.
De 14:21 eat it; or thou **m.** sell it unto an alien:
De 14:23 thou **m.** learn to fear the Lord thy God
De 15:3 Of a foreigner thou **m.** exact it again:
De 16:3 thou **m.** remember the day when thou
De 16:5 Thou **m.** not sacrifice the passover.... 3201
De 16:20 that thou **m.** live, and inherit the land
De 17:15 **m.** not set a stranger over thee,........ 3021
De 20:19 for thou **m.** eat of them, and thou shalt
De 22:3 likewise: thou **m.** not hide thyself....... 3201
De 22:7 and that thou **m.** prolong thy days.
De 23:20 a stranger thou **m.** lend upon usury:
De 23:24 **m.** eat grapes thy fill at thine own
De 23:25 **m.** pluck the ears with thine hand;
De 26:19 that thou **m.** be an holy people unto the
De 27:3 thou **m.** go in unto the land which
De 28:58 **m.** fear this glorious and fearful name,
De 30:6 with all thy soul, that thou **m.** live.
De 30:14 and in thy heart, that thou **m.** do it.
De 30:16 that thou **m.** live and multiply: and
De 30:20 That thou **m.** love the Lord thy God,
De 30:20 and that thou **m.** obey his voice, and
De 30:20 and that thou **m.** cleave upon him:
De 30:20 thou **m.** dwell in the land which the
Jos 1:7 thou **m.** observe to do according to all
Jos 1:7 **m.** prosper wheresoever thou goest.
Jos 1:8 **m.** observe to do according to all that
Jg 9:33 **m.** thou do to them as thou shalt find
Jg 11:8 that thou **m.** go with us, and fight
Jg 19:9 on your way, that thou **m.** go home
1Sa 20:13 thee away, that thou **m.** go in peace:
1Sa 24:4 **m.** do to him as it shall seem good
1Sa 28:15 **m.** make known unto me what I shall
1Sa 28:22 **m.** have strength, when thou goest on
2Sa 3:21 **m.** reign over all that thine heart
2Sa 15:34 **m.** thou for me defeat the counsel of
2Sa 22:28 that thou **m.** bring them down.
1Ki 1:12 thou **m.** save thine own life, and the
1Ki 2:3 **m.** prosper in all that thou doest, and
1Ki 2:31 thou **m.** take away the innocent blood,
1Ki 8:29 **m.** hearken unto the prayer which thy
2Ki 5:6 thou **m.** recover him of his leprosy.
2Ki 8:10 unto him, Thou **m.** certainly recover:
1Ch 22:12 **m.** keep the law of the Lord thy God.
1Ch 22:14 I prepared; and thou **m.** add thereto.
2Ch 1:11 thyself, that thou **m.** judge my people,
2Ch 18:33 that thou **m.** carry me out of the host;
Ezr 7:17 thou **m.** buy speedily with this money
Ne 1:6 that thou **m.** hear the prayer of thy
Ne 6:6 that thou **m.** be their king, according
Job 40:8 me, that thou **m.** be righteous?
Ps 32:6 thee in a time when thou **m.** be found:
Ps 45:16 thou **m.** make princes in all the earth.
Ps 94:13 That thou **m.** give him rest from the
Ps 104:27 thou **m.** give them their meat in due
Ps 130:4 with thee, that thou **m.** be feared.
Pr 2:20 thou **m.** walk in the way of good men,
Pr 5:2 That thou **m.** regard discretion, and
Pr 19:20 that thou **m.** be wise in thy latter end.
Isa 23:16 songs, that thou **m.** be remembered.
Isa 43:26 declare thou, that thou **m.** be justified.
Isa 45:3 that thou **m.** know that I, the Lord,
Isa 47:12 able to profit, if so be thou **m.** prevail.
Isa 49:6 thou **m.** be my salvation unto the end
Isa 49:9 That thou **m.** say to the prisoners, Go
Jer 4:14 wickedness, that thou **m.** be saved.
Jer 6:27 that thou **m.** know and try their way.
Jer 30:13 thy cause, that thou **m.** be bound up:
Eze 16:54 That thou **m.** bear thine own shame,
Eze 16:54 **m.** be confounded in all that thou hast
Eze 16:63 That thou **m.** remember, and be
Hab 2:15 that thou **m.** look on their nakedness!
Mk 14:12 prepare that thou **m.** eat the passover?
Lu 12:58 **that thou m. be delivered from him;**
Lu 16:2 **for thou m. be no longer steward** ...*1410*
Ac 8:37 with all thine heart, thou **m.** *1832*
Ac 24:8 **m.** take knowledge of all these things,
Ac 24:11 Because that thou **m.** understand,
1Co 7:21 but if thou **m.** be made free, use *1410*
Eph 6:3 and thou **m.** live long on the earth.
1Ti 3:15 that thou **m.** know how thou oughtest
3Jo 2 that thou **m.** prosper and be in health,
Re 3:18 **tried in the fire, that thou m. be rich;**
Re 3:18 **that thou m. be clothed, and that the**
Re 3:18 **eyes with eyesalve, that thou m. see**

MAZE See AMAZE.

MAZZAROTH (maz'-za-roth)
Job 38:32 thou bring forth **M.** in his season?...... 4216

ME See in the APPENDIX.

MEADOW See also MEADOWS.
Ge 41:2 fatfleshed; and they fed in a **m.**........... 260
Ge 41:18 well favoured; and they fed in a **m.**...... 260

MEADOWS
Jg 20:33 even out of the **m.** of Gibeah. 4629

MEAH (me'-ah)
Ne 3:1 the tower of **M.** they sanctified it,...... 3968
Ne 12:39 the tower of **M.**, even unto the 3968

MEAL See also MEALTIME.
Ge 18:6 three measures of fine **m.**, ... 7058,5560
Nu 5:15 part of an ephah of barley **m.**; 7058
1Ki 4:22 and threescore measures of **m.**,......... 7058
1Ki 17:12 but an handful of **m.** in a barrel,......... 7058
1Ki 17:14 barrel of **m.** shall not waste, neither... 7058
1Ki 17:16 he barrel of **m.** wasted not, neither 7058
2Ki 4:41 But he said, Then bring **m.**. And 7058
1Ch 12:40 meat, **m.**, cakes of figs, and bunches .. 7058
Isa 47:2 Take the millstones, and grind **m.**: 7058
Ho 8:7 stalk: the bud shall yield no **m.**:........... 7058
Mt 13:33 **and hid in three measures of m.,** *224*
Lu 13:21 **and hid in three measures of m.,** *224*

MEALTIME
Ru 2:14 her, At **m.** come thou hither,....... 6256,400

MEAN See also MEANEST; MEANETH; MEANING; MEANS; MEANT.
Ge 21:29 What **m.** these seven ewe lambs which
Ex 12:26 unto you, What **m.** ye by this service?
De 6:20 What **m.** the testimonies, and the
Jos 4:6 saying, What **m.** ye by these stones?
Jos 4:21 to come, saying, What **m.** these stones?
1Ki 18:45 came to pass in the **m.** while, ... 5704,3541
Pr 22:29 he shall not stand before **m.** men. 2823
Isa 2:9 the **m.** man boweth down, and the......... 120
Isa 3:15 **m.** ye that ye beat my people to pieces,
Isa 5:15 the **m.** man shall be brought down, ... 120
Isa 31:8 the sword, not of a **m.** man, shall........ 120
Eze 17:12 Know ye not what these things **m.**?
Eze 18:2 What **m.** ye, that ye use this proverb
Mk 9:10 rising from the dead should **m.**. *2076*
Lu 12:1 In the **m.** time, when there were
Joh 4:31 the **m.** while his disciples prayed........ *3342*
Ac 10:17 vision...he had seen should **m.**,.......... *1498*
Ac 17:20 know...what these things **m.**...... *2309,1511*
Ac 21:13 What **m.** ye to weep and to break....... *4160*
Ac 21:39 in Cilicia, a citizen of no **m.** city: *767*
Ro 2:15 thoughts the **m.** while accusing.......... *3342*
2Co 8:13 I **m.** not that other men be eased,

MEANEST
Ge 33:8 What **m.** thou by all this drove which
2Sa 16:2 unto Ziba, What **m.** thou by these?
Eze 37:18 not shew us what thou **m.** by these?
Jon 1:6 unto him, What **m.** thou, O sleeper?

MEANETH
De 29:24 what **m.** the heat of this great anger?
1Sa 4:6 What **m.** the noise of this great shout
1Sa 4:14 What **m.** the noise of this tumult?
1Sa 15:14 **m.** then this bleating of the sheep
Isa 10:7 Howbeit he **m.** not so, neither........ 1819
Mt 9:13 **go ye and learn what that m.,** *2076*
Mt 12:7 **if ye had known what this m.,** *2076*
Ac 2:12 one to another, What **m.** this?.... *2309,1511*

MEANING
Da 8:15 the vision, and sought for the **m.**,........ 998
Ac 27:2 **m.** to sail by the coasts of Asia; *3195*
1Co 14:11 if I know not the **m.** of the voice, ... *1411*

MEANS
Ex 34:7 that will by no **m.** clear the guilty;
Nu 14:18 and by no **m.** clearing the guilty,
Jg 5:22 broken by **m.** of the pransings, the
Jg 16:5 by what **m.** we may prevail against
2Sa 14:14 yet doth he devise **m.**, that his.......... 4284

1Ki 10:29 they bring them out by their **m.**......... 3027
1Ki 20:39 if by any **m.** he be missing, then shall.......
2Ch 1:17 for the kings of Syria, by their **m.**........ 3027
Ezr 4:16 by this **m.** thou shalt have no........... 6903
Ps 49:7 can by any **m.** redeem his brother,...........
Pr 6:26 For by **m.** of a whorish woman a....... 1157
Jer 5:31 the priests bear rule by their **m.**;....... 3027
Mal 1:9 this hath been by your **m.**: will he...... 3027
Mt 5:26 **Thou shalt by no m. come out** *3361*
Lu 5:18 and they sought **m.** to bring him in..........
Lu 8:36 by what **m.** he that was possessed..... *4459*
Lu 10:19 **nothing shall by any m. hurt you** .. *3364*
Joh 9:21 But by what **m.** he now seeth, we..... *4459*
Ac 4:9 by what **m.** he is made whole;.................
Ac 18:21 I must by all **m.** keep this feast......... *3843*
Ac 27:12 if by any **m.** they might attain to........ *4458*
Ro 1:10 if by any **m.** now at length I might..... *4458*
Ro 11:14 If by any **m.** I may provoke to........... *4458*
1Co 8:9 heed lest by any **m.** this liberty of...... *4458*
1Co 9:22 that I might by all **m.** save some........ *3843*
1Co 9:27 lest that by any **m.**, when I have....... *4458*
2Co 1:11 upon us by the **m.** of many persons..........
2Co 11:3 lest by any **m.**, as the serpent.......... *4458*
Ga 2:2 lest by any **m.** I should run, or had..... *4458*
Php 3:11 If by any **m.** I might attain unto......... *4458*
1Th 3:5 lest by some **m.** the tempter have...... *4458*
2Th 2:3 no man deceive you by any **m.**: *5158*
2Th 3:16 give you peace always by all **m.**......... *5158*
Heb 9:15 testament, that by **m.** of death, ... *1096*
Re 13:14 by the **m.** of those miracles which he........

MEANT
Ge 50:20 God **m.** it unto good, to bring to........ 2803
Lu 15:26 **and asked what these things m.,** ... *1498*
Lu 18:36 pass by, he asked what it **m.**. *1498*

MEANWHILE See MEAN and WHILE.

MEARAH (me'-a-rah)
Jos 13:4 **M.** that is beside the Sidonians, ... 4632

MEASURE See also MEASURED; MEASURES; MEASURING.
Ex 26:2 the curtains shall have one **m.**. 4060
Ex 26:8 curtains shall be all of one **m.**............ 4060
Le 19:35 in meteyard, in weight, or in **m.**. 4884
Nu 35:5 ye shall **m.** from without the city 4058
De 21:2 they shall **m.** unto the cities which 4058
De 25:15 and just **m.** shalt thou have: that......... 374
Jos 3:4 about two thousand cubits by **m.**:....... 4060
1Ki 6:25 were of one **m.** and one size............ 4060
1Ki 7:37 one casting, one **m.**, and one size. 4060
2Ki 7:1 shall a **m.** of fine flour be sold for 5429
2Ki 7:16 So a **m.** of fine flour was sold for a 5429
2Ki 7:18 a **m.** of fine flour for a shekel, shall.... 5429
1Ch 23:29 and for all manner of **m.** and size; 4884
2Ch 3:3 first **m.** was threescore cubits, ... 4060
Job 11:9 The **m.** thereof is longer than the 4055
Job 28:25 he weigheth the waters by **m.**. 4060
Ps 39:4 and the **m.** of my days, what it is; 4060
Ps 80:5 them tears to drink in great **m.**. 7991
Isa 5:14 opened her mouth without **m.**:.......... 2706
Isa 27:8 In **m.**, when it shooteth forth, ... 5432
Isa 40:12 the dust of the earth in a **m.**, and...... 7991
Isa 65:7 I **m.** their former work into their 4058
Jer 30:11 but I will correct thee in **m.**, and 4941
Jer 46:28 end of thee, but correct thee in **m.**; ... 4941
Jer 51:13 and the **m.** of thy covetousness........... 520
Eze 4:11 Thou shalt drink also water by **m.**, ... 4884
Eze 4:16 and they shall drink water by **m.**,....... 4884
Eze 40:10 side; they three were of one **m.**: 4060
Eze 40:10 the posts had one **m.** on this side 4060
Eze 40:21 were after the **m.** of the first gate:..... 4060
Eze 40:22 were after the **m.** of the gate that...... 4060
Eze 41:17 about within and without, by **m.**......... 4060
Eze 43:10 and let them **m.** the pattern. 4058
Eze 45:3 of this **m.** shalt thou...the length........ 4060
Eze 45:3 of this...shalt thou **m.** the length........ 4058
Eze 45:11 and the bath shall be of one **m.**, ... 8506
Eze 45:11 the **m.** thereof shall be after the........ 4971
Eze 46:22 these four corners were of one **m.**..... 4060
Eze 47:18 east side ye shall **m.** from Hauran, ... 4058
Mic 6:10 the scant **m.** that is abominable?.......... 374
Zec 2:2 To **m.** Jerusalem, to see what is........ 4058
Mt 7:2 **and with what m. ye mete, it** *3358*
Mt 23:32 **Fill ye up then the m. of your** *3358*
Mk 4:24 **With what m. ye mete, it shall be** ..*3358*
Mk 6:51 in themselves beyond **m.**, and *4053*
Mk 7:37 And were beyond **m.** astonished, ... *5249*
Mk 10:26 they were astonished out of **m.**, ... *4057*
Lu 6:38 **good m. pressed down, and** *3358*
Lu 6:38 **For with the same m. that ye** *3358*
Joh 3:34 not the Spirit by **m.** unto him. *3358*
Ro 12:3 dealt to every man the **m.** of faith...... *3358*
2Co 1:8 we were pressed out of **m.**,.............. *5236*
2Co 10:13 not boast of things without our **m.**, ... *280*
2Co 10:13 but according to the **m.** of the rule..... *3358*
2Co 10:13 to us, a **m.** to reach even unto you. ... *3358*
2Co 10:14 stretch not ourselves beyond our **m.**,........
2Co 10:15 boasting of things without our **m.**,........ *280*
2Co 11:23 in stripes above **m.**, in prisons........... *5234*
2Co 12:7 lest I should be exalted above **m.**.............
2Co 12:7 lest I should be exalted above **m.**.............
Ga 1:13 beyond **m.** I persecuted the.............. *5236*
Eph 4:7 to the **m.** of the gift of Christ............ *3358*
Eph 4:13 the **m.** of the stature of the fulness *3358*
Eph 4:16 working in the **m.** of every part, ... *3358*
Re 6:6 A **m.** of wheat for a penny, and......... *5518*
Re 11:1 Rise, and **m.** the temple of God,........ *3354*
Re 11:2 temple leave out, and **m.** it not;........ *3354*
Re 21:15 had a golden reed to **m.** the city, ... *3354*
Re 21:17 according to the **m.** of a man, that *3358*

MEASURED
Ru 3:15 it, he **m.** six measures of barley, ... 4058
2Sa 8:2 Moab, and **m.** them with a line, ... 4058
2Sa 8:2 even with two lines **m.** he to put to.... 4058
Isa 40:12 hath **m.** the waters in the hollow........ 4058
Jer 31:37 If heaven above can be **m.**, and the.... 4058
Jer 33:22 neither the sand of the sea **m.**:.......... 4058
Eze 40:5 he **m.** the breadth of the building, ... 4058
Eze 40:6 and **m.** the threshold of the gate, ... 4058
Eze 40:8 He **m.** also the porch of the gate 4058
Eze 40:9 Then **m.** he the porch of the gate, ... 4058
Eze 40:11 And he **m.** the breadth of the entry..... 4058
Eze 40:13 He **m.** then the gate from the roof..... 4058
Eze 40:19 Then he **m.** the breadth from the....... 4058
Eze 40:20 he **m.** the length thereof, and the....... 4058
Eze 40:23 **m.** from gate to gate an hundred......... 4058
Eze 40:24 and he **m.** the posts thereof and the... 4058
Eze 40:27 and he **m.** from gate to gate toward ... 4058
Eze 40:28 and he **m.** the south gate according.... 4058
Eze 40:32 and he **m.** the gate according to.......... 4058
Eze 40:35 gate, and **m.** it according to these...... 4058
Eze 40:47 So he **m.** the court, an hundred......... 4058
Eze 40:48 and **m.** each post of the porch, five 4058
Eze 41:1 and **m.** the posts, six cubits broad...... 4058
Eze 41:2 and he **m.** the length thereof, forty..... 4058
Eze 41:3 inward, and **m.** the post of the door, .. 4058
Eze 41:4 So he **m.** the length thereof, twenty .. 4058
Eze 41:5 After he **m.** the wall of the house, ... 4058
Eze 41:13 So he **m.** the house, an hundred........ 4058
Eze 41:15 And he **m.** the length of the building... 4058
Eze 42:15 the east, and **m.** it round about. 4058
Eze 42:16 He **m.** the east side with the............. 4058
Eze 42:17 He **m.** the north side, five hundred..... 4058
Eze 42:18 He **m.** the south side, five hundred 4058
Eze 42:19 and **m.** five hundred reeds with the 4058
Eze 42:20 He **m.** it by the four sides: it had a.... 4058
Eze 47:3 eastward he **m.** a thousand cubits,...... 4058
Eze 47:4, 4 Again he **m.** a thousand, and 4058
Eze 47:5 Afterward he **m.** a thousand; and 4058
Ho 1:10 which cannot be **m.** nor numbered;..... 4058
Hab 3:6 He stood, and **m.** the earth: he 4128
Mt 7:2 **mete, it shall be m. to you again** ... *488*
Mk 4:24 **ye mete, it shall be m. to you:** *3354*
Lu 6:38 **withal it shall be m. to you again** ... *488*
Re 21:16 and he **m.** the city with the reed,........ *3354*
Re 21:17 he **m.** the wall thereof, an hundred..... *3354*

MEASURES
Ge 18:6 quickly three **m.** of fine meal,............ 5429
De 25:14 not have in thine house divers **m.**,....... 374
Ru 3:15 he measured six **m.** of barley, and...........
Ru 3:17 These six **m.** of barley gave he me; ....
1Sa 25:18 five **m.** of parched corn, and an......... 5429
1Ki 4:22 one day was thirty **m.** of fine flour, ... 3734
1Ki 4:22 flour, and threescore **m.** of meal,......... 3734
1Ki 5:11 Hiram twenty thousand **m.** of wheat ... 3734
1Ki 5:11 and twenty **m.** of pure oil: 3734
1Ki 7:9 to the **m.** of hewed stones,............... 4060
1Ki 7:11 after the **m.** of hewed stones, and....... 4060
1Ki 18:32 as would contain two **m.** of seed.......... 5429
2Ki 7:1, 16 and two **m.** of barley for a shekel, ..5429
2Ki 7:18 Two **m.** of barley for a shekel, and..... 5429
2Ch 2:10 thousand **m.** of beaten wheat, and...... 3734
2Ch 2:10 twenty thousand **m.** of barley, and...... 3734
2Ch 27:5 ten thousand **m.** of wheat, and ten..... 3734
Ezr 7:22 and to an hundred **m.** of wheat, and ... 3734
Job 38:5 Who hath laid the **m.** thereof, if......... 4461
Pr 20:10 Divers weights, and divers **m.**, ... 374
Jer 13:25 the portion of thy **m.** from me,........... 4055
Eze 40:24 thereof according to these **m.**............ 4060
Eze 40:28 south gate according to these **m.**; 4060
Eze 40:29 thereof, according to these **m.**:.......... 4060
Eze 40:32 the gate according to these **m.**. 4060
Eze 40:33 thereof, were according to these **m.**: .. 4060
Eze 40:35 measured it according to these **m.**;..... 4060
Eze 43:13 these are the **m.** of the altar after...... 4060
Eze 48:16 And these shall be the **m.** thereof; 4060
Eze 48:30 four thousand and five hundred **m.**....... 4060
Eze 48:33 four thousand and five hundred **m.**:...... 4060
Eze 48:35 round about eighteen thousand **m.**: ....
Hag 2:16 one came to an heap of twenty **m.**, ...
Mt 13:33 **took, and hid in three m. of meal,** ..*4568*
Lu 13:21 **took and hid in three m. of meal,** .. *4568*
Lu 16:6 **And he said, An hundred m. of oil** .. *943*
Lu 16:7 **he said, An hundred m. of wheat** ... *2884*
Re 6:6 three **m.** of barley for a penny;.......... *5518*

MEASURING
Jer 31:39 the **m.** line shall yet go forth over...... 4060
Eze 40:3 of flax in his hand, and a **m.** reed;...... 4060
Eze 40:5 in the man's hand a **m.** reed of six 4060
Eze 42:15 made an end of **m.** the inner house, ... 4060
Eze 42:16 the east side with the **m.** reed, ... 4060
Eze 42:16, 17 with the **m.** reed round about........ 4060
Eze 42:18 hundred reeds, with the **m.** reed........ 4060
Eze 42:19 hundred reeds with the **m.** reed........ 4060
Zec 2:1 a man with a **m.** line in his hand. 4060
2Co 10:12 they **m.** themselves by themselves, ... *3354*

MEASURING-LINE See MEASURING and LINE.

MEAT See also MEATS.
Ge 1:29 seed; to you it shall be for **m.**............. 402
Ge 1:30 have given every green herb for **m.**: 402
Ge 9:3 that liveth shall be **m.** for you; 402
Ge 24:33 there was set **m.** before him....................
Ge 27:4 make me savoury **m.**, such as I...............
Ge 27:7 make me savoury **m.**, that I may ....
Ge 27:9 make them savoury **m.** for thy.................
Ge 27:14 and his mother made savoury **m.**, ...
Ge 27:17 she gave the savoury **m.** and the ....
Ge 27:31 And he also had made savoury **m.**,...........
Ge 45:23 laden with corn and bread and **m.**........ 4202
Ex 29:41 to the **m.** offering of the morning, ...
Ex 30:9 nor burnt sacrifice, nor **m.** offering; ....
Ex 40:29 burnt offering and the **m.** offering; ....
Le 2:1 when any will offer a **m.** offering..............
Le 2:3 remnant of the **m.** offering shall be............
Le 2:4 bring an oblation of a **m.** offering...............
Le 2:5 And if thy oblation be a **m.** offering...........
Le 2:6 oil thereon: it is a **m.** offering...................
Le 2:7 And if thy oblation be a **m.** offering...........
Le 2:8 thou shalt bring the **m.** offering................
Le 2:9 shall take from the **m.** offering..................
Le 2:10 that which is left of the **m.** offering...........
Le 2:11 No **m.** offering, which ye shall bring ....
Le 2:13 every oblation of thy **m.** offering ....
Le 2:13 to be lacking from thy **m.** offering: ....
Le 2:14 offer a **m.** offering of thy firstfruits ....
Le 2:14 thou shalt offer for the **m.** offering.............
Le 2:15 thereon: it is a **m.** offering.......................
Le 5:13 be the priest's, as a **m.** offering. ....
Le 6:14 this is the law of the **m.** offering: ....
Le 6:15 of the flour of the **m.** offering, ...
Le 6:15 which is upon the **m.** offering, ...
Le 6:20 flour for a **m.** offering perpetual, ...
Le 6:21 the baken pieces of the **m.** offering.............
Le 6:23 every **m.** offering for the priest...................
Le 7:9 And all the **m.** offering that is baken.........
Le 7:10 every **m.** offering, mingled with oil, ...
Le 7:37 burnt offering, of the **m.** offering,.............
Le 9:4 and a **m.** offering mingled with oil:.............
Le 9:17 he brought the **m.** offering, and took.........
Le 10:12 Take the **m.** offering that remaineth..........
Le 11:34 Of all **m.** which may be eaten, that 400
Le 14:10 deals of fine flour for a **m.** offering, ...
Le 14:20 and the **m.** offering upon the altar: ....
Le 14:21 mingled with oil for a **m.** offering,..............
Le 14:31 offering, with the **m.** offering:..................
Le 22:11 house: they shall eat of his **m.**.......... 3899
Le 22:13 she shall eat of her father's **m.**: 3899

Le 23:13 the **m.** offering thereof shall be
Le 23:16 shall offer a new **m.** offering unto
Le 23:18 the Lord, with their **m.** offering,
Le 23:37 a burnt offering, and a **m.** offering,
Le 25:6 of the land shall be **m.** for you; 402
Le 25:7 all the increase thereof be **m.** 398
Nu 4:16 and the daily **m.** offering,
Nu 6:15 and their **m.** offering, and their
Nu 6:17 shall offer also his **m.** offering,
Nu 7:13, 19,25,31,37,43,49,55,61,67,73,79
flour mingled with oil for a **m.** offering
Nu 7:87 twelve, with their **m.** offering:
Nu 8:8 young bullock with his **m.** offering,
Nu 15:4 bring a **m.** offering of a tenth deal
Nu 15:6 shalt prepare for a **m.** offering
Nu 15:9 a **m.** offering of three tenth deals of
Nu 15:24 with his **m.** offering, and his drink
Nu 18:9 every **m.** offering of theirs, and
Nu 28:5 ephah of flour for a **m.** offering,
Nu 28:8 as the **m.** offering of the morning,
Nu 28:9, 12,12 of flour for a **m.** offering,
Nu 28:13 mingled with oil for a **m.** offering
Nu 28:20 their **m.** offering shall be of flour
Nu 28:24 **m.** of the sacrifice made by fire, 3899
Nu 28:26 when ye bring a new **m.** offering
Nu 28:28 **m.** offering of flour mingled with
Nu 28:31 offering, and his **m.** offering,
Nu 29:3 their **m.** offering shall be of flour
Nu 29:6 his **m.** offering, and the daily burnt
Nu 29:6 and his **m.** offering, and their drink
Nu 29:9 their **m.** offerings shall be of flour
Nu 29:11 and the **m.** offering of it, and their
Nu 29:14 their **m.** offering shall be of flour
Nu 29:16 his **m.** offering, and his drink
Nu 29:18 their **m.** offering and their drink
Nu 29:19 the **m.** offering thereof, and their
Nu 29:21 their **m.** offering and their drink
Nu 29:22 burnt offering, and his **m.** offering,
Nu 29:24 Their **m.** offering and their drink
Nu 29:25 burnt offering, his **m.** offering, and
Nu 29:27 their **m.** offering and their drink
Nu 29:28 and his **m.** offering, and his drink
Nu 29:30 their **m.** offering and their drink
Nu 29:31 his **m.** offering, and his drink
Nu 29:33 their **m.** offering and their drink
Nu 29:34 his **m.** offering, and his drink
Nu 29:37 Their **m.** offering and their drink
Nu 29:38 and his **m.** offerings, and his drink
Nu 29:39 for your **m.** offerings, and for your
De 2:6 Ye shall buy **m.** of them for money, 400
De 2:28 Thou shalt sell me **m.** for money, 400
De 20:20 that they be not trees for **m.**, thou 3978
De 28:26 thy carcase shall be **m.** unto all 3978
Jos 22:23 burnt offering or **m.** offering,
Jos 22:29 burnt offerings, for **m.** offerings, or
Jg 1:7 off, gathered their **m.** under my table:
Jg 13:19 took a kid with a **m.** offering, and
Jg 13:23 and a **m.** offering at our hands,
Jg 14:14 Out of the eater came forth **m.**, 3978
1Sa 20:5 not fail to sit with the king at **m.**: 398
1Sa 20:24 the king sat down to eat **m.** 3899
1Sa 20:27 cometh not the son of Jesse to **m.**, 3899
1Sa 20:34 did eat no **m.** the second day of the 3899
2Sa 3:35 to eat **m.** while it was yet day, 3899
2Sa 11:8 him a mess of **m.** from the king
2Sa 12:3 it did eat of his own **m.**, and drank 6595
2Sa 13:5 Tamar come, and give me **m.**, 3899
2Sa 13:5 dress the **m.** in my sight, that I 1279
2Sa 13:7 Amnon's house, and dress him **m.** 1279
2Sa 13:10 Bring the **m.** into the chamber, 1279
1Ki 8:64, 64 offerings, and **m.** offerings,
1Ki 10:5 the **m.** of his table, and the sitting 3978
1Ki 19:8 the strength of that **m.** forty days 396
2Ki 3:20 when the **m.** offering was offered,
2Ki 16:13 burnt offering, and his **m.** offering,
2Ki 16:15 evening **m.** offering, and the king's
2Ki 16:15 and his **m.** offering, with the burnt
2Ki 16:15 their **m.** offering, and their drink
1Ch 12:40 an oxen, and **m.**, meal, cakes of 3978
1Ch 21:23 and the wheat for the **m.** offering;
1Ch 23:29 fine flour for **m.** offering, and for
2Ch 7:7 and the **m.** offerings, and the fat
2Ch 9:4 And the **m.** of his table, and the 3978
Ezr 3:7 and **m.**, and drink, and oil, unto 3978
Ezr 7:17 their **m.** offerings and their drink
Ne 10:33 for the continual **m.** offering, and
Ne 13:5 aforetime they laid the **m.** offerings,
Ne 13:9 **m.** offering and the frankincense,
Job 6:7 to touch are as my sorrowful **m.** 3899
Job 12:11 words? and the mouth taste his **m.**? 400
Job 20:14 his **m.** in his bowels is turned, it 3899
Job 20:21 There shall none of his **m.** be left; 400
Job 30:4 and juniper roots for their **m.** 3899
Job 33:20 bread, and his soul dainty **m.** 3978
Job 34:3 words, as the mouth tasteth **m.** 398
Job 36:31 people; he giveth **m.** in abundance. 400
Job 38:41 God, they wander for lack of **m.** 400
Ps 42:3 My tears have been my **m.** day 3899
Ps 44:11 us like sheep appointed for **m.**; 3978
Ps 59:15 them wander up and down for **m.**, 398
Ps 69:21 They gave me also gall for my **m.**; 1267
Ps 74:14 gavest him to be **m.** to the people 3978
Ps 78:18 heart by asking **m.** for their lust. 400
Ps 78:25 food: he sent them **m.** to the full. 6720
Ps 78:30 their **m.** was yet in their mouths, 400
Ps 79:2 servants have they given to be **m.** 3978
Ps 104:21 prey, and seek their **m.** from God. 400
Ps 104:27 give them their **m.** in due season. 400
Ps 107:18 soul abhorreth all manner of **m.**; 400
Ps 111:5 hath given **m.** unto them that fear 2964
Ps 145:15 givest them their **m.** in due season. 400
Pr 6:8 Provideth her **m.** in the summer, 3899
Pr 23:3 dainties: for they are deceitful **m.** 3899
Pr 30:22 and a fool when he is filled with **m.**; 3899
Pr 30:25 prepare their **m.** in the summer; 3899
Pr 31:15 giveth **m.** to her household, and a 2964
Isa 57:6 thou hast offered a **m.** offering
Isa 62:8 no more give thy corn to be **m.** 3978
Isa 65:25 dust shall be the serpent's **m.** 3899
Jer 7:33 carcases of this people shall be **m.** 3978
Jer 16:4 carcases shall be **m.** for the fowls 3978
Jer 17:26 and **m.** offerings, and incense, and
Jer 19:7 will I give to be **m.** for the fowls 3978
Jer 33:18 to kindle **m.** offerings, and to do
Jer 34:20 dead bodies shall be for **m.** unto 3978
La 1:11 given their pleasant things for **m.** 400
La 1:19 they sought their **m.** to relieve 400
La 4:10 were their **m.** in the destruction 1262
Eze 4:10 thy **m.** which thou shalt eat shall 3978
Eze 16:19 My **m.** also which I gave thee, 3899
Eze 29:5 given thee for **m.** to the beasts of 402
Eze 34:5 became **m.** to all the beasts of the 402
Eze 34:8 flock became **m.** to every beast of 402
Eze 34:10 that they may not be **m.** for them 402
Eze 42:13 holy things, and the **m.** offering,
Eze 44:29 They shall eat the **m.** offering, and
Eze 45:15 for a **m.** offering, and for a burnt
Eze 45:17 burnt offerings, and **m.** offerings,
Eze 45:17 and the **m.** offerings, and the burnt
Eze 45:24 he shall prepare a **m.** offering of an
Eze 45:25 according to the **m.** offering, and
Eze 46:5 **m.** offering shall be an ephah for
Eze 46:5 the **m.** offering for the lambs as he
Eze 46:7 he shall prepare a **m.** offering, an
Eze 46:11 the **m.** offering shall be an ephah
Eze 46:14 shalt prepare a **m.** offering for it
Eze 46:14 a **m.** offering continually by a
Eze 46:15 the **m.** offering, and the oil, every
Eze 46:20 they shall bake the **m.** offering;
Eze 47:12 shall grow all trees for **m.**, whose 3978
Eze 47:12 the fruit there of shall be for **m.**, 3978
Da 1:5 a daily provision of the king's **m.**, 6598
Da 1:8 with the portion of the king's **m.**, 6598
Da 1:10 hath appointed your **m.** and your 3978
Da 1:13 eat of the portion of the king's **m.**: 6598
Da 1:15 eat the portion of the king's **m.** 6598
Da 1:16 took away the portion of their **m.**, 6598
Da 4:12 much, and in it was **m.** for all: 4203
Da 4:21 much, and in it was **m.** for all; 4203
Da 11:26 feed of the portion of his **m.** shall 6598
Ho 11:4 their jaws, and I laid **m.** unto them. 398
Joe 1:9 The **m.** offering and the drink
Joe 1:13 for the **m.** offering and the drink
Joe 1:16 Is not the **m.** cut off before our 400
Joe 2:14 a **m.** offering and a drink offering
Am 5:22 offerings and your **m.** offerings,
Hab 1:16 is fat, and their **m.** plenteous. 3978
Hab 3:17 and the fields shall yield no **m.**; 400
Hag 2:12 pottage, or wine, or oil, or any **m.**, 3978
Mal 1:12 even his **m.**, is contemptible. 400
Mal 3:10 there may be **m.** in mine house, 2964
Mt 3:4 his **m.** was locusts and wild honey *5160*
Mt 6:25 **Is not the life more than m., and** *5160*
Mt 9:10 as Jesus sat at **m.** in the house,
Mt 10:10 **the workman is worthy of his m.** *5160*
Mt 14:9 and them which sat with him at **m.**,
Mt 15:37 broken **m.** that was left seven baskets
Mt 24:45 **to give them m. in due season?** *5160*
Mt 25:35 **an hungred, and ye gave me m.:** *5315*
Mt 25:42 **hungred, and ye gave me no m.:** *5315*
Mt 26:7 poured it on his head, as he sat at **m.**
Mk 2:15 as Jesus sat at **m.** in his house,
Mk 8:8 broken **m.** that was left seven baskets.
Mk 14:3 as he sat at **m.**, there came a woman
Mk 16:14 unto the eleven as they sat at **m.**,
Lu 3:11 and he that hath **m.**, let him do *1033*
Lu 7:36 Pharisee's house, and sat down to **m.**
Lu 7:37 sat at **m.** in the Pharisee's house,
Lu 7:49 they that sat at **m.** with him began to
Lu 8:55 and he commanded to give her **m.** *5315*
Lu 9:13 go and buy **m.** for all this people *1033*
Lu 11:37 and he went in, and sat down to **m.**
Lu 12:23 **The life is more than m., and the** *5160*
Lu 12:37 **and make them to sit down to m.,**
Lu 12:42 **their portion of m. in due season?** *4620*
Lu 14:10 **of them that sit at m. with thee.**
Lu 14:15 them that sat at **m.** with him heard
Lu 17:7 **the field, Go and sit down to m.?**
Lu 22:27 **is greater, he that sitteth at m., or**
Lu 22:27 **serveth? is not he that sitteth at m.?**
Lu 24:30 as he sat at **m.** with them, he took
Lu 24:41 unto them, **Have ye here any m.?** *1034*
Joh 4:8 away unto the city to buy **m.**) *5160*
Joh 4:32 **have m. to eat that ye know not** *1035*
Joh 4:34 **My m. is to do the will of him** *1033*
Joh 6:27 **not for the m. which perisheth,** *1035*
Joh 6:27 **m. which endureth unto** *1035*
Joh 6:55 **For my flesh is m. indeed,** *1035*
Joh 21:5 them, **Children, have ye any m.?** *4371*
Ac 2:46 did eat their **m.** with gladness and *5160*
Ac 9:19 received **m.**, he was strengthened *5160*
Ac 16:34 set **m.** before them, and rejoiced, *5132*
Ac 27:33 besought them all to take **m.**, *5160*
Ac 27:34 I pray you to take some **m.**: for *5160*
Ac 27:36 cheer, and they also took some **m.** *5160*
Ro 14:15 brother be grieved with thy **m.**, *1033*
Ro 14:15 Destroy not him with thy **m.**, for *1033*
Ro 14:17 the kingdom of God is not **m.** and *1035*
Ro 14:20 **m.** destroy not the work of God. *1033*
1Co 3:2 fed you with milk, and not with **m.**: *1033*
1Co 8:8 But **m.** commendeth us not to God: *1033*
1Co 8:10 sit at **m.** in the idol's temple,
1Co 8:13 if **m.** make my brother to offend, *1033*
1Co 10:3 did all eat the same spiritual **m.**; *1033*
Col 2:16 no man therefore judge you in **m.**, *1035*
Heb 5:12 of milk, and not of strong **m.** *5160*
Heb 5:14 strong **m.** belongeth to them that *5160*
Heb 12:16 morsel of **m.** sold his birthright *1035*

MEAT-OFFERING See MEAT and OFFERING.

MEATS See also BAKEMEATS.
Pr 23:6 neither desire thou his dainty **m.**:
Mk 7:19 **into the draught, purging all m.?** *1033*
Ac 15:29 abstain from **m.** offered to idols,
1Co 6:13 **M.** for the belly, and the belly for *1033*
1Co 6:13 and the belly for **m.**: but God shall *1033*
1Ti 4:3 commanding to abstain from **m.**, *1033*
Heb 9:10 Which stood only in **m.** and drinks, *1033*
Heb 13:9 not with **m.**, which have not *1033*

MEBUNNAI (me-bun'-nahee) See also SIBBECHAI.
2Sa 23:27 Anethothite, **M.** the Hushathite, 4012

MECHERATHITE (me-ker'-ath-ite)
1Ch 11:36 Hepher the **M.**, Ahijah the 4382

MEDAD (me'-dad)
Nu 11:26 and the name of the other **M.**: 4312
Nu 11:27 Eldad and **M.** do prophesy in the 4312

MEDAN (me'-dan)
Ge 25:2 Zimran, and Jokshan, and **M.**, 4091
1Ch 1:32 **M.**, and Midian, and Ishbak, and 4091

MEDDLE See also INTERMEDDLE; MEDDLED; MEDDLETH; MEDDLING.
De 2:5 **M.** not with them; for I will not 1624
De 2:19 them not, nor **m.** with them: 1624
2Ki 14:10 why shouldest thou **m.** to thy hurt, 1624
2Ch 25:19 shouldest thou **m.** to thine hurt, 1624
Pr 20:19 **m.** not with him that flattereth 6148
Pr 24:21 **m.** not with them that are given to 6148

MEDDLED
Pr 17:14 contention, before it be **m.** with 1566

MEDDLETH See also INTERMEDDLETH.
Pr 26:17 **m.** with strife belonging not to 5674

MEDDLING
2Ch 35:21 forbear thee from **m.** with God, who
Pr 20:3 strife: but every fool will be **m.** 1566

MEDE (meed) See also MEDES; MEDIAN.
Da 11:1 in the first year of Darius the **M.**, 4075

MEDEBA (med'-e-bah)
Nu 21:30 Nophah, which reacheth unto **M.** 4311
Jos 13:9 and all the plain of **M.** unto Dibon; 4311
Jos 13:16 the river, and all the plain by **M.**; 4311
1Ch 19:7 who came and pitched before **M.** 4311
Isa 15:2 shall howl over Nebo, and over **M.**: 4311

MEDES (meeds)
2Ki 17:6 Gozan, and in the cities of the **M.** 4074
2Ki 18:11 Gozan, and in the cities of the **M.**: 4074
Ezr 6:2 that is in the province of the **M.**, 4074
Es 1:19 laws of the Persians and the **M.**, 4074
Isa 13:17 I will stir up the **M.** against them, 4074
Jer 25:25 Elam, and all the kings of the **M.**, 4074
Jer 51:11 up the spirit of the kings of the **M.**: 4074
Jer 51:28 nations with the kings of the **M.**, 4074
Da 5:28 is divided, and given to the **M.** and 4076
Da 6:8,12 according to the law of the **M.** 4076
Da 6:15 O king, that the law of the **M.** and 4076
Da 9:1 Ahasuerus, of the seed of the **M.**, 4074
Ac 2:9 Parthians, and **M.**, and Elamites, *3370*

MEDIA (me'-de-ah) See also MADAI; MEDE; MEDIAN.
Es 1:3 power of Persia and **M.**, the nobles 4074
Es 1:14 the seven princes of Persia and **M.**, 4074
Es 1:18 shall the ladies of Persia and **M.** 4074
Es 10:2 of the chronicles of the kings of **M.** 4074
Isa 21:2 Go up, O Elam: besiege, O **M.**; all 4074
Da 8:20 two horns are the kings of **M.** and 4074

MEDIAN (me'-de-an) See also MEDE.
Da 5:31 Darius the **M.** took the kingdom, 4077

MEDIATOR
Ga 3:19 by angels in the hand of a **m.** *3316*
Ga 3:20 a **m.** is not...of one, but God is one. *3316*
Ga 3:20 is not a **m.** of one, but God is one.
1Ti 2:5 and one **m.** between God and men, *3316*
Heb 8:6 he is the **m.** of a better covenant, *3316*
Heb 9:15 he is the **m.** of the new testament, *3316*
Heb 12:24 Jesus the **m.** of the new covenant, *3316*

MEDICINE See also MEDICINES.
Pr 17:22 merry heart doth good like a **m.**: 1456
Eze 47:12 meat, and the leaf thereof for **m.** 8644

MEDICINES
Jer 30:3 up: thou hast no healing **m.** 7499
Jer 46:11 in vain shalt thou use many **m.**; 7499

MEDITATE See also PREMEDITATE.
Ge 24:63 went out to **m.** in the field at the
Jos 1:8 shalt **m.** therein day and night, 1897
Ps 1:2 his law doth he **m.** day and night. 1897
Ps 63:6 **m.** on thee in the night watches. 1897
Ps 77:12 I will **m.** also of all thy work, and 1897
Ps 119:15 I will **m.** in thy precepts, and have 7878
Ps 119:23 thy servant did **m.** in thy statutes. 7878
Ps 119:48 loved; and I will **m.** in thy statutes. 7878
Ps 119:78 cause: but I will **m.** in thy precepts. 7878
Ps 119:148 that I might **m.** in thy word. 7878
Ps 143:5 I **m.** on all thy works; I muse on 1897
Isa 33:18 Thine heart shall **m.** terror. Where 1897
Lu 21:14 **not to m. before what ye shall** *4304*
1Ti 4:15 **M.** upon these things; give thyself *3191*

MEDITATION
Ps 5:1 words, O Lord, consider my **m.** 1901
Ps 19:14 the **m.** of my heart, be acceptable 1902
Ps 49:3 **m.** of my heart...be understanding 1900
Ps 104:34 My **m.** of him shall be sweet: I will 7879
Ps 119:97 I thy law! it is my **m.** all the day. 7881
Ps 119:99 for thy testimonies are my **m.** 7881

MEEK
Nu 12:3 man Moses was very **m.**, above all 6035
Ps 22:26 The **m.** shall eat and be satisfied: 6035
Ps 25:9 The **m.** will he guide in judgment: 6035
Ps 25:9 and the **m.** will he teach his way. 6035
Ps 37:11 But the **m.** shall inherit the earth; 6035
Ps 76:9 to save all the **m.** of the earth. 6035
Ps 147:6 The Lord lifteth up the **m.**: he 6035
Ps 149:4 will beautify the **m.** with salvation. 6035
Isa 11:4 with equity for the **m.** of the earth: 6035
Isa 29:19 The **m.** also shall increase their joy 6035
Isa 61:1 preach good tidings unto the **m.**; 6035
Am 2:7 and turn aside the way of the **m.**: 6035
Zep 2:3 ye the Lord, all ye **m.** of the earth, 6035
Mt 5:5 **Blessed are the m.: for they shall** *4239*
Mt 11:29 **for I am m. and lowly in heart:** *4235*
Mt 21:5 thee, **m.**, and sitting upon an ass, *4239*
1Pe 3:4 ornament of a **m.** and quiet spirit, *4239*

MEEKNESS
Ps 45:4 truth and **m.** and righteousness; 6037
Zep 2:3 seek righteousness, seek **m.**: it 6038
1Co 4:21 or in love, and in the spirit of **m.**? *4236*
2Co 10:1 by the **m.** and gentleness of Christ, *4236*
Ga 5:23 **M.**, temperance: against such *4236*
Ga 6:1 such an one in the spirit of **m.**; *4236*
Eph 4:2 With all lowliness and **m.**, with *4236*
Col 3:12 of mind, **m.**, longsuffering; *4236*
1Ti 6:11 godliness, faith, love, patience, **m.** *4236*
2Ti 2:25 In **m.** instructing those that oppose *4236*
Tit 3:2 gentle, shewing all **m.** unto all men. *4236*
Jas 1:21 and receive with **m.** the engrafted *4240*
Jas 3:13 his works with **m.** of wisdom. *4240*
1Pe 3:15 that is in you with **m.** and fear: *4240*

MEET See also MEETEST; MEETETH; MEETING; MET.
Ge 2:18 will make him an help **m.** for him. 5828
Ge 2:20 was not found an help **m.** for him. 5828
Ge 14:17 king of Sodom went out to **m.** him, 7125
Ge 18:2 he ran to **m.** them from the tent 7125
Ge 19:1 seeing them rose up to **m.** them; 7125
Ge 24:17 servant ran to **m.** her, and said, Let 7125
Ge 24:65 that walketh in the field to **m.** us? 7125
Ge 29:13 he ran to **m.** him, and embraced 7125
Ge 30:16 Leah went out to **m.** him, and said, 7125
Ge 32:6 and also he cometh to **m.** thee, and 7125
Ge 33:4 Esau ran to **m.** him, and embraced 7125
Ge 46:29 went up to **m.** Israel his father, to 7125
Ex 4:14 behold, he cometh forth to **m.** thee: 7125
Ex 4:27 Go into the wilderness to **m.** Moses. 7125
Ex 8:26 Moses said, It is not **m.** so to do; 3559
Ex 18:7 went out to **m.** his father in law, 7125
Ex 19:17 out of the camp to **m.** with God; 7125
Ex 23:4 If thou **m.** thine enemy's ox or his 6293
Ex 25:22 there I will **m.** with thee, and I 3259
Ex 29:42 where I will **m.** you, to speak there 3259
Ex 29:43 I will **m.** with the children of Israel, 3259
Ex 30:6 testimony, where I will **m.**...thee: 3259
Ex 30:36 where I will **m.** with thee: it 3259
Nu 17:4 testimony, where I will **m.** with you. 3259
Nu 22:36 he went out to **m.** him unto a city 7125
Nu 23:3 the Lord will come to **m.** me: and 7125
Nu 23:15 while I **m.** the Lord yonder. 7136
Nu 31:13 to **m.** them without the camp. 7125
De 3:18 Israel, all that are **m.** for the war. 1121
Jos 2:16 lest the pursuers **m.** you; and 6293
Jos 9:11 and go to **m.** them, and say unto 7125
Jg 4:18 Jael went out to **m.** Sisera, and said 7125
Jg 4:22 Jael came out to **m.** him, and said 7125
Jg 5:30 **m.** for the necks of them that take
Jg 6:35 and they came up to **m.** them. 7125
Jg 11:31 of the doors of my house to **m.** me, 7125
Jg 11:34 came out to **m.** him with timbrels. 7125
Jg 19:3 saw him, he rejoiced to **m.** him. 7125
Ru 2:22 that they **m.** thee not in any other 6293
1Sa 10:3 and there shall **m.** thee three men 4672
1Sa 10:5 that thou shalt **m.** a company of 6293
1Sa 13:10 Saul went out to **m.** him, that he 7125
1Sa 15:12 Samuel rose early to **m.** Saul in the 7125
1Sa 17:48 drew nigh to **m.** David, that David 7125
1Sa 17:48 the army to **m.** the Philistine. 7125
1Sa 18:6 to **m.** king Saul, with tabrets, with 7125
1Sa 25:32 which sent thee this day to **m.** me: 7125
1Sa 25:34 hadst hasted and come to **m.** me, 7125
1Sa 30:21 they went forth to **m.** David, and to 7125
1Sa 30:21 **m.** the people that were with him: 7125
2Sa 6:20 of Saul came out to **m.** David, 7125
2Sa 10:5 he sent to **m.** them, because the 7125
2Sa 15:32 the Archite came to **m.** him with his 7125
2Sa 19:15 came to Gilgal, to go to **m.** the king, 7125
2Sa 19:16 the men of Judah to **m.** king David. 7125
2Sa 19:20 to go down to **m.** my lord the king. 7125
2Sa 19:24 of Saul came down to **m.** the king, 7125
2Sa 19:25 come to Jerusalem to **m.** the king, 7125
1Ki 2:8 he came down to **m.** me at Jordan, 7125
1Ki 2:19 And the king rose up to **m.** her, and 7125
1Ki 18:16 Obadiah went to **m.** Ahab, and told 7125
1Ki 18:16 him: and Ahab went to **m.** Elijah. 7125
1Ki 21:18 to go down to **m.** Ahab king of Israel, 7125
2Ki 1:3 go up to **m.** the messengers of the 7125
2Ki 1:6 There came a man up to **m.** us, and 7125
2Ki 1:7 was he which came up to **m.** you, 7125
2Ki 2:15 they came to **m.** him, and bowed 7125
2Ki 4:26 Run now, I pray thee, to **m.** her, 7125
2Ki 4:29 if thou **m.** any man, salute him not; 4672
2Ki 4:31 he went again to **m.** him, and told 7125
2Ki 5:21 down from the chariot to **m.** him, 7125
2Ki 5:26 again from his chariot to **m.** thee? 7125
2Ki 8:8 hand, and go, **m.** the man of God, 7125
2Ki 8:9 Hazael went to **m.** him, and took a 7125
2Ki 9:17 send to **m.** them, and let him say, Is 7125
2Ki 9:18 went one on horseback to **m.** him, 7125
2Ki 10:15 son of Rechab coming to **m.** him: 7125
2Ki 16:10 to Damascus to **m.** Tiglath-pileser 7125
1Ch 12:17 And David went out to **m.** them, 6440
1Ch 19:5 he sent to **m.** them: for the men 7125
2Ch 15:2 he went out to **m.** Asa, and said 6440
2Ch 19:2 Hanani the seer went out to **m.** him, 6440
Ezr 4:14 was not **m.** for us to see the king's 749
Ne 6:2 let us **m.** together in some one of 3259
Ne 6:10 us **m.** together in the house of God, 3259
Es 2:9 which were **m.** to be given her, 7200
Job 5:14 They **m.** with darkness in the 6298
Job 34:31 it is **m.** to be said unto God, I have
Job 39:21 he goeth on to **m.** the armed men. 7125
Pr 7:15 came I forth to **m.** thee, diligently 7125
Pr 11:24 that withholdeth more than is **m.**, 3476
Pr 17:12 robbed of her whelps **m.** a man, 6298
Pr 22:2 The rich and poor **m.** together: the 6298
Pr 29:13 and the deceitful man **m.** together: 6298
Isa 7:3 Isaiah, Go forth now to **m.** Ahaz, 7125
Isa 14:9 is moved for thee to **m.** thee at thy 7125
Isa 34:14 beasts of the desert shall also **m.** 6298
Isa 47:3 and I will not **m.** thee as a man. 6293
Jer 26:14 as seemeth good and **m.** unto you. 3477
Jer 27:5 unto whom it seemed **m.** unto me. 3474
Jer 41:6 forth from Mizpah to **m.** them, 7125
Jer 51:31 One post shall run to **m.** another, 7125
Jer 51:31 and one messenger to **m.** another, 7125
Eze 15:4 burned. Is it **m.** for any work? 6743
Eze 15:5 was whole, it was **m.** for no work: 6213
Eze 15:5 less shall it be **m.** yet for any work, 6213
Ho 13:8 I will **m.** them as a bear that is 6298
Am 4:12 prepare to **m.** thy God, O Israel. 7125
Zec 2:3 another angel went out to **m.** him, 7125
Mt 3:8 therefore fruits **m.** for repentance: *514*
Mt 8:34 city came out to **m.** Jesus: *4877*
Mt 15:26 **not m. to take the children's,** *2570*
Mt 25:1 **forth to m. the bridegroom** *529*
Mt 25:6 **cometh; go ye out to m. him.** *529*
Mk 7:27 **not m. to take the children's,** *2570*
Mk 14:13 **m. you a man bearing a pitcher of** *528*
Lu 14:31 **to m. him that cometh against** *528*
Lu 15:32 **m. that we should make merry,** *1163*
Lu 22:10 **a man m. you, bearing a pitcher** *4876*
Joh 12:13 and went forth to **m.** him, *5222*
Ac 26:20 and do works **m.** for repentance. *514*
Ac 28:15 to **m.** us as far as Appii forum, *529*
Ro 1:27 that recompence...which was **m.** *1163*
1Co 15:9 am not **m.** to be called an apostle, *2425*
1Co 16:4 if it be **m.** that I go also, they shall *514*
Php 1:7 is **m.** for me to think this of you *1342*
Col 1:12 hath made us **m.** to be partakers *2427*
1Th 4:17 to **m.** the Lord in the air: *529*
2Th 1:3 always for you, brethren, as it is **m.**, *514*
2Ti 2:21 and **m.** for the master's use, and *2173*
Heb 6:7 forth herbs **m.** for them by whom *2111*
2Pe 1:13 I think it **m.**, as long as I am in *1342*

MEETEST
2Ki 10:3 the best and **m.** of your master's 3477
Isa 64:5 thou **m.** him that rejoiceth and 6293

MEETETH
Ge 32:17 When Esau my brother **m.** thee, 6298
Nu 35:19 when he **m.** him, he shall slay him. 6293
Nu 35:21 slay the murderer, when he **m.** him. 6293

MEETING
1Sa 21:1 was afraid at the **m.** of David, 7125
Isa 1:13 it is inquity, even the solemn **m.** 6116

MEGIDDO (me-ghid'-do) See also MEGIDDON.
Jos 12:21 one; the king of **M.**, one; 4023
Jos 17:11 inhabitants of **M.** and her towns, ... 4023
Jg 1:27 inhabitants of **M.** and her towns: 4023
Jg 5:19 in Taanach by the waters of **M.**; 4023
1Ki 4:12 to him pertained Taanach and **M.**, ... 4023
1Ki 9:15 and Hazor, and **M.**, and Gezer. 4023
2Ki 9:27 And he fled to **M.**, and died there. 4023
2Ki 23:29 slew him at **M.**, when he had seen 4023
2Ki 23:30 him in a chariot dead from **M.**, ... 4023
1Ch 7:29 **M.** and her towns, Dor and her 4023
2Ch 35:22 came to fight in the valley of **M.**. 4023

MEGIDDON (me-ghid'-don) See also ARMAGEDDON; MEGIDDO.
Zec 12:11 mourning...in the valley of **M.**. 4023

MEHETABEEL (me-het'-a-be-el) See also MEHETABEL.
Ne 6:10 son of Delaiah the son of **M.**, ... 4105

MEHETABEL (me-het'-a-bel) See also MEHETABEEL.
Ge 36:39 wife's name was **M.**, the daughter 4105
1Ch 1:50 wife's name was **M.**, the daughter 4105

MEHIDA (me-hi'-dah)
Ezr 2:52 of Bazluth, the children of **M.**, ... 4240
Ne 7:54 of Bazlith, the children of **M.**, ... 4240

MEHIR (me'-hur)
1Ch 4:11 the brother of Shuah begat **M.**, ... 4243

MEHOLAH See ABEL-BETH-MEHOLAH; MEHOLATHITE.

MEHOLATHITE (me-ho'-lath-ite)
1Sa 18:19 given unto Adriel the **M.** to wife. 4259
2Sa 21:8 Adriel the son of Barzillai the **M.**: 4259

MEHUJAEL (me-hu'-ja-el)
Ge 4:18 and Irad begat **M.**: and **M.** begat 4232

MEHUMAN (me-hu'-man)
Es 1:10 with wine, he commanded **M.**, ... 4104

MEHUNIM (me-hu'-nim) See also MAONITE; MEHUNIMS; MEUNIM.
Ezr 2:50 of Asnah, the children of **M.**, ... 4586

MEHUNIMS (me-hu'-nims) See also MEHUNIM.
2Ch 26:7 dwelt in Gur-baal, and the **M.** 4586

ME-JARKON (me-jar'-kon)
Jos 19:46 **M.**, and Rakkon, with the border 4313

MEKONAH (me-ko'-nah)
Ne 11:28 and at **M.**, and in the villages 4368

MELATIAH (mel-a-ti'-ah)
Ne 3:7 them repaired **M.** the Gibeonite, ... 4424

MELCHI (mel'-ki) See also MELCHI-SHUA; MELCHIZEDEK.
Lu 3:24 which was the son of **M.**, which *3197*
Lu 3:28 Which was the son of **M.**, which *3197*

MELCHIAH (mel-ki'-ah) See also MALCHIAH.
Jer 21:1 unto him Pashur the son of **M.**, ... 4441

MELCHISEDEC (mel-kis'-e-dek) See also MELCHIZEDEK.
Heb 5:6 for ever after the order of **M.**. *3198*
Heb 5:10 high priest after the order of **M.**. *3198*
Heb 6:20 for ever after the order of **M.**. *3198*
Heb 7:1 For this **M.**, king of Salem, priest *3198*
Heb 7:10 of his father, when **M.** met him. *3198*
Heb 7:11 should rise after the order of **M.**, ... *3198*
Heb 7:15 for that after the similitude of **M.** *3198*
Heb 7:17 for ever after the order of **M.**. *3198*
Heb 7:21 for ever after the order of **M.**:) *3198*

MELCHI-SHUA (mel'-ki-shu'-ah) See also MALCHI-SHUA.
1Sa 14:49 Jonathan, and Ishui, and **M.**: 4444
1Sa 31:2 Jonathan, and Abinadab, and **M.**, ... 4444

MELCHIZEDEK (mel-kiz'-e-dek) See also MELCHISEDEC.
Ge 14:18 **M.** king of Salem brought forth 4442
Ps 110:4 for ever after the order of **M.**. 4442

MELEA (mel'-e-ah)
Lu 3:31 Which was the son of **M.** which *3190*

MELECH (me'-lek) See also EBED-MELECH; HAM-MELECH; NATHAN-MELECH; REGEM-MELECH.
1Ch 8:35 of Micah were, Pithon, and **M.**, ... 4429
1Ch 9:41 sons of Micah were, Pithon, and **M.**, .. 4429

MELICU (mel'-i-cu) See also MALLUCH.
Ne 12:14 Of **M.**, Jonathan; of Shebaniah, ... 4409

MELITA (mel'-i-tah)
Ac 28:1 that the island was called **M.**. *3194*

MELODY
Isa 23:16 make sweet **m.**, sing many songs, ... 5059
Isa 51:3 thanksgiving, and the voice of **m.** 2172
Am 5:23 I will not hear the **m.** of thy viols. 2172
Eph 5:19 making **m.** in your heart to the *5567*

MELONS
Nu 11:5 the **m.**, and the leeks, and the onions, ... 20

MELT See also MELTED; MELTETH; MELTING; MOLTEN.
Ex 15:15 inhabitants of Caanan shall **m.** 4127
Jos 2:11 these things, our hearts did **m.**, ... 4549
Jos 14:8 made the heart of the people **m.**: 4529
2Sa 17:10 heart of a lion, shall utterly **m.**: 4549
Ps 58:7 Let them **m.** away as waters which 3988
Ps 112:10 gnash with his teeth, and **m.** away: 4549
Isa 13:7 and every man's heart shall **m.**: 4549
Isa 19:1 heart of Egypt shall **m.** in the midst.... 4549
Jer 9:7 I will **m.** them, and try them; 6884
Eze 21:7 every heart shall **m.**, and all hands 4549
Eze 22:20 to blow the fire upon it, to **m.** it: 5413
Eze 22:20 I will leave you there, and **m.** you. 5413
Am 9:5 toucheth the land, and it shall **m.**, ... 4127
Am 9:13 wine, and all the hills shall **m.**. 4127
Na 1:5 the hills **m.**, and the earth is burned ... 4127
2Pe 3:10 elements shall **m.** with fervent *3089*
2Pe 3:12 elements shall **m.** with fervent *5080*

MELTED See also MOLTEN.
Ex 16:21 when the sun waxed hot, it **m.**. 4549
Jos 5:1 that their heart **m.**, neither was 4549
Jos 7:5 the hearts of the people **m.**, and 4549
Jg 5:5 The mountains **m.** from before 5140
1Sa 14:16 the multitude **m.** away, and they 4127
Ps 22:14 is **m.** in the midst of my bowels. 4549
Ps 46:6 he uttered his voice, the earth **m.**. 4127
Ps 97:5 hills **m.** like wax at the presence 4549
Ps 107:26 their soul is **m.** because of trouble 4127
Isa 34:3 mountains...**m.** with their blood 4549
Eze 22:21 and ye shall be **m.** in the midst 5413
Eze 22:22 As silver is **m.** in the midst of the 2046
Eze 22:22 so shall ye be **m.** in the midst 5413

MELTETH
Ps 58:8 As a snail which **m.**, let every one 8557
Ps 68:2 as wax **m.** before the fire, so let 4549
Ps 119:28 My soul **m.** for heaviness: 1811
Ps 147:18 out this word and **m.** them: he 4529
Isa 40:19 The workman **m.** a graven image, ... 5258
Jer 6:29 the founder **m.** in vain: for the 6884
Na 2:10 and the heart **m.**, and the knees 4549

MELTING
Isa 64:2 As when the **m.** fire burneth, the 2003

MELZAR (mel'-zar)
Da 1:11 Then said Daniel to **M.**, whom 4453
Da 1:16 **M.** took away the portion of their 4453

MEM (mame)
Ps 119:97 *title* [מ] **M.** ....

MEMBER See also MEMBERS.
De 23:1 or hath his privy **m.** cut off, shall not ....
1Co 12:14 For the body is not one **m.**, but *3196*
1Co 12:19 And if they were all one **m.**, where *3196*
1Co 12:26 And whether one **m.** suffer, all the *3196*
1Co 12:26 or one **m.** be honoured, all the *3196*
Jas 3:5 Even so the tongue is a little **m.**, ... *3196*

MEMBERS
Job 17:7 and all my **m.** are as a shadow. 3338
Ps 139:16 in thy book all my **m.** were written, ...
Mt 5:29, 30 **one of thy m. should perish,** *3196*
Ro 6:13 Neither yield ye your **m.** as *3196*
Ro 6:13 and your **m.** as instruments of *3196*
Ro 6:19 as ye have yielded your **m.** servants ... *3196*
Ro 6:19 so now yield your **m.** servants to *3196*
Ro 7:5 did work in our **m.** to bring forth *3196*
Ro 7:23 But I see another law in my **m.**, ... *3196*
Ro 7:23 to the law of sin which is in my **m.** ... *3196*
Ro 12:4 as we have many **m.** in one body, ... *3196*
Ro 12:4 all **m.** have not the same office: *3196*
Ro 12:5 and every one **m.** one of another. *3196*
1Co 6:15 your bodies are the **m.** of Christ? *3196*
1Co 6:15 shall I then take the **m.** of Christ, ... *3196*
1Co 6:15 and make them the **m.** of a harlot? *3196*
1Co 12:12 the body is one, and hath many **m.**, ... *3196*
1Co 12:12 and all the **m.** of that one body, ... *3196*
1Co 12:18 now hath God set the **m.** every one ... *3196*
1Co 12:20 But now are they many **m.**, yet but *3196*
1Co 12:22 much more those **m.** of the body, ... *3196*
1Co 12:23 And those **m.** of the body, which we ....
1Co 12:25 that the **m.** should have the same *3196*
1Co 12:26 suffer, all the **m.** suffer with it; *3196*
1Co 12:26 honoured, all the **m.** rejoice with it. *3196*
1Co 12:27 body of Christ, and **m.** in particular. ... *3196*
Eph 4:25 for we are **m.** one of another. *3196*
Eph 5:30 For we are **m.** of his body, of his *3196*
Col 3:5 Mortify therefore your **m.** which *3196*
Jas 3:6 so is the tongue among our **m.**, that ... *3196*
Jas 4:1 of your lusts that war in your **m.**? *3196*

MEMORIAL
Ex 3:15 is my **m.** unto all generations. 2143
Ex 12:14 day shall be unto you for a **m.**; 2146
Ex 13:9 and for a **m.** between thine eyes, ... 2146
Ex 17:14 Write this for a **m.** in a book, and 2146
Ex 28:12 the ephod for stones of **m.** unto the ... 2146
Ex 28:12 upon his two shoulders for a **m.** 2146
Ex 28:29 for a **m.** before the Lord continually 2146
Ex 30:16 it may be a **m.** unto the children 2146
Ex 39:7 stones for a **m.** to the children of 2146
Le 2:2 the priest shall burn the **m.** of it 234
Le 2:9 from the meat offering a **m.** thereof, ... 234
Le 2:16 the priest shall burn the **m.** of it, ... 234
Le 5:12 even a **m.** thereof, and burn it on the ... 234
Le 6:15 even the **m.** of it, unto the Lord. 234
Le 23:24 a **m.** of blowing of trumpets, an 2146
Le 24:7 it may be on the bread for a **m.**, ... 234
Nu 5:15 an offering of **m.**, bringing iniquity 2146
Nu 5:18 put the offering of **m.** in her hands, ... 2146
Nu 5:26 the **m.** thereof, and burn it upon 234
Nu 10:10 that they may be to you for a **m.** 2146
Nu 16:40 be a **m.** unto the children of Israel, ... 2146
Nu 31:54 for a **m.** for the children of Israel 2146
Jos 4:7 these stones shall be for a **m.** unto 2146
Ne 2:20 nor right, nor **m.**, in Jerusalem. 2146
Es 9:28 the **m.** of them perish from their 2143
Ps 9:6 their **m.** is perished with them. 2143
Ps 135:13 and thy **m.**, O Lord, throughout all 2143
Ho 12:5 God of hosts; the Lord is his **m.** 2143
Zec 6:14 for a **m.** in the temple of the Lord. 2146
Mt 26:13 **hath done, be told for a m. of.** *3422*
Mk 14:9 **shall be spoken of for a m. of.** *3422*
Ac 10:4 thine alms are come up for a **m.** *3422*

MEMORY
Ps 109:15 cut off the **m.** of them from the 2143
Ps 145:7 utter the **m.** of thy great goodness, ... 2143
Pr 10:7 The **m.** of the just is blessed: but 2143
Ec 9:5 for the **m.** of them is forgotten. 2143
Isa 26:14 and made all their **m.** to perish. 2143
1Co 15:2 if ye keep in **m.** what I preached unto ....

MEMPHIS (mem'-fis) See also NOPH.
Ho 9:6 them up, **M.** shall bury them: 4644

MEMUCAN (mem-u'-can)
Es 1:14 Meres, Mersena, and **M.**, the 4462
Es 1:16 **M.** answered before the king and 4462
Es 1:21 did according to the word of **M.**: 4462

MEN See also BONDMEN; BOWMEN; CHAPMEN; COUNTRYMEN; CRAFTSMEN; FISHERMEN; FOOTMEN; HERDMEN; HORSEMEN; HUSBANDMEN; KINSMEN; MENCHILDREN; MENPLEASERS; MEN'S; MENSERVANTS; MENSTEALERS; MERCHANTMEN; PLOWMEN; SHIPMEN; SPEARMEN; WATCHMEN; WORKMEN; WOMEN.
Ge 4:26 then began **m.** to call upon the name ....
Ge 6:1 **m.** began to multiply on the face 120
Ge 6:2 daughters of **m.** that they were fair; 120
Ge 6:4 came in unto the daughters of **m.**, ... 120
Ge 6:4 the same became mighty **m.** which 120
Ge 6:4 which were of old, **m.** of renown. 582
Ge 11:5 which the children of **m.** builded. 120
Ge 12:20 commanded his **m.** concerning 582
Ge 13:13 the **m.** of Sodom were wicked and 582
Ge 14:24 that which the young **m.** have eaten, ...
Ge 14:24 of the **m.** which went with me, by 582
Ge 17:23 male among the **m.** of Abraham's 582
Ge 17:27 all the **m.** of his house, born in the 582
Ge 18:2 and, lo, three **m.** stood by him: 582
Ge 18:16 the **m.** rose up from thence, and 582
Ge 18:22 **m.** turned their faces from thence, ... 582
Ge 19:4 the **m.** of the city, even the **m.** of 582
Ge 19:5 Where are the **m.** which came in to 582
Ge 19:8 only unto these **m.** do nothing; for 582
Ge 19:10 But the **m.** put forth their hand, and 582
Ge 19:11 smote the **m.** that were at the door 582
Ge 19:12 the **m.** said unto Lot, Hast thou here ... 582

Ge	19:16	the **m.** laid hold upon his hand, and	582
Ge	20:8	ears; and the **m.** were sore afraid.	582
Ge	22:3	took two of his young **m.** with him,	
Ge	22:5	And Abraham said unto his young **m.**,	
Ge	22:19	Abraham returned unto his young **m.**,	
Ge	24:13	the daughters of the **m.** of the city	582
Ge	24:54	he and the **m.** that were with him,	582
Ge	24:59	and Abraham's servant, and his **m.**	582
Ge	26:7	the **m.** of the place asked him of his	582
Ge	26:7	the **m.** of the place should kill me	582
Ge	29:22	together all the **m.** of the place,	582
Ge	32:6	and four hundred **m.** with him.	376
Ge	32:28	thou power with God and with **m.**,	582
Ge	33:1	and with him four hundred **m.**.	376
Ge	33:13	if **m.** should overdrive them one day,	
Ge	34:7	the **m.** were grieved, and they were	582
Ge	34:20	communed with the **m.** of their city,	582
Ge	34:21	These **m.** are peacable with us;	582
Ge	34:22	Only herein will the **m.** consent unto	582
Ge	38:21	Then he asked the **m.** of that place,	582
Ge	38:22	also the **m.** of the place said, that	582
Ge	39:11	none of the **m.** of the house there	582
Ge	39:14	she called unto the **m.** of her house,	582
Ge	41:8	of Egypt, and all the wise **m.** thereof:	
Ge	42:11	we are true **m.**; thy servants are no	
Ge	42:19	If ye be true **m.**, let one of your	
Ge	42:31	him, We are true **m.**; we are no spies:	
Ge	42:33	shall I know that ye are true **m.**;	
Ge	42:34	are no spies, but that ye are true **m.**:	
Ge	43:15	**m.** took that present, and they took	582
Ge	43:16	Bring these **m.** home, and slay, and	582
Ge	43:16	these **m.** shall dine with me at noon.	582
Ge	43:17	brought the **m.** into Joseph's house.	582
Ge	43:18	the **m.** were afraid, because they	582
Ge	43:24	brought the **m.** into Joseph's house,	582
Ge	43:33	and the **m.** marvelled one at another.	582
Ge	44:3	**m.** were sent away, they and their	582
Ge	44:4	his steward, Up, follow after the **m.**;	582
Ge	46:32	And the **m.** are shepherds, for their	582
Ge	47:2	some of his brethren, even five **m.**,	582
Ge	47:6	any **m.** of activity among them,	582
Ex	1:17	them, but saved the **m.** children alive.	
Ex	1:18	and have saved the **m.** children alive?	
Ex	2:13	two **m.** of the Hebrews strove	582
Ex	4:19	**m.** are dead which sought thy life.	582
Ex	5:9	more work be laid upon the **m.**,	582
Ex	7:11	Pharaoh also called the wise **m.** and	
Ex	10:7	let the **m.** go, that they may serve	582
Ex	10:11	go now ye that are **m.**, and serve	1397
Ex	12:33	for they said, We be all dead **m.**.	
Ex	12:37	thousand on foot that were **m.**,	1397
Ex	15:15	the mighty **m.** of Moab, trembling	
Ex	17:9	said unto Joshua, Choose us out **m.**,	582
Ex	18:21	the people able **m.**, such as fear God,	582
Ex	18:21	**m.** of truth, hating covetousness;	582
Ex	18:25	chose able **m.** out of all Israel, and	582
Ex	21:18	if **m.** strive together, and one smite	582
Ex	21:22	If **m.** strive, and hurt a woman with	582
Ex	22:31	And ye shall be holy **m.** unto me:	582
Ex	24:5	sent young **m.** of the children of Israel,	
Ex	32:28	that day about three thousand **m.**.	376
Ex	35:22	they came, both **m.** and women, as	582
Ex	36:4	And all the wise **m.**, that wrought all	
Ex	38:26	thousand and five hundred and fifty **m.**.	
Le	7:25	**m.** offer an offering made by fire	
Le	18:27	have the **m.** of the land done, which	582
Le	27:9	**m.** bring an offering unto the Lord,	
Le	27:29	which shall be devoted of **m.**, shall	120
Nu	1:5	these are the names of the **m.** that	582
Nu	1:17	And Moses and Aaron took these **m.**	582
Nu	1:44	princes of Israel, being twelve **m.**:	376
Nu	5:6	commit any sin that **m.** commit, to	120
Nu	9:6	there were certain **m.**, who were	582
Nu	9:7	And those **m.** said unto him, We are	582
Nu	11:16	Gather unto me seventy **m.** of the	376
Nu	11:24	and gathered the seventy **m.** of the	376
Nu	11:26	remained two of the **m.** in the camp,	582
Nu	11:28	servant of Moses, one of his young **m.**,	
Nu	12:3	above all the **m.** which were upon	120
Nu	13:2	Send thou **m.**, that they may search	582
Nu	13:3	all those **m.** were heads of the	582
Nu	13:16	names of the **m.** which Moses sent	582
Nu	13:21	unto Rehob, as **m.** come to Hamath	
Nu	13:31	the **m.** that went up with him said,	582
Nu	13:32	saw in it are **m.** of a great stature.	582
Nu	14:22	those **m.** which have seen my glory,	582

Nu	14:36	the **m.**, which Moses sent to search	582
Nu	14:37	those **m.** that did bring up the evil	582
Nu	14:38	the **m.** that went to search the land,	582
Nu	16:1	of Peleth, sons of Reuben, took **m.**:	
Nu	16:2	in the congregation, **m.** of renown:	582
Nu	16:14	thou put out the eyes of these **m.**?	582
Nu	16:26	from the tents of these wicked **m.**,	582
Nu	16:29	If these **m.** die the common death	
Nu	16:29	die the common death of all **m.**,	120
Nu	16:29	visited after the visitation of all **m.**;	120
Nu	16:30	these **m.** have provoked the Lord.	582
Nu	16:32	the **m.** that appertained unto Korah,	120
Nu	16:35	the two hundred and fifty **m.** that	376
Nu	18:15	be of **m.** or beasts, shall be thine:	120
Nu	22:9	said, What **m.** are these with thee?	582
Nu	22:20	If the **m.** come to call thee, rise up,	582
Nu	22:35	said unto Balaam, Go with the **m.**:	582
Nu	25:5	Slay ye every one his **m.** that were	582
Nu	26:10	devoured two hundred and fifty **m.**:	376
Nu	31:11	the prey, both of **m.** and of beasts.	120
Nu	31:21	the priest said unto the **m.** of war	582
Nu	31:28	**m.** of war which went out to battle:	582
Nu	31:32	pray which the **m.** of war had	5971
Nu	31:42	divided from the **m.** that warred,	582
Nu	31:49	have taken the sum of the **m.** of war	582
Nu	31:53	the **m.** of war had taken spoil, every	582
Nu	32:11	Surely none of the **m.** that came up	582
Nu	32:14	an increase of sinful **m.**, to augment	582
Nu	34:17	names of the **m.** which shall divide	582
Nu	34:19	And the names of the **m.** are these:	582
De	1:13	you wise **m.**, and understanding,	582
De	1:15	the chief of your tribes, wise **m.**, and	582
De	1:22	We will send **m.** before us, and they	582
De	1:23	and I took twelve **m.** of you, one of	582
De	1:35	shall not one of these **m.** of this evil	582
De	2:14	all the generation of the **m.** of war	582
De	2:16	**m.** of war were consumed and dead	582
De	2:34	utterly destroyed the **m.**, and the	4962
De	3:6	utterly destroying the **m.**, women,	4962
De	4:3	all the **m.** that followed Baal-peor,	376
De	13:13	Certain **m.**, the children of Belial,	582
De	19:17	Then both the **m.**, between whom	582
De	21:21	all the **m.** of his city shall stone him	582
De	22:21	**m.** of her city shall stone her with	582
De	25:1	there be a controversy between **m.**,	582
De	25:11	When **m.** strive together one with	582
De	27:14	say unto all the **m.** of Israel with a	376
De	29:10	officers, with all the **m.** of Israel,	376
De	29:25	Then **m.** shall say, Because they have	
De	31:12	Gather the people together, **m.**, and	582
De	32:26	of them to cease from among **m.**:	582
De	33:6	not die; and let not his **m.** be few.	4962
Jos	1:14	all the mighty **m.** of valour, and help	
Jos	2:1	sent out of Shittim two **m.** to spy	582
Jos	2:2	came **m.** in hither to night of the	582
Jos	2:3	Bring forth the **m.** that are come to	582
Jos	2:4	the woman took the two **m.**, and hid	582
Jos	2:4	There came **m.** unto me, but I wist	582
Jos	2:5	it was dark, that the **m.** went out:	582
Jos	2:5	whither the **m.** went I wot not:	582
Jos	2:7	the **m.** pursued after them the way	582
Jos	2:9	she said unto the **m.**, I know that	582
Jos	2:14	**m.** answered her, Our life for yours,	582
Jos	2:17	And the **m.** said unto her, We will be	582
Jos	2:23	the two **m.** returned, and descended	582
Jos	3:12	take you twelve **m.** out of the tribes	376
Jos	4:2	twelve **m.** out of the people, out of	582
Jos	4:4	Joshua called the twelve **m.**, whom	376
Jos	5:4	even all the **m.** of war, died in the	582
Jos	5:6	all the people that were **m.** of war,	582
Jos	6:2	thereof, and the mighty **m.** of valour.	
Jos	6:3	compass the city, all ye **m.** of war,	582
Jos	6:9	the armed **m.** went before the priests	
Jos	6:13	and the armed **m.** went before them;	
Jos	6:22	Joshua had said unto the two **m.**	582
Jos	6:23	the young **m.** that were spies went in,	
Jos	7:2	Joshua sent **m.** from Jericho to Ai,	582
Jos	7:2	And the **m.** went up and viewed Ai.	582
Jos	7:3	two or three thousand **m.** go up	376
Jos	7:4	people about three thousand **m.**:	376
Jos	7:4	and they fled before the **m.** of Ai.	582
Jos	7:5	the **m.** of Ai smote of them about	582
Jos	7:5	of them about thirty and six **m.**:	376
Jos	8:3	out thirty thousand and mighty **m.**	376
Jos	8:12	he took about five thousand **m.**, and	376

Jos	8:14	the **m.** of the city went out against	582
Jos	8:20	the **m.** of Ai looked behind them,	582
Jos	8:21	turned again, and slew the **m.** of Ai.	582
Jos	8:25	that day, both of **m.** and women,	376
Jos	8:25	thousand, even all the **m.** of Ai.	582
Jos	9:6	unto him, and to the **m.** of Israel,	376
Jos	9:7	And the **m.** of Israel said unto the	376
Jos	9:14	the **m.** took of their victuals, and	582
Jos	10:2	and all the **m.** thereof were mighty.	582
Jos	10:6	the **m.** of Gibeon sent unto Joshua	582
Jos	10:7	him, and all the mighty **m.** of valour.	
Jos	10:18	and set **m.** by it for to keep them:	582
Jos	10:24	called for all the **m.** of Israel, and	376
Jos	10:24	said unto the captains of the **m.** of war	
Jos	18:4	from among you three **m.** for each	582
Jos	18:8	the **m.** arose, and went away: and	582
Jos	18:9	the **m.** went and passed through the	582
Jos	24:11	**m.** of Jericho fought against you,	1167
Jg	1:4	of them in Bezek ten thousand **m.**.	376
Jg	3:29	at that time about ten thousand **m.**,	376
Jg	3:29	all lusty, and all **m.** of valour; and	376
Jg	3:31	of the Philistines six hundred **m.**	376
Jg	4:6	take with thee ten thousand **m.** of	376
Jg	4:10	up with ten thousand **m.** at his feet:	376
Jg	4:14	and ten thousand **m.** after him.	376
Jg	6:27	Gideon took ten **m.** of his servants,	582
Jg	6:27	household, and the **m.** of the city,	582
Jg	6:28	the **m.** of the city arose early in the	582
Jg	6:30	the **m.** of the city said unto Joash,	582
Jg	7:6	mouth, were three hundred **m.**:	376
Jg	7:7	By the three hundred **m.** that lapped	376
Jg	7:8	retained those three hundred **m.**:	376
Jg	7:11	of the armed **m.** that were in the host.	
Jg	7:16	the three hundred **m.** into three	376
Jg	7:19	the hundred **m.** that were with him,	376
Jg	7:23	the **m.** of Israel gathered themselves	376
Jg	7:24	**m.** of Ephraim gathered themselves	376
Jg	8:1	the **m.** of Ephraim said unto him,	376
Jg	8:4	three hundred **m.** that were with	376
Jg	8:5	And he said unto the **m.** of Succoth,	582
Jg	8:8	and the **m.** of Penuel answered him	582
Jg	8:8	**m.** of Succoth had answered him.	582
Jg	8:9	he spake also unto the **m.** of Penuel,	582
Jg	8:10	with them, about fifteen thousand **m.**,	
Jg	8:10	thousand **m.** that drew sword.	376
Jg	8:14	a young man of the **m.** of Succoth,	582
Jg	8:14	even threescore and seventeen **m.**	376
Jg	8:15	he came unto the **m.** of Succoth,	582
Jg	8:15	bread unto thy **m.** that are weary?	582
Jg	8:16	them he taught the **m.** of Succoth.	582
Jg	8:17	Penuel, and slew the **m.** of the city	582
Jg	8:18	What manner of **m.** were they whom	582
Jg	8:22	the **m.** of Israel said unto Gideon,	376
Jg	9:2	the ears of all the **m.** of Shechem,	1167
Jg	9:3	in the ears of all the **m.** of Shechem	1167
Jg	9:6	**m.** of Shechem gathered together,	1167
Jg	9:7	unto me, ye **m.** of Shechem, that	1167
Jg	9:18	king over the **m.** of Shechem,	1167
Jg	9:20	devour the **m.** of Shechem, and the	1167
Jg	9:20	come out from the **m.** of Shechem,	1167
Jg	9:23	Abimelech and the **m.** of Shechem;	1167
Jg	9:23	**m.** of Shechem dealt treacherously	1167
Jg	9:24	and upon the **m.** of Shechem, which	1167
Jg	9:25	the **m.** of Shechem set liers in wait	1167
Jg	9:26	**m.** of Shechem put their confidence	1167
Jg	9:28	**m.** of Hamor…father of Shechem:	582
Jg	9:36	of the mountains as if they were **m.**	582
Jg	9:39	went out before the **m.** of Shechem,	1167
Jg	9:46,	47 the **m.** of the tower of Shechem	1167
Jg	9:49	the **m.** of the tower of Shechem died	582
Jg	9:49	about a thousand **m.** and women.	376
Jg	9:51	thither fled all the **m.** and women,	582
Jg	9:54	that **m.** say not of me, A woman slew	
Jg	9:55	the **m.** of Israel saw that Abimelech	376
Jg	9:57	evil of the **m.** of Shechem did God	582
Jg	11:3	were gathered vain **m.** to Jephthah,	582
Jg	12:1	**m.** of Ephraim gathered themselves	376
Jg	12:4	together all the **m.** of Gilead,	582
Jg	12:4	the **m.** of Gilead smote Ephraim,	582
Jg	12:5	the **m.** of Gilead said unto him, Art	582
Jg	14:10	feast; for so used the young **m.** to do.	
Jg	14:18	the **m.** of the city said unto him on	582
Jg	14:19	slew thirty **m.** of them, and took	376
Jg	15:10	And the **m.** of Judah said, Why are	376
Jg	15:11	three thousand **m.** of Judah went to	376
Jg	15:15	and slew a thousand **m.** therewith.	376

Jg 15:16 of an ass have I slain a thousand **m.**..... 376
Jg 16:9 there were **m.** lying in wait, abiding..........
Jg 16:27 house was full of **m.** and women;......... 582
Jg 16:27 three thousand **m.** and women, ... 376
Jg 18:2 five **m.** from their coasts, ... 582,1121
Jg 18:2 **m.** of valour, from Zorah, and...... 582,1121
Jg 18:7 the five **m.** departed, and came to 582
Jg 18:11 six hundred **m.** appointed with 376
Jg 18:14 Then answered the five **m.** that 582
Jg 18:16 the six hundred **m.** appointed with 376
Jg 18:17 the five **m.** that went to spy out the 582
Jg 18:17 with the six hundred **m.** that were....... 376
Jg 18:22 the **m.** that were in the houses near 582
Jg 19:16 the **m.** of the place were Benjamites.... 582
Jg 19:22 **m.** of the city, certain sons of Belial,.... 582
Jg 19:25 the **m.** would not hearken to him: so.... 582
Jg 20:5 the **m.** of Gibeah rose against me,...... 1167
Jg 20:10 we will take ten **m.** of an hundred 582
Jg 20:11 all the **m.** of Israel were fathered 376
Jg 20:12 Israel sent **m.** through all the tribe....... 582
Jg 20:13 Now therefore deliver us the **m.**, the ... 582
Jg 20:15 six thousand **m.** that drew sword,........ 376
Jg 20:15 numbered seven hundred chosen **m.**..... 376
Jg 20:16 seven hundred chosen **m.** lefthanded; ... 376
Jg 20:17 **m.** of Israel, beside Benjamin, were...... 376
Jg 20:17 four hundred thousand **m.** that drew..... 376
Jg 20:17 sword: all these were **m.** of war.......... 376
Jg 20:20 the **m.** of Israel went out to battle....... 376
Jg 20:20 **m.** of Israel put themselves in array..... 376
Jg 20:21 day twenty and two thousand **m.**. 376
Jg 20:22 people the **m.** of Israel encouraged 376
Jg 20:25 again eighteen thousand **m.**; all............ 376
Jg 20:31 in the field, about thirty **m.** of Israel..... 376
Jg 20:33 all the **m.** of Israel rose up out of........ 376
Jg 20:34 thousand chosen **m.** out of all Israel, ... 376
Jg 20:35 five thousand and an hundred **m.**: 376
Jg 20:36 for the **m.** of Israel gave place to the ... 376
Jg 20:38 sign between the **m.** of Israel and........ 376
Jg 20:39 the **m.** of Israel retired in the battle, ... 376
Jg 20:39 to smite and kill the **m.** of Israel 376
Jg 20:41 when the **m.** of Israel turned again,....... 376
Jg 20:41 the **m.** of Benjamin were amazed:........ 376
Jg 20:42 their backs before the **m.** of Israel....... 376
Jg 20:44 fell...eighteen thousand **m.**; 376
Jg 20:44 all these were **m.** of valour................. 582
Jg 20:45 in the highways five thousand **m.**;........ 376
Jg 20:45 and slew two thousand **m.** of them....... 376
Jg 20:46 thousand **m.** that drew the sword; 376
Jg 20:46 all these were **m.** of valour................. 582
Jg 20:47 six hundred **m.** turned and fled to........ 376
Jg 20:48 the **m.** of Israel turned again upon 376
Jg 20:48 as well the **m.** of every city, as the.... 4974
Jg 21:1 **m.** of Israel had sworn in Mizpeh, ... 376
Jg 21:10 sent thither twelve thousand **m.** of....... 376
Ru 2:9 have I not charged the young **m.** that ....
Ru 2:9 that which the young **m.** have drawn.........
Ru 2:15 Boaz commanded his young **m.**, ...
Ru 2:21 Thou shalt keep fast by my young **m.**, ...
Ru 3:10 as thou followedst not young **m.**,..............
Ru 4:2 took ten **m.** of the elders of the city, ... 582
1Sa 2:4 The bows of the mighty **m.** are broken, ...
1Sa 2:17 the sin of the young **m.** was very great.....
1Sa 2:17 for **m.** abhorred the offering of the....... 582
1Sa 2:26 both with the Lord, and also with me. .. 582
1Sa 4:2 in the field about four thousand **m.**....... 376
1Sa 4:9 strong, and quit yourselves like **m.**, ... 582
1Sa 4:9 quit yourselves like **m.**, and fight. 582
1Sa 5:7 the **m.** of Ashdod saw that it was so, ... 582
1Sa 5:9 smote the **m.** of the city, both small..... 582
1Sa 5:12 **m.** that died not were smitten with...... 582
1Sa 6:10 the **m.** did so; and took two milch 582
1Sa 6:15 **m.** of Beth-shemesh offered burnt........ 582
1Sa 6:19 he smote the **m.** of Beth-shemesh, ... 376
1Sa 6:19 thousand and threescore and ten **m.**:.... 376
1Sa 6:20 the **m.** of Beth-shemesh said, Who 582
1Sa 7:1 And the **m.** of Kirjath-jearim came, ... 582
1Sa 7:11 the **m.** of Israel went out of Mizpeh, ... 582
1Sa 8:16 your goodliest young **m.**, and your ....
1Sa 8:22 Samuel said unto the **m.** of Israel, ... 582
1Sa 10:2 find two **m.** by Rachel's sepulchre........ 582
1Sa 10:3 there shall meet thee three **m.** going.... 582
1Sa 10:26 there went with him a band of **m.**, ...
1Sa 11:1 the **m.** of Jabesh said unto Nahash, ... 582
1Sa 11:5 him the tidings of the **m.** of Jabesh. 582
1Sa 11:8 the **m.** of Judah thirty thousand. 376
1Sa 11:9 say unto the **m.** of Jabesh-gilead, ... 376
1Sa 11:9 and shewed it to the **m.** of Jabesh; 582

1Sa 11:10 Therefore the **m.** of Jabesh said, ... 582
1Sa 11:12 bring the **m.**, that we may put them..... 582
1Sa 11:15 Saul and all the **m.** of Israel rejoiced..... 582
1Sa 13:2 Saul chose him three thousand **m.** of.........
1Sa 13:6 When the **m.** of Israel saw that they 376
1Sa 13:15 with him, about six hundred **m.**; 376
1Sa 14:2 with him were about six hundred **m.**; ... 376
1Sa 14:8 we will pass over unto these **m.**, ... 582
1Sa 14:12 the **m.** of the garrison answered........... 582
1Sa 14:14 slaughter,...was about twenty **m.**,........ 376
1Sa 14:22 all the **m.** of Israel which had hid......... 376
1Sa 14:24 the **m.** of Israel were distressed that.... 376
1Sa 15:4 and ten thousand **m.** of Judah............. 376
1Sa 17:2 And Saul and the **m.** of Israel were...... 376
1Sa 17:12 man went among **m.** for an old name.... 582
1Sa 17:19 and they, and all the **m.** of Israel, ... 376
1Sa 17:24 all the **m.** of Israel, when they saw...... 376
1Sa 17:25 the **m.** of Israel said, Have ye seen 376
1Sa 17:26 David spake to the **m.** that stood.......... 582
1Sa 17:28 heard when he spake unto the **m.**;....... 582
1Sa 17:52 the **m.** of Israel and of Judah arose, ... 582
1Sa 18:5 and Saul set him over the **m.** of war, ... 582
1Sa 18:27 arose and went, he and his **m.**, and 582
1Sa 18:27 of the Philistines two hundred **m.**; 376
1Sa 21:4 if the young **m.** have kept themselves.......
1Sa 21:5 the vessels of the young **m.** are holy, ...
1Sa 21:15 Have I need of mad **m.**, that ye have........
1Sa 22:2 with him about four hundred **m.**. 376
1Sa 22:6 and the **m.** that were with him, ... 582
1Sa 22:19 both **m.** and women, children and 376
1Sa 23:3 David's **m.** said unto him, Behold,........ 582
1Sa 23:5 So David and his **m.** went to Keilah, ... 582
1Sa 23:8 Keilah, to besiege David and his **m.**. 582
1Sa 23:11 Will the **m.** of Keilah deliver me up 1167
1Sa 23:12 Will the **m.** of Keilah deliver me and... 1167
1Sa 23:12 and my **m.** into the hand of Saul? 582
1Sa 23:13 David and his **m.**, which were about..... 582
1Sa 23:24 and his **m.** were in the wilderness 582
1Sa 23:25 also and his **m.** went to seek him. 582
1Sa 23:26 his **m.** on that side of the mountain: 582
1Sa 23:26 for Saul and his **m.** compassed David.... 582
1Sa 23:26 compassed David and his **m.** round 582
1Sa 24:2 Saul took three thousand chosen **m.**..... 376
1Sa 24:2 and went to seek David and his **m.**........ 582
1Sa 24:3 David and his **m.** remained in the 582
1Sa 24:4 And the **m.** of David said unto him,...... 582
1Sa 24:6 he said unto his **m.**, The Lord forbid.... 582
1Sa 24:22 David and his **m.** gat them up unto 582
1Sa 25:5 And David sent out ten young **m.**, and......
1Sa 25:5 David said unto the young **m.**, Get you .....
1Sa 25:8 Ask thy young **m.**, and they will shew.......
1Sa 25:8 let the young **m.** find favour in thine.........
1Sa 25:9 when David's young **m.** came, they ....
1Sa 25:11 give it unto **m.**, whom I know not 582
1Sa 25:12 So David's young **m.** turned their way,......
1Sa 25:13 David said unto his **m.**, Gird ye on 582
1Sa 25:13 after David about four hundred **m.**; 376
1Sa 25:14 But one of the young **m.** told Abigail,........
1Sa 25:15 But the **m.** were very good unto us, ... 582
1Sa 25:20 David and his **m.** came down against 582
1Sa 25:25 thine handmaid saw not the young **m.** ....
1Sa 25:27 unto the young **m.** that follow my lord.......
1Sa 26:2 three thousand chosen **m.** of Israel 376
1Sa 26:19 if they be the children of **m.**, cursed 120
1Sa 26:22 and let one of the young **m.** come over.....
1Sa 27:2 passed over with six hundred **m.**......... 376
1Sa 27:3 with Achish at Gath, he and his **m.**, ... 582
1Sa 27:8 And David and his **m.** went up, and 582
1Sa 28:1 with me to battle, thou and thy **m.**. 582
1Sa 28:8 he went, and two **m.** with him, and...... 582
1Sa 29:2 David and his **m.** passed on in the 582
1Sa 29:4 it not be with the heads of these **m.**? ... 582
1Sa 29:11 So David and his **m.** rose up early 582
1Sa 30:1 David and his **m.** were come to Ziklag.. 582
1Sa 30:3 David and his **m.** came to the city, ... 582
1Sa 30:9 six hundred **m.** that were with him, ... 376
1Sa 30:10 pursued, he and four hundred **m.**:........ 376
1Sa 30:17 save four hundred young **m.**, which....... 376
1Sa 30:21 David came to the two hundred **m.**, ... 582
1Sa 30:22 Then answered all the wicked **m.** 376
1Sa 30:22 all the wicked **m.** and...of Belial, ...
1Sa 30:31 and his **m.** were wont to haunt. 582
1Sa 31:1 the **m.** of Israel fled from before the 582
1Sa 31:6 his armourbearer, and all his **m.**, ... 582
1Sa 31:7 the **m.** of Israel...on the other side 582
1Sa 31:7 saw that the **m.** of Israel fled, and........ 582
1Sa 31:12 All the valiant **m.** arose, and went 376

2Sa 1:11 all the **m.** that were with him:............ 582
2Sa 1:15 And David called one of the young **m.**, ...
2Sa 2:3 **m.** that were with him did David 582
2Sa 2:4 And the **m.** of Judah came, and there ... 582
2Sa 2:4 **m.** of Jabesh-gilead were they that 582
2Sa 2:5 sent...unto the **m.** of Jabesh-gilead, ... 582
2Sa 2:14 Let the young **m.** now arise, and play ....
2Sa 2:17 was beaten, and the **m.** of Israel, ... 582
2Sa 2:21 lay thee hold on one of the young **m.**, ...
2Sa 2:29 Abner and his **m.** walked all that 582
2Sa 2:30 of David's servants nineteen **m.**........... 376
2Sa 2:31 of Benjamin, and of Abner's **m.**, ... 582
2Sa 2:31 hundred and threescore **m.** died. 376
2Sa 2:32 Joab and his **m.** went all night, and 582
2Sa 3:20 to Hebron, and twenty **m.** with him. 582
2Sa 3:20 the **m.** that were with him a feast........ 582
2Sa 3:34 as a man falleth before wicked **m.**, ... 1121
2Sa 3:39 these **m.** the sons of Zeruiah be too..... 582
2Sa 4:2 son had two **m.** that were captains........ 582
2Sa 4:11 wicked **m.** have slain a righteous 582
2Sa 4:12 David commanded his young **m.**, and ....
2Sa 5:6 king and his **m.** went to Jerusalem 582
2Sa 5:21 and David and his **m.** burned them...... 582
2Sa 6:1 together all the chosen **m.** of Israel, ...
2Sa 6:19 Israel, as well to the women as **m.**, ... 376
2Sa 7:9 like unto the name of the great **m.** ....
2Sa 7:14 chasten him with the rod of **m.**, ... 582
2Sa 7:14 the stripes of the children of **m.**: 120
2Sa 8:5 two and twenty thousand **m.**............... 376
2Sa 8:13 of salt, being eighteen thousand **m.**..........
2Sa 10:5 the **m.** were greatly ashamed:............. 582
2Sa 10:6 and of king Maacah a thousand **m.**, ... 376
2Sa 10:6 and of Ish-tob twelve thousand **m.**. 376
2Sa 10:7 and all the host of the mighty **m.** ....
2Sa 10:9 chose of all the choice **m.** of Israel, ...
2Sa 10:12 let us play the **m.** for our people,....... 2388
2Sa 10:18 David slew the **m.** of seven hundred.........
2Sa 11:16 where he knew...valiant **m.** were......... 582
2Sa 11:17 the **m.** of the city went out, and........... 582
2Sa 11:23 Surely the **m.** prevailed against us, ... 582
2Sa 12:1 There were two **m.** in one city; the..... 582
2Sa 13:9 said, Have out all **m.** from me............. 376
2Sa 13:32 slain all the young **m.** the king's sons; ....
2Sa 15:1 and fifty **m.** to run before him............. 376
2Sa 15:6 stole the hearts of the **m.** of Israel. 582
2Sa 15:11 with Absalom went two hundred **m.** 376
2Sa 15:13 hearts of the **m.** of Israel are after....... 376
2Sa 15:18 six hundred **m.** which came after 376
2Sa 15:22 Gittite passed over, and all his **m.**, ... 582
2Sa 16:2 summer fruit for the young **m.** to eat;.......
2Sa 16:6 all the mighty **m.** were on his right...........
2Sa 16:13 David and his **m.** went by the way,...... 582
2Sa 16:15 the **m.** of Israel, came to Jerusalem, ... 376
2Sa 16:18 this people, and all the **m.** of Israel, ... 376
2Sa 17:1 now choose out twelve thousand **m.**, ... 376
2Sa 17:8 knowest thy father and his **m.**,............ 582
2Sa 17:8 that they be mighty **m.**, and they be.........
2Sa 17:10 which be with him are valiant **m.**......... 1121
2Sa 17:12 and of all the **m.** that are with him....... 582
2Sa 17:14 Absalom and all the **m.** of Israel.......... 376
2Sa 17:24 he and all the **m.** of Israel with him...... 376
2Sa 18:7 that day of twenty thousand **m.**................
2Sa 18:15 young **m.** that bare Joab's armour.............
2Sa 18:28 which hath delivered up the **m.** 582
2Sa 19:14 the heart of all the **m.** of Judah, ... 376
2Sa 19:16 came down with the **m.** of Judah 376
2Sa 19:17 were a thousand **m.** of Benjamin.......... 376
2Sa 19:28 father's house were but dead **m.** 582
2Sa 19:35 hear any more the voice of singing **m.**........
2Sa 19:41 all the **m.** of Israel came to the........... 376
2Sa 19:41 our brethren the **m.** of Judah stolen 376
2Sa 19:41 David's **m.** with him, over Jordan? 582
2Sa 19:42 the **m.** of Judah answered the **m.** of..... 376
2Sa 19:43 the **m.** of Israel answered the **m.** of..... 376
2Sa 19:43 the words of the **m.** of Judah were 376
2Sa 19:43 than the words of the **m.** of Israel. 376
2Sa 20:2 **m.** of Judah clave unto their king, ... 376
2Sa 20:4 Assemble me the **m.** of Judah within 376
2Sa 20:5 went to assemble the **m.** of Judah: ....
2Sa 20:7 went out after him Joab's **m.**, and........ 582
2Sa 20:7 the Pelethites, and all the mighty **m.**:........
2Sa 20:11 and one of Joab's **m.** stood by him, ... 376
2Sa 21:6 seven **m.** of his sons be delivered.......... 582
2Sa 21:12 son from the **m.** of Jabesh-gilead, ... 1167
2Sa 21:17 the **m.** of David sware unto him, ... 582
2Sa 22:5 floods of ungodly **m.** made me afraid;........
2Sa 23:3 that ruleth over **m.** must be just,......... 120

2Sa	23:8	the names of the mighty **m.** whom..........	
2Sa	23:9	of the three mighty **m.** with David,..........	
2Sa	23:9	the **m.** of Israel were gone away:........	376
2Sa	23:16	three mighty **m.** brake through the..........	
2Sa	23:17	the blood of the **m.** that went in..........	582
2Sa	23:17	things did these three mighty **m.**............	
2Sa	23:20	acts, he slew two lionlike **m.** of Moab:......	
2Sa	23:22	the name among three mighty **m.**............	
2Sa	24:9	valiant **m.** that draw the sword:..........	376
2Sa	24:9	the **m.** of Judah were five hundred.......	376
2Sa	24:9	were five hundred thousand **m.**...........	376
2Sa	24:15	to Beer-sheba seventy thousand **m.**.......	376
1Ki	1:5	and fifty **m.** to run before him............	376
1Ki	1:8	mighty **m.** which belonged to David,.........	
1Ki	1:9	**m.** of Judah the king's servants:.........	582
1Ki	1:10	and the mighty **m.**, and Solomon his.........	
1Ki	2:32	two **m.** more righteous and better.......	582
1Ki	4:31	For he was wiser than all **m.**; than......	120
1Ki	5:13	the levy was thirty thousand **m.**..........	376
1Ki	8:2	**m.** of Israel assembled themselves.......	376
1Ki	8:39	the hearts of all the children of **m.**;).....	120
1Ki	9:22	but they were **m.** of war, and his........	582
1Ki	10:8	Happy are thy **m.**, happy are these......	582
1Ki	11:18	took **m.** with them out of Paran,.........	582
1Ki	11:24	And he gathered **m.** unto him, and.......	582
1Ki	12:6	Rehoboam consulted with the old **m.**,........	
1Ki	12:8	he forsook the counsel of the old **m.**,........	
1Ki	12:8	and consulted with the young **m.** that........	
1Ki	12:10	the young **m.** that were grown up with......	
1Ki	12:14	after the counsel of the young **m.**,...........	
1Ki	12:21	and fourscore thousand chosen **m.**,..........	
1Ki	13:25	**m.** passed by, and saw the carcase......	582
1Ki	18:13	hundred **m.** of the Lord's prophets.......	376
1Ki	18:22	are four hundred and fifty **m.**.............	376
1Ki	20:14	by the young **m.** of the princes of the.......	
1Ki	20:15	he numbered the young **m.** of the...........	
1Ki	20:17	the young **m.** of the princes of the..........	
1Ki	20:17	There are **m.** come out of Samaria.......	582
1Ki	20:19	So these young **m.** of the princes of.........	
1Ki	20:30	and seven thousand of the **m.** that.......	376
1Ki	20:33	Now the **m.** did diligently observe........	582
1Ki	21:10	And set two **m.**, sons of Belial, before..	582
1Ki	21:11	the **m.** of his city, even the elders.......	582
1Ki	21:13	there came in two **m.**, children of.......	582
1Ki	21:13	the **m.** of Belial witnessed against........	582
1Ki	22:6	together, about four hundred **m.**,.........	376
2Ki	2:7	fifty **m.** of the sons of the prophets......	376
2Ki	2:16	thy servants fifty strong **m.**;........	582,1121
2Ki	2:17	They sent therefore fifty **m.**; and.........	376
2Ki	2:19	the **m.** of the city said unto Elisha,......	582
2Ki	3:26	him seven hundred **m.** that drew.........	376
2Ki	4:22	me, I pray thee, one of the young **m.**,......	
2Ki	4:40	they poured out for the **m.** to eat........	582
2Ki	4:43	I set this before an hundred **m.**?.........	376
2Ki	5:22	two young **m.** of the sons of the.............	
2Ki	5:24	he let the **m.** go, and they departed.....	582
2Ki	6:20	open the eyes of these **m.**, that they........	
2Ki	7:3	there were four leprous **m.** at the........	582
2Ki	8:12	and their young **m.** wilt thou slay............	
2Ki	10:6	heads of the **m.** your master's sons,.....	582
2Ki	10:6	were with the great **m.** of the city,...........	
2Ki	10:11	all his great **m.**, and his kinsfolks, and.......	
2Ki	10:14	house, even two and forty **m.**;...........	376
2Ki	10:24	appointed fourscore **m.** without,.........	376
2Ki	10:24	any of the **m.** whom I have brought.....	582
2Ki	11:9	and they took every man his **m.** that....	582
2Ki	12:15	they reckoned not with the **m.**, into.....	582
2Ki	13:21	that, behold, they spied a band of **m.**;......	582
2Ki	15:20	of all the mighty **m.** of wealth, of each......	
2Ki	15:25	with him fifty **m.** of the Gileadites:.......	376
2Ki	17:24	of Assyria brought **m.** from Babylon,.........	
2Ki	17:30	And the **m.** of Babylon made.............	582
2Ki	17:30	the **m.** of Cuth made Nergal, and the...	582
2Ki	17:30	the **m.** of Hamath made Ashima,.........	582
2Ki	18:27	me to the **m.** which sit on the wall,.....	582
2Ki	20:14	said unto him, What said these **m.**?......	582
2Ki	23:2	and all the **m.** of Judah and all the........	376
2Ki	23:14	their places with the bones of **m.**.........	120
2Ki	23:17	the **m.** of the city told him, It is the.....	582
2Ki	24:14	all the mighty **m.** of valour, even ten........	
2Ki	24:16	And all the **m.** of might, even seven.....	582
2Ki	25:4	all the **m.** of war fled by night by the...	582
2Ki	25:19	that was set over the **m.** of war, and...	582
2Ki	25:19	and five **m.** of them that were in the....	582
2Ki	25:19	threescore **m.** of the people of the.......	376
2Ki	25:23	they and their **m.**, heard that the.........	582
2Ki	25:23	of a Maachathite, they and their **m.**......	582
2Ki	25:24	and to their **m.**, and said unto them,....	582
2Ki	25:25	royal, came, and ten **m.** with him.......	582
1Ch	4:12	These are the **m.** of Rechah.............	582
1Ch	4:22	the **m.** of Chezeba, and Joash, and.......	582
1Ch	4:42	the sons of Simeon, five hundred **m.**,...	582
1Ch	5:18	the tribe of Manasseh, of valiant **m.**,.........	
1Ch	5:18	**m.** able to bear buckler and sword,......	582
1Ch	5:21	of **m.** an hundred thousand.........	5315,120
1Ch	5:24	and Jahdiel, mighty **m.** of valour,.........	582
1Ch	5:24	famous **m.**, and heads of the house......	582
1Ch	7:2	were valiant **m.** of might in their.............	
1Ch	7:3	Joel, Ishiah, five: all of them chief **m.**........	
1Ch	7:4	for war, six and thirty thousand **m.**:..........	
1Ch	7:5	of Issachar were valiant **m.** of might,........	
1Ch	7:7,	9 fathers, mighty **m.** of valour;................	
1Ch	7:11	their fathers, mighty **m.** of valour,............	
1Ch	7:21	whom the **m.** of Gath that were born...	582
1Ch	7:40	choice and mighty **m.** of valour,...............	
1Ch	7:40	was twenty and six thousand **m.**..........	582
1Ch	8:28	fathers, by their generations, chief **m.**.......	
1Ch	8:40	of Ulam were mighty **m.** of valour,.......	582
1Ch	9:9	these **m.** were chief of the fathers.......	582
1Ch	9:13	very able **m.** for the work of the........	1368
1Ch	10:1	the **m.** of Israel fled from before the....	376
1Ch	10:7	**m.** of Israel that were in the valley......	376
1Ch	10:12	They arose, all the valiant **m.**, and.......	376
1Ch	11:10	of the mighty **m.** whom David had,...........	
1Ch	11:11	of the mighty **m.** whom David had;...........	
1Ch	11:19	shall I drink the blood of these **m.**........	582
1Ch	11:22	he slew two lionlike **m.** of Moab:............	
1Ch	11:26	the valiant **m.** of the armies were,............	
1Ch	12:1	and they were among the mighty **m.**,........	
1Ch	12:8	to the wilderness **m.** of might,...........	582
1Ch	12:8	and **m.** of war fit for the battle,..............	
1Ch	12:21	for they were all mighty **m.** of valour,.......	
1Ch	12:25	mighty **m.** of valour for the war,.............	
1Ch	12:30	mighty **m.** of valour, famous..................	
1Ch	12:32	were **m.** that had understanding of..........	
1Ch	12:38	All these **m.** of war, that could keep....	582
1Ch	16:31	and let **m.** say among the nations,...........	
1Ch	17:8	like the name of the great **m.** that are.......	
1Ch	18:5	two and twenty thousand **m.**.............	376
1Ch	19:5	told David how the **m.** were served.....	582
1Ch	19:5	for the **m.** were greatly ashamed.........	582
1Ch	19:8	and all the host of the mighty **m.**............	
1Ch	19:18	seven thousand **m.** which fought in..........	
1Ch	21:5	thousand **m.** that drew sword: and.......	376
1Ch	21:5	ten thousand **m.** that drew sword........	376
1Ch	21:14	fell of Israel seventy thousand **m.**........	376
1Ch	22:15	all manner of cunning **m.** for every..........	
1Ch	24:4	there were more chief **m.** found of.....	1397
1Ch	24:4	Eleazar there were sixteen chief **m.**..........	
1Ch	26:6	for they were mighty **m.** of valour.............	
1Ch	26:7	whose brethren were strong **m.**,........	1121
1Ch	26:8	able **m.** for strength for the service,.....	376
1Ch	26:9	had sons and brethren, strong **m.**,......	1121
1Ch	26:12	porters, even among the chief **m.**,......	1397
1Ch	26:30	and his brethren, **m.** of valour,.........	1121
1Ch	26:31	among them mighty **m.** of valour at..........	
1Ch	26:32	And his brethren, **m.** of valour,.........	1121
1Ch	28:1	the officers, and with the mighty **m.**,........	
1Ch	28:1	and with all the valiant **m.**, unto..............	
1Ch	29:24	all the princes, and the mighty **m.**,..........	
2Ch	2:2	ten thousand **m.** to bear burdens,........	376
2Ch	2:7	cunning **m.** that are with me in Judah........	
2Ch	2:14	be put to him, with thy cunning **m.**,..........	
2Ch	2:14	with the cunning **m.** of my lord David.......	
2Ch	5:3	**m.** of Israel assembled themselves.......	376
2Ch	6:18	God in very deed dwell with **m.** on......	120
2Ch	6:30	the hearts of the children of **m.**:).........	120
2Ch	8:9	but they were **m.** of war, and chief......	582
2Ch	9:7	Happy are thy **m.**, and happy are........	582
2Ch	10:6	took counsel with the old **m.**..................	
2Ch	10:8	the counsel which the old **m.** gave him,.....	
2Ch	10:8	and took counsel with the young **m.**..........	
2Ch	10:10	young **m.** that were brought up with.........	
2Ch	10:13	forsook the counsel of the old **m.**,...........	
2Ch	10:14	them after the advice of the young **m.**,.......	
2Ch	11:1	chosen **m.**, which were warriors, to..........	
2Ch	13:3	with an army of valiant **m.** of war,...........	
2Ch	13:3	four hundred thousand chosen **m.**:.......	376
2Ch	13:3	eight hundred thousand chosen **m.**,......	376
2Ch	13:3	being mighty **m.** of valour..................	
2Ch	13:7	are gathered unto him vain **m.**, the......	582
2Ch	13:15	Then the **m.** of Judah gave a shout:.....	376
2Ch	13:15	and as the **m.** of Judah shouted, it.......	376
2Ch	13:17	five hundred thousand chosen **m.**.........	376
2Ch	14:8	And Asa had an army of **m.** that bare.......	
2Ch	14:8	all these were mighty **m.** of valour..........	
2Ch	17:13	and the **m.** of war, mighty...of............	582
2Ch	17:13	mighty **m.** of valour were in Jerusalem......	
2Ch	17:14	mighty **m.** of valour three hundred...........	
2Ch	17:16	thousand mighty **m.** of valour................	
2Ch	17:17	him armed **m.** with bow and shield...........	
2Ch	18:5	of prophets four hundred **m.**, and........	376
2Ch	22:1	for the band of **m.** that came with the.......	
2Ch	23:8	and took every man his **m.** that..........	582
2Ch	24:24	came with a small company of **m.**,.......	582
2Ch	25:5	three hundred thousand choice **m.**,...........	
2Ch	25:6	thousand mighty **m.** of valour out of..........	
2Ch	26:11	Uzziah had an host of fighting **m.**,............	
2Ch	26:12	the fathers of the mighty **m.** of valour.......	
2Ch	26:15	engines, invented by cunning **m.**, to be.....	
2Ch	26:17	of the Lord, that were valiant **m.**:......	1121
2Ch	28:6	one day, which were all valiant **m.**;.....	1121
2Ch	28:14	So the armed **m.** left the captives and.......	
2Ch	28:15	**m.** which were expressed by name......	582
2Ch	31:19	the **m.** that were expressed by name,..	582
2Ch	32:3	and his mighty **m.** to stop the waters........	
2Ch	32:21	cut off all the mighty **m.** of valour...........	
2Ch	34:12	And the **m.** did the work faithfully:.......	582
2Ch	34:30	the Lord, and all the **m.** of Judah,........	376
2Ch	35:25	all the singing **m.** and the singing............	
2Ch	36:17	slew their young **m.** with the sword..........	
Ezr	1:4	**m.** of his place help him with silver,.....	582
Ezr	2:2	of the **m.** of the people of Israel:.........	582
Ezr	2:22	The **m.** of Netophah, fifty and six.......	582
Ezr	2:23	The **m.** of Anathoth, an hundred.........	582
Ezr	2:27	The **m.** of Michmas, an hundred..........	582
Ezr	2:28	**m.** of Beth-el and Ai, two hundred.......	582
Ezr	2:65	two hundred singing **m.** and singing..........	
Ezr	3:12	of the fathers, who were ancient **m.**,.........	
Ezr	4:11	the **m.** on this side of the river,..........	606
Ezr	4:21	to cause these **m.** to cease, and........	1400
Ezr	5:4	the names of the **m.** that make this....	1400
Ezr	5:10	names of the **m.** that were the chief...	1400
Ezr	6:8	expences be given unto these **m.**,......	1400
Ezr	7:28	together out of Israel chief **m.** to go.........	
Ezr	8:16	and for Meshullam, chief **m.**; also......	1400
Ezr	10:1	very great congregation of **m.** and.......	582
Ezr	10:9	all the **m.** of Judah and Benjamin.........	582
Ezr	10:17	the **m.** that had taken strange wives.....	582
Ne	1:2	came, he and certain **m.** of Judah;.......	582
Ne	2:12	night, I and some few **m.** with me;......	582
Ne	3:2	unto him builded the **m.** of Jericho.......	582
Ne	3:7	the **m.** of Gibeon, and of Mizpah,........	582
Ne	3:22	the priests, the **m.** of the plain...........	582
Ne	4:23	servants, nor the **m.** of the guard.......	582
Ne	5:5	for other **m.** have our lands and..........	582
Ne	7:7	**m.** of the people of Israel was this;......	582
Ne	7:26	The **m.** of Beth-lehem and Netophah,...	582
Ne	7:27	The **m.** of Anathoth, an hundred..........	582
Ne	7:28	The **m.** of Beth-azmaveth, forty and.....	582
Ne	7:29	**m.** of Kirjath-jearim, Chephirah,.........	582
Ne	7:30	The **m.** of Ramah and Gaba, six..........	582
Ne	7:31	the **m.** of Michmas, an hundred and.....	582
Ne	7:32	**m.** of Beth-el and Ai, an hundred.........	582
Ne	7:33	The **m.** of the other Nebo, fifty and.....	582
Ne	7:67	forty and five singing **m.** and singing.........	
Ne	8:2	congregation both of **m.** and women,....	376
Ne	8:3	before the **m.** and the women, and......	582
Ne	11:2	And the people blessed all the **m.**,.......	582
Ne	11:6	threescore and eight valiant **m.**...............	
Ne	11:14	their brethren, mighty **m.** of valour,..........	
Ne	11:14	the son of one of the great **m.**................	
Ne	13:16	There dwelt **m.** of Tyre also therein,........	
Es	1:13	Then the king said to the wise **m.**,...........	
Es	6:13	said his wise **m.** and Zeresh his wife..........	
Es	9:6	slew and destroyed five hundred **m.**.....	376
Es	9:12	and destroyed five hundred **m.** in.........	376
Es	9:15	slew three hundred **m.** at Shushan;......	376
Job	1:3	greatest of all the **m.** of the east........	1121
Job	1:19	it fell upon the young **m.**, and they..........	
Job	4:13	night, when deep sleep falleth on **m.**,...	582
Job	7:20	unto thee, O thou preserver of **m.**?.....	120
Job	11:3	thy lies make **m.** hold their peace?.....	4962
Job	11:11	For he knoweth vain **m.**: he seeth......	4962
Job	15:10	the grayheaded and very aged **m.**,............	
Job	15:18	Which wise **m.** have told from their..........	
Job	17:8	Upright **m.** shall be astonied at this,.........	
Job	22:15	which wicked **m.** have trodden?.........	4962

Job 22:29 When **m.** are cast down, then thou
Job 24:12 **M.** groan from out of the city, and 4962
Job 27:23 **M.** shall clap their hands at him, and
Job 28:4 up, they are gone away from **m.**. 582
Job 29:8 The young **m.** saw me, and hid
Job 29:21 Unto me **m.** gave ear, and waited,
Job 30:5 were driven forth from among **m.**,
Job 30:8 of fools, yea, children of base **m.**:
Job 31:31 the **m.** of my tabernacle said not, 4962
Job 32:1 So these three **m.** ceased to answer 582
Job 32:5 in the mouth of these three **m.**, 582
Job 32:9 Great **m.** are not always wise: neither
Job 33:15 when deep sleep falleth upon **m.**, 582
Job 33:16 Then he opened the ears of **m.**, and 582
Job 33:27 He looked upon **m.**, and if any say, 582
Job 34:2 Hear my words, O ye wise **m.**; and
Job 34:8 and walketh with wicked **m.**. 582
Job 34:10 unto me, ye **m.** of understanding: 582
Job 34:24 He shall break in pieces mighty **m.**
Job 34:26 He striketh them as wicked **m.** in the
Job 34:34 Let **m.** of understanding tell me, 582
Job 34:36 of his answers for wicked **m.**. 582
Job 35:12 because of the pride of evil **m.**.
Job 36:24 magnify his work, which **m.** behold. 582
Job 37:7 that all **m.** may know his work. 582
Job 37:21 And now **m.** see not the bright light
Job 37:24 **M.** do therefore fear him: he 582
Job 39:21 he goeth on to meet the armed **m.**.
Ps 4:2 O ye sons of **m.**, how long will ye 376
Ps 9:20 may know themselves to be but **m.** 582
Ps 11:4 his eyelids try, the children of **m.**. 120
Ps 12:1 fail from among the children of **m.**. 120
Ps 12:8 when the vilest **m.** are exalted. 1121,120
Ps 14:2 from heaven upon the children of **m.**, 120
Ps 17:4 Concerning the works of **m.**, by the 120
Ps 17:14 From **m.** which are thy hand, O 4962
Ps 17:14 from **m.** of the world, which have 4962
Ps 18:4 floods of ungodly **m.** made me afraid.
Ps 21:10 seed from among the children of **m.**. 120
Ps 22:6 a reproach of **m.**, and despised of 120
Ps 26:9 sinners, nor my life with bloody **m.**: 582
Ps 31:19 trust in thee before the sons of **m.**! 120
Ps 33:13 he beholdeth all the sons of **m.**. 120
Ps 36:7 children of **m.** put their trust under 120
Ps 45:2 art fairer than the children of **m.**: 120
Ps 49:10 For he seeth that wise **m.** die, likewise
Ps 49:18 and **m.** will praise thee, when thou
Ps 53:2 from heaven upon the children of **m.**, 120
Ps 55:23 deceitful **m.** shall not live out half 582
Ps 57:4 are set on fire, even the sons of **m.**, 120
Ps 58:1 ye judge uprightly, O ye sons of **m.**? 120
Ps 59:2 and save me from bloody **m.** 582
Ps 62:9 **m.** of low degree are vanity, 1121,120
Ps 62:9 **m.** of high degree are a lie: to be. 1121,376
Ps 64:9 all **m.** shall fear, and shall declare 120
Ps 66:5 his doing toward the children of **m.**. 120
Ps 66:12 caused **m.** to ride over our heads; 582
Ps 68:18 thou hast received gifts for **m.**; yea, 120
Ps 72:17 sun: and **m.** shall be blessed in him:
Ps 73:5 They are not in trouble as other **m.**; 582
Ps 73:5 are they plagued like other **m.**. 120
Ps 76:5 **m.** of might have found their hands. 582
Ps 78:31 smote down the chosen **m.** of Israel.
Ps 78:60 the tent which he placed among **m.**; 120
Ps 78:63 The fire consumed their young **m.**;
Ps 82:7 But ye shall die like **m.**, and fall like 120
Ps 83:18 That **m.** may know that thou, whose
Ps 86:14 violent **m.** have sought after my soul;
Ps 89:47 hast thou made all **m.** in vain? 1121,120
Ps 90:3 sayest, Return, ye children of **m.**. 120
Ps 105:12 they were but a few **m.** in number; 4962
Ps 107:8 Oh that **m.** would praise the Lord for
Ps 107:8 works to the children of **m.**! 120
Ps 107:15 Oh that **m.** would praise the Lord for
Ps 107:15 works to the children of **m.**! 120
Ps 107:21 Oh that **m.** would praise the Lord for
Ps 107:21 works to the children of **m.**! 120
Ps 107:31 Oh that **m.** would praise the Lord
Ps 107:31 works to the children of **m.**! 120
Ps 115:16 hath he given to the children of **m.**. 120
Ps 116:11 I said in my haste, All **m.** are liars. 120
Ps 124:2 side, when **m.** rose up against us: 120
Ps 139:19 from me therefore, ye bloody **m.** 582
Ps 141:4 works with **m.** that work iniquity: 376
Ps 145:6 **m.** shall speak of the might of thy
Ps 145:12 To make known to the sons of **m.** 120
Ps 148:12 Both young **m.**, and maidens;
Ps 148:12 and maidens; old **m.**, and children:
Pr 2:20 mayest walk in the way of good **m.**,
Pr 4:14 and go not in the way of evil **m.**.
Pr 6:30 **M.** do not despise a thief, if he steal to
Pr 7:26 many . . . **m.** have been slain by her
Pr 8:4 Unto you, O **m.**, I call; and my 376
Pr 8:31 delights were with the sons of **m.** 120
Pr 10:14 Wise **m.** lay up knowledge: but the
Pr 11:7 and the hope of unjust **m.** perisheth.
Pr 11:16 honour: and strong **m.** retain riches.
Pr 12:12 The wicked desireth the net of evil **m.**:
Pr 13:20 walketh with wise **m.** shall be wise:
Pr 15:11 the hearts of the children of **m.**? 120
Pr 16:6 fear of the Lord **m.** depart from evil.
Pr 17:6 children are the crown of old **m.**;
Pr 18:16 and bringeth him before great **m.**.
Pr 20:6 Most **m.** will proclaim every one 120
Pr 20:29 glory of young **m.** is their strength:
Pr 20:29 the beauty of old **m.** is the gray head.
Pr 22:29 he shall not stand before mean **m.**.
Pr 23:28 the transgressors among **m.**. 120
Pr 24:1 not thou envious against evil **m.**. 582
Pr 24:9 scorner is an abomination to **m.** 120
Pr 24:19 Fret not thyself because of evil **m.**,
Pr 25:1 the **m.** of Hezekiah king of Judah 582
Pr 25:6 and stand not in the place of great **m.**:
Pr 25:27 for **m.** to search their own glory is not
Pr 26:16 seven **m.** that can render a reason.
Pr 28:5 Evil **m.** understand not judgment: 582
Pr 28:7 that is a companion of riotous **m.**
Pr 28:12 When righteous **m.** do rejoice, there is
Pr 28:28 wicked rise, **m.** hide themselves: 120
Pr 29:8 Scornful **m.** bring a city into a 582
Pr 29:8 snare: but wise **m.** turn away wrath.
Pr 30:14 and the needy from among **m.**. 120
Ec 2:3 was that good for the sons of **m.**, 120
Ec 2:8 me **m.** singers and women singers,
Ec 2:8 and the delights of the sons of **m.**, 120
Ec 3:10 God hath given to the sons of **m.** 120
Ec 3:14 that **m.** should fear before him.
Ec 3:18 the estate of the sons of **m.**, that God.. 120
Ec 3:19 that which befalleth the sons of **m.** 120
Ec 6:1 sun, and it is common among **m.**: 120
Ec 7:2 for that is the end of all **m.**; and the 120
Ec 7:19 ten mighty **m.** which are in the city.
Ec 8:11 heart of the sons of **m.** is fully set 120
Ec 8:14 that there be just **m.**, unto whom it
Ec 8:14 again, there be wicked **m.**, to whom it
Ec 9:3 heart of the sons of **m.** is full of evil, 120
Ec 9:11 nor yet riches to **m.** of understanding,
Ec 9:11 nor yet favour to **m.** of skill; but time
Ec 9:12 so are the sons of **m.** snared in an 120
Ec 9:14 a little city, and few **m.** within it; 582
Ec 9:17 words of wise **m.** are heard in quiet
Ec 12:3 strong **m.** shall bow themselves, 582
Ca 3:7 threescore valiant **m.** are about it,
Ca 4:4 bucklers, all shields of mighty **m.**.
Isa 2:11 haughtiness of **m.** shall be bowed 582
Isa 2:17 haughtiness of **m.** shall be made low: 582
Isa 3:25 Thy **m.** shall fall by the sword, and 4962
Isa 5:3 and **m.** of Judah, judge, I pray you, 376
Isa 5:7 the **m.** of Judah his pleasant plant: 376
Isa 5:13 their honourable **m.** are famished, 4962
Isa 5:22 and **m.** of strength to mingle strong 582
Isa 6:12 Lord have removed **m.** far away, 120
Isa 7:13 a small thing for you to weary **m.**, 582
Isa 7:24 and with bows shall **m.** come thither;
Isa 9:3 **m.** rejoice when they divide the spoil.
Isa 9:17 shall have no joy in their young **m.**,
Isa 11:15 streams, and make **m.** go over dryshod.
Isa 13:18 shall dash the young **m.** to pieces;
Isa 19:12 where are thy wise **m.**? and let them
Isa 21:9 here cometh a chariot of **m.**, with 376
Isa 21:17 mighty **m.** of the children of Kedar,
Isa 22:2 slain **m.** are not slain with the sword,
Isa 22:6 with chariots of **m.** and horsemen, 120
Isa 23:4 neither do I nourish up young **m.**, nor
Isa 24:6 earth was burned, and few **m.** left. 582
Isa 26:19 Thy dead **m.** shall live, together with
Isa 28:14 word of the Lord, ye scornful **m.**, 582
Isa 29:11 which **m.** deliver to one that is learned,
Isa 29:13 me is taught by the precept of **m.**: 582
Isa 29:14 wisdom of their wise **m.** shall perish,
Isa 29:14 the understanding of their prudent **m.**
Isa 29:19 the poor among **m.** shall rejoice in 120
Isa 31:3 the Egyptians are **m.**, and not God; 120
Isa 31:8 and his young **m.** shall be discomfited.
Isa 35:8 the wayfaring **m.**, though fools, shall
Isa 36:12 me to the **m.** that sit upon the wall, 582
Isa 38:16 O Lord, by these things **m.** live, and in
Isa 39:3 What said these **m.**? and from 582
Isa 40:30 and the young **m.** shall utterly fall:
Isa 41:9 called thee from the chief **m.** thereof,
Isa 41:14 worm Jacob, and ye **m.** of Israel; 4962
Isa 43:4 therefore will I give **m.** for thee, 120
Isa 44:11 and the workmen, they are of **m.**: let 120
Isa 44:25 that turneth wise **m.** backward, and
Isa 45:14 and of the Sabeans, **m.** of stature, 582
Isa 45:24 even to him shall **m.** come; and all that
Isa 46:8 this, and shew yourselves **m.**: 376
Isa 51:7 fear ye not the reproach of **m.**, 582
Isa 52:14 his form more than the sons of **m.**: 120
Isa 53:3 He is despised and rejected of **m.**; 376
Isa 57:1 merciful **m.** are taken away, none 582
Isa 59:10 we are in desolate places as dead **m.**.
Isa 60:11 that **m.** may bring unto thee the forces
Isa 61:6 **m.** shall call you the Ministers of our
Isa 64:4 **m.** have not heard, nor perceived by
Isa 66:24 look upon the carcases of the **m.** 582
Jer 4:3 saith the Lord to the **m.** of Judah 376
Jer 4:4 ye **m.** of Judah and inhabitants of 376
Jer 5:5 I will get me unto the great **m.**, and
Jer 5:16 sepulchre, they are all mighty **m.**.
Jer 5:26 my people are found wicked **m.**: they
Jer 5:26 they set a trap, they catch **m.** 582
Jer 6:11 and upon the assembly of young **m.**.
Jer 6:23 set in array as **m.** for war against 376
Jer 6:30 Reprobate silver shall **m.** call them,
Jer 8:9 The wise **m.** are ashamed, they are
Jer 9:2 a lodging place of wayfaring **m.**; that
Jer 9:2 an assembly of treacherous **m.**
Jer 9:10 can **m.** hear the voice of the cattle;
Jer 9:21 and the young **m.** from the streets.
Jer 9:22 Even the carcases of **m.** shall fall. 120
Jer 10:7 among all the wise **m.** of the nations,
Jer 10:9 they are all the work of cunning **m.**.
Jer 11:2 speak unto the **m.** of Judah, and 376
Jer 11:9 is found among the **m.** of Judah, 376
Jer 11:21 the Lord of the **m.** of Anathoth, 582
Jer 11:22 the young **m.** shall die by the sword;
Jer 11:23 bring evil upon the **m.** of Anathoth, 582
Jer 15:8 against the mother of the young **m.** a
Jer 15:10 nor **m.** have lent to me on usury; yet
Jer 16:6 neither shall **m.** lament for them, nor
Jer 16:7 shall **m.** tear themselves for them in
Jer 16:7 **m.** give them the cup of consolation.
Jer 17:25 **m.** of Judah, and the inabitants of 376
Jer 18:11 speak to the **m.** of Judah, and to 376
Jer 18:21 and let their **m.** be put to death; 582
Jer 18:21 young **m.** be slain by the sword in
Jer 19:10 sight of the **m.** that go with thee, 582
Jer 26:21 the king, with all his mighty **m.**,
Jer 26:22 the king sent **m.** into Egypt, 582
Jer 26:22 and certain **m.** with him into Egypt. 582
Jer 31:13 both young **m.** and old together:
Jer 32:19 upon all the ways of the sons of **m.**: 120
Jer 32:20 and in Israel, and among other **m.**; 120
Jer 32:32 prophets, and the **m.** of Judah, and 376
Jer 32:44 **M.** shall buy fields for money, and
Jer 33:5 them with the dead bodies of **m.**, 120
Jer 34:18 give the **m.** that have transgressed 582
Jer 35:13 Go and tell the **m.** of Judah and 376
Jer 36:31 and upon the **m.** of Judah, all the 376
Jer 37:10 there remained but wounded **m.** 582
Jer 38:4 weakeneth the hands of the **m.** of 582
Jer 38:9 **m.** have done evil in all that they 582
Jer 38:10 fron hence thirty **m.** with thee, and 582
Jer 38:11 Ebed-melech took the **m.** with him, 582
Jer 38:16 give thee into the hand of these **m.** 582
Jer 39:4 saw them, and all the **m.** of war, 582
Jer 39:17 not be given into the hand of the **m.** 582
Jer 40:7 and their **m.**, heard that the king 582
Jer 40:7 had committed unto him **m.**, and 582
Jer 40:8 a Maachathite, they and their **m.** 582
Jer 40:9 sware unto them and to their **m.**, 582
Jer 41:1 of the king, even ten **m.** with him, 582
Jer 41:2 and the ten **m.** that were with him, 582
Jer 41:3 were found there, and the **m.** of war 582
Jer 41:5 from Samaria, even fourscore **m.**, 376
Jer 41:7 he, and the **m.** that were with him 582
Jer 41:8 ten **m.** were found among them that 582
Jer 41:9 cast all the dead bodies of the **m.**, 582
Jer 41:12 Then they took all the **m.**, and went 582
Jer 41:15 from Johanan with eight **m.**, and 582

Jer 41:16 even mighty **m.** of war, and the ... 582
Jer 42:17 shall it be with all the **m.** that set ... 582
Jer 43:2 Johanan...and all the proud **m.**, ... 582
Jer 43:6 Even **m.**, and women, and he ... 1397
Jer 43:9 in the sight of the **m.** of Judah; ... 582
Jer 44:15 Then all the **m.** which knew that ... 582
Jer 44:19 offerings unto her, without our **m.**? ... 582
Jer 44:20 to the **m.**, and to the women, and ... 1397
Jer 44:27 all the **m.** of Judah that are in the ... 376
Jer 46:9 and let the mighty **m.** come forth; ...
Jer 46:15 Why are thy valiant **m.** swept away? ...
Jer 46:21 Also her hired **m.** are in the midst of ...
Jer 47:2 then the **m.** shall cry, and all the ... 120
Jer 48:14 mighty and strong **m.** for the war? ... 582
Jer 48:15 his chosen young **m.** are gone down to ...
Jer 48:31 mourn for the **m.** of Kir-heres. ... 582
Jer 48:36 like pipes for the **m.** of Kir-heres: ... 582
Jer 49:15 heathen, and despised among **m.** ... 120
Jer 49:22 the heart of the mighty **m.** of Edom be ...
Jer 49:26 her young **m.** shall fall in her streets, ...
Jer 49:26 all the **m.** of war shall be cut off ... 582
Jer 49:28 and spoil the **m.** of the east. ... 1121
Jer 50:30 shall her young **m.** fall in her streets, ...
Jer 50:30 all her **m.** of war shall be cut off in ... 582
Jer 50:35 her princes, and upon her wise **m.** ...
Jer 50:36 a sword is upon her mighty **m.**; and ...
Jer 51:3 spare ye not her young **m.**; destroy ye ...
Jer 51:14 Surely I will fill thee with **m.**, as ... 120
Jer 51:30 mighty **m.** of Babylon have forborn ...
Jer 51:32 and the **m.** of war are affrighted. ... 582
Jer 51:56 her mighty **m.** are taken, every one ...
Jer 51:57 drunk her princes, and her wise **m.** ...
Jer 51:57 and her rulers, and her mighty **m.**: ...
Jer 52:7 all the **m.** of war fled, and went ... 582
Jer 52:13 all houses of the great **m.**, burned he ...
Jer 52:25 had the charge of the **m.** of war; ... 582
Jer 52:25 and seven **m.** of them that were near ... 582
Jer 52:25 **m.** of the people of the land, that ... 376
La 1:15 trodden under foot all my mighty **m.** ...
La 1:15 against me to crush my young **m.**: ...
La 1:18 my young **m.** are gone into captivity. ...
La 2:15 the city that **m.** call The perfection ...
La 2:21 my young **m.** are fallen by the sword; ...
La 3:33 nor grieve the children of **m.** ... 376
La 4:14 wandered as blind **m.** in the streets, ...
La 4:14 **m.** could not touch their garments. ...
La 5:13 they took the young **m.** to grind, and ...
La 5:14 gate, the young **m.** from their musick. ...
Eze 6:4 cast down your slain **m.** before your ...
Eze 6:13 slain **m.** shall be among their idols ...
Eze 8:11 there stood before them seventy **m.** ... 376
Eze 8:16 about five and twenty **m.**, with their ... 376
Eze 9:2 six **m.** came from the way of the ... 582
Eze 9:4 mark upon the foreheads of the **m.** ... 582
Eze 9:6 they began at the ancient **m.** which ... 582
Eze 11:1 door of the gate five and twenty **m.**; ... 376
Eze 11:2 are the **m.** that devise mischief, ... 582
Eze 11:15 thy brethren, the **m.** of thy kindred, ... 582
Eze 12:16 a few **m.** of them from the sword, ... 582
Eze 14:3 these **m.** have set up their idols in ... 582
Eze 14:14 these three **m.**, Noah, Daniel, and ... 582
Eze 14:16, 18 these three **m.** were in it, as I ... 582
Eze 15:3 will **m.** take a pin of it to hang any ...
Eze 16:17 madest to thyself images of **m.**, ... 2145
Eze 19:3 to catch the prey; it devoured **m.** ... 120
Eze 19:6 to catch the prey, and devoured **m.** ... 120
Eze 21:14 is the sword of the great **m.** that are ...
Eze 21:31 thee into the hand of brutish **m.**, ... 582
Eze 22:9 In thee are **m.** that carry tales to ... 582
Eze 23:6 rulers, all of them desirable young **m.**, ...
Eze 23:7 were the chosen **m.** of Assyria, ... 1121
Eze 23:12 horses, all of them desirable young **m.** ...
Eze 23:14 she saw **m.** pourtrayed upon the ... 582
Eze 23:23 all of them desirable young **m.**, ...
Eze 23:40 have sent for **m.** to come from far, ... 582
Eze 23:42 and with the **m.** of the common sort ... 582
Eze 23:45 the righteous **m.**, they shall judge ... 582
Eze 24:17 thy lips, and eat not the bread of **m.** ... 582
Eze 24:22 your lips, nor eat the bread of **m.** ... 582
Eze 25:4 deliver thee to the **m.** of the east ... 1121
Eze 25:10 **m.** of the east with the Ammonites, ... 1121
Eze 26:10 as **m.** enter into a city wherein is ...
Eze 26:17 that wast inhabited of seafaring **m.**, ...
Eze 27:8 thy wise **m.**, O Tyrus, that were in ...
Eze 27:9 the wise **m.** thereof were in thee thy ...
Eze 27:10 were in thine army, thy **m.** of war: ... 582
Eze 27:11 The **m.** of Arvad with thine army ... 1121
Eze 27:13 they traded the persons of **m.** and ... 120
Eze 27:15 **m.** of Dedan were thy merchants; ... 1121
Eze 27:27 all thy **m.** of war, that are in thee, ... 582
Eze 30:5 **m.** of the land that is in league, ... 1121
Eze 30:17 The young **m.** of Aven...shall fall ...
Eze 31:14 in the midst of the children of **m.**, ... 120
Eze 34:31 the flock of my pasture, are **m.**, and ... 120
Eze 35:8 fill his mountains with his slain **m.**: ...
Eze 36:10 And I will multiply **m.** upon you, ... 120
Eze 36:12 I will cause **m.** to walk upon you, ... 120
Eze 36:12 more henceforth bereave them of **m.** ...
Eze 36:13 Thou land devourest up **m.**, and ... 120
Eze 36:14 thou shalt devour **m.** no more, ... 120
Eze 36:15 Neither will I cause **m.** to hear in thee ...
Eze 36:37 increase them with **m.** like a flock ... 120
Eze 36:38 cities be filled with flocks of **m.**: ... 120
Eze 38:20 all the **m.** that are upon the face of ... 120
Eze 39:14 they shall sever out **m.** of continual ... 582
Eze 39:20 horses and chariots, with mighty **m.**, ...
Eze 39:20 and with all **m.** of war, saith the ... 376
Eze 47:15 way of Hethlon, as **m.** go to Zedad; ...
Da 2:12 to destroy all the wise **m.** of Babylon. ...
Da 2:13 forth that the wise **m.** should be slain; ...
Da 2:14 forth to slay the wise **m.** of Babylon: ...
Da 2:18 with the rest of the wise **m.** of Babylon. ...
Da 2:24 to destroy the wise **m.** of Babylon: he ...
Da 2:24 Destroy not the wise **m.** of Babylon: ...
Da 2:27 hath demanded cannot the wise **m.**, ...
Da 2:38 the children of **m.** dwell, the ... 606
Da 2:43 themselves with the seed of **m.**: ... 606
Da 2:48 over all the wise **m.** of Babylon. ...
Da 3:12 these **m.**, O king, have not ... 1400
Da 3:13 brought these **m.** before the king. ... 1400
Da 3:20 commanded the most mighty **m.** ... 1400
Da 3:21 these **m.** were bound in their coats, ... 1400
Da 3:22 the fire slew those **m.** that took up ... 1400
Da 3:23 these three **m.**, Shadrach, Meshach, ... 1400
Da 3:24 Did not we cast three **m.** bound ... 1400
Da 3:25 Lo, I see four **m.** loose, walking in ... 1400
Da 3:27 saw these **m.**, upon whose bodies ... 1400
Da 4:6 to bring in all the wise **m.** of Babylon ...
Da 4:17 High ruleth in the kingdom of **m.**, ... 606
Da 4:17 setteth up over it the basest of **m.** ... 606
Da 4:18 wise **m.** of my kingdom are not able ...
Da 4:25 they shall drive thee from **m.**, and ... 606
Da 4:25 High ruleth in the kingdom of **m.**, ... 606
Da 4:32 they shall drive thee from **m.**, and ... 606
Da 4:32 High ruleth in the kingdom of **m.**, ... 606
Da 4:33 he was driven from **m.**, and did eat ... 606
Da 5:7 and said to the wise **m.** of Babylon, ...
Da 5:8 Then came in all the king's wise **m.**: ...
Da 5:15 And now the wise **m.**, the astrologers, ...
Da 5:21 he was driven from the sons of **m.**; ... 606
Da 5:21 God ruled in the kingdom of **m.**, ... 606
Da 6:5 Then said these **m.**, We shall not ... 1400
Da 6:11 Then these **m.** assembled, and found ... 1400
Da 6:15 Then these **m.** assembled unto the ... 1400
Da 6:24 **m.** which had accused Daniel, ... 1400
Da 6:26 **m.** tremble and fear before the God ...
Da 9:7 **m.** of Judah, and to the inhabitants ... 376
Da 10:7 **m.** that were with me saw not the ... 582
Da 10:16 like the similitude of the sons of **m.** ... 120
Ho 6:7 But they like **m.** have transgressed ... 120
Ho 10:13 in the multitude of thy mighty **m.** ...
Ho 13:2 **m.** that sacrifice kiss the calves. ... 120
Joe 1:2 Hear this, ye old **m.**, and give ear, all ...
Joe 1:12 withered away from the sons of **m.** ... 120
Joe 2:7 shall run like mighty **m.**; they shall ...
Joe 2:7 shall climb the wall like **m.** of war; ... 582
Joe 2:28 your old **m.** shall dream dreams, ...
Joe 2:28 your young **m.** shall see visions: ...
Joe 3:9 war, wake up the mighty **m.**, let ... 582
Joe 3:9 let all the **m.** of war draw near; let ... 582
Am 2:11 and of your young **m.** for Nazarites. ...
Am 4:10 your young **m.** have I slain with the ...
Am 6:9 there remain ten **m.** in one house, ... 582
Am 8:13 virgins and young **m.** faint for thirst. ...
Ob 7 **m.** of thy confederacy have brought ... 582
Ob 7 the **m.** that were at peace with thee ... 582
Ob 8 even destroy the wise **m.** out of Edom, ...
Ob 9 And thy mighty **m.**, O Teman, shall be ...
Jon 1:10 were the **m.** exceedingly afraid, ... 582
Jon 1:10 For the **m.** knew that he fled from ... 582
Jon 1:13 Nevertheless the **m.** rowed hard to ... 582
Jon 1:16 the **m.** feared the Lord exceedingly, ... 582
Mic 2:8 by securely as **m.** averse from war ...
Mic 2:12 by reason of the multitude of **m.** ... 120
Mic 5:5 shepherds, and eight principal **m.** ... 120
Mic 5:7 man, nor waiteth for the sons of **m.** ... 120
Mic 6:12 rich **m.** thereof are full of violence, ...
Mic 7:2 there is none upright among **m.**: ... 120
Mic 7:6 enemies are...**m.** of his house. ... 582
Na 2:3 shield of his mighty **m.** is made red, ...
Na 2:3 red, the valiant **m.** are in scarlet: ... 582
Na 3:10 they cast lots for her honourable **m.**, ...
Na 3:10 all her great **m.** were bound in chains. ...
Hab 1:14 makest **m.** as the fishes of the sea, ... 120
Zep 1:12 punish the **m.** that are settled on ... 582
Zep 1:17 I will bring distress upon **m.**, that ... 120
Zep 1:17 that they shall walk like blind **m.**, ...
Zep 2:11 and **m.** shall worship him, every ...
Hag 1:11 and upon **m.**, and upon cattle, and ... 120
Zec 2:4 for the multitude of **m.** and cattle ... 120
Zec 3:8 for they are **m.** wondered at: for, ... 582
Zec 7:2 their **m.**, to pray before the Lord, ... 582
Zec 7:7 when **m.** inhabited the south and the ...
Zec 8:4 There shall yet old **m.** and old women ...
Zec 8:10 I set all **m.** every one against his ... 120
Zec 8:23 that ten **m.** shall take hold out of ... 582
Zec 9:17 shall make the young **m.** cheerful, ...
Zec 10:5 And they shall be as mighty **m.**, which ...
Zec 11:6 I will deliver the **m.** every one into ... 120
Zec 14:11 And **m.** shall dwell in it, and there ...
Mt 2:1 there came wise **m.** from the east to ...
Mt 2:7 he had privily called the wise **m.**, ...
Mt 2:16 saw that he was mocked of the wise **m.**, ...
Mt 2:16 had diligently enquired of the wise **m.** ...
Mt 4:19 **and I will make you fishers of m.** ... *444*
Mt 5:11 **are ye, when m. shall revile you,** ...
Mt 5:13 **and to be trodden under foot of m.** ... *444*
Mt 5:15 **Neither do m. light a candle, and** ...
Mt 5:16 **Let your light so shine before m.,** ... *444*
Mt 5:19 **and shall teach m. so, he shall be** ... *444*
Mt 6:1 **ye do not your alms before m.,** ... *444*
Mt 6:2 **that they may have glory of m.** ... *444*
Mt 6:5 **that they may be seen of m.** ... *444*
Mt 6:14 **For if ye forgive m. their** ... *444*
Mt 6:15 **if ye forgive not m. their,** ... *444*
Mt 6:16 **they may appear unto m. to fast.** ... *444*
Mt 6:18 **thou appear not unto m. to fast,** ... *444*
Mt 7:12 **ye would that m. should do to you,** ... *444*
Mt 7:16 **Do m. gather grapes of thorns,** ...
Mt 8:27 the **m.** marvelled, saying, What ... *444*
Mt 9:8 had given such power unto **m.** ... *444*
Mt 9:17 **Neither do m. put new wine into** ...
Mt 9:27 two blind **m.** followed him, crying, and ...
Mt 9:28 the house, the blind **m.** came to him: ...
Mt 10:17 **beware of m.: for they will deliver** ... *444*
Mt 10:22 **be hated of all m. for my name's** ...
Mt 10:32 **shall confess me before m., him** ... *444*
Mt 10:33 **shall deny me before m.,** ... *444*
Mt 12:31 **shall be forgiven unto m.:** ... *444*
Mt 12:31 **shall not be forgiven unto m.** ... *444*
Mt 12:36 **idle word that m. shall speak,** ... *444*
Mt 12:41 **The m. of Nineveh shall rise in** ... *435*
Mt 13:17 **righteous m. have desired to see** ...
Mt 13:25 **while m. slept, his enemy came** ... *444*
Mt 14:21 eaten were about five thousand **m.**, ... *435*
Mt 14:35 the **m.** of that place had knowledge ... *435*
Mt 15:9 **the commandments of m.** ... *444*
Mt 15:38 that did eat were four thousand **m.**, ... *435*
Mt 16:13 **Whom do m. say that I the Son of** ... *444*
Mt 16:23 **be of God, but those that be of m.** ... *444*
Mt 17:22 **be betrayed into the hands of m.:** ... *444*
Mt 19:11 **All m. cannot receive this saying,** ...
Mt 19:12 **which were made eunuchs of m.:** ... *444*
Mt 19:26 **With m. this is impossible; but** ... *444*
Mt 20:30 two blind **m.** sitting by the way side, ...
Mt 21:25 **was it? from heaven, or of m.?** ... *444*
Mt 21:26 if we shall say, Of **m.**; we fear the ... *444*
Mt 21:41 miserably destroy those wicked **m.**, ...
Mt 22:16 thou regardest not the person of **m.** ... *444*
Mt 23:5 **works they do for to be seen of m.:** ... *444*
Mt 23:7 **to be called of m., Rabbi, Rabbi.** ... *444*
Mt 23:13 **the kingdom of heaven against m.:** ... *444*
Mt 23:28 **appear righteous unto m., but** ... *444*
Mt 23:34 **unto you prophets, and wise m.,** ...
Mt 26:33 Though all **m.** shall be offended ...
Mt 28:4 did shake, and became as dead **m.** ...
Mk 1:17 **make you to become fishers of m.** ... *444*
Mk 1:37 said unto him, All **m.** seek for thee. ...
Mk 3:28 **be forgiven unto the sons of m.,** ... *444*
Mk 5:20 done for him: and all **m.** did marvel. ...
Mk 6:12 and preached that **m.** should repent. ...

Mk	6:44	loaves were about five thousand m.	435
Mk	7:7	doctrines the commandments of m.	444
Mk	7:8	ye hold the tradition of m., as the	444
Mk	7:21	out of the heart of m., proceed evil	444
Mk	8:4	man satisfy these m. with bread here	
Mk	8:24	and said, I see m. as trees, walking.	444
Mk	8:27	them, Whom do m. say that I am?	444
Mk	8:33	God, but the things that be of m.	444
Mk	9:31	is delivered into the hands of m.,	444
Mk	10:27	With m. it is impossible, but not	444
Mk	11:30	was it from heaven, or of m.?	444
Mk	11:32	if we shall say, Of m.; they feared	444
Mk	11:32	for all m. counted John, that he was a	
Mk	12:14	regardest not the person of m., but	444
Mk	13:13	of all m. for my name's sake:	
Mk	14:51	and the young m. laid hold on him:	3495
Lu	1:25	take away my reproach among m.	444
Lu	2:14	on earth peace, good will toward m.	444
Lu	3:15	all m. mused in their hearts of John,	
Lu	5:10	henceforth thou shalt catch m.	444
Lu	5:18	m. brought in a bed a man which	435
Lu	6:22	are ye, when m. shall hate you,	444
Lu	6:26	when all m. shall speak well of	444
Lu	6:31	ye would that m. should do to you,	444
Lu	6:38	shall m. give into your bosom.	
Lu	6:44	of thorns m. do not gather figs,	
Lu	7:20	When the m. were come unto him,	435
Lu	7:31	I liken the m. of this generation?	444
Lu	9:14	they were about five thousand m.	435
Lu	9:30	behold, there talked with him two m.,	435
Lu	9:32	and the two m. that stood with him.	435
Lu	9:44	be delivered into the hands of m.	444
Lu	11:31	with the m. of this generation,	435
Lu	11:32	m. of Nineve shall rise up in the	435
Lu	11:44	the m. that walk over them are	444
Lu	11:46	ye lade m. with burdens grievous	444
Lu	12:8	confess me before m., him shall	444
Lu	12:9	he that denieth me before m. shall	444
Lu	12:36	unto m. that wait for their lord,	444
Lu	12:48	to whom m. have committed much,	
Lu	13:4	they were sinners above all m.	444
Lu	13:14	six days in which m. ought to work:	
Lu	14:24	none of those m. which were	435
Lu	14:35	yet for the dunghill; but m. cast	
Lu	16:15	which justify yourselves before m.;	444
Lu	16:15	among m. is abomination	444
Lu	17:12	met him ten m. that were lepers,	435
Lu	17:34	there shall be two m. in one bed;	
Lu	17:36	Two m. shall be in the field;	
Lu	18:1	that m. ought always to pray, and not	
Lu	18:10	Two m. went up into the temple	444
Lu	18:11	that I am not as other m. are,	444
Lu	18:27	impossible with m. are possible	444
Lu	20:4	was it from heaven, or of m.?	444
Lu	20:6	if we say, Of m.; all the people will	444
Lu	20:20	which should feign themselves just m.,	
Lu	21:1	rich m. casting their gifts into the	
Lu	21:17	be hated of all m. for my name's	
Lu	22:63	the m. that held Jesus mocked him,	435
Lu	23:11	his m. of war set him at nought,	4753
Lu	24:4	two m. stood by them in shining	435
Lu	24:7	delivered into the hands of sinful m.,	444
Joh	1:4	and the life was the light of m.	444
Joh	1:7	that all m. through him might believe.	
Joh	2:10	and when m. have well drunk, then	
Joh	2:24	unto them, because he knew all m.,	
Joh	3:19	m. loved darkness rather than	444
Joh	3:26	baptizeth, and all m. come to him	
Joh	4:20	the place where m. ought to worship.	
Joh	4:28	into the city, and saith to the m.,	444
Joh	4:38	other m. laboured, and ye are	
Joh	5:23	That all m. should honour the Son,	
Joh	5:41	I receive not honour from m.	444
Joh	6:10	Jesus said, Make the m. sit down.	444
Joh	6:10	the m. sat down, in number about	435
Joh	6:14	Then those m., when they had seen	444
Joh	8:17	the testimony of two m. is true.	444
Joh	11:48	thus alone, all m. will believe on him:	
Joh	12:32	the earth, will draw all m. unto me.	
Joh	12:43	For they loved the praise of m. more	444
Joh	13:35	this shall all m. know that ye are	
Joh	15:6	m. gather them, and cast them	
Joh	17:6	manifested thy name unto the m.	444
Joh	18:3	having received a band of m. and	
Ac	1:10	two m. stood by them in white	435
Ac	1:11	m. of Galilee, why stand ye gazing	435
Ac	1:16	M. and brethren, this scripture	435
Ac	1:21	these m. which have companied with	
Ac	1:24	which knowest the hearts of all m.,	
Ac	2:5	Jews, devout m., out of every nation.	435
Ac	2:13	said, These m. are full of new wine.	
Ac	2:14	Ye m. of Judaea, and all ye that	435
Ac	2:17	your young m. shall see visions,	3495
Ac	2:17	and your old m. shall dream dreams:	
Ac	2:22	Ye m. of Israel, hear these words;	435
Ac	2:29	M. and brethren, let me freely	435
Ac	2:37	M. and brethren, what shall we do?	435
Ac	2:45	parted them to all m., as every man	
Ac	3:12	Ye m. of Israel, why marvel ye at	435
Ac	4:4	the number of the m. was about five	435
Ac	4:12	under heaven given among m.,	444
Ac	4:13	they were unlearned and ignorant m.,	444
Ac	4:16	What shall we do to these m.? for	444
Ac	4:21	all m. glorified God for that which was	
Ac	5:4	thou hast not lied unto m., but unto	444
Ac	5:6	the young m. arose, wound him up,	
Ac	5:10	the young m. came in, and found	3495
Ac	5:14	multitudes both of m. and women.)	435
Ac	5:25	the m. whom ye put in prison are	435
Ac	5:29	ought to obey God rather than m.	444
Ac	5:35	m. of Israel, take heed to yourselves	435
Ac	5:35	intend to do as touching these m.	444
Ac	5:36	to whom a number of m., about	435
Ac	5:38	Refrain from these m., and let them	444
Ac	5:38	if this counsel or this work be of m.,	444
Ac	6:3	among you seven m. of honest	435
Ac	6:11	Then they suborned m., which said,	435
Ac	7:2	M., brethren, and fathers, hearken;	435
Ac	8:2	m. carried Stephen to his burial, and	435
Ac	8:3	m. and women committed them to	435
Ac	8:12	were baptized, both m. and women.	435
Ac	9:2	whether they were m. or women, he	435
Ac	9:7	the m. which journeyed with him	435
Ac	9:38	there, they sent unto him two m.,	435
Ac	10:5	send m. to Joppa, and call for one	435
Ac	10:17	m. which were sent from Cornelius	
Ac	10:19	unto him, Behold, three m. seek thee.	435
Ac	10:21	went down to the m. which were sent	435
Ac	11:3	wentest in to m. uncircumcised, and	435
Ac	11:11	there were three m. already come	435
Ac	11:13	Send m. to Joppa, and call for	
Ac	11:20	them were m. of Cyprus and Cyrene,	435
Ac	13:15	Ye m. and brethren, if ye have any	435
Ac	13:16	M. of Israel, and ye that fear God,	435
Ac	13:26	M. and brethren, children of the	435
Ac	13:38	unto you therefore, m. and brethren,	435
Ac	13:50	women, and the chief m. of the city,	
Ac	14:11	down to us in the likeness of m.	444
Ac	14:15	We also are m. of like passions with	444
Ac	15:1	certain m. which came...from Judaea	
Ac	15:7	M. and brethren, ye know how	435
Ac	15:13	M. and brethren, hearken unto me:	435
Ac	15:17	the residue of m. might seek after	444
Ac	15:22	send chosen m. of their...company	435
Ac	15:22	Silas, chief m. among the brethren:	435
Ac	15:25	to send chosen m. unto you with our	435
Ac	15:26	M. that have hazarded their lives	444
Ac	16:17	m. are the servants of the most high	444
Ac	16:20	saying, These m., being Jews, do	444
Ac	16:35	serjeants, saying, Let those m. go.	444
Ac	17:12	were Greeks, and of m., not a few.	435
Ac	17:22	Ye m. of Athens, I perceive that in	435
Ac	17:26	made of one blood all nations of m.	444
Ac	17:30	all m. every where to repent:	444
Ac	17:31	he hath given assurance unto all m.,	
Ac	17:34	Howbeit certain m. clave unto him,	435
Ac	18:13	persuadeth m. to worship God	444
Ac	19:7	And all the m. were about twelve.	435
Ac	19:19	and burned them before all m.:	
Ac	19:29	and Aristarchus, m. of Macedonia,	
Ac	19:35	Ye m. of Ephesus, what man is there	435
Ac	19:37	ye have brought hither these m.,	435
Ac	20:26	I am pure from the blood of all m.	
Ac	20:30	of your own selves shall m. arise,	435
Ac	21:23	We have four m. which have a vow	435
Ac	21:26	Then Paul took the m., and the next	435
Ac	21:28	Crying out, M. of Israel, help: This	435
Ac	21:28	man, that teacheth all m. every where	
Ac	21:38	thousand m. that were murderers?	435
Ac	22:1	M., brethren, and fathers, hear ye	435
Ac	22:4	into prisons both m. and women.	435
Ac	22:15	thou shalt be his witness unto all m.	444
Ac	23:1	M. and brethren, I have lived in	435
Ac	23:6	M. and brethren, I am a Pharisee,	435
Ac	23:21	for him of them more than forty m.,	435
Ac	24:16	offence toward God, and toward m.	444
Ac	25:23	and principal m. of the city,	435
Ac	25:24	all m. which are here present with	435
Ac	28:17	M. and brethren, though I have	435
Ro	1:18	unrighteousness of m., who hold	444
Ro	1:27	also the m., leaving the natural use	730
Ro	1:27	m. with m. working that which is	730
Ro	2:16	God shall judge the secrets of m.	444
Ro	2:29	whose praise is not of m., but of	444
Ro	5:12	so death passed upon all m., for	444
Ro	5:18	judgment came upon all m. to	444
Ro	5:18	the free gift came upon all m. unto	444
Ro	6:19	I speak after the manner of m.	442
Ro	11:4	reserved...seven thousand m.,	435
Ro	12:16	but condescend to m. of low estate.	
Ro	12:17	things honest in the sight of all m.	444
Ro	12:18	in you, live peaceably with all m.	444
Ro	14:18	to god, and approved of m.	444
Ro	16:19	obedience is come abroad unto all m.	
1Co	1:25	foolishness of God is wiser than m.,	444
1Co	1:25	weakness of God is stronger than m.	444
1Co	1:26	that not many wise m. after the flesh,	
1Co	2:5	not stand in the wisdom of m., but	444
1Co	3:3	are ye not carnal, and walk as m.?	444
1Co	3:21	Therefore let no man glory in m.:	444
1Co	4:6	not to think of m. above that which is	
1Co	4:9	the world, and to angels, and to m.	444
1Co	7:7	that all m. were even as I myself.	444
1Co	7:23	price; be not ye the servants of m.	444
1Co	9:19	For though I be free from all m., yet	
1Co	9:22	I am made all things to all m., that I	
1Co	10:15	I speak as to wise m.; judge ye what I	
1Co	10:33	Even as I please all m. in all things,	
1Co	13:1	the tongues of m. and of angels,	444
1Co	14:2	speaketh not unto m., but unto God:	444
1Co	14:3	speaketh unto m. to edification, and	444
1Co	14:20	but in understanding be m.	5046
1Co	14:21	With m. of other tongues and other	
1Co	15:19	we are of all m. most miserable.	444
1Co	15:32	after the manner of m. I have fought	444
1Co	15:39	but there is one kind of flesh of m.,	444
1Co	16:13	faith, quit you like m., be strong	407
2Co	3:2	hearts, known and read of all m.:	444
2Co	5:11	terror of the Lord, we persuade m.;	444
2Co	8:13	mean not that other m. be eased, and	
2Co	8:21	Lord, but also in the sight of m.	444
2Co	9:13	unto them, and unto all m.;	
Ga	1:1	apostle, (not of m., neither by man,	444
Ga	1:10	For do I now persuade m., or God?	444
Ga	1:10	or do I seek to please m.? for if I yet	444
Ga	1:10	if I yet pleased m., I should not be	444
Ga	3:15	I speak after the manner of m.;	444
Ga	6:10	let us do good unto all m., especially	
Eph	3:5	made known unto the sons of m.,	444
Eph	3:9	make all m. see what is the fellowship	
Eph	4:8	captive, and gave gifts unto m.	444
Eph	4:14	by the sleight of m., and cunning	444
Eph	5:28	So ought m. to love their wives as	435
Eph	6:7	as to the Lord, and not to m.:	444
Php	2:7	and was made in the likeness of m.:	444
Php	4:5	moderation be known unto all m.	444
Col	2:8	vain deceit, after the tradition of m.,	444
Col	2:22	commandments and doctrines of m.?	444
Col	3:23	as to the Lord, and not unto m.;	444
1Th	1:5	what manner of m. we were among	
1Th	2:4	not as pleasing m., but God, which	444
1Th	2:6	Nor of m. sought we glory, neither	444
1Th	2:13	ye received it not as the word of m.,	444
1Th	2:15	not God, and are contrary to all m.:	444
1Th	3:12	toward one another, and toward all m.	
1Th	5:14	the weak, be patient toward all m.	
1Th	5:15	both among yourselves, and to all m.	
2Th	3:2	from unreasonable and wicked m.:	444
2Th	3:2	for all m. have not faith.	
1Ti	2:1	of thanks, be made for all m.;	444
1Ti	2:4	Who will have all m. to be saved,	444
1Ti	2:5	one mediator between God and m.,	444
1Ti	2:8	I will...that m. pray every where,	435
1Ti	4:10	God, who is the Saviour of all m.,	444
1Ti	5:1	and the younger m. as brethren;	
1Ti	5:24	and some m. they follow after.	444
1Ti	6:5	disputings of m. of corrupt minds,	444
1Ti	6:9	which drown m. in destruction and	444
2Ti	2:2	the same commit thou to faithful m.,	444
2Ti	2:24	be gentle unto all m., apt to teach,	
2Ti	3:2	For m. shall be lovers of their own	444

2Ti 3:8 **m.** of corrupt minds, reprobate *444*
2Ti 3:9 folly shall be manifest unto all **m.**,
2Ti 3:13 But evil **m.** and seducers shall wax *444*
2Ti 4:16 stood with me, but all **m.** forsook me:
Tit 1:8 of hospitality, a lover of good **m.**,
Tit 1:14 fables, and commandments of **m.**, *444*
Tit 2:2 That the aged **m.** be sober, grave,
Tit 2:6 Young **m.** likewise exhort to be sober
Tit 2:11 salvation hath appeared to all **m.**, *444*
Tit 3:2 shewing all meekness unto all **m.**. *444*
Tit 3:8 are good and profitable unto **m.**. *444*
Heb 5:1 high priest taken from among **m.** is *444*
Heb 5:1 for **m.** in things pertaining to God, *444*
Heb 6:16 For **m.** verily swear by the greater: *444*
Heb 7:8 And here **m.** that die receive tithes; *444*
Heb 7:28 For the law maketh **m.** high priests *444*
Heb 9:17 is of force after **m.** are dead;
Heb 9:27 it is appointed unto **m.** once to die, *444*
Heb 12:14 Follow peace with all **m.**, and holiness,
Heb 12:23 the spirits of just **m.** made perfect,
Jas 1:5 that giveth to all **m.** liberally, and
Jas 2:6 Do not rich **m.** oppress you, and draw
Jas 3:9 Therewith curse we **m.**, which are *444*
Jas 5:1 Go to now, ye rich **m.**, weep and howl
1Pe 2:4 disallowed indeed of **m.**, but chosen *444*
1Pe 2:15 silence the ignorance of foolish **m.**: *444*
1Pe 2:17 Honour all **m.**. Love the brotherhood.
1Pe 4:2 time in the flesh to the lusts of **m.**, *444*
1Pe 4:6 judged according to **m.** in the flesh, *444*
2Pe 1:21 holy **m.** of God spake as they were *444*
2Pe 3:7 and perdition of ungodly **m.**. *444*
2Pe 3:9 promise, as some **m.** count slackness;
1Jo 2:13 I write unto you, young **m.**, *3495*
1Jo 2:14 I have written unto you, young **m.**, *3495*
1Jo 5:9 If we receive the witness of **m.**, *444*
3Jo 12 Demetrius hath good report of all **m.**,
Jude 4 are certain **m.** crept in unawares, *444*
Jude 4 ungodly **m.**, turning the grace of
Re 6:15 the great **m.**, and the rich **m.**, and the
Re 6:15 the chief captains, and the mighty **m.**,
Re 8:11 and many **m.** died of the waters, *444*
Re 9:4 **m.** which have not the seal of God *444*
Re 9:6 in those days shall **m.** seek death, *444*
Re 9:7 their faces were as the faces of **m.**. *444*
Re 9:10 power was to hurt **m.** five months. *444*
Re 9:15 year, for to slay the third part of **m.**. *444*
Re 9:18 three was the third part of **m.** killed, *444*
Re 9:20 rest of the **m.** which were not killed *444*
Re 11:13 were slain of **m.** seven thousand: *444*
Re 13:13 on the earth in the sight of **m.**, *444*
Re 14:4 were redeemed from among **m.**, *444*
Re 16:2 grievous sore upon the **m.** which had *444*
Re 16:8 unto him to scorch **m.** with fire. *444*
Re 16:9 **m.** were scorched with great heat, *444*
Re 16:18 not since **m.** were upon the earth, *444*
Re 16:21 there fell upon **m.** a great hail out of *444*
Re 16:21 **m.** blasphemed God because of the *444*
Re 18:13 chariots, and slaves, and souls of **m.**. *444*
Re 18:23 were the great **m.** of the earth;
Re 19:18 the flesh of mighty **m.**, and the flesh of
Re 19:18 the flesh of all **m.**, both free and bond,
Re 21:3 the tabernacle of God is with **m.**, *444*

MENAHEM (men'-a-hem)
2Ki 15:14 **M.** the son of Gadi went up from 4505
2Ki 15:16 **M.** smote Tiphsah, and all that 4505
2Ki 15:17 began **M.** the son of Gadi to reign 4505
2Ki 15:19 **M.** gave Pul a thousand talents of 4505
2Ki 15:20 **M.** exacted the money of Israel, 4505
2Ki 15:21 the rest of the acts of **M.**, and all 4505
2Ki 15:22 And **M.** slept with his father; and 4505
2Ki 15:23 the son of **M.** began to reign over 4505

MENAN (me'-nan)
Lu 3:31 which was the son of **M.**, which *3104*

MENCHILDREN See also MEN and CHILDREN.
Ex 34:23 the year shall all your **m.** appear 2138

MEND See also AMEND; MENDING.
2Ch 24:12 brass to **m.** the house of the Lord 2388

MENDING
Mt 4:21 with...their father, **m.** their nets; *2675*
Mk 1:19 also were in the ship **m.** their nets. *2675*

MENE (me'-ne)
Da 5:25 written, **M.**, **M.**, Tekel, Upharsin 4484
Da 5:26 **M.**; God hath numbered thy 4484

MENPLEASERS
Eph 6:6 Not with eyeservice, as **m.**; but as *441*
Col 3:22 not with eyeservice, as **m.**; but in *441*

MEN'S
Ge 24:32 and the **m.** feet that were with him 582
Ge 44:1 Fill the **m.** sacks with food, as much 582
De 4:28 serve gods, the work of **m.** hands, 120
1Sa 24:9 Wherefore hearest thou **m.** words, 120
1Ki 12:13 forsook the old **m.** counsel that they
1Ki 13:2 **m.** bones shall be burnt upon thee. 120
2Ki 19:18 no gods, but the work of **m.** hands, 120
2Ki 23:20 and burned **m.** bones upon them, 120
Ps 115:4 and gold, the work of **m.** hands. 120
Ps 135:15 and gold, the work of **m.** hands. 120
Isa 37:19 no gods, but the work of **m.** hands. 120
Jer 48:41 the mighty **m.** hearts in Moab at that
Hab 2:8, 17 because of **m.** blood, and for the 120
Mt 23:4 **and lay them on m. shoulders; but** *444*
Mt 23:27 **are within full of dead m. bones,**
Lu 9:56 **is not come to destroy m. lives,** *444*
Lu 21:26 **M. hearts failing them for fear,** *444*
Ac 17:25 Neither is worshiped with **m.** hands, *444*
2Co 10:15 measure, that is, of other **m.** labours;
1Ti 5:22 neither be partaker of other **m.** sins:
1Ti 5:24 Some **m.** sins are open beforehand,
1Pe 4:15 or as a busy body in other **m.** matters.
Jude 16 having **m.** persons in admiration *4283*

MENSERVANTS
Ge 12:16 and oxen, and he asses, and **m.**, 5650
Ge 20:14 took sheep, and oxen, and **m.**, and 5650
Ge 24:35 herds, and silver, and gold, and **m.**, 5650
Ge 30:43 cattle, and maidservants, and **m.**, 5650
Ge 32:5 oxen, and asses, flocks, and **m.**, and 5650
Ex 21:7 she shall not go out as the **m.** do. 5650
De 12:12 your **m.**, and your maidservants, 5650
1Sa 8:16 he will take your **m.**, and your 5650
2Ki 5:26 and sheep, and oxen, and **m.**, and 5650
Lu 12:45 **shall begin to beat the m. and** *3816*

MENSTEALERS
1Ti 1:10 with mankind, for **m.**, for liars, *405*

MENSTRUOUS
Isa 30:22 cast them away as a **m.** cloth; 1739
La 1:17 Jerusalem is as a **m.** woman 5079
Eze 18:6 hath come near to a **m.** woman, 5079

MENTION See also MENTIONED.
Ge 40:14 and make **m.** of me unto Pharoah, 2142
Ex 23:13 make no **m.** of the name of other 2142
Jos 23:7 make **m.** of the name of their gods, 2142
1Sa 4:18 when he made **m.** of the ark of God, 2142
Job 28:18 No **m.** shall be made of coral, or of 2142
Ps 71:16 will make **m.** of thy righteousness, 2142
Ps 87:4 make **m.** of Rahab and Babylon to 2142
Isa 12:4 make **m.** that his name is exalted. 2142
Isa 19:17 every one that maketh **m.** thereof 2142
Isa 26:13 only will we make **m.** of thy name. 2142
Isa 48:1 and make **m.** of the God of Israel, 2142
Isa 49:1 hath he made **m.** of my name. 2142
Isa 62:6 ye that make **m.** of the Lord, keep 2142
Isa 63:7 **m.** the lovingkindness of the Lord, 2142
Jer 4:16 Make ye **m.** to the nations; behold, 2142
Jer 20:9 I said, I will not make **m.** of him, 2142
Jer 23:36 burden of the Lord shall ye **m.** no 2142
Am 6:10 make **m.** of the name of the Lord. 2142
Ro 1:9 **m.** of you always in my prayers; *3417*
Eph 1:16 making **m.** of you in my prayers; *3417*
1Th 1:2 making **m.** of you in our prayers; *3417*
Phm 4 **m.** of thee always in my prayers, *3417*
Heb 11:22 died, made **m.** of the departing of *3421*

MENTIONED
Jos 21:9 these cities which are here **m.** by 7121
1Ch 4:38 **m.** by their names were princes 935
2Ch 20:34 who is **m.** in the book of the kings 5927
Eze 16:56 For thy sister Sodom was not **m.** 8052
Eze 18:22 they shall not be **m.** unto him: 2142
Eze 18:24 that he hath done shall not be **m.**: 2142
Eze 33:16 hath committed shall be **m.** unto 2142

MEON See BAAL-MEON; BETH-MEON.

MEONENIM (me-on'-e-nim)
Jg 9:37 come along by the plain of **M.**. 6049

MEONOTHAI (me-on'-o-thahee)
1Ch 4:14 **M.** begat Ophrah: and Seraiah 4587

MEPHAATH (mef'-a-ath)
Jos 13:18 Jahaza, and Kedemoth, and **M.**, 4158
Jos 21:37 **M.** with her suburbs; four cities 4158
1Ch 6:79 suburbs, and **M.** with her suburbs: 4158
Jer 48:21 and upon Jahazah, and upon **M.**, 4158

MEPHIBOSHETH (me-fib'-o-sheth) See also MERIBBAAL.
2Sa 4:4 lame. And his name was **M.**. 4648
2Sa 9:6 Now when **M.**, the son of Jonathan, 4648
2Sa 9:6 And David said, **M.**. And he 4648
2Sa 9:10 **M.** thy master's son shall eat bread 4648
2Sa 9:11 As for **M.**, said the king, he shall 4648
2Sa 9:12 **M.** had a young son, whose name 4648
2Sa 9:12 of Ziba were servants unto **M.**. 4648
2Sa 9:13 So **M.** dwelt in Jerusalem: for he 4648
2Sa 16:1 Ziba the servant of **M.** met him, 4648
2Sa 16:4 are all that pertained unto **M.**. 4648
2Sa 19:24 **M.** the son of Saul came down to 4648
2Sa 19:25 wentest not thou with me, **M.**? 4648
2Sa 19:30 **M.** said unto the king, Yea, let him 4648
2Sa 21:7 But the king spared **M.**, the son of 4648
2Sa 21:8 bare unto Saul, Armoni and **M.**; 4648

MERAB (me'-rab)
1Sa 14:49 the name of the firstborn **M.**, and 4764
1Sa 18:17 Behold my elder daughter **M.**, her 4764
1Sa 18:19 pass at the time when **M.** Saul's 4764

MERAIAH (mer-a-i'-ah)
Ne 12:12 of the fathers: of Seraiah, **M.**; of 4811

MERAIOTH (me-rah'-yoth) See also MEREMOTH.
1Ch 6:6 Zerahiah, and Zerahiah begat **M.**, 4812
1Ch 6:7 **M.** begat Amariah, and Amariah 4812
1Ch 6:52 **M.** his son, Amariah his son, 4812
1Ch 9:11 the son of **M.**, the son of Ahitub, 4812
Ezr 7:3 the son of Azariah, the son of **M.**, 4812
Ne 11:11 the son of Zadok, the son of **M.**, the 4812
Ne 12:15 Of Harim, Adna; of **M.**, Helkai; 4812

MERARI (me-ra'-ri) See also MERARITES.
Ge 46:11 Levi; Gershon, Kohath, and **M.**. 4847
Ex 6:16 Gershon, and Kohath, and **M.**: 4847
Ex 6:19 the sons of **M.**; Mahali and Mushi: 4847
Nu 3:17 Gershon, and Kohath, and **M.**. 4847
Nu 3:20 the sons of **M.** by their families; 4847
Nu 3:33 **M.** was the family of the Mahlites, 4847
Nu 3:33 these are the families of **M.**. 4847
Nu 3:35 of the families of **M.** was Zuriel the 4847
Nu 3:36 custody and charge of the sons of **M.** 4847
Nu 4:29 the sons of **M.**, thou shalt number 4847
Nu 4:33, 42,45 the families of the sons of **M.**, 4847
Nu 7:8 oxen he gave unto the sons of **M.**, 4847
Nu 10:17 sons of **M.** set forward, bearing the 4847
Nu 26:57 of **M.**, the family of the Merarites. 4847
Jos 21:7 The children of **M.** by their families 4847
Jos 21:34 the families of the children of **M.**, 4847
Jos 21:40 all the cities for the children of **M.** 4847
1Ch 6:1 of Levi; Gershon, Kohath, and **M.** 4847
1Ch 6:16 of Levi; Gershon, Kohath, and **M.** 4847
1Ch 6:19 The sons of **M.**; Mahli, and Mushi 4847
1Ch 6:29 The sons of **M.**; Mahli; Libni his 4847
1Ch 6:44 sons of **M.** stood on the left hand: 4847
1Ch 6:47 the son of Mushi, the son of **M.**, 4847
1Ch 6:63 Unto the sons of **M.** were given by 4847
1Ch 6:77 Unto the rest of the children of **M.** 4847
1Ch 9:14 of Hashabiah, of the sons of **M.**; 4847
1Ch 15:6 Of the sons of **M.**; Asaiah the chief, 4847
1Ch 15:17 of the sons of **M.** their brethren, 4847
1Ch 23:6 namely, Gershon, Kohath, and **M.**. 4847
1Ch 23:21 The sons of **M.**; Mahli, and Mushi 4847
1Ch 24:26 sons of **M.** were Mahli and Mushi: 4847
1Ch 24:27 The sons of **M.** by Jaaziah; Beno, 4847
1Ch 26:10 Hosah, of the children of **M.**, had 4847
1Ch 26:19 Kore, and among the sons of **M.** 4847
2Ch 29:12 and of the sons of **M.**; Kish the son 4847
2Ch 34:12 the Levites, of the sons of **M.**; 4847
Ezr 8:19 him Jeshaiah of the sons of **M.**, 4847

MERARITES (me-ra'-rites)
Nu 26:57 of Merari, the family of the **M.**. 4848

MERATHAIM (mer-a-tha'-im)
Jer 50:21 Go up against the land of **M.**. 4850

MERCHANDISE
De 21:14 thou shalt not make **m.** of her, 6014
De 24:7 maketh **m.** of him, or selleth him; 6014
Pr 3:14 For the **m.** of it is better than the 5504
Pr 3:14 is better than the **m.** of silver, 5505

Pr 31:18 perceiveth that her **m.** is good:.......... 5504
Isa 23:18 **m.** and her hire shall be holiness........ 5504
Isa 23:18 her **m.** shall be for them that dwell..... 5504
Isa 45:14 **m.** of Ethiopia and of the Sabeans, ... 5505
Eze 26:12 riches, and make a prey of thy **m.**:...... 7404
Eze 27:9 were in thee to occupy thy **m.**. 4627
Eze 27:15 isles were the **m.** of thine hand: 5506
Eze 27:24 and made of cedar, among thy **m.**. 4819
Eze 27:27 and thy fairs, thy **m.**, thy mariners, ... 4627
Eze 27:27 calkers, and the occupiers of thy **m.**, .. 4627
Eze 27:33 multitude of thy riches and of thy **m.** ..4627
Eze 27:34 thy **m.** and all thy company in the 4627
Eze 28:16 By the multitude of thy **m.** they......... 7404
Mt 22:5 **to his farm, another to his m.**:...... *1711*
Joh 2:16 **Father's house an house of m.**. *1712*
2Pe 2:3 with feigned words make **m.** of you: ....
Re 18:11 no man buyeth their **m.** any more; *1117*
Re 18:12 **m.** of gold, and silver, and precious *1117*

MERCHANT See also MERCHANTMEN; MERCHANTS.
Ge 23:16 silver, current money with the **m.**. ....
Pr 31:24 delivereth girdles unto the **m.**............ 5503
Ca 3:6 with all powders of the **m.**?............... 7402
Isa 23:11 against the **m.** city, to destroy........... 3667
Eze 27:3 a **m.** of the people for many isles, ... 7402
Eze 27:12 Tarshish was thy **m.** by reason of 5503
Eze 27:16 Syria was thy **m.** by reason of the...... 5503
Eze 27:18 Damascus was thy **m.** in the 5503
Eze 27:20 Dedan was thy **m.** in precious 7402
Ho 12:7 He is a **m.**, the balances of deceit 3667
Zep 1:11 for all the **m.** people are cut down;..... 3667
Mt 13:45 **of heaven is like unto a m. man,**... *1713*

MERCHANTMEN See also MERCHANT and MEN.
Ge 37:28 there passed by Midianites **m.**; 5503
1Ki 10:15 Besides that he had of the **m.**, ... 8446

MERCHANTS See also MERCHANTS'.
1Ki 10:15 and of the traffick of the spice **m.**, ... 7402
1Ki 10:28 king's **m.** received the linen yarn......... 5503
2Ch 1:16 king's **m.** received the linen yarn at 5503
2Ch 9:14 which chapmen and **m.** brought.......... 5503
Ne 3:31 of the Nethinims, and of the **m.**, ... 7402
Ne 3:32 repaired the goldsmiths and the **m.**...... 7402
Ne 13:20 **m.** and sellers of all kind of ware 7402
Job 41:6 shall they depart him among the **m.**?... 3669
Isa 23:2 the **m.** of Zidon, that pass over 5503
Isa 23:8 crowning city, whose **m.** are princes, .. 5503
Isa 47:15 thou hast laboured, even thy **m.**, ... 5503
Eze 17:4 traffick; he set it in a city of **m.**........ 7402
Eze 27:13 and Mesech, they were thy **m.**:........ 7402
Eze 27:15 The men of Dedan were thy **m.**;........ 7402
Eze 27:17 land of Israel, they were thy **m.**: 7402
Eze 27:21 goats: in these were they thy **m.**. 5503
Eze 27:22 The **m.** of Sheba and Raamah,........... 7402
Eze 27:22 they were thy **m.**: they occupied in 7402
Eze 27:23 Canneh, and Eden, the **m.** of Sheba,... 7402
Eze 27:23 Asshur, and Chilmad, were thy **m.**. 7402
Eze 27:24 were thy **m.** in all sorts of things, ... 7402
Eze 27:36 **m.** among the people shall hiss at....... 5503
Eze 38:13 and Dedan, and the **m.** of Tarshish,.... 5503
Na 3:16 multiplied thy **m.** above the stars 7402
Re 18:3 the **m.** of the earth are waxed rich...... *1713*
Re 18:11 the **m.** of the earth shall weep and...... *1713*
Re 18:15 The **m.** of these things, which were *1713*
Re 18:23 **m.** were the great men of the earth; .. *1713*

MERCHANTS'
Pr 31:14 She is like the **m.** ships; she 5503

MERCIES See also MERCIES'.
Ge 32:10 worthy of the least of all the **m.**, ... 2617
2Sa 24:14 of the Lord, for his **m.** are great:....... 7356
1Ch 21:13 the Lord; for very great are his **m.**: ... 7356
2Ch 6:42 remember the **m.** of David thy 2617
Ne 9:19 thou in thy manifold **m.** forsookest...... 7356
Ne 9:27 according to thy manifold **m.** thou....... 7356
Ne 9:28 deliver them according to thy **m.**;....... 7356
Ps 25:6 O Lord, thy tender **m.** and thy.......... 7356
Ps 40:11 not thou thy tender **m.** from me, ... 7356
Ps 51:1 unto the multitude of thy tender **m.**.... 7356
Ps 69:16 to the multitude of thy tender **m.**....... 7356
Ps 77:9 he in anger shut up his tender **m.**? 7356
Ps 79:8 let thy tender **m.** speedily prevent....... 7356
Ps 89:1 I will sing of the **m.** of the Lord......... 2617
Ps 103:4 lovingkindness and tender **m.**; 7356
Ps 106:7 not the multitude of thy **m.**;.............. 2617
Ps 106:45 according to the multitude of his **m.**.... 2617
Ps 119:41 thy **m.** come also unto me, O Lord, ... 2617
Ps 119:77 Let thy tender **m.** come unto me, ... 7356
Ps 119:156 Great are thy tender **m.**, O Lord: 7356
Ps 145:9 his tender **m.** are over all his works. .. 7356
Pr 12:10 tender **m.** of the wicked are cruel. 7356
Isa 54:7 with great **m.** will I gather thee. 7356
Isa 55:3 you, even the sure **m.** of David. 2617
Isa 63:7 on them according to his **m.**, and....... 7356
Isa 63:15 of thy bowels and of thy **m.** toward 7356
Jer 16:5 Lord, even lovingkindness and **m.**. 7356
Jer 42:12 I will shew **m.** unto you, that ye may.. 7356
La 3:22 It is of the Lord's **m.** that we are 2617
La 3:32 according...the multitude of his **m.**...... 2617
Da 2:18 they would desire **m.** of the God......... 7359
Da 9:9 To the Lord our God belong **m.**............ 7356
Da 9:18 righteousnesses,...for thy great **m.**..... 7356
Ho 2:19 and in lovingkindness, and in **m.**.......... 7356
Zec 1:16 I am returned to Jerusalem with **m.**: ... 7356
Ac 13:34 will give you the sure **m.** of David...... *3741*
Ro 12:1 by the **m.** of God, that ye present........ *3628*
2Co 1:3 the Father of **m.**, and the God of all ... *3628*
Php 2:1 of the Spirit, if any bowels and **m.**,..... *3628*
Col 3:12 bowels of **m.**, kindness, humbleness ... *3628*

MERCIES'
Ne 9:31 Nevertheless for thy great **m.** sake 7356
Ps 6:4 soul: oh save me for thy **m.** sake....... 2617
Ps 31:16 servant: save me for thy **m.** sake....... 2617
Ps 44:26 help, and redeem us for thy **m.** sake. ..2617

MERCIFUL
Ge 19:16 the Lord being **m.** unto him: and........ 2551
Ex 34:6 The Lord God, **m.** and gracious, ... 7349
De 4:31 (For the Lord thy God is a **m.** God;) .. 7349
De 21:8 Be **m.**, O Lord, unto thy people 3722
De 32:43 and will be **m.** unto his land, and........ 3722
2Sa 22:26 With the **m.** thou wilt shew thyself...... 2623
2Sa 22:26 wilt shew thyself **m.**, and with the...... 2616
1Ki 20:31 the house of Israel are **m.** kings: 2617
2Ch 30:9 Lord your God is gracious and **m.**, ... 7349
Ne 9:17 ready to pardon, gracious and **m.**, ... 7349
Ne 9:31 for thou art a gracious and **m.** God..... 7349
Ps 18:25 with the **m.** thou wilt shew thyself 2623
Ps 18:25 shew thyself **m.**; with an upright 2616
Ps 26:11 redeem me, and be **m.** unto me........... 2603
Ps 37:26 He is ever **m.**, and lendeth; and his.... 2603
Ps 41:4 Lord, be **m.** unto me: heal my soul; ... 2603
Ps 41:10 But thou, O Lord, be **m.** unto me, ... 2603
Ps 56:1 Be **m.** unto me, O God: for man......... 2603
Ps 57:1 Be **m.** unto me, O God, be **m.** unto.... 2603
Ps 59:5 be not **m.** to...wicked transgressors. .. 2603
Ps 67:1 God be **m.** unto us, and bless us; 2603
Ps 86:3 Be **m.** unto me, O Lord: for I cry...... 2603
Ps 103:8 the Lord is **m.** and gracious, slow 7349
Ps 116:5 and righteous; yea, our God is **m.**...... 7355
Ps 117:2 his **m.** kindness is great toward 2617
Ps 119:58 be **m.** unto me according to thy......... 2603
Ps 119:76 **m.** kindness be for my comfort, ... 2617
Ps 119:132 be **m.** unto me, as thou usest to do.... 2603
Pr 11:17 The **m.** man doeth good to his own 2617
Isa 57:1 and **m.** men are taken away, none...... 2617
Jer 3:12 for I am **m.**, saith the Lord, and........ 2623
Joe 2:13 for he is gracious and **m.**, slow to...... 7349
Jon 4:2 art a gracious God, and **m.**, slow to.... 7349
Mt 5:7 **Blessed are the m.: for they shall**. *1655*
Lu 6:36 **m., as your Father also is m.**......... *3629*
Lu 18:13 **saying, God be m. to me a sinner**.. *2433*
Heb 2:17 be a **m.** and faithful high priest *1655*
Heb 8:12 be **m.** to their unrighteousness, ... *2436*

MERCURIUS (mer-cu'-re-us)
Ac 14:12 Barnabas, Jupiter; and Paul, **M.**. *2060*

MERCY See also MERCIES; MERCIFUL; MERCYSEAT.
Ge 19:19 and thou hast magnified thy **m.**, ... 2617
Ge 24:27 left destitute my master of his **m.** 2617
Ge 39:21 with Joseph, and shewed him **m.**,....... 2617
Ge 43:14 Almighty give you **m.** before the........ 7356
Ex 15:13 Thou in thy **m.** hast led forth the....... 2617
Ex 20:6 shewing **m.** unto thousands of them.... 2617
Ex 25:17 shalt make a **m.** seat of pure gold: 3727
Ex 25:18 them, in the two ends of the **m.** seat...3727
Ex 25:19 of the **m.** seat shall ye make the........ 3727
Ex 25:20 covering...**m.** seat with their wings,..... 3727
Ex 25:20 toward the **m.** seat shall the faces of .. 3727
Ex 25:21 put the **m.** seat above upon the ark;... 3727
Ex 25:22 with thee from above the **m.** seat, ... 3727
Ex 26:34 put the **m.** seat upon the ark of the.... 3727
Ex 30:6 **m.** seat that is over the testimony,..... 3727
Ex 31:7 the **m.** seat that is thereupon and....... 3727
Ex 33:19 shew **m.** on whom I will shew **m.**. 7355
Ex 34:7 Keeping **m.** for thousands,................ 2617
Ex 35:12 staves thereof, with the **m.** seat, ... 3727
Ex 37:6 he made the **m.** seat of pure gold: 3727
Ex 37:7 on the two ends of the **m.** seat; 3727
Ex 37:8 out of the **m.** seat made he the 3727
Ex 37:9 with their wings over the **m.** seat, ... 3727
Ex 37:9 to the **m.** seatward were the faces 3727
Ex 39:35 the staves thereof, and the **m.** seat, ... 3727
Ex 40:20 put the **m.** seat above upon the ark: ... 3727
Le 16:2 within the veil before the **m.** seat,...... 3727
Le 16:2 appear in the cloud upon the **m.** seat. ..3727
Le 16:13 the incense may cover the **m.** seat...... 3727
Le 16:14 finger upon the **m.** seat eastward; 3727
Le 16:14 before the **m.** seat shall he sprinkle 3727
Le 16:15 and sprinkle it upon the **m.** seat,....... 3727
Le 16:15 and before the **m.** seat:..................... 3727
Nu 7:89 unto him from off the **m.** seat that 3727
Nu 14:18 is longsuffering, and of great **m.**,......... 2617
Nu 14:19 unto the greatness of thy **m.**, and 2617
De 5:10 shewing **m.** unto thousands of them.... 2617
De 7:2 with them, nor shew **m.** unto them: ... 2603
De 7:9 covenant and **m.** with them that.......... 2617
De 7:12 and the **m.** which he sware unto 2617
De 13:17 of his anger, and shew thee **m.**, ... 7356
Jg 1:24 city, and we will shew thee **m.**........... 2617
2Sa 7:15 But my **m.** shall not depart away 2617
2Sa 15:20 **m.** and truth be with thee................. 2617
2Sa 22:51 sheweth **m.** to his anointed, unto 2617
1Ki 3:6 servant David my father great **m.**,....... 2617
1Ki 8:23 covenant and **m.** with thy servants 2617
1Ch 16:34 good; for his **m.** endureth for ever. 2617
1Ch 16:41 because his **m.** endureth for ever;...... 2617
1Ch 17:13 not take my **m.** away from him, as...... 2617
1Ch 28:11 and of the place of the **m.** seat, ... 3727
2Ch 1:8 hast shewed great **m.** unto David....... 2617
2Ch 5:13 good; for his **m.** endureth for ever: 2617
2Ch 6:14 shewest **m.** unto thy servants, that 2617
2Ch 7:3 good; for his **m.** endureth for ever. 2617
2Ch 7:6 because his **m.** endureth for ever,....... 2617
2Ch 20:21 Lord; for his **m.** endureth for ever. 2617
Ezr 3:11 his **m.** endureth for ever toward 2617
Ezr 7:28 hath extended **m.** unto me before........ 2617
Ezr 9:9 hath extended **m.** unto us in the 2617
Ne 1:5 keepeth covenant and **m.** for them 2617
Ne 1:11 and grant him **m.** in the sight of......... 7356
Ne 9:32 who keepest covenant and **m.**, let...... 2617
Ne 13:22 to the greatness of thy **m.**................ 2617
Job 37:13 or for his land, or for **m.**................... 2617
Ps 4:1 have **m.** upon me, and hear my 2603
Ps 5:7 house in the multitude of thy **m.**: 2617
Ps 6:2 Have **m.** upon me, O Lord; for I 2603
Ps 9:13 Have **m.** upon me, O Lord; consider... 2603
Ps 13:5 But I have trusted in thy **m.**; my 2617
Ps 18:50 and sheweth **m.** to his anointed, to..... 2617
Ps 21:7 through the **m.** of the most High........ 2617
Ps 23:6 goodness and **m.** shall follow me 2617
Ps 25:7 according to thy **m.** remember thou.... 2617
Ps 25:10 paths of the Lord are **m.** and truth..... 2617
Ps 25:16 unto me, and have **m.** upon me; 2603
Ps 27:7 have **m.** also upon me, and answer..... 2603
Ps 30:10 O Lord, and have **m.** upon me: 2603
Ps 31:7 will be glad and rejoice in thy **m.**: 2617
Ps 31:9 Have **m.** upon me, O Lord, for I am... 2603
Ps 32:10 Lord, **m.** shall compass him about. 2617
Ps 33:18 upon them that hope in his **m.**;.......... 2617
Ps 33:22 Let thy **m.**, O Lord, be upon us,........ 2617
Ps 36:5 Thy **m.**, O Lord, is in the heavens; 2617
Ps 37:21 but the righteous sheweth **m.**,........... 2603
Ps 51:1 Have **m.** upon me, O God, according .. 2603
Ps 52:8 I trust in the **m.** of God for ever 2617
Ps 57:3 God shall send forth his **m.** and his..... 2617
Ps 57:10 thy **m.** is great unto the heavens, ... 2617
Ps 59:10 The God of my **m.** shall prevent 2617
Ps 59:16 I will sing aloud of thy **m.** in the 2617
Ps 59:17 my defence, and the God of my **m.**. ... 2617
Ps 61:7 O prepare **m.** and truth, which may.... 2617
Ps 62:12 unto thee, O Lord, belongeth **m.**: 2617
Ps 66:20 my prayer, nor his **m.** from me. 2617
Ps 69:13 in the multitude of thy **m.** hear me, ... 2617
Ps 77:8 Is his **m.** clean gone for ever? doth.... 2617
Ps 85:7 Shew us thy **m.**, O Lord, and grant.... 2617
Ps 85:10 **M.** and truth are met together;.......... 2617
Ps 86:5 plenteous in **m.** unto all them that...... 2617
Ps 86:13 For great is thy **m.** toward me: and.... 2617
Ps 86:15 and plenteous in **m.** and truth........... 2617
Ps 86:16 unto me, and have **m.** upon me; 2603

Ps 89:2 said, **M.** shall be built up for ever: 2617
Ps 89:14 **m.** and truth shall go before thy........ 2617
Ps 89:24 and my **m.** shall be with him: and....... 2617
Ps 89:28 My **m.** will I keep for him for........... 2617
Ps 90:14 O satisfy us early with thy **m.**; that.... 2617
Ps 94:18 thy **m.**, O Lord, held me up............. 2617
Ps 98:3 He hath remembered his **m.** and........ 2617
Ps 100:5 is good; his **m.** is everlasting;........... 2617
Ps 101:1 will sing of **m.** and judgment: unto...... 2617
Ps 102:13 arise, and have **m.** upon Zion: for....... 7355
Ps 103:8 to anger, and plenteous in **m.**........... 2617
Ps 103:11 great is his **m.** toward them that........ 2617
Ps 103:17 But the **m.** of the Lord is from.......... 2617
Ps 106:1 good: for his **m.** endureth for ever. 2617
Ps 107:1 good: for his **m.** endureth for ever. 2617
Ps 108:4 thy **m.** is great above the heavens:...... 2617
Ps 109:12 be none to extend **m.** unto him:......... 2617
Ps 109:16 he remembered not to shew **m.**,........ 2617
Ps 109:21 because thy **m.** is good, deliver thou... 2617
Ps 109:26 O save me according to thy **m.**:.......... 2617
Ps 115:1 for thy **m.**, and for thy truth's sake. ... 2617
Ps 118:1 because his **m.** endureth for ever....... 2617
Ps 118:2, 3,4 that his **m.** endureth for ever....... 2617
Ps 118:29 good: for his **m.** endureth for ever. 2617
Ps 119:64 The earth, O Lord, is full of thy **m.**:.... 2617
Ps 119:124 thy servant according unto thy **m.**,...... 2617
Ps 123:2 God, until that he have **m.** upon us. ... 2603
Ps 123:3 Have **m.** upon us, O Lord, have **m.** ... 2603
Ps 130:7 for with the Lord there is **m.**, and...... 2617
Ps 136:1, 2,3,4,5,6 his **m.** endureth for ever. 2617
Ps 136:7, 8 for his **m.** endureth for ever:.......... 2617
Ps 136:9 for his **m.** endureth for ever. 2617
Ps 136:10, 11 for his **m.** endureth for ever: 2617
Ps 136:12 arm: for his **m.** endureth for ever. 2617
Ps 136:13, 14 for his **m.** endureth for ever: 2617
Ps 136:15, 16 for his **m.** endureth for ever. 2617
Ps 136:17, 18,19,20,21 for his **m.** endureth for.... 2617
Ps 136:22 for his **m.** endureth for ever. 2617
Ps 136:23 for his **m.** endureth for ever: 2617
Ps 136:24, 25,26 for his **m.** endureth for ever. 2617
Ps 138:8 thy **m.**, O Lord, endureth for ever: 2617
Ps 143:12 And of thy **m.** cut off mine enemies,... 2617
Ps 145:8 slow to anger, and of great **m.**.......... 2617
Ps 147:11 him, in those that hope in his **m.**. 2617
Pr 3:3 Let not **m.** and truth forsake thee: 2617
Pr 14:21 but he that hath **m.** on the poor,........ 2603
Pr 14:22 **m.** and truth shall be to them that...... 2617
Pr 14:31 honoureth him hath **m.** on the 2603
Pr 16:6 **m.** and truth iniquity is purged:.......... 2617
Pr 20:28 **M.** and truth preserve the king:......... 2617
Pr 20:28 and his throne is upholden by **m.**. 2617
Pr 21:21 righteousness and **m.** findeth life, ... 2617
Pr 28:13 and forsaketh them shall have **m.**........ 7355
Isa 9:17 shall have **m.** on their fatherless 7355
Isa 14:1 the Lord will have **m.** on Jacob, ... 7355
Isa 16:5 And in **m.** shall the throne be............ 2617
Isa 27:11 them will not have **m.** on them, ... 7355
Isa 30:18 that he may have **m.** upon you: 7355
Isa 47:6 thou didst shew them no **m.**; upon 7356
Isa 49:10 he that hath **m.** on them shall lead 7355
Isa 49:13 and will have **m.** upon his afflicted. 7355
Isa 54:8 kindness will I have **m.** on thee, ... 7355
Isa 54:10 saith the Lord that hath **m.** on thee.... 7355
Isa 55:7 and he will have **m.** upon him; and 7355
Isa 60:10 in my favour have I had **m.** on thee.... 7355
Jer 6:23 they are cruel, and have no **m.**;......... 7355
Jer 13:14 not pity, nor spare, nor have **m.**, ... 7355
Jer 21:7 neither have pity, nor have **m.**. 7355
Jer 30:18 and have **m.** on his dwellingplaces; 7355
Jer 31:20 I will surely have **m.** upon him, ... 7355
Jer 33:11 for his **m.** endureth for ever: and........ 2617
Jer 33:26 to return, and have **m.** on them.......... 7355
Jer 42:12 that he may have **m.** upon you, and.... 7355
Jer 50:42 are cruel, and will not shew **m.**: 7355
Eze 39:25 and have **m.** upon the whole house..... 7355
Da 4:27 by shewing **m.** to the poor; if it.......... 2604
Da 9:4 and **m.** to them that love him, ... 2617
Ho 1:6 no more have **m.** upon the house....... 7355
Ho 1:7 have **m.** upon the house of Judah, ... 7355
Ho 2:4 will not have **m.** upon her children;..... 7355
Ho 2:23 earth; and I will have **m.** upon her 7355
Ho 2:23 upon her that had not obtained **m.**;..... 7355
Ho 4:1 because there is no truth, nor **m.**,...... 2617
Ho 6:6 For I desired **m.**, and not sacrifice; 2617
Ho 10:12 in righteousness, reap in **m.**; break..... 2617
Ho 12:6 keep **m.** and judgment, and wait 2617
Ho 14:3 in thee the fatherless findeth **m.**. 7355
Jon 2:8 vanities forsake their own **m.**. 2617
Mic 6:8 but to do justly, and to love **m.**, ... 2617
Mic 7:18 ever, because he delighteth in **m.**........ 2617
Mic 7:20 the **m.** to Abraham, which thou 2617
Hab 3:2 known; in wrath remember **m.**, ... 7355
Zec 1:12 thou not have **m.** on Jerusalem and..... 7355
Zec 7:9 and shew **m.** and compassions........... 2617
Zec 10:6 for I have **m.** upon them: and they..... 7355
Mt 5:7 **merciful: for they shall obtain m.**. .*1653*
Mt 9:13 **I will have m., and not sacrifice:**.. *1656*
Mt 9:27 Thou son of David, have **m.** on us. *1653*
Mt 12:7 I will have **m.**, and not sacrifice, ... *1656*
Mt 15:22 Have **m.** on me, O Lord, thou son..... *1653*
Mt 17:15 Lord, have **m.** on my son: for he is.... *1653*
Mt 20:30, 31 Have **m.** on us, O Lord, thou son.. *1653*
Mt 23:23 **the law, judgment, m., and faith:**.. *1656*
Mk 10:47, 48 son of David, have **m.** on me. *1653*
Lu 1:50 his **m.** is on them that fear him *1656*
Lu 1:54 Israel, in remembrance of his **m.**;........ *1656*
Lu 1:58 Lord had shewed great **m.** upon her;.. *1656*
Lu 1:72 To perform the **m.** promised to our.... *1656*
Lu 1:78 Through the tender **m.** of our God;.... *1656*
Lu 10:37 he said, He that shewed **m.** on him. ... *1656*
Lu 16:24 **Father Abraham, have m. on me,**.. *1653*
Lu 17:13 said, Jesus, Master, have **m.** on us. ... *1653*
Lu 18:38, 39 thou son of David, have **m.** on me. .*1653*
Ro 9:15 have **m.** on whom I will have **m.**, ... *1653*
Ro 9:16 but of God that sheweth **m.**............. *1653*
Ro 9:18 Therefore hath he **m.** on whom he *1653*
Ro 9:18 on whom he will have **m.**, and on............
Ro 9:23 of his glory on the vessels of **m.**,........ *1656*
Ro 11:30 yet have now obtained **m.** through....... *1653*
Ro 11:31 that through your **m.** they also *1656*
Ro 11:31 they also may obtain **m.**................ *1653*
Ro 11:32 that he might have **m.** upon all. *1653*
Ro 12:8 that sheweth **m.**, with cheerfulness. ... *1653*
Ro 15:9 might glorify God for his **m.**;............. *1656*
1Co 7:25 that hath obtained **m.** of the Lord....... *1653*
2Co 4:1 as we have received **m.**, we faint not;..*1653*
Ga 6:16 rule, peace be on them, and **m.**,........ *1656*
Eph 2:4 But God, who is rich in **m.**, for his..... *1656*
Php 2:27 but God had **m.** on him; and not on.... *1653*
1Ti 1:2 Grace, **m.**, and peace, from God........ *1656*
1Ti 1:13 but I obtained **m.**, because I did it...... *1653*
1Ti 1:16 for this cause I obtained **m.**, that *1653*
2Ti 1:2 Grace, **m.**, and peace, from God........ *1656*
2Ti 1:16 The Lord give **m.** unto the house....... *1656*
2Ti 1:18 that he may find **m.** of the Lord in *1656*
Tit 1:4 Grace, **m.**, and peace, from God....... *1656*
Tit 3:5 but according to his **m.** he saved us,... *1656*
Heb 4:16 that we may obtain **m.**, and find.......... *1656*
Heb 10:28 Moses' law died without **m.** under...... *3628*
Jas 2:13 he shall have judgment without **m.**, ... *448*
Jas 2:13 that hath shewed no **m.**; *1656*
Jas 2:13 and **m.** rejoiceth against judgment....... *1656*
Jas 3:17 full of **m.** and good fruits, without *1656*
Jas 5:11 is very pitiful, and of tender **m.**. *3629*
1Pe 1:3 according to his abundant **m.** hath *1656*
1Pe 2:10 of God: which had not obtained **m.**, ... *1653*
1Pe 2:10 but now have obtained **m.**................ *1653*
2Jo 3 Grace be with you, **m.**, and peace,..... *1656*
Jude 2 **M.** unto you, and peace, and love, ... *1656*
Jude 21 for the **m.** of our Lord Jesus Christ.... *1656*

MERCYSEAT See also MERCY and SEAT.
Heb 9:5 of glory shadowing the **m.**; *2435*

MERED (me′-red)
1Ch 4:17 sons of Ezra were, Jether, and **M.**, ... 4778
1Ch 4:18 daughter of Pharaoh, which **M.** took. .. 4778

MEREMOTH (mer′-e-moth) See also MERAIOTH.
Ezr 8:33 by the hand of **M.** the son of Uriah 4822
Ezr 10:36 Vaniah, **M.**, Eliashib, ... 4822
Ne 3:4 them repaired **M.** the son of Urijah,.... 4822
Ne 3:21 him repaired **M.** the son of Urijah 4822
Ne 10:5 Harim, **M.**, Obadiah,........................ 4822
Ne 12:3 Shechaniah, Rehum, **M.**,.................. 4822

MERES (me′-res)
Es 1:14 **M.**, Marsena, and Memucan,............ 4825

MERIBAH (mer′-i-bah) See also MASSAH; MERIBAH-KADESH.
Ex 17:7 name of the place Massah, and **M.**, ... 4809
Nu 20:13 This is the water of **M.**; because 4809
Nu 20:24 against my word at the water of **M.**.... 4809
Nu 27:14 that is the water of **M.** in Kadesh 4809
De 33:8 didst strive at the waters of **M.**; 4809
Ps 81:7 I proved thee at the waters of **M.**...... 4809

MERIBAH-KADESH (mer′′-i-bah-ka′-desh)
De 32:51 of Israel at the waters of **M.**, ... 4809,6946

MERIB-BAAL (me-rib′-ba-al) See also MEPHIBOSHETH.
1Ch 8:34 And the son of Jonathan was **M.**; 4807
1Ch 8:34 and **M.** begat Micah. 4807
1Ch 9:40 And the son of Jonathan was **M.**: 4807
1Ch 9:40 and **M.** begat Micah. 4810

MERODACH (mer′-o-dak) See also BERODACH; EVIL-MERODACH; MERODACH-BALADAN.
Jer 50:2 **M.** is broken in pieces; 4781

MERODACH-BALADAN (mer′′-o-dak-bal′-a-dan) See also BERODACH-BALADAN.
Isa 39:1 that time **M.**, the son of Baladan,....... 4757

MEROM (me′-rom)
Jos 11:5 together at the waters of **M.**,............ 4792
Jos 11:7 against them by the waters of **M.**....... 4792

MERON See SHIMRON-MERON; MERONOTHITE.

MERONOTHITE (me-ron′-o-thite)
1Ch 27:30 the asses was Jehdeiah the **M.**: 4824
Ne 3:7 the Gibeonite, and Jadon the **M.**, ... 4824

MEROZ (me′-roz)
Jg 5:23 Curse ye **M.**, said the angel of the..... 4789

MERRILY
Es 5:14 then go thou in **m.** with the king........ 8056

MERRY See also MERRYHEARTED.
Ge 43:34 they drank, and were **m.** with him..... 7937
Jg 9:27 trode the grapes, and made **m.**,......... 1974
Jg 16:25 pass, when their hearts were **m.**,....... 2896
Jg 19:6 all night, and let thine heart be **m.**. 3190
Jg 19:9 here, that thine heart may be **m.**; 3190
Jg 19:22 they were making their hearts **m.**, ... 3190
Ru 3:7 and drunk, and his heart was **m.**,....... 3190
1Sa 25:36 Nabal's heart was **m.** within him, ... 2896
2Sa 13:28 Amnon's heart is **m.** with wine, ... 2896
1Ki 4:20 and drinking, and making **m.**. 8056
1Ki 21:7 bread, and let thine heart be **m.**: 3190
2Ch 7:10 their tents, glad and **m.** in heart 2896
Es 1:10 when the heart of the king was **m.**..... 2896
Pr 15:13 A **m.** heart maketh a cheerful............ 8056
Pr 15:15 but he that is of a **m.** heart hath a 2896
Pr 17:22 A **m.** heart doeth good like a............. 8056
Ec 8:15 to eat, and to drink, and to be **m.**:..... 8055
Ec 9:7 drink thy wine with a **m.** heart; 2896
Ec 10:19 for laughter, and wine maketh **m.**:...... 8055
Jer 30:19 the voice of them that make **m.**:........ 7832
Jer 31:4 in the dances of them that make **m.**.... 7832
Lu 12:19 **thine ease, eat, drink, and be m.**... *2165*
Lu 15:23 **kill it; and let us eat, and be m.**:.. *2165*
Lu 15:24 **is found. And they began to be m.**..*2165*
Lu 15:29 **I might make m. with my friends:**. *2165*
Lu 15:32 **was meet that we should make m.**,.*2165*
Jas 5:13 Is any **m.**? let him sing psalms. *2114*
Re 11:10 rejoice over them, and make **m.**, ... *2165*

MERRYHEARTED
Isa 24:7 languisheth, all the **m.** do sigh. ... 8056,3820

MESECH (me′-sek) See also MESHECH.
Ps 120:5 Woe is me, that I sojourn in **M.**,......... 4902

MESHA (me′-shah)
Ge 10:30 And their dwelling was from **M.**, ... 4331
2Ki 3:4 **M.**...of Moab was a sheepmaster, ... 4337
1Ch 2:42 **M.** his firstborn, which was the 4338
1Ch 8:9 and Zibia, and **M.**, and Malcham,........ 4331

MESHACH (me′-shak)
Da 1:7 Shadrach; and to Mishael, of **M.**; 4335
Da 2:49 set Shadrach, **M.**, and Abed-nego,...... 4336
Da 3:12 Shadrach, **M.**, and Abed-nego; the...... 4336
Da 3:13 bring Shadrach, **M.**, and Abed-nego. ... 4336
Da 3:14 O Shadrach, **M.**; and Abed-nego, ... 4336
Da 3:16 Shadrach, **M.**, and Abed-nego,........... 4336
Da 3:19 was changed against Shadrach, **M.**,..... 4336
Da 3:20 bind Shadrach, **M.**, and Abed-nego, ... 4336
Da 3:22 men that took up Shadrach, **M.**,......... 4336
Da 3:23 Shadrach, **M.**, and Abed-nego, fell...... 4336
Da 3:26 spake, and said, Shadrach, **M.**, and..... 4336
Da 3:26 Shadrach, **M.**, and Abed-nego,........... 4336
Da 3:28 be the God of Shadrach, **M.**, and 4336
Da 3:29 against the God of Shadrach, **M.**, ... 4336
Da 3:30 the king promoted Shadrach, **M.**, ... 4336

MESHECH (me'-shek) See also MESECH.
Ge 10:2 and Tubal, and **M.**, and Tiras. 4902
1Ch 1:5 and Tubal, and **M.**, and Tiras, 4902
1Ch 1:17 Uz, and Hul, and Gether, and **M.** 4902
Eze 27:13 and **M.**, they were thy merchants: 4902
Eze 32:26 There is **M.**, Tubal, and all her 4902
Eze 38:2 the chief prince of **M.** and Tubal, 4902
Eze 38:3 the chief prince of **M.** and Tubal: 4902
Eze 39:1 the chief prince of **M.** and Tubal: 4902

MESHELEMIAH (me-shel-e-mi'-ah) See also MESHULLAM; SHELEMIAH; SHALLUM.
1Ch 9:21 the son of **M.** was porter of the 4920
1Ch 26:1 Korhites was **M.** the son of Kore, 4920
1Ch 26:2 the sons of **M.** were, Zechariah the 4920
1Ch 26:9 **M.** had sons and brethren, strong 4920

MESHEZABEEL (me-shez'-a-be-el)
Ne 3:4 son of Berechiah, the son of **M.** 4898
1Ch 10:21 **M.**, Zadok, Juddua, 4898
1Ch 11:24 And Pethahiah the son of **M.**, of 4898

MESHILLEMITH (me-shil'-le-mith) See also MESHILLEMOTH.
1Ch 9:12 son of Meshullam, the son of **M.**, 4921

MESHILLEMOTH (me-shil'-le-moth) See also MESHILLEMITH.
2Ch 28:12 Berechiah the son of **M.**, and 4919
Ne 11:13 the son of Ahasai, the son of **M.**, 4919

MESHOBAB (me-sho'-bab)
1Ch 4:34 And **M.**, and Jamlech, and Joshah 4877

MESHULLAM (me-shul'-lam) See also MESHELLEMIAH.
2Ki 22:3 son of **M.**, the scribe, to the house 4918
1Ch 3:19 **M.**, and Hananiah, and Shelomith 4918
1Ch 5:13 and **M.**, and Sheba, and Jorai, and 4918
1Ch 8:17 And Zebadiah, and **M.**, and Hezeki, 4918
1Ch 9:7 Sallu the son of **M.**, the son of 4918
1Ch 9:8 **M.** the son of Shephathiah, the son 4918
1Ch 9:11 the son of Hilkiah, the son of **M.**, 4918
1Ch 9:12 son of **M.**, the son of Meshillemith, 4918
2Ch 34:12 **M.**, of the sons of the Kohathites, 4918
Ezr 8:16 and for Zechariah, and for **M.**, chief 4918
Ezr 10:15 and **M.** and Shabbethai the Levite 4918
Ezr 10:29 of the sons of Bani; **M.**, Malluch, 4918
Ne 3:4 And next unto them repaired **M.** 4918
Ne 3:6 and **M.** the son of Besodeiah; they 4918
Ne 3:30 repaired **M.** the son of Berechiah 4918
Ne 6:18 had taken the daughter of **M.** the 4918
Ne 8:4 Hashbadana, Zechariah, and **M.** 4918
Ne 10:7 **M.**, Abijah, Mijamin, 4918
Ne 10:20 Magpiash, **M.**, Hezir, 4918
Ne 11:7 Sallu the son of **M.**, the son of Joed, 4918
Ne 11:11 the son of Hilkiah, the son of **M.**, 4918
Ne 12:13 Of Ezra, **M.**; of Amariah, 4918
Ne 12:16 Iddo, Zechariah; of Ginnethon, **M.**; 4918
Ne 12:25 and Bakbukiah, Obadiah, **M.**, 4918
Ne 12:33 And Azariah, Ezra, and **M.**, 4918

MESHULLEMETH (me-shul'-le-meth)
2Ki 21:19 And his mother's name was **M.**, 4922

MESOBAITE (me-so'-ba-ite)
1Ch 11:47 Eliel, and Obed, and Jasiel the **M.** 4677

MESOPOTAMIA (mes-o-po-ta'-me-ah) See also ARAM and NAHARAIM.
Ge 24:10 and he arose, and went to **M.**, unto 763
De 23:4 the son of Beor of Pethor of **M.**, 763
Jg 3:8 of Chushan-rishathaim king of **M.**: 763
Jg 3:10 Chushan-rishathaim king of **M.** 763
1Ch 19:6 chariots and horsemen out of **M.**, 763
Ac 2:9 the dwellers in **M.**, and in Judaea, *3318*
Ac 7:2 father Abraham, when he was in **M.**, *3318*

MESS See also MESSES.
Ge 43:34 Benjamin's **m.** was five times so 4864
2Sa 11:8 there followed him a **m.** of meat 4864

MESSAGE
Jg 3:20 I have a **m.** from God unto thee. 1697
1Ki 20:12 when Ben-hadad heard this **m.**, as 1697
Pr 26:6 He that sendeth a **m.** by the hand 1697
Hag 1:13 in the Lord's **m.** unto the people, 4400
Lu 19:14 **him, and sent a m. after him,** *4242*
1Jo 1:5 is the **m.** which we have heard of *1860*
1Jo 3:11 is the **m.** that ye heard from the *31*

MESSENGER See also MESSENGERS.
Ge 50:16 And they sent a **m.** unto Joseph, 6680
1Sa 4:17 the **m.** answered and said, Israel 1319
1Sa 23:27 But there came a **m.** unto Saul, 4397
2Sa 11:19 And charged the **m.**, saying, When 4397
2Sa 11:22 So the **m.** went, and came and 4397
2Sa 11:23 the **m.** said unto David, Surely the 4397
2Sa 11:25 David said unto the **m.**, Thus shalt 4397
2Sa 15:13 there came a **m.** to David, saying, 5046
1Ki 19:2 Jezebel sent a **m.** unto Elijah, 4397
1Ki 22:13 And the **m.** that was gone to call 4397
2Ki 5:10 Elisha sent a **m.** unto him, saying, 4397
2Ki 6:32 ere the **m.** came to him, he said to 4397
2Ki 6:32 when the **m.** cometh, shut the door, 4397
2Ki 6:33 the **m.** came down unto him: and 4397
2Ki 9:18 The **m.** came to them, but he 4397
2Ki 10:8 And there came a **m.**, and told him, 4397
2Ch 18:12 the **m.** that went to call Micaiah 4397
Job 1:14 And there came a **m.** unto Job, and 4397
Job 33:23 If there be a **m.** with him, an 4397
Pr 13:17 A wicked **m.** falleth into mischief: 4397
Pr 17:11 a cruel **m.** shall be sent against 4397
Pr 25:13 is a faithful **m.** to them that send 6735
Isa 42:19 or deaf, as my **m.** that I sent? 4397
Jer 51:31 and one **m.** to meet another, to 5046
Eze 23:40 unto whom a **m.** was sent; and, 4397
Hag 1:13 spake Haggai the Lord's **m.** in the 4397
Mal 2:7 he is the **m.** of the Lord of hosts. 4397
Mal 3:1 I will send my **m.**, and he shall 4397
Mal 3:1 even the **m.** of the covenant, whom 4397
Mt 11:10 **I send my m. before thy face,** *32*
Mk 1:2 I send my **m.** before thy face, which *32*
Lu 7:27 **I send my m. before thy face,** *32*
2Co 12:7 the **m.** of Satan to buffet me, lest I *32*
Php 2:25 your **m.**, and he that ministered *652*

MESSENGERS
Ge 32:3 Jacob sent **m.** before him to Esau 4397
Ge 32:6 the **m.** returned to Jacob, saying, 4397
Nu 20:14 And Moses sent **m.** from Kadesh 4397
Nu 21:21 Israel sent **m.** unto Sihon king of 4397
Nu 22:5 He sent **m.** therefore unto Balaam 4397
Nu 24:12 Spake I not also to thy **m.** which 4397
De 2:26 And I sent **m.** out of the wilderness 4397
Jos 6:17 because he hid the **m.** that we sent 4397
Jos 6:25 she hid the **m.**, which Joshua sent 4397
Jos 7:22 So Joshua sent me, and they ran 4397
Jg 6:35 sent **m.** throughout all Manasseh; 4397
Jg 6:35 he sent **m.** unto Asher, and unto 4397
Jg 7:24 And Gideon sent **m.** throughout all 4397
Jg 9:31 he sent **m.** unto Abimelech privily, 4397
Jg 11:12 Jephthah sent **m.** unto the king 4397
Jg 11:13 answered unto the **m.** of Jephthah, 4397
Jg 11:14 Jephthah sent **m.** again unto the 4397
Jg 11:17 Israel sent **m.** unto the king of 4397
Jg 11:19 Israel sent **m.** unto Sihon king of 4397
1Sa 6:21 And they sent **m.** to the inhabitants 4397
1Sa 11:3 may send **m.** unto all the coasts of 4397
1Sa 11:4 then came the **m.** to Gibeah of 4397
1Sa 11:7 coasts of Israel by the hands of **m.**, 4397
1Sa 11:9 they said unto the **m.** that came 4397
1Sa 11:9 **m.** came and shewed it to the men 4397
1Sa 16:19 Wherefore Saul sent **m.** unto Jesse, 4397
1Sa 19:11 also sent **m.** unto David's house, 4397
1Sa 19:14 when Saul sent **m.** to take David, 4397
1Sa 19:15 Saul sent the **m.** again to see David, 4397
1Sa 19:16 when the **m.** were come in, behold, 4397
1Sa 19:20 And Saul sent **m.** to take David: 4397
1Sa 19:20 Spirit of God was upon the **m.** of 4397
1Sa 19:21 it was told Saul, he sent other **m.**, 4397
1Sa 19:21 Saul sent **m.** again the third time, 4397
1Sa 25:14 David sent **m.** out of the wilderness 4397
1Sa 25:42 and she went after the **m.** of David, 4397
2Sa 2:5 And David sent **m.** unto the men 4397
2Sa 3:12 And Abner sent **m.** to David on his 4397
2Sa 3:14 And David sent **m.** to Ish-bosheth 4397
2Sa 3:26 he sent **m.** after Abner, which 4397
2Sa 5:11 king of Tyre sent **m.** to David, 4397
2Sa 11:4 And David sent **m.**, and took her; 4397
2Sa 12:27 Joab sent **m.** to David, and said, 4397
1Ki 20:2 he sent **m.** to Ahab king of Israel 4397
1Ki 20:5 And the **m.** came again, and said, 4397
1Ki 20:9 he said unto the **m.** of Ben-hadad, 4397
1Ki 20:9 the **m.** departed, and brought him 4397
2Ki 1:2 he sent **m.** and said unto them, Go, 4397
2Ki 1:3 meet the **m.** of the king of Samaria, 4397
2Ki 1:5 when the **m.** turned back unto him, 4397
2Ki 1:16 as thou hast sent **m.** to enquire of 4397
2Ki 7:15 the **m.** returned, and told the king 4397
2Ki 14:8 Then Amaziah sent **m.** to Jehoash, 4397
2Ki 16:7 So Ahaz sent **m.** to Tiglath-pileser 4397
2Ki 17:4 he had sent **m.** to So king of Egypt, 4397
2Ki 19:9 he sent **m.** again unto Hezekiah, 4397
2Ki 19:14 the letter of the hand of the **m.**, and 4397
2Ki 19:23 By thy **m.** thou hast reproached the 4397
1Ch 14:1 king of Tyre sent **m.** to David, 4397
1Ch 19:2 And David sent **m.** to comfort him 4397
1Ch 19:16 worse before Israel, they sent **m.**, 4397
2Ch 36:15 their father sent to them by his **m.**, 4397
2Ch 36:16 But they mocked the **m.** of God, and 4397
Ne 6:3 I sent **m.** unto them, saying, I am 4397
Pr 16:14 wrath of a king is as **m.** of death: 4397
Isa 14:32 then answer the **m.** of the nation? 4397
Isa 18:2 saying, Go, ye swift **m.**, to a nation 4397
Isa 37:9 he heard it, he sent **m.** to Hezekiah, 4397
Isa 37:14 the letter from the hand of the **m.**, 4397
Isa 44:26 performeth the counsel of his **m.**; 4397
Isa 57:9 didst send thy **m.** far off, and didst 6735
Jer 27:3 by the hand of the **m.** which come 4397
Eze 23:16 and sent **m.** unto them into Chaldea 4397
Eze 30:9 that day shall **m.** go forth from me 4397
Na 2:13 the voice of thy **m.** shall no more be 4397
Lu 7:24 when the **m.** of John were departed, *32*
Lu 9:52 And sent **m.** before his face: and *32*
2Co 8:23 they are the **m.** of the churches, *652*
Jas 2:25 she had received the **m.**, and had *32*

MESSES
Ge 43:34 sent **m.** unto them from before 4864

MESSIAH (mes-si'-ah) see also MESSIAS.
Da 9:25 and build Jerusalem unto the **M.** 4899
Da 9:26 and two weeks shall **M.** be cut off, 4899

MESSIAS (mes-si'-as) See also MESSIAH.
Joh 1:41 unto him, We have found the **M.**, *3323*
Joh 4:25 I know that **M.** cometh, which is *3323*

MET
Ge 32:1 and the angels of God **m.** him. 6293
Ge 33:8 thou by all this drove which I **m.**? 6298
Ex 3:18 of the Hebrews hath **m.** with us: 7136
Ex 4:24 that the Lord **m.** him, and sought 6298
Ex 4:27 and **m.** him in the mount of God, 6298
Ex 5:3 of the Hebrews hath **m.** with us: 7122
Ex 5:20 And they **m.** Moses and Aaron, 6293
Nu 23:4 And God **m.** Balaam: and he said 7136
Nu 23:16 Lord **m.** Balaam, and put a word 7136
De 23:4 they **m.** you not with bread and 6923
De 25:18 How he **m.** thee by the way, and 7136
Jos 11:5 all these kings were **m.** together, 3259
Jos 17:10 **m.** together in Asher on the north, 6293
1Sa 10:10 a company of prophets **m.** him; 7125
1Sa 25:20 against her; and she **m.** them. 6298
2Sa 2:13 **m.** together by the pool of Gibeon: 6298
2Sa 16:1 servant of Mephibosheth **m.** him, 7135
2Sa 18:9 Absalom **m.** the servants of David 7122
1Ki 13:24 a lion **m.** him by the way, and slew 4672
1Ki 18:7 in the way, behold, Elijah **m.** him: 7125
2Ki 9:21 **m.** him in the portion of Naboth 4672
2Ki 10:13 **m.** with the brethren of Ahaziah 4672
Ne 13:2 **m.** not the children of Israel with 6923
Ps 85:10 Mercy and truth are **m.** together 6298
Pr 7:10 **m.** him a woman with the attire 7125
Jer 41:6 as he **m.** them, he said unto them, 6298
Am 5:19 flee from a lion, and a bear **m.** him; 6293
Mt 8:28 **m.** him two possessed with devils, *5221*
Mt 28:9 Jesus **m.** them, saying, **All hail.** *528*
Mk 5:2 there **m.** him out of the tombs a man *528*
Mk 11:4 in a place where two ways **m.**; *296*
Lu 8:27 **m.** him out of the city a certain *5221*
Lu 9:37 from the hill, much people **m.** him. *4876*
Lu 17:12 **m.** him ten men that were lepers, *528*
Joh 4:51 his servants **m.** him, and told him, *528*
Joh 11:20 was coming, went and **m.** him; *5221*
Joh 11:30 in that place where Martha **m.** him. *5221*
Joh 12:18 this cause the people also **m.** him, *5221*
Ac 10:25 was coming in, Cornelius **m.** him, *4876*
Ac 16:16 with a spirit of divination **m.** us, *528*
Ac 17:17 daily with them that **m.** with him. *3909*
Ac 20:14 when he **m.** with us at Assos, we *4820*
Ac 27:41 falling into a place where two seas **m.**,
Heb 7:1 who **m.** Abraham returning from *4876*
Heb 7:10 father, when Melchisedec **m.** him. *4876*

METE See also METED; METEYARD.
Ex 16:18 when they did **m.** it with an omer, 4058
Ps 60:6 and **m.** out the valley of Succoth. 4058

Ps 108:7 and **m.** out the valley of Succoth........ 4058
Mt 7:2 **with what measure ye m., it shall** .. *3354*
Mk 4:24 **with what measure ye m., it shall** .. *3354*
Lu 6:38 **with the same measure that ye m.** . *3354*

METED
Isa 18:2 a nation **m.** out and trodden down, ... 6978
Isa 18:7 a nation **m.** out and trodden under...... 6978
Isa 40:12 and **m.** out heaven with the span, ... 8505

METEYARD
Le 19:35 in **m.**, in weight, or in measure. 4060

METHEG-AMMAH (me''-theg-am'-mah)
2Sa 8:1 David took **M.** out of the hand of....... 4965

METHOAR See REMMON-METHOAR.

METHUSAEL (me-thu'-sa-el)
Ge 4:18 Mehujael begat **M.**: and **M.** begat 4967

METHUSELAH (me-thu'-se-lah) See also MATHUSALA.
Ge 5:21 and five years, and begat **M.**:........... 4968
Ge 5:22 walked with god after he begat **M.** 4968
Ge 5:25 **M.** lived an hundred eighty and.......... 4968
Ge 5:26 And **M.** lived after he begat Lamech 4968
Ge 5:27 the days of **M.** were nine hundred...... 4968
1Ch 1:3 Henoch, **M.**, Lamech,...................... 4968

MEUNIM (me-u'-nim) See also MEHUNIM.
Ne 7:52 the children of **M.**, the children.......... 4586

MEZEHAB (mez'-a-hab)
Ge 36:39 of Matred, the daughter of **M.**........... 4314
1Ch 1:50 of Matred, the daughter of **M.**........... 4314

MIAMIN (mi'-a-min) See also MIJAMIN; MINIAMIN.
Ezr 10:25 Malchiah, and **M.**, and Eleazar,.......... 4326
Ne 12:5 **M.**, Maadiah, Bilgah, ... 4326

MIBHAR (mib'-har)
1Ch 11:38 Nathan, **M.** the son of Haggeri, ... 4006

MIBSAM (mib'-sam)
Ge 25:13 and Kedar, and Adbeel, and **M.**, ... 4017
1Ch 1:29 then Kedar, and Adbeel, and **M.**, ... 4017
1Ch 4:25 Shallum his son, **m.** his son,............. 4017

MIBZAR (mib'-zar)
Ge 36:42 Kenaz, duke Teman, duke **M.**, ... 4014
1Ch 1:53 Kenaz, duke Teman, duke **M.**, ... 4014

MICAH (mi'-cah) See also MICAIAH; MICAH'S; MICHAH.
Jg 17:1 Ephraim, whose name was **M.**.......... 4319
Jg 17:4 and they were in the house of **M.** 4319
Jg 17:5 the man **M.** had a house of gods, ... 4318
Jg 17:8 mount Ephraim to the house of **M.**, ... 4318
Jg 17:9 **M.** said unto him, Whence comest....... 4319
Jg 17:10 **M.** said unto him, Dwell with me, ... 4319
Jg 17:12 **M.** consecrated the Levite; and 4318
Jg 17:12 priest, and was in the house of **M.** 4318
Jg 17:13 said **M.**, Now know I that the Lord.... 4318
Jg 18:2 mount Ephraim, to the house of **M.**,... 4318
Jg 18:3 they were by the house of **M.**, they ... 4318
Jg 18:4 Thus and thus dealeth **M.** with me, ... 4318
Jg 18:13 and come unto the house of **M.** 4318
Jg 18:15 even unto the house of **M.**, and......... 4318
Jg 18:22 a good way from the house of **M.**, ... 4318
Jg 18:23 said unto **M.**, What aileth thee,.......... 4318
Jg 18:26 when **M.** saw that they were too 4318
Jg 18:27 the things which **M.** had made, ... 4318
1Ch 5:5 **M.** his son, Reaia his son, Baal his..... 4318
1Ch 8:34 and Merib-baal begat **M.**.................. 4318
1Ch 8:35 the sons of **M.** were, Pithon, and....... 4318
1Ch 9:15 Mattaniah the son of **M.**, the son....... 4316
1Ch 9:40 and Merib-baal begat **M.**.................. 4318
1Ch 9:41 the sons of **M.** were, Pithon, and....... 4318
1Ch 23:20 Of the sons of Uzziel; **M.** the first,..... 4318
2Ch 34:20 Abdon the son of **M.**, and Shaphan 4318
Jer 26:18 **M.** the Morashite prophesied in 4320
Mic *general title* **M.** 4318
Mic 1:1 word of the Lord that came to **M.** 4318

MICAH'S (mi'-cahs)
Jg 18:18 And these went into **M.** house, and.... 4318
Jg 18:22 in the houses near to **M.** house 4318
Jg 18:31 they set them up **M.** graven image, ... 4318

MICAIAH (mi-ka-i'-ah) See also MICHA; MICHAIAH.
1Ki 22:8 yet one man, **M.** the son of Imlah, ... 4321
1Ki 22:9 said, Hasten hither **M.** the son of........ 4321
1Ki 22:13 messenger that was gone to call **M.**.... 4321
1Ki 22:14 **M.** said, As the Lord liveth, what 4321
1Ki 22:15 unto him **M.**, shall we go against........ 4321
1Ki 22:24 and smote **M.** on the cheek, and........ 4321
1Ki 22:25 **M.** said, Behold, thou shalt see in...... 4321
1Ki 22:26 Take **M.**, and carry him back unto....... 4321
1Ki 22:28 And **M.** said, If thou return at all in.... 4321
2Ch 18:7 the same is **M.** the son of Imla.......... 4321
2Ch 18:8 Fetch quickly **M.** the son of Imla........ 4319
2Ch 18:12 the messenger that went to call **M.** 4321
2Ch 18:13 **M.** said, As the Lord liveth, even 4321
2Ch 18:14 king said unto him, **M.**, shall we 4318
2Ch 18:23 and smote **M.** upon the cheek, and....... 4321
2Ch 18:24 **M.** said, Behold, thou shalt see on..... 4321
2Ch 18:25 Take ye **M.**, and carry him back to 4321
2Ch 18:27 **M.** said, If thou certainly return in...... 4321

MICE
1Sa 6:4 and five golden **m.**, according to the... 5909
1Sa 6:5 images of your **m.** that mar the 5909
1Sa 6:11 the coffer with the **m.** of gold and....... 5909
1Sa 6:18 the golden **m.**, according to the 5909

MICHA (mi'-cah) See also MICAH; MICAIAH.
2Sa 9:12 young son, whose name was **M.** 4316
Ne 10:11 **M.**, Rehob, Hashabiah,.................... 4316
Ne 11:17 And Mattaniah the son of **M.**, the 4316
Ne 11:22 son of Mattaniah, the son of **M.**.......... 4316

MICHAEL (mi'-ka-el)
Nu 13:13 of Asher, Sethur the son of **M.**.......... 4317
1Ch 5:13 house of their fathers were, **M.**, ... 4317
1Ch 5:14 the son of **M.**, the son of Jeshishai, ... 4317
1Ch 6:40 son of **M.**, the son of Baaseiah, the.... 4317
1Ch 7:3 **M.**, and Obadiah, and Joel, Ishiah, ... 4317
1Ch 8:16 **M.**, and Ispah, and Joha, the sons...... 4317
1Ch 12:20 **M.**, and Jozabad, and Elihu, and......... 4317
1Ch 27:18 of Issachar, Omri the son of **M.**:........ 4317
2Ch 21:2 Zechariah, and Azariah, and **M.**,......... 4317
Ezr 8:8 Zebadiah the son of **M.**, and with 4317
Da 10:13 **M.**, one of the chief princes, came 4317
Da 10:21 in these things, but **M.** your prince..... 4317
Da 12:1 at that time shall **M.** stand up,........... 4317
Jude 9 Yet **M.** the archangel, when............... *3413*
Re 12:7 **M.** and his angels fought against *3413*

MICHAH (mi'-cah) See also MICAH; MICHAIAH.
1Ch 24:24 Of the sons of Uzziel; **M.**: of the 4318
1Ch 24:24 of the sons of **M.**; Shamir................ 4318
1Ch 24:25 The brother of **M.** was Isshiah: of...... 4318

MICHAIAH (mi-ka-i'-ah) See also MICAH; MICAIAH.
2Ki 22:12 and Achbor the son of **M.**, and 4320
2Ch 13:2 His mother's name also was **M.** 4322
2Ch 17:7 and to **M.**, to teach in the cities of..... 4322
Ne 12:35 the son of **M.**, the son of Zaccur,....... 4320
Ne 12:41 Eliakim, Maaseiah, Miniamin, **M.**,....... 4320
Jer 36:11 When **M.** the son of Gemariah,.......... 4321
Jer 36:13 **M.** declared unto them all the............ 4321

MICHAL (mi'-kal) See also EGLAH.
1Sa 14:49 and the name of the younger **M.**:........ 4324
1Sa 18:20 **M.** Saul's daughter loved David:......... 4324
1Sa 18:27 Saul gave him **M.** his daughter to........ 4324
1Sa 18:28 that **M.** Saul's daughter loved him, ... 4324
1Sa 19:11 **M.** David's wife told him, saying, ... 4324
1Sa 19:12 So **M.** let David down through a 4324
1Sa 19:13 **M.** took an image, and laid it in 4324
1Sa 19:17 Saul said unto **M.**, Why hast thou........ 4324
1Sa 19:17 **M.** answered Saul, He said unto 4324
1Sa 25:44 Saul had given **M.** his daughter,......... 4324
2Sa 3:13 first bring **M.** Saul's daughter, ... 4324
2Sa 3:14 Deliver me my wife **M.**, which I 4324
2Sa 6:16 **M.** Saul's daughter looked through........ 4324
2Sa 6:20 **M.** the daughter of Saul came out 4324
2Sa 6:21 David said unto **M.**, It was before 4324
2Sa 6:23 **M.** the daughter of Saul had no........... 4324
2Sa 21:8 sons of **M.** the daughter of Saul,......... 4324
1Ch 15:29 **M.** the daughter of Saul looking 4324

MICHMAS (mik'-mas) See also MICHMASH.
Ezr 2:27 The men of **M.**, an hundred.............. 4363
Ne 7:31 The men of **M.**, an hundred.............. 4363

MICHMASH (mik'-mash) See also MICHMAS.
1Sa 13:2 thousand were with Saul in **M.** 4363
1Sa 13:5 they came up, and pitched in **M.**,........ 4363
1Sa 13:11 themselves together at **M.**;............... 4363
1Sa 13:16 the Philistines encamped in **M.** 4363
1Sa 13:23 went out to the passage of **M.**........... 4363
1Sa 14:5 situate northward over against **M.** 4363
1Sa 14:31 the Philistines that day from **M.**.......... 4363
Ne 11:31 Benjamin from Geba dwelt at **M.**.......... 4363
Isa 10:28 at **M.** he had laid up his carriages:...... 4363

MICHMETHAH (mik'-me-thah)
Jos 16:6 went out toward the sea to **M.**.......... 4366
Jos 17:7 Manasseh was from Asher to **M.**, ... 4366

MICHRI (mik'-ri)
1Ch 9:8 the son of Uzzi, the son of **M.**, ... 4381

MICHTAM (mik'-tam)
Ps 16:*title* **M.** of David.................................. 4387
Ps 56:*title* **M.** of David, when the Philistines....... 4387
Ps 57:*title* **M.** of David, when he fled from.......... 4387
Ps 58:*title* Al-taschith, **M.** of David. 4387
Ps 59:*title* **M.** of David; when Saul sent, ... 4387
Ps 60:*title* **M.** of David, to teach; when he 4387

MIDDAY
1Ki 18:29 came to pass, when **m.** was past, ... 6672
Ne 8:3 from the morning until **m.**,.......... 4276,3117
Ac 26:13 At **m.**, O king, I saw in the *2250,3319*

MIDDIN (mid'-din)
Jos 15:61 the wilderness, Beth-arabah, **M.**, ... 4081

MIDDLE See also MIDDLEMOST; MIDST.
Ex 26:28 **m.** bar in the midst of the boards....... 8432
Ex 36:33 And he made the **m.** bar to shoot 8484
Jos 12:2 from the **m.** of the river, and from..... 8432
Jg 7:19 in the beginning of the **m.** watch;....... 8484
Jg 9:37 people down by the **m.** of the land, ... 2872
Jg 16:29 took hold of the two **m.** pillars.......... 8432
1Sa 25:29 out, as out of the **m.** of a sling.......... 8432
2Sa 10:4 cut off their garments in the **m.**, ... 2677
1Ki 6:6 and the **m.** was six cubits broad,........ 8484
1Ki 6:8 door for the **m.** chamber was in the.... 8484
1Ki 6:8 winding stairs into the **m.** chamber, ... 8484
1Ki 6:8 and out of the **m.** into the third. 8484
1Ki 8:64 the king hallow the **m.** of the court..... 8432
2Ki 20:4 was gone out into the **m.** court,......... 8484
2Ch 7:7 hallowed the **m.** of the court that....... 8484
Jer 39:3 came in, and sat in the **m.** gate, ... 8484
Eze 1:16 were a wheel in the **m.** of a wheel. 8432
Eph 2:14 hath broken down the **m.** wall of........ *3320*

MIDDLEMOST
Eze 42:5 and than the **m.** of the building. 8484
Eze 42:6 lowest and the **m.** from the ground..... 8484

MIDIAN (mid'-e-an) See also MADIAN; MIDIANITE.
Ge 25:2 and Medan, and **M.**, and Ishbak, ... 4080
Ge 25:4 sons of **M.**; Ephah, and Epher, and 4080
Ge 36:35 who smote **M.** in the field of Moab,.... 4080
Ex 2:15 and dwelt in the land of **M.**: and 4080
Ex 2:16 priest of **M.** had seven daughters: 4080
Ex 3:1 his father in law, the priest of **M.**:...... 4080
Ex 4:19 the Lord said unto Moses in **M.**, Go,.. 4080
Ex 18:1 When Jethro, the priest of **M.**, ... 4080
Nu 22:4 Moab said unto the elders of **M.**, ... 4080
Nu 22:7 and the elders of **M.** departed with...... 4080
Nu 25:15 people, and of a chief house in **M.**...... 4080
Nu 25:18 the daughter of a prince of **M.**,......... 4080
Nu 31:3 and avenge the Lord of **M.**.............. 4080
Nu 31:8 they slew the kings of **M.**, beside 4080
Nu 31:8 Hur, and Reba, five kings of **M.**:......... 4080
Nu 31:9 took all the women of **M.** captives,...... 4080
Jos 13:21 Moses smote with the princes of **M.**,.. 4080
Jg 6:1 delivered them into the hand of **M.**...... 4080
Jg 6:2 the hand of **M.** prevailed against 4080
Jg 7:8 host of **M.** was beneath him in the 4080
Jg 7:13 bread tumbled into the host of **M.**, ... 4080
Jg 7:14 his hand hath God delivered **M.**, ... 4080
Jg 7:15 into your hand the host of **M.**............ 4080
Jg 7:25 and pursued **M.**, and brought the 4080
Jg 8:3 into your hands the princes of **M.**,....... 4080
Jg 8:5 Zebah and Zalmunna, kings of **M.** 4080
Jg 8:12 them, and took the two kings of **M.**,.... 4080
Jg 8:22 delivered us from the hand of **M.** 4080
Jg 8:26 that was on the kings of **M.**, and 4080
Jg 8:28 **M.** subdued before the children of...... 4080
Jg 9:17 you out of the hand of **M.**:................ 4080
1Ki 11:18 they arose out of **M.**, and came to 4080
1Ch 1:32 and Medan, and **M.**, and Ishbak,......... 4080
1Ch 1:33 the sons of **M.**; Ephah, and Epher,...... 4080
1Ch 1:46 smote **M.** in the field of Moab, ... 4080
Isa 9:4 his oppressor, as in the days of **M.** 4080
Isa 10:26 to the slaughter of **M.** at the rock 4080
Isa 60:6 the dromedaries of **M.** and Ephah;....... 4080
Hab 3:7 the curtains of the land of **M.** did 4080

MIDIANITE (mid'-e-an-ite) See also MIDIANITES; MIDIANITISH.
Nu 10:29 Hobab, the son of Raguel the **M.** 4084

MIDIANITES (mid'-e-an-ites) See also KENITES.
Ge 37:28 there passed by **M.** merchantmen;...... 4084
Ge 37:36 the **M.** sold him into Egypt unto 4092
Nu 25:17 Vex the **M.**, and smite them: 4084
Nu 31:2 the children of Israel of the **M.**; 4084
Nu 31:3 and let them go against the **M.**, ... 4080
Nu 31:7 And they warred against the **M.**,........ 4080
Jg 6:2 because of the **M.** the children of....... 4080
Jg 6:3 had sown, that the **M.** came up, ... 4080
Jg 6:6 impoverished because of the **M.**; 4080
Jg 6:7 unto the Lord because of the **M.**,....... 4080
Jg 6:11 winepress, to hide it from the **M.**....... 4080
Jg 6:13 us into the hands of the M................ 4080
Jg 6:14 Israel from the hand of the **M.**: 4080
Jg 6:16 thou shall smite the **M.** as one man. ... 4080
Jg 6:33 Then all the **M.** and the Amalekites..... 4080
Jg 7:1 host of the **M.** were on the north....... 4080
Jg 7:2 me to give the **M.** into their hands, ... 4080
Jg 7:7 deliver the **M.** into thine hand: 4080
Jg 7:12 And the **M.** and the Amalekites and.... 4080
Jg 7:23 Manasseh,...pursued after the **M.**........ 4080
Jg 7:24 saying, Come down against the **M.**, ... 4080
Jg 7:25 they took two princes of the **M.**, ... 4080
Jg 8:1 thou wentest to fight with the **M.**? 4080
Ps 83:9 Do unto them as unto the **M.**; as....... 4080

MIDIANITISH (mid''-e-an-i'-tish)
Nu 25:6 a **M.** woman in the sight of Moses, ... 4084
Nu 25:14 that was slain with the **M.** woman, ... 4084
Nu 25:15 the name of the **M.** woman that......... 4084

MIDNIGHT
Ex 11:4 About **m.** will I go out into 2676,3915
Ex 12:29 **m.** the Lord smote all the, ... 2677,3915
Jg 16:3 lay till **m.**, and arose at **m.**, ... 2677,3915
Ru 3:8 it came to pass at **m.**, that the... 2677,3915
1Ki 3:20 arose at **m.**, and took my, ... 8432,3915
Job 34:20 people shall be troubled at **m.**, ... 2676,3915
Ps 119:62 At **m.** I will rise to give thanks... 2676,3915
Mt 25:6 **at m. there was a cry made,** .. *3319,3571*
Mk 13:35 **or at m., or at the cockcrowing,**.... *3317*
Lu 11:5 **and shall go unto him at m., and**.. *3317*
Ac 16:25 at **m.** Paul and Silas prayed, and........ *3317*
Ac 20:7 and continued his speech until **m.**....... *3317*
Ac 27:27 about **m.** the shipmen deemed.... *3319,3571*

MIDST See also MIDDLE.
Ge 1:6 firmament in the **m.** of the waters,..... 8432
Ge 2:9 tree of life...in the **m.** of the garden, .. 8432
Ge 3:3 which is in the **m.** of the garden, ... 8432
Ge 15:10 and divided them in the **m.**, and laid... 8432
Ge 19:29 Lot out of the **m.** of the overthrow, ... 8432
Ge 48:16 multitude in the **m.** of the earth. 7130
Ex 3:2 of fire out of the **m.** of a bush: 8432
Ex 3:4 unto him out of the **m.** of the bush,.... 8432
Ex 3:20 which I will do in the **m.** thereof: 7130
Ex 8:22 am the Lord in the **m.** of the earth..... 7130
Ex 11:4 will I go out into the **m.** of Egypt:....... 8432
Ex 14:16 ground through the **m.** of the sea...... 8432
Ex 14:22 of Israel went into the **m.** of the sea... 8432
Ex 14:23 in after them to the **m.** of the sea, ... 8432
Ex 14:27 the Egyptians in the **m.** of the sea. 8432
Ex 14:29 upon dry land in the **m.** of the sea; 8432
Ex 15:19 on dry land in the **m.** of the sea. 8432
Ex 23:25 sickness away from the **m.** of thee. 7130
Ex 24:16 Moses out of the **m.** of the cloud. 8432
Ex 24:18 Moses went into the **m.** of the cloud, ..8432
Ex 26:28 middle bar in the **m.** of the boards 8432
Ex 27:5 may be even to the **m.** of the altar..... 2677
Ex 28:32 in the top of it, in the **m.** thereof: 8432
Ex 33:3 I will not go up in the **m.** of thee; 7130
Ex 33:5 I will come up into the **m.** of thee...... 7130
Ex 34:12 it be for a snare in the **m.** of thee:..... 7130
Ex 38:4 thereof beneath unto the **m.** of it. 2677
Ex 39:23 was an hole in the **m.** of the robe, ... 8432
Le 16:16 them in the **m.** of their uncleanness.... 8432
Nu 2:17 the Levites in the **m.** of the camp: 8432
Nu 5:3 camps, in the **m.** whereof I dwell. 8432
Nu 16:47 ran into the **m.** of the congregation;.... 8432
Nu 19:6 into the **m.** of the burning of the........ 8432
Nu 33:8 passed through the **m.** of the sea....... 8432
Nu 35:5 and the city shall be in the **m.**: this 8432
De 4:11 with fire unto the **m.** of heaven, ... 3820
De 4:12 unto you out of the **m.** of the fire: 8432
De 4:15 in Horeb out of the **m.** of the fire: 8432
De 4:33 speaking out of the **m.** of the fire,...... 8432
De 4:34 from the **m.** of another nation, by 7130
De 4:36 his words out of the **m.** of the fire. 8432
De 5:4,22 mount out of the **m.** of the fire,......... 8432
De 5:23 voice out of the **m.** of the darkness, ... 8432
De 5:24 his voice out of the **m.** of the fire: 8432
De 5:26 speaking out of the **m.** of the fire,....... 8432
De 9:10 out of the **m.** of the fire in the day..... 8432
De 10:4 out of the **m.** of the fire in the day..... 8432
De 11:3 did in the **m.** of Egypt unto Pharaoh... 8432
De 11:6 possession, in the **m.** of all Israel: 7130
De 13:5 the evil away from the **m.** of thee. 7130
De 13:16 spoil of it into the **m.** of the street 8432
De 17:20 his children, in the **m.** of Israel. 7130
De 18:15 thee a Prophet from the **m.** of thee, ... 7130
De 19:2 for thee in the **m.** of thy land, ... 8432
De 23:14 walketh in the **m.** of thy camp, ... 7130
De 32:51 in the **m.** of the children of Israel. 8432
Jos 3:17 on dry ground in the **m.** of Jordan, ... 8432
Jos 4:3 you hence out of the **m.** of Jordan, ... 8432
Jos 4:5 your God into the **m.** of Jordan, ... 8432
Jos 4:8 stones out of the **m.** of Jordan, as...... 8432
Jos 4:9 twelve stones in the **m.** of Jordan,...... 8432
Jos 4:10 the ark stood in the **m.** of Jordan, ... 8432
Jos 4:18 come up out of the **m.** of Jordan, ... 8432
Jos 7:13 accursed thing in the **m.** of thee, ... 7130
Jos 7:21 in the earth in the **m.** of my tent, ... 8432
Jos 7:23 took them out of the **m.** of the tent,.... 8432
Jos 8:13 that night into the **m.** of the valley. 8432
Jos 8:22 so they were in the **m.** of Israel, ... 8432
Jos 10:13 sun stood still in the **m.** of heaven,..... 2677
Jos 13:9, 16 city that is in the **m.** of the river, .. 8432
Jg 15:4 put a firebrand in the **m.** between 8432
Jg 18:20 and went in the **m.** of the people. 7130
Jg 20:42 they destroyed in the **m.** of them. 8432
1Sa 11:11 they came into the **m.** of the host 8432
1Sa 16:13 him in the **m.** of his brethren: and...... 7130
1Sa 18:10 prophesied in the **m.** of the house: 8432
2Sa 1:25 mighty fallen in the **m.** of the battle! ... 8432
2Sa 4:6 thither into the **m.** of the house, ... 8432
2Sa 6:17 in the **m.** of the tabernacle that 8432
2Sa 18:14 was yet alive in the **m.** of the oak. 3820
2Sa 20:12 in blood in the **m.** of the highway. 8432
2Sa 23:12 he stood in the **m.** of the ground, ... 8432
2Sa 23:20 slew a lion in the **m.** of a pit in time ... 8432
2Sa 24:5 city that lieth in the **m.** of the river 8432
1Ki 3:8 thy servant is in the **m.** of thy people . 8432
1Ki 6:27 one another in the **m.** of the house..... 8432
1Ki 8:51 from the **m.** of the furnace of iron: 8432
1Ki 20:39 went out into the **m.** of the battle; 7130
1Ki 22:35 wound into the **m.** of the chariot. 2436
2Ki 6:20 they were in the **m.** of Samaria. 8432
1Ch 11:14 themselves in the **m.** of that parcel,.... 8432
1Ch 16:1 and set it in the **m.** of the tent that.... 8432
1Ch 19:4 their garments in the **m.** hard by 2677
2Ch 6:13 had set it in the **m.** of the court: 8432
2Ch 20:14 Lord in the **m.** of the congregation; 8432
2Ch 32:4 that ran through the **m.** of the land,.... 8432
Ne 4:11 till we come in the **m.** among them, ... 8432
Ne 9:11 through the **m.** of the sea on dry 8432
Es 4:1 and went out into the **m.** of the city, .. 8432
Job 21:21 of his months is cut off in the **m.**?...... 2686
Ps 22:14 is melted in the **m.** of my bowels. 8432
Ps 22:22 in the **m.** of the congregation will I..... 8432
Ps 46:2 be carried into the **m.** of the sea;........ 3820
Ps 46:5 God is in the **m.** of her; she shall....... 7130
Ps 48:9 O God, in the **m.** of thy temple. 7130
Ps 55:10 also and sorrow are in the **m.** of it. 7130
Ps 55:11 Wickedness is in the **m.** thereof: 7130
Ps 57:6 into the **m.** whereof they are fallen..... 8432
Ps 74:4 roar in the **m.** of thy congregation; 7130
Ps 74:12 salvation in the **m.** of the earth. 7130
Ps 78:28 he let it fall in the **m.** of their camp, ... 7130
Ps 102:24 me not away in the **m.** of my days: 2677
Ps 110:2 thou in the **m.** of thine enemies. 7130
Ps 116:19 Lord's house, in the **m.** of thee, O...... 8432
Ps 135:9 and wonders in the **m.** of thee,........... 8432
Ps 136:14 Israel to pass through the **m.** of it:..... 8432
Ps 137:2 upon the willows in the **m.** thereof. 8432
Ps 138:7 Though I walk in the **m.** of trouble, ... 7130
Pr 4:21 keep them in the **m.** of thine heart..... 8432
Pr 5:14 all evil in the **m.** of the congregation... 8432
Pr 8:20 in the **m.** of the paths of judgment: 8432
Pr 14:33 that which is in the **m.** of fools is 7130
Pr 23:34 he lieth down in the **m.** of the sea,...... 3820
Pr 30:19 way of a ship in the **m.** of the sea;...... 3820
Ca 3:10 **m.** thereof being paved with love, ... 8432
Isa 4:4 the blood of Jerusalem from the **m.** 7130
Isa 5:2 and built a tower in the **m.** of it, ... 8432
Isa 5:8 be...alone in the **m.** of the earth! 7130
Isa 5:25 were torn in the **m.** of the streets...... 7130
Isa 6:5 I dwell in the **m.** of a people of......... 8432
Isa 6:12 forsaking in the **m.** of the land. 7130
Isa 7:6 and set a king in the **m.** of it, even 8432
Isa 10:23 even...in the **m.** of all the land. 7130
Isa 12:6 Holy One of Israel in the **m.** of thee... 7130
Isa 16:3 night in the **m.** of the noonday;.......... 8432
Isa 19:1 of Egypt shall melt in the **m.** of it. 7130
Isa 19:3 Egypt shall fail in the **m.** thereof; 7130
Isa 19:14 a perverse spirit in the **m.** thereof:..... 7130
Isa 19:19 Lord in the **m.** of the land of Egypt, ... 8432
Isa 19:24 a blessing in the **m.** of the land:......... 7130
Isa 24:13 it shall be in the **m.** of the land.......... 7130
Isa 24:18 cometh up out of the **m.** of the pit 8432
Isa 25:11 forth his hand in the **m.** of them, ... 7130
Isa 29:23 of mine hands, in the **m.** of him, ... 7130
Isa 30:28 shall reach to the **m.** of the neck, ... 2673
Isa 41:18 fountains in the **m.** of the valleys: 8432
Isa 52:11 go ye out of the **m.** of her; be ye 8432
Isa 58:9 thou take away from the **m.** of thee.... 8432
Isa 66:17 gardens behind one tree in the **m.**,..... 8432
Jer 6:1 flee out of the **m.** of Jerusalem, ... 7130
Jer 6:6 wholly oppression in the **m.** of her. 7130
Jer 9:6 habitation is in the **m.** of deceit;......... 8432
Jer 12:16 they be built in the **m.** of my people... 8432
Jer 14:9 thou, O Lord, art in the **m.** of us,...... 7130
Jer 17:11 leave them in the **m.** of his days, ... 2677
Jer 21:4 them into the **m.** of this city. 8432
Jer 29:8 that be in the **m.** of you, deceive 7130
Jer 30:21 shall proceed from the **m.** of them;..... 7130
Jer 37:12 thence in the **m.** of the people........... 8432
Jer 41:7 they came into the **m.** of the city, ... 8432
Jer 41:7 and cast them into the **m.** of the pit, .. 8432
Jer 46:21 her hired men are in the **m.** of her..... 7130
Jer 48:45 flame from the **m.** of Sihon, and shall........
Jer 50:8 Remove out of the **m.** of Babylon,...... 8432
Jer 50:37 people that are in the **m.** of her;........ 8432
Jer 51:1 them that dwell in the **m.** of them...... 3820
Jer 51:6 Flee out of the **m.** of Babylon, and..... 8432
Jer 51:45 people, go ye out of the **m.** of her, ... 8432
Jer 51:47 her slain shall fall in the **m.** of her. 8432
Jer 51:63 cast it into the **m.** of Euphrates: 8432
Jer 52:25 that were found in the **m.** of the city. . 8432
La 1:15 my mighty men in the **m.** of me: 7130
La 3:45 and refuse in the **m.** of the people...... 7130
La 4:13 blood of the just in the **m.** of her, ... 7130
Eze 1:4 and out of the **m.** thereof as the 8432
Eze 1:4 of amber, out of the **m.** of the fire. 8432
Eze 1:5 Also out of the **m.** thereof came the.... 8432
Eze 5:2 fire a third part in the **m.** of the city,.. 8432
Eze 5:4 and cast them into the **m.** of the fire, ..8432
Eze 5:5 I have set it in the **m.** of the nations .. 8432
Eze 5:8 judgments in the **m.** of thee in the 8432
Eze 5:10 shall eat the sons in the **m.** of thee, ... 8432
Eze 5:12 they be consumed in the **m.** of thee: .. 8432
Eze 6:7 the slain shall fall in the **m.** of you,..... 8432
Eze 7:4 abominations shall be in the **m.** of...... 8432
Eze 7:9 abominations that are in the **m.** of....... 8432
Eze 8:11 in the **m.** of them stood Jaazaniah....... 8432
Eze 9:4 him, Go through the **m.** of the city,..... 8432
Eze 9:4 through the **m.** of Jerusalem, and 8432
Eze 9:4 that be done in the **m.** thereof. 8432
Eze 10:10 wheel had been in the **m.** of a wheel. ..8432
Eze 11:7 whom ye have laid in the **m.** of it,...... 8432
Eze 11:7 bring you forth out of the **m.** of it. 8432
Eze 11:9 will bring you out of the **m.** thereof, ... 8432
Eze 11:11 ye be the flesh in the **m.** thereof; 8432
Eze 11:23 went up from the **m.** of the city,......... 8432
Eze 12:2 in the **m.** of a rebellious house, ... 8432
Eze 13:14 be consumed in the **m.** thereof: 8432
Eze 14:8 him off from the **m.** of my people;....... 8432
Eze 14:9 from the **m.** of my people Israel. 8432
Eze 15:4 ends of it, and the **m.** of it is burned. . 8432
Eze 16:53 of thy captives in the **m.** of them: 8432
Eze 17:16 in the **m.** of Babylon he shall die........ 8432
Eze 20:8 them in the **m.** of the land of Egypt.... 8432
Eze 21:32 blood shall be in the **m.** of the land;.... 8432
Eze 22:3 city sheddeth blood in the **m.** of it,..... 8432
Eze 22:7 in the **m.** of thee have they dealt by... 8432
Eze 22:9 **m.** of thee they commit lewdness....... 8432
Eze 22:13 which hath been in the **m.** of thee...... 8432
Eze 22:18 and lead, in the **m.** of the furnace; 8432
Eze 22:19 gather you into the **m.** of Jerusalem.... 8432
Eze 22:20 and tin, into the **m.** of the furnace,..... 8432
Eze 22:21 ye shall be melted in the **m.** thereof. .. 8432
Eze 22:22 is melted in the **m.** of the furnace, ... 8432
Eze 22:22 shall ye be melted in the **m.** thereof; .. 8432

Eze 22:25 of her prophets in the **m.** thereof, 8432
Eze 22:25 her many widows in the **m.** thereof. 8432
Eze 22:27 Her princes in the **m.** thereof are 7130
Eze 23:39 they done in the **m.** of mine house. 8432
Eze 24:7 For her blood is in the **m.** of her; 8432
Eze 26:5 of nets in the **m.** of the sea: 8432
Eze 26:12 and thy dust in the **m.** of the water. 8432
Eze 26:15 slaughter is made in the **m.** of thee? 8432
Eze 27:4 borders are in the **m.** of the seas, 3820
Eze 27:25 very glorious in the **m.** of the seas. 3820
Eze 27:26 broken thee in the **m.** of the seas. 3820
Eze 27:27 company which is in the **m.** of thee 8432
Eze 27:27 shall fall into the **m.** of the seas 3820
Eze 27:32 the destroyed in the **m.** of the sea? 8432
Eze 27:34 company in the **m.** of thee shall fall. 8432
Eze 28:2 seat of God, in the **m.** of the seas; 3820
Eze 28:8 that are slain in the **m.** of the seas. 3820
Eze 28:14 in the **m.** of the stones of fire. 8432
Eze 28:16 filled the **m.** of thee with violence, 8432
Eze 28:16 from the **m.** of the stones of fire 8432
Eze 28:18 forth a fire from the **m.** of thee, 8432
Eze 28:22 I will be glorified in the **m.** of thee: 8432
Eze 28:23 shall be judged in the **m.** of her by 8432
Eze 29:3 that lieth in the **m.** of his rivers, 8432
Eze 29:4 thee up out of the **m.** of thy rivers, 8432
Eze 29:12 the **m.** of the countries are desolate, 8432
Eze 29:21 of the mouth in the **m.** of them; 8432
Eze 30:7 the **m.** of the countries are desolate, 8432
Eze 30:7 the **m.** of the cities that are wasted. 8432
Eze 31:14 in the **m.** of the children of men, 8432
Eze 31:17 shadow in the **m.** of the heathen. 8432
Eze 31:18 lie in the **m.** of the uncircumcised 8432
Eze 32:20 fall in the **m.** of them that are slain 8432
Eze 32:21 speak to him out of the **m.** of hell 8432
Eze 32:25 set her a bed in the **m.** of the slain 8432
Eze 32:25 put in the **m.** of them that be slain. 8432
Eze 32:28 in the **m.** of the uncircumcised, 8432
Eze 32:32 laid in the **m.** of the uncircumcised 8432
Eze 36:23 ye have profaned in the **m.** of them; 8432
Eze 37:1 set me down in the **m.** of the valley 8432
Eze 37:26 set my sanctuary in the **m.** of them 8432
Eze 37:28 sanctuary shall be in the **m.** of them 8432
Eze 38:12 that dwell in the **m.** of the land. 2872
Eze 39:7 in the **m.** of my people Israel; 8432
Eze 41:7 chamber to the highest by the **m.** 8484
Eze 43:7 in the **m.** of the children of Israel 8432
Eze 43:9 and I will dwell in the **m.** of them 8432
Eze 46:10 And the prince in the **m.** of them, 8432
Eze 48:8 sanctuary shall be in the **m.** of it. 8432
Eze 48:10 the Lord shall be in the **m.** thereof. 8432
Eze 48:15 the city shall be in the **m.** thereof. 8432
Eze 48:21 the house shall be in the **m.** thereof. 8432
Eze 48:22 the **m.** of that which is the prince's, 8432
Da 3:6, 11 **m.** of a burning fiery furnace. 1459
Da 3:15 the **m.** of a burning fiery furnace; 1459
Da 3:21, 23 **m.** of the burning fiery furnace. 1459
Da 3:24 men bound into the **m.** of the fire? 1459
Da 3:25 loose, walking in the **m.** of the fire, 1459
Da 3:26 came forth of the **m.** of the fire. 1459
Da 4:10 behold a tree in the **m.** of the earth, 1459
Da 7:15 in my spirit in the **m.** of my body, 1459
Da 9:27 **m.** of the week he shall cause the 2677
Ho 5:4 of whoredoms is in the **m.** of them, 7130
Ho 11:9 man; the Holy One in the **m.** of thee: 7130
Joe 2:27 know that I am in the **m.** of Israel, 7130
Am 2:3 off the judge from the **m.** thereof, 7130
Am 3:9 great tumults in the **m.** thereof, 7130
Am 3:9 the oppressed in the **m.** thereof. 8432
Am 6:4 the calves out of the **m.** of the stall; 8432
Am 7:8 plumbline in the **m.** of my people 7130
Am 7:10 in the **m.** of the house of Israel: 7130
Jon 2:3 the deep, in the **m.** of the seas; 3824
Mic 2:12 as the flock in the **m.** of their fold: 8432
Mic 5:7 in the **m.** of many people as a dew 7130
Mic 5:8 in the **m.** of many people as a lion 7130
Mic 5:10 off thy horses out of the **m.** of thee, 7130
Mic 5:13 images out of the **m.** of thee; 7130
Mic 5:14 up thy groves out of the **m.** of thee: 7130
Mic 6:14 down shall be in the **m.** of thee; 7130
Mic 7:14 in the wood, in the **m.** of Carmel: 8432
Na 3:13 people in the **m.** of thee are women: 7130
Hab 2:19 is no breath at all in the **m.** of it. 7130
Hab 3:2 thy work in the **m.** of the years, 7130
Hab 3:2 in the **m.** of the years make known; 7130
Zep 2:14 shall lie down in the **m.** of her, 8432
Zep 3:5 The just Lord is in the **m.** thereof; 7130
Zep 3:11 will take away out of the **m.** of thee 7130
Zep 3:12 leave in the **m.** of thee an afflicted 7130
Zep 3:15 even the Lord, is in the **m.** of thee: 7130
Zep 3:17 thy God in the **m.** of thee is mighty; 7130
Zec 2:5 will be the glory in the **m.** of her. 8432
Zec 2:10, 11 and I will dwell in the **m.** of thee, 8432
Zec 5:4 shall remain in the **m.** of his house, 8432
Zec 5:7 that sitteth in the **m.** of the ephah. 8432
Zec 5:8 he cast it into the **m.** of the ephah; 8432
Zec 8:3 will dwell in the **m.** of Jerusalem: 8432
Zec 8:8 shall dwell in the **m.** of Jerusalem: 8432
Zec 14:1 shall be divided in the **m.** of thee. 7130
Zec 14:4 shall cleave in the **m.** thereof 2677
Mt 10:16 **as sheep in the m. of wolves:** *3319*
Mt 14:24 ship was now in the **m.** of the sea, *3319*
Mt 18:2 him, and set him in the **m.** of them, *3319*
Mt 18:20 **there am I in the m. of them.** *3319*
Mk 6:47 the ship was in the **m.** of the sea, *3319*
Mk 7:31 the **m.** of the coasts of Decapolis. *3319*
Mk 9:36 child, and set him in the **m.** of them: *3319*
Mk 14:60 the high priest stood up in the **m.**, *3319*
Lu 2:46 sitting in the **m.** of the doctors, *3319*
Lu 4:30 he passing through the **m.** of them *3319*
Lu 4:35 the devil had thrown him in the **m.**, *3319*
Lu 5:19 his couch into the **m.** before Jesus. *3319*
Lu 6:8 **up, and stand forth in the m.** *3319*
Lu 17:11 passed through the **m.** of Samaria *3319*
Lu 21:21 **are in the m. of it depart out;** *3319*
Lu 22:55 kindled a fire in the **m.** of the hall, *3319*
Lu 23:45 of the temple was rent in the **m.** *3319*
Lu 24:36 Jesus...stood in the **m.** of them, *3319*
Joh 7:14 the **m.** of the feast Jesus went up *3322*
Joh 8:3 when they had set her in the **m.**, *3319*
Joh 8:9 and the woman standing in the **m.** *3319*
Joh 8:59 going through the **m.** of them, and *3319*
Joh 19:18 either side one, and Jesus in the **m.** *3319*
Joh 20:19 came Jesus and stood in the **m.**, *3319*
Joh 20:26 stood in the **m.**, and said, **Peace be** *3319*
Ac 1:15 stood up in the **m.** of the disciples, *3319*
Ac 1:18 he burst asunder in the **m.**, and all *3319*
Ac 2:22 God did by him in the **m.** of you, *3319*
Ac 4:7 when they had set them in the **m.**, *3319*
Ac 17:22 Paul stood in the **m.** of Mars' hill, *3319*
Ac 27:21 Paul stood forth in the **m.** of them, *3319*
Php 2:15 in the **m.** of a crooked and perverse *3319*
Heb 2:12 **m.** of the church will I sing praise *3319*
Re 1:13 in the **m.** of the seven candlesticks *3319*
Re 2:1 **m. of the seven golden** *3319*
Re 2:7 **is in the m. of the paradise of** *3319*
Re 4:6 in the **m.** of the throne, and round *3319*
Re 5:6 in the **m.** of the throne and of the *3319*
Re 5:6 in the **m.** of the elders, stood a Lamb *3319*
Re 6:6 a voice in the **m.** of the four beasts *3319*
Re 7:17 which is in the **m.** of the throne *3319*
Re 8:13 flying through the **m.** of heaven, *3321*
Re 14:6 angel fly in the **m.** of heaven, *3321*
Re 19:17 fowls that fly in the **m.** of heaven, *3321*
Re 22:2 In the **m.** of the street of it, and on *3319*

MIDWIFE See also MIDWIVES.
Ge 35:17 labour, that the **m.** said unto her, 3205
Ge 38:28 **m.** took and bound upon his hand a 3205
Ex 1:16 When ye do the office of a **m.** to the 3205

MIDWIVES
Ex 1:15 of Egypt spake to the Hebrew **m.**, 3205
Ex 1:17 the **m.** feared God, and did not as 3205
Ex 1:18 the king of Egypt called for the **m.**, 3205
Ex 1:19 the **m.** said unto Pharaoh, Because 3205
Ex 1:19 ere the **m.** come in unto them. 3205
Ex 1:20 God dealt well with the **m.**: and the 3205
Ex 1:21 to pass because the **m.** feared God, 3205

MIGDAL-EL (mig'-dal-el)
Jos 19:38 And Iron, and **M.**, Horem, and 4027

MIGDAL-GAD (mig'-dal-gad)
Jos 15:37 Zenan, and Hadashah, and **M.**, 4028

MIGDOL (mig'-dol)
Ex 14:2 between **M.** and the sea, over 4024
Nu 33:7 and they pitched before **M.** 4024
Jer 44:1 land of Egypt, which dwelt at **M.**, 4024
Jer 46:14 ye in Egypt, and publish in **M.**, and 4024

MIGHT See also MIGHTEST.
Ge 12:19 so I **m.** have taken her to me to wife:
Ge 13:6 them, that they **m.** dwell together:
Ge 17:18 O that Ishmael **m.** live before thee!
Ge 26:10 **m.** lightly have lien with thy wife,
Ge 30:34 would it **m.** be according to thy word.
Ge 30:41 that they **m.** conceive among the rods.
Ge 31:27 I **m.** have sent thee away with mirth,
Ge 36:7 than that they **m.** dwell together;
Ge 37:22 that he **m.** rid him out of their hands,
Ge 43:32 Egyptians **m.** not eat bread with 3201
Ge 49:3 thou art my firstborn, my **m.**, and 3581
Ex 10:1 I **m.** shew these my signs before him:
Ex 12:33 **m.** send them out of the land in haste;
Ex 36:18 the tent together, that it **m.** be one.
Ex 39:21 **m.** be above the curious girdle of the
Ex 39:21 that the breastplate **m.** not be loosed
Le 24:12 mind of the Lord **m.** be shewed them.
Le 26:45 the heathen, that I **m.** be their God:
Nu 4:37, 41 that **m.** do service in the tabernacle
Nu 14:13 broughtest up this people in thy **m.** 3581
Nu 22:41 **m.** see the utmost part of the people.
De 2:30 that he **m.** deliver him into thy hand,
De 3:24 works, and according to thy **m.**? 1369
De 4:14 **m.** do them in the land whither ye go
De 4:36 his voice, that he **m.** instruct thee:
De 4:42 That the slayer **m.** flee thither, which
De 4:42 unto one of these cities he **m.** live:
De 5:29 that it **m.** be well with them, and with
De 6:1 **m.** do them in the land whither ye go
De 6:5 all thy soul, and with all thy **m.** 3966
De 6:23 that he **m.** bring us in, to give us the
De 6:24 that he **m.** preserve us alive, as it is at
De 8:3 he **m.** make thee know that man doth
De 8:16 **m.** humble thee, and that he **m.** prove
De 8:17 the **m.** of mine hand hath gotten 6108
De 28:32 there shall be no **m.** in thine hand 410
De 29:6 ye **m.** know that I am the Lord your
De 32:13 he **m.** eat the increase of the fields;
Jos 4:24 people of the earth **m.** know the hand
Jos 4:24 ye **m.** fear the Lord your God for ever.
Jos 11:20 that he **m.** destroy them utterly, and
Jos 11:20 and that they **m.** have no favour,
Jos 11:20 but that he **m.** destroy them, as the
Jos 20:9 killeth any person at unawares **m.** flee
Jos 22:16 ye **m.** rebel this day against the Lord?
Jos 22:24 your children **m.** speak unto our
Jos 22:27 that we **m.** do the service of the Lord
Jos 24:8 hand, that ye **m.** possess their land;
Jg 3:2 of Israel **m.** know, to teach them war,
Jg 5:31 sun when he goeth forth in his **m.** 1369
Jg 6:14 Go in this thy **m.**, and thou shalt 3581
Jg 9:24 ten sons of Jerubbaal **m.** come, and
Jg 16:30 he bowed himself with all his **m.**; 3581
Jg 18:7 **m.** put them to shame in any thing;
Ru 1:6 **m.** return from the country of Moab:
1Sa 4:4 they **m.** bring from thence the ark of
1Sa 13:10 to meet him, that he **m.** salute him.
1Sa 14:14 of land, which a yoke of oxen **m.** plow.
1Sa 18:27 that he **m.** be the king's son in law.
1Sa 20:6 of me that he **m.** run to Beth-lehem
2Sa 6:14 before the Lord with all his **m.**; 5797
2Sa 10:10 that he **m.** put them in array against
2Sa 15:4 any suit or cause **m.** come unto me,
2Sa 17:14 the Lord **m.** bring evil upon Absalom.
2Sa 17:17 they **m.** not be seen to come into 3201
2Sa 22:41 that I **m.** destroy them that hate **m.**
1Ki 2:27 that he **m.** fulfil the word of the Lord,
1Ki 7:7 for the throne where he **m.** judge,
1Ki 8:1 that they **m.** bring up the ark of the
1Ki 8:16 an house, that my name **m.** be therein;
1Ki 12:15 that he **m.** perform his saying, which
1Ki 15:17 that he **m.** not suffer any to go out or
1Ki 15:23 all the acts of Asa, and all his **m.**, 1369
1Ki 16:5 what he did, and his **m.**, are they 1369
1Ki 16:27 he did, and his **m.** that he shewed, 1369
1Ki 19:4 requested for himself that he **m.** die;
1Ki 22:7 besides, that we **m.** enquire of him?
1Ki 22:45 and his **m.** that he shewed, and 1369
2Ki 7:2 windows in heaven, **m.** this thing be?
2Ki 7:19 in heaven, **m.** such a thing be?
2Ki 10:19 he **m.** destroy the worshippers of Baal.
2Ki 10:34 and all that he did, and all his **m.**, 1369
2Ki 13:8 and all that he did, and his **m.**, are 1369
2Ki 13:12 and all that he did, and his **m.** 1369
2Ki 14:15 Jehoash which he did, and his **m.**, 1369
2Ki 14:28 and all that he did, and his **m.**, how 1369
2Ki 15:19 his hand **m.** be with him to confirm
2Ki 20:20 acts of Hezekiah, and all his **m.**, 1369
2Ki 22:17 that they **m.** provoke me to anger with
2Ki 23:10 man **m.** make his son or his daughter

2Ki 23:24 he **m.** perform the words of the law
2Ki 23:25 all his soul, and with all his **m.**, 3966
2Ki 23:33 that he **m.** not reign in Jerusalem;
2Ki 24:16 And all the men of **m.**, even seven 2428
1Ch 4:10 that thine hand **m.** be with me, and
1Ch 7:2 men of **m.** in the generations; 2428
1Ch 7:5 Issachar were valiant men of **m.**, 2428
1Ch 12:8 hold to the wilderness men of **m.**, 2428
1Ch 13:8 before God with all their **m.**, and 5797
1Ch 29:2 prepared with all my **m.** for the 3581
1Ch 29:12 and in thine hand is power and **m.**; 1369
1Ch 29:30 With all his reign and his **m.**, and 1369
2Ch 2:12 that **m.** build an house for the Lord,
2Ch 6:5 an house in, that my name **m.** be there;
2Ch 6:6 Jerusalem, that my name **m.** be there;
2Ch 10:15 that the Lord **m.** perform his word,
2Ch 11:1 he **m.** bring the kingdom again to
2Ch 16:1 he **m.** let none go out or come in to
2Ch 18:6 besides, that we **m.** enquire of him?
2Ch 20:6 hand is there not power and **m.**, 1369
2Ch 20:12 no **m.** against this great company 3581
2Ch 25:20 **m.** deliver them into the hand of their
2Ch 31:4 **m.** be encouraged in the law of the
2Ch 32:18 them; that they **m.** take the city.
2Ch 32:31 he **m.** know all that was in his heart.
2Ch 34:25 they **m.** provoke me to anger with all
2Ch 35:12 they **m.** give according to the divisions
2Ch 35:15 they **m.** not depart from their service;
2Ch 35:22 he **m.** fight with him, and hearkened
2Ch 36:22 of Jeremiah **m.** be accomplished,
Ezr 1:1 mouth of Jeremiah **m.** be fulfilled,
Ezr 5:10 **m.** write the names of the men that
Ezr 8:21 we **m.** afflict ourselves before our God,
Ne 5:3 that we **m.** buy corn, because of the
Ne 5:10 **m.** exact of them money and corn:
Ne 6:13 **m.** have matter for an evil report,
Ne 6:13 evil report, that they **m.** reproach me.
Ne 7:5 they **m.** be reckoned by genealogy.
Ne 9:24 they **m.** do with them as they would.
Ne 10:37 the same Levites **m.** have the tithes
Es 4:2 for none **m.** enter into the king's gate
Es 10:2 the acts of his power and of his **m.**, 1369
Job 6:8 that I **m.** have my request; and that
Job 9:33 us, that **m.** lay his hand upon us both.
Job 16:21 that one **m.** plead for a man with God,
Job 23:3 Oh that I knew where I **m.** find him!
Job 23:3 that I **m.** come even to his seat!
Job 23:7 the righteous **m.** dispute with him;
Job 30:2 whereto **m.** the strength of their
Job 38:13 **m.** take hold of the ends of the earth,
Job 38:13 that the wicked **m.** be shaken out of it?
Ps 18:40 that I **m.** destroy them that hate me.
Ps 68:18 the Lord God **m.** dwell among them.
Ps 76:5 none of the men of **m.** have found 2428
Ps 78:6 the generation to come **m.** know them,
Ps 78:7 That they **m.** set their hope in God,
Ps 78:8 **m.** not be as their fathers, a stubborn
Ps 105:45 that they **m.** observe his statutes, and
Ps 106:8 he **m.** make his mighty power to be
Ps 107:7 that they **m.** go to a city of habitation.
Ps 109:16 he **m.** even slay the broken in heart.
Ps 118:13 hast thrust sore at me that I **m.** fall:
Ps 119:11 heart, that I **m.** not sin against thee.
Ps 119:71 afflicted; that I **m.** learn thy statutes.
Ps 119:101 evil way, that I **m.** keep thy word.
Ps 119:148 that I **m.** meditate in thy word.
Ps 145:6 speak of the **m.** of thy terrible acts: 5807
Pr 22:21 I **m.** make thee know the certainty
Ec 2:3 I **m.** see what was that good for the
Ec 3:18 of men, that God **m.** manifest them,
Ec 3:18 they **m.** see that they themselves are
Ec 9:10 findeth to do, do it with thy **m.**; 3581
Isa 11:2 the spirit of counsel and **m.**, the 1369
Isa 28:13 that they **m.** go, and fall backward,
Isa 33:13 that are near, acknowledge my **m.** 1369
Isa 40:26 names by the greatness of his **m.**, 202
Isa 40:29 have no **m.** he increaseth strength. 202
Isa 61:3 **m.** be called trees of righteousness,
Isa 61:3 of the Lord, that he **m.** be glorified.
Isa 64:1 **m.** flow down at thy presence,
Jer 9:1 I **m.** weep day and night for the slain
Jer 9:2 I **m.** leave my people, and go from
Jer 9:23 let the mighty man glory in his **m.**, 1369
Jer 10:6 great, and thy name is great in **m.** 1369
Jer 13:11 that they **m.** be unto me for a people,
Jer 16:21 to know mine hand and my **m.**; 1369
Jer 17:23 their neck stiff, that they **m.** not hear,
Jer 19:15 necks, that they **m.** not hear my words.
Jer 20:17 my mother **m.** have been my grave,
Jer 25:7 ye **m.** provoke me to anger with the
Jer 26:19 **m.** we procure great evil against our
Jer 27:15 in my name; that I **m.** drive you out,
Jer 27:15 that ye **m.** perish, ye, and the prophets
Jer 43:3 that they **m.** put us to death, and carry
Jer 44:8 that ye **m.** cut yourselves off, and that
Jer 44:8 that ye **m.** be a curse and a reproach
Jer 49:35 bow of Elam, the chief of their **m.** 1369
Jer 51:30 their **m.** hath failed; they became 1369
Eze 17:7 that he **m.** water it by the furrows of
Eze 17:8 that it **m.** bring forth branches, and
Eze 17:8 branches, and that it **m.** bear fruit,
Eze 17:8 bear fruit, that it **m.** be a goodly vine.
Eze 17:14 That the kingdom **m.** be base, that
Eze 17:14 that it **m.** not lift itself up, but that
Eze 17:14 by keeping of his covenant it **m.** stand.
Eze 17:15 they **m.** give him horses and much
Eze 20:12 that they **m.** know that I am the Lord
Eze 20:26 that I **m.** make them desolate, to the
Eze 20:26 that they **m.** know that I am the Lord.
Eze 24:8 That it **m.** cause fury to come up to
Eze 32:29 with their **m.** are laid by them that 1369
Eze 32:30 terror they are ashamed of their **m.**; 1369
Eze 36:3 ye **m.** be a possession unto the residue
Eze 40:4 intent that I **m.** shew them unto thee
Eze 41:6 that they **m.** have hold, but they had
Da 1:4 whom they **m.** teach the learning and
Da 1:5 thereof they **m.** stand before the king.
Da 1:8 eunuchs that he **m.** not defile himself.
Da 2:20 ever: for wisdom and **m.** are his: 1370
Da 2:23 who hast given me wisdom and **m.**, 1370
Da 3:28 **m.** not serve nor worship any god,
Da 4:6 that they **m.** make known unto me the
Da 4:30 kingdom by the **m.** of my power, 8632
Da 5:2 and his concubines, **m.** drink therein.
Da 6:2 princes **m.** give accounts unto them,
Da 6:17 that the purpose **m.** not be changed
Da 8:4 so that no beasts **m.** stand before him,
Da 9:11 that they **m.** not obey thy voice;
Da 9:13 that we **m.** turn from our iniquities,
Joe 3:3 sold a girl for wine, that they **m.** drink.
Joe 3:6 ye **m.** remove them far from their
Am 1:13 that they **m.** enlarge their border:
Jon 4:5 **m.** see what would become of the city.
Jon 4:6 that it **m.** be a shadow over his head,
Mic 3:8 of judgment, and of **m.**, to declare 1369
Mic 7:16 and be confounded at all their **m.**: 1369
Hab 3:16 that I **m.** rest in the day of trouble:
Zec 4:6 Not by **m.**, nor by power, but by 2428
Zec 6:7 to go that they **m.** walk to and fro
Zec 8:9 was laid, that the temple **m.** be built.
Zec 11:10 **m.** break my covenant which I had
Zec 11:14 I **m.** break the brotherhood between
Mal 2:4 that my covenant **m.** be with Levi,
Mal 2:15 one? That he **m.** seek a godly seed.
Mt 1:22 it **m.** be fulfilled which was spoken
Mt 2:15, 23 it **m.** be fulfilled which was spoken
Mt 4:14 it **m.** be fulfilled which was spoken
Mt 8:17 it **m.** be fulfilled which was spoken
Mt 8:28 that no man **m.** pass by that way. *2480*
Mt 12:10 days? that they **m.** accuse him.
Mt 12:14 him, how they **m.** destroy him.
Mt 12:17 it **m.** be fulfilled which was spoken
Mt 13:35 it **m.** be fulfilled which was spoken
Mt 14:36 they **m.** only touch the hem of his
Mt 21:4 it **m.** be fulfilled which was spoken by
Mt 21:32 **not afterward, that ye m. believe him.**
Mt 21:34 **that they m. receive the fruits of it.**
Mt 22:15 how they **m.** entangle him in his talk.
Mt 26:4 that they **m.** take Jesus by subtilty,
Mt 26:9 this ointment **m.** have been sold for *1410*
Mt 26:56 **of the prophets m. be fulfilled.**
Mt 27:35 it **m.** be fulfilled which was spoken by
Mk 3:2 day; that they **m.** accuse him.
Mk 3:6 against him, how they **m.** destroy him.
Mk 3:14 that he **m.** send them forth to preach,
Mk 5:18 prayed him that he **m.** be with him.
Mk 6:56 they **m.** touch if it were but the border
Mk 10:51 him, Lord, that I **m.** receive my sight.
Mk 11:13 if haply he **m.** find any thing thereon:
Mk 11:18 and sought how they **m.** destroy him:
Mk 12:2 **he m. receive from the husbandmen**
Mk 14:1 scribes sought how they **m.** take him
Mk 14:5 For it **m.** have been sold for more *1410*
Mk 14:11 how he **m.** conveniently betray him.
Mk 14:35 possible, the hour **m.** pass from him.
Mk 16:1 that they **m.** come and anoint him.
Lu 1:74 enemies **m.** serve him without fear,
Lu 4:29 that they **m.** cast him down headlong.
Lu 5:19 by what way they **m.** bring him in
Lu 6:7 **m.** find an accusation against him.
Lu 6:11 another what they **m.** do to Jesus.
Lu 8:9 saying, What **m.** this parable be?
Lu 8:10 **parables; that seeing they m. not see,**
Lu 8:10 **and hearing they m. not understand.**
Lu 8:38 besought him that he **m.** be with him:
Lu 11:54 of his mouth, that they **m.** accuse him.
Lu 15:29 **that I m. make merry with my friends:**
Lu 17:6 **ye m. say unto this sycamine tree,**
Lu 19:15 **m. know how much every man had**
Lu 19:23 **I m. have required mine own with**
Lu 19:48 And could not find what they **m.** do:
Lu 20:20 that they **m.** take hold of his words,
Lu 20:20 **m.** deliver him unto the power and
Lu 22:2 scribes sought how they **m.** kill him;
Lu 22:4 how he **m.** betray him unto them.
Lu 23:23 requiring that he **m.** be crucified.
Lu 23:26 cross, that he **m.** bear it after Jesus.
Lu 24:45 they **m.** understand the scriptures,
Joh 1:7 that all men through him **m.** believe.
Joh 3:17 **the world through him m. be saved.**
Joh 5:34 **things I say, that ye m. be saved.**
Joh 5:40 **not come to me, that ye m. have life.**
Joh 6:28 that we **m.** work the works of God?
Joh 8:6 him, that they **m.** have to accuse him.
Joh 9:36 is he, Lord, that I **m.** believe on him?
Joh 9:39 **world, that they which see not m. see;**
Joh 9:39 **that they which see m. be made blind.**
Joh 10:10 **I am come that they m. have life,**
Joh 10:10 **that they m. have it more abundantly.**
Joh 10:17 **down my life, that I m. take it again.**
Joh 11:4 **that the Son of God m. be glorified**
Joh 11:57 should shew it, that they **m.** take him.
Joh 12:9 that they **m.** see Lazarus also, whom
Joh 12:10 they **m.** put Lazarus also to death;
Joh 12:38 of Esaias the prophet **m.** be fulfilled,
Joh 14:29 **when it is come to pass, ye m. believe.**
Joh 15:11 **you, that my joy m. remain in you,**
Joh 15:11 **in you, and that your joy m. be full.**
Joh 15:25 **that the word m. be fulfilled that is**
Joh 16:33 **unto you, that in me ye m. have peace.**
Joh 17:3 **they m. know thee the only true God,**
Joh 17:12 **that the scripture m. be fulfilled.**
Joh 17:13 **that they m. have my joy fulfilled in**
Joh 17:19 **that they also m. be sanctified**
Joh 18:9 That the saying **m.** be fulfilled, which
Joh 18:28 but that they **m.** eat the passover.
Joh 18:32 the saying of Jesus **m.** be fulfilled,
Joh 19:24, 28 that the scripture **m.** be fulfilled,
Joh 19:31 Pilate that their legs **m.** be broken,
Joh 19:31 and that they **m.** be taken away.
Joh 19:35 that he saith true, that ye **m.** believe.
Joh 19:38 he **m.** take away the body of Jesus:
Joh 20:31 ye **m.** believe that Jesus is the Christ,
Joh 20:31 ye **m.** have life through his name.
Ac 1:25 fell, that he **m.** go to his own place.
Ac 4:21 nothing how they **m.** punish them,
Ac 5:15 Peter passing by **m.** overshadow some
Ac 7:19 children, to the end they **m.** not live.
Ac 8:15 that they **m.** receive the Holy Ghost:
Ac 9:2 **m.** bring them bound unto Jerusalem.
Ac 9:12 **on him, that he m. receive his sight.**
Ac 9:21 that he **m.** bring them bound unto
Ac 13:42 that these words **m.** be preached to
Ac 15:17 residue of men **m.** seek after the Lord,
Ac 17:27 if haply they **m.** feel after him, and
Ac 20:24 so that I **m.** finish my course with joy,
Ac 22:24 that he **m.** know wherefore they cried
Ac 24:26 him of Paul, that he **m.** loose him:
Ac 25:21 be kept till I **m.** send him to Caesar.
Ac 25:26 had, I **m.** have somewhat to write.
Ac 26:32 man **m.** have been set at liberty, if *1410*
Ac 27:12 means they **m.** attain to Phenice, *1410*
Ro 1:10 length I **m.** have a prosperous journey
Ro 1:13 I **m.** have some fruit among you also,
Ro 3:26 that he **m.** be just, and the justifier of
Ro 4:11 that he **m.** be the father of all them
Ro 4:11 righteousness **m.** be imputed unto
Ro 4:16 it is of faith, that it **m.** be by grace;
Ro 4:16 the promise **m.** be sure to all the seed;
Ro 4:18 **m.** become the father of many nations,

Ro 5:20 entered, that the offence **m.** abound.
Ro 5:21 **m.** grace reign through righteousness
Ro 6:6 that the body of sin **m.** be destroyed,
Ro 7:13 But sins, that it **m.** appear sin, working
Ro 7:13 that sin...**m.** become exceeding sinful.
Ro 8:4 the law **m.** be fulfilled in us, who walk
Ro 8:29 he **m.** be the firstborn among many
Ro 9:11 of God according to election **m.** stand,
Ro 9:17 up, that I **m.** shew my power in thee,
Ro 9:17 my name **m.** be declared throughout
Ro 9:23 that he **m.** make known the riches of
Ro 10:1 for Israel is, that they **m.** be saved.
Ro 11:14 my flesh, and **m.** save some of them.
Ro 11:19 broken off, that I **m.** be graffed in.
Ro 11:32 that he **m.** have mercy upon all
Ro 14:9 that he **m.** be Lord both of the dead
Ro 15:4 comfort of the scriptures **m.** have hope.
Ro 15:9 Gentiles **m.** glorify God for his mercy;
Ro 15:16 up of the Gentiles **m.** be acceptable,
1Co 2:12 that we **m.** know the things that are
1Co 4:6 ye **m.** learn in us not to think of men
1Co 4:8 reign, that we also **m.** reign with you.
1Co 5:2 hath done this deed **m.** be taken away
1Co 9:19 unto all, that I **m.** gain the more.
1Co 9:20 as a Jew, that I **m.** gain the Jews;
1Co 9:20 I **m.** gain them that are under the
1Co 9:21 I **m.** gain them that are without law.
1Co 9:22 I as weak, that I **m.** gain the weak:
1Co 9:22 that I **m.** by all means save some.
1Co 9:23 that I **m.** be partaker thereof with you.
1Co 14:19 by my voice I **m.** teach others also,
2Co 1:15 that ye **m.** have a second benefit;
2Co 2:4 that ye **m.** know the love which I have
2Co 2:9 that I **m.** know the proof of you,
2Co 4:10, 11 also of Jesus **m.** be made manifest
2Co 4:15 grace **m.** through the thanksgiving of
2Co 5:4 mortality **m.** be swallowed up of life.
2Co 5:21 **m.** be made the righteousness of God
2Co 7:9 ye **m.** receive damage by us in nothing.
2Co 7:12 in the sight of God **m.** appear unto you.
2Co 8:9 that ye through his poverty **m.** be rich.
2Co 9:5 that the same **m.** be ready, as a matter
2Co 11:4 not accepted, ye **m.** well bear with him.
2Co 11:7 abasing myself that ye **m.** be exalted,
2Co 12:8 Lord thrice, that it **m.** depart from me.
Ga 1:4 he **m.** deliver us from this present evil
Ga 1:16 I **m.** preach him among the heathen;
Ga 2:4 that they **m.** bring us into bondage:
Ga 2:5 truth of the gospel **m.** continue with
Ga 2:16 **m.** be justified by the faith of Christ,
Ga 2:19 to the law, that I **m.** live unto God.
Ga 3:14 blessing of Abraham **m.** come on the
Ga 3:14 we **m.** receive the promise of the Spirit
Ga 3:22 **m.** be given to them that believe.
Ga 3:24 Christ, that we **m.** be justified by faith.
Ga 4:5 we **m.** receive the adoption of sons.
Ga 4:17 exclude you, that ye **m.** affect them.
Eph 1:10 he **m.** gather together in one all things
Eph 1:21 principality, and power, and **m.**, *1411*
Eph 2:7 he **m.** shew the exceeding riches of
Eph 2:16 **m.** reconcile both unto God in one
Eph 3:10 places **m.** be known by the church
Eph 3:16 to be strengthened with **m.** by his *1411*
Eph 3:19 **m.** be filled with all the fulness of
Eph 4:10 all heavens, that he **m.** fill all things,)
Eph 5:26 he **m.** sanctify and cleanse it with the
Eph 5:27 he **m.** present it to himself a glorious
Eph 6:10 Lord, and in the power of his **m.** *2479*
Eph 6:22 purpose, that ye **m.** know our affairs,
Eph 6:22 and that he **m.** comfort your hearts.
Php 3:4 I **m.** also have confidence in the flesh
Php 3:4 hath whereof he **m.** trust in the flesh,
Php 3:11 I **m.** attain unto the resurrection of
Col 1:9 **m.** be filled with the knowledge of his
Col 1:10 That ye **m.** walk worthy of the Lord
Col 1:11 Strengthened with all **m.**, *1411*
Col 1:18 all things he **m.** have the preeminence.
Col 2:2 their hearts **m.** be comforted, being
Col 4:8 he **m.** know your estate, and comfort
1Th 2:6 we **m.** have been burdensome, as *1410*
1Th 2:16 to the Gentiles that they **m.** be saved,
1Th 3:10 exceedingly that we **m.** see your face,
1Th 3:10 **m.** perfect that which is lacking in
2Th 2:6 that he **m.** be revealed in his time.
2Th 2:10 of the truth, that they **m.** be saved.
2Th 2:12 all **m.** be damned who believed not
2Th 3:8 **m.** not be chargeable to any of you:
1Ti 1:16 Christ **m.** shew forth all longsuffering,
2Ti 4:17 me the preaching **m.** be fully known,
2Ti 4:17 and that all the Gentiles **m.** hear:
Tit 2:14 **m.** redeem us from all iniquity, and
Tit 3:8 God **m.** be careful to maintain good
Phm 8 thought I **m.** be much bold in Christ
Phm 13 stead he **m.** have ministered unto me
Heb 2:14 through death he **m.** destroy him that
Heb 2:17 he **m.** be a merciful and faithful high
Heb 6:18 we **m.** have a strong consolation, who
Heb 9:15 are called **m.** receive the promise of
Heb 10:36 of God, ye **m.** receive the promise.
Heb 11:15 they **m.** have had an opportunity to
Heb 11:35 they **m.** obtain a better resurrection:
Heb 12:10 that we **m.** be partakers of his holiness.
Heb 12:18 unto the mount that **m.** touched,
Heb 13:12 he **m.** sanctify the people with his own
Jas 5:17 prayed earnestly that it **m.** not rain:
1Pe 1:7 **m.** be found unto praise and honour
1Pe 1:21 your faith and hope **m.** be in God.
1Pe 3:18 unjust, that he **m.** bring us to God,
1Pe 4:6 that they **m.** be judged according to
2Pe 1:4 **m.** be partaker of the divine nature
2Pe 2:11 which are greater in power and **m.**, *1411*
1Jo 2:19 they **m.** be made manifest that they
1Jo 3:8 he **m.** destroy the works of the devil.
1Jo 4:9 world, that we **m.** live through him.
3Jo 8 we **m.** be fellowhelpers to the truth.
Re 7:12 power, and **m.**, be unto our God *2479*
Re 12:14 that she **m.** fly into the wilderness,
Re 12:15 he **m.** cause her to be carried away
Re 13:17 that no man **m.** buy or sell, save *1410*
Re 16:12 the kings of the east **m.** be prepared.

MIGHTEST

De 4:35 thou **m.** know that the Lord he is God;
De 6:2 That thou **m.** fear the Lord thy God,
Jg 16:6 thou **m.** be bound to afflict thee.
Jg 16:10 thee, wherewith thou **m.** be bound.
Jg 16:13 tell me wherewith thou **m.** be bound.
1Sa 17:28 come down that thou **m.** see the battle.
Ne 9:29 that thou **m.** bring them again unto
Ps 8:2 that thou **m.** still the enemy and the
Ps 51:4 **m.** be justified when thou speakest,
Pr 22:21 thou **m.** answer the words of truth
Da 2:30 that thou **m.** know the thoughts of
Mt 15:5 **whatsoever thou m. be profited by me;**
Mk 7:11 **whatsoever thou m. be profited by me;**
Lu 1:4 thou **m.** know the certainty of those
Ac 9:17 that thou **m.** receive thy sight, and
Ro 3:4 thou **m.** be justified in thy sayings,
Ro 3:4 **m.** overcome when thou art judged
1Ti 1:3 thou **m.** charge some that they teach
1Ti 1:18 thou by them **m.** war a good warfare;

MIGHTIER

Ge 26:16 for thou are much **m.** than we. 6105
Ex 1:9 of Israel are more and **m.** than we: 6099
Nu 14:12 a greater nation and **m.** than they. 6099
De 4:38 thee greater and **m.** than thou art, 6099
De 7:1 nations greater and **m.** than thou; 6099
De 9:1 greater and **m.** than thyself, cities 6099
De 9:14 a nation **m.** and greater than they. 6099
De 11:23 nations and **m.** than yourselves. 6099
Ps 93:4 Lord on high is **m.** than the noise 117
Ec 6:10 with him that is **m.** than he. 8623
Mt 3:11 that cometh after me is **m.** than I, *2478*
Mk 1:7 cometh one **m.** than I after me, *2478*
Lu 3:16 one **m.** than I cometh, the lachet of *2478*

MIGHTIES

1Ch 11:12 who was one of the three **m.** 1368
1Ch 11:24 had the name among the three **m.** 1368

MIGHTIEST

1Ch 11:19 These things did these three **m.** 1368

MIGHTILY

De 6:3 that ye may increase **m.**, as the 3966
Jg 4:3 twenty years he **m.** oppressed the 2393
Jg 14:6 Spirit of the Lord came **m.** upon him,
Jg 15:14 Spirit of the Lord came **m.** upon him,
Jer 25:30 he shall **m.** roar upon his habitation;
Jon 3:8 sackcloth, and cry **m.** unto God: 2393
Na 2:1 loins strong, fortify thy power **m.** 3966
Ac 18:28 For he **m.** convinced the Jews, and *2159*
Ac 19:20 **m.** grew the word of God and *2596,2904*
Col 1:29 which worketh in me **m.** *1722,1411*
Re 18:2 cried **m.** with a strong voice, *1722,2479*

MIGHTY See also ALMIGHTY; MIGHTIER; MIGHTIES; MIGHTIEST.

Ge 6:4 the same became **m.** men which 1368
Ge 10:8 began to be a **m.** one in the earth. 1368
Ge 10:9 was a **m.** hunter before the Lord: 1368
Ge 10:9 the **m.** hunter before the Lord. 1368
Ge 18:18 become a great and **m.** nation, 6099
Ge 23:6 thou art a **m.** prince among us: 430
Ge 49:24 strong by the hands of the **m.** God 46
Ex 1:7 and waxed exceeding **m.**; and the 6105
Ex 1:20 multiplied, and waxed very **m.** 6105
Ex 3:19 let you go, no, not by a **m.** hand. 2389
Ex 9:28 be no more **m.** thunderings and hail; 430
Ex 10:19 turned a **m.** strong west wind, 3966
Ex 15:10 they sank as lead in the **m.** waters. 117
Ex 15:15 the **m.** men of Moab, trembling 352
Ex 32:11 great power, and with a **m.** hand? 2389
Le 19:15 nor honour the person of the **m.**: 1419
Nu 22:6 people; for they are too **m.** for me: 6099
De 3:24 thy greatness, and thy **m.** hand: 2389
De 4:34 and by war, and by a **m.** hand, 2389
De 4:37 in his sight with his **m.** power out 1419
De 5:15 out thence through a **m.** hand, and 2389
De 6:21 us out of Egypt with a **m.** hand: 2389
De 7:8 brought you out with a **m.** hand, 2389
De 7:19 **m.** hand, and the stretched out arm, 2389
De 7:21 among you, a **m.** God and terrible. 1419
De 7:23 destroy them with a **m.** destruction, 1419
De 9:26 forth out of Egypt with a **m.** hand. 2389
De 9:29 broughtest out by thy **m.** power 1419
De 10:17 a great God, a **m.**, and a terrible, 1368
De 11:2 God, his greatness, his **m.** hand, 2389
De 26:5 nation, great, **m.**, and populous: 6099
De 26:8 forth out of Egypt with a **m.** hand, 2389
De 34:12 in all that **m.** hand, and in all the 2389
Jos 1:14 armed, all the **m.** men of valour, 1368
Jos 4:24 the hand of the Lord, that it is **m.**: 2389
Jos 6:2 thereof, and the men of valour. 1368
Jos 8:3 thirty thousand **m.** men of valour, 1368
Jos 10:2 and all the men thereof were **m.** 1368
Jos 10:7 him, and all the **m.** men of valour. 1368
Jg 5:3 me have dominion over the **m.** 1368
Jg 5:22 the prancings of their **m.** ones. 47
Jg 5:23 help of the Lord against the **m.** 1368
Jg 6:12 with thee, thou **m.** men of valour. 1368
Jg 11:1 Gileadite was a **m.** man of valour, 1368
Ru 2:1 a **m.** man of wealth, of the family of 1368
1Sa 2:4 bows of the **m.** men are broken, 1368
1Sa 4:8 out of the hand of these **m.** Gods? 117
1Sa 9:1 a Benjamite, a **m.** man of power. 1368
1Sa 16:18 in playing, and a **m.** valiant man, 1368
2Sa 1:19 high places: how are the **m.** fallen! 1368
2Sa 1:21 shield of the **m.** is vilely cast away, 1368
2Sa 1:22 from the fat of the **m.**, the bow of 1368
2Sa 1:25 How are the **m.** fallen in the midst 1368
2Sa 1:27 How are the **m.** fallen, and the 1368
2Sa 10:7 and all the host of the **m.** men. 1368
2Sa 16:6 the **m.** men were on his right hand 1368
2Sa 17:8 that they be **m.** men, and they be 1368
2Sa 17:10 knoweth that thy father is a **m.** man, 1368
2Sa 20:7 the Pelethites, and all the **m.** men: 1368
2Sa 23:8 be the names of the **m.** men whom 1368
2Sa 23:9 one of the three **m.** men with David, 1368
2Sa 23:16 the three **m.** men brake through the 1368
2Sa 23:17 things did these three **m.** men. 1368
2Sa 23:22 had the name among three **m.** men. 1368
1Ki 1:8 **m.** men which belonged to David, 1368
1Ki 1:10 and the **m.** men, and Solomon his 1368
1Ki 11:28 Jeroboam was a **m.** man of valour: 1368
2Ki 5:1 he was also a **m.** man in valour, but 1368
2Ki 15:20 even of all the **m.** men of wealth, of 1368
2Ki 24:14 and all the **m.** men of valour, even 1368
2Ki 24:15 the **m.** of the land, those carried he 193
1Ch 1:10 he began to be **m.** upon the earth. 1368
1Ch 5:24 **m.** men of valour, famous men, and 1368
1Ch 7:7 their fathers, **m.** men of valour; 1368
1Ch 7:9, 11 their fathers, **m.** men of valour, 1368
1Ch 7:40 choice and **m.** men of valour, chief 1368
1Ch 8:40 of Ulam were **m.** men of valour, 1368
1Ch 11:10 of the **m.** men whom David had, 1368
1Ch 11:11 of the **m.** men whom David had; 1368
1Ch 12:1 were among the **m.** men, helpers of 1368
1Ch 12:4 a **m.** man among the thirty, and 1368
1Ch 12:21 for they were all **m.** men of valour, 1368
1Ch 12:25 **m.** men of valour for the war, seven 1368

1Ch 12:28 Zadok, a young man **m.** of valour, ... 1368
1Ch 12:30 eight hundred, **m.** men of valour, ... 1368
1Ch 19:8 and all the host of the **m.** men. 1368
1Ch 26:6 for they were **m.** men of valour. 1368
1Ch 26:31 them **m.** men of valour at Jazer of...... 1368
1Ch 27:6 who was **m.** among the thirty, and..... 1368
1Ch 28:1 the officers, and with the **m.** men, ... 1368
1Ch 29:24 all the princes, and the **m.** men, and... 1368
2Ch 6:32 thy **m.** hand, and thy stretched out..... 2389
2Ch 13:3 men, being **m.** men of valour. 1368
2Ch 13:21 But Abijah waxed **m.**, and married...... 2388
2Ch 14:8 all these were men of valour. 1368
2Ch 17:13 **m.** men of valour, were in Jerusalem. . 1368
2Ch 17:14 **m.** men of valour three hundred......... 1368
2Ch 17:16 hundred thousand **m.** men of valour.... 1368
2Ch 17:17 Eliada a **m.** man of valour, and with.... 1368
2Ch 25:6 **m.** men of valour out of Israel for 1368
2Ch 26:12 the fathers of the **m.** men of valour.... 1368
2Ch 26:13 that made war with **m.** power, to....... 2428
2Ch 27:6 So Jotham became **m.**, because he 2388
2Ch 28:7 and Zichri, a **m.** man of Ephraim, ... 1368
2Ch 32:3 and his **m.** men to stop the waters..... 1368
2Ch 32:21 cut off all the **m.** men of valour, and... 1368
Ezr 4:20 been **m.** kings also over Jerusalem, ... 8624
Ezr 7:28 before all the king's **m.** princes. 1368
Ne 3:16 and unto the house of the **m.** 1368
Ne 9:11 as a stone into the **m.** waters........... 5794
Ne 9:32 our God, the great, the **m.**, and the ... 1368
Ne 11:14 their brethren, **m.** men of valour,....... 1368
Job 5:15 and from the hand of the **m.** 2389
Job 6:23 me from the hand of the **m.**?............ 6184
Job 9:4 wise in heart, and **m.** in strength:........ 533
Job 12:19 spoiled, and overthroweth the **m.** 386
Job 12:21 weakeneth the strength of the **m.**......... 650
Job 21:7 become old, yea, are **m.** in power?...... 1396
Job 22:8 But as for the **m.** man, he had the..... 2220
Job 24:22 draweth also the **m.** with his power:...... 47
Job 34:20 the **m.** shall be taken away without........ 47
Job 34:24 break in pieces **m.** men without 3524
Job 35:9 out by reason of the arm of the **m.** 7227
Job 36:5 God is **m.**, and despiseth not any:...... 3524
Job 36:5 he is **m.** in strength and wisdom. 3524
Job 41:25 up himself, the **m.** are afraid: by 410
Ps 24:8 strong and **m.**, the Lord **m.** in battle .. 1368
Ps 29:1 Give unto the Lord, O ye **m.**,...... 1121,410
Ps 33:16 a **m.** man is not delivered by much..... 1368
Ps 45:3 sword upon thy thigh, O most **m.**, ... 1368
Ps 50:1 The **m.** God, even the Lord, hath........ 410
Ps 52:1 thou thyself in mischief, O **m.** man?.... 1368
Ps 59:3 the **m.** are gathered against me; 5794
Ps 68:33 out his voice, and that a **m.** voice. 5797
Ps 69:4 mine enemies wrongfully, are **m.**:......... 6105
Ps 74:15 the flood: thou driedst up **m.** rivers...... 386
Ps 78:65 **m.** man that shouteth by reason of..... 1368
Ps 82:1 in the congregation of the **m.**; he......... 410
Ps 89:6 who among the sons of the **m.** can 410
Ps 89:13 Thou hast a **m.** arm: strong is thy...... 1369
Ps 89:19 have laid help upon one that is **m.**;...... 1368
Ps 89:50 the reproach of all the **m.** people; 7227
Ps 93:4 yea, than the **m.** waves of the sea. 117
Ps 106:2 can utter the **m.** acts of the Lord? 1369
Ps 106:8 make his **m.** power to be known. 1369
Ps 112:2 His seed shall be **m.** upon earth:........ 1368
Ps 120:4 Sharp arrows of the **m.**, with coals..... 1368
Ps 127:4 arrows are in the hand of a **m.** man;... 1368
Ps 132:2 vowed unto the **m.** God of Jacob;.......... 46
Ps 132:5 habitation for the **m.** God of Jacob......... 46
Ps 135:10 great nations, and slew **m.** kings;....... 6099
Ps 145:4 and shall declare thy **m.** acts............ 1369
Ps 145:12 to the sons of men his **m.** acts, ... 1369
Ps 150:2 Praise him for his **m.** acts: praise....... 1369
Pr 16:32 to anger is better than the **m.**; 1368
Pr 18:18 cease, and parteth between the **m.**........ 6099
Pr 21:22 man scaleth the city of the **m.**, and 1368
Pr 23:11 For their redeemer is **m.**; he shall...... 2389
Ec 7:19 more than ten **m.** men which are 7989
Ca 4:4 bucklers, all shields of **m.** men. 1368
Isa 1:24 Lord of hosts, the **m.** One of Israel,...... 46
Isa 3:2 The **m.** man, and the man of war,...... 1368
Isa 3:25 the sword, and thy **m.** in the war....... 1369
Isa 5:15 and the **m.** man shall be humbled,........ 376
Isa 5:22 them that are **m.** to drink wine,......... 1368
Isa 9:6 Wonderful, Cousellor, The **m.** God, ... 1368
Isa 10:21 remnant of Jacob, unto the **m.** God.... 1368
Isa 10:34 and Lebanon shall fall by a **m.** one. 117
Isa 11:15 with his **m.** wind shall he shake 5868
Isa 13:3 called my **m.** ones for mine anger, ... 1368
Isa 17:12 like the rushing of **m.** waters! 3524
Isa 21:17 **m.** men of the children of Kedar, ... 1368
Isa 22:17 thee away with a **m.** captivity,........... 1397
Isa 28:2 Lord hath a **m.** and strong one, ... 2389
Isa 28:2 as a flood of **m.** waters overflowing, ... 3524
Isa 30:29 the Lord, to the **m.** One of Israel. 6697
Isa 31:8 with the sword, not of a **m.** man; 376
Isa 42:13 Lord shall go forth as a **m.** man,........ 1368
Isa 43:16 sea, and a path in the **m.** water;........ 5794
Isa 49:24 the prey be taken from the **m.**, or 1368
Isa 49:25 the captives of the **m.** shall be taken... 1368
Isa 49:26 thy Redeemer, the **m.** One of Jacob. 46
Isa 60:16 thy Redeemer, the **m.** One of Jacob. 46
Isa 63:1 speak in righteousness, **m.** to save..... 7227
Jer 5:15 it is a **m.** nation, it is an ancient.......... 386
Jer 5:16 sepulchre, they are all **m.** men. 1368
Jer 9:23 let the **m.** man glory in his might, ... 1368
Jer 14:9 as a **m.** man that cannot save? 1368
Jer 20:11 Lord is with me as a **m.** terrible one: ..1368
Jer 26:21 the king, with all his **m.** men, and all .. 1368
Jer 32:18 the Great, the **M.** God, the Lord....... 1368
Jer 32:19 Great in counsel, and **m.** in work: 7227
Jer 33:3 shew thee great and **m.** things, ... 1219
Jer 41:16 **m.** men of war, and the women, ... 1397
Jer 46:5 their **m.** ones are beaten down, ... 1368
Jer 46:6 flee away, nor the **m.** man escape;..... 1368
Jer 46:9 and let the **m.** men come forth; the.... 1368
Jer 46:12 **m.** man...stumbled against the **m.**,...... 1368
Jer 48:14 are **m.** and strong men for the war? ... 1368
Jer 48:41 the **m.** men's hearts in Moab at that... 1368
Jer 49:22 heart of the **m.** men of Edom be as.... 1368
Jer 50:9 shall be as of a **m.** expert man; 1368
Jer 50:36 a sword is upon her **m.** men; and....... 1368
Jer 51:30 The **m.** me of Babylon have forborn ... 1368
Jer 51:56 Babylon, and her **m.** men are taken, ... 1368
Jer 51:57 and her rulers, and her **m.** men: 1368
La 1:15 trodden under foot all my men.............. 47
Eze 17:13 hath also taken the **m.** of the land:....... 352
Eze 17:17 shall Pharaoh with his **m.** army.......... 1419
Eze 20:33, 34 with a **m.** hand, and with a........... 2389
Eze 31:11 hand of the **m.** one of the heathen; 410
Eze 32:12 By the swords of the **m.** will I cause .. 1368
Eze 32:21 strong among the **m.** shall speak........ 1368
Eze 32:27 not lie with the **m.** that are fallen....... 1368
Eze 32:27 terror of the **m.** in the land of the....... 1368
Eze 38:15 a great company, and a **m.** army:....... 7227
Eze 39:18 Ye shall eat the flesh of the **m.**,......... 1368
Eze 39:20 with **m.** men, and with all men of....... 1368
Da 3:20 he commanded the most **m.** men 1401
Da 4:3 and how **m.** are his wonders! 8624
Da 8:24 And his power shall be **m.**, but not..... 6105
Da 8:24 the **m.** and the holy people. 6099
Da 9:15 the land of Egypt with a **m.** hand, ... 2389
Da 11:3 And a **m.** king shall stand up, that...... 1368
Da 11:25 with a very great and **m.** army; 6099
Ho 10:13 in the multitude of thy **m.** men. 1368
Joe 2:7 They shall run like **m.** men; they 1368
Joe 3:9 Prepare war, wake up the **m.** men, ... 1368
Joe 3:11 thy **m.** ones to come down, O Lord..... 1368
Am 2:14 neither shall the **m.** deliver himself: ... 1368
Am 2:16 he that is courageous among the **m.** ... 1368
Am 5:12 transgressions and your **m.** sins: 6099
Am 5:24 and righteousness as a **m.** stream. 386
Ob 9 thy **m.** men, O Teman, shall be......... 1368
Jon 1:4 there was a **m.** temptest in the sea. ... 1419
Na 2:3 shield of his **m.** men is made red, ... 1368
Hab 1:12 O **m.** God, thou hast established........ 6697
Zep 1:14 **m.** man shall cry there bitterly. 1368
Zep 3:17 thy God in the midst of thee is **m.**; 1368
Zec 9:13 made thee as the sword of a **m.** man...1368
Zec 10:5 And they shall be as **m.** men, which ... 1368
Zec 10:7 of Ephraim shall be like a **m.** man, ... 1368
Zec 11:2 because the **m.** are spoiled: howl,........ 117
Mt 11:20 most of his **m.** works were done,........ *1411*
Mt 11:21 **if the m. works, which were done** . *1411*
Mt 11:23 **if the m. works, which have been** . *1411*
Mt 13:54 this wisdom, and these **m.** works?...... *1411*
Mt 13:58 he did not many **m.** works there........ *1411*
Mt 14:2 **m.** works do shew forth themselves ... *1411*
Mk 6:2 such **m.** works are wrought by his *1411*
Mk 6:5 he could there do no **m.** work, save ... *1411*
Mk 6:14 **m.** works do. shew forth themselves .. *1411*
Lu 1:49 he that is **m.** hath done to me great ... *1415*
Lu 1:52 put down the **m.** from their seats,....... *1413*
Lu 9:43 all amazed at the **m.** power of God..... *3168*
Lu 10:13 **if the m. works had been done in** .. *1411*
Lu 15:14 **arose a m. famine in that land;**..... *2478*
Lu 19:37 the **m.** works that they had seen; *1411*
Lu 24:19 was a prophet **m.** in deed and word.... *1415*
Ac 2:2 heaven as of a rushing **m.** wind, ... *972*
Ac 7:22 and was **m.** in words and in deeds....... *1415*
Ac 18:24 man, and **m.** in the scriptures,........... *1415*
Ro 15:19 Through **m.** signs and wonders,.......... *1411*
1Co 1:26 not many **m.**, not many noble, are...... *1415*
1Co 1:27 confound the things which are **m.**;...... *2478*
2Co 10:4 but **m.** through God to the pulling *1415*
2Co 12:12 signs, and wonders, and **m.** deeds...... *1411*
2Co 13:3 is not weak, but is **m.** in you. *1414*
Ga 2:8 **m.** in me toward the Gentiles:).......... *1754*
Eph 1:19 to the working of his **m.** power, ... *2479*
2Th 1:7 from heaven with his **m.** angels, ... *1411*
1Pe 5:6 under the **m.** hand of God, that he..... *2900*
Re 6:13 when she is shaken of a **m.** wind. *3173*
Re 6:15 chief captains, and the **m.** men, ... *1415*
Re 10:1 saw another **m.** angel come down....... *2478*
Re 16:18 so **m.** an earthquake, and so great. *5082*
Re 18:10 great city Babylon, that **m.** city! *2478*
Re 18:21 a **m.** angel took up a stone like a........ *2478*
Re 19:6 and as the voice of **m.** thunderings, ... *2478*
Re 19:18 captains, and the flesh of **m.** men,...... *2478*

MIGRON (mi'-gron)
1Sa 14:2 pomegranate tree which is in **M.**........ 4051
Isa 10:28 come to Aiath, he is passed to **M.**;..... 4051

MIJAMIN (mij'-a-min) See also MIAMIN.
1Ch 24:9 fifth to Malchijah, the sixth to **M.**,...... 4326
Ne 10:7 Meshullam, Abijah, **M.**, ... 4326

MIKLOTH (mik'-loth)
1Ch 8:32 And **M.** begat Shimeah. And 4732
1Ch 9:37 and Ahio, and Zechariah, and **M.**.......... 4732
1Ch 9:38 And **M.** begat Shimeam. And they...... 4732
1Ch 27:4 his course was **M.** also the ruler:....... 4732

MIKNEIAH (mik-ne-i'-ah)
1Ch 15:18, 21 **M.**, and Obed-edom, and Jeiel, ... 4737

MILALAI (mil'-a-lahee)
Ne 12:36 and Azarael, **M.**, Gilalai, Maai,.......... 4450

MILCAH (mil'-cah)
Ge 11:29 and the name of Nahor's wife, **M.**, ... 4435
Ge 11:29 the father of **M.**, and the father of...... 4435
Ge 22:20 **M.**, she hath also borne children 4435
Ge 22:23 these eight **M.** did bear to Nahor, ... 4435
Ge 24:15 who was born to Bethuel, son of **M.**,.. 4435
Ge 24:24 daughter of Bethuel the son of **M.**,...... 4435
Ge 24:47 son, whom **M.** bare unto him: 4435
Nu 26:33 and Noah, Hoglah, **M.**, and Tirzah..... 4435
Nu 27:1 and Hoglah, and **M.**, and Tirzah. 4435
Nu 36:11 Tirzah, and Hoglah, and **M.**, and........ 4435
Jos 17:3 and Noah, Hoglah, **M.**, and Tirzah...... 4435

MILCH See also MILK.
Ge 32:15 Thirty **m.** camels with their colts, ... 3243
1Sa 6:7 new cart, and take two **m.** kine, ... 5763
1Sa 6:10 took two **m.** kine, and tied them to 5763

MILCOM (mil'-com) See also MALCHAM; MOLECH.
1Ki 11:5 after **M.** the abomination of the.......... 4445
1Ki 11:33 and **M.** the god of the children of....... 4445
2Ki 23:13 **M.** the abomination of the children...... 4445

MILDEW
De 28:22 and with blasting, and with **m.**;.......... 3420
1Ki 8:37 if there be pestilence, blasting, **m.**,..... 3420
2Ch 6:28 pestilence, if there be blasting, or **m.**.. 3420
Am 4:9 smitten you with blasting and **m.**:........ 3420
Hag 2:17 smote you with blasting and with **m.**... 3420

MILE
Mt 5:41 **shall compel thee to go a m., go** ... *3400*

MILETUM (mi-le'-tum) See also MILETUS.
2Ti 4:20 Trophimus have I left at **M.** sick. *3399*

MILETUS (mi-le'-tus) See also MILETUM.
Ac 20:15 and the next day we came to **M.** *3399*
Ac 20:17 from **M.** he sent to Ephesus, and....... *3399*

MILK See also MILCH.
Ge 18:8 he took butter, and **m.**, and the......... 2461
Ge 49:12 wine, and his teeth white with **m.** 2461
Ex 3:8 a land flowing with **m.** and honey; 2461
Ex 3:17 a land flowing with **m.** and honey. 2461
Ex 13:5 a land flowing with **m.** and honey, ... 2461
Ex 23:19 not seethe a kid in his mother's **m.** 2461

Ex 33:3 a land flowing with **m.** and honey: 2461
Ex 34:26 not seethe a kid in his mother's **m.**. ... 2461
Le 20:24 that floweth with **m.** and honey:......... 2461
Nu 13:27 it floweth with **m.** and honey; and...... 2461
Nu 14:8 which floweth with **m.** and honey. 2461
Nu 16:13, 14 that floweth with **m.** and honey, ... 2461
De 6:3 that floweth with **m.** and honey.......... 2461
De 11:9 that floweth with **m.** and honey.......... 2461
De 14:21 not seethe a kid in his mother's **m.**. ... 2461
De 26:9, 15 that floweth with **m.** and honey. 2461
De 27:3 that floweth with **m.** and honey;......... 2461
De 31:20 that floweth with **m.** and honey;......... 2461
De 32:14 Butter of kine, and **m.** of sheep,........ 2461
Jos 5:6 that floweth with **m.** and honey.......... 2461
Jg 4:19 she opened a bottle of **m.**, and gave... 2461
Jg 5:25 asked water, and she gave him **m.**; 2461
Job 10:10 thou not poured me out as **m.**, and 2461
Job 21:24 His breasts are full of **m.**, and his 2461
Pr 27:27 have goats' **m.** enough for thy food,.... 2461
Pr 30:33 the churning of **m.** bringeth forth 2461
Ca 4:11 honey and **m.** are under thy tongue;... 2461
Ca 5:1 I have drunk my wine with my **m.**:...... 2461
Ca 5:12 rivers of waters, washed with **m.**,...... 2461
Isa 7:22 abundance of **m.** that they shall......... 2461
Isa 28:9 them that are weaned from the **m.**, ... 2461
Isa 55:1 buy wine and **m.** without money 2461
Isa 60:16 also suck the **m.** of the Gentiles, ... 2461
Isa 66:11 that ye may **m.** out, and be 4711
Jer 11:5 a land flowing with **m.** and honey, ... 2461
Jer 32:22 a land flowing with **m.** and honey; 2461
La 4:7 than snow, they were whiter than **m.**, .2461
Eze 20:6, 15 flowing with **m.** and honey,........... 2461
Eze 25:4 fruit, and they shall drink thy **m.**......... 2461
Joe 3:18 and the hills shall flow with **m.**, and.... 2461
1Co 3:2 I have fed you with **m.**, and not......... *1051*
1Co 9:7 eateth not of the **m.** of the flock?........ *1051*
Heb 5:12 become such as have need of **m.**, ... *1051*
Heb 5:13 every one that useth **m.** is unskilful.... *1051*
1Pe 2:2 desire the sincere **m.** of the word, ... *1051*

MILL See also MILLS; MILLSTONE.
Ex 11:5 maidservant that is behind the **m.**;...... 7347
Mt 24:41 **shall be grinding at the m.; the**..... *3459*

MILLET
Eze 4:9 and lentiles, and **m.**, and fitches,........ 1764

MILLIONS
Ge 24:60 the mother of thousands of **m.**,.......... 7233

MILLO (mil'-lo)
Jg 9:6 together, and all the house of **M.**, ... 4407
Jg 9:20 of Shechem, and the house of **M.**;...... 4407
Jg 9:20 and from the house of **M.**, and 4407
2Sa 5:9 David built round about from **M.** 4407
1Ki 9:15 and **m.**, and the wall of Jerusalem, ... 4407
1Ki 9:24 built for her: then did he build **M.**. 4407
1Ki 11:27 Solomon built **M.**, and repaired.......... 4407
2Ki 12:20 and slew Joash in the house of **M.**,..... 4407
1Ch 11:8 about, even from **M.** round about:...... 4407
2Ch 32:5 repaired **M.** in the city of David,........ 4407

MILLS
Nu 11:8 and ground it in **m.**, or beat it in a..... 7347

MILLSTONE See also MILLSTONES.
De 24:6 nether or the upper **m.** to pledge:...... 7347
Jg 9:53 of a **m.** upon Abimelech's head, ... 7393
2Sa 11:21 woman cast a piece of a **m.** upon him ..7393
Job 41:24 as hard as a piece of the nether **m.**. ....
Mt 18:6 **a m. were hanged about his**... *3458,3684*
Mk 9:42 **a m. were hanged about his**... *3037,3457*
Lu 17:2 **a m. were hanged about his**... *3458,3684*
Re 18:21 took up a stone like a great **m.**,.......... *3458*
Re 18:22 the sound of a **m.** shall be heard no.... *3458*

MILLSTONES
Isa 47:2 Take the **m.**, and grind meal: 7347
Jer 25:10 sound of the **m.**, and the light of........ 7347

MINCING
Isa 3:16 walking and **m.** as they go, and 2952

MIND See also MINDED; MINDFUL; MINDING; MINDS.
Ge 23:8 if it be your **m.** that I should bury...... 5315
Ge 26:35 were a grief of **m.** unto Isaac and....... 7307
Le 24:12 **m.** of the Lord might be shewed........ 6310
Nu 16:28 not done them of mine own **m.**.......... 3820
Nu 24:13 either good or bad of mine own **m.**;.... 3820
De 18:6 come with all the desire of his **m.** 5315
De 28:65 failing of eyes, and sorrow of **m.**:........ 5315
De 30:1 thou shalt call them to **m.** among....... 3824
1Sa 2:35 is in mine heart and in my **m.**:.......... 5315
1Sa 9:20 days ago, set not thy **m.** on them; 3820
1Ch 22:7 was in my **m.** to build an house......... 3824
1Ch 28:9 heart and with a willing **m.**: for.......... 5315
Ne 4:6 for the people had a **m.** to work. 3820
Job 23:13 he is in one **m.**, and who can turn him?.....
Job 34:33 Should it be according to thy **m.**?....... 5973
Ps 31:12 forgotten as a dead man out of **m.**:..... 3820
Pr 21:27 he bringeth it with a wicked **m.**? ....
Pr 29:11 A fool uttereth all his **m.**: but a 7307
Isa 26:3 peace, whose **m.** is stayed on thee:.... 3336
Isa 46:8 men: bring it again to **m.**, O ye 3820
Isa 65:17 be remembered, nor come into **m.**. 3820
Jer 3:16 Lord: neither shall it come to **m.**: 3820
Jer 15:1 yet my **m.** could not be toward this.... 5315
Jer 19:5 it, neither came it into my **m.**: 3820
Jer 32:35 neither came it into **m.**, that 3820
Jer 44:21 them, and came it not into his **m.**? 3820
Jer 51:50 let Jerusalem come into your **m.**. 3824
La 3:21 This I recall to my **m.**, therefore 3820
Eze 11:5 the things that come into your **m.**, ... 7307
Eze 20:32 that which cometh into your **m.** 7307
Eze 23:17 her **m.** was alienated from them......... 5315
Eze 23:18 then my **m.** was alienated from her, ... 5315
Eze 23:18 **m.** was alienated from her sister......... 5315
Eze 23:22 from whom thy **m.** is alienated, and.... 5315
Eze 23:28 from whom thy **m.** is alienated: 5315
Eze 38:10 shall things come into thy **m.**, ... 3824
Da 2:29 came into thy **m.** upon thy bed, ...
Da 5:20 up, and his **m.** hardened in pride,........ 7307
Hab 1:11 Then shall his **m.** change, and he 7307
Mt 22:37 **all thy soul, and with all thy m.**.. *1271*
Mk 5:15 and clothed, and in his right **m.**: *4993*
Mk 12:30 **all thy soul, and with all thy m.**,.. *1271*
Mk 14:72 Peter called to **m.** the word that *363*
Lu 1:29 and cast in her **m.** what manner of..........
Lu 8:35 Jesus, clothed, and in his right **m.**: *4993*
Lu 10:27 thy strength, and with all thy **m.**:....... *1271*
Lu 12:29 **neither be ye of doubtful m.**................
Ac 17:11 the word with all readiness of **m.**, ... *4288*
Ac 20:19 the Lord with all humility of **m.**,.................
Ro 1:28 gave them over to a reprobate **m.**,..... *3563*
Ro 7:23 warring against the law of my **m.**, ... *3563*
Ro 7:25 then with the **m.** I myself serve the ... *3563*
Ro 8:5 flesh do **m.** the things of the flesh:..... *5426*
Ro 8:7 carnal **m.** is enmity against God: *5427*
Ro 8:27 knoweth what is the **m.** of the Spirit,.. *5427*
Ro 11:34 hath known the **m.** of the Lord? *3563*
Ro 12:2 by the renewing of your **m.**, that *3563*
Ro 12:16 the same **m.** one toward another........ *5426*
Ro 12:16 **M.** not high things, but condescend *5426*
Ro 14:5 be fully persuaded in his own **m.**......... *3563*
Ro 15:6 may with one **m.** and one mouth........ *3661*
Ro 15:15 as putting you in **m.**, because of *1878*
1Co 1:10 joined together in the same **m.** *3563*
1Co 2:16 who hath known the **m.** of the Lord, .. *3563*
1Co 2:16 him? But we have the **m.** of Christ..... *3563*
2Co 7:7 mourning, your fervent **m.** toward me;.*3563*
2Co 8:12 if there be first a willing **m.**, it is *4288*
2Co 8:19 and declaration of your ready **m.**: *4288*
2Co 9:2 I know the forwardness of your **m.**,..... *4288*
2Co 13:11 be of one **m.**, live in peace; and......... *5426*
Eph 2:3 desires of the flesh and of the **m.**;...... *1271*
Eph 4:17 walk, in the vanity of the **m.**, ... *3563*
Eph 4:23 renewed in the spirit of your **m.**; *3563*
Php 1:27 with one **m.** striving together for *5590*
Php 2:2 being of one accord, of one **m.**. *5426*
Php 2:3 in lowliness of **m.** let each esteem...... *5012*
Php 2:5 Let this **m.** be in you, which was....... *5426*
Php 3:16 rule, let us **m.** the same thing. *5426*
Php 3:19 shame, who **m.** earthly things.)........... *5426*
Php 4:2 they be of the same **m.** in the Lord.... *5426*
Col 1:21 enemies in your **m.** by wicked........... *1271*
Col 2:18 vainly puffed up by his fleshly **m.**, ... *3563*
Col 3:12 humbleness of **m.**, meekness, ...
2Th 2:2 That ye be not soon shaken in **m.**,..... *3563*
2Ti 1:7 and of love, and of sound **m.**............. *4995*
Tit 1:15 their **m.** and conscience is defiled....... *3563*
Tit 3:1 Put them in **m.** to be subject to......... *5279*
Phm 14 But without thy **m.** would I do *1106*
Heb 8:10 I will put my laws into their **m.**, ... *1271*
1Pe 1:13 gird up the loins of your **m.**, be......... *1271*
1Pe 3:8 be ye all of one **m.**, having................ *3675*
1Pe 4:1 likewise with the same **m.**: for *1771*
1Pe 5:2 for filthy lucre, but of a ready **m.**;...... *4290*
Re 17:9 here is the **m.** which hath wisdom...... *3563*
Re 17:13 These have one **m.**, and shall give *1106*

MINDED See also FEEBLEMINDED; HIGHMINDED; LIKEMINDED.
Ru 1:18 she was steadfastly **m.** to go with her.......
2Ch 24:4 was **m.** to repair the house........ 5973,3820
Ezr 7:13 are **m.** of their own freewill to go up ....
Mt 1:19 was **m.** to put her away privily. *1014*
Ac 27:39 shore, into the which they were **m.**,.... *1014*
Ro 8:6 to be carnally **m.** is death; *5427*
Ro 8:6 spiritually **m.** is life and peace............ *5427*
2Co 1:15 I was **m.** to come unto you before, ... *1014*
2Co 1:17 When I therefore was thus **m.**, did...... *1011*
Gal 5:10 that ye will be none otherwise **m.**: *5426*
Php 3:15 as many as be perfect, be thus **m.**: *5426*
Php 3:15 if in any thing ye be otherwise **m.**,..... *5426*
Ti 2:6 likewise exhort to be sober **m.**.......... *4993*
Jas 1:8 A double **m.** man is unstable in all...... *1374*
Jas 4:8 purify your hearts, ye double **m.**.......... *1374*

MINDFUL See also UNMINDFUL.
1Ch 16:15 Be ye **m.** always of his covenant;....... 2142
Ne 9:17 neither were **m.** of thy wonders that... 2142
Ps 8:4 is man, that thou art **m.** of him? 2142
Ps 111:5 he will ever be **m.** of his covenant...... 2142
Ps 115:12 The Lord hath been **m.** of us: he....... 2142
Isa 17:10 hast not been **m.** of the rock of thy.... 2142
2Ti 1:4 being **m.** of thy tears that I may *3403*
Heb 2:6 is man, that thou art **m.** of him? *3403*
Heb 11:15 they had been **m.** of that country *3421*
2Pe 3:2 That ye may be **m.** of the words *3403*

MINDING
Ac 20:13 appointed, **m.** himself to go afoot. *3195*

MINDS
Jg 19:30 of it, take advice, and speak your **m.**.........
2Sa 17:9 they be chafed in their **m.**, as a........ 5315
2Ki 9:15 If it be your **m.**, then let none go 5315
Eze 24:25 whereupon they set their **m.**, their..... 5315
Eze 36:5 all their heart, with despiteful **m.**, ... 5315
Ac 14:2 made their **m.** evil affected against *5590*
Ac 28:6 changed their **m.**, and said that he..........
2Co 3:14 But their **m.** were blinded: for until *3540*
2Co 4:4 hath blinded the **m.** of them which...... *3540*
2Co 11:3 so your **m.** should be corrupted......... *3540*
Php 4:7 keep your hearts and **m.** through *3540*
1Ti 6:5 disputings of men of corrupt **m.**, ... *3563*
2Ti 3:8 men of corrupt **m.**, reprobate............ *3563*
Heb 10:16 and in their **m.** will I write them; *1271*
Heb 12:3 be wearied and faint in your **m.**. *5590*
2Pe 3:1 I stir up your pure **m.** by way of *1271*

MINE See also MY.
Ge 14:22 I have lifted up **m.** hand unto the ....
Ge 15:3 lo, one born in my house is **m.** heir.........
Ge 24:33 not eat, until I have told **m.** errand...........
Ge 24:45 I had done speaking in **m.** heart, ...
Ge 30:25 that I may go unto **m.** own place,.............
Ge 30:30 shall I provide for **m.** own house also? ......
Ge 31:10 that I lifted up **m.** eyes, and saw in a.........
Ge 31:40 and my sleep departed from **m.** eyes. ....
Ge 31:42 God hath seen **m.** affliction and the...........
Ge 31:43 cattle, and all that thou seest is **m.**:...........
Ge 41:13 me he restored unto **m.** office, and.............
Ge 44:21 me, that I may set **m.** eyes upon him. ......
Ge 48:5 came unto thee into Egypt, are **m.**;............
Ge 48:5 Reuben and Simeon, they shall be **m.**........
Ge 49:6 **m.** honour, be not thou united: for in........
Ex 7:4 bring forth **m.** armies, and my people........
Ex 7:5 I stretch forth **m.** hand upon Egypt, ...
Ex 7:17 with the rod that is in **m.** hand upon.........
Ex 13:2 both of man and of beast: it is **m.**. ....
Ex 17:9 hill with the rod of God in **m.** hand. ....
Ex 18:4 of my father, said he, was **m.** help, ...
Ex 19:5 all people: for all the earth is **m.**: ....
Ex 20:26 shalt thou go up by steps unto **m.** altar, ...
Ex 21:14 shalt take him from **m.** altar, that he.........
Ex 23:23 For **m.** Angel shall go before thee, and .....
Ex 32:34 behold, **m.** Angel shall go before thee: ......
Ex 33:23 And I will take away **m.** hand, and.............
Ex 34:19 All that open the matrix is **m.**; and............
Le 18:4 keep **m.** ordinances, to walk therein: ....
Le 18:30 Therefore shall ye keep **m.** ordinance,.......
Le 20:26 other people, that ye should be **m.**. ....
Le 22:9 shall therefore keep **m.** ordinance,.............
Le 25:23 be sold for ever: for the land is **m.**;..........
Nu 3:12 therefore the Levites shall be **m.**; ....
Nu 3:13 Because all the first born are **m.**;..............

Nu 3:13 **m.** shall they be: I am the Lord.
Nu 3:45 and the Levites shall be **m.**: I am the
Nu 8:14 of Israel: and the Levites shall be **m.**
Nu 8:17 firstborn of the children . . . are **m.**,
Nu 10:30 but I will depart to **m.** own land, and
Nu 12:7 not so, who is faithful in all **m.** house.
Nu 14:28 as ye have spoken in **m.** ears, so will I
Nu 16:28 I have not done them of **m.** own mind.
Nu 18:8 thee the charge of **m.** heave offerings
Nu 22:29 would there were a sword in **m.** hand,
Nu 23:11 I took thee to curse **m.** enemies, and
Nu 24:10 I called thee to curse **m.** enemies, and,
Nu 24:13 do either good or bad of **m.** own mind;
De 8:17 My power and the might of **m.** hand
De 10:3 having the two tables in **m.** hand.
De 26:13 the hallowed things out of **m.** house,
De 29:19 I walk in the imagination of **m.** heart,
De 32:22 For a fire is kindled in **m.** anger, and
De 32:23 I will spend **m.** arrows upon them.
De 32:41 and **m.** hand take hold on judgment;
De 32:41 will render vengeance to **m.** enemies,
De 32:42 make **m.** arrows drunk with blood,
Jos 14:7 him word again as it was in **m.** heart.
Jg 6:36 If thou wilt save Israel by **m.** hand, as
Jg 6:37 that thou wilt save Israel by **m.** hand,
Jg 7:2 saying, **M.** own hand hath saved me.
Jg 8:7 Zebah and Zalmunna unto **m.** hand,
Jg 11:30 the children of Ammon into **m.** hands,
Jg 16:17 hath not come a rasor upon **m.** head;
Jg 17:2 and spakest of also in **m.** ears, behold,
Jg 19:23 that this man is come into **m.** house,
Ru 4:6 myself, lest I mar **m.** own inheritance:
1Sa 2:1 Lord, **m.** horn is exalted in the Lord:
1Sa 2:1 mouth is enlarged over **m.** enemies;
1Sa 2:28 be my priest, to offer upon **m.** altar,
1Sa 2:29 ye at my sacrifice and at **m.** offering,
1Sa 2:33 whom I shall not cut off from **m.** altar,
1Sa 2:35 according to that which is in **m.** heart
1Sa 2:35 shall walk before **m.** anointed for ever.
1Sa 12:3 I received any bribe to blind **m.** eyes
1Sa 14:24 that I may be avenged on **m.** enemies.
1Sa 14:29 how **m.** eyes have been enlightened,
1Sa 14:43 end of the rod that was in **m.** hand,
1Sa 15:14 this bleating of the sheep in **m.** ears,
1Sa 17:46 the Lord deliver thee into **m.** hand;
1Sa 18:17 said, Let not **m.** hand be upon him,
1Sa 19:17 me so, and sent away **m.** enemy,
1Sa 20:1 what is **m.** iniquity? and what is my
1Sa 21:3 give me five loaves of bread in **m.** hand,
1Sa 21:4 is no common bread under **m.** hand,
1Sa 23:7 have delivered him into **m.** hand;
1Sa 24:6 to stretch forth **m.** hand against him,
1Sa 24:10 delivered thee to day into **m.** hand
1Sa 24:10 me kill thee: but **m.** eye spared thee;
1Sa 24:10 not put forth **m.** hand against my
1Sa 24:11 evil nor transgression in **m.** hand,
1Sa 24:12, 13 but **m.** hand shall not be upon thee,
1Sa 25:33 avenging myself with **m.** own hand.
1Sa 26:11 **m.** hand against the Lord's anointed:
1Sa 26:18 I done? or what evil is in **m.** hand?
1Sa 26:23 **m.** hand against the Lord's anointed.
1Sa 26:24 was much set by this day in **m.** eyes,
1Sa 28:2 make thee keeper of **m.** head for ever.
2Sa 5:19 wilt thou deliver them into **m.** hand?
2Sa 5:20 hath broken forth upon **m.** enemies
2Sa 6:22 and will be base in **m.** own sight:
2Sa 11:11 shall I then go into **m.** house, to eat
2Sa 14:5 woman, and **m.** husband is dead.
2Sa 14:30 See, Joab's field is near **m.**, and he 3027
2Sa 16:12 the Lord will look on **m.** affliction,
2Sa 18:12 thousand shekels of silver in **m.** hand,
2Sa 18:12 would I not put forth **m.** hand against
2Sa 18:13 wrought falsehood against **m.** own life:
2Sa 19:37 that I may die in **m.** own city, and be
2Sa 22:4 so shall I be saved from **m.** enemies.
2Sa 22:24 and have kept myself from **m.** iniquity.
2Sa 22:35 a bow of steel is broken by **m.** arms.
2Sa 22:38 I have pursued **m.** enemies, and
2Sa 22:41 also given me the necks of **m.** enemies,
2Sa 22:49 bringeth me forth from **m.** enemies:
1Ki 1:33 my son to ride upon **m.** own mule,
1Ki 1:48 throne this day, **m.** eyes even seeing it.
1Ki 2:15 knowest that the kingdom was **m.**,
1Ki 2:22 for he is **m.** elder brother; even for
1Ki 3:26 Let it be neither **m.** nor thine, but
1Ki 9:3 **m.** eyes and **m.** heart shall be there
1Ki 10:6 report that I heard in **m.** own land of
1Ki 10:7 until I came, and **m.** eyes had seen it.
1Ki 11:21 that I may go to **m.** own country.
1Ki 11:33 to do that which is right in **m.** eyes,
1Ki 14:8 that only which was right in **m.** eyes,
1Ki 20:3 Thy silver and thy gold is **m.**; thy
1Ki 20:3 children, even the goodliest, are **m.**
1Ki 21:20 Hast thou found me, O **m.** enemy?
2Ki 4:13 I dwell among **m.** own people.
2Ki 5:26 Went not **m.** heart with thee, when
2Ki 6:32 hath sent to take away **m.** head?
2Ki 10:6 If ye be **m.**, and if ye will hearken unto
2Ki 10:30 that which is right in **m.** eyes, and
2Ki 10:30 according to all that was in **m.** heart,
2Ki 18:34 delivered Samaria out of **m.** hand?
2Ki 18:35 delivered their country out of **m.** hand,
2Ki 18:35 deliver Jerusalem out of **m.** hand?
2Ki 19:28 thy tumult is come up into **m.** ears,
2Ki 19:34 for **m.** own sake, and for my servant
2Ki 20:6 will defend this city for **m.** own sake,
2Ki 20:15 All the things that are in **m.** house
2Ki 21:14 forsake the remnant of **m.** inheritance,
1Ch 12:17 me, **m.** heart shall be knit unto you:
1Ch 12:17 ye be come to betray me to **m.** enemies,
1Ch 12:17 seeing there is no wrong in **m.** hands,
1Ch 14:10 wilt thou deliver them into **m.** hand?
1Ch 14:11 in upon **m.** enemies by **m.** hand like
1Ch 16:22 Touch not **m.** anointed, and do my
1Ch 17:14 I will settle him in **m.** house and in
1Ch 17:16 and what is **m.** house, that thou hast
1Ch 22:18 inhabitants of the land into **m.** hand:
1Ch 28:2 I had in **m.** heart to build an house of
1Ch 29:3 I have of **m.** own proper good, of gold
1Ch 29:17 in the uprightness of **m.** heart I have
2Ch 7:15 Now me eyes shall be open, and
2Ch 7:15 **m.** ears attent unto the prayer that is
2Ch 7:16 **m.** eyes and...heart shall be there
2Ch 7:16 eyes and **m.** heart shall be there
2Ch 9:5 report which I heard in **m.** own land
2Ch 9:6 until I came, and **m.** eyes had seen it:
2Ch 29:10 it is in **m.** heart to make a covenant
2Ch 32:13 to deliver their lands out of **m.** hand?
2Ch 32:14 deliver his people out of **m.** hand,
2Ch 32:14 be able to deliver you out of **m.** hand?
2Ch 32:15 to deliver his people out of **m.** hand,
2Ch 32:15 your God deliver you out of **m.** hand?
2Ch 32:17 delivered their people out of **m.** hand.
2Ch 32:17 deliver his people out of **m.** hand
Ne 7:5 my God put into **m.** heart to gather
Job 3:10 womb, nor hid sorrow from **m.** eyes.
Job 4:12 and **m.** ear received a little thereof.
Job 4:16 an image was before **m.** eyes, there
Job 6:11 and what is **m.** end, that I should
Job 7:7 wind: **m.** eye shall no more see good.
Job 7:21 and take away **m.** iniquity? for now
Job 9:20 **m.** own mouth shall condemn me:
Job 9:31 and **m.** own clothes shall abhor me.
Job 10:6 That thou enquirest after **m.** iniquity.
Job 10:14 wilt not acquit me from **m.** iniquity.
Job 10:15 therefore see thou **m.** affliction;
Job 13:1 Lo, **m.** eye hath seen all this,
Job 13:1 **m.** ear hath heard and understood it.
Job 13:14 my teeth, and put my life in **m.** hand?
Job 13:15 I will maintain **m.** own ways before
Job 13:23 How many are **m.** iniquities and sins?
Job 14:17 a bag, and thou sewest up **m.** iniquity.
Job 16:4 against you, and shake **m.** head at you.
Job 16:9 **m.** enemy sharpeneth his eyes upon
Job 16:17 Not for any injustice in **m.** hands: also
Job 16:20 but **m.** eye poureth out tears unto God.
Job 17:2 and doth not **m.** eye continue in their
Job 17:7 **M.** eye also is dim by reason of
Job 17:13 If I wait, the grave is **m.** house: I
Job 19:4 erred, **m.** error remaineth with myself.
Job 19:10 **m.** hope hath he removed like a tree.
Job 19:13 **m.** acquaintance are verily estranged
Job 19:15 They that dwell in **m.** house, and my
Job 19:17 for the children's sake of my own body.
Job 19:27 **m.** eyes shall behold, and not another;
Job 27:5 till I die I will not remove **m.** integrity
Job 27:7 Let **m.** enemy be as the wicked, and
Job 31:1 I made a covenant with **m.** eyes; why
Job 31:6 that God may know **m.** integrity.
Job 31:7 and **m.** heart walked after my eyes,
Job 31:7 if any blot hath cleaved to **m.** hands;
Job 31:9 If **m.** heart have been deceived by a
Job 31:12 and would root out all **m.** increase.
Job 31:22 Then let **m.** arm fall from my shoulder
Job 31:22 and **m.** arm be broken from the bone.
Job 31:25 because **m.** hand hath gotten much;
Job 31:33 by hiding **m.** iniquity in my bosom:
Job 31:35 that **m.** adversary had written a book.
Job 32:6 and durst not shew you **m.** opinion.
Job 32:10 to me; I also will shew **m.** opinion.
Job 32:17 my part; I also will shew **m.** opinion.
Job 33:8 thou hast spoken in **m.** hearing, and
Job 40:4 I will lay my hand upon my mouth.
Job 41:11 is under the whole heaven is **m.**
Job 42:5 of the ear: but now **m.** eye seeth thee.
Ps 3:3 my glory, and the lifter up of my head.
Ps 3:7 for thou hast smitten all **m.** enemies
Ps 5:8 righteousness because of **m.** enemies;
Ps 6:7 **M.** eye is consumed because of grief;
Ps 6:7 waxeth old because of all **m.** enemies.
Ps 6:10 Let all **m.** enemies be ashamed and
Ps 7:4 him that without cause is **m.** enemy:
Ps 7:5 earth, and lay **m.** honour in the dust.
Ps 7:6 because of the rage of **m.** enemies:
Ps 7:8 according to **m.** integrity that is in me.
Ps 9:3 When **m.** enemies are turned back,
Ps 13:2 how long shall **m.** enemy be exalted
Ps 13:3 lighten **m.** eyes, lest I sleep the sleep
Ps 13:4 Lest **m.** enemy say, I have prevailed
Ps 16:5 Lord is the portion of **m.** inheritance
Ps 17:3 Thou hast proved **m.** heart; thou hast
Ps 18:3 so shall I be saved from **m.** enemies.
Ps 18:23 and I kept myself from **m.** iniquity.
Ps 18:34 a bow of steel is broken by **m.** arms.
Ps 18:37 I have pursued **m.** enemies, and
Ps 18:40 given me the necks of **m.** enemies;
Ps 18:48 He delivereth me from **m.** enemies:
Ps 23:5 me in the presence of **m.** enemies:
Ps 25:2 let not **m.** enemies triumph over me.
Ps 25:11 O Lord, pardon **m.** iniquity; for it is
Ps 25:15 **M.** eyes are ever toward the Lord; for
Ps 25:18 Look upon **m.** affliction and my pain;
Ps 25:19 Consider **m.** enemies; for they are
Ps 26:1 for I have walked in **m.** integrity: I
Ps 26:3 thy lovingkindness is before **m.** eyes:
Ps 26:6 I will wash **m.** hands in innocency: so
Ps 26:11 as for me, I will walk in **m.** integrity:
Ps 27:2 even **m.** enemies and my foes, came
Ps 27:6 now shall **m.** head be lifted up above
Ps 27:6 above **m.** enemies round about me:
Ps 27:11 in a plain path, because of **m.** enemies.
Ps 27:12 not over unto the will of **m.** enemies:
Ps 31:9 **m.** eye is consumed with grief, yea,
Ps 31:10 faileth because of **m.** iniquity, and my
Ps 31:11 was reproach among all **m.** enemies,
Ps 31:11 and a fear to **m.** acquaintance:
Ps 31:15 me from the hand of **m.** enemies, and
Ps 32:5 thee, and **m.** iniquity have I not hid.
Ps 32:8 go: I will guide thee with **m.** eye.
Ps 35:2 and buckler, and stand up for **m.** help.
Ps 35:13 prayer returned into **m.** own bosom.
Ps 35:15 But in **m.** adversity they rejoiced, and
Ps 35:19 **m.** enemies wrongfully rejoice over
Ps 35:26 together that rejoice at **m.** hurt:
Ps 38:4 For **m.** iniquities are gone over **m.** head:
Ps 38:10 as for the light of **m.** eyes, it also is
Ps 38:18 For I will declare **m.** iniquity; I will
Ps 38:19 But **m.** enemies are lively, and they
Ps 38:20 evil for good are **m.** adversaries;
Ps 39:4 Lord, make me to know **m.** end, and
Ps 39:5 and **m.** age is as nothing before thee:
Ps 40:6 desire; **m.** ears hast thou opened:
Ps 40:12 **m.** iniquities have taken hold upon me.
Ps 40:12 are more than the hairs of **m.** head:
Ps 41:5 **M.** enemies speak evil of me, When
Ps 41:9 **m.** own familiar friend, in whom I
Ps 41:11 **m.** enemy doth not triumph over me.
Ps 41:12 thou upholdest me in **m.** integrity, and
Ps 42:10 my bones, **m.** enemies reproach me;
Ps 49:4 I will incline **m.** ear to a parable: I
Ps 50:10 For every beast of the forest is **m.**,
Ps 50:11 the wild beasts of the field are **m.** 5978
Ps 50:12 for the world is **m.**, and the fulness
Ps 51:2 Wash me throughly from **m.** iniquity,
Ps 51:9 my sins, and blot out all **m.** iniquities.
Ps 54:4 Behold, God is **m.** helper: the Lord is
Ps 54:5 He shall reward evil unto **m.** enemies:
Ps 54:7 **m.** eye hath seen his desire upon **m.**
Ps 55:13 But it was thou, a man **m.** equal, my
Ps 55:13 my guide, and **m.** acquaintance.
Ps 56:2 **M.** enemies would daily swallow me.

Ps 56:9 thee, then shall **m.** enemies turn back:
Ps 59:1 Deliver me from **m.** enemies, O my
Ps 59:10 me see my desire upon **m.** enemies
Ps 60:7 Gilead is **m.**, and Manasseh is **m.**;
Ps 60:7 also is the strength of **m.** head;
Ps 69:3 **m.** eyes fail while I wait for my God
Ps 69:4 are more than the hairs of **m.** head:
Ps 69:4 me, being **m.** enemies wrongfully,
Ps 69:18 it: deliver me because of **m.** enemies.
Ps 69:19 **m.** adversaries are all before thee.
Ps 71:10 For **m.** enemies speak against me;
Ps 77:4 Thou holdest **m.** eyes waking: I am
Ps 77:6 I commune with **m.** own heart: and
Ps 88:8 Thou hast put away **m.** acquaintance
Ps 88:9 **M.** eye mourneth by reason of
Ps 88:18 and **m.** acquaintance into darkness.
Ps 89:21 **m.** arm also shall strengthen him.
Ps 92:11 **M.** eye also shall see my desire on
Ps 92:11 shall see my desire on **m.** enemies,
Ps 92:11 and **m.** ears shall hear my desire of
Ps 101:3 set no wicked thing before **m.** eyes:
Ps 101:6 **M.** eyes shall be upon the faithful of
Ps 102:8 **M.** enemies reproach me all the day;
Ps 105:15 Touch not **m.** anointed, and do my
Ps 108:8 Gilead is **m.**; Manasseh is **m.**;
Ps 108:8 also is the strength of **m.** head;
Ps 109:20 this be the reward of **m.** adversaries
Ps 109:29 Let **m.** adversaries be clothed with
Ps 116:8 soul from death, **m.** eyes from tears,
Ps 119:11 Thy word have I hid in **m.** heart, that
Ps 119:18 Open thou **m.** eyes, that I may behold
Ps 119:37 Turn away **m.** eyes from beholding
Ps 119:82 **M.** eyes fail for thy word, saying,
Ps 119:92 then have perished in **m.** affliction.
Ps 119:98 made me wiser than **m.** enemies: for
Ps 119:112 I have inclined **m.** heart to perform
Ps 119:121 justice: leave me not to **m.** oppressors.
Ps 119:123 **M.** eyes fail for thy salvation, and for
Ps 119:136 Rivers of waters run down **m.** eyes,
Ps 119:139 **m.** enemies have forgotten thy words.
Ps 119:148 **M.** eyes prevent the night watches,
Ps 119:153 Consider **m.** affliction, and deliver me:
Ps 119:157 are my persecutors and **m.** enemies;
Ps 121:1 I will lift up **m.** eyes unto the hills,
Ps 123:1 Unto thee lift I up **m.** eyes, O thou that
Ps 131:1 heart is not haughty, nor **m.** eyes lofty:
Ps 132:4 I will not give sleep to **m.** eyes,
Ps 132:4 or slumber to **m.** eyelids,
Ps 132:17 have ordained a lamp for **m.** anointed.
Ps 138:7 against the wrath of **m.** enemies,
Ps 139:2 my downsitting and **m.** uprising,
Ps 139:22 hatred: I count them **m.** enemies.
Ps 141:8 But **m.** eyes are unto thee, O God the
Ps 143:9 Deliver me, O Lord, from **m.** enemies:
Ps 143:12 And of thy mercy cut off **m.** enemies,
Pr 5:13 inclined **m.** ear to them that instructed
Pr 8:14 counsel is **m.**, and sound wisdom: I
Pr 23:15 my heart shall rejoice, even **m.** 589
Ec 1:16 I communed with **m.** own heart,
Ec 2:1 I said in **m.** heart, Go to now, I will
Ec 2:3 in **m.** heart to give myself unto wine,
Ec 2:3 acquainting **m.** heart with wisdom;
Ec 2:10 whatsoever **m.** eyes desired I kept not
Ec 3:17 I said in **m.** heart, God shall judge the
Ec 3:18 I said in **m.** heart concerning the
Ec 7:25 I applied **m.** heart to know, and to
Ec 8:16 I applied **m.** heart to know wisdom,
Ca 1:6 but **m.** own vineyard have I not kept.
Ca 2:16 My beloved is **m.**, and I am his: he
Ca 6:3 my beloved's, and my beloved is **m.**:
Ca 8:12 My vineyard, which is **m.**, is before
Isa 1:15 hands, I will hide **m.** eyes from you:
Isa 1:16 of your doings from before **m.** eyes;
Isa 1:24 Ah, I will ease me of **m.** adversaries,
Isa 1:24 and avenge me of **m.** enemies:
Isa 5:9 In **m.** ears said the Lord of hosts, Of a
Isa 6:5 **m.** eyes have seen the King, the Lord
Isa 10:5 O Assyrian, the rod of **m.** anger, and
Isa 10:5 staff in their hand is **m.** indignation.
Isa 10:25 and **m.** anger in their destruction.
Isa 13:3 called my mighty ones for **m.** anger,
Isa 16:4 Let **m.** outcasts dwell with thee,
Isa 16:11 and **m.** inward parts for Kir-haresh.
Isa 19:25 my hands, and Israel **m.** inheritance.
Isa 22:14 it was revealed in **m.** ears by the Lord
Isa 29:23 his children, the work of **m.** hands,
Isa 37:29 and thy tumult, is come into **m.** ears,
Isa 37:35 this city to save it for **m.** own sake,
Isa 38:12 **M.** age is departed, and is removed
Isa 38:14 **m.** eyes fail with looking upward: O
Isa 39:4 All that is in **m.** house have they seen:
Isa 42:1 **m.** elect, in whom my soul delighteth;
Isa 43:1 called thee by thy name; thou art **m.**.
Isa 43:25 thy transgressions for **m.** own sake,
Isa 45:4 my servant's sake, and Israel **m.** elect,
Isa 47:6 I have polluted **m.** inheritance, and
Isa 48:5 say, **M.** idol hath done them; and my
Isa 48:9 my name's sake will I defer **m.** anger,
Isa 48:11 For **m.** own sake, even for **m.** own sake,
Isa 48:13 **M.** hand also hath laid the foundation
Isa 49:22 I will lift up **m.** hand to the Gentiles,
Isa 50:4 he wakeneth **m.** ear to hear as the
Isa 50:5 The Lord God hath opened **m.** ear,
Isa 50:8 who is **m.** adversary? let him come
Isa 50:11 This shall ye have of **m.** hand; ye
Isa 51:5 and **m.** arms shall judge the people;
Isa 51:5 me, and on **m.** arm shall they trust.
Isa 51:16 covered thee in the shadow of **m.** hand,
Isa 56:5 unto them will I give in **m.** house
Isa 56:7 shall be accepted upon **m.** altar;
Isa 56:7 **m.** house shall be called an house of
Isa 60:7 come up with acceptance on **m.** altar,
Isa 63:3 for I will tread them in **m.** anger, and
Isa 63:4 the day of vengeance is in **m.** heart,
Isa 63:5 **m.** own arm brought salvation unto
Isa 63:6 tread down the people in **m.** anger,
Isa 65:9 and **m.** elect shall inherit it, and my
Isa 65:12 but did evil before **m.** eyes, and did
Isa 65:16 and because they are hid from **m.** eyes.
Isa 65:22 **m.** elect shall long enjoy the work of
Isa 66:2 all those things hath **m.** hand made,
Isa 66:4 but they did evil before **m.** eyes, and
Jer 2:7 and made **m.** heritage an abomination.
Jer 3:12 not cause **m.** anger to fall upon you:
Jer 3:15 give you pastors according to **m.** heart,
Jer 7:20 **m.** anger and my fury shall be poured
Jer 9:1 and **m.** eyes a fountain of tears, that I
Jer 11:15 hath my beloved to do in **m.** house,
Jer 12:3 me, and tried **m.** heart toward thee:
Jer 12:7 I have forsaken **m.** house, I have left
Jer 12:7 I have left **m.** heritage; I have given
Jer 12:8 **M.** heritage is unto me as a lion in the
Jer 12:9 **M.** heritage is unto me as a speckled
Jer 12:14 Lord against all **m.** evil neighbours,
Jer 13:17 and **m.** eye shall weep sore, and run
Jer 14:17 Let **m.** eyes run down with tears night
Jer 15:14 for a fire is kindled in **m.** anger, which
Jer 15:16 me the joy and rejoicing of **m.** heart:
Jer 16:17 For **m.** eyes are upon all their ways:
Jer 16:17 is their iniquity hid from **m.** eyes.
Jer 16:18 they have filled **m.** inheritance with
Jer 16:21 them to know **m.** hand and my might;
Jer 17:4 for ye have kindled a fire in **m.** anger,
Jer 18:6 potter's hand, so are ye in **m.** hand, O
Jer 20:9 his word was in **m.** heart as a burning
Jer 23:9 **M.** heart within me is broken because
Jer 24:6 I will set **m.** eyes upon them for good,
Jer 32:8 Hanameel **m.** uncle's son came to me.
Jer 32:12 the sight of Hanameel **m.** uncle's son,
Jer 32:31 been to me a provocation of **m.** anger
Jer 32:37 I have driven them in **m.** anger, and
Jer 33:5 whom I have slain in **m.** anger and in
Jer 42:18 As **m.** anger and my fury hath been
Jer 44:6 my fury and **m.** anger was poured
Jer 44:28 words shall stand, **m.**, or theirs,
Jer 48:31 **m.** heart shall mourn for the men of
Jer 48:36 **m.** heart shall sound for Moab like
Jer 48:36 and **m.** heart shall sound like pipes for
Jer 50:11 O ye destroyers of **m.** heritage,
Jer 51:25 I will stretch out **m.** hand upon thee,
La 1:16 **m.** eye, **m.** eye runneth down with
La 1:19 and **m.** elders gave up the ghost in
La 1:20 **m.** heart is turned within me; for I
La 1:21 **m.** enemies have heard of my trouble,
La 2:11 **M.** eyes do fail with tears, my bowels
La 2:22 brought up hath **m.** enemy consumed.
La 3:19 Remembering **m.** affliction and my
La 3:48 **M.** eye runneth down with rivers of
La 3:49 **M.** eye trickleth down, and ceaseth
La 3:51 **M.** eye affecteth **m.** heart because of
La 3:52 **M.** enemies chased me sore, like a
La 3:54 Waters flowed over **m.** head; then I
Eze 5:11 neither shall **m.** eye spare, neither will
Eze 5:13 Thus shall **m.** anger be accomplished,
Eze 7:3 I will send **m.** anger upon thee, and
Eze 7:4 **m.** eye shall not spare thee, neither
Eze 7:8 and accomplish **m.** anger upon thee:
Eze 7:9 And **m.** ye shall not spare, neither
Eze 8:1 as I sat in **m.** house, and the elders of
Eze 8:3 and took me by a lock of **m.** head;
Eze 8:5 up **m.** eyes the way toward the north,
Eze 8:18 **m.** eye shall not spare, neither will
Eze 8:18 they cry in **m.** ears with a loud voice,
Eze 9:1 He cried also in **m.** ears with a loud
Eze 9:5 to the others he said in **m.** hearing,
Eze 9:10 **m.** eye shall not spare, neither will I
Eze 11:20 and keep **m.** ordinances, and do them;
Eze 12:7 digged through the wall with **m.** hand;
Eze 13:9 **m.** hand shall be upon the prophets
Eze 13:13 be an overflowing shower in **m.** anger,
Eze 14:13 then will I stretch out **m.** hand upon it,
Eze 16:8 the Lord God, and thou becamest **m.**
Eze 16:18 hast set **m.** oil and **m.** incense before
Eze 17:19 surely **m.** oath that he hath despised,
Eze 18:4 Behold, all souls are **m.**; as the soul
Eze 18:4 so also the soul of the son is **m.**:
Eze 20:5 lifted up **m.** hand unto the seed of the
Eze 20:5 when I lifted up **m.** hand unto them.
Eze 20:6 that I lifted up **m.** hand unto them,
Eze 20:17 **m.** eye spared them from destroying
Eze 20:22 Nevertheless I withdrew **m.** hand,
Eze 20:23 I lifted up **m.** hand unto them also in
Eze 20:28 I lifted up **m.** hand to give it to them,
Eze 20:40 For in **m.** holy mountain, in the
Eze 20:42 I lifted up **m.** hand to give it to your
Eze 21:17 I will also smite **m.** hands together,
Eze 21:31 I will pour out **m.** indignation upon
Eze 22:8 Thou hast despised **m.** holy things,
Eze 22:13 smitten **m.** hand at thy dishonest
Eze 22:20 so will I gather you in **m.** anger and
Eze 22:26 and have profaned **m.** holy things:
Eze 22:31 I poured out **m.** indignation upon
Eze 23:4 and they were **m.**, and they bare sons
Eze 23:5 played the harlot when she was **m.**;
Eze 23:39 they done in the midst of **m.** house.
Eze 23:41 thou hast set **m.** incense and **m.** oil.
Eze 25:7 I will stretch out **m.** hand upon thee,
Eze 25:13 also stretch out **m.** hand upon Edom,
Eze 25:14 shall do in Edom according to **m.** anger
Eze 25:16 out **m.** hand upon the Philistines,
Eze 29:3 My river is **m.** own, and I have made it
Eze 29:9 The river is **m.**, and I have made it.
Eze 35:3 I will stretch out **m.** hand against thee,
Eze 35:10 and these two countries shall be **m.**,
Eze 36:7 I have lifted up **m.** hand, Surely the
Eze 36:21 But I had pity for **m.** holy name, which
Eze 36:22 but for **m.** holy name's sake, which ye
Eze 37:19 and they shall be one in **m.** hand.
Eze 43:8 I have consumed them in **m.** anger.
Eze 44:8 not kept the charge of **m.** holy things:
Eze 44:12 have I lifted up **m.** hand against them,
Eze 44:24 and my statutes in all **m.** assemblies;
Eze 47:14 I lifted up **m.** hand to give it unto your
Da 4:4 I Nebuchadnezzar was...in **m.** house,
Da 4:10 the visions of **m.** head in my bed;
Da 4:34 lifted up **m.** eyes unto heaven, and
Da 4:34 **m.** understanding returned unto me,
Da 4:36 **m.** honour and brightness returned
Da 8:3 Then I lifted up **m.** eyes, and saw, and
Da 10:5 Then I lifted up **m.** eyes, and looked,
Ho 2:5 wool and my flax, **m.** oil and my drink
Ho 2:10 none shall deliver her out of **m.** hand.
Ho 8:5 **m.** anger is kindled against them:
Ho 8:13 flesh for the sacrifices of **m.** offerings,
Ho 9:15 I will drive them out of **m.** house,
Ho 11:8 **m.** heart is turned within me, my
Ho 11:9 not execute the fierceness of **m.** anger.
Ho 13:11 I gave thee a king in **m.** anger, and
Ho 13:14 repentance shall be hid from **m.** eyes.
Ho 14:4 for **m.** anger is turned away from him
Am 1:8 I will turn **m.** hand against Ekron:
Am 9:2 hell, thence shall **m.** hand take them;
Am 9:4 I will set **m.** eyes upon them for evil,
Jon 2:2 I cried by reason of **m.** affliction unto
Mic 7:8 Rejoice not against me, O **m.** enemy:
Mic 7:10 Then she that is **m.** enemy shall see it.
Mic 7:10 **m.** eyes shall behold her: now shall
Hab 1:12 O Lord my God, **m.** Holy One? we shall

Hab 3:19 make me to walk upon **m.** high places.......
Zep 1:4 also stretch out **m.** hand upon Judah, ...
Zep 3:8 pour upon them **m.** indignation, even ....
Zep 3:10 my dispersed, shall being **m.** offering. ....
Hag 1:9 Because of **m.** house that is waste, and.....
Hag 2:8 The silver is **m.**, and the gold is **m.**, ...
Zec 1:18 Then lifted I up **m.** eyes, and saw, and .....
Zec 2:1 I lifted up **m.** eyes again, and looked,........
Zec 2:9 I will shake **m.** hand upon them, and.........
Zec 5:1 and lifted up **m.** eyes, and looked, and ......
Zec 5:9 Then lifted I up **m.** eyes, and looked, ...
Zec 6:1 and lifted up **m.** eyes, and looked, and ......
Zec 8:6 it also be marvelous in **m.** eyes? ....
Zec 9:8 I will encamp about **m.** house because.......
Zec 9:8 for now have I seen with **m.** eyes. ....
Zec 10:3 **M.** anger was kindled against the ....
Zec 11:14 I cut asunder **m.** other staff, even............
Zec 12:4 open **m.** eyes upon the house of Judah, ...
Zec 13:7 will turn **m.** hand upon the little ones. ....
Mal 1:6 I be a father, where is **m.** honour? ....
Mal 1:7 Ye offer polluted bread upon **m.** altar: ....
Mal 1:10 ye kindle fire on **m.** altar for nought. ....
Mal 3:7 are gone away from **m.** ordinances, ...
Mal 3:10 that there may be meat in **m.** house, ...
Mal 3:17 shall be **m.**, saith the Lord of hosts, ...
Mt 7:24, **26 heareth these sayings of m.**,..... *3450*
Mt 20:15 **me to do what I will with m. own?** *1699*
Mt 20:23 **not m. to give but it shall be given.** *1699*
Mt 25:27 **have received m. own with usury.** .. *1699*
Mk 9:24 I believe; help thou **m.** unbelief.......... *3450*
Mk 10:40 **on my left hand is not m. to give;**...... *1699*
Lu 1:44 thy salutation sounded in **m.** ears, ... *3450*
Lu 2:30 **m.** eyes have seen thy salvation. *3450*
Lu 9:38 my son: for he is **m.** only child. *3427*
Lu 11:6 **friend of m. in his journey is come.** *3450*
Lu 18:3 **saying, Avenge me of m. adversary.** *3450*
Lu 19:23 **have required m. own with usury?** .. *846*
Lu 19:27 **those m. enemies, which would**...... *3450*
Joh 2:4 **thee? m. hour is not yet come.**...... *3450*
Joh 5:30 **I can of m. own self do nothing;**... *1683*
Joh 5:30 **I seek not m. own will, but the**..... *1699*
Joh 6:38 **to do m. own will, but the will of..** *1699*
Joh 7:16 **My doctrine is not m., but his that.** *1699*
Joh 8:50 **I seek not m. own glory: there is** .. *3450*
Joh 9:11 made clay, and anointed **m.** eyes,....... *3450*
Joh 9:15 He put clay upon **m.** eyes, and I........ *3450*
Joh 9:30 is, and yet he hath opened **m.** eyes.... *3450*
Joh 10:14 **my sheep, and am known of m.**..... *1699*
Joh 14:24 **word which ye hear is not m., but..** *1699*
Joh 16:14 **he shall receive of m., and shall**.... *1699*
Joh 16:15 **things that the Father hath are m..** *1699*
Joh 16:15 **that he shall take of m., and shall .** *1699*
Joh 17:10 **all m. are thine, and thine, m.;**..... *1699*
Ac 11:6 which when I had fastened **m.** eyes, ...
Ac 13:22 a man after **m.** own heart, which *3450*
Ac 21:13 ye to weep and to break **m.** heart?..... *3450*
Ac 26:4 at the first among **m.** own nation *3450*
Ro 11:13 of the Gentiles, I magnify **m.** office:..... *3450*
Ro 12:19 Vengeance is **m.**; I will repay, saith.... *1698*
Ro 16:13 the Lord, and his mother and **m.**. *1700*
Ro 16:23 Gaius **m.** host, and of the whole *3450*
1Co 1:15 I had baptized in **m.** own name.......... *1699*
1Co 4:3 yea, I judge not **m.** own self. *1683*
1Co 9:2 for the seal of **m.** apostleship are *1699*
1Co 9:3 **M.** answer to them that do examine ... *1699*
1Co 10:33 not seeking **m.** own profit, but the *1683*
1Co 16:21 of me Paul with **m.** own hand............ *1699*
2Co 11:26 in perils by **m.** own countrymen, in ....
2Co 11:30 which concern **m.** infirmities............... *3450*
2Co 12:5 will not glory, but in **m.** infirmities...... *3450*
Ga 1:14 many my equals in **m.** own nation, ... *3450*
Ga 6:11 unto you with **m.** own hand............... *1699*
Php 1:4 in every prayer of **m.** for you all......... *3450*
Php 3:9 not having **m.** own righteousness, ... *1699*
2Th 3:17 of Paul with **m.** own hand, which *1699*
Tit 1:4 **m.** own son after the common faith: ....
Phm 12 him, that is, **m.** own bowels:............ *1699*
Phm 18 thee ought, put that on **m.** account;.... *1699*
Phm 19 Paul have written it with **m.** own hand, ...
Re 22:16 **sent m. angel to testify unto you**... *3450*

MINGLE See also MINGLED.
Isa 5:22 of strength to **m.** strong drink: 4537
Da 2:43 **m.** themselves with the seed of.......... 6151

MINGLED
Ex 9:24 was hail, and fire **m.** with the hail, ... 3947
Ex 29:40 of flour **m.** with the fourth part of...... 1101
Le 2:4 cakes of fine flour **m.** with oil, or 1101
Le 2:5 fine flour unleavened, **m.** with oil. 1101
Le 7:10 every meat offering, **m.** with oil,........ 1101
Le 7:12 unleavened cakes **m.** with oil, and 1101
Le 7:12 and cakes **m.** with oil, of fine flour, ... 1101
Le 9:4 and a meat offering **m.** with oil: for 1101
Le 14:10 flour for a meat offering **m.** with oil. ... 1101
Le 14:21 flour **m.** with oil for a meat offering, .. 1101
Le 19:19 not sow thy field with **m.** seed: 3610
Le 19:19 a garment **m.** of linen and woollen...... 3610
Le 23:13 tenth deals of fine flour **m.** with oil,.... 1101
Nu 6:15 cakes of fine flour **m.** with oil, and 1101
Nu 7:13, 19,25,31,37,43,49,55,61,67,73,79 full
of fine flour **m.** with oil for a............ 1101
Nu 8:8 even fine flour **m.** with oil, and........... 1101
Nu 15:4 **m.** with the fourth part of an hin of.... 1101
Nu 15:6 **m.** with the third part of an hin of...... 1101
Nu 15:9 of flour **m.** with half a hin of oil.......... 1101
Nu 28:5 **m.** with the fourth part of an hin of.... 1101
Nu 28:9, 12,12 a meat offering, **m.** with oil, ... 1101
Nu 28:13 tenth deal of flour **m.** with oil for a...... 1101
Nu 28:20 offering shall be of flour **m.** with oil: ... 1101
Nu 28:28 meat offering of flour **m.** with oil,....... 1101
Nu 29:3 offering shall be of flour **m.** with oil, ... 1101
Nu 29:9, 14 shall be of flour **m.** with oil,.......... 1101
Ezr 9:2 the holy seed have **m.** themselves...... 6148
Ps 102:9 and **m.** my drink with weeping,.......... 4537
Ps 106:35 were **m.** among the heathen, and....... 6148
Pr 9:2 she hath **m.** her wine; she hath 4537
Pr 9:5 drink the wine which I have **m.**. 4537
Isa 19:14 The Lord hath **m.** a perverse spirit 4537
Jer 25:20 And all the **m.** people, and all the....... 6154
Jer 25:24 all the kings of the **m.** people that...... 6154
Jer 50:37 upon all the **m.** people that are in the .. 6154
Ezr 30:5 all the **m.** people, and Chub, and......... 6154
Mt 27:34 him vinegar to drink **m.** with gall:....... *3396*
Mk 15:23 him to drink wine **m.** with myrrh:............
Lu 13:1 Pilate had **m.** with their sacrifices......... *3396*
Re 8:7 followed hail and fire **m.** with blood,.... *3396*
Re 15:2 it were a sea of glass **m.** with fire:..... *3396*

MINIAMIN (min'-e-a-min) See also MIAMIN.
2Ch 31:15 were Eden, and **M.**, and Jeshua,........ 4509
Ne 12:17 Of Abijah, Zichri; of **M.**,...Moadiah, ... 4509
Ne 12:41 the priests; Eliakim, Maaseiah, **M.**, ... 4509

MINISH See also DIMINISH; MINISHED.
Ex 5:19 not **m.** ought from your bricks of 1639

MINISHED See also DIMINISHED.
Ps 107:39 they are **m.** and brought low............ 4591

MINISTER See also ADMINISTER; MINISTERED; MINISTERETH; MINISTERING; MINISTERS.
Ex 24:13 rose up, and his **m.** Joshua: and......... 8334
Ex 28:1 may **m.** unto me in the priest's office, ...
Ex 28:3, 4 **m.** unto me in the priest's office............
Ex 28:35 And it shall be upon Aaron to **m.**: 8334
Ex 28:41 may **m.** unto me in the priest's office. ......
Ex 28:43 the altar to **m.** in the holy place; 8334
Ex 29:1 to **m.** unto me in the priest's office:..........
Ex 29:30 cometh...to **m.** in the holy place. 8334
Ex 29:44 sons, to **m.** to me in the priest's office......
Ex 30:20 they come near to the altar to **m.**, ... 8334
Ex 30:30 may **m.** unto me in the priest's office. ....
Ex 31:10 his sons, to **m.** in the priest's office,.........
Ex 35:19 sons, to **m.** in the priest's office. 8334
Ex 39:26 about the hem of the robe to **m.** in; ... 8334
Ex 39:41 to **m.** in the priest's office. 8334
Ex 40:13 may **m.** unto me in the priest's office. ....
Ex 40:15 may **m.** unto me in the priest's office: ....
Le 7:35 to **m.** unto the Lord in the priest's...........
Le 16:32 consecrate to **m.** in the priest's office........
Nu 1:50 and they shall **m.** unto it, and shall..... 8334
Nu 3:3 consecrated to **m.** in the priest's office. .....
Nu 3:6 priest, that they may **m.** unto him. 8334
Nu 3:31 the sanctuary wherewith they **m.**, ... 8334
Nu 4:9 thereof, wherewith they **m.** unto it:...... 8334
Nu 4:12 wherewith they **m.** in the sanctuary,... 8334
Nu 4:14 wherewith they **m.** about it, even....... 8334
Nu 8:26 But shall **m.** with their brethren in 8334
Nu 16:9 the congregation to **m.** unto them? 8334
Nu 18:2 joined unto thee, and **m.** unto thee: 8334
Nu 18:2 thou and thy sons with thee shall **m.**.........
De 10:8 before the Lord to **m.** unto him, ... 8334
De 17:12 that standeth to **m.** there before the... 8334
De 18:5 stand to **m.** in the name of the Lord, .. 8334
De 18:7 he shall **m.** in the name of the Lord.... 8334
De 21:5 God hath chosen to **m.** unto him,....... 8334
Jos 1:1 Joshua the son of Nun, Moses' **m.**,...... 8334
1Sa 2:11 And the child did **m.** unto the Lord..... 8334
1Ki 8:11 the priests could not stand to **m.** 8334
1Ch 15:2 of God, and to **m.** unto him for ever... 8334
1Ch 16:4 Levites to **m.** before the ark of the 8334
1Ch 16:37 to **m.** before ark continually, as 8334
1Ch 23:13 before the Lord, to **m.** unto him, and.. 8334
1Ch 26:12 to **m.** in the house of the Lord. 8334
2Ch 5:14 the priests could not stand to **m.** by ... 8334
2Ch 8:14 to praise and **m.** before the priests,.... 8334
2Ch 13:10 the priests, which **m.** unto the Lord, .. 8334
2Ch 23:6 and they that **m.** of the Levites; 8334
2Ch 24:14 even vessels to **m.**, and to offer 8335
2Ch 29:11 ye should **m.** unto him, and burn........ 8334
2Ch 31:2 to **m.**, and to give thanks, and to....... 8334
Ne 10:36 that **m.** in the house of our God: 8334
Ne 10:39 priests that **m.**, and the porters, ... 8334
Ps 9:8 shall **m.** judgment to the people in...... 1777
Isa 60:7 rams of Nebaioth...**m.** unto thee: 8334
Isa 60:10 and their kings shall **m.** unto thee: 8334
Jer 33:22 and the Levites that **m.** unto me........ 8334
Eze 40:46 near to the Lord to **m.** unto him. 8334
Eze 42:14 lay their garments where they **m.**; 8334
Eze 43:19 approach unto me, to **m.** unto me, ... 8334
Eze 44:11 stand before them to **m.** unto them. ... 8334
Eze 44:15 come near to me to **m.** unto me, ... 8334
Eze 44:16 near to my table, to **m.** unto me,........ 8334
Eze 44:17 **m.** in the gates of the inner court, ... 8334
Eze 44:27 inner court, to **m.** in the sanctuary, ... 8334
Eze 45:4 shall come near to **m.** unto the Lord:.. 8334
Mt 20:26 **among you, let him be your m.;**.... *1249*
Mt 20:28 **to be ministered unto, but to m.,**... *1247*
Mt 25:44 **prison, and did not m. unto thee?**.. *1247*
Mk 10:43 **among you, shall be your m.:**....... *1249*
Mk 10:45 **to be ministered unto, but to m.,**... *1247*
Lu 4:20 he gave it again to the **m.**, and sat..... *5257*
Ac 13:5 and they had also John to their **m.**...... *5257*
Ac 24:23 none...to **m.** or come unto him.......... *5256*
Ac 26:16 **to make thee a m. and a witness**... *5257*
Ro 13:4 is the **m.** of God to thee for good. *1249*
Ro 13:4 he is the **m.** of God, a revenger to..... *1249*
Ro 15:8 a **m.** of the circumcision for the *1249*
Ro 15:16 I should be the **m.** of Jesus Christ....... *3011*
Ro 15:25 Jerusalem to **m.** unto the saints. *1247*
Ro 15:27 to **m.** unto them in carnal things. *3008*
1Co 9:13 they which **m.** about holy things......... *2038*
2Co 9:10 sower both **m.** bread for your food,.... *5524*
Ga 2:17 is therefore Christ the **m.** of sin? *1249*
Eph 3:7 Whereof I was made a **m.**, according.. *1249*
Eph 4:29 it may **m.** grace unto the hearers....... *1325*
Eph 6:21 a beloved brother and faithful **m.**........ *1249*
Col 1:7 is for you a faithful **m.** of Christ;........ *1249*
Col 1:23 whereof I Paul am made a **m.**; *1249*
Col 1:25 Whereof I am made a **m.**, according ... *1249*
Col 4:7 a faithful **m.** and fellowservant in........ *1249*
1Th 3:2 our brother, and **m.** of God, and our... *1249*
1Ti 1:4 **m.** questions, rather than godly *3930*
1Ti 4:6 shalt be a good **m.** of Jesus Christ,..... *1249*
Heb 1:14 sent forth to **m.** for them who shall.... *1248*
Heb 6:10 ministered to the saints, and do **m.**. ... *1247*
Heb 8:2 A **m.** of the sanctuary, and of the *3011*
1Pe 1:12 but unto us they did **m.** the things, ... *1247*
1Pe 4:10 even so **m.** the same one to another,.. *1247*
1Pe 4:11 if any man **m.**, let him do it as of....... *1247*

MINISTERED
Nu 3:4 Ithamar **m.** in the priest's office ....
De 10:6 his son **m.** in the priest's office in.............
1Sa 2:18 Samuel **m.** before the Lord, being...... 8334
1Sa 3:1 the child Samuel **m.** unto the Lord..... 8334
2Sa 13:17 called his servant that **m.** unto him,.... 8334
1Ki 1:4 cherished the king, and **m.** to him: 8334
1Ki 1:15 the Shunammite **m.** unto the king....... 8334
1Ki 19:21 went after Elijah, and **m.** unto him. 8334
2Ki 25:14 vessels of brass wherewith they **m.**,... 8334
1Ch 6:32 **m.** before the dwelling place of the..... 8334
1Ch 28:1 companies that **m.** to the king by 8334
2Ch 22:8 of Ahaziah, that **m.** to Ahaziah, he...... 8334
Es 2:2 king's servants that **m.** unto him, ... 8334
Es 6:3 king's servants that **m.** unto him. 8334
Jer 52:18 vessels of brass wherewith they **m.**,... 8334
Eze 44:12 they **m.** unto them before their idols,.. 8334
Eze 44:19 their garments wherein they **m.**,......... 8334
Da 7:10 thousand thousands **m.** unto him, ... 8120
Mt 4:11 angels came and **m.** unto him. *1247*

Mt 8:15 and she arose, and **m.** unto them....... *1247*
Mt 20:28 **Son of man came not be m. unto,** ..*1247*
Mk 1:13 beasts; and the angels **m.** unto him. ... *1247*
Mk 1:31 left her, and she **m.** unto them.......... *1247*
Mk 10:45 **of man came not to be m. unto,**.... *1247*
Mk 15:41 followed him, and **m.** unto him;)......... *1247*
Lu 4:39 she arose and **m.** unto them. *1247*
Lu 8:3 **m.** unto him of their substance. *1247*
Ac 13:2 As they **m.** to the Lord, and fasted, ... *3008*
Ac 19:22 two of them that **m.** unto him, ... *1247*
Ac 20:34 hands have **m.** unto my necessities,.... *5256*
2Co 3:3 to be the epistle of Christ **m.** by us,... *1247*
Phil 2:25 and he that **m.** to my wants............. *3011*
Col 2:19 and bands having nourishment **m.**,...... *2023*
2Ti 1:18 things he **m.** unto me at Ephesus,...... *1247*
Phm 13 might have **m.** unto me in the bonds... *1247*
Heb 6:10 **m.** to the saints, and do minister. *1247*
2Pe 1:11 an entrance shall be **m.** unto you *2023*

MINISTERETH
2Co 9:10 Now he that **m.** seed to the sower..... *2023*
Ga 3:5 therefore that **m.** to you the Spirit, ... *2023*

MINISTERING
1Ch 9:28 had the charge of the **m.** vessels, ... 5656
Eze 44:11 of the house, and **m.** to the house:..... 8334
Mt 27:55 Jesus from Galilee, **m.** unto him:....... *1247*
Ro 12:7 Or ministry, let us wait on our **m.**:...... *1248*
Ro 15:16 the Gentiles, **m.** the gospel of God,.... *2418*
2Co 8:4 fellowship of the **m.** to the saints. *1248*
2Co 9:1 as touching the **m.** to the saints,........ *1248*
Heb 1:14 Are they not all **m.** spirits, sent......... *3010*
Heb 10:11 every priest standeth daily **m.** and...... *3008*

MINISTERS
1Ki 10:5 attendance of his **m.**, and their 8334
2Ch 9:4 attendance of his **m.**, and their 8334
Ezr 7:24 or **m.** of this house of God, ... 6399
Ezr 8:17 that they should bring unto us **m.**....... 8334
Ps 103:21 ye **m.** of his, that do his pleasure....... 8334
Ps 104:4 angels spirits; his **m.** a flaming fire: 8334
Isa 61:6 shall call you the **M.** of our God:........ 8334
Jer 33:21 with the Levites the priests, my **m.**.... 8334
Eze 44:11 they shall be **m.** in my sanctuary,....... 8334
Eze 45:4 the priests the **m.** of the sanctuary,.... 8334
Eze 45:5 the Levites, the **m.** of the house,....... 8334
Eze 46:24 with the **m.** of the house shall boil...... 8334
Joe 1:9 the priests, the Lord's **m.**, mourn. 8334
Joe 1:13 howl, ye **m.** of the altar: come, lie...... 8334
Joe 1:13 night in sackcloth, ye **m.** of my God: .. 8334
Joe 2:17 Let the priests, the **m.** of the Lord, ... 8334
Lu 1:2 eyewitnesses, and **m.** of the word;..... *5257*
Ro 13:6 for they are God's **m.**, attending........ *3011*
1Co 3:5 **m.** by whom ye believed, even as...... *1249*
1Co 4:1 account of us, as of...**m.** of Christ,...... *5257*
2Co 3:6 hath made us able **m.** of the new....... *1249*
2Co 6:4 approving ourselves as...**m.** of God, ... *1249*
2Co 11:15 thing if his **m.** also be transformed *1249*
2Co 11:15 as the **m.** of righteousness; whose *1249*
2Co 11:23 Are they **m.** of Christ? (I speak as a... *1249*
Heb 1:7 spirits, and his **m.** a flame of fire. *3011*

MINISTRATION
Lu 1:23 days of his **m.** were accomplished, ... *3009*
Ac 6:1 were neglected in the daily **m.**........... *1248*
2Co 3:7 But if the **m.** of death, written and..... *1248*
2Co 3:8 **m.** of the spirit be rather glorious?..... *1248*
2Co 3:9 if the **m.** of condemnation be glory, ... *1248*
2Co 3:9 **m.** of righteousness exceed in glory.... *1248*
2Co 9:13 Whiles by the experiment of this **m.** ... *1248*

MINISTRY
Nu 4:12 take all the instruments of **m.**,........... 8335
Nu 4:47 came to do the service of the **m.**, ... 5656
2Ch 7:6 when David praised by their **m.**; 3027
Ho 12:10 by the **m.** of the prophets................. 3027
Ac 1:17 and had obtained part of this **m.**......... *1248*
Ac 1:25 That he may take part of this **m.** *1248*
Ac 6:4 prayer, and to the **m.** of the word...... *1248*
Ac 12:25 when they had fulfilled their **m.**,......... *1248*
Ac 20:24 and the **m.**, which I have received...... *1248*
Ac 21:19 among the Gentiles by his **m.**............ *1248*
Ro 12:7 Or **m.**, let us wait on...ministering; *1248*
1Co 16:15 addicted...to the **m.** of the saints,) *1248*
2Co 4:1 Therefore seeing we have this **m.**, ... *1248*
2Co 5:18 given to us the **m.** of reconciliation; *1248*
2Co 6:3 thing, that the **m.** be not blamed:....... *1248*
Eph 4:12 for the work of the **m.**, for the.......... *1248*
Col 4:17 Take heed to the **m.** which thou hast.. *1248*
1Ti 1:12 faithful, putting me into the **m.**; *1248*
2Ti 4:5 evangelist, make full proof of thy **m.**... *1248*
2Ti 4:11 for he is profitable to me for the **m.**.. *1248*
Heb 8:6 he obtained a more excellent **m.**, ... *3009*
Heb 9:21 and all the vessels of the **m.**. *3009*

MINNI (min'-ni)
Jer 51:27 the kingdoms of Ararat, **M.**, and........ 4508

MINNITH (min'-nith)
Jg 11:33 Aroer, even till thou come to **M.**, ... 4511
Eze 27:17 traded in thy market wheat of **M.**,...... 4511

MINSTREL See also MINSTRELS.
2Ki 3:15 But now bring me a **m.** And it........... 5059
2Ki 3:15 came to pass, when the **m.** played, ... 5059

MINSTRELS
Mt 9:23 **m.** and the people making a noise, ... *834*

MINT
Mt 23:23 **ye pay the tithe of m. and anise**.... *2238*
Lu 11:42 **ye tithe m. and rue and all manner** *2238*

MIPHKAD (mif'-kad)
Ne 3:31 over against the gate **M.**, ... 4663

MIRACLE See also MIRACLES.
Ex 7:9 you, saying, Shew a **m.** for you: 4159
Mk 6:52 considered not the **m.** of the loaves: ....
Mk 9:39 **which shall do a m. in my name,** .. *1411*
Lu 23:8 hoped to have seen some **m.** done *4592*
Joh 4:54 again the second **m.** that Jesus did, ... *4592*
Joh 6:14 they had seen the **m.** that Jesus did,... *4592*
Joh 10:41 him, and said, John did no **m.**:........... *4592*
Joh 12:18 heard that he had done this **m.**.......... *4592*
Ac 4:16 notable **m.** hath been done by them.... *4592*
Ac 4:22 this **m.** of healing was shewed........... *4592*

MIRACLES
Nu 14:22 and my **m.**, which I did in Egypt......... 226
De 11:3 his **m.**, and his acts, which he did........ 226
De 29:3 the signs, and those great **m.**:........... 4159
Jg 6:13 and where be all his **m.** which our...... 6381
Joh 2:11 beginning of **m.** did Jesus in Cana....... *4592*
Joh 2:23 they saw the **m.** which he did. *4592*
Joh 3:2 can do these **m.** that thou doest, ... *4592*
Joh 6:2 because they saw his **m.** which he....... *4592*
Joh 6:26 **me, not because ye saw the m.**,..... *4592*
Joh 7:31 will he do more **m.** than these........... *4592*
Joh 9:16 man that is a sinner do such **m.**? *4592*
Joh 11:47 we? for this doeth many **m.**.............. *4592*
Joh 12:37 though he had done so many **m.** *4592*
Ac 2:22 approved of God among you by **m.**..... *1411*
Ac 6:8 did great wonders and **m.** among *4592*
Ac 8:6 and seeing the **m.** which he did. *4592*
Ac 8:13 the **m.** and signs which were done. *1411*
Ac 15:12 **m.** and wonders God had wrought...... *4592*
Ac 19:11 special **m.** by the hands of Paul: *1411*
1Co 12:10 To another the working of **m.**; to....... *1411*
1Co 12:28 after that **m.**, then gifts of healings,.... *1411*
1Co 12:29 all teachers? are all workers of **m.**? *1411*
Ga 3:5 worketh **m.** among you, doeth he it.... *1411*
Heb 2:4 and wonders, and with divers **m.**, ... *1411*
Re 13:14 those **m.** which he had power to do.... *4592*
Re 16:14 the spirits of devils, working **m.**,........ *4592*
Re 19:20 the false prophet that wrought **m.** *4592*

MIRE
2Sa 22:43 them as the **m.** of the street, and 2916
Job 8:11 Can the rush grow up without **m.**? 1207
Job 30:19 He hath cast me into the **m.**, and....... 2563
Job 41:30 sharp pointed things upon the **m.**. 2916
Ps 69:2 I sink in deep **m.**, where there is........ 3121
Ps 69:14 Deliver me out of the **m.**, and let........ 2916
Isa 10:6 down like the **m.** of the streets. 2563
Isa 57:20 whose waters cast up **m.** and dirt.. 7516
Jer 38:6 there was no water, but **m.**: 2916
Jer 38:6 so Jeremiah sunk in the **m.**. 2916
Jer 38:22 thy feet are sunk in the **m.**, and 1206
Mic 7:10 down as the **m.** of the streets. 2916
Zec 9:3 fine gold as the **m.** of the streets. 2916
Zec 10:5 enemies in the **m.** of the streets in..... 2916
2Pe 2:22 washed to her wallowing in the **m.**.. .... *1004*

MIRIAM (mir'-e-am) See also MARY.
Ex 15:20 **M.** the prophetess, the sister of........ 4813
Ex 15:21 **M.** answered them, Sing ye to the...... 4813
Nu 12:1 **M.** and Aaron spake against Moses...... 4813
Nu 12:4 unto **M.**, Come out ye three unto 4813
Nu 12:5 and called Aaron and **M.**: and they 4813
Nu 12:10 **M.** became leprous, white as snow:.... 4813
Nu 12:10 Aaron looked upon **M.**, and, behold, ... 4813
Nu 12:15 **M.** was shut out from the camp......... 4813
Nu 12:15 not till **M.** was brought in again. 4813
Nu 20:1 and **M.** died there, and was buried..... 4813
Nu 26:59 and Moses, and **M.** their sister.......... 4813
De 24:9 what the Lord thy God did unto **M.**.... 4813
1Ch 4:17 and she bare **M.**, and Shammai,......... 4813
1Ch 6:3 Aaron, and Moses, and **M.** The......... 4813
Mic 6:4 before thee Moses, Aaron, and **M.**.... 4813

MIRMA (mur'-mah)
1Ch 8:10 And Jeuz, and Shachia. and **M.**. 4821

MIRTH
Ge 31:27 have sent thee away with **m.**, and...... 8057
Ne 8:12 portions, and to make great **m.**,......... 8057
Ps 137:3 that wasted us required of us **m.**, ... 8057
Pr 14:13 and the end of that **m.** is heaviness. ... 8057
Ec 2:1 to now, I will prove thee with **m.**,...... 8057
Ec 2:2 is mad: and of **m.**, What doeth it? 8057
Ec 7:4 heart of fools is in the house of **m.**..... 8057
Ec 8:15 Then I commended **m.**, because a...... 8057
Isa 24:8 The **m.** of tabrets ceaseth, the 4885
Isa 24:11 the **m.** of the land is gone. 4885
Jer 7:34 the voice of **m.**, and the voice of 8342
Jer 16:9 and in your days, the voice of **m.**,...... 8342
Jer 25:10 will take from them the voice of **m.**,.... 8342
Eze 21:10 glitter: should we then make **m.**? 7797
Ho 2:11 will also cause all her **m.** to cease, ... 4885

MIRY
Ps 40:2 an horrible pit, out of the **m.** clay,...... 3121
Eze 47:11 But the **m.** places thereof and the...... 1207
Da 2:41 the iron mixed with **m.** clay. 2917
Da 2:43 sawest iron mixed with **m.** clay,......... 2917

MISCARRYING
Ho 9:14 give them a **m.** womb and dry........... 7921

MISCHIEF See also MISCHIEFS.
Ge 42:4 Lest peradventure **m.** befall him. 611
Ge 42:38 if **m.** befall him by the way in the 611
Ge 44:29 this also from **m.**, and **m.** befall him,.... 611
Ex 21:22 from her, and yet no **m.** follow: 611
Ex 21:23 if any **m.** follow, then thou shalt 611
Ex 32:12 For **m.** did he bring them out, to....... 7451
Ex 32:22 the people, that they are set on **m.**.... 7451
1Sa 23:9 secretly practised **m.** against him; 7451
2Sa 16:8 thou art taken in thy **m.**, because....... 7451
1Ki 11:25 beside the **m.** that Hadad did: and...... 7451
1Ki 20:7 and see how this man seeketh **m.**:...... 7451
2Ki 7:9 light, some **m.** will come upon us:...... 5771
Ne 6:2 But they thought to do me **m.**........... 7451
Es 8:3 tears to put away the **m.** of Haman 7451
Job 15:35 They conceive **m.**, and bring forth...... 5999
Ps 7:14 iniquity, and hath conceived **m.**,......... 5999
Ps 7:16 His **m.** shall return upon his own 5999
Ps 10:7 under his tongue is **m.** and vanity....... 5999
Ps 10:14 for thou beholdest **m.** and spite, to...... 5999
Ps 26:10 In whose hands is **m.**, and their......... 2154
Ps 28:3 but **m.** is in their hearts.................. 7451
Ps 36:4 He deviseth **m.** upon his bed; he......... 205
Ps 52:1 Why boastest thou thyself in **m.**,........ 7451
Ps 55:10 **m.** also and sorrow are in the midst..... 205
Ps 62:3 will ye imagine **m.** against a man? 205
Ps 94:20 thee, which frameth **m.** by a law? 5999
Ps 119:150 draw nigh that follow after **m.**: 2154
Ps 140:9 **m.** of their own lips cover them......... 5999
Pr 4:16 not, except they have done **m.**; 7489
Pr 6:14 he deviseth **m.** continually; he 7451
Pr 6:18 feet that be swift in running to **m.**,..... 7451
Pr 10:23 It is as sport to a fool to do **m.**: 2154
Pr 11:27 he that seeketh **m.**, it shall come 7451
Pr 12:21 the wicked shall be filled with **m.**. 7451
Pr 13:17 wicked messenger falleth into **m.**: 7451
Pr 17:20 a perverse tongue falleth into **m.**........ 7451
Pr 24:2 and their lips talk of **m.**.................... 5999
Pr 24:16 but the wicked shall fall into **m.**. 7451
Pr 28:14 his heart shall fall into **m.**. 7451
Isa 47:11 **m.** shall fall upon thee; thou shalt....... 1943
Isa 59:4 they conceive **m.**, and bring forth........ 5999
Eze 7:26 **M.** shall come upon **m.**, and............. 1943
Eze 11:2 these are the men that devise **m.**, ... 205
Da 11:27 king's hearts shall be to do **m.**,.......... 4827
Ho 7:15 do they imagine **m.** against me. 7451
Ac 13:10 O full of all subtilty and all **m.**,.......... *4468*

MISCHIEFS
De 32:23 I will heap **m.** upon them; I will......... 7451

Ps 52:2 Thy tongue deviseth **m.**; like a.......... 1942
Ps 140:2 Which imagine **m.** in their hearts;....... 7451

MISCHIEVOUS
Ps 21:11 they imagined a **m.** device, which....... 4209
Ps 38:12 that seek my hurt speak **m.** things, ... 1942
Pr 24:8 evil shall be called a **m.** person.......... 4209
Ec 10:13 the end of his talk is **m.** madness....... 7451
Mic 7:3 man, he uttereth his **m.** desire: 1942

MISERABLE
Job 16:2 things: **m.** comforters are ye all......... 5999
1Co 15:19 Christ, we are of all men most **m.**....... *1652*
Re 3:17 **that thou art wretched, and m.,**.... *1652*

MISERABLY
Mt 21:41 will **m.** destroy those wicked men, ... *2560*

MISERIES
La 1:7 days of her affliction and of her **m.**..... 4788
Jas 5:1 weep and howl for your **m.** that......... *5004*

MISERY See also MISERABLE; MISERIES.
Jg 10:16 was grieved for the **m.** of Israel......... 5999
Job 3:20 is light given to him that is in **m.**, ... 6001
Job 11:16 Because thou shalt forget thy **m.**, ... 5999
Pr 31:7 and remember his **m.** no more. 5999
Ec 8:6 the **m.** of man is great upon him........ 7451
La 3:19 mine affliction and my **m.**, the 4788
Ro 3:16 and **m.** are in their ways: *5004*

MISGAB (mis'-gab)
Jer 48:1 **M.** is confounded and dismayed.......... 4869

MISHAEL (mish'-a-el) See also MISHAL.
Ex 6:22 And the sons of Uzziel; **M.**, and 4332
Lev 10:4 Moses called **M.** and Elzaphan,.......... 4332
Ne 8:4 on his left hand, Pedaiah, and **M.**, ... 4332
Da 1:6 of Judah, Daniel, Hananiah, **M.**, ... 4332
Da 1:7 and to **M.**, of Meshach; and to 4332
Da 1:11 had set over Daniel, Hananiah, **M.**,..... 4332
Da 1:19 none like Daniel, Hananiah, **M.**, ... 4332
Da 2:17 the thing known to Hananiah, **M.**, ... 4332

MISHAL (mi'-shal) See also MISHAEL.
Jos 21:30 of Asher, **M.** with her suburbs, ... 4861

MISHAM (mi'-sham)
1Ch 8:12 and **M.**, and Shamed, who built.......... 4936

MISHEAL (mish'-e-al)
Jos 19:26 Alammelech, and Amad, and **M.**;........ 4861

MISHMA (mish'-mah)
Ge 25:14 And **M.**, and Dumah, and Massa, ... 4927
1Ch 1:30 **M.**, and Dumah, Massa, Hadad,......... 4927
1Ch 4:25 son, Mibsam his son, **M.** his son......... 4927
1Ch 4:26 And the sons of **M.**; Hamuel his 4927

MISHMANNAH (mish-man'-nah)
1Ch 12:10 **M.** the fourth, Jeremiah the fifth, ... 4925

MISHPAT See EN-MISHPAT.

MISHRAITES (mish'-ra-ites)
1Ch 2:53 and the Shumathites, and the **M.**;....... 4954

MISPERETH (mis-pe'-reth) See also MIZPAR.
Ne 7:7 Bilshan, **M.**, Bigvai, Nehum, ... 4559

MISREPHOTH-MAIM (mis''-re-foth-mah'-yim) See also ZAREPHATH.
Jos 11:8 unto great Zidon, and unto **M.**,.......... 4956
Jos 13:6 country from Lebanon unto **M.**, ... 4956

MISS See also AMISS; MISSED; MISSING; MISCARRYING; MISUSED.
Jg 20:16 at an hair breadth, and not **m.**........... 2398
1Sa 20:6 If thy father at all **m.** me, then.......... 6485

MISSED
1Sa 20:18 and thou shalt be **m.**, because thy...... 6485
1Sa 25:15 not hurt, neither **m.** we any thing, ... 6485
1Sa 25:21 nothing was **m.** of all that pertained.... 6485

MISSING
1Sa 25:7 neither was there ought **m.** unto........ 6485
1Ki 20:39 if by any means he be **m.**, then shall .. 6485

MIST
Ge 2:6 there went up a **m.** from the earth, ... 108
Ac 13:11 fell on him a **m.** and a darkness;.......... *887*
2Pe 2:17 the **m.** of darkness is reserved for *2217*

MISTRESS
Ge 16:4 her **m.** was despised in her eyes........ 1404
Ge 16:8 flee from the face of my **m.** Sarai....... 1404
Ge 16:9 said unto her, Return to thy **m.**, ... 1404
1Ki 17:17 the **m.** of the house, fell sick; and...... 1172
2Ki 5:3 And she said unto her **m.**, Would....... 1404
Ps 123:2 maiden unto the hand of her **m.**; 1404
Pr 30:23 handmaid that is heir to her **m.**.......... 1404
Isa 24:2 as with the maid, so with her **m.**; 1404
Na 3:4 the **m.** of witchcrafts, that selleth....... 1172

MISUSED
2Ch 36:16 and **m.** his prophets, until the........... 8591

MITE See also MITES.
Lu 12:59 **till thou hast paid the very last m.**.. *3016*

MITES
Mk 12:42 and she threw in two **m.**, which......... *3016*
Lu 21:2 widow casting in thither two **m.**......... *3016*

MITHCAH (mith'-cah)
Nu 33:28 from Tarah, and pitched in **M.**.......... 4989
Nu 33:29 they went from **M.**, and pitched in 4989

MITHNITE (mith'-nite)
1Ch 11:43 Maachah, and Joshaphat the **M.**, ... 4981

MITHREDATH (mith'-re-dath)
Ezr 1:8 by the hand of **M.** the treasurer,........ 4990
Ezr 4:7 Artaxerxes wrote Bishlam, **M.**,.......... 4990

MITRE
Ex 28:4 broidered coat, a **m.**, and a girdle: 4701
Ex 28:37 lace, that it may be upon the **m.**; 4701
Ex 28:37 the forefront of the **m.** it shall be....... 4701
Ex 28:39 shalt make the **m.** of fine linen, and.... 4701
Ex 29:6 shalt put the **m.** upon his head, and.... 4701
Ex 29:6 put the holy crown upon the **m.**.......... 4701
Ex 39:28 And a **m.** of fine linen, and goodly...... 4701
Ex 39:31 to fasten it on high upon the **m.**;......... 4701
Le 8:9 And he put the **m.** upon his head; 4701
Le 8:9 also upon the **m.**, even upon his 4701
Le 16:4 and with the linen **m.** shall he be 4701
Zec 3:5 them set a fair **m.** upon his head......... 6797
Zec 3:5 So they set a fair **m.** upon his head, ... 6797

MITYLENE (mit-i-le'-ne)
Ac 20:14 we took him in, and came to **M.**. *3412*

MIXED See also MIXT.
Ex 12:38 a **m.** multitude went up also with 6154
Ne 13:3 from Israel all the **m.** multitude.......... 6154
Pr 23:30 wine; they that go to seek **m.** wine. ... 4469
Isa 1:22 dross, thy wine **m.** with water:.......... 4107
Da 2:41 sawest the iron **m.** with miry clay. 6151
Da 2:43 thou sawest iron **m.** with miry clay,.... 6151
Da 2:43 even as iron is not **m.** with clay......... 6151
Ho 7:8 he hath **m.** himself among the 1101
Heb 4:2 not being **m.** with faith in them.......... *4786*

MIXT See also MIXED.
Nu 11:4 the **m.** multitude that was among them......

MIXTURE
Ps 75:8 the wine is red; it is full of **m.**;.......... 4538
Joh 19:39 brought a **m.** of myrrh and aloes, ... *3395*
Re 14:10 is poured out without **m.** into the *194*

MIZAR (mi'-zar)
Ps 42:6 the Hermonites, from the hill **M.**........ 4706

MIZPAH (miz'-pah) See also MIZPEH.
Ge 31:49 **M.**; for he said, the Lord watch......... 4709
1Ki 15:22 them Geba of Benjamin, and **M.**.......... 4709
2Ki 25:23 there came to Gedaliah to **M.**, even.... 4709
2Ki 25:25 Chaldees that were with him at **M.**..... 4709
2Ch 16:6 he built therewith Geba and **M.**. 4709
Ne 3:7 and of **M.**, unto the throne of the....... 4709
Ne 3:15 Col-hozeh, the ruler of part of **M.**; 4709
Ne 3:19 the son of Jeshua, the ruler of **M.**, ... 4709
Jer 40:6 Gedaliah the son of Ahikam to **M.**; 4708
Jer 40:8 they came to Gedaliah to **m.**, even..... 4708
Jer 40:10 for me, behold, I will dwell at **M.**,...... 4708
Jer 40:12 land of Judah, to Gedaliah, unto **M.**,..... 4708
Jer 40:13 the fields, came to Gedaliah to **M.**,..... 4708
Jer 40:15 spake to Gedaliah in **M.** secretly, ... 4709
Jer 41:1 Gedaliah the son of Ahikam to **M.**; 4709
Jer 41:1 they did eat bread together in **M.**...... 4709
Jer 41:3 at **M.**, and the Chaldeans that were.... 4709
Jer 41:6 went forth from **M.** to meet them, ... 4709
Jer 41:10 of the people that were in **M.**,........... 4709
Jer 41:10 all the people that remained in **M.**, ... 4709
Jer 41:14 had carried away captive from **M.**........ 4709
Jer 41:16 from **M.**, after that he had slain......... 4709
Ho 5:1 ye have been a snare on **M.**,............ 4709

MIZPAR (miz'-par) See also MISPERETH.
Ezr 2:2 Bilshan, **M.**, Bigvai, Rehum, ... 4558

MIZPEH (miz'-peh) See also MIZPAH; RAMATH-MIZPEH.
Jos 11:3 under Hermon in the land of **M.**......... 4709
Jos 11:8 unto the valley of **M.** eastward; 4708
Jos 15:38 And Dilean, and **M.**, and Joktheel, ... 4708
Jos 18:26 **M.**, and Chephirah, and Mozah, ... 4708
Jg 10:17 together, and encamped in **M.**............ 4709
Jg 11:11 all his words before the Lord in **M.**. ... 4709
Jg 11:29 and passed over **M.** of Gilead, and 4708
Jg 11:29 from **M.** of Gilead he passed over 4708
Jg 11:34 came to **M.** unto his house, and,........ 4709
Jg 20:1 land of Gilead, unto the Lord in **M.**. .. 4709
Jg 20:3 of Israel were gone up to **M.**.) 4709
Jg 21:1 the men of Israel had sworn in **M.**, ... 4709
Jg 21:5 came not up to the Lord to **M.**,......... 4709
Jg 21:8 of Israel that came not up to **M.** to 4709
1Sa 7:5 said, Gather all Israel to **M.**, and 4708
1Sa 7:6 they gathered together to **M.**,........... 4709
1Sa 7:6 Samuel judged...of Israel in **M.**.......... 4708
1Sa 7:7 were gathered together to **M.**,.......... 4708
1Sa 7:11 the men of Israel went out of **M.**, ... 4709
1Sa 7:12 and set it between **M.** and Shen, ... 4709
1Sa 7:16 to Beth-el, and Gilgal, and **M.**, and..... 4709
1Sa 10:17 together unto the Lord to **M.**;.......... 4709
1Sa 22:3 David went thence to **M.** of Moab:..... 4708

MIZRAIM (miz'-ra-im) See also ABEL-MIZRAIM; EGYPT.
Ge 10:6 sons of Ham; Cush, and **M.**, and........ 4714
Ge 10:13 And **M.** begat Ludim, and Anamim, ... 4714
1Ch 1:8 The sons of Ham; Cush, and **M.**,........ 4714
1Ch 1:11 And **M.** begat Ludim, and Anamim, ... 4714

MIZZAH (miz'-zah)
Ge 36:13 and Zerah, Shammah, and **M.**:........... 4199
Ge 36:17 Zerah, duke Shammah, duke **M.**:........ 4199
1Ch 1:37 Nahath, Zerah, Shammah, and **M.**. 4199

MNASON (na'-son)
Ac 21:16 with them one **M.** of Cyprus, an........ *3416*

MOAB (mo'-ab) See also MOABITE; PAHATH-MOAB.
Ge 19:37 a son, and called his name **M.**: 4124
Ge 36:35 who smote Midian in the field of **M.**, .. 4124
Ex 15:15 the mighty men of **M.**, trembling........ 4124
Nu 21:11 the wilderness which is before **M.**,..... 4124
Nu 21:13 for Arnon is the border of **M.**,.......... 4124
Nu 21:13 between **M.** and the Amorites. 4124
Nu 21:15 Ar, and lieth upon the border of **M.**.... 4124
Nu 21:20 in the country of **M.**, to the top of 4124
Nu 21:26 against the former king of **M.**, and 4124
Nu 21:28 it hath consumed Ar of **M.**, and the.... 4124
Nu 21:29 Woe to thee, **M.**! thou art undone,..... 4124
Nu 22:1 pitched in the plains of **M.** on this 4124
Nu 22:3 **M.** was sore afraid of the people,....... 4124
Nu 22:3 **M.** was distressed because of the...... 4124
Nu 22:4 **M.** said unto the elders of Midian,...... 4124
Nu 22:7 the elders of **M.** and the elders of...... 4124
Nu 22:8 princes of **M.** abode with Balaam........ 4124
Nu 22:10 king of **M.**, hath sent unto me,.......... 4124
Nu 22:14 the princes of **M.** rose up, and they.... 4124
Nu 22:21 and went with the princes of **M.**. 4124
Nu 22:36 out to meet him unto a city of **M.**, ... 4124
Nu 23:6 he, and all the princes of **M.**. 4124
Nu 23:7 king of **M.** hath brought me from 4124
Nu 23:17 and the princes of **M.** with him. 4124
Nu 24:17 and shall smite the corners of **M.**,...... 4124
Nu 25:1 whoredom with the daughters of **M.**. .. 4124
Nu 26:3 spake with them in the plains of **M.**. ... 4124
Nu 26:63 children of Israel in the plains of **M.**.... 4124
Nu 31:12 unto the camp at the plains of **M.**,...... 4124
Nu 33:44 in Ije-abarim, in the border of **M.**....... 4124
Nu 33:48 and pitched in the plains of **M.** by 4124
Nu 33:49 Abel-shittim in the plains of **M.**.......... 4124
Nu 33:50 spake unto Moses in...plains of **M.**..... 4124
Nu 35:1 spake unto Moses in the plains of **M.**..... 4124
Nu 36:13 children of Israel in the plains of **M.**.... 4124
De 1:5 this side Jordan, in the land of **M.**, ... 4124
De 2:8 by the way of the wilderness of **M.**. ... 4124
De 2:18 over through Ar, the coast of **M.**, ... 4124
De 29:1 children of Israel in the land of **M.**..... 4124
De 32:49 which is in the land of **M.**, that is....... 4124
De 34:1 went up from the plains of **M.** unto 4124
De 34:5 Lord died there in the land of **M.**,....... 4124
De 34:6 him in a valley in the land of **M.**, ... 4124
De 34:8 wept for Moses in the plains of **M.**..... 4124
Jos 13:32 for inheritance in the plains of **M.**,...... 4124
Jos 24:9 the son of Zippor, king of **M.**, arose ... 4124

Jg 3:12 strengthened Eglon the King of **M.** 4124
Jg 3:14 Israel served Eglon the king of **M.** 4124
Jg 3:15 present unto Eglon the king of **M.** 4124
Jg 3:17 the present unto Eglon king of **M.**: 4124
Jg 3:28 took the fords of Jordan toward **M.**, ... 4124
Jg 3:29 slew of **M.** at that time about ten 4124
Jg 3:30 **M.** was subdued that day under 4124
Jg 10:6 gods of Zidon, and the gods of **M.**, ... 4124
Jg 11:15 Israel took not away the land of **M.**, ... 4124
Jg 11:17 they sent unto the king of **M.**: but 4124
Jg 11:18 land of Edom, and the land of **M.**, ... 4124
Jg 11:18 by the east side of the land of **M.**, ... 4124
Jg 11:18 came not within the border of **M.**: 4124
Jg 11:18 for Arnon was the border of **M.** 4124
Jg 11:25 the son of Zippor, king of **M.**? 4124
Ru 1:1 to sojourn in the country of **M.**, he, ... 4124
Ru 1:2 they came into the country of **M.**, ... 4124
Ru 1:4 them wives of the women of **M.**; 4125
Ru 1:6 return from the country of **M.**: 4124
Ru 1:6 had heard in the country of **M.** how 4124
Ru 1:22 returned out of the country of **M.**: 4124
Ru 2:6 Naomi out of the country of **M.**: 4124
Ru 4:3 come again out of the country of **M.**, .. 4124
1Sa 12:9 and into the hand of the king of **M.**, ... 4124
1Sa 14:47 enemies on every side, against **M.**, ... 4124
1Sa 22:3 David went thence to Mizeph of **M.**: ... 4124
1Sa 22:3 and he said unto the king of **M.**, ... 4124
1Sa 22:4 brought them before the king of **M.**: ... 4124
2Sa 8:2 he smote **M.**, and measured them 4124
2Sa 8:12 and of **M.**, and of the children of 4124
2Sa 23:20 he slew two lionlike men of **M.**: he 4124
1Ki 11:7 for Chemosh, the abomination of **M.**, .. 4124
2Ki 1:1 **M.** rebelled against Israel after the 4124
2Ki 3:4 king of **M.** was a sheepmaster, and 4124
2Ki 3:5 the king of **M.** rebelled against the 4124
2Ki 3:7 king of **M.** hath rebelled against 4124
2Ki 3:7 go with me against **M.** to battle? 4124
2Ki 3:10 to deliver them into the hand of **M.**! ... 4124
2Ki 3:13 to deliver them into the hand of **M.** ... 4124
2Ki 3:23 now therefore, **M.**, to the spoil 4124
2Ki 3:26 king of **M.** saw that the battle 4124
1Ch 1:46 smote Midian in the field of **M.**, ... 4124
1Ch 4:22 who had the dominion in **M.**, and 4124
1Ch 8:8 begat children in the country of **M.**, ... 4124
1Ch 11:22 he slew two lionlike men of **M.**: 4124
1Ch 18:2 And he smote **M.**; and the Moabites ... 4124
1Ch 18:11 from **M.**, and from the children of 4124
2Ch 20:1 that the children of **M.**, and the 4124
2Ch 20:10 the children of Ammon and **M.** and 4124
2Ch 20:22 against the children of Ammon, **M.**, ... 4124
2Ch 20:23 children of Ammon and **M.** stood up ... 4124
Ne 13:23 of Ashdod, of Ammon, and of **M.**: 4125
Ps 60:8 **M.** is my washpot; over Edom will 4124
Ps 83:6 of **M.**, and the Hagarenes; 4124
Ps 108:9 **M.** is my washpot; over Edom will 4124
Isa 11:14 lay their hand upon Edom and **M.**; 4124
Isa 15:1 The burden of **M.** Because in the 4124
Isa 15:1 in the night Ar of **M.** is laid waste, ... 4124
Isa 15:1 in the night Kir of **M.** is laid waste, ... 4124
Isa 15:2 **M.** shall howl over Nebo, and over 4124
Isa 15:4 armed soldiers of **M.** shall cry out; 4124
Isa 15:5 My heart shall cry out for **M.**; his 4124
Isa 15:8 round about the borders of **M.**; 4124
Isa 15:9 lions upon him that escapeth of **M.**, ... 4124
Isa 16:2 the daughters of **M.** shall be at the 4124
Isa 16:4 mine outcasts dwell with thee, **M.**; 4124
Isa 16:6 We have heard of the pride of **M.**; 4124
Isa 16:7 Therefore shall **M.** howl for **M.**, ... 4124
Isa 16:11 shall sound like an harp for **M.**, and 4124
Isa 16:12 that **M.** is weary on the high place, ... 4124
Isa 16:13 Lord hath spoken concerning **M.** 4124
Isa 16:14 the glory of **M.** shall be contemned, ... 4124
Isa 25:10 **M.** shall be trodden down under 4124
Jer 9:26 **M.**, and all that are in the utmost 4124
Jer 25:21 and **M.**, and the children of Ammon, ... 4124
Jer 27:3 of Edom, and to the king of **M.**, ... 4124
Jer 40:11 when all the Jews that were in **M.**, ... 4124
Jer 48:1 Against **M.** thus saith the Lord of 4124
Jer 48:2 There shall be no more praise of **M.**: ... 4124
Jer 48:4 **M.** is destroyed; her little ones 4124
Jer 48:9 Give wings unto **M.**, that it may 4124
Jer 48:11 **M.**...been at ease from his youth, ... 4124
Jer 48:13 **M.** shall be ashamed of Chemosh, ... 4124
Jer 48:15 **M.** is spoiled, and gone up out of 4124
Jer 48:16 The calamity of **M.** is near to come, ... 4124
Jer 48:18 the spoiler of **M.** shall come upon 4124
Jer 48:20 **M.** is confounded; for it is broken 4124
Jer 48:20 ye it in Arnon, tht **M.** is spoiled, ... 4124
Jer 48:24 upon all the cities of the land of **M.**, ... 4124
Jer 48:25 The horn of **M.** is cut off, and his 4124
Jer 48:26 **M.** also shall wallow in his vomit, ... 4124
Jer 48:28 O ye that dwell in **M.**, leave the 4124
Jer 48:29 We have heard the pride of **M.**, (he 4124
Jer 48:31 Therefore will I howl for **M.**, and I 4124
Jer 48:31 and I will cry out for all **M.**; mine 4124
Jer 48:33 field, and from the land of **M.**; 4124
Jer 48:35 I will cause to cease in **M.**, saith 4124
Jer 48:36 heart shall sound for **M.** like pipes, ... 4124
Jer 48:38 upon all the housetops of **M.**, and in ... 4124
Jer 48:38 for I have broken **M.** like a vessel 4124
Jer 48:39 **M.** turned the back with shame! 4124
Jer 48:39 **M.** be a derision and a dismaying 4124
Jer 48:40 and shall spread his wings over **M.** 4124
Jer 48:41 mighty men's hearts in **M.** at that 4124
Jer 48:42 **M.** shall be destroyed from being 4124
Jer 48:43 be upon thee, O inhabitant of **M.**, ... 4124
Jer 48:44 I will bring upon it, even upon **M.**, ... 4124
Jer 48:45 and shall devour the corner of **M.**, ... 4124
Jer 48:46 Woe be unto thee, O **M.**! the people .. 4124
Jer 48:47 I bring again the captivity of **M.** 4124
Jer 48:47 Thus far is the judgment of **M.** 4124
Eze 25:8 Because that **M.** and Seir do say, ... 4124
Eze 25:9 open the side of **M.** from the cities, ... 4124
Eze 25:11 I will execute judgments upon **M.**; 4124
Da 11:41 even Edom, and **M.**, and the chief 4124
Am 2:1 For three transgressions of **M.**, ... 4124
Am 2:2 But I will send a fire upon **M.**, and 4124
Am 2:2 and **M.** shall die with tumult, with 4124
Mic 6:5 what Balak king of **M.** consulted, ... 4124
Zep 2:8 I have heard the reproach of **M.**, ... 4124
Zep 2:9 Surely **M.** shall be as Sodom, and 4124

MOABITE (mo'-ab-ite) See also MOABITES; MOABITESS; MOABITISH.
De 23:3 Ammonite or **M.** shall not enter 4125
1Ch 11:46 sons of Elnaam, and Ithmah the **M.**, ... 4125
Ne 13:1 and the **M.** shall not come into the 4125

MOABITES mo'-ab-ites)
Ge 19:37 the same is the father of the **M.** 4124
Nu 22:4 son of Zippor was king of the **M.** 4124
De 2:9 Distress not the **M.**, neither 4124
De 2:11 but the **M.** call them Emims 4125
De 2:29 **M.** which dwell in Ar, did unto me;) ... 4125
Jg 3:28 delivered your enemies the **M.** into ... 4124
2Sa 8:2 so the **M.** became David's servants, ... 4124
1Ki 11:1 of Pharaoh, women of the **M.**, ... 4125
1Ki 11:33 Chemosh the god of the **M.**, and 4124
2Ki 3:18 deliver the **M.** also into your hand 4124
2Ki 3:21 **M.** heard that the kings were come 4124
2Ki 3:22 the **M.** saw the water on the other 4124
2Ki 3:24 rose up and smote the **M.**, so that 4124
2Ki 3:24 they went forward smiting the **M.**, ... 4124
2Ki 13:20 bands of the **M.** invaded the land 4124
2Ki 23:13 Chemosh the abomination of...**M.**, ... 4124
2Ki 24:2 the Syrians, and bands of the **M.**, ... 4124
1Ch 18:2 the **M.** became David's servants, ... 4124
Ezr 9:1 the **M.**, the Egyptians, and the 4124

MOABITESS (mo'-ab-i-tess)
Ru 1:22 and Ruth the **M.**, her daughter in 4125
Ru 2:2 And Ruth the **M.** said unto Naomi, ... 4125
Ru 2:21 Ruth the **M.** said, He said unto me 4125
Ru 4:5 must buy it also of Ruth the **M.**, ... 4125
Ru 4:10 Moreover Ruth the **M.**, the wife of 4125
2Ch 24:26 the son of Shimrith a **M.** 4125

MOABITISH (mo'-ab-i-tish)
Ru 2:6 It is the **M.** damsel that came back 4125

MOADIAH (mo-ad-i'-ah) See also MAADIAH.
Ne 12:17 Zichri; of Miniamin, of **M.**, Piltai 4153

MOAN See BEMOAN.

MOCK See also MOCKED; MOCKEST; MOCKETH; MOCKING.
Ge 39:14 in an Hebrew unto us to **m.** us; 6711
Ge 39:17 unto us, came in unto me to **m.** me: ... 6711
Job 13:9 mocketh another, do ye so **m.** him? ... 2048
Job 21:3 after that I have spoken, **m.** on. 3932
Pr 1:26 I will **m.** when your fear cometh; 3932
Pr 14:9 Fools make a **m.** at sin: but among 3887
Jer 38:19 into their hand, and they **m.** me 5953
La 1:7 her, and did **m.** at her sabbaths. 7832
Eze 22:5 be far from thee, shall **m.** thee, ... 7046
Mt 20:19 **deliver him to the Gentiles to m.**,... *1702*
Mk 10:34 **they shall m. him, and shall** *1702*
Lu 14:29 **all that behold it begin to m. him**, .*1702*

MOCKED
Ge 19:14 one that **m.** unto his sons in law. 6711
Nu 22:29 the ass, Because thou hast **m.** me: 5953
Jg 16:10, 13 hast **m.** me, and told me lies: 2048
Jg 16:15 thou hast **m.** me these three times, ... 2048
1Ki 18:27 pass at noon, that Elijah **m.** them, ... 2048
2Ki 2:23 children out of the city, and **m.** him, ... 7046
2Ch 30:10 them to scorn, and **m.** them 3932
2Ch 36:16 But they **m.** the messengers of God, .. 3931
Ne 4:1 great indignation, and **m.** the Jews 3932
Job 12:4 I am as one **m.** of his neighbour, ... 7832
Mt 2:16 that he was **m.** of the wise men, ... *1702*
Mt 27:29 the knee before him, and **m.** him, ... *1702*
Mt 27:31 after that they had **m.** him, they *1702*
Mk 15:20 And when they had **m.** him, they *1702*
Lu 18:32 **be m., and spitefully entreated**, ... *1702*
Lu 22:63 and the men that held Jesus **m.** him, ... *1702*
Lu 23:11 war set him at nought, and **m.** him, ... *1702*
Lu 23:36 the soldiers also **m.** him, coming *1702*
Ac 17:32 resurrection of the dead, some **m.**: *5512*
Ga 6:7 Be not deceived; God is not **m.**: for ... *3456*

MOCKER See also MOCKERS.
Pr 20:1 Wine is a **m.**, strong drink is 3887

MOCKERS
Job 17:2 Are there not **m.** with me? and 2049
Ps 35:16 With hypocritical **m.** in feasts, they 3934
Isa 28:22 therefore be ye not **m.**, lest your 3887
Jer 15:17 sat not in the assembly of the **m.**, ... 7832
Jude 18 there should be **m.** in the last time, ... *1703*

MOCKEST
Job 11:3 when thou **m.**, shall no man make 3932

MOCKETH
Job 13:9 or as one man **m.** another, do ye so ... 2048
Job 39:22 He **m.** at fear, and is not affrighted; ... 7832
Pr 17:5 Whoso **m.** the poor reproacheth 3932
Pr 30:17 The eye that **m.** at his father, and 3932
Jer 20:7 in derision daily, every one **m.** me. 3932

MOCKING See also MOCKINGS.
Ge 21:9 she had born unto Abraham, **m.** 6711
Eze 22:4 heathen, and a **m.** to all countries. 7048
Mt 27:41 Likewise also the chief priest **m.** *1702*
Mk 15:31 Likewise also the chief priests **m.** *1702*
Ac 2:13 Others **m.** said, These men are full *5512*

MOCKINGS
Heb 11:36 trial of cruel **m.** and scourgings, ... *1701*

MODERATELY
Joe 2:23 given you the former rain **m.**, ... 6666

MODERATION
Php 4:5 Let your **m.** be known unto all *1933*

MODEST
1Ti 2:9 adorn themselves in **m.** apparel, ... *2887*

MOIST
Nu 6:3 nor eat **m.** grapes, or dried 3892

MOISTENED
Job 21:24 his bones are **m.** with marrow. 8248

MOISTURE
Ps 32:4 my **m.** is turned into the drought of 3955
Lu 8:6 **it withered...because it lacked m.** .. *2429*

MOLADAH (mo-la'-dah)
Jos 15:26 Amam, and Shema, and **M.**, ... 4137
Jos 19:2 Beer-sheba, and Sheba, and **M.**, ... 4137
1Ch 4:28 they dwelt at Beer-sheba, and **M.**, ... 4137
Ne 11:26 And at Jeshua, and at **M.**, and at 4137

MOLE See also MOLES.
Le 11:30 lizard, and the snail, and the **m.** 8580

MOLECH (mo'-lek) See also MALCHAM; MOLOCH.
Le 18:21 seed pass through the fire to **M.**, ... 4432
Le 20:2 that giveth any of his seed unto **M.**; ... 4432
Le 20:3 he hath given of his seed unto **M.**, ... 4432
Le 20:4 when he giveth of his seed unto **M.**, ... 4432
Le 20:5 to commit whoredom with **M.**, from 4432
1Ki 11:7 is before Jerusalem, and for **M.**, ... 4432
2Ki 23:10 to pass through the fire to **M.** 4432
Jer 32:35 to pass through the fire unto **M.**; 4432

MOLES
Isa 2:20 worship, to the **m.** and to the bats; 2661

MOLID (mo'-lid)
1Ch 2:29 and she bare him Ahban, and **M.** 4140

MOLLIFIED
Isa 1:6 up, neither **m.** with ointment 7401

MOLOCH (mo'-loch) See also MILCHOM; MOLECH.
Am 5:26 borne the tabernacle of your **M.** 4432
Ac 7:43 ye took up the tabernacle of **M.**, ... *3434*

MOLTEN See also MELTED.
Ex 32:4 after he had made it a **m.** calf: 4541
Ex 32:8 they have made them a **m.** calf, and 4541
Ex 34:17 Thou shalt make thee no **m.** gods. 4541
Le 19:4 nor make to yourselves **m.** gods: I 4541
Nu 33:52 and destroy all their **m.** images, and 4541
De 9:12 they have made them a **m.** image 4541
De 9:16 God, and had made you a **m.** calf: 4541
De 27:15 maketh any graven or **m.** image, an 4541
Jg 17:3,4 a graven image and a **m.** image: 4541
Jg 18:14 a graven image, and a **m.** image? 4541
Jg 18:17 the teraphim, and the **m.** image: 4541
Jg 18:18 the teraphim, and the **m.** image. 4541
1Ki 7:16 made two chapiters of **m.** brass, ... 3332
1Ki 7:23 he made a **m.** sea, ten cubits from 3332
1Ki 7:30 the laver were undersetters **m.**, at 3332
1Ki 7:33 and their spokes, were all **m.** 3332
1Ki 14:9 thee other gods, and **m.** images, ... 4541
2Ki 17:16 made them **m.** images, even two 4541
2Ch 4:2 made a **m.** sea of ten cubits from 3332
2Ch 28:2 made also **m.** images for Baalim 4541
2Ch 34:3 carved images, and the **m.** images 4541
2Ch 34:4 carved images, and the **m.** images, ... 4541
Ne 9:18 they had made them a **m.** calf, ... 4541
Job 28:2 and brass is **m.** out of the stone. 6694
Job 37:18 strong, and as a **m.** looking glass? 3332
Ps 106:19 and worshipped the **m.** image 4541
Isa 30:22 ornament of thy **m.** images of gold: 4541
Isa 41:29 **m.** images are wind and confusion. 5262
Isa 42:17 say to the **m.** images, Ye are our 4541
Isa 44:10 god, or **m.** a graven image that is 5258
Isa 48:5 my **m.** image, hath commanded 5262
Jer 10:14 for his **m.** image is falsehood, and 5262
Jer 51:17 for his **m.** image is falsehood, and 5262
Eze 24:11 the filthiness of it may be **m.** in it, ... 5413
Ho 13:2 them **m.** images of their silver, ... 4541
Mic 1:4 mountains shall be **m.** under him, ... 4549
Na 1:14 graven image and the **m.** image: 4541
Hab 2:18 the **m.** image, and a teacher of lies, ... 4541

MOMENT
Eze 33:5 up into the midst of thee in a **m.**, ... 7281
Nu 16:21 that I may consume them in a **m.** 7281
Nu 16:45 I may consume them as in a **m.** 7281
Job 7:18 morning, and try him every **m.**? 7281
Job 20:5 joy of the hypocrite but for a **m.**? 7281
Job 21:13 and in a **m.** go down to the grave. 7281
Job 34:20 In a **m.** shall they die, and the 7281
Ps 30:5 For his anger endureth but a **m.**; 7281
Ps 73:19 brought into desolation, as in a **m.**! 7281
Pr 12:19 but a lying is but for a **m.** 7281
Isa 26:20 thyself as it were for a little **m.**, ... 7281
Isa 27:3 I will water it every **m.**: lest any 7281
Isa 47:9 things shall come to thee in a **m.** in 7281
Isa 54:7 a small **m.** have I forsaken thee; 7281
Isa 54:8 I hid my face from thee for a **m.**; 7281
Jer 4:20 spoiled, and my curtains in a **m.** 7281
La 4:6 that was overthrown as in a **m.**, and 7281
Eze 26:16 and shall tremble at every **m.**, and 7281
Eze 32:10 shall tremble at every **m.**, and they 7281
Lu 4:5 kingdoms of the world in a **m.** of *4743*
1Co 15:52 In a **m.**, in the twinkling of an eye, ... *823*
2Co 4:17 affliction, which is but for a **m.**, ... *3901*

MONEY See also MONEYCHANGERS.
Ge 17:12 or bought with **m.** of any stranger, ... 3701
Ge 17:13 he that is bought with thy **m.**, must 3701
Ge 17:23 all that were bought with his **m.**, ... 3701
Ge 17:27 and bought with **m.** of the stranger, ... 3701
Ge 23:9 for as much **m.** as it is worth he 3701
Ge 23:13 I will give thee **m.** for the field; 3701
Ge 23:16 current **m.** with the merchant ....
Ge 31:15 hath quite devoured also our **m.** 3701
Ge 33:19 for an hundred pieces of **m.** 7192
Ge 42:25 to restore every man's **m.** into his 3701
Ge 42:27 he espied his **m.**; for, behold, it was 3701
Ge 42:28 My **m.** is restored; and, lo, it is 3701
Ge 42:35 man's bundle of **m.** was in his sack: 3701
Ge 42:35 their father saw the bundles of **m.**, ... 3701
Ge 43:12 And take double **m.** in your hand; 3701
Ge 43:12 the **m.** that was brought again in 3701
Ge 43:15 they took double **m.** in their hand, ... 3701
Ge 43:18 **m.** that was returned in our sacks 3701
Ge 43:21 **m.** was in the mouth of his sack, ... 3701
Ge 43:21 of his sack, our **m.** in full weight: 3701
Ge 43:22 other **m.** have we brought down in 3701
Ge 43:22 tell who put our **m.** in our sacks. 3701
Ge 43:23 in your sacks: I had your **m.** 3701
Ge 44:1 every man's **m.** in his sack's mouth. 3701
Ge 44:2 of the youngest, and his corn **m.** 3701
Ge 44:8 Behold, the **m.**, which we found in 3701
Ge 47:14 Joseph gathered up all the **m.** that 3701
Ge 47:14 Joseph brought...**m.** into Pharaoh's 3701
Ge 47:15 when **m.** failed in the land of Egypt, ... 3701
Ge 47:15 in thy presence? for the **m.** faileth. 3701
Ge 47:16 give you for your cattle, if **m.** fail. 3701
Ge 47:18 my lord, how that our **m.** is spent; 3701
Ex 12:44 man's servant that is bought for **m.**, ... 3701
Ex 21:11 shall she go out free without **m.** 3701
Ex 21:21 not be punished: for he is his **m.** 3701
Ex 21:30 If there be laid on him a sum of **m.**, ...
Ex 21:34 give **m.** unto the owner of them; 3701
Ex 21:35 the live ox, and divide the **m.** of it; 3701
Ex 22:7 deliver unto his neighbour **m.** or 3701
Ex 22:17 pay **m.** according to the dowry of 3701
Ex 22:25 If thou lend **m.** to any of my people 3701
Ex 30:16 thou shalt take the atonement **m.** 3701
Le 22:11 priest buy any soul with his **m.**, ... 3701
Le 25:37 not give him thy **m.** upon usury, ... 3701
Le 25:51 out of the **m.** that he was bought 3701
Le 27:15 fifth part of the **m.** of thy estimation 3701
Le 27:18 priest shall reckon unto him the **m.** 3701
Le 27:19 fifth part of the **m.** of thy estimation 3701
Nu 3:48 thou shalt give the **m.**, wherewith 3701
Nu 3:49 Moses took the redemption **m.** of 3701
Nu 3:50 children of Israel took he the **m.**; 3701
Nu 3:51 And Moses gave the **m.** of them that 3701
Nu 18:16 for the **m.** of five shekels, after the 3701
De 2:6 Ye shall buy meat of them for **m.**, ... 3701
De 2:6 shall also buy water of them for **m.**, ... 3701
De 2:28 Thou shalt sell me meat for **m.**, ... 3701
De 2:28 give me water for **m.**, that I may 3701
De 14:25 Then shalt thou turn it into **m.**, ... 3701
De 14:25 and bind up the **m.** in thine hand, ... 3701
De 14:26 And thou shalt bestow that **m.** for 3701
De 21:14 thou shalt not sell her at all for **m.**, ... 3701
De 23:19 usury of **m.**, usury of victuals, usury 3701
Jg 5:19 Megiddo; they took no gain of **m.** 3701
Jg 16:18 her, and brought **m.** in their hand 3701
Jg 17:4 he restored the **m.** unto his mother; 3701
1Ki 21:2 will give thee the worth of it in **m.** 3701
1Ki 21:6 him, Give me thy vineyard for **m.**; 3701
1Ki 21:15 he refused to give thee for **m.**: for 3701
2Ki 5:26 Is it a time to receive **m.**, and to 3701
2Ki 12:4 All the **m.** of the dedicated things 3701
2Ki 12:4 the **m.** of every one that passeth the 3701
2Ki 12:4 the **m.** that every man is set at, and 3701
2Ki 12:4 the **m.** that cometh into any man's 3701
2Ki 12:7 no more **m.** of your acquaintance, ... 3701
2Ki 12:8 receive no more **m.** of the people, ... 3701
2Ki 12:9 the **m.** that was brought into the 3701
2Ki 12:10 there was much **m.** in the chest, ... 3701
2Ki 12:10 the **m.** that was found in the house 3701
2Ki 12:11 And they gave the **m.**, being told, ... 3701
2Ki 12:13 **m.** that was brought into the house 3701
2Ki 12:15 the **m.** to be bestowed on workmen: 3701
2Ki 12:16 The trespass **m.** and sin **m.** was not 3701
2Ki 15:20 Menahem exacted the **m.** of Israel, ... 3701
2Ki 22:7 made with them of the **m.** that 3701
2Ki 22:9 Thy servants have gathered the **m.** 3701
2Ki 23:35 but he taxed the land to give the **m.** 3701
2Ch 24:5 of all Isarel **m.** to repair the house 3701
2Ch 24:11 they saw that there was much **m.**, ... 3701
2Ch 24:11 and gathered **m.** in abundance. 3701
2Ch 24:14 brought the rest of the **m.** before 3701
2Ch 34:9 delivered the **m.** that was brought 3701
2Ch 34:14 when they brought out the **m.** that 3701
2Ch 34:17 they have gathered together the **m.** 3701
Ezr 3:7 They gave **m.** also unto the masons, ... 3701
Ezr 7:17 mayest buy speedily with this **m.** 3702
Ne 5:4 have borrowed **m.** for the king's 3701
Ne 5:10 might exact of them **m.** and corn: 3701
Ne 5:11 also the hundredth part of the **m.**, ... 3701
Es 4:7 the **m.** that Haman had promised 3701
Job 31:39 eaten the fruits thereof without **m.**, ... 3701
Job 42:11 man also give him a piece of **m.**, ... 7192
Ps 15:5 putteth not out his **m.** to usury, ... 3701
Pro 7:20 hath taken a bag of **m.** with him, ... 3701
Ec 7:12 is a defence, and **m.** is a defence: 3701
Ec 10:19 merry: but **m.** answereth all things. 3701
Isa 43:24 bought me no sweet cane with **m.**, ... 3701
Isa 52:3 ye shall be redeemed without **m.** 3701
Isa 55:1 the waters, and he that hath no **m.**; 3701
Isa 55:1 milk without **m.** and without price. 3701
Isa 55:2 do ye spend **m.** for that which is not 3701
Jer 32:9 weighed him the **m.**, even seventeen 3701
Jer 32:10 weighed him the **m.** in the balances. 3701
Jer 32:25 Buy thee the field for **m.**, and take 3701
Jer 32:44 Men shall buy fields for **m.**, and 3701
La 5:4 We have drunken our water for **m.**; 3701
Mic 3:11 the prophets thereof divine for **m.**: 3701
Mt 17:24 that received tribute **m.** came to ....
Mt 17:27 **thou shalt find a piece of m.: that** *4715*
Mt 22:19 **Shew me the tribute m.** And they *3546*
Mt 25:18 **in the earth, and hid his lord's m.** *694*
Mt 25:27 **have put my m. to the exchangers,** *694*
Mt 28:12 they gave large **m.** unto the soldiers, ... *694*
Mt 28:15 So they took the **m.**, and did as they *694*
Mk 6:8 no bread, no **m.** in their purse: *5475*
Mk 12:41 the people cast **m.** into the treasury: *5475*
Mk 14:11 glad, and promised to give him **m.** *694*
Lu 9:3 **nor scrip, neither bread, neither m.;** *694*
Lu 19:15 **to whom he had given the m., that** *694*
Lu 19:23 **not thou my m. into the bank, that** *694*
Lu 22:5 glad, and covenanted to give him **m.** *694*
Joh 2:14 and the changers of **m.** sitting: *2773*
Joh 2:15 poured out the changers' **m.**, and *2772*
Ac 4:37 land, sold it, and brought the **m.**, ... *5536*
Ac 7:16 Abraham bought for a sum of **m.** of *694*
Ac 8:18 was given, he offered them **m.**, ... *5536*
Ac 8:20 Thy **m.** perish with thee, because *694*
Ac 8:20 of God may be purchased with **m.** *5536*
Ac 24:26 hoped also that **m.** should have *5536*
1Ti 6:10 the love of **m.** is the root of all evil: *5365*

MONEYCHANGERS
Mt 21:12 and overthrew the tables of the **m.**, ... *2855*
Mk 11:15 and overthrew the tables of the **m.**, ... *2855*

MONSTERS
La 4:3 the sea **m.** draw out the breast, ... 8577

MONTH See also MONTHS.
Ge 7:11 **m.**, the seventeenth day of the **m.**, ... 2320
Ge 8:4 the ark rested in the seventh **m.**, ... 2320
Ge 8:4 the seventeenth day of the **m.**, upon 2320
Ge 8:5 continually until the tenth **m.**: 2320
Ge 8:5 in the tenth **m.**, on the first day of the ....
Ge 8:5 on the first day of the **m.**, were the 2320
Ge 8:13 first year, in the first **m.**, the first ....
Ge 8:13 the first day of the **m.**, the waters 2320
Ge 8:14 And in the second **m.**, on the seven 2320
Ge 8:14 seven and twentieth day of the **m.**, ... 2320
Ge 29:14 abode with him the space of a **m.** 2320
Ex 12:2 This **m.** shall be unto you the 2320
Ex 12:2 be the first **m.** of the year to you. 2320
Ex 12:3 the tenth day of this **m.** they shall 2320
Ex 12:6 the fourteenth day of the same **m.**: 2320
Ex 12:18 In the first **m.**, on the fourteenth day ....
Ex 12:18 fourteenth day of the **m.** at even, ... 2320
Ex 12:18 on and twentieth day of the **m.** at 2320
Ex 13:4 This day came ye out in the **m.** Abib. 2320
Ex 13:5 shalt keep this service in this **m.** 2320
Ex 16:1 on the fifteenth day of the second **m.** 2320
Ex 19:1 In the third **m.**, when the children 2320
Ex 23:15 the time appointed of the **m.** Abib; 2320
Ex 34:18 thee, in the time of the **m.** Abib: 2320
Ex 34:18 the **m.** Abib thou camest out from 2320
Ex 40:2 first day of the first **m.** shalt thou 2320
Ex 40:17 in the first **m.** in the second year, ... 2320
Ex 40:17 on the first day of the **m.**, that the 2320
Le 16:29 seventh **m.**, on...tenth day of the **m.**, ... 2320
Le 23:5 the fourteenth day of the first **m.** at 2320
Le 23:6 on the fifteenth day of the same **m.** 2320
Le 23:24 seventh **m.**, in...first day of the **m.**, ... 2320
Le 23:27 tenth day of this seventh **m.** there 2320
Le 23:32 in the ninth day of the **m.** at even, ... 2320
Le 23:34 The fifteenth day of this seventh **m.** 2320
Le 23:39 the fifteenth day of the seventh **m.**, ... 2320
Le 23:41 shall celebrate it in the seventh **m.** 2320
Le 25:9 on the tenth day of the seventh **m.**, ... 2320
Le 27:6 from a **m.** old even unto five years. 2320

Nu 1:1, 18 on the first day of the second **m.**,.... 2320
Nu 3:15 every male from a **m.** old and.... 2320
Nu 3:22, 28,34,39 from a **m.** old and upward.... 2320
Nu 3:40 children of Israel from a **m.** old and.... 2320
Nu 3:43 names, from a **m.** old and upward,.... 2320
Nu 9:1 in the first **m.** of the second year.... 2320
Nu 9:3 In the fourteenth day of this **m.**, at.... 2320
Nu 9:5 on the fourteenth day of the first **m.**.... 2320
Nu 9:11 The fourteenth day of the second **m.**.... 2320
Nu 9:22 or a **m.**, or a year, that the cloud.... 2320
Nu 10:11 the twentieth day of the second **m.**,.... 2320
Nu 11:20 even a whole **m.**, until it come out.... 2320
Nu 11:21 flesh, that they may eat a whole **m.**.... 2320
Nu 18:16 from a **m.** old shalt thou redeem,.... 2320
Nu 20:1 the desert of Zin in the first **m.**:.... 2320
Nu 26:62 males from a **m.** old and upward:.... 2320
Nu 28:14 is the burnt offering of every **m.**.... 2320
Nu 28:16 the fourteenth day of the first **m.**.... 2320
Nu 28:17 in the fifteenth day of this **m.** is the.... 2320
Nu 29:1 And in the seventh **m.**, on the first.... 2320
Nu 29:1 first day of the **m.**, ye shall have an.... 2320
Nu 29:6 Beside the burnt offering of the **m.**,.... 2320
Nu 29:7 on the tenth day of this seventh **m.**.... 2320
Nu 29:12 the fifteenth day of the seventh **m.**.... 2320
Nu 33:3 from Rameses in the first **m.**,.... 2320
Nu 33:3 on the fifteenth day of the first **m.**;.... 2320
Nu 33:38 in the first day of the fifth **m.**.... 2320
De 1:3 eleventh **m.**, on...first day of the **m.**,.... 2320
De 16:1 Observe the **m.** of Abib, and keep.... 2320
De 16:1 for in the **m.** of Abib the Lord thy.... 2320
De 21:13 her father and her mother a full **m.**:.... 3391
Jos 4:19 on the tenth day of the first **m.**,.... 2320
Jos 5:10 on the fourteenth day of the **m.** at.... 2320
1Sa 20:27 was the second day of the **m.**, that.... 2320
1Sa 20:34 no meat the second day of the **m.**:.... 2320
1Ki 4:7 each man his **m.** in a year made.... 2320
1Ki 4:27 table, every man in his **m.**: they.... 2320
1Ki 5:14 ten thousand a **m.** by courses:.... 2320
1Ki 5:14 a **m.** they were in Lebanon, and two.... 2320
1Ki 6:1 the **m.** Zif, which is the second **m.**,.... 2320
1Ki 6:37 of the Lord laid, in the **m.** Zif:.... 3391
1Ki 6:38 in the eleventh year, in the **m.** Bul,.... 3391
1Ki 6:38 Bul, which is the eighth **m.**,.... 2320
1Ki 8:2 at the feast of the **m.** Ethanim,.... 3391
1Ki 8:2 Ethanim, which is the seventh **m.**.... 2320
1Ki 12:32 ordained a feast in the eighth **m.**,.... 2320
1Ki 12:32 on the fifteenth day of the eighth **m.**,.... 2320
1Ki 12:33 the fifteenth day of the eighth **m.**,.... 2320
1Ki 12:33 even in the **m.** which he had devised.... 2320
2Ki 15:13 he reigned a full **m.** in Samaria..... 3391
2Ki 25:1 tenth **m.**, in...tenth day of the **m.**,.... 2320
2Ki 25:3 on the ninth day of the fourth **m.**.... 2320
2Ki 25:8 fifth **m.**, on...seventh day of the **m.**,.... 2320
2Ki 25:25 it came to pass in the seventh **m.**,.... 2320
2Ki 25:27 king of Judah, in the twelfth **m.**,.... 2320
2Ki 25:27 seven and twentieth day of the **m.**,.... 2320
1Ch 12:15 went over Jordan in the first **m.**,.... 2320
1Ch 27:1 came in and went out **m.** by **m.**.... 2320
1Ch 27:2 for the first **m.** was Jashobeam the.... 2320
1Ch 27:3 captains of the host for the first **m.**.... 2320
1Ch 27:4 course of the second **m.** was Dodai.... 2320
1Ch 27:5 host for the third **m.** was Benaiah.... 2320
1Ch 27:7 for the fourth **m.** was Asahel the.... 2320
1Ch 27:8 for the fifth **m.** was Shamhuth the.... 2320
1Ch 27:9 captain for the sixth **m.** was Ira the.... 2320
1Ch 27:10 for the seventh **m.** was Helez the.... 2320
1Ch 27:11 for the eighth **m.** was Sibbecai the.... 2320
1Ch 27:12 captain for the ninth **m.** was Abiezer.... 2320
1Ch 27:13 for the tenth **m.** was Maharai the.... 2320
1Ch 27:14 for the eleventh **m.** was Benaiah.... 2320
1Ch 27:15 for the twelfth **m.** was Heldai the.... 2320
2Ch 3:2 in the second day of the second **m.**,.... 2320
2Ch 5:3 feast which was in the seventh **m.**.... 2320
2Ch 7:10 and twentieth day of the seventh **m.**.... 2320
2Ch 15:10 at Jerusalem in the third **m.**, in.... 2320
2Ch 29:3 year of his reign, in the first **m.**,.... 2320
2Ch 29:17 first day of the first **m.** to sanctify,.... 2320
2Ch 29:17 on the eighth day of the **m.** came.... 2320
2Ch 29:17 sixteenth day of the first **m.** they.... 2320
2Ch 30:2 keep the passover in the second **m.**.... 2320
2Ch 30:13 unleavened bread in the second **m.**,.... 2320
2Ch 30:15 fourteenth day of the second **m.**:.... 2320
2Ch 31:7 the third **m.** they began to lay the.... 2320
2Ch 31:7 finished them in the seventh **m.**.... 2320
2Ch 35:1 the fourteenth day of the first **m.**.... 2320
Ezr 3:1 when the seventh **m.** was come, and.... 2320
Ezr 3:6 first day of the seventh **m.** began.... 2320
Ezr 3:8 second **m.**, began Zerubbabel the.... 2320
Ezr 6:15 on the third day of the **m.** Adar,.... 3393
Ezr 6:19 the fourteenth day of the first **m.**.... 2320
Ezr 7:8 came to Jerusalem in the fifth **m.**,.... 2320
Ezr 7:9 first day of the first **m.** began he to.... 2320
Ezr 7:9 first day of the fifth **m.** came he to.... 2320
Ezr 8:31 on the twelfth day of the first **m.**,.... 2320
Ezr 10:9 the ninth **m.**, on the twentieth day.... 2320
Ezr 10:9 twentieth day of the **m.**; and all the.... 2320
Ezr 10:16 down in the first day of the tenth **m.**.... 2320
Ezr 10:17 wives by the first day of the first **m.**.... 2320
Ne 1:1 it came to pass in the **m.** Chisleu, in.... 2320
Ne 2:1 it came to pass in the **m.** Nisan, in.... 2320
Ne 6:15 twenty and fifth day of the **m.** Elul,....
Ne 7:73 and when the seventh **m.** came, the.... 2320
Ne 8:2 upon the first day of the seventh **m.**.... 2320
Ne 8:14 in the feast of the seventh **m.**:.... 2320
Ne 9:1 twenty and fourth day of this **m.**.... 2320
Es 2:16 tenth **m.**, which is the **m.** Tebeth,.... 2320
Es 3:7 the first **m.**, that is, the **m.** Nisan,.... 2320
Es 3:7 from day to day, and from **m.** to **m.**,.... 2320
Es 3:7 to the twelfth **m.**, that is,...Adar.....
Es 3:7 the twelfth...that is, the **m.** Adar..... 2320
Es 3:12 the thirteenth day of the first **m.**,.... 2320
Es 3:13 twelfth **m.**, which is the **m.** Adar,.... 2320
Es 8:9 the third **m.**, that is, the **m.** Sivan,.... 2320
Es 8:12 twelfth **m.**, which is the **m.** Adar..... 2320
Es 9:1 the twelfth **m.**, that is, the **m.** Adar,.... 2320
Es 9:15 fourteenth day also of the **m.** Adar,.... 2320
Es 9:17 the thirteenth day of the **m.** Adar;.... 2320
Es 9:19 fourteenth day of the **m.** Adar a day.... 2320
Es 9:21 the fourteenth day of the **m.** Adar,.... 2320
Es 9:22 the **m.** which was turned unto them.... 2320
Jer 1:3 Jerusalem captive in the fifth **m.**.... 2320
Jer 2:24 in her **m.** they shall find her.... 2320
Jer 28:1 the fourth year, and in the fifth **m.**,.... 2320
Jer 28:17 the same year in the seventh **m.**.... 2320
Jer 36:9 the ninth **m.**, that they proclaimed a.... 2320
Jer 36:22 in the winterhouse in the ninth **m.**:.... 2320
Jer 39:1 the tenth **m.**, came Nebuchadrezzar.... 2320
Jer 39:2 fourth **m.**, the ninth day of the **m.**,.... 2320
Jer 41:1 it came to pass in the seventh **m.**,.... 2320
Jer 52:4 tenth **m.**, in the tenth day of the **m.**,.... 2320
Jer 52:6 fourth **m.**,...the ninth day of the **m.**,.... 2320
Jer 52:12 fifth **m.**, in the tenth day of the **m.**,.... 2320
Jer 52:31 in the twelfth **m.**, in the five and.... 2320
Jer 52:31 five and twentieth day of the **m.**,.... 2320
Eze 1:1 in the thirtieth year, the fourth **m.**,....
Eze 1:1 in the fifth day of the **m.**, as I was.... 2320
Eze 1:2 In the fifth day of the **m.**, which.... 2320
Eze 8:1 in the sixth year, in the sixth **m.**,....
Eze 8:1 in the fifth day of the **m.**, as I sat.... 2320
Eze 20:1 in the seventh year, in the fifth **m.**,....
Eze 20:1 tenth day of the **m.**, that certain.... 2320
Eze 24:1 in the ninth year, in the tenth **m.**,.... 2320
Eze 24:1 in the tenth day of the **m.**, the word.... 2320
Eze 26:1 eleventh year,...first day of the **m.**,.... 2320
Eze 29:1 In the tenth year, in the tenth **m.**,....
Eze 29:1 in the twelfth day of the **m.**, the.... 2320
Eze 29:17 and twentieth year, in the first **m.**,....
Eze 29:17 in the first day of the **m.**, the word.... 2320
Eze 30:20 in the eleventh year, in the first **m.**,.... 2320
Eze 30:20 in the seventh day of the **m.**, that.... 2320
Eze 31:1 the eleventh year, in the third **m.**,....
Eze 31:1 in the first day of the **m.**, that the.... 2320
Eze 32:1 the twelfth year, in the twelfth **m.**,.... 2320
Eze 32:1 in the first day of the **m.**, that the.... 2320
Eze 32:17 year, in the fifteenth day of the **m.**,.... 2320
Eze 33:21 of our captivity, in the tenth **m.**,....
Eze 33:21 in the fifth day of the **m.**, that one.... 2320
Eze 40:1 the year, in the tenth day of the **m.**,.... 2320
Eze 45:18 saith the Lord God; in the first **m.**,....
Eze 45:18 in the first day of the **m.**, thou shalt.... 2320
Eze 45:20 shalt do the seventh day of the **m.**.... 2320
Eze 45:21 In the first **m.**, in the fourteenth....
Eze 45:21 in the fourteenth day of the **m.**, ye.... 2320
Eze 45:25 In the seventh **m.**, in the fifteenth....
Eze 45:25 in the fifteenth day of the **m.**, shall.... 2320
Da 10:4 and twentieth day of the first **m.**,.... 2320
Ho 5:7 now shall a **m.** devour them with.... 2320
Joe 2:23 and the latter rain in the first **m.**....
Hag 1:1 sixth **m.**, in the first day of the **m.**,.... 2320
Hag 1:15 and twentieth day of the sixth **m.**,.... 2320
Hag 2:1 In the seventh **m.**, in the one and....
Hag 2:1 twentieth day of the **m.**, came the.... 2320
Hag 2:10, 18 and twentieth day of the ninth **m.**,....
Hag 2:20 four and twentieth day of the **m.**,.... 2320
Zec 1:1 In the eighth **m.**, in the second year.... 2320
Zec 1:7 twentieth day the eleventh **m.**,.... 2320
Zec 1:7 which is the **m.** Sebat, in the second.... 2320
Zec 7:1 in the fourth day of the ninth **m.**,.... 2320
Zec 7:3 Should I weep in the fifth **m.**,.... 2320
Zec 7:5 in the fifth and seventh **m.**, even....
Zec 8:19 The fast of the fourth **m.**, and the fast....
Zec 11:8 shepherds also I cut off in one **m.**;.... 3391
Lu 1:26 in the sixth **m.** the angel Gabriel.... *3376*
Lu 1:36 this is the sixth **m.** with her, who.... *3376*
Re 9:15 and a day, and a **m.**, and a year, for.... *3376*
Re 22:2 and yielded her fruit every **m.**:.... *3376*

MONTHLY

Isa 47:13 the **m.** prognosticators, stand up,.... 2320

MONTHS

Ge 38:24 came to pass about three **m.** after,.... 2320
Ex 2:2 child, she hid him three **m.**.... 3391
Ex 12:2 be unto you the beginning of **m.**:.... 2320
Nu 10:10 the beginnings of your **m.**, ye shall.... 2320
Nu 28:11 the beginnings of your **m.** ye shall.... 2320
Nu 28:14 throughout the **m.** of the year..... 2320
Jg 11:37 let me alone two **m.**, that I may go.... 2320
Jg 11:38 And he sent her away for two **m.**:.... 2320
Jg 11:39 it came to pass at the end of two **m.**,.... 2320
Jg 19:2 and was there four whole **m.**.... 2320
Jg 20:47 abode in the rock Rimmon four **m.**.... 2320
1Sa 6:1 country of the Philistines seven **m.**.... 2320
1Sa 27:7 was a full year and four **m.**.... 2320
2Sa 2:11 Judah was seven years and six **m.**.... 2320
2Sa 5:5 Judah seven years and six **m.**.... 2320
2Sa 6:11 of Obed-edom the Gittite three **m.**:.... 2320
2Sa 24:8 to Jerusalem at the end of nine **m.**.... 2320
2Sa 24:13 flee three **m.** before thine enemies,.... 2320
1Ki 5:14 in Lebanon, and two **m.** at home:.... 2320
1Ki 11:16 (For six **m.** did Joab remain there.... 2320
2Ki 15:8 reign over Israel in Samaria six **m.**:.... 2320
2Ki 23:31 he reigned three **m.** in Jerusalem..... 2320
2Ki 24:8 he reigned in Jerusalem three **m.**.... 2320
1Ch 3:4 he reigned seven years and six **m.**:.... 2320
1Ch 13:14 Obed-edom in his house three **m.**.... 2320
1Ch 21:12 three **m.** to be destroyed before thy.... 2320
1Ch 27:1 throughout all the **m.** of the year,.... 2320
2Ch 36:2 he reigned three **m.** in Jerusalem..... 2320
2Ch 36:9 he reigned three **m.** and ten days.... 2320
Es 2:12 after that she had been twelve **m.**,.... 2320
Es 2:12 to wit, six **m.** with oil of myrrh, and.... 2320
Es 2:12 six **m.** with sweet odours, and with.... 2320
Job 3:6 come into the number of the **m.**.... 3391
Job 7:3 am I made to possess **m.** of vanity,.... 3391
Job 14:5 number of his **m.** are with thee,.... 2320
Job 21:21 the number of his **m.** is cut off in.... 2320
Job 29:2 Oh that I were as in **m.** past, as in.... 3391
Job 39:2 Canst thou number the **m.** that they.... 3391
Eze 39:12 seven **m.** shall the house of Israel.... 2320
Eze 39:14 after the end of seven **m.** shall they.... 2320
Eze 47:12 forth new fruit according to his **m.**,.... 2320
Da 4:29 At the end of twelve **m.** he walked.... 3393
Am 4:7 were yet three **m.** to the harvest:.... 2320
Lu 1:24 conceived, and hid herself five **m.**,.... *3376*
Lu 1:56 abode with her about three **m.**,.... *3376*
Lu 4:25 **shut up three years and six m.**,.... *3376*
Joh 4:35 **Say not ye, There are yet four m.**,.... *5072*
Ac 7:20 up in his father's house three **m.**:.... *3376*
Ac 18:11 he continued a year and six **m.**,.... *3376*
Ac 19:8 boldly for the space of three **m.**,.... *3376*
Ac 20:3 there abode three **m.** And when.... *3376*
Ac 28:11 after three **m.** we departed in a ship.... *3376*
Ga 4:10 Ye observe days, and **m.**, and times,.... *3376*
Heb 11:23 was hid three **m.** of his parents,.... *5150*
Jas 5:17 space of three years and six **m.**.... *3376*
Re 9:5 they should be tormented five **m.**:.... *3376*
Re 9:10 power was to hurt men five **m.**.... *3376*
Re 11:2 tread under foot forty and two **m.**.... *3376*
Re 13:5 him to continue forty and two **m.**.... *3376*

MONUMENTS

Isa 65:4 the graves, and lodge in the **m.**,.... 5341

MOON See also MOONS.

Ge 37:9 sun...the **m.** and the eleven stars.... 3394
De 4:19 the sun, and the **m.**, and the stars,.... 3394
De 17:3 either the sun, or **m.**, or any of the.... 3394
De 33:14 things put forth by the **m.**,.... 3391
Jos 10:12 thou, **M.**, in the valley of Ajalon..... 3394
Jos 10:13 sun stood still, and the **m.** stayed,.... 3394
1Sa 20:5 Behold, tomorrow is the new **m.**,.... 2320
1Sa 20:18 Tomorrow is the new **m.**: and thou.... 2320

1Sa 20:24 and when the new **m.** was come, ... 2320
2Ki 4:23 it is neither new **m.**, nor sabbath. ... 2320
2Ki 23:5 to the sun, and to the **m.**, and to ... 3394
Job 25:5 even to the **m.**, and it shineth not; ... 3394
Job 31:26 or the **m.** walking in brightness; ... 3394
Ps 8:3 **m.** and the stars, which thou hast ... 3394
Ps 72:5 as long as the sun and **m.** endure, ... 3394
Ps 72:7 of peace so long as the **m.** endureth. .. 3394
Ps 81:3 Blow up the trumpet in the new **m.**, ... 2320
Ps 89:37 be established for ever as the **m.**, ... 3394
Ps 104:19 He appointed the **m.** for seasons: ... 3394
Ps 121:6 thee by day, nor the **m.** by night. ... 3394
Ps 136:9 The **m.** and stars to rule by night: ... 3394
Ps 148:3 Praise ye him, sun and **m.**: praise ... 3394
Ec 12:2 **m.**, or the stars, be not darkened, ... 3394
Ca 6:10 fair is the **m.**, clear as the sun, ... 3842
Isa 3:18 and their round tires like the **m.**, ...
Isa 13:10 the **m.** shall not cause her light to ... 3394
Isa 24:23 Then the **m.** shall be confounded, ... 3842
Isa 30:26 light of the **m.** shall be as the light ... 3842
Isa 60:19 shall the **m.** give light unto thee: ... 3394
Isa 60:20 neither shall thy **m.** withdraw ... 3391
Isa 66:23 that from one new **m.** to another, ... 2320
Jer 8:2 before the sun, and the **m.**, and all ... 3394
Jer 31:35 ordinances of the **m.** and of the stars.. 3394
Eze 32:7 and the **m.** shall not give her light. ... 3394
Eze 46:1, 6 in the day of the new **m.** it shall ... 2320
Joe 2:10 the sun and the **m.** shall be dark, ... 3394
Joe 2:31 darkness, and the **m.** into blood, ... 3394
Joe 3:15 sun and the **m.** shall be darkened, ... 3394
Am 8:5 When will the new **m.** be gone, ... 2320
Hab 3:11 The sun and **m.** stood still in their ... 3394
Mt 24:29 **and the m. shall not give her light,** *4582*
Mk 13:24 **and the m. shall not give her light,** *4582*
Lu 21:25 **be signs in the sun, and in the m.,** *4582*
Ac 2:20 darkness, and the **m.** into blood, ... *4582*
1Co 15:41 sun, and another glory of the **m.**, ... *4582*
Col 2:16 or of the new **m.**, or of the sabbath ... *3561*
Re 6:12 hair, and the **m.** became as blood; ... *4582*
Re 8:12 and the third part of the **m.**, and the .. *4582*
Re 12:1 the sun, and the **m.** under her feet, ... *4582*
Re 21:23 need of the sun, neither of the **m.**, ... *4582*

MOONS
1Ch 23:31 the new **m.**, and on the set feasts, ... 2320
2Ch 2:4 on the new **m.**, and on the solemn ... 2320
2Ch 8:13 on the new **m.**, and on the solemn ... 2320
2Ch 31:3 the new **m.**, and for the set feasts, ... 2320
Ezr 3:5 both of the new **m.**, and all the set ... 2320
Ne 10:33 of the sabbaths, of the new **m.**, for ... 2320
Isa 1:13 the new **m.** and sabbaths, the ... 2320
Isa 1:14 new **m.** and your appointed feasts ... 2320
Eze 45:17 in the feasts, and in the new **m.**, ... 2320
Eze 46:3 in the sabbaths and in the new **m.**: ... 2320
Ho 2:11 her feast days, her new **m.**, and her ... 2320

MORASTHITE (mor'-ras-thite)
Jer 26:18 Micah the **M.** prophesied in the ... 4183
Mic 1:1 Lord that came to Micah the **M.** ... 4183

MORDECAI (mor'-de-cahee) See also MORDECAI'S.
Ezr 2:2 Nehemiah, Seraiah, Reelaiah, **M.**, ... 4782
Ne 7:7 Nahamani, **M.**, Bilshan, Mispereth, ... 4782
Es 2:5 a certain Jew, whose name was **M.**, ... 4782
Es 2:7 whom **M.**,...took for his own ... 4782
Es 2:10 **M.** had charged her that she should ... 4782
Es 2:11 **M.** walked every day before the ... 4782
Es 2:15 daughter of Abihail the uncle of **M.**, ... 4782
Es 2:19 then **M.** sat in the king's gate ... 4782
Es 2:20 her people; as **M.** had charged her: ... 4782
Es 2:20 Esther did the commandment of **M.**, ... 4782
Es 2:21 while **M.** sat in the king's gate, ... 4782
Es 2:22 And the thing was known to **M.**, ... 4782
Es 3:2 But **M.** bowed not, nor did him ... 4782
Es 3:3 said unto **M.**, Why transgresseth ... 4782
Es 3:5 Haman saw that **M.** bowed not, ... 4782
Es 3:6 scorn to lay hands on **M.** alone; ... 4782
Es 3:6 had shewed him the people of **M.**: ... 4782
Es 3:6 Ahasuerus, even the people of **M.** ... 4782
Es 4:1 **M.** perceived all that was done, ... 4782
Es 4:1 **M.** rent his clothes, and put on ... 4782
Es 4:4 and she sent raiment to clothe **M.**, ... 4782
Es 4:5 gave him a commandment to **M.**, ... 4782
Es 4:6 Hatach went forth to **M.** unto the ... 4782
Es 4:7 **M.** told him of all that had happened ... 4782
Es 4:9 and told Esther the words of **M.** ... 4782
Es 4:10 gave him commandment unto **M.**; ... 4782
Es 4:12 And they told to **M.** Esther's words ... 4782
Es 4:13 **M.** commanded to answer Esther, ... 4782
Es 4:15 bade them return **M.** this answer, ... 4782
Es 4:17 **M.** went his way, and did according ... 4782
Es 5:9 Haman saw **M.** in the king's gate ... 4782
Es 5:9 was full of indignation against **M.** ... 4782
Es 5:13 so long as I see **M.** the Jew sitting ... 4782
Es 5:14 that **M.** may be hanged thereon: ... 4782
Es 6:2 that **M.** had told of Bigthana and ... 4782
Es 6:3 and dignity hath been done to **M.** ... 4782
Es 6:4 the king to hang **M.** on the gallows ... 4782
Es 6:10 and do even so to **M.** the Jew, that ... 4782
Es 6:11 arrayed **M.**, and brought him on ... 4782
Es 6:12 **M.** came again to the king's gate. ... 4782
Es 6:13 If **M.** be of the seed of the Jews, ... 4782
Es 7:9 which Haman had made for **M.**, ... 4782
Es 7:10 that he had prepared for **M.** Then ... 4782
Es 8:1 And **M.** came before the king; for ... 4782
Es 8:2 from Haman, and gave it unto **M.** ... 4782
Es 8:2 Esther set **M.** over the house of ... 4782
Es 8:7 unto Esther...and to **M.** the Jew, ... 4782
Es 8:9 that **M.** commanded unto the Jews, ... 4782
Es 8:15 **M.** went out from the presence of ... 4782
Es 9:3 the fear of **M.** fell upon them. ... 4782
Es 9:4 **M.** was great in the king's house, ... 4782
Es 9:4 man **M.** waxed greater and greater ... 4782
Es 9:20 **M.** wrote these things, and sent ... 4782
Es 9:23 and as **M.** had written unto them; ... 4782
Es 9:29 and **M.** the Jew, wrote with all ... 4782
Es 9:31 **M.** the Jew and Esther the queen ... 4782
Es 10:2 declaration of the greatness of **M.**, ... 4782
Es 10:3 For **M.** the Jew was next unto king ... 4782

MORDECAI'S (mor'-de-cahees)
Es 2:22 the king thereof in **M.** name. ... 4782
Es 3:4 whether **M.** matters would stand: ... 4782

MORE See also EVERMORE; FURTHERMORE; MOREOVER.
Ge 3:1 Now the serpent was **m.** subtil than ...
Ge 8:12 returned not...unto him any **m.** ... 5750
Ge 8:21 curse the ground any **m.** for man's ... 5750
Ge 8:21 smite any **m.** everything living, as ... 5750
Ge 9:11 shall all flesh be cut off any **m.** by ... 5750
Ge 9:11 shall there any **m.** be a flood to ... 5750
Ge 9:15 waters shall no **m.** become a flood. ... 5750
Ge 17:5 thy name any **m.** be called Abram, ... 5750
Ge 29:30 he loved also Rachel **m.** than Leah, ...
Ge 32:28 name shall be called no **m.** Jacob, ... 5750
Ge 34:19 **m.** honourable than all the house ... 3513
Ge 35:10 shall not be called any **m.** Jacob, ... 5750
Ge 36:7 For their riches were **m.** than that ... 7227
Ge 37:3 loved Joseph **m.** than all his children, ...
Ge 37:4 loved him **m.** than all his brethren, ...
Ge 37:5 and they hated him yet the **m.** ... 3254
Ge 37:8 they hated him yet the **m.** for his ... 3254
Ge 37:9 I have dreamed a dream **m.**; and, ... 5750
Ge 38:26 She hath been **m.** righteous than I; ...
Ge 38:26 And he knew her again no **m.** ... 5750
Ge 44:23 you, ye shall see my face no **m.** ... 3254
Ex 1:9 of Israel are **m.** and mightier than ... 7227
Ex 1:12 But the **m.** they afflicted them, ... 3651
Ex 1:12 the **m.** they multiplied and grew ... 3651
Ex 5:7 shall no **m.** give the people straw ... 3254
Ex 5:9 there **m.** work be laid upon the men, ...
Ex 8:29 Pharaoh deal deceitfully any **m.** ... 3254
Ex 9:28 be no **m.** mighty thunderings and ...
Ex 9:29 neither shall there be any **m.** hail; ... 5750
Ex 9:34 he sinned yet **m.**, and hardened ... 3254
Ex 10:28 heed to thyself, see my face no **m.**; ... 3254
Ex 10:29 I will see thy face again no **m.** ... 5750
Ex 11:1 I bring one plague **m.** upon Pharaoh, ...
Ex 11:6 like it, nor shall be like it any **m.** ... 3254
Ex 14:13 see them again no **m.** for ever. ... 5750
Ex 16:17 and gathered, some **m.**, some less, ... 7227
Ex 30:15 The rich shall not give **m.**, and ... 7235
Ex 36:5 people bring much **m.** than enough ... 7235
Ex 36:6 man nor woman make any **m.** work ... 5750
Le 6:5 and shall add the fifth part **m.** ... 3254
Le 11:42 hath **m.** feet among all creeping ... 7235
Le 13:5 shall shut him up seven days **m.**: ... 8145
Le 13:33 that hath the scall seven days **m.**: ... 8145
Le 13:54 he shall shut it up seven days **m.**: ... 8145
Le 17:7 shall no **m.** offer their sacrifices ... 5750
Le 26:18 will punish you seven times **m.** for ... 3254
Le 26:21 bring seven times **m.** plagues upon ... 3254
Le 27:20 it shall not be redeemed any **m.** ... 5750
Nu 3:46 which are **m.** than the Levites; ... 5736
Nu 8:25 thereof, and shall serve no **m.**: ... 5750
Nu 18:5 no wrath any **m.** upon the children ... 5750
Nu 22:15 Balak sent yet again princes, **m.**, ... 7227
Nu 22:15 princes...**m.** honourable than they. ...
Nu 22:18 the Lord my God, to do less or **m.** ... 1490
Nu 22:19 the Lord will say unto me **m.** ... 3254
Nu 26:54 thou shalt give the **m.** inheritance, ... 7235
Nu 33:54 and to the **m.** ye shall give the ... 7227
Nu 33:54 ye shall give the **m.** inheritance, ... 7235
De 1:11 thousand times so many **m.** as ye ... 3254
De 3:26 speak no **m.** unto me unto me of this.. 5750
De 5:22 great voice: and he added no **m.** ... 3254
De 5:25 voice of the Lord our God any **m.**, ... 3254
De 7:7 ye were **m.** in number than any ... 7230
De 7:17 These nations are **m.** than I; how ... 7227
De 10:16 heart, and be no **m.** stiffnecked. ... 5750
De 13:11 do no **m.** any such wickedness as ... 3254
De 17:13 and do no **m.** presumptuously. ... 5750
De 17:16 henceforth return no **m.** that way. ... 5750
De 18:16 let me see this great fire any **m.**, ... 5750
De 19:9 thou add three cities **m.** for thee, ... 5750
De 19:20 commit no **m.** any such evil among ... 5750
De 20:1 and a people **m.** than thou, be not ... 7227
De 28:68 Thou shalt see it no **m.** again: ... 5750
De 31:2 I can no **m.** go out and come in: ... 5750
De 31:27 and how much **m.** after my death? ...
Jos 2:11 neither did there remain any **m.** ... 5750
Jos 5:1 was there spirit in them any **m.**, ... 5750
Jos 5:12 children of Israel manna any **m.**; ... 5750
Jos 7:12 neither will I be with you any **m.**, ... 3254
Jos 10:11 they were **m.** which died with ... 7227
Jos 23:13 will no **m.** drive out any of these ... 3254
Jg 2:19 themselves **m.** than their fathers, ...
Jg 8:28 they lifted up their heads no **m.** ... 3254
Jg 10:13 wherefore I will deliver you no **m.** ... 3254
Jg 13:21 angel of the Lord did no **m.** appear ... 3254
Jg 15:3 shall I be **m.** blameless than the ...
Jg 16:30 which he slew at his death were **m.** ... 7227
Jg 18:24 gone away: and what have I **m.**? ... 5750
Ru 1:11 are there yet any **m.** sons in my womb, ...
Ru 1:17 the Lord do so to me, and **m.** also, ... 3254
Ru 3:10 thou hast shewed **m.** kindness in the ...
1Sa 1:18 her countenance was no **m.** sad. ... 5750
1Sa 2:3 Talk no **m.** so exceeding proudly; ... 7235
1Sa 3:17 God do so to thee, and **m.** also, ... 3254
1Sa 7:13 came no **m.** into the coast of ... 3254,5750
1Sa 14:30 How much **m.**, if haply the people ... 637
1Sa 14:44 answered, God do so and **m.** also: ... 3254
1Sa 15:35 And Samuel came no **m.** to see Saul ... 3254
1Sa 18:2 go no **m.** home to his father's house. ...
1Sa 18:8 can he have **m.** but the kingdom? ... 5750
1Sa 18:29 was yet the **m.** afraid of David; ... 3254
1Sa 18:30 that David behaved himself **m.** wisely ...
1Sa 20:13 do so and much **m.** to Jonathan: ... 3254
1Sa 22:15 knew nothing of all this, less or **m.** ... 1490
1Sa 23:3 much **m.** then if we come to Keilah ...
1Sa 24:17 Thou art **m.** righteous than I: for thou ...
1Sa 25:22 **m.** also do God unto the enemies ... 3254
1Sa 25:36 she told him nothing, less or **m.**, ... 1490
1Sa 26:21 for I will no **m.** do thee harm, ... 5750
1Sa 27:1 to seek me any **m.** in any coast of ... 5750
1Sa 27:4 he sought no **m.** again for him. ... 3254
1Sa 28:15 and answereth me no **m.**, neither by ...
1Sa 30:4 until they had no **m.** power to weep. ...
2Sa 2:28 and pursed after Israel no **m.**, ... 5750
2Sa 2:28 neither fought they any **m.**, ... 3243,5750
2Sa 3:9 So do God to Abner, and **m.** also, ... 3254
2Sa 3:35 So do God to me, and **m.** also, if I ... 3254
2Sa 4:11 How much **m.**, when wicked men ...
2Sa 5:13 David took him **m.** concubines ... 5750
2Sa 6:22 And I will yet be **m.** vile than thus, ...
2Sa 7:10 place of their own, and move no **m.**; ... 5750
2Sa 7:10 of wickedness afflict them any **m.**, ... 3254
2Sa 7:20 what can David say **m.** unto thee? ... 5750
2Sa 10:19 help the children of Ammon any **m.** ... 5750
2Sa 11:25 thy battle **m.** strong against the city, ...
2Sa 14:10 shall not touch thee any **m.** ... 3254,5750
2Sa 14:11 revengers of blood to destroy...**m.**, ... 7235
2Sa 16:11 much **m.** now may this Benjamite do it? ...
2Sa 18:8 and the wood devoured **m.** people ... 7235
2Sa 19:13 God do so to me, and **m.** also, if ... 3254
2Sa 19:28 I yet to cry any **m.** unto the king? ... 5750
2Sa 19:29 Why speakest thou any **m.** of thy ... 5750
2Sa 19:35 I hear any **m.** the voice of singing ... 5750
2Sa 19:43 have also **m.** right in David than ye: ...
2Sa 20:6 do us **m.** harm than did Absalom: ...
2Sa 21:17 Thou shalt go no **m.** out with us ... 5750
2Sa 23:23 He was **m.** honourable than the thirty, ...
1Ki 2:23 God do so to me, and **m.** also, if ... 3254

Book	Ref	Context	Strong's
1Ki	2:32	who fell upon two men **m.** righteous	
1Ki	10:5	there was no **m.** spirit in her	5750
1Ki	10:10	no **m.** such abundance of spices	5750
1Ki	16:33	Ahab did **m.** to provoke the Lord	3254
1Ki	19:2	let the gods do to me, and also,	3254
1Ki	20:10	gods do so unto me, and **m.** also, if	3254
2Ki	2:12	And he saw him no **m.**: and he	5750
2Ki	2:21	thence any **m.** death or barren land.	5750
2Ki	4:6	unto her, There is not a vessel **m.**.	5750
2Ki	6:16	they that be with us are **m.** than	7227
2Ki	6:23	came no **m.** into the...of Israel.	3254,5750
2Ki	6:31	God do so and **m.** also to me, if the	3254
2Ki	9:35	they found no **m.** of her than the	3588,518
2Ki	12:7	now therefore receive no **m.** money of	5750
2Ki	12:8	consented to receive no **m.** money of	5750
2Ki	21:8	make the feet of Israel move any **m.**	3254
2Ki	21:9	seduced them to do **m.** evil than did	
2Ki	24:7	Egypt came not again any **m.** out	5750
1Ch	4:9	And Jabez was **m.** honourable than	
1Ch	11:21	he was **m.** honourable than the two;	
1Ch	14:3	David took **m.** wives at Jerusalem:	5750
1Ch	14:3	David begat **m.** sons and daughters.	5750
1Ch	17:9	place, and shall be moved no **m.**;	5750
1Ch	17:9	of wickedness waste them any **m.**,	3254
1Ch	17:18	can David speak **m.** to thee	3254,5750
1Ch	19:19	help the children of Ammon any **m.**.	5750
1Ch	21:3	hundred times so many **m.** as they	3254
1Ch	23:26	they shall no **m.** carry the tabernacle.	
1Ch	24:4	there were **m.** chief men found of	7227
2Ch	9:4	there was no **m.** spirit in her	5750
2Ch	10:11	you, I will put **m.** to your yoke:	3254
2Ch	15:19	there was no **m.** war unto the five and	
2Ch	20:25	**m.** than they could carry away:	
2Ch	25:9	is able to give thee much **m.** than	7235
2Ch	28:13	ye intend to add **m.** to our sins	
2Ch	28:22	trespass yet **m.** against the Lord:	3254
2Ch	29:34	the Levites were **m.** upright in heart	
2Ch	32:7	there be **m.** with us than with him:	7227
2Ch	32:16	spake yet **m.** against the Lord God,	
2Ch	33:8	will I any **m.** remove the foot of Israel	
2Ch	33:23	himself; but Amon trespassed **m.**	7235
2Ch	33:23	but Amon trespassed...and **m.**	
Ezr	7:20	whatsoever **m.** shall be needful	7608
Ne	2:17	that we be no **m.** a reproach.	5750
Ne	13:18	yet ye bring **m.** wrath upon Israel	3254
Ne	13:21	forth came they no **m.** on the sabbath.	
Es	1:19	Vashti come no **m.** before king	
Es	2:14	she came in unto the king no **m.**,	5750
Es	2:17	in his sight **m.** than all the virgins;	
Es	4:13	the king's house, **m.** than all the Jews.	
Es	6:6	to do honour **m.** than to myself?	3148
Job	3:21	dig for it **m.** than for hid treasures;	
Job	4:17	mortal man be **m.** just than God?	
Job	4:17	a man be **m.** pure than his maker?	
Job	7:7	mine eye shall no **m.** see good.	7725
Job	7:8	that hath seen me shall see me no **m.**:	
Job	7:9	down to the grave shall come up no **m.**.	
Job	7:10	shall return no **m.** to his house,	5750
Job	7:10	shall his place know him any **m.**	5750
Job	14:12	till the heavens be no **m.**, they shall	
Job	15:16	**m.** abominable and filthy is man,	
Job	20:9	saw him shall see him no **m.**;	3254
Job	20:9	shall his place any **m.** behold him.	5750
Job	23:12	his mouth **m.** than my necesssary food.	
Job	24:20	he shall be no **m.** remembered;	5750
Job	32:15	were amazed, they answered no **m.**:	5750
Job	32:16	stood still, and answered no **m.**;)	5750
Job	34:19	regardeth...rich **m.** than the poor?	6440
Job	34:23	not lay upon man **m.** than right;	5750
Job	34:31	chastisement, I will not offend any **m.**.	
Job	34:32	have done iniquity, I will do no **m.**	
Job	35:2	My righteousness is **m.** than God's?	3254
Job	35:11	Who teacheth us **m.** than the beasts of	
Job	41:8	remembr the battle, do no **m.**.	3254
Job	42:12	end of Job **m.** than his beginning:	
Ps	4:7	**m.** than in the time that their corn and	
Ps	10:18	the earth may no **m.** oppress.	3254,5750
Ps	19:10	**M.** to be desired are they than gold,	
Ps	39:13	before I go hence, and be no **m.**.	
Ps	40:5	are **m.** than can be numbered.	6105
Ps	40:12	are **m.** than the hairs of mine head:	6105
Ps	41:8	he lieth he shall rise up no **m.**	3254
Ps	52:3	Thou lovest evil **m.** than good; and	
Ps	69:4	**m.** than the hairs of mine head:	7231
Ps	71:14	and will yet priase thee **m.** and **m.**.	3254
Ps	73:7	have **m.** than heart could wish.	5674
Ps	74:9	there is no **m.** any prophet:	5750
Ps	76:4	Thou art **m.** glorious and excellent	
Ps	77:7	will he be favourable no **m.**?	3254,5750
Ps	78:17	they sinned yet **m.** against him by	5750
Ps	83:4	may be no **m.** in remembrace.	5750
Ps	87:2	**m.** than all the dwellings of Jacob.	
Ps	88:5	whom thou rememberest no **m.**:	5750
Ps	103:16	place thereof shall know it no **m.**.	5750
Ps	104:35	earth, and let the wicked be no **m.**	5750
Ps	115:14	Lord shall increase you **m.** and **m.**,	
Ps	119:99	**m.** understanding than all my teachers:	
Ps	119:100	I understand **m.** than the ancients,	
Ps	130:6	**m.** than they that watch for...morning:	
Ps	130:6	**m.** than they that watch for...morning.	
Ps	139:18	are **m.** in number than the sand:	7235
Pr	3:15	She is **m.** precious than rubies: and	
Pr	4:18	that shineth **m.** and **m.** unto the	1980
Pr	10:25	passeth, so is the wicked no **m.**:	
Pr	11:24	is that withholdeth **m.** than is meet,	
Pr	11:31	much **m.** the wicked and the sinner.	
Pr	12:26	is **m.** excellent than his neighbour:	
Pr	15:11	how much **m.** then the hearts of the	
Pr	17:10	A reproof entereth **m.** into a wise man	
Pr	19:7	how much **m.** do his friends go far	
Pr	21:3	justice and judgment is **m.** acceptable	
Pr	21:27	how much **m.**, when he bringeth it	
Pr	26:12	there is **m.** hope of a fool than of him.	
Pr	28:23	rebuketh a man...shall find **m.** favour	
Pr	29:20	there is **m.** hope of a fool than of him.	
Pr	30:2	Surely I am **m.** brutish than any man,	
Pr	31:7	and remember his misery no **m.**	5750
Ec	1:16	and have gotten **m.** wisdom than all	
Ec	2:9	and increased **m.** than all that were	
Ec	2:15	me; and why was I then **m.** wise?	3148
Ec	2:16	of the wise **m.** than of the fool	5973
Ec	2:25	can hasten hereunto, **m.** than I?	2351
Ec	4:2	**m.** than the living which are yet	4480
Ec	4:13	who will no **m.** be admonished.	5750
Ec	5:1	and be **m.** ready to hear, than to	7138
Ec	6:5	this hath **m.** rest than the other.	
Ec	6:8	hath the wise **m.** than the fool?	3148
Ec	7:19	**m.** than ten mighty men which are	
Ec	7:26	I find **m.** bitter than death the woman,	
Ec	9:5	neither have they any **m.** a reward;	5750
Ec	9:6	neither have they any **m.** a portion	5750
Ec	9:17	**m.** than the cry of him that ruleth	
Ec	10:10	edge, then must he put to **m.** strength:	
Ca	1:4	will remember thy love **m.** than wine:	
Ca	5:9,9	thy beloved **m.** than another beloved,	
Isa	1:5	Why should ye be, stricken any **m.**?	5750
Isa	1:5	ye will revolt **m.** [3254] and **m.**: the	
Isa	1:13	Bring no **m.** vain oblations; incense:	
Isa	2:4	shall they learn war any **m.**	5750
Isa	5:4	have been done **m.** to my vineyard,	5750
Isa	9:1	did **m.** grievously afflict her by the	
Isa	10:20	shall no **m.** again stay upon him	5750
Isa	13:12	make a man **m.** precious than fine gold;	
Isa	15:9	for I will bring **m.** upon Dimon,	3254
Isa	19:7	wither, be driven away, and be no **m.**	
Isa	23:10	Tarshish: there is no **m.** strength.	5750
Isa	23:12	Thou shalt no **m.** rejoice, O thou	3254, 5750
Isa	26:21	and shall no **m.** cover her slain.	5750
Isa	30:19	thou shalt weep no **m.**: he will be	1058
Isa	30:20	be removed into a corner any **m.**,	5750
Isa	32:5	shall be no **m.** called liberal, nor	5750
Isa	38:11	I shall be hold man no **m.** with the	
Isa	47:1	thou shalt no **m.** be called tender	3254
Isa	47:5	thou shalt no **m.** be called, The lady	3254
Isa	51:22	thou shalt no **m.** drink it again:	3254
Isa	52:1	shall no **m.** come into thee	3254,5750
Isa	52:14	was so marred **m.** than any man,	
Isa	52:14	and his form **m.** than the sons of men:	
Isa	54:1	**m.** are the children of the desolate	7227
Isa	54:4	reproach of...widowhood any **m.**.	5750
Isa	54:9	should no **m.** go over the earth;	5750
Isa	56:12	this day, and much **m.** abundant.	3499
Isa	60:18	Violence shall no **m.** be heard in	5750
Isa	60:19	sun shall be no **m.** thy light by day;	5750
Isa	60:20	Thy sun shall no **m.** go down;	5750
Isa	62:4	shalt no **m.** be termed Forsaken;	5750
Isa	62:4	land any **m.** be termed Desolate:	5750
Isa	62:8	will no **m.** give thy corn to be meat	5750
Isa	65:19	weeping shall be no **m.** heard in her,	5750
Isa	65:20	be no **m.** thence an infant of days,	5750
Jer	2:31	we will come no **m.** unto thee?	5750
Jer	3:11	herself **m.** than treacherous Judah.	
Jer	3:16	they shall say no **m.**, The ark of	5750
Jer	3:16	neither shall that be done any **m.**.	5750
Jer	3:17	walk any **m.** after the imagination	5750
Jer	7:32	it shall no **m.** be called Tophet, nor	5750
Jer	10:20	to stretch forth my tent any **m.**,	5750
Jer	11:19	name may be no **m.** remembered.	5750
Jer	16:14	that it shall no **m.** be said, The	5750
Jer	19:6	that this place shall no **m.** be called	5750
Jer	20:9	him, nor speak any **m.** in his name.	5750
Jer	22:10	he shall return no **m.**, nor see his	5750
Jer	22:11	He shall not return thither any **m.**:	5750
Jer	22:12	and shall see this land no **m.**.	5750
Jer	22:30	David, and ruling any **m.** in Judah.	5750
Jer	23:4	and they shall fear no **m.**, nor be	5750
Jer	23:7	that they shall no **m.** say, The Lord	5750
Jer	23:36	the Lord shall ye mention no **m.**;	5750
Jer	25:27	and spue, and fall, and rise no **m.**,	
Jer	30:8	no **m.** serve themselves of him.	5750
Jer	31:12	shall not sorrow any **m.** at all.	3254
Jer	31:29	In those days they shall say no **m.**,	5750
Jer	31:34	they shall teach no **m.** every man.	5750
Jer	31:34	I will remember their sin no **m.**.	5750
Jer	31:40	nor thrown down any **m.** for ever.	5750
Jer	33:24	be no **m.** a nation before them.	5750
Jer	34:10	serve themselves of them any **m.**,	5750
Jer	38:9	for there is no **m.** bread in the city.	5750
Jer	42:18	and ye shall see this place no **m.**	5750
Jer	44:26	my name shall no **m.** be named in	5750
Jer	46:23	they are **m.** than the grasshoppers,	7231
Jer	48:2	shall be no **m.** praise of Moab:	5750
Jer	49:7	Is wisdom no **m.** in Teman? is	5750
Jer	50:39	and it shall be no **m.** inhabited for	5750
Jer	51:44	not flow together any **m.** unto him:	5750
La	2:9	the law is no **m.**; her prophets also	
La	4:7	they were **m.** ruddy in body than	
La	4:15	They shall no **m.** sojourn there.	3254
La	4:16	them; he will no **m.** regard them:	3254
La	4:22	he will no **m.** carry thee away into	3254
Eze	5:6	my judgments into wickedness **m.**	4480
Eze	5:6	my statutes **m.** than the countries	4480
Eze	5:7	Because ye multiplied **m.** than the	4480
Eze	5:9	I will not do any **m.** the like,	5750
Eze	6:14	**m.** desolate than the wilderness	
Eze	12:23	shall no **m.** use it as a proverb in	5750
Eze	12:24	shall be no **m.** any vain vision nor	5750
Eze	12:25	it shall be no **m.** prolonged: for in	5750
Eze	12:28	of my words be prolonged any **m.**,	5750
Eze	13:15	the wall is no **m.**, neither they that	
Eze	13:21	shall be no **m.** in your hand to be	5750
Eze	13:23	shall see no **m.** vanity, nor divine	5750
Eze	14:11	may go no **m.** astray from me,	5750
Eze	14:11	polluted any **m.** with all their	5750
Eze	14:21	How much **m.** when I send my four	5750
Eze	15:2	is the vine tree **m.** than any tree, or	
Eze	16:41	also shalt give no hire any **m.**	5750
Eze	16:42	be quiet, and will be no **m.** angry.	5750
Eze	16:47	thou wast corrupted **m.** than they in	
Eze	16:51	thine abominations **m.** than they,	
Eze	16:52	committed **m.** abominable than	
Eze	16:52	they are **m.** righteous than thou: yea,	
Eze	16:63	and never open thy mouth any **m.**	5750
Eze	18:3	not have occasion any **m.** to use this	5750
Eze	19:9	that his voice should no **m.** be heard	5750
Eze	20:39	pollute ye my holy name no **m.** with	5750
Eze	21:5	sheath: it shall not return any **m.**.	5750
Eze	21:13	it shall be no **m.**, saith the Lord God.	
Eze	21:27	and it shall be no **m.**, until he come	
Eze	21:32	thou shalt be no **m.** remembered: for	
Eze	23:11	was **m.** corrupt in her inordinate love	
Eze	23:11	**m.** than her sister in her whoredoms.	
Eze	23:27	nor remember Egypt any **m.**	5750
Eze	24:13	purged from thy filthiness any **m.**,	5750
Eze	24:27	shalt speak, and be no **m.** dumb:	5750
Eze	26:13	of thy harps shall be no **m.** heard.	5750
Eze	26:14	thou shalt be built no **m.**: for I the	5750
Eze	26:21	thee a terror, and thou shalt be no **m.**:	
Eze	27:36	terror, and never shalt be any **m.**	
Eze	28:19	and never shalt thou be any **m.**	
Eze	28:24	shall be no **m.** a pricking brier	5750
Eze	29:15	itself any **m.** above the nations:	
Eze	29:15	that they shall no **m.** rule over the	
Eze	29:16	shall be no **m.** the confidence of	5750
Eze	30:13	shall be no **m.** a prince of land	5750
Eze	32:13	foot of man trouble them any **m.**,	5750
Eze	33:22	opened, and I was no **m.** dumb.	5750
Eze	34:10	shepherds feed themselves any **m.**;	5750

Eze 34:22 they shall no m. be a prey; and I....... 5750
Eze 34:28 they shall no m. be a prey to the....... 5750
Eze 34:29 they shall no m. be consumed with..... 5750
Eze 34:29 the shame of the heathen any m........ 5750
Eze 36:12 shalt no m. henceforth bereave.......... 5750
Eze 36:14 thou shalt devour men no m., ... 5750
Eze 36:14 neither bereave thy nations any m.,..... 5750
Eze 36:15 the shame of the heathen any m.,....... 5750
Eze 36:15 the reproach of the people any m.,...... 5750
Eze 36:15 cause thy nations to fall any m., ... 5750
Eze 36:30 ye shall receive no m. reproach of...... 5750
Eze 37:22 they shall be no m. two nations, ... 5750
Eze 37:22 into two kingdoms any m. at all. 5750
Eze 37:23 defile themselves any m. with their 5750
Eze 39:7 them pollute my holy name any m.:.... 5750
Eze 39:28 left none of them any m. there.......... 5750
Eze 39:29 I hide my face any m. from them:...... 5750
Eze 42:6 was straitened m. than the lowest..........
Eze 43:7 the house of Israel no m. defile, ... 5750
Eze 45:8 shall no m. oppress my people; 5750
Da 2:30 that I have m. than any living,........... 4481
Da 3:19 seven times m. than it was wont 5922
Da 7:20 whose look was m. stout than his 5750
Da 11:8 continue m. years than the king of...........
Ho 1:6 I will no m. have mercy upon the....... 5750
Ho 2:16 and shalt call me no m. Baali............ 5750
Ho 2:17 they shall no m. be remembered........ 5750
Ho 6:6 of God m. than burnt offerings,...............
Ho 9:15 house, I will love them no m.:........... 3254
Ho 13:2 And now they sin m. [3254] and m., and...
Ho 14:3 will we say any m. to the work of...... 5750
Ho 14:8 have I to do any m. with idols? 5750
Joe 2:2 neither shall be any m. after it, ... 3254
Joe 2:19 I will no m. make you a reproach........ 5750
Joe 3:17 strangers pass through her any m...... 5750
Am 5:2 is fallen; she shall no m. rise:........... 5750
Am 7:8 will not again pass by them any m.:.... 5750
Am 7:13 prophesy not...any m. at Bethel:......... 5750
Am 8:2 will not again pass by them any m....... 5750
Am 9:15 they shall no m. be pulled up out....... 5750
Jon 4:11 wherein are m. than sixscore 7227
Mic 4:3 shall they learn war any m.............. 5750
Mic 5:12 thou shalt have no m. soothsayers:..........
Mic 5:13 shalt no m. worship the work of 5750
Na 1:12 thee, I will affect thee no m............. 5750
Na 1:14 that no m. of thy name be sown: 5750
Na 1:15 the wicked shall no m. pass....... 3254,5750
Na 2:13 messengers shall no m. be heard. 5750
Hab 1:8 are m. fierce than the evening wolves:......
Hab 1:13 the man that is m. righteous than he?.......
Zep 3:11 thou shalt no m. be haughty....... 3254,5750
Zep 3:15 thou shalt not see evil any m. 5750
Zec 9:8 shall pass through them any m.: 5750
Zec 11:6 I will no m. pity the inhabitants 5750
Zec 13:2 they shall no m. be remembered:....... 5750
Zec 14:11 shall be no m. utter destruction; 5750
Zec 14:21 be no m. the Canaanite in the 5750
Mal 2:13 regardeth not the offering any m.,....... 5750
Mt 5:37 **is m. than these cometh of evil.** *4053*
Mt 5:47 **only, what do ye m. than others?** .. *4053*
Mt 6:25 **Is not the life m. than meat, and** .. *4119*
Mt 6:30 **shall he not much m. clothe you,** .. *3123*
Mt 7:11 **how much m. shall your Father** *3123*
Mt 10:15 **It shall be m. tolerable for the land** .*414*
Mt 10:25 **how much m. shall they call them** .*3123*
Mt 10:31 **of m. value than many sparrows.** .. *1308*
Mt 10:37 **father or mother m. than me is**....... *5228*
Mt 10:37 **loveth son or daughter m. than me**.*5228*
Mt 11:9 **unto you, and m. than a prophet**... *4055*
Mt 11:22 **be m. tolerable for Tyre and Sidon**.. *414*
Mt 11:24 **it shall be m. tolerable for the land** .*414*
Mt 12:45 **seven other spirits m. wicked than** ......
Mt 13:12 **and he shall have m. abundance:**..........
Mt 18:13 **he rejoiceth m. of that sheep, than**.*3123*
Mt 18:16 **take with thee one or two m., that**.*2089*
Mt 19:6 **are no m. twain, but one flesh** *3765*
Mt 20:10 **they should have received m.; and**..*4119*
Mt 20:31 but they cried the m., saying,........... *3185*
Mt 21:36 **other servants m. than the first:**.... *4119*
Mt 22:46 forth ask him any m. questions.......... *3765*
Mt 23:15 **make him twofold m. the child of hell**. *243*
Mt 25:20 **gained besides them five talents m.**. *243*
Mt 26:53 **give me m. than twelve legions** *4119*
Mt 27:23 but they cried out the m., saying, ... *4057*
Mk 1:45 Jesus could no m. openly enter.......... *3370*
Mk 4:24 **you that hear shall m. be given**..... *4369*
Mk 6:11 **It shall be m. tolerable for Sodom** .. *414*
Mk 7:12 **suffer him no m. to do ought for**... *3765*
Mk 7:36 but the m. he charged them, so.......... *3745*
Mk 7:36 much the m. a great deal they........... *3123*
Mk 8:14 ship with them m. than one loaf......... *1508*
Mk 9:8 they saw no man any m., save Jesus .. *3765*
Mk 9:25 **out of him, and enter no m. into**... *3370*
Mk 10:8 **are no m. twain, but one flesh**..... *3765*
Mk 10:48 he cried the m. a great deal, Thou..... *3123*
Mk 12:33 m. than all whole burnt offerings........ *4119*
Mk 12:43 **this poor widow hath cast m. in,**... *4119*
Mk 14:5 sold for m. than three hundred.......... *1833*
Mk 14:25 **drink no m. of the fruit of the** *3765*
Mk 14:31 But he spake the m. vehemently,....... *3123*
Mk 15:14 cried out...m. exceedingly, Crucify *4056*
Lu 3:13 Exact no m. than that which is *4119*
Lu 5:15 But so much the m. went there a *3123*
Lu 7:26 **you, and much m. than a prophet.** .*4055*
Lu 9:13 We have no m. but five loaves and....... *4119*
Lu 10:12 **it shall be m. tolerable in that day**.. *414*
Lu 10:14 **it shall be m. tolerable for Tyre**...... *414*
Lu 10:35 whatsoever thou spendest m., when... *4325*
Lu 11:13 **how much m. shall your heavenly** . *3123*
Lu 11:26 **seven other spirits m. wicked than** ......
Lu 12:4 **that have no m. that they can do.** .*4055*
Lu 12:7 **of m. value than many sparrows.** .. *1308*
Lu 12:23 **The life is m. than meat,** *4119*
Lu 12:23 **and the body is m. than raiment.** ....
Lu 12:24 **how much m. are ye better than** ... *3123*
Lu 12:28 **how much m. will he clothe you,** .. *3123*
Lu 12:48 **much, of him they will ask the m.** .*4055*
Lu 14:8 **lest a m. honourable man than thou**....
Lu 15:7 **m. than over ninety and nine just** ....
Lu 15:19, 21 **am no m. worthy to be called** ... *3765*
Lu 18:30 **receive manifold m. in this present**.*4179*
Lu 18:39 cried so much the m., Thou Son........ *3123*
Lu 20:36 **Neither can they die any m.: for**... *2089*
Lu 21:3 **poor widow hath cast in m. than**... *4119*
Lu 22:16 **I will not any m. eat thereof, until**.*3765*
Lu 22:44 an agony he prayed m. earnestly:....... *1617*
Lu 23:5 they were the m. fierce, saying, He ... *2001*
Joh 4:1 made and baptized m. disciples *4119*
Joh 4:41 many m. believed because of his......... *4119*
Joh 5:14 **sin no m., lest a worse thing come** .*3370*
Joh 5:18 Jews sought the m. to kill him,........... *3123*
Joh 6:66 back, and walked no m. with him....... *3765*
Joh 7:31 will he do m. miracles than these........ *4119*
Joh 8:11 **I condemn thee: go, and sin no m.** .*2001*
Joh 10:10 **they might have it m. abundantly**........
Joh 11:54 Jesus...walked no m. openly............. *2089*
Joh 12:43 praise of men m. than the praise........ *3123*
Joh 14:19 **and the world seeth me no m.:** *2089*
Joh 15:2 **that it may bring forth m. fruit** *4119*
Joh 15:4 **m. can ye, except ye abide in me**... *3761*
Joh 16:10 **my Father, and ye see me no m.;** .. *2089*
Joh 16:21 **remembereth no m. the anguish,**... *2089*
Joh 16:25 **I shall no m. speak unto you in** *2089*
Joh 17:11 **now I am no m. in the world, but** . *2089*
Joh 19:8 that saying, he was the m. afraid; *3123*
Joh 21:15 **lovest thou me m. than these?**........ *4119*
Ac 4:19 unto you m. than unto God, judge...... *3123*
Ac 5:14 were the m. added to the Lord, ... *3123*
Ac 8:39 that the eunuch saw him no m.:......... *3765*
Ac 9:22 Saul increased the m. in strength, ... *3123*
Ac 13:34 now no m. to return to corruption,..... *2001*
Ac 17:11 m. noble than those in Thessalonica,.........
Ac 18:26 him the way of God m. perfectly. *197*
Ac 19:32 m. part knew not wherefore they......... *4119*
Ac 20:25 of God, shall see my face no m. *3765*
Ac 20:35 **m. blessed to give than to receive**.. *3122*
Ac 20:38 that they should see his face no m. *3765*
Ac 22:2 to them, they kept the m. silence: *3123*
Ac 23:13 m. than forty which had made *4119*
Ac 23:15 something m. perfectly concerning *197*
Ac 23:20 somewhat of him m. perfectly. *197*
Ac 23:21 for him of them m. than forty men, ... *4119*
Ac 24:10 m. cheerfully answer for myself: *2115*
Ac 24:22 m. perfect knowledge of that way,....... *197*
Ac 25:6 among them m. than ten days, ... *4119*
Ac 27:11 m. than those things which were........ *3123*
Ac 27:12 m. part advised to depart thence........ *4119*
Ro 1:25 the creature m. than the Creator, ... *3844*
Ro 2:18 the things that are m. excellent, ...
Ro 3:7 if the truth of God hath m. abounded........
Ro 5:9 Much m. then, being now justified...... *3123*
Ro 5:10 much m., being reconciled, we shall.... *3123*
Ro 5:15 much m. the grace of God, and the..... *3123*
Ro 5:17 m. they which receive abundance *3123*
Ro 5:20 abounded, grace did much m. abound: ....
Ro 6:9 raised from the dead dieth no m.; *2089*
Ro 6:9 death hath no m. dominion over.......... *3765*
Ro 7:17 Now then it is no m. I that do it,....... *2089*
Ro 7:20 it is no m. I that do it, but sin that *2089*
Ro 8:37 m. than conquerors through him *5245*
Ro 11:6 by grace, then is it no m. of works: ... *2089*
Ro 11:6 otherwise grace is no m. grace.......... *2089*
Ro 11:6 of works, then is it no m. grace: *2089*
Ro 11:6 otherwise work is no m. work........... *2089*
Ro 11:12 how much m. their fulness? *3123*
Ro 11:24 how much m. shall these, which be *3123*
Ro 12:3 m. highly than he ought to think; *3844*
Ro 14:13 therefore judge one another any m.: ... *2001*
Ro 15:15 I have written the m. boldly unto....... *5112*
Ro 15:23 having no m. place in these parts,...... *2001*
1Co 6:3 how much m. things that pertain to *1065*
1Co 9:19 unto all, that I might gain the m. *4119*
1Co 12:22 much m. those members of the *3123*
1Co 12:22 body, which seem to be m. feeble, are......
1Co 12:23 have m. abundant comeliness *4055*
1Co 12:23 we bestow m. abundant honour; *4055*
1Co 12:24 having given m. abundant honour to.... *4055*
1Co 12:31 unto you a m. excellent way. *2596, 5236*
1Co 14:18 speak with tongues m. than ye all: *3123*
1Co 15:10 laboured m. abundantly than they....... *4055*
2Co 1:12 and m. abundantly to you-ward. *4056*
2Co 2:4 the love which I have m. abundantly... *4056*
2Co 3:9 much m. doth the ministration of........ *3123*
2Co 3:11 much m. that which remaineth is......... *3123*
2Co 4:17 for us a far m. exceeding and...... *1519,5236*
2Co 5:16 henceforth know we him no m............ *2089*
2Co 7:7 me; so that I rejoiced the m. *3123*
2Co 7:13 and exceedingly the m. joyed we *3123*
2Co 7:15 his inward affection is m. abundant..... *4056*
2Co 8:17 but being m. forward, of his own *4707*
2Co 8:22 but now much m. diligent, upon the..... *4707*
2Co 10:8 somewhat m. of our authority,........... *4055*
2Co 11:23 ministers of Christ?...I am m.; *5228*
2Co 11:23 in labors m. abundant, in stripes *4056*
2Co 11:23 in prisons m. frequent, in deaths......... *4056*
2Co 12:15 the m. abundantly I love you, the....... *4056*
Ga 1:14 being m. exceedingly zealous of the.... *4056*
Ga 3:18 of the law, it is no m. of promise:...... *2089*
Ga 4:7 thou art no m. a servant, but a son;... *2089*
Ga 4:27 the desolate hath many m. children..... *3123*
Eph 2:19 are no m. strangers and foreigners,.... *3765*
Eph 4:14 we henceforth be no m. children, ... *2001*
Eph 4:28 Let him that stole steal no m.: but..... *2001*
Php 1:9 love may abound yet m. and m. in..... *3123*
Php 1:14 are much m. bold to speak the *4056*
Php 1:24 to abide in the flesh is m. needful for ... *316*
Php 1:26 your rejoicing may be m. abundant ....
Php 2:12 but now much m. in my absence,....... *3123*
Php 2:28 I sent him . . . the m. carefully, ... *4708*
Php 3:4 he might trust in the flesh, I m.: *3123*
1Th 2:17 endeavoured the m. abundantly to...... *4056*
1Th 4:1 so ye would abound m. and m............. *3123*
1Th 4:10 that ye increase m. and m.;............. *3123*
2Ti 2:16 will increase unto m. ungodliness. *4119*
2Ti 3:4 pleasures m. than lovers of God; *3123*
Phm 16 me, but how much m. unto thee, ... *3123*
Phm 21 thou wilt also do m. than I say. *5228*
Heb 1:4 obtained a m. excellent name than............
Heb 2:1 ought to give the m. earnest heed...... *4056*
Heb 3:3 worthy of m. glory than Moses,.......... *4119*
Heb 3:3 the house hath m. honour than the...... *4119*
Heb 6:17 willing m. abundantly to shew unto..... *4054*
Heb 7:15 it is yet far m. evident: for that......... *4055*
Heb 8:6 obtained a m. excellent ministry,..............
Heb 8:12 iniquities will I remember no m.......... *2089*
Heb 9:11 a greater and m. perfect tabernacle, ...
Heb 9:14 How much m. shall the blood of......... *3123*
Heb 10:2 have had no m. conscience of sins...... *2089*
Heb 10:17 iniquities will I remember no m.......... *2089*
Heb 10:18 is, there is no m. offering for sin. *2089*
Heb 10:25 so much the m., as ye see the day *3123*
Heb 10:26 remaineth no m. sacrifice for sins,....... *2089*
Heb 11:4 unto God a m. excellent sacrifice.............
Heb 11:32 what shall I m. say? for the time *2089*
Heb 12:19 not be spoken to them any m.:......... *4369*
Heb 12:25 much m. shall not we escape, if......... *3123*
Heb 12:26 once m. I shake not the earth only,.........
Heb 12:27 And this word, Yet once m., signifieth ....
Jas 4:6 But he giveth m. grace. Wherefore *3187*
1Pe 1:7 being much m. precious than of gold.........
2Pe 1:19 having also a m. sure word of prophecy;....

Re 2:19 **the last to be m. than the first**...... *4119*
Re 3:12 **God, and he shall go no m. out**:.... *2089*
Re 7:16 hunger no **m.**, neither thirst any **m.**; .. *2089*
Re 9:12 there come two woes **m.** hereafter..... *2089*
Re 12:8 their place found any **m.** in heaven. *2089*
Re 18:11 buyeth their merchandise any **m.**:........ *3765*
Re 18:14 and thou shalt find them no **m.** at all... *3765*
Re 18:21 and shall be found no **m.** at all........... *2089*
Re 18:22 shall be heard no **m.** at all in thee; *2089*
Re 18:22 be, shall be found any **m.** in thee;...... *2089*
Re 18:22 shall be heard no **m.** at all in thee; *2089*
Re 18:23 of a candle shall shine no **m.** at all...... *2089*
Re 18:23 shall be heard no **m.** at all in thee: *2089*
Re 20:3 should deceive the nations no **m.**, ... *2089*
Re 21:1 away; and there was no **m.** sea. *2089*
Re 21:4 there shall be no **m.** death, neither..... *2089*
Re 21:4 neither shall there be any **m.** pain: *2089*
Re 22:3 there shall be no **m.** curse: but.......... *2089*

MOREH (mo'-reh)
Ge 12:6 of Sichem, unto the plain of **M.**........... 4170
De 11:30 Gilgal, beside the plains of **M.**?.......... 4170
Jg 7:1 by the hill of **M.**, in the valley. 4170

MOREOVER
Ge 24:25 She said **m.** unto him, We have both ....
Ge 32:20 say ye **m.**, Behold, thy servant.......... 1571
Ge 45:15 **M.** he kissed all his brethren, and ....
Ge 47:4 They said **m.** unto Pharaoh, For to..........
Ge 48:22 **M.** I have given to thee one portion ....
Ex 3:6 **M.** he said, I am the God of thy father,.....
Ex 3:15 God said **m.** unto Moses, Thus.......... 5750
Ex 11:3 **M.** the man Moses was very great..... 1571
Ex 18:21 **M.** thou shalt provide out of all the..........
Ex 26:1 **M.** thou shalt make the tabernacle............
Ex 30:22 **M.** the Lord spake unto Moses, saying,.....
Le 7:21 **M.** the soul that shall touch any..............
Le 7:26 **M.** ye shall eat no manner of blood,..........
Le 14:46 **M.** he that goeth into the house all...........
Le 18:20 **M.** thou shalt not lie carnally with thy ....
Le 25:45 **M.** of the children of the strangers..... 1571
Nu 13:28 and **m.** we saw the children of Anak... 1571
Nu 16:14 **M.** thou hast not brought us into a....... 637
Nu 33:56 **M.** it shall come to pass, that I...............
Nu 35:31 **M.** ye shall take no satisfaction for ....
De 1:28 **m.** we have seen the sons of the....... 1571
De 1:39 **M.** your little ones, which ye said............
De 7:20 **M.** the Lord thy God will send the..... 1571
De 28:45 **M.** all these curses shall come upon..........
De 28:60 **M.** he will bring upon thee all the.............
Jg 10:9 **M.** the children of Ammon passed ....
Ru 4:10 **M.** Ruth the Moabitess, the wife of.... 1571
1Sa 2:19 **M.** his mother made him a little...............
1Sa 12:23 **M.** as for me, God forbid that I.......... 1571
1Sa 14:21 **M.** the Hebrews that were with the..........
1Sa 17:37 David said **m.**, The Lord that..................
1Sa 20:3 And David sware **m.**, and said, Thy.... 5750
1Sa 24:11 **M.**, my father, see, yea, see the skirt .....
1Sa 28:19 **M.** the Lord will also deliver............. 1571
2Sa 7:10 **M.** I will appoint a place for my people......
2Sa 12:8 **m.** have given unto thee such and...... 3254
2Sa 15:4 Absalom said **m.**, Oh that I were made .....
2Sa 17:1 **M.** Ahithophel said unto Absalom, ...
2Sa 17:13 **M.**, if he be gotten into a city, then..... 518
2Sa 21:15 **M.** the Philistines had yet war again ....
1Ki 1:47 and **m.** the king's servants came........ 1571
1Ki 2:5 **M.** thou knowest also what Joab 1571
1Ki 2:14 He said **m.**, I have somewhat to say.........
1Ki 2:44 The king said **m.** to Shimei, Thou ....
1Ki 8:41 **M.** concerning a stranger, that is 1571
1Ki 10:18 **M.** the king made a great throne of..........
1Ki 14:14 **M.** the Lord shall raise him up a king........
2Ki 12:15 **M.** they reckoned not with the men,.........
2Ki 21:16 **M.** Manasseh shed innocent blood...... 1571
2Ki 23:15 **M.** the altar that was at Beth-el,........ 1571
2Ki 23:24 **M.** the workers with familiar............. 1571
1Ch 11:2 **m.** in time past, even when Saul........ 1571
1Ch 12:40 **M.** they that were nigh them, even.... 1571
1Ch 17:10 **M.** I will subdue all thine enemies. ....
1Ch 18:12 **M.** Abishai the son of Zeruiah slew...........
1Ch 22:15 **M.** there are workmen with thee in...........
1Ch 23:5 **M.** four thousand were porters; and.........
1Ch 25:1 **M.** David and the captains of the host........
1Ch 26:4 **M.** the sons of Obed-edom were,.............
1Ch 28:7 **M.** I will establish his kingdom.................
1Ch 29:3 **M.**, because I have set my............... 5750
2Ch 1:5 **M.** the brasen altar, that Bezaleel ....
2Ch 2:12 Huram said **m.**, Blessed be the Lord ....
2Ch 4:1 **M.** he made an altar of brass, twenty........
2Ch 4:20 **M.** the candlesticks with their lamps, ...
2Ch 6:32 **M.** concerning the stranger, which...... 1571
2Ch 7:7 **M.** Solomon hallowed the middle of...........
2Ch 9:17 **M.** the king made a great throne of..........
2Ch 17:6 **m.** he took away the high places........ 5750
2Ch 19:8 **M.** in Jerusalem did Jehoshaphat......... 1571
2Ch 21:11 **M.** he made high places in the................
2Ch 21:16 **M.** the Lord stirred up against.................
2Ch 23:9 **M.** Jehoiada the priest delivered to...........
2Ch 25:5 **M.** Amaziah gathered Judah......................
2Ch 26:9 **M.** Uzziah built towers in Jerusalem..........
2Ch 26:11 **M.** Uzziah had an host of fighting ....
2Ch 27:4 **M.** he built cities in the mountains............
2Ch 28:3 **M.** he burnt incense in the valley ....
2Ch 29:19 **M.** all the vessels, which king Ahaz ....
2Ch 29:30 **M.** Hezekiah the king and the princes ....
2Ch 31:4 **M.** he commandeth the people that.............
2Ch 32:29 **M.** he provided him cities, and..................
2Ch 35:1 **M.** Josiah kept a passover unto the...........
2Ch 36:14 **M.** all the chief of the priests, and...... 1571
Ezr 6:8 **M.** I make a decree what ye shall do........
Ezr 10:25 **M.** of Israel: of the sons of Parosh; ....
Ne 2:7 **M.** I said unto the king, If it please ....
Ne 3:6 **M.** the old gate repaired Jehoiada..............
Ne 3:26 **M.** the Nethinims dwelt in Ophel,.............
Ne 5:14 **M.** from the time that I was............. 1571
Ne 5:17 **M.** there were at my table an hundred.......
Ne 6:17 **M.** in those days the nobles of.......... 1571
Ne 9:12 **M.** thou leddest them in the day by..........
Ne 9:22 **M.** thou gavest them kingdoms and ....
Ne 11:19 **M.** the porters, Akkub, Talmon, and.........
Ne 12:8 **M.** the Levites: Jeshua, Binnui,...............
Es 5:12 Haman said **m.**, Yea, Esther the............ 637
Job 27:1 **M.** Job continued his parable, and............
Job 29:1 **M.** Job continued his parable, and............
Job 35:1 Elihu spake **m.**, and said, ...
Job 40:1 **M.** the Lord answered Job, and said, ...
Ps 19:11 **M.** by them is...servant warned:........ 1571
Ps 78:67 **M.** he refused the tabernacle of...............
Ps 105:16 **M.** he called for a famine upon the ....
Ec 3:16 **m.** I saw under the sun the place....... 5750
Ec 5:9 **M.** the profit of the earth is for all:..........
Ec 6:5 **M.** he hath not seen the sun, nor......... 1571
Ec 12:9 **m.**, because the preacher was........... 3148
Isa 3:16 **M.** the Lord saith, Because the ....
Isa 7:10 **M.** the Lord spake again unto Ahaz, ...
Isa 8:1 **M.** the Lord said unto me, Take thee ....
Isa 19:9 **M.** they that work in fine flax, and ....
Isa 29:5 **M.** the multitude of thy strangers.............
Isa 30:26 **M.** the light of the moon shall be as...........
Isa 39:8 He said **m.**, For there shall be peace ....
Jer 1:11 **M.** the word of the Lord came unto.............
Jer 2:1 **M.** the word of the Lord came to me,.......
Jer 8:4 **M.** thou shalt say unto them, Thus............
Jer 20:5 **M.** I will deliver all the strength of...........
Jer 25:10 **M.** I will take from them the voice of........
Jer 33:1 **M.** the word of the Lord came unto...........
Jer 33:23 **M.** the word of the Lord came to.............
Jer 37:18 **M.** Jeremiah said unto king Zedekiah, ...
Jer 39:7 **M.** he put out Zedekiah's eyes, and...........
Jer 40:13 **M.** Johanan the son of Kareah, and...........
Jer 44:24 **M.** Jeremiah said unto all the people, ...
Jer 48:35 **M.** I will cause to cease in Moab,.............
Eze 3:1 **M.** he said unto me, Son of man, eat........
Eze 3:10 **M.** he said unto me, Son of man, all.........
Eze 4:3 **M.** take thou unto thee an iron pan, ...
Eze 4:16 **M.** he said unto me, Son of man, ...
Eze 5:14 **M.** I will make thee waste, and a ....
Eze 7:1 **M.** the word of the Lord came unto..........
Eze 11:1 **M.** the spirit lifted me up, and.................
Eze 12:17 **M.** the word of the Lord came to me,........
Eze 16:20 **M.** thou hast taken thy sons and thy.........
Eze 16:29 hast **m.** multiplied thy fornication..............
Eze 17:11 **M.** the word of the Lord came unto,..........
Eze 19:1 **M.** take thou up a lamentation for..............
Eze 20:12 **M.** also I gave them my sabbaths,....... 1571
Eze 20:45 **M.** the word of the Lord came unto..........
Eze 22:1 **M.** the word of the Lord came unto...........
Eze 23:36 The Lord said **m.** unto me; Son of ....
Eze 23:38 **M.** this they have done unto me: 5750
Eze 28:11 **M.** the word of the Lord came unto...........
Eze 35:1 **M.** the word of the Lord came unto me,.....
Eze 36:16 **M.** the word of the Lord came unto..........
Eze 37:16 **M.**, thou son of man, take thee one..........
Eze 37:26 **M.** I will make a covenant of peace............
Eze 45:1 **m.**, when ye shall divide by lot the...........
Eze 46:18 **M.** the prince shall not take of the............
Eze 48:22 **M.** from the possession of the Levites, ...
Zec 4:8 **M.** the word of the Lord came unto.............
Zec 5:6 he said **m.**, This is their resemblance........
Mt 6:16 **M.** when ye fast, be not, as the *1161*
Mt 18:15 **M. if thy brother shall trespass**..... *1161*
Lu 16:21 **m. the dogs came and licked** .. *235, 2532*
Ac 2:26 **m.** also my flesh shall rest in hope: *2089*
Ac 11:12 **M.** these...brethren accompanied......... *1161*
Ac 19:26 **M.** ye see and hear, that not alone..... *2532*
Ro 5:20 **M.** the law entered, that...offence...... *1161*
Ro 8:30 **M.** whom he did predestinate, them.... *1161*
1Co 4:2 **M.**...required...stewards, ..*3739, 1161, 3063*
1Co 10:1 **M.**, brethren, I would not that ye *1161*
1Co 15:1 **M.**, brethren, I declare unto you......... *1161*
2Co 1:23 **M.** I call God for a record upon my *1161*
2Co 8:1 **M.**, brethren, we do you to wit of...... *1161*
1Ti 3:7 **M.** he must have a good report of...... *1161*
Heb 9:21 **M.** he sprinkled with blood............. *1161*
Heb 11:36 **m.** of bonds and imprisonments:.......... *1161*
2Pe 1:15 **M.** I will endeavour that ye *1161, 2532*

MORESHETH-GATH (mor'-e-sheth-gath) See also MORASTHITE.
Mic 1:14 shalt thou give presents to **M.**:.......... 4182

MORIAH (mo-ri'-ah)
Ge 22:2 and get thee into the land of **M.** 4179
2Ch 3:1 Lord at Jerusalem in mount **M.**,......... 4179

MORNING
Ge 1:5 evening and the **m.** were the first...... 1242
Ge 1:8 evening and the **m.** were the second... 1242
Ge 1:13 evening and the **m.** were the third 1242
Ge 1:19 evening and the **m.** were the fourth.... 1242
Ge 1:23 evening and the **m.** were the fifth 1242
Ge 1:31 evening and the **m.** were the sixth..... 1242
Ge 19:15 And when the **m.** arose, then the....... 7837
Ge 19:27 Abraham gat up early in the **m.** 1242
Ge 20:8 Abimelech rose early in the **m.**,......... 1242
Ge 21:14 Abraham rose up early in the **m.**,........ 1242
Ge 22:3 Abraham rose up early in the **m.**,........ 1242
Ge 24:54 they rose up in the **m.**, and he said,... 1242
Ge 26:31 they rose up betimes in the **m.**,......... 1242
Ge 28:18 Jacob rose up early in the **m.**, and...... 1242
Ge 29:25 that in the **m.**, behold, it was Leah:.... 1242
Ge 31:55 early in the **m.** Laban rose up, and..... 1242
Ge 40:6 Joseph came in unto them in the **m.**, .. 1242
Ge 41:8 it came to pass in the **m.** that his....... 1242
Ge 44:3 soon as the **m.** was light, the men 1242
Ge 49:27 in the **m.** he shall devour the prey, ... 1242
Ex 7:15 Get thee unto Pharaoh in the **m.**;....... 1242
Ex 8:20 Rise up early in the **m.**, and stand...... 1242
Ex 9:13 Rise up early in the **m.**, and stand....... 1242
Ex 10:13 and when it was **m.**, the east wind..... 1242
Ex 12:10 nothing of it remain until the **m.**;........ 1242
Ex 12:10 which remaineth of it until the **m.**....... 1242
Ex 12:22 the door of his house until the **m.** 1242
Ex 14:24 **m.** watch the Lord looked unto the..... 1242
Ex 14:27 his strength when the **m.** appeared;.... 1242
Ex 16:7 And in the **m.**, then ye shall see the... 1242
Ex 16:8 and in the **m.** bread to the full; for..... 1242
Ex 16:12 and in the **m.** ye shall be filled with.... 1242
Ex 16:13 in the **m.** the dew lay round about........ 1242
Ex 16:19 Let no man leave of it till the **m.**, ... 1242
Ex 16:20 some of them left of it until the **m.**,..... 1242
Ex 16:21 they gathered it every **m.**, every 1242
Ex 16:23 up for you to be kept until the **m.**...... 1242
Ex 16:24 they laid it up till the **m.**, as Moses.... 1242
Ex 18:13 from the **m.** unto the evening............ 1242
Ex 18:14 stand by thee from **m.** unto even?...... 1242
Ex 19:16 to pass on the third day in the **m.**, ... 1242
Ex 23:18 of my sacrifice remain until the **m.** 1242
Ex 24:4 and rose up early in the **m.**, and........ 1242
Ex 27:21 from evening to **m.** before the Lord:... 1242
Ex 29:34 remain unto the **m.**, then thou shalt.... 1242
Ex 29:39 one lamb thou shalt offer in the **m.**;.... 1242
Ex 29:41 to the meat offering of the **m.**, and..... 1242
Ex 30:7 thereon sweet incense every **m.**: 1242
Ex 34:2 be ready in the **m.**, and come up in..... 1242
Ex 34:2 and come up in the **m.** unto mount..... 1242
Ex 34:4 and Moses rose up early in the **m.**,.... 1242
Ex 34:25 of the passover be left unto the **m.** 1242
Ex 36:3 unto him free offerings every **m.**........ 1242
Le 6:9 upon the altar all night unto the **m.**,.... 1242
Le 6:12 shall burn wood on it every **m.**, and ... 1242
Le 6:20 perpetual, half of it in the **m.**, and...... 1242
Le 7:15 shall not leave any of it until the **m.**.... 1242

Le 9:17 beside the burnt sacrifice of the **m.**. 1242
Le 19:13 with thee all night until the **m.**.......... 1242
Le 24:3 it from the evening unto the **m.** 1242
Nu 9:12 shall leave none of it unto the **m.** 1242
Nu 9:15 the appearance of fire, until the **m.**...... 1242
Nu 9:21 cloud abode from even unto the **m.**, ... 1242
Nu 9:21 the cloud was taken up in the **m.**, ... 1242
Nu 14:40 they rose up early in the **m.**, and...... 1242
Nu 22:13, 21 Balaam rose up in the **m.**, and 1242
Nu 28:4 one lamb shalt thou offer in the **m.**,.... 1242
Nu 28:8 as the meat offering of the **m.**, and 1242
Nu 28:23 beside the burnt offering in the **m.**, ... 1242
De 16:4 even, remain all night until the **m.**..... 1242
De 16:7 thou shalt turn in the **m.**, and go 1242
De 28:67 In the **m.** thou shalt say, Would God .. 1242
De 28:67 shalt say, Would God it were **m.**!....... 1242
Jos 3:1 Joshua rose early in the **m.**; and 1242
Jos 6:12 Joshua rose early in the **m.**, and 1242
Jos 7:14 In the **m.** therefore ye shall be.......... 1242
Jos 7:16 So Joshua rose up early in the **m.**, ... 1242
Jos 8:10 And Joshua rose up early in the **m.**, ... 1242
Jg 6:28 of the city arose early in the **m.**, ... 1242
Jg 6:31 be put to death whilst it is yet **m.**: 1242
Jg 9:33 it shall be, that in the **m.**, as soon...... 1242
Jg 16:2 In the **m.**, when it is day, we shall..... 1242
Jg 19:5 when they arose early in the **m.**, ... 1242
Jg 19:8 And he arose early in the **m.** on the ... 1242
Jg 19:25 abused her all...night until the **m.**:....... 1242
Jg 19:27 And her lord rose up in the **m.**, and ... 1242
Jg 20:19 children of Israel rose up in the **m.**,..... 1242
Ru 2:7 even from the **m.** until now, that 1242
Ru 3:13 it shall be in the **m.**, that if he will 1242
Ru 3:13 Lord liveth: lie down until the **m.**......... 1242
Ru 3:14 And she lay at his feet until the **m.**: ... 1242
1Sa 1:19 they rose up in the **m.** early, and....... 1242
1Sa 3:15 And Samuel lay until the **m.**, and 1242
1Sa 5:4 they arose early on the morrow **m.**, ... 1242
1Sa 11:11 midst of the host in the **m.** watch, ... 1242
1Sa 14:36 and spoil them until the **m.** light,........ 1242
1Sa 15:12 rose early to meet Saul in the **m.**,....... 1242
1Sa 17:16 drew near **m.** and evening, and......... 7925
1Sa 17:20 David rose up early in the **m.**, and..... 1242
1Sa 19:2 take heed to thyself until the **m.**, ... 1242
1Sa 19:11 him, and to slay him in the **m.**:......... 1242
1Sa 20:35 And it came to pass in the **m.**, that.... 1242
1Sa 25:22 that pertain to him by the **m.** light...... 1242
1Sa 25:34 been left unto Nabal by the **m.** light.... 1242
1Sa 25:36 less or more, until the **m.** light.......... 1242
1Sa 25:37 it came to pass in the **m.**, when the ... 1242
1Sa 29:10 now rise up early in the **m.** with........ 1242
1Sa 29:10 as soon as ye be up early in the **m.**,... 1242
1Sa 29:11 rose up early to depart in the **m.**, ... 1242
2Sa 2:27 then in the **m.** the people had gone 1242
2Sa 11:14 And it came to pass in the **m.**, that.... 1242
2Sa 17:22 by the **m.** light there lacked not one ... 1242
2Sa 23:4 he shall be as the light of the **m.**, ... 1242
2Sa 23:4 riseth, even a **m.** without clouds; 1242
2Sa 24:11 for when David was up in the **m.**, ... 1242
2Sa 24:15 upon Israel from the **m.** even to the ... 1242
1Ki 3:21 I rose in the **m.** to give my child 1242
1Ki 3:21 when I had considered it in the **m.**, ... 1242
1Ki 17:6 him bread and flesh in the **m.**, and 1242
1Ki 18:26 of Baal from **m.** even until noon,........ 1242
2Ki 3:20 it came to pass in the **m.**, when the ... 1242
2Ki 3:22 they rose up early in the **m.**, and the.. 1242
2Ki 7:9 if we tarry till the **m.** light, some 1242
2Ki 10:8 entering in of the gate until the **m.**,.... 1242
2Ki 10:9 it came to pass in the **m.**, that he 1242
2Ki 16:15 altar burn the **m.** burnt offering, ... 1242
2Ki 19:35 and when they arose early in the **m.**,.. 1242
1Ch 9:27 and the opening thereof every **m.**........ 1242
1Ch 16:40 offering continually **m.** and evening, ... 1242
1Ch 23:30 every **m.** to thank and praise the 1242
2Ch 2:4 the burnt offerings **m.** and evening, ... 1242
2Ch 13:11 every **m.** and every evening burnt...... 1242
2Ch 20:20 they rose early in the **m.**, and went.... 1242
2Ch 31:3 the **m.** and evening burnt offerings, ... 1242
Ezr 3:3 burnt offerings **m.** and evening. 1242
Neh 4:21 the rising of the **m.** till the stars 7837
Neh 8:3 water gate from the **m.** until midday,.... 216
Job 1:5 and rose up early in the **m.**, and........ 1242
Job 4:20 are destroyed from **m.** to evening: 1242
Job 7:18 thou shouldest visit him every **m.**,....... 1242
Job 7:21 thou shalt seek me in the **m.**, but 7836
Job 11:17 shine forth, thou shalt be as the **m.**.... 1242
Job 24:17 For the **m.** is to them even as the 1242
Job 38:7 When the **m.** stars sang together, ... 1242
Job 38:12 Hast thou commanded the **m.** since 1242
Job 41:18 eyes are like the eyelids of the **m.**. 7837
Ps 5:3 voice shalt thou hear in the **m.**, ... 1242
Ps 5:3 in the **m.** will I direct my prayer........ 1242
Ps 30:5 a night, but joy cometh in the **m.**. 1242
Ps 49:14 have dominion over them in the **m.**; ... 1242
Ps 55:17 and **m.**, and at noon, will I pray,........ 1242
Ps 59:16 sing aloud of thy mercy in the **m.**:...... 1242
Ps 65:8 of the **m.** and evening to rejoice. 1242
Ps 73:14 plagued, and chastened every **m.**. 1242
Ps 88:13 in the **m.** shall my prayer prevent 1242
Ps 90:5 in the **m.** they are like grass which..... 1242
Ps 90:6 In the **m.** it flourisheth, and groweth... 1242
Ps 92:2 forth thy lovingkindness in the **m.**, ... 1242
Ps 110:3 holiness from the womb of the **m.**: 4891
Ps 119:147 prevented the dawning of the **m.**, and ....
Ps 130:6 than they that watch for the **m.**: 1242
Ps 130:6 than they that watch for the **m.**. 1242
Ps 139:9 If I take the wings of the **m.**, and 7837
Ps 143:8 hear thy lovingkindness in the **m.**; 1242
Pr 7:18 us take our fill of love until the **m.**: 1242
Pr 27:14 rising early in the **m.**, it shall be 1242
Ec 10:16 and thy princes eat in the **m.**! 1242
Ec 11:6 In the **m.** sow thy seed, and in the 1242
Ca 6:10 is she that looketh forth as the **m.**, ... 7837
Isa 5:11 them that rise up early in the **m.**, ... 1242
Isa 14:12 heaven, O Lucifer, son of the **m.**! 7837
Isa 17:11 in the **m.** shalt thou make thy seed 1242
Isa 17:14 and before the **m.** he is not. 1242
Isa 21:12 The **m.** cometh, and also the night: 1242
Isa 28:19 for **m.** by **m.** shall it pass over, by..... 1242
Isa 33:2 be thou their arm every **m.**, our 1242
Isa 37:36 when they arose early in the **m.**, ... 1242
Isa 38:13 I reckoned till **m.**, that, as a lion, so... 1242
Isa 50:4 he wakeneth **m.** by **m.**, he wakeneth.. 1242
Isa 58:8 thy light break forth as the **m.**, ... 7837
Jer 5:8 They were as fed horses in the **m.**:..... 7904
Jer 20:16 and let him hear the cry in the **m.**,..... 1242
Jer 21:12 Execute judgment in the **m.**, and 1242
La 3:23 They are new every **m.**: great is thy.. 1242
Eze 7:7 The **m.** is come unto thee, O thou..... 6843
Eze 7:10 the **m.** is gone forth; the rod hath...... 6843
Eze 12:8 the **m.** came the word of the Lord 1242
Eze 24:18 I spake unto the people in the **m.**: 1242
Eze 24:18 I did in the **m.** as I was commanded.. 1242
Eze 33:22 until he came to me in the **m.**; 1242
Eze 46:13 thou shalt prepare it every **m.**.......... 1242
Eze 46:14 a meat offering for it every **m.**, ... 1242
Eze 46:15 every **m.** for a continual...offering. 1242
Da 6:19 king arose very early in the **m.**,......... 5053
Da 8:26 vision of the evening and the **m.** 1242
Ho 6:3 going forth is prepared as the **m.**; 7837
Ho 6:4 your goodness is as a **m.** cloud,......... 1242
Ho 7:6 the **m.** it burneth as a flaming fire. 1242
Ho 10:15 in a **m.** shall the king of Israel.......... 7837
Ho 13:3 they shall be as the **m.** cloud, and...... 1242
Joe 2:2 **m.** spread upon the mountains:.......... 7837
Am 4:4 bring your sacrifices every **m.**, ... 1242
Am 4:13 that maketh the **m.** darkness, and 7837
Am 5:8 the shadow of death into the **m.**, ... 1242
Jon 4:7 when the **m.** rose the next day,......... 7837
Mic 2:1 when the **m.** is light, they practise 1242
Zep 3:5 every **m.** doth he bring his judgment... 1242
Mt 16:3 **in the m., It will be foul weather** .. *4404*
Mt 20:1 **out early in the m. to hire** ....
Mt 21:18 Now in the **m.** as he returned into *4405*
Mt 27:1 When the **m.** was come, all the chief.. *4405*
Mk 1:35 in the **m.**, rising up a great while *4404*
Mk 11:20 And in the **m.**, as they passed by,...... *4404*
Mk 13:35 **at the cockcrowing, or in the m.:** .. *4404*
Mk 15:1 in the **m.** the chief priests held......... *4404*
Mk 16:2 very early in the **m.**, the first day ....
Lu 21:38 all the people came early in the **m.** ....
Lu 24:1 very early in the **m.**, they came unto........
Joh 8:2 early in the **m.** he came again into...........
Joh 21:4 But when the **m.** was now come,....... *4405*
Ac 5:21 into the temple early in the **m.**, ...
Ac 28:23 the prophets, from **m.** till evening. *4404*
Re 2:28 **And I will give him the m. star**..... *4407*
Re 22:16 **David, and the bright and m. star.** .*3720*

MORNING-CLOUD See MORNING and CLOUD.

MORNING-LIGHT See MORNING and LIGHT.

MORNING-STAR See MORNING and STAR.

MORNING-WATCH See MORNING and WATCH.

MORROW
Ge 19:34 it came to pass on the **m.**, that the 4283
Ex 8:10 And he said, To **m.**. And he said, ... 4279
Ex 8:23 thy people: to **m.** shall this sign be..... 4279
Ex 8:29 servants, and from his people, to **m.**:.. 4279
Ex 9:5 To **m.** the Lord shall do this thing...... 4279
Ex 9:6 the Lord did that thing on the **m.**,...... 4283
Ex 9:18 to **m.** abut this time I will cause 4279
Ex 10:4 to **m.** will I bring the locusts into 4279
Ex 16:23 To **m.** is the rest of the holy sabbath.. 4279
Ex 17:9 to **m.** I will stand on the top of the 4279
Ex 18:13 pass on the **m.**, that Moses sat to...... 4283
Ex 19:10 sanctify them to day and to **m.**, ... 4279
Ex 32:5 said, To **m.** is a feast to the Lord. 4279
Ex 32:6 And they rose up early on the **m.**, ... 4283
Ex 32:30 to pass on the **m.**, that Moses said 4283
Le 7:16 on the **m.** also the remainder of it...... 4283
Le 19:6 same day ye offer it, and on the **m.**:... 4283
Le 22:30 shall leave none of it until the **m.**: 1242
Le 23:11 on the **m.** after the sabbath the 4283
Le 23:15 you from the **m.** after the sabbath, ... 4283
Le 23:16 Even unto the **m.** after the seventh.... 4283
Nu 11:18 Sanctify yourselves against to **m.**, ... 4279
Nu 14:25 To **m.** turn you, and get you into...... 4279
Nu 16:5 to **m.** the Lord will shew who are 1242
Nu 16:7 in them before the Lord to **m.**:.......... 4279
Nu 16:16 thou, and they, and Aaron, to **m.**: 4279
Nu 16:41 But on the **m.** all the congregation 4283
Nu 17:8 that on the **m.** Moses went into the 4283
Nu 22:41 to pass on the **m.**, that Balak............ 1242
Nu 33:3 on the **m.** after the passover the........ 4283
Jos 3:5 for to **m.** the Lord will do wonders...... 4279
Jos 5:11 land on the **m.** after the passover,...... 4283
Jos 5:12 the manna ceased on the **m.** after 4283
Jos 7:13 Sanctify yourselves against to **m.**: 4279
Jos 11:6 to **m.** about this time will I deliver 4279
Jos 22:18 the Lord, that to **m.** he will be wroth ..4279
Jg 6:38 for he rose up early on the **m.**, and.... 4283
Jg 9:42 to pass on the **m.**, that the people 4283
Jg 19:9 to **m.** get you early on your way,........ 4279
Jg 20:28 to **m.** I will deliver them into............ 4279
Jg 21:4 to pass on the **m.**, that the people 4283
1Sa 5:3 of Ashdod arose early on the **m.**, ... 4283
1Sa 5:4 they arose early on the **m.** morning,... 4283
1Sa 9:16 To **m.** about this time I will send 4279
1Sa 9:19 to **m.** I will let thee go, and will......... 1242
1Sa 11:9 To **m.**, by that time the sun be hot.... 4279
1Sa 11:10 To **m.** we will come out unto you, ... 4279
1Sa 11:11 it was so on the **m.**, that Saul put...... 4283
1Sa 18:10 to pass on the **m.**, that the evil 4283
1Sa 19:11 to night, to **m.** thou shalt be slain. 4279
1Sa 20:5 to **m.** is the new moon, and I should .. 4279
1Sa 20:12 sounded my father about to **m.** any 4279
1Sa 20:18 to David, To **m.** is the new moon: 4279
1Sa 20:27 came to pass on the **m.**, which was.... 4283
1Sa 28:19 to **m.** shalt thou and thy sons be........ 4279
1Sa 31:8 on the **m.**, when the Philistines 4283
2Sa 11:12 and to **m.** I will let thee depart.......... 4279
2Sa 11:12 in Jerusalem that day, and the **m.**....... 4283
1Ki 19:2 of them by to **m.** about this time. 4279
1Ki 20:6 send my servants unto thee to **m.**...... 4279
2Ki 6:28 day, and we will eat my son to **m.**. 4279
2Ki 7:1 To **m.** about this time...a measure 4279
2Ki 7:18 be to **m.** about this time in the gate 4279
2Ki 8:15 it came to pass on the **m.**, that he 4283
2Ki 10:6 me to Jezreel by to **m.** this time. 4279
1Ch 10:8 on the **m.**, when the Philistines 4283
1Ch 29:21 on the **m.** after that day, even a 4283
2Ch 20:16 To **m.** go ye down against them: 4279
2Ch 20:17 to **m.** go out against them: for the 4279
Es 2:14 on the **m.** she returned into the......... 1242
Es 5:8 will do to **m.** as the king hath said...... 4279
Es 5:12 and to **m.** am I invited unto her also... 4279
Es 5:14 to **m.** speak thou unto the king.......... 1242
Es 9:13 to do to **m.** also according unto 4279
Pr 3:28 come again, and to **m.** I will give; 4279
Pr 27:1 Boast not thyself of to **m.**; for thou.... 4279
Isa 22:13 and drink; for to **m.** we shall die. 4279
Isa 56:12 to **m.** shall be as this day, and much... 4279
Jer 20:3 to pass on the **m.**, that Pashur 4283
Zep 3:3 they gnaw not the bones till the **m.**. ... 1242
Mt 6:30 **is, and to m. is cast into the oven,**... *839*
Mt 6:34 **therefore no thought for the m.:** *839*
Mt 6:34 **for the m. shall take thought for** *839*
Mk 11:12 on the **m.**, when they were come *1887*
Lu 10:35 **And on the m. when he departed,** ... *839*
Lu 12:28 **and to m. is cast into the oven;** *839*

Lu 13:32 **and I do cures to day and to m.,** *839*
Lu 13:33 **and to m., and the day following:** *839*
Ac 4:5 to pass on the **m.**, that their rulers, *839*
Ac 10:9 On the **m.**, as they went on their *1887*
Ac 10:23 And on the **m.** Peter went away with *1887*
Ac 10:24 And the **m.** after they entered into *1887*
Ac 20:7 them, ready to depart on the **m.**; *1887*
Ac 22:30 On the **m.**, because he would have *1887*
Ac 23:15 he bring him down unto you to **m.**, *839*
Ac 23:20 down Paul to **m.** into the council, *839*
Ac 23:32 On the **m.** they left the horsemen *1887*
Ac 25:17 on the **m.** I sat on the judgment *1836*
Ac 25:22 To **m.**, said he, thou shalt hear him. *839*
Ac 25:23 And on the **m.**, when Agrippa was *1887*
1Co 15:32 us eat and drink; for to **m.** we die. *839*
Jas 4:13 To day or to **m.** we will go into such *839*
Jas 4:14 ye know not what shall be on the **m.** *839*

MORSEL See also MORSELS.
Ge 18:5 And I will fetch a **m.** of bread, and 6595
Jg 19:5 thine heart with a **m.** of bread, and 6595
Ru 2:14 bread, and dip thy **m.** in the vinegar. 6595
1Sa 2:36 piece of silver and a **m.** of bread, 3603
1Sa 28:22 let me set a **m.** of bread before 6595
1Ki 17:11 Bring me, I pray thee, a **m.** of bread 6595
Job 31:17 Or have eaten my **m.** myself alone, 6595
Pr 17:1 Better is a dry **m.**, and quietness 6595
Pr 23:8 The **m.** which thou hast eaten shalt 6595
Heb 12:16 one **m.** of meat sold his birthright. *1035*

MORSELS
Ps 147:17 He casteth forth his ice like **m.**: 6595

MORTAL See also IMMORTAL.
Job 4:17 **m.** man be more just than God? 582
Ro 6:12 therefore reign in your **m.** body, *2349*
Ro 8:11 also quicken your **m.** bodies by his *2349*
1Co 15:53 this **m.** must put on immortality. *2349*
1Co 15:54 **m.** shall have put on immortality, *2349*
2Co 4:11 be made manifest in our **m.** flesh. *2349*

MORTALITY See also IMMORTALITY.
2Co 5:4 **m.** might be swallowed up of life. *2349*

MORTALLY
De 19:11 and smite him **m.** that he die, and 5315

MORTAR See also MORTER.
Nu 11:8 or beat it in a **m.**, and baked it in 4085
Pr 27:22 thou shouldest bray a fool in a **m.** 4388

MORTER See also MORTAR.
Ge 11:3 stone, and slime had they for **m.** 2563
Ex 1:14 hard bondage, in **m.**, and in brick, 2563
Le 14:42 and he shall take other **m.**, and 6083
Le 14:45 and all the **m.** of the house; 6083
Isa 41:25 come upon princes as upon **m.**, 2563
Eze 13:10 others daubed it with untempered **m.**:
Eze 13:11 which daub it with untempered **m.**,
Eze 13:14 ye have daubed with untempered **m.**,
Eze 13:15 have daubed it with untempered **m.**,
Eze 22:28 daubed them with untempered **m.**,
Na 3:14 go into clay, and tread the **m.**, 2563

MORTGAGED
Ne 5:3 We have **m.** our lands, vineyards, 6148

MORTIFY
Ro 8:13 the Spirit do **m.** the deeds of the *2289*
Col 3:5 **M.** therefore your members which *3499*

MOSERA (mo-se'-rah) See also MOSEROTH.
De 10:6 of the children of Jaakan to **M.**: 4149

MOSEROTH (mo-se'-roth) See also MOSERA.
Nu 33:30 Hashmonah,...encamped at **M.** 4149
Nu 33:31 they departed from **M.**, and pitched 4149

MOSES (mo'-zez) See also MOSES'.
Ge *general title* Book of **M.**, Called Genesis
Ex *general title* Book Of **M.**, Called Exodus
Ex 2:10 she called his name **M.**: and she 4872
Ex 2:11 in those days, when **M.** was grown, 4872
Ex 2:14 **M.** feared, and said, Surely this 4872
Ex 2:15 this thing, he sought to slay **M.** 4872
Ex 2:15 **M.** fled from the face of Pharaoh, 4872
Ex 2:17 **M.** stood up and helped them, and 4872
Ex 2:21 **M.** was content to dwell with the 4872
Ex 2:21 he gave **M.** Zipporah his daughter. 4872
Ex 3:1 Now **M.** kept the flock of Jethro his 4872
Ex 3:3 **M.** said, I will now turn aside, and 4872
Ex 3:4 midst of the bush, and said, **M.**, **M.** 4872
Ex 3:6 **M.** hid his face; for he was afraid to 4872
Ex 3:11 **M.** said unto God, Who am I, that I 4872
Ex 3:13 **M.** said unto God, Behold, when I 4872
Ex 3:14 God said unto **M.**, I Am That I Am: 4872
Ex 3:15 God said moreover unto **M.**, Thus 4872
Ex 4:1 And **M.** answered and said, But, 4872
Ex 4:3 serpent; and **M.** fled from before it. 4872
Ex 4:4 Lord said unto **M.**, Put forth thine 4872
Ex 4:10 **M.** said unto the Lord, O my Lord, 4872
Ex 4:14 the Lord was kindled against **M.**, 4872
Ex 4:18 **M.** went and returned to Jethro his 4872
Ex 4:18 And Jethro said to **M.**, Go in peace. 4872
Ex 4:19 Lord said unto **M.** in Midian, Go, 4872
Ex 4:20 **M.** took his wife and his sons, and 4872
Ex 4:20 **M.** took the rod of God in his hand. 4872
Ex 4:21 the Lord said unto **M.**, When thou 4872
Ex 4:27 Go into the wilderness to meet **M.** 4872
Ex 4:28 **M.** told Aaron all the words of the 4872
Ex 4:29 **M.** and Aaron went and gathered 4872
Ex 4:30 the Lord had spoken unto **M.**, and 4872
Ex 5:1 afterward **M.** and Aaron went in, 4872
Ex 5:4 **M.** and Aaron, let the people from 4872
Ex 5:20 they met **M.** and Aaron, who stood 4872
Ex 5:22 **M.** returned unto the Lord, and 4872
Ex 6:1 the Lord said unto **M.**, Now shalt 4872
Ex 6:2 God spake unto **M.**, and said unto 4872
Ex 6:9 **M.** spake so unto the children of 4872
Ex 6:9 they hearkened not unto **M.** for 4872
Ex 6:10 the Lord spake unto **M.**, saying, 4872
Ex 6:12 **M.** spake before the Lord, saying, 4872
Ex 6:13 the Lord spake unto **M.** and unto 4872
Ex 6:20 and she bare him Aaron and **M.**: 4872
Ex 6:26 These are that Aaron and **M.**, to 4872
Ex 6:27 these are that **M.** and Aaron. 4872
Ex 6:28 the Lord spake unto **M.** in the land 4872
Ex 6:29 the Lord spake unto **M.**, saying, I 4872
Ex 6:30 **M.** said before the Lord, Behold, I 4872
Ex 7:1 The Lord said unto **M.**, See, I have 4872
Ex 7:6 And **M.** and Aaron did as the Lord 4872
Ex 7:7 **M.** was fourscore years old, and 4872
Ex 7:8 the Lord spake unto **M.** and unto 4872
Ex 7:10 **M.**...Aaron went in unto Pharaoh, 4872
Ex 7:14 Lord said unto **M.**, Pharaoh's heart 4872
Ex 7:19 the Lord spake unto **M.**, Say unto 4872
Ex 7:20 **M.** and Aaron did so, as the Lord 4872
Ex 8:1 the Lord spake unto **M.**, Go unto 4872
Ex 8:5 the Lord spake unto **M.**, Say unto 4872
Ex 8:8 Pharaoh called for **M.** and Aaron, 4872
Ex 8:9 **M.** said unto Pharaoh, Glory over 4872
Ex 8:12 And **M.** and Aaron went out from 4872
Ex 8:12 **M.** cried unto the Lord because of 4872
Ex 8:13 did according to the word of **M.**; 4872
Ex 8:16 Lord said unto **M.**, Say unto Aaron, 4872
Ex 8:20 Lord said unto **M.**, Rise up early 4872
Ex 8:25 called for **M.** and for Aaron, and 4872
Ex 8:26 **M.** said, It is not meet so to do; for 4872
Ex 8:29 And **M.** said, Behold, I go out from 4872
Ex 8:30 **M.** went out from Pharaoh, and 4872
Ex 8:31 did according to the word of **M.**; 4872
Ex 9:1 the Lord said unto **M.**, Go in unto 4872
Ex 9:8 Lord said unto **M.** and unto Aaron, 4872
Ex 9:8 **M.** sprinkle it toward the heaven 4872
Ex 9:10 **M.** sprinkled it up toward heaven; 4872
Ex 9:11 could not stand before **M.** because 4872
Ex 9:12 as the Lord had spoken unto **M.** 4872
Ex 9:13 Lord said unto **M.**, Rise up early 4872
Ex 9:22 Lord said unto **M.**, Stretch forth 4872
Ex 9:23 **M.** stretched forth his rod toward 4872
Ex 9:27 sent, and called for **M.** and Aaron, 4872
Ex 9:29 **M.** said unto him, As soon as I am 4872
Ex 9:33 And **M.** went out of the city from 4872
Ex 9:35 go; as the Lord had spoken by **M.** 4872
Ex 10:1 the Lord said unto **M.**, Go in unto 4872
Ex 10:3 And **M.** and Aaron came in unto 4872
Ex 10:8 **M.** and Aaron were brought again 4872
Ex 10:9 **M.** said, We will go with our young 4872
Ex 10:12 the Lord said unto **M.**, Stretch out 4872
Ex 10:13 **M.** stretched forth his rod over the 4872
Ex 10:16 Pharaoh called for **M.** and Aaron 4872
Ex 10:21 Lord said unto **M.**, Stretch out 4872
Ex 10:22 **M.** stretched forth his hand toward 4872
Ex 10:24 Pharaoh called unto **M.**, and said, 4872
Ex 10:25 **M.** said, Thou must give us also 4872
Ex 10:29 **M.** said, Thou hast spoken well, I 4872
Ex 11:1 Lord said unto **M.**, Yet will I bring 4872
Ex 11:3 **M.** was very great in the land of 4872
Ex 11:4 And **M.** said, Thus saith the Lord, 4872
Ex 11:9 Lord said unto **M.**, Pharaoh shall 4872
Ex 11:10 **M.** and Aaron did all these wonders 4872
Ex 12:1 unto **m.** and Aaron in the land of 4872
Ex 12:21 **M.** called for all the elders of Israel, 4872
Ex 12:28 Lord had commanded **M.**...Aaron, 4872
Ex 12:31 called for **M.** and Aaron by night, 4872
Ex 12:35 did according to the word of **M.**; 4872
Ex 12:43 the Lord said unto **M.** and Aaron, 4872
Ex 12:50 Lord commanded **M.** and Aaron, 4872
Ex 13:1 the Lord spake unto **M.**, saying, 4872
Ex 13:3 **M.** said unto the people, Remember 4872
Ex 13:19 **M.** took the bones of Joseph with 4872
Ex 14:1 the Lord spake unto **M.**, saying, 4872
Ex 14:11 they said unto **M.**, Because there 4872
Ex 14:13 **M.** said unto the people, Fear ye 4872
Ex 14:15 the Lord said unto **M.**, Wherefore 4872
Ex 14:21 **M.** stretched out his hand over the 4872
Ex 14:26 unto **M.**, Stretch out thine hand 4872
Ex 14:27 **M.** stretched forth his hand over 4872
Ex 14:31 the Lord, and his servant **M.** 4872
Ex 15:1 Then sang **M.** and the children of 4872
Ex 15:22 **M.** brought Israel from the Red 4872
Ex 15:24 the people murmured against **M.**, 4872
Ex 16:2 murmured against **M.** and Aaron 4872
Ex 16:4 unto **M.**, Behold, I will rain bread 4872
Ex 16:6 **M.** and Aaron said unto all the 4872
Ex 16:8 **M.** said, This shall be, when the 4872
Ex 16:9 **M.** spake unto Aaron, Say unto all 4872
Ex 16:11 the Lord spake unto **M.**, saying, 4872
Ex 16:15 And **M.** said unto them, This is the 4872
Ex 16:19 **M.** said, Let no man leave of it till 4872
Ex 16:20 they hearkened not unto **M.**; but 4872
Ex 16:20 and **M.** was wroth with them. 4872
Ex 16:22 the congregation came and told **M.** 4872
Ex 16:24 it up till the morning, as **M.** bade: 4872
Ex 16:25 And **M.** said, Eat that to day; for 4872
Ex 16:28 the Lord said unto **m.**, How long 4872
Ex 16:32 **M.** said, This is the thing which 4872
Ex 16:33 **M.** said unto Aaron, Take a pot, 4872
Ex 16:34 As the Lord commanded **M.**, so 4872
Ex 17:2 the people did chide with **M.**, and 4872
Ex 17:2 **M.** said unto them, why chide ye 4872
Ex 17:3 people murmured against **M.**, and 4872
Ex 17:4 **M.** cried unto the Lord, saying, 4872
Ex 17:5 Lord said unto **M.**, Go on before 4872
Ex 17:6 **M.** did so in the sight of the elders 4872
Ex 17:9 **M.** said unto Joshua, Choose us 4872
Ex 17:10 Joshua did as **m.** had said to him, 4872
Ex 17:10 **M.**, Aaron, and Hur went up to the 4872
Ex 17:11 when **M.** held up his hand, that 4872
Ex 17:14 the Lord said unto **M.**, Write this 4872
Ex 17:15 **M.** built an altar, and called the 4872
Ex 18:1 of all that God had done for **M.**, 4872
Ex 18:5 wife unto **M.** in the wilderness, 4872
Ex 18:6 he said unto **M.**, I thy father in law 4872
Ex 18:7 **M.** went out to meet his father in 4872
Ex 18:8 **M.** told his father in law all that 4872
Ex 18:13 that **M.** sat to judge the people: 4872
Ex 18:13 stood by **M.** from the morning unto 4872
Ex 18:15 And **M.** said unto his father in law, 4872
Ex 18:24 **M.** hearkened to the voice of his 4872
Ex 18:25 **M.** chose able men out of all Israel, 4872
Ex 18:26 hard causes they brought unto **M.**, 4872
Ex 18:27 **M.** let his father in law depart; 4872
Ex 19:3 And **M.** went up unto God, and the 4872
Ex 19:7 **M.** came and called for the elders 4872
Ex 19:8 And **M.** returned the words of the 4872
Ex 19:9 the Lord said unto **M.**, Lo, I come 4872
Ex 19:9 **M.** told the words of the people 4872
Ex 19:10 Lord said unto **M.**, Go unto the 4872
Ex 19:14 And **M.** went down from the mount 4872
Ex 19:17 **M.** brought forth the people out of 4872
Ex 19:19 **M.** spake, and God answered him 4872
Ex 19:20 Lord called **M.** up to the top of the 4872
Ex 19:20 top of the mount; and **M.** went up 4872
Ex 19:21 the Lord said unto **M.**, Go down, 4872
Ex 19:23 **M.** said unto the Lord, The people 4872
Ex 19:25 **M.** went down unto the people, and 4872
Ex 20:19 said unto **M.**, Speak thou with us, 4872
Ex 20:20 **M.** said unto the people, Fear not: 4872
Ex 20:21 and **M.** drew near unto the thick 4872
Ex 20:22 the Lord said unto **M.**, Thus thou 4872
Ex 24:1 unto **M.**, Come up unto the Lord, 4872
Ex 24:2 **M.** alone shall come near the Lord: 4872
Ex 24:3 **M.** came and told the people all 4872

Ex	24:4	**M.** wrote all the words of the Lord,	4872
Ex	24:6	**M.** took half of the blood, and put	4872
Ex	24:8	**M.** took the blood, and sprinkled it	4872
Ex	24:9	Then went up **M.**, and Aaron, and	4872
Ex	24:12	Lord said unto **M.**, Come up to me	4872
Ex	24:13	And **M.** rose up, and his minister	4872
Ex	24:13	**M.** went up into the mount of God.	4872
Ex	24:15	**M.** went up into the mount, and a	4872
Ex	24:16	he called unto **M.** out of the midst	4872
Ex	24:18	**M.** went into the midst of the cloud,	4872
Ex	24:18	**M.** was in the mount forty days	4872
Ex	25:1	the Lord spake unto **M.**, saying,	4872
Ex	30:11,	17 the Lord spake unto **M.**, saying,	4872
Ex	30:22	the Lord spake unto **M.**, saying,	4872
Ex	30:34	the Lord said unto **M.**, Take unto	4872
Ex	31:1,	12 the Lord spake unto **M.**, saying,	4872
Ex	31:18	And he gave unto **M.**, when he had	4872
Ex	32:1	the people saw that **M.** delayed to	4872
Ex	32:1	for as for this **M.**, the man that	4872
Ex	32:7	Lord said unto **M.**, Go, get thee	4872
Ex	32:9	the Lord said unto **M.**, I have seen	4872
Ex	32:11	**M.** besought the Lord his God, and	4872
Ex	32:15	**M.** turned and went down from the	
Ex	32:17	as they shouted, he said unto **M.**,	4872
Ex	32:21	And **M.** said unto Aaron, What did	4872
Ex	32:23	for as for this **M.**, the man that	4872
Ex	32:25	when **M.** saw that the people were	4872
Ex	32:26	**M.** stood in the gate of the camp,	4872
Ex	32:28	did according to the word of **M.**:	4872
Ex	32:29	**M.** had said, Consecrate yourselves	4872
Ex	32:30	**M.** said unto the people, Ye have	4872
Ex	32:31	**M.** returned unto the Lord, and	4872
Ex	32:33	the Lord said unto **M.**, Whosoever	4872
Ex	33:1	Lord said unto **M.**, Depart, and go	4872
Ex	33:5	Lord had said unto **M.**, Say unto	4872
Ex	33:7	And **M.** took the tabernacle, and	4872
Ex	33:8	**M.** went out unto the tabernacle,	4872
Ex	33:8	his tent door, and looked after **M.**,	4872
Ex	33:9	**M.** entered into the tabernacle, the	4872
Ex	33:9	and the Lord talked with **M.**.	4872
Ex	33:11	Lord spake unto **M.** face to face,	4872
Ex	33:12	**M.** said unto the Lord, See, thou	4872
Ex	33:17	Lord said unto **M.**, I will do this	4872
Ex	34:1	Lord said unto **M.**, Hew thee two	4872
Ex	34:4	**M.** rose up early in the morning,	4872
Ex	34:8	**M.** made haste, and bowed his	4872
Ex	34:27	the Lord said unto **M.**, Write thou	4872
Ex	34:29	**M.** came down from mount Sinai	4872
Ex	34:29	**M.** wist not that the skin of his face	4872
Ex	34:30	all the children of Israel saw **M.**,	4872
Ex	34:31	**M.** called unto them; and Aaron	4872
Ex	34:31	him: and **M.** talked with them	4872
Ex	34:33	**M.** had done speaking with them,	4872
Ex	34:34	when **M.** went in before the Lord	4872
Ex	34:35	of Israel saw the face of **M.**, that	4872
Ex	34:35	**M.** put the vail upon his face again,	4872
Ex	35:1	**M.** gathered all the congregation	4872
Ex	35:4	**M.** spake unto all the congregation	4872
Ex	35:20	departed from the presence of **M.**.	4872
Ex	35:29	to be made by the hand of **M.**.	4872
Ex	35:30	**M.** said unto the children of Israel,	4872
Ex	36:2	**M.** called Bezaleel and Aholiab,	4872
Ex	36:3	they received of **M.** all the offering,	4872
Ex	36:5	they spake unto **M.**, saying, The	4872
Ex	36:6	**M.** gave commandment, and they	4872
Ex	38:21	to the commandment of **M.**, for	4872
Ex	38:22	all that the Lord commanded **M.**.	4872
Ex	39:1,	5,7,21,26,29,31 Lord commanded **M.**.	4872
Ex	39:32	all that the Lord commanded **M.**,	4872
Ex	39:33	brought the tabernacle unto **M.**,	4872
Ex	39:42	all that the Lord commanded **M.**,	4872
Ex	39:43	**M.** did look upon all the work, and,	4872
Ex	39:43	they done it: and **M.** blessed them.	4872
Ex	40:1	the Lord spake unto **M.**, saying,	4872
Ex	40:16	Thus did **M.**: according to all that	4872
Ex	40:18	**M.** reared up the tabernacle, and	4872
Ex	40:19	it; as the Lord commanded **M.**.	4872
Ex	40:21	as the Lord commanded **M.**.	4872
Ex	40:23	as the Lord commanded **M.**.	4872
Ex	40:25,	27,29 the Lord commanded **M.**.	4872
Ex	40:31	**M.** and Aaron and his sons washed	4872
Ex	40:32	as the Lord commanded **M.**.	4872
Ex	40:33	gate. So **M.** finished the work.	4872
Ex	40:35	**M.** was not able to enter into the	4872
Le	*general*	*title* Book Of **M.**, Called Leviticus	
Le	1:1	the Lord called unto **M.**, and spake	4872
Le	4:1	the Lord spake unto **M.**, saying,	4872
Le	5:14	the Lord spake unto **M.**, saying,	4872
Le	6:1,8,	19,24 the Lord spake unto **M.**,	4872
Le	7:22,	28 the Lord spake unto **M.**, saying,	4872
Le	7:38	Which the Lord commanded **M.** in	4872
Le	8:1	the Lord spake unto **M.**, saying,	4872
Le	8:4	**M.** did as the Lord commanded	4872
Le	8:5	**M.** said unto the congregation,	4872
Le	8:6	**M.** brought Aaron and his sons,	4872
Le	8:9	as the Lord commanded **M.**.	4872
Le	8:10	And **M.** took the anointing oil, and	4872
Le	8:13	**M.** brought Aaron's sons, and put	4872
Le	8:13	them; as the Lord commanded **M.**	4872
Le	8:15	**M.** took the blood, and put it upon	4872
Le	8:16	and **M.** burned it upon the altar.	4872
Le	8:17	camp; as the Lord commanded **M.**	4872
Le	8:19	and **M.** sprinkled the blood upon the	4872
Le	8:20	**M.** burnt the head, and the pieces,	4872
Le	8:21	**M.** burnt the whole ram upon the	4872
Le	8:21	Lord; as the Lord commanded **M.**.	4872
Le	8:23	**M.** took of the blood of it, and put	4872
Le	8:24	**M.** put of the blood upon the tip of	4872
Le	8:24	and **M.** sprinkled the blood upon the	4872
Le	8:28	**M.** took them from off their hands,	4872
Le	8:29	**M.** took the breast, and waved it	4872
Le	8:29	part; as the Lord commanded **M.**.	4872
Le	8:30	**M.** took of the anointing oil, and of	4872
Le	8:31	**M.** said unto Aaron and to his sons,	4872
Le	8:36	Lord commanded by the hand of **M.**.	4872
Le	9:1	that **M.** called Aaron and his sons,	4872
Le	9:5	brought that which **M.** commanded	4872
Le	9:6	**M.** said, This is the thing which the	4872
Le	9:7	**M.** said unto Aaron, Go unto the	4872
Le	9:10	altar; as the Lord commanded **M.**	4872
Le	9:21	before the Lord; as **M.** commanded.	4872
Le	9:23	And **M.** and Aaron went into the	4872
Le	10:3	**M.** said unto Aaron, This is it that	4872
Le	10:4	**M.** called Mishael and Elzaphan,	4872
Le	10:5	out of the camp; as **M.** had said.	4872
Le	10:6	And **M.** said unto Aaron, and unto	4872
Le	10:7	did according to the word of **M.**.	4872
Le	10:11	unto them by the hand of **M.**	4872
Le	10:12	And **M.** spake unto Aaron, and unto	4872
Le	10:16	**M.** diligently sought the goat of the	4872
Le	10:19	Aaron said unto **M.**, Behold, this	4872
Le	10:20	And when **M.** heard that, he was	4872
Le	11:1	Lord spake unto **M.** and to Aaron,	4872
Le	12:1	the Lord spake unto **M.**, saying,	4872
Le	13:1	the Lord spake unto **M.** and Aaron,	4872
Le	14:1	the Lord spake unto **M.**, saying,	4872
Le	14:33	the Lord spake unto **M.** and unto	4872
Le	15:1	Lord spake unto **M.** and to Aaron,	4872
Le	16:1	Lord spake unto **M.** after the death	4872
Le	16:2	And the Lord said unto **M.**, Speak	4872
Le	16:34	did as the Lord commanded **M.**.	4872
Le	17:1	the Lord spake unto **M.**, saying,	4872
Le	18:1	the Lord spake unto **M.**, saying,	4872
Le	19:1	the Lord spake unto **M.**, saying,	4872
Le	20:1	the Lord spake unto **M.**, saying,	4872
Le	21:1	And the Lord said unto **M.**, Speak	4872
Le	21:16	the Lord spake unto **M.**, saying,	4872
Le	21:24	**M.** told it unto Aaron, and to his	4872
Le	22:1,	17,26, spake unto **m.**, saying,	4872
Le	23:1,	9,23,26,33 spake unto **M.**, saying	4872
Le	23:44	**M.** declared unto the children of	4872
Le	24:1	the Lord spake unto **M.**, saying,	4872
Le	24:11	they brought him unto **M.**: (and his	4872
Le	24:13	the Lord spake unto **M.**, saying,	4872
Le	24:23	And **M.** spake unto the children of	4872
Le	24:23	did as the Lord commanded **M.**,	4872
Le	25:1	Lord spake unto **M.** in mount Sinai,	4872
Le	26:46	in mount Sinai by the hand of **M.**.	4872
Le	27:1	the Lord spake unto **M.**, saying,	4872
Le	27:34	which the Lord commanded **M.** for	4872
Nu	*general*	*title* Book Of **M.**, Called Numbers	
Nu	1:1	And the Lord spake unto **M.** in the	4872
Nu	1:17	And **M.** and Aaron took these men	4872
Nu	1:19	As the Lord commanded **M.**, so he	4872
Nu	1:44	which **M.** and Aaron numbered,	4872
Nu	1:48	For the Lord had spoken unto **M.**,	4872
Nu	1:54	all that the Lord commanded **M.**,	4872
Nu	2:1	the Lord spake unto **M.** and unto	4872
Nu	2:33	Israel; as the Lord commanded **M.**	4872
Nu	2:34	all that the Lord commanded **M.**:	4872
Nu	3:1	the generations of Aaron and **M.**	4872
Nu	3:1	the Lord spake with **M.** in mount Sinai	
Nu	3:5,	11 the Lord spake unto **M.**, saying,	4872
Nu	3:14	And the Lord spake unto **M.** in the	4872
Nu	3:16	**M.** numbered them according to	4872
Nu	3:38	congregation eastward, shall be **M.**,	4872
Nu	3:39	which **M.** and Aaron numbered at	4872
Nu	3:40	the Lord said unto **M.**, Number all	4872
Nu	3:42	And **M.** numbered, as the Lord	4872
Nu	3:44	the Lord spake unto **M.**, saying,	4872
Nu	3:49	**M.** took the redemption money of	4872
Nu	3:51	**M.** gave the money of them that	4872
Nu	3:51	Lord, as the Lord commanded **M.**.	4872
Nu	4:1,	17 Lord spake unto **M.** and unto	4872
Nu	4:21	the Lord spake unto **M.**, saying,	4872
Nu	4:34	**M.** and Aaron and the chief of the	4872
Nu	4:37	which **M.** and Aaron did number	4872
Nu	4:37	of the Lord by the hand of **M.**	4872
Nu	4:41	whom **M.** and Aaron did number	4872
Nu	4:45	whom **M.** and Aaron numbered	4872
Nu	4:45	word of the Lord by the hand of **M.**.	4872
Nu	4:46	whom **M.** and Aaron and the chief	4872
Nu	4:49	were numbered by the hand of **M.**,	4872
Nu	4:49	him, as the Lord commanded **M.**	4872
Nu	5:1	the Lord spake unto **M.**, saying	4872
Nu	5:4	as the Lord spake unto **M.**, so did	4872
Nu	5:11	the Lord spake unto **M.**, saying,	4872
Nu	6:1,	22 the Lord spake unto **M.**, saying,	4872
Nu	7:1	**M.** had fully set up the tabernacle,	4872
Nu	7:4	the Lord spake unto **M.**, saying,	4872
Nu	7:6	**M.** took the wagons and the oxen,	4872
Nu	7:11	the Lord said unto **M.**, They shall	4872
Nu	7:89	**M.** was gone into the tabernacle of	4872
Nu	8:1	the Lord spake unto **M.**, saying,	4872
Nu	8:3	as the Lord commanded **M.**.	4872
Nu	8:4	which the Lord had shewed **M.**, so	4872
Nu	8:5	the Lord spake unto **M.**, saying,	4872
Nu	8:20	And **M.**, and Aaron, and all the	4872
Nu	8:20	Lord commanded **M.** concerning	4872
Nu	8:22	had commanded **M.** concerning the	4872
Nu	8:23	the Lord spake unto **M.**, saying,	4872
Nu	9:1	And the Lord spake unto **M.** in the	4872
Nu	9:4	And **M.** spake unto the children of	4872
Nu	9:5	all that the Lord commanded **M.**,	4872
Nu	9:6	came before **M.** and before Aaron	4872
Nu	9:8	**M.** said unto them, Stand still, and	4872
Nu	9:9	the Lord spake unto **M.**, saying,	4872
Nu	9:23	of the Lord by the hand of **M.**	4872
Nu	10:1	the Lord spake unto **M.**, saying,	4872
Nu	10:13	of the Lord by the hand of **M.**	4872
Nu	10:29	And **M.** said unto Hobab, the son of	4872
Nu	10:35	that **M.** said, Rise up, Lord, and let	4872
Nu	11:2	And the people cried unto **M.**; and	4872
Nu	11:2	**M.** prayed unto the Lord, the fire	4872
Nu	11:10	Then **M.** heard the people weep	4872
Nu	11:10	greatly; **M.** also was displeased	4872
Nu	11:11	**M.** said unto the Lord, Wherefore	4872
Nu	11:16	the Lord said unto **M.**, Gather unto	4872
Nu	11:21	**M.** said, The people, among whom	4872
Nu	11:23	said unto **M.**, Is the Lord's hand	4872
Nu	11:24	**M.** went out, and told the people the	4872
Nu	11:27	ran a young man, and told **M.**, and	4872
Nu	11:28	the son of Nun, the servant of **M.**,	4872
Nu	11:28	answered and said, My lord **M.**,	4872
Nu	11:29	**M.** said unto him, Enviest thou for	4872
Nu	11:30	**M.** gat him into the camp, he and	4872
Nu	12:1	Aaron spake against **M.** because of	4872
Nu	12:2	Lord indeed spoken only by **M.**?	4872
Nu	12:3	the man **M.** was very meek, above	4872
Nu	12:4	the Lord spake suddenly unto **M.**,	4872
Nu	12:7	My servant **M.** is not so, who is	4872
Nu	12:8	to speak against my servant **M.**?	4872
Nu	12:11	And Aaron said unto **M.**, Alas, my	4872
Nu	12:13	**M.** cried unto the Lord, saying,	4872
Nu	12:14	And the Lord said unto **M.**, If her	4872
Nu	13:1	the Lord spake unto **M.**, saying,	4872
Nu	13:3	**M.** by the commandment of the	4872
Nu	13:16	which **M.** sent to spy out the land.	4872
Nu	13:16	**M.** called Oshea the son of Nun	4872
Nu	13:17	**M.** sent them to spy out the land	4872
Nu	13:26	And they went and came to **M.**, and	4872
Nu	13:30	Caleb stilled the people before **M.**,	4872
Nu	14:2	Israel murmured against **M.** and	4872
Nu	14:5	**M.** and Aaron fell on their faces	4872
Nu	14:11	the Lord said unto **M.**, How long	4872
Nu	14:13	And **M.** said unto the Lord, Then	4872
Nu	14:26	the Lord spake unto **M.** and unto	4872
Nu	14:36	the men, which **M.** sent to search	4872
Nu	14:39	**M.** told these sayings unto all the	4872
Nu	14:41	And **M.** said, Wherefore now do ye	4872

Book	Ref	Context	Strong's
Nu	14:44	**M.**, departed not out of the camp	4872
Nu	15:1,	17 the Lord spake unto **M.**, saying,	4872
Nu	15:22	the Lord hath spoken unto **M.**,	4872
Nu	15:23	commanded you by the hand of **M.**,	4872
Nu	15:23	day that the Lord commanded **M.**,	
Nu	15:33	brought him unto **M.** and Aaron,	4872
Nu	15:35	the Lord said unto **M.**, The man	4872
Nu	15:36	died; as the Lord commanded **M.**	4872
Nu	15:37	the Lord spake unto **M.**, saying,	4872
Nu	16:2	And they rose up before **M.**, with	4872
Nu	16:3	themselves together against **M.** and	4872
Nu	16:4	when **M.** heard it, he fell upon his	4872
Nu	16:8	**M.** said unto Korah, Hear, I pray	4872
Nu	16:12	And **M.** sent to call Dathan and	4872
Nu	16:15	**M.** was very wroth, and said unto	4872
Nu	16:16	**M.** said unto Korah, Be thou and	4872
Nu	16:18	of the congregation with **M.** and	4872
Nu	16:20	the Lord spake unto **M.** and unto	4872
Nu	16:23	the Lord spake unto **M.**, saying,	4872
Nu	16:25	**M.** rose up and went unto Dathan	4872
Nu	16:28	**M.** said, Hereby ye shall know that	4872
Nu	16:36	the Lord spake unto **M.**, saying,	4872
Nu	16:40	Lord said to him by the hand of **M.**.	4872
Nu	16:41	murmured against **M.** and against	4872
Nu	16:42	gathered against **M.** and against	4872
Nu	16:43	And **M.** and Aaron came before the	4872
Nu	16:44	the Lord spake unto **M.**, saying,	4872
Nu	16:46	**M.** said unto Aaron, Take a censer,	4872
Nu	16:47	Aaron took as **M.** commanded, and	4872
Nu	16:50	returned unto **M.** unto the door of	4872
Nu	17:1	the Lord spake unto **M.**, saying,	4872
Nu	17:6	And **M.** spake unto the children of	4872
Nu	17:7	**M.** laid up the rods before the Lord	4872
Nu	17:8	**M.** went into the tabernacle of	4872
Nu	17:9	**M.** brought out all the rods from	4872
Nu	17:10	Lord said unto **M.**, Bring Aaron's	4872
Nu	17:11	**M.** did so: as the Lord commanded	4872
Nu	17:12	children of Israel spake unto **M.**,	4872
Nu	18:25	the Lord spake unto **M.**, saying,	4872
Nu	19:1	the Lord spake unto **M.** and unto	4872
Nu	20:2	together against **M.** and against	4872
Nu	20:3	And the people chode with **M.**, and	4872
Nu	20:6	And **M.** and Aaron went from the	4872
Nu	20:7	the Lord spake unto **M.**, saying,	4872
Nu	20:9	**M.** took the rod from before the	4872
Nu	20:10	And **M.** and Aaron gathered the	4872
Nu	20:11	**M.** lifted up his hand, and with his	4872
Nu	20:12	the Lord spake unto **M.** and Aaron,	4872
Nu	20:14	**M.** sent messengers from Kadesh	4872
Nu	20:23	spake unto **M.** and Aaron in mount	4872
Nu	20:27	**M.** did as the Lord commanded:	4872
Nu	20:28	**M.** stripped Aaron of his garments,	4872
Nu	20:28	**M.** and Eleazar came down from	4872
Nu	21:5	spake against God, and against **M.**,	4872
Nu	21:7	Therefore the people came to **M.**,	4872
Nu	21:7	And **M.** prayed for the people.	4872
Nu	21:8	the Lord said unto **M.**, Make thee	4872
Nu	21:9	**M.** made a serpent of brass, and	4872
Nu	21:16	whereof the Lord spake unto **M.**,	4872
Nu	21:32	**M.** sent to spy out Jaazer, and they	4872
Nu	21:34	Lord said unto **M.**, Fear him not:	4872
Nu	25:4	the Lord said unto **M.**, Take all the	4872
Nu	25:5	**M.** said unto the judges of Israel,	4872
Nu	25:6	woman into the sight of **M.**, and in	4872
Nu	25:10,	16 the Lord spake unto **M.**, saying,	4872
Nu	26:1	the Lord spake unto **M.**, and unto	4872
Nu	26:3	**M.** and Eleazar the priest spake	4872
Nu	26:4	as the Lord commanded **M.** and the	4872
Nu	26:9	who strove against **M.** and against	4872
Nu	26:52	the Lord spake unto **M.**, saying,	4872
Nu	26:59	bare unto Amram Aaron and **M.**,	4872
Nu	26:63	they that were numbered by **M.** and	4872
Nu	26:64	was not a man of them whom **M.**	4872
Nu	27:2	they stood before **M.**, and before	4872
Nu	27:5	**M.** brought their cause before the	4872
Nu	27:6	the Lord spake unto **M.**, saying,	4872
Nu	27:11	as the Lord commanded **M.**.	4872
Nu	27:12	said unto **M.**, Get thee up into this	4872
Nu	27:15	**M.** spake unto the Lord, saying,	4872
Nu	27:18	the Lord said unto **M.**, Take thee	4872
Nu	27:22	**M.** did as the Lord commanded him:	4872
Nu	27:23	commanded by the hand of **M.**	4872
Nu	28:1	the Lord spake unto **M.**, saying,	4872
Nu	29:40	And **M.** told the children of Israel	4872
Nu	29:40	all that the Lord commanded **M.**.	4872
Nu	30:1	And **M.** spake unto the heads of the	4872
Nu	30:16	which the Lord commanded **M.**,	4872
Nu	31:1	the Lord spake unto **M.**, saying,	4872
Nu	31:3	**M.** spake unto the people, saying,	4872
Nu	31:6	And **M.** sent them to the war, a	4872
Nu	31:7	as the Lord commanded **M.**; and	4872
Nu	31:12	the prey, and the spoil, unto **M.**,	4872
Nu	31:13	**M.**, and Eleazar the priest, and all	4872
Nu	31:14	**M.** was wroth with the officers of	4872
Nu	31:15	**M.** said unto them, Have ye saved	4872
Nu	31:21	which the Lord commanded **M.**;	4872
Nu	31:25	the Lord spake unto **M.**, saying,	4872
Nu	31:31	**M.** and Eleazar the priest did as the	4872
Nu	31:31	did as the Lord commanded **M.**.	4872
Nu	31:41	**M.** gave the tribute, which was the	4872
Nu	31:41	priest, as the Lord commanded **M.**.	4872
Nu	31:42	which **M.** divided from the men that	4872
Nu	31:47	**M.** took one portion of fifty, both of	4872
Nu	31:47	Lord; as the Lord commanded **M.**.	4872
Nu	31:48	of hundreds, came near unto **M.**:	4872
Nu	31:49	they said unto **M.**, Thy servants	4872
Nu	31:51,	54 **M.** and Eleazar the priest took	4872
Nu	32:2	Reuben came and spake unto **M.**,	4872
Nu	32:6	**M.** said unto the children of Gad	4872
Nu	32:20	**M.** said unto them, If ye will do	4872
Nu	32:25	children of Reuben spake unto **M.**,	4872
Nu	32:28	**M.** commanded Eleazar the priest,	4872
Nu	32:29	**M.** said unto them, If the children	4872
Nu	32:33	**M.** gave unto them, even to the	4872
Nu	32:40	**M.** gave Gilead unto Machir the son	4872
Nu	33:1	their armies under the hand of **M.**	4872
Nu	33:2	And **M.** wrote their goings out	4872
Nu	33:50	Lord spake unto **M.** in the plains of	4872
Nu	34:1	the Lord spake unto **M.**, saying,	4872
Nu	34:13	And **M.** commanded the children of	4872
Nu	34:16	the Lord spake unto **M.**, saying,	4872
Nu	35:1	Lord spake unto **M.** in the plains of	4872
Nu	35:9	the Lord spake unto **M.**, saying,	4872
Nu	36:1	came near, and spake before **M.**,	4872
Nu	36:5	And **M.** commanded the children of	4872
Nu	36:10	Even as the Lord commanded **M.**,	4872
Nu	36:13	commanded by the hand of **M.** unto	4872
De	*general*	*title* Book Of **M.**, Called Deuteronomy	
De	1:1	which **M.** spake unto all Israel on	4872
De	1:3	that **M.** spake unto the children	4872
De	1:5	Moab, began **M.** to declare this law,	4872
De	4:41	**M.** severed three cities on this side	4872
De	4:44	**M.** set before the children of Israel:	4872
De	4:45	which **M.** spake unto the children	4872
De	4:46	**M.** and the children of Israel smote,	4872
De	5:1	**M.** called all Israel, and said unto	4872
De	27:1	And **M.** with the elders of Israel	4872
De	27:9	And **M.** and the priests the Levites	4872
De	27:11	**M.** charged the people the same	4872
De	29:1	which the Lord commanded **M.** to	4872
De	29:2	**M.** called unto all Israel, and said	4872
De	31:1	And **M.** went and spake these words	4872
De	31:7	**M.** called unto Joshua, and said	4872
De	31:9	**M.** wrote this law, and delivered it	4872
De	31:10	And **M.** commanded them, saying,	4872
De	31:14	the Lord said unto **M.**, Behold, thy	4872
De	31:14	And **M.** and Joshua went, and	4872
De	31:16	the Lord said unto **M.**, Behold, thou	4872
De	31:22	**M.** therefore wrote this song the	4872
De	31:24	**M.** had made an end of writing the	4872
De	31:25	That **M.** commanded the Levites,	4872
De	31:30	And **M.** spake in the ears of all the	4872
De	32:44	**M.** came and spake all the words of	4872
De	32:45	**M.** made an end of speaking all	4872
De	32:48	And the Lord spake unto **M.** that	4872
De	33:1	**M.** the man of God blessed the	4872
De	33:4	**M.** commanded us a law, even the	4872
De	34:1	And **M.** went up from the plains of	4872
De	34:5	So **M.** the servant of the Lord died	4872
De	34:7	**M.** was an hundred and twenty	4872
De	34:8	the children of Israel wept for **M.**	4872
De	34:8	and mourning for **M.** were ended.	4872
De	34:9	**M.** had laid his hands upon him:	4872
De	34:9	and did as the Lord commanded **M.**	4872
De	34:10	prophet since in Israel like unto **M.**,	4872
De	34:12	terror which **M.** shewed in the	4872
Jos	1:1	after the death of **M.** the servant of	4872
Jos	1:2	**M.** my servant is dead; now	4872
Jos	1:3	given unto you, as I said unto **M.**	4872
Jos	1:5	as I was with **M.**, so I will be with	4872
Jos	1:7	which **M.** my servant commanded	4872
Jos	1:13	Remember the word which **M.** the	4872
Jos	1:14	in the land which **M.** gave you on	4872
Jos	1:15	which **M.** the Lord's servant gave	4872
Jos	1:17	we hearkened unto **M.** in all things,	4872
Jos	1:17	be with thee, as he was with **M.**	4872
Jos	3:7	as I was with **M.**, so I will be with	4872
Jos	4:10	to all that **M.** commanded Joshua:	4872
Jos	4:12	of Israel, as **M.** spake unto them:	4872
Jos	4:14	they feared him, as they feared **M.**,	4872
Jos	8:31	As **M.** the servant of the Lord	4872
Jos	8:31	written in the book of the law of **M.**,	4872
Jos	8:32	the stones a copy of the law of **M.**,	4872
Jos	8:33	as **M.** the servant of the Lord had	4872
Jos	8:35	a word of all that **M.** commanded,	4872
Jos	9:24	commanded his servant **M.** to give	4872
Jos	11:12	as **M.** the servant of the Lord	4872
Jos	11:15	As the Lord commanded **M.** his	4872
Jos	11:15	so did **M.** command Joshua, and so	4872
Jos	11:15	of all that the Lord commanded **M.**	4872
Jos	11:20	them, as the Lord commanded **M.**	4872
Jos	11:23	to all that the Lord said unto **M.**;	4872
Jos	12:6	did **M.** the servant of the Lord and	4872
Jos	12:6	**M.** the servant of the Lord gave it	4872
Jos	13:8	inheritance, which **M.** gave them,	4872
Jos	13:8	as **M.** the servant of the Lord gave	4872
Jos	13:12	for these did **M.** smite, and cast	4872
Jos	13:15	And **M.** gave unto the tribe of the	4872
Jos	13:21	whom **M.** smote with the princes of	4872
Jos	13:24	**M.** gave inheritance unto the tribe	4872
Jos	13:29	**M.** gave inheritance unto the half	4872
Jos	13:32	countries which **M.** did distribute	4872
Jos	13:33	Levi **M.** gave not any inheritance:	4872
Jos	14:2	commanded by the hand of **M.**, for	4872
Jos	14:3	**M.** had given the inheritance of two	4872
Jos	14:5	As the Lord commanded **M.**, so	4872
Jos	14:6	the thing that the Lord said unto **M.**	4872
Jos	14:7	**M.** the servant of the Lord sent me	4872
Jos	14:9	And **M.** sware on that day, saying,	4872
Jos	14:10	the Lord spake this word unto **M.**,	4872
Jos	14:11	I was in the day that **M.** sent me:	4872
Jos	17:4	Lord commanded **M.** to give us an	4872
Jos	18:7	**M.** the servant of the Lord gave	4872
Jos	20:2	spake unto you by the hand of **M.**:	4872
Jos	21:2	commanded by the hand of **M.** to	4872
Jos	21:8	commanded by the hand of **M.**	4872
Jos	22:2	all that **M.** the servant of the Lord	4872
Jos	22:4	**M.** the servant of the Lord gave	4872
Jos	22:5	**M.** the servant of the Lord charged	4872
Jos	22:7	**M.** had given possession in Bashan:	4872
Jos	22:9	word of the Lord by the hand of **M.**.	4872
Jos	23:6	written in the book of the law of **M.**,	4872
Jos	24:5	I sent **M.** also and Aaron, and	4872
Jg	1:20	Hebron unto Caleb, as **M.** said:	4872
Jg	3:4	their fathers by the hand of **M.**	4872
Jg	4:11	of Hobab the father in law of **M.**,	4872
1Sa	12:6	Lord that advanced **M.** and Aaron,	4872
1Sa	12:8	then the Lord sent **M.** and Aaron,	4872
1Ki	2:3	as it is written in the law of **M.**,	4872
1Ki	8:9	stone, which **M.** put there at Horeb,	4872
1Ki	8:53	as thou spakest by the hand of **M.**	4872
1Ki	8:56	he promised by the hand of **M.** his	4872
2Ki	14:6	in the book of the law of **M.**,	4872
2Ki	18:4	brasen serpent that **M.** had made:	4872
2Ki	18:6	which the Lord commanded **M.**	4872
2Ki	18:12	that **M.** the servant of the Lord	4872
2Ki	21:8	that my servant **M.** commanded	4872
2Ki	23:25	according to all the law of **M.**;	4872
1Ch	6:3	children of Amram; Aaron, and **M.**,	4872
1Ch	6:49	to all that **M.** the servant of God	4872
1Ch	15:15	as **M.** commanded according to	4872
1Ch	21:29	which **M.** made in the wilderness,	4872
1Ch	22:13	which the Lord charged **M.** with	4872
1Ch	23:13	sons of Amram; Aaron and **M.**:	4872
1Ch	23:14	concerning **M.** the man of God,	4872
1Ch	23:15	The sons of **M.** were, Gershom, and	4872
1Ch	26:24	the son of Gershom, the son of **M.**,	4872
2Ch	1:3	**M.**...servant of the Lord had made	4872
2Ch	5:10	two tables which **M.** put therein	4872
2Ch	8:13	to the commandment of **M.**,	4872
2Ch	23:18	as it is written in the law of **M.**,	4872
2Ch	24:6	commandment of **M.** the servant of	4872
2Ch	24:9	that **M.** the servant of God laid upon	4872
2Ch	25:4	written in the law in the book of **M.**,	4872
2Ch	30:16	to the law of **M.** the man of God;	4872
2Ch	33:8	the ordinances by the hand of **M.**	4872
2Ch	34:14	of the law of the Lord given by **M.**	4872
2Ch	35:6	word of the Lord by the hand of **M.**	4872

2Ch 35:12 as it is written in the book of **M.**....... 4872
Ezr 3:2 in the law of **M.** the man of God........ 4872
Ezr 6:18 as it is written in the book of **M.**....... 4872
Ezr 7:6 a ready scribe in the law of **M.**,......... 4872
Ne 1:7 thou commandest thy servant **M.**....... 4872
Ne 1:8 thou commandest thy servant **M.**,....... 4872
Ne 8:1 to bring the book of the law of **M.**,.... 4872
Ne 8:14 the Lord had commanded by **M.**,....... 4872
Ne 9:14 by the hand of **M.** thy servant:......... 4872
Ne 10:29 was given by **M.** the servant of God,.. 4872
Ne 13:1 that day they read in the book of **M.**.. 4872
Ps 77:20 flock by the hand of **M.** and Aaron..... 4872
Ps 90:*title* A Prayer of **M.** the man of God......... 4872
Ps 99:6 **M.** and Aaron among his priests,......... 4872
Ps 103:7 He made known his ways unto **M.**,....... 4872
Ps 105:26 He sent **M.** his servant; and Aaron..... 4872
Ps 106:16 They envied **M.** also in the camp,...... 4872
Ps 106:23 had not **M.** his chosen stood before.... 4872
Ps 106:32 it went ill with **M.** for their sakes:...... 4872
Isa 63:11 the days of old, **M.**, and his people,.... 4872
Isa 63:12 led them by the right hand of **M.**........ 4872
Jer 15:1 **M.** and Samuel stood before me,........ 4872
Da 9:11 in the law of **M.** the servant of God,... 4872
Da 9:13 As it is written in the law of **M.**,....... 4872
Mic 6:4 I sent before thee **M.**, Aaron, and...... 4872
Mal 4:4 ye the law of **M.** my servant, which.... 4872
Mt 8:4 **offer the gift that M. commanded,** .*3475*
Mt 17:3 appeared unto them **M.** and Elias....... *3475*
Mt 17:4 one for thee, and one for **M.**, and...... *3475*
Mt 19:7 Why did **M.** then command to give..... *3475*
Mt 19:8 **M. because of the hardness of**....... *3475*
Mt 22:24 **M.** said, If a man die, having no....... *3475*
Mk 1:44 **those things which M. commanded,***3475*
Mk 7:10 **M. said, Honour thy father and**..... *3475*
Mk 9:4 appeared unto them Elias with **M.**:..... *3475*
Mk 9:5 one for thee, and one for **M.**, and...... *3475*
Mk 10:3 them, **What did M. command you?**..*3475*
Mk 10:4 **M.** suffered...a bill of divorcement,..... *3475*
Mk 12:19 **M.** wrote...If a man's brother die,...... *3475*
Mk 12:26 **have ye not read in the book of M.**,*3475*
Lu 2:22 the law of **M.** were accomplished,...... *3475*
Lu 5:14 **according as M. commanded, for a**.*3475*
Lu 9:30 two men, which were **M.** and Elias:.... *3475*
Lu 9:33 one for thee, and one for **M.**, and...... *3475*
Lu 16:29 **They have M. and the prophets;**.... *3475*
Lu 16:31 **they hear not M. and the prophets,** *3475*
Lu 20:28 **M.** wrote...If any man's brother die,... *3475*
Lu 20:37 **even M. shewed at the bush,**......... *3475*
Lu 24:27 And beginning at **M.** and all the......... *3475*
Lu 24:44 **were written in the law of M.,**...... *3475*
Joh 1:17 For the law was given by **M.**, but...... *3475*
Joh 1:45 found him, of whom **M.** in the law,...... *3475*
Joh 3:14 **as M. lifted up the serpent in the**.. *3475*
Joh 5:45 **you, even M., in whom ye trust**..... *3475*
Joh 5:46 **For had ye believed M., ye would**.. *3475*
Joh 6:32 **M. gave you not that bread from**... *3475*
Joh 7:19 **Did not M. give you the law, and**... *3475*
Joh 7:22 **M....gave unto you circumcision;**... *3475*
Joh 7:22 **(not because it is of M., but of**...... *3475*
Joh 7:23 **law of M. should not be broken;**.... *3475*
Joh 8:5 **M.** in the law commanded us, that...... *3475*
Joh 9:29 We know that God spake unto **M.**:...... *3475*
Ac 3:22 For **M.** truly said unto the fathers,..... *3475*
Ac 6:11 blasphemous words against **M.**,.......... *3475*
Ac 6:14 the customs which **M.** delivered us..... *3475*
Ac 7:20 In which time **M.** was born, and........ *3475*
Ac 7:22 **M.** was learned in all the wisdom....... *3475*
Ac 7:29 Then fled **M.** at this saying, and........ *3475*
Ac 7:31 When **M.** saw it, he wondered at....... *3475*
Ac 7:32 Then **M.** trembled, and durst not....... *3475*
Ac 7:35 This **M.** whom they refused, saying,... *3475*
Ac 7:37 This is that **M.**, which said unto the... *3475*
Ac 7:40 for as for this **M.**, which brought us... *3475*
Ac 7:44 had appointed, speaking unto **M.**,....... *3475*
Ac 13:39 not be justified by the law of **M.**........ *3475*
Ac 15:1 circumcised after the manner of **M.**,... *3475*
Ac 15:5 command...to keep the law of **M.**....... *3475*
Ac 15:21 **M.** of old time hath in every city........ *3475*
Ac 21:21 among the Gentiles to forsake **M.**,..... *3475*
Ac 26:22 the prophets and **M.** did say should.... *3475*
Ac 28:23 both out of the law of **M.**, and out..... *3475*
Ro 5:14 death reigned from Adam to **M.**,........ *3475*
Ro 9:15 he saith to **M.**, I will have mercy....... *3475*
Ro 10:5 **M.** describeth the righteousness......... *3475*
Ro 10:19 First **M.** saith, I will provoke you....... *3475*
1Co 9:9 For it is written in the law of **M.**,...... *3475*
1Co 10:2 all baptized unto **M.** in the cloud........ *3475*
2Co 3:7 not stedfastly behold the face of **M.**..... *3475*
2Co 3:13 not as **M.**, which put a vail over his.... *3475*
2Co 3:15 unto this day, when **M.** is read,......... *3475*
2Ti 3:8 Jannes and Jambres withstood **M.**,...... *3475*
Heb 3:2 as also **M.** was faithful in all his......... *3475*
Heb 3:3 worthy of more glory than **M.**,.......... *3475*
Heb 3:5 And **M.** verily was faithful in all his..... *3475*
Heb 3:16 all that came out of Egypt by **M.**........ *3475*
Heb 7:14 of which tribe **M.** spake nothing......... *3475*
Heb 8:5 as **M.** was admonished of God when... *3475*
Heb 9:19 when **M.** had spoken every precept.... *3475*
Heb 11:23 By faith **M.**, when he was born, was.. *3475*
Heb 11:24 By faith **M.**, when he was come to..... *3475*
Heb 12:21 that **M.** said, I exceedingly fear and.... *3475*
Jude 9 he disputed about the body of **M.**,....... *3475*
Re 15:3 sing the song of **M.** the servant of..... *3475*

MOSES' (mo'-zez)

Ex 17:12 **M.** hands were heavy; and they......... 4872
Ex 18:1 priest of Midian, **M.** father in law,...... 4872
Ex 18:2 Then Jethro, **M.** father in law, took.... 4872
Ex 18:2 took Zipporah, **M.** wife, after he........ 4872
Ex 18:5 **M.** father in law, came with his......... 4872
Ex 18:12 **M.** father in law, took a burnt.......... 4872
Ex 18:12 to eat bread with **M.** father in law...... 4872
Ex 18:14 **M.** father in law saw all that he did.... 4872
Ex 18:17 And **M.** father in law said unto him,.... 4872
Ex 32:19 **M.** anger waxed hot, and he cast....... 4872
Ex 34:29 two tables of testimony in **M.** hand,.... 4872
Ex 34:35 that the skin of **M.** face shone: and.... 4872
Le 8:29 ram of consecration it was **M.** part;.... 4872
Nu 10:29 the Midianite, **M.** father in law,......... 4872
Jos 1:1 Joshua the son of Nun, **M.** minister,... 4872
Jg 1:16 of the Kenite, **M.** father in law,......... 4872
Mt 23:2 **and the Pharisees sit in M. seat:**... *3475*
Joh 9:28 disciple; but we are **M.** disciples......... *3475*
Heb 10:28 that despised **M.** law died without...... *3475*

MOST See also ALMOST; FOREMOST; HINDERMOST; HINDMOST; INNERMOST; MIDDLEMOST; NETHERMOST; OUTMOST; UTMOST; UTTERMOST.

Ge 14:18 was the priest of the **m.** high God...... 5945
Ge 14:19 be Abram of the **m.** high God,........... 5945
Ge 14:20 blessed be the **m.** high God, which...... 5945
Ge 14:22 unto the Lord, the **m.** high God,........ 5945
Ex 26:33 the holy place and the **m.** holy.......... 6944
Ex 26:34 the testimony in the **m.** holy place...... 6944
Ex 29:37 and it shall be an altar **m.** holy:......... 6944
Ex 30:10 it is **m.** holy unto the Lord.............. 6944
Ex 30:29 them, that they may be **m.** holy:........ 6944
Ex 30:36 thee: it shall be unto you **m.** holy....... 6944
Ex 40:10 and it shall be an altar **m.** holy.......... 6944
Le 2:3,10 a thing **m.** holy of the offerings.......... 6944
Le 6:17 it is **m.** holy, as is the sin offering,..... 6944
Le 6:25 killed before the Lord: it is **m.** holy.... 6944
Le 6:29 shall eat thereof: it is **m.** holy.......... 6944
Le 7:1 the trespass offering: it is **m.** holy...... 6944
Le 7:6 eaten in the holy place: it is **m.** holy... 6944
Le 10:12 beside the altar: for it is **m.** holy....... 6944
Le 10:17 the holy place, seeing it is **m.** holy,.... 6944
Le 14:13 the trespass offering: it is **m.** holy:..... 6944
Le 21:22 both of the **m.** holy, and of the holy.. 6944
Le 24:9 is **m.** holy unto him of the offerings.... 6944
Le 27:28 every devoted thing is **m.** holy unto.... 6944
Nu 4:4 about the **m.** holy things:................. 6944
Nu 4:19 approach unto the **m.** holy things:...... 6944
Nu 18:9 shall be thine of the **m.** holy things,.... 6944
Nu 18:9 be **m.** holy for thee and thy sons....... 6944
Nu 18:10 In the **m.** holy place shalt thou eat..... 6944
Nu 24:16 knew the knowledge of the **m.** High,.. 6944
De 32:8 When the **m.** High divided to the....... 6944
2Sa 22:14 and the **m.** High uttered his voice...... 6944
2Sa 23:19 Was he not **m.** honourable of three?.........
1Ki 6:16 oracle, even for the **m.** holy place...... 6944
1Ki 7:50 the inner house, the **m.** holy place,..... 6944
1Ki 8:6 of the house, to the **m.** holy place,..... 6944
1Ch 6:49 all the work of the place **m.** holy,....... 6944
1Ch 23:13 should sanctify the **m.** holy things,...... 6944
2Ch 3:8 And he made the **m.** holy house,......... 6944
2Ch 3:10 in the **m.** holy house he made two..... 6944
2Ch 4:22 doors thereof for the **m.** holy place,.... 6944
2Ch 5:7 into the **m.** holy place, even under..... 6944
2Ch 31:14 the Lord, and the **m.** holy things........ 6944
Ezr 2:63 should not eat of the **m.** holy things,.........
Ne 7:65 should not eat of the **m.** holy things,... 6944
Es 6:9 one of the king's **m.** noble princes,..... 6579
Job 34:17 thou condemn him that is **m.** just?...... 3524
Ps 7:17 to the name of the Lord **m.** high....... 5945
Ps 9:2 to thy name, O thou **m.** high............ 5945
Ps 21:6 hast made him **m.** blessed for ever:.........
Ps 21:7 the mercy of the **m.** High he shall...... 5945
Ps 45:3 sword upon thy thigh, O **m.** mighty,.........
Ps 46:4 of the tabernacles of the **m.** High....... 5945
Ps 47:2 For the Lord **m.** high is terrible; he.... 5945
Ps 50:14 pay thy vows unto the **m.** High:........ 5945
Ps 56:2 against me, O thou **m.** High............. 4791
Ps 57:2 I will cry unto God **m.** high; unto....... 5945
Ps 73:11 there knowledge in the **m.** High?....... 5945
Ps 77:10 of the right hand of the **m.** High........ 5945
Ps 78:17 by provoking the **M.** High in the........ 5945
Ps 78:56 and provoked the **m.** high God, and.... 5945
Ps 82:6 you are children of the **m.** High......... 5945
Ps 83:18 art the **m.** High over all the earth...... 5945
Ps 91:1 in the secret place of the **m.** High....... 5945
Ps 91:9 even the **m.** High, thy habitation;........ 5945
Ps 92:1 praises unto thy name, O **m.** High:...... 5945
Ps 92:8 thou, Lord, art **M.** high for evermore........
Ps 107:11 the counsel of the **m.** High:.............. 5945
Pr 20:6 **M.** men will proclaim every one......... 7230
Ca 5:11 His head is as the **m.** fine gold,......... 3800
Ca 5:16 His mouth is **m.** sweet: yea, he is...........
Ca 8:6 which hath a **m.** vehement flame..............
Isa 14:14 clouds; I will be like the **m.** High....... 5945
Isa 26:7 **m.** upright, dost weigh the path of the......
Jer 6:26 an only son, **m.** bitter lamentation:...........
Jer 50:31 I am against thee, O thou **m.** proud,.........
Jer 50:32 the **m.** proud shall stumble and fall,..........
La 3:35 man before the face of the **m.** High,... 5945
La 3:38 Out of the mouth of the **m.** High........ 5945
La 4:1 how is the **m.** fine gold changed!........ 2896
Eze 2:7 forbear: for they are **m.** rebellious...........
Eze 23:12 and rulers clothed **m.** gorgeously,............
Eze 33:28 For I will lay the land **m.** desolate,..........
Eze 33:29 when I have laid the land **m.** desolate.......
Eze 35:3 and I will make thee **m.** desolate.............
Eze 35:7 I make mount Seir **m.** desolate,......... 8077
Eze 41:4 unto me, This is the **m.** holy place..... 6944
Eze 42:13 Lord shall eat the **m.** holy things:....... 6944
Eze 42:13 shall they lay the **m.** holy things,....... 6944
Eze 43:12 round about shall be **m.** holy............ 6944
Eze 44:13 holy things, in the **m.** holy place:....... 6944
Eze 45:3 sanctuary and the **m.** holy place......... 6944
Eze 48:12 be unto them a thing **m.** holy............ 6944
Da 3:20 commanded the **m.** mighty men......... 2429
Da 3:26 ye servants of the **m.** high God,........ 5943
Da 4:17 may know that the **m.** High ruleth...... 5943
Da 4:24 this is the decree of the **m.** High,...... 5943
Da 4:25, 32 know that the **m.** High ruleth in..... 5943
Da 4:34 and I blessed the **m.** High, and I........ 5943
Da 5:18 **m.** high God gave Nebuchadnezzar...... 5943
Da 5:21 knew that the **m.** high God ruled...... 5943
Da 7:18 saints of the **m.** High shall take......... 5946
Da 7:22 given to the saints of the **m.** High;..... 5946
Da 7:25 great words against the **m.** High,....... 5943
Da 7:25 wear out the saints of the **m.** High,...... 5946
Da 7:27 of the saints of the **m.** High, whose.... 5945
Da 9:24 and to anoint the **m.** Holy................. 6944
Da 11:15 mount, and take the **m.** fenced cities:.......
Da 11:39 he do in the **m.** strong holds with...... 4581
Ho 7:16 return, but not to the **m.** High:......... 5920
Ho 11:7 they called them to the **m.** High,........ 5920
Ho 12:14 provoked him to anger **m.** bitterly:..... 8563
Mic 7:4 the **m.** upright is sharper than a thorn.......
Mt 11:20 **m.** of his mighty works were done,..... *4118*
Mk 5:7 thou Son of the **m.** high God? I......... *5310*
Lu 1:1 are **m.** surely believed among us,.............
Lu 1:3 in order, **m.** excellent Theophilus,...... *2903*
Lu 7:42 **which of them will love him m.?**... *4119*
Lu 7:43 that he, to whom he forgave **m.**........ *4119*
Lu 8:28 Jesus, thou Son of God **m.** high?........ *5310*
Ac 7:48 **m.** High dwelleth not in temples........ *5310*
Ac 16:17 the servants of the **m.** high God,....... *5310*
Ac 20:38 Sorrowing **m.** of all for the words....... *3122*
Ac 23:26 unto the **m.** excellent governor.......... *2903*
Ac 24:3 and in all places, **m.** noble Felix,........ *2903*
Ac 26:5 that after the **m.** straitest sect of our........
Ac 26:25 I am not mad, **m.** noble Festus;......... *2903*
1Co 14:27 let it be by two, or at the **m.** by three,*4119*
1Co 15:19 we are of all men **m.** miserable...............
2Co 12:9 **M.** gladly therefore will I rather.......... *2236*
Heb 7:1 Salem, priest of the **m.** high God,...... *5310*
Jude 20 yourselves on your **m.** holy faith,.......... *40*
Re 18:12 manner vessels of **m.** precious wood,........
Re 21:11 was like unto a stone **m.** precious,..........

MOST-HIGH See MOST and HIGH.

MOST-HOLY See MOST and HOLY.

MOTE
Mt 7:3 **m. that is in thy brother's eye,**...... *2595*
Mt 7:4 **pull out the m. out of thine eye;**... *2595*
Mt 7:5 **the m. out of thy brother's eye**...... *2595*
Lu 6:41 **the m. that is in thy brother's eye,**. *2595*
Lu 6:42 **out the m. that is in thine eye,**..... *2595*
Lu 6:42 **m. that is in thy brother's eye**........ *2595*

MOTH See also MOTHEATEN.
Job 4:19 which are crushed before the m.? 6211
Job 13:28 as a garment that is m. eaten............ 6211
Job 27:18 He buildeth his house as a m., and..... 6211
Ps 39:11 beauty to consume away like a m.:..... 6211
Isa 50:9 garment; the m. shall eat them up...... 6211
Isa 51:8 For the m. shall eat them up like a 6211
Ho 5:12 will I be unto Ephraim as a m., ... 6211
Mt 6:19 **where m. and rust doth corrupt,**.... *4597*
Mt 6:20 **where neither m. nor rust doth**..... *4597*
Lu 12:33 **neither m. corrupteth**.................. *4597*

MOTHEATEN See also MOTH and EATEN.
Jas 5:2 and your garments are m.. .... *4598*

MOTHER See also GRANDMOTHER; MOTHERS'; MOTHERS.
Ge 2:24 a man leave his father and his m., ... 517
Ge 3:20 because she was the m. of all living. 517
Ge 17:16 and she shall be a m. of nations;..............
Ge 20:12 but not the daughter of my m.; and 517
Ge 21:21 his m. took him a wife out of the......... 517
Ge 24:53 and to her m. precious things. 517
Ge 24:55 her m. said, Let the damsel abide........ 517
Ge 24:60 be thou the m. of thousands of...............
Ge 24:67 her into his m. Sarah's tent, and 517
Ge 27:11 And Jacob said to Rebekah his m.,........ 517
Ge 27:13 his m. said unto him, Upon me be 517
Ge 27:14 and brought them to his m.: and 517
Ge 27:14 and his m. made savoury meat, such.... 517
Ge 28:5 of Rebekah, Jacob's and Esau's m........ 517
Ge 28:7 Jacob obeyed his father and his m.,....... 517
Ge 30:14 and brought them unto his m. Leah..... 517
Ge 32:11 me, and the m. with the children......... 517
Ge 37:10 I and thy m. and thy brethren indeed ... 517
Ge 44:20 he alone is left of his m., and his........ 517
Ex 2:8 maid went and called the child's m.. 517
Ex 20:12 Honour thy father and thy m.: that 517
Ex 21:15 that smiteth his father, or his m., ... 517
Ex 21:17 he that curseth his father, or his m.,..... 517
Le 18:7 father, or the nakedness of thy m.,...... 517
Le 18:7 she is thy m.: thou shalt not.............. 517
Le 18:9 of thy father, or daughter of thy m., ... 517
Le 19:3 Ye shall fear every man his m., and..... 517
Le 20:9 that curseth his father or his m........... 517
Le 20:9 he hath cursed his father or his m.; 517
Le 20:14 If a man take a wife and her m., it is ... 517
Le 21:2 for his m., and for his father, and for ... 517
Le 21:11 himself for his father, or for his m.; 517
Nu 6:7 unclean for his father, or for his m.,...... 517
Nu 26:59 whom her m. bare to Levi in Egypt:.........
De 5:16 Honour thy father and thy m., as 517
De 13:6 the son of thy m., or thy son, or thy ... 517
De 21:13 bewail her father and her m. a full 517
De 21:18 of his father, or the voice of his m.,...... 517
De 21:19 father and his m. lay hold on him,........ 517
De 22:15 father of the damsel, and her m., ... 517
De 27:16 setteth light by his father or his m....... 517
De 27:22 father, or the daughter of his m.. 517
De 27:23 he that lieth with his m. in law. 2859
De 33:9 said unto his father and to his m., ... 517
Jos 2:13 save alive my father, and my m., ... 517
Jos 2:18 shalt bring thy father, and thy m., ... 517
Jos 6:23 and her father, and her m., and her...... 517
Jg 5:7 arose, that I arose a m. in Israel....... 517
Jg 5:28 The m. of Sisera looked out at a......... 517
Jg 8:19 brethren, even the sons of my m.: 517
Jg 14:2 up, and told his father and his m., ... 517
Jg 14:3 Then his father and his m. said unto 517
Jg 14:4 But his father and his m. knew not...... 517
Jg 14:5 his father and his m., to Timnath,........ 517
Jg 14:6 he told not...his m. what he had done. ..517
Jg 14:9 came to his father and m., and he 517
Jg 14:16 have not told it my father nor my m., .. 517
Jg 17:2 he said unto his m., The eleven.......... 517
Jg 17:2 his m. said, Blessed be thou of the...... 517
Jg 17:3 hundred shekels of silver to his m.. 517
Jg 17:3 his m. said, I had wholly dedicated....... 517
Jg 17:4 he restored the money unto his m.; 517
Jg 17:4 his m. took two hundred shekels of...... 517
Ru 1:14 and Orpah kissed her m. in law; 2545
Ru 2:11 hast done unto thy m. in law since 2545
Ru 2:11 hast left thy father and thy m., ... 517
Ru 2:18 her m. in law saw what she had 2545
Ru 2:19 And her m. in law said unto her, ... 2545
Ru 2:19 And she shewed her m. in law with.... 2545
Ru 2:23 and dwelt with her m. in law............ 2545
Ru 3:1 Naomi her m. in law said unto her, ... 2545
Ru 3:6 to all that her m. in law bade her....... 2545
Ru 3:16 when she came to her m. in law, ... 2545
Ru 3:17 Go not empty unto thy m. in law. 2545
1Sa 2:19 his m. made him a little coat, and........ 517
1Sa 15:33 so shall thy m. be childless among....... 517
1Sa 22:3 Let my father and my m., I pray......... 517
2Sa 17:25 sister to Zeruiah Joab's m.. 517
2Sa 19:37 grave of my father and of my m.. 517
2Sa 20:19 to destroy a city and a m. in Israel: 517
1Ki 1:6 and his m. bare him after Absalom. ....
1Ki 1:11 unto Bath-sheba the m. of Solomon,..... 517
1Ki 2:13 to Bath-sheba the m. of Solomon......... 517
1Ki 2:19 a seat to be set for the king's m.; 517
1Ki 2:20 king said unto her, Ask on, my m.:....... 517
1Ki 2:22 answered and said unto his m., ... 517
1Ki 3:27 no wise slay it: she is the m. thereof. .. 517
1Ki 15:13 And also Maachah his m., even her...... 517
1Ki 17:23 and delivered him unto his m.: 517
1Ki 19:20 pray thee, kiss my father and my m.,... 517
1Ki 22:52 his father, and in the way of his m.,...... 517
2Ki 3:2 not like his father, and like his m.:....... 517
2Ki 3:13 and to the prophets of thy m.. And...... 517
2Ki 4:19 said to a lad, Carry him to his m.. 517
2Ki 4:20 and brought him to his m., he sat........ 517
2Ki 4:30 And the m. of the child said, As the..... 517
2Ki 9:22 thy m. Jezebel and her witchcrafts....... 517
2Ki 11:1 Athaliah the m. of Ahaziah saw 517
2Ki 24:12 his m., and his servants, and his 517
2Ki 24:15 and the king's m., and the king's......... 517
1Ch 2:26 Atarah, she was the m. of Onam.......... 517
1Ch 4:9 and his m. called his name Jabez, ... 517
2Ch 15:16 Maachah the m. of Asa the king, he..... 517
2Ch 22:3 for his m. was his counsellor to do 517
2Ch 22:10 Athaliah the m. of Ahaziah saw that 517
Es 2:7 she had neither father nor m., and....... 517
Es 2:7 when her father and m. were dead, ... 517
Job 17:14 Thou art my, m. and my sister. 517
Ps 27:10 my father and m. forsake me,............ 517
Ps 35:14 as one that mourneth for his m.. 517
Ps 51:5 and in sin did my m. conceive me........ 517
Ps 109:14 not the sin of his m. be blotted out...... 517
Ps 113:9 and to be a joyful m. of children. 517
Ps 131:2 as a child that is weaned of his m.: 517
Pr 1:8 and forsake not the law of thy m.: 517
Pr 4:3 only beloved in the sight of my m.. 517
Pr 6:20 and forsake not the law of thy m.: 517
Pr 10:1 foolish son is the heaviness of his m..... 517
Pr 15:20 but a foolish man despiseth his m.. 517
Pr 19:26 chaseth away his m., is a son that....... 517
Pr 20:20 Whoso curseth his father or his m., ... 517
Pr 23:22 despise not thy m. when she is old...... 517
Pr 23:25 Thy father and thy m. shall be glad,..... 517
Pr 28:24 Whoso robbeth his father or his m.,..... 517
Pr 29:15 to himself bringeth his m. to shame. 517
Pr 30:11 father, and doth not bless their m.. 517
Pr 30:17 despiseth to obey his m., the ravens.... 517
Pr 31:1 prophecy that his m. taught him.......... 517
Ca 3:11 wherewith his m. crowned him in 517
Ca 6:9 she is the only one of her m., she is.... 517
Ca 8:1 that sucked the breasts of my m.! 517
Ca 8:5 there thy m. brought thee forth: 517
Isa 8:4 to cry, My father, and my m., the....... 517
Isa 49:1 from the bowels of my m. hath he........ 517
Isa 50:1 transgressions is your m. put away...... 517
Isa 66:13 As one whom his m. comforteth, so...... 517
Jer 15:8 against the m. of the young men a....... 517
Jer 15:10 Woe is me, my m., that thou hast....... 517
Jer 16:7 for their father or for their m............. 517
Jer 20:14 not the day wherein my m. bare me 517
Jer 20:17 my m. might have been my grave,....... 517
Jer 22:26 thee out, and thy m. that bare thee, ... 517
Jer 50:12 Your m. shall be sore confounded; 517
Eze 16:3 an Amorite, and thy m. an Hittite. 517
Eze 16:44 As is the m., so is her daughter......... 517
Eze 16:45 your m. was an Hittite, and your......... 517
Eze 19:2 And say, What is thy m.? A lioness: 517
Eze 19:10 Thy m. is like a vine in thy blood, ... 517
Eze 22:7 they set light by father and m.: in 517
Eze 23:2 women, the daughters of one m.: 517
Eze 44:25 but for father, or for m., or for son, ... 517
Ho 2:2 Plead with your m., plead: for she....... 517
Ho 2:5 For their m. hath played the harlot: 517
Ho 4:5 the night, and I will destroy thy m....... 517
Ho 10:14 m. was dashed in pieces upon her 517
Mic 7:6 daughter riseth up against her m., ... 517
Mic 7:6 in law against her m. in law; 2545
Zec 13:3,3 father and his m. that begat him.......... 517
Mt 1:18 as his m. Mary was espoused to........ *3384*
Mt 2:11 the young child with Mary his m.,........ *3384*
Mt 2:13 take the young child and his m., ... *3384*
Mt 2:14 took the young child and his m. by..... *3384*
Mt 2:20 take the young child and his m., ... *3384*
Mt 2:21 took the young child and his m., ... *3384*
Mt 8:14 he saw his wife's m. laid, and sick...... *3994*
Mt 10:35 **and the daughter against her m.,** .. *3384*
Mt 10:35 **in law against her m. in law** *3994*
Mt 10:37 **loveth father or m. more than**........ *3384*
Mt 12:46 his m. and his brethren stood............ *3384*
Mt 12:47 thy m. and thy brethren stand........... *3384*
Mt 12:48 **Who is my m.? and who are my**.... *3384*
Mt 12:49 **behold my m. and my brethren!** *3384*
Mt 12:50 **is my brother, and sister, and m..** . *3384*
Mt 13:55 son? is not his m. called Mary? *3384*
Mt 14:8 being before instructed of her m., ... *3384*
Mt 14:11 and she brought it to her m.. .... *3384*
Mt 15:4 **saying, Honour thy father and m.:** . *3384*
Mt 15:4 **that curseth father or m., let him** . *3384*
Mt 15:5 **shall say to his father or his m.,** *3384*
Mt 15:6 **honour not his father or his m.,**.... *3384*
Mt 19:5 **shall a man leave father and m.,**... *3384*
Mt 19:19 **Honour thy father and thy m.:**...... *3384*
Mt 19:29 **father, or m., or wife, or children,** . *3384*
Mt 20:20 to him the m. of Zebedee's children.... *3384*
Mt 27:56 Mary the m. of James and Joses,......... *3384*
Mt 27:56 and the m. of Zebedee's children.......... *3384*
Mk 1:30 But Simon's wife's m. lay sick of a..... *3994*
Mk 3:31 then his brethren and his m., ... *3384*
Mk 3:32 thy m. and thy brethren without *3384*
Mk 3:33 **Who is my m., or my brethren?**...... *3384*
Mk 3:34 **Behold my m. and my brethren!**.... *3384*
Mk 3:35 **my brother, and my sister, and m..** *3384*
Mk 5:40 father and the m. of the damsel,........ *3384*
Mk 6:24 said unto her m., What shall I ask? *3384*
Mk 6:28 and the damsel gave it to her m.. .... *3384*
Mk 7:10 **Honour thy father and thy m.;**...... *3384*
Mk 7:10 **Whoso curseth father or m., let**.... *3384*
Mk 7:11 **man shall say to his father or m.,** . *3384*
Mk 7:12 **do ought for his father or his m.;** .. *3384*
Mk 10:7 **a man leave his father and m.,**....... *3384*
Mk 10:19 **not, Honour thy father and m.**...... *3384*
Mk 10:29 **sisters, or father, or m., or wife,**... *3384*
Mk 15:40 Mary the m. of James the less and..... *3384*
Mk 15:47 Mary the m. of Joses beheld where he......
Mk 16:1 Mary the m. of James, and Salome..........
Lu 1:43 the m. of my Lord should come to......... *3384*
Lu 1:60 his m. answered and said, Not so; *3384*
Lu 2:33 Joseph and his m. marvelled at.......... *3384*
Lu 2:34 and said unto Mary his m., Behold, ... *3384*
Lu 2:43 Joseph and his m. knew not of it........ *3384*
Lu 2:48 and his m. said unto him, Son, why.... *3384*
Lu 2:51 his m. kept all these sayings in her *3384*
Lu 4:38 Simon's wife's m. was taken with........ *3994*
Lu 7:12 the only son of his m., and she *3384*
Lu 7:15 and he delivered him to his m.. .... *3384*
Lu 8:19 Then came to him his m. and his *3384*
Lu 8:20 Thy m. and thy brethren stand.......... *3384*
Lu 8:21 **My m. and my brethren are these..** *3384*
Lu 8:51 father and the m. of the maiden.......... *3384*
Lu 12:53 **the m. against the daughter, and**... *3384*
Lu 12:53 **and the daughter against the m.;**... *3384*
Lu 12:53 **m. in law against the daughter**..... *3994*
Lu 12:53 **in law against the m. in law**.......... *3994*
Lu 14:26 **hate not his father, and m., and**.... *3384*
Lu 18:20 **Honour thy father and thy m.**..........
Lu 24:10 Joanna, and Mary the m. of James,...........
Joh 2:1 and the m. of Jesus was there:.......... *3384*
Joh 2:3 m. of Jesus saith unto him, They *3384*
Joh 2:5 His m. saith unto the servants,.......... *3384*
Joh 2:12 and his m., and his brethren, and....... *3384*
Joh 6:42 whose father and m. we know? how... *3384*
Joh 19:25 stood by the cross of Jesus his m.. .... *3384*

Joh 19:26 When Jesus therefore saw his **m.**,...... *3384*
Joh 19:26 he saith unto his **m.**, **Woman,**.......... *3384*
Joh 19:27 he to the disciple, **Behold thy m.!**.... *3384*
Ac 1:14 and Mary the **m.** of Jesus, and with.... *3384*
Ac 12:12 the house of Mary the **m.** of John,..... *3384*
Ro 16:13 in the Lord, and his **m.** and mine....... *3384*
Ga 4:26 is free, which is the **m.** of us all........ *3384*
Eph 5:31 shall a man leave his father and **m.**...... *3384*
Eph 6:2 Honour thy father and **m.**, which........ *3384*
2Ti 1:5 Lois, and thy **m.** Eunice; and I.......... *3384*
Heb 7:3 Without father, without **m.**, without...... *282*
Re 17:5 Great, The **M.** of Harlots And........... *3384*

MOTHER-IN-LAW See MOTHER and LAW.

MOTHER'S
Ge 24:28 told them of her **m.** house these......... 517
Ge 24:67 was comforted after his **m.** death......... 517
Ge 27:29 let thy **m.** sons bow down to thee:...... 517
Ge 28:2 the house of Bethuel thy **m.** father;..... 517
Ge 28:2 daughters of Laban thy **m.** brother....... 517
Ge 29:10 daughter of Laban his **m.** brother,....... 517
Ge 29:10 the sheep of Laban his **m.** brother,....... 517
Ge 29:10 the flock of Laban his **m.** brother......... 517
Ge 43:29 his brother Benjamin, his **m.** son,........ 517
Ex 23:19 shalt not seethe a kid in his **m.** milk..... 517
Ex 34:26 shalt not seethe a kid in his **m.** milk..... 517
Le 18:13 the nakedness of thy **m.** sister:......... 517
Le 18:13 for she is thy **m.** near kinswoman........ 517
Le 20:17 or his **m.** daughter, and see her.......... 517
Le 20:19 the nakedness of thy **m.** sister, nor...... 517
Le 24:11 (and his **m.** name was Shelomith,......... 517
Nu 12:12 he cometh out of his **m.** womb............ 517
De 14:21 shalt not seethe a kid in his **m.** milk..... 517
Jg 9:1 to Shechem unto his **m.** brethren,......... 517
Jg 9:1 family of the house of his **m.** father,..... 517
Jg 9:3 his **m.** brethren spake of him in the..... 517
Jg 16:17 unto God from my **m.** womb: if I......... 517
Ru 1:8 Go, return each to her **m.** house:........ 517
1Sa 20:30 the confusion of thy **m.** nakedness?...... 517
1Ki 11:26 whose **m.** name was Zeruah, a............ 517
1Ki 14:21, 31 And his **m.** name was Naamah........ 517
1Ki 15:2, 10 And his **m.** name was Maachah,...... 517
1Ki 22:42 And his **m.** name was Azubah the........ 517
2Ki 8:26 And his **m.** name was Athaliah, the...... 517
2Ki 12:1 **m.** name was Zibiah of Beer-sheba....... 517
2Ki 14:2 And his **m.** name was Jehoaddan of...... 517
2Ki 15:2 And his **m.** name was Jecholiah of........ 517
2Ki 15:33 And his **m.** name was Jerusha, the....... 517
2Ki 18:2 **m.** name also was Abi, the daughter..... 517
2Ki 21:1 And his **m.** name was Hephzi-bah........ 517
2Ki 21:19 his **m.** name was Meshullemeth,.......... 517
2Ki 22:1 and his **m.** name was Jedidah, the........ 517
2Ki 23:31 And his **m.** name was Hamutal, the...... 517
2Ki 23:36 And his **m.** name was Zebudah, the...... 517
2Ki 24:8 And his **m.** name was Nehushta, the.... 517
2Ki 24:18 And his **m.** name was Hamutal, the...... 517
2Ch 12:13 And his **m.** name was Naamah an........ 517
2Ch 13:2 His **m.** name also was Michaiah the...... 517
2Ch 20:31 And his **m.** name was Azubah the........ 517
2Ch 22:2 His **m.** name also was Athaliah the....... 517
2Ch 24:1 His **m.** name also was Zibiah of.......... 517
2Ch 25:1 And his **m.** name was Jehoaddan of...... 517
2Ch 26:3 His **m.** name also was Jecoliah of........ 517
2Ch 27:1 His **m.** name also was Jerushah, the..... 517
2Ch 29:1 And his **m.** name was Abijah, the........ 517
Job 1:21 Naked came I out of my **m.** womb,....... 517
Job 3:10 shut not up the doors of my **m.** womb, ...
Job 31:18 guided her from my **m.** womb;)........... 517
Ps 22:9 when I was upon my **m.** breasts.......... 517
Ps 22:10 thou art my God from my **m.** belly....... 517
Ps 50:20 thou slanderest thine own **m.** son........ 517
Ps 69:8 and an alien unto my **m.** children......... 517
Ps 71:6 that took me out of my **m.** bowels:...... 517
Ps 139:13 hast covered me in my **m.** womb......... 517
Ec 5:15 As he came forth of his **m.** womb,........ 517
Ca 1:6 my **m.** children were angry with me;..... 517
Ca 3:4 had brought him into my **m.** house,....... 517
Ca 8:2 and bring thee into my **m.** house,........ 517
Isa 50:1 is the bill of your **m.** divorcement,....... 517
Jer 52:1 And his **m.** name was Hamutal the........ 517
Eze 16:45 Thou art thy **m.** daughter, that........... 517
Mt 19:12 **were so born from their m. womb:** .*3384*
Lu 1:15 Ghost, even from his **m.** womb,........ *3384*
Joh 3:4 the second time into his **m.** womb,...... *3384*
Joh 19:25 And his **m.** sister, Mary the wife of.... *3384*
Ac 3:2 man lame from his **m.** womb was....... *3384*
Ac 14:8 being a cripple from his **m.** womb,..... *3384*
Ga 1:15 separated me from my **m.** womb,........ *3384*

MOTHERS See also MOTHERS'.
Isa 49:23 and their queens thy nursing **m.**:.............
Jer 16:3 concerning their **m.** that bare them,..... 517
La 2:12 They say to their **m.**, Where is corn..... 517
La 5:3 fatherless, our **m.** are as widows......... 517
Mk 10:30 **and sisters, and m., and children,** ..*3384*
1Ti 1:9 of fathers and murderers of **m.**,......... *3389*
1Ti 5:2 The elder women as **m.**; the............. *3384*

MOTHERS'
La 2:12 poured out into their **m.** bosom........... 517

MOTIONS
Ro 7:5 the **m.** of sin, which were by the....... *3804*

MOULDY
Jos 9:5 their provision was dry and **m.**.......... 5350
Jos 9:12 now, behold, it is dry, and it is **m.**:.... 5350

MOUNT See also MOUNTAIN; MOUNTED; MOUNTING; MOUNTS.
Ge 10:30 unto Sephar a **m.** of the east............ 2022
Ge 14:6 And the Horites in their **m.** Seir,....... 2042
Ge 22:14 in the **m.** of the Lord it shall be......... 2022
Ge 31:21 set his face toward the **m.** Gilead....... 2022
Ge 31:23 they overtook him in the **m.** Gilead.... 2022
Ge 31:25 had pitched his tent in the **m.**:........... 2022
Ge 31:25 Laban…pitched in the **m.** of Gilead..... 2022
Ge 31:54 Jacob offered sacrifice upon the **m.**,.... 2022
Ge 31:54 and tarried all night in the **m.**........... 2022
Ge 36:8 Thus dwelt Esau in **m.** Seir: Esau...... 2022
Ge 36:9 father of the Edomites in **m.** Seir:...... 2022
Ex 4:27 went, and met him in the **m.** of God,.. 2022
Ex 18:5 he encamped at the **m.** of God:.......... 2022
Ex 19:2 there Israel camped before the **m.**...... 2022
Ex 19:11 sight of all the people upon **m.** Sinai... 2022
Ex 19:12 that ye go not up into the **m.**, or....... 2022
Ex 19:12 whosoever toucheth the **m.** shall be.... 2022
Ex 19:13 long, they shall come up to the **m.**..... 2022
Ex 19:14 Moses went down from the **m.** unto.... 2022
Ex 19:16 and a thick cloud upon the **m.**, and.... 2022
Ex 19:17 stood at the nether part of the **m.**...... 2022
Ex 19:18 **m.** Sinai was altogether on a smoke,... 2022
Ex 19:18 and the whole **m.** quaked greatly........ 2022
Ex 19:20 the Lord came down upon **m.** Sinai,.... 2022
Ex 19:20 on the top of the **m.**: and the Lord..... 2022
Ex 19:20 called Moses up to the top of the **m.**;. 2022
Ex 19:23 people cannot come up to **m.** Sinai:.... 2022
Ex 19:23 us, saying, Set bounds about the **m.**,.. 2022
Ex 24:12 Moses, Come up to me into the **m.**,... 2022
Ex 24:13 Moses went up into the **m.** of God...... 2022
Ex 24:15 And Moses went up into the **m.**,....... 2022
Ex 24:15 and a cloud covered the **m.**............... 2022
Ex 24:16 of the Lord abode upon **m.** Sinai,....... 2022
Ex 24:17 devouring fire on the top of the **m.**..... 2022
Ex 24:18 cloud, and gat him up into the **m.**:..... 2022
Ex 24:18 Moses was in the **m.** forty days and.... 2022
Ex 25:40 which was shewed thee in the **m.**...... 2022
Ex 26:30 which was shewed thee in the **m.**,..... 2022
Ex 27:8 as it was shewed thee in the **m.**, so.... 2022
Ex 31:18 communing with him upon **m.** Sinai,.... 2022
Ex 32:1 delayed to come down out of the **m.**,.. 2022
Ex 32:15 turned, and went down from the **m.**,.. 2022
Ex 32:19 and brake them beneath the **m.**......... 2022
Ex 33:6 of their ornaments by the **m.** Horeb... 2022
Ex 34:2 up in the morning unto **m.** Sinai,........ 2022
Ex 34:2 there to me in the top of the **m.**......... 2022
Ex 34:3 man be seen throughout all the **m.**;.... 2022
Ex 34:3 flocks nor herds feed before that **m.**... 2022
Ex 34:4 and went up unto **m.** Sinai, as........... 2022
Ex 34:29 Moses came down from **m.** Sinai......... 2022
Ex 34:29 when he came down from the **m.**,...... 2022
Ex 34:32 had spoken with him in **m.** Sinai........ 2022
Le 7:38 Lord commanded Moses in **m.** Sinai,... 2022
Le 25:1 Lord spake unto Moses in **m.** Sinai,.... 2022
Le 26:46 in **m.** Sinai by the hand of Moses....... 2022
Le 27:34 for the children of Israel in **m.** Sinai.... 2022
Nu 3:1 Lord spake with Moses in **m.** Sinai...... 2022
Nu 10:33 departed from the **m.** of the Lord...... 2022
Nu 20:22 Kadesh, and came unto **m.** Hor.......... 2022
Nu 20:23 unto Moses and Aaron in **m.** Hor,....... 2022
Nu 20:25 and bring them up unto **m.** Hor:......... 2022
Nu 20:27 and they went up into **m.** Hor in the... 2022
Nu 20:28 died there in the top of the **m.**:......... 2022
Nu 20:28 Eleazar came down from the **m.**......... 2022
Nu 21:4 they journeyed from **m.** Hor by the.... 2022
Nu 27:12 Get thee up into this **m.** Abarim,....... 2022
Nu 28:6 ordained in **m.** Sinai for a sweet......... 2022
Nu 33:23 and pitched in **m.** Shapher................ 2022
Nu 33:24 And they removed from **m.** Shapher,.. 2022
Nu 33:37 Kadesh, and pitched in **m.** Hor,......... 2022
Nu 33:38 the priest went up into **m.** Hor at...... 2022
Nu 33:39 years old when he died in **m.** Hor....... 2022
Nu 33:41 they departed from **m.** Hor, and......... 2022
Nu 34:7 ye shall point out for you **m.** Hor:...... 2022
Nu 34:8 From **m.** Hor ye shall point out.......... 2022
De 1:2 from Horeb by the way of **m.** Seir..... 2022
De 1:6 have dwelt long enough in this **m.**:..... 2022
De 1:7 go to the **m.** of the Amorites, and...... 2022
De 2:1 we compassed **m.** Seir many days........ 2022
De 2:5 I have given **m.** Seir unto Esau for..... 2022
De 3:8 the river of Arnon unto **m.** Hermon;... 2022
De 3:12 the river Arnon, and half **m.** Gilead,... 2022
De 4:48 unto **m.** Sion, which is Hermon,.......... 2022
De 5:4 with you face to face in the **m.** out...... 2022
De 5:5 fire, and went not up into the **m.**;)...... 2022
De 5:22 unto all your assembly in the **m.**......... 2022
De 9:9 When I was gone up into the **m.** to.... 2022
De 9:9 I abode in the **m.** forty days and........ 2022
De 9:10 the Lord spake with you in the **m.**...... 2022
De 9:15 turned and came down from the **m.**,... 2022
De 9:15 and the **m.** burned with fire: and........ 2022
De 9:21 brook that descended out of the **m.**.... 2022
De 10:1 and come up unto me into the **m.**,...... 2022
De 10:3 the first, and went up into the **m.**,...... 2022
De 10:4 the Lord spake unto you in the **m.**...... 2022
De 10:5 came down from the **m.**, and put......... 2022
De 10:10 I stayed in the **m.**, according to the.... 2022
De 11:29 put the blessing upon **m.** Gerizim,...... 2022
De 11:29 and the curse upon **m.** Ebal.............. 2022
De 27:4 in **m.** Ebal, and thou shalt plaister...... 2022
De 27:12 stand upon **m.** Gerizim to bless the.... 2022
De 27:13 shall stand upon **m.** Ebal to curse;...... 2022
De 32:49 unto **m.** Nebo, which is in the land..... 2022
De 32:50 die in the **m.** whither thou goest up,... 2022
De 32:50 Aaron thy brother died in **m.** Hor,...... 2022
De 33:2 he shined forth from **m.** Paran, and.... 2022
Jos 8:30 the Lord God of Israel in **m.** Ebal,...... 2022
Jos 8:33 of them over against **m.** Gerizim,....... 2022
Jos 8:33 half of them over against **m.** Ebal;...... 2022
Jos 11:17 from the **m.** Halak, that goeth up....... 2022
Jos 11:17 of Lebanon under **m.** Hermon:........... 2022
Jos 12:1 the river Arnon unto **m.** Hermon,....... 2022
Jos 12:5 And reigned in **m.** Hermon, and in...... 2022
Jos 12:7 Lebanon even unto the **m.** Halak,....... 2022
Jos 13:5 from Baal-gad under **m.** Hermon......... 2022
Jos 13:11 all **m.** Hermon, and all Bashan unto.... 2022
Jos 13:19 Zareth-Sharhar in…**m.** of the valley,.... 2022
Jos 15:9 went out to the cities of **m.** Ephron;... 2022
Jos 15:10 from Baalah westward unto **m.** Seir,... 2022
Jos 15:10 along unto the side of **m.** Jearim........ 2022
Jos 15:11 And passed along to **m.** Baalah, and.... 2022
Jos 16:1 Jericho throughout **m.** Beth-el,........... 2022
Jos 17:15 if **m.** Ephraim be too narrow for......... 2022
Jos 19:50 Timnath-serah in **m.** Ephraim:........... 2022
Jos 20:7 Kedesh in Galilee in **m.** Naphtali,........ 2022
Jos 20:7 and Shechem in **m.** Ephraim, and......... 2022
Jos 21:21 with her suburbs in **m.** Ephraim,......... 2022
Jos 24:4 I gave unto Esau **m.** Seir, to possess.. 2022
Jos 24:30 which is in **m.** Ephraim, on the.......... 2022
Jos 24:33 was given him in **m.** Ephraim............. 2022
Jg 1:35 Amorites would dwell in **m.** Heres...... 2022
Jg 2:9 in the **m.** of Ephraim, on the............. 2022
Jg 3:3 Hivites that dwell in **m.** Lebanon,........ 2022
Jg 3:3 from **m.** Baal-hermon unto the........... 2022
Jg 3:27 went down with him from the **m.**,...... 2022
Jg 4:5 Ramah and Beth-el in **m.** Ephraim:..... 2022
Jg 4:6 Go and draw toward **m.** Tabor, and.... 2022
Jg 4:12 Abinoam was gone up to **m.** Tabor..... 2022
Jg 4:14 Barak went down from **m.** Tabor,....... 2022
Jg 7:3 and depart early from **m.** Gilead......... 2022
Jg 7:24 throughout all **m.** Ephraim, saying,..... 2022
Jg 9:7 and stood in the top of **m.** Gerizim,..... 2022
Jg 9:48 gat him up to **m.** Zalmon, he and....... 2022
Jg 10:1 he dwelt in Shamir in **m.** Ephraim...... 2022
Jg 12:15 in the **m.** of the Amalekites............... 2022
Jg 17:1 there was a man of **m.** Ephraim,......... 2022
Jg 17:8 and he came to **m.** Ephraim to the...... 2022
Jg 18:2 when they came to **m.** Ephraim, to..... 2022
Jg 18:13 passed thence unto **m.** Ephraim,......... 2022
Jg 19:1 on the side of **m.** Ephraim, who......... 2022
Jg 19:16 which was also of **m.** Ephraim;.......... 2022

Jg 19:18 toward the side of **m.** Ephraim; 2022
1Sa 1:1 of **m.** Ephraim, and his name was 2022
1Sa 9:4 he passed through **m.** Ephraim, 2022
1Sa 13:2 in Michmash and in **m.** Beth-el, and 2022
1Sa 14:22 had hid themselves in **m.** Ephraim, 2022
1Sa 31:1 and fell down slain in **m.** Gilboa. 2022
1Sa 31:8 his three sons fallen in **m.** Gilboa. 2022
2Sa 1:6 by chance upon **m.** Gilboa, behold, 2022
2Sa 15:30 went up by the ascent of **m.** Olivet,
2Sa 15:32 David was come to the top of the **m.**,
2Sa 20:21 but a man of **m.** Ephraim, Sheba 2022
1Ki 4:8 The son of Hur, in **m.** Ephraim: 2022
1Ki 12:25 built Shechem in **m.** Ephraim, and 2022
1Ki 18:19 to me all Israel unto **m.** Carmel, 2022
1Ki 18:20 prophets together unto **m.** Carmel. 2022
1Ki 19:8 nights unto Horeb the **m.** of God. 2022
1Ki 19:11 stand upon the **m.** before the Lord. 2022
2Ki 2:25 he went from thence to **m.** Carmel, 2022
2Ki 4:25 unto the man of God to **m.** Carmel. 2022
2Ki 5:22 from **m.** Ephraim two young men 2022
2Ki 19:31 and they that escape out of **m.** Zion: 2022
2Ki 23:13 right hand of the **m.** of corruption, 2022
2Ki 23:16 sepulchres...were there in the **m.**, 2022
1Ch 4:42 five hundred men, went to **m.** Seir, 2022
1Ch 5:23 and Senir, and unto **m.** Hermon. 2022
1Ch 6:67 Shechem in **m.** Ephraim with her 2022
1Ch 10:1 and fell down slain in **m.** Gilboa. 2022
1Ch 10:8 and his sons fallen in **m.** Gilboa. 2022
2Ch 3:1 the Lord at Jerusalem in **m.** Moriah, 2022
2Ch 13:4 Abijah stood up upon **m.** Zemaraim, 2022
2Ch 13:4 which is in **m.** Ephraim, and said, 2022
2Ch 15:8 he had taken from **m.** Ephraim, 2022
2Ch 19:4 from Beer-sheba to **m.** Ephraim, 2022
2Ch 20:10 of Ammon and Moab and **m.** Seir, 2022
2Ch 20:22 of Ammon, Moab, and **m.** Seir, 2022
2Ch 20:23 against the inhabitants of **m.** Seir, 2022
2Ch 33:15 altars that he had built in the **m.** of 2022
Ne 8:15 Go forth unto the **m.**, and fetch 2022
Ne 9:13 camest down also upon **m.** Sinai, 2022
Job 20:6 excellency **m.** up to the heavens, 5927
Job 39:27 the eagle **m.** up at thy command, 1361
Ps 48:2 joy of the whole earth, is **m.** Zion, 2022
Ps 48:11 **m.** Zion rejoice, let the daughters 2022
Ps 74:2 **m.** Zion, wherein thou hast dwelt. 2022
Ps 78:68 Judah, the **m.** Zion which he loved. 2022
Ps 107:26 They **m.** up to the heaven, they go 5927
Ps 125:1 in the Lord shall be as **m.** Zion, 2022
Ca 4:1 goats, that appear from **m.** Gilead. 2022
Isa 4:5 every dwelling place of **m.** Zion, 2022
Isa 8:18 of hosts, which dwelleth in **m.** Zion. 2022
Isa 9:18 **m.** up like the lifting up of smoke. 55
Isa 10:12 his whole work upon **m.** Zion and 2022
Isa 10:32 the **m.** of the daughter of Zion, 2022
Isa 14:13 upon the **m.** of the congregation, 2022
Isa 16:1 unto the **m.** of the daughter of Zion. 2022
Isa 18:7 of the Lord of hosts, the **m.** Zion. 2022
Isa 24:23 Lord of hosts shall reign in **m.** Zion, 2022
Isa 27:13 Lord in the holy **m.** at Jerusalem. 2022
Isa 28:21 shall rise up as in **m.** Perazim, he 2022
Isa 29:3 lay siege against thee with a **m.**, 4674
Isa 29:8 be, that fight against **m.** Zion. 2022
Isa 31:4 come down to fight for **m.** Zion, and 2022
Isa 37:32 they that escape out of **m.** Zion: 2022
Isa 40:31 shall **m.** up with wings as eagles; 5927
Jer 4:15 affliction from **m.** Ephraim. 2022
Jer 6:6 and cast a **m.** against Jerusalem: 5550
Jer 31:6 upon the **m.** Ephraim shall cry, 2022
Jer 50:19 upon **m.** Ephraim and Gilead. 2022
Jer 51:53 Babylon should **m.** up to heaven, 5927
Eze 4:2 against it, and cast a **m.** against it: 5550
Eze 10:16 wings to **m.** up from the earth, the 7311
Eze 21:22 to cast a **m.**, and to build a fort. 5550
Eze 26:8 cast a **m.** against thee, and lift up 5550
Eze 35:2 man, set thy face against **m.** Seir, 2022
Eze 35:3 Behold, O **m.** Seir, I am against 2022
Eze 35:7 will I make **m.** Seir most desolate, 2022
Eze 35:15 thou shalt be desolate, O **m.** Seir, 2022
Da 11:15 north shall come, and cast up a **m.**, 5550
Joe 2:32 in **m.** Zion and in Jerusalem shall 2022
Ob 8 understanding out of the **m.** of 2022
Ob 9 every one of the **m.** of Esau may be 2022
Ob 17 upon **m.** Zion shall be deliverance, 2022
Ob 19 south shall possess the **m.** of Esau; 2022
Ob 21 saviours shall come up on **m.** Zion 2022
Ob 21 to judge the **m.** of Esau; and the 2022
Mic 4:7 shall reign over them in **m.** Zion 2022
Hab 3:3 and the Holy One from **m.** Paran. 2022
Zec 14:4 in that day upon the **m.** of Olives, 2022
Zec 14:4 the **m.** of Olives shall cleave in the 2022
Mt 21:1 Bethphage, unto the **m.** of Olives, *3735*
Mt 24:3 as he sat upon the **m.** of Olives, the *3735*
Mt 26:30 they went out into the **m.** of Olives. *3735*
Mk 11:1 and Bethany, at the **m.** of Olives, *3735*
Mk 13:3 And as he sat upon the **m.** of Olives *3735*
Mk 14:26 they went out into the **m.** of Olives. *3735*
Lu 19:29 Bethany, at the **m.** called...Olives, *3735*
Lu 19:29 at...the **m.** of Olives, he sent two
Lu 19:37 at the descent of the **m.** of Olives, *3735*
Lu 21:37 he went out, and abode in the **m.** *3735*
Lu 21:37 out, and abode in...the **m.** of Olives.
Lu 22:39 as he was wont, to the **m.** of Olives; *3735*
Joh 8:1 Jesus went unto the **m.** of Olives. *3735*
Ac 1:12 from the **m.** called Olivet, which is *3735*
Ac 7:30 to him in the wilderness of **m.** Sina *3735*
Ac 7:38 which spake to him in the **m.** Sina, *3735*
Ga 4:24 the one from the **m.** Sinai, which *3735*
Ga 4:25 For this Agar is **m.** Sinai in Arabia, *3735*
Heb 8:5 the pattern shewed to thee in the **m.** *3735*
Heb 12:18 unto the **m.** that might be touched, *3735*
Heb 12:22 ye are come unto **m.** Sion, and unto *3735*
2Pe 1:18 we were with him in the holy **m.**. *3735*
Re 14:1 lo, a Lamb stood on the **m.** Sion, *3735*

MOUNTAIN See also MOUNTAINS.
Ge 12:8 unto a **m.** on the east of Beth-el, 2022
Ge 14:10 they that remained fled to the **m.** 2022
Ge 19:17 escape to the **m.**, lest thou be 2022
Ge 19:19 I cannot escape to the **m.**, lest some 2022
Ge 19:30 and dwelt in the **m.**, and his two 2022
Ex 3:1 and came to the **m.** of God, even to 2022
Ex 3:12 ye shall serve God upon this **m.** 2022
Ex 15:17 in the **m.** of thine inheritance, in 2022
Ex 19:3 Lord called unto him out of the **m.**, 2022
Ex 20:18 of the trumpet, and the **m.** smoking: 2022
Nu 13:17 southward, and go up into the **m.**: 2022
Nu 14:40 gat them up into the top of the **m.**, 2022
De 1:19 the way of the **m.** of the Amorites, 2022
De 1:20 come unto the **m.** of the Amorites, 2022
De 1:24 turned and went up into the **m.**, 2022
De 1:44 Amorites, which dwelt in that **m.**, 2022
De 2:3 Ye have compassed this **m.** long 2022
De 3:25 that goodly **m.**, and Lebanon. 2022
De 4:11 came near and stood under the **m.**; 2022
De 4:11 and the **m.** burned with fire unto the 2022
De 5:23 (for the **m.** did burn with fire,) that 2022
De 32:49 Get thee up into this **m.** Abarim, 2022
De 33:19 shall call the people unto the **m.**; 2022
De 34:1 plains of Moab unto the **m.** of Nebo, 2022
Jos 2:16 Get you to the **m.**, lest the pursuers 2022
Jos 2:22 came unto the **m.**, and abode there 2022
Jos 2:23 descended from the **m.**, and passed 2022
Jos 11:16 and the plain, and the **m.** of Israel, 2022
Jos 14:12 therefore give me this **m.**, whereof 2022
Jos 15:8 border went up to the top of the **m.** 2022
Jos 17:18 But the **m.** shall be thine; for it is 2022
Jos 18:16 came down to the end of the **m.** 2022
Jos 20:7 which is Hebron, in the **m.** of Judah. 2022
Jg 1:9 Canaanites, that dwelt in the **m.**, 2022
Jg 1:19 drave out the inhabitants of the **m.**; 2022
Jg 1:34 the children of Dan into the **m.**: 2022
Jg 3:27 a trumpet in the **m.** of Ephraim, 2022
1Sa 17:3 the Philistines stood on a **m.** on the 2022
1Sa 17:3 Israel stood on a **m.** on the other 2022
1Sa 23:14 remained in a **m.** in the wilderness 2022
1Sa 23:26 Saul went on this side of the **m.**, 2022
1Sa 23:26 and his men on that side of the **m.**: 2022
2Ki 2:16 cast him upon some **m.**, or into 2022
2Ki 6:17 behold, the **m.** was full of horses 2022
2Ch 2:2 thousand to hew in the **m.**, and 2022
2Ch 2:18 thousand to be hewers in the **m.** 2022
Job 14:18 the **m.** falling cometh to nought, 2022
Ps 11:1 my soul, Flee as a bird to your **m.**? 2022
Ps 30:7 hast made my **m.** to stand strong: 2042
Ps 48:1 our God, in the **m.** of his holiness. 2022
Ps 78:54 to this **m.**, which his right hand had 2022
Ca 4:6 I will get me to the **m.** of myrrh, 2022
Isa 2:2 the **m.** of the Lord's house shall be 2022
Isa 2:3 let us go up to the **m.** of the Lord, 2022
Isa 11:9 hurt nor destroy in all my holy **m.**: 2022
Isa 13:2 ye up a banner upon the high **m.**, 2022
Isa 25:6 in this **m.** shall the Lord of hosts 2022
Isa 25:7 he will destroy in this **m.** the face 2022
Isa 25:10 For in this **m.** shall the hand of the 2022
Isa 30:17 as a beacon upon the top of a **m.**, 2022
Isa 30:25 there shall be upon every high **m.**, 2022
Isa 30:29 to come into the **m.** of the Lord, 2022
Isa 40:4 and every **m.** and hill shall be made 2022
Isa 40:9 get thee up into the high **m.**: O 2022
Isa 56:7 them will I bring to my holy **m.**, 2022
Isa 57:7 Upon a lofty and high **m.** hast thou 2022
Isa 57:13 land, and shall inherit my holy **m.**; 2022
Isa 65:11 that forget my holy **m.**, that 2022
Isa 65:25 hurt nor destroy in all my holy **m.**, 2022
Isa 66:20 beasts, to my holy **m.** Jerusalem, 2022
Jer 3:6 she is gone up upon every high **m.** 2022
Jer 16:16 they shall hunt them from every **m.**, 2022
Jer 17:3 O my **m.** in the field, I will give thy 2042
Jer 26:18 the **m.** of the house as the high 2022
Jer 31:23 of justice, and **m.** of holiness. 2022
Jer 50:6 they have gone from **m.** to hill, they 2022
Jer 51:25 I am against thee, O destroying **m.**, 2022
Jer 51:25 and will make thee a burnt **m.**. 2022
La 5:18 Because of the **m.** of Zion, which 2022
Eze 11:23 stood upon the **m.** which is on the 2022
Eze 17:22 will plant it upon an high **m.** and 2022
Eze 17:23 In the **m.** of the height of Israel 2022
Eze 20:40 For in mine holy **m.** in the 2022
Eze 20:40 in the **m.** of the height of Israel, 2022
Eze 28:14 thou wast upon the holy **m.** of God; 2022
Eze 28:16 as profane out of the **m.** of God: 2022
Eze 40:2 and set me upon a very high **m.**, 2022
Eze 43:12 Upon the top of the **m.** the whole 2022
Da 2:35 the image became a great **m.**, 2906
Da 2:45 cut out of the **m.** without hands, 2906
Da 9:16 thy city Jerusalem, thy holy **m.**: 2022
Da 9:20 my God for the holy **m.** of my God; 2022
Da 11:45 the seas in the glorious holy **m.**; 2022
Joe 2:1 and sound an alarm in my holy **m.**: 2022
Joe 3:17 God dwelling in Zion, my holy **m.**: 2022
Am 4:1 that are in the **m.** of Samaria, 2022
Am 6:1 and trust in the **m.** of Samaria, 2022
Ob 16 as ye have drunk upon my holy **m.**, 2022
Mic 3:12 and the **m.** of the house as the high 2022
Mic 4:1 that the **m.** of the house of the Lord 2022
Mic 4:2 let us go up to the **m.** of the Lord, 2022
Mic 7:12 from sea to sea, and from **m.** to **m.** 2022
Zep 3:11 be haughty because of my holy **m.**. 2022
Hag 1:8 Go up to the **m.**, and bring wood, 2022
Zec 4:7 Who art thou, O great **m.**? before 2022
Zec 8:3 **m.** of the Lord of hosts the holy **m.**. 2022
Zec 14:4 half of the **m.** shall remove toward 2022
Mt 4:8 up into an exceeding high **m.**, *3735*
Mt 5:1 multitudes, he went up into a **m.**: *3735*
Mt 8:1 he was come down from the **m.**, *3735*
Mt 14:23 went up into a **m.** apart to pray: *3735*
Mt 15:29 went up into a **m.**, and sat down *3735*
Mt 17:1 them up into an high **m.** apart, *3735*
Mt 17:9 as they came down from the **m.**, *3735*
Mt 17:20 **ye shall say unto this m., Remove.** *3735*
Mt 21:21 **also if ye shall say unto this m.,** *3735*
Mt 28:16 Galilee, into a **m.** where Jesus had *3735*
Mk 3:13 And he goeth up into a **m.**, and *3735*
Mk 6:46 he departed into a **m.** to pray. *3735*
Mk 9:2 leadeth them up into an high **m.** *3735*
Mk 9:9 as they came down from the **m.**, he *3735*
Mk 11:23 **whosoever shall say unto this m.,** *3735*
Lu 3:5 every **m.** and hill shall be brought *3735*
Lu 4:5 taking him up into an high **m.**, *3735*
Lu 6:12 that he went out into a **m.** to pray, *3735*
Lu 8:32 of many swine feeding on the **m.**: *3735*
Lu 9:28 and went up into a **m.** to pray. *3735*
Joh 4:20 Our fathers worshipped in this **m.**; *3735*
Joh 4:21 **when ye shall neither in this m.,** *3735*
Joh 6:3 And Jesus went up into a **m.**, and *3735*
Joh 6:15 again into a **m.** himself alone. *3735*
Heb 12:20 if so much as a beast touch the **m.**, *3735*
Re 6:14 every **m.** and island were moved *3735*
Re 8:8 as it were a great **m.** burning with *3735*
Re 21:10 in the spirit to a great and high **m.**, *3735*

MOUNTAINS
Ge 7:20 prevail; and the **m.** were covered. 2022
Ge 8:4 the month, upon the **m.** of Ararat. 2022
Ge 8:5 month, were the tops of the **m.** seen. 2022
Ge 22:2 burnt offering upon one of the **m.** 2022
Ex 32:12 them out, to slay them in the **m.**, 2022
Nu 13:29 and the Amorites, dwell in the **m.**: 2022
Nu 23:7 Aram, out of the **m.** of the east, 2042
Nu 33:47 and pitched in the **m.** of Abarim, 2022
Nu 33:48 departed from the **m.** of Abarim, 2022
De 2:37 nor unto the cities in the **m.**, nor 2022

De 12:2 their gods, upon the high **m.**, and 2022
De 32:22 on fire the foundations of the **m.**........ 2022
De 33:15 the chief things of the ancient **m.**, ... 2042
Jos 10:6 the Amorites that dwell in the **m.**....... 2022
Jos 11:2 that were on the north of the **m.**, ... 2022
Jos 11:3 and the Jebusite in the **m.**, and to...... 2022
Jos 11:21 cut off the Anakims from the **m.**, ... 2022
Jos 11:21 and from all the **m.** of Judah, and....... 2022
Jos 11:21 and from all the **m.** of Israel:............ 2022
Jos 12:8 In the **m.**, and in the valleys, and....... 2022
Jos 15:48 And in the **m.**, Shamir, and Jattir, ... 2022
Jos 18:12 went up through the **m.** westward;..... 2022
Jg 5:5 **m.** melted from before the Lord, ... 2022
Jg 6:2 them the dens which are in the **m.**, ... 2022
Jg 9:25 in wait for him in the top of the **m.**, ... 2022
Jg 9:36 people down from the top of the **m.**. .. 2022
Jg 9:36 Thou seest the shadow of the **m.** as... 2022
Jg 11:37 may go up and down upon the **m.**, ... 2022
Jg 11:38 bewailed her virginity upon the **m.**...... 2022
1Sa 26:20 doth hunt a partridge in the **m.**.......... 2022
2Sa 1:21 Ye **m.** of Gilboa, let there be no 2022
1Ki 5:15 thousand hewers in the **m.**;............... 2022
1Ki 19:11 great and strong wind rent the **m.**,..... 2022
2Ki 19:23 come up to the height of the **m.**, to.... 2022
1Ch 12:8 as swift as the roes upon the **m.**;....... 2022
2Ch 18:16 all Israel scattered upon the **m.**, ... 2022
2Ch 21:11 high places in the **m.** of Judah, ... 2022
2Ch 26:10 and vine dressers in the **m.**, and in 2022
2Ch 27:4 he built cities in the **m.** of Judah, ... 2022
Job 9:5 Which removeth the **m.**, and they 2022
Job 24:8 are wet with the showers of the **m.**,.... 2022
Job 28:9 he overturneth the **m.** by the roots. ... 2022
Job 39:8 The range of the **m.** is his pastures,... 2022
Job 40:20 Surely the **m.** bring him forth food, ... 2022
Ps 36:6 righteousness is like the great **m.**;...... 2042
Ps 46:2 the **m.** be carried into the midst 2022
Ps 46:3 **m.** shake with the swelling thereof. 2022
Ps 50:11 I know all the fowls of the **m.**: and..... 2022
Ps 65:6 by his strength setteth fast the **m.**; 2022
Ps 72:3 The **m.** shall bring peace to the......... 2022
Ps 72:16 in the earth upon the top of the **m.**; ... 2022
Ps 76:4 and excellent than the **m.** of prey........ 2042
Ps 83:14 as the flame setteth the **m.** on fire; 2022
Ps 87:1 His foundation is in the holy **m.**. 2042
Ps 90:2 Before the **m.** were brought forth, ... 2022
Ps 104:6 the waters stood above the **m.**. 2022
Ps 104:8 They go up by the **m.**; they go down.. 2022
Ps 114:4 The **m.** skipped like rams, and the..... 2022
Ps 114:6 Ye **m.**, that ye skipped like rams; 2022
Ps 125:2 the **m.** are round about Jerusalem, ... 2022
Ps 133:3 descended upon the **m.** of Zion:......... 2042
Ps 144:5 touch the **m.**, and they shall............. 2022
Ps 147:8 maketh grass to grow upon the **m.**..... 2022
Ps 148:9 **M.**, and all hills; fruitful trees, and....... 2022
Pr 8:25 Before the **m.** were settled, before 2022
Pr 27:25 and herbs of the **m.** are gathered....... 2022
Ca 2:8 he cometh leaping upon the **m.**,.......... 2022
Ca 2:17 young hart upon the **m.** of Bether...... 2022
Ca 4:8 dens, from the **m.** of the leopards...... 2042
Ca 8:14 young hart upon the **m.** of spices. 2022
Isa 2:2 established in the top of the **m.**, ... 2022
Isa 2:14 upon all the high **m.**, and upon all....... 2022
Isa 13:4 noise of a multitude in the **m.**, like..... 2022
Isa 14:25 upon my **m.** tread him under foot:...... 2022
Isa 17:13 shall be chased as the chaff of the **m.** .. 2022
Isa 18:3 he lifteth up an ensign on the **m.**; 2022
Isa 18:6 together unto the fowls of the **m.**,...... 2022
Isa 22:5 the walls, and of crying to the **m.**. 2022
Isa 34:3 the **m.** shall be melted with their 2022
Isa 37:24 I come up to the height of the **m.**, ... 2022
Isa 40:12 weighed the **m.** in scales, and the 2022
Isa 41:15 thou shalt thresh the **m.**, and beat...... 2022
Isa 42:11 them shout from the top of the **m.**. 2022
Isa 42:15 I will make waste **m.** and hills, and..... 2022
Isa 44:23 break forth into singing, ye **m.**, O...... 2022
Isa 49:11 I will make all my **m.** a way, and 2022
Isa 49:13 break forth into singing, O **m.**: for...... 2022
Isa 52:7 How beautiful upon the **m.** are the 2022
Isa 54:10 For the **m.** shall depart, and the 2022
Isa 55:12 the **m.** and the hills shall break.......... 2022
Isa 64:1 that the **m.** might flow down at thy 2022
Isa 64:3 the **m.** flowed down at thy presence.... 2022
Isa 65:7 have burned incense upon the **m.**,...... 2022
Isa 65:9 out of Judah an inheritor of my **m.**:..... 2022
Jer 3:23 hills, and from the multitude of **m.**:..... 2022
Jer 4:24 I beheld the **m.**, and, lo, they........... 2022
Jer 9:10 For the **m.** will I take up a weeping.... 2022
Jer 13:16 your feet stumble upon the dark **m.**,... 2022
Jer 17:26 and from the **m.**, and from the 2022
Jer 31:5 vines upon the **m.** of Samaria: 2022
Jer 32:44 Judah, and in the cities of the **m.**, ... 2022
Jer 33:13 In the cities of the **m.**, in the cities 2022
Jer 46:18 Surely as Tabor is among the **m.**, ... 2022
Jer 50:6 have turned them away on the **m.**:..... 2022
La 4:19 they pursued us upon the **m.**, they..... 2022
Eze 6:2 thy face toward the **m.** of Israel,........ 2022
Eze 6:3 Ye **m.** of Israel, hear the word of....... 2022
Eze 6:3 Thus saith the Lord God to the **m.**,.... 2022
Eze 6:13 in all the tops of the **m.**, and under.... 2022
Eze 7:7 not the sounding again of the **m.**. 2022
Eze 7:16 and shall be on the **m.** like doves...... 2022
Eze 18:6 And hath not eaten upon the **m.**, ... 2022
Eze 18:11 but even hath eaten upon the **m.**, ... 2022
Eze 18:15 That hath not eaten upon the **m.**,....... 2022
Eze 19:9 be heard upon the **m.** of Israel. 2022
Eze 22:9 and in thee they eat upon the **m.**: 2022
Eze 31:12 upon the **m.** and in all the valleys...... 2022
Eze 32:5 I will lay thy flesh upon the **m.**, ... 2022
Eze 32:6 thou swimmest, even to the **m.**; 2022
Eze 33:28 the **m.** of Israel shall be desolate, ... 2022
Eze 34:6 sheep wandered through all the **m.**, ... 2022
Eze 34:13 feed them upon the **m.** of Israel......... 2022
Eze 34:14 upon the high **m.** of Israel shall.......... 2022
Eze 34:14 they feed upon the **m.** of Israel. 2022
Eze 35:8 will fill his **m.** with his slain men: 2022
Eze 35:12 spoken against the **m.** of Israel, ... 2022
Eze 36:1 prophesy unto the **m.** of Israel, and.... 2022
Eze 36:1, 4 Ye **m.** of Israel, hear the word 2022
Eze 36:4 Thus saith the Lord God to the **m.**,.... 2022
Eze 36:6 say unto the **m.**, and to the hills, ... 2022
Eze 36:8 O **m.** of Israel, ye shall shoot forth..... 2022
Eze 37:22 in the land upon the **m.** of Israel;....... 2022
Eze 38:8 people, against the **m.** of Israel,......... 2022
Eze 38:20 and the **m.** shall be thrown down, ... 2022
Eze 38:21 against him throughout all my **m.**, ... 2022
Eze 39:2 bring thee upon the **m.** of Israel: 2022
Eze 39:4 shalt fall upon the **m.** of Israel,.......... 2022
Eze 39:17 sacrifice upon the **m.** of Israel, that.... 2022
Ho 4:13 sacrifice upon the tops of the **m.**,....... 2022
Ho 10:8 they shall say to the **m.**, Cover us; 2022
Joe 2:2 the morning spread upon the **m.**: 2022
Joe 2:5 noise of chariots on the tops of **m.** 2022
Joe 3:18 the **m.** shall drop down new wine,...... 2022
Am 3:9 yourselves upon the **m.** of Samaria, ... 2022
Am 4:13 For, lo, he that formeth the **m.**, and... 2022
Am 9:13 and the **m.** shall drop sweet wine,...... 2022
Jon 2:6 went down to the bottoms of the **m.**;.. 2022
Mic 1:4 the **m.** shall be molten under him, ... 2022
Mic 4:1 be established in the top of the **m.**, ... 2022
Mic 6:1 Arise, contend thou before the **m.**,..... 2022
Mic 6:2 Hear ye, O **m.**, the Lord's................ 2022
Na 1:5 The **m.** quake at him, and the hills..... 2022
Na 1:15 Behold upon the **m.** the feet of him.... 2022
Na 3:18 thy people is scattered upon the **m.**,... 2022
Hab 3:6 the everlasting **m.** were scattered, ... 2042
Hab 3:10 **m.** saw thee, and they trembled: 2022
Hag 1:11 upon the land, and upon the **m.**, ... 2022
Zec 6:1 chariots out from between two **m.**;..... 2022
Zec 6:1 and the **m.** were **m.** of brass. 2022
Zec 14:5 ye shall flee to the valley of the **m.**; ... 2022
Zec 14:5 for the valley of the **m.** shall reach..... 2022
Mal 1:3 laid his **m.** and his heritage waste....... 2022
Mt 18:12 **goeth into the m., and seeketh** *3735*
Mt 24:16 **be in Judaea flee into the m.:** *3735*
Mk 5:5 night and day, he was in the **m.**,......... *3735*
Mk 5:11 there nigh unto the **m.** a great herd.... *3735*
Mk 13:14 **that be in Judaea flee to the m.:** ... *3735*
Lu 21:21 **are in Judaea flee to the m.;** *3735*
Lu 23:30 **begin to say to the m., Fall on**...... *3735*
1Co 13:2 faith, so that I could remove **m.**,........ *3735*
Heb 11:38 wandered in deserts, and in **m.**,......... *3735*
Re 6:15 dens and in the rocks of the **m.**; *3735*
Re 6:16 said to the **m.** and rocks, Fall on us, .. *3735*
Re 16:20 away, and the **m.** were not found....... *3735*
Re 17:9 The seven heads are seven **m.**, on..... *3735*

MOUNTED
Eze 10:19 **m.** up from the earth in my sight: 7426

MOUNTING
Isa 15:5 for by the **m.** up of Luhith with 4608

MOUNTS
Jer 32:24 the **m.**, they are come unto the......... 5550
Jer 33:4 which are thrown down by the **m.**,..... 5550
Eze 17:17 by casting up **m.**, and building 5550

MOURN See also MOURNED; MOURNETH; MOURNFULLY; MOURNING.
Ge 23:2 Abraham came to **m.** for Sarah, ... 5594
1Sa 16:1 How long wilt thou **m.** for Saul, ... 56
2Sa 3:31 sackscloth, and **m.** before Abner. 5594
1Ki 13:29 to the city, to **m.** and to bury him...... 5594
1Ki 14:13 And all Israel shall **m.** for him, and..... 5594
Ne 8:9 Lord your God; **m.** not, nor weep.......... 56
Job 2:11 together to come to **m.** with him 5110
Job 5:11 those which **m.** may be exalted.......... 6937
Job 14:22 and his soul within him shall **m.**. 56
Ps 55:2 I **m.** in my complaint, and make a 7300
Pr 5:11 And thou **m.** at the last, when they.... 5098
Pr 29:2 wicked beareth rule, the people **m.**. 584
Ec 3:4 a time to **m.**, and a time to dance; 5594
Isa 3:26 her gates shall lament and **m.**; and 56
Isa 16:7 of Kir-hareseth shall ye **m.**; 1897
Isa 19:8 The fishers also shall **m.**, and all 578
Isa 38:14 I did **m.** as a dove: mine eyes fail 1897
Isa 59:11 like bears, and **m.** sore like doves:...... 1897
Isa 61:2 of our God; to comfort all that **m.**; 57
Isa 61:3 To appoint unto them that **m.** in 57
Isa 66:10 joy with her, all ye that **m.** for her:....... 56
Jer 4:28 For this shall the earth **m.**, and the 56
Jer 12:4 How long shall the land **m.**, and the....... 56
Jer 48:31 shall **m.** for the men of Kir-heres....... 1897
La 1:4 The ways of Zion do **m.**, because.......... 57
Eze 7:12 the buyer rejoice, nor the seller **m.**: 56
Eze 7:27 The king shall **m.**, and the prince.......... 56
Eze 24:16 neither shalt thou **m.** nor weep,......... 5594
Eze 24:23 ye shall not **m.** nor weep; but ye 5594
Eze 24:23 and **m.** one toward another............... 5098
Eze 31:15 I caused Lebanon to **m.** for him, ... 6937
Ho 4:3 Therefore shall the land **m.**, and 56
Ho 10:5 the people thereof shall **m.** over it,........ 56
Joe 1:9 the priests, the Lord's ministers, **m.**...... 56
Am 1:2 habitations of the shepherds shall **m.**,...... 56
Am 8:8 every one **m.** that dwelleth therein?....... 56
Am 9:5 and all that dwell therein shall **m.**: 56
Zec 12:10 and they shall **m.** for him, as one....... 5594
Zec 12:12 land shall **m.**, every family apart; 5594
Mt 5:4 **Blessed are they that m.: for they** ..*3996*
Mt 9:15 **children of the bridechamber m.,** .. *3996*
Mt 24:30 **shall all the tribes of the earth m.,** .*2875*
Lu 6:25 **now! for ye shall m. and weep.** *3996*
Jas 4:9 Be afflicted, and **m.**, and weep: let..... *3996*
Re 18:11 earth shall weep and **m.** over her;...... *3996*

MOURNED
Ge 37:34 loins, and **m.** for his son many days....... 56
Ge 50:3 Egyptians **m.** for him threescore 1058
Ge 50:10 there they **m.** with a great and.......... 5594
Ex 33:4 heard these evil tidings, they **m.**: 56
Nu 14:39 of Israel: and the people **m.** greatly. 56
Nu 20:29 they **m.** for Aaron thirty days,........... 1058
1Sa 15:35 nevertheless Samuel **m.** for Saul: 56
2Sa 1:12 And they **m.**, and wept, and fasted..... 5594
2Sa 11:26 was dead, she **m.** for her husband....... 5594
2Sa 13:37 And David **m.** for his son every day. 56
2Sa 14:2 that had a long time **m.** for the dead:..... 56
1Ki 13:30 and they **m.** over him, saying,............ 5594
1Ki 14:18 and all Israel **m.** for him, according..... 5594
1Ch 7:22 Ephraim their father **m.** many days,....... 56
2Ch 35:24 Judah and Jerusalem **m.** for Josiah. 56
Ezr 10:6 he **m.** because of the transgression of.... 56
Ne 1:4 I...wept, and **m.** certain days, and......... 56
Zec 7:5 When ye fasted and **m.** in the............ 5594
Mt 11:17 **we have m. unto you, and ye have**..*2354*
Mr 16:10 with him, as they **m.** and wept. *3996*
Lu 7:32 **we have m. to you, and ye have** *2354*
1Co 5:2 and have not rather **m.**, that he......... *3996*

MOURNER See also MOURNERS.
2Sa 14:2 I pray thee, feign thyself to be a **m.**,..... 56

MOURNERS
Job 29:25 army, as one that comforteth the **m.**...... 57
Ec 12:5 and the **m.** go about the streets;........ 5594
Isa 57:18 comforts unto him and to his **m.**. 57
Hos 9:4 be unto them as the bread of **m.**; 205

MOURNETH
2Sa 19:1 king weepeth and **m.** for Absalom. 56
Ps 35:14 as one that **m.** for his mother............... 57
Ps 88:9 Mine eye **m.** by reason of 1669
Isa 24:4 The earth **m.** and fadeth away, the........ 56

Isa 24:7 new wine **m.**, the vine languisheth,........ 56
Isa 33:9 the earth **m.** and languisheth: 56
Jer 12:11 and being desolate it **m.** unto me; 56
Jer 14:2 Judah **m.**, and the gates thereof........... 56
Jer 23:10 for because of swearing the land **m.**;...... 56
Joe 1:10 The field is wasted, the land **m.**; for...... 56
Zec 12:10 for him, as one **m.** for his only son,.... 5594

MOURNFULLY

Mal 3:14 that we have walked **m.** before the..... 6941

MOURNING

Ge 27:41 The days of **m.** for my father are at 60
Ge 37:35 down into the grave unto my son **m.**. 57
Ge 50:4 when the days of his **m.** were past,.... 1086
Ge 50:10 made a **m.** for his father seven days. 60
Ge 50:11 saw the **m.** in the floor of Atad, they..... 60
Ge 50:11 is a grievous **m.** to the Egyptians:......... 60
De 26:14 I have not eaten thereof in my **m.**, ... 205
De 34:8 and **m.** for Moses were ended............. 60
2Sa 11:27 when the **m.** was past, David sent 60
2Sa 14:2 put on now **m.** apparel, and anoint......... 60
2Sa 19:2 that day was turned into **m.** unto all 60
Es 4:3 great **m.** among the Jews,...fasting, ... 60
Es 6:12 Haman hasted to his house **m.**, and....... 57
Es 9:22 to joy, and from **m.** into a good day:...... 60
Job 3:8 who are ready to raise up their **m.**..... 3882
Job 30:28 I went **m.** without the sun: I stood..... 6937
Job 30:31 My harp also is turned to **m.**, and my.... 60
Ps 30:11 turned for me my **m.** into dancing: 4553
Ps 38:6 greatly; I go **m.** all the day long........ 6937
Ps 42:9 go I **m.** because of the oppression...... 6937
Ps 43:2 go I **m.** because of the oppression...... 6937
Ec 7:2 better to go to the house of **m.**, than..... 60
Ec 7:4 of the wise is in the house of **m.**;.......... 60
Isa 22:12 hosts call to weeping, and to **m.**, ... 4553
Isa 51:11 and sorrow and **m.** shall flee away. 585
Isa 60:20 the days of thy **m.** shall be ended. 60
Isa 61:3 beauty for ashes, the oil of joy for **m.**, ... 60
Jer 6:26 make thee **m.**, as for an only son,......... 60
Jer 9:17 call for the **m.** women, that they......... 6969
Jer 16:5 not into the house of **m.**, neither 4798
Jer 16:7 men tear themselves for them in **m.**,..... 60
Jer 31:13 I will turn their **m.** into joy, and will 60
La 2:5 in the daughter of Judah **m.** and......... 8386
La 5:15 ceased; our dance is turned into **m.**....... 60
Eze 2:10 lamentations, and **m.**, and woe. 1899
Eze 7:16 all of them **m.**, every one for his 1993
Eze 24:17 to cry, make no **m.** for the dead, ... 60
Eze 31:15 down to the grave I caused a **m.**: 56
Da 10:2 I Daniel was **m.** three full weeks.......... 56
Joe 2:12 and with weeping, and with **m.**: 4553
Am 5:16 shall call the husbandman to **m.**, ... 60
Am 8:10 And I will turn your feasts into **m.**, ... 60
Am 8:10 will make it as the **m.** of an only son, ... 60
Mic 1:8 like the dragons, and **m.** as the owls...... 60
Mic 1:11 not forth in the **m.** of Beth-ezel; 4553
Zec 12:11 there be great **m.** in Jerusalem, ... 4553
Zec 12:11 as the **m.** of Hadadrimmon in the 4553
Mt 2:18 and great **m.**, Rachel weeping for....... *3602*
2Co 7:7 your **m.**, your fervent mind toward..... *3602*
Jas 4:9 laughter be turned to **m.**, and your..... *3997*
Re 18:8 day, death, and **m.**, and famine;......... *3997*

MOUSE See also MICE.

Le 11:29 the weasel, and the **m.**, and the 5909
Isa 66:17 and the **m.**, shall be consumed 5909

MOUTH See also MOUTHS.

Ge 4:11 hath opened her **m.** to receive thy 6310
Ge 8:11 in her **m.** was an olive leaf pluckt....... 6310
Ge 24:57 the damsel, and enquire at her **m.**...... 6310
Ge 29:2 great stone was upon the well's **m.**. ... 6310
Ge 29:3 rolled the stone from the well's **m.**,.... 6310
Ge 29:3 the stone again upon the well's **m.** 6310
Ge 29:8 roll the stone from the well's **m.**; 6310
Ge 29:10 rolled the stone from the well's **m.**,..... 6310
Ge 42:27 for, behold, it was in his sack's **m.**. 6310
Ge 43:12 again in the **m.** of your sacks, carry.... 6310
Ge 43:21 money was in the **m.** of his sack,........ 6310
Ge 44:1 every man's money in his sack's **m.**.... 6310
Ge 44:2 in the sack's **m.** of the youngest, ... 6310
Ge 45:12 it is my **m.** that speaketh unto you. 6310
Ex 4:11 him, Who hath made man's **m.**? or 6310
Ex 4:12 and I will be with thy **m.**, and teach ... 6310
Ex 4:15 unto him, and put words in his **m.**:...... 6310
Ex 4:15 will be with thy **m.**, and with his **m.**,.. 6310
Ex 4:16 he shall be to thee instead of a **m.**, ... 6310
Ex 13:9 the Lord's law may be in thy **m.**: 6310
Ex 23:13 neither let it be heard out of thy **m.**.. .. 6310
Nu 12:8 With him will I speak **m.** to **m.**, even ..6310
Nu 16:30 thing, and the earth open her **m.**, ... 6310
Nu 16:32 earth opened her **m.**, and swallowed.... 6310
Nu 22:28 the Lord opened the **m.** of the ass, ... 6310
Nu 22:38 the word that God putteth in my **m.**,.. 6310
Nu 23:5 the Lord put a word in Balaam's **m.**..... 6310
Nu 23:12 which the Lord hath put in my **m.**?..... 6310
Nu 23:16 Balaam, and put a word in his **m.**,...... 6310
Nu 26:10 earth opened her **m.**, and swallowed... 6310
Nu 30:2 to all that proceedeth out of his **m.**...... 6310
Nu 32:24 hath proceeded out of your **m.**. 6310
Nu 35:30 put to death by the **m.** of witnesses: .. 6310
De 8:3 of the **m.** of the Lord doth man live.... 6310
De 11:6 earth opened her **m.**, and swallowed... 6310
De 17:6 At the **m.** of two witnesses, or three.. 6310
De 17:6 at the **m.** of one witness he shall not .. 6310
De 18:18 and will put my words in his **m.**;........ 6310
De 19:15 sinneth: at the **m.** of two witnesses,... 6310
De 19:15 or at the **m.** of three witnesses, shall...6310
De 23:23 thou hast promised with thy **m.**. 6310
De 30:14 is very nigh unto thee, in thy **m.**, ... 6310
De 32:1 hear, O earth, the words of my **m.**. ... 6310
Jos 1:8 law shall not depart out of thy **m.**; 6310
Jos 6:10 any word proceed out of your **m.**,...... 6310
Jos 9:14 not counsel at the **m.** of the Lord. 6310
Jos 10:18 stones upon the **m.** of the cave, and... 6310
Jos 10:22 Open the **m.** of the cave and bring..... 6310
Jos 10:27 laid great stones in the cave's **m.**,...... 6310
Jg 7:6 putting their hand to their **m.**, were.... 6310
Jg 9:38 Where is now thy **m.**, wherewith....... 6310
Jg 11:35 I have opened my **m.** unto the Lord, .. 6310
Jg 11:36 hast opened thy **m.** unto the Lord,..... 6310
Jg 11:36 hath proceeded out of thy **m.**; 6310
Jg 18:19 lay thine hand upon thy **m.**, and go..... 6310
1Sa 1:12 the Lord, that Eli marked her **m.**........ 6310
1Sa 2:1 my **m.** is enlarged over mine............ 6310
1Sa 2:3 not arrogancy come out of your **m.**:.... 6310
1Sa 14:26 but no man put his hand to his **m.**:...... 6310
1Sa 14:27 honeycomb,...put his hand to his **m.**; .. 6310
1Sa 17:35 him, and delivered it out of his **m.**:..... 6310
2Sa 1:16 thy **m.** hath testified against thee, ... 6310
2Sa 14:3 So Joab put the words in her **m.**. 6310
2Sa 14:19 words in the **m.** of thine handmaid:..... 6310
2Sa 17:19 spread a covering over the well's **m.**,... 6310
2Sa 18:25 be alone, there is tidings in his **m.**. 6310
2Sa 22:9 and fire out of his **m.** devoured:........ 6310
1Ki 7:31 And the **m.** of it within the chapiter.... 6310
1Ki 7:31 but the **m.** thereof was round after...... 6310
1Ki 7:31 also upon the **m.** of it were gravings... 6310
1Ki 8:15 spake with his **m.** unto David my....... 6310
1Ki 8:24 thou spakest also with thy **m.**, and..... 6310
1Ki 13:21 hast disobeyed the **m.** of the Lord,..... 6310
1Ki 17:24 word of the Lord in thy **m.** is truth. ... 6310
1Ki 19:18 every **m.** which hath not kissed him.... 6310
1Ki 22:13 good unto the king with one **m.**: 6310
1Ki 22:22 spirit in the **m.** of all his prophets. 6310
1Ki 22:23 in the **m.** of all these thy prophets, ... 6310
2Ki 4:34 child, and put his **m.** upon his **m.**,........ 6310
1Ch 16:12 and the judgments of his **m.**;............. 6310
2Ch 6:4 he spake with his **m.** to my father...... 6310
2Ch 6:15 and spakest with thy **m.**, and hast...... 6310
2Ch 18:21 spirit in the **m.** of all his prophets. 6310
2Ch 18:22 in the **m.** of these thy prophets, and... 6310
2Ch 35:22 words of Necho from the **m.** of God, .. 6310
2Ch 36:12 speaking from the **m.** of the Lord....... 6310
2Ch 36:21 of the Lord by the **m.** of Jeremiah,..... 6310
2Ch 36:22 Lord spoken by the **m.** of Jeremiah 6310
Ezr 1:1 of the Lord by the **m.** of Jeremiah...... 6310
Ne 9:20 not thy manna from their **m.**, and....... 6310
Es 7:8 word went out of the king's **m.**, and... 6310
Job 3:1 After this opened Job his **m.**, and....... 6310
Job 5:15 from their **m.**, and from the hand of ... 6310
Job 5:16 hope, and iniquity stoppeth her **m.**. 6310
Job 7:11 Therefore I will not refrain my **m.**;..... 6310
Job 8:2 the words of thy **m.** be like a strong... 6310
Job 8:21 Till he fill thy **m.** with laughing, ... 6310
Job 9:20 mine own **m.** shall condemn me: 6310
Job 12:11 words? and the **m.** taste his meat? 2441
Job 15:5 For thy **m.** uttereth thine iniquity,...... 6310
Job 15:6 Thine own **m.** condemneth thee, ... 6310
Job 15:13 lettest such words go out of thy **m.**? .. 6310
Job 15:30 by the breath of his **m.** shall he go..... 6310
Job 16:5 would strengthen you with my **m.**, ... 6310
Job 16:10 have gaped upon me with their **m.**; 6310
Job 19:16 I intreated him with my **m.**.............. 6310
Job 20:12 wickedness be sweet in his **m.**, ... 6310
Job 20:13 not; but keep it still within his **m.**: 2441
Job 21:5 and lay your hand upon your **m.**......... 6310
Job 22:22 I pray thee, the law from his **m.**,....... 6310
Job 23:4 and fill my **m.** with arguments. 6310
Job 23:12 have esteemed the words of his **m.**.... 6310
Job 29:9 and laid their hand on their **m.**........... 6310
Job 29:10 cleaved to the roof of their **m.**........... 2441
Job 29:23 they opened their **m.** wide as for 6310
Job 31:27 or my **m.** hath kissed my hand: 6310
Job 31:30 have I suffered my **m.** to sin by.......... 2441
Job 32:5 no answer in the **m.** of these three 6310
Job 33:2 Behold, now I have opened my **m.**, ... 6310
Job 33:2 my tongue hath spoken in my **m.**. 2441
Job 34:3 trieth words, as the **m.** tasteth meat... 2441
Job 35:16 doth Job open his **m.** in vain;............ 6310
Job 37:2 the sound that goeth out of his **m.**. 6310
Job 40:4 I will lay mine hand upon my **m.**. 6310
Job 40:23 he can draw up Jordan into his **m.**..... 6310
Job 41:19 Out of his **m.** go burning lamps,......... 6310
Job 41:21 and a flame goeth out of his **m.**. 6310
Ps 5:9 there is no faithfulness in their **m.**;..... 6310
Ps 8:2 Out of...**m.** of babes and sucklings...... 6310
Ps 10:7 His **m.** is full of cursing and deceit 6310
Ps 17:3 that my **m.** shall not transgress. 6310
Ps 17:10 with their **m.** they speak proudly........ 6310
Ps 18:8 and fire out of his **m.** devoured:......... 6310
Ps 19:14 Let the words of my **m.**, and the....... 6310
Ps 22:21 Save me from the lion's **m.**: for......... 6310
Ps 32:9 whose **m.** must be held in with bit 5716
Ps 33:6 of them by the breath of his **m.**. 6310
Ps 34:1 shall continually be in my **m.**. 6310
Ps 35:21 they opened their **m.** wide against...... 6310
Ps 36:3 The words of his **m.** are iniquity 6310
Ps 37:30 The **m.** of the righteous speaketh....... 6310
Ps 38:13 dumb man that openeth not his **m.**. 6310
Ps 38:14 and in whose **m.** are no reproofs........ 6310
Ps 39:1 I will keep my **m.** with a bridle,......... 6310
Ps 39:9 I was dumb, I opened not my **m.**;........ 6310
Ps 40:3 he hath put a new song in my **m.**,....... 6310
Ps 49:3 My **m.** shall speak of wisdom; and...... 6310
Ps 50:16 that...take my covenant in thy **m.**?..... 6310
Ps 50:19 Thou givest thy **m.** to evil, and thy 6310
Ps 51:15 my **m.** shall shew forth thy praise. 6310
Ps 54:2 give ear to the words of my **m.**. 6310
Ps 55:21 The words of his **m.** were smoother... 6310
Ps 58:6 Break their teeth, O God, in their **m.**: .6310
Ps 59:7 they belch out with their **m.**:............. 6310
Ps 59:12 the sin of their **m.** and the words....... 6310
Ps 62:4 they bless with their **m.**, but they....... 6310
Ps 63:5 my **m.** shall praise thee with joyful...... 6310
Ps 63:11 the **m.** of them that speak lies shall.... 6310
Ps 66:14 and my **m.** hath spoken, when I was... 6310
Ps 66:17 I cried unto him with my **m.**, and....... 6310
Ps 69:15 not the pit shut her **m.** upon me. 6310
Ps 71:8 Let my **m.** be filled with thy praise...... 6310
Ps 71:15 My **m.** shall shew forth thy.............. 6310
Ps 73:9 set their **m.** against the heavens, ... 6310
Ps 78:1 your ears to the words of my **m.**. 6310
Ps 78:2 I will open my **m.** in a parable: I........ 6310
Ps 78:36 they did flatter him with their **m.**, ... 6310
Ps 81:10 open thy **m.** wide, and I will fill it. 6310
Ps 89:1 with my **m.** will I make known thy 6310
Ps 103:5 satisfieth thy **m.** with good things;...... 5716
Ps 105:5 and the judgments of his **m.**;............ 6310
Ps 107:42 and all iniquity shall stop her **m.**....... 6310
Ps 109:2 For the **m.** of the wicked and the....... 6310
Ps 109:2 the **m.** of the deceitful are opened...... 6310
Ps 109:30 greatly praise the Lord with my **m.**; ... 6310
Ps 119:13 all the judgments of thy **m.**. 6310
Ps 119:43 word of truth utterly out of my **m.**;.... 6310
Ps 119:72 The law of thy **m.** is better unto me... 6310
Ps 119:88 shall I keep the testimony of thy **m.**. .. 6310
Ps 119:103 yea, sweeter than honey to my **m.**!..... 6310
Ps 119:108 the freewill offerings of my **m.**, O 6310
Ps 119:131 I opened my **m.**, and panted: for I 6310
Ps 126:2 was our **m.** filled with laughter, ... 6310
Ps 137:6 tongue cleave to the roof of my **m.**; ... 2441
Ps 138:4 they hear the words of thy **m.**........... 6310
Ps 141:3 Set a watch, O Lord, before my **m.**;... 6310
Ps 141:7 are scattered at the grave's **m.**,......... 6310
Ps 144:8 Whose **m.** speaketh vanity, and 6310
Ps 144:11 whose **m.** speaketh vanity, and.......... 6310
Ps 145:21 My **m.** shall speak the praise of the.... 6310
Ps 149:6 high praises of God be in their **m.**,..... 1627
Pr 2:6 out of his **m.** cometh knowledge 6310
Pr 4:5 decline from the words of my **m.**. 6310
Pr 4:24 put away from thee a froward **m.**,...... 6310

Pr 5:3 and her **m.** is smoother than oil: ... 2441
Pr 5:7 not from the words of my **m.** ... 6310
Pr 6:2 snared with the words of thy **m.**, ... 6310
Pr 6:2 art taken with the words of thy **m.** ... 6310
Pr 6:12 man, walketh with a froward **m.** ... 6310
Pr 7:24 and attend to the words of my **m.** ... 6310
Pr 8:7 For my **m.** shall speak truth; and ... 2441
Pr 8:8 All the words of my **m.** are in ... 6310
Pr 8:13 way, and the froward **m.**, do I hate. ... 6310
Pr 10:6 covereth the **m.** of the wicked. ... 6310
Pr 10:11 The **m.** of a righteous man is a well ... 6310
Pr 10:11 covereth the **m.** of the wicked. ... 6310
Pr 10:14 but the **m.** of the foolish is near ... 6310
Pr 10:31 The **m.** of the just bringeth forth ... 6310
Pr 10:32 but the **m.** of the wicked speaketh ... 6310
Pr 11:9 An hypocrite with his **m.** destroyeth ... 6310
Pr 11:11 overthrown by the **m.** of the wicked. ... 6310
Pr 12:6 the **m.** of the upright shall deliver ... 6310
Pr 12:14 with good by the fruit of his **m.**: ... 6310
Pr 13:2 shall eat good by the fruit of his **m.**: ... 6310
Pr 13:3 He that keepeth his **m.** keepeth his ... 6310
Pr 14:3 In the **m.** of the foolish is a rod of ... 6310
Pr 15:2 but the **m.** of fools poureth out ... 6310
Pr 15:14 but the **m.** of fools feedeth on ... 6310
Pr 15:23 hath joy by the answer of his **m.**: ... 6310
Pr 15:28 the **m.** of the wicked poureth out ... 6310
Pr 16:10 king: his **m.** transgresseth not in ... 6310
Pr 16:23 heart of the wise teacheth his **m.**, ... 6310
Pr 16:26 for his **m.** craveth it of him. ... 6310
Pr 18:4 The words of a man's **m.** are as ... 6310
Pr 18:6 and his **m.** calleth for strokes. ... 6310
Pr 18:7 A fool's **m.** is his destruction, and ... 6310
Pr 18:20 satisfied with the fruit of his **m.**; ... 6310
Pr 19:24 much as bring it to his **m.** again. ... 6310
Pr 19:28 and the **m.** of the wicked devoureth ... 6310
Pr 20:17 his **m.** shall be filled with gravel. ... 6310
Pr 21:23 Whoso keepeth his **m.** and his ... 6310
Pr 22:14 The **m.** of strange women is a deep ... 6310
Pr 24:7 he openeth not his **m.** in the gate. ... 6310
Pr 26:7,9 so is a parable in the **m.** of fools. ... 6310
Pr 26:15 him to bring it again to his **m.** ... 6310
Pr 26:28 and a flattering **m.** worketh ruin. ... 6310
Pr 27:2 praise thee, and not thine own **m.**; ... 6310
Pr 30:20 she eateth, and wipeth her **m.**, and ... 6310
Pr 30:32 evil, lay thine hand upon thy **m.** ... 6310
Pr 31:8 Open thy **m.** for the dumb in the ... 6310
Pr 31:9 Open thy **m.**, judge righteously, ... 6310
Pr 31:26 She openeth her **m.** with wisdom; ... 6310
Ec 5:2 Be not rash with thy **m.**, and let not ... 6310
Ec 5:6 Suffer not thy **m.** to cause thy flesh ... 6310
Ec 6:7 All the labour of man is for his **m.**, ... 6310
Ec 10:12 The words of a wise man's **m.** are ... 6310
Ec 10:13 beginning of the words of his **m.** ... 6310
Ca 1:2 kiss me with the kisses of his **m.**: ... 6310
Ca 5:16 His **m.** is most sweet; yea, he is ... 2441
Ca 7:9 And the roof of thy **m.** like the best ... 2441
Isa 1:20 the **m.** of the Lord hath spoken it. ... 6310
Isa 5:14 opened her **m.** without measure: ... 6310
Isa 6:7 he laid it upon my **m.**, and said, Lo, ... 6310
Isa 9:12 shall devour Israel with open **m.** ... 6310
Isa 9:17 and every **m.** speaketh folly. For ... 6310
Isa 10:14 wing, or opened the **m.**, or peeped. ... 6310
Isa 11:4 the earth with the rod of his **m.**, ... 6310
Isa 19:7 by the **m.** of the brooks, and every ... 6310
Isa 29:13 people draw near me with their **m.**, ... 6310
Isa 30:2 and have not asked at my **m.**; to ... 6310
Isa 34:16 for my **m.** it hath commanded, and ... 6310
Isa 40:5 the **m.** of the Lord hath spoken it. ... 6310
Isa 45:23 the word is gone out of my **m.** in ... 6310
Isa 48:3 and they went forth out of my **m.**, ... 6310
Isa 49:2 made my **m.** like a sharp sword; ... 6310
Isa 51:16 I have put my words in thy **m.**, ... 6310
Isa 53:7 afflicted, ye he opened not his **m.**: ... 6310
Isa 53:7 is dumb, so he openeth not his **m.** ... 6310
Isa 53:9 neither was any deceit in his **m.** ... 6310
Isa 55:11 be that goeth forth out of my **m.**: ... 6310
Isa 57:4 against whom make ye a wide **m.**, ... 6310
Isa 58:14 the **m.** of the Lord hath spoken it. ... 6310
Isa 59:21 words, which I have put in thy **m.**, ... 6310
Isa 59:21 shall not depart out of thy **m.**, nor ... 6310
Isa 59:21 nor out of the **m.** of thy seed, nor ... 6310
Isa 59:21 nor out of the **m.** of thy seed's seed, ... 6310
Isa 62:2 the **m.** of the Lord shall name. ... 6310
Jer 1:9 forth his hand, and touched my **m.** ... 6310
Jer 1:9 I have put my words in thy **m.** ... 6310
Jer 5:14 I will make my words in thy **m.** fire, ... 6310
Jer 7:28 and is cut off from their **m.** ... 6310
Jer 9:8 to his neighbour with his **m.**, but ... 6310
Jer 9:12 the **m.** of the Lord hath spoken, ... 6310
Jer 9:20 your ear receive the word of his **m.**, ... 6310
Jer 12:2 thou art near in their **m.**, and far ... 6310
Jer 15:19 the vile, thou shalt be as my **m.**: ... 6310
Jer 23:16 and not out of the **m.** of the Lord. ... 6310
Jer 32:4 and shall speak with him **m.** to **m.**, ... 6310
Jer 34:3 he shall speak with thee **m.** to **m.**, ... 6310
Jer 36:4 wrote from the **m.** of Jeremiah all ... 6310
Jer 36:6 thou hast written from my **m.**, the ... 6310
Jer 36:17 write all these words at his **m.**? ... 6310
Jer 36:18 these words unto me with his **m.**, ... 6310
Jer 36:27 wrote at the **m.** of Jeremiah, ... 6310
Jer 36:32 therein from the **m.** of Jeremiah ... 6310
Jer 44:17 thing goeth forth out of our own **m.**, ... 6310
Jer 44:26 be named in the **m.** of any man of ... 6310
Jer 45:1 in a book at the **m.** of Jeremiah, ... 6310
Jer 48:28 nest in the sides of the hole's **m.** ... 6310
Jer 51:44 bring forth out of his **m.** that which ... 6310
La 2:16 have opened their **m.** against thee: ... 6310
La 3:29 He putteth his **m.** in the dust; if so ... 6310
La 3:38 Out of the **m.** of the most High ... 6310
La 4:4 cleaveth to the roof of his **m.** for ... 2441
Eze 2:8 open thy **m.**, and eat that I give ... 6310
Eze 3:2 So I opened my **m.**, and he caused ... 6310
Eze 3:3 and it was in my **m.** as honey for ... 6310
Eze 3:17 hear the word at my **m.**, and give ... 6310
Eze 3:26 tongue cleave to the roof of thy **m.**, ... 2441
Eze 3:27 I will open thy **m.**, and thou shalt ... 6310
Eze 4:14 there abominable flesh into my **m.** ... 6310
Eze 16:56 was not mentioned by thy **m.** in ... 6310
Eze 16:63 and never open thy **m.** any more ... 6310
Eze 21:22 open the **m.** in the slaughter, to lift ... 6310
Eze 24:27 thy **m.** be opened to him which is ... 6310
Eze 29:21 the opening of the **m.** in the midst ... 6310
Eze 33:7 thou shalt hear the word at my **m.**, ... 6310
Eze 33:22 had opened my **m.**, until he came ... 6310
Eze 33:22 my **m.** was opened, and I was no ... 6310
Eze 33:31 with their **m.** they shew much love, ... 6310
Eze 34:10 will deliver my flock from their **m.**, ... 6310
Eze 35:13 Thus with your **m.** ye have boasted ... 6310
Da 3:26 near to the **m.** of the burning fiery ... 8651
Da 4:31 the word was in the king's **m.**, ... 6433
Da 6:17 and laid upon the **m.** of the den; ... 6433
Da 7:5 and it had three ribs in the **m.** of it ... 6433
Da 7:8 and a **m.** speaking great things. ... 6433
Da 7:20 a **m.** that spake very great things. ... 6433
Da 10:3 came flesh nor wine in my **m.**, ... 6310
Da 10:16 then I opened my **m.**, and spake, ... 6310
Ho 2:17 the names of Baalim out of her **m.**, ... 6310
Ho 6:5 slain them by the words of my **m.**: ... 6310
Ho 8:1 Set the trumpet to thy **m.**. He ... 2441
Joe 1:5 for it is cut off from your **m.** ... 6310
Am 3:12 out of the **m.** of the lion two legs, ... 6310
Mic 4:4 **m.** of the Lord of hosts hath spoken ... 6310
Mic 6:12 tongue is deceitful in their **m.** ... 6310
Mic 7:5 keep the doors of thy **m.** from her ... 6310
Mic 7:16 shall lay their hand upon their **m.**, ... 6310
Na 3:12 even fall into the **m.** of the eater. ... 6310
Zep 3:13 tongue be found in their **m.**: for ... 6310
Zec 5:8 weight of lead upon the **m.** thereof. ... 6310
Zec 8:9 words by the **m.** of the prophets, ... 6310
Zec 9:7 take away his blood out of his **m.**, ... 6310
Zec 14:12 shall consume away in their **m.** ... 6310
Mal 2:6 The law of truth was in his **m.**, and ... 6310
Mal 2:7 they should seek the law at his **m.**: ... 6310
Mt 4:4 **proceedeth out of the m. of God** ... *4750*
Mt 5:2 he opened his **m.**, and taught them, ... *4750*
Mt 12:34 **of the heart the m. speaketh.** ... *4750*
Mt 13:35 I will open my **m.** in parables; I will ... *4750*
Mt 15:8 **nigh unto me with their m.,** ... *4750*
Mt 15:11 **which goeth into the m. defileth** ... *4750*
Mt 15:11 **that which cometh out of the m.,** ... *4750*
Mt 15:17 **entereth in at the m. goeth into** ... *4750*
Mt 15:18 **which proceed out of the m. come** ... *4750*
Mt 17:27 **when thou hast opened his m.,** ... *4750*
Mt 18:16 **the m. of two or three witnesses** ... *4750*
Mt 21:16 **of the m. of babes and sucklings** ... *4750*
Lu 1:64 his **m.** was opened immediately, and ... *4750*
Lu 1:70 spake by the **m.** of his holy prophets, ... *4750*
Lu 4:22 which proceeded out of his **m.**. And ... *4750*
Lu 6:45 **of the heart his m. speaketh.** ... *4750*
Lu 11:54 to catch something out of his **m.**, ... *4750*
Lu 19:22 **thine own m. will I judge thee,** ... *4750*
Lu 21:15 **I will give you a m. and wisdom,** ... *4750*
Lu 22:71 ourselves have heard of his own **m.** ... *4750*
Joh 19:29 upon hyssop, and put it to his **m.** ... *4750*
Ac 1:16 the Holy Ghost by the **m.** of David ... *4750*
Ac 3:18 by the **m.** of all his prophets, that ... *4750*
Ac 3:21 by the **m.** of all his holy prophets ... *4750*
Ac 4:25 by the **m.** of thy servant David hast ... *4750*
Ac 8:32 shearer, so opened he not his **m.**: ... *4750*
Ac 8:35 Philip opened his **m.**, and began at ... *4750*
Ac 10:34 Then Peter opened his **m.**, and said, ... *4750*
Ac 11:8 hath at any time entered into my **m.** ... *4750*
Ac 15:7 the Gentiles by my **m.** should hear ... *4750*
Ac 15:27 tell you the same things by **m.** ... *3056*
Ac 18:14 was now about to open his **m.**, ... *4750*
Ac 22:14 shouldest hear the voice of his **m.** ... *4750*
Ac 23:2 by him to smite him on the **m.** ... *4750*
Ro 3:14 Whose **m.** is full of cursing and ... *4750*
Ro 3:19 that every **m.** may be stopped, and ... *4750*
Ro 10:8 word is nigh thee, even in thy **m.**: ... *4750*
Ro 10:9 confess with thy **m.** the Lord Jesus, ... *4750*
Ro 10:10 and with the **m.** confession is made ... *4750*
Ro 15:6 one mind and one **m.** glorify God, ... *4750*
1Co 9:9 shalt not muzzle the **m.** of the ox ...
2Co 6:11 our **m.** is open unto you, our ... *4750*
2Co 13:1 In the **m.** of two or three witnesses ... *4750*
Eph 4:29 proceed out of your **m.**, but that ... *4750*
Eph 6:19 that I may open my **m.** boldly, to ... *4750*
Col 3:8 communication out of your **m.** ... *4750*
2Th 2:8 consume with the spirit of his **m.**, ... *4750*
2Ti 4:17 delivered out of the **m.** of the lion. ... *4750*
Jas 3:10 of the same **m.** proceedeth blessing ... *4750*
1Pe 2:22 neither was guile found in his **m.**: ... *4750*
Jude 16 **m.** speaketh great swelling words, ... *4750*
Re 1:16 and out of his **m.** went a sharp ... *4750*
Re 2:16 **them with the sword of my m.** ... *4750*
Re 3:16 **hot, I will spue thee out of my m.** ... *4750*
Re 9:19 For their power is in their **m.**, and ... *4750*
Re 10:9 shall be in thy **m.** sweet as honey. ... *4750*
Re 10:10 it was in my **m.** sweet as honey: ... *4750*
Re 11:5 fire proceedeth out of their **m.**, and ... *4750*
Re 12:15 cast out of his **m.** water as a flood ... *4750*
Re 12:16 earth opened her **m.**, and swallowed ... *4750*
Re 12:16 which the dragon cast out of his **m.** ... *4750*
Re 13:2 and his **m.** as the **m.** of a lion: and ... *4750*
Re 13:5 him a **m.** speaking great things and ... *4750*
Re 13:6 And he opened his **m.** in blasphemy ... *4750*
Re 14:5 And in their **m.** was found no guile: ... *4750*
Re 16:13 come out of the **m.** of the dragon, ... *4750*
Re 16:13 and out of the **m.** of the beast, ... *4750*
Re 16:13 out of the **m.** of the false prophet. ... *4750*
Re 19:15 out of his **m.** goeth a sharp sword. ... *4750*
Re 19:21 sword proceeded out of his **m.**: ... *4750*

MOUTHS

Ge 44:8 which we found in our sacks' **m.**, ... 6310
De 31:19 put it in their **m.**, that this song ... 6310
De 31:21 out of the **m.** of their seed: for I ... 6310
Ps 22:13 They gaped upon me with their **m.**, ... 6310
Ps 78:30 their meat was yet in their **m.**, ... 6310
Ps 115:5 They have **m.**, but they speak not: ... 6310
Ps 135:16 They have **m.**, but they speak not; ... 6310
Ps 135:17 is there any breath in their **m.** ... 6310
Isa 52:15 the kings shall shut their **m.** at him: ... 6310
Jer 44:25 have both spoken with your **m.**, and ... 6310
La 3:46 our enemies have opened their **m.** ... 6310
Da 6:22 angel, and hath shut the lions' **m.**, ... 6433
Mic 3:5 he that putteth not into their **m.**, ... 6310
Tit 1:11 Whose **m.** must be stopped, who ... *1993*
Heb 11:33 promises, stopped the **m.** of lions, ... *4750*
Jas 3:3 we put bits in the horses' **m.**, that ... *4750*
Re 9:17 and out of their **m.** issued fire and ... *4750*
Re 9:18 which issued out of their **m.** ... *4750*

MOVE See also MOVEABLE; MOVED; MOVETH; MOVING; REMOVE.

Ex 11:7 shall not a dog **m.** his tongue, ... 2782
Le 11:10 of all that **m.** in the waters, and of ... 8318
De 23:25 thou shalt not **m.** a sickle unto thy ... 5130
De 32:21 I will **m.** them to jealousy with those ...
Jg 13:25 Spirit of the Lord began to **m.** him ... 6470
2Sa 7:10 of their own, and **m.** no more; ... 7264
2Ki 21:8 will I make the feet of Israel **m.** ... 5110
2Ki 23:18 alone; let no man **m.** his bones. ... 5128
Jer 10:4 and with hammers, that it **m.** not. ... 6328
Mic 7:17 they shall **m.** out of their holes ... 7264
Mt 23:4 **will not m. them with one of their** ... *2795*
Ac 17:28 in him we live, and **m.**, and have ... *2795*
Ac 20:24 none of these things **m.** me, ... *3056,4160*

MOVEABLE See also UNMOVEABLE.

Pr 5:6 her ways are **m.**, that thou canst ... 5128

MOVED See also MOVEDST; REMOVED.
Ge 1:2 the Spirit of God **m.** upon the face 7363
Ge 7:21 And all flesh died that **m.** upon the 7430
De 32:21 They have **m.** me to jealousy with that......
Jos 10:21 none **m.** his tongue against any of 2782
Jos 15:18 she **m.** him to ask of her father a....... 5496
Jg 1:14 she **m.** him to ask of her father a....... 5496
Ru 1:19 all the city was **m.** about them, ... 1949
1Sa 1:13 only her lips **m.**, but her voice was 5128
2Sa 18:33 the king was much **m.**, and went 7264
2Sa 22:8 the foundations of heaven **m.** and 7264
2Sa 24:1 he **m.** David against them to say, ... 5496
1Ch 16:30 shall be stable, that it be not **m.**. 4131
1Ch 17:9 place, and shall be **m.** no more; 7264
2Ch 18:31 God **m.** them to depart from him. 5496
Ezr 4:15 they have **m.** sedition within the 5648
Es 5:9 he stood not up, nor **m.** for him, ... 2111
Job 37:1 my heart…is **m.** out of his place. 5425
Job 41:23 in themselves; they cannot be **m.**....... 4131
Ps 10:6 said in his heart, I shall not be **m.**:...... 4131
Ps 13:4 trouble me rejoice when I am **m.**. 4131
Ps 15:5 doeth these things shall never be **m.**... 4131
Ps 16:8 at my right hand, I shall not be **m.**. ... 4131
Ps 18:7 foundations also of the hills **m.**.......... 7264
Ps 21:7 the most High he shall not be **m.**. 4131
Ps 30:6 I said, I shall never be **m.**. 4131
Ps 46:5 she shall not be **m.**: God shall help..... 4131
Ps 46:6 raged, the kingdoms were **m.**: he....... 4131
Ps 55:22 never suffer the righteous to be **m.**.... 4131
Ps 62:2 defence; I shall not be greatly **m.**....... 4131
Ps 62:6 he is my defence; I shall not be **m.**. ... 4131
Ps 66:9 and suffereth not our feet to be **m.**. ... 4132
Ps 68:8 Sinai itself was **m.** at the presence of........
Ps 78:58 **m.** him to jealousy with their graven.........
Ps 93:1 is stablished, that it cannot be **m.**....... 4131
Ps 96:10 established that is shall not be **m.**: 4131
Ps 99:1 cherubims; let the earth be **m.**. 5120
Ps 112:6 Surely he shall not be **m.** for ever:..... 4131
Ps 121:3 He will not suffer thy foot to be **m.**:... 4132
Pr 12:3 of the righteous shall not be **m.**. 4131
Ca 5:4 and my bowels were **m.** for him. 1993
Isa 6:4 posts of the door **m.** at the voice 5128
Isa 7:2 his heart was **m.**, and the heart of 5128
Isa 7:2 the trees of the wood are **m.** with........ 5128
Isa 10:14 there was none that **m.** the wing, ... 5074
Isa 14:9 Hell from beneath is **m.** for thee 7264
Isa 19:1 the idols of Egypt shall be **m.** at 5128
Isa 24:19 the earth is **m.** exceedingly.............. 4132
Isa 40:20 graven image, that shall not be **m.**. 4131
Isa 41:7 with nails, that it should not be **m.**. 4131
Jer 4:24 and all the hills **m.** lightly.................. 7043
Jer 25:16 And they shall drink, and be **m.**, ... 1607
Jer 46:7 whose waters are **m.** as the rivers?.... 1607
Jer 46:8 his waters are **m.** like the rivers; 1607
Jer 49:21 The earth is **m.** at the noise of.......... 7493
Jer 50:46 taking of Babylon the earth is **m.**, ... 7493
Da 8:7 he was **m.** with choler against him,...........
Da 11:11 of the south shall be **m.** with choler,.........
Mt 9:36 was **m.** with compassion on them, ... *4697*
Mt 14:14 **m.** with compassion toward them, ... *4697*
Mt 18:27 **servant was m. with compassion,** .. *4697*
Mt 20:24 were **m.** with indignation against *23*
Mt 21:10 all the city was **m.**, saying, Who is..... *4579*
Mk 1:41 Jesus, **m.** with compassion, put.......... *4697*
Mk 6:34 and was **m.** with compassion toward ... *4697*
Mk 15:11 But the chief priests **m.** the people, ... *383*
Ac 2:25 hand, that I should not be **m.**: *4531*
Ac 7:9 the patriarchs, **m.** with envy, sold...... *2206*
Ac 17:5 Jews which believed not, **m.** with........ *2206*
Ac 21:30 And all the city was **m.**, and the *2795*
Col 1:23 and be not **m.** away from the hope..... *3334*
1Th 3:3 no man should be **m.** by these........... *4525*
Heb 11:7 By faith Noah,…**m.** with fear, ... *2125*
Heb 12:28 a kingdom which cannot be **m.**, ... *761*
2Pe 1:21 they were **m.** by the Holy Ghost. *5342*
Re 6:14 every mountain and island were **m.**...... *2795*

MOVEDST
Job 2:3 thou **m.** me against him, to destroy 5496

MOVER
Ac 24:5 and a **m.** of sedition among all the *2795*

MOVETH See also REMOVETH.
Ge 1:21 and every living creature that **m.**, ... 7430
Ge 1:28 over every living thing that **m.** upon ... 7430
Ge 9:2 upon all that **m.** upon the earth, and ... 7430
Le 11:46 living creature that **m.** in the waters, .. 7430
Job 40:17 He **m.** his tail like a cedar: the 2654
Ps 69:34 seas,…every thing that **m.** therein. 7430
Pr 23:31 the cup, when it **m.** itself aright.......... 1980
Eze 47:9 every thing that liveth, which **m.**,....... 8317

MOVING See also REMOVING.
Ge 1:20 the **m.** creature that hath life, ... 8318
Ge 9:3 Every **m.** thing that liveth shall be...... 7430
Job 16:5 the **m.** of my lips should asswage....... 5205
Pr 16:30 **m.** his lips he bringeth evil to............ 7169
Joh 5:3 waiting for the **m.** of the water.......... *2796*

MOWER
Ps 129:7 the **m.** filleth not his hand: nor 7114

MOWINGS
Am 7:1 latter growth after the king's **m.**. 1488

MOWN
Ps 72:6 down like rain upon the **m.** grass: 1488

MOZA (mo'-zah)
1Ch 2:46 concubine, bare Haran, and **M.**, ... 4162
1Ch 8:36 and Zimri; and Zimri begat **M.**, ... 4162
1Ch 8:37 **M.** begat Binea: Rapha was his.......... 4162
1Ch 9:42 and Zimri; and Zimri begat **M.**; 4162
1Ch 9:43 And **M.** begat Binea; and Rephaiah..... 4162

MOZAH (mo'-zah)
Jos 18:26 Mizpeh, and Chephirah, and **M.**, ... 4681

MUCH See also INASMUCH; FORASMUCH; FORSOMUCH.
Ge 23:9 for as **m.** money as it is worth he shall .....
Ge 26:16 for thou art **m.** mightier than we........ 3966
Ge 30:43 had **m.** cattle, and maidservants, ... 7227
Ge 34:12 Ask me never so **m.** dowry 3966,7235
Ge 41:49 corn as the sand of the sea, very **m.**, . 7235
Ge 43:34 mess was five times so **m.** as any of .. 7235
Ge 44:1 with food, as **m.** as they can carry,...... 834
Ge 50:20 this day, to save **m.** people alive........ 7227
Ex 12:38 and herds, even very **m.** cattle........... 3515
Ex 12:42 a night to be **m.** observed unto the..........
Ex 14:28 remained not so **m.** as one of them. ... 5704
Ex 16:5 be twice as **m.** as they gather daily...... 834
Ex 16:18 gathered **m.** had nothing over, and 7235
Ex 16:22 day they gathered twice as **m.** bread, ...
Ex 30:23 of sweet cinnamon half so **m.**, even.... 4276
Ex 36:5 The people bring **m.** more than 7235
Ex 36:7 the work to make it, and too **m.**. 3498
Le 7:10 of Aaron have, one as **m.** as another. ....
Le 13:7 But if the scab spread **m.** abroad 6581
Le 13:22 if it spread **m.** abroad in the skin, ... 6581
Le 13:27 it be spread **m.** abroad in the skin, ... 6581
Le 13:35 if the scall spread **m.** in the skin........ 6581
Le 14:21 if he be poor, and cannot get so **m.**;.........
Nu 16:3 Ye take too **m.** upon you, seeing 7227
Nu 16:7 Ye take too **m.** upon you, ye sons of.. 7227
Nu 20:20 out against him with **m.** people, ... 3515
Nu 21:4 of the people was **m.** discouraged....... 7114
Nu 21:6 and **m.** people of Israel died............. 7227
De 2:5 land,…not so **m.** as a foot breadth; 5704
De 3:19 (for I know that ye have **m.** cattle,).... 7227
De 28:38 carry **m.** seed out into the field, ... 7227
De 31:27 and how **m.** more after my death?............
Jos 11:4 **m.** people, even as the sand that is.... 7227
Jos 13:1 yet very **m.** land to be possessed....... 7235
Jos 19:9 of Judah was too **m.** for them:........... 7227
Jos 22:8 with **m.** riches unto your tents, and.... 7227
Jos 22:8 with very **m.** cattle, with silver, and .. 7227
Jos 22:8 iron, and with very **m.** raiment: 7235
Ru 1:13 it grieveth me **m.** for your sakes 3966
1Sa 2:16 then take as **m.** as thy soul desireth; ....
1Sa 14:30 How **m.** more, if haply the people........ 637
1Sa 14:30 **m.** greater slaughter among the ....
1Sa 18:30 so that his name was **m.** set by. 3966
1Sa 19:2 Saul's son delighted **m.** in David:........ 3966
1Sa 20:13 do so and **m.** more to Jonathan:......... 3254
1Sa 23:3 how **m.** more then if we come to 637
1Sa 26:24 as thy life was **m.** set by this day 1431
1Sa 26:24 so let my life be **m.** set by in the....... 1431
2Sa 4:11 How **m.** more, when wicked men 637
2Sa 8:8 David took exceeding **m.** brass. 7235
2Sa 13:34 there came **m.** people by the way 7227
2Sa 14:25 to be so **m.** praised as Absalom for 3966
2Sa 16:11 **m.** more now may this Benjamite 637
2Sa 17:12 there shall not be left so **m.** as one. ... 1571
2Sa 18:33 the king was **m.** moved, and went up........
1Ki 4:29 and understanding exceeding **m.**,........ 7235
1Ki 8:27 how **m.** less this house that I have 637
1Ki 10:2 very **m.** gold, and precious stones:..... 7227
1Ki 12:28 It is too **m.** for you to go up to 7227
2Ki 5:13 how **m.** rather then, when he 637,3588
2Ki 10:18 little; but Jehu shall serve him **m.**........ 7235
2Ki 12:10 there was **m.** money in the chest, ... 7225
2Ki 21:6 he wrought **m.** wickedness in the....... 7235
2Ki 21:16 shed innocent blood very **m.**, till he.... 7235
1Ch 18:8 brought David very **m.** brass, ... 7227
1Ch 20:2 brought also exceeding **m.** spoil 7235
1Ch 22:4 brought **m.** cedar wood to David. 7230
1Ch 22:8 thou hast shed **m.** blood upon the 7227
2Ch 2:16 Lebanon, as **m.** as thou shalt need: 3605
2Ch 6:18 how **m.** less this house which I have 637
2Ch 14:13 they carried away very **m.** spoil. 7235
2Ch 14:14 was exceeding **m.** spoil in them. 7235
2Ch 17:13 **m.** business in the cities of Judah: 7227
2Ch 20:25 gathering of the spoil, it was so **m.**. ... 7227
2Ch 24:11 they saw that there was **m.** money,.... 7227
2Ch 25:9 Lord is able to give thee **m.** more...... 7235
2Ch 25:13 of them, and took **m.** spoil................ 7227
2Ch 26:10 he had **m.** cattle, both in the low 7227
2Ch 27:3 on the wall of Ophel he built **m.**......... 7230
2Ch 27:5 So **m.**…the children of Ammon pay 1931
2Ch 28:8 took also away **m.** spoil from them, ... 7227
2Ch 30:13 assembled at Jerusalem **m.** people...... 7227
2Ch 32:4 was gathered **m.** people together, ... 7227
2Ch 32:4 Assyria come, and find **m.** water? 7227
2Ch 32:15 how **m.** less shall your God......... 637,3588
2Ch 32:27 Hezekiah had exceeding **m.** riches...... 7235
2Ch 32:29 had given him substance very **m.**. 7227
2Ch 33:6 wrought **m.** evil in the sight of the 7235
2Ch 36:14 transgressed very **m.** after all the 7227
Ezr 7:22 and salt without prescribing how **m.**,........
Ezr 10:13 it is a time of **m.** rain, and we are...........
Ne 4:10 decayed, and there is **m.** rubbish; 7235
Ne 6:16 **m.** cast down in their own eyes: 3966
Ne 9:37 it yieldeth **m.** increase unto the 7235
Es 1:18 shall there arise too **m.** contempt 1767
Job 4:19 How **m.** less in them that dwell in 637
Job 9:14 How **m.** less shall I answer him, .. 637,3588
Job 15:10 men, **m.** elder than thy father. 3524
Job 15:16 How **m.** more abominable and filthy..........
Job 25:6 How **m.** less man, that is a worm? 637
Job 31:25 because mine hand had gotten **m.**;....... 3524
Job 34:19 How **m.** less to him that accepteth not......
Job 42:10 gave Job twice as **m.** as he…before. 634
Ps 19:10 than gold, yea, than **m.** fine gold:....... 7227
Ps 33:16 is not delivered by **m.** strength.......... 7230
Ps 35:18 will praise thee among **m.** people. 6079
Ps 119:14 thy testimonies, as **m.** as in all riches. ......
Ps 119:107 I am afflicted very **m.**: quicken 3966
Pr 7:21 With…**m.** fair speech she caused........ 7230
Pr 11:31 **m.** more the wicked and the sinner...... 637
Pr 13:23 **M.** food is in the tillage of the 7230
Pr 14:4 **m.** increase is by the strength of 7230
Pr 15:6 of the righteous is **m.** treasure: 7227
Pr 15:11 how **m.** more then the hearts of the..... 637
Pr 16:16 How **m.** better is it to get wisdom than.....
Pr 17:7 fool: **m.** less do lying lips a prince........ 637
Pr 19:7 how **m.** more do his friends go far 637
Pr 19:10 **m.** less for a servant to have rule 637
Pr 19:24 not so **m.** as bring it to his mouth...... 1571
Pr 21:27 how **m.** more, when he bringeth it....... 637
Pr 25:16 eat so **m.** as is sufficient for thee, ... 1767
Pr 25:27 It is not good to eat **m.** honey:........... 7235
Ec 1:18 in **m.** wisdom is **m.** grief: and he 7230
Ec 5:12 sweet, whether he eat little or **m.**:..... 7235
Ec 5:17 he hath **m.** sorrow and wrath with...... 7235
Ec 5:20 he shall not **m.** remember the days 7235
Ec 7:16 Be not righteous over **m.**; neither 7235
Ec 7:17 Be not over **m.** wicked, neither be..... 7235
Ec 9:18 but one sinner destroyeth **m.** good. 7235
Ec 10:18 By **m.** slothfulness the building ....
Ec 12:12 and **m.** study is a weariness of the 7235
Ca 4:10 how **m.** better is thy love than wine! ....
Isa 21:7 hearkened diligently with **m.** heed: 7227
Isa 30:33 pile thereof is fire and **m.** wood; 7235
Isa 56:12 this day, and **m.** more abundant. 3966
Jer 2:22 with nitre, and take thee **m.** sope, ... 7235
Jer 2:36 Why gaddest thou about so **m.** to 3966
Jer 40:12 wine and summer fruits very **m.**. 7335
Eze 14:21 How **m.** more when I send my four 637
Eze 15:5 how **m.** less shall it be meet........ 637,3588
Eze 17:15 give him horses and **m.** people. 7227
Eze 22:5 which art infamous and **m.** vexed. 7227
Eze 23:32 had in derision; it containeth **m.**. 4767
Eze 26:7 and companies, and **m.** people. 7227

Eze 33:31 their mouth they shew **m.** love,...............
Da 4:12, 21 fair, and the fruit thereof **m.**,......... 7690
Da 7:5 thus unto it, Arise, devour **m.** flesh.... 7690
Da 7:28 my cogitations **m.** troubled me, and.... 7690
Da 11:13 with a great army and with **m.** riches........
Joe 2:6 the people shall be **m.** pained:...................
Jon 4:11 their left hand; and also **m.** cattle?...... 7227
Na 2:10 and **m.** pain is in all loins,..................... 2479
Hag 1:6 Ye have sown **m.**, and bring in........... 7235
Hag 1:9 Ye looked for **m.**, and lo, it came to... 7235
Mal 3:13 have we spoken so **m.** against thee?.........
Mt 6:7 **be heard for their m. speaking**...... *4180*
Mt 6:26 **Are ye not m. better than they?**..... *3123*
Mt 6:30 **shall he not m. more clothe you, O** *4183*
Mt 7:11 **how m. more shall your Father**..... *4214*
Mt 10:25 **how m. more shall they call them** ..*4214*
Mt 12:12 **How m. then is a man better than**..*4214*
Mt 13:5 **where they had not m. earth: and** . *4183*
Mt 15:33 so **m.** bread in the wilderness, as......... *5118*
Mt 26:9 might have been sold for **m.**, and....... *4183*
Mk 1:45 out, and began to publish it **m.**,......... *4183*
Mk 2:2 no, not so **m.** as about the door: *3366*
Mk 3:20 they could not so **m.** as eat bread...... *3383*
Mk 4:5 **ground, where it had not m. earth;** *4183*
Mk 5:10 he besought him **m.** that he would....... *4183*
Mk 5:21 side, **m.** people gathered unto him:...... *4183*
Mk 5:24 and **m.** people followed him, and........ *4183*
Mk 6:31 they had no leisure so **m.** as to eat. ....
Mk 6:34 when he came out, saw **m.** people, ... *4183*
Mk 7:36 so **m.** the more a great deal they......... *3123*
Mk 10:14 Jesus saw it, he was **m.** displeased,...... *23*
Mk 10:41 they began to be **m.** displeased with...... *23*
Mk 12:41 and many that were rich cast in **m.**. ... *4183*
Lu 5:15 so **m.** the more went there a fame..... *3123*
Lu 6:3 **Have ye not read so m. as this,**..... *3761*
Lu 6:34 **to sinners, to receive as m. again**...*2470*
Lu 7:11 went with him, and **m.** people. *4183*
Lu 7:12 **m.** people of the city was with her. *2425*
Lu 7:26 **you, and m. more than a prophet**...*4055*
Lu 7:47 **are forgiven; for she loved m.:** *4183*
Lu 8:4 **m.** people were gathered together,..... *4183*
Lu 9:37 from the hill, **m.** people met him......... *4183*
Lu 10:40 was cumbered about **m.** serving,........ *4183*
Lu 11:13 **how m. more shall your heavenly**.. *4214*
Lu 12:19 **m. goods laid up for many years;** .. *4183*
Lu 12:24 **how m. more are ye better than**.... *4214*
Lu 12:28 **m. more will he clothe you, O ye** .. *4214*
Lu 12:48 **unto whomsoever m. is given, of**... *4183*
Lu 12:48 **given, of him shall be m. required:**.*4183*
Lu 12:48 **to whom men have committed m.,**..*4183*
Lu 16:5 **How m. owest thou unto my lord?**. *4214*
Lu 16:7 **another, And how m. owest thou?** . *4214*
Lu 16:10 **is least is faithful also in m.:**........ *4183*
Lu 16:10 **in the least is unjust also in m.**..... *4183*
Lu 18:13 **not lift up so m. as his eyes unto**.. *3761*
Lu 18:39 but he cried so **m.** the more, Thou *4183*
Lu 19:15 **how m. every man had gained by** ....
Lu 24:4 were **m.** perplexed thereabout,.......... *1280*
Joh 3:23 because there was **m.** water there: *4183*
Joh 6:10 there was **m.** grass in the place......... *4183*
Joh 6:11 of the fishes as **m.** as they would........ *3745*
Joh 7:12 **m.** murmuring among the people........ *4183*
Joh 12:9 **M.** people of the Jews therefore *4183*
Joh 12:12 **m.** people that were come to the....... *4183*
Joh 12:24 **if it die, it bringeth forth m. fruit**..*4183*
Joh 14:30 **I will not talk m. with you: for**.... *4183*
Joh 15:5 **the same bringeth forth m. fruit:** .. *4183*
Joh 15:8 **glorified, that ye bear m. fruit;**..... *4183*
Ac 5:8 whether ye sold the land for so **m.**? ... *5118*
Ac 5:8 And she said, Yea, for so **m.**............. *5118*
Ac 5:37 drew away **m.** people after him:.......... *2425*
Ac 7:5 it, no, not s **m.** as to set his foot on:.........
Ac 9:13 how **m.** evil he hath done to thy........ *3745*
Ac 10:2 which gave **m.** alms to the people, ... *4183*
Ac 11:24 and **m.** people was added unto the *2425*
Ac 11:26 the church, and taught **m.** people. *2425*
Ac 14:22 through **m.** tribulation enter into *4183*
Ac 15:7 when there had been **m.** disputing,..... *4183*
Ac 16:16 brought her masters **m.** gain by......... *4183*
Ac 18:10 **for I have m. people in this city**..... *4183*
Ac 18:27 helped them **m.** which had believed *4183*
Ac 19:2 have not so **m.** as heard whether....... *3761*
Ac 19:26 and turned away **m.** people, saying..... *2425*
Ac 20:2 had given them **m.** exhortation, he *4183*
Ac 26:24 **m.** learning doth make thee mad. *4183*
Ac 27:9 Now when **m.** time was spent, and..... *2425*
Ac 27:10 will be with hurt and **m.** damage,....... *4183*
Ac 27:16 had **m.** work to come by the boat; *3433*
Ro 1:15 So, as **m.** as in me is, I am ready...... *3588*
Ro 3:2 **M.** every way: chiefly, because.......... *4183*
Ro 5:9 **M.** more then, being now justified...... *4183*
Ro 5:10 **m.** more, being reconciled, we shall.... *4183*
Ro 5:15 **m.** more the grace of God, and the *4183*
Ro 5:17 **m.** more they which receive...grace.... *4183*
Ro 5:20 grace did **m.** more abound: *5248*
Ro 9:22 endured with **m.** longsuffering the *4183*
Ro 11:12 how **m.** more their fulness?............... *4124*
Ro 11:24 how **m.** more shall these, which be *4124*
Ro 12:18 as **m.** as lieth in you, live peaceably.... *3588*
Ro 15:22 I have been **m.** hindered from *5248*
Ro 16:6 who bestowed **m.** labour on us. *4183*
Ro 16:12 which laboured **m.** in the Lord........... *4183*
1Co 2:3 and in fear, and in **m.** trembling. *4183*
1Co 5:1 fornication as is not so **m.** as............ *3761*
1Co 6:3 **m.** more things that pertain to this..... *3386*
1Co 12:22 **m.** more those members of the *4183*
1Co 16:19 Priscilla salute you **m.** in the Lord,..... *4183*
2Co 2:4 out of **m.** affliction and anguish of....... *4183*
2Co 3:9 **m.** more doth the ministration of........ *4183*
2Co 3:11 **m.** more that which remaineth is........ *4183*
2Co 6:4 in **m.** patience, in afflictions, in *4183*
2Co 8:4 Praying us with **m.** intreaty that......... *4183*
2Co 8:15 had gathered **m.** had nothing over; *4183*
2Co 8:22 things, but now **m.** more diligent,....... *4183*
Php 1:14 **m.** more bold to speak the word........ *4056*
Php 2:12 but now **m.** more in my absence, ... *4183*
1Th 1:5 Holy Ghost, and in **m.** assurance;....... *4183*
1Th 1:6 received the word in **m.** affliction, ... *4183*
1Th 2:2 gospel of God with **m.** contention. *4183*
1Ti 3:8 not given to **m.** wine, not greedy of ... *4183*
2Ti 4:14 the coppersmith did me **m.** evil:.......... *4183*
Tit 2:3 false accusers, not given to **m.** wine, .. *4183*
Phm 8 though I might be **m.** bold in Christ.... *4183*
Phm 16 how **m.** more unto thee, both in the ... *4214*
Heb 1:4 made so **m.** better than the angels, ... *5118*
Heb 7:22 By so **m.** was Jesus made a surety..... *5118*
Heb 8:6 by how **m.** also he is the mediator *3745*
Heb 9:14 How **m.** more shall the blood of......... *4214*
Heb 10:25 so **m.** the more, as ye see the day..... *5118*
Heb 10:29 how **m.** sorer punishment, suppose..... *4214*
Heb 12:9 we not **m.** rather be in subjection....... *4183*
Heb 12:20 if so **m.** as a beast touch the............. *2579*
Heb 12:25 **m.** more shall not we escape, if we.... *4183*
Jas 5:16 of a righteous man availeth **m.**........... *4183*
1Pe 1:7 being **m.** more precious than of gold... *4183*
2Pe 2:18 the flesh, through **m.** wantonness,............
Re 5:4 I wept **m.**, because no man was *4183*
Re 8:3 was given unto him **m.** incense,......... *4183*
Re 18:7 How **m.** she hath glorified herself,...... *3745*
Re 18:7 so **m.** torment and sorrow give her: ... *5118*
Re 19:1 I heard a great voice of **m.** people...... *4183*

MUFFLERS
Isa 3:19 and the bracelets, and the **m.**,............ 7479

MULBERRY
2Sa 5:23 them over against the **m.** trees.......... 1057
2Sa 5:24 a going in the tops of the **m.** trees, ... 1057
1Ch 14:14 them over against the **m.** trees.......... 1057
1Ch 14:15 of going in the tops of the **m.** trees, ... 1057

MULBERRY-TREES See MULBERRY and TREES.

MULE See also MULES.
2Sa 13:29 every man gat him up upon his **m.**, ... 6505
2Sa 18:9 And Absalom rode upon a **m.**, and...... 6505
2Sa 18:9 the **m.** went under the thick boughs ... 6505
2Sa 18:9 **m.** that was under him went away...... 6505
1Ki 1:33 my son to ride upon mine own **m.**,...... 6506
1Ki 1:38 to ride upon king David's **m.**, ... 6506
1Ki 1:44 him to ride upon the king's **m.**:.......... 6506
Ps 32:9 ye not as the horse, or as the **m.**, ... 6505
Zec 14:15 the plague of the horse, of the **m.**,...... 6505

MULES See also MULES'.
Ge 36:24 found the **m.** in the wilderness, ... 3222
1Ki 10:25 armour, and spices, horses, and **m.**, ... 6505
1Ki 18:5 to save the horses and the **m.** alive, ... 6505
1Ch 12:40 on asses, and on camels, and on **m.**, .. 6505
2Ch 9:24 harness, and spices, horses, and **m.**, .. 6505
Ezr 2:66 their **m.**, two hundred forty and......... 6505
Ne 7:68 their **m.**, two hundred forty and......... 6505
Es 8:10 on horseback, and riders on **m.**, ... 7409
Es 8:14 posts that rode upon **m.** and camels.... 7409
Isa 66:20 and in litters, and upon **m.**, and......... 6505
Eze 27:14 with horses and horsemen and **m.**. 6505

MULES'
2Ki 5:17 servant two **m.** burden of earth?........ 6505

MULTIPLIED See also MULTIPLIEDST.
Ge 47:27 and grew, and **m.** exceedingly. 7235
Ex 1:7 **m.**, and waxed exceedingly mighty; 7235
Ex 1:12 them, the more they **m.** and grew...... 7235
Ex 1:20 people **m.**, and waxed very mighty. 7235
Ex 11:9 my wonders may be **m.** in the land..... 7235
De 1:10 The Lord your God hath **m.** you,........ 7235
De 8:13 and thy silver and thy gold is **m.**,....... 7235
De 8:13 and all that thou hast is **m.**; 7235
De 11:21 That your days may be **m.**, and the.... 7235
Jos 24:3 **m.** his seed, and gave him Isaac. 7235
1Ch 5:9 their cattle were **m.** in the land of...... 7235
Job 27:14 If his children be **m.**, it is for the....... 7235
Job 35:6 or if thy transgressions be **m.**, ... 7231
Ps 16:4 Their sorrows shall be **m.** that 7235
Ps 38:19 that hate me wrongfully are **m.**.......... 7231
Ps 107:38 also, so that they are **m.** greatly;....... 7235
Pr 9:11 For by me thy days shall be **m.**,........ 7235
Pr 29:16 When the wicked are **m.**, ... 7235
Isa 9:3 Thou hast **m.** the nation, and not....... 7235
Isa 59:12 our transgressions are **m.** before........ 7231
Jer 3:16 when ye be **m.** and increased in......... 7235
Eze 5:7 ye **m.** more than the nations that....... 1995
Eze 11:6 Ye have **m.** your slain in this city,...... 7235
Eze 16:25 passed by, and **m.** thy whoredoms. 7235
Eze 16:29 hast moreover **m.** thy fornication........ 7235
Eze 16:51 thou hast **m.** thine abominations......... 7235
Eze 21:15 may faint, and their ruins be **m.**:........ 7235
Eze 23:19 she **m.** her whoredoms, in calling........ 7235
Eze 31:5 boughs were **m.**, and his branches...... 7235
Eze 35:13 have **m.** your words against me: 6280
Da 4:1 the earth; Peace be **m.** unto you........ 7680
Da 6:25 the earth; Peace be **m.** unto you........ 7680
Ho 2:8 and oil, and **m.** her silver and gold, ... 7235
Ho 8:14 and Judah hath **m.** fenced cities:......... 7235
Ho 12:10 **m.** visions, and used similitudes, ... 7235
Na 3:16 **m.** thy merchants above the stars 7235
Ac 6:1 number of the disciples was **m.**,......... *4129*
Ac 6:7 of the disciples **m.** in Jerusalem *4129*
Ac 7:17 the people grew and **m.** in Egypt, ... *4129*
Ac 9:31 comfort of the Holy Ghost, were **m.**.. *4129*
Ac 12:24 But the word of God grew and **m.**. *4129*
1Pe 1:2 Grace unto you, and peace, be **m.**...... *4129*
2Pe 1:2 Grace and peace be **m.** unto you........ *4129*
Jude 2 unto you, and peace, and love, be **m.**. *4129*

MULTIPLIEDST
Ne 9:23 children also **m.** thou as stars........... 7235

MULTIPLIETH
Job 9:17 and **m.** my wounds without cause...... 7235
Job 34:37 us, and **m.** his words against God. 7235
Job 35:16 he **m.** words without knowledge......... 3527

MULTIPLY See also MULTIPLIED; MULTIPLIETH; MULTIPLYING.
Ge 1:22 Be fruitful, and **m.**, and fill the 7235
Ge 1:22 seas, and let fowl **m.** in the earth....... 7235
Ge 1:28 Be fruitful, and **m.**, and replenish....... 7235
Ge 3:16 I will greatly **m.** thy sorrow and thy ... 7235
Ge 6:1 men began to **m.** on the face of the..... 7231
Ge 8:17 be fruitful, and **m.** upon the earth....... 7235
Ge 9:1 Be fruitful, and **m.**, and replenish....... 7235
Ge 9:7 be ye fruitful, and **m.**; bring forth....... 7235
Ge 9:7 in the earth, and **m.** therein. 7235
Ge 16:10 I will **m.** thy seed exceedingly, that.... 7235
Ge 17:2 thee, and will **m.** thee exceedingly...... 7235
Ge 17:20 and will **m.** him exceedingly; 7235
Ge 22:17 I will **m.** thy seed as the stars of the.. 7235
Ge 26:4 make thy seed to **m.** as the stars of... 7235
Ge 26:24 and **m.** thy seed for my servant......... 7235
Ge 28:3 and make thee fruitful, and **m.** thee, ... 7235
Ge 35:11 be fruitful and **m.**; a nation and a 7235
Ge 48:4 will make thee fruitful, and **m.** thee, ... 7235
Ex 1:10 lest they **m.**, and it come to pass,...... 7235
Ex 7:3 **m.** my signs and my wonders in the 7235
Ex 23:29 beast of the field **m.** against thee. 7227
Ex 32:13 I will **m.** your seed as the stars of 7235
Le 26:9 and make you fruitful, and **m.** you, ... 7235
De 7:13 thee, and bless thee, and **m.** thee: 7235
De 8:1 that ye may live, and **m.**, and go in.... 7235
De 8:13 when thy herds and thy flocks **m.**, ... 7235
De 13:17 compassion upon thee, and **m.** thee, ... 7235

De 17:16 he shall not **m.** horses to himself, ... 7235
De 17:16 to the end that he should **m.** horses: .. 7235
De 17:17 Neither shall he **m.** wives to himself, .. 7235
De 17:17 **m.** to himself silver and gold. 7235
De 28:63 you to do you good, and to **m.** you; ... 7235
De 30:5 good, and **m.** thee above thy fathers... 7235
De 30:16 that thou mayest live and **m.**:.............. 7235
1Ch 4:27 neither did all their family **m.**, like...... 7235
Job 29:18 and I shall **m.** my days as the sand..... 7235
Jer 30:19 I will **m.** them, and they shall not....... 7235
Jer 33:22 so will I **m.** the seed of David my...... 7235
Eze 16:7 I have caused thee to **m.** as the bud... 7233
Eze 36:10 And I will **m.** men upon you, all......... 7235
Eze 36:11 I will **m.** upon you man and beast;...... 7235
Eze 36:30 And I will **m.** the fruit of the tree, ... 7235
Eze 37:26 and I will place them, and **m.** them,.... 7235
Am 4:4 at Gilgal **m.** transgression; and 7235
2Co 9:10 **m.** your seed sown, and increase *4129*
Heb 6:14 and multiplying I will **m.** thee. *4129*

MULTIPLYING

Ge 22:17 in **m.** I will multiply thy seed as......... 7235
Heb 6:14 thee, and **m.** I will multiply thee. *4129*

MULTITUDE See also MULTITUDES.

Ge 16:10 it shall not be numbered for **m.**. 7230
Ge 28:3 thou mayest be a **m.** of people; 6951
Ge 30:30 and it is now increased unto a **m.**;....... 7230
Ge 32:12 which cannot be numbered for **m.**. 7230
Ge 48:4 I will make of thee a **m.** of people;..... 6951
Ge 48:16 let them grow into a **m.** in the midst .. 7230
Ge 48:19 seed shall become a **m.** of nations. 4393
Ex 12:38 mixed **m.** went up also with them; 7227
Ex 23:2 shalt not follow a **m.** to do evil; 7227
Le 25:16 According to the **m.** of years thou...... 7230
Nu 11:4 the mixt **m.** that was among them 628
Nu 32:1 Gad had a very great **m.** of cattle: 7227
De 1:10 day as the stars of heaven for **m.**......... 7230
De 10:22 thee as the stars of heaven for **m.**. 7230
De 28:62 were as the stars of heaven for **m.**:.... 7230
Jos 11:4 that is upon the sea shore in **m.**, ... 7230
Jg 4:7 army, which his chariots and his **m.**; ... 1995
Jg 6:5 they came as grasshoppers for **m.**;..... 7230
Jg 7:12 valley like grasshoppers for **m.**; 7230
Jg 7:12 as the sand by the sea side for **m.**. 7230
1Sa 13:5 sand which is on the sea shore in **m.**: . 7230
1Sa 14:16 and, behold, the **m.** melted away, ... 1995
2Sa 6:19 even among the whole **m.** of Israel,.... 1995
2Sa 17:11 the sand that is by the sea for **m.**; 7230
1Ki 3:8 be numbered nor counted for **m.**......... 7230
1Ki 4:20 the sand which is by the sea in **m.**, ... 7230
1Ki 8:5 not be told nor numbered for **m.**......... 7230
1Ki 20:13 Hast thou seen all this great **m.**? 1995
1Ki 20:28 deliver all this great **m.** into thine............
2Ki 7:13 they are as all the **m.** of Israel that 1995
2Ki 7:13 even as all the **m.** of the Israelites 1995
2Ki 19:23 With the **m.** of my chariots I am......... 7393
2Ki 25:11 with the remnant of the **m.**, did......... 1995
2Ch 1:9 like the dust of the earth in **m.**.......... 7227
2Ch 5:6 not be told nor numbered for **m.**........ 7230
2Ch 13:8 and ye be a great **m.**, and there are.... 1995
2Ch 14:11 in thy name we go against this **m.**...... 1995
2Ch 20:2 cometh a great **m.** against thee.......... 1995
2Ch 20:15 dismayed by reason of this great **m.**; .. 1995
2Ch 20:24 wilderness, they looked unto the **m.**, .. 1995
2Ch 28:5 and carried away a great **m.** of them.........
2Ch 30:18 For a **m.** of the people, even many 4768
2Ch 32:7 nor for all the **m.** that is with him: 1995
Ne 13:3 from Israel all the mixed **m.**.............. 6154
Es 5:11 riches, and the **m.** of his children, ... 7230
Es 10:3 accepted of the **m.** of his brethren,..... 7230
Job 11:2 not the **m.** of words be answered?..... 7230
Job 31:34 Did I fear a great **m.**, or did the........ 1995
Job 32:7 **m.** of years should teach wisdom. 7230
Job 33:19 **m.** of his bones with strong pain: 7379
Job 35:9 By reason of the **m.** of oppressions 7230
Job 39:7 He scorneth the **m.** of the city, ... 1995
Ps 5:7 thy house in the **m.** of thy mercy:...... 7230
Ps 5:10 in the **m.** of their transgressions; 7230
Ps 33:16 no king saved by the **m.** of an host; ... 7230
Ps 42:4 for I had gone with the **m.**, I went...... 5519
Ps 42:4 praise, with a **m.** that kept holyday..... 1995
Ps 49:6 in the **m.** of their riches;.................. 7230
Ps 51:1 unto the **m.** of thy tender mercies...... 7230
Ps 68:30 of spearmen, the **m.** of the bulls, ... 5712
Ps 69:13 in the **m.** of thy mercy hear me,........ 7230
Ps 69:16 to the **m.** of thy tender mercies:......... 7230
Ps 74:19 unto the **m.** of the wicked: forget....... 2416
Ps 94:19 In the **m.** of my thoughts within......... 7230
Ps 97:1 let the **m.** of isles be glad thereof. 7227
Ps 106:7 not the **m.** of thy mercies; but 7230
Ps 106:45 according to the **m.** of his mercies...... 7230
Ps 109:30 I will praise him among the **m.**. 7227
Pr 10:19 In the **m.** of words there wanteth 7230
Pr 11:14 in the **m.** of counsellors there is 7230
Pr 14:28 In the **m.** of people is the king's 7230
Pr 15:22 in the **m.** of counsellors they are........ 7230
Pr 20:15 There is gold, and a **m.** of rubies:...... 7230
Pr 24:6 in **m.** of counsellors there is safety..... 7230
Ec 5:3 cometh through the **m.** of business;.... 7230
Ec 5:3 a fool's voice is known by **m.** of......... 7230
Ec 5:7 For in the **m.** of dreams and many 7230
Isa 1:11 the **m.** of your sacrifices unto me? 7230
Isa 5:13 and their **m.** dried up with thirst. 1995
Isa 5:14 their glory, and their **m.**, and their..... 1995
Isa 13:4 The noise of a **m.** in the mountains, ... 1995
Isa 16:14 contemned, with all that great **m.**;...... 1995
Isa 17:12 Woe to the **m.** of many people, ... 1995
Isa 29:5 Moreover the **m.** of thy strangers...... 1995
Isa 29:5 the **m.** of the terrible ones shall be..... 1995
Isa 29:7 the **m.** of all the nations that fight 1995
Isa 29:8 So shall the **m.** of all the nations be,... 1995
Isa 31:4 a **m.** of shepherds is called forth........ 4393
Isa 32:14 the **m.** of the city shall be left; the..... 1995
Isa 37:24 By the **m.** of my chariots am I 7230
Isa 47:9 and for the **m.** of thy sorceries, ... 7230
Isa 47:12 and with the **m.** of thy sorceries, ... 7230
Isa 47:13 wearied in the **m.** of thy counsels....... 7230
Isa 60:6 The **m.** of camels shall cover thee,...... 8229
Isa 63:7 and according to the **m.** of his........... 7230
Jer 3:23 and from the **m.** of mountains:........... 1995
Jer 10:13 is a **m.** of waters in the heavens, ... 1995
Jer 12:6 they have called a **m.** after thee:........ 4392
Jer 30:14 one, for the **m.** of thine iniquity; 7230
Jer 30:15 for the **m.** of thine iniquity:............... 7230
Jer 44:15 a great **m.**, even all the people 6951
Jer 46:25 I will punish the **m.** of No, and........... 582
Jer 49:32 and the **m.** of their cattle a spoil:......... 527
Jer 51:16 is a **m.** of waters in the heavens; 527
Jer 51:42 covered with the **m.** of the waves......... 527
Jer 52:15 of Babylon, and the rest of the **m.**........ 527
La 1:5 for the **m.** of her transgressions:........ 7230
La 3:32 according to the **m.** of his mercies...... 7230
Eze 7:11 shall remain, nor of their **m.**, nor....... 1995
Eze 7:12 wrath is upon all the **m.** thereof......... 1995
Eze 7:13 is touching the whole **m.** thereof, ... 1995
Eze 7:14 wrath is upon all the **m.** thereof......... 1995
Eze 14:4 according to the **m.** of his idols;......... 7230
Eze 19:11 height with the **m.** of her branches..... 7230
Eze 23:42 a voice of a **m.** being at ease was 1995
Eze 27:12 of the **m.** of all kind of riches; 7230
Eze 27:16 by reason of the **m.** of the wares....... 7230
Eze 27:18 thy merchant in the **m.** of the wares... 7230
Eze 27:18 making, for the **m.** of all riches;......... 7230
Eze 27:33 the earth with the **m.** of thy riches 7230
Eze 28:16 By the **m.** of thy merchandise they..... 7230
Eze 28:18 by the **m.** of thine iniquities, by......... 7230
Eze 29:19 he shall take her **m.**, and take her...... 1995
Eze 30:4 and they shall take away her **m.**, ... 1995
Eze 30:10 make the **m.** of Egypt to cease by 1995
Eze 30:15 and I will cut off the **m.** of No........... 1995
Eze 31:2 king of Egypt, and to his **m.**; Whom... 1995
Eze 31:5 long because of the **m.** of waters, ... 7227
Eze 31:9 him fair by the **m.** of his branches:..... 7230
Eze 31:18 This is Pharaoh and all his **m.**, ... 1995
Eze 32:12 mighty will I cause thy **m.** to fall,....... 1995
Eze 32:12 all the **m.** thereof shall be destroyed... 1995
Eze 32:16 even for Egypt, and for all her **m.**,...... 1995
Eze 32:18 of man, wail for the **m.** of Egypt,....... 1995
Eze 32:24 There is Elam and all her **m.** round.... 1995
Eze 32:25 midst of the slain with all her **m.**........ 1995
Eze 32:26 is Meshech, Tubal, and all her **m.** 1995
Eze 32:31 shall be comforted over all his **m.**,...... 1995
Eze 32:32 even Pharaoh and all his **m.**, saith 1995
Eze 39:11 shall they bury Gog and all his **m.**: 1995
Eze 47:9 there shall be a very great **m.** of fish,.......
Da 10:6 of his words like the voice of a **m.**. 1995
Da 11:10 shall assemble a **m.** of great forces:.... 1995
Da 11:11 and he shall set forth a great **m.**;....... 1995
Da 11:11 the **m.** shall be given into his hand. 1995
Da 11:12 when he hath taken away the **m.**, ... 1995
Da 11:13 shall set forth a **m.** greater than 1995
Hos 9:7 mad, for the **m.** of thine iniquity, ... 7230
Hos 10:1 according to the **m.** of his fruit he...... 7230
Hos 10:13 way, in the **m.** of thy mighty men. 7230
Mic 2:12 noise by reason of the **m.** of men............
Na 3:3 and there is a **m.** of slain, and a......... 7230
Na 3:4 Because of the **m.** of the whoredoms.. 7230
Zec 2:4 the **m.** of man and cattle therein: 7230
Mt 13:2 the whole **m.** stood on the shore. *3793*
Mt 13:34 things spake Jesus unto the **m.** in....... *3793*
Mt 13:36 Then Jesus sent the **m.** away, and *3793*
Mt 14:5 put him to death, he feared the **m.**,.... *3793*
Mt 14:14 went forth, and saw a great **m.**, ... *3793*
Mt 14:15 send the **m.** away, that they may....... *3793*
Mt 14:19 he commanded the **m.** to sit down...... *3793*
Mt 14:19 disciples, and...disciples to the **m.**...... *3793*
Mt 15:10 And he called the **m.**, and said unto.... *3793*
Mt 15:31 Insomuch that the **m.** wondered,........ *3793*
Mt 15:32 **I have compassion on the m.**,......... *3793*
Mt 15:33 wilderness, as to fill so great a **m.**?.... *3793*
Mt 15:35 he commanded the **m.** to sit down........ *3793*
Mt 15:36 disciples, and...disciples to the **m.**...... *3793*
Mt 15:39 And he sent away the **m.**, and took.... *3793*
Mt 17:14 And when they were come to the **m.**,.. *3793*
Mt 20:29 Jericho, a great **m.** followed him. *3793*
Mt 20:31 And the **m.** rebuked them, because *3793*
Mt 21:8 And a very great **m.** spread their....... *3793*
Mt 21:11 And the **m.** said, This is Jesus the *3793*
Mt 21:46 hands on him, they feared the **m.**........ *3793*
Mt 22:33 And when the **m.** heard this, they...... *3793*
Mt 23:1 Then spake Jesus to the **m.**, and to.... *3793*
Mt 26:47 with him a great **m.** with swords........ *3793*
Mt 27:20 **m.** that they should ask Barabbas,...... *3793*
Mt 27:24 washed his hands before the **m.**,........ *3793*
Mk 2:13 and all the **m.** resorted unto him,....... *3793*
Mk 3:7 a great **m.** from Galilee followed........ *4128*
Mk 3:8 a great **m.**, when they had heard....... *4128*
Mk 3:9 wait on him because of the **m.**,........... *3793*
Mk 3:20 And the **m.** cometh together again,...... *3793*
Mk 3:32 And the **m.** sat about him, and they.... *3793*
Mk 4:1 was gathered unto him a great **m.**,..... *3793*
Mk 4:1 and the whole **m.** was by the sea on... *3793*
Mk 4:36 when they had sent away the **m.**, ... *3793*
Mk 5:31 Thou seest the **m.** thronging thee, ... *3793*
Mk 7:33 And he took him aside from the **m.**, ... *3793*
Mk 8:1 those days the **m.** being very great, ... *3793*
Mk 8:2 **I have compassion on the m.**,......... *3793*
Mk 9:14 he saw a great **m.** about them, and *3793*
Mk 9:17 one of the **m.** answered and said,........ *3793*
Mk 14:43 with him a great **m.** with swords........ *3793*
Mk 15:8 the **m.** crying aloud began to desire.... *3793*
Lu 1:10 **m.** of the people were praying........... *4128*
Lu 2:13 a **m.** of the heavenly host praising...... *4128*
Lu 3:7 **m.** that came forth to be baptized *3793*
Lu 5:6 they inclosed a great **m.** of fishes:...... *4128*
Lu 5:19 bring him in because of the **m.**, ... *3793*
Lu 6:17 and a great **m.** of people out of all..... *4128*
Lu 6:19 the whole **m.** sought to touch him;: *3793*
Lu 8:37 Then the whole **m.** of the country...... *4128*
Lu 8:45 the **m.** throng thee and press thee, ... *3793*
Lu 9:12 Send the **m.** away, that they may....... *3793*
Lu 9:16 the disciples to set before the **m.**........ *3793*
Lu 12:1 an innumerable **m.** of people, ... *3461*
Lu 18:36 hearing the **m.** pass by, he asked....... *3793*
Lu 19:37 whole **m.** of the disciples began to...... *4128*
Lu 19:39 the Pharisees from among the **m.**....... *3793*
Lu 22:6 unto them in the absence of the **m.**..... *3793*
Lu 22:47 while he yet spake, behold a **m.**, ... *3793*
Lu 23:1 And the whole **m.** of them arose,....... *4128*
Joh 5:3 lay a great **m.** of impotent folk, ... *4128*
Joh 5:13 away, a **m.** being in that place........... *3793*
Joh 6:2 a great **m.** followed him, because *3793*
Joh 21:6 able to draw it for the **m.** of fishes..... *4128*
Ac 2:6 abroad, the **m.** came together, and..... *4128*
Ac 4:32 the **m.** of them that believed were *4128*
Ac 5:16 came also a **m.** out of the cities......... *4128*
Ac 6:2 called the **m.** of the disciples unto *4128*
Ac 6:5 the saying pleased the whole **m.**: *4128*
Ac 14:1 that a great **m.** both of the Jews........ *4128*
Ac 14:4 But the **m.** of the city was divided: *4128*
Ac 15:12 Then all the **m.** kept silence, and....... *4128*
Ac 15:30 they had gathered the **m.** together, ... *4128*
Ac 16:22 **m.** rose up together against them:...... *3793*
Ac 17:4 of the devout Greeks a great **m.**,........ *4128*
Ac 19:9 spake evil of that way before the **m.**,.. *4128*
Ac 19:33 they drew Alexander out of the **m.**,..... *3793*
Ac 21:22 the **m.** must needs come together:..... *4128*
Ac 21:34 thing, some another, among...**m.**:........ *3793*
Ac 21:36 the **m.** of the people followed after,.... *4128*
Ac 23:7 Sadducees: and the **m.** was divided..... *4128*
Ac 24:18 neither with **m.**, nor with tumult. *3793*

Ac 25:24 about whom all the **m.** of the Jews..... *4128*
Heb 11:12 many as the stars of the sky in **m.**,..... *4128*
Jas 5:20 death, and shall hide a **m.** of sins....... *4128*
1Pe 4:8 for charity shall cover the **m.** of sins... *4128*
Re 7:9 a great **m.**, which no man could......... *3793*
Re 19:6 as it were the voice of a great **m.**,..... *3793*

MULTITUDES
Eze 32:20 the sword: draw her and all her **m.**.... 1995
Joe 3:14 **M.**, **m.** in the valley of decision:........ 1995
Mt 4:25 followed him great **m.** of people........ *3793*
Mt 5:1 And seeing the **m.**, he went up into..... *3793*
Mt 8:1 mountain, great **m.** followed him........ *3793*
Mt 8:18 Jesus saw great **m.** about him,........... *3793*
Mt 9:8 But when the **m.** saw it, they............ *3793*
Mt 9:33 and the **m.** marvelled, saying, It........ *3793*
Mt 9:36 But when he saw the **m.**, he was........ *3793*
Mt 11:7 Jesus began to say unto the **m.**......... *3793*
Mt 12:15 and great **m.** followed him, and he...... *3793*
Mt 13:2 great **m.** were gathered together........ *3793*
Mt 14:22 side, while he sent the **m.** away:........ *3793*
Mt 14:23 when he had sent the **m.** away, he...... *3793*
Mt 15:30 great **m.** came unto him, having......... *3793*
Mt 19:2 And great **m.** followed him; and he...... *3793*
Mt 21:9 And the **m.** that went before, and...... *3793*
Mt 26:55 same hour said Jesus to the **m.**,........ *3793*
Lu 5:15 great **m.** came together to hear,........ *3793*
Lu 14:25 there went great **m.** with him: and...... *3793*
Ac 5:14 Lord, **m.** both of men and women.)...... *4128*
Ac 13:45 when the Jews saw the **m.**, they......... *3793*
Re 17:15 are peoples, and **m.**, and nations,........ *3793*

MUNITION See also MUNITIONS.
Isa 29:7 that fight against her and her **m.**,....... 4685
Na 2:1 keep the **m.**, watch the way, make..... 4694

MUNITIONS
Isa 33:16 defence shall be the **m.** of rocks:....... 4679

MUPPIN (mup'-pim) See also SHUPPIM.
Ge 46:21 and Rosh, **M.**, and Huppim, and........ 4649

MURDER See also MURDERS.
Ps 10:8 places doth he **m.** the innocent:......... 2026
Ps 94:6 stranger, and **m.** the fatherless.......... 7523
Jer 7:9 Will ye steal, **m.**, and commit........... 7523
Ho 6:9 company of priests **m.** in the way....... 7523
Mt 19:18 Jesus said, **Thou shalt do no m.**,..... *5407*
Mk 15:7 committed **m.** in the insurrection........ *5408*
Lu 23:19 and for **m.**, was cast into prison.)....... *5408*
Lu 23:25 and **m.** was cast into prison, whom...... *5408*
Ro 1:29 full of envy, **m.**, debate, deceit,......... *5408*

MURDERER See also MURDERERS.
Nu 35:16 of iron, so that he die, he is a **m.**:...... 7523
Nu 35:16 the **m.** shall surely be put to death..... 7523
Nu 35:17 he may die, and he die, he is a **m.**:.... 7523
Nu 35:17 the **m.** shall surely be put to death..... 7523
Nu 35:18 he may die, and he die, he is a **m.**:.... 7523
Nu 35:18 the **m.** shall surely be put to death..... 7523
Nu 35:19 of blood himself shall slay the **m.**:...... 7523
Nu 35:21 for he is a **m.**: the revenger of blood.. 7523
Nu 35:21 shall slay the **m.**, when he meeteth.... 7523
Nu 35:30 the **m.** shall be put to death by the..... 7523
Nu 35:31 no satisfaction for the life of a **m.**,...... 7523
2Ki 6:32 this son of a **m.** hath sent to take...... 7523
Job 24:14 **m.** rising with the light killeth the....... 7523
Ho 9:13 bring forth his children to the **m.**........ 2026
Joh 8:44 **He was a m. from the beginning**,..... *443*
Ac 3:14 desired a **m.** to be granted unto.......... *5406*
Ac 28:4 No doubt this man is a **m.**, whom,....... *5406*
1Pe 4:15 let none of you suffer as a **m.**, or as... *5406*
1Jo 3:15 hateth his brother is a **m.**: and ye........ *443*
1Jo 3:15 know that no **m.** hath eternal life......... *443*

MURDERERS
2Ki 14:6 children of the **m.** he slew not:.......... 5221
Isa 1:21 lodged in it; but now **m.**................... 7523
Jer 4:31 my soul is wearied because of **m.**......... 2026
Mt 22:7 **armies, and destroyed those m.**,..... *5406*
Ac 7:52 been now the betrayers and **m.**:.......... *5406*
Ac 21:38 four thousand men that were **m.**?........ *4607*
1Ti 1:9 and profane, for **m.** of fathers........... *3964*
1Ti 1:9 and **m.** of mothers, for manslayers....... *3389*
Re 21:8 and the abominable, and **m.**, and........ *5406*
Re 22:15 and whoremongers, and **m.**, and......... *5406*

MURDERS
Mt 15:19 **heart proceed evil thoughts, m.**..... *5408*
Mk 7:21 **adulteries, fornications, m.**,.......... *5408*
Ga 5:21 Envyings, **m.**, drunkenness,.............. *5408*
Re 9:21 Neither repented they of their **m.**,..... *5408*

MURMUR See also MURMURED; MURMURING.
Ex 16:7 are we, that ye **m.** against us?.......... 3885
Ex 16:8 which ye **m.** against him: and........... 3885
Nu 14:27 congregation which **m.** against me?..... 3885
Nu 14:27 Israel, which they **m.** against me........ 3885
Nu 14:36 congregation to **m.** against him,.......... 3885
Nu 16:11 is Aaron, that ye **m.** against him?....... 3885
Nu 17:5 whereby they **m.** against you............. 3885
Joh 6:43 them, **M. not among yourselves**...... *1111*
1Co 10:10 Neither **m.** ye, as some of them also.. *1111*

MURMURED
Ex 15:24 And the people **m.** against Moses,....... 3885
Ex 16:2 children of Israel **m.** against Moses..... 3885
Ex 17:3 and the people **m.** against Moses,...... 3885
Nu 14:2 children of Israel **m.** against Moses..... 3885
Nu 14:29 upward, which have **m.** against me,..... 3885
Nu 16:41 children of Israel **m.** against Moses..... 3885
De 1:27 And ye **m.** in your tents, and said,..... 7279
Jos 9:18 And all...**m.** against the princes.......... 3885
Ps 106:25 But **m.** in their tents, and.................. 7279
Isa 29:24 they that **m.** shall learn doctrine......... 7279
Mt 20:11 **they m. against the goodman of**.... *1111*
Mk 14:5 poor. And they **m.** against her........... *1690*
Lu 5:30 Pharisees **m.** against his disciples,...... *1111*
Lu 15:2 And the Pharisees and scribes **m.**,...... *1234*
Lu 19:7 And when they saw it, they all **m.**...... *1234*
Joh 6:41 The Jews then **m.** at him, because...... *1111*
Joh 6:61 himself that his disciples **m.** at it,...... *1111*
Joh 7:32 that the people **m.** such things............ *1111*
1Co 10:10 as some of them also **m.**, and were..... *1111*

MURMURERS
Jude 16 These are **m.**, complainers,............... *1113*

MURMURING See also MURMURINGS.
Joh 7:12 was much **m.** among the people......... *1112*
Ac 6:1 there arose a **m.** of the Grecians....... *1112*

MURMURINGS
Ex 16:7 heareth your **m.** against the Lord:...... 8519
Ex 16:8 for that the Lord heareth your **m.**........ 8519
Ex 16:8 your **m.** are not against us, but......... 8519
Ex 16:9 Lord: for he hath heard your **m.**........ 8519
Ex 16:12 have heard the **m.** of the children of... 8519
Nu 14:27 have heard the **m.** of the children of... 8519
Nu 17:5 me the **m.** of the children of Israel,..... 8519
Nu 17:10 quite take away their **m.** from me,..... 8519
Php 2:14 Do all things without **m.** and............ *1112*

MURRAIN
Ex 9:3 there shall be a very grievous **m.**........ 1698

MUSE See also MUSED; MUSING.
Ps 143:5 I **m.** on the work of thy hands........... 7878

MUSED
Lu 3:15 all men **m.** in their hearts of John,...... *1260*

MUSHI (mu'-shi) See also MUSHITES.
Ex 6:19 sons of Merari; Mahali and **M.**:.......... 4187
Nu 3:20 by their families; Mahli, and **M.**.......... 4187
1Ch 6:19 The sons of Merari; Mahli, and **M.**...... 4187
1Ch 6:47 the son of **M.**, the son of Merari,....... 4187
1Ch 23:21 sons of Merari; Mahli, and **M.**........... 4187
1Ch 23:23 sons of **M.**; Mahli, and Eder, and........ 4187
1Ch 24:26 sons of Merari were Mahli and **M.**:...... 4187
1Ch 24:30 sons also of **M.**; Mahli, and Eder,...... 4187

MUSHITES (mu'-shites)
Nu 3:33 and the family of the **M.**: these.......... 4188
Nu 26:58 family of the **M.**, the family of the...... 4188

MUSIC See MUSICK.

MUSICAL
1Ch 16:42 and with **m.** instruments of God......... 7892
Ne 12:36 with the **m.** instruments of David....... 7892
Ec 2:8 as **m.** instruments, and that of all....... 7705

MUSICIAN See also MUSICIANS.
Ps 4:*title* To the chief **M.** on Neginoth,............ 5329
Ps 5:*title* To the chief **M.** upon Nehiloth,........... 5329
Ps 6:*title* To the chief **M.** on Neginoth............. 5329
Ps 8:*title* To the chief **M.** upon Gittith,............ 5329
Ps 9:*title* To the chief **M.** upon Muth-labben,...... 5329
Ps 11:*title* To the chief **M.**, A Psalm of.............. 5329
Ps 12:*title* To the chief **M.** upon Sheminith,......... 5329
Ps 13:*title* To the chief **M.**, A Psalm of.............. 5329
Ps 14:*title* To the chief **M.**, A Psalm of.............. 5329
Ps 18:*title* To the chief **M.**, A Psalm of.............. 5329
Ps 19:*title* To the chief **M.**, A Psalm of.............. 5329
Ps 20:*title* To the chief **M.**, A Psalm of.............. 5329
Ps 21:*title* To the chief **M.**, A Psalm of.............. 5329
Ps 22:*title* To the chief **M.** upon Aijeleth............ 5329
Ps 31:*title* To the chief **M.**, A Psalm of.............. 5329
Ps 36:*title* To the chief **M.**, A Psalm of.............. 5329
Ps 39:*title* To the chief **M.**, even to.................. 5329
Ps 40:*title* To the chief **M.**, A Psalm of.............. 5329
Ps 41:*title* To the chief **M.**, A Psalm of.............. 5329
Ps 42:*title* To the chief **M.**, Maschil, for............ 5329
Ps 44:*title* To the chief **M.** for the sons of.......... 5329
Ps 45:*title* To the chief **M.** upon Shoshannim,...... 5329
Ps 46:*title* To the chief **M.** for the sons of.......... 5329
Ps 47:*title* To the chief **M.**, A Psalm for.............. 5329
Ps 49:*title* To the chief **M.**, A Psalm for.............. 5329
Ps 51:*title* To the chief **M.**, A Psalm of.............. 5329
Ps 52:*title* To the chief **M.**, Maschil, A.............. 5329
Ps 53:*title* To the chief **M.** upon Mahalath,.......... 5329
Ps 54:*title* To the chief **M.** on Neginoth,............ 5329
Ps 55:*title* To the chief **M.** on Neginoth,............ 5329
Ps 56:*title* To the chief **M.** upon Jonath-............ 5329
Ps 57:*title* To the chief **M.**, Al-taschith,............ 5329
Ps 58:*title* To the chief **M.**, Al-taschith,............ 5329
Ps 59:*title* To the chief **M.**, Al-taschith,............ 5329
Ps 60:*title* To the chief **M.** upon Shushan-........... 5329
Ps 61:*title* To the chief **M.** upon Neginah,.......... 5329
Ps 62:*title* To the chief **M.**, to Jeduthun,............ 5329
Ps 64:*title* To the chief **M.**, A Psalm of.............. 5329
Ps 65:*title* To the chief **M.**, A Psalm and............ 5329
Ps 66:*title* To the chief **M.**, A Song or............... 5329
Ps 67:*title* To the chief **M.** on Neginoth............. 5329
Ps 68:*title* To the chief **M.**, a Psalm or.............. 5329
Ps 69:*title* To the chief **M.** upon Shoshannim,...... 5329
Ps 70:*title* To the chief **M.**, A Psalm of.............. 5329
Ps 75:*title* To the chief **M.**, Al-taschith,............ 5329
Ps 76:*title* To the chief **M.** on Neginoth,............ 5329
Ps 77:*title* To the chief **M.**, to Jeduthun,............ 5329
Ps 80:*title* To...chief **M.** upon Shoshannim-......... 5329
Ps 81:*title* To the chief **M.** upon Gittith,............ 5329
Ps 84:*title* To the chief **M.** upon Gittith,............ 5329
Ps 85:*title* To the chief **M.**, A Psalm for.............. 5329
Ps 88:*title* to the chief **M.** upon Mahalath............ 5329
Ps 109:*title* To the chief **M.**, A Psalm of.............. 5329
Ps 139:*title* To the chief **M.**, A Psalm of.............. 5329
Ps 140:*title* To the chief **M.**, A Psalm of.............. 5329

MUSICIANS
Re 18:22 of harpers, and **m.**, and of pipers,...... *3451*

MUSICK
1Sa 18:6 with joy, and with instruments of **m.**........
1Ch 15:16 singers with instruments of **m.**.......... 7892
2Ch 5:13 cymbals and instruments of **m.**,.......... 7892
2Ch 7:6 instruments of **m.** of the Lord,........... 7892
2Ch 23:13 the singers with instruments of **m.**,.... 7892
2Ch 34:12 could skill of instruments of **m.**,......... 7892
Ec 12:4 all the daughters of **m.** shall be.......... 7892
La 3:63 their rising up; I am their **m.**............. 4485
La 5:14 gate, the young men from their **m.**...... 5058
Da 3:5 dulcimer, and all kinds of **m.**, ye......... 2170
Da 3:7 psaltery, and all kinds of **m.**, all........... 2170
Da 3:10, 15 dulcimer, and all kinds of **m.**,......... 2170
Da 6:18 neither were instruments of **m.**...............
Am 6:5 to themselves instruments of **m.**,........ 7892
Lu 15:25 **house, he heard m. and dancing**.... *4858*

MUSING
Ps 39:3 while I was **m.** the fire burned:.......... 1901

MUST
Ge 17:13 **m.** needs be circumcised:......................
Ge 24:5 **m.** I needs bring my son again unto..........
Ge 29:26 Laban said, It **m.** not be so done in.........
Ge 30:16 Thou **m.** come in unto me; for surely........
Ge 43:11 If it **m.** be so now, do this; take of the.....
Ge 47:29 the time drew nigh that Israel **m.** die:.......
Ex 10:9 for we **m.** hold a feast unto the Lord.........
Ex 10:25 Thou **m.** give us also sacrifices and..........
Ex 10:26 thereof **m.** we take to serve the Lord.......
Ex 10:26 not with what we **m.** serve the Lord,........
Ex 12:16 save that which every man **m.** eat,...........
Ex 18:20 **m.** walk, and the work that they **m.** do.....
Le 11:32 it **m.** be put into water, and it shall be......
Le 23:6 days ye **m.** eat unleavened bread..............
Nu 6:21 so he **m.** do after the law of his................
Nu 18:22 Neither **m.** the children of Israel.............
Nu 20:10 **m.** we fetch you water out of this............
Nu 23:12 **M.** I not take heed to speak that.............

Nu 23:26 that the Lord speaketh, that I **m.** do?
De 1:22 again by what way we **m.** go up,
De 4:22 But I **m.** die in this land,
De 4:22 I **m.** not go over Jordan: but ye
De 12:18 **m.** eat them before the Lord thy God
De 31:7 thou **m.** go with this people unto the
De 31:14 thy days approach that thou **m.** die:
Jos 3:4 know the way by which ye **m.** go:
Jos 22:18 that ye **m.** turn away this day from
Jg 13:16 thou **m.** offer it unto the Lord.
Jg 21:17 There **m.** be an inheritance for them
Ru 4:5 thou **m.** buy it also of Ruth the
1Sa 14:43 was in mine hand, and, lo, I **m.** die.
2Sa 14:14 we **m.** needs die, and are as water
2Sa 23:3 that ruleth over men **m.** be just,
2Sa 23:7 touch them **m.** be fenced with iron
1Ki 18:27 he sleepeth, and **m.** be awaked.
1Ch 17:11 that thou **m.** go to be with thy fathers,
1Ch 22:5 Lord **m.** be exceedingly magnifical,
Ezr 10:12 As thou hast said, so **m.** we do 5921
Ps 32:9 mouth **m.** be held in with bit and
Pr 18:24 hath friends **m.** shew himself friendly:
Pr 19:19 deliver him, yet thou **m.** do it again.
Ec 10:10 edge, then **m.** he put to more strength:
Ca 8:12 O Solomon, **m.** have a thousand, and
Isa 28:10 For precept **m.** be upon precept,
Jer 10:5 they **m.** needs be borne, because thy
Jer 10:19 Truly this is a grief, and I **m.** bear it.
Eze 34:18 but ye **m.** tread down with your feet
Eze 34:18 ye **m.** foul the residue with your feet?
Mt 16:21 that he **m.** go unto Jerusalem, *1163*
Mt 17:10 scribes that Elias **m.** first come? *1163*
Mt 18:7 **it m. needs be that offences come;** *318*
Mt 24:6 **all these things m. come to pass,** *1163*
Mt 26:54 **be fulfilled, that thus it m. be?** *1163*
Mk 2:22 **new wine m. be put into new.**
Mk 8:31 Son of man **m.** suffer many things, *1163*
Mk 9:11 the scribes that Elias **m.** first come? *1163*
Mk 9:12 **man, that he m. suffer many,**
Mk 13:7 **for such things m. needs be; but** *1163*
Mk 13:10 **the gospel m. first be published** *1163*
Mk 14:49 **but the scriptures m. be fulfilled.** *2443*
Lu 2:49 **that I m. be about my Father's** *1163*
Lu 4:43 **I m. preach the kingdom of God** *1163*
Lu 5:38 **wine m. be put into new bottles;**
Lu 9:22 **Son of man m. suffer many things,** *1163*
Lu 13:33 **Nevertheless I m. walk to-day,** *1163*
Lu 14:18 **and I m. needs go and see it:** *2192*
Lu 17:25 **first m. he suffer many things,** *1163*
Lu 19:5 **for the day I m. abide at thy** *1163*
Lu 21:9 **these things m. first come to pass;** *1163*
Lu 22:7 when the passover **m.** be killed. *1163*
Lu 22:37 **m. yet be accomplished in me.** *1163*
Lu 23:17 (he **m.** release one unto them at
Lu 24:7 Son of man **m.** be delivered into *1163*
Lu 24:44 **all things m. be fulfilled, which** *1163*
Joh 3:7 **unto thee, Ye m. be born again.** *1163*
Joh 3:14 **so m. the Son of man be lifted up:** *1163*
Joh 3:30 He **m.** increase, but I...decrease. *1163*
Joh 3:30 He...increase, but I **m.** decrease.
Joh 4:4 he **m.** needs go through Samaria.
Joh 4:24 **m. worship him in spirit and in** *1163*
Joh 9:4 **I m. work the works of him that** *1163*
Joh 10:16 **them also I m. bring, and they** *1163*
Joh 12:34 The Son of man **m.** be lifted up? *1163*
Joh 20:9 he **m.** rise again from the dead. *1163*
Ac 1:16 **m.** needs have been fulfilled, *1163*
Ac 1:22 **m.** one be ordained to be a witness *1163*
Ac 3:21 Whom the heaven **m.** receive until *1163*
Ac 4:12 men, whereby we **m.** be saved. *1163*
Ac 9:6 **shall be told thee what thou m. do.** *1163*
Ac 9:16 **he m. suffer for my name's sake.** *1163*
Ac 14:22 **m.** through much tribulation enter *1163*
Ac 15:24 souls, saying, Ye **m.** be circumcised,
Ac 16:30 Sirs, what **m.** I do to be saved? *1163*
Ac 17:3 Christ **m.** needs have suffered, *1163*
Ac 18:21 I **m.** by all means keep this feast *1163*
Ac 19:21 been there, I **m.** also see Rome. *1163*
Ac 21:22 the multitude **m.** needs come *1163*
Ac 23:11 **so m. thou bear witness also at** *1163*
Ac 27:24 thou **m.** be brought before Caesar: *1163*
Ac 27:26 **m.** be cast upon a certain island. *1163*
Ro 13:5 ye **m.** needs be subject, not only
1Co 5:10 for then **m.** ye needs go out of the *3784*
1Co 11:19 there **m.** be also heresies among *1163*
1Co 15:25 For he **m.** reign, till he hath put all *1163*
1Co 15:53 corruptible **m.** put on incorruption,
1Co 15:53 this mortal **m.** put on immortality.
2Co 5:10 For we **m.** all appear before the *1163*
2Co 11:30 If I **m.** needs glory, I will glory of *1163*
1Ti 3:2 A bishop then **m.** be blameless, the *1163*
1Ti 3:7 Moreover he **m.** have a good report *1163*
1Ti 3:8 Likewise **m.** the deacons be grave, not
1Ti 3:11 Even so **m.** their wives be grave, not
2Ti 2:6 laboureth **m.** be first partaker of *1163*
2Ti 2:24 servant of the Lord **m.** not strive; *1163*
Tit 1:7 For a bishop **m.** be blameless, as *1163*
Tit 1:11 Whose mouths **m.** be stopped, who *1163*
Heb 4:6 remaineth that some **m.** enter therein,
Heb 9:16 there **m.** also of necessity be the
Heb 9:26 For then **m.** he often have suffered *1163*
Heb 11:6 he that cometh to God **m.** believe *1163*
Heb 13:17 as they that **m.** give account, that
1Pe 4:17 judgment **m.** begin at the house of
2Pe 1:14 shortly I **m.** put off this my tabernacle,
Re 1:1 which **m.** shortly come to pass; *1163*
Re 4:1 thee things which **m.** be hereafter. *1163*
Re 10:11 Thou **m.** prophesy again before *1163*
Re 11:5 he **m.** in this manner be killed. *1163*
Re 13:10 sword **m.** be killed with the sword. *1163*
Re 17:10 he **m.** continue a short space. *1163*
Re 20:3 after that he **m.** be loosed a little *1163*
Re 22:6 things which **m.** shortly be done. *1163*

MUSTARD
Mt 13:31 **heaven is like a grain of m. seed,** *4615*
Mt 17:20 **have faith as a grain of m. seed,** *4615*
Mk 4:31 **It is like a grain of m. seed,** *4615*
Lu 13:19 **It is like a grain of m. seed,** *4615*
Lu 17:6 **ye had faith as a grain of m.,** *4615*

MUSTARD-SEED See MUSTARD and SEED.

MUSTERED
2Ki 25:19 which **m.** the people of the land, 6633
Jer 52:25 host, who **m.** the people of the land; 6633

MUSTERETH
Isa 13:4 the Lord of hosts **m.** the host of 6485

MUTABILITY See IMMUTABILITY.

MUTABLE See IMMUTABLE.

MUTH-LABBEN (muth-lab'-ben)
Ps 9:*title* To the chief Musician upon **M.**, 4192

MUTTER See also MUTTERED.
Isa 8:19 wizards that peep, and that **m.**: 1897

MUTTERED
Isa 59:3 your tongue hath **m.** perverseness. 1897

MUTUAL
Ro 1:12 **m.** faith both of you and me. *1722,240*

MUZZLE
De 25:4 not **m.** the ox when he treadeth 2629
1Co 9:9 not **m.** the mouth of the ox that *5392*
1Ti 5:18 not **m.** the ox that treadeth out *5392*

MY See in the APPENDIX; also MINE; MYSELF.

MYRA (mi'-rah)
Ac 27:5 we came to **M.**, a city of Lycia. *3460*

MYRRH
Ge 37:25 bearing spicery and balm and **m.**, 3910
Ge 43:11 spices, and **m.**, nuts, and almonds: 3910
Ex 30:23 of pure **m.** five hundred shekels, 4753
Es 2:12 six months with oil of **m.**, and six 4753
Ps 45:8 thy garments smell of **m.**, and aloes, 4753
Pr 7:17 I have perfumed my bed with **m.**, 4753
Ca 1:13 A bundle of **m.** is my well beloved 4753
Ca 3:6 of smoke, perfumed with **m.** and 4753
Ca 4:6 will get me to the mountain of **m.**, 4753
Ca 4:14 **m.** and aloes, with all the chief 4753
Ca 5:1 gathered my **m.** with my spice; I 4753
Ca 5:5 my hands dropped with **m.**, and my 4753
Ca 5:5 my fingers with sweet smelling **m.**, 4753
Ca 5:13 lilies, dropping sweet smelling **m.**, 4753
Mt 2:11 gold, and frankincense, and **m.** *4666*
Mk 15:23 to drink wine mingled with **m.**: *4669*
Joh 19:39 a mixture of **m.** and aloes, about *4666*

MYRTLE
Ne 8:15 **m.** branches, and palm branches, 1918
Isa 41:19 the shittah tree, and the **m.**, and 1918
Isa 55:13 brier shall come up the **m.** tree: 1918
Zec 1:8 he stood among the **m.** trees that 1918
Zec 1:10 man that stood among the **m.** trees 1918
Zec 1:11 that stood among the **m.** trees, and 1918

MYRTLE-TREE See MYRTLE and TREE.

MYSELF
Ge 3:10 because I was naked; and I hid **m.**
Ge 22:16 By **m.** have I sworn, saith the Lord,
Ex 19:4 wings, and brought you unto **m.**
Nu 8:17 land of Egypt I sanctified them for **m.**
Nu 12:6 I the Lord will make **m.** known unto
De 1:9 I am not able to bear you **m.** alone:
De 1:12 How can I **m.** alone bear your
De 10:5 I turned **m.** and came down from the
Jg 16:20 at other times before, and shake **m.**
Ru 4:6 I cannot redeem it for **m.**, lest I mar
1Sa 13:12 I forced **m.** therefore, and offered a
1Sa 20:5 that I may hide **m.** in the field unto
1Sa 25:33 avenging **m.** with mine own hand.
2Sa 18:2 surely go forth with you **m.** also. 589
2Sa 22:24 and have kept **m.** from mine iniquity.
1Ki 18:15 I will surely show **m.** unto him to-day.
1Ki 22:30 I will disguise **m.**, and enter into the
2Ki 5:18 and I bow **m.** in the house of Rimmon:
2Ki 5:18 when I bow down **m.** in the house of
2Ch 7:12 place to **m.** for a house of sacrifice.
2Ch 18:29 I will disguise **m.**, and will go to the
Ne 5:7 Then I consulted with **m.**, and I
Es 5:12 banquet that she had prepared but **m.**
Es 6:6 delight to do honour more than to **m.**?
Job 6:10 I would harden **m.** in sorrow; let him
Job 7:20 thee, so that I am a burden to **m.**?
Job 9:20 If I justify **m.**, mine own mouth shall
Job 9:27 off my heaviness, and comfort **m.**
Job 9:30 If I wash **m.** with snow water, and
Job 10:1 I will leave my complaint upon **m.**;
Job 13:20 then will I not hide **m.** from thee.
Job 19:4 erred, mine error remaineth with **m.**
Job 19:27 Whom I shall see for **m.**, and mine
Job 31:17 have eaten my morsel **m.** alone, and
Job 31:29 or lifted up **m.** when evil found him:
Job 42:6 I abhor **m.**, and repent in dust and
Ps 18:23 and I kept **m.** from mine iniquity.
Ps 35:14 I behaved **m.** as though he had been
Ps 55:12 then I would have hid **m.** from him:
Ps 57:8 and harp: I **m.** will awake early.
Ps 101:2 behave **m.** wisely in a perfect way.
Ps 108:2 and harp: I **m.** will awake early.
Ps 109:4 adversaries: but I give **m.** unto prayer.
Ps 119:16 I will delight **m.** in thy statutes: I will
Ps 119:47 will delight **m.** in thy commandments,
Ps 119:52 old, O Lord; and I have comforted **m.**
Ps 131:1 do I exercise **m.** in great matters,
Ps 131:2 I have behaved and quieted **m.**, 5315
Ec 2:3 in mine heart to give **m.** unto wine,
Ec 2:12 I turned **m.** to behold wisdom, and
Ec 2:14 I **m.** perceived also that one event 589
Ec 2:19 I have shewed **m.** wise under the sun.
Isa 33:10 I be exalted; now will I lift up **m.**
Isa 42:14 I have been still, and refrained **m.**:
Isa 43:21 This people have I formed for **m.**; they
Isa 44:24 spreadeth abroad the earth by **m.**;
Isa 45:23 I have sworn by **m.**, the word is gone
Jer 8:18 I would comfort **m.** against sorrow,
Jer 21:5 I **m.** will fight against you with an 589
Jer 22:5 words, I swear by **m.**, saith the Lord,
Jer 49:13 I have sworn by **m.**, saith the Lord,
Eze 14:7 I the Lord will answer him by **m.**:
Eze 20:5 made **m.** known unto them in the land
Eze 20:9 sight I made **m.** known unto them,
Eze 29:3 mine own, and I have made it for **m.**
Eze 35:11 I will make **m.** known among them,
Eze 38:23 will I magnify **m.**, and sanctify **m.**;
Da 10:3 neither did I anoint **m.** at all, till
Mic 6:6 and bow **m.** before the high God?
Hab 3:16 I trembled in **m.**, that I might rest
Zec 7:3 separating **m.**, as I have done these
Lu 7:7 I **m.** worthy to come unto thee: *1683*
Lu 24:39 **hands and my feet, that it is I m.**
Joh 5:31 **If I bear witness of m., my witness** *1683*
Joh 7:17 **of God, or whether I speak of m.** *1683*
Joh 7:28 **I am not come of m., but he that** *1683*
Joh 8:14 **Though I bear record of m., yet** *1683*
Joh 8:18 **I am one that bear witness of m.,** *1683*
Joh 8:28 **he, and that I do nothing of m.;** *1683*
Joh 8:42 **neither came I of m., but he sent** *1683*
Joh 8:54 **If I honour m., my honour is** *1683*

Joh 10:18 **from me, but I lay it down of m.** ...*1683*
Joh 12:49 **For I have not spoken of m.; but** .. *1683*
Joh 14:3 **again, and receive you unto m.;** *1683*
Joh 14:10 **speak unto you I speak not of m.:**. *1683*
Joh 14:21 **him, and will manifest m. to him**.. *1683*
Joh 17:19 **for their sakes I sanctify m., that** . *1683*
Ac 10:26 saying, Stand up; I **m.** also am a man. ......
Ac 20:24 count I my life dear unto **m.**, so *1683*
Ac 24:10 the more cheerfully answer for **m.**:..... *1683*
Ac 24:16 And herein do I exercise **m.**, to have........
Ac 25:22 Festus, I would also hear the man **m.**......
Ac 26:2 I think **m.** happy, king Agrippa, ... *1683*
Ac 26:2 I shall answer for **m.** this day before.........
Ac 26:9 I verily thought with **m.**, that I.......... *1683*
Ro 7:25 the mind I **m.** serve the law of God;.........
Ro 9:3 could wish that **m.** were accursed........ *846*
Ro 11:4 reserved to **m.** seven thousand............ *1683*
Ro 15:14 I **m.** also am persuaded of you, my...........
Ro 16:2 succourer of many, and of **m.** also. *846*
1Co 4:4 For I know nothing by **m.**; yet am *1683*
1Co 4:6 I have in a figure transferred to **m.** *1683*
1Co 7:7 that all men were even as I **m.**.......... *1683*
1Co 9:19 I made **m.** servant unto all, that I *1683*
1Co 9:27 to others, I **m.** should be a castaway. ....
2Co 2:1 But I determined this with **m.**, ... *1683*
2Co 10:1 Now I Paul **m.** beseech you by the..........
2Co 11:7 an offence in abasing **m.** that ye......... *1683*
2Co 11:9 kept **m.** from being burdensome......... *1683*
2Co 11:9 unto you, and so will I keep **m.**.......... *1683*
2Co 11:16 me, that I may boast **m.** a little. ....
2Co 12:5 of **m.** I will not glory, but in mine *1683*
2Co 12:13 it be that I **m.** was not burdensome..........
Ga 2:18 I make **m.** a transgressor. *1683*
Php 2:24 that I also **m.** shall come shortly. ....
Php 3:13 I count not **m.** to have apprehended: ....
Phm 17 a partner, receive him as **m.**............ *1691*

MYSIA (miz'-ye-ah)
Ac 16:7 After they were come to **M.**, they *3463*
Ac 16:8 passing by **M.** came down to Troas. ... *3463*

MYSTERIES
Mt 13:11 **the m. of the kingdom of heaven,**.. *3466*
Lu 8:10 **the m. of the kingdom of God:**...... *3466*
1Co 4:1 and stewards of the **m.** of God. *3466*
1Co 13:2 and understand all **m.**, and all............ *3466*
1Co 14:2 in the spirit he speaketh **m.**.............. *3466*

MYSTERY See also MYSTERIES.
Mk 4:11 **the m. of the kingdom of God:**...... *3466*
Ro 11:25 ye should be ignorant of this **m.**,......... *3466*
Ro 16:25 to the revelation of the **m.**, which...... *3466*
1Co 2:7 speak the wisdom of God in a **m.**,....... *3466*
1Co 15:51 I shew you a **m.**; We shall not all......... *3466*
Eph 1:9 known unto us the **m.** of his will,....... *3466*
Eph 3:3 he made known unto me the **m.**; *3466*
Eph 3:4 my knowledge in the **m.** of Christ) *3466*
Eph 3:9 what is the fellowship of the **m.**,........ *3466*
Eph 5:32 This is a great **m.**: but I speak.......... *3466*
Eph 6:19 make known the **m.** of the gospel, ... *3466*
Col 1:26 even the **m.** which hath been hid *3466*
Col 1:27 glory of this **m.** among the Gentiles;... *3466*
Col 2:2 acknowledgment of the **m.** of God, ... *3466*
Col 4:3 to speak the **m.** of Christ, for which.... *3466*
2Th 2:7 **m.** of iniquity doth already work:........ *3466*
1Ti 3:9 Holding the **m.** of the faith in a.......... *3466*
1Ti 3:16 great is the **m.** of godliness:............. *3466*
Re 1:20 **The m. of the seven stars which**.... *3466*
Re 10:7 the **m.** of God should be finished,....... *3466*
Re 17:5 written, **M.**, Babylon The Great,........ *3466*
Re 17:7 will tell thee the **m.** of the woman,..... *3466*

N.

NAAM (na'-am)
1Ch 4:15 of Jephunneh; Iru, Elah, and **N.**: 5277

NAAMAH (na'-a'-mah) See also NAAMATHITE.
Ge 4:22 the sister of Tubal-cain was **N.**.......... 5279
Jos 15:41 Gederoth, Beth-dagon, and **N.**,.......... 5279
1Ki 14:21, 31 And his mother's name was **N.**....... 5279
2Ch 12:13 And his mother's name was **N.** an...... 5279

NAAMAN (na'-a-man) See also NAAMAN'S; NAAMITES.
Ge 46:21 **N.**, Ehi, and Rosh, Muppim, and........ 5283
Nu 26:40 the sons of Bela were Ard and **N.**:...... 5283
Nu 26:40 Ardites: and of **N.**, the family of 5283
2Ki 5:1 Now **N.**, captain of the host of the 5283
2Ki 5:6 sent **N.** my servant to thee, that.......... 5283
2Ki 5:9 So **N.** came with his horses and......... 5283
2Ki 5:11 But **N.** was wroth, and went away, ... 5283
2Ki 5:17 And **N.** said, Shall there not then, ... 5283
2Ki 5:20 master hath spared **N.** this Syrian, ... 5283
2Ki 5:21 So Gehazi followed after **N.**. And 5283
2Ki 5:21 when **N.** saw him running after.......... 5283
2Ki 5:23 And **N.** said, Be content, take two 5283
2Ki 5:27 leprosy therefore of **N.** shall cleave..... 5283
1Ch 8:4 And Abishua, and **N.**, and Ahoah,....... 5283
1Ch 8:7 And **N.**, and Ahiah, and Gera, he 5283
Lu 4:27 **cleansed, saving N. the Syrian**. *3497*

NAAMAN'S (na'-a-mans)
2Ki 5:2 maid; and she waited on **N.** wife. 5283

NAAMATHITE (na'-a-math-ite)
Job 2:11 the Shuhite, and Zophar the **N.**:......... 5284
Job 11:1 Then answered Zophar the **N.**, ... 5284
Job 20:1 Then answered Zophar the **N.**, ... 5284
Job 42:9 Shuhite and Zophar the **N.** went,........ 5284

NAAMITES (na'-a-mites)
Nu 26:40 of Naaman, the family of the **N.**......... 5280

NAARAH (na'-a-rah) See also NAARAN; NAARATH.
1Ch 4:5 had two wives, Helah and **N.**............ 5292
1Ch 4:6 And **N.** bare him Ahuzam, and........... 5292
1Ch 4:6 These were the sons of **N.**............... 5292

NAARAI (na'-a-rahee) See also PAARAI.
1Ch 11:37 Carmelite, **N.** the son of Ezbai, ... 5293

NAARAN (na'-a-ran) See also NAARATH.
1Ch 7:28 eastward **N.**, and westward Gezer,..... 5295

NAARATH (na'-a-rath) See also NAARAH; NAARAN.
Jos 16:7 and to **N.**, and came to Jericho, ... 5292

NAASHON (na'-a-shon) See also NAHSHON.
Ex 6:23 Amminadab, sister of **N.**, to wife;....... 5177

NAASSON (na'-as-son) See also NAASHON.
Mt 1:4 Aminadab begat **N.**; and **N.**............... *3476*
Lu 3:32 Salmon, which was the son of **N.**, ... *3476*

NABAL (na'-bal) See also NABAL'S.
1Sa 25:3 Now the name of the man was **N.**;..... 5037
1Sa 25:4 that **N.** did shear his sheep............... 5037
1Sa 25:5 and go to **N.**, and greet him in my..... 5037
1Sa 25:9 they spake to **N.** according to all....... 5037
1Sa 25:10 **N.** answered David's servants, and..... 5037
1Sa 25:19 But she told not her husband **N.**. 5037
1Sa 25:25 regard this man of Belial, even **N.**:..... 5037
1Sa 25:25 **N.** is his name, and folly is with.......... 5037
1Sa 25:26 that seek evil to my lord, be as **N.**...... 5037
1Sa 25:34 there had not been left unto **N.** by..... 5037
1Sa 25:36 Abigail came to **N.**; and, behold, ... 5037
1Sa 25:37 when the wine was gone out of **N.**,.... 5037
1Sa 25:38 the Lord smote **N.**, that he died. 5037
1Sa 25:39 David heard that **N.** was dead, ... 5037
1Sa 25:39 my reproach from the hand of **N.**, ... 5037
1Sa 25:39 the wickedness of **N.** upon his own..... 5037
1Sa 30:5 the wife of **N.** the Carmelite. 5037
2Sa 3:3 the wife of **N.** the Carmelite; 5037

NABAL'S (na'-balz)
1Sa 25:14 young men told Abigail, **N.** wife, ... 5037
1Sa 25:36 **N.** heart was merry within him, ... 5037
1Sa 27:3 Abigail the Carmelitess, **N.** wife......... 5037
2Sa 2:2 Abigail **N.** wife the Carmelite............ 5037

NABAS See BARNABAS.

NABOTH (na'-both)
1Ki 21:1 **N.** the Jezreelite had a vineyard, ... 5022
1Ki 21:2 Ahab spake unto **N.**, saying, Give 5022
1Ki 21:3 **N.** said to Ahab, The Lord forbid it 5022
1Ki 21:4 which **N.** the Jezreelite had spoken..... 5022
1Ki 21:6 I spake unto **N.** the Jezreelite, and..... 5022
1Ki 21:7 the vineyard of **N.** the Jezreelite. 5022
1Ki 21:8 were in his city, dwelling with **N.**....... 5022
1Ki 21:9 set **N.** on high among the people:....... 5022
1Ki 21:12 set **N.** on high among the people......... 5022
1Ki 21:13 against him, even against **N.**, in.......... 5022
1Ki 21:13 **N.** did blaspheme God and the.......... 5022
1Ki 21:14 saying, **N.** is stoned, and is dead........ 5022
1Ki 21:15 Jezebel heard that **N.** was stoned, ... 5022
1Ki 21:15 possession of the vineyard of **N.** the... 5022
1Ki 21:15 for **N.** is not alive, but dead............ 5022
1Ki 21:16 when Ahab heard that **N.** was dead, ... 5022
1Ki 21:16 to go down to the vineyard of **N.**....... 5022
1Ki 21:18 he is in the vineyard of **N.**, whither.... 5022
1Ki 21:19 where dogs licked the blood of **N.**....... 5022
2Ki 9:21 in the portion of **N.** the Jezreelite....... 5022
2Ki 9:25 in the portion of the field of **N.** the..... 5022
2Ki 9:26 seen yesterday the blood of **N.**,......... 5022

NACHON'S (na'-kons) See also CHIDON.
2Sa 6:6 they came to **N.** threshingfloor, ... 5225

NACHOR (na'-kor) See also NAHOR.
Jos 24:2 Abraham, and the father of **N.**: 5152
Lu 3:34 Thara, which was the son of **N.**, ... *3493*

NADAB (na'-dab)
Ex 6:23 to wife; and she bare him **N.**, and...... 5070
Ex 24:1 the Lord, thou, and Aaron, **N.**, and 5070
Ex 24:9 went up Moses, and Aaron, **N.**, and... 5070
Ex 28:1 office, even Aaron, **N.** and Abihu, ... 5070
Le 10:1 **N.** and Abihu, the sons of Aaron,....... 5070
Nu 3:2 the names of the sons of Aaron; **N.**.... 5070
Nu 3:4 **N.** and Abihu died before the Lord, ... 5070
Nu 26:60 And unto Aaron was born **N.**, and..... 5070
Nu 26:61 And **N.** and Abihu died, when they..... 5070
1Ki 14:20 **N.** his son reigned in his stead. 5070
1Ki 15:25 **N.** the son of Jeroboam began to........ 5070
1Ki 15:27 for **N.** and all Israel laid siege to........ 5070
1Ki 15:31 the rest of the acts of **N.**, and all....... 5070
1Ch 2:28 sons of Shammai; **N.**, and Abishur. 5070
1Ch 2:30 sons of **N.**; Seled, and Appaim:.......... 5070
1Ch 6:3 sons also of Aaron; **N.**, and Abihu, ... 5070
1Ch 8:30 Zur, and Kish, and Baal, and **N.**,......... 5070
1Ch 9:36 Kish, and Baal, and Ner, and **N.**,........ 5070
1Ch 24:1 The sons of Aaron; **N.**, and Abihu, ... 5070
1Ch 24:2 **N.** and Abihu died before their........... 5070

NADIB See AMMI-NADIB.

NAGGAE See NAGGE.

NAGGE (nag'-e) See also NEARIAH.
Lu 3:25 of Esli, which was the son of **N.**, ... *3477*

NAHALAL (na'-ha-lal) See also NAHALLAL; NAHALOL.
Jos 21:35 **N.** with her suburbs; four cities. 5096

NAHALIEL (na-ha'-le-el)
Nu 21:19 And from Mattanah to **N.**: 5160
Nu 21:19 and from **N.** to Bamoth: 5160

NAHALLAL (na'-hal-el) See also NAHALAL.
Jos 19:15 Kattath, and **N.**, and Shimron, ... 5096

NAHALOL (na'-ha-lol) See also NAHALAL.
Jg 1:30 Kitron, nor the inhabitants of **N.**; 5096

NAHAM (na'-ham) See also ISHBAH.
1Ch 4:19 the sister of **N.**, the father of........... 5163

NAHAMANI (na-ham'-a-ni)
Ne 7:7 Azariah, Raamiah, **N.**, Mordecai, ... 5167

NAHARAI (na'-ha-rahee) See also NAHARI.
1Ch 11:39 the Ammonite, **N.** the Berothite,........ 5171

NAHARAIM See ARAM-NAHARAIM.

NAHARI (na'-ha-ri) See also NAHARAI.
2Sa 23:37 **N.** the Beerothite, armourbearer........ 5171

NAHASH (na'-hash) See also IR-NAHASH.
1Sa 11:1 Then **N.** the Ammonite came up, ... 5176
1Sa 11:1 the men of Jabesh said unto **N.**,......... 5176
1Sa 11:2 **N.** the Ammonite answered them, ... 5176
1Sa 12:12 that **N.** the king of the children of 5176
2Sa 10:2 kindness unto Hanun the son of **N.**,.... 5176
2Sa 17:25 in to Abigail the daughter of **N.**,......... 5176
2Sa 17:27 that Shobi the son of **N.** of Rabbah..... 5176

1Ch 19:1 that **N.** the king of the children of 5176
1Ch 19:2 kindness unto Hanun the son of **N.**,.... 5176

NAHATH (na'-hath) See also TOHU.
Ge 36:13 the sons of Reuel; **N.**, and Zerah, ... 5184
Ge 36:17 duke **N.**, duke Zerah, duke 5184
1Ch 1:37 **N.**, Zerah, Shammah, and Mizzah....... 5184
1Ch 6:26 Zophai his son, and **N.** his son,.......... 5184
2Ch 31:13 and Azaziah, and **N.**, and Asahel, ... 5184

NAHBI (nah'-bi)
Nu 13:14 of Naphtali, **N.** the son of Vophsi. 5147

NAHOR (na'-hor) See also NACHOR; NAHOR'S.
Ge 11:22 lived thirty years, and begat **N.**: 5152
Ge 11:23 Serug lived after he begat **N.** two 5152
Ge 11:24 **N.** lived nine and twenty years, ... 5152
Ge 11:25 **N.** lived after he begat Terah an......... 5152
Ge 11:26 and begat Abram, **N.**, and Haran........ 5152
Ge 11:27 begat Abram, **N.**, and Haran: and....... 5152
Ge 11:29 Abram and **N.** took them wives: 5152
Ge 22:20 born children unto thy brother **N.**;...... 5152
Ge 22:23 these eight Milcah did bear to **N.**, ... 5152
Ge 24:10 Mesopotamia, unto the city of **N.**. 5152
Ge 24:15 the wife of **N.**, Abraham's brother, ... 5152
Ge 24:24 of Milcah, which she bare unto **N.**..... 5152
Ge 29:5 Know ye Laban the son of **N.**? 5152
Ge 31:53 God of **N.**, the God of their father,..... 5152
1Ch 1:26 Serug, **N.**, Terah, ... 5152

NAHOR'S (na'-hors)
Ge 11:29 and the name of **N.** wife, Milcah, ... 5152
Ge 24:47 The daughter of Bethuel, **N.** son,....... 5152

NAHSHON (nah'-shon) See also NAASHON; NAASHON.
Nu 1:7 **N.** the son of Amminadab. 5177
Nu 2:3 **N.** the son of Amminadab shall be 5177
Nu 7:12 his offering the first day was **N.**......... 5177
Nu 7:17 of **N.** the son of Amminadab............. 5177
Nu 10:14 was **N.** the son of Amminadab. 5177
Ru 4:20 begat **N.**, and **N.** begat Salmon,......... 5177
1Ch 2:10 and Amminadab begat **N.**, prince........ 5177
1Ch 2:11 **N.** begat Salma, and Salma begat 5177

NAHUM (na'-hum) See also NAUM.
Na *general title* **N.**.. 5151
Na 1:1 the vision of **N.** the Elkoshite. 5151

NAIL See also NAILING; NAILS.
Jg 4:21 Heber's wife took a **n.** of the tent, ... 3489
Jg 4:21 and smote the **n.** into his temples, ... 3489
Jg 4:22 dead, and the **n.** was in his temples..... 3489
Jg 5:26 She put her hand to the **n.**, and her ... 3489
Ezr 9:8 to give us a **n.** in his holy place, ... 3489
Isa 22:23 fasten him as a **n.** in a sure place;...... 3489
Isa 22:25 **n.** that is fastened in the sure place.... 3489
Zec 10:4 out of him the **n.**, out of him the 3489

NAILING
Col 2:14 out of the way, **n.** it to his cross: *4338*

NAILS
De 21:12 shave her head, and pare her **n.**; 6856
1Ch 22:3 iron in abundance for the **n.** for 4548
2Ch 3:9 weight of the **n.** was fifty shekels....... 4548
Ec 12:11 as **n.** fastened by the masters of.......... 4930
Isa 41:7 and he fastened it with **n.**, that it....... 4548
Jer 10:4 it with **n.** and with hammers, that 4548
Da 4:33 and his **n.** like birds' claws. 2953
Da 7:19 were of iron, and his **n.** of brass; 2953
Joh 20:25 in his hands the print of the **n.**, ... *2247*
Joh 20:25 my finger into the print of the **n.**, ... *2247*

NAIN (nane)
Lu 7:11 that he went into a city called **N.**; *3484*

NAIOTH (nah'-yoth)
1Sa 19:18 Samuel went and dwelt in **N.**............. 5121
1Sa 19:19 Behold, David is at **N.** in Ramah. 5121
1Sa 19:22 Behold, they be at **N.** in Ramah......... 5121
1Sa 19:23 he went thither to **N.** in Ramah: 5121
1Sa 19:23 until he came to **N.** in Ramah. 5121
1Sa 20:1 David fled from **N.** in Ramah, and 5121

NAKED
Ge 2:25 they were both **n.**, the man and......... 6174
Ge 3:7 knew that they were **n.**; and they 5903
Ge 3:10 I was afraid, because I was **n.**;.......... 5903
Ge 3:11 Who told thee that thou wast **n.**? 5903
Ex 32:25 saw that the people were **n.**, ... 6544
Ex 32:25 had made them **n.** unto their shame.... 6544
1Sa 19:24 lay down **n.** all that day and all 6174
2Ch 28:15 all that were **n.** among them, and....... 4636
2Ch 28:19 Israel; for he made Judah **n.**,............. 6544
Job 1:21 **N.** came I out of my mother's.......... 6174
Job 1:21 and **n.** shall I return thither: the 6174
Job 22:6 stripped the **n.** of their clothing.......... 6174
Job 24:7 the **n.** to lodge without clothing, ... 6174
Job 24:10 him to go **n.** without clothing, and...... 6174
Job 26:6 Hell is **n.** before him, and................ 6174
Ec 5:15 **n.** shall he return to go as he came, ... 6174
Isa 20:2 he did so, walking **n.** and barefoot...... 6174
Isa 20:3 servant Isaiah hath walked **n.** and....... 6174
Isa 20:4 young and old, **n.** and barefoot, ... 6174
Isa 58:7 when thou seest the **n.**, that thou 6174
La 4:21 and shalt make thyself **n.**.................. 6168
Eze 16:7 whereas thou wast **n.** and bare. 5903
Eze 16:22 youth, when thou wast **n.** and bare,.... 5903
Eze 16:39 jewels, and leave these **n.** and bare.... 5903
Eze 18:7 hath covered the **n.** with a garment; ... 5903
Eze 18:16 hath covered the **n.** with a garment, ... 5903
Eze 23:29 and shall leave thee **n.** and bare:........ 5903
Ho 2:3 Lest I strip her **n.**, and set her as...... 6174
Am 2:16 the mighty shall flee away **n.** in 6174
Mic 1:8 howl, I will go stripped and **n.**: 6174
Mic 1:11 of Saphir, having thy shame **n.**: 6181
Hab 3:9 Thy bow was made quite **n.**,.............. 5783
Mt 25:36 **N., and ye clothed me: I was sick**.. *1131*
Mt 25:38 **thee in? or n., and clothed thee?** ... *1131*
Mt 25:43 **n., and ye clothed me not: sick,** *1131*
Mt 25:44 **or n., or sick, or in prison, and**..... *1131*
Mk 14:51 linen cloth cast about his **n.** body; *1131*
Mk 14:52 linen cloth, and fled from them **n.**....... *1131*
Joh 21:7 coat unto him, (for he was **n.**,) and *1131*
Ac 19:16 out of that house **n.** and wounded. *1131*
1Co 4:11 hunger, and thirst, and are **n.**,............ *1130*
2Co 5:3 clothed we shall not be found **n.**. *1131*
Heb 4:13 all things are **n.** and opened unto *1131*
Jas 2:15 If a brother or sister be **n.**, and.......... *1131*
Re 3:17 **and poor, and blind, and n.:**........... *1131*
Re 16:15 lest he walk **n.**, and they see his *1131*
Re 17:16 and shall make her desolate and **n.**, ... *1131*

NAKEDNESS
Ge 9:22 Canaan, saw the **n.** of his father, ... 6172
Ge 9:23 and covered the **n.** of their father;....... 6172
Ge 9:23 and they saw not their father's **n.**....... 6172
Ge 42:9, 12 to see the **n.** of the land ye are..... 6172
Ex 20:26 they **n.** be not discovered thereon....... 6172
Ex 28:42 them linen breeches to cover their **n.**; .6172
Le 18:6 of kin to him, to uncover their **n.**: 6172
Le 18:7 **n.** of thy father, or the **n.** of thy........ 6172
Le 18:7 thou shalt not uncover her **n.**. 6172
Le 18:8 The **n.** of thy father's wife shalt......... 6172
Le 18:8 not uncover: it is thy father's **n.**. 6172
Le 18:9 The **n.** of thy sister, the daughter...... 6172
Le 18:9 their **n.** thou shalt not uncover. 6172
Le 18:10 The **n.** of thy son's daughter, or of..... 6172
Le 18:10 their **n.** thou shalt not uncover: 6172
Le 18:10 uncover: for theirs is thine own **n.**. 6172
Le 18:11 **n.** of thy father's wife's daughter,....... 6172
Le 18:11 sister, thou shalt not uncover her **n.**... 6172
Le 18:12 uncover the **n.** of thy father's sister: .. 6172
Le 18:13 the **n.** of thy mother's sister: 6172
Le 18:14 the **n.** of thy father's brother,........... 6172
Le 18:15 the **n.** of thy daughter in law:............ 6172
Le 18:15 wife; thou shalt not uncover her **n.**...... 6172
Le 18:16 uncover the **n.** of thy brother's wife:.... 6172
Le 18:16 brother's wife: it is thy brother's **n.**.... 6172
Le 18:17 not uncover the **n.** of a woman and 6172
Le 18:17 daughter, to uncover her **n.**; for 6172
Le 18:18 vex her, to uncover her **n.**, besides.... 6172
Le 18:19 unto a woman to uncover her **n.**; 6172
Le 20:11 uncovered his father's **n.**: both of....... 6172
Le 20:17 and see her **n.**, and she see his **n.**;.... 6172
Le 20:17 he hath uncovered his sister's **n.**;........ 6172
Le 20:18 sickness and shall uncover her **n.**; 6172
Le 20:19 the **n.** of thy mother's sister, nor........ 6172
Le 20:20 he hath uncovered his uncle's **n.**: 6172
Le 20:21 he hath uncovered his brother's **n.**; 6172
De 28:48 hunger, and in thirst, and in **n.**, ... 5903
1Sa 20:30 the confusion of thy mother's **n.**? 6172
Isa 47:3 Thy **n.** shall be uncovered, yea, thy.... 6172
La 1:8 because they have seen her **n.**: yea,... 6172
Eze 16:8 skirt over thee, and covered thy **n.**: ... 6172
Eze 16:36 and thy **n.** discovered through thy....... 6172
Eze 16:37 and will discover thy **n.** unto them,..... 6172
Eze 16:37 them, that they may see all thy **n.**. 6172
Eze 22:10 they discovered their father's **n.**:........ 6172
Eze 23:10 These discovered her **n.**: they took.... 6172
Eze 23:18 discovered her **n.**: then my mind........ 6172
Eze 23:29 the **n.** of thy whoredoms shall be 6172
Ho 2:9 and my flax given to cover her **n.**....... 6172
Na 3:5 and I will shew the nations thy **n.**, ... 4626
Hab 2:15 that thou mayest look on their **n.**! 4589
Ro 8:35 famine, or **n.**, or peril, or sword?....... *1132*
2Co 11:27 in fastings often, in cold and **n.**. *1132*
Re 3:18 **the shame of thy n. do not appear;** .*1132*

NAME See also NAMED; NAME'S; NAMES; NAMETH; SURNAME.
Ge 2:11 **n.** of the first is Pison: that is it......... 8034
Ge 2:13 the **n.** of the second river is Gihon: 8034
Ge 2:14 the **n.** of the third river is Hiddekel: ... 8034
Ge 2:19 creature, that was the **n.** thereof. 8034
Ge 3:20 And Adam called his wife's **n.** Eve;..... 8034
Ge 4:17 **n.** of the city, after the **n.** of his son, . 8034
Ge 4:19 wives: the **n.** of the one was Adah, ... 8034
Ge 4:19 Adah, and the **n.** of the other Zillah. ... 8034
Ge 4:21 his brother's **n.** was Jubal: he was...... 8034
Ge 4:25 bare a son, and called his **n.** Seth:...... 8034
Ge 4:26 a son; and he called his **n.** Enos: 8034
Ge 4:26 men to call upon the **n.** of the Lord.... 8034
Ge 5:2 and called their **n.** Adam, in the......... 8034
Ge 5:3 his image; and called his **n.** Seth: 8034
Ge 5:29 And he called his **n.** Noah, saying,...... 8034
Ge 10:25 two sons: the **n.** of one was Peleg; 8034
Ge 10:25 and his brother's **n.** was Joktan......... 8034
Ge 11:4 and let us make us a **n.**, lest we be.... 8034
Ge 11:9 is the **n.** of it called Babel; because 8034
Ge 11:29 the **n.** of Abram's wife was Sarai;....... 8034
Ge 11:29 the **n.** of Nahor's wife, Milcah, the..... 8034
Ge 12:2 bless thee, and make thy **n.** great; 8034
Ge 12:8 and called upon the **n.** of the Lord...... 8034
Ge 13:4 Abram called on the **n.** of the Lord...... 8034
Ge 16:1 an Egyptian, whose **n.** was Hagar. 8034
Ge 16:11 son, and shalt call his **n.** Ishmael;....... 8034
Ge 16:13 she called the **n.** of the Lord that....... 8034
Ge 16:15 Abram called his son's **n.**, which 8034
Ge 17:5 thy **n.** any more be called Abram, ... 8034
Ge 17:5 but thy **n.** shall be Abraham;............. 8034
Ge 17:15 thou shalt not call her **n.** Sarai, ... 8034
Ge 17:15 Sarai, but Sarah shall her **n.** be.......... 8034
Ge 17:19 and thou shalt call his **n.** Isaac: 8034
Ge 19:22 the **n.** of the city was called Zoar. 8034
Ge 19:37 bare a son, and called his **n.** Moab: 8034
Ge 19:38 a son, and called his **n.** Ben-ammi: 8034
Ge 21:3 Abraham called the **n.** of his son........ 8034
Ge 21:33 called there on the **n.** of the Lord, ... 8034
Ge 22:14 the **n.** of that place Jehovah-jireh:....... 8034
Ge 22:24 concubine, whose **n.** was Reumah, ... 8034
Ge 24:29 a brother, and his **n.** was Laban:......... 8034
Ge 25:1 a wife, and her **n.** was Keturah. 8034
Ge 25:25 and they called his **n.** Esau. 8034
Ge 25:26 his **n.** was called Jacob: and Isaac....... 8034
Ge 25:30 therefore was his **n.** called Edom. 8034
Ge 26:20 he called the **n.** of the well Esek;....... 8034
Ge 26:21 and he called the **n.** of it Sitnah. 8034
Ge 26:22 he called the **n.** of it Rehoboth; and.... 8034
Ge 26:25 called upon the **n.** of the Lord, and..... 8034
Ge 26:33 the **n.** of the city is Beer-sheba 8034
Ge 28:19 called the **n.** of that place Beth-el:....... 8034
Ge 28:19 **n.** of that city was called Luz at the.... 8034
Ge 29:16 the **n.** of the elder was Leah, and 8034
Ge 29:16 the **n.** of the younger was Rachel....... 8034
Ge 29:32 a son, and she called his **n.** Reuben: ... 8034
Ge 29:33 also: and she called his **n.** Simeon. 8034
Ge 29:34 therefore was his **n.** called Levi. 8034
Ge 29:35 she called his **n.** Judah; and left 8034
Ge 30:6 son: therefore called she his **n.** Dan.... 8034
Ge 30:8 and she called his **n.** Naphtali, ... 8034
Ge 30:11 cometh: and she called his **n.** Gad. 8034
Ge 30:13 blessed: and she called his **n.** Asher. .. 8034
Ge 30:18 and she called his **n.** Issachar. 8034
Ge 30:20 sons: and she called his **n.** Zebulun..... 8034
Ge 30:21 daughter, and called her **n.** Dinah. 8034
Ge 30:24 she called his **n.** Joseph; and said, ... 8034
Ge 31:48 was the **n.** of it called Galeed; 8034
Ge 32:2 the **n.** of that place Mahanaim. 8034
Ge 32:27 What is thy **n.**? And he said, Jacob..... 8034
Ge 32:28 **n.** shall be called no more Jacob,........ 8034
Ge 32:29 said, Tell me, I pray thee, thy **n.**......... 8034
Ge 32:29 it that thou dost ask after my **n.**? 8034
Ge 32:30 called the **n.** of the place Peniel: 8034
Ge 33:17 **n.** of the place is called Succoth, ... 8034
Ge 35:8 the **n.** of it was called Allon-bachuth.... 8034
Ge 35:10 said unto him, Thy **n.** is Jacob: 8034

Ge 35:10 thy **n.** shall not be called any more..... 8034
Ge 35:10 Jacob, but Israel shall be thy **n.**: 8034
Ge 35:10 and he called his **n.** Israel................. 8034
Ge 35:15 And Jacob called the **n.** of the place.... 8034
Ge 35:18 she called his **n.** Ben-oni: but his 8034
Ge 36:32 the **n.** of his city was Dinhabah.......... 8034
Ge 36:35 and the **n.** of his city was Avith.......... 8034
Ge 36:39 stead: and the **n.** of his city was Pau; . 8034
Ge 36:39 and his wife's **n.** was Mehetabel, the .. 8034
Ge 38:1 Adullamite, whose **n.** was Hirah......... 8034
Ge 38:2 Canaanite, whose **n.** was Shuah;........ 8034
Ge 38:3 bare a son; and he called his **n.** Er..... 8034
Ge 38:4 a son; and she called his **n.** Onan....... 8034
Ge 38:5 bare a son; and called his **n.** Shelah: ... 8034
Ge 38:6 his firstborn, whose **n.** was Tamar. 8034
Ge 38:29 therefore his **n.** was called Pharez...... 8034
Ge 38:30 hand: and his **n.** was called Zarah....... 8034
Ge 41:45 And Pharaoh called Joseph's **n.**........... 8034
Ge 41:51 Joseph called the **n.** of the firstborn.... 8034
Ge 41:52 **n.** of the second called he Ephraim:.... 8034
Ge 48:6 called after the **n.** of their brethren..... 8034
Ge 48:16 and let my **n.** be named on them, ... 8034
Ge 48:16 the **n.** of my fathers Abraham and...... 8034
Ge 50:11 the **n.** of it was called Abel-mizraim, ... 8034
Ex 1:15 which the **n.** of the one was Shiphrah,..8034
Ex 1:15 and the **n.** of the other Puah:............ 8034
Ex 2:10 son. And she called his **n.** Moses:...... 8034
Ex 2:22 son, and he called his **n.** Gershom:..... 8034
Ex 3:13 shall say to me, What is his **n.**?......... 8034
Ex 3:15 this is my **n.** for ever, and this is........ 8034
Ex 5:23 I came to Pharaoh to speak in thy **n.**,. 8034
Ex 6:3 Jacob, by the **n.** of God Almighty, ...
Ex 6:3 by my **n.** Jehovah was I not known..... 8034
Ex 9:16 and that my **n.** may be declared.......... 8034
Ex 15:3 is a man of war: the Lord is his **n.**..... 8034
Ex 15:23 the **n.** of it was called Marah............. 8034
Ex 16:31 Israel called the **n.** thereof Manna: 8034
Ex 17:7 called the **n.** of the place Massah, ... 8034
Ex 17:15 called the **n.** of it Jehovah-nissi: 8034
Ex 18:3 the **n.** of the one was Gershom; for.... 8034
Ex 18:4 And the **n.** of the other was Eliezer;... 8034
Ex 20:7 the **n.** of the Lord thy God in vain; 8034
Ex 20:7 guiltless that taketh his **n.** in vain....... 8034
Ex 20:24 in all places where I record my **n.** I.... 8034
Ex 23:13 no mention of the **n.** of other gods, ... 8034
Ex 23:21 transgressions: for my **n.** is in him. 8034
Ex 28:21 every one with his **n.** shall they be..... 8034
Ex 31:2 called by **n.** Bezaleel the son of Uri, ... 8034
Ex 33:12 I know thee by **n.**, and thou hast....... 8034
Ex 33:17 in my sight, and I know thee by **n.**...... 8034
Ex 33:19 proclaim the **n.** of the Lord before...... 8034
Ex 34:5 and proclaimed the **n.** of the Lord. 8034
Ex 34:14 the Lord, whose **n.** is Jealous, is a..... 8034
Ex 35:30 the Lord hath called by **n.** Bezaleel..... 8034
Ex 39:14 of a signet, every one with his **n.**,...... 8034
Le 18:21 shalt thou profane the **n.** of thy God: .. 8034
Le 19:12 ye shall not swear by my **n.** falsely,..... 8034
Le 19:12 shalt thou profane the **n.** of thy God: .. 8034
Le 20:3 and to profane my holy **n.**................ 8034
Le 21:6 and not profane the **n.** of their God: ... 8034
Le 22:2 that they profane not my holy **n.** in 8034
Le 22:32 Neither shall ye profane my holy **n.**;... 8034
Le 24:11 son blasphemed the **n.** of the Lord, ... 8034
Le 24:11 his mother's **n.** was Shelomith, the..... 8034
Le 24:16 that blasphemeth the **n.** of the Lord,... 8034
Le 24:16 he blasphemeth the **n.** of the Lord, ... 8034
Nu 4:32 **n.** ye shall reckon the instruments....... 8034
Nu 6:27 shall put my **n.** upon the children of.... 8034
Nu 11:3 called the **n.** of the place Taberah: 8034
Nu 11:26 camp, the **n.** of the one was Eldad, ... 8034
Nu 11:26 and the **n.** of the other Medad:............ 8034
Nu 11:34 **n.** of that place Kibroth-hattaavah:...... 8034
Nu 17:2 thou every man's **n.** upon his rod....... 8034
Nu 17:3 Aaron's **n.** upon the rod of Levi: 8034
Nu 21:3 called the **n.** of the place Hormah....... 8034
Nu 25:14 the **n.** of the Israelite that was slain,... 8034
Nu 25:15 And the **n.** of the Midianitish woman... 8034
Nu 26:46 the **n.** of the daughter of Asher was ... 8034
Nu 26:59 **n.** of Amram's wife was Jochebed,...... 8034
Nu 27:4 the **n.** of our father be done away...... 8034
Nu 32:42 and called it Nobah, after his own **n.**... 8034
De 3:14 and called them after his own **n.**, ... 8034
De 5:11 the **n.** of the Lord thy God in vain: 8034
De 5:11 guiltless that taketh his **n.** in vain....... 8034
De 6:13 serve him, and shalt swear by his **n.**... 8034
De 7:24 destroy their **n.** from under heaven: ... 8034
De 9:14 blot out their **n.** from under heaven: ... 8034
De 10:8 and to bless in his **n.**, unto this day.... 8034
De 10:20 thou cleave, and swear by his **n.**........ 8034
De 12:5 of all your tribes to put his **n.** there,... 8034
De 12:11 to cause his **n.** to dwell there;........... 8034
De 12:21 God hath chosen to put his **n.** there ... 8034
De 14:23 he shall choose to place his **n.** there, .. 8034
De 14:24 God shall choose to set his **n.** there, .. 8034
De 16:2 shall choose to place his **n.** there. 8034
De 16:6 God shall choose to place his **n.** in, ... 8034
De 16:11 hath chosen to place his **n.** there. 8034
De 18:5 to minister in the **n.** of the Lord, ... 8034
De 18:7 shall minister in the **n.** of the Lord..... 8034
De 18:19 words which he shall speak in my **n.**,... 8034
De 18:20 presume to speak a word in my **n.**,.... 8034
De 18:20 shall speak in the **n.** of other gods,..... 8034
De 18:22 speaketh in the **n.** of the Lord, if...... 8034
De 21:5 and to bless in the **n.** of the Lord; 8034
De 22:14 bring up an evil **n.** upon her, and....... 8034
De 22:19 hath brought up an evil **n.** upon a....... 8034
De 25:6 shall succeed in the **n.** of his brother .. 8034
De 25:6 that his **n.** be not put out of Israel. 8034
De 25:7 up unto his brother a **n.** in Israel, ... 8034
De 25:10 And his **n.** shall be called in Israel, ... 8034
De 26:2 shall choose to place his **n.** there. 8034
De 26:19 in praise, and in **n.**, and in honour;..... 8034
De 28:10 thou art called by the **n.** of the Lord;.. 8034
De 28:58 fear this glorious and fearful **n.**, ... 8034
De 29:20 blot out his **n.** from under heaven. 8034
De 32:3 I will publish the **n.** of the Lord: 8034
Jos 5:9 the **n.** of the place is called Gilgal....... 8034
Jos 7:9 and cut off our **n.** from the earth: 8034
Jos 7:9 what wilt thou do unto thy great **n.**?... 8034
Jos 7:26 the **n.** of that people was called, The.. 8034
Jos 9:9 of the **n.** of the Lord thy God: for....... 8034
Jos 14:15 And the **n.** of Hebron before was...... 8034
Jos 15:15 and the **n.** of Debir before was.......... 8034
Jos 19:47 Dan, after the **n.** of Dan their father... 8034
Jos 21:9 which are here mentioned by **n.**,......... 8034
Jos 23:7 make mention of the **n.** of their gods, ..8034
Jg 1:10 (now the **n.** of Hebron before was...... 8034
Jg 1:11 and the **n.** of Debir before was.......... 8034
Jg 1:17 the **n.** of the city was called Hormah... 8034
Jg 1:23 the **n.** of the city before was Luz.)..... 8034
Jg 1:26 city, and called the **n.** thereof Luz:..... 8034
Jg 1:26 which is the **n.** thereof unto this day.... 8034
Jg 2:5 called the **n.** of that place Bochim:...... 8034
Jg 8:31 son, whose **n.** he called Abimelech. 8034
Jg 13:2 the Danites, whose **n.** was Manoah; ... 8034
Jg 13:6 he was, neither told he me his **n.**:...... 8034
Jg 13:17 What is thy **n.**, that when thy sayings. 8034
Jg 13:18 Why askest thou thus after my **n.**, ... 8034
Jg 13:24 a son, and called his **n.** Samson: 8034
Jg 15:19 wherefore he called the **n.** thereof...... 8034
Jg 16:4 of Sorek, whose **n.** was Delilah.......... 8034
Jg 17:1 Ephraim, whose **n.** was Micah.......... 8034
Jg 18:29 they called the **n.** of the city Dan, ... 8034
Jg 18:29 after the **n.** of Dan their father, who... 8034
Jg 18:29 howbeit the **n.** of the city was Laish... 8034
Ru 1:2 the **n.** of the man was Elimelech, ... 8034
Ru 1:2 and the **n.** of his wife Naomi, and....... 8034
Ru 1:2 the **n.** of his two sons Mahlon and...... 8034
Ru 1:4 Moab; the **n.** of the one was Orpah, ... 8034
Ru 1:4 and the **n.** of the other Ruth: and....... 8034
Ru 2:1 of Elimelech; and his **n.** was Boaz. 8034
Ru 2:19 The man's **n.** with whom I wrought.... 8034
Ru 4:5, 10 to raise up the **n.** of the dead upon .8034
Ru 4:10 the **n.** of the dead be not cut off from..8034
Ru 4:14 that his **n.** may be famous in Israel..... 8034
Ru 4:17 women her neighbours gave it a **n.**,..... 8034
Ru 4:17 Naomi; and they called his **n.** Obed: ... 8034
1Sa 1:1 and his **n.** was Elkanah, the son of..... 8034
1Sa 1:2 the **n.** of the one was Hannah, and..... 8034
1Sa 1:2 and the **n.** of the other Peninnah:....... 8034
1Sa 1:20 bare a son, and called his **n.** Samuel, .. 8034
1Sa 7:12 and called the **n.** of it Eben-ezer, ... 8034
1Sa 8:2 Now the **n.** of his firstborn was Joel; .. 8034
1Sa 8:2 and the **n.** of his second, Abiah:......... 8034
1Sa 9:1 whose **n.** was Kish, the son of Abiel,... 8034
1Sa 9:2 he had a son, whose **n.** was Saul, a.... 8034
1Sa 14:4 and the **n.** of the one was Bozez,....... 8034
1Sa 14:4 and the **n.** of the other Seneh. 8034
1Sa 14:49 these; the **n.** of the firstborn Merab, .. 8034
1Sa 14:49 and the **n.** of the younger Michal: 8034
1Sa 14:50 the **n.** of Saul's wife was Ahinoam, ... 8034
1Sa 14:50 the **n.** of the captain of his host was... 8034
1Sa 16:3 unto me him whom I **n.** unto thee. 559
1Sa 17:12 whose **n.** was Jesse; and he had........ 8034
1Sa 17:23 the Philistine of Gath, Goliath by **n.**,... 8034
1Sa 17:45 to thee in the **n.** of the Lord of hosts, .8034
1Sa 18:30 Saul; so that his **n.** was much set by. .. 8034
1Sa 20:42 both of us in the **n.** of the Lord......... 8034
1Sa 21:7 and his **n.** was Doeg, an Edomite,...... 8034
1Sa 24:21 wilt not destroy my **n.** out of my 8034
1Sa 25:3 Now the **n.** of the man was Nabal: 8034
1Sa 25:3 and the **n.** of his wife Abigail: and...... 8034
1Sa 25:5 go to Nabal, and greet him in my **n.**: .. 8034
1Sa 25:9 to all those words in the **n.** of David,.. 8034
1Sa 25:25 even Nabal: for as his **n.** is, so is he; . 8034
1Sa 25:25 Nabal is his **n.**, and folly is with him: .. 8034
1Sa 28:8 him up, whom I shall **n.** unto thee. 559
2Sa 3:7 a concubine, whose **n.** was Rizpah,..... 8034
2Sa 4:2 the **n.** of the one was Baanah, and..... 8034
2Sa 4:2 the **n.** of the other Rechab, the 8034
2Sa 4:4 lame. And his **n.** was Mephibosheth.... 8034
2Sa 5:20 the **n.** of that place Baal-perazim........ 8034
2Sa 6:2 **n.** is called by the **n.** of the Lord of ... 8034
2Sa 6:8 called the **n.** of the place Perez-uzzah ....
2Sa 6:18 the people in the **n.** of the Lord of..... 8034
2Sa 7:9 and have made thee a great **n.**, ... 8034
2Sa 7:9 like unto the **n.** of the great men....... 8034
2Sa 7:13 He shall build an house for my **n.**,...... 8034
2Sa 7:23 to make him a **n.**, and to do for you... 8034
2Sa 7:26 thy **n.** be magnified for ever, saying,... 8034
2Sa 8:13 And David gat him a **n.** when he........ 8034
2Sa 9:2 Saul a servant whose **n.** was Ziba....... 8034
2Sa 9:12 a young son, whose **n.** was Micha. 8034
2Sa 12:24 a son, and he called his **n.** Solomon: ... 8034
2Sa 12:25 and he called his **n.** Jedidiah, ... 8034
2Sa 12:28 the city, and it be called after my **n.**... 8034
2Sa 13:1 a fair sister, whose **n.** was Tamar; 8034
2Sa 13:3 had a friend, whose **n.** was Jonadab, ... 8034
2Sa 14:7 not leave to my husband neither **n.**...... 8034
2Sa 14:27 one daughter, whose **n.** was Tamar: ... 8034
2Sa 16:5 whose **n.** was Shimei, the son of Gera: 8034
2Sa 17:25 whose **n.** was Ithra an Israelite,......... 8034
2Sa 18:18 I have no son to keep my **n.** in.......... 8034
2Sa 18:18 he called the pillar after his own **n.**:.... 8034
2Sa 20:1 man of Belial, whose **n.** was Sheba,..... 8034
2Sa 20:21 Sheba the son of Bichri by **n.**, hath 8034
2Sa 22:50 and I will sing praises unto thy **n.**. 8034
2Sa 23:18 them, and had the **n.** among three...... 8034
2Sa 23:22 had the **n.** among three mighty men. .. 8034
1Ki 1:47 God make the **n.** of Solomon better.... 8034
1Ki 1:47 of Solomon better than thy **n.**, and..... 8034
1Ki 3:2 house built unto the **n.** of the Lord,.... 8034
1Ki 5:3 house unto the **n.** of the Lord his....... 8034
1Ki 5:5 house unto the **n.** of the Lord my 8034
1Ki 5:5 he shall build an house unto my **n.**. 8034
1Ki 7:21 and called the **n.** thereof Jachin:........ 8034
1Ki 7:21 pillar, and called the **n.** thereof Boaz... 8034
1Ki 8:16 house, that thy **n.** might be therein: ... 8034
1Ki 8:17 an house for the **n.** of the Lord God... 8034
1Ki 8:18 heart to build an house unto my **n.**, ... 8034
1Ki 8:19 he shall build the house unto my **n.**. ... 8034
1Ki 8:20 an house for the **n.** of the Lord God... 8034
1Ki 8:29 thou hast said, My **n.** shall be there: .. 8034
1Ki 8:33 thee, and confess thy **n.**, and pray, ... 8034
1Ki 8:35 confess thy **n.**, and turn from their..... 8034
1Ki 8:42 (For they shall hear of thy great **n.**, ... 8034
1Ki 8:43 people of the earth may know thy **n.**, ..8034
1Ki 8:43 I have builded, is called by thy **n.**....... 8034
1Ki 8:44 house that I have built for thy **n.**: 8034
1Ki 8:48 house which I have built for thy **n.**: 8034
1Ki 9:3 built, to put my **n.** there for ever;...... 8034
1Ki 9:7 which I have hallowed for my **n.**, ... 8034
1Ki 10:1 concerning the **n.** of the Lord, she..... 8034
1Ki 11:26 whose mother's **n.** was Zeruah, a....... 8034
1Ki 11:36 have chosen me to put my **n.** there.... 8034
1Ki 13:2 the house of David, Josiah by **n.**; 8034
1Ki 14:21 tribes of Israel, to put his **n.** there. 8034
1Ki 14:21, 31 his mother's **n.** was Naamah an 8034
1Ki 15:2, 10 his mother's **n.** was Maachah, the.. 8034
1Ki 16:24 the **n.** of the city which he built,........ 8034
1Ki 16:24 after the **n.** of Shemer, owner of the .. 8034
1Ki 18:24 And call ye on the **n.** of your gods, ... 8034
1Ki 18:24 and I will call on the **n.** of the Lord: ... 8034
1Ki 18:25 call on the **n.** of your gods, but put 8034
1Ki 18:26 and called on the **n.** of Baal from 8034
1Ki 18:31 came, saying, Israel shall be thy **n.**:..... 8034
1Ki 18:32 built an altar in the **n.** of the Lord:..... 8034
1Ki 21:8 So she wrote letters in Ahab's **n.**,...... 8034

1Ki 22:16 which is true in the **n.** of the Lord? 8034
1Ki 22:42 And his mother's **n.** was Azubah 8034
2Ki 2:24 cursed them in the **n.** of the Lord. 8034
2Ki 5:11 call on the **n.** of the Lord his God, ... 8034
2Ki 8:26 And his mother's **n.** was Athaliah, ... 8034
2Ki 12:1 And his mother's **n.** was Zibiah of 8034
2Ki 14:2 his mother's **n.** was Jehoaddan of 8034
2Ki 14:7 called the **n.** of it Joktheel unto this 8034
2Ki 14:27 he would blot out the **n.** of Israel 8034
2Ki 15:2 his mother's **n.** was Jecholiah of 8034
2Ki 15:33 And his mother's **n.** was Jerusha, ... 8034
2Ki 18:2 His mother's **n.** also was Abi, the 8034
2Ki 21:1 his mother's **n.** was Hephzi-bah. 8034
2Ki 21:4 said, In Jerusalem will I put my **n.** 8034
2Ki 21:7 of Israel, will I put my **n.** for ever: 8034
2Ki 21:19 his mother's **n.** was Meshullemeth, ... 8034
2Ki 22:1 And his mother's **n.** was Jedidah, ... 8034
2Ki 23:27 which I said, My **n.** shall be there. 8034
2Ki 23:31 And his mother's **n.** was Hamutal, ... 8034
2Ki 23:34 and turned his **n.** to Jehoiakim, and 8034
2Ki 23:36 And his mother's **n.** was Zebudah, ... 8034
2Ki 24:8 And his mother's **n.** was Nehushta, ... 8034
2Ki 24:17 and changed his **n.** to Zedekiah. 8034
2Ki 24:18 And his mother's **n.** was Hamutal, ... 8034
1Ch 1:19 sons: the **n.** of the one was Peleg; 8034
1Ch 1:19 and his brother's **n.** was Joktan. 8034
1Ch 1:43 and the **n.** of his city was Dinhabah. ... 8034
1Ch 1:46 and the **n.** of his city was Avith. 8034
1Ch 1:50 and the **n.** of his city was Pai; 8034
1Ch 1:50 and his wife's **n.** was Mehetabel, ... 8034
1Ch 2:26 wife, whose **n.** was Atarah; she was ... 8034
1Ch 2:29 the **n.** of the wife of Abishur was 8034
1Ch 2:34 an Egyptian, whose **n.** was Jarha 8034
1Ch 4:3 **n.** of their sister was Hazelelponi: 8034
1Ch 4:9 and his mother called his **n.** Jabez, ... 8034
1Ch 4:41 these written by **n.** came in the days .. 8034
1Ch 7:15 whose sister's **n.** was Maachah;) 8034
1Ch 7:15 the **n.** of the second...Zelophehad: 8034
1Ch 7:16 son, and she called his **n.** Peresh; 8034
1Ch 7:16 the **n.** of his brother was Sheresh; 8034
1Ch 7:23 he called his **n.** Beriah, because it 8034
1Ch 8:29 whose wife's **n.** was Maachah: 8034
1Ch 9:35 whose wife's **n.** was Maachah: 8034
1Ch 11:20 them, and had a **n.** among the three. .. 8034
1Ch 11:24 the **n.** among the three mighties. 8034
1Ch 12:31 which were expressed by **n.**, to 8034
1Ch 13:6 cherubims, whose **n.** is called on it. 8034
1Ch 14:11 the **n.** of that place Baal-perazim. 8034
1Ch 16:2 the people in the **n.** of the Lord. 8034
1Ch 16:8 call upon his **n.**, make known his 8034
1Ch 16:10 Glory ye in his holy **n.**: let the heart ... 8034
1Ch 16:29 the Lord the glory due unto his **n.**: 8034
1Ch 16:35 we may give thanks to thy holy **n.**, ... 8034
1Ch 16:41 who were expressed by **n.**, to give 8034
1Ch 17:8 thee a **n.** like the **n.** of the great men. 8034
1Ch 17:21 to make thee a **n.** of greatness and 8034
1Ch 17:24 thy **n.** may be magnified for ever, ... 8034
1Ch 21:19 he spake in the **n.** of the Lord. 8034
1Ch 22:7 unto the **n.** of the Lord my God: 8034
1Ch 22:8 shalt not build an house unto my **n.**, ... 8034
1Ch 22:9 for his **n.** shall be Solomon, and I 8034
1Ch 22:10 He shall built an house for my **n.**; 8034
1Ch 22:19 is to be built to the **n.** of the Lord. 8034
1Ch 23:13 him, and to bless in his **n.** for ever. 8034
1Ch 28:3 shalt not built an house for my **n.**, ... 8034
1Ch 29:13 thee, and praise thy glorious **n.**. 8034
1Ch 29:16 build thee an house for thine holy **n.** ... 8034
2Ch 2:1 an house for the **n.** of the Lord, ... 8034
2Ch 2:4 build an house to the **n.** of the Lord ... 8034
2Ch 3:17 **n.** of that on the right hand Jachin, ... 8034
2Ch 3:17 and the **n.** of that on the left Boaz. 8034
2Ch 6:5 house in, that my **n.** might be there; .. 8034
2Ch 6:6 Jerusalem,...my **n.** might be there; 8034
2Ch 6:7 an house for the **n.** of the Lord God ... 8034
2Ch 6:8 heart to build an house for my **n.**, ... 8034
2Ch 6:9 he shall build the house for my **n.**. 8034
2Ch 6:10 the house for the **n.** of the Lord God.. 8034
2Ch 6:20 that thou wouldest put thy **n.** there; ... 8034
2Ch 6:24 and shall return and confess thy **n.**, ... 8034
2Ch 6:26 and confess thy **n.**, and turn from 8034
2Ch 6:33 people of the earth may know thy **n.**, ..8034
2Ch 6:33 I have built is called by thy **n.**. 8034
2Ch 6:34 house which I have built for thy **n.**; 8034
2Ch 6:38 house which I have built for thy **n.**: 8034
2Ch 7:14 people, which are called by my **n.**, ... 8034
2Ch 7:16 that my **n.** may be there for ever: 8034
2Ch 7:20 which I have sanctified for my **n.**, ... 8034
2Ch 12:13 tribes of Israel, to put his **n.** there. 8034
2Ch 12:13 And his mother's **n.** was Naamah 8034
2Ch 13:2 His mother's name also was Michaiah. ..8034
2Ch 14:11 and in thy **n.** we go against this 8034
2Ch 18:15 truth to me in the **n.** of the Lord? 8034
2Ch 20:8 thee a sanctuary therein for thy **n.**, ... 8034
2Ch 20:9 presence, (for thy **n.** is in this house,) .8034
2Ch 20:26 the **n.** of the same place was called, ... 8034
2Ch 20:31 And his mother's **n.** was Azubah 8034
2Ch 22:2 His mother's **n.** also was Athaliah. 8034
2Ch 24:1 His mother's **n.** also was Zibiah of 8034
2Ch 25:1 And his mother's **n.** was Jehoaddan. 8034
2Ch 26:3 His mother's **n.** also was Jecoliah of 8034
2Ch 26:8 his **n.** spread abroad even to the 8034
2Ch 26:15 And his **n.** spread far abroad; for 8034
2Ch 27:1 His mother's **n.** also was Jerushah, ... 8034
2Ch 28:9 Lord was there, whose **n.** was Oded: . 8034
2Ch 28:15 which were expressed by **n.** rose up, .. 8034
2Ch 29:1 And his mother's **n.** was Abijah, ... 8034
2Ch 31:19 the men that were expressed by **n.**, ... 8034
2Ch 33:4 Jerusalem shall my **n.** be for ever. 8034
2Ch 33:7 of Israel, will I put my **n.** for ever: 8034
2Ch 33:18 spake to him in the **n.** of the Lord 8034
2Ch 36:4 and turned his **n.** to Jehoiakim. 8034
Ezr 2:61 Gileadite,...was called after their **n.**: ... 8034
Ezr 5:1 in the **n.** of the God of Israel, even 8036
Ezr 5:14 one, whose **n.** was Sheshbazzar, ... 8036
Ezr 6:12 hath caused his **n.** to dwell there 8036
Ezr 8:20 all of them were expressed by **n.**. 8034
Ne 1:9 I have chosen to set my **n.** there. 8034
Ne 1:11 servants, who desire to fear thy **n.**: 8034
Ne 7:63 to wife, and was called after their **n.** ... 8034
Ne 9:5 and blessed be thy glorious **n.**, ... 8034
Ne 9:7 and gavest him the **n.** of Abraham; 8034
Ne 9:10 So didst thou get thee a **n.**, as it is 8034
Es 2:5 whose **n.** was Mordecai, the son of 8034
Es 2:14 her, and that she were called by **n.**. ... 8034
Es 2:22 the king thereof in Mordecai's **n.** 8034
Es 3:12 in the **n.** of king Ahasuerus was it 8034
Es 8:8 as it liketh you, in the king's **n.**, ... 8034
Es 8:8 which is written in the king's **n.**, ... 8034
Es 8:10 he wrote in the king Ahasuerus' **n.**, ... 8034
Es 9:26 days Purim after the **n.** of Pur. 8034
Job 1:1 whose **n.** was Job; and that man 8034
Job 1:21 away; blessed be the **n.** of the Lord. .. 8034
Job 18:17 he shall have no **n.** in the street. 8034
Job 42:14 called the **n.** of the first, Jemima; 8034
Job 42:14 and the **n.** of the second, Kezia; 8034
Job 42:14 the **n.** of the third, Keren-happuch. 8034
Ps 5:11 them also that love thy **n.** be joyful 8034
Ps 7:17 will sing praise to the **n.** of the Lord ... 8034
Ps 8:1,9 excellent is thy **n.** in all the earth! 8034
Ps 9:2 I will sing praise to thy **n.**, O thou 8034
Ps 9:5 thou hast put out their **n.** for ever. 8034
Ps 9:10 they that know thy **n.** will put their 8034
Ps 18:49 and sing praises unto thy **n.**. 8034
Ps 20:1 **n.** of the God of Jacob defend thee; 8034
Ps 20:5 in the **n.** of our God we will set up 8034
Ps 20:7 we will remember the **n.** of the Lord .. 8034
Ps 22:22 declare thy **n.** unto my brethren: 8034
Ps 29:2 the Lord the glory due unto his **n.**; 8034
Ps 33:21 we have trusted in his holy **n.**. 8034
Ps 34:3 me, and let us exalt his **n.** together. ... 8034
Ps 41:5 When shall he die, and his **n.** perish? .. 8034
Ps 44:5 through thy **n.** will we tread them 8034
Ps 44:8 day long, and praise thy **n.** for ever. ... 8034
Ps 44:20 we have forgotten the **n.** of our God,.. 8034
Ps 45:17 will make thy **n.** to be remembered 8034
Ps 48:10 According to thy **n.**, O God, so is 8034
Ps 52:9 I will wait on thy **n.**; for it is good 8034
Ps 54:1 Save me, O God, by thy **n.**, and 8034
Ps 54:6 I will praise thy **n.**, O Lord; for it is ... 8034
Ps 61:5 heritage of those that fear thy **n.**. 8034
Ps 61:8 I sing praise unto thy **n.** for ever, ... 8034
Ps 63:4 I will lift up my hands in thy **n.** 8034
Ps 66:2 Sing forth the honour of his **n.**: 8034
Ps 66:4 unto thee; they shall sing to thy **n.** 8034
Ps 68:4 unto God, sing praises to his **n.**: 8034
Ps 68:4 upon the heavens by his **n.** Jah, ... 8034
Ps 69:30 will praise the **n.** of God with a song, ..8034
Ps 69:36 that love his **n.** shall dwell therein. 8034
Ps 72:17 His **n.** shall endure for ever: 8034
Ps 72:17 his **n.** shall be continued as long as 8034
Ps 72:19 blessed be his glorious **n.** for ever: 8034
Ps 74:7 the dwelling place of thy **n.** to the 8034
Ps 74:10 enemy blaspheme thy **n.** for ever? 8034
Ps 74:18 people have blasphemed thy **n.**. 8034
Ps 74:21 let the poor and needy praise thy **n.**. .. 8034
Ps 75:1 thy **n.** is near thy wondrous works 8034
Ps 76:1 God known: his **n.** is great in Israel. ... 8034
Ps 79:6 that have not called upon thy **n.** 8034
Ps 79:9 salvation, for the glory of thy **n.**: 8034
Ps 80:18 us, and we will call upon thy **n.**. 8034
Ps 83:4 that the **n.** of Israel be no more in 8034
Ps 83:16 shame; that they may seek thy **n.**, ... 8034
Ps 83:18 thou, whose **n.** alone is Jehovah, ... 8034
Ps 86:9 O Lord; and shall glorify thy **n.** 8034
Ps 86:11 truth: unite my heart to fear thy **n.**. ... 8034
Ps 86:12 I will glorify thy **n.** for evermore. 8034
Ps 89:12 and Hermon shall rejoice in thy **n.** 8034
Ps 89:16 In thy **n.** shall they rejoice all the 8034
Ps 89:24 in my **n.** shall his horn be exalted. 8034
Ps 91:14 high, because he hath known my **n.**. ... 8034
Ps 92:1 to sing praises unto thy **n.**, O most 8034
Ps 96:2 Sing unto the Lord, bless his **n.**; 8034
Ps 96:8 the Lord the glory due unto his **n.**: 8034
Ps 99:3 praise thy great and terrible **n.**; 8034
Ps 99:6 among them that call upon his **n.**; 8034
Ps 100:4 thankful unto him, and bless his **n.**. 8034
Ps 102:15 shall fear the **n.** of the Lord, and 8034
Ps 102:21 declare the **n.** of the Lord in Zion, ... 8034
Ps 103:1 that is within me, bless his holy **n.**. 8034
Ps 105:1 call upon his **n.**: make known his 8034
Ps 105:3 Glory ye in his holy **n.**: let the 8034
Ps 106:47 to give thanks unto thy holy **n.**, and ... 8034
Ps 109:13 following let their **n.** be blotted out. 8034
Ps 111:9 ever: holy and reverend is his **n.**. 8034
Ps 113:1 Lord, praise the **n.** of the Lord. 8034
Ps 113:2 Blessed be the **n.** of the Lord from 8034
Ps 113:3 same the Lord's **n.** is to be praised. ... 8034
Ps 115:1 but unto thy **n.** give glory, for thy 8034
Ps 116:4 called I upon the **n.** of the Lord; 8034
Ps 116:13 and call upon the **n.** of the Lord. 8034
Ps 116:17 and will call upon the **n.** of the Lord. .. 8034
Ps 118:10 in the **n.** of the Lord will I destroy 8034
Ps 118:11, 12 the **n.** of the Lord I will destroy 8034
Ps 118:26 that cometh in the **n.** of the Lord: 8034
Ps 119:55 I have remembered thy **n.**, O Lord, ... 8034
Ps 119:132 to do unto those that love thy **n.**. 8034
Ps 122:4 give thanks unto the **n.** of the Lord. ... 8034
Ps 124:8 Our help is in the **n.** of the Lord, ... 8034
Ps 129:8 we bless you in the **n.** of the Lord. 8034
Ps 135:1 Praise ye the **n.** of the Lord; praise 8034
Ps 135:3 sing praises unto his **n.**; for it is 8034
Ps 135:13 Thy **n.**, O Lord, endureth for ever; 8034
Ps 138:2 praise thy **n.** for thy lovingkindness 8034
Ps 138:2 magnified thy word above all thy **n.**. ... 8034
Ps 139:20 and thine enemies take thy **n.** in vain. ....
Ps 140:13 shall give thanks unto thy **n.**: 8034
Ps 142:7 of prison, that I may praise thy **n.**: 8034
Ps 145:1 I will bless thy **n.** for ever and ever. .. 8034
Ps 145:2 and I will praise thy **n.** for ever and 8034
Ps 145:21 let all flesh bless his holy **n.** for ever .. 8034
Ps 148:5, 13 them praise the **n.** of the Lord: 8034
Ps 148:13 for his **n.** alone is excellent; his 8034
Ps 149:3 Let them praise his **n.** in the dance: ... 8034
Pr 10:7 but the **n.** of the wicked shall rot. 8034
Pr 18:10 **n.** of the Lord is a strong tower: 8034
Pr 21:24 Proud and haughty scorner is his **n.**, ... 8034
Pr 22:1 A good **n.** is rather to be chosen 8034
Pr 30:4 is his **n.**, and what is his son's **n.**, ... 8034
Pr 30:9 and take the **n.** of my God in vain. 8034
Ec 6:4 and his **n.** shall be covered with 8034
Ec 7:1 A good **n.** is better than precious 8034
Ca 1:3 thy **n.** is as ointment poured forth, ... 8034
Isa 4:1 only let us be called by thy **n.**, to 8034
Isa 7:14 son, and shall call his **n.** Immanuel. 8034
Isa 8:3 Call his **n.** Maher-shalal-hash-baz. 8034
Isa 9:6 his **n.** shall be called Wonderful, ... 8034
Isa 12:4 Praise the Lord, call upon his **n.**, ... 8034
Isa 12:4 mention that his **n.** is exalted. 8034
Isa 14:22 cut off from Babylon the **n.**, and 8034
Isa 18:7 to the place of the **n.** of the Lord. 8034
Isa 24:15 even the **n.** of the Lord God of 8034
Isa 25:1 will exalt thee, I will praise thy **n.**; 8034
Isa 26:8 the desire of our soul is to thy **n.**, ... 8034
Isa 26:13 will we make mention of thy **n.** 8034
Isa 29:23 of him, they shall sanctify my **n.**, ... 8034
Isa 30:27 the **n.** of the Lord cometh from far, ... 8034
Isa 41:25 the sun shall he call upon my **n.**: 8034
Isa 42:8 I am the Lord: that is my **n.**: and 8034
Isa 43:1 thee, I have called thee by thy **n.**; 8034
Isa 43:7 every one that is called by my **n.**: 8034
Isa 44:5 shall call himself by the **n.** of Jacob; 8034

Isa	44:5	himself by the **n.** of Israel	8034
Isa	45:3	the Lord, which call thee by thy **n.**,	8034
Isa	45:4	I have even called thee by thy **n.**:	8034
Isa	47:4	the Lord of hosts is his **n.**, the	8034
Isa	48:1	are called by the **n.** of Israel, and	8034
Isa	48:1	which swear by the **n.** of the Lord,	8034
Isa	48:2	Israel; The Lord of hosts is his **n.**	8034
Isa	48:11	for how should my **n.** be polluted? and	
Isa	48:19	his **n.** should not have been cut off	8034
Isa	49:1	hath he made mention of my **n.**.	8034
Isa	50:10	let him trust in the **n.** of the Lord,	8034
Isa	51:15	roared: The Lord of hosts is his **n.**	8034
Isa	52:5	and my **n.** continually every day is	8034
Isa	52:6	my people shall know my **n.**:	8034
Isa	54:5	the Lord of hosts is his **n.**; and thy	8034
Isa	55:13	and it shall be to the Lord for a **n.**,	8034
Isa	56:5	and a **n.** better than of sons and of	8034
Isa	56:5	I will give them an everlasting **n.**,	8034
Isa	56:6	him, and to love the **n.** of the Lord,	8034
Isa	57:15	eternity, whose **n.** is Holy; I dwell	8034
Isa	59:19	shall they fear the **n.** of the Lord	8034
Isa	60:9	unto the **n.** of the Lord thy God,	8034
Isa	62:2	thou shalt be called by a new **n.**,	8034
Isa	62:2	the mouth of the Lord shall **n.**.	8034
Isa	63:12	to make himself an everlasting **n.**?	8034
Isa	63:14	to make thyself a glorious **n.**.	8034
Isa	63:16	redeemer; thy **n.** is from everlasting	8034
Isa	63:19	they were not called by thy **n.**	8034
Isa	64:2	thy **n.** known to thine adversaries,	8034
Isa	64:7	is none that calleth upon thy **n.**,	8034
Isa	65:1	nation that was not called by my **n.**.	8034
Isa	65:15	leave your **n.** for a curse unto my	8034
Isa	65:15	and call his servants by another **n.**:	8034
Isa	66:22	shall your seed and your **n.** remain.	8034
Jer	3:17	unto it, to the **n.** of the Lord, to	8034
Jer	7:10, 11	house, which is called by my **n.**,	8034
Jer	7:12	where I set my **n.** at the first, and	8034
Jer	7:14	house, which is called by my **n.**,	8034
Jer	7:30	the house which is called by my **n.**,	8034
Jer	10:6	great, and thy **n.** is great in might	8034
Jer	10:16	The Lord of hosts is his **n.**.	8034
Jer	10:25	the families that call not on thy **n.**:	8034
Jer	11:16	The Lord called thy **n.**, A green	8034
Jer	11:19	his **n.** may be no more remembered.	8034
Jer	11:21	Prophesy not in the **n.** of the Lord,	8034
Jer	12:16	of my people, to swear by my **n.**,	8034
Jer	13:11	unto me for a people, and for a **n.**,	8034
Jer	14:9	and we are called by thy **n.**; leave	8034
Jer	14:14	prophets prophesy lies in my **n.**:	8034
Jer	14:15	prophets that prophesy in my **n.**,	8034
Jer	15:16	for I am called by thy **n.**, O Lord	8034
Jer	16:21	shall know that my **n.** is The Lord.	8034
Jer	20:3	Lord hath not called thy **n.** Pashur,	8034
Jer	20:9	him, nor speak any more in his **n.**.	8034
Jer	23:6	his **n.** whereby he shall be called,	8034
Jer	23:25	that prophesy lies in my **n.**, saying,	8034
Jer	23:27	to forget my **n.** by their dreams	8034
Jer	23:27	have forgotten my **n.** for Baal.	8034
Jer	25:29	the city which is called by my **n.**,	8034
Jer	26:9	prophesied in the **n.** of the Lord,	8034
Jer	26:16	spoken to us in the **n.** of the Lord	8034
Jer	26:20	prophesied in the **n.** of the Lord,	8034
Jer	27:15	yet they prophesy a lie in my **n.**;	8034
Jer	29:9	prophesy falsely unto you in my **n.**:	8034
Jer	29:21	prophesy a lie unto you in my **n.**;	8034
Jer	29:23	have spoken lying words in my **n.**,	8034
Jer	29:25	hast sent letters in thy **n.** unto all	8034
Jer	31:35	roar; The Lord of hosts is his **n.**:	8034
Jer	32:18	God, The Lord of hosts, is his **n.**,	8034
Jer	32:20	and hast made thee a **n.**, as at this	8034
Jer	32:34	the house which is called by my **n.**,	8034
Jer	33:2	to establish it; the Lord is his **n.**;	8034
Jer	33:9	it shall be to me a **n.** of joy, a praise	8034
Jer	33:16	is the **n.** wherewith she shall be called,	
Jer	34:15	house which is called by my **n.**:	8034
Jer	34:16	But ye turned and polluted my **n.**,	8034
Jer	37:13	was there, whose **n.** was Irijah,	8034
Jer	44:16	unto us in the **n.** of the Lord, we	8034
Jer	44:26	I have sworn, by my great **n.**, saith	8034
Jer	44:26	that my **n.** shall no more be named	8034
Jer	46:18	King, whose **n.** is the Lord of hosts,	8034
Jer	48:15	King, whose **n.** is the Lord of hosts,	8034
Jer	48:17	all ye that know his **n.**, say, How is	8034
Jer	50:34	strong; the Lord of hosts is his **n.**:	8034
Jer	51:19	the Lord of hosts is his **n.**.	8034
Jer	51:57	King, whose **n.** is the Lord of hosts.	8034
Jer	52:1	his mother's **n.** was Hamutal the	8034
La	3:55	I called upon thy **n.**, O Lord, out of	8034
Eze	20:29	And the **n.** thereof is called Bamah	8034
Eze	20:39	but pollute ye my holy **n.** no more	8034
Eze	24:2	man, write thee the **n.** of the day,	8034
Eze	36:20	they went, they profaned my holy **n.**,	8034
Eze	36:21	But I had pity for mine holy **n.**,	8034
Eze	36:23	I will sanctify my great **n.**, which	8034
Eze	39:7	So will I make my holy **n.** known in	8034
Eze	39:7	them pollute my holy **n.** any more:	8034
Eze	39:16	**n.** of the city shall be Hamonah.	8034
Eze	39:25	and will be jealous for my holy **n.**;	8034
Eze	43:7	my holy **n.**, shall the house of Israel	8034
Eze	43:8	even defiled my holy **n.** by their	8034
Eze	48:35	**n.** of the city from that day shall be	8034
Da	1:7	unto Daniel the **n.** of Belteshazzar;	8034
Da	2:20	Blessed be the **n.** of God for ever	8036
Da	2:26	Daniel, whose **n.** was Belteshazzar,	8036
Da	4:8	me, whose **n.** was Belteshazzar,	8036
Da	4:8	according to the **n.** of my god, and	8036
Da	4:19	Daniel, whose **n.** was Belteshazzar,	8036
Da	9:6	spake in thy **n.** to our kings, our	8034
Da	9:18	the city which is called by thy **n.**:	8034
Da	9:19	and thy people are called by thy **n.**	8034
Da	10:1	whose **n.** was called Belteshazzar;	8034
Ho	1:4	said unto him, Call his **n.** Jezreel;	8034
Ho	1:6	unto him, Call her **n.** Lo-ruhamah:	8034
Ho	1:9	said God, Call his **n.** Lo-ammi:	8034
Ho	2:17	more be remembered by their **n.**.	8034
Joe	2:26	praise the **n.** of the Lord your God,	8034
Joe	2:32	shall call on the **n.** of the Lord shall	8034
Am	2:7	same maid, to profane my holy **n.**:	8034
Am	4:13	Lord, The God of hosts, is his **n.**	8034
Am	5:8	of the earth: The Lord is his **n.**:	8034
Am	5:27	Lord, whose **n.** is the God of hosts.	8034
Am	6:10	make mention of the **n.** of the Lord.	8034
Am	9:6	of the earth: The Lord is his **n.**.	8034
Am	9:12	heathen, which are called by my **n.**,	8034
Mic	4:5	walk every one in the **n.** of his god,	8034
Mic	4:5	we will walk in the **n.** of the Lord	8034
Mic	5:4	in the majesty of the **n.** of the Lord.	8034
Mic	6:9	the man of wisdom shall see thy **n.**:	8034
Na	1:14	that no more of thy **n.** be sown: out	8034
Zep	1:4	the **n.** of the Chemarims with the	8034
Zep	3:9	all call upon the **n.** of the Lord,	8034
Zep	3:12	shall trust in the **n.** of the Lord.	8034
Zep	3:20	I will make you a **n.** and a praise	8034
Zec	5:4	him that sweareth falsely by my **n.**:	8034
Zec	6:12	the man whose **n.** is The Branch;	8034
Zec	10:12	shall walk up and down in his **n.**,	8034
Zec	13:3	speakest lies in the **n.** of the Lord:	8034
Zec	13:9	they shall call on my **n.**, and I will	8034
Zec	14:9	there be one Lord, and his **n.** one.	8034
Mal	1:6	you, O priests, that despise my **n.**.	8034
Mal	1:6	Wherein have we despised thy **n.**?	8034
Mal	1:11	same my **n.** shall be great among	8034
Mal	1:11	incense shall be offered unto my **n.**,	8034
Mal	1:11	for my **n.** shall be great among the	8034
Mal	1:14	and my **n.** is dreadful among the	8034
Mal	2:2	to heart, to give glory unto my **n.**,	8034
Mal	2:5	me, and was afraid before my **n.**.	8034
Mal	3:16	Lord, and that thought upon his **n.**	8034
Mal	4:2	But unto you that fear my **n.** shall	8034
Mt	1:21	and thou shalt call his **n.** Jesus	*3686*
Mt	1:23	they shall call his **n.** Emmanuel,	*3686*
Mt	1:25	son: and he called his **n.** Jesus	*3686*
Mt	6:9	**art in heaven, Hallowed be thy n.**	*3686*
Mt	7:22	**have we not prophesied in thy n.?**	*3686*
Mt	7:22	**and in thy n. have cast out devils?**	*3686*
Mt	7:22	**in thy n. done many wonderful**	*3686*
Mt	10:41	**a prophet in the n. of a prophet**	*3686*
Mt	10:41	**man in the n. of a righteous man**	*3686*
Mt	10:42	**water only in the n. of a disciple,**	*3686*
Mt	12:21	in his **n.** shall the Gentiles trust.	*3686*
Mt	18:5	**one such little child in my n.**	*3686*
Mt	18:20	**are gathered together in my n.,**	*3686*
Mt	21:9	that cometh in the **n.** of the Lord;	*3686*
Mt	23:39	**that cometh in the n. of the Lord**	*3686*
Mt	24:5	**many shall come in my n., saying,**	*3686*
Mt	27:32	a man of Cyrene, Simon by **n.**: him	*3686*
Mt	28:19	**them in the n. of the Father, and**	*3686*
Mk	5:9	**What is thy n.?** And he answered,	*3686*
Mk	5:9	My **n.** is Legion: for we are many.	*3686*
Mk	5:22	of the synagogue, Jairus by **n.**;	*3686*
Mk	6:14	(for his **n.** was spread abroad:) and	*3686*
Mk	9:37	**one of such children in my n.,**	*3686*
Mk	9:38	saw one casting out devils in thy **n.**,	*3686*
Mk	9:39	**which shall do a miracle in my n.,**	*3686*
Mk	9:41	**a cup of water to drink in my n.,**	*3686*
Mk	11:9	that cometh in the **n.** of the Lord:	*3686*
Mk	11:10	that cometh in the **n.** of the Lord:	*3686*
Mk	13:6	**many shall come in my n., saying,**	*3686*
Mk	16:17	**In my n. shall they cast out devils;**	*3686*
Lu	1:5	of Aaron, and her **n.** was Elisabeth.	*3686*
Lu	1:13	son, and thou shalt call his **n.** John.	*3686*
Lu	1:27	to a man whose **n.** was Joseph, of	*3686*
Lu	1:27	David; and the virgin's **n.** was Mary.	*3686*
Lu	1:31	a son, and shalt call his **n.** Jesus.	*3686*
Lu	1:49	me great things; and holy is his **n.**.	*3686*
Lu	1:59	Zacharias, after the **n.** of his father.	*3686*
Lu	1:61	thy kindred that is called by this **n.**	*3686*
Lu	1:63	and wrote, saying, His **n.** is John.	*3686*
Lu	2:21	the child, his **n.** was called Jesus,	*3686*
Lu	2:25	Jerusalem, whose **n.** was Simeon;	*3686*
Lu	6:22	**cast out your n. as evil, for the**	*3686*
Lu	8:30	asked him, saying, **What is thy n.?**	*3686*
Lu	9:48	**this child in my n. receiveth**	*3686*
Lu	9:49	saw one casting out devils in thy **n.**;	*3686*
Lu	10:17	are subject unto us through thy **n.**	*3686*
Lu	11:2	**art in heaven, Hallowed be thy n.**	*3686*
Lu	13:35	**that cometh in the n. of the Lord**	*3686*
Lu	19:38	that cometh in the **n.** of the Lord:	*3686*
Lu	21:8	**many shall come in my n., saying,**	*3686*
Lu	24:18	one of them, whose **n.** was Cleopas,	*3686*
Lu	24:47	**be preached in his n. among all**	*3686*
Joh	1:6	sent from God, whose **n.** was John.	*3686*
Joh	1:12	even to them that believe on his **n.**:	*3686*
Joh	2:23	feast day, many believed in his **n.**,	*3686*
Joh	3:18	**not believed in the n. of the only**	*3686*
Joh	5:43	**I am come in my Father's n., and**	*3686*
Joh	5:43	**another shall come in his own n.,**	*3686*
Joh	10:3	**he calleth his own sheep by n.,**	*3686*
Joh	10:25	**works that I do in my Father's n.,**	*3686*
Joh	12:13	that cometh in the **n.** of the Lord.	*3686*
Joh	12:28	**Father, glorify thy n..** Then came	*3686*
Joh	14:13	**whatsoever ye shall ask in my n.,**	*3686*
Joh	14:14	**If ye shall ask any thing in my n.,**	*3686*
Joh	14:26	**the Father will send in my n.,**	*3686*
Joh	15:16	**shall ask of the Father in my n.,**	*3686*
Joh	16:23	**shall ask the Father in my n., he**	*3686*
Joh	16:24	**have ye asked nothing in my n.:**	*3686*
Joh	16:26	**At that day ye shall ask in my n.:**	*3686*
Joh	17:6	**manifested thy n. unto the men**	*3686*
Joh	17:11	**keep through thine own n. those**	*3686*
Joh	17:12	**in the world, I kept them in thy n.:**	*3686*
Joh	17:26	**I have declared unto them thy n.,**	*3686*
Joh	18:10	ear. The servant's **n.** was Malchus.	*3686*
Joh	20:31	ye might have life through his **n.**	*3686*
Ac	2:21	shall call on the **n.** of the Lord shall	*3686*
Ac	2:38	one of you in the **n.** of Jesus Christ	*3686*
Ac	3:6	the **n.** of Jesus Christ of Nazareth	*3686*
Ac	3:16	his **n.** through faith in his **n.** hath	*3686*
Ac	4:7	or by what **n.**, have ye done this?	*3686*
Ac	4:10	the **n.** of Jesus Christ of Nazareth,	*3686*
Ac	4:12	there is none other **n.** under heaven	*3686*
Ac	4:17	henceforth to no man in this **n.**.	*3686*
Ac	4:18	at all nor teach in the **n.** of Jesus.	*3686*
Ac	4:30	by the **n.** of thy holy child Jesus.	*3686*
Ac	5:28	that ye should not teach in this **n.**?	*3686*
Ac	5:40	should not speak in the **n.** of Jesus,	*3686*
Ac	5:41	worthy to suffer shame for his **n.**.	*3686*
Ac	7:58	man's feet, whose **n.** was Saul.	*2564*
Ac	8:12	of God, and the **n.** of Jesus Christ,	*3686*
Ac	8:16	baptized in the **n.** of the Lord Jesus.)	*3686*
Ac	9:14	to bind all that call on thy **n.**.	*3686*
Ac	9:15	**to bear my n. before the Gentiles,**	*3686*
Ac	9:21	called on this **n.** in Jerusalem,	*3686*
Ac	9:27	at Damascus in the **n.** of Jesus.	*3686*
Ac	9:29	boldly in the **n.** of the Lord Jesus,	*3686*
Ac	10:43	that through his **n.** whosoever	*3686*
Ac	10:48	to be baptized in the **n.** of the Lord.	*3686*
Ac	13:6	a Jew, whose **n.** was Bar-jesus:	*3686*
Ac	13:8	(for so is his **n.** by interpretation)	*3686*
Ac	15:14	take out of them a people for his **n.**	*3686*
Ac	15:17	upon whom my **n.** is called, saith	*3686*
Ac	15:26	lives for the **n.** of our Lord Jesus	*3686*
Ac	16:18	in the **n.** of Jesus Christ to come out	*3686*
Ac	19:5	baptized in the **n.** of the Lord Jesus.	*3686*
Ac	19:13	spirits the **n.** of the Lord Jesus,	*3686*
Ac	19:17	**n.** of the Lord Jesus was magnified.	*3686*
Ac	21:13	Jerusalem for the **n.** of the Lord	*3686*
Ac	22:16	sins, calling on the **n.** of the Lord.	*3686*
Ac	26:9	things contrary to the **n.** of Jesus of	*3686*
Ac	28:7	the island, whose **n.** was Publius;	*3686*
Ro	1:5	faith among all nations, for his **n.**:	*3686*

Ref		Context	No.
Ro	2:24	the n. of God is blasphemed among	3686
Ro	9:17	and that my n. might be declared	3686
Ro	10:13	shall call upon the n. of the Lord	3686
Ro	15:9	the Gentiles, and sing unto thy n..	3686
1Co	1:2	call upon the n. of Jesus Christ	3686
1Co	1:10	by the n. of our Lord Jesus Christ,	3686
1Co	1:13	were ye baptized in the n. of Paul?	3686
1Co	1:15	that I had baptized in mine own n..	3686
1Co	5:4	In the n. of our Lord Jesus Christ,	3686
1Co	6:11	in the n. of the Lord Jesus, and by	3686
Eph	1:21	and every n. that is named, not	3686
Eph	5:20	in the n. of our Lord Jesus Christ;	3686
Php	2:9	him a n. which is above every n.:	3686
Php	2:10	That at the n. of Jesus every knee	3686
Col	3:17	do all in the n. of the Lord Jesus,	3686
2Th	1:12	That the n. of our Lord Jesus	3686
2Th	3:6	in the n. of our Lord Jesus Christ,	3686
1Ti	6:1	that the n. of God and his doctrine	3686
2Ti	2:19	one that nameth the n. of Christ	3686
Heb	1:4	a more excellent n. than they	3686
Heb	2:12	declare thy n. unto my brethren,	3686
Heb	6:10	which ye have shewed toward his n.,	3686
Heb	13:15	of our lips giving thanks to his n..	3686
Jas	2:7	n. by the which ye are called?	3686
Jas	5:10	have spoken in the n. of the Lord,	3686
Jas	5:14	him with oil in the n. of the Lord:	3686
1Pe	4:14	be reproached for the n. of Christ,	3686
1Jo	3:23	believe on the n. of his Son Jesus	3686
1Jo	5:13	believe on the n. of the Son of God;	3686
1Jo	5:13	believe on the n. of the Son of God.	3686
3Jo	14	thee. Greet the friends by n..	3686
Re	2:13	**thou holdest fast my n., and hast**	3686
Re	2:17	**and in the stone a new n. written,**	3686
Re	3:1	**thou hast a n. that thou livest,**	3686
Re	3:5	**not blot out his n. out of the book**	3686
Re	3:5	**confess his n. before my Father,**	3686
Re	3:8	**and hast not denied my n..**	3686
Re	3:12	**n. of my God, and the n. of the**	3686
Re	3:12	**I will write upon him my new n.**	3686
Re	6:8	his n. that sat on him was Death,	3686
Re	8:11	n. of the star is called Wormwood:	3686
Re	9:11	whose n. in the Hebrew tongue is	3686
Re	9:11	Greek tongue hath his n. Apollyon.	3686
Re	11:18	and them that fear thy n., small and	3686
Re	13:1	upon his heads the n. of blasphemy.	3686
Re	13:6	against God, to blaspheme his n.,	3686
Re	13:17	had the mark, or the n. of the beast,	3686
Re	13:17	the beast, or the number of his n.	3686
Re	14:1	having his Father's n. written in	3686
Re	14:11	receiveth the mark of his n..	3686
Re	15:2	and over the number of his n.,	3686
Re	15:4	O Lord, and glorify thy n.? for thou	3686
Re	16:9	and blasphemed the n. of God,	3686
Re	17:5	upon her forehead was a n. written,	3686
Re	19:12	and he had a n. written, that no	3686
Re	19:13	his n. is called The Word of God.	3686
Re	19:16	and on his thigh a n. written, King	3686
Re	22:4	his n. shall be in their foreheads.	3686

NAMED See also SURNAMED.

Ref		Context	No.
Ge	23:16	which he had n. in the audience	1696
Ge	27:36	Is not he rightly n. Jacob?	7121,8034
Ge	48:16	and let my name be n. on them,	7121
Jos	2:1	into an harlot's house, n. Rahab,	8034
1Sa	4:21	And she n. the child I-chabod,	7121
1Sa	17:4	n. Goliath, of Gath, whose height	8034
1Sa	22:20	the son of Ahitub, n. Abiathar,	8034
2Ki	17:34	of Jacob, whom he n. Israel;	8034
1Ch	23:14	sons were n. of the tribe of Levi.	7121
Ec	6:10	which hath been is n. already,	8034,7121
Isa	61:6	be n. the Priests of the Lord:	7121
Jer	44:26	my name shall no more be n. in	7121
Da	5:12	whom the king n. Belteshazzar:	8036
Am	6:1	which are n. chief of the nations,	5344
Mic	2:7	thou that art n. the house of Jacob,	559
Mt	9:9	a man, n. Matthew, sitting at the	3004
Mt	27:57	a rich man of Arimathaea, n. Joseph,	3686
Mk	14:32	a place which was n. Gethsemane:	3686
Mk	15:7	there was one n. Barabbas, which	3004
Lu	1:5	a certain priest n. Zacharias, of	3686
Lu	1:26	unto a city of Galilee, n. Nazareth,	3686
Lu	2:21	which was so n. of the angel	2564
Lu	5:27	forth, and saw a publican, n. Levi,	3686
Lu	6:13	twelve, whom also he n. apostles;	3687
Lu	6:14	Simon, (whom he also n. Peter,)	3687
Lu	8:41	there came a man n. Jairus, and he	3686
Lu	10:38	woman n. Martha received him into	3686
Lu	16:20	**was a certain beggar n. Lazarus,**	3686
Lu	19:2	there was a man n. Zacchaeus,	2564
Lu	23:50	behold, there was a man n. Joseph,	3686
Joh	3:1	of the Pharisees, n. Nicodemus,	3686
Joh	11:1	a certain man was sick, n. Lazarus,	
Joh	11:49	And one of them, n. Caiaphas, being	
Ac	5:1	But a certain man n. Ananias,	3686
Ac	5:34	a Pharisee, n. Gamaliel, a doctor	3686
Ac	9:10	disciple at Damascus, n. Ananias;	3686
Ac	9:12	**a man n. Ananias coming in,**	3686
Ac	9:33	he found a certain man n. Aeneas.	3686
Ac	9:36	Joppa a certain disciple n. Tabitha,	3686
Ac	11:28	stood up one of them n. Agabus,	3686
Ac	12:13	damsel came to hearken, n. Rhoda.	3686
Ac	16:1	disciple was there, n. Timotheus,	3686
Ac	16:14	woman n. Lydia, a seller of purple,	3686
Ac	17:34	a woman n. Damaris, and others	3686
Ac	18:2	Jew n. Aquila, born in Pontus,	3686
Ac	18:7	a certain man's house, n. Justus,	3686
Ac	18:24	And a certain Jew n. Apollos, born	3686
Ac	19:24	man n. Demetrius, a silversmith,	3686
Ac	20:9	a certain young man n. Eutychus,	3686
Ac	21:10	Judaea a certain prophet, n. Agabus.	3686
Ac	24:1	with a certain orator n. Tertullus,	
Ac	27:1	other prisoners unto one n. Julius,	3686
Ro	15:20	gospel, not where Christ was n.,	3687
1Co	5:1	so much as n. among the Gentiles,	3687
Eph	1:21	and every man that is n., not only	3687
Eph	3:15	family in heaven and earth is n.,	3687
Eph	5:3	let it not be once n. among you,	3687

NAMELY

Ref		Context	No.
Le	1:10	be of the flocks, n., of the sheep,	
Nu	1:32	Of the children of Joseph, n., of the	
Nu	9:15	n., the tent of the testimony:	
Nu	13:11	Of the tribe of Joseph, n., of the tribe	
Nu	31:8	that were slain; n., Evi, and Rekem,	
De	4:43	N., Bezer in the wilderness, in the	
De	13:7	N., of the gods of the people which	
De	20:17	n., the Hittites, and the Amorites, the	
Jg	3:3	N., five lords of the Philistines, and	
Jg	8:35	to the house of Jerubbaal, n., Gideon,	
1Ch	6:57	they gave the cities of Judah, n.,	
1Ch	6:61	tribe, n., out of the half tribe of	
1Ch	9:23	n., the house of the tabernacle, by	
1Ch	23:6	the sons of Levi, n., Gershon, Kohath,	
Ezr	10:18	n., of the sons of Jeshua the son of	
Ne	12:35	n., Zechariah the son of Jonathan, the	
Es	8:12	n., upon the thirteenth day of the	
Ec	5:13	n., riches kept for the owners thereof	
Isa	7:20	n., by them beyond the river, by	
Jer	26:22	n., Elnathan the son of Achbor, and	
Mk	12:31	**And the second is like, n. this, Thou**	
Ac	15:22	n., Judas surnamed Barsabas, and	
Ro	13:9	n., Thou shalt love thy neighbour	1722

NAME'S

Ref		Context	No.
1Sa	12:22	his people for his great n. sake:	8034
1Ki	8:41	out of a far country for thy n. sake;	8034
2Ch	6:32	a far country for thy great n. sake,	8034
Ps	23:3	of righteousness for his n. sake.	8034
Ps	25:11	For thy n. sake, O Lord, pardon	8034
Ps	31:3	therefore for thy n. sake lead me,	8034
Ps	79:9	away our sins, for thy n. sake.	8034
Ps	106:8	he saved them for his n. sake, that	8034
Ps	109:21	O God the Lord, for thy n. sake:	8034
Ps	143:11	Quicken me, O Lord, for thy n. sake:	8034
Isa	48:9	For my n. sake will I defer mine	8034
Isa	66:5	cast you out for my n. sake, said,	8034
Jer	14:7	us, do thou it for thy n. sake:	8034
Jer	14:21	Do not abhor us, for thy n. sake,	8034
Eze	20:9,	14 But I wrought for my n. sake,	8034
Eze	20:22	and wrought for my n. sake, that it	8034
Eze	20:44	wrought with you for my n. sake,	8034
Eze	36:22	but for mine holy n. sake, which ye	8034
Mt	10:22	**hated of all men for my n. sake:**	3686
Mt	19:29	**children, or lands, for my n. sake,**	3686
Mt	24:9	**of all nations for my n. sake**	3686
Mk	13:13	**be hated of all men for my n. sake:**	3686
Lu	21:12	**kings and rulers for my n. sake.**	3686
Lu	21:17	**be hated of all men for my n. sake.**	3686
Joh	15:21	**they do unto you for my n. sake,**	3686
Ac	9:16	**he must suffer for my n. sake**	3686
1Jo	2:12	are forgiven you for his n. sake,	3686
3Jo	7	that for his n. sake they went forth,	3686
Re	2:3	**and for my n. sake hast laboured,**	3686

NAMES

Ref		Context	No.
Ge	2:20	Adam gave n. to all cattle, and to	8034
Ge	25:13	are the n. of the sons of Ishmael,	8034
Ge	25:13	by their n., according to their	8034
Ge	25:16	of Ishmael, and these are their n.,	8034
Ge	26:18	called their n. after the n. by which	8034
Ge	36:10	are the n. of Esau's sons; Eliphaz	8034
Ge	36:40	the n. of the dukes that came of	8034
Ge	36:40	after their places, by their n.; Duke	8034
Ge	46:8	are the n. of the children of Israel,	8034
Ex	1:1	are the n. of the children of Israel,	8034
Ex	6:16	these are the n. of the sons of Levi	8034
Ex	28:9	them the n. of the children of Israel:	8034
Ex	28:10	Six of their n. on one stone, and the	8034
Ex	28:10	six n. of the rest on the other stone,	8034
Ex	28:11	with the n. of the children of Israel:	8034
Ex	28:12	shall bear their n. before the Lord	8034
Ex	28:21	with the n. of the children of Israel,	8034
Ex	28:21	twelve, according to their n., like	8034
Ex	28:29	bear the n. of the children of Israel	8034
Ex	39:6	with the n. of the children of Israel.	8034
Ex	39:14	to the n. of the children of Israel,	8034
Ex	39:14	twelve, according to their n., like	8034
Nu	1:2	with the number of their n., every	8034
Nu	1:5	n. of the men that shall stand with	8034
Nu	1:17	which are expressed by their n.:	8034
Nu	1:18,	20,22,24,26,28,30,32,34,36,38,40,42 according to the number of the n.	8034
Nu	3:2	are the n. of the sons of Aaron;	8034
Nu	3:3	are the n. of the sons of Aaron, the	8034
Nu	3:17	were the sons of Levi by their n.;	8034
Nu	3:18	are the n. of the sons of Gershon	8034
Nu	3:40	and take the number of their n..	8034
Nu	3:43	firstborn males by the number of n.,	8034
Nu	13:4	these were their n.: of the tribe	8034
Nu	13:16	n. of the men which Moses sent	8034
Nu	26:33	and the n. of the daughters of	8034
Nu	26:53	according to the number of n..	8034
Nu	26:55	the n. of the tribes of their fathers	8034
Nu	27:1	these are the n. of his daughters;	8034
Nu	32:38	(their n. being changed,) and	8034
Nu	32:38	gave other n. unto the cities which	8034
Nu	34:17	These are the n. of the men which	8034
Nu	34:19	the n. of the men are these: of the	8034
De	12:3	the n. of them out of that place,	8034
Jos	17:3	these are the n. of his daughters,	8034
1Sa	14:49	the n. of his two daughters were	8034
1Sa	17:13	the n. of his three sons that went	8034
2Sa	5:14	n. of those that were born unto him	8034
2Sa	23:8	These be the n. of the mighty men	8034
1Ki	4:8	And these are their n.: The son of	8034
1Ch	4:38	mentioned by their n. were princes	8034
1Ch	6:17	be the n. of the sons of Gershom;	8034
1Ch	6:65	cities, which are called by their n..	8034
1Ch	8:38	had six sons, whose n. are these,	8034
1Ch	9:44	had six sons, whose n. are these,	8034
1Ch	14:4	are the n. of his children which he	8034
1Ch	23:24	by number of n. by their polls, that	8034
Ezr	5:4	What are the n. of the men that	8036
Ezr	5:10	We asked their n. also, to certify	8036
Ezr	5:10	we might write the n. of the men	8036
Ezr	8:13	whose n. are these, Eliphelet,	8034
Ezr	10:16	and all of them by their n., were	8034
Ps	16:4	nor take up their n. into my lips.	8034
Ps	49:11	call their lands after their own n..	8034
Ps	147:4	he calleth them all by their n.	8034
Isa	40:26	he calleth them all by n. by the	8034
Eze	23:4	the n. of them were Aholah the	8034
Eze	23:4	were their n.; Samaria is Aholah,	8034
Eze	48:1	Now these are the n. of the tribes.	8034
Eze	48:31	after the n. of the tribes of Israel:	8034
Da	1:7	the prince of the eunuchs gave n.:	8034
Ho	2:17	I will take away the n. of Baalim	8034
Zec	13:2	will cut off the n. of the idols out of	8034
Mt	10:2	the n. of the twelve apostles are	3686
Lu	10:20	**your n. are written in heaven**	3686
Ac	1:15	(the number of the n. together were	3686
Ac	18:15	if it be a question of words and n.,	3686
Php	4:3	whose n. are in the book of life.	3686
Re	3:4	**hast a few n. even in Sardis which**	3686
Re	13:8	whose n. are not written in the	3686
Re	17:3	full of n. of blasphemy, having	3686
Re	17:8	whose n. were not written in the	3686
Re	21:12	angels, and n. written thereon,	3686
Re	21:12	are the n. of the twelve tribes of the	
Re	21:14	them the n. of the twelve apostles	3686

NAMETH
2Ti 2:19 one that **n.** the name of Christ *3687*

NANGAE See NAGGE.

NAOMI (na'-o-mee) See also NAOMI'S.
Ru 1:2 and the name of his wife **N.**, and 5281
Ru 1:8 **N.** said unto her two daughters in...... 5281
Ru 1:11 **N.** said, Turn again, my daughters:..... 5281
Ru 1:19 them, and they said, Is this **N.**?........ 5281
Ru 1:20 them, Call me not **N.**, call me Mara:... 5281
Ru 1:21 why then call ye me **N.**, seeing the 5281
Ru 1:22 So **N.** returned, and Ruth the........... 5281
Ru 2:1 **N.** had a kinsman of her husband's, ... 5281
Ru 2:2 Ruth the Moabitess said unto **N.**,....... 5281
Ru 2:6 damsel that came back with **N.** 5281
Ru 2:20 **N.** said unto her daughter in law, ... 5281
Ru 2:20 **N.** said unto her, The man is near...... 5281
Ru 2:22 **N.** said unto Ruth her daughter in...... 5281
Ru 3:1 **N.** her mother in law said unto her,.... 5281
Ru 4:3 he said unto the kinsman, **N.**, that...... 5281
Ru 4:5 buyest the field of the hand of **N.**,...... 5281
Ru 4:9 and Mahlon's, of the hand of **N.**......... 5281
Ru 4:14 women said unto **N.**, Blessed be......... 5281
Ru 4:16 **N.** took the child, and laid it in her..... 5281
Ru 4:17 saying, There is a son born to **N.**; 5281

NAOMI'S (na'-o-meze)
Ru 1:3 And Elimelech **N.** husband died;......... 5281

NAPHISH (na'-fish) See also NEPHISH.
Ge 25:15 Tema, Jetur, **N.**, and Kedemah:......... 5305
1Ch 1:31 Jetur, **N.**, and Kedemah. These......... 5305

NAPHTALI (naf'-ta-li) See also NEPHTHALIM.
Ge 30:8 and she called his name **N.** 5321
Ge 35:25 Rachel's handmaid; Dan, and **N.**: 5321
Ge 46:24 And the sons of **N.**; Jahzeel, and........ 5321
Ge 49:21 **N.** is a hind let loose: he giveth......... 5321
Ex 1:4 Dan, and **N.**, Gad, and Asher. 5321
Nu 1:15 Of **N.**; Ahira the son of Enan. 5321
Nu 1:42 Of the children of **N.**, throughout 5321
Nu 1:43 of them, even of the tribe of **N.**,........ 5321
Nu 2:29 Then the tribe of **N.**: and the............ 5321
Nu 2:29 captain of the children of **N.** shall 5321
Nu 7:78 Ahira...prince of the children of **N.**, ... 5321
Nu 10:27 of the children of **N.** was Ahira.......... 5321
Nu 13:14 Of the tribe of **N.**, Nahbi the son of.... 5321
Nu 26:48 the sons of **N.** after their families:...... 5321
Nu 26:50 These are the families of **N.**............ 5321
Nu 34:28 of the tribe of the children of **N.**, ... 5321
De 27:13 Asher, and Zebulun, Dan, and **N.**......... 5321
De 33:23 of **N.** he said, O **N.**, satisfied with...... 5321
De 34:2 all **N.**, and the land of Ephraim, ... 5321
Jos 19:32 lot came out to the children of **N.**, ... 5321
Jos 19:32 for the children of **N.** according to...... 5321
Jos 19:39 children of **N.** according to their......... 5321
Jos 20:7 Kedesh in Galilee in mount **N.**,.......... 5321
Jos 21:6 and out of the tribe of **N.**, and out 5321
Jos 21:32 out of the tribe of **N.**, Kedesh in........ 5321
Jg 1:33 did **N.** drive out the inhabitants......... 5321
Jg 4:6 thousand men of the children of **N.**...... 5321
Jg 4:10 called Zebulun and **N.** to Kedesh;....... 5321
Jg 5:18 Zebulun and **N.** were a people that..... 5321
Jg 6:35 and unto Zebulun, and unto **N.**;.......... 5321
Jg 7:23 themselves together out of **N.**, and..... 5321
1Ki 4:15 Ahimaaz was in **N.**; he also took........ 5321
1Ki 7:14 a widow's son of the tribe of **N.**,........ 5321
1Ki 15:20 Cinneroth, with all the land of **N.**...... 5321
2Ki 15:29 all the land of **N.**, and carried them 5321
1Ch 2:2 Joseph, and Benjamin, **N.**, Gad, ... 5321
1Ch 6:62 and out of the tribe of **N.**, and out 5321
1Ch 6:76 And out of the tribe of **N.**; Kedesh..... 5321
1Ch 7:13 The sons of **N.**; Jahziel, and Guni,...... 5321
1Ch 12:34 And of **N.** a thousand captains, and...... 5321
1Ch 12:40 unto Issachar and Zebulun and **N.**,....... 5321
1Ch 27:19 of **N.**, Jerimoth the son of Azriel: 5321
2Ch 16:4 and all the store cities of **N.**............ 5321
2Ch 34:6 and Simeon, even unto **N.**, with......... 5321
Ps 68:27 of Zebulun, and the princes of **N.**....... 5321
Isa 9:1 land of Zebulun and the land of **N.**,...... 5321
Eze 48:3 unto the west side, a portion for **N.**..... 5321
Eze 48:4 And by the border of **N.**, from the 5321
Eze 48:34 one gate of Asher, one gate of **N.**...... 5321

NAPHTUHIM (naf'-too-him)
Ge 10:13 Anamim, and Lehabim, and **N.**,.......... 5320
1Ch 1:11 Anamim, and Lehabim, and **N.**,.......... 5320

NAPKIN
Lu 19:20 **which I have kept laid up in a n.**: . *4676*
Joh 11:44 face was bound about with a **n.**......... *4676*
Joh 20:7 And the **n.**, that was about his head, .. *4676*

NARCISSUS (nar-sis'-sus)
Ro 16:11 that be of the household of **N.**,.......... *3488*

NARD See SPIKENARD.

NARROW See also NARROWED; NARROWER.
Nu 22:26 further, and stood in a **n.** place,......... 6862
Jos 17:15 mount Ephraim be too **n.** for thee......... 213
1Ki 6:4 he made windows of **n.** lights............. 331
Pr 23:27 and a strange woman is a **n.** pit.......... 6862
Isa 49:19 even now be too **n.** by reason of 3334
Eze 40:16 **n.** windows to the little chambers, ... 331
Eze 41:16 posts, and the **n.** windows, and the....... 331
Eze 41:26 were **n.** windows and palm trees 331
Mt 7:14 **is the gate, and n. is the way,**....... *2346*

NARROWED
1Ki 6:6 he made **n.** rests round about,........... 4052

NARROWER
Isa 28:20 covering **n.** than that he can wrap 6887

NARROWLY
Job 13:27 and lookest **n.** unto all my paths; 8104
Isa 14:16 that see thee shall **n.** look upon thee, ...

NATHAN (na'-than) See also NATHAN-MELECH.
2Sa 5:14 Shammuah, and Shobab, and **N.**, ... 5416
2Sa 7:2 the king said unto **N.** the prophet,...... 5416
2Sa 7:3 And **N.** said unto the king, Go, do....... 5416
2Sa 7:4 the word of the Lord came unto **N.**, ... 5416
2Sa 7:17 vision, so did **N.** speak unto David. 5416
2Sa 12:1 And the Lord sent **N.** unto David....... 5416
2Sa 12:5 he said to **N.**, As the Lord liveth, ... 5416
2Sa 12:7 And **N.** said to David, Thou art the 5416
2Sa 12:13 David said unto **N.**, I have sinned...... 5416
2Sa 12:13 **N.** said unto David, The Lord also....... 5416
2Sa 12:15 And **N.** departed unto his house.......... 5416
2Sa 12:25 sent by the hand of **N.** the prophet;.... 5416
2Sa 23:36 Igal the son of **N.** of Zobah, Bani 5416
1Ki 1:8 **N.** the prophet, and Shimei, and 5416
1Ki 1:10 **N.** the prophet, and Benaiah, and....... 5416
1Ki 1:11 **N.** spake unto Bath-sheba the........... 5416
1Ki 1:22 king, **N.** the prophet also came in....... 5416
1Ki 1:23 saying, Behold **N.** the prophet. 5416
1Ki 1:24 And **N.** said, My lord, O king, hast 5416
1Ki 1:32 the priest, and **N.** the prophet, and 5416
1Ki 1:34 priest and **N.** the prophet anoint 5416
1Ki 1:38, 44 the priest, and **N.** the prophet,...... 5416
1Ki 1:45 **N.** the prophet have anointed him....... 5416
1Ki 4:5 the son of **N.** was over the officers: ... 5416
1Ki 4:5 Zabud the son of **N.** was principal....... 5416
1Ch 2:36 Attai begat **N.**, and **N.** begat............ 5416
1Ch 3:5 Shimea, and Shobab, and **N.**, and....... 5416
1Ch 11:38 Joel the brother of **N.**, Mibhar the...... 5416
1Ch 14:4 and Shobab, **N.**, and Solomon............ 5416
1Ch 17:1 that David said to **N.** the prophet, ... 5416
1Ch 17:2 **N.** said unto David, Do all that is 5416
1Ch 17:3 word of God came to **N.**, saying, ... 5416
1Ch 17:15 vision, so did **N.** speak unto David. 5416
1Ch 29:29 and in the book of **N.** the prophet, ... 5416
2Ch 9:29 in the book of **N.** the prophet, and 5416
2Ch 29:25 king's seer, and **N.** the prophet: 5416
Ezr 8:16 for **N.**, and for Zechariah, and for....... 5416
Ezr 10:39 Shelemiah, and **N.**, and Adaiah,........... 5416
Ps 51:*title* **N.** the prophet came unto him, ... 5416
Zec 12:12 the family of the house of **N.** a part,... 5416
Lu 3:31 which was the son of **N.**, which *3481*

NATHANAEL (na-than'-a-el) See also BARTHOLOMEW.
Joh 1:45 Philip findeth **N.**, and saith unto......... *3482*
Joh 1:46 **N.** said unto him, Can there any *3482*
Joh 1:47 Jesus saw **N.** coming to him, and *3482*
Joh 1:48 **N.** saith unto him, Whence knowest.... *3482*
Joh 1:49 **N.** answered and saith unto him,........ *3482*
Joh 21:2 Didymus, and **N.** of Cana in Galilee, ... *3482*

NATHAN-MELECH (na''-than-me'-lek)
2Ki 23:11 chamber of **N.** the chamberlain, ... 5419

NATION See also NATIONS.
Ge 12:2 I will make of thee a great **n.**, and 1471
Ge 15:14 also that **n.**, whom they shall serve, ... 1471
Ge 17:20 and I will make him a great **n.**......... 1471
Ge 18:18 become a great and mighty **n.**, and..... 1471
Ge 20:4 wilt thou slay also a righteous **n.**? 1471
Ge 21:13 of the bondwoman will I make a **n.**,.... 1471
Ge 21:18 for I will make him a great **n.**............ 1471
Ge 35:11 a **n.** and a company of nations shall..... 1471
Ge 46:3 I will there make of thee a great **n.**: ... 1471
Ex 9:24 land of Egypt since it became a **n.**...... 1471
Ex 19:6 kingdom of priests, and an holy **n.**...... 1471
Ex 21:8 to sell her unto a strange **n.** he 5971
Ex 32:10 and I will make of thee a great **n.** 1471
Ex 33:13 consider that this **n.** is thy people. 1471
Ex 34:10 done in all the earth, nor in any **n.**: 1471
Le 18:26 neither any of your own **n.**, nor any..... 249
Le 20:23 not walk in the manners of the **n.**, ... 1471
Nu 14:12 and will make of thee a greater **n.**...... 1471
De 4:6 Surely this great **n.** is a wise and....... 1471
De 4:7 what **n.** is there so great, who hath.... 1471
De 4:8 what **n.** is there so great, that hath.... 1471
De 4:34 a **n.** from the midst of another **n.**,...... 1471
De 9:14 I will make of thee a **n.** mightier........ 1471
De 26:5 with a few, and became there a **n.**, ... 1471
De 28:33 shall a **n.** which thou knowest not 5971
De 28:36 unto a **n.** which neither thou nor........ 1471
De 28:49 Lord shall bring a **n.** against thee....... 1471
De 28:49 a **n.** whose tongue thou shalt not 1471
De 28:50 A **n.** of fierce countenance, which....... 1471
De 32:21 them to anger with a foolish **n.**......... 1471
De 32:28 For they are a **n.** void of counsel,...... 1471
2Sa 7:23 what one **n.** in the earth is like thy..... 1471
1Ki 18:10 there is no **n.** or kingdom, whither..... 1471
1Ki 18:10 took an oath of the kingdom and **n.**, ... 1471
2Ki 17:29 every **n.** made gods of their own, ... 1471
2Ki 17:29 every **n.** in their cities wherein they ... 1471
1Ch 16:20 And when they went from **n.** to **n.**,... 1471
1Ch 17:21 what one **n.** in the earth is like thy..... 1471
2Ch 15:6 **n.** was destroyed of **n.**, and city of..... 1471
2Ch 32:15 for no god of any **n.** or kingdom was .. 1471
Job 34:29 done against a **n.**, or against a man 1471
Ps 33:12 Blessed is the **n.** whose God is the 1471
Ps 43:1 my cause against an ungodly **n.**:......... 1471
Ps 83:4 let us cut them off from being a **n.**; 1471
Ps 105:13 they went from one **n.** to another, ... 1471
Ps 106:5 rejoice in the gladness of thy **n.**, ... 1471
Ps 147:20 He hath not dealt so with any **n.**:....... 1471
Pr 14:34 Righteousness exalteth a **n.**: but 1471
Isa 1:4 Ah sinful **n.**, a people laden with........ 1471
Isa 2:4 **n.** shall not lift up sword against **n.**, ... 1471
Isa 9:3 Thou hast multiplied the **n.**, and......... 1471
Isa 10:6 send him against an hypocritical **n.**,...... 1471
Isa 14:32 answer the messengers of the **n.**?...... 1471
Isa 18:2 to a **n.** scattered and peeled, to a 1471
Isa 18:2 a **n.** meted out and trodden down,...... 1471
Isa 18:7 a **n.** meted out and trodden under...... 1471
Isa 26:2 that the righteous **n.** which keepeth.... 1471
Isa 26:15 Thou hast increased the **n.**, O Lord,... 1471
Isa 26:15 O Lord, thou hast increased the **n.**:..... 1471
Isa 49:7 to him whom the **n.** abhorreth, to 1471
Isa 51:4 and give ear unto me, O my **n.**: 3816
Isa 55:5 shalt call a **n.** that thou knowest 1471
Isa 58:2 as a **n.** that did righteousness, and..... 1471
Isa 60:12 **n.** and kingdom that will not serve...... 1471
Isa 60:22 and a small one a strong **n.**: I the 1471
Isa 65:1 **n.** that was not called by my name..... 1471
Isa 66:8 or shall a **n.** be born at once? for as... 1471
Jer 2:11 Hath a **n.** changed their gods, which... 1471
Jer 5:9 my soul be avenged on such a **n.** as ... 1471
Jer 5:15 I will bring a **n.** upon you from far,..... 1471
Jer 5:15 it is a mighty **n.**, it is an ancient **n.**,... 1471
Jer 5:15 a **n.** whose language thou knowest 1471
Jer 5:29 my soul be avenged on such a **n.** as ... 1471
Jer 6:22 a great **n.** shall be raised from the...... 1471
Jer 7:28 is a **n.** that obeyeth not the voice of... 1471
Jer 9:9 my soul be avenged on such a **n.** as ... 1471
Jer 12:17 pluck up and destroy that **n.**, saith 1471
Jer 18:7 I shall speak concerning a **n.**, and....... 1471
Jer 18:8 If that **n.**, against whom I have.......... 1471
Jer 18:9 I shall speak concerning a **n.**, and....... 1471
Jer 25:12 the king of Babylon, and that **n.**,........ 1471
Jer 25:32 evil shall go forth from **n.** to **n.**, and... 1471
Jer 27:8 the **n.** and kingdom which will not 1471
Jer 27:8 that **n.** will I punish, saith the Lord, ... 1471
Jer 27:13 against the **n.** that will not serve........ 1471
Jer 31:36 shall cease from being a **n.** before 1471
Jer 33:24 that they should be no more a **n.** 1471
Jer 48:2 and let us cut it off from being a **n.** ... 1471
Jer 49:31 get you up unto the wealthy **n.**,......... 1471
Jer 49:36 shall be no **n.** whither the outcasts 1471
Jer 50:3 there cometh up a **n.** against her, ... 1471

Jer 50:41 a great **n.**, and many kings shall be 1471
La 4:17 watched for a **n.** that could not save... 1471
Eze 2:3 a rebellious **n.** that hath rebelled........ 1471
Eze 37:22 I will make them one **n.** in the land.... 1471
Da 3:29 every people, **n.**, and language,........... 524
Da 8:22 shall stand up out of the **n.**,............. 1471
Da 12:1 as never was since there was a **n.** 1471
Joe 1:6 For a **n.** is come up upon my land,..... 1471
Am 6:14 I will raise up against you a **n.**, O 1471
Mic 4:3 **n.** shall not lift...sword against **n.**,...... 1471
Mic 4:7 that was cast far off a strong **n.**:........ 1471
Hab 1:6 Chaldeans, that bitter and hasty **n.**, ... 1471
Zep 2:1 gather together, O **n.** not desired;....... 1471
Zep 2:5 sea coast, the **n.** of the Cherethites!... 1471
Hag 2:14 So is this people, and so is this **n.**...... 1471
Mal 3:9 have robbed me, even this whole **n.**. .. 1471
Mt 21:43 **to a n. bringing forth the fruits** *1484*
Mt 24:7 **For n. shall rise against n., and**.... *1484*
Mk 7:26 a Greek, a Syrophenician by **n.**;......... *1085*
Mk 13:8 **For n. shall rise against n., and**.... *1484*
Lu 7:5 he loveth our **n.**, and he hath built *1484*
Lu 21:10 unto then, **N. shall rise against n.**,.. *1484*
Lu 23:2 found this fellow perverting the **n.**,..... *1484*
Joh 11:48 take away both our place and **n.**. *1484*
Joh 11:50 and that the whole **n.** perish not. *1484*
Joh 11:51 that Jesus should die for that **n.**;........ *1484*
Joh 11:52 And not for that **n.** only, but that....... *1484*
Joh 18:35 Thine own **n.** and the chief priests *1484*
Ac 2:5 men, out of every **n.** under heaven..... *1484*
Ac 7:7 **n.** to whom they shall be in bondage... *1484*
Ac 10:22 report among all the **n.** of the Jews, ... *1484*
Ac 10:28 or come unto one of another **n.**;.......... *246*
Ac 10:35 in every **n.** he that feareth him,......... *1484*
Ac 24:2 worthy deeds are done unto this **n.** *1484*
Ac 24:10 of many years a judge unto this **n.**, ... *1484*
Ac 24:17 I came to bring alms to my **n.**, and *1484*
Ac 26:4 among mine own **n.** at Jerusalem,....... *1484*
Ac 28:19 that I had ought to accuse my **n.** of.... *1484*
Ro 10:19 and by a foolish **n.** I will anger you..... *1484*
Ga 1:14 many my equals in mine own **n.**,......... *1085*
Php 2:15 of a crooked and perverse **n.**, ... *1074*
1Pe 2:9 an holy **n.**, a peculiar people; *1484*
Re 5:9 and tongue, and people, and **n.**;......... *1484*
Re 14:6 every **n.**, and kindred, and tongue,..... *1484*

NATIONS

Ge 10:5 after their families, in their **n.**........... 1471
Ge 10:20 in their countries, and in their **n.**........ 1471
Ge 10:31 in their lands, after their **n.**.............. 1471
Ge 10:32 after their generations, in their **n.**: 1471
Ge 10:32 were the **n.** divided in the earth......... 1471
Ge 14:1 king of Elam, and Tidal king of **n.**; 1471
Ge 14:9 Elam, and with Tidal king of **n.**,......... 1471
Ge 17:4 thou shalt be a father of many **n.**. 1471
Ge 17:5 father of many **n.** have I made thee.... 1471
Ge 17:6 I will make **n.** of thee, and kings........ 1471
Ge 17:16 and she shall be a mother of **n.**; 1471
Ge 18:18 the **n.** of earth shall be blessed.......... 1471
Ge 22:18 all the **n.** of the earth be blessed; 1471
Ge 25:16 twelve princes according to their **n.**...... 523
Ge 25:23 Two **n.** are in thy womb, and two...... 1471
Ge 26:4 all the **n.** of the earth be blessed; 1471
Ge 27:29 thee, and **n.** bow down to thee:......... 3816
Ge 35:11 a company of **n.** shall be of thee, ... 1471
Ge 48:19 seed shall become a multitude of **n.**.... 1471
Ex 34:24 I will cast out the **n.** before thee,....... 1471
Le 18:24 for in all these the **n.** are defiled....... 1471
Le 18:28 spued out the **n.** that were before...... 1471
Nu 14:15 the **n.** which have heard the fame 1471
Nu 23:9 shall not be reckoned among the **n.**. .. 1471
Nu 24:8 he shall eat up the **n.** his enemies, ... 1471
Nu 24:20 Amalek was the first of the **n.**;.......... 1471
De 2:25 the **n.** that are under the whole 5971
De 4:6 understanding...the sight of the **n.**,..... 5971
De 4:19 unto all **n.** under the whole heaven..... 5971
De 4:27 shall scatter you among the **n.**,.......... 5971
De 4:38 To drive out **n.** from before thee....... 1471
De 7:1 hath cast out many **n.** before thee,..... 1471
De 7:1 seven **n.** greater and mightier than...... 1471
De 7:17 These **n.** are more than I; how can 1471
De 7:22 God will put out those **n.** before thee.. 1471
De 8:20 As the **n.** which the Lord destroyeth .. 1471
De 9:1 possess **n.** greater and mightier than... 1471
De 9:4, 5 but for the wickedness of these **n.**.... 1471
De 11:23 will the Lord drive out all these **n.**..... 1471
De 11:23 possess greater **n.** and mightier than... 1471
De 12:2 the **n.** which ye shall possess served .. 1471
De 12:29 God shall cut off the **n.** from before.... 1471
De 12:30 How did these **n.** serve their gods?.... 1471
De 14:2 all the **n.** that are upon the earth. 5971
De 15:6 and thou shalt lend unto many **n.**, ... 1471
De 15:6 and thou shalt reign over many **n.**, ... 1471
De 17:14 like as all the **n.** that are about me;.... 1471
De 18:9 after the abominations of those **n.**. 1471
De 18:14 these **n.**, which thou shalt possess, ... 1471
De 19:1 Lord thy God hath cut off the **n.**,........ 1471
De 20:15 are not of the cities of these **n.**. 1471
De 26:19 And to make thee high above all **n.** 1471
De 28:1 on high above all **n.** of the earth: 1471
De 28:12 and thou shalt lend unto many **n.**, ... 1471
De 28:37 all **n.** whither the Lord shall lead....... 5971
De 28:65 among these **n.** shalt thou find no........ 1471
De 29:16 and how we came through the **n.** 1471
De 29:18 to go and serve the gods of these **n.**;. 1471
De 29:24 Even all **n.** shall say, Wherefore 1471
De 30:1 call them to mind among all the **n.**,..... 1471
De 30:3 and gather thee from all the **n.**,........ 5971
De 31:3 destroy these **n.** from before thee,..... 1471
De 32:8 the Most High divided to the **n.** their.. 1471
De 32:43 Rejoice, O ye **n.**, with his people: 1471
Jos 12:23 one; the king of the **n.** of Gilgal,........ 1471
Jos 23:3 God hath done unto all these **n.**.......... 1471
Jos 23:4 divided unto you by lot these **n.** that... 1471
Jos 23:4 with all the **n.** that I have cut off, ... 1471
Jos 23:7 That ye come not among these **n.**,..... 1471
Jos 23:9 from before you great **n.** and strong: .. 1471
Jos 23:12 cleave unto the remnant of these **n.**,... 1471
Jos 23:13 no more drive out any of these **n.**...... 1471
Jg 2:21 **n.** which Joshua left when he died: 1471
Jg 2:23 Therefore the Lord left those **n.**, ... 1471
Jg 3:1 these are the **n.** which the Lord left, .. 1471
1Sa 8:5 a king to judge us like all the **n.**......... 1471
1Sa 8:20 That we also may be like all the **n.**;..... 1471
1Sa 27:8 those **n.** were of old the inhabitants..........
2Sa 7:23 Egypt, from the **n.** and their gods?..... 1471
2Sa 8:11 dedicated of all **n.** which he subdued; .. 1471
1Ki 4:31 his fame was in all **n.** round about. 1471
1Ki 11:2 **n.** concerning which the Lord said...... 1471
1Ki 14:24 to all the abominations of the **n.**......... 1471
2Ki 17:26 The **n.** which thou hast removed,....... 1471
2Ki 17:33 manner of the **n.** whom they carried... 1471
2Ki 17:41 So these **n.** feared the Lord, and 1471
2Ki 18:33 of the gods of the **n.** delivered at all... 1471
2Ki 19:12 Have the gods of the **n.** delivered...... 1471
2Ki 19:17 destroyed the **n.** and their lands,........ 1471
2Ki 21:9 to do more evil than did the **n.**.......... 1471
1Ch 14:17 brought the fear of him upon all **n.**. 1471
1Ch 16:24 marvellous works among all **n.**.......... 5971
1Ch 16:31 and let men say among the **n.**, The 1471
1Ch 17:21 by driving out **n.** from before thy....... 1471
1Ch 18:11 that he brought from all these **n.**;....... 1471
2Ch 7:20 and a byword among all **n.**............... 5971
2Ch 13:9 manner of the **n.** of other lands? 5971
2Ch 32:13 the gods of the **n.** of those lands......... 1471
2Ch 32:14 there among all the gods of those **n.**... 1471
2Ch 32:17 the gods of the **n.** of other lands........ 1471
2Ch 32:23 was magnified in the sight of all **n.** 1471
Ezr 4:10 the rest of the **n.** whom the great 524
Ne 1:8 scatter you abroad among the **n.**: 5971
Ne 9:22 gavest them kingdoms and **n.**, ... 5971
Ne 13:26 among many **n.** was there no king...... 1471
Job 12:23 He increaseth the **n.**, and destroyeth .. 1471
Job 12:23 he enlargeth the **n.**, and straiteneth.... 1471
Ps 9:17 hell, and all the **n.** that forget God. 1471
Ps 9:20 **n.** may know themselves to be but..... 1471
Ps 22:27 the kindreds of the **n.** shall worship.... 1471
Ps 22:28 he is the governor among the **n.**. 1471
Ps 47:3 us, and the **n.** under our feet. 3816
Ps 57:9 I will sing unto thee among the **n.**. 3816
Ps 66:7 for ever; his eyes behold the **n.**:....... 1471
Ps 67:2 thy saving health among all **n.**. 1471
Ps 67:4 let the **n.** be glad and sing for joy: 3816
Ps 67:4 and govern the **n.** upon earth. 3816
Ps 72:11 before him: all **n.** shall serve him. 1471
Ps 72:17 in him: all **n.** shall call him blessed...... 1471
Ps 82:8 earth: for thou shalt inherit all **n.**. 1471
Ps 86:9 All **n.**...thou hast made shall come...... 1471
Ps 96:5 all the gods of the **n.** are idols:.......... 5971
Ps 106:27 their seed also among the **n.**, and 1471
Ps 106:34 They did not destroy the **n.**,............ 5971
Ps 108:3 praises unto thee among the **n.**......... 3816
Ps 113:4 The Lord is high above all **n.**, and...... 1471
Ps 117:1 O praise the Lord, all ye **n.**: praise 1471
Ps 118:10 All **n.** compassed me about: but in...... 1471
Ps 135:10 smote great **n.**, and slew mighty........ 1471
Pr 24:24 people curse, **n.** shall abhor him:........ 3816
Isa 2:2 hills; and all **n.** shall flow unto it......... 1471
Isa 2:4 And he shall judge among the **n.**, ... 1471
Isa 5:26 lift up an ensign to the **n.** from far, ... 1471
Isa 9:1 beyond Jordan, in Galilee of the **n.**. 1471
Isa 10:7 to destroy and cut off **n.** not a few..... 1471
Isa 11:12 he shall set up an ensign for the **n.**, ... 1471
Isa 13:4 kingdoms of **n.** gathered together: 1471
Isa 14:6 he that ruled the **n.** in anger, is......... 1471
Isa 14:9 their thrones all the kings of the **n.**. ... 1471
Isa 14:12 ground, which didst weaken the **n.**! 1471
Isa 14:18 the kings of the **n.**, even all of them, .. 1471
Isa 14:26 is stretched out upon all the **n.**......... 1471
Isa 17:12 and to the rushing of **n.**, that make 3816
Isa 17:13 The **n.** shall rush like the rushing of... 3816
Isa 23:3 revenue; and she is a mart of **n.**. 1471
Isa 25:3 city of the terrible **n.** shall fear thee. .. 1471
Isa 25:7 the vail that is spread over all **n.**........ 1471
Isa 29:7 the multitude of all the **n.** that fight 1471
Isa 29:8 shall the multitude of all the **n.** be, ... 1471
Isa 30:28 sift the **n.** with the sieve of vanity:...... 1471
Isa 33:3 up of thyself the **n.** were scattered..... 1471
Isa 34:1 Come near, ye **n.**, to hear; and 1471
Isa 34:2 of the Lord is upon all **n.**, and his 1471
Isa 36:18 any of the gods of the **n.** delivered..... 1471
Isa 37:12 Have the gods of the **n.** delivered 1471
Isa 37:18 Assyria have laid waste all the **n.**,........ 776
Isa 40:15 the **n.** are as a drop of a bucket, ... 1471
Isa 40:17 All **n.** before him are as nothing;........ 1471
Isa 41:2 to his foot, gave the **n.** before him, ... 1471
Isa 43:9 Let all the **n.** be gathered together,.... 1471
Isa 45:1 holden, to subdue **n.** before him;........ 1471
Isa 45:20 ye that are escaped of the **n.**; they..... 1471
Isa 52:10 holy arm in the eyes of all the **n.**; 1471
Isa 52:15 So shall he sprinkle many **n.**; the 1471
Isa 55:5 **n.** that knew not thee shall run.......... 1471
Isa 60:12 those **n.** shall be utterly wasted. 1471
Isa 61:11 to spring forth before all the **n.**.......... 1471
Isa 64:2 the **n.** may tremble at thy presence!... 1471
Isa 66:18 I will gather all **n.** and tongues; 1471
Isa 66:19 that escape of them unto the **n.**, ... 1471
Isa 66:20 the Lord out of all **n.** upon horses, ... 1471
Jer 1:5 ordained thee a prophet unto the **n.**.... 1471
Jer 1:10 have this day set thee over the **n.**...... 1471
Jer 3:17 all the **n.** shall be gathered unto it,..... 1471
Jer 3:19 goodly heritage of the hosts of **n.**? 1471
Jer 4:2 and the **n.** shall bless themselves in.... 1471
Jer 4:16 Make ye mention to the **n.**; behold,.... 1471
Jer 6:18 Therefore hear, ye **n.**, and know, ... 1471
Jer 9:26 for all these **n.** are uncircumcised, ... 1471
Jer 10:7 would not fear thee, O King of **n.**?..... 1471
Jer 10:7 among all the wise men of the **n.**, ... 1471
Jer 10:10 and the **n.** shall not be able to abide ... 1471
Jer 22:8 And many **n.** shall pass by this city..... 1471
Jer 25:9 against all these **n.** round about, ... 1471
Jer 25:11 and these **n.** shall serve the king......... 1471
Jer 25:13 hath prophesied against all the **n.**. 1471
Jer 25:14 many **n.** and great kings shall serve.... 1471
Jer 25:15 and cause all the **n.**, to whom I send .. 1471
Jer 25:17 and made all the **n.** to drink, unto 1471
Jer 25:31 Lord hath a controversy with the **n.**, .. 1471
Jer 26:6 a curse to all the **n.** of the earth. 1471
Jer 27:7 all **n.** shall serve him, and his son, ... 1471
Jer 27:7 many **n.** and great kings shall serve.... 1471
Jer 27:11 the **n.** that bring their neck under 1471
Jer 28:11 of Babylon from the neck of all **n.** 1471
Jer 28:14 iron upon the neck of all these **n.**,...... 1471
Jer 29:14 I will gather you from all the **n.**, ... 1471
Jer 29:18 among all the **n.** whither I have 1471
Jer 30:11 I make a full end of all **n.** whither I 1471
Jer 31:7 shout among the chief of the **n.**: 1471
Jer 31:10 Hear the word of the Lord, O ye **n.**, .. 1471
Jer 33:9 honour before all the **n.** of the earth, .. 1471
Jer 36:2 Judah, and against all the **n.**, from...... 1471
Jer 43:5 that were returned from all **n.**, ... 1471
Jer 44:8 among all the **n.** of the earth?........... 1471
Jer 46:12 The **n.** have heard of thy shame, ... 1471
Jer 46:28 I will make a full end of all the **n.**....... 1471
Jer 50:2 Declare ye among the **n.**,...publish, ... 1471
Jer 50:9 an assembly of great **n.** from the 1471
Jer 50:12 the hindermost of the **n.** shall be a 1471
Jer 50:23 become a desolation among the **n.**!..... 1471
Jer 50:46 and the cry is heard among the **n.**...... 1471
Jer 51:7 the **n.** have drunken of her wine; 1471

Jer 51:7 her wine; therefore the **n.** are mad..... 1471
Jer 51:20 thee will I break in pieces the **n.**,....... 1471
Jer 51:27 blow the trumpet among the **n.**,......... 1471
Jer 51:27 prepare the **n.** against her, call......... 1471
Jer 51:28 Prepare against her the **n.** with the.... 1471
Jer 51:41 an astonishment among the **n.**! 1471
Jer 51:44 the **n.** shall not flow together any....... 1471
La 1:1 that she was great among the **n.**,........ 1471
Eze 5:5 I have set it in the midst of the **n.** 1471
Eze 5:6 into wickedness more than the **n.**,........ 1471
Eze 5:7 multiplied more than the **n.** that......... 1471
Eze 5:7 according to the judgments of the **n.**.... 1471
Eze 5:8 midst of thee in the sight of the **n.**..... 1471
Eze 5:14 a reproach among the **n.** that are....... 1471
Eze 5:15 unto the **n.** that are round about........ 1471
Eze 6:8 escape the sword among the **n.**, ... 1471
Eze 6:9 shall remember me among the **n.**........ 1471
Eze 12:15 I shall scatter them among the **n.**,...... 1471
Eze 19:4 The **n.** also heard of him; he was....... 1471
Eze 19:8 the **n.** set against him on every 1471
Eze 25:10 not be remembered among the **n.**. 1471
Eze 26:3 and will cause many **n.** to come up..... 1471
Eze 26:5 and it shall become a spoil to the **n.**. .. 1471
Eze 28:7 upon thee, the terrible of the **n.**: 1471
Eze 29:12 scatter the Egyptians among the **n.**, ... 1471
Eze 29:15 exalt itself any more above the **n.**: 1471
Eze 29:15 they shall no more rule over the **n.**. ... 1471
Eze 30:11 the terrible of the **n.**, shall be........... 1471
Eze 30:23, 26 scatter...Egyptians among...**n.**,...... 1471
Eze 31:6 under his shadow dwelt all great **n.**. .. 1471
Eze 31:12 And strangers, the terrible of the **n.**, .. 1471
Eze 31:16 I made the **n.** to shake at the sound... 1471
Eze 32:2 Thou art like a young lion of the **n.**, ... 1471
Eze 32:9 bring thy destruction among the **n.**,.... 1471
Eze 32:12 the terrible of the **n.**, all of them: 1471
Eze 32:16 the daughters of the **n.** shall lament..... 1471
Eze 32:18 and the daughters of the famous **n.**,.... 1471
Eze 35:10 said, These two **n.** and these two 1471
Eze 36:13 up men, and hast bereaved thy **n.**; 1471
Eze 36:14 neither bereave thy **n.** any more,....... 1471
Eze 36:15 thou cause thy **n.** to fall any more,...... 1471
Eze 37:22 and they shall be no more two **n.**,...... 1471
Eze 38:8 but it is brought forth out of the **n.**, ... 1471
Eze 38:12 that are gathered out of the **n.**, ... 1471
Eze 38:23 be known in the eyes of many **n.**,....... 1471
Eze 39:27 in them in the sight of many **n.**;........ 1471
Da 3:4 O people, **n.**, and languages,............... 524
Da 3:7 the people, the **n.**,...the languages,...... 524
Da 4:1 unto all people, **n.**, and languages, ... 524
Da 5:19 him, all people, **n.**, and languages, ... 524
Da 6:25 Darius wrote unto all people, **n.**, ... 524
Da 7:14 that all people, **n.**, and languages, ... 524
Ho 8:10 they have hired among the **n.**,........... 1471
Ho 9:17 shall be wanderers among the **n.**........ 1471
Joe 3:2 I will also gather all **n.**, and will........ 1471
Joe 3:2 they have scattered among the **n.**, ... 1471
Am 6:1 which are named chief of the **n.**, to.... 1471
Am 9:9 the house of Israel among all **n.**,........ 1471
Mic 4:2 many **n.** shall come, and say, Come,... 1471
Mic 4:3 people,...rebuke strong **n.** afar off;..... 1471
Mic 4:11 many **n.** are gathered against thee,...... 1471
Mic 7:16 **n.** shall see and be confounded at....... 1471
Na 3:4 selleth **n.** through her whoredoms, ... 1471
Na 3:5 I will shew the **n.** thy nakedness,........ 1471
Hab 1:17 not spare continually to slay the **n.**?.... 1471
Hab 2:5 but gathereth unto him all **n.**, and 1471
Hab 2:8 thou hast spoiled many **n.**, all the....... 1471
Hab 3:6 beheld, and drove asunder the **n.**; 1471
Zep 2:14 midst of her, all the beasts of the **n.**:.. 1471
Zep 3:6 I have cut off the **n.**: their towers....... 1471
Zep 3:8 determination is to gather the **n.**,....... 1471
Hag 2:7 And I will shake all **n.**, and the.......... 1471
Hag 2:7 and the desire of all **n.** shall come: 1471
Zec 2:8 me unto the **n.** which spoiled you:..... 1471
Zec 2:11 many **n.** shall be joined to the Lord.... 1471
Zec 7:14 all the **n.** whom they knew not. 1471
Zec 8:22 **n.** shall come to seek the Lord of...... 1471
Zec 8:23 hold out of all languages of the **n.**,...... 1471
Zec 12:9 **n.** that come against Jerusalem. 1471
Zec 14:2 gather all **n.** against Jerusalem to 1471
Zec 14:3 go forth, and fight against those **n.**,.... 1471
Zec 14:16 **n.** which came against Jerusalem........ 1471
Zec 14:19 punishment of all **n.** that come not...... 1471
Mal 3:12 all **n.** shall call you blessed: for ye....... 1471
Mt 24:9 **ye shall be hated of all n. for my ..** *1484*
Mt 24:14 **world for a witness unto all n.;**..... *1484*
Mt 25:32 **before him shall be gathered all n.:** *1484*
Mt 28:19 **Go ye therefore, and teach all n.,**.. *1484*
Mk 11:17 **called of all n. the house of prayer!** *1484*
Mk 13:10 **first be published among all n.**..... *1484*
Lu 12:30 **do the n. of the world seek after:** .. *1484*
Lu 21:24 **be led away captive into all n.:** *1484*
Lu 21:25 **and upon the earth distress of n.,**.. *1484*
Lu 24:47 **preached in his name among all n.,** *1484*
Ac 13:19 when he had destroyed seven **n.** in *1484*
Ac 14:16 all **n.** to walk in their own ways.......... *1484*
Ac 17:26 made of one blood all **n.** of men......... *1484*
Ro 1:5 obedience to the faith among all **n.**, ... *1484*
Ro 4:17 made thee a father of many **n.**,)......... *1484*
Ro 4:18 become the father of many **n.**,........... *1484*
Ro 16:26 known to all **n.** for the obedience *1484*
Ga 3:8 In thee shall all **n.** be blessed............. *1484*
Re 2:26 **him will I give power over the n.** .. *1484*
Re 7:9 no man could number, of all **n.**, ... *1484*
Re 10:11 many peoples, and **n.**, and tongues,.... *1484*
Re 11:9 people...kindreds...tongues and **n.**....... *1484*
Re 11:18 the **n.** were angry, and thy wrath........ *1484*
Re 12:5 was to rule all **n.** with a rod of iron: ... *1484*
Re 13:7 all kindreds, and tongues, and **n.**......... *1484*
Re 14:8 she made all **n.** drink of the wine *1484*
Re 15:4 for all **n.** shall come and worship......... *1484*
Re 16:19 parts, and the cities of the **n.** fell: *1484*
Re 17:15 peoples, and multitudes, and **n.**,......... *1484*
Re 18:3 For all **n.** have drunk of the wine....... *1484*
Re 18:23 thy sorceries were all **n.** deceived. *1484*
Re 19:15 that with it he should smite the **n.**:..... *1484*
Re 20:3 he should deceive the **n.** no more, ... *1484*
Re 20:8 and shall go out to deceive the **n.** *1484*
Re 21:24 And the **n.** of them which are saved ... *1484*
Re 21:26 glory and honour of the **n.** into it. *1484*
Re 22:2 tree were for the healing of the **n.**. *1484*

NATIVE

Jer 22:10 no more, nor see his **n.** country. 4138

NATIVITY

Ge 11:28 father Terah in the land of his **n.**,...... 4138
Ru 2:11 thy mother, and the land of thy **n.**,..... 4138
Jer 46:16 people and to the land of our **n.**,......... 4138
Eze 16:3 and thy **n.** is of the land of Canaan; 4138
Eze 16:4 as for thy **n.**, in the day thou wast..... 4138
Eze 21:30 wast created, in the land of thy **n.**...... 4351
Eze 23:15 of Chaldea, the land of their **n.**: 4138

NATURAL

De 34:7 not dim, nor his **n.** force abated......... 3893
Ro 1:26 women did change the **n.** use into...... *5446*
Ro 1:27 leaving the **n.** use of the woman, ... *5446*
Ro 1:31 without **n.** affection, implacable, ...
Ro 11:21 spared not the **n.** branches, ... *2596,5449*
Ro 11:24 these, which be the **n.** branches, .*2596,5449*
1Co 2:14 But the **n.** man receiveth not the....... *5591*
1Co 15:44 It is sown a **n.** body; it is raised a...... *5591*
1Co 15:44 There is a **n.** body, and there is a...... *5591*
1Co 15:46 is spiritual, but that which is **n.**;......... *5591*
2Ti 3:3 Without **n.** affection, trucebreakers, ...
Jas 1:23 beholding his **n.** face in a glass: *1083*
2Pe 2:12 But these, as **n.** brute beasts, made... *5446*

NATURALLY

Php 2:20 who will **n.** care for your state. *1103*
Jude 10 what they know **n.**, as brute beasts, ... *5447*

NATURE

Ro 1:26 use into that which is against **n.**:........ *5449*
Ro 2:14 do by **n.** the things contained in the.... *5449*
Ro 2:27 not uncircumcision which is by **n.**, ... *5449*
Ro 11:24 of the olive tree which is wild by **n.**,.... *5449*
Ro 11:24 and wert graffed contrary to **n.** into.... *5449*
1Co 11:14 Doth not even **n.** itself teach you, ... *5449*
Ga 2:15 We who are Jews by **n.**, and not.......... *5449*
Ga 4:8 unto them which by **n.** are no gods. *5449*
Eph 2:3 were by **n.** the children of wrath,........ *5449*
Heb 2:16 he took not on him the **n.** of angels; ....
Jas 3:6 and setteth on fire the course of **n.**; ... *1078*
2Pe 1:4 be partakers of the divine **n.**,............ *5449*

NAUGHT See also NOUGHT.

2Ki 2:19 water is **n.**, and the ground barren. 7451
Pr 20:14 It is **n.**, it is **n.**, saith the buyer:......... 7451

NAUGHTINESS

1Sa 17:28 pride, and the **n.** of thine heart;......... 7455
Pr 11:6 shall be taken in their own **n.**............ 1942
Jas 1:21 all filthiness and superfluity of **n.**, ... *2549*

NAUGHTY

Pr 6:12 A **n.** person, a wicked man,............. 1100
Pr 17:4 a liar giveth ear to a **n.** tongue.......... 1942
Jer 24:2 the other basket had very **n.** figs, ... 7451

NAUM (na'-um) See also NAHUM.

Lu 3:25 of Amos, which was the son of **N.**,...... *3486*

NAVEL

Job 40:16 his force is in the **n.** of his belly. 8306
Pr 3:8 It shall be health to thy **n.**, and 8270
Ca 7:2 Thy **n.** is like a round goblet, ... 8326
Eze 16:4 thou wast born thy **n.** was not cut,..... 8270

NAVES

1Ki 7:33 axletrees, and their **n.**, and their........ 1354

NAVY

1Ki 9:26 King Solomon made a **n.** of ships......... 590
1Ki 9:27 Hiram sent in the **n.** his servants,........ 590
1Ki 10:11 the **n.** also of Hiram, that brought........ 590
1Ki 10:22 a **n.** of Tharshish with the **n.** of 590
1Ki 10:22 once in three years came the **n.** of 590

NAY See also NO.

Ge 18:15 he said, **N.**; but thou didst laugh. 3808
Ge 19:2 And they said, **N.**: but we will............ 3808
Ge 23:11 **N.**, my lord, hear me: the field give ... 3808
Ge 33:10 Jacob said, **N.**, I pray thee, if now 408
Ge 42:10 **N.**, my lord, but to buy food are......... 3808
Ge 42:12 **N.**, but to see the nakedness of......... 3808
Nu 22:30 do so unto thee? And he said, **N.**......... 3808
Jos 5:14 said, **N.**; but as captain of the host..... 3808
Jos 24:21 said unto Joshua, **N.**; but we will........ 3808
Jg 12:5 thou an Ephraimite? If he said, **N.**; 3808
Jg 19:23 **N.**, my brethren,...I pray you, do........ 408
Jg 19:23 **n.**, I pray you, do not so wickedly;...........
Ru 1:13 **n.**, my daughters; for it grieveth me 408
1Sa 2:16 **N.**; but thou shalt give it me now:...........
1Sa 2:24 **N.**, my sons; for it is no good............ 408
1Sa 8:19 **N.**; but we will have a king over........ 3808
1Sa 10:19 unto him, **N.**, but set a king over us.........
1Sa 12:12 **N.**; but a king shall reign over us: 3808
2Sa 13:12 **N.**, my brother, do not force me; 408
2Sa 13:25 **N.**, my son, let us not all now go, ... 408
2Sa 16:18 Hushai said unto Absalom, **N.**; 3808
2Sa 24:24 the king said unto Araunah, **N.**; 3808
1Ki 2:17 (for he will not say thee **n.**,) that he give...
1Ki 2:20 I pray thee, say me not **n.**. And 6440
1Ki 2:20 my mother: for I will not say thee **n.**........
1Ki 2:30 he said, **N.**; but I will die here. 3808
1Ki 3:22 And the other woman said, **N.**; but..... 3808
1Ki 3:23 saith, **N.**; but thy son is the dead,....... 3808
2Ki 3:13 king of Israel said unto him, **N.**: 408
2Ki 4:16 said, **N.**, my lord, thou man of God,..... 408
2Ki 20:10 **n.**, but let the shadow return 3808
1Ch 21:24 And king David said to Ornan, **N.**;...... 3808
Jer 6:15 **n.**, they were not at all ashamed,....... 1571
Jer 8:12 **n.**, they were not at all ashamed,....... 1571
Mt 5:37 **be, Yea, yea; N., n.:** *3756*
Mt 13:29 **he said, N.; lest while ye gather**.... *3756*
Lu 12:51 **I tell you, N.; but rather division:** ..*3780*
Lu 13:3, 5 **you, N.: but, except ye repent,** ... *3780*
Lu 16:30 **And he said, N., father Abraham:**.. *3780*
Joh 7:12 **N.**; but he deceiveth the people........... *3756*
Ac 16:37 **n.** verily; but let them come............. *3756*
Ro 3:27 works? **N.**: but by the law of faith. *3780*
Ro 7:7 **N.**, I had not known sin, but by the *235*
Ro 8:37 **N.**, in all these things we are more *235*
Ro 9:20 **N.** but, O man, who art thou that *3304*
1Co 6:8 **N.**, ye do wrong, and defraud, and....... *235*
1Co 12:22 **N.**, much more those members of the .. *235*
2Co 1:17 there should be yea yea, and **n. n.**? ... *3756*
2Co 1:18 word toward you was not yea and **n.**. ..*3756*
2Co 1:19 was not yea and **n.**, but in him was.... *3756*
Jas 5:12 your yea be yea; and your **n.**, **n.**; *3756*

NAZARENE (naz-a-reen') See also NAZARENES.

Mt 2:23 prophets, He shall be called a **N.**. *3480*

NAZARENES (naz-a-reens')

Ac 24:5 a ringleader of the sect of the **N.**: *3480*

NAZARETH (naz'-a-reth) See also NAZARENE.

Mt 2:23 came and dwelt in a city called **N.**: *3478*
Mt 4:13 And leaving **N.**, he came and dwelt..... *3478*
Mt 21:11 Jesus the prophet of **N.** of Galilee. *3478*
Mt 26:71 fellow was also with Jesus of **N.**.......... *3478*
Mk 1:9 that Jesus came from **N.** of Galilee, ... *3478*
Mk 1:24 to do with thee, thou Jesus of **N.**?...... *3478*
Mk 10:47 he heard that it was Jesus of **N.**, ... *3478*
Mk 14:67 thou also wast with Jesus of **N.**. *3478*

Mk 16:6 Ye seek Jesus of **N.**, which was......... *3478*
Lu 1:26 unto a city of Galilee, named **N.**,......... *3478*
Lu 2:4 from Galilee, out of the city of **N.**, ... *3478*
Lu 2:39 into Galilee, to their own city **N.**......... *3478*
Lu 2:51 down with them, and came to **N.**, ... *3478*
Lu 4:16 he came to **N.**, where he had been...... *3478*
Lu 4:34 to do with thee, thou Jesus of **N.**?......... *3478*
Lu 18:37 told him, that Jesus of **N.** passeth by. ..*3478*
Lu 24:19 Concerning Jesus of **N.**, which was...... *3478*
Joh 1:45 Jesus of **N.**, the son of Joseph. *3478*
Joh 1:46 any good thing come out of **N.**? *3478*
Joh 18:5 They answered him, Jesus of **N.**........ *3478*
Joh 18:7 **seek ye? And they said, Jesus of N.**... *3478*
Joh 19:19 Jesus Of **N.** The King Of The Jews. ... *3478*
Ac 2:22 Jesus of **N.**, a man approved of God... *3478*
Ac 3:6 In the name of Jesus Christ of **N.**........ *3478*
Ac 4:10 by the name of Jesus Christ of **N.**, ... *3478*
Ac 6:14 this Jesus of **N.** shall destroy this....... *3478*
Ac 10:38 How God anointed Jesus of **N.** with.... *3478*
Ac 22:8 me, **I am Jesus of N., whom thou**.. *3478*
Ac 26:9 contrary to the name of Jesus of **N.**... *3478*

NAZARITE (naz'-a-rite) See also NAZARITES.
Nu 6:2 themselves to vow a vow of a **N.**,...... 5139
Nu 6:13 And this is the law of the **N.**, when.... 5139
Nu 6:18 the **N.** shall shave the head of his 5139
Nu 6:19 put them upon the hands of the **N.**,.... 5139
Nu 6:20 after that the **N.** may drink wine........ 5139
Nu 6:21 the law of the **N.** who hath vowed,...... 5139
Jg 13:5 the child shall be a **N.** unto God......... 5139
Jg 13:7 for the child shall be a **N.** to God....... 5139
Jg 16:17 I have been a **N.** unto God from my... 5139

NAZARITES (naz'-a-rites)
La 4:7 Her **N.** were purer than snow, ... 5139
Am 2:11 and of your young men for **N.**.......... 5139
Am 2:12 But ye gave the **N.** wine to drink;....... 5139

NEAH (ne'-ah)
Jos 19:13 out to Remmon-methoar to **N.**;.......... 5269

NEAPOLIS (ne-ap'-o-lis)
Ac 16:11 and the next day to **N.**;.................... *3496*

NEAR See also NEARER; NEXT; NIGH.
Ge 12:11 was come **n.** to enter into Egypt,....... 7126
Ge 18:23 Abraham drew **n.**, and said, Wilt........ 5066
Ge 19:9 Lot, and came **n.** to break the door.... 5066
Ge 19:20 this city is **n.** to flee unto, and it is 7138
Ge 20:4 Abimelech had not come **n.** her: 7126
Ge 27:21 unto Jacob, Come **n.**, I pray thee,....... 5066
Ge 27:22 Jacob went **n.** unto Isaac his father;.... 5066
Ge 27:25 Bring it **n.** to me, and I will eat of 5066
Ge 27:25 he brought it **n.** to him, and he did..... 5066
Ge 27:26 Come **n.** now, and kiss me, my son.... 5066
Ge 27:27 he came **n.**, and kissed him: and he.... 5066
Ge 29:10 Jacob went **n.**, and rolled the stone 5066
Ge 33:3 until he came **n.** to his brother. 5066
Ge 33:6 Then the handmaidens came **n.**,......... 5066
Ge 33:7 Leah also with her children came **n.**,..... 5066
Ge 33:7 after came Joseph **n.** and Rachel, ... 5066
Ge 37:18 even before he came **n.** unto them, ... 7126
Ge 43:19 came **n.** to the steward to Joseph's..... 5066
Ge 44:18 Then Judah came **n.** unto him, and...... 5066
Ge 45:4 brethren, Come **n.** to me, I pray you...5066
Ge 45:4 they came **n.**. And he said, I am........ 5066
Ge 45:10 and thou shalt be **n.** unto me, thou,.... 7138
Ge 48:10 And he brought them **n.** unto him; 5066
Ge 48:13 and brought them **n.** unto him. 5066
Ex 12:48 then let him come **n.** and keep it; 7126
Ex 13:17 Philistines, although that was **n.**;........ 7138
Ex 14:20 the one came not **n.** the other all....... 7126
Ex 16:9 of Israel, Come **n.** before the Lord:.... 7126
Ex 19:22 also, which come **n.** to the Lord, ... 5066
Ex 20:21 drew **n.** unto the thick darkness.......... 5066
Ex 24:2 Moses alone shall come **n.** the Lord: .. 5066
Ex 28:43 come **n.** unto the altar to minister......... 5066
Ex 30:20 come **n.** to the altar to minister, ... 5066
Ex 40:32 when they came **n.** unto the altar,...... 7126
Le 9:5 all the congregation drew **n.** and........ 7126
Le 10:4 Come **n.**, carry your brethren from 7126
Le 10:5 So they went **n.**, and carried them 7126
Le 18:6 to any that is **n.** of kin to him, to....... 7607
Le 18:12 she is thy father's **n.** kinswoman. 7607
Le 18:13 she is thy mother's **n.** kinswoman. 7607
Le 18:17 for they are her **n.** kinswomen: 7608
Le 20:19 he uncovereth his **n.** kin: they........... 7607
Le 21:2 for his kin, that is **n.** unto him,.......... 7138
Nu 3:6 Bring the tribe of Levi **n.**, and.......... 7138
Nu 5:16 the priest shall bring her **n.**, and........ 7138
Nu 16:5 cause him to come **n.** unto him:......... 7126
Nu 16:5 will he cause to come **n.** unto him...... 7126
Nu 16:9 to bring you **n.** to himself to do......... 7138
Nu 16:10 he hath brought thee **n.** to him, ... 7138
Nu 16:40 come **n.** to offer incense before 7126
Nu 17:13 cometh any thing **n.** unto the 7138
Nu 26:3 of Moab by Jordan **n.** Jericho, saying,........
Nu 26:63 plains of Moab by Jordan **n.** Jericho. ....
Nu 31:12 Moab, which are by Jordan **n.** Jericho........
Nu 31:48 of hundreds, came **n.** unto Moses; 5066
Nu 32:16 they came **n.** unto him, and said, ... 5066
Nu 33:48 plains of Moab by Jordan **n.** Jericho ....
Nu 33:50 plains of Moab by Jordan **n.** Jericho, ...
Nu 34:15 this side Jordan **n.** Jericho eastward, ...
Nu 35:1 plains of Moab by Jordan **n.** Jericho ....
Nu 36:1 came **n.**, and spake before Moses, ... 5066
Nu 36:13 plains of Moab by Jordan **n.** Jericho. ....
De 1:22 ye came **n.** unto me every one of 7126
De 4:11 ye came **n.** and stood under the......... 7126
De 5:23 that ye came **n.** unto me, even all....... 7126
De 5:27 Go thou **n.**, and hear all that the........ 7126
De 16:21 any trees **n.** unto the altar of the......... 681
De 21:5 the sons of Levi shall come **n.**;.......... 5066
De 25:11 the wife of the one draweth **n.** for...... 7126
Jos 3:4 come not **n.** unto it, that ye may 7126
Jos 10:24 Come **n.**, put your feet upon the......... 7126
Jos 10:24 they came **n.**, and put their feet 7126
Jos 15:46 all that lay **n.** Ashdod, with their......... 3027
Jos 17:4 they came **n.** before Eleazar the 7126
Jos 18:13 **n.** the hill that lieth on the south......... 5921
Jos 21:1 Then came **n.** the heads of the.......... 7126
Jg 18:22 were in the houses **n.** to Micah's 5973
Jg 19:13 and let us draw **n.** to one of these 7126
Jg 20:24 And the children of Israel came **n.**...... 7126
Jg 20:34 knew not that evil was **n.** them. 5060
Ru 2:20 The man is **n.** of kin unto us, one...... 7138
Ru 3:9 handmaid; for thou art a **n.** kinsman..........
Ru 3:12 it is true that I am thy **n.** kinsman:...........
1Sa 4:19 was with child, **n.** to be delivered:............
1Sa 7:10 the Philistines drew **n.** to battle......... 5066
1Sa 9:18 then Saul drew **n.** to Samuel in the...... 5066
1Sa 10:20 all the tribes of Israel to come **n.**,...... 7126
1Sa 10:21 the tribe of Benjamin to come **n.** by 7126
1Sa 14:36 Let us draw **n.** hither unto God. 7126
1Sa 14:38 Draw ye **n.** hither, all the chief of 5066
1Sa 17:16 the Philistine drew **n.** morning and 5066
1Sa 17:40 and he drew **n.** to the Philistine......... 5066
1Sa 17:41 Philistine came on and drew **n.**........... 7126
1Sa 30:21 when David came **n.** to the people, ... 5066
2Sa 1:15 and said, Go **n.**, and fall upon him. 5066
2Sa 14:30 See Joab's field is **n.** mine, and he 413
2Sa 18:25 And he came apace, and drew **n.**. 7126
2Sa 19:42 the king is **n.** of kin to us:................ 7138
2Sa 20:16 Come **n.** hither, that I may speak........ 7126
2Sa 20:17 And when he was come **n.** unto her, .. 7126
1Ki 8:46 the land of the enemy, far or **n.**;......... 7138
1Ki 18:30 all the people, Come **n.** unto me........ 5066
1Ki 18:30 all the people came **n.** unto him. 5066
1Ki 18:36 Elijah the prophet came **n.**, and 5066
1Ki 21:2 because it is **n.** unto my house: 7138
1Ki 22:24 the son of Chenaanah went **n.**, and...... 5066
2Ki 4:27 Gehazi came **n.** to thrust her away...... 5066
2Ki 5:13 And his servants came **n.**, and........... 5066
2Ch 6:36 captives unto a land far off or **n.**; 7138
2Ch 18:23 the son of Chenaanah came **n.**,........... 5066
2Ch 21:16 that were **n.** the Ethiopians:.............. 3027
2Ch 29:31 come **n.** and bring sacrifices and 5066
Es 5:2 So Esther drew **n.**, and touched 7126
Es 9:1 drew **n.** to be put in execution, ... 5060
Job 31:37 a prince would I go **n.** unto him. 7126
Job 33:22 his soul draweth **n.** unto the grave, ... 7126
Job 41:16 One is so **n.** to another, that no air.... 5066
Ps 22:11 not far from me; for trouble is **n.**;........ 7138
Ps 32:9 bridle, lest they come **n.** unto thee...... 7126
Ps 73:28 is good for me to draw **n.** to God: 7132
Ps 75:1 name is **n.** thy wondrous works.......... 7138
Ps 107:18 draw **n.** unto the gates of death. 5060
Ps 119:151 Thou art **n.**, O Lord; and all thy 7138
Ps 119:169 Let my cry come **n.** before thee, ... 7126
Ps 148:14 of Israel, a people **n.** unto him........... 7138
Pr 7:8 through the street **n.** her corner;.......... 681
Pr 10:14 of the foolish is **n.** destruction. 7138
Pr 27:10 for better is a neighbour that is **n.**....... 7138
Isa 13:22 and her time is **n.** to come, and her ... 7138
Isa 26:17 **n.** the time of her delivery, is in 7126
Isa 29:13 draw **n.** me with their mouth, and 5066
Isa 33:13 ye that are **n.**, acknowledge my........... 7138
Isa 34:1 Come **n.**, ye nations, to hear; and....... 7126
Isa 41:1 let them come **n.**; then let them 5066
Isa 41:1 let us come **n.** together to................ 7126
Isa 41:5 of the earth were afraid, drew **n.**, ... 7126
Isa 45:20 draw **n.** together, ye that are............ 5066
Isa 45:21 Tell ye, and bring them **n.**; yea, let.... 5066
Isa 46:13 I bring **n.** thy righteousness; it 7126
Isa 48:16 Come ye **n.** unto me, hear ye this;...... 7126
Isa 50:8 He is **n.** that justifieth me; who 7138
Isa 50:8 adversary? let him come **n.** to me...... 5066
Isa 51:5 My righteousness is **n.**; my.............. 7138
Isa 54:14 for it shall not come **n.** thee............. 7126
Isa 55:6 call ye upon him while he is **n.**. 7138
Isa 56:1 for my salvation is **n.** to come, and.... 7138
Isa 57:3 But draw **n.** hither, ye sons of the 7126
Isa 57:19 is far off, and to him that is **n.**,.......... 7138
Isa 65:5 come not **n.** to me; for I am holier..... 5066
Jer 12:2 thou art **n.** in their mouth, and 7138
Jer 25:26 the kings of the north, far and **n.**, ... 7138
Jer 30:21 will cause him to draw **n.**, and he........ 7126
Jer 42:1 even unto the greatest, came **n.**, ... 5066
Jer 46:3 and shield, and draw **n.** to battle......... 5066
Jer 48:16 calamity of Moab is **n.** to come,.......... 7138
Jer 48:24 cities of the land of Moab, far or **n.**.... 7138
Jer 52:25 that were **n.** the king's person,.......... 7200
La 3:57 Thou drewest **n.** in the day that I 7126
La 4:18 our end is **n.**, our days are fulfilled;.... 7126
Eze 6:12 that is **n.** shall fall by the sword;......... 7138
Eze 7:7 is come, the day of trouble is **n.** 7138
Eze 7:12 time is come, the day draweth **n.**:...... 5060
Eze 9:1 charge over the city to draw **n.**, ... 7126
Eze 9:6 come not **n.** any man upon whom......... 5066
Eze 11:3 Which say, It is not **n.**; let us............ 7138
Eze 18:6 come **n.** to a menstruous woman,....... 7126
Eze 22:4 hast caused thy days to draw **n.**, ... 7126
Eze 22:5 Those that be **n.**, and those that.......... 7138
Eze 30:3 For the day is **n.**, even the day of...... 7138
Eze 30:3 the day of the Lord is **n.**, a cloudy...... 7138
Eze 40:46 **n.** to the Lord to minister unto.......... 7131
Eze 44:13 they shall not come **n.** unto me, ... 5066
Eze 44:13 come **n.** to any of my holy things,....... 5066
Eze 44:15 **n.** to me to minister unto me, ... 7126
Eze 44:16 and they shall come **n.** to my table,..... 7126
Eze 45:4 come **n.** to minister unto the Lord:..... 7131
Da 3:8 time certain Chaldeans came **n.**,......... 7127
Da 3:26 **n.** to the mouth of the burning 7127
Da 6:12 came **n.**, and spake before the king.... 7127
Da 7:13 they brought him **n.** before him. 7127
Da 7:16 I came **n.** unto one of them that 7127
Da 8:17 So he came **n.** where I stood: and....... 681
Da 9:7 and unto all Israel, that are **n.**, ... 7138
Joe 3:9 let all the men of war draw **n.**;.......... 5066
Joe 3:14 the day of the Lord is **n.** in the 7138
Am 6:3 the seat of violence to come **n.**;.......... 5066
Ob 15 day of the Lord is **n.** upon all the........ 7138
Zep 1:14 great day of the Lord is **n.**, it is **n.**, ... 7138
Zep 3:2 Lord; she drew not **n.** to her God........ 7126
Mal 3:5 I will come **n.** to you to judgment; 7126
Mt 21:34 **when the time of the fruit drew n.**, *1448*
Mt 24:33 **these things, know that it is n.**,.... *1451*
Mk 13:28 **leaves, ye know that summer is n.**: *1451*
Lu 15:1 Then drew **n.** unto him all the........... *1448*
Lu 18:40 when he was come **n.**, he asked him, ..*1448*
Lu 19:41 when he was come **n.**, he beheld *1448*
Lu 21:8 **the time draweth n.: go ye not**....... *1448*
Lu 22:47 drew **n.** unto Jesus to kiss him. *1448*
Lu 24:15 Jesus himself drew **n.**, and went *1448*
Joh 3:23 baptizing in Ænon **n.** to Salim,........... *1451*
Joh 4:5 **n.** to the parcel of ground that........... *4139*
Joh 11:54 a country **n.** to the wilderness,........... *1451*
Ac 7:31 and as he drew **n.** to behold it, the *4334*
Ac 8:29 Philip, Go **n.**, and join thyself to this... *4334*
Ac 9:3 journeyed, he came **n.** Damascus: *1448*
Ac 10:24 together his kinsmen and **n.** friends...... *316*
Ac 21:33 chief captain came **n.**, and took him,... *1448*
Ac 23:15 ever he come **n.**, are ready to kill him. *1448*
Ac 27:27 that they drew **n.** to some country; *4317*
Heb 10:22 Let us draw **n.** with a true heart........ *4334*

NEARER
Ru 3:12 there is a kinsman **n.** than I. 7138
Ro 13:11 is our salvation **n.** than when we........ *1452*

NEARIAH (ne-a-ri'-ah) See also NAGGE.
1Ch 3:22 and Bariah, and **N.**, and Shaphat, ... 5294

1Ch 3:23 And the sons of N.; Elioenai, and....... 5294
1Ch 4:42 and N., and Rephaiah, and Uzziel, ... 5294

NEATH See BENEATH; UNDERNEATH.

NEBAI (ne'-bahee)
Ne 10:19 Hariph, Anathoth, N., ... 5109

NEBAIOTH (ne-bah'-yoth) See also NEBAJOTH.
1Ch 1:29 The firstborn of Ishmael, N.;............ 5032
Isa 60:7 the rams of N. shall minister unto 5032

NEBAJOTH (ne-ba'-joth) See also NEBAIOTH.
Ge 25:13 the firstborn of Ishmael, N.; and........ 5032
Ge 28:9 son, the sister of N., to be his wife.... 5032
Ge 36:3 Ishmael's daughter, sister of N., ... 5032

NEBALLAT (ne-bal'-lat)
Ne 11:34 Hadid, Zeboim, N., ... 5041

NEBAT (ne'-bat)
1Ki 11:26 And Jeroboam the son of N., an......... 5028
1Ki 12:2 when Jeroboam the son of N., who..... 5028
1Ki 12:15 unto Jeroboam the son of N.. 5028
1Ki 15:1 of king Jeroboam the son of N.......... 5028
1Ki 16:3 house of Jeroboam the son of N......... 5028
1Ki 16:26 the way of Jeroboam the son of N., ... 5028
1Ki 16:31 the sins of Jeroboam the son of N., ... 5028
1Ki 21:22 house of Jeroboam the son of N., ... 5028
1Ki 22:52 the way of Jeroboam the son of N., ... 5028
2Ki 3:3 the sins of Jeroboam the son of N., ... 5028
2Ki 9:9 house of Jeroboam the son of N., ... 5028
2Ki 10:29 the sins of Jeroboam the son of N., ... 5028
2Ki 13:2, 11 sins of Jeroboam the son of N., ... 5028
2Ki 14:24 the sins of Jeroboam the son of N., ... 5028
2Ki 15:9, 18,24,28 of Jeroboam the son of N., ... 5028
2Ki 17:21 made Jeroboam the son of N. king:..... 5028
2Ki 23:15 which Jeroboam the son of N., who 5028
2Ch 9:29 against Jeroboam the son of N.?......... 5028
2Ch 10:2 when Jeroboam the son of N., who..... 5028
2Ch 10:15 spake...to Jeroboam the son of N....... 5028
2Ch 13:6 Yet Jeroboam the son of N., the 5028

NEBO (ne'-bo) See also PISGAH; SAMGAR-NEBO.
Nu 32:3 and Shebam, and N., and Beon,......... 5015
Nu 32:38 N., and Baal-meon, (their names........ 5015
Nu 33:47 mountains of Abarim, before N.. 5015
De 32:49 mount N., which is in the land of 5015
De 34:1 of Moab unto the mountain of N., ... 5015
1Ch 5:8 dwelt in Aroer, even unto N. and....... 5015
Ezr 2:29 The children of N., fifty and two. 5015
Ezr 10:43 the sons of N.; Jeiel, Mattithiah. 5015
Ne 7:33 men of the other N., fifty and two...... 5015
Isa 15:2 Moab shall howl over N., and over...... 5015
Isa 46:1 Bel boweth down, N. stoopeth, ... 5015
Jer 48:1 Woe unto N.! for it is spoiled: 5015
Jer 48:22 upon N., and upon Beth-diblathaim, ... 5015

NEBUCHADNEZZAR (neb-u-kad-nez'-zar) See also NEBUCHADREZZAR.
2Ki 24:1 N. king of Babylon came up, and........ 5019
2Ki 24:10 servants of N. king of Babylon........... 5019
2Ki 24:11 N. king of Babylon came against 5019
2Ki 25:1 that N. king of Babylon came, he, ... 5019
2Ki 25:8 is the nineteenth year of king N......... 5019
2Ki 25:22 whom N. king of Babylon had left,...... 5019
1Ch 6:15 and Jerusalem by the hand of N.. 5019
2Ch 36:6 Against him came up N. king of 5019
2Ch 36:7 N. also carried of the vessels of the ... 5019
2Ch 36:10 king N. sent, and brought him to 5019
2Ch 36:13 he also rebelled against king N., ... 5019
Ezr 1:7 which N. had brought forth out of 5019
Ezr 2:1 whom N. the king of Babylon had....... 5019
Ezr 5:12 he gave them into the hand of N........ 5020
Ezr 5:14 which N. took out of the temple 5020
Ezr 6:5 N. took forth out of the temple.......... 5020
Ne 7:6 N. the king of Babylon had carried 5019
Es 2:6 N. the king of Babylon had carried 5019
Jer 27:6 all these lands into the hand of N.. 5019
Jer 27:8 which will not serve the same N......... 5019
Jer 27:20 Which N. king of Babylon took not, ... 5019
Jer 28:3 that N. king of Babylon took away...... 5019
Jer 28:11 Even so will I break the yoke of N..... 5019
Jer 28:14 they may serve N. king of Babylon;..... 5019
Jer 29:1 whom N. had carried away captive 5019
Jer 29:3 of Judah sent unto Babylon to N. 5019
Jer 34:1 when N. king of Babylon, and all........ 5019
Jer 39:5 up to N. king of Babylon to Riblah...... 5019
Da 1:1 came N. king of Babylon unto............ 5019
Da 1:18 eunuchs brought them in before N...... 5019
Da 2:1 the second year of the reign of N., ... 5019
Da 2:1 N. dreamed dreams, wherewith 5019
Da 2:28 maketh known to the king N. 5020
Da 2:46 the king N. fell upon his face, and 5020
Da 3:1 N. the king made an image of gold, ... 5020
Da 3:2 N. the king sent to gather together 5020
Da 3:2 the image which N. the king had......... 5020
Da 3:3 image that N. the king had set up; 5020
Da 3:3 the image that N. had set up............ 5020
Da 3:5 image that N. the king hath set up: 5020
Da 3:7 image that N. the king had set up. 5020
Da 3:9 They spake and said to the king N., ... 5020
Da 3:13 N. in his rage and fury commanded..... 5020
Da 3:14 N. spake and said unto them, Is it..... 5020
Da 3:16 O N., we are not careful to answer..... 5020
Da 3:19 Then was N. full of fury, and the 5020
Da 3:24 Then N. the king was astonied, ... 5020
Da 3:26 N. came near to the mouth of the...... 5020
Da 3:28 N. spake, and said, Blessed be the...... 5020
Da 4:1 N. the king, unto all people,............. 5020
Da 4:4 I N. was at rest in mine house, and.... 5020
Da 4:18 This dream I king N. have seen......... 5020
Da 4:28 All this came upon the king N.. 5020
Da 4:31 O king N., to thee it is spoken; The... 5020
Da 4:33 was the thing fulfilled upon N.: 5020
Da 4:34 days I N. lifted up mine eyes unto..... 5020
Da 4:37 I N. praise and extol and honour........ 5020
Da 5:2 which his father N. had taken out....... 5020
Da 5:11 whom the king N. thy father, the....... 5020
Da 5:18 God gave N. thy father a kingdom,...... 5020

NEBUCHADREZZAR (neb-u-kad-rez'-zar) See also NEBUCHADNEZZAR.
Jer 21:2 N. king of Babylon maketh war.......... 5019
Jer 21:7 the hand of N. king of Babylon,......... 5019
Jer 22:25 the hand of N. king of Babylon, ... 5019
Jer 24:1 that N. king of Babylon had carried..... 5019
Jer 25:1 the first year of N. king of Babylon; ... 5019
Jer 25:9 N. the king of Babylon, my servant, ... 5019
Jer 29:21 deliver them into the hand of N. 5019
Jer 32:1 which was the eighteenth year of N.... 5019
Jer 32:28 Chaldeans, and into the hand of N..... 5019
Jer 35:11 when N. king of Babylon came up 5019
Jer 37:1 whom N. king of Babylon made 5019
Jer 39:1 came N. king of Babylon and all......... 5019
Jer 39:11 N. king of Babylon gave charge 5019
Jer 43:10 I will send and take N. the king of 5019
Jer 44:30 king of Judah into the hand of N......... 5019
Jer 46:2 N. king of Babylon smote in the......... 5019
Jer 46:13 N. king of Babylon should come......... 5019
Jer 46:26 into the hand of N. king of Babylon, ... 5019
Jer 49:28 N. king of Babylon shall smite, ... 5019
Jer 49:30 for N. king of Babylon hath broken..... 5019
Jer 51:34 N. the king of Babylon hath 5019
Jer 52:4 N. king of Babylon came, he and....... 5019
Jer 52:12 the nineteenth year of N. king of 5019
Jer 52:28 the people whom N. carried away 5019
Jer 52:29 In the eighteenth year of N. he 5019
Jer 52:30 the three and twentieth year of N. 5019
Eze 26:7 I will bring upon Tyrus N. king of 5019
Eze 29:18 N. king of Babylon caused his army.... 5019
Eze 29:19 will give the land of Egypt unto N. 5019
Eze 30:10 to cease by the hand of N. king of 5019

NEBUSHASBAN (neb-u-shas'-ban)
Jer 39:13 captain of the guard sent, and N., ... 5021

NEBUZAR-ADAN (neb-u-zar'-a-dan)
2Ki 25:8 came N., captain of the guard, a 5018
2Ki 25:11 did N. the captain of the guard 5018
2Ki 25:20 N. captain of the guard took these,..... 5018
Jer 39:9 Then N. the captain of the guard 5018
Jer 39:10 N. the captain of the guard left of 5018
Jer 39:11 to N. the captain of the guard, ... 5018
Jer 39:13 So N. the captain of the guard sent, ... 5018
Jer 40:1 that N. the captain of the guard......... 5018
Jer 41:10 whom N. the captain of the guard 5018
Jer 43:6 that N. the captain of the guard.......... 5018
Jer 52:12 came N., captain of the guard,........... 5018
Jer 52:15 N. the captain of the guard carried 5018
Jer 52:16 But N. the captain of the guard left 5018
Jer 52:26 N. the captain of the guard took 5018
Jer 52:30 N. the captain of the guard carried...... 5018

NECESSARY
Job 23:12 his mouth more than my n. food. 2706
Ac 13:46 It was n. that the word of God *316*
Ac 15:28 burden than these n. things; *1876*
Ac 28:10 such things as were n........ *4314,3588,5532*
1Co 12:22 seem to be more feeble, are n.......... *316*
2Co 9:5 Therefore I thought it n. to exhort *316*
Php 2:25 Yet I supposed it n. to send to you....... *316*
Tit 3:14 maintain good works for n. uses, ... *316*
Heb 9:23 was therefore n. that the patterns *318*

NECESSITIES
Ac 20:34 hands have ministered unto my n., ... *5532*
2Co 6:4 much patience, in affliction, in n., ... *318*
2Co 12:10 reproaches, in n., in persecutions, ... *318*

NECESSITY See also NECESSITIES.
Lu 23:17 (For of n. he must release one *2192,318*
Ro 12:13 Distributing to the n. of saints, ... *5532*
1Co 7:37 stedfast in his heart, having no n., ... *318*
1Co 9:16 for n. is laid upon me; yea, woe is....... *318*
2Co 9:7 not grudgingly, or of n.: for God *318*
Php 4:16 sent once and again unto my n.. .... *5532*
Phm 14 not be as it were of n., but willingly..... *318*
Heb 7:12 there is made of n. a change also *318*
Heb 8:3 wherefore it is of n. that this man *316*
Heb 9:16 there must also of n. be the death....... *318*

NECHO (ne'-ko) See also PHARAOH-NECHOH.
2Ch 35:20 N. king of Egypt came up to fight 5224
2Ch 35:22 the words of N. from the mouth of....... 5224
2Ch 36:4 N. took Jehoahaz his brother, and 5224

NECHOH See NECHO.

NECK See also NECKS; STIFFNECKED.
Ge 27:16 and upon the smooth of his n.. 6677
Ge 27:40 shalt break his yoke from off thy n.... 6677
Ge 33:4 and fell on his n., and kissed him: 6677
Ge 41:42 and put a gold chain about his n.; 6677
Ge 45:14 fell upon his brother Benjamin's n.,..... 6677
Ge 45:14 and Benjamin wept upon his n.. 6677
Ge 46:29 fell on his n., and he wept on his n..... 6677
Ge 49:8 shall be in the n. of thine enemies;..... 6203
Ex 13:13 it, then thou shalt break his n.. 6203
Ex 34:20 not, then shalt thou break his n.. 6203
Le 5:8 and wring off his head from his n., ... 6203
De 21:4 shall strike off the heifer's n. there..... 6203
De 28:48 put a yoke of iron upon thy n., ... 6677
De 31:27 thy rebellion, and thy stiff n.; 6203
1Sa 4:18 and his n. brake, and he died: for 4665
2Ki 17:14 like to the n. of their fathers, that...... 6203
2Ch 36:13 he stiffened his n., and hardened........ 6203
Ne 9:29 hardened their n., and would not......... 6203
Job 15:26 runneth upon him, even on his n., ... 6677
Job 16:12 he hath also taken me by my n., ... 6203
Job 39:19 thou clothed his n. with thunder? 6677
Job 41:22 In his n. remaineth strength, and 6677
Ps 75:5 on high: speak not with a stiff n.......... 6677
Pr 1:9 thy head, and chains about thy n........ 1621
Pr 3:3 bind them about thy n.; write............ 1621
Pr 3:22 unto thy soul, and grace to thy n.. 1621
Pr 6:21 heart, and tie them about thy n.. 1621
Pr 29:1 often reproved hardeneth his n., ... 6203
Ca 1:10 jewels, thy n. with chains of gold. 6677
Ca 4:4 Thy n. is like the tower of David 6677
Ca 4:9 eyes, with one chain of thy n.. 6677
Ca 7:4 Thy n. is as a tower of ivory; 6677
Isa 8:8 over, he shall reach even to the n.; 6677
Isa 10:27 and his yoke from off thy n., and 6677
Isa 30:28 shall reach to the midst of the n., ... 6677
Isa 48:4 and thy n. is an iron sinew, and......... 6203
Isa 52:2 thyself from the bands of thy n., ... 6677
Isa 66:3 a lamb, as if he cut off a dog's n.; 6202
Jer 7:26 their ear, but hardened their n.. 6202
Jer 17:23 their ear, but made their n. stiff, ... 6202
Jer 27:2 yokes, and put them upon thy n., ... 6677
Jer 27:8 will not put their n. under the yoke.... 6677
Jer 27:11 that bring their n. under the yoke 6677
Jer 28:10 from off the prophet Jeremiah's n., ... 6677
Jer 28:11 n. of all nations within the space 6677
Jer 28:12 off the n. of the prophet Jeremiah, ... 6677
Jer 28:14 a yoke of iron upon the n. of all......... 6677
Jer 30:8 will break his yoke from off thy n., ... 6677
La 1:14 wreathed, and come up upon my n.. ... 6677
Eze 16:11 thy hands, and a chain on thy n.. 1627
Da 5:7, 16,29 chain of gold about his n., ... 6676
Hos 10:11 but I passed over upon her fair n., ... 6676
Hab 3:13 the foundation unto the n.. Selah. 6676
Mt 18:6 **were hanged about his n., and** *5137*
Mk 9:42 **were hanged about his n., and he**.. *5137*
Lu 15:20 **and fell on his n., and kissed him.** .*5137*
Lu 17:2 **were hanged about his n., and he**.. *5137*

Ac 15:10 a yoke upon the **n.** of the disciples, ... *5137*
Ac 20:37 and fell on Paul's **n.**, and kissed him, .. *5137*

NECKS
Jos 10:24 feet upon the **n.** of these kings......... 6677
Jos 10:24 put their feet upon the **n.** of them...... 6677
Jg 5:30 the **n.** of them that take the spoil? 6677
Jg 8:21 that were on their camels' **n.**. 6677
Jg 8:26 that were about their camels' **n.**......... 6677
2Sa 22:41 given me the **n.** of mine enemies, ... 6203
2Ki 17:14 not hear, but hardened their **n.**,......... 6203
Ne 3:5 put not their **n.** to the work of 6677
Ne 9:16 proudly, and hardened their **n.**,......... 6203
Ne 9:17 but hardened their **n.**, and in their...... 6203
Ps 18:40 given me the **n.** of mine enemies; 6203
Isa 3:16 walk with stretched forth **n.** and 1627
Jer 19:15 they have hardened their **n.**, that....... 6203
Jer 27:12 Bring your **n.** under the yoke of 6677
La 5:5 Our **n.** are under persecution: we 6677
Eze 21:29 upon the **n.** of them that are slain, ... 6677
Mic 2:3 which ye shall not remove your **n.**;...... 6677
Ro 16:4 for my life laid down their own **n.**. *5137*

NECROMANCER
De 18:11 spirits, or a wizard, or a **n.**,....... 1875,4191

NEDABIAH (ned-a-bi'-ah)
1Ch 3:18 Jecaniah, Hoshama, and **N.**. 5072

NEED See also NEEDED; NEEDEST; NEEDETH; NEEDFUL; NEEDS.
De 15:8 lend him sufficient for his **n.**, in 4270
1Sa 21:15 Have I **n.** of mad men, that ye 2638
2Ch 2:16 Lebanon, as much as thou shalt **n.**. 6878
2Ch 20:17 Ye shall not **n.** to fight in this battle:........
Ezr 6:9 that which they have **n.** of, both 2818
Pr 31:11 that he shall have no **n.** of spoil. 2637
Mt 3:14 I have **n.** to be baptized of thee,.......... *5532*
Mt 6:8 **what things ye have n. of,** *5532*
Mt 6:32 **ye have n. of all these things** *5535*
Mt 9:12 **be whole n. not a physician,** .. *2192,5532*
Mt 14:16 **They n. not depart; give ye** *2192,5532*
Mt 21:3 **say The Lord hath n. of them;** *5532*
Mt 26:25 further **n.** have we of witnesses? *5532*
Mk 2:17 **whole have no n. of the physician,** .*5532*
Mk 2:25 **what David did, when he had n.,** ... *5532*
Mk 11:3 **ye that the Lord hath n. of him;** ... *5532*
Mk 14:63 **n.** we any further witnesses? *2192,5532*
Lu 5:31 **are whole n. not a physician;** . *2192,5532*
Lu 9:11 healed them that had **n.** of healing...... *5532*
Lu 12:30 **that ye have n. of these things**...... *5535*
Lu 15:7 **which n. no repentance.** *2192,5532*
Lu 19:31 **Because the Lord hath n. of him**... *5532*
Lu 19:34 they said, The Lord hath **n.** of him..... *5532*
Lu 22:71 What **n.** we any further witness? .*2192,5532*
Joh 13:29 that we have **n.** of against the feast;... *5532*
Ac 2:45 to all men, as every man had **n.**. *5532*
Ac 4:35 every man according as he had **n.**. *5532*
Ro 16:2 business she hath **n.** of you: for......... *5535*
1Co 7:36 and **n.** so require, let him do what *3784*
1Co 12:21 the hand, I have no **n.** of thee:.......... *5532*
1Co 12:21 to the feet, I have no **n.** of you. *5532*
1Co 12:24 For our comely parts have no **n.**......... *5532*
2Co 3:1 or **n.** we, as some others, epistles *5535*
Php 4:12 both to abound and to suffer **n.**...............
Php 4:19 my God shall supply all your **n.**.......... *5532*
1Th 1:8 we **n.** not to speak any thing...... *2192,5532*
1Th 4:9 love ye **n.** not that I write unto you:... *5532*
1Th 5:1 ye have no **n.** that I write unto you.... *5532*
Heb 4:16 and find grace to help in time of **n.**..... *2121*
Heb 5:12 ye have **n.** that one teach you.......... *5532*
Heb 5:12 are become such as have **n.** of milk,... *5532*
Heb 7:11 further **n.** was there that another....... *5532*
Heb 10:36 For ye have **n.** of patience, that,........ *5532*
1Pe 1:6 though now for a season, if **n.** be,...... *1163*
1Jo 2:27 **n.** not that any man teach you:... *2192,5532*
1Jo 3:17 and seeth his brother have **n.**, and *5532*
Re 3:17 **goods, and have n. of nothing;** *5532*
Re 21:23 And the city had no **n.** of the sun,....... *5532*
Re 22:5 they **n.** no candle, neither light... *2192,5532*

NEEDED
Joh 2:25 **n.** not that any should testify...... *2192,5532*
Ac 17:25 hands, as though he **n.** any thing,....... *4326*

NEEDEST
Joh 16:30 **n.** not that any man should ask... *2192,5532*

NEEDETH
Ge 33:15 And he said, What **n.** it? let me find ....
Lu 11:8 **and give him as many as he n.**...... *5535*
Joh 13:10 **n. not save to wash his feet,** .. *2192,5532*
Eph 4:28 he may have to give to him that **n.**..... *5532*
2Ti 2:15 workman that **n.** not to be ashamed, ... *422*
Heb 7:27 Who **n.** not daily, as those high.... *2192,318*

NEEDFUL
Ezr 7:20 be **n.** for the house of thy God, ... 2819
Lu 10:42 **But one thing is n.: and Mary** *5532*
Ac 15:5 That it was **n.** to circumcise them, ... *1163*
Php 1:24 abide in the flesh is more **n.** for you..... *316*
Jas 2:16 things which are **n.** to the body; *2006*
Jude 3 it was **n.** for me to write unto you,...... *318*

NEEDLE See also NEEDLE'S; NEEDLEWORK.
Mt 19:24 **to go through the eye of a n.,** *4476*
Mk 10:25 **to go through the eye of a n.,** *4476*

NEEDLE'S
Lu 18:25 **a camel to go through a n. eye.** *4476*

NEEDLEWORK
Ex 26:36 linen, wrought with **n.**. 4639,7551
Ex 27:16 fine twined linen, wrought with **n.**. 7551
Ex 28:39 thou shalt make the girdle of **n.**. 7551
Ex 36:37 scarlet and fine twined linen, of **n.**;..... 7551
Ex 38:18 for the gate of the court was **n.**,........ 7551
Ex 39:29 blue, and purple, and scarlet, of **n.**;.... 7551
Jg 5:30 a prey of divers colours of **n.**, ... 7553
Jg 5:30 divers colours of **n.** on both sides,...... 7553
Ps 45:14 unto the king in raiment of **n.**. 7553

NEEDS
Ge 17:13 money, must **n.** be circumcised:......... 4135
Ge 19:9 and he will **n.** be a judge: 8199
Ge 24:5 must I **n.** bring thy son again unto...... 7725
Ge 31:30 though thou wouldest **n.** be gone, ...
2Sa 14:14 For we must **n.** die, and are as waters......
Jer 10:5 they must **n.** be borne, because they.......
Mt 18:7 **for it must n. be that offences** *318*
Mk 13:7 **for such things must n. be; but the** .....
Lu 14:18 **and I must n. go and see it:** *318*
Joh 4:4 he must **n.** go through Samaria. ....
Ac 1:16 this scripture must **n.** have been.............
Ac 17:3 that Christ must **n.** have suffered, ...
Ac 21:22 the multitude must **n.** come *3843*
Ro 13:5 ye must **n.** be subject, not only........... *318*
1Co 5:10 then must ye **n.** go out of the world. ....
2Co 11:30 If I must **n.** glory, I will glory of.............

NEEDY
De 15:11 to thy poor, and to thy **n.**, in thy land.... 34
De 24:14 an hired servant that is poor and **n.**,...... 34
Job 24:4 They turn the **n.** out of the way: 34
Job 24:14 with the light killeth the poor and **n.**, ... 34
Ps 9:18 the **n.** shall not alway be forgotten: 34
Ps 12:5 of the poor, for the sighing of the **n.**,..... 34
Ps 35:10 the **n.** from him that spoileth him?......... 34
Ps 37:14 to cast down the poor and **n.**, and to..... 34
Ps 40:17 But I am poor and **n.**; yet the Lord......... 34
Ps 70:5 I am poor and **n.**: make haste unto........ 34
Ps 72:4 he shall save the children of the **n.**, ... 34
Ps 72:12 shall deliver the **n.** when he crieth;........ 34
Ps 72:13 He shall spare the poor and **n.**, and....... 34
Ps 72:13 and shall save the souls of the **n.**. 34
Ps 74:21 let the poor and **n.** praise thy name. 34
Ps 82:3 do justice to the afflicted and **n.**......... 7326
Ps 82:4 Deliver the poor and **n.**: rid them.......... 34
Ps 86:1 Lord, hear me: for I am poor and **n.**...... 34
Ps 109:16 but persecuted the poor and **n.** man, ... 34
Ps 109:22 For I am poor and **n.**, and my heart 34
Ps 113:7 and lifteth the **n.** out of the dunghill;...... 34
Pr 30:14 earth, and the **n.** from among men. 34
Pr 31:9 plead the cause of the poor and **n.**. 34
Pr 31:20 forth her hands to the **n.**..................... 34
Isa 10:2 turn aside the **n.** from judgment,......... 1800
Isa 14:30 and the **n.** shall lie down in safety: 34
Isa 25:4 a strength to the **n.** in his distress, ... 34
Isa 26:6 the poor, and the steps of the **n.**. 1800
Isa 32:7 even when the **n.** speaketh right. 34
Isa 41:17 When the poor and **n.** seek water, ... 34
Jer 5:28 the right of the **n.** do they not judge...... 34
Jer 22:16 judged the cause of the poor and **n.**;...... 34
Eze 16:49 the hand of the poor and **n.**. 34
Eze 18:12 Hath oppressed the poor and **n.**,........... 34
Eze 22:29 and have vexed the poor and **n.**,........... 34
Am 4:1 oppress the poor, which crush the **n.**,.... 34
Am 8:4 this, O ye that swallow up the **n.**, ... 34
Am 8:6 and the **n.** for a pair of shoes; 34

NEESINGS
Job 41:18 By his **n.** a light doth shine, and 5846

NEGINAH (neg'-i-nah) See also NEGINOTH.
Ps 61:*title* To the chief Musician upon **N.**,.......... 5058

NEGINOTH (neg'-i-noth) See also NEGINAH.
Ps 4:*title* To the chief Musician on **N.**,............. 5058
Ps 6:*title* To the chief Musician on **N.**,............. 5058
Ps 54:*title* To the chief Musician on **N.**,............. 5058
Ps 55:*title* To the chief Musician on **N.**,............. 5058
Ps 67:*title* To the chief Musician on **N.**,............. 5058
Ps 76:*title* To the chief Musician on **N.**,............. 5058

NEGLECT See also NEGLECTED; NEGLECTING.
Mt 18:17 **And if he shall n. to hear them,**.... *3878*
Mt 18:17 **but if he n. to hear the church,**..... *3878*
1Ti 4:14 **N.** not the gift that is in thee,............ *272*
Heb 2:3 escape, if we **n.** so great salvation;...... *272*

NEGLECTED
Ac 6:1 were **n.** in the daily ministration......... *3865*

NEGLECTING
Col 2:23 and humility, and **n.** of the body; *857*

NEGLIGENT
2Ch 29:11 My sons, be not now **n.**: for the........ 7952
2Pe 1:12 I will not be **n.** to put you always *272*

NEGO See ABED-NEGO.

NEHELAMITE (ne-hel'-am-ite)
Jer 29:24 also speak to Shemaiah the **N.**,.......... 5161
Jer 29:32 Lord concerning Shemaiah the **N.**;...... 5161
Jer 29:32 I will punish Shemaiah the **N.**, ... 5161

NEHEMIAH (ne-he-mi'-ah)
Ezr 2:2 with Zerubbabel: Jeshua, **N.**, ... 5166
Ne *general title* The Book Of **N.** 5166
Ne 1:1 words of **N.** the son of Hachaliah. 5166
Ne 3:16 him repaired **N.** the son of Azbuk,...... 5166
Ne 7:7 came with Zerubbabel, Jeshua, **N.**, ... 5166
Ne 8:9 **N.**, which is the Tirshatha, and.......... 5166
Ne 10:1 that sealed were, **N.**, the Tirshatha, ... 5166
Ne 12:26 and in the days of **N.** the governor, ... 5166
Ne 12:47 in the days of **N.**, gave the portions.... 5166

NEHILOTH (ne'-hi-loth)
Ps 5:*title* To the chief Musician upon **N.**,.......... 5155

NEHUM (ne'-hum) See also REHUM.
Ne 7:7 Bilshan, Mispereth, Bigvai, **N.**, ... 5149

NEHUSHTA (ne-hush'-tah)
2Ki 24:8 And his mother's name was **N.**, ... 5179

NEHUSHTAN (ne-hush'-tan)
2Ki 18:4 incense to it: and he called it **N.**. 5180

NEIEL (ne-i'-el)
Jos 19:27 and **N.**, and goeth out to Cabul.......... 5272

NEIGHBOUR See also NEIGHBOUR'S; NEIGHBOURS.
Ex 3:22 woman shall borrow of her **n.**,........... 7934
Ex 11:2 let every man borrow of his **n.**, ... 7453
Ex 11:2 and every woman of her **n.**, jewels..... 7468
Ex 12:4 him and his **n.** next unto his house..... 7934
Ex 20:16 bear false witness against thy **n.**. 7453
Ex 21:14 come presumptuously upon his **n.**,...... 7453
Ex 22:7 man shall deliver unto his **n.** money.... 7453
Ex 22:9 he shall pay double unto his **n.**. 7453
Ex 22:10 If a man deliver unto his **n.** an ass, ... 7453
Ex 22:14 if a man borrow ought of his **n.**, ... 7453
Ex 32:27 companion, and every man his **n.**. 7138
Le 6:2 and lie unto his **n.** in that which......... 5997
Le 6:2 violence, or hath deceived his **n.**;....... 5997
Le 19:13 Thou shalt not defraud thy **n.**, ... 7453
Le 19:15 shalt thou judge thy **n.**.................... 5997
Le 19:16 stand against the blood of thy **n.**. 7453
Le 19:17 shalt in any wise rebuke thy **n.**,.......... 5997
Le 19:18 thou shalt love thy **n.** as thyself:......... 7453
Le 24:19 a man cause a blemish in his **n.**; 5997
Le 25:14 And if thou sell ought unto thy **n.**,...... 5997
Le 25:15 the jubile thou shalt buy of thy **n.**,...... 5997
De 4:42 which should kill his **n.** unawares,....... 7453
De 5:20 bear false witness against thy **n.**. 7453
De 15:2 that lendeth ought unto his **n.** shall..... 7453
De 15:2 he shall not exact it of his **n.**, or of.... 7453
De 19:4 Whoso killeth his **n.** ignorantly, ... 7453
De 19:5 man goeth into the wood with his **n.**.... 7453
De 19:5 lighteth upon his **n.**, that he die; 7453
De 19:11 But if any man hate his **n.**, and lie...... 7453
De 22:26 when a man riseth against his **n.**, ... 7453

De 23:25 into the standing corn of thy n.,......... 7453
De 27:24 be he that smiteth his n. secretly........ 7453
Jos 20:5 because he smote his n. unwittingly,.... 7453
Ru 4:7 off his shoe, and gave it to his n........ 7453
1Sa 15:28 and hath given it to a n. of thine,....... 7453
1Sa 28:17 given it to thy n., even to David:....... 7453
2Sa 12:11 and give them unto thy n., and he...... 7453
1Ki 8:31 If any man trespass against his n., ... 7453
1Ki 20:35 said unto his n. in the word of the 7453
2Ch 6:22 If a man sin against his n., and an...... 7453
Job 12:4 I am as one mocked of his n., who..... 7453
Job 16:21 God, as a man pleadeth for his n.! 7453
Ps 12:2 speak vanity every one with his n.. 7453
Ps 15:3 his tongue, nor doeth evil to his n., ... 7453
Ps 15:3 up a reproach against his n.. 7138
Ps 101:5 Whoso privily slandereth his n., ... 7453
Pr 3:28 Say not unto thy n., Go, and come..... 7453
Pr 3:29 Devise not evil against thy n., ... 7453
Pr 11:9 with his mouth destroyeth his n.. 7453
Pr 11:12 is void of wisdom despiseth his n.. 7453
Pr 12:26 is more excellent than his n.: 7453
Pr 14:20 poor is hated even of his own n.. 7453
Pr 14:21 He that despiseth his n. sinneth:........ 7453
Pr 16:29 A violent man enticeth his n., and...... 7453
Pr 18:17 his n. cometh and searcheth him. 7453
Pr 19:4 the poor is separated from his n.. 7453
Pr 21:10 his n. findeth no favour in his eyes. 7453
Pr 24:28 Be not a witness against thy n. 7453
Pr 25:8 when thy n. hath put thee to shame. .. 7453
Pr 25:9 Debate thy cause with thy n. 7453
Pr 25:18 beareth false witness against his n...... 7453
Pr 26:19 So is the man that deceiveth his n.,.... 7453
Pr 27:10 better is a n. that is near than a........ 7934
Pr 29:5 that flattereth his n. spreadeth a........ 7453
Ec 4:4 for this a man is envied of his n.......... 7453
Isa 3:5 by another, and every one by his n. ... 7453
Isa 19:2 and every one against his n.; 7453
Isa 41:6 They helped every one his n.; and..... 7453
Jer 6:21 the n. and his friend shall perish. 7934
Jer 7:5 between a man and his n.;................ 7453
Jer 9:4 Take ye heed every one of his n., ... 7453
Jer 9:4 every n. will walk with slanders......... 7453
Jer 9:5 they will deceive every one his n., ... 7453
Jer 9:8 speaketh peaceably to his n. with....... 7453
Jer 9:20 and every one her n. lamentation. 7468
Jer 22:8 they shall say every man to his n.,...... 7453
Jer 23:27 which they tell every man to his n., ... 7453
Jer 23:30 my words every one from his n.. 7453
Jer 23:35 shall ye say every one to his n., and .. 7453
Jer 31:34 teach no more every man his n., ... 7453
Jer 34:15 liberty every man to his n.; and ye..... 7453
Jer 34:17 brother, and every man to his n.. 7453
Jer 49:18 Gomorrah and the n. cities thereof, ... 7934
Jer 50:40 Gomorrah and the n. cities thereof, ... 7934
Hab 2:15 unto him that giveth his n. drink, ... 7453
Zec 3:10 ye call every man his n. under the 7453
Zec 8:10 all men every one against his n.......... 7453
Zec 8:16 ye every man the truth to his n.; 7453
Zec 8:17 evil in your hearts against his n.; 7453
Zec 14:13 every one on the hand of his n., and .. 7453
Zec 14:13 rise up against the hand of his n.. 7453
Mt 5:43 **been said, Thou shalt love thy n.,..** *4139*
Mt 19:19 **Thou shalt love thy n. as thyself...** *4139*
Mt 22:39 **Thou shalt love thy n. as thyself...** *4139*
Mk 12:31 **Thou shalt love thy n. as thyself...** *4139*
Mk 12:33 and to love his n. as himself, is *4139*
Lu 10:27 all thy mind; and thy n. as thyself. *4139*
Lu 10:29 said unto Jesus, And who is my n.? *4139*
Lu 10:36 **was n. unto him that fell among...** *4139*
Ac 7:27 he that did his n. wrong thrust him *4139*
Ro 13:9 Thou shalt love thy n. as thyself. *4139*
Ro 13:10 Love worketh no ill to his n.:............ *4139*
Ro 15:2 Let every one of us please his n., ... *4139*
Gal 5:14 Thou shalt love thy n. as thyself. *4139*
Eph 4:25 speak every man truth with his n.. .... *4139*
Heb 8:11 shall not teach every man his n., ... *4139*
Jas 2:8 Thou shalt love thy n. as thyself, ... *4139*

NEIGHBOUR'S

Ex 20:17 Thou shalt not covet thy n. house, ... 7453
Ex 20:17 thou shalt not covet thy n. wife, ... 7453
Ex 20:17 his ass, nor anything that is thy n.. 7453
Ex 22:8 have put his hand unto his n. goods.... 7453
Ex 22:11 not put his hand unto his n. goods;...... 7453
Ex 22:26 If thou at all take thy n. raiment 7453
Le 18:20 not lie carnally with thy n. wife, to..... 5997
Le 20:10 adultery with his n. wife,.................. 7453
Le 25:14 or buyest ought of thy n. hand, ye 5997
De 5:21 shalt thou desire thy n. wife, ... 7453
De 5:21 shalt thou covet thy n. house, his 7453
De 5:21 his ass, or any thing that is thy n...... 7453
De 19:14 shalt not remove thy n. landmark, ... 7453
De 22:24 he hath humbled his n. wife: 7453
De 23:24 thou comest into thy n. vineyard, ... 7453
De 23:25 a sickle unto thy n. standing corn....... 7453
De 27:17 he that removeth his n. landmark. 7453
Job 31:9 or if I have laid wait at my n. door; 7453
Pr 6:29 So he that goeth in to his n. wife; 7453
Pr 25:17 thy foot from thy n. house; lest he..... 7453
Jer 5:8 every one neighed after his n. wife..... 7453
Jer 22:13 useth his n. service without wages, ... 7453
Eze 18:6 neither hath defiled his n. wife,......... 7453
Eze 18:11 mountains, and defiled his n. wife,...... 7453
Eze 18:15 Israel, hath not defiled his n. wife, ... 7453
Eze 22:11 abomination with his n. wife; and 7453
Eze 33:26 and ye defile every one his n. wife: 7453
Zec 11:6 the men every one into his n. hand, ... 7453

NEIGHBOURS See also NEIGHBOURS'.

Jos 9:16 they heard that they were their n., ... 7138
Ru 4:17 the women her n. gave it a name,...... 7934
2Ki 4:3 vessels abroad of all thy n., even....... 7934
Ps 28:3 which speak peace to their n., but...... 7453
Ps 31:11 but especially among my n., and 7934
Ps 44:13 makest us a reproach to our n., a 7934
Ps 79:4 We are become a reproach to our n., ..7934
Ps 79:12 And render unto our n. sevenfold....... 7934
Ps 80:6 Thou makest us a strife unto our n.. .. 7934
Ps 89:41 him: he is a reproach to his n.. 7934
Jer 12:14 against all mine evil n., that touch...... 7934
Jer 49:10 his brethren, and his n., and he is...... 7934
Eze 16:26 the Egyptians thy n., great of flesh; ... 7934
Eze 22:12 thou hast greedily gained of thy n. 7453
Eze 23:5 her lovers, on the Assyrians her n., ... 7138
Eze 23:12 doted upon the Assyrians her n., ... 7138
Lu 1:58 And her n. and her cousins heard....... *4040*
Lu 14:12 **thy kinsmen, nor thy rich n.......** *1069*
Lu 15:6 **calleth together his friends and n.,.** *1069*
Lu 15:9 **she calleth her friends and her n...** *1069*
Joh 9:8 The n. therefore, and they which....... *1069*

NEIGHBOURS'

Jer 29:23 adultery with their n. wives, and........ 7453

NEIGHED

Jer 5:8 every one n. after his neighbour's 6670

NEIGHING See also NEIGHINGS.

Jer 8:16 sound of the n. of his strong ones; 4684

NEIGHINGS

Jer 13:27 seen thine adulteries, and thy n., ... 4684

NEITHER

Ge 3:3 not eat of it, n. shall ye touch it, ... 3808
Ge 8:21 n. will I again smite any more every... 3808
Ge 9:11 n. shall all flesh be cut off any more ... 3808
Ge 9:11 n. shall there any more be a flood...... 3808
Ge 17:5 N. shall thy name any more be.......... 3808
Ge 19:17 thee, n. stay thou in all the plain; 408
Ge 21:26 this thing: n. didst thou tell me,.......... 3808
Ge 21:26 me, n. yet heard I of it, but to day. ... 3808
Ge 22:12 n. do thou any thing unto him: 408
Ge 24:16 n. had any man known her: and......... 3808
Ge 29:7 n. is it time that the cattle should 3808
Ge 39:9 n. hath he kept back any thing from ... 3808
Ge 45:6 there shall n. be earing nor harvest...... 369
Ex 4:8 n. hearken to the voice of the first..... 3808
Ex 4:9 signs, n. hearken unto thy voice, ... 3808
Ex 4:10 n. heretofore, nor since thou hast 1571
Ex 5:2 Lord, n. will I let Israel go. 1571,3808
Ex 5:23 n. hast thou delivered thy people 3808
Ex 7:22 n. did he hearken unto them; as 3808
Ex 7:23 n. did he set his heart to this........... 3808
Ex 8:32 also, n. would he let the people......... 3808
Ex 9:29 n. shall there be any more hail; 3808
Ex 9:35 n. would he let the children of............ 3808
Ex 10:6 n. thy fathers, nor thy fathers' 3808
Ex 10:14 they, n. after them shall be such........ 3808
Ex 10:23 n. rose any from his place for............ 3808
Ex 12:39 n. had...prepared...victual.......... 1571,3808
Ex 12:46 n. shall ye break a bone thereof......... 3808
Ex 13:7 n. shall there be leaven seen with...... 3808
Ex 16:24 n. was there any worm therein.......... 3808
Ex 20:23 n. shall ye make unto you gods of...... 3808
Ex 20:26 N. shalt thou go up by steps unto 3808
Ex 22:21 n. vex a stranger, nor oppress him:..... 3808
Ex 22:25 n. shalt thou lay upon him usury. 3808
Ex 22:31 n. shall ye eat any flesh that is torn..... 3808
Ex 23:2 n. shalt thou speak in a cause to........ 3808
Ex 23:3 N. shalt thou countenance a poor 3808
Ex 23:13 n. let it be heard out of thy mouth. 3808
Ex 23:18 n. shall the fat of my sacrifice........... 3808
Ex 24:2 n. shall the people go up with him...... 3808
Ex 30:9 n. shall ye pour drink offering............ 3808
Ex 30:32 n. shall ye make any other like it, ... 3808
Ex 32:18 n. is it the voice of them that cry for ... 369
Ex 34:3 n. let any man be seen throughout....... 408
Ex 34:3 n. let the flocks nor herds feed 408
Ex 34:24 n. shall any man desire thy land,........ 3808
Ex 34:25 n. shall the sacrifice of the feast of...... 3808
Ex 34:28 he did n. eat bread, nor drink water. .. 3808
Ex 36:6 Let n. man nor woman make any 408
Le 2:13 n. shalt thou suffer the salt of the...... 3808
Le 3:17 that ye eat n. fat nor blood. 3808
Le 5:11 n. shall he put any frankincense 3808
Le 7:18 n. shall it be imputed unto him that 3808
Le 10:6 n. rend your clothes; lest ye die, and.. 3808
Le 11:43 n. shall ye make yourselves unclean.... 3808
Le 11:44 n. shall ye defile yourselves with........ 3808
Le 17:12 n. shall any stranger...eat blood......... 3808
Le 18:3 n. shall ye walk in their ordinances..... 3808
Le 18:17 n. shalt thou take her son's.............. 3808
Le 18:18 N. shalt thou take a wife to her......... 3808
Le 18:21 n. shalt thou profane the name of....... 3808
Le 18:23 N. shalt thou lie with any beast to....... 3808
Le 18:23 n. shall any woman stand before a...... 3808
Le 18:26 n. any of your own nation, nor any...........
Le 19:9 n. shalt thou gather the gleanings of ....
Le 19:10 n. shalt thou gather every grape of..... 3808
Le 19:11 Ye shall not steal, n. deal falsely, ... 3808
Le 19:11 deal falsely, n. lie one to another. 3808
Le 19:12 n. shalt thou profane the name of thy........
Le 19:13 not defraud thy neighbour, n. rob....... 3808
Le 19:16 n. shalt thou stand against the........... 3808
Le 19:19 n. shall a garment mingled of linen 3808
Le 19:26 n. shall ye use enchantment, nor......... 3808
Le 19:27 n. shalt thou mar the corners of thy ... 3808
Le 19:31 n. seek after wizards, to be defiled...... 408
Le 21:5 n. shall they shave off the corner....... 3808
Le 21:7 n. shall they take a woman put away .. 3808
Le 21:11 N. shall he go in to any dead body, ... 3808
Le 21:12 N. shall he go out of the sanctuary, ... 3808
Le 21:15 N. shall he profane his seed among..... 3808
Le 22:24 n. shall ye make any offering............. 3808
Le 22:25 N. from a stranger's hand shall ye...... 3808
Le 22:32 N. shall ye profane my holy name; 3808
Le 23:14 ye shall eat n. bread, nor parched 3808
Le 23:22 n. shalt thou gather any gleaning........ 3808
Le 25:4 thou shalt n. sow thy field, nor.......... 3808
Le 25:5 n. gather the grapes of thy vine......... 3808
Le 25:11 n. reap that which groweth of itself 3808
Le 26:1 n. rear you up a standing image,........ 3808
Le 26:1 n. shall ye set up any image of.......... 3808
Le 26:6 n. shall the sword go through your..... 3808
Le 26:20 n. shall the trees of the land yield 3808
Le 26:44 them away, n. will I abhor them, ... 3808
Le 27:33 good or bad, n. shall he change it: 3808
Nu 1:49 n. take the sum of them among the.... 3808
Nu 5:13 n. she be taken with the manner;........ 3808
Nu 6:3 n. shall he drink any liquor of............ 3808
Nu 11:19 days, n. ten days, nor twenty days;.... 3808
Nu 14:9 n. fear ye the people of the land; 408
Nu 14:23 n. shall any of them that provoked 3808
Nu 16:15 them, n. have I hurt one of them....... 3808
Nu 18:3 that n. they, nor ye also, die. 3808,1571
Nu 18:20 n. shalt thou have any part among...... 3808
Nu 18:22 N. must the children of Israel........... 3808
Nu 18:32 n. shall ye pollute the holy things....... 3808
Nu 20:5 n. is there any water to drink. 369
Nu 20:17 n. will we drink of the water of thy.... 3808
Nu 21:5 is no bread, n. is there any water;....... 369
Nu 23:19 n. the son of man, that he should............
Nu 23:21 n. hath he seen perverseness in 3808
Nu 23:23 n. is there any divination against 3808
Nu 23:25 N. curse them at all, nor bless ... 1571,3808
Nu 35:23 not his enemy, n. sought his harm: 3808
Nu 36:9 N. shall the inheritance remove.......... 3808
De 1:21 thee; fear not, n. be discouraged. 408
De 1:29 Dread not, n. be afraid of them. 3808
De 1:42 unto them, Go not up, n. fight; 3808
De 2:9 n. contend with them in battle: 408

De 2:27 I will **n.** turn unto the right hand........ 3808
De 4:2 **n.** shall ye diminish ought from it, ... 3808
De 4:28 **n.** see, nor hear, nor eat, nor smell.... 3808
De 4:31 not forsake thee, **n.** destroy thee,...... 3808
De 5:18 **N.** shalt thou commit adultery........... 3808
De 5:19 **N.** shalt thou steal. 3808
De 5:20 **N.** shalt thou bear false witness......... 3808
De 5:21 **N.** shalt thou desire thy neighbour's.... 3808
De 5:21 **n.** shalt thou covet thy neighbour's..... 3808
De 7:3 **N.** shalt thou make marriages with..... 3808
De 7:16 them: **n.** shalt thou serve their gods;.. 3808
De 7:26 **N.** shalt thou bring an abomination...... 3808
De 8:3 not, **n.** did thy fathers know;............ 3808
De 8:4 old upon thee, **n.** did thy foot swell, ... 3808
De 9:9 I **n.** did eat bread nor drink water:..... 3808
De 9:18 I did **n.** eat bread, nor drink water, ... 3808
De 13:8 **n.** shall thine eye pity him, ... 3808
De 13:8 eye pity him, **n.** shalt thou spare,....... 3808
De 13:8 spare, **n.** shalt thou conceal him:......... 3808
De 16:4 **n.** shall there any thing of the flesh, ... 3808
De 16:19 not respect persons, **n.** take a gift:..... 3808
De 16:22 **N.** shalt thou set thee up any image; .. 3808
De 17:17 **N.** shall he multiply wives to............ 3808
De 17:17 **n.** shall he greatly multiply...silver...... 3808
De 18:16 **n.** let me see this great fire any more,.3808
De 20:3 **n.** be ye terrified because of them; 408
De 21:4 valley, which is **n.** eared nor sown, ... 3808
De 21:7 this blood, **n.** have our eyes seen it.... 3808
De 22:5 **n.** shall a man put on a woman's........ 3808
De 24:5 **n.** shall he be charged with any 3808
De 24:15 **n.** shall the sun go down upon it;....... 3808
De 24:16 **n.** shall the children be put to death.... 3808
De 26:13 commandments, **n.** have I forgotten.... 3808
De 26:14 **n.** have I taken away ought thereof.... 3808
De 28:36 **n.** thou nor thy fathers have known; ... 3808
De 28:39 **n.** drink of the wine, nor gather the.... 3808
De 28:64 **n.** thou nor thy fathers have known, ... 3808
De 28:65 **n.** shall...sole of thy foot have rest:.... 3808
De 29:6 **n.** have ye drunk wine or strong........ 3808
De 29:14 **N.** with you only do I make this......... 3808
De 30:11 not hidden from thee, **n.** is it far off. .. 3808
De 30:13 **N.** is it beyond the sea, that thou....... 3808
De 31:8 he will not fail thee, **n.** forsake thee: .. 3808
De 31:8 thee: fear not, **n.** be dismayed............ 3808
De 32:28 **n.** is there any understanding in 369
De 32:39 **n.** is there any that can deliver out of... 369
De 33:9 **n.** did...acknowledge his brethren,........ 3808
Jos 1:9 be not afraid, **n.** be thou dismayed:...... 408
Jos 2:11 **n.** did...remain any more courage....... 3808
Jos 5:1 **n.** was there spirit in them any more, . 3808
Jos 5:1 **n.** was there spirit in them any more, . 3808
Jos 5:12 **n.** had the children of Israel manna...... 3808
Jos 6:10 **n.** shall any word proceed out of your. 3808
Jos 7:12 **n.** will I be with you any more, ... 3808
Jos 8:1 Fear not, **n.** be thou dismayed: 408
Jos 11:14 them, **n.** left they any to breathe. 3808
Jos 23:7 **n.** make mention of the name of 3808
Jos 23:7 **n.** serve them, nor bow yourselves 3808
Jg 1:27 **N.** did Manasseh drive out the........... 3808
Jg 1:29 **N.** did Ephraim drive out the............. 3808
Jg 1:30 **N.** did Zebulun drive out the 3808
Jg 1:31 **N.** did Asher drive out the................ 3808
Jg 1:33 **N.** did Naphtali drive out the............. 3808
Jg 2:23 **n.** delivered he them into the hand..... 3808
Jg 6:4 for Israel, **n.** sheep, nor ox, nor ass. ....
Jg 8:23 you, **n.** shall my son rule over you: 3808
Jg 8:35 **N.** shewed they kindness to the......... 3808
Jg 11:34 her he had **n.** son nor daughter........... 369
Jg 13:6 he was, **n.** told he me his name:........ 3808
Jg 13:7 drink, **n.** eat any unclean thing: 408
Jg 13:14 **n.** let her drink wine or strong drink, ... 408
Jg 13:23 **n.** would he have shewed us all......... 3808
Jg 20:8 **n.** will we any of us turn into his 3808
Ru 2:8 **n.** go from hence, but abide,...... 1571,3808
1Sa 1:15 I have drunk **n.** wine nor strong 3808
1Sa 2:2 **n.** is there any rock like our God......... 369
1Sa 3:7 **n.** was the word of the Lord yet.............
1Sa 4:20 answered not, **n.** did she regard it...... 3808
1Sa 5:5 **n.** the priests of Dagon, nor any........ 3808
1Sa 12:4 **n.** hast thou taken ought of any 3808
1Sa 13:22 was **n.** sword nor spear found in the... 3808
1Sa 16:8, 9 **N.** hath the Lord chosen......... 1571,3808
1Sa 20:27 to meat, **n.** yesterday, nor to-day?..... 1571
1Sa 21:8 **n.** brought my sword nor my..... 1571,3808
1Sa 24:11 is **n.** evil nor transgression in mine 369
1Sa 25:7 **n.** was there ought missing unto 3808
1Sa 25:15 not hurt, **n.** missed we any thing, ... 3808
1Sa 26:12 man saw it, nor knew it, **n.** awaked: 369
1Sa 27:9 and left **n.** man nor woman alive,....... 3608
1Sa 27:11 saved **n.** man nor woman alive,.......... 3608
1Sa 28:6 **n.** by dreams, nor by Urim, nor by 1571
1Sa 28:15 **n.** by prophets, nor by dreams: 1571
1Sa 30:15 that thou wilt **n.** kill me, nor deliver..... 518
1Sa 30:19 **n.** small nor great, **n.** sons nor.......... 4480
1Sa 30:19 **n.** spoil, nor anything that they had.... 4480
2Sa 1:21 dew, **n.** let there be rain, upon you,..... 408
2Sa 2:28 no more, **n.** fought they any more...... 3808
2Sa 7:10 **n.** shall the children of wickedness...... 3808
2Sa 7:22 **n.** is there any God beside thee, ... 369
2Sa 12:17 not, **n.** did he eat bread with them. 3808
2Sa 13:22 his brother Amnon **n.** good nor bad: ... 3808
2Sa 14:7 **n.** name nor remainder upon the........ 1115
2Sa 14:14 **n.** doth God respect any person:........ 3808
2Sa 18:3 **n.** if half of us died, will they care 518
2Sa 19:6 regardest **n.** princes nor servants: 369
2Sa 19:19 **n.** do thou remember that which thy 408
2Sa 19:24 **n.** dressed his feet, nor trimmed........ 3808
2Sa 20:1 **n.** have we inheritance in the son of... 3808
2Sa 21:4 **n.** for us shalt thou kill any man in....... 369
2Sa 21:10 **n.** the birds of the air to rest on 3808
2Sa 24:24 **n.** will I offer burnt offerings unto 3808
1Ki 3:11 **n.** hast asked riches for thyself,......... 3808
1Ki 3:12 **n.** after thee shall any arise like......... 3808
1Ki 3:26 Let it be **n.** mine nor thine,....... 1571,3808
1Ki 5:4 that there is **n.** adversary nor evil........ 369
1Ki 6:7 there was **n.** hammer nor axe nor....... 3808
1Ki 7:47 **n.** was the weight of the brass found.. 3808
1Ki 11:2 **n.** shall they come in unto you:.......... 3808
1Ki 12:16 **n.** have we inheritance in the son of... 3808
1Ki 13:8, 16 **n.** will I eat bread nor drink water ..3808
1Ki 16:11 **n.** of his kinsfolks, nor of his friends. ....
1Ki 17:14 waste, **n.** shall the cruse of oil fail, ... 3808
1Ki 17:16 not, **n.** did the cruse of oil fail, ... 3808
1Ki 18:29 was **n.** voice, nor any to answer,.......... 369
1Ki 22:31 Fight **n.** with small nor great, save...... 3808
2Ki 3:17 not see wind, **n.** shall ye see rain;....... 3808
2Ki 4:23 it is **n.** new moon, nor sabbath. 3808
2Ki 4:31 but there was **n.** voice, nor hearing...... 369
2Ki 5:17 offer **n.** burnt offering nor sacrifice..... 3808
2Ki 6:19 is not the way, **n.** is this the city: 3808
2Ki 7:10 was no man there, **n.** voice of man, ... 369
2Ki 10:14 forty men; **n.** left he any of them....... 3808
2Ki 12:8 **n.** to repair the breaches of the......... 1115
2Ki 13:7 **N.** did he leave of the people to......... 3808
2Ki 13:23 **n.** cast he them from his presence 3808
2Ki 17:34 **n.** do they after their statutes, or........ 369
2Ki 17:38 forget: **n.** shall ye fear other gods...... 3808
2Ki 18:30 **N.** let Hezekiah make you trust in 408
2Ki 21:8 **N.** will I make the feet of Israel......... 3808
2Ki 23:25 **n.** after him arose there any like........ 3808
1Ch 4:27 **n.** did all their family multiply, like....... 3808
1Ch 17:9 **n.** shall the children of wickedness...... 3808
1Ch 17:20 **n.** is there any God beside thee, ... 369
1Ch 19:19 **n.** would the Syrians help the............ 3808
1Ch 27:24 **n.** was the number put in the............ 3808
2Ch 1:11 enemies, **n.** yet hast asked long life;... 3808
2Ch 1:12 **n.** shall there any after thee have....... 3808
2Ch 6:5 **n.** chose I any man to be a ruler........ 3808
2Ch 9:9 **n.** was there any such spice as the..... 3808
2Ch 13:20 **N.** did Jeroboam recover strength...... 3808
2Ch 20:12 **n.** know we what to do: but our 3808
2Ch 25:4 **n.** shall the children die for the.......... 3808
2Ch 26:18 **n.** shall it be for thine honour from..... 3808
2Ch 30:3 **n.** had the people gathered 3808
2Ch 32:15 on this manner, **n.** yet believe him:...... 408
2Ch 33:8 **N.** will I any more remove the foot 3808
2Ch 34:2 declined **n.** to the right hand, nor....... 3808
2Ch 34:28 **n.** shall thine eyes see all the evil...... 3808
2Ch 35:18 **n.** did all the kings of Israel keep....... 3808
Ezr 9:12 **n.** take their daughters unto your 408
Ezr 10:13 **n.** is this a work of one day or two: ... 3808
Ne 2:12 **n.** told I any man what my God had.... 3808
Ne 2:12 **n.** was there any beast with me, ... 369
Ne 2:16 **n.** had I as yet told it to the Jews, ... 3808
Ne 4:11 They shall not know, **n.** see, till we.... 3808
Ne 4:23 So **n.** I, nor my brethren, nor my........ 369
Ne 5:5 **n.** is it in our power to redeem them; .. 369
Ne 5:16 this wall, **n.** bought we any land:........ 3808
Ne 8:10 **n.** be ye sorry; for the joy of the......... 408
Ne 8:11 for the day is holy; **n.** be ye grieved. ... 408
Ne 9:17 **n.** were mindful of thy wonders 3808
Ne 9:19 **n.** the pillar of fire by night, to shew.........
Ne 9:34 **N.** have our kings, our princes, ... 3808
Ne 9:35 **n.** turned they from their wicked........ 3808
Es 2:7 for she had **n.** father nor mother, ... 369
Es 3:8 people; **n.** keep they the king's laws:.... 369
Es 4:16 **n.** eat nor drink three days, night........ 408
Job 3:4 **n.** let the light shine upon it. 408
Job 3:9 **n.** let it see the dawning of the day:..... 408
Job 3:26 I was not in safety, **n.** had I rest, ... 3808
Job 3:26 **n.** was I quiet; yet trouble came. 3808
Job 5:4 **n.** is there any to deliver them........... 369
Job 5:6 **n.** doth trouble spring out of the........ 3808
Job 5:21 **n.** shalt...be afraid of destruction........ 3808
Job 5:22 **n.** shalt thou be afraid of the beasts..... 408
Job 7:10 **n.** shall his place know him any......... 3808
Job 8:20 man, **n.** will he help the evil doers; 3808
Job 9:33 **N.** is there any daysman betwixt........ 3808
Job 15:29 **n.** shall his substance continue,.......... 3808
Job 15:29 **n.** shall he prolong the perfection....... 3808
Job 18:19 He shall **n.** have son nor nephew....... 3808
Job 20:9 **n.** shall his place any more behold...... 3808
Job 21:9 **n.** is the rod of God upon them. 3808
Job 23:12 **N.** have I gone back from the........... 3808
Job 23:17 **n.** hath he covered the darkness from.......
Job 28:13 **n.** is it found in the land of the.......... 3808
Job 28:15 **n.** shall silver be weighed for the....... 3808
Job 28:19 **n.** shall it be valued with pure gold...... 3808
Job 31:30 **N.** have I suffered my mouth to sin.... 3808
Job 32:9 **n.** do the aged understand judgment. ....
Job 32:14 **n.**...answer him with...speeches......... 3808
Job 32:21 **n.** let me give flattering titles unto 3808
Job 33:7 **n.** shall my hand be heavy upon.......... 3808
Job 33:9 innocent; **n.** is there iniquity in me. 3808
Job 34:12 **n.**...the Almighty pervert judgment..... 3808
Job 35:13 **n.** will the Almighty regard it. 3808
Job 36:26 **n.** can the number of his year be........ 3808
Job 39:7 **n.** regardeth he the crying of the....... 3808
Job 39:17 **n.**...imparted to her understanding...... 3808
Job 39:22 **n.** turneth he back from the sword. 3808
Job 39:24 **n.** believeth he that it is the sound..... 3808
Ps 5:4 **n.** shall evil dwell with thee.............. 3808
Ps 6:1 thine anger, **n.** chasten me in thy....... 3808
Ps 16:10 **n.** wilt thou suffer thine Holy One...... 3808
Ps 18:37 **n.** did I turn again till they were 3808
Ps 22:24 **n.** hath he hid his face from him; 3808
Ps 26:4 **n.** will I go in with dissemblers......... 3808
Ps 27:9 leave me not, **n.** forsake me, O God.... 408
Ps 33:17 **n.**...deliver any by...great strength. 3808
Ps 35:19 **n.** let them wink with the eye that hate.....
Ps 37:1 **n.** be thou envious against the 408
Ps 38:1 **n.** chasten me in thy hot displeasure.........
Ps 38:3 **n.** is there any rest in my bones 369
Ps 44:3 **n.** did their own arm save them:........ 3808
Ps 44:6 my bow, **n.** shall my sword save me... 3808
Ps 44:17 **n.** have we dealt falsely in thy........... 3808
Ps 44:18 **n.** have our steps declined from thy..........
Ps 55:12 **n.** was it he that hated me that 3808
Ps 69:15 **n.** let the deep swallow me up, and...... 408
Ps 73:5 **n.** are they plagued like other men..... 3808
Ps 74:9 **n.** is there among us any that............ 3808
Ps 75:6 promotion cometh **n.** from the east,.... 3808
Ps 78:37 **n.** were...steadfast in his covenant. 3808
Ps 81:9 **n.** shalt thou worship any strange....... 3808
Ps 82:5 know not, **n.** will they understand; 3808
Ps 86:8 **n.** are there any works like unto 369
Ps 91:10 **n.** shall any plague come nigh thy...... 3808
Ps 92:6 not; **n.** doth a fool understand this...... 3808
Ps 94:7 **n.** shall the God of Jacob regard it...... 3808
Ps 94:14 **n.** will he forsake his inheritance......... 3808
Ps 103:9 **n.** will he keep his anger for ever. 3808
Ps 109:12 **n.** let there be any to favour his.......... 408
Ps 115:7 **n.** speak they through their throat...... 3808
Ps 115:17 **n.** any that go down into silence. 3808
Ps 121:4 Israel shall **n.** slumber nor sleep. 3804
Ps 129:8 **N.** do they which go by say, The....... 3808
Ps 131:1 **n.** do I exercise myself in great......... 3808
Ps 135:17 **n.** is there any breath in their............ 369
Pr 2:19 **n.** take they hold of the paths of life. ....
Pr 3:11 **n.** be weary of his correction: 408
Pr 3:25 **n.** of the desolation of the wicked,...........
Pr 4:5 **n.** decline from the words of my.......... 408
Pr 6:25 **n.** let her take thee with her eyelids. ... 408
Pr 6:35 **n.** will he rest content, though........... 3808
Pr 15:12 him: **n.** will he go unto the wise. 3808
Pr 22:22 **n.** oppress the afflicted in the gate: 3808
Pr 23:6 **n.** desire thou his dainty meats: 408
Pr 24:1 evil men, **n.** desire to be with them; 408
Pr 24:19 **n.** be thou envious at the wicked;........ 408
Pr 27:10 **n.** go into thy brother's house in the 408
Pr 30:3 I **n.** learned wisdom, nor have the...... 3808

Pr 30:8 give me **n.** poverty nor riches; feed 408
Ec 1:11 **n.** shall there be any remembrance..... 3808
Ec 4:8 he hath **n.** child nor brother:........ 1571,369
Ec 4:8 **n.** is his eye satisfied with riches; 3808
Ec 4:8 **n.** saith he, For whom do I labour,..........
Ec 5:6 **n.** say thou before the angel, that........ 408
Ec 6:10 **n.** may he contend with him that........ 3808
Ec 7:16 much; **n.** make thyself over wise: 408
Ec 7:17 much wicked, **n.** be thou foolish: 408
Ec 8:8 **n.** hath...power in the day of death: 369
Ec 8:8 **n.** shall wickedness deliver those........ 3808
Ec 8:13 **n.** shall he prolong his days, which..... 3808
Ec 8:16 there is that **n.** day nor night....... 1571,369
Ec 9:5 **n.** have they any more a reward;.. 1571,369
Ec 9:6 **n.** have they any more a portion... 1571,369
Ec 9:11 **n.** yet bread to the wise, nor yet....... 3808
Ca 8:7 love, **n.** can the floods drown it: 3808
Isa 1:6 **n.** bound up, **n.** mollified with........... 3808
Isa 1:23 **n.** doth the cause of the widow.......... 3808
Isa 2:4 **n.** shall they learn war any more.......... 3808
Isa 2:7 **n.** is there...end of their treasures; 3808
Isa 2:7 **n.** is there any end of their chariots:... 3808
Isa 3:7 my house is **n.** bread nor clothing: 369
Isa 5:12 **n.** consider the operation of his.......... 3808
Isa 5:27 **n.** shall the girdle of their loins be...... 3808
Isa 7:4 **n.** be fainthearted for the two tails...... 408
Isa 7:7 stand, **n.** shall it come to pass.......... 3808
Isa 7:12 not ask, **n.** will I tempt the Lord........ 3808
Isa 8:12 **n.** fear ye their fear, nor be afraid...... 3808
Isa 9:13 **n.** do they seek the Lord of hosts....... 3808
Isa 9:17 **n.**...have mercy on their fatherless 3808
Isa 10:7 not so, **n.** doth his heart think so;..... 3808
Isa 11:3 **n.** reprove after the hearing of his...... 3808
Isa 13:20 **n.** shall it be dwelt in from............... 3808
Isa 13:20 **n.** shall the Arabian pitch tent............ 3808
Isa 13:20 **n.** shall the shepherds make their....... 3808
Isa 16:10 singing, **n.** shall there be shouting; 3808
Isa 17:8 **n.** shall respect that which his 3808
Isa 19:15 **N.** shall there be any work for........... 3808
Isa 22:11 **n.** had respect unto him that............. 3808
Isa 23:4 **n.** do I nourish up young men, nor..... 3808
Isa 26:18 **n.** have the inhabitants of the.......... 1077
Isa 28:27 **n.** is a cart wheel turned about upon... 1077
Isa 29:22 **n.** shall his face now wax pale. 3808
Isa 31:1 One of Israel, **n.** seek the Lord! 3808
Isa 33:20 **n.** shall any of the cords thereof 1077
Isa 33:21 **n.** shall gallant ship pass thereby......... 3808
Isa 36:15 **N.** let Hezekiah make you trust in 408
Isa 40:28 earth, fainteth not, **n.** is weary?......... 3808
Isa 42:8 **n.** my praise to graven images................
Isa 42:24 **n.** were they obedient unto his law..... 3808
Isa 43:2 **n.** shall the flame kindle upon thee. 3808
Isa 43:10 formed, **n.** shall there be after me....... 3808
Isa 43:18 things, **n.** consider the things of old. 408
Isa 43:23 **n.** hast thou honoured me with.......... 3808
Isa 43:24 **n.** hast thou filled me with the fat 3808
Isa 44:8 Fear ye not, **n.** be afraid: have not 408
Isa 44:19 heart, **n.** is there knowledge nor......... 4808
Isa 47:7 **n.** didst remember the latter end 4808
Isa 47:8 **n.** shall I know the loss of children: 4808
Isa 49:10 **n.** shall the heat nor sun smite 4808
Isa 50:5 not rebellious, **n.** turned away back. ... 4808
Isa 51:7 **n.** be ye afraid of their revilings. 408
Isa 51:18 **n.** is there any that taketh her by........ 369
Isa 53:9 **n.** was any deceit in his mouth. 3808
Isa 54:4 **n.** be thou confounded; for thou 408
Isa 54:10 **n.** shall the covenant of my peace 3808
Isa 55:8 **n.** are your ways my ways, saith 3808
Isa 56:3 **N.** let the son of the strangers,........... 408
Isa 56:3 **n.** let the eunuch say, Behold, I am 408
Isa 57:16 **n.** will I be always wroth: for the....... 3808
Isa 59:1 **n.** his ear heavy, that it cannot hear. .. 3808
Isa 59:6 **n.** shall they cover themselves with.... 3808
Isa 59:9 from us, **n.** doth justice overtake us: .. 3808
Isa 60:19 **n.** for brightness shall the moon......... 3808
Isa 60:20 **n.** shall thy moon withdraw itself:....... 3808
Isa 62:4 **n.**...thy land any more be termed......... 3808
Isa 64:4 **n.** hath the eye seen, O God, besides. 3808
Isa 64:9 **n.** remember iniquity for ever: 408
Isa 66:19 my fame, **n.** have seen my glory;....... 3808
Isa 66:24 die, **n.** shall their fire be quenched; 3808
Jer 2:6 **N.** said they, Where is the Lord 3808
Jer 3:16 the Lord: **n.** shall it come to mind:..... 3808
Jer 3:16 **n.** shall they remember it; 3808
Jer 3:16 **n.** shall they visit it; 3808
Jer 3:16 **n.** shall that be done any more. 3808
Jer 3:17 **n.** shall they walk any more after....... 3808
Jer 4:28 repent, **n.** will I turn back from it....... 3808
Jer 5:12 not he; **n.** shall evil come upon us;..... 3808
Jer 5:12 **n.** shall we see sword nor famine:...... 3808
Jer 5:15 **n.** understandest what they say. 3808
Jer 5:24 **N.** say they in their heart, Let us 3808
Jer 6:15 ashamed, **n.** could they blush: 1571,3808
Jer 7:6 **n.** walk after other gods to your 3808
Jer 7:16 **n.** lift up cry nor prayer for them, ... 408
Jer 7:16 them, **n.** make intercession to me:....... 408
Jer 7:31 them not, **n.** came it into my heart..... 3808
Jer 8:12 all ashamed, **n.** could they blush:......... 3808
Jer 9:10 **n.** can men hear the voice of the 3808
Jer 9:13 obeyed my voice, **n.** walked therein;... 3808
Jer 9:16 **n.** they nor their fathers have........... 3808
Jer 9:23 **n.** let the mighty man glory in his........ 408
Jer 10:5 **n.** also is it in them to do good. ... 1571,369
Jer 11:14 **n.** lift up a cry or prayer for them: 408
Jer 14:13 sword, **n.** shall ye have famine; 3808
Jer 14:14 not, **n.** have I commanded them,........ 3808
Jer 14:14 them, **n.** spake unto them:................ 3808
Jer 15:10 I have **n.** lent us usury, nor men 3808
Jer 16:2 a wife, **n.** shalt thou have sons or 3808
Jer 16:4 lamented; **n.** shall they be buried; 3808
Jer 16:5 **n.** go to lament nor bemoan them: 3808
Jer 16:6 **n.** shall men lament for them, nor 3808
Jer 16:7 **N.** shall men tear themselves for........ 3808
Jer 16:7 **n.** shall men give them the cup of 3808
Jer 16:13 know not, **n.** ye nor your fathers; ....
Jer 16:17 **n.** is their iniquity hid from mine 3808
Jer 17:8 **n.** shall cease from yielding fruit......... 3808
Jer 17:16 **n.** have I desired the woeful day;....... 3808
Jer 17:22 **N.** carry forth a burden out of your 3808
Jer 17:22 the sabbath day, **n.** do ye any work,... 3808
Jer 17:23 obeyed not, **n.** inclined their ear, ... 3808
Jer 18:23 **n.** blot out their sin from thy sight, ... 408
Jer 19:4 **n.** they nor their fathers have............ 3808
Jer 19:5 spake it, **n.** came it into my mind:...... 3808
Jer 21:7 them, **n.** have pity, nor have mercy.... 3808
Jer 22:3 **n.** shed innocent blood in this place...... 408
Jer 22:10 ye not for the dead, **n.** bemoan him; 408
Jer 23:4 **n.** shall they be lacking, saith the....... 3808
Jer 25:33 lamented, **n.** gathered, nor buried; 3808
Jer 29:8 **n.** hearken to your dreams which......... 408
Jer 29:32 **n.** shall he behold the good that I....... 3808
Jer 30:10 **n.** be dismayed, O Israel: for, lo, I 408
Jer 32:23 thy voice, **n.** walked in thy law; 3808
Jer 32:35 them not, **n.** came it into my mind, ... 3808
Jer 33:18 **N.** shall the priests the Levites.......... 3808
Jer 33:22 **n.** the sand of the sea measured: 3808
Jer 34:14 not unto me, **n.** inclined their ear....... 3808
Jer 35:6 drink no wine, **n.** ye nor your sons...........
Jer 35:7 **N.** shall ye build house, nor sow 3808
Jer 35:9 **n.** have we vineyard, nor field, nor..... 3808
Jer 36:24 **n.** the king, nor any of his servants..........
Jer 37:2 **n.** he, nor his servants, nor the......... 3808
Jer 38:16 **n.** will I give thee into the hand of....... 518
Jer 42:13 **n.** obey the voice of the Lord your..... 1115
Jer 44:3 knew not, **n.** they, ye, nor your fathers.....
Jer 44:10 **n.** have they feared, nor walked in 3808
Jer 48:11 **n.** hath he gone into captivity: 3808
Jer 49:18 **n.** shall a son of man dwell in it. 3808
Jer 49:31 which have **n.** gates nor bars 3808
Jer 50:39 **n.** shall it be dwelt in from............... 3808
Jer 50:40 **n.** shall any son of man dwell 3808
Jer 51:43 **n.** doth any son of man pass 3808
Jer 51:62 remain it in, **n.** man nor beast, ... 1115
Eze 2:6 them, **n.** be afraid of their words,........ 408
Eze 3:9 not, **n.** be dismayed at their looks, ... 3808
Eze 4:14 **n.** came there abominable flesh into.... 3808
Eze 5:7 **n.** have kept my judgments, ... 3808
Eze 5:7 **n.** have done according to the 3808
Eze 5:11 thee; **n.** shall mine eye spare, ... 1571
Eze 5:11 eye spare, **n.** will I have any pity. 3808
Eze 7:4 not spare thee, **n.** will I have pity: 3808
Eze 7:9 shall not spare, **n.** will I have pity: 3808
Eze 7:11 **n.** shall there be wailing for them....... 3808
Eze 7:13 **n.** shall any strengthen himself in 3808
Eze 7:19 their souls, **n.** fill their bowels: 3808
Eze 8:18 shall not spare, **n.** will I have pity: 3808
Eze 9:5 not your eye spare, **n.** have ye pity: 408
Eze 9:10 shall not spare, **n.** will I have pity, ... 3808
Eze 11:11 **n.** shall ye be the flesh in the midst..........
Eze 11:12 **n.** executed my judgments, but.......... 3808
Eze 13:5 **n.** made up the hedge for the house of.....
Eze 13:9 **n.** shall they be written in the 3808
Eze 13:9 **n.** shall they enter into the land of...... 3808
Eze 13:15 is no more, **n.** they that daubed it; 369
Eze 14:11 **n.** be polluted any more with all......... 3808
Eze 14:16 shall deliver **n.** sons nor daughters;....... 518
Eze 14:18 shall deliver **n.** sons nor daughters, ... 3808
Eze 14:20 shall deliver **n.** son nor daughter;......... 518
Eze 16:4 **n.** wast thou washed in water to........ 3808
Eze 16:16 shall not come, **n.** shall it be so. 3808
Eze 16:49 **n.** did she strengthen the hand of....... 3808
Eze 16:51 **N.** hath Samaria committed half of...... 3808
Eze 17:17 **N.** shall Pharaoh with his mighty 3808
Eze 18:6 **n.** hath lifted up his eyes to the......... 3808
Eze 18:6 **n.** hath defiled his neighbour's 3808
Eze 18:6 **n.** hath come near to a menstruous 3808
Eze 18:8 usury, **n.** hath taken any increase,...... 3808
Eze 18:15 **n.** hath lifted up his eyes to the......... 3808
Eze 18:16 **N.** hath oppressed any, hath not 3808
Eze 18:16 pledge, **n.** hath spoiled by violence, ... 3808
Eze 18:20 **n.** shall the father bear the iniquity..... 3808
Eze 20:8 **n.** did they forsake the idols of.......... 3808
Eze 20:17 **n.** did I make an end of them in the ... 3808
Eze 20:18 **n.** observe their judgments, nor 408
Eze 20:21 **n.** kept my judgments to do them, ... 3808
Eze 22:26 **n.** have they shewed difference.......... 3808
Eze 23:8 **N.** left she her whoredoms brought 3808
Eze 24:14 **n.** will I spare, **n.** will I repent; 3808
Eze 24:16 yet **n.** shalt thou mourn nor weep, ... 3808
Eze 24:16 weep, **n.** shall thy tears run down. 3808
Eze 29:11 **n.** shall it be inhabited forty years. 3808
Eze 29:15 **n.** shall it exalt itself any more 3808
Eze 31:14 **n.** shoot up their top among the......... 3808
Eze 31:14 **n.** their trees stand up in their 3808
Eze 32:13 **n.** shall the foot of man trouble.......... 3808
Eze 33:12 **n.** shall the righteous be able to live ... 3808
Eze 34:4 **n.** have ye healed that which was......... 3808
Eze 34:4 **n.** have ye bound up that which was.... 3808
Eze 34:4 **n.** have ye brought again that which.... 3808
Eze 34:4 **n.** have ye sought that which was 3808
Eze 34:8 **n.** did my shepherds search for my..... 3808
Eze 34:10 flock; **n.** shall the shepherds feed 3808
Eze 34:28 **n.** shall the beast of the land devour ... 3808
Eze 34:29 **n.** bear the shame of the heathen......... 3808
Eze 36:14 **n.** bereave thy nations any more,....... 3808
Eze 36:15 **N.** will I cause men to hear in thee 3808
Eze 36:15 **n.** shalt thou bear the reproach of...... 3808
Eze 36:15 **n.** shalt thou cause thy nations to....... 3808
Eze 37:22 **n.** shall they be divided into two 3808
Eze 37:23 **N.** shall they defile themselves any..... 3808
Eze 38:11 walls, and having **n.** bars nor gates, ... 369
Eze 39:10 **n.** cut down any out of the forests; 3808
Eze 39:29 **N.** will I hide my face any more.......... 3808
Eze 43:7 more defile, **n.** they, nor their kings, ...
Eze 44:20 **N.** shall they shave their heads,......... 3808
Eze 44:21 **N.** shall any priest drink wine,........... 3808
Eze 44:22 **N.** shall they take for their wives a..... 3808
Eze 47:12 fade, **n.** shall the fruit thereof be......... 3808
Eze 48:14 they shall not sell of it, **n.** exchange, .. 3808
Da 3:27 **n.** were their coats changed, nor........ 3809
Da 6:4 **n.** was there any error or fault found.. 3809
Da 6:18 **n.** were instruments of musick.......... 3809
Da 8:4 **n.** was there any that could deliver 369
Da 9:6 **N.** have we hearkened unto thy.......... 3808
Da 9:10 **N.** have we obeyed the voice of the ... 3808
Da 10:3 **n.** came flesh nor wine in my mouth, .. 3808
Da 10:3 **n.** did I anoint myself at all, till.......... 3808
Da 10:17 in me, **n.** is there breath left in me. ... 3808
Da 11:6 **n.** shall he stand, nor his arm: but...... 3808
Da 11:15 withstand, **n.** his chosen people,.......... 369
Da 11:15 **n.** shall there be any strength to 369
Da 11:17 not stand on his side, **n.** be for him.... 3808
Da 11:20 destroyed, **n.** in anger, nor in battle. .. 3808
Da 11:37 **N.** shall he regard the God of his 3808
Ho 2:2 not my wife, **n.** am I her husband: 3808
Ho 4:15 Gilgal, **n.** go ye up to Beth-aven,......... 408
Ho 9:4 **n.** shall they be pleasing unto him: 3808
Ho 14:3 **n.** will we say any more to the work .. 3808
Joe 2:2 like, **n.** shall be any more after it, ... 3808
Joe 2:8 **N.** shall one thrust another; they........ 3808
Am 2:14 **n.** shall the mighty deliver himself: 3808
Am 2:15 **N.** shall he stand that handleth the 3808
Am 2:15 **n.** shall he that rideth the horse......... 3808
Am 5:22 **n.** will I regard the peace offerings 3808
Am 7:14 prophet, **n.** was I a prophet's son;...... 3808
Ob 12 **n.** shouldest thou have rejoiced 408
Ob 12 **n.** shouldest thou have spoken 408
Ob 14 **N.** shouldest thou have stood in the 408

Ob 14 n. shouldest thou have delivered up ... 408
Jon 3:7 Let n. man nor beast, herd nor ... 369
Jon 4:10 not laboured, n. madest it grow; ... 3808
Mic 2:3 your necks; n. shall ye go haughtily: ... 3808
Mic 4:3 n. shall they learn war any more ... 3808
Mic 4:12 n. understand they his counsel: ... 3808
Hab 2:5 a proud man, n. keepeth at home, ... 3808
Hab 3:17 n. shall fruit be in the vines; ... 369
Zep 1:12 will not do good, n. will he do evil. ... 3808
Zep 1:18 N. their silver nor their gold shall ... 3808
Zep 3:13 n. shall a deceitful tongue be found ... 3808
Zec 8:10 n. was there any peace to him that ... 369
Zec 11:16 n. shall seek the young one, nor ... 3808
Zec 13:4 n. shall they wear a rough garment ... 3808
Mal 1:10 n. do ye kindle fire on mine altar ... 3808
Mal 1:10 n. will I accept an offering at your ... 3808
Mal 3:11 n. shall your vine cast her fruit ... 3808
Mal 4:1 shall leave them n. root nor branch. ...
Mt 5:15 N. do men light a candle, and put . 3761
Mt 5:34 n. by heaven; for it is God's ... 3383
Mt 5:35 n. by Jerusalem; for it is the city .. 3383
Mt 5:36 N. shalt thou swear by thy head, ... 3383
Mt 6:15 n. will your Father forgive your ... 3761
Mt 6:20 n. moth nor rust doth corrupt, and 3777
Mt 6:26 n. do they reap, nor gather into ... 3761
Mt 6:28 they toil not, n. do they spin: ... 3761
Mt 7:6 n. cast ye your pearls before swine, 3366
Mt 7:18 n. can a corrupt tree bring forth ... 3761
Mt 9:17 N. do men put new wine into old .. 3761
Mt 10:9 Provide n. gold, nor silver, nor ... 3361
Mt 10:10 journey, n. two coats, n. shoes, ... 3366
Mt 11:18 John came n. eating nor drinking, .3383
Mt 11:27 n. knoweth any man the Father, ... 3761
Mt 12:4 n. for them which were with him, ..3761
Mt 12:19 n. shall any man hear his voice in ... 3761
Mt 12:32 be forgiven him, n. in this world, .. 3777
Mt 12:32 world, n. in the world to come ... 3777
Mt 13:13 hear not, n. do they understand ... 3761
Mt 16:9 n. remember the five loaves of the .3761
Mt 16:10 N. the seven loaves of the four ... 3761
Mt 21:27 N. tell I you by what authority I ... 3761
Mt 22:16 n. carest thou for any man: ... 2532,3756
Mt 22:30 n. marry, nor...given in marriage, .3777
Mt 22:46 n. durst any man from that day ... 3761
Mt 23:10 N. be ye called masters: for one ... 3366
Mt 23:13 men: for ye n. go in yourselves, ... 3761
Mt 23:13 n. suffer ye them that are entering 3756
Mt 24:18 N. let him which is in the field ... 3361
Mt 24:20 the winter, n. on the sabbath day: . 3366
Mt 25:13 ye know n. the day nor the hour ... 3383
Mk 4:22 n. was any thing kept secret, but .. 3761
Mk 5:4 n. could any man tame him. ... 2532,3762
Mk 8:14 n. had they in the ship with ... 2532,3762
Mk 8:17 perceive ye not yet, n. understand? 3761
Mk 8:26 N. go into the town, nor tell it to .. 3366
Mk 11:26 n. will your Father which is in ... 3761
Mk 11:33 N. do I tell you by what authority .3761
Mk 12:21 her, and died, n. left he any seed: ... 3761
Mk 12:24 scriptures, n. the power of God? ... 3366
Mk 12:25 n. marry, nor...given in marriage; . 3777
Mk 13:11 shall speak, n. do ye premeditate: . 3366
Mk 13:15 n. enter therein, to take any thing .3366
Mk 13:19 unto this time, n. shall be. ... 3756,3361
Mk 13:32 heaven, n. the Son, but the Father .3761
Mk 14:40 n. wist they what to answer ... 2532,3756
Mk 14:59 But n. so did their witness agree ... 3761
Mk 14:68 n. understand I what thou sayest. ... 3761
Mk 16:8 n. said they any thing to any ... 2532,3762
Mk 16:13 residue: n. believed they them. ... 3761
Lu 1:15 n. wine nor strong drink; ... 3756,3361
Lu 3:14 to no man, n. accuse any falsely; ... 3366
Lu 6:43 n. doth a corrupt tree bring forth .. 3761
Lu 7:7 n. thought I myself worthy to come ... 3761
Lu 7:33 came n. eating bread nor drinking .3383
Lu 8:17 n. any thing hid, that shall not be ..3761
Lu 8:27 n. abode in any house, but in ... 2532,3756
Lu 8:43 n. could be healed of any, ... 3756
Lu 9:3 journey, n. staves, nor scrip, n. ... 3383
Lu 9:3 n. scrip, n. bread, n. money; ... 3383
Lu 9:3 money; n. have two coats apiece ... 3383
Lu 10:4 Carry n. purse, nor scrip, nor ... 3361
Lu 11:33 secret place, n. under a bushel, ... 3761
Lu 12:2 n. hid, that shall not be known. ...
Lu 12:22 n. for the body, what ye shall put ..3366
Lu 12:24 ravens: for they n. sow nor reap; ... 3756
Lu 12:24 which n. have storehouse nor barn; 3756
Lu 12:29 drink, n. be ye of doubtful mind ... 3361
Lu 12:33 approacheth, n. moth corrupteth ... 3761
Lu 12:47 n. did according to his will, shall .. 3366
Lu 14:12 thy brethren, n. thy kinsmen, nor . 3366
Lu 14:35 It is n. fit for the land, nor yet for .3777
Lu 15:29 n. transgressed I at any time thy .. 3763
Lu 16:26 n. can they pass to us, that would ..3366
Lu 16:31 n. will they be persuaded, though .. 3761
Lu 17:21 N. shall they say, Lo here! or, lo .. 3761
Lu 18:2 feared not God, n. regarded man: .. 3366
Lu 18:34 n. knew they the things which ... 2532,3756
Lu 20:8 N. tell I you by what authority I ... 3761
Lu 20:21 n. acceptest thou the person ... 2532,3756
Lu 20:35 n. marry, nor...given in marriage: . 3777
Lu 20:36 N. can they die any more: for ... 3777
Joh 1:25 Christ, nor Elias, n. that prophet? ...
Joh 3:20 light, n. cometh to the light, . 2532,3756
Joh 4:15 thirst not, n. come hither to draw. ... 3366
Joh 4:21 shall n. in this mountain, nor yet .. 3777
Joh 5:37 n. heard his voice at any time, ... 3777
Joh 6:24 was not there, n. his disciples, ... 3761
Joh 7:5 n. did his brethren believe in him. ... 3761
Joh 8:11 N. do I condemn thee: go, and sin ..3761
Joh 8:19 Ye n. know me, nor my Father: ... 3777
Joh 8:42 n. came I of myself, but he sent ... 3761
Joh 9:3 N. hath this man sinned, nor his ... 3777
Joh 10:28 n. shall any man pluck them ..2532,3756
Joh 13:16 n. he that is sent greater than he .. 3761
Joh 14:17 it seeth him not, n. knoweth him: ..3761
Joh 14:27 be troubled, n. let it be afraid ... 3366
Joh 17:20 N. pray I for these alone, but for .. 3366
Ac 2:27 n. wilt thou suffer thine Holy One ... 3761
Ac 2:31 n. his flesh did see corruption. ... 3761
Ac 4:12 N. is there salvation in any ... 2532,3756
Ac 4:32 n. said any of them that ought of ... 3761
Ac 4:34 N. was there any among them ... 3761
Ac 8:21 Thou hast n. part nor lot in this ... 3756
Ac 9:9 sight, and n. did eat nor drink. ... 3756
Ac 15:10 n. our fathers nor we were able to ... 3777
Ac 16:21 us to receive, n. to observe, being ... 3761
Ac 17:25 N. is worshipped with men's ... 3761
Ac 19:37 which are n. robbers of churches, ... 3777
Ac 20:24 n. count I my life dear unto ... 3761
Ac 21:21 n. to walk after the customs. ... 3366
Ac 23:8 resurrection, n. angel, nor spirit: ... 3366
Ac 23:12 they would n. eat nor drink till ... 3383
Ac 23:21 they will n. eat nor drink till they ... 3383
Ac 24:12 they n. found me in the temple ... 3777
Ac 24:12 any man, n. raising up the people, ... 2228
Ac 24:12 n. in the synagogue, nor in the ... 2228
Ac 24:13 N. can they prove the things ... 2228
Ac 24:18 in the temple, n. with multitude, ... 3756
Ac 25:8 N. against the law of the Jews, ... 3777
Ac 25:8 n. against the temple, nor yet ... 3777
Ac 27:20 when n. sun nor stars in many ... 3383
Ac 28:21 We n. received letters out of Judaea ... 3777
Ac 28:21 n. any of the brethren that came ... 3777
Ro 1:21 him not as God, n. were thankful; ... 2228
Ro 2:28 n. is that circumcision, which is ... 3761
Ro 4:19 n. yet the deadness of Sarah's womb: ...
Ro 6:13 N. yield ye your members as ... 3366
Ro 8:7 to the law of God, n. indeed can be ... 3761
Ro 8:38 n. death, nor life, nor angels, nor ... 3777
Ro 9:7 N., because they are the seed of ... 3761
Ro 9:11 n. having done any good or evil, ... 3366
Ro 14:21 It is good n. to eat flesh, nor to ... 3361
1Co 2:9 n. have entered into the heart ... 2532,3756
1Co 2:14 n. can he know them, because ... 2532,3756
1Co 3:2 bear it, n. yet now are ye able. ... 235,3777
1Co 3:7 n. is he that planteth any thing, ... 3777
1Co 3:7 n. he that watereth; but God that ... 3777
1Co 5:8 n. with the leaven of malice and ... 3366
1Co 6:9 n. fornicators, nor idolaters, nor ... 3777
1Co 8:8 for n., if we eat, are we the better; ... 3777
1Co 8:8 n., if we eat not, are we the worse ... 3777
1Co 9:15 n. have I written these things, that it ...
1Co 10:7 N. be ye idolaters, as were some ... 3366
1Co 10:8 N. let us commit fornication, as ... 3366
1Co 10:9 N. let us tempt Christ, as some of ... 3366
1Co 10:10 N. murmur ye, as some of them ... 3366
1Co 10:32 n. to the Jews, nor to the Gentiles, ...
1Co 11:9 N. was the man created for ... 2542,3756
1Co 11:11 n. is the man without the woman, ... 3777
1Co 11:11 n. the woman without the man, ... 3777
1Co 11:16 custom, n. the churches of God. ... 3761
1Co 15:50 of God; n. doth corruption inherit ... 3761
Ga 1:1 n. by man, but by Jesus Christ, and ... 3761
Ga 1:12 For I n. received it of man, ... 3761
Ga 1:12 n. was I taught it, but by the Lord ... 3777
Ga 1:17 N. went I up to Jerusalem to them ... 3761
Ga 2:3 n. Titus, who was with me, being a ... 3761
Ga 3:28 There is n. Jew nor Greek, there ... 3756
Ga 3:28 there is n. bond nor free, there is ... 3756
Ga 3:28 there is n. male nor female: for ye ... 3756
Ga 5:6 n. circumcision availeth any thing, ... 3777
Ga 6:13 For n. they themselves who are ... 3761
Ga 6:15 n. circumcision availeth any thing, ... 3777
Eph 4:27 N. give place to the devil. ... 3383
Eph 5:4 N. filthiness, nor foolish ... 2532,3756
Eph 6:9 n. is there respect of persons ... 2532,3756
Php 2:16 run in vain, n. laboured in vain. ... 3761
Col 3:11 Where there is n. Greek nor Jew, ... 3756
1Th 2:5 n. at any time used we flattering ... 3777
1Th 2:6 glory, n. of you, nor yet of others, ... 3777
2Th 2:2 n. by spirit, nor by word, nor by ... 3383
2Th 3:8 N. did we eat any man's bread for ... 3761
2Th 3:10 would not work, n. should he eat. ... 3366
1Ti 1:4 N. give heed to fables and endless ... 3366
1Ti 1:7 understanding n. what they say, ... 3383
1Ti 5:22 n. be partaker of other men's sins: ... 3366
Heb 4:13 N. is there any creature that ... 2532,3756
Heb 7:3 n. beginning of days, nor end of ... 3383
Heb 9:12 N. by the blood of goats and ... 3761
Heb 9:18 n. the first testament was dedicated ... 3761
Heb 10:8 not, n. hadst pleasure therein; ... 3761
Jas 1:13 evil, n. tempteth he any man: ... 2582,3762
Jas 1:17 variableness, n. shadow of turning ... 2228
Jas 5:12 brethren, swear not, n. by heaven, ... 3383
Jas 5:12 n. by earth, n. by any other oath: ... 3383
1Pe 2:22 n. was guile found in his mouth: ... 3761
1Pe 3:14 of their terror, n. be troubled; ... 3366
1Pe 5:3 N. as being lords over God's ... 3366
2Pe 1:8 shall n. be barren nor unfruitful ... 3756
1Jo 2:15 n. the things that are in the world ... 3366
1Jo 3:6 hath not seen him, n. known him. ... 3761
1Jo 3:10 God, n. he that loveth not his brother ...
1Jo 3:18 us not love in word, n. in tongue; ... 3366
2Jo 10 your house, n. bid him God speed: ... 3366
3Jo 10 n. doth he himself receive the ... 3777
Re 3:15 that thou art n. cold nor hot: ... 3777
Re 3:16 art lukewarm, and n. cold nor hot, 3777
Re 5:3 nor in earth, n. under the earth, ... 3761
Re 5:3 to open the book, n. to look thereon. ..3761
Re 5:4 read the book, n. to look thereon ... 3777
Re 7:3 Hurt not the earth, n. the sea, nor ... 3383
Re 7:16 no more, n. thirst any more; ... 3761
Re 7:16 n. shall the sun light on them, nor ... 3761
Re 9:4 n. any green thing, n. any tree; but ...
Re 9:20 which n. can see, nor hear, nor ... 3777
Re 9:21 N. repented they of their ... 2532,3756
Re 12:8 n. was there place found any more ... 3777
Re 20:4 worshipped the beast, n. his image, ... 3777
Re 20:4 n....received his mark upon ... 2532,3756
Re 21:4 more death, n. sorrow, nor crying, ... 3777
Re 21:4 n. shall there be any more pain: for ...
Re 21:23 sun, n. of the moon, to shine in it: ... 3761
Re 21:27 n. whatsoever worketh abomination, ...
Re 22:5 need no candle, n. light of the sun; ...

NEKEB (ne'-keb)
Jos 19:33 N., and Jabneel, unto Lakum; ... 5346

NEKODA (ne-ko'-dah)
Ezr 2:48 of Rezin, the children of N., ... 5353
Ezr 2:60 children of N., six hundred fifty ... 5353
Ne 7:50 of Rezin, the children of N., ... 5353
Ne 7:62 children of N., six hundred forty ... 5353

NEMUEL (ne-mu'-el) See also JEMUEL; NEMUELITES.
Nu 26:9 sons of Eliab; N., and Dathan, ... 5241
Nu 26:12 of N., the family of the Nemuelites: ... 5241
1Ch 4:24 sons of Simeon were, N. and Jamin, ... 5241

NEMUELITES (ne-mu'-el-ites)
Nu 26:12 of Nemuel, the family of the N.: ... 5242

NEPHEG (ne'-feg)
Ex 6:21 sons of Izhar; Korah, and N., and ... 5298
2Sa 5:15 Ibhar also, and Elishua, and N., ... 5298
1Ch 3:7 And Nogah, and N., and Japhia, ... 5298
1Ch 14:6 And Nogah, and N., and Japhia, ... 5298

NEPHEW See also NEPHEWS.
Job 18:19 neither have son nor n. among ... 5220
Isa 14:22 and son, and n., saith the Lord ... 5220

NEPHEWS
Jg 12:14 he had forty sons and thirty **n.**, 1121
1Ti 5:4 if any widow have children or **n.**, *1549*

NEPHISH (ne'-fish) See also NAPHISH.
1Ch 5:19 Hagarites, with Jetur, and **N.**, 5305

NEPHISHESIM (ne-fish'-e-sim) See also NEPHUSIM.
Ne 7:52 of Meunim, the children of **N.**, 5300

NEPHTHALIM (nef'-tha-lim) See also NAPHTALI.
Mt 4:13 in the borders of Zabulon and **N.**: *3508*
Mt 4:15 and the land of **N.**, by the way of *3508*
Re 7:6 **N.** were sealed twelve thousand. *3508*

NEPHTOAH (nef-to'-ah)
Jos 15:9 the fountain of the water of **N.**, 5318
Jos 18:15 went out to the well of waters of **N.**: 5318

NEPHUSIM (ne-fu'-sim) See also NEPHISHESIM.
Ezr 2:50 of Mehunim, the children of **N.**, 5304

NER (nur)
1Sa 14:50 Abner, the son on **N.**, Saul's uncle. 5369
1Sa 14:51 **N.** the father of Abner was the son 5369
1Sa 26:5 Abner the son **N.**, the captain of 5369
1Sa 26:14 and to Abner the son of **N.**, saying, 5369
2Sa 2:8 Abner the son of **N.**, captain of 5369
2Sa 2:12 And Abner the son of **N.**, and the 5369
2Sa 3:23 son of **N.** came to the king, and he 5369
2Sa 3:25 Thou knowest Abner the son of **N.**, 5369
2Sa 3:28 the blood of Abner the son of **N.**: 5369
2Sa 3:37 king to slay Abner the son of **N.**: 5369
1Ki 2:5 unto Abner the son of **N.**, and unto 5369
1Ki 2:32 Abner the son of **N.**, captain of the 5369
1Ch 8:33 **N.** begat Kish, and Kish begat Saul, 5369
1Ch 9:36 Kish, and Baal, and **N.**, and Nadab, 5369
1Ch 9:39 **N.** begat Kish; and Kish begat 5369
1Ch 26:28 and Abner the son of **N.**, and Joab 5369

NEREUS (ne'-re-us)
Ro 16:15 Salute Philologus, and Julia, **N.**, *3517*

NERGAL (nur'-gal) See also NERGAL-SHAREZER.
2Ki 17:30 and the men of Cuth made **N.**, and 5370

NERGAL-SHAREZER (nur''-gal-sha-re'-zur)
Jer 39:3 sat in the middle gate, even **N.**, 5371
Jer 39:3 **N.**, Rab-mag, with all the residue 5371
Jer 39:13 **N.**, Rab-mag, and all the king of 5371

NERI (ne'-ri)
Lu 3:27 Salathiel, which was the son of **N.**, *3518*

NERIAH (ne-ri'-ah)
Jer 32:12, 16 unto Baruch the son of **N.**, 5374
Jer 36:4 called Baruch the son of **N.**: and 5374
Jer 36:8 Baruch the son of **N.** did according 5374
Jer 36:14 the son of **N.** took the roll in his 5374
Jer 36:32 to Baruch the scribe, the son of **N.**; 5374
Jer 43:3 son of **N.** setteth thee on against us, 5374
Jer 43:6 prophet, and Baruch the son of **N.**: 5374
Jer 45:1 spake unto Baruch the son of **N.**, 5374
Jer 51:59 commanded Seraiah the son of **N.**, 5374

NERO (ne'-ro)
2Ti *subscr.* when Paul was brought before **N.** *3505*

NEST See also NESTS.
Nu 24:21 and thou puttest thy **n.** in a rock 7064
Du 22:6 If a bird's **n.** chance to be before 7064
Du 32:11 As an eagle stirreth up her **n.**, 7064
Job 29:18 Then I said, I shall die in my **n.**, 7064
Job 39:27 command, and make her **n.** on high? 7064
Ps 84:3 the swallow a **n.** for herself, where 7064
Pr 27:8 a bird that wandereth from her **n.**, 7064
Isa 10:14 as a **n.** the riches of the people: 7064
Isa 16:2 a wandering bird cast out of the **n.**, 7064
Isa 34:15 shall the great owl make her **n.**, 7077
Jer 22:23 that makest thy **n.** in the cedars, 7077
Jer 48:28 like the dove that maketh her **n.** in 7077
Jer 49:16 make thy **n.** as high as the eagle, 7064
Ob 4 thou set thy **n.** among the stars, 7064
Hab 2:9 that he may set his **n.** on high, that 7064

NESTS
Ps 104:17 Where the birds make their **n.**: as 7077
Eze 31:6 heaven made their **n.** in his boughs, 7077
Mt 8:20 **and the birds of the air have n.;** *2682*
Lu 9:58 **holes, and birds of the air have n.;** *2682*

NET See also NETS; NETWORK.
Ex 27:4 upon the **n.** shalt thou make four 7568
Ex 27:5 the **n.** may be even to the midst of 7568
Job 18:8 he is cast into a **n.** by his own feet, 7568
Job 19:6 hath compassed me with his **n.** 4685
Ps 9:15 in the **n.** which they hid is their 7568
Ps 10:9 when he draweth him into his **n.** 7568
Ps 25:15 he shall pluck my feet out of the **n.** 7568
Ps 31:4 me out of the **n.** that they have laid 7568
Ps 35:7 they hid for me their **n.** in a pit, 7568
Ps 35:8 **n.** that he hath hid catch himself: 7568
Ps 57:6 have prepared a **n.** for my steps; 7568
Ps 66:11 Thou broughtest us into the **n.**; 4685
Ps 140:5 have spread a **n.** by the wayside; 7568
Pr 1:17 **n.** is spread in the sight of any bird. 7568
Pr 12:12 wicked desireth the **n.** of evil men: 4686
Pr 29:5 spreadeth a **n.** for his feet. 7568
Ec 9:12 fishes that are taken in an evil **n.**, 4686
Isa 51:20 the streets, as a wild bull in a **n.**: 4364
La 1:13 he hath spread a **n.** for my feet, he 7568
Eze 12:13 My **n.** also will I spread upon him, 7568
Eze 17:20 And I will spread my **n.** upon him, 7568
Eze 19:8 and spread their **n.** over him: he 7568
Eze 32:3 I will therefore spread out my **n.** 7568
Eze 32:3 they shall bring thee up in my **n.** 2764
Ho 5:1 and a **n.** spread upon Tabor. 7568
Ho 7:12 go, I will spread my **n.** upon them; 7568
Mic 7:2 every man his brother with a **n.** 2764
Hab 1:15 they catch them in their **n.**, and 2764
Hab 1:16 they sacrifice unto their **n.**, and 2764
Hab 1:17 Shall they therefore empty their **n.**, 2764
Mt 4:18 brother, casting a **n.** into the sea: *293*
Mt 13:47 **kingdom of heaven is like a n.,** *4522*
Mk 1:16 brother, casting a **n.** into the sea: *293*
Lu 5:5 at thy word I will let down the **n.** *1350*
Lu 5:6 of fishes: and their **n.** break. *1350*
Joh 21:6 **Cast the n. on the right side of the** *1350*
Joh 21:8 cubits,) dragging the **n.** with fishes. *1350*
Joh 21:11 drew the **n.** to the land full of fishes, *1350*
Joh 21:11 many, yet was not the **n.** broken. *1350*

NETHANEEL (ne-than'-e-el)
Nu 1:8 of Issachar; **N.** the son of Zuar. 5417
Nu 2:5 **N.** the son of Zuar shall be captain 5417
Nu 7:18 the second day **N.** the son of Zuar, 5417
Nu 7:23 the offering of **N.** the son of Zuar. 5417
Nu 10:15 Issachar was **N.** the son of Zuar. 5417
1Ch 2:14 **N.** the fourth, Raddai the fifth, 5417
1Ch 15:24 **N.**, and Amasai, and Zechariah, 5417
1Ch 24:6 Shemaiah the son of **N.** the scribe, 5417
1Ch 26:4 Sacar the fourth, and **N.** the fifth, 5417
2Ch 17:7 to **N.**, and to Michaiah, to teach in 5417
2Ch 35:9 and Shemaiah and **N.**, his brethren, 5417
Ezr 10:22 Ishmael, **N.**, Jozabad, and Elasah 5417
Ne 12:21 Hashabiah; of Jedaiah, **N.** 5417
Ne 12:36 **N.**, and Judah, Hanani, with the 5417

NETHANIAH (neth-a-ni'-ah)
2Ki 25:23 even Ishmael the son of **N.**, and 5418
2Ki 25:25 month, that Ishmael the son of **N.**, 5418
1Ch 25:2 and **N.**, and Asarelah, the sons of 5418
1Ch 25:12 The fifth to **N.**, he, his sons, and 5418
2Ch 17:8 Levites, even Shemaiah, and **N.**, 5418
Jer 36:14 princes sent Jehudi the son of **N.**, 5418
Jer 40:8 Mizpah, even Ishmael the son of **N.**, 5418
Jer 40:14 Ishmael the son of **N.** to slay thee? 5418
Jer 40:15 I will slay Ishmael the son of **N.**, 5418
Jer 41:1 Ishmael the son of **N.** the son of 5418
Jer 41:2 arose Ishmael the son **N.**, and the 5418
Jer 41:6 Ishmael the son of **N.** went forth 5418
Jer 41:7 Ishmael the son of **N.** slew them, 5418
Jer 41:9 Ishmael the son of **N.** filled it with 5418
Jer 41:10 Ishmael the son of **N.** carried them 5418
Jer 41:11 Ishmael the son of **N.** had done, 5418
Jer 41:12 to fight with Ishmael the son of **N.**, 5418
Jer 41:15 But Ishmael the son of **N.** escaped 5418
Jer 41:16 from Ishmael the son of **N.**, from 5418
Jer 41:18 the son of **N.** had slain Gedaliah 5418

NETHER See also NETHERMOST.
Ex 19:17 stood at the **n.** part of the mount. 8482
De 24:6 take the **n.** or the upper millstone 7347
Jos 15:19 upper springs, and the **n.** springs. 8482
Jos 16:3 the coast of Beth-horon the **n.**, 8481
Jos 18:13 the south side of the **n.** Beth-horon. 8481
Jg 1:15 upper springs and the **n.** springs. 8482
1Ki 9:17 Gezer, and Beth-horon the **n.**, 8481
1Ch 7:24 who built Beth-horon the **n.**, and 8481
2Ch 8:5 the upper, and Beth-horon the **n.**, 8481
Job 41:24 hard as a piece of the **n.** millstone. 8482
Eze 31:14 death, to the **n.** parts of the earth, 8482
Eze 31:16 in the **n.** parts of the earth. 8482
Eze 31:18 Eden unto the **n.** parts of the earth: 8482
Eze 32:18 unto the **n.** parts of the earth, with 8482
Eze 32:24 into the **n.** parts of the earth, which 8482

NETHERMOST
1Ki 6:6 **n.** chamber was five cubits broad, 8481

NETHINIMS (neth'-in-ims)
1Ch 9:2 the priests, Levites, and the **N.** 5411
Ezr 2:43 The **N.**: the children of Ziha, the 5411
Ezr 2:58 All the **N.**, and the children of 5411
Ezr 2:70 and the **N.**, dwelt in their cities, 5411
Ezr 7:7 and the **N.**, unto Jerusalem, in the 5411
Ezr 7:24 **N.**, or ministers of this house of 5412
Ezr 8:17 his brethren the **N.**, at the place 5411
Ezr 8:20 Also of the **N.**, whom David and 5411
Ezr 8:20 two hundred and twenty **N.**: all 5411
Ne 3:26 Moreover the **N.** dwelt in Ophel, 5411
Ne 3:31 Malchiah...unto the place of the **N.**, 5411
Ne 7:46 The **N.**: the children of Ziha, the 5411
Ne 7:60 All the **N.**, and the children of 5411
Ne 7:73 people, and the **N.**, and all Israel, 5411
Ne 10:28 the porters, the singers, the **N.**, 5411
Ne 11:3 and the **N.**, and the children of 5411
Ne 11:21 But the **N.** dwelt in Ophel: and 5411
Ne 11:21 Ziha and Gispa were over the **N.** 5411

NETOPHAH (ne-to'-fah) See also NETOPHATHITE.
Ezr 2:22 The men of **N.**, fifty and six. 5199
Ne 7:26 The men of Beth-lehem and **N.**, 5199

NETOPHATHI (ne-to'-fa-thi) See also NETOPHATHITE.
Ne 12:28 and from the village of **N.**; 5200

NETOPHATHITE (ne-to'-fa-thite) See also NETOPHATHI; NETOPHATHITES.
2Sa 23:28 the Ahohite, Maharai the **N.**, 5200
2Sa 23:29 Heleb the son of Baanah, a **N.**, 5200
2Ki 25:23 the son of Tanhumeth the **N.**, 5200
1Ch 11:30 Maharai the **N.**, Heled the son 5200
1Ch 11:30 Heled the son of Baanah the **N.**, 5200
1Ch 27:13 tenth month was Maharai the **N.**, 5200
1Ch 27:15 twelfth month was Heldai the **N.**, 5200
Jer 40:8 sons of Ephai the **N.**, and Jezaniah 5200

NETOPHATHITES (ne-to'-fa-thites)
1Ch 2:54 of Salma; Beth-lehem, and the **N.**, 5200
1Ch 9:16 dwelt in the villages of the **N.** 5200

NETS
1Ki 7:17 **n.** of checker work, and wreaths 7638
Ps 141:10 the wicked fall into their own **n.**, 4365
Ec 7:26 whose heart is snares and **n.**, and 2764
Isa 19:8 that spread **n.** upon the waters 4364
Eze 26:5 be a place for the spreading of **n.** 2764
Eze 26:14 shalt be a place to spread **n.** upon; 2764
Eze 47:10 shall be a place to spread forth **n.**; 2764
Mt 4:20 they straightway left their **n.**, and *1350*
Mt 4:21 their father, mending their **n.**; and *1350*
Mk 1:18 straightway they forsook their **n.**, *1350*
Mk 1:19 were in the ship mending their **n.** *1350*
Lu 5:2 them, and were washing their **n.** *1350*
Lu 5:4 **let down your n. for a draught.** *1350*

NETTLES
Job 30:7 under the **n.** they were gathered. 2738
Pr 24:31 **n.** have covered the face thereof, 2738
Isa 34:13 **n.** and brambles in the fortresses 7057
Ho 9:6 their silver, **n.** shall possess them: 7057
Zep 2:9 the breeding of **n.**, and saltpits, 2738

NETWORK See also NETWORKS.
Ex 27:4 for it a grate of **n.** of brass; 4639,7568
Ex 38:4 for the altar a brasen grate of **n.**, 4639,7568
1Ki 7:28 rows round about upon the one **n.**, 7639
1Ki 7:20 the belly which was by the **n.**: and 7639
1Ki 7:42 rows of pomegranates for one **n.**, 7639
Jer 52:22 **n.** and pomegranates upon the 7639
Jer 52:23 all the pomegranates upon the **n.** 7639

NETWORKS
1Ki 7:41 the two **n.**, to cover the two bowls 7639
1Ki 7:42 pomegranates for the two **n.**, even 7639
Isa 19:9 and they that weave **n.**, shall be 2355

NEVER See also NEVERTHELESS.
Ge 34:12 Ask me **n.** so much dowry and gift,
Ge 41:19 such as I **n.** saw in all the land of 3808
Le 6:13 upon the altar; it shall **n.** go out. 3808
Nu 19:2 and upon which **n.** came yoke: 3808
De 15:11 poor shall **n.** cease out of the land: 3808

Jg 2:1 **n.** break my covenant with 3808,5769
Jg 14:3 **n.** a woman among the daughters 369
Jg 16:7 green withs that were **n.** dried, ... 3808
Jg 16:11 new ropes that were **n.** occupied, ... 3808
2Sa 12:10 sword shall **n.** depart......... 3808,5704,5769
2Ch 18:7 he **n.** prophesied good unto me, ... 369
2Ch 21:17 so that there was **n.** a son left him, ... 3808
Job 3:16 as infants which **n.** saw light. 3808
Job 9:30 and make my hands **n.** so clean; 1253
Job 21:25 soul, and **n.** eateth with pleasure........ 3808
Ps 10:6 for I shall **n.** be in adversity. 1755
Ps 10:11 his face; he will **n.** see it. 1074,5331
Ps 15:5 these things shall **n.** be moved. .. 3808,5769
Ps 30:6 I said, I shall **n.** be moved......... 3808,5769
Ps 31:1 let me **n.** be ashamed:............... 408,3808
Ps 49:19 they shall **n.** see light. 5704,5331,3808
Ps 55:22 **n.** suffer the righteous to be 3808,5769
Ps 58:5 of charmers, charming **n.** so wisely..........
Ps 71:1 trust: let me **n.** be put to........... 408,5769
Ps 119:93 I will **n.** forget thy precepts: 5769,3808
Pr 10:30 righteous shall **n.** be removed: ... 5769,1077
Pr 27:20 Hell and destruction are **n.** full;.......... 3808
Pr 27:20 the eyes of man are **n.** satisfied. 3808
Pr 30:15 three things that are **n.** satisfied, ... 3808
Isa 13:20 It shall **n.** be inhabited, ... 3808,5331
Isa 14:20 seed of evildoers shall **n.** be........ 3808,5769
Isa 25:2 be no city; it shall **n.** be built. 5769,3808
Isa 56:11 dogs which can **n.** have enough,......... 3808
Isa 62:6 shall **n.** hold their peace day nor 3808
Isa 63:19 thou **n.** barest rule over them; ... 5769,3808
Jer 20:11 confusion shall **n.** be forgotten........... 3808
Jer 33:17 shall **n.** want a man to sit upon........... 3808
Eze 16:63 and **n.** open thy mouth any more 3808
Eze 26:21 shalt thou **n.** be found again, ... 3808,5769
Eze 27:36 and **n.** shalt be any more........... 5704,5769
Eze 28:19 and **n.** shalt thou be any.......... 5704,5769
Da 2:44 which shall **n.** be destroyed:....... 5957,3809
Da 12:1 such as **n.** was since there was a....... 3808
Joe 2:26, 27 and my people shall **n.** be...... 3808,5769
Am 8:7 **n.** forget any of their works. 518,5331
Am 8:14 shall fail, and **n.** rise up again. 3808
Hab 1:4 judgment doth **n.** go forth:......... 3808,5331
Mt 7:23 **I n. knew you: depart from me,** *3763*
Mt 9:33 saying, It was **n.** so seen in Israel....... *3763*
Mt 21:16 **have ye n. read, Out of the mouth**..*3763*
Mt 21:42 **Did ye n. read in the scriptures,**.... *3763*
Mt 26:33 of thee, yet I will **n.** be offended........ *3763*
Mt 27:14 answered him to **n.** a word;....... *3761,1520*
Mk 2:12 We **n.** saw it on this fashion............. *3763*
Mk 2:25 **Have ye n. read what David did,** ... *3763*
Mk 3:29 **hath n. forgiveness,** .. *3756,1519,3588,165*
Mk 9:43, 45 **that n. shall be quenched:** *3756*
Mk 11:2 **colt tied, whereon n. man sat,** *3762,4455*
Mk 14:21 **that man if he had n. been born**.... *3756*
Lu 15:29 **and yet thou n. gavest me a kid,**... *3763*
Lu 19:30 **tied, whereon yet n. man sat:**....... *3762*
Lu 23:29 **and the wombs that n. bare,** *3756*
Lu 23:29 **and the paps which n. gave suck**... *3756*
Lu 23:53 wherein **n.** man before was laid. *3764*
Joh 4:14 **give...shall n. thirst;** .. *3364,1519,3588,165*
Joh 6:35 **that cometh to me shall n. hunger;**. *165*
Joh 6:35 **believeth on me shall n.**.......... *3364,4455*
Joh 7:15 man letters, having **n.** learned? *3361*
Joh 7:46 **N.** man spake like this man............... *3763*
Joh 8:33 **n.** in bondage to any man: *3762,4455*
Joh 8:51 **saying...shall n. see**.. *3364,1519,3588,165*
Joh 8:52 shall **n.** taste of death. ..*3364,1519,3588,165*
Joh 10:28 **shall n. perish,** *3364,1519,3588,165*
Joh 11:26 **in me shall n.**............ *3364,1519,3588,165*
Joh 13:8 Thou shalt **n.** wash my..*3364,1519,3588,165*
Joh 19:41 wherein was **n.** man yet laid. *3764*
Ac 10:14 **n.** eaten any thing that is common...... *3763*
Ac 14:8 mother's womb, who **n.** had walked:... *3763*
1Co 13:8 Charity **n.** faileth: but whether........... *3763*
2Ti 3:7 **n.** able to come to the knowledge *3368*
Heb 10:1 can **n.** with those sacrifices which........ *3763*
Heb 10:11 which can **n.** take away sins: *3763*
Heb 13:5 I will **n.** leave thee, nor forsake......... *3364*
2Pe 1:10 these things, ye shall **n.** fall: *3364,4219*

NEVERTHELESS

Ex 32:34 **n.** in the day when I visit I will...............
Le 11:4 **N.** these shall ye not eat of them 389
Le 11:36 **N.** a fountain or pit, wherein there........ 389
Nu 13:28 **N.** the people be strong that dwell....... 657
Nu 14:44 **n.** the ark of the covenant of the.............
Nu 18:15 **n.** the firstborn of man shalt thou 389
Nu 24:22 **N.** the Kenite shall be wasted, ... 3588,518
Nu 31:23 **n.** it shall be purified with the............ 389
De 14:7 **N.** these ye shall not eat of them 389
De 23:5 **N.** the Lord thy God would not..............
Jos 13:13 **N.** the children of Israel expelled not ....
Jos 14:8 **N.** my brethren that went up with...........
Jg 1:33 **n.** the inhabitants of Beth-shemesh..........
Jg 2:16 **N.** the Lord raised up judges, which ....
1Sa 8:19 **N.** the people refused to obey the ....
1Sa 15:35 **n.** Samuel mourned for Saul: and........ 3588
1Sa 20:26 **N.** Saul spake not any thing that ....
1Sa 29:6 day: **n.** the lords favour thee not.............
2Sa 5:7 **N.** David took the strong hold of.............
2Sa 17:18 **N.** a lad saw them, and told Absalom: ....
2Sa 23:16 **n.** he would not drink thereof, ...
1Ki 8:19 **N.** thou shalt not build the house; 7535
1Ki 15:4 **N.** for David's sake did the Lord........ 3588
1Ki 15:14 **n.** Asa's heart was perfect with 7535
1Ki 15:23 **N.** in the time of his old age he 7535
1Ki 22:43 **n.** the high places were not taken........ 389
2Ki 2:10 **n.**, if thou see me when I am taken..........
2Ki 3:3 **N.** he cleaved unto the sins of........... 7535
2Ki 13:6 **N.** they departed not from the sins 389
2Ki 23:9 **N.** the priests of the high places.......... 389
1Ch 11:5 **N.** David took the castle of Zion,..............
1Ch 21:4 **N.** the king's word prevailed against..........
2Ch 12:8 **N.** they shall be his servants;.............. 3588
2Ch 15:17 **n.** the heart of Asa was perfect all 7535
2Ch 19:3 **N.** there are good things found in.......... 61
2Ch 30:11 **N.** divers of Asher and Manasseh 389
2Ch 33:17 **N.** the people did sacrifice still in 61
2Ch 35:22 **N.** Josiah would not turn his face............
Ne 4:9 **N.** we made our prayer unto our God, ...
Ne 9:26 **N.** they were disobedient, and.................
Ne 9:31 **N.** for thy great mercies' sake thou ....
Ne 13:26 **n.** even him did outlandish women...... 1571
Es 5:10 **N.** Haman refrained himself: and ....
Ps 31:22 **n.** thou heardest the voice of my......... 403
Ps 49:12 **N.** man being in honour abideth.............
Ps 73:23 **N.** I am continually with thee:..................
Ps 78:36 **N.** they did flatter him with their..............
Ps 89:33 **N.** my lovingkindness will I not...............
Ps 106:8 **N.** he saved them for his name's...............
Ps 106:44 **N.** he regarded their affliction, when.........
Pr 19:21 **n.** the counsel of the Lord, that...............
Ec 9:16 **n.** the poor man's wisdom is despised, ...
Isa 9:1 **N.** the dimness shall not be such.......... 3588
Jer 5:18 **N.** in those days, saith the Lord, ... 1571
Jer 26:24 **N.** the hand of Ahikam the son of......... 389
Jer 28:7 **N.** hear thou now this word that I 389
Jer 36:25 **N.** Elnathan and Delaiah and.............. 1571
Eze 3:21 **N.** if thou warn the righteous man, ...
Eze 16:60 **N.** I will remember my covenant..............
Eze 20:17 **N.** mine eye spared them from ....
Eze 20:22 **N.** I withdrew mine hand, and ....
Eze 33:9 **N.**, if thou warn the wicked of his ....
Da 4:15 **N.** leave the stump of his roots in...... 1297
Jon 1:13 **N.** the men rowed hard to bring it to........
Mt 14:9 **n.** for the oath's sake, and them ....
Mt 26:39 **n. not as I will, but as thou wilt**... *4133*
Mt 26:64 **n. I say unto you, Hereafter shall**..*4133*
Mk 14:36 **n. not what I will, but what thou**... *235*
Lu 5:5 **n.** at thy word I will let down the *1161*
Lu 13:33 **N. I must walk to day, and**........... *4133*
Lu 18:8 **N. when the Son of man cometh,** .. *4133*
Lu 22:42 **n. not my will, but thine, be done**..*4133*
Joh 11:15 **may believe; n. let us go unto him**...*235*
Joh 12:42 **N.** among the chief rulers.......... *3676,3305*
Joh 16:7 **N. I tell you the truth; It is**........... *235*
Ac 14:17 **N.** he left not himself without *2544*
Ac 27:11 **N.** the centurion believed the *1161*
Ro 5:14 **N.** death reigned from Adam to........... *235*
Ro 15:15 **N.**, brethren, I have written the *1161*
1Co 7:2 **N.**, to avoid fornication, let every....... *1161*
1Co 7:28 **N.** such shall have trouble in the........ *1161*
1Co 7:37 **N.** he that standeth stedfast in his....... *1161*
1Co 9:12 **N.** we have not used this power;........ *235*
1Co 11:11 **N.** neither is the man without the......... *4133*
2Co 3:16 **N.**, when it shall turn to the Lord, ... *1161*
2Co 7:6 **N.** God, that comforteth those that...... *235*
2Co 12:16 **n.**, being crafty, I caught you with....... *235*
Ga 2:20 **n.** I live; yet not I, but Christ *1161*
Ga 4:30 **N.** what saith the scripture? Cast.......... *235*
Eph 5:33 **N.**, let every one of you...so love *4133*
Php 1:24 **N.** to abide in the flesh is more *1161*
Php 3:16 **N.**, whereto we have already *4133*
2Ti 1:12 **n.** I am not ashamed: for I know *235*
2Ti 2:19 **N.** the foundation of God standeth...... *3305*
Heb 12:11 **n.** afterward it yieldeth the *1161*
2Pe 3:13 **N.** we, according to his promise,........ *1161*
Re 2:4 **N. I have somewhat against thee,**... *235*

NEW See also NEWBORN; NEWS; RENEW.

Ex 1:8 arose up a **n.** king over Egypt, ... 2319
Le 23:16 a **n.** meat offering unto the Lord. 2319
Le 26:10 forth the old because of the **n.**. 2319
Nu 16:30 But if the Lord make a **n.** thing, ... 1278
Nu 28:26 a **n.** meat offering unto the Lord, ... 2319
De 20:5 is there that hath built a **n.** house, ... 2319
De 22:8 When thou buildest a **n.** house,........... 2319
De 24:5 When a man hath taken a **n.** wife, ... 2319
De 32:17 not, to **n.** gods that came newly up, ... 2319
Jos 9:13 of wine, which we filled, were **n.**; 2319
Jg 5:8 They chose **n.** gods; then was war..... 2319
Jg 15:13 they bound him with two **n.** cords, ... 2319
Jg 15:15 he found a **n.** jawbone of an ass, ... 2961
Jg 16:11 If they bind me fast with **n.** ropes 2319
Jg 16:12 Delilah therefore took **n.** ropes, ... 2319
1Sa 6:7 Now therefore make a **n.** cart, and...... 2319
1Sa 20:5 Behold, to morrow is the **n.** moon,..... 2320
1Sa 20:18 To morrow is the **n.** moon: and......... 2320
1Sa 20:24 and when the **n.** moon was come, ... 2320
2Sa 6:3 set the ark of God upon a **n.** cart,....... 2319
2Sa 6:3 sons of Abinadab, drave the **n.** cart. ... 2319
2Sa 21:16 he being girded with a **n.** sword,......... 2319
1Ki 11:29 had clad himself with a **n.** garment; 2319
1Ki 11:30 Ahijah caught the **n.** garment that....... 2319
2Ki 2:20 Bring me a **n.** cruse, and put salt....... 2319
2Ki 4:23 it is neither **n.** moon, nor sabbath. 2320
1Ch 13:7 carried the ark of God in a **n.** cart...... 2319
1Ch 23:31 in the **n.** moons, and on the set.......... 2320
2Ch 2:4 on the **n.** moons, and on the solemn... 2320
2Ch 8:13 on the **n.** moons, and on the solemn... 2320
2Ch 20:5 of the Lord, before the **n.** court,......... 2319
2Ch 31:3 and for the **n.** moons, and for the 2320
Ezr 3:5 offering, both of the **n.** moons, and..... 2320
Ezr 6:4 stones, and a row of **n.** timber; 2323
Ne 10:33 of the sabbaths, of the **n.** moons, ... 2320
Ne 10:39 offering of the corn, of the **n.** wine,.... 8492
Ne 13:5 the tithes of the corn, the **n.** wine,...... 8492
Ne 13:12 tithe of the corn and the **n.** wine......... 8492
Job 32:19 it is ready to burst like **n.** bottles. 2319
Ps 33:3 Sing unto him a **n.** song; play............ 2319
Ps 40:3 hath put a **n.** song in my mouth, ... 2319
Ps 81:3 up the trumpet in the **n.** moon, ... 2320
Ps 96:1 O sing unto the Lord a **n.** song: 2319
Ps 98:1 O sing unto the Lord a **n.** song; for.... 2319
Ps 144:9 I will sing a **n.** song unto thee, O........ 2319
Ps 149:1 Sing unto the Lord a **n.** song, and...... 2319
Pr 3:10 presses...burst out with **n.** wine. 8492
Ec 1:9 there is no **n.** thing under the sun. 2319
Ec 1:10 it may be said, See, this is **n.**? it 2319
Ca 7:13 of pleasant fruits, **n.** and old, which 2319
Isa 1:13 the **n.** moons and sabbaths, the 2320
Isa 1:14 Your **n.** moons and your appointed 2320
Isa 24:7 The **n.** wine mourneth, the vine........... 8492
Isa 41:15 a **n.** sharp threshing instrument 2319
Isa 42:9 to pass, and **n.** things do I declare: 2319
Isa 42:10 Sing unto the Lord a **n.** song, and....... 2319
Isa 43:19 Behold, I will do a **n.** thing; now it..... 2319
Isa 48:6 shewed thee **n.** things from this.......... 2319
Isa 62:2 thou shalt be called by a **n.** name, ... 2319
Isa 65:8 the **n.** wine is found in the cluster, ... 8492
Isa 65:17 create **n.** heavens and a **n.** earth: 2319
Isa 66:22 as the **n.** heavens and the **n.** earth,.... 2319
Isa 66:23 that from one **n.** moon to another, ... 2320
Jer 26:10 down in the entry of the **n.** gate 2319
Jer 31:22 hath created a **n.** thing in the earth, ... 2319
Jer 31:31 I will make a **n.** covenant with the...... 2319
Jer 36:10 at the entry of the **n.** gate of the 2319
La 3:23 They are **n.** every morning: great 2319
Eze 11:19 I will put a **n.** spirit within you; 2319
Eze 18:31 make you a **n.** heart and a **n.** spirit: ... 2319
Eze 36:26 A **n.** heart also will I give you, and..... 2319
Eze 36:26 a **n.** spirit will I put within you: 2319
Eze 45:17 in the feasts, and in the **n.** moons, ... 2320
Eze 46:1 day of the **n.** moon it shall be opened. .2320
Eze 46:3 the sabbaths and in the **n.** moons....... 2320
Eze 46:6 in the day of the **n.** moon it shall be ... 2320
Eze 47:12 shall bring forth **n.** fruit according...... 1069
Ho 2:11 her feast days, her **n.** moons, and....... 2320
Ho 4:11 and **n.** wine take away the heart. 8492
Ho 9:2 and the **n.** wine shall fail in her......... 8492

Joe 1:5 because of the n. wine; for it is cut.........
Joe 1:10 the n. wine is dried up, the oil.......... 8492
Joe 3:18 mountains shall drop down n. wine, ...
Am 8:5 When will the n. moon be gone, ... 2320
Hag 1:11 upon the n. wine,...upon the oil......... 8492
Zec 9:17 cheerful, and n. wine the maids.......... 8492
Mt 9:16 of n. cloth unto an old garment, for..46
Mt 9:17 men put n. wine into old bottles:... 3501
Mt 9:17 they put n. wine into...bottles,...... 3501
Mt 9:17 they put...wine into n. bottles,...... 2537
Mt 13:52 of his treasure things n. and old... 2537
Mt 26:28 is my blood of the n. testament,.... 2537
Mt 26:29 day when I drink it n. with you.... 2537
Mt 27:60 And laid it in his own n. tomb, which.. 2537
Mk 1:27 is this? What n. doctrine is this?........ 2537
Mk 2:21 piece of n. cloth on an old garment:..46
Mk 2:21 else the n. piece that filled it up... 2537
Mk 2:22 putteth n. wine into old bottles:.... 3501
Mk 2:22 the n. wine doth burst...bottles,.... 3501
Mk 2:22 n. wine must be put into...bottles...3501
Mk 2:22 wine must be put into n. bottles.... 2537
Mk 14:24 is my blood of the n. testament,.... 2537
Mk 14:25 drink it n. in the kingdom of God..2537
Mk 16:17 they shall speak with n. tongues;.. 2537
Lu 5:36 piece of a n. garment upon an old;.2537
Lu 5:36 then both the n. maketh a rent,.... 2537
Lu 5:36 of the n. agreeth not with the old.. 2537
Lu 5:37 putteth n. wine into old bottles;.... 3501
Lu 5:37 else the n. wine will burst...bottles,3501
Lu 5:38 n. wine must be put into...bottles;..3501
Lu 5:38 wine must be put into n. bottles;... 2537
Lu 5:39 old wine straightway desireth n.:.. 2537
Lu 22:20 This cup is the n. testament in my.2537
Joh 13:34 A n. commandment I give unto..... 2537
Joh 19:41 and in the garden a n. sepulchre, ... 2537
Ac 2:13 These men are full of n. wine. 1098
Ac 17:19 we know what this n. doctrine,.......... 2537
Ac 17:21 to tell, or to hear some n. thing.) 2537
1Co 5:7 that ye may be a n. lump, as ye........ 3501
1Co 11:25 This cup is the n. testament in my.2537
2Co 3:6 able ministers of the n. testament; 2537
2Co 5:17 be in Christ, he is a n. creature:........ 2537
2Co 5:17 behold, all things are become n.......... 2537
Ga 6:15 uncircumcision, but a n. creature........ 2537
Eph 2:15 in himself of twain one n. man,.......... 2537
Eph 4:24 that ye put on the n. man, which 2537
Col 2:16 or of the n. moon, or of the sabbath... 3561
Col 3:10 have put on the n. man, which is....... 3501
Heb 8:8 I will make a n. covenant with the...... 2537
Heb 8:13 A n. covenant, he hath made the....... 2537
Heb 9:15 the mediator of the n. testament,....... 2537
Heb 10:20 By a n. and living way, which he 4372
Heb 12:24 the mediator of the n. covenant, ... 3501
2Pe 3:13 look for n. heavens and a n. earth, ... 2537
1Jo 2:7 I write no n. commandment unto 2537
1Jo 2:8 n. commandment I write unto you, ... 2537
2Jo 5 I wrote a n. commandment unto........ 2537
Re 2:17 in the stone a n. name written,...... 2537
Re 3:12 city of my God,...is n. Jerusalem,.. 2537
Re 3:12 I will write upon him my n. name..2537
Re 5:9 they sung a n. song, saying, Thou....... 2537
Re 14:3 And they sung as it were a n. song..... 2537
Re 21:1 I saw a n. heaven and a n. earth:...... 2537
Re 21:2 I...saw the holy city, n. Jerusalem,..... 2537
Re 21:5 said, Behold, I make all things n. 2537

NEWBORN
1Pe 2:2 As n. babes, desire the sincere........... 738

NEWLY
De 32:17 new gods that came n. up, whom....... 7138
Jg 7:19 they had but n. set the watch: 6965

NEW-MOON See NEW and MOON.

NEWNESS
Ro 6:4 we also should walk in n. of life......... 2538
Ro 7:6 that we should serve in n. of spirit, ... 2538

NEWS
Pr 25:25 so is good n. from a far country. 8052

NEXT
Ge 17:21 thee at this set time in the n. year. 312
Ex 12:4 his neighbour n. unto his house 7138
Nu 2:5 those that do pitch n. unto him shall.........
Nu 11:32 all that night, and all the n. day, ... 4283
Nu 27:11 his kinsman that is n. to him of 7138
De 213 city which is n. unto the slain man, ... 7138
De 213:6 city, that are n. unto the slain man,.... 7138
Ru 2:20 of kin unto us, one of our n. kinsmen. ......
1Sa 17:13 n. unto him Abinadab, and the........... 4932
1Sa 23:17 Israel, I shall be n. unto thee;........... 4932
1Sa 30:17 unto the evening of the n. day:.......... 4283
2Ki 6:29 I said unto her on the n. day, Give...... 312
1Ch 5:12 Joel the chief,...Shapham the n., ... 4932
1Ch 16:5 the chief, and n. to him Zechariah, ... 4932
2Ch 17:15 And n. to him was Jehohanan..... 5921,3027
2Ch 17:16 n. him was Amasiah the son of... 5921,3027
2Ch 17:18 And n. him was Jehozabad, and .. 5921,3027
2Ch 28:7 Elkanah that was n. to the king. 4932
2Ch 31:12 and Shimei his brother was the n.. 4932
2Ch 31:15 and n. him were Eden, and........ 5921,3027
Ne 3:2 n. unto him builded the men of... 5921,3027
Ne 3:2 n. to them builded Zaccur the..... 5921,3027
Ne 3:4 n....them repaired Meremoth..... 5921,3027
Ne 3:4 n....them repaired Meshullam..... 5921,3027
Ne 3:4 n. unto them repaired Zadok......... 5921,3027
Ne 3:5 n. unto them the Tekoites......... 5921,3027
Ne 3:7 n. unto them repaired Melatiah... 5921,3027
Ne 3:8 N. unto him repaired Uzziel the.. 5921,3027
Ne 3:8 N....also repaired Hananiah........ 5921,3027
Ne 3:9 n....them repaired Rephaiah........ 5921,3027
Ne 3:10 n. unto them repaired Jedaiah....... 5921,3027
Ne 3:10 n. unto him repaired Hattush...... 5921,3027
Ne 3:12 n. unto him repaired Shallum...... 5921,3027
Ne 3:17 N....him repaired Hashabiah, ... 5921,3027
Ne 3:19 And n. to him repaired Ezer the. 5921,3027
Ne 13:13 n. to them was Hanan...son of... 5921,3027
Ex 1:14 the n. unto him was Carshena, ... 7138
Ex 10:3 Jew was n. unto king Ahasuerus, ... 4932
Jon 4:7 when the morning rose the n. day,..... 4283
Mt 27:62 Now the n. day, that followed the...... 1887
Mk 1:38 Let us go into the n. towns, that I.2192
Lu 9:37 that on the n. day, when they were.... 1836
Joh 1:29 n. day John seeth Jesus coming......... 1887
Joh 1:35 the n. day after John stood, and......... 1887
Joh 12:12 On the n. day much people that......... 1887
Ac 4:3 put them in hold unto the n. day: 839
Ac 7:26 the n. day he shewed himself unto 1966
Ac 13:42 preached to them the n. sabbath. 3342
Ac 13:44 the n. sabbath day came almost.......... 2064
Ac 14:20 n. day he departed with Barnabas 1887
Ac 16:11 Samothracia,...n. day to Neapolis; 1966
Ac 20:15 came the n. day over against Chios; ... 1966
Ac 20:15 the n. day we arrived at Samos, ... 2087
Ac 20:15 and the n. day we came to Miletus..... 2192
Ac 21:8 the n. day we that were of Paul's 1887
Ac 21:26 the n. day purifying himself with......... 2192
Ac 25:6 the n. day sitting on the judgment...... 1887
Ac 27:3 the n. day we touched at Sidon. 2087
Ac 27:18 the n. day they lightened the ship; 1836
Ac 28:13 we came the n. day to Puteoli:.......... 1206

NEZIAH (ne-zi'-ah)
Ezr 2:54 children of N., the children of............ 5335
Ne 7:56 children of N., the children of............ 5335

NEZIB (ne'-zib)
Jos 15:43 Jiphtah, and Ashnah, and N., ... 5334

NIBHAZ (nib'-haz)
2Ki 17:31 the Avites made N. and Tartak,.......... 5026

NIBSHAN (nib'-shan)
Jos 15:62 And N., and the city of Salt, and........ 5044

NICANOR (ni-ca'-nor)
Ac 6:5 Prochorus, and N., and Timon,.......... 3527

NICODEMUS (nic-o-de'-mus)
Joh 3:1 a man of the Pharisees, named N.,...... 3530
Joh 3:4 N. saith unto him, How can a man 3530
Joh 3:9 N. answered and said unto him,.......... 3530
Joh 7:50 N. saith unto them, (he that came...... 3530
Joh 19:39 And there came also N., which at 3530

NICOLAITANES (nic-o-la'-i-tans)
Re 2:6 thou hatest the deeds of the N.,..... 3531
Re 2:15 that hold the doctrine of the N.,... 3531

NICOLAS (nic'-o-las)
Ac 6:5 and N. a proselyte of Antioch:........... 3532

NICOPOLIS (ni-cop'-o-lis)
Tit 3:12 diligent to come unto me to N.:.......... 3533
Tit *subscr.* Cretians, from N. of......................... 3533

NIGER (ni'-jur) See also SIMEON.
Ac 13:1 and Simeon that was called N.,.......... 3526

NIGH See also NEAR.
Ge 47:29 time drew n. that Israel must die....... 7126
Ex 3:5 Draw not n. hither: put off thy.......... 7126
Ex 14:10 when Pharaoh drew n., the children.... 7126
Ex 24:2 Lord: but they shall not come n.;........ 5066
Ex 32:19 soon as he came n. unto the camp, ... 7126
Ex 34:30 they were afraid to come n. him.......... 5066
Ex 34:32 all the children of Israel came n.: 5066
Le 10:3 be sanctified in them that come n........ 7138
Le 21:3 sister a virgin, that is n. unto him, ... 7138
Le 21:21 shall come n. to offer the offerings..... 5066
Le 21:21 not come n. to offer the bread of......... 5066
Le 21:23 nor come n. unto the altar, because.... 5066
Le 25:49 any that is n. of kin unto him of......... 7607
Nu 1:51 stranger that cometh n. shall be......... 7126
Nu 3:10, 38 stranger that cometh n. shall be 7126
Nu 8:19 children of Israel come n. unto 5066
Nu 18:3 they shall not come n. the vessels...... 7126
Nu 18:4 a stranger shall not come n. unto....... 7126
Nu 18:7 stranger that cometh n. shall be......... 7126
Nu 18:22 come n. the tabernacle of the............ 7126
Nu 24:17 I shall behold him, but not n.: there ... 7126
De 1:7 unto all the places n. thereunto,......... 7934
De 2:19 when thou comest n. over against 7126
De 4:7 who hath God so n. unto them, as 7126
De 13:7 n. unto thee, or far off from thee, ... 7126
De 20:2 when ye are come n. unto the battle, ..7126
De 20:10 thou comest n. unto a city to fight 7126
De 22:2 if thy brother be not n. unto thee, ... 7126
De 30:14 But the word is very n. unto thee,..... 7126
Jos 8:11 went up, and drew n., and came......... 5066
1Sa 17:48 came and drew n. to meet David, ... 7126
2Sa 10:13 Joab drew n., and the people that 5066
2Sa 11:20 approached ye so n. unto the city............
2Sa 11:21 why went ye n. the wall? then say....... 5066
2Sa 15:5 any man came n. to him to do him..... 7126
1Ki 2:1 the days of David drew n. that he...... 7126
1Ki 8:59 be n. unto the Lord our God day and.. 7126
1Ch 12:40 Moreover they that were n. them, ... 7126
1Ch 19:14 drew n. before the Syrians unto......... 5066
Es 9:20 king Ahasuerus, both n. and far, ... 7126
Ps 32:6 they shall not come n. unto him.......... 5060
Ps 34:18 n. unto them that are of a broken 7126
Ps 69:18 Draw n. unto my soul, and.............. 7126
Ps 73:2 gone; my steps had well n. slipped...... 4952
Ps 85:9 his salvation is n. them that fear 7138
Ps 88:3 my life draweth n. unto the grave, ... 5060
Ps 91:7 but it shall not come n. thee. 5066
Ps 91:10 any plague come n. thy dwelling. 7126
Ps 119:150 draw n. that follow after mischief 7126
Ps 145:18 n. unto all them that call upon him, ... 7138
Pr 5:8 come not n. the door of her house: 7126
Ec 12:1 nor the years draw n., when thou...... 5060
Isa 5:19 of the Holy One of Israel draw n. 7126
Joe 2:1 Lord cometh, for it is n. at hand;....... 7126
Mt 15:8 draweth n. unto me with their...... 1448
Mt 15:29 came n. unto the sea of Galilee; 3844
Mt 21:1 when they drew n. unto Jerusalem, ... 1448
Mt 24:32 ye know that summer is n.:............ 1451
Mk 2:4 not come n. unto him for the press, ...
Mk 5:11 there was n. unto the mountains........ 4314
Mk 5:21 him: and he was n. unto the sea. 3844
Mk 11:1 And when they came n. to Jerusalem, ...
Mk 13:29 come to pass, know that it is n.,... 1451
Lu 7:12 when he came n. to the gate of......... 1448
Lu 10:9,11 kingdom of God is come n. unto... 1448
Lu 15:25 he came and drew n. to the house,.1448
Lu 18:35 as he was come n. unto Jericho, ... 1448
Lu 19:11 because he was n. to Jerusalem, ... 1451
Lu 19:29 when he was come n. to Bethphage ... 1448
Lu 19:37 when he was come n., even not at..... 1448
Lu 21:20 that the desolation thereof is n.,... 1448
Lu 21:28 for your redemption draweth n.. ... 1448
Lu 21:30 that summer is now n. at hand...... 1451
Lu 21:31 the kingdom of God is n. at hand...1451
Lu 22:1 feast of unleavened bread drew n.,..... 1448
Lu 24:28 And they drew n. unto the village, ... 1448
Joh 6:4 a feast of the Jews, was n.. 1451
Joh 6:19 sea, and drawing n. unto the ship:...... 1451
Joh 6:23 n. unto the place where they did......... 1451
Joh 11:18 Bethany was n. unto Jerusalem,......... 1451
Joh 11:55 the Jews' passover was n. at hand:...... 1451
Joh 19:20 Jesus was crucified...n. to the city:..... 1451
Joh 19:42 for the sepulchre was n. at hand. 1451
Ac 7:17 the time of the promise drew n., ... 1448
Ac 9:38 as Lydda was n. to Joppa, and the 1451

Ac 10:9 drew **n.** unto the city, Peter went...... *1448*
Ac 22:6 was come **n.** unto Damascus about..... *1448*
Ac 27:8 **n.** whereunto was the city of Lasea..... *1451*
Ro 10:8 The word is **n.** thee, even in thy....... *1451*
Eph 2:13 are made **n.** by the blood of Christ..... *1451*
Eph 2:17 afar off, and to them that were **n.**...... *1451*
Php 2:27 indeed he was sick **n.** unto death: *3897*
Php 2:30 work of Christ he was **n.** unto death,.. *1448*
Heb 6:8 rejected, and is **n.** unto cursing;......... *1451*
Heb 7:19 by the which we draw **n.** unto God..... *1448*
Jas 4:8 Draw **n.** to God, and he will draw **n.**.. *1448*
Jas 5:8 the coming of the Lord draweth **n.**..... *1448*

NIGHT See also MIDNIGHT; NIGHTS; YESTERNIGHT.
Ge 1:5 and the darkness he called **N.**........... 3915
Ge 1:14 to divide the day from the **n.**; and...... 3915
Ge 1:16 the lesser light to rule the **n.**: he 3915
Ge 1:18 to rule over the day and over the **n.**,.. 3915
Ge 8:22 and day and **n.** shall not cease........... 3915
Ge 14:15 he and his servants, by **n.**, and smote..3915
Ge 19:2 tarry all **n.**, and wash your feet, and ye.....
Ge 19:2 but we will abide in the street all **n.**..........
Ge 19:5 men which came in to thee this **n.**? 3915
Ge 19:33 made their father drink wine that **n.**:... 3915
Ge 19:34 make him drink wine this **n.** also;....... 3915
Ge 19:35 made their father drink wine that **n.**..... 3915
Ge 20:3 came to Abimelech in a dream by **n.**,.. 3915
Ge 24:54 that were with him, and tarried all **n.**;.......
Ge 26:24 appeared unto him the same **n.**,......... 3915
Ge 28:11 tarried there all **n.**, because the sun ....
Ge 30:15 Therefore he shall lie with thee to **n.**.. 3915
Ge 30:16 And he lay with her that **n.**.............. 3915
Ge 31:24 Laban the Syrian in a dream by **n.**,...... 3915
Ge 31:39 stolen by day, or stolen by **n.**.......... 3915
Ge 31:40 consumed me, and the frost by **n.**;..... 3915
Ge 31:54 bread, and tarried all **n.** in the mount........
Ge 32:13 And he lodged there that same **n.**;..... 3915
Ge 32:21 lodged that **n.** in the company........... 3915
Ge 32:22 he rose up that **n.**, and took his two... 3915
Ge 40:5 each man his dream in one **n.**, each.... 3915
Ge 41:11 And we dreamed a dream in one **n.**,... 3915
Ge 46:2 God spake...in the visions of the **n.**,.... 3915
Ge 49:27 and at **n.** he shall divide the spoil........ 6153
Ex 10:13 land all that day, and all that **n.**;......... 3915
Ex 12:8 they shall eat the flesh in that **n.**,........ 3915
Ex 12:12 through the land of Egypt this **n.**,....... 3915
Ex 12:30 And Pharaoh rose up in the **n.**, he,..... 3915
Ex 12:31 called for Moses and Aaron by **n.**,....... 3915
Ex 12:42 It is a **n.** to be much observed unto.... 3915
Ex 12:42 that **n.** of the Lord to be observed..... 3915
Ex 13:21 by **n.** in a pillar of fire, to give.......... 3915
Ex 13:21 them light; to go by day and **n.**: 3915
Ex 13:22 by day, nor the pillar of fire by **n.**,...... 3915
Ex 14:20 it gave light by **n.** to these: so that.... 3915
Ex 14:20 came not near the other all the **n.**...... 3915
Ex 14:21 by a strong east wind all that **n.**,........ 3915
Ex 40:38 and fire was on it by **n.**, in the sight... 3915
Le 6:9 the burning upon the altar all **n.**.......... 3915
Le 6:20 morning, and half thereof at **n.**.......... 6153
Le 8:35 day and **n.** seven days, and keep 3915
Le 11:16 And the owl, and the **n.** hawk, and...... 8464
Le 19:13 abide with thee all **n.** until...morning.........
Nu 9:16 and the appearance of fire by **n.**.......... 3915
Nu 9:21 whether it was by day or by **n.** that ... 3915
Nu 11:9 dew fell upon the camp in the **n.**,........ 3915
Nu 11:32 up all that day, and all that **n.**, and..... 3915
Nu 14:1 cried; and the people wept that **n.**...... 3915
Nu 14:14 cloud, and in a pillar of fire by **n.**....... 3915
Nu 22:8 said unto them, Lodge here this **n.**,.... 3915
Nu 22:19 tarry ye also here this **n.**, that I......... 3915
Nu 22:20 And God came unto Balaam at **n.**,....... 3915
De 1:33 in fire by **n.**, to shew you by what..... 3915
De 14:15 the owl, and the **n.** hawk, and the...... 8464
De 16:1 thee forth out of Egypt by **n.**............ 3915
De 16:4 even, remain all **n.** until the morning.........
De 21:23 shall not remain all **n.** upon the tree, ...
De 23:10 that chanceth him by **n.**, then.............. 3915
De 28:66 and thou shalt fear day and **n.**, and..... 3915
Jos 1:8 shalt meditate therein day and **n.**, ... 3915
Jos 2:2 there came men in hither to **n.** of 3915
Jos 4:3 place, where ye shall lodge this **n.**....... 3915
Jos 8:3 valour, and sent them away by **n.**...... 3915
Jos 8:9 Joshua lodged that **n.** among the 3915
Jos 8:13 Joshua went that **n.** into the midst...... 3915
Jos 10:9 and went up from Gilgal all **n.**........... 3915
Jg 6:25 And it came to pass the same **n.**,........ 3915
Jg 6:27 do it by day, that he did it by **n.**........ 3915
Jg 6:40 And God did so that **n.**: for it was...... 3915
Jg 7:9 And it came to pass the same **n.**,...... 3915
Jg 9:32 Now therefore up by **n.**, thou and...... 3915
Jg 9:34 people that were with him, by **n.**, ... 3915
Jg 16:2 laid wait for him all **n.** in the gate....... 3915
Jg 16:2 and were quiet all the **n.**, saying, ... 3915
Jg 19:6 content, I pray thee, and tarry all **n.**,........
Jg 19:9 evening, I pray you tarry all **n.**:...............
Jg 19:10 But the man would not tarry hat **n.**, ...
Jg 19:13 to one of these places to lodge all **n.**, ...
Jg 19:25 and abused her all the **n.** until........... 3915
Jg 20:5 house round about upon me by **n.**, ... 3915
Ru 1:12 I should have an husband also to **n.**,... 3915
Ru 3:2 he winnoweth barley to **n.** in the........ 3915
Ru 3:13 Tarry this **n.**, and it shall be in.......... 3915
1Sa 14:34 every man his ox with him that **n.**,..... 3915
1Sa 14:36 go down after the Philistines by **n.**, ... 3915
1Sa 15:11 and he cried unto the Lord all **n.**......... 3915
1Sa 15:16 the Lord hath said to me this **n.**....... 3915
1Sa 19:10 and David fled, and escaped that **n.**.... 3915
1Sa 19:11 If thou save not thy life to **n.**, to 3915
1Sa 19:24 naked all that day and all that **n.**........ 3915
1Sa 25:16 a wall unto us both by **n.** and day, ... 3915
1Sa 26:7 Abishai came to the people by **n.**: 3915
1Sa 28:8 and they came to the woman by **n.**:..... 3915
1Sa 28:20 no bread all the day, nor all the **n.**..... 3915
1Sa 28:25 rose up, and went away that **n.**......... 3915
1Sa 31:12 valiant men arose, and went all **n.**,..... 3915
2Sa 2:29 and his men walked all that **n.**........... 3915
2Sa 2:32 And Joab and his men went all **n.**,...... 3915
2Sa 4:7 them away through the plain all **n.**...... 3915
2Sa 7:4 And it came to pass after **n.**, that 3915
2Sa 12:16 went in, and lay all **n.** upon the earth........
2Sa 17:1 and pursue after David this **n.**: 3915
2Sa 17:16 Lodge not this **n.** in the plains of 3915
2Sa 19:7 not tarry one with thee this **n.**: 3915
2Sa 21:10 day, nor the beasts of the field by **n.**.. 3915
1Ki 3:5 to Solomon in a dream by **n.**: and 3915
1Ki 3:19 this woman's child died in the **n.**;.......... 3915
1Ki 8:29 open toward this house **n.** and day, ... 3915
1Ki 8:59 unto the Lord our God day and **n.**,..... 3915
2Ki 6:14 they came by **n.**, and compassed........ 3915
2Ki 7:12 the king arose in the **n.**, and said....... 3915
2Ki 8:21 and he arose by **n.**, and smote the..... 3915
2Ki 19:35 it came to pass that **n.**, that the 3915
2Ki 25:4 all the men of war fled by **n.** by the ... 3915
1Ch 9:33 employed in that work day and **n.**..... 3915
1Ch 17:3 it came to pass the same **n.**, that....... 3915
2Ch 1:7 In that **n.** did God appear unto 3915
2Ch 6:20 open upon this house day and **n.**,....... 3915
2Ch 7:12 Lord appeared to Solomon by **n.**,....... 3915
2Ch 21:9 he rose up by **n.**, and smote the........ 3915
2Ch 35:14 burnt offerings and the fat until **n.**;..... 3915
Ne 1:6 I pray before thee now, day and **n.**, ... 3915
Ne 2:12 I arose in the **n.**, I and some few....... 3915
Ne 2:13 I went out by **n.** by the gate of the..... 3915
Ne 2:15 went I up in the **n.** by the brook,...... 3915
Ne 4:9 a watch against them day and **n.**,........ 3915
Ne 4:22 in the **n.** they may be a guard to us, .. 3915
Ne 6:10 in the **n.** will they come to slay 3915
Ne 9:12 in the **n.** by a pillar of fire, to give..... 3915
Ne 9:19 neither the pillar of fire by **n.**, to 3915
Es 4:16 eat nor drink three days, **n.** or day:.... 3915
Es 6:1 On that **n.** could not the king sleep,.... 3915
Job 3:3 the **n.** in which it was said, There...... 3915
Job 3:6 As for that **n.**, let darkness seize....... 3915
Job 3:7 let that **n.** be solitary, let no joyful..... 3915
Job 4:13 thoughts from the visions of the **n.**,.... 3915
Job 5:14 grope in the noonday as in the **n.**....... 3915
Job 7:4 shall I arise, and the **n.** be gone?....... 6153
Job 17:12 They change the **n.** into day: the....... 3915
Job 20:8 chased away as a vision of the **n.**....... 3915
Job 24:14 needy, and in the **n.** is as a thief........ 3915
Job 26:10 the day and **n.** come to an end.......... 2822
Job 27:20 stealeth him away in the **n.**............... 3915
Job 29:19 the dew lay all **n.** upon my branch...........
Job 30:17 bones are pierced in me in the **n.**......... 3915
Job 33:15 In a dream, in a vision of the **n.**, ... 3915
Job 34:25 and he overturneth them in the **n.**,..... 3915
Job 35:10 maker, who giveth songs in the **n.**; 3915
Job 36:20 Desire not the **n.**, when people are 3915
Ps 1:2 law doth he meditate day and **n.**........ 3915
Ps 6:6 all the **n.** make I my bed to swim; 3915
Ps 16:7 also instruct me in the **n.** seasons...... 3915
Ps 17:3 thou hast visited me in the **n.**; thou.... 3915
Ps 19:2 and **n.** unto **n.** sheweth knowledge..... 3915
Ps 22:2 and in the **n.** season, and am not 3915
Ps 30:5 weeping may endure for a **n.**, but 6153
Ps 32:4 day and **n.** thy hand was heavy.......... 3915
Ps 42:3 have been my meat day and **n.**,......... 3915
Ps 42:8 in the **n.** his song shall be with.......... 3915
Ps 55:10 Day and **n.** they go about it upon....... 3915
Ps 63:6 meditate on thee in the **n.** watches...........
Ps 74:16 day is thine, the **n.** also is thine:....... 3915
Ps 77:2 my sore ran in the **n.**, and ceased....... 3915
Ps 77:6 to remembrance my song in the **n.**:.... 3915
Ps 78:14 and all the **n.** with a light of fire......... 3915
Ps 88:1 I have cried day and **n.** before thee: ... 3915
Ps 90:4 is past, and as a watch in the **n.**........ 3915
Ps 91:5 not be afraid for the terror by **n.**; 3915
Ps 92:2 and thy faithfulness every **n.**,............ 3915
Ps 104:20 Thou makest darkness, and it is **n.**:.... 3915
Ps 105:39 and fire to give light in the **n.**............ 3915
Ps 119:55 O Lord, in the **n.**, and have kept 3915
Ps 119:148 Mine eyes prevent the **n.** watches,...........
Ps 121:6 thee by day, nor the moon by **n.**........ 3915
Ps 134:1 which by **n.** stand in the house of....... 3915
Ps 136:9 The moon and stars to rule by **n.**:...... 3915
Ps 139:11 even the **n.** shall be light about me..... 3915
Ps 139:12 thee; but the **n.** shineth as the day:.... 3915
Pr 7:9 evening, in the black and dark **n.**: 3915
Pr 31:15 She riseth also while it is yet **n.**, ... 3915
Pr 31:18 her candle goeth not out by **n.**......... 3915
Ec 2:23 his heart taketh not rest in the **n.**...... 3915
Ec 8:16 neither day nor **n.** seeth sleep with.... 3915
Ca 1:13 he shall lie all **n.** betwixt my breasts..........
Ca 3:1 By **n.** on my bed I sought him........... 3915
Ca 3:8 his thigh because of fear in the **n.**...... 3915
Ca 5:2 my locks with the drops of the **n.**...... 3915
Isa 4:5 the shining of a flaming fire by **n.**:...... 3915
Isa 5:11 that continue until **n.**, till wine.......... 5399
Isa 15:1 in the **n.** Ar of Moab is laid waste,..... 3915
Isa 15:1 in the **n.** Kir of Moab is laid waste, ... 3915
Isa 16:3 make thy shadow as the **n.** in the 3915
Isa 21:4 the **n.** of my pleasure hath he........... 5399
Isa 21:11, 11 Watchman, what of the **n.**?........... 3915
Isa 21:12 morning cometh, and also the **n.**:....... 3915
Isa 26:9 soul have I desired thee in the **n.**;...... 3915
Isa 27:3 hurt it, I will keep it **n.** and day......... 3915
Isa 28:19 it pass over, by day and by **n.**:.......... 3915
Isa 29:7 shall be as a dream of a **n.** vision....... 3915
Isa 30:29 Ye shall have a song, as in the **n.** 3915
Isa 34:10 shall not be quenched **n.** nor day;....... 3915
Isa 38:12, 13 from day even to **n.** wilt thou........ 3915
Isa 59:10 stumble at noon day as in the **n.**;....... 5399
Isa 60:11 they shall not be shut day nor **n.**; 3915
Isa 62:6 never hold their peace day nor **n.**:...... 3915
Jer 6:5 Arise, and let us go by **n.**, and let....... 3915
Jer 9:1 that I might weep day and **n.** for........ 3915
Jer 14:8 that turneth aside to tarry for a **n.**? ....
Jer 14:17 run down with tears **n.** and day, ... 3915
Jer 16:13 shall ye serve other gods day and **n.**;.. 3915
Jer 31:35 and of the stars for a light by **n.**,...... 3915
Jer 33:20 and my covenant of the **n.**, and that ... 3915
Jer 33:20 not be day and **n.** in their seasons;..... 3915
Jer 33:25 my covenant be not with day and **n.**, .. 3915
Jer 36:30 the heat, and in the **n.** to the frost...... 3915
Jer 39:4 and went forth out of the city by **n.**,... 3915
Jer 49:9 if thieves by **n.**, they will destroy....... 3915
Jer 52:7 went forth out of the city by **n.** by...... 3915
La 1:2 She weepeth sore in the **n.**, and her... 3915
La 2:18 run down like a river day and **n.**: 3915
La 2:19 Arise, cry out in the **n.**: in the 3915
Da 2:19 revealed unto Daniel in a vision.......... 3916
Da 5:30 In that **n.** was Belshazzar the king...... 3916
Da 6:18 palace, and passed the **n.** fasting: 956
Da 7:2 I was in my vision by **n.**, and,........... 3916
Da 7:7 After this I saw in the **n.** visions,....... 3916
Da 7:13 I saw in the **n.** visions, and, behold, ... 3916
Ho 4:5 also shall fall with thee in the **n.**, ... 3915
Ho 7:6 their baker sleepeth all the **n.**; in 3915
Joe 1:13 lie all **n.** in sackcloth, ye ministers of.........
Am 5:8 and maketh the day dark with **n.**:.........
Ob 5 thieves came to thee, if robbers by **n.**,.3915
Jon 4:10 up in a **n.**, and perished in a **n.**: 3915
Mic 3:6 Therefore **n.** shall be unto you, ... 3915
Zec 1:8 I saw by **n.**, and behold a man........... 3915
Zec 14:7 not day, nor **n.**: but it shall come....... 3915
Mt 2:14 young child and his mother by **n.**, ... *3571*
Mt 14:25 in the fourth watch of the **n.** Jesus *3571*
Mt 26:31 **be offended because of me this n**... *3571*
Mt 26:34 **That this n., before the cock**......... *3571*

Mt 27:64 his disciples come by **n.**, and steal...... *3571*
Mt 28:13 Say ye, His disciples came by **n.**,....... *3571*
Mk 4:27 **should sleep, and rise n. and day,..** *3571*
Mk 5:5 always, **n.** and day, he was in the *3571*
Mk 6:48 about the fourth watch of the **n.** he *3571*
Mk 14:27 **be offended because of me this n.:.** *3571*
Mk 14:30 **That this day, even in this n.,.......** *3571*
Lu 2:8 keeping watch over their flock by **n.**.. *3571*
Lu 2:37 fastings and prayers **n.** and day......... *3571*
Lu 5:5 we have toiled all the **n.**, and have *3571*
Lu 6:12 continued all **n.** in prayer to God........ *1273*
Lu 12:20 **this n. thy soul shall be required...** *3571*
Lu 17:34 **in that n. there shall be two men ..** *3571*
Lu 18:7 **which cry day and n. unto him, ...** *3571*
Lu 21:37 at **n.** he went out, and abode in the.... *3571*
Joh 3:2 same came to Jesus by **n.**, and said.... *3571*
Joh 7:50 (he that came to Jesus by **n.**, being *3571*
Joh 9:4 **the n. cometh, when no man can ..** *3571*
Joh 11:10 **But if a man walk in the n., he ....** *3571*
Joh 13:30 immediately out: and it was **n.**............ *3571*
Joh 19:39 at the first came to Jesus by **n.**, and... *3571*
Joh 21:3 and that **n.** they caught nothing.......... *3571*
Ac 5:19 angel...by **n.** opened the prison.......... *3571*
Ac 9:24 watched the gates day and **n.** to *3571*
Ac 9:25 Then the disciples took him by **n.**, ... *3571*
Ac 12:6 the same **n.** Peter was sleeping.......... *3571*
Ac 16:9 vision appeared to Paul in the **n.**;......... *3571*
Ac 16:33 took them the same hour of the **n.**,..... *3571*
Ac 17:10 sent away Paul and Silas by **n.** unto.... *3571*
Ac 18:9 spake the Lord to Paul in the **n.** by..... *3571*
Ac 20:31 not to warn every one **n.** and day *3571*
Ac 23:11 the **n.** following the Lord stood by...... *3571*
Ac 23:23 hundred, at the third hour of the **n.**;... *3571*
Ac 23:31 brought him by **n.** to Antipatris.......... *3571*
Ac 26:7 serving God day and **n.**, hope to......... *3571*
Ac 27:23 there stood by me this **n.** the angel.... *3571*
Ac 27:27 when the fourteenth **n.** was come, ... *3571*
Ro 13:12 The **n.** is far spent, the day is at *3571*
1Co 11:23 same **n.** in which he was betrayed...... *3571*
2Co 11:25 a **n.** and a day I have been in the....... *3574*
1Th 2:9 labouring **n.** and day, because we....... *3571*
1Th 3:10 **N.** and day praying exceedingly.......... *3571*
1Th 5:2 Lord so cometh as a thief in the **n.**.. ... *3571*
1Th 5:5 we are not of the **n.**, nor of darkness. .*3571*
1Th 5:7 For they that sleep sleep in the **n.**; *3571*
1Th 5:7 be drunken are drunken in the **n.**........ *3571*
2Th 3:8 with labour and travail **n.** and day,...... *3571*
1Ti 5:5 supplications and prayers **n.** and......... *3571*
2Ti 1:3 of thee in my prayers **n.** and day; *3571*
2Pe 3:10 Lord will come as a thief in the **n.**;..... *3571*
Re 4:8 they rest not day and **n.**, saying, ... *3571*
Re 7:15 serve him day and **n.** in his temple:..... *3571*
Re 8:12 third part of it, and the **n.** likewise. *3571*
Re 12:10 them before our God day and **n.**.......... *3571*
Re 14:11 they have no rest day nor **n.**, who *3571*
Re 20:10 be tormented day and **n.** for ever....... *3571*
Re 21:25 day: for there shall be no **n.** there...... *3571*
Re 22:5 And there shall be no **n.** there; and.... *3571*

NIGHT-HAWK See NIGHT and HAWK.

NIGHTS
Ge 7:4 the earth forty days and forty **n.**;....... 3915
Ge 7:12 the earth forty days and forty **n.**........ 3915
Ex 24:18 the mount forty days and forty **n.**........ 3915
Ex 34:28 the Lord forty days and forty **n.**; 3915
De 9:9 the mount forty days and forty **n.**,....... 3915
De 9:11 the end of forty days and forty **n.**. 3915
De 9:18 at the first, forty days and forty **n.**:.... 3915
De 9:25 the Lord forty days and forty **n.**, ... 3915
De 10:10 first time, forty days and forty **n.**;...... 3915
1Sa 30:12 any water, three days and three **n.**...... 3915
1Ki 19:8 of that meat forty days and forty **n.**.... 3915
Job 2:13 ground seven days and seven **n.**, ... 3915
Job 7:3 wearisome **n.** are appointed to me....... 3915
Isa 21:8 and I am set in my ward whole **n.**:...... 3915
Jon 1:17 of the fish three days and three **n.**. 3915
Mt 4:2 had fasted forty days and forty **n.**,....... *3571*
Mt 12:40 **and three n. in the whale's belly; ..** *3571*
Mt 12:40 **three n. in the heart of the earth...** *3571*

NIGHT-VISION See NIGHT and VISION.

NIGHT-WATCHES See NIGHT and WATCHES.

NIMRAH (nim'-rah) See also BETH-NIMRAH.
Nu 32:3 **N.**, and Heshbon, and Elealeh, ... 5247

NIMRIM (nim'-rim)
Isa 15:6 the waters of **N.** shall be desolate: 5249
Jer 48:34 waters also of **N.** shall be desolate. 5249

NIMROD (nim'-rod)
Ge 10:8 Cush begat **N.**: he began to be a 5248
Ge 10:9 **N.** the mighty hunter before the 5248
1Ch 1:10 Cush begat **N.**: he began to be.......... 5248
Mic 5:6 land of **N.** in the entrances thereof: 5248

NIMSHI (nim'-shi)
1Ki 19:16 the son of **N.** shalt thou anoint 5250
2Ki 9:2 son of Jehoshaphat the son of **N.**,........ 5250
2Ki 9:14 son of Jehoshaphat the son of **N.**......... 5250
2Ki 9:20 the driving of Jehu the son o f **N.**;....... 5250
2Ch 22:7 against Jehu the son of **N.**, whom....... 5250

NINE See also NINETEEN.
Ge 5:5 that Adam lived were **n.** hundred 8672
Ge 5:8 of Seth were **n.** hundred and twelve ... 8672
Ge 5:11 of Enos were **n.** hundred and five 8672
Ge 5:14 of Cainan were **n.** hundred and ten...... 8672
Ge 5:20 of Jared were **n.** hundred sixty and...... 8672
Ge 5:27 were **n.** hundred sixty and **n.** years: ... 8672
Ge 9:29 of Noah were **n.** hundred and fifty...... 8672
Ge 11:19 Reu two hundred and **n.** years, and.... 8672
Ge 11:24 Nahor lived **n.** and twenty years, ... 8672
Ge 17:1 Abram was ninety years old and **n.**,.... 8672
Ge 17:24 Abraham was ninety years...and **n.**,.... 8672
Ex 38:24 offering, was twenty and **n.** talents,.... 8672
Le 25:8 be unto thee forty and **n.** years. 8672
Nu 1:23 Simeon, were fifty and **n.** thousand..... 8672
Nu 2:13 fifty and **n.** thousand and three 8672
Nu 29:26 And on the fifth day **n.** bullocks, ... 8672
Nu 34:13 to give unto the **n.** tribes, and to 8672
De 3:11 **n.** cubits was the length thereof,........ 8672
Jos 13:7 an inheritance unto the **n.** tribes, ... 8672
Jos 14:2 for the **n.** tribes, and for the half 8672
Jos 15:32 the cities are twenty and **n.**, with........ 8672
Jos 15:44 **n.** cities with their villages................ 8672
Jos 15:54 Zior; **n.** cities with their villages......... 8672
Jos 21:16 **n.** cities out of those two tribes......... 8672
Jg 4:3 he had **n.** hundred chariots of iron;....... 8672
Jg 4:13 even **n.** hundred chariots of iron, ... 8672
2Sa 24:8 Jerusalem at the end of **n.** months...... 8672
2Ki 14:2 and reigned twenty and **n.** years in..... 8672
2Ki 15:13 the **n.** and thirtieth year of Uzziah...... 8672
2Ki 15:17 **n.** and thirtieth year of Azariah.......... 8672
2Ki 17:1 in Samaria over Israel **n.** years........... 8672
2Ki 18:2 he reigned twenty and **n.** years in...... 8672
1Ch 3:8 and Eliada, and Eliphelet, **n.**.............. 8672
1Ch 9:9 **n.** hundred and fifty and six............... 8672
2Ch 25:1 he reigned twenty and **n.** years in...... 8672
2Ch 29:1 he reigned **n.** and twenty years in...... 8672
Ezr 1:9 of silver, **n.** and twenty knives, ... 8672
Ezr 2:8 of Zattu, **n.** hundred forty and five...... 8672
Ezr 2:36 **n.** hundred seventy and three............ 8672
Ezr 2:42 in all an hundred thirty and **n.**.......... 8672
Ne 7:38 thousand **n.** hundred and thirty. 8672
Ne 7:39 **n.** hundred seventy and three............ 8672
Ne 11:1 and **n.** parts to dwell in other cities. ... 8672
Ne 11:8 Sallai, **n.** hundred twenty and eight..... 8672
Mt 18:12 **he not leave the ninety and n., and** *1768*
Mt 18:13 **and n. which went not astray........** *1768*
Lu 15:4 **ninety and n. in the wilderness, ...** *1768*
Lu 15:7 **over ninety and n. just persons, ...** *1768*
Lu 17:17 **ten cleansed? but where are the n.?** *1767*

NINE HUNDRED See NINE and HUNDRED.

NINETEEN
Ge 11:25 an hundred and **n.** years,........... 8672,6240
Jos 19:38 **n.** cities with their villages............ 8672,6240
2Sa 2:30 of David's servants **n.** men and... 8672,6240

NINETEENTH
2Ki 25:8 which is the **n.** year of king 8672,6240
1Ch 24:16 The **n.** to Pethahiah, the........... 8672,6240
1Ch 25:26 The **n.** to Mallothi, he, his sons,..8672,6240
Jer 52:12 the **n.** year of Nebuchadrezzar.... 8672,6240

NINETY
Gen 5:9 Enos lived **n.** years, and begat 8673
Gen 5:17 eight hundred **n.** and five years:.......... 8673
Gen 5:30 Noah five hundred **n.** and five years,.... 8673
Gen 17:1 when Abram was **n.** years old and...... 8673
Gen 17:17 Sarah, that is **n.** years old, bear? 8673
Gen 17:24 Abraham was **n.** years old and nine, ... 8673
1Sa 4:15 Now Eli was **n.** and eight years old; ... 8673
1Ch 9:6 their brethren, six hundred and **n.**...... 8673
Ezr 2:16 of Ater of Hezekiah, **n.** and eight. 8673
Ezr 2:20 The children of Gibbar, **n.** and five. 8673
Ezr 2:58 were three hundred **n.** and two. 8673
Ezr 8:35 for all Israel, **n.** and six rams, ... 8673
Ne 7:21 of Ater of Hezekiah, **n.** and eight. 8673
Ne 7:25 The children of Gibeon, **n.** and five...... 8673
Ne 7:60 were three hundred **n.** and two. 8673
Jer 52:23 there were **n.** and six pomegranates ... 8673
Eze 4:5 days, three hundred and **n.** days: 8673
Eze 4:9 hundred and **n.** days shalt thou eat..... 8673
Eze 41:12 and the length thereof **n.** cubits. 8673
Da 12:11 thousand two hundred and **n.** days....... 8673
Mt 18:12 **doth he not leave the n. and nine,.** *1768*
Mt 18:13 **n. and nine which went not astray.** *1768*
Lu 15:4 **doth not leave the n. and nine in ..** *1768*
Lu 15:7 **than over n. and nine just persons,** *1768*

NINEVE (nin'-e-ve) See also NINEVEH; NINEVITES.
Lu 11:32 **The men of N. shall rise up in ......** *3535*

NINEVEH (nin'-e-veh) See also NINEVE.
Ge 10:11 forth Asshur, and builded **N.**, and...... 5210
Ge 10:12 And Resen between **N.** and Calah: 5210
2Ki 19:36 and returned, and dwelt at **N.** 5210
Isa 37:37 and returned, and dwelt at **N.**. 5210
Jon 1:2 go to **N.**, that great city, and cry 5210
Jon 3:2 Arise, go unto **N.**, that great city,...... 5210
Jon 3:3 So Jonah arose, and went unto **N.**,..... 5210
Jon 3:3 **N.** was an exceeding great city of 5210
Jon 3:4 days, and **N.** shall be overthrown. 5210
Jon 3:5 So the people of **N.** believed God,...... 5210
Jon 3:6 word came unto the king of **N.**, and.... 5210
Jon 3:7 published through **N.** by the decree 5210
Jon 4:11 should not I spare **N.**, that great........ 5210
Na 1:1 The burden of **N.**. The book of the 5210
Na 2:8 **N.** is of old like a pool of water: 5210
Na 3:7 thee, and say, **N.** is laid waste: 5210
Zep 2:13 will make **N.** a desolation, and dry...... 5210
Mt 12:41 **men of N. shall rise in judgment ...** *3536*

NINEVITES (nin'-e-vites)
Lu 11:30 **as Jonas was a sign unto the N.,...** *3536*

NINTH
Le 23:32 in the **n.** day of the month at even, ... 8672
Le 25:22 yet of old fruit until the **n.** year; 8671
Nu 7:60 On the **n.** day Abidan the son of.......... 8671
2Ki 17:6 In the **n.** year of Hoshea the king 8671
2Ki 18:10 is the **n.** year of Hoshea king of......... 8672
2Ki 25:1 to pass in the **n.** year of his reign, ... 8671
2Ki 25:3 on the **n.** day of the fourth month 8672
1Ch 12:12 the eighth, Elzabad the **n.**,................ 8671
1Ch 24:11 The **n.** to Jeshuah, the tenth to 8671
1Ch 25:16 The **n.** to Mattaniah, he, his sons, ... 8671
1Ch 27:12 The **n.** captain for the **n.** month was... 8671
2Ch 16:12 Asa in the thirty and **n.** year of 8672
Ezr 10:9 It was the **n.** month, on the............. 8671
Jer 36:9 king of Judah, in the **n.** month........... 8671
Jer 36:22 in the winterhouse in the **n.** month: 8671
Jer 39:1 In the **n.** year of Zedekiah king of...... 8671
Jer 39:2 the **n.** day of the month, the city 8672
Jer 52:4 to pass in the **n.** year of his reign, ... 8671
Jer 52:6 in the **n.** day of the month, the........ 8672
Eze 24:1 Again in the **n.** year, in the tenth....... 8671
Hag 2:10, 18 twentieth day of the **n.** month, ... 8671
Zec 7:1 in the fourth day of the **n.** month, ... 8671
Mt 20:5 **out about he sixth and n. hour,......** *1766*
Mt 27:45 over all the land unto the **n.** hour....... *1766*
Mt 27:46 the **n.** hour Jesus cried with a loud..... *1766*
Mk 15:33 the whole land until the **n.** hour. *1766*
Mk 15:34 the **n.** hour Jesus cried with a loud...... *1766*
Lu 23:44 over all the earth until the **n.** hour. *1766*
Ac 3:1 hour of prayer, being the **n.** hour....... *1766*
Ac 10:3 vision evidently about the **n.** hour....... *1766*
Ac 10:30 and at the **n.** hour I prayed in my *1766*
Re 21:20 the eighth, beryl; the **n.**, a topaz; *1766*

NISAN (ni'-san) See also ABIB.
Ne 2:1 it came to pass in the month **N.**,......... 5212
Es 3:7 first month, that is, the month **N.**, ... 5212

NISROCH (nis'-rok)
2Ki 19:37 worshipping in the house of **N.** 5268
Isa 37:38 worshipping in the house of **N.** 5268

NISSI See JEHOVAH-NISSI.

NITRE
Pr 25:20 as vinegar upon **n.**, so is he that........ 5247
Jer 2:22 though thou wash thee with **n.**, ... 5247

NO See also NAY; NONE; NOTHING.
Ge 8:9 dove found **n.** rest for the sole of....... 3808
Ge 9:15 waters shall **n.** more become a flood... 3808
Ge 11:30 Sarai was barren; she had **n.** child. 369
Ge 13:8 unto Lot, Let there be **n.** strife,.......... 408
Ge 15:3 to me thou hast given **n.** seed: and, ... 3808
Ge 16:1 Abram's wife bare him **n.** children: 3808
Ge 26:29 That thou wilt do us **n.** hurt, as we.... 3808
Ge 30:1 that she bare Jacob **n.** children,........... 369
Ge 31:50 my daughters, **n.** man is with us;....... 3808
Ge 32:28 name shall be called **n.** more Jacob, ... 3808
Ge 37:22 said unto them, Shed **n.** blood, but..... 3808
Ge 37:22 and lay **n.** hand upon him; that he 3808
Ge 37:24 was empty, there was **n.** water in it. .. 3808
Ge 37:32 whether it be thy son's coat or **n.**. 3808
Ge 38:21 There was **n.** harlot in this place........ 3808
Ge 38:22 there was **n.** harlot in this place......... 3808
Ge 38:26 And he knew her again **n.** more......... 3808
Ge 40:8 and there is **n.** interpreter of it. 369
Ge 41:44 thee shall **n.** man lift up his hand........ 3808
Ge 42:11 true men, thy servants are **n.** spies.... 3808
Ge 42:31 We are true men; we are **n.** spies:..... 3808
Ge 42:34 shall I know that ye are **n.** spies, ... 3808
Ge 44:23 you, ye shall see my face **n.** more...... 3808
Ge 45:1 there stood **n.** man with him, while 3808
Ge 47:4 have **n.** pasture for their flocks; 369
Ge 47:13 there was **n.** bread in all the land; 369
Ex 2:12 when he saw that there was **n.** man,..... 369
Ex 3:19 you go, **n.**, not by a mighty hand. 3808
Ex 5:7 **n.** more give the people straw to.......... 3808
Ex 5:16 is **n.** straw given unto thy servants, ... 369
Ex 5:18 there shall **n.** straw be given you, ... 3808
Ex 8:22 that **n.** swarms of flies shall be.......... 1115
Ex 9:26 of Israel were, was there **n.** hail. 3808
Ex 9:28 be **n.** more mighty thunderings and....... 3808
Ex 9:28 you go, and ye shall stay **n.** longer..... 3808
Ex 10:14 there were **n.** such locusts as they, ... 3808
Ex 10:28 heed to thyself, see my face **n.** more;..3808
Ex 10:29 I will see thy face again **n.** more........ 3808
Ex 12:16 **n.** manner of work shall be done in..... 3808
Ex 12:19 be **n.** leaven found in your houses: 3808
Ex 12:43 there shall **n.** stranger eat thereof: 3808
Ex 12:48 **n.** uncircumcised person shall at......... 3808
Ex 13:3 shall **n.** leaven bread be eaten. 3808
Ex 13:7 **n.** leavened bread be seen with thee,.. 3808
Ex 14:11 there were **n.** graves in Egypt, hast..... 369
Ex 14:13 see them again **n.** more for ever......... 3808
Ex 15:22 wilderness, and found **n.** water. 3808
Ex 16:4 they will walk in my law, or **n.**. 3808
Ex 16:18 he that gathered little had **n.** lack; 3808
Ex 16:19 **n.** man leave of it till the morning. 408
Ex 16:29 **n.** man go out of his place on the 408
Ex 17:1 **n.** water for the people to drink. 369
Ex 20:3 have **n.** other gods before me. 3808
Ex 21:8 strange nation...shall have **n.** power,... 3808
Ex 21:22 her, and yet **n.** mischief follow:.......... 3808
Ex 22:2 there shall **n.** blood be shed for him..... 369
Ex 22:10 or driven away, **n.** man seeing it: 369
Ex 23:8 And thou shalt take **n.** gift: for 3808
Ex 23:13 make **n.** mention of the name of 3808
Ex 23:32 shalt make **n.** covenant with them, ... 3808
Ex 30:9 offer **n.** strange incense thereon,......... 3808
Ex 30:12 there be **n.** plague among them, ... 3808
Ex 33:4 and **n.** man did put on him his 3808
Ex 33:20 for there shall **n.** man see me, and..... 3808
Ex 34:3 **n.** man shall come up with thee, ... 3808
Ex 34:7 will by **n.** means clear the guilty; 3808
Ex 34:14 thou shalt worship **n.** other god: 3808
Ex 34:17 shalt make thee **n.** molten gods. 3808
Ex 35:3 shall kindle **n.** fire throughout your 3808
Le 2:11 **N.** meat offering, which ye shall......... 3808
Le 2:11 for ye shall burn **n.** leaven, nor any.... 3808
Le 5:11 he shall put **n.** oil upon it, neither 3808
Le 6:30 And **n.** sin offering, whereof any of..... 3808
Le 7:23 ye shall eat **n.** manner of fat, of ox,.... 3808
Le 7:24 use: but ye shall in **n.** wise eat of it. .. 3808
Le 7:26 ye shall eat **n.** manner of blood,......... 3808
Le 11:12 Whatsoever hath **n.** fins or scales 369
Le 12:4 she shall touch **n.** hallowed thing,....... 3808
Le 13:21 there be **n.** white hairs therein, and..... 369
Le 13:26 be **n.** white hair in the bright spot, ... 369
Le 13:26 it be **n.** lower than the other skin, ... 369
Le 13:31 and that there is **n.** black hair in it;...... 369
Le 13:32 and there be in it **n.** yellow hair,......... 3808
Le 16:17 shall be **n.** man in the tabernacle........ 3808
Le 16:29 do **n.** work at all, whether it be one ... 3808
Le 17:7 shall **n.** more offer their sacrifices 3808
Le 17:12 **N.** soul of you shall eat blood, ... 3808
Le 17:14 eat the blood of **n.** manner of flesh: 3808
Le 19:15, 35 Ye shall do **n.** unrighteousness 3808
Le 20:14 there be **n.** wickedness among you..... 3808
Le 21:3 him, which hath had **n.** husband: 3808
Le 21:21 **N.** man that hath a blemish of the seed .....
Le 22:10 **n.** stranger eat of the holy thing: 3808
Le 22:13 or divorced, and have **n.** child, and 369
Le 22:13 there shall **n.** stranger eat thereof. 3808
Le 22:21 there shall be **n.** blemish therein. 3808
Le 23:3 ye shall do **n.** work therein: it is the.... 3808
Le 23:7, 8, 21 ye shall do **n.** servile work.. 3605,3808
Le 23:25 Ye shall do **n.** servile work 3605,3808
Le 23:28 do **n.** work in that same day: 3808
Le 23:31 Ye shall do **n.** manner of work: it....... 3808
Le 23:35, 36 ye shall do **n.** servile work 3605,3808
Le 25:31 which have **n.** wall round about 369
Le 25:36 Take thou **n.** usury of him, or............. 408
Le 26:1 you **n.** idols nor graven image, ... 3808
Le 26:37 have **n.** power to stand before your.... 3808
Le 27:26 firstling, **n.** man shall sanctify it; 3808
Le 27:28 **n.** devoted thing,...shall be sold... 3605,3808
Nu 1:53 be **n.** wrath upon the congregation 3808
Nu 3:4 of Sinai, and they had **n.** children: 3808
Nu 5:8 have **n.** kinsmen to recompense the 369
Nu 5:13 and there be **n.** witness against her...... 369
Nu 5:15 he shall pour **n.** oil upon it, nor 3808
Nu 5:19 If **n.** man have lain with thee, and...... 3808
Nu 6:3 shall drink **n.** vinegar of wine, or........ 3808
Nu 6:5 shall **n.** rasor come upon his head: 3808
Nu 6:6 Lord...shall come at **n.** dead body. 3808
Nu 8:19 be **n.** plague among the children of..... 3808
Nu 8:25 thereof, and shall serve **n.** more: 3808
Nu 8:26 the charge, and shall do **n.** service. 3808
Nu 14:18 by **n.** means clearing the guilty, ... 3808
Nu 16:40 that **n.** stranger, which is not of the ... 3808
Nu 18:5 be **n.** wrath any more upon the 3808
Nu 18:20 have **n.** inheritance in their land, ... 3808
Nu 18:23 of Israel they have **n.** inheritance. 3808
Nu 18:24 they shall have **n.** inheritance. 3808
Nu 18:32 ye shall bear **n.** sin by reason of it, ... 3808
Nu 19:2 without spot, wherein is **n.** blemish,..... 369
Nu 19:15 hath **n.** covering bound upon it, is........ 369
Nu 20:2 was **n.** water for the congregation: 3808
Nu 20:5 it is **n.** place of seed, or of figs, or..... 3808
Nu 21:5 there is **n.** bread, neither is there....... 369
Nu 22:26 where was **n.** way to turn either to...... 369
Nu 23:23 there is **n.** enchantment against 3808
Nu 26:33 the son of Hepher had **n.** sons, but 3808
Nu 26:62 was **n.** inheritance given them 3808
Nu 27:3 in his own sin, and had **n.** sons.......... 3808
Nu 27:4 family, because he hath **n.** son?........... 369
Nu 27:8 If a man die, and have **n.** son, then...... 369
Nu 27:9 And if he have **n.** daughter, then ye..... 369
Nu 27:10 And if he have **n.** brethren, then ye 369
Nu 27:11 And if his father have **n.** brethren, ... 369
Nu 27:17 as sheep which have **n.** shepherd......... 369
Nu 28:18 shall do **n.** manner of servile work...... 3808
Nu 28:25 ye shall do **n.** servile work. 3605,3808
Nu 28:26 ye shall do **n.** servile work: 3605,3808
Nu 29:1 ye shall do **n.** servile work: it is . 3605,3808
Nu 29:12 ye shall do **n.** servile work, and.. 3605,3808
Nu 29:35 ye shall do **n.** servile work 3605,3808
Nu 33:14 was **n.** water for the people to drink... 3808
Nu 35:31 shall take **n.** satisfaction for the life..... 3808
Nu 35:32 ye shall take **n.** satisfaction for him..... 3808
De 1:39 **n.** knowledge between good and evil, .. 3808
De 2:5 **n.**, not so much as a foot breadth;............
De 3:26 speak **n.** more unto me of this 408
De 4:12 the words, but saw **n.** similitude;.......... 369
De 4:15 ye saw **n.** manner of similitude on...... 3808
De 5:22 great voice: and he added **n.** more. 3808
De 7:2 shalt make **n.** covenant with them, ... 3808
De 7:16 eye shall have **n.** pity upon them:........ 3808
De 7:24 there shall **n.** man be able to stand..... 3808
De 8:2 keep his commandments, or **n.**. 3808
De 8:15 drought, where there was **n.** water;..... 369
De 10:9 Levi hath **n.** part nor inheritance........ 3808
De 10:16 heart, and be **n.** more stiffnecked........ 3808
De 11:17 that there be **n.** rain, and that the....... 3808
De 11:25 **n.** man shall be able to stand before ... 3808
De 12:12 as he hath **n.** part nor inheritance 369
De 13:11 do **n.** more any such wickedness........ 3808
De 14:27, 29 he hath **n.** part nor inheritance........ 369
De 15:4 there shall be **n.** poor among you;....... 3808
De 15:19 do **n.** work with the firstling of thy..... 3808
De 16:3 thou shalt eat **n.** leavened bread 3808
De 16:4 shall be **n.** leavened bread seen 3808
De 16:8 God: thou halt do **n.** work therein. 3808
De 17:13 and do **n.** more presumptuously. 3808
De 17:16 henceforth return **n.** more that way. ... 3808
De 18:1 the tribe of Levi, shall have **n.** part 3808
De 18:2 they have **n.** inheritance among.......... 3808
De 19:20 commit **n.** more any such evil........... 3808
De 20:12 if it will make **n.** peace with thee, ... 3808
De 21:14 be, if thou have **n.** delight in her, ... 3808
De 22:26 the damsel **n.** sin worthy of death:....... 369
De 23:14 he see **n.** unclean thing in thee, ... 3808
De 23:17 be **n.** whore of the daughters of......... 3808
De 23:22 to vow, it shall be **n.** sin in thee. 3808
De 24:1 that she find **n.** favour in his eyes, ... 3808
De 24:6 **N.** man shall take the nether or the.... 3808
De 25:5 one of them die, and have **n.** child, ... 369
De 28:26 and **n.** man shall fray them away. 369
De 28:29 and **n.** man shall save thee. 369
De 28:32 shall be **n.** might in thine hand. 369
De 28:65 nations shalt thou find **n.** ease, ... 3808
De 28:68 Thou shalt see it **n.** more again: 3808
De 28:68 and **n.** man shall buy you. 369
De 31:2 I can **n.** more go out and come in: 3808
De 32:12 there was **n.** strange god with him....... 369
De 32:20 children in whom is **n.** faith.............. 3808
De 32:39 am he, and there is **n.** god with me: 369
De 34:6 **n.** man knoweth of his sepulchre........ 3808
Jos 8:20 they had **n.** power to flee this way 3808
Jos 8:31 which **n.** man hath lift up any iron: 3808
Jos 10:14 there was **n.** day like that before it..... 3808
Jos 11:20 that they might have **n.** favour,.......... 1115
Jos 14:4 they gave **n.** part unto the Levites 3808
Jos 17:3 the son of Manasseh, had **n.** sons, ... 3808
Jos 18:7 Levites have **n.** part among you;......... 3808
Jos 22:25 Gad; ye have **n.** part in the Lord:........ 369
Jos 22:27 come, Ye have **n.** part in the Lord....... 369
Jos 23:9 **n.** man hath been able to stand.......... 3808
Jos 23:13 God will **n.** more drive out any of 3808
Jg 2:2 **n.** league with the inhabitants of......... 3808
Jg 4:20 man here? that thou shalt say, **N.**........ 369
Jg 5:19 they took **n.** gain of money............... 3808
Jg 6:4 and left **n.** sustenance for Israel, ... 3808
Jg 8:28 they lifted up their heads **n.** more. 3808
Jg 10:13 I will deliver you **n.** more................ 3808
Jg 11:39 had vowed; and she knew **n.** man. 3808
Jg 13:5 **n.** rasor shall come on his head: 3808
Jg 13:7 now drink **n.** wine nor strong drink, ... 408
Jg 13:21 of the Lord did **n.** more appear.......... 3808
Jg 15:13 they spake unto him, saying, **N.**;........ 3808
Jg 17:6 days there was **n.** king in Israel, ... 369
Jg 18:1 there was **n.** king in Israel: and in 369
Jg 18:7 was **n.** magistrate in the land, that....... 369
Jg 18:7 and had **n.** business with any man........ 369
Jg 18:10 where there is **n.** want of any thing 369
Jg 18:28 And there was **n.** deliverer, because 369
Jg 18:28 had **n.** business with any man; and....... 369
Jg 19:1 when there was **n.** king in Israel, ... 369
Jg 19:15 was **n.** man that took them into his...... 369
Jg 19:18 **n.** man that receiveth me to house........ 369
Jg 19:19 there is **n.** want of any thing............... 369
Jg 19:30 **n.** such deed done nor seen from....... 3808
Jg 21:12 virgins, that had known **n.** man by...... 3808
Jg 21:25 days there was **n.** king in Israel; 369
1Sa 1:2 but Hannah had **n.** children................ 369
1Sa 1:11 shall **n.** rasor come upon his head. 3808
1Sa 1:15 answered and said, **N.**, my lord, ... 3808
1Sa 1:18 her countenance was **n.** more sad. 3808
1Sa 2:3 Talk **n.** more so exceeding proudly; 408
1Sa 2:9 by strength shall **n.** man prevail. 3808
1Sa 2:24 for it is **n.** good report that I hear:..... 3808
1Sa 3:1 days; there was **n.** open vision............ 369
1Sa 6:7 on which there hath come **n.** yoke,..... 3808
1Sa 7:13 **n.** more into the coast of Israel: 3808
1Sa 10:14 we saw that they were **n.** where, ... 369
1Sa 10:27 him, and brought him **n.** presents....... 3808
1Sa 11:3 then, if there be **n.** man to save us,..... 369
1Sa 13:19 Now there was **n.** smith found.......... 3808
1Sa 14:6 is **n.** restraint to the Lord to save 369
1Sa 14:26 **n.** man put his hand to his mouth: 369
1Sa 15:35 Samuel came **n.** more to see Saul 3808
1Sa 17:32 Let **n.** man's heart fail because of........ 408
1Sa 17:50 was **n.** sword in the hand of David....... 369
1Sa 18:2 would let him go **n.** more home to 3808
1Sa 20:15 **n.**, not when the Lord hath cut off..........

1Sa 20:21 there is peace to thee, and **n.** hurt; 369
1Sa 20:34 eat **n.** meat the second day of the.... 3808
1Sa 21:1 thou alone, and **n.** man with thee? 369
1Sa 21:2 Let **n.** man know any thing of the.... 408
1Sa 21:4 **n.** common bread under mine hand,.... 369
1Sa 21:6 **n.** bread there but the shewbread, ... 3808
1Sa 21:9 for there is **n.** other save that here.... 369
1Sa 25:31 this shall be **n.** grief unto thee,.... 3808
1Sa 26:12 gat them away, and **n.** man saw it, ... 369
1Sa 26:21 for I will **n.** more do thee harm, ... 3808
1Sa 27:4 he sought **n.** more again for him. 3808
1Sa 28:10 there shall **n.** punishment happen.... 518
1Sa 28:15 me, and answereth me **n.** more, ... 3808
1Sa 28:20 and there was **n.** strength in him; 3808
1Sa 28:20 he had eaten **n.** bread all the day, ... 3808
1Sa 29:3 found **n.** fault in him since he fell 3808
1Sa 30:4 they had **n.** more power to weep.... 369
1Sa 30:12 he had eaten **n.** bread, nor drunk.... 3808
2Sa 1:21 let there be **n.** dew, neither let.... 408
2Sa 2:28 and pursued after Israel **n.** more, ... 3808
2Sa 6:23 the daughter of Saul had **n.** child.... 3808
2Sa 7:10 of their own, and move **n.** more; 3808
2Sa 12:6 thing, and because he had **n.** pity.... 3808
2Sa 13:12 **n.** such thing ought to be done in.... 3808
2Sa 13:16 said unto him, There is **n.** cause: 408
2Sa 14:25 head there was **n.** blemish in him.... 3808
2Sa 15:3 there is **n.** man deputed of the king 369
2Sa 15:26 I have **n.** delight in thee; behold, ... 3808
2Sa 18:13 there is **n.** matter hid from the king,.... 3808
2Sa 18:18 I have **n.** son to keep my name in 369
2Sa 18:20 day thou shalt bear **n.** tidings, ... 3808
2Sa 18:22 that thou hast **n.** tidings ready? 369
2Sa 20:1 We have **n.** part in David, neither.... 369
2Sa 20:10 Amasa took **n.** heed to the sword 3808
2Sa 21:4 will have **n.** silver nor gold of Saul, ... 369
2Sa 21:17 go **n.** more out with us to battle, ... 3808
1Ki 1:1 with clothes, but he gat **n.** heat. 3808
1Ki 3:2 was **n.** house built unto the name.... 3808
1Ki 3:18 **n.** stranger with us in the house,.... 369
1Ki 3:22 said, **N.**; but the dead is thy son,.... 3808
1Ki 3:26 living child, and in **n.** wise slay it. 408
1Ki 3:27 living child, and in **n.** wise slay it: 3808
1Ki 6:18 was cedar; there was **n.** stone sen.... 369
1Ki 8:16 I chose **n.** city out of all the tribes 3808
1Ki 8:23 Israel, there is **n.** God like thee, ... 369
1Ki 8:35 is shut up, and there is **n.** rain, ... 3808
1Ki 8:46 there is **n.** man that sinneth not,) 369
1Ki 9:22 did Solomon make **n.** bondmen: 3808
1Ki 10:5 there was **n.** more spirit in her.... 3808
1Ki 10:10 there came **n.** more such abundance 3808
1Ki 10:12 there came **n.** such almug trees, nor.... 3808
1Ki 13:9 Eat **n.** bread, nor drink water, nor 3808
1Ki 13:17 shalt eat **n.** bread nor drink water 3808
1Ki 13:22 Eat **n.** bread, and drink **n.** water;.... 408
1Ki 17:7 there had been **n.** rain in the land. 3808
1Ki 17:17 that there was **n.** breath left in him. 3808
1Ki 18:10 there is **n.** nation or kingdom,.... 518
1Ki 18:23, 23 on wood, and put **n.** fire under: 3808
1Ki 18:25 your gods, but put **n.** fire under.... 3808
1Ki 18:26 there was **n.** voice, nor any that.... 369
1Ki 21:4 his face, and would eat **n.** bread. 3808
1Ki 21:5 so sad, that thou eatest **n.** bread?.... 369
1Ki 22:17 These have **n.** master: let them.... 3808
1Ki 22:18 prophesy **n.** good concerning me, ... 3808
1Ki 22:47 There was then **n.** king in Edom: 369
2Ki 1:16 is **n.** God in Israel to inquire of his 369
2Ki 1:17 of Judah; because he had **n.** son.... 3808
2Ki 2:12 And he saw him **n.** more: and he 3808
2Ki 3:9 there was **n.** water for the host, and 3808
2Ki 4:14 she hath **n.** child, and her husband.... 369
2Ki 4:41 And there was **n.** harm in the pot. 3808
2Ki 5:15 that there is **n.** God in all the earth,.... 369
2Ki 5:25 Thy servant went **n.** whither.... 3808
2Ki 6:23 came **n.** more into the land of Israel. 3808
2Ki 7:5 behold, there was **n.** man there.... 369
2Ki 7:10 there was **n.** man there, neither.... 369
2Ki 9:35 **n.** more of her than the skull, and.... 3808
2Ki 10:31 Jehu took **n.** heed to walk in the law.... 3808
2Ki 12:7 receive **n.** more money of your.... 408
2Ki 12:8 to receive **n.** more money of the.... 1115
2Ki 17:4 **n.** present to the king of Assyria,.... 3808
2Ki 19:18 were **n.** gods, but the work of men's.... 3808
2Ki 22:7 was **n.** reckoning made with them 3808
2Ki 23:10 that **n.** man might make his son or.... 1115
2Ki 23:18 alone; let **n.** man move his bones. 408
2Ki 23:25 him was there **n.** king before him,.... 3808
2Ki 25:3 **n.** bread for the people of the land. 3808
1Ch 2:34 Now Sheshan had **n.** sons, but 3808
1Ch 12:17 there is **n.** wrong in mine hands,.... 3808
1Ch 16:21 suffered **n.** man to do them wrong: 3808
1Ch 16:22 and do my prophets **n.** harm.... 408
1Ch 17:9 place, and shall be moved **n.** more; 3808
1Ch 22:16 and the iron, there is **n.** number.... 369
1Ch 23:22 Eleazar died, and had **n.** sons, but.... 3808
1Ch 23:26 shall **n.** more carry the tabernacle,.... 369
1Ch 24:2 their father, and had **n.** children: 3808
1Ch 24:28 came Eleazar, who had **n.** sons.... 3808
2Ch 6:5 I chose **n.** city among all the tribes.... 3808
2Ch 6:14 is **n.** God like thee in the heaven,.... 369
2Ch 6:26 is shut up, and there is **n.** rain, ... 3808
2Ch 6:36 there is **n.** man which sinneth not,).... 369
2Ch 7:13 up heaven that there be **n.** rain, ... 3808
2Ch 8:9 Solomon make **n.** servants for his.... 3808
2Ch 9:4 there was **n.** more spirit in her.... 3808
2Ch 13:9 a priest of them that are **n.** gods. 3808
2Ch 14:6 and he had **n.** war in those years;.... 369
2Ch 14:11 or with them that have **n.** power: 369
2Ch 15:5 was **n.** peace to him that went out,.... 369
2Ch 15:19 was **n.** more war unto the five and.... 3808
2Ch 17:10 made **n.** war against Jehoshaphat.... 3808
2Ch 18:16 sheep that have **n.** shepherd: and.... 369
2Ch 18:16 These have **n.** master; let them.... 3808
2Ch 19:7 **n.** iniquity with the Lord our God, ... 369
2Ch 20:12 **n.** might against this great company 369
2Ch 21:19 people made **n.** burning for him, ... 3808
2Ch 22:9 **n.** power to keep still the kingdom.... 369
2Ch 32:15 **n.** good of any nation or kingdom.... 3808
2Ch 35:18 was **n.** passover like to that kept 3808
2Ch 36:16 people, till there was **n.** remedy.... 369
2Ch 36:17 **n.** compassion upon young man or.... 3808
Ezr 4:16 **n.** portion on this side of the river.... 3809
Ezr 9:14 should be **n.** remnant nor escaping?.... 369
Ezr 10:6 he did eat **n.** bread, nor drink.... 3808
Ne 2:14 there was **n.** place for the beast.... 369
Ne 2:17 that we be **n.** more a reproach. 3808
Ne 2:20 ye have **n.** portion, nor right, nor.... 369
Ne 6:1 there was **n.** breach left therein; 3808
Ne 6:8 **n.** such things done as thou sayest, ... 3808
Ne 13:19 there should **n.** burden be brought.... 3808
Ne 13:21 came they **n.** more on the Sabbath. 3808
Ne 13:26 was there **n.** king like him, who was.... 3808
Es 1:19 Vashti come **n.** more before king 3808
Es 2:14 came in unto the king **n.** more,.... 3808
Es 5:12 let **n.** man come in with the king.... 3808
Es 8:8 king's ring, may **n.** man reverse. 369
Es 9:2 and **n.** man could withstand them; 3808
Job 3:7 let **n.** joyful voice come therein. 408
Job 4:18 he put **n.** trust in his servants; 3808
Job 5:19 seven there shall **n.** evil touch thee. 3808
Job 7:7 mine eye shall **n.** more see good.... 3808
Job 7:8 hath seen me shall see me **n.** more. 3808
Job 7:9 the grave shall come up **n.** more.... 3808
Job 7:10 shall return **n.** more to his house, ... 3808
Job 9:25 they flee away, they see **n.** good. 3808
Job 10:18 the ghost, and **n.** eye had seen me!.... 3808
Job 11:3 shall **n.** man make thee ashamed? 369
Job 12:2 **N.** doubt but ye are the people, ... 551
Job 12:14 man, and there can be **n.** opening. 3808
Job 12:24 a wilderness where there is **n.** way. 3808
Job 13:4 ye are all physicians of **n.** value.... 457
Job 14:12 till the heavens be **n.** more, they 1115
Job 15:3 wherewith he can do **n.** good?.... 3808
Job 15:15 he putteth **n.** trust in his saints;.... 3808
Job 15:19 **n.** stranger passed among them. 3808
Job 15:28 in houses which **n.** man inhabiteth, ... 3808
Job 16:18 blood, and let my cry have **n.** place.... 408
Job 18:17 shall have **n.** name in the street.... 3808
Job 19:7 aloud, but there is **n.** judgment.... 3808
Job 19:16 servant, and he gave me **n.** answer;.... 3808
Job 20:9 saw him shall see him **n.** more; 3808
Job 20:21 shall **n.** man look for his goods. 3808
Job 23:6 **N.**; but he would put strength in.... 3808
Job 24:7 they have **n.** covering in the cold.... 369
Job 24:15 saying, **N.** eye shall see me: and.... 3808
Job 24:20 he shall be **n.** more remembered;.... 3808
Job 24:22 riseth up, and **n.** man is sure of life.... 3808
Job 26:2 thou the arm that hath **n.** strength? 3808
Job 26:3 counselled him that hath **n.** wisdom?.... 3808
Job 26:6 and destruction hath **n.** covering.... 369
Job 28:7 is a path which **n.** fowl knoweth,.... 3808
Job 28:18 **N.** mention shall be made of coral, ... 3808
Job 30:13 my calamity, they have **n.** helper. 3808
Job 30:17 season: and my sinews take **n.** rest.... 3808
Job 32:3 because they had found **n.** answer,.... 3808
Job 32:5 there was **n.** answer in the mouth 369
Job 32:15 amazed, they answered **n.** more: 3808
Job 32:16 stood still, and answered **n.** more;).... 3808
Job 32:19 belly is as wine which hath **n.** vent;.... 3808
Job 34:22 is **n.** darkness, nor shadow of death, ... 369
Job 34:32 done iniquity, I will do **n.** more.... 3808
Job 36:16 place, where there is **n.** straitness;.... 3808
Job 36:19 **n.** not gold, nor all the forces of.... 3808
Job 38:11 shalt thou come, but **n.** further:.... 3808
Job 38:26 on the earth, where **n.** man is; on.... 3808
Job 38:26 wilderness, wherein there is **n.** man; 3808
Job 40:5 twice; but I will proceed **n.** further. 3808
Job 41:8 remember the battle, do **n.** more.... 408
Job 41:16 that **n.** air can come between them.... 3808
Job 42:2 that **n.** thought can be withholden.... 3808
Job 42:15 all the land were **n.** women found.... 3808
Ps 3:2 There is **n.** help for him in God.... 369
Ps 5:9 is **n.** faithfulness in their mouth; 369
Ps 6:5 in death there is **n.** remembrance of.... 369
Ps 10:18 man of...earth may **n.** more oppress. 1077
Ps 14:1 said in his heart, There is **n.** God.... 369
Ps 14:3 is none that doeth good, **n.**, not one....
Ps 14:4 workers of iniquity **n.** knowledge? 3808
Ps 19:3 There is **n.** speech nor language,.... 369
Ps 22:6 But I am a worm, and **n.** man; a.... 3808
Ps 23:4 I will fear **n.** evil: for thou art with.... 3808
Ps 32:2 and in whose spirit there is **n.** guile. 369
Ps 32:9 mule, which have **n.** understanding:.... 369
Ps 33:16 is **n.** king saved by the multitude of.... 369
Ps 34:9 is **n.** want to them that fear him.... 369
Ps 36:1 is **n.** fear of God before his eyes.... 369
Ps 38:3 There is **n.** soundness in my flesh 369
Ps 38:7 there is **n.** soundness in my flesh. 369
Ps 38:14 and in whose mouth are **n.** reproofs. 369
Ps 39:13 before I go hence, and be **n.** more.... 369
Ps 40:17 make **n.** tarrying, O my God.... 408
Ps 41:8 he lieth he shall rise up **n.** more. 3808
Ps 50:9 will take **n.** bullock out of thy house, ... 3808
Ps 53:1 said in his heart, There is **n.** God.... 369
Ps 53:3 is none that doeth good, **n.**, not one....
Ps 53:4 workers of iniquity **n.** knowledge? 3808
Ps 53:5 in great fear, where **n.** fear was: 3808
Ps 55:19 Because they have **n.** changes, ... 369
Ps 63:1 thirsty land, where **n.** water is; 1097
Ps 69:2 mire, where there is **n.** standing:.... 369
Ps 70:5 O Lord, make **n.** tarrying.... 408
Ps 72:12 also, and him that hath **n.** helper. 369
Ps 73:4 there are **n.** bands in their death: 369
Ps 74:9 signs: there is **n.** more any prophet: 369
Ps 77:7 and will he be favourable **n.** more? 3808
Ps 78:64 their widows made **n.** lamentation.... 3808
Ps 81:9 shall **n.** strange god be in thee; 3808
Ps 83:4 may be **n.** more in remembrance.... 3808
Ps 84:11 **n.** good thing will he withhold from.... 3808
Ps 88:4 am as a man that hath **n.** strength: 369
Ps 88:5 whom thou rememberest **n.** more: 3808
Ps 91:10 There shall **n.** evil befall thee, ... 3808
Ps 92:15 there is **n.** unrighteousness in him. 3808
Ps 101:3 **n.** wicked thing before mine eyes: 3808
Ps 102:27 and thy years shall have **n.** end. 3808
Ps 103:16 thereof shall know it **n.** more. 3808
Ps 104:35 and let the wicked be **n.** more. 369
Ps 105:14 suffered **n.** man to do them wrong: 3808
Ps 105:15 and do my prophets **n.** harm.... 408
Ps 107:4 way; they found **n.** city to dwell in. 3808
Ps 107:40 wilderness, where there is **n.** way.... 3808
Ps 119:3 They also do **n.** iniquity: they walk.... 3808
Ps 142:4 was **n.** man that would know me: 369
Ps 142:4 failed me; **n.** man cared for my soul. 369
Ps 143:2 shall **n.** man living be justified.... 3808
Ps 144:14 that there be **n.** breaking in, nor 369
Ps 144:14 be **n.** complaining in our streets. 369
Ps 146:3 son of man, in whom there is **n.** help. 369
Pr 1:24 out my hand, and **n.** man regarded;.... 369
Pr 3:30 if he have done thee **n.** harm.... 3808
Pr 6:7 Which having **n.** guide, overseer, ... 369
Pr 8:24 When there were **n.** depths, I was.... 369
Pr 8:24 **n.** fountains abounding with water. 369
Pr 10:22 and he addeth **n.** sorrow with it.... 3808
Pr 10:25 passeth, so is the wicked **n.** more: 369
Pr 11:14 Where **n.** counsel is, the people fall:.... 369
Pr 12:21 shall **n.** evil happen to the just:.... 3808
Pr 12:28 pathway thereof there is **n.** death. 408
Pr 14:4 Where **n.** oxen are, the crib is.... 369

Pr	17:16	seeing he hath **n.** heart to it?	369
Pr	17:20	a froward heart findeth **n.** good:	3808
Pr	17:21	and the father of a fool hath **n.** joy.	3808
Pr	18:2	hath **n.** delight in understanding,	3808
Pr	21:10	findeth **n.** favour in his eyes.	3808
Pr	21:30	is **n.** wisdom nor understanding nor	369
Pr	22:24	Make **n.** friendship with an angry	408
Pr	24:20	be **n.** reward to the evil man; the	3808
Pr	25:28	hath **n.** rule over his own spirit is	369
Pr	26:20	Where **n.** wood is, there the fire	657
Pr	26:20	so where there is **n.** talebearer, the	369
Pr	28:1	wicked flee when **n.** man pursueth:	369
Pr	28:3	sweeping rain which leaveth **n.** food.	369
Pr	28:17	flee to the pit; let **n.** man stay him.	408
Pr	28:24	and saith, It is **n.** transgression;	369
Pr	29:9	he rage or laugh, there is **n.** rest.	369
Pr	29:18	Where there is **n.** vision, the people	369
Pr	30:20	saith, I have done **n.** wickedness	3808
Pr	30:27	The locusts have **n.** king, yet go	369
Pr	30:31	against whom there is **n.** rising up.	510
Pr	31:7	and remember his misery **n.** more	3808
Pr	31:11	that he shall have **n.** need of spoil.	3808
Ec	1:9	there is **n.** new thing under the sun.	369
Ec	1:11	is **n.** remembrance of former things;	369
Ec	2:11	there was **n.** profit under the sun.	369
Ec	2:16	there is **n.** remembrance of the wise	369
Ec	3:11	**n.** man can find out the work that	1097
Ec	3:12	know that there is **n.** good in them,	369
Ec	3:19	a man hath **n.** preeminence above a	369
Ec	4:1	and they had **n.** comforter; and on	369
Ec	4:1	power; but they had **n.** comforter.	369
Ec	4:8	yet is there **n.** end of all his labour;	369
Ec	4:13	who will **n.** more be admonished.	3808
Ec	4:16	There is **n.** end of all the people,	369
Ec	5:4	for he hath **n.** pleasure in fools:	369
Ec	6:3	and also that he have **n.** burial;	3808
Ec	6:6	told, yet he hath seen **n.** good:	3808
Ec	7:21	Also take **n.** heed unto all words	808
Ec	8:5	commandment shall feel **n.** evil	3808
Ec	8:8	There is **n.** man that hath power	369
Ec	8:8	there is **n.** discharge in that war;	369
Ec	8:15	hath **n.** better thing under the sun,	369
Ec	9:1	**n.** man knoweth either love or	369
Ec	9:8	and let thy head lack **n.** ointment.	408
Ec	9:10	for there is **n.** work, nor device, nor	369
Ec	9:15	yet **n.** man remembered that same	3808
Ec	10:11	and a babbler is **n.** better.	369
Ec	10:20	not the king, **n.** not in thy thought;	408
Ec	12:1	say, I have **n.** pleasure in them;	369
Ec	12:12	making many books there is **n.** end;	369
Ca	4:7	my love; there is **n.** spot in thee.	369
Ca	5:6	him; but he gave me **n.** answer.	3808
Ca	8:8	sister, and she hath **n.** breasts:	369
Isa	1:6	head there is **n.** soundness in it;	369
Isa	1:13	Bring **n.** more vain oblations;	3808
Isa	1:30	and as a garden that hath **n.** water.	369
Isa	5:6	clouds that they rain **n.** rain upon it.	
Isa	5:8	field to field, till there be **n.** place,	675
Isa	5:13	because they have **n.** knowledge:	1097
Isa	8:20	because there is **n.** light in them.	369
Isa	9:7	and peace there shall be **n.** end,	369
Isa	9:17	have **n.** joy in their young men,	3808
Isa	9:19	fire: **n.** man shall spare his brother.	3808
Isa	10:15	lift up itself, as if it were **n.** wood.	3808
Isa	10:20	shall **n.** more again stay upon him	3808
Isa	13:14	as a sheep that **n.** man taketh up:	369
Isa	13:18	shall have **n.** pity on the fruit of	3808
Isa	14:8	**n.** feller is come up against us.	3808
Isa	15:6	faileth, there is **n.** green thing.	3808
Isa	16:10	vineyards there shall be **n.** singing,	3808
Isa	16:10	tread out **n.** wine in their presses;	3808
Isa	19:7	be driven away, and be **n.** more.	369
Isa	23:1	that there is **n.** house, **n.** entering in:	
Isa	23:10	Tarshish: there is **n.** more strength	369
Isa	23:12	Thou shalt **n.** more rejoice, O thou	3808
Isa	23:12	there also shalt thou have **n.** rest.	3808
Isa	24:10	is shut up, that **n.** man may come in.	
Isa	25:2	a palace of strangers to be **n.** city;	
Isa	26:21	and shall **n.** more cover her slain.	3808
Isa	27:11	it is a people of **n.** understanding:	3808
Isa	27:11	them will shew them **n.** favour.	3808
Isa	28:8	so that there is **n.** place clean.	1097
Isa	29:16	it, He had **n.** understanding?	3808
Isa	30:7	help in vain, and to **n.** purpose:	7385
Isa	30:16	ye said, **N.**; for we will flee upon	3808
Isa	30:19	thou shalt weep **n.** more: he will	3808
Isa	32:5	shall be **n.** more called liberal, nor	3808
Isa	33:8	the cities, he regardeth **n.** man.	3808
Isa	33:21	shall go **n.** galley with oars,	1077
Isa	34:16	**n.** one of these shall fail, none	3808
Isa	35:9	**N.** lion shall be there, nor any	3808
Isa	37:19	they were **n.** gods, but the work of	3808
Isa	38:11	I shall behold man **n.** more with the	3808
Isa	40:20	impoverished that he hath **n.**	3808
Isa	40:28	**n.** searching of his understanding.	369
Isa	40:29	**n.** might he increaseth strength.	369
Isa	41:28	I beheld, and there was **n.** man;	369
Isa	41:28	and there was **n.** counsellor, that,	369
Isa	43:10	me there was **n.** God formed,	3808
Isa	43:11	and beside me there is **n.** saviour.	369
Isa	43:12	was **n.** strange god among you:	369
Isa	43:24	me **n.** sweet cane with money,	3808
Isa	44:6	last; and beside me there is **n.** God.	369
Isa	44:8	yea, there is **n.** God; I know not any.	369
Isa	44:12	he drinketh **n.** water, and is faint.	3808
Isa	45:5	else, there is **n.** God besides me:	369
Isa	45:9	or thy work, He hath **n.** hands?	369
Isa	45:14	there is none else, there is **n.** God.	657
Isa	45:20	have **n.** knowledge that set up the	3808
Isa	45:21	and there is **n.** God else beside me;	369
Isa	47:1	there is **n.** throne, O daughter of the	369
Isa	47:1	thou shalt **n.** more be called tender	3808
Isa	47:5	thou shalt **n.** more be called, The	3808
Isa	47:6	thou didst shew them **n.** mercy;	3808
Isa	48:22	There is **n.** peace, saith the Lord,	369
Isa	50:2	when I came, was there **n.** man?	369
Isa	50:2	or have I **n.** power to deliver? behold,	369
Isa	50:2	stinketh, because there is **n.** water,	369
Isa	50:10	in darkness, and hath **n.** light? let	369
Isa	51:22	thou shalt **n.** more drink it again:	3808
Isa	52:1	there shall **n.** more come unto thee	3808
Isa	52:11	thence, touch **n.** unclean thing;	408
Isa	53:2	he hath **n.** form nor comeliness;	3808
Isa	53:2	**n.** beauty that we should desire him.	3808
Isa	53:9	because he had done **n.** violence,	3808
Isa	54:9	waters of Noah should **n.** more go over	
Isa	54:17	**N.** weapon that is formed against	3808
Isa	55:1	and he that hath **n.** money; come	369
Isa	57:1	and **n.** man layeth it to heart: and	369
Isa	57:10	saidst thou not, There is **n.** hope:	
Isa	57:21	There is **n.** peace, saith my God, to	369
Isa	58:3	and thou takest **n.** knowledge?	3808
Isa	59:8	is **n.** judgment in their goings:	369
Isa	59:10	and we grope as if we had **n.** eyes:	369
Isa	59:15	him that there was **n.** judgment.	369
Isa	59:16	And he saw that there was **n.** man,	369
Isa	59:16	that there was **n.** intercessor:	369
Isa	60:15	so that **n.** man went through thee,	369
Isa	60:18	Violence shall **n.** more be heard in	3808
Isa	60:19	The sun shall be **n.** more thy light	3808
Isa	60:20	Thy sun shall **n.** more go down;	3808
Isa	62:4	shalt **n.** more be termed Forsaken;	3808
Isa	62:7	give him **n.** rest, till he establish,	408
Isa	62:8	**n.** more give thy corn to be meat	518
Isa	65:19	of weeping shall be **n.** more heard	3808
Isa	65:20	shall be **n.** more thence an infant	3808
Jer	2:6	a land that **n.** man passed through,	3808
Jer	2:6	and where **n.** man dwelt?	3808
Jer	2:11	their gods, which are yet **n.** gods?	3808
Jer	2:13	cisterns, that can hold **n.** water.	3808
Jer	2:25	but thou saidst, There is **n.** hope:	
Jer	2:25	**n.**; for I have loved strangers, and	3808
Jer	2:30	they received **n.** correction: your	3808
Jer	2:31	we will come **n.** more unto thee?	3808
Jer	3:3	and there hath been **n.** latter rain;	3808
Jer	3:16	the Lord, they shall say **n.** more,	3808
Jer	4:22	to do good they have **n.** knowledge.	3808
Jer	4:23	the heavens, and they had **n.** light.	369
Jer	4:25	and, lo, there was **n.** man, and all	369
Jer	5:7	sworn by them that are **n.** gods:	3808
Jer	6:10	reproach; they have **n.** delight in it.	3808
Jer	6:14	peace; when there is **n.** peace.	369
Jer	6:23	they are cruel, and have **n.** mercy;	3808
Jer	7:32	it shall **n.** more be called Tophet,	3808
Jer	7:32	in Tophet, till there be **n.** place.	369
Jer	8:6	**n.** man repented...of his wickedness,	369
Jer	8:11	Peace, peace; when there is **n.** peace.	369
Jer	8:13	there shall be **n.** grapes on the vine,	369
Jer	8:15	looked for peace, but **n.** good came;	369
Jer	8:22	Is there **n.** balm in Gilead? is there	369
Jer	8:22	is there **n.** physician there? why	369
Jer	10:14	and there is **n.** breath in them.	3808
Jer	11:19	name may be **n.** more remembered:	3808
Jer	11:23	there shall be **n.** remnant of them:	3808
Jer	12:11	because **n.** man layeth it to heart.	369
Jer	12:12	the land: **n.** flesh shall have peace.	369
Jer	14:3	to the pits, and found **n.** water;	3808
Jer	14:4	for there was **n.** rain in the earth,	3808
Jer	14:5	it, because there was **n.** grass.	3808
Jer	14:6	did fail, because there was **n.** grass.	369
Jer	14:19	us, and there is **n.** healing for us?	369
Jer	14:19	for peace, and there is **n.** good; and	369
Jer	16:14	that it shall **n.** more be said, The	3808
Jer	16:19	things, wherein there is **n.** profit.	369
Jer	16:20	himself, and they are **n.** gods?	3808
Jer	17:21	bear **n.** burden on the sabbath day,	408
Jer	17:24	in **n.** burden through the gates of	1115
Jer	17:24	sabbath day, to do **n.** work therein;	1115
Jer	18:12	There is **n.** hope: but we will walk	
Jer	19:6	shall **n.** more be called Tophet,	3808
Jer	19:11	till there be **n.** place to bury.	369
Jer	22:3	do **n.** wrong, do **n.** violence to the	408
Jer	22:10	for he shall return **n.** more, nor	3808
Jer	22:12	and shall see this land **n.** more.	3808
Jer	22:28	he a vessel wherein is **n.** pleasure?	363
Jer	22:30	**n.** man of his seed shall prosper,	3808
Jer	23:4	and they shall fear **n.** more, nor be	3808
Jer	23:7	shall **n.** more say, The Lord liveth,	3808
Jer	23:17	heart, **N.** evil shall come upon you.	3808
Jer	23:36	the Lord shall ye mention **n.** more;	3808
Jer	25:6	hands; and I will do you **n.** hurt.	3808
Jer	25:27	and spue, and fall, and rise **n.** more,	3808
Jer	25:35	shepherds shall have **n.** way to flee,	4480
Jer	30:8	and strangers shall **n.** more serve	3808
Jer	30:13	up: thou hast **n.** healing medicines.	369
Jer	30:17	Zion, whom **n.** man seeketh after.	369
Jer	31:29	those days they shall say **n.** more,	3808
Jer	31:34	shall teach **n.** more every man his	3808
Jer	31:34	I will remember their sin **n.** more.	3808
Jer	33:24	be **n.** more a nation before them.	
Jer	35:6	they said, W will drink **n.** wine:	3808
Jer	35:6	Ye shall drink **n.** wine, neither ye	3808
Jer	35:8	us, to drink **n.** wine all our days,	1115
Jer	36:19	and let **n.** man know where ye be.	408
Jer	38:6	the dungeon there was **n.** water,	369
Jer	38:9	there is **n.** more bread in the city.	369
Jer	38:24	Let **n.** man know of these words,	408
Jer	39:12	well to him, and do him **n.** harm;	408
Jer	40:15	and **n.** man shall know it:	3808
Jer	41:4	Gedaliah, and **n.** man knew it,	3808
Jer	42:14	Saying, **N.**, but we will go into the	3808
Jer	42:14	where we shall see **n.** war, nor hear	3808
Jer	42:18	and ye shall see this place **n.** more.	3808
Jer	44:2	and **n.** man dwelleth therein,	369
Jer	44:5	burn **n.** incense unto other gods.	1115
Jer	44:17	and were well, and saw **n.** evil.	3808
Jer	44:22	that the Lord could **n.** longer bear	3808
Jer	44:26	my name shall **n.** more be named	518
Jer	45:3	in my sighing, and I find **n.** rest.	3808
Jer	48:2	shall be **n.** more praise of Moab:	369
Jer	48:8	city, and **n.** city shall escape:	3808
Jer	48:33	their shouting shall be **n.** shouting.	3808
Jer	48:38	like a vessel wherein is **n.** pleasure.	369
Jer	49:1	Hath Israel **n.** sons? hath he **n.** heir?	369
Jer	49:7	Is wisdom **n.** more in Teman? is	369
Jer	49:18	**n.** man shall abide there, neither	3808
Jer	49:33	there shall **n.** man abide there, nor	3808
Jer	49:36	there shall be **n.** nation whither the	3808
Jer	50:14	shoot at her, spare **n.** arrows: for	408
Jer	50:39	be **n.** more inhabited for ever;	3808
Jer	50:40	so shall **n.** man abide there, neither	3808
Jer	51:17	and there is **n.** breath in them.	3808
Jer	51:43	a land wherein **n.** man dwelleth,	3808
Jer	52:6	there was **n.** bread for the people	3808
La	1:3	the heathen, she findeth **n.** rest:	3808
La	1:6	like harts that find **n.** pasture, and	3808
La	1:9	wonderfully: she had **n.** comforter.	369
La	2:9	the Gentiles: the law is **n.** more;	369
La	2:9	also find **n.** vision from the Lord,	3808
La	2:18	give thyself **n.** rest: let not the	408
La	4:4	and **n.** man breaketh it unto them.	369
La	4:6	and **n.** hands stayed on her.	3808
La	4:15	They shall **n.** more sojourn there.	3808
La	4:16	he will **n.** more regard them: they	3808
La	4:22	will **n.** more carry thee away into	3808
La	5:5	we labour, and have **n.** rest.	3808
Eze	12:23	shall **n.** more use it as a proverb in	3808
Eze	12:24	shall be **n.** more any vain vision	3808
Eze	12:25	it shall be **n.** more prolonged: for	3808

Eze 13:10 and there was n. peace; and one........ 369
Eze 13:15 The wall is n. more, neither they......... 369
Eze 13:16 and there is n. peace, saith the Lord.... 369
Eze 13:21 shall be n. more in your hand to........ 3808
Eze 13:23 ye shall see n. more vanity, nor 3808
Eze 14:11 of Israel may go n. more astray......... 3808
Eze 14:15 n. man may pass through because...... 1097
Eze 15:5 whole, it was meet for n. work: 3808
Eze 16:34 and n. reward is given unto thee:....... 3808
Eze 16:41 also shalt give n. hire any more......... 3808
Eze 16:42 quiet, and will be n. more angry. 3808
Eze 18:32 I have n. pleasure in the death of....... 3808
Eze 19:9 voice should n. more be heard upon ... 3808
Eze 19:14 hath n. strong rod to be a sceptre....... 3808
Eze 20:39 pollute ye my holy name n. more....... 3808
Eze 21:13 it shall be n. more, saith the Lord...... 3808
Eze 21:27 it shall be n. more, until he come....... 3808
Eze 21:32 thou shalt be n. more remembered:..... 3808
Eze 22:26 put n. difference between the holy 3808
Eze 24:6 by piece; let n. lot fall upon it. 3808
Eze 24:17 make n. mourning for the dead, ... 3808
Eze 24:27 speak, and shall be n. more dumb: 3808
Eze 26:13 thy harps shall be n. more heard........ 3808
Eze 26:14 thou shalt be built n. more: for I......... 3808
Eze 26:21 terror, and thou shalt be n. more: 369
Eze 28:3 there is n. secret...they can hide 3808
Eze 28:9 thou shalt be a man, and n. God, ... 3808
Eze 28:24 shall be n. more a pricking brier 3808
Eze 29:11 N. foot of man shall pass through........ 3808
Eze 29:15 shall n. more rule over the nations. 3808
Eze 29:16 shall be n. more the confidence of...... 3808
Eze 29:18 yet had he n. wages, nor his army, ... 3808
Eze 30:13 there shall be n. more a prince of 3808
Eze 33:11 I have n. pleasure in the death of........ 518
Eze 33:22 opened, and I was n. more dumb. 3808
Eze 34:5 because there is n. shepherd: and...... 1097
Eze 34:8 because there was n. shepherd, ... 369
Eze 34:22 they shall n. more be a prey; and 3808
Eze 34:28 they shall n. more be a prey to the..... 3808
Eze 34:29 shall be n. more consumed with......... 3808
Eze 36:12 shalt n. more henceforth bereave 3808
Eze 36:14 thou shalt devour men n. more,......... 3808
Eze 36:29 it, and lay n. famine upon you. 3808
Eze 36:30 receive n. more reproach of famine 3808
Eze 37:8 but there was n. breath in them.......... 369
Eze 37:22 they shall be n. more two nations, ... 3808
Eze 39:10 shall take n. wood out of the field,..... 3808
Eze 43:7 the house of Israel n. more defile,....... 3808
Eze 44:2 n. man shall enter in by it; because.... 3808
Eze 44:9 N. stranger, uncircumcised in........... 3808
Eze 44:17 and n. wool shall come upon them,..... 3808
Eze 44:25 come at n. dead person to defile 3808
Eze 44:25 sister that hath had n. husband,......... 3808
Eze 44:28 give them n. possession in Israel: 3808
Eze 45:8 shall n. more oppress my people;....... 3808
Da 1:4 Children in whom was n. blemish,.......... 369
Da 2:10 therefore there is n. king, ... 3606,3809
Da 2:35 n. place was found for them:...... 3606,3809
Da 3:25 of the fire, and they have n. hurt;...... 3809
Da 3:27 whose bodies the fire had n. power, ... 3809
Da 3:29 is n. other God that can deliver......... 3809
Da 4:9 and n. secret troubleth thee,...... 3606,3809
Da 6:2 the king should have n. damage......... 3809
Da 6:15 is, That n. decree nor statute 3606,3809
Da 6:22 O king, have I done n. hurt. 3809
Da 6:23 n. manner of hurt was found...... 3606,3809
Da 8:4 n. beasts might stand before him, ... 3808
Da 8:7 was n. power in the ram to stand 3808
Da 10:3 I ate n. pleasant bread, neither.......... 3808
Da 10:8 there remained n. strength in me:...... 3808
Da 10:8 corruption,...I retained n. strength. 3808
Da 10:16 and I have retained n. strength.......... 3808
Da 10:17 there remained n. strength in me,....... 3808
Ho 1:6 I will n. more have mercy upon the.... 3808
Ho 2:16 and shalt call me n. more Baali.......... 3808
Ho 2:17 shall n. more be remembered by........ 3808
Ho 4:1 there is n. truth, nor mercy, nor......... 369
Ho 4:4 Yet let n. man strive, nor reprove....... 408
Ho 4:6 that thou shalt be n. priest to me:...........
Ho 8:7 the whirlwind: it hath n. stalk: 369
Ho 8:7 the bud shall yield n. meal: if so be...... 369
Ho 8:8 as a vessel wherein is n. pleasure........ 369
Ho 9:15 I will love them n. more; all their......... 3808
Ho 9:16 dried up, they shall bear n. fruit: 1077
Ho 10:3 We have n. king, because we feared.... 369
Ho 13:4 thou shalt know n. god but me:......... 3808
Ho 13:4 for there is n. saviour beside me......... 369

Joe 1:18 because they have n. pasture; yea, ... 369
Joe 2:19 will n. more make you a reproach........ 3808
Joe 3:17 shall n. strangers pass through her..... 3808
Am 3:4 in the forest, when he hath n. prey? 369
Am 3:5 the earth, where n. gin is for him:....... 369
Am 5:2 is fallen; she shall n. more rise:......... 3808
Am 5:20 very dark, and n. brightness in it?....... 3808
Am 6:10 and he shall say, N.. Then shall 657
Am 7:14 I was n. A prophet, neither was I a.... 3808
Am 9:15 they shall n. more be pulled up out 3808
Mic 3:7 lips; for there is n. answer of God....... 369
Mic 4:9 is there n. king in thee? is thy........... 369
Mic 5:12 shalt have n. more soothsayers:......... 3808
Mic 5:13 shalt n. more worship the work of....... 3808
Mic 7:1 there is n. cluster to eat: my soul 369
Na 1:12 thee, I will afflict thee n. more. 3808
Na 1:14 that n. more of thy name be sown: 3808
Na 1:15 wicked shall n. more pass through....... 3808
Na 2:13 messengers shall n. more be heard,.... 3808
Na 3:18 and n. man gathereth them................. 369
Na 3:19 There is n. healing of thy bruise;......... 369
Hab 1:14 that have n. ruler over them?........... 3808
Hab 2:19 is n. breath at all in the midst of it. 369
Hab 3:17 fields shall yield n. meat; and the....... 3808
Hab 3:17 there shall be n. herd in the stalls:..... 3808
Zep 2:5 that there shall be n. inhabitant. 369
Zep 3:5 but the unjust knoweth n. shame. 3808
Zep 3:6 so that there is n. man, that there..... 1097
Zep 3:11 thou shalt n. more be haughty........... 3808
Hag 2:12 the priests answered and said, N.. 3808
Zec 1:21 so that n. man did lift up his head: 3808
Zec 4:5, 13 these be? And I said, N., my lord...3808
Zec 7:14 that n. man passed through nor ....
Zec 8:10 there was n. hire for man, nor any....... 3808
Zec 8:17 neighbour; and love n. false oath:....... 3808
Zec 9:8 oppressor shall pass through............. 3808
Zec 9:11 out of the pit wherein is n. water......... 3808
Zec 10:2 because there was n. shepherd. 639
Zec 11:6 I will n. more pity the inhabitants....... 3808
Zec 13:2 they shall n. more be remembered: 3808
Zec 13:5 he shall say, I am n. prophet, I am 3808
Zec 14:11 shall be n. more utter destruction; 3808
Zec 14:17 even upon them shall be n. rain......... 3808
Zec 14:18 and come not, that have n. rain; 3808
Zec 14:21 shall be n. more the Canaanite in....... 3808
Mal 1:10 I have n. pleasure in you, saith.......... 639
Mt 5:18 **shall in n. wise pass from the law,** .3364
Mt 5:20 **in n. case enter into the kingdom**.. 3364
Mt 5:26 **shalt by n. means come out thence,**3364
Mt 6:1 **otherwise ye have n. reward of**...... 3756
Mt 6:24 **N. man can serve two masters:**...... 3762
Mt 6:25 **Take n. thought for your life,** 3361
Mt 6:31 **Therefore take n. thought, saying,** .3361
Mt 6:34 **Take...n. thought for the morrow:**..3361
Mt 8:4 unto him, **See thou tell n. man;** 3367
Mt 8:10 **so great faith, n., not in Israel**....... 3761
Mt 8:28 **n.** man might pass by that way.......... 3361
Mt 9:16 **N. man putteth a piece of new** 3762
Mt 9:30 saying, **See that n. man know it**..... 3762
Mt 9:36 as sheep having **n.** shepherd. 3361
Mt 10:19 **n. thought how or what ye shall** ... 3361
Mt 10:42 **shall in n. wise lose his reward**....... 3364
Mt 11:27 **n. man knoweth the Son, but the** .. 3762
Mt 12:39 **there shall n. sign be given to it,**... 3756
Mt 13:5 **they had n. deepness of earth:**....... 3361
Mt 13:6 **they had n. root, they withered** 3361
Mt 16:4 **there shall n. sign be given unto it,**3756
Mt 16:7 is because we have taken **n.** bread. 3756
Mt 16:8 **because ye have brought n. bread?** .3756
Mt 16:20 tell **n.** man that he was Jesus the....... 3762
Mt 17:8 they saw **n.** man, save Jesus only. 3762
Mt 17:9 **Tell the vision to n. man, until the**.3762
Mt 19:6 **are n. more twain, but one flesh**... 3765
Mt 19:18 **Thou shalt do n. murder, Thou** 3756
Mt 20:7 **Because n. man hath hired us**....... 3762
Mt 20:13 **said, Friend, I do thee n. wrong:**... 3756
Mt 21:19 unto it, **Let n. fruit grow on thee** ... 3371
Mt 22:23 say that there is **n.** resurrection,......... 3361
Mt 22:24 If a man die, having **n.** children,.......... 3361
Mt 22:25 having **n.** issue, left his wife unto....... 3361
Mt 22:46 **n.** man was able to answer him a....... 3762
Mt 23:9 **And call n. man your father upon** ..3361
Mt 24:4 **Take heed that n. man deceive** 3361
Mt 24:21 **to this time, n., nor ever shall be**.. 3361
Mt 24:22 **there should n. flesh be saved:** 3756,3956
Mt 24:36 **day and hour knoweth n. man,** 3762
Mt 24:36 **n., not the angels of heaven, but**... 3761

Mt 25:3 **lamps, and took n. oil with them:** . 3756
Mt 25:42 **hungred, and ye gave me n. meat:**. 3756
Mt 25:42 **thirsty, and ye gave me n. drink:** .. 3756
Mt 26:55 **temple, and ye laid n. hold on me**. 3756
Mk 1:45 could **n.** more openly enter into......... 3371
Mk 2:2 was **n.** room to receive them, ... 3370
Mk 2:2 **n.**, not so much as about the door:...........
Mk 2:17 **have n. need of the physician, but**. 3756
Mk 2:21 **N. man also seweth a piece of**...... 3762
Mk 2:22 **n. man putteth new wine into old**.. 3762
Mk 3:27 **N. man can enter into a strong**..... 3762
Mk 4:5 **because it had n. depth of earth:**... 3361
Mk 4:6 **because it had n. root, it withered**. 3361
Mk 4:7 **choked it, and it yielded n. fruit**.... 3756
Mk 4:17 **have n. root in themselves, and so**. 3756
Mk 4:40 **how is it that ye have n. faith?** 3756
Mk 5:3 and **n.** man could bind him,............... 3762
Mk 5:3 bind him, **n.**, not with chains,............ 3777
Mk 5:37 he suffered **n.** man to follow him,........ 3762
Mk 5:43 that **n.** man should know it; and......... 3367
Mk 6:5 he could there do **n.** mighty work, ... 3762
Mk 6:8 **n.** script, **n.** bread, **n.** money in 3361
Mk 6:31 had **n.** leisure so much as to eat. 3761
Mk 7:12 **suffer him n. more to do ought for**.3765
Mk 7:24 and would have **n.** man know it: 3762
Mk 7:36 them that they should tell **n.** man:...... 3367
Mk 8:12 **shall n. sign be given unto this** 1487
Mk 8:16 It is because we have **n.** bread.......... 3756
Mk 8:17 **ye, because ye have n. bread?**......... 3756
Mk 8:30 they should tell **n.** man of him. 3367
Mk 9:3 **n.** fuller on earth can white them. 3756
Mk 9:8 saw **n.** man any more, save Jesus...... 3762
Mk 9:9 tell **n.** man what things they had......... 3367
Mk 9:25 **him, and enter n. more into him**.. 3371
Mk 9:39 **n. man which shall do a miracle** ... 3762
Mk 10:8 **are n. more twain, but one flesh**.. 3765
Mk 10:29 **is n. man that hath left house, or** ..3762
Mk 11:14 **N. man eat fruit of thee hereafter** .3367
Mk 12:14 art true, and carest for **n.** man: 3762
Mk 12:18 which say there is **n.** resurrection; 3361
Mk 12:19 behind him, and leave **n.** children, ... 3361
Mk 12:20 took a wife, and dying left **n.** seed. 3756
Mk 12:22 the seven had her, and left **n.** seed: ... 3756
Mk 12:34 **n.** man after that durst ask him 3762
Mk 13:11 **take n. thought beforehand what** .. 3361
Mk 13:20 **days, n. flesh should be saved:** 3756,3956
Mk 13:32 **and that hour knoweth n. man,**..... 3762
Mk 13:32 **n., not the angels which are in**............
Mk 14:25 **I will drink n. more of the fruit**.... 3765
Lu 1:7 they had **n.** child, because that.......... 3756
Lu 1:33 his kingdom there shall be **n.** end....... 3756
Lu 2:7 was **n.** room for them in the inn. 3756
Lu 3:13 Exact **n.** more than that which is 3367
Lu 3:14 Do violence to **n.** man, neither 3367
Lu 4:24 **N. prophet is accepted in his own**.. 3762
Lu 5:14 **he charged him to tell n. man: but** .3367
Lu 5:36 **N. man putteth a piece of a new** ... 3762
Lu 5:37 **n. man putteth new wine into old**.. 3762
Lu 5:39 **N. man also having drunk old wine**3762
Lu 7:9 so great faith, **n.**, not in Israel.......... 3761
Lu 7:44 **gavest me n. water for my feet:**..... 3756
Lu 7:45 **Thou gavest me n. kiss: but this**.... 3756
Lu 8:13 **and these have n. root, which for**.. 3756
Lu 8:14 **and bring n. fruit to perfection**. 3756
Lu 8:16 **N. man, when he hath lighted a**.... 3762
Lu 8:27 and ware **n.** clothes, neither abode..... 3756
Lu 8:51 he suffered **n.** man to go in, save....... 3762
Lu 8:56 should tell **n.** man what was done........ 3367
Lu 9:13 We have **n.** more but five loaves........ 3756
Lu 9:21 them to tell **n.** man that thing;........... 3367
Lu 9:36 and told **n.** man in those days any....... 3762
Lu 9:62 **N. man, having put his hand to**..... 3762
Lu 10:4 **and salute n. man by the way**....... 3367
Lu 10:22 **n. man knoweth who the Son is,** ... 3762
Lu 11:20 **n. doubt the kingdom of God is** 686
Lu 11:29 **and there shall n. sign be given it,** .3756
Lu 11:33 **N. man, when he hath lighted a**.... 3762
Lu 11:36 **of light, having n. part dark,** ..3365,5100
Lu 12:4 **have n. more that they can**.... 3365,5100
Lu 12:11 **ye n. thought how or what thing**... 3361
Lu 12:17 **I have n. room where to bestow** 3756
Lu 12:22 **Take n. thought for your life,** 3361
Lu 12:33 **not, where n. thief approacheth,** ... 3756
Lu 13:11 and could in **n.** wise lift up herself...... 3361
Lu 15:7 **persons, which need n. repentance**. 3756
Lu 15:16 **eat: and n. man gave unto him**. 3762
Lu 15:19, 21 **am n. more worthy to be called** .3765

Lu 16:2 **thou mayest be n. longer steward**... 3756
Lu 16:13 **N. servant can serve two masters:** . 3762
Lu 18:17 **child shall in n. wise enter therein.** 3364
Lu 18:29 **is n. man that hath left house, or** .. 3762
Lu 20:22 to give tribute unto Caesar, or n.? ... 3756
Lu 20:31 and they left n. children, and died. ... 3756
Lu 22:36 **and he that hath n. sword, let him.** 3361
Lu 22:53 **forth n. hands against me:**... 3756
Lu 23:4 people, I find n. fault in this man. ... 3762
Lu 23:14 have found n. fault in this man... 3762
Lu 23:15 N., nor yet Herod: for I sent... 235
Lu 23:22 found n. cause of death in him:... 3762
Joh 1:18 N. man hath seen God at any time; ... 3762
Joh 1:21 prophet? And he answered, N.. ... 3756
Joh 1:47 **Israelite...in whom is n. guile!** ... 3756
Joh 2:3 saith unto him, They have n. wine. ... 3756
Joh 3:2 for n. man can do these miracles ... 3762
Joh 3:13 **n. man hath ascended up to**... 3762
Joh 3:32 n. man receiveth his testimony. ... 3762
Joh 4:9 n. dealings with the Samaritans... 3756
Joh 4:17 and said, I have n. husband... 3756
Joh 4:17 **hast well said, I have n. husband:** .. 3756
Joh 4:27 n. man said, What seekest thou?... 3762
Joh 4:38 **whereon ye bestowed n. labour:**... 3756
Joh 4:44 hath n. honour in his own country. ... 3756
Joh 5:7 I have n. man, when the water is ... 3756
Joh 5:14 **sin n. more, lest a worse thing**... 3371
Joh 5:22 **For the Father judgeth n. man,** ... 3762
Joh 6:37 **to me I will in n. wise cast out.** ... 3364
Joh 6:44 **N. man can come to me, except** ... 3762
Joh 6:53 **his blood, ye have n. life in you.** ... 3756
Joh 6:65 **that n. man can come unto me,** ... 3762
Joh 6:66 and walked n. more with him. ... 3765
Joh 7:4 n. man...doeth any thing in secret, ... 3762
Joh 7:13 n. man spake openly of him for fear... 3762
Joh 7:18 **and n. unrighteousness is in him**... 3756
Joh 7:27 n. man knoweth whence he is. ... 3762
Joh 7:30 but n. man laid hands on him,... 3762
Joh 7:44 but n. man laid hands on him... 3762
Joh 7:52 out of Galilee ariseth n. prophet... 3756
Joh 8:10 **hath n. man condemned thee?**... 3762
Joh 8:11 She said, N. man, Lord. And ... 3762
Joh 8:11 **condemn thee: go, and sin n. more.** 3371
Joh 8:15 **after the flesh; I judge n. man.**... 3762
Joh 8:20 and n. man laid hands on him; for ... 3762
Joh 8:37 **my word hath n. place in you.** ... 3756
Joh 8:44 **because there is n. truth in him.**... 3756
Joh 9:4 **cometh, when n. man can work.** ... 3762
Joh 9:25 Whether he be a sinner or n., I know...
Joh 9:41 **were blind, ye should have n. sin:** . 3756
Joh 10:18 **N. man taketh it from me, but I** ... 3762
Joh 10:29 **n. man is able to pluck them out** .. 3762
Joh 10:41 and said, John did n. miracle: ... 3762
Joh 11:10 **because there is n. light in him.**... 3756
Joh 11:54 walked n. more openly among ... 3765
Joh 13:8 **not, thou hast n. part with me.**... 3756
Joh 13:28 n. man at the table knew for what... 3762
Joh 14:6 **n. man cometh unto the Father,** .. 3762
Joh 14:19 **and the world seeth me n. more;** ... 3765
Joh 15:4 **n. more can ye, except ye abide** ... 3761
Joh 15:13 **Greater love hath n. man than**... 3762
Joh 15:22 **they have n. cloke for their sin.**... 3756
Joh 16:10 **Father, and ye see me n. more;**... 3765
Joh 16:21 **remembereth n. more the anguish,** . 3765
Joh 16:22 **your joy n. man taketh from you.** .. 3762
Joh 16:25 **shall n. more speak...in proverbs,** .. 3765
Joh 16:29 plainly, and speakest n. proverb... 3762
Joh 17:11 **now I am n. more in the world.**... 3765
Joh 18:38 them, I find in him n. fault at all, ... 3762
Joh 19:4 know what I find n. fault in him. ... 3762
Joh 19:6 him: for I find n. fault in him... 3756
Joh 19:9 But Jesus gave him n. answer. ... 3756
Joh 19:11 **have n. power at all against me,** ... 3756
Joh 19:15 We have n. king but Caesar... 3756
Joh 21:5 **any meat? They answered him, N.**... 3756
Ac 1:20 and let n. man dwell therein:... 3361
Ac 4:17 spread n. further among the people, ... 3361
Ac 4:17 henceforth to n. man in this name. ... 3367
Ac 5:13 durst n. man join himself to them:... 3762
Ac 5:23 opened, we found n. man within. ... 3762
Ac 7:5 n., not so much as to set his foot on: ...
Ac 7:5 him, when as yet he had n. child. ... 3756
Ac 7:11 and our fathers found n. sustenance... 3756
Ac 8:39 that the eunuch saw him n. more:... 3765
Ac 9:7 hearing a voice, but seeing n. man. ... 3367
Ac 9:8 eyes were opened, he saw n. man: ... 3762
Ac 10:34 God is n. respecter of persons: ... 3756
Ac 12:18 n. small stir among the soldiers, ... 3756
Ac 13:28 found n. cause of death in him,... 3367
Ac 13:34 n. more to return to corruption, ... 3371
Ac 13:37 raised again, saw n. corruption. ... 3756
Ac 13:41 which ye shall in n. wise believe, ... 3364
Ac 15:2 Barnabas had n. small dissension... 3756
Ac 15:9 n. difference between us and them, ... 3762
Ac 15:24 we gave n. such commandment: ... 3756
Ac 15:28 you n. greater burden than these... 3367
Ac 16:28 Do thyself n. harm: for we are all... 3367
Ac 18:10 **n. man shall set on thee to hurt**... 3762
Ac 18:15 I will be n. judge of such matters... 3756
Ac 19:23 arose n. small stir about that way. ... 3756
Ac 19:24 n. small gain unto the craftsmen; ... 3756
Ac 19:26 saying that they be n. gods, which ... 3756
Ac 19:40 n. cause whereby we may give... 3367
Ac 20:25 ye all,...shall see my face n. more... 3765
Ac 20:33 I have coveted n. man's silver, or... 3762
Ac 20:38 they should see his face n. more... 3765
Ac 21:25 that they observe n. such thing, ... 3367
Ac 21:39 Cilicia, a citizen of n. mean city: ... 3756
Ac 23:8 say that there is n. resurrection,... 3361
Ac 23:9 We find n. evil in this man: but if... 3762
Ac 23:22 See thou tell n. man that thou hast... 3367
Ac 25:10 to the Jews have I done n. wrong, ... 3762
Ac 25:11 n. man may deliver me unto them. ... 3762
Ac 25:26 I have n. certain thing to write... 3756
Ac 27:20 and n. small tempest lay on us, ... 3756
Ac 27:22 shall be n. loss of any man's life ... 3762
Ac 28:2 people shewed us n. little kindness:... 3756
Ac 28:4 N. doubt this man is a murderer, ...
Ac 28:5 into the fire, and felt n. harm. ... 3762
Ac 28:6 and saw n. harm come to him, ... 3367
Ac 28:18 there was n. cause of death in me... 3762
Ac 28:31 confidence, n. man forbidding him. ... 209
Ro 2:11 is n. respect of person with God... 3756
Ro 3:9 are we better than they? N.,... 3756
Ro 3:9 we better than they?...in n. wise: ... 3843
Ro 3:10 There is none righteous, n., not one:... 3756
Ro 3:12 is none that doeth good, n., not one. ...
Ro 3:18 There is n. fear of God before ... 3756
Ro 3:20 n. flesh be justified in his ... 3756,3956
Ro 3:22 believe: for there is n. difference: ... 3756
Ro 4:15 wrath: for where n. law is, there ... 3756
Ro 4:15 law is, there is n. transgression... 3761
Ro 5:13 not imputed when there is n. law. ... 3361
Ro 6:9 from the dead dieth n. more; ... 3765
Ro 6:9 hath n. more dominion over him. ... 3765
Ro 7:3 so that she is n. adulteress, though... 3361
Ro 7:17 Now then it is n. more I that do it, ... 3765
Ro 7:18 my flesh) dwelleth n. good thing: ... 3756
Ro 7:20 it is n. more I that do it, but sin... 3765
Ro 8:1 therefore now n. condemnation... 3762
Ro 10:12 is n. difference between the Jew... 3756
Ro 10:19 jealousy by them that are n. people, ... 3756
Ro 11:6 grace, then is it n. more of works:... 3765
Ro 11:6 otherwise grace is n. more grace. ... 3765
Ro 11:6 of works, then is it n. more grace:... 3765
Ro 11:6 otherwise work is n. more work. ... 3765
Ro 12:17 Recompense to n. man evil for evil... 3367
Ro 13:1 For there is n. power but of God:... 3756
Ro 13:8 Owe n. man any thing, but to love... 3367
Ro 13:10 worketh n. ill to his neighbour:... 3756
Ro 14:7 and n. man dieth to himself... 3762
Ro 14:13 that n. man put a stumblingblock... 3361
Ro 15:23 now having n. more place in these ... 3371
1Co 1:7 So that ye come behind in n. gift; ... 3367
1Co 1:10 there be n. divisions among you;... 3361
1Co 1:29 n. flesh...glory in his presence. .. 3361,3956
1Co 2:11 things of God knoweth n. man... 3762
1Co 2:15 yet he himself is judged of n. man... 3762
1Co 3:11 other foundation can n. man lay ... 3762
1Co 3:18 Let n. man deceive himself. If... 3367
1Co 3:21 Therefore let n. man glory in men... 3367
1Co 4:6 that n. one of you be puffed up for... 3361
1Co 4:11 and have n. certain dwellingplace; ... 790
1Co 5:11 with such an one n. not to eat...
1Co 6:5 n., not one that shall be able to...
1Co 7:25 virgins I have n. commandment ... 3756
1Co 7:37 in his heart, having n. necessity, ... 3361
1Co 8:13 I will eat n. flesh while the world... 3364
1Co 9:10 For our sakes, n. doubt, this is ... 1063
1Co 10:13 hath n. temptation taken you but... 3756
1Co 10:24 Let n. man seek his own, but... 3367
1Co 10:25, 27 asking n. question for conscience ... 3367
1Co 11:16 we have n. such custom, neither... 3756
1Co 12:3 that n. man speaking by the Spirits... 3762
1Co 12:3 that n. man can say that Jesus is ... 3762
1Co 12:21 to the hand, I have n. need of thee: ... 3756
1Co 12:21 to the feet, I have n. need of you... 3756
1Co 12:24 For our comely parts have n. need:... 3756
1Co 12:25 should be n. schism in the body;... 3361
1Co 13:5 easily provoked, thinketh n. evil;... 3756
1Co 14:2 for n. man understandeth him;... 3762
1Co 14:28 But if there be n. interpreter, let... 3361
1Co 15:12 there is n. resurrection of the dead?... 3756
1Co 15:13 there be n. resurrection of the dead, .. 3756
1Co 16:2 there be n. gatherings when I come. .. 3361
1Co 16:11 Let n. man therefore despise him:... 3361
2Co 2:13 I had n. rest in my spirit, because... 3756
2Co 3:10 had n. glory in this respect, by... 3761
2Co 5:16 know we n. man after the flesh: ... 3762
2Co 5:16 henceforth know we him n. more... 3765
2Co 5:21 to be sin for us, who knew n. sin; ... 3361
2Co 6:3 Giving n. offence in any thing,... 3367
2Co 7:2 us; we have wronged n. man, ... 3762
2Co 7:2 we have corrupted n. man; we have... 3762
2Co 7:2 man, we have defrauded n. man. ... 3762
2Co 7:5 our flesh had n. rest, but we were... 3762
2Co 8:15 had gathered little had n. lack... 3756
2Co 8:20 that n. man should blame us in... 3361
2Co 11:9 I was chargeable to n. man: ... 3762
2Co 11:10 n. man shall stop me of this... 3756,3762
2Co 11:14 And n. marvel; for Satan himself... 3762
2Co 11:15 it is n. great thing if his ministers ... 3762
2Co 11:16 again, Let n. man think me a fool;... 3367
2Co 13:7 pray to God that ye do n. evil; ... 3361,3367
Ga 2:5 by subjection, n., not for an hour;...
Ga 2:6 were, it maketh n. matter to me:... 3762
Ga 2:6 God accepteth n. man's person:)... 3756
Ga 2:16 law shall n. flesh be justified. ... 3756,3956
Ga 3:11 that n. man is justified by the law ... 3762
Ga 3:15 n. man disannulleth, or addeth... 3762
Ga 3:18 the law, it is n. more of promise:... 3765
Ga 3:25 are n. longer under a schoolmaster... 3765
Ga 4:7 art n. more a servant, but a son;... 3765
Ga 4:8 them which by nature are n. gods. ... 3361
Ga 5:4 Christ is become of n. effect unto ... 2673
Ga 5:23 against such there is n. law... 3756
Ga 6:17 henceforth let n. man trouble me: ... 3367
Eph 2:12 having n. hope, and without God... 3361
Eph 2:19 therefore ye are n. more strangers... 3765
Eph 4:14 we henceforth be n. more children, ... 3371
Eph 4:28 Let him that stole steal n. more: ... 3371
Eph 4:29 Let n. corrupt communication... 3956,3361
Eph 5:5 ye know, that n. whoremonger,.. 3956,3756
Eph 5:6 Let n. man deceive you with vain... 3367
Eph 5:11 n. fellowship with the unfruitful... 3361
Eph 5:29 For n. man ever yet hated his own ... 3762
Php 2:7 But made himself of n. reputation,... 5013
Php 2:20 For I have n. man likeminded,... 3762
Php 3:3 have n. confidence in the flesh... 3756
Php 4:15 n. church communicated with me ... 3762
Col 2:16 Let n. man therefore judge you in... 3361
Col 2:18 n. man beguile you of your reward... 3367
Col 3:25 and there is n. respect of persons... 3756
1Th 3:1 when we could n. longer forbear, ... 3371
1Th 3:3 n. man should be moved by these... 3367
1Th 3:5 when I could n. longer forbear,... 3371
1Th 4:6 n. man go beyond and defraud his... 3361
1Th 4:13 even as others which have n. hope... 3361
1Th 5:1 have n. need that I write unto you. ... 3756
2Th 2:3 Let n. man deceive you by any... 3361
2Th 3:14 have n. company with him, that... 3361
1Ti 1:3 that they teach n. other doctrine,... 3361
1Ti 3:3 Not given to wine, n. striker, not ... 3361
1Ti 4:12 Let n. man despise thy youth; but... 3367
1Ti 5:22 Lay hands suddenly on n. man,... 3367
1Ti 5:23 Drink n. longer water, but use a... 3371
1Ti 6:16 which n. man can approach unto; ... 3762
1Ti 6:16 whom n. man hath seen, nor can see:... 3762
2Ti 2:4 N. man that warreth entangleth ... 3762
2Ti 2:14 strive not about words to n. profit,... 3762
2Ti 3:9 they shall proceed n. further: for ... 3756
2Ti 4:16 answer n. man stood with me, ... 3762
Tit 1:7 not given to wine, n. striker, not... 3361
Tit 2:8 having n. evil thing to say of you. ... 3367
Tit 2:15 authority. Let n. man despise thee. ... 3367
Tit 3:2 To speak evil of n. man, to be ... 3367
Tit 3:2 man, to be n. brawlers, but gentle,... 269
Heb 5:4 n. man taketh this honour unto... 3756
Heb 6:13 he could sware by n. greater, he ... 3762
Heb 7:13 of which n. man gave attendance... 3762
Heb 8:7 should n. place have been sought... 3756

Heb 8:12 will I remember **n.** more. *3364*
Heb 9:17 otherwise it is of **n.** strength at all *3361*
Heb 9:22 shedding of blood is **n.** remission *3756*
Heb 10:2 had **n.** more conscience of sins. *3367*
Heb 10:6 for sin thou hast had **n.** pleasure. *3756*
Heb 10:17 iniquities will I remember **n.** more. *3361*
Heb 10:18 there is **n.** more offering for sin. *3765*
Heb 10:26 remaineth **n.** more sacrifice for sins, *3765*
Heb 10:38 soul shall have **n.** pleasure in him. *3756*
Heb 12:11 Now **n.** chastening for the *3956,3756*
Heb 12:14 without which **n.** man shall see the *3762*
Heb 12:17 for he found **n.** place of repentance, *3756*
Heb 13:10 whereof they have **n.** right to eat *3756*
Heb 13:14 here we have **n.** continuing city, *3756*
Jas 1:11 the sun is **n.** sooner risen with a
Jas 1:13 Let **n.** man say when he is tempted, *3367*
Jas 1:17 with whom is **n.** variableness, *3756*
Jas 2:11 Now if thou commit **n.** adultery, *3756*
Jas 2:13 mercy, that hath shewed **n.** mercy; *3361*
Jas 3:8 the tongue can **n.** man tame; it is *3762*
Jas 3:12 so can **n.** fountain both yield salt *3762*
1Pe 2:22 Who did **n.** sin, neither was guile *3756*
1Pe 3:10 his lips that they speak **n.** guile: *3361*
1Pe 4:2 That he **n.** longer should live the *3371*
2Pe 1:20 **n.** prophecy of the scripture *3956,3756*
1Jo 1:5 and in him is **n.** darkness at all. *3756*
1Jo 1:8 If we say that we have **n.** sin, we *3756*
1Jo 2:7 I write **n.** new commandment unto *3756*
1Jo 2:19 **n.** doubt have continued with us:
1Jo 2:21 and that **n.** lie is of the truth. *3956,3756*
1Jo 2:27 and his truth, and is **n.** lie, and *3956,3756*
1Jo 3:5 our sins; and in him is **n.** sin. *3956,3756*
1Jo 3:7 children, let **n.** man deceive you: *3367*
1Jo 3:15 **n.** murderer hath eternal life *3956,3756*
1Jo 4:12 **N.** man hath seen God at any *3762*
1Jo 4:18 There is **n.** fear in love; but *3756*
3Jo 4 **n.** greater joy than to hear that my *3756*
Re 2:17 **which n. man knoweth saving he** *3762*
Re 3:7 **openeth, and n. man shutteth,** *3762*
Re 3:7 **and shutteth, and n. man openeth;** *3762*
Re 3:8 **open door, and n. man can shut it:** *3762*
Re 3:11 **hast, that n. man take thy crown** *3367*
Re 3:12 **and he shall go n. more out: and I** *3364*
Re 5:3 **n.** man in heaven, nor in earth, *3762*
Re 5:4 because **n.** man was found worthy *3762*
Re 7:9 which **n.** man could number, of all *3762*
Re 7:16 They shall hunger **n.** more, *3756*
Re 10:6 that there should be time **n.** longer: *3756*
Re 13:17 And that **n.** man might buy or sell, *3361*
Re 14:3 and **n.** man could learn that song *3762*
Re 14:5 in their mouth was found **n.** guile: *3756*
Re 14:11 they have **n.** rest day nor night, *3756*
Re 15:8 and **n.** man was able to enter into *3762*
Re 17:12 have received **n.** kingdom as yet; *3768*
Re 18:7 I sit a queen, and am **n.** widow, *3756*
Re 18:7 widow, and shall see **n.** sorrow. *3364*
Re 18:11 **n.** man buyeth their merchandise *3762*
Re 18:14 thou shalt find them **n.** more at all. *3364*
Re 18:21 and shall be found **n.** more at all. *3364*
Re 18:22 shall be heard **n.** more at all in thee; *3364*
Re 18:22 **n.** craftsman, of whatsoever *3956,3364*
Re 18:22 shall be heard **n.** more at all in thee: *3364*
Re 18:23 shall shine **n.** more at all in thee; *3364*
Re 18:23 bride shall be heard **n.** more at all *3364*
Re 19:12 name written, that **n.** man knew, *3762*
Re 20:3 should deceive the nations **n.** more, *3361*
Re 20:6 the second death hath **n.** power, *3756*
Re 20:11 there was found **n.** place for them. *3756*
Re 21:1 away; and there was **n.** more sea. *3756*
Re 21:4 and there shall be **n.** more death, *3756*
Re 21:22 And I saw **n.** temple therein: for *3756*
Re 21:23 And the city had **n.** need of the sun, *3756*
Re 21:25 for there shall be **n.** night there. *3756*
Re 21:27 there shall in **n.** wise enter into it *3364*
Re 22:3 And there shall be **n.** more curse: *3756*
Re 22:5 And there shall be **n.** night there; *3756*
Re 22:5 they need **n.** candle, neither light *3756*

NO (no) See also POPULOUS.
Jer 46:25 will punish the multitude of **N.**, 4996
Eze 30:14 and will execute judgments in **N.**, 4996
Eze 30:15 I will cut off the multitude of **N.** 4996
Eze 30:16 pain, and **N.** shall be rent asunder, 4996
Na 3:8 Art thou better than populous **N.**, 4996

NOADIAH (no-a-di'-ah)
Ezr 8:33 Jeshua, and **N.** the son of Binnui, 5129
Ne 6:14 and on the prophetess **N.**, and the 5129

NOAH (no'-ah) See also NOAH'S; NOE.
Ge 5:29 he called his name **N.**, saying, 5146
Ge 5:30 after he begat **N.** five hundred 5146
Ge 5:32 And **N.** was five hundred years old: 5146
Ge 5:32 **N.** began Shem, Ham, and Japheth. 5146
Ge 6:8 **N.** found grace in the eyes of the 5146
Ge 6:9 These are the generations of **N.**: 5146
Ge 6:9 **N.** was a just man and perfect in 5146
Ge 6:9 and **N.** walked with God. 5146
Ge 6:10 **N.** begat three sons, Shem, Ham, 5146
Ge 6:13 And God said unto **N.**, The end of 5146
Ge 6:22 Thus did **N.**; according to all that 5146
Ge 7:1 the Lord said unto **N.**, Come thou 5146
Ge 7:5 **N.** did according unto all that the 5146
Ge 7:6 **N.** was six hundred years old when 5146
Ge 7:7 **N.** went in, and his sons, and his 5146
Ge 7:9 two and two unto **N.** into the ark, 5146
Ge 7:9 female, as God had commanded **N.** 5146
Ge 7:13 In the selfsame day entered **N.**, 5146
Ge 7:13 Ham, and Japheth, the sons of **N.**, 5146
Ge 7:15 they went in unto **N.** into the ark, 5146
Ge 7:23 **N.** only remained alive, and they 5146
Ge 8:1 God remembered **N.**, and every 5146
Ge 8:6 **N.** opened the window of the ark 5146
Ge 8:11 so **N.** knew that the waters were 5146
Ge 8:13 **N.** removed the covering of the ark, 5146
Ge 8:15 And God spake unto **N.**, saying, 5146
Ge 8:18 **N.** went forth, and his sons, and 5146
Ge 8:20 **N.** builded an altar unto the Lord; 5146
Ge 9:1 God blessed **N.** and his sons, and 5146
Ge 9:8 God spake unto **N.**, and to his sons 5146
Ge 9:17 God said unto **N.**, This is the token 5146
Ge 9:18 the sons of **N.**, that went forth of 5146
Ge 9:19 These are the three sons of **N.**: and 5146
Ge 9:20 **N.** began to be an husbandman, 5146
Ge 9:24 **N.** awoke from his wine, and knew 5146
Ge 9:28 And **N.** lived after the flood three 5146
Ge 9:29 the days of **N.** were nine hundred 5146
Ge 10:1 the generations of the sons of **N.**, 5146
Ge 10:32 are the families of the sons of **N.**, 5146
Nu 26:33 Zelophehad were Mahlah, and **N.**, 5270
Nu 27:1 of his daughters; Mahlah, **N.**, 5270
Nu 36:11 **N.**, the daughters of Zelophehad, 5270
Jos 17:3 of his daughters, Mahlah, and **N.**, 5270
1Ch 1:4 **N.**, Shem, Ham, and Japheth. 5146
Isa 54:9 is as the waters of **N.** unto me: 5146
Isa 54:9 waters of **N.** should no more go 5146
Eze 14:14 three men, **N.**, Daniel, and Job, 5146
Eze 14:20 Though **N.**, Daniel, and Job, were 5146
Heb 11:7 By faith **N.**, being warned by God *3575*
1Pe 3:20 of God waited in the days of **N.**, *3575*
2Pe 2:5 but saved **N.** the eighth person, a *3575*

NOAH'S (no'-ahz)
Ge 7:11 the six hundredth year of **N.** life, 5146
Ge 7:13 and **N.** wife, and three wives of his 5146

NOB (nob)
1Sa 21:1 came David to **N.** to Abimelech 5011
1Sa 22:9 I saw the son of Jesse coming to **N.**, 5011
1Sa 22:11 house, the priests that were in **N.**: 5011
1Sa 22:19 And **N.**, the city of the priests, smote 5011
Ne 11:32 And at Anathoth, **N.**, Ananiah, 5011
Isa 10:32 yet shall he remain at **N.** that day: 5011

NOBAH (no'-bah) See also KENAH; NOPHAH.
Nu 32:42 And **N.** went and took Kenath, 5025
Nu 32:42 called it **N.**, after his own name. 5025
Jg 8:11 dwelt in tents on the east of **N.** 5025

NOBLE See also NOBLEMAN; NOBLES.
Ezr 4:10 whom the great and Asnapper 3358
Es 6:9 one of the king's most **n.** princes, 6579
Jer 2:21 Yet I had planted thee a **n.** vine, wholly
Ac 17:11 These were more **n.** than those in *2104*
Ac 24:3 and in all places, most **n.** Felix, *2908*
Ac 26:25 said, I am not mad, most **n.** Festus; *2908*
1Co 1:26 mighty, not many **n.**, are called; *2104*

NOBLEMAN
Lu 19:12 **A certain n. went into a far** *2104,444*
Joh 4:46 there was a certain **n.**, whose son *937*
Joh 4:49 The **n.** saith unto him, Sir, come *937*

NOBLES
Ex 24:11 the **n.** of the children of Israel. 678
Nu 21:18 the **n.** of the people digged it, by 5081
Jg 5:13 have dominion over the **n.** among 117
1Ki 21:8 to the **n.** that were in his city, 2715
1Ki 21:11 the elders and the **n.** who were the 2715
2Ch 23:20 captains of hundreds, and the **n.**, 117
Ne 2:16 nor to the priests, nor to the **n.**, 2715
Ne 3:5 but their **n.** put not their necks to 117
Ne 4:14 rose up, and said unto the **n.**, and 2715
Ne 4:19 And I said unto the **n.**, and to the 2715
Ne 5:7 I rebuked the **n.**, and the rulers, and 2715
Ne 6:17 the **n.** of Judah sent many letters 2715
Ne 7:5 heart to gather together the **n.**, 2715
Ne 10:29 clave to their brethren, their **n.**, 117
Ne 13:17 I contended with the **n.** of Judah, 2715
Es 1:3 **n.** and princes of the provinces, 6579
Job 29:10 The **n.** held their peace, and their 5057
Ps 83:11 Make their **n.** like Oreb, and like 5081
Ps 149:8 and their **n.** with fetters of iron; 3513
Pr 8:16 By me princes rule, and **n.**, even 5081
Ec 10:17 when thy king is the son of **n.**, and 2715
Isa 13:2 may go into the gates of the **n.** 5081
Isa 34:12 call the **n.** thereof to the kingdom, 2715
Isa 43:14 have brought down all their **n.**, 1281
Jer 14:3 their **n.** have sent their little ones to 117
Jer 27:20 the **n.** of Judah and Jerusalem; 2715
Jer 30:21 their **n.** shall be of themselves, 117
Jer 39:6 Babylon slew all the **n.** of Judah. 2715
Jon 3:7 the decree of the king and his **n.**, 1419
Na 3:18 thy **n.** shall dwell in the dust: thy 117

NOD (nod)
Ge 4:16 dwelt in the land of **N.**, on the 5113

NODAB (no'-dab)
1Ch 5:19 with Jetur, and Nephish, and **N.** 5114

NOE (no'-e) See also NOAH.
Mt 24:37 **as the days of N. were, so shall** *3575*
Mt 24:38 **day that N. entered into the ark,** *3575*
Lu 3:36 which was the son of **N.**, which *3575*
Lu 17:26 **as it was in the days of N., so shall** *3575*
Lu 17:27 **day that N. entered into the ark,** *3575*

NOGAH (no'-gah)
1Ch 3:7 And **N.**, and Nepheg, and Japhia, 5052
1Ch 14:6 And **N.**, and Nepheg, and Japhia, 5052

NOHAH (no'-hah)
1Ch 8:2 **N.** the fourth, and Rapha the fifth. 5119

NOISE See also NOISED.
Ex 20:18 and the **n.** of the trumpet, and the 6963
Ex 32:17 Joshua heard the **n.** of the people 6963
Ex 32:17 There is a **n.** of war in the camp. 6963
Ex 32:18 the **n.** of them that sing do I hear. 6963
Jos 6:10 nor make any **n.** with your voice, 8085
Jg 5:11 delivered from the **n.** of archers 6963
1Sa 4:6 heard the **n.** of the shout, they 6963
1Sa 4:6 meaneth the **n.** of this great shout 6963
1Sa 4:14 when Eli heard the **n.** of the crying, 6963
1Sa 4:14 What meaneth the **n.** of this tumult? 6963
1Sa 14:19 the **n.** that was in the host of the 1995
1Ki 1:41 **n.** of the city being in an uproar? 6963
1Ki 1:45 This is the **n.** that ye have heard. 6963
2Ki 7:6 the Syrians to hear a **n.** of chariots, 6963
2Ki 7:6 **n.** of horses, even the **n.** of a great 6963
2Ki 11:13 Athaliah heard the **n.** of the guard 6963
1Ch 15:28 making a **n.** with psalteries and 8085
2Ch 23:12 when Athaliah heard the **n.** of the 6963
Ezr 3:13 discern the **n.** of the shout of joy 6963
Ezr 3:13 the **n.** of the weeping of the people: 6963
Ezr 3:13 shout, and the **n.** was heard afar off. 6963
Job 36:29 or the **n.** of his tabernacle? 8663
Job 36:33 **n.** thereof sheweth concerning it, 7452
Job 37:2 Hear attentively the **n.** of his voice, 7267
Ps 33:3 song; play skilfully with a loud **n.** 8643
Ps 42:7 deep at the **n.** of thy waterspouts: 6963
Ps 55:2 in my complaint, and make a **n.**; 1949
Ps 59:6 they make a **n.** like a dog, and go 1993
Ps 59:14 let them make a **n.** like a dog, 1993
Ps 65:7 Which stilleth the **n.** of the seas, 7588
Ps 65:7 **n.** of their waves, and the tumult of 7588
Ps 66:1 Make a joyful **n.** unto God, all ye
Ps 81:1 make a joyful **n.** unto the God of
Ps 93:4 than the **n.** of many waters, yea, 6963
Ps 95:1 let us make a joyful **n.** to the rock of
Ps 95:2 a joyful **n.** unto him with psalms.
Ps 98:4 Make a joyful **n.** unto the Lord, all
Ps 98:4 make a loud **n.**, and rejoice, and 6476
Ps 98:6 make a joyful **n.** before the Lord, the
Ps 100:1 Make a joyful **n.** unto the Lord, all ye
Isa 9:5 of the warrior is with confused **n.**,

Isa 13:4 **n.** of a multitude in the mountains, 6963
Isa 13:4 tumultuous **n.** of the kingdoms of 6963
Isa 14:11 the grave, and the **n.** of thy viols: 1998
Isa 17:12 make a **n.** like the **n.** of the seas; 1993
Isa 24:8 the **n.** of them that rejoice endeth, 7588
Isa 24:18 who fleeth from the **n.** of the fear 6963
Isa 25:5 bring down the **n.** of strangers, as 7588
Isa 29:6 and with earthquake, and great **n.**, 6963
Isa 31:4 abase himself for the **n.** of them: 1995
Isa 33:3 At the **n.** of the tumult the people 6963
Isa 66:6 A voice of **n.** from the city, a voice 7588
Jer 4:19 my heart maketh a **n.** in me; I 1993
Jer 4:29 flee for the **n.** of the horsemen 6963
Jer 10:22 Behold, the **n.** of the bruit is come, 6963
Jer 11:16 with the **n.** of a great tumult he 6963
Jer 25:31 A **n.** shall come even to the ends of 7588
Jer 46:17 Pharaoh king of Egypt is but a **n.**; 7588
Jer 47:3 the **n.** of the stamping of the hoofs 6963
Jer 49:21 is moved at the **n.** of their fall; 6963
Jer 49:21 at the cry the **n.** thereof was heard 6963
Jer 50:46 At the **n.** of the taking of Babylon 6963
Jer 51:55 a **n.** of their voice is uttered: 7588
La 2:7 a **n.** in the house of the Lord, 6963
Eze 1:24 went, I heard the **n.** of their wings, 6963
Eze 1:24 like the **n.** of great waters, as the 6963
Eze 1:24 of speech, as the **n.** of an host: 6963
Eze 3:13 I heard also the **n.** of the wings of 6963
Eze 3:13 the **n.** of the wheels over against 6963
Eze 3:13 them, and a **n.** of a great rushing. 6963
Eze 19:7 thereof, by the **n.** of his roaring 6963
Eze 26:10 shake at the **n.** of the horsemen, 6963
Eze 26:13 cause the **n.** of thy songs to cease; 1995
Eze 37:7 as I prophesied, there was a **n.**, 6963
Eze 43:2 voice was like a **n.** of many waters: 6963
Joe 2:5 Like the **n.** of chariots on the tops of 6963
Joe 2:5 like the **n.** of a flame of fire that 6963
Am 5:23 away from me the **n.** of thy songs; 1995
Mic 2:12 make a great **n.** by reason of the 1949
Na 3:2 The **n.** of a whip, and the **n.** of the 6963
Zep 1:10 the **n.** of a cry from the fish gate, 6963
Zec 9:15 and make a **n.** as through wine; 6963
Mt 9:23 minstrels and...people make a **n.**, *2350*
2Pe 3:10 shall pass away with a great **n.**, *4500*
Re 6:1 heard, as it were the **n.** of thunder, *5456*

NOISED

Jos 6:27 his fame was **n.** throughout all the
Mk 2:1 it was **n.** that he was in the house. *191*
Lu 1:65 all these sayings were **n.** abroad *1255*
Ac 2:6 when this was **n.** abroad, the *1096,5408*

NOISOME

Ps 91:3 fowler, and from the **n.** pestilence. 1942
Eze 14:15 I cause **n.** beasts to pass through 7451
Eze 14:21 the **n.** beast, and the pestilence, 7451
Re 16:2 fell a **n.** and grievous sore upon the *2556*

NON (non) See also NUN.

1Ch 7:27 **N.** his son, Jehoshuah his son 5126

NONE See also NO and ONE.

Ge 23:6 **n.** of us shall withhold from 376,3808
Ge 28:17 is **n.** other but the house of God, 369
Ge 39:9 is **n.** greater in this house than I; 369
Ge 39:11 there was **n.** of the men of the house 369
Ge 41:8 there was **n.** that could interpret 369
Ge 41:15 and there is **n.** that can interpret it: 369
Ge 41:24 was **n.** that could declare it to me 369
Ge 41:39 there is **n.** so discreet and wise as 369
Ex 8:10 is **n.** like unto the Lord our God 369
Ex 9:14 there is **n.** like me in all the earth. 369
Ex 9:24 **n.** like it in all the land of Egypt 3808
Ex 11:6 such as there was **n.** like it, nor 3808
Ex 12:22 **n.** of you shall go out at the door of 3808
Ex 15:26 put **n.** of these diseases upon thee, 3808
Ex 16:26 the sabbath, in it there shall be **n.** 3808
Ex 16:27 for to gather, and they found **n.** 3808
Ex 23:15 **n.** shall appear before me empty:) 3808
Ex 34:20 **n.** shall appear before me empty. 3808
Le 18:6 **N.** of you shall approach to any 376,3808
Le 21:1 shall **n.** be defiled for the dead 3808
Le 22:30 leave **n.** of it until the morrow: 3808
Le 25:26 if the man have **n.** to redeem it, and 3808
Le 26:6 down, and **n.** shall make you afraid: 369
Le 26:17 ye shall flee when **n.** pursueth you. 369
Le 26:36 they shall fall when **n.** pursueth. 369
Le 26:37 before a sword, when **n.** pursueth: 369
Le 27:29 **N.** devoted, which shall be 3606,3808
Nu 7:9 the sons of Kohath he gave **n.**: 3808
Nu 9:12 leave **n.** of it unto the morning, nor 3808
Nu 21:35 until there was **n.** left him alive: 1115
Nu 30:8 she bound her soul, of **n.** effect: 6565
Nu 32:11 Surely **n.** of the men that came up
De 2:34 of every city, we left **n.** to remain: 3808
De 3:3 smote him until **n.** was left to him 1115
De 4:35 God; there is **n.** else beside him 369
De 4:39 the earth beneath: there is **n.** else. 369
De 5:7 shalt have **n.** other gods before me.
De 7:15 **n.** of the evil diseases of Egypt, 3808
De 22:27 cried, and there was **n.** to save her. 369
De 28:31 thou shalt have **n.** to rescue them 369
De 28:66 have **n.** assurance of thy life: 3808
De 32:36 and there is **n.** shut up, or left 657
De 33:26 is **n.** like unto the God of Jeshurun, 369
Jos 6:1 Israel: **n.** went out, and **n.** came in 369
Jos 8:22 let **n.** of them remain or escape 1115
Jos 9:23 **n.** of you be freed from being 3808
Jos 10:21 **n.** moved his tongue against any 3808
Jos 10:28 were therein; he let **n.** remain: 3808
Jos 10:30 therein; he let **n.** remain in it; 3808
Jos 10:33 he had left him **n.** remaining 1115
Jos 10:37 he left **n.** remaining, according 3808
Jos 10:39 therein; he left **n.** remaining: as 3808
Jos 10:40 he left **n.** remaining, but utterly 3808
Jos 11:8 they left them **n.** remaining, 1115
Jos 11:13 Israel burned **n.** of them, save 3808
Jos 11:22 **n.** of the Anakims left in the land 3808
Jos 13:14 of Levi he gave **n.** inheritance; 3808
Jos 14:3 gave **n.** inheritance among them 3808
Jg 19:28 let us be going. But **n.** answered 369
Jg 21:8 came **n.** to the camp from 3808,376
Jg 21:9 were **n.** of the inhabitants of 369,376
Ru 4:4 is **n.** to redeem it beside thee; and 369
1Sa 2:2 There is **n.** holy as the Lord: for 369
1Sa 2:2 for there is **n.** besides thee: neither 369
1Sa 3:19 **n.** of his words fall to the ground. 3808
1Sa 10:24 **n.** like him among all the people? 369
1Sa 14:24 **n.** of the people tasted any food 3808
1Sa 21:9 David said, There is **n.** like that; 369
1Sa 22:8 is **n.** that sheweth me that my son
1Sa 22:8 is **n.** of you that is sorry for me, or 369
2Sa 7:22 for there is **n.** like thee, neither is 369
2Sa 14:6 and there was **n.** to part them, but 369
2Sa 14:19 **n.** can turn to the right hand or to 376
2Sa 14:25 was **n.** to be so much praised 3808,376
2Sa 18:12 Beware that **n.** touch the young man
2Sa 22:42 looked, but there was **n.** to save; 369
1Ki 3:12 there was **n.** like thee before thee, 3808
1Ki 8:60 is God, and that there is **n.** else 369
1Ki 10:21 were of pure gold; **n.** were of silver: 369
1Ki 12:20 was **n.** that followed the house of 3808
1Ki 15:22 all Judah; **n.** was exempted: 369
1Ki 21:25 But there was **n.** like unto Ahab, 3808
2Ki 5:16 I will receive **n.**. And he urged him
2Ki 6:12 his servants said, **N.**, my lord, O 3808
2Ki 9:10 and there shall be **n.** to bury her. 369
2Ki 9:15 let **n.** go forth nor escape out of the 408
2Ki 10:11 until he left him **n.** remaining 1115
2Ki 10:19 his priests; let **n.** be wanting: 376,408
2Ki 10:23 be here with you **n.** of the servants
2Ki 10:25 and slay them; let **n.** come forth 408
2Ki 17:18 was **n.** left but the tribe of Judah 3808
2Ki 18:5 after him was **n.** like him among 3808
2Ki 24:14 **n.** remained, save the poorest sort 3808
1Ch 15:2 **N.** ought to carry the ark of God 3808
1Ch 17:20 O Lord, there is **n.** like thee, 369
1Ch 23:17 Eliezer had **n.** other sons; but 3808
1Ch 29:15 a shadow, and there is **n.** abiding 369
2Ch 1:12 such as **n.** of the kings have had 3808
2Ch 9:11 **n.** such seen before in the land of 3808
2Ch 9:20 were of pure gold: **n.** were of silver; 369
2Ch 10:16 we have **n.** inheritance in the son 3808
2Ch 16:1 let **n.** go out or come in to Asa 1115
2Ch 20:6 that **n.** is able to withstand thee? 369
2Ch 20:24 fallen to the earth, and **n.** escaped. 369
2Ch 23:6 let **n.** come into the house of the 408
2Ch 23:19 that **n.** which was unclean in any 3808
Ezr 8:15 found there **n.** of the sons of Levi 3808
Ne 4:23 **n.** of us put off our clothes, saving 369
Es 1:8 **n.** did compel: for so the king had 369
Es 4:2 **n.** might enter into the king's gate 369
Job 1:8 there is **n.** like him in the earth, 369
Job 2:3 there is **n.** like him in the earth, 369
Job 2:13 and **n.** spake a word unto him: for 369
Job 3:9 dark; let it look for light but have **n.**, 369
Job 10:7 there is **n.** that can deliver out of 369
Job 11:19 down, and **n.** shall make thee afraid; 369
Job 18:15 tabernacle, because it is **n.** of his: 1097
Job 20:21 There shall **n.** of his meat be left; 369
Job 29:12 and him that had **n.** to help him. 3808
Job 32:12 was **n.** of you that convinced Job, 369
Job 35:10 **n.** saith, Where is God my maker, 3808
Job 35:12 they cry, but **n.** giveth answer, 3808
Job 41:10 **N.** is so fierce that dare stir him up: 3808
Ps 7:2 pieces, while there is **n.** to deliver. 369
Ps 10:15 his wickedness till thou find **n.**. 1077
Ps 14:1 works, there is **n.** that doeth good. 369
Ps 14:3 is **n.** that doeth good, no, not one. 369
Ps 18:41 cried, but there was **n.** to save them: 369
Ps 22:11 is near; for there is **n.** to help 369
Ps 22:29 and **n.** can keep alive his own soul. 3808
Ps 25:3 **n.** that wait on thee be ashamed: 3808
Ps 33:10 devices of the people of **n.** effect. 5106
Ps 34:22 **n.** of them that trust in him shall 3808
Ps 37:31 heart; **n.** of his steps shall slide. 3808
Ps 49:7 **N.** of them can by any means 376,3808
Ps 50:22 pieces, and there be **n.** to deliver. 369
Ps 53:1 iniquity: there is **n.** that doeth good. 369
Ps 53:3 there is **n.** that doeth good, no, not 369
Ps 69:20 some to take pity, but there was **n.**; 369
Ps 69:20 and for comforters, but I found **n.**. 3808
Ps 69:25 and let **n.** dwell in their tents 408
Ps 71:11 him; for there is **n.** to deliver him 369
Ps 73:25 is **n.** upon earth that I desire 3808
Ps 76:5 **n.** of the men of might have found 3808
Ps 79:3 and there was **n.** to bury them 369
Ps 81:11 voice; and Israel would **n.** of me. 3808
Ps 86:8 the gods there is **n.** like unto thee, 369
Ps 107:12 fell down, and there was **n.** to help. 369
Ps 109:12 be **n.** to extend mercy unto him: 408
Ps 139:16 as yet there was **n.** of them 3808,259
Pr 1:25 and would **n.** of my reproof: 3808
Pr 1:30 They would **n.** of my counsel: they 3808
Pr 2:19 **N.** that go unto her return again, 3808
Pr 3:31 and choose **n.** of his ways. 408
Ca 4:2 twins, and **n.** is barren among them. 369
Isa 1:31 together, and **n.** shall quench them. 369
Isa 5:27 **N.** shall be weary nor stumble 369
Isa 5:27 them; **n.** shall slumber nor sleep; 3808
Isa 5:29 away safe, and **n.** shall deliver it 369
Isa 10:14 there was **n.** that moved the wing, 3808
Isa 14:6 is persecuted, and **n.** hindereth 1097
Isa 14:31 **n.** shall be alone in his appointed 369
Isa 17:2 down, and **n.** shall make them afraid. 369
Isa 22:22 so he shall open, and **n.** shall shut; 369
Isa 22:22 and he shall shut, and **n.** shall open 369
Isa 34:10 **n.** shall pass through it for ever and 369
Isa 34:12 the kingdom, but **n.** shall be there, 369
Isa 34:16 fail, **n.** shall want her mate: 802,3808
Isa 41:17 needy seek water, and there is **n.**, 369
Isa 41:26 yea, there is **n.** that sheweth, 369
Isa 41:26 yea, there is **n.** that declareth, 369
Isa 41:26 there is **n.** that heareth your words 369
Isa 42:22 are for a prey, and **n.** delivereth; 369
Isa 42:22 for a spoil, and **n.** saith, Restore. 369
Isa 43:13 is **n.** that can deliver out of my hand: 369
Isa 44:19 And **n.** considereth in his heart, 3808
Isa 45:5 I am the Lord, and there is **n.** else, 369
Isa 45:6 west, that there is **n.** beside me 657
Isa 45:6 I am the Lord, and there is **n.** else. 369
Isa 45:14 and there is **n.** else, there is no God 369
Isa 45:18 I am the Lord; and there is **n.** else. 369
Isa 45:21 a Saviour; there is **n.** beside me 369
Isa 45:22 for I am God, and there is **n.** else. 369
Isa 46:9 for I am God, and there is **n.** else; 369
Isa 46:9 I am God, and there is **n.** like me, 657
Isa 47:8 heart, I am, and **n.** else besides me; 657
Isa 47:10 thou hast said, **N.** seeth me. Thy 369
Isa 47:10 heart, I am, and **n.** else besides me. 657
Isa 47:15 to his quarter; **n.** shall save thee. 369
Isa 50:2 I called, was there **n.** to answer? 369
Isa 51:18 is **n.** to guide her among all the sons 369
Isa 57:1 **n.** considering that the righteous is 369
Isa 59:4 **n.** calleth for justice, nor any 369
Isa 59:11 look for judgment, but there is **n.**; 369
Isa 63:3 people there was **n.** with me; 369,376
Isa 63:5 looked, and there was **n.** to help; 369
Isa 63:5 that there was **n.** to uphold: 369
Isa 64:7 is **n.** that calleth upon thy name, 369
Isa 66:4 when I called, **n.** did answer; 369
Jer 4:4 fire, and burn that **n.** can quench it, 369
Jer 4:22 and they have **n.** understanding: 3808

Jer 7:33 and **n.** shall fray them away. 369
Jer 9:10 **n.** can pass through them; 1097,376
Jer 9:12 that **n.** passeth through? 1997
Jer 9:22 and **n.** shall gather them. 369
Jer 10:6 as there is **n.** like unto thee, O Lord 369
Jer 10:7 kingdoms, there is **n.** like unto thee. 369
Jer 10:20 there is **n.** to stretch forth my tent 369
Jer 13:19 be shut up, and **n.** shall open them: 369
Jer 14:16 they shall have **n.** to bury them, 369
Jer 21:12 and burn that **n.** can quench it, 369
Jer 23:14 **n.** doth return from...wickedness: 1115
Jer 30:7 day is great, so that **n.** is like it: 369
Jer 30:10 quiet, and **n.** shall make him afraid. 369
Jer 30:13 There is **n.** to plead thy cause, that 369
Jer 34:9 **n.** should serve himself of them, 1115
Jer 34:10 **n.** should serve themselves of them 1115
Jer 35:14 for unto this day they drink **n.**, 3808
Jer 36:30 shall have **n.** to sit upon the throne 3808
Jer 42:17 **n.** of them shall remain or escape 3808
Jer 44:7 Judah, to leave you **n.** to remain; 1115
Jer 44:14 that **n.** of the remnant of Judah, 3808
Jer 44:14 **n.** shall return but such as shall 3808
Jer 46:27 ease, and **n.** shall make him afraid. 369
Jer 48:33 **n.** shall tread with shouting; 3808
Jer 49:5 and **n.** shall gather up him that 369
Jer 50:3 and **n.** shall dwell therein; they 3808
Jer 50:9 man; **n.** shall return in vain. 3808
Jer 50:20 sought for, and there shall be **n.**; 369
Jer 50:29 round about; let **n.** thereof escape: 408
Jer 50:32 and fall, and **n.** shall raise him up: 369
Jer 51:62 that **n.** shall remain in it, neither 1115
La 1:2 lovers she hath **n.** to comfort her: 369
La 1:4 **n.** come to the solemn feasts: all 1997
La 1:7 of the enemy, and **n.** did help her: 369
La 1:17 and there is **n.** to comfort her: the 369
La 1:21 I sigh: there is **n.** to comfort me: 369
La 2:22 of the Lord's anger **n.** escaped 3808
La 5:8 is **n.** that doth deliver us out of 369
Eze 7:11 **n.** of them shall remain, nor of 3808
Eze 7:14 ready; but **n.** goeth to the battle: 369
Eze 7:25 seek peace, and there shall be **n.**. 369
Eze 12:28 **n.** of my words be prolonged any 3808
Eze 16:5 **N.** eye pitied thee, to do any of 3808
Eze 16:34 **n.** followeth thee to commit 3808
Eze 18:7 pledge, hath spoiled **n.** by violence, 3808
Eze 22:30 not destroy it: but I found **n.** 3808
Eze 31:14 end that **n.** of all the trees by the 3808
Eze 33:16 **N.** of his sins...he hath committed 3808
Eze 33:28 that **n.** shall pass through. 369
Eze 34:6 **n.** did search or seek after them. 369
Eze 34:28 and **n.** shall make them afraid. 369
Eze 39:26 land, and **n.** made them afraid. 369
Eze 39:28 left **n.** of them any more there. 3808
Da 1:19 them all was found **n.** like Daniel, 3808
Da 2:11 **n.** other than can shew it before 3809
Da 4:35 **n.** can stay his hand, or say unto 3809
Da 6:4 could find **n.** occasion nor fault; 3809
Da 8:7 **n.** that could deliver the ram out 3808
Da 8:27 at the vision, but **n.** understood it. 369
Da 10:21 is **n.** that holdeth with me in these 369
Da 11:16 and **n.** shall stand before him: and 369
Da 11:45 to his end, and **n.** shall help him. 369
Da 12:10 **n.** of the wicked shall understand; 3808
Ho 2:10 and **n.** shall deliver her out of mine 3808
Ho 5:14 take away and **n.** shall rescue him. 369
Ho 7:7 **n.** among them that calleth unto 369
Ho 11:7 High, **n.** at all would exalt him. 3808
Ho 12:8 **n.** iniquity in me that were sin. 3808
Joe 2:27 the Lord your God, and **n.** else: 369
Am 5:2 land; there is **n.** to raise her up. 369
Am 5:6 there be **n.** to quench it in Beth-el. 369
Ob 7 there is **n.** understanding in him. 369
Mic 2:5 **n.** that shall cast a cord by lot in 3808
Mic 3:11 us? **n.** evil can come upon us. 3808
Mic 4:4 **n.** shall make them afraid: for the 369
Mic 5:8 in pieces, and **n.** can deliver. 369
Mic 7:2 and there is **n.** upright among men: 369
Na 2:8 they cry; but **n.** shall look back. 369
Na 2:9 for there is **n.** end of the store and 369
Na 2:11 whelp, and **n.** make them afraid? 369
Na 3:3 and there is **n.** end of their corpses; 369
Zep 2:15 I am, and there is **n.** beside me: 657
Zep 3:6 streets waste, that **n.** passeth by: 1097
Zep 3:6 man, that there is **n.** inhabitant. 369
Zep 3:13 and **n.** shall make them afraid. 369
Hag 1:6 ye clothe you, but there is **n.** warm; 369
Zec 7:10 let **n.** of you imagine evil against 408
Zec 8:17 let **n.** of you imagine evil in your 408
Mal 2:15 let **n.** deal treacherously against 408
Mt 12:43 **seeking rest, and findeth n.** *3756*
Mt 15:6 **commandment of God of n. effect** *208*
Mt 19:17 **there is n. good but one, that is,** *3762*
Mt 26:60 But found **n.**: yea, though many *3756*
Mt 26:60 witnesses came, yet found they **n.**. *3756*
Mk 7:13 **Making...word of God of n. effect** *208*
Mk 10:18 **is n. good but one, that is, God.** *3762*
Mk 12:31 **is n. other commandment greater.** *3756*
Mk 12:32 God; and there is **n.** other but he: *3756*
Mk 14:55 to put him to death; and found **n.**. *3756*
Lu 1:61 is **n.** of thy kindred that is called *3762*
Lu 3:11 him impart to him that hath **n.**; *3361*
Lu 4:26 **unto n. of them was Elias sent,** *3762*
Lu 4:27 **n. of them was cleansed, saving** *3762*
Lu 11:24 **seeking rest; and finding n., he** *3361*
Lu 13:6 **sought fruit thereon, and found n.,** *3756*
Lu 13:7 **fruit on this fig tree, and find n.** *3756*
Lu 14:24 **n. of those men which were bidden** *3762*
Lu 18:19 **n. is good, save one, that is, God.** *3762*
Lu 18:34 they understood **n.** of these things: *3762*
Joh 6:22 that there was **n.** other boat there, *3756*
Joh 7:19 **n. of you keepeth the law? Why go** *3762*
Joh 8:10 saw **n.** but the woman, he said *3367*
Joh 15:24 **the works which n. other man did,** *3762*
Joh 16:5 **n. of you asketh me, Whither** *3762*
Joh 17:12 **and n. of them is lost, but the son** *3762*
Joh 18:9 thou gavest me have I lost **n.** *3762*
Joh 21:12 **n.** of the disciples durst ask him, *3762*
Ac 3:6 said, Silver and gold have I **n.**; *3756*
Ac 4:12 is **n.** other name under heaven *3777*
Ac 7:5 he gave him **n.** inheritance in it, *3756*
Ac 8:16 yet he was fallen upon **n.** of them: *3762*
Ac 8:24 **n.** of these things which ye have *3367*
Ac 11:19 word to **n.** but unto the Jews only. *3367*
Ac 18:17 Gallio cared for **n.** of these things. *3762*
Ac 20:24 But **n.** of these things move *3762*
Ac 24:23 forbid **n.** of his acquaintance to *3367*
Ac 25:11 but if there be **n.** of these things *3762*
Ac 25:18 they brought **n.** accusation of such *3762*
Ac 26:22 saying **n.** other things than those *3762*
Ac 26:26 persuaded that **n.** of these *5100,3756,3762*
Ro 3:10 there is **n.** righteous, no, not one: *3756*
Ro 3:11 There is **n.** that understandeth, *3756*
Ro 3:11 there is **n.** that seeketh after God. *3756*
Ro 3:12 there is **n.** that doeth good, no, not *3756*
Ro 4:14 and the promise made of **n.** effect: *2673*
Ro 8:9 the Spirit of Christ, he is **n.** of his *3756*
Ro 9:6 word of God hath taken **n.** effect. *1601*
Ro 14:7 For **n.** of us liveth to himself, and *3762*
1Co 1:14 thank God that I baptized **n.** of you, *3762*
1Co 1:17 cross...should be made of **n.** effect. *2758*
1Co 2:8 **n.** of the princes of this world *3762*
1Co 7:29 wives be as though they had **n.**; *3361*
1Co 8:4 there is **n.** other God but one. *3762*
1Co 9:15 But I have used **n.** of these things: *3762*
1Co 10:32 Give **n.** offence, neither to...Jews, *677*
1Co 14:10 **n.** of them is without signification. *3762*
2Co 1:13 we write **n.** other things unto you, *3756*
Ga 1:19 But other of the apostles saw I **n.**, *3756*
Ga 3:17 make the promise of **n.** effect. *208*
Ga 5:10 ye will be **n.** otherwise minded; *3762*
1Th 5:15 **n.** render evil for evil unto any *3361,5100*
1Ti 5:14 give **n.** occasion to the adversary *3361*
1Pe 4:15 let **n.** of you suffer as a murderer, *3387*
1Jo 2:10 is **n.** occasion of stumbling in him. *3756*
Re 2:10 **Fear n. of those things which thou** *3367*
Re 2:24 **put upon you n. other burden.** *3367*

NOON See also AFTERNOON; NOONDAY; NOONTIDE.
Ge 43:16 men shall dine with me at **n.**. 6672
Ge 43:25 present against Joseph came at **n.**: 6672
2Sa 4:5 Ish-bosheth, who lay on a bed at **n.**. 6672
1Ki 18:26 Baal from morning even until **n.**, 6672
1Ki 18:27 it came to pass at **n.**, that Elijah 6672
1Ki 20:16 And they went out at **n.**. But 6672
2Ki 4:20 he sat on her knees till **n.**, and then 6672
Ps 55:17 Evening, and morning, and at **n.**, 6672
Ca 1:7 thou makest thy flock to rest at **n.**: 6672
Isa 58:10 and thy darkness be as the **n.** day: 6672
Isa 59:10 we stumble at **n.** day as in the 6672
Jer 6:4 her; arise, and let us go up at **n.**. 6672
Am 8:9 will cause the sun to go down at **n.**, 6672
Zep 2:4 shall drive out Ashdod at the **n.** day, 6672
Ac 22:6 nigh unto Damascus about **n.**, *3314*

NOONDAY See also NOON and DAY.
De 28:29 And thou shalt grope at **n.**, as the 6672
Job 5:14 and grope in the **n.** as in the night. 6672
Job 11:17 age shall be clearer than the **n.**; 6672
Ps 37:6 light, and thy judgment as the **n.** 6672
Ps 91:6 the destruction that wasteth at **n.** 6672
Isa 16:3 as the night in the midst of the **n.**; 6672
Jer 15:8 of the young men a spoiler at **n.**: 6672

NOONTIDE
Jer 20:16 and the shouting at **n.**; 6256,6672

NOPH (nof) See also MEMPHIS.
Isa 19:13 the princes of **N.** are deceived; 5297
Jer 2:16 the children of **N.** and Tahapanes 5297
Jer 44:1 and at Tahpanhes, and at **N.**, and 5297
Jer 46:14 publish in **N.** and in Tahpanhes: 5297
Jer 46:19 for **N.** shall be waste and desolate 5297
Eze 30:13 their images to cease out of **N.**; 5297
Eze 30:16 and **N.** shall have distresses daily. 5297

NOPHAH (no'-fah) See also NOBAH.
Nu 21:30 them waste even unto **N.**, which 5302

NOR
Ge 19:33 when she lay down, **n.** when she arose.
Ge 19:35 when she lay down, **n.** when she arose.
Ge 21:23 me, **n.** with my son, **n.** with my son's
Ge 45:5 grieved, **n.** angry with yourselves, 408
Ge 45:6 shall neither be earing **n.** harvests.
Ge 49:10 Judah, **n.** a lawgiver from between
Ex 4:1 me, **n.** hearken unto my voice: 3808
Ex 4:10 **n.** since thou hast spoken unto thy 1571
Ex 10:6 thy fathers, **n.** thy father's fathers 3808
Ex 11:6 none like it, **n.** be like it any more. 3808
Ex 12:9 of it raw, **n.** sodden at all with water,
Ex 13:22 by day, **n.** the pillar of fire by night,
Ex 20:5 thyself to them, **n.** serve them: 3808
Ex 20:10 thou, **n.** thy son, **n.** thy daughter,
Ex 20:10 thy manservant, **n.** thy maidservant,
Ex 20:10 **n.** thy cattle, **n.** thy stranger that is
Ex 20:17 **n.** his manservant, **n.** his maidservant,
Ex 20:17 **n.** his ox, **n.** his ass, **n.** any thing that is
Ex 22:21 vex a stranger, **n.** oppress him: 3808
Ex 22:28 **n.** curse the ruler of thy people. 3808
Ex 23:24 gods, **n.** serve them, **n.** do after their 3808
Ex 23:26 nothing cast their young, **n.** be barren,
Ex 23:32 covenant with them, **n.** with their gods.
Ex 30:9 **n.** burnt sacrifice, **n.** meat offering;
Ex 34:3 **n.** herds feed before that mount. 408
Ex 34:10 in all the earth, **n.** in any nation:
Ex 34:28 neither eat bread, **n.** drink water. 3808
Ex 36:6 **n.** woman make any more work 408
Le 2:11 shall burn no leaven, **n.** any honey,
Le 3:17 that ye eat neither fat **n.** blood.
Le 10:9 Do not drink wine **n.** strong drink,
Le 10:9 **n.** thy sons with thee, when ye go
Le 11:12 hath no fins **n.** scales in the waters,
Le 11:26 clovenfooted, **n.** cheweth the cud, 369
Le 12:4 thing, **n.** come into the sanctuary, 3808
Le 13:34 **n.** be in sight deeper than the skin;
Le 17:16 wash them not, **n.** bathe his flesh; 3808
Le 18:26 your own nation, **n.** any stranger that
Le 19:4 **n.** make to yourselves molten 3808
Le 19:14 **n.** put a stumblingblock before the 3808
Le 19:15 **n.** honour the person of the mighty: 3808
Le 19:18 **n.** bear any grudge against the 3808
Le 19:20 redeemed, **n.** freedom given her; 3808
Le 19:26 use enchantment, **n.** observe times. 3808
Le 19:28 dead, **n.** print any marks upon you: 3808
Le 20:19 sister, **n.** of thy father's sister;
Le 21:5 **n.** make...cuttings in their flesh. 3808
Le 21:10 his head, **n.** rend his clothes; 3808
Le 21:11 **n.** defile himself for his father, or 3808
Le 21:12 **n.** profane the sanctuary of his God; 3808
Le 21:23 vail, **n.** come nigh unto the altar, 3808
Le 22:22 **n.** make an offering by fire of them 3808
Le 23:14 **n.** parched corn, **n.** green ears, until
Le 25:4 thy field, **n.** prune thy vineyard. 3808
Le 25:11 **n.** gather the grapes in it of thy vine 3808
Le 25:20 not sow, **n.** gather in our increase. 3808
Le 25:37 **n.** lend him thy victuals for increase. 3808
Le 26:1 shall make no idols **n.** graven image,
Le 27:10 shall not alter it, **n.** change it, a 3808
Nu 5:15 it, **n.** put frankincense thereon; 3808
Nu 6:3 **n.** eat moist grapes, or dried. 3808
Nu 9:12 morning, **n.** break any bone of it: 3808
Nu 11:19 one day, **n.** two days, **n.** five days, 3808

Nu 11:19 neither ten days, **n.** twenty days; 3808
Nu 18:3 that neither they, **n.** ye also, die.
Nu 20:17 turn to the right hand, **n.** to the left,
Nu 23:25 them at all, **n.** bless them at all. 3808
De 1:45 your voice, **n.** give ear unto you. 3808
De 2:19 them not, **n.** meddle with them; 408
De 2:27 turn unto the right hand **n.** to the left.
De 2:37 **n.** unto any place of the river Jabbok,
De 2:37 **n.** unto the cities in the mountains,
De 2:37 **n.** unto whatsoever the Lord our God
De 4:28 see, **n.** hear, **n.** eat, **n.** smell. 3808
De 4:31 thee, **n.** forget the covenant of thy 3808
De 5:9 thyself unto them, **n.** serve them: 3808
De 5:14 work, thou, **n.** thy son, **n.** thy daughter,
De 5:14 **n.** thy manservant, **n.** thy maidservant,
De 5:14 **n.** thine ox, **n.** thine ass, **n.** any of thy
De 5:14 **n.** thy servant that is within thy gates;
De 7:2 them, **n.** shew mercy unto them: 3808
De 7:3 **n.** his daughter shalt thou take 3808
De 7:7 his love upon you, **n.** choose you, 3808
De 7:25 **n.** take it unto thee, lest thou be
De 9:9 did eat bread **n.** drink water: 3808
De 9:18 neither eat bread, **n.** drink water, 3808
De 9:23 him not, **n.** hearkened to his voice. 3808
De 9:27 **n.** to their wickedness, **n.** to their sin:
De 10:9 Levi hath no part **n.** inheritance with
De 10:17 not persons, **n.** taketh reward: 3808
De 12:12 hath no part **n.** inheritance with you.
De 12:17 **n.** any of thy vows which thou vowest,
De 12:17 **n.** thy freewill offerings, or heave
De 12:32 add thereto, **n.** diminish from it. 3808
De 13:6 hast not known, thou, **n.** thy fathers;
De 13:8 unto him, **n.** hearken unto him; 3808
De 14:1 **n.** make any baldness between your 3808
De 14:8 flesh, **n.** touch their dead carcase. 3808
De 14:27 hath no part **n.** inheritance with thee.
De 14:29 hath no part **n.** inheritance with thee,)
De 15:7 **n.** shut thine hand from thy poor 3808
De 15:19 **n.** shear the firstling of thy sheep. 3808
De 17:11 thee, to the right hand, **n.** to the left.
De 17:16 **n.** cause the people to return to 3808
De 18:1 no part **n.** inheritance with Israel:
De 18:22 thing follow not, **n.** come to pass, 3808
De 21:4 which is neither eared **n.** sown, and 3808
De 22:30 wife, **n.** discover his father's skirt. 3808
De 23:6 seek their peace **n.** their prosperity
De 23:17 **n.** a sodomite of the sons of Israel. 3808
De 24:17 the stranger, **n.** of the fatherless:
De 24:17 **n.** take a widow's raiment to 3808
De 26:14 **n.** given ought thereof for the dead: 3808
De 28:36 neither thou **n.** thy father have known;
De 28:39 of the wine, **n.** gather the grapes; 3808
De 28:50 old, **n.** shew favour to the young: 3808
De 28:64 neither thou **n.** thy fathers have known,
De 29:23 **n.** beareth, **n.** any grass groweth 3808
De 31:6 fear not, **n.** be afraid of them: for 408
De 31:6 will not fail thee, **n.** forsake thee. 3808
De 33:9 brethren, **n.** knew his own children: 3808
De 34:7 dim, **n.** his natural force abated. 3808
Jos 1:5 I will not fail thee, **n.** forsake thee. 3808
Jos 6:10 shall not shout, **n.** make any noise. 3808
Jos 10:25 Fear not, **n.** be dismayed, be strong 408
Jos 13:13 Geshurites, **n.** the Maachathites: 408
Jos 22:19 the Lord, **n.** rebel against us, in 408
Jos 22:26 for burnt offering, **n.** for sacrifice: 3808
Jos 22:28 for burnt offerings, **n.** for sacrifices; 3808
Jos 23:7 gods, **n.** cause to swear by them: 3808
Jos 23:7 them, **n.** bow yourselves unto them, 3808
Jos 24:12 with thy sword, **n.** with thy bow. 3808
Jos 24:19 your transgressions **n.** your sins.
Jg 1:27 her towns, **n.** Taanach and her towns,
Jg 1:27 **n.** the inhabitants of Dor and her
Jg 1:27 **n.** the inhabitants of Ibleam and her
Jg 1:27 **n.** the inhabitants of Megiddo and her
Jg 1:30 **n.** the inhabitants of Nahalol; but the
Jg 1:31 **n.** the inhabitants of Zidon, **n.** of Ahlab,
Jg 1:31 **n.** of Achzib, **n.** of Helbah,
Jg 1:31 **n.** of Aphik, **n.** of Rehob:
Jg 1:33 **n.** the inhabitants of Beth-anath;
Jg 2:10 not the Lord, **n.** yet the works 1571
Jg 2:19 doings, **n.** from their stubborn way.
Jg 6:4 Israel, neither sheep, **n.** ox, **n.** ass.
Jg 11:15 **n.** the land of the children of Ammon:
Jg 11:34 he had neither son **n.** daughter. 176
Jg 13:4 and drink not wine **n.** strong drink,
Jg 13:7 now drink no wine **n.** strong drink,
Jg 13:14 drink, **n.** eat any unclean thing: 408
Jg 13:23 **n.** would as at this time have told 3908
Jg 14:16 not told it my father **n.** my mother, 3908
Jg 19:30 was no such deed done **n.** seen from 3908
1Sa 1:15 drunk neither wine **n.** strong drink,
1Sa 3:14 with sacrifice **n.** offering for ever.
1Sa 5:5 **n.** any that come into Dagon's house,
1Sa 12:4 not defrauded us, **n.** oppressed us, 3808
1Sa 12:21 which cannot profit **n.** deliver; for 3808
1Sa 13:22 **n.** spear found in the hand of any of
1Sa 15:29 of Israel will not lie **n.** repent: 3808
1Sa 20:27 meat, neither yesterday, **n.** to day? 1571
1Sa 20:31 not be established, **n.** thy kingdom.
1Sa 21:8 my sword **n.** my weapons with me, 1571
1Sa 22:15 **n.** to all the house of my father:
1Sa 24:11 there is neither evil **n.** transgression
1Sa 25:31 thee, **n.** offence of heart unto my lord,
1Sa 26:12 no man saw it, **n.** knew it, neither 369
1Sa 27:9 and left neither man **n.** woman alive,
1Sa 27:11 saved neither man **n.** woman alive,
1Sa 28:6 dreams, **n.** by Urim, **n.** by prophets. 1571
1Sa 28:15 neither by prophets, **n.** by dreams: 1571
1Sa 28:18 **n.** executedst his fierce wrath 3808
1Sa 28:20 no bread all the day, **n.** all the night.
1Sa 30:12 no bread, **n.** drunk any water, 3808
1Sa 30:15 **n.** deliver me into the hands of my 518
1Sa 30:19 small **n.** great, neither sons **n.** 5703
1Sa 30:19 **n.** any thing that they had taken 5703
2Sa 1:21 rain, upon you, **n.** fields of offerings:
2Sa 2:19 not to the right hand **n.** to the left.
2Sa 3:34 bound, **n.** thy feet put into fetters: 3808
2Sa 13:22 brother Amnon neither good **n.** bad:
2Sa 14:7 name **n.** remainder upon the earth.
2Sa 19:6 regardest neither princes **n.** servants:
2Sa 19:24 **n.** trimmed his beard, **n.** washed 3808
2Sa 21:4 **n.** gold of Saul, **n.** of his house;
2Sa 21:10 **n.** the beasts of the field by night.
1Ki 3:8 numbered **n.** counted for multitude.
1Ki 3:11 **n.** hast asked the life of thine 3808
1Ki 3:26 Let it be neither mine **n.** thine, but
1Ki 5:4 neither adversary **n.** evil occurrent. 369
1Ki 6:7 that there was neither hammer **n.** axe
1Ki 6:7 **n.** any tool of iron heard in the house,
1Ki 8:5 told **n.** numbered for multitude. 3808
1Ki 8:57 let him not leave us, **n.** forsake us: 408
1Ki 10:12 trees, **n.** were seen unto this day. 3808
1Ki 12:24 up, **n.** fight against your brethren 3808
1Ki 13:8 will I eat bread **n.** drink water in 3808
1Ki 13:9 Eat no bread, **n.** drink water, 3808
1Ki 13:9 **n.** turn again by the same way 3808
1Ki 13:16 return with thee, **n.** go in with thee:
1Ki 13:16 bread **n.** drink water with thee in 3808
1Ki 13:17 eat no bread **n.** drink water there, 3808
1Ki 13:17 **n.** turn again to go by the way that 3808
1Ki 13:28 eaten the carcase, **n.** torn the ass. 3808
1Ki 16:11 of his kinsfolks, **n.** of his friends.
1Ki 17:1 shall not be dew **n.** rain these years,
1Ki 18:26 was no voice, **n.** any that answered. 369
1Ki 18:29 **n.** any to answer, **n.** any that 369
1Ki 20:8 Hearken not unto him, **n.** consent. 3808
1Ki 22:31 Fight neither with small **n.** great,
2Ki 3:14 not look toward thee, **n.** see thee. 518
2Ki 4:23 is neither new moon, **n.** Sabbath. 3808
2Ki 4:31 there was neither voice, **n.** hearing. 369
2Ki 5:17 offering **n.** sacrifice unto other gods,
2Ki 6:10 himself there, not once **n.** twice. 3808
2Ki 9:15 go forth **n.** escape out of the city
2Ki 14:6 **n.** the children be put to death for 3808
2Ki 14:26 **n.** any left, **n.** any helper for Israel. 369
2Ki 17:35 gods, **n.** bow yourselves to them, 3808
2Ki 17:35 **n.** serve them, **n.** sacrifice to them: 3808
2Ki 18:5 Judah, **n.** any that were before him.
2Ki 18:12 would not hear them, **n.** do them. 3808
2Ki 19:32 this city, **n.** shoot an arrow there, 3808
2Ki 19:32 **n.** come before it with shield, 3808
2Ki 19:32 with shield, **n.** cast a bank against it.
2Ki 20:13 in his house, **n.** in all his dominion,
2Ki 23:22 Israel, **n.** in all the days of the kings
2Ki 23:22 of Israel, **n.** of the kings of Judah;
1Ch 21:24 **n.** offer burnt offerings without cost.
1Ch 22:13 courage; dread not, **n.** be dismayed. 408
1Ch 23:26 **n.** any vessels of it for the service
1Ch 28:20 fear not, **n.** be dismayed: for the 408
1Ch 28:20 will not fail thee, **n.** forsake thee, 3808
2Ch 1:11 or honour, **n.** the life of thine enemies,
2Ch 5:6 told **n.** numbered for multitude. 3808
2Ch 6:14 thee in the heaven, **n.** in the earth;
2Ch 11:4 up, **n.** fight against your brethren: 3808
2Ch 15:5 that went out, **n.** to him that came in,
2Ch 19:7 **n.** respect of persons, **n.** taking of gifts.
2Ch 20:15 afraid **n.** dismayed by reason of 408
2Ch 20:17 fear not, **n.** be dismayed; to morrow 408
2Ch 21:12 **n.** in the ways of Asa king of Judah,
2Ch 29:7 incense **n.** offered burnt offerings 3808
2Ch 32:7 **n.** dismayed for the king of Assyria, 408
2Ch 32:7 **n.** for all the multitude that is with
2Ch 32:15 **n.** persuade you on this manner, 408
2Ch 34:2 to the right hand, **n.** to the left.
Ezr 9:12 **n.** seek their peace or their wealth 3808
Ezr 9:14 should be no remnant **n.** escaping?
Ezr 10:6 did eat no bread, **n.** drink water: 3808
Ne 1:7 **n.** the statutes, **n.** the judgments,
Ne 2:16 Jews, **n.** to the priests, **n.** to the nobles,
Ne 2:16 **n.** to the rulers, **n.** to the rest that did
Ne 2:20 no portion, **n.** right, **n.** memorial, in
Ne 4:23 I, **n.** my brethren, **n.** my servants,
Ne 4:23 **n.** the men of the guard which
Ne 7:61 their father's house, **n.** their seed,
Ne 8:9 your God; mourn not, **n.** weep. 408
Ne 9:31 consume them, **n.** forsake them; 3808
Ne 9:34 priests, **n.** our fathers, kept thy law, 3808
Ne 9:34 thy law, **n.** hearkened unto thy 3808
Ne 10:30 **n.** take their daughters for our 3808
Ne 13:25 **n.** take their daughters unto your 518
Es 2:7 for she had neither father **n.** mother,
Es 2:10 not shewed her people **n.** her kindred:
Es 2:20 yet shewed her kindred **n.** her people;
Es 3:2 bowed not, **n.** did him reverence. 3808
Es 3:5 bowed not, **n.** did him reverence,
Es 4:16 neither eat **n.** drink three days, 408
Es 5:9 stood not up, **n.** moved for him, 3808
Es 9:28 **n.** the memorial of them perish. 3808
Job 1:22 not, **n.** charged God foolishly. 3808
Job 3:10 womb, **n.** hid sorrow from mine eyes.
Job 7:19 **n.** let me alone till I swallow 3808
Job 14:12 **n.** be raised out of their sleep. 3808
Job 18:19 son **n.** nephew among his people, 3808
Job 18:19 **n.** any remaining in his dwellings. 3808
Job 24:13 **n.** abide in the paths thereof. 3808
Job 27:4 **n.** tongue utter deceit. 518
Job 28:8 it, **n.** the fierce lion passed by it. 3808
Job 34:19 **n.** regardeth the rich more than 3808
Job 34:22 no darkness, **n.** shadow of death, 369
Job 36:19 gold, **n.** all the forces of strength. 3808
Job 41:12 **n.** his power, **n.** his comely proportion.
Job 41:26 spear, the dart, **n.** the habergeon.
Ps 1:1 **n.** standeth in the way of sinners, 3808
Ps 1:1 **n.** sitteth in the seat of the scornful. 3808
Ps 1:5 **n.** sinners in the congregation of the
Ps 15:3 **n.** doeth evil to his neighbour, 3808
Ps 15:3 **n.** taketh up a reproach against his 3808
Ps 15:5 **n.** taketh reward against the 3808
Ps 16:4 **n.** take up their names into my 1077
Ps 19:3 There is no speech **n.** language, 369
Ps 22:24 despised **n.** abhored the affliction. 3808
Ps 24:4 unto vanity, **n.** sworn deceitfully. 3808
Ps 25:7 of my youth, **n.** my transgression:
Ps 26:9 sinners, **n.** my life with bloody men:
Ps 28:5 Lord, **n.** the operation of his hands,
Ps 37:25 forsaken, **n.** his seed begging bread.
Ps 37:33 **n.** condemn him when he is 3808
Ps 40:4 proud, **n.** such as turn aside to lies. 3808
Ps 49:7 **n.** given to God a ransom for him: 3808
Ps 50:9 thy house, **n.** he goats out of thy folds.
Ps 59:3 my transgression, **n.** for my sin, 3808
Ps 66:20 my prayer, **n.** his mercy from me.
Ps 75:6 **n.** from the west, **n.** from the south,
Ps 78:42 **n.** the day when he delivered them.
Ps 89:22 **n.** the son of wickedness afflict him. 3808
Ps 89:33 **n.** suffer my faithfulness to fail. 3808
Ps 89:34 **n.** alter the thing that is gone out of 3808
Ps 91:5 **n.** for the arrow that flieth by day;
Ps 91:6 **N.** for the pestilence that walketh
Ps 91:6 **n.** for the destruction that wasteth at
Ps 103:10 **n.** rewarded us according to our 3808
Ps 121:4 Israel shall neither slumber **n.** sleep. 3808
Ps 121:6 thee by day, **n.** the moon by night.
Ps 129:7 **n.** he that bindeth sheaves his bosom.
Ps 131:1 not haughty, **n.** mine eyes lofty:; 3808
Ps 132:3 of my house, **n.** go up into my bed;
Ps 144:14 be no breaking in, **n.** going out; 369
Ps 146:3 trust in princes, **n.** in the son of man,
Pr 4:27 not to the right hand **n.** to the left:
Pr 5:13 **n.** inclined mine ear to them that 3808
Pr 6:4 thine eyes, **n.** slumber to thine eyelids.

Pr 8:26 had not made the earth, n. the fields, ...
Pr 8:26 n. the highest part of the dust of the ....
Pr 17:26 good, n. to strike princes for equity.........
Pr 21:30 no...n. understanding n. counsel.......... 369
Pr 30:3 n. have the knowledge of the holy...........
Pr 30:8 give me neither poverty n. riches;...........
Pr 31:3 n. thy ways to that which destroyeth........
Pr 31:4 wine; n. for princes strong drink: 408
Ec 1:8 n. the ear filled with hearing. 3808
Ec 3:14 to it, n. any thing taken from it:.......... 369
Ec 4:8 yea, he hath neither child n. brother:........
Ec 5:10 n. he that loveth abundance with.............
Ec 6:5 seen the sun, n. known any thing:...... 3808
Ec 8:16 neither day n. night seeth sleep..............
Ec 9:10 n. device, n. knowledge, n. wisdom, ...
Ec 9:11 swift, n. the battle to the strong, ... 3808
Ec 9:11 n....riches to men of understanding, ... 3808
Ec 9:11 n. yet favour to men of skill;............ 3808
Ec 11:5 n. how the bones do grow in the womb.....
Ec 12:1 n. the years draw nigh, when thou ....
Ec 12:2 n. the clouds return after the rain: ....
Ca 2:7 n. awake my love, till he please. 518
Ca 3:5 n. awake my love, till he please. 518
Ca 8:4 n. awake my love, until he please.............
Isa 3:7 house is neither bread n. clothing: 369
Isa 5:6 it shall not be pruned, n. digged; 3808
Isa 5:27 be weary n. stumble among them;...... 3808
Isa 5:27 none shall slumber n. sleep;.............. 3808
Isa 5:27 n. the latchet of their shoes be.......... 3808
Isa 8:12 fear ye their fear, n. be afraid. 3808
Isa 11:9 not hurt n. destroy in all my holy....... 3808
Isa 14:21 they do not rise, n. possess the land, ...
Isa 14:21 n. fill the face of the world with cities. ......
Isa 22:2 with the sword, n. dead in battle. 3808
Isa 23:4 travail not, n. bring forth children,...... 3808
Isa 23:4 up young men, n. bring up virgins. ....
Isa 23:18 shall not be treasured n. laid up;........ 3808
Isa 28:28 n. break it with the wheel of his cart, ...
Isa 28:28 n. bruise it with his horsemen. 3808
Isa 30:5 not profit them, n. be an help........... 3808
Isa 30:5 be an help n. profit, but a shame, ... 3808
Isa 31:4 n. abase himself for the noise of 3808
Isa 32:5 n. the churl said to be bountiful. 3808
Isa 34:10 It shall not be quenched night n. day; ....
Isa 35:9 n. any ravenous beast shall go up....... 1077
Isa 37:33 this city, n. shoot an arrow there,...... 3808
Isa 37:33 n. come before it with shields, ... 3808
Isa 37:33 n. cast a bank against it. 3808
Isa 39:2 in his house, n. in all his dominion,..........
Isa 40:16 n. the beasts thereof sufficient for 369
Isa 42:2 He shall not cry, n. lift up, ... 3808
Isa 42:2 n. cause his voice to be heard in the .. 3808
Isa 42:4 He shall not fail n. be discouraged,..... 3808
Isa 43:23 n. wearied thee with incense............. 3808
Isa 44:9 witnesses; they see not, n. know;...... 1077
Isa 44:18 have not known n. understood........... 3808
Isa 44:19 knowledge n. understanding to........... 3808
Isa 44:20 n. say, Is there not a lie in my right... 3808
Isa 45:13 captives, not for price n. reward,....... 3808
Isa 45:17 shall not be ashamed n. confounded.... 3808
Isa 46:7 n. save him out of his trouble............ 3808
Isa 47:14 coal to warm at, n. fire to sit before it. ....
Isa 48:1 not in truth, n. in righteousness......... 3808
Isa 48:19 cut off n. destroyed from before me. .. 3808
Isa 49:10 They shall not hunger n. thirst; 3808
Isa 49:10 shall the heat n. sun smite them: 3808
Isa 51:14 pit, n. that his bread should fail. 3808
Isa 52:12 go out with haste, n. go by flight: 3808
Isa 53:2 he hath no form n. comeliness; and 3808
Isa 54:9 not be wroth with thee, n. rebuke thee.....
Isa 57:11 me, n. laid it to thy heart?................ 3808
Isa 58:13 ways, n. finding thine own pleasure, ...
Isa 58:13 n. speaking thine own words:.................
Isa 59:4 justice, n. any pleadeth for truth:......... 369
Isa 59:21 mouth, n. out of the mouth of thy seed,....
Isa 59:21 n. out of the mouth of thy seed's seed,.....
Isa 60:11 they shall not be shut day n. night;..........
Isa 60:18 wasting n. destruction within thy.............
Isa 62:6 never hold their peace day n. night:..........
Isa 64:4 not heard, n. perceived by the ear, ... 3808
Isa 65:17 be remembered, n. come into mind. ... 3808
Isa 65:19 heard in her, n. the voice of crying. ....
Isa 65:20 n. an old man that hath not filled his.........
Isa 65:23 in vain, n. bring forth for trouble;....... 3808
Isa 65:25 not hurt n. destroy in all my holy....... 3808
Jer 4:11 my people, not to fan, n. to cleanse, .. 3808
Jer 5:4 Lord, n. the judgment of their God..........
Jer 5:12 neither shall we see sword n. famine: ....
Jer 6:19 my words, n. to my law, but rejected it. ...
Jer 6:20 n. your sacrifices sweet unto me........ 3808
Jer 6:25 into the field, n. walk by the way; 408
Jer 7:16 lift up cry n. prayer for them,............. 408
Jer 7:22 n. commanded them in the day.......... 3808
Jer 7:24 hearkened not, n. inclined their ear, ... 3808
Jer 7:26 not unto me, n. inclined their ear,...... 3808
Jer 7:28 their God, n. receiveth correction: 3808
Jer 7:32 n. the valley of the son of Hinnom,...........
Jer 8:2 not be gathered, n. be buried;........... 3808
Jer 8:13 on the vine, n. figs on the fig tree,...... 369
Jer 9:16 they n. their fathers have known:.............
Jer 11:8 obeyed not, n. inclined their ear, ... 3808
Jer 13:14 not pity, n. spare, n. have mercy, ... 3808
Jer 14:16 wives, n. their sons, n. their daughters:....
Jer 15:10 n. men have lent to me on usury, ... 3808
Jer 15:17 assembly of the mockers, n. rejoiced; ......
Jer 16:2 shalt thou have sons n. daughters ....
Jer 16:5 go to lament n. bemoan them: for...... 3808
Jer 16:6 lament for them, n. cut themselves, ... 3808
Jer 16:6 n. make themselves bald for them:..... 3808
Jer 16:13 know not, neither ye n. your fathers;........
Jer 17:21 n. bring it in by the gates of ....
Jer 17:23 not hear, n. receive instruction.......... 1115
Jer 18:18 the priest, n. counsel from the wise, ...
Jer 18:18 the wise, n. the word from the prophet.....
Jer 19:4 they n. their fathers have known,.............
Jer 19:4 have known, n. the kings of Judah,............
Jer 19:5 I commanded not, n. spake it, ... 3808
Jer 19:6 n. The valley of the son of Hinnom, ...
Jer 20:9 n. speak any more in his name. 3808
Jer 21:7 neither have pity, n. have mercy........ 3808
Jer 22:3 stranger, the fatherless, n. the widow, ...
Jer 22:10 no more, n. see his native country. ....
Jer 23:4 shall fear no more, n. be dismayed,.... 3808
Jer 23:32 sent them not, n. commanded them;... 3808
Jer 25:4 n. inclined your ear to hear.............. 3808
Jer 25:33 neither gathered, n. buried; 3808
Jer 25:35 n. the principal of the flock to escape........
Jer 27:9 n. to your diviners, n. to...dreamers, ...
Jer 27:9 n. to...enchanters, n. to...sorcerers, ...
Jer 31:40 n. thrown down any more for ever..... 3808
Jer 35:6 wine, neither ye, n. your sons for ever: ....
Jer 35:7 shall ye build house, n. sow seed, ... 3808
Jer 35:7 n. plant vineyard, n. have any: 3808
Jer 35:8 our wives, our sons, n. our daughters;......
Jer 35:9 N. to build houses for us to dwell 1115
Jer 35:9 have we vineyard, n. field, n. seed: ....
Jer 35:15 your ear, n. hearkened unto me......... 3808
Jer 36:24 not afraid, n. rent their garments, ... 3808
Jer 36:24 the king, n. any of his servants that ....
Jer 37:2 he, n. his servants, n. the people of the....
Jer 37:19 come against you, n. against this land? .....
Jer 42:14 n. hear the sound of the trumpet, ... 3808
Jer 42:14 trumpet, n. have hunger of bread;...... 3808
Jer 42:21 n. any thing for the which he hath............
Jer 44:3 not, neither they, ye, n. your fathers........
Jer 44:5 n. inclined their ear to turn from........ 3808
Jer 44:10 have they feared, n. walked in my...... 3808
Jer 44:10 in my law, n. in my statutes, ...
Jer 44:23 voice of the Lord, n. walked in...law,.. 3808
Jer 44:23 n. in his statutes, n. in his testimonies;.....
Jer 46:6 away, n. the mighty man escape;......... 408
Jer 49:31 which have neither gates n. bars........ 3808
Jer 49:33 n. any son of man dwell in it............ 3808
Jer 51:5 been forsaken, n. Judah of his God, ...
Jer 51:26 a corner, n. a stone for foundations; ....
Jer 51:62 remain in it, neither man n. beast,...........
La 2:22 anger none escaped n. remained: ....
La 3:33 n. grieve the children of men. ....
Eze 2:6 n. be dismayed at their looks,............ 408
Eze 3:18 n. speakest to warn the wicked 3808
Eze 3:19 wickedness, n. from his wicked way, ...
Eze 7:11 n. of their multitude, n. of any of........ 3808
Eze 7:12 buyer rejoice, n. the seller mourn:....... 408
Eze 12:24 any vain vision n. flattering divination ....
Eze 13:23 more vanity, n. divine divinations: 3808
Eze 14:16 deliver neither sons n. daughters;......... 508
Eze 14:18 shall deliver neither sons n. daughters,......
Eze 14:20 deliver neither son n. daughter;........... 518
Eze 16:4 not salted at all, n. swaddled at all. 3808
Eze 16:47 n. done after their abominations: ....
Eze 16:48 hath not done, she n. her daughters, ...
Eze 18:17 hath not received usury n. increase, ...
Eze 20:18 n. defile yourselves with their idols: 408
Eze 20:44 n. according to your corrupt doings, ...
Eze 22:24 cleansed, n. rained upon in the day..... 3808
Eze 23:27 n. remember Egypt any more. 3808
Eze 24:16 neither shalt thou mourn n. weep,...... 3808
Eze 24:22 your lips, n. eat the bread of men. 3808
Eze 24:23 ye shall not mourn n. weep; but ye..... 3808
Eze 28:24 n. any grieving thorn of all that are..........
Eze 29:5 be brought together, n. gathered: 3808
Eze 29:11 n. foot of beast shall pass through...... 3808
Eze 29:18 yet had he no wages, n. his army, ...
Eze 31:8 n. any tree in the garden of God..............
Eze 32:13 n. the hoofs of beasts trouble them. ... 3808
Eze 37:23 idols, n. with their detestable things, ...
Eze 37:23 n. with any of their transgressions:...........
Eze 38:11 walls, and having neither bars n. gates, ...
Eze 43:7 defile, neither they, n. their kings, ...
Eze 43:7 n. by the carcases of their kings in...........
Eze 44:9 in heart, n. uncircumcised in flesh, ...
Eze 44:13 n. to come near to any of my holy ....
Eze 44:20 n. suffer their locks to grow long; 3808
Eze 44:22 a widow, n. her that is put away:.............
Eze 48:14 n. alienate the firstfruits of the 3808
Da 1:8 n. with the wine which he drank: ....
Da 2:10 there is no king, lord, n. ruler,.................
Da 3:12, 14,18 n. worship the golden image 3809
Da 3:27 n. was an hair of their head singed,..... 3809
Da 3:27 n. the smell of fire had passed on 3809
Da 3:28 n. worship any god, except their........ 3809
Da 5:8 n. make known to the king the.................
Da 5:10 n. let thy countenance be changed: 408
Da 5:23 which see not, n. hear, n. know;....... 3809
Da 6:4 could find none occasion n. fault;........ 3809
Da 6:13 n. the decree that thou hast signed, ...
Da 6:15 n. statute which the king establisheth........
Da 10:3 came flesh n. wine in any mouth,....... 3808
Da 11:4 n. according to his dominion which 3808
Da 11:6 neither shall he stand, n. his arm: ....
Da 11:20 neither in anger, n. in battle. 3808
Da 11:24 have not done, n. his fathers' fathers; ....
Da 11:37 of his fathers, n. the desire of women,......
Da 11:37 n. regard any god: for he shall 3808
Ho 1:7 by bow, n. by sword, n. by battle,...........
Ho 1:7 battle, by horses, n. by horsemen. ....
Ho 1:10 cannot be measured n. numbered;...... 3808
Ho 4:1 because there is no truth, n. mercy, ... 369
Ho 4:1 n. knowledge of God in the land. 369
Ho 4:4 no man strive, n. reprove another: 408
Ho 4:14 n. your spouses when they commit...........
Ho 4:15 n. swear, The Lord liveth. 408
Ho 5:13 you, n. cure you of your wound......... 3808
Ho 7:10 their God, n. seek him for all this. 3808
Am 5:5 not Beth-el, n. enter into Gilgal, ... 3808
Am 8:11 of bread, n. a thirst for water, but 3808
Am 9:10 evil shall not overtake n. prevent us. ....
Ob 13 n....laid hands on their substance.......... 408
Jon 3:7 man n. beast, herd n. flock, taste any.......
Jon 3:7 let them not feed, n. drink water:........ 408
Mic 5:7 n. waiteth for the sons of men. 3808
Zep 1:6 the Lord, n. enquired for him............ 3808
Zep 1:18 silver n. their gold shall be able to 1571
Zep 3:13 not do iniquity, n. speak lies; 3808
Zec 1:4 did not hear, n. hearken unto me,...... 3808
Zec 4:6 Not by might, n. by power, but by..... 3808
Zec 7:10 not the window, n. the fatherless, the.......
Zec 7:10 the stranger, n. the poor; and let.............
Zec 7:14 no man passed through n. returned: ....
Zec 8:10 hire for man, n. any hire for beast;...... 369
Zec 11:16 one, n. heal that that is broken,......... 3808
Zec 11:16 n. feed that that standeth still: but 3808
Zec 14:6 the light shall not be clear, n. dark: ....
Zec 14:7 to the Lord, not day, n. night: 3808
Mal 4:1 leave them neither root n. branch. ....
Mt 5:35 **N. by the earth; for it is his**......... *3383*
Mt 6:20 **neither moth n. rust doth corrupt,** .*3777*
Mt 6:20 **do not break through n. steal:**....... *3761*
Mt 6:25 **n. yet for your body, what ye shall**.*3366*
Mt 6:26 **do they reap, n. gather into barns;** .*3761*
Mt 10:9 **neither gold, n. silver, n. brass in**.. *3366*
Mt 10:10 **N. scrip for your journey, neither** ..*3361*
Mt 10:10 **coats, neither shoes, n. yet staves:** .*3366*
Mt 10:14 **receive you, n. hear your words,** ... *3366*
Mt 10:24 **n. the servant above his lord**........ *3761*
Mt 11:18 **came neither eating n. drinking,** ... *3383*
Mt 12:19 He shall not strive, n. cry; neither *3761*
Mt 22:29 **scriptures, n. the power of God**..... *3366*
Mt 22:30 **marry, n. are given in marriage,** ... *3777*
Mt 24:21 **this time, no, n. ever shall be**. *3364,3761*

Mt 25:13 **day n. the hour wherein the Son**... *3761*
Mk 6:11 **shall not receive you, n. hear you,** .*3366*
Mk 8:26 **town, n. tell it to any in the town.**.*3366*
Mk 12:25 **marry, n. are given in marriage;** ... *3777*
Lu 1:15 drink neither wine **n.** strong drink; *2532*
Lu 6:44 **n. of a bramble bush gather they** .. *3761*
Lu 7:33 **eating bread n. drinking wine;** *3383*
Lu 9:3 **staves, n. scrip, neither bread,** *3383*
Lu 10:4 **neither purse, n. scrip, n. shoes:** ... *3361*
Lu 12:24 **for they neither sow n. reap;**......... *3761*
Lu 12:24 **neither have storehouses n. barn;**... *3761*
Lu 14:12 **not thy friends, n. thy brethren,**.... *3364*
Lu 14:12 **kinsmen, n. thy rich neighbours;**... *3364*
Lu 14:35 **the land, n. yet for the dunghill;**... *3777*
Lu 17:23 **go not after them, n. follow them.** .*3364*
Lu 18:4 **I fear not God, n. regard man;**...... *3756*
Lu 20:35 **marry, n. are given in marriage:** ... *3777*
Lu 21:15 **not be able to gainsay n. resist.** *3761*
Lu 22:68 **will not answer me, n. let me go**... *2228*
Lu 23:15 No, **n.** yet Herod: for I sent you to.... *3761*
Joh 1:13 of blood, **n.** of the will of the flesh, ... *3761*
Joh 1:13 **n.** of the will of man, but of God........ *3761*
Joh 1:25 thou be not that Christ, **n.** Elias, ... *3777*
Joh 4:21 **this mountain, n. yet at Jerusalem,** *3777*
Joh 5:37 **at any time, n. seen his shape**....... *3777*
Joh 8:19 **neither know me, n. my Father:**.... *3777*
Joh 9:3 **this man sinned, n. his parents:** *3777*
Joh 11:50 **N.** consider that it is expedient.......... *3761*
Joh 12:40 **n.** understand with their hearts,.......... *2532*
Joh 16:3 **have not known the Father, n. me.** *3761*
Ac 4:18 all **n.** teach in the name of Jesus. *3366*
Ac 8:21 neither part **n.** lot in this matter: *3761*
Ac 9:9 sight, and neither did eat **n.** drink. *3761*
Ac 13:27 **n.** yet the voices of the prophets *2532*
Ac 15:10 fathers **n.** we were able to bear? *3777*
Ac 19:37 **n.** yet blasphemers of your goddess.... *3777*
Ac 23:8 neither angel, **n.** spirit: but the.......... *3383*
Ac 23:12, 21 neither eat **n.** drink till they had..........
Ac 24:12 in the synagogues, **n.** in the city: *3777*
Ac 24:18 with multitude, **n.** with tumult. *3761*
Ac 25:8 the temple, **n.** yet against Caesar,...... *3777*
Ac 27:20 neither sun **n.** stars in many days......... *3383*
Ro 8:38 neither death, **n.** life, **n.** angels,......... *3777*
Ro 8:38 **n.** principalities, **n.** powers, ... *3777*
Ro 8:38 **n.** things present, **n.** things to come,.. *3777*
Ro 8:39 **N.** height, **n.** depth, **n.** any other....... *3777*
Ro 9:16 willeth, **n.** of him that runneth, ... *3761*
Ro 14:21 to eat flesh, **n.** to drink wine,........... *3366*
Ro 14:21 **n.** any thing whereby thy brother....... *3366*
1Co 2:6 **n.** of the princes of this world, that *3761*
1Co 2:9 hath not seen, **n.** ear heard, ... *2532,3756*
1Co 6:9 **n.** idolaters, **n.** adulterers,............... *3777*
1Co 6:9 **n.** effeminate, **n.** abusers of............. *3777*
1Co 6:10 **N.** thieves, **n.** covetous,................... *3777*
1Co 6:10 **n.** drunkards, **n.** revilers,.................. *3756*
1Co 6:10 **n.** extortioners, shall inherit the......... *3756*
1Co 10:32 **n.** to the Gentiles, **n.** to the church.... *2532*
1Co 12:21 **n.** again the head to the feet, I.......... *2228*
2Co 4:2 **n.** handling the word of God............. *3366*
2Co 7:12 **n.** for his cause...suffered wrong,....... *3777*
Ga 3:28 There is neither Jew **n.** Greek,.......... *3761*
Ga 3:28 there is neither bond **n.** free, ... *3761*
Ga 3:28 there is neither male **n.** female: *3761*
Ga 4:14 flesh ye despised not, **n.** rejected;...... *3761*
Ga 5:6 any thing, **n.** uncircumcision; *3777*
Ga 6:15 any thing, **n.** uncircumcision, but......... *3777*
Eph 5:4 Neither filthiness, **n.** foolish talking, ... *2532*
Eph 5:4 **n.** jesting, which are not.................. *2228*
Eph 5:5 **n.** unclean person, **n.** covetous man,... *2228*
Col 3:11 there is neither Greek **n.** Jew........... *2532*
Col 3:11 circumcision **n.** uncircumcision, ... *2532*
Col 3:11 Barbarian, Scythian, bond **n.** free: ....
1Th 2:3 not of deceit, **n.** of uncleanness, ... *3761*
1Th 2:3 of uncleanness, **n.** of guile, ... *3777*
1Th 2:5 know, **n.** a cloke of covetousness;...... *3777*
1Th 2:6 **N.** of men sought we glory, neither *3777*
1Th 2:6 **n.** yet of others, when we might have..*3777*
1Th 5:5 not of the night, **n.** of darkness. *3761*
2Th 2:2 **n.** by word, **n.** by letter as from us,... *3383*
1Ti 1:7 they say, **n.** whereof they affirm. *3383*
1Ti 2:12 **n.** to usurp authority over the *3761*
1Ti 6:16 no man hath seen, **n.** can see: to....... *3761*
1Ti 6:17 **n.** trust in uncertain riches, but *3366*
2Ti 1:8 of our Lord, **n.** of me his prisoner:..... *3366*
Heb 7:3 beginning of days, **n.** end of life;........ *3383*
Heb 9:25 **N.** yet that he should offer himself *3761*
Heb 12:5 **n.** faint when thou art rebuked of...... *3366*
Heb 12:18 **n.** unto blackness, and darkness,........ *2532*
Heb 13:5 never leave thee, **n.** forsake *3761,3364*
2Pe 1:8 neither be barren **n.** unfruitful in *3761*
Re 3:15 **that thou art neither cold n. hot:** .. *3777*
Re 3:16 **lukewarm, and neither cold n. hot,** *3777*
Re 5:3 no man in heaven, **n.** in earth,........... *3761*
Re 7:1 **n.** on the sea, **n.** on any tree........... *3383*
Re 7:3 neither the sea, **n.** the trees, till........ *3383*
Re 7:16 the sun light on them, **n.** any heat...... *3761*
Re 9:20 neither can see, **n.** hear, **n.** walk: *3777*
Re 9:21 their murders, **n.** of their sorceries,..... *3777*
Re 9:21 sorceries, **n.** of their fornication, ... *3777*
Re 9:21 their fornication, **n.** of their thefts. *3777*
Re 14:11 and they have no rest day **n.** night, ... *2532*
Re 21:4 death, neither sorrow, **n.** crying,........ *3777*

NORTH See also NORTHERN; NORTHWARD.
Ge 28:14 and to the **n.**, and to the south:......... 6828
Ex 26:20 **n.** side there shall be twenty boards: .. 6828
Ex 26:35 shalt put the table on the **n.** side. 6828
Ex 27:11 for the **n.** side in length there shall..... 6828
Ex 36:25 which is toward the **n.** corner,........... 6828
Ex 38:11 for the **n.** side the hangings were an.... 6828
Nu 2:25 camp of Dan shall be on the **n.** side.... 6828
Nu 34:7 And this shall be your **n.** border: 6828
Nu 34:9 this shall be your **n.** border:.............. 6828
Nu 35:5 on the **n.** side two thousand cubits; 6828
Jos 8:11 and pitched on the **n.** side of Ai: 6828
Jos 8:13 host that was on the **n.** of the city, ... 6828
Jos 11:2 were on the **n.** of the mountains, ... 6828
Jos 15:5 their border in the **n.** quarter was 6828
Jos 15:6 along by the **n.** of Beth-arabah;.......... 6828
Jos 15:10 which is Chesalon, on the **n.** side, ... 6828
Jos 16:6 sea to Michmethah on the **n.** side; 6828
Jos 17:9 also was on the **n.** side of the river, ... 6828
Jos 17:10 met together in Asher on the **n.**, ... 6828
Jos 18:5 shall abide in their coasts on the **n.**. ... 6828
Jos 18:12 their border on the **n.** side was from .. 6828
Jos 18:12 to the side of Jericho on the **n.** side,... 6828
Jos 18:16 in the valley of the giants on the **n.**, ... 6828
Jos 18:17 And was drawn from the **n.**, and....... 6828
Jos 18:19 were at the **n.** bay of the salt sea 6828
Jos 19:14 compasseth it on the **n.** side to.......... 6828
Jos 19:27 toward the **n.** side of Beth-emek,....... 6828
Jos 24:30 on the **n.** side of the hill of Gaash. 6828
Jg 2:9 on the **n.** side of the hill Gaash.......... 6828
Jg 7:1 Midianites were on the **n.** side 6828
Jg 21:19 which is on the **n.** side of Beth-el,...... 6828
1Ki 7:25 oxen, three looking toward the **n.**, ... 6828
2Ki 16:14 put it on the **n.** side of the altar......... 6828
1Ch 9:24 toward the east, west, **n.**, and south. . 6828
2Ch 4:4 oxen, three looking toward the **n.**, ... 6828
Job 26:7 He stretcheth out the **n.** over the 6828
Job 37:9 whirlwind: and cold out of the **n.**........ 4215
Job 37:22 Fair weather cometh out of the **n.**:..... 6828
Ps 48:2 mount Zion, on the sides of the **n.**, ... 6828
Ps 89:12 **n.** and the south thou hast created..... 6828
Ps 107:3 from the **n.**, and from the south......... 6828
Pr 25:23 The **n.** wind driveth away rain:.......... 6828
Ec 1:6 and turneth about unto the **n.**;........... 6828
Ec 11:3 toward the south, or toward the **n.**,.... 6828
Ca 4:16 Awake, O **n.** wind; and come, thou 6828
Isa 14:13 congregation, in the sides of the **n.**.... 6828
Isa 14:31 shall come from the **n.** a smoke, ... 6828
Isa 41:25 I have raised up one from the **n.**,........ 6828
Isa 43:6 I will say to the **n.**, Give up; and to ... 6828
Isa 49:12 these from the **n.** and from the west; ..6828
Jer 1:13 the face thereof is toward the **n.**......... 6828
Jer 1:14 Out of the **n.** an evil shall break......... 6828
Jer 1:15 families of the kingdoms of the **n.**,...... 6828
Jer 3:12 proclaim these words toward the **n.**,... 6828
Jer 3:18 out of the land of the **n.** to the land.... 6828
Jer 4:6 for I will bring evil from the **n.**, and.... 6828
Jer 6:1 for evil appeareth out of the **n.**, and ... 6828
Jer 6:22 people cometh from the **n.** country, ... 6828
Jer 10:22 commotion out of the **n.** country, ... 6828
Jer 13:20 behold them that come from the **n.**..... 6828
Jer 16:15 of Israel from the land of the **n.**,........ 6828
Jer 23:8 of Israel out of the **n.** country, ... 6828
Jer 25:9 and take all the families of the **n.**, ... 6828
Jer 25:26 all the kings of the **n.**, far and near, ... 6828
Jer 31:8 will bring them from the **n.** country, ... 6828
Jer 46:6 stumble, and fall toward the **n.** by...... 6828
Jer 46:10 hath a sacrifice in the **n.** country........ 6828
Jer 46:20 cometh; it cometh out of the **n.**......... 6828
Jer 46:24 into the hand of the people of the **n.**... 6828
Jer 47:2 Behold, waters rise up out of the **n.**,... 6828
Jer 50:3 out of the **n.**...cometh up a nation...... 6828
Jer 50:9 great nations from the **n.** country:...... 6828
Jer 50:41 a people shall come from the **n.**,........ 6828
Jer 51:48 shall come unto her from the **n.**,........ 6828
Eze 1:4 a whirlwind came out of the **n.**, ... 6828
Eze 8:3 gate that looketh toward the **n.**;......... 6828
Eze 8:5 eyes now the way toward the **n.**........ 6828
Eze 8:5 mine eyes the way toward the **n.**, ... 6828
Eze 8:14 house which was toward the **n.**;......... 6828
Eze 9:2 gate, which lieth toward the **n.**, ... 6828
Eze 20:47 all faces from the south to the **n.** 6828
Eze 21:4 all flesh from the south to the **n.**......... 6828
Eze 26:7 a king of kings, from the **n.**, with....... 6828
Eze 32:30 There be the princes of the **n.**, all...... 6828
Eze 38:6 of Togarmah of the **n.** quarters,.......... 6828
Eze 38:15 from thy place out of the **n.** parts, ... 6828
Eze 39:2 cause thee to come up from **n.** parts, ..6828
Eze 40:20 court that looked toward the **n.**, ... 6828
Eze 40:23 over against the gate toward the **n.**,... 6828
Eze 40:35 And he brought me to the **n.** gate,...... 6828
Eze 40:40 goeth up to the entry of the **n.** gate, .. 6828
Eze 40:44 which was at the side of the **n.** gate; .. 6828
Eze 40:44 having the prospect toward the **n.**. 6828
Eze 40:46 whose prospect is toward the **n.**......... 6828
Eze 41:11 one door toward the **n.**, and another... 6828
Eze 42:1 utter court, the way toward the **n.**: 6828
Eze 42:1 before the building toward the **n.**. 6828
Eze 42:2 an hundred cubits was the **n.** door,..... 6828
Eze 42:4 cubit; and their doors toward the **n.**.... 6828
Eze 42:11 chambers which were toward the **n.**, .. 6828
Eze 42:13 The **n.** chambers and the south 6828
Eze 42:17 measured the **n.** side, five hundred.... 6828
Eze 44:4 brought...me the way of the **n.** gate.... 6828
Eze 46:9 entering in by the way of the **n.** gate.. 6828
Eze 46:9 go forth by the way of the **n.** gate: 6828
Eze 46:19 priests, which looked toward the **n.**.... 6828
Eze 47:15 of the land toward the **n.** side, from ... 6828
Eze 47:17 Damascus, and the **n.** northward,....... 6828
Eze 47:17 of Hamath. And this is the **n.** side...... 6828
Eze 48:1 From the **n.** end to the coast of the ... 6828
Eze 48:10 toward the **n.** five and twenty 6828
Eze 48:16 the **n.** side four thousand and five 6828
Eze 48:17 toward the **n.** two hundred and.......... 6828
Eze 48:30 goings out of the city on the **n.** side, .. 6828
Da 11:6 shall come to the king of the **n.** to 6828
Da 11:7 the fortress of the king of the **n.**,........ 6828
Da 11:8 more years than the king of the **n.**...... 6828
Da 11:11 him, even with the king of the **n.**: 6828
Da 11:13 For the king of the **n.** shall return, ... 6828
Da 11:15 So the king of the **n.** shall come, ... 6828
Da 11:40 and the king of the **n.** shall come 6828
Da 11:44 tidings...out of the **n.** shall trouble...... 6828
Am 8:12 and from the **n.** even to the east, ... 6828
Zep 2:13 stretch out his hand against the **n.**,...... 6828
Zec 2:6 and flee from the land of the **n.**, ... 6828
Zec 6:6 therein go forth into the **n.** country; ... 6828
Zec 6:8 these that go toward the **n.** country.... 6828
Zec 6:8 quieted my spirit in the **n.** country. 6828
Zec 14:4 half...shall remove toward the **n.**,........ 6828
Lu 13:29 **from the n., and from the south,**... *1005*
Ac 27:12 toward the south west and **n.** west..... *5566*
Re 21:13 on the **n.** three gates; on the south.... *1005*

NORTHERN
Jer 15:12 Shall iron break the **n.** iron and.......... 6828
Joe 2:20 far off from you the **n.** army, ... 6830

NORTHWARD See also NORTH and TOWARD.
Ge 13:14 from the place where thou art **n.**, ... 6828
Ex 40:22 upon the side of the tabernacle **n.**, ... 6828
Le 1:11 shall kill it on the side of the altar **n.** .. 6828
Nu 3:35 pitch on the side of the tabernacle **n.**. . 6828
De 2:3 mountain long enough: turn you **n.**. ... 6828
De 3:27 lift up thine eyes westward, and **n.**,.... 6828
Jos 13:3 even unto the borders of Ekron **n.**, ... 6828
Jos 15:7 and so **n.**, looking toward Gilgal,........ 6828
Jos 15:8 end of the valley of the giants **n.**........ 6828
Jos 15:11 went out unto the side of Ekron **n.**...... 6828
Jos 17:10 **n.** it was Manasseh's, and the sea...... 6828
Jos 18:18 the side over against Arabah **n.**, ... 6828
Jos 18:19 along to the side of Beth-hoglah **n.**..... 6828
Jg 12:1 themselves together, and went **n.**, ... 6828

1Sa 14:5 situate n. over against Michmash, ... 6828
1Ch 26:14 cast lots; and his lot came out n.. 6828
1Ch 26:17 n. four a day, southward four a day, ... 6828
Eze 8:5 behold n. at the gate of the altar........ 6828
Eze 40:19 an hundred cubits eastward and n....... 6828
Eze 47:2 he me out of the way of the gate n., .. 6828
Eze 47:17 of Damascus, and the north n.,......... 6828
Eze 48:1 the border of Damascus n., to the...... 6828
Eze 48:31 three gates n.; one gate of Reuben, ... 6828
Da 8:4 the ram pushing westward, and n.,...... 6828

NORTH-WEST See NORTH and WEST.

NOSE See also NOSES.
Le 21:18 or a lame, or he that hath a flat n., ... 2763
2Ki 19:28 I will put my hook in thy n., and......... 639
Job 40:24 eyes: his n. pierceth through snares..... 639
Job 41:2 Canst thou put an hook into his n.?...... 639
Pr 30:33 the wringing of the n. bringeth forth..... 639
Ca 7:4 they n. is as the tower of Lebanon 639
Ca 7:8 and the smell of thy n. like apples; 639
Isa 3:21 The rings, and n. jewels, ... 639
Isa 37:29 therefore will I put my hook in thy n.,.. 639
Isa 65:5 These are a smoke in my n., a fire...... 639
Eze 8:17 lo, they put the branch to their n.. 639
Eze 23:25 they shall take away thy n. and thine.... 639

NOSE-JEWELS See NOSE and JEWELS.

NOSES
Ps 115:6 n. have they, but they smell not:......... 639
Eze 39:11 it shall stop the n. of the passengers: ....

NOSTRILS
Ge 2:7 into his n. the breath of life; and 639
Ge 7:22 in whose n. was the breath of life,....... 639
Ex 15:8 with the blast of thy n. thy waters....... 639
Nu 11:20 month, until it come out at your n., ... 639
2Sa 22:9 There went up a smoke out of his n., .. 639
2Sa 22:16 at the blast of the breath of his n.. 639
Job 4:9 by the breath of his n. are they........... 639
Job 27:3 and the spirit of God is in my n.;.......... 639
Job 39:20 the glory of his n. is terrible. 5170
Job 41:20 Out of his n. goeth smoke, as out...... 5156
Ps 18:8 went up a smoke out of his n., ... 639
Ps 18:15 at the blast of the breath of thy n......... 639
Isa 2:22 from man, whose breath is in his n. 639
La 4:20 The breath of our n., the anointed....... 639
Am 4:10 your camps to come up unto your n..... 639

NOT See in the APPENDIX; also CANNOT; NOTWITHSTANDING.

NOTABLE
Da 8:5 goat had a n. horn between his.......... 2380
Da 8:8 and for it came up four n. ones 2380
Mt 27:16 a n. prisoner, called Barabbas............ 1978
Ac 2:20 great and n. day of the Lord come: 2016
Ac 4:16 indeed a n. miracle hath been done..... 1110

NOTE See also NOTABLE; NOTED.
Isa 30:8 in a table, and n. it in a book, ... 2710
Ro 16:7 who are of n. among the apostles,....... 1978
2Th 3:14 n. that man, and have no company 4598

NOTED
Da 10:21 is n. in the scripture of truth:............ 7559

NOTHING See also NAUGHT.
Ge 11:6 n. will be restrained from............ 3808,3605
Ge 19:8 only unto these men do n.; for... 3808,1697
Ge 26:29 have done unto thee n. but good,........ 7535
Ge 40:15 and here also have I done n....... 3808,3972
Ex 9:4 n. die of all that is the children's......... 3808
Ex 12:10 ye shall let n. of it remain until.......... 3808
Ex 12:20 Ye shall eat n. leavened; in all your.... 3808
Ex 16:18 that gathered much had n. over, ... 3808
Ex 21:2 seventh he shall go out free for n.. 2600
Ex 22:3 if he have n., then he shall be sold...... 369
Ex 23:26 There shall n. cast their young, ... 3808
Nu 6:4 eat n. that is made of the vine tree, ... 3808
Nu 11:6 is n. at all, beside this manna, ... 369,3605
Nu 16:26 and touch n. of theirs, lest ye...... 408,3605
Nu 22:16 Let n., I pray thee, hinder thee 408
De 2:7 with thee; thou hast lacked n.. 3808
De 20:16 save alive n. that breatheth:....... 3808,3605
De 22:26 the damsel thou shalt do n.;....... 3808,1697
De 28:55 he hath n. left him in the siege.......... 3605
Jos 11:15 left n. undone of all that the....... 3808,1697
Jg 3:2 such as before knew n. thereof;......... 3808
Jg 7:14 is n. else save the sword of Gideon 369
Jg 14:6 and he had n. in his hand:.......... 3972,369
1Sa 3:18 every whit, and hid n. from him......... 3808
1Sa 20:2 father will do n. either great 3808,1697
1Sa 22:15 thy servant knew n. of all this, ... 3808,1697
1Sa 25:21 so that n. was missed of all that . 3808,3972
1Sa 25:36 she told him n., less or more, ... 3808,1697
1Sa 27:1 there is n. better for me than that....... 369
1Sa 30:19 And there was n. lacking to them,....... 3808
2Sa 12:3 But the poor man had n., save..... 369,3605
2Sa 24:24 offer...that which doth cost me n.. 2600
1Ki 4:27 in his month: they lacked n........ 3808,1697
1Ki 8:9 There was n. in the ark save the 369
1Ki 10:21 n. accounted of in the days of 3808,3972
1Ki 11:22 country? And he answered, N. 3808
1Ki 18:43 looked, and said, There is n....... 3808,3972
1Ki 22:16 tell me n. but that which is true 3808
2Ki 10:10 fall unto the earth n. of the word of.... 3808
2Ki 20:13 there was n. in his house, nor.... 3808,1697
2Ki 20:15 there is n. among my treasures 1697
2Ki 20:17 n. shall be left, saith the Lord. ... 3808,1697
2Ch 5:10 There was n. in the ark save the 369
2Ch 9:2 n. hid from Solomon which 3808,1697
2Ch 14:11 said, Lord, it is n. with thee to help..... 369
2Ch 18:15 thou say n. but the truth to me 3808
Ezr 4:3 Ye have n. to do with us to build....... 3808
Ne 2:2 this is n. else but sorrow of heart........ 369
Ne 5:8 peace, and found n. to answer........... 3808
Ne 5:12 them, and will require n. of them;...... 3808
Ne 8:10 unto them for whom n. is prepared: ... 3808
Ne 9:21 wilderness, so that they lacked n.; 3808
Es 2:15 required n. but what Hegai........ 3808,1697
Es 5:13 Yet all this availeth me n., so long....... 369
Es 6:3 There is n. done for him.......... 3808,1697
Es 6:10 n. fail of all that thou hast spoken. 1697
Job 6:18 aside; they go to n., and perish. 8414
Job 6:21 now ye are n.; ye see my casting 3808
Job 8:9 are but of yesterday, and know n.,..... 3808
Job 24:25 liar, and make my speech n. worth?..... 408
Job 26:7 and hangeth the earth upon n........... 1099
Job 34:9 It profiteth a man n. that he............. 3808
Ps 17:3 hast tried me, and shalt find n.; 1077
Ps 19:6 is n. hid from the heat thereof. 369
Ps 39:5 and mine age is as n. before thee:....... 369
Ps 49:17 dieth he shall carry n. away: 3808,3605
Ps 119:165 law: and n. shall offend them. 369
Pr 8:8 is n. froward or perverse in them. 369
Pr 9:13 is simple, and knoweth n........... 1077,4100
Pr 10:2 Treasures of wickedness profit n........ 3808
Pr 13:4 the sluggard desireth, and hath n......... 369
Pr 13:7 himself rich, yet hath n.:........... 3808,3605
Pr 20:4 shall he beg in harvest and have n.. 369
Pr 22:27 If thou hast n. to pay, why should 369
Ec 2:24 There is n. better for a man, than 369
Ec 3:14 n. can be put to it, nor any thing......... 369
Ec 3:22 is n. better, than that a man should 369
Ec 5:14 and there is n. in his hand......... 3808,3972
Ec 5:15 and shall take n. of his labour,.... 3808,3972
Ec 6:2 so that he wanteth n. for his soul........ 369
Ec 7:14 man should find n. after him....... 3808,3972
Isa 34:12 and all her princes shall be n.. 657
Isa 39:2 there was n. in his house, nor.... 3808,1697
Isa 39:4 is n. among my treasures that.... 3808,1697
Isa 39:6 n. shall be left, saith the Lord. ... 3808,1697
Isa 40:17 All nations before him are as n.;.......... 369
Isa 40:17 counted to him less than n., ... 657,8414
Isa 40:23 That bringeth the princes to n. 369
Isa 41:11 confounded: they shall be as n.; 369
Isa 41:12 that war against thee shall be as n.,..... 369
Isa 41:24 Behold, ye are of n., and your work 369
Isa 41:29 are all vanity; their works are n.; 657
Isa 44:10 image that is profitable for n.?........... 1115
Jer 10:24 anger, lest thou bring me to n.............. 4591
Jer 13:7 it was profitable for n........... 3808,3605
Jer 13:10 girdle, which is good for n.......... 3808,3605
Jer 32:17 there is n. too hard for thee: 3808,1697
Jer 32:23 n. of all that thou commandedst 3808
Jer 38:14 thee a thing; hide n. from me...... 408,1697
Jer 39:10 of the people, which had n.,........ 3808,3972
Jer 42:4 I will keep n. back from you. 3808,1697
Jer 50:26 her utterly: let n. of her be left........... 408
La 1:12 Is it n. to you, all ye that pass by?..... 3808
Eze 13:3 their own spirit, and have seen n.! 1115
Da 4:35 of the earth are reputed as n.: 3809
Joe 2:3 yea, and n. shall escape them............ 3808
Am 3:4 out of his den, if he have taken n.? 1115
Am 3:5 earth, and have taken n. at all?.......... 3808
Am 3:7 the Lord God will do n., but....... 3808,1697
Hag 2:3 your eyes in comparison of it as n.?..... 369
Mt 5:13 it is thenceforth good for n., but... 3762
Mt 10:26 there is n. covered, that shall not.. 3762
Mt 15:32 three days, and have n. to eat:3756,5100
Mt 17:20 n. shall be impossible unto you...... 3762
Mt 21:19 found n. thereon, but leaves only, ... 3762
Mt 23:16 shall swear by the temple, it is n.; .3762
Mt 23:18 shall swear by the altar, it is n.;.. 3762
Mt 26:62 said unto him, Answerest thou n.? 3762
Mt 27:12 priests and elders, he answered n.. 3762
Mt 27:19 thou n. to do with that just man: 3367
Mt 27:24 Pilate saw that he could prevail n.,..... 3762
Mk 1:44 See thou say n. to any man: but ... 3367
Mk 4:22 there is n. hid, which shall.... 3756,5100
Mk 5:26 was n. bettered, but rather grew....... 3367
Mk 6:8 should take n. for their journey,......... 3367
Mk 6:36 for they have n. to eat. 3756,5100
Mk 7:15 There is n. from without a man,... 3762
Mk 8:1 and having n. to eat, Jesus called......... 3385
Mk 8:2 three days, and have n. to eat.3756,5100
Mk 9:29 This kind can come forth by n.,.... 3762
Mk 11:13 came to it, he found n. but leaves;..... 3762
Mk 14:60 Jesus, saying, Answerest thou n.?...... 3762
Mk 14:61 he held his peace, and answered n.. ... 3762
Mk 15:3 things: but he answered n.. 3756,3762
Mk 15:4 again, saying, Answerest thou n.? 3756,3762
Mk 15:5 Jesus yet answered n.; so that... 3756,3762
Lu 1:37 n. shall be impossible. 3756,3956,4487
Lu 4:2 And in those days he did eat n........... 3762
Lu 5:5 all the night, and have taken n............ 3762
Lu 6:35 and lend, hoping for n. again;....... 3367
Lu 7:42 And when they had n. to pay, he... 3361
Lu 8:17 n. is secret, that shall not be made.3756
Lu 9:3 Take n. for your journey, neither.. 3367
Lu 10:19 n. shall by any means hurt you.... 3762
Lu 11:6 I have n. to set before him?... 3756,3739
Lu 12:2 there is n. covered, that shall not.. 3762
Lu 22:35 ye any thing? And they said, N.. 3762
Lu 23:9 words; but he answered him n.. 3762
Lu 23:15 n. worthy of death is done unto him. .. 3762
Lu 23:41 but this man hath done n. amiss. 3762
Joh 3:27 A man can receive n., except it be..... 3762
Joh 4:11 Sir, thou hast n. to draw with, ... 3777
Joh 5:19 The Son can do n. of himself, but ..3762
Joh 5:30 I can of mine own self do n.:..3756,3762
Joh 6:12 that remain, that n. be lost:... 3361,5100
Joh 6:39 hath given me I should lose n., 3361,848
Joh 6:63 quickeneth; the flesh profiteth n.: . 3762
Joh 7:26 boldly, and they say n. unto him. 3762
Joh 8:28 am he, and that I do n. of myself;. 3762
Joh 8:54 I honour myself, my honour is n... 3762
Joh 9:33 man were not of God, he could do n... 3762
Joh 11:49 unto them, Ye know n. at all,........... 3756
Joh 12:19 Perceive ye how ye prevail n.?......... 3762
Joh 14:30 world cometh, and hath n. in me.. 3762
Joh 15:5 fruit: for without me ye can do n... 3762
Joh 16:23 And in that day ye shall ask me n..3762
Joh 16:24 have ye asked n. in my name:....... 3762
Joh 18:20 resort; and in secret have I said n..3762
Joh 21:3 and that night they caught n............. 3762
Ac 4:14 them, they could say n. against it....... 3762
Ac 4:21 finding n. how they might punish........ 3367
Ac 10:20 and go with them, doubting n............ 3367
Ac 11:8 n. common or unclean hath........ 3956,3763
Ac 11:12 me go with them, n. doubting. 3367
Ac 17:21 spent their time in n. else, but 3762
Ac 19:36 to be quiet, and to do n. rashly. 3367
Ac 20:20 kept back n. that was profitable......... 3762
Ac 21:24 informed concerning thee, are n.;....... 3762
Ac 23:14 will eat n. until we have slain Paul....... 3367
Ac 23:29 to have n. laid to his charge worthy.... 3367
Ac 25:25 had committed n. worthy of death, ... 3367
Ac 26:31 This man doeth n. worthy of death..... 3762
Ac 27:33 continued fasting, having taken n........ 3367
Ac 28:17 committed n. against the people,........ 3762
Ro 14:14 that there is n. unclean of itself: 3762
1Co 1:19 will bring to n. the understanding......... 114
1Co 4:4 For I know n. by myself; yet am I..... 3762
1Co 4:5 Therefore judge n. before the time..... 3385
1Co 7:19 Circumcision is n., and................... 3762
1Co 7:19 and uncircumcision is n., but the........ 3762
1Co 8:2 he knoweth n. yet as he ought to 3762
1Co 8:4 that an idol is n. in the world, ... 3762
1Co 9:16 the gospel, I have n. to glory of: 3756
1Co 13:2 and have not charity, I am n.............. 3762
1Co 13:3 not charity, it profiteth me n............. 3762
2Co 6:10 as having n., and yet possessing........ 3367

2Co 7:9 might receive damage by us in **n.**....... *3367*
2Co 8:15 had gathered much had **n.** over;......... *3756*
2Co 12:11 for in **n.** am I behind the very.......... *3762*
2Co 12:11 chiefest apostles, though I be **n.**........ *3762*
2Co 13:8 we can do **n.** against the truth,... *3756,5100*
Ga 2:6 in conference added **n.** to me:........... *3762*
Ga 4:1 a child, differeth **n.** from a servant, ... *3762*
Ga 5:2 Christ shall profit you **n.**.................... *3762*
Ga 6:3 to be something, when he is **n.**, ... *3367*
Php 1:20 that in **n.** I shall be ashamed, ... *3762*
Php 1:28 in **n.** terrified by your adversaries: *3367*
Php 2:3 Let **n.** be done through strife or *3367*
Php 4:6 Be careful for **n.**; but in every thing ... *3367*
1Th 4:12 and that ye may have lack of **n.**.......... *3367*
1Ti 4:4 God is good, and **n.** to be refused,..... *3762*
1Ti 5:21 another, doing **n.** by partiality............ *3367*
1Ti 6:4 He is proud, knowing **n.**, but doting.... *3367*
1Ti 6:7 For we brought **n.** into this world, ... *3762*
1Ti 6:7 certain we can carry **n.** out........ *3761,5100*
Tit 1:15 defiled and unbelieving is **n.** pure; *3762*
Tit 3:13 that **n.** be wanting unto them. *3367*
Phm 14 without thy mind would I do **n.**;......... *3762*
Heb 2:8 he left **n.** that is not put under him..... *3762*
Heb 7:14 of which tribe Moses spake **n.**............ *3762*
Heb 7:19 For the law made **n.** perfect, but the.. *3762*
Jas 1:4 be perfect and entire, wanting **n.**.. ...... *3367*
Jas 1:6 let him ask in faith, **n.** wavering:........ *3367*
3Jo 7 forth, taking **n.** of the Gentiles. *3367*
Re 3:17 **with goods, and have need of n.;** ... *3762*

NOTICE
2Sa 3:36 all the people took **n.** of it, and it....... 5234
2Co 9:5 bounty, whereof ye had **n.** before,...... *4293*

NOTWITHSTANDING
Ex 16:20 **N.** they hearkened not unto Moses;..........
Ex 21:21 **N.**, if he continue a day or two, he...... 389
Le 25:32 **N.** the cities of the Levites, and..............
Le 27:28 **N.** no devoted thing, that a man.......... 389
Nu 26:11 **N.** the children of Korah died not.............
Nu 26:55 **N.** the land shall be divided by lot: ....
De 1:26 **N.** ye would not go up, but rebelled ....
De 12:15 **N.** thou mayest kill and eat flesh........ 7535
Jos 22:19 **N.**, if the land of your possession 389
Jg 4:9 **n.** the journey that thou takest shall..... 657
Jg 9:5 **n.** yet Jotham the youngest son ....
1Sa 2:25 **N.** they hearkened not unto the ....
1Sa 20:8 **n.**, if there be in me iniquity, slay ....
1Sa 29:9 **n.** the princes of the Philistines 389
2Sa 24:4 **N.** the king's word prevailed against..........
1Ki 11:12 **N.** in thy days I will not do it for......... 389
2Ki 17:14 **N.** they would not hear, but...................
2Ki 23:26 **N.** the Lord turned not from the 389
2Ch 6:9 **N.** thou shalt not build the house; 7535
2Ch 32:26 **N.** Hezekiah humbled himself for..............
Jer 35:14 **n.** I have spoken unto you, rising.............
Eze 20:21 **N.** the children rebelled against me:..........
Mic 7:13 **N.** the land shall be desolate ....
Mt 2:22 **n.**, being warned of God in a dream,.........
Mt 11:11 **n. he that is least in the kingdom** ....
Mt 17:27 **N., lest we should offend them,** ....
Lu 10:11 **n. be ye sure of this, that the** *4133*
Lu 10:20 **N. in this rejoice not, that the** *4133*
Ac 15:34 **N.** it pleased Silas to abide there.............
Ac 24:4 **N.**, that I be not further tedious...............
Php 1:18 **n.**, every way, whether in................ *4133*
Php 4:14 **N.** ye have well done, that ye did *4133*
1Ti 2:15 **N.** shall she be saved in childbearing,........
2Ti 4:17 **N.** the Lord stood with me, and................
Jas 2:16 **n.** ye give them not those things.............
Rev 2:20 **N. I have a few things against thee,** *.235*

NOUGHT See also NAUGHT; NOTHING.
Ge 29:15 thou therefore serve me for **n.**?......... 2600
De 13:17 cleave **n.** of the cursed thing 408,3972
De 15:9 brother, and thou givest him **n.**;.......... 3808
De 28:63 destroy you, and to bring you to **n.**;... 8045
Ne 4:15 had brought their counsel to **n.**,......... 6565
Job 1:9 said, Doth Job fear God for **n.**?......... 2600
Job 8:22 place of the wicked shall come to **n.**..... 369
Job 14:18 the mountain falling cometh to **n.**, ... 5034
Job 22:6 a pledge from thy brother for **n.**, ... 2600
Ps 33:10 the counsel of the heathen to **n.**: 6331
Ps 44:12 Thou sellest thy people for **n.**, ... 3808,1952
Pr 1:25 ye have set at **n.** all my counsel, ... 6544
Isa 8:10 together, and it shall come to **n.**;........ 6565
Isa 29:20 the terrible one is brought to **n.**,........ 656
Isa 29:21 turn aside the just for a thing of **n.**........ 8414
Isa 41:12 be as nothing, and as a thing of **n.**....... 657
Isa 41:24 of nothing, and your work of **n.**:.......... 659
Isa 49:4 I have spent my strength for **n.**,........ 8414
Isa 52:3 Ye have sold yourselves for **n.**; 2600
Isa 52:5 my people is taken away for **n.**? 2600
Jer 14:14 and a thing of **n.**, and the deceit of...... 434
Am 5:5 and Beth-el shall come to **n.**.............. 205
Am 6:13 which rejoice in a thing of **n.**,..... 3808,1697
Mal 1:10 you that would shut the doors for **n.**? ....
Mal 1:10 ye kindle fire on mine altar for **n.**....... 2600
Mk 9:12 **many things, and be set at n** *1847*
Lu 23:11 with his men of war set him at **n.**, ... *1848*
Ac 4:11 is the stone which was set at **n.** of..... *1848*
Ac 5:36 were scattered, and brought to **n.**...... *3762*
Ac 5:38 work be of men, it will come to **n.**: *2647*
Ac 19:27 craft is in danger to be set at **n.**;........ *557*
Ro 14:10 why dost thou set at **n.** thy brother? .. *1848*
1Co 1:28 not, to bring to **n.** things that are:...... *2673*
1Co 2:6 of this world, that come to **n.**:.......... *2673*
2Th 3:8 did we eat any man's bread for **n.**; *1432*
Re 18:17 hour so great riches is come to **n.**...... *2049*

NOURISH See also NOURISHED; NOURISHETH; NOURISHING.
Ge 45:11 And there will I **n.** thee; for yet 3557
Ge 50:21 I will **n.** you, and your little ones. 3557
Isa 7:21 a man shall **n.** a young cow, and........ 2421
Isa 23:4 neither do I **n.** up young men, nor 1431
Isa 44:14 an ash, and the rain doth **n.** it. 1431

NOURISHED
Ge 47:12 And Joseph **n.** his father, and his 3557
2Sa 12:3 which he had bought and **n.** up: 2421
Isa 1:2 I have **n.** and brought up children,...... 1431
Eze 19:2 **n.** her whelps among young lions. 7235
Ac 7:20 **n.** up in his father's house three.......... *397*
Ac 7:21 him up, and **n.** him for her own son. *397*
Ac 12:20 their country was **n.** by the king's...... *5142*
1Ti 4:6 **n.** up in the words of faith and of...... *1789*
Jas 5:5 ye have **n.** your hearts, as in a day *5142*
Re 12:14 her place, where she is **n.** for a time,. *5142*

NOURISHER
Ru 4:15 thy life, and a **n.** of thine old age; 3557

NOURISHETH
Eph 5:29 **n.** and cherisheth it, even as the........ *1625*

NOURISHING
Da 1:5 so **n.** them three years, that at the 1431

NOURISHMENT
Col 2:19 having **n.** ministered, and knit........... *2023*

NOVICE
1Ti 3:6 Not a **n.**, lest being lifted up with....... *3504*

NOW
Ge 2:23 This is **n.** bones of my bones, and...... 6471
Ge 3:1 **N.** the serpent was more subtil than.........
Ge 3:22 and **n.**, lest he put forth his hand, ... 6258
Ge 4:11 **n.** art thou cursed from the earth,...... 6258
Ge 10:1 **N.** these are the generations of the ....
Ge 11:6 **n.** nothing will be restrained from....... 6258
Ge 11:27 **N.** these are the generations of...............
Ge 12:1 **N.** the Lord had said unto Abram, Get......
Ge 12:11 Behold **n.**, I know...thou art a fair...... 4994
Ge 12:19 **n.** therefore behold thy wife, take 6258
Ge 13:14 Lift up **n.** thine eyes, and look from..........
Ge 15:5 Look **n.** toward heaven, and tell......... 4994
Ge 16:1 **N.** Sarai, Abram's wife, bare him no ....
Ge 16:2 **n.**, the Lord hath restrained me.......... 4994
Ge 18:3 if **n.** I have found favour in thy 4994
Ge 18:11 **N.** Abraham and Sarah were old and ....
Ge 18:21 I will go down **n.**, and see whether 4994
Ge 18:27, 31 Behold **n.**, I have taken upon me... 4994
Ge 19:2 Behold **n.**, my lords, turn in, I pray.... 4994
Ge 19:8 Behold **n.**, I have two daughters........ 4994
Ge 19:9 **n.** will we deal worse with thee, ... 6288
Ge 19:19 Behold **n.**, thy servant hath found 4994
Ge 19:20 Behold **n.**, this city is near to flee...... 4994
Ge 20:7 **N.**...restore the man his wife; 6258
Ge 21:23 **N.** therefore swear unto me here....... 6258
Ge 22:2 Take **n.** thy son, thine only son......... 4994
Ge 22:12 for **n.** I know that thou fearest God,... 6258
Ge 24:42 if **n.** thou do prosper my way........... 4994
Ge 24:49 **n.** if ye will deal kindly and truly........ 6258
Ge 25:12 **N.** these are the generations of...............
Ge 26:22 **n.** the Lord hath made room for us, ... 6258
Ge 26:28 Let there be **n.** an oath betwixt us,.... 4994
Ge 26:29 thou art **n.** the blessed of the Lord..... 6258
Ge 27:2 he said, Behold **n.** I am old.............. 4994
Ge 27:3 **N.** therefore take, I pray thee ....
Ge 27:8 **N.** therefore my son, obey my voice........
Ge 27:9 Go **n.** to the flock and fetch me ....
Ge 27:26 Come near **n.**, and kiss me, my son. .. 4994
Ge 27:36 **n.** he hath taken...my blessing........... 6258
Ge 27:37 shall I do **n.** unto thee, my son?.......... 645
Ge 27:43 **N.** therefore, my son, obey my 6258
Ge 29:32 **n.** therefore my husband will love....... 6258
Ge 29:34 **N.** this time will my husband...... 6471,6258
Ge 29:35 said, **N.** will I praise the Lord: ... 6471,6258
Ge 30:20 **n.** will my husband dwell with me,...... 6471
Ge 30:30 it is **n.** increased unto a multitude;............
Ge 30:30 **n.** when shall I provide for mine 6258
Ge 31:12 Lift up **n.** thine eyes, and see, all....... 4994
Ge 31:13 **n.** arise, get thee out from this.......... 6258
Ge 31:16 **n.** then, whatsoever God hath said..... 6258
Ge 31:25 **N.** Jacob had pitched his tent in the ....
Ge 31:28 hast **n.** done foolishly in so doing. 6258
Ge 31:30 **n.**, though thou wouldest needs be...... 6258
Ge 31:34 **N.** Rachel had taken the images, and ....
Ge 31:42 hadst sent me away **n.** empty............ 6258
Ge 31:44 **N.** therefore come thou, let us 6258
Ge 32:4 Laban, and stayed there until **n.**:........ 6258
Ge 32:10 and **n.** I am become two bands.......... 6258
Ge 33:10 **n.** I have found grace in thy sight,...... 4994
Ge 33:15 Let me **n.** leave with thee some of..... 4994
Ge 34:5 **n.** his sons were with his cattle in the.......
Ge 35:22 **N.** the sons of Jacob were twelve:............
Ge 36:1 **N.** these are the generations of Esau, ...
Ge 37:3 **N.** Israel loved Joseph more than all ....
Ge 37:20 Come **n.** therefore, and let us slay 6258
Ge 37:32 know **n.** whether it be thy son's 4994
Ge 41:33 **N.** therefore let Pharaoh look out ....
Ge 42:1 **N.** when Jacob saw that there was..............
Ge 43:10 surely **n.** we had returned this........... 6258
Ge 43:11 If it must be so **n.**, do this; take of...... 645
Ge 44:10 **N.** also let it be according unto.......... 6258
Ge 44:30 **N.** therefore when I come to thy 6258
Ge 44:33 **N.** therefore, I pray thee, let thy....... 6258
Ge 45:5 **N.** therefore be not grieved, nor........ 6258
Ge 45:8 So **n.** it was not you that sent me...... 6258
Ge 45:19 **N.** thou art commanded, this do ye;..........
Ge 46:30 **N.** let me die, since I have seen........ 6471
Ge 46:34 from our youth even until **n.**, both...... 6258
Ge 47:4 **n.** therefore, we pray thee, let thy..... 6258
Ge 47:29 If **n.** I have found grace in thy sight.... 4994
Ge 48:5 And **n.** thy two sons, Ephraim and 6258
Ge 48:10 **N.** the eyes of Israel were dim for age,.....
Ge 50:4 **n.** I have found grace in your eyes, ... 4994
Ge 50:5 **N.** therefore let me go up, I pray....... 6258
Ge 50:17 Forgive, I pray...**n.**, the trespass 4994
Ge 50:17 **n.**, we pray...forgive the trespass 4994
Ge 50:21 **N.** therefore fear ye not: I will 6258
Ex 1:1 **N.** these are the names of the children......
Ex 1:8 **N.** there arose up a new king over...........
Ex 2:15 **N.** when Pharaoh heard this thing,............
Ex 2:16 **N.** the priest of Midian had seven.............
Ex 3:1 **N.** Moses kept the flock of Jethro ....
Ex 3:3 I will **n.** turn aside, and see this 4994
Ex 3:9 **N.** therefore, behold, the cry of......... 6258
Ex 3:10 Come **n.** therefore, and I will send 6258
Ex 3:18 **n.** let us go, we beseech thee, three .. 6258
Ex 4:6 Put **n.** thine hand into thy bosom. 4994
Ex 4:12 **N.** therefore go, and I will be with..... 6258
Ex 5:5 the people of the land **n.** are many, ... 6258
Ex 5:18 Go therefore **n.**, and work; for.......... 6258
Ex 6:1 **N.** shalt thou see what I will do to 6258
Ex 7:11 **n.** the magicians of Egypt, they ....
Ex 9:15 For **n.** I will stretch out my hand, ... 6258
Ex 9:18 foundation thereof even until **n.**.......... 6258
Ex 9:19 Send therefore **n.**, and gather thy 6258
Ex 10:11 go **n.** ye that are men, and serve........ 4994
Ex 10:17 **N.** therefore forgive, I pray thee,....... 6258
Ex 11:2 Speak **n.** in the ears of the people,..... 4994
Ex 12:40 **N.** the sojourning of the children of..........
Ex 16:36 **N.** an omer is the tenth part of an............
Ex 18:11 **N.** I know that the Lord is greater..... 6258
Ex 18:19 Hearken **n.** unto my voice, I will......... 6258
Ex 19:5 **N.** therefore, if ye will obey my......... 6258
Ex 21:1 **N.** these are the judgments which...... 6258
Ex 29:38 **N.** this is that which thou shalt offer... 6258
Ex 32:10 **N.** therefore let me alone, that my..... 6258
Ex 32:30 and **n.** I will go up unto the Lord;..... 6258
Ex 32:32 **n.**, if thou wilt forgive their sin--;...... 6258
Ex 32:34 Therefore **n.** go, lead the people........ 6258
Ex 33:5 **n.** put off thy ornaments from thee,.... 6258
Ex 33:13 **N.** therefore, I pray thee, if I have.... 6258

Ex 33:13 shew me **n.** thy way, that I may........ 4994
Ex 34:9 **n.** I have found grace in thy sight,...... 4994
Nu 11:6 But **n.** our soul is dried away: 6258
Nu 11:23 shalt see **n.** whether my word shall 6258
Nu 12:3 (**N.** the man Moses was very meek, ...
Nu 12:6 Hear **n.** my words: If there be a........ 4994
Nu 12:13 Heal her **n.**, O God, I beseech thee. .. 4994
Nu 13:20 **N.** the time was the time of the..............
Nu 13:22 (**N.** Hebron was built seven years ....
Nu 14:15 **N.** if thou shalt kill all this people as ....
Nu 14:17 **n.**, I beseech thee, let the power of... 6258
Nu 14:19 people, from Egypt even until **n.**........ 2008
Nu 14:22 tempted me **n.** these ten times,......... 2088
Nu 14:25 (**N.** the Amalekites and the Canaanites ......
Nu 14:41 Wherefore **n.** do ye transgress the..... 2088
Nu 16:1 **N.** Korah, the son of Izhar, the son of......
Nu 16:49 **N.** they that died in the plague were.........
Nu 20:10 Hear **n.**, ye rebels; must we fetch...... 4994
Nu 22:4 **N.** shall this company lick up all......... 6258
Nu 22:6 Come **n.** therefore, I pray thee,......... 6258
Nu 22:11 the earth: come **n.**, curse me them; ... 6258
Nu 22:19 **N.** therefore, I pray you, tarry ye...... 6258
Nu 22:22 **N.** he was riding upon his ass, and his ......
Nu 22:29 hand, for **n.** would I kill thee............ 6258
Nu 22:33 surely **n.** also I had slain thee, and..... 6258
Nu 22:34 **n.** therefore, if it displease thee, I...... 6258
Nu 22:38 have I **n.** any power at all to say 6258
Nu 24:11 Therefore **n.** flee thou to thy place:.... 6258
Nu 24:14 **n.**, behold, I go unto my people:........ 6258
Nu 24:17 I shall see him, but not **n.**: I shall 6258
Nu 25:14 **N.** the name of the Israelite that was.........
Nu 31:17 **N.** therefore kill every male............. 6258
Nu 31:43 (**N.** the half that pertained unto the..........
Nu 32:1 **N.** the children of Reuben and the...........
De 2:13 **N.** rise up, said I, and get you........... 6258
De 4:1 **N.** therefore hearken, O Israel, ... 6258
De 4:32 ask **n.** of the days that are past, ... 4994
De 5:25 **N.** therefore why should we die?........ 6258
De 6:1 **N.** these are the commandments, the........
De 10:12 **n.**, Israel, what doth the Lord thy...... 6258
De 10:22 **n.** the Lord thy God hath made thee... 6258
De 26:10 And **n.**, behold, I have brought the..... 6258
De 31:19 **N.** therefore write ye this song for..... 6258
De 31:21 even **n.**, before I have brought.......... 3117
De 32:39 See **n.** that I, even I, am he, and....... 6258
Jos 1:1 **N.** after the death of Moses the..............
Jos 1:2 **n.** therefore arise, go over this.......... 6258
Jos 2:12 **N.** therefore, I pray you, swear........ 6258
Jos 3:12 **N.** therefore take you twelve men........ 6258
Jos 5:5 **N.** all the people that came out.......... 3588
Jos 5:14 the host of the Lord am I **n.** come...... 6258
Jos 6:1 **N.** Jericho was straitly shut up................
Jos 7:19 tell me **n.** what thou hast done; 4994
Jos 8:11 **n.** there was a valley between them ....
Jos 9:6 **n.** therefore make ye a league 6258
Jos 9:11 **n.** make ye a league with us. 6258
Jos 9:12 but **n.**, behold, it is dry, and it is 6258
Jos 9:17 **N.** their cities were Gibeon, and ....
Jos 9:19 **n.** therefore we may not touch 6258
Jos 9:23 **N.** therefore ye are cursed, and......... 6258
Jos 9:25 **n.**, behold, we are in thine hand: 6258
Jos 10:1 **N.** it came to pass, when Adoni-zedec.......
Jos 12:1 **N.** these are the kings of the land, ...
Jos 13:1 **N.** Joshua was old and stricken in............
Jos 13:7 **N.** therefore divide this land for 6258
Jos 14:10 **n.**, behold, the Lord hath kept me....... 6258
Jos 14:10 **n.**, lo, I am this day fourscore and 6258
Jos 14:11 even so is my strength **n.**, for war,..... 6258
Jos 14:12 **N.** therefore give me this mountain,.... 6258
Jos 17:8 **N.** Manasseh had the land of..................
Jos 18:21 **N.** the cities of the tribe of the children.....
Jos 22:4 **n.** the Lord your God hath given........ 6258
Jos 22:4 **n.** return ye, and get you unto your ... 6258
Jos 22:7 **N.** to the one half of the tribe of............
Jos 22:26 Let us **n.** prepare to build us an 4994
Jos 22:31 **n.** ye have delivered the children of 227
Jos 24:14 **N.** therefore fear the Lord, and 6258
Jos 24:23 **N.** therefore put away, said he, the 6258
Jg 1:1 **N.** after the death of Joshua it came ....
Jg 1:8 **N.** the children of Judah had fought...........
Jg 1:10 (**n.** the name of Hebron before was ....
Jg 1:23 (**N.** the name of the city before was ....
Jg 3:1 **N.** these are the nations which the ....
Jg 4:11 **N.** Heber the Kenite, which was of ....
Jg 6:13 **n.** the Lord hath forsaken us, and 6258
Jg 6:17 If **n.** I have found grace in thy........... 4994
Jg 6:39 it **n.** be dry only upon the fleece;....... 4994
Jg 7:3 **N.** therefore go to, proclaim in 6288
Jg 8:2 I done **n.** in comparison of you? 6288
Jg 8:6 and Zalmunna **n.** in thine hand, ... 6258
Jg 8:10 **N.** Zebah and Zalmunna were in...............
Jg 8:15 and Zalmunna **n.** in thine hand, ... 6258
Jg 9:16 **N.** therefore, if ye have done truly..... 6258
Jg 9:32 **N.** therefore up by night, thou and 6258
Jg 9:38 Where is **n.** thy mouth, wherewith...... 645
Jg 9:38 go out, I pray **n.**, and fight with......... 6258
Jg 11:1 **N.** Jephthah the Gileadite was a ....
Jg 11:7 and why are ye come unto me **n.**........ 6258
Jg 11:8 Therefore we turn again to thee **n.**,...... 6258
Jg 11:13 **n.** therefore restore those lands.......... 6258
Jg 11:23 So **n.** the Lord God of Israel hath 6258
Jg 11:25 **n.** art thou anything better than 6258
Jg 12:6 they unto him, Say **n.** Shibboleth:....... 4994
Jg 13:3 Behold **n.**, thou art barren, and 4994
Jg 13:4 **N.** therefore beware, I pray thee, ... 6258
Jg 13:7 **n.** drink no wine nor strong drink,...... 6258
Jg 13:12 said, **N.** let thy words come to pass. .. 6258
Jg 14:2 **n.** therefore get her for me to wife. ... 6258
Jg 14:12 I will **n.** put forth a riddle unto 4994
Jg 15:3 **N.** shall I be more blameless than 6471
Jg 15:18 **n.** shall I die for thirst, and fall......... 6258
Jg 16:9 **N.** there were men lying in wait,.............
Jg 16:10 **n.** tell me, I pray thee, wherewith...... 6258
Jg 16:27 **N.** the house was full of men and............
Jg 17:3 **n.** therefore I will restore it unto 6258
Jg 17:13 **N.** know I that the Lord will do me 6258
Jg 18:14 **n.** therefore consider what ye have..... 6258
Jg 19:9 **n.** the day draweth toward evening,..... 4994
Jg 19:18 am **n.** going to the house of the Lord;.......
Jg 19:22 **N.** as they were making their hearts.........
Jg 19:24 them I will bring out **n.**, and 4994
Jg 20:3 (**N.** the children of Benjamin heard ....
Jg 20:9 **n.** this shall be the thing which 6258
Jg 20:13 **N.** therefore deliver us the men,........ 6258
Jg 20:38 **N.** there was an appointed sign...............
Jg 21:1 **N.** the men of Israel had sworn in............
Ru 1:1 **N.** it came to pass in the days when.........
Ru 2:2 Let me **n.** go to the field, and 4994
Ru 2:7 even from the morning until **n.**, ... 6258
Ru 3:2 and **n.** is not Boaz of our kindred, ... 6258
Ru 3:11 **n.**, my daughter, fear not; I will do 6258
Ru 3:12 **n.** it is true...I am thy near kinsman: .. 6258
Ru 4:7 **N.** this was the manner in former time......
Ru 4:18 **n.** these are the generations of Pharez: .....
1Sa 1:1 **N.** there was a certain man of ....
1Sa 1:9 **N.** Eli the priest sat upon a seat by a........
1Sa 1:13 **N.** Hannah, she spake in her heart; ....
1Sa 2:12 **N.** the sons of Eli were the sons of ....
1Sa 2:16 but thou shalt give it me **n.**: 3588,6258
1Sa 2:22 **N.** Eli was very old, and heard all that ......
1Sa 2:30 **n.** the Lord saith, Be it far from 6258
1Sa 3:7 **N.** Samuel did not yet know the Lord, ...
1Sa 4:1 **n.** Israel went out against the..................
1Sa 4:15 **N.** Eli was ninety and eight years old; ....
1Sa 6:7 **N.** therefore make a new cart, and..... 6258
1Sa 8:2 **N.** the name of his firstborn was Joel; ....
1Sa 8:5 **n.** make us a king to judge us like...... 6258
1Sa 8:9 **N.** therefore hearken unto their 6258
1Sa 9:1 **N.** there was a man of Benjamin, ...
1Sa 9:3 Take **n.** one of the servants with 4994
1Sa 9:6 Behold **n.**, there is in this city a 4994
1Sa 9:6 to pass: **n.** let us go thither; 6258
1Sa 9:9 he that is **n.** called a prophet was....... 3117
1Sa 9:12 make haste **n.**, for he came to day 6258
1Sa 9:13 **N.** therefore get you up; for about 6258
1Sa 9:15 **N.** the Lord had told Samuel in his ....
1Sa 10:19 **N.** therefore present yourselves......... 6258
1Sa 12:2 **n.**, behold, the king walketh before..... 6258
1Sa 12:7 **N.** therefore stand still, that I may 6258
1Sa 12:10 **n.** deliver us out of the hand of our 6258
1Sa 12:13 **N.** therefore behold the king whom..... 6258
1Sa 12:16 **N.**...stand and see this great thing,...... 6258
1Sa 13:12 come down **n.** upon me to Gilgal,........ 6258
1Sa 13:13 **n.** would the Lord have established..... 6258
1Sa 13:14 **n.** thy kingdom shall not continue: 6258
1Sa 13:19 **N.** there was so smith found ....
1Sa 14:1 **N.** it came to pass upon a day, that ....
1Sa 14:17 Number **n.**, and see who is gone 4994
1Sa 14:30 there not been **n.** a much greater 6258
1Sa 14:49 **N.** the sons of Saul were Jonathan, ...
1Sa 15:1 **n.** therefore hearken thou unto 6258
1Sa 15:3 **N.** go and smite Amalek, and 6258
1Sa 15:25 **N.** therefore, I pray thee, pardon....... 6258
1Sa 15:30 yet honour me **n.**, I pray thee, ... 6258
1Sa 16:12 **N.** he was ruddy, and withal of a.............
1Sa 16:15 Behold **n.**, an evil spirit from God 4994
1Sa 16:16 our Lord **n.** command thy servants, ... 4994
1Sa 16:17 Provide me **n.** a man that can play 4994
1Sa 17:1 **N.** the Philistines gathered together..........
1Sa 17:12 **N.** David was the son of that..................
1Sa 17:17 Take **n.** for thy brethren an ephah......... 4994
1Sa 17:19 **N.** Saul, and they, and all the men of........
1Sa 17:29 David said, What have I **n.** done?....... 6258
1Sa 18:22 **n.** therefore be the king's son in 6258
1Sa 19:2 **n.** therefore, I pray thee, take heed ... 6258
1Sa 20:29 and **n.**, if I have found favour in......... 6258
1Sa 20:31 **n.** send and fetch him unto me, ... 6258
1Sa 20:36 Run, find out **n.** the arrows which...... 4994
1Sa 21:3 **N.**...what is under thine hand? ....
1Sa 21:7 **N.** a certain man of the servants of..........
1Sa 22:6 (**n.** Saul abode in Gibeah under a tree ....
1Sa 22:7 Hear **n.**, ye Benjamites; will the 4994
1Sa 22:12 said, Hear **n.**, thou son of Ahitub. 4994
1Sa 23:20 **N.** therefore, O king, come down....... 6258
1Sa 24:20 And **n.**, behold, I know well that....... 6258
1Sa 24:21 Swear **n.** therefore unto me by the...... 6258
1Sa 25:3 **N.** the name of the man was Nabal;.... 6258
1Sa 25:7 **n.** I have heard that thou hast 6258
1Sa 25:7 **n.** thy shepherds which were with us, ...
1Sa 25:10 be many servants **n.** a days that break ....
1Sa 25:17 **N.** therefore know and consider 6258
1Sa 25:21 **N.** David had said, Surely in vain have ......
1Sa 25:26 **N.** therefore, my lord, as the Lord..... 6258
1Sa 25:26 **n.** let thine enemies, and they that..... 6258
1Sa 25:27 And **n.** this blessing which thine......... 6258
1Sa 26:8 **n.** therefore let me smite him, I 6258
1Sa 26:11 take thou **n.** the spear that is at his.... 6258
1Sa 26:16 **n.** see where the king's spear is, ... 6258
1Sa 26:19 **N.** therefore, I pray thee, let my 6258
1Sa 26:20 **N.** therefore, let not my blood fall 6258
1Sa 27:1 I shall **n.** perish one day by the 6258
1Sa 27:5 have **n.** found grace in thine eyes,...... 4994
1Sa 28:3 **N.** Samuel was dead, and all Israel ....
1Sa 28:22 **N.** therefore, I pray thee, hearken 6258
1Sa 29:1 **N.** the Philistines gathered together..........
1Sa 29:7 Wherefore **n.** return, and go in.......... 6258
1Sa 29:10 **n.** rise up early in the morning 6258
1Sa 31:1 **N.** the Philistines fought against ....
2Sa 1:1 **N.** it came to pass after the death of.........
2Sa 2:6 **n.** the Lord shew kindness and.......... 6258
2Sa 2:7 **n.** let your hands be strengthened, ... 6258
2Sa 2:14 Let the young men **n.** arise, and........ 4994
2Sa 3:1 **N.** there was long war between the..........
2Sa 3:18 **N.** then do it: for the Lord hath......... 6258
2Sa 4:11 not therefore **n.** require his blood....... 6258
2Sa 7:2 See **n.**, I dwell in an house of........... 4994
2Sa 7:8 **N.** therefore so shalt thou say 6258
2Sa 7:25 **n.**, O Lord God, the word that thou ... 6258
2Sa 7:28 **n.**, O Lord God, thou art that God,.... 6258
2Sa 7:29 Therefore **n.** let it please thee to 6258
2Sa 9:6 **N.** when Mephibosheth, the son of...........
2Sa 9:10 **N.** Ziba had fifteen sons and twenty..........
2Sa 12:10 **N.** therefore the sword shall 6258
2Sa 12:23 **n.** he is dead, wherefore should.......... 6258
2Sa 12:28 **N.** therefore gather the rest of the...... 6258
2Sa 13:7 Go **n.** to thy brother Amnon's 4994
2Sa 13:13 **N.** therefore, I pray thee, speak 6258
2Sa 13:17 Put **n.** this woman out from me, ... 4994
2Sa 13:20 but hold **n.** thy peace, my sister: 6258
2Sa 13:24 said, Behold **n.**, thy servant hath 4994
2Sa 13:25 Nay, my son, let us not all **n.** go, ... 4994
2Sa 13:28 **N.** Absalom had commanded his ....
2Sa 13:28 **n.** when Amnon's heart is merry........ 4994
2Sa 13:33 **N.** therefore let not my lord the 6258
2Sa 14:1 **N.** Joab the son of Zeruiah perceived ....
2Sa 14:2 and put on **n.** mourning apparel,......... 4994
2Sa 14:15 **N.** therefore that I am come to.......... 6258
2Sa 14:15 I will **n.** speak unto the king; it.......... 4994
2Sa 14:17 the king shall **n.** be comfortable: 4994
2Sa 14:18 said, Let my lord the king **n.** speak. ... 4994
2Sa 14:21 Behold **n.**, I have done this thing: 4994
2Sa 14:32 **n.**...let me see the king's face; 6258
2Sa 15:34 so will I **n.** also be thy servant: 6258
2Sa 16:11 more **n.** may this Benjamite do it?...... 6258
2Sa 17:1 Let me **n.** choose out twelve 4994
2Sa 17:5 Call **n.** Hushai the Archite also, ... 4994
2Sa 17:9 he is hid **n.** in some pit, or in some.... 6258
2Sa 17:16 **N.** therefore send quickly, and tell...... 6258
2Sa 17:17 **N.** Jonathan and Ahimaaz stayed by ....
2Sa 18:3 **n.** thou art worth ten thousand of....... 6258

2Sa 18:3 therefore **n.** it is better that than....... 6258
2Sa 18:18 **N.** Absalom in his lifetime had taken........
2Sa 18:19 Let me **n.** run, and fear the king........ 4994
2Sa 19:7 **N.** therefore arise, go forth, and........ 6258
2Sa 19:7 befell thee from thy youth until **n.**...... 6258
2Sa 19:9 and **n.** he is fled out of the land for.... 6258
2Sa 19:10 **N.** therefore why speak ye not a........ 6258
2Sa 19:32 **N.** Barzillai was a very aged man,............
2Sa 20:6 **N.** shall Sheba the son of Bichri......... 6258
2Sa 20:23 **N.** Joab was over all the host of..............
2Sa 21:2 (**n.** the Gibeonites were not of the...........
2Sa 23:1 **N.** these be the last words of David. ....
2Sa 24:2 go **n.** through all the tribes of............ 4994
2Sa 24:3 **N.** the Lord thy God add unto the...........
2Sa 24:10 and **n.**, I beseech thee, O Lord,........ 6258
2Sa 24:13 **n.** advise, and see what answer I....... 6258
2Sa 24:14 fall **n.** into the hand of the Lord;........ 4994
2Sa 24:16 is enough: stay **n.** thine hand. 6258
1Ki 1:1 **N.** king David was old and stricken..........
1Ki 1:12 **N.** therefore come, let me, I pray....... 6258
1Ki 1:18 And **n.**, behold, Adonijah reigneth;...... 6258
1Ki 1:18 **n.**, my lord the king, thou knowest..... 6258
1Ki 2:1 **N.** the days of David drew night that.. 6258
1Ki 2:9 **N.**...hold him not guiltless: for........... 6258
1Ki 2:16 **n.** I ask one petition of thee, deny..... 6258
1Ki 2:24 **N.** therefore, as the Lord liveth,........ 6258
1Ki 3:7 And **n.**, O Lord my God, thou hast.... 6258
1Ki 5:4 **n.** the Lord my God hath given me.... 6258
1Ki 5:6 **N.** therefore command thou that........ 6258
1Ki 8:25 Therefore **n.**, Lord God of Israel, ... 6258
1Ki 8:26 And **n.**, O God of Israel, let thy........ 6258
1Ki 9:11 (**N.** Hiram the king of Tyre had..............
1Ki 10:14 **N.** the weight of gold that came to...........
1Ki 12:4 **n.** therefore make thou the.............. 6258
1Ki 12:11 **n.** whereas my father did lade you...... 6258
1Ki 12:16 **n.** see to thine own house, David....... 6258
1Ki 12:26 **N.** shall the kingdom return to the...... 6258
1Ki 13:6 Intreat **n.** the face of the Lord........... 4994
1Ki 13:11 **N.** there dwelt an old prophet in.............
1Ki 14:14 that day: but what? even **n.**............. 6258
1Ki 14:29 **N.** the rest of the acts of Rehoboam,........
1Ki 15:1 **N.** in the eighteenth year of king..............
1Ki 15:7 **N.** the rest of the acts of Abijam, and..........
1Ki 15:31 **N.** the rest of the acts of Nadab, and........
1Ki 16:5 **N.** the rest of the acts of Baasha, ...
1Ki 16:14 **N.** the rest of the acts of Elah, and..........
1Ki 16:20 **N.** the rest of the acts of Zimri, and.........
1Ki 16:27 **N.** the rest of the acts of Omri which.......
1Ki 17:24 **N.** by this I know that thou art a....... 6258
1Ki 18:3 (**N.** Obadiah feared the Lord greatly:.........
1Ki 18:11, 14 **n.** thou sayest, Go, tell thy.......... 6258
1Ki 18:19 **N.** therefore send, and gather to......... 6258
1Ki 18:43 And said to his servant, Go up **n.**,..... 4994
1Ki 19:4 **n.**, O Lord, take away my life;.......... 6258
1Ki 20:31 Behold **n.**, we have heard that the..... 4994
1Ki 20:33 **N.** the men did diligently observe............
1Ki 21:7 Dost thou **n.** govern the kingdom....... 6258
1Ki 22:13 Behold **n.**, the words of the.............. 4994
1Ki 22:23 **N.** therefore, behold, the Lord.......... 6258
1Ki 22:39 **N.** the rest of the acts of Ahab, and.........
1Ki 22:45 **N.** the rest of the acts of Jehoshaphat, ...
2Ki 1:4 **N.** therefore thus saith the Lord, ...
2Ki 1:5 Why are ye **n.** turned back?.............. 2088
2Ki 1:14 my life **n.** be precious in thy sight...... 6258
2Ki 1:18 **N.** the rest of the acts of Ahaziah............
2Ki 2:16 **n.**, there be with thy servants.......... 4994
2Ki 3:1 **N.** Jehoram the son of Ahab began to........
2Ki 3:15 But **n.** bring me a minstrel. And........ 6258
2Ki 3:23 **n.** therefore, Moab, to the spoil......... 6258
2Ki 4:1 **N.** there cried a certain woman of............
2Ki 4:9 Behold **n.**, I perceive that this is....... 4994
2Ki 4:13 Say **n.** unto her, Behold, thou hast...... 4994
2Ki 4:26 Run **n.**, I pray thee, to meet her, ... 6258
2Ki 5:1 **N.** Naaman, captain of the host of............
2Ki 5:6 **N.** when this letter is come unto......... 6258
2Ki 5:8 let him come **n.** to me, and he.......... 4994
2Ki 5:15 **n.** I know that there is no god in....... 4994
2Ki 5:15 **n.** therefore, I pray thee, take a........ 6258
2Ki 5:22 even **n.** there be come to me from..... 6258
2Ki 6:1 Behold **n.**, the place where we.......... 4994
2Ki 7:4 **N.** therefore come, and let us fall........ 6258
2Ki 7:9 **n.** therefore come, that we may go..... 6258
2Ki 7:12 will **n.** shew you what the Syrians...... 4994
2Ki 7:19 **N.**, behold, if the Lord should make.........
2Ki 8:6 she left the land, even until **n.**........... 6258
2Ki 9:12 they said, It is false; tell us **n.**........... 4994
2Ki 9:14 (**N.** Joram had kept Ramoth-gilead, ...
2Ki 9:26 **N.** therefore take and cast him.......... 6258
2Ki 9:34 Go, see **n.** this cursed woman, and.... 4994
2Ki 10:2 **N.** as soon as this letter cometh......... 6258
2Ki 10:6 **N.** the king's sons, being seventy......... 6258
2Ki 10:10 Know **n.** that there shall fall unto......... 645
2Ki 10:19 **N.** therefore call unto me all the........ 6258
2Ki 10:34 **N.** the rest of the acts of Jehu, and all......
2Ki 12:7 **n.** therefore receive no more............ 6258
2Ki 13:8 **N.** the rest of the acts of Jehoahaz..... 6258
2Ki 13:14 **N.** Elisha was fallen sick of his...............
2Ki 13:19 **n.** thou shalt smite Syria...thrice........ 6258
2Ki 14:15 **N.** the rest of the acts of Jehoash............
2Ki 14:19 **N.** they made a conspiracy against............
2Ki 14:28 **N.** the rest of the acts of Jeroboam, ...
2Ki 15:36 **N.** the rest of the acts of Jotham, ...
2Ki 16:19 **N.** the rest of the acts of Ahaz which........
2Ki 18:1 **N.** it came to pass in the third year..........
2Ki 18:13 **N.** in the fourteenth year of king..............
2Ki 18:19 them, Speak ye **n.** to Hezekiah,......... 4994
2Ki 18:20 **N.** on whom dost thou trust, that....... 6258
2Ki 18:21 **N.**, behold, thou trustest upon the...... 6258
2Ki 18:23 **N.** therefore, I pray thee, give.......... 6258
2Ki 18:25 Am I **n.** come up without the Lord..... 6258
2Ki 19:19 **N.** therefore, O Lord our God, I........ 6258
2Ki 19:25 **n.** have I brought it to pass, that....... 6258
2Ki 20:3 remember **n.** how I have walked......... 4994
2Ki 21:17 **N.** the rest of the acts of Manasseh,.........
2Ki 21:25 **N.** the rest of the acts of Amon which......
2Ki 22:14 (**n.** she dwelt in Jerusalem in the.............
2Ki 23:28 **N.** the rest of the acts of Josiah, and........
2Ki 24:5 **N.** the rest of the acts of Jehoiakim, ...
2Ki 25:4 (**n.** the Chaldees were against the............
2Ki 25:11 **N.** the rest of the people that were..........
1Ch 1:32 **N.** the sons of Keturah, Abraham's...........
1Ch 1:43 **N.** these are the kings that reigned..........
1Ch 2:34 **n.** Sheshan had no sons, but..................
1Ch 2:42 **N.** the sons of Caleb the brother of..........
1Ch 3:1 **N.** these were the sons of David,............
1Ch 5:1 **N.** the sons of Reuben the firstborn..........
1Ch 6:54 **N.** these are their dwelling places............
1Ch 7:1 **N.** the sons of Issachar were, Tola,..........
1Ch 8:1 **N.** Benjamin begat Bela his firstborn,........
1Ch 9:2 **N.** the first inhabitants that dwelt in..........
1Ch 10:1 **N.** the Philistines fought against..............
1Ch 11:15 **N.** three of the thirty captains went..........
1Ch 12:1 **N.** these are they that came to David.......
1Ch 14:1 **N.** Hiram the king of Tyre sent..............
1Ch 14:4 **N.** these are the names of his................
1Ch 17:1 **N.** it came to pass, as David sat in...........
1Ch 17:7 **N.** therefore thus shalt thou say......... 6258
1Ch 17:23 Therefore **n.**, Lord, let the thing........ 6258
1Ch 17:26 And **n.**, Lord, thou art God, and........ 6258
1Ch 17:27 **N.** therefore let it please thee to......... 6258
1Ch 18:1 **N.** after this it came to pass, that............
1Ch 18:9 **N.** when Tou king of Hamath heard..........
1Ch 19:1 **N.** it came to pass after this, that............
1Ch 19:10 **N.** when Joab saw that the battle............
1Ch 21:8 but **n.**, I beseech thee, do away........ 6258
1Ch 21:12 **N.** therefore advise thyself what........ 6258
1Ch 21:13 let me fall **n.** into the hand of the....... 4994
1Ch 21:15 is enough, stay **n.** thine hand. 6258
1Ch 21:20 **N.** Ornan was threshing wheat.................
1Ch 22:5 **n.** make preparations for it. So.......... 4994
1Ch 22:11 **N.**, my son, the Lord be with............ 6258
1Ch 22:14 **N.**, behold, in my trouble I have.............
1Ch 22:19 **N.** set your heart and your soul......... 6258
1Ch 23:3 **N.** the Levites were numbered from...........
1Ch 23:14 **N.** concerning Moses the man of God, ...
1Ch 24:1 **N.** these are the divisions of the sons.......
1Ch 24:7 **N.** the first lot came forth to..................
1Ch 25:9 **N.** the first lot came forth for Asaph.........
1Ch 27:1 **N.** the children of Israel after their..........
1Ch 28:8 **N.** therefore in the sight of all.......... 6258
1Ch 28:10 Take heed **n.**; for the Lord hath........ 6258
1Ch 29:2 **N.** I have prepared with all my might........
1Ch 29:13 **N.** therefore, our God, we thank........ 6258
1Ch 29:17 **n.** have I seen with joy thy people, ... 6258
1Ch 29:20 **N.** bless the Lord your God. And....... 4994
1Ch 29:29 **N.** the acts of David the king, first..........
2Ch 1:9 **N.**, O Lord God, let thy promise....... 6258
2Ch 1:10 me **n.** wisdom and knowledge,........... 6258
2Ch 2:7 Send me **n.** therefore a man cunning... 6258
2Ch 2:13 And **n.** I have sent a cunning man, ... 6258
2Ch 2:15 **N.** therefore the wheat, and the......... 6258
2Ch 3:3 **N.** these are the things wherein...............
2Ch 6:7 **N.** it was in the heart of David my..........
2Ch 6:16 **N.** therefore, O Lord God of Israel,.... 6258
2Ch 6:17 **N.** then, O Lord God of Israel, let..... 6258
2Ch 6:40 **N.**, my God, let, I beseech thee,....... 6258
2Ch 6:41 **N.** therefore arise, O Lord God,........ 6258
2Ch 7:1 **N.** when Solomon had made an end..........
2Ch 7:15 **N.** mine eyes shall be open, and........ 6258
2Ch 7:16 For **n.** have I chosen and sanctified.... 6258
2Ch 8:16 **N.** all the work of Solomon was..............
2Ch 9:13 **N.** the weight of gold that came to..........
2Ch 9:29 **N.** the rest of the acts of Solomon,..........
2Ch 10:4 **n.** therefore ease thou somewhat....... 6258
2Ch 10:16 **n.**, David, see to thine own house...... 6258
2Ch 12:15 **N.** the acts of Rehoboam, first and..........
2Ch 13:1 **N.** in the eighteenth year of king............
2Ch 13:8 And **n.** ye think to withstand the........ 6258
2Ch 15:3 **N.** for a long season Israel hath been........
2Ch 18:1 **n.** Jehoshaphat had riches and.................
2Ch 18:22 **N.** therefore, behold, the Lord.......... 6258
2Ch 18:30 **N.** the king of Syria had commanded.........
2Ch 19:7 **n.** let the fear of the Lord be............ 6258
2Ch 20:10 **n.**, behold, the children of Ammon...... 6258
2Ch 20:34 **N.** the rest of the acts of Jehoshaphat, ...
2Ch 21:1 **N.** Jehoshaphat slept with his fathers,........
2Ch 21:4 **N.** when Jehoram was risen up to............
2Ch 23:12 **N.** when Athaliah heard the noise of.........
2Ch 24:11 **N.** it came to pass, that at what time........
2Ch 24:17 **N.** after the death of Jehoiada came.........
2Ch 24:27 **N.** concerning his sons, and the..............
2Ch 25:3 **N.** it came to pass, when the.................
2Ch 25:14 **N.** it came to pass, after that.................
2Ch 25:19 abide **n.** at home; why shouldest........ 6258
2Ch 25:26 **N.** the rest of the acts of Amaziah,...........
2Ch 25:27 **N.** after the time that Amaziah did............
2Ch 26:22 **N.** the rest of the acts of Uzziah, first.......
2Ch 27:7 **N.** the rest of the acts of Jotham, and.......
2Ch 28:10 And **n.** ye purpose to keep under....... 6258
2Ch 28:11 **N.** hear me therefore, and deliver...... 6258
2Ch 28:26 **N.** the rest of his acts and of all his..........
2Ch 29:5 Levites, sanctify **n.** yourselves,.......... 6258
2Ch 29:10 **N.** it is in mine heart to make a......... 6258
2Ch 29:11 My sons, be not **n.** negligent: for....... 6258
2Ch 29:17 **N.** they began on the first day of the........
2Ch 29:31 **N.**...have consecrated yourselves......... 6258
2Ch 30:8 **N.** be ye not stiffnecked as your........ 6258
2Ch 31:1 **N.** when all this was finished, all.............
2Ch 32:15 **N.** therefore let not Hezekiah............ 6258
2Ch 32:32 **N.** the rest of the acts of Hezekiah,..........
2Ch 33:14 **N.** after this he built a wall without..........
2Ch 33:18 **N.** the rest of the acts of Manasseh,.........
2Ch 34:8 **N.** in the eighteenth year of his reign,.......
2Ch 34:22 (**n.** she dwelt in Jerusalem in the.............
2Ch 35:3 serve **n.** the Lord your God, and....... 6258
2Ch 35:26 **N.** the rest of the acts of Josiah, and........
2Ch 36:8 **N.** the rest of the acts of Jehoiakim, ...
2Ch 36:22 **N.** in the first year of Cyrus king of..........
Ezr 1:1 **N.** in the first year of Cyrus king of..........
Ezr 2:1 **N.** these are the children of the..............
Ezr 3:8 **N.** in the second year of their coming.........
Ezr 4:1 **N.** when the adversaries of Judah and.......
Ezr 4:13 Be it known **n.** unto the king, that, ... 3705
Ezr 4:14 **N.** because we have maintenance....... 3705
Ezr 4:21 Give ye **n.** commandment to cause...... 3705
Ezr 4:22 Take heed **n.** that ye fail not to do...........
Ezr 4:23 **N.** when the copy of king.................. 116
Ezr 5:16 until **n.** hath it been in building, ... 3705
Ezr 5:17 **N.** therefore, if it seem good to the.... 3705
Ezr 6:6 **N.** therefore, Tatnai, governor........... 3705
Ezr 7:1 **N.** after these things, in the reign of.........
Ezr 7:11 **N.** this is the copy of the letter that.........
Ezr 8:1 These are **n.** the chief of their fathers,......
Ezr 8:33 **N.** on the fourth day was the silver..........
Ezr 9:1 **N.** when these things were done, the.......
Ezr 9:8 And **n.** for a little space grace hath..... 6258
Ezr 9:10 **n.**, O our God, what shall we say...... 6258
Ezr 9:12 **N.**...give not your daughters unto....... 6258
Ezr 10:1 **N.** when Ezra had prayed, and when.........
Ezr 10:2 land: yet **n.** here is hope in Israel...... 6258
Ezr 10:3 **N.**...let us make a covenant with....... 6258
Ezr 10:11 **N.** therefore make confession unto..... 6258
Ezr 10:14 Let **n.** our rulers of all the.............. 4994
Ne 1:6 Let thine ear **n.** be attentive, and....... 4994
Ne 1:6 which I pray before thee **n.**, day......... 3117
Ne 1:10 **N.** these are thy servants and thy.........
Ne 1:11 let **n.** thine ear be attentive to the..... 4994
Ne 2:1 **N.** I had not been beforetime sad in.........

Ne 2:9 **N.** the king had sent captains of the...
Ne 4:3 **N.** Tobiah the Ammonite was by him, ...
Ne 5:5 **n.** our flesh is as the flesh of our... 6258
Ne 5:18 **N.** that which was prepared for me...
Ne 6:1 **N.** it came to pass, when Sanballat, ...
Ne 6:7 **n.** shall it be reported to the king... 6258
Ne 6:6 Come **n.** therefore, and let us take... 6258
Ne 6:9 **N.** therefore, O God, strengthen my... 6258
Ne 7:1 **N.** it came to pass, when the wall was...
Ne 7:4 **N.** the city was large and great: but...
Ne 9:1 **N.** in the twenty and fourth day of...
Ne 9:32 **N.** therefore, our God, the great,... 6258
Ne 10:1 **N.** those that sealed were, Nehemiah,...
Ne 11:3 **N.** these are the chief of the province...
Ne 12:1 **N.** these are the priests and the...
Ne 13:3 **N.** it came to pass, when they had...
Es 1:1 **N.** it came to pass in the days of...
Es 2:5 **N.** in Shushan the palace there was a...
Es 2:12 **N.** when every maid's turn was come...
Es 2:15 **N.** when the turn of Esther, the...
Es 3:4 **N.** it came to pass, when they spake...
Es 5:1 **N.** it came to pass on the third day, ...
Es 6:4 **N.** Haman was come into the outward...
Es 6:6 **N.** Haman thought in his heart, To...
Es 9:1 **N.** in the twelfth month, that is, the...
Es 9:12 **n.** what is thy petition? and it shall...
Job 1:6 **N.** there was a day when the sons of...
Job 1:11 But put forth thine hand **n.**, and... 4994
Job 2:5 But put forth thine hand **n.**, and... 4994
Job 2:11 **N.** when Job's three friends heard of...
Job 3:13 For **n.** should I have lain still and... 6258
Job 4:5 But **n.** it is come upon thee, and... 6258
Job 4:12 **N.** a thing was secretly brought to me, ...
Job 5:1 Call **n.**, if there be any that will... 4994
Job 6:3 For **n.** it would be heavier than the... 6258
Job 6:21 For **n.** ye are nothing; ye see my... 6258
Job 6:28 **N.** therefore be content, look upon... 6258
Job 7:21 for **n.** shall I sleep in the dust; and... 6258
Job 8:6 surely **n.** he would awake for thee,... 6258
Job 9:25 **N.** my days are swifter than a post:...
Job 12:7 But ask **n.** the beasts, and they... 4994
Job 13:6 Hear **n.** my reasoning, and hearken... 4994
Job 13:18 Behold **n.**, I have ordered my cause;.. 4994
Job 13:19 for **n.**, if I hold my tongue, I shall... 6258
Job 14:16 For **n.** thou numberest my steps:... 6258
Job 16:7 But **n.** he hath made me weary:... 6258
Job 16:19 Also **n.**, behold, my witness is in... 6258
Job 17:3 Lay down **n.**, put me in a surety... 4994
Job 17:10 you all, do ye return, and come **n.**... 4994
Job 17:15 And where is **n.** my hope? as for... 645
Job 19:6 Know **n.** that God hath overthrown... 645
Job 19:23 Oh that my words were **n.** written!... 645
Job 22:21 Acquaint **n.** thyself with him, and... 4994
Job 24:25 if it be not so **n.**, who will make... 645
Job 30:1 **n.** they that are younger than I... 6258
Job 30:9 And **n.** am I their song, yea, I am... 6258
Job 30:16 **n.** my soul is poured out upon me;... 6258
Job 32:4 **N.** Elihu had waited till Job had spoken,...
Job 32:14 **N.** he hath not directed his words...
Job 33:2 **n.** I have opened my mouth, my... 4994
Job 34:16 If **n.** thou hast understanding, hear...
Job 35:15 But **n.**, because it is not so, he hath... 6258
Job 37:21 And **n.** men see not the bright light... 6258
Job 38:3 Gird up **n.** thy loins like a man;... 4994
Job 40:7 Gird up thy loins **n.** like a man: I... 4994
Job 40:10 Deck thyself **n.** with majesty and... 4994
Job 40:15 Behold **n.** behemoth, which I made... 4994
Job 40:16 Lo **n.**, his strength is in his loins,... 4994
Job 42:5 ear; but **n.** mine eye seeth thee... 6258
Job 42:8 take unto you **n.** seven bullocks... 6258
Ps 2:10 Be wise **n.** therefore, O ye kings: be.. 6258
Ps 12:5 sighing of the needy, **n.** will I arise,... 6258
Ps 17:11 have **n.** compassed us in our steps:... 6258
Ps 20:6 **N.** know I that the Lord saveth his... 6258
Ps 27:6 And **n.** shall mine head be lifted up... 6258
Ps 37:25 I have been young, and **n.** am old; yet...
Ps 39:7 And **n.**, Lord, what wait I for? my... 6258
Ps 41:8 and **n.** that he lieth he shall rise up no...
Ps 50:22 **N.** consider this, ye that forget... 4994
Ps 71:18 **N.** also when I am old and...
Ps 74:6 **n.** they break down the carved... 6258
Ps 115:2 say, Where is **n.** their God?... 4994
Ps 116:14, 18 pay my vows unto the Lord **n.**... 4994
Ps 118:2 Let Israel **n.** say, that his mercy... 4994
Ps 118:3 Let the house of Aaron **n.** say, that... 4994
Ps 118:4 Let them **n.** that fear the Lord say,... 4994
Ps 118:25 Save **n.**, I beseech thee, O Lord: O... 4994
Ps 118:25 I beseech thee, send **n.** prosperity... 4994
Ps 119:67 astray: but **n.** have I kept thy word... 6258
Ps 122:8 I will **n.** say, Peace be within thee... 4994
Ps 124:1 was on our side, **n.** may Israel say;... 4994
Ps 129:1 from my youth, may Israel **n.** say:... 4994
Pr 5:7 Hear me **n.** therefore, O ye... 6258
Pr 6:3 Do this **n.**, my son, and deliver... 645
Pr 7:12 **N.** is she without, **n.** in the streets,... 6471
Pr 7:24 Hearken unto me **n.** therefore, O... 6258
Pr 8:32 **N.** therefore hearken unto me, O... 6258
Ec 2:1 Go to **n.**, I will prove thee with... 4994
Ec 2:16 which **n.** is in the days to come... 3528
Ec 3:15 That which hath been is **n.**; and... 3528
Ec 9:6 and their envy, is **n.** perished;... 3528
Ec 9:7 for God **n.** accepteth thy works... 3528
Ec 9:15 **N.** there was found in it a poor wise...
Ec 12:1 Remember **n.** thy Creator in the days...
Ca 3:2 I will rise **n.**, and go about the... 4994
Ca 7:8 **N.** also thy breasts shall be as... 4994
Isa 1:18 Come **n.**, and let us reason... 4994
Isa 1:21 lodged in it; but **n.** murderers... 6258
Isa 5:1 **N.** will I sing to my wellbeloved... 4994
Isa 5:3 **n.**, O inhabitants of Jerusalem,... 6258
Isa 5:5 **n.** go to; I will tell you what I will... 6258
Isa 7:3 Go forth **n.** to meet Ahaz, thou,... 4994
Isa 7:13 said, Hear ye **n.**, O house of David:... 4994
Isa 8:7 **N.** therefore, behold, the Lord...
Isa 16:14 **n.** the Lord hath spoken, saying,... 6258
Isa 19:12 men? and let them tell thee **n.**,... 4994
Isa 22:1 What aileth thee **n.**, that thou art... 645
Isa 28:22 **N.** therefore be ye not mockers... 6258
Isa 29:22 Jacob shall not **n.** be ashamed,... 6258
Isa 29:22 neither shall his face **n.** wax pale...
Isa 30:8 **N.** go, write it before them in a... 6258
Isa 31:3 **N.** the Egyptians are men, and not...
Isa 33:10 **N.** will I rise, saith the Lord;... 6258
Isa 33:10 the Lord; **n.** will I be exalted;... 6258
Isa 33:10 be exalted; **n.** will I lift up myself... 6258
Isa 36:1 **N.** it came to pass in the fourteenth...
Isa 36:4 Say ye **n.** to Hezekiah, Thus saith... 4994
Isa 36:5 **n.** on whom dost thou trust, that... 6258
Isa 36:8 **N.** therefore give pledges, I pray... 6258
Isa 36:10 And am I **n.** come up without the... 6258
Isa 37:20 **N.** therefore, O Lord our God, save... 6258
Isa 37:26 **n.** have I brought it to pass, that... 6258
Isa 38:3 Remember **n.**, O Lord, I beseech... 4994
Isa 42:14 **n.** will I cry like a travailing woman;...
Isa 43:1 **n.** thus saith the Lord that created... 6258
Isa 43:19 **n.** it shall spring forth; shall ye not... 6258
Isa 44:1 Yet **n.** hear, O Jacob my servant;... 6258
Isa 47:8 hear **n.** this, thou that art given to... 6258
Isa 47:12 Stand **n.** with thine enchantments,... 4994
Isa 47:13 Let **n.** the astrologers, the... 4994
Isa 48:7 They are created **n.**, and not from... 6258
Isa 48:16 and **n.** the Lord God, and his Spirit,... 6258
Isa 49:5 **n.**, saith the Lord that formed me... 6258
Isa 49:19 even **n.** be too narrow by reason... 6258
Isa 51:21 hear **n.** this, thou afflicted, and... 4994
Isa 52:5 **N.** therefore, what have I here,... 6258
Isa 64:8 **n.**, O Lord, thou art our father; we... 6258
Jer 2:18 **n.** what hast thou to do in the way... 6258
Jer 4:12 **n.** also will I give sentence against... 6258
Jer 4:31 Woe is me **n.**! for my soul is... 4994
Jer 5:1 and see **n.**, and know, and seek in... 4994
Jer 5:21 Hear **n.** this, O foolish people, and... 4994
Jer 5:24 Let us **n.** fear the Lord our God,... 4994
Jer 7:12 But go ye **n.** unto my place which... 4994
Jer 7:13 **n.**, because ye have done all these... 4994
Jer 14:10 he will **n.** remember their iniquity,... 4994
Jer 17:15 the word of the Lord? let it come **n.**... 4994
Jer 18:11 **N.** therefore go to, speak to the... 6258
Jer 18:11 return...**n.** every one from his evil... 4994
Jer 18:13 Ask ye **n.** among the heathen, who... 4994
Jer 20:1 **N.** Pashur the son of Immer the...
Jer 25:5 Turn ye again **n.** every one from... 4994
Jer 26:8 **N.** it came to pass, when Jeremiah...
Jer 26:13 Therefore **n.** amend your ways... 6258
Jer 27:6 And **n.** have I given all these lands... 6258
Jer 27:16 shall **n.** shortly be brought again... 6258
Jer 27:18 **n.** make intercession to the Lord... 4994
Jer 28:7 hear thou **n.** this word that I speak... 4994
Jer 28:15 Hear **n.**, Hananiah; The Lord hath... 4994
Jer 29:1 **N.** these are the words of the letter...
Jer 29:27 **N.** therefore why hast thou not... 6258
Jer 30:6 Ask ye **n.**, and see whether a man... 4994
Jer 32:16 **N.** when I had delivered the evidence...
Jer 32:36 **n.** therefore thus saith the Lord,... 6258
Jer 34:10 **N.** when all the princes, and all the...
Jer 34:15 ye were **n.** turned, and had done... 3117
Jer 35:15 Return ye **n.** every man from his... 4994
Jer 36:15 Sit down **n.**, and read it in our ears... 4994
Jer 36:16 **N.** it came to pass, when they had...
Jer 36:17 Tell us **n.**, How didst thou write... 4994
Jer 36:22 **N.** the king sat in the winterhouse in...
Jer 37:3 Pray **n.** unto the Lord our God for... 4994
Jer 37:4 **N.** Jeremiah came in and went out...
Jer 37:19 Where are **n.** your prophets which...
Jer 37:20 hear **n.**, I pray thee, O my lord the... 6254
Jer 38:7 **N.** when Ebed-melech the Ethiopian,...
Jer 38:12 Put **n.** these old cast clouts and... 4994
Jer 38:25 Declare unto us **n.** what thou hast... 4994
Jer 39:11 **n.** Nebuchadrezzar king of Babylon...
Jer 39:15 **N.** the word of the Lord came unto...
Jer 40:3 **N.** the Lord hath brought it, and...
Jer 40:4 **n.**, behold, I loose thee this day... 6258
Jer 40:5 **N.** while he was not yet gone back, he...
Jer 40:7 **N.** when all the captains of the forces...
Jer 41:1 **N.** it came to pass in the seventh...
Jer 41:9 **N.** the pit wherein Ishmael had cast...
Jer 41:13 **N.** it came to pass, that when all the...
Jer 42:15 **n.** therefore hear the word of the... 6258
Jer 42:21 **n.** I have this day declared it to you;...
Jer 42:22 **N.** therefore know certainly that... 6258
Jer 44:7 Therefore **n.** thus saith the Lord,... 6258
Jer 45:3 Woe is me **n.**! for the Lord hath... 4994
Jer 52:7 (**n.** the Chaldeans were by the city...
Jer 52:12 **N.** in the fifth month, in the tenth day...
Eze 1:1 **N.** it came to pass in the thirtieth...
Eze 1:15 **N.** as I held the living creatures,...
Eze 4:14 even till **n.** have I not eaten of that... 6258
Eze 7:3 **N.** is the end come upon thee,... 6258
Eze 7:8 **N.** will I shortly pour out my fury... 6258
Eze 8:5 Son of man, lift up thine eyes **n.**... 4994
Eze 8:8 me, Son of man, dig **n.** in the wall:... 4994
Eze 10:3 **N.** the cherubims stood on the right...
Eze 16:8 **N.** when I passed by thee, and looked...
Eze 17:12 Say **n.** to the rebellious house,... 4994
Eze 18:14 **N.**, lo, if he beget a son, that seeth all...
Eze 18:25 Hear **n.**, O house of Israel; Is not... 4994
Eze 19:5 **N.** when she saw that she had waited,...
Eze 19:13 **n.** she is planted in the wilderness,... 6258
Eze 22:2 **N.**, thou son of man, wilt thou judge,...
Eze 23:43 Will they **n.** commit whoredoms... 6258
Eze 26:2 be replenished, **n.** she is laid waste:...
Eze 26:18 **N.** shall the isles tremble in the... 6258
Eze 27:2 **N.**, thou son of man, take up a...
Eze 33:22 **N.** the hand of the Lord was upon me...
Eze 38:12 desolate places that are **n.** inhabited,...
Eze 39:25 **N.** will I bring again the captivity... 6258
Eze 41:12 **N.** the building that was before the...
Eze 42:5 **N.** the upper chambers were shorter:...
Eze 42:15 **N.** when he had made an end of...
Eze 43:9 **N.** let them put away their... 6258
Eze 46:12 **N.** when the prince shall prepare... 3588
Eze 47:7 **N.** when I had returned, behold, at...
Eze 48:1 **N.** these are the names of the tribes...
Da 1:6 **N.** among these were of the children...
Da 1:9 **N.** God had brought Daniel into favour...
Da 1:18 **N.** at the end of the days that the king...
Da 2:23 made known unto me **n.** what we... 3705
Da 2:23 **n.** made known unto us the king's... 3705
Da 3:15 **N.** if ye be ready that at what time... 3705
Da 4:18 **N.** thou, O Belteshazzar, declare...
Da 4:37 **N.** I Nebuchadnezzar praise and... 3705
Da 5:10 **N.** the queen by reason of the words...
Da 5:12 **n.** let Daniel be called, and he will... 3705
Da 5:15 **n.** the wise men, the astrologers,... 3705
Da 5:16 **n.** if thou canst read the writing,... 3705
Da 6:8 **N.**, O king, establish the decree,... 3705
Da 6:10 **N.** when Daniel knew that the... 1768
Da 6:16 **N.** the king spake and said unto... 116
Da 8:18 **N.** as he was speaking with me, I was...
Da 8:22 **N.** that being broken, whereas four...
Da 9:15 And **n.**, O Lord our God, that hast... 6258
Da 9:17 **N.** therefore, O our God, hear the... 6258
Da 9:22 I am **n.** come forth to give thee skill... 6258
Da 10:11 for unto thee am I **n.** sent:... 6258
Da 10:14 **N.** I am come to make thee...
Da 10:20 **n.** will I return to fight with the... 6258
Da 11:2 And **n.** will I shew thee the truth... 6258
Da 11:34 **N.** when they shall fall, they shall be...
Ho 1:8 **N.** when she had weaned Lo-ruhamah,...
Ho 2:7 then was it better with me than **n.**... 6258

Ho 2:10 **n.** will I discover her lewdness in....... 6258
Ho 4:16 **n.** the Lord will feed them as a lamb .. 6258
Ho 5:3 for **n.**, O Ephraim, thou committest.........
Ho 5:7 **n.** shall **n.** month devour them 6258
Ho 7:2 **n.** their own doings have beset them ....
Ho 8:8 **n.** shall they be among the Gentiles as......
Ho 8:10 **n.** will I gather them, and they.......... 6258
Ho 8:13 **n.** will he remember their iniquity,...... 6258
Ho 10:2 **n.** shall they be found faulty: he......... 6258
Ho 10:3 **n.** they shall say, We have no king,.... 6258
Ho 13:2 And **n.** they sin more and more, and... 6258
Joe 2:12 Therefore also **n.**, saith the Lord. 6258
Am 6:7 Therefore **n.** shall they go captive...... 6258
Am 7:16 **N.** therefore hear thou the word 6258
Jon 1:1 **N.** the word of the Lord came unto ....
Jon 1:17 **N.** the Lord...prepared a great fish...........
Jon 3:3 **N.** Nineveh was an exceeding great ....
Jon 4:3 **n.**, O Lord, take, I beseech thee, ... 6258
Mic 4:9 **N.** why dost thou cry out aloud? is...... 6258
Mic 4:10 **n.** shalt thou go...out of the city, ... 6258
Mic 4:11 **N.** also many nations are gathered...... 6258
Mic 5:1 **N.** gather thyself in troops, O 6258
Mic 5:4 **n.** shall he be great unto the ends...... 6258
Mic 6:1 Hear ye **n.** what the Lord saith; 4994
Mic 6:5 remember **n.** what Balak king of........ 4994
Mic 7:4 **n.** shall be their perplexity................ 6258
Mic 7:10 **n.** shall she be trodden down as the ... 6258
Na 1:13 **n.** will I break his yoke from off......... 6258
Hag 1:5 **N.** therefore thus saith the Lord of...... 6258
Hag 2:2 Speak **n.** to Zerubbabel the son of...... 4994
Hag 2:3 and how do ye see it **n.**? is it not 6258
Hag 2:4 Yet **n.** be strong, O Zerubbabel, ... 6258
Hag 2:11 Ask **n.** the priests concerning the....... 4994
Hag 2:15 **n.**, I pray...consider from this day...... 4994
Hag 2:18 Consider **n.** from this day and 4994
Zec 1:4 Turn ye **n.** from your evil ways, ... 4994
Zec 3:3 **N.** Joshua was clothed with filthy.............
Zec 3:8 Hear **n.**, O Joshua the high priest,...... 4994
Zec 5:5 Lift up **n.** thine eyes, and see what 4994
Zec 8:11 **n.** I will not be unto the residue 6258
Zec 9:8 for **n.** have I seen with mine eyes...... 6258
Mal 1:8 offer it **n.** unto thy governor; will........ 4994
Mal 1:9 **n.**, I pray you, beseech God that 6258
Mal 2:1 **n.**, O ye priests, this commandment ... 6258
Mal 3:10 and prove me **n.** herewith, saith 4994
Mal 3:15 And **n.** we call the proud happy; 6258
Mt 1:18 **N.** the birth of Jesus Christ was on 1161
Mt 1:22 **N.** all this was done, that it might 1161
Mt 2:1 **N.** when Jesus was born in............... 1161
Mt 3:10 **n.** also the ax is laid unto the root...... 2236
Mt 3:15 **Suffer it to be so n.: for thus it 737**
Mt 4:12 **N.** when Jesus had heard that............ 1161
Mt 8:18 **N.** when Jesus saw great.................. 1161
Mt 9:18 saying, My daughter is even **n.** dead: ... 737
Mt 10:2 **N.** the names of the twelve............... 1161
Mt 11:2 **N.** when John had heard in the 1161
Mt 11:12 **until n. the kingdom of heaven 737**
Mt 14:15 place, and the time is **n.** past; 2236
Mt 14:24 But the ship was **n.** in the midst of 2236
Mt 15:32 **continue with me n. three days, ... 2236**
Mt 21:18 **N.** in the morning as he returned....... 1161
Mt 22:25 **N.** there were with us seven............ 1161
Mt 24:32 **N. learn a parable of the fig tree;.. 1161**
Mt 26:6 **N.** when Jesus was in Bethany, in...... 1161
Mt 26:17 **N.** the first day of the feast of........... 1161
Mt 26:20 **N.** when the even was come, he sat... 1161
Mt 26:45 **Sleep on n., and take your rest: 3063**
Mt 26:48 **N.** he that betrayed him gave............ 1161
Mt 26:53 **that I cannot n. pray to my Father, .737**
Mt 26:59 **N.** the chief priests, and elders,...............
Mt 26:65 **n.** ye have heard his blasphemy. 3568
Mt 26:69 **N.** Peter sat without in the palace: 1161
Mt 27:15 **N.** at that feast the governor was....... 1161
Mt 27:42 him **n.** come down from the cross, ... 3568
Mt 27:43 let him deliver him **n.**, if he will.......... 3568
Mt 27:45 **N.** from the sixth hour there was....... 1161
Mt 27:54 **N.** when the centurion, and they....... 1161
Mt 27:62 **N.** the next day, that followed the...... 1161
Mt 28:11 **N.** when they were going, behold,...... 1161
Mk 1:14 **N.** after that John was put in............ 1161
Mk 1:16 **N.** as he walked by the sea of Galilee, ...
Mk 4:37 into the ship, so that it was **n.** full...... 2235
Mk 5:11 **N.** there was there nigh unto the 1161
Mk 6:35 when the day was **n.** far spent, ... 2236
Mk 6:35 place, and **n.** the time is far passed: ... 2236
Mk 8:2 **have n. been with me three days, .. 2236**
Mk 8:14 **N.** the disciples had forgotten to 2532
Mk 10:30 **an hundredfold n. in this time. 3568**
Mk 11:11 **n.** the eventide was come, he went.... 2236
Mk 12:20 **N.** there were seven brethren: and..... 3767
Mk 13:12 **N. the brother shall betray the...... 1161**
Mk 13:28 **N. learn a parable of the fig tree;.. 1161**
Mk 14:41 **Sleep on n., and take your rest: it. 3063**
Mk 15:6 **N.** at that feast he released unto........ 1161
Mk 15:32 Christ...descend **n.** from the cross, ... 3568
Mk 15:42 And **n.** when the even was come, ... 2236
Mk 16:9 **N.** when Jesus was risen early the 1161
Lu 1:7 both were **n.** well stricken in years...........
Lu 1:57 **N.** Elisabeth's full time came that....... 1161
Lu 2:15 Let us **n.** go even unto Bethlehem, ... 1211
Lu 2:29 **n.** lettest thou thy servant depart....... 3568
Lu 2:41 **N.** his parents went to Jerusalem 2532
Lu 3:1 **N.** in the fifteenth year of the reign.... 1161
Lu 3:9 **n.** also the axe is laid unto the root.... 2236
Lu 3:21 **N.** when all the people were 1161
Lu 4:40 **N.** when the sun was setting, all........ 1161
Lu 5:4 **N.** when he had left speaking, he 1161
Lu 6:21 **Blessed are ye that hunger n.: for ..3568**
Lu 6:21 **Blessed are ye that weep n.: for ye.3568**
Lu 6:25 **Woe unto you that laugh n.! for ye 3568**
Lu 7:1 **N.** when he had ended all his 1161
Lu 7:6 he was **n.** not far from the house, ... 2236
Lu 7:12 **N.** when he came nigh to the gate....... 1161
Lu 7:39 **N.** when the Pharisee which had........ 1161
Lu 8:11 **N. the parable is this: The seed is ..1161**
Lu 8:22 **N.** it came to pass on a certain day, ... 2532
Lu 8:38 **N.** the man out of whom the devils...... 1161
Lu 9:7 **N.** Herod the tetrarch heard of all..... 1161
Lu 10:36 **which n. of these three, thinkest... 3767**
Lu 10:38 **N.** it came to pass, as they went, ... 1161
Lu 11:7 **the door is n. shut, and my........... 2236**
Lu 11:39 **N. do ye Pharisees make clean the .3568**
Lu 14:17 **Come; for all things are n. ready.. 2236**
Lu 15:25 **N. his elder son was in the field:... 1161**
Lu 16:25 **n. he is comforted, and thou art.... 3568**
Lu 18:22 **N.** when Jesus heard these things, ... 1161
Lu 19:37 even **n.** at the descent of the mount... 2236
Lu 19:42 **n. they are hid from thine eyes...... 3568**
Lu 20:37 **N. that the dead are raised, even... 1161**
Lu 21:30 **when they n. shoot forth, ye see ... 2236**
Lu 21:30 **that summer is n. night at hand.... 2236**
Lu 22:1 **N.** the feast of unleavened bread........ 1161
Lu 22:36 **But n., he that hath a purse, let ... 3568**
Lu 23:47 **N.** when the centurion saw what......... 1161
Lu 24:1 **N.** upon the first day of the week, ... 2532
Joh 1:44 **N.** Philip was of Bethsaida, the.......... 1161
Joh 2:8 **Draw out n., and bear unto the..... 3568**
Joh 2:10 hast kept the good wine until **n.**.......... 737
Joh 2:23 **N.** when he was in Jerusalem at......... 1161
Joh 4:6 **N.** Jacob's well was there. Jesus 1161
Joh 4:18 **he whom thou n. hast is not thy ... 3568**
Joh 4:23 **the hour cometh, and n. is, when.. 3568**
Joh 4:42 **N.** we believe, not because of thy...... 3765
Joh 4:43 **N.** after two days he departed........... 1161
Joh 4:51 And as he was **n.** going down, his...... 2236
Joh 5:2 **N.** there is at Jerusalem by the.......... 1161
Joh 5:6 been **n.** a long time in that case,......... 2236
Joh 5:25 **The hour is coming, and n. is, ... 3568**
Joh 6:10 **N.** there was much grass in the......... 1160
Joh 6:16 And when even was **n.** come, his............
Joh 6:17 it was **n.** dark, and Jesus was not 2236
Joh 7:2 **N.** the Jews' feast of tabernacles......... 1161
Joh 7:14 **N.** about the midst of the feast.......... 2236
Joh 8:5 **N.** Moses in the law commanded........ 1161
Joh 8:40 **But n. ye seek to kill me, a man... 3568**
Joh 8:52 **N.** we know that thou hast a devil...... 3568
Joh 9:19 blind? how then doth he **n.** see?.......... 737
Joh 9:21 by what means he **n.** seeth, we.......... 3568
Joh 9:25 that, whereas I was blind, **n.** I see. 737
Joh 9:31 **N.** we know that God heareth not 1161
Joh 9:41 **n. ye say, We see; therefore your .. 3568**
Joh 11:1 **N.** a certain man was sick, named...... 1161
Joh 11:5 **N.** Jesus loved Martha, and her 1161
Joh 11:18 **N.** Bethany was nigh...Jerusalem,...... 1161
Joh 11:22 that even **n.**, whatsoever thou wilt 3568
Joh 11:30 **N.** Jesus was not yet come into the.... 1161
Joh 11:57 **N.** both the chief priests and the...... 1161
Joh 12:27 **N. is my soul troubled; and what ...3568**
Joh 12:31 **N. is the judgment of this world;... 3568**
Joh 12:31 **n. shall the prince of this world be .3568**
Joh 13:1 **N.** before the feast of the passover, ... 1161
Joh 13:2 devil having **n.** put into the heart 2236
Joh 13:7 **What I do thou knowest not n.;...... 737**
Joh 13:19 **N. I tell you before it come, that,... 737**
Joh 13:23 **N.** there was leaning on Jesus'........... 1161
Joh 13:28 **N.** no man at the table knew for........ 1161
Joh 13:31 **N. is the Son of man glorified,....... 3568**
Joh 13:33 **ye cannot come; so n. I say to you. .737**
Joh 13:36 **go, thou canst not follow me n.; ... 3568**
Joh 13:37 Lord, why cannot I follow thee **n.**? 737
Joh 14:29 **n. I have told you before it come .. 3568**
Joh 15:3 **N. ye are clean through the word.. 2236**
Joh 15:22 **n. they have no cloke for their sin. 3568**
Joh 15:24 **n. have they both seen and hated .. 3568**
Joh 16:5 **n. I go my way to him that sent ... 3568**
Joh 16:12 **you, but ye cannot bear them n...... 737**
Joh 16:19 **N.** Jesus knew that they were 3767
Joh 16:22 **ye n. therefore have sorrow: but I ..3568**
Joh 16:29 Lo, **n.** speakest thou plainly, and........ 3568
Joh 16:30 **N.** are we sure that thou knowest...... 3568
Joh 16:31 answered them, **Do ye n. believe?.... 737**
Joh 16:32 **the hour cometh, yea, is n. come, . 3568**
Joh 17:5 **n., O Father, glorify thou me with .3568**
Joh 17:7 **N. they have known that all things 3568**
Joh 17:11 **And n. I am no more in the world, .3765**
Joh 17:13 **And n. come I to thee; and these... 3568**
Joh 18:14 **N.** Caiaphas was he, which gave 1161
Joh 18:24 **N.** Annas had sent him bound............ 3767
Joh 18:36 **n. is my kingdom not from hence.. 3568**
Joh 18:40 **N.** Barabbas was a robber. 1161
Joh 19:23 **n.** the coat was without seam, woven . 1161
Joh 19:25 **N.** there stood by the cross of Jesus... 1161
Joh 19:28 all things were **n.** accomplished,......... 2236
Joh 19:29 **N.** there was set a vessel full of 3767
Joh 19:41 **N.** in the place where he was............ 1161
Joh 21:4 when the morning was **n.** come, ... 2236
Joh 21:6 **n.** they were not able to draw it......... 3765
Joh 21:7 **N.** when Simon Peter heard............... 3767
Joh 21:10 **the fish which ye have n. caught... 3568**
Joh 21:14 This is **n.** the third time that Jesus..... 2236
Ac 1:18 **N.** this man purchased a field 3767
Ac 2:6 **N.** when this was noised abroad,........ 1161
Ac 2:33 this, which ye **n.** see and hear........... 3568
Ac 2:37 **N.** when they heard this they were 1161
Ac 3:1 **N.** Peter and John went up together... 1161
Ac 3:17 **n.**, brethren, I wot that through......... 3568
Ac 4:3 next day: for it was **n.** eventide.......... 2236
Ac 4:13 **N.**, when they saw the boldness of..... 1161
Ac 4:29 **n.**, Lord, behold their threatenings: 3568
Ac 5:24 **N.** when the high priest and the.......... 1161
Ac 5:38 **n.** I say unto you, Refrain from 3568
Ac 7:4 into this land, wherein ye **n.** dwell....... 3568
Ac 7:11 **N.** there came a dearth all over 1161
Ac 7:34 **n.** come, I will send thee into............ 3568
Ac 7:52 whom ye have been **n.** the betrayers .. 3568
Ac 8:14 **N.** when the apostles which were....... 1161
Ac 9:36 **N.** there was at Joppa a certain 1161
Ac 10:5 **n.** send men to Joppa, and call for...... 3568
Ac 10:17 **N.** while Peter doubted in himself....... 1161
Ac 10:33 **N.** therefore are we all here.............. 3568
Ac 11:19 **N.** they which were scattered............ 3767
Ac 12:1 **N.** about that time Herod the king....... 1161
Ac 12:11 **N.** I know of a surety, that the.......... 3568
Ac 12:18 **N.** as soon as it was day, there 1161
Ac 13:1 **N.** there were in the church that........ 1161
Ac 13:11 **n.**, behold, the hand of the Lord is..... 3568
Ac 13:13 **N.** when Paul and his company 1161
Ac 13:34 **n.** no more to return to corruption, he ......
Ac 13:43 **N.** when the congregation was........... 1161
Ac 15:10 **N.** therefore why tempt ye God, to.... 3568
Ac 16:6 **N.** ...they had gone throughout......... 1161
Ac 16:36 **n.** therefore depart, and go in peace... 3568
Ac 16:37 **n.** do they thrust us out privily?......... 3568
Ac 17:1 **N.** when they had passed through 1161
Ac 17:16 **N.** while Paul waited for them at......... 1161
Ac 17:30 **n.** commandeth all men everywhere.... 3568
Ac 18:14 was **n.** about to open his mouth,........ 1161
Ac 20:22 **n.**, behold, I go bound in the spirit..... 3568
Ac 20:25 And **n.**, behold, I know that ye all,..... 3568
Ac 20:32 **n.**, brethren, I commend you to God, . 3568
Ac 21:3 **N.** when we had discovered 1161
Ac 22:1 ye my defence which I make **n.**.......... 3568
Ac 22:16 **n.** why tarriest thou? arise, and......... 3568
Ac 23:15 **N.** therefore ye with the counsel........ 3568
Ac 23:21 and **n.** are they ready, looking for a.... 3568
Ac 24:13 things whereof they **n.** accuse me. 3568
Ac 24:17 **N.** after many years I came to.......... 1161
Ac 25:1 **N.** when Festus was come into.......... 3767
Ac 26:6 **n.** I stand and am judged for the........ 3568

Ac 26:17 **Gentiles, unto whom n. I send** *3568*
Ac 27:9 **N.** when much time was spent, and.... *1161*
Ac 27:9 when sailing was **n.** dangerous,.......... *2235*
Ac 27:9 the fast was **n.** already past, ... *2235*
Ac 27:22 And **n.** I exhort you to be of good...... *3568*
Ro 1:10 if by any means **n.** at length I............ *2236*
Ro 1:13 **N.** I would not have you ignorant, ... *1161*
Ro 3:19 **N.** we know that what things soever... *1161*
Ro 3:21 But **n.** the righteousness of God *3568*
Ro 4:4 **N.** to him that worketh is the............ *1161*
Ro 4:19 not his own body **n.** dead, when *2236*
Ro 4:23 **N.** it was not written for his sake....... *1161*
Ro 5:9 being **n.** justified by his blood, ... *3568*
Ro 5:11 we have **n.** received the atonement. ... *3568*
Ro 6:8 **N.** if we be dead with Christ, we *1161*
Ro 6:19 even so **n.** yield your members.......... *3568*
Ro 6:21 things whereof ye are **n.** ashamed?..... *3568*
Ro 6:22 But **n.** being made free from sin, ... *3570*
Ro 7:6 **n.** we are delivered from the law, ... *3570*
Ro 7:17 **N.** then it is no more I that do it, ... *3570*
Ro 7:20 **N.** if I do that I would not, it is no..... *1161*
Ro 8:1 therefore **n.** no condemnation to *3568*
Ro 8:9 **N.** if any man have not the Spirit *1161*
Ro 8:22 in pain together until **n.**.................. *3568*
Ro 11:12 **n.** if the fall of them be the riches...... *1161*
Ro 11:30 God, yet have **n.** obtained mercy *3568*
Ro 11:31 so have these also **n.** not believed,..... *3568*
Ro 13:11 **n.** it is high time to awake out of *2236*
Ro 13:11 for **n.** is our salvation nearer than *3568*
Ro 14:15 **n.** walkest thou not charitably............ *3765*
Ro 15:5 **N.** the God of patience and............... *1161*
Ro 15:8 **N.** I say that Jesus Christ was a *1160*
Ro 15:13 **N.** the God of hope fill you with all..... *1161*
Ro 15:23 **n.** having no more place in these........ *3570*
Ro 15:25 **n.** I go unto Jerusalem to minister...... *3570*
Ro 15:30 **N.** I beseech you, brethren, for the.... *1161*
Ro 15:33 **N.** the God of peace be with you all. .. *1161*
Ro 16:17 **N.** I beseech you, brethren, mark *1161*
Ro 16:25 **N.** to him that is of power to stablish.. *1161*
Ro 16:26 But **n.** is made manifest, and by *3568*
1Co 1:10 **N.** I beseech you, brethren, by the *1161*
1Co 1:12 **N.** this I say, that every one of you.... *1161*
1Co 2:12 **N.** we have received, not the spirit *1161*
1Co 3:2 bear it, neither yet **n.** are ye able. *3568*
1Co 3:8 **N.** he that planteth and he that.......... *1161*
1Co 3:12 **N.** if any man build upon this............ *1161*
1Co 4:7 **n.** if thou didst receive it, why *2532*
1Co 4:8 **N.** ye are full, **n.** ye are rich, ye *2236*
1Co 4:18 **N.** some are puffed up, as though I *1161*
1Co 5:11 **n.** I have written unto you not to....... *3570*
1Co 6:7 **N.** therefore there is utterly a........... *2236*
1Co 6:13 **N.** the body is not for fornication, ... *1161*
1Co 7:1 **N.** concerning the things whereof ye... *1161*
1Co 7:14 unclean; but **n.** are they holy............ *3568*
1Co 7:25 **N.** concerning virgins I have no *1161*
1Co 8:1 **N.** as touching things offered unto...... *1161*
1Co 9:25 **N.** they do it to obtain a...crown; *367*
1Co 10:6 **N.** these things were our examples,.... *1161*
1Co 10:11 **N.** all these things happened unto....... *1161*
1Co 11:2 **N.** I praise you, brethren, that ye *1161*
1Co 11:17 **N.** is this that I declare unto you I *1161*
1Co 12:1 **N.** concerning spiritual gifts,............. *1161*
1Co 12:4 **N.** there are diversities of gifts, but.... *1161*
1Co 12:18 **n.** hath God set the members every ... *3570*
1Co 12:20 But **n.** are they many members, ... *3568*
1Co 12:27 **N.** ye are the body of Christ, and *1161*
1Co 13:12 **n.** we see through a glass, darkly; *737*
1Co 13:12 **N.** I know in part; but then shall I *737*
1Co 13:13 And **n.** abideth faith, hope, charity,..... *3570*
1Co 14:6 **N.**, brethren, if I come unto you......... *3570*
1Co 15:12 **N.** if Christ be preached that he......... *1161*
1Co 15:20 **n.** is Christ risen from the dead, ... *3570*
1Co 15:50 **N.** this I say, brethren, that flesh......... *1161*
1Co 16:1 **N.** concerning the collection for the *1161*
1Co 16:5 **N.** I will come unto you, when I *1161*
1Co 16:7 I will not see you **n.** by the way;.......... *737*
1Co 16:10 **N.** if Timotheus come, see that he *1161*
2Co 1:21 **N.** he which stablisheth us with you.... *1161*
2Co 2:14 **N.** thanks be unto God, which........... *1161*
2Co 3:17 **N.** the Lord is that Spirit: and........... *1161*
2Co 5:5 **N.** he that hath wrought us for the..... *1161*
2Co 5:16 yet **n.** henceforth know we him no *3568*
2Co 5:20 **N.** then we are ambassadors for *3767*
2Co 6:2 behold, **n.** is the accepted time; *3568*
2Co 6:2 behold, **n.** is the day of salvation.)....... *3568*
2Co 6:13 **N.** for a recompence in the same, ... *1161*
2Co 7:9 **N.** I rejoice, not that ye were made.... *3568*
2Co 8:11 **N.** therefore perform the doing of *3570*
2Co 8:14 **n.** at this time your abundance........... *3568*
2Co 8:22 but **n.** much more diligent, upon *3570*
2Co 9:10 **N.** he that ministereth seed to........... *1161*
2Co 10:1 **N.** I Paul myself beseech you by the... *1161*
2Co 12:6 but **n.** I forbear, lest any man should ....
2Co 13:2 being absent **n.** I write to them *3568*
2Co 13:7 **N.** I pray to God that ye do no evil; ... *1161*
Ga 1:9 As we said before, so say I **n.** again, ... *737*
Ga 1:10 For do I **n.** persuade men, or God? *737*
Ga 1:20 **N.** the things which I write unto *2236*
Ga 1:23 **n.** preacheth that faith which once *3568*
Ga 2:20 the life which I **n.** live in the flesh...... *3568*
Ga 3:3 are ye **n.** made perfect by the flesh?... *3568*
Ga 3:16 **N.** to Abraham and his seed were *1161*
Ga 3:20 **N.** a mediator is not a mediator of...... *1161*
Ga 4:1 **N.** I say, That the heir, as long as *2236*
Ga 4:9 But **n.**, after that ye have known *3568*
Ga 4:20 I desire to be present with you **n.**, ... *737*
Ga 4:25 to Jerusalem which **n.** is, and is *3568*
Ga 4:28 **N.** we, brethren, as Isaac was, are..... *1161*
Ga 4:29 after the Spirit, even so it is **n.**. *3568*
Ga 5:19 **N.** the works of the flesh are *1161*
Eph 2:2 the spirit that **n.** worketh in the......... *3568*
Eph 2:13 But **n.** in Christ Jesus ye who *3570*
Eph 2:19 **N.**...ye are no more strangers........... *3767*
Eph 3:5 **n.** revealed unto his holy apostles....... *3568*
Eph 3:10 **n.** unto the principalities and *3568*
Eph 3:20 **N.** unto him that is able to do............ *1161*
Eph 4:9 (**N.** that he ascended, what is it but.... *1161*
Eph 5:8 but **n.** are ye light in the Lord:.......... *3568*
Php 1:5 gospel from the first day until **n.**; *3568*
Php 1:20 so **n.** also Christ shall be magnified...... *3568*
Php 1:30 saw in me, and **n.** hear to be in me.... *3568*
Php 2:12 but **n.** much more in my absence, ... *3568*
Php 3:18 **n.** tell you even weeping, that they *3568*
Php 4:10 **n.** at the last your care of me hath...... *2236*
Php 4:15 **N.** ye Philippians know also, that........ *1161*
Php 4:20 **N.** unto God and our Father be glory.. *1161*
Col 1:21 works, yet **n.** hath he reconciled........ *3570*
Col 1:24 **n.** rejoice in my sufferings for you, ... *3568*
Col 1:26 **n.** is made manifest to his saints: *3570*
Col 3:8 **n.** ye also put off all these; anger,....... *3570*
1Th 3:6 **n.** when Timotheus came from you *737*
1Th 3:8 For **n.** we live, if ye stand fast in....... *3568*
1Th 3:11 **N.** God himself and our Father, and.... *1161*
1Th 5:14 **N.** we exhort you, brethren, warn....... *1161*
2Th 2:1 **N.** we beseech you, brethren, by the.. *1161*
2Th 2:6 And **n.** ye know what withholdeth *3568*
2Th 2:7 only he who **n.** letteth will let, ... *737*
2Th 2:16 **N.** our Lord Jesus Christ himself, ... *1161*
2Th 3:6 **N.** we command you, brethren, in *1161*
2Th 3:12 **N.** them that are such we command.... *1161*
2Th 3:16 **N.** the Lord of peace himself give *1161*
1Ti 1:5 **N.** the end of the commandment is *1161*
1Ti 1:17 **N.** unto the King eternal, immortal, ... *1161*
1Ti 4:1 **N.** the Spirit speaketh expressly, ... *1161*
1Ti 4:8 promise of the life that **n.** is, and *3568*
1Ti 5:5 **N.** she that is a widow indeed, and..... *1161*
2Ti 1:10 But is **n.** made manifest by the.......... *3568*
2Ti 3:8 **N.** as Jannes and Jambres................ *1161*
2Ti 4:6 For I am **n.** ready to be offered, ... *2236*
Phm 9 **n.** also a prisoner of Jesus Christ. *3570*
Phm 11 but **n.** profitable to thee and to me: *3570*
Phm 16 Not **n.** as a servant, but above a......... *3765*
Heb 2:8 **n.** we see not yet all things put *3568*
Heb 7:4 **N.** consider how great this man *1161*
Heb 8:1 **N.** of the things which we have *1161*
Heb 8:6 But **n.** hath he obtained a more *3570*
Heb 8:13 **N.** that which decayeth and............... *1161*
Heb 9:5 we cannot **n.** speak particularly........... *3568*
Heb 9:6 **N.** when these things were thus *1161*
Heb 9:24 **n.** to appear in the presence of........... *3568*
Heb 9:26 **n.** once in the end of the world hath... *3568*
Heb 10:18 **N.** where remission of these is, ... *1161*
Heb 10:38 **N.** the just shall live by faith: but *1161*
Heb 11:1 **N.** faith is the substance of things *1161*
Heb 11:16 **n.** they desire a better country, ... *3570*
Heb 12:11 **N.** no chastening for the present *1161*
Heb 12:26 **n.** he hath promised, saying, Yet.......... *3568*
Heb 13:20 **N.** the God of peace, that brought....... *1161*
Jas 2:11 **N.** if thou commit no adultery, yet....... *1161*
Jas 4:13 Go to **n.**, ye that say, To day or *3568*
Jas 4:16 **n.** ye rejoice in your boastings: all...... *3568*
Jas 5:1 Go to **n.**, ye rich men, weep and *3568*
1Pe 1:6 through **n.** for a season, if need be, ... *737*
1Pe 1:8 in whom, though **n.** ye see him not,..... *737*
1Pe 1:12 which are **n.** reported unto you by *3568*
1Pe 2:10 people, but are **n.** the people of God: ..*3568*
1Pe 2:10 mercy, but **n.** have obtained mercy..... *3568*
1Pe 2:25 are **n.** returned unto the Shepherd *3568*
1Pe 3:21 even baptism doth also **n.** save us...... *3568*
2Pe 2:3 **n.** of a long time lingereth not, ...
2Pe 3:1 beloved, I **n.** write unto you; in *2236*
2Pe 3:7 and the earth, which are **n.**,................ *3568*
2Pe 3:18 him be glory both **n.** and for ever. *3568*
1Jo 2:8 past, and the true light **n.** shineth. *2235*
1Jo 2:9 brother, is in darkness even until **n.**..... *737*
1Jo 2:18 even **n.** are there many antichrists; *3568*
1Jo 2:28 **n.**, little children, abide in him; *3568*
1Jo 3:2 Beloved, **n.** are we the sons of God, .. *3568*
1Jo 4:3 even **n.** already is it in the world. *3568*
2Jo 5 And **n.** I beseech thee, lady, not as.... *3568*
Jude 24 **N.** unto him that is able to keep *1161*
Jude 25 and power, both **n.** and ever. *3568*
Re 12:10 **N.** is come salvation, and strength. *737*

NOW-A-DAYS See NOW and DAYS.

NO-WISE See NO and WISE.

NUMBER See also NUMBERED; NUMBERETH; NUMBERING; NUMBERS.

Ge 13:16 man can **n.** the dust of the earth,....... 4487
Ge 15:5 stars, if thou be able to **n.** them: 5608
Ge 34:30 being few in **n.**, they shall gather 4557
Ge 41:49 numbering; for it was without **n.**. 4557
Ex 12:4 it according to the **n.** of the souls;...... 4373
Ex 16:16 according to he **n.** of your persons; 4557
Ex 23:26 land: the **n.** of thy days I will fulfil....... 4557
Ex 30:12 children of Israel after their **n.**,.......... 6485
Le 15:13 he shall **n.** to himself seven days........ 5608
Le 15:28 she shall **n.** to herself seven days,...... 5608
Le 23:16 seventh sabbath shall ye **n.** fifty......... 5608
Le 25:8 thou shalt **n.** seven sabbaths of........... 5608
Le 25:15 to the **n.** of years after the jubile 4557
Le 25:15 unto the **n.** of years of the fruits........ 4557
Le 25:16 to the **n.** of the years of the fruits...... 4557
Le 25:50 be according unto the **n.** of years,....... 4557
Le 26:22 your cattle, and make you few in **n.**;.........
Nu 1:2 fathers, with the **n.** of their names, ... 4557
Nu 1:3 shall **n.** them by their armies............. 6485
Nu 1:18, 20,22,24,26,28,30,32,34,36,38,40,42
according to the **n.** of the names,............
Nu 1:49 thou shalt not **n.** the tribe of Levi, ... 6485
Nu 3:15 **N.** the children of Levi after the 6485
Nu 3:15 old and upward shalt thou **n.** them...... 6485
Nu 3:22 according to the **n.** of all the males,.... 4557
Nu 3:28 In the **n.** of all the males, from a 4557
Nu 3:34 according to the **n.** of all the males,.... 4557
Nu 3:40 **N.** all the firstborn of the males of..... 6485
Nu 3:40 and take the **n.** of their names........... 4557
Nu 3:43 firstborn males by the **n.** of names, ... 4557
Nu 3:48 odd **n.** of them is to be redeemed, ... 5736
Nu 4:23 fifty years old shalt thou **n.** them; 6485
Nu 4:29 shalt **n.** them after their families, ... 6485
Nu 4:30 fifty years old shalt thou **n.** them, ... 6485
Nu 4:37 which Moses and Aaron did **n.**........... 6485
Nu 4:41 whom Moses and Aaron did **n.** 6485
Nu 14:29 of you, according to your whole **n.**, ... 4557
Nu 14:34 **n.** the days in which ye searched 4557
Nu 15:12 According to the **n.**...ye...prepare, ... 4557
Nu 15:12 do to every one according to their **n.**.. 4557
Nu 23:10 the **n.** of the fourth part of Israel?....... 4557
Nu 26:53 according to the **n.** of names. 4557
Nu 29:18, 21,24,27,30,33,37 shall be according
to their **n.**, after the........................ 4557
Nu 31:36 was in **n.** three hundred thousand....... 4557
De 4:27 be left few in **n.** among the heathen,... 4557
De 7:7 ye were more in **n.** than any people; ....
De 16:9 Seven weeks shalt thou **n.** unto......... 5608
De 16:9 begin to **n.** the seven weeks from...... 5608
De 25:2 to his fault, by a certain **n.**. 4557
De 28:62 And ye shall be left few in **n.**, whereas .....
De 32:8 the **n.** of the children of Israel. 4557
Jos 4:5,8 **n.** of the tribes of the children of 4557
Jg 6:5 and their camels were without **n.**: 4557
Jg 7:6 the **n.** of them that lapped, putting 4557
Jg 7:12 and their camels were without **n.**, ... 4557
Jg 21:23 them wives, according to their **n.**, ... 4557
1Sa 6:4 **n.** of the lords of the Philistines: 4557
1Sa 6:18 **n.** of all the cities of the Philistines..... 4557
1Sa 14:17 **N.** now, and see who is gone from..... 6485
2Sa 2:15 over the **n.** twelve of Benjamin,......... 4557
2Sa 21:20 foot six toes, four and twenty in **n.**; ... 4557

2Sa 24:1 to say, Go, **n.** Israel and Judah......... 4487
2Sa 24:2 Beer-sheba, and **n.** ye the people,...... 6485
2Sa 24:2 I may know the **n.** of the people....... 4557
2Sa 24:4 the king, to **n.** the people of Israel..... 6485
2Sa 24:9 the sum of the **n.** of the people......... 4662
1Ki 18:31 to the **n.** of the tribes of the sons of... 4557
1Ki 20:25 And **n.** thee an army, like the army.... 4487
1Ch 7:2 whose **n.** was in the days of David..... 4557
1Ch 7:9 And the **n.** of them, after their.......... 3187
1Ch 7:40 **n.** throughout the genealogy....... 4557,3187
1Ch 11:11 **n.** of the mighty men whom David...... 4557
1Ch 21:1 and provoked David to **n.** Israel......... 4487
1Ch 21:2 Go, **n.** Israel from Beer-sheba even.... 5608
1Ch 21:2 and bring the **n.** of them to me,......... 4557
1Ch 21:5 the sum of the **n.** of the people......... 4662
1Ch 22:16 brass, and the iron, there is no **n.**...... 4557
1Ch 23:3 their **n.** by their polls, man by man,.... 4557
1Ch 23:24 counted by **n.** of names of their......... 4557
1Ch 23:31 feasts, by **n.**, according to the order... 4557
1Ch 25:1 the **n.** of the workmen according to.... 4557
1Ch 25:7 the **n.** of them, with their brethren..... 4557
1Ch 27:1 the children of Israel after their **n.**,...... 4557
1Ch 27:23 But David took not the **n.** of them..... 4557
1Ch 27:24 the son of Zeruiah began to **n.**,.......... 4487
1Ch 27:24 was the **n.** put in the account of........ 4557
2Ch 12:3 people were without **n.** that came...... 4557
2Ch 26:11 according to the **n.** of their account.... 4557
2Ch 26:12 whole **n.** of the chief of the fathers..... 4557
2Ch 29:32 And the **n.** of the burnt offerings,....... 4557
2Ch 30:24 **n.** of priests sanctified themselves...........
2Ch 35:7 to the **n.** of thirty thousand, and........ 4557
Ezr 1:9 And this is the **n.** of them: thirty....... 4557
Ezr 2:2 the **n.** of the men of the people of...... 4557
Ezr 3:4 the daily burnt offerings by **n.**,.......... 4557
Ezr 6:17 to the **n.** of the tribes of Israel.......... 4510
Ezr 8:34 By **n.** and by weight of every one:..... 4557
Ne 7:7 **n.**, I say, of the men of the people..... 4557
Es 9:11 day the **n.** of those that were slain..... 4557
Job 1:5 according to the **n.** of them all.......... 4557
Job 3:6 not come into the **n.** of the months.... 4557
Job 5:9 marvellous things without **n.**:............. 4557
Job 9:10 out; yea, and wonders without **n.**......... 4557
Job 14:5 the **n.** of his months are with thee,.... 4557
Job 15:20 and the **n.** of years is hidden to the.... 4557
Job 21:21 the **n.** of his months is cut off in the... 4557
Job 25:3 Is there any **n.** of his armies? and...... 4557
Job 31:37 unto him the **n.** of my steps; as a...... 4557
Job 34:24 in pieces mighty men without **n.**,...... 2714
Job 36:26 can the **n.** of his years be searched.... 4557
Job 38:21 because the **n.** of thy days is great?... 4557
Job 38:37 Who can **n.** the clouds in wisdom?...... 5608
Job 39:2 Canst thou **n.** the months that they.... 5608
Ps 90:12 So teach us to **n.** our days, that........ 4487
Ps 105:12 they were but a few men in **n.**;......... 4557
Ps 105:34 caterpillars, and that without **n.**,........ 4557
Ps 139:18 they are more in **n.** than the sand:...........
Ps 147:4 He telleth the **n.** of the stars; he....... 4557
Ca 6:8 concubines, and virgins without **n.**...... 4557
Isa 21:17 the residue of the **n.** of archers,........ 4557
Isa 40:26 that bringeth out their host by **n.**:...... 4557
Isa 65:11 the drink offering unto that **n.**......... 4507
Isa 65:12 will I **n.** you to the sword, and ye...... 4487
Jer 2:28 according to the **n.** of thy cities......... 4557
Jer 2:32 have forgotten me days without **n.**..... 4557
Jer 11:13 For according to the **n.** of thy cities.... 4557
Jer 11:13 according to the **n.** of the streets....... 4557
Jer 44:28 a small **n.** that escape the sword........ 4557
Eze 4:4 according to the **n.** of the days that.... 4557
Eze 4:5 according to the **n.** of the days,......... 4557
Eze 4:9 according to the **n.** of the days that.... 4557
Eze 5:3 shalt also take thereof a few in **n.**,..... 4557
Da 9:2 by books the **n.** of the years,............ 4557
Ho 1:10 the **n.** of the children of Israel shall.... 4557
Joe 1:6 my land, strong, and without **n.**,........ 4557
Na 3:3 of slain, and a great **n.** of carcases;..........
Mk 10:46 disciples and a great **n.** of people,...... *3793*
Lu 22:3 being of the **n.** of the twelve............. *706*
Joh 6:10 sat down, in **n.** about five thousand...... *706*
Ac 1:15 (the **n.** of names together were......... *3793*
Ac 4:4 the **n.** of the men was about five......... *706*
Ac 5:36 to whom a **n.** of men, about four......... *706*
Ac 6:1 the **n.** of the disciples was multiplied,........
Ac 6:7 the **n.** of the disciples multiplied in....... *706*
Ac 11:21 and a great **n.** believed, and turned...... *706*
Ac 16:5 the faith, and increased in **n.** daily........ *706*
Ro 9:27 the **n.** of the children of Israel be......... *706*
2Co 10:12 dare not make ourselves of the **n.**,..... *1469*
1Ti 5:9 not a widow be taken into the **n.**....... *2639*
Re 5:11 the **n.** of them was ten thousand........ *706*
Re 7:4 I heard the **n.** of them which were........ *706*
Re 7:9 multitude, which no man could **n.**,........ *705*
Re 9:16 the **n.** of the army of the horsemen..... *706*
Re 9:16 and I heard the **n.** of them................ *706*
Re 13:17 of the beast, or the **n.** of his name...... *706*
Re 13:18 count the **n.** of the beast: for it is........ *706*
Re 13:18 the beast: for it is the **n.** of a man;...... *706*
Re 13:18 his **n.** is Six hundred threescore.......... *706*
Re 15:2 mark, and over the **n.** of his name,...... *706*
Re 20:8 **n.** of whom is as the sand of the sea.... *706*

NUMBERED

Ge 13:16 then shall thy seed also be **n.**........... 4487
Ge 16:10 it shall not be **n.** for multitude.......... 5608
Ge 32:12 which cannot be **n.** for multitude........ 5608
Ex 30:13, 14 among them that are **n.**,............. 6485
Ex 38:25 And the silver of them that were **n.**..... 6485
Ex 38:26 for every one that went to be **n.**,........ 6485
Nu 1:19 so he **n.** them in the wilderness of..... 6485
Nu 1:21 Those that were **n.** of them, even...... 6485
Nu 1:22 fathers, those that were **n.** of them,.... 6485
Nu 1:23, 25,27,29,31,33,35,37,39,41,43 Those that were **n.** of them,...................... 6485
Nu 1:44 These are those that were **n.**,........... 6485
Nu 1:44 which Moses and Aaron **n.**, and the.... 6485
Nu 1:45 So were all those that were **n.** of....... 6485
Nu 1:46 they that were **n.** were six hundred.... 6485
Nu 1:47 fathers were not **n.** among them........ 6485
Nu 2:4 and those that were **n.** of them,........ 6485
Nu 2:6, 8 and those that were **n.** thereof,....... 6485
Nu 2:9 that were **n.** in the camp of Judah...... 6485
Nu 2:11 and those that were **n.** thereof,......... 6485
Nu 2:13, 15 and those that were **n.** of them,.... 6485
Nu 2:16 that were **n.** in the camp of Reuben.... 6485
Nu 2:19, 21,23 those that were **n.** of them,...... 6485
Nu 2:24 All that were **n.** of the camp of......... 6485
Nu 2:26, 28,30 those that were **n.** of them,...... 6485
Nu 2:31 that were **n.** in the camp of Dan........ 6485
Nu 2:32 were **n.** of the children of Israel by.... 6485
Nu 2:32 all those that were **n.** of the camps.... 6485
Nu 2:33 the Levites were not **n.** among the...... 6485
Nu 3:16 And Moses **n.** them according to the.. 6485
Nu 3:22 that were **n.** of them, according to..... 6485
Nu 3:22 that were **n.** of them were seven....... 6485
Nu 3:34 And those that were **n.** of them,........ 6485
Nu 3:39 that were **n.** of the Levites, which..... 6485
Nu 3:39 Levites, which Moses and Aaron **n.**..... 6485
Nu 3:42 Moses **n.**, and the Lord commanded... 6485
Nu 3:43 of those that were **n.** of them, were... 6485
Nu 4:34 **n.** the sons of the Kohathites after..... 6485
Nu 4:36 those that were **n.** of them by their.... 6485
Nu 4:37 they that were **n.** of the families........ 6485
Nu 4:38 And those that were **n.** of the sons..... 6485
Nu 4:40 Even those that were **n.** of them,....... 6485
Nu 4:41 they that were **n.** of the families of..... 6485
Nu 4:42 those that were **n.** of the families of... 6485
Nu 4:44 Even those that were **n.** of them....... 6485
Nu 4:45 those that were **n.** of the families....... 6485
Nu 4:45 Moses and Aaron **n.** according to....... 6485
Nu 4:46 those that were **n.** of the Levites,....... 6485
Nu 4:46 Aaron and the chief of Israel **n.**,........ 6485
Nu 4:48 Even those that were **n.** of them,....... 6485
Nu 4:49 they were **n.** by the hand of Moses,... 6485
Nu 4:49 thus were they **n.** of him, as the........ 6485
Nu 7:2 and were over them that were **n.**,........ 6485
Nu 14:29 all that were **n.** of you, according....... 6485
Nu 26:7 that were **n.** of them were forty and... 6485
Nu 26:18, 22,25,27,34 that were **n.** of them,...... 6485
Nu 26:37 according to those that were **n.** of...... 6485
Nu 26:41 that were **n.** of them were forty........ 6485
Nu 26:43 to those that were **n.** of them,.......... 6485
Nu 26:47 to those that were **n.** of them;.......... 6485
Nu 26:50 and they that were **n.** of them were... 6485
Nu 26:51 the **n.** of the children of Israel, six..... 6485
Nu 26:54 to those that were **n.** of him............. 6485
Nu 26:57 are they that were **n.** of the Levites... 6485
Nu 26:62 that were **n.** of them were twenty...... 6485
Nu 26:62 were not **n.** among the children of...... 6485
Nu 26:63 are they that were **n.** by Moses and... 6485
Nu 26:63 who **n.** the children of Israel in the..... 6485
Nu 26:64 Moses and Aaron the priest **n.**,......... 6485
Nu 26:64 when they **n.** the children of Israel..... 6485
Jos 8:10 and **n.** the people, and went up, he.... 6485
Jg 20:15 the children of Benjamin were **n.**........ 6485
Jg 20:15 were **n.** seven hundred chosen men.... 6485
Jg 20:17 were **n.** four hundred thousand.......... 6485
Jg 21:9 For the people were **n.**, and, behold,.. 6485
1Sa 11:8 And when he **n.** them in Bezek, the... 6485
1Sa 13:15 Saul **n.** the people that were present.. 6485
1Sa 14:17 when they had **n.**, behold, Jonathan.... 6485
1Sa 15:4 together, and **n.** them in Telaim,......... 6485
2Sa 18:1 David **n.** the people that were with..... 6485
2Sa 24:10 after that he had **n.** the people.......... 5608
1Ki 3:8 be **n.** nor counted for multitude.......... 4487
1Ki 8:5 not be told nor **n.** for multitude.......... 4487
1Ki 20:15 he **n.** the young men of the princes.... 6485
1Ki 20:15 after them he **n.** all the people,.......... 6485
1Ki 20:26 year, that Ben-hadad **n.** the Syrians,... 6485
1Ki 20:27 children of Israel were **n.**, and were... 6485
2Ki 3:6 the same time, and **n.** all Israel.......... 6485
1Ch 21:17 commanded the people to be **n.**?......... 4487
1Ch 23:3 the Levites were **n.** from the age........ 5608
1Ch 23:27 the Levites were **n.** from twenty........ 4557
2Ch 2:17 Solomon **n.** all the strangers that........ 5608
2Ch 2:17 David his father had **n.** them; and...... 5608
2Ch 5:6 not be told nor **n.** for multitude.......... 4487
2Ch 25:5 he **n.** them from twenty years old........ 6485
Ezr 1:8 and **n.** them unto Sheshbazzar, the..... 5608
Ps 40:5 them, they are more than can be **n.**.... 5608
Ec 1:15 which is wanting cannot be **n.**............ 4487
Isa 22:10 have **n.** the houses of Jerusalem,........ 5608
Isa 53:12 he was **n.** with the transgressors;...... 4487
Jer 33:22 the host of heaven cannot be **n.**,......... 5608
Da 5:26 God hath **n.** thy kingdom, and............ 4483
Ho 1:10 which cannot be measured nor **n.**;....... 5608
Mt 10:30 **very hairs of your head are all n.**.. *705*
Mk 15:28 he was **n.** with the transgressors....... *3049*
Lu 12:7 **very hairs of your head are all n.**.. *705*
Ac 1:17 For he was **n.** with us, and had.......... *2674*
Ac 1:26 he was **n.** with the eleven apostles..... *4785*

NUMBEREST

Ex 30:12 the Lord, when thou **n.** them;........... 6485
Ex 30:12 among them, when thou **n.** them........ 6485
Job 14:16 For now thou **n.** my steps: dost........ 5608

NUMBERING

Ge 41:49 sea, very much, until he left **n.**;......... 5608
2Ch 2:17 after the **n.** where with David his....... 5610

NUMBERS

Nu *general* *title* Book of Moses, Called **N.**........... 4057
1Ch 12:23 the **n.** of the bands that were............ 4557
2Ch 17:14 the **n.** of them according to the......... 6486
Ps 71:15 for I know not the **n.** thereof............ 5615

NUN (nun) See also NON.

Ex 33:11 his servant Joshua, the son of **N.**,...... 5126
Nu 11:28 Joshua the son of **N.**, the servant....... 5126
Nu 13:8 of Ephraim, Oshea the son of **N.**......... 5126
Nu 13:16 Moses called Oshea the son of **N.**....... 5126
Nu 14:6 Joshua the son of **N.**, and Caleb......... 5126
Nu 14:30 Jephunneh,...Joshua the son of **N.**...... 5126
Nu 14:38 Joshua the son of **N.**, and Caleb......... 5126
Nu 26:65 Jephunneh,...Joshua the son of **N.**...... 5126
Nu 27:18 Take thee Joshua the son of **N.**, a...... 5126
Nu 32:12 Kenezite, and Joshua the son of **N.**:.... 5126
Nu 32:28 Joshua the son of **N.**, and the chief..... 5126
Nu 34:17 priest, and Joshua the son of **N.**......... 5126
De 1:38 But Joshua the son of **N.**, which......... 5126
De 31:23 gave Joshua the son of **N.** a charge,... 5126
De 32:44 he, and Hoshea the son of **N.**............ 5126
De 34:9 the son of **N.** was full of the spirit...... 5126
Jos 1:1 spake unto Joshua the son of **N.**,........ 5126
Jos 2:1 Joshua the son of **N.** sent out of........ 5126
Jos 2:23 and came to Joshua the son of **N.**,...... 5126
Jos 6:6 the son of **N.** called the priests,......... 5126
Jos 14:1 priest, and Joshua the son of **N.**,........ 5126
Jos 17:4 before Joshua the son of **N.**, and........ 5126
Jos 19:49 inheritance to Joshua the son of **N.**..... 5126
Jos 19:51 priest, and Joshua the son of **N.**,......... 5126
Jos 21:1 and unto Joshua the son of **N.**,.......... 5126
Jos 24:29 Joshua the son of **N.**, the servant....... 5126
Jg 2:8 Joshua the son of **N.**, the servant of... 5126
1Ki 16:34 he spake by Joshua the son of **N.**........ 5126
Ne 8:17 the days of Jeshua the son of **N.**......... 5126
Ps 119:105 *title* [ב] **N.**...

NURSE See also NURSED; NURSING.

Ge 24:59 Rebekah their sister, and her **n.**,....... 3243
Ge 35:8 But Deborah Rebekah's **n.** died, and... 3243

Ex 2:7 to thee a **n.** of the Hebrew women,.... 3243
Ex 2:7 that she may **n.** the child for thee?...... 3243
Ex 2:9 this child away, and **n.** it for me, ... 3243
Ru 4:16 her bosom, and became **n.** unto it......... 539
2Sa 4:4 and his **n.** took him up, and fled: 539
2Ki 11:2 they hid him, even him and his **n.**, ... 3243
2Ch 22:11 him and his **n.** in a bedchamber. 3243
1Th 2:7 as a **n.** cherisheth her children;.......... *5162*

NURSED
Ex 2:9 woman took the child, and **n.** it. 5134
Isa 60:4 daughters shall be **n.** at thy side.......... 539

NURSING
Nu 11:12 as a **n.** father beareth the sucking........ 539
Isa 49:23 And kings shall be thy **n.** fathers, ... 539
Isa 49:23 and their queens thy **n.** mothers: 3243

NURTURE
Eph 6:4 **n.** and admonition of the Lord. *3809*

NUTS
Ge 43:11 spices, and myrrh, **n.**, and almonds:..... 992
Ca 6:11 went down into the garden of **n.** to 93

NYMPHAS (nim'-fas)
Col 4:15 which are in Laodicea, and **N.**, ... *3564*

O.

O See in the APPENDIX; also OH.

OAK See also OAKS.
Ge 35:4 Jacob hid them under the **o.** which....... 424
Ge 35:8 buried beneath Beth-el under an **o.**: 437
Jos 24:26 set it up there under an **o.**, that was.... 427
Jg 6:11 under an **o.** which was in Ophrah,........ 424
Jg 6:19 brought it out unto him under the **o.**, ... 424
2Sa 18:9 under the thick boughs of a great **o.**,.... 424
2Sa 18:9 and his head caught hold of the **o.**,....... 424
2Sa 18:10 I saw Absalom hanged in an **o.**........... 424
2Sa 18:14 was yet alive in the midst of the **o.**..... 424
1Ki 13:14 and found him sitting under an **o.**;........ 424
1Ch 10:12 buried their bones under the **o.** in......... 424
Isa 1:30 shall be as an **o.** whose leaf fadeth,...... 424
Isa 6:13 and as an **o.**, whose substance is in...... 437
Isa 44:14 taketh the cypress and the **o.**, which.... 437
Eze 6:13 and under every thick **o.**, the place...... 424

OAKS
Isa 1:29 be ashamed of the **o.** which ye have..... 352
Isa 2:13 up, and upon all the **o.** of Bashan,........ 437
Eze 27:6 Of the **o.** of Bashan have they made..... 437
Ho 4:13 hills, under **o.** and poplars and elms,..... 437
Am 2:9 and he was strong as the **o.**; yet I....... 437
Zec 11:2 howl, O ye **o.** of Bashan; for the......... 437

OAR See also OARS.
Eze 27:29 And all that handle the **o.**, the........... 4880

OARS
Isa 33:21 wherein shall go no galley with **o.**...... ,7885
Eze 27:6 Bashan have they made thine **o.**;........ 4880

OATH See also OATH'S; OATHS.
Ge 24:8 shalt be clear from this my **o.**............ 7621
Ge 24:41 shalt thou be clear from this my **o.**, ... 423
Ge 24:41 one, thou shalt be clear from my **o.** 423
Ge 26:3 I will perform the **o.** which I 7621
Ge 26:28 Let there be now an **o.** betwixt us,...... 423
Ge 50:25 Joseph took an **o.** of the children......... 7650
Ex 22:11 an **o.** of the Lord be between them 7621
Le 5:4 a man shall pronounce with an **o.**, ... 7621
Nu 5:19 priest shall charge her by an **o.**,......... 7650
Nu 5:21 the woman with an **o.** of cursing, ... 7621
Nu 5:21 Lord make thee a curse and an **o.**...... 7621
Nu 30:2 swear on **o.** to bind his soul with a..... 7621
Nu 30:10 her soul by a bond with an **o.**;........... 7621
Nu 30:13 every binding **o.** to afflict the soul, ... 7621
De 7:8 he would keep the **o.** which he had..... 7621
De 29:12 into his **o.**, which the Lord thy God 423
De 29:14 do I make this covenant and this **o.**;..... 423
Jos 2:17 will be blameless of this thine **o.** 7621
Jos 2:20 then we will be quit of thine **o.**.......... 7621
Jos 9:20 because of the **o.** which we sware...... 7621
Jg 21:5 had made a great **o.** concerning him.... 7621
1Sa 14:26 mouth: for the people feared the **o.**... 7621
1Sa 14:27 charged the people with the **o.**: 7650
1Sa 14:28 straitly charged...people with an **o.**, ... 7650
2Sa 21:7 Lord's **o.** that was between them, ... 7621
1Ki 2:43 thou not kept the **o.** of the Lord, ... 7621
1Ki 8:31 an **o.** be laid upon him to cause him 423
1Ki 8:31 **o.** come before thine altar in this 423
1Ki 18:10 he took an **o.** of the kingdom and........ 7650
2Ki 11:4 took an **o.** of them in the house of 7650
1Ch 16:16 Abraham, and of his **o.** unto Isaac; 7621
2Ch 6:22 an **o.** be laid upon him to make him....... 423
2Ch 6:22 the **o.** come before the altar in this 423
2Ch 15:15 And all Judah rejoiced at the **o.**: 7621
Ne 5:12 priests, and took an **o.** of them,.......... 7650
Ne 10:29 entered into a curse, and into an **o.**, ... 7621
Ps 105:9 Abraham, and his **o.** unto Isaac;.......... 7621
Ec 8:2 and that in regard of the **o.** of God. 7621
Ec 9:2 sweareth, as he that feareth an **o.**...... 7621
Jer 11:5 That I may perform the **o.** which I 7621
Eze 16:59 despised the **o.** in breaking the........... 423
Eze 17:13 him, and hath taken an **o.** of him: 423
Eze 17:16 whose **o.** he despised, and whose 423
Eze 17:18 he despised the **o.** by breaking the....... 423
Eze 17:19 surely mine **o.** that he hath despised, ... 423
Da 9:11 the **o.** that is written in the law of...... 7621
Zec 8:17 his neighbour; and love no false **o.**:...... 7621
Mt 14:7 he promised with an **o.** to give her..... *3727*
Mt 26:72 he denied with an **o.**, I do not know ... *3727*
Lu 1:73 **o.** which he sware to our father......... *3727*
Ac 2:30 God had sworn with an **o.** to him,...... *3727*
Ac 23:21 have bound themselves with an **o.**,......... *332*
Heb 6:16 an **o.** for confirmation is to them *3727*
Heb 6:17 his counsel, confirmed it by an **o.**: *3727*
Heb 7:20 without an **o.** he was made priest:...... *3728*
Heb 7:21 priests were made without an **o.**; *3728*
Heb 7:21 but this with an **o.** by him that said *3728*
Heb 7:28 the word of the **o.**, which was since ... *3728*
Jas 5:12 the earth, neither by any other **o.**: *3727*

OATH'S
Mt 14:9 nevertheless for the **o.** sake, and *3727*
Mk 6:26 yet for his **o.** sake, and for their *3727*

OATHS
Eze 21:23 sight, to them that have sworn **o.** 7621
Hab 3:9 according to the **o.** of the tribes,......... 7621
Mt 5:33 **perform unto the Lord thine o.** *3727*

OBADIAH (o-ba-di'-ah)
1Ki 18:3 And Ahab called **O.**, which was the..... 5662
1Ki 18:3 (Now **O.** feared the Lord greatly:....... 5662
1Ki 18:4 **O.** took an hundred prophets, and 5662
1Ki 18:5 And Ahab said unto **O.**, Go into the.... 5662
1Ki 18:6 **O.** went another way by himself......... 5662
1Ki 18:7 And as **O.** was in the way, behold,..... 5662
1Ki 18:16 So **O.** went to meet Ahab, and told 5662
1Ch 3:21 the sons of Arnan, the sons of **O.**, ... 5662
1Ch 7:3 Michael, and **O.**, and Joel, Ishiah,....... 5662
1Ch 8:38 and Sheariah, and **O.**, and Hanan........ 5662
1Ch 9:16 **O.** the son of Shemaiah, the son of....... 5662
1Ch 9:44 and Sheariah, and **O.**, and Hanan:......... 5662
1Ch 12:9 Ezer the first, **O.** the second, Eliab 5662
1Ch 27:19 Of Zebulun, Ishmaiah the son of **O.**: ... 5662
2Ch 17:7 and to **O.**, and to Zechariah, and to 5662
2Ch 34:12 overseers...were Jahath and **O.**,......... 5662
Ezr 8:9 **O.** the son of Jehiel, and with him....... 5662
Ne 10:5 Harim, Meremoth, **O.**,...................... 5662
Ne 12:25 **O.**, Meshullam, Talmon, Akkub,.......... 5662
Ob *general* *title* **O.**..
Ob 1 The vision of **O.**. Thus saith the 5662

OBAL (o'-bal)
Ge 10:28 And **O.**, and Abimael, and Sheba, ... 5745

OBED (o'-bed) See also OBED-EDOM.
Ru 4:17 and they called his name **O.**: he......... 5744
Ru 4:21 begat Boaz, and Boaz begat **O.**,.......... 5744
Ru 4:22 **O.** begat Jesse, and Jesse begat......... 5744
1Ch 2:12 Boaz begat **O.**, and **O.** begat Jesse,.... 5744
1Ch 2:37 begat Ephlal, and Ephlal begat **O.**,....... 5744
1Ch 2:38 And **O.** begat Jehu, and Jehu begat..... 5744
1Ch 11:47 and **O.**, and Jasiel the Mesobaite......... 5744
1Ch 26:7 and **O.**, Elzabad, whose brethren 5744
2Ch 23:1 and Azariah the son of **O.**, and 5744
Mt 1:5 begat **O.** of Ruth; and **O.** begat *5601*
Lu 3:32 of Jesse, which was the son of **O.**, ... *5601*

OBED-EDOM (o''-bed-e'-dom)
2Sa 6:10 into the house of **O.** the Gittite.......... 5654
2Sa 6:11 continued in the house of **O.** the 5654
2Sa 6:11 the Lord blessed **O.**, and all his 5654
2Sa 6:12 Lord hath blessed the house of **O.**,..... 5654
2Sa 6:12 from the house of **O.** into the city of... 5654
1Ch 13:13 carried it aside into the house of **O.**.... 5654
1Ch 13:14 God remained with the family of **O.** 5654
1Ch 13:14 the Lord blessed the house of **O.**,...... 5654
1Ch 15:18 and **O.**, and Jeiel, the porters........... 5654
1Ch 15:21 and **O.**, and Jeiel, and Azaziah, with...... 5654
1Ch 15:24 **O.** and Jehiah were doorkeepers 5654
1Ch 15:25 Lord out of the house of **O.** with joy... 5654
1Ch 16:5 and Eliab, and Benaiah, and **O.**........... 5654
1Ch 16:38 **O.** with their brethren, threescore...... 5654
1Ch 16:38 **O.** also the son of Jeduthun and......... 5654
1Ch 26:4 Moreover the sons of **O.** were, ... 5654
1Ch 26:8 All these of the sons of **O.**: they and .. 5654
1Ch 26:8 were threescore and two of **O.**........... 5654
1Ch 26:15 To **O.** southward; and to his sons 5654
2Ch 25:24 found in the house of God with **O.**,...... 5654

OBEDIENCE See also DISOBEDIENCE.
Ro 1:5 **o.** to the faith among all nations, ... *5218*
Ro 5:19 so by the **o.** of one shall many be *5218*
Ro 6:16 death, or of **o.** unto righteousness?..... *5218*
Ro 16:19 For your **o.** is come abroad unto all.... *5218*
Ro 16:26 to all nations for the **o.** of faith: *5218*
1Co 14:34 are commanded to be under **o.**, ... *5293*
2Co 7:15 he remembereth the **o.** of you all, ... *5218*
2Co 10:5 every thought to the **o.** of Christ; *5218*
2Co 10:6 when your **o.** is fulfilled.................... *5218*
Phm 21 Having confidence in thy **o.** I wrote *5218*
Heb 5:8 yet learned he **o.** by the things.......... *5218*
1Pe 1:2 unto **o.** and sprinkling of the blood...... *5218*

OBEDIENT See also DISOBEDIENT.
Ex 24:7 Lord...said will we do, and be **o.**......... 8085
Nu 27:20 the children of Israel may be **o.** 8085
De 4:30 and shalt be **o.** unto his voice;........... 8085
De 8:20 ye would not be **o.** unto the voice 8085
2Sa 22:45 they hear, they shall be **o.** unto me. ... 8085
Pr 25:12 so is a wise reprover upon an **o.** ear... 8085
Isa 1:19 If ye be willing and **o.**, ye shall eat...... 8085
Isa 42:24 neither were they **o.** unto his law...... 8085
Ac 6:7 of the priests were **o.** to the faith. *5219*
Ro 15:18 to make the Gentiles **o.**, by word....... *5218*
2Co 2:9 whether ye be **o.** in all things............ *5255*
Eph 6:5 **o.** to them that are your masters *5219*
Php 2:8 and became **o.** unto death, even......... *5255*
Tit 2:5 good, **o.** to their own husbands,......... *5293*
Tit 2:9 to be **o.** unto their own masters,........ *5293*
1Pe 1:14 As **o.** children, not fashioning *5218*

OBEISANCE
Ge 37:7 about, and made **o.** to my sheaf......... 7812
Ge 37:9 moon and the eleven stars made **o.** ... 7812
Ge 43:28 down their heads, and made **o.**......... 7812
Ex 18:7 meet his father in law, and did **o.**,...... 7812
2Sa 1:2 that he fell to the earth, and did **o.**..... 7812
2Sa 14:4 her face to the ground, and did **o.**, ... 7812
2Sa 15:5 man came nigh to him to do him **o.**, ... 7812
1Ki 1:16 Bath-sheba bowed, and did **o.** unto..... 7812
2Ch 24:17 of Judah, and made **o.** to the king....... 7812

OBEY See also DISOBEYED; OBEYED; OBEYETH; OBEYING.
Ge 27:8 my son, **o.** my voice according to....... 8085
Ge 27:13 only **o.** my voice, and go fetch me...... 8085
Ge 27:43 my son, **o.** my voice; and arise, flee ... 8085
Ex 5:2 should **o.** his voice to let Israel go? 8085
Ex 19:5 if ye will **o.** my voice indeed, and....... 8085
Ex 23:21 Beware of him, and **o.** his voice,........ 8085
Ex 23:22 if thou shalt indeed **o.** his voice,......... 8085
De 11:27 if ye **o.** the commandments of the 8085
De 11:28 if ye will not **o.** the commandments 8085
De 13:4 commandments, and **o.** his voice,........ 8085
De 21:18 will not **o.** the voice of his father,....... 8085
De 21:20 rebellious, he will not **o.** our voice;..... 8085
De 27:10 **o.** the voice of the Lord thy God, ... 8085
De 28:62 wouldest not **o.** the voice of the......... 8085
De 30:2 shalt **o.** his voice according to all........ 8085

De 30:8 return and **o.** the voice of the Lord, ... 8085
De 30:20 and that thou mayest **o.** his voice, ... 8085
Jos 24:24 we serve, and his voice will we **o.** 8085
1Sa 8:19 refused to **o.** the voice of Samuel; 8085
1Sa 12:14 serve him, and **o.** his voice, and not ... 8085
1Sa 12:15 ye will not **o.** the voice of the Lord, ... 8085
1Sa 15:19 didst thou not **o.** the voice of the 8085
1Sa 15:22 to **o.** is better than sacrifice, and to 8085
Ne 9:17 refused to **o.**, neither were mindful 8085
Job 36:11 If they **o.** and serve him, they shall 8085
Job 36:12 But if they **o.** not, they shall perish 8085
Ps 18:44 they hear of me, they shall **o.** me: 8085
Pr 30:17 and despiseth to **o.** his mother, ... 3349
Isa 11:14 children of Ammon shall **o.** them. 4928
Jer 7:23 **O.** my voice, and I will be your 8085
Jer 11:4 **O.** my voice, and do them according ... 8085
Jer 11:7 and protesting, saying, **O.** my voice 8085
Jer 12:17 if they will not **o.**, I will utterly 8085
Jer 18:10 in my sight, that it **o.** not my voice, ... 8085
Jer 26:13 **o.** the voice of the Lord your God; 8085
Jer 35:14 but **o.** their father's commandment: 8085
Jer 38:20 **O.**, I beseech thee, the voice of the ... 8085
Jer 42:6 we will **o.** the voice of the Lord our ... 8085
Jer 42:6 when we **o.** the voice of the Lord 8085
Jer 42:13 neither **o.** the voice of the Lord your .. 8085
Da 7:27 dominions shall serve and **o.** him. 8086
Da 9:11 that they might not **o.** thy voice; 8085
Zec 6:15 diligently **o.** the voice of the Lord 8085
Mt 8:27 even the winds and the sea **o.** him! *5219*
Mk 1:27 unclean spirits, and they do **o.** him. *5219*
Mk 4:41 even the wind and the sea **o.** him? *5219*
Lu 8:25 winds and water, and they **o.** him. *5219*
Lu 17:6 **in the sea; and it should o. you** *5219*
Ac 5:29 ought to **o.** God rather than men. *3980*
Ac 5:32 God hath given to them that **o.** him. ... *3980*
Ac 7:39 our fathers would not **o.**, ... *5255,1036*
Ro 2:8 and do not **o.** the truth, but *544*
Ro 2:8 the truth, but **o.** unrighteousness, ... *3982*
Ro 6:12 ye should **o.** it in the lusts thereof. *5219*
Ro 6:12 yield yourselves servants to **o.**, ... *5218*
Ro 6:16 his servants ye are to whom ye **o.**; *5219*
Ga 3:1 that ye should not **o.** the truth. *3982*
Ga 5:7 that ye should not **o.** the truth? *3982*
Eph 6:1 Children, **o.** your parents in the *5219*
Col 3:20 Children, **o.** your parents in all *5219*
Col 3:22 **o.** in all things your masters *5219*
2Th 1:8 that **o.** not the gospel of our Lord *5219*
2Th 3:14 if any man **o.** not our word by this *5219*
Tit 3:1 to **o.** magistrates, to be ready to *3980*
Heb 5:9 salvation unto all them that **o.** *5219*
Heb 13:17 **O.** them that have the rule over *3982*
Jas 3:3 horses' mouths, that they may **o.** *3982*
1Pe 3:1 if any **o.** not the word, they also *544*
1Pe 4:17 them that **o.** not the gospel of God? *544*

OBEYED See also DISOBEYED; OBEYEDST.
Ge 22:18 because thou hast **o.** my voice. 8085
Ge 26:5 Because that Abraham **o.** my voice, ... 8085
Ge 28:7 Jacob **o.** his father and his mother, ... 8085
Jos 5:6 they **o.** not the voice of the Lord: 8085
Jos 22:2 **o.** my voice in all that I commanded 8085
Jg 2:2 but ye have not **o.** my voice: why 8085
Jg 6:10 dwell: but ye have not **o.** my voice. 8085
1Sa 15:20 Yea, I have **o.** the voice of the Lord, .. 8085
1Sa 15:24 the people, and **o.** their voice. 8085
1Sa 28:21 thine handmaid hath **o.** thy voice, ... 8085
1Ki 20:36 hast not **o.** the voice of the Lord, ... 8085
2Ki 18:12 they **o.** not the voice of the Lord 8085
1Ch 29:23 prospered; and all Israel **o.** him. 8085
2Ch 11:4 they **o.** the words of the Lord, and 8085
Pr 5:13 have not **o.** the voice of my teachers, ..8085
Jer 3:13 ye have not **o.** my voice, saith the 8085
Jer 3:25 have not **o.** the voice of the Lord our ..8085
Jer 9:13 and have not **o.** my voice, neither 8085
Jer 11:8 Yet they **o.** not, nor inclined their 8085
Jer 17:23 they **o.** not, neither inclined their 8085
Jer 32:23 but they **o.** not thy voice, neither 8085
Jer 34:10 more, then they **o.**, and let them go. .. 8085
Jer 35:8 we **o.** the voice of Jonadab the son 8085
Jer 35:10 we have dwelt in tents, and have **o.**, .. 8085
Jer 35:18 **o.** the commandment of Jonadab 8085
Jer 40:3 the Lord, and have not **o.** his voice, ... 8085
Jer 42:21 not **o.** the voice of the Lord your 8085
Jer 43:4 **o.** not the voice of the Lord, to dwell ..8085
Jer 43:7 they **o.** not the voice of the Lord: 8085
Jer 44:23 have not **o.** the voice of the Lord, ... 8085
Da 9:10 Neither have we **o.** the voice of the 8085
Da 9:14 he doeth: for we **o.** not his voice. 8085
Zep 3:2 She **o.** not the voice; she received 8085
Hag 1:12 **o.** the voice of the Lord their God, ... 8085
Ac 5:36 as many as **o.** him, were scattered, ... *3982*
Ac 5:37 as many as **o.** him, were dispersed. *3982*
Ro 6:17 have **o.** from the heart that form *5219*
Ro 10:16 they have not all **o.** the gospel. *5219*
Php 2:12 my beloved, as ye have always **o.**, ... *5219*
Heb 11:8 By faith Abraham...**o.**; *5219*
1Pe 3:6 Even as Sara **o.** Abraham, calling *5219*

OBEYEDST
1Sa 28:18 thou **o.** not the voice of the Lord, ... 8085
Jer 22:21 youth, that thou **o.** not my voice. 8085

OBEYETH
Isa 50:10 that **o.** the voice of his servant, ... 8085
Jer 7:28 a nation that **o.** not the voice of the 8085
Jer 11:3 Cursed be the man that **o.** not the 8085

OBEYING
Jg 2:17 **o.** the commandments of the Lord; 8085
1Sa 15:22 as in **o.** the voice of the Lord? 8085
1Pe 1:22 purified your souls in **o.** the truth *5218*

OBIL (o'-bil)
1Ch 27:30 Over the camels also was **O.** the 179

OBJECT
Ac 24:19 **o.**, if they had ought against me. *2723*

OBLATION See also OBLATIONS.
Le 2:4 thou bring an **o.** of a meat offering 7133
Le 2:5, 7 if thy **o.** be a meat offering baken 7133
Le 2:12 for the **o.** of the firstfruits, ye shall 7133
Le 2:13 every **o.** of thy meat offering shalt 7133
Le 3:1 And if his **o.** be a sacrifice of peace 7133
Le 7:14 one out of the whole **o.** for an heave .. 7133
Le 7:29 shall bring his **o.** unto the Lord of 7133
Le 22:18 that will offer his **o.** for all his vows, ... 7133
Nu 18:9 every **o.** of theirs, every meat 7133
Nu 31:50 We have therefore brought an **o.** 7133
Isa 19:21 and shall do sacrifice and **o.**; yea, ... 4503
Isa 40:20 so impoverished that he hath no **o.** 8641
Isa 66:3 he that offereth an **o.**, as if he 4503
Jer 14:12 they offer burnt offering and an **o.**, ... 4503
Eze 44:30 every **o.** all, of every sort of 8641
Eze 45:1 ye shall offer an **o.** unto the Lord, ... 8641
Eze 45:6 against the **o.** of the holy portion: 8641
Eze 45:7 side of the **o.** of the holy portion, ... 8641
Eze 45:7 before the **o.** of the holy portion, ... 8641
Eze 45:13 This is the **o.** that ye shall offer; 8641
Eze 45:16 give this **o.** for the prince in Israel. 8641
Eze 48:9 The **o.** that ye shall offer unto the 8641
Eze 48:10 for the priests, shall be this holy **o.**; ... 8641
Eze 48:12 this **o.** of the land that is offered 8642
Eze 48:18 against the **o.** of the holy portion. 8641
Eze 48:20 All the **o.** shall be five and twenty 8641
Eze 48:20 shall offer the holy **o.** foursquare, ... 8641
Eze 48:21 and on the other of the holy **o.**, ... 8641
Eze 48:21 five and twenty thousand of the **o.** 8641
Eze 48:21 and it shall be the holy **o.**; and the 8641
Da 2:46 should offer an **o.** and sweet odours 4541
Da 9:21 about the time of the evening **o.**. 4503
Da 9:27 the sacrifice and the **o.** to cease, ... 4503

OBLATIONS
Le 7:38 children of Israel to offer their **o.** 7133
2Ch 31:14 to distribute the **o.** of the Lord, ... 8641
Isa 1:13 Bring no more vain **o.**; incense is 4503
Eze 20:40 and the firstfruits of your **o.**, ... 4864
Eze 44:30 of every sort of your **o.**, shall be 8641

OBOTH (o'-both)
Nu 21:10 set forward, and pitched in **O.**. 88
Nu 21:11 they journeyed from **O.**, and pitched 88
Nu 33:43 from Punon, and pitched in **O.** 88
Nu 33:44 they departed from **O.**, and pitched 88

OBSCURE
Pr 20:20 shall be put out in **o.** darkness. 380

OBSCURITY
Isa 29:18 eyes of the blind shall see out of **o.**, ... 652
Isa 58:10 then shall thy light rise in **o.**, and 2822
Isa 59:9 we wait for light, but behold **o.**; 2822

OBSERVATION
Lu 17:20 **of God cometh not with o.:** *3907*

OBSERVE See also OBSERVED; OBSERVEST; OBSERVETH.
Ex 12:17 **o.** the feast of unleavened bread; 8104
Ex 12:17 ye **o.** this day in your generations 8104
Ex 12:24 shall **o.** this thing for an ordinance 8104
Ex 31:16 **o.** the sabbath throughout their 6213
Ex 34:11 **O.** thou that which I command 8104
Ex 34:22 thou shalt **o.** the feast of weeks, ... 6213
Le 19:26 ye use enchantment, nor **o.** times. 6049
Le 19:37 shall ye **o.** all my statutes, and 8104
Nu 28:2 shall ye **o.** to offer unto me in their 8104
De 5:32 shall **o.** to do therefore as the Lord 8104
De 6:3 O Israel, and **o.** to do it; that it 8104
De 6:25 **o.** to do all these commandments 8104
De 8:1 commandments...shall ye **o.** to do, ... 8104
De 11:32 ye shall **o.** to do all the statutes 8104
De 12:1 which ye shall **o.** to do in the land, ... 8104
De 12:28 **O.** and hear all these words which 8104
De 12:32 soever I command you, **o.** to do it: 8104
De 15:5 to **o.** to do all these commandments 8104
De 16:1 **O.** the mouth of Abib, and keep the 8104
De 16:12 thou shalt **o.** and do these statutes. 8104
De 16:13 shalt **o.** the feast of tabernacles 6213
De 17:10 thou shalt **o.** to do according to all 8104
De 24:8 of leprosy, that thou **o.** diligently, ... 8104
De 24:8 them, so ye shall **o.** to do. 8104
De 28:1 to **o.** and to do...his commandments ... 8104
De 28:13 thee this day, to **o.** and to do them: ... 8104
De 28:15 to **o.** to do all his commandments 8104
De 28:58 wilt not **o.** to do all the words of. 8104
De 31:12 **o.** to do all the words of this law: 8104
De 32:46 command your children to **o.** to do, ... 8104
Jos 1:7,8 thou mayest **o.** to do according to 8104
Jg 13:14 all that I commanded her let her **o.** 8104
1Ki 20:33 Now the men did diligently **o.** 5172
2Ki 17:37 ye shall **o.** to do for evermore; 8104
2Ki 21:8 only if they will **o.** to do according 8104
2Ch 7:17 and shalt **o.** my statutes and my 8104
Ne 1:5 him and **o.** his commandments: 8104
Ne 10:29 to **o.** and do all the commandments 8104
Ps 105:45 That they might **o.** his statutes, ... 8104
Ps 107:43 is wise, and will **o.** these things, ... 8104
Ps 119:34 I shall **o.** it with my whole heart. 8104
Pr 23:26 and let thine eyes **o.** my ways. 5341
Jer 8:7 the swallow **o.** the time of their 8104
Eze 20:18 neither **o.** their judgments, nor 8104
Eze 37:24 and **o.** my statutes, and do them. 8104
Ho 13:7 as a leopard by the way will I **o.** 7789
Jon 2:8 They that **o.** lying vanities forsake 8104
Mt 23:3 **whatsoever they bid you o., that** ... *5083*
Mt 23:3 **that o. and do; but do not ye** *5083*
Mt 28:20 **Teaching them to o. all things** *5083*
Ac 16:21 to receive, neither to **o.**, being *4160*
Ac 21:25 that they **o.** no such thing, save *5083*
Ga 4:10 Ye **o.** days, and months, and *3906*
1Ti 5:21 that thou **o.** these things without *5442*

OBSERVED
Ge 37:11 him; but his father **o.** the saying. 8104
Ex 12:42 is a night to be much **o.** unto the 8107
Ex 12:42 is that night of the Lord to be **o.** of 8107
Nu 15:22 not **o.** all these commandments, ... 6213
De 33:9 they have **o.** thy word, and kept 8104
2Sa 11:16 to pass, when Joab **o.** the city, ... 8104
2Ki 21:6 through the fire, and **o.** times, ... 6049
2Ch 33:6 also he **o.** times, and used 6049
Ho 14:8 I have heard him, and **o.** him: I 7789
Mk 6:20 just man and a holy, and **o.** him; *4933*
Mk 10:20 all these have I **o.** from my youth. *5442*

OBSERVER See also OBSERVERS.
De 18:10 an **o.** of times, or an enchanter, ... 6049

OBSERVERS
De 18:14 hearkened unto **o.** of times, and 6049

OBSERVEST
Isa 42:20 many things, but thou **o.** not; 8104

OBSERVETH
Ec 11:4 He that **o.** the wind shall not sow; 8104

OBSTINATE
De 2:30 his spirit, and made his heart **o.**, ... 553
Isa 48:4 Because I knew that thou art **o.**, ... 7186

OBTAIN See also OBTAINED; OBTAINETH; OBTAINING.
Ge 16:2 be that I may **o.** children by her. 1129
Pr 8:35 and shall **o.** favour of the Lord. 6329
Isa 35:10 they shall **o.** joy and gladness, and 5381
Isa 51:11 they shall **o.** gladness and joy; and 5381
Da 11:21 and **o.** the kingdom by flatteries. 2388
Mt 5:7 **merciful: for they shall o. mercy** ... *1653*

Lu 20:35 **accounted worthy to o. that world,** *5177*
Ro 11:31 mercy they also may **o.** mercy. *1653*
1Co 9:24 the prize? So run, that ye may **o.**, *2638*
1Co 9:25 do it to **o.** a corruptible crown; *2983*
1Th 5:9 to **o.** salvation by our Lord Jesus *4047*
2Ti 2:10 that they may also **o.** the salvation *5177*
Heb 4:16 that we may **o.** mercy, and find *2983*
Heb 11:35 might **o.** a better resurrection: *5177*
Jas 4:2 and desire to have, and cannot **o.**: *2013*

OBTAINED
Ne 13:6 certain days **o.** I leave of the king: 7592
Es 2:9 him, and she **o.** kindness of him; 5375
Es 2:15 Esther **o.** favour in the sight of all 5375
Es 2:17 she **o.** grace and favour in his 5375
Es 5:2 that she **o.** favour in his sight: 5375
Ho 2:23 upon her that had not **o.** mercy; 5375
Ac 1:17 and had **o.** part of this ministry. *2975*
Ac 22:28 With a great sum **o.** I this freedom. *2932*
Ac 26:22 Having therefore **o.** help of God, I *5177*
Ac 27:13 that they had **o.** their purpose, *2902*
Ro 11:7 Israel hath not **o.** that which he *2013*
Ro 11:7 but the election hath **o.** it, and the *2013*
Ro 11:30 **o.** mercy through their unbelief: *1653*
1Co 7:25 one that hath **o.** mercy of the Lord *1653*
Eph 1:11 also we have **o.** an inheritance, *2820*
1Ti 1:13 but I **o.** mercy, because I did it *1653*
1Ti 1:16 Howbeit for this cause I **o.** mercy, *1653*
Heb 1:4 by inheritance **o.** a more excellent *2816*
Heb 6:15 endured, he **o.** the promise. *2013*
Heb 8:6 he **o.** a more excellent ministry, *5177*
Heb 9:12 **o.** eternal redemption for us. *2147*
Heb 11:2 by it the elders **o.** a good report. *3140*
Heb 11:4 **o.** witness that he was righteous, *3140*
Heb 11:33 **o.** promises, stopped the mouths of *2013*
Heb 11:39 **o.** a good report through faith, *3140*
1Pe 2:10 of God: which had not **o.** mercy, *1653*
1Pe 2:10 but now have **o.** mercy. *1653*
2Pe 1:1 that have **o.** like precious faith *2975*

OBTAINETH
Pr 12:2 A good man **o.** favour of the Lord: 6329
Pr 18:22 thing, and **o.** favour of the Lord. 6329

OBTAINING
2Th 2:14 to the **o.** of the glory of our Lord *4047*

OCCASION See also OCCASIONED; OCCASIONS.
Ge 43:18 that he may seek **o.** against us, and 1556
Jg 9:33 to do them as thou shalt find **o.** 4672
Jg 14:4 sought an **o.** against…Philistines: 8385
1Sa 10:7 thee, that thou do as **o.** serve thee; 4672
2Sa 12:14 given great **o.** to the enemies of the
Ezr 7:20 which thou shalt have **o.** to bestow, 5308
Jer 2:24 in her **o.** who can turn her away? 8385
Eze 18:3 have **o.** any more to use this proverb
Da 6:4 sought to find **o.** against Daniel 5931
Da 6:4 they could find none **o.** nor fault; 5931
Da 6:5 not find any **o.** against this Daniel, 5931
Ro 7:8,11 taking **o.** by the commandment, *874*
Ro 14:13 or an **o.** to fall in his brother's way. *4625*
2Co 5:12 give you **o.** to glory on our behalf, *874*
2Co 8:8 by **o.** of the forwardness of others, *1223*
2Co 11:12 cut off **o.** from them which desire **o.**; *874*
Ga 5:13 use not liberty for an **o.** to the flesh, *874*
1Ti 5:14 give none **o.** to the adversary to *874*
1Jo 2:10 is none **o.** of stumbling in him. *4625*

OCCASIONED
1Sa 22:22 **o.** the death of all the persons 5437

OCCASIONS
De 22:14 And give **o.** of speech against her, 5949
De 22:17 hath given **o.** of speech against her, 5949
Job 33:10 Behold, he findeth **o.** against me, 8569

OCCUPATION
Ge 46:33 and shall say, What is your **o.**? 4639
Ge 47:3 unto his brethren, What is your **o.**? 4639
Jon 1:8 What is thine **o.**? and whence 4399
Ac 18:3 by their **o.** they were tentmakers. *5078*
Ac 19:25 together with the workmen of like **o.**, *5078*

OCCUPIED
Ex 38:24 the gold that was **o.** for the work 6213
Jg 16:11 new ropes that never were **o.**, 6213,4399
Eze 27:16 they **o.** in thy fairs with emeralds, 5414
Eze 27:19 going to and fro **o.** in thy fairs: 5414
Eze 27:21 they **o.** with thee in lambs, and 5503
Eze 27:22 they **o.** in thy fairs with chief of 5414
Heb 13:9 them that have been **o.** therein. *4043*

OCCUPIERS
Eze 27:27 and the **o.** of thy merchandise, 6148

OCCUPIETH
1Co 14:16 that **o.** the room of unlearned *378*

OCCUPY See also OCCUPIED; OCCUPIETH.
Eze 27:9 in thee to **o.** thy merchandise. 6148
Lu 19:13 **and said unto them, O. till I come.** *4231*

OCCURRENT
1Ki 5:4 is neither adversary nor evil **o.** 6294

OCRAN (o'-cran)
Nu 1:13 Of Asher; Pagiel the son of **O.** 5918
Nu 2:27 Asher shall be Pagiel the son of **O.** 5918
Nu 7:72 Pagiel the son of **O.**, prince of the 5918
Nu 7:77 the offering of Pagiel the son of **O.** 5918
Nu 10:26 of Asher was Pagiel the son of **O.** 5918

ODD
Nu 3:48 the **o.** number…is to be redeemed, 5736

ODED (o'-ded)
2Ch 15:1 came upon Azariah the son of **O.**: 5752
2Ch 15:8 and the prophecy of **O.** the prophet, 5752
2Ch 28:9 Lord was there, whose name was **O.**: 5752

ODIOUS
1Ch 19:6 had made themselves **o.** to David, 887
Pr 30:23 **o.** woman when she is married; 8130

ODOUR See also ODOURS.
Joh 12:3 filled with the **o.** of the ointment. *3744*
Php 4:18 an **o.** of a sweet smell, a sacrifice *3744*

ODOURS
Le 26:31 smell the savour of your sweet **o.** 5207
2Ch 16:14 bed which was filled with sweet **o.** 1314
Es 2:12 and six months with sweet **o.**, and 1314
Jer 34:5 thee, so shall they burn **o.** for thee;
Da 2:46 an oblation and sweet **o.** unto him. 5208
Re 5:8 golden vials full of **o.**, which are *2368*
Re 18:13 cinnamon, and **o.**, and ointments, *2368*

OF See in the APPENDIX; also HEREOF; OFF; THEREOF; WHEREOF.

OFF See also OFFSCOURING; OFFSPRING.
Ge 7:4 from **o.** the face of the earth. 5921
Ge 8:3 waters returned from **o.** the earth 5921
Ge 8:7 were dried up from **o.** the earth. 5921
Ge 8:8 from **o.** the face of the ground; 5921
Ge 8:11 mouth was an olive leaf pluck **o.**:
Ge 8:11 were abated from **o.** the earth. 5921
Ge 8:13 were dried up from **o.** the earth: 5921
Ge 9:11 shall all flesh be cut **o.** any more by
Ge 11:8 and they left **o.** to build the city.
Ge 17:14 soul shall be cut **o.** from his people;
Ge 17:22 he left **o.** talking with him, and God
Ge 21:16 down over against him a good way **o.**,
Ge 22:4 up his eyes, and saw the place afar **o.**
Ge 24:64 saw Isaac, she lighted **o.** the camel. 5921
Ge 27:40 break his yoke from **o.** thy neck. 5921
Ge 37:18 And when they saw him afar **o.**, even
Ge 38:14 her widow's garments **o.** from her, 5921
Ge 40:19 lift up thy head from **o.** thee, 5921
Ge 40:19 shall eat thy flesh from **o.** thee. 5921
Ge 41:42 took **o.** his ring from his hand,
Ge 44:4 out of the city, and not yet far **o.**,
Ex 2:4 his sister stood afar **o.**, to wit what
Ex 3:5 put **o.** thy shoes from **o.** thy feet; for
Ex 4:25 and cut **o.** the foreskin of her son,
Ex 9:15 thou shalt be cut **o.** from the earth.
Ex 12:15 that soul shall be cut **o.** from Israel.
Ex 12:19 shall be cut **o.** from the congregation
Ex 14:25 And took **o.** their chariot wheels, that
Ex 20:18 saw it, they removed, and stood afar **o.**
Ex 20:21 the people stood afar **o.**, and Moses
Ex 23:23 the Jebusites; and I will cut them **o.**
Ex 24:1 of Israel; and worship ye afar **o.**
Ex 30:33, 38 shall even be cut **o.** from his people.
Ex 31:14 shall be cut **o.** from among his people.
Ex 32:2 Break **o.** the golden earrings, which are
Ex 32:3 people brake **o.** the golden earrings
Ex 32:24 hath any gold, let them break it **o.**
Ex 33:5 now put **o.** thy ornaments from thee,
Ex 33:7 the camp, afar **o.** from the camp.
Ex 34:34 he took the vail **o.**, until he came out.
Le 1:15 and wring **o.** his head, and burn it on
Le 3:9 he take **o.** hard by the backbone;
Le 4:8 take **o.** from it…the fat of the bullock
Le 4:10 As it was taken **o.** from the bullock
Le 4:31 fat is taken away from **o.** the sacrifice
Le 5:8 and wring **o.** his head from his neck,
Le 6:11 And he shall put **o.** his garments, and
Le 7:20, 21 soul shall be cut **o.** from his people.
Le 7:25 it shall be cut **o.** from his people.
Le 7:27 soul shall be cut **o.** from his people.
Le 7:34 from **o.** the sacrifices of their peace
Le 8:28 took them from **o.** their hands, 5921
Le 13:40 man whose hair is fallen **o.** his head,
Le 13:41 hair fallen **o.** from the part of his head
Le 14:8 shave **o.** all his hair, and wash himself
Le 14:9 he shall shave all his hair **o.** his head
Le 14:9 even all his hair he shall shave **o.**:
Le 14:41 that they scrape **o.** without the city
Le 16:12 coals of fire from **o.** the altar. 5921
Le 16:23 shall put **o.** the linen garments, which
Le 17:4 shall be cut **o.** from among his people:
Le 17:9 shall be cut **o.** from among his people.
Le 17:10 will cut him **o.** from among his people.
Le 17:14 whosoever eateth it shall be cut **o.**
Le 18:29 be cut **o.** from among their people.
Le 19:8 shall be cut **o.** from among his people.
Le 20:3 will cut him **o.** from among his people;
Le 20:5 against his family, and will cut him **o.**,
Le 20:6 will cut him **o.** from among his people.
Le 20:17 be cut **o.** in the sight of their people:
Le 20:18 be cut **o.** from among their people.
Le 21:5 they shave **o.** the corner of their beard,
Le 22:3 shall be cut **o.** from my presence:
Le 23:29 shall be cut **o.** from among his people.
Nu 2:2 far **o.** about the tabernacle of the
Nu 4:18 Cut ye not **o.** the tribe of the families
Nu 7:89 unto him from **o.** the mercy seat 5921
Nu 9:10 or be in a journey afar **o.**, yet he shall
Nu 9:13 shall be cut **o.** from among his people:
Nu 10:11 taken up from **o.** the tabernacle 5921
Nu 12:10 departed from **o.** the tabernacle; 5921
Nu 15:30 shall be cut **o.** from among his people.
Nu 15:31 that soul shall utterly be cut **o.**;
Nu 16:46 put fire therein from **o.** the altar, 5921
Nu 19:13 that soul shall be cut **o.** from Israel:
Nu 19:20 cut **o.** from among the congregation,
De 4:26 utterly perish from **o.** the land 5921
De 6:15 thee from **o.** the face of the earth. 5921
De 11:17 ye perish … from **o.** the good land 5921
De 12:29 shall cut **o.** the nations from before
De 13:7 nigh unto thee, or far **o.** from thee,
De 19:1 Lord thy God hath cut **o.** the nations,
De 20:15 cities which are very far **o.** from thee,
De 21:4 strike **o.** the heifer's neck there in the
De 21:13 of her captivity from **o.** her, 5921
De 23:1 or hath his privy member cut **o.**,
De 25:9 loose his shoe from **o.** his foot, 5921
De 25:12 Then thou shalt cut **o.** her hand, thine
De 28:21 consumed thee from **o.** the land, 5921
De 28:63 shall be plucked from **o.** the land 5921
De 30:11 hidden from thee, neither is it far **o.**
Jos 3:13 the waters of Jordan shall be cut **o.**
Jos 3:16 the salt sea, failed, and were cut **o.**
Jos 4:7 the waters of Jordan were cut **o.**
Jos 4:7 the waters of Jordan were cut **o.**
Jos 5:9 the reproach of Egypt from **o.** you. 5921
Jos 5:15 loose thy shoe from **o.** thy foot; for 5921
Jos 7:9 and cut **o.** our name from the earth:
Jos 10:27 they took them down **o.** the trees, 5921
Jos 11:21 and cut **o.** the Anakims from the
Jos 15:18 and she lighted **o.** her ass; and 5921
Jos 23:4 with all the nations that I have cut **o.**,
Jos 23:13 ye perish from **o.** this good land 5921
Jos 23:15 you from **o.** this good land which 5921
Jos 23:16 quickly from **o.** the good land 5921
Jg 1:6 caught him, and cut **o.** his thumbs
Jg 1:7 thumbs and their great toes cut **o.**,
Jg 1:14 and she lighted from **o.** her ass; 5921
Jg 4:15 lighted down from **o.** his chariot, 5921
Jg 5:26 smote Sisera, she smote **o.** his head,
Jg 13:20 toward heaven from **o.** the altar, 5921
Jg 15:14 his bands loosed from **o.** his hands. 5921
Jg 16:12 from **o.** his arms like a thread. 5921
Jg 16:19 caused him to shave **o.** the seven locks
Jg 21:6 is one tribe cut **o.** from Israel this day.
Ru 2:20 Lord, who hath not left **o.** his kindness
Ru 4:7 a man plucked **o.** his shoe, and gave it
Ru 4:8 it for thee. So he drew **o.** his shoe.

Ru 4:10 that the name of the dead be not cut **o.**
1Sa 2:31 come, that I will cut **o.** thine arm,
1Sa 2:33 I shall not cut **o.** from mine altar,
1Sa 4:18 fell from **o.** the seat backward by 5921
1Sa 5:4 hands were cut **o.** upon the threshold;
1Sa 6:5 will lighten his hand from **o.** you, 5921
1Sa 6:5 and from **o.** your gods, 5921
1Sa 6:5 and from **o.** your land. 5921
1Sa 17:39 them. And David put them **o.** him. 5921
1Sa 17:51 him, and cut **o.** his head therewith.
1Sa 19:24 And he stripped **o.** his clothes also,
1Sa 20:15 cut **o.** thy kindness from my house
1Sa 20:15 when the Lord hath cut **o.** the enemies
1Sa 24:4 and cut **o.** the skirt of Saul's robe
1Sa 24:5 because he had cut **o.** Saul's skirt
1Sa 24:11 for in that I cut **o.** the skirt of thy robe,
1Sa 24:21 thou wilt not cut **o.** my seed after me,
1Sa 25:23 lighted **o.** the ass, and fell before 5921
1Sa 26:13 and stood on the top of an hill afar **o.**;
1Sa 28:9 hath cut **o.** those that have familiar
1Sa 31:9 And they cut **o.** his head, and
1Sa 31:9 and stripped **o.** his armour, and
2Sa 4:12 and cut **o.** their hands and their feet,
2Sa 7:9 have cut **o.** all thine enemies out of
2Sa 10:4 shaved **o.** the one half of their beards,
2Sa 10:4 cut **o.** their garments in the middle,
2Sa 11:2 that David arose from **o.** his bed, 5921
2Sa 11:24 shooters shot from **o.** the wall upon 5921
2Sa 12:30 their king's crown from **o.** his head, 5921
2Sa 15:17 and tarried in a place that was far **o.**
2Sa 16:9 over, I pray thee, and take **o.** his head
2Sa 20:22 cut **o.** the head of Sheba the son of
1Ki 9:7 will I cut **o.** Israel out of the land
1Ki 11:16 he had cut **o.** every male in Edom:)
1Ki 13:34 house of Jeroboam, even to cut it **o.**,
1Ki 13:34 it from **o.** the face of the earth.
1Ki 14:10 will cut **o.** from Jeroboam him that
1Ki 14:14 cut **o.** the house of Jeroboam that day:
1Ki 15:21 that he left **o.** building of Ramah, and
1Ki 18:4 Jezebel cut **o.** the prophets of the Lord,
1Ki 20:11 boast himself as he that putteth it **o.**
1Ki 21:21 and will cut **o.** from Ahab him that
2Ki 1:16 shalt not come down **o.** that bed on
2Ki 2:7 went, and stood to view afar **o.**:
2Ki 4:25 man of God saw her afar **o.**, that he
2Ki 9:8 and I will cut **o.** from Ahab him that
2Ki 16:17 Ahaz cut **o.** the borders of the bases,
2Ki 16:17 removed the laver from **o.** them; 5921
2Ki 16:17 the sea from **o.** the brasen oxen 5921
2Ki 18:16 cut **o.** the gold from the doors of the
2Ki 23:27 and will cast **o.** this city Jerusalem
1Ch 17:8 have cut **o.** all thine enemies from
1Ch 19:4 and cut **o.** their garments in the midst
1Ch 20:2 of their king from **o.** his head, 5921
1Ch 28:9 forsake him, he will cast thee **o.** for ever...
2Ch 6:36 captives unto a land far **o.** or near;
2Ch 11:14 cast them **o.** from executing the
2Ch 16:5 he left **o.** building of Ramah, and let
2Ch 20:25 which they stripped **o.** for themselves,
2Ch 22:7 anointed to cut **o.** the house of Ahab
2Ch 26:21 was cut **o.** from the house of the Lord:
2Ch 32:21 angel, which cut **o.** all the mighty men
Ezr 3:13 and the noise was heard afar **o.**.
Ezr 9:3 plucked **o.** the hair of my head and of
Ne 4:23 none of us put **o.** our clothes, saving
Ne 4:23 every one put them **o.** for washing.
Ne 5:10 I pray you, let us leave **o.** this usury.
Ne 12:43 joy of Jerusalem was heard...afar **o.**.
Ne 13:25 and plucked **o.** their hair, and made
Es 8:2 And the king took **o.** his ring, which
Job 2:12 lifted up their eyes afar **o.**, and knew
Job 4:7 or where were the righteous cut **o.**?
Job 6:9 let loose his hand, and cut me **o.**!
Job 8:14 Whose hope shall be cut **o.**, and whose
Job 9:27 I will leave **o.** my heaviness, and
Job 11:10 If he cut **o.**, and shut up, or gather
Job 15:4 Yea, thou castest **o.** fear, and
Job 15:33 shake **o.** his unripe grape as the vine,
Job 15:33 shall cast **o.** his flower as the olive.
Job 17:11 my purposes are broken **o.**, even the
Job 18:16 and above shall his branch be cut **o.**
Job 21:21 of his months is cut **o.** in the midst?
Job 23:17 I was not cut **o.** before the darkness,
Job 24:24 cut **o.** as the tops of the ears of corn.
Job 32:15 no more: they left **o.** speaking.
Job 36:20 when people are cut **o.** in their place.
Job 36:25 may see it; man may behold it afar **o.**.
Job 39:25 and he smelleth the battle afar **o.**,
Job 39:29 the prey, and her eyes behold afar **o.**
Ps 10:1 Why standest thou afar **o.**, O Lord?
Ps 12:3 Lord shall cut **o.** all flattering lips,
Ps 30:11 thou hast put **o.** my sackcloth, and
Ps 31:22 I am cut **o.** from before thine eyes:
Ps 34:16 cut **o.** the remembrance of them from
Ps 36:3 he hath left **o.** to be wise, and to do
Ps 37:9 For evildoers shall be cut **o.**: but
Ps 37:22 that be cursed of him shall be cut **o.**.
Ps 37:28 the seed of the wicked shall be cut **o.**.
Ps 37:34 when the wicked are cut **o.**, thou shalt
Ps 37:38 the end of the wicked shall be cut **o.**.
Ps 38:11 sore; and my kinsman stand afar **o.**.
Ps 43:2 why dost thou cast me **o.**? why go I
Ps 44:9 But thou hast cast **o.**, and put us to
Ps 44:23 O Lord? arise, cast us not **o.** for ever.
Ps 54:5 enemies: cut them **o.** in thy truth.
Ps 55:7 Lo, then would I wander far **o.**, and
Ps 60:1 O God, thou hast cast us **o.**, thou hast
Ps 60:10 thou, O God, which hadst cast us **o.**?
Ps 65:5 of them that are afar **o.** upon the sea:
Ps 71:9 Cast me not **o.** in the time of old age;
Ps 74:1 why hast thou cast us **o.** for ever?
Ps 75:10 horns of the wicked also will I cut **o.**;
Ps 76:12 He shall cut **o.** the spirit of princes:
Ps 77:7 Will the Lord cast **o.** for ever? and will
Ps 83:4 let us cut them **o.** from being a nation;
Ps 88:5 and they are cut **o.** from thy hand.
Ps 88:14 why castest thou **o.** my soul? why
Ps 88:16 over me; thy terrors have cut me **o.**
Ps 89:38 But thou hast cast **o.** and abhorred,
Ps 90:10 for it is soon cut **o.**, and we fly away.
Ps 94:14 the Lord will not cast **o.** his people,
Ps 94:23 cut them **o.** in their...wickedness;
Ps 94:23 the Lord our God shall cut them **o.**.
Ps 101:5 his neighbour, him will I cut **o.**:
Ps 101:8 I may cut **o.** all the wicked doers from
Ps 108:11 not thou, O God, who hast cast us **o.**?
Ps 109:13 Let his posterity be cut **o.**; and in the
Ps 109:15 he may cut **o.** the memory of them.
Ps 138:6 but the proud he knoweth afar **o.**.
Ps 139:2 understandest my thought afar **o.**.
Ps 143:12 of thy mercy cut **o.** mine enemies,
Pr 2:22 wicked shall be cut **o.** from the earth,
Pr 17:14 leave **o.** contention, before it be
Pr 23:18 thine expectation shall not be cut **o.**.
Pr 24:14 and thy expectation shall not be cut **o.**.
Pr 26:6 the hand of a fool cutteth **o.** the feet,
Pr 27:10 that is near than a brother far **o.**.
Pr 30:14 to devour the poor from **o.** the earth,
Ec 7:24 That which is far **o.**, and exceeding
Ca 5:3 I have put **o.** my coat; how shall I put
Isa 6:6 with the tongs from **o.** the altar: 5921
Isa 9:14 will cut **o.** from Israel head and tail,
Isa 10:7 heart to destroy and cut **o.** nations
Isa 10:27 taken away from **o.** thy shoulder, 5921
Isa 10:27 and his yoke from **o.** thy neck, 5921
Isa 11:13 adversaries of Judah shall be cut **o.**:
Isa 14:22 cut **o.** from Babylon the name, and
Isa 14:25 shall his yoke depart from **o.** them, 5921
Isa 14:25 depart from **o.** their shoulders. 5921
Isa 15:2 be baldness, and every beard cut **o.**
Isa 17:13 rebuke them, and they shall flee far **o.**,
Isa 18:5 cut **o.** the sprigs with pruning hooks,
Isa 20:2 the sackcloth from **o.** thy loins, 5921
Isa 20:2 and put **o.** thy shoe from thy foot.
Isa 22:25 that was upon it shall be cut **o.**:
Isa 23:7 feet shall carry her afar **o.** to sojourn.
Isa 25:8 wipe away tears from **o.** all faces; 5921
Isa 25:8 he take away from **o.** all the earth: 5921
Isa 27:11 withered, they shall be broken **o.**:
Isa 27:12 beat **o.** from the channel of the river
Isa 29:20 all that watch for iniquity are cut **o.**:
Isa 33:9 and Carmel shake **o.** their fruits.
Isa 33:13 Hear, ye that are far **o.**, what I have
Isa 33:17 behold the land that is very far **o.**
Isa 34:4 as the leaf falleth **o.** from the vine, and
Isa 38:10 I said in the cutting **o.** of my days,
Isa 38:12 cut **o.** like a weaver my life: he will
Isa 38:12 he will cut me **o.** with pining sickness:
Isa 46:13 it shall not be far **o.**, and my salvation
Isa 47:11 thou shalt not be able to put it **o.**:
Isa 48:9 refrain for thee, that I cut thee not **o.**.
Isa 48:19 his name should not have been cut **o.**
Isa 50:6 to them that plucked **o.** the hair:
Isa 53:8 for he was cut **o.** out of the land of the
Isa 55:13 everlasting sign...shall not be cut **o.**
Isa 56:5 everlasting name,...shall not be cut **o.**.
Isa 57:9 and didst send thy messengers far **o.**,
Isa 57:19 Peace, peace to him that is far **o.**, and
Isa 59:11 for salvation, but it is far **o.** from us.
Isa 59:14 backward, and justice standeth afar **o.**:
Isa 66:3 a lamb, as if he cut **o.** a dog's neck;
Isa 66:19 to the isles afar **o.**, that have not heard
Jer 7:28 perished,...is cut **o.** from their mouth.
Jer 7:29 Cut **o.** thine hair, O Jerusalem,...cast
Jer 9:21 to cut **o.** the children from without,
Jer 11:19 cut him **o.** from the land of the living,
Jer 23:23 saith the Lord, and not a God afar **o.**?
Jer 24:10 they be consumed from **o.** the land 5921
Jer 28:10 **o.** the prophet Jeremiah's neck, 5921
Jer 28:12 **o.** the neck of the prophet Jeremiah 5921
Jer 28:16 thee from **o.** the face of the earth; 5921
Jer 30:8 break his yoke from **o.** thy neck, 5921
Jer 31:10 and declare it in the isles afar **o.**, and
Jer 31:37 I will also cast **o.** all the seed of Israel
Jer 33:24 he hath even cast them **o.**? thus they
Jer 38:27 So they left **o.** speaking with him; for
Jer 44:7 to cut **o.** from you man and woman,
Jer 44:8 that ye might cut yourselves **o.**, and
Jer 44:11 you for evil, and to cut **o.** all Judah.
Jer 44:18 since we left **o.** to burn incense to the
Jer 46:27 behold, I will save thee from afar **o.**.
Jer 47:4 And to cut **o.** from Tyrus and Zidon
Jer 47:5 Askelon is cut **o.** with the remnant of
Jer 48:2 let us cut it **o.** from being a nation
Jer 48:25 The horn of Moab is cut **o.**, and his
Jer 49:26 men of war shall be cut **o.** in that day,
Jer 49:30 Flee, get you far **o.**, dwell deep, O ye
Jer 50:16 Cut **o.** the sower from Babylon, and
Jer 50:30 men of war shall be cut **o.** in that day,
Jer 51:6 be not cut **o.** in her iniquity; for this is
Jer 51:50 remember the Lord afar **o.**, and let
Jer 51:62 to cut it **o.**, that none shall remain in
La 2:3 He hath cut **o.** in his fierce anger all
La 2:7 The Lord hath cast **o.** his altar, he
La 3:17 removed my soul far **o.** from peace:
La 3:31 For the Lord will not cast **o.** for ever:
La 3:53 have cut **o.** my life in the dungeon,
La 3:54 mine head; then I said, I am cut **o.**
Eze 6:12 that is far **o.** shall die of the pestilence;
Eze 8:6 I should go far **o.** from my sanctuary?
Eze 10:18 departed from **o.** the threshold of 5921
Eze 11:16 cast them far **o.** among the heathens,
Eze 12:27 of the times that are afar **o.**.
Eze 14:8 will cut him **o.** from the midst of my
Eze 14:13 and will cut **o.** man and beast from it:
Eze 14:17 so that I cut **o.** man and beast from it:
Eze 14:19 blood, to cut **o.** from it man and beast:
Eze 14:21 to cut **o.** from it man and beast?
Eze 17:4 cropped **o.** the top of his young twigs,
Eze 17:9 and cut **o.** the fruit thereof, that it
Eze 17:17 building forts, to cut **o.** many persons:
Eze 17:22 I will crop **o.** from the top of his young
Eze 18:17 hath taken **o.** his hand from the poor,
Eze 21:3 will cut **o.** from thee the righteous and
Eze 21:4 I will cut **o.** from thee the righteous
Eze 21:26 the diadem, and take **o.** the crown:
Eze 23:34 thereof,...pluck **o.** thine own breasts:
Eze 25:7 and I will cut thee **o.** from the people,
Eze 25:13 and will cut **o.** man and beast from it;
Eze 25:16 and I will cut **o.** the Cherethims, and
Eze 26:16 and put **o.** their broidered garments:
Eze 29:8 and cut **o.** man and beast out of thee.
Eze 30:15 and I will cut **o.** the multitude of No.
Eze 31:12 terrible of the nations, have cut him **o.**,
Eze 35:7 will cut **o.** from him that passeth out
Eze 37:11 is lost: we are cut **o.** for our parts.
Eze 44:19 shall put **o.** their garments wherein
Da 4:14 down the tree, and cut **o.** his branches,
Da 4:14 shake **o.** his leaves, and scatter his
Da 4:27 and break **o.** thy sins by righteousness,
Da 9:7 that are near, and that are far **o.**,
Da 9:26 two weeks shall Messiah be cut **o.**,
Ho 4:10 have left **o.** to take heed to the Lord.
Ho 8:3 hath cast **o.** the thing that is good:
Ho 8:4 them idols, that they may be cut **o.**.
Ho 8:5 Thy calf, O Samaria, hath cast thee **o.**:
Ho 10:7 Samaria, her king is cut **o.** as the foam.
Ho 10:15 the king of Israel utterly be cut **o.**
Ho 11:4 take **o.** the yoke on their jaws, 5921
Joe 1:5 wine; for it is cut **o.** from your mouth.
Joe 1:9 is cut **o.** from the house of the Lord;

Joe 1:16 Is not the meat cut **o.** before our eyes,.....
Joe 2:20 far **o.** from you the northern army,..........
Joe 3:8 to the Sabeans, to a people far **o.**:...........
Am 1:5 cut **o.** the inhabitant from the plain of........
Am 1:8 cut **o.** the inhabitant from Ashdod,............
Am 1:11 and did cast **o.** all pity, and his anger........
Am 2:3 I will cut **o.** the judge from the midst.........
Am 3:14 the horns of the altar shall be cut **o.**,........
Am 5:7 leave **o.** righteousness in the earth,..........
Am 9:8 it from **o.** the face of the earth;......... 5921
Ob 5 (how art thou cut **o.**!) would they not........
Ob 9 of Esau may be cut **o.** by slaughter.........
Ob 10 and thou shalt be cut **o.** for ever...........
Ob 14 to cut **o.** those of his that did escape;.......
Mic 2:8 ye pull **o.** the robe with the garment.........
Mic 3:2 who pluck **o.** the skin from **o.** them,.........
Mic 3:2 their flesh from **o.** their bones;.......... 5921
Mic 3:3 and flay their skin from **o.** them;........ 5921
Mic 4:3 rebuke strong nations afar **o.**; and.........
Mic 4:7 that was cast far **o.** a strong nation:..........
Mic 5:9 and all thine enemies shall be cut **o.**,.........
Mic 5:10 cut **o.** thy horses out of the midst of.........
Mic 5:11 And I will cut **o.** the cities of thy land,......
Mic 5:12 cut **o.** witchcrafts out of thine hand;..........
Mic 5:13 Thy graven images also will I cut **o.**,........
Na 1:13 will I break his yoke from **o.** thee,..... 5921
Na 1:14 thy gods will I cut **o.** the graven image......
Na 1:15 through thee; he is utterly cut **o.**...........
Na 2:13 I will cut **o.** thy prey from the earth,........
Na 3:15 the sword shall cut thee **o.**, it shall eat......
Hab 2:10 thy house by cutting **o.** many people,........
Hab 3:17 the flock shall be cut **o.** from the fold,........
Zep 1:2 all things from **o.** the land,......... 5921,6440
Zep 1:3 cut **o.** man from **o.** the land,...... 5921,6440
Zep 1:4 I will cut **o.** the remnant of Baal from.......
Zep 1:11 all they that bear silver are cut **o.**...........
Zep 3:6 I have cut **o.** the nations: their towers......
Zep 3:7 their dwelling should not be cut **o.**,...........
Zec 5:3 every one that stealeth shall be cut **o.**........
Zec 5:3 every one that sweareth shall be cut **o.**.....
Zec 6:15 that are far **o.** shall come and build...........
Zec 9:6 will cut **o.** the pride of the Philistines.........
Zec 9:10 I will cut **o.** the chariot from Ephraim,.......
Zec 9:10 and the battle bow shall be cut **o.**:............
Zec 10:6 be as though I had not cast them **o.**:...........
Zec 11:8 Three shepherds also I cut **o.** in one.........
Zec 11:9 that is to be cut **o.**, let it be cut **o.**;..........
Zec 11:16 shall not visit those that be cut **o.**,..........
Zec 13:2 cut **o.** the names of the idols out of the.....
Zec 13:8 parts therein shall be cut **o.** and die;.........
Zec 14:2 shall not be cut **o.** from the city..............
Mal 2:12 will cut **o.** the man that doeth this,............
Mt 5:30 **right hand offend thee, cut it o.,**... *1581*
Mt 8:30 a good way **o.** from them a herd......... *575*
Mt 10:14 **city, shake o. the dust of your feet.** *1621*
Mt 18:8 **thy foot offend thee, cut them o.,**.. *1581*
Mt 26:51 high priest's, and smote **o.** his ear....... *851*
Mt 26:58 Peter followed him afar **o.** unto the...... *575*
Mt 27:31 they took the robe **o.** from him,......... *1562*
Mt 27:55 women were...beholding afar **o.**,.......... *575*
Mk 5:6 when he saw Jesus afar **o.**, he ran........ *575*
Mk 6:11 **shake o. the dust under your feet**.. *1621*
Mk 9:43 **if thy hand offend thee, cut it o.**:... *609*
Mk 9:45 **if thy foot offend thee, cut it o.**:.... *609*
Mk 11:8 cut down branches **o.** the trees.......... *1537*
Mk 11:13 seeing a fig tree afar **o.** having leaves,......
Mk 14:47 of the high priest, and cut **o.** his ear,... *609*
Mk 14:54 Peter followed him afar **o.**, even.......... *575*
Mk 15:20 they took **o.** the purple from him,......... *609*
Mk 15:40 were also women looking on afar **o.**:.... *575*
Lu 9:5 **shake o. the very dust from your**.... *660*
Lu 10:11 **on us, we do wipe o. against you:**... *631*
Lu 14:32 **the other is yet a great way o.,**....... *631*
Lu 15:20 **when he was yet a great way o.,**....... *568*
Lu 16:23 **and seeth Abraham afar o., and**...... *575*
Lu 17:12 that were lepers, which stood afar **o.**........
Lu 18:13 **publican, standing afar o., would**.........
Lu 22:50 high priest, and cut **o.** his right ear...... *851*
Lu 22:54 house. And Peter followed afar **o.**...........
Lu 23:49 him from Galilee, stood afar **o.**,.................
Joh 11:18 Jerusalem, about fifteen furlongs **o.**...... *575*
Joh 18:10 servant, and cut **o.** his right ear........... *609*
Joh 18:26 his kinsman whose ear Peter cut **o.**,....... *609*
Ac 2:39 to all that are afar **o.**, even as many.........
Ac 7:33 Put **o.** thy shoes from thy feet; for..... *3089*
Ac 12:7 his chains fell **o.** from his hands......... *1601*
Ac 13:51 shook **o.** the dust of their feet........... *1621*
Ac 16:22 the magistrates rent **o.** their clothes,.. *4048*
Ac 22:23 cried out, and cast **o.** their clothes,..... *4496*
Ac 27:32 soldiers cut **o.** the ropes of the boat,.... *609*
Ac 27:32 ropes of the boat, and let her fall **o.**.. *1601*
Ac 28:5 he shook **o.** the beast into the fire,...... *660*
Ro 11:17 if some of the branches be broken **o.**.. *1575*
Ro 11:19 The branches were broken **o.**, that I.... *1575*
Ro 11:20 of unbelief they were broken **o.**,........ *1575*
Ro 11:22 otherwise thou also shalt be cut **o.**.... *1581*
Ro 13:12 let us...cast **o.** the work of darkness,... *659*
2Co 11:12 I may cut **o.** occasion from them........ *1581*
Ga 5:12 were even cut **o.** which trouble you..... *609*
Eph 2:13 were far **o.** are made nigh by the....... *3112*
Eph 2:17 peace to you which were afar **o.**, and........
Eph 4:22 ye put **o.** concerning the former.......... *659*
Col 2:11 putting **o.** the body of the sins of the.... *554*
Col 3:8 But now ye also put **o.** all these:......... *659*
Col 3:9 put **o.** the old man with his deeds;....... *554*
1Ti 5:12 they have cast **o.** their first faith.......... *114*
Heb 11:13 but having seen them afar **o.**, and were.....
2Pe 1:9 things is blind, and cannot see afar **o.**,........
2Pe 1:14 I must put **o.** this my tabernacle,......... *595*
Re 18:10 Standing afar **o.** for the fear of her....... *575*
Re 18:15 shall stand afar **o.** for the fear of......... *575*
Re 18:17 many as trade by sea, stood afar **o.**,.... *575*

OFFENCE See also OFFENCES.
1Sa 25:31 thee, nor **o.** of heart unto my lord,..... 4383
Isa 8:14 a rock of **o.** to both the houses of...... 4383
Ho 5:15 till they acknowledge their **o.**, and........ 816
Mt 16:23 **Satan: thou art an o. unto me:**...... *4625*
Mt 18:7 **that man by whom the o. cometh!**. *4625*
Ac 24:16 conscience void of **o.** toward God,....... *677*
Ro 5:15 not as the **o.**, so also is the free........ *3900*
Ro 5:15 through...**o.** of one many be dead,...... *3900*
Ro 5:17 if by one man's **o.** death reigned........ *3900*
Ro 5:18 as by the **o.** of one judgment came..... *3900*
Ro 5:20 entered, that the **o.** might abound...... *3900*
Ro 9:33 a stumblingstone and rock of **o.**:........ *4625*
Ro 14:20 for that man who eateth with **o.**......... *4348*
1Co 10:32 Give none **o.**, neither to the Jews,....... *677*
2Co 6:3 Giving no **o.** in any thing, that the...... *4349*
2Co 11:7 committed an **o.** in abasing myself........ *266*
Ga 5:11 then is the **o.** of the cross ceased........ *4625*
Php 1:10 and without **o.** till the day of Christ;..... *677*
1Pe 2:8 of stumbling, and a rock of **o.**,........... *4625*

OFFENCES
Ec 10:4 for yielding pacifieth great **o.**............ 2399
Mt 18:7 **Woe unto the world because of o.!** *4625*
Mt 18:7 **for it must needs be that o. come**.. *4625*
Lu 17:1 **impossible but that o. will come:**... *4625*
Ro 4:25 Who was delivered for our **o.**, and...... *3900*
Ro 5:16 the free gift is of many **o.** unto.......... *3900*
Ro 16:17 them which cause divisions and **o.**...... *4625*

OFFEND See also OFFENDED.
Job 34:31 I will not **o.** any more:..................... 2254
Ps 73:15 I should **o.** against the generation........ 898
Ps 119:165 law: and nothing shall **o.** them.......... 4383
Jer 2:3 all that devour him shall **o.**; evil........... 816
Jer 50:7 We **o.** not, because they have sinned.... 816
Ho 4:15 play the harlot, yet let not Judah **o.**;..... 816
Hab 1:11 he shall pass over, and **o.**, imputing..... 816
Mt 5:29 **if thy right eye o. thee, pluck it**.... *4624*
Mt 5:30 **if thy right hand o. thee, cut it off,** *4624*
Mt 13:41 **of his kingdom all things that o.,**.. *4625*
Mt 17:27 **lest we should o. them, go thou to** . *4624*
Mt 18:6 **shall o. one of these little ones**..... *4624*
Mt 18:8 **if thy hand or thy foot o. thee, cut.** *4624*
Mt 18:9 **And if thine eye o. thee, pluck it**... *4624*
Mk 9:42 **shall o. one of these little ones**..... *4624*
Mk 9:43 **And if thy hand o. thee, cut it off:**. *4624*
Mk 9:45 **And if thy foot o. thee, cut it off:**.. *4624*
Mk 9:47 **And if thine eye o. thee, pluck it**... *4624*
Lu 17:2 **should o. one of these little ones**... *4624*
Joh 6:61 said unto them, **Doth this o. you?**.... *4624*
1Co 8:13 if meat make my brother to **o.**,.......... *4624*
1Co 8:13 lest I make my brother to **o.**............. *4624*
Jas 2:10 the whole law, yet **o.** in one point,..... *4417*
Jas 3:2 For in many things we **o.** all............. *4417*
Jas 3:2 If any man **o.** not in word, the.......... *4417*

OFFENDED
Ge 20:9 what have I **o.** thee, that thou.......... 2398
Ge 40:1 baker had **o.** their lord the king of...... 2398
2Ki 18:14 saying, I have **o.**; return from me:..... 2398
2Ch 28:13 have **o.** against the Lord already,......... 819
Pr 18:19 A brother **o.** is harder to be won....... 6586
Jer 37:18 What have I **o.** against thee, or......... 2398
Eze 25:12 and hath greatly **o.**, and revenged........ 816
Ho 13:1 but when he **o.** in Baal, he died........... 816
Mt 11:6 **whosoever shall not be o. in me.**... *4624*
Mt 13:21 **of the word, by and by he is o.**.... *4624*
Mt 13:57 And they were **o.** in him. But Jesus.... *4624*
Mt 15:12 thou that the Pharisees were **o.**,......... *4624*
Mt 24:10 **And then shall many be o., and**..... *4624*
Mt 26:31 **All ye shall be o. because of me**.... *4624*
Mt 26:33 Though all men shall be **o.** because..... *4624*
Mt 26:33 of thee, yet will I never be **o.**.......... *4624*
Mk 4:17 **sake, immediately they are o.**....... *4624*
Mk 6:3 with us? And they were **o.** at him...... *4624*
Mk 14:27 **All ye shall be o. because of me**.... *4624*
Mk 14:29 Although all shall be **o.**, yet will not.... *4624*
Lu 7:23 **whosoever shall not be o. in me.**.... *4624*
Joh 16:1 **unto you, that ye should not be o.**..*4624*
Ac 25:8 Caesar, have I **o.** any thing at all......... *264*
Ro 14:21 brother stumbleth, or is **o.**, or.......... *4624*
2Co 11:29 weak? who is **o.**, and I burn not?....... *4624*

OFFENDER See also OFFENDERS.
Isa 29:21 That make a man an **o.** for a word,.... 2398
Ac 25:11 if I be an **o.**, or have committed........... *91*

OFFENDERS
1Ki 1:21 son Solomon shall be counted **o.**....... 2400

OFFER See also OFFERED; OFFERETH; OFFERING.
Ge 22:2 **o.** him there for a burnt offering........ 5927
Ex 22:29 not delay to **o.** the first of thy ripe..........
Ex 23:18 not **o.** the blood of my sacrifice.......... 2076
Ex 29:36 thou shalt **o.** every day a bullock........ 6213
Ex 29:38 which thou shalt **o.** upon the altar;...... 6213
Ex 29:39 lamb thou shalt **o.** in the morning;...... 6213
Ex 29:39 other lamb thou shalt **o.** at even:....... 6213
Ex 29:41 other lamb thou shalt **o.** at even,....... 6213
Ex 30:9 **o.** no strange incense thereon,........... 5927
Ex 34:25 not **o.** the blood of my sacrifice.......... 7819
Ex 35:24 that did **o.** an offering of silver.......... 7311
Le 1:3 him **o.** a male without blemish:......... 7126
Le 1:3 shall **o.** it of his own voluntary will..... 7126
Le 2:1 when any will **o.** a meat offering........ 7126
Le 2:12 ye shall **o.** them unto the Lord:.......... 7126
Le 2:13 thine offerings thou shalt **o.** salt........ 7126
Le 2:14 **o.** a meat offering of thy firstfruits...... 7126
Le 2:14 thou shalt **o.** for the meat offering...... 7126
Le 3:1 offering, if he **o.** it of the herd;.......... 7126
Le 3:1 he shall **o.** it without blemish before.... 7126
Le 3:3 shall **o.** of the sacrifice of the peace..... 7126
Le 3:6 he shall **o.** it without blemish............ 7126
Le 3:7 If he **o.** a lamb for his offering, then... 7126
Le 3:7 then shall he **o.** it before the Lord...... 7126
Le 3:9 **o.** of the sacrifice of the peace........... 7126
Le 3:12 then he shall **o.** it before the Lord...... 7126
Le 3:14 he shall **o.** thereof his offering,......... 7126
Le 4:14 shall **o.** a young bullock for the sin,.... 7126
Le 5:8 who shall **o.** that which is for the sin... 7126
Le 5:10 **o.** the second for a burnt offering,...... 6213
Le 6:14 Aaron shall **o.** it before the Lord,........ 7126
Le 6:20 which they shall **o.** unto the Lord in.... 7126
Le 6:21 shalt thou **o.** for a sweet savour......... 7126
Le 6:22 is anointed in his stead shall **o.** it:...... 6213
Le 7:3 he shall **o.** of it all the fat thereof;...... 7126
Le 7:11 which he shall **o.** unto the Lord......... 7126
Le 7:12 If he **o.** it for a thanksgiving, then..... 7126
Le 7:12 **o.** with the sacrifice of thanksgiving.... 7126
Le 7:13 **o.** for his offering leavened bread....... 7126
Le 7:14 **o.** one out of the whole oblation......... 7126
Le 7:25 men **o.** an offering made by fire unto... 7126
Le 7:38 to **o.** their oblations unto the Lord,..... 7126
Le 9:2 and **o.** them before the Lord............. 7126
Le 9:7 **o.** thy sin offering, and thy burnt........ 6213
Le 9:7 **o.** the offering of the people, and....... 6213
Le 12:7 Who shall **o.** it before the Lord,......... 7126
Le 14:12 **o.** him for a trespass offering, and....... 7126
Le 14:19 the priest shall **o.** the sin offering,...... 6213
Le 14:20 priest shall **o.** the burnt offering......... 5927
Le 14:30 shall **o.** the one of the turtledoves,..... 6213
Le 15:15 And the priest shall **o.** them, the........ 6213
Le 15:30 shall **o.** the one for a sin offering,...... 6213
Le 16:6 **o.** his bullock of the sin offering,....... 7126
Le 16:9 fell, and **o.** him for a sin offering........ 6213
Le 16:24 forth, and **o.** his burnt offering,.......... 6213
Le 17:4 to **o.** an offering unto the Lord.......... 7126
Le 17:5 which they **o.** in the open field,.......... 2076
Le 17:5 **o.** them for peace offerings unto........ 2076

Le	17:7	**o.** their sacrifices unto devils,	2076
Le	17:9	to **o.** it unto the Lord; even that	6213
Le	19:5	ye **o.** a sacrifice of peace offerings	2076
Le	19:5	Lord, ye shall **o.** it at your own will.	2076
Le	19:6	be eaten the same day ye **o.** it,	2077
Le	21:6	bread of their God, they do **o.**	7126
Le	21:17	approach to **o.** the bread of his God.	7126
Le	21:21	nigh to **o.** the offerings of the Lord.	7126
Le	21:21	nigh to **o.** the bread of his God.	7126
Le	22:15	Israel, which they **o.** unto the Lord;	7311
Le	22:18	that will **o.** his oblation for all his	7126
Le	22:18	will **o.** unto the Lord for a burnt	7126
Le	22:19	Ye shall **o.** at your own will a male	
Le	22:20	a blemish, that shall ye not **o.**:	7126
Le	22:22	ye shall not **o.** these unto the Lord,	7126
Le	22:23	thou **o.** for a freewill offering;	6213
Le	22:24	not **o.** unto the Lord that which	7126
Le	22:25	shall ye **o.** the bread of your God	7126
Le	22:29	when ye will **o.** a sacrifice of	2076
Le	22:29	the Lord, **o.** it at your own will.	2076
Le	23:8	shall **o.** an offering made by fire	7126
Le	23:12	ye shall **o.** that day when ye wave	6213
Le	23:16	shall **o.** a new meat offering unto	7126
Le	23:18	shall **o.** with the bread seven lambs	7126
Le	23:25,	27,36,36,37 **o.** an offering...by fire	7126
Le	27:11	do not **o.** a sacrifice unto the Lord,	7126
Nu	5:25	the Lord, and **o.** it upon the altar:	7126
Nu	6:11	shall **o.** the one for a sin offering,	6213
Nu	6:14	shall **o.** his offering unto the Lord,	7126
Nu	6:16	shall **o.** his sin offering, and his	6213
Nu	6:17	shall **o.** the ram for a sacrifice of	6213
Nu	6:17	shall **o.** also his meat offering, and	6213
Nu	7:11	They shall **o.** their offering, each	7126
Nu	7:18	of Zuar, prince of Issachar, did **o.**	7126
Nu	7:24	of the children of Zebulun, did **o.**	
Nu	7:30	of the children of Reuben, did **o.**	
Nu	7:36	of the children of Simeon, did **o.**	
Nu	8:11	Aaron shall **o.** the Levites before	5130
Nu	8:12	shalt **o.** the one for a sin offering,	6213
Nu	8:13	**o.** them for an offering unto the	5130
Nu	8:15	them, and **o.** them for an offering.	5130
Nu	9:7	not **o.** an offering of the Lord in	7126
Nu	15:7	**o.** the third part of an hin of wine,	7126
Nu	15:14	will **o.** an offering made by fire,	6213
Nu	15:19	ye shall **o.** up an heave offering	7311
Nu	15:20	**o.** up a cake of the first of your	7311
Nu	15:24	shall **o.** one young bullock for a	6213
Nu	16:40	come near to **o.** incense before	
Nu	18:12	which they shall **o.** unto the Lord,	5414
Nu	18:19	children of Israel **o.** unto the Lord,	7311
Nu	18:24	they **o.** as an heave offering unto	7311
Nu	18:26	shall **o.** up an heave offering of it	7311
Nu	18:28	ye also shall **o.** an heave offering	7311
Nu	18:29	ye shall **o.** every heave offering of	7311
Nu	28:2	**o.** unto me in their due season.	7126
Nu	28:3	which ye shall **o.** unto the Lord;	7126
Nu	28:4	lamb shalt thou **o.** in the morning,	6213
Nu	28:4	other lamb shalt thou **o.** at even;	6213
Nu	28:8	other lamb shalt thou **o.** at even:	6213
Nu	28:8	thou shalt **o.** it, a sacrifice made by	6213
Nu	28:11	ye shall **o.** a burnt offering unto	7126
Nu	28:19	ye shall **o.** a sacrifice made by fire	7126
Nu	28:20	tenth deals shall ye **o.** for a bullock,	6213
Nu	28:21	A several tenth deal shalt thou **o.** for	6213
Nu	28:23	**o.** these beside the burnt offering	6213
Nu	28:24	this manner ye shall **o.** daily,	6213
Nu	28:27	ye shall **o.** the burnt offering for	7126
Nu	28:31	shall **o.** them beside the continual	6213
Nu	29:2	shall **o.** a burnt offering for a sweet	6213
Nu	29:8	shall **o.** a burnt offering unto the	7126
Nu	29:13	And ye shall **o.** a burnt offering, a	7126
Nu	29:17	shall **o.** twelve young bullocks, two	
Nu	29:36	But ye shall **o.** a burnt offering,	7126
De	12:13	thou **o.** not thy burnt offerings in	5927
De	12:14	thou shalt **o.** thy burnt offerings,	5927
De	12:27	thou shalt **o.** thy burnt offerings,	6213
De	18:3	from them that **o.** a sacrifice,	2076
De	27:6	**o.** burnt offerings thereon unto	5927
De	27:7	thou shalt **o.** peace offerings, and	2076
De	33:19	shall **o.** sacrifices of righteousness:	2076
Jos	22:23	**o.** thereon burnt offering or meat	5927
Jos	22:23	if to **o.** peace offerings thereon, let	6213
Jg	3:18	made an end to **o.** the present,	7126
Jg	6:26	**o.** a burnt sacrifice with the wood	5927
Jg	11:31	I will **o.** it up for a burnt offering.	5927
Jg	13:16	if thou wilt **o.** a burnt offering,	6213
Jg	13:16	thou must **o.** it unto the Lord.	5927
Jg	16:23	**o.** a great sacrifice unto Dagon	2076
1Sa	1:21	went up to **o.** unto the Lord the	2076
1Sa	2:19	husband to **o.** the yearly sacrifice.	2076
1Sa	2:28	to **o.** upon mine altar, to burn	5927
1Sa	10:8	unto thee, to **o.** burnt offerings,	5927
2Sa	24:12	the Lord, I **o.** thee three things;	5190
2Sa	24:22	take and **o.** up what seemeth good	5927
2Sa	24:24	will I **o.** burnt offerings unto the	5927
1Ki	3:4	did Solomon **o.** upon that altar.	5927
1Ki	9:25	did Solomon **o.** burnt offerings	5927
1Ki	13:2	upon thee shall he **o.** the priests	2076
2Ki	5:17	**o.** neither burnt offering nor	6213
2Ki	10:24	to **o.** sacrifices and burnt offerings,	6213
1Ch	16:40	**o.** burnt offerings unto the Lord	5927
1Ch	21:10	the Lord, I **o.** thee three things:	5186
1Ch	21:24	nor **o.** burnt offerings without	5927
1Ch	23:31	**o.** all burnt sacrifices unto the	5927
1Ch	29:14	should be able to **o.** so willingly	
1Ch	29:17	here, to **o.** willingly unto thee.	
2Ch	23:18	**o.** the burnt offerings of the Lord,	5927
2Ch	24:14	to minister, and to **o.** withal, and	5927
2Ch	29:21	to **o.** them on the altar of the Lord.	5927
2Ch	29:27	to **o.** the burnt offering upon the	5927
2Ch	35:12	**o.** unto the Lord, as it is written.	7126
2Ch	35:16	**o.** burnt offerings upon the altar	5927
Ezr	3:2	to **o.** burnt offerings thereon, as it	5927
Ezr	3:6	**o.** burnt offerings unto the Lord.	5927
Ezr	6:10	may **o.** sacrifices of sweet savours	7127
Ezr	7:17	and **o.** them upon the altar of the	7127
Job	42:8	and **o.** up for yourselves a burnt	5927
Ps	4:5	**O.** the sacrifices of righteousness,	2076
Ps	16:4	offerings of blood will I not **o.**,	5258
Ps	27:6	**o.** in his tabernacle sacrifices of	2076
Ps	50:14	**O.** unto God thanksgiving; and	2076
Ps	51:19	they **o.** bullocks upon thine altar.	5927
Ps	66:15	will **o.** unto thee burnt sacrifices of	5927
Ps	66:15	I will **o.** bullocks with goats.	6213
Ps	72:10	Sheba and Seba shall **o.** gifts.	7126
Ps	116:17	I will **o.** to thee the sacrifice of	2076
Isa	57:7	wentest thou up to **o.** sacrifice.	2076
Jer	11:12	gods unto whom they **o.** incense:	
Jer	14:12	**o.** burnt offering and an oblation,	5927
Jer	33:18	before me to **o.** burnt offerings,	5927
Eze	6:13	where they did **o.** sweet savour	5414
Eze	20:31	For when ye **o.** your gifts, when	5375
Eze	43:18	**o.** burnt offerings thereon, and to	5927
Eze	43:22	second day thou shalt **o.** a kid	7126
Eze	43:23	thou shalt **o.** a young bullock	7126
Eze	43:24	thou shalt **o.** them before the Lord,	7126
Eze	43:24	**o.** them up for a burnt offering	5927
Eze	44:7	**o.** my bread, the fat and the blood,	7126
Eze	44:15	**o.** unto me the fat and the blood,	7126
Eze	44:27	he shall **o.** his sin offering, saith	7126
Eze	45:1	shall **o.** an oblation unto the Lord,	7311
Eze	45:13	is the oblation that ye shall **o.**;	7311
Eze	45:14	ye shall **o.** the tenth part of a bath	
Eze	46:4	offering that the prince shall **o.**	7126
Eze	48:8	be the offering which ye shall **o.**	7311
Eze	48:9	oblation that ye shall **o.** unto the	7311
Eze	48:20	**o.** the holy oblation foursquare,	7311
Da	2:46	**o.** an oblation and sweet odours	5260
Ho	9:4	not **o.** wine offerings to the Lord,	5258
Am	4:5	And **o.** a sacrifice of thanksgiving	6999
Am	5:22	Though ye **o.** me burnt offerings	5927
Hag	2:14	which they **o.** there is unclean.	7126
Mal	1:7	Ye **o.** polluted bread upon mine	5066
Mal	1:8	if ye **o.** the blind for sacrifice, is it	5066
Mal	1:8	if ye **o.** the lame and sick, is it not	5066
Mal	1:8	**o.** it now unto thy governor; will	7126
Mal	3:3	may **o.** unto the Lord an offering	5066
Mt	5:24	**and then come and o. thy gift**	*4374*
Mt	8:4	**o. the gift that Moses commanded,**	*4374*
Mk	1:44	**o. for thy cleansing those things**	*4374*
Lu	2:24	to **o.** a sacrifice according to that	*1325*
Lu	5:14	**o. for thy cleansing, according as**	*4374*
Lu	6:29	**on the one cheek o. also the other;**	*3930*
Lu	11:12	**an egg, will he o. him a scorpion?**	*1929*
Heb	5:1	**o.** both gifts and sacrifices	*4374*
Heb	5:3	so also for himself, to **o.** for sins.	*4374*
Heb	7:27	to **o.** up sacrifice, first for his own	*399*
Heb	8:3	ordained to **o.** gifts and sacrifices:	*4374*
Heb	8:3	man have somewhat also to **o.**	*4374*
Heb	8:4	that **o.** gifts according to the law:	*4374*
Heb	9:25	that he should **o.** himself often,	*4374*
Heb	13:15	let us **o.** the sacrifice of praise to	*399*
1Pe	2:5	to **o.** up spiritual sacrifices,	*399*
Re	8:3	**o.** it with the prayers of all saints	*1325*

OFFERED

Ge	8:20	**o.** burnt offerings on the altar.	5927
Ge	22:13	and **o.** him up for a burnt offering	5927
Ge	31:54	**o.** sacrifice upon the mount, and	2076
Ge	46:1	and **o.** sacrifices unto the God of his	2076
Ex	24:5	of Israel, which **o.** burnt offerings,	5927
Ex	32:6	**o.** burnt offerings, and brought	5927
Ex	35:22	man that **o.**...an offering of gold	5130
Ex	35:22	every man...**o.** an offering of gold	
Ex	40:29	**o.** upon it the burnt offering and	5927
Le	7:8	burnt offering which he hath **o.**	7126
Le	7:15	eaten the same day that it is **o.**;	7133
Le	9:15	slew it, and **o.** it for sin, as the	2398
Le	9:16	and **o.** it according to the manner.	6213
Le	10:1	**o.** strange fire before the Lord,	7126
Le	10:19	day have they **o.** their sin offering	7126
Le	16:1	when they **o.** before the Lord, and	7126
Nu	3:4	they **o.** strange fire before the Lord,	7126
Nu	7:2	over them that were numbered, **o.**:	7126
Nu	7:10	**o.** for dedicating of the altar in	7126
Nu	7:10	**o.** their offering before the altar.	7126
Nu	7:12	he that **o.** his offering the first day	7126
Nu	7:19	He **o.** for his offering one silver	7126
Nu	7:42	prince of the children of Gad, **o.**:	
Nu	7:48	prince of the children of Ephraim, **o.**:	
Nu	7:54	On the eighth day **o.** Gamaliel the	
Nu	7:60	prince of the children of Benjamin, **o.**:	
Nu	7:66	prince of the children of Dan, **o.**:	
Nu	7:72	prince of the children of Asher, **o.**:	
Nu	7:78	prince of the children of Naphtali, **o.**:	
Nu	8:21	and Aaron **o.** them as an offering	5130
Nu	16:35	and fifty men that **o.** incense.	7126
Nu	16:38	for they **o.** them before the Lord,	7126
Nu	16:39	they that were burnt had **o.**; and	7126
Nu	22:40	And Balak **o.** oxen and sheep,	2076
Nu	23:2	and Balaam **o.** on every altar a	5927
Nu	23:4	**o.** upon every altar a bullock and	5927
Nu	23:14,	30 **o.** a bullock and a ram on every	5927
Nu	26:61	**o.** strange fire before the Lord.	7126
Nu	28:15	offering unto the Lord shall be **o.**,	6213
Nu	28:24	**o.** beside the continual burnt	6213
Nu	31:52	gold of the offering that they **o.**	7311
Jos	8:31	they **o.** thereon burnt offerings	5927
Jg	5:2	the people willingly **o.** themselves.	
Jg	5:9	**o.** themselves willingly among the	
Jg	6:28	bullock was **o.** upon the altar	5927
Jg	13:19	**o.** it upon a rock unto the Lord:	5927
Jg	20:26	and **o.** burnt offerings and peace	5927
Jg	21:4	and **o.** burnt offerings and peace	5927
1Sa	1:4	the time was that Elkanah **o.**,	2076
1Sa	2:13	that, when any man **o.** sacrifice,	2076
1Sa	6:14	**o.** the kine a burnt offering unto	5927
1Sa	6:15	of Beth-shemesh **o.** burnt offerings	5927
1Sa	7:9	lamb, and **o.** it for a burnt offering	5927
1Sa	13:9	And he **o.** the burnt offering	5927
1Sa	13:12	therefore, and **o.** a burnt offering.	5927
2Sa	6:17	David **o.** burnt offerings and peace	5927
2Sa	15:12	from Giloh, while he **o.** sacrifices.	2076
2Sa	24:25	and **o.** burnt offerings and peace	5927
1Ki	3:15	Lord, and **o.** up burnt offerings,	5927
1Ki	3:15	**o.** peace offerings, and made a	6213
1Ki	8:62	him, **o.** sacrifice before the Lord.	2076
1Ki	8:63	And Solomon **o.** a sacrifice of peace	2076
1Ki	8:63	he **o.** unto the Lord, two and twenty	2076
1Ki	8:64	there he **o.** burnt offerings, and	6213
1Ki	12:32	in Judah, and he **o.** upon the altar.	5927
1Ki	12:33	So he **o.** upon the altar which he	5927
1Ki	12:33	he **o.** upon the altar, and burnt	5927
1Ki	22:43	the people **o.** and burnt incense	2076
2Ki	3:20	when the meat offering was **o.**,	5927
2Ki	3:27	**o.** him for a burnt offering upon	5927
2Ki	16:12	to the altar, and **o.** thereon.	5927
1Ch	6:49	his sons **o.** upon the altar of the	6999
1Ch	15:26	they **o.** seven bullocks and seven	2076
1Ch	16:1	they **o.** burnt sacrifices and peace	7126
1Ch	21:26	and **o.** burnt offerings and peace	5927
1Ch	29:6	of the king's work, **o.** willingly,	
1Ch	29:9	rejoiced, for that they **o.** willingly,	
1Ch	29:9	with perfect heart they **o.** willingly	
1Ch	29:17	have willingly **o.** all these things:	
1Ch	29:21	**o.** burnt offerings unto the Lord,	5927
2Ch	1:6	**o.** a thousand burnt offerings upon	5927
2Ch	4:6	such things as they **o.** for the	4639
2Ch	7:4	**o.** sacrifices before the Lord.	2076
2Ch	7:5	And king Solomon **o.** a sacrifice of	2076
2Ch	7:7	there he **o.** burnt offerings, and the	6213
2Ch	8:12	Solomon **o.** burnt offerings unto	5927

2Ch 15:11 **o.** unto the Lord the same time, 2076
2Ch 17:16 willingly **o.** himself unto the Lord;
2Ch 24:14 And they **o.** burnt offerings in the 5927
2Ch 29:7 incense nor **o.** burnt offerings 5927
Ezr 1:6 beside all that was willingly **o.**
Ezr 2:68 **o.** freely for the house of God to
Ezr 3:3 they **o.** burnt offerings thereon 5927
Ezr 3:4 **o.** the daily burnt offerings by number,
Ezr 3:5 **o.** the continual burnt offering,
Ezr 3:5 willingly **o.** a freewill offering 5068
Ezr 6:3 the place where they **o.** sacrifices, 1684
Ezr 6:17 **o.** at the dedication of this house 7127
Ezr 7:15 freely **o.** unto the God of Israel, 5069
Ezr 8:25 all Israel there present, had **o.**: 7311
Ezr 8:35 **o.** burnt offerings unto the God of 7126
Ezr 10:19 they **o.** a ram of the flock for their
Ne 11:2 willingly **o.** themselves to dwell at
Ne 12:43 that day they **o.** great sacrifices, 2076
Job 1:5 **o.** burnt offerings according to 5927
Isa 57:6 thou hast **o.** a meat offering. 5927
Isa 66:3 oblation, as if he **o.** swine's blood; 5927
Jer 32:29 they have **o.** incense unto Baal, 6999
Eze 20:28 and they **o.** there their sacrifices, 2076
Eze 48:12 this oblation of the land that is **o.** 8641
Da 11:18 the reproach **o.** by him to cease;
Am 5:25 Have ye **o.** unto me sacrifices and 5066
Jon 1:16 **o.** a sacrifice unto the Lord, and 2076
Mal 1:11 in every place incense shall be **o.** 5066
Ac 7:41 and **o.** sacrifice unto the idol, and *321*
Ac 7:42 have ye **o.** to me slain beasts and *4374*
Ac 8:18 was given, he **o.** them money, *4374*
Ac 15:29 ye abstain from meats **o.** to idols, *1494*
Ac 21:25 themselves from things **o.** to idols, *1494*
Ac 21:26 until that an offering should be **o.** *4374*
1Co 8:1 as touching things **o.** unto idols, *1494*
1Co 8:4 are **o.** in sacrifice unto idols, *1494*
1Co 8:7 eat it as a thing **o.** unto an idol; *1494*
1Co 8:10 those things which are **o.** to idols; *1494*
1Co 10:19 **o.** in sacrifice to idols is any thing? *1494*
1Co 10:28 This is **o.** in sacrifice unto idols, *1494*
Php 2:17 and if I be **o.** upon the sacrifice *4689*
2Ti 4:6 For I am now ready to be **o.**, and *4689*
Heb 5:7 when he had **o.** up prayers and *4374*
Heb 7:27 he did once, when he **o.** up himself.
Heb 9:7 which he **o.** for himself, and for *4374*
Heb 9:9 were **o.** both gifts and sacrifices,
Heb 9:14 **o.** himself without spot to God, *4374*
Heb 9:28 once **o.** to bear the sins of many; *4374*
Heb 10:1 they **o.** year by year continually *4374*
Heb 10:2 they not have ceased to be **o.**? *4374*
Heb 10:8 therein; which are **o.** by the law; *4374*
Heb 10:12 he had **o.** one sacrifice for sins *4374*
Heb 11:4 By faith Abel **o.** unto God a more *4374*
Heb 11:17 when he was tried, **o.** up Isaac: *4374*
Heb 11:17 **o.** up his only begotten son, *4374*
Jas 2:21 when he had **o.** Isaac his son upon *399*

OFFERETH
Le 6:26 The priest that **o.** it for sin shall 2398
Le 7:8 that **o.** any man's burnt offering 7126
Le 7:9 shall be the priest's that **o.** it. 7126
Le 7:16 same day that he **o.** his sacrifice: 7126
Le 7:18 it be imputed unto him that **o.** it: 7126
Le 7:29 He that **o.** the sacrifice of his peace 7126
Le 7:33 **o.** the blood of the peace offerings, 7126
Le 17:8 that **o.** a burnt offering or sacrifice, 5926
Le 21:8 for he **o.** the bread of thy God: he 7126
Le 22:21 **o.** a sacrifice of peace offerings unto 7126
Nu 15:4 that **o.** his offering unto the Lord 7126
Ps 50:23 Whoso **o.** praise glorifieth me: 2076
Isa 66:3 he that **o.** an oblation, as if he 5927
Jer 48:35 him that **o.** in the high places, and 5927
Mal 2:12 that **o.** an offering unto the Lord 5066

OFFERING See also OFFERINGS.
Ge 4:3 the ground an **o.** unto the Lord 4503
Ge 4:4 respect unto Abel and to his **o.**: 4503
Ge 4:5 and to his **o.** he had not respect. 4503
Ge 22:2 and offer him there for a burnt **o.**
Ge 22:3 and clave the wood for the burnt **o.**,
Ge 22:6 took the wood of the burnt **o.**, and
Ge 22:7 where is the lamb for a burnt **o.**?
Ge 22:8 himself a lamb for a burnt **o.**: so
Ge 22:13 a burnt **o.** in the stead of his son.
Ge 35:14 and he poured a drink **o.** thereon,
Ex 18:12 took a burnt **o.** and sacrifices for
Ex 25:2 Israel, that they bring me an **o.**: 8641
Ex 25:2 with his heart ye shall take my **o.**. 8641
Ex 25:3 the **o.** which ye shall take of them; 8641
Ex 29:14 without the camp: it is a sin **o.**.
Ex 29:18 it is a burnt **o.** unto the Lord: it is
Ex 29:18 an **o.** made by fire unto the Lord.
Ex 29:24 for a wave **o.** before the Lord.
Ex 29:25 them upon the altar for a burnt **o.**,
Ex 29:25 an **o.** made by fire unto the Lord.
Ex 29:26 wave it for a wave **o.** before the Lord:
Ex 29:27 sanctify the breast of the wave **o.**,
Ex 29:27 shoulder of the heave **o.**, which is 8641
Ex 29:28 of Israel; for it is an heave **o.**: 8641
Ex 29:28 be an heave **o.** from the children 8641
Ex 29:28 even their heave **o.** unto the Lord. 8641
Ex 29:36 every day a bullock for a sin **o.**
Ex 29:40 of an hin of wine for a drink **o.**.
Ex 29:41 to the meat **o.** of the morning, 4503
Ex 29:41 according to the drink **o.** thereof,
Ex 29:41 an **o.** made by fire unto the Lord.
Ex 29:42 This shall be a continual burnt **o.**
Ex 30:9 nor burnt sacrifice, nor meat **o.**; 4503
Ex 30:9 neither shall ye pour drink **o.**
Ex 30:10 year with the blood of the sin **o.**
Ex 30:13 shekel shall be the **o.** of the Lord 8641
Ex 30:14 shall give an **o.** unto the Lord 8641
Ex 30:15 when they give an **o.** unto the Lord, 8641
Ex 30:20 minister, to burn **o.** made by fire
Ex 30:28 altar of burnt **o.** with all his vessels,
Ex 31:9 the altar of burnt **o.** with all his
Ex 35:5 among you an **o.** unto the Lord: 8641
Ex 35:5 let him bring it, an **o.** of the Lord; 8641
Ex 35:16 The altar of burnt **o.**, with his
Ex 35:21 they brought the Lord's **o.** to the 8641
Ex 35:22 that offered offered an **o.** of gold
Ex 35:24 did offer an **o.** of silver and brass 8641
Ex 35:24 and brass brought the Lord's **o.**: 8641
Ex 35:29 of Israel brought a willing **o.** unto
Ex 36:3 they received of Moses all the **o.**, 8641
Ex 36:6 work for the **o.** of the sanctuary. 8641
Ex 38:1 altar of burnt **o.** of shittim wood:
Ex 38:24 holy place, even the gold of the **o.**, 8573
Ex 38:29 the brass of the **o.** was seventy 8573
Ex 40:6 set the altar of the burnt **o.** before
Ex 40:10 anoint the altar of the burnt **o.**,
Ex 40:29 the altar of burnt **o.** by the door
Ex 40:29 offered upon it the burnt **o.** and the
Ex 40:29 and offered upon it...the meat **o.**; 4503
Le 1:2 of you bring an **o.** unto the Lord, 7133
Le 1:2 ye shall bring your **o.** of the cattle, 7133
Le 1:3 If his **o.** be a burnt sacrifice of the 7133
Le 1:4 upon the head of the burnt **o.**;
Le 1:6 he shall flay the burnt **o.**, and cut
Le 1:9 an **o.** made by fire, of a sweet
Le 1:10 if his **o.** be of the flocks, namely, 7133
Le 1:13 an **o.** made by fire, of a sweet
Le 1:14 for his **o.** to the Lord be of fowls, 7133
Le 1:14 he shall bring his **o.** of turtledoves, 7133
Le 1:17 an **o.** made by fire, of a sweet
Le 2:1 will offer a meat **o.** unto the Lord, 7133
Le 2:1 Lord, his **o.** shall be of fine flour; 7133
Le 2:2 to be an **o.** made by fire, of a sweet
Le 2:3 of the meat **o.** shall be Aaron's 4503
Le 2:4 of a meat **o.** baken in the oven, 4503
Le 2:5 be a meat **o.** baken in a pan, it 4503
Le 2:6 pour oil thereon: it is a meat **o.**. 4503
Le 2:7 be a meat **o.** baken in a fryingpan, 4503
Le 2:8 thou shalt bring the meat **o.** that is 4503
Le 2:9 priest shall take from the meat **o.** 4503
Le 2:9 it is an **o.** made by fire, of a sweet
Le 2:10 is left of the meat **o.** shall be 4503
Le 2:11 No meat **o.**, which ye shall bring 4503
Le 2:11 in any **o.** of the Lord made by fire.
Le 2:13 thy meat **o.** shalt thou season 4503
Le 2:13 to be lacking from thy meat **o.**: 4503
Le 2:14, 14 offer a meat **o.** of thy firstfruits 4503
Le 2:15 thereon: it is a meat **o.**. 4503
Le 2:16 is an **o.** made by fire unto the Lord.
Le 3:1 oblation be a sacrifice of peace **o.**,
Le 3:2 his hand upon the head of his **o.**, 7133
Le 3:3 offer of the sacrifice of the peace **o.**,
Le 3:3 an **o.** made by fire unto the Lord;
Le 3:5 it is an **o.** made by fire, of a sweet
Le 3:6 if his **o.** for a sacrifice of peace 7133
Le 3:6 sacrifice of peace **o.** unto the Lord
Le 3:7 If he offer a lamb for his **o.**, then 7133
Le 3:8 his hand upon the head of his **o.**, 7133
Le 3:9 offer of the sacrifice of the peace **o.**
Le 3:9 an **o.** made by fire unto the Lord;
Le 3:11 it is the food of the **o.** made by fire
Le 3:12 if he **o.** be a goat, then he shall 7133
Le 3:14 And he shall offer thereof his **o.**, 7133
Le 3:14 an **o.** made by fire unto the Lord;
Le 3:16 it is the food of the **o.** made by fire
Le 4:3 blemish unto the Lord for a sin **o.**.
Le 4:7 bottom of the altar of the burnt **o.**,
Le 4:8 fat of the bullock for the sin **o.**;
Le 4:10 upon the altar of the burnt **o.**.
Le 4:18 bottom of the altar of the burnt **o.**,
Le 4:20 did with the bullock for a sin **o.**,
Le 4:21 it is a sin **o.** for the congregation.
Le 4:23 he shall bring his **o.**, a kid of the 7133
Le 4:24 where they kill the burnt **o.** before
Le 4:24 before the Lord: it is a sin **o.**.
Le 4:25 take of the blood of the sin **o.** with
Le 4:25 the horns of the altar of burnt **o.**,
Le 4:25 bottom of the altar of burnt **o.**.
Le 4:28 he shall bring his **o.**, a kid of the 7133
Le 4:29 hand upon the head of the sin **o.**,
Le 4:29 and slay the sin **o.** in the place of
Le 4:29 in the place of the burnt **o.**.
Le 4:30 the horns of the altar of burnt **o.**,
Le 4:32 And if he bring a lamb for a sin **o.**, 7133
Le 4:33 hand upon the head of the sin **o.**,
Le 4:33 and slay it for a sin **o.**, in the
Le 4:33 place where they kill the burnt **o.**.
Le 4:34 blood of the sin **o.** with his finger,
Le 4:34 the horns of the altar of burnt **o.**,
Le 5:6 bring his trespass **o.** unto the Lord 817
Le 5:6 or a kid of the goats, for a sin **o.**;
Le 5:7 one for a sin **o.**, and the other
Le 5:7 and the other for a burnt **o.**.
Le 5:8 that which is for the sin **o.** first,
Le 5:9 sprinkle of the blood of the sin **o.**
Le 5:9 bottom of the altar: it is a sin **o.**.
Le 5:10 offer the second for a burnt **o.**,
Le 5:11 that sinned shall bring for his **o.** 7133
Le 5:11 an ephah of fine flour for a sin **o.**;
Le 5:11 thereon: for it is a sin **o.**.
Le 5:12 fire unto the Lord: it is a sin **o.**.
Le 5:13 shall be the priest's, as a meat **o.**, 4503
Le 5:15 of the sanctuary, for a trespass **o.**:
Le 5:16 him with the ram of the trespass **o.**,
Le 5:18 thy estimation, for a trespass **o.**, unto
Le 5:19 It is a trespass **o.**: he hath certainly
Le 6:5 in the day of his trespass **o.**.
Le 6:6 bring his trespass **o.** unto the Lord,
Le 6:6 with thy estimation, of a trespass **o.**,
Le 6:9 This is the law of the burnt **o.**:
Le 6:9 It is the burnt **o.**, because of the
Le 6:10 with the burnt **o.** on the altar, and
Le 6:12 lay the burnt **o.** in order upon it;
Le 6:14 And this is the law of the meat **o.**: 4503
Le 6:15 the flour of the meat **o.**, and of the 4503
Le 6:15 which is upon the meat **o.**, and 4503
Le 6:17 it is most holy, as is the sin **o.**,
Le 6:17 most holy, as is...the trespass **o.**.
Le 6:20 is the **o.** of Aaron and of his sons, 7133
Le 6:20 fine flour for a meat **o.** perpetual, 4503
Le 6:21 and the baken pieces of the meat **o.** 4503
Le 6:23 every meat **o.** for the priest shall be 4503
Le 6:25 saying, This is the law of the sin **o.**:
Le 6:25 place where the burnt **o.** is killed
Le 6:25 the sin **o.** be killed before the Lord:
Le 6:30 no sin **o.**, whereof any of the blood
Le 7:1 this is the law of the trespass **o.**:
Le 7:2 place where they kill the burnt **o.**
Le 7:2 shall they kill the trespass **o.**: and
Le 7:5 upon the altar for an **o.** made by fire
Le 7:5 fire unto the Lord: it is a trespass **o.**.
Le 7:7 As the sin **o.** is, so is the trespass
Le 7:7 so is the trespass **o.**: there is one
Le 7:8 that offereth any man's burnt **o.**,
Le 7:8 the burnt **o.** which he hath offered.
Le 7:9 meat **o.** that is baken in the oven, 4503
Le 7:10 every meat **o.**, mingled with oil, 4503
Le 7:13 offer for his **o.** leavened bread 7133
Le 7:14 for an heave **o.** unto the Lord, and 8641
Le 7:16 if the sacrifice of his **o.** be a vow, 7133
Le 7:16 or a voluntary **o.**, it shall be eaten the
Le 7:25 offer an **o.** made by fire unto the Lord,
Le 7:30 waved for a wave **o.** before the Lord.
Le 7:32 for an heave **o.** of the sacrifices of 8641
Le 7:37 This is the law of the burnt **o.**,
Le 7:37 This is the law of...the meat **o.**, 4503

Le 7:37 This is the law of...the sin **o.**,
Le 7:37 This is the law of...the trespass **o.**,
Le 8:2 and a bullock for the sin **o.**, and
Le 8:14 brought the bullock for the sin **o.**:
Le 8:14 head of the bullock for the sin **o.**.
Le 8:18 brought the ram for the burnt **o.**: 5930
Le 8:21 an **o.** made by fire unto the Lord;
Le 8:27 them for a wave **o.** before the Lord.
Le 8:28 on the altar upon the burnt **o.**:
Le 8:28 an **o.** made by fire unto the Lord.
Le 8:29 waved it for a wave **o.** before the Lord:
Le 9:2 Take thee a young calf for a sin **o.**,
Le 9:2 and a ram for a burnt **o.**, without
Le 9:3 ye a kid of the goats for a sin **o.**;
Le 9:3 without blemish, for a burnt **o.**;
Le 9:4 and a meat **o.** mingled with oil: 4503
Le 9:7 unto the altar, and offer thy sin **o.**,
Le 9:7 and thy burnt **o.**, and make an
Le 9:7 and offer the **o.** of the people, and 7133
Le 9:8 slew the calf of the sin **o.**, which
Le 9:10 caul above the liver of the sin **o.**,
Le 9:12 he slew the burnt **o.**; and Aaron's
Le 9:13 presented the burnt **o.** unto him,
Le 9:14 them upon the burnt **o.** on the altar.
Le 9:15 And he brought the people's **o.**, 7133
Le 9:15 took the goat, which was the sin **o.**
Le 9:16 he brought the burnt **o.**, and offered it
Le 9:17 he brought the meat **o.**, and took 4503
Le 9:21 waved for a wave **o.** before the Lord;
Le 9:22 and came down from **o.** of the sin 6213
Le 9:22 of the sin **o.**, and the burnt
Le 9:22 and the burnt **o.**, and peace offerings.
Le 9:24 upon the altar the burnt **o.** and
Le 10:12 Take the meat **o.** that remaineth 4503
Le 10:15 wave it for a wave **o.** before the Lord;
Le 10:16 sought the goat of the sin **o.**, and,
Le 10:17 have ye not eaten the sin **o.** in the
Le 10:19 day have they offered their sin **o.**
Le 10:19 and their burnt **o.** before the Lord;
Le 10:19 if I had eaten the sin **o.** to day,
Le 12:6 of the first year for a burnt **o.**,
Le 12:6 or a turtledove, for a sin **o.**, unto
Le 12:8 pigeons; the one for the burnt **o.**,
Le 12:8 and the other for a sin **o.**: and
Le 14:10 deals of fine flour for a meat **o.**,
Le 14:12 lamb, and offer him for a trespass **o.**,
Le 14:12 them for a wave **o.** before the Lord:
Le 14:13 place where he shall kill the sin **o.**
Le 14:13 and the burnt **o.**, in the holy place:
Le 14:13 for as the sin **o.** is the priest's,
Le 14:13 so is the trespass **o.**: it is most holy:
Le 14:14 some of the blood of the trespass **o.**,
Le 14:17 upon the blood of the trespass **o.**:
Le 14:19 the priest shall offer the sin **o.**,
Le 14:19 he shall kill the burnt **o.**:
Le 14:20 the priest shall offer the burnt **o.**
Le 14:20 and the meat **o.** upon the altar: 4503
Le 14:21 lamb for a trespass **o.** to be waved,
Le 14:21 mingled with oil for a meat **o.**, 4503
Le 14:22 and the one shall be a sin **o.**,
Le 14:22 and the other a burnt **o.**.
Le 14:24 take the lamb of the trespass **o.**,
Le 14:24 them for a wave **o.** before the Lord:
Le 14:25 shall kill the lamb of the trespass **o.**,
Le 14:25 some of the blood of the trespass **o.**,
Le 14:28 place of the blood of the trespass **o.**:
Le 14:31 is able to get, the one for a sin **o.**,
Le 14:31 and the other for a burnt **o.**, with
Le 14:31 with the meat **o.**: and the priest 4503
Le 15:15 offer them, the one for a sin **o.**,
Le 15:15 and the other for a burnt **o.**; and
Le 15:30 shall offer the one for a sin **o.**,
Le 15:30 and the other for a burnt **o.**; and
Le 16:3 with a young bullock for a sin **o.**,
Le 16:3 and a ram for a burnt **o.**.
Le 16:5 two kids of the goats for a sin **o.**,
Le 16:5 and one ram for a burnt **o.**.
Le 16:6 shall offer his bullock of the sin **o.**,
Le 16:9 lot fell, and offer him for a sin **o.**
Le 16:11 bring the bullock of the sin **o.**,
Le 16:11 kill the bullock of the sin **o.** which
Le 16:15 shall he kill the goat of the sin **o.**,
Le 16:24 come forth, and offer his burnt **o.**,
Le 16:24 and the burnt **o.** of the people, and
Le 16:25 fat of the sin **o.** shall he burn upon
Le 16:27 And the bullock for the sin **o.**, and
Le 16:27 and the goat for the sin **o.**, whose

Le 17:4 to offer an **o.** unto the Lord before 7133
Le 17:8 offereth a burnt **o.** or sacrifice,
Le 19:21 bring his trespass **o.** unto the Lord,
Le 19:21 even a ram for a trespass **o.**.
Le 19:22 with the ram of the trespass **o.** before
Le 22:12 not eat of an **o.** of the holy things. 8641
Le 22:18 offer unto the Lord for a burnt **o.**;
Le 22:21 or a freewill **o.** in beeves or sheep,
Le 22:22 nor make an **o.** by fire of them
Le 22:23 mayest thou offer for a freewill **o.**;
Le 22:24 neither shall ye make any **o.** thereof
Le 22:27 an **o.** made by fire unto the Lord.
Le 23:8 an **o.** made by fire unto the Lord
Le 23:12 year for a burnt **o.** unto the Lord.
Le 23:13 meat **o.** thereof shall be two tenth 4503
Le 23:13 an **o.** made by fire unto the Lord for a
Le 23:13 drink **o.** thereof shall be of wine,
Le 23:14 have brought an **o.** unto your God: 7133
Le 23:15 ye brought the sheaf of the wave **o.**;
Le 23:16 offer a new meat **o.** unto the Lord. 4503
Le 23:18 be for a burnt **o.** unto the Lord,
Le 23:18 with their meat **o.**, and their 4503
Le 23:18 even an **o.** made by fire, of sweet
Le 23:19 one kid of the goats for a sin **o.**,
Le 23:20 for a wave **o.** before the Lord,
Le 23:25, 27 an **o.** made by fire unto the Lord.
Le 23:36, 36 an **o.** made by fire unto the Lord:
Le 23:37 an **o.** made by fire unto the Lord,
Le 23:37 unto the Lord, a burnt **o.**,
Le 23:37 and a meat **o.**, a sacrifice, 4503
Le 24:7 even an **o.** made by fire unto the Lord.
Le 27:9 men bring an **o.** unto the Lord, 7133
Nu 4:16 incense, and the daily meat **o.**, 4503
Nu 5:9 every **o.** of all the holy things of 8641
Nu 5:15 and he shall bring her **o.** for her, 7133
Nu 5:15 thereon; for it is an **o.** of jealousy, 4503
Nu 5:15 **o.** of memorial, bringing iniquity 4503
Nu 5:18 the **o.** of memorial in her hands, 4503
Nu 5:18 which is the jealousy **o.**: and the 4503
Nu 5:25 jealousy **o.** out of a woman's hand, 4503
Nu 5:25 shall wave the **o.** before the Lord, 4503
Nu 5:26 shall take an handful of the **o.**, 4503
Nu 6:11 shall offer the one for a sin **o.**,
Nu 6:11 and the other for a burnt **o.**, and
Nu 6:12 of the first year for a trespass **o.**:
Nu 6:14 shall offer his **o.** unto the Lord, 7133
Nu 6:14 without blemish for a burnt **o.**, and
Nu 6:14 year without blemish for a sin **o.**,
Nu 6:15 and their meat **o.**, and their drink 4503
Nu 6:16 Lord, and shall offer his sin **o.**,
Nu 6:16 offer his sin...and his burnt **o.**:
Nu 6:17 priest shall offer also his meat **o.**, 4503
Nu 6:17 also his meat...and his drink **o.**.
Nu 6:20 them for a wave **o.** before the Lord:
Nu 6:21 **o.** unto the Lord for...separation, 7133
Nu 7:3 brought their **o.** before the Lord, 7133
Nu 7:10 offered their **o.** before the altar 7133
Nu 7:11 They shall offer their **o.**, each 7133
Nu 7:12 he that offered his **o.** the first day 7133
Nu 7:13 his **o.** was one silver charger, the 7133
Nu 7:13 mingled with oil for a meat **o.**: 4503
Nu 7:15 of the first year, for a burnt **o.**:
Nu 7:16 One kid of the goats for a sin **o.**:
Nu 7:17 this was the **o.** of Nahshon the 7133
Nu 7:19 for his **o.** one silver charger, the 7133
Nu 7:19 mingled with oil for a meat **o.**: 4503
Nu 7:21 of the first year, for a burnt **o.**:
Nu 7:22 One kid of the goats for a sin **o.**:
Nu 7:23 was the **o.** of Nethaneel the son 7133
Nu 7:25 His **o.** was one silver charger, the 7133
Nu 7:25 mingled with oil for a meat **o.**: 4503
Nu 7:27 of the first year, for a burnt **o.**:
Nu 7:28 One kid of the goats for a sin **o.**:
Nu 7:29 the **o.** of Eliab the son of Helon. 7133
Nu 7:31 His **o.** was one silver charger of 7133
Nu 7:31 mingled with oil for a meat **o.**: 4503
Nu 7:33 of the first year, for a burnt **o.**:
Nu 7:34 One kid of the goats for a sin **o.**:
Nu 7:35 this was the **o.** of Elizur the son of 7133
Nu 7:37 His **o.** was one silver charger, 7133
Nu 7:37 mingled with oil for a meat **o.**: 4503
Nu 7:39 of the first year, for a burnt **o.**:
Nu 7:40 One kid of the goats for a sin **o.**:
Nu 7:41 this was the **o.** of Shelumiel the 7133
Nu 7:43 His **o.** was one silver charger of the 7133
Nu 7:43 mingled with oil for a meat **o.**: 4503
Nu 7:45 of the first year, for a burnt **o.**:

Nu 7:46 One kid of the goats for a sin **o.**:
Nu 7:47 this was the **o.** of Eliasaph the 7133
Nu 7:49 His **o.** was one silver charger, the 7133
Nu 7:49 mingled with oil for a meat **o.**: 4503
Nu 7:51 of the first year, for a burnt **o.**:
Nu 7:52 One kid of the goats for a sin **o.**:
Nu 7:53 this was the **o.** of Elishama the 7133
Nu 7:55 His **o.** was one silver charger of 7133
Nu 7:55 mingled with oil for a meat **o.**: 4503
Nu 7:57 of the first year, for a burnt **o.**:
Nu 7:58 One kid of the goats for a sin **o.**:
Nu 7:59 this was the **o.** of Gamaliel the 7133
Nu 7:61 His **o.** was one silver charger, the 7133
Nu 7:61 mingled with oil for a meat **o.**: 4503
Nu 7:63 of the first year, for a burnt **o.**:
Nu 7:64 One kid of the goats for a sin **o.**:
Nu 7:65 this was the **o.** of Abidan the son 7133
Nu 7:67 His **o.** was one silver charger, the 7133
Nu 7:67 mingled with oil for a meat **o.**: 4503
Nu 7:69 of the first year, for a burnt **o.**:
Nu 7:70 One kid of the goats for a sin **o.**:
Nu 7:71 this was the **o.** of Ahiezer the son 7133
Nu 7:73 His **o.** was one silver charger, the 7133
Nu 7:73 mingled with oil for a meat **o.**: 4503
Nu 7:75 of the first year, for a burnt **o.**:
Nu 7:76 One kid of the goats for a sin **o.**:
Nu 7:77 this was the **o.** of Pagiel the son 7133
Nu 7:79 His **o.** was one silver charger, the 7133
Nu 7:79 mingled with oil for a meat **o.**: 4503
Nu 7:81 of the first year, for a burnt **o.**:
Nu 7:82 One kid of the goats for a sin **o.**:
Nu 7:83 this was the **o.** of Ahira the son of 7133
Nu 7:87 the burnt **o.** were twelve bullocks,
Nu 7:87 year twelve, with their meat **o.**: 4503
Nu 7:87 kids of the goats for sin **o.** twelve.
Nu 8:8 a young bullock with his meat **o.**, 4503
Nu 8:8 bullock shalt thou take for a sin **o.**.
Nu 8:11 for an **o.** of the children of Israel, 8573
Nu 8:12 shalt offer the one for a sin **o.**,
Nu 8:12 other for a burnt **o.**, unto the Lord,
Nu 8:13 offer them for an **o.**, unto the Lord. 8573
Nu 8:15 them, and offer them for an **o.**. 8573
Nu 8:21 them as an **o.** before the Lord; and 8573
Nu 9:7 we may not offer an **o.** of the Lord 7133
Nu 9:13 he brought not the **o.** of the Lord 7133
Nu 15:3 will make an **o.** by fire unto the Lord
Nu 15:3 Lord, a burnt **o.**, or a sacrifice in
Nu 15:3 or in a freewill **o.**, or in your
Nu 15:4 that offereth his **o.** unto the Lord 7133
Nu 15:4 bring a meat **o.** of a tenth deal of 4503
Nu 15:5 of an hin of wine for a drink **o.** shalt
Nu 15:5 with the burnt **o.** or sacrifice, for one
Nu 15:6 prepare for a meat **o.** two tenth 4503
Nu 15:7 for a drink **o.** thou shalt offer the
Nu 15:8 preparest a bullock for a burnt **o.**,
Nu 15:9 a meat **o.** of three tenth deals of 4503
Nu 15:10 for a drink **o.** half an hin of wine,
Nu 15:10 **o.** made by fire, of a sweet savour
Nu 15:13 after this manner, in **o.**...by fire, 7126
Nu 15:13, 14 an **o.** made by fire, of a sweet
Nu 15:19 offer up an heave **o.** unto the Lord. 8641
Nu 15:20 first of your dough for an heave **o.**: 8641
Nu 15:20 the heave **o.** of the threshingfloor, 8641
Nu 15:21 an heave **o.** in your generations. 8641
Nu 15:24 one young bullock for a burnt **o.**,
Nu 15:24 unto the Lord, with his meat **o.**, 4503
Nu 15:24 and his drink **o.**, according to the
Nu 15:24 One kid of the goats for a sin **o.**.
Nu 15:25 and they shall bring their **o.**, a 7133
Nu 15:25 and their sin **o.** before the Lord,
Nu 15:27 goat of the first year for a sin **o.**.
Nu 16:15 Respect not thou their **o.**: I have 4503
Nu 18:9 of theirs, every meat **o.** of theirs, 4503
Nu 18:9 and every sin **o.** of theirs, and
Nu 18:9 every trespass **o.** of theirs, which they
Nu 18:11 the heave **o.** of their gift, with all 8641
Nu 18:17 their fat for an **o.** made by fire,
Nu 18:24 they offer as an heave **o.** unto the 8641
Nu 18:26 ye shall offer up an heave **o.** of it 8641
Nu 18:27 your heave **o.** shall be reckoned 8641
Nu 18:28 offer an heave **o.** unto the Lord 8641
Nu 18:28 Lord's heave **o.** to Aaron the priest. 8641
Nu 18:29 offer every heave **o.** of the Lord, 8641
Nu 23:3 unto Balak, Stand by thy burnt **o.**,
Nu 23:15 Balak, Stand here by thy burnt **o.**,
Nu 23:17 he stood by his burnt **o.**, and the
Nu 28:2 My **o.**, and my bread for my 7133

Nu	28:3	This is the **o.** made by fire which ye	
Nu	28:3	by day, for a continual burnt **o.**.	
Nu	28:5	of an ephah of flour for a meat **o.**,	4503
Nu	28:6	a continual burnt **o.**, which was	
Nu	28:7	the drink **o.** thereof shall be the	
Nu	28:7	unto the Lord for a drink **o.**.	
Nu	28:8	as the meat **o.** of the morning,	4503
Nu	28:8	and as the drink **o.** thereof, thou	
Nu	28:9	tenth deals of flour for a meat **o.**,	4503
Nu	28:9	with oil, and the drink **o.** thereof:	
Nu	28:10	is the burnt **o.** of every sabbath,	
Nu	28:10	beside the continual burnt **o.**,	
Nu	28:10	and his drink **o.**.	
Nu	28:11	offer a burnt **o.** unto the Lord;	
Nu	28:12,	12 tenth deals of flour...a meat **o.**,	4503
Nu	28:13	oil for a meat **o.** unto one lamb;	4503
Nu	28:13	for a burnt **o.** of a sweet savour, a	
Nu	28:14	is the burnt **o.** of every month	
Nu	28:15	one kid of the goats for a sin **o.**	
Nu	28:15	beside the continual burnt **o.**,	
Nu	28:15	and his drink **o.**.	
Nu	28:19	made by fire for a brunt **o.** unto	
Nu	28:20	meat **o.** shall be of flour mingled	4503
Nu	28:22	one goat for a sin **o.**, to make an	
Nu	28:23	the burnt **o.** in the morning,	
Nu	28:23	which is for a continual burnt **o.**.	
Nu	28:24	beside the continual burnt **o.**,	
Nu	28:24	and his drink **o.**.	
Nu	28:26	when ye bring a new meat **o.** unto	4503
Nu	28:27	the burnt **o.** for a sweet savour	
Nu	28:28	meat **o.** of flour mingled with oil,	4503
Nu	28:31	beside the continual burnt **o.**,	
Nu	28:31	and his meat **o.**, (they shall be	4503
Nu	29:2	offer a burnt **o.** for a sweet savour	
Nu	29:3	meat **o.** shall be of flour mingled	4503
Nu	29:5	one kid of the goats for a sin **o.**,	
Nu	29:6	Beside the burnt **o.** of the month,	
Nu	29:6	and his meat **o.**,	4503
Nu	29:6	and the daily burnt **o.**,	
Nu	29:6	and his meat **o.**,	4503
Nu	29:8	offer a burnt **o.** unto the Lord for a	
Nu	29:9	meat **o.** shall be of flour mingled	4503
Nu	29:11	One kid of the goats for a sin **o.**;	
Nu	29:11	beside the sin **o.** of atonement,	
Nu	29:11	and the continual burnt **o.**,	
Nu	29:11	and the meat **o.** of it, and their	4503
Nu	29:13	offer a burnt **o.**, a sacrifice made	
Nu	29:14	meat **o.** shall be of flour mingled	4503
Nu	29:16	And one kid of the goats for a sin **o.**;	
Nu	29:16	beside the continual burnt **o.**,	
Nu	29:16	his meat **o.**,	4503
Nu	29:16	and his drink **o.**.	
Nu	29:18	And their meat **o.** and their drink	4503
Nu	29:19	one kid of the goats for a sin **o.**;	
Nu	29:19	beside the continual burnt **o.**, and	
Nu	29:19	and the meat **o.** thereof, and their	4503
Nu	29:21	And their meat **o.** and their drink	4503
Nu	29:22	And one goat for a sin **o.**; beside	
Nu	29:22	beside the continual burnt **o.**,	
Nu	29:22	and his meat **o.**,	4503
Nu	29:22	and his drink **o.**.	
Nu	29:24	Their meat **o.** and their drink	4503
Nu	29:25	And one kid of the goats for a sin **o.**;	
Nu	29:25	beside the continual burnt **o.**,	
Nu	29:25	his meat **o.**,	4503
Nu	29:25	and his drink **o.**.	
Nu	29:27	And their meat **o.** and their drink	4503
Nu	29:28	And one goat for a sin **o.**; beside	
Nu	29:28	beside the continual burnt **o.**,	
Nu	29:28	and his meat **o.**,	4503
Nu	29:28	and his drink **o.**.	
Nu	29:30	and their meat **o.** and their drink	4503
Nu	29:31	And one goat for a sin **o.**; beside	
Nu	29:31	beside the continual burnt **o.**,	
Nu	29:31	his meat **o.**,	4503
Nu	29:31	and his drink **o.**.	
Nu	29:33	And their meat **o.** and their drink	4503
Nu	29:34	And one goat for a sin **o.**; beside	
Nu	29:34	beside the continual burnt **o.**,	
Nu	29:34	his meat **o.**,	4503
Nu	29:34	and his drink **o.**.	
Nu	29:36	ye shall offer a burnt **o.**, a sacrifice	
Nu	29:37	Their meat **o.** and their drink	4503
Nu	29:38	And one goat for a sin **o.**; beside	
Nu	29:38	beside the continual burnt **o.**,	
Nu	29:38	and his meat **o.**,	4503
Nu	29:38	and his drink **o.**.	
Nu	31:29	for an heave **o.** of the Lord.	8641
Nu	31:41	which was the Lord's heave **o.**,	8641
Nu	31:52	the gold of the **o.** that they offered.	8641
De	12:11	and the heave **o.** of your hand, and	8641
De	12:17	offerings, or heave **o.** of thine hand:	8641
De	16:10	with a tribute of a freewill **o.**	
De	23:23	a freewill **o.**, according as thou hast	
Jos	22:23	to offer thereon burnt **o.** or meat	
Jos	22:23	offer thereon burnt...or meat **o.**,	4503
Jos	22:26	an altar, not for burnt **o.**, nor for	
Jg	11:31	and I will offer it up for a burnt **o.**.	
Jg	13:16	and if thou wilt offer a burnt **o.**,	
Jg	13:19	Manoah took a kid with a meat **o.**,	4503
Jg	13:23	would not have received a burnt **o.**	
Jg	13:23	and a meat **o.** at our hands,	4503
1Sa	2:17	for men abhorred the **o.** of the Lord.	4503
1Sa	2:29	ye at my sacrifice and at mine **o.**,	4503
1Sa	3:14	purged with sacrifice nor **o.** for ever.	4503
1Sa	6:3	in any wise return him a trespass **o.**:	
1Sa	6:4	What shall be the trespass **o.** which	
1Sa	6:8	which ye return him for a trespass **o.**,	
1Sa	6:14	offered the kine a burnt **o.** unto	
1Sa	6:17	returned for a trespass **o.** unto the	
1Sa	7:9	lamb, and offered it for a burnt **o.**	
1Sa	7:10	as Samuel was **o.** up the burnt	5927
1Sa	7:10	the burnt **o.**, the Philistines drew	
1Sa	13:9	said, Bring hither a burnt **o.** to me,	
1Sa	13:9	And he offered the burnt **o.**.	
1Sa	13:10	soon as he had made an end of **o.**	5927
1Sa	13:10	the burnt **o.**, behold, Samuel	
1Sa	13:12	therefore, and offered a burnt **o.**.	
1Sa	26:19	against me, let him accept an **o.**:	4503
2Sa	6:18	as David had made an end of **o.**	5927
1Ki	18:29,	36 the **o.** of the evening sacrifice,	5927
2Ki	3:20	when the meat **o.** was offered,	4503
2Ki	3:27	offered him for a burnt **o.** upon	
2Ki	5:17	offer neither burnt **o.** nor sacrifice	
2Ki	10:25	soon as he had made an end of **o.**	6213
2Ki	10:25	the burnt **o.**, that Jehu said to the	
2Ki	16:13	And he burnt his burnt **o.**, and his	
2Ki	16:13	and his meat **o.**, and poured his	4503
2Ki	16:13	and poured his drink **o.**, and	
2Ki	16:15	altar burn the morning burnt **o.**,	
2Ki	16:15	and the evening meat **o.**, and the	4503
2Ki	16:15	burnt sacrifice, and his meat **o.**,	4503
2Ki	16:15	with the burnt **o.** of all the people	
2Ki	16:15	meat **o.**, and their drink offerings;	4503
2Ki	16:15	it all the blood of the burnt **o.**,	
1Ch	6:49	upon the altar of the burnt **o.**,	
1Ch	16:2	when David had made an end of **o.**	5927
1Ch	16:29	bring an **o.**, and come before him:	4503
1Ch	16:40	upon the altar of the burnt **o.**	
1Ch	21:23	and the wheat for the meat **o.**;	4503
1Ch	21:26	by fire upon the altar of burnt **o.**.	
1Ch	21:29	and the altar of the burnt **o.**, were at	
1Ch	22:1	this is the altar of the burnt **o.** for	
1Ch	23:29	and for the fine flour for meat **o.**,	4503
2Ch	4:6	as they offered for the burnt **o.**	
2Ch	7:1	and consumed the burnt **o.** and the	
2Ch	8:13	**o.** according to the commandment	5927
2Ch	29:18	and the altar of burnt **o.**, with all the	
2Ch	29:21	goats, for a sin **o.** for the kingdom,	
2Ch	29:23	goats for the sin **o.** before the king	
2Ch	29:24	king commanded that the burnt **o.**	
2Ch	29:24	and the sin **o.** should be made for	
2Ch	29:27	offer the burnt **o.** upon the altar.	
2Ch	29:27	And when the burnt **o.** began, the	
2Ch	29:28	until the burnt **o.** was finished.	
2Ch	29:29	when they had made an end of **o.**,	5927
2Ch	29:32	all these were for a burnt **o.** to the	
2Ch	29:35	drink offerings for every burnt **o.**.	
2Ch	30:22	**o.** peace offerings, and making	2076
2Ch	35:14	Aaron were busied in **o.** of burnt	5927
Ezr	1:4	freewill **o.** for the house of God	
Ezr	3:5	offered the continual burnt **o.**,	
Ezr	3:5	that willingly offered a freewill **o.**	
Ezr	6:17	for a sin **o.** for all Israel, twelve	
Ezr	7:16	with the freewill **o.** of the people,	
Ezr	7:16	**o.** willingly for the house of their God	
Ezr	8:25	even the **o.** of the house of our God,	8641
Ezr	8:28	silver and the gold are a freewill **o.**	
Ezr	8:35	twelve he goats for a sin **o.**:	
Ezr	8:35	this was a burnt **o.** unto the Lord.	
Ne	10:33	and for the continual meat **o.**,	4503
Ne	10:33	and for the continual burnt **o.** of the	
Ne	10:34	for the wood **o.**, to bring it into	7133
Ne	10:39	shall bring the **o.** of the corn,	8641
Ne	13:9	the meat **o.** and the frankincense.	4503
Ne	13:31	And for the wood **o.**, at times	7133
Job	42:8	offer up for yourselves a burnt **o.**;	
Ps	40:6	and **o.** thou didst not desire;	4503
Ps	40:6	burnt **o.**...hast thou not required.	
Ps	40:6	and sin **o.** hast thou not required.	
Ps	51:16	thou delightest not in burnt **o.**.	
Ps	51:19	with burnt **o.** and whole burnt **o.**:	
Ps	96:8	bring an **o.**, and come into his	4503
Isa	40:16	beasts sufficient for a burnt **o.**.	
Isa	43:23	caused thee to serve with an **o.**,	4503
Isa	53:10	shalt make his soul an **o.** for sin,	
Isa	57:6	them hast thou poured a drink **o.**,	
Isa	57:6	thou hast offered a meat **o.**.	4503
Isa	61:8	I hate robbery for burnt **o.**;	
Isa	65:11	furnish the drink **o.** unto that number.	
Isa	66:20	brethren for an **o.** unto the Lord	4503
Isa	66:20	bring an **o.** in a clean vessel into	4503
Jer	11:17	me to anger in **o.** incense unto Baal.	
Jer	14:12	when they offer burnt **o.** and an	
Eze	20:28	the provocation of their **o.**:	7133
Eze	40:38	where they washed the burnt **o.**	
Eze	40:39	side, to slay thereon the burnt **o.** and	
Eze	40:39	to slay thereon...the sin **o.** and	
Eze	40:39	to slay thereon...the trespass **o.**.	
Eze	40:42	of hewn stone for the burnt **o.**,	
Eze	40:42	slew the burnt **o.** and the sacrifice.	
Eze	40:43	the tables was the flesh of the **o.**.	7133
Eze	42:13	most holy things, and the meat **o.**,	4503
Eze	42:13	and the sin **o.**, and the	
Eze	42:13	and the trespass **o.**; for the place	
Eze	43:19	a young bullock for a sin **o.**.	
Eze	43:21	take the bullock also of the sin **o.**,	
Eze	43:22	goats without blemish for a sin **o.**;	
Eze	43:24	shall offer them up for a burnt **o.**	
Eze	43:25	every day a goat for a sin **o.**:	
Eze	44:11	they shall slay the burnt **o.** and	
Eze	44:27	he shall offer his sin **o.**, saith the	
Eze	44:29	They shall eat the meat **o.**, and	4503
Eze	44:29	They shall eat...the sin **o.**, and	
Eze	44:29	They shall eat...the trespass **o.**;	
Eze	45:15	pastures of Israel; for a meat **o.**,	4503
Eze	45:15	and for a burnt **o.**, and for peace	
Eze	45:17	he shall prepare the sin **o.**,	
Eze	45:17	he shall prepare...the meat **o.**,	4503
Eze	45:17	he shall prepare...the burnt **o.**,	
Eze	45:19	shall take of the blood of the sin **o.**,	
Eze	45:22	of the land a bullock for a sin **o.**	
Eze	45:23	prepare a burnt **o.** to the Lord,	
Eze	45:23	kid of the goats daily for a sin **o.**	
Eze	45:24	he shall prepare a meat **o.** of an	4503
Eze	45:25	seven days, according to the sin **o.**,	
Eze	45:25	and according to the burnt **o.**, and	
Eze	45:25	and according to the meat **o.**, and	4503
Eze	46:2	priests shall prepare his burnt **o.**	
Eze	46:4	the burnt **o.** that the prince shall offer	
Eze	46:5	the meat **o.** shall be an ephah for	4503
Eze	46:5	and the meat **o.** for the lambs as he	4503
Eze	46:7	And he shall prepare a meat **o.**, an	4503
Eze	46:11	the meat **o.** shall be an ephah to a	4503
Eze	46:12	shall prepare a voluntary burnt **o.**	
Eze	46:12	he shall prepare his burnt **o.** and	
Eze	46:13	Thou shalt daily prepare a burnt **o.**	
Eze	46:14	And thou shalt prepare a meat **o.**	4503
Eze	46:14	a meat **o.** continually by a perpetual	4503
Eze	46:15	prepare the lamb, and the meat **o.**,	4503
Eze	46:15	morning for a continual burnt **o.**.	
Eze	46:20	priests shall boil the trespass **o.**	
Eze	46:20	priests shall boil...the sin **o.**,	
Eze	46:20	where they shall bake the meat **o.**;	4503
Eze	48:8	be the **o.** which ye shall offer of	8641
Joe	1:9	The meat **o.** and the	4503
Joe	1:9	drink **o.** is cut off from the house	
Joe	1:13	my God: for the meat **o.** and the	4503
Joe	1:13	drink **o.** is withholden from the	
Joe	2:14	behind him; even a meat **o.** and a	4503
Joe	2:14	drink **o.** unto the Lord your God.	
Zep	3:10	my dispersed, shall bring mine **o.**	4503
Mal	1:10	neither will I accept an **o.** at your	4503
Mal	1:11	unto my name, and a pure **o.**:	4503
Mal	1:13	thus ye brought an **o.**: should I	4503
Mal	2:12	and him that offereth an **o.** unto the	4503
Mal	2:13	he regardeth not the **o.** any more,	4503
Mal	3:3	the Lord an **o.** in righteousness.	4503
Mal	3:4	the **o.** of Judah and Jerusalem be	4503

Lu 23:36 coming to him, and **o.** him vinegar, *4374*
Ac 21:26 until that an **o.** should be offered *4376*
Ro 15:16 the **o.** up of the Gentiles might be *4376*
Eph 5:2 hath given himself for us an **o.** and *4376*
Heb 10:5 Sacrifice and **o.** thou wouldest not, *4376*
Heb 10:8 Sacrifice and **o.** and burnt offerings *4376*
Heb 10:8 and **o.** for sin thou wouldest not,
Heb 10:10 through the **o.** of the body of Jesus *4376*
Heb 10:11 **o.** oftentimes the same sacrifices, *4374*
Heb 10:14 by one **o.** he hath perfected for ever *4376*
Heb 10:18 these is, there is no more **o.** for sin. *4376*

OFFERINGS

Ge 8:20 and offered burnt **o.** on the altar.
Ex 10:25 give us also sacrifices and burnt **o.**,
Ex 20:24 shalt sacrifice thereon thy burnt **o.**,
Ex 20:24 thy peace **o.**, thy sheep, and thine
Ex 24:5 Israel, which offered burnt **o.**, and
Ex 24:5 sacrificed peace **o.** of oxen unto 2077
Ex 29:28 of the sacrifice of their peace **o.**,
Ex 32:6 the morrow, and offered burnt **o.**,
Ex 32:6 and brought peace **o.**; and the people
Ex 36:3 brought yet unto him free **o.** every
Le 2:3,10 the **o.** of the Lord made by fire.
Le 2:13 with all thine **o.**...shalt offer salt 7133
Le 4:10 bullock of the sacrifice of peace **o.**:
Le 4:26 the fat of the sacrifice of peace **o.**:
Le 4:31 from off the sacrifice of peace **o.**;
Le 4:35 from the sacrifice of the peace **o.**;
Le 4:35 the **o.** made by fire unto the Lord:
Le 5:12 the **o.** made by fire unto the Lord:
Le 6:12 thereon the fat of the peace **o.**.
Le 6:17 their portion of my **o.** made by fire;
Le 6:18 the **o.** of the Lord made by fire:
Le 7:11 the law of the sacrifice of peace **o.**,
Le 7:13 of thanksgiving of his peace **o.**.
Le 7:14 sprinkleth the blood of the peace **o.**.
Le 7:15, 18 of the sacrifice of his peace **o.**
Le 7:20, 21 flesh of the sacrifice of peace **o.**,
Le 7:29 offereth the sacrifice of his peace **o.**
Le 7:29 of the sacrifice of his peace **o.**.
Le 7:30 the **o.** of the Lord made by fire,
Le 7:32 of the sacrifices of your peace **o.**
Le 7:33 offereth the blood of the peace **o.**,
Le 7:34 off the sacrifices of their peace **o.**,
Le 7:35 out of the **o.** of the Lord made by fire,
Le 7:37 of the sacrifice of the peace **o.**;
Le 9:4 a bullock and a ram for peace **o.**,
Le 9:18 the ram for a sacrifice of peace **o.**,
Le 9:22 the burnt offering, and peace **o.**.
Le 10:12 the **o.** of the Lord made by fire,
Le 10:14 out of the sacrifices of peace **o.** of the
Le 10:15 with the **o.** made by fire of the fat,
Le 17:5 offer them for peace **o.** unto the 2077
Le 19:5 offer a sacrifice of peace **o.** unto
Le 21:6 for the **o.** of the Lord made by fire,
Le 21:21 the **o.** of the Lord made by fire:
Le 22:18 vows, and for all his freewill **o.**, which
Le 22:21 offereth a sacrifice of peace **o.** unto
Le 23:18 and their drink **o.**, even an
Le 23:19 year for a sacrifice of peace **o.**
Le 23:37 offering, a sacrifice, and drink **o.**,
Le 23:38 and beside all your freewill **o.**,
Le 24:9 of the **o.** of the Lord made by fire
Nu 6:14 ram without blemish for peace **o.**,
Nu 6:15 meat offering, and their drink **o.**
Nu 6:17 the ram for a sacrifice of peace **o.**
Nu 6:18 under the sacrifice of the peace **o.**
Nu 7:17, 23,29,35,41,47,53,59,65,71,77,83
And for a sacrifice of peace **o.**,
Nu 7:88 oxen for the sacrifice of the peace **o.**
Nu 10:10 the trumpets over your burnt **o.**,
Nu 10:10 over the sacrifices of your peace **o.**;
Nu 15:8 a vow, or peace **o.** unto the Lord:
Nu 18:8 mine heave **o.** of all the hallowed 8641
Nu 18:11 the wave **o.** of the children of Israel:
Nu 18:19 All the heave **o.** of the holy things, 8641
Nu 28:14 their drink **o.** shall be half an hin
Nu 28:31 without blemish) and their drink **o.**.
Nu 29:6 meat offering, and their drink **o.**,
Nu 29:11 offering of it, and their drink **o.**
Nu 29:18 and their drink **o.** for the bullocks, for
Nu 29:19 offering thereof, and their drink **o.**
Nu 29:21, 24,27,30,33 and their drink **o.** for the
Nu 29:37 and their drink **o.** for the bullock,
Nu 29:39 your vows, and your freewill **o.**,
Nu 29:39 for your burnt **o.**, and for your
Nu 29:39 for your meat **o.**, and for your 4503
Nu 29:39 and for your drink **o.**, and for your
Nu 29:39 and for your peace **o.**
De 12:6 ye shall bring your burnt **o.**, and
De 12:6 tithes, and heave **o.** of your hand,
De 12:6 your vows, and your freewill **o.**,
De 12:11 your burnt **o.**, and your sacrifices,
De 12:13 offer not thy burnt **o.** in every place
De 12:14 there thou shalt offer thy burnt **o.**,
De 12:17 thou vowest, freewill **o.**, or heave
De 12:27 And thou shalt offer thy burnt **o.**,
De 18:1 eat the **o.** of the Lord made by fire,
De 27:6 shalt not offer burnt **o.** thereon
De 27:7 thou shalt offer peace **o.**, and shalt
De 32:38 drank the wine of their drink **o.**?
Jos 8:31 they offered thereon burnt **o.** unto
Jos 8:31 unto the Lord, and sacrificed peace **o.**.
Jos 22:23 or if to offer peace **o.** thereon, let 2077
Jos 22:27 Lord before him with our burnt **o.**,
Jos 22:27 sacrifices, and with our peace **o.**;
Jos 22:28 not for burnt **o.**, nor for sacrifices;
Jos 22:29 to build an altar for burnt **o.**, for
Jos 22:29 for meat **o.**, or for sacrifices, 4503
Jg 20:26 until even, and offered burnt **o.**
Jg 20:26 and peace **o.** before the Lord.
Jg 21:4 an altar, and offered burnt **o.** and
Jg 21:4 an altar, and offered...peace **o.**.
1Sa 2:28 thy father all the **o.** made by fire of
1Sa 2:29 chiefest of all the **o.** of Israel my 4503
1Sa 6:15 of Beth-shemesh offered burnt **o.**
1Sa 10:8 down unto thee, to offer burnt **o.**,
1Sa 10:8 to sacrifice sacrifices of peace **o.**:
1Sa 11:15 sacrificed sacrifices of peace **o.**
1Sa 13:9 burnt offering to me, and peace **o.**
1Sa 15:22 Lord as great delight in burnt **o.**
2Sa 1:21 be rain, upon you, nor fields of **o.**: 8641
2Sa 6:17 for it: and David offered burnt **o.**
2Sa 6:17 and peace **o.** before the Lord.
2Sa 6:18 made an end of offering burnt **o.**
2Sa 6:18 and peace **o.**, he blessed the people
2Sa 24:24 neither will I offer burnt **o.** unto
2Sa 24:25 unto the Lord, and offered burnt **o.**
2Sa 24:25 and peace **o.**. So the Lord was
1Ki 3:4 a thousand burnt **o.** did Solomon
1Ki 3:15 the Lord, and offered up burnt **o.**,
1Ki 3:15 and offered peace **o.**, and made a
1Ki 8:63 offered a sacrifice of peace **o.**,
1Ki 8:64 for there he offered burnt **o.**,
1Ki 8:64 for there he offered...and meat **o.**, 4503
1Ki 8:64 and the fat of the peace **o.**:
1Ki 8:64 too little to receive the burnt **o.**,
1Ki 8:64 too little to receive the...meat **o.**, 4503
1Ki 8:64 and the fat of the peace **o.**
1Ki 9:25 year did Solomon offer burnt **o.**
1Ki 9:25 and peace **o.** upon the altar which he
2Ki 10:24 in to offer sacrifices and burnt **o.**,
2Ki 16:13 sprinkled the blood of his peace **o.**
2Ki 16:15 meat offering, and their drink **o.**;
1Ch 16:1 sacrifices and peace **o.** before God
1Ch 16:2 an end of offering the burnt **o.** and
1Ch 16:2 and the peace **o.**, he blessed the people
1Ch 16:40 To offer burnt **o.** unto the Lord
1Ch 21:23 give thee the oxen also for burnt **o.**,
1Ch 21:24 nor offer burnt **o.** without cost
1Ch 21:26 unto the Lord, and offered burnt **o.**
1Ch 21:26 and peace **o.**, and called upon the
1Ch 29:21 and offered burnt **o.** unto the Lord,
1Ch 29:21 with their drink **o.**, and sacrifices
2Ch 1:6 a thousand burnt **o.** upon it.
2Ch 2:4 the burnt **o.** morning and evening,
2Ch 7:7 Lord: for there he offered burnt **o.**,
2Ch 7:7 and the fat of the peace **o.**, because
2Ch 7:7 was not able to receive the burnt **o.**,
2Ch 7:7 and the meat **o.**, and the fat 4503
2Ch 8:12 Then Solomon offered burnt **o.**
2Ch 23:18 to offer the burnt **o.** of the Lord
2Ch 24:14 And they offered burnt **o.** in the house
2Ch 29:7 nor offered burnt **o.** in the holy place
2Ch 29:31 bring sacrifices and thank **o.** into the
2Ch 29:31 brought in sacrifices and thank **o.**;
2Ch 29:31 as were of a free heart burnt **o.**
2Ch 29:32 And the number of the burnt **o.**,
2Ch 29:34 they could not flay all the burnt **o.**:
2Ch 29:35 the burnt **o.** were in abundance
2Ch 29:35 with the fat of the peace **o.**, and
2Ch 29:35 drink **o.** for every burnt offering.
2Ch 30:15 and brought in the burnt **o.** into the
2Ch 30:22 feast seven days, offering peace **o.**, 2077
2Ch 31:2 the priests and Levites for burnt **o.**
2Ch 31:2 and for peace **o.**, to minister, and
2Ch 31:3 of his substance for the burnt **o.**,
2Ch 31:3 the morning and evening burnt **o.**,
2Ch 31:3 and the burnt **o.** for the sabbaths,
2Ch 31:10 the people began to bring the **o.** 8641
2Ch 31:12 brought in the **o.** and the tithes 8641
2Ch 31:14 was over the freewill **o.** of God, 8641
2Ch 33:16 and sacrificed thereon peace **o.** 2077
2Ch 33:16 and thank **o.**, and commanded
2Ch 35:7 and kids, all for the passover **o.**,
2Ch 35:8 unto the priests for the passover **o.**
2Ch 35:9 gave unto the Levites for passover **o.**
2Ch 35:12 they removed the burnt **o.**, that they
2Ch 35:13 but the other holy **o.** sod they in pots,
2Ch 35:14 were busied in offering of burnt **o.**
2Ch 35:16 to offer burnt **o.** upon the altar of
Ezr 3:2 to offer burnt **o.** thereon, as it is
Ezr 3:3 they offered burnt **o.** thereon unto
Ezr 3:3 even burnt **o.** morning and evening.
Ezr 3:4 and offered the daily burnt **o.** by
Ezr 3:6 they to offer burnt **o.** unto the Lord.
Ezr 6:9 for the burnt **o.** of the God of heaven,
Ezr 7:17 rams, lambs, with their meat **o.** 4503
Ezr 7:17 and their drink **o.**, and offer them
Ezr 8:35 offered burnt **o.** unto the God of Israel,
Ne 10:33 for the sin **o.** to make an atonement
Ne 10:37 firstfruits of our dough, and our **o.**, 8641
Ne 12:44 for the treasures, for the **o.**, for 8641
Ne 13:5 aforetime they laid the meat **o.**, 4503
Ne 13:5 porters; and the **o.** of the priests. 4503
Job 1:5 offered burnt **o.** according to the
Ps 16:4 their drink **o.** of the blood will I not offer,
Ps 20:3 Remember all thy **o.**, and accept 4503
Ps 50:8 for thy sacrifices or thy burnt **o.**,
Ps 66:13 go into thy house with burnt **o.**:
Ps 119:108 thee, the freewill **o.** of my mouth,
Pro 7:14 I have peace **o.** with me; this day
Isa 1:11 I am full of the burnt **o.** of rams,
Isa 43:23 me the small catttle of thy burnt **o.**;
Isa 56:7 their burnt **o.** and their sacrifices
Jer 6:20 your burnt **o.** are not acceptable,
Jer 7:18 pour out drink **o.** unto other gods, 5262
Jer 7:21 Put your burnt **o.** unto your
Jer 7:22 concerning burnt **o.** or sacrifices:
Jer 17:26 from the south, bringing burnt **o.**,
Jer 17:26 and sacrifices, and meat **o.**, and 4503
Jer 19:5 sons with fire for burnt **o.** unto
Jer 19:13 out drink **o.** unto other gods
Jer 32:29 out drink **o.** unto other gods,
Jer 33:18 a man before me to offer burnt **o.**,
Jer 33:18 and to kindle meat **o.**, and to do 4503
Jer 41:5 with **o.** and incense in their hand, 4503
Jer 44:17, 18 to pour out drink **o.** unto her,
Jer 44:19 and poured out drink **o.** unto her,
Jer 44:19 and poured out drink **o.** unto her,
Jer 44:25 and to pour out drink **o.** unto her:
Eze 20:28 poured out there their drink **o.**
Eze 20:40 and there will I require your **o.**, 8641
Eze 43:18 make it, to offer burnt **o.** thereon,
Eze 43:27 the priests shall make your burnt **o.**
Eze 43:27 upon the altar, and your peace **o.**;
Eze 45:15 burnt offering, and for peace **o.**, to
Eze 45:17 the prince's part to give burnt **o.**
Eze 45:17 and meat **o.**, 4503
Eze 45:17 and drink **o.**, in the feasts, and in
Eze 45:17 and the peace **o.**, to make reconciliation
Eze 46:2 burnt offering and his peace **o.**, and
Eze 46:12 or peace **o.** voluntarily unto the
Eze 46:12 burnt offering and his peace **o.**, as he
Hos 6:6 of God more than burnt **o.**.
Hos 8:13 flesh for the sacrifices of mine **o.**, 1890
Hos 9:4 shall not offer wine **o.** to the Lord,
Am 4:5 proclaim and publish the free **o.**:
Am 5:22 Thou ye offer me burnt **o.** and
Am 5:22 meat **o.**, I will not accept them: 4503
Am 5:22 the peace **o.** of your fat beasts.
Am 5:25 **o.** in the wilderness forty years, 4503
Mic 6:6 I come before him with burnt **o.**,
Mal 3:8 we robbed thee? In tithes and **o.** 8641
Mk 12:33 all whole burnt **o.** and sacrifices. *3646*
Lu 21:4 **cast in unto the o. of God:** *1435*
Ac 24:17 bring alms to my nation, and **o.** *4376*
Heb 10:6 In burnt **o.** and sacrifices for sin *3646*
Heb 10:8 and burnt **o.** and offering for sin *3646*

OFFICE See also OFFICES.
Ge 41:13 me he restored unto mine o., and...... 3653
Ex 1:16 the o. of a midwife to the Hebrew...........
Ex 28:1 minister unto me in the priest's o.,..........
Ex 28:3, 4,41 unto me in the priest's o.................
Ex 29:1 minister unto me in the priest's o.:..........
Ex 29:9 and the priest's o. shall be theirs for.........
Ex 29:44 minister to me in the priest's o...............
Ex 30:30 minister unto me in the priest's o............
Ex 31:10 sons, to minister in the priest's o.,..........
Ex 35:19 sons, to minister in the priest's o............
Ex 39:41 to minister in the priest's o....................
Ex 40:13 minister unto me in the priest's o............
Ex 40:15 minister unto me in the priest's o.:..........
Le 7:35 unto the Lord in the priest's o.;............
Le 16:32 in the priest's o. in his father's ....
Nu 3:3 to minister in the priest's o......................
Nu 3:4 ministered in the priest's o. in the...........
Nu 3:10 they shall wait on their priest's o.............
Nu 4:16 And to the o. of Eleazar the son of 6486
Nu 18:7 keep your priest's o. for everything..........
Nu 18:7 I have given your priest's o. unto you......
De 10:6 in the priest's o. in his stead..................
1Ch 6:10 priest's o. in the temple that....................
1Ch 6:32 waited on their o. according to 5656
1Ch 9:22 the seer did ordain in their set o.............
1Ch 9:26 were in their set o., and were over..........
1Ch 9:31 had the set o. over the things that...........
1Ch 23:28 their o. was to wait on the sons of..... 4612
1Ch 24:2 Ithamar executed the priest's o...............
2Ch 11:14 from executing the priest's o. unto ....
2Ch 24:11 was brought unto the king's o. by 6486
2Ch 31:15 the cities of the priest, in their set o., ...
2Ch 31:18 for in their set o. they sanctified.............
Ne 13:13 and their o. was to distribute unto............
Ps 109:8 few; and let another take his o.. 6486
Eze 44:13 to do the o. of a priest unto me,.............
Lu 1:8 while he executed the priest's o......... *2407*
Lu 1:9 to the custom of the priest's o.,......... *2405*
Ro 11:13 of the Gentiles, I magnify mine o.: *1248*
Ro 12:4 all members have not the same o.: *4234*
1Ti 3:1 If a man desire the o. of a bishop,....... *1984*
1Ti 3:10 let them use the o. of a deacon, ... *1247*
1Ti 3:13 that have used the o. of a deacon....... *1247*
Heb 7:5 receive the o. of the priesthood, ... *2405*

OFFICER See also OFFICERS.
Ge 37:36 unto Potiphar, and o. of Pharaoh's,..... 5631
Ge 39:1 and Potiphar, and o. of Pharaoh,.......... 5631
Jg 9:28 of Jerubbaal? and Zebul his o.?........... 6496
1Ki 4:5 the son of Nathan was principal o.,...... 5324
1Ki 4:19 the only o. which was in the land....... 5333
1Ki 22:9 the king of Israel called an o., and...... 5631
2Ki 8:6 appointed unto her a certain o.,.......... 5631
2Ki 25:19 he took an o. that was set over the.... 5631
2Ch 24:11 priest's o. came and emptied the........ 6496
Mt 5:25 **the judge deliver thee to the o.,**..... *5257*
Lu 12:58 **the judge deliver thee to the o.,**..... *4233*
Lu 12:58 **and the o. cast thee into prison**..... *4233*

OFFICERS
Ge 40:2 was wroth against two of his o., ... 5631
Ge 40:7 asked Pharaoh's o. that were with...... 5631
Ge 41:34 let him appoint o. over the land, ... 6496
Ex 5:6 of the people, and their o., saying, ... 7860
Ex 5:10 of the people went out, and their o.,.... 7860
Ex 5:14 And the o. of the children of Israel,.... 7860
Ex 5:15 the o. of the children of Israel came ... 7860
Ex 5:19 the o. of the children of Israel did....... 7860
Nu 11:16 of the people, and o. over them;......... 7860
Nu 31:14 was wroth with the o. of the host, ... 6485
Nu 31:48 o. which were over thousands of.......... 6485
De 1:15 tens, and o. among your tribes. 7860
De 16:18 Judges and o. shalt thou make thee 7860
De 20:5 the o. shall speak unto the people, ... 7860
De 20:8 the o. shall speak further unto the...... 7860
De 20:9 when the o. have made an end of......... 7860
De 29:10 your o., with all the men of Israel, ... 7860
De 31:28 elders of your tribes, and your o.,....... 7860
Jos 1:10 Joshua commanded the o. of the 7860
Jos 3:2 that the o. went through the host;...... 7860
Jos 8:33 all Israel, and their elders, and o.,....... 7860
Jos 23:2 for their judges, and for their o.,......... 7860
Jos 24:1 for their judges, and for their o.;......... 7860
1Sa 8:15 give to his o., and to his servants. 5631
1Ki 4:5 the son of Nathan was over the o.: 5324
1Ki 4:7 had twelve o. over all Israel, which 5324
1Ki 4:27 those o. provided victual for king 5324
1Ki 4:28 they unto the place where the o. were, ...
1Ki 5:16 the chief of Solomon's o. which............ 5324
1Ki 9:23 o. that were over Solomon's work,...... 5324
2Ki 11:15 the hundreds, the o. of the host, ... 6485
2Ki 11:18 priest appointed o. over the house....... 6486
2Ki 24:12 and his princes, and his o.: and.......... 5631
2Ki 24:15 king's wives, and his o., and the 5631
1Ch 23:4 six thousand were o. and judges: 7860
1Ch 26:29 over Israel, for o. and judges. 7860
1Ch 26:30 o. among them of Israel on this........... 6486
1Ch 27:1 their o. that served the king in........... 7860
1Ch 28:1 with the o., and with the mighty......... 5631
2Ch 8:10 the chief of king Solomons o.,............ 5324
2Ch 18:8 of Israel called for one of his o., ... 5631
2Ch 19:11 the Levites shall be o. before you. 7860
2Ch 34:13 there were scribes, and o., and 7860
Es 1:8 to all the o. of his house, that 7227
Es 2:3 king appoint o. in all the provinces...... 6496
Es 9:3 o. of the king, helped the Jews;.......... 6213
Isa 60:17 I will also make thy o. peace, and 6486
Jer 29:26 be o. in the house of the Lord,........... 6496
Joh 7:32 chief priests sent o. to take him......... *5257*
Joh 7:45 came the o. of the chief priests and.... *5257*
Joh 7:46 The o. answered, Never man spake.... *5257*
Joh 18:3 received a band of men and o. from.... *5257*
Joh 18:12 and o. of the Jews took Jesus, and *5257*
Joh 18:18 the servants and o. stood there, ... *5257*
Joh 18:22 one of the o. which stood by struck.... *5257*
Joh 19:6 priests therefore and o. saw him,........ *5257*
Ac 5:22 But when the o. came, and found........ *5257*
Ac 5:26 Then went the captain with the o.,...... *5257*

OFFICES
1Sa 2:36 pray thee, into one of the priest's o.,........
1Ch 24:3 according to their o. in their............. 6486
2Ch 7:6 And the priests waited on their o.:...... 4931
2Ch 23:18 the o. of the house of the Lord 6486
Ne 13:14 of my God, and for the o. thereof. 4929

OFFSCOURING
La 3:45 made us as the o. and refuse in.......... 5501
1Co 4:13 the o. off all things unto this day......... *4067*

OFFSPRING
Job 5:25 thine o. as the grass of the earth. 6631
Job 21:8 and their o. before their eyes. 6631
Job 27:14 o. shall not be satisfied with bread...... 6631
Job 31:8 eat; yea, let my o. be rooted out. 6631
Isa 22:24 o. and the issue, all vessels of small ... 6631
Isa 44:3 and my blessing upon thine o.: 6631
Isa 48:19 the o. of thy bowels like the gravel 6631
Isa 61:9 and their o. among the people: 6631
Isa 65:23 the Lord, and their o. with them........ 6631
Ac 17:28 have said, For we are also his o.. ...... *1085*
Ac 17:29 then as we are the o. of God, we *1085*
Re 22:16 **I am the root and the o. of David,**. *1085*

OFT See also OFTEN; OFTTIMES.
2Ki 4:8 as o. as he passed by, he turned 1767
Job 21:17 How o. is the candle of...wicked put out!...
Job 21:17 how o. cometh their destruction upon........
Ps 78:40 How o. did they provoke him in...............
Mt 9:14 do we and the Pharisees fast o.,........... *4183*
Mt 17:15 into the fire, and o. into the water. *4178*
Mt 18:21 how o. shall my brother sin against..... *4212*
Mk 7:3 they wash their hands o., eat not,....... *4435*
Ac 26:11 And I punished them o. in every........ *4178*
1Co 11:25 **this do ye, as o. as ye drink it, in** . *3740*
2Co 11:23 more frequent, in deaths o................ *4178*
2Ti 1:16 he o. refreshed me, and was not........ *4178*
Heb 6:7 in the rain that cometh o. upon it,...... *4178*

OFTEN See also OFTENER; OFTENTIMES.
Pr 29:1 He, that being o. reproved hardenth ....
Mal 3:16 they that feared the Lord spake o. one......
Mt 23:37 **how o. would I have gathered thy** . *4212*
Mk 5:4 been o. bound with fetters and *4178*
Lu 5:33 the disciples of John fast o., and *4437*
Lu 13:34 **how o. would I have gathered thy** . *4212*
1Co 11:26 For as o. as ye eat this bread, and..... *3740*
2Co 11:26 In journeyings o., in perils of............ *3740*
2Co 11:27 watchings o., in hunger and thirst,...... *3740*
2Co 11:27 fastings o., in cold and nakedness....... *3740*
Php 3:18 walk, of whom I have told you o., ... *3740*
1Ti 5:23 sake and thine o. infirmities. *4437*
Heb 9:25 that he should offer himself o., as *4178*
Heb 9:26 For then must he o. have suffered *4178*
Re 11:6 with all plagues, as o. as they will. *3740*

OFTENER
Ac 24:26 wherefore he sent for him the o., ... *4437*

OFTENTIMES See also OFTTIMES.
Job 33:29 these things worketh God o....... 6471,7969
Ec 7:22 For o. also thine own heat......... 6471,7227
Lu 8:29 o. it had caught him: and he....... *4183,5550*
Ro 1:13 o. I purposed to come unto you, ... *4178*
2Co 8:22 o. proved diligent in many things,....... *4178*
Heb 10:11 and offering o. the same sacrifices, ... *4178*

OFTTIMES
Mk 17:15 for o. he falleth into the fire, and....... *4178*
Mk 9:22 o. it hath cast him into the fire, ... *4178*
Joh 18:2 Jesus o. resorted thither with his *4178*

OG (og)
Nu 21:33 O. the king of Bashan went out 5747
Nu 32:33 the kingdom of O. king of Bashan,...... 5747
De 1:4 and O. the king of Bashan, which....... 5747
De 3:1 O. the king of Bashan came out......... 5747
De 3:3 God delivered into our hands O. 5747
De 3:4 the kingdom of O. in Bashan. 5747
De 3:10 of the kingdom of O. in Bashan......... 5747
De 3:11 only O. king of Bashan remained....... 5747
De 3:13 Bashan, being the kingdom of O.,........ 5747
De 4:47 and the land of O. king of Bashan,...... 5747
De 29:7 and O. the king of Bashan, came....... 5747
De 31:4 as he did to Sihon and to O., kings..... 5747
Jos 2:10 Sihon and O., whom ye utterly.......... 5747
Jos 9:10 and to O. king of Bashan, which 5747
Jos 12:4 the coast of O. king of Bashan,........... 5747
Jos 13:12 All the kingdom of O. in Bashan,........ 5747
Jos 13:30 the kingdom of O. king of Bashan,....... 5747
Jos 13:31 of the kingdom of O. in Bashan,......... 5747
1Ki 4:19 and of O. king of Bashan; and he 5747
Ne 9:22 and the land of O. king of Bashan........ 5747
Ps 135:11 and O. king of Bashan, and all the...... 5747
Ps 136:20 And O. the king of Bashan: for his 5747

OH
Ge 18:30, 32 O. let not the Lord be angry,......... 4994
Ge 19:18 unto them, O., not so, my Lord: 4994
Ge 19:20 O., let me escape thither, (is it not 4994
Ge 44:18 O. my lord, let thy servant, I pray....... 994
Ec 32:31 O., this people have sinned a great 577
Jg 6:13 O. my Lord, if the Lord be with us,..... 994
Jg 6:15 O. my Lord, wherewith shall I save 994
1Sa 1:26 O. my lord, as thy soul liveth, my 994
2Sa 15:4 O. that I were made judge in the land,......
2Sa 23:15 O. that one would give me drink of the .....
1Ch 4:10 O. that thou wouldest bless me........... 518
1Ch 11:17 O. that one would give me drink of the .....
Job 6:2 O. that my grief were thoroughly....... 3863
Job 6:8 O. that I might have my request; and ....
Job 10:18 O. that I had given up the ghost, and........
Job 11:5 o. that God would speak, and open his......
Job 19:23 O. that my words were now written! ....
Job 19:23 o. that they were printed in a book! ....
Job 23:3 O. that I knew where I might find him! .....
Job 29:2 O. that I were as in months past, as in .....
Job 31:31 O. that we had of his flesh! we cannot ......
Job 31:35 O. that one would hear me! behold,..........
Ps 6::4 o. save me for thy mercies' sake.............
Ps 7:9 O. let the wickedness of the 4994
Ps 14:7 O. that the salvation of Israel were...........
Ps 31:19 O. how great is thy goodness, which ....
Ps 53:6 O. that the salvation of Israel were...........
Ps 55:6 O. that I had wings like a dove! for ....
Ps 81:13 O. that my people had hearkened....... 3863
Ps 107:8, 15,21,31 O. that men would praise ....
Isa 64:1 O. that thou wouldest rend the.......... 3863
Jer 9:1 O. that my head were waters, and ....
Jer 9:2 O. that I had in the wilderness a.............
Jer 44:4 O., do not this abominable thing......... 4994

OHAD (o'-had)
Ge 46:10 Jemuel, and Jamin, and O., and 161
Ex 6:15 Jemuel, and Jamin, and O., and 161

OHEL (o'-hel)
1Ch 3:20 And Hashubah, and O., and............... 169

OIL See also OILED.
Ge 28:18 and poured o. upon the top of it. 8081
Ge 35:14 thereon, and he poured o. thereon. 8081
Ex 25:6 O. for the light, spices for 8081
Ex 25:6 spices for anointing o., and for............. 8081
Ex 27:20 pure o. olive beaten for the light, ... 8081
Ex 29:2 cakes unleavened tempered with o., ... 8081

Ex	29:2	wafers unleavened anointed with o.:	8081
Ex	29:7	shalt thou take the anointing o.,	8081
Ex	29:21	the altar, and of the anointing, o.	8081
Ex	29:40	fourth part of an hin of beaten o.;	8081
Ex	30:24	sanctuary, and of o. olive an hin:	8081
Ex	30:25	make it an o. of holy ointment, an	8081
Ex	30:25	it shall be an holy anointing o.	8081
Ex	30:31	be an holy anointing o. unto me	8081
Ex	31:11	the anointing o., and sweet incense	8081
Ex	35:8	And o. for the light, and spices for	8081
Ex	35:8	and spices for anointing o., and for	8081
Ex	35:14	his lamps, with the o. for the light,	8081
Ex	35:15	and the anointing o., and the sweet	8081
Ex	35:28	And spice, and o. for the light,	8081
Ex	35:28	and for the anointing o., and for	8081
Ex	37:29	And he made the holy anointing o.,	
Ex	39:37	vessels thereof, and the o. for light,	8081
Ex	39:38	and the anointing o., and the sweet	8081
Ex	40:9	thou shalt take the anointing o.,	8081
Le	2:1	he shall pour o. upon it, and put	8081
Le	2:2	and of the o. thereof, with all the	8081
Le	2:4	cakes of fine flour mingled with o.,	8081
Le	2:4	unleavened wafers anointed with o.	8081
Le	2:5	flour unleavened, mingled with o.	8081
Le	2:6	it in pieces, and pour o. thereon:	8081
Le	2:7	shall be made of fine flour with o.	8081
Le	2:15	And thou shalt put o. upon it, and	8081
Le	2:16	thereof, and part of the o. thereof,	8081
Le	5:11	he shall put no o. upon it, neither	8081
Le	6:15	meat offering, and of the o. thereof,	8081
Le	6:21	In a pan it shall be made with o.;	8081
Le	7:10	meat offering, mingled with o.,	8081
Le	7:12	unleavened cakes mingled with o.,	8081
Le	7:12	unleavened wafers anointed with o.,	8081
Le	7:12	and cakes mingled with o., of fine	8081
Le	8:2	the garments, and the anointing o.,	8081
Le	8:10	Moses took the anointing o., and	8081
Le	8:12	he poured of the anointing o. upon	8081
Le	8:30	Moses took of the anointing o., and	8081
Le	9:4	meat offering mingled with o.: for	8081
Le	10:7	anointing o. of the Lord is upon you.	8081
Le	14:10	mingled with o., and one log of o.	8081
Le	14:12	trespass offering, and the log of o.,	8081
Le	14:15	shall take some of the log of o., and	8081
Le	14:16	shall dip his right finger in the o.	8081
Le	14:16	sprinkle of the o. with his finger	8081
Le	14:17	the rest of the o. that is in his hand	8081
Le	14:18	the remnant of the o. that is in the	8081
Le	14:21	deal of fine flour mingled with o.	8081
Le	14:21	for a meat offering, and a log of o.;	8081
Le	14:24	trespass offering, and the log of o.,	8081
Le	14:26	priest shall pour of the o. into the	8081
Le	14:27	some of the o. that is in his left	8081
Le	14:28	priest shall put of the o. that is in	8081
Le	14:29	rest of the o. that is in the priest's	8081
Le	21:10	head the anointing o. was poured,	8081
Le	21:12	the crown of the anointing o. of his	8081
Le	23:13	deals of fine flour mingled with o.,	8081
Le	24:2	pure o. olive beaten for the light,	8081
Nu	4:9	snuffdishes, and all the o. vessels	8081
Nu	4:16	pertaineth the o. for the light,	8081
Nu	4:16	meat offering, and the anointing o.	8081
Nu	5:15	he shall pour no o. upon it, nor put	8081
Nu	6:15	cakes of fine flour mingled with o.,	8081
Nu	6:15	unleavened bread anointed with o.,	8081
Nu	7:13,	19,25,31,37,43,49,55,61,67,73,79 mingled with o. for a meat offering:	
Nu	8:8	even fine flour mingled with o., and	8081
Nu	11:8	of it as the taste of fresh o.	8081
Nu	15:4	with the fourth part of an hin of o.	8081
Nu	15:6	with the third part of an hin of o.	8081
Nu	15:9	flour mingled with half an hin of o.	8081
Nu	18:12	the best of the o., and all the best of	8081
Nu	28:5	fourth part of an hin of beaten o.	8081
Nu	28:9,	12,12, meat offering, mingled with o.,	8081
Nu	28:13	tenth deal of flour mingled with o.:	8081
Nu	28:20	shall be of flour mingled with o.,	8081
Nu	28:28	offering of flour mingled with o.,	8081
Nu	29:3,	9,14 be of flour mingled with o.,	8081
Nu	35:25	was anointed with the holy o.	8081
De	7:13	corn, and thy wine, and thine o.,	3323
De	8:8	a land of o. olive, and honey;	8081
De	11:14	corn, and thy wine, and thine o.	3323
De	12:17	thy corn, or of thy wine, or of thy o.,	3323
De	14:23	corn, of thy wine, and of thine o.,	3323
De	18:4	corn, of thy wine, and of thine o.,	3323
De	28:40	not anoint thyself with the o.;	8081
De	28:51	leave thee either corn, wine, or o.,	3323
De	32:13	rock, and o. out of the flinty rock;	8081
De	33:24	and let him dip his foot in o.	8081
1Sa	10:1	Samuel took a vial of o., and poured	8081
1Sa	16:1	fill thine horn with o., and go, I will	8081
1Sa	16:13	Then Samuel took the horn of o.,	8081
2Sa	1:21	he had not been anointed with o.	8081
2Sa	14:2	anoint not thyself with o., but be as	8081
1Ki	1:39	the priest took an horn of o. out of	8081
1Ki	5:11	and twenty measures of pure o.:	8081
1Ki	17:12	in a barrel, and a little o. in a cruse:	8081
1Ki	17:14	neither shall the cruse of o. fail,	8081
1Ki	17:16	not, neither did the cruse of o. fail,	8081
2Ki	4:2	thing in the house, save a pot of o.	8081
2Ki	4:6	a vessel more. And the o. stayed.	8081
2Ki	4:7	Go, sell the o., and pay thy debt,	8081
2Ki	9:1	take this box of o. in thine hand,	8081
2Ki	9:3	Then take the box of o., and pour it	8081
2Ki	9:6	and he poured the o. on his head,	8081
2Ki	18:32	a land of o. olive and of honey,	3323
1Ch	9:29	flour, and the wine, and the o.,	8081
1Ch	12:40	bunches of raisins, and wine, and o.,	8081
1Ch	27:28	over the cellars of o. was Joash:	8081
2Ch	2:10	and twenty thousand baths of o.	8081
2Ch	2:15	the barely, the o., and the wine	8081
2Ch	11:11	store of victual, and of o. and wine	8081
2Ch	31:5	of corn, wine, and o., and honey,	3323
2Ch	32:28	increase of corn, and wine, and o.;	3323
Ezr	3:7	meat, and drink, and o., unto them	8081
Ezr	6:9	salt, wine, and o., according to	4887
Ezr	7:22	to an hundred baths of o., and salt	4887
Neh	5:11	the corn, the wine, and the o., that	3323
Neh	10:37	of wine and of o., unto the priests,	3323
Neh	10:39	the new wine, and the o., unto the	3323
Neh	13:5	new wine, and the o. which was	3323
Neh	13:12	wine and the o. unto the treasuries,	3323
Es	2:12	wit, six months with o. of myrrh,	8081
Job	24:11	Which make o. within their walls,	6671
Job	29:6	rock poured me out rivers of o.;	8081
Ps	23:5	thou anointest my head with o.;	8081
Ps	45:7	anointed thee with...o. of gladness	8081
Ps	55:21	his words were softer than o., yet	8081
Ps	89:20	with my holy o. have I anointed him:	8081
Ps	92:10	I shall be anointed with fresh o.	8081
Ps	104:15	o. to make his face to shine, and	8081
Ps	109:18	water, and like o. into his bones.	8081
Ps	141:5	it shall be an excellent o., which	8081
Pr	5:3	and her mouth is smoother than o.:	8081
Pr	21:17	he that loveth wine and o. shall not	8081
Pr	21:20	and o. in the dwelling of the wise;	8081
Isa	41:19	and the myrtle, and the o. tree;	8081
Isa	61:3	ashes the o. of joy for mourning,	8081
Jer	31:12	for wine, and for o., and for the	3323
Jer	40:10	wine, and summer fruits, and o.,	8081
Jer	41:8	of barley, and of o., and of honey.	8081
Eze	16:9	thee, and I anointed thee with o.	8081
Eze	16:13	eat fine flour, and honey, and o.:	8081
Eze	16:18	hast set mine o. and mine incense	8081
Eze	16:19	thee, fine flour, and o., and honey,	8081
Eze	23:41	hast set mine incense and mine o.	8081
Eze	27:17	and honey, and o., and balm.	8081
Eze	32:14	and cause their rivers to run like o.,	8081
Eze	45:14	the ordinance of o., the bath of o.,	8081
Eze	45:24	ram, and an hin of o. for an ephah.	8081
Eze	45:25	offering, and according to the o.	8081
Eze	46:5,	7,11 and an hin of o. to an ephah.	8081
Eze	46:14	and the third part of an hin of o., to	8081
Eze	46:15	and the meat offering, and the o.,	8081
Ho	2:5	and my flax, mine o. and my drink.	8081
Ho	2:8	I gave her corn, and wine, and o.,	3323
Ho	2:22	the corn, and the wine, and the o.;	3323
Ho	12:1	and o. is carried into Egypt.	8081
Joe	1:10	is dried up, the o. languisheth.	3323
Joe	2:19	send you corn, and wine, and o.,	3323
Joe	2:24	shall overflow with wine and o.	3323
Mic	6:7	with ten thousands of rivers of o.?	8081
Mic	6:15	thou shalt not anoint thee with o.;	8081
Hag	1:11	the new wine and upon the o.,	3323
Hag	2:12	bread or pottage or wine, or o., or	8081
Zec	4:12	empty the golden o. out of themselves?	
Mt	25:3	**lamps, and took no o. with them:**	*1637*
Mt	25:4	**wise took o. in their vessels with**	*1637*
Mt	25:8	**Give us of your o.; for our lamps**	*1637*
Mk	6:13	anointed with o. many that were	*1637*
Lu	7:46	**My head with o. thou didst not**	*1637*
Lu	10:34	**wounds, pouring in o. and wine,**	*1637*
Lu	16:6	**said, An hundred measures of o.**	*1637*
Heb	1:9	anointed thee with...o. of gladness	*1637*
Jas	5:14	anointing him with o. in the name	*1637*
Re	6:6	thou hurt not the o. and the wine	*1637*
Re	18:13	and wine, and o., and fine flour, and	*1637*

OILED

Ex	29:23	bread, and one cake of o. bread,	8081
Le	8:26	a cake of o. bread, and one wafer,	8081

OIL-OLIVE See OIL and OLIVE.

OIL-TREE See OIL and TREE.

OINTMENT See also OINTMENTS.

Ex	30:25	shalt make it an oil of holy o., an o.	4888
Ex	30:25	an o. compound after the art	7545
2Ki	20:13	the spices, and the precious o.,	8081
1Ch	9:30	sons of the priests made the o. of	4842
Job	41:31	he maketh the sea like a pot of o.	4841
Ps	133:2	like the precious o. upon the head,	8081
Pr	27:9	O. and perfume rejoice the heart:	8081
Pr	27:16	and the o. of his right hand, which	8081
Ec	7:1	name is better than precious o.;	8081
Ec	9:8	white; and let thy head lack no o.	8081
Ec	10:1	flies cause the o. of the apothecary	8081
Ca	1:3	thy name is as o. poured forth,	8081
Isa	1:6	bound up, neither mollified with o.	8081
Isa	39:2	and the spices, and the precious o.,	8081
Isa	57:9	thou wentest to the king with o.,	8081
Mt	26:7	alabaster box of very precious o.,	*3464*
Mt	26:9	For this o. might have been sold for	*3464*
Mt	26:12	**hath poured this o. on my body,**	*3464*
Mk	14:3	alabaster box of o. of spikenard	*3464*
Mk	14:4	Why was this waste of the o. made?	*3464*
Lu	7:37	brought an alabaster box of o.,	*3464*
Lu	7:38	feet, and anointed them with the o.	*3464*
Lu	7:46	**hath anointed my feet with o.**	*3464*
Joh	11:2	which anointed the Lord with o.,	*3464*
Joh	12:3	Mary a pound of o. of spikenard,	*3464*
Joh	12:3	was filled with the odour of the o.	*3464*
Joh	12:5	Why was not this o. sold for three	*3464*

OINTMENTS

Ca	1:3	of the savour of thy good o. thy	8081
Ca	4:10	the smell of thine o. than all spices!	8081
Am	6:6	anoint themselves with the chief o.:	8081
Lu	23:56	and prepared spices and o.; and	*3464*
Re	18:13	cinnamon, and odours, and o., and	*3464*

OLD See also ELDER; ELDEST.

Ge	5:32	Noah was five hundred years o.:	1121
Ge	6:4	mighty men which were of o.,	5769
Ge	7:6	Noah was six hundred years o.	1121
Ge	11:10	Shem was an hundred years o.,	1121
Ge	12:4	Abram was seventy and five years o.	1121
Ge	15:9	Take...an heifer of three years o.,	8027
Ge	15:9	and a she goat of three years o.,	8027
Ge	15:9	and a ram of three years o., and a	8027
Ge	15:15	shalt be buried in a good o. age.	7872
Ge	16:16	was fourscore and six years o.,	1121
Ge	17:1	when Abram was ninety years o.	1121
Ge	17:12	he that is eight days o. shall be	1121
Ge	17:17	him that is an hundred years o.?	1121
Ge	17:17	Sarah, that is ninety years o., bear?	1323
Ge	17:24	Abraham was ninety years o. and	1121
Ge	17:25	Ishmael...was thirteen years o.,	1121
Ge	18:11	Now Abraham and Sarah were o.	2205
Ge	18:12	After I am waxed o. shall I have	1086
Ge	18:12	pleasure, my lord being o. also?	2204
Ge	18:13	a surety bear a child, which am o.?	2204
Ge	19:4	house round, both o. and young,	2205
Ge	19:31	unto the younger, Our father is o.,	2204
Ge	21:2	bare Abraham a son in his o. age,	2208
Ge	21:4	his son Isaac being eight days o.,	1121
Ge	21:5	Abraham was an hundred years o.,	1121
Ge	21:7	have born him a son in his o. age.	2208
Ge	23:1	and seven and twenty years o.:	2416
Ge	24:1	Abraham was o., and well stricken	2204
Ge	24:36	son to my master when she was o.:	2209
Ge	25:8	ghost, and died in a good o. age,	7872
Ge	25:8	an o. man, and full of years; and	2205
Ge	25:20	Isaac was forty years o. when he	1121
Ge	25:26	Isaac was three score years o. when	1121
Ge	26:34	Esau was forty years o. when he	1121
Ge	27:1	when Isaac was o., and his eyes	2204
Ge	27:2	I am o., I know not the day of my	2204
Ge	35:29	people, being o. and full of days:	2205
Ge	37:2	Joseph, being seventeen years o.,	1121

Ge 37:3 he was the son of his **o.** age: 2208
Ge 41:46 Joseph, being seventeen years **o.**, 1121
Ge 43:27 well, the **o.** man of whom ye spake? 2205
Ge 44:20 We have a father, an **o.** man, and 2205
Ge 44:20 a child of his **o.** age, a little one; 2208
Ge 47:8 Jacob, How **o.** art thou? 3113,8140,3117
Ge 49:9 as a lion, and as an **o.** lion; 3833
Ge 50:26 being an hundred and ten years **o.**: 1121
Ex 7:7 Moses was fourscore years **o.**, and 1121
Ex 7:7 Aaron fourscore and three years **o.**, 1121
Ex 10:9 go with our young and with our **o.**, 2205
Ex 30:14 from twenty years **o.** and above, 1121
Ex 38:26 from twenty years **o.** and upward, 1121
Le 13:11 It is an **o.** leprosy in the skin of 3462
Le 19:32 and honour the face of the **o.** man, 2205
Le 25:22 eat yet of **o.** fruit until the ninth 3465
Le 25:22 come in ye shall eat of the **o.** store. 3465
Le 26:10 And ye shall eat **o.** store, and bring 3462
Le 26:10 forth the **o.** because of the new. 3465
Le 27:3 years **o.** even unto sixty years **o.**, 1121
Le 27:5 years **o.** even unto twenty years **o.**, 1121
Le 27:6 a month **o.** even unto five years **o.**, 1121
Le 27:7 it be from sixty years **o.** and above; 1121
Nu 1:3 From twenty years **o.** and upward, 1121
Nu 1:18, 20,22,24,26,28,30,32,34,36,38,40,42,45
from twenty years **o.** and 1121
Nu 3:15 male from a month **o.** and upward 1121
Nu 3:22, 28,34,39,40,43 from a month **o.** and 1121
Nu 4:3 From thirty years **o.** and upward 1121
Nu 4:3 even unto fifty years **o.**, all that 1121
Nu 4:23 From thirty years **o.** and upward 1121
Nu 4:23 until fifty years **o.** shalt thou 1121
Nu 4:30 From thirty years **o.** and upward 1121
Nu 4:30 even unto fifty years **o.** shalt thou 1121
Nu 4:35 From thirty years **o.** and upward 1121
Nu 4:35 even unto fifty years **o.**, every one 1121
Nu 4:39 From thirty years **o.** and upward 1121
Nu 4:39 even unto fifty years **o.**, every one 1121
Nu 4:43 From thirty years **o.** and upward 1121
Nu 4:43 even unto fifty years **o.**, every one 1121
Nu 4:47 From thirty years **o.** and upward 1121
Nu 4:47 even unto fifty years **o.**, every one 1121
Nu 8:24 from twenty and five years **o.** and 1121
Nu 14:29 from twenty years **o.** and upward, 1121
Nu 18:16 from a month **o.** shalt thou redeem, 1121
Nu 26:2 from twenty years **o.** and upward, 1121
Nu 26:4 from twenty years **o.** and upward; 1121
Nu 26:62 males from a month **o.** and upward: 1121
Nu 32:11 from twenty years **o.** and upward, 1121
Nu 32:11 from twenty years **o.** and upward, 1121
Nu 33:39 and twenty years **o.** and upward: 1121
Nu 33:39 and twenty and three years **o.** 1121
De 2:20 giants dwelt therein in **o.** time; 6440
De 8:4 raiment waxed not **o.** upon thee, 1086
De 19:14 they of **o.** time have set in thine 7223
De 28:50 not regard the person of the **o.**, 2205
De 29:5 clothes are not waxen **o.** upon you, 1086
De 29:5 shoe is not waxen **o.** upon thy foot. 1086
De 31:2 an hundred and twenty years **o.** 1121
De 32:7 Remember the days of **o.**, consider 5769
De 34:7 an hundred and twenty years **o.** 1121
Jos 5:11 did eat of the **o.** corn of the land 5669
Jos 5:12 after they had eaten of the **o.** corn 5669
Jos 6:21 man and woman, young and **o.**, 5288
Jos 9:4 and took **o.** sacks upon their asses, 1087
Jos 9:4 and wine bottles, **o.**, and rent, and 1087
Jos 9:5 And **o.** shoes and clouted upon their 1087
Jos 9:5 feet, and **o.** garments upon them 1087
Jos 9:13 shoes are become **o.** by reason of 1086
Jos 13:1 Now Joshua was **o.** and stricken in 2204
Jos 13:1 Thou art **o.** and stricken in years, 2204
Jos 14:7 Forty years **o.** was I when Moses 1121
Jos 14:10 this day fourscore and five years **o.** 1121
Jos 23:1 that Joshua waxed **o.** and stricken 2204
Jos 23:2 them, I am **o.** and stricken in age: 2204
Jos 24:2 the other side of the flood in **o.** time, 5769
Jos 24:29 being an hundred and ten years **o.** 1121
Jg 2:8 being an hundred and ten years **o.** 1121
Jg 6:25 the second bullock of seven years **o.**,
Jg 8:32 Gideon...died in a good **o.** age, 7872
Jg 19:16 came an **o.** man from his work 2205
Jg 19:7 and the **o.** man said, Whither goest 2205
Jg 19:20 And the **o.** man said, Peace be with 2205
Jg 19:22 the master of the house, the **o.** man, 2205
Ru 1:12 I am too **o.** to have an husband. 2204
Ru 4:15 and a nourisher of thine **o.** age: 7872
1Sa 2:22 Now Eli was very **o.**, and heard 2204
1Sa 2:31 not be an **o.** man in thine house 2205
1Sa 2:32 not be an **o.** man in thine house for 2205
1Sa 4:15 Eli was ninety and eight years **o.**; 1121
1Sa 4:18 for he was an **o.** man, and heavy. 2204
1Sa 8:1 came to pass, when Samuel was **o.**, 2204
1Sa 8:5 Behold, thou art **o.**, and thy sons 2204
1Sa 12:2 and I am **o.** and grayheaded; and, 2204
1Sa 17:12 man went among men for an **o.** man 2204
1Sa 27:8 nations were of **o.** inhabitants 5769
1Sa 28:14 she said, An **o.** man cometh up; 2205
2Sa 2:10 Saul's son was forty years **o.** when 1121
2Sa 4:4 was five years **o.** when the tidings 1121
2Sa 5:4 David was thirty years **o.** when he 1121
2Sa 19:32 aged man, even fourscore years **o.**: 1121
2Sa 19:35 I am this day fourscore years **o.**: 1121
2Sa 20:18 They were wont to speak in **o.** time, 7223
1Ki 1:1 king David was **o.** and stricken in 2204
1Ki 1:15 chamber: and the king as very **o.**; 2204
1Ki 11:4 to pass, when Solomon was **o.**, 2209
1Ki 12:6 consulted with the **o.** men, that 2205
1Ki 12:8 forsook the counsel of the **o.** men 2205
1Ki 12:13 forsook the **o.** men's counsel that 2205
1Ki 13:11 dwelt an **o.** prophet in Beth-el; 2205
1Ki 13:25 the city where the **o.** prophet dwelt 2205
1Ki 13:29 and the **o.** prophet came to the city, 2205
1Ki 14:21 was forty and one years **o.** when 1121
1Ki 15:23 time of his **o.** age he was diseased 2209
1Ki 22:42 was thirty and five years **o.** when 1121
2Ki 4:14 no child, and her husband is **o.** 2204
2Ki 8:17 Thirty and two years **o.** was he 1121
2Ki 8:26 and twenty years **o.** was Ahaziah 1121
2Ki 11:21 Seven years **o.** was Jehoash when 1121
2Ki 14:2 He was twenty and five years **o.** 1121
2Ki 14:21 Azariah, which was sixteen years **o.**, 1121
2Ki 15:2 Sixteen years **o.** was he when he 1121
2Ki 15:33 Five and twenty years **o.** was he 1121
2Ki 16:2 Twenty years **o.** was Ahaz when he 1121
2Ki 18:2 Twenty and five years **o.** was he 1121
2Ki 21:1 Manasseh was twelve years **o.** when 1121
2Ki 21:19 Amon was twenty and two years **o.** 1121
2Ki 22:1 Josiah was eight years **o.** when he 1121
2Ki 23:31 was twenty and three years **o.** when 1121
2Ki 23:36 and twenty and five years **o.** when 1121
2Ki 24:8 Jehoiachin was eighteen years **o.** 1121
2Ki 24:18 was twenty and one years **o.** when 1121
1Ch 2:21 when he was threescore years **o.**; 1121
1Ch 4:40 they of Ham had dwelt there of **o.** 6440
1Ch 23:1 So when David was **o.** and full of 2204
1Ch 23:27 from twenty years **o.** and above: 1121
1Ch 27:23 from twenty years **o.** and under: 1121
1Ch 29:28 And he died in a good **o.** age, full 7872
2Ch 10:6 took counsel with the **o.** men that 2205
2Ch 10:8 the counsel which the **o.** men gave 2205
2Ch 10:13 forsook the counsel of the **o.** men, 2205
2Ch 12:13 was one and forty years **o.** when 1121
2Ch 20:31 was thirty and five years **o.** when 1121
2Ch 21:5 was thirty and two years **o.** when 1121
2Ch 21:20 Thirty and two years **o.** was he 1121
2Ch 22:2 Forty and two years **o.** was Ahaziah 1121
2Ch 24:1 Joash was seven years **o.** when he 1121
2Ch 24:15 But Jehoiada waxed **o.**, and was 2204
2Ch 24:15 an hundred and thirty years **o.** 1121
2Ch 25:1 was twenty and five years **o.** when 1121
2Ch 25:5 from twenty years **o.** and above, 1121
2Ch 26:1 Uzziah, who was sixteen years **o.**, 1121
2Ch 26:3 Sixteen years **o.** was Uzziah when 1121
2Ch 27:1 was twenty and five years **o.** when 1121
2Ch 27:8 was five and twenty years **o.** when 1121
2Ch 28:1 was twenty years **o.** when he began 1121
2Ch 29:1 he was five and twenty years **o.**, 1121
2Ch 31:16 from three years **o.** and upward, 1121
2Ch 31:17 from twenty years **o.** and upward, 1121
2Ch 33:1 Manasseh was twelve years **o.** 1121
2Ch 33:21 Amon was two and twenty years **o.** 1121
2Ch 34:1 Josiah was eight years **o.** when he 1121
2Ch 36:2 was twenty and three years **o.** when 1121
2Ch 36:5 was twenty and five years **o.** when 1121
2Ch 36:9 Jehoiachin was eight years **o.** when 1121
2Ch 36:11 was one and twenty years **o.** when 1121
2Ch 36:17 **o.** man, or him that stooped for 2205
Ezr 3:8 from twnety years **o.** and upward, 1121
Ezr 4:15 within the same of **o.** time: 5957
Ezr 4:19 this city of **o.** time hath made 5957
Ne 3:6 **o.** gate repaired Jehoiada the son 3465
Ne 9:21 their clothes waxed not **o.**, and 1086
Ne 12:39 Ephraim, and above the **o.** gate, 3465
Ne 12:46 the days of David and Asaph of **o.** 6924
Es 3:13 all Jews, both young and **o.**, little 2205
Job 4:11 **o.** lion perisheth for lack of prey,
Job 14:8 root thereof wax **o.** in the earth, 2204
Job 20:4 Knowest thou not this of **o.**, since 5703
Job 21:7 do the wicked live, become **o.**, yea, 6275
Job 22:15 the **o.** way which wicked men have 5769
Job 30:2 me, in whom **o.** age was perished?
Job 32:6 I am young, and ye are very **o.**; 3453
Job 42:17 died, being **o.** and full of days. 2205
Ps 6:7 it waxeth **o.** because of all mine 6275
Ps 25:6 for they have been ever of **o.** 5769
Ps 32:3 my bones waxed **o.** through my 1086
Ps 37:25 have been young, and now am **o.**; 2204
Ps 44:1 in their days in the times of **o.** 6924
Ps 55:19 them, even he that abideth of **o.** 6924
Ps 68:33 of heavens, which were of **o.**; 6924
Ps 71:9 me not off in the time of **o.** age; 2209
Ps 71:18 when I am **o.** and grayheaded, O 2209
Ps 74:2 which thou hast purchased of **o.**; 6924
Ps 74:12 For God is my King of **o.**, working 6924
Ps 77:5 I have considered the days of **o.**, 6924
Ps 77:11 will remember thy wonders of **o.** 6924
Ps 78:2 I will utter dark sayings of **o.**: 6924
Ps 92:14 still bring forth fruit in **o.** age; 7872
Ps 93:2 Thy throne is established of **o.**: 227
Ps 102:25 Of **o.** hast thou laid the foundation 6440
Ps 102:26 them shall wax **o.** like a garment; 1086
Ps 119:52 remembered thy judgments of **o.**, 5769
Ps 119:152 have known of **o.** that thou hast 6924
Ps 143:5 I remember the days of **o.**; I 6924
Ps 148:12 maidens; **o.** men, and children: 2205
Pr 8:22 of his way, before his works of **o.** 227
Pr 17:6 children are the crown of **o.** men; 2205
Pr 20:29 beauty of **o.** men is the gray head. 2205
Pr 22:6 when he is **o.**, he will not depart 2204
Pr 23:10 Remove not the **o.** landmark; and 5769
Pr 23:22 not thy mother when she is **o.** 2204
Ec 1:10 it hath been already of **o.** time, 5769
Ec 4:13 child than an **o.** and foolish king, 2205
Ca 7:13 of pleasant fruits, new and **o.**, 3465
Isa 15:5 Zoar, an heifer of three years **o.**: 7992
Isa 20:4 Ethiopians captives, young and **o.**, 2205
Isa 22:11 walls for the water of the **o.** pool: 3465
Isa 25:1 thy counsels of **o.** are faithfulness 7350
Isa 30:6 whence come...young and **o.** lion, 3918
Isa 30:33 For Tophet is ordained of **o.**; yea, 865
Isa 43:18 neither consider the things of **o.**, 6931
Isa 46:4 And even to your **o.** age I am he; 2209
Isa 46:9 Remember the former things of **o.**: 5769
Isa 50:9 all shall wax **o.** as a garment; 1086
Isa 51:6 earth shall wax **o.** like a garment, 1086
Isa 51:9 days, in the generations of **o.** 5769
Isa 57:11 not I held my peace even of **o.**, and 5769
Isa 58:12 shall build the **o.** waste places: 5769
Isa 61:4 they shall build the **o.** wastes, 5769
Isa 63:9 and carried them all the days of **o.** 5769
Isa 63:11 Then he remembered the days of **o.**, 5769
Isa 65:20 an **o.** man hath not filled his 2205
Isa 65:20 shall die an hundred years **o.**; 1121
Isa 65:20 sinner being an hundred years **o.** 1121
Jer 2:20 of **o.** time I have broken thy yoke, 5769
Jer 6:16 and see, and ask for the **o.** paths, 5769
Jer 28:8 been before me and before thee of **o.** 5769
Jer 31:3 The Lord hath appeared of **o.** unto 7350
Jer 31:13 both young men and **o.** together: 2205
Jer 38:11 **o.** cast clouts and **o.** rotten rags, 1094
Jer 38:12 Put now these **o.** cast clouts and 1094
Jer 46:26 be inhabited, as in the days of **o.**, 6924
Jer 48:34 as an heifer of three years **o.**: 7992
Jer 51:22 I break in pieces **o.** and young; 2205
Jer 52:1 was one and twenty years **o.** when 1121
La 1:7 that she had in the days of **o.**, 6924
La 2:17 had commanded in the days of **o.**: 6924
La 2:21 The young and the **o.** lie on the 2205
La 3:4 and my skin hath he made **o.**; 1086
La 3:6 places, as they that be dead of **o.** 5769
La 5:21 turned; renew our days as of **o.** 6924
Eze 9:6 Slay utterly **o.** and young, both 2205
Eze 23:43 her that was **o.** in adulteries, 1087
Eze 25:15 to destroy it for the **o.** hatred; 5769
Eze 26:20 the pit, with the people of **o.** time, 5769
Eze 26:20 the earth, in places desolate of **o.**, 5769
Eze 36:11 settle you after your **o.** estates, 6927
Eze 38:17 of whom I have spoken in **o.** time 6931
Da 5:31 about three score and two years **o.** 1247
Joe 1:2 Hear this, ye **o.** men, and give ear, 2205
Joe 2:28 your **o.** men shall dream dreams, 2205

Am 9:11 I will build it as in the days of **o.**: 5769
Mic 5:2 goings forth have been from of **o.**, 6924
Mic 6:6 offerings, with calves of a year **o.**? 1121
Mic 7:14 and Gilead, as in the days of **o.** 5769
Mic 7:20 our fathers from the days of **o.** 6924
Na 2:8 But Nineveh is of **o.** like a pool of 3117
Na 2:11 the lion, even the **o.** lion, walked,
Zec 8:4 yet **o.** men and **o.** women dwell in 2205
Mal 3:4 as in the days of **o.**, and as in 5769
Mt 2:16 from two years **o.** and under, 1332
Mt 5:21 **that it was said by them of o. time,** 744
Mt 5:27 **that it was said by them of o. time,** 744
Mt 5:33 **hath been said by them of o. time,** 744
Mt 9:16 **of new cloth unto an o. garment,** 3820
Mt 9:17 **men put new wine into o. bottles:** 3820
Mt 13:52 **of his treasure things new and o.** 3820
Mk 2:21 **of new cloth on an o. garment:** 3820
Mk 2:21 **it up taketh away from the o.,** 3820
Mk 2:22 **putteth new wine into o. bottles:** 3820
Lu 1:18 for I am an **o.** man, and my wife 4246
Lu 1:36 also conceived a son in her **o.** age: 1094
Lu 2:42 And when he was twelve years **o.**,
Lu 5:36 **of a new garment upon an o.;** 3820
Lu 5:36 **the new agreeth not with the o.** 3820
Lu 5:37 **putteth new wine into o. bottles;** 3820
Lu 5:39 **No man also having drunk o. wine** 3820
Lu 5:39 **new: for he saith, The o. is better.** 3820
Lu 9:8 one of the **o.** prophets was risen 744
Lu 9:19 one of the **o.** prophets is risen again. 744
Lu 12:33 **yourselves bags which wax not o.,** 3822
Joh 3:4 can a man be born when he is **o.**? 1088
Joh 8:57 Thou art not yet fifty years **o.**, and
Joh 21:18 **when thou shalt be o., thou shalt** 1095
Ac 2:17 your **o.** men shall dream dreams: 4245
Ac 4:22 For the man was above forty years **o.**,
Ac 7:23 when he was full forty years **o.**, it 5550
Ac 15:21 Moses of **o.** time hath in every city 744
Ac 21:16 Mnason of Cyprus, an **o.** disciple, 744
Ro 4:19 he was about an hundred years **o.**, 1541
Ro 6:6 our **o.** man is crucified with him 3820
1Co 5:7 Purge out therefore the **o.** leaven, 3820
1Co 5:8 not with **o.** leaven, neither with the 3820
2Co 3:14 in the reading of the **o.** testament; 3820
2Co 5:17 creature: **o.** things are past away; 744
Eph 4:22 That ye put off...the **o.** man, which 3820
Col 3:9 that ye have put off the **o.** man 3820
1Ti 4:7 refuse profane and **o.** wives' fables, 1126
1Ti 5:9 number under threescore years **o.**,
Heb 1:11 shall wax **o.** as doth a garment; 3822
Heb 8:13 covenant, he hath made the first **o.** 3822
Heb 8:13 that which decayeth and waxeth **o.** 1095
1Pe 3:5 in the **o.** time the holy women also, 4218
2Pe 1:9 he was purged from his **o.** sins. 3819
2Pe 1:21 came not in **o.** time by the will of 4218
2Pe 2:5 spared not the **o.** world, but saved 744
2Pe 3:5 word of God the heavens were of **o.**, 1597
1Jo 2:7 an **o.** commandment which ye had 3820
1Jo 2:7 The **o.** commandment is the word 3820
Jude 4 who were before of **o.** ordained to 3819
Re 12:9 that **o.** serpent, called the Devil, 744
Re 20:2 that **o.** serpent, which is the devil, 744

OLD AGE See OLD and AGE.

OLDNESS
Ro 7:6 and not in the **o.** of the letter. 3821

OLIVE See also OLIVES; OLIVEYARDS.
Ge 8:11 in her mouth was an **o.** leaf pluckt 2132
Ex 27:20 that they bring thee pure oil **o.** 2132
Ex 30:24 the sanctuary, and of oil **o.** an hin: 2132
Le 24:2 they bring unto thee pure oil **o.** 2132
De 6:11 **o.** trees, which thou plantedst not; 2132
De 8:8 a land of oil **o.**, and honey; 2132
De 24:20 When thou beatest thine **o.** tree, 2132
De 28:40 Thou shalt have **o.** trees throughout 2132
De 28:40 for thine **o.** shall cast his fruit. 2132
Jg 9:8 they said unto the **o.** tree, Reign 2132
Jg 9:9 But the **o.** tree said unto them, 2132
1Ki 6:23 he made two cherubims of **o.** tree, 8081
1Ki 6:31 the oracle he made doors of **o.** tree: 8081
1Ki 6:32 The two doors also were of **o.** tree; 8081
1Ki 6:33 door of the temple posts of **o.** tree, 8081
2Ki 18:32 a land of oil **o.** and of honey, 2132
1Ch 27:28 over the **o.** trees and the sycomore 2132
Ne 8:15 and fetch **o.** branches, and pine 2132
Job 15:33 shall cast off his flower as the **o.** 2132
Ps 52:8 am like a green **o.** tree in the house 2132
Ps 128:3 thy children like **o.** plants round 2132
Isa 17:6 in it, as the shaking of an **o.** tree, 2132
Isa 24:13 shall be as the shaking of an **o.** tree, 2132
Jer 11:16 called thy name, A green **o.** tree, 2132
Hos 14:6 his beauty shall be as the **o.** tree, 2132
Am 4:9 trees and your **o.** trees increased, 2132
Hab 3:17 the labour of the **o.** shall fail, and 2132
Hab 2:19 the pomegranate, and the **o.** tree, 2132
Zec 4:3 two **o.** trees by it, one upon the right 2132
Zec 4:11 What are these two **o.** trees upon 2132
Zec 4:12 What be these two **o.** branches 2132
Ro 11:17 and thou, being a wild **o.** tree, wert 65
Ro 11:17 the root and fatness of the **o.** tree; 1636
Ro 11:24 if thou wert cut out of the **o.** tree 65
Ro 11:24 to nature into a good **o.** tree: 2565
Ro 11:24 be graffed into their own **o.** tree? 1636
Jas 3:12 tree, my brethren, bear **o.** berries? 1636
Re 11:4 These are the two **o.** trees, and the 1636

OLIVE-BERRIES See OLIVE and BERRIES.

OLIVE-BRANCHES See OLIVE and BRANCHES.

OLIVE-LEAF See OLIVE and LEAF.

OLIVES
Jg 15:5 corn, with the vineyards and **o.** 2132
Mic 6:15 thou shalt tread the **o.**, but thou 2132
Zec 14:4 in that day upon the mount of **O.**, 2132
Zec 14:4 the Mount of **O.** shall cleave in the 2132
Mt 21:1 Bethphage, unto the mount of **O.**, 1636
Mt 24:3 And as he sat upon the mount of **O.**, 1636
Mt 26:30 they went out into the mount of **O.** 1636
Mk 11:1 and Bethany, at the mount of **O.**, 1636
Mk 13:3 And as he sat upon the mount of **O.** 1636
Mk 14:26 they went out into the mount of **O.** 1636
Lu 19:29 the mount called the mount of **O.**, 1636
Lu 19:37 at the descent of the mount of **O.**, 1636
Lu 21:37 that is called the mount of **O.** 1636
Lu 22:39 as he was wont, to the mount of **O.**; 1636
Joh 8:1 Jesus went unto the mount of **O.** 1636

OLIVET See also MOUNT and OLIVES.
2Sa 15:30 up by the ascent of mount **O.**, 2132
Ac 1:12 from the mount called **O.**, which 1638

OLIVE-TREE See OLIVE and TREE.

OLIVEYARD See also OLIVEYARDS.
Ex 23:11 with thy vineyard and with thy **o.** 2132

OLIVEYARDS
Jos 24:13 vineyard and **o.** which ye planted 2132
1Sa 8:14 and your **o.**, even the best of them, 2132
2Ki 5:26 and to receive garments, and **o.**, 2132
Ne 5:11 vineyards, their **o.**, and their houses, 2132
Ne 9:25 **o.**, and fruit trees in abundance: 2132

OLYMPAS (o-lim'-pas)
Ro 16:15 and **O.**, and all the saints which 3632

OMAR (o'-mar)
Ge 36:11 sons of Eliphaz were Teman, **O.**, 201
Ge 36:15 duke Teman, duke **O.**, duke Zepho, 201
1Ch 1:36 The sons of Eliphaz; Teman, and **O.**, 201

OMEGA (o'-me-gah)
Re 1:8 **I am Alpha and O., the beginning** 5598
Re 1:11 **I am Alpha and O., the first and** 5598
Re 21:6 **I am Alpha and O., the beginning** 5598
Re 22:13 **I am Alpha and O., the beginning** 5598

OMER See also OMERS.
Ex 16:16 an **o.** for every man, according to 6016
Ex 16:18 when they did mete it with an **o.**, 6016
Ex 16:32 Fill an **o.** of it to be kept for your 6016
Ex 16:33 a pot, and put an **o.** full of manna 6016
Ex 16:36 an **o.** is the tenth part of an ephah. 6016

OMERS
Ex 16:22 much bread, two **o.** for one man: 6016

OMITTED
Mt 23:23 **o....weightier matters of the law,** 863

OMNIPOTENT
Re 19:6 for the Lord God **o.** reigneth. 3841

OMRI (om'-ri)
1Ki 16:16 made **O.**,...captain of the host, king 6018
1Ki 16:17 **O.** went up from Gibbethon, and all 6018
1Ki 16:21 him king; and half followed **O.** 6018
1Ki 16:22 people that followed **O.** prevailed 6018
1Ki 16:22 so Tibni died, and **O.** reigned. 6018
1Ki 16:23 began **O.** to reign over Israel, twelve 6018
1Ki 16:25 **O.** wrought evil in the eyes of the 6018
1Ki 16:27 rest of the acts of **O.** which he did 6018
1Ki 16:28 **O.** slept with his fathers, and was 6018
1Ki 16:29 began Ahab the son of **O.** to reign 6018
1Ki 16:29 Ahab the son of **O.** reigned over 6018
1Ki 16:30 Ahab the son of **O.** did evil in the 6018
2Ki 8:26 Athaliah, the daughter of **O.** king 6018
1Ch 7:8 and **O.**, and Jerimoth, and Abiah, 6018
1Ch 9:4 the son of Ammihud, the son of **O.**, 6018
1Ch 27:18 of Issachar, **o.** the son of Michael: 6018
2Ch 22:2 was Athaliah the daughter of **O.** 6018
Mic 6:16 the statues of **O.** are kept, and all 6018

ON See also ANON; ONWARD; THEREON; UPON; WHEREON.
Ge 2:2 **o.** the seventh day God ended his work
Ge 2:2 he rested **o.** the seventh day from all
Ge 4:15 Cain, vengeance shall be taken **o.** him
Ge 4:16 in the land of Nod, **o.** the east of Eden.
Ge 6:1 multiply **o.** the face of the earth, 5921
Ge 6:6 that he had made man **o.** the earth, 5921
Ge 8:4 **o.** the seventeenth day of the month, 5921
Ge 8:5 month, **o.** the first day of the month, 5921
Ge 8:9 **o.** the face of the whole earth: 5921
Ge 8:14 **o.** the seven and twentieth day of the
Ge 8:20 offered burnt offerings **o.** the altar.
Ge 12:8 unto a mountain **o.** the east of Beth-el,
Ge 12:8 Beth-el **o.** the west, and Hai **o.** the east:
Ge 12:9 going **o.** still toward the south.
Ge 13:3 he went **o.** his journeys from the south
Ge 13:4 Abram called **o.** the name of the Lord.
Ge 14:15 which is **o.** the left hand of Damascus.
Ge 17:3 Abram fell **o.** his face: and God 5921
Ge 18:5 your hearts; after that ye shall pass **o.**:
Ge 18:16 with them to bring them **o.** the way.
Ge 19:2 rise up early, and go **o.** your ways.
Ge 19:34 And it came to pass **o.** the morrow,
Ge 20:9 brought **o.** me and **o.** my kingdom 5921
Ge 21:14 Hagar, putting it **o.** her shoulder, 5921
Ge 21:33 called there **o.** the name of the Lord,
Ge 22:4 Then **o.** the third day Abraham lifted
Ge 22:9 him **o.** the altar upon the wood. 5921
Ge 24:33 mine errand. And he said, Speak **o.**
Ge 24:45 with her pitcher **o.** her shoulder; 5921
Ge 25:26 and his hand took hold **o.** Esau's heel;
Ge 28:12 behold a ladder set up **o.** the earth,
Ge 28:12 of God ascending and descending **o.** it.
Ge 28:20 bread to eat, and raiment to put **o.**,
Ge 29:1 Then Jacob went **o.** his journey, and
Ge 31:22 it was told Laban **o.** the third day that
Ge 32:1 Jacob went **o.** his way, and the angels
Ge 32:19 **O.** this manner shall ye speak unto
Ge 33:4 fell **o.** his neck, and kissed him: 5921
Ge 33:14 and I will lead **o.** softly, according as
Ge 33:16 Esau returned that day **o.** his way
Ge 34:25 And it came to pass **o.** the third day,
Ge 37:23 of many colours that was **o.** him; 5921
Ge 38:9 wife, that he spilled it **o.** the ground,
Ge 38:19 put **o.** the garments of her widowhood.
Ge 40:14 think **o.** me when it shall be well with
Ge 40:16 three white baskets **o.** my head: 5921
Ge 40:19 thee, and shall hang thee **o.** a tree; 5921
Ge 43:31 himself, and said, Set **o.** bread.
Ge 43:32 And they set **o.** for him by himself,
Ge 44:14 they fell before him **o.** the ground.
Ge 44:34 evil that shall come **o.** my father.
Ge 46:29 fell **o.** his neck, and wept **o.** his neck 5921
Ge 48:16 and let my name be named **o.** them,
Ge 49:26 they shall be **o.** the head of Joseph,
Ge 49:26 and **o.** the crown of the head of him
Ex 1:10 Come **o.**, let us deal wisely with them;
Ex 2:6 And she had compassion **o.** him, 5921
Ex 2:11 brethren, and looked **o.** their burdens:
Ex 4:3 And he said, Cast it **o.** the ground.
Ex 4:3 he cast it **o.** the ground, and it became
Ex 6:28 came to pass **o.** the day when the Lord
Ex 8:4 the frogs shall come up both **o.** thee,
Ex 12:7 and strike it **o.** the two side posts 5921
Ex 12:7 **o.** the upper door post of the houses, 5921
Ex 12:11 your shoes **o.** your feet, and your staff
Ex 12:18 **o.** the fourteenth day of the month at
Ex 12:23 lintel, and **o.** the two side posts, 5921
Ex 12:29 of Pharaoh that sat **o.** this throne 5921
Ex 12:37 six hundred thousand **o.** foot that
Ex 14:16 Israel shall go **o.** dry ground through
Ex 14:22, 29 **o.** their right hand and **o.** their
Ex 15:14 hold **o.** the inhabitants of Palestina.

De 9:10 **o.** them was written according to 5921
De 10:2 I will write **o.** the tables the words 5921
De 10:4 he wrote **o.** the tables, according to 5921
De 11:30 they not **o.** the other side Jordan, by
De 16:8 **o.** the seventh day shall be a solemn
De 2:19 father and his mother lay hold **o.** him,
De 2:22 and thou hang him **o.** a tree: 5921
De 22:5 man put **o.** a woman's garment:
De 22:6 way in any tree, or **o.** the ground, 5921
De 22:28 and lay hold **o.** her, and lie with her,
De 23:11 shall be, when evening cometh **o.**,
De 26:7 voice, and looked **o.** our affliction,
De 27:2 **o.** the day when ye shall pass over
De 28:1 set thee **o.** high above all nations 5921
De 28:2 these blessings shall come **o.** thee, 5921
De 30:7 and **o.** them that hate thee, which 5921
De 32:11 them, beareth them **o.** her wings: 5921
De 32:13 rise **o.** the high places of the earth, 5921
De 32:22 set **o.** fire the foundations of the
De 32:41 mine hand take hold **o.** judgment;
De 33:26 help, and in his excellency **o.** the sky.
Jos 1:14 Moses gave you **o.** this side Jordan;
Jos 1:15 servant gave you **o.** this side Jordan
Jos 2:10 that were **o.** the other side Jordan,
Jos 2:19 his blood shall be **o.** our head, if any
Jos 3:17 of the Lord stood firm **o.** dry ground
Jos 3:17 Israelites passed over **o.** dry ground,
Jos 4:14 **O.** that day the Lord magnified
Jos 4:19 up out of Jordan **o.** the tenth day
Jos 4:22 came over this Jordan **o.** dry land.
Jos 5:1 were **o.** the side of Jordan westward,
Jos 5:10 kept the passover **o.** the fourteenth
Jos 5:11 the old corn of the land **o.** the morrow
Jos 5:12 And the manna ceased **o.** the morrow
Jos 5:14 Joshua fell **o.** his face to the earth, 413
Jos 6:7 Pass **o.**, and compass the city, and
Jos 6:7 armed pass **o.** before the ark of the 413
Jos 6:8 horns passed **o.** before the Lord, 413
Jos 6:9 the priests going **o.**, and blowing
Jos 6:13 before the ark of the Lord went **o.** 413
Jos 6:13 priests going **o.**, and blowing with 413
Jos 6:15 And it came to pass **o.** the seventh day,
Jos 6:15 **o.** that day they compassed the city
Jos 7:2 Beth-aven, **o.** the east side of Beth-el,
Jos 7:7 and dwelt **o.** the other side Jordan!
Jos 8:8 city, that ye shall set the city **o.** fire:
Jos 8:9 Beth-el and Ai, **o.** the west side of Ai:
Jos 8:11 and pitched **o.** the north side of Ai:
Jos 8:12 and Ai, **o.** the west side of the city.
Jos 8:13 host that was **o.** the north of the city,
Jos 8:13 liers in wait **o.** the west of the city,
Jos 8:19 and hasted and set the city **o.** fire.
Jos 8:22 some **o.** this side, and some **o.** that
Jos 8:24 all fallen **o.** the edge of the sword,
Jos 8:29 he hanged **o.** a tree until eventide: 5921
Jos 8:33 stood **o.** this side the ark and **o.** that
Jos 9:1 kings which were **o.** this side Jordan,
Jos 9:12 of our houses **o.** the day we came forth
Jos 9:17 came unto their cities **o.** the third day.
Jos 10:26 and hanged them **o.** five trees: 5921
Jos 10:32 Israel, which took it **o.** the second day,
Jos 10:35 they took it **o.** that day, and smote
Jos 11:2 were **o.** the north of the mountains,
Jos 11:2 and in the borders of Dor **o.** the west,
Jos 11:3 Canaanite **o.** the east and **o.** the west,
Jos 12:1 their land **o.** the other side Jordan
Jos 12:1 Hermon, and all the plain **o.** the east:
Jos 12:3 to the sea of Chinneroth **o.** the east,
Jos 12:3 the plain, even the salt sea **o.** the east,
Jos 12:7 smote **o.** this side Jordan **o.** the west,
Jos 13:16 is **o.** the bank of the river Arnon, 5921
Jos 13:27 sea of Chinnereth **o.** the other side
Jos 13:32 of Moab, or the other side Jordan,
Jos 14:3 an half tribe **o.** the other side Jordan:
Jos 14:9 And Moses sware **o.** that day, saying,
Jos 15:3 and ascended up **o.** the south side
Jos 15:7 which is **o.** the south side of the river:
Jos 15:10 which is Chesalon, **o.** the north side,
Jos 15:10 and passed **o.** to Timnah:
Jos 16:1 unto the water of Jericho **o.** the east,
Jos 16:5 inheritance **o.** the east side was
Jos 16:6 the sea to Michmethah **o.** the north
Jos 16:6 passed by it **o.** the east to Janohah;
Jos 17:5 which were **o.** the other side Jordan;
Jos 17:7 went along **o.** the right hand unto 413
Jos 17:8 Tappuah **o.** the border of Manasseh 413
Jos 17:9 also was **o.** the north side of the river,
Jos 17:10 met together in Asher **o.** the north,
Jos 17:10 and in Issachar **o.** the east.
Jos 18:5 shall abide in their coast **o.** the south,
Jos 18:5 shall abide in their coasts **o.** the north.
Jos 18:7 inheritance beyond Jordan **o.** the east,
Jos 18:12 border **o.** the north side was from
Jos 18:12 to the side of Jericho **o.** the north side,
Jos 18:13 lieth **o.** the south side of the nether
Jos 18:15 and the border went out **o.** the west,
Jos 18:16 in the valley of the giants **o.** the north,
Jos 18:16 to the side of Jebusi **o.** the south,
Jos 18:20 was the border of it **o.** the east side.
Jos 19:13 passeth **o.** along **o.** the east to
Jos 19:14 it **o.** the north side to Hannathon:
Jos 19:27 goeth out to Cabul **o.** the left hand,
Jos 19:34 reacheth to Zebulun **o.** the south side,
Jos 19:34 reacheth to Asher **o.** the west side,
Jos 20:8 **o.** the other side Jordan by Jericho
Jos 22:4 gave you **o.** the other side Jordan.
Jos 22:7 brethren **o.** this side Jordan westward.
Jos 22:20 **o.** all the congregation of Israel? 5921
Jos 24:2 dwelt **o.** the other side of the flood
Jos 24:8 which dwelt **o.** the other side Jordan;
Jos 24:14 served **o.** the other side of the flood,
Jos 24:15 were **o.** the other side of the flood,
Jos 24:30 **o.** the north side of the hill of Gaash.
Jg 1:8 of the sword, and set the city **o.** fire.
Jg 2:9 **o.** the north side of the hill Gaash.
Jg 3:25 lord was fallen down dead **o.** the earth.
Jg 4:15 his chariot, and fled away **o.** his feet.
Jg 4:17 fled away **o.** his feet to the tent of
Jg 4:23 God subdued **o.** that day Jabin the
Jg 5:1 Barak the son of Abinoam **o.** that day,
Jg 5:10 Speak, ye that ride **o.** white asses, ye
Jg 5:15 he was sent **o.** foot into the valley.
Jg 5:17 Asher continued **o.** the sea shore, and
Jg 5:30 colours of needlework **o.** both side,
Jg 6:32 **o.** that day he called him Jerubbaal,
Jg 6:37 if the dew be **o.** the fleece only, 5921
Jg 6:38 for he rose up early **o.** the morrow,
Jg 6:40 there was dew **o.** all the ground. 5921
Jg 7:1 were **o.** the north side of them, by
Jg 7:17 them, Look **o.** me, and do likewise:
Jg 7:18 also **o.** every side of all the camp,
Jg 7:25 to Gideon **o.** the other side Jordan.
Jg 8:11 dwelt in tents **o.** the east of Nobah
Jg 8:21 that were **o.** their camels' necks.
Jg 8:26 that was **o.** the kings of Midian, 5921
Jg 8:34 of all their enemies **o.** every side:
Jg 9:8 went forth **o.** a time to anoint a king
Jg 9:42 And it came to pass **o.** the morrow,
Jg 9:48 took it, and laid it **o.** his shoulder, 5921
Jg 9:49 and set the hold **o.** fire upon them;
Jg 10:4 sons that rode **o.** thirty ass colts, 5921
Jg 10:8 that were **o.** the other side Jordan
Jg 11:18 pitched **o.** the other side of Arnon,
Jg 12:14 **o.** threescore and ten ass colts: 5921
Jg 13:5 no rasor shall come **o.** his head: 5921
Jg 13:19 and Manoah and his wife looked **o.**.
Jg 13:20 And Manoah and his wife looked **o.** it,
Jg 13:20 and fell **o.** their faces to the 5921
Jg 14:9 in his hands and went **o.** eating,
Jg 14:15, 17 came to pass **o.** the seventh day,
Jg 14:18 of the city said unto him **o.** the seventh
Jg 15:5 when he had set the brands **o.** fire,
Jg 15:18 and called **o.** the Lord, and said, 413
Jg 16:29 and **o.** which it was borne up, 5921
Jg 19:1 **o.** the side of mount Ephraim,
Jg 19:5 **o.** the fourth day, when they arose
Jg 19:8 early in the morning **o.** the fifth day
Jg 19:9 to morrow get you early **o.** your way,
Jg 19:14 they passed **o.** and went their way;
Jg 19:29 a knife, and laid hold **o.** his concubine,
Jg 20:30 the children of Benjamin **o.** the third
Jg 20:48 also they set **o.** fire all the cities that
Jg 21:4 And it came to pass **o.** the morrow,
Jg 21:19 which is **o.** the north side of Beth-el,
Jg 21:19 **o.** the east side of the highway that
Jg 21:19 Shechem, and **o.** the south of Lebonah.
Ru 1:7 went **o.** the way to return unto the
Ru 2:3 hap was to light **o.** a part of the field
Ru 2:9 Let thine eyes be **o.** the field that they
Ru 2:10 she fell **o.** her face, and bowed 5921
Ru 3:15 of barley, and laid it **o.** her: 5921
1Sa 1:11 look **o.** the affliction of thine handmaid,
1Sa 2:26 And the child Samuel grew **o.**, and
1Sa 2:34 two sons, **o.** Hophni and Phinehas; 413
1Sa 5:3 of Ashdod arose early **o.** the morrow,
1Sa 5:4 arose early **o.** the morrow morning,
1Sa 5:5 tread **o.** the threshold of Dagon 5921
1Sa 6:4 plague was **o.** you all, and **o.** your lords.
1Sa 6:7 **o.** which there hath come no yoke, 5921
1Sa 6:15 and put them **o.** the great stone: 413
1Sa 7:6 before the Lord, and fasted **o.** that day,
1Sa 7:10 with a great thunder **o.** that day
1Sa 9:20 days ago, set not thy mind **o.** them;
1Sa 9:20 **o.** whom is all the desire of Israel?
1Sa 9:20 Is it not **o.** thee, and **o.** all thy father's
1Sa 9:27 **o.** before us, (and he passed **o.**,)
1Sa 10:3 thou go **o.** forward from thence,
1Sa 11:2 **O.** this condition will I make a
1Sa 11:7 fear of the Lord fell **o.** the people, 5921
1Sa 11:11 And it was so **o.** the morrow, that Saul
1Sa 12:11 hand of your enemies **o.** every side,
1Sa 13:5 sand which is **o.** the sea shore in 5921
1Sa 14:1 garrison, that is **o.** the other side.
1Sa 14:4 there was a sharp rock **o.** the one side,
1Sa 14:4 and a sharp rock **o.** the other side:
1Sa 14:16 they went **o.** beating down one
1Sa 14:19 Philistines went **o.** and increased:
1Sa 14:24 I may be avenged **o.** mine enemies.
1Sa 14:32 calves, and slew them **o.** the ground:
1Sa 14:40 he unto all Israel, Be ye **o.** one side,
1Sa 14:40 my son will be **o.** the other side.
1Sa 14:47 against all his enemies **o.** every side,
1Sa 15:12 is gone about, and passed **o.**, and
1Sa 15:16 and he said unto him, Say **o.**.
1Sa 15:18 the Lord sent thee **o.** a journey, and
1Sa 16:6 were come, that he looked **o.** Eliab,
1Sa 16:7 Look not **o.** his countenance, or 413
1Sa 16:7 or **o.** the height of his stature;
1Sa 16:7 looketh **o.** the outward appearance,
1Sa 16:7 but the Lord looketh **o.** the heart.
1Sa 16:16 who is a cunning player **o.** an harp:
1Sa 17:3 stood **o.** a mountain **o.** the one side, 413
1Sa 17:3 stood **o.** a mountain **o.** the other 413
1Sa 17:41 Philistine came **o.** and drew near
1Sa 18:10 And it came to pass **o.** the morrow,
1Sa 18:24 saying, **O.** this manner spake David.
1Sa 19:23 and he went **o.**, and prophesied,
1Sa 20:20 shoot three arrows **o.** the side thereof,
1Sa 20:21 the arrows are **o.** this side of thee,
1Sa 20:27 And it came to pass **o.** the morrow,
1Sa 20:41 fell **o.** his face to the ground, and
1Sa 21:13 scrabbled **o.** the doors of the gate, 5921
1Sa 22:18 and slew **o.** that day fourscore and five
1Sa 23:19 which is **o.** the south of Jeshimon?
1Sa 23:21 Lord; for ye have compassion **o.** me.
1Sa 23:24 the plain **o.** the south of Jeshimon. 413
1Sa 23:26 Saul went **o.** this side of the mountain,
1Sa 23:26 his men **o.** that side of the mountain:
1Sa 24:7 out of the cave, and went **o.** his way.
1Sa 25:13 men, Gird ye **o.** every man his sword.
1Sa 25:13 they girded **o.** every man his sword;
1Sa 25:13 and David also girded **o.** his sword:
1Sa 25:14 our master; and he railed **o.** them.
1Sa 25:18 of figs, and laid them **o.** asses. 5921
1Sa 25:19 Go **o.** before me; behold, I come
1Sa 25:20 it was so, as she rode **o.** the ass, 5921
1Sa 25:23 and fell before David **o.** her face, 5921
1Sa 25:41 bowed herself **o.** her face to the earth,
1Sa 26:13 and stood **o.** the top of an hill afar 5921
1Sa 26:25 So David went **o.** his way, and Saul
1Sa 27:11 Lest they should tell **o.** us, saying, 5921
1Sa 28:8 himself, and put **o.** other raiment,
1Sa 28:20 fell straightway all along **o.** the earth,
1Sa 28:22 strength; when thou goest **o.** thy way.
1Sa 29:2 Philistines passed **o.** by hundred,
1Sa 29:2 his men passed **o.** in the rereward
1Sa 30:1 were come to Ziklag **o.** the third day,
1Sa 30:2 them away, and went **o.** their way.
1Sa 31:7 were **o.** the other side of the valley,
1Sa 31:7 that were **o.** the other side Jordan,
1Sa 31:8 And it came to pass **o.** the morrow,
2Sa 1:2 It came even to pass **o.** the third day,
2Sa 1:10 the bracelet that was **o.** his arm, 5921
2Sa 1:11 Then David took hold **o.** his clothes,
2Sa 1:24 who put **o.** ornaments of gold upon
2Sa 2:13 the one **o.** the one side of the pool 5921
2Sa 2:13 other **o.** the other side of the pool 5921
2Sa 2:21 lay thee hold **o.** one of the young men.

2Sa 2:25 and stood **o.** the top of an hill........... 5921
2Sa 3:12 sent messengers to David **o.** his behalf,.....
2Sa 3:29 Let it rest **o.** the head of Joab,.......... 5921
2Sa 3:29 Joab, and **o.** all his father's house;........ 413
2Sa 3:29 is a leper, or that leaneth **o.** a staff,..........
2Sa 3:29 or that falleth **o.** the sword, or that..........
2Sa 4:5 who lay **o.** a bed at noon.......................
2Sa 4:7 lay **o.** his bed in his bedchamber,....... 5921
2Sa 5:8 David said **o.** that day, Whosoever...........
2Sa 5:10 And David went **o.**, and grew great,.........
2Sa 6:5 **o.** all manner of instruments made of........
2Sa 6:5 even **o.** harps, and **o.** psalteries, and........
2Sa 6:5 **o.** timbrels,...**o.** cornets,...**o.** cymbals.......
2Sa 8:7 were **o.** the servants of Hadadezer,...... 413
2Sa 9:3 yet a son, which is lame **o.** his feet.........
2Sa 9:6 come unto David, he fell **o.** his face,... 5921
2Sa 9:13 table; and was lame **o.** both his feet.........
2Sa 11:13 at even he went out to lie **o.** his bed........
2Sa 12:18 And it came to pass **o.** the seventh day,....
2Sa 12:30 and it was set **o.** David's head.......... 5921
2Sa 13:5 Lay thee down **o.** thy bed, and make.. 5921
2Sa 13:19 Tamar put ashes **o.** her head, and...... 5921
2Sa 13:19 of divers colours that was **o.** her,....... 5921
2Sa 13:19 and laid her hand **o.** her head,........... 5921
2Sa 13:19 her head, and went **o.** crying..................
2Sa 13:31 his garments, and lay **o.** the earth;...........
2Sa 14:2 and put **o.** now mourning apparel,.............
2Sa 14:3 and speak **o.** this manner unto him...........
2Sa 14:4 she fell **o.** her face to the ground,...... 5921
2Sa 14:9 be **o.** me, and **o.** my father's house:... 5921
2Sa 14:12 lord the king. And he said, Say **o.**...........
2Sa 14:14 and are as water spilt **o.** the ground,........
2Sa 14:22 Joab fell to the ground **o.** his face,....... 413
2Sa 14:26 because the hair was heavy **o.** him,.... 5921
2Sa 14:30 hath barley there; go and set it **o.** fire.......
2Sa 14:30 Absalom's servants set the field **o.** fire.....
2Sa 14:31 have thy servants set my field **o.** fire?.......
2Sa 14:33 bowed himself **o.** his face to the......... 5921
2Sa 15:6 And **o.** this manner did Absalom to all.......
2Sa 15:18 his servants passed **o.** beside him;............
2Sa 15:18 Gath, passed **o.** before the king...............
2Sa 15:33 If thou passest **o.** with me, then..............
2Sa 16:2 be for the king's household to ride **o.**;.......
2Sa 16:6 were **o.** his right hand and **o.** his left........
2Sa 16:12 the Lord will look **o.** mine affliction,..........
2Sa 16:13 Shimei went along **o.** the hill's side...........
2Sa 17:12 as the dew falleth **o.** the ground:........ 5921
2Sa 19:40 Then the king went **o.** to Gilgal,..............
2Sa 19:40 and Chimham went **o.** with him:................
2Sa 20:8 Joab's garment that he had put **o.** was.......
2Sa 20:13 all the people went **o.** after Joab,.............
2Sa 21:10 birds of the air to rest **o.** them.......... 5921
2Sa 21:20 that had **o.** every hand six fingers,............
2Sa 21:20 and **o.** every foot six toes, four and..........
2Sa 22:4 I will call **o.** the Lord, who is worthy........
2Sa 22:49 also hast lifted me up **o.** high..................
2Sa 23:1 man who was raised up **o.** high,...............
2Sa 24:5 in Aroer, **o.** the right side of the city........
2Sa 24:20 servants coming **o.** toward him:...............
2Sa 24:20 the king **o.** his face upon the ground.........
1Ki 1:20 shall sit **o.** the throne of my lord....... 5921
1Ki 1:27 who should sit **o.** the throne of my lord.....
1Ki 1:46 Solomon sitteth **o.** the throne of......... 5921
1Ki 1:48 hath given one to sit **o.** my throne..... 5921
1Ki 1:50 caught hold **o.** the horns of the altar.........
1Ki 1:51 caught hold **o.** the horns of the altar,.........
1Ki 2:4 a man **o.** the throne of Israel............ 5921
1Ki 2:5 and in his shoes that were **o.** his feet........
1Ki 2:14 unto thee. And she said, Say **o.**.................
1Ki 2:15 that all Israel set their faces **o.** me,.... 5921
1Ki 2:16 And she said unto him, Say **o.**..................
1Ki 2:19 her, and sat down **o.** his throne,........ 5921
1Ki 2:19 and she sat **o.** his right hand..................
1Ki 2:20 said unto her, Ask **o.**, my mother:............
1Ki 2:24 **o.** the throne of David my father,....... 5921
1Ki 2:28 caught hold **o.** the horns of the altar.........
1Ki 2:37 be, that **o.** the day thou goest out,..........
1Ki 2:42 certain, **o.** the day thou goest out,............
1Ki 3:6 him a son to sit **o.** his throne, as....... 5921
1Ki 4:24 all the region **o.** this side the river,..........
1Ki 4:24 all the kings **o.** this side the river:...........
1Ki 4:24 peace **o.** all sides round about him...........
1Ki 4:29 the sand that is **o.** the sea shore........ 5921
1Ki 5:3 which were about him **o.** every side,........
1Ki 5:4 God hath given me rest **o.** every side,......
1Ki 6:10 **o.** the house with timber of cedar,...........
1Ki 6:15 covered them **o.** the inside with wood,......
1Ki 6:16 twenty cubits **o.** the sides of the house,....
1Ki 7:3 beams, that lay **o.** forty five pillars,..........
1Ki 7:9 so **o.** the outside toward the great...... 5704
1Ki 7:28 work of the borders was **o.** this manner:......
1Ki 7:29 **o.** the borders that were between...... 5921
1Ki 7:35 **o.** the top of the base the ledges...... 5921
1Ki 7:36 **o.** the plates of the ledges thereof,..... 5921
1Ki 7:36 **o.** the borders thereof, he graved....... 5921
1Ki 7:39 bases **o.** the right side of the house,... 5921
1Ki 7:39 five **o.** the left side of the house:....... 5921
1Ki 7:39 he set the sea **o.** the right side of the.......
1Ki 7:41 were **o.** the top of the two pillars:...... 5921
1Ki 7:43 bases, and ten lavers **o.** the bases;..... 5921
1Ki 7:49 of pure gold, five **o.** the right side,...........
1Ki 7:49 and five **o.** the left; before the oracle,.......
1Ki 8:20 and sit **o.** the throne of Israel,........... 5921
1Ki 8:23 heaven above, or **o.** earth beneath,..... 5921
1Ki 8:25 sight to sit **o.** the throne of Israel;..... 5921
1Ki 8:27 will God indeed dwell **o.** the earth?..... 5921
1Ki 8:50 they may have compassion **o.** them:.........
1Ki 8:54 arose...from kneeling **o.** his knees...... 5921
1Ki 8:66 **O.** the eighth day he sent the people........
1Ki 9:26 **o.** the shore of the Red sea, in the..... 5921
1Ki 10:9 to set thee **o.** the throne of Israel:..... 5921
1Ki 10:19 and there were stays **o.** either side..........
1Ki 10:19 **o.** the place of the seat, and two......... 413
1Ki 10:20 twelve lions stood there **o.** the one side....
1Ki 10:20 and **o.** the other upon the six steps:.........
1Ki 11:30 the new garment that was **o.** him,...... 5921
1Ki 12:32 **o.** the fifteenth day of the month, like.......
1Ki 13:4 from the altar, saying, Lay hold **o.** him......
1Ki 14:23 **o.** every high hill, and under............. 5921
1Ki 16:11 soon as he sat **o.** his throne, that he... 5921
1Ki 16:24 and built **o.** the hill, and called the....... 853
1Ki 18:7 he knew him, and fell **o.** his face,....... 5921
1Ki 18:23, 23 and lay it **o.** wood, and put no fire. 5921
1Ki 18:24 And call ye **o.** the name of your gods,.......
1Ki 18:24 and I will call **o.** the name of the Lord:......
1Ki 18:25 and call **o.** the name of your gods, but......
1Ki 18:26 and called **o.** the name of Baal from..........
1Ki 18:33 pieces, and laid him **o.** the wood,....... 5921
1Ki 18:33 pour it **o.** the burnt sacrifice and on.... 5921
1Ki 18:39 people saw it, they fell **o.** their faces:..5921
1Ki 18:46 the hand of the Lord was **o.** Elijah;...... 413
1Ki 19:6 there was a cake baken **o.** the coals,.........
1Ki 19:15 Go, return **o.** thy way to the wilderness....
1Ki 20:11 Let not him that girdeth **o.** his harness......
1Ki 20:20 king of Syria escaped **o.** an horse....... 5921
1Ki 20:31 put sackcloth **o.** our loins, and rope..........
1Ki 20:32 So they girded sackcloth **o.** their loins,......
1Ki 20:32 and put ropes **o.** their heads, and............
1Ki 21:9, 12 set Naboth **o.** high among the.............
1Ki 22:10 of Judah sat each **o.** his throne,......... 5921
1Ki 22:10 having put **o.** their robes,......................
1Ki 22:19 I saw the Lord sitting **o.** his throne,... 5921
1Ki 22:19 standing by him **o.** his right hand and.......
1Ki 22:19 his right hand and **o.** his left....................
1Ki 22:20 And one said **o.** this manner,...................
1Ki 22:20 and another said **o.** that manner...............
1Ki 22:24 and smote Micaiah **o.** the cheek,........ 5921
1Ki 22:30 battle; but put thou **o.** thy robes.............
2Ki 1:4, 6 that bed **o.** which thou art gone up,..........
2Ki 1:9 behold, he sat **o.** the top of an hill...... 5921
2Ki 1:13 and fell **o.** his knees before Elijah,...... 5921
2Ki 1:16 that bed **o.** which thou art gone up,..........
2Ki 2:6 leave thee. And they two went **o.**...........
2Ki 2:8 they two went over **o.** dry ground............
2Ki 2:11 and they still went **o.**, and talked,.............
2Ki 2:15 spirit of Elijah doth rest **o.** Elisha....... 5921
2Ki 2:24 he turned back, and looked **o.** them,..........
2Ki 3:11 water **o.** the hands of Elijah............. 5921
2Ki 3:21 that were able to put **o.** armour,.............
2Ki 3:22 water **o.** the other side as red as............
2Ki 3:25 **o.** every good piece of land cast every......
2Ki 4:8 And it fell **o.** a day, that Elisha passed......
2Ki 4:10 little chamber, I pray thee, **o.** the wall;.....
2Ki 4:11 it fell **o.** a day, that he came thither..........
2Ki 4:18 it fell **o.** a day, that he went out to his......
2Ki 4:20 he sat **o.** her knees till noon, and........ 5921
2Ki 4:21 him **o.** the bed of the man of God,..... 5921
2Ki 4:31 Gehazi passed **o.** before them, and...........
2Ki 4:38 Set **o.** the great pot, and seethe..............
2Ki 5:2 and she waited **o.** Naaman's wife.............
2Ki 5:11 and call **o.** the name of the Lord his.........
2Ki 5:18 and he leaneth **o.** my hand, and I....... 5921
2Ki 6:29 I said unto her **o.** the next day, Give........
2Ki 6:31 head of Elisha...shall stand **o.** him...... 5921
2Ki 7:2 lord **o.** whose hand the king leaned..... 5921
2Ki 7:17 the lord **o.** whose hand he leaned to... 5921
2Ki 8:12 their strong holds wilt thou set **o.** fire,......
2Ki 8:15 And it came to pass **o.** the morrow,..........
2Ki 8:15 in water, and spread it **o.** his face,..... 5921
2Ki 9:3 box of oil, and pour it **o.** his head,...... 5921
2Ki 9:6 and he poured the oil **o.** his head,........ 413
2Ki 9:13 it under him **o.** the top of the stairs,.... 413
2Ki 9:17 watchman **o.** the tower in Jezreel,...... 5921
2Ki 9:18 went one **o.** horseback to meet him,.........
2Ki 9:19 sent out a second **o.** horseback, which......
2Ki 9:32 and said, Who is **o.** my side? who?...... 854
2Ki 9:33 **o.** the wall, and **o.** the horses............ 413
2Ki 10:3 and set him **o.** his father's throne,...... 5921
2Ki 10:15 he lighted **o.** Jehonadab the son of....... 854
2Ki 10:30 shall sit **o.** the throne of Israel.......... 5921
2Ki 11:5 of you that enter in **o.** the sabbath shall.....
2Ki 11:7 of all you that go forth **o.** the sabbath,......
2Ki 11:9 that were to come in **o.** the sabbath,........
2Ki 11:9 that should go out **o.** the sabbath,............
2Ki 11:16 they laid hands **o.** her; and she went.........
2Ki 11:19 he sat **o.** the throne of the kings........ 5921
2Ki 12:9 **o.** the right side as one cometh into..........
2Ki 12:15 money to be bestowed **o.** workmen:.........
2Ki 13:21 revived, and stood up **o.** his feet.......... 5921
2Ki 13:23 had compassion **o.** them, and had............
2Ki 14:4 and burnt incense **o.** the high places.........
2Ki 14:20 And they brought him **o.** horses:........ 5921
2Ki 15:4 burnt incense still **o.** the high places.........
2Ki 15:12 shall sit **o.** the throne of Israel........... 5921
2Ki 16:4 **o.** the hills and under every green...... 5921
2Ki 16:14 put it **o.** the north side of the altar..... 5921
2Ki 18:14 which thou puttest **o.** me will I bear... 5921
2Ki 18:20 **o.** whom dost thou trust, that thou..... 5921
2Ki 18:21 **o.** which if a man lean, it will go into.. 5921
2Ki 18:21 of Egypt unto all that trust **o.** him...... 5921
2Ki 18:23 be able **o.** thy part to set riders upon........
2Ki 18:24 put thy trust **o.** Egypt for chariots...... 5921
2Ki 18:26 of the people that are **o.** the wall....... 5921
2Ki 18:27 me to the men which sit **o.** the wall,... 5921
2Ki 19:22 and lifted up thine eyes **o.** high?..............
2Ki 19:26 as the grass **o.** the house tops, and as......
2Ki 20:5 **o.** the third day thou shalt go up unto.......
2Ki 20:7 laid it **o.** the boil, and he recovered.... 5921
2Ki 23:8 which were **o.** a man's left hand at..... 5921
2Ki 23:12 were **o.** the top of the upper chamber. 5921
2Ki 23:13 were **o.** the right hand of the mount.........
2Ki 25:3 **o.** the ninth day of the fourth month.........
2Ki 25:8 **o.** the seventh day of the month,............
2Ki 25:27 **o.** the seven and twentieth day of the.......
1Ch 4:10 And Jabez called **o.** the God of Israel,.......
1Ch 6:32 then they waited **o.** their office...............
1Ch 6:39 Asaph, who stood **o.** his right hand,..... 5921
1Ch 6:44 of Merari stood **o.** the left hand:........ 5921
1Ch 6:49 offering, and **o.** the altar of incense,.... 5921
1Ch 6:78 **o.** the other side Jordan by Jericho,.... 5921
1Ch 6:78 **o.** the east of Jordan, were given them.....
1Ch 10:5 fell likewise **o.** the sword, and died..... 5921
1Ch 10:8 And it came to pass **o.** the morrow,.........
1Ch 12:18 Thine are we, David, and **o.** thy side,.......
1Ch 12:37 And **o.** the other side of Jordan, of the......
1Ch 12:40 brought bread **o.** asses, and **o.** camels,......
1Ch 12:40 and **o.** mules, and **o.** oxen, and meat,.......
1Ch 13:6 Lord,...whose name is called **o.** it...........
1Ch 14:2 his kingdom was lifted up **o.** high,............
1Ch 15:20 with psalteries **o.** Alamoth;............... 5921
1Ch 15:21 harps **o.** the Shiminith to excel......... 5921
1Ch 16:7 **o.** that day David delivered first this.........
1Ch 18:7 were **o.** the servants of Hadarezer,...... 5921
1Ch 20:6 six **o.** each hand, and six **o.** each foot:......
1Ch 21:17 be **o.** me and **o.** my father's house:..........
1Ch 21:17 not **o.** thy people, that they should be.......
1Ch 22:18 he not given you rest **o.** every side?.........
1Ch 23:28 was to wait **o.** the sons of Aaron.............
1Ch 23:31 the new moons, and **o.** the set feasts,.......
1Ch 26:30 them of Israel **o.** this side Jordan.............
1Ch 29:15 our days **o.** the earth are as a........... 5921
1Ch 29:21 the Lord, **o.** the morrow after that day,.....
1Ch 29:22 and drink before the Lord **o.** that day........
1Ch 29:23 Solomon sat **o.** the throne of the........ 5921
1Ch 29:25 **o.** any king before him in Israel......... 5921
2Ch 2:4 **o.** the sabbaths, and **o.** the new moons,....
2Ch 2:4 and **o.** the solemn feasts of the Lord.........
2Ch 3:7 and graved cherubims **o.** the walls...... 5921
2Ch 3:13 they stood **o.** their feet, and their...... 5921
2Ch 3:15 chapiter that was **o.** the top of each.... 5921
2Ch 3:16 put them **o.** the heads of the pillars;... 5921

2Ch 3:16 and put them **o.** the chains
2Ch 3:17 the pillars...one **o.** the right hand,
2Ch 3:17 and the other **o.** the left; and called
2Ch 3:17 name of that **o.** the right hand Jachin,
2Ch 3:17 and the name of that **o.** the left Boaz.
2Ch 4:6 lavers, and put five **o.** the right hand,
2Ch 4:6 and five **o.** the left, to wash in them:
2Ch 4:7 candlesticks...five **o.** the right hand,
2Ch 4:7 and five **o.** the left.
2Ch 4:8 ten tables,...five **o.** the right side,
2Ch 4:8 and five **o.** the left.
2Ch 4:10 he set the sea **o.** the right side of the
2Ch 4:12 were **o.** the top of the two pillars, 5921
2Ch 4:12 which were **o.** the top of the pillars; 5921
2Ch 4:13 pomegranates **o.** the two wreaths;
2Ch 4:13 rows of pomegranates **o.** each wreath,
2Ch 6:10 and am set **o.** the throng of Israel, 5921
2Ch 6:18 deed dwell with men **o.** the earth? 5921
2Ch 7:6 the priests waited **o.** their offices:
2Ch 7:10 **o.** the three and twentieth day of the
2Ch 7:22 of Egypt, and laid hold **o.** other gods,
2Ch 8:12 offerings unto the Lord **o.** the altar 5921
2Ch 8:13 **o.** the sabbaths, and **o.** the new moons,
2Ch 8:13 and **o.** the solemn feasts, three times
2Ch 9:8 in thee to set thee **o.** his throne, 5921
2Ch 9:18 stays **o.** each side of the sitting place,
2Ch 9:19 twelve lions stood there **o.** the one side
2Ch 9:19 and **o.** the other upon the six steps.
2Ch 10:12 came to Rehoboam **o.** the third day,
2Ch 10:12 Come again to me **o.** the third day.
2Ch 11:12 strong, having Judah...**o.** his side
2Ch 14:7 he hath given us rest **o.** every side.
2Ch 14:11 for we rest **o.** thee, and in thy 5921
2Ch 16:7 thou hast relied **o.** the king of Syria, 5921
2Ch 16:7 and not relied **o.** the Lord thy God, 5921
2Ch 16:8 because thou didst rely **o.** the Lord, 5921
2Ch 17:19 These waited **o.** the king, beside
2Ch 18:9 sat either of them **o.** his throne, 5921
2Ch 18:18 **o.** [5921] his right hand and **o.** his left
2Ch 18:24 Behold, thou shalt see **o.** that day
2Ch 18:29 battle; but put thou **o.** thy robes.
2Ch 20:2 from beyond the sea **o.** this side Syria;
2Ch 20:19 of Israel with a loud voice **o.** high.
2Ch 20:26 And **o.** the fourth day they assembled
2Ch 20:29 of God was **o.** all the kingdoms 5921
2Ch 23:4 part of you entering **o.** the sabbath,
2Ch 23:8 that were to come in **o.** the sabbath,
2Ch 23:8 that were to go out **o.** the sabbath:
2Ch 23:15 So they laid hands **o.** her; and when
2Ch 24:25 slew him **o.** his bed, and he died: 5921
2Ch 26:15 **o.** the towers and upon the bulwarks, 5921
2Ch 27:3 **o.** the wall of Ophel he built much.
2Ch 28:4 **o.** the hills, and under every green 5921
2Ch 29:17 began **o.** the first day of the first month
2Ch 29:17 **o.** the eighth day of the month came
2Ch 29:21 offer them **o.** the altar of the Lord. 5921
2Ch 29:22 the blood, and sprinkled it **o.** the altar:
2Ch 30:15 **o.** the fourteenth day of the second
2Ch 32:15 nor persuade you **o.** this manner,
2Ch 32:17 to rail **o.** the Lord God of Israel,
2Ch 32:18 of Jerusalem that were **o.** the wall, 5921
2Ch 32:22 other, and guided them **o.** every side.
2Ch 33:14 **o.** the west side of Gihon, in the valley,
2Ch 34:4 that were **o.** high above them,
2Ch 35:1 **o.** the fourteenth day of the first
2Ch 36:15 **o.** his people, and **o.** his dwelling 5921
Ezr 4:10 the rest that are **o.** this side the river,
Ezr 4:11 the men **o.** this side the river, and
Ezr 4:16 have no portion **o.** this side the river.
Ezr 5:3,6 governor **o.** this side the river, and
Ezr 5:6 which were **o.** this side the river, sent
Ezr 5:8 the walls, and this work goeth fast **o.**,
Ezr 6:13 Tatnai, governor **o.** this side the river,
Ezr 6:15 **o.** the third day of the month Adar, 5705
Ezr 7:9 and **o.** the first day of the fifth month
Ezr 8:31 **o.** the twelfth day of the first month,
Ezr 8:33 Now **o.** the fourth day was the silver
Ezr 8:36 the governors **o.** this side the river:
Ezr 10:9 **o.** the twentieth day of the month;
Ne 2:14 went **o.** to the gate of the fountain, 413
Ne 3:7 of the governor **o.** this side the river.
Ne 3:13 cubits **o.** the wall unto the dung gate.
Ne 4:13 the wall, and **o.** the higher places,
Ne 4:17 They which builded **o.** the wall, and
Ne 4:22 a guard to us, and labour **o.** the day.
Ne 6:14 and **o.** the prophetess Noadiah, and
Ne 8:4 and Maaseiah, **o.** his right hand; 5921
Ne 8:4 and **o.** his left hand, Pedaiah, and
Ne 8:13 And **o.** the second day were gathered
Ne 8:18 and **o.** the eighth day was a solemn
Ne 9:10 Pharaoh, and **o.** all his servants,
Ne 9:10 and **o.** all the people of his land:
Ne 9:11 the midst of the sea **o.** the dry land;
Ne 9:32 that hath come upon us, **o.** our kings.
Ne 9:32 **o.** our princes, and **o.** our priests, and
Ne 9:32 **o.** our prophets, and **o.** our fathers,
Ne 9:32 and **o.** all thy people, since the time
Ne 10:31 victuals **o.** the sabbath day to sell,
Ne 10:31 **o.** the sabbath, or **o.** the hold day:
Ne 12:31 went **o.** the right hand upon the wall
Ne 13:1 **O.** that day they read in the book of
Ne 13:15 treading wine presses **o.** the sabbath,
Ne 13:15 into Jerusalem **o.** the sabbath day;
Ne 13:16 sold **o.** the sabbath unto the children
Ne 13:19 be brought in **o.** the sabbath day.
Ne 13:21 ye do so again, I will lay hands **o.** you.
Ne 13:21 came they no more **o.** the sabbath.
Es 1:2 Ahasuerus sat **o.** the throne of his 5921
Es 1:10 **O.** the seventh day, when the heart of
Es 1:11 beauty: for she was fair to look **o.**
Es 2:14 **o.** the morrow she returned into the
Es 2:21 to lay hand **o.** the king Ahasuerus.
Es 2:23 they were both hanged **o.** a tree: 5921
Es 3:6 scorn to lay hands **o.** Mordecai alone;
Es 3:12 **o.** the thirteenth day of the first
Es 4:1 and put **o.** sackcloth with ashes,
Es 5:1 Now it came to pass **o.** the third day,
Es 5:1 Esther put **o.** her royal apparel,
Es 6:1 **O.** that night could not the king sleep,
Es 6:2 to lay hand **o.** the king Ahasuerus.
Es 6:4 to hang Mordecai **o.** the gallows 5921
Es 6:9 bring him **o.** horseback through
Es 6:11 brought him **o.** horseback through
Es 7:2 said unto Esther **o.** the second day
Es 7:10 hanged Haman **o.** the gallows 5921
Es 8:1 **O.** that day did the king Ahasuerus
Es 8:9 Sivan, **o.** the three and twentieth day
Es 8:10 sent letters by posts **o.** horseback,
Es 8:10 riders **o.** mules, camels, and young
Es 8:13 avenge themselves **o.** their enemies.
Es 8:14 hastened and pressed **o.** by the king's
Es 9:1 **o.** the thirteenth day of the same,
Es 9:2 to lay hand **o.** such as sought their
Es 9:10 **o.** the spoil laid they not their hand.
Es 9:11 **O.** that day the number of those that
Es 9:15 **o.** the fourteenth day also of the
Es 9:15 **o.** the prey they laid not their hand.
Es 9:16 they laid not their hands **o.** the prey.
Es 9:17 **O.** the thirteenth day of the month
Es 9:17 **o.** the fourteenth day of the same.
Es 9:18 together **o.** the thirteenth day thereof.
Es 9:18 and **o.** the fourteenth day thereof;
Es 9:18 and **o.** the fifteenth day of the same.
Es 9:25 should be hanged **o.** the gallows. 5921
Job 1:10 about all that he hath **o.** every side?
Job 4:13 when deep sleep falleth **o.** men, 5921
Job 5:11 set up **o.** high those that be low;
Job 9:11 he passeth **o.** also, but I perceive
Job 13:13 and let come **o.** me what will.
Job 15:26 runneth upon him, even **o.** his neck,
Job 15:27 maketh collops of fat **o.** his flanks.
Job 16:16 and **o.** my eyelids is the shadow of 5921
Job 16:19 heaven, and my record is **o.** high.
Job 17:9 righteous also shall hold **o.** his way,
Job 18:11 shall make him afraid **o.** every side,
Job 19:10 He hath destroyed me **o.** every side,
Job 21:3 and after that I have spoken, mock **o.**
Job 21:6 trembling taketh hold **o.** my flesh.
Job 23:9 **O.** the left hand, where he doth work.
Job 23:9 he hideth himself **o.** the right hand,
Job 24:20 the worm shall feed sweetly **o.** him;
Job 27:17 but the just shall put it **o.**, and the
Job 27:20 Terrors take hold **o.** him as waters,
Job 29:9 and laid their hand **o.** their mouth.
Job 29:14 I put **o.** righteousness, and it
Job 29:24 If I laughed **o.** them, they believed 413
Job 31:2 of the Almighty from **o.** high?
Job 36:2 I have yet to speak **o.** God's behalf.
Job 36:7 with kings are they **o.** the throne;
Job 36:16 which should be set **o.** thy table
Job 36:17 judgment and justice take hold **o.** thee.
Job 37:6 to the snow. Be thou **o.** the earth;
Job 38:26 To cause it to rain **o.** the earth, 5921
Job 38:26 **o.** the wilderness, wherein there
Job 39:18 time she lifteth up herself **o.** high,
Job 39:21 goeth **o.** to meet the armed men.
Job 39:27 command, and make her nest **o.** high?
Job 39:28 She dwelleth and abideth **o.** the rock,
Job 40:12 Look **o.** every one that is proud, and
Ps 4:*title* To the chief Musician **o.** Neginoth,
Ps 6:*title* To the chief Musician **o.** Neginoth
Ps 7:7 therefore return thou **o.** high.
Ps 12:8 The wicked walk **o.** every side, when
Ps 21:3 a crown of pure gold **o.** his head.
Ps 22:8 he trusted **o.** the Lord that he 413
Ps 25:3 that wait **o.** thee be ashamed:
Ps 25:5 **o.** thee do I wait all the day.
Ps 25:21 preserve me; for I wait **o.** thee.
Ps 27:14 Wait **o.** the Lord: be of good
Ps 27:14 heart: wait, I say, **o.** the Lord.
Ps 31:13 fear was **o.** every side: while they took
Ps 35:17 Lord, how long wilt thou look **o.**?
Ps 37:34 Wait **o.** the Lord, and keep his
Ps 48:2 mount Zion, **o.** the sides of the north,
Ps 49:14 the grave; death shall feed **o.** them;
Ps 52:9 and I will wait **o.** thy name; for
Ps 54:*title* To the chief Musician **o.** Neginoth,
Ps 55:*title* To the chief Musician **o.** Neginoth,
Ps 57:4 even among them that are set **o.** fire,
Ps 63:6 meditate **o.** thee in the night watches.
Ps 65:12 the little hills rejoice **o.** every side.
Ps 66:6 went through the flood **o.** foot:
Ps 67:*title* To the chief Musician **o.** Neginoth,
Ps 68:18 Thou hast ascended **o.** high, thou
Ps 68:21 one as goeth **o.** still in his trespasses,
Ps 68:25 the players **o.** instruments followed
Ps 69:6 Let not them that wait **o.** thee, O
Ps 69:29 salvation, O God, set me up **o.** high.
Ps 71:21 and comfort me **o.** every side.
Ps 75:5 Lift not up your horn **o.** high:
Ps 76:*title* To the chief Musician **o.** Neginoth,
Ps 78:53 And he led them **o.** safely so that
Ps 79:1 they have laid Jerusalem **o.** heaps.
Ps 81:3 appointed, **o.** our solemn feast day.
Ps 82:5 they walk **o.** in darkness: all the
Ps 83:14 the flame setteth the mountains **o.** fire;
Ps 87:7 players **o.** instruments shall be there:
Ps 91:14 I will set him **o.** high, because he hath
Ps 92:11 shall see my desire **o.** mine enemies,
Ps 93:4 The Lord **o.** high is mightier than
Ps 104:32 He looketh **o.** the earth, and it
Ps 107:41 Yet setteth he the poor **o.** high from
Ps 113:5 Lord our God, who dwelleth **o.** high,
Ps 118:6 The Lord is **o.** my side; I will not fear:
Ps 119:59 I thought **o.** my ways, and turned my
Ps 119:84 thou execute judgment **o.** them that
Ps 119:143 and anguish have taken hold **o.** me:
Ps 124:1,2 been the Lord who was **o.** our side,
Ps 142:4 I looked **o.** my right hand, and beheld,
Ps 143:5 I meditate **o.** all thy works;
Ps 143:5 I muse **o.** the work of thy hands.
Pr 4:25 Let thine eyes look right **o.**, and let
Pr 5:5 to death; her steps take hold **o.** hell.
Pr 9:14 **o.** a seat in the high places of the 5921
Pr 9:15 who go right **o.** their ways:
Pr 14:21 he that hath mercy **o.** the poor, happy
Pr 14:31 honoureth him hath mercy **o.** the poor.
Pr 15:14 mouth of fools feedeth **o.** foolishness.
Pr 20:22 but wait **o.** the Lord, and he shall
Pr 22:3 simple pass **o.**, and are punished.
Pr 27:12 simple pass **o.**, and are punished.
Pr 27:18 he that waiteth **o.** his master
Ec 2:3 and to lay hold **o.** folly, till I might see
Ec 2:11 I looked **o.** all the works that my hands
Ec 2:11 **o.** the labour that I had laboured to do:
Ec 4:1 **o.** the side of their oppressors there
Ca 2:12 The flowers appear **o.** the earth; the
Ca 3:1 By night **o.** my bed I sought him 5921
Ca 5:3 off my coat; how shall I put it **o.**?
Isa 7:25 **o.** all hills that shall be digged with
Isa 9:17 have mercy **o.** their fatherless and
Isa 9:20 he shall snatch **o.** the right hand, 5921
Isa 9:20 and he shall eat **o.** the left hand, 5921
Isa 10:12 upon mount Zion and **o.** Jerusalem,
Isa 11:8 shall play **o.** the hole of the asp, 5921
Isa 11:8 put his hand **o.** the cockatrice' den. 5921
Isa 13:18 have no pity **o.** the fruit of the womb;
Isa 14:1 the Lord will have mercy **o.** Jacob,
Isa 15:2 **o.** all their heads shall be baldness,
Isa 15:3 **o.** the tops of their houses, and in 5921
Isa 16:12 Moab is weary **o.** the high place, 5921

Isa 18:3 the world, and dwellers **o.** the earth,
Isa 18:3 lifteth up an ensign **o.** the mountains;
Isa 22:16 him out a sepulchre **o.** high,
Isa 24:18 the windows from **o.** high are open,
Isa 24:21 of the high ones that are **o.** high,
Isa 25:6 fat things, a feast of wine **o.** the lees,
Isa 25:6 of wines **o.** the lees well refined
Isa 26:3 peace, whose mind is stayed **o.** thee:
Isa 26:5 down them that dwell **o.** high; 4791
Isa 27:11 the women come, and set them **o.** fire;
Isa 27:11 them will not have mercy **o.** them,
Isa 28:1 are **o.** the head of the fat valleys of
Isa 28:4 is **o.** the head of the fat valley, 5921
Isa 28:20 that a man can stretch himself **o.** it:
Isa 30:17 and as an ensign **o.** an hill 5921
Isa 31:1 and stay **o.** horses, and trust in 5921
Isa 31:4 the young lion roaring **o.** his prey, 5921
Isa 32:15 be poured upon us from **o.** high,
Isa 32:19 shall hail, coming down **o.** the forest;
Isa 33:5 exalted; for he dwelleth **o.** high:
Isa 33:16 He shall dwell **o.** high; his place of
Isa 36:5 now **o.** whom dost thou trust, that 5921
Isa 36:6 of this broken reed, **o.** Egypt; 5921
Isa 36:8 be able **o.** thy part to set riders upon
Isa 36:9 put thy trust **o.** Egypt for chariots 5921
Isa 36:11 of the people that are **o.** the wall. 5921
Isa 37:23 and lifted up thine eyes **o.** high?
Isa 37:27 as the grass **o.** the housetops, and as
Isa 40:26 Lift up your eyes **o.** high, and
Isa 42:25 it hath set him **o.** fire round about,
Isa 44:20 He feedeth **o.** ashes; a deceived heart
Isa 47:1 of Babylon, sit **o.** the ground: 5921
Isa 48:14 he will do his pleasure **o.** Babylon, and
Isa 48:14 and his arm shall be **o.** the Chaldeans
Isa 49:10 hath mercy **o.** them shall lead them,
Isa 49:15 compassion **o.** the son of her womb?
Isa 49:18 bind them **o.** thee, as a bride doeth.
Isa 51:5 and **o.** mine arm shall they trust. 413
Isa 51:9 put **o.** strength, O arm of the Lord;
Isa 52:1 awake; put **o.** thy strength, O Zion;
Isa 52:1 put **o.** thy beautiful garments, O
Isa 53:6 hath laid **o.** him the iniquity of us all
Isa 54:3 forth **o.** the right hand and **o.** the left;
Isa 54:8 kindness will I have mercy **o.** thee,
Isa 54:10 the Lord that hath mercy **o.** thee.
Isa 56:2 the son of man that layeth hold **o.** it;
Isa 57:17 he went **o.** frowardly in the way
Isa 58:4 your voice to be heard **o.** high.
Isa 58:13 doing thy pleasure **o.** my holy day;
Isa 59:17 For he put **o.** righteousness as a
Isa 59:17 put **o.** the garments of vengeance
Isa 60:7 up with acceptance **o.** mine altar, 5921
Isa 60:10 in my favour have I had mercy **o.** thee.
Isa 63:7 all that the Lord hath bestowed **o.** us,
Isa 63:7 which he hath bestowed **o.** them
Jer 4:7 destroyer of the Gentiles is **o.** his way;
Jer 5:9,29 soul be avenged **o.** such a nation
Jer 6:23 They shall lay hold **o.** bow and spear;
Jer 6:25 of the enemy and fear is **o.** every side.
Jer 7:29 up a lamentation **o.** high places; 5921
Jer 8:13 there shall be no grapes **o.** the vine,
Jer 8:13 nor figs **o.** the fig tree, and the leaf
Jer 8:21 astonishment hath taken hold **o.** me.
Jer 9:9 my soul be avenged **o.** such a nation
Jer 10:25 the families that call not **o.** thy name:
Jer 11:20 let me see thy vengeance **o.** them: for
Jer 12:15 and have compassion **o.** them, and will
Jer 13:2 girdle...and put it **o.** my loins. 5921
Jer 13:27 thine abominations **o.** the hills in 5921
Jer 15:10 I have neither lent **o.** usury, nor men
Jer 15:10 nor men have lent to me **o.** usury; yet
Jer 17:11 As the partridge sitteth **o.** eggs, and
Jer 17:21 bear no burden **o.** the sabbath day,
Jer 17:22 out of your houses **o.** the sabbath day,
Jer 17:24 gates of this city **o.** the sabbath day,
Jer 17:25 riding in chariots and **o.** horses, they
Jer 17:27 gates of Jerusalem **o.** the sabbath day;
Jer 18:3 he wrought a work **o.** the wheels. 5921
Jer 20:3 And it came to pass **o.** the morrow,
Jer 20:10 defaming of many, fear **o.** every side.
Jer 20:10 and we shall take our revenge **o.** him.
Jer 20:12 let me see thy vengeance **o.** them:
Jer 22:4 riding in chariots and **o.** horses, he,
Jer 23:12 they shall be driven **o.**, and fall
Jer 25:29 to bring evil **o.** the city which is called
Jer 25:30 The Lord shall roar from **o.** high,

Jer 30:6 man with his hands **o.** his loins, 5921
Jer 30:18 and have mercy **o.** his dwellingplaces;
Jer 31:29 children's teeth are set **o.** edge.
Jer 31:30 grape, his teeth shall be set **o.** edge.
Jer 32:29 shall come and set fire **o.** this city,
Jer 33:26 to return, and have mercy **o.** them.
Jer 36:22 there was a fire **o.** the hearth burning
Jer 36:23 into the fire that was **o.** the hearth, 413
Jer 36:23 in the fire that was **o.** the hearth. 5921
Jer 38:22 Thy friends have set thee **o.**, and
Jer 43:3 of Neriah setteth thee **o.** against us,
Jer 43:12 as a shepherd putteth **o.** his garment;
Jer 46:4 spears, and put **o.** the brigandines.
Jer 48:11 and he hath settled **o.** his lees, and 413
Jer 49:23 there is sorrow **o.** the sea; it cannot be
Jer 49:24 flee, and fear hath seized **o.** her:
Jer 49:29 cry unto them, Fear is **o.** every side
Jer 50:6 turned them away **o.** the mountains:
Jer 50:19 he shall feed **o.** Carmel and Bashan,
Jer 52:23 and six pomegranates **o.** a side;
La 1:2 and her tears are **o.** her cheeks: 5921
La 2:21 young and the old lie **o.** the ground in
La 4:6 moment, and no hands stayed **o.** her
Eze 1:8 their wings **o.** their four sides; 5921
Eze 1:10 the face of a lion, **o.** the right side: 413
Eze 1:10 had the face of an ox **o.** the left side;
Eze 1:23 two, which covered **o.** this side,
Eze 1:23 two, which covered **o.** that side,
Eze 3:23 of Chebar: and I fell **o.** my face. 5921
Eze 4:6 lie again **o.** thy right side, and thou 5921
Eze 7:16 and shall be **o.** the mountains like 413
Eze 10:3 cherubims stood **o.** the right side of
Eze 11:23 which is **o.** the east side of the city.
Eze 16:11 thy hands and a chain **o.** thy neck. 5921
Eze 16:12 I put a jewel **o.** thy forehead, and 5921
Eze 16:15 fornications **o.** every one that passed
Eze 16:33 they may come unto thee **o.** every side
Eze 18:2 children's teeth are set **o.** edge?
Eze 19:8 nations set against him **o.** every side
Eze 21:16 **o.** the right hand, or **o.** the left,
Eze 23:5 doted **o.** her lovers, **o.** the Assyrians 413
Eze 23:7 and with all **o.** whom she doted:
Eze 23:22 bring them against thee **o.** every side;
Eze 24:3 Set **o.** a pot, set it **o.**, and also pour
Eze 24:10 Heap **o.** wood, kindle the fire, consume
Eze 24:17 put **o.** thy shoes upon thy feet, and
Eze 25:9 his cities which are **o.** his frontiers,
Eze 26:17 their terror to be **o.** all that haunt it!
Eze 28:23 by the sword upon her **o.** every side;
Eze 31:4 the deep set him **o.** high with her rivers
Eze 33:32 and can play well **o.** an instrument:
Eze 36:3 and swallowed you up **o.** every side,
Eze 37:21 and will gather them **o.** every side,
Eze 39:6 I will send a fire **o.** Magog, and among
Eze 39:9 shall set **o.** fire and burn the weapons,
Eze 39:11 the passengers **o.** the east of the sea:
Eze 39:17 gather yourselves **o.** every side to my
Eze 40:2 was as the frame of a city **o.** the south.
Eze 40:5 a wall **o.** the outside of the house
Eze 40:10 three **o.** this side, and three **o.** that
Eze 40:10 measure **o.** this side and **o.** that side.
Eze 40:12 was one cubit **o.** this side, and the
Eze 40:12 space was one cubit **o.** that side:
Eze 40:12 chambers were six cubits **o.** this side,
Eze 40:12 and six cubits **o.** that side.
Eze 40:21 three **o.** this side and three **o.** that side;
Eze 40:26 it had palm trees, one **o.** this side,
Eze 40:26 and another **o.** that side, upon the
Eze 40:34, 37 **o.** this side, and **o.** that side:
Eze 40:39 the gate were two tables **o.** this side,
Eze 40:39 and two tables **o.** that side, to slay
Eze 40:40 **o.** the other side, which was at the 413
Eze 40:41 Four tables were **o.** this side, and four
Eze 40:41 tables **o.** that side, by the side of the
Eze 40:48 of the porch, five cubits **o.** this side,
Eze 40:48 and five cubits **o.** that side:
Eze 40:48 the gate was three cubits **o.** this side,
Eze 40:48 and three cubits **o.** that side.
Eze 40:49 pillars by the posts, one **o.** this side,
Eze 40:49 and another **o.** that side.
Eze 41:1 post, six cubits broad **o.** the one side,
Eze 41:1 and six cubits broad **o.** the other side,
Eze 41:2 door were five cubits **o.** the one side,
Eze 41:2 and five cubits **o.** the other side: and
Eze 41:5, 10 round about the house **o.** every side.
Eze 41:15 **o.** the one side and **o.** the other side,
Eze 41:16 round about **o.** their three stories,

Eze 41:19 toward the palm tree **o.** the one side,
Eze 41:19 toward the palm tree **o.** the other side:
Eze 41:20 made, and **o.** the wall of the temple.
Eze 41:25 **o.** them, **o.** the doors of the temple, 413
Eze 41:26 **o.** the one side and **o.** the other side,
Eze 41:26 **o.** the sides of the porch, and upon 413
Eze 42:7 court **o.** the forepart of the chambers,
Eze 42:9 was the entry **o.** the east side, as one
Eze 42:14 and shall put **o.** other garments,
Eze 43:20 and put it **o.** the four horns of it, 5921
Eze 43:20 and **o.** the four corners of the settle, 413
Eze 43:22 **o.** the second day thou shalt offer a kid
Eze 44:19 they shall put **o.** other garments;
Eze 45:7 **o.** the one side and **o.** the other side of
Eze 46:1 but **o.** the sabbath it shall be opened,
Eze 46:12 offerings, as he did **o.** the sabbath day:
Eze 46:19 was a place **o.** the two sides westward
Eze 47:2 there ran out waters **o.** the right side.
Eze 47:2 trees **o.** the one side and **o.** the other.
Eze 47:12 **o.** this side and **o.** that side, shall
Eze 48:16 **o.** the east side four thousand and
Eze 48:21 **o.** the one side and **o.** the other of the
Eze 48:30 goings out of the city **o.** the north side,
Da 3:27 the smell of fire had passed **o.** them.
Da 6:14 set his heart **o.** Daniel to deliver 5922
Da 7:5 it raised up itself **o.** one side, and it
Da 8:5 west **o.** the face of the whole earth,
Da 8:18 I was in a deep sleep **o.** my face 5921
Da 10:9 was I in a deep sleep **o.** my face, and 5921
Da 11:17 she shall not stand **o.** his side, neither
Da 11:31 And arms shall stand **o.** his part, and
Da 12:5 one **o.** this side of the bank of the
Da 12:5 **o.** that side of the bank of the river.
Ho 4:8 set their heart **o.** their iniquity. 413
Ho 5:1 ye have been a snare **o.** Mizpah, and
Ho 6:3 if we follow **o.** to know the Lord:
Ho 10:5 priest thereof that rejoiced **o.** it, 5921
Ho 10:8 thistle shall come up **o.** their altars: 5921
Ho 10:8 Cover us; and to the hills, Fall **o.** us 5921
Ho 11:4 that take off the yoke **o.** their jaws, 5921
Ho 11:6 the sword shall abide **o.** his cities,
Ho 12:1 Ephraim feedeth **o.** wind, and
Ho 12:6 and wait **o.** thy God continually.
Joe 2:5 chariots **o.** the tops of mountains 5921
Joe 2:7 shall march every one **o.** his ways,
Joe 2:32 shall call **o.** the name of the Lord
Am 1:7 I will send a fire **o.** the wall of Gaza,
Am 1:10 I will send a fire **o.** the wall of Tyrus,
Am 2:7 of the earth **o.** the head of the poor,
Am 5:19 leaned his hand **o.** the wall, and a 5921
Ob 11 that thou stoodest **o.** the other side,
Ob 12 have looked **o.** the day of thy brother
Ob 13 not have looked **o.** their affliction
Ob 13 have laid hands **o.** their substance
Ob 21 saviours shall come up **o.** mount Zion
Jon 3:5 put **o.** sackcloth, from the greatest
Jon 4:5 and sat **o.** the east side of the city, and
Jon 4:10 Thou hast had pity **o.** the gourd, 5921
Mic 2:13 and the Lord **o.** the head of them.
Na 1:2 will take vengeance **o.** his adversaries,
Hab 1:13 evil, and canst not look **o.** iniquity: 413
Hab 2:9 that he may set his nest **o.** high,
Hab 2:15 mayest look **o.** their nakedness! 5921
Hab 2:16 spewing shall be **o.** thy glory. 5921
Hab 3:10 and lifted up his hands **o.** high.
Hab 3:19 singer **o.** my stringed instruments.
Zep 1:9 those that leap **o.** the threshold, 5921
Zep 1:12 men that are settled **o.** their lees: 5921
Zec 1:12 thou not have mercy **o.** Jerusalem
Zec 1:12 and **o.** the cities of Judah,
Zec 5:3 cut off as **o.** this side according to it;
Zec 5:3 cut off as **o.** that side according to it.
Zec 10:5 riders **o.** horses shall be confounded.
Zec 12:6 **o.** the right hand and **o.** the left: 5921
Zec 13:9 they shall call **o.** my name, and I will
Zec 14:4 which is before Jerusalem **o.** the east,
Zec 14:13 every one **o.** the hand of his neighbour,
Mal 1:10 kindle fire **o.** mine altar for nought
Mt 1:18 of Jesus Christ was **o.** this wise: *3779*
Mt 1:20 while he thought **o.** these things, *1760*
Mt 4:5 him **o.** a pinnacle of the temple, *1909*
Mt 4:21 And going **o.** from thence, he saw
Mt 5:14 **A city that is set o. an hill cannot** *1883*
Mt 5:15 **a bushel, but o. a candlestick;** *1909*
Mt 5:28 **whosoever looketh o. a woman to**
Mt 5:39 **shall smite thee o. thy right cheek,** *1909*
Mt 5:45 **to rise o. the evil and...the good,** *1909*

Mt 5:45 evil and o. the good, and sendeth
Mt 5:45 rain o. the just and...the unjust. 1909
Mt 5:45 the just and o. the unjust.
Mt 6:25 your body, what ye shall put o. 1746
Mt 9:2 sick of the palsy, lying o. a bed: 1909
Mt 9:6 hath power o. earth to forgive sins, 1909
Mt 9:27 Thou son of David, have mercy o. us
Mt 9:36 moved with compassion o. them, 4012
Mt 10:29 them shall not fall o. the ground 1909
Mt 10:34 I am come to send peace o. earth: 1909
Mt 12:1 that time Jesus went o. the sabbath
Mt 12:5 that o. the sabbath days the priests
Mt 12:10 it lawful to heal o. the sabbath days?
Mt 12:11 if it fall into a pit o. the sabbath day,
Mt 12:11 will he not lay hold o. it, and lift it
Mt 12:12 lawful to do well o. the sabbath days
Mt 13:2 whole multitude stood o. the shore, 1909
Mt 14:3 For Herod had laid hold o. John,
Mt 14:13 followed him o. foot out of...cities. 3979
Mt 14:19 multitude to set down o. the grass, 1909
Mt 14:25 went unto them, walking o. the sea. 1909
Mt 14:26 disciples saw him walking o. the sea, 1909
Mt 14:28 bid me come unto thee o. the water. 1909
Mt 14:29 walked o. the water, to go to Jesus. 1909
Mt 15:22 Have mercy o. me, O Lord, thou son
Mt 15:32 have compassion o. the multitude, 1909
Mt 15:35 multitude to set down o. the ground. 1909
Mt 16:19 whatsoever thou shalt bind o. 1909
Mt 16:19 whatsoever thou shall loose o. 1909
Mt 17:6 they fell o. their face, and were sore 1909
Mt 17:15 Lord, have mercy o. my son: for he is
Mt 18:18 Whatsoever ye shall bind o. earth, 1909
Mt 18:18 whatsoever ye shall loose o. earth, 1909
Mt 18:19 if two of you shall agree o. earth 1909
Mt 18:28 and he laid hands o. him, and took
Mt 18:33 had compassion o. thy fellow servant,
Mt 18:33 even as I had pity o. thee?
Mt 19:13 he should put his hands o. them, 2007
Mt 19:15 And he laid his hands o. them, and 2007
Mt 20:21 sit, the one o. thy right hand, 1537
Mt 20:21 and the other o. the left, in thy 1537
Mt 20:23 sit o. my right hand, and o. my 1537
Mt 20:30, 31 Have mercy o. us, O Lord, thou
Mt 20:34 So Jesus had compassion o. them, and
Mt 21:7 and put o. them their clothes, and 1883
Mt 21:19 fruit grow o. thee henceforward 1537
Mt 21:38 and let us seize o. his inheritance.
Mt 21:44 whosoever shall fall o. this stone 1909
Mt 21:44 o. whomsoever it shall fall, it will. 1909
Mt 21:46 when they sought to lay hands o. him,
Mt 22:11 had not o. a wedding garment: 1746
Mt 22:40 O. these two commandments hang 1722
Mt 22:44 Sit thou o. my right hand, till I 1537
Mt 23:4 and lay them o. men's shoulders; 1909
Mt 24:17 is o. the housetop not come down 1909
Mt 24:20 winter, neither o. the sabbath day 1722
Mt 25:33 set the sheep o. his right hand, 1537
Mt 25:33 right hand, but the goats o. the 1537
Mt 25:34 say unto them o. his right hand, 1537
Mt 25:41 also unto them o. the left hand, 1537
Mt 26:5 Not o. the feast day, lest there be 1722
Mt 26:7 poured it o. his head, as he sat at 1909
Mt 26:12 poured this ointment o. my body, 1909
Mt 26:39 and fell o. his face, and prayed, 1909
Mt 26:45 Sleep o. now, and take your rest:
Mt 26:50 they, and laid hands o. Jesus, 1909
Mt 26:55 the temple, and ye laid no hold o. me
Mt 26:57 they that had laid hold o. Jesus led
Mt 26:64 sitting o. the right hand of power, 1537
Mt 27:19 was set down o. the judgment seat, 1909
Mt 27:25 blood be o. us, and o. our children. 1909
Mt 27:28 him, and put o. him a scarlet robe. 4060
Mt 27:30 reed, and smote him o. the head 1519
Mt 27:31 and put his own raiment o. him, 1746
Mt 27:38 with him, one o. the right hand, 1537
Mt 27:38 right hand, and another o. the left. 1537
Mt 27:48 vinegar, and put it o. a reed, and 4060
Mk 1:21 o. the sabbath day he entered into
Mk 2:10 hath power o. earth to forgive sins, 1909
Mk 2:12 We never saw it o. this fashion.
Mk 2:21 of new cloth o. an old garment: 1909
Mk 2:23 the corn fields o. the sabbath day; 1722
Mk 2:24 why do they o. the sabbath day that 1722
Mk 3:2 would heal him o. the sabbath day;
Mk 3:4 lawful to do good o. the sabbath days,
Mk 3:5 had looked round about o. them with
Mk 3:9 that a small ship should wait o. him 4342
Mk 3:21 of it, they went out to lay hold o. him:
Mk 3:34 looked round about o. them which sat
Mk 4:1 was by the sea o. the land. 1909
Mk 4:5 And some fell o. stony ground, 1909
Mk 4:8 And other fell o. good ground, 1519
Mk 4:16 which are sown o. stony ground; 1909
Mk 4:20 which are sown o. good ground; 1909
Mk 4:21 and not to be set o. a candlestick? 1909
Mk 4:38 part of the ship, asleep o. a pillow: 1909
Mk 5:19 and hath had compassion o. thee.
Mk 5:23 thee, come and lay thy hands o. her, 2007
Mk 6:9 sandals; and not put o. two coats. 1746
Mk 6:21 Herod o. his birthday made a supper
Mk 6:47 the sea, and he alone o. the land. 1909
Mk 8:2 have compassion o. the multitude, 1909
Mk 8:6 people to sit down o. the ground: 1909
Mk 8:23 when he had spit o. his eyes, and 1519
Mk 8:33 about and looked o. his disciples,
Mk 9:3 no fuller o. earth can white them. 1909
Mk 9:20 he fell o. the ground, and wallowed 1909
Mk 9:22 have compassion o. us, and help us. 1909
Mk 9:40 is not against us is o. our part. 5228
Mk 10:37 we may sit, one o. thy right hand, 1537
Mk 10:37 other o. thy left hand, in thy glory. 1537
Mk 10:40 But to set o. my right hand and 1537
Mk 10:40 o. my left hand is not mine to 1537
Mk 10:47 thou son of David, have mercy o. me.
Mk 10:48 Thou son of David, have mercy o. me.
Mk 11:7 and cast their garments o. him; 1911
Mk 11:12 o. the morrow, when they were come
Mk 12:12 And they sought to lay hold o. him,
Mk 12:36 Sit thou o. my right hand, till I 1537
Mk 13:15 that is o. the housetop not go 1909
Mk 14:2 Not o. the feast day, lest there be 1722
Mk 14:3 box, and poured it o. his head. 2596
Mk 14:6 hath wrought a good work o. me 1722
Mk 14:35 and fell o. the ground, and prayed 1909
Mk 14:41 Sleep o. now, and take your rest:
Mk 14:46 they laid their hands o. him, and 1909
Mk 14:51 and the young men laid hold o. him:
Mk 14:62 sitting o. the right hand of power, 1537
Mk 14:65 And some began to spit o. him, and 1716
Mk 15:19 they smote him o. the head with a reed,
Mk 15:20 and put his own clothes o. him, and 1746
Mk 15:27 thieves; the one o. his right hand, 1537
Mk 15:27 hand, and the other o. his left. 1537
Mk 15:29 that passed by railed o. him, wagging
Mk 15:36 of vinegar, and put it o. a reed, and 4060
Mk 15:40 were also women looking o. afar off:
Mk 16:5 young man sitting o. the right side, 1722
Mk 16:18 they shall lay hands o. the sick, 1909
Mk 16:19 and sat o. the right hand of God. 1537
Lu 1:11 standing o. the right side of the altar 1537
Lu 1:25 the days wherein he looked o. me, 1896
Lu 1:50 his mercy is o. them that fear him.
Lu 1:59 o. the eighth day they came to 1722
Lu 1:65 fear came o. all that dwelt round 1909
Lu 1:78 the dayspring from o. high hath visited
Lu 2:14 o. earth peace, good will toward 1909
Lu 4:9 set him o. a pinnacle of the temple, 1909
Lu 4:16 the synagogue o. the sabbath day, 1722
Lu 4:20 the synagogue were fastened o. him.
Lu 4:31 taught them o. the sabbath days. 1722
Lu 4:40 and he laid his hands o. every one 2007
Lu 5:12 who seeing Jesus fell o. his face, 1909
Lu 5:17 it came to pass o. a certain day, 1722
Lu 6:1 came to pass o. the second sabbath 1722
Lu 6:2 lawful to do o. the sabbath days? 1722
Lu 6:6 to pass also o. another sabbath, 1722
Lu 6:7 he would heal o. the sabbath day; 1722
Lu 6:9 lawful o. the sabbath days to do good,
Lu 6:20 lifted up his eyes o. his disciples, 1519
Lu 6:29 him smiteth thee o. the one cheek 1909
Lu 6:48 and laid the foundation o. a rock: 1909
Lu 7:13 saw her, he had compassion o. her, 1909
Lu 7:16 And there came a fear o. all: and they
Lu 7:40 thee. And he saith, Master, say o.
Lu 8:8 And other fell o. good ground, and 1519
Lu 8:13 They o. the rock are they, which, 1909
Lu 8:15 that o. the good ground are they, 1722
Lu 8:16 but setteth it o. a candlestick, 1909
Lu 8:22 it came to pass o. a certain day, 1722
Lu 8:23 down a storm of wind o. the lake; 1519
Lu 8:32 swine feeding o. the mountain: 1722
Lu 9:37 came to pass, that o. the next day, 1722
Lu 10:11 which cleaveth o. us, we do wipe off
Lu 10:19 tread o. serpents and scorpions, 1883
Lu 10:31 him, he passed by o. the other side.
Lu 10:32 at the place, came and looked o. him,
Lu 10:32 and passed by o. the other side.
Lu 10:33 saw him, he had compassion o. him,
Lu 10:34 and set him o. his own beast, and 1909
Lu 10:35 o. the morrow when he departed, 1909
Lu 10:37 He that shewed mercy o. him. 3326
Lu 11:33 a bushel, but o. a candlestick, 1909
Lu 12:22 for the body, what ye shall put o., 1746
Lu 12:49 am come to send fire o. the earth; 1519
Lu 12:51 I am come to give peace o. earth? 1722
Lu 13:7 come seeking fruit o. this fig tree, 1722
Lu 13:10 of the synagogues o. the sabbath. 1722
Lu 13:13 And he laid his hands o. her: and 2007
Lu 13:14 that Jesus had healed o. the sabbath
Lu 13:14 be healed, and not o. the sabbath day.
Lu 13:15 o. the sabbath loose his ox or his ass
Lu 13:16 from this bond o. the sabbath day?
Lu 14:1 Pharisees to eat bread o. the sabbath.
Lu 14:3 Is it lawful to heal o. the sabbath day?
Lu 14:5 pull him out o. the sabbath day? 1722
Lu 15:5 he layeth it o. his shoulders, 1909
Lu 15:20 fell o. his neck, and kissed him. 1909
Lu 15:22 the best robe, and put it o. him: 1746
Lu 15:22 o. his hand, and shoes o. his feet: 1519
Lu 16:24 Father Abraham, have mercy o. me,
Lu 17:13 said, Jesus, Master, have mercy o. us.
Lu 17:16 fell down o. his face at his feet, 1909
Lu 18:8 shall he find faith o. the earth? 1909
Lu 18:32 spitefully entreated,...spitted o.: 1716
Lu 18:38 thou son of David, have mercy o. me.
Lu 18:39 Thou Son of David, have mercy o. me.
Lu 19:43 and keep thee in o. every side, 3840
Lu 20:1 to pass, that o. one of those days, 1722
Lu 20:18 o. whomsoever it shall fall, it will. 1909
Lu 20:19 hour sought to lay hands o. him; 1909
Lu 20:42 Lord, Sit thou o. my right hand, 1537
Lu 21:12 they shall lay their hands o. you, 1909
Lu 21:26 which are coming o. the earth. 1904
Lu 21:35 as a snare shall it come o. all them 1909
Lu 21:35 dwell o. the face of the whole 1909
Lu 22:21 betrayeth me is with me o. the 1909
Lu 22:30 o. thrones judging the twelve 1909
Lu 22:64 they struck him o. the face, and
Lu 22:69 sit o. the right hand of the power 1537
Lu 23:26 and o. him they laid the cross, that 2007
Lu 23:30 say to the mountains, Fall o. us; 1909
Lu 23:33 malefactors, one o. the right hand, 1537
Lu 23:33 right hand, and the other o. the left, 1537
Lu 23:39 which were hanged railed o. him,
Lu 23:54 preparation,...the sabbath drew o. 2020
Lu 24:49 be endued with power from o. high.
Joh 1:12 to them that believe o. his name: 1519
Joh 1:33 descending, and remaining o. him, 1909
Joh 2:11 and his disciples believed o. him. 1519
Joh 3:18 believeth o. him is not condemned: 1519
Joh 3:36 believeth o. the Son hath everlasting 1519
Joh 3:36 the wrath of God abideth o. him. 1909
Joh 4:6 his journey, sat thus o. the well: 1909
Joh 4:35 up your eyes, and look o. the fields;
Joh 4:39 the Samaritans...believed o. him. 1519
Joh 5:9 o. the same day was the sabbath. 1722
Joh 5:16 these things o. the sabbath day. 1722
Joh 5:24 and believeth o. him that sent me,
Joh 6:2 he did o. them that were diseased. 1909
Joh 6:19 they see Jesus walking o. the sea, 1909
Joh 6:22 which stood o. the other side of the sea
Joh 6:25 found him o. the other side of the sea,
Joh 6:29 believe o. him whom he hath sent. 1519
Joh 6:35 believeth o. me shall never thirst. 1519
Joh 6:40 the Son, and believeth o. him, 1519
Joh 6:47 believeth o. me hath everlasting 1519
Joh 7:22 ye o. the sabbath day circumcise 1722
Joh 7:23 a man o. the sabbath day receive 1722
Joh 7:23 whit whole o. the sabbath day? 1722
Joh 7:30 but no man laid hands o. him, 1909
Joh 7:31 of the people believed on him, 1519
Joh 7:38 He that believeth o. me, as the 1519
Joh 7:39 that believe o. him should receive: 1519
Joh 7:44 but no man laid hands o. him. 1909
Joh 7:48 of the Pharisees believed o. him? 1519
Joh 8:6 with his finger wrote o. the ground, 1519
Joh 8:8 down, and wrote o. the ground. 1519
Joh 8:20 and no man laid hands o. him; for his

Joh 8:30 these words, many believed o. him..... 1519
Joh 8:31 to those Jews which believed o. him, ...
Joh 9:6 spat o. the ground, and made clay...... 5476
Joh 9:35 **thou believe o. the Son of God?**..... 1519
Joh 9:36 Lord, that I might believe o. him?...... 1519
Joh 10:42 And many believed o. him there......... 1519
Joh 11:45 which Jesus did, believed o. him. 1519
Joh 11:48 alone, all men will believe o. him:....... 1519
Joh 12:11 went away, and believed o. Jesus....... 1519
Joh 12:12 O. the next day much people that............
Joh 12:15 cometh, sitting o. an ass's colt.......... 1909
Joh 12:37 them, yet they believed not o. him: 1519
Joh 12:42 rulers also many believed o. him; 1519
Joh 12:44 and said, **He that believeth o. me,**... 1519
Joh 12:44 **believeth not o. me, but o. him**....... 1519
Joh 12:46 **believeth o. me should not abide in** 1519
Joh 13:22 the disciples looked one o. another, ... 1519
Joh 13:23 leaning o. Jesus' bosom one of his...... 1722
Joh 13:25 he then lying o. Jesus' breast 1909
Joh 14:12 **He that believeth o. me, the works.** 1519
Joh 16:9 **sin, because they believe not o. me;** 1519
Joh 17:4 **I have glorified thee o. the earth;**.. 1909
Joh 17:20 **believe o. me through their word;**.. 1519
Joh 19:2 of thorns, and put it o. his head,........ 2007
Joh 19:2 and they put o. him a purple robe, ... 4016
Joh 19:18 other with him, o. either side one, ... 1782
Joh 19:19 a title, and put it o. the cross........... 1909
Joh 19:31 upon the cross o. the sabbath day, ... 1722
Joh 19:37 look o. him whom they pierced.......... 1519
Joh 20:22 had said this, he breathed o. them,...... 1720
Joh 21:1 and o. this wise shewed he himself..........
Joh 21:4 come, Jesus stood o. the shore:......... 1519
Joh 21:6 **net o. the right side of the ship,**.... 1519
Joh 21:20 also leaned o. his breast at supper,..... 1909
Ac 2:18 And o. my servants and 1909
Ac 2:18 o. my handmaidens I will pour........... 1909
Ac 2:21 shall call o. the name of the Lord....... 1941
Ac 2:25 for he is o. my right hand, that I 1537
Ac 2:30 up Christ to sit o. his throne;............ 1909
Ac 2:34 Lord, Sit thou o. my right hand, ... 1537
Ac 3:4 him with John, said, Look o. us. 1519
Ac 3:12 or why look ye so earnestly o. us, ... 1909
Ac 4:3 they laid hands o. them, and put ....
Ac 4:5 And it came to pass o. the morrow, ... 1909
Ac 4:22 o. whom this miracle of healing.......... 1909
Ac 5:5 great fear came o. all them that......... 1909
Ac 5:15 and laid them o. beds and couches,..... 1909
Ac 5:18 laid their hands o. the apostles, ... 1909
Ac 5:30 whom ye slew and hanged o. a tree.... 1909
Ac 6:6 prayed, they laid...hands o. them. 2007
Ac 6:15 council, looking stedfastly o. him, ... 1519
Ac 7:5 no, not so much as to set his foot o.: ....
Ac 7:6 And God spake o. this wise, That his........
Ac 7:54 gnashed o. him with their teeth. 1909
Ac 7:55 standing o. the right hand of God, ... 1537
Ac 7:56 standing o. the right hand of God. 1537
Ac 8:17 laid they their hands o. them,............ 1909
Ac 8:18 laying o. the apostles' hands.............. 1936
Ac 8:19 o. whomsoever I lay hands, he may.... 2007
Ac 8:36 And as they went o. their way, ... 2596
Ac 8:39 and he went o. his way rejoicing..............
Ac 9:12 **putting his hand o. him, that he**... 2007
Ac 9:14 to bind all that call o. thy name,...............
Ac 9:17 and putting his hands o. him said,....... 1909
Ac 9:21 called o. this name in Jerusalem, ... 1941
Ac 10:4 And when he looked o. him, he was ....
Ac 10:7 soldier of them that waited o. him...... 4342
Ac 10:9 O. the morrow, as they went o. their ....
Ac 10:19 While Peter thought o. the vision, ... 4012
Ac 10:23 o. the morrow Peter went away with........
Ac 10:39 they slew and hanged o. a tree:......... 1909
Ac 10:44 Holy Ghost fell o. all them which 1909
Ac 10:45 o. the Gentiles also was poured out.... 1909
Ac 11:15 Holy Ghost fell o. them, as o. us at ... 1909
Ac 11:17 us, who believed o. the Lord Jesus...... 1909
Ac 12:7 he smote Peter o. the side, and raised......
Ac 12:8 thyself, and bind o. thy sandals.......... 5265
Ac 12:10 out, and passed o. through one street; ......
Ac 13:3 and laid their hands o. them, ... 2007
Ac 13:9 Holy Ghost, set his eyes o. him,........ 1519
Ac 13:11 fell o. him a mist and a darkness;....... 1909
Ac 13:14 into the synagogue o. the sabbath day, ...
Ac 13:15 exhortation for the people, say o...............
Ac 13:34 he said o. this wise, I will give you..........
Ac 13:36 fell o. sleep, and was laid unto his............
Ac 14:10 voice, Stand upright o. thy feet.......... 1909
Ac 14:23 the Lord, o. whom they believed. 1519
Ac 15:3 being brought o. their way by the............
Ac 16:13 o. the sabbath we went out of the city......
Ac 16:31 Believe o. the Lord Jesus Christ, ... 1909
Ac 17:5 and set all the city o. an uproar, ...
Ac 17:26 to dwell o. all the face of the earth,.... 1909
Ac 18:8 believed o. the Lord with all his...............
Ac 18:10 **man shall set o. thee to hurt thee:** 2007
Ac 19:4 believe o. him which should come....... 1519
Ac 19:4 after him, that is, o. Christ Jesus....... 1519
Ac 19:6 the Holy Ghost came o. them; and..... 1909
Ac 19:16 the evil spirit was leaped o. them,...... 1909
Ac 19:17 fear fell o. them all, and the name...... 1909
Ac 20:7 them, ready to depart o. the morrow;.......
Ac 20:10 Paul went down, and fell o. him,........ 1968
Ac 20:37 wept sore, and fell o. Paul's neck,...... 1909
Ac 21:3 Cyprus, we left it o. the left hand, ...
Ac 21:5 brought us o. our way, with wives 1909
Ac 21:5 we kneeled down o. the shore, and.... 1909
Ac 21:23 men which have a vow o. them; 1909
Ac 21:27 the people, and laid hands o. him, ... 1909
Ac 21:40 licence Paul stood o. the stairs, ... 1909
Ac 22:16 calling o. the name of the Lord.......... 1941
Ac 22:19 them that believed o. thee:............... 1909
Ac 22:30 O. the morrow, because he would............
Ac 23:2 by him to smite him o. the mouth. ....
Ac 23:24 beasts, that they may set Paul o., ... 1913
Ac 23:32 O. the morrow they left the horsemen ......
Ac 25:6 day sitting o. the judgment seat......... 1909
Ac 25:17 any delay o. the morrow I sat 1909
Ac 25:17 I sat o. the judgment seat,................ 1909
Ac 25:23 o. the morrow, when Agrippa was............
Ac 27:20 and no small tempest lay o. us, ... 1945
Ac 27:33 while the day was coming o., Paul............
Ac 27:44 And the rest, some o. boards,........... 1909
Ac 27:44 some o. broken pieces of the ship. 1909
Ac 28:3 of sticks, and laid them o. the fire,..... 1909
Ac 28:3 the heat, and fastened o. his hand...... 2510
Ac 28:4 venomous beast hang o. his hand,....... 1537
Ac 28:8 laid his hands o. him, and healed........ 2007
Ro 4:5 believeth o. him that justifieth the 1909
Ro 4:24 if we believe o. him that raised up...... 1909
Ro 9:15 I will have mercy o. whom I will.............
Ro 9:15 will have compassion o. whom I will..........
Ro 9:18 hath he mercy o. whom he will have.........
Ro 9:23 his glory o. the vessels of mercy, ... 1909
Ro 9:33 whosoever believeth o. him shall........ 1909
Ro 10:6 is of faith speaketh o. this wise, Say........
Ro 10:11 Whosoever believeth o. him shall 1909
Ro 10:14 they call o. him in whom they have 1941
Ro 11:22 God: o. them which fell, severity; 1909
Ro 12:7 let us wait o. our ministering:............ 1722
Ro 12:7 or he that teacheth, o. teaching; 1722
Ro 12:8 he that exhorteth, o. exhortation:........ 1722
Ro 12:20 shalt heap coals of fire o. his head...... 1909
Ro 13:12 let us put o. the armour of light......... 1746
Ro 13:14 put ye o. the Lord Jesus Christ, ... 1746
Ro 15:3 that reproached thee fell o. me.......... 1909
Ro 15:24 be brought o. my way thitherward...........
Ro 16:6 who bestowed much labour o. us. 1519
Ro 16:19 am glad therefore o. your behalf: 1909
1Co 1:4 my God always o. your behalf, for...... 4012
1Co 11:10 woman to have power o. her head...... 1909
1Co 14:25 so falling down o. his face he will...... 1909
1Co 15:53 must put o. incorruption, ... 1746
1Co 15:53 this mortal must put o. immortality..... 1746
1Co 15:54 shall have put o. incorruption,............ 1746
1Co 15:54 mortal shall have put o. immortality, ... 1746
1Co 16:6 bring me o. my journey whithersoever ......
1Co 16:17 that which was lacking o. your part...........
2Co 1:11 be given by many o. our behalf........... 5228
2Co 1:16 be brought o. my way toward Judaea. ....
2Co 4:8 We are troubled o. every side, yet....... 1722
2Co 5:12 occasion to glory o. our behalf,.......... 5228
2Co 6:7 o. the right hand and o. the left, ...
2Co 7:5 but we were troubled o. every side; ... 1722
2Co 8:1 o. the churches of Macedonia; 1722
2Co 8:24 and of our boasting o. your behalf. 5228
2Co 10:7 ye look o. things after the outward 991
2Co 11:20 if a man smite you o. the face. 1519
Ga 3:13 is every one that hangeth o. a tree:.... 1909
Ga 3:14 might come o. the Gentiles............... 1519
Ga 3:27 into Christ have put o. Christ............ 1746
Ga 6:16 peace be o. them, and mercy, and...... 1909
Eph 1:10 in heaven, and which are o. earth;...... 1909
Eph 4:8 When he ascended up o. high, he....... 5311
Eph 4:24 And that ye put o. the new man, ... 1746
Eph 6:3 thou mayest live long o. the earth...... 1909
Eph 6:11 Put o. the whole armour of God, ... 1746
Eph 6:14 o. the breastplate of righteousness; 1746
Php 1:29 not only to believe o. him, but also..... 1519
Php 2:4 not every man o. his own things, but........
Php 2:4 every man also o. the things of others. .....
Php 2:27 mercy o. him; and not o. him only,...........
Php 2:27 o. me also, lest I should have sorrow........
Php 4:8 be any praise, think o. these things. ....
Col 3:1 sitteth o. the right hand of God. 1722
Col 3:2 affection o. things above, not o. things ......
Col 3:2 things above, not...o. the earth.......... 1909
Col 3:6 o. the children of disobedience:.......... 1909
Col 3:10 And have put o. the new man, which.. 1746
Col 3:12 Put o. therefore, as the elect of God, ..1746
Col 3:14 above all these things put o. charity,.........
1Th 5:8 putting o. the breastplate of faith........ 1746
2Th 1:8 vengeance o. them that know not God, ...
1Ti 1:16 believe o. him to life everlasting......... 1909
1Ti 1:18 prophecies...went before o. thee, ... 1909
1Ti 3:16 believed o. in the world, received up ....
1Ti 4:14 with the laying o. of the hands of....... 1936
1Ti 5:22 Lay hands suddenly o. no man,.......... 2007
1Ti 6:12 lay hold o. eternal life, whereunto 1949
1Ti 6:19 they may lay hold o. eternal life......... 1949
2Ti 1:6 thee by the putting o. of my hands....... 1936
2Ti 2:22 call o. the Lord out of a pure heart. ... 1941
Tit 3:6 Which he shed o. us abundantly......... 1909
Tit 3:13 lawyer and Apollos o. their journey...........
Phm 18 ought, put that o. mine account; 1677
Heb 1:3 sat down o. the right hand of the........ 1722
Heb 1:3 right hand of the Majesty o. high; 1722
Heb 1:13 Sit o. my right hand, until I make....... 1537
Heb 2:16 not o. him the nature of angels;.......... 1949
Heb 2:16 took o. him the seed of Abraham. 1949
Heb 4:4 place of the seventh day o. this wise, ...
Heb 5:2 can have compassion o. the ignorant, ...
Heb 5:2 and o. them that are out of the way;.........
Heb 6:1 let us go o. unto perfection; not..............
Heb 6:2 baptisms, and of laying o. of hands, ... 1936
Heb 8:1 o. the right hand of the throne of....... 1722
Heb 8:4 if he were o. the earth, he should....... 1909
Heb 9:10 carnal ordinances, imposed o. them...........
Heb 10:12 sat down o. the right hand of God;..... 1722
Heb 11:13 strangers and pilgrims o....earth......... 1909
Heb 12:25 refused him that spoke o. earth, ... 1909
Jas 3:6 and setteth o. fire the cause of nature;.....
Jas 3:6 of nature; and it is set o. fire of hell. ....
Jas 4:14 know not what shall be o. the morrow. .....
Jas 5:5 have lived in pleasure o. the earth,..... 1909
Jas 5:17 and it rained not o. the earth by the... 1909
1Pe 1:17 And if ye call o. the Father, who 1941
1Pe 2:6 that believeth o. him shall not be 1909
1Pe 2:24 our sins in his own body o. the tree, .. 1909
1Pe 3:3 of gold, or of putting o. of apparel;..... 1745
1Pe 3:22 and is o. the right hand of God;......... 1722
1Pe 4:14 o. their part he is evil spoken of, ... 2596
1Pe 4:14 but o. your part he is glorified........... 2596
1Pe 4:16 let him glorify God o. this behalf. 1722
2Pe 3:12 being o. fire shall be dissolved,................
1Jo 3:23 should believe o. the name of his Son ....
1Jo 5:10 He that believeth o. the Son of God ... 1519
1Jo 5:13, 13 believe o. the name of the Son...... 1519
3Jo 6 if thou bring forward o. their journey ....
Jude 20 up yourselves o. your most holy faith,.......
Re 1:10 was in the Spirit o. the Lord's day, ... 1722
Re 3:3 **I will come o. thee as a thief, and**..1909
Re 4:2 heaven, and one sat o. the throne...... 1909
Re 4:4 had o. their heads crowns of gold....... 1909
Re 4:9 thanks to him that sat o. the throne,... 1909
Re 4:10 before him that sat o. the throne, ... 1909
Re 5:1 hand of him that sat o. the throne 1909
Re 5:1 written within and o. the backside, ... 1909
Re 5:10 and we shall reign o. the earth. 1909
Re 5:13 is in heaven, and o. the earth, and 1722
Re 6:2 and he that sat o. him had a bow; 1909
Re 6:5 he that sat o. him had a pair of.......... 1909
Re 6:8 name that sat o. him was Death,........ 1883
Re 6:10 o. [575] them that dwell o....earth? 1909
Re 6:16 the mountains and rocks, Fall o. us, ... 1909
Re 6:16 of him that sitteth o. the throne,........ 1909
Re 7:1 angels standing o. the four corners...... 1909
Re 7:1 wind should not blow o. the earth, ... 1909
Re 7:1 the earth, nor o. the sea, nor............ 1909
Re 7:1 the sea, nor o. any tree. 1909
Re 7:11 before the throne o. their faces, ... 1909

Re 7:15 he that sitteth **o.** the throne shall....... *1909*
Re 7:16 neither shall the sun light **o.** them, ... *1909*
Re 9:7 and **o.** their heads were as it were..... *1909*
Re 9:17 and them that sat **o.** them, having...... *1909*
Re 10:2 sea, and his left foot **o.** the earth, ... *1909*
Re 11:10 them that dwelt **o.** the earth. *1909*
Re 11:16 which sat before God **o.** their seats, ... *1909*
Re 13:13 down from heaven **o.** the earth in....... *1519*
Re 13:14 them that dwell **o.** the earth by *1909*
Re 13:14 to them that dwell **o.** the earth, ... *1909*
Re 14:1 a Lamb stood **o.** the mount Sion, ... *1909*
Re 14:6 unto them that dwell **o.** the earth, ... *1909*
Re 14:14 having **o.** his head a golden crown, ... *1909*
Re 14:15 voice to him that sat **o.** the cloud, ... *1909*
Re 14:16 And he that sat **o.** the cloud thrust..... *1909*
Re 14:16 thrust in his sickle **o.** the earth; *1909*
Re 15:2 stand **o.** the sea of glass, having *1909*
Re 17:8 dwell **o.** the earth shall wonder, ... *1909*
Re 17:9 **o.** which the woman sitteth. *1909*
Re 18:19 they cast dust **o.** their heads, and *1909*
Re 18:20 for God hath avenged you **o.** her......... *1537*
Re 19:4 God that sat **o.** the throne, saying, ... *1909*
Re 19:12 and **o.** his head were many crowns; *1909*
Re 19:16 hath **o.** his vesture and **o.** his thigh *1909*
Re 19:18 and of them that sit **o.** them, and....... *1909*
Re 19:19 against him that sat **o.** the horse, ... *1909*
Re 20:2 he laid hold **o.** the dragon, that old...........
Re 20:6 **o.** such the second death hath no *1909*
Re 20:9 up **o.** the breadth of the earth, ... *1909*
Re 20:11 white throne, and him that sat **o.** it, ... *1909*
Re 21:13 **O.** the east three gates; *575*
Re 21:13 **o.** the north three gates;.................... *575*
Re 21:13 **o.** the south three gates; *575*
Re 21:13 and **o.** the west three gates................ *575*
Re 22:2 and **o.** either side of the river, was...... *1909*

ON (on)
Ge 41:45 daughter of Poti-pherah priest of **O.**. 204
Ge 41:50 daughter of Poti-pherah priest of **O.**. 204
Ge 46:20 daughter of Poti-pherah priest of **O.** 204
Nu 16:1 and **O.**, the son of Peleth, sons of 203

ONAM (o'-nam)
Ge 36:23 and Ebal, Shepho, and **O.**.................. 208
1Ch 1:40 and Ebal, Shephi, and **O.**. 208
1Ch 2:26 Atarah; she was the mother of **O.**........ 208
1Ch 2:28 the sons of **O.** were, Shammai, and....... 208

ONAN (o'-nan)
Ge 38:4 a son; and she called his name **O.**......... 209
Ge 38:8 Judah said unto **O.**, Go in unto thy....... 209
Ge 38:9 **O.** knew that the seed should not be.... 209
Ge 46:12 the sons of Judah; Er, and **O.**, and....... 209
Ge 46:12 and **O.** died in the land of Canaan. 209
Nu 26:19 The sons of Judah were Er and **O.**:....... 209
Nu 26:19 and **O.** died in the land of Canaan. 209
1Ch 2:3 The sons of Judah; Er, and **O.**, and...... 209

ONCE
Ge 18:32 and I will speak yet but this **o.**: 6471
Ex 10:17 I pray thee, my sin only this **o.**, ... 6471
Ex 30:10 upon the horns of it **o.** in a year.......... 259
Ex 30:10 **o.** in the year shall he make 259
Le 16:34 of Israel for all their sins **o.** a year....... 259
Nu 13:30 Let us go up at **o.**, and possess it;..........
De 7:22 mayest not consume them at **o.**, ... 4118
Jos 6:3 and go round about the city **o.**. 259
Jos 6:11 compassed the city, going about it **o.**:... 259
Jos 6:14 day they compassed the city **o.**, ... 259
Jg 6:39 me, and I will speak but this **o.**: 6471
Jg 6:39 prove,...but this **o.** with the fleece; 6471
Jg 16:18 Come up this **o.**, for he hath shewed .. 6471
Jg 16:28 me, I pray thee, only this **o.**, O God, ..6471
Jg 16:28 be at **o.** avenged of the Philistines............
1Sa 26:8 spear even to the earth at **o.**, ... 6471,259
1Ki 10:22 **o.** in three years came the navy of....... 259
2Ki 6:10 saved himself there, not **o.** nor twice.... 259
2Ch 9:21 every three years **o.** came the ships..... 259
Ne 5:18 and **o.** in ten days store of all sorts...... 996
Ne 13:20 lodged without Jerusalem **o.** or 6471
Job 33:14 For God speaketh **o.**, yea twice, yet 259
Job 40:5 **O.** have I spoken; but I will not.......... 259
Ps 62:11 God hath spoken **o.**; twice have I 259
Ps 74:6 carved work thereof at **o.** with axes..........
Ps 76:7 in thy sight when **o.** thou art angry?..... 227
Ps 89:35 **O.** have I sworn by my holiness that.... 259
Pr 28:18 perverse in his ways shall fall at **o.**. 259
Isa 42:14 I will destroy and devour at **o.**........... 3162
Isa 66:8 or shall a nation be born at **o.**? 6471
Jer 10:18 inhabitants of the land at this **o.**, ... 6471
Jer 13:27 made clean? when shall it **o.** be? 5750
Jer 16:21 I will this **o.** cause them to know, ... 6471
Hag 2:6 Yet **o.**, it is a little while, and I will...... 259
Lu 13:25 **When o. the master of the house is**.....
Lu 23:18 they cried out all at **o.**, saying, ... *3826*
Ro 6:10 that he died, he died unto sin **o.**: *2178*
Ro 7:9 I was alive without the law **o.**: but *4218*
1Co 15:6 above five hundred brethren at **o.**;...... *2178*
2Co 11:25 I beaten with rods, **o.** was I stoned,..... *530*
Ga 1:23 the faith which **o.** he destroyed.......... *4218*
Eph 5:3 let it not be **o.** named among you,....... *3366*
Php 4:16 **o.** and again unto my necessity............ *530*
1Th 2:18 unto you, even I Paul, **o.** and again; *530*
Heb 6:4 for those who were **o.** enlightened, ... *530*
Heb 7:27 for this he did **o.**, when he offered *2178*
Heb 9:7 the high priest alone **o.** every year,....... *530*
Heb 9:12 he entered in **o.** into the holy place, ... *2178*
Heb 9:26 **o.** in the end of the world hath he *530*
Heb 9:27 it is appointed unto men **o.** to die, ... *530*
Heb 9:28 So Christ was **o.** offered to bear the *530*
Heb 10:2 worshippers **o.** purged should have........ *530*
Heb 10:10 the body of Jesus Christ **o.** for all....... *2178*
Heb 12:26 **o.** more I shake not the earth only,...... *530*
Heb 12:27 this word, Yet **o.** more, signifieth the ... *530*
1Pe 3:18 Christ also hath **o.** suffered for sins, ... *530*
1Pe 3:20 when **o.** the longsuffering of God *530*
Jude 3 faith which was **o.** delivered unto the.... *530*
Jude 5 though ye **o.** knew this, how that the ... *530*

ONE See also NONE; ONE'S; ONES.
Ge 1:9 be gathered together unto **o.** place,...... 259
Ge 2:21 he took **o.** of his ribs, and closed up..... 259
Ge 2:24 his wife: and they shall be **o.** flesh. 259
Ge 3:6 a tree to be desired to make **o.** wise, ...
Ge 3:22 the man is become as **o.** of us, to........ 259
Ge 4:14 every **o.** that findeth me shall slay...........
Ge 4:19 the name of the **o.** was Adah, and 259
Ge 10:5 every **o.** after his tongue, after their 376
Ge 10:8 began to be a mighty **o.** in the earth. ....
Ge 10:25 sons: the name of **o.** was Peleg; 259
Ge 11:1 was of **o.** language, and of **o.** speech. ... 259
Ge 11:3 they said **o.** to another, Go to, let us ... 376
Ge 11:6 Lord said, behold, the people is **o.**,....... 259
Ge 11:6 and they have all **o.** language; and........ 259
Ge 11:7 not understand **o.** another's speech. 376
Ge 13:11 themselves the **o.** from the other......... 376
Ge 14:13 And there came **o.** that had escaped, ...
Ge 15:3 lo, **o.** born in my house is mine heir. ....
Ge 15:10 laid each piece **o.** against another: ....
Ge 19:9 This **o.** fellow came in to sojourn, ... 259
Ge 19:14 But he seemed as **o.** that mocked ....
Ge 19:20 to flee unto, and it is a little **o.**: ....
Ge 19:20 escape thither, (is it not a little **o.**?)..........
Ge 21:15 cast the child under **o.** of the shrubs. ... 259
Ge 22:2 upon **o.** of the mountains which I......... 259
Ge 24:41 if they give not thee **o.**, thou shalt...........
Ge 25:23 the **o.** people shall be stronger than..........
Ge 26:10 **o.** of the people might lightly have 259
Ge 26:26 and Ahuzzath **o.** of his friends, and ....
Ge 26:31 morning, and sware **o.** to another: 376
Ge 27:29 cursed be every **o.** that curseth thee, ...
Ge 27:38 Hast thou but **o.** blessing, my 259
Ge 27:45 deprived also of you both in **o.** day? 259
Ge 30:33 every **o.** that is not speckled and 3605
Ge 30:35 and every **o.** that had some white in it, ...
Ge 31:49 when we are absent **o.** from another. ... 376
Ge 32:8 If Esau come to the **o.** company, ... 259
Ge 33:13 if men should overdrive them **o.** day,.... 259
Ge 34:14 sister to **o.** that is uncircumcised; 376
Ge 34:16 you, and we will become **o.** people......... 259
Ge 34:22 dwell with us, to be **o.** people, ... 259
Ge 37:19 they said **o.** to another, Behold, this..... 376
Ge 38:28 that the **o.** put out his hand: and.............
Ge 40:5 each man his dream in **o.** night, ... 259
Ge 41:5 ears of corn came up upon **o.** stalk, ... 259
Ge 41:11 And we dreamed a dream in **o.** night, ... 259
Ge 41:22 seven ears came up in **o.** stalk, full 259
Ge 41:25 The dream of Pharaoh is **o.**: God......... 259
Ge 41:26 are seven years: the dream is **o.**. 259
Ge 41:38 Can we find such a **o.** as this is, a man .....
Ge 42:1 sons, Why do ye look **o.** upon another? .....
Ge 42:11 We are all **o.** man's sons; we are......... 259
Ge 42:13 the sons of **o.** man in the land of 259
Ge 42:13 day with our father, and **o.** is not. 259
Ge 42:16 Send **o.** of you, and let him fetch......... 259
Ge 42:19 let **o.** of your brethren be bound in 259
Ge 42:21 And they said **o.** to another, We are 376
Ge 42:27 And as **o.** of them opened his sack....... 259
Ge 42:28 saying **o.** to another, What is this 376
Ge 42:32 **o.** is not, and the youngest is this......... 259
Ge 42:33 leave **o.** of your brethren here with...... 259
Ge 43:33 the men marvelled **o.** at another. 376
Ge 44:20 and a child of his old age, a little **o.**; ....
Ge 44:28 And the **o.** went out from me, and....... 259
Ge 47:21 to cities from **o.** end of the borders ....
Ge 48:1 **o.** told Joseph, Behold, thy father is..........
Ge 48:2 **o.** told Jacob, and said, Behold, thy son.....
Ge 48:22 given to thee **o.** portion above thy 259
Ge 49:16 people, as **o.** of the tribes of Israel. 259
Ge 49:28 every **o.** according to his blessing 376
Ex 1:15 the name of the **o.** was Shiphrah, ... 259
Ex 2:6 This is **o.** of the Hebrews' children. ....
Ex 2:11 smiting an Hebrew, **o.** of his brethren. ......
Ex 6:25 **o.** of the daughters of Putiel to wife;.........
Ex 8:31 his people; there remained not **o.**. 259
Ex 9:6 of the children of Israel died not **o.**. 259
Ex 9:7 not **o.** of the cattle of the Israelites...... 259
Ex 10:5 **o.** cannot be able to see the earth: ....
Ex 10:19 remained not **o.** locust in all the 259
Ex 10:23 They saw not **o.** another, neither......... 376
Ex 11:1 **o.** plague more upon Pharaoh,............ 259
Ex 12:18 until the **o.** and twentieth day of the..... 259
Ex 12:30 house where there was not **o.** dead. ....
Ex 12:46 In **o.** house shall it be eaten; thou......... 259
Ex 12:48 shall be as **o.** that is born in the land: ....
Ex 12:49 **O.** law shall be to him that is............. 259
Ex 14:7 and captains over every **o.** of them...........
Ex 14:20 **o.** came not near the other all the...... 2088
Ex 14:28 remained not so much as **o.** of them...... 259
Ex 16:15 they said **o.** to another, It is manna:..... 376
Ex 16:22 much bread, two omers for **o.** man: 259
Ex 17:12 **o.** [259] on the **o.** side, and there 2088
Ex 18:3 the name of the **o.** was Gershom;........ 259
Ex 18:16 I judge between **o.** and another, ... 376
Ex 21:18 and **o.** smite another with a stone, or.......
Ex 21:35 And if **o.** man's ox hurt another's, ...
Ex 23:29 out from before thee in **o.** year; 259
Ex 24:3 the people answered with **o.** voice, ... 259
Ex 25:12 two rings shall be in the **o.** side of it, ... 259
Ex 25:19 make **o.** [259] cherub on the **o.** end,... 2088
Ex 25:20 their faces shall look **o.** to another:..........
Ex 25:32 of the candlestick out of the **o.** side,...... 259
Ex 25:33 a knop and a flower in **o.** branch;......... 259
Ex 25:36 shall be **o.** beaten work of pure gold..... 259
Ex 26:2 length of **o.** curtain shall be eight......... 259
Ex 26:2 breadth of **o.** curtain four cubits:......... 259
Ex 26:2 every **o.** of the curtains shall have............
Ex 26:2 the curtains shall have **o.** measure. 259
Ex 26:3 be coupled together **o.** to another; 802
Ex 26:3 shall be coupled **o.** to another. 802
Ex 26:4 blue upon the edge of the **o.** curtain...... 259
Ex 26:5 shalt thou make in the **o.** curtain, ... 259
Ex 26:5 loops may take hold **o.** of another. 802
Ex 26:6 taches: and it shall be **o.** tabernacle...... 259
Ex 26:8 length of **o.** curtain shall be thirty 259
Ex 26:8 breadth of **o.** curtain four cubits: ....
Ex 26:8 curtains shall be all of **o.** measure. 259
Ex 26:10 loops on the edge of the **o.** curtain....... 259
Ex 26:11 the tent together, that it may be **o.**....... 259
Ex 26:13 And a cubit on the **o.** side, and a cubit ......
Ex 26:16 shall be the breadth of **o.** board........... 259
Ex 26:17 tenons shall there be in **o.** board, ... 259
Ex 26:17 set in order **o.** against another: 802
Ex 26:19 two sockets under **o.** board for his....... 259
Ex 26:21 two sockets under **o.** board, and two.... 259
Ex 26:24 above the head of it unto **o.** ring: 259
Ex 26:25 two sockets under **o.** board, and two.... 259
Ex 26:26 of the **o.** side of the tabernacle,........... 259
Ex 27:9 and hundred cubits long for **o.** side:...... 259
Ex 27:14 The hanging of **o.** side of the gate...........
Ex 28:10 Six of their names on **o.** stone, and....... 259
Ex 28:21 every **o.** with his name shall they be 376
Ex 29:1 Take **o.** young bullock, and two........... 259
Ex 29:3 thou shalt put them into **o.** basket,....... 259
Ex 29:15 Thou shalt also take **o.** ram; and 259
Ex 29:23 **o.** loaf of bread, and **o.** cake of oiled 259
Ex 29:23 and **o.** wafer out of the basket of the.... 259
Ex 29:39 The **o.** lamb thou shalt offer in the....... 259
Ex 29:40 And with the **o.** lamb a tenth deal of 259
Ex 30:13 every **o.** that passeth among them that......
Ex 30:14 Every **o.** that passeth among them ....
Ex 31:14 every **o.** that defileth it shall surely be .....

Ex 32:15 on the **o.** side and on the other were
Ex 33:7 that every **o.** which sought the Lord
Ex 34:15 and **o.** call thee, and thou eat of his
Ex 35:21 every **o.** whose heart stirred him up,
Ex 35:21 and every **o.** whom his spirit made
Ex 35:24 Every **o.** that did offer an offering of
Ex 36:2 even every **o.** whose heart stirred him
Ex 36:9 length of **o.** curtain was twenty and 259
Ex 36:9 breadth of **o.** curtain four cubits:
Ex 36:9 the curtains were all of **o.** size 259
Ex 36:10 the five curtains **o.** unto another: 259
Ex 36:10 curtains he coupled **o.** unto another 259
Ex 36:11 loops of blue on the edge of **o.** curtain 259
Ex 36:12 Fifty loops made he in **o.** curtain, 259
Ex 36:12 the loops held **o.** curtain to another 259
Ex 36:13 coupled the curtains **o.** unto another 259
Ex 36:13 taches: so it became **o.** tabernacle. 259
Ex 36:15 of **o.** curtain was thirty cubits, 259
Ex 36:15 cubits was the breadth of **o.** curtain: 259
Ex 36:15 the eleven curtains were of **o.** size 259
Ex 36:18 the tent together, that it might be **o.** 259
Ex 36:21 breadth of a board **o.** cubit and a half.
Ex 36:22 **O.** board had two tenons, equally 259
Ex 36:22 equally distant **o.** from another: 259
Ex 36:24 under **o.** board for his two tenons, 259
Ex 36:26 silver; two sockets under **o.** board, 259
Ex 36:29 at the head thereof, to **o.** ring: 259
Ex 36:31 of the **o.** side of the tabernacle, 259
Ex 36:33 boards from the **o.** end to the other
Ex 37:3 even two rings upon the **o.** side of it, 259
Ex 37:6 **o.** cubit and half the breadth thereof.
Ex 37:7 beaten out of **o.** piece made he them,
Ex 37:8 **O.** cherub on the end on this side, 259
Ex 37:9 seat, with their faces **o.** to another; 376
Ex 37:18 candlestick out of the **o.** side thereof,
Ex 37:19 fashion of almonds in **o.** branch, 259
Ex 37:22 it was **o.** beaten work of pure gold 259
Ex 38:14 The hangings of the **o.** side of the gate
Ex 38:26 every **o.** that went to be numbered,
Ex 39:14 of a signet, every **o.** with his name, 376
Le 4:27 if any **o.** of the common people sin 5315
Le 5:4 then he shall be guilty in **o.** of these 259
Le 5:5 shall be guilty in **o.** of these things, 259
Le 5:7 **o.** for a sin offering, and the other 259
Le 5:13 sin that he hath sinned in **o.** of these, 259
Le 6:18 every **o.** that toucheth them shall be
Le 7:7 there is **o.** law for them: the priest 259
Le 7:10 Aaron have, **o.** as much as another. 376
Le 7:14 offer **o.** out of the whole oblation 259
Le 8:26 he took **o.** unleavened cake, and a 259
Le 8:26 a cake of oiled bread, and **o.** wafer, 259
Le 11:26 every **o.** that touched them shall be
Le 12:8 the **o.** for the burnt offering, and the 259
Le 13:2 or unto **o.** of his sons the priests: 259
Le 14:5 that **o.** of the birds be killed 259
Le 14:10 and **o.** ewe lamb of the first year 259
Le 14:10 mingled with oil, and **o.** log of oil 259
Le 14:12 And the priest shall take **o.** he lamb, 259
Le 14:21 take **o.** lamb for a trespass offering 259
Le 14:21 **o.** tenth deal of fine flour mingled 259
Le 14:22 the **o.** shall be a sin offering, and the 259
Le 14:30 shall offer the **o.** of the turtledoves, 259
Le 14:31 the **o.** for a sin offering, and the 259
Le 14:50 And he shall kill the **o.** of the birds 259
Le 15:15 the **o.** for a sin offering, and the 259
Le 15:30 shall offer the **o.** for a sin offering, 259
Le 16:5 and **o.** ram for a burnt offering 259
Le 16:8 **o.** lot for the Lord, and the other lot 259
Le 16:27 **o.** carry forth without the camp;
Le 16:29 whether it be **o.** of your own country,
Le 17:15 whether it be **o.** of your own country,
Le 18:30 any **o.** of these abominable customs,
Le 19:8 every **o.** that eateth it shall bear his
Le 19:11 falsely, neither lie **o.** to another 376
Le 19:34 be unto you as **o.** born among you,
Le 20:9 every **o.** that curseth his father or 376
Le 22:28 kill it and her young both in **o.** day 259
Le 23:18 and **o.** young bullock, and two rams: 259
Le 23:19 ye shall sacrifice **o.** kid of the goats 259
Le 24:5 two tenth deals shall be in **o.** cake. 259
Le 24:22 Ye shall have **o.** manner of law, as 259
Le 24:22 stranger, as for **o.** of your own country:
Le 25:14 ye shall not oppress **o.** another: 376
Le 25:17 not therefore oppress **o.** another; 376
Le 25:46 shall not rule **o.** over another with 376
Le 25:48 **o.** of his brethren may redeem him: 259
Le 26:26 shall bake your bread in **o.** oven, 259
Le 26:37 And they shall fall **o.** upon another, 376
Nu 1:4 every **o.** head of the house of his 376
Nu 1:41 were forty and **o.** thousand and 259
Nu 1:44 each **o.** was for the house of his 259
Nu 2:16 fifty and **o.** thousand and four 259
Nu 2:28 forty and **o.** thousand and five 259
Nu 2:34 every **o.** after their families, 376
Nu 4:19 appoint them every **o.** to his service 376
Nu 4:30, 35,39,43 every **o.** that entereth into
Nu 4:47 every **o.** that came to do the service
Nu 4:49 every **o.** according to his service, 376
Nu 5:2 and every **o.** that hath an issue, and
Nu 6:11 shall offer the **o.** for a sin offering, 259
Nu 6:14 **o.** he lamb of the first year without 259
Nu 6:14 **o.** ewe lamb of the first year without 259
Nu 6:14 **o.** ram without blemish for peace 259
Nu 6:19 and **o.** unleavened cake out of the 259
Nu 6:19 and **o.** unleavened wafer, and shall 259
Nu 7:3 of the princes, and for each **o.** an ox:
Nu 7:13 his offering was **o.** silver charger, 259
Nu 7:13 **o.** silver bowl of seventy shekels, 259
Nu 7:14 **O.** spoon of ten shekels of gold, full 259
Nu 7:15 **O.** young bullock, **o.** ram, **o.** lamb 259
Nu 7:16 **O.** kid of the goats for a sin offering: 259
Nu 7:19 for his offering **o.** silver charger, 259
Nu 7:19 **o.** silver bowl of seventy shekels, 259
Nu 7:20 **O.** spoon of gold of ten shekels, full 259
Nu 7:21 **O.** young bullock, **o.** ram, **o.** lamb 259
Nu 7:22 **O.** kid of the goats for a sin offering: 259
Nu 7:25 His offering was **o.** silver charger, 259
Nu 7:25 **o.** silver bowl of seventy shekels, 259
Nu 7:26 **O.** golden spoon of ten skekels, full 259
Nu 7:27 **O.** young bullock, **o.** ram, **o.** lamb 259
Nu 7:28 **O.** kid of the goats for a sin offering: 259
Nu 7:31 His offering was **o.** silver charger of 259
Nu 7:31 **o.** silver bowl of seventy shekels, 259
Nu 7:33 **O.** golden spoon of ten shekels, full 259
Nu 7:33 **O.** young bullock, **o.** ram, **o.** lamb 259
Nu 7:34 **O.** kid of the goats for a sin offering: 259
Nu 7:37 His offering was **o.** silver charger, 259
Nu 7:37 **o.** silver bowl of seventy shekels, 259
Nu 7:38 **O.** golden spoon of ten shekels, full 259
Nu 7:39 **O.** young bullock, **o.** ram, **o.** lamb 259
Nu 7:40 **O.** kid of the goats for a sin offering: 259
Nu 7:43 His offering was **o.** silver charger 259
Nu 7:44 **O.** golden spoon of ten shekels, full 259
Nu 7:45 **O.** young bullock, **o.** ram, **o.** lamb 259
Nu 7:46 **O.** kid of the goats for a sin offering: 259
Nu 7:49 His offering was **o.** silver charger 259
Nu 7:49 **o.** silver bowl of seventy shekels, 259
Nu 7:50 **O.** golden spoon of ten shekels, full 259
Nu 7:51 **O.** young bullock, **o.** ram, **o.** lamb 259
Nu 7:52 **O.** kid of the goats for a sin offering: 259
Nu 7:55 His offering was **o.** silver charger of 259
Nu 7:55 **o.** silver bowl of seventy shekels, 259
Nu 7:56 **O.** golden spoon of ten shekels, full 259
Nu 7:57 **O.** young bullock, **o.** ram, **o.** lamb 259
Nu 7:58 **O.** kid of the goats for a sin offering: 259
Nu 7:61 His offering was **o.** silver charger, 259
Nu 7:61 **o.** silver bowl of seventy shekels, 259
Nu 7:62 **O.** golden spoon of ten shekels, full 259
Nu 7:63 **O.** young bullock, **o.** ram, **o.** lamb 259
Nu 7:64 **O.** kid of the goats for a sin offering: 259
Nu 7:67 His offering was **o.** silver charger, 259
Nu 7:67 **o.** silver bowl of seventy shekels, 259
Nu 7:68 **O.** golden spoon of ten shekels, full 259
Nu 7:69 **O.** young bullock, **o.** ram, **o.** lamb 259
Nu 7:70 **O.** kid of the goats for a sin offering: 259
Nu 7:73 His offering was **o.** silver charger, 259
Nu 7:73 **o.** silver bowl of seventy shekels, 259
Nu 7:74 **O.** golden spoon of ten shekels, full 259
Nu 7:75 **O.** young bullock, **o.** ram, **o.** lamb 259
Nu 7:76 **O.** kid of the goats for a sin offering: 259
Nu 7:79 His offering was **o.** silver charger, 259
Nu 7:79 **o.** silver bowl of seventy shekels, 259
Nu 7:80 **O.** golden spoon of ten shekels, full 259
Nu 7:81 **O.** young bullock, **o.** ram, **o.** lamb 259
Nu 7:82 **O.** kid of the goats for a sin offering: 259
Nu 7:89 the voice of **o.** speaking unto him
Nu 8:12 shalt offer the **o.** for a sin offering, 259
Nu 9:14 ye shall have **o.** ordinance, both for 259
Nu 10:4 if they blow but with **o.** trumpet, 259
Nu 11:19 Ye shall not eat **o.** day, nor two days, 259
Nu 11:26 the name of the **o.** was Eldad, and 259
Nu 11:28 **o.** of his young men, answered and
Nu 12:12 Let her not be as **o.** dead, of whom
Nu 13:2 man, every **o.** a ruler among them.
Nu 13:23 a branch with **o.** cluster of grapes, 259
Nu 14:4 And they said **o.** to another, Let us 376
Nu 14:15 shalt kill all this people as **o.** man, 259
Nu 15:5 offering or sacrifice, for **o.** lamb 259
Nu 15:11 be done for **o.** bullock, or for **o.** ram, 259
Nu 15:12 ye do to every **o.** according to their 259
Nu 15:15 **O.** ordinance shall be both for you 259
Nu 15:16 **O.** law and **o.** manner shall be for 259
Nu 15:24 **o.** young bullock for a burnt offering, 259
Nu 15:24 **o.** kid of the goats for a sin offering. 259
Nu 15:29 **o.** law for him that sinneth through 259
Nu 16:3 the congregation are holy, every **o.**
Nu 16:15 I have not taken **o.** ass from them, 259
Nu 16:15 neither have I hurt **o.** of them 259
Nu 16:22 shall **o.** man sin, and wilt thou be 259
Nu 17:2 take of every **o.** of them a rod
Nu 17:3 **o.** rod shall be for the head of the 259
Nu 17:6 every **o.** of their princes gave him a
Nu 17:6 a rod apiece, for each prince **o.**, 259
Nu 18:11 every **o.** that is clean in thy house
Nu 18:13 every **o.** that is clean in thine house
Nu 19:3 and **o.** shall slay her before his face:
Nu 19:5 **o.** shall burn the heifer in his sight;
Nu 19:16 whosoever toucheth **o.** that is slain
Nu 19:18 bone, or **o.** slain, or **o.** dead, or a grave:
Nu 21:8 that every **o.** that is bitten, when he
Nu 25:5 Slay ye every **o.** his men that were 376
Nu 25:6 **o.** of the children of Israel came and 376
Nu 26:54 to every **o.** shall his inheritance be 376
Nu 28:4 The **o.** lamb shalt thou offer in the 259
Nu 28:7 fourth part of an hin for the **o.** lamb: 259
Nu 28:11 and **o.** ram, seven lambs of the first 259
Nu 28:12 mingled with oil, for **o.** bullock; 259
Nu 28:12 mingled with oil, for **o.** ram; 259
Nu 28:13 for a meat offering unto **o.** lamb; 259
Nu 28:15 **o.** kid of the goats for a sin offering 259
Nu 28:19 **o.** ram, and seven lambs of the first 259
Nu 28:22 **o.** goat for a sin offering, to make 259
Nu 28:27 **o.** ram, seven lambs of the first year; 259
Nu 28:28 three tenth deals unto **o.** bullock, 259
Nu 28:28 two tenth deals unto **o.** ram, 259
Nu 28:29 A several tenth deal unto **o.** lamb, 259
Nu 28:30 And **o.** kid of the goats, to make an 259
Nu 29:2 **o.** young bullock, **o.** ram, and seven 259
Nu 29:4 And **o.** tenth deal for 259
Nu 29:4 tenth deal for **o.** lamb, throughout 259
Nu 29:5 **o.** kid of the goats for a sin offering, 259
Nu 29:8 **o.** young bullock, **o.** ram, and seven 259
Nu 29:9 and two tenth deals to **o.** ram, 259
Nu 29:10 A several tenth deal for **o.** lamb, 259
Nu 29:11 **O.** kid of the goats for a sin offering; 259
Nu 29:16, 19 And **o.** kid of the goats for a sin 259
Nu 29:22 **o.** goat for a sin offering; beside the 259
Nu 29:25 **o.** kid of the goats for a sin offering; 259
Nu 29:28, 31,34 And **o.** goat for a sin offering; 259
Nu 29:36 **o.** bullock, **o.** ram, seven lambs of 259
Nu 29:38 **o.** goat for a sin offering; beside the 259
Nu 31:28 **o.** soul of five hundred, both of the 259
Nu 31:30 thou shalt take **o.** portion of fifty, of 259
Nu 31:34 threescore and **o.** thousand asses 259
Nu 31:39 Lord's tribute was threescore and **o.** 259
Nu 31:47 Moses took **o.** portion of fifty, both 259
Nu 31:49 and there lacketh not **o.** man of us,
Nu 34:18 shall take **o.** prince of every tribe, 259
Nu 35:8 every **o.** shall give of his cities unto 376
Nu 35:15 **o.** that killeth any person unawares
Nu 35:30 **o.** witness shall not testify against 259
Nu 36:7 for every **o.** of the children of Israel 376
Nu 36:8 be wife unto **o.** of the family of the 259
Nu 36:9 remove from **o.** tribe to another tribe;
Nu 36:9 every **o.** of the tribes of the children 376
De 1:22 ye came near unto me every **o.** of you,
De 1:23 twelve men of you, **o.** of a tribe: 259
De 1:35 there shall not **o.** of these men of 376
De 2:36 there was not **o.** city too strong for us:
De 4:4 are alive every **o.** of you this day.
De 4:32 from the **o.** side of heaven unto the
De 4:42 that fleeing unto **o.** of these cities he 259
De 6:4 Israel: The Lord our God is **o.** Lord: 259
De 12:14 Lord shall choose in **o.** of thy tribes, 259
De 13:7 from the **o.** end of the earth even unto
De 13:12 shalt hear say in **o.** of thy cities, 259
De 15:7 a poor man of **o.** of thy brethren 259
De 17:6 at the mouth of **o.** witness he shall 259
De 17:15 **o.** from among thy brethren shalt thou
De 18:10 any **o.** that maketh his son or his
De 19:5 he shall flee unto **o.** of those cities, 259

De 19:11 die, and fleeth into **o.** of these cities: 259
De 19:15 **O.** witness shall not rise up against 259
De 21:1 If **o.** be found slain in the land which
De 21:15 two wives, **o.** beloved, and another 259
De 23:16 he shall choose in **o.** of thy gates, 259
De 24:5 but he shall be free at home **o.** year, 259
De 25:5 dwell together, and **o.** of them die, 259
De 25:11 men strive together **o.** with another, 259
De 25:11 and the wife of the **o.** draweth near 259
De 28:7 shall come out against thee **o.** way, 259
De 28:25 shalt go out **o.** way against them, 259
De 28:57 And toward her young **o.** that cometh
De 28:64 from **o.** end of the earth even unto
De 32:30 How should **o.** chase a thousand, 259
De 33:3 every **o.** shall receive of thy words
De 33:8 and thy Urim be with thy holy **o.**,
Jos 9:2 and with Israel, with **o.** accord 259
Jos 10:2 a great city, as **o.** of the royal cities, 259
Jos 10:42 land did Joshua take at **o.** time, 259
Jos 12:9 The king of Jericho, **o.**; 259
Jos 12:9 of Ai, which is beside Beth-el, **o.**; 259
Jos 12:10 The king of Jerusalem, **o.**; 259
Jos 12:10 the king of Hebron, **o.**; 259
Jos 12:11 The king of Jarmuth, **o.**; 259
Jos 12:11 the king of Lachish, **o.**; 259
Jos 12:12 The king of Eglon, **o.**; 259
Jos 12:12 the king of Gezer, **o.**; 259
Jos 12:13 The king of Debir, **o.**; 259
Jos 12:13 the king of Geder, **o.**; 259
Jos 12:14 The king of Hormah, **o.**; 259
Jos 12:14 the king of Arad, **o.**; 259
Jos 12:15 The king of Libnah, **o.**; 259
Jos 12:15 the king of Adullam, **o.**; 259
Jos 12:16 The king of Makkedah, **o.**; 259
Jos 12:16 the king of Beth-el, **o.**; 259
Jos 12:17 The king of Tappuah, **o.**; 259
Jos 12:17 the king of Hepher, **o.**; 259
Jos 12:18 The king of Aphek, **o.**; 259
Jos 12:18 the king of Lasharon, **o.**; 259
Jos 12:19 The king of Madon, **o.**; 259
Jos 12:19 the king of Hazor, **o.**; 259
Jos 12:20 The king of Shimron-meron, **o.**; 259
Jos 12:20 the king of Achshaph, **o.**; 259
Jos 12:21 The king of Taanach, **o.**; 259
Jos 12:21 the king of Megiddo, **o.**; 259
Jos 12:22 The king of Kedesh, **o.**; 259
Jos 12:22 the king of Jokneam of Carmel, **o.**; 259
Jos 12:23 king of Dor in the coast of Dor. **o.**; 259
Jos 12:23 the king of the nations of Gilgal, **o.**; 259
Jos 12:24 The king of Tirzah, **o.**; 259
Jos 12:24 all the kings thirty and **o.**. 259
Jos 13:31 to the **o.** half of the children of Machir
Jos 17:14 Why hast thou given me but **o.** lot 259
Jos 17:14 and **o.** portion to inherit, seeing I 259
Jos 17:17 thou shalt not have **o.** lot only: 259
Jos 20:4 that doth flee unto **o.** of those cities 259
Jos 21:42 cities were every **o.** with their suburbs
Jos 22:7 the **o.** half of the tribe of Manasseh
Jos 22:14 each **o.** was an head of the house of 376
Jos 23:10 **O.** man of you shall chase a 259
Jos 23:14 not **o.** thing hath failed of all the 259
Jos 23:14 and not **o.** thing hath failed thereof 259
Jg 6:16 smite the Midianites as **o.** man 259
Jg 6:29 they said **o.** to another, Who hath 376
Jg 6:31 because **o.** hath cast down his altar
Jg 7:5 Every **o.** that lappeth of the water
Jg 7:5 every **o.** that boweth down upon his
Jg 8:18 each **o.** resembled the children of a 259
Jg 9:2 over you, or that **o.** reign over you? 259
Jg 9:5 and ten persons, upon **o.** stone: 259
Jg 9:18 and ten persons, upon **o.** stone, 259
Jg 10:18 princes of Gilead said **o.** to another, 376
Jg 11:35 thou art **o.** of them that trouble me:
Jg 12:7 was buried in **o.** of the cities of Gilead.
Jg 16:5 will give thee every **o.** of us eleven 376
Jg 16:29 of the **o.** with his right hand, and of 259
Jg 17:5 and consecrated **o.** of his sons, who 259
Jg 17:11 man was unto him as **o.** of his sons 259
Jg 18:19 be a priest unto the house of **o.** man, 259
Jg 19:13 let us draw near to **o.** of these places 259
Jg 20:1 was gathered together as **o.** man, 259
Jg 20:8 And all the people arose as **o.** man, 259
Jg 20:11 the city, knit together as **o.** man. 259
Jg 20:16 every **o.** could sling stones at an hair
Jg 20:31 **o.** goeth up to the house of God, 259
Jg 21:3 be to day **o.** tribe lacking in Israel? 259
Jg 21:6 **o.** tribe cut off from Israel this day. 259
Jg 21:8 What **o.** is there of the tribes of 259
Ru 1:4 the name of the **o.** was Orpah, and 259
Ru 2:13 like unto **o.** of thine handmaidens 259
Ru 2:20 kin unto us, **o.** of our next kinsmen
Ru 3:14 rose up before **o.** could know another.
Ru 4:1 Ho, such a **o.**! turn aside, sit down 492
1Sa 1:2 the name of the **o.** was Hannah, 259
1Sa 1:24 and **o.** ephah of flour, and a bottle of 259
1Sa 2:25 If **o.** man sin against another, the
1Sa 2:34 in **o.** day they shall die both of them. 259
1Sa 2:36 every **o.** that is left in thine house
1Sa 2:36 thee, into **o.** of the priests' offices, 259
1Sa 3:11 every **o.** that heareth it shall tingle.
1Sa 6:4 for **o.** plague was on you all, and on 259
1Sa 6:17 the Lord; for Ashdod **o.**, for Gaza **o.**, 259
1Sa 6:17 Askelon **o.**, for Gath **o.**, for Ekron **o.**; 259
1Sa 9:3 now **o.** of the servants with thee, 259
1Sa 10:3 **o.** carrying three kids, and another 259
1Sa 10:11 people said **o.** to another, What is 376
1Sa 10:12 **o.** of the same place answered and 376
1Sa 11:7 and they came out with **o.** consent 259
1Sa 13:1 Saul reigned **o.** year; and when he had
1Sa 13:17 **o.** company turned unto the way 259
1Sa 14:4 was a sharp rock on the **o.** side, 2088
1Sa 14:4 the name of the **o.** was Bozez, and 259
1Sa 14:5 The forefront of the **o.** was situate 259
1Sa 14:16 they went on beating down **o.** another
1Sa 14:28 Then answered **o.** of the people, and
1Sa 14:40 Be ye on **o.** side, and I and Jonathan 259
1Sa 14:45 there shall not **o.** hair of his head fall
1Sa 16:18 Then answered **o.** of the servants, 259
1Sa 17:3 stood on a mountain on the **o.** side, 2088
1Sa 17:7 **o.** bearing a shield went before him.
1Sa 17:36 Philistine shall be as **o.** of them, 259
1Sa 18:7 women answered **o.** another as they
1Sa 18:21 my son in law in the **o.** of the twain
1Sa 19:22 And **o.** said, Behold, they be at Naioth
1Sa 20:15 every **o.** from the face of the earth. 376
1Sa 20:41 times; and they kissed **o.** another, 376
1Sa 20:41 wept **o.** with another, until David 376
1Sa 21:11 did they not sing **o.** to another of him
1Sa 22:2 And every **o.** that was in distress, 376
1Sa 22:2 and every **o.** that was in debt, and 376
1Sa 22:2 and every **o.** that was discontented, 376
1Sa 22:7 son of Jesse give every **o.** of you fields
1Sa 22:20 **o.** of the sons of Ahimelech the son 259
1Sa 25:14 **o.** of the young men told Abigail, 259
1Sa 26:15 came **o.** of the people in to destroy 259
1Sa 26:20 as when **o.** doth hunt a partridge in
1Sa 26:22 let **o.** of the young men come over 259
1Sa 27:1 perish **o.** day by the hand of Saul; 259
1Sa 29:5 they sang **o.** to another in dances,
2Sa 1:15 David called **o.** of the young men, 259
2Sa 2:13 the **o.** [428] on the **o.** side of the pool, 2088
2Sa 2:16 And they caught every **o.** his fellow 376
2Sa 2:21 thee hold on **o.** of the young men, 259
2Sa 2:25 and became **o.** troop, and stood on 259
2Sa 2:27 every **o.** from following his brother. 376
2Sa 3:13 **o.** thing I require of thee, that is, 259
2Sa 3:29 house of Joab **o.** that hath an issue,
2Sa 4:2 the name of the **o.** was Baanah, 259
2Sa 4:10 When **o.** told me, saying, Behold, Saul
2Sa 6:19 as men, to every **o.** a cake of bread, 376
2Sa 6:19 departed every **o.** to his house 376
2Sa 6:20 **o.** of the vain fellows shamelessly 259
2Sa 7:23 what **o.** nation in the earth is like 259
2Sa 8:2 and with **o.** full line to keep alive
2Sa 9:11 at my table, as **o.** of the king's sons 259
2Sa 10:4 and shaved off **o.** half of their beards,
2Sa 11:3 **o.** said, Is not this Bath-sheba, the
2Sa 11:25 the sword devoureth **o.** as well as 2088
2Sa 12:1 There were two men in **o.** city; the 259
2Sa 12:1 city; the **o.** rich, and the other poor. 259
2Sa 12:3 had nothing, save **o.** little ewe lamb, 259
2Sa 13:13 shalt be as **o.** of the fools in Israel. 259
2Sa 13:30 sons, and there is not **o.** of them left. 259
2Sa 14:6 but the **o.** smote the other, and slew 259
2Sa 14:11 not **o.** hair of thy son fall to the earth.
2Sa 14:12 speak **o.** word unto my lord the king
2Sa 14:13 speak this thing as **o.** which is faulty,
2Sa 14:27 and **o.** daughter, whose name was 259
2Sa 15:2 Thy servant is **o.** of the tribes of 259
2Sa 15:31 and **o.** told David, saying, Ahithophel
2Sa 17:12 there shall not be left so much as **o.**. 259
2Sa 17:13 be not **o.** small stone found there 1571
2Sa 17:22 lacked not **o.** of them that was not 259
2Sa 18:17 all Israel fled every **o.** to his tent 376
2Sa 19:7 not tarry **o.** with thee this night: 376
2Sa 19:14 Judah, even as the heart of **o.** man; 259
2Sa 20:11 And **o.** of Joab's men stood by him, 376
2Sa 20:12 every **o.** that came by him stood still.
2Sa 20:19 I am **o.** of them that are peaceable and
2Sa 23:8 hundred, whom he slew at **o.** time 259
2Sa 23:9 **o.** of the three mighty men with David,
2Sa 23:15 Oh that **o.** would give me drink of the
2Sa 23:24 brother of Joab was **o.** of the thirty;
2Sa 24:12 choose thee **o.** of them, that I may 259
1Ki 1:48 hath given **o.** to sit on my throne this
1Ki 2:16 I ask **o.** petition of thee, deny me 259
1Ki 2:20 I desire **o.** small petition of thee; 259
1Ki 3:17 And the **o.** woman said, O my lord, 259
1Ki 3:17 I and this woman dwell in **o.** house; 259
1Ki 3:23 The **o.** saith, This is my son that 2063
1Ki 3:25 half to the **o.**, and half to the other. 259
1Ki 4:22 Solomon's provision for **o.** day was 259
1Ki 6:24 five cubits was the **o.** wing of the 259
1Ki 6:24 from the uttermost part of the **o.** wing
1Ki 6:25 half to the **o.**, and half to the other. 259
1Ki 6:26 of the **o.** cherub was ten cubits, and 259
1Ki 6:27 so that the wing of the **o.** touched 259
1Ki 6:27 touched the **o.** wall, and the wing
1Ki 6:27 touched **o.** another in the midst of 3671
1Ki 6:34 leaves of the **o.** door were folding, 259
1Ki 7:7 from **o.** side of the floor to the other.
1Ki 7:16 of the **o.** chapiter was five cubits, 259
1Ki 7:17 seven for the **o.** chapiter, and seven 259
1Ki 7:18 round about upon the **o.** network, 259
1Ki 7:23 cubits from the **o.** brim to the other:
1Ki 7:27 cubits was the length of **o.** base, 259
1Ki 7:34 to the four corners of **o.** base: and 259
1Ki 7:36 to the proportion of every **o.**, 376
1Ki 7:37 **o.** casting, **o.** measure, and **o.** size. 259
1Ki 7:38 **o.** laver contained forty baths: and 259
1Ki 7:38 upon every **o.** of the ten bases **o.** laver. 259
1Ki 7:42 of pomegranates for **o.** network, 259
1Ki 7:44 **o.** sea, and twelve oxen under the 259
1Ki 8:56 **o.** word of all his good promise, 259
1Ki 9:8 every **o.** that passeth by it shall be
1Ki 10:14 that came to Solomon in **o.** year 259
1Ki 10:16 shekels of gold went to **o.** target. 259
1Ki 10:17 pound of gold went to **o.** shield: 259
1Ki 10:20 twelve lions stood...on the **o.** side 2088
1Ki 11:13 give **o.** tribe to thy son for David my 259
1Ki 11:32 have **o.** tribe for my servant David's 259
1Ki 11:36 And unto his son will I give **o.** tribe, 259
1Ki 12:29 And he set the **o.** in Beth-el, and the 259
1Ki 12:30 went to worship before the **o.**, even 259
1Ki 13:33 and he became **o.** of the priests of the
1Ki 14:21 was forty and **o.** years old when he 259
1Ki 15:10 And forty and **o.** years reigned he in 259
1Ki 16:11 left him not **o.** that pisseth against a
1Ki 18:6 Ahab went **o.** way by himself, and 259
1Ki 18:23 choose **o.** bullock for themselves, 259
1Ki 18:25 you **o.** bullock for yourselves, and 259
1Ki 18:40 of Baal; let not **o.** of them escape. 376
1Ki 19:2 not thy life as the life of **o.** of them 259
1Ki 20:20 and they slew every **o.** his man: 376
1Ki 20:29 thousand footmen in **o.** day 259
1Ki 22:8 There is yet **o.** man, Micaiah the 259
1Ki 22:13 good unto the king with **o.** mouth: 259
1Ki 22:13 thee, be like the word of **o.** of them, 259
1Ki 22:20 And **o.** said on this manner, and
1Ki 22:28 Hearken, O people, every **o.** of you
1Ki 22:38 **o.** washed the chariot in the pool of
2Ki 3:11 **o.** the king of Israel's servants 259
2Ki 3:23 and they have smitten **o.** another: 376
2Ki 4:22 **o.** of the young men, and **o.** of the 259
2Ki 4:39 **o.** went out into the field to gather 259
2Ki 5:4 **o.** went in, and told his lord, saying,
2Ki 6:3 **o.** said, Be content, I pray thee, and 259
2Ki 6:5 as **o.** was felling a beam, the axe 259
2Ki 6:12 **o.** of his servants said, None, my 259
2Ki 7:3 they said **o.** to another, Why sit we 376
2Ki 7:6 and they said **o.** to another, Lo, the 376
2Ki 7:8 they went into **o.** tent, and did eat 259
2Ki 7:9 they said **o.** to another, We do not 376
2Ki 7:13 **o.** of his servants answered and 259
2Ki 8:26 he reigned **o.** year in Jerusalem 259
2Ki 9:1 prophet called **o.** of the children of 259
2Ki 9:11 and **o.** said unto him, Is all well?
2Ki 9:18 went **o.** on horseback to meet him,

2Ki 10:21 was full from **o.** end to another.
2Ki 12:4 of every **o.** that passeth the account,
2Ki 12:9 side as **o.** cometh into the house of...... 376
2Ki 14:8 let us look **o.** another in the face.
2Ki 14:11 looked **o.** another in the face at.
2Ki 14:23 and reigned forty and **o.** years. 259
2Ki 17:27 Carry thither **o.** of the priests whom 259
2Ki 17:28 then **o.** of the priests whom they......... 259
2Ki 18:24 turn away the face of **o.** captain of....... 259
2Ki 18:31 vine, and every **o.** of his fig tree, ... 376
2Ki 18:31 drink ye every **o.** the waters of his...... 376
2Ki 19:22 even against the Holy **O.** of Israel
2Ki 21:16 Jerusalem from **o.** end to another;
2Ki 22:1 thirty and **o.** years in Jerusalem........... 259
2Ki 23:35 every **o.** according to his taxation, ... 376
2Ki 24:18 was twenty and **o.** years old when he... 259
2Ki 25:16 two pillars, **o.** sea, and the bases......... 259
2Ki 25:17 height of the **o.** pillar was eighteen....... 259
1Ch 1:19 sons: the name of the **o.** Peleg; 259
1Ch 9:31 Mattithiah, **o.** of the Levites,
1Ch 10:13 of **o.** that had a familiar spirit,
1Ch 11:11 hundred slain by him at **o.** time. 259
1Ch 11:12 who was **o.** of the three mighties.
1Ch 11:17 **o.** would give me drink of the water
1Ch 12:14 **o.** of the least was over an hundred, ... 259
1Ch 12:25 war, seven thousand and **o.** hundred.
1Ch 12:38 of **o.** heart to make David king............ 259
1Ch 16:3 And he dealt to every **o.** of Israel,....... 376
1Ch 16:3 to every **o.** a loaf of bread, and a......... 376
1Ch 16:20 from **o.** kingdom to another people:
1Ch 17:5 and from **o.** tabernacle to another.
1Ch 17:21 what **o.** nation in the earth is like 259
1Ch 21:10 things: choose thee **o.** of them that...... 259
1Ch 23:10 therefore they were in **o.** reckoning, ... 259
1Ch 24:5 divided by lot, **o.** sort with another; 428
1Ch 24:6 **o.** of the Levites, wrote them before
1Ch 24:6 **o.** principal household being taken 259
1Ch 24:6 Eleazar, and **o.** taken for Ithamar.
1Ch 24:17 The **o.** and twentieth to Jachin, the...... 259
1Ch 25:28 The **o.** and twentieth to Hothir, he, ... 259
1Ch 26:12 having wards **o.** against another,
1Ch 27:18 Elihu, **o.** of the brethren of David:
1Ch 29:7 **o.** hundred thousand talents of iron.
2Ch 3:11 **o.** wing of the...cherub was five 259
2Ch 3:11 wing of the **o.** cherub was five cubits,
2Ch 3:12 **o.** wing of the other cherub was five
2Ch 3:17 **o.** on the right hand, and the other 259
2Ch 4:15 **O.** sea, and twelve oxen under it......... 259
2Ch 5:13 trumpeters and singers were as **o.**,....... 259
2Ch 5:13 **o.** sound to be heard in praising and..... 259
2Ch 6:29 every **o.** shall know his own sore
2Ch 7:21 to every **o.** that passeth by it; so
2Ch 9:6 **o.** half of the greatness of thy wisdom.
2Ch 9:13 that came to Solomon in **o.** year......... 259
2Ch 9:15 of beaten gold went to **o.** target. 259
2Ch 9:16 shekels of gold went to **o.** shield. 259
2Ch 9:19 twelve lions stood there on the **o.** side
2Ch 12:13 was **o.** and forty years old when he...... 259
2Ch 16:13 died in the **o.** and fortieth year of 259
2Ch 18:7 There is yet **o.** man, by whom we 259
2Ch 18:8 Israel called for **o.** of his officers,......... 259
2Ch 18:12 good to the king with **o.** assent; 259
2Ch 18:12 be like **o.** of theirs, and speak thou 259
2Ch 18:19 **o.** spake saying after this manner, and.
2Ch 20:23 every **o.** helped to destroy another.
2Ch 22:2 he reigned **o.** year in Jerusalem. 259
2Ch 25:17 Come, let us see **o.** another in the face.
2Ch 25:21 and they saw **o.** another in the face,
2Ch 26:11 Hananiah, **o.** of the king's captains.
2Ch 28:6 and twenty thousand in **o.** day,............. 259
2Ch 30:12 was to give them **o.** heart to do the..... 259
2Ch 30:17 for every **o.** that was not clean,
2Ch 30:18 saying, The good Lord pardon every **o.**
2Ch 31:16 every **o.** that entereth into the house
2Ch 32:12 Ye shall worship before **o.** altar, ... 259
2Ch 34:1 in Jerusalem **o.** and thirty years........... 259
2Ch 35:24 in **o.** of the sepulchres of his fathers.
2Ch 36:11 Zedekiah was **o.** and twenty years 259
Ezr 2:1 and Judah, every **o.** unto his city; 376
Ezr 2:26 Gaba, six hundred twenty and **o.**........ 259
Ezr 2:69 and **o.** thousand drams of gold,
Ezr 2:69 and **o.** hundred priests' garments.
Ezr 3:1 together as **o.** man to Jerusalem........... 259
Ezr 3:5 every **o.** that willingly offered a
Ezr 5:14 and they were delivered unto **o.**,
Ezr 6:5 every **o.** to his place, and place them
Ezr 8:34 By number and by weight of every **o.**:
Ezr 9:4 every **o.** that trembled at the words of
Ezr 9:11 filled it form **o.** end to another with
Ezr 10:2 **o.** of the sons of Elam, answered and
Ezr 10:13 is this a work of **o.** day or two: for...... 259
Ne 1:2 Hanani, **o.** of my brethren, came, he 259
Ne 3:8 the son of **o.** of the apothecaries,
Ne 3:28 every **o.** over against his house........... 376
Ne 4:15 to the wall, every **o.** unto his work. 376
Ne 4:17 every **o.** with...hands wrought in.
Ne 4:17 with **o.** of his hands wrought in the 259
Ne 4:18 every **o.** had his sword girded by......... 376
Ne 4:19 upon the wall, **o.** far from another.
Ne 4:22 Let every **o.** with his servant lodge...... 376
Ne 4:23 every **o.** put them off for washing........ 376
Ne 5:7 exact usury, every **o.** of his brother. 376
Ne 5:18 prepared for me daily was **o.** ox and..... 259
Ne 6:2 together in some **o.** the villages
Ne 7:3 every **o.** in his watch and every **o.**....... 376
Ne 7:6 and to Judah, every **o.** unto his city;..... 376
Ne 7:30 Gaba, six hundred twenty and **o.**. 259
Ne 7:37 Ono, seven hundred twenty and **o.**........ 259
Ne 7:63 took **o.** of the daughters of Barzillai
Ne 8:1 themselves together as **o.** man........... 259
Ne 8:16 every **o.** upon the roof of his house,..... 376
Ne 9:3 their God **o.** fourth part of the day;
Ne 10:28 every **o.** having knowledge, and having
Ne 11:1 cast lots, to bring **o.** of ten to dwell..... 259
Ne 11:3 dwelt every **o.** in his possession in....... 376
Ne 11:14 Zabdiel, the son of **o.** of the great men.
Ne 11:20 Judah, every **o.** in his inheritance......... 376
Ne 12:31 **o.** went on the right hand upon the
Ne 13:10 work, were fled every **o.** to his field. ... 376
Ne 13:28 and **o.** of the sons of Joiada, the son of
Ne 13:30 Levites, every **o.** in his business; 376
Es 1:7 being diverse **o.** from another,).......... 3627
Es 3:13 children and women, in **o.** day, even 259
Es 4:5 Hatach, **o.** of the king's chamberlains,
Es 4:11 is **o.** law of his to put him to death, ... 259
Es 6:9 to the hand of **o.** of the king's most 376
Es 7:9 **o.** of the chamberlains, said before....... 259
Es 8:12 **o.** day in all the provinces of king 259
Es 9:19 of sending portions **o.** to another. 376
Es 9:22 of sending portions **o.** to another, ... 376
Job 1:1 **o.** that feared God, and eschewed evil.
Job 1:4 in their houses, every **o.** his day; 376
Job 1:8 **o.** that feareth God, and escheweth
Job 2:3 **o.** that feareth God, and escheweth
Job 2:10 Thou speakest as **o.** of the foolish......... 259
Job 2:11 came every **o.** from his own place;....... 376
Job 2:12 they rent every **o.** his mantle, and....... 376
Job 5:2 man, and envy slayeth the silly **o.**.
Job 6:10 concealed the words of the Holy **O.**.
Job 6:26 and the speeches of **o.** that is desperate, ...
Job 9:3 cannot answer him **o.** of a thousand...... 259
Job 9:22 This is **o.** thing, therefore I said it. 259
Job 12:4 I am as **o.** mocked of his neighbour.
Job 13:9 as **o.** mocketh another, do ye so mock
Job 14:3 open thine eyes upon such an **o.**,
Job 14:4 thing out of an unclean? not **o.**. 259
Job 16:21 **o.** might plead for a man with God,
Job 17:10 I cannot find **o.** wise man among you.
Job 19:11 me unto him as **o.** of his enemies.
Job 21:23 **O.** dieth in his full strength, being
Job 23:13 he is in **o.** mind, and who can turn....... 259
Job 24:6 They reap every **o.** his corn in the
Job 24:17 if **o.** know them, they are in the terrors ....
Job 29:25 as **o.** that comforteth the mourners.
Job 31:15 did not **o.** fashion us in the womb?....... 259
Job 31:35 Oh that **o.** would hear me! behold,
Job 33:23 interpreter, **o.** among a thousand, ... 259
Job 40:11 and behold every **o.** that is proud, and
Job 40:12 Look on every **o.** that is proud,
Job 41:9 shall not **o.** be cast down even at the
Job 41:16 **O.** is so near to another, that no air.... 259
Job 41:17 They are joined **o.** to another, they...... 376
Job 41:32 **o.** would think the deep to be hoary.
Job 42:11 and every **o.** an earring of gold. 376
Ps 12:2 They speak vanity every **o.** with his..... 376
Ps 14:3 is none that doeth good, no, not **o.** 259
Ps 16:10 thine Holy **O.** to see corruption.
Ps 27:4 **O.** thing have I desired of the Lord,..... 259
Ps 29:9 doth every **o.** speak of his glory.
Ps 32:6 For this shall every **o.** that is godly
Ps 34:20 bones: not **o.** of them is broken. 259
Ps 35:14 as **o.** that mourneth for his mother.
Ps 49:16 thou afraid when **o.** is made rich,......... 376
Ps 50:21 I was altogether such an **o.** as thyself:
Ps 53:3 Every **o.** of them is gone back: they
Ps 53:3 is none that doeth good, no, not **o.**. 259
Ps 58:8 let every o. of them pass away:
Ps 63:11 every **o.** that sweareth by him shall
Ps 64:6 inward thought of every **o.** of them, ... 376
Ps 68:21 hairy scalp of such an **o.** as goeth on.
Ps 68:30 every **o.** submit himself with pieces of.
Ps 71:18 thy power to every **o.** that is to come.
Ps 71:22 the harp, O thou Holy **O.** of Israel.
Ps 73:20 As a dream when **o.** awaketh; so,
Ps 75:7 he putteth down **o.** and setteth up
Ps 78:41 and limited the Holy **o.** of Israel.
Ps 78:65 the Lord awaked as **o.** out of sleep,
Ps 82:7 men, and fall like of **o.** the princes. 259
Ps 83:5 consulted together with **o.** consent:
Ps 84:7 every **o.** of them in Zion appeareth
Ps 89:10 Rahab in pieces, as **o.** that is slain;
Ps 89:18 the Holy **O.** of Israel is our king.
Ps 89:19 spakest in vision to thy holy **o.**,
Ps 89:19 laid help upon **o.** that is mighty;
Ps 89:19 exalted **o.** chosen out of the people.
Ps 105:13 they went from **o.** nation to another,
Ps 105:13 from **o.** kingdom to another people;
Ps 105:37 not **o.** feeble person among their
Ps 106:11 there was not **o.** of them left. 259
Ps 115:8 so is every **o.** that trusteth in them.
Ps 119:160 every **o.** of thy righteous judgments
Ps 119:162 thy word, as **o.** that findeth great spoil.
Ps 128:1 Blessed is every **o.** that feareth the
Ps 135:18 so is every **o.** that trusteth in them.
Ps 137:3 saying, Sing us **o.** the songs of Zion.
Ps 141:7 as when **o.** cutteth and cleaveth wood
Ps 145:4 **o.** generation shall praise thy works
Pr 1:14 among us; let us all have **o.** purse: 259
Pr 1:19 the ways of every **o.** that is greedy of.
Pr 3:18 happy is every **o.** that retaineth her.
Pr 6:11 thy poverty come as **o.** that travelleth,
Pr 6:28 Can **o.** go upon hot coals, and his 376
Pr 8:30 by him as **o.** brought up with him:
Pr 15:12 scorner loveth not **o.** that reproveth
Pr 16:5 Every **o.** that is proud in heart is an
Pr 17:14 strife is as when **o.** letteth out water:
Pr 19:25 reprove **o.** that hath understanding,
Pr 20:6 proclaim every **o.** his own goodness: 376
Pr 21:5 every **o.** that is hasty only to want.
Pr 22:26 Be not thou **o.** of them that strike
Pr 24:34 poverty come as **o.** that travelleth;
Pr 26:17 like **o.** that taketh a dog by the ears.
Ec 1:4 **O.** generation passeth away, and
Ec 2:14 **o.** event happeneth to them all. 259
Ec 3:19 even **o.** thing befalleth them: as 2088
Ec 3:19 as the **o.** dieth, so dieth the other;...... 2088
Ec 3:19 they have all **o.** breath; so that a 259
Ec 3:20 All go unto **o.** place; all are of the........ 259
Ec 4:8 There is **o.** alone, and there is not a 259
Ec 4:9 Two are better than **o.**; because........... 259
Ec 4:10 they fall, the **o.** will lift up his fellow:.... 259
Ec 4:11 heat: but how can **o.** be warm alone? ... 259
Ec 4:12 if **o.** prevail against him two shall......... 259
Ec 5:18 and comely for **o.** to eat and to drink,
Ec 6:6 no good: do not all go to **o.** place?....... 259
Ec 7:14 set the **o.** over against the other,....... 2088
Ec 7:27 counting **o.** by **o.**, to find out the......... 259
Ec 7:28 **o.** man among a thousand have I 259
Ec 8:9 a time wherein **o.** man ruleth over.
Ec 9:2 there is **o.** event to the righteous, ... 259
Ec 9:3 that there is **o.** event unto all: yea, ... 259
Ec 9:18 but **o.** sinner destroyeth much good. 259
Ec 10:3 he saith to every **o.** that he is a fool.
Ec 10:15 labour of the foolish wearieth every **o.**
Ec 12:11 which are given from **o.** shepherd. 259
Ca 1:7 as **o.** that turneth aside by the flocks
Ca 2:10 Rise up, my love, my fair **o.**, and come
Ca 2:13 Arise, my love, my fair **o.**, and come
Ca 4:2 whereof every **o.** bear twins, and none
Ca 4:9 my heart with **o.** of thine eyes, ... 259
Ca 4:9 thine eyes, with **o.** chain of thy neck. ... 259
Ca 6:6 whereof every **o.** beareth twins,........... 259
Ca 6:6 there is not **o.** barren among them....... 259
Ca 6:9 My dove, my undefiled is but **o.**;.......... 259
Ca 6:9 she is the only **o.** of her mother, ... 259
Ca 6:9 choice **o.** of her that bare her. 259
Ca 8:10 in his eyes as **o.** that found favour.
Ca 8:11 every **o.** for the fruit thereof was to..... 376
Isa 1:4 provoked the Holy **O.** of Israel
Isa 1:23 every **o.** loveth gifts, and followeth
Isa 1:24 Lord of hosts, the might **O.** of Israel,

Book	Ref	Context	No.
Isa	2:12	shall be upon every **o.** that is proud	
Isa	2:12	and upon every **o.** that is lifted up;	
Isa	2:20	made each **o.** for himself to worship,	
Isa	3:5	be oppressed, every **o.** by another,	376
Isa	3:5	and every **o.** by his neighbour: the	376
Isa	4:1	women shall take hold of **o.** man,	259
Isa	4:3	even every **o.** that is written among	
Isa	5:10	acres of vineyard shall yield **o.** bath,	259
Isa	5:19	counsel of the Holy **O.** of Israel	
Isa	5:24	the word of the Holy **O.** of Israel.	
Isa	5:30	and if **o.** look unto the land, behold	
Isa	6:2	seraphims: each **o.** had six wings:	259
Isa	6:3	**o.** cried unto another, and said, Holy,	
Isa	6:6	Then flew **o.** of the seraphims unto	259
Isa	7:22	every **o.** eat that is left in the land.	
Isa	9:14	and tail, branch and rush, in **o.** day.	259
Isa	9:17	every **o.** is an hypocrite and an evildoer,	
Isa	10:14	and as **o.** gathereth eggs that are left,	
Isa	10:17	fire, and his Holy **O.** for a flame;	
Isa	10:17	his thorns and his briers in **o.** day;	259
Isa	10:20	Lord, the Holy **O.** of Israel, in truth.	
Isa	10:34	and Lebanon shall fall by a mighty **o.**	
Isa	12:6	for great is the Holy **O.** of Israel	
Isa	13:8	they shall be amazed **o.** at another;	376
Isa	13:14	and flee every **o.** into his own land.	
Isa	13:15	Every **o.** that is found shall be thrust	
Isa	13:15	every **o.** that is joined unto them.	
Isa	14:18	in glory, every **o.** in his own house.	376
Isa	14:32	shall **o.** then answer the messengers	
Isa	15:3	and in their streets, every **o.** shall howl,	
Isa	16:7	howl for Moab, every **o.** shall howl: for	
Isa	17:7	respect to the Holy **O.** of Israel.	
Isa	19:2	fight every **o.** against his brother,	376
Isa	19:2	and every **o.** against his neighbour;	376
Isa	19:17	every **o.** that maketh mention thereof	
Isa	19:18	**o.** shall be called, The city of	259
Isa	19:20	send them a saviour, and a great **o.**,	
Isa	23:15	according to the days of **o.** king:	259
Isa	27:12	ye shall be gathered **o.** by **o.**, O ye	259
Isa	28:2	the Lord hath a mighty and strong **o.**,	
Isa	29:4	be, as of **o.** that hath a familiar spirit,	
Isa	29:11	men deliver to **o.** that is learned,	
Isa	29:19	rejoice in the Holy **O.** of Israel.	
Isa	29:20	terrible **o.** is brought to nought,	
Isa	29:23	and sanctify the Holy **O.** of Jacob,	
Isa	30:11	cause the Holy **O.** of Israel to cease	
Isa	30:12	thus saith the Holy **O.** of Israel,	
Isa	30:15	Lord God, the Holy **O.** of Israel;	
Isa	30:17	**O.** thousand shall flee at the rebuke	259
Isa	30:17	shall flee at the rebuke of **o.**; at the	259
Isa	30:29	when **o.** goeth with a pipe to come	
Isa	30:29	to the mighty **O.** of Israel.	
Isa	31:1	not unto the Holy **O.** of Israel,	
Isa	33:20	not **o.** of the stakes thereof shall ever	
Isa	34:15	be gathered, every **o.** with her mate.	
Isa	34:16	no **o.** of these shall fail, none shall	259
Isa	36:9	turn away the face **o.** captain of	259
Isa	36:16	and eat ye every **o.** of his vine,	376
Isa	36:16	and every **o.** of his fig tree, and	376
Isa	36:16	drink ye every **o.** the waters of his	376
Isa	37:23	even against the Holy **O.** of Israel.	
Isa	40:25	shall I be equal? saith the Holy **O.**.	
Isa	40:26	is strong in power; not **o.** faileth.	376
Isa	41:6	They helped every **o.** his neighbour;	376
Isa	41:6	every **o.** said to his brother, Be of	376
Isa	41:14	redeemer, the Holy **O.** of Israel.	
Isa	41:16	shalt glory in the Holy **O.** of Israel.	
Isa	41:20	the Holy **O.** of Israel hath created it.	
Isa	41:25	I have raised up **o.** from the north,	
Isa	41:27	give to Jerusalem **o.** that bringeth	
Isa	43:3	the Holy **O.** of Israel, thy Saviour:	
Isa	43:7	every **o.** that is called by my name:	
Isa	43:14	redeemer, the Holy **O.** of Israel;	
Isa	43:15	I am the Lord, your Holy **O.**, the	
Isa	44:5	**O.** shall say, I am the Lord's; and	
Isa	45:11	the Lord, the Holy **O.** of Israel,	
Isa	45:24	Surely, shall **o.** say, in the Lord have	
Isa	46:7	**o.** shall cry unto him yet can he not	
Isa	47:4	is his name, the Holy **O.** of Israel.	
Isa	47:9	come to thee in a moment in **o.** day,	259
Isa	47:15	wander every **o.** to his quarter;	376
Isa	48:17	Redeemer, the Holy **O.** of Israel;	
Isa	49:7	Redeemer of Israel, and his Holy **O.**,	
Isa	49:7	the Holy **O.** of Israel, and he shall	
Isa	49:26	thy Redeemer, the Mighty **O.** of Jacob.	
Isa	53:6	turned every **o.** to his own way;	376
Isa	54:5	Redeemer the Holy **O.** of Israel;	
Isa	55:1	Ho, every **o.** that thirsteth, come ye	
Isa	55:5	and for the Holy **O.** of Israel; for	
Isa	56:6	every **o.** that keepeth the sabbath	
Isa	56:11	their own way, every **o.** for his gain,	376
Isa	57:2	each **o.** walking in his uprightness.	
Isa	57:15	lofty **O.** that inhabiteth eternity,	
Isa	60:9	God, and to the Holy **O.** of Israel,	
Isa	60:14	The Zion of the Holy **O.** of Israel.	
Isa	60:16	thy Redeemer, the mighty **O.** of Jacob.	
Isa	60:22	A little **o.** shall become a thousand,	
Isa	60:22	and a small **o.** a strong nation:	
Isa	65:8	and **o.** saith, Destroy it not; for a	
Isa	66:8	be made to bring forth in **o.** day?	259
Isa	66:13	As **o.** whom his mother comforteth,	376
Isa	66:17	in the gardens, behind **o.** tree in the	259
Isa	66:23	that from **o.** new moon to another,	
Isa	66:23	and from **o.** sabbath to another,	
Jer	1:15	shall set every **o.** his throne at the	376
Jer	3:14	I will take you **o.** of a city, and two	259
Jer	5:6	every **o.** that goeth out thence shall be	
Jer	5:8	morning: every **o.** neighed after his	376
Jer	6:3	they shall feed every **o.** in his place.	376
Jer	6:13	them every **o.** is given to covetousness;	
Jer	6:13	the priest every **o.** dealeth falsely.	
Jer	8:6	every **o.** turned to his course, as the	
Jer	8:10	for every **o.** from the least even unto	
Jer	8:10	the priest every **o.** dealeth falsely.	
Jer	9:4	ye heed every **o.** of his neighbour,	376
Jer	9:5	will deceive every **o.** his neighbour,	376
Jer	9:8	**o.** speaketh peaceably to his	
Jer	9:20	every **o.** her neighbour lamentation.	
Jer	10:3	for **o.** cutteth a tree out of the forest,	
Jer	11:8	walked every **o.** in the imagination	376
Jer	12:12	devour from the **o.** end of the land	
Jer	13:14	will dash them **o.** against another,	376
Jer	15:10	yet every **o.** of them doth curse me.	
Jer	16:12	walk every **o.** after the imagination	376
Jer	18:11	return ye now every **o.** from his evil	376
Jer	18:12	we will every **o.** do the imagination	376
Jer	18:16	every **o.** that passeth thereby shall be	
Jer	19:8	every **o.** that passeth thereby shall be	
Jer	19:9	eat every **o.** the flesh of his friend	376
Jer	19:11	as **o.** breaketh a potter's vessel, that	
Jer	20:7	in derision daily, every **o.** mocketh me,	
Jer	20:11	is with me as a mighty terrible **o.**:	
Jer	22:7	thee, every **o.** with his weapons:	376
Jer	23:17	they say unto every **o.** that walketh	
Jer	23:30	steal my words every **o.** from his	376
Jer	23:35	ye say every **o.** to his neighbour,	376
Jer	23:35	and every **o.** to his brother, What	376
Jer	24:2	**O.** basket had very good figs, even	259
Jer	25:5	now every **o.** from his evil way,	376
Jer	25:26	north, far and near, **o.** with another,	376
Jer	25:33	at that day from **o.** end of the earth	
Jer	30:14	with the chastisement of a cruel **o.**, for	
Jer	30:16	thine adversaries, every **o.** of them,	
Jer	31:30	But every **o.** shall die for his own	376
Jer	32:19	give every **o.** according to his ways,	376
Jer	32:39	will give them **o.** heart, and **o.** way,	259
Jer	34:10	every **o.** should let his manservant,	376
Jer	34:10	every **o.** his maidservant, go free,	376
Jer	34:17	liberty, every **o.** to his brother, and	376
Jer	35:2	into **o.** of the chambers, and give	259
Jer	36:7	will return every **o.** from his evil way:	
Jer	36:16	they were afraid both **o.** and other,	376
Jer	38:7	**o.** of the eunuchs which was in the	376
Jer	46:16	to fall, yea, **o.** fell upon another:	376
Jer	49:17	every **o.** that goeth by it shall be	
Jer	50:13	every **o.** that goeth by Babylon shall	
Jer	50:16	shall turn every **o.** to his people,	376
Jer	50:16	shall flee every **o.** to his own land.	376
Jer	50:29	Lord, against the Holy **O.** of Israel.	
Jer	50:42	every **o.** put in array, like a man to the	
Jer	51:5	sin against the Holy **O.** of Israel.	
Jer	51:9	go every **o.** into his own country:	376
Jer	51:31	**O.** post shall run to meet another, and	
Jer	51:31	and **o.** messenger to meet another, to	
Jer	51:31	that his city is taken at **o.** end,	
Jer	51:46	a rumour shall both come **o.** year, and	
Jer	51:56	every **o.** of their bows is broken: for	
Jer	52:1	Zedekiah was **o.** and twenty years	259
Jer	52:20	**o.** sea, and twelve brasen bulls that	259
Jer	52:21	of **o.** pillar was eighteen cubits;	259
Jer	52:22	height of **o.** chapiter was five cubits,	259
Eze	1:6	And every **o.** had four faces, and	259
Eze	1:6	faces, and every **o.** had four wings.	259
Eze	1:9	wings were joined **o.** to another;	802
Eze	1:9	they went every **o.** straight forward.	376
Eze	1:11	wings of every **o.** were joined **o.** to	376
Eze	1:12	they went every **o.** straight forward:	376
Eze	1:15	behold **o.** wheel upon the earth by	259
Eze	1:16	and they four had **o.** likeness: and	259
Eze	1:23	straight, the **o.** toward the other:	802
Eze	1:23,	23 every **o.** had two, which covered	376
Eze	1:28	and I heard a voice of **o.** that spake.	
Eze	3:13	creatures that touched **o.** another,	802
Eze	4:8	turn thee from **o.** side to another,	
Eze	4:9	fitches, and put them in **o.** vessel,	259
Eze	4:17	and be astonied **o.** with another,	376
Eze	7:16	mourning, every **o.** for his iniquity.	376
Eze	9:2	**o.** man among them was clothed	259
Eze	10:7	**o.** cherub stretched forth his hand	
Eze	10:9	**o.** wheel by...cherub, and another	259
Eze	10:10	wheel by **o.** cherub, and another	
Eze	10:10	they four had **o.** likeness, as if a	259
Eze	10:14	every **o.** had four faces: the first face	259
Eze	10:19	every **o.** stood at the door of the east	
Eze	10:21	Every **o.** had four faces apiece, and	259
Eze	10:21	faces apiece, and every **o.** four wings;	259
Eze	10:22	they went every **o.** straight forward.	376
Eze	11:5	into your mind, every **o.** of them.	
Eze	11:19	And I will give them **o.** heart, and	259
Eze	13:10	and **o.** built up a wall, and, lo, others	
Eze	14:7	For every **o.** of the house of Israel,	376
Eze	15:7	they shall go out form **o.** fire, and	
Eze	16:15	on every **o.** that passed by; his it was.	
Eze	16:25	thy feet to every **o.** that passed by,	
Eze	16:44	Behold, every **o.** that useth proverbs	
Eze	17:22	top of his young twigs a tender **o.**,	
Eze	18:10	the like to any **o.** of these things,	259
Eze	18:30	every **o.** according to his ways,	376
Eze	19:3	she brought up **o.** of her whelps:	259
Eze	20:39	Go ye, serve ye every **o.** his idols,	376
Eze	21:16	Go thee **o.** way or other, either on the	
Eze	21:19	shall come forth out of **o.** land:	259
Eze	22:6	every **o.** were in thee to their power	376
Eze	22:11	And **o.** hath committed abomination.	
Eze	23:2	women, the daughters of **o.** mother:	259
Eze	23:13	defiled, that they took both **o.** way,	259
Eze	24:23	and mourn **o.** toward another.	376
Eze	31:11	hand of the mighty **o.** of the heathen;	
Eze	33:20	judge...every **o.** after his own ways	376
Eze	33:21	**o.** that escaped out of Jerusalem	
Eze	33:24	Abraham was **o.**, and he inherited	259
Eze	33:26	ye defile every **o.** his neighbour's	376
Eze	33:30	houses, and speak **o.** to another,	2297
Eze	33:30	every **o.** to his brother, saying,	376
Eze	33:32	song of **o.** that hath a pleasant voice,	
Eze	34:23	will set up **o.** shepherd over them,	259
Eze	37:16	son of man, take thee **o.** stick, and	259
Eze	37:17	join them **o.** to another into **o.** stick;	259
Eze	37:17	they shall become **o.** in thine hand.	259
Eze	37:19	of Judah, and make them **o.** stick,	259
Eze	37:19	and they shall be **o.** in mine hand.	259
Eze	37:22	make them **o.** nation in the land	259
Eze	37:22	**o.** king shall be king to them all:	259
Eze	37:24	and they all shall have **o.** shepherd:	259
Eze	39:7	am the Lord, the Holy **O.** in Israel.	
Eze	40:5	the breadth of the building, **o.** reed;	259
Eze	40:5	and the height, **o.** reed.	259
Eze	40:6	the gate, which was **o.** reed broad;	259
Eze	40:6	the gate, which was **o.** reed broad.	259
Eze	40:7	little chamber was **o.** reed long,	259
Eze	40:7	and **o.** reed broad; and between the	259
Eze	40:7	of the gate within was **o.** reed.	259
Eze	40:8	porch of the gate within, **o.** reed.	259
Eze	40:10	they three were of **o.** measure: and	259
Eze	40:10	posts had **o.** measure on this side	259
Eze	40:12	the little chamber was **o.** cubit on	259
Eze	40:12	and the space was **o.** cubit on that side;	
Eze	40:13	from the roof of **o.** little chamber to	
Eze	40:26	it had palm trees, **o.** on this side,	259
Eze	40:40	as **o.** goeth up to the entry of the north	
Eze	40:42	an half broad, and **o.** cubit high:	259
Eze	40:44	**o.** at the side of the east gate having	259
Eze	40:49	**o.** on this side, and another on that	259
Eze	41:1	six cubits broad on the **o.** side,	
Eze	41:2	were five cubits on the **o.** side, and	
Eze	41:6	**o.** over another, and thirty in order;	
Eze	41:11	was left **o.** door toward the north,	259
Eze	41:15	the galleries thereof on the **o.** side	

Eze 41:19 toward the palm tree on the o. side,
Eze 41:21 the appearance of the o. as the
Eze 41:24 two leaves for the o. door, and two 259
Eze 41:26 and palm trees on the o. side and on
Eze 42:4 breadth inward, a way of o. cubit; 259
Eze 42:9 as o. goeth into them from the utter
Eze 42:12 the east, as o. entereth into them.
Eze 43:14 two cubits, and the breadth o. cubit. 259
Eze 43:14 four cubits, and the breadth o. cubit;
Eze 45:7 be for the prince on the o. side and
Eze 45:7 be over against o. of the portions, 259
Eze 45:11 and the bath shall be of o. measure, 259
Eze 45:15 o. lamb out of the flock, out of two 259
Eze 45:20 the month for every o. that erreth, 376
Eze 46:12 o. shall then open him the gate that
Eze 46:12 his going forth o. shall shut the gate.
Eze 46:17 his inheritance to o. of his servants, 259
Eze 46:22 four corners were of o. measure. 259
Eze 47:7 many trees on the o. side and on the
Eze 47:14 inherit it, o. as well as another: 376
Eze 48:1 of Hethlon, as o. goeth to Hamath,
Eze 48:8 in length as o. of the other parts, 259
Eze 48:21 on the o. side and on the other of the
Eze 48:31 gates northward; o. gate of Reuben, 259
Eze 48:31 o. gate of Judah, o. gate of Levi. 259
Eze 48:32 three gates; and o. gate of Joseph, 259
Eze 48:32 o. gate of Benjamin, o. gate of Dan. 259
Eze 48:33 and three gates; o. gate of Simeon, 259
Eze 48:33 o. gate of Issachar, o. gate of Zebulun 259
Eze 48:34 their three gates; o. gate of Gad, 259
Eze 48:34 o. gate of Asher, o. gate of Naphtali. 259
Da 2:9 there is but o. decree for you: 2298
Da 2:43 they shall not cleave o. to another, 1836
Da 3:19 heat the furnace o. seven times 2298
Da 4:13 and an holy o. came down from
Da 4:19 was astonied for o. hour, and 2298
Da 4:23 and an holy o. coming down from
Da 5:6 knees smote o. against another. 1668
Da 7:3 the sea, diverse o. from another. 1668
Da 7:5 and it raised up itself on o. side, 2298
Da 7:13 o. like the Son of man came with the
Da 7:16 near unto o. of them that stood 2298
Da 8:3 but o. was higher than the other, 259
Da 8:9 out of o. of them came forth a little 259
Da 8:13 Then I heard o. saint speaking, and 259
Da 9:27 the covenant with many for o. week: 259
Da 10:13 withstood me o. and twenty days: 259
Da 10:13 lo, Michael, o. of the chief princes, 259
Da 10:16 o. like the similitude of the sons of
Da 10:18 touched me o. like the appearance
Da 11:5 shall be strong, and o. of his princes;
Da 11:7 roots shall o. stand up in his estate,
Da 11:10 and o. shall certainly come, and
Da 11:27 they shall speak lies at o. table; 259
Da 12:1 every o. that shall be found written in
Da 12:5 the o. on this side of the bank of 259
Da 12:6 o. said to the man clothed in linen,
Ho 1:11 and appoint themselves o. head, 259
Ho 4:3 every o. that dwelleth therein shall
Ho 11:9 and Holy O. in the midst of thee:
Joe 2:7 shall march every o. on his ways, 376
Joe 2:8 Neither shall o. thrust another; 376
Joe 2:8 shall walk ever every o. in his path: 1397
Am 3:5 o. take up a snare from the earth,
Am 4:7 I caused it to rain upon o. city, and 259
Am 4:7 o. piece was rained upon, and the 259
Am 4:8 three cities wandered unto o. city, 259
Am 6:9 if there remain ten men in o. house, 259
Am 6:12 rock? will o. plow there with oxen?
Am 8:8 every o. mourn that dwelleth therein?
Ob 9 every o. of the mount of Esau may 376
Ob 11 even thou wast as o. of them. 259
Jon 1:7 And they said every o. to his fellow, 376
Jon 3:8 turn every o. from his evil way, and 376
Mic 2:4 shall o. take up a parable against you,
Mic 4:5 every o. in the name of his god, 376
Na 1:11 There is o. come out of thee, that
Na 2:4 shall justle o. against another in the
Hab 1:12 O Lord my God, mine Holy O.? 6918
Hab 3:3 and the Holy O. from mount Paran. 6918
Zep 2:11 every o. from his place, even all 376
Zep 2:15 every o. that passeth by her shall hiss,
Zep 3:9 Lord, to serve him with o. consent. 259
Hag 2:1 o. and twentieth day of the month, 259
Hag 2:12 If o. bear holy flesh in the skirt of
Hag 2:13 If o. that is unclean by a dead body
Hag 2:16 o. came to an heap of twenty measures,
Hag 2:16 o. came to the pressfat for to draw
Hag 2:22 every o. by the sword of his brother. 376
Zec 3:9 upon o. stone shall be seven eyes: 259
Zec 3:9 the iniquity of that land in o. day. 259
Zec 4:3 o. upon the right side of the bowl, 259
Zec 5:3 every o. that stealeth shall be cut off
Zec 5:3 every o. that sweareth shall be cut off
Zec 8:10 men every o. against his neighbour. 376
Zec 8:21 the inhabitants of o. city shall go to 259
Zec 10:1 rain, to every o. grass in the field. 376
Zec 11:6 every o. into his neighbour's hand, 376
Zec 11:7 two staves; the o. I called Beauty, 259
Zec 11:8 shepherds...I cut off in o. month; 259
Zec 11:9 rest eat every o. the flesh of another. 802
Zec 11:16 neither shall seek the young o., nor
Zec 12:10 as o. mourneth for his only son, and
Zec 12:10 as o. that is in bitterness for his
Zec 13:4 be ashamed every o. of his vision, 376
Zec 13:6 And o. shall say unto him, What are
Zec 14:7 But it shall be o. day which shall be 259
Zec 14:9 there be o. Lord, and his name o. 259
Zec 14:13 lay hold every o. on the hand of his 376
Zec 14:16 that every o. that is left of all the
Mal 2:3 and o. shall take you away with it.
Mal 2:10 Have we not all o. father? hath 259
Mal 2:10 hath not o. God created us? why do 259
Mal 2:15 And did not he make o.? Yet had he 259
Mal 2:15 And wherefore o.? That he might 259
Mal 2:16 for o. covereth violence with his
Mal 2:17 Every o. that doeth evil is good in the
Mal 3:16 the Lord spake often o. to another: 376
Mt 3:3 voice of o. crying in the wilderness,
Mt 5:18 heaven and earth pass, o. jot or 1520
Mt 5:18 o. tittle shall in no wise pass 3391
Mt 5:19 shall break o. of these least 3391
Mt 5:29, 30 should o. of thy members 1520
Mt 5:36 not make o. hair white or black 3391
Mt 6:24 for either he will hate the o., and 1520
Mt 6:24 or else he will hold to the o., and 1520
Mt 6:27 can add o. cubit unto his stature? 1520
Mt 6:29 was not arrayed like o. of these 1520
Mt 7:8 every o. that asketh receiveth; and
Mt 7:21 Not every o. that saith unto me,
Mt 7:26 every o. that heareth these sayings
Mt 7:29 he taught them as o. having authority,
Mt 10:29 and o. of them shall not fall on 1520
Mt 10:42 o. of these little ones a cup of 1520
Mt 12:6 place is o. greater than the temple.
Mt 12:11 that shall have o. sheep, and if it 1520
Mt 12:22 unto him o. possessed with a devil,
Mt 12:29 can o. enter into a strong man's 5100
Mt 12:47 Then o. said unto him, Behold, thy 5100
Mt 13:19 When any o. heareth the word of
Mt 13:19 then cometh the wicked o., and
Mt 13:38 are the children of the wicked o.;
Mt 13:46 had found o. pearl of great price, 1520
Mt 16:14 Jeremias, or o. of the prophets. 1520
Mt 17:4 here three tabernacles, o. for thee, 3391
Mt 17:4 and o. for Moses, and o. for Elias. 3391
Mt 18:5 shall receive o. such little child in 1520
Mt 18:6 shall offend o. of these little ones 1520
Mt 18:9 thee to enter into life with o. eye, 3442
Mt 18:10 despise not o. of these little ones; 1520
Mt 18:12 o. of them be gone astray, doth 1520
Mt 18:14 o. of these little ones should 1520
Mt 18:16 take with thee o. or two more, 1520
Mt 18:24 o. was brought unto him, which 1520
Mt 18:28 found o. of his fellowservants, 1520
Mt 18:35 forgive not every o. his brother
Mt 19:5 and they twain shall be o. flesh? 3391
Mt 19:6 are no more twain, but o. flesh 3391
Mt 19:16 o. came and said unto him, Good 1520
Mt 19:17 is none good but o., that is, God: 1520
Mt 19:29 And every o. that hath forsaken
Mt 20:12 last have wrought but o. hour, 3391
Mt 20:13 he answered o. of them, and said, 1520
Mt 20:21 may sit, the o. on thy right hand, 1520
Mt 21:24 I also will ask you o. thing, 1520
Mt 21:35 took his servants, and beat o., 3739
Mt 22:5 their ways, o. to his farm, 3538,3303
Mt 22:35 o. of them, which was a lawyer, 1520
Mt 23:4 not move them with o. of their
Mt 23:8 o. is your Master, even Christ; 1520
Mt 23:9 for o. is your Father, which is in 1520
Mt 23:10 for o. is your Master, even Christ. 1520
Mt 23:15 and land to make o. proselyte, 1520
Mt 24:2 not be left here o. stone upon
Mt 24:10 and shall betray o. another, 240
Mt 24:10 another, and shall hate o. another 240
Mt 24:31 from o. end of heaven to the other.
Mt 24:40, 41 o. shall be taken, and the other 1520
Mt 25:15 unto o. he gave five talents, 3739,3303
Mt 25:15 another two, and to another o.; 1520
Mt 25:18 he that had received o. went and 1520
Mt 25:24 had received the o. talent 1520
Mt 25:29 every o. that hath shall be given,
Mt 25:32 separate them o. from another, as 240
Mt 25:40 it unto o. of the least of these my 1520
Mt 25:45 it not to o. of the least of these, 1520
Mt 26:14 Then o. of the twelve, called Judas 1520
Mt 26:21 you, that o. of you shall betray 1520
Mt 26:22 every o. of them to say unto him,
Mt 26:40 ye not watch with me o. hour? 3391
Mt 26:47 lo, Judas, o. of the twelve, came 1520
Mt 26:51 o. of them which were with Jesus 1520
Mt 26:73 Peter, Surely thou also art o. of them:
Mt 27:38 o. on the right hand, and another 1520
Mt 27:48 And straightway o. of them ran, 1520
Mk 1:3 voice of o. crying in the wilderness,
Mk 1:7 cometh o. mightier than I after me,
Mk 1:22 taught them as o. that had authority,
Mk 1:24 who thou art, the Holy O. of God.
Mk 2:3 bringing o. sick of the palsy, which
Mk 4:41 said o. to another, What manner 240
Mk 5:22 o. of the rulers of the synagogue, 1520
Mk 6:15 prophet, or as o. of the prophets. 1520
Mk 7:14 Hearken unto me every o. of you,
Mk 7:32 bring unto him o. that was deaf,
Mk 8:14 ship with them more than o. loaf. 1520
Mk 8:28 and others, O. of the prophets. 1520
Mk 9:5 three tabernacles: o. for thee. 3391
Mk 9:5 and o. for Moses, and o. for Elias.
Mk 9:10 questioning o. with another what
Mk 9:17 o. of the multitude answered and 1520
Mk 9:26 and he was as o. dead; insomuch
Mk 9:37 receive o. of such children in my 1520
Mk 9:38 o. casting out devils in thy name, 5100
Mk 9:42 shall offend o. of these little ones 1520
Mk 9:47 into the kingdom of God with o. 3442
Mk 9:49 every o. shall be salted with fire,
Mk 9:50 and have peace o. with another. 240
Mk 10:8 And they twain shall be o. flesh: 3391
Mk 10:8 are no more twain, but o. flesh.
Mk 10:17 came o. running, and kneeled to 1520
Mk 10:18 is none good but o., that is, God. 1520
Mk 10:21 O. thing thou lackest: go thy 1520
Mk 10:37 we may sit, o. on thy right hand, 1520
Mk 11:29 I will also ask of you o. question, 1520
Mk 12:6 Having yet therefore o. son, his 1520
Mk 12:28 o. of the scribes came, and having 1520
Mk 12:29 The Lord our God is o. Lord: 1520
Mk 12:32 there is o. God; and there is none 1520
Mk 13:1 o. of his disciples saith unto him, 1520
Mk 13:2 not be left o. stone upon another,
Mk 14:10 Judas Iscariot, o. of the twelve, 1520
Mk 14:18 O. of you which eateth with me 1520
Mk 14:19 to say unto him o. by o., Is it I? 1520
Mk 14:20 It is o. of the twelve, that dippeth 1520
Mk 14:37 couldest thou not watch o. hour? 3391
Mk 14:43 cometh Judas, o. of the twelve, 1520
Mk 14:47 o. of them that stood by drew a 1520
Mk 14:66 o. of the maids of the high priest: 3391
Mk 14:69 that stood by, This is o. of them.
Mk 14:70 to Peter, Surely thou art o. of them:
Mk 15:6 he released unto them o. prisoner, 1520
Mk 15:7 And there was o. named Barabbas,
Mk 15:21 they compel o. Simon a Cyrenian, 5100
Mk 15:27 the o. on his right hand, and the 1520
Mk 15:36 O. ran and filled a sponge full of 1520
Lu 2:3 taxed, every o. into his own city.
Lu 2:15 the shepherds said o. to another, 240
Lu 2:36 there was o. Anna, a prophetess,
Lu 3:4 voice of o. crying in the wilderness,
Lu 3:16 but o. mightier than I cometh, the
Lu 4:34 who thou art; the Holy O. of God.
Lu 4:40 laid his hands on every o. of them, 1520
Lu 5:3 And he entered into o. of the ships, 1520
Lu 6:9 unto them, I will ask you o. thing; 5100
Lu 6:11 communed o. with another what 240
Lu 6:29 on the o. cheek offer also the other;
Lu 6:40 every o. that is perfect shall be as
Lu 7:8 I say unto o., Go, and he goeth; 5129
Lu 7:32 calling o. to another, and saying, 240
Lu 7:36 o. of the Pharisees desired him 5100

Book	Ref	Context	No.
Lu	7:41	the o. owed five hundred pence,	1520
Lu	8:25	wondered, saying o. to another,	240
Lu	8:42	For he had o. only daughter, about	
Lu	8:49	cometh o. from the ruler of the	5100
Lu	9:8	o. of the old prophets was risen	1520
Lu	9:19	that o. of the old prophets is risen	5100
Lu	9:33	three tabernacles; o. for thee,	3391
Lu	9:33	and o. for Moses, and o. for Elias:	3391
Lu	9:43	wondered every o. at all things	3956
Lu	9:49	o. casting out devils in thy name;	5100
Lu	10:42	But o. thing is needful: and Mary	1520
Lu	11:1	o. of his disciples said unto him,	5100
Lu	11:4	forgive every o. that is indebted	
Lu	11:10	every o. that asketh receiveth; and	
Lu	11:45	Then answered o. of the lawyers,	5100
Lu	11:46	burdens with o. of your fingers	1520
Lu	12:1	that they trode o. upon another, he	240
Lu	12:6	not o. of them is forgotten before	1520
Lu	12:13	o. of the company said unto him,	5100
Lu	12:25	can add to his stature o. cubit?	1520
Lu	12:27	was not arrayed like o. of these,	1520
Lu	12:52	shall be five in o. house divided,	1520
Lu	13:10	teaching in o. of the synagogues	3391
Lu	13:15	not each o. of you on the sabbath	
Lu	13:23	Then said o. unto him, Lord, are	5100
Lu	14:1	house of o. of the chief Pharisees	5100
Lu	14:15	o. of them that sat at meat with	5100
Lu	14:18	o. consent began to make excuse	3391
Lu	15:4	he lose o. of them, doth not leave	1520
Lu	15:7	over o. sinner that repenteth,	1520
Lu	15:8	if she lose o. piece, doth not light	3391
Lu	15:10	God over o. sinner that repenteth	1520
Lu	15:19	me as o. of thy hired servants	1520
Lu	15:26	he called o. of the servants, and	1520
Lu	16:5	every o. of his lord's debtors	1520
Lu	16:13	either he will hate the o., and	1520
Lu	16:13	or else he will hold to the o., and	1520
Lu	16:17	than o. tittle of the law to fail	3391
Lu	16:30	if o. went unto them from the	5100
Lu	16:31	though o. rose from the dead	5100
Lu	17:2	should offend o. of these little	1520
Lu	17:15	And o. of them, when he saw that	1520
Lu	17:22	shall desire to see o. of the days	3391
Lu	17:24	out of the o. part under heaven,	
Lu	17:34	there shall be two men in o. bed;	3391
Lu	17:34	the o. shall be taken, and the	1520
Lu	17:35	the o. shall be taken, and the	3391
Lu	17:36	the o. shall be taken, and the	1520
Lu	18:10	the o. a Pharisee, and the other a	1520
Lu	18:14	for every o. that exalteth himself	
Lu	18:19	none is good, save o., that is, God	1520
Lu	18:22	Yet lackest thou o. thing: sell all	1520
Lu	19:26	unto every o. which hath shall be	
Lu	19:44	leave in thee o. stone upon another;	
Lu	20:1	on o. of those days, as he taught	3391
Lu	20:3	I will also ask you o. thing; and	1520
Lu	21:6	shall not be left o. stone upon	
Lu	22:36	him sell his garment, and buy o.	
Lu	22:47	was called Judas, o. of the twelve,	1520
Lu	22:50	o. of them smote the servant of the	1520
Lu	22:59	about the space of o. hour after	3391
Lu	23:14	as o. that perverteth the people: and	
Lu	23:17	release o. unto them at the feast.)	1520
Lu	23:26	away, they laid hold upon o. Simon,	5100
Lu	23:33	o. on the right hand, and the	3739,3303
Lu	23:39	o. of the malefactors which were	1520
Lu	24:17	these that ye have o. to another,	240
Lu	24:18	the o. of them, whose name was	1520
Lu	24:32	they said o. to another, Did not our	240
Joh	1:23	voice of o. crying in the wilderness,	
Joh	1:26	there standeth o. among you, whom	
Joh	1:40	O. of the two which heard John	1520
Joh	3:8	so is every o. that is born of the	
Joh	3:20	every o. that doeth evil hateth the	
Joh	4:33	said the disciples o. to another,	240
Joh	4:37	O. soweth, and another reapeth	243
Joh	5:44	which receive honour o. of another,	240
Joh	5:45	there is o. that accuseth you, even	
Joh	6:7	every o. of them may take a little.	
Joh	6:8	O. of his disciples, Andrew, Simon	1520
Joh	6:22	save that o. whereinto his disciples	1520
Joh	6:40	every o. which seeth the Son, and	
Joh	6:70	twelve,, and o. of you is a devil?	1520
Joh	6:71	betray him, being o. of the twelve.	1520
Joh	7:21	unto them, I have done o. work,	1520
Joh	7:50	Jesus by night, being o. of them,)	1520
Joh	8:9	went out o. by o., beginning at the	1520
Joh	8:18	am o. that bear witness of myself,	
Joh	8:41	we have o. Father, even God.	1520
Joh	8:50	there is o. that seeketh and judgeth	
Joh	9:25	o. thing I know, that, whereas I	1520
Joh	9:32	the eyes of o. that was born blind.	
Joh	10:16	there shall be o. fold, and	3391
Joh	10:16	there shall be...o. shepherd	1520
Joh	10:30	I and my Father are o.	1520
Joh	11:49	o. of them named Caiaphas, being	1520
Joh	11:50	o. man should die for the people,	1520
Joh	11:52	together in o. the children of God	1520
Joh	12:2	Lazarus was o. of them that sat at	1520
Joh	12:4	o. of his disciples, Judas Iscariot,	1520
Joh	12:48	my words, hath o. that judgeth him:	
Joh	13:14	also ought to wash o. another's	240
Joh	13:21	that o. of you shall betray me	1520
Joh	13:22	the disciples looked o. on another,	240
Joh	13:23	on Jesus' bosom o. of his disciples,	1520
Joh	13:34	unto you, That ye love o. another;	240
Joh	13:34	you, that ye also love o. another	240
Joh	13:35	if ye have love o. to another	240
Joh	15:12	That ye love o. another, as I have	240
Joh	15:17	you, that ye love o. another	240
Joh	17:11	me, that they may be o., as we	1520
Joh	17:21	That they all may be o.; as thou,	1520
Joh	17:21	that they also may be o. in us:	1520
Joh	17:22	they may be o., even as we are o.:	1520
Joh	17:23	they may be made perfect in o.;	1520
Joh	18:14	o. man should die for the people.	1520
Joh	18:17	thou also o. of this man's disciples?	
Joh	18:22	o. of the officers which stood by	1520
Joh	18:25	Art not thou also o. of his disciples?	
Joh	18:26	O. of the servants of the high	1520
Joh	18:37	Every o. that is of the truth	
Joh	18:39	release unto you o. at the passover:	1520
Joh	19:18	on either side o., and Jesus in the	
Joh	19:34	But o. of the soldiers with a spear	1520
Joh	20:12	the o. at the head, and the other at	1520
Joh	20:24	Thomas, o. of the twelve, called	1520
Joh	21:25	if they should be written every o.,	1520
Ac	1:14	continued with o. accord in prayer	3661
Ac	1:22	must o. be ordained to be a witness	1520
Ac	2:1	they were all with o. accord in	3661
Ac	2:1	all with...accord in o. place	3858,848
Ac	2:7	marvelled, saying o. to another,	240
Ac	2:12	in doubt, saying o. to another,	243
Ac	2:27	thine Holy O. to see corruption	
Ac	2:38	and be baptized every o. of you in	
Ac	2:46	daily with o. accord in the temple,	3661
Ac	3:14	ye denied the Holy O. and the Just,	
Ac	3:26	turning away every o. of you from	
Ac	4:24	their voice to God with o. accord,	3661
Ac	4:32	were of o. heart and of...soul:	
Ac	4:32	were of...heart and of o. soul:	3391
Ac	5:12	with o. accord in Solomon's porch.	3661
Ac	5:16	and they were healed every o.	
Ac	5:25	came o. and told them, saying,	5100
Ac	5:34	stood there up o. in the council, a	5100
Ac	7:24	seeing o. of them suffer wrong, he	5100
Ac	7:26	would have set them at o. again,	1515
Ac	7:26	why do ye wrong o. to another?	240
Ac	7:52	before of the coming of the Just O.; of	
Ac	7:57	and ran upon him with o. accord,	3661
Ac	8:6	the people with o. accord gave heed	3661
Ac	8:9	that himself was some great o.:	
Ac	9:11	the house of Judas for o. called Saul,	
Ac	9:43	in Joppa with o. Simon a tanner.	5100
Ac	10:2	o. that feared God with all his house,	
Ac	10:5	men to Joppa, and call for o. Simon,	
Ac	10:6	lodgeth with o. Simon a tanner,	5100
Ac	10:22	a just man, and o. that feareth God,	
Ac	10:28	or come unto o. of another nation;	
Ac	10:32	the house of o. Simon a tanner by the	
Ac	11:28	stood up o. of them named Agabus,	1520
Ac	12:10	and passed on through o. street;	3391
Ac	12:20	they came with o. accord to him,	3661
Ac	13:25	there cometh o. after me, whose	
Ac	13:35	thine Holy O. to see corruption	
Ac	15:25	being assembled with o. accord,	3661
Ac	15:39	departed asunder o. from the other:	240
Ac	17:7	that there is another king, o. Jesus.	
Ac	17:26	hath made of o. blood all nations	1520
Ac	17:27	he be not far from every o. of us:	1520
Ac	18:7	o. that worshipped God, whose house	
Ac	18:12	made insurrection with o. accord	3361
Ac	19:9	daily in the school of o. Tyrannus.	5100
Ac	19:14	there were seven sons of o. Sceva, a	
Ac	19:29	with o. accord into the theatre	3661
Ac	19:32	cried o. thing, and some another:	3303
Ac	19:34	all with o. voice about the space of	3391
Ac	19:38	let them implead o. another.	240
Ac	20:31	ceased not to warn every o. night	1520
Ac	21:6	had taken our leave o. of another,	240
Ac	21:7	and abode with them o. day.	3391
Ac	21:8	evangelist, which was o. of the seven:	
Ac	21:16	with them o. Mnason of Cyprus,	5100
Ac	21:26	be offered for every o. of them.	1520
Ac	21:34	some cried o. thing, and some another,	
Ac	22:12	And o. Ananias, a devout man	5100
Ac	22:14	know his will, and see that Just O.,	
Ac	23:6	that the o. part were Sadducees,	1520
Ac	23:17	Paul called o. of the centurions	1520
Ac	24:21	Except it be for this o. voice, that	3391
Ac	25:19	and of o. Jesus, which was dead,	5100
Ac	27:1	other prisoners unto o. named Julius,	
Ac	27:2	o. Aristarchus, a Macedonian of	
Ac	28:2	a fire, and receive us every o.,	
Ac	28:13	after o. day the south wind blew,	3391
Ac	28:25	that Paul had spoken o. word,	1520
Ro	1:16	salvation to every o. that believeth;	
Ro	1:27	in their lust o. toward another;	240
Ro	2:15	accusing or...excusing o. another;)	240
Ro	2:28	is not a Jew, which is o. outwardly;	
Ro	2:29	But he is a Jew, which is o. inwardly;	
Ro	3:10	There is none righteous, no, not o.:	1520
Ro	3:12	is none that doeth good, no, not o.	1520
Ro	3:30	Seeing it is o. God, which shall	1520
Ro	5:7	for a righteous man will o. die:	5100
Ro	5:12	as by o. man sin entered into the	1520
Ro	5:15	the offence of o. many be dead,	1520
Ro	5:15	which is by o. man, Jesus Christ,	1520
Ro	5:16	not as it was by o. that sinned, so	1520
Ro	5:16	was by o. to condemnation, but the	1520
Ro	5:17	by o. man's offence death reigned	1520
Ro	5:17	man's offence death reigned by o.;	1520
Ro	5:17	reign in life by o., Jesus Christ.)	1520
Ro	5:18	by the offence of o. judgment came	1520
Ro	5:18	the righteousness of o. the free gift	1520
Ro	5:19	as by o. man's disobedience many	1520
Ro	5:19	by the obedience of o. shall many be	1520
Ro	9:10	Rebecca also had conceived by o.,	1520
Ro	9:21	lump to make o. vessel unto honour,	
Ro	10:4	law for righteousness to every o.	3956
Ro	12:4	have many members in o. body,	1520
Ro	12:5	being many, are o. body in Christ,	1520
Ro	12:5	every o. members...of another.	1520
Ro	12:5	members o. of another.	240
Ro	12:10	kindly affectioned o. to another	240
Ro	12:10	in honour preferring o. another;	240
Ro	12:16	of the same mind o. toward another.	240
Ro	13:8	any thing, but to love o. another:	240
Ro	14:2	For o. believeth that he may eat all	3789
Ro	14:5	O. man esteemeth...day above	3739,3303
Ro	14:5	man esteemeth o. day above another:	
Ro	14:12	every o. of us shall give account of	
Ro	14:13	not...judge o. another any more:	240
Ro	14:19	wherewith o. may edify another	240
Ro	15:2	every o. of us please his neighbour	
Ro	15:5	be likeminded o. toward another	240
Ro	15:6	That ye may with o. mind...mouth	3661
Ro	15:6	with...mind and o. mouth glorify	1520
Ro	15:7	Wherefore receive ye o. another,	240
Ro	15:14	able also to admonish o. another.	240
Ro	16:16	Salute o. another with an holy kiss.	240
1Co	1:12	that every o. of you saith, I am of	
1Co	3:4	For while o. saith, I am of Paul;	5100
1Co	3:8	and he that watereth are o.:	1520
1Co	4:6	no o. of you be puffed up for o.	1520
1Co	5:1	o. should have his father's wife.	5100
1Co	5:5	To deliver such an o. unto Satan	
1Co	5:11	with such an o. no not to eat.	
1Co	6:5	not o. that shall be able to judge	
1Co	6:7	ye go to law with o. another.	1438
1Co	6:16	is joined to an harlot is o. body?	1520
1Co	6:16	two, saith he, shall be o. flesh.	3391
1Co	6:17	is joined unto the Lord is o. spirit.	1520
1Co	7:5	Defraud ye not o. the other, except	240
1Co	7:7	o. after this manner, and	3739,3303
1Co	7:17	as the Lord hath called every o., so	
1Co	7:25	as o. that hath obtained mercy of the	
1Co	8:4	there is none other God but o.	1520
1Co	8:6	But to us there is but o. God, the	1520
1Co	8:6	o. Lord Jesus Christ, by whom are	1520
1Co	9:24	run all, but o. receiveth the prize?	1520

1Co 9:26 fight I, not as **o.** that beateth the air:........
1Co 10:8 and fell in **o.** day three and twenty..... *3391*
1Co 10:17 many are **o.** bread, and **o.** body:........ *1520*
1Co 10:17 are all partakers of that **o.** bread........ *1520*
1Co 11:5 is even all **o.** as if she were shaven.... *1520*
1Co 11:20 come together...into **o.** place, ... *3588,846*
1Co 11:21 eating every **o.** taketh before other..........
1Co 11:21 **o.** is hungry, and another is....... *3739,3303*
1Co 11:33 together to eat, tarry **o.** for another..... *240*
1Co 12:8 For to **o.** is given by the Spirit... *3739,3303*
1Co 12:11 that **o.** and the selfsame Spirit, ... *1520*
1Co 12:12 as the body is **o.**, and hath many *1520*
1Co 12:12 the members of that **o.** body, being.... *1520*
1Co 12:12 many, are **o.** body: so also is Christ. .. *1520*
1Co 12:13 For by **o.** Spirit are we all baptized..... *1520*
1Co 12:13 into **o.** body, whether we be Jews or.. *1520*
1Co 12:13 been all made to drink **o.** Spirit......... *1520*
1Co 12:14 For the body is not **o.** member, but.... *1520*
1Co 12:18 every **o.** of them in the body, as it..... *1520*
1Co 12:19 if they were all **o.** member, where *1520*
1Co 12:20 many members, yet but **o.** body. *1520*
1Co 12:25 have the same care **o.** for another. *240*
1Co 12:26 whether **o.** member suffer, all the...... *1520*
1Co 12:26 or **o.** member be honoured, all the..... *1520*
1Co 14:23 be come together into **o.** place,.... *3588,846*
1Co 14:24 come in **o.** that believeth not, or........ *5100*
1Co 14:24 or **o.** unlearned, he is convinced of..........
1Co 14:26 every **o.** of you hath a psalm, hath ....
1Co 14:27 by course; and let **o.** interpret........... *1520*
1Co 14:31 For ye may all prophesy **o.** by.... *2596,1520*
1Co 14:31 ye may all prophesy...by **o.**,.............. *1520*
1Co 15:8 of me also, as of **o.** born out of due time...
1Co 15:39 there is **o.** kind of flesh of men, ... *243*
1Co 15:40 the glory of the celestial is **o.**, and *2087*
1Co 15:41 There is **o.** glory of the sun, and....... *243*
1Co 15:41 **o.** star differeth from another star in.........
1Co 16:2 every **o.** of you lay by him in store,..........
1Co 16:16 to every **o.** that helpeth with us, ...
1Co 16:20 ye **o.** another with an holy kiss. *240*
2Co 2:7 such a **o.** should be swallowed up............
2Co 2:16 To the **o.** we are the savour of.......... *3303*
2Co 5:10 every **o.** may receive the things done........
2Co 5:14 that if **o.** died for all, then were all..... *1520*
2Co 10:11 Let such an **o.** think this, that, ...
2Co 11:2 have espoused you to **o.** husband, ... *1520*
2Co 11:24 received I forty stripes save **o.**.......... *3391*
2Co 12:2 **o.** caught up to the third heaven. ....
2Co 12:5 Of such an **o.** will I glory: yet of..............
2Co 13:11 be of **o.** mind, live in peace; and... *3588,846*
2Co 13:12 Greet **o.** another with an holy kiss. *240*
Ga 3:10 Cursed is every **o.** that continueth............
Ga 3:13 Cursed is every **o.** that hangeth on...........
Ga 3:16 as of **o.**, And to thy seed, which is..... *1520*
Ga 3:20 not a mediator of **o.**, but God is **o.**..... *1520*
Ga 3:28 for ye are all **o.** in Christ Jesus......... *1520*
Ga 4:22 **o.** by a bondmaid, the other by a *1520*
Ga 4:24 the **o.** from the mount Sinai, which..... *3391*
Ga 5:13 flesh, but by love serve **o.** another...... *240*
Ga 5:14 all the law is fulfilled in **o.** word, ... *1520*
Ga 5:15 if ye bite and devour **o.** another, ... *240*
Ga 5:15 ye be not consumed **o.** of another........ *240*
Ga 5:17 are contrary the **o.** to the other: so *240*
Ga 5:26 **o.** another, envying **o.** another. *240*
Ga 6:1 restore such an **o.** in the spirit of..........
Ga 6:2 Bear ye **o.** another's burdens, and *240*
Eph 1:10 gather together in **o.** all things................
Eph 2:14 who hath made both **o.**, and hath *1520*
Eph 2:15 in himself of twain **o.** new man, so..... *1520*
Eph 2:16 both unto God in **o.** body by the........ *1520*
Eph 2:18 access by **o.** Spirit unto the Father..... *1520*
Eph 4:2 forbearing **o.** another in love;.............. *240*
Eph 4:4 There is **o.** body, and **o.** Spirit, even.. *1520*
Eph 4:4 called in **o.** hope of your calling;......... *3391*
Eph 4:5 **O.** Lord,...faith, **o.** baptism,.............. *1520*
Eph 4:5 Lord, **o.** faith,...baptism, ... *3391*
Eph 4:6 **O.** God and Father of all, who is........ *1520*
Eph 4:7 unto every **o.** of us is given grace........ *1520*
Eph 4:25 for we are members **o.** of another. *240*
Eph 4:32 And be ye kind **o.** to another, ... *240*
Eph 4:32 forgiving **o.** another, even as God....... *1438*
Eph 5:21 Submitting yourselves **o.** to another...... *240*
Eph 5:31 wife, and they two shall be **o.** flesh. ... *3391*
Eph 5:33 let every **o.** of you in particular..............
Php 1:16 The **o.** preach Christ of contention, ... *3303*
Php 1:27 that ye stand fast in **o.** spirit, with...... *1520*
Php 1:27 with **o.** mind striving together........... *3391*
Php 2:2 the same love, being **o.** accord, ... *4861*
Php 2:2 love, being...of **o.** mind............. *3888,1520*
Php 3:13 this **o.** thing I do, forgetting those...... *1520*
Col 3:9 Lie not **o.** to another, seeing that........ *240*
Col 3:13 Forbearing **o.** another, and................. *240*
Col 3:13 forgiving **o.** another, if any man *1438*
Col 3:15 also ye are called in **o.** body; and....... *1520*
Col 3:16 and admonishing **o.** another in............ *1438*
Col 4:9 and beloved brother, who is **o.** of you. ......
Col 4:12 Epaphras, who is **o.** of you, a servant.......
1Th 2:11 and charged every **o.** of you, as a *1520*
1Th 3:12 abound in love **o.** toward another, ... *240*
1Th 4:4 every **o.** of you should know how............
1Th 4:9 taught of God to love **o.** another.......... *240*
1Th 4:18 comfort **o.** another with these words. ... *240*
1Th 5:11 edify **o.** another, even as also ye........ *1520*
2Th 1:3 charity of every **o.** of you all toward... *1520*
1Ti 2:5 there is **o.** God, and **o.** mediator......... *1520*
1Ti 3:2 husband of **o.** wife, vigilant, sober, ... *3391*
1Ti 3:4 **O.** that ruleth well his own house,............
1Ti 3:12 deacons be the husbands of **o.** wife,.... *3391*
1Ti 5:9 having been the wife of **o.** man, ... *1520*
1Ti 5:21 without preferring **o.** before another,.........
2Ti 2:19 every **o.** that nameth the name of..........
Tit 1:6 blameless, the husband of **o.** wife, ... *3391*
Tit 1:12 **O.** of themselves, even a prophet....... *5100*
Tit 3:3 envy, hateful, and hating **o.** another...... *240*
Phm 9 being such an **o.** as Paul the aged,............
Heb 2:6 But **o.** in a certain place testified,....... *5100*
Heb 2:11 who are sanctified are all of **o.**:.......... *1520*
Heb 3:13 exhort **o.** another daily, while it *1438*
Heb 5:12 ye have need that **o.** teach you again ....
Heb 5:13 For every **o.** that useth milk is ....
Heb 6:11 every **o.** of you do shew the same............
Heb 10:12 he had offed **o.** sacrifice for sins.......... *3391*
Heb 10:14 by **o.** offering he hath perfected for *3391*
Heb 10:24 us consider **o.** another to provoke........ *240*
Heb 10:25 but exhorting **o.** another: and so much ....
Heb 11:12 Therefore spring there even of **o.**, ... *1520*
Heb 12:16 who for **o.** morsel of meat sold his *3391*
Heb 13:14 continuing city,...we seek **o.** to come. ....
Jas 2:10 yet offend in **o.** point, he is guilty....... *1520*
Jas 2:16 **o.** of you say unto them, Depart in..... *5100*
Jas 2:19 believest that there is **o.** God; thou *1520*
Jas 4:11 Speak not evil **o.** another, ... *240*
Jas 4:12 There is **o.** lawgiver, who is able to.... *1520*
Jas 5:9 Grudge not **o.** against another, ... *240*
Jas 5:16 Confess your faults **o.** to another, ... *240*
Jas 5:16 pray **o.** for another, that ye may be *240*
Jas 5:19 the truth, and **o.** convert him; *5100*
1Pe 1:22 love **o.** another with a pure heart......... *240*
1Pe 3:8 Finally, be ye all of **o.** mind, having.... *3675*
1Pe 3:8 having compassion **o.** for another,............
1Pe 4:9 hospitality **o.** to another without *240*
1Pe 4:10 minister the same **o.** to another, ... *1438*
1Pe 5:5 all of you be subject **o.** to another,....... *240*
1Pe 5:14 Greet ye **o.** another with a kiss of *240*
2Pe 3:8 be not ignorant of this **o.** thing, ... *1520*
2Pe 3:8 that **o.** day is with the Lord as a......... *3391*
2Pe 3:8 and a thousand years as **o.** day.......... *3391*
1Jo 1:7 have fellowship **o.** with another, ... *3391*
1Jo 2:13 ye have overcome the wicked **o.**..............
1Jo 2:14 and ye have overcome the wicked **o.**. ....
1Jo 2:20 ye have an unction from the Holy **O.**, ...
1Jo 2:29 every **o.** that doeth righteousness............
1Jo 3:11 that we should love **o.** another. *240*
1Jo 3:12 Not as Cain, who was of that wicked **o.**,.....
1Jo 3:23 and love **o.** another, as he gave us....... *240*
1Jo 4:7 Beloved, let us love **o.** another: for...... *240*
1Jo 4:7 every **o.** that loveth is born of God,..........
1Jo 4:11 ye ought also to love **o.** another. *240*
1Jo 4:12 If we love **o.** another, God dwelleth..... *240*
1Jo 5:1 every **o.** that loveth him that begat...........
1Jo 5:7 Ghost: and these three are **o.**. *1520*
1Jo 5:8 blood: and these three agree in **o.**...... *1520*
1Jo 5:18 and that wicked **o.** toucheth him not. ....
2Jo 5 beginning, that we love **o.** another. *240*
Re 1:13 midst...**o.** like unto the Son of man,..........
Re 2:23 **I will give unto every o. of you**..........
Re 4:2 in heaven, and **o.** sat on the throne. ....
Re 5:5 And **o.** of the elders saith unto me, ... *1520*
Re 5:8 having every **o.** of them harps, and...........
Re 6:1 the Lamb opened **o.** of the seals, ... *3391*
Re 6:1 **o.** of the four beasts saying, Come..... *1520*
Re 6:4 that they should kill **o.** another:........... *240*
Re 6:11 robes were given unto every **o.** of............
Re 7:13 **o.** of the elders answered, saying....... *1520*
Re 9:12 **O.** woe is past; and, behold, there *3391*
Re 11:10 and shall send gifts **o.** to another; *240*
Re 13:3 I saw **o.** of his heads as it were......... *3391*
Re 14:14 cloud **o.** sat like unto the Son of man, ...
Re 15:7 **o.** of the four beasts gave unto the..... *1520*
Re 17:1 there came **o.** of the seven angels...... *1520*
Re 17:10 five are fallen, and **o.** is, and the........ *1520*
Re 17:12 as kings **o.** hour with the beast. *3391*
Re 17:13 These have **o.** mind, and shall give..... 3391
Re 18:8 shall her plagues come in **o.** day, ... 3391
Re 18:10 in **o.** hour is thy judgment come......... 3391
Re 18:17 in **o.** hour so great riches is come...... 3391
Re 18:19 for in **o.** hour is she made desolate..........
Re 21:9 unto me **o.** of the seven angels.......... *1520*
Re 21:21 every several gate was of **o.** pearl:..... *1520*

ONE'S

Ec 7:1 day of death than the day of **o.** birth. ....
Ac 16:26 and every **o.** bands were loosed..............

ONES

Ge 34:29 all their little **o.**, and their wives took........
Ge 43:8 we, and thou, and also our little **o.**. ....
Ge 45:19 the land of Egypt for your little **o.**, ...
Ge 46:5 their little **o.**, and their wives, in the........
Ge 47:24 and for food for your little **o.**...............
Ge 50:8 only their little **o.**, and their flocks,...........
Ge 50:21 I will nourish you, and your little **o.**. ....
Ex 10:10 as I will let you go, and your little **o.**; ....
Ex 10:24 let your little **o.** also go with you.............
Nu 14:31 But your little **o.**, which ye said should........
Nu 31:9 of Midian captives, and their little **o.**, ...
Nu 31:17 kill every male among the little **o.**,............
Nu 32:16 our cattle, and cities for our little **o.**: ....
Nu 32:17 little **o.** shall dwell in the fenced cities ....
Nu 32:24 Build your cities for your little **o.**, and.......
Nu 32:26 Our little **o.**, our wives, our flocks, and.....
De 1:39 your little **o.**, which ye said should be a.....
De 2:34 women, and the little **o.**, of every city,.......
De 3:19 But your wives, and your little **o.**, and ....
De 20:14 But the women, and the little **o.**, and.......
De 22:6 whether they be young **o.**, or eggs, and ....
De 29:11 Your little **o.**, your wives, and thy...........
Jos 1:14 Your wives, your little **o.**, and your ....
Jos 8:35 with the women, and the little **o.**, and.......
Jg 5:22 the pransings of their mighty **o.**. ....
Jg 18:21 and put the little **o.** and the cattle............
2Sa 15:22 and all the little **o.** that were with him......
1Ch 16:13 ye children of Jacob, his chosen **o.**..........
2Ch 20:13 with their little **o.**, their wives, ...
2Ch 31:18 all their little **o.**, their wives, and their .....
Ezr 8:21 and for our little **o.**, and for all our ....
Es 8:11 assault them, both little **o.** and women, ...
Job 21:11 send forth their little **o.** like a flock,..........
Job 38:41 when his young **o.** cry unto God, they.......
Job 39:3 bring forth their young **o.**, they cast ....
Job 39:4 Their young **o.** are in good liking, they.....
Job 39:16 She is hardened against her young **o.**,.......
Job 39:30 Her young **o.** also suck up blood: and.........
Ps 10:10 that the poor may fall by his strong **o.**.......
Ps 83:3 and consulted against thy hidden **o.**..........
Ps 137:9 dasheth thy little **o.** against the stones.......
Pr 1:22 How long, ye simple **o.**, will ye love ....
Pr 7:7 among the simple **o.**, I discerned.............
Isa 5:17 the waste places of the fat **o.** shall...........
Isa 10:16 hosts, send among his fat **o.** leanness;.......
Isa 10:33 high **o.** of stature shall be hewn down; .....
Isa 11:7 their young **o.** shall lie down together:.......
Isa 13:3 I have commanded my sanctified **o.**, I ....
Isa 13:3 called my mighty **o.** for mine anger,..........
Isa 14:9 thee, even all the chief **o.** of the earth; .....
Isa 24:21 shall punish the host of the high **o.**..........
Isa 25:4 the blast of the terrible **o.** is as a storm ....
Isa 25:5 of the terrible **o.** shall be brought low. ......
Isa 29:5 of the terrible **o.** shall be as chaff that.......
Isa 32:11 be troubled, ye careless **o.**: strip you, ...
Isa 33:7 valiant **o.** shall cry without: their ....
Isa 57:15 to revive the heart of the contrite **o.**..........
Jer 2:33 also taught the wicked **o.** thy ways. ....
Jer 8:16 sound of the neighing of his strong **o.**;.......
Jer 14:3 have sent their little **o.** to the waters: ....
Jer 46:5 and their mighty **o.** are beaten down........
Jer 48:4 her little **o.** have caused a cry to be.........
Jer 48:45 of the head of the tumultuous **o.**. 1121
La 4:3 they give suck to their young **o.**:..............
Da 4:17 the demand by the word of the holy **o.**:.....
Da 8:8 for it came up four notable **o.**...................
Da 11:17 and upright **o.** with him; thus shall he........

Joe 3:11 cause thy mighty o. to come down,
Zec 4:14 These are the two anointed o., that
Zec 13:7 will turn mine hand upon the little o.
Mt 10:42 **of these little o. a cup of cold water**
Mt 18:6 **shall offend one of these little o.**
Mt 18:10 **ye despise not one of these little o.;**
Mt 18:14 **one of these little o. should perish**
Mk 9:42 **shall offend one of these little o. that**
Mk 10:42 **their great o. exercise authority upon**
Lu 17:2 **He should offend one of these little o.**

ONESIMUS (O-nes'-i-mus)
Col 4:9 O., a faithful and beloved brother, *3682*
Col *subscr* Colossians by Tychicus and O. *3682*
Phm 10 I beseech thee for my son O., *3682*
Phm *subscr* to Philemon, by O. a servant. *3682*

ONESIPHORUS (o-ne-sif'-o-rus)
2Ti 1:16 give mercy unto the house of O.; *3683*
2Ti 4:19 Aquila, and the household of O. *3683*

ONI See BEN-ONI.

ONIONS
Nu 11:5 leeks, and the o., and the garlick: 1211

ONLY
Ge 6:5 his heart was o. evil continually. 7535
Ge 7:23 Noah o. remained alive, and they 389
Ge 14:24 Save o. that which the young men 7535
Ge 19:8 eyes: o. unto these men do nothing; 7535
Ge 22:2 now thy son, thine o. son Isaac, 3173
Ge 22:12 thy son, thine o. son from me 3162
Ge 22:16 withheld thy son, thine o. son: 3173
Ge 24:8 o. bring not my son thither again. 7535
Ge 27:13 o. obey my voice, and go fetch 389
Ge 34:22 O. herein will the men consent 389
Ge 34:23 o. let us consent unto them, and 389
Ge 41:40 o. in the throne will I be greater 7535
Ge 47:22 O. the land of the priests bought 7535
Ge 47:26 except the land of the priests o., 905
Ge 50:8 o. their little ones, and the 7535
Ex 8:9 they may remain in the river o.? 7535
Ex 8:11 they shall remain in the river o. 7535
Ex 8:28 o. ye shall not go very far away: 7535
Ex 9:26 O. in the land of Goshen, where 7535
Ex 10:17 forgive, . . . my sin o. this once, and 389
Ex 10:17 take away from me this death o. 7535
Ex 10:24 o. let your flocks and your herds 7535
Ex 12:16 that o. may be done of you. 905
Ex 21:19 o. he shall pay for the loss of his 7535
Ex 22:20 unto any god, save unto the Lord o., 905
Ex 22:27 For that is his covering o., it is his 905
Le 21:23 O. he shall not go in unto the vail, 389
Le 27:26 O. the firstling of the beasts, which 389
Nu 1:49 O. thou shalt not number the tribe 389
Nu 12:2 indeed spoken o. by Moses? 7535
Nu 14:9 O. rebel not ye against the Lord, 389
Nu 18:3 o. they shall not come nigh the 389
Nu 20:19 I will o., without doing any thing 7535
Nu 22:35 o. the word that I shall speak unto
Nu 31:22 O. the gold, and the silver, the 389
Nu 36:6 o. to the family of the tribe of their 389
De 2:28 o. I will pass through on my feet; 7535
De 2:35 O. the cattle we took for a prey 7535
De 2:37 O. unto the land of the children of 7535
De 3:11 O. Og king of Bashan remained of 7535
De 4:9 O. take heed to thyself, and keep 7535
De 4:12 similitude; o. ye heard a voice. 2108
De 8:3 that man doth not live by bread o., 905
De 10:15 O. the Lord had a delight in thy 7535
De 12:16 O. ye shall not eat the blood; ye 7535
De 12:23 O. be sure that thou eat not the 7535
De 12:26 O. thy holy things which thou hast, 7535
De 15:5 O. if thou carefully hearken unto 7535
De 15:23 O. thou shalt not eat the blood 7535
De 20:20 O. the trees which thou knowest 7535
De 22:25 man o. that lay with her shall die: 905
De 28:13 and thou shalt be above o., and 7535
De 28:29, 33 thou shalt be o. oppressed and 389
De 29:14 with you o. do I make this covenant 905
Jos 1:7 O. be thou strong and very 7535
Jos 1:17 o. the Lord thy God be with thee, 7535
Jos 1:18 o. be strong and of a good courage 7535
Jos 6:15 o. on that day they compassed the 7535
Jos 6:17 o. Rahab the harlot shall live, she 7535
Jos 6:24 o. the silver, and the gold, and the 7535
Jos 8:2 o. the spoil thereof, and the cattle 7535
Jos 8:27 O. the cattle and the spoil of the 7535
Jos 11:13 none of them, save Hazor o.; 905
Jos 11:22 o. in Gaza, in Gath, and in Ashdod, 7535
Jos 13:6 o. divide thou it by lot unto the 7535
Jos 13:14 O. unto the tribe of Levi he gave 7535
Jos 17:17 thou shalt not have one lot o.:
Jg 3:2 O. that the generations of the 7535
Jg 6:37 and if the dew be on the fleece o., 905
Jg 6:39 it now be dry o. upon the fleece, 905
Jg 6:40 for it was dry upon the fleece o., 905
Jg 10:15 deliver us o., we pray thee, this 389
Jg 11:34 she was his o. child; beside her 3173
Jg 16:28 and strengthen me,...o. this once, 389
Jg 19:20 me; o. lodge not in the street. 7535
1Sa 1:13 o. her lips moved, but her voice 7535
1Sa 1:23 o. the Lord establish his word 389
1Sa 5:4 o. the stump of Dagon was left to 7535
1Sa 7:3 unto the Lord, and serve him o. 905
1Sa 7:4 Ashtaroth, and served the Lord o. 905
1Sa 12:24 O. fear the Lord, and serve him in 389
1Sa 18:17 o. be thou valiant for me, and fight 389
1Sa 20:14 shalt not o. while yet I live shew me
1Sa 20:39 o. Jonathan and David knew the 389
2Sa 13:32 king's sons; for Ammon o. is dead: 905
2Sa 13:33 are dead: for Ammon o. is dead. 905
2Sa 17:2 flee; and I will smite the king o.: 905
2Sa 20:21 deliver him o. and I will depart 905
2Sa 23:10 returned after him o. to spoil. 389
1Ki 3:2 O. the people sacrificed in high 7535
1Ki 3:3 o. he sacrificed and burnt incense 7535
1Ki 4:19 o. officer which was in the land. 259
1Ki 8:39 (for thou, even thou o., knowest 905
1Ki 12:20 David, but the tribe of Judah o. 905
1Ki 14:8 to do that o. which was right in 7535
1Ki 14:13 he o. of Jeroboam shall come to 905
1Ki 15:5 save o. in the matter of Uriah the 7535
1Ki 18:22 even I o., remain a prophet of the 905
1Ki 19:10, 14 and I, even I o., am left; and 905
1Ki 22:31 save o. with the king of Israel. 905
2Ki 3:25 o. in Kir-haraseth left they the stones
2Ki 10:23 but the worshippers of Baal o. 905
2Ki 17:18 none left but the tribe of Judah o. 905
2Ki 19:19 thou art the Lord God, even thou o. 905
2Ki 21:8 o. if they will observe to do 7535
1Ch 22:12 O. the Lord give thee wisdom and
2Ch 2:6 save o. to burn sacrifice before him?
2Ch 6:30 (for thou o. knowest the hearts of the 905
2Ch 18:30 save o. with the king of Israel. 905
2Ch 33:17 yet unto the Lord their God o. 7535
Ezr 10:15 O. Jonathan the son of Asahel and 389
Es 1:16 not done wrong to the king o. 905
Job 1:12 o. upon himself put not forth 3535
Job 1:15, 16,17,19 I o. am escaped alone 7535
Job 13:20 O. do not two things unto me: 389
Job 34:29 a nation, or against a man o.: 3162
Ps 4:8 Lord, o. makest me dwell in safety. 910
Ps 51:4 Against thee, thee o., have I sinned, 905
Ps 62:2 He o. is my rock and my salvation; 389
Ps 62:4 They o. consult to cast him down 389
Ps 62:5 My soul, wait thou o. upon God; 389
Ps 62:6 He o. is my rock and my salvation: 389
Ps 71:16 thy righteousness, even of thine o. 905
Ps 72:18 who o. doeth wondrous things. 905
Ps 91:8 O. with thine eyes shalt thou 7535
Pr 4:3 tender and o. beloved in the sight 3173
Pr 5:17 Let them be o. and I will depart 905
Pr 11:23 desire of the righteous is o. good: 389
Pr 13:10 O. by pride cometh contention: 7535
Pr 14:23 of the lips tendeth o. to penury. 389
Pr 17:11 An evil man seeketh o. rebellion: 389
Pr 21:5 diligent tend o. to plenteousness; 389
Pr 21:5 every one that is hasty o. to want. 389
Ec 7:29 this o. have I found, that God hath 905
Ca 6:9 she is the o. one of her mother, she
Isa 4:1 o. let us be called by thy name, to 7535
Isa 26:13 by thee o. will we make mention 905
Isa 28:19 o. to understand the report. 7535
Isa 37:20 thou art the Lord, even thou o. 905
Jer 3:13 O. acknowledge thine iniquity, 389
Jer 6:26 thee mourning, as for an o. son, 3173
Jer 32:30 children of Judah have o. done evil 389
Jer 32:30 have o. provoked me to anger with 389
Eze 7:5 God; An evil, an o. evil, behold, is 259
Eze 14:16 they o. shall be delivered, but the 905
Eze 14:18 o. shall be delivered themselves. 905
Eze 44:20 they shall o. poll their heads. 3697
Am 3:2 You o. have I known of all the 7535
Am 8:10 it as the mourning for his o. son, and 3173
Zec 12:10 one mourneth for his o. son, and 3173
Mt 4:10 **God, and him o. shalt thou serve** *3441*
Mt 5:47 **And if ye salute your brethren o.,** *3440*
Mt 8:8 speak the word o., and my servant *3440*
Mt 10:42 **a cup of cold water o. in the** *3440*
Mt 12:4 **with him, but o. for the priests?** *3441*
Mt 14:36 o. touch the hem of his garment: *3440*
Mt 17:8 they saw no man, save Jesus o. *3441*
Mt 21:19 nothing thereon, but leaves o., *3440*
Mt 21:21 **not o. do this which is done to** *3440*
Mt 24:36 **of heaven, but my Father o.** *3441*
Mk 2:7 who can forgive sins but God o.? *1520*
Mk 5:36 **Be not afraid, o. believe,** *3440*
Mk 6:8 for their journey, save a staff o.; *3440*
Mk 9:8 save Jesus o. with themselves. *3441*
Lu 4:8 **God, and him o. shalt thou serve** *3441*
Lu 7:12 the o. son of his mother, and she *3439*
Lu 8:42 For he had one o. daughter, about *3439*
Lu 8:50 **Fear not: believe o., and she shall** *3440*
Lu 9:38 my son: for he is mine o. child. *3439*
Lu 24:18 thou o. a stranger in Jerusalem, *3441*
Joh 1:14 as of the o. begotten of the Father,) *3439*
Joh 1:18 the o. begotten Son, which is in the *3439*
Joh 3:16 **he gave his o. begotten Son, that** *3439*
Joh 3:18 **name of the o. begotten Son of** *3439*
Joh 5:18 he not o. had broken the sabbath, *3440*
Joh 5:44 **honour that cometh from God o.?** *3441*
Joh 11:52 And not for that nation o., but *3440*
Joh 12:9 they came not for Jesus' sake o. *3440*
Joh 13:9 Lord, not my feet o., but also my *3440*
Joh 17:3 **might know thee the o. true God,** *3441*
Ac 8:16 o. they were baptized in the name *3440*
Ac 11:19 word to none but unto the Jews o. *3440*
Ac 18:25 knowing o. the baptism of John. *3440*
Ac 19:27 not o. this our craft is in danger to *3440*
Ac 21:13 I am ready not to be bound o., but *3440*
Ac 21:25 save o. that they keep themselves from
Ac 26:29 not o. thou, but also all that hear *3440*
Ac 27:10 not o. of the lading and ship, but *3440*
Ro 1:32 not o. do the same, but have *3440*
Ro 3:29 Is he the God of the Jews o.? is he *3440*
Ro 4:9 then upon the circumcision o., or
Ro 4:12 who are not of the circumcision o., *3440*
Ro 4:16 not to that o. which is of the law, *3440*
Ro 5:3 And not o. so, but we glory in *3440*
Ro 5:11 not o. so, but we also joy in God *3440*
Ro 8:23 And not o. they, but ourselves also, *3440*
Ro 9:10 And not o. this; but when Rebecca *3440*
Ro 9:24 not of the Jews o., but also of the *3440*
Ro 13:5 needs be subject, not o. for wrath, *3440*
Ro 16:4 unto whom not o. I give thanks, *3441*
Ro 16:27 to God o. wise, be glory through *3441*
1Co 7:39 to whom she will; o. in the Lord. *3440*
1Co 9:6 Or I o. and Barnabas, have not we *3441*
1Co 14:36 from you? or came it unto you o.? *3441*
1Co 15:19 If in this life o. we have hope in *3440*
2Co 7:7 and not by his coming o., but by *3440*
2Co 8:10 not o. to do, but also to be forward *3440*
2Co 8:19 And not that o., but who was also *3440*
2Co 8:21 not o. in the sight of the Lord, but *3440*
2Co 9:12 not o. supplieth the want of the *3440*
Ga 1:23 they had heard o., That he which *3440*
Ga 2:10 O. they would that we should *3440*
Ga 3:2 This o. would I learn of you, *3440*
Ga 4:18 not o. when I am present with you. *3440*
Ga 5:13 o. use not liberty for an occasion to *3440*
Ga 6:12 o. lest they...suffer persecution *3440*
Eph 1:21 not o. in this world, but also in that *3440*
Php 1:27 O. let your conversation be as it *3440*
Php 1:29 not o. to believe on him, but also to *3440*
Php 2:12 obeyed, not as in my presence o., *3440*
Php 2:27 and not on him o., but on me also, *3440*
Php 4:15 giving and receiving, but ye o. *3441*
Col 4:11 These o. are my fellowworkers *3441*
1Th 1:5 came not unto you in word o., but *3440*
1Th 1:8 not o. in Macedonia and Achaia, *3440*
1Th 2:8 not the gospel of God o., but also *3440*
2Th 2:7 o. he who now letteth will let, until *3440*
1Ti 1:17 the o. wise God, be honour and *3441*
1Ti 5:13 not o. idle, but tattlers also and *3440*
1Ti 6:15 is the blessed and o. Potentate, *3441*
1Ti 6:16 Who o. hath immortality, dwelling *3441*
2Ti 2:20 there are not o. vessels of gold and *3440*
2Ti 4:8 and not to me o., but unto all them *3440*
2Ti 4:11 O. Luke is with me. Take Mark, *3441*
Heb 9:10 stood o. in meats and drinks, and *3440*

Heb 11:17 offered up his o. begotten son, ... *3439*
Heb 12:26 once more I shake not the earth o., ... *3440*
Jas 1:22 of the word, and not hearers o., ... *3440*
Jas 2:24 man is justified, and not by faith o. ... *3440*
1Pe 2:18 not o. to the good and gentle, but ... *3440*
1Jo 2:2 and not for ours o., but also for ... *3440*
1Jo 4:9 God sent his o. begotten Son into ... *3439*
1Jo 5:6 not by water o., but by water and ... *3440*
2Jo 1:1 and not I o., but also all they that ... *3441*
Jude 4 denying the o. Lord God, and our ... *3441*
Jude 25 To the o. wise God our Saviour, be ... *3441*
Re 9:4 o. those men which have not the ... *3441*
Re 15:4 for thou o. art holy: for all nations ... *3441*

ONLY-BEGOTTEN See ONLY and BEGOTTEN.

ONO (o'-no)
1Ch 8:12 who built O., and Lord, with the ... 207
Ezr 2:33 The children of Lord, Hadid, and O., ... 207
Ne 6:2 one of the villages in the plain of O. ... 207
Ne 7:37 The children of Lod, Hadid, and O., ... 207
Ne 11:35 Lod and O., the valley of craftsmen. ... 207

ONWARD
Ex 40:36 of Israel went o. in all their journeys: ...

ONYCHA (on'-e-kah)
Ex 30:34 stacte, and o., and galbanum; ... 7827

ONYX (o'-nix)
Ge 2:12 there is bdellium and the o. stone. ... 7718
Ex 25:7 O. stones, and stones to be set in ... 7718
Ex 28:9 And thou shalt take two o. stones, ... 7718
Ex 28:20 the fourth row a beryl, and an o., ... 7718
Ex 35:9 o. stones, and stones to be set for ... 7718
Ex 35:27 And the rulers brought o. stones, ... 7718
Ex 39:6 they wrought o. stones inclosed in ... 7718
Ex 39:13 row, a beryl, an o., and a jasper: ... 7718
1Ch 29:2 o. stones, and stones to be set, ... 7718
Job 28:16 gold of Ophir, with the precious o., ... 7718
Eze 28:13 the beryl, the o., and the jasper, ... 7718

OPEN See also OPENED; OPENEST; OPENETH; OPENING.
Ge 1:20 in the o. firmament of heaven. ... 6440
Ge 38:14 sat in an o. place, which is by the ... 5869
Ex 21:33 if a man shall o. a pit, or if a man ... 6605
Le 14:7 living bird loose into the o. field. ... 6440
Le 14:53 bird out of the city into the o. fields, ... 6440
Le 17:5 which they offer in the o. field, even ... 6440
Nu 8:16 instead of such as o. every womb, ... 6363
Nu 16:30 and the earth o. her mouth, and ... 6475
Nu 19:15 And every o. vessel, which hath no ... 6605
Nu 19:16 slain with a sword in the o. fields, ... 6440
Nu 24:3 man whose eyes are o. hath said: ... 8365
Nu 24:4 a trance, but having his eyes o.: ... 1540
Nu 24:15 man whose eyes are o. hath said: ... 8365
Nu 24:16 a trance, but having his eyes o.: ... 1540
De 15:8 shalt o. thine hand wide unto him, ... 6605
De 15:11 shalt o. thine hand wide unto thy ... 6605
De 20:11 answer of peace, and o. unto thee, ... 6605
De 28:12 shall o. unto thee his good treasure, ... 6605
Jos 8:17 they left the city o., and pursued ... 6605
Jos 10:22 O. the mouth of the cave, and bring ... 6605
1Sa 3:1 those days; there was no o. vision. ... 6555
2Sa 11:11 lord, are encamped in the o. fields; ... 6440
1Ki 6:18 carved with knops and o. flowers: ... 6358
1Ki 6:29 palm trees and o. flowers, within ... 6358
1Ki 6:32 and palm trees and o. flowers, and ... 6358
1Ki 6:35 and palm trees and o. flowers: ... 6358
1Ki 8:29 thine eyes maybe o. toward this ... 6605
1Ki 8:52 That thine eyes may be o. unto the ... 6605
2Ki 6:17 Lord, I pray thee, o. his eyes, that ... 6491
2Ki 6:20 Lord, o. the eyes of these men, ... 6491
2Ki 9:3 Then o. the door, and flee, and ... 6605
2Ki 13:17 he said, O. the window eastward. ... 6605
2Ki 19:16 o., Lord, thine eyes, and see: and ... 6491
2Ch 6:20 That thine eyes may be o. upon ... 6605
2Ch 6:40 let, I beseech thee, thine eyes be o., ... 6605
2Ch 7:15 Now mine eyes shall be o., and ... 6605
Ne 1:6 and thine eyes o., that thou mayest ... 6605
Ne 6:5 time with an o. letter in his hand; ... 6605
Job 11:5 speak, and o. his lips against thee; ... 6605
Job 14:3 dost thou o. thine eyes upon such ... 6491
Job 32:20 I will o. my lips and answer. ... 6605
Job 34:26 men in the o. sight of others; ... 4725
Job 35:16 doth Job o. his mouth in vain; ... 6475
Job 41:14 Who can o. the doors of his face? ... 6605
Ps 5:9 their throat is an o. sepulchre; they ... 6605
Ps 34:15 and his ears are o. unto their cry. ...
Ps 49:4 I will o. my dark saying upon the ... 6605
Ps 51:15 O Lord, o. thou my lips; and my ... 6605
Ps 78:2 I will o. my mouth in a parable: ... 6605
Ps 81:10 o. thy mouth wide, and I will fill it. ...
Ps 118:19 O.... the gates of righteousness: ... 6605
Ps 119:18 O. thou mine eyes, that I may ... 1540
Pr 13:16 but a fool layeth o. his folly. ... 6566
Pr 20:13 o. thine eyes, and thou shalt be ... 6491
Pr 27:5 O. rebuke is better than secret ... 1540
Pr 31:8 O. thy mouth for the dumb in the ... 6605
Pr 31:9 O. thy mouth, judge righteously, ... 6605
Ca 5:2 O. to me, my sister, my love, my ... 6605
Ca 5:5 I rose up to o. to my beloved; and ... 6605
Isa 9:12 shall devour Israel with o. mouth. ... 3605
Isa 22:22 so he shall o., and none shall shut; ... 6605
Isa 22:22 and he shall shut, and none shall o.. ... 6605
Isa 24:18 the windows from on high are o., ... 6605
Isa 26:2 O. ye the gates, that the righteous ... 6605
Isa 28:24 doth he o. and break the clods of ... 6605
Isa 37:17 o. thine eyes, O Lord, and see: and ... 6491
Isa 41:18 I will o. rivers in high places, and ... 6605
Isa 42:7 To o. the blind eyes, to bring out ... 6491
Isa 45:1 to o. before him the two leaved ... 6605
Isa 45:8 let the earth o., and let them bring ... 6605
Isa 60:11 thy gates shall be o. continually; ... 6605
Jer 5:16 Their quiver is as an o. sepulchre, ... 6605
Jer 9:22 fall as dung upon the o. field, and ... 6440
Jer 13:19 shut up, and none shall o. them: ... 6605
Jer 32:11 custom, and that which was o.: ... 1540
Jer 32:14 and this evidence which is o.; and ... 1540
Jer 32:19 thine eyes are o. upon all the ways ... 6491
Jer 50:26 utmost border, o. her storehouses: ... 6605
Eze 2:8 o. thy mouth, and eat that I give ... 6475
Eze 3:27 I will o. thy mouth, and thou shalt ... 6605
Eze 16:5 thou wast cast out in the o. field, ... 6440
Eze 16:63 and never o. thy mouth any more ... 6610
Eze 21:22 to o. the mouth in the slaughter, ... 6605
Eze 25:9 I will o. the side of Moab from the ... 6605
Eze 29:5 thou shalt fall upon the o. fields; ... 6440
Eze 32:4 cast thee forth upon the o. field, ... 6440
Eze 33:27 him that is in the o. field will I give ... 6440
Eze 37:2 were very many in the o. valley; ... 6440
Eze 37:12 I will o. your graves, and cause ... 6605
Eze 39:5 Thou shalt fall upon the o. field: ... 6440
Eze 46:12 one shall then o. him the gate that ... 6605
Da 6:10 and his windows being o. in his ... 6606
Da 9:18 o. thine eyes, and behold our ... 6491
Na 3:13 set wide o. unto thine enemies: ... 6605
Zec 11:1 O. thy doors, O Lebanon, that the ... 6605
Zec 12:4 I will o. mine eyes upon the house ... 6491
Mal 3:10 I will not o. you the windows of ... 6605
Mt 13:35 I will o. my mouth in parables; I ... *455*
Mt 25:11 **saying, Lord, Lord, o. to us.** ... *455*
Lu 12:36 **may o. unto him immediately.** ... *455*
Lu 13:25 **door, saying, Lord, Lord, o. unto** ... *455*
Joh 1:51 **Hereafter ye shall see heaven o.,** ... *455*
Joh 10:21 Can a devil o. the eyes of the blind? ... *455*
Ac 16:27 sleep, and seeing the prison doors o., ... *455*
Ac 18:14 Paul was now about to o. his mouth, ... *455*
Ac 19:38 the law is o., and there are deputies: ... *71*
Ac 26:18 **To o. their eyes, and to turn them** ... *455*
Ro 3:13 Their throat is an o. sepulchre; ... *455*
2Co 3:18 with o. face beholding as in a glass ... *343*
2Co 6:11 our mouth is o. unto you, our heart ... *455*
Eph 6:19 that I may o. my mouth boldly, ... *1722,457*
Col 4:3 that God would o. unto us a door of ... *455*
1Ti 5:24 men's sins are o. beforehand, ... *4271*
Heb 6:6 afresh, and put him to an o. shame ... *3856*
1Pe 3:12 and his ears are o. unto their prayers: ...
Re 3:8 **I have set before thee an o. door,** ... *455*
Re 3:20 **hear my voice, and o. the door,** ... *455*
Re 5:2 Who is worthy to o. the book, and to ... *455*
Re 5:3 no man...was able to o. the book, ... *455*
Re 5:4 worthy to o. and to read the book, ... *455*
Re 5:5 hath prevailed to o. the book, and ... *455*
Re 5:9 the book, and to o. the seals thereof: ... *455*
Re 10:2 he had in his hand a little book o.: ... *455*
Re 10:8 and take the little book which is o. ... *455*

OPENED
Ge 3:5 thereof, then your eyes shall be o., ... 6491
Ge 3:7 And the eyes of them both were o., ... 6491
Ge 4:11 which hath o. her mouth to receive ... 6475
Ge 7:11 the windows of heaven were o.. ... 6605
Ge 8:6 that Noah o. the window of the ark ... 6605
Ge 21:19 God o. her eyes, and she saw a ... 6491
Ge 29:31 Leah was hated, he o. her womb: ... 6605
Ge 30:22 hearkened to her, and o. her womb. ... 6605
Ge 41:56 Joseph o. all the storehouses, and ... 6605
Ge 42:27 as one of them o. his sack to give ... 6605
Ge 43:21 we o. our sacks, and, behold, every ... 6605
Ge 44:11 ground, and o. every man his sack. ... 6605
Ex 2:6 she had o. it, she saw the child: ... 6605
Nu 16:32 earth o. her mouth, and swallowed ... 6605
Nu 22:28 the Lord o. the mouth of the ass, ... 6605
Nu 22:31 the Lord o. the eyes of Balaam, ... 1540
Nu 26:10 earth O. her mouth, and swallowed ... 6605
De 11:6 earth o. her mouth, and swallowed ... 6475
Jg 3:25 he o. not the doors of the parlour; ... 6605
Jg 3:25 they took a key, and o. them: ... 6605
Jg 4:19 she o. a bottle of milk, and gave ... 6605
Jg 11:35 I have o. my mouth unto the Lord, ... 6475
Jg 11:36 hast o. thy mouth unto the Lord, ... 6475
Jg 19:27 o. the doors of the house, and went ... 6605
1Sa 3:15 o. the doors of the house of the Lord. ... 6605
2Ki 4:35 times, and the child o. his eyes. ... 6491
2Ki 6:17 Lord o. the eyes of the young man; ... 6491
2Ki 6:20 Lord o. their eyes, and they saw; ... 6491
2Ki 9:10 And he o. the door and fled. ... 6605
2Ki 13:17 window eastward. And he o. it. ... 6605
2Ki 15:16 because they o. not to him, ... 6605
2Ch 29:3 o. the doors of the house of the ... 6605
Ne 7:3 Let not the gates of Jerusalem be o. ... 6605
Ne 8:5 Ezra o. the book in the sight of all ... 6605
Ne 8:5 when he o. it, all the people stood ... 6605
Ne 13:19 that they should not be o. till after ... 6605
Job 3:1 After this o. Job his mouth, and ... 6605
Job 29:23 they o. their mouth wide as for the ... 6473
Job 31:32 but I o. my doors to the traveller. ... 6605
Job 33:2 Behold, now I have o. my mouth, ... 6605
Job 38:17 Have the gates of death been o. ... 1540
Ps 35:21 they o. their mouth wide against ...
Ps 39:9 I was dumb, I o. not my mouth; ... 6605
Ps 40:6 mine ears hast thou o.: burnt ... 3738
Ps 78:23 above, and o. the doors of heaven, ... 6605
Ps 105:41 He o. the rock, and the waters ... 6605
Ps 106:17 earth o. and swallowed up Dathan, ... 6605
Ps 109:2 the mouth of the deceitful are o. ... 6605
Ps 119:131 I o. my mouth, and panted: ... 6473
Ca 5:6 I o. to my beloved; but my beloved ... 6605
Isa 5:14 o. her mouth without measure: ... 6473
Isa 10:14 moved the wing, or o. the mouth, ... 6475
Isa 14:17 o. not the house of his prisoners? ... 6605
Isa 35:5 the eyes of the blind shall be o., ... 6491
Isa 48:8 time that thine ear was not o. ... 6605
Isa 50:5 The Lord God hath o. mine ear, ... 6605
Isa 53:7 afflicted, yet he o. not his mouth: ... 6605
Jer 20:12 for unto thee have I o. my cause. ... 1540
Jer 50:25 The Lord hath o. his armoury, ... 6605
La 2:16 enemies have o. their mouths ... 6475
La 3:46 our enemies have o. their mouths ... 6475
Eze 1:1 the heavens were o., and I saw ... 6605
Eze 3:2 I o. my mouth, and he caused me to ... 6605
Eze 16:25 and hast o. thy feet to every one ... 6589
Eze 24:27 In that day shall thy mouth be o. ... 6605
Eze 33:22 had o. my mouth, until he came to ... 6605
Eze 33:22 and my mouth was o., and I was no ... 6605
Eze 37:13 when I have o. your graves, O my ... 6605
Eze 44:2 gate shall be shut, it shall not be o., ... 6605
Eze 46:1 on the sabbath it shall be o., and in ... 6605
Eze 46:1 day of the new moon it shall be o.. ... 6605
Da 7:10 was set, and the books were o.. ... 6606
Da 10:16 then I o. my mouth, and spake, ... 6605
Na 2:6 The gates of the rivers shall be o., ... 6605
Zec 13:1 shall be a fountain o. to the house ... 6605
Mt 2:11 when they had o. their treasures, ... *455*
Mt 3:16 the heavens were o. unto him, and ... *455*
Mt 5:2 he o. his mouth, and taught them, ... *455*
Mt 7:7 **knock, and it shall be o. unto you:** ... *455*
Mt 7:8 **to him that knocketh it shall be o.** ... *455*
Mt 9:30 their eyes were o.; and Jesus straitly ... *455*
Mt 17:27 **and when thou hast o. his mouth,** ... *455*
Mt 20:33 him, Lord, that our eyes may be o.. ... *455*
Mt 27:52 graves were o.; and many bodies ... *455*
Mk 1:10 he saw the heavens o., and the ... *4977*
Mk 7:34 him, **Ephphatha,** that is, Be o.. ... *1272*
Mk 7:35 straightway his ears were o., and ... *1272*
Lu 1:64 his mouth was o. immediately, ... *455*
Lu 3:21 and praying, the heaven was o., ... *455*
Lu 4:17 And when he had o. the book, he ... *380*
Lu 11:9 **knock, and it shall be o. unto you.** ... *455*
Lu 11:10 **to him that knocketh it shall be o.** ... *455*

Lu 24:31 their eyes were **o.**, and they knew..... *1272*
Lu 24:32 while he **o.** to us the scriptures?........ *1272*
Lu 24:45 Then **o.** he their understanding, ... *1272*
Joh 9:10 unto him, How were thine eyes **o.**?...... *455*
Joh 9:14 Jesus made the clay, and **o.** his eyes.... *455*
Joh 9:17 of him, that he hath **o.** thine eyes?....... *455*
Joh 9:21 who hath **o.** his eyes, we know not:..... *455*
Joh 9:26 did he to thee? how **o.** he thine eyes? .. *455*
Joh 9:30 he is, and yet he hath **o.** mine eyes. *455*
Joh 9:32 that any man **o.** the eyes of one that.... *455*
Joh 11:37 man, which **o.** the eyes of the blind,.... *455*
Ac 5:19 Lord by night **o.** the prison doors, ... *455*
Ac 5:23 when we had **o.**, we found no man....... *455*
Ac 7:56 Behold, I see the heavens **o.**, and......... *455*
Ac 8:32 his shearer, so **o.** he not his mouth:..... *455*
Ac 8:35 Then Philip **o.** his mouth, and began..... *455*
Ac 9:8 when his eyes were **o.**, he saw no....... *455*
Ac 9:40 she **o.** her eyes: when she saw........... *455*
Ac 10:11 saw heaven **o.**, and a certain vessel *455*
Ac 10:34 Then Peter **o.** his mouth, and said, ... *455*
Ac 12:10 which **o.** to them of his own accord:..... *455*
Ac 12:14 she **o.** not the gate for gladness, but..... *455*
Ac 12:16 and when they had **o.** the door, and..... *455*
Ac 14:27 **o.** the door of faith unto the Gentiles.... *455*
Ac 16:14 whose heart the Lord **o.**, that she...... *1272*
Ac 16:26 immediately all the doors were **o.**, ... *455*
1Co 16:9 door and effectual is **o.** unto me, ... *455*
2Co 2:12 a door was **o.** unto me of the Lord, ... *455*
Heb 4:13 all things are naked and **o.** unto *5136*
Re 4:1 behold, a door was **o.** in heaven: *455*
Re 6:1 when the Lamb **o.** one of the seals, ... *455*
Re 6:3 And when he had **o.** the second seal, ... *455*
Re 6:5 And when he had **o.** the third seal, ... *455*
Re 6:7 and when he had **o.** the fourth seal, ... *455*
Re 6:9 And when he had **o.** the fifth seal, ... *455*
Re 6:12 when he had **o.** the sixth seal, ... *455*
Re 8:1 and when he had **o.** the seventh seal,... *455*
Re 9:2 And he **o.** the bottomless pit; and........ *455*
Re 11:19 the temple of God was **o.** in heaven, ... *455*
Re 12:16 earth **o.** her mouth, and swallowed....... *455*
Re 13:6 **o.** his mouth in blasphemy against........ *455*
Re 15:5 of the testimony in heaven was **o.**:........ *455*
Re 19:11 And I saw heaven **o.**, and behold a *455*
Re 20:12 before God; and the books were **o.**:..... *455*
Re 20:12 another book was **o.**, which is the........ *455*

OPENEST
Ps 104:28 thou **o.** thine hand, they are filled....... 6605
Ps 145:16 Thou **o.** thine hand, and satisfiest....... 6605

OPENETH
Ex 13:2 whatsoever **o.** the womb among........ 6363
Ex 13:12 unto the Lord all that **o.** the matrix, ... 6363
Ex 13:15 to the Lord all that **o.** the matrix, ... 6363
Ex 34:19 All that **o.** the matrix is mine; and...... 6363
Nu 3:12 all the firstborn that **o.** the matrix 6363
Nu 18:15 thing that **o.** the matrix in all flesh,..... 6363
Job 27:19 he **o.** his eyes, and he is not............ 6491
Job 33:16 he **o.** the ears of men, and sealeth 1540
Job 36:10 He **o.** also their ear to discipline, ... 1540
Job 36:15 and **o.** their ears in oppression........... 1540
Ps 38:13 dumb man that **o.** not his mouth 6605
Ps 146:8 The Lord **o.** the eyes of the blind: 6491
Pr 13:3 he that **o.** wide his lips shall have....... 6589
Pr 24:7 he **o.** not his mouth in the gate.......... 6605
Pr 31:26 She **o.** her mouth with wisdom; 6605
Isa 53:7 is dumb, so he **o.** not his mouth. 6605
Eze 20:26 the fire all that **o.** the womb,............ 6363
Lu 2:23 Every male that **o.** the womb shall..... *1272*
Joh 10:3 **him the porter o.; and the sheep**..... *455*
Re 3:7 **he that o., and no man shutteth;** *455*
Re 3:7 **and shutteth, and no man o.;** *455*

OPENING See also OPENINGS.
1Ch 9:27 and the **o.** thereof every morning....... 4668
Job 12:14 up a man, and there can be no **o.**........ 6605
Pr 8:6 **o.** of my lips shall be right things. 4669
Isa 42:20 **o.** the ears, but he heareth not.......... 6491
Isa 61:1 **o.** of the prison to them that are........ 6495
Eze 29:21 will give thee the **o.** of the mouth 6610
Ac 17:3 **O.** and alleging, that Christ must........ *1272*

OPENINGS
Pr 1:21 concourse in the **o.** of the gates:........ 6607

OPENLY
Ge 38:21 that was **o.** by the way side?............ 5879
Ps 98:2 righteousness hath he **o.** shewed in ....
Mt 6:4 **shall reward thee o.** *1722,3588,5318*
Mt 6:6 **shall reward thee o.** *1722,3588,5318*
Mt 6:18 **shall reward thee o.** *1722,3588,5318*
Mk 1:45 no more **o.** enter into the city, ... *5320*
Mk 8:32 And he spake that saying **o.**.............. *3954*
Joh 7:4 himself seeketh to be known **o.**.. ..*1722,3954*
Joh 7:10 not **o.**, but as it were in secret........... *5320*
Joh 7:13 no man spake **o.** of him for fear of *3954*
Joh 11:54 walked no more **o.** among the Jews; ... *3954*
Joh 18:20 **I spake o. to the world; I ever**....... *3954*
Ac 10:40 the third day, and shewed him **o.**; *1717*
Ac 16:37 have beaten us **o.** uncondemned,......... *1219*
Col 2:15 he made a shew of them **o.**, ... *1722,3954*

OPERATION See also OPERATIONS.
Ps 28:5 the Lord, nor the **o.** of his hands, ... 4639
Isa 5:12 neither consider the **o.** of his hands. ... 4639
Col 2:12 through the faith of the **o.** of God,...... *1753*

OPERATIONS
1Co 12:6 there are diversities of **o.**, but it is..... *1755*

OPHEL (o'-fel)
2Ch 27:3 on the wall of **O.** he built much......... 6077
2Ch 33:14 and compassed about **O.**, and raised ... 6077
Ne 3:26 the Nethinims dwelt in **O.**, unto......... 6077
Ne 3:27 lieth out, even unto the wall of **O.**...... 6077
Ne 11:21 but the Nethinims dwelt in **O.**: 6077

OPHIR (o'-fur)
Ge 10:29 And **O.**, and Havilah, and Jobab:.......... 211
1Ki 9:28 they came to **O.**, and fetched from....... 211
1Ki 10:11 Hiram, that brought gold from **O.**, ... 211
1Ki 10:11 brought in from **O.** great plenty of 211
1Ki 22:48 ships of Tharshish to go to **O.** for........ 211
1Ch 1:23 And **O.**, and Havilah, and Jobab.......... 211
1Ch 29:4 talents of gold, of the gold of **O.**,.......... 211
2Ch 8:18 with the servants of Solomon to **O.**, ... 211
2Ch 9:10 which brought gold from **O.**, brought..... 211
Job 22:24 the gold of **O.** as the stones of the 211
Job 28:16 cannot be valued with the gold of **O.**, ... 211
Ps 45:9 did stand the queen in gold of **O.**......... 211
Isa 13:12 man than the golden wedge of **O.**......... 211

OPHNI (of'-ni)
Jos 18:24 Chephar-haammonai, and **O.**, and 6078

OPHRAH (of'-rah) See also APHRAH.
Jos 18:23 And Avim, and Parah, and **O.**,........... 6084
Jg 6:11 sat under an oak which was in **O.**,...... 6084
Jg 6:24 it is yet in **O.** of the Abi-ezrites......... 6084
Jg 8:27 and put it in his city, even in **O.**: 6084
Jg 8:32 sepulchre of Joash his father, in **O.**..... 6084
Jg 9:5 went unto his father's house at **O.**,..... 6084
1Sa 13:17 unto the way that leadeth to **O.**,.......... 6084
1Ch 4:14 And Meonothai begat **O.**; and........... 6084

OPINION See also OPINIONS.
Job 32:6 and durst not shew you mine **o.**.......... 1843
Job 32:10 to me; I also will shew mine **o.**.......... 1843
Job 32:17 my part, I also will shew mine **o.**....... 1843

OPINIONS
1Ki 18:21 How long halt ye between two **o.**? 5587

OPPORTUNITY
Mt 26:16 time he sought **o.** to betray him......... *2120*
Lu 22:6 sought **o.** to betray him unto them *2120*
Ga 6:10 As we have therefore **o.**, let us do..... *2540*
Php 4:10 were also careful, but ye lacked **o.**........ *170*
Heb 11:15 have had **o.** to have returned. *2540*

OPPOSE See also OPPOSED; OPPOSEST; OPPPOSETH.
2Ti 2:25 instructing those that **o.** themselves; *475*

OPPOSED
Ac 18:6 And when they **o.** themselves, and....... *498*

OPPOSEST
Job 30:21 hand thou **o.** thyself against me.......... 7852

OPPOSETH
2Th 2:4 Who **o.** and exalteth himself above....... *480*

OPPOSITIONS
1Ti 6:20 and **o.** of science falsely so called:........ *477*

OPPRESS See also OPPRESSED; OPPRESSETH; OPPRESSING.
Ex 3:9 wherewith the Egyptians **o.** them....... 3905
Ex 22:21 neither vex a stranger, nor **o.** him:..... 3905
Ex 23:9 Also thou shalt not **o.** a stranger:....... 3905
Le 25:14 hand, ye shall not **o.** one another:....... 3238
Le 25:17 shall not therefore **o.** one another;...... 3238
De 23:16 him best: thou shalt not **o.** him.......... 3238
De 24:14 Thou shalt not **o.** an hired servant...... 6231
Jg 10:12 and the Maonites, did **o.** you;............ 3905
Job 10:3 unto thee that thou shouldest **o.**,......... 6231
Ps 10:18 man of the earth may no more **o.**....... 6206
Ps 17:9 From the wicked that **o.** me, from...... 7703
Ps 119:122 for good: let not the proud **o.** me....... 6231
Pr 22:22 neither **o.** the afflicted in the gate:...... 1792
Isa 49:26 I will feed them that **o.** thee with....... 3238
Jer 7:6 If ye **o.** not the stranger, the 6231
Jer 30:20 and I will punish all that **o.** them. 3905
Eze 45:8 shall no more **o.** my people; and........ 3238
Ho 12:7 are in his hand: he loveth to **o.**.......... 6231
Am 4:1 which **o.** the poor, which crush the..... 6231
Mic 2:2 so they **o.** a man and his house, ... 6231
Zec 7:10 **o.** not the widow, nor the fatherless, .. 6231
Mal 3:5 that **o.** the hireling in his wages, ... 6231
Jas 2:6 Do not rich men **o.** you, and draw....... *2616*

OPPRESSED
De 28:29 thou shalt be only **o.** and spoiled......... 6231
De 28:33 thou shalt be only **o.** and crushed....... 6231
Jg 2:18 by reason of them that **o.** them 3905
Jg 4:3 mightily **o.** the children of Israel......... 3905
Jg 6:9 out of the hand of all that **o.** you,....... 3905
Jg 10:8 and **o.** the children of Israel: 7533
1Sa 10:18 kingdoms, and of them that **o.** you: 3905
1Sa 12:3 whom have I **o.**? or of whose hand..... 7533
1Sa 12:4 hast not defrauded us, nor **o.** us, ... 7533
2Ki 13:4 because the king of Syria **o.** them. 3905
2Ki 13:22 But Hazael king of Syria **o.** Israel....... 3905
2Ch 16:10 And Asa **o.** some of the people.......... 7533
Job 20:19 **o.** and hath forsaken the poor;........... 7533
Job 35:9 they make the **o.** to cry: they cry out.......
Ps 9:9 also will be a refuge for the **o.**,.......... 1790
Ps 10:18 To judge the fatherless and the **o.**,..... 1790
Ps 74:21 O let not the **o.** return ashamed:........ 1790
Ps 103:6 and judgment for all that are **o.**.......... 6231
Ps 106:42 Their enemies also **o.** them, and........ 3905
Ps 146:7 executeth judgment for the **o.**:........... 6231
Ec 4:1 the tears of such as were **o.**, ... 6231
Isa 1:17 seek judgment, relieve the **o.**, ... 2541
Isa 3:5 And the people shall be **o.**, every....... 5065
Isa 23:12 no more rejoice, O thou **o.** virgin, ... 6231
Isa 38:14 O Lord, I am **o.**; undertake for me..... 6234
Isa 52:4 Assyrian **o.** them without cause. 6231
Isa 53:7 He was **o.**, and he was afflicted, ... 5065
Isa 58:6 to let the **o.** go free, and that ye 7533
Jer 50:33 and the children of Judah were **o.**........ 6231
Eze 18:7 hath not **o.** any, but hath restored....... 3238
Eze 18:12 Hath **o.** the poor and needy, hath....... 3238
Eze 18:16 Neither hath **o.** nay, hath not 3238
Eze 18:18 because he cruelly **o.**, spoiled his 6231
Eze 22:29 have **o.** the stranger wrongfully.......... 6231
Ho 5:11 Ephraim is **o.** and broken in 6231
Am 3:9 and the **o.** in the midst thereof. 6217
Ac 7:24 and avenged him that was **o.**, and *2669*
Ac 10:38 all that were **o.** of the devil;............. *2616*

OPPRESSETH
Nu 10:9 against the enemy that **o.** you, ... 6887
Ps 56:1 me up; he fighting daily **o.** me. 3905
Pr 14:31 He that **o.** the poor reproacheth......... 6231
Pr 22:16 He that **o.** the poor to increase his..... 6231
Pr 28:3 A poor man that **o.** the poor is like..... 6231

OPPRESSING
Jer 46:16 our nativity, from the **o.** sword.......... 3238
Jer 50:16 for fear of the **o.** sword they shall...... 3238
Zep 3:1 filthy and polluted, to the **o.** city! 3238

OPPRESSION See also OPPRESSIONS.
Ex 3:9 the **o.** wherewith the Egyptians 3906
De 26:7 and our labour, and our **o.**: 3906
2Ki 13:4 he saw the **o.** of Israel, because the ... 3906
Job 36:15 and openeth their ears in **o.**............ 3906
Ps 12:5 For the **o.** of the poor, for the........... 7701
Ps 42:9 because of the **o.** of the enemy? 3906
Ps 43:2 because of the **o.** of the enemy? 3906
Ps 44:24 forgettest our affliction and our **o.**?..... 3906
Ps 55:3 because of the **o.** of the wicked: 6125
Ps 62:10 Trust not in **o.**, and become not 6233
Ps 73:8 and speak wickedly concerning **o.**: 6233
Ps 107:39 brought low through **o.**, affliction,....... 6115
Ps 119:134 Deliver me from the **o.** of man: 6233
Ec 5:8 If thou seest the **o.** of the poor, ... 6233
Ec 7:7 Surely **o.** maketh a wise man mad;..... 6233
Isa 5:7 for judgment, but behold **o.**;.............. 4939
Isa 30:12 despise this word, and trust in **o.**......... 6233
Isa 54:14 thou shalt be far from **o.**; for thou....... 6233
Isa 59:13 speaking **o.** and revolt, concerning...... 6233

Jer 6:6 she is wholly **o.** in the midst of her. ... 6233
Jer 22:17 and for **o.**, and for violence, to do it. .. 6233
Eze 22:7 they dealt by **o.** with the stranger: 6233
Eze 22:29 people of the land have used **o.**, ... 6233
Eze 46:18 of the people's inheritance by **o.**,........ 3238

OPPRESSIONS

Job 35:9 By reason of the multitude of **o.** 6217
Ec 4:1 the **o.** that are done under the sun: 6217
Isa 33:15 he that despiseth the gain of **o.**,......... 4642

OPPRESSOR See also OPPRESSORS.

Job 3:18 they hear not the voice of the **o.**........ 5065
Job 15:20 number of years is hidden to the **o.**.... 6184
Ps 72:4 and shall break in pieces the **o.**.......... 6231
Pr 3:31 Envy thou not the **o.**, and.......... 376,2555
Pr 28:16 understanding is also a great **o.**:........ 4642
Isa 9:4 of his shoulder, the rod of his **o.**,........ 5065
Isa 14:4 and say, How hath the **o.** ceased! 5065
Isa 51:13 day because of the fury of the **o.**, ... 6693
Isa 51:13 and where is the fury of the **o.**?......... 6693
Jer 21:12 spoiled out of the hand of the **o.**, ... 6231
Jer 22:3 spoiled out of the hand of the **o.**: 6216
Jer 25:38 because of the fierceness of the **o.**, ... 3238
Zec 9:8 no **o.** shall pass through them........... 5065
Zec 10:4 bow, out of him every **o.** together...... 5065

OPPRESSORS

Job 27:13 and the heritage of **o.**, which they...... 6184
Ps 54:3 and **o.** seek after my soul: they 6184
Ps 119:121 justice: leave me not to mine **o.**......... 6231
Ec 4:1 side of their **o.** there was power; 6231
Isa 3:12 children are their **o.**, and women........ 5065
Isa 14:2 and they shall rule over their **o.**......... 5065
Isa 16:4 **o.** are consumed out of the land......... 7429
Isa 19:20 unto the Lord because of the **o.**,......... 3905

OR See also NOR.

Ge 13:9 **o.** if thou depart to the right hand, ...
Ge 17:12 **o.** bought with money of any stranger, ...
Ge 24:21 his journey prosperous **o.** not. ....
Ge 24:49 to the right hand, **o.** to the left. 176
Ge 24:50 cannot speak unto thee bad **o.** good. 176
Ge 26:11 that toucheth this man **o.** his wife............
Ge 27:21 thou be my very son Esau **o.** not. ....
Ge 30:1 Give me children, **o.** else I die................
Ge 31:14 yet any portion **o.** inheritance for us ....
Ge 31:24, 29 to Jacob either good **o.** bad.......... 5704
Ge 31:39 stolen by day, **o.** stolen by night.............
Ge 31:43 daughters, **o.** unto their children.......... 176
Ge 31:50 **o.** if thou shalt take other wives..............
Ge 37:8 **o.** shalt thou indeed have dominion ....
Ge 37:32 whether it be thy son's coat **o.** no. ....
Ge 39:10 her, to lie by her, **o.** to be with her..........
Ge 41:44 no man lift up his hand **o.** foot in.............
Ge 42:16 **o.** else by the life of Pharaoh...................
Ge 44:8 of thy lord's house silver **o.** gold? 176
Ge 44:16 speak? **o.** how shall we clear ourselves? ....
Ge 44:19 Have ye a father, **o.** a brother? 176
Ex 4:11 mouth? **o.** who maketh the dumb, ... 176
Ex 4:11 **o.** deaf, **o.** the seeing, **o.** the blind? 176
Ex 5:3 with pestilence, **o.** with the sword. 176
Ex 10:15 the trees, **o.** in the herbs of the field, ...
Ex 11:7 his tongue, against man **o.** beast: 5704
Ex 12:5 out from the sheep, **o.** from the goats:......
Ex 12:19 he be a stranger, **o.** born in the land.........
Ex 16:4 they will walk in my law, **o.** no. ....
Ex 17:7 Is the Lord among us, **o.** not? ....
Ex 19:12 the mount, **o.** touch the border of it: ....
Ex 19:13 whether it be beast **o.** man, it shall..........
Ex 19:13 surely be stones, **o.** shot through; 176
Ex 20:4 **o.** any likeness of any thing that is...........
Ex 20:4 **o.** that is in the earth beneath, **o.** that ......
Ex 21:4 have born him sons **o.** daughters; 176
Ex 21:6 to the door, **o.** unto the door post; 176
Ex 21:15 that smiteth his father, **o.** his mother. ....
Ex 21:16 him, **o.** if he be found in his hand, ...
Ex 21:17 that curseth his father, **o.** his mother, ...
Ex 21:18 with a stone, **o.** with his fist, and 176
Ex 21:20 man smite his servant, **o.** his maid, ... 176
Ex 21:21 if he continue a day **o.** two, he........... 176
Ex 21:26 his servant, **o.** the eye of his maid, ... 176
Ex 21:27 tooth, **o.** his maidservant's tooth; 176
Ex 21:28 If an ox gore a man **o.** a woman, ... 176
Ex 21:29 he hath killed a man **o.** woman; 176
Ex 21:31 a son, **o.** have gored a daughter, ... 176
Ex 21:32 a manservant **o.** a maidservant; 176
Ex 21:33 **o.** if a man shall dig a pit, and not........ 176
Ex 21:33 it, and an ox **o.** an ass fall therein; 176
Ex 21:36 **O.** if it be known that the ox hath........ 176
Ex 22:1 ox, **o.** a sheep, and kill it, **o.** sell it; 176
Ex 22:4 whether it be ox, **o.** ass, **o.** sheep; 5704
Ex 22:5 a field **o.** vineyard to be eaten, and...... 176
Ex 22:6 **o.** the standing corn, **o.** the field, be 176
Ex 22:7 neighbour money **o.** stuff to keep,........ 176
Ex 22:9 **o.** for any manner of lost thing,...............
Ex 22:10 **o.** an ox, **o.** a sheep, **o.** any beast, to .. 176
Ex 22:10 **o.** be hurt, **o.** driven away, no man...... 176
Ex 22:14 it be hurt, **o.** die, the owner thereof..... 176
Ex 22:22 afflict any widow, **o.** fatherless child..........
Ex 23:4 enemy's ox **o.** his ass going astray, ... 176
Ex 28:43 **o.** when they come near unto the 176
Ex 29:34 the consecrations, **o.** of the bread, ...
Ex 30:20 **o.** when they come near to the altar..... 176
Ex 30:33 **o.** whosoever putteth any of it upon a ....
Ex 34:19 whether ox **o.** sheep, that is male. ....
Le 1:10 **o.** of the goats, for a burnt sacrifice; 176
Le 1:14 of turtledoves, **o.** of young pigeons. 176
Le 2:4 **o.** unleavened wafers anointed with...........
Le 3:1 whether it be a male **o.** female, he ....
Le 3:6 male **o.** female, he shall offer it 176
Le 4:23 **O.** if his sin, wherein he hath............. 176
Le 4:28 **O.** if his sin, which he hath sinned, ... 176
Le 5:1 whether he hath seen **o.** known of it; ... 176
Le 5:2 **O.** if a soul touch any unclean thing,..... 176
Le 5:2 **o.** a carcase of unclean cattle, ... 176
Le 5:2 **o.** the carcase of unclean creeping........ 176
Le 5:3 **O.** if he touch the uncleanness of......... 176
Le 5:4 **O.** if a soul swear, pronouncing with..... 176
Le 5:4 his lips to do evil, **o.** to go good, ... 176
Le 5:6 lamb **o.** a kid of the goats, for a sin 176
Le 5:7, 11 turtledoves, **o.** two young pigeons, .. 176
Le 6:2 him to keep, **o.** in fellowship,.............. 176
Le 6:2 **o.** in a thing taken away by violence, ... 176
Le 6:2 **o.** hath deceived his neighbour; 176
Le 6:3 **O.** have found that which was lost, ... 176
Le 6:4 away, **o.** the thing which he hath......... 176
Le 6:4 **o.** that which was delivered him to....... 176
Le 6:4 **o.** the lost thing which he found, ... 176
Le 6:5 **O.** all that about which he hath........... 176
Le 7:16 be a vow, **o.** a voluntary offering, it 176
Le 7:21 man, **o.** any unclean beast, **o.** any........ 176
Le 7:23 of fat, of ox, **o.** of sheep, **o.** of goat. ....
Le 7:26 whether it be of fowl **o.** of beast, in..........
Le 11:4 cud, **o.** of them that divide the hoof: ....
Le 11:32 wood, **o.** raiment, **o.** skin, **o.** sack, ... 176
Le 11:35 it be oven, **o.** ranges for pots, they ....
Le 11:36 fountain **o.** pit, wherein there is plenty ......
Le 11:42 **o.** whatsoever hath more feet............ 5704
Le 12:6 fulfilled, for a son, **o.** for a daughter,.........
Le 12:6 young pigeon, **o.** a turtledove, for a 176
Le 12:7 that hath born a male **o.** a female. 176
Le 12:8 two turtles, **o.** two young pigeons;....... 176
Le 13:2 a rising, a scab, **o.** bright spot, and...... 176
Le 13:2 **o.** unto one of his sons the priests: 176
Le 13:16 **O.** if the raw flesh turn again, and 176
Le 13:19 white rising, **o.** a bright spot, white,..... 176
Le 13:24 **O.** if there be any flesh, in the skin...... 176
Le 13:24 spot, somewhat reddish, **o.** white; 176
Le 13:29 If a man **o.** woman have a plague......... 176
Le 13:29 plague upon the head **o.** the beard; 176
Le 13:30 a leprosy upon the head **o.** beard......... 176
Le 13:38 **o.** also a woman have in the skin of 176
Le 13:42 in the bald head, **o.** bald forehead, ... 176
Le 13:42 his bald head, **o.** his bald forehead. 176
Le 13:43 bald head, **o.** in his bald forehead,........ 176
Le 13:47 garment, **o.** a linen garment;............... 176
Le 13:48 warp, **o.** woof; of linen, **o.** of woollen; .. 176
Le 13:48 skin, **o.** in any thing made of skin; 176
Le 13:49 **o.** reddish in the garment, **o.**...skin, ... 176
Le 13:49 **o.** in the woof, **o.** in any thing of skin; .. 176
Le 13:51 warp, **o.** in the woof, **o.** in a skin, ... 176
Le 13:51 **o.** in any work that is made of.................
Le 13:52 **o.** woof, in woollen **o.** in linen, **o.** any .. 176
Le 13:53 **o.** in the woof, **o.** in any thing of skin;.. 176
Le 13:55 whether it be bare within **o.** without. ....
Le 13:56 of the garment, **o.** out of the skin, ... 176
Le 13:56 **o.** out of the warp, **o.** out of the woof: ..176
Le 13:57 **o.** in the woof, **o.** in any thing of......... 176
Le 13:58 **o.** woof, **o.** whatsoever thing of skin 176
Le 13:59 **o.** linen, either in the warp, **o.** woof,.... 176
Le 13:59 **o.** any thing of skins, to pronounce 176
Le 13:59 clean, **o.** to pronounce it unclean. 176
Le 14:22 turtledoves, **o.** two young pigeons,........ 176
Le 14:30 **o.** of the young pigeons, such as he 176
Le 14:37 hollow strakes, greenish **o.** reddish, ... 176
Le 15:3 **o.** his flesh be stopped from his........... 176
Le 15:14 turtledoves, **o.** two young pigeons,........ 176
Le 15:23 **o.** on any thing whereon she sitteth, ... 176
Le 15:25 **o.** if it run beyond the time of her 176
Le 15:29 two turtles, **o.** two young pigeons,........ 176
Le 16:29 **o.** a stranger that sojourneth among..........
Le 17:3 an ox, **o.** lamb, **o.** goat, in the camp, ... 176
Le 17:3 **o.** that killeth it out of the camp, ... 176
Le 17:8 **o.** of the strangers which sojourn ....
Le 17:8 a burnt offering **o.** sacrifice,................ 176
Le 17:10, 13 **o.** of the strangers that sojourn...........
Le 17:13 catcheth any beast **o.** fowl that may 176
Le 17:15 **o.** that which was torn with beasts, ...
Le 17:15 of your own country, **o.** a stranger, ...
Le 18:7 father, **o.** the nakedness of thy mother, ...
Le 18:9 father, **o.** daughter of thy mother,........ 176
Le 18:9 be born at home, **o.** born abroad, ... 176
Le 18:10 **o.** of thy daughter's daughter, even...... 176
Le 18:17 **o.** her daughter's daughter, to ....
Le 19:35 in meteyard, in weight, **o.** in measure. ......
Le 20:2 **o.** of the strangers that sojourn in ....
Le 20:9 curseth his father **o.** his mother shall ....
Le 20:9 cursed his father **o.** his mother; ....
Le 20:17 **o.** his mother's daughter, and see 176
Le 20:25 **o.** by fowl, **o.** by any manner of living.......
Le 20:27 A man also **o.** woman hath a............... 176
Le 20:27 **o.** that is a wizard, shall surely be put.......
Le 21:7 a wife that is a whore, **o.** profane;............
Le 21:11 for his father, **o.** for his mother; ....
Le 21:14 **o.** a divorced woman, **o.** profane, ...
Le 21:14 **o.** an harlot, these shall he not take:..........
Le 21:18 blind man, **o.** a lame, **o.** he that 176
Le 21:18 flat nose, **o.** any thing superfluous,........ 176
Le 21:19 **O.** a man that is brokenfooted,............ 176
Le 21:19 is brokenfooted, **o.** brokenhanded,........ 176
Le 21:20 **O.** crookbackt, **o.** a dwarf, ... 176
Le 21:20 **o.** that hath a blemish in his eye, ... 176
Le 21:20 a blemish in his eye, **o.** be scurvy, ...
Le 21:20 **o.** scabbed **o.** hath his stones.............. 176
Le 22:4 is a leper, **o.** hath a running issue; 176
Le 22:4 **o.** a man whose seed goeth from him; .. 176
Le 22:5 **O.** whosoever toucheth any creeping 176
Le 22:5 **o.** man of whom he may take............. 176
Le 22:8 dieth of itself, **o.** is torn with beasts, ...
Le 22:10 of the priest, **o.** an hired servant,............
Le 22:13 daughter be a widow, **o.** divorced,............
Le 22:16 **O.** suffer them to bear the iniquity of........
Le 22:18 Israel, **o.** of the strangers in Israel, ...
Le 22:19 beeves, of the sheep, **o.** of the goats. ....
Le 22:21 **o.** a freewill offering in beeves 176
Le 22:21 a freewill offering in beeves **o.** sheep, ...
Le 22:22 **o.** broken, **o.** maimed, **o.** having a 176
Le 22:22 **o.** scurvy, **o.** scabbed ye shall not........ 176
Le 22:23 bullock **o.** a lamb that hath any thing........
Le 22:23 superfluous **o.** lacking in his parts, ...
Le 22:24 bruised, **o.** crushed, **o.** broken, **o.** cut; .....
Le 22:27 a bullock, **o.** a sheep, **o.** goat, is 176
Le 22:28 whether it be cow **o.** ewe, ye shall 176
Le 25:14 **o.** buyest ought of thy neighbour's 176
Le 25:35 he be a stranger, **o.** a sojourner; that.......
Le 25:36 thou no usury of him, **o.** increase: but.......
Le 25:47 the sojourner **o.** stranger wax rich by thee,.
Le 25:47 the stranger **o.** sojourner by thee, ...
Le 25:49 **o.** his uncle's son, may redeem him,..... 176
Le 25:49 **o.** any that is nigh of kin unto him...........
Le 25:49 **o.** if he be able, he may redeem.......... 176
Le 26:15 **o.** if your soul abhor my judgments,..........
Le 27:10 good for a bad, **o.** a bad for a good: 176
Le 27:12 value it, whether it be good **o.** bad: ....
Le 27:14 estimate it, whether it be good **o.** bad: .....
Le 27:20 **o.** if he have sold the field to..................
Le 27:26 whether it be ox **o.** sheep: it is the...... 176
Le 27:27 **o.** if it be not redeemed, then it..............
Le 27:28 possession, shall be sold **o.** redeemed: ......
Le 27:30 **o.** of the fruit of the tree, is the Lord's: ....
Le 27:32 the tithe of the herd, **o.** of the flock,.........
Le 27:33 not search whether it be good **o.** bad, ...
Nu 5:6 a man **o.** woman shall commit any........ 176
Nu 5:14 **o.** if the spirit of jealousy come upon.... 176
Nu 5:30 **O.** when the spirit of jealousy 176
Nu 6:2 either man **o.** woman shall separate...... 176
Nu 6:3 **o.** wine, **o.** vinegar of strong drink, ...
Nu 6:3 grapes, nor eat moist grapes, **o.** dried.......
Nu 6:7 for his father, **o.** for his mother, ...
Nu 6:7 for his brother, **o.** for his sister, when ......
Nu 6:10 two turtles, **o.** two young pigeons, ... 176
Nu 9:10 **o.** of your posterity shall be unclean.........

Book	Ref.	Context	No.
Nu	9:10	**o.** be in a journey afar off, yet he	176
Nu	9:21	**o.** by night that the cloud was taken	
Nu	9:22	**O.** whether it were two days,	
Nu	9:22	**o.** a month, **o.** a year, that the cloud	176
Nu	11:8	it in mills, **o.** beat it in a mortar,	176
Nu	11:22	**o.** shall all the fish of the sea be	
Nu	11:23	shall come to pass unto thee **o.** not.	
Nu	13:18	be strong **o.** weak, few **o.** many;	
Nu	13:19	dwell in, whether it be good **o.** bad;	
Nu	13:19	whether in tents, **o.** in strong holds;	
Nu	13:20	whether it be fat **o.** lean, whether	
Nu	13:20	there be wood therein **o.** not.	
Nu	14:2	**o.** would God we had died in this	
Nu	15:3	**o.** a sacrifice in performing a vow,	176
Nu	15:3	a vow, **o.** in a freewill offering,	176
Nu	15:3	**o.** in your solemn feasts, to make a	176
Nu	15:3	the Lord, of the herd, **o.** of the flock:	176
Nu	15:5	with the burnt offering **o.** sacrifice,	176
Nu	15:6	**O.** for a ram, thou shalt prepare for	176
Nu	15:8	**o.** for a sacrifice in performing a vow,	176
Nu	15:8	**o.** peace offering unto the Lord:	176
Nu	15:11	for one bullock, **o.** for one ram,	
Nu	15:11	**o.** for a lamb, **o.** a kid.	176
Nu	15:14	**o.** whosoever be among you in your	176
Nu	15:30	he be born in the land, **o.** a stranger,	
Nu	16:14	**o.** given us inheritance of fields and	
Nu	16:29	**o.** if they be visited after the	176
Nu	18:15	whether it be of men **o.** beasts, shall	176
Nu	18:17	of a cow, **o.** the firstling of a sheep,	
Nu	18:17	**o.** the firstling of a goat, thou shalt	176
Nu	19:16	the open fields, **o.** a dead body,	
Nu	19:16	**o.** a bone of a man,	
Nu	19:16	**o.** a grave, shall be unclean seven	
Nu	19:18	that touched a bone, **o.** one slain,	
Nu	19:18	**o.** one dead. **o.** a grave:	176
Nu	20:5	it is no place of seed, **o.** of figs,	
Nu	20:5	**o.** of vines, **o.** of pomegranates;	
Nu	20:17	the fields, **o.** through the vineyards,	
Nu	21:22	into the fields, **o.** into the vineyards;	
Nu	22:18	Lord my God, to do less **o.** more.	176
Nu	22:26	either to the right hand **o.** to the left.	
Nu	23:8	**o.** how shall I defy, whom the Lord	
Nu	23:19	**o.** hath he spoken, and shall he not	
Nu	24:13	good **o.** bad of mine own mind;	176
Nu	30:2	**o.** swear an oath to bind his soul	176
Nu	30:5	**o.** of her bonds wherewith she hath	
Nu	30:6	**o.** uttered ought out of her lips,	176
Nu	30:10	**o.** bound her soul by a bond with an	176
Nu	30:12	**o.** concerning the bond of her soul,	
Nu	30:13	it, **o.** her husband may make it void.	
Nu	30:14	**o.** all her bonds, which are upon	
Nu	32:19	on yonder side Jordan, **o.** forward;	
Nu	35:18	**O.** if he smite him with an hand	176
Nu	35:20	**o.** hurl at him by laying of wait,	176
Nu	35:21	**o.** in enmity smite him with his	176
Nu	35:22	**o.** have cast upon him any thing	176
Nu	35:23	**O.** with any stone, wherewith a	176
De	3:24	God is there in heaven **o.** in earth,	
De	4:16	the likeness of male **o.** female,	176
De	4:23,	25 image, **o.** the likeness of anything,	
De	4:32	is, **o.** hath been heard like it?	176
De	4:34	**O.** hath God assayed to go and take	176
De	5:8	image, **o.** any likeness of anything	
De	5:8	above, **o.** that is in the earth beneath,	
De	5:8	**o.** that is in the waters beneath the	
De	5:21	**o.** his manservant, **o.** his maidservant,	
De	5:21	ox, **o.** his ass, **o.** anything that is thy	
De	5:32	aside to the right hand **o.** to the left.	
De	7:14	be male **o.** female barren among you,	
De	7:14	among you, **o.** among your cattle.	
De	7:25	the silver **o.** gold that is on them,	
De	8:2	keep his commandments, **o.** no.	
De	9:5	**o.** for the uprightness of thine heart,	
De	12:17	thy corn, **o.** of thy wine, **o.** of thy oil,	
De	12:17	**o.** the firstlings of thy herds,	
De	12:17	**o.** of thy flock, nor any of thy vows	
De	12:17	**o.** heave offering of thine hand:	
De	13:1	prophet, **o.** a dreamer of dreams,	176
De	13:1	and giveth thee a sign **o.** a wonder,	176
De	13:2	the sign **o.** the wonder come to pass,	
De	13:3	prophet, **o.** that dreamer of dreams:	176
De	13:5	prophet, **o.** that dreamer of dreams,	176
De	13:6	mother, **o.** thy son, **o.** thy daughter,	
De	13:6	daughter, **o.** the wife of thy bosom,	176
De	13:6	**o.** thy friend, which is as thine own	176
De	13:7	nigh unto thee, **o.** far off from thee,	176
De	14:7	**o.** of them that divide the cloven hoof;	
De	14:21	**o.** thou mayest sell it unto an alien:	176
De	14:24	**o.** if the place be too far from thee,	
De	14:26	for oxen, **o.** for sheep, **o.** for wine,	
De	14:26	**o.** for strong drink,	
De	14:26	**o.** for whatsoever thy soul desireth:	
De	15:2	it of his neighbour, **o.** of his brother;	
De	15:12	man, **o.** an Hebrew woman, be sold	176
De	15:21	therein, as if it be lame, **o.** blind,	176
De	15:21	**o.** have any ill blemish, thou shalt	
De	17:1	bullock, **o.** sheep, wherein is blemish,	
De	17:1	**o.** any evilfavouredness: for that	
De	17:2	man **o.** woman, that hath wrought	
De	17:3	sun, **o.** moon, **o.** any of the host of	176
De	17:5	bring forth that man **o.** that woman,	176
De	17:5	gates, even that man **o.** that woman,	176
De	17:6	two witnesses, **o.** three witnesses,	176
De	17:12	the Lord thy God, **o.** unto the judge,	176
De	17:20	to the right hand, **o.** to the left:	
De	18:3	sacrifice, whether it be ox **o.** sheep;	
De	18:10	son **o.** his daughter to pass through	
De	18:10	**o.**...useth divinations, **o.** an observer	
De	18:10	of times, **o.** an enchanter, **o.** a witch,	
De	18:11	**O.** a charmer, **o.** a consulter with	
De	18:11	spirits, **o.** a wizard, **o.** a necromancer.	
De	18:20	**o.** that shall speak in the name of	
De	19:15	man for any iniquity, **o.** for any sin,	
De	19:15	**o.** at the mouth of three witnesses,	
De	21:18	his father, **o.** the voice of his mother,	
De	22:1	brother's ox **o.** his sheep go astray,	176
De	22:2	**o.** if thou know him not, then thou	
De	22:4	ass **o.** his ox fall down by the way,	176
De	22:6	way in any tree, **o.** on the ground,	176
De	22:6	whether they be young ones, **o.** eggs,	176
De	22:6	upon the young, **o.** upon the eggs,	176
De	23:1	**o.** hath his privy member cut off,	
De	23:3	An Ammonite **o.** Moabite shall not	
De	23:18	**o.** the price of a dog, into the house of	
De	24:3	**o.** if the latter husband die, which	176
De	24:6	**o.** the upper millstone to pledge:	
De	24:7	merchandise of him **o.** selleth him;	
De	24:14	**o.** of thy strangers that are in thy	
De	27:15	maketh any graven **o.** molten image,	
De	27:16	light by his father **o.** his mother.	
De	27:22	**o.** the daughter of his mother.	176
De	28:14	day, to the right hand, **o.** to the left,	
De	28:51	leave thee either corn, wine, **o.** oil,	
De	28:51	**o.** the increase of thy kine,	
De	28:51	**o.** flocks of thy sheep, until he have	
De	29:6	have ye drunk wine **o.** strong drink:	
De	29:18	man, **o.** woman, **o.** family, **o.** tribe,	176
De	32:36	and there is none shut up, **o.** left.	
Jos	1:7	it to the right hand **o.** to the left,	
Jos	5:13	thou for us, **o.** for our adversaries?	
Jos	7:3	two **o.** three thousand men go up	176
Jos	8:17	was not a man left in Ai **o.** Beth-el,	
Jos	8:20	power to flee this way **o.** that way:	
Jos	8:22	let none of them remain **o.** escape.	
Jos	10:14	no day like that before it **o.** after it,	
Jos	22:22	in rebellion, **o.** if in transgression.	
Jos	22:23	**o.** if to offer thereon burnt offering	
Jos	22:23	burnt offering **o.** meat offering,	
Jos	22:23	**o.** if to offer peace offerings thereon,	
Jos	22:28	so say to us **o.** to our generations in	
Jos	22:29	for meat offerings, **o.** for sacrifices,	
Jos	23:6	to the right hand **o.** to the left;	
Jos	24:15	flood, **o.** the gods of the Amorites,	
Jg	2:22	as their fathers did keep it, **o.** not.	
Jg	5:8	a shield **o.** spear seen among forty	
Jg	5:30	prey; to every man a damsel **o.** two;	
Jg	9:2	you, **o.** that one reign over you?	
Jg	11:25	**o.** did he ever fight against them,	
Jg	13:14	let her drink wine **o.** strong drink,	
Jg	14:3	brethren, **o.** among all my people,	
Jg	14:6	he told not his father **o.** his mother.	
Jg	18:19	**o.** that thou be a priest unto a	176
Jg	19:13	all night, in Gibeah, **o.** in Ramah.	176
Jg	20:28	my brother, **o.** shall I cease?	176
Jg	21:22	fathers **o.** their brethren come	176
Ru	1:16	**o.** to return from following after thee:	
Ru	3:10	young men, whether poor **o.** rich.	
1Sa	2:14	pan, **o.** kettle, **o.** caldron, **o.** pot;	176
1Sa	6:12	aside to the right hand **o.** to the left;	
1Sa	12:3	I taken? **o.** whose ass have I taken?	
1Sa	12:3	I taken? **o.** whom have defrauded?	
1Sa	12:3	**o.** of whose hand have I received any	
1Sa	13:19	make them swords **o.** spears:	176
1Sa	14:6	Lord to save by many **o.** by few.	176
1Sa	14:52	any strong man, **o.** any valiant man,	
1Sa	16:7	**o.** on the height of his stature;	
1Sa	18:18	life, **o.** my father's family in Israel,	
1Sa	20:2	do nothing either great **o.** small,	176
1Sa	20:10	**o.** what if thy father answer thee	176
1Sa	20:12	to-morrow any time, **o.** the third day,	
1Sa	21:3	mine hand, **o.** what there is present.	176
1Sa	21:8	under thine hand spear **o.** sword?	176
1Sa	22:8	**o.** sheweth unto me that my son hath	
1Sa	22:15	nothing of all this, less **o.** more.	176
1Sa	25:31	**o.** that my lord hath avenged himself:	
1Sa	25:36	she told him nothing, less **o.** more,	
1Sa	26:10	him; **o.** his day shall come to die;	176
1Sa	26:10	**o.** he shall descend into battle,	
1Sa	26:18	I done? **o.** what evil is in mine hand?	
1Sa	29:3	with me these days, **o.** these years.	176
1Sa	30:2	slew not any, either great **o.** small,	
2Sa	2:21	to thy right hand **o.** to thy left,	176
2Sa	3:23	on the sword, **o.** that lacketh bread.	
2Sa	3:29	that hath an issue, **o.** that is a leper,	
2Sa	3:29	is a leper, **o.** that leaneth on a staff,	
2Sa	3:29	staff, **o.** that falleth on the sword,	
2Sa	3:35	if I taste bread, **o.** aught else, till	176
2Sa	14:19	turn to the right hand **o.** to the left	
2Sa	15:4	man which hath any suite **o.** cause	
2Sa	15:21	whether in death **o.** life, even there	
2Sa	17:9	in some pit, **o.** in some other place:	176
2Sa	19:35	taste what I eat **o.** what I drink?	854
2Sa	19:42	cost? **o.** hath he given us any gift?	
2Sa	20:20	that I should swallow up **o.** destroy.	
2Sa	24:13	**o.** wilt thou flee three months before	
2Sa	24:13	**o.** that there be three days' pestilence.	
1Ki	3:7	I know not how to go out **o.** come in.	
1Ki	8:23	in heaven above, **o.** on earth beneath,	
1Ki	8:37	locust, **o.** if there be caterpiller;	
1Ki	8:38	any man, **o.** by all thy people Israel,	
1Ki	8:46	the land of the enemy, far **o.** near;	176
1Ki	9:6	from following me, ye **o.** your children,	
1Ki	15:17	suffer any to go out **o.** come in to Asa	
1Ki	18:10	there is no nation **o.** kingdom, whither	
1Ki	18:27	**o.** he is pursuing, **o.** he is on a journey,	
1Ki	18:27	a journey, **o.** peradventure he sleepeth,	
1Ki	20:18	**o.** whether they be come out for war,	
1Ki	20:39	**o.** else thou shalt pay a talent of	176
1Ki	21:2	**o.**, if it seem good to thee, I will give	176
1Ki	21:6	**o.** else, if it please thee, I will give	
1Ki	22:6	to battle, **o.** shall I forbear?	
1Ki	22:15	to battle, **o.** shall we forbear?	
2Ki	2:16	some mountain, **o.** into some valley.	176
2Ki	2:21	thence anymore death **o.** barren land.	
2Ki	4:13	king, **o.** to the captain of the host?	176
2Ki	6:27	barnfloor, **o.** out of the winepress?	176
2Ki	9:32	to him out two **o.** three eunuchs.	
2Ki	12:13	any vessels of gold, **o.** vessels of silver,	
2Ki	13:19	have smitten five **o.** six times;	176
2Ki	17:34	statutes, **o.** after their ordinances,	
2Ki	17:34	**o.** after the law and commandment	
2Ki	20:9	degrees, **o.** go back ten degrees?	
2Ki	22:2	to the right hand **o.** to the left.	
2Ki	23:10	son **o.** his daughter to pass through	
1Ch	21:12	**o.** three months to be destroyed	
1Ch	21:12	**o.** else three days the sword of the	
2Ch	1:11	not asked riches, wealth, **o.** honour,	
2Ch	6:28	**o.** mildew, locust **o.** caterpillers;	
2Ch	6:28	sore **o.** whatsoever sickness there be;	
2Ch	6:29	what prayer **o.** what supplication	
2Ch	6:29	of any man, **o.** all thy people Israel,	
2Ch	6:36	captives unto a land far off **o.** near;	176
2Ch	7:13	**o.** if I command the locusts to	
2Ch	7:13	**o.** if I send pestilence among my	
2Ch	8:15	matter, **o.** concerning the treasures.	
2Ch	14:11	**o.** with them that have no power:	
2Ch	15:13	to death, whether small **o.** great,	5704
2Ch	15:13	great, whether man **o.** woman.	5704
2Ch	16:1	let none go out **o.** come in to Asa king	
2Ch	18:5,	14 to battle, **o.** shall I forbear?	
2Ch	18:30	Fight ye not with small **o.** great,	854
2Ch	20:9	judgment, **o.** pestilence, **o.** famine,	
2Ch	32:15	for no god of any nation **o.** kingdom	
2Ch	36:17	upon young man **o.** maiden,	
2Ch	36:17	old man, **o.** him that stooped for age:	
Ezr	7:24	**o.** ministers of this house of God,	
Ezr	7:24	to impose toll, tribute, **o.** custom,	
Ezr	7:26	be unto death, **o.** to banishment,	2006
Ezr	7:26	**o.** to confiscation of goods,	2006
Ezr	7:26	of goods, **o.** imprisonment.	
Ezr	9:12	nor seek their peace **o.** their wealth.	

Ezr 10:13 is this a work of one day **o.** two:
Ne 2:16 not whether I went, **o.** what I did;
Ne 5:8 brethren? **o.** shall they be sold unto us?
Ne 10:31 bring ware **o.** any victuals on the
Ne 10:31 on the sabbath, **o.** on the holy day:
Ne 13:20 without Jerusalem once **o.** twice.
Ne 13:25 unto your sons, **o.** for yourselves.
Es 4:11 whosoever, whether man **o.** woman,
Es 4:16 eat nor drink three days, night **o.** day:
Es 8:6 **o.** how can I endure to see the
Es 9:12 **o.** what is thy request further? and it
Job 3:12 **o.** why the breasts that I should suck?
Job 3:15 **O.** with princes that had gold, who 176
Job 3:16 **O.** as an hidden untimely birth I had 176
Job 4:7 **o.** where were the righteous cut off?
Job 6:5 **o.** loweth the ox over his fodder?
Job 6:6 **o.** is there any taste in the white of
Job 6:12 of stones? **o.** is my flesh of brass?
Job 6:22 **o.**, Give a reward for me of your
Job 6:23 **O.**, Deliver me from the enemy's
Job 6:23 **o.**, Redeem me from the hand of the
Job 7:12 Am I a sea, **o.** a whale, that thou
Job 8:3 **o.** doth the Almighty pervert justice?
Job 10:4 flesh? **o.** seest thou as man seeth?
Job 11:10 off, and shut up, **o.** gather together,
Job 12:8 **O.** speak to the earth, and it shall 176
Job 13:9 **o.** as one man mocketh another, do
Job 13:22 **o.** let me speak, and answer thou 176
Job 15:3 **o.** with speeches wherewith he can do
Job 15:7 **o.** wast thou made before the hills
Job 16:3 **o.** what emboldeneth thee that thou 176
Job 22:3 **o.** is it gain to him that thou
Job 22:11 **O.** darkness, that thou canst not 176
Job 25:4 **o.** how can he be clean that is born of
Job 28:16 the precious onyx, **o.** the sapphire.
Job 28:18 shall be made of coral, **o.** of pearls:
Job 31:5 **o.** if my foot hath hasted to deceit;
Job 31:9 **o.** if I have laid wait at my neighbour's
Job 31:13 my manservant **o.** of my maidservant,
Job 31:16 **o.** have caused the eyes of the widow
Job 31:17 **O.** have eaten my morsel myself
Job 31:19 clothing, **o.** any poor without covering:
Job 31:24 **o.** have said to the fine gold, Thou art
Job 31:26 **o.** the moon walking in brightness;
Job 31:27 **o.** my mouth hath kissed my hand:
Job 31:29 **o.** lifted up myself when evil found
Job 31:34 **o.** did the contempt of families terrify
Job 31:38 **o.** that the furrow likewise thereof
Job 31:39 **o.** have caused the owners thereof to
Job 32:12 Job, **o.** that answered his words:
Job 34:13 **o.** who hath disposed the whole world?
Job 34:29 a nation, **o.** against a man only:
Job 34:33 thou refuse, **o.** whether thou choose;
Job 35:6 **o.** if thy transgressions be multiplied,
Job 35:7 **o.** what receiveth he of thine hand? 176
Job 36:23 **o.** who can say, Thou hast wrought
Job 36:29 clouds, **o.** the noise of his tabernacle?
Job 37:13 correction, **o.** for his land, **o.** for mercy.
Job 38:5 **o.** who hath stretched the line upon 176
Job 38:6 **o.** who laid the corner stone thereof; 176
Job 38:8 **O.** who shut up the sea with doors,
Job 38:16 **o.** hast thou walked into the search of
Job 38:17 **o.** hast thou seen the doors of the
Job 38:21 **o.** because the number of thy days is
Job 38:22 **o.** hast thou seen the treasures of the
Job 38:25 **o.** the way for the lightning of thunder;
Job 38:28 **o.** who hath begotten the drops of 176
Job 38:31 **o.** loose the bands of Orion? 176
Job 38:32 **o.** canst thou guide Arcturus with his
Job 38:36 **o.** who hath given understanding 176
Job 38:37 **o.** who can stay the bottles of heaven,
Job 38:39 **o.** fill the appetite of the young lions,
Job 39:1 **o.** canst thou mark when the hinds do
Job 39:2 **o.** knowest thou the time when they
Job 39:5 **o.** who hath loosed the bands of the
Job 39:9 to serve thee, **o.** abide by thy crib?
Job 39:10 **o.** will he harrow the valleys after
Job 39:11 **o.** wilt thou leave thy labour to him?
Job 39:13 **o.** wings and feathers unto the
Job 39:15 **o.** that the wild beast may break them.
Job 40:9 **o.** canst thou thunder with a voice like
Job 41:1 **o.** his tongue with a cord which thou
Job 41:2 **o.** bore his jaw through with a thorn?
Job 41:5 **o.** wilt thou bind him for thy maidens?
Job 41:7 irons? **o.** his head with fish spears?
Job 41:13 **o.** who can come to him with his
Job 41:20 as out of a seething pot **o.** caldron.

Ps 18:31 **o.** who is a rock save our God?
Ps 24:3 **o.** who shall stand in his holy place?
Ps 32:9 Be ye not as the horse, **o.** as the mule,
Ps 35:14 he had been my friend **o.** brother:
Ps 44:20 **o.** stretched out our hands to a stranger
Ps 50:8 thy sacrifices **o.** thy burnt offerings,
Ps 50:13 of bulls, **o.** drink the blood of goats?
Ps 50:16 **o.** that thou shouldest take my
Ps 66:*title* the chief Musician, A song **o.** Psalm.
Ps 67:*title* on Neginoth, A Psalm **o.** Song.
Ps 68:*title* Musician, A Psalm **o.** Song of David.
Ps 69:31 than an ox **o.** bullock that hath horns
Ps 75:*title* A Psalm **o.** Song of Asaph.
Ps 76:*title* A Psalm **o.** Song of Asaph.
Ps 87:*title* A Psalm **o.** Song for the sons of
Ps 88:*title* A Song **o.** Psalm for the sons of
Ps 88:11 **o.** thy faithfulness in destruction?
Ps 89:8 **o.** to thy faithfulness round about
Ps 90:2 **o.** ever thou hadst formed the earth
Ps 92:*title* A Psalm **o.** Song for the sabbath day.
Ps 94:16 **o.** who will stand up for me against
Ps 108:*title* A Song **o.** Psalm of David.
Ps 120:3 **o.** what shall be done unto thee, thou
Ps 131:1 matters, **o.** in things too high for me.
Ps 132:4 mine eyes, **o.** slumber to mine eyelids,
Ps 139:7 **o.** whither shall I flee from thy
Ps 144:3 **o.** the son of man, that thou makest
Pr 6:7 having no guide, overseer, **o.** ruler,
Pr 7:22 **o.** as a fool to the correction of the
Pr 8:8 nothing froward **o.** perverse in them.
Pr 8:23 the beginning, **o.** ever the earth was.
Pr 20:20 curseth his father **o.** his mother,
Pr 22:26 **o.** of them that are sureties for debts.
Pr 23:34 **o.** as he that lieth upon the top of a
Pr 28:24 robbeth his father **o.** his mother, and
Pr 29:9 whether he rage **o.** laugh, there is no
Pr 30:4 up into heaven, **o.** descended?
Pr 30:9 **o.** lest I be poor and steal, and take
Pr 30:32 **o.** if thou hast thought evil, lay
Ec *general* *title* Ecclesiastes: **O.**, The Preacher.
Ec 2:19 he shall be a wise man **o.** a fool? 176
Ec 2:25 **o.** who else can hasten her unto, more
Ec 5:12 whether he eat little **o.** much: but
Ec 9:1 no man knoweth either love **o.** hatred
Ec 11:3 **o.** toward the north, in the place
Ec 11:6 shall prosper, either this **o.** that, 176
Ec 11:6 **o.** whether they both shall be alike
Ec 12:2 sun, **o.** the light, **o.** the moon, **o.** the
Ec 12:6 **O.** ever the silver cord be loosed, 5704
Ec 12:6 **o.** the golden bowl be broken,
Ec 12:6 **o.** the pitcher be broken at the
Ec 12:6 **o.** the wheel broken at the cistern.
Ec 12:14 it be good, **o.** whether it be evil.
Ca 2:9 is like a roe **o.** a young hart: 176
Ca 2:17 be thou like a roe **o.** young hart 176
Ca 6:12 **O.** ever I was aware, my soul made me
Ca 8:14 thou like to a roe **o.** to a young hart 176
Isa 1:11 bullocks, **o.** of lambs, **o.** of he goats.
Isa 7:11 the depth, **o.** into the height above. 176
Isa 10:14 wing, **o.** opened the mouth, **o.** peeped.
Isa 10:15 **o.** shall the saw magnify itself
Isa 10:15 **o.** as if the staff should lift up itself,
Isa 17:6 two **o.** three berries in the top of the
Isa 17:6 four **o.** five in the outmost fruitful
Isa 17:8 made, either the groves, **o.** the images.
Isa 19:15 head **o.** tail, branch **o.** rush, may do.
Isa 27:5 **O.** let him take hold of my strength, 176
Isa 27:7 **o.** is he slain according to the
Isa 29:8 **o.** as when a thirsty man dreameth,
Isa 29:16 **o.** shall the thing framed say of him
Isa 30:14 **o.** to take water withal out of the pit.
Isa 38:14 Like a crane **o.** a swallow, so did I
Isa 40:13 **o.** being his counseller hath taught
Isa 40:18 **o.** what likeness will ye compare unto
Isa 40:25 ye liken me, **o.** shall I be equal?
Isa 41:22 them; **o.** declare us things for to come.
Isa 41:23 do good, **o.** do evil, that we may be
Isa 42:19 **o.** deaf, as my messenger that I sent?
Isa 43:9 **o.** let them hear, and say, It is truth.
Isa 44:10 a god, **o.** molten a graven image
Isa 45:9 thou? **o.** thy work, He hath no hands?
Isa 45:10 **o.** to the woman, What hast thou
Isa 49:24 **o.** the lawful captive delivered?
Isa 50:1 **o.** which of my creditors is it to 176
Isa 50:2 **o.** have I no power to deliver?
Isa 57:11 hast thou been afraid **o.** feared,
Isa 66:8 **o.** shall a nation be born at once?

Jer 2:18 **o.** what hast thou to do in the way of
Jer 2:32 her ornaments, **o.** a bride her attire?
Jer 7:22 burnt offerings **o.** sacrifices:
Jer 11:14 neither lift up a cry **o.** prayer for them:
Jer 11:19 like a lamb **o.** an ox that is brought
Jer 13:23 his skin, **o.** the leopard his spots?
Jer 14:22 **o.** can the havens give showers?
Jer 15:5 **o.** who shall bemoan thee?
Jer 15:5 **o.** who shall go aside to ask how thou
Jer 16:2 sons **o.** [*some eds.* NOR] daughters in order
Jer 16:7 for their father **o.** for their mother.
Jer 16:10 against us? **o.** what is our iniquity?
Jer 16:10 **o.** what is our sin that we have
Jer 18:14 **o.** shall the cold flowing waters that
Jer 20:17 **o.** that my mother might have been
Jer 21:13 us? **o.** who shall enter into our
Jer 22:18 saying, Ah my brother! **o.**, Ah sister!
Jer 22:18 him, saying, Ah lord! **o.**, Ah his glory!
Jer 23:33 people, **o.** the prophet, **o.** a priest, 176
Jer 32:43 It is desolate without man **o.** beast;
Jer 34:9 being an Hebrew **o.** an Hebrewess,
Jer 36:23 Jehudi had read three **o.** four leaves,
Jer 37:18 against thee, **o.** against thy servants,
Jer 37:18 thy servants, **o.** against this people,
Jer 40:5 **o.** go wheresoever it seemeth 176
Jer 42:6 it be good, **o.** whether it be evil, we
Jer 42:17 none of them shall remain **o.** escape
Jer 44:14 sojourn there, shall escape **o.** remain,
Jer 44:28 words shall stand, mine **o.** theirs.
Jer 48:24 cities of the land of Moab, far **o.** near.
Eze 2:5 hear, **o.** whether they will forbear,
Eze 2:7 hear, **o.** whether they will forbear:
Eze 3:11 hear **o.** whether they will forbear.
Eze 4:14 dieth of itself, **o.** is torn in pieces;
Eze 14:7 **o.** of the stranger that sojourneth in
Eze 14:17 **O.** if I bring a sword upon that 176
Eze 14:19 **O.** if I send a pestilence into that 176
Eze 15:2 **o.** than a branch which is among
Eze 15:3 **o.** will men take a pin of it to hang
Eze 17:9 without great power **o.** many people
Eze 17:15 **o.** shall he break the covenant, and be
Eze 21:16 Go thee one way **o.** other, either on the
Eze 21:16 either on the right hand, **o.** on the left,
Eze 22:14 **o.** can thine hands be strong, in the
Eze 34:6 and none did search **o.** seek after them.
Eze 44:22 **o.** a widow that had a priest before.
Eze 44:25 but for father, **o.** for mother,
Eze 44:25 **o.** for son, **o.** for daughter, for brother,
Eze 44:25 **o.** for sister that hath had no husband, 1011
Eze 44:31 **o.** torn, whether it be fowl **o.** beast.
Eze 46:12 burnt offering **o.** peace offerings
Da 2:10 magician, **o.** astrologer, **o.** Chaldean.
Da 4:19 dream, **o.** the interpretation thereof,
Da 4:35 **o.** say unto him, What doest thou?
Da 6:4 there any error **o.** fault found in him.
Da 6:7, 12 ask a petition of any God **o.** man.
Da 6:24 **o.** ever they came at the bottom of
Da 11:29 not be as the former, **o.** as the latter.
Joe 1:2 **o.** even in the days of your fathers?
Am 3:12 lion two legs, **o.** a piece of an ear; 176
Am 4:8 two **o.** three cities wandered unto one
Am 5:19 **o.** went into the house, and leaned his
Am 6:2 **o.** their border greater than your
Mic 6:7 **o.** with ten thousands of rivers of oil?
Hag 2:12 his skirt do touch bread, **o.** pottage,
Hag 2:12 **o.** wine, **o.** oil, **o.** any meat, shall it be
Zec 8:10 to him that went out **o.** came in
Mal 1:8 with thee, **o.** accept thy person? 176
Mal 2:13 **o.** receiveth it with good will at your
Mal 2:17 **o.**, Where is the God of judgment? 176
Mt 5:17 **destroy the law, o. the prophets:** *2228*
Mt 5:18 **one jot o. one tittle shall in no** *2228*
Mt 5:36 **not make one hair white o. black** *2228*
Mt 6:24 **o. else he will hold to the one,** *2228*
Mt 6:25 **ye shall eat, o. what ye shall drink;**
Mt 6:31 **we eat? o., What shall we drink?** *2228*
Mt 6:31 **o. Wherewithal shall we be** *2228*
Mt 7:4 **O. how wilt thou say to thy** *2228*
Mt 7:9 **O. what man is there of you,** *2228*
Mt 7:10 **O. if he ask a fish, will he give** *2532*
Mt 7:16 **of thorns, o. figs of thistles?** *2228*
Mt 9:5 **thee; o. to say, Arise, and walk?** *2228*
Mt 10:11 **into whatsoever city o. town ye** *2228*
Mt 10:14 **depart out of that house o. city,** *2228*
Mt 10:19 **thought how o. what ye shall** *2228*
Mt 10:37 **He that loveth father o. mother** *2228*
Mt 10:37 **he that loveth son o. daughter** *2228*

Mt 11:3 come, o. do we look for another? 2228
Mt 12:5 O. have ye not read in the law, 2228
Mt 12:25 every city o. house divided 2228
Mt 12:29 O. else how can one enter into a 2228
Mt 12:33 o. else make the tree corrupt, and 2228
Mt 13:21 tribulation o. persecution ariseth 2228
Mt 15:4 He that curseth father o. mother, 2228
Mt 15:5 say to his father o. his mother, It 2228
Mt 15:6 honour not his father o. his 2228
Mt 16:14 Jeremias, o. one of the prophets. 2228
Mt 16:26 soul? o. what shall a man give in 2228
Mt 17:25 the earth take custom o. tribute? 2228
Mt 17:25 own children, o. of strangers? 2228
Mt 18:8 if thy hand o. thy foot offend 2228
Mt 18:8 to enter into life halt o. maimed, 2228
Mt 18:8 having two hands o. two feet 2228
Mt 18:16 take with thee one o. two more, 2228
Mt 18:16 mouth of two o. three witnesses 2228
Mt 18:20 where two o. three are gathered 2228
Mt 19:29 houses, o. brethren, o. sisters, 2228
Mt 19:29 o. father o. mother, 2228
Mt 19:29 father,...mother, o. wife, 2228
Mt 19:29 o. children, o. lands, for my 2228
Mt 21:25 was it from heaven, o. of men? 2228
Mt 22:17 to give tribute unto Caesar, o. not? 2228
Mt 23:17 o. the temple that sanctifieth the 2228
Mt 23:19 o. the altar that sanctifieth the 2228
Mt 24:23 you, Lo, here is Christ, o. there; 2228
Mt 25:37 o. thirsty, and gave thee drink? 2228
Mt 25:38 thee in? o. naked, and clothed 2228
Mt 25:39 O. when saw we thee sick, 2228
Mt 25:39 o. in prison, and came unto thee? 2228
Mt 25:44 hungred, o. athirst, o. a stranger, 2228
Mt 25:44 o. naked, o. sick, o. in prison, 2228
Mt 27:17 o. Jesus which is called Christ? 2228
Mk 2:9 o. to say, Arise, and take up thy 2228
Mk 3:4 on the sabbath days, o. to do evil? 2228
Mk 3:4 to save life, o. to kill? But they 2228
Mk 3:33 is my mother, o. my brethren? 2228
Mk 4:17 affliction o. persecution ariseth 2228
Mk 4:21 under a bushel, o. under a bed? 2228
Mk 4:30 o. with what comparison shall we 2228
Mk 6:15 a prophet, o. as one of the prophets. 2228
Mk 6:56 into villages, o. cities, o. country, 2228
Mr 7:10 Whoso curseth father o. mother, 2228
Mk 7:11 shall say to his father o. mother, 2228
Mk 7:12 ought for his father o. his mother; 2228
Mk 8:37 O. what shall a man give in 2228
Mk 10:29 that hath left house, o. brethren, 2228
Mk 10:29 o. sisters, o. father, o. mother, 2228
Mk 10:29 father,...mother, o. wife, 2228
Mk 10:29 o. children, o. lands, for my sake, 2228
Mk 11:30 was it from heaven, o. of men? 2228
Mk 12:14 to give tribute to Caesar, o. not? 2228
Mk 12:15 Shall we give, o. shall we not give? 2228
Mk 13:21 here is Christ; o., lo, he is there; 2228
Mk 13:35 cometh, at even, o. at midnight, 2228
Mk 13:35 midnight, o. at the cockcrowing, 2228
Mk 13:35 cockcrowing, o. in the morning 2228
Lu 2:24 turtledoves, o. two young pigeons. 2228
Lu 3:15 whether he were the Christ, o. not;
Lu 5:23 o. to say, Rise up and walk? 2228
Lu 6:9 days to do good, o. to do evil? 2228
Lu 6:9 evil? to save life, o. to destroy it? 2228
Lu 7:19, 20 come? o. look we for another? 2228
Lu 8:16 vessel, o. putteth it under a bed; 2228
Lu 9:25 and lose himself, o. be cast away? 2228
Lu 11:11 o. if ye ask a fish, will he for a fish
Lu 11:12 O. if he shall ask an egg, 2228,2532
Lu 12:11 how o. what thing ye shall 2228
Lu 12:11 shall answer, o. what ye shall 2228
Lu 12:14 me a judge o. a divider over you? 2228
Lu 12:29 shall eat, o. what ye shall drink, 2228
Lu 12:38 watch, o. come in the third 2532
Lu 12:41 this parable unto us, o. even to all? 2228
Lu 13:4 O. those eighteen, upon whom 2228
Lu 13:15 loose his ox o. his ass from the 2228
Lu 14:5 an ass o. an ox fallen into a pit, 2228
Lu 14:12 thou makest a dinner o. a supper, 2228
Lu 14:31 O. what king, going to make war 2228
Lu 14:32 O. else, while the other is yet a 1161
Lu 16:13 o. else he will hold to the one 2228
Lu 17:7 servant plowing o. feeding cattle, 2228
Lu 17:21 they say, Lo here! o., lo there! 2228
Lu 17:23 to you, See here; o., see there: 2228
Lu 18:11 o. even as this publican. 2228
Lu 18:29 o. parents, o. brethren, o. wife, 2228
Lu 18:29 o. children, for the kingdom of 2228
Lu 20:2 o. who is he that gave thee this 2228
Lu 20:4 was it from heaven, o. of men? 2228
Lu 20:22 to give tribute unto Caesar, o. no? 2228
Lu 22:27 sitteth at meat, o. he that serveth? 2228
Joh 2:6 two o. three firkins apiece. 2228
Joh 4:27 o., Why talkest thou with her? 2228
Joh 6:19 five and twenty o. thirty furlongs, 2228
Joh 7:17 God, o. whether I speak of myself 2228
Joh 7:48 of the rulers o. of the Pharisees 2228
Joh 9:2 did sin, this man, o. his parents, 2228
Joh 9:21 o. who hath opened his eyes, we 2228
Joh 9:25 Whether he be a sinner o. no, I know
Joh 13:29 o., that he should give something 2228
Joh 14:11 o. else believe me for the very 1161
Joh 18:34 o. did others tell it thee of me? 2228
Ac 1:7 to know the times o. the seasons, 2228
Ac 3:12 o. why look ye so earnestly on us, 2228
Ac 3:12 by our own power o. holiness we 2228
Ac 4:7 By what power, o. by what name, 2228
Ac 4:34 were possessors of lands o. houses 2228
Ac 5:38 this counsel o. this work be of men, 2228
Ac 7:49 o. what is the place of my rest? 2228
Ac 8:34 of himself, o. of some other man? 2228
Ac 9:2 whether they were men o. women, 2532
Ac 10:14 thing that is common o. unclean. 2228
Ac 10:28 o. come unto one of another nation; 2228
Ac 10:28 call any man common o. unclean. 2228
Ac 11:8 for nothing common o. unclean hath 2228
Ac 17:21 to tell, o. to hear some new thing.) 2532
Ac 17:29 like unto gold, o. silver, o. stone, 2228
Ac 18:14 of wrong o. wicked lewdness, 2228
Ac 19:12 the sick handkerchiefs o. aprons, 2228
Ac 20:33 no man's silver, o. gold, o. apparel. 2228
Ac 23:9 a spirit o. an angel hath spoken to 2228
Ac 23:15 o. ever he come near, are ready to 4253
Ac 23:29 worthy of death o. of bonds. 2228
Ac 24:20 O. else let these same here say, if 2228
Ac 24:23 to minister o. come unto him. 2228
Ac 25:11 o. have committed any thing 2532
Ac 26:31 worthy of death o. of bonds. 2228
Ac 28:6 o. fallen down dead suddenly: 2228
Ac 28:17 people, o. customs of our fathers, 2228
Ac 28:21 shewed o. spake any harm of thee. 2228
Ro 2:4 O. despisest thou the riches of his 2228
Ro 2:15 accusing o. else excusing one 2228
Ro 3:1 o. what profit is there of 2228
Ro 4:9 o. upon the uncircumcision also? 2228
Ro 4:10 circumcision, o. in uncircumcision? 2228
Ro 4:13 was not to Abraham, o. to his seed, 2228
Ro 6:16 o. of obedience unto righteousness 2228
Ro 8:35 o. distress, o. persecution, o. famine, 2228
Ro 8:35 o. nakedness, o. peril, o. sword? 2228
Ro 9:11 having done any good o. evil, that 2228
Ro 10:7 O., Who shall descend into the deep? 2228
Ro 11:34 o. who hath been his counsellor? 2228
Ro 11:35 O. who hath first given to him, and 2228
Ro 12:7 O. ministry, let us wait on our 1535
Ro 12:7 o. he that teacheth, on teaching; 1535
Ro 12:8 O. he that exhorteth, on 1535
Ro 14:4 own master he standeth o. falleth. 2228
Ro 14:8 whether we live therefore, o. die, 5037
Ro 14:10 o. why dost thou set at nought 2228
Ro 14:13 a stumblingblock o. an occasion 2228
Ro 14:21 brother stumbleth, o. is offended, 2228
Ro 14:21 is offended, o. is made weak. 2228
1Co 1:13 o. were ye baptized in the name of 2228
1Co 2:1 excellency of speech o. of wisdom, 2228
1Co 3:22 Paul, o. Apollos, o. Cephas, 1535
1Co 3:22 o. the world, o. life, o. death, 1535
1Co 3:22 o. things present, o. things to come; 1535
1Co 4:3 o. you, o. of man's judgment: 2228
1Co 4:21 come unto you with a rod, o. in love, 2228
1Co 5:10 this world, o. with the covetous, 2228
1Co 5:10 the covetous, o. extortioners, 2228
1Co 5:10 the covetous, o. with idolaters; 2228
1Co 5:11 be a fornicator, o. covetous, 2228
1Co 5:11 o. an idolater, o. a railer, 2228
1Co 5:11 o. a drunkard, o. an extortioner; 2228
1Co 7:11 o. be reconciled to her husband: 2228
1Co 7:15 A brother o. a sister is not under 2228
1Co 7:16 o. how knowest thou, O man, 2228
1Co 8:5 whether in heaven o. in earth, 1535
1Co 9:6 O. I only and Barnabas, have not 2228
1Co 9:7 o. who feedeth a flock, and eateth 2228
1Co 9:8 o. saith not the law the same also? 2228
1Co 9:10 O. saith he it altogether for our 2228
1Co 10:19 o. that which is offered in sacrifice 2228
1Co 10:31 eat, o. drink, o. whatsoever ye do, 1535
1Co 11:4 Every man praying o. prophesying, 2228
1Co 11:5 woman that prayeth o. prophesieth 2228
1Co 11:6 for a woman to be shorn o. shaven, 2228
1Co 11:22 o. despise ye the church of God, 2228
1Co 12:13 whether we be Jews o. Gentiles, 1535
1Co 12:13 whether we be bond o. free; 1535
1Co 12:26 o. one member be honoured, all 1535
1Co 13:1 brass, o. a tinkling cymbal. 2228
1Co 14:6 by revelation, o. by knowledge, 2228
1Co 14:6 o. by prophesying, o. by doctrine? 2228
1Co 14:7 giving sound, whether pipe o. harp, 1535
1Co 14:7 be known what is piped o. harped? 2228
1Co 14:23 that are unlearned, o. unbelievers, 2228
1Co 14:24 believeth not, o. one unlearned, 2228
1Co 14:27 be by two, o. at the most by three, 2228
1Co 14:29 the prophets speak two o. three, 2228
1Co 14:36 from you, o. came it unto you only? 2228
1Co 14:37 himself to be a prophet, o. spiritual, 2228
1Co 15:11 whether it were I o. they, so we 1535
1Co 15:37 o. wheat, o. of some other grain: 2228
2Co 1:6 o. whether we be comforted, it is 1535
2Co 1:13 than what ye read o. acknowledge; 2228
2Co 1:17 o. the things that I purpose, do I 2228
2Co 3:1 o. need we, as some others, 2228,3361
2Co 3:1 o. letters of commendation from 2228
2Co 5:9 that, whether present o. absent, 1535
2Co 5:10 done, whether it be good o. bad. 1535
2Co 5:13 o. whether we be sober, it is for your 1535
2Co 6:15 o. what part hath he that believeth 2228
2Co 8:23 o. our brethren be enquired of, 1535
2Co 9:7 not grudgingly, o. of necessity: 2228
2Co 10:12 o. compare ourselves with some 2228
2Co 11:4 o. if ye receive another spirit, which 2228
2Co 11:4 o. another gospel, which ye have 2228
2Co 12:2 o. whether out of the body I cannot 1535
2Co 12:3 in the body, o. out of the body, 1535
2Co 12:6 me to be, o. that he heareth of me. 2228
2Co 13:1 the mouth of two o. three witnesses 2532
Ga 1:8 o. an angel from heaven, preach 2228
Ga 1:10 do I now persuade men, o. God? 2228
Ga 1:10 o. do I seek to please men? for if I 2228
Ga 2:2 I should run, o. had run, in vain. 2228
Ga 3:2,5 the law, o. by the hearing of faith? 2228
Ga 3:15 disannulleth, o. addeth thereto. 2228
Ga 4:9 God, o. rather are known of God, 1161
Eph 3:20 above all that we ask o. think, 2228
Eph 5:3 all uncleanness, o. covetousness, 2228
Eph 5:27 spot, o. wrinkle, o. any such thing; 2228
Eph 6:8 Lord, whether he be bond o. free. 1535
Php 1:18 whether in pretence, o. in truth, 1535
Php 1:20 whether it be by life, o. by death. 1535
Php 1:27 come and see you, o. else be absent, 1535
Php 2:3 done through strife o. vainglory; 2228
Col 1:16 they be thrones, o. dominions, 1535
Col 1:16 o. principalities, o. powers: 1535
Col 1:20 things in earth, o. things in heaven. 1535
Col 2:16 judge you in meat, o. in drink, 2228
Col 2:16 o. in respect of a holyday, 2228
Col 2:16 o. of the new moon, o....the sabbath 2228
Col 3:17 ye do in word o. in deed, do all in 2228
1Th 2:19 hope, o. joy, o. crown of rejoicing? 2228
1Th 5:10 that, whether we wake o. sleep, 1535
2Th 2:2 shaken in mind, o. be troubled, 3383
2Th 2:4 called God, o. that is worshipped; 2228
2Th 2:15 whether by word, o. our epistle. 1535
1Ti 2:9 o. gold, o. pearls, o. costly array; 2228
1Ti 5:4 widow have children o. nephews, 2228
1Ti 5:16 any man o. woman that believeth 2228
1Ti 5:19 but before two o. three witnesses. 2228
Tit 1:6 not accused of riot o. unruly. 2228
Tit 3:12 Artemas unto thee, o. Tychicus, 2228
Phm 18 wronged thee, o. oweth thee ought, 2228
Heb 2:6 o. the son of man, that thou visitest 2228
Heb 10:28 under two o. three witnesses: 2228
Heb 12:16 any fornicator, o. profane person, 2228
Heb 12:20 o. thrust through with a dart: 2228
Jas 2:3 o. sit here under my footstool: 2228
Jas 2:15 If a brother o. sister be naked, and 2228
Jas 4:13 To day o. to morrow we will go into 2228
Jas 4:15 we shall live, and do this, o. that. 2228
1Pe 1:11 what, o. what manner of time the 2228
1Pe 2:14 O. unto governors, as unto them 1535
1Pe 3:3 of gold, o. of putting on of apparel: 2228

1Pe 3:9 evil for evil, **o.** railing for railing: *2228*
1Pe 4:15 **o.** as a thief, **o.** as an evildoer, *2228*
1Pe 4:15 **o.** as a busybody in other men's *2228*
Re 2:5, 16 **o. else I will come unto thee** *1161*
Re 3:15 **I would thou wert cold o. hot:)** *2228*
Re 13:16 right hand, **o.** in their foreheads: *2228*
Re 13:17 that no man might buy **o.** sell, save *2228*
Re 13:17 the mark, **o.** the name of the beasts. *2228*
Re 13:17 beast, **o.** the number of his name. *2228*
Re 14:9 mark in his forehead, **o.** in his hand, *2228*
Re 20:4 their foreheads, **o.** in their hands; *2532*
Re 21:27 abomination, **o.** maketh a lie; *2532*

ORACLE See also ORACLES.
2Sa 16:23 had enquired at the **o.** of God: 1697
1Ki 6:5 both of the temple and of the **o.**: 1687
1Ki 6:16 them for it within, even for the **o.**, 1687
1Ki 6:19 And the **o.** he prepared in the house 1687
1Ki 6:20 the **o.** in the forepart was twenty 1687
1Ki 6:21 by the chains of gold before the **o.**; 1687
1Ki 6:22 altar that was by the **o.** he overlaid 1687
1Ki 6:23 the **o.** he made two cherubims of 1687
1Ki 6:31 entering of the **o.** he made doors 1687
1Ki 7:49 and five on the left, before the **o.**, 1687
1Ki 8:6 his place, into the **o.** of the house, 1687
1Ki 8:8 out in the holy place before the **o.**, 1687
2Ch 3:16 he made chains, as in the **o.**, and 1687
2Ch 4:20 after the manner before the **o.**, of 1687
2Ch 5:7 his place, to the **o.** of the house, 1687
2Ch 5:9 seen from the ark before the **o.**; 1687
Ps 28:2 up my hands toward thy holy **o.** 1687

ORACLES
Ac 7:38 the lively **o.** to give unto us: *3051*
Ro 3:2 were committed the **o.** of God. *3051*
Heb 5:12 the first principles of the **o.** of God; *3051*
1Pe 4:11 let him speak as the **o.** of God; *3051*

ORATION
Ac 12:21 throne, and made an **o.** unto them. *1215*

ORATOR
Isa 3:3 artificer, and the eloquent **o.**. 3908
Ac 24:1 with a certain **o.** named Tertullus, *4489*

ORCHARD See also ORCHARDS.
Ca 4:13 plants are an **o.** of pomegranates, 6508

ORCHARDS
Ec 2:5 I made me gardens and **o.**, and I 6508

ORDAIN See ORDAINED; ORDAINETH.
1Ch 9:22 the seer did **o.** in their set office. 3245
1Ch 17:9 Also I will **o.** a place for my people 7760
Isa 26:12 Lord, thou wilt **o.** peace for us: 8239
1Co 7:17 walk. And so **o.** I in all churches. *1299*
Ti 1:5 and **o.** elders in every city, as I *2525*

ORDAINED
Nu 28:6 was **o.** in mount Sinai for a sweet 6213
1Ki 12:32 And Jeroboam **o.** a feast in the eighth 6213
1Ki 12:33 **o.** a feast unto the children of Israel: 6213
2Ki 23:5 had **o.** to burn incense in the 5414
2Ch 11:15 And he **o.** him priests for the high 5975
2Ch 23:18 with singing, as it was **o.** by David.
2Ch 29:27 the instruments **o.** by David king of
Es 9:27 The Jews **o.**, and took upon them, 6965
Ps 8:2 thou **o.** strength because of thine 3245
Ps 8:3 and the stars, which thou hast **o.**; 3559
Ps 81:5 This he **o.** in Joseph for a 7760
Ps 132:17 have **o.** a lamp for mine anointed. 6186
Isa 30:33 Tophet is **o.** of old; yea, for the 6186
Jer 1:5 and I **o.** thee a prophet unto the 5414
Da 2:24 Arioch, whom the king had **o.** 4483
Hab 1:12 thou hast **o.** them for judgment; 7760
Mk 3:14 **o.** twelve, that they should be with *4160*
Joh 15:16 **I have chosen you, and o. you,** *5087*
Ac 1:22 must one be **o.** to be a witness *1096*
Ac 10:42 was **o.** of God to be the Judge of *3724*
Ac 13:48 as were **o.** to eternal life believed. *5021*
Ac 14:23 when they had **o.** them elders in *5500*
Ac 16:4 were **o.** of the apostles and elders *2919*
Ac 17:31 by that man whom he hath **o.**; *3724*
Ro 7:10 which was **o.** to life, I found to be
Ro 13:1 the powers that be are **o.** of God. *5021*
1Co 2:7 God **o.** before the world unto our *4304*
1Co 9:14 Lord **o.** that they which preach *1299*
Ga 3:19 was **o.** by angels in the hand of a *1299*
Eph 2:10 **o.** that we should walk in them. *4282*
1Ti 2:7 Whereunto I am **o.** a preacher, *5087*
2Ti *subscr.* **o.** the first bishop of the church *5500*
Tit *subscr.* **o.** the first bishop of the church *5500*
Heb 5:1 **o.** for men in things pertaining to *2525*
Heb 8:3 every high priest is **o.** to offer gifts *2525*
Heb 9:6 when these things were thus **o.**, *2680*
Jude 4 who were before of old **o.** to this *4270*

ORDAINETH
Ps 7:13 he **o.** his arrows against the 6466

ORDER See also ORDERED; ORDERETH; ORDERINGS.
Ge 22:9 there, and laid the wood in **o.** 6186
Ex 26:17 set in **o.** one against another: 7947
Ex 27:21 Aaron and his sons shall **o.** it from 6186
Ex 39:37 even with the lamps to be set in **o.**, 4634
Ex 40:4 the table, and set in **o.** the things 6186
Ex 40:4 that are to be set in **o.** upon it; 6187
Ex 40:23 And he set the bread in **o.** upon it 6186
Le 1:7 lay the wood in **o.** upon the fire: 6186
Le 1:8 and the fat in **o.** upon the wood 6186
Le 1:12 and the priest shall lay them in **o.** 6186
Le 6:12 lay the burnt offering in **o.** upon it; 6186
Le 24:3 shall Aaron **o.** it from the evening 6186
Le 24:4 shall **o.** the lamps upon the pure 6186
Le 24:8 every sabbath he shall set it in **o.** 6186
Jos 2:6 she had laid in **o.** upon the roof. 6186
Jg 13:12 How shall we **o.** the child, and 4941
2Sa 17:23 city, and put his household in **o.**, 6680
1Ki 18:33 And he put the wood in **o.**, and cut 6186
1Ki 20:14 he said, Who shall **o.** the battle? 631
2Ki 20:1 the Lord, Set thine house in **o.**; 6680
2Ki 23:4 and the priests of the second **o.**,
1Ch 6:32 their office according to their **o.** 4941
1Ch 15:13 we sought him not after the due **o.** 4941
1Ch 23:31 according to the **o.** commanded 4941
1Ch 25:2 according to the **o.** of the king. 3027
1Ch 25:6 according to the king's **o.** to Asaph, 3027
2Ch 8:14 according to the **o.** of David his 4941
2Ch 13:11 shewbread also set they in **o.** upon
2Ch 29:35 house of the Lord was set in **o.** 3559
Job 10:22 shadow of death, without any **o.**, 5468
Job 23:4 I would **o.** my cause before him, 6186
Job 33:5 set thy words in **o.** before me, 6186
Job 37:19 **o.** our speech by reason of darkness. 6186
Ps 40:5 be reckoned up in **o.** unto thee: 6186
Ps 50:21 and set them in **o.** before thine eyes. 6186
Ps 110:4 ever after the **o.** of Melchizedek. 1700
Ps 119:133 **O.** my steps in thy word: and let 3559
Ec 12:9 out, and set in **o.** many proverbs. 8626
Isa 9:7 kingdom, to **o.** it, and to establish 3559
Isa 38:1 the Lord, Set thine house in **o.**: 6680
Isa 44:7 declare it, and set it in **o.** for me, 6186
Jer 46:3 **O.** ye the buckler and shield, and 6186
Eze 41:6 over another, and thirty in **o.**; 6471
Lu 1:1 in **o.** a declaration of those things *1299*
Lu 1:3 to write unto thee in **o.**, most *2517*
Lu 1:8 before God in the **o.** of his course, *5010*
Ac 11:4 and expounded it by **o.** unto them, *2517*
Ac 18:23 of Galatia and Phrygia in **o.**, *2517*
1Co 11:34 rest will I set in **o.** when I come. *1299*
1Co 14:40 things be done decently and in **o.** *5010*
1Co 15:23 every man in his own **o.**; Christ *5001*
1Co 16:1 as I have given **o.** to the churches *1299*
Col 2:5 joying and beholding your **o.**, and *5010*
Tit 1:5 set in **o.** the things that are wanting, *1930*
Heb 5:6 ever after the **o.** of Melchisedec. *5010*
Heb 5:10 priest after the **o.** of Melchisedec. *5010*
Heb 6:20 ever after the **o.** of Melchisedec. *5010*
Heb 7:11 rise after the **o.** of Melchisedec, *5010*
Heb 7:11 not be called after the **o.** of Aaron? *5010*
Heb 7:17 ever after the **o.** of Melchisedec. *5010*
Heb 7:21 ever after the **o.** of Melchisedec:) *5010*

ORDERED
Jg 6:26 top of this rock, in the **o.** place, 4634
2Sa 23:5 covenant, **o.** in all things and 6186
Job 13:18 I have **o.** my cause; I know that 6186
Ps 37:23 of a good man are **o.** by the Lord: 3559

ORDERETH
Ps 50:23 to him that **o.** his conversation 7760

ORDERINGS
1Ch 24:19 the **o.** of them in their service to 6486

ORDERLY See also DISORDERLY.
Ac 21:24 that thou thyself also walkest **o.**, *4748*

ORDINANCE See also ORDINANCES.
Ex 12:14 keep it a feast by an **o.** for ever. 2708
Ex 12:17 your generations by an **o.** for ever. 2708
Ex 12:24 observe this thing for an **o.** to thee 2706
Ex 12:43 This is the **o.** of the passover: 2708
Ex 13:10 therefore keep this **o.** in his season 2708
Ex 15:25 for them a statute and an **o.**, and 4941
Le 18:30 Therefore shall ye keep mine **o.**, 4931
Le 22:9 They shall therefore keep mine **o.**, 4931
Nu 9:14 according to the **o.** of the passover, 2708
Nu 9:14 ye shall have one **o.**, both for the 2708
Nu 10:8 shall be to you for an **o.** for ever 2708
Nu 15:15 One **o.** shall be both for you of the 2708
Nu 15:15 an **o.** for ever in your generations: 2708
Nu 18:8 and to thy sons, by an **o.** for ever. 2706
Nu 19:2 This is the **o.** of the law which the 2708
Nu 31:21 This is the **o.** of the law which the 2708
Jos 24:25 a statute and an **o.** in Shechem. 4941
1Sa 30:25 it a statute and an **o.** for Israel 4941
2Ch 2:4 This is an **o.** for ever to Israel.
2Ch 35:13 with fire according to the **o.**: but 4941
2Ch 35:25 and made them an **o.** in Israel: 2706
Ezr 3:10 after the **o.** of David king of Israel. 3027
Ps 99:7 and the **o.** that he gave them. 2706
Isa 24:5 the laws, changed the **o.**, broken 2706
Isa 58:2 forsook not the **o.** of their God: 4941
Eze 45:14 Concerning the **o.** of oil, the bath 2706
Eze 46:14 by a perpetual **o.** unto the Lord. 2708
Mal 3:14 is it that we have kept his **o.**, 4931
Ro 13:2 the power, resisteth the **o.** of God: *1296*
1Pe 2:13 Submit...to every **o.** of man for *2937*

ORDINANCES
Ex 18:20 thou shalt teach them **o.** and laws, 2706
Le 18:3 neither shall ye walk in their **o.** 2708
Le 18:4 and keep mine **o.**, to walk therein: 2708
Nu 9:12 all the **o.** of the passover they shall 2708
2Ki 17:34 or after their **o.**, or after the law 4941
2Ki 17:37 And the statutes, and the **o.**, and 4941
2Ch 33:8 and the **o.** by the hand of Moses. 4941
Ne 10:32 Also we made **o.** for us, to charge 4687
Job 38:33 Knowest thou the **o.** of heaven? 2708
Ps 119:91 this day according to thine **o.**: 4941
Isa 58:2 they ask of me the **o.** of justice; 4941
Jer 31:35 the **o.** of the moon and of the stars 2708
Jer 31:36 If those **o.** depart from before me, 2706
Jer 33:25 not appointed the **o.** of heaven and 2708
Eze 11:20 and keep mine **o.**, and do them: 4941
Eze 43:11 all the **o.** thereof, and all the forms 2708
Eze 43:11 and all the **o.** thereof, and do them. 2708
Eze 43:18 These are the **o.** of the altar in the 2708
Eze 44:5 concerning all the **o.** of the house 2708
Mal 3:7 ye are gone away from mine **o.**, 2706
Lu 1:6 and **o.** of the Lord blameless. *1345*
1Co 11:2 keep the **o.**, as I delivered them to *3862*
Eph 2:15 commandments contained in **o.**; *1378*
Col 2:14 Blotting out the handwriting of **o.** *1378*
Col 2:20 in the world, are ye subject to **o.**, *1379*
Heb 9:1 had also **o.** of divine service, and *1345*
Heb 9:10 divers washings, and carnal **o.**, *1345*

ORDINARY
Eze 16:27 and have diminished thine **o.** food, 2706

OREB (o'-reb)
Jg 7:25 of the Midianites, **O.** and Zeeb; 6157
Jg 7:25 and they slew **O.** upon the rock **O.**, 6157
Jg 7:25 brought the heads of **O.** and Zeeb to 6157
Jg 8:3 the princes of Midian, **O.** and Zeeb: 6157
Ps 83:11 Make their nobles like **O.**, and like 6157
Isa 10:26 slaughter of Midian at the rock of **O.**: 6157

OREGIM See JAARE-OREGIM.

OREN (o'-ren)
1Ch 2:25 and Bunah, and **O.**, and Ozem, and 767

ORGAN See also ORGANS.
Ge 4:21 such as handle the harp and **o.** 5748
Job 21:12 and rejoice at the sound of the **o.** 5748
Job 30:31 and my **o.** into the voice of them 5748

ORGANS
Ps 150:4 with stringed instruments and **o.** 5748

ORION (o-ri'-on)
Job 9:9 Arcturus, **O.**, and Pleiades, and 3685
Job 38:31 Pleiades, or loose the bands of **O.**? 3685
Am 5:8 that maketh the seven stars and **O.**, 3685

ORNAMENT See also ORNAMENTS.
Pr 1:9 be an **o.** of grace unto thy head, 3880
Pr 4:9 give to thine head an **o.** of grace: 3880

Pr 25:12 gold, and an **o.** of fine gold, ... 2481
Isa 30:22 the **o.** of thy molten images of gold:..... 642
Isa 49:18 thee with them all, as with an **o.**,........ 5716
Eze 7:20 As for the beauty of his **o.**, he set 5716
1Pe 3:4 the **o.** of a meek and quiet spirit, ...

ORNAMENTS
Ex 33:44 and no man did put on him his **o.**. 5716
Ex 33:5 now put off thy **o.** from thee, that...... 5716
Ex 33:6 stripped themselves of their **o.** by...... 5716
Jg 8:21 and took away the **o.** that were on..... 7720
Jg 8:26 beside **o.**, and collars, and purple 7720
2Sa 1:24 put on **o.** of gold upon your apparel. ... 5716
Isa 3:18 their tinkling **o.** about their feet, ... 5914
Isa 3:20 bonnets, and the **o.** of the legs, ... 6807
Isa 61:10 decketh himself with **o.**, ... 6287
Jer 2:32 Can a maid forget her **o.**, or a........... 5716
Jer 4:30 thou deckest thee with **o.** of gold, ... 5716
Eze 16:7 and thou art come to excellent **o.**:...... 5716
Eze 16:11 I decked thee also with **o.**, and I........ 5716
Eze 23:40 eyes, and deckedst thyself with **o.**,...... 5716

ORNAN (or'-nan) See also ARAUNAH.
1Ch 21:15, 18 threshingfloor of **O.** the Jebusite...... 771
1Ch 21:20 **O.** turned back, and saw the angel;...... 771
1Ch 21:20 Now **O.** was threshing wheat............. 771
1Ch 21:21 as David came to **O.**, **O.** looked and..... 771
1Ch 21:22 Then David said to **O.**, Grant me the ... 771
1Ch 21:23 **O.** said unto David, Take it to thee,..... 771
1Ch 21:24 So David said to **O.**, Nay; but I will..... 771
1Ch 21:25 So David gave to **O.** for the place six... 771
1Ch 21:28 threshingfloor of **O.** the Jebusite, ... 771
2Ch 3:1 threshingfloor of **O.** the Jebusite.......... 771

ORPAH (or'-pah)
Ru 1:4 the name of the one was **O.**, and....... 6204
Ru 1:14 and **O.** kissed her mother in law; 6204

ORPHANS
La 5:3 We are **o.** and fatherless, our........... 3490

OSEE (o'-see) See also HOSEA; JOSHUA; OSHEA.
Ro 9:25 As he saith also in **O.**, I will call *5617*

OSHEA (o-she'-ah) See also HOSHEA; OSEE.
Nu 13:8 of Ephraim, **O.** the son of Nun. 1954
Nu 13:16 called **O.** the son of Nun Jehoshua...... 1954

OSPRAY
Le 11:13 and the ossifrage, and the **o.**,............ 5822
De 14:12 and the ossifrage, and the **o.**,............ 5822

OSSIFRAGE
Le 11:13 eagle, and the **o.**, and the ospray, ... 6538
De 14:12 eagle, and the **o.**, and the ospray, ... 6538

OSTRICH See also OSTRICHES.
Job 39:13 wings and feathers unto the **o.**? 5133

OSTRICHES
La 4:3 cruel, like the **o.** in the wilderness...... 3283

OTHER See also ANOTHER; OTHERS; OTHERWISE.
Ge 4:19 and the name of the **o.** Zillah............ 8145
Ge 8:10, 12 And he stayed yet **o.** seven days;.... 312
Ge 13:11 themselves the one from the **o.**........... 251
Ge 20:16 that are with thee, and with all **o.**.............
Ge 26:23 shall be stronger than the **o.** people;.........
Ge 28:17 is none **o.** but the house of God,.............
Ge 29:27 serve with me yet seven **o.** years........ 312
Ge 29:30 served with him yet seven **o.** years...... 312
Ge 31:50 if thou shalt take **o.** wives beside ....
Ge 32:8 then the **o.** company which is left.............
Ge 41:3 seven **o.** kine came up after them........ 312
Ge 41:3 stood by the **o.** kine upon the brink..........
Ge 41:19 seven **o.** kine came up after them, ... 312
Ge 43:14 he may send away your **o.** brother,....... 312
Ge 43:22 **o.** money have we brought down in...... 312
Ge 47:21 of Egypt even to the **o.** end thereof..........
Ex 1:15 and the name of the **o.** Puah: 8145
Ex 4:7 it was turned again as his **o.** flesh............
Ex 14:20 one came not near the **o.** all the 2088
Ex 17:12 one side, and the **o.** on the...side; 259
Ex 17:12 one side, and the...on the **o.** side;...... 2088
Ex 18:4 And the name of the **o.** was Eliezer; 259
Ex 18:7 asked each **o.** of their welfare;............ 7453
Ex 20:3 shalt have no **o.** gods before me.......... 312
Ex 23:13 no mention of the name of **o.** gods,...... 312
Ex 25:12 and two rings in the **o.** side of it......... 8145
Ex 25:19 one end, and the **o.** cherub on the 259
Ex 25:19 and the...cherub on the **o.** end: 2088
Ex 25:32 the candlestick out of the **o.** side:....... 8145
Ex 25:33 made like almonds in the **o.** branch, ... 259
Ex 26:3 **o.** five curtains shall be coupled one to......
Ex 26:13 and a cubit on the **o.** side of that 2088
Ex 26:27 of the **o.** side of the tabernacle, ... 8145
Ex 27:15 on the **o.** side shall be hangings 8145
Ex 28:10 the **o.** six names of the rest on the..........
Ex 28:10 names of the rest on the **o.** stone, ...
Ex 28:25 the **o.** two ends of the two wreathen ....
Ex 28:27 two **o.** rings of gold thou shalt make, ...
Ex 28:27 against the **o.** coupling thereof, ...
Ex 29:19 And thou shalt take the **o.** ram; 8145
Ex 29:39 the **o.** lamb thou shalt offer at even: ... 8145
Ex 29:41 the **o.** lamb thou shalt offer at even, ... 8145
Ex 30:32 neither shall ye make any **o.** like it, ...
Ex 32:15 and on the **o.** were they written. 2088
Ex 34:14 For thou shalt worship no **o.** god:........ 312
Ex 36:10 and the **o.** five curtains he coupled...........
Ex 36:25 for the **o.** side of the tabernacle, ... 8145
Ex 36:32 of the **o.** side of the tabernacle, ... 8145
Ex 36:33 boards from the one end to the **o.**...... 8145
Ex 37:3 and two rings upon the **o.** side of it. ... 8145
Ex 37:8 cherub on the **o.** end of that side: ....
Ex 37:18 out of the **o.** side thereof:................ 8145
Ex 38:15 for the **o.** side of the court gate, ... 8145
Ex 39:20 And they made two **o.** golden rings, ...
Ex 39:20 over against the **o.** coupling thereof, ...
Le 5:7 and the **o.** for a burnt offering............. 259
Le 6:11 put on **o.** garments, and carry forth...... 312
Le 7:24 beasts, may be used in any **o.** use:...........
Le 8:22 And he brought the **o.** ram, the 8145
Le 11:23 But all **o.** flying creeping things, which ......
Le 12:8 and the **o.** for a sin offering: 259
Le 13:26 and it be no lower than the **o.** skin, but.....
Le 14:22 offering, and the **o.** a burnt offering...... 259
Le 14:31 and the **o.** for a burnt offering,............ 259
Le 14:42 they shall take **o.** stones, and put 312
Le 14:42 and he shall take **o.** morter, and.......... 312
Le 15:15, 30 and the **o.** for a burnt offering;........ 259
Le 16:8 and the **o.** lot for the scapegoat............ 259
Le 18:18 beside the **o.** in her life time.................
Le 20:24 have separated you from **o.** people. ....
Le 20:26 and have severed you from **o.** people, ...
Le 25:53 the **o.** shall not rule with rigour over.........
Nu 6:11 and the **o.** for a burnt offering, ... 259
Nu 8:12 and the **o.** for a burnt offering, ... 259
Nu 10:21 and the **o.** did set up the tabernacle..........
Nu 11:26 and the name of the **o.** Medad:.......... 8145
Nu 11:31 were a day's journey on the **o.** side, ... 3541
Nu 21:13 and pitched on the **o.** side of Arnon, ... 5676
Nu 24:1 he went not, as at **o.** times, to seek for ....
Nu 28:4,8 **o.** lamb shalt thou offer at even; 8145
Nu 32:38 and give **o.** names unto the cities ....
Nu 36:3 to any of the sons of the **o.** tribes 259
Nu 4:32 the one side of heaven unto the **o.**, ...
De 5:7 shalt have none **o.** gods before me....... 312
De 6:14 Ye shall not go after **o.** gods, of the..... 312
De 7:4 me, that they may serve **o.** gods:........ 312
De 8:19 walk after **o.** gods, and serve them, ... 312
De 11:16 and ye turn aside, and serve **o.** gods,.... 312
De 11:28 to go after **o.** gods, which ye have not.. 312
De 11:30 Are they not on the **o.** side Jordan, ... 5676
De 13:2 Let us go after **o.** gods, which thou 312
De 13:6 Let us go and serve **o.** gods, which 312
De 13:7 even unto the **o.** end of the earth;............
De 13:13 Let us go and serve **o.** gods, which 312
De 17:3 And hath gone and served **o.** gods, ... 312
De 18:20 shall speak in the name of **o.** gods, ... 312
De 28:14 to go after **o.** gods to serve them. 312
De 28:36 and there shalt thou serve **o.** gods,...... 312
De 28:64 one end of the earth even unto the **o.**; .....
De 28:64 and there thou shalt serve **o.** gods,...... 312
De 29:26 For they went and served **o.** gods, ... 312
De 30:17 and worship **o.** gods, and serve them; .. 312
De 31:18 in that they are turned unto **o.** gods..... 312
De 31:20 then will they turn unto **o.** gods, ... 312
Jos 2:10 Amorites,...on the **o.** side Jordan, ... 5676
Jos 7:7 and dwelt on the **o.** side Jordan! 5676
Jos 8:22 the **o.** issued out of the city against...... 428
Jos 11:19 of Gibeon: all **o.** they took in battle. ....
Jos 12:1 their land on the **o.** side Jordan.......... 5676
Jos 13:27 on the **o.** side Jordan eastward. 5676
Jos 13:32 of Moab, on the **o.** side Jordan, ... 5676
Jos 14:3 an half tribe on the **o.** side Jordan: 5676
Jos 17:5 which were on the **o.** side Jordan; 5676
Jos 20:8 And on the **o.** side Jordan by Jericho... 5676
Jos 21:27 out of the **o.** half tribe of Manasseh..........
Jos 22:4 Lord gave you on...**o.** side Jordan. 5676
Jos 22:7 unto the **o.** half thereof gave Joshua..........
Jos 23:16 have gone and served **o.** gods, and 312
Jos 24:2 dwelt on the **o.** side of the flood in..... 5676
Jos 24:2 of Nachor: and they served **o.** gods...... 312
Jos 24:3 from the **o.** side of the flood,............. 5676
Jos 24:8 which dwelt on the **o.** side Jordan;....... 5676
Jos 24:14 served on the **o.** side of the flood,....... 5676
Jos 24:15 that were on the **o.** side of the flood,.. 5676
Jos 24:16 forsake the Lord, to serve **o.** gods;...... 312
Jg 2:12 followed **o.** gods, of the gods of the 312
Jg 2:17 they went a whoring after **o.** gods, ... 312
Jg 2:19 in following **o.** gods to serve them, ... 312
Jg 7:7 and let all the **o.** people go every man.......
Jg 7:25 to Gideon on the **o.** side Jordan. 5676
Jg 9:44 and the two **o.** companies ran upon all.......
Jg 10:8 that were on the **o.** side Jordan in...... 5676
Jg 10:13 forsaken me, and served **o.** gods: 312
Jg 11:18 and pitched on the **o.** side of Arnon, ... 5676
Jg 13:10 unto me, that came unto me the **o.** day.....
Jg 16:17 become weak, and be like any **o.** man. ......
Jg 16:20 I will go out as at **o.** times before, ...
Jg 16:29 hand, and of the **o.** with his left............ 259
Jg 20:30 array against Gibeah, as at **o.** times..........
Jg 20:31 kill, as at **o.** times, in the highways, ...
Jg 20:31 and the **o.** to Gibeah in the field, ... 259
Ru 1:4 and the name of the **o.** Ruth: 8145
Ru 2:22 they meet thee not in any **o.** field......... 312
1Sa 1:2 and the name of the **o.** Peninnah:....... 8145
1Sa 3:10 and called as at **o.** times, Samuel,.............
1Sa 8:8 forsaken me, and served **o.** gods, ... 312
1Sa 14:1 garrison, that is on the **o.** side........... 5676
1Sa 14:4 and a sharp rock on the **o.** side: 2088
1Sa 14:4 and the name of the **o.** Seneh............. 259
1Sa 14:5 **o.** southward over against Gibeah. 259
1Sa 14:40 my son will be on the **o.** side.............. 259
1Sa 17:3 stood on a mountain on the **o.** side:.... 2088
1Sa 18:10 played with his hand, as at **o.** times: ....
1Sa 19:21 he sent **o.** messengers, and they......... 312
1Sa 20:25 king sat upon his seat, as at **o.** times, ...
1Sa 21:9 for there is no **o.** save that here.......... 312
1Sa 26:13 Then David went over to the **o.** side, ..5676
1Sa 26:19 the Lord, saying, Go, serve **o.** gods..... 312
1Sa 28:8 himself, and put on **o.** raiment,............ 312
1Sa 30:20 which they drave before those **o.** cattle, ...
1Sa 31:7 were on the **o.** side of the valley,........ 5676
1Sa 31:7 they that were on the **o.** side Jordan,.. 5676
2Sa 1:24 clothed you in scarlet, with **o.** delights,......
2Sa 2:13 the **o.** on the...side of the pool........... 428
2Sa 2:13 the...on the **o.** side of the pool. 2088
2Sa 4:2 and the name of the **o.** Rechab, ... 8145
2Sa 12:1 city; the one rich, and the **o.** poor. 259
2Sa 13:16 this evil is...greater than the **o.**............. 312
2Sa 14:6 but the one smote the **o.**, and slew....... 259
2Sa 17:9 now in some pit, or in some **o.** place: ....
2Sa 24:22 and **o.** instruments of the oxen for...........
1Ki 3:22 the **o.** woman said, Nay; but the 312
1Ki 3:23 the **o.** saith, Nay; but thy son is 2063
1Ki 3:25 half to the one, and half to the **o.**. 259
1Ki 3:26 But the **o.** said, Let it be neither 2063
1Ki 6:24 cubits the **o.** wing of the cherub:........ 8145
1Ki 6:24 unto the uttermost part of the **o.** 3671
1Ki 6:25 And the **o.** cherub was ten cubits:....... 8145
1Ki 6:26 and so was it of the **o.** cherub............ 8145
1Ki 6:27 of the **o.** cherub touched the **o.** wall; .. 8145
1Ki 6:34 the two leaves of the **o.** door were..... 8145
1Ki 7:6 the **o.** pillars and the thick beam were.......
1Ki 7:7 from one side of the floor to the **o.**...........
1Ki 7:16 height of the **o.** chapiter was five 8145
1Ki 7:17 and seven for the **o.** chapiter............ 8145
1Ki 7:18 and so did he for the **o.** chapiter. 8145
1Ki 7:20 round about upon the **o.** chapiter........ 8145
1Ki 7:23 cubits from the one brim to the **o.**:...........
1Ki 9:6 but go and serve **o.** gods, and............ 312
1Ki 9:9 and have taken hold upon **o.** gods, ... 312
1Ki 10:20 one side and on the **o.** upon the six.... 2088
1Ki 11:4 turned away his heart after **o.** gods: 312
1Ki 11:10 that he should not go after **o.** gods: 312
1Ki 12:29 Beth-el, and the **o.** put he in Dan. 259
1Ki 14:9 hast gone and made thee **o.** gods,......... 312
1Ki 18:23 I will dress the **o.** bullock, and lay 259
1Ki 20:29 pitched one over against the **o.** 428
2Ki 3:22 saw the water on the **o.** side as red ... 5048
2Ki 5:17 offering nor sacrifice unto **o.** gods, ... 312
2Ki 12:7 Jehoiada the priest, and the **o.** priests, ...
2Ki 17:7 of Egypt, and had feared **o.** gods, ... 312

2Ki 17:35 Ye shall not fear o. gods, nor bow....... 312
2Ki 17:37 and ye shall not fear o. gods.............. 312
2Ki 17:38 forget; neither shall ye fear o. gods...... 312
2Ki 22:17 have burned incense unto o. gods,........ 312
1Ch 6:78 on the o. side Jordan by Jericho,........ 5676
1Ch 9:32 And o. of their brethren, of the..............
1Ch 12:37 And on the o. side of Jordan, of the.... 5676
1Ch 23:17 Eliezer had none o. sons; but the........ 312
2Ch 3:11 o. wing was likewise five cubits,.......... 312
2Ch 3:11 reaching to the wing of the o. cherub. .. 312
2Ch 3:12 one wing of the o. cherub was five...... 259
2Ch 3:12 the o. wing was five cubits also,.......... 312
2Ch 3:12 joining to the wing of the o. cherub..... 312
2Ch 3:17 right hand, and the o. on the left;........ 259
2Ch 7:19 you, and shall go and serve o. gods,..... 312
2Ch 7:22 laid hold on o. gods, and worshipped.... 312
2Ch 9:19 and on the o. upon the six steps........ 2088
2Ch 13:9 the manner of the nations of o. lands?.......
2Ch 20:1 with them o. beside the Ammonites,.........
2Ch 25:12 And o. ten thousand left alive did the........
2Ch 28:25 places to burn incense unto o. gods,...... 312
2Ch 29:34 and until the o. priests had sanctified........
2Ch 30:23 took counsel to keep o. seven days:..... 312
2Ch 30:23 they kept o. seven days with gladness.......
2Ch 32:13 done unto all the people of o. lands?.........
2Ch 32:17 gods of the nations of o. lands have..........
2Ch 32:22 from the hand of all o., and guided...........
2Ch 34:12 and o. of the Levites, all that could..........
2Ch 34:25 have burned incense unto o. gods,........ 312
2Ch 35:13 the o. holy offerings sod they in pots,.......
Ezr 1:10 and ten, and o. vessels a thousand....... 312
Ezr 2:31 The children of the o. Elam, a............ 312
Ne 3:11 repaired the o. piece, and...tower...... 8145
Ne 3:20 earnestly repaired the o. piece,.......... 8145
Ne 4:16 o. half of them held both the spears,.........
Ne 4:17 with the o. hand held a weapon........... 259
Ne 5:5 o. men have our lands...vineyards........ 312
Ne 7:33 The men of the o. Nebo, fifty and....... 312
Ne 7:34 children of the o. Elam, a thousand...... 312
Ne 11:1 with nine parts to dwell in o. cities..........
Ne 12:38 the o. company of them that gave...... 8145
Es 2:12 and with o. things for the purifying...........
Es 9:16 the o. Jews that were in the king's..... 7605
Job 8:12 down, it withereth before any o. herb.......
Job 24:24 they are taken out of the way as all o.,.....
Ps 73:5 They are not in trouble as o. men;...........
Ps 73:5 neither are they plagued like o. men.........
Ps 85:10 and peace have kissed each o.................
Ec 3:19 as the one dieth, so dieth the o.;........ 2088
Ec 6:5 this hath more rest than the o.............. 2088
Ec 7:14 set the one over against the o.,.......... 2088
Isa 26:13 o. lords beside thee have had dominion......
Isa 49:20 shalt have, after thou hast lost the o.,........
Jer 1:16 have burned incense unto o. gods,........ 312
Jer 7:6 walk after o. gods to your hurt:.......... 312
Jer 7:9 after o. gods whom ye know not;......... 312
Jer 7:18 out drink offerings unto o. gods........... 312
Jer 11:10 went after o. gods to serve them:........ 312
Jer 12:12 the land even to the o. end of the land:.....
Jer 13:10 walk after o. gods, to serve them,........ 312
Jer 16:11 have walked after o. gods, and have..... 312
Jer 16:13 shall ye serve o. gods day and night;.... 312
Jer 19:4 burned incense in it unto o. gods,......... 312
Jer 19:13 out drink offerings unto o. gods........... 312
Jer 22:9 and worshipped o. gods, and served..... 312
Jer 24:2 o. basket had very naughty figs,.......... 259
Jer 25:6 go not after o. gods to serve them,...... 312
Jer 25:33 even unto the o. end of the earth:...........
Jer 32:20 and in Israel, and among o. men; and........
Jer 32:29 out drink offerings unto o. gods,........... 312
Jer 35:15 go not after o. gods to serve them,...... 312
Jer 36:16 they were afraid both one and o.,........ 7453
Jer 44:3 burn incense, and to serve o. gods,...... 312
Jer 44:5 to burn no incense unto o. gods.......... 312
Jer 44:8 burning incense unto o. gods in the...... 312
Jer 44:15 had burned incense unto o. gods,.......... 312
Eze 1:23 straight, the one toward the o.:........... 269
Eze 16:34 from o. women in thy whoredoms,...........
Eze 21:16 Go thee one way or o., either on the........
Eze 40:6 the o. threshold of the gate, which....... 259
Eze 40:40 on the o. side, which was at the.......... 312
Eze 41:1 and six cubits on the o. side, which.... 6311
Eze 41:2 side, and five cubits on the o. side:..... 6311
Eze 41:15 on the o. side, an hundred cubits,....... 6311
Eze 41:19 toward the palm tree on the o. side:... 6311
Eze 41:21 the one as the appearance of the o...........
Eze 41:24 door, and two leaves for the o. door.... 312
Eze 41:26 on the one side and on the o. side,..... 6311
Eze 42:14 shall put on o. garments, and shall....... 312
Eze 44:19 and they shall put on o. garments;....... 312
Eze 45:7 and on the o. side of the oblation........ 2088
Eze 47:7 trees on the one side and on the o..... 2088
Eze 48:8 in length as one of the o. parts, from........
Eze 48:21 and on the o. of the holy oblation,....... 2088
Da 2:11 there is none o. that can shew it......... 321
Da 2:44 shall not be left to o. people, but......... 321
Da 3:21 and their hats, and their o. garments,.......
Da 3:29 is no o. God that can deliver after....... 321
Da 7:20 and of the o. which came up, and........ 317
Da 8:3 but one was higher than the o.,......... 8145
Da 12:5 behold, there stood o. two, the one..... 312
Da 12:5 the o. on that side of the bank of......... 259
Ho 3:1 who look to o. gods, and love............ 312
Ho 9:1 not, O Israel, for joy, as o. people:..........
Ho 13:10 where is any o. that may save thee in.......
Ob 11 day...thou stoodest on the o. side,..... 5048
Zec 4:3 the o. upon the left side thereof.......... 259
Zec 11:7 Beauty, and the o. I called Bands;....... 259
Zec 11:14 Then I cut asunder mine o. staff......... 8145
Mt 4:21 he saw o. two brethren, James the...... 243
Mt 5:39 **cheek, turn to him the o. also........ 243**
Mt 6:24 **will hate the one, and love the o.;. 2087**
Mt 6:24 **to the one, and despise the o......... 2087**
Mt 8:18 to depart unto the o. side................ 4008
Mt 8:28 when he was come to the o. side....... 4008
Mt 12:13 it was restored whole, like as the o..... 243
Mt 12:45 **with himself seven o. spirits.......... 2087**
Mt 13:8 **But o. fell into good ground, and.... 243**
Mt 14:22 to go before him unto the o. side,....... 4008
Mt 16:5 disciples were come to the o. side,...... 4008
Mt 20:21 the o. on the left, in thy kingdom....... 1520
Mt 21:36 **he sent o. servants more than the... 243**
Mt 21:41 his vineyard unto o. husbandmen,........ 243
Mt 22:4 **Again, he sent forth o. servants,...... 243**
Mt 23:23 **and not to leave the o. undone...... 2548**
Mt 24:31 **from one end of heaven to the o.... 1565**
Mt 24:40, **41 shall be taken, and the o. left... 1520**
Mt 25:11 **Afterward came also the o. virgins, 3062**
Mt 25:16 **and made them o. five talents........ 243**
Mt 25:17 **received two, he also gained o........ 243**
Mt 25:20 **came and brought o. five talents,.... 243**
Mt 25:22 **gained two o. talents beside them... 243**
Mt 27:61 Mary Magdalene, and the o. Mary,...... 243
Mt 28:1 Mary Madalene and the o. Mary to...... 243
Mk 3:5 hand was restored whole as the o........ 243
Mk 4:8 **o. fell on good ground, and did....... 243**
Mk 4:19 **the lusts of o. things entering in,.. 3062**
Mk 4:35 **Let us pass over unto the o. side... 4008**
Mk 4:36 were also with him o. little ships........ 243
Mk 5:1 over unto the o. side of the sea,......... 4008
Mk 5:21 again by ship unto the o. side,........... 4008
Mk 6:45 to the o. side before unto Bethsaida, .. 4008
Mk 7:4 And many o. things there be, which..... 243
Mk 7:8 **and many o. such like things ye do..243**
Mk 8:13 ship again departed to the o. side........ 4008
Mk 10:37 hand, and the o. on thy left hand,...... 1520
Mk 12:31 **is none o. commandment greater.... 243**
Mk 12:32 God; and there is none o. but he:......... 243
Mk 15:27 right hand, and the o. on his left.......... 1520
Mk 15:41 and many o. women which came up...... 243
Lu 3:18 many o. things in his exhortation........ 2087
Lu 4:43 **kingdom of God to o. cities also:.... 2087**
Lu 5:7 partners, which were in the o. ship,... 2087
Lu 6:10 hand was restored whole as the o........ 243
Lu 6:29 **on the one cheek offer also the o.;.. 243**
Lu 7:41 **hundred pence, and the o. fifty..... 2087**
Lu 8:8 **And o. fell on good ground, and.... 2087**
Lu 8:22 **over unto the o. side of the lake.... 4008**
Lu 10:1 Lord appointed o. seventy also,......... 2087
Lu 10:31 **him, he passed by on the o. side.... 492**
Lu 10:32 **him, and passed by on the o. side... 492**
Lu 11:26 **seven o. spirits more wicked than.. 2087**
Lu 11:42 **and not to leave the o. undone...... 2548**
Lu 14:32 **while the o. is yet a great way off,. 846**
Lu 16:13 **will hate the one, and love the o.;. 2087**
Lu 16:13 **hold to the one, and despise the o. .2087**
Lu 17:24 **unto the o. part under heaven; so........**
Lu 17:34 **be taken, and the o. shall be left... 2087**
Lu 17:35 **one shall be taken, and the o. left..2087**
Lu 17:36 **one shall be taken, and the o. left..2087**
Lu 18:10 **a Pharisee, and the o. a publican...2087**
Lu 18:11 **thee, that I am not as o. men are,. 3062**
Lu 18:14 **house justified rather than the o... 1565**
Lu 22:65 many o. things blasphemously............ 2087
Lu 23:32 And there were also two o.,............. 2087
Lu 23:33 right hand, and the o. on the left....... 3739
Lu 23:40 But the o. answering rebuked him,...... 2087
Lu 24:10 o. women that were with them,......... 3062
Joh 4:38 **o. men laboured, and ye are entered 243**
Joh 6:22 stood on the o. side of the sea.......... 4008
Joh 6:22 that there was none o. boat there,........ 243
Joh 6:23 came o. boats from Tiberias nigh......... 243
Joh 6:25 him on the o. side of the sea,............ 4008
Joh 10:1 **but climbeth up some o. way, the... 237**
Joh 10:16 **o. sheep I have, which are not of.... 243**
Joh 15:24 **the works which none o. man did,.. 243**
Joh 18:16 Then went out that o. disciple,............ 243
Joh 19:18 crucified him, and two o. with him,...... 243
Joh 19:32 the o. which was crucified with him...... 243
Joh 20:2 to the o. disciple, whom Jesus loved,.... 243
Joh 20:3 went forth, and that o. disciple, and..... 243
Joh 20:4 and the o. disciple did outrun Peter,...... 243
Joh 20:8 Then went in also that o. disciple,....... 243
Joh 20:12 at the head, and the o. at the feet,..... 1520
Joh 20:25 o. disciples therefore said unto him,..... 243
Joh 20:30 And many o. signs truly did Jesus........ 243
Joh 21:2 Zebedee, and two o. of his disciples..... 243
Joh 21:8 the o. disciples came in a little ship;..... 243
Joh 21:25 also many o. things which Jesus did,..... 243
Ac 2:4 began to speak with o. tongues,.......... 2087
Ac 2:40 with many o. words did he testify...... 2087
Ac 4:12 Neither is there salvation in any o.:...... 243
Ac 4:12 none o. name under heaven given...... 2087
Ac 5:29 Peter and the o. apostles answered..........
Ac 8:34 of himself, or of some o. man?.......... 2087
Ac 15:2 Barnabas, and certain o. of them,........ 243
Ac 15:39 departed asunder one from the o.:....... 240
Ac 17:9 security of Jason, and of the o.,......... 3062
Ac 17:18 o. some, He seemeth to be a setter.........
Ac 19:39 any thing concerning o. matters,......... 2087
Ac 23:6 Sadducees, and the o. Pharisees,........ 2087
Ac 26:22 saying none o. things than those........ 1622
Ac 27:1 Paul and certain o. prisoners unto...... 2087
Ro 1:13 also, even as among o. Gentiles.......... 3062
Ro 8:39 nor any o. creature, shall be able......... 2087
Ro 13:9 if there be any o. commandment,........ 2087
1Co 1:16 know not whether I baptized any o...... 243
1Co 3:11 o. foundation can no man lay than........ 243
1Co 7:5 Defraud ye not one the o., except it.... 240
1Co 8:4 that there is none o. God but one........ 2087
1Co 9:5 as well as o. apostles, and as the...... 3062
1Co 10:29 I say, not thine own, but of the o...... 2087
1Co 11:21 one taketh before o. his own supper:........
1Co 14:17 well, but the o. is not edified............. 2087
1Co 14:21 With men of o. tongues and...lips....... 2084
1Co 14:21 With men of...tongues and o. lips....... 2087
1Co 14:29 two or three, and let the o. judge........ 243
1Co 15:37 of wheat, or of some o. grain:............ 3062
2Co 1:13 we write none o. things unto you,........ 243
2Co 2:16 and to the o. the savour of life unto.... 3739
2Co 8:13 I mean not that o. men be eased,......... 243
2Co 10:15 that is, of o. men's labours; but.......... 245
2Co 11:8 I robbed o. churches, taking wages...... 243
2Co 12:13 ye were inferior to o. churches,.......... 3062
2Co 13:2 and to all o., that, if I come again,..... 3062
Ga 1:8 any o. gospel unto you than that...we.......
Ga 1:9 any o. gospel unto you than that ye..........
Ga 1:19 But o. of the apostles saw I none,....... 2087
Ga 2:13 the o. Jews dissembled likewise......... 3062
Ga 4:22 bondmaid, the o. by a freewoman....... 1520
Ga 5:17 these are contrary the one to the o...... 240
Eph 3:5 in o. ages was not made known......... 2087
Eph 4:17 henceforth walk not as o. Gentiles...... 3062
Php 1:13 all the palace, and in all o. places;...... 3062
Php 1:17 But the o. of love, knowing that I am ......
Php 2:3 esteem o. better than themselves........ 240
Php 3:4 any o. man thinketh that he hath......... 243
Php 4:3 and with o. my fellowlabourers,......... 3062
2Th 1:3 you all toward each o. aboundeth;........ 240
1Ti 1:3 that they teach no o. doctrine,............ 2085
1Ti 1:10 be any o. thing that is contrary to...... 2087
1Ti 5:22 be partakers of o. men's sins:............ 245
Jas 5:12 the earth, neither by any o. oath:........ 243
1Pe 4:15 as a busybody in o. men's matters........ 244
2Pe 3:16 as they do also the o. scriptures,........ 3062
Re 2:24 **will put upon you none o. burden... 243**
Re 8:13 by reason of the o. voices of the........ 3062
Re 17:10 one is, and the o. is not yet come;...... 243

OTHERS
Job 8:19 and out of the earth shall **o.** grow........ 312
Job 31:10 and let **o.** bow down upon her............ 312
Job 34:24 number, and set **o.** in their stead.......... 312
Job 34:26 as wicked men in the open sight of **o.**;......
Ps 49:10 perish, and leave their wealth to **o.**...... 312
Pr 5:9 Lest thou give thine honour unto **o.**, ... 312
Ec 7:22 thou thyself likewise hast cursed **o.**,..... 312
Isa 56:8 Yet will I gather **o.** to him, beside...........
Jer 6:12 houses shall be turned unto **o.**, with..... 312
Jer 8:10 will I give their wives unto **o.**, and....... 312
Eze 9:5 to the **o.** he said in mine hearing, ... 428
Eze 13:6 and they have made **o.** to hope that..........
Eze 13:10 **o.** daubed it with untempered morter; ....
Da 7:19 which was diverse from all the **o.**, ...
Da 11:4 plucked up, even for **o.** beside those. ... 312
Mt 5:47 **only, what do ye more than o.?** ....
Mt 15:30 dumb, maimed, and many **o.**, and *2087*
Mt 16:14 and **o.**, Jeremias, or one of the......... 2087
Mt 20:3 **o. standing idle in the marketplace,** *243*
Mt 20:6 **out, and found o. standing idle,** *243*
Mt 21:8 **o.** cut down branches from the trees, ... *243*
Mt 26:67 **o.** smote him with the palms of......... *3588*
Mt 27:42 He saved **o.**; himself he cannot *243*
Mk 6:15 **O.** said, That it is Elias. *243*
Mk 6:15 And **o.** said, That it is a prophet, or..... *243*
Mk 8:28 Elias; and **o.**, One of the prophets. *243*
Mk 11:8 **o.** cut down branches off the trees,...... *243*
Mk 12:5 **and him they killed, and many o.;** .. *243*
Mk 12:9 **and will give the vineyard unto o.**... *243*
Mk 15:31 He saved **o.**; himself he cannot save..... *243*
Lu 5:29 of publicans and of **o.** that sat down *243*
Lu 8:3 and many **o.**, which ministered.......... *2087*
Lu 8:10 **but to o. in parables; that seeing**... *3062*
Lu 9:8 of **o.**, that one of the old prophets *243*
Lu 9:19 **o.** say, that one of the old prophets *243*
Lu 11:16 And **o.**, tempting him, sought of......... *2087*
Lu 18:9 were righteous, and despised **o.**:......... *3062*
Lu 20:16 **and shall give the vineyard to o.**..... *243*
Lu 23:35 He saved **o.**; let him save himself, ... *243*
Lu 24:1 prepared, and certain **o.** with them. ....
Joh 7:12 He is a good man: **o.** said, Nay;.......... *243*
Joh 7:41 **O.** said, This is the Christ. But.......... *243*
Joh 9:9 This is he: **o.** said, He is like him:....... *243*
Joh 9:16 **O.** said, How can a man that is a.......... *243*
Joh 10:21 **O.** said, These are not the words of..... *243*
Joh 12:29 **o.** said, An angel spake to him. *243*
Joh 18:34 **thyself, or did o. tell it thee of me?** . *243*
Ac 2:13 **O.** mocking said, These men are........ *2087*
Ac 15:35 word of the Lord, with many **o.** also... *2087*
Ac 17:32 and **o.** said, We will hear thee again.... *3588*
Ac 17:34 named Damaris, and **o.** with them. *2087*
Ac 28:9 **o.** also, which had diseases in the....... *3062*
1Co 9:2 If I be not an apostle unto **o.**, yet........ *243*
1Co 9:12 If **o.** be partakers of this power over.... *243*
1Co 9:27 means, when I have preached to **o.**,..... *243*
1Co 14:19 by my voice I might teach **o.** also, ... *243*
2Co 3:1 or need we, as some **o.**, epistles of..........
2Co 8:8 occasion of the forwardness of **o.**, ... *2087*
Eph 2:3 the children of wrath, even as **o.**......... *3062*
Php 2:4 man also on the things of **o.**.............. *2087*
1Th 2:6 glory, neither of you, nor yet of **o.**, ... *243*
1Th 4:13 even as **o.** which have no hope.......... *3062*
1Th 5:6 let us not sleep, as do **o.**; but let........ *3062*
1Ti 5:20 before all, that **o.** also may fear. *3062*
2Ti 2:2 who shall be able to teach **o.** also....... *2087*
Heb 9:25 place every year with blood of **o.**:........ *245*
Heb 11:35 and **o.** were tortured, not accepting...... *243*
Heb 11:36 **o.** had trial of cruel mockings and........ *2087*
Jude 23 And **o.** save with fear, pulling............ *3739*

OTHERWISE
1Sa *general title* Samuel, **O.** Called, The First............
2Sa *general title* Samuel, **O.** Called, The Second..........
2Sa 18:13 **O.** I should have wrought.................. 176
1Ki 1:21 **O.** it shall come to pass, when my...........
2Ch 30:18 passover **o.** than it was written.......... 3808
Ps 38:16 lest **o.** they should rejoice over me:..........
Mt 6:1 **o. ye have no reward of your** *1490*
Lu 5:36 **if o., then both the new maketh a** . *1490*
Ro 11:6 works: **o.** grace is no more grace....... *1893*
Ro 11:6 grace: **o.** work is no more work......... *1893*
Ro 11:22 **o.** thou also shalt be cut off............... *1893*
2Co 11:16 if **o.**, yet as a fool receive me, that *1490*
Ga 5:10 that ye will be none **o.** minded: *243*
Php 3:15 if in any thing ye be **o.** minded, ... *2088*
1Ti 5:25 and they that are **o.** cannot be hid. *247*
1Ti 6:3 If any man teach **o.**, and consent........ *2085*
Heb 9:17 **o.** it is of no strength at all while *1893*

OTHNI (oth'-ni)
1Ch 26:7 The sons of Shemaiah; **O.**, and......... 6273

OTHNIEL (oth'-ne-el)
Jos 15:17 **O.** the son of Kenaz, the brother....... 6274
Jg 1:13 And **O.** the son of Kenaz, Caleb's 6274
Jg 3:9 even **O.** the son of Kenaz, Caleb's 6274
Jg 3:11 and **O.** the son of Kenaz died........... 6274
1Ch 4:13 And the sons of Kenaz; **O.**, and......... 6274
1Ch 4:13 and the sons of **O.**; Hathath............. 6274
1Ch 27:15 Heldai the Netophathite, of **O.**:.......... 6274

OUCHES
Ex 28:11 make them to be set in **o.** of gold. 4865
Ex 28:13 And thou shalt make **o.** of gold; 4865
Ex 28:14 fasten...wreathen chains to the **o.**....... 4865
Ex 28:25 thou shalt fasten in the two **o.**, and 4865
Ex 39:6 onyx stones inclosed in **o.** of gold,...... 4865
Ex 39:13 they were inclosed in **o.** of gold in...... 4865
Ex 39:16 they made two **o.** of gold, and two..... 4865
Ex 39:18 chains they fastened in the two **o.**, ... 4865

OUGHT See also AUGHT; NOUGHT; OUGHTEST.
Ge 20:9 hast done deeds unto me that **o.** not to.....
Ge 34:7 which thing **o.** not to be done.................
Ge 39:6 he knew not **o.** he had, save............. 3972
Ge 47:18 there is not **o.** left in the sight of my ....
Ex 5:8 ye shall not diminish **o.** thereof: ....
Ex 5:11 yet not **o.** of your work shall be......... 1697
Ex 5:19 shall not minish **o.** from your bricks ....
Ex 12:46 shalt not carry forth **o.** of the flesh ....
Ex 22:14 if a man borrow **o.** of his neighbour, ...
Ex 29:34 **o.** of the flesh of the consecrations, ...
Le 4:2,27 things which **o.** not to be done,...............
Le 11:25 whosoever beareth **o.** of the carcase ....
Le 19:6 and if **o.** remain until the third day,...........
Le 25:14 if thou sell **o.** unto thy neighbour,....... 4465
Le 25:14 or buyest **o.** of thy neighbour's hand. ....
Le 27:31 man will at all redeem **o.** of his tithes,.......
Nu 15:24 if **o.** be committed by ignorance ....
Nu 15:30 the soul that doeth **o.** presumptuously, ...
Nu 30:6 vowed, or uttered **o.** out of her lips,.........
De 4:2 neither shall ye diminish **o.** from it,..........
De 15:2 that lendeth **o.** unto his neighbour ....
De 26:14 neither have I taken away **o.** thereof.........
De 26:14 nor given **o.** thereof for the dead:............
Jos 21:45 failed not **o.** of any good thing 1697
Ru 1:17 if **o.** but death part thee and me..............
1Sa 12:4 taken **o.** of any man's hand. 3972
1Sa 12:5 have not found **o.** in my hand. 3972
1Sa 25:7 there **o.** missing unto them, ... 3972
1Sa 30:22 we will not give them **o.** of the spoil.........
2Sa 3:35 If I taste bread, or **o.** else, ... 3972
2Sa 13:12 no such thing **o.** to be done in Israel:........
2Sa 14:10 said, Whosoever saith **o.** unto thee, ...
2Sa 14:19 **o.** that my lord the king hath spoken:........
1Ch 12:32 times, to know what Israel **o.** to do; ....
1Ch 15:2 none **o.** to carry the ark of God but..........
2Ch 13:5 **O.** ye not to know that the Lord God ....
Ne 5:9 **o.** ye not to walk in the fear of God..........
Ps 76:11 presents unto him that **o.** to be feared. .....
Mt 5:23 **thy brother hath o. against thee;**... *5100*
Mt 21:3 **And if any man say o. unto you,** ... *5100*
Mt 23:23 **these o. ye to have done, and not** .. *1163*
Mk 7:12 **do o. for his father or his mother;**..*3762*
Mk 8:23 him, he asked him if he saw **o.**.......... *5100*
Mk 11:25 **forgive, if ye have o. against any:** . *5100*
Mk 13:14 **prophet, standing where it o. not,** . *1163*
Lu 11:42 **these o. ye to have done, and not** .. *1163*
Lu 12:12 **the same hour what we o. to say**... *1163*
Lu 13:14 six days in which men **o.** to work:...... *1163*
Lu 13:16 **o. not this woman, being a** *1163*
Lu 18:1 that men **o.** always to pray, and not.... *1163*
Lu 24:26 **O. not Christ to have suffered**....... *1163*
Joh 4:20 the place where men **o.** to worship..... *1163*
Joh 4:33 any man brought him **o.** to eat? ....
Joh 13:14 **also o. to wash one another's feet.** .*3784*
Joh 19:7 a law, and by our law he **o.** to die,..... *3784*
Ac 4:32 **o.** of the things which he possessed..... *5100*
Ac 5:29 **o.** to obey God rather than men......... *1163*
Ac 17:29 **o.** not to think that the Godhead *3784*
Ac 19:36 ye **o.** to be quiet, and to do nothing.... *1163*
Ac 20:35 labouring ye **o.** to support the weak,... *1163*
Ac 21:21 **o.** not to circumcise their children, ...
Ac 24:19 Who **o.** to have been here before *1163*
Ac 24:19 object, if they had **o.** against me. *5100*
Ac 25:10 seat, where I **o.** to be judged: *1163*
Ac 25:24 that he **o.** not to live any longer......... *1163*
Ac 26:9 I **o.** to do many things contrary to...... *1163*
Ac 28:19 I had **o.** to accuse my nation of.......... *5100*
Ro 8:26 what we should pray for as we **o.**: *1163*
Ro 12:3 more highly than he **o.** to think;......... *1163*
Ro 15:1 strong **o.** to bear the infirmities of...... *3784*
1Co 8:2 nothing yet as he **o.** to know............. *1163*
1Co 11:7 indeed **o.** not to cover his head,......... *3784*
1Co 11:10 cause **o.** the woman to have power...... *3784*
2Co 2:3 from them of whom I **o.** to rejoice;..... *1163*
2Co 2:7 ye **o.** rather to forgive him, and..............
2Co 12:11 for I **o.** to have been commended....... *3784*
2Co 12:14 **o.** not to lay up for the parents,......... *3784*
Eph 5:28 So **o.** men to love their wives as........ *3784*
Eph 6:20 may speak boldly, as I **o.** to speak. *1163*
Col 4:4 make it manifest, as I **o.** to speak. *1163*
Col 4:6 how ye **o.** to answer every man......... *1163*
1Th 4:1 how ye **o.** to walk and to please God, . *1163*
2Th 3:7 know how ye **o.** to follow us: *1163*
1Ti 5:13 speaking things which they **o.** not....... *1163*
Tit 1:11 teaching things which they **o.** not, ... *1163*
Phm 18 wronged thee, or oweth thee **o.**,....... *5100*
Heb 2:1 **o.** to give the more earnest heed *1163*
Heb 5:3 by reason hereof he **o.**, as for the...... *3784*
Heb 5:12 for the time ye **o.** to be teachers, ... *3784*
Jas 3:10 these things **o.** not so to be............. *5534*
Jas 4:15 For that ye **o.** to say, If the Lord will.......
2Pe 3:11 what manner of persons **o.** ye to be ... *1163*
1Jo 2:6 **o.** himself also so to walk, even as..... *3784*
1Jo 3:16 we **o.** to lay down our lives for the..... *3784*
1Jo 4:11 us, we **o.** also to love one another. *3784*
3Jo 8 We therefore **o.** to receive such, that.. *3784*

OUGHTEST
1Ki 2:9 knowest what thou **o.** to do unto him; ....
Mt 25:27 **o. therefore to have put my money** .*1163*
Ac 10:6 shall tell thee what thou **o.** to do........ *1163*
1Ti 3:15 know how thou **o.** to behave thyself.... *1163*

OUR See in the APPENDIX; also OURS; OURSELVES.

OURS See also OURSELVES.
Ge 26:20 herdmen, saying, The water is **o.**:...........
Ge 31:16 hath taken from our father, that is **o.**, ...
Ge 34:23 and every beast of theirs be **o.**?...............
Nu 32:32 on this side Jordan may be **o.**.................
1Ki 22:3 Know ye that Ramoth in Gilead is **o.**, ...
Eze 36:2 even the ancient high places are **o.** in........
Mk 12:7 **and the inheritance shall be o.**....... *2257*
Lu 20:14 **that the inheritance may be o.**....... *2257*
1Co 1:2 Christ our Lord, both theirs and **o.**:.... *2257*
2Co 1:14 as ye also are **o.** in the day of the...... *2257*
Tit 3:14 let **o.** also learn to maintain good........ *2251*
1Jo 2:2 and not for **o.** only, but also for......... *2251*

OURSELVES
Ge 37:10 to bow down **o.** to thee to the earth?........
Ge 44:16 we speak? or how shall we clear **o.**? ....
Nu 32:17 we **o.** will go ready armed before 587
De 2:35 we took cattle for a prey unto **o.**,............
De 3:7 of the cities, we took for a prey to **o.**.......
1Sa 14:8 and we will discover **o.** unto them. ....
1Ch 19:13 and let us behave **o.** valiantly for our ....
Ezr 4:3 but we **o.** together will build unto 587
Ezr 8:21 we might afflict **o.** before our God, ...
Ne 10:32 to charge **o.** yearly with the third............
Job 34:4 let us know among **o.** what is good............
Ps 83:12 Let us take to **o.** the houses of God ....
Ps 100:3 that hath made us, and not we **o.**; 587
Pr 7:18 morning: let us solace **o.** with loves. ....
Isa 28:15 and under falsehood have we hid **o.**: ....
Isa 56:12 and we will fill **o.** with strong drink; ....
Jer 50:5 Come, and let us join **o.** to the Lord.........
Lu 22:71 we **o.** have heard of his own mouth. ....
Joh 4:42 for we have heard him **o.**, and know.........
Ac 6:4 will give **o.** continually to prayer,.............
Ac 23:14 have bound **o.** under a great curse, ... *1438*
Ro 8:23 but **o.** also, which have the first fruits.......
Ro 8:23 of the Spirit, even we **o.** groan................
Ro 8:23 groan within **o.**, waiting for the.......... *1438*
Ro 15:1 of the weak, and not to please **o.**........ *1438*
1Co 11:31 For if we would judge **o.**, we should.... *1438*
2Co 1:4 we **o.** are comforted of God. ....
2Co 1:9 we had the sentence of death in **o.**,.... *1438*
2Co 1:9 that we should not trust in **o.**, but...... *1438*

2Co 3:1 Do we begin again to commend **o.**? *1438*
2Co 3:5 that we are sufficient of **o.** to think..... *1438*
2Co 3:5 to think any thing as of **o.**; but our..... *1438*
2Co 4:2 commending **o.** to every man's *1438*
2Co 4:5 For we preach not **o.**, but Christ *1438*
2Co 4:5 **o.** your servants for Jesus' sake......... *1438*
2Co 5:12 we commend not **o.** again unto you,.... *1438*
2Co 5:13 whether we be beside **o.**, it is to God:......
2Co 6:4 approving **o.** as the ministers of......... *1438*
2Co 7:1 let us cleanse **o.** from all filthiness...... *1438*
2Co 10:12 we dare not make **o.** of the number,... *1438*
2Co 10:12 or compare **o.** with some that........... *1438*
2Co 10:14 stretch not **o.** beyond our measure,.... *1438*
2Co 12:19 think ye that we excuse **o.** unto you?........
Ga 2:17 if...we **o.** also are found sinners, is..........
1Th 2:10 we behaved **o.** among you that believe: .....
2Th 1:4 we **o.** glory in you in the churches....... *846*
2Th 3:7 behaved not **o.** disorderly among you; ....
2Th 3:9 to make **o.** an ensample unto you....... *1438*
Tit 3:3 we **o.** also were sometimes foolish, ... *2249*
Heb 10:25 the assembling of **o.** together, ... *1438*
1Jo 1:8 we deceive **o.**, and the truth is not..... *1438*

OUT See in the APPENDIX; also OUTCAST; OUTER; OUTGOINGS; OUTLANDISH; OUTLIVED; OUTMOST; OUTRAGEOUS; OUTRUN; OUTSIDE; OUTSTRETCHED; OUTWARD; OUTWENT; THEREOUT; THROUGHOUT; UTMOST; UTTER; WITHOUT.

OUTCAST See also OUTCASTS.
Jer 30:17 they called thee an **O.**, saying, ... 5080

OUTCASTS
Ps 147:2 gathereth together the **o.** of Israel...... 1760
Isa 11:12 and shall assemble the **o.** of Israel,...... 1760
Isa 16:3 hide the **o.**; bewray not him that........ 5080
Isa 16:4 Let mine **o.** dwell with thee, Moab;..... 5080
Isa 27:13 and the **o.** in the land of Egypt, ... 5080
Isa 56:8 which gathereth the **o.** of Israel 1760
Jer 49:36 the **o.** of Elam shall not come............ 5080

OUTER See also UTTER.
Eze 10:5 was heard even to the **o.** court,.......... 2435
Mt 8:12 **shall be cast out into o. darkness:** ..*1857*
Mt 22:13 **and cast him into o. darkness;** *1857*
Mt 25:30 **servant into o. darkness: there** *1857*

OUTGOINGS
Jos 17:9 and the **o.** of it were at the sea: 8444
Jos 17:18 and the **o.** of it shall be thine:.......... 8444
Jos 18:19 **o.** of the border were at the north 8444
Jos 19:14 the **o.** thereof are in the valley of....... 8444
Jos 19:22 **o.** of their border were at Jordan: 8444
Jos 19:29 the **o.** thereof are at the sea from...... 8444
Jos 19:33 and the **o.** thereof were at Jordan:...... 8444
Ps 65:8 the **o.** of the morning and evening...... 4161

OUTLANDISH
Ne 13:26 him did **o.** women cause to sin. 5237

OUTLIVED
Jg 2:7 the elders that **o.** Joshua, ... 748,3117,310

OUTMOST See also UTMOST.
Ex 26:10 curtain that is **o.** in the coupling,......... 7020
Nu 34:3 **o.** coast of the salt sea eastward:....... 7097
De 30:4 out unto the **o.** parts of heaven,......... 7097
Isa 17:6 in the **o.** fruitful branches thereof, ...

OUTRAGEOUS
Pr 27:4 Wrath is cruel, and anger is **o.**; 7858

OUTRUN
Joh 20:4 the other disciple did **o.** Peter, ... *4370,5032*

OUTSIDE
Jg 7:11 unto the **o.** of the armed men............ 7097
Jg 7:17 when I come to the **o.** of the camp,.... 7097
Jg 7:19 came unto the **o.** of the camp in the ... 7097
1Ki 7:9 on the **o.** toward the great court. 2351
Eze 40:5 behold a wall on the **o.** of the house ... 2351
Mt 23:25 **ye make clean the o. of the cup** *1855*
Mt 23:26 **the o. of them may be clean also**.... *1623*
Lu 11:39 **make clean the o. of the cup and** .. *1855*

OUTSTRETCHED
De 26:8 a mighty hand, and with an **o.** arm, ... 5186
Jer 21:5 fight against you with an **o.** hand........ 5186
Jer 27:5 by my great power by my **o.** arm,....... 5186

OUTWARD
Nu 35:4 from the wall of the city and **o.**.......... 2435
1Sa 16:7 man looketh on the **o.** appearance, ... 5869
1Ch 26:29 for the **o.** business over Israel, ... 2435
Ne 11:16 had the oversight of the **o.** business.... 2435
Es 6:4 Haman was come into the **o.** court 2435
Eze 40:17 brought he me into the **o.** court, ... 2435
Eze 40:20 the gate of the **o.** court that looked 2435
Eze 40:34 arches...were toward the **o.** court; 2435
Eze 44:1 way of the gate of the **o.** sanctuary 2435
Mt 23:27 **which indeed appear beautiful o.,** .. *1855*
Ro 2:28 which is **o.** in the flesh:...... *1722,3588,5318*
2Co 4:16 though our **o.** man perish, yet the...... *1854*
2Co 10:7 on things after the **o.** appearance? *4383*
1Pe 3:3 **o.** adorning of plaiting the hair, ... *1855*

OUTWARDLY
Mt 23:38 **so ye also o. appear righteous** *1855*
Ro 2:28 is not a Jew, which is one **o.**;..... *1722,5318*

OUTWENT
Mk 6:33 out of all cities, and **o.** them, and....... *4281*

OVEN See also OVENS.
Le 2:4 of a meat offering baken in the **o.**,....... 8574
Le 7:9 offering that is baken in the **o.**,.......... 8574
Le 11:35 whether it be **o.**, or ranges for pots,... 8574
Le 26:26 shall bake your bread in one **o.**,......... 8574
Ps 21:9 Thou shalt make them as a fiery **o.** 8574
La 5:10 skin was black like an **o.** because 8574
Ho 7:4 as an **o.** heated by the baker, who 8574
Ho 7:6 made ready their heart like an **o.**, ... 8574
Ho 7:7 They are all hot as an **o.**, and have 8574
Mal 4:1 cometh, that shall burn as an **o.**; 8574
Mt 6:30 **and to morrow is cast into the o.,** ..*2823*
Lu 12:28 **and to morrow is cast into the o.;** ..*2823*

OVENS
Ex 8:3 and into thine **o.**, and into thy............ 8574

OVER See also MOREOVER; OVERCHARGE; OVERCOME; OVERDRIVE; OVERFLOW; OVERLAY; OVERLIVED; OVERMUCH; OVERPASS; OVERPLUS; OVERRAN; OVERSEE; OVERSHADOW; OVERSIGHT; OVERSPREAD; OVERTAKE; OVERTHROW; OVERTURN; OVERWHELM; PASSOVER.
Ge 1:18 to rule **o.** the day and **o.** the night,..........
Ge 1:26 have dominion **o.** the fish of the sea,.........
Ge 1:26 **o.** the fowl of the air, and **o.** the cattle,.....
Ge 1:26 **o.** all the earth,and **o.** every creeping........
Ge 1:28 **o.** the fish of the sea, and **o.** the fowl ....
Ge 1:28 and **o.** every living thing that moveth ....
Ge 3:16 thy husband, and he shall rule **o.** thee. ......
Ge 4:7 his desire, and thou shalt rule **o.** him. ....
Ge 8:1 made a wind to pass **o.** the earth, ... 5921
Ge 9:14 when I bring a cloud **o.** the earth, ... 5921
Ge 21:16 and sat her down **o.** against him......... 5048
Ge 21:16 she sat **o.** against him, and lift up....... 5048
Ge 24:2 house, that ruled **o.** all that he had, ...
Ge 25:25 out red, all **o.** like an hairy garment; ....
Ge 27:29 be lord **o.** thy brethren, and let thy ....
Ge 31:21 he rose up, and passed **o.** the river, ... 5674
Ge 31:52 I will not pass **o.** this heap to thee, ... 5674
Ge 31:52 thou shalt not pass **o.** this heap and.... 5674
Ge 32:10 my staff I passed **o.** this Jordan; 5674
Ge 32:16 Pass **o.** before me, and put a space 5674
Ge 32:21 So went the present **o.** before him: 5674
Ge 32:22 and passed **o.** the ford Jabbok............ 5674
Ge 32:23 them **o.** the brook, and sent **o.** that.... 5674
Ge 32:31 as he passed **o.** Penuel the sun rose 5674
Ge 33:3 And he passed **o.** before them, and 5674
Ge 33:14 thee, pass **o.** before his servant: 5674
Ge 36:31 any king **o.** the children of Israel. ....
Ge 37:8 Shalt thou indeed reign **o.** us? 5921
Ge 37:8 thou indeed have dominion **o.** us?............
Ge 39:4 made him overseer **o.** his house,......... 5921
Ge 39:5 his house, and **o.** all that he had, ... 5921
Ge 41:33 and set him **o.** the land of Egypt........ 5921
Ge 41:34 let him appoint officers **o.** the land,...... 5921
Ge 41:40 Thou shalt be **o.** my house, and........ 5921
Ge 41:41 set thee **o.** all the land of Egypt......... 5921
Ge 41:43 him ruler **o.** all the land of Egypt. 5921
Ge 41:45 went out **o.** all the land of Egypt........ 5921
Ge 41:56 was **o.** all the face of the earth: 5921
Ge 42:6 Joseph was...governor **o.** the land, ... 5921
Ge 45:26 he is governor **o.** all the land of Egypt. .....
Ge 47:6 then make them rulers **o.** my cattle. ... 5921
Ge 47:20 the famine prevailed **o.** them: 5921
Ge 47:26 made it a law **o.** the land of Egypt........ 5921
Ge 49:22 whose branches run **o.** the wall:......... 5921
Ex 1:8 there arose up a new king **o.** Egypt,... 5921
Ex 1:11 they did set **o.** them taskmasters 5921
Ex 2:14 thee a prince and a judge **o.** us? 5921
Ex 5:14 taskmasters had set **o.** them, ... 5921
Ex 8:5 hand with thy rod **o.** the streams, ... 5921
Ex 8:5 **o.** the rivers, and **o.** the ponds, and ... 5921
Ex 8:6 his hand **o.** the waters of Egypt;........ 5921
Ex 8:9 said unto Pharaoh, Glory **o.** me: 5921
Ex 10:12 out thine hand **o.** the land of Egypt..... 5921
Ex 10:13 forth his rod **o.** the land of Egypt,...... 5921
Ex 10:14 went up **o.** all the land of Egypt,........ 5921
Ex 10:21 be darkness **o.** the land of Egypt,........ 5921
Ex 12:13 I see the blood, I will pass **o.** you, ... 5921
Ex 12:23 the Lord will pass **o.** the door, and..... 5921
Ex 12:27 passed **o.** the houses of the children ... 5921
Ex 14:2 the sea, **o.** against Baal-zephon: 6440
Ex 14:7 and captains **o.** every one of them....... 5921
Ex 14:16 stretch out thine hand **o.** the sea,....... 5921
Ex 14:21 stretched out his hand **o.** the sea; 5921
Ex 14:26 Stretch out thine hand **o.** the sea, ... 5921
Ex 14:27 stretched forth his hand **o.** the sea, ... 5921
Ex 15:16 till thy people pass **o.**, O Lord,.......... 5674
Ex 15:16 till the people pass **o.**, which thou 5674
Ex 16:18 gathered much had nothing **o.**,........... 5736
Ex 16:23 that which remaineth **o.** lay up for...... 5736
Ex 18:21 and place such **o.** them, to be........... 5921
Ex 18:25 and made them heads **o.** the people,... 5921
Ex 25:27 **O.** against the border shall the.......... 5980
Ex 25:37 may give light **o.** against it......... 5921,5676
Ex 26:12 **o.** the backside of the tabernacle........ 5921
Ex 26:13 hang **o.** the side of the tabernacle....... 5921
Ex 26:35 candlestick **o.** against the table on 5227
Ex 28:27 **o.** against the other coupling 5980
Ex 30:6 mercy seat that is **o.** the testimony, ... 5921
Ex 36:14 hair for the tent **o.** the tabernacle:....... 5921
Ex 37:9 with their wings **o.** the mercy seat, ... 5980
Ex 37:14 **O.** against the border were the rings, . 5980
Ex 39:20 **o.** against the other coupling 5980
Ex 40:19 abroad the tent **o.** the tabernacle,....... 5921
Ex 40:24 congregation, **o.** against the table, ... 5227
Ex 40:36 taken up from **o.** the tabernacle, ... 5921
Le 14:5 an earthen vessel **o.** running water: 5921
Le 14:6 was killed **o.** the running water:......... 5921
Le 14:50 an earthen vessel **o.** running water: 5921
Le 16:21 confess **o.** him all the iniquities of...... 5921
Le 25:43 shalt not rule **o.** him with rigour:.............
Le 25:46 but **o.** your brethren the children of..........
Le 25:46 not rule one **o.** another with rigour..........
Le 25:53 shall not rule with rigour **o.** him..............
Le 26:16 I will even appoint **o.** you terror,.............
Le 26:17 they that hate you shall reign **o.** you; ....
Nu 1:50 the Levites **o.** the tabernacle of 5921
Nu 1:50 and **o.** all the vessels thereof, and...... 5921
Nu 1:50 and **o.** all things that belong to it:....... 5921
Nu 3:32 be chief **o.** the chief of the Levites, ...
Nu 3:49 of them that were **o.** and above 5736
Nu 4:6 shall spread **o.** it a cloth wholly of...... 4605
Nu 5:30 him, and he be jealous **o.** his wife,...........
Nu 7:2 were **o.** them that were numbered, ... 5975
Nu 8:2 **o.** against the candlestick.......... 5922,6440
Nu 8:3 **o.** against the candlestick,.......... 5922,6440
Nu 10:10 trumpets **o.** your burnt offerings, ... 5921
Nu 10:10 **o.** the sacrifices of your peace offerings; ....
Nu 10:14 **o.** his host was Nahshon the son of..... 5921
Nu 10:15, 16 **o.** the host of the tribe of the 5921
Nu 10:18 **o.** his host was Elizur the son of........ 5921
Nu 10:19, 20 **o.** the host of the tribe of the 5921
Nu 10:22 **o.** his host was Elishama the son of.... 5921
Nu 10:23, 24 **o.** the host of the tribe of the 5921
Nu 10:25 **o.** his host was Ahiezer the son of 5921
Nu 10:26, 27 **o.** the host of the tribe of the 5921
Nu 11:16 of the people, and officers **o.** them; ....
Nu 14:14 that thy cloud standeth **o.** them, ... 5921
Nu 16:13 thyself altogether a prince **o.** us?......... 5921
Nu 22:5 earth, and they abide **o.** against me: ....
Nu 25:15 he was head **o.** a people, and of a...........
Nu 27:16 set a man **o.** the congregation, ... 5921
Nu 31:14 with the captains **o.** thousands, and...........
Nu 31:14 and captains **o.** hundreds which came ....
Nu 31:48 which were **o.** thousands of the host, ...
Nu 32:5 and bring us not **o.** Jordan. 5674
Nu 32:7 from going **o.** into the land which 5674
Nu 32:21 will go all of you armed **o.** Jordan....... 5674
Nu 32:27 But thy servants will pass **o.**, every.... 5674
Nu 32:29 will pass with you **o.** Jordan, every...... 5674
Nu 32:30 will not pass **o.** with you armed, ... 5674
Nu 32:32 will pass **o.** armed before the Lord..... 5674
Nu 33:51 When ye are passed **o.** Jordan into 5674
Nu 35:10 ye be come **o.** Jordan into the land..... 5674
De 1:1 the plain **o.** against the Red sea, ... 4136

De 1:13 and I will make them rulers **o.** you. ....
De 1:15 and made them heads **o.** you,........... 5921
De 1:15 **o.** thousands...captains **o.** hundreds, ...
De 1:15 captains **o.** fifties, and captains **o.** tens, ...
De 2:13 and get you **o.** the brook Zered. 5674
De 2:13 And we went **o.** the brook Zered. 5674
De 2:14 we were come **o.** the brook Zered, ... 5674
De 2:18 Thou art to pass **o.** through Ar, the.... 5674
De 2:19 **o.** against the children of Ammon, ... 4136
De 2:24 and pass **o.** the river Arnon: 5674
De 2:29 until I shall pass **o.** Jordan into the 5674
De 3:18 pass **o.** armed before your brethren.... 5674
De 3:25 let me go **o.**, and see the good land.... 5674
De 3:27 for thou shalt not go **o.** this Jordan. 5674
De 3:28 he shall go **o.** before this people, ... 5674
De 3:29 in the valley **o.** against Beth-peor. 4136
De 4:14 land whither ye go **o.** to possess it. 5674
De 4:21 that I should not go **o.** Jordan, and 5674
De 4:22 this land, I must not go **o.** Jordan:...... 5674
De 4:22 but ye shall go **o.**, and possess that.... 5674
De 4:26 ye go **o.** Jordan to possess it; ye 5674
De 4:46 in the valley **o.** against Beth-peor, ... 4136
De 9:1 to pass **o.** Jordan this day, to go......... 5674
De 9:3 God is he that goeth **o.** before thee;... 5674
De 11:30 the champaign **o.** against Gilgal, ... 4136
De 11:31 ye shall pass **o.** Jordan to go in to...... 5674
De 12:10 when ye go **o.** Jordan, and dwell........ 5674
De 15:6 and thou shalt reign **o.** many nations, ...
De 15:6 but they shall not reign **o.** thee. ....
De 17:14 I will set a king **o.** me, like as all....... 5921
De 17:15 in any wise set him king **o.** thee, ... 5921
De 17:15 shalt thou set king **o.** thee: thou 5921
De 17:15 mayest not set a stranger **o.** thee, ... 5921
De 21:6 shall wash their hands **o.** the heifer..... 5921
De 24:20 thou shalt not go **o.** the boughs again:.......
De 27:2 day when ye shall pass **o.** Jordan........ 5674
De 27:3 this law, when thou art passed **o.**,...... 5674
De 27:4 shall be when ye be gone **o.** Jordan, ... 5674
De 27:12 when ye are come **o.** Jordan; 5674
De 28:23 And thy heaven that is **o.** thy head..... 5921
De 28:36 king which thou shalt set **o.** thee,....... 5921
De 28:63 Lord rejoiced **o.** you to do you good, .. 5921
De 28:63 will rejoice **o.** you to destroy you, ... 5921
De 30:9 the Lord will again rejoice **o.** thee 5921
De 30:9 good, as he rejoiced **o.** thy fathers: 5921
De 30:13 Who shall go **o.** the sea for us, and 5674
De 30:18 passest **o.** Jordan...to possess it........ 5674
De 31:2 Thou shalt not go **o.** this Jordan......... 5674
De 31:3 he will go **o.** before thee, and he 5674
De 31:3 Joshua, he shall go **o.** before thee, ... 5674
De 31:13 ye go **o.** Jordan to possess it.............. 5674
De 31:15 stood **o.** the door of the tabernacle..... 5921
De 32:11 her nest, fluttereth **o.** her young, ... 5921
De 32:47 ye go **o.** Jordan to possess it............. 5674
De 32:49 that is **o.** against Jericho;........... 5921,6440
De 34:1 that is **o.** against Jericho............ 5921,6440
De 34:4 but thou shalt not go **o.** thither.......... 5674
De 34:6 of Moab, **o.** against Beth-peor: 4136
Jos 1:2 arise, go **o.** this Jordan, thou,............ 5674
Jos 1:11 days ye shall pass **o.** this Jordan, ... 5674
Jos 2:23 passed **o.**, and came to Joshua the...... 5674
Jos 3:1 lodged there before they passed **o.**...... 5674
Jos 3:6 and pass **o.** before the people. And..... 5674
Jos 3:11 all the earth passeth **o.** before you 5674
Jos 3:14 from their tents, to pass **o.** Jordan,..... 5674
Jos 3:16 passed **o.** right against Jericho. 5674
Jos 3:17 Israelites passed **o.** on dry ground,..... 5674
Jos 3:17 people were passed clean **o.** Jordan. ... 5674
Jos 4:1 people were clean passed **o.** Jordan, ... 5674
Jos 4:3 ye shall carry them **o.** with you, ... 5674
Jos 4:5 Pass **o.** before the ark of the Lord..... 5674
Jos 4:7 when it passed **o.** Jordan, the........... 5674
Jos 4:8 and carried them **o.** with them unto.... 5674
Jos 4:10 the people hasted and passed **o.**......... 5674
Jos 4:11 all the people were clean passed **o.**,.... 5674
Jos 4:11 that the ark of the Lord passed **o.**,..... 5674
Jos 4:12 tribe of Manasseh, passed **o.** armed...... 5674
Jos 4:13 prepared for war passed **o.** before...... 5674
Jos 4:18 flowed **o.** all his banks, as they did..... 5921
Jos 4:22 came **o.** this Jordan on dry land. 5674
Jos 4:23 before you, until ye were passed **o.**,... 5674
Jos 4:23 before us, until we were gone **o.**: 5674
Jos 5:1 of Israel, until we were passed **o.**, ... 5674
Jos 5:13 there stood a man **o.** against him 5048
Jos 7:7 all brought this people **o.** Jordan,........ 5674
Jos 7:26 **o.** him a great heap of stones unto..... 5921
Jos 8:31 **o.** which no man hath lift up any 5921
Jos 8:33 of them **o.** against mount Gerizim, ... 413
Jos 8:33 them **o.** against mount Ebal; 413,4136
Jos 9:1 great sea **o.** against Lebanon, ... 413,4136
Jos 18:13 went **o.** from thence toward Luz, ... 5674
Jos 18:17 which is **o.** against the going up......... 5227
Jos 18:18 toward the side **o.** against Arabah....... 4136
Jos 22:11 **o.** against the land of Canaan, ... 413,4136
Jos 22:19 pass ye **o.** unto the land of the.......... 5674
Jos 24:11 ye went **o.** Jordan, and came unto...... 5674
Jg 3:28 and suffered not a man to pass **o.**. 5674
Jg 5:13 dominion **o.** the nobles among..................
Jg 5:13 made me have dominion **o.** the mighty.......
Jg 6:33 gathered together, and went **o.**,.......... 5674
Jg 8:4 came to Jordan, and passed **o.**,.......... 5674
Jg 8:22 Rule thou **o.** us, both thou, and thy..........
Jg 8:23 said unto them, I will not rule **o.** you, ...
Jg 8:23 neither shall my son rule **o.** you:.............
Jg 8:23 the Lord shall rule **o.** you. ....
Jg 9:2 and ten persons, reign **o.** you, or that.......
Jg 9:2 or that one reign **o.** you? remember ....
Jg 9:8 a time to anoint a king **o.** them;......... 5921
Jg 9:8 the olive tree, Reign thou **o.** us. 5921
Jg 9:9 and go to be promoted **o.** the trees?... 5921
Jg 9:10 fig tree, Come thou, and reign **o.** us.... 5921
Jg 9:11 and go to be promoted **o.** the trees?... 5921
Jg 9:12 vine, Come thou, and reign **o.** us. 5921
Jg 9:13 and go to be promoted **o.** the trees?... 5921
Jg 9:14 Come thou, and reign **o.** us.............. 5921
Jg 9:15 in truth ye anoint me king **o.** you, ... 5921
Jg 9:18 king **o.** the men of Shechem:............ 5921
Jg 9:22 had reigned three years **o.** Israel,......... 5921
Jg 9:26 brethren, and went **o.** to Shechem:..... 5674
Jg 10:9 of Ammon passed **o.** Jordan to........... 5674
Jg 10:18 head **o.** all the inhabitants of Gilead..........
Jg 11:8 head **o.** all the inhabitants of Gilead..........
Jg 11:11 him head and captain **o.** them:........... 5921
Jg 11:29 and he passed **o.** Gilead, and............ 5674
Jg 11:29 and passed **o.** Mizpeh of Gilead,......... 5674
Jg 11:29 **o.** unto the children of Ammon: 5674
Jg 11:32 So Jephthah passed **o.** unto the......... 5674
Jg 12:1 passedst thou **o.** to fight against......... 5674
Jg 12:3 passed **o.** against the children of 5674
Jg 12:5 were escaped said, Let me go **o.**; 5674
Jg 14:4 the Philistines had dominion **o.** Israel.........
Jg 15:11 that the Philistines are rulers **o.** us?.........
Jg 19:10 and came **o.** against Jebus, which 5227
Jg 19:12 Israel; we will pass **o.** to Gibeah. 5674
Jg 20:43 down with ease **o.** against Gibeah....... 5227
Ru 2:5 servant that was set **o.** the reapers, ... 5921
Ru 2:6 servant that was set **o.** the reapers 5921
Ru 3:9 thy skirt **o.** thine handmaid; for.......... 5921
1Sa 2:1 mouth is enlarged **o.** mine enemies;.... 5921
1Sa 8:1 that he made his sons judges **o.** Israel......
1Sa 8:7 that I should not reign **o.** them. 5921
1Sa 8:9 the king that shall reign **o.** them. 5921
1Sa 8:11 of the king that shall reign **o.** you:..........
1Sa 8:12 **o.** thousands, and captains **o.** fifties; ....
1Sa 8:19 but we will have a king **o.** us;........... 5921
1Sa 9:16 to be captain **o.** my people Israel, ... 5921
1Sa 9:17 of this same shall reign **o.** my people. ....
1Sa 10:1 to be captain **o.** his inheritance? 5921
1Sa 10:19 unto him, Nay, but set a king **o.** us. ... 5921
1Sa 11:12 he that said, Shall Saul reign **o.** us? 5921
1Sa 12:1 me, and have made a king **o.** you....... 5921
1Sa 12:12 Nay; but a king shall reign **o.** us: 5921
1Sa 12:13 the Lord hath set a king **o.** you. 5921
1Sa 12:14 also the king that reigneth **o.** you....... 5921
1Sa 13:1 he had reigned two years **o.** Israel, ... 5921
1Sa 13:7 of the Hebrews went **o.** Jordan to 5674
1Sa 13:14 him to be captain **o.** his people, ... 5921
1Sa 14:1, 4 go **o.** to the Philistines' garrison, ... 5674
1Sa 14:5 northward **o.** against Michmash, ... 4136
1Sa 14:5 other southward **o.** against Gibeah...... 4136
1Sa 14:6 and let us go **o.** unto the garrison 5674
1Sa 14:8 we will pass **o.** unto these men, and... 5674
1Sa 14:23 battle passed **o.** unto Beth-aven......... 5674
1Sa 14:47 Saul took the kingdom **o.** Israel,......... 5921
1Sa 15:1 anoint thee to be king **o.** his people, ... 5921
1Sa 15:1 to anoint thee to be king...**o.** Israel; ....
1Sa 15:7 that is **o.** against Egypt............ 5921,6440
1Sa 15:17 Lord anointed thee king **o.** Israel? 5921
1Sa 15:26 thee from being king **o.** Israel........... 5921
1Sa 15:35 he had made Saul king **o.** Israel. 5921
1Sa 16:1 him from reigning **o.** Israel: fill.......... 5921
1Sa 17:50 David prevailed **o.** the Philistine......... 4480
1Sa 18:5 Saul set him **o.** the men of war,......... 5921
1Sa 18:13 made him his captain **o.** a thousand;..........
1Sa 19:20 standing as appointed **o.** them,........... 5921
1Sa 22:2 he became a captain **o.** them: and 5921
1Sa 22:9 was set **o.** the servants of Saul,......... 5921
1Sa 23:17 and thou shalt be king **o.** Israel,......... 5921
1Sa 25:30 have appointed thee ruler **o.** Israel; ....
1Sa 26:13 David went **o.** to the other side, ... 5674
1Sa 26:22 let one of the young men come **o.**......... 5674
1Sa 27:2 passed **o.** with the six hundred men.... 5674
1Sa 30:10 could not go **o.** the brook Besor. 5674
2Sa 1:17 lamentation **o.** Saul,...**o.** Jonathan....... 5921
2Sa 1:24 daughters of Israel, weep **o.** Saul,........ 413
2Sa 2:4 David king **o.** the house of Judah........ 5921
2Sa 2:7 have anointed me king **o.** them. 5921
2Sa 2:8 and brought him **o.** to Mahanaim;....... 5674
2Sa 2:9 king **o.** Gilead, and **o.** the Ashurites, ... 413
2Sa 2:9 and **o.** Jezreel, and **o.** Ephraim, ... 1591
2Sa 2:9 and **o.** Benjamin, and **o.** all Israel. 5921
2Sa 2:10 when he began to reign **o.** Israel,....... 5921
2Sa 2:11 in Hebron **o.** the house of Judah......... 5921
2Sa 2:15 arose and went **o.** by number............ 5674
2Sa 2:29 the plain, and passed **o.** Jordan, ... 5674
2Sa 3:10 of David **o.** Israel and **o.** Judah, ... 5921
2Sa 3:17 in times past to be king **o.** you: 5921
2Sa 3:21 reign **o.** all that thine heart desireth. ....
2Sa 3:33 And the king lamented **o.** Abner, ... 413
2Sa 3:34 all the people wept again **o.** him. 5921
2Sa 4:12 them up **o.** the pool in Hebron........... 5921
2Sa 5:2 when Saul was king **o.** us, thou 5921
2Sa 5:2 thou shalt be a captain **o.** Israel. 5921
2Sa 5:3 they anointed David king **o.** Israel. 5921
2Sa 5:5 he reigned **o.** Judah seven years 5921
2Sa 5:5 thirty and three years **o.** all Israel 5921
2Sa 5:12 had established him king **o.** Israel, ... 5921
2Sa 5:17 had anointed David king **o.** Israel,....... 5921
2Sa 5:23 **o.** against the mulberry trees. 4136
2Sa 6:21 me ruler **o.** the people of the Lord, ... 5921
2Sa 6:21 the people of the Lord, **o.** Israel: 5921
2Sa 7:8 to be ruler **o.** my people, **o.** Israel: 5921
2Sa 7:11 judges to be **o.** my people Israel. 5921
2Sa 7:26 Lord of hosts is the God **o.** Israel: 5921
2Sa 8:15 And David reigned **o.** all Israel;.......... 5921
2Sa 8:16 the son of Zeruiah was **o.** the host: 5921
2Sa 8:18 Benaiah...was **o.** both the Cherethites.......
2Sa 10:17 together, and passed **o.** Jordan, ... 5674
2Sa 12:7 I anointed thee king **o.** Israel,............ 5921
2Sa 15:22 David said to Ittai, Go and pass **o.**. 5674
2Sa 15:22 Ittai the Gittite passed **o.**, and all....... 5674
2Sa 15:23 voice, and all the people passed **o.**: 5674
2Sa 15:23 himself passed **o.** the brook Kidron,.... 5674
2Sa 15:23 all the people passed **o.**, toward the.... 5674
2Sa 16:9 let me go **o.**, I pray thee, and take...... 5674
2Sa 16:13 on the hill's side **o.** against him, ... 5980
2Sa 17:16 wilderness, but speedily pass **o.**; 5674
2Sa 17:19 a covering **o.** the well's mouth, ... 5921
2Sa 17:20 be gone **o.** the brook of water. 5674
2Sa 17:21 and pass quickly **o.** the water: 5674
2Sa 17:22 him, and they passed **o.** Jordan: 5674
2Sa 17:22 them that was not gone **o.** Jordan....... 5674
2Sa 17:24 And Absalom passed **o.** Jordan,.......... 5674
2Sa 18:1 and captains of hundreds **o.** them. 5921
2Sa 18:8 **o.** the face of all the country: 5921
2Sa 18:24 went up to the roof **o.** the gate........... 413
2Sa 18:33 up to the chamber **o.** the gate, ... 5921
2Sa 19:10 Absalom, whom we anointed **o.** us,....... 5921
2Sa 19:15 to conduct the king **o.** Jordan. 5674
2Sa 19:17 went **o.** Jordan before the king. 6743
2Sa 19:18 there went **o.** a ferry boat to carry..... 5674
2Sa 19:18 to carry **o.** the king's household,........ 5674
2Sa 19:18 the king, as he was come **o.** Jordan; ... 5674
2Sa 19:22 that I am this day king **o.** Israel?........ 5921
2Sa 19:31 and went **o.** Jordan with the king,....... 5674
2Sa 19:31 the king, to conduct him **o.** Jordan...... 5674
2Sa 19:33 Come thou **o.** with me, and I will....... 5674
2Sa 19:36 will go a little way **o.** Jordan with....... 5674
2Sa 19:37 let him go **o.** with my lord the king; ... 5674
2Sa 19:38 Chimham shall go **o.** with me, and...... 5674
2Sa 19:39 And all the people went **o.** Jordan....... 5674
2Sa 19:39 And when the king was come **o.**, the.. 5674
2Sa 19:41 David's men with him, **o.** Jordan? 5674
2Sa 20:21 shall be thrown to thee **o.** the wall. 1157
2Sa 20:23 Joab was **o.** all the host of Israel: 413
2Sa 20:23 Benaiah...was **o.** the Cherethites........ 5921
2Sa 20:23 Cherethites and **o.** the Pelethites: 5921
2Sa 20:24 And Adoram was **o.** the tribute:......... 5921
2Sa 22:30 by my God have I leaped **o.** a wall. ....
2Sa 23:3 He that ruleth **o.** men must be just,..........

2Sa 23:23 And David set him **o.** his guard.......... 413
2Sa 24:5 And they passed **o.** Jordan, and......... 5674
1Ki 1:34 anoint him there king **o.** Israel:.......... 5921
1Ki 1:35 to be ruler **o.** Israel and **o.** Judah........ 5921
1Ki 2:11 days that David reigned **o.** Israel........ 5921
1Ki 2:35 of Jehoiada in his room **o.** the host:.... 5921
1Ki 2:37 and passest **o.** the brook Kidron,....... 5674
1Ki 4:1 Solomon was king **o.** all Israel........... 5921
1Ki 4:4 the son of Jehoiada was **o.** the host:... 5921
1Ki 4:5 son of Nathan was **o.** the officers:...... 5921
1Ki 4:6 And Ahishar was **o.** the household:...... 5921
1Ki 4:6 the son of Abda was **o.** the tribute...... 5921
1Ki 4:7 had twelve officers **o.** all Israel,......... 5921
1Ki 4:21 And Solomon reigned **o.** all kingdoms........
1Ki 4:24 **o.** all the region on this side the river,......
1Ki 4:24 **o.** all the kings on this side the river:........
1Ki 5:7 a wise son **o.** this great people.......... 5921
1Ki 5:14 and Adoniram was **o.** the levy........... 5921
1Ki 5:16 officers which were **o.** the work,.......... 5921
1Ki 5:16 which ruled **o.** the people that wrought......
1Ki 6:1 year of Solomon's reign **o.** Israel,........ 5921
1Ki 7:20 **o.** against the belly which was by........ 5980
1Ki 7:39 eastward **o.** against the south............ 4136
1Ki 8:7 two wings **o.** the place of the ark,....... 413
1Ki 8:16 David to be **o.** my people Israel........... 5921
1Ki 9:23 officers that were **o.** Solomon's work,.. 5921
1Ki 9:23 bear rule **o.** the people that wrought.........
1Ki 11:24 and became captain **o.** a band, when.........
1Ki 11:25 Israel, and reigned **o.** Syria.............. 5921
1Ki 11:28 **o.** all the charge of the house of Joseph......
1Ki 11:37 and shalt be king **o.** Israel................. 5921
1Ki 11:42 reigned in Jerusalem **o.** all Israel......... 5921
1Ki 12:17 Judah, Rehoboam reigned **o.** them........ 5921
1Ki 12:18 Adoram, who was **o.** the tribute;.......... 5921
1Ki 12:20 and made him king **o.** all Israel:.......... 5921
1Ki 13:30 mourned **o.** him, saying, Alas, my...... 5921
1Ki 14:2 that I should be king **o.** this people..... 5921
1Ki 14:7 thee prince **o.** my people Israel,.......... 5921
1Ki 14:14 shall raise him up a king **o.** Israel,...... 5921
1Ki 15:1 of Nebat reigned Abijam **o.** Judah........ 5921
1Ki 15:9 king of Israel reigned Asa **o.** Judah...... 5921
1Ki 15:25 Nadab...began to reign **o.** Israel.......... 5921
1Ki 15:25 and reigned **o.** Israel two years........... 5921
1Ki 15:33 to reign **o.** all Israel in Tirzah,........... 5921
1Ki 16:2 thee prince **o.** my people Israel;.......... 5921
1Ki 16:8 Elah...to reign **o.** Israel in Tirzah,...... 5921
1Ki 16:16 king **o.** Israel that day in the camp..... 5921
1Ki 16:18 and burnt the king's house **o.** him....... 5921
1Ki 16:23 Judah began Omri to reign **o.** Israel,... 5921
1Ki 16:29 began Ahab...to reign **o.** Israel:.......... 5921
1Ki 16:29 Ahab...reigned **o.** Israel in Samaria...... 5921
1Ki 19:15 anoint Hazael to be king **o.** Syria:......... 5921
1Ki 19:16 thou anoint to be king **o.** Israel:.......... 5921
1Ki 20:29 pitched one **o.** against the other......... 5227
1Ki 22:31 captains that had rule **o.** his chariots,........
1Ki 22:41 of Asa began to reign **o.** Judah........... 5921
1Ki 22:51 began to reign **o.** Israel in Samaria...... 5921
1Ki 22:51 and reigned two years **o.** Israel........... 5921
2Ki 2:8 they two went **o.** on dry ground........ 5674
2Ki 2:9 to pass, when they were gone **o.**,....... 5674
2Ki 2:14 and thither: and Elisha went **o.**......... 5674
2Ki 3:1 began to reign **o.** Israel in Samaria...... 5921
2Ki 5:11 and strike his hand **o.** the place,......... 413
2Ki 8:13 that thou shalt be king **o.** Syria.......... 5921
2Ki 8:20 and made a king **o.** themselves........... 5921
2Ki 8:21 So Joram went **o.** to Zair, and all....... 5674
2Ki 9:3 have anointed thee king **o.** Israel........ 5921
2Ki 9:6 anointed thee king **o.** the people......... 413
2Ki 9:6 people of the Lord, even **o.** Israel........ 413
2Ki 9:12 I have anointed thee king **o.** Israel...... 413
2Ki 9:29 began Ahaziah to reign **o.** Judah......... 5921
2Ki 10:5 And he that was **o.** the house, and...... 5921
2Ki 10:5 he that was **o.** the city, the elders...... 5921
2Ki 10:22 unto him that was **o.** the vestry,......... 5921
2Ki 10:36 Jehu reigned **o.** Israel in Samaria........ 5921
2Ki 11:3 And Athaliah did reign **o.** the land....... 5921
2Ki 11:4 and fetched the rulers **o.** hundreds,..........
2Ki 11:9 And the captains **o.** the hundreds did........
2Ki 11:10 to the captains **o.** hundreds did the...........
2Ki 11:18 officers **o.** the house of the Lord........ 5921
2Ki 11:19 And he took the rulers **o.** hundreds,.........
2Ki 13:1, 10 to reign **o.** Israel in Samaria,......... 5921
2Ki 13:14 and wept **o.** his face, and said, O my.. 5921
2Ki 15:5 the king's son was **o.** the house,......... 5921
2Ki 15:8 reign **o.** Israel in Samaria six............. 5921
2Ki 15:17 the son of Gadi to reign **o.** Israel,...... 5921
2Ki 15:23, 27 to reign **o.** Israel in Samaria,......... 5921
2Ki 17:1 of Elah to reign in Samaria **o.** Israel.... 5921
2Ki 18:18, 37 which was **o.** the household,......... 5921
2Ki 19:2 which was **o.** the household,............. 5921
2Ki 21:13 will stretch **o.** Jerusalem the line of..... 5921
2Ki 25:19 that was set **o.** the men of war,......... 5921
2Ki 25:22 **o.** them he made Gedaliah...ruler....... 5921
1Ch 1:43 king reigned **o.** the children of Israel;........
1Ch 5:11 of God dwelt **o.** against them............ 5048
1Ch 6:31 David set **o.** the service of song......... 5921
1Ch 8:32 in Jerusalem, **o.** against them............ 5048
1Ch 9:19 were **o.** the work of the service,......... 5921
1Ch 9:19 being **o.** the host of the Lord,........... 5921
1Ch 9:20 was the ruler **o.** them in time past,.... 5921
1Ch 9:26 **o.** the chambers and treasuries.......... 5921
1Ch 9:31 **o.** the things that were made in the.... 5921
1Ch 9:32 were **o.** the shewbread, to prepare..... 5921
1Ch 9:38 **o.** against their brethren.................. 5048
1Ch 11:2 shalt be ruler **o.** my people Israel...... 5921
1Ch 11:3 they anointed David king **o.** Israel,..... 5921
1Ch 11:25 and David set him **o.** his guard.......... 5921
1Ch 12:4 among the thirty, and **o.** the thirty;.... 5921
1Ch 12:14 one of the least was **o.** an hundred,..........
1Ch 12:14 and the greatest **o.** a thousand.................
1Ch 12:15 are they that went **o.** Jordan in.......... 5674
1Ch 12:38 to make David king **o.** all Israel:......... 5921
1Ch 14:2 had confirmed him king **o.** Israel,........ 5921
1Ch 14:8 was anointed king **o.** all Israel,........... 5921
1Ch 14:14 **o.** against the mulberry trees............ 4136
1Ch 15:25 and the captains **o.** thousands, went to......
1Ch 17:7 be ruler **o.** my people Israel:............. 5921
1Ch 17:10 judges to be **o.** my people Israel........ 5921
1Ch 18:14 So David reigned **o.** all Israel, and...... 5921
1Ch 18:15 the son of Zeruiah was **o.** the host;.... 5921
1Ch 18:17 was **o.** the Cherethites and the.......... 5921
1Ch 19:17 all Israel, and passed **o.** Jordan,......... 5674
1Ch 21:16 hand stretched out **o.** Jerusalem.......... 5921
1Ch 22:10 of his kingdom **o.** Israel for ever......... 5921
1Ch 23:1 Solomon his son king **o.** Israel........... 5921
1Ch 24:31 cast lots **o.** against their brethren....... 5980
1Ch 24:31 **o.** against their younger brethren......... 5980
1Ch 26:20 Ahijah was **o.** the treasures of the...... 5921
1Ch 26:20 **o.** the treasures of the dedicated.............
1Ch 26:22 which were **o.** the treasures of the..... 5921
1Ch 26:26 brethren were **o.** all the treasures...... 5921
1Ch 26:26 captains **o.** thousands and hundreds,........
1Ch 26:29 for the outward business **o.** Israel,...... 5921
1Ch 26:32 made rulers **o.** the Reubenites, the...... 5921
1Ch 27:2 **O.** the first course for the first.......... 5921
1Ch 27:4 **o.** the course of the second month...... 5921
1Ch 27:16 Furthermore **o.** the tribes of Israel:.... 5921
1Ch 27:25 And **o.** the king's treasures was......... 5921
1Ch 27:25 and **o.** the storehouses in the fields,.... 5921
1Ch 27:26 **o.** them that did the work of the........ 5921
1Ch 27:27 And **o.** the vineyards was Shimei........ 5921
1Ch 27:27 **o.** the increase of the vineyards for.... 5921
1Ch 27:28 **o.** the olive trees and the sycomore..... 5921
1Ch 27:28 and **o.** the cellars of oil was Joash:..... 5921
1Ch 27:29 **o.** the herds that fed in Sharon was.... 5921
1Ch 27:29 **o.** the herds that were in the valleys... 5921
1Ch 27:30 **O.** the camels also was Obil the......... 5921
1Ch 27:30 and **o.** the asses was Jehdeiah the...... 5921
1Ch 27:31 And **o.** the flocks was Jaziz the.......... 5921
1Ch 28:1 and the captains **o.** the thousands,...........
1Ch 28:1 and captains **o.** the hundreds, and............
1Ch 28:1 the stewards **o.** all the substance and........
1Ch 28:4 to be king **o.** Israel for ever:............. 5921
1Ch 28:4 me to make me king **o.** all Israel:....... 5921
1Ch 28:5 the kingdom of the Lord **o.** Israel...... 5921
1Ch 29:3 **o.** and above all that I have prepared.. 5921
1Ch 29:12 of thee, and thou reignest **o.** all:........ 4605
1Ch 29:26 son of Jesse reigned **o.** all Israel........ 5921
1Ch 29:27 time that he reigned **o.** Israel was...... 5921
1Ch 29:30 and the times that went **o.** him,......... 5674
1Ch 29:30 **o.** Israel, and **o.** all the kingdoms of.... 5921
2Ch 1:9 thou hast made me king **o.** a people..... 5921
2Ch 1:11 **o.** whom I have made thee king:......... 5921
2Ch 1:13 congregation, and reigned **o.** Israel..... 5921
2Ch 2:11 he hath made thee king **o.** them......... 5921
2Ch 4:10 the east end, **o.** against the south...... 4136
2Ch 5:8 their wings **o.** the place of the ark,..... 5921
2Ch 6:5 to be a ruler **o.** my people Israel:....... 5921
2Ch 6:6 David to be **o.** my people Israel.......... 5921
2Ch 6:36 them **o.** before their enemies,........... 6440
2Ch 8:10 and fifty, that bare rule **o.** the people........
2Ch 9:8 made he thee king **o.** them, to do...... 5921
2Ch 9:26 And he reigned **o.** all the kings from.........
2Ch 9:30 Jerusalem **o.** all Israel forty years....... 5921
2Ch 10:17 Judah, Rehoboam reigned **o.** them....... 5921
2Ch 10:18 Hadoram that was **o.** the tribute;....... 5921
2Ch 13:1 began Abijah to reign **o.** Judah........... 5921
2Ch 13:5 gave the kingdom **o.** Israel to David.... 5921
2Ch 19:11 chief priest is **o.** you in all matters..... 5921
2Ch 20:6 rulest not thou **o.** all the kingdoms of........
2Ch 20:27 made them to rejoice **o.** their enemies.......
2Ch 20:31 Jehoshaphat reigned **o.** Judah: he......... 5921
2Ch 22:12 and Athaliah reigned **o.** the land.......... 5921
2Ch 23:14 of hundreds that were set **o.** the host.......
2Ch 25:5 and made them captains **o.** thousands,.......
2Ch 25:5 and captains **o.** hundreds, according..........
2Ch 26:21 his son was **o.** the king's house,......... 5921
2Ch 31:12 **o.** which Cononiah the Levite was...... 5921
2Ch 31:14 was **o.** the freewill offerings of God,... 5921
2Ch 32:6 he set captains of war **o.** the people,.. 5921
2Ch 32:11 to give **o.** yourselves to die by famine.......
2Ch 34:13 were **o.** the bearers of burdens,......... 5921
2Ch 36:4 Eliakim his brother king **o.** Judah........ 5921
2Ch 36:10 his brother king **o.** Judah and............. 5921
Ezr 4:10 and noble Asnapper brought **o.**,.......... 1541
Ezr 4:20 mighty kings also **o.** Jerusalem,.......... 5922
Ezr 4:20 ruled **o.** all countries beyond the..............
Ezr 9:6 are increased **o.** our head, and........... 4605
Ne 2:7 convey me **o.** till I come...Judah;......... 5674
Ne 3:10 even **o.** against the house. And........... 5048
Ne 3:16 **o.** against the sepulchres of David,...... 5048
Ne 3:19 piece **o.** against the going up to the.... 5048
Ne 3:23 and Hashub **o.** against their house...... 5048
Ne 3:25 **o.** against the turning of the wall,....... 5048
Ne 3:26 the place **o.** against the water gate..... 5048
Ne 3:27 **o.** against the great tower that........... 5048
Ne 3:28 every one **o.** against his house........... 5048
Ne 3:29 son of Immer **o.** against his house....... 5048
Ne 3:30 of Berechiah **o.** against his chamber.... 5048
Ne 3:31 **o.** against the gate of Miphkad, and.... 5048
Ne 5:15 servants bare rule **o.** the people:........ 5921
Ne 7:2 of the palace, charge **o.** Jerusalem:..... 5921
Ne 7:3 one to be **o.** against his house........... 5048
Ne 9:28 so that they had the dominion **o.** them:.....
Ne 9:37 the kings whom thou hast set **o.** us:.... 5921
Ne 9:37 they have dominion **o.** our bodies,....... 5921
Ne 9:37 and **o.** our cattle, at their pleasure,...... 5921
Ne 11:9 of Senuah was second **o.** the city........ 5921
Ne 11:21 and Gispa were **o.** the Nethinims......... 5921
Ne 11:22 the singers were **o.** the business of..... 5048
Ne 12:8 which was **o.** the thanksgiving, he....... 5921
Ne 12:9 **o.** against them in the watches........... 5048
Ne 12:24 their brethren **o.** against them,.......... 5980
Ne 12:24 man of God, ward **o.** against ward....... 5980
Ne 12:37 gate, which was **o.** against them,......... 5048
Ne 12:38 gave thanks went **o.** against them,...... 4136
Ne 12:44 **o.** the chambers for the treasures,....... 5921
Ne 13:13 I made treasurers **o.** the treasuries,..... 5921
Ne 13:26 God made him king **o.** all Israel:........ 5921
Es 1:1 **o.** an hundred and seven and twenty.........
Es 3:12 that were **o.** every province, and......... 5921
Es 5:1 house, **o.** against the king's house;...... 5227
Es 5:1 **o.** against the gate of the house......... 5227
Es 8:2 Mordecai **o.** the house of Haman......... 5921
Es 9:1 Jews hoped to have power **o.** them,..........
Es 9:1 had rule **o.** them that hated them;)..........
Job 6:5 or loweth the ox **o.** his fodder?........... 5921
Job 7:12 that thou settest a watch **o.** me?......... 5921
Job 14:16 dost thou not watch **o.** my sin?........... 5921
Job 16:11 me **o.** into the hands of the wicked...... 5921
Job 26:7 out the north **o.** the empty place,........ 5921
Job 34:13 hath given him a charge **o.** the earth?.......
Job 41:34 king **o.** all the children of pride.......... 5921
Job 42:11 comforted him **o.** all the evil that........ 5921
Ps 8:6 dominion **o.** the works of thy hands;.........
Ps 12:4 lips are our own: who is lord **o.** us?..........
Ps 13:2 mine enemy be exalted **o.** me?........... 5921
Ps 18:29 and by my God have I leaped **o.** a wall......
Ps 19:13 let them not have dominion **o.** me:...........
Ps 23:5 my head with oil; my cup runneth **o.**.........
Ps 25:2 let not mine enemies triumph **o.** me..........
Ps 27:12 not **o.** unto the will of mine enemies:.........
Ps 30:1 hast not made my foes to rejoice **o.** me.....
Ps 35:19 enemies wrongfully rejoice **o.** me:..........
Ps 35:24 and let them not rejoice **o.** me................
Ps 38:4 iniquities are gone **o.** mine head:........ 5674
Ps 38:16 otherwise they should rejoice **o.** me:.........
Ps 41:11 enemy doth not triumph **o.** me........... 5921

Ps 42:7 and thy billows are gone o. me. 5921
Ps 47:2 he is a great King o. all the earth. 5921
Ps 47:8 God reigneth o. the heathen: God 5921
Ps 49:14 upright shall have dominion o. them
Ps 60:8 o. Edom will I cast out my shoe: 5921
Ps 65:13 valleys...are covered o. with corn; 5848
Ps 66:12 hast caused men to ride o. our heads;
Ps 68:34 his excellency is o. Israel, and his 5921
Ps 78:50 gave their life o. to the pestilence; 5462
Ps 78:62 his people o. also unto the sword; 5462
Ps 83:18 art the most high o. all the earth. 5921
Ps 88:16 Thy fierce wrath goeth o. me; thy 5674
Ps 91:11 shall give his angels charge o. thee,
Ps 103:16 For the wind passeth o. it, and it 5674
Ps 103:19 heavens; and his kingdom ruleth o. all.
Ps 104:9 bound that they may not pass o.; 5674
Ps 106:41 they that hated them ruled o. them.
Ps 108:9 o. Edom will I cast out my shoe; 5921
Ps 108:9 o. Philistia will I triumph.
Ps 109:6 Set thou a wicked man o. him: and 5921
Ps 110:6 wound the heads o. many countries. 5921
Ps 118:18 hath not given me o. unto death. 5414
Ps 119:133 any iniquity have dominion o. me.
Ps 124:4 the stream had gone o. our soul: 5674
Ps 124:5 proud waters had gone o. our soul. 5674
Ps 145:9 tender mercies are o. all his works. 5921
Pr 17:2 A wise servant shall have rule o. a son
Pr 19:10 for a servant to have rule o. princes.
Pr 19:11 glory to pass o. a transgression. 5921
Pr 20:26 and bringeth the wheel o. them. 5921
Pr 22:7 The rich ruleth o. the poor, and the
Pr 24:31 lo, it was all grown o. with thorns. 5927
Pr 25:28 that hath no rule o. his own spirit is
Pr 28:15 a wicked ruler o. the poor people. 5921
Ec 1:12 I the Preacher was king o. Israel 5921
Ec 2:19 yet shall he have rule o. all my labour
Ec 7:14 hath set...one o. against the other, 5980
Ec 7:16 Be not righteous o. much; neither 7235
Ec 7:16 neither make thyself o. wise: why 3148
Ec 7:17 Be not o. much wicked, neither be 7235
Ec 8:8 power o. the spirit to retain the spirit:
Ec 8:9 one man ruleth o. another to his own
Ca 2:4 and his banner o. me was love. 5921
Ca 2:11 is past, the rain is o. and gone; 2498
Isa 3:4 princes, and babes shall rule o. them.
Isa 3:12 oppressors, and women rule o. them.
Isa 8:7 shall come up o. all his channels, 5921
Isa 8:7 channels, and go o. all his banks: 5921
Isa 8:8 he shall overflow and go o., he 5674
Isa 10:29 They are gone o. the passage: they 5674
Isa 11:15 he shake his hand o. the river, 5921
Isa 11:15 and make men go o. dryshod. 1869
Isa 14:2 and they shall rule o. their oppressors.
Isa 15:2 shall howl o. Nebo, and o. Medeba: 5921
Isa 16:8 out, they are gone o. the sea. 5674
Isa 19:4 Egyptians will I give o. into the 5534
Isa 19:4 and a fierce king shall rule o. them,
Isa 19:16 of hosts, which he shaketh o. it. 5921
Isa 22:15 Shebna, which is o. the house, and 5921
Isa 23:2 of Zidon, that pass o. the sea. 5674
Isa 23:6 Pass ye o. to Tarshish; howl, ye 5674
Isa 23:11 stretched out his hand o. the sea, 5921
Isa 23:12 of Zidon: arise, pass o. to Chittim; 5674
Isa 25:7 of the covering cast o. all people, 5921
Isa 25:7 vail that is spread o. all nations. 5921
Isa 26:13 beside thee have had dominion o. us:
Isa 28:19 by morning shall it pass o., 5674
Isa 31:5 it; and passing o. he will preserve it.
Isa 31:9 he shall pass o. to his strong hold 5674
Isa 35:8 the unclean shall not pass o. it; 5674
Isa 36:3 son, which was o. the house, 5921
Isa 36:22 Hilkiah, that was o. the household, 5921
Isa 37:2 Eliakim, who was o. the household, 5921
Isa 40:19 goldsmith spreadeth it o. with gold,
Isa 40:27 is passed o. from my God? 5674
Isa 41:2 him, and made him rule o. kings?
Isa 45:14 stature, shall come o. unto thee, 5674
Isa 45:14 in chains they shall come o., and 5674
Isa 47:2 the thigh, pass o. the rivers. 5674
Isa 51:10 a way for the ransomed to pass o.? 5674
Isa 51:23 Bow down, that we may go o.: 5674
Isa 51:23 as the street, to them that went o.. 5674
Isa 52:5 that rule o. them make them to howl,
Isa 54:9 should no more go o. the earth; 5674
Isa 62:5 bridegroom rejoiceth o. the bride, 5921
Isa 62:5 so shall thy God rejoice o. thee. 5921
Isa 63:19 thou never barest rule o. them; they

Jer 1:10 this day set thee o. the nations 5921
Jer 1:10 and o. the kingdoms to root out, 5921
Jer 2:10 pass o. the isles of Chittim, and 5674
Jer 5:6 leopard shall watch o. their cities: 5921
Jer 5:22 roar, yet can they not pass o. it? 5674
Jer 6:17 Also I set watchmen o. you, 5921
Jer 13:21 to be captains, and as chief o. thee: 5921
Jer 15:3 I will appoint o. them four kinds, 5921
Jer 23:4 And I will set up shepherds o. them 5921
Jer 31:28 that like as I have watched o. them, 5921
Jer 31:28 so will I watch o. them, to build, 5921
Jer 31:39 shall yet go forth o. against it 5048
Jer 32:41 rejoice o. them to do them good, 5921
Jer 33:26 to be rulers o. the seed of Abraham, 413
Jer 40:5 made governor o. the cities of Judah,
Jer 40:11 that he had set o. them Gedaliah 5921
Jer 41:2 Babylon had made governor o. the land.
Jer 41:10 to go o. to the Ammonites. 5674
Jer 43:10 spread his royal pavilion o. them. 5921
Jer 44:27 I will watch o. them for evil, 5921
Jer 48:32 thy plants are gone o. the sea, 5674
Jer 48:40 shall spread his wings o. Moab. 413
Jer 49:19 man, that I may appoint o. her? 413
Jer 49:22 and spread his wings o. Bozrah; 5921
Jer 50:44 man, that I may appoint o. her? 413
La 2:17 thine enemy to rejoice o. thee, 5921
La 3:54 Waters flowed o. mine head; then I 5921
La 5:8 Servants have ruled o. us: there is
Eze 1:20, 21 were lifted up o. against them: 5980
Eze 1:22 stretched forth o. their heads 5921
Eze 1:25 firmament that was o. their heads, 5921
Eze 1:26 firmament that was o. their heads 5921
Eze 3:13 of the wheels o. against them, 5980
Eze 9:1 them that have charge o. the city to
Eze 10:1 o. them as it were a sapphire 5921
Eze 10:2 and scatter them o. the city. 5921
Eze 10:4 stood o. the threshold of the house; 5921
Eze 10:18 house, and stood o. the cherubims. 5921
Eze 10:19 God of Israel was o. them above. 5921
Eze 11:22 God of Israel was o. them above. 5921
Eze 16:8 and I spread my skirt o. thee, and 5921
Eze 16:27 have stretched out my hand o. thee, 5921
Eze 19:8 and spread their net o. him: he 5921
Eze 20:33 fury poured out, will I rule o. you:
Eze 27:32 for thee, and lament o. thee, 5921
Eze 29:15 shall no more rule o. the nations. 5921
Eze 32:3 therefore spread out my net o. thee 5921
Eze 32:8 of heaven will I make dark o. thee, 5921
Eze 32:31 be comforted o. all his multitude, 5921
Eze 34:23 I will set up one shepherd o. them, 5921
Eze 37:24 my servant, shall be king o. them; 5921
Eze 40:18 o. against the length of the gates 5980
Eze 40:23 was o. against the gate toward the 5048
Eze 41:6 one o. another, and thirty in order; 413
Eze 41:15 o. against the separate place 413,6440
Eze 41:16 three stories, o. against the door, 5048
Eze 42:1 was o. against the separate place, 5048
Eze 42:3 O. against the twenty cubits which 5048
Eze 42:3 o. against the pavement which was 5048
Eze 42:7 without o. against the chambers, 5980
Eze 42:10 o. against the separate place, 413,6440
Eze 42:10 and o. against the building.
Eze 45:6 o. against the oblation of the holy 5980
Eze 45:7 be o. against one of the portions, 5980
Eze 46:9 but shall go forth o. against it. 5226
Eze 47:5 a river that I could not pass o.: 5674
Eze 47:5 a river that could not be passed o.. 5674
Eze 47:20 a man come o. against Hamath. 5227
Eze 48:13 o. against the border of the 5980
Eze 48:15 o. against the five and twenty. 5922,6440
Eze 48:18, 18 o. against the oblation of the 5980
Eze 48:21, 21 o. against the five and 5922,6440
Eze 48:21 o. against the portions for the 5980
Da 1:11 had set o. Daniel, Hananiah, 5921
Da 2:38 and hath made thee ruler o. them all.
Da 2:39 which shall bear rule o. all the earth.
Da 2:48 o. the whole province of Babylon, 5922
Da 2:48 o. all the wise men of Babylon. 5922
Da 2:49 o. the affairs of the province of 5922
Da 3:12 o. the affairs of the province of 5921
Da 4:16 and let seven times pass o. him. 5922
Da 4:17 setteth up o. it the basest of men. 5922
Da 4:23 field, till seven times pass o. him; 5922
Da 4:25, 32 seven times shall pass o. thee, 5922
Da 5:5 wrote o. against the candlestick 6903
Da 5:21 appointeth o. it whomsoever he 5922
Da 6:1 to set o. the kingdom an hundred 5922

Da 6:1 should be o. the whole kingdom;
Da 6:2 And o. these three presidents; 5924
Da 6:3 to set him o. the whole realm. 5922
Da 9:1 o. the realm of the Chaldeans; 5921
Da 11:39 he shall cause them to rule o. many,
Da 11:40 and shall overflow and pass o.. 5674
Da 11:43 o. the treasures of gold and of silver,
Da 11:43 o. all the precious things of Egypt:
Ho 10:5 people thereof shall mourn o. it, 5921
Ho 10:11 I passed o. upon her fair neck: 5674
Ho 12:4 he had power o. the angel, and 413
Joe 2:17 that the heathen should rule o. them:
Ob 12 rejoiced o. the children of Judah
Jon 2:3 and thy waves passed o. me. 5674
Jon 4:6 and made it to come up o. Jonah, 5921
Jon 4:6 it might be a shadow o. his head, 5921
Mic 3:6 sun shall go down o. the prophets, 5921
Mic 3:6 and the day shall be dark o. them. 5921
Mic 4:7 Lord shall reign o. them in mount 5921
Na 3:19 thee shall clap their hands o. thee: 5921
Hab 1:11 and he shall pass o., and offend, 5674
Hab 1:14 things, that have no ruler o. them?
Hab 2:19 it is laid o. with gold and silver,
Zep 3:17 he will rejoice o. thee with joy; 5921
Zep 3:17 he will joy o. thee with singing. 5921
Hag 1:10 heaven o. you is stayed from dew, 5921
Zec 1:21 up their horn o. the land of Judah 413
Zec 5:3 o. the face of the whole earth: 5921
Zec 9:14 And the Lord shall be seen o. them, 5921
Zec 14:9 Lord shall be king o. all the earth: 5921
Mt 2:9 o. where the young child was. *1883*
Mt 9:1 passed o., and came into his own *1276*
Mt 10:23 **have gone o. the cities of Israel,** *5055*
Mt 14:34 And when they were gone o., they *1276*
Mt 20:25 **Gentiles exercise dominion o. them,**
Mt 21:2 **Go into the village o. against you,** *561*
Mt 24:45 **hath made ruler o. his household,** *1909*
Mt 24:47 **make him ruler o. all his goods** *1909*
Mt 25:21 **hast been faithful o. a few things,** *1909*
Mt 25:21 **make thee ruler o. many things:** *1909*
Mt 25:23 **hast been faithful o. a few things,** *1909*
Mt 25:23 **make thee ruler o. many things:** *1909*
Mt 27:37 set up o. his head his accusation *1883*
Mt 27:45 there was darkness o. all the land *1909*
Mt 27:61 sitting o. against the sepulchre. *561*
Mk 4:35 **Let us pass o. unto the other side.** *1330*
Mk 5:1 o. unto the other side of the sea,
Mk 5:21 Jesus was passed o. again by ship *1276*
Mk 6:7 gave them power o. unclean spirits;
Mk 6:53 And when they had passed o., they *1276*
Mk 10:42 **are accounted to rule o. the Gentiles**
Mk 10:42 **Gentiles exercise lordship o. them;**
Mk 11:2 **into the village o. against you:** *2713*
Mk 12:41 Jesus sat o. against the treasury, *2713*
Mk 13:3 of Olives o. against the temple, *2713*
Mk 15:26 of his accusation was written o., *1924*
Mk 15:33 was darkness o. the whole land *1909*
Mk 15:39 which stood o. against him, *1537,1727*
Lu 1:33 o. the house of Jacob for ever; *1909*
Lu 2:8 watch o. their flock by night. *1909*
Lu 4:10 give his angels charge o. thee, *4012*
Lu 4:39 he stood o. her, and rebuked the *1883*
Lu 6:38 **shaken together, and running o.,** *5240*
Lu 8:22 **o. unto the other side of the lake.** *1330*
Lu 8:26 which is o. against Galilee. *495*
Lu 9:1 power and authority o. all devils, *1909*
Lu 10:19 **and o. all the power of the enemy:** *1909*
Lu 11:42 **pass o. judgment and...love of God:** *3928*
Lu 11:44 **that walk o. them are not aware** *1883*
Lu 12:14 **me a judge or a divider o. you?** *1909*
Lu 12:42 **shall make ruler o. his household,** *1909*
Lu 12:44 **make him ruler o. all that he hath.** *1909*
Lu 15:7 **o. one sinner that repenteth,** *1909*
Lu 15:7 **more than o. ninety and nine just** *1909*
Lu 15:10 **God o. one sinner that repenteth** *1909*
Lu 19:14 **not have this man to reign o. us,** *1909*
Lu 19:17 **have thou authority o. ten cities.** *1883*
Lu 19:19 **to him, Be thou also o. five cities.** *1883*
Lu 19:27 **not that I should reign o. them,** *1909*
Lu 19:30 **ye into the village o. against you;** *2713*
Lu 19:41 he beheld the city, and wept o. it, *1909*
Lu 22:25 **Gentiles exercise lordship o. them;**
Lu 23:38 written o. him in letters of Greek, *1909*
Lu 23:44 was a darkness o. all the earth *1909*
Joh 6:1 Jesus went o. the sea of Galilee, *4008*
Joh 6:13 remained o. and above unto them *4052*
Joh 6:17 o. the sea toward Capernaum. *4008*

Joh 17:2 **hast given him power o. all flesh,**
Joh 18:1 his disciples o. the brook Cedron, *4008*
Ac 6:3 we may appoint o. this business. *1909*
Ac 7:10 made him governor o. Egypt and *1909*
Ac 7:11 there came a dearth o. all the land *1909*
Ac 7:16 were carried o. into Sychem, and *3346*
Ac 7:27 thee a ruler and a judge o. us? *1909*
Ac 8:2 made great lamentation o. him. *1909*
Ac 16:9 Come o. into Macedonia, and help *1224*
Ac 18:23 went o. all the country of Galatia *1330*
Ac 19:13 call o. them which had evil spirits *1909*
Ac 20:2 when he had gone o. those parts, *1330*
Ac 20:15 the next day o. against Chios; and *481*
Ac 20:28 o. the which the Holy Ghost hath *1722*
Ac 21:2 a ship sailing o. unto Phenicia, *1276*
Ac 27:5 we had sailed o. the sea of Cilicia *1277*
Ac 27:7 were come o. against Cnidus, the *2596*
Ac 27:7 under Crete, o. against Salmone; *2596*
Ro 1:28 gave them o. to a reprobate mind, *3860*
Ro 5:14 even o. them that had not sinned *1909*
Ro 6:9 death hath no more dominion o. him.
Ro 6:14 sin shall not have dominion o. you:
Ro 7:1 hath dominion o. a man as long as he
Ro 9:5 who is o. all, God blessed for ever. *1909*
Ro 9:21 Hath not the potter power o. the clay,
Ro 10:12 the same Lord o. all is rich unto all
Ro 15:12 shall rise to reign o. the Gentiles;
1Co 7:37 but hath power o. his own will, *4012*
1Co 9:12 be partakers of this power o. you,
2Co 1:24 that we have dominion o. your faith,
2Co 3:13 Moses, which put a vail o. his face, *1909*
2Co 8:15 had gathered much had nothing o.; *4121*
2Co 11:2 am jealous o. you with godly jealousy:
Eph 1:22 him to be the head o. all things to *5228*
Eph 4:19 themselves o. unto lasciviousness, *3860*
Col 2:15 them openly, triumphing o. them in it.
1Th 3:7 were comforted o. you in all our *1909*
1Th 5:12 you, and are o. you in the Lord, *4291*
1Ti 2:12 nor to usurp authority o. the man, but
Heb 2:7 set him o. the works of thy hands: *1909*
Heb 3:6 Christ as a son o. his own house; *1909*
Heb 9:5 And o. it the cherubims of glory *5231*
Heb 10:21 an high priest o. the house of God; *1909*
Heb 13:7 them which have the rule o. you,
Heb 13:17 Obey them that have the rule o. you,
Heb 13:24 all them that have the rule o. you,
Jas 5:14 let them pray o. him, anointing *1909*
1Pe 3:12 of the Lord are o. the righteous, *1909*
1Pe 5:3 as being lords o. God's heritage, *2634*
Jude 7 giving themselves o. to fornication, *1608*
Re 2:26 **will I give power o. the nations:** *1909*
Re 6:8 o. the fourth part of the earth, *1909*
Re 9:11 they had a king o. them, which is *1909*
Re 11:6 o. waters to turn them to blood, *1909*
Re 11:10 the earth shall rejoice o. them, *1909*
Re 13:7 was given him o. all kindreds, and *1909*
Re 14:18 the altar, which had power o. fire; *1909*
Re 15:2 had gotten the victory o. the beast, *1537*
Re 15:2 and o. his image, and o. his mark, *1537*
Re 15:2 and o. the number of his name, *1537*
Re 16:9 which hath power o. these plagues: *1909*
Re 17:18 reigneth o. the kings of the earth. *1909*
Re 18:11 earth shall weep and mourn o. her; *1909*
Re 18:20 Rejoice o. her, thou heaven, and ye *1909*

OVERCAME
Ac 19:16 o. them, and prevailed against *2634*
Re 3:21 **even as I also o., and am set down** *3528*
Re 12:11 o. him by the blood of the Lamb, *3528*

OVERCHARGE See also OVERCHARGED.
2Co 2:5 in part: that I may not o. you all. *1912*

OVERCHARGED
Lu 21:34 **your hearts be o. with surfeiting,** *925*

OVERCOME See also OVERCAME; OVERCOMETH.
Ge 49:19 Gad, a troop shall o. him: 1464
Ge 49:19 but he shall o. at the last. 1464
Ex 32:18 of them that cry for being o.: but 2476
Nu 13:30 it; for we are well able to o. it. 3201
Nu 22:11 I shall be able to o. them, and 3898
2Ki 16:5 Ahaz, but could not o. him. 3898
Ca 6:5 from me, for they have o. me: 7292
Isa 28:1 of them that are o. with wine! 1986
Jer 23:9 like a man whom wine hath o., 5674
Lu 11:22 **shall come upon him, and o. him,** *3528*
Joh 16:33 **of good cheer; I have o. the world.** *3528*
Ro 3:4 mightest o. when thou art judged. *3528*
Ro 12:21 Be not o. of evil, *3528*
Ro 12:21 but o. evil with good. *3528*
2Pe 2:19 for of whom a man is o., of the *2274*
2Pe 2:20 again entangled therein, and o., *2274*
1Jo 2:13 because ye have o. the wicked one. *3528*
1Jo 2:14 and ye have o. the wicked one. *3528*
1Jo 4:4 little children, and have o. them: *3528*
Re 11:7 and shall o. them, and kill them. *3528*
Re 13:7 with the saints, and to o. them: *3528*
Re 17:14 Lamb, and the Lamb shall o. them: *3528*

OVERCOMETH
1Jo 5:4 is born of God o. the world: and *3528*
1Jo 5:4 is the victory that o. the world, *3528*
1Jo 5:5 Who is he that o. the world, but *3528*
Re 2:7 **To him that o. will I give to eat of** *3528*
Re 2:11 **He that o. shall not be hurt of the** *3528*
Re 2:17 **To him that o. will I give to eat of** *3528*
Re 2:26 **he that o., and keepeth my works** *3528*
Re 3:5 **He that o., the same shall be** *3528*
Re 3:12 **Him that o. will I make a pillar in** *3528*
Re 3:21 **To him that o. will I grant to sit** *3528*
Re 21:7 He that o. shall inherit all things; *3528*

OVERDRIVE
Ge 33:13 if men should o. them one day, 1849

OVERFLOW See also OVERFLOWED; OVERFLOWETH; OVERFLOWING; OVERFLOWN.
De 11:4 water of the Red sea to o. them 6687
Ps 69:2 waters, where the floods o. me. 7857
Ps 69:15 Let not the waterflood o. me, 7857
Isa 8:8 he shall o. and go over, he shall 7857
Isa 10:22 decreed shall o. with righteousness. 7857
Isa 28:17 waters shall o. the hiding place. 7857
Isa 43:2 the rivers, they shall not o. thee: 7857
Jer 47:2 shall o. the land, and all that is 7857
Da 11:10 one shall certainly come, and o., 7857
Da 11:26 destroy him, and his army shall o.: 7857
Da 11:40 and shall o. and pass over. 7857
Joe 2:24 the fats shall o. with wine and oil. 7783
Joe 3:13 for the press is full, the fats o.; 7783

OVERFLOWED
Ps 78:20 gushed out, and the streams o.; 7857
2Pe 3:6 was, being o. with water, perished: *2626*

OVERFLOWETH
Jos 3:15 Jordan o. all his banks all the 4390

OVERFLOWING
Job 28:11 He bindeth the floods from o.; 1065
Job 38:25 watercourse for the o. of waters, 7858
Isa 28:2 a flood of mighty waters o., shall 7857
Isa 28:15, 18 when the o. scourge shall pass 7857
Isa 30:28 And his breath, as an o. stream, 7857
Jer 47:2 and shall be an o. flood, and shall 7857
Eze 13:11 there shall be an o. shower; and 7857
Eze 13:13 be an o. shower in mine anger, 7857
Eze 38:22 an o. rain, and great hailstones, 7857
Hab 3:10 the o. of the water passed by: the 2230

OVERFLOWN
1Ch 12:15 when it had o. all his banks; and 4390
Job 22:16 foundation was o. with a flood: 3332
Da 11:22 shall they be o. from before him, 7857

OVERLAID
Ex 26:32 of shittim wood o. with gold: 6823
Ex 36:34 he o. the boards with gold, and 6823
Ex 36:34 the bars, and o. the bars with gold. 6823
Ex 36:36 wood, and o. them with gold: 6823
Ex 36:38 and he o. their chapiters and their 6823
Ex 37:2 And he o. it with pure gold within 6823
Ex 37:4 wood, and o. them with gold. 6823
Ex 37:11 he o. it with pure gold, and made 6823
Ex 37:15 o. them with gold, to bear the table. 6823
Ex 37:26 And he o. it with pure gold, both 6823
Ex 37:28 wood, and o. them with gold. 6823
Ex 38:2 the same: and he o. it with brass. 6823
Ex 38:6 wood, and o. them with brass. 6823
Ex 38:28 o. their chapiters, and filleted them. 6823
1Ki 3:19 in the night; because she o. it. 7901
1Ki 6:20 and he o. it with pure gold; and 6823
1Ki 6:21 Solomon o. the house within with 6823
1Ki 6:21 the oracle; and he o. it with gold. 6823
1Ki 6:22 the whole house he o. with gold, 6823
1Ki 6:22 altar...by the oracle he o. with gold. 6823
1Ki 6:28 And he o. the cherubims with gold. 6823
1Ki 6:30 floor of the house he o. with gold, 6823
1Ki 6:32 flowers, and o. them with gold, 6823
1Ki 10:18 ivory, and o. it with the best gold. 6823
2Ki 18:16 Hezekiah king of Judah had o., 6823
2Ch 3:4 and he o. it within with pure gold. 6823
2Ch 3:5 which he o. with fine gold, and set 2645
2Ch 3:7 He o. also the house, the beams, 2645
2Ch 3:8 cubits: and he o. it with fine gold, 2645
2Ch 3:9 o. the upper chambers with gold. 2645
2Ch 3:10 work, and o. them with gold. 6823
2Ch 4:9 and o. the doors of them with brass. 6823
2Ch 9:17 of ivory, and o. it with pure gold. 6823
Ca 5:14 as bright ivory o. with sapphires. 5968
Heb 9:4 covenant o. round about with gold, *4028*

OVERLAY See also OVERLAID.
Ex 25:11 thou shalt o. it with pure gold, 6823
Ex 25:11 within and without shalt thou o. it, 6823
Ex 25:13 wood, and o. them with gold. 6823
Ex 25:24 thou shalt o. it with pure gold, and 6823
Ex 25:28 wood, and o. them with gold, 6823
Ex 26:29 thou shalt o. the boards with gold, 6823
Ex 26:29 thou shalt o. the bars with gold. 6823
Ex 26:37 o. them with gold, and their hooks 6823
Ex 27:2 and thou shalt o. it with brass. 6823
Ex 27:6 wood, and o. them with brass. 6823
Ex 30:3 shalt o. it with pure gold, the top 6823
Ex 30:5 wood, and o. them with gold. 6823
1Ch 29:4 to o. the walls of the houses 2902

OVERLAYING
Ex 38:17 the o. of their chapiters of silver; 6826
Ex 38:19 the o. of their chapiters and their 6826

OVERLIVED
Jos 24:31 the elders that o. Joshua, 748,3117,310

OVERMUCH
2Co 2:7 be swallowed up with o. sorrow. *4055*

OVERPASS See also OVERPAST.
Jer 5:28 they o. the deeds of the wicked: 5674

OVERPAST
Ps 57:1 until these calamities be o. 5674
Isa 26:20 until the indignation be o.. 5674

OVERPLUS
Le 25:27 and restore the o. unto the man to 5736

OVERRAN
2Sa 18:23 way of the plain, and o. Cushi. 5674

OVERRUNNING
Na 1:8 But with an o. flood he will make 5674

OVERSEE
1Ch 9:29 also were appointed to o. the vessels,
2Ch 2:2 and six hundred to o. them. 5329

OVERSEER See also OVERSEERS.
Ge 39:4 he made him o. over his house, 6485
Ge 39:5 he had made him o. in his house, 6485
Ne 11:9 the son of Zichri was their o.: 6496
Ne 11:14 their o. was Zabdiel, the son of one 6496
Ne 11:22 o. also of the Levites at Jerusalem 6496
Ne 12:42 sang loud, with Jezrahiah their o.. 6496
Pr 6:7 having no guide, o., or ruler, 7860

OVERSEERS
2Ch 2:18 o. to set the people a work. 5329
2Ch 31:13 o. under the hand of Cononiah 6496
2Ch 34:12 the o. of them were Jahath and 6485
2Ch 34:13 o. of all that wrought the work in 5329
2Ch 34:17 it into the hand of the o., and to 6485
Ac 20:28 the Holy Ghost hath made you o., *1985*

OVERSHADOW See also OVERSHADOWED.
Lu 1:35 power of the Highest shall o. thee: *1982*
Ac 5:15 Peter passing by might o. some *1982*

OVERSHADOWED
Mt 17:5 behold, a bright cloud o. them: *1982*
Mk 9:7 there was a cloud that o. them: *1982*
Lu 9:34 there came a cloud, and o. them: *1982*

OVERSIGHT
Ge 43:12 hand; peradventure it was an o. 4870
Nu 3:32 o. of them that keep the charge of 6486
Nu 4:16 the o. of all the tabernacle, and of 6486
2Ki 12:11 the o. of the house of the Lord: 6485
2Ki 22:5 the o. of the house of the Lord: 6485
2Ki 22:9 the o. of the house of the Lord. 6485
1Ch 9:23 had the o. of the gates of the house 5921
2Ch 34:10 the o. of the house of the Lord, 6485

Ne 11:16 had the **o.** of the outward business 5921
Ne 13:4 having the **o.** of the chamber of 5414
1Pe 5:2 among you, taking the **o.** thereof, *1983*

OVERSPREAD See also OVERSPREADING.
Ge 9:19 of them was the whole earth **o.** 5310

OVERSPREADING
Da 9:27 and for the **o.** of abominations he 3671

OVERTAKE See also OVERTAKE; OVERTAKETH.
Ge 44:4 when thou dost **o.** them, say unto 5381
Ex 15:9 enemy said, I will pursue, I will **o.**, 5381
De 19:6 while his heart is hot, and **o.** him, 5381
De 28:2 shall come on thee, and **o.** thee, 5381
De 28:15 shall come upon thee, and **o.** thee: 5381
De 28:45 and shall pursue thee, and **o.** thee, 5381
Jos 2:5 them quickly; for ye shall **o.** them. 5381
1Sa 30:8 after this troop? shall I **o.** them? 5381
1Sa 30:8 for thou shalt surely **o.** them, and 5381
2Sa 15:14 lest he **o.** us suddenly, and bring 5381
Isa 59:9 from us, neither doth justice **o.** us: 5381
Jer 42:16 sword, which ye feared, shall **o.** you 5381
Ho 2:7 lovers, but she shall not **o.** them; 5381
Ho 10:9 children of iniquity did not **o.** them. 5381
Am 9:10 evil shall not **o.** nor prevent us. 5066
Am 9:13 the plowman shall **o.** the reaper, 5066
1Th 5:4 that day should **o.** you as a thief. *2638*

OVERTAKEN
Ps 18:37 mine enemies, and **o.** them: 5381
Ga 6:1 Brethren, if a man be **o.** in a fault, *4301*

OVERTAKETH
1Ch 21:12 sword of thine enemies **o.** thee; 5381

OVERTHREW
Ge 19:15 And he **o.** those cities, and all the 2015
Ge 19:29 he **o.** the cities in which Lot dwelt. 2015
Ex 14:27 and the Lord **o.** the Egyptians in 5287
De 29:23 which the Lord **o.** in his anger, 2015
Ps 136:15 But **o.** Pharaoh and his host in the 5286
Isa 13:19 God **o.** Sodom and Gomorrah, 4114
Jer 20:16 be as the cities which the Lord **o.**, 2015
Jer 50:40 As God **o.** Sodom and Gomorrah 4114
Am 4:11 as God **o.** Sodom and Gomorrah. 4114
Mt 21:12 **o.** the tables of…moneychangers, *2690*
Mk 11:15 **o.** the tables of the moneychangers, *2690*
Joh 2:15 changers' money, and **o.** the tables; *390*

OVERTHROW See also OVERTHREW; OVERTHROWETH; OVERTHROWN.
Ge 19:21 also, that I will not **o.** this city, 2015
Ge 19:29 sent Lot out of the midst of the **o.**, 2018
Ex 23:24 but thou shalt utterly **o.** them, 2040
De 12:3 ye shall **o.** their altars, and break 5422
De 29:23 therein, like the **o.** of Sodom, and 4114
2Sa 10:3 and to spy it out, and to **o.** it? 2015
2Sa 11:25 strong against the city, and **o.** it: 2040
1Ch 19:3 and to **o.**, and to spy out the land? 2015
Ps 106:26 to **o.** them in the wilderness: 5307
Ps 106:27 To **o.** their seed also among the 5307
Ps 140:4 have purposed to **o.** my goings. 1760
Ps 140:11 hunt the violent man to **o.** him. 4073
Pr 18:5 to **o.** the righteous in judgment. 5186
Jer 49:18 in the **o.** of Sodom and Gomorrah 4114
Hag 2:22 I will **o.** the throne of kingdoms, 2015
Hag 2:22 I will **o.** the chariots, and those 2015
Ac 5:39 if it be of God, ye cannot **o.** it; *2647*
2Ti 2:18 already; and **o.** the faith of some. *396*
2Pe 2:6 condemned them with an **o.**, *2692*

OVERTHROWETH
Job 12:19 away spoiled, and **o.** the mighty. 5557
Pr 13:6 but wickedness **o.** the sinner. 5557
Pr 21:12 but God **o.** the wicked for their 5557
Pr 22:12 **o.** the words of the transgressor. 5557
Pr 29:4 but he that receiveth gifts **o.** it. 2040

OVERTHROWN
Ex 15:7 hast **o.** them that rose up against 2040
Jg 9:40 and many were **o.** and wounded, 5307
2Sa 17:9 some of them be **o.** at the first. 5307
2Ch 14:13 and the Ethiopians were **o.**, that 5307
Job 19:6 Know now that God hath **o.** me, 5791
Ps 141:6 judges are **o.** in stony places, 8058
Pr 11:11 it is **o.** by the mouth of the wicked. 2040
Pr 12:7 The wicked are **o.**, and are not: 2015
Pr 14:11 house of the wicked shall be **o.**: 8045
Isa 1:7 it is desolate, as **o.** by strangers. 4114
Jer 18:23 but let them be **o.** before thee; 3782
La 4:6 that was **o.** as in a moment, and 2015
Da 11:41 and many countries shall be **o.**: 3782
Am 4:11 I have **o.** some of you, as God 2015
Jon 3:4 days, and Nineveh shall be **o.** 2015
1Co 10:5 for they were **o.** in the wilderness. *2693*

OVERTOOK
Ge 31:23 they **o.** him in the mount Gilead. 1692
Ge 31:25 Then Laban **o.** Jacob. Now 5381
Ge 44:6 And he **o.** them, and he spake unto 5381
Ex 14:9 and **o.** them encamping by the sea, 5381
Jg 18:22 and **o.** the children of Dan. 1692
Jg 20:42 but the battle **o.** them; and them 1692
2Ki 25:5 and **o.** him in the plains of Jericho: 5381
Jer 39:5 **o.** Zedekiah in the plains of Jericho: 5381
Jer 52:8 **o.** Zedekiah in the plains of Jericho; 5381
La 1:3 **o.** her between the straits. 5381

OVERTURN See also OVERTURNED; OVERTURNETH.
Job 12:15 them out, and they **o.** the earth. 2015
Eze 21:27 I will **o.**, **o.**, **o.**, it: and it shall be 5754

OVERTURNED
Jg 7:13 and **o.** it, that the tent lay along. 2015

OVERTURNETH
Job 9:5 not: which **o.** them in his anger; 2015
Job 28:9 he **o.** the mountains by the roots. 2015
Job 34:25 and he **o.** them in the night, so 2015

OVERWHELM See also OVERWHELMED.
Job 6:27 Yea, ye **o.** the fatherless, and ye 5307

OVERWHELMED
Ps 55:5 upon me, and horror hath **o.** me. 3680
Ps 61:2 unto thee, when my heart is **o.**: 5848
Ps 77:3 and my spirit was **o.** Selah. 5848
Ps 78:53 not: but the sea **o.** their enemies. 3680
Ps 102:*title* of the afflicted, when he is **o.**, 5848
Ps 124:4 Then the waters had **o.** us, the 7857
Ps 142:3 When my spirit was **o.** within me, 5848
Ps 143:4 is my spirit **o.** within me; my 5848

OWE See also OWED; OWEST; OWETH.
Ro 13:8 **O.** no man any thing, but to love *3784*

OWED
Mt 18:24 **o. him ten thousand talents.** *3781*
Mt 18:28 **which o. him an hundred pence:** *3784*
Lu 7:41 **the one o. five hundred pence, and** *3784*

OWEST
Mt 18:28 **saying, Pay me that thou o.** *3784*
Lu 16:5 **How much o. thou unto my lord?** *3784*
Lu 16:7 **another, And how much o. thou?** *3784*
Phm 19 **o.** unto me even thine own self. *4359*

OWETH
Phm 18 wronged thee, or **o.** thee ought, *3784*

OWL See also OWLS.
Le 11:16 the **o.**, and the night hawk, 1323,3284
Le 11:17 the little **o.**, and the cormorant, 3563
Le 11:17 the cormorant, and the great **o.**, 3244
De 14:15 the **o.**, and the night hawk, 1323,3284
De 14:16 the little **o.**, and the…swan, 3563
De 14:16 and the great **o.**, and the swan, 3244
Ps 102:6 I am like an **o.** of the desert. 3563
Isa 34:11 the **o.** also and the raven shall 3244
Isa 34:14 screech **o.** also shall rest there, 3917
Isa 34:15 shall the great **o.** make her nest, 7091

OWLS
Job 30:29 and a companion to **o.** 1323,3284
Isa 13:21 and **o.** shall dwell there, and 1323,3284
Isa 34:13 dragons, and a court for **o.** 1323,3284
Isa 43:20 me, the dragons and the **o.**: 1323,3284
Jer 50:39 and the **o.** shall dwell therein: 1323,3284
Mic 1:8 and mourning as the **o.** 1323,3284

OWN See also OWNETH.
Ge 1:27 So God created man in his **o.** image,
Ge 5:3 begat a son in his **o.** likeness,
Ge 14:14 trained servants, born in his **o.** house,
Ge 15:4 come forth out of thine **o.** bowels
Ge 30:25 that I may go unto mine **o.** place, and
Ge 30:30 shall I provide for mine **o.** house also?
Ge 30:40 and he put his **o.** flocks by themselves,
Ge 47:24 four parts shall be your **o.**, for seed
Ex 5:16 but the fault is in thine **o.** people
Ex 18:27 and he went his way into his **o.** land.
Ex 21:36 for ox; and the dead shall be his **o.**
Ex 22:5 man's field; of the best of his **o.** field,
Ex 22:5 and of the best of his **o.** vineyard,
Ex 32:13 to whom thou swarest by thine **o.** self,
Le 1:3 shall offer it of his **o.** voluntary will
Le 7:30 His **o.** hands…bring the offerings
Le 14:15 into the palm of his **o.** left hand: 3548
Le 14:26 into the palm of his **o.** left hand: 3548
Le 16:29 it be one of your **o.** country, or a 249
Le 17:15 whether it be one of your **o.** country, 249
Le 18:10 for theirs is thine **o.** nakedness.
Le 18:26 neither any of your **o.** nation, nor 249
Le 19:5 Lord, ye shall offer it at your **o.** will.
Le 21:14 take a virgin of his **o.** people to wife.
Le 22:19 offer at your **o.** will a male without
Le 22:29 unto the Lord, offer it at your **o.** will.
Le 24:22 as for one of your **o.** country: for I 249
Le 25:5 which groweth of its **o.** accord of thy
Le 25:41 and shall return unto his **o.** family,
Nu 1:52 their tents, every man by his **o.** camp,
Nu 1:52 and every man by his **o.** standard,
Nu 2:2 shall pitch by his **o.** standard, with
Nu 10:30 but I will depart to mine **o.** land, and
Nu 13:33 were in our **o.** sight as grasshoppers,
Nu 15:39 that ye seek not after your **o.** heart
Nu 15:39 and your **o.** eyes, after which ye use to
Nu 16:28 have not done them of mine **o.** mind.
Nu 16:38 of these sinners against their **o.** souls,
Nu 24:13 do either good or bad of mine **o.** mind:
Nu 27:3 but died in his **o.** sin, and had no sons
Nu 32:42 and called it Nobah, after his **o.** name.
Nu 36:9 shall keep himself to his **o.** inheritance.
De 3:14 and called them after his **o.** name,
De 12:8 man whatsoever is right in his **o.** eyes.
De 13:6 or thy friend, which is as thine **o.** soul,
De 22:2 shalt bring it unto thine **o.** house,
De 23:24 eat grapes thy fill at thine **o.** pleasure;
De 24:13 sleep in his **o.** raiment, and bless thee:
De 24:16 shall be put to death for his **o.** sin.
De 28:53 shalt eat the fruit of thine **o.** body,
De 33:9 brethren, nor knew his **o.** children:
Jos 7:11 have put it even among their **o.** stuff.
Jos 20:6 come unto his **o.** city, and unto his
Jos 20:6 and unto his **o.** house, unto the city
Jg 2:19 they ceased not from their **o.** doings,
Jg 7:2 saying, Mine **o.** hand hath saved me.
Jg 8:29 Joash went and dwelt in his **o.** house
Jg 17:6 that which was right in his **o.** eyes.
Jg 21:25 that which was right in his **o.** eyes.
Ru 4:6 lest I mar mine **o.** inheritance:
1Sa 2:20 And they went unto their **o.** home.
1Sa 5:11 and let it go again to his **o.** place,
1Sa 6:9 way of his **o.** coast to Beth-shemesh,
1Sa 13:14 sought him a man after his **o.** heart,
1Sa 14:46 the Philistines went to their **o.** place.
1Sa 15:17 thou wast little in thine **o.** sight,
1Sa 18:1 Jonathan loved him as his **o.** soul.
1Sa 18:3 because he loved him as his **o.** soul.
1Sa 20:17 for he loved him as he loved his **o.** soul.
1Sa 20:30 the son of Jesse to thine **o.** confusion,
1Sa 25:26 avenging thyself with thine **o.** hand,
1Sa 25:33 avenging myself with mine **o.** hand.
1Sa 25:39 wickedness of Nabal upon his **o.** head.
1Sa 28:3 buried him in Ramah,…in his **o.** city.
2Sa 4:11 a righteous person in his **o.** house
2Sa 6:22 and will be base in mine **o.** sight:
2Sa 7:10 they may dwell in a place of their **o.**,
2Sa 7:21 sake, and according to thine **o.** heart,
2Sa 12:3 it did eat of his **o.** meat, and drank of
2Sa 12:3 drank of his **o.** cup, and lay in his
2Sa 12:4 take of his **o.** flock and of his **o.** herd,
2Sa 12:11 against thee out of thine **o.** house,
2Sa 12:20 then he came to his **o.** house; and
2Sa 14:24 said, Let him turn to his **o.** house,
2Sa 14:24 So Absalom returned to his **o.** house,
2Sa 17:11 go to battle in thine **o.** person.
2Sa 18:13 wrought falsehood against mine **o.** life:
2Sa 18:18 he called the pillar after his **o.** name:
2Sa 19:28 them that did eat at thine **o.** table.
2Sa 19:30 come again in peace unto his **o.** house.
2Sa 19:37 that I may die in mine **o.** city, and be
2Sa 19:39 him; and he returned unto his **o.** place.
2Sa 23:21 hand, and slew him with his **o.** spear.
1Ki 1:12 that thou mayest save thine **o.** life, and
1Ki 1:33 my son to ride upon mine **o.** mule,
1Ki 2:23 spoken this word against his **o.** life.
1Ki 2:26 thee to Anathoth, unto thine **o.** fields;

1Ki 2:32 return his blood upon his **o.** head,
1Ki 2:34 buried in his **o.** house in the wilderness,
1Ki 2:37 thy blood shall be upon thine **o.** head.
1Ki 2:44 thy wickedness upon thine **o.** head;
1Ki 3:1 made an end of building his **o.** house,
1Ki 7:1 Solomon was building his **o.** house
1Ki 8:38 every man the plague of his **o.** heart,
1Ki 9:15 house of the Lord, and his **o.** house,
1Ki 10:6 I heard in mine **o.** land of thy acts
1Ki 10:13 she turned and went to her **o.** country,
1Ki 11:19 him to wife the sister of his **o.** wife,
1Ki 11:21 that I may go to mine **o.** country.
1Ki 11:22 thou seekest to go to thine **o.** country?
1Ki 12:16 now see to thine **o.** house, David.
1Ki 12:33 which he had devised of his **o.** heart;
1Ki 13:30 And he laid his carcase in his **o.** grave;
1Ki 14:12 therefore, get thee to thine **o.** house:
1Ki 17:19 abode, and laid him upon his **o.** bed.
1Ki 22:36 city, and every man to his **o.** country.
2Ki 2:12 he took hold of his **o.** clothes, and rent
2Ki 3:27 him, and returned to their **o.** land.
2Ki 4:13 I dwell among mine **o.** people.
2Ki 12:18 and his **o.** hallowed things, and all the
2Ki 14:6 man shall be put to death for his **o.** sin.
2Ki 17:23 away out of their **o.** land to Assyria
2Ki 17:29 every nation made gods of their **o.**,
2Ki 17:33 the Lord, and served their **o.** gods,
2Ki 18:27 they may eat their **o.** dung, and drink
2Ki 18:27 and drink their **o.** piss with you?
2Ki 18:31 then eat ye every man of his **o.** vine,
2Ki 18:32 you away to a land like your **o.** land,
2Ki 19:7 and shall return to his **o.** land; and
2Ki 19:7 him to fall by the sword in his **o.** land.
2Ki 19:34 this city, to save it, for mine **o.** sake,
2Ki 20:6 I will defend this city for mine **o.** sake,
2Ki 21:18 buried in the garden of his **o.** house,
2Ki 21:23 him, and slew the king in his **o.** house.
2Ki 23:30 and buried him in his **o.** sepulchre.
1Ch 11:23 hand, and slew him with his **o.** spear.
1Ch 17:19 according to thine **o.** heart, hast thou
1Ch 17:21 went to redeem to be his **o.** people,
1Ch 17:22 thou make thine **o.** people for ever;
1Ch 29:3 I have of mine **o.** proper good, of gold
1Ch 29:14 and of thine **o.** have we given thee.
1Ch 29:16 of thine hand, and is all thine **o.**.
2Ch 6:23 his way upon his **o.** head;
2Ch 6:29 know his **o.** sore and his **o.** grief,
2Ch 7:11 in his **o.** house, he prosperously
2Ch 8:1 house of the Lord, and his **o.** house,
2Ch 9:5 I heard in mine **o.** land of thine acts,
2Ch 9:12 and went away to her **o.** land, she
2Ch 10:16 and now, David, see to thine **o.** house.
2Ch 16:14 they buried him in his **o.** sepulchres,
2Ch 24:25 his **o.** servants conspired against him
2Ch 25:4 but every man shall die for his **o.** sin.
2Ch 25:15 their **o.** people out of thine hand?
2Ch 31:1 to his possession, into their **o.** cities.
2Ch 32:21 with shame of face to his **o.** land.
2Ch 32:21 they that came forth of his **o.** bowels
2Ch 33:20 and they buried him in his **o.** house:
2Ch 33:24 him, and slew him in his **o.** house
Ezr 7:13 are minded of their **o.** freewill to
Ne 4:4 their reproach upon their **o.** head,
Ne 6:8 feignest them out of thine **o.** heart.
Ne 6:16 were much cast down in their **o.** eyes:
Es 1:22 man should bear rule in his **o.** house,
Es 2:7 were dead, took for his **o.** daughter.
Es 9:25 Jews, should return upon his **o.** head,
Job 2:11 they came every one from his **o.** place;
Job 5:13 taketh the wise in their **o.** craftiness:
Job 9:20 mine **o.** mouth shall condemn me:
Job 9:31 and mine **o.** clothes shall abhor me.
Job 13:15 maintain mine **o.** ways before him.
Job 15:6 Thine **o.** mouth condemneth thee, and
Job 15:6 yea, thine **o.** lips testify against thee.
Job 18:7 his **o.** counsel shall cast him down.
Job 18:8 For he is cast into a net by his **o.** feet,
Job 19:17 the children's sake of mine **o.** body.
Job 20:7 shall perish for ever like his **o.** dung:
Job 32:1 he was righteous in his **o.** eyes.
Job 40:14 that thine **o.** right hand can save thee.
Ps 4:4 commune with your **o.** heart upon
Ps 5:10 let them fall by their **o.** counsels;
Ps 7:16 mischief shall return upon his **o.** head,
Ps 7:16 shall come down upon his **o.** pate.
Ps 9:15 which they hid is their **o.** foot taken.
Ps 9:16 is snared in the work of his **o.** hands.

Ps 12:4 our lips are our **o.**: who is lord over
Ps 15:4 He that sweareth to his **o.** hurt, and
Ps 17:10 They are inclosed in their **o.** fat: with
Ps 20:4 Grant thee according to thine **o.** heart,
Ps 21:13 exalted, Lord, in thine **o.** strength:
Ps 22:29 and none can keep alive his **o.** soul.
Ps 33:12 he hath chosen for his **o.** inheritance.
Ps 35:13 prayer returned into mine **o.** bosom.
Ps 36:2 he flattereth himself in his **o.** eyes,
Ps 37:15 sword shall enter into their **o.** heart,
Ps 41:9 mine **o.** familiar friend, in whom I
Ps 44:3 land in possession by their **o.** sword,
Ps 44:3 neither did their **o.** arm save them:
Ps 45:10 forget also thine **o.** people, and thy
Ps 49:11 call their lands after their **o.** names.
Ps 50:20 thou slanderest thine **o.** mother's son.
Ps 64:8 their **o.** tongue to fall upon themselves:
Ps 67:6 God, even our **o.** God, shall bless us.
Ps 74:22 Arise, O God, plead thine **o.** cause:
Ps 77:6 I commune with mine **o.** heart: and
Ps 78:29 for he gave them their **o.** desire;
Ps 78:52 his **o.** people to go forth like sheep,
Ps 81:12 gave them up unto their **o.** hearts' lust:
Ps 81:12 and they walked in their **o.** counsels.
Ps 94:23 bring upon them their **o.** iniquity,
Ps 94:23 cut them off in their **o.** wickedness;
Ps 106:39 were they defiled with their **o.** works,
Ps 106:39 a whoring with their **o.** inventions.
Ps 106:40 that he abhorred his **o.** inheritance.
Ps 109:29 their **o.** confusion as with a mantle,
Ps 138:8 forsake not the works of thine **o.** hands.
Ps 140:9 mischief of their **o.** lips cover them.
Ps 141:10 Let the wicked fall into their **o.** nets,
Pr 1:18 And they lay wait for their **o.** blood;
Pr 1:18 they lurk privily for their **o.** lives.
Pr 1:31 they eat of the fruit of their **o.** way,
Pr 1:31 and be filled with their **o.** devices.
Pr 3:5 lean not unto thine **o.** understanding.
Pr 3:7 Be not wise in thine **o.** eyes: fear the
Pr 5:15 Drink water out of thine **o.** cistern,
Pr 5:15 running waters out of thine **o.** well.
Pr 5:17 Let them be only thine **o.**, and not
Pr 5:22 His **o.** inquities shall take the wicked
Pr 6:32 that doeth it destroyeth his **o.** soul.
Pr 8:36 that sinneth…wrongeth his **o.** soul:
Pr 11:5 wicked shall fall by his **o.** wickedness.
Pr 11:6 shall be taken in their **o.** naughtiness.
Pr 11:17 merciful man doeth good to his **o.** soul:
Pr 11:19 evil pursueth it to his **o.** death.
Pr 11:29 He that troubleth his **o.** house shall
Pr 12:15 way of a fool is right in his **o.** eyes:
Pr 14:10 heart knoweth his **o.** bitterness; 5315
Pr 14:14 in heart shall be filled with his **o.** ways:
Pr 14:20 poor is hated even of his **o.** neighbour:
Pr 15:27 greedy of gain troubleth his **o.** house;
Pr 15:32 instruction despiseth his **o.** soul:
Pr 16:2 ways of a man are clean in his **o.** eyes;
Pr 18:11 as an high wall in his **o.** conceit.
Pr 18:17 is first in his **o.** cause seemeth just;
Pr 19:8 that getteth wisdom loveth his **o.** soul:
Pr 19:16 commandment keepeth his **o.** soul;
Pr 20:2 to anger sinneth against his **o.** soul.
Pr 20:6 proclaim every one his **o.** goodness:
Pr 20:24 a man then understand his **o.** way?
Pr 21:2 way of a man is right in his **o.** eyes:
Pr 23:4 be rich: cease from thine **o.** wisdom.
Pr 25:27 to search their **o.** glory is not glory
Pr 25:28 he that hath no rule over his **o.** spirit
Pr 26:5 lest he be wise in his **o.** conceit.
Pr 26:12 thou a man wise in his **o.** conceit?
Pr 26:16 sluggard is wiser in his **o.** conceit
Pr 27:2 praise thee, and not thine **o.** mouth;
Pr 27:2 a stranger, and not thine **o.** lips.
Pr 27:10 Thine **o.** friend, and thy father's friend,
Pr 28:10 he shall fall himself into his **o.** pit:
Pr 28:11 rich man is wise in his **o.** conceit;
Pr 28:26 that trusteth in his **o.** heart is a fool:
Pr 29:24 partner with a thief hateth his **o.** soul:
Pr 30:12 that are pure in their **o.** eyes, and yet
Pr 31:31 let her **o.** works praise her in the gates.
Ec 1:16 I communed with mine **o.** heart,
Ec 3:22 a man should rejoice in his **o.** works;
Ec 4:5 hands together, and eateth his **o.** flesh.
Ec 7:22 thine **o.** heart knoweth that thou thyself
Ec 8:9 ruleth over another to his **o.** hurt.
Ca 1:6 but mine **o.** vineyard have I not kept.
Isa 2:8 worship the work of their **o.** hands,

Isa 2:8 that which their **o.** fingers have made:
Isa 4:1 saying, We will eat our **o.** bread,
Isa 4:1 and wear our **o.** apparel: only let us
Isa 5:21 them that are wise in their **o.** eyes,
Isa 5:21 eyes, and prudent in their **o.** sight!
Isa 9:20 eat every man the flesh of his **o.** arm:
Isa 13:14 shall every man turn to his **o.** people,
Isa 13:14 and flee every one into his **o.** land.
Isa 14:1 Israel, and set them in their **o.** land:
Isa 14:18 lie in glory, every one in his **o.** house.
Isa 23:7 her **o.** feet shall carry her afar off to
Isa 31:7 which your **o.** hands have made unto
Isa 36:12 they may eat their **o.** dung, and drink
Isa 36:12 dung, and drink their **o.** piss with you?
Isa 36:16 every one the waters of his **o.** cistern;
Isa 36:17 you away to a land like your **o.** land,
Isa 37:7 a rumour, and return to his **o.** land;
Isa 37:7 to fall by the sword in his **o.** land.
Isa 37:35 this city to save it for mine **o.** sake,
Isa 43:25 thy transgressions for mine **o.** sake,
Isa 44:9 they are their **o.** witness; they see
Isa 48:11 mine **o.** sake, even for mine **o.** sake,
Isa 49:26 that oppress thee with their **o.** flesh;
Isa 49:26 shall be drunken with their **o.** blood,
Isa 53:6 have turned every one to his **o.** way;
Isa 56:11 they all look to their **o.** way, every one
Isa 58:7 hide not thyself from thine **o.** flesh?
Isa 58:13 honour him, not doing thine **o.** ways,
Isa 58:13 nor finding thine **o.** pleasure,
Isa 58:13 nor speaking thine **o.** words:
Isa 63:5 mine **o.** arm brought salvation unto
Isa 65:2 was not good; after their **o.** thoughts;
Isa 66:3 Yea, they have chosen their **o.** ways,
Jer 1:16 worshipped the works of their **o.** hands.
Jer 2:19 Thine **o.** wickedness shall correct
Jer 2:30 **o.** sword hath devoured your prophets,
Jer 7:19 to the confusion of their **o.** faces?
Jer 9:14 after the imagination of their **o.** heart,
Jer 18:12 but we will walk after our **o.** devices,
Jer 23:8 and they shall dwell in their **o.** land.
Jer 23:16 they speak a vision of their **o.** heart,
Jer 23:17 after the imagination of his **o.** heart,
Jer 23:26 prophets of the deceit of their **o.** heart;
Jer 25:7 works of your hands to your **o.** hurt.
Jer 25:14 to the works of their **o.** hands.
Jer 27:11 will I let remain still in their **o.** land,
Jer 30:18 shall be builded upon her **o.** heap,
Jer 31:17 shall come again to their **o.** border.
Jer 31:30 every one shall die for his **o.** iniquity:
Jer 37:7 return to Egypt into their **o.** land.
Jer 42:12 cause you to return to your **o.** land.
Jer 44:9 their wives, and your **o.** wickedness,
Jer 44:17 thing goeth forth out of our **o.** mouth,
Jer 46:16 and let us go again to our **o.** people,
Jer 50:16 they shall flee every one to his **o.** land.
Jer 51:9 let us go every one into his **o.** country:
Jer 52:27 away captive out of his **o.** land.
La 4:10 women have sodden their **o.** children:
Eze 11:21 their way upon their **o.** heads,
Eze 13:2 that prophesy out of their **o.** hearts,
Eze 13:3 prophets, that follow their **o.** spirit,
Eze 13:17 which prophesy out of their **o.** heart;
Eze 14:5 the house of Israel in their **o.** heart,
Eze 14:14 should deliver but their **o.** souls
Eze 14:20 shall but deliver their **o.** souls.
Eze 16:6 saw thee polluted in thine **o.** blood,
Eze 16:15 thou didst trust in thine **o.** beauty,
Eze 16:52 bear thine **o.** shame for thy sins that
Eze 16:54 thou mayest bear thine **o.** shame,
Eze 17:19 will I recompense upon his **o.** head.
Eze 20:26 And I polluted them in their **o.** gifts,
Eze 20:43 shall lothe yourselves in your **o.** sight
Eze 22:31 their **o.** way have I recompensed upon
Eze 23:34 thereof, and pluck off thine **o.** breasts:
Eze 29:3 My river is mine **o.**, and I have made
Eze 32:10 every man for his **o.** life, in the day
Eze 33:4 his blood shall be upon his **o.** head.
Eze 33:13 if he trust to his **o.** righteousness,
Eze 34:13 and will bring them to their **o.** land,
Eze 36:17 house of Israel dwelt in their **o.** land,
Eze 36:17 they defiled it by their **o.** way and by
Eze 36:24 and will bring you into your **o.** land.
Eze 36:31 shall ye remember your **o.** evil ways,
Eze 36:31 shall lothe yourselves in your **o.** sight
Eze 36:32 and confounded for your **o.** ways,
Eze 37:14 and I shall place you in your **o.** land:

Eze 37:21 and bring them into their o. land:
Eze 39:28 have gathered them unto their o. land,
Eze 46:18 inheritance out of his o. possession:
Da 3:28 worship any god, except their o. God
Da 6:17 the king sealed it with his o. signet,
Da 8:24 be mighty, but not by his o. power:
Da 9:19 defer not, for thine o. sake, O my God:
Da 11:9 and shall return into his o. land.
Da 11:16 shall do according to his o. will, 7522
Da 11:18 a prince for his o. behalf shall cause
Da 11:18 without his o. reproach he shall cause
Da 11:19 face toward the fort of his o. land:
Da 11:28 do exploits, and return to his o. land.
Ho 7:2 now their o. doings have beset them.
Ho 10:6 shall be ashamed of his o. counsel.
Ho 11:6 them, because of their o. counsels.
Ho 13:2 according to their o. understanding,
Joe 3:4 your recompence upon your o. head;
Joe 3:7 your recompence upon your o. head:
Am 6:13 taken to us horns by our o. strength?
Am 7:11 led away captive out of their o. land.
Ob 15 shall return upon thine o. head.
Jon 2:8 lying vanities forsake their o. mercy.
Mic 7:6 enemies are the men of his o. house.
Hag 1:9 ye run every man unto his o. house.
Zec 5:11 and set there upon her o. base.
Zec 11:5 and their o. shepherds pity them not.
Zec 12:6 be inhabited again in her o. place,
Mal 3:17 a man spareth his o. son that serveth
Mt 2:12 departed into their o. country another
Mt 7:3 the beam that is in thine o. eye?
Mt 7:4 behold, a beam is in thine o. eye?
Mt 7:5 cast out the beam out of thine o.
Mt 9:1 over, and came into his o. city. 2398
Mt 10:36 foes shall be they of his o. household
Mt 13:54 he was come into his o. country,
Mt 13:57 in his o. country, and in his o. house
Mt 16:26 whole world, and lose his o. soul?
Mt 17:25 of their o. children, or of strangers?
Mt 20:15 to do what I will with mine o.?
Mt 25:14 who called his o. servants, and 2398
Mt 25:27 have received mine o. with usury
Mt 27:31 and put his o. raiment on him, and
Mt 27:60 And laid it in his o. new tomb, which
Mk 6:1 and came into his o. country;
Mk 6:4 but in his o. country and among
Mk 6:4 his o. kin, and in his o. house
Mk 7:9 that ye may keep your o. tradition
Mk 8:3 away fasting to their o. houses,
Mk 8:36 whole world, and lose his o. soul?
Mk 15:20 and put his o. clothes on him, 2398
Lu 1:23 he departed to his o. house.
Lu 1:56 and returned to her o. house.
Lu 2:3 be taxed, every one into his o. city, 2398
Lu 2:35 sword pierce through thy o. soul also
Lu 2:39 into Galilee, to their o. city Nazareth.
Lu 4:24 is accepted in his o. country
Lu 5:25 lay, and departed to his o. house,
Lu 5:29 him a great feast in his o. house:
Lu 6:41 the beam that is in thine o. eye? 2398
Lu 6:42 not the beam that is in thine o. eye?
Lu 6:42 first the beam out of thine o. eye,
Lu 6:44 every tree is known by his o. fruit 2398
Lu 8:39 Return to thine o. house, and shew
Lu 9:26 when he shall come in his o. glory,
Lu 10:34 and set him on his o. beast, and 2398
Lu 14:26 his o. life also, he cannot be my 1438
Lu 16:12 shall give you that which is your o.?
Lu 18:7 shall not God avenge his o. elect,
Lu 19:22 Out of thine o. mouth I judge thee,
Lu 19:23 have required mine o. with usury?
Lu 21:30 know of your o. selves that summer
Lu 22:71 ourselves have heard of his o. 1438
Joh 1:11 He came unto his o., and his
Joh 1:11 and his o. received him not.
Joh 1:41 first findeth his o. brother Simon,
Joh 4:41 more believed because of his o. word;
Joh 4:44 hath no honour in his o. country. 2398
Joh 5:30 I can of mine o. self do nothing:
Joh 5:30 I seek not mine o. will, but the
Joh 5:43 another shall come in his o. name, 2398
Joh 6:38 not to do mine o. will, but the will
Joh 7:18 of himself seeketh his o. glory: 2398
Joh 7:53 every man went unto his o. house.
Joh 8:9 being convicted by their o. conscience,
Joh 8:44 a lie, he speaketh of his o.: 2398
Joh 8:50 I seek not mine o. glory: there is
Joh 10:3 he calleth his o. sheep by name, 2398
Joh 10:4 when he putteth forth his o. sheep, 2398
Joh 10:12 whose o. the sheep are not, 2398
Joh 13:1 loved his o. which were in the world, 2398
Joh 15:19 world, the world would love his o. 2398
Joh 16:32 be scattered, every man to his o., 2398
Joh 17:5 glorify thou me with thine o. self 4572
Joh 17:11 keep through thine o. name those
Joh 18:35 Thine o. nation and the chief priests
Joh 19:27 disciple took her unto his o. home. 2398
Joh 20:10 away again unto their o. home. 1438
Ac 1:7 Father hath put in his o. power 2398
Ac 1:25 that he might go to his o. place. 2398
Ac 2:6 them speak in his o. language. 2398
Ac 2:8 we every man in our o. tongue, 2398
Ac 3:12 by our o. power or holiness we had 2398
Ac 4:23 they went to their o. company, 2398
Ac 4:32 which he possessed was his o.; 2398
Ac 5:4 it remained, was it not thine o.?
Ac 5:4 sold, was it not in thine o. power?
Ac 7:21 and nourished him for her o. son. 1438
Ac 7:41 In the works of their o. hands.
Ac 12:10 opened to them of his o. accord: 848
Ac 13:22 a man after mine o. heart, which
Ac 13:36 he had served his o. generation by 2398
Ac 14:16 all nations to walk in their o. ways. 848
Ac 15:22 send chosen men of their o. company
Ac 17:28 also of your o. poets have said, 2596
Ac 18:6 Your blood be upon your o. heads;
Ac 20:28 hath purchased with his o. blood. 2398
Ac 20:30 Also of your o. selves shall men arise,
Ac 21:11 and bound his o. hands and feet, 848
Ac 25:19 against him of their o. superstition, 2398
Ac 26:4 mine o. nation at Jerusalem,
Ac 27:19 day we cast out with our o. hands 849
Ac 28:30 years in his o. hired house, and 2398
Ro 1:24 through the lusts of their o. hearts,
Ro 1:24 to dishonour their o. bodies between
Ro 4:19 he considered not his o. body now 1438
Ro 8:3 God sending his o. Son in the 1438
Ro 8:32 that spared not his o. Son, but 2398
Ro 10:3 to establish their o. righteousness, 2398
Ro 11:24 be graffed into their o. olive tree? 2398
Ro 11:25 should be wise in your o. conceits; 1438
Ro 12:16 Be not wise in your o. conceits 1438
Ro 14:4 to his o. master he standeth or 2398
Ro 14:5 be fully persuaded in his o. mind. 2398
Ro 16:4 my life laid down their o. necks: 1438
Ro 16:18 our Jesus Christ, but their o. belly: 1438
1Co 1:15 I had baptized in mine o. name.
1Co 3:8 man shall receive his o. reward. 2398
1Co 3:8 reward according to his o. labour. 2398
1Co 3:19 taketh the wise in their o. craftiness.
1Co 4:3 yea, I judge not mine o. self. 1683
1Co 4:12 labour, working with our o. hands: 2398
1Co 6:14 also raise up us by his o. power. 848
1Co 6:18 sinneth against his o. body. 2398
1Co 6:19 of God, and ye are not your o.? 1438
1Co 7:2 let every man have his o. wife, and 1438
1Co 7:2 every woman have her o. husband. 2398
1Co 7:4 wife hath not power of her o. body, 2398
1Co 7:4 hath not power of his o. body, but 2398
1Co 7:35 And this I speak for your o. profit; 846
1Co 7:37 but hath power over his o. will, 2398
1Co 9:7 warfare any time at his o. charges? 2398
1Co 10:24 Let no man seek his o., but every 1438
1Co 10:29 Conscience, I say, not thine o., but of 1438
1Co 10:33 not seeking mine o. profit, but the 1683
1Co 11:21 taketh before other his o. supper: 2398
1Co 13:5 seeketh not her o., is not easily 1438
1Co 15:23 But every man in his o. order: 2398
1Co 11:38 him, and to every seed his o. body 2398
1Co 16:21 of me Paul with mine o. hand. 1699
2Co 6:12 ye are straitened in your o. bowels.
2Co 8:5 gave their o. selves to the Lord,
2Co 8:17 of his o. accord he went unto you. 830
2Co 11:26 in perils by mine o. countrymen, in
2Co 13:5 be in the faith, prove your o. selves.
2Co 13:5 Know ye not your o. selves, how that
Ga 1:14 many my equals in mine o. nation,
Ga 4:15 would have plucked out your o. eyes,
Ga 6:4 let every man prove his o. work, 1438
Ga 6:5 man shall bear his o. burden. 2398
Ga 6:11 unto you with mine o. hand.
Eph 1:11 after the counsel of his o. will: 848
Eph 1:20 set him at his o. right hand in the 848
Eph 5:22 yourselves unto your o. husbands, 2398
Eph 5:24 the wives be to their o. husbands 2398
Eph 5:28 love their wives as their o. bodies. 1438
Eph 5:29 no man ever yet hated his o. flesh; 1438
Php 2:4 not every man on his o. things, 1438
Php 2:12 work out your o. salvation with fear 1438
Php 2:21 For all seek their o., not the
Php 3:9 having mine o. righteousness, 1699
Col 3:18 yourselves unto your o. husbands, 2398
1Th 2:8 of God only, but also our o. souls, 1438
1Th 2:14 like things of your o. countrymen, 2398
1Th 2:15 Lord Jesus, and their o. prophets, 2398
1Th 4:11 be quiet, and to do your o. business, 2398
1Th 4:11 and to work with your o. hands, 2398
2Th 3:12 they work, and eat their o. bread. 1438
2Th 3:17 of Paul with mine o. hand, which
1Ti 1:2 Timothy, my o. son in the faith: 1103
1Ti 3:4 One that ruleth well his o. house, 2398
1Ti 3:5 know not how to rule his o. house, 2398
1Ti 3:12 children and their o. houses well. 2398
1Ti 5:8 if any provide not for his o., and 2398
1Ti 5:8 specially for those of his o. house, 2398
1Ti 6:1 count their o. masters worthy of 2398
2Ti 1:9 according to his o. purpose and 2398
2Ti 3:2 men shall be lovers of their o. selves,
2Ti 4:3 after their o. lusts shall they heap 2398
Tit 1:4 o. son after the common faith: 1103
Tit 1:12 even a prophet of their o., said, 2398
Tit 2:5 good, obedient to their o. husbands, 2398
Tit 2:9 be obedient unto their o. masters, 2398
Phm 12 him, that is, mine o. bowels:
Phm 19 have written it with mine o. hand,
Phm 19 unto me even thine o. self besides. 4572
Heb 2:4 Holy Ghost, according to his o. will?
Heb 3:6 Christ as a son over his o. house; 848
Heb 4:10 also hath ceased from his o. works, 848
Heb 7:27 up sacrifice, first for his o. sins, 2398
Heb 9:12 but by his o. blood he entered in 2398
Heb 12:10 chastened...after their o. pleasure; 848
Heb 13:12 the people with his o. blood, 2398
Jas 1:14 he is drawn away of his o. lust, and 2398
Jas 1:18 Of his o. will begat he us with the
Jas 1:22 hearers only, deceiving your o. selves.
Jas 1:26 tongue, but deceiveth his o. heart, 848
1Pe 2:24 Who his o. self bare our sins in his 848
1Pe 2:24 our sins in his o. body on the tree,
1Pe 3:1 in subjection to your o. husbands; 2398
1Pe 3:5 subjection unto their o. husbands: 2398
2Pe 2:12 perish in their o. corruption; 848
2Pe 2:13 themselves with their o. deceivings 848
2Pe 2:22 dog is turned to his o. vomit again; 2398
2Pe 3:3 scoffers, walking after their o. lusts, 2398
2Pe 3:16 scriptures, unto their o. destruction. 2398
2Pe 3:17 fall from your o. stedfastness. 2398
1Jo 3:12 Because his o. works were evil, and
Jude 6 but left their o. habitation, he 2398
Jude 13 sea, foaming out their o. shame; 1438
Jude 16 walking after their o. lusts; and 848
Jude 18 walk after their o. ungodly lusts, 1438
Re 1:5 us from our sins in his o. blood, 848

OWNER See also OWNERS.

Ex 21:28 but the o. of the ox shall be quit 1167
Ex 21:29 and it hath been testified to his o., 1167
Ex 21:29 and his o. also shall be put to death 1167
Ex 21:34 The o. of the pit shall make it good, 1167
Ex 21:34 give money unto the o. of them; 1167
Ex 21:36 and his o. hath not kept him in; he 1167
Ex 22:11 and the o. of it shall accept thereof, 1167
Ex 22:12 shall make restitution unto the o. 1167
Ex 22:14 the o. thereof being not with it, he 1167
Ex 22:15 the o. thereof be with it, he shall not 1167
1Ki 16:24 the name of Shemer, o. of the hill, 113
Isa 1:3 The ox knoweth his o., and the 7069
Ac 27:11 the master and the o. of the ship, 3490

OWNERS

Job 31:39 the o. thereof to lose their life: 1167
Pr 1:19 taketh away the life of the o. 1167
Ec 5:11 good is there to the o. thereof, 1167
Ec 5:13 riches kept for the o. thereof to 1167
Lu 19:33 the o. thereof said unto them, 2962

OWNETH

Le 14:35 And he that o. the house shall come
Ac 21:11 bind the man that o. this girdle, 2076

OX See also OXEN.
Ex 20:17 nor his **o.**, nor his ass, nor any.......... 7794
Ex 21:28 If an **o.** gore a man or a woman,........ 7794
Ex 21:28 then the **o.** shall be surely stoned,....... 7794
Ex 21:28 the owner of the **o.** shall be quit. 7794
Ex 21:29 **o.** were wont to push with his horn.... 7794
Ex 21:29 the **o.** shall be stoned, and his........... 7794
Ex 21:32 If the **o.** shall push a manservant........ 7794
Ex 21:32 silver, and the **o.** shall be stoned........ 7794
Ex 21:33 and an **o.** or an ass fall therein; 7794
Ex 21:35 And if one man's **o.** hurt another's,..... 7794
Ex 21:35 then they shall sell the live **o.**, and..... 7794
Ex 21:35 the dead **o.** also they shall divide.............
Ex 21:36 the **o.** hath used to push in time 7794
Ex 21:36 in; he shall surely pay **o.** for **o.**;......... 7794
Ex 22:1 If a man shall steal an **o.**, or a.......... 7794
Ex 22:1 he shall restore five oxen for an **o.**,.... 7794
Ex 22:4 whether it be **o.**, or ass, or sheep;..... 7794
Ex 22:9 whether it be for **o.**, for ass, for........ 7794
Ex 22:10 his neighbour an ass, or an **o.**, or....... 7794
Ex 23:4 meet thine enemy's **o.** or his ass........ 7794
Ex 23:12 that thine **o.** and thine ass may......... 7794
Ex 34:19 thy cattle, whether **o.** or sheep,......... 7794
Le 7:23 shall eat no manner of fat, of **o.**, ... 7794
Le 17:3 that killeth an **o.**, or lamb, or goat,..... 7794
Le 27:26 whether it be **o.**, or sheep: it is the.... 7794
Nu 7:3 princes, and for each one an **o.**:.......... 7794
Nu 22:4 as the **o.** licketh up the grass of the ... 7794
De 5:14 thine **o.**, nor thine ass, nor any of...... 7794
De 5:21 his **o.**, or his ass, or any thing that..... 7794
De 14:4 ye shall eat: the **o.**, the sheep, and 7794
De 14:5 and the wild **o.**, and the chamois. 8377
De 18:3 sacrifice, whether it be **o.** or sheep; ... 7794
De 22:1 brother's **o.** or his sheep go astray, ... 7794
De 22:4 thy brother's ass or his **o.** fall down.... 7794
De 22:10 not plow with an **o.** and an ass 7794
De 25:4 shalt not muzzle the **o.** when he 7794
De 28:31 Thine **o.** shall be slain before thine 7794
Jos 6:21 and **o.**, and sheep, and ass, with the.... 7794
Jg 3:31 hundred men with an **o.** goad: 1241
Jg 6:4 for Israel, neither sheep, nor **o.**,......... 7794
1Sa 12:3 whose **o.** have I taken? or whose ass.. 7794
1Sa 14:34 Bring me hither every man his **o.**,........ 7794
1Sa 14:34 brought every man his **o.** with him..... 7794
1Sa 15:3 infant and suckling, **o.** and sheep, ... 7794
Ne 5:18 was one **o.** and six choice sheep; 7794
Job 6:5 or loweth the **o.** over his fodder? 7794
Job 24:3 take the widow's **o.** for a pledge. 7794
Job 40:15 thee; he eateth grass as an **o.**.......... 1241
Ps 69:31 please the Lord better than an **o.**....... 7794
Ps 106:20 similitude of an **o.** that eateth grass. ... 7794
Pr 7:22 as an **o.** goeth to the slaughter, or..... 7794
Pr 14:4 increase is by the strength of the **o.**.. 7794
Pr 15:17 a stalled **o.** and hatred therewith. 7794
Isa 1:3 The **o.** knoweth his owner, and the 7794
Isa 11:7 the lion shall eat straw like the **o.**, ... 1241
Isa 32:20 the feet of the **o.** and the ass. 7794
Isa 66:3 He that killeth an **o.** is as if he slew ... 7794
Jer 11:19 I was like a lamb or an **o.** that is......... 441
Eze 1:10 they four had the face of an **o.** on 7794
Lu 13:15 **the sabbath loose his o. or his ass.** *1016*
Lu 14:5 **an ass or an o. fallen into a pit,...** *1016*
1Co 9:9 not muzzled the mouth of the **o.** that .. *1016*
1Ti 5:18 not muzzled the **o.** that treadeth out... *1016*

OXEN
Ge 12:16 and he had sheep, and **o.**, and he....... 1241
Ge 20:14 Abimelech took sheep, and **o.**, and..... 1241
Ge 21:27 And Abraham took sheep and **o.**,......... 1241
Ge 32:5 And I have **o.**, and asses, flocks, ... 7794
Ge 34:28 took their sheep, and their **o.**, and 1241
Ex 9:3 upon the **o.**, and upon the sheep: 1241
Ex 20:24 offerings, thy sheep, and thine **o.**: 1241
Ex 22:1 he shall restore five **o.** for an ox, ... 1241
Ex 22:30 shalt thou do with thine **o.**, and 7794
Ex 24:5 peace offerings of **o.** unto the Lord..... 6499
Nu 7:3 six covered wagons, and twelve **o.**; 1241
Nu 7:6 Moses took the wagons and the **o.**, ... 1241
Nu 7:7 Two wagons and four **o.** he gave 1241
Nu 7:8 four wagons and eight **o.** he gave 1241
Nu 7:17, 23,29,35,41,47,53,59,65,71,77,83
two **o.**, five rams, five he goats, ... 1241
Nu 7:87 All the **o.** for the burnt offering.......... 1241
Nu 7:88 all the **o.** for the sacrifice of the......... 1241
Nu 22:40 Balak offered **o.** and sheep, and sent... 1241
Nu 23:1 and prepare me here seven **o.** and 6499
De 14:26 for **o.**, or for sheep, or for wine, or.... 1241
Jos 7:24 and his **o.**, and his asses, and his 7794
1Sa 11:7 he took a yoke of **o.**, and hewed........ 1241
1Sa 11:7 so shall it be done unto his **o.**........... 1241
1Sa 14:14 land, which a yoke of **o.** might plow..........
1Sa 14:32 took sheep, and **o.**, and calves, and.... 1241
1Sa 15:9 the best of the sheep, and of the **o.**,.... 1241
1Sa 15:14 the lowing of the **o.** which I hear?...... 1241
1Sa 15:15 the best of the sheep and of the **o.**,..... 1241
1Sa 15:21 took of the spoil, sheep and **o.**, the 1241
1Sa 22:19 **o.**, and asses, and sheep, with the 7794
1Sa 27:9 took away the sheep, and the **o.**, ... 1241
2Sa 6:6 took hold of it; for the **o.** shook it. 1241
2Sa 6:13 paces, he sacrificed **o.** and fatlings...... 7794
2Sa 24:22 here be **o.** for burnt sacrifice, and...... 1241
2Sa 24:22 instruments of the **o.** for wood. 1241
2Sa 24:24 and the **o.** for fifty shekels of silver. ... 1241
1Ki 1:9 Adonijah slew sheep and **o.** and fat ... 1241
1Ki 1:19 And he hath slain **o.** and fat cattle 7794
1Ki 1:25 hath slain **o.** and fat cattle and sheep... 7794
1Ki 4:23 Ten fat **o.**, and twenty **o.** out of the ... 1241
1Ki 7:25 It stood upon twelve **o.**,three 1241
1Ki 7:29 were lions, **o.**, and cherubims:........... 1241
1Ki 7:29 and beneath the lions and **o.** were 1241
1Ki 7:44 sea, and twelve **o.** under the sea; 1241
1Ki 8:5 sacrificing sheep and **o.**, that could 1241
1Ki 8:63 two and twenty thousand **o.**, and an..... 1241
1Ki 19:19 was plowing with twelve yoke of **o.** ....
1Ki 19:20 And he left the **o.**, and ran after 1241
1Ki 19:21 took a yoke of **o.**, and slew them, ... 1241
1Ki 19:21 flesh with the instruments of the **o.**, ... 1241
2Ki 5:26 vineyards, and sheep, and **o.**, and 1241
2Ki 16:17 the brasen **o.** that were under it, ... 1241
1Ch 12:40 and on mules, and on **o.**, and meat, ... 1241
1Ch 12:40 and wine, and oil, and **o.**, and sheep.... 1241
1Ch 13:9 hold the ark; for the **o.** stumbled......... 1241
1Ch 21:23 thee the **o.** also for burnt offerings, ... 1241
2Ch 4:3 under it was the similitude of **o.**,......... 1241
2Ch 4:3 Two rows of **o.** were cast, when it..... 1241
2Ch 4:4 It stood upon twelve **o.**, three........... 1241
2Ch 4:15 One sea, and twelve **o.** under it.......... 1241
2Ch 5:6 sacrificed sheep and **o.**, which could.... 1241
2Ch 7:5 of twenty and two thousand **o.**,........... 1241
2Ch 15:11 had brought, seven hundred **o.** and..... 1241
2Ch 18:2 Ahab killed sheep and **o.** for him in..... 1241
2Ch 29:33 six hundred **o.** and three thousand....... 1241
2Ch 31:6 brought in the tithe of **o.** and sheep,... 1241
2Ch 35:8 small cattle, and three hundred **o.**. 1241
2Ch 35:9 small cattle, and five hundred **o.**.......... 1241
2Ch 35:12 Moses. And so did they with the **o.**..... 1241
Job 1:3 camels. and five hundred yoke of **o.**,.... 1241
Job 1:14 The **o.** were plowing, and the asses.... 1241
Job 42:12 camels, and a thousand yoke of **o.**,..... 1241
Ps 8:7 All sheep and **o.**, yea, and the beasts ... 504
Ps 144:14 our **o.** may be strong to labour;........... 441
Pr 14:4 Where no **o.** are, the crib is clean: 5091
Isa 7:25 shall be for the sending forth of **o.**,...... 7794
Isa 22:13 joy and gladness, slaying **o.**, and 1241
Isa 30:24 The **o.** likewise and the young asses 504
Jer 51:23 the husbandman and his yoke of **o.**; ....
Da 4:25, 32 make thee to eat grass as **o.**,......... 8450
Da 4:33 and did eat grass as **o.**, and his 8450
Da 5:21 they fed him with grass like **o.**, and.... 8450
Am 6:12 rock? will one plow there with **o.**?...... 1241
Mt 22:4 **my o. and my fatlings are killed,**. *5022*
Lu 14:19 **I have bought five yoke of o., and** *1016*
Joh 2:14 that sold **o.** and sheep and doves, ... *1016*
Joh 2:15 temple, and the sheep, and the **o.**; *1016*
Ac 14:13 **o.** and garlands unto the gates,........... *5022*
1Co 9:9 corn. Doth God take care for **o.**? *1016*

OX-GOAD See OX and GOAD.

OZEM (o'-zem)
1Ch 2:15 **O.** the sixth, David the seventh:.......... 684
1Ch 2:25 and Oren, and **O.**, and Ahijah............. 684

OZIAS (o-zi'-as) See also UZZIAH.
Mt 1:8 begat Joram, and Joram begat **O.**; *3604*
Mt 1:9 And **O.** begat Joatham; and............... *3604*

OZNI (oz'-ni) See also OZNITES.
Nu 26:16 Of **O.**, the family of the Oznites: 244

OZNITES (oz'-nites)
Nu 26:16 Of Ozni, the family of the **O.**: of.......... 244

P.

PAANEAH See ZAPH-NATH-PAANEAH.

PAARI (pa'-ar-ahee) See also NOARAI.
2Sa 23:35 the Carmelite, **P.** the Arbite, ... 6474

PACATIANA (pa-ca-she-a'-nah)
1Ti *subscr.* the chiefest city of Phrygia **P.**. *3818*

PACES See also APACE.
2Sa 6:13 ark of the Lord had gone six **p.**, ... 6806

PACIFIED
Es 7:10 Then was the king's wrath **p.**. 7918
Eze 16:63 when I am **p.** toward thee for all........ 3722

PACIFIETH
Pr 21:14 A gift in secret **p.** anger: and a.......... 3711
Ec 10:4 for yielding **p.** great offences. 3240

PACIFY See also PACIFIED; PACIFIETH.
Pr 16:14 death: but a wise man will **p.** it.......... 3722

PADAN (pa'-dan) See also PADAN-ARAM.
Ge 48:7 as for me, when I came from **P.**, ... 6307

PADAN-ARAM (pa''-dan-a'-ram)
Ge 25:20 of Bethuel the Syrian of **P.**, ... 6307
Ge 28:2 go to **P.**, to the house of Bethuel....... 6307
Ge 28:5 he went to **P.** unto Laban, son of....... 6307
Ge 28:6 Jacob, and sent him away to **P.**, ... 6307
Ge 28:7 his mother, and was gone to **P.**; 6307
Ge 31:18 which he had gotten in **P.**, for to go... 6307
Ge 33:18 of Canaan, when he came from **P.**;..... 6307
Ge 35:9 again when he came out of **P.**, and..... 6307
Ge 35:26 which were born to him in **P.**............ 6307
Ge 46:15 which she bare unto Jacob in **P.**, ... 6307

PADDLE
De 23:13 shalt have a **p.** upon thy weapon; 3489

PADON (pa'-don)
Ezr 2:44 of Siaha, the children of **P.**, ... 6303
Ne 7:47 children of Sia, the children of **P.**, ... 6303

PAGIEL (pa'-ghe-el)
Nu 1:13 Of Asher; **P.** the son of Ocran. 6295
Nu 2:27 Asher shall be **P.** the son of Ocran..... 6295
Nu 7:72 eleventh day **P.** the son of Ocran,...... 6295
Nu 7:77 the offering of **P.** the son of Ocran..... 6295
Nu 10:26 of Asher was **P.** the son of Ocran. 6295

PAHATH-MOAB (pa''-hath-mo'-ab)
Ezr 2:6 children of **P.**, of the children........... 6355
Ezr 8:4 Of the sons of **P.**; Elihoenai the......... 6355
Ezr 10:30 And of the sons of **P.**; Adna, and....... 6355
Ne 3:11 and Hashub the son of **P.**, repaired 6355
Ne 7:11 The children of **P.**, of the children...... 6355
Ne 10:14 The chief of the people; Parosh, **P.**, ... 6355

PAI (pa'-i) See also PAU.
1Ch 1:50 and the name of his city was **P.**; 6464

PAID See also PAYED.
Ezr 4:20 and custom, was **p.** unto them. 3052
Jon 1:3 so he **p.** the fare thereof, and went 5414
Mt 5:26 **thou hast p. the uttermost farthing.** *591*
Lu 12:59 **till thou hast p. the very last mite** . *591*

PAIN See also PAINED; PAINFUL; PAINS.
Job 14:22 his flesh upon him shall have **p.**, ... 3510
Job 15:20 wicked man travaileth with **p.** all his..........
Job 33:19 He is chastened also with **p.** upon 4341
Job 33:19 multitude of his bones with strong **p.**: ....
Ps 25:18 upon mine affliction and my **p.**; 5999
Ps 48:6 and **p.**, as of a woman in travail. 2427
Isa 13:8 in **p.** as a woman that travaileth: 2342
Isa 21:3 are my loins filled with **p.**; pangs........ 2479
Isa 26:17 the time of her delivery, is in **p.**, ... 2342
Isa 26:18 been with child, we have been in **p.**,... 2342
Isa 66:7 before her **p.** came, she was............ 2256
Jer 6:24 and **p.**, as of a woman in travail. 2427
Jer 12:13 they have put themselves to **p.**,......... 2470

Jer 15:18 Why is my p. perpetual, and my 3511
Jer 22:23 the p. as of a woman in travail! 2427
Jer 30:23 all with p. upon the head of the 2342
Jer 51:8 take balm for her p., if so be she........ 4341
Eze 30:4 and great p. shall be in Ethiopia,........ 2479
Eze 30:9 great p. shall come upon them,.......... 2479
Eze 30:16 Sin shall have great p., and No.......... 2342
Mic 4:10 Be in p., and labour to bring forth,....... 2342
Na 2:10 and much p. is in all loins, and the 2479
Ro 8:22 and travaileth in p. together until now........
Re 16:10 they gnawed their tongues for p.,........ *4192*
Re 21:4 neither shall there be any more p.:...... *4192*

PAINED
Ps 55:4 My heart is sore p. within me: and..... 2342
Isa 23:5 be sorely p. at the report of Tyre. 2342
Jer 4:19 bowels! I am p. at my very heart;...... 3176
Joe 2:6 face the people shall be much p.: 2342
Re 12:2 in birth, and p. to be delivered........... *928*

PAINFUL
Ps 73:16 to know this, it was too p. for me;..... 5999

PAINFULNESS
2Co 11:27 In weariness and p., in watchings....... *3449*

PAINS
1Sa 4:19 travailed; for her p. came upon her...... 6735
Ps 116:3 the p. of hell gat hold upon me:......... 4712
Ac 2:24 up, having loosed the p. of death: *5604*
Re 16:11 because of their p. and their sores, ... *4192*

PAINTED See also PAINTEDST.
2Ki 9:30 she p. her face, and tired her..... 7760,6320
Jer 22:14 with cedar, and p. with vermilion. 4886

PAINTEDST
Eze 23:40 p. thy eyes, and deckedst thyself....... 3583

PAINTING
Jer 4:30 thou rentest thy face with p., in......... 6320

PAIR See also REPAIR.
Am 2:6 silver, and the poor for a p. of shoes;.......
Am 8:6 and the needy for a p. of shoes;..............
Lu 2:24 A p. of turtledoves, or two young....... *2201*
Re 6:5 had a p. of balances in his hand. *2218*

PALACE See also PALACES.
1Ki 16:18 into the p. of the king's house,............ 759
1Ki 21:1 hard by the p. of Ahab king of.......... 1964
2Ki 15:25 in the p. of the king's house, with........ 759
2Ki 20:18 in the p. of the king of Babylon. 1964
1Ch 29:1 p. is not for man, but for the Lord..... 1002
1Ch 29:19 these things, and to build the p.,........ 1002
2Ch 9:11 of the Lord, and to the king's p., ... 1004
Ezr 4:14 maintenance from the king's p.,......... 1964
Ezr 6:2 p. that is in the province of the 1002
Ne 1:1 year, as I was in Shushan the p.,........ 1002
Ne 2:8 make beams for the gates of the p. 1002
Ne 7:2 and Hananiah the ruler of the p.,......... 1002
Es 1:2 which was in Shushan the p., ... 1002
Es 1:5 were present in Shushan the p., ... 1002
Es 1:5 of the garden of the king's p.; 1055
Es 2:3 young virgins unto Shushan the p.,..... 1002
Es 2:5 Now in Shushan the p. there was a 1002
Es 2:8 together unto Shushan the p., to......... 1002
Es 3:15 decree was given in Shushan the p....... 1002
Es 7:7 his wrath went into the p. garden:...... 1055
Es 7:8 king returned out of the p. garden...... 1055
Es 8:14 was given at Shushan the p............... 1002
Es 9:6 in Shushan the p. the Jews slew 1002
Es 9:11 that were slain in Shushan the p. 1002
Es 9:12 hundred men in Shushan the p.,.......... 1002
Ps 45:15 they shall enter into the king's p......... 1964
Ps 144:12 after the similitude of a p.:................ 1964
Ca 8:9 will build upon her a p. of silver:........ 2918
Isa 25:2 a p. of strangers to be no city; it......... 759
Isa 39:7 in the p. of the king of Babylon. 1964
Jer 30:18 p. shall remain after the manner.......... 759
Da 1:4 in them to stand in the king's p., ... 1964
Da 4:4 house, and flourishing in my p.: 1965
Da 4:29 he walked in the p. of the kingdom..... 1965
Da 5:5 of the wall of the king's p.: and 1965
Da 6:18 Then the king went to his p., and 1965
Da 8:2 that I was at Shushan in the p., ... 1002
Da 11:45 shall plant the tabernacles of the p....... 643
Am 4:3 and ye shall cast them into the p.,...... 2038
Na 2:6 and the p. shall be dissolved. 1964
Mt 26:3 unto the p. of the high priest, who....... *833*
Mt 26:58 afar off unto the high priest's p., ... *833*
Mt 26:69 Now Peter sat without in the p.: *833*
Mk 14:54 even into the p. of the high priest:....... *833*
Mk 14:66 And as Peter was beneath in the p., ... *833*
Lu 11:21 strong man armed keepeth his p.,... *833*
Joh 18:15 Jesus into the p. of the high priest....... *833*
Php 1:13 in Christ are manifest in all the p., ... *4232*

PALACES
2Ch 36:19 burnt all the p. thereof with fire, ... 759
Ps 45:8 and cassia, out of the ivory p., ... 1964
Ps 48:3 is known in her p. for a refuge............ 759
Ps 48:13 well her bulwarks, consider her p.; 759
Ps 78:69 he built his sanctuary like high p., ...
Ps 122:7 walls, and prosperity within thy p. 759
Pr 30:28 with her hands, and is in kings' p....... 1964
Isa 13:22 and dragons in their pleasant p.: 1964
Isa 23:13 they raised up the p. thereof; and........ 759
Isa 32:14 Because the p. shall be forsaken;......... 759
Isa 34:13 And thorns shall come up in her p., ... 759
Jer 6:5 by night, and let us destroy her p....... 759
Jer 9:21 and is entered into our p., to cut off 759
Jer 17:27 it shall devour the p. of Jerusalem,....... 759
Jer 49:27 shall consume the p. of Ben-hadad. 759
La 2:5 he hath swallowed up all her p.: 759
La 2:7 of the enemy the walls of her p.;......... 759
Eze 19:7 he knew their desolate p., and he laid.......
Eze 25:4 and they shall set their p. in thee,...... 2918
Ho 8:14 and it shall devour the p. thereof. 759
Am 1:4 shall devour the p. of Ben-hadad.......... 759
Am 1:7 which shall devour the p. thereof:......... 759
Am 1:10 which shall devour the p. thereof. 759
Am 1:12 which shall devour the p. of Bozrah....... 759
Am 1:14 it shall devour the p. thereof, with....... 759
Am 2:2 and it shall devour the p. of Kirioth:..... 759
Am 2:5 it shall devour the p. of Jerusalem........ 759
Am 3:9 Publish in the p. at Ashdod, and......... 759
Am 3:9 and in the p. in the land of Egypt, ... 759
Am 3:10 up violence and robbery in their p......... 759
Am 3:11 thee, and thy p. shall be spoiled. 759
Am 6:8 I abhor...Jacob, and hate his p.: 759
Mic 5:5 and when he shall tread in our p.,......... 759

PALAL (pa'-lal)
Ne 3:25 P. the son of Uzai, over against......... 6420

PALE
Isa 29:22 neither shall his face now wax p......... 2357
Re 6:8 I looked, and behold a p. horse:.......... *5515*

PALENESS
Jer 30:6 and all faces are turned into p.? 3420

PALESTINA (pal-es-ti'-nah) See also PALESTINE; PHILISTIA.
Ex 15:14 hold on the inhabitants of P.. 6429
Isa 14:29 Rejoice not thou, whole P., because ... 6429
Isa 14:31 city; thou, whole P., art dissolved:..... 6429

PALESTINE (pal'-es-tine) See also PALESTINA.
Joe 3:4 Zidon, and all the coasts of P.?.......... 6429

PALET See BETH-PALET.

PALLU (pal'-lu) See also PALLUITES; PHALLU.
Ex 6:14 Hanoch, and P., Hezron, and............ 6396
Nu 26:5 of P., the family of the Palluites:......... 6396
Nu 26:8 And the sons of P.; Eliab. 6396
1Ch 5:3 Hanoch, and P., Hezron, and............ 6396

PALLUITES (pal'-lu-ites)
Nu 26:5 of Pallu, the family of the P.: 6384

PALM See also PALMS.
Ex 15:27 and threescore and ten p. trees: 8558
Le 14:15, 26 into the p. of his own left hand:..... 3709
Le 23:40 branches of p. trees, goodly trees,..... 8558
Nu 33:9 and threescore and ten p. trees;.......... 8558
De 34:3 Jericho, the city of p. trees, unto......... 8558
Jg 1:16 went up out of the city of p. trees 8558
Jg 3:13 and possessed the city of p. trees. 8558
Jg 4:5 under the p. tree of Deborah 8560
1Ki 6:29, 32 cherubims and p. trees and open.... 8561
1Ki 6:32 cherubims, and upon he p. trees. 8561
1Ki 6:35 cherubims and p. trees and open......... 8561
1Ki 7:36 cherubims, lions, and p. trees,........... 8561
2Ch 3:5 and set thereon p. trees and chains. ... 8561
2Ch 28:15 to Jericho, the city of p. trees, ... 8558
Ne 8:15 myrtle branches, and p. branches,....... 8558
Ps 92:12 shall flourish like the p. tree:............. 8558
Ca 7:7 This thy stature is like to a p. tree,..... 8558
Ca 7:8 I said, I will go up to the p. tree, ... 8558
Jer 10:5 They are upright as the p. tree, ... 8560
Eze 40:16 and upon each post were p. trees. 8561
Eze 40:22 and their arches, and their p. trees,.... 8561
Eze 40:26 and it had p. trees, one on this side, .. 8561
Eze 40:31, 34,37 p. trees were upon the posts.... 8561
Eze 41:18 made with cherubims and p. trees,...... 8561
Eze 41:18 that a p. tree was between a cherub... 8561
Eze 41:19 toward the p. tree on the one side,..... 8561
Eze 41:19 toward the p. tree on the other side:.. 8561
Eze 41:20 were cherubims and p. trees made, ... 8561
Eze 41:25 cherubims and p. trees, like as were.... 8561
Eze 41:26 were narrow windows and p. trees..... 8561
Joe 1:12 the p. tree also, and the apple tree, ... 8558
Joh 12:13 Took branches of p. trees, and.......... *5404*
Joh 18:22 struck Jesus with the p. of his.......... *4475*

PALM-BRANCHES See PALM and BRANCHES.

PALMERWORM
Joe 1:4 That which the p. hath left hath......... 1501
Joe 2:25 and the caterpiller, and the p.,........... 1501
Am 4:9 increased, the p. devoured them: 1501

PALMS
1Sa 5:4 both the p. of his hands were cut....... 3709
2Ki 9:35 the feet, and the p. of her hands......... 3709
Isa 49:16 graven...upon the p. of my hands;...... 3709
Da 10:10 knees and upon the p. of my hands. ... 3709
Mt 26:67 smote him with...p. of their hands,..... *4474*
Mk 14:65 smote him with...p. of their hands...... *4475*
Re 7:9 robes, and p. in their hands;............ *5404*

PALM-TREE See PALM and TREE.

PALSIES
Ac 8:7 and many taken with p., and that 3886

PALSY See also PALSIES.
Mt 4:24 lunatick, and those that had...p.;......... *3885*
Mt 8:6 servant lieth at home sick of the p., ... *3885*
Mt 9:2 brought to him a man sick of the p.,.... *3885*
Mt 9:2 faith said unto the sick of the p.;......... *3885*
Mt 9:6 (then saith he to the sick of the p.,)... *3885*
Mk 2:3 him, bringing one sick of the p., ... *3885*
Mk 2:4 bed wherein the sick of the p. lay. *3885*
Mk 2:5 he said unto the sick of the p., Son, .. *3885*
Mk 2:9 easier to say to the sick of the p., ... *3885*
Mk 2:10 sins, (he saith to the sick of the p.,).. *3885*
Lu 5:18 a man which was taken with a p.: *3886*
Lu 5:24 (he said unto the sick of the p.,) I *3886*
Ac 9:33 eight years, and was sick of the p.. ..... *3886*

PALTI (pal'-ti)
Nu 13:9 of Benjamin, P. the son of Raphu....... 6406

PALTIEL (pal'-te-el) See also PHALTIEL.
Nu 34:26 of Issachar, P. the son of Azzan. 6409

PALTITE (pal'-tite) See also PELONITE.
2Sa 23:26 Helez the P., Ira the son of............. 6407

PAMPHYLIA (pam-fil'-e-ah)
Ac 2:10 Phyrgia, and P., in Egypt, and *3828*
Ac 13:13 Paphos, they came to Perga in P.: *3828*
Ac 14:24 Pisidia, they came to P.. .... *3828*
Ac 15:38 who departed from them from P.,...... *3828*
Ac 27:5 sailed over the sea of Cilicia and P., ... *3828*

PAN See also PANS; FRYINGPANS.
Le 2:5 be a meat offering baken in a p.,........ 4227
Le 6:21 In a p. it shall be made with oil;......... 4227
Le 7:9 and in the p., shall be the priest's 4227
1Sa 2:14 he struck it into the p., or kettle, ... 3595
2Sa 13:9 she took a p., and poured them 4958
1Ch 23:29 for that which is baked in the p., ... 4227
Eze 4:3 take thou unto thee an iron p., ... 4227

PANGS
Isa 13:8 p. and sorrows shall take hold of........ 6735
Isa 21:3 p. have taken hold upon me, as 6735
Isa 21:3 the p. of a woman that travaileth:........ 6735
Isa 26:17 in pain, and crieth out in her p.; 2256
Jer 22:23 thou be when p. come upon thee, ... 2256
Jer 48:41 as the heart of a woman in her p.: 6887
Jer 49:22 as the heart of a woman in her p.. 6887
Jer 50:43 and p. as of a woman in travail. 2427
Mic 4:9 p. have taken thee as a woman in 2427

PANNAG (pan'-nag)
Eze 27:17 market wheat of Minnith, and P.,....... 6436

PANS See also FRYINGPANS.
Ex 27:3 make his p. to receive his ashes, ... 5518

Nu 11:8 baked it in **p.**, and made cakes of 6517
1Ch 9:31 things that were made in the **p.** 2281
2Ch 35:13 in caldrons, and in **p.**, and divided 6745

PANT See also PANTED; PANTETH.
Am 2:7 That **p.** after the dust of the earth 7602

PANTED
Ps 119:131 I opened my mouth, and **p.**: for I 7602
Isa 21:4 My heart **p.**, fearfulness 8582

PANTETH
Ps 38:10 My heart **p.**, my strength faileth 5503
Ps 42:1 the hart **p.** after the water brooks, 6165
Ps 42:1 so **p.** my soul after thee, O God. 6165

PAPER
Isa 19:7 The **p.** reeds by the brooks, by the 6169
2Jo 12 would not write with **p.** and ink: *5489*

PAPER-REEDS See PAPER and REEDS.

PAPHOS (pa'-fos)
Ac 13:6 had gone through the isle unto **P.**, *3974*
Ac 13:13 and his company loosed from **P.**, *3974*

PAPS
Eze 23:21 Egyptians for the **p.** of thy youth. 7699
Lu 11:27 the **p.** which thou hast sucked *3149*
Lu 23:29 **and the p. which never gave suck.** *3149*
Re 1:13 about the **p.** with a golden girdle. *3149*

PARABLE See also PARABLES.
Nu 23:7 And he took up his **p.**, and said, 4912
Nu 23:18 he took up his **p.**, and said, Rise up, 4912
Nu 24:3, 15 And he took up his **p.**, and said, 4912
Nu 24:20 he took up his **p.**, and said, Amalek 4912
Nu 24:21 took up his **p.**, and said, Strong is 4912
Nu 24:23 he took up his **p.**, and said, Alas, 4912
Job 27:1 Moreover Job continued his **p.**, 4912
Job 29:1 Moreover Job continued his **p.**, 4912
Ps 49:4 I will incline mine ear to a **p.**: I will 4912
Ps 78:2 I will open my mouth in a **p.**: I will 4912
Pr 26:7,9 so is a **p.** in the mouth of fools. 4912
Eze 17:2 speak a **p.** unto the house of Israel; 4912
Eze 24:3 utter a **p.** unto the rebellious house, 4912
Mic 2:4 shall one take up a **p.** against you, 4912
Hab 2:6 all these take up a **p.** against him, 4912
Mt 13:18 **ye therefore the p. of the sower.** *3850*
Mt 13:24, 31 Another **p.** put he forth unto *3850*
Mt 13:33 Another **p.** spake he unto them; *3850*
Mt 13:34 without a **p.** spake he not unto them: *3850*
Mt 13:36 Declare unto us the **p.** of the tares *3850*
Mt 15:15 unto him, Declare unto us this **p.** *3850*
Mt 21:33 **Hear another p.: There was a** *3850*
Mt 24:32 **Now learn a p. of the fig tree;** *3850*
Mk 4:10 with the twelve asked of him the **p.** *3850*
Mk 4:13 unto them, **Know ye not this p.?** *3850*
Mk 4:34 without a **p.** spake he not unto them: *3850*
Mk 7:17 asked him concerning the **p.** *3850*
Mk 12:12 he had spoken the **p.** against them: *3850*
Mk 13:28 **Now learn a p. of the fig tree;** *3850*
Lu 5:36 And he spake also a **p.** unto them; *3850*
Lu 6:39 And he spake a **p.** unto them, **Can** *3850*
Lu 8:4 out of every city, he spake by a **p.**: *3850*
Lu 8:9 him, saying, What might this **p.** be? *3850*
Lu 8:11 **Now the p. is this: The seed is the.** *3850*
Lu 12:16 he spake a **p.** unto them, saying, *3850*
Lu 12:41 Lord, speakest thou this **p.** unto us, *3850*
Lu 13:6 He spake also this **p.**; **A certain** *3850*
Lu 14:7 he put forth a **p.** to those which *3850*
Lu 15:3 he spake this **p.** unto them, saying, *3850*
Lu 18:1 he spake a **p.** unto them to this end, *3850*
Lu 18:9 And he spake this **p.** unto certain *3850*
Lu 19:11 he added and spake a **p.**, because *3850*
Lu 20:9 he to speak to the people this **p.**; *3850*
Lu 20:19 had spoken this **p.** against them *3850*
Lu 21:29 And he spake to them a **p.**: **Behold** *3850*
Joh 10:6 This **p.** spake Jesus unto them *3942*

PARABLES
Eze 20:49 say of me, Doth he not speak **p.**? 4912
Mt 13:3 many things unto them in **p.**, *3850*
Mt 13:10 Why speakest thou unto them in **p.**? *3850*
Mt 13:13 **Therefore speak I to them in p.:** *3850*
Mt 13:34 Jesus unto the multitude in **p.**; *3850*
Mt 13:35 saying, I will open my mouth in **p.**; *3850*
Mt 13:53 when Jesus had finished these **p.**, *3850*
Mt 21:45 and Pharisees had heard his **p.**, *3850*
Mt 22:1 and spake unto them again by **p.**, *3850*
Mk 3:23 and said unto them in **p.**, **How can** *3850*
Mk 4:2 he taught them many things by **p.**, *3850*
Mk 4:11 **all these things are done in p.:** *3850*
Mk 4:13 **and how then will ye know all p.?** *3850*
Mk 4:33 many such **p.** spake he the word *3850*
Mk 12:1 he began to speak unto them by **p.** *3850*
Lu 8:10 **to others in p.; that seeing they** *3850*

PARADISE
Lu 23:43 **To day shalt thou be with me in p.** *3857*
2Co 12:4 How that he was caught up into **p.**, *3857*
Re 2:7 **is in the midst of the p. of God.** *3857*

PARAH (pa'-rah)
Jos 18:23 And Avim, and **P.**, and Ophrah, 6511

PARAMOURS
Eze 23:20 she doted upon their **p.**, whose 6370

PARAN (pa'-ran) See also EL-PARAN.
Ge 21:21 he dwelt in the wilderness of **P.**: 6290
Nu 10:12 cloud rested in the wilderness of **P.** 6290
Nu 12:16 and pitched in the wilderness of **P.** 6290
Nu 13:3 them from the wilderness of **P.**: 6290
Nu 13:26 unto the wilderness of **P.**, to 6290
De 1:1 Red sea, between **P.**, and Tophel, 6290
De 33:2 he shined forth from mount **P.**, and 6290
1Sa 25:1 went down to the wilderness of **P.** 6290
1Ki 11:18 arose out of Midian, and came to **P.**: 6290
1Ki 11:18 they took men with them out of **P.**, 6290
Hab 3:3 and the Holy One from mount **P.** 6290

PARBAR (par'-bar)
1Ch 26:18 At **P.** westward, four at the 6503
1Ch 26:18 at the causeway, and two at **P.** 6503

PARCEL
Ge 33:19 he bought a **p.** of a field, where he 2513
Jos 24:32 in a **p.** of ground which Jacob bought 2513
Ru 4:3 selleth a **p.** of land, which was our 2513
1Ch 11:13 was a **p.** of ground full of barley; 2513
1Ch 11:14 themselves in the midst of that **p.**, 2513
Joh 4:5 the **p.** of ground that Jacob gave *5564*

PARCHED
Le 23:14 eat neither bread, nor **p.** corn, nor 7039
Jos 5:11 and **p.** corn in the selfsame day
Ru 2:14 he reached her **p.** corn, and she 7039
1Sa 17:17 brethren an ephah of this **p.** corn, 7039
1Sa 25:18 and five measures of **p.** corn, and an 7039
2Sa 17:28 and barley, and flour, and **p.** corn, 7039
2Sa 17:28 beans, and lentiles, and **p.** pulse, 7039
Isa 35:7 **p.** ground shall become a pool, 8273
Jer 17:6 shall inhabit the **p.** places in the 2788

PARCHMENTS
2Ti 4:13 the books, but especially the **p.** *3200*

PARDON See also PARDONED; PARDONETH.
Ex 23:21 will not **p.** your transgressions: 5375
Ex 34:9 and **p.** our iniquity and our sin, 5545
Nu 14:19 **P.**, I beseech thee, the iniquity of 5545
1Sa 15:25 I pray thee, **p.** my sin, and turn 5375
2Ki 5:18 this thing the Lord **p.** thy servant, 5545
2Ki 5:18 Lord **p.** thy servant in this thing. 5545
2Ki 24:4 blood; which the Lord would not **p.** 5545
2Ch 30:18 The good Lord **p.** every one 3722
Ne 9:17 but thou art a God ready to **p.**, 5547
Job 7:21 dost thou not **p.** my transgression, 5375
Ps 25:11 O Lord, **p.** mine iniquity; for it is 5545
Isa 55:7 our God, for he will abundantly **p.** 5545
Jer 5:1 seeketh the truth; and I will **p.** it. 5545
Jer 5:7 How shall I **p.** thee for this? thy 5545
Jer 33:8 and I will **p.** all their iniquities, 5545
Jer 50:20 for I will **p.** them whom I reserve. 5545

PARDONED
Nu 14:20 I have **p.** according to thy word: 5545
Isa 40:2 that her iniquity is **p.**: for she 7521
La 3:42 have rebelled: thou hast not **p.** 5545

PARDONETH
Mic 7:18 like unto thee, that **p.** iniquity, 5375

PARE
De 21:12 shave her head, and **p.** her nails; 6213

PARENTS
Mt 10:21 **shall rise up against their p., and** *1118*
Mk 13:12 **shall rise up against their p., and** *1118*
Lu 2:27 the **p.** brought in the child Jesus, *1118*
Lu 2:41 his **p.** went to Jerusalem every year *1118*
Lu 8:56 And her **p.** were astonished: but he *1118*
Lu 18:29 **hath left house, or p., or brethren,** *1118*
Lu 21:16 **ye shall be betrayed both by p.,** *1118*
Joh 9:2 who did sin, this man, or his **p.**, *1118*
Joh 9:3 **hath this man sinned, nor his p.:** *1118*
Joh 9:18 until they called the **p.** of him that *1118*
Joh 9:20 His **p.** answered them and said, We *1118*
Joh 9:22 These words spake his **p.**, because *1118*
Joh 9:23 Therefore said his **p.**, He is of age; *1118*
Ro 1:30 of evil things, disobedient to **p.**, *1118*
2Co 12:14 ought not to lay up for the **p.**, but *1118*
2Co 12:14 but the **p.** for the children. *1118*
Eph 6:1 Children, obey your **p.** in the Lord: *1118*
Col 3:20 obey your **p.** in all things: for *1118*
1Ti 5:4 at home, and to requite their **p.**: *4269*
2Ti 3:2 disobedient to **p.**, unthankful, *1118*
Heb 11:23 was hid three months of his **p.**, *3962*

PAREZ See RIMMON-PAREZ.

PARLOUR See also PARLOURS.
Jg 3:20 and he was sitting in a summer **p.**, 5944
Jg 3:23 shut the doors of the **p.** upon him, 5944
Jg 3:24 the doors of the **p.** were locked, 5944
Jg 3:25 he opened not the doors of the **p.**; 5944
1Sa 9:22 and brought them into the **p.**, and 3957

PARLOURS
1Ch 28:11 and of the inner **p.** thereof, and of 2315

PARMASHTA (par-mash'-tah)
Es 9:9 And **P.**, and Arisai, and Aridai, 6534

PARMENAS (par'-me-nas)
Ac 6:5 and Timon, and **P.**, and Nicolas a *3937*

PARNACH (par'-nak)
Nu 34:25 Zebulun, Elizaphan the son of **P.** 6535

PAROSH (pa'-rosh) See also PHAROSH.
Ezr 2:3 The children of **P.**, two thousand 6551
Ezr 10:25 of the sons of **P.**; Ramiah, and 6551
Ne 3:25 After him Pedaiah the son of **P.** 6551
Ne 7:8 The children of **P.**, two thousand 6551
Ne 10:14 The chief of the people; **P.**, 6551

PARSHANDATHA (par-shan'-da-thah)
Es 9:7 **P.**, and Dalphon, and Aspatha, 6577

PART See also APART; DEPART; FOREPART; IMPART; PARTAKEST; PARTED; PARTETH; PARTING; PARTS.
Ge 41:34 up the fifth **p.** of the land of Egypt
Ge 47:24 shall give the fifth **p.** unto Pharaoh,
Ge 47:26 that Pharaoh should have the fifth **p.**;
Ex 16:36 an omer is the tenth **p.** of an ephah.
Ex 19:17 stood at the nether **p.** of the mount.
Ex 29:26 the Lord: and it shall be thy **p.** 4490
Ex 29:40 the fourth **p.** of an hin of beaten oil;
Ex 29:40 and the fourth **p.** of an hin of wine for
Le 1:16 cast it beside the altar on the east **p.**,
Le 2:6 Thou shalt **p.** it in pieces, and pour 6626
Le 2:16 of it, **p.** of the beaten corn thereof, and
Le 2:16 and **p.** of the oil thereof, with all the
Le 5:11 his offering the tenth **p.** of a ephah
Le 5:16 and shall add the fifth **p.** thereto, and
Le 6:5 shall add the fifth **p.** more thereto,
Le 6:20 the tenth **p.** of an ephah of fine flour
Le 7:33 have the right shoulder for his **p.** 4940
Le 8:29 of consecration it was Moses' **p.**; 4940
Le 11:35 whereupon any **p.** of their carcase
Le 11:37 And if any **p.** of their carcase fall upon
Le 11:38 any **p.** of their carcase fall thereon,
Le 13:41 from the **p.** of his head toward his face,
Le 22:14 he shall put the fifth **p.** thereof unto it,
Le 23:13 be of wine, the fourth **p.** of an hin.
Le 27:13 fifth **p.** thereof unto thy estimation.
Le 27:15 he shall add the fifth **p.** of the money
Le 27:16 unto the Lord some **p.** of a field of
Le 27:19 he shall add the fifth **p.** of the money
Le 27:27 and shall add a fifth **p.** of it thereto:
Le 27:31 shall add thereto the fifth **p.** thereof.
Nu 5:7 and add unto it the fifth **p.** thereof,
Nu 5:15 tenth **p.** of an ephah of barley meal;
Nu 15:4 with the fourth **p.** of an hin of oil.
Nu 15:5 the fourth **p.** of an hin of wine for
Nu 15:6 with the third **p.** of an hin of oil.
Nu 15:7 offer the third **p.** of an hin of wine,
Nu 18:20 thou have any **p.** among them: 2506
Nu 18:20 I am thy **p.** and thine inheritance 2506
Nu 18:26 the Lord, even a tenth **p.** of the tithe. 2506

Nu 18:29 even the hallowed **p.** thereof out of it
Nu 22:41 might see the utmost **p.** of the people.
Nu 23:10 the number of the fourth **p.** of Israel?
Nu 23:13 shalt see but the utmost **p.** of them,
Nu 28:5 And a tenth **p.** of an ephah of flour
Nu 28:5 the fourth **p.** of an hin of beaten oil.
Nu 28:7 fourth **p.** of an hin for the one lamb:
Nu 28:14 and the third **p.** of an hin unto a ram,
Nu 28:14 the fourth **p.** of an hin unto a lamb:
De 10:9 Levi hath no **p.** nor inheritance 2506
De 12:12 no **p.** nor inheritance with you. 2506
De 14:27 no **p.** nor inheritance with thee. 2506
De 14:29 no **p.** nor inheritance with thee,) 2506
De 18:1 no **p.** nor inheritance with Israel: 2506
De 33:21 he provided the first **p.** for himself,
Jos 14:4 they gave no **p.** unto the Levites 2506
Jos 15:1 the uttermost **p.** of the south coast.
Jos 15:5 the sea at the uttermost **p.** of Jordan:
Jos 15:13 a **p.** among the children of Judah, 2506
Jos 18:7 the Levites have no **p.** among you; 2506
Jos 19:9 for the **p.** of the children of Judah 2506
Jos 22:25 ye have no **p.** in the Lord: so shall 2506
Jos 22:27 to come, Ye have no **p.** in the Lord. 2506
Ru 1:17 if ought but death **p.** thee and me. 6504
Ru 2:3 hap was to light on a **p.** of the field 2513
Ru 3:13 perform unto thee the **p.** of a kinsman,
Ru 3:13 well; let him do the kinsman's **p.**:
Ru 3:13 will not do the **p.** of a kinsman to thee,
Ru 3:13 will I do the **p.** of a kinsman to thee,
1Sa 9:8 the fourth **p.** of a shekel of silver:
1Sa 14:2 tarried in the uttermost **p.** of Gibeah
1Sa 23:20 and our **p.** shall be to deliver him into
1Sa 30:24 as his **p.** is that goeth down to the 2506
1Sa 30:24 his **p.** be that tarrieth by the stuff: 2506
1Sa 30:24 by the stuff: they shall **p.** alike. 2505
2Sa 14:6 there was none to **p.** them, but 5337
2Sa 18:2 sent forth a third **p.** of the people
2Sa 18:2 and a third **p.** under the hand of Ittai
2Sa 20:1 We have no **p.** in David, neither 2506
1Ki 6:24 the uttermost **p.** of the one wing unto
1Ki 6:24 the uttermost **p.** of the other were ten
1Ki 6:31 side posts were a fifth **p.** of the wall.
1Ki 6:33 of olive tree, a fourth **p.** of the wall.
2Ki 6:25 the fourth **p.** of a cab of dove's dung
2Ki 7:5 come to the uttermost **p.** of the camp
2Ki 7:8 came to the uttermost **p.** of the camp,
2Ki 11:5 A third **p.** of you that enter in on the
2Ki 11:6 a third **p.** shall be at the gate of Sur:
2Ki 11:6 and a third **p.** at the gate behind the
2Ki 18:23 be able on thy **p.** to set riders upon
1Ch 12:29 the greatest **p.** of them had kept the
2Ch 23:4 A third **p.**... entering on the sabbath,
2Ch 23:5 And a third **p.** shall be at the king's
2Ch 23:5 and a third **p.** at the gate of the
2Ch 29:16 went into the inner **p.** of the house
Ne 1:9 unto the uttermost **p.** of the heaven,
Ne 3:9 ruler of the half **p.** of Jerusalem. 6418
Ne 3:12 ruler of the half **p.** of Jerusalem, 6418
Ne 3:14 the ruler of **p.** of Beth-haccerem; 6418
Ne 3:15 the ruler of **p.** of Mizpah; he 6418
Ne 3:16 the ruler of the half **p.** of Beth-zur, 6418
Ne 3:17 of the half **p.** of Keilah, in his **p.** 6418
Ne 3:18 the ruler of the half **p.** of Keilah 6418
Ne 5:11 also the hundredth **p.** of the money,
Ne 9:3 Lord their God one fourth **p.** of the day;
Ne 9:3 and another fourth **p.** they confessed,
Ne 10:32 yearly with the third **p.** of a shekel
Job 32:17 I said, I will answer also my **p.**, 2506
Job 41:6 **p.** him among the merchants? 2673
Ps 5:9 their inward **p.** is very wickedness;
Ps 22:18 **p.** my garments among them, 2505
Ps 51:6 hidden **p.** thou shalt make me to know
Ps 118:7 The Lord taketh my **p.** with them
Pr 8:26 highest **p.** of the dust of the world
Pr 8:31 in the habitable **p.** of his earth;
Pr 17:2 shall have **p.** of the inheritance 2505
Isa 7:18 uttermost **p.** of the rivers of Egypt,
Isa 24:16 From the uttermost **p.** of the earth
Isa 36:8 able on thy **p.** to set riders upon them.
Isa 44:16 He burneth **p.** thereof in the fire; 2677
Isa 44:16 with **p.** thereof he eateth flesh; 2677
Isa 44:19 I have burned **p.** of it in the fire; 2677
Eze 4:11 by measure, the sixth **p.** of an hin:
Eze 5:2 Thou shalt burn with fire a third **p.**
Eze 5:2 and thou shalt take a third **p.**, and
Eze 5:2 a third **p.** thou shalt scatter in the
Eze 5:12 A third **p.** of thee shall die with the
Eze 5:12 third **p.** shall fall by the sword round
Eze 5:12 scatter a third **p.** into all the winds,
Eze 39:2 and leave but the sixth **p.** of thee,
Eze 45:11 may contain the tenth **p.** of an homer.
Eze 45:11 the ophah the tenth **p.** of an homer:
Eze 45:13, 13 sixth **p.** of an ephah of an homer
Eze 45:14 offer the tenth **p.** of a bath out of the
Eze 45:17 prince's **p.** to give burnt offerings,
Eze 46:14 morning, the sixth **p.** of an ephah,
Eze 46:14 and the third **p.** of an hin of oil, to
Da 1:2 with **p.** of the vessels of the house 7117
Da 2:33 his feet **p.** of iron and **p.** of clay. 4481
Da 2:41 **p.** of potters' clay, and **p.** of iron, 4481
Da 2:42 the toes of the feet were **p.** of iron, 4481
Da 2:42 **p.** of clay, so the kingdom shall be 4481
Da 5:5 the king saw the **p.** of the hand 6447
Da 5:24 the **p.** of the hand sent from him; 6447
Da 11:31 And arms shall stand on his **p.**,
Joe 2:20 his hinder **p.** toward the utmost sea,
Am 7:4 great deep, and did eat up a **p.** 2506
Zec 13:9 bring the third **p.** through the fire,
Mk 4:38 he was in the hinder **p.** of the ship,
Mk 9:40 **he that is not against us is on our p.**
Mk 13:27 **from the uttermost p. of the earth**
Mk 13:27 **to the uttermost p. of heaven.**
Lu 10:42 **Mary hath chosen that good p.,** *3310*
Lu 11:36 **be full of light, having no p. dark,** *3313*
Lu 11:39 **but your inward p. is full of ravening.**
Lu 17:24 **out of the one p. under heaven,**
Lu 17:24 **unto the other p. under heaven;**
Joh 13:8 **thee not, thou hast no p. with me.** *3313*
Joh 19:23 four parts, to every soldier a **p.**; *3313*
Ac 1:8 **unto the uttermost p. of the earth.**
Ac 1:17 had obtained **p.** of this ministry. *2819*
Ac 1:25 he may take **p.** of this ministry *2819*
Ac 5:2 And kept back **p.** of the price, his wife
Ac 5:2 brought a certain **p.**, and laid it at *3313*
Ac 5:3 keep back **p.** of the price of the land?
Ac 8:21 neither **p.** not lot in this matter: *3310*
Ac 14:4 and **p.** held with the Jews,
Ac 14:4 and **p.** with the apostles.
Ac 16:12 chief city of that **p.** of Macedonia, *3310*
Ac 19:32 more **p.** knew not wherefore they were
Ac 23:6 that the one **p.** were Sadducees, *3313*
Ac 23:9 were of the Pharisees' **p.** arose, *3313*
Ac 27:12 the more **p.** advised to depart thence
Ac 27:41 hinder **p.** was broken with the *4403*
Ro 11:25 in **p.** is happened to Israel, until *3313*
1Co 12:24 honour to that **p.** which lacked:
1Co 13:9 know in **p.**, and we prophesy in **p.** *3313*
1Co 13:10 which is in **p.** shall be done away. *3313*
1Co 13:12 now I know in **p.**; but then shall I *3313*
1Co 15:6 the greater **p.** remain unto this *4119*
1Co 16:17 lacking on your **p.** they have supplied.
2Co 1:14 ye have acknowledged us in **p.**, *3313*
2Co 2:5 he hath not grieved me, but in **p.**: *3313*
2Co 6:15 or what **p.** hath he that believeth *3310*
Eph 4:16 in the measure of every **p.**, *3313*
Tit 2:8 is of the contrary **p.** may be ashamed,
Heb 2:14 likewise took **p.** of the same; *3348*
Heb 7:2 Abraham gave a tenth **p.** of all; *3307*
1Pe 4:14 on their **p.** he is evil spoken of, but on
1Pe 4:14 of, but on your **p.** he is glorified.
Re 6:8 them over the fourth **p.** of the earth,
Re 8:7 and the third **p.**, of trees was burnt up,
Re 8:8 the third **p.** of the sea became blood;
Re 8:9 And the third **p.** of the creatures
Re 8:9 and the third **p.** of the ships were
Re 8:10 fell upon the third **p.** of the rivers,
Re 8:11 the third **p.** of the waters became
Re 8:12 the third **p.** of the sun was smitten,
Re 8:12 smitten, and the third **p.** of the moon,
Re 8:12 moon, and the third **p.** of the stars;
Re 8:12 as the third **p.** of them was darkened,
Re 8:12 the day shone not for a third **p.** of it,
Re 9:15 year, for to slay the third **p.** of men.
Re 9:18 three was the third **p.** of men killed,
Re 11:13 and the tenth **p.** of the city fell, and in
Re 12:4 the third **p.** of the stars of heaven,
Re 20:6 hath **p.** in the first resurrection: *3313*
Re 21:8 liars, shall have their **p.** in the lake *3313*
Re 22:19 away his **p.** out of the book of life, *3313*

PARTAKER See also PARTAKERS.
Ps 50:18 and hast been **p.** with adulterers. 2506
1Co 9:10 in hope should be **p.** of his hope. *3348*
1Co 9:23 I might be **p.** thereof with you. *4791*
1Co 10:30 if I by grace be a **p.**, why am I evil *3348*
1Ti 5:22 neither be **p.** of other men's sins: *2841*
2Ti 1:8 be thou **p.** of the afflictions of the *4777*
2Ti 2:6 must be first **p.** of the fruits. *3335*
1Pe 5:1 a **p.** of the glory that shall be *2844*
2Jo 11 God speed is **p.** of his evil deeds. *2841*

PARTAKERS
Mt 23:30 **we would not have been p. with** *2844*
Ro 15:27 made **p.** of their spiritual things, *2841*
1Co 9:12 be **p.** of this power over you, are *3348*
1Co 9:13 at the altar are **p.** with the altar? *4829*
1Co 10:17 for we are all **p.** of that one bread. *3348*
1Co 10:18 eat of the sacrifices **p.** of the altar? *2844*
1Co 10:21 ye cannot be **p.** of the Lord's table, *3348*
2Co 1:7 that as ye are **p.** of the sufferings, *2844*
Eph 3:6 **p.** of his promise in Christ by the *4830*
Eph 5:7 Be not ye therefore **p.** with them. *4830*
Php 1:7 gospel, ye are all **p.** of my grace. *4791*
Col 1:12 us meet to be **p.** of the inheritance *3310*
1Ti 6:2 and beloved, **p.** of the benefit. *482*
Heb 2:14 as the children are **p.** of flesh and *2841*
Heb 3:1 **p.** of the heavenly calling, consider *3353*
Heb 3:14 For we are made **p.** of Christ, if we *3353*
Heb 6:4 were made **p.** of the Holy Ghost, *3353*
Heb 12:8 whereof all are **p.**, then are ye *3353*
Heb 12:10 we might be **p.** of his holiness. *3335*
1Pe 4:13 ye are **p.** of Christ's sufferings; *2841*
2Pe 1:4 might be **p.** of the divine nature, *2844*
Re 18:4 that ye be not **p.** of her sins, and *4790*

PARTAKEST
Ro 11:17 them **p.** of the root and fatness *1096,4791*

PARTED See also DEPARTED; IMPARTED.
Ge 2:10 and from thence it was **p.**, and 6504
2Ki 2:11 of fire, and **p.** them both asunder; 6504
2Ki 2:14 waters, they **p.** hither and thither: 2673
Job 38:24 By what way is the light **p.**, which 2505
Joe 3:2 among the nations, and **p.** my land. 2505
Mt 27:35 and **p.** his garments, casting lots: *1266*
Mt 27:35 They **p.** my garments among them, *1266*
Mk 15:24 they **p.** his garments, casting lots *1266*
Lu 23:34 they **p.** his raiment, and cast lots. *1266*
Lu 24:51 he was **p.** from them, and carried *1339*
Joh 19:24 They **p.** my raiment among them, *1266*
Ac 2:45 **p.** them to all men, as every man *1266*

PARTETH
Le 11:3 Whatsoever **p.** the hoof, and is 6536
De 14:6 And every beast that **p.** the hoof, 6536
Pr 18:18 cease, and **p.** between the mighty. 6504

PARTHIANS (par-the'-uns)
Ac 2:9 **P.**, and Medes, and Elamites, and *3934*

PARTIAL
Mal 2:9 but have been **p.** in the law, 5375,6440
Jas 2:4 Are ye not then **p.** in yourselves, *1252*

PARTIALITY
1Ti 5:21 another, doing nothing by **p.** *4346*
Jas 3:17 of mercy and good fruits, without **p.**, *87*

PARTICULAR
1Co 12:27 of Christ, and members in **p.** *3313*
Eph 5:33 every one of you in **p.** so love *3588,1520*

PARTICULARLY
Ac 21:19 he declared **p.** what *1520,1538,2596*
Heb 9:5 we cannot now speak **p.** *2596,3313*

PARTIES
Ex 22:9 cause of both **p.** shall come before the

PARTING See also DEPARTING.
Eze 21:21 Babylon stood at the **p.** of the way, 517

PARTITION
1Ki 6:21 made a **p.** by the chains of gold. 5674
Eph 2:14 broken down the middle wall of **p.** *5418*

PARTLY
Da 2:42 shall be **p.** strong, and **p.** broken. 7118
1Co 11:18 you; and I **p.** believe it. *3313,5100*
Heb 10:33 **P.**, whilst ye were made a *5124,3303*
Heb 10:33 **p.**, whilst ye became companions *1161*

PARTNER See also PARTNERS.
Pr 29:24 Whoso is **p.** with a thief hateth his 2505
2Co 8:23 he is my **p.** and fellowhelper *2844*
Phm 17 If thou count me therefore a **p.**, *2844*

PARTNERS

Lu 5:7 And they beckoned unto their **p.**, ... *3353*
Lu 5:10 Zebedee, which were **p.** with Simon... *2844*

PARTRIDGE

1Sa 26:20 as when one doth hunt a **p.** in the... 7124
Jer 17:11 the **p.** sitteth on eggs, and hatcheth... 7124

PARTS

Ge 47:24 four **p.** shall be your own, for seed... 3027
Ex 33:23 hand, and thou shalt see my back **p.** ...
Le 1:8 Aaron's sons, shall lay the **p.**, the ... 5409
Le 22:23 thing superfluous or lacking in his **p.**, ...
Nu 10:5 lie on the east **p.** shall go forward. ...
Nu 11:1 were in the uttermost **p.** of the camp. ...
Nu 31:27 divide the prey into two **p.**; between...
De 19:3 giveth thee to inherit, into three **p.**, ...
De 30:4 out unto the outmost **p.** of heaven, ...
Jos 18:5 they shall divide it into seven **p.**... 2506
Jos 18:6 describe the land into seven **p.**, ... 2506
Jos 18:9 it by cities into seven **p.** in a book, ... 2506
1Sa 5:9 they had emerods in their secret **p.** ...
2Sa 19:43 and said, We have ten **p.** in the king, ...
1Ki 6:38 throughout all the **p.** thereof, and... 1697
1Ki 7:25 and all their hinder **p.** were inward. ...
1Ki 16:21 of Israel divided into two **p.** ... 2677
2Ki 11:7 two **p.** of all you that go forth on ... 3027
2Ch 4:4 and all their hinder **p.** were inward. ...
Ne 11:1 nine **p.** to dwell in other cities. ... 3027
Job 26:14 these are **p.** of his ways: but how ... 7098
Job 38:36 hath put wisdom in the inward **p.**? ...
Job 41:12 I will not conceal his **p.**, nor his... 905
Ps 2:8 uttermost **p.** of the earth for thy ...
Ps 51:6 thou desirest truth in the inward **p.** ...
Ps 63:9 shall go into the lower **p.** of the earth. ...
Ps 65:8 dwell in the uttermost **p.** are afraid...
Ps 78:66 he smote his enemies in the hinder **p.** ...
Ps 136:13 which divided the Red sea into **p.**: ... 1506
Ps 139:9 dwell in the uttermost **p.** of the sea; ...
Ps 139:15 wrought in the lowest **p.** of the earth. ...
Pr 18:8 into the innermost **p.** of the belly. ...
Pr 20:27 searching all the inward **p.** of the belly. ...
Pr 20:30 so do stripes the inward **p.** of the belly. ...
Pr 26:22 into the innermost **p.** of the belly. ...
Isa 3:17 the Lord will discover their secret **p.** ...
Isa 16:11 and mine inward **p.** for Kir-haresh. ...
Isa 44:23 shout, ye lower **p.** of the earth: ...
Jer 31:33 I will put my law in their inward **p.**, ...
Jer 34:18 and passed between the **p.** thereof, ... 1335
Jer 34:19 passed between the **p.** of the calf; ... 1335
Eze 26:20 set thee in the low **p.** of the earth, ...
Eze 31:14 death, to the nether **p.** of the earth, ...
Eze 31:16 comforted in the nether **p.** of the earth. ...
Eze 31:18 Eden unto the nether **p.** of the earth: ...
Eze 32:18 unto the nether **p.** of the earth, with...
Eze 32:24 into the nether **p.** of the earth, which...
Eze 37:11 we are cut off for our **p.** ...
Eze 38:15 from thy place out of the north **p.**, ... 3411
Eze 39:2 thee to come up from the north **p.**, ... 3411
Eze 48:8 in length as one of the other **p.**, ... 2506
Zec 13:8 two **p.** therein shall be cut off and ... 6310
Mt 2:22 he turned aside into the **p.** of Galilee: ...
Mt 12:42 **from the uttermost p. of the earth to** ...
Mk 8:10 came into the **p.** of Dalmanutha... *3313*
Lu 11:31 **from the utmost p. of the earth** ...
Joh 19:23 his garments, and made four **p.**, ... *3313*
Ac 2:10 and in the **p.** of Libya about Cyrene, ... *3313*
Ac 20:2 when he had gone over those **p.**, ... *3313*
Ro 15:23 having no more place in these **p.**, ... *2825*
1Co 12:23 our uncomely **p.** have more abundant ...
1Co 12:24 For our comely **p.** have no need: but ...
Eph 4:9 first into the lower **p.** of the earth? ... *3313*
Re 16:19 great city was divided into three **p.**, ... *3313*

PARUAH (par'-u-ah)

1Ki 4:17 Jehoshaphat the son of **P.**, in ... 6515

PARVAIM (par-va'-im)

2Ch 3:6 and the gold was gold of **P.**. ... 6516

PAS See PAS-DAMMIM.

PASACH (pa'-sak)

1Ch 7:33 sons of Japhlet; **P.**, and Bimhal, ... 6457

PAS-DAMMIM (pas-dam'-mim)

1Ch 11:13 He was with David at **P.**, and... 6450

PASEAH (pa-se'-ah) See also PHASEAH.

1Ch 4:12 Eshton begat Beth-rapha, and **P.**, ... 6454
Ezr 2:49 children of Uzza, the children of **P.**, ... 6454
Ne 3:6 repaired Jehoiada the son of **P.**, ... 6454

PASHUR (pash'-ur)

1Ch 9:12 the son of Jeroham, the son of **P.**, ... 6583
Ezr 2:38 The children of **P.**, a thousand two... 6583
Ezr 10:22 And of the sons of **P.**; Elioenai, ... 6583
Ne 7:41 The children of **P.**, a thousand two... 6583
Ne 10:3 **P.**, Amariah, Malchijah, ... 6583
Ne 11:12 the son of **P.**, the son of Malchiah, ... 6583
Jer 20:1 **P.** the son of Immer the priest, ... 6583
Jer 20:2 **P.** smote Jeremiah the prophet, ... 6583
Jer 20:3 **P.** brought forth Jeremiah out of ... 6583
Jer 20:3 Lord hath not called thy name **P.**, ... 6583
Jer 20:6 **P.**,...all that dwell in thine house... 6583
Jer 21:1 king Zedekiah sent unto him **P.** ... 6583
Jer 38:1 and Gedaliah the son of **P.**, and ... 6583
Jer 38:1 and **P.** the son of Malchiah, ... 6583

PASS See also COMPASS; OVERPASS; PASSED; PASSEST; PASSETH; PASSING; PASSOVER; PAST; TRESPASS.

Ge 4:3 in process of time it came to **p.**, ...
Ge 4:8 and it came to **p.**, when they were in the ..
Ge 4:14 it shall come to **p.**, that every one...
Ge 6:1 it came to **p.**, when men began to...
Ge 7:10 it came to **p.** after seven days, that ...
Ge 8:1 made a wind to **p.** over the earth, ... 5674
Ge 8:6 came to **p.** at the end of forty days, ...
Ge 8:13 it came to **p.** in the six hundredth...
Ge 9:14 And it shall come to **p.**, when I bring a ...
Ge 11:2 it came to **p.**, as they journeyed...
Ge 12:11 And it came to **p.**, when he was come ...
Ge 12:12 Therefore it shall come to **p.**, when the...
Ge 12:14 And it came to **p.**, that, when Abram ...
Ge 14:1 it came to **p.** in the days of Amraphel ...
Ge 15:17 And it came to **p.**, that, when the sun...
Ge 18:3 **p.** not away, I pray thee, from thy ... 5674
Ge 18:5 hearts; after that ye shall **p.** on: ... 5674
Ge 19:17 it came to **p.**, when they had brought...
Ge 19:29 it came to **p.**, when God had destroyed...
Ge 19:34 And it came to **p.** on the morrow, that...
Ge 20:13 it came to **p.**, when God caused me...
Ge 21:22 And it came to **p.** at that time, that ...
Ge 22:1, 20 And it come to **p.** after these things, ...
Ge 24:14 And let it come to **p.** that the damsel...
Ge 24:15 And it came to **p.**, before he had done ...
Ge 24:22 And it came to **p.**, as the camels had ...
Ge 24:30 And it came to **p.**, when he saw the ...
Ge 24:43 it shall come to **p.**, that when the virgin ...
Ge 24:52 And it came to **p.**, that, when...
Ge 25:11 to **p.** after the death of Abraham, ...
Ge 26:8 came to **p.**, when he had been there...
Ge 26:32 And it came to **p.** the same day, ...
Ge 27:1 And it came to **p.**, that when Isaac ...
Ge 27:30 it came to **p.**, as soon as Isaac had...
Ge 27:40 it shall come to **p.** when thou shalt ...
Ge 29:10 came to **p.**, when Jacob saw Rachel ...
Ge 29:13 it came to **p.**, when Laban heard...
Ge 29:23 it came to **p.** in the evening, that ...
Ge 29:25 it came to **p.** that in the morning, ...
Ge 30:25 And it came to **p.**, when Rachel had ...
Ge 30:32 will **p.** through all thy flock to day, ... 5674
Ge 30:41 And it came to **p.**, whensoever the...
Ge 31:10 it came to **p.** at the time that the...
Ge 31:52 I will not **p.** over this heap to thee, ... 5674
Ge 31:52 thou shalt not **p.** over this heap ... 5674
Ge 32:16 **P.** over before me, and put a space... 5674
Ge 33:14 thee, **p.** over before his servant: ... 5674
Ge 34:25 And it came to **p.** on the third day, ...
Ge 35:17 And it came to **p.**, when she was in...
Ge 35:18 And it came to **p.**, as her soul was...
Ge 35:22 it came to **p.**, when Israel dwelt in ...
Ge 37:23 And it came to **p.**, when Joseph was...
Ge 38:1 And it came to **p.** at that time, that ...
Ge 38:9 and it came to **p.**, when he went in ...
Ge 38:24 And it came to **p.** about three months ...
Ge 38:27 And it came to **p.** in the time of her ...
Ge 38:28 And it came to **p.**, when she travailed, ...
Ge 38:29 it came to **p.**, as he drew back his...
Ge 39:5 And it came to **p.** from the time that he ...
Ge 39:7 And it came to **p.** after these things, ...
Ge 39:10 And it came to **p.**, as she spake to ...
Ge 39:11 And it came to **p.** about this time, ...
Ge 39:13 And it came to **p.**, when she saw that...
Ge 39:15 And it came to **p.**, when he heard that ...
Ge 39:18 And it came to **p.**, as I lifted up my...
Ge 39:19 And it came to **p.**, when his master...
Ge 40:1 And it came to **p.** after these things, ...
Ge 40:20 And it came to **p.** the third day, which ...
Ge 41:1 And it came to **p.** at the end of two...
Ge 41:8 And it came to **p.** in the morning...
Ge 41:13 And it came to **p.**, as he interpreted ...
Ge 41:32 and God will shortly bring it to **p.**... 6213
Ge 42:35 And it came to **p.** as they emptied...
Ge 43:2 it came to **p.**, when they had eaten...
Ge 43:21 it came to **p.**, when we came to the ...
Ge 44:24 And it came to **p.** when we came up...
Ge 44:31 It shall come to **p.**, when he seeth ...
Ge 46:33 it shall come to **p.**, when Pharaoh shall...
Ge 47:24 And it shall come to **p.** in the increase, ...
Ge 48:1 And it came to **p.** after these things, ...
Ge 50:20 to bring to **p.**, as it is this day, ... 6213
Ex 1:10 and it come to **p.**, that, when there ...
Ex 1:21 it came to **p.**, because the midwives ...
Ex 2:11 it came to **p.** in those days, when...
Ex 2:23 And it came to **p.** in process of time, ...
Ex 3:21 it shall come to **p.**, that, when ye go, ...
Ex 4:8, 9 come to **p.**, if they will not believe...
Ex 4:24 it came to **p.** by the way in the inn, ...
Ex 6:28 it came to **p.** on the day when the...
Ex 12:12 For I will **p.** through the land of... 5674
Ex 12:13 I see the blood, I will **p.** over you, ... 6452
Ex 12:23 the Lord will **p.** through to smite ... 5674
Ex 12:23 the Lord will **p.** over the door, and... 6452
Ex 12:25 And it shall come to **p.**, when ye be ...
Ex 12:26 And it shall come to **p.**, when your...
Ex 12:29 it came to **p.**, that at midnight the...
Ex 12:41 it came to **p.** at the end of the four ...
Ex 12:41 even the selfsame day it came to **p.**, ...
Ex 12:51 And it came to **p.** the selfsame day, ...
Ex 13:15 came to **p.**, when Pharaoh would...
Ex 13:17 it came to **p.**, when Pharaoh had...
Ex 14:24 it came to **p.**, that in the morning...
Ex 15:16 till thy people **p.** over, O Lord, ... 5674
Ex 15:16 till the people **p.** over, which thou ... 5674
Ex 16:5 come to **p.**, that on the sixth day ...
Ex 16:10 And it came to **p.**, as Aaron spake...
Ex 16:13 came to **p.**, that at even the quails ...
Ex 16:22 it came to **p.**, that on the sixth day...
Ex 16:27 it came to **p.**, that there went out ...
Ex 17:11 And it came to **p.** when Moses held up ...
Ex 18:13 And it came to **p.** on the morrow, ...
Ex 19:16 it came to **p.** on the third day in the ...
Ex 22:27 it shall come to **p.**, when he crieth ...
Ex 32:19 it came to **p.**, as soon as he came ...
Ex 32:30 it came to **p.** on the morrow, that ...
Ex 33:7 it came to **p.**, that every one which ...
Ex 33:8 it came to **p.**, when Moses went out...
Ex 33:9 And it came to **p.**, as Moses entered ...
Ex 33:19 make all my goodness **p.** before... 5674
Ex 33:22 come to **p.**, while my glory passeth ...
Ex 33:22 thee with my hand while I **p.** by: ... 5674
Ex 34:29 it came to **p.**, when Moses came...
Ex 40:17 it came to **p.** in the first month in...
Le 9:1 came to **p.** on the eighth day, that...
Le 18:21 seed **p.** through the fire to Molech, ... 5674
Nu 5:27 come to **p.**, that, if she be defiled, ...
Nu 7:1 came to **p.** on the day that Moses ...
Nu 10:11 it came to **p.** on the twentieth day of ...
Nu 10:35 And it came to **p.**, when the ark set ...
Nu 11:23 shall come to **p.** unto thee or not. ...
Nu 11:25 it came to **p.**, that, when the spirit...
Nu 16:31 came to **p.**, as he had made an end ...
Nu 16:42 came to **p.**, when the congregation ...
Nu 17:5 it shall come to **p.**, that the man's rod, ...
Nu 17:8 it came to **p.**, that on the morrow ...
Nu 20:17 Let us **p.**, I pray thee, through thy... 5674
Nu 20:17 we will not **p.** through the fields, or... 5674
Nu 20:18 Thou shalt not **p.** by me, lest I... 5674
Nu 21:8 come to **p.**, that every one that is...
Nu 21:9 came to **p.**, that if a serpent had...
Nu 21:22 Let me **p.** through thy land: we ... 5674
Nu 21:23 Israel to **p.** through his border: ... 5674
Nu 22:41 it came to **p.** on the morrow, that ...
Nu 26:1 it came to **p.** after the plague, that ...
Nu 27:7 of their father to **p.** unto them. ... 5674
Nu 27:8 his inheritance to **p.** unto his ... 5674
Nu 32:27 But thy servants will **p.** over, every ... 5674
Nu 32:29 will **p.** with you over Jordan, every... 5674
Nu 32:30 will not **p.** over with you armed, ... 5674
Nu 32:32 We will **p.** over armed before the... 5674
Nu 33:55 then it shall come to **p.**, that those ...
Nu 33:56 come to **p.**, that I shall do unto you, ...
Nu 34:4 of Akrabbim, and **p.** on to Zin: ... 5674
Nu 34:4 Hazar-addar, and **p.** on to Azmon: ... 5674
De 1:3 it came to **p.** in the fortieth year, ...

Book	Ref	Context	No.
De	2:4	Ye are to **p.** through the coast of	5674
De	2:16	it came to **p.**, when all the men of	
De	2:18	Thou art to **p.** over through Ar,	5674
De	2:24	and **p.** over the river Arnon:	5674
De	2:27	Let me **p.** through thy land: I will	5674
De	2:28	only I will **p.** through on my feet;	5674
De	2:29	shall **p.** over Jordan into the land	5674
De	2:30	Sihon...would not let us **p.** by him:	5674
De	3:18	ye shall **p.** over armed before your	5674
De	5:23	it came to **p.**, when ye heard the	
De	7:12	it shall come to **p.**, if ye hearken to	
De	9:1	Thou art to **p.** over Jordan this	5674
De	9:11	it came to **p.** at the end of forty days	
De	11:13	And it shall come to **p.**, if ye shall	
De	11:29	it shall come to **p.**, when the Lord	
De	11:31	ye shall **p.** over Jordan to go in to	5674
De	13:2	the sign or the wonder come to **p.**,	
De	18:10	daughter to **p.** through the fire,	5674
De	18:19	shall come to **p.**, that whosoever	
De	18:22	thing follow not, nor come to **p.**,	
De	24:1	it come to **p.** that she find no favour	
De	27:2	day when ye shall **p.** over Jordan	5674
De	28:1	it shall come to **p.**, if thou shalt	
De	28:15	it shall come to **p.**, if thou wilt not	
De	28:63	it shall come to **p.**, that as the Lord	
De	29:19	it come to **p.**, when he heareth the	
De	30:1	it shall come to **p.**, when all these	
De	31:21	shall come to **p.**, when many evils	
De	31:24	it came to **p.**, when Moses made an	
Jos	1:1	it came to **p.**, that the Lord spake	
Jos	1:11	**P.** through the host, and command	5674
Jos	1:11	ye shall **p.** over this Jordan, to go	5674
Jos	1:14	but ye shall **p.** before your brethren	5674
Jos	2:5	it came to **p.** about the time of	
Jos	3:2	it came to **p.** after three days, that	
Jos	3:6	and **p.** over before the people	5674
Jos	3:13	come to **p.**, as soon as the soles of	
Jos	3:14	it came to **p.**, when the people	5674
Jos	3:14	from their tents, to **p.** over Jordan,	5674
Jos	4:1	it came to **p.**, when all the people	
Jos	4:5	**P.** over before the ark of the	5674
Jos	4:11	it came to **p.**, when all the people	
Jos	4:18	And it came to **p.**, when the priests	
Jos	5:1	it came to **p.**, when all the kings of	
Jos	5:8	And it came to **p.**, when they had	
Jos	5:13	it came to **p.**, when Joshua was by	
Jos	6:5	come to **p.**, that when they make a	
Jos	6:7	**P.** on, and compass the city, and	5674
Jos	6:7	let him that is armed **p.** on before	5674
Jos	6:8	it came to **p.**, when Joshua had	
Jos	6:15	And it came to **p.** on the seventh day,	
Jos	6:16	And it came to **p.** at the seventh time,	
Jos	6:20	came to **p.**, when the people heard	
Jos	8:5	come to **p.**, when they come out	
Jos	8:14	it came to **p.**, when the king of Ai	
Jos	8:24	came to **p.**, when Israel had made	
Jos	9:1	it came to **p.**, when all the kings	
Jos	9:16	came to **p.** at the end of three days	
Jos	10:1	it came to **p.**, when Adoni-zedec	
Jos	10:11	came to **p.**, as they fled from before	
Jos	10:20	And it came to **p.**, when Joshua and	
Jos	10:24	And it came to **p.**, when they brought	
Jos	10:27	And it came to **p.** at the time of the	
Jos	11:1	And it came to **p.**, when Jabin king	
Jos	15:18	it came to **p.**, as she came unto him,	
Jos	17:13	it came to **p.**, when the children of	
Jos	21:45	the house of Israel; all came to **p.**	935
Jos	22:19	then **p.** ye over unto the land of	5674
Jos	23:1	it came to **p.** a long time after that	
Jos	23:14	all are come to **p.** unto you, and	
Jos	23:15	come to **p.**, that as all good things	
Jos	24:29	And it came to **p.** after these things,	
Jg	1:1	the death of Joshua it came to **p.**,	
Jg	1:14	And it came to **p.**, when she came	
Jg	1:28	And it came to **p.**, when Israel was	
Jg	2:4	it came to **p.**, when the angel of the	
Jg	2:19	it came to **p.**, when the judge was	
Jg	3:27	And it came to **p.**, when he was come,	
Jg	3:28	and suffered not a man to **p.** over.	5674
Jg	6:7	it came to **p.**, when the children of	
Jg	6:25	And it came to **p.** the same night,	
Jg	7:9	And it came to **p.** the same night,	
Jg	8:33	it came to **p.**, as soon as Gideon was	
Jg	9:42	it came to **p.** on the morrow, that	
Jg	11:4	And it came to **p.** in process of time,	
Jg	11:17	Let me, I pray thee, **p.** through thy	5674
Jg	11:19	Let us **p.**, we pray thee, through	5674
Jg	11:20	But Sihon trusted not Israel to **p.**	5674
Jg	11:35	And it came to **p.**, when he saw her,	
Jg	11:39	it came to **p.** at the end of two months,	
Jg	13:12	said, Now let thy words come to **p.**	935
Jg	13:17	when thy sayings come to **p.** we may	935
Jg	13:20	it came to **p.**, when the flame went	
Jg	14:11	And it came to **p.**, when they saw him,	
Jg	14:15	And it came to **p.** on the seventh day,	
Jg	14:17	and it came to **p.** on the seventh day,	
Jg	15:1	But it came to **p.** in a while after,	
Jg	15:17	it came to **p.**, when he had made an	
Jg	16:4	it came to **p.** afterward, that he loved	
Jg	16:16	it came to **p.**, when she pressed him	
Jg	16:25	it came to **p.**, when their hearts were	
Jg	19:1	And it came to **p.** in those days, when	
Jg	19:5	And it came to **p.** on the fourth day,	
Jg	19:12	Israel; we will **p.** over to Gibeah.	5674
Jg	21:3	why is this come to **p.** in Israel,	
Jg	21:4	And it came to **p.** on the morrow, that	
Ru	1:1	Now it came to **p.** in the days when	
Ru	1:19	it came to **p.**, when they were come	
Ru	3:8	And it came to **p.** at midnight, that	
1Sa	1:12	And it came to **p.**, as she continued	
1Sa	1:20	it came to **p.**, when the time was	
1Sa	2:36	it shall come to **p.**, that every one	
1Sa	3:2	it came to **p.** at that time, when Eli	
1Sa	4:18	And it came to **p.**, when he made	
1Sa	5:10	And it came to **p.**, as the ark of God	
1Sa	7:2	And it came to **p.**, while the ark abode	
1Sa	8:1	it came to **p.**, when Samuel was old,	
1Sa	9:6	that he saith cometh surely to **p.**	
1Sa	9:26	it came to **p.** about the spring of	
1Sa	9:27	Bid the servant **p.** on before us,	5674
1Sa	10:5	it shall come to **p.**, when thou art	
1Sa	10:9	And all those signs came to **p.** that day,	
1Sa	10:11	it came to **p.**, when all that knew him	
1Sa	11:11	and it came to **p.**, that they which	
1Sa	13:10	it came to **p.**, that as soon as he had	
1Sa	13:22	So it came to **p.** in the day of battle,	
1Sa	14:1	Now it came to **p.** upon a day, that	
1Sa	14:8	we will **p.** over unto these men,	5674
1Sa	14:19	And it came to **p.**, while Saul talked	
1Sa	16:6	And it came to **p.**, when they were	
1Sa	16:8	and made him **p.** before Samuel.	5674
1Sa	16:9	Then Jesse made Shammah to **p.** by.	5674
1Sa	16:10	made seven of his sons to **p.** before	5674
1Sa	16:16	shall come to **p.**, when the evil spirit	
1Sa	16:23	it came to **p.**, when the evil spirit	
1Sa	17:48	it came to **p.**, when the Philistine	
1Sa	18:1	it came to **p.**, when he had made an	
1Sa	18:6	it came to **p.** as they came, when	
1Sa	18:10	And it came to **p.** on the morrow, that	
1Sa	18:19	came to **p.** at the time when Merab	
1Sa	18:30	it came to **p.**, after they went forth,	
1Sa	20:27	And it came to **p.** on the morrow,	
1Sa	20:35	it came to **p.** in the morning, that	
1Sa	23:6	And it came to **p.**, when Abiathar	
1Sa	23:23	it shall come to **p.**, if he be in the land,	
1Sa	24:1	And it came to **p.**, when Saul was	
1Sa	24:5	it came to **p.** afterward, that David's	
1Sa	24:16	And it came to **p.**, when David had	
1Sa	25:30	it shall come to **p.**, when the Lord	
1Sa	25:37	it came to **p.** in the morning, when	
1Sa	25:38	it came to **p.** about ten days after,	
1Sa	28:1	And it came to **p.** in those days, that	
1Sa	30:1	And it came to **p.**, when David and his	
1Sa	31:8	it came to **p.** on the morrow, when	
2Sa	1:1	it came to **p.** after the death of Saul,	
2Sa	1:2	It came even to **p.** on the third day,	
2Sa	2:1	it came to **p.** after this, that David	
2Sa	2:23	it came to **p.**, that as many as came	
2Sa	3:6	And it came to **p.**, while there was	
2Sa	4:4	it came to **p.**, as she made haste to	
2Sa	7:1	it came to **p.**, when the king sat in	
2Sa	7:4	And it came to **p.** that night, that	
2Sa	8:1	it came to **p.**, that David smote the	
2Sa	10:1	came to **p.** after this, that the king	
2Sa	11:1	And it came to **p.**, after the year	
2Sa	11:2	came to **p.** in an eveningtide, that	
2Sa	11:14	it came to **p.** in the morning, that	
2Sa	11:16	it came to **p.**, when Joab observed	
2Sa	12:18	it came to **p.** on the seventh day,	
2Sa	12:31	them **p.** through the brickkiln:	5674
2Sa	13:1	And it came to **p.** after this, that	
2Sa	13:23	came to **p.** after two full years,that	
2Sa	13:30	came to **p.**, while they were in the	
2Sa	13:36	came to **p.**, as soon as he had made	
2Sa	15:1	And it came to **p.** after this, that	
2Sa	15:7	And it came to **p.** after forty years, that	
2Sa	15:22	David said to Ittai, Go and **p.** over.	5674
2Sa	15:32	came to **p.**, that when David was	
2Sa	16:16	it came to **p.**, when Hushai the	
2Sa	17:9	will come to **p.**, when some of them	
2Sa	17:16	speedily **p.** over; lest the king be	5674
2Sa	17:21	it came to **p.**, after they were	
2Sa	17:21	and **p.** quickly over the water: for	5674
2Sa	17:27	came to **p.**, when David was come	
2Sa	19:25	it came to **p.**, when he was come	
2Sa	21:18	it came to **p.** after this, that there	
1Ki	1:21	come to **p.**, when my lord the king	
1Ki	2:39	came to **p.** at the end of three years,	
1Ki	3:18	came to **p.** the third day after that	
1Ki	5:7	it came to **p.**, when Hiram heard	
1Ki	6:1	it came to **p.** in the four hundred	
1Ki	8:10	And it came to **p.**, when the priests	
1Ki	9:1	it came to **p.**, when Solomon had	
1Ki	9:10	it came to **p.** at the end of twenty	
1Ki	11:4	came to **p.**, when Solomon was old,	
1Ki	11:15	it came to **p.**, when David was in	
1Ki	11:29	it came to **p.** at that time when	
1Ki	12:2	came to **p.**, when Jeroboam the son	
1Ki	12:20	it came to **p.**, when all Israel heard	
1Ki	13:4	it came to **p.**, when king Jeroboam	
1Ki	13:20	it came to **p.**, as they sat at the table,	
1Ki	13:23	it came to **p.**, after he had eaten	
1Ki	13:31	came to **p.**, after he had buried him,	
1Ki	13:32	of Samaria, shall surely come to **p.**	
1Ki	14:25	came to **p.** in the fifth year of king	
1Ki	15:21	it came to **p.**, when Baasha heard	
1Ki	15:29	came to **p.**, when he reigned, that	
1Ki	16:11	came to **p.**, when he began to reign,	
1Ki	16:18	it came to **p.**, when Zimri saw that	
1Ki	16:31	it came to **p.**, as if it had been a	
1Ki	17:7	it came to **p.** after a while, that the	
1Ki	17:17	came to **p.** after these things, that	
1Ki	18:1	it came to **p.** after many days, that	
1Ki	18:6	between them to **p.** throughout it:	5674
1Ki	18:12	come to **p.**, as soon as I am gone	
1Ki	18:17	came to **p.**, when Ahab saw Elijah,	
1Ki	18:27	it came to **p.** at noon, that Elijah	
1Ki	18:29	came to **p.**, when midday was past,	
1Ki	18:36	And it came to **p.** at the time of the	
1Ki	18:44	came to **p.** at the seventh time, that	
1Ki	18:45	came to **p.** in the mean while, that	
1Ki	19:17	come to **p.**, that him that escapeth	
1Ki	20:12	came to **p.**, when Benhadad heard	
1Ki	20:26	came to **p.** at the return of the year,	
1Ki	21:1	it came to **p.** after these things,	
1Ki	21:15	it came to **p.**, when Jezebel heard	
1Ki	21:16	came to **p.**, when Ahab heard that	
1Ki	21:27	came to **p.**, when Ahab heard those	
1Ki	22:2	it came to **p.** in the third year, that	
1Ki	22:32,	33 came to **p.**, when the captains of	
2Ki	2:1	And it came to **p.**, when the Lord	
2Ki	2:9	it came to **p.**, when they were gone	
2Ki	2:11	it came to **p.**, as they still went on,	
2Ki	3:5	came to **p.**, when Ahab was dead,	
2Ki	3:15	it came to **p.**, when the minstrel	
2Ki	3:20	it came to **p.** in the morning, when	
2Ki	4:6	it came to **p.**, when the vessels were	
2Ki	4:25	it came to **p.**, when the man of God	
2Ki	4:40	came to **p.**, as they were eating of	
2Ki	5:7	came to **p.**, when the king of Israel	
2Ki	6:9	that thou **p.** not such a place; for	5674
2Ki	6:20	came to **p.**, when they were come	
2Ki	6:24	And it came to **p.** after this, that	
2Ki	6:30	it came to **p.**, when the king heard	
2Ki	7:18	came to **p.** as the man of God had	
2Ki	8:3	came to **p.** at the seven years' end,	
2Ki	8:5	it came to **p.**, as he was telling the	
2Ki	8:15	came to **p.** on the morrow, that he	
2Ki	9:22	came to **p.**, when Joram saw Jehu,	
2Ki	10:7	it came to **p.**, when the letter came	
2Ki	10:9	it came to **p.** in the morning, that	
2Ki	10:25	came to **p.**, as soon as he had made	
2Ki	13:21	came to **p.**, as they were burying a	
2Ki	14:5	came to **p.**, as soon as the kingdom	
2Ki	15:12	generation. And so it came to **p.**	
2Ki	16:3	made his son to **p.** through...fire,	5674
2Ki	17:17	their daughters to **p.** through...fire,	5674
2Ki	18:1	it came to **p.** in the third year of	
2Ki	18:9	it came to **p.** in the fourth year of	
2Ki	19:1	it came to **p.**, when king Hezekiah	

2Ki 19:25 now have I brought it to **p.**, that..........
2Ki 19:35 it came to **p.**, that night, that the..........
2Ki 19:37 came to **p.**, as he was worshipping..........
2Ki 20:4 it came to **p.**, afore Isaiah was gone..........
2Ki 21:6 made his son **p.** through the fire, ... 5674
2Ki 22:3 came to **p.** in the eighteenth year..........
2Ki 22:11 it came to **p.**, when the king had..........
2Ki 23:10 daughter to **p.** through the fire to....... 5674
2Ki 24:20 it came to **p.** in Jerusalem and..........
2Ki 25:1 it came to **p.** in the ninth year of..........
2Ki 25:25 it came to **p.** in the seventh month, ...
2Ki 25:27 it came to **p.** in the seventh and..........
1Ch 10:8 it came to **p.** on the morrow, when..........
1Ch 15:26 it came to **p.**, when God helped the..........
1Ch 15:29 And it came to **p.**, as the ark of the..........
1Ch 17:1 it came to **p.**, as David sat in his..........
1Ch 17:3 it came to **p.** the same night, that..........
1Ch 17:11 it shall come to **p.**, when thy days..........
1Ch 18:1 after this it came to **p.**, that David..........
1Ch 19:1 Now it came to **p.** after this, that..........
1Ch 20:1 it came to **p.**, that after the year..........
1Ch 20:4 it came to **p.** after this, that there..........
2Ch 5:11 And it came to **p.**, when the priests..........
2Ch 5:13 came even to **p.**, as the trumpeters..........
2Ch 8:1 it came to **p.** at the end of twenty..........
2Ch 10:2 it came to **p.**, when Jeroboam the..........
2Ch 12:1 it came to **p.**, when Rehoboam had..........
2Ch 12:2 it came to **p.**, that in the fifth year..........
2Ch 13:15 it came to **p.**, that God smote..........
2Ch 16:5 came to **p.**, when Baasha heard it,..........
2Ch 18:31 it came to **p.**, when the captains of..........
2Ch 18:32 came to **p.**, that, when the captains..........
2Ch 20:1 came to **p.** after this also, that the..........
2Ch 21:19 came to **p.**, that in process of time, ...
2Ch 22:8 came to **p.**, that, when Jehu was..........
2Ch 24:4 it came to **p.** after this, that Joash..........
2Ch 24:11 came to **p.**, that at what time the..........
2Ch 24:23 came to **p.** at the end of the year,..........
2Ch 25:3 came to **p.**, when the kingdom was..........
2Ch 25:14 came to **p.**, after that Amaziah was..........
2Ch 25:16 came to **p.**, as he talked with him,..........
2Ch 33:6 his children to **p.** through the fire....... 5674
2Ch 34:19 it came to **p.**, when the king had..........
Ne 1:1 it came to **p.** in the month Chisleu,..........
Ne 1:4 it came to **p.**, when I heard these..........
Ne 2:1 it came to **p.** in the month Nisan, ...
Ne 2:14 beast that was under me to **p.**.......... 5674
Ne 4:1 came to **p.**, that when Sanballat..........
Ne 4:7 it came to **p.**, that when Sanballat,..........
Ne 4:12 it came to **p.**, that when the Jews..........
Ne 4:15 it came to **p.**, when our enemies..........
Ne 4:16 it came to **p.** from that time forth,..........
Ne 6:1 Now it came to **p.**, when Sanballat, ...
Ne 6:16 it came to **p.**, that when all our..........
Ne 7:1 it came to **p.**, when the wall was..........
Ne 13:3 it came to **p.**, when they had heard..........
Ne 13:19 came to **p.**, that when the gates of..........
Es 1:1 came to **p.** in the days of Ahasuerus, ...
Es 2:8 came to **p.**, when the king's...decree..........
Es 3:4 came to **p.**, when they spake daily..........
Es 5:1 it came to **p.** on the third day, that..........
Job 6:15 the stream of brooks they **p.** away; 5674
Job 11:16 remember it as waters that **p.** away:.... 5674
Job 14:5 his bounds that he cannot **p.**; 5674
Job 19:8 fenced up my way that I cannot **p.**. 5674
Job 34:20 troubled at midnight, and **p.** away:...... 5674
Ps 37:5 him; and he shall bring it to **p.**....... 6213
Ps 37:7 who bringeth wicked devices to **p.**....... 6213
Ps 58:8 let every one of them **p.** away:.......... 1980
Ps 78:13 and caused them to **p.** through; 5674
Ps 80:12 which **p.** by the way do pluck her? 5674
Ps 89:41 All that **p.** by the way spoil him: he.... 5674
Ps 104:9 a bound that they may not **p.** over: 5674
Ps 136:14 made Israel to **p.** through the midst.... 5674
Ps 148:6 made a decree which shall not **p.**. 5674
Pr 4:15 Avoid it, **p.** not by it, turn from it, ... 5674
Pr 4:15 turn from it, and **p.** away.......... 5674
Pr 8:29 should not **p.** his commandment: 5674
Pr 16:30 his lips he bringeth evil to **p.**.......... 3615
Pr 19:11 glory to **p.** over a transgression. 5674
Pr 22:3 but the simple **p.** on,...are punished.... 5674
Pr 27:12 but the simple **p.** on,...are punished.... 5674
Isa 2:2 it shall come to **p.** in the last days,..........
Isa 3:24 come to **p.**, that instead of sweet..........
Isa 4:3 shall come to **p.**, that he that is left..........
Isa 7:1 it came to **p.** in the days of Ahaz the..........
Isa 7:7 stand, neither shall it come to **p.**..........
Isa 7:18, 21 it shall come to **p.** in that day,..........
Isa 7:22 shall come to **p.**, for the abundance..........
Isa 7:23 And it shall come to **p.** in that day,..........
Isa 8:8 And he shall **p.** through Judah;.......... 2498
Isa 8:21 they shall **p.** through it, hardly.......... 5674
Isa 8:21 come to **p.**, that when they shall..........
Isa 10:12 shall come to **p.**, that when the Lord..........
Isa 10:20, 27 it shall come to **p.** in that day,..........
Isa 11:11 And it shall come to **p.** in that day,..........
Isa 14:3 And it shall come to **p.** in the day..........
Isa 14:24 have thought, so shall it come to **p.**;..........
Isa 16:12 it shall come to **p.**, when it is seen..........
Isa 17:4 And in that day it shall come to **p.**,..........
Isa 21:1 whirlwinds in...south **p.** through; 2498
Isa 22:7 shall come to **p.**, that thy choicest..........
Isa 22:20 And it shall come to **p.** in that day,..........
Isa 23:2 of Zidon, that **p.** over the sea,.......... 5674
Isa 23:6 **P.** ye over to Tarshish; howl, ye 5674
Isa 23:10 **P.** through thy land as a river, O 5674
Isa 23:12 arise, **p.** over to Chittim; there also.... 5674
Isa 23:15 come to **p.** in that day, that Tyre..........
Isa 23:17 come to **p.** after the end of seventy..........
Isa 24:18 And it shall come to **p.** that he who..........
Isa 24:21 And it shall come to **p.** in that day,..........
Isa 27:12, 13 it shall come to **p.** in that day,..........
Isa 28:15, 18 the overflowing scourge shall **p.**..... 5674
Isa 28:19 morning by morning shall it **p.** over, ... 5674
Isa 28:21 bring to **p.** his act, his strange act. 5674
Isa 30:32 where the grounded staff shall **p.**, ... 4569
Isa 31:9 he shall **p.** over to his strong hold...... 5674
Isa 33:21 neither...gallant ship **p.** thereby.......... 5674
Isa 34:10 none shall **p.** through it for ever......... 5674
Isa 35:8 the unclean shall not **p.** over it; 5674
Isa 36:1 came to **p.** in the fourteenth year..........
Isa 37:1 it came to **p.**, when king Hezekiah..........
Isa 37:26 now have I brought it to **p.**, that..........
Isa 37:38 came to **p.**, as he was worshipping..........
Isa 42:9 the former things are come to **p.**,..........
Isa 46:11 spoken it, I will also bring it to **p.**; ....
Isa 47:2 the thigh, **p.** over the rivers.......... 5674
Isa 48:3 suddenly, and they came to **p.**..........
Isa 48:5 it came to **p.** I shewed it thee: lest..........
Isa 51:10 a way for the ransomed to **p.** over?.... 5674
Isa 65:24 come to **p.**, that before they call, ...
Isa 66:23 it shall come to **p.**, that from one..........
Jer 2:10 For **p.** over the isles of Chittim, ... 5674
Jer 3:9 it came to **p.** through the lightness..........
Jer 3:16 come to **p.**, when ye be multiplied..........
Jer 4:9 it shall come to **p.** at that day, saith..........
Jer 5:19 shall come to **p.**, when ye shall say, ...
Jer 5:22 perpetual decree,...it cannot **p.** it: 5674
Jer 5:22 they roar, yet can they not **p.** over it? .5674
Jer 8:13 them shall **p.** away from them. 5674
Jer 9:10 so that none can **p.** through them;...... 5674
Jer 12:15 come to **p.**, after that I have plucked..........
Jer 12:16 shall come to **p.**, if they will diligently..........
Jer 13:6 it came to **p.** after many days, that..........
Jer 15:2 it shall come to **p.**, if they say unto..........
Jer 15:14 thee to **p.** with thine enemies into...... 5674
Jer 16:10 shall come to **p.**, when thou shalt..........
Jer 17:24 come to **p.**, if ye diligently hearken..........
Jer 20:3 it came to **p.** on the morrow, that..........
Jer 22:8 many nations shall **p.** by this city,....... 5674
Jer 25:12 come to **p.**, when seventy years..........
Jer 26:8 it came to **p.**, when Jeremiah had..........
Jer 27:8 it shall come to **p.**, that the nation..........
Jer 28:1 it came to **p.** the same year, in the..........
Jer 28:9 of the prophet shall come to **p.**,..........
Jer 30:8 shall come to **p.** in that day, saith..........
Jer 31:28 shall come to **p.**, that like as I have..........
Jer 32:24 thou hast spoken is come to **p.**;..........
Jer 32:35 daughters to **p.** through the fire......... 5674
Jer 33:13 flocks **p.** again under the hands of...... 5674
Jer 35:11 came to **p.**, when Nebuchadrezzar..........
Jer 36:1 it came to **p.** in the fourth year of..........
Jer 36:9 And it came to **p.** in the fifth year of..........
Jer 36:16 it came to **p.**, when they had heard..........
Jer 36:23 it came to **p.**, that when Jehudi had..........
Jer 37:11 came to **p.**, that when the army of..........
Jer 39:4 came to **p.**, that when Zedekiah the..........
Jer 41:1 it came to **p.** in the seventh month, ...
Jer 41:4 came to **p.** the second day after he..........
Jer 41:6 and it came to **p.**, as he met them,..........
Jer 41:13 came to **p.**, that when all the people..........
Jer 42:4 come to **p.** that whatsoever thing..........
Jer 42:7 And it came to **p.** after ten days, ...
Jer 42:16 it shall come to **p.**, that the sword,..........
Jer 43:1 it came to **p.**, that when Jeremiah..........
Jer 49:39 shall come to **p.** in the latter days, ...
Jer 51:43 neither doth any son of man **p.** 5674
Jer 52:3 came to **p.** in Jerusalem and Judah,..........
Jer 52:4 came to **p.** in the ninth year of his..........
Jer 52:31 came to **p.** in the seven and thirtieth..........
La 1:12 it nothing to you, all ye that **p.** by?..... 5674
La 2:15 that **p.** by clap their hands at thee; 5674
La 3:37 and it cometh to **p.**, when the Lord..........
La 3:44 our prayer should not **p.** through.......... 5674
La 4:21 cup also shall **p.** through unto thee: 5674
Eze 1:1 it came to **p.** in the thirtieth year, ...
Eze 3:16 came to **p.** at the end of seven days, ...
Eze 5:1 and cause it to **p.** upon thine head...... 5674
Eze 5:14 thee, in the sight of all that **p.** by....... 5674
Eze 5:17 and blood shall **p.** through thee; 5674
Eze 8:1 And it came to **p.** in the sixth year, ...
Eze 9:8 came to **p.**, while they were slaying..........
Eze 10:6 And it came to **p.** that when he had..........
Eze 11:13 it came to **p.**, when I prophesied,..........
Eze 12:25 I shall speak shall come to **p.**; 6213
Eze 14:15 noisome beasts to **p.** through the 5674
Eze 14:15 no man may **p.** through because......... 5674
Eze 16:21 to cause them to **p.** through the fire ... 5674
Eze 16:23 And it came to **p.** after all thy..........
Eze 20:1 And it came to **p.** in the seventh year, ...
Eze 20:26 caused to **p.** through the fire all......... 5674
Eze 20:31 your sons to **p.** through the fire, ... 5674
Eze 20:37 will cause you to **p.** under the rod, ... 5674
Eze 21:7 cometh, and shall be brought to **p.**, ...
Eze 23:37 to **p.** for them through the fire, to...... 5674
Eze 24:14 it shall come to **p.**, and I will do it;..........
Eze 26:1 it came to **p.** in the eleventh year,..........
Eze 29:11 No foot of man shall **p.** through it,...... 5964
Eze 29:11 nor foot of beast shall **p.** through it,.... 5964
Eze 29:17 And it came to **p.** in the seven and..........
Eze 30:20 it came to **p.** in the eleventh year,..........
Eze 31:1 it came to **p.** in the eleventh year,..........
Eze 32:1 it came to **p.** in the twelfth year, in..........
Eze 32:17 came to **p.** also in the twelfth year, ...
Eze 32:19 Whom dost thou **p.** in beauty? go..........
Eze 33:21 it came to **p.** in the twelfth year of..........
Eze 33:28 desolate,...none shall **p.** through.......... 5674
Eze 33:33 And when this cometh to **p.**, (lo, it..........
Eze 37:2 me to **p.** by them round about: 5674
Eze 38:10 come to **p.**, that at the same time..........
Eze 38:18 it shall come to **p.** at the same time..........
Eze 39:11 shall come to **p.** in that day, that..........
Eze 39:15 the passengers that **p.** through the 5674
Eze 44:17 And it shall come to **p.**, that when..........
Eze 46:21 and caused me to **p.** by the four 5674
Eze 47:5 was a river that I could not **p.** over: ... 5674
Eze 47:9 it shall come to **p.**, that every thing..........
Eze 47:10 it shall come to **p.**, that the fishers..........
Eze 47:22 come to **p.**, that ye shall divide it by..........
Eze 47:23 shall come to **p.**, that in what tribe..........
Da 2:29 what should come to **p.** hereafter: ....
Da 2:29 to thee what shall come to **p.**..........
Da 2:45 what shall come to **p.** hereafter:..........
Da 4:16 and let seven times **p.** over him......... 2499
Da 4:23 field, till seven times **p.** over him; 2499
Da 4:25, 32 and seven times shall **p.** over thee, .2499
Da 7:14 dominion, which shall not **p.** away,...... 5709
Da 8:2 came to **p.**, when I saw, that I was..........
Da 8:15 came to **p.**, when I, even I Daniel, ...
Da 11:10 and overflow, and **p.** through:.......... 5674
Da 11:40 and shall overflow and **p.** over. 5674
Ho 1:5 shall come to **p.** at that day, that..........
Ho 1:10 shall come to **p.**, that in the place..........
Ho 2:21 come to **p.** in that day, I will hear, ...
Joe 2:28 it shall come to **p.** afterward, that..........
Joe 2:32 it shall come to **p.**, that whosoever..........
Joe 3:17 shall no strangers **p.** through her........ 5674
Joe 3:18 it shall come to **p.** in that day, that..........
Am 5:5 Gilgal, and **p.** not to Beer-sheba:........ 5674
Am 5:17 for I will **p.** through thee, saith the..... 5674
Am 6:2 **P.** ye unto Calneh, and see; and......... 5674
Am 6:9 come to **p.**, if there remain ten..........
Am 7:2 it came to **p.**, that when they had..........
Am 7:8 not again **p.** by them any more: 5674
Am 8:2 not again **p.** by them any more. 5674
Am 8:9 And it shall come to **p.** in that day,..........
Jon 4:8 came to **p.**, when the sun did arise,..........
Mic 1:11 **P.** ye away, thou inhabitant of.......... 5674
Mic 2:8 the garment from them that **p.** by 5674

Mic 2:13 and their king shall **p.** before them, 5674
Mic 4:1 in the last days it shall come to **p.**,
Mic 5:10 And it shall come to **p.** in that day,
Na 1:12 down, when he shall **p.** through. 5674
Na 1:15 wicked shall no more **p.** through 5674
Na 3:7 come to **p.**, that all they that look
Hab 1:11 mind change, and he shall **p.** over, 5674
Zep 1:8 shall come to **p.** in the day of the
Zep 1:10 And it shall come to **p.** in that day,
Zep 1:12 And it shall come to **p.** at that time,
Zep 2:2 before the day **p.** as the chaff, 5674
Zec 3:4 caused thine iniquity to **p.** from 5674
Zec 6:15 And this shall come to **p.**, if ye will
Zec 7:1 it came to **p.** in the fourth year of
Zec 7:13 it is come to **p.**, that as he cried,
Zec 8:13 it shall come to **p.**, that as ye were
Zec 8:20 yet come to **p.**, that there shall come
Zec 8:23 shall come to **p.**, that ten men shall
Zec 9:8 and no oppressor shall **p.** through 5674
Zec 10:11 **p.** through the sea with affliction, 5674
Zec 12:9 it shall come to **p.** in that day, that
Zec 13:2 And it shall come to **p.** in that day,
Zec 13:2 the unclean spirit to **p.** out of the 5674
Zec 13:3 it shall come to **p.**, that when any
Zec 13:4 it shall come to **p.** in that day, that
Zec 13:8 it shall come to **p.**, that in all the land,
Zec 14:6, 13 it shall come to **p.** in that day, that
Zec 14:7 but it shall come to **p.**, that at evening
Zec 14:16 it shall come to **p.**, that every one that
Mt 5:18 **Till heaven and earth p., one jot** *3928*
Mt 5:18 **one tittle shall in no wise p. from** *3928*
Mt 7:28 came to **p.**, when Jesus had ended
Mt 8:28 that no man might **p.** by that way *3928*
Mt 9:10 came to **p.**, as Jesus sat at meat in
Mt 11:1 came to **p.**, when Jesus had made
Mt 13:53 it came to **p.**, that when Jesus had
Mt 19:1 it came to **p.**, that when Jesus had
Mt 24:6 **all these things must come to p.,**
Mt 24:34 **This generation shall not p., till all** *3928*
Mt 24:35 **Heaven and earth shall p. away,** *3928*
Mt 24:35 **but my words shall not p. away.** *3928*
Mt 26:1 And it came to **p.**, when Jesus had
Mt 26:39 **possible, let this cup p. from me:** *3928*
Mt 26:42 **if this cup may not p. away** *3928*
Mk 1:9 it came to **p.** in those days, that
Mk 2:15 it came to **p.**, that, as Jesus sat at
Mk 2:23 it came to **p.**, that he went through
Mk 4:4 **came to p., as he sowed, some fell**
Mk 4:35 **Let us p. over unto the other side** *1330*
Mk 11:23 **which he saith shall come to p.;**
Mk 13:29 **shall see these things come to p.,**
Mk 13:30 **this generation shall not p., till all** *3928*
Mk 13:31 **Heaven and earth shall p. away:** *3928*
Mk 13:31 **but my words shall not p. away.** *3928*
Mk 14:35 the hour might **p.** from him. *3928*
Lu 1:8 came to **p.**, that while he executed
Lu 1:23 came to **p.**, that, as soon as the days
Lu 1:41 it came to **p.**, that, when Elisabeth
Lu 1:59 came to **p.**, that on the eighth day
Lu 2:1 And it came to **p.** in those days, that
Lu 2:15 came to **p.**, as the angels were gone
Lu 2:15 see this thing which is come to **p.**,
Lu 2:46 it came to **p.**, that after three days
Lu 3:21 it came to **p.**, that Jesus also being
Lu 5:1 it came to **p.**, that, as the people
Lu 5:12 came to **p.**, when he was in a certain
Lu 5:17 it came to **p.** on a certain day, as he
Lu 6:1 it came to **p.** on the second sabbath
Lu 6:6 came to **p.** also on another sabbath,
Lu 6:12 it came to **p.** in those days, that he
Lu 7:11 it came to **p.** the day after, that he
Lu 8:1 And it came to **p.** afterward, that
Lu 8:22 it came to **p.** on a certain day, that
Lu 8:40 it came to **p.**, that, when Jesus was
Lu 9:18 came to **p.**, as he was alone praying,
Lu 9:28 it came to **p.** about an eight days
Lu 9:33 came to **p.**, as they departed from
Lu 9:37 it came to **p.**, that on the next day,
Lu 9:51 came to **p.**, when the time was come
Lu 9:57 came to **p.**, that, as they went in the
Lu 10:38 it came to **p.**, as they went, that he
Lu 11:1 came to **p.**, that, as he was praying
Lu 11:14 came to **p.**, when the devil was gone
Lu 11:27 came to **p.**, as he spake these things,
Lu 11:42 **p. over judgment and the love of** *3928*
Lu 12:55 **will be heat; and it cometh to p.**
Lu 14:1 it came to **p.**, as he went into the
Lu 16:17 **easier for heaven and earth to p.,** *3928*
Lu 16:22 **it came to p., that the beggar died,**
Lu 16:26 **which would p. from hence to you** *1224*
Lu 16:26 **neither can they p. to us, that** *1276*
Lu 17:11 And it came to **p.**, as he went to
Lu 17:14 it came to **p.**, that, as they went,
Lu 18:35 it came to **p.**, that as he was come
Lu 18:36 And hearing the multitude **p.** by, *1279*
Lu 19:4 see him: for he was to **p.** that way *1330*
Lu 19:15 it came to **p.**, that when he was
Lu 19:29 it came to **p.**, when he was come
Lu 20:1 it came to **p.**, that on one of those
Lu 21:7 when these things shall come to **p.**?
Lu 21:9 **these things must first come to p.;**
Lu 21:28 **these things begin to come to p.,**
Lu 21:31 **when ye see these things come to p.,**
Lu 21:32 **This generation shall not p. away,** *3928*
Lu 21:33 **Heaven and earth shall p. away:** *3928*
Lu 21:33 **but my words shall not p. away.** *3928*
Lu 21:36 **these things that shall come to p.,**
Lu 24:4 it came to **p.**, as they were much
Lu 24:12 himself at that which was come to **p.**.
Lu 24:15 And it came to **p.**, that, while they
Lu 24:18 are come to **p.** there in these days?
Lu 24:30 it came to **p.**, as he sat at meat with
Lu 24:51 it came to **p.**, while he blessed them,
Joh 13:19 **when it is come to p., ye may believe.**
Joh 14:29 **I have told you before it come to p.,**
Joh 14:29 **that, when it is come to p., ye might**
Joh 15:25 **But this cometh to p., that the word**
Ac 2:17 it shall come to **p.** in the last days,
Ac 2:21 it shall come to **p.**, that whosoever
Ac 3:23 it shall come to **p.**, that every soul,
Ac 4:5 it came to **p.** on the morrow, that
Ac 9:32 And it came to **p.**, as Peter passed *1330*
Ac 9:37 it came to **p.** in those days, that
Ac 9:43 it came to **p.**, that he tarried many
Ac 11:26 And it came to **p.**, that a whole year
Ac 11:28 came to **p.** in the days of Claudius
Ac 14:1 it came to **p.** in Iconium, that they
Ac 16:16 it came to **p.**, as we went to prayer,
Ac 18:27 he was disposed to **p.** into Achaia, *1330*
Ac 19:1 came to **p.**, that, while Apollos was
Ac 21:1 it came to **p.**, that after we were
Ac 22:6 it came to **p.**, that, as I made my
Ac 22:17 it came to **p.**, that, when I was come
Ac 27:44 so it came to **p.**, that they escaped
Ac 28:8 came to **p.**, that the father of Publius
Ac 28:17 it came to **p.**, that after three days
Ro 9:26 it shall come to **p.**, that in the place
1Co 7:36 if she **p.** the flower of her age, *5230*
1Co 15:54 shall be brought to **p.** the saying
1Co 16:5 I shall **p.** through Macedonia: *1330*
1Co 16:5 for I do **p.** through Macedonia. *1330*
2Co 1:16 And to **p.** by you into Macedonia, *1330*
1Th 3:4 even as it came to **p.**, and ye know.
Jas 1:10 of the grass he shall **p.** away. *3928*
1Pe 1:17 **p.** the time of your sojourning here *390*
2Pe 3:10 the heavens shall **p.** away with a *3928*
Re 1:1 which must shortly come to **p.**;

PASSAGE See also PASSAGES.

Nu 20:21 Edom refused to give Israel **p.** 5674
Jos 22:11 at the **p.** of the children of Israel. 1552
1Sa 13:23 went out to the **p.** of Michmash. 4569
Isa 10:29 They are gone over the **p.**: they 4569

PASSAGES

Jg 12:5 Gileadites took the **p.** of Jordan 4569
Jg 12:6 and slew him at the **p.** of Jordan: 4569
1Sa 14:4 between the **p.**, by which Jonathan 4569
Jer 22:20 cry from the **p.**: for all thy lovers 5676
Jer 51:32 And that the **p.** are stopped, and 4569

PASSED See also COMPASSED; PASSEDST; PAST; TRESPASSED.

Ge 12:6 And Abram **p.** through the land 5674
Ge 15:17 a burning lamp that **p.** between 5674
Ge 31:21 he rose up, and **p.** over the river, 5674
Ge 32:10 with my staff I **p.** over this Jordan; 5674
Ge 32:22 sons, and **p.** over the ford Jabbok 5674
Ge 32:31 as he **p.** over Penuel the sun rose 5674
Ge 33:3 he **p.** over before them, and bowed 5674
Ge 37:28 **p.** by Midianites merchantmen; 5674
Ex 12:27 **p.** over the houses of the children 6452
Ex 34:6 And the Lord **p.** by before him, 5674
Nu 14:7 which we **p.** through to search it 5674
Nu 20:17 left, until we have **p.** thy borders. 5674
Nu 33:8 and **p.** through the midst of the sea 5674
Nu 33:51 are **p.** over Jordan into the land of 5674
De 2:8 when we **p.** by from our brethren 5674
De 2:8 and **p.** by the way of the wilderness 5674
De 27:3 of this law, when thou art **p.** over, 5674
De 29:16 the nations through which ye **p.** by; 5674
Jos 2:23 **p.** over, and came to Joshua the 5674
Jos 3:1 lodged there before they **p.** over 5674
Jos 3:4 ye have not **p.** this way heretofore. 5674
Jos 3:16 people **p.** over...against Jericho. 5674
Jos 3:17 the Israelites **p.** over on dry ground, 5674
Jos 3:17 people were **p.** clean over Jordan. 5674
Jos 4:1 people were clean **p.** over Jordan, 5674
Jos 4:7 when it **p.** over Jordan, the waters 5674
Jos 4:10 and the people hasted and **p.** over. 5674
Jos 4:11 all the people were clean **p.** over, 5674
Jos 4:11 the ark of the Lord **p.** over, and the 5674
Jos 4:12 tribe of Manasseh, **p.** over armed 5674
Jos 4:13 thousand prepared for war **p.** over 5674
Jos 4:23 until ye were **p.** over, as the Lord 5674
Jos 5:1 until we were **p.** over, that their 5674
Jos 6:8 priests...**p.** on before the Lord, 5674
Jos 10:29 Then Joshua **p.** from Makkedah, 5674
Jos 10:31 And Joshua **p.** from Libnah, and 5674
Jos 10:34 Lachish Joshua **p.** unto Eglon, 5674
Jos 15:3 and **p.** along to Zin, and ascended 5674
Jos 15:3 and **p.** along to Hezron, and went 5674
Jos 15:4 From thence it **p.** toward Azmon, 5674
Jos 15:6 **p.**...by the north of Beth-arabah; 5674
Jos 15:7 the border **p.** toward the waters of 5674
Jos 15:10 and **p.** along unto the side of mount 5674
Jos 15:10 and **p.** on to Timnah: 5674
Jos 15:11 **p.** along to mount Baalah, and went 5674
Jos 16:6 and **p.** by it on the east to Janohah; 5674
Jos 18:9 men went and **p.** through the land, 5674
Jos 18:18 And **p.** along toward the side over 5674
Jos 18:19 And the border **p.** along to the side 5674
Jos 24:17 all the people through whom we **p.**: 5674
Jg 3:26 and **p.** beyond the quarries, and 5674
Jg 8:4 Gideon came to Jordan, and **p.** over, 5674
Jg 10:9 children of Ammon **p.** over Jordan 5674
Jg 11:29 he **p.** over Gilead, and Manasseh, 5674
Jg 11:29 and **p.** over Mizpeh of Gilead, and 5674
Jg 11:29 **p.** over unto the children of Ammon 5674
Jg 11:32 Jephthah **p.** over unto the children 5674
Jg 12:3 and **p.** over against the children of 5674
Jg 18:13 **p.** thence unto mount Ephraim, 5674
Jg 19:14 And they **p.** on and went their way; 5674
1Sa 9:4 And he **p.** through mount Ephraim, 5674
1Sa 9:4 and **p.** through the land of Shalisha, 5674
1Sa 9:4 they **p.** through the land of Shalim, 5674
1Sa 9:4 **p.** through the land of...Benjamites, 5674
1Sa 9:27 pass on before us, (and he **p.** on,) 5674
1Sa 14:23 the battle **p.** over unto Beth-aven. 5674
1Sa 15:12 and **p.** on, and gone down to Gilgal 5674
1Sa 27:2 **p.** over with the six hundred men 5674
1Sa 29:2 the Philistines **p.** on by hundreds, 5674
1Sa 29:2 and his men **p.** on in the rereward 5674
2Sa 2:29 the plain, and **p.** over Jordan, and 5674
2Sa 10:17 Israel together, and **p.** over Jordan, 5674
2Sa 15:18 all his servants **p.** on beside him; 5674
2Sa 15:18 from Gath, **p.** on before the king 5674
2Sa 15:22 And Ittai the Gittite **p.** over, and all 5674
2Sa 15:23 voice, and all the people **p.** over: 5674
2Sa 15:23 himself **p.** over the brook Kidron, 5674
2Sa 15:23 Kidron, and all the people **p.** over, 5674
2Sa 17:22 with him, and they **p.** over Jordan: 5674
2Sa 17:24 And Absalom **p.** over Jordan, he 5674
2Sa 24:5 they **p.** over Jordan, and pitched 5674
1Ki 13:25 And, behold, men **p.** by, and saw the 5674
1Ki 19:11 And, behold, the Lord **p.** by, and a 5674
1Ki 19:19 and Elijah **p.** by him, and cast his 5674
1Ki 20:39 as the king **p.** by, he cried unto the 5674
2Ki 4:8 on a day, that Elisha **p.** to Shunem, 5674
2Ki 4:8 that as oft as he **p.** by, he turned 5674
2Ki 4:31 Gehazi **p.** on before them, and laid 5674
2Ki 6:30 and he **p.** by upon the wall, and the 5674
2Ki 14:9 there **p.** by a wild beast that was 5674
1Ch 19:17 all Israel, and **p.** over Jordan, and 5674
2Ch 9:22 king Solomon **p.** all the kings of 1431
2Ch 25:18 and there **p.** by a wild beast that 5674
2Ch 30:10 So the posts **p.** from city to city 5674
Job 4:15 Then a spirit **p.** before my face; 2498
Job 9:26 are **p.** away as the swift ships: 2498
Job 15:19 and no stranger **p.** among them. 5674
Job 28:8 it, nor the fierce lion **p.** by it 5710
Ps 18:12 was before him his thick clouds **p.**, 5674

Ps 37:36 Yet he **p.** away, and, lo, he was 5674
Ps 48:4 assembled, they **p.** by together.......... 5674
Ps 90:9 all our days are **p.** away in thy........... 6437
Ca 3:4 but a little that I **p.** from them,.......... 5674
Isa 10:28 come to Aiath, he is **p.** to Migron; 5674
Isa 40:27 judgment is **p.** over from my God? 5674
Isa 41:3 He pursued them, and **p.** safely; 5674
Jer 2:6 a land that no man **p.** through, and..... 5674
Jer 11:15 and the holy flesh is **p.** from thee? 5674
Jer 34:18 and **p.** between the parts thereof, ... 5674
Jer 34:19 **p.** between the parts of the calf; 5674
Jer 46:17 he hath **p.** the time appointed............ 5674
Eze 16:6 when I **p.** by thee, and saw thee......... 5674
Eze 16:8 Now when I **p.** by thee, and looked..... 5674
Eze 16:15 on every one that **p.** by; his it........... 5674
Eze 16:25 thy feet to every one that **p.** by,........ 5674
Eze 36:34 in the sight of all that **p.** by............... 5674
Eze 47:5 a river that could not be **p.** over........ 5674
Da 3:27 the smell of fire had **p.** on them.......... 5709
Da 6:18 to his palace, and **p.** the night fasting: ....
Ho 10:11 but I **p.** over upon her fair neck: I...... 5674
Jon 2:3 billows and thy waves **p.** over me. 5674
Mic 2:13 up, and have **p.** through the gate, ... 5674
Na 3:19 not thy wickedness **p.** continually? 5674
Hab 3:10 the overflowing of the water **p.** by:...... 5674
Zec 7:14 no man **p.** through nor returned:........ 5674
Mt 9:1 entered into a ship, and **p.** over,........ *1276*
Mt 9:9 And as Jesus **p.** forth from thence,..... *3855*
Mt 20:30 when they heard that Jesus **p.** by,...... *3855*
Mt 27:39 And they that **p.** by reviled him, ... *3899*
Mk 2:14 as he **p.** by, he saw Levi the son......... *3855*
Mk 5:21 Jesus was **p.** over again by ship......... *1276*
Mk 6:35 place, and now the time is far **p.**:.............
Mk 6:48 sea, and would have **p.** by them......... *3928*
Mk 6:53 And when they had **p.** over, they....... *1276*
Mk 9:30 thence, and **p.** through Galilee; *3899*
Mk 11:20 as they **p.** by, they saw the fig tree...... *3899*
Mk 15:21 one Simon a Cyrenian, who **p.** by,...... *3855*
Mk 15:29 And they that **p.** by railed on him,...... *3899*
Lu 10:31 **saw him, he p. by on the other side** *492*
Lu 10:32 **him, and p. by on the other side**.... *492*
Lu 17:11 **p.** through the midst of Samaria......... *1330*
Lu 19:1 entered and **p.** through Jericho........... *1330*
Joh 5:24 **but is p. from death unto life**....... *3327*
Joh 8:59 the midst of them, and so **p.** by......... *3855*
Joh 9:1 and as Jesus **p.** by, he saw a man *3855*
Ac 9:32 Peter **p.** throughout all quarters......... *1330*
Ac 12:10 out, and **p.** on through one street;...... *4281*
Ac 14:24 they had **p.** throughout Pisidia, ... *1330*
Ac 15:3 **p.** through Phenice and Samaria, ... *1330*
Ac 17:1 they had **p.** through Amphipolis......... *1353*
Ac 17:23 For as I **p.** by, and beheld your......... *1330*
Ac 19:1 Paul having **p.** through the upper........ *1330*
Ac 19:21 when he had **p.** through Macedonia..... *1330*
Ro 5:12 so death **p.** upon all men, for that *1330*
1Co 10:1 cloud, and all **p.** through the sea; *1330*
2Co 5:17 old things are **p.** away; behold, all...... *3928*
Heb 4:14 priest, that is **p.** into the heavens,...... *1330*
Heb 11:29 faith they **p.** through he Red sea........ *1224*
1Jo 3:14 we have **p.** from death unto life, ... *3327*
Re 21:1 and the first earth were **p.** away;......... *3928*
Re 21:4 for the former things are **p.** away. *565*

PASSEDST
Jg 12:1 **p.** thou over to fight against the........ 5674

PASSENGERS
Pr 9:15 **p.** who go right on their ways: ... 5674,1870
Eze 39:11 the valley of the **p.** on the east of...... 5674
Eze 39:11 and it shall stop the noses of the **p.**:... 5674
Eze 39:14 land to bury with the **p.** those that..... 5674
Eze 39:15 the **p.** that pass through the land,....... 5674

PASSEST See also COMPASSEST.
De 3:21 all the kingdoms whither thou **p.**....... 5674
De 30:18 **p.** over Jordan to go to possess it. 5674
2Sa 15:33 If thou **p.** on with me, then thou........ 5674
1Ki 2:37 out, and **p.** over the brook Kidron,..... 5674
Isa 43:2 When thou **p.** through the waters,...... 5674

PASSETH See also COMPASSETH.
Ex 30:13 them, every one that **p.** among.......... 5674
Ex 30:14 Every one that **p.** among them that.... 5674
Ex 33:22 while my glory **p.** by, that I will put.... 5674
Le 27:32 whatsoever **p.** under the rod, the....... 5674
Jos 3:11 **p.** over before you into Jordan........... 5674
Jos 16:2 **p.** along unto the borders of Archi...... 5674
Jos 19:13 from thence **p.** on along on the east.... 5674
1Ki 9:8 one that **p.** by it shall be astonished,... 5674
2Ki 4:9 of God, which **p.** by us continually...... 5674
2Ki 12:4 of every one that **p.** the account, ... 5674
2Ch 7:21 to every one that **p.** by it; so that...... 5674
Job 9:11 he **p.** on also, but I perceive him 2498
Job 14:20 for ever against him, and he **p.**:......... 1980
Job 30:15 my welfare **p.** away as a cloud........... 5674
Job 37:21 the wind **p.**, and cleanseth them......... 5674
Ps 8:8 **p.** through the paths of the seas. 5674
Ps 78:39 a wind that **p.** away, and cometh........ 1980
Ps 103:16 For the wind **p.** over it, and it is........ 5674
Ps 144:4 days are as a shadow that **p.** away. 5674
Pr 10:25 As the whirlwind **p.**, so is the............ 5674
Pr 26:17 He that **p.** by, and meddleth with....... 5674
Ec 1:4 One generation **p.** away, and............ 1980
Isa 29:5 shall be as chaff that **p.** away:............ 5674
Jer 9:12 wilderness, that none **p.** through?....... 5674
Jer 13:24 scatter them as the stubble that **p.**..... 5674
Jer 18:16 that **p.** thereby shall be astonished,..... 5674
Jer 19:8 that **p.** thereby shall be astonished...... 5674
Eze 35:7 and cut off from it him that **p.** out...... 5674
Ho 13:3 and as the early dew that **p.** away,..... 1980
Mic 7:18 and **p.** by the transgression of the...... 5674
Zep 2:15 every one that **p.** by her shall hiss, ... 5674
Zep 3:6 their streets waste, that none **p.** by:... 5674
Zec 9:8 army, because of him that **p.** by,........ 5674
Lu 18:37 that Jesus of Nazareth **p.** by.............. *3928*
1Co 7:31 the fashion of this world **p.** away........ *3855*
Eph 3:19 love of Christ, which **p.** knowledge,.... *5235*
Php 4:7 God, which **p.** all understanding, ... *5242*
1Jo 2:17 the world **p.** away, and the lust *3855*

PASSING See also COMPASSING; TRESPASSING.
Jg 19:18 We are **p.** from Beth-lehem-judah....... 5674
2Sa 1:26 was wonderful, **p.** the love of women........
2Sa 15:24 people had done **p.** out of the city. 5674
2Ki 6:26 king of Israel was **p.** by upon the 5674
Ps 84:6 Who **p.** through the valley of Baca...... 5674
Pr 7:8 **P.** through the street near her 5674
Isa 31:5 and **p.** over he will preserve it.......... 5674
Eze 39:14 **p.** through the land to bury with 5674
Lu 4:30 he **p.** through the midst of them *1330*
Ac 5:15 the shadow of Peter **p.** by might........ *2064*
Ac 8:40 **p.** through he preached in all the........ *1330*
Ac 16:8 **p.** by Mysia came down to Troas. *3928*
Ac 27:8 hardly **p.** it, came unto a place........... *3881*

PASSION See also PASSIONS; COMPASSION.
Ac 1:3 shewed himself alive after his **p.** *3958*

PASSIONS See also COMPASSIONS.
Ac 14:15 We also are men of like **p.** with you, .. *3663*
Jas 5:17 a man subject to like **p.** as we are,..... *3663*

PASSOVER See also PASSOVERS.
Ex 12:11 eat it in haste: it is the Lord's **p.** 6453
Ex 12:21 to your families, and kill the **p.** 6453
Ex 12:27 It is the sacrifice of the Lord's **p.**,...... 6453
Ex 12:43 This is the ordinance of the **p.**:.......... 6453
Ex 12:48 and will keep the **p.** to the Lord, ... 6453
Ex 34:25 of the **p.** be left unto the morning. 6453
Le 23:5 first month at even is the Lord's **p.**... 6453
Nu 9:2 keep the **p.** at his appointed season. ... 6453
Nu 9:4 Israel, that they should keep the **p.**. ... 6453
Nu 9:5 kept the **p.** on the fourteenth day....... 6453
Nu 9:6 could not keep the **p.** on that day:...... 6453
Nu 9:10 he shall keep the **p.** unto the Lord. 6453
Nu 9:12 ordinances of the **p.** they shall keep.... 6453
Nu 9:13 and forbeareth to keep the **p.**,........... 6453
Nu 9:14 and will keep the **p.** unto the Lord; 6453
Nu 9:14 according to the ordinance of the **p.**,... 6453
Nu 28:16 first month is the **p.** of the Lord. 6453
Nu 33:3 morrow after the **p.** the children 6453
De 16:1 keep the **p.** unto the Lord thy God:.... 6453
De 16:2 shalt therefore sacrifice the **p.** 6453
De 16:5 Thou mayest not sacrifice the **p.** 6453
De 16:6 thou shalt sacrifice the **p.** at even,...... 6453
Jos 5:10 kept the **p.** on the fourteenth day....... 6453
Jos 5:11 land on the morrow after the **p.**,........ 6453
2Ki 23:21 Keep the **p.** unto the Lord your God, ..6453
2Ki 23:22 there was not holden such a **p.** from... 6453
2Ki 23:23 this **p.** was holden to the Lord in....... 6453
2Ch 30:1 to keep the **p.** unto the Lord God 6453
2Ch 30:2 to keep the **p.** in the second month. ... 6453
2Ch 30:5 to keep the **p.** unto the Lord God 6453
2Ch 30:15 killed the **p.** on the fourteenth day...... 6453
2Ch 30:18 yet did they eat the **p.** otherwise 6453
2Ch 35:1 Josiah kept a **p.** unto the Lord in........ 6453
2Ch 35:1 killed the **p.** on the fourteenth day...... 6453
2Ch 35:6 kill the **p.**, and sanctify yourselves,..... 6453
2Ch 35:7 and kids, all for the **p.** offerings, ... 6453
2Ch 35:8 unto the priests for the **p.** offerings 6453
2Ch 35:9 unto the Levites for **p.** offerings......... 6453
2Ch 35:11 they killed the **p.**, and the priests....... 6453
2Ch 35:13 And they roasted the **p.** with fire 6453
2Ch 35:16 to keep the **p.**, and to offer burnt....... 6453
2Ch 35:17 that were present kept the **p.** at that.. 6453
2Ch 35:18 was no **p.** like to that kept in Israel.... 6453
2Ch 35:18 keep such a **p.** as Josiah kept, ... 6453
2Ch 35:19 the reign of Josiah was this **p.** kept..... 6453
Ezr 6:19 children of the captivity kept the **p.** 6453
Ezr 6:20 killed the **p.** for all the children of....... 6453
Eze 45:21 of the month, ye shall have the **p.**,..... 6453
Mt 26:2 **two days is the feast of the p.**,...... *3957*
Mt 26:17 we prepare for thee to eat the **p.**? *3957*
Mt 26:18 **I will keep the p. at thy house**...... *3957*
Mt 26:19 them; and they made ready the **p.**...... *3957*
Mk 14:1 two days was the feast of the **p.**, ... *3957*
Mk 14:12 when they killed the **p.**, his disciples... *3957*
Mk 14:12 prepare that thou mayest eat the **p.**? .. *3957*
Mk 14:14 **I shall eat the p. with my**............ *3957*
Mk 14:16 them: and they made ready the **p.**...... *3957*
Lu 2:41 every year at the feast of the **p.**. *3957*
Lu 22:1 drew nigh, which is called the **P.**. *3957*
Lu 22:7 bread, when the **p.** must be killed. *3957*
Lu 22:8 **Go and prepare us the p., that we**..*3957*
Lu 22:11 **I shall eat the p. with my**............ *3957*
Lu 22:13 them: and they made ready the **p.**...... *3957*
Lu 22:15 **I have desired to eat this p. with**.. *3957*
Joh 2:13 And the Jews' **p.** was at hand, and *3957*
Joh 2:23 when he was in Jerusalem at the **p.**,... *3957*
Joh 6:4 the **p.**, a feast of the Jews, was nigh... *3957*
Joh 11:55 And the Jews' **p.** was nigh at hand:.... *3957*
Joh 11:55 went...up to Jerusalem before the **p.**,.. *3957*
Joh 12:1 Jesus six days before the **p.** came to... *3957*
Joh 13:1 Now before the feast of the **p.**, when.. *3957*
Joh 18:28 but that they might eat the **p.**. *3957*
Joh 18:39 release unto you one at the **p.**........... *3957*
Joh 19:14 And it was the preparation of the **p.**, .. *3957*
1Co 5:7 Christ our **p.** is sacrificed for us:........ *3957*
Heb 11:28 Through faith he kept the **p.**, and....... *3957*

PASSOVERS
2Ch 30:17 the charge of the killing of the **p.** 6453

PAST See also OVERPASSED; PASSED.
Ge 50:4 the days of his mourning were **p.**, ... 5674
Ex 21:29 to push with his horn in time **p.**,....... 8032
Ex 21:36 the ox hath used to push in time **p.**, ... 8032
Nu 21:22 way, until we be **p.** thy borders......... 5674
De 2:10 Emims dwelt therein in times **p.**,...............
De 4:32 ask now of the days that are **p.**, ... 7223
De 4:42 and hated him not in times **p.**; and 8032
De 19:4 whom he hated not in time **p.**;............ 8032
De 19:6 as he hated him not in time **p.**............ 8032
1Sa 15:32 Surely the bitterness of death is **p.**..... 5493
1Sa 19:7 was in his presence, as in times **p.**..... 8032
2Sa 3:17 for David in times **p.** to be king.......... 8032
2Sa 5:2 in time **p.**, when Saul was king over ... 8032
2Sa 11:27 And when the mourning was **p.**,.......... 5493
2Sa 16:1 when David was a little **p.** the top...... 5674
1Ki 18:29 came to pass when midday was **p.**,..... 5674
1Ch 9:20 was the ruler over them in time **p.**,..........
1Ch 11:2 time **p.**, even when Saul was king, ... 8032
Job 9:10 doeth great things **p.** finding out; 369
Job 14:13 me secret, until thy wrath be **p.**, ... 7725
Job 17:11 My days are **p.**, my purposes are....... 5674
Job 29:2 Oh that I were as in months **p.**,......... 6924
Ps 90:4 are but as yesterday when it is **p.**, ... 5674
Ec 3:15 God requireth that which is **p.**. 7291
Ca 2:11 the winter is **p.**, the rain is over 5674
Jer 8:20 harvest is **p.**, the summer is ended,.... 5674
Mt 14:15 place, and the time is now **p.**; *3928*
Mk 16:1 when the sabbath was **p.**, Mary......... *1230*
Lu 9:36 the voice was **p.**, Jesus was found...... *1096*
Ac 12:10 **p.** the first and the second ward, ... *1330*
Ac 14:16 in times **p.** suffered all nations........... *3944*
Ac 27:9 because the fast was...already **p.**,......... *3928*
Ro 3:25 the remission of sins that are **p.**,......... *4266*
Ro 11:30 in times **p.** have not believed God, ...
Ro 11:33 and his ways **p.** finding out!............... *421*
Ga 1:13 heard of my conversation in time **p.**..........
Ga 1:23 he which persecuted us in times **p.**..........
Ga 5:21 as I have also told you in time **p.**, ... *4302*
Eph 2:2 Wherein in time **p.** ye walked..................

Eph 2:3 all had our conversation in times **p.**....
Eph 2:11 that ye, being in time **p.** Gentiles ....
Eph 4:19 Who being **p.** feeling have given *524*
2Ti 2:18 that the resurrection is **p.** already;.... *1096*
Phm 11 in time **p.** was to thee unprofitable, ...
Heb 1:1 spake in time **p.** unto the fathers.... *3819*
Heb 11:11 of a child when she was **p.** age, ... *3844*
1Pe 2:10 Which in time **p.** were not a people, ...
1Pe 4:3 the time **p.** of our life may suffice.... *3928*
1Jo 2:8 because the darkness is **p.**, and *3855*
Re 9:12 One woe is **p.**; and, behold, there.... *565*
Re 11:14 The second woe is **p.**; and, behold,.... *565*

PASTOR See also PASTORS.
Jer 17:16 have not hastened from being a **p.**.... 7462

PASTORS
Jer 2:8 **p.** also transgressed against me, ... 7462
Jer 3:15 will give you **p.** according to mine 7462
Jer 10:21 **p.** are become brutish, and have 7462
Jer 12:10 Many **p.**...destroyed my vineyard, ... 7462
Jer 22:22 The wind shall eat up all thy **p.**,.... 7462
Jer 23:1 Woe be unto the **p.** that destroy 7462
Jer 23:2 against the **p.** that feed my people;.... 7462
Eph 4:11 and some, **p.** and teachers;.... *4166*

PASTURE See also PASTURES.
Ge 47:4 servants have no **p.** for their flocks;.... 4829
1Ch 4:39 valley, to seek **p.** for their flocks.... 4829
1Ch 4:40 And they found fat **p.** and good, and 4829
1Ch 4:41 there was **p.** there for their flocks.... 4829
Job 39:8 range of the mountains is his **p.**, ... 4829
Ps 74:1 smoke against the sheep of thy **p.**?.... 4830
Ps 79:13 we, thy people and sheep of thy **p.**.... 4830
Ps 95:7 the people of his **p.**, and the sheep.... 4830
Ps 100:3 his people, and the sheep of his **p.**.... 4830
Isa 32:14 a joy of wild asses, a **p.** of flocks; 4829
Jer 23:1 and scatter the sheep of my **p.**! 4830
Jer 25:36 for the Lord hath spoiled their **p.**.... 4830
La 1:6 become like harts that find no **p.**, ... 4829
Eze 34:14 I will feed them in a good **p.**, and.... 4829
Eze 34:14 and in a fat **p.** shall they feed upon.... 4829
Eze 34:18 you to have eaten up the good **p.**,.... 4829
Eze 34:31 ye my flock, the flock of my **p.**,.... 4830
Ho 13:6 According to their **p.**, so were they.... 4830
Joe 1:18 perplexed, because they have no **p.**; 4829
Joh 10:9 **shall go in and out, and find p.**.... *3542*

PASTURES
1Ki 4:23 and twenty oxen out of the **p.**, ... 7471
Ps 23:2 maketh me to lie down in green **p.**.... 4999
Ps 65:12 drop upon the **p.** of the wilderness: 4999
Ps 65:13 The **p.** are clothed with flocks; 3733
Isa 30:23 day shall thy cattle feed in large **p.**.... 3733
Isa 49:9 their **p.** shall be in all high places. 4830
Eze 34:18 your feet the residue of your **p.**?.... 4829
Eze 45:15 hundred, out of the fat **p.** of Israel; 4945
Joe 1:19 devoured the **p.** of the wilderness, ... 4999
Joe 1:20 devoured the **p.** of the wilderness. 4999
Joe 2:22 the **p.** of the wilderness do spring, ... 4999

PATARA (pat'-a-rah)
Ac 21:1 Rhodes, and from thence unto **P.**.... *3959*

PATE
Ps 7:16 shall come down upon his own **p.**.... 6936

PATH See also PATHS; PATHWAY.
Ge 49:17 an adder in the **p.**, that biteth the.... 734
Nu 22:24 angel of the Lord stood in a **p.** of.... 4934
Job 28:7 is a **p.** which no fowl knoweth, and.... 5410
Job 30:13 They mar my **p.**, they set forward 5410
Job 41:32 He maketh a **p.** to shine after him;.... 5410
Ps 16:11 Thou wilt shew me the **p.** of life:.... 734
Ps 27:11 O Lord, and lead me in a plain **p.**, ... 734
Ps 77:19 sea, and thy **p.** in the great waters,.... 7635
Ps 119:35 Make me to go in the **p.** of thy.... 5410
Ps 119:105 my feet, and a light unto my **p.**.... 5410
Ps 139:3 Thou compassest my **p.** and my 734
Ps 142:3 me, then thou knewest my **p.**.... 5410
Pr 1:15 them; refrain thy foot from their **p.**.... 5410
Pr 2:9 and equity; yea, every good **p.**.... 4570
Pr 4:14 Enter not into the **p.** of the wicked, ... 734
Pr 4:18 the **p.** of the just is as the shining.... 734
Pr 4:26 Ponder the **p.** of thy feet, and let.... 4570
Pr 5:6 shouldest ponder the **p.** of life,.... 734
Isa 26:7 dost weigh the **p.** of the just.... 4570
Isa 30:11 of the way, turn aside out of the **p.**,.... 734
Isa 40:14 taught him in the **p.** of judgment,.... 734
Isa 43:16 and a **p.** in the mighty waters;.... 5410
Joe 2:8 shall walk every one in his **p.**:.... 4546

PATHROS (path'-ros) See also PATHRUSIM.
Isa 11:11 and from Egypt, and from **P.**, and.... 6624
Jer 44:1 at Noph, and in the country of **P.**,.... 6624
Jer 44:15 dwelt in the land of Egypt, in **P.**,.... 6624
Eze 29:14 them to return into the land of **P.**, ... 6624
Eze 30:14 And I will make **P.** desolate, and.... 6624

PATHRUSIM (path-ru'-sim)
Ge 10:14 And **P.**, and Casluhim, (out of 6625
1Ch 1:12 And **P.**, and Casluhim, (of whom.... 6625

PATHS
Job 6:18 **p.** of their way are turned aside; 734
Job 8:13 So are the **p.** of all that forget God; 734
Job 13:27 lookest narrowly unto all my **p.**; 734
Job 19:8 and he hath set darkness in my **p.**.... 5410
Job 24:13 thereof, nor abide in the **p.** thereof.... 5410
Job 33:11 the stocks, he marketh all my **p.**. 734
Job 38:20 know the **p.** to the house thereof?.... 5410
Ps 8:8 passeth through the **p.** of the seas. 734
Ps 17:4 me from the **p.** of the destroyer.... 734
Ps 17:5 Hold up my goings in thy **p.**, that.... 4570
Ps 23:3 me in the **p.** of righteousness for 4570
Ps 25:4 thy ways, O Lord; teach me thy **p.**.... 734
Ps 25:10 All the **p.** of the Lord are mercy 734
Ps 65:11 goodness; and thy **p.** drop fatness. 4570
Pr 2:8 He keepeth the **p.** of judgment, and.... 734
Pr 2:13 leave the **p.** of uprightness, to walk.... 734
Pr 2:15 and they froward in their **p.**: 4570
Pr 2:18 death, and her **p.** unto the dead.... 4570
Pr 2:19 take they hold of the **p.** of life.... 734
Pr 2:20 and keep the **p.** of the righteous.... 734
Pr 3:6 him, and he shall direct thy **p.**.... 734
Pr 3:17 and all her **p.** are peace.... 5410
Pr 4:11 wisdom; I have led thee in right **p.**.... 4570
Pr 7:25 her ways, go not astray in her **p.**.... 5410
Pr 8:2 by the way in the places of the **p.**.... 5410
Pr 8:20 in the midst of the **p.** of judgment: 5410
Isa 2:3 his ways, and we will walk in his **p.** 734
Isa 3:12 err, and destroy the way of thy **p.**.... 734
Isa 42:16 in **p.** that they have not known: 5410
Isa 58:12 the restorer of **p.** to dwell in.... 5410
Isa 59:7 and destruction are in their **p.**.... 4546
Isa 59:8 they have made them crooked **p.**: 5410
Jer 6:16 and ask for the old **p.**, where is the.... 5410
Jer 18:15 in their ways from the ancient **p.**,.... 7635
Jer 18:15 walk in **p.**, in a way not cast up;.... 5410
La 3:9 stone, he hath made my **p.** crooked.... 5410
Ho 2:6 wall, that she shall not find her **p.**.... 5410
Mic 4:2 ways, and we will walk in his **p.**: 734
Mt 3:3 of the Lord, make his **p.** straight.... *5147*
Mk 1:3 of the Lord, make his **p.** straight.... *5147*
Lu 3:4 of the Lord, make his **p.** straight.... *5147*
Heb 12:13 made straight **p.** for your feet, lest.... *5163*

PATHWAY
Pr 12:28 in the **p.** thereof...is no death.... 1870,5410

PATIENCE
Mt 18:26 **Lord, have p. with me, and I will** *3114*
Mt 18:29 **Have p. with me, and I will pay** *3114*
Lu 8:15 **it, and bring forth fruit with p.** *5281*
Lu 21:19 **In your p. possess ye your souls**.... *5281*
Ro 5:3 that tribulation worketh **p.**; *5281*
Ro 5:4 And **p.**, experience; and experience, ... *5281*
Ro 8:25 not, then do we with **p.** wait for it. *5281*
Ro 15:4 **p.** and comfort of the scriptures.... *5281*
Ro 15:5 Now the God of **p.** and consolation.... *5281*
2Co 6:4 the ministers of God, in much **p.**, in *5281*
2Co 12:12 were wrought among you in all **p.**, ... *5281*
Col 1:11 unto all **p.** and longsuffering with.... *5281*
1Th 1:3 and **p.** of hope in our Lord Jesus.... *5281*
2Th 1:4 for your **p.** and faith in all your.... *5281*
1Ti 6:11 godliness, faith, love, **p.**, meekness. *5281*
2Ti 3:10 faith, longsuffering, charity, **p.**, ... *5281*
Tit 2:2 sound in faith, in charity, in **p.**.... *5281*
Heb 6:12 faith and **p.** inherit the promises.... *3115*
Heb 10:36 For ye have need of **p.**, that, after.... *5281*
Heb 12:1 let us run with **p.** the race that is.... *5281*
Jas 1:3 the trying of your faith worketh **p.**.... *5281*
Jas 1:4 But let **p.** have her perfect work,.... *5281*
Jas 5:7 and hath long **p.** for it, until he.... *3114*
Jas 5:10 of suffering affliction, and of **p.**.... *3115*
Jas 5:11 Ye have heard of the **p.** of Job,.... *5281*
2Pe 1:6 temperance **p.**; and to **p.** godliness;.... *5281*
Re 1:9 the kingdom and **p.** of Jesus Christ, ... *5281*
Re 2:2 **works, and thy labour, and thy p.,** .*5281*
Re 2:3 **hast p., and for my name's sake**.... *5281*
Re 2:19 **faith, and thy p., and thy works;**.... *5281*
Re 3:10 thou hast kept the word of my **p.**,.... *5281*
Re 13:10 it the **p.** and the faith of the saints. *5281*
Re 14:12 Here is the **p.** of the saints: here.... *5281*

PATIENT
Ec 7:8 **p.** in spirit is better than the proud 750
Ro 2:7 by **p.** continuance in well doing.... *5281*
Ro 12:12 in hope; **p.** in tribulation; *5278*
1Th 5:14 the weak, be **p.** toward all men. *3114*
2Th 3:5 and into the **p.** waiting for Christ.... *5281*
1Ti 3:3 **p.**, not a brawler, not covetous;.... *1933*
2Ti 2:24 gentle unto all men, apt to teach, **p.**,.... *420*
Jas 5:7 Be **p.** therefore, brethren, unto the *3114*
Jas 5:8 Be ye also **p.**; stablish your hearts: *3114*

PATIENTLY
Ps 37:7 in the Lord, and wait **p.** for him:.... 2342
Ps 40:1 I waited **p.** for the Lord; and he 6960
Ac 26:3 I beseech thee to hear me **p.**.... *3116*
Heb 6:15 And so, after he had **p.** endured, ... *3114*
1Pe 2:20 for your faults, ye shall take it **p.**?.... *5278*
1Pe 2:20 ye take it **p.**, this as acceptable with.... *5278*

PATMOS (pat'-mos)
Re 1:9 was in the isle that is called **P.**, ... *3963*

PATRIARCH See also PATRIARCHS.
Ac 2:29 speak unto you of the **p.** David,.... *3966*
Heb 7:4 the **p.** Abraham gave the tenth of.... *3966*

PATRIARCHS
Ac 7:8 and Jacob begat the twelve **p.**.... *3966*
Ac 7:9 And the **p.**, moved with envy, sold.... *3966*

PATRIMONY
De 18:8 which cometh of the sale of his **p.**.... 5921,1

PATROBAS (pat'-ro-bas)
Ro 16:14 **P.**, Hermes, and the brethren.... *3969*

PATTERN See also PATTERNS.
Ex 25:9 after the **p.** of the tabernacle, and.... 8403
Ex 25:9 the **p.** of all the instruments thereof,.... 8403
Ex 25:40 **p.**,...shewed thee in the mount.... 8403
Nu 8:4 the **p.** which the Lord had shewed.... 4758
Jos 22:28 the **p.** of the altar of the Lord, ... 8403
2Ki 16:10 fashion of the altar, and the **p.** of it, ... 8403
1Ch 28:11 **p.** of the porch, and of the houses.... 8403
1Ch 28:12 the **p.** of all that he had by the spirit,.... 8403
1Ch 28:18 and gold for the **p.** of the chariot of.... 8403
1Ch 28:19 me, even all the works of this **p.**. 8403
Eze 43:10 and let them measure the **p.**. 8508
1Ti 1:16 **p.** to them which should hereafter *5296*
Tit 2:7 showing thyself a **p.** of good works:.... *5179*
Heb 8:5 the **p.** shewed to thee in the mount.... *5179*

PATTERNS
Heb 9:23 **p.** of things in the heavens should *5262*

PAU (pa'-u) See also PAI.
Ge 36:39 and the name of his city was **P.**;.... 6464

PAUL (pawl) See also PAUL'S; PAULUS; SAUL.
Ac 13:9 Saul, (who also is called **P.**,) filled.... *3972*
Ac 13:13 when **P.** and his company loosed.... *3972*
Ac 13:16 Then **P.** stood up, and beckoning.... *3972*
Ac 13:43 followed **P.** and Barnabas: who, ... *3972*
Ac 13:45 things which were spoken by **P.**, ... *3972*
Ac 13:46 Then **P.** and Barnabas waxed bold,.... *3972*
Ac 13:50 raised persecution against **P.** and *3972*
Ac 14:9 The same heard **P.** speak: who *3972*
Ac 14:11 the people saw that **P.** had done, ... *3972*
Ac 14:12 and **P.**, Mercurius, because he was.... *3972*
Ac 14:14 when the apostles, Barnabas and **P.**,.... *3972*
Ac 14:19 having stoned **P.**, drew him out of.... *3972*
Ac 15:2 **P.** and Barnabas had no small.... *3972*
Ac 15:2 determined that **P.** and Barnabas,.... *3972*
Ac 15:12 gave audience to Barnabas and **P.**, ... *3972*
Ac 15:22 to Antioch with **P.** and Barnabas; *3972*
Ac 15:25 with our beloved Barnabas and **P.**, ... *3972*
Ac 15:35 **P.** also and Barnabas continued in *3972*
Ac 15:36 **P.** said unto Barnabas, Let us go.... *3972*
Ac 15:38 **P.** thought not good to take him *3972*
Ac 15:40 And **P.** chose Silas, and departed, ... *3972*
Ac 16:3 would **P.** have to go forth with him; *3972*
Ac 16:9 vision appeared to **P.** in the night; *3972*
Ac 16:14 the things which were spoken of **P.**.... *3972*
Ac 16:17 The same followed **P.** and us, and.... *3972*
Ac 16:18 But **P.**, being grieved, turned and *3972*
Ac 16:19 they taught **P.** and Silas, and drew.... *3972*

Ac 16:25 at midnight **P.** and Silas prayed, ... 3972
Ac 16:28 **P.** cried with a loud voice, saying, ... 3972
Ac 16:29 and fell down before **P.** and Silas, ... 3972
Ac 16:36 this saying to **P.**, The magistrates ... 3972
Ac 16:37 But **P.** said unto them, They have ... 3972
Ac 17:2 And **P.**, as his manner was, went in ... 3972
Ac 17:4 and consorted with **P.** and Silas; ... 3972
Ac 17:10 sent away **P.** and Silas by night ... 3972
Ac 17:13 God was preached of **P.** at Berea, ... 3972
Ac 17:14 sent away **P.** to go as it were to the .. 3972
Ac 17:15 they that conducted **P.** brought him ... 3972
Ac 17:16 while **P.** waited for them at Athens, ... 3972
Ac 17:22 **P.** stood in the midst of Mars' hill, ... 3972
Ac 17:33 So **P.** departed from among them ... 3972
Ac 18:1 After these things **P.** departed from ... 3972
Ac 18:5 **P.** was pressed in the spirit, and ... 3972
Ac 18:9 spake the Lord to **P.** in the night by ... 3972
Ac 18:12 with one accord against **P.**, and ... 3972
Ac 18:14 when **P.** was now about to open his ... 3972
Ac 18:18 And **P.** after this tarried there yet a ... 3972
Ac 19:1 **P.** having passed through the upper ... 3972
Ac 19:4 Then said **P.**, John verily baptized ... 3972
Ac 19:6 when **P.** had laid his hands upon ... 3972
Ac 19:11 miracles by the hands of **P.**: ... 3972
Ac 19:13 you by Jesus whom **P.** preacheth. ... 3972
Ac 19:15 Jesus I know, and **P.** I know; but ... 3972
Ac 19:21 **P.** purposed in the spirit, when he ... 3972
Ac 19:26 this **P.** hath persuaded and turned ... 3972
Ac 19:30 And when **P.** would have entered in ... 3972
Ac 20:1 **P.** called unto him the disciples ... 3972
Ac 20:7 **P.** preached unto them, ready to ... 3972
Ac 20:9 as **P.** was long preaching, he sunk ... 3972
Ac 20:10 And **P.** went down, and fell on him, ... 3972
Ac 20:13 there intending to take in **P.**: for ... 3972
Ac 20:16 **P.**...determined to sail by Ephesus, ... 3972
Ac 21:4 who said to **P.** through the Spirit, ... 3972
Ac 21:13 Then **P.** answered, What mean ye ... 3972
Ac 21:18 **P.** went in with us unto James; ... 3972
Ac 21:26 **P.** took the men, and the next day ... 3972
Ac 21:29 **P.** had brought into the temple.) ... 3972
Ac 21:30 they took **P.**, and drew him out of ... 3972
Ac 21:32 the soldiers, they left beating of **P.** ... 3972
Ac 21:37 as **P.** was to be led into the castle, ... 3972
Ac 21:39 But **P.** said, I am a man which am ... 3972
Ac 21:40 **P.** stood on the stairs, and beckoned .. 3972
Ac 22:25 **P.** said unto the centurion that ... 3972
Ac 22:28 And **P.** said, But I was free born. ... 3972
Ac 22:30 and brought **P.** down, and set him ... 3972
Ac 23:1 **P.**, earnestly beholding the council, ... 3972
Ac 23:3 Then said **P.** unto him, God shall ... 3972
Ac 23:5 Then said **P.**, I wist not, brethren, ... 3972
Ac 23:6 **P.** perceived that the one part were ... 3972
Ac 23:10 lest **P.** should have been pulled in ... 3972
Ac 23:11 and said, **Be of good cheer P.** ... 3972
Ac 23:12 eat nor drink till they had killed **P.**. ... 3972
Ac 23:14 eat nothing until we have slain **P.** ... 3972
Ac 23:16 entered into the castle, and told **P.** ... 3972
Ac 23:17 **P.** called one of the centurions unto ... 3972
Ac 23:18 **P.** the prisoner called me unto him, ... 3972
Ac 23:20 wouldest bring down **P.** to morrow ... 3972
Ac 23:24 that they may set **P.** on, and bring ... 3972
Ac 23:31 took **P.**, and brought him by night ... 3972
Ac 23:33 presented **P.** also before him ... 3972
Ac 24:1 informed the governor against **P.** ... 3972
Ac 24:10 Then **P.**, after that the governor ... 3972
Ac 24:23 commanded a centurion to keep **P.**, ... 3972
Ac 24:24 he sent for **P.**, and heard him ... 3972
Ac 24:26 should have been given him of **P.**, ... 3972
Ac 24:27 the Jews a pleasure, left **P.** bound ... 3972
Ac 25:2 the Jews informed him against **P.**, ... 3972
Ac 25:4 **P.** should be kept at Caesarea, and ... 3972
Ac 25:6 seat commanded **P.** to be brought ... 3972
Ac 25:7 grievous complaints against **P.** ... 3972
Ac 25:9 answered **P.**, and said, Wilt thou go ... 3972
Ac 25:10 Then said **P.**, I stand at Caesar's ... 3972
Ac 25:19 dead, whom **P.** affirmed to be alive. ... 3972
Ac 25:21 **P.** had appealed to be reserved ... 3972
Ac 25:23 morrow...**P.** was brought forth ... 3972
Ac 26:1 Then Agrippa said unto **P.**, Thou ... 3972
Ac 26:1 **P.** stretched forth the hand, and ... 3972
Ac 26:24 **P.**, thou art beside thyself; much ... 3972
Ac 26:28 Agrippa said unto **P.**, Almost thou ... 3972
Ac 26:29 **P.** said, I would to God, that not ... 3972
Ac 27:1 they delivered **P.** and certain other ... 3972
Ac 27:3 Julius courteously entreated **P.**, ... 3972
Ac 27:9 already past, **P.** admonished them, ... 3972
Ac 27:11 things which were spoken by **P.**. ... 3972
Ac 27:21 **P.** stood forth in the midst of them, ... 3972
Ac 27:24 Fear not, **P.**; thou must be brought ... 3972
Ac 27:31 **P.** said to the centurion and to the ... 3972
Ac 27:33 **P.** besought them all to take meat, ... 3972
Ac 27:43 the centurion, willing to save **P.**, ... 3972
Ac 28:3 **P.** had gathered a bundle of sticks, ... 3972
Ac 28:8 to whom **P.** entered in, and prayed, ... 3972
Ac 28:15 whom when **P.** saw, he thanked ... 3972
Ac 28:16 **P.** was suffered to dwell by himself ... 3972
Ac 28:17 days **P.** called the chief of the Jews ... 3972
Ac 28:25 after that **P.** had spoken one word, ... 3972
Ac 28:30 **P.** dwelt two whole years in his ... 3972
Ro general *title* **P.** . . . To The Romans. ... 3972
Ro 1:1 **P.**, a servant of Jesus Christ, called ... 3972
1Co general *title* **P.** . . . To The Corinthians. ...
1Co 1:1 **P.**, called to be an apostle of Jesus ...
1Co 1:12 every one of you saith, I am of **P.**; ...
1Co 1:13 was **P.** crucified for you? or were ...
1Co 1:13 were ye baptized in the name of **P.**? ...
1Co 3:4 For while one saith, I am of **P.**; ...
1Co 3:5 Who then is **P.**, and who is Apollos, ...
1Co 3:22 Whether **P.**, or Apollos, or Cephas, ...
1Co 16:21 of me **P.** with mine own hand ... 3972
2Co general *title* **P.** . . . To The Corinthians. ... 3972
2Co 1:1 **P.**, an apostle of Jesus Christ by the ... 3972
2Co 10:1 Now I **P.** myself beseech you by ... 3972
Ga general *title* **P.** . . . To the Galatians. ... 3972
Ga 1:1 **P.**, an apostle, (not of men, neither ... 3972
Ga 5:2 Behold, I **P.** say unto you, that if ... 3972
Eph general *title* **P.** . . . To The Ephesians. ... 3972
Eph 1:1 **P.**, an apostle of Jesus Christ by ... 3972
Eph 3:1 For this cause I **P.**, the prisoner of ... 3972
Php general *title* **P.** . . . To the Philippians. ... 3972
Php 1:1 **P.** and Timotheus, the servants of ... 3972
Col general *title* **P.** . . . To The Colossians. ... 3972
Col 1:1 **P.**, an apostle of Jesus Christ by ... 3972
Col 1:23 whereof I **P.** am made a minister: ... 3972
Col 4:18 salutation by the hand of me **P.** ... 3972
1Th general *title* **P.** . . . To The Thessalonians. ... 3972
1Th 1:1 **P.**, and Silvanus, and Timotheus, ... 3972
1Th 2:18 *you, even I* **P.**, once and again; ... 3972
2Th general *title* **P.** . . . To The Thessalonians. ... 3972
2Th 1:1 **P.**, and Silvanus, and Timotheus, ... 3972
2Th 3:17 The salutation of **P.** with mine own ... 3972
1Ti general *title* **P.** . . . The Apostle To Timothy. ... 3972
1Ti 1:1 **P.**, an apostle of Jesus Christ by ... 3972
2Ti general *title* **P.** . . . The Apostle To Timothy. ... 3972
2Ti 1:1 **P.**, an apostle of Jesus Christ by ... 3972
2Ti *subscr.* **P.** was brought before Nero ... 3972
Tit general *title* The Epistle Of **P.** To Titus. ... 3972
Tit 1:1 **P.**, a servant of God, and an ... 3972
Phm title Epistle Of **P.** To Philemon. ... 3972
Phm 1 **P.**, a prisoner of Jesus Christ, and ... 3972
Phm 9 being such an one as **P.** the aged, ... 3972
Phm 19 I **P.** have written it with mine own ... 3972
Heb general *title* **P.** . . . To The Hebrews. ... 3972
2Pe 3:15 even as our beloved brother **P.** ... 3972

PAUL'S (pawls)
Ac 19:29 **P.** companions in travel, they ... 3972
Ac 20:37 fell on **P.** neck, and kissed him, ... 3972
Ac 21:8 that were of **P.** company departed, ... 3972
Ac 21:11 took **P.** girdle, and bound his own ... 3972
Ac 23:16 And when **P.** sister's son heard of ... 3972
Ac 25:14 declared **P.** cause unto the king, ... 3972

PAULUS See also PAUL.
Ac 13:7 deputy of the country, Sergius **P.**, ... 3972

PAVED
Ex 24:10 were a **p.** work of a sapphire stone, ... 3840
Ca 3:10 midst thereof being **p.** with love, ... 7528

PAVEMENT
2Ki 16:17 it, and put it upon a **p.** of stones ... 4837
2Ch 7:3 faces to the ground upon the **p.**, ... 7531
Es 1:6 a **p.** of red, and blue, and white, ... 7531
Eze 40:17 **p.** made for the court round about: ... 7531
Eze 40:17 thirty chambers were upon the **p.** ... 7531
Eze 40:18 And the **p.** by the side of the gates ... 7531
Eze 40:18 of the gates was the lower **p.** ... 7531
Eze 42:3 **p.** which was for the utter court, ... 7531
Joh 19:13 in a place that is called the **P.**, ... 3038

PAVILION See also PAVILIONS.
Ps 18:11 his **p.** round about him were dark ... 5521
Ps 27:5 he shall hide me in his **p.**: in the ... 5520
Ps 31:20 shalt keep him secretly in a **p.** ... 5521
Jer 43:10 shall spread his royal **p.** over them. ... 8237

PAVILIONS
2Sa 22:12 he made darkness **p.** round about ... 5521
1Ki 20:12 drinking, he and the kings in the **p.**, ... 5521
1Ki 20:16 drinking himself drunk in the **p.**, ... 5521

PAW See also PAWETH; PAWS.
2Sa 17:37 delivered me out of...**p.** of the lion, ... 3027
2Sa 17:37 and out of the **p.** of the bear, he will .. 3027

PAWETH
Job 39:21 He **p.** in the valley, and rejoiceth ... 2658

PAWS
Le 11:27 And whatsoever goeth upon his **p.**, ... 3709

PAY See also PAID; PAYED; PAYETH; REPAY.
Ex 21:19 he shall **p.** for the loss of his time, ... 5414
Ex 21:22 he shall **p.** as the judges determine ... 5414
Ex 21:36 he shall surely **p.** ox for ox; and ... 7999
Ex 22:7 thief be found, let him **p.** double. ... 7999
Ex 22:9 **p.** double unto his neighbour. ... 7999
Ex 22:17 **p.** money according to the dowry ... 8254
Nu 20:19 thy water, then I will **p.** for it: ... 5414,4377
De 23:21 thou shalt not slack to **p.** it: for ... 7999
2Sa 15:7 let me go and **p.** my vow, which I ... 7999
1Ki 20:39 else thou shalt **p.** a talent of silver ... 8254
2Ki 4:7 Go, sell the oil, and **p.** thy debt, ... 7999
2Ch 8:8 make to **p.** tribute until this day ... 5927
2Ch 27:5 children of Ammon **p.** unto him, ... 7725
Ezr 4:13 will they not **p.** toll, tribute, and ... 5415
Es 3:9 will **p.** ten thousand talents of silver ... 8254
Es 4:7 that Haman had promised to **p.** to ... 8254
Job 22:27 thee, and thou shalt **p.** thy vows. ... 7999
Ps 22:25 **p.** my vows before them that fear ... 7999
Ps 50:14 and **p.** thy vows unto the most High: .. 7999
Ps 66:13 offerings: I will **p.** thee my vows, ... 7999
Ps 76:11 Vow, and **p.** unto the Lord your God: . 7999
Ps 116:14, 18, **p.** my vows unto the Lord now ... 7999
Pr 19:17 he hath given will he **p.** him again. ... 7999
Pr 22:27 If thou hast nothing to **p.**, why ... 7999
Ec 5:4 a vow unto God, defer not to **p.** it; ... 7999
Ec 5:4 **p.** that which thou hast vowed ... 7999
Ec 5:5 thou shouldest vow and not **p.** ... 7999
Jon 2:9 I will **p.** that that I have vowed ... 7999
Mt 17:24 Doth not your master **p.** tribute? ... 5055
Mt 18:25 **forasmuch as he had not to p., his** .. 591
Mt 18:26 **with me, and I will p. thee all.** ... 591
Mt 18:28 **saying, P. me that thou owest.** ... 591
Mt 18:29 **with me, and I will p. thee all.** ... 591
Mt 18:30 **prison, till he should p. the debt.** ... 591
Mt 18:34 **should p. all that was due unto him.** 591
Mt 23:23 **for ye p. tithe of mint and anise** ... 586
Lu 7:42 **when they had nothing to p., he** ... 591
Ro 13:6 For this cause **p.** ye tribute also: ... 5055

PAYED See also PAID; REPAYED.
Pr 7:14 me; this day have I **p.** my vows ... 7999
Heb 7:9 tithes, **p.** tithes in Abraham ... 1183

PAYETH See also REPAYETH.
Ps 37:21 borroweth, and **p.** not again: ... 7999

PAYMENT
Mt 18:25 **that he had, and p. to be made.** ... 591

PAZZEZ See BETH-PAZZEZ.

PE (pay)
Ps 119:129 *title* [פ] **P.** ...

PEACE See also PEACEABLE; PEACEMAKERS.
Ge 15:15 thou shalt go to thy fathers in **p.**; ... 7965
Ge 24:21 man wondering at her held his **p.**, ... 2790
Ge 26:29 and have sent thee away in **p.**: ... 7965
Ge 26:31 and they departed from him in **p.** ... 7965
Ge 28:21 again to my father's house in **p.**; ... 7965
Ge 34:5 Jacob held his **p.** until they were ... 2790
Ge 41:16 give Pharaoh an answer of **p.** ... 7965
Ge 43:23 And he said, **P.** be to you, fear not: ... 7965
Ge 44:17 get you up in **p.** unto your father. ... 7965
Ex 4:18 And Jethro said to Moses, Go in **p.** ... 7965
Ex 14:14 you, and ye shall hold your **p.** ... 2790
Ex 18:23 shall also go to their place in **p.** ... 7965
Ex 20:24 offerings, and thy **p.** offerings, ... 8002
Ex 24:5 sacrificed **p.** offerings of oxen unto ... 8002
Ex 29:28 of the sacrifice of their **p.** offerings, ... 8002
Ex 32:6 offerings, and brought **p.** offerings; ... 8002
Le 3:1 be a sacrifice of **p.** offering, if he ... 8002
Le 3:3 of the sacrifice of the **p.** offering ... 8002
Le 3:6 a sacrifice of **p.** offering unto the ... 8002
Le 3:9 of the sacrifice of the **p.** offering ... 8002

Le 4:10 of the sacrifice of **p.** offerings: and...... 8002
Le 4:26 fat of the sacrifice of **p.** offerings:....... 8002
Le 4:31 off the sacrifice of **p.** offerings: and..... 8002
Le 4:35 the sacrifice of the **p.** offerings; 8002
Le 6:12 thereon the fat of the **p.** offerings....... 8002
Le 7:11 law of the sacrifice of **p.** offerings,...... 8002
Le 7:13 of thanksgiving of his **p.** offerings. 8002
Le 7:14 the blood of the **p.** offerings. 8002
Le 7:15, 18 of the sacrifice of his **p.** offerings ... 8002
Le 7:20, 21 of the sacrifice of **p.** offerings, ... 8002
Le 7:29 the sacrifice of his **p.** offerings unto 8002
Le 7:29 of the sacriice of his **p.** offerings. 8002
Le 7:32 the sacrifices of your **p.** offerings. 8002
Le 7:33 the blood of the **p.** offerings, and 8002
Le 7:34 the sacrifices of their **p.** offerings, ... 8002
Le 7:37 of the sacrifice of the **p.** offerings;...... 8002
Le 9:4 bullock and a ram for **p.** offerings, ... 8002
Le 9:18 ram for a sacrifice of **p.** offerings,....... 8002
Le 9:22 the burnt offering, and **p.** offerings. 8002
Le 10:3 glorified. And Aaron held his **p.**......... 1826
Le 10:14 out of the sacrifices of **p.** offerings..... 8002
Le 17:5 them for **p.** offerings unto the Lord. ... 8002
Le 19:5 ye offer a sacrifice of **p.** offerings 8002
Le 22:21 offereth a sacrifice of **p.** offerings 8002
Le 23:19 year for a sacrifice of **p.** offerings. 8002
Le 26:6 I will give **p.** in the land, and ye......... 7965
Nu 6:14 without blemish for **p.** offerings,......... 8002
Nu 6:17 ram for a sacrifice of **p.** offerings......... 8002
Nu 6:18 the sacrifice of the **p.** offerings. 8002
Nu 6:26 upon thee, and give thee **p.**. 7965
Nu 7:17, 23,29,35,41,47,53,59,65,71,77,83
sacrifice of **p.** offerings, two oxen.............
Nu 7:88 for the sacrifice of the **p.** offerings...... 8002
Nu 10:10 the sacrifices of your **p.** offerings; 8002
Nu 15:8 vow, or **p.** offerings unto the Lord: 8002
Nu 25:12 give unto him my covenant of **p.**: 7965
Nu 29:39 offerings, and for your **p.** offerings...... 8002
Nu 30:4 her father shall hold his **p.** at her; 2790
Nu 30:7 held his **p.** at her in the day that........ 2790
Nu 30:11 held his **p.** at her, and disallowed her.. 2790
Nu 30:14 hold his **p.** at her from day to day; 2790
Nu 30:14 he held his **p.** at her in the day.......... 2790
De 2:26 king of Heshbon with words of **p.**,....... 7965
De 20:10 against it, then proclaim **p.** unto it...... 7965
De 20:11 if it make thee answer of **p.**, and 7965
De 20:12 if it will make no **p.** with thee, but 7999
De 23:6 Thou shalt not seek their **p.** nor 7965
De 27:7 And thou shalt offer **p.** offerings,........ 8002
De 29:19 I shall have **p.**, though I walk in......... 7965
Jos 8:31 Lord, and sacrificed **p.** offerings. 8002
Jos 9:15 Joshua made **p.** with them, and.......... 7965
Jos 10:1 Gibeon had made **p.** with Israel,......... 7999
Jos 10:4 for it hath made **p.** with Joshua.......... 7999
Jos 10:21 to Joshua at Makkedah in **p.**:............. 7965
Jos 11:19 There was not a city that made **p.**...... 7999
Jos 22:23 or if to offer **p.** offerings thereon,....... 8002
Jos 22:27 sacrifices, and with our **p.** offerings;.... 8002
Jg 4:17 was **p.** between Jabin the king of........ 7965
Jg 6:23 him, **P.** be unto thee; fear not:......... 7965
Jg 8:9 When I come again in **p.**, I will........... 7965
Jg 11:31 I return in **p.** from the children of 7965
Jg 18:6 the priest said unto them, Go in **p.**:..... 7965
Jg 18:19 they said unto him, Hold thy **p.**, ... 2790
Jg 19:20 the old man said, **P.** be with thee; 7965
Jg 20:26 and **p.** offerings before the Lord......... 8002
Jg 21:4 burnt offerings and **p.** offerings. 8002
1Sa 1:17 Eli answered and said, Go in **p.**: 7965
1Sa 7:14 **p.** between Israel and the Amorites. ... 7965
1Sa 10:8 sacrifice sacrifices of **p.** offerings: 8002
1Sa 10:27 no presents. But he held his **p.**.......... 2790
1Sa 11:15 sacrificed sacrifices of **p.** offerings....... 8002
1Sa 13:9 offering to me, and **p.** offerings.......... 8002
1Sa 20:7 is well; thy servant shall have **p.**: 7965
1Sa 20:13 away, that thou mayest go in **p.**:........ 7965
1Sa 20:21 for there is **p.** to thee, and no hurt;.... 7965
1Sa 20:42 Jonathan said to David, Go in **p.**,........ 7965
1Sa 25:6 in prosperity, **P.** be both to thee,........ 7965
1Sa 25:6 and **p.** be to thine house,.................. 7965
1Sa 25:6 and **p.** be unto all that thou hast. 7965
1Sa 25:35 Go up in **p.** to thine house; see, I...... 7965
1Sa 29:7 now return, and go in **p.**, that thou..... 7965
2Sa 3:21 Abner away; and he went in **p.**.......... 7965
2Sa 3:22 him away, and he was gone in **p.**. 7965
2Sa 3:23 him away, and he is gone in **p.**. 7965
2Sa 6:17 and **p.** offerings before the Lord........ 8002
2Sa 6:18 burnt offerings and **p.** offerings, ... 8002
2Sa 10:19 made **p.** with Israel, and served......... 7999
2Sa 13:20 but hold now thy **p.**, my sister: he 2790
2Sa 15:9 the king said unto him, Go in **p.**.......... 7965
2Sa 15:27 return into the city in **p.**, and your 7965
2Sa 17:3 so all the people shall be in **p.**. 7965
2Sa 19:24 until the day he came again in **p.**. 7965
2Sa 19:30 again in **p.** unto his own house........... 7965
2Sa 24:25 burnt offerings and **p.** offerings. 8002
1Ki 2:5 shed the blood of war in **p.**, and 7965
1Ki 2:6 head go down to the grave in **p.**. 7965
1Ki 2:33 there be **p.** for ever from the Lord..... 7965
1Ki 3:15 offered **p.** offerings, and made a.......... 8002
1Ki 4:24 and he had **p.** on all sides round......... 7965
1Ki 5:12 **p.** between Hiram and Solomon;........... 7965
1Ki 8:63 offered a sacrifice of **p.** offerings, ... 8002
1Ki 8:64 and the fat of the **p.** offerings: 8002
1Ki 8:64 and the fat of the **p.** offerings. 8002
1Ki 9:25 **p.** offerings upon the altar which 8002
1Ki 20:18 Whether they be come out for **p.**, ... 7965
1Ki 22:17 every man to his house in **p.**. 7965
1Ki 22:27 of affliction, until I come in **p.**. 7965
1Ki 22:28 If thou return at all in **p.**, the Lord..... 7965
1Ki 22:44 Jehoshaphat made **p.** with the............ 7999
2Ki 2:3,5 Yea, I know it; hold ye your **p.**.......... 2814
2Ki 5:19 And he said unto him, go in **p.**. 7965
2Ki 7:9 good tidings, and we hold our **p.**: 2814
2Ki 9:17 them, and let him say, Is it **p.**?.......... 7965
2Ki 9:18 said, Thus saith the king, Is it **p.**?...... 7965
2Ki 9:18 What hast thou to do with **p.**? 7965
2Ki 9:19 said, Thus saith the king, Is it **p.**?...... 7965
2Ki 9:19 What hast thou to do with **p.**? 7965
2Ki 9:22 Jehu, that he said, Is it **p.**, Jehu? 7965
2Ki 9:22 And he answered, What **p.**, so long.... 7965
2Ki 9:31 Had Zimri **p.**, who slew his master?.... 7965
2Ki 16:13 the blood of his **p.** offerings,.............. 8002
2Ki 18:36 But the people held their **p.**, and....... 2790
2Ki 20:19 good, if **p.** and truth be in my days? ... 7965
2Ki 22:20 be gathered into thy grave in **p.**;......... 7965
1Ch 12:18 son of Jesse: **p.**, **p.** be unto thee, ... 7965
1Ch 12:18 thee, and **p.** be to thine helpers;........ 7965
1Ch 16:1 offered...**p.** offerings before God. 8002
1Ch 16:2 burnt offerings and the **p.** offerings, ... 8002
1Ch 19:19 made **p.** with David, and became......... 7999
1Ch 21:26 burnt offerings and **p.** offerings, ... 8002
1Ch 22:9 give **p.** and quietness unto Israel......... 7965
2Ch 7:7 and the fat of **p.** offerings, ... 8002
2Ch 15:5 was no **p.** to him that went out,......... 7965
2Ch 18:16 return...every man to his house in **p.**.. 7965
2Ch 18:26 of affliction, until I return in **p.**........... 7965
2Ch 18:27 If thou certainly return in **p.**, then....... 7965
2Ch 19:1 of Judah returned to his house in **p.**..... 7965
2Ch 29:35 with the fat of the **p.** offerings,.......... 8002
2Ch 30:22 seven days, offering **p.** offerings,......... 8002
2Ch 31:2 burnt offerings and for **p.** offerings,..... 8002
2Ch 33:16 **p.** offerings and thank offerings, ... 8002
2Ch 34:28 be gathered to thy grave in **p.**, ... 7965
Ezr 4:17 unto the rest beyond the river, **P.**,...... 8001
Ezr 5:7 thus; Unto Darius the king, all **p.**. 8001
Ezr 7:12 unto Ezra the priest,...perfect **p.**,..............
Ezr 9:12 nor seek their **p.** or their wealth........ 7965
Ne 5:8 Then held they their **p.**, and found 2790
Ne 8:11 Hold your **p.**, for the day is holy;....... 2013
Es 4:14 if thou altogether holdest thy **p.**......... 2790
Es 9:30 with words of **p.** and truth, ... 7965
Es 10:3 and speaking **p.** to all his seed. 7965
Job 5:23 of the field shall be at **p.** with thee..... 7999
Job 5:24 that thy tabernacle shall be in **p.**; 7965
Job 11:3 thy lies make men hold their **p.**? 2790
Job 13:5 ye would altogether hold your **p.**!........ 2790
Job 13:13 Hold your **p.**, let me alone, that I........ 2790
Job 22:21 now thyself with him, and be at **p.**: 7999
Job 25:2 he maketh **p.** in his high places. 7965
Job 29:10 the nobles held their **p.**, and their 6963
Job 33:31 me: hold thy **p.**, and I will speak........ 2790
Job 33:33 hold thy **p.**, and I shall teach thee 2790
Ps 4:8 both lay me down in **p.**, and sleep: 7965
Ps 7:4 unto him that was at **p.** with me; 7999
Ps 28:3 which speak **p.** to their neighbours 7965
Ps 29:11 Lord will bless his people with **p.**. 7965
Ps 34:14 and do good; seek **p.**, and pursue it.... 7965
Ps 35:20 For they speak not **p.**: but they......... 7965
Ps 37:11 themselves in the abundance of **p.**. 7965
Ps 37:37 for the end of that man is **p.**. 7965
Ps 39:2 dumb with silence, I held my **p.**,........ 2814
Ps 39:12 hold not thy **p.** at my tears: for I....... 2790
Ps 55:18 He that delivered my soul in **p.**.......... 7965
Ps 55:20 against such as be at **p.** with him: 7965
Ps 72:3 mountains...bring **p.** to the people, ... 7965
Ps 72:7 abundance of **p.** so long as the moon... 7965
Ps 83:1 hold not thy **p.**, and be not still,......... 2790
Ps 85:8 he will speak **p.** unto his people, ... 7965
Ps 85:10 righteousness and **p.** have kissed........ 7965
Ps 109:1 Hold not thy **p.**, O God of my 2790
Ps 119:165 Great **p.** have they which love 7965
Ps 120:6 long dwelt with him that hateth **p.**. 7965
Ps 120:7 I am for **p.**: but when I speak, they.... 7965
Ps 122:6 Pray for the **p.** of Jerusalem: they 7965
Ps 122:7 **P.** be within thy walls, and 7965
Ps 122:8 I will now say, **P.** be within thee. 7965
Ps 125:5 iniquity: but **p.** shall be upon Israel. 7965
Ps 128:6 children, and **p.** upon Israel.............. 7965
Ps 147:14 He maketh **p.** in thy borders, and....... 7965
Pr 3:2 long life, and **p.**, shall they add to 7965
Pr 3:17 and all her paths are **p.**. 7965
Pr 7:14 I have **p.** offerings with me; this 8002
Pr 11:12 of understanding holdeth his **p.**. 2790
Pr 12:20 but to the counsellors of **p.** is joy. 7965
Pr 16:7 his enemies to be at **p.** with him. 7999
Pr 17:28 Even a fool, when he holdeth his **p.**,.... 2790
Ec 3:8 a time of war, and a time of **p.**. 7965
Isa 9:6 Father, The Prince of **P.**. 7965
Isa 9:7 increase of his government and **p.** 7965
Isa 26:3 wilt keep him in perfect **p.**, whose...... 7965
Isa 26:12 Lord, thou wilt ordain **p.** for us:......... 7965
Isa 27:5 that he may make **p.** with me;........... 7965
Isa 27:5 me; and he shall make **p.** with me. 7965
Isa 32:17 work of righteousness shall be **p.**; 7965
Isa 33:7 the ambassadors of **p.** shall weep 7965
Isa 36:21 they held their **p.**, and answered........ 2790
Isa 38:17 for **p.** I had great bitterness: but........ 7965
Isa 39:8 shall be **p.** and truth in my days......... 7965
Isa 42:14 I have long time holden my **p.**; 2814
Isa 45:7 I make **p.**, and create evil: I the 7965
Isa 48:18 then had thy **p.** been as a river, and... 7965
Isa 48:22 There is no **p.**, saith the Lord, unto ... 7965
Isa 52:7 good tidings, that publisheth **p.**; 7965
Isa 53:5 chastisement of our **p.** was upon 7965
Isa 54:10 the covenant of my **p.** be removed, ... 7965
Isa 54:13 great shall be the **p.** of thy children. ... 7965
Isa 55:12 with joy, and be led forth with **p.**: 7965
Isa 57:2 He shall enter into **p.**: they shall........ 7965
Isa 57:11 have not I held my **p.** even of old, ... 2814
Isa 57:19 **P.**, **p.** to him that is far off, and to..... 7965
Isa 57:21 There is no **p.**, saith my God, to the .. 7965
Isa 59:8 The way of **p.** they know not; and...... 7965
Isa 59:8 goeth therein shall not know **p.**.......... 7965
Isa 60:17 I will also make thy officers **p.**, and 7965
Isa 62:1 Zion's sake will I not hold my **p.**, ... 2814
Isa 62:6 never hold their **p.** day nor night: 2814
Isa 64:12 wilt thou hold thy **p.**, and afflict us 2814
Isa 66:12 I will extend **p.** to her like a river, ... 7965
Jer 4:10 Ye shall have **p.**; whereas the sword... 7965
Jer 4:19 I cannot hold my **p.**, because thou....... 2790
Jer 6:14 saying, **P.**, **p.**; when there is no **p.**. ... 7965
Jer 8:11 saying, **P.**, **p.**; when there is no **p.**. ... 7965
Jer 8:15 We looked for **p.**, but no good came; .. 7965
Jer 12:5 in the land of **p.**, wherein thou........... 7965
Jer 12:12 of the land: no flesh shall have **p.**. 7965
Jer 14:13 will give you assured **p.** in this place... 7965
Jer 14:19 looked for **p.**, and there is no good;.... 7965
Jer 16:5 taken away my **p.** from this people, ... 7965
Jer 23:17 Lord hath said, Ye shall have **p.**;........ 7965
Jer 28:9 prophet which prophesieth of **p.**, ... 7965
Jer 29:7 seek the **p.** of the city whither I have . 7965
Jer 29:7 in the **p.** thereof shall ye have **p.**. 7965
Jer 29:11 thoughts of **p.**, and not of evil, to....... 7965
Jer 30:5 of trembling, of fear, and not of **p.**. 7965
Jer 33:6 the abundance of **p.** and truth. 7965
Jer 34:5 But thou shalt die in **p.**: and with........ 7965
Jer 43:12 he shall go forth from thence in **p.**...... 7965
La 3:17 removed my soul far off from **p.**: 7965
Eze 7:25 they shall seek **p.**, and there shall 7965
Eze 13:10 saying, **P.**; and there was no **p.**;........ 7965
Eze 13:16 which see visions of **p.** for her, and.... 7965
Eze 13:16 there is no **p.**, saith the Lord God...... 7965
Eze 34:25 make with them a covenant of **p.**, ... 7965
Eze 37:26 make a covenant of **p.** with them; 7965
Eze 43:27 the altar, and your **p.** offerings; 8002
Eze 45:15 burnt offering, and for **p.** offerings,...... 8002
Eze 45:17 burnt offering, and the **p.** offerings, ... 8002
Eze 46:2 burnt offering and his **p.** offerings, ... 8002
Eze 46:12 burnt offering or **p.** offerings 8002

Eze 46:12 burnt offering and his p. offerings,....... 8002
Da 4:1 earth: P. be multiplied unto you......... 8001
Da 6:25 earth; P. be multiplied unto you......... 8001
Da 8:25 and by p. shall destroy many;............ 7962
Da 10:19 p. be unto thee, be strong, yea, be.... 7965
Am 5:22 the p. offerings of your fat beasts....... 8002
Ob 7 men that were at p. with thee have.... 7965
Mic 3:5 bite with their teeth, and cry, P.; 7965
Mic 5:5 this man shall be the p., when the...... 7965
Na 1:15 good tidings, that publisheth p.! 7965
Zep 1:7 Hold thy p. at the presence of the...... 2013
Hag 2:9 in this place will I give p., saith 7965
Zec 6:13 the counsel of p. shall be between......... 7965
Zec 8:10 was there any p. to him that went...... 7965
Zec 8:16 execute...judgment of truth and p....... 7965
Zec 8:19 therefore love the truth and p.. 7965
Zec 9:10 he shall speak p. unto the heathen:..... 7965
Mal 2:5 covenant...with him of life and p.; 7965
Mal 2:6 he walked with me in p. and equity, ... 7965
Mt 10:13 **worthy, let your p. come upon it:**.. *1515*
Mt 10:13 **worthy, let your p. return to you**. . *1515*
Mt 10:34 **I am come to send p. on earth:**..... *1515*
Mt 10:34 **I came not to send p., but a sword**. *1515*
Mt 20:31 because they should hold their p. *4623*
Mt 26:63 But Jesus held his p.. And the high *4623*
Mk 1:25 **Hold thy p., and come out of him**. .*5392*
Mk 3:4 **or to kill?** But they held their p.. ..... *4623*
Mk 4:39 and said unto the sea, **P., be still**. *4623*
Mk 5:34 **go p., and be whole of thy plague**...*1515*
Mk 9:34 But they held their p.: for by the....... *4623*
Mk 9:50 **and have p. one with another**........ *1518*
Mk 10:48 him that he should hold his p.:......... *4623*
Mk 14:61 held his p., and answered nothing........ *4623*
Lu 1:79 to guide our feet into the way of p.. ... *1515*
Lu 2:14 on earth p., good will toward men...... *1515*
Lu 2:29 lettest thou thy servant depart in p.,... *1515*
Lu 4:35 **Hold thy p., and come out of him**. .*5392*
Lu 7:50 **faith hath saved thee; go in p.**.... *1515*
Lu 8:48 **hath made thee whole; go in p.**.... *1515*
Lu 10:5 **first say, P. be to this house**........ *1515*
Lu 10:6 **And if the son of p. be there, your**.*1515*
Lu 10:6 **your p. shall rest upon it: if not, it***1515*
Lu 11:21 **his palace, his goods are in p.:**....... *1515*
Lu 12:51 **that I am come to give p. on earth?***1515*
Lu 14:4 And they held their p.. And he *2270*
Lu 14:32 **and desireth conditions of p.**.......... *1515*
Lu 18:39 him, that he should hold his p.:......... *4623*
Lu 19:38 p. in heaven,...glory in the highest. *1515*
Lu 19:40 **if these should hold their p., the**... *4623*
Lu 19:42 **things which belong unto thy p.!**... *1515*
Lu 20:26 at his answer, and held their p.. .... *4601*
Lu 24:36 saith unto them, **P. be unto you**....... *1515*
Joh 14:27 **P. I leave with you, my p. I give**... *1515*
Joh 16:33 **you, that in me ye might have p.**. ..*1515*
Joh 20:19 saith unto them, **P. be unto you**...... *1515*
Joh 20:21 Jesus to them again, **P. be unto you:***1515*
Joh 20:26 the midst, and said, **P. be unto you**. . *1515*
Ac 10:36 preaching p. by Jesus Christ:............. *1515*
Ac 11:18 held their p., and glorified God, ... *2270*
Ac 12:17 with the hand to hold their p.,........... *4601*
Ac 12:20 desired p.; because their country *1515*
Ac 15:13 after they had held their p., James *4601*
Ac 15:33 were let go in p. from the brethren *1515*
Ac 16:36 now therefore depart, and go in p.. .... *1515*
Ac 18:9 **but speak, and hold not thy p.:**...... *4623*
Ro 1:7 Grace to you and p. from God our *1515*
Ro 2:10 But glory, honour, and p., to every..... *1515*
Ro 3:17 the way of p. have they not known:.... *1515*
Ro 5:1 we have p. with god through our *1515*
Ro 8:6 be spiritually minded is life and p........ *1515*
Ro 10:15 that preach the gospel of p., and........ *1515*
Ro 14:17 but righteousness, and p., and joy *1515*
Ro 14:19 after the things which make for p.,...... *1515*
Ro 15:13 you with all joy and p. in believing,..... *1515*
Ro 15:33 Now the God of p. be with you all. *1515*
Ro 16:20 God of p. shall bruise Satan under....... *1515*
1Co 1:3 Grace be unto you, and p., from God.. *1515*
1Co 7:15 cases: but God hath called us to p....... *1515*
1Co 14:30 sitteth by, let the first hold his p........ *4601*
1Co 14:33 the author of confusion, but of p., ... *1515*
1Co 16:11 but conduct him forth in p., that he *1515*
2Co 1:2 to you and p. from God our Father,..... *1515*
2Co 13:11 comfort, be of one mind, live in p.; *1518*
2Co 13:11 of love and p. shall be with you. *1515*
Ga 1:3 Grace be to you and p. from God....... *1515*
Ga 5:22 the fruit of the Spirit is love, joy, p., .. *1515*
Ga 6:16 p. be on them, and mercy, and upon... *1515*
Eph 1:2 Grace be to you, and p., from God..... *1515*
Eph 2:14 For he is our p., who hath made......... *1515*
Eph 2:15 twain one new man, so making p.; *1515*
Eph 2:17 preached p. to you which were afar *1515*
Eph 4:3 unity of the Spirit in the bond of p....... *1515*
Eph 6:15 the preparation of the gospel of p.;..... *1515*
Eph 6:23 P. be to the brethren, and love *1515*
Php 1:2 Grace be unto you, and p., from God.. *1515*
Php 4:7 the p. of God, which passeth all.......... *1515*
Php 4:9 and the God of p. shall be with you. ... *1515*
Col 1:2 Grace be unto you, and p., from God.. *1515*
Col 1:20 made p. through the blood of his......... *1517*
Col 3:15 the p. of God rule in your hearts, ... *1515*
1Th 1:1 Grace be unto you, and p., from God.. *1515*
1Th 5:3 when they shall say, P. and safety; *1515*
1Th 5:13 And be at p. among yourselves.......... *1518*
1Th 5:23 And the very God of p. sanctify you ... *1515*
2Th 1:2 Grace unto you, and p., from God...... *1515*
2Th 3:16 the Lord of p. himself give you p....... *1515*
1Ti 1:2 mercy, and p., from God our Father... *1515*
2Ti 1:2 mercy, and p., from God the Father ... *1515*
2Ti 2:22 righteousness, faith, charity, p., ... *1515*
Tit 1:4 mercy, and p., from God the Father ... *1515*
Phm 3 Grace to you, and p., from God our ... *1515*
Heb 7:2 King of Salem, which is, King of p.; ... *1515*
Heb 11:31 she had received the spies with p....... *1515*
Heb 12:14 Follow p. with all men, and.............. *1515*
Heb 13:20 the God of p., that brought again *1515*
Jas 2:16 Depart in p., be ye warmed and *1515*
Jas 3:18 is sown in p. of them that make p..... *1515*
1Pe 1:2 Christ: Grace unto you, and p., be..... *1515*
1Pe 3:11 good; let him seek p., and ensue it..... *1515*
1Pe 5:14 P. be with you all that are in Christ.... *1515*
2Pe 1:2 Grace and p. be multiplied unto *1515*
2Pe 3:14 that ye may be found of him in p., ... *1515*
2Jo 3 Grace be with you, mercy, and p., ... *1515*
3Jo 14 P. be to thee. Our friends salute *1515*
Jude 2 you, and p., and love, be multiplied. ... *1515*
Re 1:4 Grace be unto you, and p., from him .. *1515*
Re 6:4 thereon to take p. from the earth,...... *1515*

PEACEABLE
Ge 34:21 These men are p. with us;................ 8003
2Sa 20:19 that are p. and faithful in Israel: 7999
1Ch 4:40 land was wide, and quiet, and p.; 7961
Isa 32:18 shall dwell in a p. habitation, and........ 7965
Jer 25:37 the p. habitations are cut down.......... 7965
1Ti 2:2 we may lead a quiet and p. life in....... *2272*
Heb 12:11 the p. fruit of righteousness unto *1516*
Jas 3:17 first pure, then p., gentle, and easy.... *1516*

PEACEABLY
Ge 37:4 and could not speak p. unto him......... 7965
Jg 11:13 now...restore those lands again p.. 7965
Jg 21:13 Rimmon, and to call p. unto them....... 7965
1Sa 16:4 coming, and said, Comest thou p.? 7965
1Sa 16:5 And he said, P.: I am come to 7965
1Ki 2:13 And she said, Comest thou p.? 7965
1Ki 2:13 And he said, P.............................. 7965
1Ch 12:17 If ye be come p. unto me to help me,. 7965
Jer 9:8 one speaketh p. to his neighbour........ 7965
Da 11:21 he shall come in p., and obtain 7962
Da 11:24 He shall enter p. even upon the.......... 7962
Ro 12:18 lieth in you, live p. with all men......... *1518*

PEACEMAKERS
Mt 5:9 **Blessed are the p.: for they shall**... *1518*

PEACE-OFFERING See PEACE and OFFERING.

PEACOCKS
1Ki 10:22 and silver, ivory, and apes, and p....... 8500
2Ch 9:21 and silver, ivory, and apes, and p....... 8500
Job 39:13 thou the goodly wings unto the p.?..... 7443

PEARL See also PEARLS.
Mt 13:46 **he had found one p. of great price**.*3135*
Re 21:21 every several gate was of one p.: *3135*

PEARLS
Job 28:18 shall be made of coral, or of p.......... 1378
Mt 7:6 **cast ye your p. before swine**,......... *3135*
Mt 13:45 **merchant man, seeking goodly p.** .. *3135*
1Ti 2:9 hair, or gold, or p., or costly array;.... *3135*
Re 17:4 gold and precious stones and p., ... *3135*
Re 18:12 and precious stones, and of p., and..... *3135*
Re 18:16 gold, and precious stones, and p.! *3135*
Re 21:21 the twelve gates were twelve p.; *3135*

PECULIAR
Ex 19:5 ye shall be a p. treasure unto me....... 5459
De 14:2 thee to be a p. people unto himself,..... 5459
De 26:18 thee this day to be his p. people,....... 5459
Ps 135:4 and Israel for his p. treasure............. 5459
Ec 2:8 and the p. treasure of kings and of..... 5459
Tit 2:14 a p. people, zealous of good works. *4041*
1Pe 2:9 an holy nation, a p. people;........ *1519,4047*

PEDAHEL (ped'-a-hel)
Nu 34:28 Naphtali, P. the son of Ammihud........ 6300

PEDAHZUR (pe-dah'-zur)
Nu 1:10 Manasseh; Gamaliel the son of P.. 6301
Nu 2:20 shall be Gamaliel the son of P.. 6301
Nu 7:54 day offered Gamaliel the son of P.,...... 6301
Nu 7:59 offering of Gamaliel the son of P......... 6301
Nu 10:23 was Gamaliel the son of P.. 6301

PEDAIAH (pe-dah'-yah)
2Ki 23:36 the daughter of P. of Rumah............. 6305
1Ch 3:18 Malchiram also, and P., and.............. 6305
1Ch 3:19 the sons of P. were, Zerubbabel, ... 6305
1Ch 27:20 of Manasseh, Joel the son of P.: 6305
Ne 3:25 After him P. the son of Parosh.......... 6305
Ne 8:4 on his left hand, P., and Mishael,....... 6305
Ne 11:7 the son of Joed, the son of P., the..... 6305
Ne 13:13 the scribe, and of the Levites, P.:...... 6305

PEDIGREES
Nu 1:18 they declared their p. after their 3205

PEELED See also PILLED.
Isa 18:2 to a nation scattered and p., to a 4178
Isa 18:7 of a people scattered and p., and 4178
Eze 29:18 bald, and every shoulder was p.:........ 4803

PEEP See also PEEPED.
Isa 8:19 and unto wizards that p., and that 6850

PEEPED
Isa 10:14 wing, or opened the mouth, or p........ 6850

PEKAH (pe'-kah)
2Ki 15:25 But P. the son of Remaliah, a 6492
2Ki 15:27 P. the son of Remaliah began to 6492
2Ki 15:29 In the days of P. king of Israel.......... 6492
2Ki 15:30 made a conspiracy against P. the 6492
2Ki 15:31 And the rest of the acts of P., and..... 6492
2Ki 15:32 In the second year of P. the son of.... 6492
2Ki 15:37 Syria, and P. the son of Remaliah. 6492
2Ki 16:1 In the seventeenth year of P. the 6492
2Ki 16:5 P. son of Remaliah king of Israel........ 6492
2Ch 28:6 For P. the son of Remaliah slew in..... 6492
Isa 7:1 P. the son of Remaliah, king of.......... 6492

PEKAHIAH (pe-ka-hi'-ah)
2Ki 15:22 P. his son reigned in his stead.......... 6494
2Ki 15:23 P. the son of Menahem began to 6494
2Ki 15:26 And the rest of the acts of P., and..... 6494

PEKOD (pe'-kod)
Jer 50:21 and against the inhabitants of P.:........ 6489
Eze 23:23 all the Chaldeans, P., and Shoa,.......... 6489

PELAIAH (pel-a-i'-ah)
1Ch 3:24 and Eliashib, and P., and Akkub,......... 6411
Ne 8:7 P., and the Levites, caused the......... 6411
Ne 10:10 Shebaniah, Hodijah, Kelita, P., ... 6411

PELALIAH (pel-a-li'-ah)
Ne 11:12 the son of Jeroham, the son of P., ... 6421

PELATIAH (pel-a-til'-ah)
1Ch 3:21 the sons of Hananiah; P., and........... 6410
1Ch 4:42 having for their captains P., and......... 6410
Ne 10:22 P., Hanan, Anaiah,.......................... 6410
Eze 11:1 and P. the son of Benaiah, princes 6410
Eze 11:13 that P. the son of Benaiah died.......... 6410

PELEG (pe'-leg) See also PHALEG.
Ge 10:25 two sons: the name of one was P.; 6389
Ge 11:16 four and thirty years, and begat P.: 6389
Ge 11:17 And Eber lived after he begat P. 6389
Ge 11:18 P. lived thirty years, and begat.......... 6389
Ge 11:19 P. lived after he begat Reu two......... 6389
1Ch 1:19 sons: the name of the one was P.: 6389
1Ch 1:25 Eber, P., Reu,................................. 6389

PELET (pe'-let) See also BETH-PALET.
1Ch 2:47 Gesham, and P., and Ephah, and 6404
1Ch 12:3 and P., the sons of Azmaveth; 6404

PELETH (pe'-leth)
Nu 16:1 and On, the son of P., sons of 6431
1Ch 2:33 the sons of Jonathan; P., and 6431

PELETHITES (pel'-e-thites)
2Sa 8:18 both the Cherethites and the **P.**; ... 6432
2Sa 15:18 and all the **P.**, and all the Gittites, ... 6432
2Sa 20:7 the **P.**, and all the mighty men: ... 6432
2Sa 20:23 the Cherethites and over the **P.**: ... 6432
1Ki 1:38 and the **P.**, went down, and caused ... 6432
1Ki 1:44 the Cherethites, and the **P.**, and ... 6432
1Ch 18:17 over the Cherethites and the **P.**; ... 6432

PELICAN
Le 11:18 and the **p.**, and the gier eagle, ... 6893
De 14:17 And the **p.**, and the gier eagle, and ... 6893
Ps 102:6 I am like a **p.** of the wilderness: ... 6893

PELONITE (pel'-o-nite) See also PALTITE.
1Ch 11:27 the Harorite, Helez the **P.**, ... 6397
1Ch 11:36 the Mecherathite, Ahijah the **P.**, ... 6397
1Ch 27:10 seventh month was Helez the **P.** ... 6397

PEN See also PENKNIFE.
Jg 5:14 they that handle the **p.** of the ... 7626
Job 19:24 they were graven with an iron **p.** ... 5842
Ps 45:1 tongue is the **p.** of a ready writer ... 5842
Isa 8:1 roll, and write in it with a man's **p.** ... 2747
Jer 8:8 it; the **p.** of the scribes is in vain. ... 5842
Jer 17:1 Judah is written with a **p.** of iron, ... 5842
3Jo 13 with ink and **p.** write unto thee: ... *2563*

PENCE
Mt 18:28 **which owed him an hundred p.:** ... *1220*
Mk 14:5 for more than three hundred **p.**, ... *1220*
Lu 7:41 **the one owed five hundred p., and** *1220*
Lu 10:35 **he took out two p., and gave them** .*1220*
Joh 12:5 ointment sold for three hundred **p.**, ... *1220*

PENIEL (pe-ni'-el) See also PENUEL.
Ge 32:30 called the name of the place **P.**: ... 6439

PENINNAH (pe-nin'-nah)
1Sa 1:2 and the name of the other **P.**: ... 6444
1Sa 1:2 and **P.** had children, but Hannah ... 6444
1Sa 1:4 offered, he gave to **P.** his wife, ... 6444

PENKNIFE
Jer 36:23 leaves, he cut it with the **p.**, and ... 8593

PENNY See also PENNYWORTH; PENCE.
Mt 20:2 **with the labourers for a p. a day,** .. *1220*
Mt 20:9 **hour, they received every man a p.** .*1220*
Mt 20:10 **likewise received every man a p.** .. *1220*
Mt 20:13 **not thou agree with me for a p.?** ... *1220*
Mt 22:19 And they brought unto him a **p.**. ... *1220*
Mk 12:15 **bring me a p., that I may see it.** ... *1220*
Lu 20:24 **Shew me a p.. Whose image and** ... *1220*
Re 6:6 A measure of wheat for a **p.**, and ... *1220*
Re 6:6 three measures of barley for a **p.**; ... *1220*

PENNYWORTH
Mk 6:37 and buy two hundred **p.** of bread, ... *1220*
Joh 6:7 Two hundred **p.** of bread is not ... *1220*

PENTECOST (pen'-te-cost)
Ac 2:1 the day of **P.** was fully come, ... *4005*
Ac 20:16 to be at Jerusalem the day of **P.**. ... *4005*
1Co 16:8 I will tarry at Ephesus until **P.**. ... *4005*

PENUEL (pe-nu'-el) See also PENIEL.
Ge 32:31 as he passed over **P.** the sun rose ... 6439
Jg 8:8 he went up thence to **P.**, and spake ... 6439
Jg 8:8 and the men of **P.** answered him ... 6439
Jg 8:9 he spake also unto the men of **P.**, ... 6439
Jg 8:17 And he beat down the tower of **P.**, ... 6439
1Ki 12:25 went out from thence, and built **P.** ... 6439
1Ch 4:4 and **P.** the father of Gedor, and ... 6439
1Ch 8:25 and **P.**, the sons of Shashak; ... 6439

PENURY
Pr 14:23 talk of the lips tendeth only to **p.**. ... 4270
Lu 21:4 **but she of her p. hath cast in all** ... *5303*

PEOPLE See also PEOPLE'S; PEOPLES.
Ge 11:6 Lord said, Behold, the **p.** is one, ... 5971
Ge 14:16 and the women also, and the **p.** ... 5971
Ge 17:14 soul shall be cut off from his **p.**; ... 5971
Ge 17:16 nations; kings of **p.** shall be of her ... 5971
Ge 19:4 all the **p.** from every quarter: ... 5971
Ge 23:7 bowed himself to the **p.** of the land, ... 5971
Ge 23:11 in the presence of the sons of my **p.** ... 5971
Ge 23:12 bowed down himself before the **p.** ... 5971
Ge 23:13 the audience of the **p.** of the land, ... 5971
Ge 25:8 years; and was gathered to his **p.** ... 5971
Ge 25:17 died; and was gathered unto his **p.**. ... 5971
Ge 25:23 and two manner of **p.** shall be ... 3816
Ge 25:23 the one **p.** shall be stronger than ... 3816
Ge 25:23 be stronger than the other **p.**; and ... 3816
Ge 26:10 one of the **p.** might lightly have ... 5971
Ge 26:11 And Abimelech charged all his **p.**, ... 5971
Ge 27:29 Let **p.** serve thee, and nations bow ... 5971
Ge 28:3 thou mayest be a multitude of **p.**; ... 5971
Ge 29:1 into the land of the **p.** of the east. ... 1121
Ge 32:7 divided the **p.** that was with him, ... 5971
Ge 34:16 you, and we will become one **p.** ... 5971
Ge 34:22 for to dwell with us, to be one **p.** ... 5971
Ge 35:6 and all the **p.** that were with him. ... 5971
Ge 35:29 was gathered unto his **p.**, being ... 5971
Ge 41:40 thy word shall all my **p.** be ruled: ... 5971
Ge 41:55 the **p.** cried to Pharaoh for bread: ... 5971
Ge 42:6 and he it was that sold to all the **p.** ... 5971
Ge 47:21 as for the **p.**, he removed them to ... 5971
Ge 47:23 Then Joseph said unto the **p.**, ... 5971
Ge 48:4 will make of thee a multitude of **p.**; ... 5971
Ge 48:19 know it: he also shall become a **p.**, ... 5971
Ge 49:10 shall the gathering of the **p.** be. ... 5971
Ge 49:16 Dan shall judge his **p.**, as one of ... 5971
Ge 49:29 I am to be gathered unto my **p.**: ... 5971
Ge 49:33 and was gathered unto his **p.** ... 5971
Ge 50:20 is this day, to save much **p.** alive. ... 5971
Ex 1:9 And he said unto his **p.**, Behold, ... 5971
Ex 1:9 the **p.** of the children of Israel are ... 5971
Ex 1:20 the **p.** multiplied, and waxed very ... 5971
Ex 1:22 And Pharaoh charged all his **p.**, ... 5971
Ex 3:7 surely seen the affliction of my **p.** ... 5971
Ex 3:10 bring forth my **p.** the children of ... 5971
Ex 3:12 thou hast brought forth the **p.** out ... 5971
Ex 3:21 will give this **p.** favour in the sight ... 5971
Ex 4:16 be thy spokesman unto the **p.**: ... 5971
Ex 4:21 that he shall not let the **p.** go. ... 5971
Ex 4:30 did the signs in the sight of the **p.** ... 5971
Ex 4:31 And the **p.** believed: and when they ... 5971
Ex 5:1 Let my **p.** go, that they may hold a ... 5971
Ex 5:4 Aaron, let the **p.** from their works? ... 5971
Ex 5:5 the **p.** of the land now are many, ... 5971
Ex 5:6 same day the taskmasters of the **p.**, ... 5971
Ex 5:7 Ye shall no more give the **p.** straw ... 5971
Ex 5:10 the taskmasters of the **p.** went out, ... 5971
Ex 5:10 officers, and they spake to the **p.**, ... 5971
Ex 5:12 So the **p.** were scattered abroad ... 5971
Ex 5:16 but the fault is in thine own **p.** ... 5971
Ex 5:22 hast thou so evil entreated this **p.**? ... 5971
Ex 5:23 name, he hath done evil to this **p.**; ... 5971
Ex 5:23 hast thou delivered thy **p.** at all. ... 5971
Ex 6:7 I will take you to me for a **p.**, and I ... 5971
Ex 7:4 and my **p.** the children of Israel, ... 5971
Ex 7:14 he refuseth to let the **p.** go. ... 5971
Ex 7:16 Let my **p.** go, that they may serve ... 5971
Ex 8:1 Let my **p.** go, that they may serve ... 5971
Ex 8:3 of thy servants, and upon thy **p.**, ... 5971
Ex 8:4 up both on thee, and upon thy **p.**, ... 5971
Ex 8:8 the frogs from me, and from my **p.**; ... 5971
Ex 8:8 and I will let the **p.** go, that they ... 5971
Ex 8:9 and for thy servants, and for thy **p.**, ... 5971
Ex 8:11 from thy servants, and from thy **p.**; ... 5971
Ex 8:20 Let my **p.** go, that they may serve ... 5971
Ex 8:21 Else, if thou wilt not let my **p.** go, ... 5971
Ex 8:21 upon thy servants, and upon thy **p.**, ... 5971
Ex 8:22 of Goshen, in which my **p.** dwell, ... 5971
Ex 8:23 division between my **p.** and thy **p.**: ... 5971
Ex 8:29 from his servants, and from his **p.**, ... 5971
Ex 8:29 the **p.** go to sacrifice to the Lord. ... 5971
Ex 8:31 from his servants, and from his **p.**; ... 5971
Ex 8:32 also, neither would he let the **p.** go. ... 5971
Ex 8:1 Let my **p.** go, that they may serve ... 5971
Ex 8:7 and he did not let the **p.** go. ... 5971
Ex 8:13 Let my **p.** go, that they may serve ... 5971
Ex 8:14 upon thy servants, and upon thy **p.**; ... 5971
Ex 8:15 I may smite thee and thy **p.** with ... 5971
Ex 8:17 exaltest thou thyself against my **p.**, ... 5971
Ex 8:27 and I and my **p.** are wicked. ... 5971
Ex 10:3 let my **p.** go, that they may serve ... 5971
Ex 10:4 Else, if thou refuse to let my **p.** go, ... 5971
Ex 11:2 Speak now in the ears of the **p.**, and .. 5971
Ex 11:3 the Lord gave the **p.** favour in the ... 5971
Ex 11:3 servants, and in the sight of the **p.**. ... 5971
Ex 11:8 out, and all the **p.** that follow thee: ... 5971
Ex 12:27 **p.** bowed the head and worshipped. ... 5971
Ex 12:31 get you forth from among my **p.**, ... 5971
Ex 12:33 Egyptians were urgent upon the **p.**, ... 5971
Ex 12:34 **p.** took their dough before it was ... 5971
Ex 12:36 the Lord gave the **p.** favour in the ... 5971
Ex 13:3 Moses said unto the **p.**, Remember ... 5971
Ex 13:17 when Pharaoh had let the **p.** go, ... 5971
Ex 13:17 Lest peradventure the **p.** repent ... 5971
Ex 13:18 God led the **p.** about, through the ... 5971
Ex 13:22 of fire by night, from before the **p.** ... 5971
Ex 14:5 the king of Egypt that the **p.** fled: ... 5971
Ex 14:5 servants was turned against the **p.**, ... 5971
Ex 14:6 chariot, and took his **p.** with him: ... 5971
Ex 14:13 Moses said unto the **p.**, Fear ye ... 5971
Ex 14:31 the **p.** feared the Lord, and believed ... 5971
Ex 15:13 in thy mercy hast led forth the **p.** ... 5971
Ex 15:14 **p.** shall hear, and be afraid: sorrow ... 5971
Ex 15:16 still as a stone; till thy **p.** pass over ... 5971
Ex 15:16 O Lord, till the **p.** pass over, which ... 5971
Ex 15:24 the **p.** murmured against Moses, ... 5971
Ex 16:4 and the **p.** shall go out and gather ... 5971
Ex 16:27 there went out some of the **p.** on ... 5971
Ex 16:30 So the **p.** rested on the seventh day ... 5971
Ex 17:1 was no water for the **p.** to drink. ... 5971
Ex 17:2 the **p.** did chide with Moses, and ... 5971
Ex 17:3 the **p.** thirsted there for water; and ... 5971
Ex 17:3 the **p.** murmured against Moses, ... 5971
Ex 17:4 What shall I do unto this **p.**? they ... 5971
Ex 17:5 Go on before the **p.**, and take with ... 5971
Ex 17:6 out of it, that the **p.** may drink. ... 5971
Ex 17:13 discomfited Amalek and his **p.** with ... 5971
Ex 18:1 for Moses, and for Israel his **p.**, ... 5971
Ex 18:10 hath delivered the **p.** from under ... 5971
Ex 18:13 that Moses sat to judge the **p.**: and ... 5971
Ex 18:13 and the **p.** stood by Moses from the ... 5971
Ex 18:14 in law saw all that he did to the **p.**, ... 5971
Ex 18:14 thing that thou doest to the **p.**? ... 5971
Ex 18:14 and all the **p.** stand by thee from ... 5971
Ex 18:15 the **p.** come unto me to enquire of ... 5971
Ex 18:18 thou, and this **p.** that is with thee: ... 5971
Ex 18:19 Be thou for the **p.** to God-ward, ... 5971
Ex 18:21 provide out of all the **p.** able men, ... 5971
Ex 18:22 let them judge the **p.** at all seasons: ... 5971
Ex 18:23 this **p.** shall also go to their place ... 5971
Ex 18:25 and made them heads over the **p.**, ... 5971
Ex 18:26 they judged the **p.** at all seasons: ... 5971
Ex 19:5 treasure unto me above all **p.**: for ... 5971
Ex 19:7 and called for the elders of the **p.**, ... 5971
Ex 19:8 all the **p.** answered together, and ... 5971
Ex 19:8 Moses returned the words of the **p.** ... 5971
Ex 19:9 that the **p.** may hear when I speak ... 5971
Ex 19:9 Moses told the words of the **p.** unto ... 5971
Ex 19:10 Go unto the **p.**, and sanctify them ... 5971
Ex 19:11 come down in the sight of all the **p.** ... 5971
Ex 19:12 set bounds unto the **p.** round about, ... 5971
Ex 19:14 down from the mount unto the **p.**, ... 5971
Ex 19:14 sanctified the **p.**; and they washed ... 5971
Ex 19:15 said unto the **p.**, Be ready against ... 5971
Ex 19:16 that all the **p.** that was in the camp ... 5971
Ex 19:17 Moses brought forth the **p.** out of ... 5971
Ex 19:21 Go down, charge the **p.**, lest they ... 5971
Ex 19:23 The **p.** cannot come up to mount ... 5971
Ex 19:24 let not the priests and the **p.** break ... 5971
Ex 19:25 Moses went down unto the **p.**, and ... 5971
Ex 20:18 all the **p.** saw the thunderings, and ... 5971
Ex 20:18 when the **p.** saw it, they removed, ... 5971
Ex 20:20 Moses said unto the **p.**, Fear not: ... 5971
Ex 20:21 the **p.** stood afar off, and Moses ... 5971
Ex 22:25 If thou lend money to any of my **p.** ... 5971
Ex 22:28 gods, now curse the ruler of thy **p.**. ... 5971
Ex 23:11 that the poor of thy **p.** may eat: and ... 5971
Ex 23:27 will destroy all the **p.** to whom thou ... 5971
Ex 24:2 neither shall the **p.** go up with him. ... 5971
Ex 24:3 Moses came and told the **p.** all the ... 5971
Ex 24:3 and all the **p.** answered with one ... 5971
Ex 24:7 and read in the audience of the **p.**: ... 5971
Ex 24:8 blood, and sprinkled it on the **p.**, ... 5971
Ex 30:33 shall even be cut off from his **p.** ... 5971
Ex 30:38 shall even be cut off from his **p.** ... 5971
Ex 31:14 shall be cut off from among his **p.**. ... 5971
Ex 32:1 when the **p.** saw that Moses delayed .. 5971
Ex 32:1 **p.** gathered themselves together ... 5971
Ex 32:3 the **p.** brake off the golden earrings ... 5971
Ex 32:6 the **p.** sat down to eat and drink, ... 5971
Ex 32:7 for thy **p.**, which thou broughtest ... 5971
Ex 32:9 unto Moses, I have seen this **p.**, ... 5971
Ex 32:9 and, behold, it is a stiffnecked **p.**: ... 5971
Ex 32:11 thy wrath wax hot against thy **p.**, ... 5971
Ex 32:12 repent of this evil against thy **p.** ... 5971
Ex 32:14 which he thought to do unto his **p.**. ... 5971
Ex 32:17 Joshua heard the noise of the **p.** as ... 5971
Ex 32:21 Aaron, What did this **p.** unto thee, ... 5971
Ex 32:22 thou knowest the **p.**, that they are ... 5971
Ex 32:25 Moses saw that the **p.** were naked; ... 5971
Ex 32:28 there fell of the **p.** that day about ... 5971

Ex 32:30 Moses said unto the **p.**, Ye have........ 5971
Ex 32:31 Oh, this **p.** have sinned a great sin,.... 5971
Ex 32:34 lead the **p.** unto the place of which..... 5971
Ex 32:35 the Lord plagued the **p.**, because....... 5971
Ex 33:1 the **p.** which thou hast brought up...... 5971
Ex 33:3 for thou art a stiffnecked **p.**: lest I...... 5971
Ex 33:4 when the **p.** heard these evil tidings,... 5971
Ex 33:5 of Israel, Ye are a stiffnecked **p.**:....... 5971
Ex 33:8 all the **p.** rose up, and stood every....... 5971
Ex 33:10 And all the **p.** saw the cloudy pillar..... 5971
Ex 33:10 all the **p.** rose up and worshipped,...... 5971
Ex 33:12 sayest unto me, Bring up this **p.**:....... 5971
Ex 33:13 consider that this nation is thy **p.**...... 5971
Ex 33:16 that I and thy **p.** have found grace...... 5971
Ex 33:16 shall we be separated, I and thy **p.**..... 5971
Ex 33:16 from all the **p.** that are upon the........ 5971
Ex 34:9 among us; for it is a stiffnecked **p.**;.... 5971
Ex 34:10 before all thy **p.** I will do marvels,...... 5971
Ex 34:10 all the **p.** among which thou art.......... 5971
Ex 36:5 **p.** bring much more than enough........ 5971
Ex 36:6 **p.** were restrained from bringing........ 5971
Le 4:3 sin according to the sin of the **p.**;...... 5971
Le 4:27 if any one of the common **p.** sin......... 5971
Le 7:20, 21 soul shall be cut off from his **p.**..... 5971
Le 7:25 eateth it shall be cut off from his **p.**.... 5971
Le 7:27 that soul shall be cut off from his **p.**.... 5971
Le 9:7 for thyself, and for the **p.**: and.......... 5971
Le 9:7 and offer the offering of the **p.**, and.... 5971
Le 9:15 which was the sin offering for the **p.**,.. 5971
Le 9:18 offerings, which was for the **p.**: and.... 5971
Le 9:22 lifted up his hand toward the **p.**,....... 5971
Le 9:23 and came out, and blessed the **p.**:....... 5971
Le 9:23 of the Lord appeared unto all the **p.**..... 5971
Le 9:24 when all the **p.** saw, they shouted,..... 5971
Le 10:3 before all the **p.** I will be glorified....... 5971
Le 10:6 lest wrath come upon all the **p.**:......... 5712
Le 16:15 the sin offering, that is for the **p.**,...... 5971
Le 16:24 and the burnt offering of the **p.**,......... 5971
Le 16:24 atonement for himself, and...the **p.**..... 5971
Le 16:33 for all the **p.** of the congregation........ 5971
Le 17:4 shall be cut off from among his **p.**:..... 5971
Le 17:9 shall be cut off from among his **p.**...... 5971
Le 17:10 will cut him off from among his **p.**..... 5971
Le 18:29 shall be cut off from among their **p.**.... 5971
Le 19:8 shall be cut off from among his **p.**..... 5971
Le 19:16 down as a talebearer among thy **p.**:.... 5971
Le 19:18 against the children of thy **p.**, but...... 5971
Le 20:2 the **p.** of the land shall stone him....... 5971
Le 20:3 will cut him off from among his **p.**;..... 5971
Le 20:4 the **p.** of the land do any ways hide.... 5971
Le 20:5 with Molech, from among their **p.**..... 5971
Le 20:6 will cut him off from among his **p.**..... 5971
Le 20:17 cut off in the sight of their **p.**:.... 1121,5971
Le 20:18 shall be cut off from among their **p.**.... 5971
Le 20:24 have separated you from other **p.**....... 5971
Le 20:26 severed you from other **p.**, that ye..... 5971
Le 21:1 defiled for the dead among his **p.**:..... 5971
Le 21:4 being a chief man among his **p.**, to..... 5971
Le 21:14 take a virgin of his own **p.** to wife...... 5971
Le 21:15 he profane his seed among his **p.**:...... 5971
Le 23:29 shall be cut off from among his **p.**..... 5971
Le 23:30 will I destroy from among his **p.**....... 5971
Le 26:12 be your God, and ye shall be my **p.**.... 5971
Nu 5:21 a curse and an oath among thy **p.**,...... 5971
Nu 5:27 shall be a curse among her **p.**........... 5971
Nu 9:13 shall be cut off from among his **p.**:..... 5971
Nu 11:1 And when the **p.** complained, it.......... 5971
Nu 11:2 the **p.** cried unto Moses; and when..... 5971
Nu 11:8 the **p.** went about, and gathered it,..... 5971
Nu 11:10 Then Moses heard the **p.** weep......... 5971
Nu 11:11 the burden of all this **p.** upon me?...... 5971
Nu 11:12 Have I conceived all this **p.**? have I.... 5971
Nu 11:13 I have flesh to give unto all this **p.**?.... 5971
Nu 11:14 am not able to bear all this **p.** alone,... 5971
Nu 11:16 knowest to be the elders of the **p.**,.... 5971
Nu 11:17 bear the burden of the **p.** with thee,... 5971
Nu 11:18 And say thou unto the **p.**, Sanctify...... 5971
Nu 11:21 The **p.**, among whom I am, are six..... 5971
Nu 11:24 told the **p.** the words of the Lord,...... 5971
Nu 11:24 seventy men of the elders of the **p.**,... 5971
Nu 11:29 that all the Lord's **p.** were prophets,... 5971
Nu 11:32 the **p.** stood up all that day, and all..... 5971
Nu 11:33 the Lord was kindled against the **p.**,... 5971
Nu 11:33 Lord smote the **p.** with a very great... 5971
Nu 11:34 there they buried the **p.** that lusted.... 5971
Nu 11:35 the **p.** journeyed...unto Hazeroth;....... 5971
Nu 12:15 **p.** journeyed not till Miriam was......... 5971
Nu 12:16 the **p.** removed from Hazeroth, and.... 5971
Nu 13:18 **p.** that dwelleth therein, whether....... 5971
Nu 13:28 **p.** be strong that dwell in the land,..... 5971
Nu 13:30 Caleb stilled the **p.** before Moses,..... 5971
Nu 13:31 be not able to go up against the **p.**;.... 5971
Nu 13:32 the **p.** that we saw in it are men of a.. 5971
Nu 14:1 cried; and the **p.** wept that night......... 5971
Nu 14:9 neither fear ye the **p.** of the land;...... 5971
Nu 14:11 How long will this **p.** provoke me?...... 5971
Nu 14:13 broughtest up this **p.** in thy might...... 5971
Nu 14:14 that thou Lord art among this **p.**,....... 5971
Nu 14:15 shalt kill all this **p.** as one man,.......... 5971
Nu 14:16 Lord was not able to bring this **p.**....... 5971
Nu 14:19 the iniquity of this **p.** according.......... 5971
Nu 14:19 and as thou hast forgiven this **p.**,....... 5971
Nu 14:39 Israel: and the **p.** mourned greatly...... 5971
Nu 15:26 seeing all the **p.** were in ignorance..... 5971
Nu 15:30 shall be cut off from among his **p.**..... 5971
Nu 16:41 Ye have killed the **p.** of the Lord....... 5971
Nu 16:47 plague was begun among the **p.**:........ 5971
Nu 16:47 and made an atonement for the **p.**..... 5971
Nu 20:1 and the **p.** abode in Kadesh; and........ 5971
Nu 20:3 And the **p.** chode with Moses, and..... 5971
Nu 20:20 came out against him with much **p.**,..... 5971
Nu 20:24 Aaron shall be gathered unto his **p.**:.... 5971
Nu 20:26 Aaron shall be gathered unto his **p.**,.... 5971
Nu 21:2 If thou wilt indeed deliver this **p.**........ 5971
Nu 21:4 of the **p.** was much discouraged......... 5971
Nu 21:5 And the **p.** spake against God, and..... 5971
Nu 21:6 sent fiery serpents among the **p.**,....... 5971
Nu 21:6 and they bit the **p.**; and much........... 5971
Nu 21:6 and much **p.** of Israel died............... 5971
Nu 21:7 Therefore the **p.** came to Moses,....... 5971
Nu 21:7 us. And Moses prayed for the **p.**...... 5971
Nu 21:16 Gather the **p.** together, and I will....... 5971
Nu 21:18 the nobles of the **p.** digged it, by the.. 5971
Nu 21:23 Sihon gathered all his **p.** together,...... 5971
Nu 21:29 thou art undone, O **p.** of Chemosh:.... 5971
Nu 21:33 out against them, he, and all his **p.**,... 5971
Nu 21:34 him into thy hand, and all his **p.**,........ 5971
Nu 21:35 him, and his sons, and all his **p.**,........ 5971
Nu 22:3 And Moab was sore afraid of the **p.**,... 5971
Nu 22:5 of the land of the children of his **p.**,.... 5971
Nu 22:5 there is a **p.** come out from Egypt;.... 5971
Nu 22:6 I pray thee, curse me this **p.**; for....... 5971
Nu 22:11 there is a **p.** come out of Egypt,........ 5971
Nu 22:12 them; thou shalt not curse the **p.**:....... 5971
Nu 22:17 I pray thee, curse me this **p.**............ 5971
Nu 22:41 might see the utmost part of the **p.**.... 5971
Nu 23:9 the **p.** shall dwell alone, and shall....... 5971
Nu 23:24 the **p.** shall rise up as a great lion,..... 5971
Nu 24:14 And now, behold, I go unto my **p.**:..... 5971
Nu 24:14 I will advertise thee what this **p.**........ 5971
Nu 24:14 shall do to thy **p.** in the latter days..... 5971
Nu 25:1 **p.** began to commit whoredom with.... 5971
Nu 25:2 called the **p.** unto the sacrifices of..... 5971
Nu 25:2 **p.** did eat, and bowed down to their... 5971
Nu 25:4 Take all the heads of the **p.**, and........ 5971
Nu 25:15 he was head over a **p.**, and of a.......... 523
Nu 26:4 Takethe sum of the **p.**, from twenty.........
Nu 27:13 also shalt be gathered unto thy **p.**,..... 5971
Nu 31:2 shalt thou be gathered unto thy **p.**....... 5971
Nu 31:3 Moses spake unto the **p.**, saying,....... 5971
Nu 32:15 and ye shall destroy all this **p.**.......... 5971
Nu 33:14 was no water for the **p.** to drink........ 5971
De 1:28 The **p.** is greater and taller than we;... 5971
De 2:4 And command thou the **p.**, saying,...... 5971
De 2:10 a **p.** great, and many, and tall, as....... 5971
De 2:16 and dead from among the **p.**,............. 5971
De 2:21 A **p.** great, and many, and tall, as...... 5971
De 2:32 out against us, he and all his **p.**,........ 5971
De 2:33 him, and his sons, and all his **p.**........ 5971
De 3:1 out against us, he and all his **p.**,........ 5971
De 3:2 I will deliver him, and all his **p.**,......... 5971
De 3:3 the king of Bashan, and all his **p.**:...... 5971
De 3:28 for he shall go over before this **p.**,..... 5971
De 4:6 is a wise and understanding **p.**.......... 5971
De 4:10 Gather me the **p.** together, and I....... 5971
De 4:20 to be unto him a **p.** of inheritance,...... 5971
De 4:33 Did ever **p.** hear the voice of God...... 5971
De 5:28 the voice of the words of this **p.**,....... 5971
De 6:14 the gods of the **p.** which are round..... 5971
De 7:6 thou art an holy **p.** unto the Lord....... 5971
De 7:6 to be a special **p.** unto himself,.......... 5971
De 7:6 above all **p.** that are upon the face...... 5971
De 7:7 were more in number than any **p.**;..... 5971
De 7:7 for ye were the fewest of all **p.**:....... 5971
De 7:14 Thou shalt be blessed above all **p.**:..... 5971
De 7:16 thou shalt consume all the **p.** which.... 5971
De 7:19 all the **p.** of whom thou art afraid....... 5971
De 9:2 A **p.** great and tall, the children of....... 5971
De 9:6 for thou art a stiffnecked **p.**............. 5971
De 9:12 for thy **p.** which thou hast brought...... 5971
De 9:13 I have seen this **p.**, and, behold, it...... 5971
De 9:13 and, behold, it is a stiffnecked **p.**:....... 5971
De 9:26 not thy **p.** and thine inheritance,......... 5971
De 9:27 unto the stubbornness of this **p.**,........ 5971
De 9:29 are thy **p.** and thine inheritance,......... 5971
De 10:11 take thy journey before the **p.**, that.... 5971
De 10:15 even you above all **p.**, as it is this...... 5971
De 13:7 of the gods of the **p.** which are.......... 5971
De 13:9 afterwards the hand of all the **p.**........ 5971
De 14:2 thou art an holy **p.** unto the Lord....... 5971
De 14:2 hath chosen thee to be a peculiar **p.**... 5971
De 14:21 thou art an holy **p.** unto the Lord....... 5971
De 16:18 judge the **p.** with just judgment.......... 5971
De 17:7 afterward the hands of all the **p.**........ 5971
De 17:13 And all the **p.** shall hear, and fear,...... 5971
De 17:16 cause the **p.** to return to Egypt,........ 5971
De 18:3 be the priest's due from the **p.**,......... 5971
De 20:1 a **p.** more than thou, be not afraid...... 5971
De 20:2 approach and speak unto the **p.**,......... 5971
De 20:5 the officers shall speak unto the **p.**,.... 5971
De 20:8 shall speak further unto the **p.**, and.... 5971
De 20:9 an end of speaking unto the **p.**,.......... 5971
De 20:9 captains of the armies to lead the **p.**... 5971
De 20:11 that all the **p.** that is found therein..... 5971
De 20:16 of the cities of these **p.**, which the..... 5971
De 21:8 merciful, O Lord, unto thy **p.** Israel,.... 5971
De 21:8 lay not innocent blood unto thy **p.** of... 5971
De 26:15 from heaven, and bless thy **p.** Israel,.. 5971
De 26:18 thee this day to be his peculiar **p.**,..... 5971
De 26:19 mayest be an holy **p.** unto the Lord.... 5971
De 27:1 elders of Israel commanded the **p.**,..... 5971
De 27:9 thou art become the **p.** of the Lord..... 5971
De 27:11 Moses charged the **p.** the same day,.... 5971
De 27:12 upon mount Gerizim to bless the **p.**,... 5971
De 27:15 the **p.** shall answer and say, Amen..... 5971
De 27:16, 17,18,19,20,21,22,23,24,25,26
And all the **p.** shall say, Amen........... 5971
De 28:9 thee an holy **p.** unto himself, as he..... 5971
De 28:10 all **p.** of the earth shall see that......... 5971
De 28:32 shall be given unto another **p.**, and..... 5971
De 28:64 shall scatter thee among all **p.**,.......... 5971
De 29:13 thee to day for a **p.** unto himself,....... 5971
De 31:7 must go with this **p.** unto the land...... 5971
De 31:12 Gather the **p.** together, men, and....... 5971
De 31:16 and this **p.** will rise up, and go a........ 5971
De 32:6 the Lord, O foolish **p.** and unwise?..... 5971
De 32:8 set the bounds of the **p.** according....... 5971
De 32:9 For the Lord's portion is his **p.**;......... 5971
De 32:21 with those which are not a **p.**;........... 5971
De 32:36 Lord shall judge his **p.**, and repent..... 5971
De 32:43 Rejoice, O ye nations, with his **p.**:...... 5971
De 32:43 unto his land, and to his **p.**.............. 5971
De 32:44 of this song in the ears of the **p.**,........ 5971
De 32:50 up, and be gathered unto thy **p.**; as.... 5971
De 32:50 Hor, and was gathered unto his **p.**:..... 5971
De 33:3 Yea, he loved the **p.**; all his saints...... 5971
De 33:5 the heads ofthe **p.** and the tribes of.... 5971
De 33:7 Judah, and bring him unto his **p.**:....... 5971
De 33:17 he shall push the **p.** together to the.... 5971
De 33:19 shall call the **p.** unto the mountain:..... 5971
De 33:21 he came with the heads of the **p.**,....... 5971
De 33:29 O **p.** saved by the Lord, the shield...... 5971
Jos 1:2 thou, and all this **p.**, unto the land....... 5971
Jos 1:6 unto this **p.** shalt thou divide for an.... 5971
Jos 1:10 commanded the officers of the **p.**,...... 5971
Jos 1:11 the host, and commanded the **p.**,........ 5971
Jos 3:3 they commanded the **p.**, saying,......... 5971
Jos 3:5 Joshua said unto the **p.**, Sanctify......... 5971
Jos 3:6 and pass over before the **p.** And....... 5971
Jos 3:6 covenant, and went before the **p.**........ 5971
Jos 3:14 the **p.** removed from their tents to..... 5971
Jos 3:14 ark of the covenant before the **p.**;...... 5971
Jos 3:16 and the **p.** passed over right against.... 5971
Jos 3:17 **p.** were passed clean over Jordan....... 1471
Jos 4:1 **p.** were clean passed over Jordan,...... 1471
Jos 4:2 Take you twelve men out of the **p.**,..... 5971
Jos 4:10 Joshua to speak unto the **p.**,............. 5971
Jos 4:10 and the **p.** hasted and passed over...... 5971

Jos	4:11	all the **p.** were clean passed over,	5971
Jos	4:11	priests, in the presence of the **p.**.	5971
Jos	4:19	And the **p.** came up out of Jordan	5971
Jos	4:24	all the **p.** of the earth might know	5971
Jos	5:4	All the **p.** that came out of Egypt,	5971
Jos	5:5	**p.** that came out were circumcised:	5971
Jos	5:5	**p.** that were born in the wilderness	5971
Jos	5:6	all the **p.** that were men of war,	1471
Jos	5:8	had done circumcising all the **p.**,	1471
Jos	6:5	**p.** shall shout with a great shout;	5971
Jos	6:5	the **p.** shall ascend up every man	5971
Jos	6:7	And he said unto the **p.**, Pass on,	5971
Jos	6:8	Joshua had spoken unto the **p.**,	5971
Jos	6:10	And Joshua had commanded the **p.**,	5971
Jos	6:16	Joshua said unto the **p.**, Shout; for	5971
Jos	6:20	**p.** shouted when the priests blew	5971
Jos	6:20	**p.** heard the shout of the trumpet,	5971
Jos	6:20	the **p.** shouted with a great shout,	5971
Jos	6:20	so that the **p.** went up into the city, ...	5971
Jos	7:3	unto him, Let not all the **p.** go up;	5971
Jos	7:3	not all the **p.** to labour thither;	5971
Jos	7:4	went up thither of the **p.** about	5971
Jos	7:5	the hearts of the **p.** melted, and	5971
Jos	7:7	at all brought this **p.** over Jordan,	5971
Jos	7:13	sanctify the **p.**, and say, Sanctify	5971
Jos	8:1	take all the **p.** of war with thee,	5971
Jos	8:1	the king of Ai, and his **p.**, and his	5971
Jos	8:3	Joshua arose, and all the **p.** of war,	5971
Jos	8:5	**p.** that are with me, will approach	5971
Jos	8:9	lodged that night among the **p.**.	5971
Jos	8:10	and numbered the **p.**, and went up,	5971
Jos	8:10	elders of Israel, before the **p.** to Ai.	5971
Jos	8:11	And all the **p.**,...went up, and drew	5971
Jos	8:11	even the **p.** of war that were with	5971
Jos	8:13	when they had set the **p.**, even all	5971
Jos	8:14	to battle, he and all his **p.**, at a	5971
Jos	8:16	the **p.** that were in Ai were called	5971
Jos	8:20	the **p.** that fled to the wilderness	5971
Jos	8:33	they should bless the **p.** of Israel.	5971
Jos	10:7	he, and all the **p.** of war with him,	5971
Jos	10:13	stayed, until the **p.** had avenged	1471
Jos	10:21	**p.** returned to the camp to Joshua	5971
Jos	10:33	and Joshua smote him and his **p.**,	5971
Jos	11:4	and their hosts with them, much **p.**	5971
Jos	11:7	came, and all the **p.** of war with him,	5971
Jos	14:8	made the heart of the **p.** melt: but	5971
Jos	17:14	I am a great **p.**, forasmuch as the	5971
Jos	17:15	If thou be a great **p.**, then get thee	5971
Jos	17:17	Thou art a great **p.**, and hast great	5971
Jos	24:2	Joshua said unto all the **p.**, Thus	5971
Jos	24:16	**p.** answered and said, God forbid	5971
Jos	24:17	the **p.** through whom we passed:	5971
Jos	24:18	drave out from before us all the **p.**,	5971
Jos	24:19	Joshua said unto the **p.**, Ye cannot	5971
Jos	24:21	**p.** said unto Joshua, Nay; but we	5971
Jos	24:22	And Joshua said unto the **p.**, Ye are	5971
Jos	24:24	**p.** said unto Joshua, The Lord our	5971
Jos	24:25	made a covenant with the **p.** that	5971
Jos	24:27	Joshua said unto all the **p.**, Behold,	5971
Jos	24:28	Joshua let the **p.** depart, every man	5971
Jg	1:16	they went and dwelt among the **p.**	5971
Jg	2:4	**p.** lifted up their voice, and wept	5971
Jg	2:6	when Joshua had let the **p.** go, the	5971
Jg	2:7	the **p.** served the Lord all the days	5971
Jg	2:12	the gods of the **p.** that were round	5971
Jg	2:20	**p.** hath transgressed my covenant	1471
Jg	3:18	away the **p.** that bare the present.	5971
Jg	4:13	and all the **p.** that were with him,	5971
Jg	5:2	the **p.** willingly offered themselves.	5971
Jg	5:9	themselves willingly among the **p.**.	5971
Jg	5:11	the **p.** of the Lord go down to the	5971
Jg	5:13	over the nobles among the **p.**: the	5971
Jg	5:14	thee, Benjamin, among thy **p.**;	5971
Jg	5:18	were a **p.** that jeoparded their lives	5971
Jg	7:1	the **p.** that were with him, rose up	5971
Jg	7:2	The **p.** that are with thee are too	5971
Jg	7:3	go to, proclaim in the ears of the **p.**,	5971
Jg	7:3	of the **p.** twenty and two thousand;	5971
Jg	7:4	Gideon, The **p.** are yet too many;	5971
Jg	7:5	down the **p.** unto the water: and	5971
Jg	7:6	the rest of the **p.** bowed down upon	5971
Jg	7:7	the other **p.** go every man unto his	5971
Jg	7:8	the **p.** took victuals in their hand,	5971
Jg	8:5	of bread unto the **p.** that follow me;	5971
Jg	9:29	to God this **p.** were under my hand!	5971
Jg	9:32	thou and the **p.** that is with thee,	5971
Jg	9:33	when he and the **p.** that is with him	5971
Jg	9:34	the **p.** that were with him, by night,	5971
Jg	9:35	up, and the **p.** that were with him,	5971
Jg	9:36	And when Gaal saw the **p.**, he said	5971
Jg	9:36	there come **p.** down from the top of	5971
Jg	9:37	come **p.** down by the middle of the	5971
Jg	9:38	this the **p.** that thou hast despised?	5971
Jg	9:42	that the **p.** went out into the field;	5971
Jg	9:43	took the **p.**, and divided them into	5971
Jg	9:43	**p.** were come forth out of the city;	5971
Jg	9:44	ran upon all the **p.**...in the fields,	5971
Jg	9:45	he took the city, and slew the **p.**	5971
Jg	9:48	and all the **p.** that were with him;	5971
Jg	9:48	said unto the **p.** that were with him,	5971
Jg	9:49	all the **p.** likewise cut down every	5971
Jg	10:18	the **p.** and princes of Gilead said	5971
Jg	11:11	the **p.** made him head and captain	5971
Jg	11:20	Sihon gathered all his **p.** together,	5971
Jg	11:21	and all his **p.** into the hand of Israel,	5971
Jg	11:23	Amorites from before his **p.** Israel,	5971
Jg	12:2	I and my **p.** were at great strife with	5971
Jg	14:3	never a woman...among all my **p.**,	5971
Jg	14:16	a riddle unto the children of my **p.**,	5971
Jg	14:17	the riddle to the children of her **p.**	5971
Jg	16:24	when the **p.** saw him, they praised	5971
Jg	16:30	upon the lords, and upon all the **p.**	5971
Jg	18:7	came to Laish, and saw the **p.**	5971
Jg	18:10	ye shall come unto a **p.** secure, and	5971
Jg	18:20	and went in the midst of the **p.**	5971
Jg	18:27	Laish, unto a **p.** that were at quiet	5971
Jg	20:2	the chief of all the **p.**, even all the	5971
Jg	20:2	in the assembly of the **p.** of God,	5971
Jg	20:8	all the **p.** arose as one man, saying,	5971
Jg	20:10	to fetch victual for the **p.**, that they	5971
Jg	20:16	Among all this **p.** there were seven	5971
Jg	20:22	the **p.** the men of Israel encouraged	5971
Jg	20:26	all the **p.**, went up, and came unto	5971
Jg	20:31	Benjamin went out against the **p.**,	5971
Jg	20:31	they began to smite of the **p.**, and	5971
Jg	21:2	the **p.** came to the house of God, and	5971
Jg	21:4	the morrow, that the **p.** rose early,	5971
Jg	21:9	the **p.** were numbered, and, behold,	5971
Jg	21:15	the **p.** repented them for Benjamin,	5971
Ru	1:6	the Lord had visited his **p.** in giving	5971
Ru	1:10	we will return with thee unto thy **p.**.	5971
Ru	1:15	sister in law is gone...unto her **p.**,	5971
Ru	1:16	thy **p.** shall be my **p.**, and thy God	5971
Ru	2:11	unto a **p.** which thou knewest not	5971
Ru	3:11	all the city of my **p.** doth know that	5971
Ru	4:4	and before the elders of my **p.**. If	5971
Ru	4:9	unto the elders, and unto all the **p.**,	5971
Ru	4:11	all the **p.** that were in the gate, and	5971
1Sa	2:13	the priest's custom with the **p.** was,	5971
1Sa	2:23	of your evil dealings by all this **p.**	5971
1Sa	2:24	ye make the Lord's **p.** to transgress.	5971
1Sa	2:29	of all the offerings of Israel my **p.**?	5971
1Sa	4:3	the **p.** were come into the camp,	5971
1Sa	4:4	So the **p.** sent to Shiloh, that they	5971
1Sa	4:17	also a great slaughter among the **p.**,	5971
1Sa	5:10	of Israel to us, to slay us and our **p.**	5971
1Sa	5:11	that it slay us not, and our **p.**: for	5971
1Sa	6:6	did they not let the **p.** go, and they	
1Sa	6:19	he smote of the **p.** fifty thousand	5971
1Sa	6:19	the **p.** lamented, because the Lord	5971
1Sa	6:19	Lord had smitten many of the **p.**	5971
1Sa	8:7	Hearken unto the voice of the **p.**	5971
1Sa	8:10	the words of the Lord unto the **p.**	5971
1Sa	8:19	the refused to obey the voice of	5971
1Sa	8:21	Samuel heard all the words of the **p.**,	5971
1Sa	9:2	he was higher than any of the **p.**	5971
1Sa	9:12	there is a sacrifice of the **p.** to day	5971
1Sa	9:13	for the **p.** will not eat until he come,	5971
1Sa	9:16	him to be captain over my **p.** Israel,	5971
1Sa	9:16	save my **p.** out of the hand of the	5971
1Sa	9:16	I have looked upon my **p.**, because	5971
1Sa	9:17	this same shall reign over my **p.**.	5971
1Sa	9:24	since I said, I have invited the **p.**.	5971
1Sa	10:11	the **p.** said one to another, What is	5971
1Sa	10:17	And Samuel called the **p.** together	5971
1Sa	10:23	when he stood among the **p.**, he was	5971
1Sa	10:23	higher than any of the **p.** from his	5971
1Sa	10:24	Samuel said to all the **p.**, See ye him	5971
1Sa	10:24	is none like him among all the **p.**?	5971
1Sa	10:24	the **p.** shouted, and said, God save	5971
1Sa	10:25	Samuel told the **p.** the manner of the	5971
1Sa	10:25	Samuel sent all the **p.** away, every	5971
1Sa	11:4	the tidings in the ears of the **p.**:	5971
1Sa	11:4	all the **p.** lifted up their voices, and	5971
1Sa	11:5	What aileth the **p.** that they weep?	5971
1Sa	11:7	the fear of the Lord fell on the **p.**,	5971
1Sa	11:11	put the **p.** in three companies; and	5971
1Sa	11:12	the **p.** said unto Samuel, Who is he	5971
1Sa	11:14	said Samuel to the **p.**, Come, and let	5971
1Sa	11:15	all the **p.** went to Gilgal; and there	5971
1Sa	12:6	Samuel said unto the **p.**, It is the	5971
1Sa	12:18	all the **p.** greatly feared the Lord	5971
1Sa	12:19	all the **p.** said unto Samuel, Pray	5971
1Sa	12:20	Samuel said unto the **p.**, Fear not:	5971
1Sa	12:22	the Lord will not forsake his **p.** for	5971
1Sa	12:22	pleased the Lord to make you his **p.**.	5971
1Sa	13:2	the rest of the **p.** he sent every man	5971
1Sa	13:4	**p.** were called together after Saul	5971
1Sa	13:5	**p.** as the sand which is on the sea	5971
1Sa	13:6	a strait (for the **p.** were distressed,)	5971
1Sa	13:6	the **p.** did hide themselves in caves,	5971
1Sa	13:7	all the **p.** followed him trembling.	5971
1Sa	13:8	and the **p.** were scattered from him.	5971
1Sa	13:11	that the **p.** were scattered from me,	5971
1Sa	13:14	him to be captain over his **p.**,	5971
1Sa	13:15	numbered the **p.** that were present	5971
1Sa	13:16	the **p.** that were present with them,	5971
1Sa	13:22	found in the hand of any of the **p.**	5971
1Sa	14:2	the **p.** that were with him were	5971
1Sa	14:3	the **p.** knew not that Jonathan was	5971
1Sa	14:15	in the field, and among all the **p.**:	5971
1Sa	14:17	said Saul unto the **p.** that were with	5971
1Sa	14:20	Saul and all the **p.** that were with	5971
1Sa	14:24	for Saul had adjured the **p.**, saying,	5971
1Sa	14:24	so none of the **p.** tasted any food.	5971
1Sa	14:26	the **p.** were come into the wood,	5971
1Sa	14:26	mouth: for the **p.** feared the oath.	5971
1Sa	14:27	father charged the **p.** with the oath:	5971
1Sa	14:28	Then answered one of the **p.**, and	5971
1Sa	14:28	straitly charged the **p.** with an oath,	5971
1Sa	14:28	this day. And the **p.** were faint.	5971
1Sa	14:30	haply the **p.** had eaten freely to day	5971
1Sa	14:31	Aijalon: and the **p.** were very faint.	5971
1Sa	14:32	the **p.** flew upon the spoil, and took	5971
1Sa	14:32	the **p.** did eat them with the blood	5971
1Sa	14:33	Behold, the **p.** sin against the Lord,	5971
1Sa	14:34	Disperse yourselves among the **p.**,	5971
1Sa	14:34	all the **p.** brought every man his ox	5971
1Sa	14:38	near hither, all the chief of the **p.**:	5971
1Sa	14:39	was not a man among all the **p.** that	5971
1Sa	14:40	**p.** said unto Saul, Do what seemeth	5971
1Sa	14:41	were taken: but the **p.** escaped	5971
1Sa	14:45	**p.** said unto Saul, Shall Jonathan	5971
1Sa	14:45	**p.** rescued Jonathan, that he died	5971
1Sa	15:1	anoint thee to be king over his **p.**,	5971
1Sa	15:4	Saul gathered the **p.** together, and	5971
1Sa	15:8	utterly destroyed all the **p.** with	5971
1Sa	15:9	Saul and the **p.** spared Agag, and	5971
1Sa	15:15	the **p.** spared the best of the sheep	5971
1Sa	15:21	the **p.** took of the spoil, sheep and	5971
1Sa	15:24	because I feared the **p.**, and obeyed	5971
1Sa	15:30	thee, before the elders of my **p.**,	5971
1Sa	17:27	**p.** answered him after this manner,	5971
1Sa	17:30	the **p.** answered him again after the	5971
1Sa	18:5	accepted in the sight of all the **p.**,	5971
1Sa	18:13	went out and came in before the **p.**.	5971
1Sa	23:8	Saul called all the **p.** together to	5971
1Sa	26:5	the **p.** pitched round about him.	5971
1Sa	26:7	Abishai came to the **p.** by night:	5971
1Sa	26:7	Abner and the **p.** lay...about him.	5971
1Sa	26:14	David cried to the **p.**, and to Abner	5971
1Sa	26:15	came one of the **p.** in to destroy the	5971
1Sa	27:12	his **p.** Israel utterly to abhor him;	5971
1Sa	30:4	David...the **p.** that were with him	5971
1Sa	30:6	for the **p.** spake of stoning him,	5971
1Sa	30:6	soul of all the **p.** was grieved, every	5971
1Sa	30:21	to meet the **p.** that were with him:	5971
1Sa	30:21	when David came near to the **p.**, he	5971
1Sa	31:9	of their idols, and among the **p.**.	5971
2Sa	1:4	that the **p.** are fled from the battle,	5971
2Sa	1:4	many of the **p.** also are fallen and	5971
2Sa	1:12	his son, and for the **p.** of the Lord,	5971
2Sa	2:26	bid the **p.** return from following	5971
2Sa	2:27	in the morning the **p.** had gone up,	5971
2Sa	2:28	a trumpet, and all the **p.** stood still,	5971
2Sa	2:30	he had gathered all the **p.** together,	5971
2Sa	3:18	I will save my **p.** Israel out of the	5971
2Sa	3:31	David said to Joab, and to all the **p.**	5971
2Sa	3:32	grave of Abner; and all the **p.** wept.	5971
2Sa	3:34	And all the **p.** wept again over him.	5971
2Sa	3:35	the **p.** came to cause David to eat	5971

Book	Ref	Context	No.
2Sa	3:36	all the **p.** took notice of it, and it	5971
2Sa	3:36	the king did pleased all the **p.**	5971
2Sa	3:37	all the **p.** and all Israel understood	5971
2Sa	5:2	Thou shalt feed my **p.** Israel, and	5971
2Sa	5:12	kingdom for his **p.** Israel's sake	5971
2Sa	6:2	David arose,...went with all the **p.**	5971
2Sa	6:18	he blessed the **p.** in the name of the	5971
2Sa	6:19	And he dealt among all the **p.**, even	5971
2Sa	6:19	**p.** departed every one to his house	5971
2Sa	6:21	me ruler over the **p.** of the Lord,	5971
2Sa	7:7	I commanded to feed my **p.** Israel,	5971
2Sa	7:8	to be ruler over my **p.**, over Israel:	5971
2Sa	7:10	appoint a place for my **p.** Israel,	5971
2Sa	7:11	judges to be over my **p.** Israel, and	5971
2Sa	7:23	nation in the earth is like thy **p.**,	5971
2Sa	7:23	whom God went to redeem for a **p.**	5971
2Sa	7:23	for thy land, before thy **p.**, which	5971
2Sa	7:24	confirmed to thyself thy **p.** Israel	5971
2Sa	7:24	Israel to be a **p.** unto thee for ever:	5971
2Sa	8:15	judgment and justice unto all his **p.**	5971
2Sa	10:10	the rest of the **p.** he delivered into	5971
2Sa	10:12	and let us play the men for our **p.**,	5971
2Sa	10:13	and the **p.** that were with him,	5971
2Sa	11:7	how Joab did, and how the **p.** did,	5971
2Sa	11:17	and there fell some of the **p.** of the	5971
2Sa	12:28	gather the rest of the **p.** together,	5971
2Sa	12:29	David gathered all the **p.** together,	5971
2Sa	12:31	he brought forth the **p.** that were	5971
2Sa	12:31	David and all the **p.** returned unto	5971
2Sa	13:34	there came much **p.** by the way of	5971
2Sa	14:13	such a thing against the **p.** of God?	5971
2Sa	14:15	because the **p.** have made me afraid:	5971
2Sa	15:12	for the **p.** increased continually	5971
2Sa	15:17	went forth, and all the **p.** after him.	5971
2Sa	15:23	and all the **p.** passed over: the king	5971
2Sa	15:23	all the **p.** passed over, toward the	5971
2Sa	15:24	until all the **p.** had done passing	5971
2Sa	15:30	all the **p.** that was with him covered	5971
2Sa	16:6	all the **p.** and all the mighty men	5971
2Sa	16:14	and all the **p.** that were with him,	5971
2Sa	16:15	Absalom, and all the **p.** the men of	5971
2Sa	16:18	this **p.**, and all the men of Israel,	5971
2Sa	17:2	the **p.** that are with him shall flee;	5971
2Sa	17:3	will bring back all the **p.** unto thee:	5971
2Sa	17:3	so all the **p.** shall be in peace.	5971
2Sa	17:8	war, and will not lodge with the **p.**	5971
2Sa	17:9	There is a slaughter among the **p.**	5971
2Sa	17:16	and all the **p.** that are with him.	5971
2Sa	17:22	and all the **p.** that were with him,	5971
2Sa	17:29	and for the **p.** that were with him,	5971
2Sa	17:29	The **p.** is hungry, and weary, and	5971
2Sa	18:1	David numbered the **p.** that were	5971
2Sa	18:2	sent forth a third part of the **p.**	5971
2Sa	18:2	And the king said unto the **p.**, I will	5971
2Sa	18:3	the **p.** answered, Thou shalt not go	5971
2Sa	18:4	all the **p.** came out by hundreds	5971
2Sa	18:5	all the **p.** heard when the king gave	5971
2Sa	18:6	**p.** went out into the field against	5971
2Sa	18:7	Where the **p.** of Israel were slain	5971
2Sa	18:8	wood devoured more **p.** that day	5971
2Sa	18:16	and the **p.** returned from pursuing	5971
2Sa	18:16	Israel: for Joab held back the **p.**	5971
2Sa	19:2	into mourning unto all the **p.**	5971
2Sa	19:2	**p.** heard say that day how the king	5971
2Sa	19:3	the **p.** gat them by stealth that day	5971
2Sa	19:3	**p.** being ashamed steal away when	5971
2Sa	19:8	they told unto all the **p.**, saying,	5971
2Sa	19:8	And all the **p.** came before the king:	5971
2Sa	19:9	all the **p.** were at strife throughout	5971
2Sa	19:39	And all the **p.** went over Jordan.	5971
2Sa	19:40	the **p.** of Judah conducted the king,	5971
2Sa	19:40	king, and also half the **p.** of Israel.	5971
2Sa	20:12	man saw that all the **p.** stood still,	5971
2Sa	20:13	the **p.** went on after Joab, to pursue	376
2Sa	20:15	**p.** that were with Joab battered	5971
2Sa	20:22	the woman went unto all the **p.** in	5971
2Sa	22:28	And the afflicted **p.** thou wilt save:	5971
2Sa	22:44	from the strivings of my **p.**, thou	5971
2Sa	22:44	**p.** which I knew not shall serve me.	5971
2Sa	22:48	bringeth down the **p.** under me,	5971
2Sa	23:10	**p.** returned after him only to spoil.	5971
2Sa	23:11	and the **p.** fled from the Philistines.	5971
2Sa	24:2	Beer-sheba, and number ye the **p.**,	5971
2Sa	24:2	I may know the number of the **p.**	5971
2Sa	24:3	the Lord thy God add unto the **p.**,	5971
2Sa	24:4	king, to number the **p.** of Israel.	5971
2Sa	24:9	up the sum of the number of the **p.**	5971
2Sa	24:10	after that he had numbered the **p.**	5971
2Sa	24:15	there died of the **p.** from Dan even	5971
2Sa	24:16	to the angel that destroyed the **p.**,	5971
2Sa	24:17	he saw the angel that smote the **p.**,	5971
2Sa	24:21	plague may be stayed from the **p.**	5971
1Ki	1:39	the **p.** said, God save king Solomon.	5971
1Ki	1:40	And all the **p.** came up after him,	5971
1Ki	1:40	the **p.** piped with pipes, and rejoiced	5971
1Ki	3:2	the **p.** sacrificed in high places,	5971
1Ki	3:8	thy servant is in the midst of thy **p.**	5971
1Ki	3:8	which thou hast chosen, a great **p.**,	5971
1Ki	3:9	understanding heart to judge thy **p.**,	5971
1Ki	3:9	able to judge this thy so great a **p.**?	5971
1Ki	4:34	And there came of all **p.** to hear the	5971
1Ki	5:7	David a wise son over this great **p.**	5971
1Ki	5:16	ruled over the **p.** that wrought in	5971
1Ki	6:13	and will not forsake my **p.** Israel.	5971
1Ki	8:16	that I brought forth my **p.** Israel	5971
1Ki	8:16	chose David to be over my **p.** Israel.	5971
1Ki	8:30	thy servant, and of thy **p.** Israel,	5971
1Ki	8:33	When thy **p.** Israel be smitten down	5971
1Ki	8:34	and forgive the sin of thy **p.** Israel,	5971
1Ki	8:36	of thy servants, and of thy **p.** Israel,	5971
1Ki	8:36	land, which thou hast given to thy **p.**	5971
1Ki	8:38	by any man, or by all thy **p.** Israel,	5971
1Ki	8:41	stranger, that is not of thy **p.** Israel,	5971
1Ki	8:43	**p.** of the earth may know thy name,	5971
1Ki	8:43	to fear thee, as do thy **p.** Israel;	5971
1Ki	8:44	If thy **p.** go out to battle against	5971
1Ki	8:50	And forgive thy **p.** that have sinned	5971
1Ki	8:51	be thy **p.**, and thine inheritance,	5971
1Ki	8:52	the supplication of thy **p.** Israel,	5971
1Ki	8:53	from among all the **p.** of the earth,	5971
1Ki	8:56	hath given rest unto his **p.** Israel,	5971
1Ki	8:59	cause of his **p.** Israel at all times,	5971
1Ki	8:60	all the **p.** of the earth may know,	5971
1Ki	8:66	the eighth day he sent the **p.** away:	5971
1Ki	8:66	his servant, and for Israel his **p.**	5971
1Ki	9:7	proverb and a byword among all **p.**	5971
1Ki	9:20	**p.** that were left of the Amorites,	5971
1Ki	9:23	bare rule over the **p.** that wrought	5971
1Ki	12:5	again to me. And the **p.** departed.	5971
1Ki	12:6	advise that I may answer this **p.**?	5971
1Ki	12:7	thou wilt be a servant unto this **p.**	5971
1Ki	12:9	give ye that we may answer this **p.**,	5971
1Ki	12:10	Thus shalt thou speak unto this **p.**	5971
1Ki	12:12	and all the **p.** came to Rehoboam	5971
1Ki	12:13	the king answered the **p.** roughly,	5971
1Ki	12:15	the king hearkened not unto the **p.**;	5971
1Ki	12:16	the **p.** answered the king, saying,	5971
1Ki	12:23	to the remnant of the **p.**, saying,	5971
1Ki	12:27	If this **p.** go up to do sacrifice in	5971
1Ki	12:27	then shall the heart of this **p.** turn	5971
1Ki	12:30	the **p.** went to worship before the	5971
1Ki	12:31	made priests of the lowest of the **p.**,	5971
1Ki	13:33	made again of the lowest of the **p.**	5971
1Ki	14:2	that I should be king over this **p.**	5971
1Ki	14:7	I exalted thee from among the **p.**,	5971
1Ki	14:7	made thee prince over my **p.** Israel,	5971
1Ki	16:2	made thee prince over my **p.** Israel;	5971
1Ki	16:2	and hast made my **p.** Israel to sin,	5971
1Ki	16:15	And the **p.** were encamped against	5971
1Ki	16:16	**p.** that were encamped heard say,	5971
1Ki	16:21	**p.** of Israel divided into two parts:	5971
1Ki	16:21	half of the **p.** followed Tibni the son	5971
1Ki	16:22	the **p.** that followed Omri prevailed	5971
1Ki	16:22	against the **p.** that followed Tibni	5971
1Ki	18:21	Elijah came unto all the **p.**, and	5971
1Ki	18:21	the **p.** answered him not a word.	5971
1Ki	18:22	Then said Elijah unto the **p.**, I,	5971
1Ki	18:24	the **p.** answered and said, It is well	5971
1Ki	18:30	Elijah said unto all the **p.**, Come	5971
1Ki	18:30	And all the **p.** came near unto him.	5971
1Ki	18:37	that this **p.** may know that thou art	5971
1Ki	18:39	when all the **p.** saw it, they fell on	5971
1Ki	19:21	gave unto the **p.**, and they did eat.	5971
1Ki	20:8	all the **p.** said unto him, Hearken	5971
1Ki	20:10	for all the **p.** that follow me	5971
1Ki	20:15	after them he numbered all the **p.**,	5971
1Ki	20:42	go for his life, and thy **p.** for his **p.**	5971
1Ki	21:9	set Naboth on high among the **p.**	5971
1Ki	21:12	set Naboth on high among the **p.**	5971
1Ki	21:13	Naboth, in the presence of the **p.**,	5971
1Ki	22:4	I am as thou art, my **p.** as thy **p.**,	5971
1Ki	22:28	Hearken, O **p.**, every one of you.	5971
1Ki	22:43	for the **p.** offered and burnt incense	5971
2Ki	3:7	I am as thou art, my **p.** as thy **p.**,	5971
2Ki	4:13	I dwell among mine own **p.**	5971
2Ki	4:41	Pour out for the **p.**, that they may	5971
2Ki	4:42	Give unto the **p.**, that they may eat.	5971
2Ki	4:43	Give the **p.**, that they may eat: for	5971
2Ki	6:18	Smite this **p.**, I pray thee, with	1471
2Ki	6:30	the **p.** looked, and, behold, he had	5971
2Ki	7:16	the **p.** went out, and spoiled the	5971
2Ki	7:17, 20	**p.** trode upon him in the gate	5971
2Ki	8:21	and the **p.** fled into their tents.	5971
2Ki	9:6	have anointed thee king over the **p.**	5971
2Ki	10:9	said to all the **p.**, Ye be righteous:	5971
2Ki	10:18	Jehu gathered all the **p.** together,	5971
2Ki	11:13	the noise of the guard and of the **p.**,	5971
2Ki	11:13	came to the **p.** into the temple of	5971
2Ki	11:14	and all the **p.** of the land rejoiced,	5971
2Ki	11:17	Lord and the king and the **p.**, that	5971
2Ki	11:17	that they should be the Lord's **p.**;	5971
2Ki	11:17	between the king also and the **p.**	5971
2Ki	11:18	all the **p.** of the land went into the	5971
2Ki	11:19	guard, and all the **p.** of the land;	5971
2Ki	11:20	And all the **p.** of the land rejoiced.	5971
2Ki	12:3	**p.** still sacrificed and burnt incense	5971
2Ki	12:8	to receive no more money of the **p.**,	5971
2Ki	13:7	did he leave of the **p.** to Jehoahaz	5971
2Ki	14:4	**p.** did sacrifice and burnt incense	5971
2Ki	14:21	all the **p.** of Judah took Azariah,	5971
2Ki	15:4	the **p.** sacrificed and burnt incense	5971
2Ki	15:5	house, judging the **p.** of the land.	5971
2Ki	15:10	smote him before the **p.**, and slew	5971
2Ki	15:35	**p.** sacrificed and burned incense	5971
2Ki	16:9	and carried the **p.** of it captive to Kir,	
2Ki	16:15	offering of all the **p.** of the land,	5971
2Ki	18:26	ears of the **p.** that are on the wall.	5971
2Ki	18:36	But the **p.** held their peace, and	5971
2Ki	20:5	tell Hezekiah the captain of my **p.**	5971
2Ki	21:24	the **p.** of the land slew all them that	5971
2Ki	21:24	**p.** of the land made Josiah his son	5971
2Ki	22:4	keepers...have gathered of the **p.**	5971
2Ki	22:13	and for the **p.**, and for all Judah,	5971
2Ki	23:2	and all the **p.**, both small and great:	5971
2Ki	23:3	And all the **p.** stood to the covenant.	5971
2Ki	23:6	the graves of the children of the **p.**	5971
2Ki	23:21	And the king commanded all the **p.**,	5971
2Ki	23:30	the **p.** of the land took Jehoahaz	5971
2Ki	23:35	and the gold of the **p.** of the land,	5971
2Ki	24:14	the poorest sort of the **p.** of the land.	5971
2Ki	25:3	was no bread for the **p.** of the land.	5971
2Ki	25:11	Now the rest of the **p.** that were left	5971
2Ki	25:19	which mustered the **p.** of the land,	5971
2Ki	25:19	threescore men of the **p.** of the land	5971
2Ki	25:22	for the **p.** that remained in the land	5971
2Ki	25:26	And all the **p.**, both small and great,	5971
1Ch	5:25	after the gods of the **p.** of the land,	5971
1Ch	10:9	unto their idols, and to the **p.**	5971
1Ch	11:2	Thou shalt feed my **p.** Israel, and	5971
1Ch	11:2	shalt be ruler over my **p.** Israel.	5971
1Ch	11:13	**p.** fled from before the Philistines,	5971
1Ch	13:4	was right in the eyes of all the **p.**	5971
1Ch	14:2	up on high, because of his **p.** Israel.	5971
1Ch	16:2	blessed the **p.** in the name of the	5971
1Ch	16:8	known his deeds among the **p.**	5971
1Ch	16:20	from one kingdom to another **p.**;	5971
1Ch	16:26	For all the gods of the **p.** are idols:	5971
1Ch	16:28	ye kindreds of the **p.**, give unto the	5971
1Ch	16:36	**p.** said, Amen, and praised the Lord.	5971
1Ch	16:43	**p.** departed every man to his house:	5971
1Ch	17:6	whom I commanded to feed my **p.**,	5971
1Ch	17:7	shouldest be ruler over my **p.** Israel:	5971
1Ch	17:9	will ordain a place for my **p.** Israel,	5971
1Ch	17:10	commanded judges to be over my **p.**	5971
1Ch	17:21	in the earth is like thy **p.** Israel,	5971
1Ch	17:21	went to redeem to be his own **p.**,	5971
1Ch	17:21	driving out nations...before thy **p.**,	5971
1Ch	17:22	thy **p.** Israel didst thou make thine	5971
1Ch	17:22	thou make thine own **p.** for ever;	5971
1Ch	18:14	judgment and justice among...his **p.**	5971
1Ch	19:7	the king of Maachah and his **p.**;	5971
1Ch	19:11	the rest of the **p.** he delivered unto	5971
1Ch	19:13	let us behave...valiantly for our **p.**,	5971
1Ch	19:14	Joab and the **p.** that were with him.	5971
1Ch	20:3	brought out the **p.** that were in it,	5971
1Ch	20:3	all the **p.** returned to Jerusalem.	5971
1Ch	21:2	to Joab and to the rulers of the **p.**,	5971
1Ch	21:3	Lord make his **p.** an hundred times	5971

1Ch 21:5 gave the sum of the number of the **p.**. 5971
1Ch 21:17 commanded the **p.** to be numbered?.... 5971
1Ch 21:17 but not on thy **p.**, that they should..... 5971
1Ch 21:22 plague may be stayed from the **p.**. 5971
1Ch 22:18 before the Lord, and before his **p.**,..... 5971
1Ch 23:25 of Israel hath given rest unto his **p.**, ... 5971
1Ch 28:2 Hear me, my brethren, and my **p.**....... 5971
1Ch 28:21 princes and all the **p.** will be wholly..... 5971
1Ch 29:9 Then the **p.** rejoiced, for that they 5971
1Ch 29:14 But who am I, and what is my **p.**,...... 5971
1Ch 29:17 and now have I seen with joy thy **p.**, .. 5971
1Ch 29:18 the thoughts of the heart of thy **p.**, ... 5971
2Ch 1:9 king over a **p.** like the dust of the...... 5971
2Ch 1:10 go out and come in before this **p.**....... 5971
2Ch 1:10 who can judge this thy **p.**, that is so.... 5971
2Ch 1:11 that thou mayest judge my **p.**, over.... 5971
2Ch 2:11 Because the Lord hath loved his **p.**,.... 5971
2Ch 2:18 overseers to set the **p.** a work. 5971
2Ch 6:5 forth my **p.** out of the land of Egypt ... 5971
2Ch 6:5 man to be a ruler over my **p.** Israel:... 5971
2Ch 6:6 have chosen David to be over my **p.**... 5971
2Ch 6:21 of thy servant, and of thy **p.** Israel, ... 5971
2Ch 6:24 if thy **p.** Israel be put to the worse..... 5971
2Ch 6:25 and forgive the sin of thy **p.** Israel,..... 5971
2Ch 6:27 the sin of thy servants, and of thy **p.** ... 5971
2Ch 6:27 given unto thy **p.** for an inheritance. ... 5971
2Ch 6:29 of any man, or of all thy **p.** Israel,...... 5971
2Ch 6:32 which is not of thy **p.** Israel, but is..... 5971
2Ch 6:33 that all **p.** of the earth may know 5971
2Ch 6:33 and fear thee, as doth thy **p.** Israel,.... 5971
2Ch 6:34 If thy **p.** go out to war against their.... 5971
2Ch 6:39 forgive thy **p.** which have sinned........ 5971
2Ch 7:4 Then the king and all the **p.** offered.... 5971
2Ch 7:5 the king and all the **p.** dedicated......... 5971
2Ch 7:10 he sent the **p.** away unto their tents, .. 5971
2Ch 7:10 and to Solomon, and to Israel his **p.**.... 5971
2Ch 7:13 if I send pestilence among my **p.**;....... 5971
2Ch 7:14 If my **p.**, which are called by my......... 5971
2Ch 8:7 the **p.** that were left of the Hittites,.... 5971
2Ch 8:10 and fifty, that bare rule over the **p.**. ... 5971
2Ch 10:5 three days. And the **p.** departed. 5971
2Ch 10:6 ye me to return answer to this **p.**?..... 5971
2Ch 10:7 If thou be kind to this **p.**, and please... 5971
2Ch 10:9 we may return answer to this **p.**,....... 5971
2Ch 10:10 Thus shalt thou answer the **p.** that..... 5971
2Ch 10:12 So Jeroboam and all the **p.** came to 5971
2Ch 10:15 the king hearkened not unto the **p.**...... 5971
2Ch 10:16 the **p.** answered the king, saying,....... 5971
2Ch 12:3 **p.** were without number that came 5971
2Ch 13:17 And Abijah and his **p.** slew them........ 5971
2Ch 14:13 Asa and the **p.** that were with him 5971
2Ch 16:10 And Asa oppressed some of the **p.**....... 5971
2Ch 17:9 cities of Judah, and taught the **p.**....... 5971
2Ch 18:2 and for the **p.** that he had with him, ... 5971
2Ch 18:3 am as thou art, and my **p.** as thy **p.**; .. 5971
2Ch 18:27 And he said, Hearken, all ye **p.**. 5971
2Ch 19:4 he went out again through the **p.** 5971
2Ch 20:7 of this land before thy **p.** Israel,......... 5971
2Ch 20:21 when he had consulted with the **p.**, ... 5971
2Ch 20:25 Jehoshaphat and his **p.** came to take ... 5971
2Ch 20:33 the **p.** had not prepared their hearts ... 5971
2Ch 21:14 plague will the Lord smite thy **p.**,........ 5971
2Ch 21:19 And his **p.** made no burning for him,... 5971
2Ch 23:5 all the **p.** shall be in the courts of....... 5971
2Ch 23:6 the **p.** shall keep the watch of the 5971
2Ch 23:10 he set all the **p.**, every man having..... 5971
2Ch 23:12 Athaliah heard the noise of the **p.**....... 5971
2Ch 23:12 she came to the **p.** into the house 5971
2Ch 23:13 and all the **p.** of the land rejoiced, ... 5971
2Ch 23:16 between him, and between all the **p.**,.. 5971
2Ch 23:16 that they should be the Lord's **p.**. 5971
2Ch 23:17 all the **p.** went to the house of Baal,... 5971
2Ch 23:20 nobles, and the governors of the **p.**, ... 5971
2Ch 23:20 and all the **p.** of the land, and........... 5971
2Ch 23:21 And all the **p.** of the land rejoiced:...... 5971
2Ch 24:10 the princes and all the **p.** rejoiced,...... 5971
2Ch 24:20 priest, which stood above the **p.**, ... 5971
2Ch 24:23 destroyed all the princes of the **p.**....... 5971
2Ch 24:23 the princes...from among the **p.**, ... 5971
2Ch 25:11 And Amaziah...led forth his **p.**, and..... 5971
2Ch 25:15 thou sought after the gods of the **p.**,.... 5971
2Ch 25:15 which could not deliver their own **p.** ... 5971
2Ch 26:1 all the **p.** of Judah took Uzziah,.......... 5971
2Ch 26:21 house, judging the **p.** of the land. 5971
2Ch 27:2 And the **p.** did yet corruptly............. 5971
2Ch 29:36 Hezekiah rejoiced, and all the **p.**, ... 5971
2Ch 29:36 that God had prepared the **p.**: for....... 5971
2Ch 30:3 neither had the **p.** gathered.............. 5971
2Ch 30:13 assembled at Jerusalem much **p.**......... 5971
2Ch 30:18 a multitude of the **p.**, even many of..... 5971
2Ch 30:20 to Hezekiah, and healed the **p.**. 5971
2Ch 30:27 Levites arose and blessed the **p.**;....... 5971
2Ch 31:4 he commanded the **p.** that dwelt in..... 5971
2Ch 31:8 blessed the Lord, and his **p.** Israel. 5971
2Ch 31:10 the **p.** began to bring the offerings...........
2Ch 31:10 for the Lord hath blessed his **p.**;........ 5971
2Ch 32:4 was gathered much **p.** together......... 5971
2Ch 32:6 he set captains of war over the **p.**,..... 5971
2Ch 32:8 And the **p.** rested themselves upon..... 5971
2Ch 32:13 done unto all the **p.** of other lands?..... 5971
2Ch 32:14 that could deliver his **p.** out of mine.... 5971
2Ch 32:15 able to deliver his **p.** out of mine........ 5971
2Ch 32:17 not delivered their **p.** out of mine....... 5971
2Ch 32:17 the God of Hezekiah deliver his **p.**...... 5971
2Ch 32:18 unto the **p.** of Jerusalem that were 5971
2Ch 32:19 the gods of the **p.** of the earth, ... 5971
2Ch 33:10 spake to Manasseh, and to his **p.**: 5971
2Ch 33:17 the **p.** did sacrifice still in the high...... 5971
2Ch 33:25 the **p.** of the land slew all them that ... 5971
2Ch 33:25 **p.** of the land made Josiah his son 5971
2Ch 34:30 and all the **p.**, great and small: 5971
2Ch 35:3 Lord your God, and his **p.** Israel,....... 5971
2Ch 35:5 families of your brethren the **p.**, . 1121,5971
2Ch 35:7 And Josiah gave to the **p.**, of...... 1121,5971
2Ch 35:8 princes gave willingly unto the **p.**, ... 5971
2Ch 35:12 of the families of the **p.**, to........ 1121,5971
2Ch 35:13 them speedily among all the **p.**.. 1121,5971
2Ch 36:1 the **p.** of the land took Jehoahaz the.... 5971
2Ch 36:14 priests, and the **p.**, transgressed........ 5971
2Ch 36:15 because he had compassion on his **p.**, . 5971
2Ch 36:16 of the Lord arose against his **p.**, ... 5971
2Ch 36:23 is there among you of all his **p.**? 5971
Ezr 1:3 is there among you of all his **p.**? 5971
Ezr 2:2 of the men of the **p.** of Israel: 5971
Ezr 2:70 and the Levites, and some of the **p.**, .. 5971
Ezr 3:1 **p.** gathered themselves together 5971
Ezr 3:3 because of the **p.** of those countries:... 5971
Ezr 3:11 the **p.** shouted with a great shout,...... 5971
Ezr 3:13 the **p.** could not discern the noise....... 5971
Ezr 3:13 the noise of the weeping of the **p.**:...... 5971
Ezr 3:13 for the **p.** shouted with a loud shout, .. 5971
Ezr 4:4 **p.** of the land weakened the hands...... 5971
Ezr 4:4 the hands of the **p.** of Judah, and 5971
Ezr 5:12 carried the **p.** away into Babylon. 5972
Ezr 6:12 dwell there destroy all kings and **p.**, ... 5972
Ezr 7:13 that all they of the **p.** of Israel, and 5972
Ezr 7:16 with the freewill offering of the **p.**, ... 5972
Ezr 7:25 may judge all the **p.** that are beyond... 5972
Ezr 8:15 I viewed the **p.**, and the priests, ... 5971
Ezr 8:36 they furthered the **p.**, and the house... 5971
Ezr 9:1 The **p.** of Israel, and the priests, ... 5971
Ezr 9:1 separated...from...**p.** of the lands, ... 5971
Ezr 9:2 mingled with...**p.** of those lands: 5971
Ezr 9:11 the filthiness of the **p.** of the lands, ... 5971
Ezr 9:14 with the **p.** of these abominations?...... 5971
Ezr 10:1 children: for the **p.** wept very sore..... 5971
Ezr 10:2 strange wives of the **p.** of the land: 5971
Ezr 10:9 **p.** sat in the street of the house of..... 5971
Ezr 10:11 separate...from the **p.** of the land,...... 5971
Ezr 10:13 But the **p.** are many, and it is a time.. 5971
Ne 1:10 these are thy servants and thy **p.**,...... 5971
Ne 4:6 for the **p.** had a mind to work........... 5971
Ne 4:13 I even set the **p.** after their families.... 5971
Ne 4:14, 19 rulers, and to the rest of the **p.**,.... 5971
Ne 4:22 at the same time said I unto the **p.**,..... 5971
Ne 5:1 And there was a great cry of the **p.**.... 5971
Ne 5:13 the **p.** did according to this promise. ... 5971
Ne 5:15 me were chargeable unto the **p.**,........ 5971
Ne 5:15 their servants bare rule over the **p.**..... 5971
Ne 5:18 the bondage was heavy upon this **p.**..... 5971
Ne 5:19 to all that I have done for this **p.**. 5971
Ne 7:4 but the **p.** were few therein, and the .. 5971
Ne 7:5 nobles, and the rulers, and the **p.**,....... 5971
Ne 7:7 number,...of...men of the **p.** of Israel.. 5971
Ne 7:72 that which the rest of the **p.** gave 5971
Ne 7:73 and the singers, and some of the **p.**,.... 5971
Ne 8:1 **p.** gathered themselves together 5971
Ne 8:3 ears of all the **p.** were attentive......... 5971
Ne 8:5 the book in the sight of all the **p.**; 5971
Ne 8:5 (for he was above all the **p.**;) when 5971
Ne 8:5 he opened it, all the **p.** stood up: 5971
Ne 8:6 And all the **p.** answered, Amen,......... 5971
Ne 8:7 caused the **p.** to understand the law:... 5971
Ne 8:7 law: and the **p.** stood in their place..... 5971
Ne 8:9 and the Levites that taught the **p.**, ... 5971
Ne 8:9 said unto all the **p.**, This day is holy ... 5971
Ne 8:9 For all the **p.** wept, when they heard.. 5971
Ne 8:11 So the Levites stilled all the **p.**,......... 5971
Ne 8:12 all the **p.** went their way to eat, and... 5971
Ne 8:13 the chief of the fathers of all the **p.**, ... 5971
Ne 8:16 So the **p.** went forth, and brought 5971
Ne 9:10 and on all the **p.** of his land:............. 5971
Ne 9:24 their kings, and the **p.** of the land, ... 5971
Ne 9:30 into the hand of the **p.** of the lands..... 5971
Ne 9:32 on our fathers, and on all thy **p.**,........ 5971
Ne 10:14 The chief of the **p.**; Parosh,............. 5971
Ne 10:28 And the rest of the **p.**, the priests,..... 5971
Ne 10:28 separated...from the **p.** of the lands.... 5971
Ne 10:30 daughters unto the **p.** of the land,...... 5971
Ne 10:31 And if the **p.** of the land bring ware.... 5971
Ne 10:34 the priests, the Levites, and the **p.**, ... 5971
Ne 11:1 rulers of the **p.** dwelt at Jerusalem: 5971
Ne 11:1 the rest of the **p.** also cast lots, to..... 5971
Ne 11:2 And the **p.** blessed all the men, that ... 5971
Ne 11:24 in all matters concerning the **p.**.......... 5971
Ne 12:30 purified themselves, and...the **p.**, ... 5971
Ne 12:38 and the half of the **p.** upon the wall, ... 5971
Ne 13:1 of Moses in the audience of the **p.**; 5971
Ne 13:24 according to the language of each **p.**. .. 5971
Es 1:5 the king made a feast unto all the **p.**... 5971
Es 1:11 shew...**p.** and...princes her beauty:..... 5971
Es 1:16 the **p.** that are in all the provinces..... 5971
Es 1:22 and to every **p.** after their language,... 5971
Es 1:22 to the language of every **p.**.............. 5971
Es 2:10 Esther had not shewed her **p.** nor...... 5971
Es 2:20 yet shewed her kindred nor her **p.**; 5971
Es 3:6 had shewed him the **p.** of Mordecai: ... 5971
Es 3:6 Ahasuerus, even the **p.** of Mordecai.... 5971
Es 3:8 is a certain **p.** scattered abroad and 5971
Es 3:8 among the **p.** in all the provinces........ 5971
Es 3:8 their laws are diverse from all **p.**;....... 5971
Es 3:11 silver is given to thee, the **p.** also, ... 5971
Es 3:12 to the rulers of every **p.** of every....... 5971
Es 3:12 to every **p.** after their language;......... 5971
Es 3:14 province was published unto all **p.**, ... 5971
Es 4:8 make request before him for her **p.**. ... 5971
Es 4:11 **p.** of the king's provinces, do know, ... 5971
Es 7:3 petition, and my **p.** at my request: 5971
Es 7:4 For we are sold, I and my **p.**, to be 5971
Es 8:6 the evil that shall come unto my **p.**? ... 5971
Es 8:9 unto every **p.** after their language,...... 5971
Es 8:11 all the power of the **p.** and province.... 5971
Es 8:13 province was published unto all **p.**, ... 5971
Es 8:17 of the **p.** of the land became Jews; 5971
Es 9:2 for the fear of them fell upon all **p.**. 5971
Es 10:3 seeking the wealth of his **p.**, and........ 5971
Job 12:2 No doubt but ye are the **p.**, and 5971
Job 12:24 of the chief of the **p.** of the earth,...... 5971
Job 17:6 made me also a byword of the **p.**; 5971
Job 18:19 have son nor nephew among his **p.**,.... 5971
Job 34:20 the **p.** shall be troubled at midnight,.... 5971
Job 34:30 reign not, lest the **p.** be ensnared. 5971
Job 36:20 when **p.** are cut off in their place. 5971
Job 36:31 For by them judgeth he the **p.**; he 5971
Ps 2:1 and the **p.** imagine a vain thing? 3816
Ps 3:6 be afraid of ten thousands of **p.**,.......... 5971
Ps 3:8 Lord: thy blessing is upon thy **p.**......... 5971
Ps 7:7 congregation of the **p.** compass.......... 3816
Ps 7:8 The Lord shall judge the **p.**............... 5971
Ps 9:8 shall minister judgment to the **p.**......... 3816
Ps 9:11 declare among the **p.** his doings. 5971
Ps 14:4 who eat up my **p.** as they eat bread, .. 5971
Ps 14:7 back the captivity of his **p.**, Jacob....... 5971
Ps 18:27 For thou wilt save the afflicted **p.**;....... 5971
Ps 18:43 me from the strivings of the **p.**;......... 5971
Ps 18:43 a **p.** whom I have not known shall...... 5971
Ps 18:47 me, and subdueth the **p.** under me. 5971
Ps 22:6 of men, and despised of the **p.**. 5971
Ps 22:31 righteousness unto a **p.** that shall 5971
Ps 28:9 Save thy **p.**, and bless thine............. 5971
Ps 29:11 Lord will give strength unto his **p.**;..... 5971
Ps 29:11 Lord will bless his **p.** with peace. 5971
Ps 33:10 the devices of the **p.** of none effect. ... 5971
Ps 33:12 **p.** whom he hath chosen for his own... 5971
Ps 35:18 I will praise thee among much **p.**........ 5971
Ps 44:2 thou didst afflict the **p.**, and cast 3816
Ps 44:12 Thou sellest thy **p.** for nought, and...... 5971
Ps 44:14 shaking of the head among the **p.**....... 3816
Ps 45:5 whereby the **p.** fall under thee........... 5971
Ps 45:10 forget also thine own **p.**, and thy........ 5971
Ps 45:12 the rich among the **p.** shall intreat 5971

Book	Ref.	Context	No.
Ps	45:17	shall the **p.** praise thee for ever and	5971
Ps	47:1	O clap your hands, all ye **p.**; shout;	5971
Ps	47:3	He shall subdue the **p.** under us,	5971
Ps	47:9	The princes of the **p.** are gathered	5971
Ps	47:9	even the **p.** of the God of Abraham:	5971
Ps	49:1	Hear this, all ye **p.**; give ear, all	5971
Ps	50:4	the earth, that he may judge his **p.**.	5971
Ps	50:7	Hear, O my **p.**, and I will speak;	5971
Ps	53:4	who eat up my **p.** as they eat bread:	5971
Ps	53:6	back the captivity of his **p.**, Jacob	5971
Ps	56:7	in thine anger cast down the **p.**,	5971
Ps	57:9	praise thee, O Lord, among the **p.**	5971
Ps	59:11	Slay them not, lest my **p.** forget:	5971
Ps	60:3	hast shewed thy **p.** hard things:	5971
Ps	62:8	ye **p.**, pour out your heart before	5971
Ps	65:7	waves, and the tumult of the **p.**.	3816
Ps	66:8	O bless our God, ye **p.**, and make	5971
Ps	67:3	Let the **p.** praise thee, O God; let	5971
Ps	67:3	O God; let all the **p.** praise thee.	5971
Ps	67:4	thou shalt judge the **p.** righteously,	5971
Ps	67:5	Let the **p.** praise thee, O God; let	5971
Ps	67:5	O God; let all the **p.** praise thee.	5971
Ps	68:7	thou wentest forth before thy **p.**,	5971
Ps	68:22	bring my **p.** again from the depths of	
Ps	68:30	the bulls, with the calves of the **p.**,	5971
Ps	68:30	thou the **p.** that delight in war.	5971
Ps	68:35	strength and power unto his **p.**.	5971
Ps	72:2	judge thy **p.** with righteousness.	5971
Ps	72:3	shall bring peace to the **p.**, and the	5971
Ps	72:4	He shall judge the poor of the **p.**,	5971
Ps	73:10	Therefore his **p.** return hither: and	5971
Ps	74:14	and gavest him to be meat to the **p.**	5971
Ps	74:18	the foolish **p.** have blasphemed thy	5971
Ps	77:14	declared thy strength among the **p.**	5971
Ps	77:15	with thine arm redeemed thy **p.**,	5971
Ps	77:20	Thou leddest thy **p.** like a flock by	5971
Ps	78:1	Give ear, O my **p.**, to my law:	5971
Ps	78:20	also? can he provide flesh for his **p.**?	5971
Ps	78:52	his own **p.** to go forth like sheep,	5971
Ps	78:62	gave his **p.** over also unto the sword;	5971
Ps	78:71	brought him to feed Jacob his **p.**,	5971
Ps	79:13	we thy **p.** and sheep of thy pasture	5971
Ps	80:4	angry against the prayer of thy **p.**?	5971
Ps	81:8	O my **p.**, and I will testify unto thee:	5971
Ps	81:11	**p.** would not hearken to my voice;	5971
Ps	81:13	Oh that my **p.** had hearkened unto	5971
Ps	83:3	taken crafty counsel against thy **p.**,	5971
Ps	85:2	hast forgiven the iniquity of thy **p.**,	5971
Ps	85:6	that thy **p.** may rejoice in thee?	5971
Ps	85:8	for he will speak peace unto his **p.**,	5971
Ps	87:6	count when he writeth up the **p.**,	5971
Ps	89:15	the **p.** that know the joyful sound:	5971
Ps	89:19	exalted one chosen out of the **p.**.	5971
Ps	89:50	the reproach of all the mighty **p.**;	5971
Ps	94:5	They break in pieces thy **p.**, O	5971
Ps	94:8	ye brutish among the **p.**: and ye	5971
Ps	94:14	For the Lord will not cast off his **p.**,	5971
Ps	95:7	we are the **p.** of his pasture, and	5971
Ps	95:10	It is a **p.** that do err in their heart,	5971
Ps	96:3	heathen, his wonders among all **p.**.	5971
Ps	96:7	O ye kindreds of the **p.**, give unto	5971
Ps	96:10	he shall judge the **p.** righteously.	5971
Ps	96:13	and the **p.** with his truth.	5971
Ps	97:6	and all the **p.** see his glory.	5971
Ps	98:9	the world, and the **p.** with equity.	5971
Ps	99:1	Lord reigneth; let the **p.** tremble:	5971
Ps	99:2	and he is high above all the **p.**.	5971
Ps	100:3	we are his **p.**, and the sheep of his	5971
Ps	102:18	the **p.** which shall be created shall	5971
Ps	102:22	When the **p.** are gathered together,	5971
Ps	105:1	known his deeds among the **p.**	5971
Ps	105:13	from one kingdom to another **p.**;	5971
Ps	105:20	even the ruler of the **p.**, and let	5971
Ps	105:24	he increased his **p.** greatly; and	5971
Ps	105:25	He turned their heart to hate his **p.**,	5971
Ps	105:40	The **p.** asked, and he brought quails,	
Ps	105:43	he brought forth his **p.** with joy,	5971
Ps	105:44	they inherited the labour of the **p.**;	3816
Ps	106:4	that thou bearest unto thy **p.**:	5971
Ps	106:40	of the Lord kindled against his **p.**,	5971
Ps	106:48	let all the **p.** say, Amen. Praise ye	5971
Ps	107:32	also in the congregation of the **p.**,	5971
Ps	108:3	praise thee, O Lord, among the **p.**	5971
Ps	110:3	Thy **p.** shall be willing in the day	5971
Ps	111:6	He hath shewed his **p.** the power of	5971
Ps	111:9	He sent redemption unto his **p.**: he	5971
Ps	113:8	even with the princes of his **p.**.	5971
Ps	114:1	from a **p.** of strange language;	5971
Ps	116:14	now in the presence of all his **p.**.	5971
Ps	116:18	now in the presence of all his **p.**,	5971
Ps	117:1	ye nations: praise him, all ye **p.**.	523
Ps	125:2	so the Lord is round about his **p.**	5971
Ps	135:12	an heritage unto Israel his **p.**.	5971
Ps	135:14	the Lord will judge his **p.**, and he	5971
Ps	136:16	led his **p.** through the wilderness:	5971
Ps	144:2	who subdueth my **p.** under me.	5971
Ps	144:15	Happy is that **p.**, that is in such a	5971
Ps	144:15	happy is that **p.**, whose God is the	5971
Ps	148:11	Kings of the earth, and all **p.**;	3816
Ps	148:14	also exalteth the horn of his **p.**,	5971
Ps	148:14	of Israel, a **p.** near unto him.	5971
Ps	149:4	the Lord taketh pleasure in his **p.**	5971
Ps	149:7	and punishments upon the **p.**;	3816
Pr	11:14	Where no counsel is, the **p.** fall:	5971
Pr	11:26	corn, the **p.** shall curse him: but	3816
Pr	14:28	of **p.** is the king's honour: but in	5971
Pr	14:28	the want of **p.** is the destruction	3816
Pr	14:34	but sin is a reproach to any **p.**.	3816
Pr	24:24	him shall the **p.** curse, nations	5971
Pr	28:15	is a wicked ruler over the poor **p.**	5971
Pr	29:2	are in authority, the **p.** rejoice: but	5971
Pr	29:2	wicked beareth rule, the **p.** mourn.	5971
Pr	29:18	there is no vision, the **p.** perish:	5971
Pr	30:25	The ants are a **p.** not strong, yet	5971
Ec	4:16	There is no end of all the **p.**, even	5971
Ec	12:9	he still taught the **p.** knowledge;	5971
Isa	1:3	not know, my **p.** doth not consider.	5971
Isa	1:4	nation, a **p.** laden with iniquity,	5971
Isa	1:10	law of our God, ye **p.** of Gomorrah.	5971
Isa	2:3	many **p.** shall go and say, Come	5971
Isa	2:4	nations, and shall rebuke many **p.**	5971
Isa	2:6	Therefore thou hast forsaken thy **p.**	5971
Isa	3:5	And the **p.** shall be oppressed, every	5971
Isa	3:7	make me not a ruler of the **p.**	5971
Isa	3:12	As for my **p.**, children are their	5971
Isa	3:12	O my **p.**, they which lead thee cause	5971
Isa	3:13	plead, and standeth to judge the **p.**	5971
Isa	3:14	judgment with the ancients of his **p.**,	5971
Isa	3:15	What mean ye that ye beat my **p.**	5971
Isa	5:13	my **p.** are gone into captivity,	5971
Isa	5:25	of the Lord kindled against his **p.**,	5971
Isa	6:5	the midst of a **p.** of unclean lips:	5971
Isa	6:9	Go, and tell this **p.**, Hear ye indeed,	5971
Isa	6:10	Make the heart of this **p.** fat, and	5971
Isa	7:2	heart of his **p.**, as the trees of the	5971
Isa	7:8	be broken, that it be not a **p.**.	5971
Isa	7:17	bring upon thee, and upon thy **p.**,	5971
Isa	8:6	**p.** refuseth the waters of Shiloah	5971
Isa	8:9	Associate yourselves, O ye **p.**, and	5971
Isa	8:11	should not walk in the way of this **p.**,	5971
Isa	8:12	all them to whom this **p.** shall say,	5971
Isa	8:19	should not a **p.** seek unto their God?	5971
Isa	9:2	The **p.** that walked in darkness have	5971
Isa	9:9	the **p.** shall know, even Ephraim	5971
Isa	9:13	the **p.** turneth not unto him that	5971
Isa	9:16	the leaders of this **p.** cause them to	5971
Isa	9:19	**p.** shall be as the fuel of the fire:	5971
Isa	10:2	the right from the poor of my **p.**,	5971
Isa	10:6	against the **p.** of my wrath will I	5971
Isa	10:13	have removed the bounds of the **p.**,	5971
Isa	10:14	as a nest the riches of the **p.**:	5971
Isa	10:22	though thy **p.** Israel be as the sand	5971
Isa	10:24	O my **p.** that dwellest in Zion, be	5971
Isa	11:10	shall stand for an ensign of the **p.**;	5971
Isa	11:11	to recover the remnant of his **p.**,	5971
Isa	11:16	highway for the remnant of his **p.**,	5971
Isa	12:4	declare his doings among the **p.**,	5971
Isa	13:4	The noise...like as of a great **p.**;	5971
Isa	13:14	shall every man turn to his own **p.**,	5971
Isa	14:2	the **p.** shall take them, and bring	5971
Isa	14:6	He who smote the **p.** in wrath with	5971
Isa	14:20	destroyed thy land, and slain thy **p.**	5971
Isa	14:32	the poor of his **p.** shall trust in it.	5971
Isa	17:12	Woe to the multitude of many **p.**,	5971
Isa	18:2	to a **p.** terrible from their beginning	5971
Isa	18:7	hosts of a **p.** scattered and peeled,	5971
Isa	18:7	a **p.** terrible from their beginning	5971
Isa	19:25	saying, Blessed be Egypt my **p.**,	5971
Isa	22:4	spoiling of the daughter of my **p.**.	5971
Isa	23:13	this **p.** was not, till the Assyrian	5971
Isa	24:2	as with the **p.**, so with the priest;	5971
Isa	24:4	haughty **p.** of the earth do languish.	5971
Isa	24:13	the midst of the land among the **p.**,	5971
Isa	25:3	shall the strong **p.** glorify thee, the	5971
Isa	25:6	make unto...**p.** a feast of fat things,	5971
Isa	25:7	of the covering cast over all **p.**,	5971
Isa	25:8	rebuke of his **p.** shall he take away	5971
Isa	26:11	be ashamed for their envy at the **p.**;	5971
Isa	26:20	**p.**, enter thou into thy chambers,	5971
Isa	27:11	for it is a **p.** of no understanding:	5971
Isa	28:5	beauty, unto the residue of his **p.**,	5971
Isa	28:11	tongue will he speak to this **p.**.	5971
Isa	28:14	rule this **p.** which is in Jerusalem	5971
Isa	29:13	**p.** draw near me with their mouth,	5971
Isa	29:14	a marvellous work among this **p.**.	5971
Isa	30:5	all ashamed of a **p.** that could not	5971
Isa	30:6	to a **p.** that shall not profit them.	5971
Isa	30:9	That this is a rebellious **p.**, lying	5971
Isa	30:19	For the **p.** shall dwell in Zion at	5971
Isa	30:26	bindeth up the breach of his **p.**, and	5971
Isa	30:28	bridle in the jaws of the **p.**, causing	5971
Isa	32:13	Upon the land of my **p.** shall come	5971
Isa	32:18	my **p.** shall dwell in a peaceable	5971
Isa	33:3	the noise of the tumult the **p.** fled;	5971
Isa	33:12	**p.** shall be as the burnings of lime:	5971
Isa	33:19	Thou shalt not see a fierce **p.**,	5971
Isa	33:19	a **p.** of a deeper speech than thou	5971
Isa	33:24	the **p.** that dwell therein shall be	5971
Isa	34:1	hearken, ye **p.**: let the earth hear,	3816
Isa	34:5	and upon the **p.** of my curse, to	5971
Isa	36:11	ears of the **p.** that are on the wall.	5971
Isa	40:1	comfort ye my **p.**, saith your God.	5971
Isa	40:7	upon it: surely the **p.** is grass.	5971
Isa	41:1	let the **p.** renew their strength:	3816
Isa	42:5	he that giveth breath unto the **p.**	5971
Isa	42:6	give thee for a covenant of the **p.**,	5971
Isa	42:22	But this is a **p.** robbed and spoiled;	5971
Isa	43:4	men for thee, and **p.** for thy life.	3816
Isa	43:8	Bring...the blind **p.** that have eyes,	5971
Isa	43:9	and let the **p.** be assembled: who	3816
Isa	43:20	the desert, to give drink to my **p.**,	5971
Isa	43:21	This **p.** have I formed for myself;	5971
Isa	44:7	since I appointed the ancient **p.**?	5971
Isa	47:6	I was wroth with my **p.**, I have	5971
Isa	49:1	hearken, ye **p.**, from far; The Lord	3816
Isa	49:8	give thee for a covenant of the **p.**,	5971
Isa	49:13	for the Lord hath comforted his **p.**,	5971
Isa	49:22	and set up my standard to the **p.**:	5971
Isa	51:4	Hearken unto me, my **p.**; and give	5971
Isa	51:4	to rest for a light of the **p.**	5971
Isa	51:5	and mine arms shall judge the **p.**;	5971
Isa	51:7	the **p.** in whose heart is my law;	5971
Isa	51:16	and say unto Zion, Thou art my **p.**.	5971
Isa	51:22	that pleadeth the cause of his **p.**,	5971
Isa	52:4	My **p.** went down aforetime into	5971
Isa	52:5	my **p.** is taken away for nought?	5971
Isa	52:6	my **p.** shall know my name:	5971
Isa	52:9	for the Lord hath comforted his **p.**,	5971
Isa	53:8	for the transgression of my **p.** was	5971
Isa	55:4	given him for a witness to the **p.**,	3816
Isa	55:4	leader and commander to the **p.**	3816
Isa	56:3	utterly separated me from his **p.**:	5971
Isa	56:7	called an house of prayer for all **p.**	5971
Isa	57:14	block out of the way of my **p.**	5971
Isa	58:1	shew my **p.** their transgression,	5971
Isa	60:2	earth, and gross darkness the **p.**	3816
Isa	60:21	Thy **p.** also shall be all righteous:	5971
Isa	61:9	and their offspring among the **p.**	5971
Isa	62:10	gates; prepare ye the way of the **p.**;	5971
Isa	62:10	stones; lift up a standard for the **p.**	5971
Isa	62:12	they shall call them, The holy **p.**,	5971
Isa	63:3	of the **p.** there was none with me:	5971
Isa	63:6	tread down the **p.** in mine anger,	5971
Isa	63:8	they are my **p.**, children that will	5971
Isa	63:11	the days of old, Moses, and his **p.**,	5971
Isa	63:14	so didst thou lead thy **p.**, to make	5971
Isa	63:18	**p.** of thy holiness have possessed	5971
Isa	64:9	we beseech thee, we are all thy **p.**	5971
Isa	65:2	all the day unto a rebellious **p.**,	5971
Isa	65:3	A **p.** that provoketh me to anger	5971
Isa	65:10	in, for my **p.** that have sought me.	5971
Isa	65:18	a rejoicing, and her **p.** a joy.	5971
Isa	65:19	in Jerusalem, and joy in my **p.**	5971
Isa	65:22	days of a tree are the days of my **p.**,	5971
Jer	1:18	and against the **p.** of the land.	5971
Jer	2:11	my **p.** have changed their glory for	5971
Jer	2:13	my **p.** have committed two evils;	5971
Jer	2:31	wherefore say my **p.**, We are lords;	5971
Jer	2:32	yet my **p.** have forgotten me days	5971
Jer	4:10	thou hast greatly deceived this **p.**	5971
Jer	4:11	it be said to this **p.** and to Jerusalem,	5971

Jer 4:11 toward the daughter of my **p.**, not...... 5971
Jer 4:22 For my **p.** is foolish, they have not..... 5971
Jer 5:14 this **p.** wood, and it shall devour........ 5971
Jer 5:21 Hear not this, O foolish **p.**, and......... 5971
Jer 5:23 But this **p.** hath a revolting and a....... 5971
Jer 5:26 among my **p.** are found wicked men:... 5971
Jer 5:31 and my **p.** love to have it so: and....... 5971
Jer 6:14 of the daughter of my **p.** slightly, ... 5971
Jer 6:19 I will bring evil upon this **p.**, even...... 5971
Jer 6:21 lay stumblingblocks before this **p.**, ... 5971
Jer 6:22 a **p.** cometh from the north country, ... 5971
Jer 6:26 O daughter of my **p.**, gird thee with ... 5971
Jer 6:27 tower and a fortress among my **p.**,...... 5971
Jer 7:12 for the wickedness of my **p.** Israel....... 5971
Jer 7:16 Therefore pray not thou for this **p.**,.... 5971
Jer 7:23 be your God, and ye shall be my **p.**:... 5971
Jer 7:33 carcases of this **p.** shall be meat for.... 5971
Jer 8:5 is this **p.** of Jerusalem slidden back..... 5971
Jer 8:7 but my **p.** know not the judgment of... 5971
Jer 8:11 of the daughter of my **p.** slightly, ... 5971
Jer 8:19 of the cry of the daughter of my **p.** 5971
Jer 8:21 the daughter of my **p.** am I hurt; 5971
Jer 8:22 of the daughter of my **p.** recovered?... 5971
Jer 9:1 the slain of the daughter of my **p.**! 5971
Jer 9:2 I might leave my **p.**, and go from....... 5971
Jer 9:7 I do for the daughter of my **p.**? 5971
Jer 9:15 I will feed them, even this **p.**, with..... 5971
Jer 10:3 For the customs of the **p.** are vain: 5971
Jer 11:4 so shall ye be my **p.**, and I will be 5971
Jer 11:14 pray not thou for this **p.**, neither........ 5971
Jer 12:14 have caused my **p.** Israel to inherit:.... 5971
Jer 12:16 diligently learn the ways of my **p.**,...... 5971
Jer 12:16 they taught my **p.** to swear by Baal;... 5971
Jer 12:16 they be built in the midst of my **p.**. 5971
Jer 13:10 This evil **p.**, which refuse to hear....... 5971
Jer 13:11 they might be unto me for a **p.**, and... 5971
Jer 14:10 Thus saith the Lord unto his **p.**, ... 5971
Jer 14:11 Pray not for this **p.** for their good. 5971
Jer 14:16 the **p.** to whom they prophesy shall.... 5971
Jer 14:17 virgin daughter of my **p.** is broken...... 5971
Jer 15:1 mind could not be toward this **p.**:....... 5971
Jer 15:7 I will destroy my **p.**, since they 5971
Jer 15:20 unto this **p.** a fenced brazen wall........ 5971
Jer 16:5 taken away my peace from this **p.**, ... 5971
Jer 16:10 shalt shew these **p.** all these words, ... 5971
Jer 17:19 in the gate of the children of the **p.**, ... 5971
Jer 18:15 Because my **p.** hath forgotten me,...... 5971
Jer 19:1 and take of the ancients of the **p.**, ... 5971
Jer 19:11 so will I break this **p.** and this city, ... 5971
Jer 19:14 Lord's house; and said to all the **p.**,.... 5971
Jer 21:7 the **p.**, and such as are left in this....... 5971
Jer 21:8 unto this **p.** thou shalt say, Thus........ 5971
Jer 22:2 thy **p.** that enter in by these gates: 5971
Jer 22:4 he, and his servants, and his **p.**. 5971
Jer 23:2 against the pastors that feed my **p.**;.... 5971
Jer 23:13 and caused my **p.** Israel to err........... 5971
Jer 23:22 had caused my **p.** to hear my words, .. 5971
Jer 23:27 to cause my **p.** to forget my name...... 5971
Jer 23:32 and cause my **p.** to err by their lies,... 5971
Jer 23:32 they shall not profit this **p.** at all, ... 5971
Jer 23:33 when this **p.**, or the prophet, or a...... 5971
Jer 23:34 prophet, and the priest, and the **p.**, ... 5971
Jer 24:7 they shall be my **p.**, and I will be....... 5971
Jer 25:1 concerning all the **p.** of Judah in......... 5971
Jer 25:2 spake unto all the **p.** of Judah, and...... 5971
Jer 25:19 and his princes, and all his **p.**; 5971
Jer 25:20 And all the mingled **p.**, and all the...........
Jer 25:24 mingled **p.** that dwell in the desert, ...
Jer 26:7 the **p.** heard Jeremiah speaking.......... 5971
Jer 26:8 end of speaking...unto all the **p.**,....... 5971
Jer 26:8 prophets and all the **p.** took him,........ 5971
Jer 26:9 **p.** were gathered against Jeremiah...... 5971
Jer 26:11 unto the princes and to all the **p.**, ... 5971
Jer 26:12 unto all the princes and to all the **p.**,... 5971
Jer 26:16 said the princes and all the **p.** unto...... 5971
Jer 26:17 spake to all the assembly of the **p.**, ... 5971
Jer 26:18 and spake to all the **p.** of Judah,......... 5971
Jer 26:23 into the graves of the common **p.**....... 5971
Jer 26:24 hand of the **p.** to put him to death...... 5971
Jer 27:12 and serve him and his **p.**, and live. 5971
Jer 27:13 Why will ye die, thou and thy **p.**, by.... 5971
Jer 27:16 to the priests and to all this **p.**, ... 5971
Jer 28:1 of the priests and of all the **p.**, ... 5971
Jer 28:5 and in the presence of all the **p.** that... 5971
Jer 28:7 ears, and in the ears of all the **p.**; 5971
Jer 28:11 spake in the presence of all the **p.**,..... 5971
Jer 28:15 thou makest this **p.** to trust in a lie. ... 5971
Jer 29:1 to all the **p.** whom Nebuchadnezzar..... 5971
Jer 29:16 all the **p.** that dwelleth in this city, ... 5971
Jer 29:25 all the **p.** that are at Jerusalem, ... 5971
Jer 29:32 have a man to dwell among this **p.**; 5971
Jer 29:32 the good that I will do for my **p.**,....... 5971
Jer 30:3 again the capitivity of my **p.** Israel...... 5971
Jer 30:22 ye shall be my **p.**, and I will be your... 5971
Jer 31:1 of Israel, and they shall be my **p.**....... 5971
Jer 31:2 The **p.** which were left of the sword... 5971
Jer 31:7 Lord, save thy **p.**, the remnant of...... 5971
Jer 31:14 my **p.** shall be satisfied with my......... 5971
Jer 31:33 their God, and they shall be my **p.**. 5971
Jer 32:21 brought forth thy **p.** Israel out of........ 5971
Jer 32:38 And they shall be my **p.**, and I will..... 5971
Jer 32:42 all this great evil upon this **p.**, so....... 5971
Jer 33:24 thou not what this **p.** have spoken, ... 5971
Jer 33:24 they have despised my **p.**, that they... 5971
Jer 34:1 all the **p.**, fought against Jerusalem, ... 5971
Jer 34:8 had made a covenant with all the **p.**.... 5971
Jer 34:10 when all the princes, and all the **p.**, ... 5971
Jer 34:19 priests, and all the **p.** of the land,....... 5971
Jer 35:16 this **p.** hath not hearkened unto me: ... 5971
Jer 36:6 words of the Lord in...ears of the **p.**.... 5971
Jer 36:7 hath pronounced against this **p.**......... 5971
Jer 36:9 the Lord to all the **p.** in Jerusalem,..... 5971
Jer 36:9 the **p.** that came from the cities of..... 5971
Jer 36:10 house, in the ears of all the **p.**........... 5971
Jer 36:13 read the book in the ears of the **p.**..... 5971
Jer 36:14 thou hast read in the ears of the **p.**, ... 5971
Jer 37:2 nor the **p.** of the land, did hearken..... 5971
Jer 37:4 in and went out among the **p.**:........... 5971
Jer 37:12 thence in the midst of the **p.**............. 5971
Jer 37:18 thy servants, or against this **p.**, ... 5971
Jer 38:1 had spoken unto all the **p.**, saying, ... 5971
Jer 38:4 the hands of all the **p.**, in speaking..... 5971
Jer 38:4 seeketh not the welfare of this **p.**,...... 5971
Jer 39:8 and the houses of the **p.**, with fire,..... 5971
Jer 39:9 the remnant of the **p.** that remained.... 5971
Jer 39:9 the rest of the **p.** that remained......... 5971
Jer 39:10 the guard left of the poor of the **p.**, ... 5971
Jer 39:14 home: so he dwelt among the **p.**........ 5971
Jer 40:5 and dwell with him among the **p.**:........ 5971
Jer 40:6 among the **p.** that were left in the...... 5971
Jer 41:10 the residue of the **p.** that were in....... 5971
Jer 41:10 all the **p.** that remained in Mizpah, ... 5971
Jer 41:13 all the **p.** which were with Ishmael..... 5971
Jer 41:14 **p.** that Ishmael had carried away........ 5971
Jer 41:16 the remnant of the **p.** whom he had.... 5971
Jer 42:1 the **p.** from the least even unto the 5971
Jer 42:8 all the **p.** from the least even to the ... 5971
Jer 43:1 end of speaking unto all the **p.** all...... 5971
Jer 43:4 **p.**, obeyed not the voice of the Lord,.. 5971
Jer 44:15 **p.** that dwelt in the land of Egypt,...... 5971
Jer 44:20 Then Jeremiah said unto all the **p.**, ... 5971
Jer 44:20 all the **p.** which had given him that..... 5971
Jer 44:21 princes, and the **p.** of the land, did..... 5971
Jer 44:24 Jeremiah said unto all the **p.**, and....... 5971
Jer 46:16 let us go again to our own **p.**, and to.. 5971
Jer 46:24 into the hand of the **p.** of the north. ... 5971
Jer 48:42 shall be destroyed from being a **p.**,..... 5971
Jer 48:46 the **p.** of Chemosh perisheth: for........ 5971
Jer 49:1 Gad, and his **p.** dwell in his cities?...... 5971
Jer 50:6 My **p.** hath been lost sheep: their 5971
Jer 50:16 they shall turn every one to his **p.**,...... 5971
Jer 50:37 mingled **p.** that are in the midst of............
Jer 50:41 a **p.** shall come from the north, and.... 5971
Jer 51:45 My **p.**, go ye out of the midst of her, . 5971
Jer 51:58 the **p.** shall labour in vain, and the...... 5971
Jer 52:6 was no bread for the **p.** of the land..... 5971
Jer 52:15 captive certain of the poor of the **p.**,.... 5971
Jer 52:15 residue of the **p.** that remained in........ 5971
Jer 52:25 who mustered the **p.** of the land; 5971
Jer 52:25 men of the **p.** of the land, that were... 5971
Jer 52:28 **p.** whom Nebuchadrezzar carried........ 5971
La 1:1 city sit solitary, that was full of **p.**!..... 5971
La 1:7 **p.** fell into the hand of the enemy,...... 5971
La 1:11 all her **p.** sigh, they seek bread; 5971
La 1:18 hear, I pray you, all **p.**, and behold..... 5971
La 2:11 of the daughter of my **p.**; 5971
La 3:14 I was a derision to all my **p.**; and....... 5971
La 3:45 and refuse in the midst of the **p.**........ 5971
La 3:48 of the daughter of my **p.**. 5971
La 4:3 the daughter of my **p.** is become........ 5971
La 4:6 daughter of my **p.** is greater than....... 5971
La 4:10 of the daughter of my **p.**. 5971
Eze 3:5 not sent to a **p.** of a strange speech... 5971
Eze 3:6 to many **p.** of a strange speech and.... 5971
Eze 3:11 unto the children of thy **p.**, and.......... 5971
Eze 7:27 the **p.** of the land shall be troubled: 5971
Eze 11:1 the son of Benaiah, princes of the **p.**... 5971
Eze 11:17 will even gather you from the **p.**, and.. 5971
Eze 11:20 they shall be my **p.**, and I will be....... 5971
Eze 12:19 say unto the **p.** of the land, Thus....... 5971
Eze 13:9 not be in the assembly of my **p.**,........ 5971
Eze 13:10 because they have seduced my **p.**, ... 5971
Eze 13:17 against the daughters of thy **p.**, ... 5971
Eze 13:18 Will ye hunt the souls of my **p.**, and... 5971
Eze 13:19 will ye pollute me among my **p.** for..... 5971
Eze 13:19 lying to my **p.** that hear your lies?...... 5971
Eze 13:21 and deliver my **p.** out of your hand,..... 5971
Eze 13:23 deliver my **p.** out of your hand: 5971
Eze 14:8 him off from the midst of my **p.**;........ 5971
Eze 14:9 him from the midst of my **p.** Israel..... 5971
Eze 14:11 they may be my **p.**, and I may be 5971
Eze 17:9 many **p.** to pluck it up by the roots 5971
Eze 17:15 might give him horses and much **p.**..... 5971
Eze 18:18 which is not good among his **p.**, lo, ... 5971
Eze 20:34 I will bring you out from the **p.**,......... 5971
Eze 20:35 you into the wilderness of the **p.**,....... 5971
Eze 20:41 when I bring you out from the **p.**, ... 5971
Eze 21:12 for it shall be upon my **p.**, it shall....... 5971
Eze 21:12 of the sword shall be upon my **p.**: 5971
Eze 22:29 **p.** of the land have used oppression,... 5971
Eze 23:24 and with an assembly of **p.**, which...... 5971
Eze 24:18 spake unto the **p.** in the morning:....... 5971
Eze 24:19 the **p.** said unto me, Wilt thou not...... 5971
Eze 25:7 I will cut thee off from the **p.**, and..... 5971
Eze 25:14 Edom by the hand of my **p.** Israel: 5971
Eze 26:2 broken that was the gates of the **p.**;... 5971
Eze 26:7 and companies, and much **p.**............... 5971
Eze 26:11 he shall slay thy **p.** by the sword, ... 5971
Eze 26:20 into the pit, with the **p.** of old time,.... 5971
Eze 27:3 merchant of the **p.** for many isles,...... 5971
Eze 27:33 of the seas, thou filledst many **p.**; 5971
Eze 27:36 merchants among the **p.** shall hiss...... 5971
Eze 28:19 that know thee among the **p.** shall...... 5971
Eze 28:25 **p.** among whom they are scattered,.... 5971
Eze 29:13 gather the Egyptians from the **p.**........ 5971
Eze 30:5 all the mingled **p.**, and Chub, and............
Eze 30:11 He and his **p.** with him, the 5971
Eze 31:12 the **p.** of the earth are gone down...... 5971
Eze 32:3 thee with a company of many **p.**; 5971
Eze 32:9 will also vex the hearts of many **p.**, ... 5971
Eze 32:10 will make many **p.** amazed at thee,..... 5971
Eze 33:2 speak to the children of thy **p.**, and.... 5971
Eze 33:2 **p.** of the land take a man of their....... 5971
Eze 33:3 blow the trumpet, and warn the **p.**: 5971
Eze 33:6 trumpet, and the **p.** be not warned; 5971
Eze 33:12 say unto the children of thy **p.**, The.... 5971
Eze 33:17 Yet the children of thy **p.** say, The..... 5971
Eze 33:30 children of thy **p.** still are talking....... 5971
Eze 33:31 come unto thee as the **p.** cometh, ... 5971
Eze 33:31 they sit before thee as my **p.**, and...... 5971
Eze 34:13 I will bring them out from the **p.**,........ 5971
Eze 34:30 even the house of Israel, are my **p.**,... 5971
Eze 36:3 talkers, and are an infamy of the **p.**: ... 5971
Eze 36:8 yield your fruit to my **p.** of Israel; 5971
Eze 36:12 walk upon you, even my **p.** Israel;...... 5971
Eze 36:15 the reproach of the **p.** any more, ... 5971
Eze 36:20 these are the **p.** of the Lord, and....... 5971
Eze 36:28 ye shall be my **p.**, and I will be your... 5971
Eze 37:12 O my **p.**, I will open your graves, ... 5971
Eze 37:13 have opened your graves, O my **p.**,.... 5971
Eze 37:18 children of thy **p.** shall speak unto...... 5971
Eze 37:23 so shall they be my **p.**, and I will....... 5971
Eze 37:27 their God, and they shall be my **p.**. 5971
Eze 38:6 his bands; and many **p.** with thee. 5971
Eze 38:8 gathered out of many **p.**, against........ 5971
Eze 38:9 thy bands, and many **p.** with thee....... 5971
Eze 38:12 the **p.** that are gathered out of the 5971
Eze 38:14 my **p.** of Israel dwelleth safely, ... 5971
Eze 38:15 and many **p.** with thee, all of them..... 5971
Eze 38:16 come up against my **p.** of Israel, ... 5971
Eze 38:22 the many **p.** that are with him, an 5971
Eze 39:4 bands, and the **p.** that is with thee: 5971
Eze 39:7 known in the midst of my **p.** Israel; 5971
Eze 39:13 all the **p.** of the land shall bury 5971
Eze 39:27 brought them again from the **p.**,......... 5971
Eze 42:14 those things which are for the **p.**........ 5971
Eze 44:11 sacrifice for the **p.**, and they shall....... 5971
Eze 44:19 even into the utter court to the **p.**,..... 5971

Eze	44:19	shall not sanctify the **p.** with their	5971
Eze	44:23	shall teach my **p.** the difference	5971
Eze	45:8	shall no more oppress my **p.**; and	5971
Eze	45:9	away your exactions from my **p.**,	5971
Eze	45:16	the **p.** of the land shall give this	5971
Eze	45:22	prepare for himself and all the **p.**	5971
Eze	46:3	the **p.** of the land shall worship at	5971
Eze	46:9	when the **p.** of the land shall come	5971
Eze	46:18	my **p.** be not scattered every man	5971
Eze	46:20	the utter court, to sanctify the **p.**	5971
Eze	46:24	shall boil the sacrifice of the **p.**	5971
Da	2:44	kingdom...not be left to other **p.**,	5972
Da	3:4	O **p.**, nations, and languages,	5972
Da	3:7	all the **p.** heard the sound of the	5972
Da	3:7	all the **p.**, the nations, and the	5972
Da	3:29	That every **p.**, nation,...language,	5972
Da	4:1	the king, unto all **p.**, nations, and	5972
Da	5:19	him, all **p.**, nations, and languages,	5972
Da	6:25	Darius wrote unto all **p.**, nations,	5972
Da	7:14	that all **p.**, nations, and languages,	5972
Da	7:27	be given to the **p.** of the saints of	5972
Da	8:24	destroy the mighty and the holy **p.**	5971
Da	9:6	fathers, and to all the **p.** of the land	5971
Da	9:15	that hast brought thy **p.** forth out	5971
Da	9:16	Jerusalem and thy **p.** are become	5971
Da	9:19	and thy **p.** are called by thy name.	5971
Da	9:20	my sin and the sin of my **p.** Israel,	5971
Da	9:24	upon thy **p.** and upon thy holy	5971
Da	9:26	the **p.** of the prince that shall come	5971
Da	10:14	what shall befall thy **p.** in the	5971
Da	11:14	the robbers of thy **p.** shall exalt	5971
Da	11:15	neither his chosen **p.**, neither shall	5971
Da	11:23	become strong with a small **p.**	1471
Da	11:32	but the **p.** that do know their God	5971
Da	11:33	among the **p.** shall instruct many:	5971
Da	12:1	standeth for the children of thy **p.**:	5971
Da	12:1	that time thy **p.** shall be delivered,	5971
Da	12:7	to scatter the power of the holy **p.**,	5971
Ho	1:9	for ye are not my **p.**, and I will not	5971
Ho	1:10	Ye are not my **p.**, there it shall be	5971
Ho	2:23	say to them which were not my **p.**,	5971
Ho	2:23	Thou art my **p.**; and they shall say,	5971
Ho	4:4	for thy **p.** are as they that strive	5971
Ho	4:6	My **p.** are destroyed for lack of	5971
Ho	4:8	They eat up the sin of my **p.**, and	5971
Ho	4:9	there shall be, like **p.**, like priest:	5971
Ho	4:12	My **p.** ask counsel at their stocks,	5971
Ho	4:14	**p.** that doth not understand shall	5971
Ho	6:11	I returned the captivity of my **p.**	5971
Ho	7:8	hath mixed himself among the **p.**;	5971
Ho	9:1	not, O Israel, for joy, as other **p.**:	5971
Ho	10:5	the **p.** thereof shall mourn over it,	5971
Ho	10:10	**p.** shall be gathered against them,	5971
Ho	10:14	shall a tumult arise among thy **p.**,	5971
Ho	11:7	my **p.** are bent to backsliding from	5971
Joe	2:2	a great **p.** and a strong; there hath	5971
Joe	2:5	as a strong **p.** set in battle array	5971
Joe	2:6	face the **p.** shall be much pained:	5971
Joe	2:16	Gather the **p.**, sanctify the	5971
Joe	2:17	Spare thy **p.**, O Lord, and give not	5971
Joe	2:17	should they say among the **p.**,	5971
Joe	2:18	jealous for his land, and pity his **p.**	5971
Joe	2:19	will answer and say unto his **p.**,	5971
Joe	2:26, 27	my **p.** shall never be ashamed.	5971
Joe	3:2	there for my **p.** and for my heritage	5971
Joe	3:3	And they have cast lots for my **p.**;	5971
Joe	3:8	to the Sabeans, to a **p.** far off:	1471
Joe	3:16	the Lord will be the hope of his **p.**,	5971
Am	1:5	**p.** of Syria shall go into captivity	5971
Am	3:6	the city, and the **p.** not be afraid?	5971
Am	7:8	in the midst of my **p.** Israel:	5971
Am	7:15	Go, prophesy unto my **p.** Israel.	5971
Am	8:2	end is come upon my **p.** of Israel;	5971
Am	9:10	All the sinners of my **p.** shall die	5971
Am	9:14	bring again the captivity of my **p.**	5971
Ob	13	have entered into the gate of my **p.**	5971
Jon	1:8	country? and of what **p.** art thou?	5971
Jon	3:5	So the **p.** of Nineveh believed God,	582
Mic	1:2	Hear, all ye **p.**; hearken, O earth,	5971
Mic	1:9	he is come unto the gate of my **p.**,	5971
Mic	2:4	hath changed the portion of my **p.**:	5971
Mic	2:8	Even of late my **p.** is risen up as an	5971
Mic	2:9	women of my **p.** have ye cast out	5971
Mic	2:11	shall even be the prophet of this **p.**	5971
Mic	3:3	Who also eat the flesh of my **p.**, and	5971
Mic	3:5	the prophets that make my **p.** err,	5971
Mic	4:1	the hills; and **p.** shall flow unto it.	5971
Mic	4:3	he shall judge among many **p.**,	5971
Mic	4:5	**p.** will walk every one in the name	5971
Mic	4:13	thou shalt beat in pieces many **p.**:	5971
Mic	5:7	of many **p.** as a dew from the Lord,	5971
Mic	5:8	in the midst of many **p.** as a lion	5971
Mic	6:2	hath a controversy with his **p.**, and	5971
Mic	6:3	O my **p.**, what have I done unto	5971
Mic	6:5	O my **p.**, remember now what	5971
Mic	6:16	shall bear the reproach of my **p.**	5971
Mic	7:14	Feed thy **p.** with thy rod, the flock	5971
Na	3:13	**p.** in the midst of thee are women:	5971
Na	3:18	**p.** is scattered upon the mountains,	5971
Hab	2:5	and heapeth unto him all **p.**:	5971
Hab	2:8	remnant of the **p.** shall spoil thee;	5971
Hab	2:10	thy house by cutting off many **p.**,	5971
Hab	2:13	the **p.** shall labour in the very fire,	5971
Hab	2:13	and the **p.** shall weary themselves	3816
Hab	3:13	forth for the salvation of thy **p.**,	5971
Hab	3:16	when he cometh up unto the **p.**, he	5971
Zep	1:11	all the merchant **p.** are cut down;	5971
Zep	2:8	they have reproached my **p.**, and	5971
Zep	2:9	residue of my **p.** shall spoil them,	5971
Zep	2:9	remnant of my **p.** shall possess	1471
Zep	2:10	magnified themselves against...**p.**	5971
Zep	3:9	I turn to the **p.** a pure language,	5971
Zep	3:12	of thee an afflicted and poor **p.**,	5971
Zep	3:20	a praise among all **p.** of the earth,	5971
Hag	1:2	This **p.** say, The time is not come,	5971
Hag	1:12	with the remnant of the **p.**, obeyed	5971
Hag	1:12	and the **p.** did fear before the Lord	5971
Hag	1:13	in the Lord's message unto the **p.**,	5971
Hag	1:14	spirit of all the remnant of the **p.**;	5971
Hag	2:2	priest, and to the residue of the **p.**,	5971
Hag	2:4	and be strong, all ye **p.** of the land,	5971
Hag	2:14	So is this **p.**, and so is this nation	5971
Zec	2:11	in that day, and shall be my **p.**:	5971
Zec	7:5	Speak unto all the **p.** of the land,	5971
Zec	8:6	the remnant of this **p.** in these days,	5971
Zec	8:7	I will save my **p.** from the east	5971
Zec	8:8	shall be my **p.**, and I will be their	5971
Zec	8:11	not be unto the residue of this **p.** as	5971
Zec	8:12	remnant of this **p.** to possess all	5971
Zec	8:20	that there shall come **p.**, and the	5971
Zec	8:22	many **p.** and strong nations shall	5971
Zec	9:16	in that day as the flock of his **p.**:	5971
Zec	10:9	And I will sow them among the **p.**:	5971
Zec	11:10	which I had made with all the **p.**	5971
Zec	12:2	unto all the **p.** round about, when	5971
Zec	12:3	a burdensome stone for all **p.**: all	5971
Zec	12:3	though all the **p.** of the earth be	1471
Zec	12:4	smite every horse of the **p.** with	5971
Zec	12:6	shall devour all the **p.** round about,	5971
Zec	13:9	hear them: I will say, It is my **p.**:	5971
Zec	14:2	residue of the **p.** shall not be cut off	5971
Zec	14:12	Lord will smite all the **p.** that have	5971
Mal	1:4	The **p.** against whom the Lord hath	5971
Mal	2:9	base before all the **p.**, according	5971
Mt	1:21	shall save his **p.** from their sins.	*2992*
Mt	2:4	and scribes of the **p.** together, he	*2992*
Mt	2:6	Governor,...shall rule my **p.** Israel.	*2992*
Mt	4:16	The **p.** which sat in darkness saw	*2992*
Mt	4:23	all manner of disease among the **p.**	*2992*
Mt	4:24	they brought unto him all sick **p.**	
Mt	4:25	great multitudes of **p.** from Galilee,	
Mt	7:28	**p.** were astonished at his doctrine:	*3793*
Mt	9:23	and the **p.** making a noise,	*3793*
Mt	9:25	when the **p.** were put forth, he went	*3793*
Mt	9:35	and every disease among the **p.**	*2992*
Mt	12:23	all the **p.** were amazed, and said,	*3793*
Mt	12:46	While he yet talked to the **p.**,	*3793*
Mt	14:13	and when the **p.** had heard thereof,	*3793*
Mt	15:8	**p. draweth nigh unto me with their**	*2992*
Mt	21:23	the elders of the **p.** came unto him	*2992*
Mt	21:26	shall say, Of men; we fear the **p.**;	*3793*
Mt	26:3	scribes, and the elders of the **p.**,	*2992*
Mt	26:5	there be an uproar among the **p.**	*2992*
Mt	26:47	chief priests and elders of the **p.**	*2992*
Mt	27:1	and elders of the **p.** took counsel	*2992*
Mt	27:15	to release unto the **p.** a prisoner,	*3793*
Mt	27:25	Then answered all the **p.**, and said,	*2992*
Mt	27:64	him away, and say unto the **p.**,	*2992*
Mk	5:21	side, much **p.** gathered unto him:	*3793*
Mk	5:24	and much **p.** followed him, and	*3793*
Mk	6:33	And the **p.** saw them departing, and	*3793*
Mk	6:34	saw much **p.**, and was moved with	*3793*
Mk	6:45	while he sent away the **p.**	*3793*
Mk	7:6	**p. honoureth me with their lips,**	*2992*
Mk	7:14	he had called all the **p.** unto him,	*3793*
Mk	7:17	entered into the house from the **p.**,	*3793*
Mk	8:6	commanded the **p.** to sit down on	*3793*
Mk	8:6	and they did set them before the **p.**	*3793*
Mk	8:34	he had called the **p.** unto him with	*3793*
Mk	9:15	And straightway all the **p.**, when	*3793*
Mk	9:25	Jesus saw that the **p.** came running	*3793*
Mk	10:1	and the **p.** resort unto him again;	*3793*
Mk	10:46	disciples and a great number of **p.**,	*3793*
Mk	11:18	**p.** was astonished at his doctrine	*3793*
Mk	11:32	say, Of men; they feared the **p.**:	*2992*
Mk	12:12	lay hold on him, but feared the **p.**;	*3793*
Mk	12:37	the common **p.** heard him gladly.	*3793*
Mk	12:41	beheld how the **p.** cast money into	*3793*
Mk	14:2	lest there be an uproar of the **p.**	*2992*
Mk	15:11	But the chief priests moved the **p.**,	*3793*
Mk	15:15	so Pilate, willing to content the **p.**,	*3793*
Lu	1:10	multitude of the **p.** were praying	*2992*
Lu	1:17	ready a **p.** prepared for the Lord	*2992*
Lu	1:21	And the **p.** waited for Zacharias,	*2992*
Lu	1:68	hath visited and redeemed his **p.**,	*2992*
Lu	1:77	knowledge of salvation unto his **p.**	*2992*
Lu	2:10	great joy, which shall be to all **p.**	*2992*
Lu	2:31	prepared before the face of all **p.**;	*2992*
Lu	2:32	and the glory of thy **p.** Israel.	*2992*
Lu	3:10	And the **p.** asked him, saying,	*3793*
Lu	3:15	And as the **p.** were in expectation,	*2992*
Lu	3:18	preached he unto the **p.**	*2992*
Lu	3:21	Now when all the **p.** were baptized,	*2992*
Lu	4:42	the **p.** sought him, and came unto	*3793*
Lu	5:1	**p.** pressed upon him to hear the	*3793*
Lu	5:3	and taught the **p.** out of the ship,	*3793*
Lu	6:17	multitude of **p.** out of all Judaea	*2992*
Lu	7:1	sayings in the audience of the **p.**,	*2992*
Lu	7:9	said unto the **p.** that followed	*3793*
Lu	7:11	went with him, and much **p.**	*3793*
Lu	7:12	much **p.** of the city was with her.	*3793*
Lu	7:16	and, That God hath visited his **p.**	*2992*
Lu	7:24	speak unto the **p.** concerning	*3798*
Lu	7:29	And all the **p.** that heard him, and	*2992*
Lu	8:4	And when much **p.** were gathered	*3793*
Lu	8:40	the **p.** gladly received him: for	*3793*
Lu	8:42	as he went the **p.** thronged him.	*3793*
Lu	8:47	declared unto him before all the **p.**	*2992*
Lu	9:11	And the **p.**, when they knew it,	*3793*
Lu	9:13	go and buy meat for all this **p.**	*2992*
Lu	9:18	saying, **Whom say the p. that I**	*3793*
Lu	9:37	from the hill, much **p.** met him.	*3793*
Lu	11:14	dumb spake; and the **p.** wondered.	*3793*
Lu	11:29	when the **p.** were gathered thick	*3793*
Lu	12:1	an innumerable multitude of **p.**,	*3793*
Lu	12:54	he said also to the **p.**, **When ye see**	*3793*
Lu	13:14	said unto the **p.**, There are six days	*3793*
Lu	13:17	the **p.** rejoiced for all the glorious	*3793*
Lu	18:43	all the **p.**, when they saw it, gave	*2992*
Lu	19:47	chief of the **p.** sought to destroy	*2992*
Lu	19:48	the **p.** were very attentive to hear	*2992*
Lu	20:1	as he taught the **p.** in the temple,	*2992*
Lu	20:6	say, Of men; all the **p.** will stone us:	*2992*
Lu	20:9	he to speak to the **p.** this parable;	*2992*
Lu	20:19	and they feared the **p.**: for they	*2992*
Lu	20:26	take hold of his words before the **p.**:	*2992*
Lu	20:45	in the audience of all the **p.** he said	*2992*
Lu	21:23	**the land, and wrath upon this p.**	*2992*
Lu	21:38	all the **p.** came early in the morning	*2992*
Lu	22:2	kill him; for they feared the **p.**	*2992*
Lu	22:66	the elders of the **p.** and the chief	*2992*
Lu	23:4	to the chief priests and to the **p.**,	*3793*
Lu	23:5	He stirreth up the **p.**, teaching	*2992*
Lu	23:13	priests and the rulers and the **p.**,	*2992*
Lu	23:14	me, as one that perverteth the **p.**:	*2992*
Lu	23:27	followed him a great company of **p.**,	*2992*
Lu	23:35	And the **p.** stood beholding. And	*2992*
Lu	23:48	And all the **p.** that came together	*3793*
Lu	24:19	and word before God and all the **p.**;	*2992*
Joh	6:22	**p.** which stood on the other side	*3793*
Joh	6:24	**p.** therefore saw that Jesus was	*3793*
Joh	7:12	much murmuring among the **p.**	*3793*
Joh	7:12	said, Nay; but he deceiveth the **p.**:	*3793*
Joh	7:20	**p.** answered and said, Thou hast a	*3793*
Joh	7:31	many of the **p.** believed on him,	*3793*
Joh	7:32	heard that the **p.** murmured such	*3793*
Joh	7:40	Many of the **p.**, therefore, when	*3793*
Joh	7:43	was a division among the **p.**	*3793*
Joh	7:49	this **p.** who knoweth not the law are	*3793*
Joh	8:2	all the **p.** came unto him; and he sat	*2992*
Joh	11:42	**because of the p. which stand by I**	*3793*

Joh 11:50 that one man should die for the **p.**,...... *2992*
Joh 12:9 Much **p.** of the Jews therefore knew... *3793*
Joh 12:12 next day much **p.** that were come to... *3793*
Joh 12:17 The **p.** therefore that was with him *3793*
Joh 12:18 For this cause the **p.** also met him, ... *3793*
Joh 12:29 the **p.** therefore, that stood by, and.... *3793*
Joh 12:34 **p.** answered him, We have heard....... *3793*
Joh 18:14 that one man should die for the **p.**...... *2992*
Ac 2:47 and having favour with all the **p.**. *2992*
Ac 3:9 the **p.** saw him walking and praising.... *2992*
Ac 3:11 all the **p.** ran together unto them in.... *2992*
Ac 3:12 he answered unto the **p.**, Ye men of.... *2992*
Ac 3:23 be destroyed from among the **p.**. *2992*
Ac 4:1 And as they spake unto the **p.**, the..... *2992*
Ac 4:2 grieved that they taught the **p.**, and.... *2992*
Ac 4:8 Ye rulers of the **p.**, and elders of....... *2992*
Ac 4:10 you all, and to all the **p.** of Israel, ... *2992*
Ac 4:17 it spread no further among the **p.**, ... *2992*
Ac 4:21 punish them, because of the **p.**: for *2992*
Ac 4:25 and the **p.** imagine vain things? *2992*
Ac 4:27 **p.** of Israel, were gathered together, .. *2992*
Ac 5:12 and wonders wrought among the **p.**; ... *2992*
Ac 5:13 them: but the **p.** magnified them. *2992*
Ac 5:20 and speak in the temple to the **p.**........ *2992*
Ac 5:25 in the temple, and teaching the **p.**. *2992*
Ac 5:26 they feared the **p.**, lest they should *2992*
Ac 5:34 had in reputation among all the **p.**,....... *2992*
Ac 5:37 and drew away much **p.** after him:......... *2992*
Ac 6:8 wonders and miracles among the **p.**. ... *2992*
Ac 6:12 stirred up the **p.**, and the elders, ... *2992*
Ac 7:17 the **p.** grew and multiplied in Egypt, ... *2992*
Ac 7:34 seen the affliction of my **p.**.............. *2992*
Ac 8:6 the **p.** with one accord gave heed........ *3793*
Ac 8:9 and bewitched the **p.** of Samaria,........ *1484*
Ac 10:2 which gave much alms to the **p.**,........ *2992*
Ac 10:41 Not to all the **p.**, but unto witnesses... *2992*
Ac 10:42 commanded us to preach unto the **p.**,.. *2992*
Ac 11:24 much **p.** was added unto the Lord. *3793*
Ac 11:26 with the church, and taught much **p.**. .. *3793*
Ac 12:4 Easter to bring him forth to the **p.**. *2992*
Ac 12:11 expectation of the **p.** of the Jews........ *2992*
Ac 12:22 the **p.** gave a shout, saying, It is........ *1218*
Ac 13:15 any word of exhortation for the **p.**,...... *2992*
Ac 13:17 God of this **p.** of Israel chose our....... *2992*
Ac 13:17 exalted the **p.** when they dwelt as...... *2992*
Ac 13:24 of repentance to all the **p.** of Israel..... *2992*
Ac 13:31 who are his witnesses unto the **p.**. *2992*
Ac 14:11 the **p.** saw what Paul had done, ... *3793*
Ac 14:13 have done sacrifice with the **p.**. *3793*
Ac 14:14 and ran in among the **p.**, crying out, ... *3793*
Ac 14:18 scarce restrained they the **p.**, that,..... *3793*
Ac 14:19 who persuaded the **p.**, and having *3793*
Ac 15:14 take out of them a **p.** for his name. *2992*
Ac 17:5 sought to bring them out to the **p.**. *1218*
Ac 17:8 And they troubled the **p.** and the *3793*
Ac 17:13 thither also, and stirred up the **p.**........ *3793*
Ac 18:10 **for I have much p. in this city.**..... *2992*
Ac 19:4 saying unto the **p.**, that they should.... *2992*
Ac 19:26 and turned away much **p.**, saying *3793*
Ac 19:30 would have entered in unto the **p.**, ... *1218*
Ac 19:33 have made his defence unto the **p.**. *1218*
Ac 19:35 the townclerk had appeased the **p.**,...... *3793*
Ac 21:27 stirred up all the **p.**, and laid hands..... *3793*
Ac 21:28 against the **p.**, and the law, and......... *2992*
Ac 21:30 was moved, and the **p.** ran together: .. *2992*
Ac 21:35 soldiers for the violence of the **p.**. *3793*
Ac 21:36 For the multitude of the **p.** followed.... *2992*
Ac 21:39 thee, suffer me to speak unto the **p.**... *2992*
Ac 21:40 beckoned with the hand unto the **p.**. ... *2992*
Ac 23:5 not speak evil of the ruler of thy **p.**. ... *2992*
Ac 24:12 neither raising up the **p.**, neither in..... *3793*
Ac 26:17 **Delivering thee from the p., and**.... *2992*
Ac 26:23 should shew light unto the **p.**,and....... *2992*
Ac 28:2 barbarous **p.** shewed us no little...............
Ac 28:17 committed nothing against the **p.**,........ *2992*
Ac 28:26 Go unto this **p.**, and say, Hearing ye .. *2992*
Ac 28:27 the heart of this **p.** is waxed gross, ... *2992*
Ro 9:25 also in Osee, I will call them my **p.**, ... *2992*
Ro 9:25 which were not my **p.**; and her.......... *2992*
Ro 9:26 said unto them, Ye are not my **p.**;...... *2992*
Ro 10:19 to jealousy by them that are no **p.**,...... *1484*
Ro 10:21 a disobedient and gainsaying **p.**. *2992*
Ro 11:1 then, Hath God cast away his **p.**?........ *2992*
Ro 11:2 God hath not cast away his **p.** which... *2992*
Ro 15:10 Rejoice, ye Gentiles, with his **p.**. *2992*
Ro 15:11 Gentiles; and laud him, all ye **p.**......... *2992*
1Co 10:7 The **p.** sat down to eat and drink, ... *2992*
1Co 14:21 other lips will I speak unto this **p.**; *2992*
2Co 6:16 their God, and they shall be my **p.**. *2992*
Tit 2:14 a peculiar **p.**, zealous of good works. .. *2992*
Heb 2:17 reconciliation for the sins of the **p.**...... *2992*
Heb 4:9 therefore a rest to the **p.** of God. *2992*
Heb 5:3 as for the **p.**, so also for himself, to.... *2992*
Heb 7:5 to take tithes of the **p.** according........ *2992*
Heb 7:11 (for under it the **p.** received the law,) .. *2992*
Heb 8:10 God, and they shall be to me a **p.**: *2992*
Heb 9:7 himself, and for the errors of the **p.**:.... *2992*
Heb 9:19 spoken every precept to all the **p.**...... *2992*
Heb 9:19 sprinkled...the book, and all the **p.**, ... *2992*
Heb 10:30 again, The Lord shall judge his **p.**........ *2992*
Heb 11:25 suffer affliction with the **p.** of God, ... *2992*
Heb 13:12 sanctify the **p.** with his own blood, ... *2992*
1Pe 2:9 an holy nation, a peculiar **p.**; that *2992*
1Pe 2:10 Which in time past were not a **p.**, ... *2992*
1Pe 2:10 but are now the **p.** of God: which....... *2992*
2Pe 2:1 false prophets also among the **p.**, ... *2992*
Jude 5 having saved the **p.** out of...Egypt,...... *2992*
Re 5:9 and tongue, and **p.**, and nation:.......... *2992*
Re 7:9 and kindreds, and **p.**, and tongues, ... *2992*
Re 11:9 And they of the **p.** and kindreds and ... *2992*
Re 14:6 and kindred, and tongue, and **p.**, ... *2992*
Re 18:4 Come out of her, my **p.**, that ye be.... *2992*
Re 19:1 a great voice of much **p.** in heaven, ... *3793*
Re 21:3 with them, and they shall be his **p.**, ... *2992*

PEOPLE'S
Le 9:15 And he brought the **p.** offering,........... 5971
Eze 46:18 shall not take of the **p.** inheritance...... 5971
Mt 13:15 **For this p. heart is waxed gross,** ... *2992*
Heb 7:27 his own sins, and then for the **p.**:....... *2992*

PEOPLES
Re 10:11 prophesy again before many **p.**, ... *2992*
Re 17:15 where the whore sitteth, are **p.**, and... *2992*

PEOR (pe'-or) See also BAAL-PEOR; BETH-PEOR; PEOR'S.
Nu 23:28 Balaam unto the top of **P.**,................ 6465
Nu 25:18 beguiled you in the matterof **P.**,.......... 6465
Nu 31:16 against the Lord in the matter of **P.**, .. 6465
Jos 22:17 Is the iniquity of **P.** too little for us, ... 6465

PEOR'S
Nu 25:18 the day of the plague for **P.** sake. 6465

PERADVENTURE
Ge 18:24 **P.** there be fifty righteous within......... 194
Ge 18:28 **P.** there shall lack five of the fifty........ 194
Ge 18:29 **P.** there shall be forty found there......... 194
Ge 18:30 **P.** there shall thirty be found there. 194
Ge 18:31 **P.** there shall be twenty found there. ... 194
Ge 18:32 **P.** ten shall be found there. And......... 194
Ge 24:5 **P.** the woman will not be willing to....... 194
Ge 24:39 **P.** the woman will not follow me 194
Ge 27:12 my father **p.** will feel me, and I shall 194
Ge 31:31 **P.** thou wouldest take by force.......... 6435
Ge 32:20 his face; **p.** he will accept of me. 194
Ge 38:11 Lest **p.** he die also, as his brethren ....
Ge 42:4 said, Lest **p.** mischief befall him. ....
Ge 43:12 your hand; **p.** it was an oversight:........ 194
Ge 44:34 lest **p.** I see the evil that shall come ....
Ge 50:15 Joseph will **p.** hate us, and will 3863
Ex 13:17 God said, Lest **p.** the people repent..........
Ex 32:30 **p.** I shall make an atonement for 194
Nu 22:6 **p.** I shall prevail, that we may smite..... 194
Nu 22:11 **p.** I shall be able to overcome them, ... 194
Nu 23:3 **p.** the Lord will come to meet me: 194
Nu 23:27 **p.** it will please God that thou mayest... 194
Jos 9:7 **P.** ye dwell among us; and how........... 194
1Sa 6:5 **p.** he will lighten his hand from off......... 194
1Sa 9:6 **p.** he can shew us our way that we...... 194
1Ki 18:5 **p.** we may find grass to save the......... 194
1Ki 18:27 **p.** he sleepeth, and must be awaked..... 194
1Ki 20:31 of Israel: **p.** he will save thy life. 194
2Ki 2:16 lest **p.** the Spirit of the Lord hath.............
Jer 20:10 **P.** he will be enticed, and we shall........ 194
Ro 5:7 yet **p.** for a good man some would *5029*
2Ti 2:25 if God **p.** will give them repentance *3379*

PERAZIM (per'-a-zim) See also BAAL-PERAZIM.
Isa 28:21 Lord shall rise up as in mount **P.**, ... *3379*

PERCEIVE See also PERCEIVED; PERCEIVEST; PERCEIVETH; PERCEIVING.
De 29:4 hath not given you an heart to **p.**, ... 3045
Jos 22:31 day we **p.** that the Lord is among us, ..3045
1Sa 12:17 **p.** and see that your wickedness is..... 3045
2Sa 19:6 for this day I **p.**, that if Absalom........ 3045
2Ki 4:9 I **p.** that this is an holy man of God, ... 3045
Job 9:11 he passeth on also, but I **p.** him not..... 995
Job 23:8 and backward, but I cannot **p.** him: 995
Pr 1:2 to **p.** the words of understanding;............
Ec 3:22 I **p.** that there is nothing better, ... 7200
Isa 6:9 not; and see ye indeed, but **p.** not...... 3045
Isa 33:19 deeper speech than thou canst **p.**; 8085
Mt 13:14 **ye shall see, and shall not p.**:....... *1492*
Mk 4:12 **seeing they may see, and not p.**; ... *1492*
Mk 7:18 **Do ye not p., that whatsoever** *3539*
Mk 8:17 **p. ye not yet, neither understand?** . *3539*
Lu 8:46 **I p. that virtue is gone out of me**.. *1097*
Joh 4:19 Sir, I **p.** that thou art a prophet. *2334*
Joh 12:19 **P.** ye how ye prevail nothing? *2334*
Ac 8:23 For I **p.** that thou art in the gall of..... *3708*
Ac 10:34 I **p.** that God is no respecter of......... *2638*
Ac 17:22 I **p.** that in all things ye are too *2334*
Ac 27:10 I **p.**...this voyage will be with hurt...... *2334*
Ac 28:26 and seeing ye shall see, and not **p.**:.... *1492*
2Co 7:8 **p.** that the same epistle hath made....... *991*
1Jo 3:16 Hereby **p.** we the love of God, ... *1097*

PERCEIVED
Ge 19:33, 35 he **p.** not when she lay down, ... 3045
Jg 6:22 Gideon **p.** that he was an angel.......... 7200
1Sa 3:8 And Eli **p.** that the Lord had called 995
1Sa 28:14 And Saul **p.** that it was Samuel, ... 3045
2Sa 5:12 David **p.**...the Lord had established..... 3045
2Sa 12:19 David **p.** that the child was dead:........ 995
2Sa 14:1 **p.** that the king's heart was toward...... 3045
1Ki 22:33 **p.** that it was not the king of Israel 7200
1Ch 14:2 David **p.**...the Lord had confirmed...... 3045
2Ch 18:32 **p.**...it was not the king of Israel,........ 7200
Ne 6:12 I **p.** that god had not sent him;........... 5234
Ne 6:16 **p.** that this work was wrought of 3045
Ne 13:10 **p.** that the portions of the Levites...... 3045
Es 4:1 Mordecai **p.** all that was done,........... 3045
Job 38:18 thou **p.**the breadth of the earth? 995
Ec 1:17 I **p.** that this also is vexation of 3045
Ec 2:14 and I myself **p.** also that one event..... 3045
Isa 64:4 have not heard, nor **p.** by the ear,....... 238
Jer 23:18 and hath **p.** and heard his word? 7200
Jer 38:27 him; for the matter was not **p.**. 8085
Mt 16:8 Which when Jesus **p.**, he said unto *1097*
Mt 21:45 they **p.** that he spake of them. *1097*
Mt 22:18 Jesus **p.** their wickedness, and said..... *1097*
Mk 2:8 when Jesus **p.** in his spirit that *1921*
Lu 1:22 they **p.** that he had seen a vision *1921*
Lu 5:22 when Jesus **p.** their thoughts, he......... *1921*
Lu 9:45 hid from them, that they **p.** it not: *143*
Lu 20:19 **p.** that he had spoken this parable *1097*
Lu 20:23 But he **p.** their craftiness, and said..... *2657*
Joh 6:15 **p.**...they would come and take him..... *1097*
Ac 4:13 **p.** that they were unlearned and.......... *2638*
Ac 23:6 **p.**...the one part were Sadducees,...... *1097*
Ac 23:29 I **p.** to be accused of questions of....... *2147*
Ga 2:9 **p.** the grace that was given unto *1097*

PERCEIVEST
Pr 14:7 **p.** not in him the lips of knowledge..... 3045
Lu 6:41 **p. not the beam that is in thine** *2657*

PERCEIVETH
Job 14:21 low, but he **p.** it not of them. 995
Job 33:14 once, yea twice, yet man **p.** it not...... 7789
Pr 31:18 **p.** that her merchandise is good: 2938

PERCEIVING
Mk 12:28 **p.** that he had answered them well, ... *1492*
Lu 9:47 Jesus, **p.** the thought of their heart,.... *1492*
Ac 14:9 **p.** that he had faith to be healed, ... *1492*

PERDITION
Joh 17:12 **of them is lost, but the son of p.**; ... *684*
Php 1:28 is to them an evident token of **p.**,......... *684*
2Th 2:3 of sin be revealed, the son of **p.**;.......... *684*
1Ti 6:9 drown men in destruction and **p.**.......... *684*
Heb 10:39 not of them who draw back unto **p.**;...... *684*
2Pe 3:7 of judgment and **p.** of ungodly men....... *684*
Re 17:8 of the bottomless pit, and go into **p.**:.... *684*
Re 17:11 is of the seven, and goeth into **p.**. *684*

PERES (pe'-res) See also UPHARSIN.
Da 5:28 **P.**; Thy kingdom is divided, and......... 6537

PERESH (pe'-resh)
1Ch 7:16 a son, and she called his name **P.**; 6570

PEREZ (pe'-rez) See also PEREZ-UZZAH; PHARES.
1Ch 27:3 Of the children of **P.** was the chief..... 6557

Ne 11:4 of Mahalaleel, of the children of **P.**; 6557
Ne 11:6 sons of **P.** that dwelt at Jerusalem...... 6557

PEREZ-UZZA (pe″-rez-uz′-zah) See also PEREZ-UZZAH.
1Ch 13:11 that place is called **P.** to this day. 6560

PEREZ-UZZAH (pe″-rez-uz′-zah) See also PEREZ-UZZA.
2Sa 6:8 name of the place **P.** to this day. 6560

PERFECT See also PERFECTED; PERFECTING; UNPERFECT.
Ge 6:9 Noah was a just man and **p.** in his...... 8549
Ge 17:1 walk before me, and be thou **p.** 8549
Le 22:21 sheep, it shall be **p.** to be accepted; ... 8549
De 18:13 shalt be **p.** with the Lord thy God. 8549
De 25:15 shalt have a **p.** and just weight, ... 8003
De 25:15 a **p.** and just measure shalt thou 8003
De 32:4 He is the Rock, his work is **p.**:........... 8549
1Sa 14:41 Lord God of Israel, Give a **p.** lot......... 8549
2Sa 22:31 As for God, his way is **p.**; the word ... 8549
2Sa 22:33 power: and he maketh my way **p.**. 8549
1Ki 8:61 Let your heart therefore be **p.**........... 8003
1Ki 11:4 his heart was not **p.** with the Lord..... 8003
1Ki 15:3 his heart was not **p.** with the Lord..... 8003
1Ki 15:14 nevertheless Asa's heart was **p.**.......... 8003
2Ki 20:3 thee in truth and with a **p.** heart, ... 8003
1Ch 12:38 came with a **p.** heart to Hebron, ... 8003
1Ch 28:9 serve him with a **p.** heart and with..... 8003
1Ch 29:9 with **p.** heart they offered willingly...... 8003
1Ch 29:19 unto Solomon my son a **p.** heart, ... 8003
2Ch 4:21 made he of gold, and that **p.** gold;...... 4357
2Ch 15:17 heart of Asa was **p.** all his days. 8003
2Ch 16:9 them whose heart is **p.** toward him...... 8003
2Ch 19:9 faithfully, and with a **p.** heart............ 8003
2Ch 25:2 of the Lord, but not with a **p.** heart.... 8003
Ezr 7:12 unto Ezra the priest,...**p.** peace, ... 1585
Job 1:1 and that man was **p.** and upright, ... 8535
Job 1:8 a **p.** and an upright man, one that....... 8535
Job 2:3 a **p.** and an upright man, one that....... 8535
Job 8:20 God will not cast away a **p.** man, ... 8535
Job 9:20 if I say, I am **p.**, it shall also prove...... 8535
Job 9:21 Though I were **p.**, yet would I not 8535
Job 9:22 destroyeth the **p.** and the wicked....... 8535
Job 22:3 that thou makest thy ways **p.**?.......... 8552
Job 36:4 he that is **p.** in knowledge is with....... 8549
Job 37:16 of him which is **p.** in knowledge?......... 8549
Ps 18:30 As for God, his way is **p.**: the.......... 8549
Ps 18:32 strength, and maketh my way **p.**......... 8549
Ps 19:7 law of the Lord is **p.**, converting........ 8549
Ps 37:37 Mark the **p.** man, and behold the 8535
Ps 64:4 they may shoot in secret at the **p.**:....... 8535
Ps 101:2 behave myself wisely in a **p.** way. 8549
Ps 101:2 within my house with a **p.** heart......... 8537
Ps 101:6 he that walketh in a **p.** way, he 8549
Ps 138:8 will **p.** that which concerneth me: 1584
Ps 139:22 I hate them with **p.** hatred: I............ 8503
Pr 2:21 land, and the **p.** shall remain in it. 8549
Pr 4:18 more and more unto the **p.** day. 3559
Pr 11:5 righteousness of the **p.** shall direct 8549
Isa 18:5 when the bud is **p.**, and the sour 8552
Isa 26:3 Thou wilt keep him in **p.** peace, whose......
Isa 38:3 thee in truth and with a **p.** heart, ... 8003
Isa 42:19 who is blind as he that is **p.**, and 7999
Eze 16:14 it was **p.** through my comeliness, ... 3632
Eze 27:3 thou hast said, I am of **p.** beauty,........ 3632
Eze 27:11 they have made thy beauty **p.**. 3634
Eze 28:12 full of wisdom, and **p.** in beauty.......... 3632
Eze 28:15 Thou wast **p.** in thy ways from the..... 8549
Mt 5:48 **Be ye therefore p., even as your**.... *5046*
Mt 5:48 **Father which is in heaven is p.**..... *5046*
Mt 19:21 **If thou wilt be p., go and sell that** .*5046*
Lu 1:3 having had **p.** understanding of all *199*
Lu 6:40 **that is p. shall be as his master.** ... *2675*
Joh 17:23 **that they may be made p. in one;**.. *5048*
Ac 3:16 hath given him this **p.** soundness........ *3647*
Ac 22:3 **p.** manner of the law of the fathers, ... *195*
Ac 24:22 more **p.** knowledge of that way, ... *197*
Ro 12:2 and acceptable, and **p.**, will of God...... *5046*
1Co 2:6 wisdom among them that are **p.**:.......... *5046*
1Co 13:10 But when that which is **p.** is come,..... *5046*
2Co 12:9 **strength is made p. in weakness**.... *5048*
2Co 13:11 Be **p.**, be of good comfort, be of....... *2675*
Ga 3:3 are ye now made **p.** by the flesh? *2005*
Eph 4:13 unto a **p.** man, unto the measure *5046*
Php 3:12 attained, either were already **p.**: *5048*
Php 3:15 Let us therefore, as many as be **p.**,..... *5046*
Col 1:28 every man **p.** in Christ Jesus: *5046*
Col 4:12 that ye may stand **p.** and complete *5046*
1Th 3:10 might **p.** that which is lacking *2675*
2Ti 3:17 That the man of God may be **p.**, ... *739*
Heb 2:10 the captain of their salvation **p.**.......... *5048*
Heb 5:9 And being made **p.**, he became the..... *5048*
Heb 7:19 For the law made nothing **p.**, but....... *5048*
Heb 9:9 make him that did the service **p.**,....... *5048*
Heb 9:11 a greater and more **p.** tabernacle,....... *5046*
Heb 10:1 make the comers thereunto **p.**............ *5048*
Heb 11:40 without us should not be made **p.**....... *5048*
Heb 12:23 to the spirits of just men made **p.**. *5048*
Heb 13:21 Make you **p.** in every good work *2675*
Jas 1:4 But let patience have her **p.** work, ... *5046*
Jas 1:4 be **p.** and entire, wanting nothing. *5046*
Jas 1:17 and every **p.** gift is from above, ... *5046*
Jas 1:25 looketh into the **p.** law of liberty. *5046*
Jas 2:22 and by works was faith made **p.**? *5048*
Jas 3:2 not in word, the same is a **p.** man,..... *5046*
1Pe 5:10 suffered a while, make you **p.**,........... *2675*
1Jo 4:17 Herein is our love made **p.**, that *5048*
1Jo 4:18 but **p.** love casteth out fear:.............. *5046*
1Jo 4:18 that feareth is not made **p.** in love...... *5048*
Re 3:2 **have not found thy works p.** *4137*

PERFECTED
2Ch 8:16 So the house of the Lord was **p.**........ 8003
2Ch 24:13 and the work was **p.** by them, ... 5927,724
Eze 27:4 thy builders have **p.** thy beauty.......... 3634
Mt 21:16 **and sucklings thou hast p. praise?**..*2675*
Lu 13:32 **and the third day I shall be p.**..... *5048*
Heb 10:14 by one offering he hath **p.** for ever..... *5048*
1Jo 2:5 in him verily is the love of God **p.**:..... *5048*
1Jo 4:12 in us, and his love is **p.** in us. *5048*

PERFECTING
2Co 7:1 **p.** holiness in the fear of God. *2005*
Eph 4:12 For the **p.** of the saints, for the......... *2677*

PERFECTION See also PERFECTNESS.
Job 11:7 find out the Almighty unto **p.**? 8503
Job 15:29 shall he prolong the **p.** thereof.......... 4512
Job 28:3 darkness, and searcheth out all **p.**: 8503
Ps 50:2 Out of Zion, the **p.** of beauty,............ 4359
Ps 119:96 I have seen an end of all **p.**:............. 8502
Isa 47:9 shall come upon thee in their **p.**......... 8537
La 2:15 The **p.** of beauty, The joy of the......... 3632
Lu 8:14 **this life, and bring no fruit to p.**... *5052*
2Co 13:9 this also we wish, even your **p.**. *2676*
Heb 6:1 of Christ, let us go on unto **p.**; *5051*
Heb 7:11 **p.** were by the Levitical priesthood,.... *5050*

PERFECTLY
Jer 23:20 latter days ye shall consider it **p.**......... 998
Mt 14:36 as touched were made **p.** whole.......... *1295*
Ac 18:26 unto him the way of God more **p.**........ *197*
Ac 23:15 would enquire something more **p.** *197*
Ac 23:20 enquire somewhat of him more **p.**.......... *197*
1Co 1:10 but that ye be **p.** joined together........ *2675*
1Th 5:2 know **p.** that the day of the Lord......... *199*

PERFECTNESS See also PERFECTION.
Col 3:14 on charity, which is the bond of **p.**. *5047*

PERFORM See also PERFORMED; PERFORMETH; PERFORMING.
Ge 26:3 I will **p.** the oath which I sware 6965
Ex 18:18 art not able to **p.** it thyself alone........ 6213
Nu 4:23 all that enter in to **p.** the service,........ 6633
De 4:13 which he commanded you to **p.**,.......... 6213
De 9:5 may **p.** the word which the Lord.......... 6965
De 23:23 of thy lips thou shalt keep and **p.**; 6213
De 25:5 **p.** the duty of an husband's brother ....
De 25:7 **p.** the duty of my husband's brother. ....
Ru 3:13 **p.** unto thee the part of a kinsman,...........
1Sa 3:12 day I will **p.** against Eli all things........ 6965
2Sa 14:15 **p.** the request of his handmaid........... 6213
1Ki 6:12 then will I **p.** my word with thee,........ 6965
1Ki 12:15 Lord, that he might **p.** his saying, ... 6965
2Ki 23:3 to **p.** the words of this covenant 6965
2Ki 23:24 he might **p.** the words of the law, ... 6965
2Ch 10:15 that the Lord might **p.** his word,......... 6965
2Ch 34:31 to **p.** the words of the covenant.......... 6213
Es 5:8 my petition, and to **p.** my request, ... 6213
Job 5:12 their hands cannot **p.** their enterprise........
Ps 21:11 device, which they are not able to **p.**. ......
Ps 61:8 ever, that I may daily **p.** my vows....... 7999
Ps 119:106 I have sworn, and I will **p.** it,........... 6965
Ps 119:112 heart to **p.** thy statutes alway,.......... 6213
Isa 9:7 zeal of the Lord of hosts will **p.** this. .. 6213
Isa 19:21 vow a vow unto the Lord, and **p.** it. ... 7999
Isa 44:28 and shall **p.** all my pleasure: 7999
Jer 1:12 for I will hasten my word to **p.** it. 6213
Jer 11:5 **p.** the oath which I have sworn.......... 6965
Jer 28:6 Lord **p.** thy words which thou hast 6965
Jer 29:10 and **p.** my good word toward you, ... 6965
Jer 33:14 will **p.** that good thing which I have 6965
Jer 44:25 We will surely **p.** our vows that 6213
Jer 44:25 your vows, and surely **p.** your vows. .. 6213
Eze 12:25 will I say the word, and will **p.** it, ... 6213
Mic 7:20 Thou wilt **p.** the truth to Jacob, ... 5414
Na 1:15 thy solemn feasts, **p.** thy vows: 7999
Mt 5:33 **shalt p. unto the Lord thine oaths:** ..*591*
Lu 1:72 **p.** the mercy promised to our............. *4160*
Ro 4:21 promised, he was able also to **p.**......... *4160*
Ro 7:18 how to **p.** that which is good I find..... *2716*
2Co 8:11 Now therefore **p.** the doing of it; *2005*
Php 1:6 will **p.** it until the day of Jesus........... *2005*

PERFORMANCE
Lu 1:45 there shall be a **p.** of those things *5050*
2Co 8:11 so there may be a **p.** also out of *2005*

PERFORMED
1Sa 15:11 hath not **p.** my commandments. 6965
1Sa 15:13 **p.** the commandment of the Lord. 6965
2Sa 21:14 **p.** all that the king commanded. 6213
1Ki 8:20 And the Lord hath **p.** his word 6965
2Ch 6:10 The Lord therefore hath **p.** his word... 6965
Ne 9:8 and hast **p.** thy words; for thou art...... 6965
Es 1:15 she hath not **p.** the commandment....... 6213
Es 5:6 half of the kingdom it shall be **p.**. 6213
Es 7:2 and it shall be **p.**, even to the half....... 6213
Ps 65:1 and unto thee shall the vow be **p.**. 7999
Isa 10:12 the Lord hath **p.** his whole work......... 1214
Jer 23:20 have **p.** the thoughts of his heart:....... 6965
Jer 30:24 he have **p.** the intents of his heart:...... 6965
Jer 34:18 not **p.** the words of the covenant 6965
Jer 35:14 The words of Jonadab...are **p.**; 6965
Jer 35:16 **p.** the commandment of their father, ... 6965
Jer 51:29 purpose of the Lord shall be **p.**.......... 6965
Eze 37:14 the Lord have spoken it, and **p.** it, ... 6213
Lu 1:20 day that these things shall be **p.**,......... *1096*
Lu 2:39 **p.** all things according to the law........ *5055*
Ro 15:28 When therefore I have **p.** this,........... *2005*

PERFORMETH
Ne 5:13 that **p.** not this promise, even thus..... 6965
Job 23:14 **p.** the thing that is appointed for........ 7999
Ps 57:2 unto God that **p.** all things for me. 1584
Isa 44:26 **p.** the counsel of his messengers;........ 7999

PERFORMING
Nu 15:3 offering, or a sacrifice in **p.** a vow, ... 6381
Nu 15:8 or for a sacrifice in **p.** a vow, ... 6381

PERFUME See also PERFUMED; PERFUMES.
Ex 30:35 And thou shalt make it a **p.**, a 7004
Ex 30:37 for the **p.** which thou shalt make, ... 7004
Pr 27:9 Ointment and **p.** rejoice the heart: 7004

PERFUMED
Pr 7:17 have **p.** my bed with myrrh, aloes, ... 5130
Ca 3:6 **p.** with myrrh and frankincense,......... 6999

PERFUMES
Isa 57:9 and didst increase thy **p.**, and........... 7547

PERGA (pur′-gah)
Ac 13:13 they came to **P.** in Pamphylia: *4011*
Ac 13:14 when they departed from **P.**, they...... *4011*
Ac 14:25 they had preached the word in **P.**, ... *4011*

PERGAMOS (pur′-ga-mos)
Re 1:11 **and unto P., and unto Thyatira,**.... *4010*
Re 2:12 **angel of the church in P. write;**.... *4010*

PERHAPS
Ac 8:22 if **p.** the thought of thine heart may...... *686*
2Co 2:7 lest **p.** such...should be swallowed...... *3381*
Phm 15 For **p.** he...departed for a season, ... *5029*

PERIDA (per-i′-dah) See also PERUDA.
Ne 7:57 of Sophereth, the children of **P.**, ... 6514

PERIL See also PERILS.
La 5:9 got our bread with the **p.** of our lives,.......
Ro 8:35 or nakedness, or **p.**, or sword? *2794*

PERILOUS
2Ti 3:1 the last days **p.** times shall come........ *5467*

PERILS
2Co 11:26 in **p.** of waters, in **p.** of robbers......... *2794*
2Co 11:26 in **p.** by mine own countrymen,.......... *2794*

2Co 11:26 by the heathen, in **p.** in the city,........ *2794*
2Co 11:26 in the city, in **p.** in the wilderness,..... *2794*
2Co 11:26 in the wilderness, in **p.** in the sea,..... *2794*
2Co 11:26 the sea, in **p.** among false brethren;.... *2794*

PERISH See also PERISHED; PERISHETH; PERISHING.
Ge 41:36 land **p.** not through the famine........... 3772
Ex 19:21 Lord to gaze, and many of them **p.**...... 5307
Ex 21:26 or the eye of his maid, that it **p.**;....... 7843
Le 26:38 And ye shall **p.** among the heathen,........ 6
Nu 17:12 Behold, we die, we **p.**, we all **p.**.......... 6
Nu 24:20 latter end shall be that he **p.** for ever...... 8
Nu 24:24 Eber, and he also shall **p.** for ever.......... 8
De 4:26 shall soon utterly **p.** from off the land...... 6
De 8:19 you, this day that ye shall surely **p.**......... 6
De 8:20 so shall ye **p.**; because ye would not....... 6
De 11:17 ye **p.** quickly from off the good land........ 6
De 26:5 A Syrian ready to **p.** was my father,........ 6
De 28:20 destroyed, and until thou **p.** quickly;........ 6
De 28:22 they shall pursue thee until thou **p.**......... 6
De 30:18 you this day, that ye shall surely **p.**,........ 6
Jos 23:13 until ye **p.** from off this good land........... 6
Jos 23:16 shall **p.** quickly from off the good........... 6
Jg 5:31 So let all thine enemies **p.**, O Lord:........ 6
1Sa 26:10 shall descend into battle, and **p.**......... 5595
1Sa 27:1 **p.** one day by the hand of Saul:.......... 5595
2Ki 9:8 For the whole house of Ahab shall **p.**:...... 6
Es 3:13 to kill, and to cause to **p.**, all Jews,........ 6
Es 4:16 according to the law: and if I **p.**, I **p.**........ 6
Es 7:4 to be destroyed, to be slain, and to **p.**,..... 6
Es 8:11 to destroy, to slay, and to cause to **p.**,..... 6
Es 9:28 nor the memorial of them **p.** from....... 5486
Job 3:3 Let the day **p.** wherein I was born,.......... 6
Job 4:9 By the blast of God they **p.**, and by........ 6
Job 4:20 **p.** for ever without any regarding it......... 6
Job 6:18 aside; they go to nothing, and **p.**........... 6
Job 8:13 and the hypocrite's hope shall **p.**:........... 6
Job 18:17 His remembrance shall **p.** from the.......... 6
Job 20:7 he shall **p.** for ever like his own dung...... 6
Job 29:13 blessing of him that was ready to **p.**........ 6
Job 31:19 have seen any **p.** for want of clothing...... 6
Job 34:15 All flesh shall **p.** together, and man..... 1478
Job 36:12 they shall **p.** by the sword, and.......... 5674
Ps 1:6 but the way of the ungodly shall **p.**......... 6
Ps 2:12 lest he be angry, and ye **p.** from the....... 6
Ps 9:3 they shall fall and **p.** at thy presence....... 6
Ps 9:18 expectation of the poor shall not **p.**......... 6
Ps 37:20 the wicked shall **p.**, and the enemies....... 6
Ps 41:5 When shall he die, and his name **p.**?........ 6
Ps 49:10 the fool and the brutish person **p.**,.......... 6
Ps 49:12 not: he is like the beasts that **p.**........ 1820
Ps 49:20 not, is like the beasts that **p.**........... 1820
Ps 68:2 let the wicked **p.** at...presence of God..... 6
Ps 73:27 they that are far from thee shall **p.**:........ 6
Ps 80:16 **p.** at the rebuke of thy countenance......... 6
Ps 83:17 let them be put to shame and **p.**:........... 6
Ps 92:9 Lord, for, lo, thine enemies shall **p.**;........ 6
Ps 102:26 They shall **p.**, but thou shalt endure:....... 6
Ps 112:10 the desire of the wicked shall **p.**............ 6
Ps 146:4 in that very day his thoughts **p.**............. 6
Pr 10:28 expectation of the wicked shall **p.**.......... 6
Pr 11:7 man dieth, his expectation shall **p.**:.......... 6
Pr 11:10 the wicked **p.**, there is shouting............ 6
Pr 19:9 and he that speaketh lies shall **p.**............ 6
Pr 21:28 A false witness shall **p.**: but the man....... 6
Pr 28:28 when they **p.**, the righteous increase........ 6
Pr 29:18 there is no vision, the people **p.**:........ 6544
Pr 31:6 drink unto him that is ready to **p.**,.......... 6
Ec 5:14 But those riches **p.** by evil travail:.......... 6
Isa 26:14 and made all their memory to **p.**............ 6
Isa 27:13 ready to **p.** in the land of Assyria,.......... 6
Isa 29:14 wisdom of their wise men shall **p.**,.......... 6
Isa 41:11 they that strive with thee shall **p.**.......... 6
Isa 60:12 that will not serve thee shall **p.**;............ 6
Jer 4:9 that the heart of the king shall **p.**,........... 6
Jer 6:21 neighbour and his friend shall **p.**............ 6
Jer 10:11 they shall **p.** from the earth, and............ 7
Jer 10:15 time of their visitation they shall **p.**......... 6
Jer 18:18 the law shall not **p.** from the priest,........ 6
Jer 27:10 drive you out, and ye should **p.**............. 6
Jer 27:15 drive you out, and that ye might **p.**,........ 6
Jer 40:15 and the remnant in Judah **p.**?................ 6
Jer 48:8 the valley also shall **p.**, and the plain....... 6
Jer 51:18 time of their visitation they shall **p.**........ 6
Eze 7:26 but the law shall **p.** from the priest,........ 6
Eze 25:7 cause thee to **p.** out of the countries:....... 6
Da 2:18 Daniel and his fellows should not **p.**......... 7
Am 1:8 the remnant of the Philistines shall **p.**,..... 6
Am 2:14 the flight shall **p.** from the swift,............ 6
Am 3:15 the houses of ivory shall **p.**, and the........ 6
Jon 1:6 will think upon us, that we **p.** not........... 6
Jon 1:14 let us not **p.** for this man's life, and......... 6
Jon 3:9 from his fierce anger, that we **p.** not?...... 6
Zec 9:5 and the king shall **p.** from Gaza,............ 6
Mt 5:29, 30 **one of thy members should p.**,.... *622*
Mt 8:25 him, saying, Lord, save us: we **p.**......... *622*
Mt 9:17 **runneth out, and the bottles p.**:...... *622*
Mt 18:14 **one of these little ones should p.**..... *622*
Mt 26:52 **the sword shall p. with the sword**.. *622*
Mk 4:38 Master, carest thou not that we **p.**?..... *622*
Lu 5:37 **be spilled, and the bottles shall p.**.... *622*
Lu 8:24 saying, Master, master, we **p.**........... *622*
Lu 13:3, 5 **repent, ye shall all likewise p.**..... *622*
Lu 13:33 **that a prophet p. out of Jerusalem**.. *622*
Lu 15:17 **and to spare, and I p. with hunger!**. *622*
Lu 21:18 **shall not an hair of your head p.**.... *622*
Joh 3:15 **believeth in him should not p.**,....... *622*
Joh 3:16 **believeth in him should not p.**,....... *622*
Joh 10:28 **and they shall never p., neither**...... *622*
Joh 11:50 and that the whole nation **p.** not.......... *622*
Ac 8:20 Thy money **p.** with thee,..... *1510,1519,684*
Ac 13:41 ye despisers, and wonder, and **p.**:....... *853*
Ro 2:12 law shall also **p.** without law:............. *622*
1Co 1:18 cross is to them that **p.** foolishness;..... *622*
1Co 8:11 shall the weak brother **p.**, for whom..... *622*
2Co 2:15 that are saved, and in them that **p.**:..... *622*
2Co 4:16 but though our outward man **p.**,......... *1311*
Col 2:22 Which all are to **p.** with the using;)..... *5356*
2Th 2:10 unrighteousness in them that **p.**;.......... *622*
Heb 1:11 They shall **p.**; but thou remainest;....... *622*
2Pe 2:12 utterly **p.** in their own corruption;...... *2704*
2Pe 3:9 not willing that any should **p.**, but........ *622*

PERISHED
Nu 16:33 **p.** from among the congregation............ 6
Nu 21:30 Heshbon is **p.** even unto Dibon,............. 6
Jos 22:20 man **p.** not alone in his iniquity.......... 1478
2Sa 1:27 fallen, and the weapons of war **p.**!.......... 6
Job 4:7 thee, who ever **p.**, being innocent?.......... 6
Job 30:2 profit me, in whom old age was **p.**?......... 6
Ps 9:6 their memorial is **p.** with them.............. 6
Ps 10:16 the heathen are **p.** out of his land........... 6
Ps 83:10 Which **p.** at En-dor: they became....... 8045
Ps 119:92 should then have **p.** in mine affliction....... 6
Ec 9:6 hatred, and their envy, is now **p.**;........... 6
Jer 7:28 truth is **p.**, and is cut off from their......... 6
Jer 48:36 riches that he hath gotten are **p.**........... 6
Jer 49:7 is counsel **p.** from the prudent?.............. 6
La 3:18 and my hope is **p.** from the Lord:............ 6
Joe 1:11 because the harvest of the field is **p.**....... 6
Jon 4:10 up in a night, and **p.** in a night:............ 6
Mic 4:9 no king in thee? is thy counsellor **p.**?...... 6
Mic 7:2 The good man is **p.** out of the earth:........ 6
Mt 8:32 into the sea, and **p.** in the waters......... *599*
Lu 11:51 **p. between the altar and the temple**: *622*
Ac 5:37 he also **p.**; and all, even as many......... *622*
1Co 15:18 are fallen asleep in Christ are **p.**......... *622*
Heb 11:31 By faith the harlot Rahab **p.** not........ *4881*
2Pe 3:6 being overflowed with water, **p.**:......... *622*
Jude 11 and **p.** in the gainsaying of Core.......... *622*

PERISHETH
Job 4:11 The old lion **p.** for lack of prey, and........ 6
Pr 11:7 and the hope of unjust men **p.**................ 6
Ec 7:15 just man that **p.** in his righteousness,....... 6
Isa 57:1 righteous **p.**, and no man layeth............. 6
Jer 9:12 for what the land **p.** and is burned up...... 6
Jer 48:46 the people of Chemosh **p.**: for thy.......... 6
Joh 6:27 **Labour not for the meat which p.**,.. *622*
Jas 1:11 and the grace of the fashion of it **p.**:..... *622*
1Pe 1:7 more precious than of gold that **p.**,...... *622*

PERISHING
Job 33:18 and his life from **p.** by the sword...... 5674

PERIZZITE (per'-iz-zite) See also PERIZZITES.
Ge 13:7 the **P.** dwelled then in the land,......... 6522
Ex 33:2 and the Hittite, and the **P.**,............. 6522
Ex 34:11 and the Hittite, and the **P.**,............. 6522
Jos 9:1 Amorite, the Canaanite, the **P.**,......... 6522
Jos 11:3 **P.**, and...Jebusite in the mountains,.... 6522

PERIZZITES (per'-iz-zites)
Ge 15:20 Hittites, and the **P.**, and the............ 6522
Ge 34:30 among the Canaanites and the **P.**:...... 6522
Ex 3:8 the **P.**, and the Hivites, and the......... 6522
Ex 3:17 the **P.**, and the Hivites, and the......... 6522
Ex 23:23 and the Hittites, and the **P.**, and........ 6522
De 7:1 the **P.**, and the Hivites, and the........... 6522
De 20:17 and the **P.**, the Hivites, and the.......... 6522
Jos 3:10 and the **P.**, and the Girgashites,......... 6522
Jos 12:8 the **P.**, the Hivites, and the.............. 6522
Jos 17:15 in the land of the **P.** and of the.......... 6522
Jos 24:11 the Amorites, and the **P.**, and the...... 6522
Jg 1:4 Canaanites and the **P.** into their.......... 6522
Jg 1:5 slew the Canaanites and the **P.**.......... 6522
Jg 3:5 Hittites, and Amorites, and **P.**,........... 6522
1Ki 9:20 **P.**, Hivites, and Jebusites, which........ 6522
2Ch 8:7 the **P.**, and the Hivites, and the.......... 6522
Ezr 9:1 the Canaanites, the Hittites, the **P.**,... 6522
Ne 9:8 Hittites, the Amorites, and the **P.**,..... 6522

PERJURED
1Ti 1:10 for liars, for **p.** persons, and if.......... *1965*

PERMISSION
1Co 7:6 But I speak this by **p.**, and not of...... *4774*

PERMIT See also PERMITTED.
1Co 16:7 a while with you, if the Lord **p.**......... *2010*
Heb 6:3 And this will we do, if God **p.**............ *2010*

PERMITTED
Ac 26:1 Thou art **p.** to speak for thyself......... *2010*
1Co 14:34 it is not **p.** unto them to speak;.......... *2010*

PERNICIOUS
2Pe 2:2 many shall follow their **p.** ways;........... *684*

PERPETUAL
Ge 9:12 is with you, for **p.** generations:.......... 5769
Ex 29:9 shall be theirs for a **p.** statute:.......... 5769
Ex 30:8 a **p.** incense before the Lord............. 8548
Ex 31:16 generations, for a **p.** covenant........... 5769
Le 3:17 a **p.** statute for your generations........ 5769
Le 6:20 fine flour for a meat offering **p.**,......... 8548
Le 24:9 Lord made by fire by a **p.** statute....... 5769
Le 25:34 sold; for it is their **p.** possession........ 5769
Nu 19:21 it shall be a **p.** statute unto them,....... 5769
Ps 9:6 destructions are come to a **p.** end:..... 5331
Ps 74:3 thy feet unto the **p.** desolations;........ 5331
Ps 78:66 he put them to a **p.** reproach............ 5769
Jer 5:22 bound of the sea by a **p.** decree,........ 5769
Jer 8:5 slidden back by a **p.** backsliding?........ 5331
Jer 15:18 Why is my pain **p.**, and my wound...... 5331
Jer 18:16 land desolate, and a **p.** hissing;......... 5769
Jer 23:40 and a **p.** shame, which shall not......... 5769
Jer 25:9 and an hissing, and **p.** desolations....... 5769
Jer 25:12 and will make it **p.** desolations........... 5769
Jer 49:13 the cities thereof shall be **p.** wastes.... 5769
Jer 50:5 to the Lord in a **p.** covenant that....... 5769
Jer 51:39 and sleep a **p.** sleep, and not wake,.... 5769
Jer 51:57 shall sleep a **p.** sleep, and not wake,... 5769
Eze 35:5 Because thou hast had a **p.** hatred,..... 5769
Eze 35:9 will make thee **p.** desolations, and...... 5769
Eze 46:14 by a **p.** ordinance unto the Lord.......... 5769
Hab 3:6 scattered, the **p.** hills did bow:.......... 5769
Zep 2:9 and saltpits, and a **p.** desolation:........ 5769

PERPETUALLY
1Ki 9:3 mine heart shall be there **p.**....... 3605,3117
2Ch 7:16 mine heart shall be there **p.**....... 3605,3117
Am 1:11 all pity, and his anger did tear **p.**,........ 5703

PERPLEXED
Es 3:15 drink; but the city Shushan was **p.**....... 943
Joe 1:18 the herds of cattle are **p.**, because....... 943
Lu 9:7 And he was **p.**, because that it was.... *1280*
Lu 24:4 as they were much **p.** thereabout,...... *1280*
2Co 4:8 we are **p.**, but not in despair;............. *639*

PERPLEXITY
Isa 22:5 and of **p.** by the Lord God of hosts.... 3998
Mic 7:4 cometh; now shall be their **p.**............ 3998
Lu 21:25 **earth distress of nations, with p.**;... *640*

PERSECUTE See also PERSECUTED; PERSECUTEST; PERSECUTING.
Job 19:22 Why do ye **p.** me as God, and are...... 7291
Job 19:28 Why **p.** we him, seeing the root of..... 7291
Ps 7:1 save me from all them that **p.** me,..... 7291
Ps 7:5 Let the enemy **p.** my soul, and.......... 7291
Ps 10:2 in his pride doth **p.** the poor:............ 1814
Ps 31:15 enemies,...from them that **p.** me......... 7291
Ps 35:3 the way against them that **p.** me:....... 7291
Ps 35:6 let the angel of the Lord **p.** them........ 7291
Ps 69:26 they **p.** him who thou hast smitten;.... 7291

Ps 71:11 forsaken him: p. and take him; 7291
Ps 83:15 So p. them with thy tempest, and 7291
Ps 119:84 judgment on them that p. me? 7291
Ps 119:86 they p. me wrongfully; help thou 7291
Jer 17:18 them be confounded that p. me, 7291
Jer 29:18 I will p. them with the sword, 7291,310
La 3:66 P. and destroy them in anger 7291
Mt 5:11 **men shall revile you, and p. you.** *1377*
Mt 5:44 **despitefully use you, and p. you;** *1377*
Mt 10:23 **when they p. you in this city, flee.** *1377*
Mt 23:34 **and p. them from city to city:** *1377*
Lu 11:49 **of them they shall slay and p.:** *1559*
Lu 21:12 **their hands on you, and p. you,** *1377*
Joh 5:16 therefore did the Jews p. Jesus, *1377*
Joh 15:20 **me, they will also p. you;** *1377*
Ro 12:14 Bless them which p. you: bless, and *1377*

PERSECUTED
De 30:7 that hate thee, which p. thee. 7291
Ps 109:16 but p. the poor and needy man, 7291
Ps 119:161 have p. me without a cause: but 7291
Ps 143:3 For the enemy hath p. my soul; he 7291
Isa 14:6 ruled the nations in anger, is p., 4783
La 3:43 covered with anger, and p. us: 7291
Mt 5:10 **are p. for righteousness' sake:** *1377*
Mt 5:12 **so p. they the prophets which were** *1377*
Joh 15:20 **If they have p. me, they will also** *1377*
Ac 7:52 prophets have not your fathers p.? *1377*
Ac 22:4 And I p. this way unto the death, *1377*
Ac 26:11 I p. them even unto strange cities. *1377*
1Co 4:12 we bless; being p., we suffer it: *1377*
1Co 15:9 because I p. the church of God. *1377*
2Co 4:9 P., but not forsaken; cast down, *1377*
Ga 1:13 measure I p. the church of God, *1377*
Ga 1:23 he which p. us in times past now *1377*
Ga 4:29 p. him that was born after the *1377*
1Th 2:15 own prophets, and have p. us; *1559*
Re 12:13 p. the woman which brought forth *1377*

PERSECUTEST
Ac 9:4 him, **Saul, Saul, why p. thou me?** *1377*
Ac 9:5 said, **I am Jesus whom thou p.:** *1377*
Ac 22:7 me, **Saul, Saul, why p. thou me?** *1377*
Ac 22:8 **Jesus of Nazareth, whom thou p.** *1377*
Ac 26:14 **Saul, Saul, why p. thou me? it is** *1377*
Ac 26:15 he said, **I am Jesus whom thou p.** *1377*

PERSECUTING
Php 3:6 Concerning zeal, p. the church; *1377*

PERSECUTION See also PERSECUTIONS.
La 5:5 Our necks are under p.: we 7291
Mt 13:21 **or p. ariseth because of the word,** *1375*
Mk 4:17 **or p. ariseth for the word's sake,** *1375*
Ac 8:1 was a great p. against the church *1375*
Ac 11:19 the p. that arose about Stephen *2347*
Ac 13:50 and raised p. against Paul and *1375*
Ro 8:35 shall tribulation, or distress, or p., *1375*
Ga 5:11 circumcision, why do I...suffer p.? *1377*
Ga 6:12 suffer p. for the cross of Christ. *1377*
2Ti 3:12 godly in Christ Jesus shall suffer p. *1377*

PERSECUTIONS
Mk 10:30 **and children, and lands, with p.;** *1375*
2Co 12:10 p., in distresses for Christ's sake: *1375*
2Th 1:4 faith in all your p. and tribulations *1375*
2Ti 3:11 P., afflictions, which came unto me *1375*
2Ti 3:11 at Lystra; what p. I endured: *1375*

PERSECUTOR See also PERSECUTORS.
1Ti 1:13 before a blasphemer, and a p., *1376*

PERSECUTORS
Ne 9:11 p. thou threwest into the deeps, 7291
Ps 7:13 his arrows against the p. 1814
Ps 119:157 are my p. and mine enemies; 7291
Ps 142:6 very low: deliver me from my p.; 7291
Jer 15:15 me, and revenge me of my p.; 7291
Jer 20:11 therefore my p. shall stumble, and 7291
La 1:3 all her p. overtook her between 7291
La 4:19 Our p. are swifter than the eagles 7291

PERSEVERANCE
Eph 6:18 with all p. and supplication for *4343*

PERSIA (per'-she-ah) See also ELAM; PERSIAN.
2Ch 36:20 the reign of the kingdom of P.: 6539
2Ch 36:22 the first year of Cyrus king of P., 6539
2Ch 36:22 up the spirit of Cyrus king of P., 6539
2Ch 36:23 Thus saith Cyrus king of P., All the 6539
Ezr 1:1 the first year of Cyrus king of P., 6539
Ezr 1:1 up the spirit of Cyrus king of P., 6539
Ezr 1:2 saith Cyrus king of P., The Lord 6539
Ezr 1:8 did Cyrus king of P. bring forth 6539
Ezr 3:7 that they had of Cyrus king of P. 6539
Ezr 4:3 the king of P. hath commanded us 6539
Ezr 4:5 all the days of Cyrus king of P., 6539
Ezr 4:5 the reign of Darius king of P. 6539
Ezr 4:7 wrote...unto Artaxerxes king of P.; 6539
Ezr 4:24 of the reign of Darius king of P. 6540
Ezr 6:14 Darius, and Artaxerxes king of P. 6540
Ezr 7:1 the reign of Artaxerxes king of P., 6539
Ezr 9:9 us in the sight of the kings of P., 6539
Es 1:3 the power of P. and Media, the 6539
Es 1:14 the seven princes of P. and Media, 6539
Es 1:18 shall the ladies of P. and Media say 6539
Es 10:2 of the kings of Media and P.? 6539
Eze 27:10 They of P. and of Lud and of Phut 6539
Eze 38:5 P., Ethiopia, and Libya with them; 6539
Da 8:20 are the kings of Media and P. 6539
Da 10:1 the third year of Cyrus king of P. 6539
Da 10:13 But the prince of the kingdom of P. 6539
Da 10:13 remained...with the kings of P. 6539
Da 10:20 to fight with the prince of P.: 6539
Da 11:2 stand up yet three kings in P.; 6539

PERSIAN (pur'-she-un) See also PERSIANS.
Ne 12:22 to the reign of Darius the P. 6542
Da 6:28 and in the reign of Cyrus the P., 6523

PERSIANS (pur'-she-uns) See also ELAMITES.
Es 1:19 the laws of the P. and the Medes, 6539
Da 5:28 and given to the Medes and P. 6540
Da 6:8, 12 to the law of the Medes and P., 6540
Da 6:15 that the law of the Medes and P. is, 6540

PERSIS (pur'-sis)
Ro 16:12 Salute the beloved P., which *4069*

PERSON See also PERSONS.
Ge 39:6 Joseph was a goodly p., and well
Ex 12:48 no uncircumcised p. shall eat thereof.
Le 19:15 not respect the p. of the poor. 6440
Le 19:15 nor honour the p. of the mighty: 6440
Nu 5:6 the Lord, and that p. be guilty; 5315
Nu 19:17 for an unclean p. they shall take of
Nu 19:18 And a clean p. shall take hyssop, 376,120
Nu 19:19 And the clean p. shall sprinkle upon
Nu 19:22 whatsoever the unclean p. toucheth
Nu 31:19 whosoever hath killed any p., and 5315
Nu 35:11 which killeth any p. at unawares. 5315
Nu 35:15 one that killeth any p. unawares 5315
Nu 35:30 Whoso killeth any p., the murderer 5315
Nu 35:30 shall not testify against any p. to 5315
De 15:22 and the clean p. shall eat it alike,
De 27:25 reward to slay an innocent p. 5315
De 28:50 shall not regard the p. of the old, 6440
Jos 20:3 that killeth any p. unawares and 5315
Jos 20:9 that whosoever killeth any p. at 5315
1Sa 9:2 of Israel a goodlier p. than he: 376
1Sa 16:18 prudent in matters, and a comely p., 376
1Sa 25:35 voice, and have accepted thy p. 6440
2Sa 4:11 men have slain a righteous p. in 376
2Sa 14:14 neither doth God respect any p.: 5315
2Sa 17:11 thou go to battle in thine own p. 6440
Job 13:8 Will ye accept his p.? will ye 6440
Job 22:29 up; and he shall save the humble p.
Job 32:21 I pray you, accept any man's p., 6440
Ps 15:4 In whose eyes a vile p. is contemned;
Ps 49:10 the fool and the brutish p. perish,
Ps 101:4 from me: I will not know a wicked p.
Ps 105:37 not one feeble p. among their tribes.
Pr 6:12 A naughty p., a wicked man, 120
Pr 18:5 to accept the p. of the wicked, 6440
Pr 24:8 shall be called a mischievous p. 1167
Pr 28:17 violence to the blood of any p. 5315
Isa 32:5 The vile p. shall be no more called
Isa 32:6 the vile p. will speak villany, and his
Jer 43:6 every p. that Nebuzar-adan the 5315
Jer 52:25 them that were near the king's p., 6440
Eze 16:5 to the lothing of thy p., in the day 5315
Eze 33:6 and take any p. from among them, 5315
Eze 44:25 shall come at no dead p. to defile 120
Da 11:21 in his estate shall stand up a vile p.,
Mal 1:8 or accept thy p.? saith the Lord 6440
Mt 22:16 thou regardest not the p. of men. *4383*
Mt 27:24 innocent of the blood of this just p.:
Mk 12:14 thou regardest not the p. of men, *4383*
Lu 20:21 neither acceptest thou the p. of any, *4383*
1Co 5:13 from among yourselves that wicked p.
2Co 2:10 forgave I it in the p. of Christ; *4383*
Ga 2:6 to me: God accepteth no man's p.:) *4383*
Eph 5:5 nor unclean p., nor covetous man, who
Heb 1:3 and the express image of his p. *5287*
Heb 12:16 any fornicator, or profane p., as Esau,
2Pe 2:5 but saved Noah the eighth p., a

PERSONS
Ge 14:21 said unto Abram, Give me the p., 5315
Ge 36:6 and all the p. of his house, and his 5315
Ex 16:16 according to the number of your p.; 5315
Le 27:2 the p. shall be for the Lord by thy 5315
Nu 19:18 and upon the p. that were there, 5315
Nu 31:28 soul of five hundred, both of the p., 120
Nu 31:30 take one portion of fifty, of the p., of 120
Nu 31:35 and two thousand p. in all, 5315,120
Nu 31:40 the p. were sixteen thousand; 5315,120
Nu 31:40 tribute was thirty and two p. 5315,120
Nu 31:46 And sixteen thousand p.;) 5315,120
De 1:17 shall not respect p. in judgment; 6440
De 10:17 which regardeth not p., nor taketh 6440
De 10:22 Egypt with threescore and ten p.; 5315
De 16:19 thou shalt not respect p., neither 6440
Jg 9:2 which are threescore and ten p., 376
Jg 9:4 Abimelech hired vain and light p., 582
Jg 9:5 being threescore and ten p., upon 376
Jg 9:18 threescore and ten p., upon one 376
Jg 20:39 of the men of Israel about thirty p.: 376
1Sa 9:22 bidden, which were about thirty p. 376
1Sa 22:18 five p. that did wear a linen ephod. 376
1Sa 22:22 of all the p. of thy father's house. 5315
2Ki 10:6 the king's sons, being seventy p., 376
2Ki 10:7 slew seventy p., and put their heads 376
2Ch 19:7 nor respect of p., nor taking of 6440
Job 13:10 you, if ye do secretly accept p. 6440
Job 34:19 that accepteth not the p. of princes, 6440
Ps 26:4 I have not sat with vain p., neither 4962
Ps 82:2 and accept the p. of the wicked? 6440
Pr 12:11 he that followeth vain p. is void of
Pr 24:23 not good to have respect of p. in 6440
Pr 28:19 after vain p. shall have poverty
Pr 28:21 To have respect of p. is not good: 6440
Jer 52:29 eight hundred thirty and two p.: 5315
Jer 52:30 seven hundred forty and five p.: 5315
Jer 52:30 the p. were four thousand and six 5315
La 4:16 respected not the p. of the priests, 6440
Eze 17:17 building forts, to cut off many p.: 5315
Eze 27:13 traded the p. of men and vessels 5315
Jon 4:11 are more than sixscore thousand p. 120
Zep 3:4 are light and treacherous p.: 582
Mal 1:9 means: will he regard your p.? 6440
Lu 15:7 **than over ninety and nine just p.,**
Ac 10:34 that God is no respecter of p.: *4381*
Ac 17:17 with the Jews, and with the devout p.,
Ro 2:11 there is no respect of p. with God. *4382*
2Co 1:11 upon us by the means of many p. *4383*
Eph 6:9 is there respect of p. with him. *4382*
Col 3:25 done: and there is no respect of p. *4382*
1Ti 1:10 for liars, for perjured p., and if *678*
Jas 2:1 Lord of glory, with respect of p. *4382*
Jas 2:9 if ye have respect to p., ye commit *4380*
1Pe 1:17 who without respect of p. judgeth *678*
2Pe 3:11 what manner of p. ought ye to be in
Jude 16 having men's p. in admiration *4383*

PERSUADE See also PERSUADED; PERSUADEST; PERSUADETH; PERSUADING.
1Ki 22:20 Who shall p. Ahab, that he may 6601
1Ki 22:21 the Lord, and said, I will p. him. 6601
1Ki 22:22 Thou shalt p. him, and prevail 6601
2Ch 32:11 Doth not Hezekiah p. you to give 5496
2Ch 32:15 you, nor p. you on this manner, 5496
Isa 36:18 Beware lest Hezekiah p. you, 5496
Mt 28:14 we will p. him, and secure you, *3982*
2Co 5:11 the terror of the Lord, we p. men; *3982*
Ga 1:10 For do I now p. men, or God? or *3982*

PERSUADED
2Ch 18:2 and p. him to go up with him to 5496
Pr 25:15 By long forbearing is a prince p., 6601
Mt 27:20 and elders p. the multitude that *3982*
Lu 16:31 **neither will they be p., though one** *3982*
Lu 20:6 they be p. that John was a prophet. *3982*
Ac 13:43 p. them to continue in the grace of *3982*
Ac 14:19 who p. the people, and, having *3982*
Ac 18:4 and p. the Jews and the Greeks. *3982*
Ac 19:26 p. and turned away much people, *3982*

Ac 21:14 And when he would not be **p.**, we...... *3982*
Ac 26:26 I am **p.** that none of these things....... *3982*
Ro 4:21 And being fully **p.** that, what he......... *4135*
Ro 8:38 For I am **p.**, that neither death,......... *3982*
Ro 14:5 man be fully **p.** in his own mind. *4135*
Ro 14:14 and am **p.** by the Lord Jesus, that...... *3982*
Ro 15:14 also am **p.** of you, my brethren,......... *3982*
2Ti 1:5 and I am **p.** that in thee also. *3982*
2Ti 1:12 and am **p.** that he is able to keep....... *3982*
Heb 6:9 we are **p.** better things of you, and *3982*
Heb 11:13 were **p.** of them, and embraced......... *3982*

PERSUADEST
Ac 26:28 thou **p.** me to be a Christian. *3982*

PERSUADETH
2Ki 18:32 unto Hezekiah, when he **p.** you,......... 5496
Ac 18:13 This fellow **p.** men to worship God *374*

PERSUADING
Ac 19:8 and **p.** the things concerning the *3982*
Ac 28:23 **p.** them concerning Jesus, both out..... *3982*

PERSUASION
Ga 5:8 **p.** cometh not of him that calleth........ *3988*

PERTAIN See also APPERTAIN; PERTAINED; PERTAINETH; PERTAINING; PURTENANCE.
Le 7:20 peace offerings, that **p.** unto the Lord, ...
Le 7:21 offerings, which **p.** unto the Lord. ....
1Sa 25:22 if I leave of all that **p.** to him by the ....
Ro 15:17 in those things which **p.** to God. ....
1Co 6:3 much more things that **p.** to this life? ....
2Pe 1:3 unto us all things that **p.** unto life ....

PERTAINED
Nu 31:43 half that **p.** unto the congregation ....
Jos 24:33 in a hill that **p.** to Phinehas his son, ...
Jg 6:11 that **p.** unto Joash the Abi-ezrite: ....
1Sa 25:21 was missed of all that **p.** unto him: ....
2Sa 2:15 which **p.** to Ish-bosheth the son of............
2Sa 9:9 **p.** to Saul and to all his house........... 1961
2Sa 16:4 are all that **p.** unto Mephibosheth. ....
1Ki 4:10 to him **p.** Sochoh, and all the land of.........
1Ki 4:12 to him **p.** Taanach and Megiddo, and..........
1Ki 4:13 to him **p.** the towns of Jair the son of.........
1Ki 4:13 to him also **p.** the region of Argob,...........
1Ki 7:48 all the vessels that **p.** unto the house........
2Ki 24:7 all that **p.** to the king of Egypt.................
1Ch 9:27 thereof every morning **p.** to them............
1Ch 11:31 that **p.** to the children of Benjamin,..........
2Ch 12:4 the fenced cities which **p.** to Judah, ...
2Ch 34:33 that **p.** to the children of Israel, ...

PERTAINETH
Le 14:32 get that which **p.** to his cleansing. ....
Nu 4:16 the priest **p.** the oil for the light, ...
De 22:5 wear that which **p.** unto a man, ... 3627
1Sa 27:6 Ziklag **p.** unto the kings of Judah......... 1961
2Sa 6:12 Obed-edom, and all that **p.** unto him, ...
Ro 9:4 to whom **p.** the adoption, and the............
Heb 7:13 are spoken **p.** to another tribe, ... *3348*

PERTAINING
Jos 13:31 were **p.** unto the children of Machir..........
1Ch 26:32 every matter **p.** to God, and affairs............
Ac 1:3 things **p.** to the kingdom of God:....... *4012*
Ro 4:1 as **p.** to the flesh, hath found? ....
1Co 6:4 judgments of things **p.** to this life, ...
Heb 2:17 high priest in things **p.** to God, ...
Heb 5:1 ordained for men in things **p.** to God,........
Heb 9:9 perfect, as **p.** to the conscience; ....

PERUDA (per'-u-dah) See also PERIDA.
Ezr 2:55 of Sophereth, the children of **P.**,........ 6514

PERVERSE
Nu 22:32 because thy way is **p.** before me:......... 3399
De 32:5 are a **p.** and crooked generation. 6141
1Sa 20:30 son of the **p.** rebellious woman, ... 5753
Job 6:30 my taste discern **p.** things? 1942
Job 9:20 perfect, it shall also prove me **p.**........ 6140
Pr 4:24 and **p.** lips put far from thee............. 3891
Pr 8:8 is nothing froward or **p.** in them......... 6141
Pr 12:8 is of a **p.** heart shall be despised. 5753
Pr 14:2 is **p.** in his ways despiseth him. 3868
Pr 17:20 a **p.** tongue falleth into mischief.......... 2015
Pr 19:1 he that is **p.** in his lips, and...a fool 6141
Pr 23:33 thine heart shall utter **p.** things. 8419
Pr 28:6 he that is **p.** in his ways, though 6141
Pr 28:18 **p.** in his ways shall fall at once. 6140
Isa 19:14 The Lord hath mingled a **p.** spirit....... 5773
Mt 17:17 said, **O faithless and p. generation,** .*1294*
Lu 9:41 said, **O faithless and p. generation,** .*1294*
Ac 20:30 men arise, speaking **p.** things, to......... *1294*
Php 2:15 midst of a crooked and **p.** nation, ... *1294*
1Ti 6:5 **P.** disputings of men of corrupt.......... *3859*

PERVERSELY
2Sa 19:19 that which thy servant did **p.** the........ 5753
1Ki 8:47 We have sinned,and have done **p.**,...... 5753
Ps 119:78 for they dealt **p.** with me without 5791

PERVERSENESS
Nu 23:21 neither hath he seen **p.** in Israel: 5999
Pr 11:3 **p.** of transgressors shall destroy 5558
Pr 15:4 **p.** therein is a breach in the spirit. 5558
Isa 30:12 trust in oppression and **p.**, and 3868
Isa 59:3 your tongue hath muttered **p.**............ 5766
Eze 9:9 of blood, and the city full of **p.**:........... 4297

PERVERT See also PERVERTED; PERVERTETH; PERVERTING.
De 16:19 and **p.** the words of the righteous....... 5557
De 24:17 **p.** the judgment of the stranger, ... 5186
Job 8:3 Doth God **p.** judgment? 5791
Job 8:3 or doth the Almighty **p.** justice? 5791
Job 34:12 will the Almighty **p.** judgment. 5791
Pr 17:23 bosom to **p.** the ways of judgment...... 5186
Pr 31:5 forget...law, and **p.** the judgment 8138
Mic 3:9 abhor judgment, and **p.** all equity........ 6140
Ac 13:10 to **p.** the right ways of the Lord? *1294*
Ga 1:7 and would **p.** the gospel of Christ....... *3344*

PERVERTED
1Sa 8:3 and took bribes, and **p.** judgment. 5186
Job 33:27 sinned, and **p.**...which was right,........ 5753
Isa 47:10 thy knowledge, it hath **p.** thee; 7725
Jer 3:21 they have **p.** their way, and they........ 5753
Jer 23:36 **p.** the words of the living God, ... 2015

PERVERTETH
Ex 23:8 and **p.** the words of the righteous...... 5557
De 27:19 cursed be he that **p.** the judgment 5186
Pr 10:9 that **p.** his ways shall be known. 6140
Pr 19:3 foolishness of man **p.** his way: 5557
Lu 23:14 unto me, as one that **p.** the people; *654*

PERVERTING
Ec 5:8 violent **p.** of judgment and justice ....
Lu 23:2 We found this fellow **p.** the nation, ... *1294*

PESTILENCE See also PESTILENCES.
Ex 5:3 he fall upon us with **p.**, or with the...... 1698
Ex 9:15 smite thee and thy people with **p.**; 1698
Le 26:25 I will send the **p.** among you; and 1698
Nu 14:12 I will smite them with the **p.**, and 1698
De 28:21 shall make the **p.** cleave unto thee,..... 1698
2Sa 24:13 there be three days' **p.** in thy land? 1698
2Sa 24:15 So the Lord sent a **p.** upon Israel....... 1698
1Ki 8:37 be in the land famine, if there be **p.**,... 1698
1Ch 21:12 even the **p.**, in the land, and the........ 1698
1Ch 21:14 So the Lord sent **p.** upon Israel: 1698
2Ch 6:28 if there be **p.**, if there be blasting,...... 1698
2Ch 7:13 or if I send **p.** among my people; 1698
2Ch 20:9 sword, judgment, or **p.**, or famine, ... 1698
Ps 78:50 but gave their life over to the **p.**; 1698
Ps 91:3 fowler, and from the noisome **p.** 1698
Ps 91:6 for the **p.** that walketh in darkness; 1698
Jer 14:12 and by the famine, and by the **p.**........ 1698
Jer 21:6 they shall die of a great **p.**.................. 1698
Jer 21:7 as are left in this city from the **p.**,....... 1698
Jer 21:9 and by the famine, and by the **p.**:........ 1698
Jer 24:10 famine, and the **p.**, among them,........ 1698
Jer 27:8 with the famine, and with the **p.** 1698
Jer 27:13 sword, by the famine, and by the **p.**, .. 1698
Jer 28:8 of war, and of evil, and of **p.**.............. 1698
Jer 29:17 the sword, the famine, and the **p.**, ... 1698
Jer 29:18 the famine, and with the **p.**, and 1698
Jer 32:24 famine, and of the **p.**: and what 1698
Jer 32:36 and by the famine, and by the **p.**;........ 1698
Jer 34:17 sword, to the **p.**, and to the famine; ... 1698
Jer 38:2 sword, by the famine, and by the **p.**: .. 1698
Jer 42:17 sword, by the famine, and by the **p.**: .. 1698
Jer 42:22 sword, by the famine, and by the **p.**, .. 1698
Jer 44:13 sword, by the famine, and by the **p.**: .. 1698
Eze 5:12 A third part...shall die with the **p.**,...... 1698
Eze 5:17 **p.** and blood shall pass through 1698
Eze 6:11 sword, by the famine, and by the **p.** .. 1698
Eze 6:12 He that is far off shall die of the **p.**;.... 1698
Eze 7:15 and the **p.** and the famine within: 1698
Eze 7:15 famine and **p.** shall devour him........... 1698
Eze 12:16 from the famine, and from the **p.**; 1698
Eze 14:19 Or if I send a **p.** into that land, and 1698
Eze 14:21 the noisome beast, and the **p.**, to....... 1698
Eze 28:23 I will send into her **p.**, and blood........ 1698
Eze 33:27 and in the caves shall die of the **p.**..... 1698
Eze 38:22 against him with **p.** and with blood;..... 1698
Am 4:10 I have sent among you the **p.** after..... 1698
Hab 3:5 Before him went the **p.**, and 1698

PESTILENCES
Mt 24:7 **p., and earthquakes, in divers** *3061*
Lu 21:11 **divers places, and famines, and p.;** .*3061*

PESTILENT
Ac 24:5 have found this man a **p.** fellow,......... *3061*

PESTLE
Pr 27:22 a mortar among wheat with a **p.**,......... 5940

PETER (pe'-tur) See also CEPHAS; PETER'S; SIMON.
Mt 4:18 And Simon called **P.**, and Andrew *4074*
Mt 10:2 The first, Simon, who is called **P.**,...... *4074*
Mt 14:28 **P.** answered him and said, Lord,........ *4074*
Mt 14:29 when **P.** was come down out of the.... *4074*
Mt 15:15 Then answered **P.** and said unto *4074*
Mt 16:16 And Simon **P.** answered and said, ... *4074*
Mt 16:18 **That thou art P., and upon this** *4074*
Mt 16:22 **P.** took him, and began to rebuke *4074*
Mt 16:23 said unto **P.**, **Get thee behind me,** ... *4074*
Mt 17:1 Jesus taketh **P.**, James, and John *4074*
Mt 17:4 Then answered **P.**, and said unto........ *4074*
Mt 17:24 received tribute money came to **P.**,.... *4074*
Mt 17:26 **P.** saith unto him, Of strangers.......... *4074*
Mt 18:21 Then came **P.** to him, and said,.......... *4074*
Mt 19:27 answered **P.** and said unto him, ... *4074*
Mt 26:33 **P.** answered and said unto him, ... *4074*
Mt 26:35 **P.** said unto him, Though I should...... *4074*
Mt 26:37 **P.** and the two sons of Zebedee, ... *4074*
Mt 26:40 saith unto **P.**, **What, could ye not**...... *4074*
Mt 26:58 **P.** followed him afar off unto the...... *4074*
Mt 26:69 Now **P.** sat without in the palace: *4074*
Mt 26:73 said to **P.**, Surely thou also art one *4074*
Mt 26:75 **P.** remembered the word of Jesus,..... *4074*
Mk 3:16 And Simon he surnamed **P.**;............... *4074*
Mk 5:37 to follow him, save **P.**, and James, ... *4074*
Mk 8:29 **P.** answereth and saith unto him, ... *4074*
Mk 8:32 **P.** took him, and began to rebuke *4074*
Mk 8:33 he rebuked **P.**, saying, **Get thee** *4074*
Mk 9:2 Jesus taketh with him **P.**, and............ *4074*
Mk 9:5 **P.** answered and said to Jesus,........... *4074*
Mk 10:28 **P.** began to say unto him, Lo, we...... *4074*
Mk 11:21 **P.** calling to remembrance saith *4074*
Mk 13:3 **P.** and James and John...Andrew......... *4074*
Mk 14:29 **P.** said unto him, Although all........... *4074*
Mk 14:33 he taketh with him **P.** and James......... *4074*
Mk 14:37 saith unto **P.**, **Simon, sleepest thou?** .*4074*
Mk 14:54 **P.** followed him afar off, even into...... *4074*
Mk 14:66 **P.** was beneath in the palace, there.... *4074*
Mk 14:67 when she saw **P.** warming himself,..... *4074*
Mk 14:70 said again to **P.**, Surely thou art *4074*
Mk 14:72 **P.** called to mind the word that *4074*
Mk 16:7 tell his disciples and **P.** that he *4074*
Lu 5:8 When Simon **P.** saw it, he fell down ... *4074*
Lu 6:14 Simon, (whom he also named **P.**,)....... *4074*
Lu 8:45 **P.** and they that were with him *4074*
Lu 8:51 suffered no man to go in, save **P.**,...... *4074*
Lu 9:20 **P.** answering said, The Christ of......... *4074*
Lu 9:28 he took **P.** and John and James,.......... *4074*
Lu 9:32 But **P.** and they that were with him..... *4074*
Lu 9:33 **P.** said unto Jesus, Master, it is *4074*
Lu 12:41 **P.** said unto him, Lord, speakest *4074*
Lu 18:28 Then **P.** said, Lo, we have left all, ... *4074*
Lu 22:8 And he sent **P.** and John, saying, ... *4074*
Lu 22:34 **I tell thee, P., the cock shall not** .. *4074*
Lu 22:54 house. And **P.** followed afar off.......... *4074*
Lu 22:55 together, **P.** sat down among them..... *4074*
Lu 22:58 them. And **P.** said, Man, I am not...... *4074*
Lu 22:60 **P.** said, Man, I know not what thou ... *4074*
Lu 22:61 Lord turned, and looked upon **P.**........ *4074*
Lu 22:61 **P.** remembered the word of the........ *4074*
Lu 22:62 And **P.** went out, and wept bitterly. ... *4074*
Lu 24:12 Then arose **P.**, and ran unto the........ *4074*
Joh 1:44 Bethsaida,...city of Andrew and **P.**.... *4074*
Joh 6:68 Simon **P.** answered him, Lord, to........ *4074*
Joh 13:6 Then cometh he to Simon **P.**: and....... *4074*
Joh 13:6 **P.** saith unto him, Lord, dost thou...........
Joh 13:8 **P.** saith unto him, Thou shalt *4074*
Joh 13:9 Simon **P.** saith unto him, Lord, not..... *4074*

Joh 13:24 Simon **P.** therefore beckoned to........ *4074*
Joh 13:36 Simon **P.** said unto him, Lord,............ *4074*
Joh 13:37 **P.** said unto him, Lord, why cannot.... *4074*
Joh 18:10 Simon **P.** having a sword drew it, ... *4074*
Joh 18:11 said Jesus unto **P.**, Put up thy......... *4074*
Joh 18:15 And Simon **P.** followed Jesus, and....... *4074*
Joh 18:16 **P.** stood at the door without. Then *4074*
Joh 18:16 kept the door, and brought in **P.**........ *4074*
Joh 18:17 damsel that kept the door unto **P.**,...... *4074*
Joh 18:18 **P.** stood with them, and warmed *4074*
Joh 18:25 And Simon **P.** stood and warmed *4074*
Joh 18:26 his kinsman whose ear **P.** cut off, ... *4074*
Joh 18:27 **P.** then denied again: and................ *4074*
Joh 20:2 runneth, and cometh to Simon **P.**,...... *4074*
Joh 20:3 **P.** therefore went forth, and that *4074*
Joh 20:4 the other disciple did outrun **P.**,......... *4074*
Joh 20:6 cometh Simon **P.** following him, ... *4074*
Joh 21:2 together Simon **P.**, and Thomas......... *4074*
Joh 21:3 Simon **P.** saith unto them, I go a....... *4074*
Joh 21:7 loved saith unto **P.**, It is the Lord..... *4074*
Joh 21:7 **P.** heard that it was the Lord,........... *4074*
Joh 21:11 Simon **P.** went up, and drew the........ *4074*
Joh 21:15 Jesus saith to Simon **P.**, Simon,......... *4074*
Joh 21:17 **P.** was grieved because he said......... *4074*
Joh 21:20 **P.**, turning about, seeth the.............. *4074*
Joh 21:21 **P.** seeing him saith to Jesus, Lord,..... *4074*
Ac 1:13 where abode both **P.**, and James,...... *4074*
Ac 1:15 **P.** stood up in the midst of the.......... *4074*
Ac 2:14 **P.**, standing up with the eleven, ... *4074*
Ac 2:37 unto **P.** and to the rest of the *4074*
Ac 2:38 Then **P.** said unto them, Repent, ... *4074*
Ac 3:1 **P.** and John went up together into...... *4074*
Ac 3:3 seeing **P.** and John about to go.......... *4074*
Ac 3:4 **P.**, fastening his eyes upon him *4074*
Ac 3:6 **P.** said, Silver and gold have I........... *4074*
Ac 3:11 which was healed held **P.** and John, ... *4074*
Ac 3:12 when **P.** saw it he answered unto *4074*
Ac 4:8 **P.**, filled with the Holy Ghost, said..... *4074*
Ac 4:13 saw the boldness of **P.** and John, ... *4074*
Ac 4:19 **P.** and John answered and said *4074*
Ac 5:3 **P.** said, Ananias, why hath Satan *4074*
Ac 5:8 **P.** answered unto her, Tell me.......... *4074*
Ac 5:9 **P.** said unto her, How is it that *4074*
Ac 5:15 the shadow of **P.** passing by might...... *4074*
Ac 5:29 **P.** and the other apostles answered.... *4074*
Ac 8:14 they sent unto them **P.** and John:....... *4074*
Ac 8:20 But **P.** said unto him, Thy money *4074*
Ac 9:32 **P.** passed throughout all quarters, ... *4074*
Ac 9:34 **P.** said unto him, Aeneas, Jesus.......... *4074*
Ac 9:38 disciples had heard that **P.** was.......... *4074*
Ac 9:39 Then **P.** arose and went with them..... *4074*
Ac 9:40 **P.** put them all forth, and kneeled...... *4074*
Ac 9:40 and when she saw **P.**, she sat up....... *4074*
Ac 10:5 one Simon, whose surname is **P.**:....... *4074*
Ac 10:9 **P.** went up upon the housetop to....... *4074*
Ac 10:13 voice to him, Rise, **P.**; kill and eat. *4074*
Ac 10:14 **P.** said, Not so, Lord; for I have *4074*
Ac 10:17 **P.** doubted in himself what this.......... *4074*
Ac 10:18 which was surnamed **P.**, were............ *4074*
Ac 10:19 While **P.** thought on the vision, the *4074*
Ac 10:21 **P.** went down to the men which........ *4074*
Ac 10:23 morrow **P.** went away with them, ... *4074*
Ac 10:25 as **P.** was coming in, Cornelius met...... *4074*
Ac 10:26 **P.** took him up, saying, Stand up; *4074*
Ac 10:32 Simon, whose surname is **P.**; *4074*
Ac 10:34 **P.** opened his mouth, and said, Of...... *4074*
Ac 10:44 **P.** yet spake these words, the Holy.... *4074*
Ac 10:45 as many as came with **P.**,................ *4074*
Ac 10:46 magnify God. Then answered **P.**, ... *4074*
Ac 11:2 **P.** was come up to Jerusalem, ... *4074*
Ac 11:4 **P.** rehearsed the matter from the....... *4074*
Ac 11:7 unto me, Arise, **P.**; slay and eat. *4074*
Ac 11:13 for Simon, whose surname is **P.**; *4074*
Ac 12:3 proceeded further to take **P.** also....... *4074*
Ac 12:5 **P.** therefore was kept in prison: *4074*
Ac 12:6 **P.**...sleeping between two soldiers, ... *4074*
Ac 12:7 he smote **P.** on the side, and raised ... *4074*
Ac 12:11 when **P.** was come to himself, he....... *4074*
Ac 12:13 as **P.** knocked at the door of the........ *4074*
Ac 12:14 told how **P.** stood before the gate. *4074*
Ac 12:16 But **P.** continued knocking: and......... *4074*
Ac 12:18 soldiers, what was become of **P.**......... *4074*
Ac 15:7 **P.** rose up, and said unto them,........ *4074*
Ga 1:18 I went up to Jerusalem to see **P.**,...... *4074*
Ga 2:7 of the circumcision was unto **P.**; *4074*
Ga 2:8 he that wrought effectually in **P.** *4074*
Ga 2:11 But when **P.** was come to Antioch, ... *4074*
Ga 2:14 I said unto **P.** before them all,........... *4074*
1Pe *general* *title* First Epistle General Of **P.**......... *4074*
1Pe 1:1 **P.**, an apostle of Jesus Christ,.......... *4074*
2Pe *general* *title* Second Epistle General Of **P.**...... *4074*
2Pe 1:1 Simon **P.**, a servant and an apostle..... *4074*

PETER'S (pe'-turz)
Mt 8:14 Jesus was come into **P.** house,.......... *4074*
Joh 1:40 him, was Andrew, Simon **P.** brother... *4074*
Joh 6:8 Andrew, Simon **P.** brother, saith........ *4074*
Ac 12:14 And when she knew **P.** voice, she...... *4074*

PETHAHIAH (peth-a-hi'-ah)
1Ch 24:16 nineteenth to **P.**, the twentieth......... 6611
Ezr 10:23 Kelaiah, (the same is Kelita,) **P.**, ... 6611
Ne 9:5 Hodijah, Shebaniah, and **P.**, said 6611
Ne 11:24 And **P.** the son of Meshezabeel, of..... 6611

PETHOR (pe'-thor)
Nu 22:5 unto Balaam the son of Beor to **P.**, ... 6604
De 23:4 Balaam the son of Beor of **P.** of 6604

PETHUEL (pe-thu'-el)
Joe 1:1 that come to Joel the son of **P.**.......... 6602

PETITION See also PETITIONS.
1Sa 1:17 God of Israel grant thee thy **p.** 7596
1Sa 1:27 Lord hath given me my **p.** which I...... 7596
1Ki 2:16 I ask one **p.** of thee, deny me not...... 7596
1Ki 2:20 said, I desire one small **p.** of thee; 7596
Es 5:6 What is thy **p.**? and it shall be.......... 7596
Es 5:7 and said, My **p.** and my request is; 7596
Es 5:8 if it please the king to grant my **p.**, ... 7596
Es 7:2 What is thy **p.**, queen Esther? and 7596
Es 7:3 let my life be given me at my **p.**,....... 7596
Es 9:12 now what is thy **p.**? and it shall be 7596
Da 6:7 shall ask a **p.** of any God or man........ 1159
Da 6:12 that shall ask a **p.** of any God or man........
Da 6:13 maketh his **p.** three times a day......... 1159

PETITIONS
Ps 20:5 banners: the Lord fulfil all thy **p.**........ 4862
1Jo 5:15 have the **p.** that we desired of him....... *155*

PEULTHAI (pe-ul'-thahee)
1Ch 26:5 the seventh, **P.** the eighth:.............. 6469

PHALEC (fa'-lek) See also PELEG.
Lu 3:35 which was the son of **P.**, which......... *5317*

PHALLU (fal'-lu) See also PALLU.
Ge 46:9 sons of Reuben; Hanoch, and **P.**, ... 6396

PHALTI (fal'-ti) See also PHALTIEL.
1Sa 25:44 his daughter, David's wife, to **P.**........ 6406

PHALTIEL (fal'-te-el) See also PHALTI.
2Sa 3:15 even from **P.** the son of Laish........... 6409

PHANUEL (fan-u'-el)
Lu 2:36 a prophetess, the daughter of **P.**,....... *5323*

PHARAOH (fa'-ra-o) See also PHARAOH'S; PHARAOH-HOPHRA; PHARAOH-NECHO.
Ge 12:15 The princes also of **P.** saw her, ... 6547
Ge 12:15 and commended her before **P.**:.......... 6547
Ge 12:17 the Lord plagued **P.** and his house 6547
Ge 12:18 **P.** called Abram, and said, What is..... 6547
Ge 12:20 **P.** commanded his men concerning..... 6547
Ge 39:1 Potiphar, an officer of **P.**, captain...... 6547
Ge 40:2 **P.** was wroth against two of his......... 6547
Ge 40:13 days shall **P.** lift up thine head,.......... 6547
Ge 40:14 and make mention of me unto **P.**, ... 6547
Ge 40:17 of all manner of bakemeats for **P.**;...... 6547
Ge 40:19 three days shall **P.** lift up thy head 6547
Ge 41:1 of full two years, that **P.** dreamed: 6547
Ge 41:4 favoured and fat kine. So **P.** awoke. ... 6547
Ge 41:7 and **P.** awoke, and, behold, it was a ... 6547
Ge 41:8 and **P.** told them his dream; but 6547
Ge 41:8 that could interpret them unto **P.**......... 6547
Ge 41:9 Then spake the chief butler unto **P.**,... 6547
Ge 41:10 **P.** was wroth with his servants,.......... 6547
Ge 41:14 Then **P.** sent and called Joseph,......... 6547
Ge 41:14 his raiment, and came in unto **P.**........ 6547
Ge 41:15 And **P.** said unto Joseph, I have.......... 6547
Ge 41:16 Joseph answered **P.**, saying, It is 6547
Ge 41:16 shall give **P.** an answer of peace. 6547
Ge 41:17 **P.** said unto Joseph, In my dream, ... 6547
Ge 41:25 And Joseph said unto **P.**,.................. 6547
Ge 41:25 The dream of **P.** is one; God hath...... 6547
Ge 41:25 shewed **P.** what he is about to do. 6547
Ge 41:28 thing which I have spoken unto **P.**:..... 6547
Ge 41:28 is about to do he sheweth unto **P.**...... 6547
Ge 41:32 dream was doubled unto **P.** twice;...... 6547
Ge 41:33 let **P.** look out a man discreet and...... 6547
Ge 41:34 Let **P.** do this, and let him appoint...... 6547
Ge 41:35 lay up corn under the hand of **P.**,....... 6547
Ge 41:37 the thing was good in the eyes of **P.**, ..6547
Ge 41:38 **P.** said unto his servants, Can we...... 6547
Ge 41:39 **P.** said unto Joseph, Forasmuch as..... 6547
Ge 41:41 **P.** said unto Joseph, See, I have set... 6547
Ge 41:42 **P.** took off his ring from his hand,...... 6547
Ge 41:44 And **P.** said unto Joseph, I am **P.**, ... 6547
Ge 41:45 And **P.** called Joseph's name 6547
Ge 41:46 years old when he stood before **P.**....... 6547
Ge 41:46 went out from the presence of **P.**, ... 6547
Ge 41:55 the people cried to **P.** for bread:....... 6547
Ge 41:55 **P.** said unto all the Egyptians, Go...... 6547
Ge 42:15 By the life of **P.** ye shall not go forth.. 6547
Ge 42:16 by the life of **P.** surely ye are spies.... 6547
Ge 44:18 servant: for thou art even as **P.**......... 6547
Ge 45:2 and the house of **P.** heard. 6547
Ge 45:8 he hath made me a father to **P.**, ... 6547
Ge 45:16 pleased **P.** well, and his servants. 6547
Ge 45:17 **P.** said unto Joseph, Say unto thy 6547
Ge 45:21 to the commandment of **P.**,............... 6547
Ge 46:5 which **P.** had sent to carry him........... 6547
Ge 46:31 I will go up, and shew **P.**, and say 6547
Ge 46:33 to pass, when **P.** shall call you, ... 6547
Ge 47:1 Joseph came and told **P.**, and said, ... 6547
Ge 47:2 men, and presented them unto **P.**...... 6547
Ge 47:3 **P.** said unto his brethren, What is...... 6547
Ge 47:3 they said unto **P.**, Thy servants......... 6547
Ge 47:4 They said moreover to **P.**, For to...... 6547
Ge 47:5 **P.** spake unto Joseph, saying, Thy 6547
Ge 47:7 before **P.**: and Jacob blessed **P.**......... 6547
Ge 47:8 **P.** said unto Jacob, How old art......... 6547
Ge 47:9 Jacob said unto **P.**, the days of the..... 6547
Ge 47:10 And Jacob blessed **P.**, and went......... 6547
Ge 47:10 and went out from before **P.**............. 6547
Ge 47:11 of Rameses, as **P.** had commanded..... 6547
Ge 47:19 our land will be servants unto **P.**:....... 6547
Ge 47:20 bought all the land of Egypt for **P.**; 6547
Ge 47:22 had a portion assigned them of **P.**, ... 6547
Ge 47:22 did eat their portion which **P.** gave..... 6547
Ge 47:23 have bought you this day...for **P.**:....... 6547
Ge 47:24 ye shall give the fifth part unto **P.**,...... 6547
Ge 47:26 that **P.** should have the fifth part;....... 6547
Ge 50:4 Joseph spake unto the house of **P.**, ... 6547
Ge 50:4 speak, I pray you, in the ears of **P.**,..... 6547
Ge 50:6 **P.** said, Go up, and bury thy father, ... 6547
Ge 50:7 him went up all the servants of **P.**,.... 6547
Ex 1:11 they built for **P.** treasure cities,......... 6547
Ex 1:19 the midwives said unto **P.**, Because.... 6547
Ex 1:22 **P.** charged all his people, saying, ... 6547
Ex 2:5 daughter of **P.** came down to wash...... 6547
Ex 2:15 Now when **P.** heard this thing, he...... 6547
Ex 2:15 Moses fled from the face of **P.**, and.... 6547
Ex 3:10 I will send thee unto **P.**, that thou...... 6547
Ex 3:11 Who am I, that I should go unto **P.**,.... 6547
Ex 4:21 thou do all those wonders before **P.**, .. 6547
Ex 4:22 thou shalt say unto **P.**, Thus saith...... 6547
Ex 5:1 and Aaron went in, and told **P.**,......... 6547
Ex 5:2 **P.** said, Who is the Lord, that I.......... 6547
Ex 5:5 **P.** said, Behold, the people of the...... 6547
Ex 5:6 And **P.** commanded the same day......... 6547
Ex 5:10 Thus saith **P.**, I will not give you....... 6547
Ex 5:15 of Israel came and cried unto **P.**, ... 6547
Ex 5:20 way, as they came forth from **P.**:........ 6547
Ex 5:21 to be abhorred in the eyes of **P.**,....... 6547
Ex 5:23 I came to **P.** to speak in thy name, ... 6547
Ex 6:1 shalt thou see what I will do to **P.**: 6547
Ex 6:11 Go in, speak unto **P.** king of Egypt, ... 6547
Ex 6:12 how then shall **P.** hear me, who am.... 6547
Ex 6:13 Israel, and unto **P.** king of Egypt, ... 6547
Ex 6:27 which spake to **P.** king of Egypt, ... 6547
Ex 6:29 speak thou unto **P.** king of Egypt....... 6547
Ex 6:30 and how shall **P.** hearken unto me? 6547
Ex 7:1 See, I have made thee a god to **P.**:..... 6547
Ex 7:2 thy brother shall speak unto **P.**,......... 6547
Ex 7:4 But **P.** shall not hearken unto you,..... 6547
Ex 7:7 old, when they spake unto **P.**............ 6547
Ex 7:9 When **P.** shall speak unto you, ... 6547
Ex 7:9 Take thy rod, and cast it before **P.**, ... 6547
Ex 7:10 Moses and Aaron went in unto **P.**,..... 6547
Ex 7:10 Aaron cast down his rod before **P.**, ... 6547
Ex 7:11 Then **P.** also called the wise men....... 6547
Ex 7:15 Get thee unto **P.** in the morning: 6547
Ex 7:20 were in the river, in the sight of **P.**,... 6547
Ex 7:23 **P.** turned and went into his house,..... 6547

Ex 8:1 Go unto **P.**, and say unto him, Thus... 6547
Ex 8:8 **P.** called for Moses and Aaron,... 6547
Ex 8:9 Moses said unto **P.**, Glory over me:... 6547
Ex 8:12 and Aaron went out from **P.**:... 6547
Ex 8:12 which he had brought against **P.**... 6547
Ex 8:15 when **P.** saw that there was respite,... 6547
Ex 8:19 Then the magicians said unto **P.**,... 6547
Ex 8:20 the morning, and stand before **P.**;... 6547
Ex 8:24 swarm of flies into the house of **P.**,... 6547
Ex 8:25 **P.** called for Moses and for Aaron,... 6547
Ex 8:28 **P.** said, I will let you go, that ye... 6547
Ex 8:29 swarms of flies may depart from **P.**,... 6547
Ex 8:29 let not **P.** deal deceitfully any more... 6547
Ex 8:30 And Moses went out from **P.**, and... 6547
Ex 8:31 the swarms of flies from **P.**,... 6547
Ex 8:32 **P.** hardened his heart at this time... 6547
Ex 9:1 Go in unto **P.**, and tell him, Thus... 6547
Ex 9:7 **P.** sent, and, behold, there was not... 6547
Ex 9:7 And the heart of **P.** was hardened,... 6547
Ex 9:8 toward...heaven in the sight of **P.**,... 6547
Ex 9:10 of the furnace, and stood before **P.**;... 6547
Ex 9:12 the Lord hardened the heart of **P.**,... 6547
Ex 9:13 stand before **P.**, and say unto him,... 6547
Ex 9:20 the Lord among the servants of **P.**,... 6547
Ex 9:27 **P.** sent, and called for Moses and... 6547
Ex 9:33 Moses went out of the city from **P.**,... 6547
Ex 9:34 when **P.** saw that the rain and the... 6547
Ex 9:35 heart of **P.** was hardened, neither... 6547
Ex 10:1 said unto Moses, Go in unto **P.**:... 6547
Ex 10:3 Moses and Aaron came in unto **P.**,... 6547
Ex 10:6 himself, and went out from **P.**... 6547
Ex 10:8 Aaron were brought again unto **P.**:... 6547
Ex 10:16 **P.** called for Moses and Aaron in... 6547
Ex 10:18 he went out from **P.**, and intreated... 6547
Ex 10:24 **P.** called unto Moses, and said, Go... 6547
Ex 10:28 **P.** said unto him, Get thee from... 6547
Ex 11:1 I bring one plague more upon **P.**,... 6547
Ex 11:5 firstborn of **P.** that sitteth upon his... 6547
Ex 11:8 went out from **P.** in a great anger... 6547
Ex 11:9 **P.** shall not hearken unto you;... 6547
Ex 11:10 did all these wonders before **P.**:... 6547
Ex 12:29 the firstborn of **P.** that sat on his... 6547
Ex 12:30 **P.** rose up in the night, he, and all... 6547
Ex 13:15 **P.** would hardly let us go, that the... 6547
Ex 13:17 when **P.** had let the people go, that... 6547
Ex 14:3 **P.** will say of the children of Israel,... 6547
Ex 14:4 I will be honoured upon **P.**, and... 6547
Ex 14:5 heart of **P.** and of his servants was... 6547
Ex 14:8 The Lord hardened the heart of **P.**... 6547
Ex 14:9 all the horses and chariots of **P.**,... 6547
Ex 14:10 when **P.** drew nigh, the children of... 6547
Ex 14:17 and I will get me honour upon **P.**,... 6547
Ex 14:18 I have gotten me honour upon **P.**,... 6547
Ex 14:28 all the host of **P.** that came into the... 6547
Ex 15:19 the horse of **P.** went in with his... 6547
Ex 18:4 delivered me from the sword of **P.**:... 6547
Ex 18:8 all that the Lord had done unto **P.**... 6547
Ex 18:10 and out of the hand of **P.**, who hath... 6547
De 6:22 and sore, upon Egypt, upon **P.**, and... 6547
De 7:8 from the hand of **P.** king of Egypt... 6547
De 7:18 what the Lord thy God did unto **P.**,... 6547
De 11:3 did in the midst of Egypt unto **P.**... 6547
De 29:2 eyes in the land of Egypt unto **P.**,... 6547
De 34:11 to do in the land of Egypt to **P.**, and.. 6547
1Sa 6:6 and **P.** hardened their hearts?... 6547
1Ki 3:1 made affinity with **P.** king of Egypt,... 6547
1Ki 9:16 **P.** king of Egypt had gone up, and... 6547
1Ki 11:1 together with the daughter of **P.**,... 6547
1Ki 11:18 to Egypt, unto **P.** king of Egypt;... 6547
1Ki 11:19 great favour in the sight of **P.**, so... 6547
1Ki 11:20 household among the sons of **P.**... 6547
1Ki 11:21 Hadad said to **P.**, Let me depart,... 6547
1Ki 11:22 Then **P.** said unto him, But what... 6547
2Ki 17:7 under the hand of **P.** king of Egypt,... 6547
2Ki 18:21 so is **P.** king of Egypt unto all that... 6547
2Ki 23:35 gave the silver and the gold to **P.**;... 6547
2Ki 23:35 to the commandment of **P.**:... 6547
1Ch 4:18 sons of Bithiah the daughter of **P.**,... 6547
2Ch 8:11 the daughter of **P.** out of the city of... 6547
Ne 9:10 signs and wonders upon **P.**, and... 6547
Ps 135:9 the midst of thee, O Egypt, upon **P.**,... 6547
Ps 136:15 **P.** and his host in the Red sea:... 6547
Isa 19:11 wise counsellers of **P.** is become... 6547
Isa 19:11 how say ye unto **P.**, I am the son of.. 6547
Isa 30:2 themselves in the strength of **P.**,... 6547
Isa 30:3 the strength of **P.** be your shame,... 6547
Isa 36:6 so is **P.** king of Egypt to all that... 6547
Jer 25:19 **P.** king of Egypt, and his servants,... 6547
Jer 46:17 **P.** king of Egypt is but a noise;... 6547
Jer 46:25 punish the multitude of No, and **P.**,... 6547
Jer 46:25 even **P.**, and all them that trust in... 6547
Jer 47:1 before that **P.** smote Gaza... 6547
Eze 17:17 shall **P.** with his mighty army and... 6547
Eze 29:2 thy face against **P.** king of Egypt;... 6547
Eze 29:3 I am against thee, **P.** king of Egypt,... 6547
Eze 30:21 have broken the arm of **P.** king of... 6547
Eze 30:22 I am against **P.** king of Egypt,... 6547
Eze 30:25 and the arms of **P.** shall fall down;... 6547
Eze 31:2 speak unto **P.** king of Egypt, and... 6547
Eze 31:18 This is **P.** and all his multitude,... 6547
Eze 32:2 lamentation for **P.** king of Egypt,... 6547
Eze 32:31 **P.** shall see them, and shall be... 6547
Eze 32:31 even **P.** and all his army slain by the .. 6547
Eze 32:32 even **P.** and all his multitude,... 6547
Ac 7:10 in the sight of **P.** king of Egypt;... *5328*
Ac 7:13 kindred was made known unto **P.**... *5328*
Ro 9:17 For the scripture saith unto **P.**,... *5328*

PHARAOH-HOPHRA (fa''-ra-o-hof'-rah)
Jer 44:30 I will give **P.** king of Egypt into... 6548

PHARAOH-NECHO (fa''-ra-o-ne'-ko) See also PHARAOH-NECHOH.
Jer 46:2 against the army of **P.** king of... 6549

PHARAOH-NECHOH (fa''-ra-o-ne'-ko) See also PHARAOH-NECHO.
2Ki 23:29 **P.** king of Egypt went up against... 6549
2Ki 23:33 **P.** put him in bands at Riblah in... 6549
2Ki 23:34 **P.** made Eliakim the son of Josiah... 6549
2Ki 23:35 to his taxation, to give it unto **P.**... 6549

PHARAOH'S (fa'-ra-oze)
Ge 12:15 woman was taken into **P.** house... 6547
Ge 37:36 unto Potiphar, an officer of **P.**, and... 6547
Ge 40:7 he asked **P.** officers that were with... 6547
Ge 40:11 **P.** cup was in my hand: and I took... 6547
Ge 40:11 and pressed them into **P.** cup,... 6547
Ge 40:11 and I gave the cup into **P.** hand... 6547
Ge 40:13 shalt deliver **P.** cup into his hand,... 6547
Ge 40:20 third day, which was **P.** birthday,... 6547
Ge 40:21 and he gave the cup into **P.** hand:... 6547
Ge 45:16 fame thereof was heard in **P.** house,... 6547
Ge 47:14 brought the money into **P.** house... 6547
Ge 47:20 over them: so the land became **P.**... 6547
Ge 47:25 my lord, and we will be **P.** servants. .. 6547
Ge 47:26 priests only, which became not **P.**... 6547
Ex 2:7 Then said his sister to **P.** daughter,... 6547
Ex 2:8 And **P.** daughter said unto her, Go... 6547
Ex 2:9 **P.** daughter said unto her, Take... 6547
Ex 2:10 she brought him unto **P.** daughter,... 6547
Ex 5:14 **P.** taskmasters had set over them,... 6547
Ex 7:3 And I will harden **P.** heart, and... 6547
Ex 7:13 And he hardened **P.** heart, that he... 6547
Ex 7:14 **P.** heart was hardened, he refuseth... 6547
Ex 7:22 **P.** heart was hardened, neither... 6547
Ex 8:19 and **P.** heart was hardened, and he... 6547
Ex 10:7 **P.** servants said... How long... 6547
Ex 10:11 were driven out from **P.** presence... 6547
Ex 10:20, 27 the Lord hardened **P.** heart,... 6547
Ex 11:3 Egypt, in the sight of **P.** servants,... 6547
Ex 11:10 the Lord hardened **P.** heart, so that... 6547
Ex 14:4 I will harden **P.** heart, that he shall... 6547
Ex 14:23 sea, even all **P.** horses, his chariots,... 6547
Ex 15:4 **P.** chariots and...hosts hath he cast... 6547
De 6:21 We were **P.** bondmen in Egypt;... 6547
1Sa 2:27 they were in Egypt in **P.** house?... 6547
1Ki 3:1 and took **P.** daughter, and brought... 6547
1Ki 7:8 made also an house for **P.** daughter,... 6547
1Ki 9:24 **P.** daughter came up out of the city... 6547
1Ki 11:20 Tahpenes weaned in **P.** house:... 6547
1Ki 11:20 and Genubath was in **P.** household... 6547
Ca 1:9 company of horses in **P.** chariots... 6547
Jer 37:5 **P.** army was come...out of Egypt:... 6547
Jer 37:7 **P.** army, which has come forth to... 6547
Jer 37:11 Jerusalem for fear of **P.** army, from... 6547
Jer 43:9 which is at the entry of **P.** house... 6547
Eze 30:24 but I will break **P.** arms, and he... 6547
Ac 7:21 **P.** daughter took him up, and... *5328*
Heb 11:24 be called the son of **P.** daughter;... *5328*

PHARES fa'-rez) See also PHAREZ.
Mt 1:3 And Judas begat **P.** and Zara of... *5329*
Mt 1:3 **P.** begat Esrom; and Esrom begat... *5329*
Lu 3:33 Esrom, which was the son of **P.**,... *5329*

PHAREZ (fa'-rez) See also PEREZ; PHARES; PHARZITES.
Ge 38:29 therefore his name was called **P.**... 6557
Ge 46:12 and Shelah, and **P.**, and Zarah:... 6557
Ge 46:12 sons of **P.** were Hezron and Hamul... 6557
Nu 26:20 of **P.**, the family of the Pharzites:... 6557
Nu 26:21 sons of **P.** were; of Hezron, the... 6557
Ru 4:12 thy house be like the house of **P.**,... 6557
Ru 4:18 the generations of **P.**: **P.** begat... 6557
1Ch 2:4 his daughter in law bare him **P.**... 6557
1Ch 2:5 sons of **P.**; Hezron, and Hamul... 6557
1Ch 4:1 **P.**, Hezron, and Carmi, and Hur,... 6557
1Ch 9:4 children of **P.** the son of Judah... 6557

PHARISEE (far'-i-see) See also PHARISEE'S; PHARISEES.
Mt 23:26 **Thou blind P., cleanse first that**... *5330*
Lu 7:39 the **P.** which had bidden him saw it,... *5330*
Lu 11:37 **P.** besought him to dine with him:... *5330*
Lu 11:38 when the **P.** saw it, he marveled... *5330*
Lu 18:10 **one a P., and the other a publican.** *5330*
Lu 18:11 **The P. stood and prayed thus with** *5330*
Ac 5:34 a **P.**, named Gamaliel, a doctor of... *5330*
Ac 23:6 Men and brethren, I am a **P.**,... *5330*
Ac 23:6 the son of a **P.**: of the hope and... *5330*
Ac 26:5 sect of our religion I lived a **P.**... *5330*
Php 3:5 as touching the law, a **P.**;... *5330*

PHARISEE'S (far'-i-seze)
Lu 7:36 he went into the **P.** house, and sat... *5330*
Lu 7:37 Jesus sat at meat in the **P.** house,... *5330*

PHARISEES (far'-i-seze) See also PHARISEES'.
Mt 3:7 saw many of the **P.** and Sadducees... *5330*
Mt 5:20 **righteousness of the scribes and P.**, *5330*
Mt 9:11 when the **P.** saw it, they said unto... *5330*
Mt 9:14 Why do we and the **P.** fast oft, but... *5330*
Mt 9:34 the **P.** said, He casteth out devils... *5330*
Mt 12:2 But when the **P.** saw it, they said... *5330*
Mt 12:14 the **P.** went out, and held a council... *5330*
Mt 12:24 when the **P.** heard it, they said,... *5330*
Mt 12:38 certain of the scribes and of the **P.**... *5330*
Mt 15:1 Then came to Jesus scribes and **P.**,... *5330*
Mt 15:12 thou that the **P.** were offended,... *5330*
Mt 16:1 **P.** also with the Sadducees came,... *5330*
Mt 16:6, 11 **beware of the leaven of the P.**... *5330*
Mt 16:12 but of the doctrine of the **P.** and of... *5330*
Mt 19:3 **P.** also came unto him, tempting... *5330*
Mt 21:45 and **P.** had heard his parables,... *5330*
Mt 22:15 Then went the **P.**, and took counsel... *5330*
Mt 22:34 the **P.** had heard that he had put... *5330*
Mt 22:41 the **P.** were gathered together,... *5330*
Mt 23:2 **scribes and the P. sit in Moses'**... *5330*
Mt 23:13, 14,15,23,25,27,29 **P., hypocrites!**... *5330*
Mt 27:62 chief priests and **P.** came together... *5330*
Mk 2:16 the scribes and **P.** saw him eat with... *5330*
Mk 2:18 of John and of the **P.** used to fast:... *5330*
Mk 2:18 disciples of John and of the **P.** fast,... *5330*
Mk 2:24 **P.** said unto him, Behold, why do... *5330*
Mk 3:6 the **P.** went forth, and straightway... *5330*
Mk 7:1 came together unto him the **P.**,... *5330*
Mk 7:3 For the **P.**, and all the Jews, except... *5330*
Mk 7:5 Then the **P.** and scribes asked him,... *5330*
Mk 8:11 **P.** came...and began to question... *5330*
Mk 8:15 **beware of the leaven of the P.**,... *5330*
Mk 10:2 the **P.** came to him, and asked him,... *5330*
Mk 12:13 send unto him certain of the **P.**... *5330*
Lu 5:17 were **P.** and doctors of the law... *5330*
Lu 5:21 scribes and the **P.** began to reason,... *5330*
Lu 5:30 their scribes and **P.** murmured... *5330*
Lu 5:33 likewise the disciples of the **P.**;... *5330*
Lu 6:2 certain of the **P.** said unto them,... *5330*
Lu 6:7 the scribes and **P.** watched him,... *5330*
Lu 7:30 **P.** and lawyers rejected the counsel... *5330*
Lu 7:36 one of the **P.** desired him that he... *5330*
Lu 11:39 **do ye P. make clean the outside of.** *5330*
Lu 11:42 **woe unto you, P.! for ye tithe mint** *5330*
Lu 11:43 **Woe unto you, P.! for ye love the..** *5330*
Lu 11:44 **Woe unto you, scribes and P.**,... *5330*
Lu 11:53 **P.** began to urge him vehemently,... *5330*
Lu 12:1 **Beware ye of the leaven of the P.**, *5330*
Lu 13:31 day there came certain of the **P.**,... *5330*
Lu 14:1 house of one of the chief **P.** to eat... *5330*
Lu 14:3 spake unto the lawyers and **P.**,... *5330*
Lu 15:2 And the **P.** and scribes murmured,... *5330*
Lu 16:14 **P.** also, who were covetous, heard... *5330*
Lu 17:20 when he was demanded of the **P.**,... *5330*
Lu 19:39 the **P.** from among the multitude... *5330*
Joh 1:24 which were sent were of the **P.**... *5330*
Joh 3:1 man of the **P.**, named Nicodemus,... *5330*

Joh 4:1 Lord knew how the **P.** had heard....... 5330
Joh 7:32 **P.** heard that the people murmured.... 5330
Joh 7:32 **P.** and...chief priests sent officers...... 5330
Joh 7:45 officers to the chief priests and **P.**;..... 5330
Joh 7:47 answered them the **P.**, Are ye also.... 5330
Joh 7:48 rulers or of the **P.** believed on him?... 5330
Joh 8:3 and **P.** brought unto him a woman...... 5330
Joh 8:13 The **P.** therefore said unto him,......... 5330
Joh 9:13 They brought to the **P.** him that........ 5330
Joh 9:15 the **P.** also asked him how he had...... 5330
Joh 9:16 said some of the **P.**, This man is not.. 5330
Joh 9:40 some of the **P.** which were with him... 5330
Joh 11:46 went their ways to the **P.**, and told.... 5330
Joh 11:47 gathered the chief priests and...**P.**...... 5330
Joh 11:57 the **P.** had given a commandment,...... 5330
Joh 12:19 The **P.** therefore said among............ 5330
Joh 12:42 of the **P.** they did not confess him,...... 5330
Joh 18:3 officers from the...priests and **P.**,....... 5330
Ac 15:5 of the sect of the **P.** which believed,... 5330
Ac 23:6 were Sadducees, and the other **P.**,..... 5330
Ac 23:7 a dissension between the **P.** and........ 5330
Ac 23:8 nor spirit: but the **P.** confess both...... 5330

PHARISEES' (far'-i-seez)
Ac 23:9 scribes that were of the **P.** part......... 5330

PHAROSH (fa'-rosh)
Ezr 8:3 of Shechaniah, of the sons of **P.**;........ 6551

PHARPAR (far'-par)
2Ki 5:12 and **P.**, rivers of Damascus,............. 6554

PHARZITES (far'-zites)
Nu 26:20 of Pharez, the family of the **P.**: of...... 6558

PHASEAH (fa-se'-ah) See also PASEAH.
Ne 7:51 of Uzza, the children of **P.**,............... 6454

PHEBE (fe'-be)
Ro 16:1 I commend unto you **P.** our sister,..... 5402
Ro *subscr.* sent by **P.** servant of the church at.... 5402

PHELET See BETH-PHELET.

PHENICE (fe-ni'-se) See also PHENICIA.
Ac 11:19 Stephen travelled as far as **P.**,.......... 5403
Ac 15:3 passed through **P.** and Samaria,......... 5403
Ac 27:12 means they might attain to **P.**,.......... 5405

PHENICIA (fe-nish'-e-ah) See also PHENICE.
Ac 21:2 finding a ship sailing...unto **P.**,........... 5403

PHIAL See VIAL.

PHICHOL (fi'-kol)
Ge 21:22 **P.** the chief captain of his host......... 6369
Ge 21:32 **P.** the chief captain of his host,......... 6369
Ge 26:26 **P.** the chief captain of his army......... 6369

PHILADELPHIA (fil-a-del'-fe-ah)
Re 1:11 **and unto Sardis, and unto P., and.** 5359
Re 3:7 **angel of the church in P. write;**.... 5359

PHILEMON (fi-le'-mon)
Phm *gen* *title* The Epistle Of Paul To **P.**........ 5371
Phm 1 unto **P.** our dearly beloved, and......... 5371
Phm *subscr* Written from Rome to **P.**, by............ 5371

PHILETUS (fi-le'-tus)
2Ti 2:17 of whom is Hymenaeus and **P.**;......... 5372

PHILIP (fil'-ip) See also PHILIP'S.
Mt 10:3 **P.**, and Bartholomew; Thomas,.......... 5376
Mk 3:18 Andrew, and **P.**, and Bartholomew,.... 5376
Lu 3:1 his brother **P.** tetrarch of Ituraea....... 5376
Lu 6:14 and John, **P.** and Bartholomew,.......... 5376
Joh 1:43 findeth **P.**, and saith unto him,.......... 5376
Joh 1:44 Now **P.** was of Bethsaida, the city..... 5376
Joh 1:45 **P.** findeth Nathanael, and saith.......... 5376
Joh 1:46 **P.** saith unto him, Come and see....... 5376
Joh 1:48 **Before that P. called thee, when**... 5376
Joh 6:5 he saith unto **P.**, **Whence shall we**... 5376
Joh 6:7 **P.** answered him, Two hundred......... 5376
Joh 12:21 same came therefore to **P.**,which....... 5376
Joh 12:22 **P.** cometh and telleth Andrew: and..... 5376
Joh 12:22 again Andrew and **P.** tell Jesus......... 5376
Joh 14:8 **P.** saith unto him, Lord, shew us....... 5376
Joh 14:9 **yet hast thou not known me, P.?**... 5376
Ac 1:13 **P.**, and Thomas, Bartholomew,.......... 5376
Ac 6:5 **P.**, and Prochorus, and Nicanor,....... 5376
Ac 8:5 **P.** went down to...city of Samaria,..... 5376
Ac 8:6 unto those things which **P.** spake,...... 5376
Ac 8:12 when they believed **P.** preaching........ 5376
Ac 8:13 baptized, he continued with **P.**,.......... 5376
Ac 8:26 angel of the Lord spake unto **P.**,......... 5376
Ac 8:29 Then the Spirit said unto **P.**, Go........ 5376
Ac 8:30 **P.** ran thither to him, and heard........ 5376
Ac 8:31 he desired **P.** that he would come...... 5376
Ac 8:34 And the eunuch answered **P.**, and...... 5376
Ac 8:35 **P.** opened his mouth, and began........ 5376
Ac 8:37 **P.** said, If thou believest with all........ 5376
Ac 8:38 the water, both **P.** and the eunuch;.... 5376
Ac 8:39 Spirit of the Lord caught away **P.**,...... 5376
Ac 8:40 But **P.** was found at Azotus: and........ 5376
Ac 21:8 unto the house of **P.** the evangelist,... 5376

PHILIPPI (fil-ip'-pi) See also PHILIPPIANS.
Mt 16:13 into the coasts of Caesarea **P.**,.......... 5375
Mk 8:27 into the towns of Caesarea **P.**:.......... 5375
Ac 16:12 And from thence to **P.**, which is........ 5375
Ac 20:6 And we sailed away from **P.** after...... 5375
1Co *subscr* Corinthians was written from **P.**......... 5375
2Co *subscr* Corinthians was written from **P.**......... 5375
Php 1:1 in Christ Jesus which are at **P.**,......... 5375
1Th 2:2 as ye know, at **P.**, we were bold in.... 5375

PHILIPPIANS (fil-ip'-pe-uns)
Php *general* *title* Epistle Of Paul . . . To The **P.**.... 5374
Php 4:15 Now ye **P.** know also, that in the....... 5374
Php *subscr.* It was written to the **P.** from Rome.........

PHILIP'S (fil'-ips)
Mt 14:3 Herodias' sake, his brother **P.** wife..... 5376
Mk 6:17 Herodias' sake, his brother **P.** wife:.... 5376
Lu 3:19 for Herodias his brother **P.** wife,........ 5376

PHILISTIA (fil-is'-te-ah) See also PALESTINE; PHILISTINE.
Ps 60:8 **P.**, triumph thou because of me.......... 6429
Ps 87:4 behold **P.**, and Tyre, with Ethiopia;.... 6429
Ps 108:9 my shoe; over **P.** will I triumph......... 6429

PHILISTIM (fil-is'-tim) See also PHILISTINES.
Ge 10:14 Casluhim, (out of whom came **P.**,)...... 6430

PHILISTINE (fil-is'-tin) See also PHILISTINES.
1Sa 17:8 am not I a **P.**,and ye servants to....... 6430
1Sa 17:10 **P.** said, I defy the armies of Israel..... 6430
1Sa 17:11 Israel heard those words of the **P.**,.... 6430
1Sa 17:16 **P.** drew near morning and evening,.... 6430
1Sa 17:23 up the champion, the **P.** of Gath,....... 6430
1Sa 17:26 done to the man that killeth this **P.**,... 6430
1Sa 17:26 for who is this uncircumcised **P.**,....... 6430
1Sa 17:32 will go and fight with this **P.**........... 6430
1Sa 17:33 art not able to go against this **P.**........ 6430
1Sa 17:36 uncircumcised **P.** shall be as one........ 6430
1Sa 17:37 me out of the hand of this **P.**........... 6430
1Sa 17:40 hand: and he drew near to the **P.**..... 6430
1Sa 17:41 **P.** came on and drew near unto......... 6430
1Sa 17:42 **P.** looked about, and saw David,........ 6430
1Sa 17:43 the **P.** said unto David, Am I a dog,... 6430
1Sa 17:43 the **P.** cursed David by his gods........ 6430
1Sa 17:44 the **P.** said to David, Come to me,..... 6430
1Sa 17:45 said David to the **P.**, Thou comest...... 6430
1Sa 17:48 the **P.** arose, and came and drew...... 6430
1Sa 17:48 toward the army to meet the **P.**........ 6430
1Sa 17:49 and smote the **P.** in his forehead,....... 6430
1Sa 17:50 prevailed over the **P.** with a sling,...... 6430
1Sa 17:50 and smote the **P.**, and slew him:........ 6430
1Sa 17:51 David ran, and stood upon the **P.**....... 6430
1Sa 17:54 And David took the head of the **P.**,.... 6430
1Sa 17:55 saw David go forth against the **P.**,..... 6430
1Sa 17:57 from the slaughter of the **P.**,............ 6430
1Sa 17:57 before Saul with the head of the **P.**.... 6430
1Sa 18:6 from the slaughter of the **P.**,............ 6430
1Sa 19:5 life in his hand, and slew the **P.**,........ 6430
1Sa 21:9 The sword of Goliath the **P.**, whom.... 6430
1Sa 22:10 him the sword of Goliath the **P.**......... 6430
2Sa 21:17 and smote the **P.**, and killed him....... 6430

PHILISTINES (fil-is'-tinz) See also PHILISTIM; PHILISTINES'.
Ge 21:32 returned into the land of the **P.**........ 6430
Ge 26:1 unto Abimelech king of the **P.**........... 6430
Ge 26:8 Abimelech king of the **P.** looked......... 6430
Ge 26:14 servants: and the **P.** envied him......... 6430
Ge 26:15 **P.** had stopped them, and filled.......... 6430
Ge 26:18 the **P.** had stopped them after the...... 6430
Ex 13:17 the way of the land of the **P.**,........... 6430
Ex 23:31 sea even unto the sea of the **P.**,........ 6430
Jos 13:2 all the borders of the **P.**, and all......... 6430
Jos 13:3 five lords of the **P.**; the..................... 6430
Jg 3:3 Namely, five lords of the **P.**, and....... 6430
Jg 3:31 slew of the **P.** six hundred men.......... 6430
Jg 10:6 the gods of the **P.**, and forsook the.... 6430
Jg 10:7 sold them into the hands of the **P.**,.... 6430
Jg 10:11 of Ammon, and from the **P.**?............ 6430
Jg 13:1 into the hand of the **P.** forty years...... 6430
Jg 13:5 Israel out of the hand of the **P.**......... 6430
Jg 14:1 Timnath of the daughters of the **P.**..... 6430
Jg 14:2 Timnath of the daughters of the **P.**:.... 6430
Jg 14:3 a wife of the uncircumcised **P.**?......... 6430
Jg 14:4 sought an occasion against the **P.**:...... 6430
Jg 14:4 the **P.** had dominion over Israel......... 6430
Jg 15:3 I be more blameless than the **P.**,...... 6430
Jg 15:5 go into the standing corn of the **P.**,.... 6430
Jg 15:6 the **P.** said, Who hath done this?....... 6430
Jg 15:6 the **P.** came up, and burnt her and..... 6430
Jg 15:9 **P.** went up, and pitched in Judah,....... 6430
Jg 15:11 not that the **P.** are rulers over us?..... 6430
Jg 15:12 deliver thee into the hand of the **P.**..... 6430
Jg 15:14 Lehi, the **P.** shouted against him:....... 6430
Jg 15:20 judged Israel in the days of the **P.**....... 6430
Jg 16:5 lords of the **P.** came up unto her,...... 6430
Jg 16:8 lords of the **P.** brought up to her....... 6430
Jg 16:9, 12,14, The **P.** be upon thee, Samson.. 6430
Jg 16:18 and called for the lords of the **P.**,....... 6430
Jg 16:18 lords of the **P.** came up unto her,...... 6430
Jg 16:20 The **P.** be upon thee, Samson........... 6430
Jg 16:21 **P.** took him, and put out his eyes,..... 6430
Jg 16:23 the lords of the **P.** gathered them....... 6430
Jg 16:27 all the lords of the **P.** were there;...... 6430
Jg 16:28 may be at once avenged of the **P.**...... 6430
Jg 16:30 Samson said, Let me die with the **P.**..6430
1Sa 4:1 went out against the **P.** to battle,....... 6430
1Sa 4:1 and the **P.** pitched in Aphek............. 6430
1Sa 4:2 **P.** put themselves in array against...... 6430
1Sa 4:2 Israel was smitten before the **P.**:....... 6430
1Sa 4:3 smitten us to day before the **P.**?........ 6430
1Sa 4:6 when the **P.** heard the noise of the.... 6430
1Sa 4:7 the **P.** were afraid, for they said,....... 6430
1Sa 4:9 quit yourselves like men, O ye **P.**,..... 6430
1Sa 4:10 **P.** fought, and Israel was smitten,...... 6430
1Sa 4:17 and said, Israel is fled before the **P.**,.. 6430
1Sa 5:1 And the **P.** took the ark of God, and.. 6430
1Sa 5:2 When the **P.** took the ark of God,...... 6430
1Sa 5:8 and gathered all the lords of the **P.**.... 6430
1Sa 5:11 together all the lords of the **P.**, and.... 6430
1Sa 6:1 the country of the **P.** seven months.... 6430
1Sa 6:2 the **P.** called for the priests and........ 6430
1Sa 6:4 the number of the lords of the **P.**:....... 6430
1Sa 6:12 the lords of the **P.** went after them.... 6430
1Sa 6:16 the five lords of the **P.** had seen it,.... 6430
1Sa 6:17 emerods which the **P.** returned for..... 6430
1Sa 6:18 the number of all the cities of the **P.**.. 6430
1Sa 6:21 **P.** have brought again the ark of........ 6430
1Sa 7:3 deliver you out of the hand of the **P.**.. 6430
1Sa 7:7 **P.** heard that the children of Israel..... 6430
1Sa 7:7 the lords of the **P.** went up against..... 6430
1Sa 7:7 heard it, they were afraid of the **P.**.... 6430
1Sa 7:8 save us out of the hand of the **P.**....... 6430
1Sa 7:10 the **P.** drew near to battle against...... 6430
1Sa 7:10 thunder on that day upon the **P.**,....... 6430
1Sa 7:11 pursued the **P.**, and smote them,........ 6430
1Sa 7:13 So the **P.** were subdued, and they..... 6430
1Sa 7:13 hand of the Lord was against the **P.**... 6430
1Sa 7:14 which the **P.** had taken from Israel..... 6430
1Sa 7:14 deliver out of the hand of the **P.**........ 6430
1Sa 9:16 my people out of the hand of the **P.**:.. 6430
1Sa 10:5 where is the garrison of the **P.**:......... 6430
1Sa 12:9 Hazor, and into the hand of the **P.**,.... 6430
1Sa 13:3 smote the garrison of the **P.** that....... 6430
1Sa 13:3 was in Geba, and the **P.** heard of it.... 6430
1Sa 13:4 had smitten a garrison of the **P.**,........ 6430
1Sa 13:4 had in abomination with the **P.**........... 6430
1Sa 13:5, 11 the **P.** gathered themselves.......... 6430
1Sa 13:12 **P.** will come down now upon me to.... 6430
1Sa 13:16 but the **P.** encamped in Michmash...... 6430
1Sa 13:17 camp of the **P.** in three companies:.... 6430
1Sa 13:19 for the **P.** said, Lest the Hebrews..... 6430
1Sa 13:20 the Israelites went down to the **P.**,..... 6430
1Sa 13:23 the garrison of the **P.** went out to...... 6430
1Sa 14:11 unto the garrison of the **P.**: and......... 6430
1Sa 14:11 the **P.** said, Behold, the Hebrews....... 6430
1Sa 14:19 of the **P.** went on and increased:....... 6430
1Sa 14:21 Hebrews that were with the **P.**......... 6430
1Sa 14:22 when they heard that the **P.** fled,....... 6430
1Sa 14:30 greater slaughter among the **P.**?........ 6430
1Sa 14:31 they smote the **P.** that day from........ 6430
1Sa 14:36 us go down after the **P.** by night,...... 6430
1Sa 14:37 God, Shall I go down after the **P.**?...... 6430
1Sa 14:46 went up from following the **P.**:.......... 6430
1Sa 14:46 and the **P.** went to their own place..... 6430

1Sa 14:47 kings of Zobah, and against the **P.**: 6430
1Sa 14:52 war against the **P.** all the days of 6430
1Sa 17:1 **P.** gathered together their armies 6430
1Sa 17:2 the battle in array against the **P.** 6430
1Sa 17:3 **P.** stood on a mountain on the one 6430
1Sa 17:4 champion out of the camp of the **P.**, 6430
1Sa 17:19 valley of Elah, fighting with the **P.** 6430
1Sa 17:21 the **P.** had put the battle in array, 6430
1Sa 17:23 name, out of the armies of the **P.**, 6430
1Sa 17:46 carcases of the hosts of the **P.** this 6430
1Sa 17:51 **P.** saw their champion was dead, 6430
1Sa 17:52 and shouted, and pursued the **P.**, 6430
1Sa 17:52 the wounded of the **P.** fell down by 6430
1Sa 17:53 returned from chasing after the **P.**, 6430
1Sa 18:17 let the hand of the **P.** be upon him 6430
1Sa 18:21 hand of the **P.** may be against him. 6430
1Sa 18:25 but an hundred foreskins of the **P.**, 6430
1Sa 18:25 David fall by the hand of the **P.** 6430
1Sa 18:27 slew of the **P.** two hundred men; 6430
1Sa 18:30 the princes of the **P.** went forth: 6430
1Sa 19:8 fought with the **P.**, and slew them 6430
1Sa 23:1 Behold, the **P.** fight against Keilah, 6430
1Sa 23:2 Shall I go and smite these **P.**? 6430
1Sa 23:2 Go, and smite the **P.**, and save 6430
1Sa 23:3 against the armies of the **P.**? 6430
1Sa 23:4 will deliver the **P.** into thine hand 6430
1Sa 23:5 to Keilah, and fought with the **P.**, 6430
1Sa 23:27 for the **P.** have invaded the land. 6430
1Sa 23:28 David, and went against the **P.**: 6430
1Sa 24:1 was returned from following the **P.**, 6430
1Sa 27:1 escape into the land of the **P.**; and 6430
1Sa 27:7 David dwelt in the country of the **P.** 6430
1Sa 27:11 dwelleth in the country of the **P.** 6430
1Sa 28:1 **P.** gathered their armies together 6430
1Sa 28:4 **P.** gathered themselves together, 6430
1Sa 28:5 when Saul saw the host of the **P.**, 6430
1Sa 28:15 for the **P.** make war against me, 6430
1Sa 28:19 with thee into the hand of the **P.**: 6430
1Sa 28:19 of Israel into the hand of the **P.** 6430
1Sa 29:1 the **P.** gathered together all their 6430
1Sa 29:2 the lords of the **P.** passed on by 6430
1Sa 29:3 Then said the princes of the **P.**, 6430
1Sa 29:3 said unto the princes of the **P.**, Is 6430
1Sa 29:4 of the **P.** were wroth with him; 6430
1Sa 29:4 the princes of the **P.** said unto him, 6430
1Sa 29:7 displease not the lords of the **P.** 6430
1Sa 29:9 the princes of the **P.** have said, He 6430
1Sa 29:11 to return into the land of the **P.** 6430
1Sa 29:11 And the **P.** went up to Jezreel. 6430
1Sa 30:16 had taken out of the land of the **P.**, 6430
1Sa 31:1 Now the **P.** fought against Israel: 6430
1Sa 31:1 of Israel fled from before the **P.**, 6430
1Sa 31:2 the **P.** followed hard upon Saul and 6430
1Sa 31:2 **P.** slew Jonathan, and Abinadab, 6430
1Sa 31:7 and the **P.** came and dwelt in them. 6430
1Sa 31:8 when the **P.** came to strip the slain, 6430
1Sa 31:9 into the land of the **P.** round about. 6430
1Sa 31:11 that which the **P.** had done to Saul: 6430
2Sa 1:20 lest the daughters of the **P.** rejoice, 6430
2Sa 3:14 for an hundred foreskins of the **P.** 6430
2Sa 3:18 Israel out of the hand of the **P.**, and 6430
2Sa 5:17 **P.** heard that they had anointed 6430
2Sa 5:17 all the **P.** came up to seek David; 6430
2Sa 5:18 The **P.** also came and spread 6430
2Sa 5:19 saying, Shall I go up to the **P.**? 6430
2Sa 5:19 deliver the **P.** into thine hand. 6430
2Sa 5:22 And the **P.** came up yet again, and 6430
2Sa 5:24 thee, to smite the host of the **P.** 6430
2Sa 5:25 smote the **P.** from Geba until thou 6430
2Sa 8:1 smote the **P.**, and subdued them: 6430
2Sa 8:1 out of the hand of the **P.** 6430
2Sa 8:12 children of Ammon, and of the **P.**, 6430
2Sa 19:9 us out of the hand of the **P.**; 6430
2Sa 21:12 where the **P.** had hanged them, 6430
2Sa 21:12 the **P.** had slain Saul in Gilboa: 6430
2Sa 21:15 **P.** had yet war again with Israel; 6430
2Sa 21:15 him, and fought against the **P.**: 6430
2Sa 21:18 again a battle with the **P.** at Gob: 6430
2Sa 21:19 again a battle in Gob with the **P.**, 6430
2Sa 23:9 with David, when they defied the **P.** 6430
2Sa 23:10 smote the **P.** until his hand was 6430
2Sa 23:11 **P.**...gathered together into a troop, 6430
2Sa 23:11 and the people fled from the **P.** 6430
2Sa 23:12 and defended it, and slew the **P.**: 6430
2Sa 23:13 of the **P.** pitched in the valley 6430
2Sa 23:14 of the **P.** was then in Beth-lehem. 6430
2Sa 23:16 brake through the host of the **P.**, 6430

1Ki 4:21 the river unto the land of the **P.**, 6430
1Ki 15:27 which belonged to the **P.**; 6430
1Ki 16:15 which belonged to the **P.** 6430
2Ki 8:2 sojourned in the land of the **P.** 6430
2Ki 8:3 returned out of the land of the **P.**: 6430
2Ki 18:8 He smote the **P.**, even unto Gaza, 6430
1Ch 1:12 Casluhim, (of whom came the **P.**,) 6430
1Ch 10:1 Now the **P.** fought against Israel; 6430
1Ch 10:1 of Israel fled from before the **P.**, 6430
1Ch 10:2 the **P.** followed hard after Saul, 6430
1Ch 10:2 **P.** slew Jonathan, and Abinadab, 6430
1Ch 10:7 and the **P.** came and dwelt in them. 6430
1Ch 10:8 the **P.** came to strip the slain, 6430
1Ch 10:9 and sent into the land of the **P.** 6430
1Ch 10:11 all that the **P.** had done to Saul, 6430
1Ch 11:13 the **P.** were gathered together 6430
1Ch 11:13 the people fled from before the **P.** 6430
1Ch 11:14 and delivered it, and slew the **P.**; 6430
1Ch 11:15 host of the **P.** encamped in the 6430
1Ch 11:18 brake through the host of the **P.**, 6430
1Ch 12:19 with the **P.** against Saul to battle: 6430
1Ch 12:19 lords of the **P.** upon advisement 6430
1Ch 14:8 **P.** heard that David was anointed 6430
1Ch 14:8 all the **P.** went up to seek David. 6430
1Ch 14:9 the **P.** came and spread themselves 6430
1Ch 14:10 Shall I go up against the **P.**? 6430
1Ch 14:13 the **P.** yet again spread themselves 6430
1Ch 14:15 thee to smite the host of the **P.** 6430
1Ch 14:16 smote the host of the **P.** from 6430
1Ch 18:1 David smote the **P.**, and subdued 6430
1Ch 18:1 towns out of the hand of the **P.** 6430
1Ch 18:11 Ammon, and from the **P.**, and from 6430
1Ch 20:4 arose war at Gezer with the **P.**: 6430
1Ch 20:5 there was war again with the **P.**: 6430
2Ch 9:26 river even unto the land of the **P.**, 6430
2Ch 17:11 **P.** brought Jehoshaphat presents, 6430
2Ch 21:16 Jehoram the spirit of the **P.**, 6430
2Ch 26:6 warred against the **P.**, and brake 6430
2Ch 26:6 about Ashdod, and among the **P.** 6430
2Ch 26:7 God helped him against the **P.**, 6430
2Ch 28:18 The **P.** also had invaded the cities 6430
Ps 56:*title* when the **P.** took him in Gath. 6430
Ps 83:7 **P.** with the inhabitants of Tyre; 6430
Isa 2:6 and are soothsayers like the **P.**, 6430
Isa 9:12 Syrians before, and the **P.** behind; 6430
Isa 11:14 shoulders of the **P.** toward the west; 6430
Jer 25:20 all the kings of the land of the **P.**, 6430
Jer 47:1 the prophet against the **P.**, 6430
Jer 47:4 day that cometh to spoil all the **P.**, 6430
Jer 47:4 the Lord will spoil the **P.**, the 6430
Eze 16:27 the daughters of the **P.**, which are 6430
Eze 16:57 the daughters of the **P.**, which 6430
Eze 25:15 the **P.** have dealt by revenge, 6430
Eze 25:16 stretch out mine hand upon the **P.**, 6430
Am 1:8 remnant of the **P.** shall perish, 6430
Am 6:2 then go down to Gath of the **P.**: 6430
Am 9:7 **P.** from Caphtor, and the Syrians 6430
Ob 19 and they of the plain the **P.**: and 6430
Zep 2:5 O Canaan, the land of the **P.**, I will 6430
Zec 9:6 I will cut off the pride of the **P.** 6430

PHILISTINES' (fil-is'-tinz)
Ge 21:34 Abraham sojourned in the **P.** land 6430
1Sa 14:1 let us go over to the **P.** garrison, 6430
1Sa 14:4 to go over unto the **P.** garrison, 6430
1Ch 11:16 **P.** garrison was then at Beth-lehem. 6430

PHILOLOGUS (fil-ol'-o-gus)
Ro 16:15 Salute **P.**, and Julia, Nereus, and *5378*

PHILOSOPHERS
Ac 17:18 Then certain **p.** of the Epicureans, *5386*

PHILOSOPHY
Col 2:8 spoil you through **p.** and...deceit *5385*

PHINEHAS (fin'-e-has) See also PHINEHAS'.
Ex 6:25 she bare him **P.**: these are the 6372
Nu 25:7 And when **P.**, the son of Eleazar, 6372
Nu 25:11 **P.**, the son of Eleazar, the son of 6372
Nu 31:6 **P.** the son of Eleazar the priest, 6372
Jos 22:13 **P.** the son of Eleazar the priest, 6372
Jos 22:30 when **P.** the priest, and the princes 6372
Jos 22:31 **P.** the son of Eleazar the priest 6372
Jos 22:32 **P.** the son of Eleazar the priest, 6372
Jos 24:33 a hill that pertained to **P.** his son, 6372
Jg 20:28 **P.**, the son of Eleazar, the son of 6372
1Sa 1:3 the two sons of Eli, Hophni and **P.**, 6372
1Sa 2:34 thy two sons, on Hophni and **P.**; 6372
1Sa 4:4 the two sons of Eli, Hophni and **P.**, 6372
1Sa 4:11 of Eli, Hophni and **P.**, were slain. 6372
1Sa 4:17 sons also, Hophni and **P.**, are dead, 6372
1Sa 14:3 Ichabod's brother, the son of **P.**, 6372
1Ch 6:4 Eleazar begat **P.**, **P.** begat Abishua, 6372
1Ch 6:50 Aaron; Eleazar his son, **P.** his son, 6372
1Ch 9:20 **P.** the son of Eleazar was the ruler 6372
Ezr 7:5 The son of Abishua, the son of **P.**, 6372
Ezr 8:2 Of the sons of **P.**; Gershom: of the 6372
Ezr 8:33 with him was Eleazar the son of **P.**; 6372
Ps 106:30 stood up **P.**,...executed judgment: 6372

PHINEHAS' (fin'-e-has)
1Sa 4:19 And his daughter in law, **P.** wife, 6372

PHLEGON (fle'-gon)
Ro 16:14 Salute Asyncritus, **P.**, Hermas, *5393*

PHOEBE See PHEBE.

PHOENICE See PHENICE.

PHOENICIA See PHENICIA.

PHOENICIAN See PHENICIAN.

PHRYGIA (frij'-e-ah)
Ac 2:10 **P.**, and Pamphylia, in Egypt, and *5435*
Ac 16:6 when they had gone throughout **P.** *5435*
Ac 18:23 all the country of Galatia and **P.** *5435*
1Ti *subscr* chiefest city of **P.** Pacatiana. *5435*

PHURAH (fu'-rah)
Jg 7:10 go thou with **P.** thy servant down 6513
Jg 7:11 went he down with **P.** his servant 6513

PHUT (fut) See also PUT.
Ge 10:6 and Mizraim, and **P.**, and Canaan. 6316
Eze 27:10 of Persia and of Lud and of **P.** 6316

PHUVAH (fu'-vah) See also PUAH.
Ge 46:13 sons of Issachar; Tola, and **P.**, 6312

PHYGELLUS (fi-jel'-lus)
2Ti 1:15 of whom are **P.** and Hermogenes. *5436*

PHYLACTERIES
Mt 23:5 **they make broad their p., and** *5440*

PHYSICIAN See also PHYSICIANS.
Jer 8:22 in Gilead; is there no **p.** there? 7495
Mt 9:12 **They that be whole need not a p.,** *2395*
Mk 2:17 **are whole have no need of the p.,** *2395*
Lu 4:23 **me this proverb, P., heal thyself:** *2395*
Lu 5:31 **They that are whole need not a p.;** *2395*
Col 4:14 Luke, the beloved **p.**, and Demas, *2395*

PHYSICIANS
Ge 50:2 commanded his servants the **p.** 7495
Ge 50:2 and the **p.** embalmed Israel. 7495
2Ch 16:12 sought not to the Lord, but to the **p.** 7495
Job 13:4 of lies, ye are all **p.** of no value. 7495
Mk 5:26 suffered many things of many **p.**, *2395*
Lu 8:43 had spent all her living upon **p.**, *2395*

PI See PI-BESETH; PI-HAHIROTH.

PI-BESETH (pi-be'-zeth)
Eze 30:17 The young men of Aven and of **P.** 6364

PICK
Pr 30:17 ravens of the valley shall **p.** it out, 5365

PICTURES
Nu 33:52 destroy all their **p.**, and destroy 4906
Pr 25:11 is like apples of gold in **p.** of silver. 4906
Isa 2:16 Tarshish,...upon all pleasant **p.** 7914

PIECE See also APIECE; PIECES.
Ge 15:10 laid each **p.** one against another: 1335
Ex 37:7 of gold, beaten out of one **p.** made 4749
Nu 10:2 of a whole **p.** shalt thou make them:
Jg 9:53 woman cast a **p.** of a millstone 6400
1Sa 2:36 crouch to him for a **p.** of silver and 95
1Sa 2:36 that I may eat a **p.** of bread. 6595
1Sa 30:12 gave him a **p.** of a cake of figs, 6400
2Sa 6:19 of bread, and a good **p.** of flesh, 829
2Sa 11:21 a woman cast a **p.** of a millstone 6400
2Sa 23:11 a **p.** of ground full of lentiles: 2513
2Ki 3:19 and mar every good **p.** of land with 2513
2Ki 3:25 on every good **p.** of land cast every 2513
1Ch 16:3 of bread, and a good **p.** of flesh, 829
Ne 3:11 repaired the other **p.**, and the 4060
Ne 3:19 another **p.** over against the going 4060
Ne 3:20 earnestly repaired the other **p.**, 4060
Ne 3:21 Urijah the son of Koz another **p.**, 4060

Ne 3:24 the son of Henadad another **p.**, 4060
Ne 3:27 the Tekoites repaired another **p.**, 4060
Ne 3:30 the sixth son of Zalaph, another **p.** 4060
Job 41:24 as a **p.** of the nether millstone. 6400
Job 42:11 man also gave him a **p.** of money,
Pr 6:26 a man is brought to a **p.** of bread: 3603
Pr 28:21 for a **p.** of bread that man will 6595
Ca 4:3 are like a **p.** of a pomegranate 6400
Ca 6:7 As a **p.** of a pomegranate are thy 6400
Jer 37:21 give him daily a **p.** of bread out 3603
Eze 24:4 thereof into it, even every good **p.**, 5409
Eze 24:6 bring it out **p.** by **p.**; let no lot fall 5409
Am 3:12 the lion two legs, or a **p.** of an ear; 915
Am 4:7 one **p.** was rained upon, and the
Am 4:7 **p.** whereupon it rained not withered.
Mt 9:16 **putteth a p. of new cloth unto an** *1915*
Mt 17:27 **mouth, thou shalt find a p. of money:**
Mk 2:21 **seweth a p. of new cloth on an old** *1915*
Mk 2:21 **the new p. that filled it up taketh** *4138*
Lu 5:36 **putteth a p. of a new garment** *1915*
Lu 5:36 **the p. that was taken out of the** *1915*
Lu 14:18 **I have bought a p. of ground, and**
Lu 15:8 **if she lose one p., doth not light a.** *1406*
Lu 15:9 **have found the p. which I had lost.** *1406*
Lu 24:42 gave him a **p.** of a broiled fish, *3313*

PIECES See also SHOULDERPIECES.
Ge 15:17 that passed between those **p.**, 1506
Ge 20:16 thy brother a thousand **p.** of silver:
Ge 33:19 father, for an hundred **p.** of money.
Ge 37:28 Ishmeelites for twenty **p.** of silver:
Ge 37:33 Joseph is without doubt rent in **p.**
Ge 44:28 and I said, Surely he is torn in **p.**;
Ge 45:22 he gave three hundred **p.** of silver,
Ex 15:6 Lord, hath dashed in **p.** the enemy.
Ex 22:13 If it be torn in **p.**, then let him bring
Ex 29:17 And thou shalt cut the ram in **p.**, 5409
Ex 29:17 put them unto his **p.**, and unto his 5409
Le 1:6 burnt offering, and cut it into his **p.** 5409
Le 1:12 he shall cut it into his **p.**, with his 5409
Le 2:6 Thou shalt part it in **p.**, and pour 6595
Le 6:21 the baken **p.** of the meat offering 6595
Le 8:20 he cut the ram into **p.**; and Moses 5409
Le 8:20 the head, and the **p.**, and the fat. 5409
Le 9:13 with the **p.** thereof, and the head: 5409
Jos 24:32 Shechem for an hundred **p.** of silver:
Jg 9:4 him threescore and ten **p.** of silver
Jg 16:5 of us eleven hundred **p.** of silver.
Jg 19:29 with her bones, into twelve **p.**, 5409
Jg 20:6 my concubine, and cut her in **p.**,
1Sa 2:10 of the Lord shall be broken to **p.**;
1Sa 11:7 yoke of oxen, and hewed them in **p.**,
1Sa 15:33 Samuel hewed Agag in **p.** before the
1Ki 11:30 on him, and rent it in twelve **p.**: 7168
1Ki 11:31 to Jeroboam, Take thee ten **p.**: 7168
1Ki 18:23 and cut it in **p.**, and lay it on wood,
1Ki 18:33 and cut the bullock in **p.**, and laid
1Ki 19:11 brake in **p.** the rocks before the Lord:
2Ki 2:12 clothes, and rent them in two **p.** 7168
2Ki 5:5 silver, and six thousand **p.** of gold,
2Ki 6:25 was sold for fourscore **p.** of silver,
2Ki 6:25 of dove's dung for five **p.** of silver.
2Ki 11:18 and his images brake they in **p.**
2Ki 18:4 brake in **p.** the brasen serpent that
2Ki 23:14 he brake in **p.** the images, and cut
2Ki 24:13 cut in **p.** all the vessels of gold which
2Ki 25:13 did the Chaldees break in **p.**, and
2Ch 23:17 brake his altars and his images in **p.**,
2Ch 25:12 that they all were broken in **p.**
2Ch 28:24 cut in **p.** the vessels of the house of
2Ch 31:1 brake the images in **p.**, and cut
2Ch 34:4 the molten images, he brake in **p.**,
Job 16:12 me by my neck, and shaken me to **p.**,
Job 19:2 soul, and brake me in **p.** with words?
Job 34:24 brake in **p.** mighty men without
Job 40:18 His bones are as strong **p.** of brass;
Ps 2:9 dash them in **p.** like a potter's vessel.
Ps 7:2 my soul like a lion, rending it in **p.**,
Ps 50:22 that forget God, lest I tear you in **p.**,
Ps 58:7 his arrows, let them be as cut in **p.**
Ps 68:30 submit himself with **p.** of silver: 7518
Ps 72:4 and shall break in **p.** the oppressor.
Ps 74:14 breakest the heads of leviathan in **p.**,
Ps 89:10 Thou hast broken Rahab in **p.**, as one
Ps 94:5 They break in **p.** thy people, O Lord,
Ca 8:11 was to bring a thousand **p.** of silver.
Isa 3:15 mean ye that ye beat my people to **p.**,
Isa 8:9 ye shall be broken in **p.**; and give ear,
Isa 8:9 and ye shall be broken in **p.**; gird
Isa 8:9 yourselves...ye shall be broken in **p.**
Isa 13:16 children also shall be dashed to **p.**
Isa 13:18 also shall dash the young men to **p.**;
Isa 30:14 potter's vessel that is broken in **p.**;
Isa 45:2 I will break in **p.** the gates of brass,
Jer 5:6 goeth out thence shall be torn in **p.**:
Jer 23:29 hammer that breaketh the rock in **p.**?
Jer 50:2 Merodach is broken in **p.**; her idols
Jer 50:2 her images are broken in **p.**
Jer 51:20 thee will I break in **p.** the nations,
Jer 51:21 break in **p.** the horse and his rider;
Jer 51:21 break in **p.** the chariot and his rider;
Jer 51:22 will I break in **p.** man and woman;
Jer 51:22 will I break in **p.** old and young;
Jer 51:22 break in **p.** the young man and the
Jer 51:23 break in **p.** with thee the shepherd and
Jer 51:23 will I break in **p.** the husbandman
Jer 51:23 I break in **p.** captains and rulers.
La 3:11 aside my ways, and pulled me in **p.**:
Eze 4:14 that dieth of itself, or is torn in **p.**;
Eze 13:19 of barley and for **p.** of bread, 6595
Eze 24:4 Gather the **p.** thereof into it, even 5409
Da 2:5 ye shall be cut in **p.**, and your 1917
Da 2:34 of iron and clay, and brake them to **p.**
Da 2:35 and the gold, broken to **p.** together,
Da 2:40 forasmuch as iron breaketh in **p.** and
Da 2:40 these, shall it break in **p.** and bruise.
Da 2:44 it shall break in **p.** and consume all
Da 2:45 and that it break in **p.** the iron, the
Da 3:29 and Abed-nego, shall be cut in **p.**, 1917
Da 6:24 and brake all their bones in **p.** or
Da 7:7 it devoured and brake in **p.**, and
Da 7:19 which devoured, brake in **p.**, and
Da 7:23 shall tread it down, and break it in **p.**
Ho 3:2 her to me for fifteen **p.** of silver,
Ho 8:6 of Samaria shall be broken in **p.**
Ho 10:14 mother was dashed in **p.** upon her
Ho 13:16 their infants shall be dashed in **p.**,
Mic 1:7 images thereof shall be beaten to **p.**,
Mic 3:3 their bones, and chop them in **p.**,
Mic 4:13 thou shalt beat in **p.** many people:
Mic 5:8 treadeth down, and teareth in **p.**,
Na 2:1 He that dasheth in **p.** is come up
Na 2:12 The lion did tear in **p.** enough for his
Na 3:10 young children also were dashed in **p.**
Zec 11:12 for my price thirty **p.** of silver.
Zec 11:13 And I took the thirty **p.** of silver, and
Zec 11:16 the fat, and tear their claws in **p.**
Zec 12:3 themselves with it shall be cut in **p.**,
Mt 26:15 with him for thirty **p.** of silver.
Mt 27:3 brought again the thirty **p.** of silver
Mt 27:5 cast down the **p.** of silver in the
Mt 27:6 the chief priests took the silver **p.**,
Mt 27:9 And they took the thirty **p.** of silver
Mk 5:4 by him, and the fetters broken in **p.**,
Lu 15:8 **woman having ten p. of silver,** *1406*
Ac 19:19 found it fifty thousand **p.** of silver.
Ac 23:10 should have been pulled in **p.** of *1288*
Ac 27:44 and some on broken **p.** of the ship.

PIERCE See also PIERCED; PIERCETH; PIERCING.
Nu 24:8 **p.** them through with his arrows. 4272
2Ki 18:21 it will go into his hand, and **p.** it: 5344
Isa 36:6 it will go into his hand, and **p.** it: 5344
Lu 2:35 shall **p.** through thy own soul also,) *1330*

PIERCED
Jg 5:26 had **p.** and stricken through his 4272
Job 30:17 My bones are **p.** in me in the night 5365
Ps 22:16 me: they **p.** my hands and my feet. 738
Zec 12:10 look upon me whom they have **p.**, 1856
Joh 19:34 soldiers with a spear **p.** his side, *3572*
Joh 19:37 shall look on him whom they **p.** *1574*
1Ti 6:10 **p.** themselves through with many *4044*
Re 1:7 him, and they also which **p.** him: *1574*

PIERCETH
Job 40:24 eyes: his nose **p.** through snares. 5344

PIERCING See also PIERCINGS.
Isa 27:1 punish leviathan the **p.** serpent, 1281
Heb 4:12 **p.** even to the dividing asunder of *1338*

PIERCINGS
Pr 12:18 speaketh like the **p.** of a sword: 4094

PIETY
1Ti 5:4 them learn first to show **p.** at *2151*

PIGEON See also PIGEONS.
Ge 15:9 and a turtledove, and a young **p.** 1469
Le 12:6 and a young **p.**, or a turtledove, 3123

PIGEONS
Le 1:14 of turtledoves, or of young **p.** 3123
Le 5:7, 11 two turtledoves, or two young **p.**, 3123
Le 12:8 bring two turtles, or two young **p.**; 3123
Le 14:22 two turtledoves, or two young **p.**, 3123
Le 14:30 the turtledoves, or of the young **p.**, 3123
Le 15:14 two turtledoves, or two young **p.**, 3123
Le 15:29 her two turtles, or two young **p.**, 3123
Nu 6:10 bring two turtles, or two young **p.**, 3123
Lu 2:24 of turtledoves, or two young **p.** *4058*

PI-HAHIROTH (pi-ha-hi'-roth)
Ex 14:2 they turn and encamp before **P.**, 6367
Ex 14:9 sea, beside **P.**, before Baal-zephon. 6367
Nu 33:7 Etham, and turned again unto **P.**, 6367
Nu 33:8 And they departed from before **P.**, 6367

PILATE (pi'-lut)
Mt 27:2 him to Pontius **P.** the governor. *4091*
Mt 27:13 said **P.** unto him, Hearest thou not *4091*
Mt 27:17 **P.** said unto them, Whom will ye *4091*
Mt 27:22 **P.** saith unto them, What shall I do *4091*
Mt 27:24 When **P.** saw that he could prevail *4091*
Mt 27:58 went to **P.**, and begged the body of *4091*
Mt 27:58 Then **P.** commanded the body to be *4091*
Mt 27:62 Pharisees came together unto **P.**, *4091*
Mt 27:65 **P.** said unto them, Ye have a *4091*
Mk 15:1 him away, and delivered him to **P.** *4091*
Mk 15:2 **P.** asked him, Art thou the King of *4091*
Mk 15:4 And **P.** asked him again, saying, *4091*
Mk 15:5 nothing; so that **P.** marvelled. *4091*
Mk 15:9 **P.** answered them, saying, Will ye *4091*
Mk 15:12 **P.** answered and said again unto *4091*
Mk 15:14 **P.** said unto them, Why, what evil *4091*
Mk 15:15 And so **P.**, willing to content the *4091*
Mk 15:43 went in boldly unto **P.**, and craved *4091*
Mk 15:44 **P.** marvelled if he were already *4091*
Lu 3:1 Pontius **P.** being governor of *4091*
Lu 13:1 blood **P.** had mingled with their *4091*
Lu 23:1 of them arose, and led him unto **P.** *4091*
Lu 23:3 And **P.** asked him, saying, Art thou *4091*
Lu 23:4 said **P.** to the chief priests and to *4091*
Lu 23:6 When **P.** heard of Galilee, he asked *4091*
Lu 23:11 robe, and sent him again to **P.** *4091*
Lu 23:12 **P.** and Herod were made friends *4091*
Lu 23:13 **P.**, when he had called together *4091*
Lu 23:20 **P.** therefore, willing to release *4091*
Lu 23:24 **P.** gave sentence that it should be *4091*
Lu 23:52 This man went unto **P.**, and begged *4091*
Joh 18:29 **P.** then went out unto them, and *4091*
Joh 18:31 Then said **P.** unto them, Take ye *4091*
Joh 18:33 **P.** entered into the judgment hall *4091*
Joh 18:35 **P.** annswered, Am I a Jew? Thine *4091*
Joh 18:37 **P.** therefore said unto him, Art thou *4091*
Joh 18:38 **P.** saith unto him, What is truth? *4091*
Joh 19:1 Then **P.** therefore took Jesus, and *4091*
Joh 19:4 **P.** therefore went forth again, and *4091*
Joh 19:5 **P.** saith unto them, Behold the man!
Joh 19:6 **P.** saith unto them, Take ye him, *4091*
Joh 19:8 **P.** therefore heard that saying, *4091*
Joh 19:10 Then saith **P.** unto him, Speakest *4091*
Joh 19:12 thenceforth **P.** sought to release *4091*
Joh 19:13 **P.** therefore heard that saying, *4091*
Joh 19:15 **P.** saith unto them, Shall I crucify *4091*
Joh 19:19 **P.** wrote a title, and put it on the *4091*
Joh 19:21 the chief priests of the Jews to **P.**, *4091*
Joh 19:22 **P.** answered, What I have written *4091*
Joh 19:31 besought **P.** that their legs might *4091*
Joh 19:38 besought **P.** that he might take *4091*
Joh 19:38 of Jesus: and **P.** gave him leave. *4091*
Ac 3:13 denied him in the presence of **P.**, *4091*
Ac 4:27 both Herod, and Pontius **P.**, with *4091*
Ac 13:28 they **P.** that he should be slain. *4091*
1Ti 6:13 before Pontius **P.** witnessed a good *4091*

PILDASH (pil'-dash)
Ge 22:22 and Hazo, and **P.**, and Jidlaph, 6394

PILE
Isa 30:33 **p.** thereof is fire and much wood; 4071
Eze 24:9 will even make the **p.** for fire great. 4071

PILEHA (pil'-e-hah)
Ne 10:24 Hallohesh, **P.**, Shobek 6401

PILESER See TIGLATH-PILESER.

PILGRIM See PILGRIMS.

PILGRIMAGE
Ge 47:9 The days of the years of my **p.** are 4033
Ge 47:9 my fathers in the days of their **p.**....... 4033
Ex 6:4 land of Canaan, the land of their **p.**, ... 4033
Ps 119:54 my songs in the house of my **p.**......... 4033

PILGRIMS
Heb 11:13 strangers and **p.** on the earth. *3927*
1Pe 2:11 I beseech you as strangers and **p.**, ... *3927*

PILLAR See also PILLARS.
Ge 19:26 him, and she became a **p.** of salt,....... 5333
Ge 28:18 his pillows, and set it up for a **p.**,....... 4676
Ge 28:22 this stone, which I have set for a **p.**, .. 4676
Ge 31:13 where thou anointedst the **p.**, and...... 4676
Ge 31:45 took a stone, and set it up for a **p.**...... 4676
Ge 31:51 this heap, and behold this **p.**, which 4676
Ge 31:52 this **p.** be witness, that I will not 4676
Ge 31:52 not pass over this heap and this **p.**..... 4676
Ge 35:14 And Jacob set up a **p.** in the place 4676
Ge 35:14 talked with him, even a **p.** of............ 4678
Ge 35:20 And Jacob set a **p.** upon her grave: 4676
Ge 35:20 that is the **p.** of Rachel's grave 4678
Ex 13:21 them by day in a **p.** of a cloud, to 5982
Ex 13:21 by night in a **p.** of fire, to give them... 5982
Ex 13:22 took not away the **p.** of the cloud........ 5982
Ex 13:22 by day, nor the **p.** of fire by night, ... 5982
Ex 14:19 the **p.** of the cloud went from before... 5982
Ex 14:24 through the **p.** of fire and of the......... 5982
Ex 33:9 the cloudy **p.** descended, and stood 5982
Ex 33:10 the people saw the cloudy **p.** stand..... 5982
Nu 12:5 Lord came down in the **p.** of the........ 5982
Nu 14:14 them, by day time in a **p.** of a cloud, .. 5982
Nu 14:14 and in a **p.** of fire by night. 5982
De 31:15 the tabernacle in a **p.** of a cloud: 5982
De 31:15 **p.** of the cloud stood over the door 5982
Jg 9:6 of the **p.** that was in Shechem. 5324
Jg 20:40 out of the city with a **p.** of smoke, ... 5982
2Sa 18:18 and reared up for himself a **p.**, ... 4678
2Sa 18:18 he called the **p.** after his own name: ... 4678
1Ki 7:21 set up the right **p.**, and called the 5982
1Ki 7:21 he set up the left **p.**, and called 5982
2Ki 11:14 the king stood by a **p.**, as the........... 5982
2Ki 23:3 the king stood by a **p.**, and made a...... 5982
2Ki 25:17 the one **p.** was eighteen cubits, ... 5982
2Ki 25:17 the second **p.** with wreathen work...... 5982
2Ch 23:13 the king stood at his **p.** at the 5982
Ne 9:12 them in the day by a cloudy **p.**; 5982
Ne 9:12 and in the night by a **p.** of fire, ... 5982
Ne 9:19 **p.** of the cloud departed not from........ 5982
Ne 9:19 neither the **p.** of fire by night, to 5982
Ps 99:7 spake unto them in the cloudy **p.**: 5982
Isa 19:19 a **p.** at the border thereof to the........ 4676
Jer 1:18 defenced city, and an iron **p.**, and....... 5982
Jer 52:21 of one **p.** was eighteen cubits; 5982
Jer 52:22 The second **p.** also and the 5982
1Ti 3:15 the **p.** and ground of the truth. *4769*
Re 3:12 **a p. in the temple of my God,**....... *4769*

PILLARS
Ex 24:4 **p.**, according to the twelve tribes....... 4676
Ex 26:32 it upon four **p.** of shittim wood 5982
Ex 26:37 hanging five **p.** of shittim wood, ... 5982
Ex 27:10 twenty **p.** thereof and their twenty....... 5982
Ex 27:10 the hooks of the **p.**, and their fillets 5982
Ex 27:11 twenty **p.** and their twenty sockets..... 5982
Ex 27:11 hooks of the **p.** and their fillets of....... 5982
Ex 27:12 their **p.** ten, and their sockets ten. 5982
Ex 27:14, 15 their **p.** three, and their sockets 5982
Ex 27:16 **p.** shall be four, and their sockets 5982
Ex 27:17 All the **p.** round about the court......... 5982
Ex 35:11 his bars, his **p.**, and his sockets, ... 5982
Ex 35:17 his **p.**, and their sockets, and the 5982
Ex 36:36 thereunto four **p.** of shittim wood. 5982
Ex 36:38 the five **p.** of it with their hooks: 5982
Ex 38:10 Their **p.** were twenty, and their......... 5982
Ex 38:10 the hooks of the **p.** and their fillets..... 5982
Ex 38:11 their **p.** were twenty, and their.......... 5982
Ex 38:11 hooks of the **p.** and their fillets of....... 5982
Ex 38:12 their **p.** ten, and their sockets ten; 5982
Ex 38:12 hooks of the **p.** and their fillets of....... 5982
Ex 38:14, 15 their **p.** three, and their sockets 5982
Ex 38:17 the sockets for the **p.** were of brass; .. 5982
Ex 38:17 hooks of the **p.** and their fillets of....... 5982
Ex 38:17 all the **p.** of the court were filleted 5982
Ex 38:19 their **p.** were four, and their sockets... 5982
Ex 38:28 shekels he made hooks for the **p.**,....... 5982
Ex 39:33 bars, and his **p.**, and his sockets; 5982
Ex 39:40 his **p.**, and his sockets, and the 5982
Ex 40:18 bars thereof, and reared up his **p.**....... 5982
Nu 3:36 and the **p.** thereof, and the sockets 5982
Nu 3:37 the **p.** of the court round about,......... 5982
Nu 4:31 bars thereof, and the **p.** thereof, ... 5982
Nu 4:32 the **p.** of the court round about,......... 5982
De 12:3 break their **p.**,burn their groves 4676
Jg 16:25 and they set him between the **p.**........ 5982
Jg 16:26 Suffer me that I may feel the **p.**......... 5982
Jg 16:29 took hold of the two middle **p.**........... 5982
1Sa 2:8 the **p.** of the earth are the Lord's,...... 4690
1Ki 7:2 upon four rows of cedar **p.**,............... 5982
1Ki 7:2 with cedar beams upon the **p.**.............. 5982
1Ki 7:3 lay on forty five **p.**, fifteen in a row. ... 5982
1Ki 7:6 And he made a porch of **p.**; the 5982
1Ki 7:6 the other **p.** and the thick beam 5982
1Ki 7:15 he cast two **p.** of brass, of eighteen.... 5982
1Ki 7:16 to set upon the tops of the **p.**:............ 5982
1Ki 7:17 which were upon the top of the **p.**;...... 5982
1Ki 7:18 And he made the **p.**, and two rows..... 5982
1Ki 7:19 the top of the **p.** were of lily work 5982
1Ki 7:20 And the chapiters upon the two **p.**....... 5982
1Ki 7:21 the **p.** in the porch of the temple: 5982
1Ki 7:22 the top of the **p.** was lily work: 5982
1Ki 7:22 so was the work of the **p.** finished...... 5982
1Ki 7:41 The two **p.**, and the two bowls of...... 5982
1Ki 7:41 that were on the top of the two **p.**; 5982
1Ki 7:41 which were upon the top of the **p.**;..... 5982
1Ki 7:42 the chapiters that were upon the **p.**; ... 5982
1Ki 10:12 king made of the almug trees **p.**......... 4552
2Ki 18:16 **p.** which Hezekiah king of Judah 547
2Ki 25:13 **p.** of brass that were in the house...... 5982
2Ki 25:16 The two **p.**, one sea, and the bases.... 5982
1Ch 18:8 made the brasen sea, and the **p.**, ... 5982
2Ch 3:15 he made before the house two **p.**......... 5982
2Ch 3:16 put them on the heads of the **p.**;........ 5982
2Ch 3:17 reared up the **p.** before the temple,.... 5982
2Ch 4:12 the two **p.**, and the pommels, and...... 5982
2Ch 4:12 were on the top of the two **p.**, ... 5982
2Ch 4:12 which were on the top of the **p.**;......... 5982
2Ch 4:13 chapiters which were upon the **p.**....... 5982
Es 1:6 to silver rings and **p.** of marble: 5982
Job 9:6 place, and the **p.** thereof tremble. 5982
Job 26:11 The **p.** of heaven tremble and are 5982
Ps 75:3 are dissolved: I bear up the **p.** of it. ... 5982
Pr 9:1 she hath hewn out her seven **p.**:.......... 5982
Ca 3:6 of the wilderness like **p.** of smoke, ... 8490
Ca 3:10 He made the **p.** thereof of silver, ... 5982
Ca 5:15 His legs are as **p.** of marble, set......... 5982
Jer 27:19 concerning the **p.**, and concerning....... 5982
Jer 52:17 **p.** of brass that were in the house...... 5982
Jer 52:20 The two **p.**, one sea, and twelve......... 5982
Jer 52:21 concerning the **p.**, the height of 5982
Eze 40:49 and there were **p.** by the posts, one... 5982
Eze 42:6 had not **p.** as the **p.** of the courts: 5982
Joe 2:30 blood, and fire, and **p.** of smoke......... 8490
Ga 2:9 and John, who seemed to be **p.**, ... *4769*
Re 10:1 the sun, and his feet as **p.** of fire: *4769*

PILLED See also PEELED.
Ge 30:37 and **p.** white strakes in them, and 6478
Ge 30:38 rods which he had **p.** before the......... 6478

PILLOW See also PILLOWS.
1Sa 19:13 a **p.** of goats' hair for his bolster, ... 3523
1Sa 19:16 a **p.** of goats' hair for his bolster. 3523
Mk 4:38 part of the ship, asleep on a **p.**: *4344*

PILLOWS
Ge 28:11 that place, and put them for his **p.**,...... 4763
Ge 28:18 the stone that he had put for his **p.**, ... 4763
Eze 13:18 women that sew **p.** in all armholes,..... 3704
Eze 13:20 I am against your **p.**, wherewith ye 3704

PILNESER See TILGATH-PILNESER.

PILOTS
Eze 27:8 that were in thee, were thy **p.**. 2259
Eze 27:27 thy mariners, and thy **p.**, thy 2259
Eze 27:28 at the sound of the cry of thy **p.**......... 2259
Eze 27:29 all the **p.** of the sea, shall come 2259

PILTAI (pil'-tahee)
Ne 12:17 of Miniamin, of Moadiah, **P.**; 6408

PIN See also PINS.
Jg 16:14 she fastened it with the **p.**, and 3489
Jg 16:14 went away with the **p.** of the beam,.... 3489
Eze 15:3 take a **p.** of it to hang any vessel....... 3489

PINE See also PINETH; PINING.
Le 26:39 that are left of you shall **p.** away........ 4743
Le 26:39 shall they **p.** away with them............ 4743
Ne 8:15 fetch olive branches, and **p.** 6086,8081
Isa 41:19 the desert the fir tree, and the **p.**, ... 8410
Isa 60:13 unto thee, the fir tree, the **p.** tree, ... 8410
La 4:9 these **p.** away, stricken through......... 2100
Eze 24:23 shall **p.** away for your iniquities, ... 4743
Eze 33:10 upon us, and we **p.** away in them,...... 4743

PINETH
Mk 9:18 with his teeth, and **p.** away;............. *3583*

PINING
Isa 38:12 he will cut me off with **p.** sickness:..... 1803

PINNACLE
Mt 4:5 setteth him on a **p.** of the temple,...... *4419*
Lu 4:9 and set him on a **p.** of the temple, ... *4419*

PINON (pi'-non)
Ge 36:41 Aholibamah, duke Elah, duke **P.**,........ 6373
1Ch 1:52 Aholibamah, duke Elah, duke **P.**,........ 6373

PINS
Ex 27:19 thereof, and all the **p.** thereof, and..... 3489
Ex 27:19 the **p.** of the court shall be of brass.... 3489
Ex 35:18 The **p.** of the tabernacle, and the....... 3489
Ex 35:18 the **p.** of the court, and their cords,..... 3489
Ex 38:20 all the **p.** of the tabernacle, and of..... 3489
Ex 38:31 and all the **p.** of the tabernacle, ... 3489
Ex 38:31 all the **p.** of the court round about...... 3489
Ex 39:40 his cords, and his **p.**, and all the 3489
Nu 3:37 and their **p.**, and their cords............. 3489
Nu 4:32 and their **p.**, and their cords,............. 3489
Isa 3:22 the wimples, and the crisping **p.**,..............

PIPE See also PIPED; PIPES.
1Sa 10:5 with a tabret, and a **p.**, and a harp, ... 2485
Isa 5:12 viol, the tabret, and **p.**, and wine, ... 2485
Isa 30:29 one goeth with a **p.** to come into the .. 2485
1Co 14:7 giving sound, whether **p.** or harp, ... *836*

PIPED
1Ki 1:40 and the people **p.** with pipes, and....... 2490
Mt 11:17 **We have p. unto you, and ye have**.. *832*
Lu 7:32 **We have p. unto you, and ye have**.. *832*
1Co 14:7 it be known what is **p.** or harped?........ *832*

PIPERS
Re 18:22 harpers, and musicians, and of **p.**......... *834*

PIPES
1Ki 1:40 and the people piped with **p.**, and....... 2485
Jer 48:36 heart shall sound for Moab like **p.**, ... 2485
Jer 48:36 mine heart shall sound like **p.** for 2485
Eze 28:13 of thy tabrets and of thy **p.** was......... 5345
Zec 4:2 seven **p.** to the seven lamps which..... 4166
Zec 4:12 two golden **p.** empty the golden......... 6804

PIRAM (pi'-ram)
Jos 10:3 and unto **P.** king of Jarmuth, and........ 6502

PIRATHON (pir'-a-thon) See also PIRATHONITE.
Jg 12:15 Was buried in **P.** in the land of.......... 6552

PIRATHONITE (pir'-a-thon-ite)
Jg 12:13 son of Hillel, a **P.**, judged Israel......... 6553
Jg 12:15 Abdon the son of Hillel the **P.** died,.... 6553
2Sa 23:30 Benaiah the **P.**, Hiddai of the 6553
1Ch 11:31 of Benjamin, Benaiah the **P.**,............. 6553
1Ch 27:14 month was Benaiah the **P.**, of the 6553

PISGAH (piz'-gah) See also ASHDOTH-PISGAH; NEBO.
Nu 21:20 top of **P.**, which looketh toward......... 6449
Nu 23:14 field of Zophim, to the top of **P.**, ... 6449
De 3:27 Get thee up into the top of **P.**, and 6449
De 4:49 the plain, under the springs of **P.**..... 6449
De 34:1 the top of **P.**, that is over against 6449

PISIDIA (pi-sid'-e-ah)
Ac 13:14 they came to Antioch in **P.**, and......... *4099*
Ac 14:24 they had passed throughout **P.**, ... *4099*

PISON (pi'-son)
Ge 2:11 The name of the first is **P.**: that........ 6376

PISPAH (piz'-pah)
1Ch 7:38 Jephunneh, and **P.**, and Ara. 6462

PISS See also PISSETH.
2Ki 18:27 and drink their own **p.** with you?........ 7890
Isa 36:12 and drink their own **p.** with you?........ 7890

PISSETH
1Sa 25:22, 34 any that **p.** against the wall. 8366

1Ki 14:10 him that **p.** against the wall, and 8366
1Ki 16:11 him not one that **p.** against a wall, 8366
1Ki 21:21 Ahab him that **p.** against a wall, 8366
2Ki 9:8 Ahab him that **p.** against the wall, 8366

PIT See also PITS.
Ge 37:20 him, and cast him into some **p.**, 953
Ge 37:22 but cast him into this **p.** that is in 953
Ge 37:24 took him, and cast him into a **p.**: 953
Ge 37:24 **p.** was empty, there was no water 953
Ge 37:28 and lifted up Joseph out of the **p.**, 953
Ge 37:29 And Reuben returned unto the **p.**; 953
Ge 37:29 behold, Joseph was not in the **p.**; 953
Ex 21:33 And if a man shall open a **p.**, or 953
Ex 21:33 if a man shall dig a **p.**, and not cover 953
Ex 21:34 owner of the **p.** shall make it good, 953
Le 11:36 Nevertheless a fountain or **p.**, 953
Nu 16:30 they go down quick into the **p.**; 7585
Nu 16:33 went down alive into the **p.**, and 7585
2Sa 17:9 he is hid now in some **p.**, or in 6354
2Sa 18:17 cast him into a great **p.** in the wood, 6354
2Sa 23:20 and slew a lion in the midst of a **p.** 953
2Ki 10:14 slew them at the **p.** of the shearing 953
1Ch 11:22 slew a lion in a **p.** in a snowy day. 953
Job 6:27 and ye dig a **p.** for your friend.
Job 17:16 go down to the bars of the **p.**, 7585
Job 33:18 keepeth back his soul from the **p.**, 7845
Job 33:24 him from going down to the **p.**: 7845
Job 33:28 his soul from going into the **p.**, 7845
Job 33:30 To bring back his soul from the **p.**, 7845
Ps 7:15 He made a **p.**, and digged it, and 953
Ps 9:15 heathen are sunk down in the **p.** 7845
Ps 28:1 like them that go down into the **p.** 953
Ps 30:3 that I should not go down to the **p.** 953
Ps 30:9 blood, when I go down to the **p.**? 7845
Ps 35:7 they hid for me their net in a **p.**, 7845
Ps 40:2 me up also out of an horrible **p.**, 953
Ps 55:23 down into the **p.** of destruction: 875
Ps 57:6 they have digged a **p.** before me, 7882
Ps 69:15 let not the **p.** shut her mouth upon 875
Ps 88:4 with them that go down into the **p.**: 953
Ps 88:6 Thou hast laid me in the lowest **p.**, 953
Ps 94:13 the **p.** be digged for the wicked. 7845
Ps 143:7 unto them that go down into the **p.** 953
Pr 1:12 as those that go down into the **p.**: 953
Pr 22:14 of strange women is a deep **p.**: 7745
Pr 23:27 a strange woman is a narrow **p.**. 875
Pr 26:27 Whoso diggeth a **p.** shall fall 7845
Pr 28:10 shall fall himself into his own **p.**: 7816
Pr 28:17 doeth violence...shall flee to the **p.**; 953
Ec 10:8 He that diggeth a **p.** shall fall into 1475
Isa 14:15 down to hell, to the sides of the **p.**. 953
Isa 14:19 that go down to the stones of the **p.**; 953
Isa 24:17 Fear, and the **p.**, and the snare, 6354
Isa 24:18 noise of...fear shall fall into the **p.**; 6354
Isa 24:18 cometh up out of the midst of the **p.** 6354
Isa 24:22 as prisoners are gathered in the **p.**, 953
Isa 30:14 to take water withal out of the **p.** 1360
Isa 38:17 it from the **p.** of corruption: 7845
Isa 38:18 that go down into the **p.** cannot hope. 953
Isa 51:1 hole of the **p.** whence ye are digged. 953
Isa 51:14 that he should not die in the **p.**, 7845
Jer 18:20 they have digged a **p.** for my soul. 7745
Jer 18:22 have digged a **p.** to take me, 7743,7882
Jer 41:7 cast them into the midst of the **p.**, 953
Jer 41:9 the **p.** wherein Ishmael had cast all 953
Jer 48:43 Fear, and the **p.**, and the snare, 6354
Jer 48:44 from the fear shall fall into the **p.**; 6354
Jer 48:44 and he that getteth up out of the **p.** 6354
Eze 19:4 he was taken in their **p.**, and 7845
Eze 19:8 over him: he was taken in their **p.** 7845
Eze 26:20 with them that descend into the **p.**, 953
Eze 26:20 with them that go down to the **p.**, 953
Eze 28:8 shall bring thee down to the **p.**, 7845
Eze 31:14 with them that go down to the **p.**. 953
Eze 31:16 with them that descend into the **p.**: 953
Eze 32:18 with them that go down into the **p.**. 953
Eze 32:23 graves are set in the sides of the **p.**, 953
Eze 32:24 with them that go down to the **p.**: 953
Eze 32:25 with them that go down to the **p.**: 953
Eze 32:29, 30 with them that go down to the **p.**. 953
Zec 9:11 out of the **p.** wherein is no water. 953
Mt 12:11 **it fall into a p. on the sabbath day,** *999*
Lu 14:5 **an ass or an ox fallen into a p.** *5421*
Re 9:1 given the key of the bottomless **p.**. *5421*
Re 9:2 And he opened the bottomless **p.**; *5421*
Re 9:2 there arose a smoke out of the **p.**, *5421*
Re 9:2 by reason of the smoke of the **p.**. *5421*
Re 9:11 is the angel of the bottomless **p.**,
Re 11:7 ascendeth out of the bottomless **p.**
Re 17:8 ascend out of the bottomless **p.**, and
Re 20:1 having the key of the bottomless **p.**
Re 20:3 And cast him into the bottomless **p.**,

PITCH See also PITCHED.
Ge 6:14 shalt **p.** it within and without 3722
Ge 6:14 it within and without with **p.** 3724
Ex 2:3 daubed it with slime and with **p.**, 2203
Nu 1:52 of Israel shall **p.** their tents, 2583
Nu 1:53 the Levites shall **p.** round about 2583
Nu 2:2 shall **p.** by his own standard, 2583
Nu 2:2 of the congregation shall they **p.**. 2583
Nu 2:3 Judah **p.** throughout their armies: 2583
Nu 2:5 And those that do **p.** next unto him 2583
Nu 2:12 And those which **p.** by him shall be 2583
Nu 3:23 shall **p.** behind the tabernacle 2583
Nu 3:29, 35 **p.** on the side of the tabernacle 2583
De 1:33 you out a place to **p.** your tents in, 2583
Jos 4:20 of Jordan, did Joshua **p.** in Gilgal. 6965
Isa 13:20 neither shall the Arabian **p.** tent 167
Isa 34:9 thereof shall be turned into **p.**, 2203
Isa 34:9 thereof shall become burning **p.**. 2203
Jer 6:3 shall **p.** their tents against her 8628

PITCHED
Ge 12:8 east of Beth-el, and **p.** his tent, 5186
Ge 13:12 and **p.** his tent toward Sodom. 167
Ge 26:17 **p.** his tent in the valley of Gerar, 2583
Ge 26:25 an altar...and **p.** his tent there: 5186
Ge 31:25 Jacob had **p.** his tent in the mount: 8628
Ge 31:25 Laban...**p.** in the mount of Gilead. 8628
Ge 33:18 and **p.** his tent before the city. 2583
Ex 17:1 **p.** in Rephidim: and there was no 2583
Ex 19:2 and had **p.** in the wilderness; and 2583
Ex 33:7 and **p.** it without the camp, 5186
Nu 1:51 when the tabernacle is to be **p.**, 2583
Nu 2:34 so they **p.** by their standards, and 2583
Nu 9:17 children of Israel **p.** their tents. 2583
Nu 9:18 commandment of the Lord they **p.**: 2583
Nu 12:16 and **p.** in the wilderness of Paran. 2583
Nu 21:10 Israel set forward, and **p.** in Oboth. 2583
Nu 21:11 **p.** at Ije-abarim, in the wilderness 2583
Nu 21:12 and **p.** in the valley of Zared. 2583
Nu 21:13 and **p.** on the other side of Arnon, 2583
Nu 22:1 and **p.** in the plains of Moab on this 2583
Nu 33:5 from Rameses, and **p.** in Succoth. 2583
Nu 33:6 from Succoth, and **p.** in Etham, 2583
Nu 33:7 and they **p.** before Migdol. 2583
Nu 33:8 of Etham, and **p.** in Marah. 2583
Nu 33:9 ten palm trees; and they **p.** there. 2583
Nu 33:15 and **p.** in the wilderness of Sinai. 2583
Nu 33:16 Sinai, and **p.** in Kibroth-hattaavah. 2583
Nu 33:18 from Hazeroth, and **p.** in Rithmah. 2583
Nu 33:19 Rithmah, and **p.** in Rimmon-parez. 2583
Nu 33:20 Rimmon-parez, and **p.** in Libnah. 2583
Nu 33:21 from Libnah, and **p.** at Rissah. 2583
Nu 33:22 from Rissah, and **p.** in Kehelathah. 2583
Nu 33:23 and **p.** in mount Shapher. 2583
Nu 33:25 Haradah, and **p.** in Makheloth. 2583
Nu 33:27 from Tahath, and **p.** at Tarah. 2583
Nu 33:28 from Tarah, and **p.** in Mithcah. 2583
Nu 33:29 from Mithcah,...**p.** in Hashmonah, 2583
Nu 33:31 Moseroth, and **p.** in Bene-jaakan. 2583
Nu 33:33 Hor-hagidgad, and **p.** in Jotbathah. 2583
Nu 33:36 and **p.** in the wilderness of Zin, 2583
Nu 33:37 Kadesh, and **p.** in mount Hor; 2583
Nu 33:41 mount Hor, and **p.** in Zalmonah. 2583
Nu 33:42 from Zalmonah, and **p.** in Punon. 2583
Nu 33:43 from Punon, and **p.** in Oboth. 2583
Nu 33:44 from Oboth, and **p.** in Ije-abarim, 2583
Nu 33:45 from Iim, and **p.** in Dibon-gad. 2583
Nu 33:47 and **p.** in the mountains of Abarim, 2583
Nu 33:48 **p.** in the plains of Moab by Jordan 2583
Nu 33:49 **p.** by Jordan, from Beth-jesimoth. 2583
Jos 8:11 and **p.** on the north side of Ai: 2583
Jos 11:5 **p.** together at the waters of Merom, 2583
Jg 4:11 and **p.** his tent unto the plain of 5186
Jg 6:33 and **p.** in the valley of Jezreel. 2583
Jg 7:1 and **p.** beside the well of Harod: 2583
Jg 11:18 and **p.** on the other side of Arnon, 2583
Jg 11:20 and **p.** in Jahaz, and fought against 2583
Jg 15:9 the Philistines...**p.** in Judah, 2583
Jg 18:12 and **p.** in Kirjath-jearim, in Judah: 2583
1Sa 4:1 battle, and **p.** beside Eben-ezer; 2583
1Sa 4:1 and the Philistines **p.** in Aphek. 2583
1Sa 13:5 they came up, and **p.** in Michmash, 2583
1Sa 17:1 **p.** between Shochoh and Azekah 2583
1Sa 17:2 **p.** by the valley of Elah, and set the 2583
1Sa 26:3 And Saul **p.** in the hill of Hachilah, 2583
1Sa 26:5 to the place where Saul had **p.**: 2583
1Sa 26:5 and the people **p.** round about him. 2583
1Sa 28:4 and came and **p.** in Shunem: and 2583
1Sa 28:4 together, and they **p.** in Gilboa. 2583
1Sa 29:1 **p.** by a fountain which is in Jezreel. 2583
2Sa 6:17 tabernacle that David had **p.** for it; 5186
2Sa 17:26 Absalom **p.** in the land of Gilead. 2583
2Sa 23:13 **p.** in the valley of Rephaim. 2583
2Sa 24:5 passed over Jordan, and **p.** in Aroer, 2583
1Ki 20:27 children of Israel **p.** before them 2583
1Ki 20:29 they **p.** one over against the other, 2583
2Ki 25:1 Jerusalem, and **p.** against it; 2583
1Ch 15:1 the ark of God, and **p.** it for a tent. 5186
1Ch 16:1 of the tent that David had **p.** for it: 5186
1Ch 19:7 who came and **p.** before Medeba. 2583
2Ch 1:4 had **p.** a tent for it at Jerusalem. 5186
Jer 52:4 Jerusalem, and **p.** against it, 2583
Heb 8:2 which the Lord **p.**, and not man. *4078*

PITCHER See also PITCHERS.
Ge 24:14 Let down thy **p.**, I pray thee, that 3537
Ge 24:15 with her **p.** upon her shoulder. 3537
Ge 24:16 well, and filled her **p.**, and came up. 3537
Ge 24:17 thee, drink a little water of thy **p.**. 3537
Ge 24:18 and let down her **p.** upon her hand, 3537
Ge 24:20 and emptied her **p.** into the trough, 3537
Ge 24:43 a little water of thy **p.** to drink; 3537
Ge 24:45 forth with her **p.** on her shoulder; 3537
Ge 24:46 let down her **p.** from her shoulder, 3537
Ec 12:6 or the **p.** be broken at the fountain, 3537
Mk 14:13 **you a man bearing a p. of water;** *2765*
Lu 22:10 **meet you, bearing a p. of water;** *2765*

PITCHERS
Jg 7:16 every man's hand, with empty **p.**, 3537
Jg 7:16 and lamps within the **p.**. 3537
Jg 7:19 and brake the **p.** that were in their 3537
Jg 7:20 brake the **p.**, and held the lamps 3537
La 4:2 are they esteemed as earthen **p.**, 5035

PITHOM (pi'-thom)
Ex 1:11 treasure cities, **P.** and Raamses. 6619

PITHON (pi'-thon)
1Ch 8:35 the sons of Micah were, **P.**, and 6377
1Ch 9:41 the sons of Micah were, **P.**, and 6377

PITIED
Ps 106:46 He made them also to be **p.** of all 7356
La 2:2 of Jacob, and hath not **p.**: 2550
La 2:17 hath thrown down, and hath not **p.**: 2550
La 2:21 anger; thou hast killed, and not **p.**. 2550
La 3:43 thou hast slain, thou hast not **p.**. 2550
Eze 16:5 None eye **p.** thee, to do any of 2347

PITIETH
Ps 103:13 Like as a father **p.** his children. 7355
Ps 103:13 so the Lord **p.** them that fear him. 7355
Eze 24:21 eyes, and that which your soul **p.**; 4263

PITIFUL
La 4:10 The hands of the **p.** women have 7362
Jas 5:11 the Lord is very **p.**, and of tender *4184*
1Pe 3:8 love as brethren, be **p.**, be *2155*

PITS See also SALTPITS; SLIMEPITS.
1Sa 13:6 rocks, and in high places, and in **p.**. 953
Ps 119:85 The proud have digged **p.** for me, 7882
Ps 140:10 be cast into the fire; into deep **p.**,
Jer 2:6 through a land of deserts and...**p.**, 7745
Jer 14:3 they came to the **p.**, and found no 1356
La 4:20 the Lord, was taken in their **p.**, 7825

PITY See also PITIED; PITIETH; PITIFUL.
De 7:16 eye shall have no **p.** upon them: 2347
De 13:8 neither shall thine eye **p.** him, 2347
De 19:13 Thine eye shall not **p.** him, but thou 2347
De 19:21 thine eye shall not **p.**; but life shall 2347
De 25:12 her hand, thine eye shall not **p.** her. 2347
2Sa 12:6 thing, and because he had no **p.**. 2550
Job 6:14 is afflicted **p.** should be shewed. 2617
Job 19:21 Have **p.** upon me, have **p.** upon me, 2603
Ps 69:20 I looked for some to take **p.**, but 5110
Pr 19:17 He that hath **p.** upon the poor 2603
Pr 28:8 it for him that will **p.** the poor. 2603
Isa 13:18 no **p.** on the fruit of the womb; 7355
Isa 63:9 and in his **p.** he redeemed them; 2551

Jer 13:14 I will not **p.**, nor spare, nor have 2550
Jer 15:5 For who shall have **p.** upon thee, O 2550
Jer 21:7 neither have **p.**, nor have mercy. 2550
Eze 5:11 spare, neither will I have any **p.** 2550
Eze 7:4 spare thee, neither will I have **p.**: 2550
Eze 7:9 not spare, neither will I have **p.**: 2550
Eze 8:18 not spare, neither will I have **p.**: 2550
Eze 9:5 your eye spare, neither have ye **p.**: 2550
Eze 9:10 not spare, neither will I have **p.**, 2550
Eze 36:21 But I had **p.** for mine holy name, 2550
Joe 2:18 for his land, and **p.** his people. 2550
Am 1:11 the sword, and did cast off all **p.**, 7356
Jon 4:10 Thou hast had **p.** on the gourd, 2347
Zec 11:5 their own shepherds **p.** them not. 2550
Zec 11:6 no more **p.** the inhabitants of the 2550
Mt 18:33 **fellowservant,...I had p. on thee?** *1653*

PLACE See also BURYINGPLACE; COUCHINGPLACE; DWELLINGPLACE; FEEDINGPLACE; MARKETPLACE; PLACED; PLACES; THRESHINGPLACE.

Ge 1:9 be gathered together unto one **p.**, 4725
Ge 12:6 the land unto the **p.** of Sichem, 4725
Ge 13:3 unto the **p.** where his tent had been 4725
Ge 13:4 Unto the **p.** of the altar, which he 4725
Ge 13:14 look from the **p.** where thou art 4725
Ge 18:24 spare the **p.** for the fifty righteous 4725
Ge 18:26 will spare all the **p.** for their sakes. 4725
Ge 18:33 and Abraham returned unto his **p.** 4725
Ge 19:12 the city, bring them out of this **p.**: 4725
Ge 19:13 we will destroy this **p.**, because the 4725
Ge 19:14 and said, Up, get you out of this **p.**; 4725
Ge 19:27 **p.** where he stood before the Lord: 4725
Ge 20:11 the fear of God is not in this **p.**; 4725
Ge 20:13 at every **p.** whither we shall come, 4725
Ge 21:31 he called that **p.** Beer-sheba; 4725
Ge 22:3 the **p.** of which God had told him. 4725
Ge 22:4 up his eyes, and saw the **p.** afar off. 4725
Ge 22:9 the **p.** which God had told him of; 4725
Ge 22:14 the name of that **p.** Jehovah-jireh: 4725
Ge 26:7 men of the **p.** asked him of his wife; 4725
Ge 26:7 men of the **p.** should kill me for 4725
Ge 28:11 he lighted upon a certain **p.**, and 4725
Ge 28:11 he took of the stones of that **p.**, and 4725
Ge 28:11 and lay down in that **p.** to sleep. 4725
Ge 28:16 Surely the Lord is in this **p.**; and I 4725
Ge 28:17 and said, How dreadful is this **p.**! 4725
Ge 28:19 called the name of that **p.** Beth-el: 4725
Ge 29:3 upon the well's mouth in his **p.** 4725
Ge 29:22 together all the men of the **p.**, and 4725
Ge 30:25 that I may go unto mine own **p.**, 4725
Ge 31:55 departed, and returned unto his **p.** 4725
Ge 32:2 the name of that **p.** Mahanaim. 4725
Ge 32:30 called the name of the **p.** Peniel: 4725
Ge 33:17 the name of the **p.** is called Succoth 4725
Ge 35:7 altar, and called the **p.** El-beth-el: 4725
Ge 35:13 in the **p.** where he talked with him. 4725
Ge 35:14 in the **p.** where he talked with him, 4725
Ge 35:15 the **p.** where God spake with him, 4725
Ge 38:14 herself, and sat in an open **p.**, 6607
Ge 38:21 Then he asked the men of that **p.**, 4725
Ge 38:21 said, There was no harlot in this **p.**.
Ge 38:22 also the men of the **p.** said, that 4725
Ge 38:22 that there was no harlot in this **p.**.
Ge 39:20 **p.** where the king's prisoners were 4725
Ge 40:3 the **p.** where Joseph was bound. 4725
Ge 40:13 head, and restore thee unto thy **p.**: 3653
Ge 48:9 whom God hath given me in this **p.**.
Ge 50:19 Fear not: for am I in the **p.** of God?
Ex 3:5 **p.** whereon thou standest is holy 4725
Ex 3:8 unto the **p.** of the Canaanites, and 4725
Ex 10:23 rose any from his **p.** for three days: 8478
Ex 13:3 the Lord brought you out from this **p.**:
Ex 15:17 the **p.**, O Lord, which thou hast 4349
Ex 16:29 abide ye every man in his **p.**, let no 8478
Ex 16:29 let no man go out of his **p.** on the 4725
Ex 17:7 called the name of the **p.** Massah, 4725
Ex 18:21 **p.** such over them, to be rulers of 7760
Ex 18:23 shall also go to their **p.** in peace. 4725
Ex 21:13 thee a **p.** whither he shall flee. 4725
Ex 23:20 into the **p.** which I have prepared. 4725
Ex 26:33 between the holy **p.** and the most holy.
Ex 26:34 of the testimony in the most holy **p.**.
Ex 28:29 when he goeth in unto the holy **p.**,
Ex 28:35 he goeth in unto the holy **p.** before the
Ex 28:43 the altar to minister in the holy **p.**;
Ex 29:30 congregation to minister in the holy **p.**
Ex 29:31 and seethe his flesh in the holy **p.**. 4725
Ex 31:11 oil, and sweet incense for the holy **p.**:
Ex 32:34 lead the people unto the **p.** of which
Ex 33:21 there is a **p.** by me, and thou shalt 4725
Ex 35:19 to do service in the holy **p.**, the holy
Ex 38:24 work in all the work of the holy **p.**,
Ex 39:1 to do service in the holy **p.**, and made
Ex 39:41 to do service in the holy **p.**, and the
Le 1:16 east part, by the **p.** of the ashes, 4725
Le 4:12 without the camp unto a clean **p.**, 4725
Le 4:24 kill it in the **p.** where they kill the 4725
Le 4:29 in the **p.** of the burnt offering. 4725
Le 4:33 sin offering in the **p.** where they kill 4725
Le 6:11 without the camp unto a clean **p.** 4725
Le 6:16 shall it be eaten in the holy **p.**; 4725
Le 6:25 the **p.** where the burnt offering is 4725
Le 6:26 in the holy **p.** shall it be eaten, in 4725
Le 6:27 it was sprinkled in the holy **p.**. 4725
Le 6:30 to reconcile withal in the holy **p.**,
Le 7:2 In the **p.** where they kill the burnt 4725
Le 7:6 it shall be eaten in the holy **p.**: it 4725
Le 10:13 shall eat it in the holy **p.**, because 4725
Le 10:14 shoulder shall ye eat in a clean **p.**; 4725
Le 10:17 eaten the sin offering in the holy **p.**, 4725
Le 10:18 not brought in within the holy **p.**:
Le 10:18 indeed have eaten it in the holy **p.**,
Le 13:19 **p.** of the boil...be a white rising, 4725
Le 13:23 But if the bright spot stay in his **p.**,
Le 13:28 And if the bright spot stay in his **p.**, 8478
Le 14:13 the **p.** where he shall kill the sin 4725
Le 14:13 the burnt offering, in the holy **p.**: 4725
Le 14:28 the **p.** of the blood of the trespass 4725
Le 14:40 shall cast them into an unclean **p.** 4725
Le 14:41 without the city into an unclean **p.**: 4725
Le 14:42 put them in the **p.** of those stones; 8478
Le 14:45 out of the city into an unclean **p.**. 4725
Le 16:2 times into the holy **p.** within the vail
Le 16:3 shall Aaron come into the holy **p.**:
Le 16:16 make an atonement for the holy **p.**,
Le 16:17 make an atonement in the holy **p.**,
Le 16:20 an end of reconciling the holy **p.**
Le 16:23 put on when he went into the holy **p.**,
Le 16:24 his flesh with water in the holy **p.**, 4725
Le 16:27 make atonement in the holy **p.**,
Le 24:9 they shall eat in the holy **p.**: 4725
Nu 2:17 man in his **p.** by their standards. 3027
Nu 9:17 **p.** where the cloud abode, there 4725
Nu 10:14 In the first **p.** went the standard of
Nu 10:29 journeying unto the **p.** of which 4725
Nu 10:33 to search out a resting **p.** for them.
Nu 11:3 the name of the **p.** Taberah: 4725
Nu 11:34 of that **p.** Kibroth-hattaavah: 4725
Nu 13:24 **p.** was called the brook Eschol, 4725
Nu 14:40 **p.** which the Lord hath promised: 4725
Nu 18:10 In the most holy **p.** shalt thou eat it;
Nu 18:31 ye shall eat it in every **p.**, ye and 4725
Nu 19:9 without the camp in a clean **p.**, 4725
Nu 20:5 to bring us in unto the evil **p.**? 4725
Nu 20:5 it is no **p.** of seed, or of figs, or of 4725
Nu 21:3 called the name of the **p.** Hormah. 4725
Nu 22:26 and stood in a narrow **p.**, where 4725
Nu 23:3 thee. And he went to an high **p.**.
Nu 23:13 thee, with me unto another **p.**, 4725
Nu 23:27 I will bring thee unto another **p.**: 4725
Nu 24:11 Therefore now flee thou to thy **p.**: 4725
Nu 24:25 and went and returned to his **p.**: 4725
Nu 28:7 holy **p.** shalt thou cause the strong
Nu 32:1 behold, the **p.** was a **p.** for cattle; 4725
Nu 32:17 have brought them unto their **p.**: 4725
Nu 33:54 be in the **p.** where his lot falleth;
De 1:31 went, until ye come into this **p.**. 4725
De 1:33 you out a **p.** to pitch your tents 4725
De 2:37 unto any **p.** of the river Jabbok, 3027
De 9:7 until ye came unto this **p.**, ye 4725
De 11:5 until ye came into this **p.**; 4725
De 11:24 Every **p.** whereon the soles of your 4725
De 12:3 the names of them out of that **p.** 4725
De 12:5 **p.** which the Lord your God shall 4725
De 12:11 a **p.** which the Lord your God shall 4725
De 12:13 thy burnt offerings in every **p.** that 4725
De 12:14 the **p.** which the Lord shall choose 4725
De 12:18 **p.** which the Lord thy God shall 4725
De 12:21 the **p.** which the Lord thy God hath 4725
De 12:26 the **p.** which the Lord shall choose: 4725
De 14:23 before the Lord thy God, in the **p.** 4725
De 14:23 choose to **p.** his name there, 7931
De 14:24 or if the **p.** be too far from thee, 4725
De 14:25 unto the **p.** which the Lord thy God 4725
De 15:20 by year in the **p.** which the Lord 4725
De 16:2 the **p.** which the Lord shall choose 4725
De 16:2 shall choose to **p.** his name there. 7931
De 16:6 at the **p.** which the Lord thy God 4724
De 16:6 shall choose to **p.** his name in, 7931
De 16:7 shalt roast and eat it in the **p.** 4725
De 16:11 in the **p.** which the Lord thy God 4725
De 16:11 hath chosen to **p.** his name there. 7931
De 16:15 **p.** which the Lord shall choose: 4725
De 16:16 in the **p.** which he shall choose; 4725
De 17:8 arise, and get thee up into the **p.** 4725
De 17:10 they of that **p.** which the Lord 4725
De 18:6 the **p.** which the Lord shall choose; 4725
De 21:19 city, and unto the gate of his **p.**; 4725
De 23:12 have a **p.** also without the camp, 4725
De 23:16 **p.** which he shall choose in one of 4725
De 26:2 go unto the **p.** which the Lord 4725
De 26:2 shall choose to **p.** his name there. 7931
De 26:9 hath brought us into this **p.**, and 4725
De 27:15 and putteth it in a secret **p.**.
De 29:7 And when ye came unto this **p.**, 4725
De 31:11 in the **p.** which he shall choose, 4725
Jos 1:3 Every **p.** that the sole of your foot 4725
Jos 3:3 then ye shall remove from your **p.**, 4725
Jos 4:3 of the **p.** where the priests' feet stood
Jos 4:3 leave them in the lodging **p.**, where ye
Jos 4:8 unto the **p.** where they lodged, and
Jos 4:9 **p.** where the feet of the priests which
Jos 4:18 of Jordan returned unto their **p.**, 4725
Jos 5:9 the name of the **p.** is called Gilgal 4725
Jos 5:15 **p.** whereon thou standest is holy. 4725
Jos 7:26 **p.** was called, The valley of Achor, 4725
Jos 8:19 arose quickly out of their **p.**, and 4725
Jos 9:27 in the **p.** which he should choose. 4725
Jos 20:4 give him a **p.**, that he may dwell 4725
Jg 2:5 called the name of that **p.** Bochim: 4725
Jg 6:26 top of this rock, in the ordered **p.**, 4634
Jg 7:7 people go every man unto his **p.**. 4725
Jg 7:21 stood every man in his **p.** round. 8478
Jg 9:55 departed every man unto his **p.**. 4725
Jg 11:19 thee through thy land into my **p.**. 4725
Jg 15:17 and called that **p.** Ramath-lehi. 4725
Jg 15:19 an hollow **p.** that was in the jaw,
Jg 17:8 to sojourn where he could find a **p.**:
Jg 17:9 I go to sojourn where I may find a **p.**
Jg 18:3 and what makest thou in this **p.**?
Jg 18:10 **p.** where there is no want of any 4725
Jg 18:12 called that **p.** Mahaneh-dan unto 4725
Jg 19:16 men of the **p.** were Benjamites. 4725
Jg 19:28 rose up, and got him unto his **p.**. 4725
Jg 20:22 **p.** where they put themselves in 4725
Jg 20:33 of Israel rose up out of their **p.**, 4725
Jg 20:36 Israel gave **p.** to the Benjamites, 4725
Jg 21:19 in a **p.** which is on the north side of
Ru 1:7 forth out of the **p.** where she was, 4725
Ru 3:4 mark the **p.** where he shall lie, 4725
Ru 4:10 and from the gate of his **p.**: ye are 4725
1Sa 3:2 Eli was laid down in his **p.**, and his 4725
1Sa 3:9 Samuel went and lay down in his **p.**. 4725
1Sa 5:3 Dagon, and set him in his **p.** again. 4725
1Sa 5:11 let it go again to his own **p.**, that it 4725
1Sa 6:2 wherewith we shall send it to his **p.** 4725
1Sa 9:12 of the people to day in the high **p.**:
1Sa 9:13 before he go up to the high **p.** to eat:
1Sa 9:14 them, for to go up to the high **p.**.
1Sa 9:19 go up before me unto the high **p.**;
1Sa 9:22 sit in the chiefest **p.** among them 4725
1Sa 9:25 down from the high **p.** into the city,
1Sa 10:5 coming down from the high **p.** with a
1Sa 10:12 And one of the same **p.** answered and
1Sa 10:13 prophesying, he came to the high **p.**.
1Sa 12:8 and made them dwell in this **p.**. 4725
1Sa 14:9 we will stand still in our **p.**, and 8478
1Sa 14:46 Philistines went to their own **p.**. 4725
1Sa 15:12 behold, he set him up a **p.**, and is 3027
1Sa 19:2 and abide in a secret **p.**, and hide
1Sa 20:19 **p.** where thou didst hide thyself 4725
1Sa 20:25 side, and David's **p.** was empty. 4725
1Sa 20:27 month, that David's **p.** was empty: 4725
1Sa 20:37 lad was come to the **p.** of the arrow 4725
1Sa 20:41 arose out of a **p.** toward the south,
1Sa 21:2 my servants to such and such a **p.**. 4725
1Sa 23:22 and see his **p.** where his haunt is, 4725
1Sa 23:28 called that **p.** Sela-hammahlekoth. 4725
1Sa 26:5 to the **p.** where Saul had pitched: 4725
1Sa 26:5 David beheld the **p.** where Saul lay, 4725
1Sa 26:25 way, and Saul returned to his **p.**. 4725

1Sa 27:5 them give me a **p.** in some town........ 4725
1Sa 29:4 he may go again to his **p.** which......... 4725
2Sa 2:16 **p.** was called Helkath-hazzurim, ... 4725
2Sa 2:23 there, and died in the same **p.**:.......... 8478
2Sa 2:23 came to the **p.** where Asahel fell........ 4725
2Sa 5:20 name of that **p.** Baal-perazim............ 4725
2Sa 6:8 the name of the **p.** Perez-uzzah 4725
2Sa 6:17 ark of the Lord, and set it in his **p.**, ... 4725
2Sa 7:10 I will appoint a **p.** for my people 4725
2Sa 7:10 they may dwell in a **p.** of their own, ... 8478
2Sa 11:16 assigned Uriah unto a **p.** where.......... 4725
2Sa 15:17 tarried in a **p.** that was far off........... 1004
2Sa 15:19 return to thy **p.**, and abide with......... 4725
2Sa 15:21 what **p.** my lord the king shall be, ... 4725
2Sa 17:9 in some pit, or in some other **p.**: 4725
2Sa 17:12 come upon him in some **p.** where he... 4725
2Sa 18:18 called unto this day, Absalom's **p.**........ 3027
2Sa 19:39 and he returned unto his own **p.**. 4725
2Sa 22:20 brought me forth also into a large **p.**: ....
2Sa 23:7 burned with fire in the same **p.**.......... 7675
1Ki 3:4 for that was the great high **p.**: a ....
1Ki 4:12 unto the **p.** that is beyond Jokneam:..........
1Ki 4:28 brought they unto the **p.** where 4725
1Ki 5:9 the **p.** that thou shalt appoint me,........ 4725
1Ki 6:16 the oracle, even for the most holy **p.**. ....
1Ki 7:50 of the inner house, the most holy **p.**, ...
1Ki 8:6 covenant of the Lord unto his **p.**, ... 4725
1Ki 8:6 to the most holy **p.**, even under the ....
1Ki 8:7 two wings over the **p.** of the ark,....... 4725
1Ki 8:8 out in the holy **p.** before the oracle,...........
1Ki 8:10 priests were come out of the holy **p.**, ...
1Ki 8:13 a settled **p.** for thee to abide in for...........
1Ki 8:21 I have set there a **p.** for the ark. 4725
1Ki 8:29 the **p.** of which thou hast said, My 4725
1Ki 8:29 servant shall make toward this **p.**....... 4725
1Ki 8:30 when they shall pray toward this **p.** 4725
1Ki 8:30 hear thou in heaven thy dwelling **p.** 4725
1Ki 8:35 if they pray toward this **p.**, and.......... 4725
1Ki 8:39 thou in heaven thy dwelling **p.**, ... 4349
1Ki 8:43 Hear thou in heaven thy dwelling **p.**,.... 4349
1Ki 8:49 prayer...in heaven thy dwelling **p.**,...... 4349
1Ki 10:19 on either side on the **p.** of the seat, ... 4725
1Ki 11:7 build an high **p.** for Chemosh, the............
1Ki 13:8 bread nor drunk water in this **p.** 4725
1Ki 13:16 drink water with thee in this **p.**.......... 4725
1Ki 13:22 bread and drunk water in the **p.**, ... 4725
1Ki 20:24 kings away, every man out of his **p.**, .. 4725
1Ki 21:19 **p.** where dogs licked the blood of....... 4725
1Ki 22:10 in a void **p.** in the entrance of the 4725
2Ki 5:11 and strike his hand over the **p.**, and.... 4725
2Ki 6:1 **p.** where we dwell with thee is too..... 4725
2Ki 6:2 let us make us a **p.** there, where we .. 4725
2Ki 6:6 fell it? And he shewed him the **p.**........ 4725
2Ki 6:8 and such a **p.** shall be my camp. 4725
2Ki 6:9 Beware that thou pass not such a **p.**;.. 4725
2Ki 6:10 king of Israel sent to the **p.** which...... 4725
2Ki 18:25 Lord against this **p.** to destroy it? 4725
2Ki 22:16 Behold, I will bring evil upon this **p.**, .. 4725
2Ki 22:17 shall be kindled against this **p.**, and..... 4725
2Ki 22:19 what I spake against this **p.**, and........ 4725
2Ki 22:20 evil which I will bring upon this **p.**...... 4725
2Ki 23:15 the high **p.** which Jeroboam the son of.........
2Ki 23:15 altar and the high **p.** he brake down,.........
2Ki 23:15 burned the high **p.**, and stamped it ....
1Ch 6:32 the dwelling **p.** of the tabernacle of...........
1Ch 6:49 for all the work of the **p.** most holy. ....
1Ch 13:11 **p.** is called Perez-uzza to this day. 4725
1Ch 14:11 the name of that **p.** Baal-perazim. 4725
1Ch 15:1 and prepared a **p.** for the ark of God, ..4725
1Ch 15:3 up the ark of the Lord unto his **p.**. 4725
1Ch 15:12 unto the **p.** that I have prepared for it........
1Ch 16:27 and gladness are in his **p.**. 4725
1Ch 16:39 Lord in the high **p.** that was at Gibeon, ...
1Ch 17:9 ordain a **p.** for my people Israel, ... 4725
1Ch 17:9 and they shall dwell in their **p.**, and.... 8478
1Ch 21:22 me the **p.** of this threshingfloor,......... 4725
1Ch 21:25 to Ornan for the **p.** six hundred 4725
1Ch 21:29 that season in the high **p.** at Gibeon...........
1Ch 23:32 and the charge of the holy **p.**, and the.......
1Ch 28:11 and of the **p.** of the mercy seat, ... 1004
2Ch 1:3 to the high **p.** that was at Gibeon;............
2Ch 1:4 **p.** which David had prepared for it:...........
2Ch 1:13 to the high **p.** that was at Gibeon ....
2Ch 3:1 **p.** that David had prepared in the....... 4725
2Ch 4:22 doors thereof for the most holy **p.**, ...
2Ch 5:7 covenant of the Lord unto his **p.**, ... 4725
2Ch 5:7 into the most holy **p.**, even under the ....
2Ch 5:8 their wings over the **p.** of the ark, ... 4725
2Ch 5:11 priests were come out of the holy **p.** .. 4725
2Ch 6:2 and a **p.** for thy dwelling for ever....... 4349
2Ch 6:20 the **p.** whereof thou hast said that...... 4725
2Ch 6:20 thy servant prayeth toward this **p.**...... 4725
2Ch 6:21 they shall make toward this **p.**: 4725
2Ch 6:21 hear thou from thy dwelling **p.**, even... 4725
2Ch 6:26 yet if they pray toward this **p.**, and 4725
2Ch 6:30 thou from heaven thy dwelling **p.**, ... 4349
2Ch 6:33, 39 even from thy dwelling **p.**, and...... 4349
2Ch 6:40 the prayer that is made in this **p.**. 4725
2Ch 6:41 arise, O Lord God, into thy resting **p.**,......
2Ch 7:12 have chosen this **p.** to myself for 4725
2Ch 7:15 the prayer that is made in this **p.**. 4725
2Ch 9:18 stays on each side of the sitting **p.**, ... 4725
2Ch 18:9 they sat in a void **p.** at the entering in ......
2Ch 20:26 name of the same **p.** was called, ... 4725
2Ch 24:11 it, and carried it to his **p.** again.......... 4725
2Ch 29:5 forth the filthiness out of the holy **p.**.........
2Ch 29:7 in the holy **p.** unto the God of Israel. ....
2Ch 30:16 they stood in their **p.** after their......... 5977
2Ch 30:27 came up to his holy dwelling **p.**,...............
2Ch 34:24 I will bring evil upon this **p.**, and........ 4725
2Ch 34:25 shall be poured out upon this **p.**,......... 4725
2Ch 34:27 heardest his words against this **p.**,...... 4725
2Ch 34:28 evil that I will bring upon this **p.**. 4725
2Ch 34:31 the king stood in his **p.**, and made...... 5977
2Ch 35:5 stand in the holy **p.** according to the.........
2Ch 35:10 the priests stood in their **p.**, and....... 5977
2Ch 35:15 the sons of Asaph were in their **p.**, ... 4612
2Ch 36:15 on his people, and on his dwelling **p.**..........
Ezr 1:4 whosoever remaineth in any **p.**.......... 4725
Ezr 1:4 men of his **p.** help him with silver, ... 4725
Ezr 2:68 house of God to set it up in his **p.**...... 4349
Ezr 5:15 house of God be builded in his **p.**........ 870
Ezr 6:3 the **p.** where they offered sacrifices,..... 870
Ezr 6:5 at Jerusalem, every one to his **p.**, ... 870
Ezr 6:5 and **p.** them in the house of God........ 5182
Ezr 6:7 build this house of God in his **p.**. 870
Ezr 8:17 Iddo the chief at the **p.** Casiphia,........ 4725
Ezr 8:17 the Nethinims, at the **p.** Casiphia, ... 4725
Ezr 9:8 and to give us a nail in his holy **p.**,..... 4725
Ne 1:9 unto the **p.** that I have chosen to....... 4725
Ne 2:3 the **p.** of my fathers' sepulchres, ... 1004
Ne 2:14 there was no **p.** for the beast that...... 4725
Ne 3:16 **p.** over against the sepulchres of David, ...
Ne 3:26 **p.** over against the water gate toward.......
Ne 3:31 son unto the **p.** of the Nethinims,....... 1004
Ne 4:20 In what **p.**...ye hear the sound of....... 4725
Ne 8:7 and the people stood in their **p.**. 5977
Ne 9:3 they stood up in their **p.**, and read 5977
Ne 13:11 together, and set them in their **p.**. 5977
Es 2:9 best **p.** of the house of the women. ....
Es 4:14 arise to the Jews from another **p.**;...... 4725
Es 7:8 into the **p.** of the banquet of wine; 1004
Job 2:11 came every one from his own **p.**;........ 4725
Job 6:17 they are consumed out of their **p.**. 4725
Job 7:10 shall his **p.** know him any more.......... 4725
Job 8:17 heap, and seeth the **p.** of stones. 1004
Job 8:18 If he destroy him from his **p.**, then..... 4725
Job 8:22 the dwelling **p.** of the wicked shall............
Job 9:6 shaketh the earth out of her **p.**, ... 4725
Job 14:18 and the rock is removed out of his **p.**.. 4725
Job 16:18 blood, and let my cry have no **p.**......... 4725
Job 18:4 the rock be removed out of his **p.**?..... 4725
Job 18:21 the **p.** of him that knoweth not God.... 4725
Job 20:9 shall his **p.** any more behold him. 4725
Job 26:7 out the north over the empty **p.**, ... 8414
Job 27:21 a storm hurleth him out of his **p.**........ 4725
Job 27:23 and shall hiss him out of his **p.**. 4725
Job 28:1 and a **p.** for gold where they fine it. ... 4725
Job 28:6 stones of it are the **p.** of sapphires: 4725
Job 28:12, 20 is the **p.** of understanding?........... 4725
Job 28:23 and he knoweth the **p.** thereof,.......... 4725
Job 36:16 thee out of the strait into a broad **p.**,........
Job 36:20 when people are cut off in their **p.**...... 8478
Job 37:1 my heart...is moved out of his **p.**........ 4725
Job 38:10 And brake up for it my decreed **p.**,...........
Job 38:12 the dayspring to know his **p.**;............ 4725
Job 38:19 darkness, where is the **p.** thereof,...... 4725
Job 39:28 the crag of the rock, and the strong **p.**......
Job 40:12 tread down the wicked in their **p.**....... 8478
Ps 18:11 He made darkness his secret **p.**; his ....
Ps 18:19 me forth also into a large **p.**;............ 4800
Ps 24:3 or who shall stand in his holy **p.**? 4725
Ps 26:8 **p.** where thine honour dwelleth......... 4725
Ps 26:12 My foot standeth in an even **p.**; in............
Ps 32:7 Thou art my hiding **p.**; thou shalt ....
Ps 33:14 the **p.** of his habitation he looketh....... 4349
Ps 37:10 shalt diligently consider his **p.**,........... 4725
Ps 44:19 broken us in the **p.** of dragons,.......... 4725
Ps 46:4 holy **p.** of the tabernacles of the most ....
Ps 52:5 pluck thee out of thy dwelling **p.**, ...
Ps 66:12 broughtest us out into a wealthy **p.**...........
Ps 68:17 them, as in Sinai, in the holy **p.**. ....
Ps 74:7 the dwelling **p.** of thy name to the...........
Ps 76:2 and his dwelling **p.** in Zion. ....
Ps 79:7 and laid waste his dwelling **p.**. ....
Ps 81:7 thee in the secret **p.** of thunder: ....
Ps 90:1 Lord, thou hast been our dwelling **p.**.........
Ps 91:1 He that dwelleth in the secret **p.** of..........
Ps 103:16 **p.** thereof shall know it no more. 4725
Ps 104:8 the **p.** which thou hast founded for 4725
Ps 118:5 me, and set me in a large **p.**. ....
Ps 119:114 Thou art my hiding **p.** and my ....
Ps 132:5 until I find out a **p.** for the Lord,........ 4725
Pr 1:21 She crieth in the chief **p.** of concourse,......
Pr 14:26 his children shall have a **p.** of refuge. ....
Pr 15:3 eyes of the Lord are in every **p.**, ... 4725
Pr 24:15 righteous; spoil not his resting **p.** ....
Pr 25:6 stand not in the **p.** of great men: 4725
Pr 27:8 man that wandereth from his **p.**. 4725
Ec 1:5 hasteth to his **p.** where he arose........ 4725
Ec 1:7 **p.** from whence the rivers come, ... 4725
Ec 3:16 under the sun the **p.** of judgment, ... 4725
Ec 3:16 **p.** of righteousness, that iniquity 4725
Ec 3:20 All go unto one **p.**; all are of the........ 4725
Ec 6:6 no good: do not all go to one **p.**? 4725
Ec 8:10 and gone from the **p.** of the holy,....... 4725
Ec 10:4 up against thee, leave not thy **p.**;....... 4725
Ec 10:6 dignity, and the rich sit in low **p.**..............
Ec 11:3 in the **p.** where the tree falleth,.......... 4725
Isa 4:5 every dwelling **p.** of mount Zion, ...
Isa 4:6 and for a **p.** of refuge, and for a..............
Isa 5:8 field to field, till there be no **p.**. 4725
Isa 7:23 that every **p.** shall be, where there..... 4725
Isa 13:13 earth shall remove out of her **p.**,........ 4725
Isa 14:2 them, and bring them to their **p.**: 4725
Isa 16:12 that Moab is weary on the high **p.**,..........
Isa 18:4 I will consider in my dwelling **p.**...............
Isa 18:7 the **p.** of the name of the Lord of......... 4725
Isa 22:23 fasten him as a nail in a sure **p.**; 4725
Isa 22:25 nail that is fastened in the sure **p.** 4725
Isa 25:5 strangers, as the heat in a dry **p.**; ....
Isa 26:21 cometh out of his **p.** to punish the...... 4725
Isa 28:8 so that there is no **p.** clean.............. 4725
Isa 28:17 waters shall overflow the hiding **p.**............
Isa 28:25 barley and the rye in their **p.**? 1367
Isa 30:32 **p.** where the grounded staff shall.............
Isa 32:2 a man shall be as an hiding **p.** from..........
Isa 32:2 as rivers of water in a dry **p.**, as the ....
Isa 32:19 and the city shall be low in a low **p.**,.........
Isa 33:16 his **p.** of defence shall be the...................
Isa 33:21 will be unto us a **p.** of broad rivers..... 4725
Isa 34:14 there, and find for herself a **p.** of rest. ......
Isa 35:1 solitary **p.** shall be glad for them; ....
Isa 45:19 secret, in a dark **p.** of the earth:........ 4725
Isa 46:7 carry him, and set him in his **p.**, ... 8478
Isa 46:7 from his **p.** shall he not remove: 4725
Isa 46:13 and I will **p.** salvation in Zion for 5414
Isa 49:20 ears, The **p.** is too straight for me: 4725
Isa 49:20 give **p.** to me that I may dwell. 4725
Isa 54:2 Enlarge the **p.** of thy tent, and let...... 4725
Isa 56:5 **p.** and a name better than of sons...... 3027
Isa 57:15 I dwell in the high and holy **p.**, with..........
Isa 60:13 beautify the **p.** of my sanctuary;......... 4725
Isa 60:13 make the **p.** of my feet glorious. 4725
Isa 65:10 valley of Achor a **p.** for the herds to.........
Isa 66:1 and where is the **p.** of my rest?......... 4725
Jer 4:7 he is gone forth from his **p.** to............ 4725
Jer 4:26 lo, the fruitful **p.** was a wilderness,..........
Jer 6:3 they shall feed every one in his **p.**...... 3027
Jer 7:3 will cause you to dwell in this **p.**. 4725
Jer 7:6 shed not innocent blood in this **p.**,...... 4725
Jer 7:7 will I cause you to dwell in this **p.**, ... 4725
Jer 7:12 unto my **p.** which was in Shiloh,......... 4725
Jer 7:14 unto the **p.** which I gave to you.......... 4725
Jer 7:20 shall be poured out upon this **p.**, ... 4725
Jer 7:32 bury in Tophet, till there be no **p.**. 4725
Jer 9:2 lodging **p.** of wayfaring men: that I...........
Jer 13:7 took the girdle from the **p.** where 4725

Jer 14:13 give you assured peace in this **p.**. 4725
Jer 16:2 have sons or daughters in this **p.**. 4725
Jer 16:3 daughters that are born in this **p.**, 4725
Jer 16:9 will cause to cease out of this **p.** 4725
Jer 17:12 is the **p.** of our sanctuary. 4725
Jer 18:14 waters that come from another **p.** be
Jer 19:3 I will bring evil upon this **p.**, the 4725
Jer 19:4 me, and have estranged this **p.**, 4725
Jer 19:4 this **p.** with the blood of innocents; 4725
Jer 19:6 **p.** shall no more be called Tophet, 4725
Jer 19:7 of Judah and Jerusalem in this **p.**; 4725
Jer 19:11 Tophet, till there be no **p.** to bury 4725
Jer 19:12 Thus will I do unto this **p.**, saith 4725
Jer 19:13 shall be defiled as the **p.** of Tophet, 4725
Jer 22:3 shed innocent blood in this **p.**. 4725
Jer 22:11 which went forth out of this **p.**; 4725
Jer 22:12 he shall die in the **p.** whither they 4725
Jer 24:5 whom I have sent out of this **p.** into 4725
Jer 27:22 up, and restore them to this **p.**. 4725
Jer 28:3 will I bring again into this **p.** all 4725
Jer 28:3 of Babylon took away from this **p.**, 4725
Jer 28:4 will bring again to this **p.** Jeconiah 4725
Jer 28:6 captive, from Babylon into this **p.** 4725
Jer 29:10 in causing you to return to this **p.**. 4725
Jer 29:14 bring you again into the **p.** whence 4725
Jer 32:37 will bring them again unto this **p.**, 4725
Jer 33:10 there shall be heard in this **p.**, 4725
Jer 33:12 Again in this **p.**, which is desolate 4725
Jer 38:9 like to die for hunger in the **p.** 8478
Jer 40:2 pronounced this evil upon this **p.**. 4725
Jer 42:18 and ye shall see this **p.** no more. 4725
Jer 42:22 in the **p.** whither ye desire to go 4725
Jer 44:29 I will punish you in this **p.**, that ye 4725
Jer 51:62 thou hast spoken against this **p.**, 4725
Eze 3:12 the glory of the Lord from his **p.**. 4725
Eze 6:13 the **p.** where they did offer sweet 4725
Eze 7:22 they shall pollute my secret **p.**:
Eze 10:11 **p.** whither the head looked they 4725
Eze 12:3 from thy **p.** to another **p.** in their 4725
Eze 16:24 also built unto thee an eminent **p.**
Eze 16:24 made thee an high **p.** in every street.
Eze 16:25 thy high **p.** at every head of the way,
Eze 16:31 eminent **p.** in the head of every way,
Eze 16:31 makest thine high **p.** in every street;
Eze 16:39 shall throw down thine eminent **p.**,
Eze 17:16 the **p.** where the king dwelleth 4725
Eze 20:29 is the high **p.** whereunto ye go?
Eze 21:19 choose thou a **p.**, choose it at the 3027
Eze 21:30 I will judge thee in the **p.** where 4725
Eze 26:5 shall be a **p.** for the spreading of nets
Eze 26:14 shalt be a **p.** to spread nets upon;
Eze 37:14 I shall **p.** you in your own land: 3241
Eze 37:26 I will **p.** them, and multiply them, 5414
Eze 38:15 come from thy **p.** out of the north 4725
Eze 39:11 give unto God a **p.** there of graves 4725
Eze 41:4 unto me, This is the most holy **p.**.
Eze 41:9 was the **p.** of the side chambers 1004
Eze 41:11 were toward the **p.** that was left.
Eze 41:11 the breadth of the **p.** that was left 4725
Eze 41:12 the separate **p.** at the end toward the
Eze 41:13 and the separate **p.**, and the building,
Eze 41:14 and of the separate **p.** toward the east,
Eze 41:15 the separate **p.** which was behind it,
Eze 42:1 that was over against the separate **p.**,
Eze 42:10 over against the separate **p.**, and over
Eze 42:13 which are before the separate **p.**, they
Eze 42:13 trespass offering; for the **p.** is holy. 4725
Eze 42:14 shall they not go out of the holy **p.**
Eze 42:20 the sanctuary and the profane **p.**.
Eze 43:7 Son of man, the **p.** of my throne, 4725
Eze 43:7 the **p.** of the soles of my feet, where 4725
Eze 43:13 this shall be the higher **p.** of the altar
Eze 43:21 he shall burn it in the appointed **p.** of
Eze 44:13 my holy things, in the most holy **p.**:
Eze 45:3 the sanctuary and the most holy **p.**.
Eze 45:4 it shall be a **p.** for their houses, 4725
Eze 45:4 and an holy **p.** for the sanctuary.
Eze 46:19 there was a **p.** on the two sides 4725
Eze 46:20 the **p.** where the priests shall boil 4725
Eze 47:10 they shall be a **p.** to spread forth nets;
Eze 48:15 shall be a profane **p.** for the city, for
Da 2:35 no **p.** was found for them: and the 870
Da 8:11 **p.** of his sanctuary was cast down. 4349
Da 11:31 they shall **p.** the abomination that 5414
Ho 1:10 **p.** where it was said unto them 4725
Ho 4:16 will feed them as a lamb in a large **p.**
Ho 5:15 I will go and return to my **p.**, till 4725
Ho 9:13 Tyrus, is planted in a pleasant **p.**:
Ho 11:11 and I will **p.** them in their houses, 3427
Ho 13:13 **p.** of the breaking forth of children.
Joe 3:7 I will raise them out of the **p.** 4725
Am 8:3 be many dead bodies in every **p.**; 4725
Mic 1:3 the Lord cometh forth out of his **p.**, 4725
Mic 1:4 that are poured down a steep **p.**.
Na 1:8 an utter end of the **p.** thereof, 4725
Na 3:17 **p.** is not known where they are. 4725
Zep 1:4 the remnant of Baal from this **p.**, 4725
Zep 2:11 worship him every one from his **p.**, 4725
Zep 2:15 a **p.** for beasts to lie down in! every
Hag 2:9 and in this **p.** will I give peace, 4725
Zec 6:12 and he shall grow up out of his **p.**, 8478
Zec 10:6 I will bring them again to **p.** them; 3427
Zec 10:10 and **p.** shall not be found for them.
Zec 12:6 be inhabited again in her own **p.**, 8478
Zec 14:10 be lifted up, and inhabited in her **p.**, 8478
Zec 14:10 gate unto the **p.** of the first gate, 4725
Mal 1:11 in every **p.** incense shall be offered. 4725
Mt 8:32 violently down a steep **p.** into the sea,
Mt 9:24 He said unto them, **Give p.: for the** *402*
Mt 12:6 **in this p. is one...than the temple.** *5602*
Mt 14:13 by ship into a desert **p.** apart: *5117*
Mt 14:15 This is a desert **p.**, and the time is *5117*
Mt 14:35 the men of that **p.** had knowledge *5117*
Mt 17:20 **Remove hence to yonder p.; and it**
Mt 24:15 **the prophet, stand in the holy p.,** *5117*
Mt 26:36 them unto a **p.** called Gethsemane, *5564*
Mt 26:52 **Put up again thy sword into his p.:** *5117*
Mt 27:33 come unto a **p.** called Golgotha. *5117*
Mt 27:33 that is to say, a **p.** of a skull, *5117*
Mt 28:6 Come see the **p.** where the Lord lay. *5117*
Mk 1:35 departed into a solitary **p.**, and *5117*
Mk 5:13 violently down a steep **p.** into the sea,
Mk 6:10 **p. soever ye enter into an house,** *3699*
Mk 6:10 **abide till ye depart from that p.** *1564*
Mk 6:31 **yourselves apart into a desert p.,** *5117*
Mk 6:32 they departed into a desert **p.** by *5117*
Mk 6:35 This is a desert **p.**, and now the *5117*
Mk 11:4 without in a **p.** where two ways met;
Mk 12:1 **and digged a p. for the winefat, and**
Mk 14:32 to a **p.** which..named Gethsemane: *5564*
Mk 15:22 bring him unto the **p.** Golgotha, *5117*
Mk 15:22 being interpreted, The **p.** of a skull. *5117*
Mk 16:6 behold the **p.** where they laid him. *5117*
Lu 4:17 found the **p.** where it was written, *5117*
Lu 4:37 went out into every **p.** of the country. *5117*
Lu 4:42 departed and went into a desert **p.**; *5117*
Lu 8:33 violently down a steep **p.** into the
Lu 9:10 aside privately into a desert **p.** *5117*
Lu 9:12 for we are here in a desert **p.**. *5117*
Lu 10:1 his face into every city and **p.**, *5117*
Lu 10:32 **a Levite, when he was at the p.** *5117*
Lu 11:1 as he was praying in a certain **p.**, *5117*
Lu 11:33 **a candle, putteth it in a secret p.**
Lu 14:9 **and say to thee, Give this man p.:** *5117*
Lu 16:28 **also come into this p. of torment.** *5117*
Lu 19:5 And when Jesus came to the **p.**, he *5117*
Lu 22:40 when he was at the **p.**, he said unto *5117*
Lu 23:5 beginning from Galilee to this **p.** *5602*
Lu 23:33 And when they were come to the **p.**, *5117*
Joh 4:20 in Jerusalem is the **p.** where men *5117*
Joh 5:13 away, a multitude being in that **p.** *5117*
Joh 6:10 there was much grass in the **p.** *5117*
Joh 6:23 unto the **p.** where they did eat *5117*
Joh 8:37 **my word hath no p. in you.** *5562*
Joh 10:40 **p.** where John at first baptized; *5117*
Joh 11:6 still in the same **p.** where he was. *5117*
Joh 11:30 in that **p.** where Martha met him. *5117*
Joh 11:41 from the **p.** where the dead was laid.
Joh 11:48 take away both our **p.** and nation. *5117*
Joh 14:2 **you. I go to prepare a p. for you.** *5117*
Joh 14:3 **if I go and prepare a p. for you,** *5117*
Joh 18:2 which betrayed him, knew the **p.**: *5117*
Joh 19:13 in a **p.** that is called the Pavement, *5117*
Joh 19:17 his cross went forth into a **p.**
Joh 19:17 called the **p.** of a skull, which is *5117*
Joh 19:20 the **p.** where Jesus was crucified *5117*
Joh 19:41 the **p.** where he was crucified there *5117*
Joh 20:7 wrapped together in a **p.** by itself. *5117*
Ac 1:25 fell, that he might go to his own **p.** *5117*
Ac 2:1 were all with one accord in one **p.**
Ac 4:31 the **p.** was shaken where they *5117*
Ac 6:13 words against this holy **p.**, and the *5117*
Ac 6:14 of Nazareth shall destroy this **p.**, *5117*
Ac 7:7 come forth, and serve me in this **p.** *5117*
Ac 7:33 the **p.** where thou standest is holy *5117*
Ac 7:49 Lord: or what is the **p.** of my rest? *5117*
Ac 8:32 **p.** of the scripture which he read *4042*
Ac 12:17 departed, and went into another **p.** *5117*
Ac 21:12 and they of that **p.**, besought him *1786*
Ac 21:28 people, and the law, and this **p.**: *5117*
Ac 21:28 and hath polluted this holy **p.** *5117*
Ac 25:23 was entered into the **p.** of hearing. *201*
Ac 27:8 a **p.** which is called The fair havens; *5117*
Ac 27:41 into a **p.** where two seas met, *5117*
Ro 9:26 **p.** where it was said unto them, *5117*
Ro 12:19 but rather give **p.** unto wrath: *5117*
Ro 15:23 having no more **p.** in these parts, *5117*
1Co 1:2 that in every **p.** call upon the name *5117*
1Co 11:20 come together therefore into one **p.**,
1Co 14:23 church be come together into one **p.**,
2Co 2:14 his knowledge by us in every **p.** *5117*
Ga 2:5 whom we gave **p.** by subjection, *1502*
Eph 4:27 Neither give **p.** to the devil. *5117*
1Th 1:8 in every **p.** your faith to God-ward *5117*
Heb 2:6 But one in a certain **p.** testified,
Heb 4:4 spake in a certain **p.** of the seventh
Heb 4:5 And in this **p.** again, If they shall
Heb 5:6 As he saith also in another **p.**, Thou
Heb 8:7 no **p.** have been sought for the *5117*
Heb 9:12 he entered in once into the holy **p.**,
Heb 9:25 high priest entereth into the holy **p.**
Heb 11:8 he was called to go out into a **p.** *5117*
Heb 12:17 for he found no **p.** of repentance, *5117*
Jas 2:3 Sit thou here in a good **p.**; and
Jas 3:11 at the same **p.** sweet water and *3692*
2Pe 1:19 a light that shineth in a dark **p.**, *5117*
Re 2:5 **thy candlestick out of this p.** *5117*
Re 12:6 she hath a **p.** prepared of God, *5117*
Re 12:8 was their **p.** found any more *5117*
Re 12:14 into her **p.**, where she is nourished *5117*
Re 16:16 a **p.** called in the Hebrew tongue *5117*
Re 20:11 and there was found no **p.** for them. *5117*

PLACED

Ge 3:24 he **p.** at the east of the garden of 7931
Ge 47:11 And Joseph **p.** his father and his 3427
1Ki 12:32 and he **p.** in Beth-el the priests of 5975
2Ki 17:6 **p.** them in Halah and in Habor by 3427
2Ki 17:24 **p.** them in the cities of Samaria 3427
2Ki 17:26 **p.** in the cities of Samaria, know 3427
2Ch 1:14 which he **p.** in the chariot cities, 3240
2Ch 4:8 **p.** them in the temple, five on the 3240
2Ch 17:2 he **p.** forces in all the fenced cities 5414
Job 20:4 old, since man was **p.** upon earth, 7760
Ps 78:60 the tent which he **p.** among men; 7931
Isa 5:8 they may be **p.** alone in the midst 3427
Jer 5:22 have **p.** the sand for the bound of 776
Eze 17:5 he **p.** it by great waters, and set 3947

PLACES See also MARKETPLACES.

Ge 28:15 keep thee in all **p.** whither thou goest,
Ge 36:40 to their families after their **p.**, 4725
Ex 20:24 **p.** where I record my name I will 4725
Ex 25:27 be for **p.** of the staves to bear the 1004
Ex 26:29 rings of gold for **p.** for the bars: 1004
Ex 30:4 they shall be for **p.** for the staves 1004
Ex 36:34 rings of gold to be **p.** for the bars, 1004
Ex 37:14 **p.** for the staves to bear the table. 1004
Ex 37:27 **p.** for the staves to bear it withal. 1004
Ex 38:5 of brass, to be **p.** for the staves. 1004
Le 26:30 I will destroy your high **p.**, and cut
Nu 21:28 the lords of the high **p.** of Arnon.
Nu 22:41 him up into the high **p.** of Baal,
Nu 33:52 and quite pluck down all their high **p.**:
De 1:7 and unto all the **p.** nigh thereunto,
De 12:2 Ye shall utterly destroy all the **p.**, 4725
De 32:13 ride on the high **p.** of the earth,
De 33:29 thou shalt tread upon their high **p.**
Jos 5:8 they abode in their **p.** in the camps 8478
Jg 5:11 of archers in the **p.** of drawing water,
Jg 5:18 the death in the high **p.** of the field
Jg 19:13 one of these **p.** to lodge all night, 4725
Jg 20:33 Israel came forth out of their **p.**, 4725
1Sa 7:16 and judged Israel in all those **p.** 4725
1Sa 13:6 in rocks, and in high **p.**, and in pits
1Sa 23:23 of all the lurking **p.** where he hideth
1Sa 30:31 to all the **p.** where David himself 4725
2Sa 1:19 of Israel is slain upon thy high **p.**:
2Sa 1:25 thou wast slain in thine high **p.**.
2Sa 7:7 In all the **p.** wherein I have walked
2Sa 22:34 feet: and setteth me upon my high **p.**

2Sa 22:46 shall be afraid out of their close **p.**
1Ki 3:2 Only the people sacrificed in high **p.**,
1Ki 3:3 only he...burnt incense in high **p.**.
1Ki 12:31 And he made an house of high **p.**, and
1Ki 12:32 priests of the high **p.** which he...made
1Ki 13:2 he offer the priests of the high **p.**
1Ki 13:32 against all the houses of the high **p.**
1Ki 13:33 lowest...people, priests of the high **p.**:
1Ki 13:33 one of the priests of the high **p.**.
1Ki 14:23 For they also built them high **p.**, and
1Ki 15:14 But the high **p.** were not removed:
1Ki 22:43 the high **p.** were not taken away;
1Ki 22:43 and burnt incense yet in the high **p.**.
2Ki 12:3 But the high **p.** were not taken away:
2Ki 12:3 and burnt incense in the high **p.**.
2Ki 14:4 the high **p.** were not taken away:
2Ki 14:4 and burnt incense on the high **p.**.
2Ki 15:4 that the high **p.** were not removed:
2Ki 15:4 and burnt incense still on the high **p.**.
2Ki 15:35 the high **p.** were not removed:
2Ki 15:35 burned incense still in the high **p.**.
2Ki 16:4 burnt incense in the high **p.**, and on
2Ki 17:9 built them high **p.** in all their cities,
2Ki 17:11 they burnt incense in all the high **p.**,
2Ki 17:29 put them in the houses of the high **p.**
2Ki 17:32 lowest of them priests of the high **p.**,
2Ki 17:32 for them in the houses of the high **p.**.
2Ki 18:4 He removed the high **p.**, and brake the
2Ki 18:22 whose high **p.** and...altars Hezekiah
2Ki 19:24 I dried up all the rivers of besieged **p.**
2Ki 21:3 For he built up again the high **p.**
2Ki 23:5 in the high **p.** in the cities of Judah,
2Ki 23:5 and in the **p.** round about Jerusalem;
2Ki 23:8 defiled the high **p.** where the priests
2Ki 23:8 brake down the high **p.** of the gates
2Ki 23:9 the priests of the high **p.** came not up
2Ki 23:13 high **p.** that were before Jerusalem,
2Ki 23:14 filled their **p.** with...bones of men. 4725
2Ki 23:19 all the houses of the high **p.** that were
2Ki 23:20 he slew all the priests of the high **p.**
1Ch 6:54 dwelling **p.** throughout their castles
2Ch 8:11 the **p.** are holy, whereunto the ark of
2Ch 11:15 ordained him priests for the high **p.**,
2Ch 14:3 of the strange gods, and the high **p.**,
2Ch 14:5 away...the high **p.** and the images:
2Ch 15:17 But the high **p.** were not taken away
2Ch 17:6 he took away the high **p.** and groves
2Ch 20:33 the high **p.** were not taken away:
2Ch 21:11 he made high **p.** in the mountains
2Ch 28:4 burnt incense in the high **p.**, and on
2Ch 28:25 he made high **p.** to burn incense
2Ch 31:1 threw down the high **p.** and the altars
2Ch 32:12 taken away his high **p.** and his altars,
2Ch 33:3 For he built again the high **p.** which
2Ch 33:17 people did sacrifice still in the high **p.**,
2Ch 33:19 and the **p.** wherein he built high 4725
2Ch 33:19 wherein he built high **p.**, and set up
2Ch 34:3 purge...Jerusalem from the high **p.**,
Ne 4:12 From all **p.** whence ye shall return 4725
Ne 4:13 set I in the lower **p.** behind the wall, .. 4725
Ne 4:13 and on the higher **p.**, I even set
Ne 12:27 sought the Levites out of all...**p.**, 4725
Job 3:14 built desolate **p.** for themselves; 2723
Job 20:26 darkness shall be hid in his secret **p.**:
Job 21:28 are the dwelling **p.** of the wicked? 168
Job 25:2 him, he maketh peace in his high **p.**.
Job 37:8 into dens, and remain in their **p.**. 4585
Ps 10:8 in the lurking **p.** of the villages:
Ps 10:8 in the secret **p.** doth he murder the
Ps 16:6 lines are fallen unto me in pleasant **p.**;
Ps 17:12 were a young lion lurking in secret **p.**.
Ps 18:33 feet, and setteth me upon my high **p.**.
Ps 18:45 and be afraid out of their close **p.**
Ps 49:11 their dwelling **p.** to all generations;
Ps 68:35 thou art terrible out of thy holy **p.**:
Ps 73:18 thou didst set them in slippery **p.**:
Ps 74:20 the dark **p.** of the earth are full of the
Ps 78:58 provoked him...with their high **p.**,
Ps 95:4 his hand are the deep **p.** of the earth:
Ps 103:22 works in all **p.** of his dominion: 4725
Ps 105:41 they ran in the dry **p.** like a river.
Ps 109:10 bread also out of their desolate **p.**.
Ps 110:6 shall fill the **p.** with the dead bodies;
Ps 135:6 in earth, in the seas, and all deep **p.**.
Ps 141:6 judges are overthrown in stony **p.**, 3027
Pr 8:2 She standeth in the top of high **p.**,
Pr 8:2 by the way in the **p.** of the paths. 1004
Pr 9:3 crieth upon the highest **p.** of the city,
Pr 9:14 on a seat in the high **p.** of the city,
Ca 2:14 the rock, in the secret **p.** of the stairs,
Isa 5:17 and the waste **p.** of the fat ones shall
Isa 15:2 to Bajith, and to Dibon, the high **p.**,
Isa 32:18 sure dwellings, and in quiet resting **p.**;
Isa 36:7 whose high **p.** and...altars Hezekiah
Isa 37:25 up all the rivers of the besieged **p.**
Isa 40:4 made straight, and the rough **p.** plain:
Isa 41:18 I will open rivers in high **p.**, and
Isa 44:26 I will raise up the decayed **p.** thereof:
Isa 45:2 and make the crooked **p.** straight:
Isa 45:3 and hidden riches of secret **p.**,
Isa 49:9 their pastures shall be in all high **p.**.
Isa 49:19 For thy waste and thy desolate **p.**,
Isa 51:3 he will comfort all her waste **p.**; and
Isa 52:9 together, ye waste **p.** of Jerusalem:
Isa 58:12 be of thee shall build the old waste **p.**:
Isa 58:14 to ride upon the high **p.** of the earth,
Isa 59:10 we are in desolate **p.** as dead men
Jer 3:2 Lift up thine eyes unto the high **p.**,
Jer 3:21 A voice was heard upon the high **p.**,
Jer 4:11 wind of the high **p.** in the wilderness
Jer 4:12 a full wind from those **p.** shall come
Jer 5:1 and seek in the broad **p.** thereof, if
Jer 7:29 and take up a lamentation on high **p.**;
Jer 7:31 they have built the high **p.** of Tophet,
Jer 8:3 in all the **p.** whither I have driven 4725
Jer 12:12 The spoilers are come upon all high **p.**
Jer 13:17 my soul shall weep in secret **p.** for
Jer 14:6 wild asses did stand in the high **p.**,
Jer 17:3 to the spoil, and thy high **p.** for sin,
Jer 17:6 but shall inhabit the parched **p.** in the
Jer 17:26 and from the **p.** about Jerusalem, 5439
Jer 19:5 have built also the high **p.** of Baal,
Jer 23:10 the pleasant **p.** of the wilderness are
Jer 23:24 Can any hide himself in secret **p.** that
Jer 24:9 all **p.** whither I shall drive them. 4725
Jer 26:18 of the house as the high **p.** of a forest.
Jer 29:14 all the **p.** whither I have driven 4725
Jer 32:35 And they built the high **p.** of Baal,
Jer 32:44 and in the **p.** about Jerusalem, and in
Jer 33:13 and in the **p.** about Jerusalem, and in
Jer 40:12 all **p.** whither they were driven, 4725
Jer 45:5 for a prey in all **p.** whither thou 4725
Jer 48:35 him that offereth in the high **p.**, and
Jer 49:10 bare, I have uncovered his secret **p.**,
La 2:6 hath destroyed his **p.** of the assembly:
La 3:6 He hath set me in dark **p.**, as they that
La 3:10 in wait, and as a lion in secret **p.**.
Eze 6:3 you, and I will destroy your high **p.**.
Eze 6:6 and the high **p.** shall be desolate;
Eze 7:24 and their holy **p.** shall be defiled.
Eze 16:16 and deckedst thy high **p.** with divers
Eze 16:39 and shall break down thy high **p.**:
Eze 21:2 and drop thy word toward the holy **p.**,
Eze 26:20 parts of the earth, in **p.** desolate of old,
Eze 34:12 deliver them out of all **p.** where 4725
Eze 34:13 in all the inhabited **p.** of the country.
Eze 34:26 the **p.** round about my hill a blessing:
Eze 36:2 even the ancient high **p.** are ours in
Eze 36:36 that I the Lord build the ruined **p.**,
Eze 38:12 desolate **p.** that are now inhabited,
Eze 38:20 and the steep **p.** shall fall, and every
Eze 43:7 of their kings in their high **p.**.
Eze 46:23 was made with boiling **p.** under the
Eze 46:24 These are the **p.** of them that boil, 1004
Eze 47:11 But the miry **p.** thereof and the
Da 11:24 upon the fattest **p.** of the province;
Ho 9:6 the pleasant **p.** for their silver, nettles
Ho 10:8 The high **p.** also of Aven, the sin of
Am 4:6 and want of bread in all your **p.**: 4725
Am 4:13 upon the high **p.** of the earth,
Am 7:9 the high **p.** of Isaac shall be desolate,
Mic 1:3 tread upon the high **p.** of the earth.
Mic 1:5 and what are the high **p.** of Judah?
Mic 3:12 the house as the high **p.** of the forest.
Hab 3:19 make me to walk upon mine high **p.**.
Zec 3:7 I will give thee **p.** to walk among
Mal 1:4 will return and build the desolate **p.**;
Mt 12:43 **he walketh through dry p., seeking** *5117*
Mt 13:5 **Some fell upon stony p., where they**
Mt 13:20 **that received the seed into stony p.,**
Mt 24:7 **and earthquakes, in divers p..** *5117*
Mk 1:45 city, but was without in desert **p.**: *5117*
Mk 13:8 **shall be earthquakes in divers p.,..** *5117*
Lu 11:24 **he walketh through dry p., seeking** *5117*
Lu 21:11 **earthquakes shall be in divers p.,..** *5117*
Ac 24:3 We accept it always, and in all **p.**, *3837*
Eph 1:3 blessings in heavenly **p.** in Christ:
Eph 1:20 his own right hand in the heavenly **p.**,
Eph 2:6 in heavenly **p.** in Christ Jesus:
Eph 3:10 in heavenly **p.** might be known by
Eph 6:12 spiritual wickedness in high **p.**.
Php 1:13 all the palace, and in all other **p.**;
Heb 9:24 into the holy **p.** made with hands,
Re 6:14 island were moved out of their **p.**. *5117*

PLAGUE See also PLAGUED; PLAGUES.
Ex 11:1 bring one **p.** more upon Pharaoh, 5061
Ex 12:13 **p.** shall not be upon you to destroy 5063
Ex 30:12 that there be no **p.** among them, 5063
Le 13:2 of his flesh like the **p.** of leprosy; 5061
Le 13:3 shall look on the **p.** in the skin of 5061
Le 13:3 the hair in the **p.** is turned white, 5061
Le 13:3 **p.** in sight be deeper than the skin 5061
Le 13:3 skin of his flesh, it is a **p.** of leprosy:.. 5061
Le 13:4 up him that hath the **p.** seven days: 5061
Le 13:5 if the **p.** in his sight be at a stay, 5061
Le 13:5 and the **p.** spread not in the skin; 5061
Le 13:6 behold, if the **p.** be somewhat dark, 5061
Le 13:6 **p.** spread not in the skin, the priest 5061
Le 13:9 When the **p.** of leprosy is in a man, 5061
Le 13:12 hath the **p.** from his head even to 5061
Le 13:13 pronounce him clean that hath...**p.** 5061
Le 13:17 if the **p.** be turned into white; then 5061
Le 13:17 pronounce him clean that hath...**p.**: 5061
Le 13:20 **p.** of leprosy broken out of the boil 5061
Le 13:22 pronounce him unclean: it is a **p.**. 5061
Le 13:25, 27 unclean: it is the **p.** of leprosy. 5061
Le 13:29 or woman have a **p.** upon the head 5061
Le 13:30 Then the priest shall see the **p.**: and,.. 5061
Le 13:31 the priest look on the **p.** of the scall, .. 5061
Le 13:31 up him that hath the **p.** of the scall 5061
Le 13:32 day the priest shall look on the **p.**: 5061
Le 13:44 unclean; his **p.** is in his head. 5061
Le 13:45 And the leper in whom the **p.** is, his 5061
Le 13:46 days wherein the **p.** shall be in him. 5061
Le 13:47 garment...that the **p.** of leprosy is in,.. 5061
Le 13:49 if the **p.** be greenish or reddish in 5061
Le 13:49 it is a **p.** of leprosy, and shall be 5061
Le 13:50 the priest shall look upon the **p.**, 5061
Le 13:50 up it that hath the **p.** seven days: 5061
Le 13:51 look on the **p.** on the seventh day: 5061
Le 13:51 if the **p.** be spread in the garment, 5061
Le 13:51 the **p.** is a fretting leprosy; it is 5061
Le 13:52 thing of skin, wherein the **p.** is: 5061
Le 13:53 the **p.** be not spread in the garment, 5061
Le 13:54 wash the thing wherein the **p.** is, 5061
Le 13:55 the priest shall look on the **p.**, after 5061
Le 13:55 the **p.** have not changed his colour, 5061
Le 13:55 colour, and the **p.** be not spread; 5061
Le 13:56 the **p.** be somewhat dark after the 5061
Le 13:57 it is a spreading **p.**: thou shalt burn
Le 13:57 shalt burn that wherein the **p.** is 5061
Le 13:58 if the **p.** be departed from them, 5061
Le 13:59 This is the law of the **p.** of leprosy 5061
Le 14:3 if the **p.** of leprosy be healed in the 5061
Le 14:32 him in whom is the **p.** of leprosy, 5061
Le 14:34 I put the **p.** of leprosy in a house of 5061
Le 14:35 there is as it were a **p.** in the house:.. 5061
Le 14:36 the priest go into it to see the **p.**, 5061
Le 14:37 he shall look on the **p.**, and, behold, 5061
Le 14:37 if the **p.** be in the walls of the house 5061
Le 14:39 **p.** be spread in the walls of the 5061
Le 14:40 away the stones in which the **p.** is, 5061
Le 14:43 if the **p.** come again, and break out 5061
Le 14:44 if the **p.** be spread in the house, it 5061
Le 14:48 the **p.** hath not spread in the house, 5061
Le 14:48 clean, because the **p.** is healed. 5061
Le 14:54 law for all manner of **p.** of leprosy, 5061
Nu 8:19 there be no **p.** among the children 5063
Nu 11:33 the people with a very great **p.** 4347
Nu 14:37 died by the **p.** before the Lord. 4046
Nu 16:46 from the Lord; the **p.** is begun. 5063
Nu 16:47 the **p.** was begun among the people: 5063
Nu 16:48 the living; and the **p.** was stayed. 4046
Nu 16:49 Now they that died in the **p.** were 4046
Nu 16:50 congregation: and the **p.** was stayed. 4046
Nu 25:8 **p.** was stayed from the children of 4046
Nu 25:9 and those that died in the **p.** were 4046
Nu 25:18 slain in the day of the **p.** for Peor's 4046
Nu 26:1 it came to pass after the **p.**, that the 4046

Nu 31:16 was a **p.** among the congregation....... 4046
De 24:8 Take heed in the **p.** of leprosy, that.... 5061
De 28:61 Also every sickness, and every **p.**,..... 4347
Jos 22:17 was a **p.** in the congregation of the..... 5063
1Sa 6:4 for one **p.** was on you all, and on...... 4046
2Sa 24:21 **p.** may be stayed from the people...... 4046
2Sa 24:25 and the **p.** was stayed from Israel...... 4046
1Ki 8:37 of their cities; whatsoever **p.**,............ 5061
1Ki 8:38 every man the **p.** of his own heart,...... 5061
1Ch 21:22 **p.** may be stayed from the people...... 4046
2Ch 21:14 **p.** will the Lord smite thy people,...... 4046
Ps 89:23 face, and **p.** them that hate him......... 5063
Ps 91:10 neither shall any **p.** come nigh thy...... 5061
Ps 106:29 and the **p.** brake in upon them........... 4046
Ps 106:30 judgment: and so the **p.** was stayed.... 4046
Zec 14:12 this shall be the **p.** wherewith the...... 4046
Zec 14:15 be the **p.** of the horse, of the mule,.... 4046
Zec 14:15 shall be in these tents, as this **p.**....... 4046
Zec 14:18 there shall be the **p.**, wherewith the.... 4046
Mk 5:29 that she was healed of that **p.**........... *3148*
Mk 5:34 **in peace, and be whole of thy p.**...... *3148*
Re 16:21 God because of the **p.** of the hail;...... *4127*
Re 16:21 the **p.** thereof was exceeding great..... *4127*

PLAGUED
Ge 12:17 Lord **p.** Pharaoh and his house.......... 5060
Ex 32:35 the Lord **p.** the people, because......... 5062
Jos 24:5 I **p.** Egypt, according to that which..... 5062
1Ch 21:17 thy people that they should be **p.**....... 4046
Ps 73:5 neither are they **p.** like other men...... 5060
Ps 73:14 all the day long have I been **p.**,......... 5060

PLAGUES
Ge 12:17 plagued Pharaoh...with great **p.**.......... 5061
Ex 9:14 at this time send all my **p.** upon......... 4046
Le 26:21 seven times more **p.** upon you............ 4347
De 28:59 Lord will make thy **p.** wonderful,......... 4347
De 28:59 and the **p.** of thy seed, even great **p.**,. 4347
De 29:22 when they see the **p.** of that land,....... 4347
1Sa 4:8 smote the Egyptians with all the **p.**....... 4347
Jer 19:8 hiss because of all the **p.** thereof......... 4347
Jer 49:17 and shall hiss at all the **p.** thereof........ 4347
Jer 50:13 be astonished, and hiss at all her **p.**..... 4347
Ho 13:14 O death, I will be thy **p.**; O grave,...... 1698
Mk 3:10 to touch him, as many as had **p.**......... *3148*
Lu 7:21 many of their infirmities and **p.**,.......... *3148*
Re 9:20 which were not killed by these **p.**........ *4127*
Re 11:6 and to smite the earth with all **p.**,....... *4127*
Re 15:1 angels having the seven last **p.**;.......... *4127*
Re 15:6 of the temple, having the seven **p.**,..... *4127*
Re 15:8 seven **p.** of the seven angels were...... *4127*
Re 16:9 which hath power over these **p.**:......... *4127*
Re 18:4 and that ye receive not of her **p.**......... *4127*
Re 18:8 shall her **p.** come in one day, death,.... *4127*
Re 21:9 seven vials full of the seven last **p.**,.... *4127*
Re 22:18 God shall add unto him the **p.** that...... *4127*

PLAIN See also PLAINS.
Ge 11:2 found a **p.** in the land of Shinar;......... 1237
Ge 12:6 of Sichem, unto the **p.** of Moreh.......... 436
Ge 13:10 and beheld all the **p.** of Jordan,.......... 3603
Ge 13:11 Lot chose him all the **p.** of Jordan;...... 3603
Ge 13:12 Lot dwelled in the cities of the **p.**........ 3603
Ge 13:18 came and dwelt in the **p.** of Mamre,...... 436
Ge 14:13 for he dwelt in the **p.** of Mamre the...... 436
Ge 19:17 neither stay thou in all the **p.**;............ 3603
Ge 19:25 those cities, and all the **p.**, and all...... 3603
Ge 19:28 and toward all the land of the **p.**,........ 3603
Ge 19:29 God destroyed the cities of the **p.**,...... 3603
Ge 25:27 Jacob was a **p.** man, dwelling in.......... 8535
De 1:1 in the **p.** over against the Red sea,...... 6160
De 1:7 places nigh thereunto, in the **p.**,.......... 6160
De 2:8 the way of the **p.** from Elath, and....... 6160
De 3:10 the cities of the **p.**, and all Gilead,....... 4334
De 3:17 **p.** also, and Jordan, and the coast........ 6160
De 3:17 even unto the sea of the **p.**, even the.. 6160
De 4:43 the wilderness, in the **p.** country,....... 4334
De 4:49 **p.** on this side Jordan eastward,.......... 6160
De 4:49 even unto the sea of the **p.**, under...... 6160
De 34:3 **p.** of the valley of Jericho, the city...... 3603
Jos 3:16 down toward the sea of the **p.**,........... 6160
Jos 8:14 at a time appointed, before the **p.**;...... 6160
Jos 11:16 Goshen, and the valley, and the **p.**,..... 6160
Jos 12:1 Hermon, and all the **p.** on the east:..... 6160
Jos 12:3 the **p.** to the sea of Chinneroth on....... 6160
Jos 12:3 and unto the sea of the **p.**, even the.... 6160
Jos 13:9 all the **p.** of Medeba unto Dibon;......... 4334
Jos 13:16 the river, and all the **p.** by Medeba;.... 4334
Jos 13:17 and all her cities that are in the **p.**;...... 4334
Jos 13:21 all the cities of the **p.**, and all the....... 4334
Jos 20:8 Bezer in the wilderness upon the **p.**..... 4334
Jg 4:11 his tent unto the **p.** of Zaanaim,........... 436
Jg 9:6 by the **p.** of the pillar that was in......... 436
Jg 9:37 come along by the **p.** of Meonenim....... 436
Jg 11:33 and unto the **p.** of the vineyards,.......... 58
1Sa 10:3 thou shalt come to the **p.** of Tabor,....... 436
1Sa 23:24 the **p.** on the south of Jeshimon......... 6160
2Sa 2:29 all that night through the **p.**,.............. 6160
2Sa 4:7 them away through the **p.** all night...... 6160
2Sa 15:28 tarry in the **p.** of the wilderness,........ 6160
2Sa 18:23 Ahimaaz ran by the way of the **p.**,........ 3603
1Ki 7:46 In the **p.** of Jordan did the king.......... 3603
1Ki 20:23 let us fight against them in the **p.**,...... 4334
1Ki 20:25 we will fight against them in the **p.**..... 4334
2Ki 14:25 of Hamath unto the sea of the **p.**,....... 6160
2Ki 25:4 king went the way toward the **p.**......... 6160
2Ch 4:17 In the **p.** of Jordan did the king........... 3603
Ne 3:22 the priests, the men of the **p.**........... 3603
Ne 6:2 one of the villages in the **p.** of Ono..... 1237
Ne 12:28 **p.** country round about Jerusalem,....... 3603
Ps 27:11 lead me in a **p.** path, because of........ 4334
Pr 8:9 all **p.** to him that understandeth,......... 5228
Pr 15:19 way of the righteous is made **p.**.......... 5549
Isa 28:25 he hath made **p.** the face thereof,....... 7737
Isa 40:4 straight, and the rough places **p.**:....... 1237
Jer 17:26 of Benjamin, and from the **p.**,............. 8219
Jer 21:13 of the valley, and rock of the **p.**,........ 4334
Jer 39:4 and he went out the way of the **p.**..... 6160
Jer 48:8 and the **p.** shall be destroyed, as......... 4334
Jer 48:21 is come upon the **p.** country;.............. 4334
Jer 52:7 they went by the way of the **p.**........... 6160
Eze 3:22 Arise, go forth into the **p.**, and I......... 1237
Eze 3:23 arose, and went forth into the **p.**:........ 1237
Eze 8:4 to the vision that I saw in the **p.**......... 1237
Da 3:1 he set it up in the **p.** of Dura, in the... 1236
Am 1:5 the inhabitant from the **p.** of Aven,...... 1237
Ob 19 and they of the **p.** the Philistines:....... 8219
Hab 2:2 vision, and make it **p.** upon tables,........ 874
Zec 4:7 thou shalt become a **p.**: and he........... 4334
Zec 7:7 inhabited the south and the **p.**?........... 8219
Zec 14:10 All the land shall be turned as a **p.**..... 6160
Mk 7:35 tongue was loosed, and he spake **p.**...... *3723*
Lu 6:17 and stood in the **p.**, and the........ *5117,3977*

PLAINLY
Ex 21:5 if the servant shall **p.** say, I love......... 559
De 27:8 all the words of this law very **p.**.......... 874
1Sa 2:27 **p.** appear unto the house of thy.......... 1540
1Sa 10:16 He told up **p.** that the asses were...... 5046
Ezr 4:18 sent unto us hath been **p.** read.......... 6568
Isa 32:4 shall be ready to speak **p.**................ 6703
Joh 10:24 If thou be the Christ, tell us **p.**.......... *3954*
Joh 11:14 Then said Jesus unto them **p.**,........... *3954*
Joh 16:25 **I shall shew you p. of the Father**.. *3954*
Joh 16:29 him, Lo, now speakest thou **p.**,.......... *3954*
Heb 11:14 declare **p.** that they seek a country..... *1718*

PLAINNESS
2Cor 3:12 hope, we use great **p.** of speech:........ *3954*

PLAINS
Ge 18:1 unto him in the **p.** of Mamre:.............. 436
Nu 22:1 and pitched in the **p.** of Moab on........ 6160
Nu 26:3 spake with them in the **p.** of Moab...... 6160
Nu 26:63 children of Israel in the **p.** of Moab by. 6160
Nu 31:12 unto the camp at the **p.** of Moab,....... 6160
Nu 33:48 and pitched in the **p.** of Moab by........ 6160
Nu 33:49 unto Abel-shittim in the **p.** of Moab.... 6160
Nu 33:50 spake unto Moses in the **p.** of Moab... 6160
Nu 35:1 spake unto Moses in the **p.** of Moab... 6160
Nu 36:13 children of Israel in the **p.** of Moab..... 6160
De 11:30 Gilgal, beside the **p.** of Moreh?........... 436
De 34:1 Moses went up from the **p.** of Moab... 6160
De 34:8 wept for Moses in the **p.** of Moab...... 6160
Jos 4:13 unto battle, to the **p.** of Jericho......... 6160
Jos 5:10 month at even in the **p.** of Jericho....... 6160
Jos 11:2 and of the **p.** south of Chinneroth,....... 6160
Jos 12:8 and in the **p.**, and in the springs,........ 6160
Jos 13:32 for inheritance in the **p.** of Moab,........ 6160
2Sa 17:16 night in the **p.** of the wilderness,........ 6160
2Ki 25:5 overtook him in the **p.** of Jericho:........ 6160
1Ch 27:28 trees that were in the low **p.** was...... 8219
2Ch 9:27 trees that are in the low **p.** in........... 8219
2Ch 26:10 in the low country, and in the **p.**:....... 4334
Jer 39:5 Zedekiah in the **p.** of Jericho:............. 6160
Jer 52:8 Zedkiah in the **p.** of Jericho;.............. 6160

PLAISTER See also PLAISTERED.
Le 14:42 morter, and shall **p.** the house........... 2902
De 27:2 great stones, and **p.** them with.......... 7874
De 27:2 great stones, and...them with **p.**:......... 7875
De 27:4 Ebal, and thou shalt **p.** them with....... 7874
De 27:4 Ebal, and thou shalt...them with **p.**..... 7875
Isa 38:21 and lay it for a **p.** upon the boil,......... 4799
Da 5:5 **p.** of the wall fo the king's palace:...... 1528

PLAISTERED
Le 14:43 the house, and after it is **p.**;.............. 2902
Le 14:48 the house, after the house was **p.**:...... 2902

PLAITING See also PLATTED.
1Pe 3:3 outward adorning of **p.** the hair,.......... *1708*

PLANES
Isa 44:13 he fitteth it with **p.**, and he............. 4741

PLANETS
2Ki 23:5 and to the **p.**, and to all the hosts...... 4208

PLANKS
1Ki 6:15 floor of the house with **p.** of fir.......... 6763
Eze 41:25 thick **p.** upon the face of...porch........ 6086
Eze 41:26 of the house, and thick **p.**................ 5646

PLANT See also PLANTED; PLANTETH; PLANTING; PLANTS; SUPPLANT.
Ge 2:5 every **p.** of the field before it was...... 7880
Ex 15:17 shalt bring them in, and **p.** them........ 5193
De 16:21 shalt not **p.** thee a grove of any......... 5193
De 28:30 thou shalt **p.** a vineyard, and shalt...... 5193
De 28:39 Thou shalt **p.** vineyards, and dress...... 5193
2Sa 7:10 my people Israel, and will **p.** them,..... 5193
2Ki 19:29 sow ye, and reap, and **p.** vineyards,... 5193
1Ch 17:9 my people Israel, and will **p.** them,..... 5193
Job 14:9 and bring forth boughs like a **p.**........ 5194
Ps 107:37 sow the fields, and **p.** vineyards,........ 5193
Ec 3:2 a time to **p.**, and a time to pluck up.... 5193
Isa 5:7 the men of Judah his pleasant **p.**:........ 5194
Isa 17:10 shalt thou **p.** pleasant plants, and........ 5193
Isa 17:11 shalt thou make thy **p.** to grow,.......... 5194
Isa 37:30 ye, and reap, and **p.** vineyards,........... 5193
Isa 41:19 will **p.** in the wilderness the cedar,...... 5414
Isa 51:16 that I may **p.** the heavens, and lay...... 5193
Isa 53:2 grow up before him as a tender **p.**,...........
Isa 65:21 they shall **p.** vineyards, and eat........... 5193
Isa 65:22 they shall not **p.**, and another eat:....... 5193
Jer 1:10 to throw down, to build, and to **p.**...... 5193
Jer 2:21 art turned into the degenerate **p.** of..........
Jer 18:9 a kingdom, to build and to **p.** it;.......... 5193
Jer 24:6 and I will **p.** them, and not pluck........ 5193
Jer 29:5 **p.** gardens, and eat the fruit of them;.. 5193
Jer 29:28 **p.** gardens, and eat the fruit of them.. 5193
Jer 31:5 yet **p.** vines upon the mountains......... 5193
Jer 31:5 the planters shall **p.**, and shall eat...... 5193
Jer 31:28 over them, to build, and to **p.**, saith.... 5193
Jer 32:41 I will **p.** them in this land assuredly.... 5193
Jer 35:7 nor sow seed, nor **p.** vineyard, nor..... 5193
Jer 42:10 I will **p.** you, and not pluck you up:.... 5193
Eze 17:22 **p.** it upon an high mountain and......... 8362
Eze 17:23 of the height of Israel will I **p.** it:...... 8362
Eze 28:26 build houses, and **p.** vineyards;.......... 5193
Eze 34:29 raise up for them a **p.** of renown,........ 4302
Eze 36:36 and **p.** that that was desolate:............ 5193
Da 11:45 **p.** the tabernacles of his palace.......... 5193
Am 9:14 and they shall **p.** vineyards, and......... 5193
Am 9:15 and I will **p.** them upon their land,....... 5193
Zep 1:13 and they shall **p.** vineyards, but.......... 5193
Mt 15:13 **p., which my heavenly Father**....... *5451*

PLANTATION
Eze 17:7 water it by the furrows of her **p.**....... 4302

PLANTED See also PLANTEDST; SUPPLANTED.
Ge 2:8 Lord God **p.** a garden eastward.......... 5193
Ge 9:20 husbandman, and he **p.** a vineyard:...... 5193
Ge 21:33 Abraham **p.** a grove in Beer-sheba,...... 5193
Le 19:23 shall have **p.** all manner of trees......... 5193
Nu 24:6 lign aloes which the Lord hath **p.**,....... 5193
De 20:6 man is he that hath **p.** a vineyard,....... 5193
Jos 24:13 oliveyards which ye **p.** not do ye eat... 5193
Ps 1:3 shall be like a tree **p.** by the rivers...... 8362
Ps 80:8 cast out the heathen, and **p.** it........... 5193
Ps 80:15 which thy right hand hath **p.**, and........ 5193
Ps 92:13 that be **p.** in the house of the............ 8362
Ps 94:9 He that **p.** the ear, shall he not.......... 5193

Ps 104:16 of Lebanon, which he hath **p.**; 5193
Ec 2:4 me houses; I **p.** me vineyards: 5193
Ec 2:5 and I **p.** trees in them of all kinds of 5193
Ec 3:2 a time to pluck up that which is **p.**; 5193
Isa 5:2 **p.** it with the choicest vine, and 5193
Isa 40:24 they shall not be **p.**; yea, they shall 5193
Jer 2:21 I had **p.** thee a noble vine, wholly 5193
Jer 11:17 the Lord of hosts, that **p.** thee, hath 5193
Jer 12:2 Thou hast **p.** them, yea, they have 5193
Jer 17:8 shall be as a tree **p.** by the waters, 8362
Jer 45:4 which I have **p.** I will pluck up, 5193
Eze 17:5 of the land, and **p.** it in a fruitful field;
Eze 17:8 It was **p.** in a good soil by great 8362
Eze 17:10 behold, being **p.**, shall it prosper? 8362
Eze 19:10 in thy blood, **p.** by the waters: 8362
Eze 19:13 And now she is **p.** in the wilderness, 8362
Ho 9:13 Tyrus, is **p.** in a pleasant place: 8362
Am 5:11 ye have **p.** pleasant vineyards, but 5193
Mt 15:13 **my heavenly Father hath not p.,** *5452*
Mt 21:33 **which p. a vineyard, and hedged it** *5452*
Mk 12:1 **A certain man p. a vineyard, and** *5452*
Lu 13:6 **had a fig tree p. in his vineyard;** *5452*
Lu 17:6 **the root, and be thou p. in the sea;** *5452*
Lu 17:28 **they sold, they p., they builded:** *5452*
Lu 20:9 **A certain man p. a vineyard, and** *5452*
Ro 6:5 **p.** together in the likeness of his *4854*
1Co 3:6 I have **p.**, Apollos watered; but *5452*

PLANTEDST
De 6:11 and olive trees, which thou **p.** not; 5193
Ps 44:2 with thy hand, and **p.** them; how 5193

PLANTERS
Jer 31:5 the **p.** shall plant, and shall eat 5193

PLANTETH
Pr 31:16 of her hands she **p.** a vineyard 5198
Isa 44:14 he **p.** an ash, and the rain doth 5198
1Co 3:7 neither is he that **p.** any thing, *5452*
1Co 3:8 Now he that **p.** and he that watereth *5452*
1Co 9:7 who **p.** a vineyard, and eateth not *5452*

PLANTING See also PLANTINGS.
Isa 60:21 the branch of my **p.**, the work of 4302
Isa 61:3 the **p.** of the Lord, that he might 4302

PLANTINGS
Mic 1:6 the field, and as **p.** of a vineyard: 4302

PLANTS
1Ch 4:23 that dwelt among **p.** and hedges: 5194
Ps 128:3 children like olive **p.** round about 8363
Ps 144:12 our sons may be as **p.** grown up 5195
Ca 4:13 **p.** are…orchard of pomegranates, 7973
Isa 16:8 broken down the principal **p.** 8291
Isa 17:10 shalt thou plant pleasant **p.**, and 5194
Jer 48:32 thy **p.** are gone over the sea, they 5189
Eze 31:4 rivers running round about…**p.**, 4302

PLASTER See PLAISTER.

PLAT See also PLAITING; PLATTED.
2Ki 9:26 I will requit thee in this **p.**, saith 2513
2Ki 9:26 cast him into the **p.** of ground, 2513

PLATE See also PLATES.
Ex 28:36 thou shalt make a **p.** of pure gold, 6731
Ex 39:30 they made the **p.** of the holy crown 6731
Le 8:9 forefront, did he put the golden **p.**, 6731

PLATES
Ex 39:3 they did beat the gold into thin **p.**, 6341
Nu 16:38 let them make them broad **p.** for 6341
Nu 16:39 were made broad **p.** for a covering
1Ki 7:30 brasen wheels, and **p.** of brass: 5633
1Ki 7:36 For on the **p.** of the ledges thereof, 3871
Jer 10:9 Silver spread into **p.** is brought from

PLATTED See also PLAITING.
Mt 27:29 they had **p.** a crown of thorns, *4120*
Mk 15:17 **p.** a crown of thorns, and put it *4120*
Joh 19:2 the soldiers **p.** a crown of thorns, *4120*

PLATTER
Mt 23:25 **outside of the cup and of the p.,** *3953*
Mt 23:26 **which is within the cup and p.,** *3953*
Lu 11:39 **the outside of the cup and the p.;** *4094*

PLAY See also PLAYED; PLAYETH; PLAYING.
Ex 32:6 and to drink, and rose up to **p.** 6711
De 22:21 to **p.** the whore in her father's house:
1Sa 16:16 he shall **p.** with his hand, and 5059
1Sa 16:17 me now a man that can **p.** well, 5059
1Sa 21:15 to **p.** the mad man in my presence?
2Sa 2:14 men now arise, and **p.** before us. 7832
2Sa 6:21 therefore will I **p.** before the Lord 7832
2Sa 10:12 and let us **p.** the men for our people,
Job 40:20 where all the beasts of the field **p.** 7832
Job 41:5 thou **p.** with him as with a bird? 7832
Ps 33:3 **p.** skillfully with a loud noise. 5059
Ps 104:26 thou hast made to **p.** therein. 7832
Isa 11:8 shall **p.** on the hole of the asp, 8173
Eze 33:32 and can **p.** well on an instrument: 5059
Ho 3:3 thou shalt not **p.** the harlot, and thou
Ho 4:15 **p.** the harlot, yet let not Judah offend;
1Co 10:7 eat and drink, and rose up to **p.** *3815*

PLAYED See also DISPLAYED; PLAYEDST.
Ge 38:24 daughter in law hath **p.** the harlot;
Jg 19:2 concubine **p.** the whore against him,
1Sa 16:23 an harp, and **p.** with his hand: 5059
1Sa 18:7 answered one another as they **p.**, 7832
1Sa 18:10 David **p.** with his hand, as at other 5059
1Sa 19:9 and David **p.** with his hand. 5059
1Sa 26:21 I have **p.** the fool, and have erred
2Sa 6:5 house of Israel **p.** before the Lord 7832
2Ki 3:15 came to pass, when the minstrel **p.**, 5059
1Ch 13:8 David and all Israel **p.** before God 7832
Jer 3:1 thou hast **p.** the harlot with many
Jer 3:6 tree, and there hath **p.** the harlot.
Jer 3:8 not, but went and **p.** the harlot also.
Eze 16:28 Thou hast **p.** the whore also with the
Eze 16:28 yea, thou hast **p.** the harlot with them,
Eze 23:5 Aholah **p.** the harlot when she was
Eze 23:19 had **p.** the harlot in the land of Egypt.
Ho 2:5 For their mother hath **p.** the harlot:

PLAYEDST
Eze 16:15 **p.** the harlot because of thy renown,
Eze 16:16 **p.** the harlot thereupon: the like

PLAYER See also PLAYERS.
1Sa 16:16 who is a cunning **p.** on a harp: 5059

PLAYERS
Ps 68:25 **p.** on instruments followed after; 5059
Ps 87:7 **p.** on instruments shall be there: 2490

PLAYETH
Eze 23:44 go in unto a woman that **p.** the harlot:

PLAYING
Le 21:9 she profane herself by **p.** the whore,
1Sa 16:18 Beth-lehemite that is cunning in **p.**, 5059
1Ch 15:29 saw king David dancing and **p.**: 7832
Ps 68:25 were the damsels **p.** with timbrels.
Jer 2:20 tree thou wanderest, **p.** the harlot.
Eze 16:41 cause thee to cease from **p.** the harlot,
Zec 8:5 boys and girls **p.** in the streets 7832

PLEA
De 17:8 between **p.** and **p.**, and between 1779

PLEAD See also IMPLEAD; PLEADED; PLEADETH; PLEADINGS.
Jg 6:31 Will ye **p.** for Baal? will ye save 7378
Jg 6:31 he that will **p.** for him, let him be 7378
Jg 6:31 let him **p.** for himself, because one 7378
Jg 6:32 Let Baal **p.** against him, because 7378
1Sa 24:15 and **p.** my cause, and deliver me 7378
Job 9:19 who shall set me a time to **p.**?
Job 13:19 Who is he that will **p.** with me? 7378
Job 16:21 one might **p.** for a man with God, 3198
Job 19:5 and **p.** against me my reproach: 3198
Job 23:6 Will he **p.** against me with his 7378
Ps 35:1 **P.** my cause, O Lord, with them 7378
Pr 43:1 Judge me, O God, and **p.** my cause 7378
Pr 74:22 Arise, O God, **p.** thine own cause: 7378
Pr 119:154 **P.** my cause, and deliver me: 7378
Pr 22:23 the Lord will **p.** their cause, and 7378
Pr 23:11 he shall **p.** their cause with thee. 7378
Pr 31:9 **p.** the cause of the poor and needy. 1777
Isa 1:17 the fatherless, **p.** for the widow. 7378
Isa 3:13 The Lord standeth up to **p.**, and 7378
Isa 43:26 remembrance: let us **p.** together: 8199
Isa 66:16 will the Lord **p.** with all flesh: 8199
Jer 2:9 I will yet **p.** with you, saith the 7378
Jer 2:9 your children's children will I **p.** 7378
Jer 2:29 Wherefore will ye **p.** with me? ye 7378
Jer 2:35 I will **p.** with thee, because thou 8199
Jer 12:1 thou, O Lord, when I **p.** with thee: 7378
Jer 25:31 he will **p.** with all flesh; he will 8199
Jer 30:13 There none to **p.** thy cause, that 1777
Jer 50:34 he shall thoroughly **p.** their cause, 7378
Jer 51:36 Behold, I will **p.** thy cause, and take 7378
Eze 17:20 and will **p.** with him there for his 8199
Eze 20:35 will I **p.** with you face to face. 8199
Eze 20:36 so will I **p.** with you, saith the Lord. 8199
Eze 38:22 will **p.** against him with pestilence 8199
Ho 2:2 **P.** with your mother, **p.**: for she is 7378
Joe 3:2 **p.** with them there for my people 8199
Mic 6:2 people, and he will **p.** with Israel. 3198
Mic 7:9 until he **p.** my cause, and execute 7378

PLEADED
1Sa 25:39 the Lord that hath **p.** the cause 7378
La 3:58 thou hast **p.** the causes of my soul; 7378
Eze 20:36 Like as I **p.** with your fathers in 8199

PLEADETH
Job 16:21 as a man **p.** for his neighbour!
Isa 51:22 that **p.** the cause of his people, 7378
Isa 59:4 for justice, nor any **p.** for truth: 8199

PLEADINGS
Job 13:6 and hearken to the **p.** of my lips. 7379

PLEASANT
Ge 2:9 every tree that is **p.** to the sight, 2530
Ge 3:6 it was **p.** to the eyes, and a tree 8378
Ge 49:15 good, and the land that it was **p.**; 5276
2Sa 1:23 and Jonathan were lovely and **p.** 5273
2Sa 1:26 very **p.** hast thou been unto me: 5276
1Ki 20:6 whatsoever is **p.** in thine eyes, 4261
2Ki 2:19 situation of this city is **p.**, as my 2896
2Ch 32:27 and for all manner of **p.** jewels; 2532
Ps 16:6 are fallen unto me in **p.** places; 5273
Ps 81:2 the **p.** harp with the psaltery. 5273
Ps 106:24 they despised the **p.** land, they 2532
Ps 133:1 how **p.** it is for brethren to dwell 5273
Ps 135:3 praises unto his name; for it is **p.** 5273
Ps 147:1 praises unto our God; for it is **p.**: 5273
Pr 2:10 and knowledge is **p.** to thy soul; 5276
Pr 5:19 be as the loving hind and **p.** roe; 2580
Pr 9:17 and bread eaten in secret is **p.** 5276
Pr 15:26 the words of the pure are **p.** words. 5278
Pr 16:24 **P.** words are as an honeycomb, 5278
Pr 22:18 **p.** thing if thou keep them within 5273
Pr 24:4 with all precious and **p.** riches. 5273
Ec 11:7 a **p.** thing it is for the eyes to 2896
Ca 1:16 thou art fair, my beloved, yea, **p.** 5273
Ca 4:13 of pomegranates, with **p.** fruits; 4022
Ca 4:16 his garden, and eat his **p.** fruits. 4022
Ca 7:6 How fair and how **p.** art thou, O 5276
Ca 7:13 gates are all manner of **p.** fruits, 4022
Isa 2:16 Tarshish, and upon all **p.** pictures. 2532
Isa 5:7 the men of Judah his **p.** plant: 8191
Isa 13:22 and dragons in their **p.** palaces: 6027
Isa 17:10 shalt thou plant **p.** plants, and 2532
Isa 32:12 for the teats, for the **p.** fields, 2531
Isa 54:12 and all thy borders of **p.** stones. 2656
Isa 64:11 all our **p.** things are laid waste. 4261
Jer 3:19 and give thee a **p.** land, a goodly 2532
Jer 12:10 **p.** portion a desloate wilderness. 2532
Jer 23:10 **p.** places of the wilderness are 4999
Jer 25:34 and ye shall fall like a **p.** vessel. 2532
Jer 31:20 my dear son? is he a **p.** child? 8191
La 1:7 all her **p.** things that she had in 4262
La 1:10 his hand upon all her **p.** things: 4621
La 1:11 have given their **p.** things for meat 4622
La 2:4 slew all that were **p.** to the eye 4622
Eze 26:12 walls, and destroy thy **p.** houses: 2532
Eze 33:32 song of one that hath a **p.** voice, 3303
Da 8:9 the east, and toward the **p.** land. 6643
Da 10:3 I ate no **p.** bread, neither came 2530
Da 11:38 precious stones, and **p.** things. 2530
Ho 9:6 **p.** places for their silver, nettles 4261
Ho 9:13 Tyrus, is planted in a **p.** place: 5116
Ho 13:15 the treasure of all **p.** vessels. 2532
Joe 3:5 temples my goodly **p.** things: 4261
Am 5:11 ye have planted **p.** vineyards, but 2531
Mic 2:9 ye cast out from their **p.** houses; 8588
Na 2:9 glory out of all the **p.** furniture. 2532
Zec 7:14 for they laid the **p.** land desolate. 2532
Mal 3:4 of Judah and Jerusalem be **p.** 6148

PLEASANTNESS
Pr 3:17 Her ways are ways of **p.**, and all 5278

PLEASE See also DISPLEASE; PLEASED; PLEASETH; PLEASING.
Ex 21:8 If she **p.** not her master, who 7451,5869
Nu 23:27 peradventure it will **p.** God 3477,5869
1Sa 20:13 if it **p.** my father to do thee evil, 3190

2Sa 7:29 **p.** thee to bless the house of thy 2974
1Ki 21:6 else, if it **p.** thee, I will give thee 2655
1Ch 17:27 **p.** thee to bless the house of thy 2974
2Ch 10:7 kind to this people, and **p.** them, ... 7521
Ne 2:5 If it **p.** the king, and if thy servant 2895
Ne 2:7 If it **p.** the king, let letters be 2895
Es 1:19 it **p.** the king, let there go a royal 2895
Es 3:9 If it **p.** the king, let it be written 2895
Es 5:8 it **p.** the king to grant my petition, ... 2895
Es 7:3 if it **p.** the king, let my life be given ... 2895
Es 8:5 it **p.** the king, and if I have found 2896
Es 9:13 If it **p.** the king, let it be granted 2896
Job 6:9 it would **p.** God to destroy me; 2974
Job 20:10 children shall seek to **p.** the poor, ... 7521
Ps 69:31 shall **p.** the Lord better than an ox 3190
Pr 16:7 When a man's ways **p.** the Lord, ... 7521
Ca 2:7 up, nor awake my love, till he **p.**. 2654
Ca 3:5 up, nor awake my love, till he **p.**. 2654
Ca 8:4 up, nor awake my love, until he **p.**. 2654
Isa 2:6 **p.** themselves in the children of 5606
Isa 55:11 shall accomplish that which I **p.**, ... 2654
Isa 56:4 and choose the things that **p.** me, ... 2654
Joh 8:29 **do always those things that p. him.** .*701*
Ro 8:8 that are in the flesh cannot **p.** God. *700*
Ro 15:1 the weak, and not to **p.** ourselves. *700*
Ro 15:2 Let every one of us **p.** his neighbour *700*
1Co 7:32 the Lord, how he may **p.** the Lord: *700*
1Co 7:33 the world, how he may **p.** his wife. *700*
1Co 7:34 world, how she may **p.** her husband. *700*
1Co 10:33 Even as I **p.** all men in all things, ... *700*
Ga 1:10 men, or God? or do I seek to **p.** men? . *700*
1Th 2:15 they **p.** not God, and are contrary *700*
1Th 4:1 how ye ought to walk and to **p.** God, ... *700*
2Ti 2:4 he may **p.** him who hath chosen him *700*
Tit 2:9 to **p.** them well in all things; *2001,1511*
Heb 11:6 faith it is impossible to **p.** him: *2100*

PLEASED See also DISPLEASED.
Ge 28:8 daughter of Canaan **p.** not 7451,5869
Ge 33:10 of God, and thou wast **p.** with me. 7521
Ge 34:18 And their words **p.** Hamor, ... 3190,5869
Ge 45:16 and it **p.** Pharaoh well, and his 3190,5869
Nu 24:1 Balaam saw that it **p.** the Lord 2895
De 1:23 And the saying **p.** me well: 3190,5869
Jos 22:30 of Manasseh spake, it **p.** them 3190,5869
Jos 22:33 thing **p.** the children of Israel; 3190,5869
Jg 13:23 If the Lord was **p.** to kill us, he 2654
Jg 14:7 and she **p.** Samson well 3477,5869
1Sa 12:22 hath **p.** the Lord to make you his 2974
1Sa 18:20 Saul, and the thing **p.** him 3477,5869
1Sa 18:26 it **p.** David well to be the king's .. 3477,5869
2Sa 3:36 notice of it, and it **p.** them: 3190,5869
2Sa 3:36 whatsoever the king did **p.** all 2896,5869
2Sa 17:4 the saying **p.** Absalom well, ... 3477,5869
2Sa 19:6 day, then it had **p.** thee well. 3477,5869
1Ki 3:10 the speech **p.** the Lord, that 3190,5869
1Ki 9:1 desire which he was **p.** to do, ... 2654
1Ki 9:12 him; and they **p.** him not. 3477,5869
2Ch 30:4 the thing **p.** the king and all 3477,5869
Ne 2:6 So it **p.** the king to send me; and I 3190
Es 1:21 **p.** the king and the princes; 3190,5869
Es 2:4 And the thing **p.** the king; 3190,5869
Es 2:9 And the maiden **p.** him, and 3190,5869
Es 5:14 And the thing **p.** Haman; and he 3190
Ps 40:13 Be **p.**, O Lord, to deliver me: O 7521
Ps 51:19 shalt thou be **p.** with the sacrifices 2654
Ps 115:3 hath done whatsoever he hath **p.** 2654
Ps 135:6 Whatsoever the Lord **p.**, that did 2654
Isa 42:21 Lord is well **p.** for his righteousness ... 2654
Isa 53:10 Yet it **p.** the Lord to bruise him; 2654
Da 6:1 It **p.** Darius to set over the 8232
Jon 1:14 O Lord, hast done as it **p.** thee. 2654
Mic 6:7 Lord be **p.** with thousands of rams, ... 7521
Mal 1:8 will he be **p.** with thee, or accept 7521
Mt 3:17 beloved Son, in whom I am well **p.** *2106*
Mt 12:18 beloved, in whom my soul is well **p.**: .. *2106*
Mt 14:6 danced before them, and **p.** Herod. *700*
Mt 17:5 beloved Son, in whom I am well **p.**; *2106*
Mk 1:11 beloved Son, in whom I am well **p.** *2106*
Mk 6:22 came in, and danced, and **p.** Herod *700*
Lu 3:22 beloved Son; in thee I am well **p.** *2106*
Ac 6:5 the saying **p.** the whole multitude: *700*
Ac 12:3 And because he saw it **p.** the Jews, ... *701*
Ac 15:22 Then **p.** it the apostles and elders, ... *1380*
Ac 15:34 it **p.** Silas to abide there still. *1380*
Ro 15:3 For even Christ **p.** not himself; *700*
Ro 15:26 For it hath **p.** them of Macedonia *2106*
Ro 15:27 It hath **p.** them verily; and their *2106*
1Co 1:21 it **p.** God by the foolishness of *2106*
1Co 7:12 and she be **p.** to dwell with him, ... *4909*
1Co 7:13 if he be **p.** to dwell with her, let *4909*
1Co 10:5 many of them God was not well **p.**: *2106*
1Co 12:18 in the body, as it hath **p.** him. *2309*
1Co 15:38 giveth it a body as it hath **p.** him, ... *2309*
Gal 1:10 for if I yet **p.** men, I should not be *700*
Gal 1:15 But when it **p.** God, who separated *2106*
Col 1:19 it **p.** the Father that in him should *2106*
Heb 11:5 had this testimony, that he **p.** God. *2100*
Heb 13:16 with such sacrifices God is well **p.** *2100*
2Pe 1:17 beloved son, in whom I am well **p.** *2106*

PLEASERS See MENPLEASERS.

PLEASETH
Ge 16:6 hand; do to her as it **p.** thee. 2896,5869
Ge 20:15 thee: dwell where it **p.** thee 2896,5869
Jg 14:3 for me; for she **p.** me well 3477,5869
Es 2:4 the maiden which **p.** the king 3190,5869
Ec 7:26 whoso **p.** God shall escape 2896,6440
Ec 8:3 for he doeth whatsoever **p.** him. 2654

PLEASING See also WELLPLEASING.
Es 8:5 the king, and I be **p.** in his eyes, ... 2896
Ho 9:4 neither shall they be **p.** unto him: 6148
Col 1:10 walk worthy of the Lord unto all **p.**, ... *699*
Col 3:20 this is well **p.** unto the Lord. ....
1Th 2:4 not as **p.** men, but God, which trieth *700*
1Jo 3:22 those things that are **p.** in his sight. *701*

PLEASURE See also DISPLEASURE; PLEASURES.
Ge 18:12 I am waxed old shall I have **p.**, ... 5730
De 23:24 eat grapes thy fill at thine own **p.**; 5315
1Ch 29:17 heart, and hast **p.** in uprightness. 7521
Ezr 5:17 and let the king send his **p.** to us 7470
Ezr 10:11 God of your fathers, and do his **p.**: 7522
Ne 9:37 and over our cattle, at their **p.**, ... 7522
Es 1:8 do according to every man's **p.**. 7522
Job 21:21 For what **p.** hath he in his house 2656
Job 21:25 soul, and never eateth with **p.**. 2896
Job 22:3 Is it any **p.** to the Almighty, that 2656
Ps 5:4 God that hath **p.** in wickedness: 2655
Ps 35:27 **p.** in the prosperity of his servant. 2655
Ps 51:18 Do good in thy good **p.** unto Zion: 7522
Ps 102:14 thy servants take **p.** in her stones, ... 7521
Ps 103:21 ye ministers of his, that do his **p.** 7522
Ps 105:22 To bind his princes at his **p.**; and 5315
Ps 111:2 of all them that have **p.** therein. 2656
Ps 147:10 taketh not **p.** in the legs of a man. 7521
Ps 147:11 Lord taketh **p.** in them that fear 7521
Ps 149:4 the Lord taketh **p.** in his people: 7521
Pr 21:17 that loveth **p.** shall be a poor man; 8057
Ec 2:1 therefore enjoy **p.**: and, behold, ... 2896
Ec 5:4 pay it; for he hath no **p.** in fools: 2656
Ec 12:1 thou shalt say, I have no **p.** in them; .. 2656
Isa 21:4 the night of my **p.** hath he turned 2837
Isa 44:28 and shall perform all my **p.**: 2656
Isa 46:10 shall stand, and I will do all my **p.**: 2656
Isa 48:14 he will do his **p.** on Babylon, and 2656
Isa 53:10 **p.** of the Lord shall prosper in his 2656
Isa 58:3 in the day of your fast ye find **p.**, ... 2656
Isa 58:13 from doing thy **p.** on my holy day; 2656
Isa 58:13 own ways, nor finding thine own **p.**, ... 2656
Jer 2:24 snuffeth up the wind at her **p.** 185,5315
Jer 22:28 is he a vessel wherein is no **p.**? 2656
Jer 34:16 he had set at liberty at there **p.**, ... 5315
Jer 48:38 like a vessel wherein is no **p.**, ... 2656
Eze 16:37 with whom thou hast taken **p.**, ... 6148
Eze 18:23 Have I any **p.** at all that the wicked 2654
Eze 18:32 no **p.** in the death of him that dieth, ... 2654
Eze 33:11 no **p.** in the death of the wicked; 2654
Ho 8:8 as a vessel wherein is no **p.** 2656
Hag 1:8 I will take **p.** in it, and I will be 7521
Mal 1:10 I have no **p.** in you, saith the Lord 2656
Lu 12:32 **your Father's good p. to give you** .. *2106*
Ac 24:27 willing to shew the Jews a **p.**, ... *5485*
Ac 25:9 Festus, willing to do the Jews a **p.**, ... *5485*
Ro 1:32 but have **p.** in them that do them. *4909*
2Co 12:10 Therefore I take **p.** in infirmities, ... *2106*
Eph 1:5 according to the good **p.** of his will, ... *2107*
Eph 1:9 according to his good **p.** which he *2107*
Php 2:13 both to will and to do of his good **p.** .. *2107*
2Th 1:11 all the good **p.** of his goodness, ... *2107*
2Th 2:12 but had **p.** in unrighteousness. *2106*
1Ti 5:6 But she that liveth in **p.** is dead *4684*
Heb 10:6 sacrifices...thou hast had no **p.**. *2106*
Heb 10:8 not, neither hadst **p.** therein; *2106*
Heb 10:38 my soul shall have no **p.** in him *2106*
Heb 12:10 chastened...after their own **p.**; *3588,1380*
Jas 5:5 Ye have lived in **p.** on the earth, ... *5171*
2Pe 2:13 count it **p.** to riot in the day time. *2237*
Re 4:11 and for thy **p.** they are and were *2307*

PLEASURES
Job 36:11 in prosperity, and their years in **p.**. 5273
Ps 16:11 hand there are **p.** for evermore 5273
Ps 36:8 them drink of the river of thy **p.**. 5730
Isa 47:8 thou that art given to **p.**, that 5719
Lu 8:14 **cares and riches and p. of this life**, *2237*
2Ti 3:4 lovers of **p.** more than lovers of *5569*
Tit 3:3 serving divers lusts and **p.**, living *2237*
Heb 11:25 to enjoy the **p.** of sin for a season; *2237*

PLEDGE See also PLEDGES.
Ge 38:17 Wilt thou give me a **p.**, till thou 6162
Ge 38:18 he said, What **p.** shall I give thee? 6162
Ge 38:20 his **p.** from the woman's hand: 6162
Ex 22:26 thy neighbour's raiment to **p.**, ... 2254
De 24:6 nether or the upper millstone to **p.**: 2254
De 24:6 for he taketh a man's life to **p.**. 2254
De 24:10 go into his house to fetch his **p.** 5667
De 24:11 bring out the **p.** abroad unto thee. 5667
De 24:12 thou shalt not sleep with his **p.**: 5667
De 24:13 shalt deliver him the **p.** again when 5667
De 24:17 take the widow's raiment to **p.**: 2254
1Sa 17:18 brethren fare, and take their **p.** 6161
Job 22:6 taken a **p.** from thy brother for 2254
Job 24:3 they take the widow's ox for a **p.** 2254
Job 24:9 breast, and take a **p.** of the poor 2254
Pr 20:16 a **p.** of him for a strange woman. 2254
Pr 27:13 a **p.** of him for a strange woman. 2254
Eze 18:7 hath restored to the debtor his **p.**, ... 2258
Eze 18:12 hath not restored the **p.**, and hath 2258
Eze 18:16 hath not withholden the **p.**, neither 2258
Eze 33:15 If the wicked restore the **p.**, give 2258
Am 2:8 clothes laid to **p.** by every altar, ... 2254

PLEDGES
2Ki 18:23 give **p.** to my lord...king of Assyria, ... 6148
Isa 36:8 give **p.**, I pray thee, to my master 6148

PLEIADES (ple'-ya-dez)
Job 9:9 maketh Arcturus, Orion, and **P.**, ... 3598
Job 38:31 bind the sweet influences of **P.**, ... 3598

PLENISH See REPLENISH.

PLENTEOUS
Ge 41:34 of Egypt in the seven **p.** years. 7647
Ge 41:47 And in the seven **p.** years the earth 7647
De 28:11 Lord shall make thee **p.** in goods, ... 3498
De 30:9 make thee **p.** in every work of thine ... 3498
2Ch 1:15 gold at Jerusalem as **p.** as stones, ...
Ps 86:5 **p.** in mercy unto all them that call 7227
Ps 86:15 and **p.** in mercy and truth. 7227
Ps 103:8 slow to anger, and **p.** in mercy. 7227
Ps 130:7 and with him is **p.** redemption. 7235
Isa 30:23 earth, and it shall be fat and **p.**: 8082
Hab 1:16 portion is fat, and their meat **p.**. 1277
Mt 9:37 **The harvest truly is p., but the** *4183*

PLENTEOUSNESS
Ge 41:53 the seven years of **p.**, that was in 7647
Pr 21:5 of the diligent tend only to **p.**; 4195

PLENTIFUL
Ps 68:9 Thou, O God, didst send a **p.** rain, ... 5071
Isa 16:10 away, and joy out of the **p.** field; 3759
Jer 2:7 I brought you into a **p.** country, ... 3759
Jer 48:33 gladness is taken from the **p.** field, ... 3759

PLENTIFULLY
Job 26:3 hast thou **p.** declared the thing 7230
Ps 31:23 and **p.** rewardeth the proud doer. 3499
Lu 12:16 **certain rich man brought forth p.**: .*2164*

PLENTY See also PLENTIFUL.
Ge 27:28 the earth, and **p.** of corn and wine: 7230
Ge 41:29 come seven years of great **p.** 7647
Ge 41:30 the **p.** shall be forgotten in the land 7647
Ge 41:31 **p.** shall not be known in the land 7647
Le 11:36 pit, wherein there is **p.** of water, ... 4723
1Ki 10:11 Ophir great **p.** of almug trees, ... 7235
2Ch 31:10 enough to eat, and have left **p.**: 7230
Job 22:25 and thou shalt have **p.** of silver. 8443
Job 37:23 in judgment, and in **p.** of justice: 7230
Pr 3:10 So shall thy barns be filled with **p.**, ... 7647

Pr 28:19 his land shall have **p.** of bread: 7646
Jer 44:17 for then had we **p.** of victuals, and 7646
Joe 2:26 And ye shall eat in **p.**, and be 398

PLOT See PLAT.

PLOTTETH
Ps 37:12 The wicked **p.** against the just, ... 2161

PLOUGH See also PLOW.
Lu 9:62 **man, having put his hand to the p.,** .*723*

PLOW See also EAR; PLOUGH; PLOWED; PLOWETH; PLOWING; PLOWMAN; PLOWSHARES.
De 22:10 Thou shalt not **p.** with an ox and........ 2790
1Sa 14:14 land, which a yoke of oxen might **p.**..........
Job 4:8 I have seen, they that **p.** iniquity,....... 2790
Pr 20:4 sluggard will not **p.** by reason of 2790
Isa 28:24 the plowman **p.** all day to sow?.......... 2790
Ho 10:11 Judah shall **p.**, and Jacob shall.......... 2790
Am 6:12 rock? will one **p.** there with oxen?...... 2790
1Co 9:10 he that ploweth should **p.** in hope; *722*

PLOWED
Jg 14:18 If ye had not **p.** with my heifer, ... 2790
Ps 129:3 The plowers **p.** upon my back: 2790
Jer 26:18 Zion shall be **p.** like a field, and 2790
Ho 10:13 Ye have **p.** wickedness, ye have 2790
Mic 3:12 Zion for your sake be **p.** as a field, ... 2790

PLOWERS
Ps 129:3 The **p.** plowed upon my back: they..... 2790

PLOWETH
1Co 9:10 he that **p.** should plow in hope; *722*

PLOWING
1Ki 19:19 was **p.** with twelve yoke of oxen........ 2790
Job 1:14 The oxen were **p.**, and the asses......... 2790
Pr 21:4 and the **p.** of the wicked, is sin.......... 5215
Lu 17:7 **having a servant p. or feeding** *722*

PLOWMAN See also PLOWMEN.
Isa 28:24 Doth the **p.** plow all day to sow?........ 2790
Am 9:13 the **p.** shall overtake the reaper, ... 2790

PLOWMEN
Isa 61:5 sons of the alien shall be your **p.** 406
Jer 14:4 **p.** were ashamed, they covered their.... 406

PLOWSHARES
Isa 2:4 shall beat their swords into **p.**, and 855
Joe 3:10 Beat your **p.** into swords, and your...... 855
Mic 4:3 shall beat their swords into **p.**, and 855

PLUCK See also PLUCKED; PLUCKETH; PLUCKT.
Le 1:16 **p.** away his crop with his feathers, ... 5493
Nu 33:52 **p.** down all their high places:............ 8045
De 23:25 thou mayest **p.** the ears with thine 6998
2Ch 7:20 will I **p.** them up by the roots out 5428
Job 24:9 **p.** the fatherless from the breast, ... 1497
Ps 25:15 he shall **p.** my feet out of the net....... 3318
Ps 52:5 **p.** thee out of thy dwelling place, ... 5255
Ps 74:11 right hand? **p.** it out of thy bosom. 3615
Ps 80:12 which pass by the way do **p.** her?........ 717
Ec 3:2 time to **p.** up that which is planted; 6131
Jer 12:14 I will **p.** them out of their land,.......... 5428
Jer 12:14 and **p.** out the house of Judah from..... 5428
Jer 12:17 **p.** up and destroy that nation,............ 5428
Jer 18:7 to **p.** up, and to pull down, and to...... 5428
Jer 22:24 hand, yet would I **p.** thee thence;....... 5423
Jer 24:6 plant them, and not **p.** them up.......... 5428
Jer 31:28 to **p.** up, and to break down, and to ... 5428
Jer 42:10 will plant you, and not **p.** you up: 5428
Jer 45:4 which I have planted I will **p.** up, ... 5428
Eze 17:9 to **p.** it up by the roots thereof.......... 5375
Eze 23:34 **p.** off thine own breasts: and............ 5423
Mic 3:2 **p.** off their skin from off them, ... 1497
Mic 5:14 And I will **p.** up thy groves out of 5428
Mt 5:29 **right eye offend thee, p. it out,**..... *1808*
Mt 12:1 and began to **p.** the ears of corn, ... *5089*
Mt 18:9 **thine eye offend thee, p. it out,**..... *1807*
Mk 2:23 they went, to **p.** the ears of corn. *5089*
Mk 9:47 **if thine eye offend thee, p. it out:** ..*1544*
Joh 10:28 **any man p. them out of my hand....** *726*
Joh 10:29 **to p. them out of my Father's hand.** *726*

PLUCKED See also PLUCKT.
Ex 4:7 **p.** it out of his bosom, and, behold, ... 3318
De 28:63 ye shall be **p.** from off the land.......... 5255
Ru 4:7 a man **p.** off his shoe, and gave it 8025
2Sa 23:21 **p.** the spear out of the Egyptian's 1497
1Ch 11:23 **p.** the spear out of the Egyptian's 1497
Ezr 9:3 **p.** off the hair of my head and of........ 4803
Ne 13:25 **p.** off their hair, and made them.......... 4803
Job 29:17 and **p.** the spoil out of his teeth. 7993
Isa 50:6 cheeks to them that **p.** off the hair: 4803
Jer 6:29 for the wicked are not **p.** away. 5423
Jer 12:15 I have **p.** them out I will return, ... 5428
Jer 31:40 it shall not be **p.** up, nor thrown 5428
Eze 19:12 she was **p.** up in fury, she was cast.... 5428
Da 7:4 till the wings thereof were **p.**, ... 4804
Da 7:8 the first horns **p.** up by the roots:...... 6132
Da 11:4 for his kingdom shall be **p.** up,........... 5428
Am 4:11 a firebrand **p.** out of the burning: 5337
Zec 3:2 not this a brand **p.** out of the fire?....... 5337
Mk 5:4 had been **p.** asunder by him, and........ *1288*
Lu 6:1 his disciples **p.** the ears of corn, ... *5089*
Lu 17:6 **Be thou p. up by the root, and be** ..*1610*
Ga 4:15 would have **p.** out your own eyes,...... *1846*
Jude 12 twice dead, **p.** up by the roots;.......... *1610*

PLUCKETH
Pr 14:1 foolish **p.** it down with her hands......... 2040

PLUCKT See also PLUCKED.
Ge 8:11 her mouth was an olive leaf **p.** off: 2965

PLUMBLINE
Am 7:7 made by a **p.**, with a **p.** in his hand...... 594
Am 7:8 what seest thou? And I said, A **p.**........ 594
Am 7:8 I will set a **p.** in the midst of my 594

PLUMMET
2Ki 21:13 and the **p.** of the house of Ahab:........ 4949
Isa 28:17 line, and righteousness to the **p.**: 4949
Zec 4:10 shall see the **p.** in the hand of........ 68,913

PLUNGE
Job 9:31 Yet shalt thou **p.** me in the ditch,....... 2881

PLUS See OVERPLUS.

PLY See REPLY; SUPPLY.

POCHERETH (po-ke'-reth)
Ezr 2:57 the children of **P.** of Zebaim,............ 6380
Ne 7:59 the children of **P.** of Zebaim,............ 6380

POETS
Ac 17:28 also of your own **p.** have said,.......... *4163*

POINT See also APPOINT; POINTED; POINTS.
Ge 25:32 said, Behold, I am at the **p.** to die:..... 1980
Nu 34:7 ye shall **p.** out for you mount Hor: 8376
Nu 34:8 mount Hor ye shall **p.** out your.......... 8376
Nu 34:10 ye shall **p.** out your east border 184
Jer 17:1 and with the **p.** of a diamond: 6856
Eze 21:15 have set the **p.** of the sword against 19
Mk 5:23 daughter lieth at the **p.** of death:........ *2079*
Joh 4:47 son: for he was at the **p.** of death. *3195*
Jas 2:10 yet offend in one **p.**, he is guilty of all. ......

POINTED See also APPOINTED.
Job 41:30 sharp **p.** things upon the mire............ 2742

POINTS
Ec 5:16 in all **p.** as he came, so shall he......... 5980
Heb 4:15 was in all **p.** tempted like as we are,.........

POISON
De 32:24 with the **p.** of serpents of the dust. 2534
De 32:33 Their wine is the **p.** of dragons, and ... 2534
Job 6:4 **p.** whereof drinketh up my spirit: 2534
Job 20:16 He shall suck the **p.** of asps: the........ 7219
Ps 58:4 Their **p.** is like the **p.** of a serpent: 2534
Ps 140:3 adders' **p.** is under their lips............. 2534
Ro 3:13 the **p.** of asps is under their lips: *2447*
Jas 3:8 an unruly evil, full of deadly **p.**........... *2447*

POLE
Nu 21:8 fiery serpent, and set it upon a **p.**: 5251
Nu 21:9 of brass, and put it upon a **p.**, ... 5251

POLICY
Da 8:25 through his **p.**...shall cause craft......... 7922

POLISHED
Ps 144:12 **p.** after the similitude of a palace:....... 2404
Isa 49:2 hid me, and made me a **p.** shaft;........ 1305
Da 10:6 his feet like in colour to **p.** brass,....... 7044

POLISHING
La 4:7 rubies, their **p.** was of sapphire:......... 1508

POLL See also POLLED; POLLS.
Nu 3:47 take five shekels apiece by the **p.**,...... 1538
Eze 44:20 they shall only **p.** their heads............. 3697
Mic 1:16 **p.** thee for thy delicate children; 1494

POLLED
2Sa 14:26 And when he **p.** his head, (for it 1548
2Sa 14:26 at every year's end that he **p.** it; 1548
2Sa 14:26 heavy on him, therefore he **p.** it:) 1548

POLLS
Nu 1:2 names, every male by their **p.**; 1538
Nu 1:18 years old and upward, by their **p.**....... 1538
Nu 1:20, 22 number of the names, by their **p.**,.. 1538
1Ch 23:3 their number by their **p.**, man by 1538
1Ch 23:24 by number of names by their **p.**,........ 1538

POLLUTE See also POLLUTED; POLLUTING.
Nu 18:32 neither shall ye **p.** the holy things....... 2490
Nu 35:33 So ye shall not **p.** the land wherein..... 2610
Jer 7:30 is called by my name, to **p.** it............ 2930
Eze 7:21 for a spoil; and they shall **p.** it........... 2490
Eze 7:22 and they shall **p.** my secret place: 2490
Eze 13:19 And will ye **p.** me among my people ... 2490
Eze 20:31 ye **p.** yourselves with all your idols,.... 2930
Eze 20:39 **p.** ye my holy name no more with...... 2490
Eze 39:7 I will not let them **p.** my holy name.... 2490
Eze 44:7 to **p.** it, even my house, when ye 2490
Da 11:31 shall **p.** the sanctuary of strength, ... 2490

POLLUTED
Ex 20:25 thy tool upon it, thou hast **p.** it.......... 2490
2Ki 23:16 burned...upon the altar, and **p.** it,........ 2930
2Ch 36:14 **p.** the house of the Lord, which he..... 2930
Ezr 2:62 as **p.**, put from the priesthood. 1351
Ne 7:64 as **p.**, put from the priesthood. 1351
Ps 106:38 and the land was **p.** with blood. 2610
Isa 47:6 I have **p.** mine inheritance, and......... 2490
Isa 48:11 how should my name be **p.**? and I...... 2490
Jer 2:23 How canst thou say, I am not **p.**, I..... 2930
Jer 3:1 shall not that land be greatly **p.**? 2610
Jer 3:2 and thou hast **p.** the land with thy...... 2610
Jer 34:16 But ye turned and **p.** my name, ... 2490
La 2:2 he hath **p.** the kingdom and the 2490
La 4:14 have **p.** themselves with blood, so...... 1351
Eze 4:14 soul hath not been **p.**; for, from.......... 2930
Eze 14:11 neither be **p.** any more with all......... 2930
Eze 16:6 saw thee **p.** in thine own blood,........... 947
Eze 16:22 naked and bare,...**p.** in thy blood. 947
Eze 20:9 should not be **p.** before...heathen,...... 2490
Eze 20:13 and my sabbaths they greatly **p.**:........ 2490
Eze 20:14 should not be **p.** before...heathen,...... 2490
Eze 20:16 my statutes, but **p.** my sabbaths: 2490
Eze 20:21 they **p.** my sabbaths: then I said,........ 2490
Eze 20:22 be **p.** in the sight of the heathen, ... 2490
Eze 20:24 had **p.** my sabbaths, and their eyes...... 2490
Eze 20:26 I **p.** them in their own gifts, in........... 2930
Eze 20:30 Are ye **p.** after the manner of your..... 2930
Eze 23:17 she was **p.** with them, and her mind... 2930
Eze 23:30 because thou art **p.** with their idols..... 2930
Eze 36:18 idols wherewith they had **p.** it: 2930
Ho 6:8 iniquity, and is **p.** with blood. 6121
Ho 9:4 all that eat thereof shall be **p.**:........... 2930
Am 7:17 and thou shalt die in a **p.** land:........... 2931
Mic 2:10 because it is **p.**, it shall destroy 2930
Zep 3:1 Woe to her that is filthy and **p.**, to..... 1351
Zep 3:4 her priests have **p.** the sanctuary, ... 2490
Mal 1:7 Ye offer **p.** bread upon mine altar;...... 1351
Mal 1:7 ye say, Wherein have we **p.** thee?...... 1351
Mal 1:12 The table of the Lord is **p.**; and the.... 1351
Ac 21:28 temple,...hath **p.** this holy place. *2840*

POLLUTING
Isa 56:2,6 keepeth the sabbath from **p.** it,.......... 2490

POLLUTION See POLLUTIONS.
Eze 22:10 her that was set apart for **p.**. 2931

POLLUTIONS
Ac 15:20 that they abstain from **p.** of idols, ... *234*
2Pe 2:20 have escaped the **p.** of the world *3393*

POLLUX (pol'-lux)
Ac 28:11 whose sign was Castor and **P.**........... *1359*

POMEGRANATE See POMEGRANATES.
Ex 28:34 bell and a **p.**, a golden bell and a **p.**,... 7416
Ex 39:26 A bell and a **p.**, a bell and a **p.**, ... 7416
1Sa 14:2 under a **p.** tree which is in Migron: 7416
Ca 4:3 thy temples are like a piece of a **p.**...... 7416
Ca 6:7 As a piece of a **p.** are thy temples....... 7416
Ca 8:2 spiced wine of the juice of my **p.**........ 7416
Joe 1:12 the **p.** tree, the palm tree also, and.... 7416
Hag 2:19 the **p.**, and the olive tree, hath not..... 7416

POMEGRANATE-TREE See POMEGRANATE and TREE.

POMEGRANATES
Ex 28:33 thou shalt make **p.** of blue, and of 7416
Ex 39:24 upon the hems of the robe **p.** of blue, 7416
Ex 39:25 and put the bells between the **p.** 7416
Ex 39:25 robe, round about between the **p.**; 7416
Nu 13:23 they brought of the **p.**, and of the 7416
Nu 20:5 or of figs, or of vines, or of **p.**; 7416
De 8:8 and vines, and fig trees, and **p.**; 7416
1Ki 7:18 that were upon the top, with **p.**: 7416
1Ki 7:20 upon the two pillars had **p.** also above,
1Ki 7:20 and the **p.** were two hundred in 7416
1Ki 7:42 And four hundred **p.** for the two 7416
1Ki 7:42 two rows of **p.** for one network, 7416
2Ki 25:17 **p.** upon the chapiter round about, 7416
2Ch 3:16 and made an hundred **p.**, and put 7416
2Ch 4:13 hundred **p.** on the two wreaths; 7416
2Ch 4:13 two rows of **p.** on each wreath, 7416
Ca 4:13 Thy plants are an orchard of **p.**, 7416
Ca 6:11 vine flourished, and the **p.** budded. 7416
Ca 7:12 grape appear, and the **p.** bud forth: 7416
Jer 52:22 **p.** upon the chapiters round about, 7416
Jer 52:22 and the **p.** were like unto these. 7416
Jer 52:23 were ninety and six **p.** on a side; 7416
Jer 52:23 and all the **p.** upon the network 7416

POMMELS
2Ch 4:12 and the **p.**, and the chapiters 1543
2Ch 4:12, 13 cover the two **p.** of the chapiters 1543

POMP
Isa 5:14 and their multitude, and their **p.**, 7588
Isa 14:11 Thy **p.** is brought down to the 1347
Eze 7:24 make the **p.** of the strong to cease; 1347
Eze 30:18 the **p.** of her strength shall cease 1347
Eze 32:12 they shall spoil the **p.** of Egypt, 1347
Eze 33:28 the **p.** of her strength shall cease; 1347
Ac 25:23 come, and Bernice, with great **p.**, *5325*

PONDER See PONDERED; PONDERETH.
Pr 4:26 **P.** the path of thy feet, and let all 6424
Pr 5:6 thou shouldest **p.** the path of life, 6424

PONDERED
Lu 2:19 things, and **p.** them in her heart *4820*

PONDERETH
Pr 5:21 the Lord, and he **p.** all his goings. 6424
Pr 21:2 eyes: but the Lord **p.** the hearts. 8505
Pr 24:12 not he that **p.** the heart consider it? 8505

PONDS
Ex 7:19 upon their rivers, and upon their **p.**, 98
Ex 8:5 over the rivers, and over the **p.**, 98
Isa 19:10 all that make sluices and **p.** for fish. 99

PONTIUS (pon'-she-us)
Mt 27:2 him to **P.** Pilate the governor. *4194*
Lu 3:1 **P.** Pilate being governor of Judaea, *4194*
Ac 4:27 both Herod, and **P.** Pilate, with the *4194*
1Ti 6:13 before **P.** Pilate witnessed a good *4194*

PONTUS (pon'-tus)
Ac 2:9 and Cappadocia, in **P.**, and Asia, *4195*
Ac 18:2 Jew named Aquila, born in **P.**, *4195*
1Pe 1:1 strangers scattered throughout **P.**, *4195*

POOL See also POOLS.
2Sa 2:13 met together by the **p.** of Gibeon: 1295
2Sa 2:13 the one on the one side of the **p.**, 1295
2Sa 2:13 other on the other side of the **p.** 1295
2Sa 4:12 them up over the **p.** in Hebron. 1295
1Ki 22:38 the chariot in the **p.** of Samaria; 1295
2Ki 18:17 by the conduit of the upper **p.**, 1295
2Ki 20:20 how he made a **p.**, and a conduit, 1295
Ne 2:14 the fountain, and to the king's **p.**: 1295
Ne 3:15 **p.** of Siloah by the king's garden. 1295
Ne 3:16 and to the **p.** that was made, and 1295
Isa 7:3 end of the conduit of the upper **p.** 1295
Isa 22:9 together the waters of the lower **p.** 1295
Isa 22:11 two walls for the water of the old **p.**: 1295
Isa 35:7 parched ground shall become a **p.**, 98
Isa 36:2 by the conduit of the upper **p.** 1295
Isa 41:18 make the wilderness a **p.** of water, 98
Na 2:8 Nineveh is…like a **p.** of water: 1295
Joh 5:2 there is…by the sheep market a **p.**, *2861*
Joh 5:4 down at a certain season into the **p.**, *2861*
Joh 5:7 is troubled, to put me into the **p.**: *2861*
Joh 9:7 him, **Go, wash in the p. of Siloam,** *2861*
Joh 9:11 Go to the **p.** of Siloam, and wash: *2861*

POOLS
Ex 7:19 and upon all their **p.** of water, 4723
Ps 84:6 a well; the rain also filleth the **p.** 1293
Ec 2:6 I made me **p.** of water, to water 1295
Isa 14:23 for the bittern, and **p.** of water: 98
Isa 42:15 islands, and I will dry up the **p.** 98

POOR See also POORER; POOREST.
Ge 41:19 kine…**p.** and very ill favoured and 1800
Ex 22:25 lend…to any of my people that is **p.** 6041
Ex 23:3 shalt thou countenance a **p.** man 1800
Ex 23:6 not wrest the judgment of thy **p.** 34
Ex 23:11 that the **p.** of thy people may eat: 34
Ex 30:15 more, and the **p.** shall not give less 1800
Le 14:21 if he be **p.**, and cannot get so much; 1800
Le 19:10 leave them for the **p.** and stranger: 6041
Le 19:15 not respect the person of the **p.**, 1800
Le 23:22 thou shalt leave them unto the **p.**, 6041
Le 25:25 If thy brother be waxen **p.**, and 4134
Le 25:35 And if thy brother be waxen **p.**, and 4134
Le 25:39 that dwelleth by thee be waxen **p.**, 4134
Le 25:47 brother that dwelleth by him wax **p.**, 4134
De 15:4 there shall be no **p.** among you; 34
De 15:7 If there be among you a **p.** man 34
De 15:7 shut thine hand from thy **p.** brother: 34
De 15:9 eye be evil against thy **p.** brother, 34
De 15:11 **p.** shall never cease out of the land: 34
De 15:11 to thy **p.**, and to thy needy, in thy 6041
De 24:12 And if the man be **p.**, thou shalt not 6041
De 24:14 oppress an hired servant that is **p.** 6041
De 24:15 he is **p.**, and setteth his heart upon 6041
Jg 6:15 my family is **p.** in Manasseh, and 1800
Ru 3:10 not young men, whether **p.** or rich. 1800
1Sa 2:7 The Lord maketh **p.**, and maketh 3423
1Sa 2:8 raiseth up the **p.** out of the dust, 1800
1Sa 18:23 seeing that I am a **p.** man, and 7326
2Sa 12:1 city; the one rich, and the other **p.** 7326
2Sa 12:3 But the **p.** man had nothing, save 7326
2Sa 12:4 took the **p.** man's lamb, and dressed 7326
2Ki 25:12 **p.** of the land to be vinedressers 1803
Es 9:22 one to another, and gifts to the **p.** 34
Job 5:15 he saveth the **p.** from the sword, 34
Job 5:16 So the **p.** hath hope, and iniquity 1800
Job 20:10 children shall seek to please the **p.**, 1800
Job 20:19 oppressed and hath forsaken the **p.**; 1800
Job 24:4 **p.** of the earth hide themselves 6035
Job 24:9 breast, and take a pledge of the **p.** 6041
Job 24:14 rising with the light killeth the **p.** 6041
Job 29:12 I delivered the **p.** that cried, and 6041
Job 29:16 I was a father to the **p.**: and the 34
Job 30:25 was not my soul grieved for the **p.**? 34
Job 31:16 withheld the **p.** from their desire, 1800
Job 31:19 clothing, or any **p.** without covering; 34
Job 34:19 the rich more than the **p.**? 1800
Job 34:28 the cry of the **p.** to come unto him, 1800
Job 36:6 wicked: but giveth right to the **p.** 6041
Job 36:15 delivereth the **p.** in his affliction, 6041
Ps 9:18 expectation of the **p.** shall not 6035,6041
Ps 10:2 in his pride doth persecute the **p.**: 6041
Ps 10:8 eyes are privily set against the **p.** 2489
Ps 10:9 he lieth in wait to catch the **p.**: 6041
Ps 10:9 doth catch the **p.** when he draweth 6041
Ps 10:10 the **p.** may fall by his strong ones. 2489
Ps 10:14 **p.** committeth himself unto thee; 2489
Ps 12:5 For the oppression of the **p.**, 6041
Ps 14:6 have shamed the counsel of the **p.**, 6041
Ps 34:6 This **p.** man cried, and the Lord 6041
Ps 35:10 deliverest the **p.** from him that is too 6041
Ps 35:10 the **p.** and the needy from him that 6041
Ps 37:14 bow, to cast down the **p.** and needy, 6041
Ps 40:17 I am **p.** and needy; yet the Lord 6041
Ps 41:1 is he that considereth the **p.**: 1800
Ps 49:2 low and high, rich and **p.**, together. 34
Ps 68:10 prepared of thy goodness for the **p.** 6041
Ps 69:29 But I am **p.** and sorrowful: let thy 6041
Ps 69:33 For the Lord heareth the **p.**, and 34
Ps 70:5 I am **p.** and needy: make haste 6041
Ps 72:2 and thy **p.** with judgment. 6041
Ps 72:4 He shall judge the **p.** of the people, 6041
Ps 72:12 **p.** also, and him that had no helper. 6041
Ps 72:13 He shall spare the **p.** and needy, 1800
Ps 74:19 forget not…congregation of thy **p.** 6041
Ps 74:21 the **p.** and needy praise thy name. 6041
Ps 82:3 Defend the **p.** and fatherless: do 1800
Ps 82:4 Deliver the **p.** and needy: rid them 1800
Ps 86:1 hear me: for I am **p.** and needy. 6041
Ps 107:41 Yet setteth he the **p.** on high from 34
Ps 109:16 persecuted the **p.** and needy man, 6041
Ps 109:22 For I am **p.** and needy, and my 6041
Ps 109:31 stand at the right hand of the **p.**, 34
Ps 112:9 dispersed, he hath given to the **p.**; 34
Ps 113:7 raiseth up the **p.** out of the dust, 1800
Ps 132:15 I will satisfy her **p.** with bread. 34
Ps 140:12 the afflicted, and the right of the **p.** 34
Pr 10:4 He becometh **p.** that dealeth with 7326
Pr 10:15 the destruction of the **p.** is their 1800
Pr 13:7 there is that maketh himself **p.**, 7326
Pr 13:8 but the **p.** heareth not rebuke. 7326
Pr 13:23 Much food is in the tillage of the **p.**: 7326
Pr 14:20 The **p.** is hated even of his own 7326
Pr 14:21 he that hath mercy on the **p.**, 6035,6041
Pr 14:31 that oppresseth the **p.** reproacheth 1800
Pr 14:31 him hath mercy on the **p.** 34
Pr 17:5 Whoso mocketh the **p.** reproacheth 7326
Pr 18:23 The **p.** useth intreaties; but the 7326
Pr 19:1 Better is the **p.** that walketh in his 7326
Pr 19:4 **p.** is separated from his neighbour. 1800
Pr 19:7 brethren of the **p.** do hate him: 7326
Pr 19:17 that hath pity upon the **p.** lendeth 1800
Pr 19:22 and a **p.** man is better than a liar. 7326
Pr 21:13 stoppeth his ears at…cry of the **p.**, 1800
Pr 21:17 loveth pleasure shall be a **p.** man: 4270
Pr 22:2 The rich and **p.** meet together: 7326
Pr 22:7 The rich ruleth over the **p.**, and the 7326
Pr 22:9 he giveth of his bread to the **p.** 1800
Pr 22:16 that oppresseth the **p.** to increase 1800
Pr 22:22 Rob not the **p.**, because he is **p.**: 1800
Pr 28:3 A **p.** man that oppresseth the 7326
Pr 28:3 A…man that oppresseth the **p.** 1800
Pr 28:6 Better is the **p.** that walketh in his 1800
Pr 28:8 it for him that will pity the **p.** 1800
Pr 28:11 but the **p.** that hath understanding 1800
Pr 28:15 a wicked ruler over the **p.** people. 1800
Pr 28:27 that giveth unto the **p.** shall not 7326
Pr 29:7 considereth the cause of the **p.**: 1800
Pr 29:13 The **p.** and the deceitful man meet 7326
Pr 29:14 king that faithfully judgeth the **p.**, 1800
Pr 30:9 or lest I be **p.**, and steal, and take 3423
Pr 30:14 devour the **p.** from off the earth, 6041
Pr 31:9 plead the cause of the **p.** and needy. 6041
Pr 31:20 She stretched out her hand to the **p.**; 6041
Ec 4:13 Better is a **p.** and a wise child 4542
Ec 4:14 born in his kingdom becometh **p.** 7326
Ec 5:8 thou seest the oppression of the **p.**, 7326
Ec 6:8 what hath the **p.**, that knoweth to 6041
Ec 9:15 was found in it a **p.** wise man, 4542
Ec 9:15 remembered that same **p.** man. 4542
Ec 9:16 the **p.** man's wisdom is despised, 4542
Isa 3:14 spoil of the **p.** is in your houses. 6041
Isa 3:15 pieces, and grind the faces of the **p.**? 6041
Isa 10:2 the right from the **p.** of my people, 6041
Isa 10:30 be heard unto Laish, O **p.** Anathoth. 6041
Isa 11:4 righteousness shall he judge the **p.**, 1800
Isa 14:30 the firstborn of the **p.** shall feed, 1800
Isa 14:32 **p.** of his people shall trust in it. 6041
Isa 25:4 thou hast been a strength to the **p.**, 1800
Isa 26:6 it down, even the feet of the **p.**, 6041
Isa 29:19 the **p.** among men shall rejoice in 34
Isa 32:7 to destroy the **p.** with lying 6035,6041
Isa 41:17 the **p.** and needy seek water, 6041
Isa 58:7 **p.** that are cast out to thy house? 6041
Isa 66:2 that is **p.** and of a contrite spirit, 6041
Jer 2:34 of the souls of the **p.** innocents: 34
Jer 5:4 said, Surely these are **p.**; they are 1800
Jer 20:13 delivered the soul of the **p.** from the 34
Jer 22:16 He judged the cause of the **p.** and 6041
Jer 39:10 guard left of the **p.** of the people, 1800
Jer 40:7 and of the **p.** of the land, of them 1803
Jer 52:15 certain of the **p.** of the people, and 1803
Jer 52:16 the **p.** of the land for vinedressers 1803
Eze 16:49 the hand of the **p.** and needy. 6041
Eze 18:12 Hath oppressed the **p.** and needy, 6041
Eze 18:17 hath taken off his hand from the **p.**, 6041
Eze 22:29 and have vexed the **p.** and needy: 6041
Da 4:27 by shewing mercy to the **p.**; if it 6033
Am 2:6 silver, and the **p.** for a pair of shoes; 34
Am 2:7 of the earth on the head of the **p.**, 1800
Am 4:1 which oppress the **p.**, which crush 1800
Am 5:11 as your treading is upon the **p.**, and 1800
Am 5:12 turn aside the **p.** in the gate from 34
Am 8:4 the **p.** of the land to fail, 6035,6041
Am 8:6 That we may buy the **p.** for silver, 1800
Hab 3:14 was as to devour the **p.** secretly. 6041
Zep 3:12 of thee an afflicted and **p.** people, 1800
Zec 7:10 widow,…the stranger, nor the **p.**; 6041

Zec 11:7 even you, O **p.** of the flock. 6041
Zec 11:11 **p.** of the flock that waited upon me 6041
Mt 5:3 Blessed are the **p.** in spirit: for *4434*
Mt 11:5 the **p.** have the gospel preached to. *4434*
Mt 19:21 that thou hast, and give to the **p.**, *4434*
Mt 26:9 sold for much, and given to the **p.** *4434*
Mt 26:11 ye have the **p.** always with you; *4434*
Mk 10:21 thou hast, and give to the **p.**, and *4434*
Mk 12:42 there came a certain **p.** widow, *4434*
Mk 12:43 this **p.** widow hath cast more in, *4434*
Mk 14:5 and have been given to the **p.** *4434*
Mk 14:7 ye have the **p.** with you always, *4434*
Lu 4:18 me to preach the gospel to the **p.**; *4434*
Lu 6:20 Blessed be ye **p.**: for yours is the *4434*
Lu 7:22 to the **p.** the gospel is preached. *4434*
Lu 14:13 thou makest a feast, call the **p.**, *4434*
Lu 14:21 and bring in hither the **p.**, and the *4434*
Lu 18:22 hast, and distribute unto the **p.**, *4434*
Lu 19:8 half of my goods I give to the **p.**; *4434*
Lu 21:2 **p.** widow casting in thither two *3998*
Lu 21:3 **p.** widow hath cast in more than *4434*
Joh 12:5 hundred pence, and given to the **p.**? *4434*
Joh 12:6 he said, not that he cared for the **p.**; *4434*
Joh 12:8 **p.** always ye have with you; but *4434*
Joh 13:29 he should give something to the **p.** *4434*
Ro 15:26 **p.** saints which are at Jerusalem. *4434*
1Co 13:3 I bestow all my goods to feed the **p.**, *4434*
2Co 6:10 as **p.**, yet making many rich; as *4434*
2Co 8:9 yet for your sakes he became **p.**, *4433*
2Co 9:9 abroad; he hath given to the **p.**: *3993*
Ga 2:10 that we should remember the **p.**; *4434*
Jas 2:2 in also a **p.** man in vile raiment; *4434*
Jas 2:3 say to the **p.**, Stand thou there, or *4434*
Jas 2:5 not God chosen the **p.** of this world *4434*
Jas 2:6 But ye have despised the **p.** Do *4434*
Re 3:17 miserable, and **p.**, and blind, and *4434*
Re 13:16 great, rich and **p.**, free and bond, *4434*

POORER
Le 27:8 if he be **p.** than thy estimation, 4134

POOREST
2Ki 24:14 **p.** sort of the people of the land. 1803

POPLAR See also POPLARS.
Ge 30:37 Jacob took him rods of green **p.**, 3839

POPLARS
Ho 4:13 hills, under oaks and **p.** and elms, 3839

POPULOUS
De 26:5 a nation, great, mighty, and **p.**: 7227
Na 3:8 Art thou better than **p.** No, that 527

PORATHA (por'-a-thah)
Es 9:8 And **P.**, and Adalia, and Aridatha, 6334

PORCH See also PORCHES.
Jg 3:23 Ehud went forth through the **p.**, 4528
1Ki 6:3 **p.** before the temple of the house, 197
1Ki 7:6 he made a **p.** of pillars; the length 197
1Ki 7:6 and the **p.** was before them: and the 197
1Ki 7:7 Then he made a **p.** for the throne 197
1Ki 7:7 judge, even the **p.** of judgment: 197
1Ki 7:8 had another court within the **p.**, 197
1Ki 7:8 had taken to wife, like unto this **p.** 197
1Ki 7:12 Lord, and for the **p.** of the house. 197
1Ki 7:19 pillars were of lily work in the **p.**, 197
1Ki 7:21 the pillars in the **p.** of the temple: 197
1Ch 28:11 to Solomon...the pattern of the **p.**, 197
2Ch 3:4 **p.** that was in the front of the house, 197
2Ch 8:12 which he had built before the **p.** 197
2Ch 15:8 that was before the **p.** of the Lord. 197
2Ch 29:7 have shut up the doors of the **p.**, and 197
2Ch 29:17 came they to the **p.** of the Lord: 197
Eze 8:16 between the **p.** and the altar, were 197
Eze 40:7 **p.** of the gate within was one reed. 197
Eze 40:8 He measured also the **p.** of the gate. 197
Eze 40:9 Then measured he the **p.** of the gate, 197
Eze 40:9 and the **p.** of the gate was inward. 197
Eze 40:15 the face of the **p.** of the inner gate 197
Eze 40:39 in the **p.** of the gate were two tables, 197
Eze 40:40 which was at the **p.** of the gate, 197
Eze 40:48 brought me to the **p.** of the house, 197
Eze 40:48 measured each post of the **p.**, five 197
Eze 40:49 length of the **p.** was twenty cubits, 197
Eze 41:25 thick planks upon the face of the **p.** 197
Eze 41:26 the other side, on the sides of the **p.**, 197
Eze 44:3 he shall enter by the way of the **p.** 197
Eze 46:2 shall enter by the way of the **p.** of 197
Eze 46:8 he shall go in by the way of the **p.** 197
Joe 2:17 weep between the **p.** and the altar, 197
Mt 26:71 when he was gone out into the **p.**, *4440*
Mk 14:68 And he went out into the **p.**; and *4259*
Joh 10:23 in the temple in Solomon's **p.** *4745*
Ac 3:11 in the **p.** that is called Solomon's, *4745*
Ac 5:12 all with one accord in Solomon's **p.** *4745*

PORCHES
Eze 41:15 temple, and the **p.** of the court; 197
Joh 5:2 tongue Beth sda, having five **p.** *4745*

PORCIUS (por'-she-us)
Ac 24:27 after two years **P.** Festus came *4201*

PORT See also REPORT; SUPPORT.
Ne 2:13 dragon well, and to the dung **p.**, 8179

PORTER See also PORTERS.
2Sa 18:26 the watchman called unto the **p.**, 7778
2Ki 7:10 and called unto the **p.** of the city: 7778
1Ch 9:21 was **p.** of the door of the tabernacle 7778
2Ch 31:14 the **p.** toward the east, was over the 7778
Mk 13:34 and commanded the **p.** to watch. *2377*
Joh 10:3 To him the **p.** openeth; and the *2377*

PORTERS
2Ki 7:11 he called the **p.**; and they told it 7778
1Ch 9:17 the **p.** were, Shallum, and Akkub, 7778
1Ch 9:18 **p.** in the companies of the children 7778
1Ch 9:22 were chosen to be **p.** in the gates 7778
1Ch 9:24 In four quarters were the **p.**, 7778
1Ch 9:26 these Levites, the four chief **p.**, 7778
1Ch 15:18 and Obed-edom, and Jeiel, the **p.** 7778
1Ch 16:38 of Jeduthun and Hosah to be **p.**: 7778
1Ch 16:42 And the sons of Jeduthun were **p.** 8179
1Ch 23:5 Moreover four thousand were **p.**; 7778
1Ch 26:1 Concerning the divisions of the **p.**: 7778
1Ch 26:12 these were the divisions of the **p.**, 7778
1Ch 26:19 These are the divisions of the **p.** 7778
2Ch 8:14 **p.** also by their courses at every 7778
2Ch 23:4 the Levites, shall be **p.** of the doors; 7778
2Ch 23:19 set the **p.** at the gates of the house 7778
2Ch 34:13 were scribes, and officers, and **p.** 7778
2Ch 35:15 and the **p.** waited at every gate; they 7778
Ezr 2:42 children of the **p.**: the children of 7778
Ezr 2:70 people, and the singers, and the **p.**, 7778
Ezr 7:7 Levites, and the singers, and the **p.**, 7778
Ezr 7:24 priests and Levites, singers, **p.**, 8652
Ezr 10:24 and of the **p.**; Shallum, and 7778
Ne 7:1 **p.** and the singers and the Levites 7778
Ne 7:45 The **p.**: the children of Shallum, 7778
Ne 7:73 priests, and the Levites, and the **p.**, 7778
Ne 10:28 the priests, the Levites, the **p.**, the 7778
Ne 10:39 the priests that minister, and the **p.**, 7778
Ne 11:19 Moreover the **p.**, Akkub, Talmon, 7778
Ne 12:25 were **p.** keeping the ward at the 7778
Ne 12:45 the **p.** kept the ward of their God, 7778
Ne 12:47 portions of the singers and the **p.** 7778
Ne 13:5 Levites, and the singers, and the **p.**; 7778

PORTION See also PORTIONS.
Ge 14:24 the **p.** of the men which went with 2506
Ge 14:24 and Mamre: let them take their **p.** 2506
Ge 31:14 yet any **p.** or inheritance for us in 2506
Ge 47:22 the priests had a **p.** assigned them 2706
Ge 47:22 did eat their **p.** which Pharaoh gave 2706
Ge 48:22 to thee one **p.** above thy brethren, 7926
Le 6:17 given it unto them for their **p.** of 2506
Le 7:35 This is the **p.** of the anointing of Aaron,
Nu 31:30 thou shalt take one **p.** of fifty, of the 270
Nu 31:36 **p.** of them that went out to war, 2506
Nu 31:47 Moses took one **p.** of fifty, both of 270
De 21:17 a double **p.** of all that he hath: 6310
De 32:9 For the Lord's **p.** is his people; 2506
De 33:21 in a **p.** of the lawgiver, was he 2513
Jos 17:14 but one lot and one **p.** to inherit, 2256
Jos 19:9 of the **p.** of the children of Judah 2256
1Sa 1:5 unto Hannah he gave a worthy **p.**; 4490
1Sa 9:23 Bring the **p.** which I gave thee, of 4490
1Ki 12:16 What **p.** have we in David? neither 2506
2Ki 2:9 double **p.** of thy spirit be upon me. 6310
2Ki 9:10 eat Jezebel in the **p.** of Jezreel, 2506
2Ki 9:21 met him in the **p.** of Naboth the 2513
2Ki 9:25 him in the **p.** of the field of Naboth 2513
2Ki 9:36 In the **p.** of Jezreel shall dogs eat 2506
2Ki 9:37 face of the field in the **p.** of Jezreel; 2506
2Ch 10:16 saying, What **p.** have we in David? 2506
2Ch 28:21 For Ahaz took away a **p.** out of the 2505
2Ch 31:3 also the king's **p.** of his substance 4521
2Ch 31:4 **p.** of the priests and the Levites, 4521
2Ch 31:16 his daily **p.** for their service in 1697
Ezr 4:16 have no **p.** on this side the river. 2508
Ne 2:20 but ye have no **p.**, nor right, nor 2506
Ne 11:23 a certain **p.** should be for the singers,
Ne 12:47 and the porters, every day his **p.**: 1697
Job 20:29 the **p.** of a wicked man from God, 2506
Job 24:18 their **p.** is cursed in the earth: he 2513
Job 26:14 but how little a **p.** is heard of him? 1697
Job 27:13 the **p.** of a wicked man with God, 2506
Job 31:2 what **p.** of God is there from above? 2506
Ps 11:6 this shall be the **p.** of their cup. 4521
Ps 16:5 Lord is the **p.** of mine inheritance 4490
Ps 17:14 which have their **p.** in this life, 2506
Ps 63:10 sword: they shall be a **p.** for foxes. 4521
Ps 73:26 of my heart, and my **p.** for ever. 2506
Ps 119:57 Thou art my **p.**, O Lord: I have 2506
Ps 142:5 and my **p.** in the land of the living. 2506
Pr 31:15 and a **p.** to her maidens. 2706
Ec 2:10 this was my **p.** of all my labour. 2506
Ec 2:21 therein shall he leave it for his **p.** 2506
Ec 3:22 in his own works; for that is his **p.**: 2506
Ec 5:18 God giveth him: for it is his **p.** 2506
Ec 5:19 to eat thereof, and to take his **p.**, 2506
Ec 9:6 neither have they any more a **p.** 2506
Ec 9:9 for that is thy **p.** in this life, and in 2506
Ec 11:2 Give a **p.** to seven, and also to eight; 2506
Isa 17:14 This is the **p.** of them that spoil us, 2506
Isa 53:12 I divide him a **p.** with the great, 2506
Isa 57:6 stones of the stream is thy **p.**; 2506
Isa 61:7 they shall rejoice in their **p.**: 2506
Jer 10:16 **p.** of Jacob is not like them: for he 2506
Jer 12:10 have trodden my **p.** under foot, 2513
Jer 12:10 pleasant **p.** a desolate wilderness. 2513
Jer 13:25 the **p.** of thy measures from me, 4490
Jer 51:19 The **p.** of Jacob is not like them; 2506
Jer 52:34 day a **p.** until the day of his death, 1697
La 3:24 The Lord is my **p.**, saith my soul; 2506
Eze 45:1 unto the Lord, an holy **p.** of the land:
Eze 45:4 The holy **p.** of the land shall be for
Eze 45:6 against the oblation of the holy **p.**:
Eze 45:7 And a **p.** shall be for the prince on the
Eze 45:7 other side of the oblation of the holy **p.**,
Eze 45:7 before the oblation of the holy **p.**, and
Eze 48:1 are his sides east and west, a **p.** for Dan:
Eze 48:2 side unto the west side, a **p.** for Asher.
Eze 48:3 unto the west side, a **p.** for Naphtali.
Eze 48:4 unto the west side, a **p.** for Manasseh.
Eze 48:5 unto the west side, a **p.** for Ephraim.
Eze 48:6 unto the west side, a **p.** for Reuben.
Eze 48:7 unto the west side, a **p.** for Judah.
Eze 48:18 against the oblation of the holy **p.**
Eze 48:18 against the oblation of the holy **p.**;
Eze 48:23 west side, Benjamin shall have a **p.**
Eze 48:24 the west side, Simeon shall have a **p.**
Eze 48:25 side unto the west side, Issachar a **p.**
Eze 48:26 side unto the west side, Zebulun a **p.**
Eze 48:27 east side unto the west side, Gad a **p.**
Da 1:8 with the **p.** of the king's meat, nor 6598
Da 1:13 eat of the **p.** of the king's meat: 6598
Da 1:15 did eat the **p.** of the king's meat. 6598
Da 1:16 took away the **p.** of their meat, and 6598
Da 4:15 let his **p.** be with the beasts in the 2508
Da 4:23 let his **p.** be with the beasts of the 2508
Da 11:26 they that feed of the **p.** of his meat 6598
Mic 2:4 hath changed the **p.** of my people: 2506
Hab 1:16 by them their **p.** is fat, and their 2506
Zec 2:12 Lord shall inherit Judah his **p.** in 2506
Mt 24:51 him his **p.** with the hypocrites: *3313*
Lu 12:42 their **p.** of meat in due season? *4620*
Lu 12:46 him his **p.** with the unbelievers. *3313*
Lu 15:12 give me the **p.** of goods that falleth *3313*

PORTIONS
De 18:8 shall have like **p.** to eat, besides 2506
Jos 17:5 fell ten **p.** to Manasseh, besides 2256
1Sa 1:4 her sons and her daughters **p.**: 4490
2Ch 31:19 give **p.** to all the males among the 4490
Ne 8:10 and send **p.** unto them for whom 4490
Ne 8:12 and to send **p.**, and to make great 4490
Ne 12:44 **p.** of the law for the priests and 4521
Ne 12:47 gave the **p.** of the singers and the 4521
Ne 13:10 the **p.** of the Levites had not been 4521
Es 9:19 and of sending **p.** one to another. 4490
Es 9:22 and of sending **p.** one to another, 4490
Eze 45:7 shall be over against one of the **p.**, 2506
Eze 47:13 Israel: Joseph shall have two **p.** 2256

Eze 48:21 over against the **p.** for the prince: 2506
Eze 48:29 these are their **p.**, saith the Lord 4256
Ho 5:7 month devour them with their **p.**......... 2506

PORTRAY See POURTRAY.

POSSESS See also DISPOSSESS; POSSESSED; POSSESSEST; POSSESSETH; POSSESSING.

Ge 22:17 shall **p.** the gate of his enemies;......... 3423
Ge 24:60 let thy seed **p.** the gate of those........ 3423
Le 20:24 give it unto you to **p.** it, a land that.... 3423
Nu 13:30 Let us go up at once, and **p.** it; 3423
Nu 14:24 he went; and his seed shall **p.** it. 3423
Nu 27:11 of his family, and he shall **p.** it: 3423
Nu 33:53 I have given you the land to **p.** it. 3423
De 1:8 **p.** the land which the Lord sware....... 3423
De 1:21 go up and **p.** it, as the Lord God of.... 3423
De 1:39 will I give it, and they shall **p.** it. 3423
De 2:24 begin to **p.** it, and contend with......... 3423
De 2:31 begin to **p.**, that thou mayest 3423
De 3:18 hath given you this land to **p.** it: 3423
De 3:20 until they also **p.** the land which......... 3423
De 4:1 go in and **p.** the land which the.......... 3423
De 4:5 in the land whither ye go to **p.** it. 3423
De 4:14 the land whither ye go over to **p.** it.... 3423
De 4:22 shall go over, and **p.** that good land. ... 3423
De 4:26 ye go over Jordan to **p.** it; ye shall..... 3423
De 5:31 the land which I give them to **p.** it. 3423
De 5:33 days in the land which ye shall **p.**........ 3423
De 6:1 in the land whither ye go to **p.** it: 3423
De 6:18 mayest go in and **p.** the good land...... 3423
De 7:1 the land whither thou goest to **p.** it, ... 3423
De 8:1 and go in and **p.** the land which the 3423
De 9:1 **p.** nations greater and mightier 3423
De 9:4 hath brought me in to **p.** this land: 3423
De 9:5 heart, dost thou go to **p.** their land:.... 3423
De 9:6 land to **p.** it for thy righteousness;...... 3423
De 9:23 and **p.** the land which I have given 3423
De 10:11 they may go in and **p.** the land, ... 3423
De 11:8 be strong, and go in and **p.** the land, .. 3423
De 11:8 the land, whither ye go to **p.** it;......... 3423
De 11:10 whither thou goest in to **p.** it, is 3423
De 11:11 the land, whither ye go to **p.** it, is a.... 3423
De 11:23 **p.** greater nations and mightier 3423
De 11:29 the land whither thou goest to **p.** it, ... 3423
De 11:31 over Jordan to go in to **p.** the land 3423
De 11:31 you, and ye shall **p.** it, and dwell........ 3423
De 12:1 of thy fathers giveth thee to **p.** it, ... 3423
De 12:2 nations which ye shall **p.** served......... 3423
De 12:29 whither thou goest to **p.** them, and..... 3423
De 15:4 thee for an inheritance to **p.** it: 3423
De 17:14 shalt **p.** it, and shalt dwell therein,...... 3423
De 18:14 these nations, which thou shalt **p.**,....... 3423
De 19:2, 14 Lord thy God giveth thee to **p.** it... 3423
De 21:1 Lord thy God giveth thee to **p.** it, ... 3423
De 23:20 land whither thou goest to **p.** it.......... 3423
De 25:19 giveth thee an inheritance to **p.** it,...... 3423
De 28:21 land, whither thou goest to **p.** it......... 3423
De 28:63 land whither thou goest to **p.** it.......... 3423
De 30:5 possessed, and thou shalt **p.** it;.......... 3423
De 30:16 land whither thou goest to **p.** it.......... 3423
De 30:18 passest over Jordan to go to **p.** it........ 3423
De 31:3 before thee, and thou shalt **p.** them: ... 3423
De 31:13 whither ye go over Jordan to **p.** it. 3423
De 32:47 whither ye go over Jordan to **p.** it. 3423
De 33:23 **p.** thou the west and the south........... 3423
Jos 1:11 this Jordan, to go in to **p.** the land,..... 3423
Jos 1:11 Lord your God giveth you to **p.** it. 3423
Jos 18:3 long are ye slack to go to **p.** the land,. 3423
Jos 23:5 ye shall **p.** their land, as the Lord 3423
Jos 24:4 gave unto Esau mount Seir, to **p.** it;... 3423
Jos 24:8 hand, that ye might **p.** their land; 3423
Jg 2:6 unto his inheritance to **p.** the land. 3423
Jg 11:23 Israel, and shouldest thou **p.** it? 3423
Jg 11:24 Wilt not thou **p.** that which 3423
Jg 11:24 Chemosh thy god giveth thee to **p.**? ... 3423
Jg 11:24 out from before us, them will we **p.**.... 3423
Jg 18:9 to go, and to enter to **p.** the land....... 3423
1Ki 21:18 whither he is gone down to **p.** it. 3423
1Ch 28:8 that ye may **p.** this good land, and...... 3423
Ezr 9:11 The land, unto which ye go to **p.** it, ... 3423
Neh 9:15 they should go in to **p.** the land 3423
Neh 9:23 that they should go in to **p.** it............ 3423
Job 7:3 I made to **p.** months of vanity, ... 5157
Job 13:26 to **p.** the iniquities of my youth.......... 3423
Isa 14:2 house of Israel shall **p.** them in......... 5157
Isa 14:21 do not rise, nor **p.** the land, nor 3423
Isa 34:11 and the bittern shall **p.** it; the owl...... 3423
Isa 34:17 they shall **p.** it forever, from............. 3423
Isa 57:13 his trust in me shall **p.** the land, ... 5157
Isa 61:7 their land they shall **p.**...double: 3423
Jer 30:3 their fathers, and they shall **p.** it. 3423
Eze 7:24 and they shall **p.** their houses: 3423
Eze 33:25 blood: and shall ye **p.** the land? 3423
Eze 33:26 wife: and shall ye **p.** the land? 3423
Eze 35:10 shall be mine, and we will **p.** it; 3423
Eze 36:12 and they shall **p.** thee, and thou......... 3423
Da 7:18 **p.** the kingdom for ever, even for 2631
Ho 9:6 their silver, nettles shall **p.** them:....... 3423
Am 2:10 to **p.** the land of the Amorite............ 3423
Am 9:12 they may **p.** the remnant of Edom,..... 3423
Ob 17 of Jacob shall **p.** their possessions....... 3423
Ob 19 south shall **p.** the mount of Esau;....... 3423
Ob 19 they shall **p.** the fields of Ephraim, ... 3423
Ob 19 and Benjamin shall **p.** Gilead. ....
Ob 20 shall **p.** that of the Canaanites,...............
Ob 20 shall **p.** the cities of the south............ 423
Hab 1:6 **p.** the dwellingplaces that are not......... 423
Zep 2:9 remnant of my people shall **p.**............ 5157
Zec 8:12 this people to **p.** all these things. 5157
Lu 18:12 **I give tithes of all that I p.**........... *2932*
Lu 21:19 **In your patience p. ye your souls.** ..*2932*
1Th 4:4 **p.** his vessel in sanctification and........ *2932*

POSSESSED See also DISPOSSESSED.

Nu 21:24 and **p.** his land from Arnon unto......... 3423
Nu 21:35 them alive: and they **p.** his land. 3423
De 3:12 this land which we **p.** at that time, ... 3423
De 4:47 they **p.** his land, and the land of Og.... 3423
De 30:5 the land which thy fathers **p.**,............ 3423
Jos 1:15 they also have **p.** the land which 3423
Jos 12:1 **p.** their land on the other side 3423
Jos 13:1 yet very much land to be **p.**.............. 3423
Jos 19:47 the edge of the sword, and **p.** it, ... 3423
Jos 21:43 and they **p.** it, and dwelt therein. 3423
Jos 22:9 possession, whereof they were **p.**, ... 270
Jg 3:13 and **p.** the city of palm trees. 3423
Jg 11:21 **p.** all the land of the Amorites, ... 3423
Jg 11:22 **p.** all the coasts of the Amorites, ... 3423
2Ki 17:24 **p.** Samaria, and dwelt in the cities...... 3423
Ne 9:22 so they **p.** the land of Sihon, and........ 3423
Ne 9:24 children went in and **p.** the land, ... 3423
Ne 9:25 **p.** houses full of all goods, wells......... 3423
Ps 139:13 For thou hast **p.** my reins: thou......... 7069
Pr 8:22 Lord **p.** me in the beginning of 7069
Isa 63:18 people of thy holiness have **p.** it......... 3423
Jer 32:15 shall be **p.** again in this land. 7069
Jer 32:23 And they came in, and **p.** it; but 3423
Da 7:22 that the saints **p.** the kingdom. 2631
Mt 4:24 those which were **p.** with devils, ... *1139*
Mt 8:16 many that were **p.** with devils; *1139*
Mt 8:28 there met him two **p.** with devils, ... *1139*
Mt 8:33 befallen to the **p.** of the devils. *1139*
Mt 9:32 him a dumb man **p.** with a devil. *1139*
Mt 12:22 one **p.** with a devil, blind, and........... *1139*
Mk 1:32 and them that were **p.** with devils. *1139*
Mk 5:15 see him that was **p.** with the devil,..... *1139*
Mk 5:16 to him that was **p.** with the devil,...... *1139*
Mk 5:18 had been **p.** with the devil prayed........ *1139*
Lu 8:36 was **p.** of the devils was healed. *1139*
Ac 4:32 aught of the things which he **p.**........... *5224*
Ac 8:7 of many that were **p.** with them:........ *2192*
Ac 16:16 damsel **p.** with a spirit of divination..... *2192*
1Co 7:30 that buy, as though they **p.** not;......... *2722*

POSSESSEST

De 26:1 and **p.** it, and dwellest therein; 3423

POSSESSETH

Nu 36:8 daughter, that **p.** an inheritance.......... 3423
Lu 12:15 **abundance of...things which he p.** . *5224*

POSSESSING

2Co 6:10 nothing, and yet **p.** all things. *2722*

POSSESSION See also POSSESSIONS.

Ge 17:8 Canaan, for an everlasting **p.**; 272
Ge 23:4 me a **p.** of a buryingplace with you,...... 272
Ge 23:9 **p.** of a buryingplace amongst you......... 272
Ge 23:18 Unto Abraham for a **p.** in the 4736
Ge 23:20 Abraham for a **p.** of a buryingplace....... 272
Ge 26:14 had **p.** of flocks, and **p.** of herds, ... 4735
Ge 36:43 habitations in the land of their **p.**: 272
Ge 47:11 them a **p.** in the land of Egypt, ... 272
Ge 48:4 seed after thee for an everlasting **p.**...... 272
Ge 49:30 Hittite for a **p.** of a buryingplace.......... 272
Ge 50:13 the field for a **p.** of a buryingplace........ 272
Le 14:34 Canaan, which I give to you for a **p.**,..... 272
Le 14:34 in a house of the land of your **p.**;.......... 272
Le 25:10 shall return every man unto his **p.**, ... 272
Le 25:13 shall return every man unto his **p.** 272
Le 25:24 all the land of your **p.** ye shall grant..... 272
Le 25:25 and hath sold away some of his **p.**, ... 272
Le 25:27 it; that he may return unto his **p.** 272
Le 25:28 and he shall return unto his **p.**............ 272
Le 25:32 the houses of the cities of their **p.**, ... 272
Le 25:33 the city of his **p.**, shall go out in the..... 272
Le 25:33 **p.** among the children of Israel............ 272
Le 25:34 be sold; for it is their perpetual **p.** 272
Le 25:41 unto the **p.** of his fathers shall he 272
Le 25:45 your land: and they shall be your **p.** 272
Le 25:46 after you, to inherit them for a **p.**; 272
Le 27:16 some part of a field of his **p.**, then....... 272
Le 27:21 the **p.** thereof shall be the priest's. 272
Le 27:22 which is not of the fields of his **p.**: 272
Le 27:24 whom the **p.** of the land did belong. 272
Le 27:28 his **p.** shall be sold or redeemed: 272
Nu 24:18 And Edom shall be a **p.**, Seir also 3424
Nu 24:18 Seir also shall be a **p.** for his............ 3424
Nu 26:56 According to the lot shall the **p.**......... 5159
Nu 27:4 Give unto us therefore a **p.** among....... 272
Nu 27:7 shalt surely give them a **p.** of an 272
Nu 32:5 be given unto thy servants for a **p.**, ... 272
Nu 32:22 shall be your **p.** before the Lord.......... 272
Nu 32:29 them the land of Gilead for a **p.**:.......... 272
Nu 32:32 **p.** of our inheritance on this side 272
Nu 35:2 the inheritance of their **p.** cities to 272
Nu 35:8 of the **p.** of the children of Israel: 272
Nu 35:28 shall return into the land of his **p.** 272
De 2:5 mount Seir unto Esau for a **p.** 3425
De 2:9 not give thee of their land for a **p.**;..... 3425
De 2:9 unto the children of Lot for a **p.**.......... 3425
De 2:12 land of his **p.**, which the Lord gave..... 3425
De 2:19 of the children of Ammon any **p.**; 3425
De 2:19 it unto the children of Lot for a **p.**....... 3425
De 3:20 ye return every man unto his **p.**, ... 3425
De 11:6 the substance that was in their **p.**,....... 7272
De 32:49 unto the children of Israel for a **p.**: 272
Jos 1:15 return unto the land of your **p.**, ... 3425
Jos 12:6 gave it for a **p.** unto the Reubenites,.... 3425
Jos 12:7 for a **p.** according to their divisions;.... 3425
Jos 13:29 this was the **p.** of the half tribe of...........
Jos 21:12 the son of Jephunneh for his **p.**.. 272
Jos 21:41 the **p.** of the children of Israel were..... 272
Jos 22:4 unto the land of your **p.**, which.......... 272
Jos 22:7 Moses had given **p.** in Bashan: ....
Jos 22:9 to the land of their **p.**, whereof they..... 272
Jos 22:19 if the land of your **p.** be unclean, ... 272
Jos 22:19 unto the land of the **p.** of the Lord,...... 272
Jos 22:19 dwelleth, and take **p.** among us: 270
1Ki 21:15 **p.** of the vineyard of Naboth the 3423
1Ki 21:16 the Jezreelite, to take **p.** of it. 3423
1Ki 21:19 Hast thou killed, and also taken **p.**? 3423
1Ch 28:1 **p.** of the king, and of his sons, ... 4735
2Ch 11:14 left their suburbs and their **p.**, ... 272
2Ch 20:11 to come to cast us out of thy **p.**, ... 3425
2Ch 31:1 every man to his **p.**, into their 272
Ne 11:3 every one in his **p.** in their cities, ... 272
Ps 2:8 parts of the earth for thy **p.**................ 272
Ps 44:3 got not the land in **p.** by their own..... 3423
Ps 69:35 may dwell there, and have it in **p.**...... 3423
Ps 83:12 ourselves the houses of God in **p.**...... 3423
Pr 28:10 shall have good things in **p.**.............. 5157
Isa 14:23 also make it a **p.** for the bittern, ... 4180
Eze 11:15 unto us is this land given in **p.**........... 4181
Eze 25:4 to the men of the east for a **p.**, ... 4181
Eze 25:10 and will give them in **p.**, that the 4181
Eze 36:2 ancient high places are ours in **p.**: 4181
Eze 36:3 might be a **p.** unto the residue of........ 4181
Eze 36:5 appointed my land into their **p.** 4181
Eze 44:28 them no **p.** in Israel: I am their **p.**....... 272
Eze 45:5 for a **p.** for twenty chambers. 272
Eze 45:6 ye shall appoint the **p.** of the city......... 272
Eze 45:7 and of the **p.** of the city, before the 272
Eze 45:7 before the **p.** of the city, from the 272
Eze 45:8 In the land shall be his **p.** in Israel: 272
Eze 46:16 it shall be their **p.** by inheritance. 272
Eze 46:18 to thrust them out of their **p.**; but 272
Eze 46:18 sons inheritance out of his own **p.**:....... 272
Eze 46:18 not scattered every man from his **p.**...... 272
Eze 48:20 foursquare, with the **p.** of the city........ 272
Eze 48:21 and of the **p.** of the city, over............ 272
Eze 48:22 Moreover, from the **p.** of the Levites, .. 272
Eze 48:22 Levites, and from the **p.** of the city,..... 272

Ac 5:1 with Sapphira his wife, sold a **p.**, *2933*
Ac 7:5 he would give it to him for a **p.**, *2697*
Ac 7:45 Jesus into the **p.** of the Gentiles, *2697*
Eph 1:14 redemption of the purchased **p.**, *4047*

POSSESSIONS
Ge 34:10 therein,and get you **p.** therein. 270
Ge 47:27 and they had **p.** therein, and grew, 270
Nu 32:30 have **p.** among you in the land. 270
1Sa 25:2 Maon, whose **p.** were in Carmel; 4639
1Ch 7:28 And their **p.** and habitations were, 272
1Ch 9:2 that dwelt in their **p.** in their cities 272
2Ch 32:29 cities, and **p.** of flocks and herds in 4735
Ec 2:7 great **p.** of great and small cattle 4735
Ob 17 of Jacob shall possess their **p.** 4180
Mt 19:22 sorrowful: for he had great **p.** *2933*
Mk 10:22 grieved: for he had great **p.** *2933*
Ac 2:45 And sold their **p.** and goods, and *2933*
Ac 28:7 quarters were **p.** of the chief man *5564*

POSSESSOR See also POSSESSORS.
Ge 14:19 high God, **p.** of heaven and earth: 7069
Ge 14:22 God, the **p.** of heaven and earth, 7069

POSSESSORS
Zec 11:5 Whose **p.** slay them, and hold 7069
Ac 4:34 **p.** of lands or houses sold them, *2935*

POSSIBLE See also IMPOSSIBLE.
Mt 19:26 **but with God all things are p.** *1415*
Mt 24:24 **if it were p., they shall deceive** *1415*
Mt 26:39 **it be p., let this cup pass from me:** *1415*
Mk 9:23 **things are p. to him that believeth** *1415*
Mk 10:27 **God: for with God all things are p.** *1415*
Mk 13:22 **if it were p., even the elect,** *1415*
Mk 14:35 if it were **p.**, the hour might pass *1415*
Mk 14:36 **Father, all things are p. unto thee;** *1415*
Lu 18:27 **impossible with men are p. with** *1415*
Ac 2:24 not **p.** that he should be holden of it. *1415*
Ac 20:16 it were **p.** for him, to be at Jerusalem. *1415*
Ac 27:39 if it were **p.**, to thrust in the ship. *1410*
Ro 12:18 If it be **p.**, as much as lieth in you, *1415*
Ga 4:15 if it had been **p.**, ye would have *1415*
Heb 10:4 it is not **p.** that the blood of bulls *102*

POST See also POSTS.
Ex 12:7 on the upper door **p.** of the houses, 4947
Ex 21:6 to the door, or unto the door **p.**; 4201
1Sa 1:9 upon a seat by a **p.** of the temple 4201
Job 9:25 Now my days are swifter than a **p.** 7323
Jer 51:31 One **p.** shall run to meet another, 7323
Eze 40:14 the **p.** of the court round about the 352
Eze 40:16 and upon each **p.** were palm trees. 352
Eze 40:48 and measured each **p.** of the porch, 352
Eze 41:3 and measured the **p.** of the door, two 352
Eze 43:8 their **p.** by my posts, and the wall 4201
Eze 46:2 and shall stand by the **p.** of the gate, 4201

POSTERITY
Ge 45:7 to preserve you a **p.** in the earth, 7611
Nu 9:10 you or of your **p.** shall be unclean 1755
1Ki 16:3 I will take away the **p.** of Baasha, 310
1Ki 16:3 and the **p.** of his house; and will 310
1Ki 21:21 will take away thy **p.**, and will cut 310
Ps 49:13 yet their **p.** approve their sayings. 310
Ps 109:13 Let his **p.** be cut off; and in the 319
Da 11:4 and not to his **p.**, nor according to 319
Am 4:2 hooks, and your **p.** with fishhooks. 319

POSTS
Ex 12:7 and strike it on the two side **p.** 4201
Ex 12:22 and the two side **p.** with the blood 4201
Ex 12:23 the lintel, and on the two side **p.**, 4201
De 6:9 write them upon the **p.** of thy house, 4201
De 11:20 write them upon the door **p.** of 4201
Jg 16:3 gate of the city, and the two **p.**, 4201
1Ki 6:31 lintel and side **p.** were a fifth part 4201
1Ki 6:33 for the door of the temple **p.** of olive 4201
1Ki 7:5 all the doors and **p.** were square, 4201
2Ch 3:7 beams, the **p.**, and...walls thereof, 5592
2Ch 30:6 **p.** went with the letters from the 7323
2Ch 30:10 the **p.** passed from city to city 7323
Es 3:13 the letters were sent by **p.** into all 7323
Es 3:15 The **p.** went out, being hastened by 7323
Es 8:10 and sent letters by **p.** on horseback, 7323
Es 8:14 So the **p.** that rode upon mules and 7323
Pr 8:34 waiting at the **p.** of my doors. 4201
Isa 6:4 the **p.** of the door moved at the 520
Isa 57:8 Behind the doors also and the **p.** 4201
Eze 40:9 and the **p.** thereof, two cubits; and 352
Eze 40:10 **p.** had one measure on this side and 352
Eze 40:14 made also **p.** of threescore cubits, 352
Eze 40:16 **p.** within the gate round about, 352
Eze 40:21 the **p.** thereof and the arches thereof 352
Eze 40:24 he measured the **p.** thereof and the 352
Eze 40:26 on that side, upon the **p.** thereof. 352
Eze 40:29 chambers thereof, and the **p.** thereof, 352
Eze 40:31 palm trees were upon the **p.** thereof: 352
Eze 40:33 chambers thereof, and the **p.** thereof 352
Eze 40:34 palm trees were upon the **p.** thereof, 352
Eze 40:36 chambers thereof, the **p.** thereof, 352
Eze 40:37 **p.** thereof were toward the utter 352
Eze 40:37 palm trees were upon the **p.** thereof, 352
Eze 40:38 thereof were by the **p.** of the gates, 352
Eze 40:49 there were pillars by the **p.**, one on 352
Eze 41:1 measured the **p.**, six cubits broad on 352
Eze 41:16 door **p.**, and the narrow windows, 5592
Eze 41:21 The **p.** of the temple were squared, 4201
Eze 43:8 their post by my **p.**, and the wall 4201
Eze 45:19 and put it upon the **p.** of the house, 4201
Eze 45:19 upon the **p.** of the gate of the inner 4201
Am 9:1 the door, that the **p.** may shake: 5592

POT See also POTS; POTSHERD; WASHPOT; WATERPOT.
Ex 16:33 Take a **p.**, and put an omer full of 6803
Le 6:28 if it be sodden in a brasen **p.**, it 3627
Jg 6:19 and he put the broth in a **p.**, and 6517
1Sa 2:14 pan, or kettle, or caldron, or **p.**; 6517
2Ki 4:2 thing in the house, save a **p.** of oil. 610
2Ki 4:38 his servant, Set on the great **p.**, 5518
2Ki 4:39 shred them into the **p.** of pottage: 5518
2Ki 4:40 man of God, there is death in the **p.** 5518
2Ki 4:41 meal. And he cast it into the **p.**; 5518
2Ki 4:41 And there was no harm in the **p.** 5518
Job 41:20 as out of a seething **p.** or caldron. 1731
Job 41:31 maketh the deep to boil like a **p.** 5518
Job 41:31 the sea like a **p.** of ointment.
Pr 17:3 The fining **p.** is for silver, and the 4715
Pr 27:21 As the fining **p.** for silver, and the 4715
Ec 7:6 the crackling of thorns under a **p.**, 5518
Jer 1:13 I said, I see a seething **p.**; and the 5518
Eze 24:3 Set on a **p.**, set it on, and also 5518
Eze 24:6 to the **p.** whose scum is therein, 5518
Mic 3:3 chop them in pieces, as for the **p.**, 5518
Zec 14:21 every **p.** in Jerusalem and in Judah 5518
Heb 9:4 was the golden **p.** that had manna, *4713*

POTENT See IMPOTENT.

POTENTATE
1Ti 6:15 who is the blessed and only **P.**, the *1413*

POTI See POTI-PHERAH.

POTIPHAR (pot'i-far)
Ge 37:36 sold him into Egypt unto **P.**, an 6318
Ge 39:1 **P.**, an officer of Pharaoh, captain 6318

POTI-PHERAH (po-tif'e-rah)
Ge 41:45 the daughter of **P.** priest of On 6319
Ge 41:50 the daughter of **P.** priest of On bare 6319
Ge 46:20 the daughter of **P.** priest of On bare 6319

POTS See also WATERPOTS.
Ex 16:3 when we sat by the flesh **p.**, and 5518
Ex 38:3 **p.**, and the shovels, and the basons, 5518
Le 11:35 whether it be oven, or ranges for **p.**,
1Ki 7:45 the **p.**, and the shovels, and the 5518
2Ki 25:14 the **p.**, and the shovels, and the 5518
2Ch 4:11 And Huram made the **p.**, and the 5518
2Ch 4:16 The **p.** also, and the shovels, and the 5518
2Ch 35:13 other holy offerings sod they in **p.**, 5518
Ps 58:9 Before your **p.** can feel the thorns, 5518
Ps 68:13 Though ye have lien among the **p.**, 8240
Ps 81:6 hands were delivered from the **p.** 1731
Jer 35:5 of the Rechabites **p.** full of wine, 1375
Zec 14:20 **p.** in the Lord's house shall be like 5518
Mk 7:4 **p.**, brasen vessels, and of tables. *3582*
Mk 7:8 **as the washing of p. and cups:** *3582*

POTSHERD See also POTSHERDS.
Job 2:8 he took him a **p.** to scrape himself 2789
Ps 22:15 My strength is dried up like a **p.**; 2789
Pr 26:23 and a wicked heart are like a **p.** 2789
Isa 45:9 Let the **p.** strive with the potsherds 2789

POTSHERDS
Isa 45:9 Let the potsherd strive with the **p.** 2789

POTTAGE
Ge 25:29 And Jacob sod **p.**: and Esau came 5138
Ge 25:30 I pray thee, with that same red **p.**;
Ge 25:34 gave Esau bread and **p.** of lentiles; 5138
2Ki 4:38 and seethe **p.** for the sons of the 5138
2Ki 4:39 and shred them into the pot of **p.** 5138
2Ki 4:40 pass, as they were eating of the **p.**, 5138
Hag 2:12 with his skirt do touch bread, or **p.**, 5138

POTTER See also POTTER'S; POTTERS.
Isa 41:25 morter, and as the **p.** treadeth clay. 3335
Isa 64:8 we are the clay, and thou our **p.**; 3335
Jer 18:4 was marred in the hand of the **p.** 3335
Jer 18:4 as seemed good to the **p.** to make it 3335
Jer 18:6 cannot I do with you as this **p.**? 3335
La 4:2 the work of the hands of the **p.**! 3335
Zec 11:13 said unto me, Cast it unto the **p.** 3335
Zec 11:13 cast them to the **p.** in the house of 3335
Ro 9:21 not the **p.** power over the clay, *2763*
Re 2:27 **as the vessels of a p. shall they be** *2764*

POTTER'S
Ps 2:9 them in pieces like a **p.** vessel. 3335
Isa 29:16 shall be esteemed as the **p.** clay: 3335
Jer 18:2 Arise, and go down to the **p.** house, 3335
Jer 18:3 I went down to the **p.** house, and, 3335
Jer 18:6 Behold, as the clay is in the **p.** hand, 3335
Jer 19:1 Go and get a **p.** earthen bottle, and 3335
Jer 19:11 city, as one breaketh a **p.** vessel, 3335
Da 2:41 part of **p.** clay, and part of iron, 6353
Mt 27:7 bought with them the **p.** field, to *2763*
Mt 27:10 And gave them for the **p.** field, as *2763*

POTTERS See also POTTERS'.
1Ch 4:23 These were the **p.**, and those that 3335

POTTERS'
Isa 30:14 **p.** vessel that is broken in pieces; 3335

POUND See also POUNDS.
1Ki 10:17 three **p.** of gold went to one shield: 4488
Ezr 2:69 five thousand **p.** of silver, and one 4488
Ne 7:71 and two hundred **p.** of silver. 4488
Ne 7:72 gold, and two thousand **p.** of silver, 4488
Lu 19:16 **thy p. hath gained ten pounds** *3414*
Lu 19:18 **thy p. hath gained five pounds** *3414*
Lu 19:20 **here is thy p., which I have kept** *3414*
Lu 19:24 **Take from him the p., and give it** *3414*
Joh 12:3 a **p.** of ointment of spikenard. *3046*
Joh 19:39 aloes, about a hundred **p.** weight. *3046*

POUNDS
Lu 19:13 **and delivered them ten p.,** *3414*
Lu 19:16 **thy pound hath gained ten p.** *3414*
Lu 19:18 **thy pound hath gained five p.** *3414*
Lu 19:24 **and give it to him that hath ten p.** *3414*
Lu 19:25 **unto him, Lord, he hath ten p.** *3414*

POUR See also POURED; POURETH; POURING.
Ex 4:9 river, and **p.** it upon the dry land: 8210
Ex 29:7 and **p.** it upon his head, and anoint 3332
Ex 29:12 **p.** all the blood beside the bottom 8210
Ex 30:9 shall ye **p.** drink offering thereon. 5258
Le 2:1 and he shall **p.** oil upon it, and put 3332
Le 2:6 part it in pieces, and **p.** oil thereon: 3332
Le 4:7 shall **p.** all the blood of the bullock 8210
Le 4:18 **p.** out all the blood at the bottom 8210
Le 4:25 shall **p.** out his blood at the bottom 8210
Le 4:30 **p.** out all the blood thereof at the 8210
Le 4:34 shall **p.** out all the blood thereof at 8210
Le 14:15 **p.** it into the palm of his own left 3332
Le 14:18 he shall **p.** upon the head of him 5414
Le 14:26 priest shall **p.** of the oil into the 3332
Le 14:41 they shall **p.** out the dust that they 8210
Le 17:13 shall even **p.** out the blood thereof, 8210
Nu 5:15 he shall **p.** no oil upon it, nor put 3332
Nu 24:7 **p.** the water out of his buckets, 5140
De 12:16 shall **p.** it upon the earth as water. 8210
De 12:24 shalt **p.** it upon the earth as water. 8210
De 15:23 shalt **p.** it upon the ground as water. 8210
Jg 6:20 this rock, and **p.** out the broth. 8210
1Ki 18:33 and **p.** it on the burnt sacrifice, 3332
2Ki 4:4 **p.** out into all those vessels, and 3332
2Ki 4:41 **P.** out for the people, that they may 3332
2Ki 9:3 the box of oil, and **p.** it on his head, 3332
Job 36:27 they **p.** down rain according to the 2212
Ps 42:4 things, I **p.** out my soul in me: 8210
Ps 62:8 **p.** out your heart before him: God 8210
Ps 69:24 **P.** out thine indignation upon them, 8210
Ps 79:6 **P.** out thy wrath upon the heathen 8210
Pr 1:23 I will **p.** out my spirit unto you, I 5042
Isa 44:3 **p.** water upon him that is thirsty, 3332
Isa 44:3 I will **p.** my spirit upon thy seed, 3332

Isa 45:8 the skies **p.** down righteousness:........ 5140
Jer 6:11 **p.** it out upon the children abroad,...... 8210
Jer 7:18 to **p.** out drink offerings unto other..... 5258
Jer 10:25 **P.** out thy fury upon the heathen....... 8210
Jer 14:16 will **p.** their wickedness upon them. 8210
Jer 18:21 **p.** out their blood by the force of....... 5064
Jer 44:17, 18,19,25 **p.** out drink offerings unto.... 5258
La 2:19 **p.** out thine heart like water.............. 8210
Eze 7:8 I shortly **p.** out my fury upon thee, ... 8210
Eze 14:19 and **p.** my fury upon it in blood,.... 8210
Eze 20:8 I will **p.** out my fury upon them, ... 8210
Eze 20:13 **p.** out my fury upon them in the........ 8210
Eze 20:21 I would **p.** out my fury upon them,...... 8210
Eze 21:31 **p.** out mine indignation upon thee,...... 8210
Eze 24:3 set it on, and also **p.** water into it:..... 3332
Eze 30:15 And I will **p.** my fury upon Sin, the 8210
Ho 5:10 **p.** out my wrath upon them like......... 8210
Joe 2:28 will **p.** out my spirit upon all flesh;...... 8210
Joe 2:29 those days will I **p.** out my spirit........ 8210
Mic 1:6 I will **p.** down the stones thereof........ 5064
Ze 3:8 to **p.** upon them mine indignation,......... 8210
Zec 12:10 I will **p.** upon the house of David, ... 8210
Mal 3:10 heaven, and **p.** you out a blessing,...... 7324
Ac 2:17 **p.** out of my Spirit upon all flesh: *1632*
Ac 2:18 **p.** out in those days of my Spirit;....... *1632*
Re 16:1 **p.** out the vials of the wrath of God.... *1632*

POURED See also POUREDST.
Ge 28:18 pillar, and **p.** oil upon the top of it. 3332
Ge 35:14 and he **p.** a drink offering thereon, ... 5258
Ge 35:14 and he **p.** oil thereon....................... 3332
Ex 9:33 the rain was not **p.** upon the earth. 5413
Ex 30:32 Upon man's flesh shall it not be **p.**,...... 3251
Le 4:12 place, where the ashes are **p.** out, ... 8211
Le 4:12 where the ashes are **p.** out shall he.... 8211
Le 8:12 And he **p.** of the anointing oil upon..... 3332
Le 8:15 **p.** the blood at the bottom of the 3332
Le 9:9 **p.** out the blood at the bottom of....... 3332
Le 21:10 whose head the anointing oil was **p.**,... 3332
Nu 28:7 cause the strong wine to be **p.** 5258
De 12:27 **p.** out upon the altar of the Lord 8210
1Sa 1:15 **p.** out my soul before the Lord.......... 8210
1Sa 7:6 water, and **p.** it out before the Lord, .. 8210
1Sa 10:1 vial of oil, and **p.** it upon his head,...... 3332
2Sa 13:9 a pan, and **p.** them out before him;...... 3332
2Sa 23:16 thereof, but **p.** it out unto the Lord. ... 5258
1Ki 13:3 that are upon it shall be **p.** out. 8210
1Ki 13:5 and the ashes **p.** out from the altar,.... 8210
2Ki 3:11 **p.** water on the hands of Elijah. 3332
2Ki 4:5 the vessels to her; and she **p.** out....... 3332
2Ki 4:40 So they **p.** out for the men to eat. 3332
2Ki 9:6 he **p.** the oil on his head, and said...... 3332
2Ki 16:13 **p.** his drink offering, and sprinkled...... 5258
1Ch 11:18 drink of it, but **p.** it out to the Lord.... 5258
2Ch 12:7 my wrath shall not be **p.** out upon...... 5413
2Ch 34:21 wrath of the Lord that is **p.** out upon.. 5413
2Ch 34:25 my wrath shall be **p.** out upon this...... 5413
Job 3:24 roarings are **p.** out like the waters...... 5413
Job 10:10 Hast thou not **p.** me out as milk, ... 5413
Job 29:6 the rock **p.** me out rivers of oil;......... 6694
Job 30:16 now my soul is **p.** out upon me;......... 8210
Ps 22:14 I am **p.** out like water, and all my...... 8210
Ps 45:2 grace is **p.** into thy lips: therefore 3332
Ps 77:17 The clouds **p.** out water: the skies..... 2229
Ps 142:2 **p.** out my complaint before him;......... 8210
Ca 1:3 thy name is as ointment **p.** forth, ... 7324
Isa 26:16 they **p.** out a prayer when thy........... 6694
Isa 29:10 hath **p.** out upon you the spirit 5258
Isa 32:15 spirit be **p.** upon us from on high, ... 6168
Isa 42:25 **p.** upon him the fury of his anger, ... 8210
Isa 53:12 hath **p.** out his soul unto death: 6168
Isa 57:6 hast thou **p.** a drink offering, thou 8210
Jer 7:20 my fury shall be **p.** out upon this......... 5413
Jer 19:13 **p.** out drink offerings unto other 5258
Jer 32:29 **p.** out drink offerings unto other 5258
Jer 42:18 and my fury hath been **p.** forth.......... 5413
Jer 42:18 so shall my fury be **p.** forth upon 5413
Jer 44:6 fury and mine anger was **p.** forth,....... 5413
Jer 44:19 **p.** out drink offerings unto her,.......... 5258
La 2:4 Zion: he **p.** out his fury like fire......... 8210
La 2:11 my liver is **p.** upon the earth, for....... 8210
La 2:12 **p.** out into their mothers' bosom. 8210
La 4:1 **p.** out in the top of every street. 8210
La 4:11 he hath **p.** out his fierce anger, and..... 8210
Eze 16:36 Because thy filthiness was **p.** out, ... 8210
Eze 20:28 **p.** out there their drink offerings. 5258
Eze 20:33 with fury **p.** out, will I rule over 8210
Eze 20:34 out arm, and with fury **p.** out. 8210
Eze 22:22 Lord have **p.** out my fury upon you. ... 8210
Eze 22:31 I **p.** out mine indignation upon........... 8210
Eze 23:8 and **p.** their whoredom upon her. 8210
Eze 24:7 she **p.** it not upon the ground, to....... 8210
Eze 36:18 Wherefore I **p.** my fury upon them..... 8210
Eze 39:29 **p.** out my spirit upon the house......... 8210
Da 9:11 therefore the curse is **p.** upon us, ... 5413
Da 9:27 shall be **p.** upon the desolate............. 5413
Mic 1:4 waters that are **p.** down a steep 5064
Na 1:6 his fury is **p.** out like fire, and the...... 5413
Zep 1:17 blood shall be **p.** out as dust, and....... 8210
Mt 26:7 ointment, and **p.** it on his head, ... *2708*
Mt 26:12 **hath p. this ointment on my body,**.. *906*
Mk 14:3 the box, and **p.** it on his head............ *2708*
Joh 2:15 and **p.** out the changers' money. *1632*
Ac 10:45 **p.** out the gift of the Holy Ghost......... *1632*
Re 14:10 **p.** out without mixture into the......... *2767*
Re 16:2 **p.** out his vial upon the earth;............ *1632*
Re 16:3 angel **p.** out his vial upon the sea; *1632*
Re 16:4 **p.** out his vial upon the rivers and...... *1632*
Re 16:8 angel **p.** out his vial upon the sun;...... *1632*
Re 16:10 angel **p.** out his vial upon the seat...... *1632*
Re 16:12 **p.** out his vial upon the great river..... *1632*
Re 16:17 angel **p.** out his vial into the air; *1632*

POUREDST
Eze 16:15 **p.** out thy fornications on every 8210

POURETH
Job 12:21 He **p.** contempt upon princes, and...... 8210
Job 16:13 **p.** out my gall upon the ground. 8210
Job 16:20 mine eye **p.** out tears unto God. 1811
Ps 75:8 **p.** out of the same: but the dregs....... 5064
Ps 102:*title* **p.** out his complaint before the 8210
Ps 107:40 He **p.** contempt upon princes, and...... 8210
Pr 15:2 mouth of fools **p.** out foolishness. 5042
Pr 15:28 of the wicked **p.** out evil things.......... 5042
Am 5:8 **p.** them out upon the face of the........ 8210
Am 9:6 **p.** them out upon the face of the........ 8210
Joh 13:5 After that he **p.** water into a bason, ... *906*

POURING
Eze 9:8 **p.** out of thy fury upon Jerusalem?...... 8210
Lu 10:34 **p. in oil and wine, and set him on his** ·

POURTRAY See also POURTRAYED.
Eze 4:1 and **p.** it upon the city, even............. 2710

POURTRAYED
Eze 8:10 **p.** upon the wall round about............. 2707
Eze 23:14 she saw men **p.** upon the wall, ... 2707
Eze 23:14 the Chaldeans **p.** with vermilion, ... 2710

POVERTY
Ge 45:11 and all that thou hast, come to **p.**....... 3423
Pr 6:11 thy **p.** come as one that travelleth, ... 7389
Pr 10:15 destruction of the poor is their **p.**....... 7389
Pr 11:24 than is meet, but it tendeth to **p.** 4270
Pr 13:18 **P.** and shame shall be to him that...... 7389
Pr 20:13 not sleep, lest thou come to **p.**; 3423
Pr 23:21 and the glutton shall come to **p.**:........ 3423
Pr 24:34 thy **p.** come as one that travelleth; 7389
Pr 28:19 vain persons shall have **p.** enough....... 7389
Pr 28:22 not that **p.** shall come upon him. 2639
Pr 30:8 give me neither **p.** nor riches; 7389
Pr 31:7 Let him drink, and forget his **p.**, ... 7389
2Co 8:2 deep **p.** abounded unto the riches....... *4432*
2Co 8:9 ye through his **p.** might be rich........... *4432*
Re 2:9 **thy works, and tribulation, and p.,** *4432*

POWDER See also POWDERS.
Ex 32:20 it in the fire, and ground it to **p.**, ... 1854
De 28:24 the rain of thy land **p.** and dust:............ 80
2Ki 23:6 and stamped it small to **p.**, and.......... 6083
2Ki 23:6 the **p.** thereof upon the graves of....... 6083
2Ki 23:15 stamped it small to **p.**, and burned...... 6083
2Ch 34:7 beaten the graven images into **p.**,........ 1854
Mt 21:44 **shall fall, it will grind him to p.** ... *3039*
Lu 20:18 **shall fall, it will grind him to p.** ... *3039*

POWDERS
Ca 3:6 with all **p.** of the merchant?.................. 81

POWER See also POWERFUL; POWERS.
Ge 31:6 with all my **p.** I have served your....... 3581
Ge 31:29 the **p.** of my hand to do you hurt:......... 410
Ge 32:28 prince hast **p.** with God and with........ 8280
Ge 49:3 dignity, and the excellency of **p.**:........ 5794
Ex 9:16 up, for to shew in thee my **p.**;............ 3581
Ex 15:6 O Lord, is become glorious in **p.**:......... 3581
Ex 21:8 strange nation he shall have no **p.**, ... 4910
Ex 32:11 the land of Egypt with great **p.**, ... 3581
Le 26:19 will break the pride of your **p.**; 5797
Le 26:37 **p.** to stand before your enemies......... 8617
Nu 14:17 let the **p.** of my lord be great,........... 3581
Nu 22:38 now any **p.** at all to say any thing? 3201
De 4:37 with his mighty **p.** out of Egypt; 3581
De 8:17 My **p.** and the might of mine hand....... 3581
De 8:18 that giveth thee **p.** to get wealth, ... 3581
De 9:29 broughtest out by thy mighty **p.**.......... 3581
De 32:36 he seeth that their **p.** is gone, and...... 3027
Jos 8:20 **p.** to flee this way or that way: 3027
Jos 17:17 a great people, and has great **p.**:......... 3581
1Sa 9:1 a Benjamite, a mighty man of **p.**. 2428
1Sa 30:4 until they had no more **p.** to weep...... 3581
2Sa 22:33 God is my strength and **p.**: and 2428
2Ki 17:36 the land of Egypt with great **p.**........... 3581
2Ki 19:26 their inhabitants were of small **p.**,........ 3027
1Ch 20:1 Joab led forth the **p.** of the army,........ 2428
1Ch 29:11 and the **p.**, and the glory, and the 1369
1Ch 29:12 in thine hand is **p.** and might; 3581
2Ch 14:11 or with them that have no **p.**:.............. 3581
2Ch 20:6 in thine hand is there not **p.** and 3581
2Ch 22:9 no **p.** to keep still the kingdom. 3581
2Ch 25:8 God hath **p.** to help, and to cast 3581
2Ch 26:13 that made war with mighty **p.**, to....... 3581
2Ch 32:9 Lachish, and all his **p.** with him,)......... 4475
Ezr 4:23 them to cease by force and **p.**. 2429
Ezr 8:22 his **p.** and his wrath is against all........ 5797
Ne 1:10 hast redeemed by thy great **p.**,........... 3581
Ne 5:5 is it in our **p.** to redeem them; 3027
Es 1:3 **p.** of Persia and Media, the nobles 2428
Es 8:11 **p.** of the people and province that...... 2428
Es 9:1 Jews hoped to have **p.** over them,........ 7980
Es 10:2 the acts of his **p.** and of his might, ... 8633
Job 1:12 all that he hath is in thy **p.**; only........ 3027
Job 5:20 in war from the **p.** of the sword.......... 3027
Job 21:7 old, yea, are mighty in **p.**?................ 2428
Job 23:6 against me with his great **p.**?............. 3581
Job 24:22 draweth also the mighty with his **p.**: ... 3581
Job 26:2 thou helped him that is without **p.**?..... 3581
Job 26:12 He divideth the sea with his **p.**, ... 3581
Job 26:14 but the thunder of his **p.** who can........ 1369
Job 36:22 Behold, God exalteth by his **p.**: 3581
Job 37:23 he is excellent in **p.**, and in................ 3581
Job 41:12 not conceal his parts, nor his **p.**,......... 1369
Ps 21:13 so will we sing and praise thy **p.**......... 1369
Ps 22:20 my darling from the **p.** of the dog....... 3027
Ps 37:35 I have seen the wicked in great **p.**, ... 6184
Ps 49:15 my soul from the **p.** of the grave: 3027
Ps 59:11 scatter them by thy **p.**; and bring........ 2428
Ps 59:16 But I will sing of thy **p.**; yea, I.......... 5797
Ps 62:11 this; that **p.** belongeth unto God......... 5797
Ps 63:2 To see thy **p.** and thy glory, so as I... 5797
Ps 65:6 mountains; being girded with **p.**: 1369
Ps 66:3 through the greatness of thy **p.** 5797
Ps 66:7 He ruleth by his **p.** for ever; his 1369
Ps 68:35 giveth strength and **p.** unto his 8592
Ps 71:18 thy **p.** to every one that is to come. ... 1369
Ps 78:26 by his **p.** he brought in the south....... 5797
Ps 79:11 according to the greatness of thy **p.**...... 2220
Ps 90:11 knoweth the **p.** of thine anger? 5797
Ps 106:8 make his mighty **p.** to be known. 1369
Ps 110:3 shall be willing in the day of thy **p.**, ... 2428
Ps 111:6 his people the **p.** of his works, ... 3581
Ps 145:11 thy kingdom, and talk of thy **p.**;.......... 1369
Ps 147:5 Great is our Lord, and of great **p.**: 3581
Ps 150:1 him in the firmament of his **p.**. 5797
Pr 3:27 it is in the **p.** of thine hand to do it. 410
Pr 18:21 and life are in the **p.** of the tongue: 3027
Ec 4:1 of their oppressors there was **p.**; 3581
Ec 5:19 hath given him **p.** to eat thereof,........ 7980
Ec 6:2 God giveth him not **p.** to eat thereof,.. 7980
Ec 8:4 the word of a king is, there is **p.**: 7983
Ec 8:8 no man that hath **p.** over the spirit...... 7989
Ec 8:8 hath he **p.** in the day of death:........... 7983
Isa 37:27 their inhabitants were of small **p.**,....... 3027
Isa 40:26 might, for that he is strong in **p.**; 3581
Isa 40:29 He giveth **p.** to the faint; and to 3581
Isa 43:17 and horse, the army and the **p.**;......... 5808
Isa 47:14 deliver...from the **p.** of the flame: 3027
Isa 50:2 redeem? or have I no **p.** to deliver?..... 3581
Jer 10:12 He hath made the earth by his **p.**,....... 3581
Jer 27:5 my great **p.** and by my outstretched ... 3581
Jer 32:17 by thy great **p.** and stretched out....... 3581
Jer 51:15 He hath made the earth by his **p.**,....... 3581

Eze 17:9 without great p. or many people 2220
Eze 22:6 in thee to their p. to shed blood. 2220
Eze 30:6 pride of her p. shall come down: 5797
Da 2:37 given thee a kingdom, p., and 2632
Da 3:27 whose bodies the fire had no p., 7981
Da 4:30 kingdom by the might of my p., 2632
Da 6:27 Daniel from the p. of the lions. 3028
Da 8:6 ran unto him in the fury of his p. 3581
Da 8:7 there was no p. in the ram to stand 3581
Da 8:22 out of the nation, but not in his p. 3581
Da 8:24 And his p. shall be mighty, but not 3581
Da 8:24 be mighty, but not by his own p.: 3581
Da 11:6 shall not retain the p. of the arm; 3581
Da 11:25 shall stir up his p. and his courage 3581
Da 11:43 have p. over the treasures of gold 4910
Da 12:7 to scatter the p. of the holy people, 3027
Ho 12:3 his strength he had p. with God: 8280
Ho 12:4 Yea, he had p. over the angel, and 7786
Ho 13:14 ransom…from the p. of the grave; 3027
Mic 2:1 because it is in the p. of their hand. 410
Mic 3:8 I am full of p. by the spirit of the 3581
Na 1:3 is slow to anger, and great in p., 3581
Na 2:1 loins, strong, fortify thy p. mightily 3581
Hab 1:11 imputing this his p. unto his god. 3581
Hab 2:9 be delivered from the p. of evil! 3709
Hab 3:4 and there was the hiding of his p. 5797
Zec 4:6 Not by might, nor by p., but by my 3581
Zec 9:4 he will smite her p. in the sea; 2428
Mt 6:13 **kingdom, and the p., and the** *1411*
Mt 9:6 **Son of man hath p. on earth to** *1849*
Mt 9:8 which had given such p. unto men. *1849*
Mt 10:1 he gave them p. against unclean *1849*
Mt 22:29 **the scriptures, nor the p. of God** *1411*
Mt 24:30 **of heaven with p. and great glory** *1411*
Mt 26:64 **sitting on the right hand of p.,** *1411*
Mt 28:18 **All p. is given unto me in heaven** *1849*
Mk 2:10 **Son of man hath p. on earth to** *1849*
Mk 3:15 And to have p. to heal sicknesses, *1849*
Mk 6:7 gave them p. over unclean spirits; *1849*
Mk 9:1 **the kingdom of God come with p.** *1411*
Mk 12:24 **scriptures, neither the p. of God?** *1411*
Mk 13:26 **the clouds with great p. and glory.** *1411*
Mk 14:62 **sitting on the right hand of p.,** *1411*
Lu 1:17 him in the spirit and p. of Elias, to *1411*
Lu 1:35 p. of the Highest shall overshadow *1411*
Lu 4:6 All this p. will I give thee, and the *1849*
Lu 4:14 returned in the p. of the Spirit into *1411*
Lu 4:32 doctrine: for his word was with p. *1849*
Lu 4:36 authority and p. he commandeth *1411*
Lu 5:17 p. of the Lord was present to heal *1411*
Lu 5:24 **Son of man hath p. upon earth to** *1849*
Lu 9:1 p. and authority over all devils, *1411*
Lu 9:43 amazed at the mighty p. of God. *3168*
Lu 10:19 **unto you p. to tread on serpents** *1849*
Lu 10:19 **and over all the p. of the enemy:** *1411*
Lu 12:5 **killed hath p. to cast into hell;** *1849*
Lu 20:20 p. and authority of the governor. *746*
Lu 21:27 **of man coming in a cloud with p.** *1411*
Lu 22:53 **your hour, and the p. of darkness.** *1849*
Lu 22:69 **on the right hand of the p. of God.** *1411*
Lu 24:49 **be endued with p. from on high.** *1411*
Joh 1:12 he p. to become the sons of God, *1849*
Joh 10:18 **I have p. to lay it down, and I** *1849*
Joh 10:18 **and I have p. to take it again.** *1849*
Joh 17:2 **hast given him p. over all flesh,** *1849*
Joh 19:10 not that I have p. to crucify thee, *1849*
Joh 19:10 thee, and have p. to release thee? *1849*
Joh 19:11 **have no p. at all against me,** *1849*
Ac 1:7 **the Father hath put in his own p.** *1849*
Ac 1:8 **But ye shall receive p., after that** *1411*
Ac 3:12 by our own p. or holiness we had *1411*
Ac 4:7 By what p., or by what name, have *1411*
Ac 4:33 great p. gave the apostles witness *1411*
Ac 5:4 sold, was it not in thine own p.? *1849*
Ac 6:8 Stephen, full of faith and p., did *1411*
Ac 8:10 This man is the great p. of God. *1411*
Ac 8:19 Saying, Give me also this p., that *1849*
Ac 10:38 with the Holy Ghost and with p.: *1411*
Ac 26:18 **and from the p. of Satan unto God,** *1849*
Ro 1:4 to be the Son of God with p., *1411*
Ro 1:16 it is the p. of God unto salvation *1411*
Ro 1:20 even his eternal p. and Godhead; *1411*
Ro 9:17 that I might shew my p. in thee, *1411*
Ro 9:21 not the potter p. over the clay, *1849*
Ro 9:22 wrath, and to make his p. known, *1415*
Ro 13:1 For there is no p. but of God: the *1849*
Ro 13:2 therefore resisteth the p., *1849*
Ro 13:3 thou then not be afraid of the p.? *1849*
Ro 15:13 through the p. of the Holy Ghost. *1411*
Ro 15:19 by the p. of the Spirit of God; so *1411*
Ro 16:25 to him that is of p. to stablish you *1410*
1Co 1:18 which are saved it is the p. of God. *1411*
1Co 1:24 Christ the p. of God, and the *1411*
1Co 2:4 demonstration of…Spirit and of p.: *1411*
1Co 2:5 of men, but in the p. of God. *1411*
1Co 4:19 which are puffed up, but the p. *1411*
1Co 4:20 of God is not in word, but in p. *1411*
1Co 5:4 with the p. of our Lord Jesus Christ, *1411*
1Co 6:12 not be brought under the p. of any. *1850*
1Co 6:14 will also raise up us by his own p. *1411*
1Co 7:4 wife hath not p. of her own body, *1850*
1Co 7:4 hath not p. of his own body, but *1850*
1Co 7:37 but hath p. over his own will, and *1849*
1Co 9:4 Have we not p. to eat and to drink? *1849*
1Co 9:5 Have we not p. to lead…a sister, *1849*
1Co 9:6 have not we p. to forbear working? *1849*
1Co 9:12 be partakers of this p. over you, *1849*
1Co 9:12 we have not used this p.; but *1849*
1Co 9:18 I abuse not my p. in the gospel. *1849*
1Co 11:10 the woman to have p. on her head *1849*
1Co 15:24 all rule and all authority and p. *1411*
1Co 15:43 in weakness; it is raised in p.: *1411*
2Co 4:7 excellency of the p. may be of God, *1411*
2Co 6:7 the word of truth, by the p. of God, *1411*
2Co 8:3 For to their p., I bear record, yea, *1411*
2Co 8:3 beyond their p. they were willing *1411*
2Co 12:9 the p. of Christ may rest upon me. *1411*
2Co 13:4 yet he liveth by the p. of God. *1411*
2Co 13:4 him by the p. of God toward you. *1411*
2Co 13:10 according to the p. which the Lord *1849*
Eph 1:19 the exceeding greatness of his p. *1411*
Eph 1:19 to the working of his mighty p., *2904*
Eph 1:21 all principality, and p., and might, *1849*
Eph 2:2 to the prince of the p. of the air, *1849*
Eph 3:7 by the effectual working of his p. *1411*
Eph 3:20 to the p. that worketh in us, *1411*
Eph 6:10 Lord, and in the p. of his might. *2904*
Php 3:10 him, and the p. of his resurrection, *1411*
Col 1:11 according to his glorious p., unto *2904*
Col 1:13 us from the p. of darkness, and *1849*
Col 2:10 the head of all principality and p.: *1849*
1Th 1:5 but also in p., and in the Holy *1411*
2Th 1:9 Lord, and from the glory of his p.; *2479*
2Th 1:11 and the work of faith with p.: *1411*
2Th 2:9 all p. and signs and lying wonders, *1411*
2Th 3:9 Not because we have not p., but to *1849*
1Ti 6:16 be honour and p. everlasting. *2904*
2Ti 1:7 of p., and of love, and of a sound *1411*
2Ti 1:8 gospel according to the p. of God; *1411*
2Ti 3:5 but denying the p. thereof: from *1411*
Heb 1:3 all things by the word of his p., *1411*
Heb 2:14 him that had the p. of death, that *2904*
Heb 7:16 but after the p. of an endless life. *1411*
1Pe 1:5 kept by the p. of God through faith *1411*
2Pe 1:3 as his divine p. hath given unto us *1411*
2Pe 1:16 you the p. and coming of our Lord *1411*
2Pe 2:11 are greater in p. and might, bring *2479*
Jude 25 and majesty, dominion and p., *1849*
Re 2:26 **will I give p. over the nations:** *1849*
Re 4:11 to receive glory and honour and p.: *1411*
Re 5:12 Lamb that was slain to receive p., *1411*
Re 5:13 and honour, and glory, and p., be *2904*
Re 6:4 p. was given to him that sat thereon
Re 6:8 p. was given unto them over the *1849*
Re 7:12 p., and might, be unto our God *1411*
Re 9:3 and unto them was given p., as *1849*
Re 9:3 the scorpions of the earth have p. *1849*
Re 9:10 p. was to hurt men five months. *1849*
Re 9:19 their p. is in their mouth, and in *1849*
Re 11:3 I will give p. unto my two witnesses,
Re 11:6 have p. to shut heaven, that it *1849*
Re 11:6 have p. over waters to turn them to *1849*
Re 11:17 hast taken to thee thy great p., *1411*
Re 12:10 our God, and the p. of his Christ: *1849*
Re 13:2 the dragon gave him his p., and *1411*
Re 13:4 which gave p. unto the beast: and *1849*
Re 13:5 p. was given unto him to continue *1849*
Re 13:7 and p. was given him over all *1849*
Re 13:12 he exerciseth all the p. of the first *1849*
Re 13:14 miracles which he had p. to do in *1325*
Re 13:15 And he had p. to give life unto the *1325*
Re 14:18 the altar, which had p. over fire; *1849*
Re 15:8 the glory of God, and from his p.; *1411*
Re 16:8 p. was given unto him to scorch men
Re 16:9 which hath p. over these plagues: *1849*
Re 17:12 receive p. as kings one hour with *1849*
Re 17:13 p. and strength unto the beast. *1411*
Re 18:1 from heaven, having great p.; *1849*
Re 19:1 honour, and p., unto the Lord our *1411*
Re 20:6 such the second death hath no p., *1849*

POWERFUL
Ps 29:4 The voice of the Lord is p.; the 3581
2Co 10:10 his letters,…are weighty and p.; *2478*
Heb 4:12 the word of God is quick, and p., *1756*

POWERS
Mt 24:29 **p. of the heavens shall be shaken:** *1411*
Mk 13:25 **the p. that are in heaven shall be** *1411*
Lu 12:11 **unto magistrates, and p., take ye** *1849*
Lu 21:26 **the p. of heaven shall be shaken.** *1411*
Ro 8:38 angels, nor principalities, nor p., *1411*
Ro 13:1 soul be subject unto the higher p. *1849*
Ro 13:1 the p. that be are ordained of God. *1849*
Eph 3:10 and p. in heavenly places might be *1849*
Eph 6:12 against principalities, against p., *1849*
Col 1:16 dominions, or principalities, or p.: *1849*
Col 2:15 having spoiled principalities and p., *1849*
Ti 3:1 be subject to principalities and p., *1849*
Heb 6:5 and the p. of the world to come, *1411*
1Pe 3:22 p. being made subject unto him. *1411*

PRACTICES
2Pe 2:14 they have exercised with covetous p.;

PRACTISE See also PRACTICES; PRACTISED.
Ps 141:4 to p. wicked works with men that 5953
Isa 32:6 to p. hypocrisy, and to utter error 6213
Da 8:24 and shall prosper, and p., and shall 6213
Mic 2:1 when the morning is light, they p. it, 6213

PRACTISED
1Sa 23:9 Saul secretly p. mischief against 2790
Da 8:12 ground; and it p., and prospered. 6213

PRAETORIUM (pre-to'-re-um)
Mk 15:16 him away into the hall, called P.; *4232*

PRAISE See also PRAISED; PRAISES; PRAISETH; PRAISING.
Ge 29:35 she said, Now will I p. the Lord: 3034
Ge 49:8 art he whom thy brethren shall p.: 3034
Le 19:24 shall be holy to p. the Lord withal. 1974
De 10:21 He is thy p., and he is thy God, 8416
De 26:19 in p., and in name, and in honour; 8416
Jg 5:2 P. ye the Lord for the avenging 1288
Jg 5:3 will sing p. to the Lord God of Israel.
1Ch 16:4 and p. the Lord God of Israel: 1984
1Ch 16:35 thy holy name, and glory in thy p. 8416
1Ch 23:5 made, said David, to p. therewith. 1984
1Ch 23:30 morning to thank and p. the Lord, 1984
1Ch 25:3 to give thanks and to p. the Lord. 1984
1Ch 29:13 thee, and p. thy glorious name. 1984
2Ch 7:6 the king had made to p. the Lord, 3034
2Ch 8:14 p. and minister before the priests, 1984
2Ch 20:19 stood up to p. the Lord God of 1984
2Ch 20:21 should p. the beauty of holiness, 1984
2Ch 20:21 the army, and to say, P. the Lord; 3034
2Ch 20:22 when they began to sing and to p., 8416
2Ch 23:13 and such as taught to sing p. 1984
2Ch 29:30 Levites to sing p. unto the Lord 1984
2Ch 31:2 to p. in the gates of the tents of the 1984
Ezr 3:10 p. the Lord, after the ordinance of 1984
Ne 9:5 exalted above all blessing and p. 8416
Ne 12:24 to p. and to give thanks, according 1984
Ne 12:46 songs of p. and thanksgiving unto 8416
Ps 7:17 I will p. the Lord according to his 3034
Ps 7:17 sing p. to the name of the Lord
Ps 9:1 I will p. thee, O Lord, with my 3034
Ps 9:2 I will sing p. to thy name, O thou
Ps 9:14 I may shew forth all thy p. in the 8416
Ps 21:13 so will we sing and p. thy power. 2167
Ps 22:22 of the congregation will I p. thee. 1984
Ps 22:23 Ye that fear the Lord, p. him; all 1984
Ps 22:25 My p. shall be of thee in the great 8416
Ps 22:26 shall p. the Lord that seek him: 1984
Ps 28:7 and with my song will I p. him. 3034
Ps 30:9 Shall the dust p. thee? shall it 3034
Ps 30:12 that my glory may sing p. to thee,
Ps 33:1 for p. is comely for the upright. 8416
Ps 33:2 P. the Lord with harp: sing unto 3034
Ps 34:1 his p. shall continually be in my 8416
Ps 35:18 I will p. thee among much people. 1984
Ps 35:28 and of thy p. all the day long. 8416
Ps 40:3 my mouth, even p. unto our God: 8416

Ps 42:4 with the voice of joy and **p.**, with....... 8426
Ps 42:5 shall yet **p.** him for the help of.......... 3034
Ps 42:11 for I shall yet **p.** him, who is the........ 3034
Ps 43:4 upon the harp will I **p.** thee, O God.... 3034
Ps 43:5 for I shall yet **p.** him, who is the........ 3034
Ps 44:8 day long, and **p.** thy name for ever..... 3034
Ps 45:17 shall the people **p.** thee for ever 3034
Ps 48:10 thy **p.** unto the ends of the earth: 8416
Ps 49:18 and men will **p.** thee, when thou 3034
Ps 50:23 Whoso offereth **p.** glorifieth me: 8426
Ps 51:15 my mouth shall shew forth thy **p.**........ 8416
Ps 52:9 I will **p.** thee for ever, because.......... 3034
Ps 54:6 I will **p.** thy name, O Lord; for it is.... 3034
Ps 56:4 In God I will **p.** his word, in God I...... 1984
Ps 56:10 In God will I **p.** his word: in the......... 1984
Ps 56:10 in the Lord will I **p.** his word. 1984
Ps 57:7 is fixed: I will sing and give **p.**......... 2167
Ps 57:9 I will **p.** thee, O Lord, among the 3034
Ps 61:8 I sing **p.** unto thy name for ever, ...
Ps 63:3 than life, my lips shall **p.** thee........... 7623
Ps 63:5 shall **p.** thee with joyful lips:............. 1984
Ps 65:1 **P.** waiteth for thee, O God, in 8416
Ps 66:2 of his name: make his **p.** glorious. 8416
Ps 66:8 make the voice of his **p.** to be heard:.. 8416
Ps 67:3 Let the people **p.** thee, O God; let..... 3034
Ps 67:3 O God; let all the people **p.** thee........ 3034
Ps 67:5 Let the people **p.** thee, O God; let...... 3034
Ps 67:5 O God; let all the people **p.** thee........ 3034
Ps 69:30 **p.** the name of God with a song,........ 1984
Ps 69:34 Let the heaven and earth **p.** him, ... 1984
Ps 71:6 my **p.** shall be continually of thee. 8416
Ps 71:8 Let my mouth be filled with thy **p.** 8416
Ps 71:14 will yet **p.** thee more and more.......... 8416
Ps 71:22 will also **p.** thee with the psaltery,...... 3034
Ps 74:21 the poor and needy **p.** thy name. 1984
Ps 76:10 the wrath of man shall **p.** thee: 3034
Ps 79:13 forth thy **p.** to all generations. 8416
Ps 86:12 I will **p.** thee, O Lord my God, with 3034
Ps 88:10 shall the dead arise and **p.** thee? 3034
Ps 89:5 the heavens shall **p.** thy wonders, ... 3034
Ps 98:4 noise, and rejoice, and sing **p.**. ....
Ps 99:3 **p.** thy great and terrible name; 3034
Ps 100:*title* A Psalm of **p.**.................................. 8426
Ps 100:4 and into his courts with **p.**: 8416
Ps 102:18 shall be created shall **p.** the Lord. 1984
Ps 102:21 in Zion, and his **p.** in Jerusalem;.......... 8416
Ps 104:33 I will sing **p.** to my God while I ....
Ps 104:35 Lord, O my soul. **P.** ye the Lord. 1984
Ps 105:45 and keep his laws. **P.** ye the Lord...... 1984
Ps 106:1 **P.** ye the Lord. O give thanks........... 1984
Ps 106:2 who can shew forth all his **p.**? 8416
Ps 106:12 they his words; they sang his **p.**. 8416
Ps 106:47 holy name, and to triumph in thy **p.**.... 8416
Ps 106:48 people say, Amen. **P.** ye the Lord. 1984
Ps 107:8, 15,21,31 Oh that men would **p.**........... 3034
Ps 107:32 and **p.** him in the assembly of the....... 1984
Ps 108:1 I will sing and give **p.**, even with 2167
Ps 108:3 I will **p.** thee, O Lord, among the 3034
Ps 109:1 not thy peace, O God of thy **p.**;......... 8416
Ps 109:30 **p.** the Lord with my mouth;.............. 3034
Ps 109:30 will **p.** him among the multitude. 1984
Ps 111:1 **P.** ye the Lord, I will 1984
Ps 111:1 **p.** the Lord with my whole heart,....... 3034
Ps 111:10 his **p.** endureth for ever. 8416
Ps 112:1 **P.** ye the Lord. Blessed is the 1984
Ps 113:1 **P.** ye the Lord. **P.**, O ye servants..... 1984
Ps 113:1 the Lord, **p.** the name of the Lord. 1984
Ps 113:9 mother of children. **P.** ye the Lord..... 1984
Ps 115:17 The dead **p.** not the Lord, neither...... 1984
Ps 115:18 forth...for evermore. **P.** the Lord......... 1984
Ps 116:19 thee, O Jerusalem. **P.** ye the Lord..... 1984
Ps 117:1 O **p.** the Lord, all ye nations: 1984
Ps 117:1 ye nations: **p.** him, all ye people. 7623
Ps 117:2 endureth for ever. **P.** ye the Lord...... 1984
Ps 118:19 into them, and I will **p.** the Lord: 3034
Ps 118:21 I will **p.** thee: for thou hast heard........ 3034
Ps 118:28 Thou art my God, and I will **p.** thee: .. 3034
Ps 119:7 **p.** thee with uprightness of heart,...... 3034
Ps 119:164 Seven times a day do I **p.** thee.......... 1984
Ps 119:171 My lips shall utter **p.**, when thou 8416
Ps 119:175 my soul live, and it shall **p.** thee; 1984
Ps 135:1 **P.** ye the Lord. **P.** ye the name 1984
Ps 135:1 **p.** him, O ye servants of the Lord...... 1984
Ps 135:3 **P.** the Lord; for the Lord is good: 1984
Ps 135:21 at Jerusalem. **P.** ye the Lord............ 1984
Ps 138:1 will **p.** thee with my whole heart: 3034
Ps 138:1 the gods will I sing **p.** unto thee. 2167
Ps 138:2 **p.** thy name for...lovingkindness......... 3034
Ps 138:4 the kings of the earth shall **p.** thee, ... 3034
Ps 139:14 I will **p.** thee; for I am fearfully.......... 3034
Ps 142:7 of prison, that I may **p.** thy name:...... 3034
Ps 145:*title* David's Psalm of **p.**. 8416
Ps 145:2 I will **p.** thy name for ever and.......... 1984
Ps 145:4 generation shall **p.** thy works to......... 7623
Ps 145:10 All thy works shall **p.** thee, O............ 3034
Ps 145:21 shall speak the **p.** of the Lord:........... 8416
Ps 146:1 **P.** ye the Lord. **P.** the Lord, O......... 1984
Ps 146:2 While I live I will **p.** the Lord: I will ... 1984
Ps 146:10 all generations. **P.** ye the Lord. 1984
Ps 147:1 **P.** ye the Lord: for it is good to........ 1984
Ps 147:1 it is pleasant; and **p.** is comely.......... 8416
Ps 147:7 sing **p.** upon the harp unto our................
Ps 147:12 **P.** the Lord, O Jerusalem; 7623
Ps 147:12 Jerusalem; **p.** thy God, O Zion........... 1984
Ps 147:20 not known them. **P.** ye the Lord........ 1984
Ps 148:1 **P.** ye the Lord. **P.** ye the Lord.......... 1984
Ps 148:1 the heavens: **p.** him in the heights...... 1984
Ps 148:2 **P.** ye him, all his angels: 1984
Ps 148:2 his angels: **p.** ye him, all his hosts...... 1984
Ps 148:3 **P.** ye him, sun and moon: 1984
Ps 148:3 moon: **p.** him, all ye stars of light:...... 1984
Ps 148:4 **P.** him, ye heavens of heavens, and.... 1984
Ps 148:5 Let them **p.** the name of the Lord:..... 1984
Ps 148:7 **P.** the Lord from the earth, ye.......... 1984
Ps 148:13 Let them **p.** the name of the Lord:..... 1984
Ps 148:14 people, the **p.** of all his saints;........... 8416
Ps 148:14 near unto him. **P.** ye the Lord........... 1984
Ps 149:1 **P.** ye the Lord. Sing unto the Lord..... 1984
Ps 149:1 and his **p.** in the congregation of 8416
Ps 149:3 Let them **p.** his name in the............. 1984
Ps 149:9 have all his saints. **P.** ye the Lord...... 1984
Ps 150:1 **P.** ye the Lord............................... 1984
Ps 150:1 **P.** God in his sanctuary: 1984
Ps 150:1 **p.** him in the firmament of his........... 1984
Ps 150:2 **P.** him for his mighty acts; 1984
Ps 150:2 **p.** him according to his excellent 1984
Ps 150:3 **P.** him with the sound of the............. 1984
Ps 150:3 **p.** him with the psaltery and harp. 1984
Ps 150:4 **P.** him with the timbrel and dance:..... 1984
Ps 150:4 **p.** him with stringed instruments 1984
Ps 150:5 **P.** him upon the loud cymbals:........... 1984
Ps 150:5 **p.** him upon the high sounding........... 1984
Ps 150:6 that hath breath **p.** the Lord............. 1984
Ps 150:6 the Lord. **P.** ye the Lord. 1984
Pr 27:2 Let another man **p.** thee, and not........ 1984
Pr 27:21 for gold; so is a man to his **p.**. 4110
Pr 28:4 that forsake the law **p.** the wicked:..... 1984
Pr 31:31 her own works **p.** her in the gates. 1984
Isa 12:1 O Lord, I will **p.** thee: though 3034
Isa 12:4 **P.** the Lord, call upon his name, ... 3034
Isa 25:1 I will **p.** thy name; for thou hast 3034
Isa 38:18 For the grave cannot **p.** thee, death.... 3034
Isa 38:19 living, the living, he shall **p.** thee,....... 3034
Isa 42:8 neither my **p.** to graven images. 8416
Isa 42:10 his **p.** from the end of the earth,........ 8416
Isa 42:12 and declare his **p.** in the islands. 8416
Isa 43:21 myself; they shall shew forth my **p.**.... 8416
Isa 48:9 and for my **p.** will I refrain for thee, ... 8416
Isa 60:18 walls Salvation, and thy gates **P.**........ 8416
Isa 61:3 garment of **p.** for the spirit of.......... 8416
Isa 61:11 **p.** to spring forth before all the.......... 8416
Isa 62:7 make Jerusalem a **p.** in the earth......... 8416
Isa 62:9 it shall eat it, and **p.** the Lord;.......... 1984
Jer 13:11 and for a **p.**, and for a glory: 8416
Jer 17:14 I shall be saved: for thou art my **p.**. ... 8416
Jer 17:26 sacrifices of **p.** unto the house of........ 8426
Jer 20:13 **p.** ye the Lord: for he hath............... 1984
Jer 31:7 **p.** ye, and say, O Lord, save thy....... 1984
Jer 33:9 a **p.** and an honour before all the........ 8416
Jer 33:11 **P.** the Lord of hosts: for the Lord 3034
Jer 33:11 shall bring the sacrifice of **p.** into........ 8426
Jer 48:2 shall be no more **p.** of Moab: 8416
Jer 49:25 is the city of **p.** not left, the city of 8416
Jer 51:41 how is the **p.** of the whole earth........ 8416
Da 2:23 I thank thee, and **p.** thee, O thou....... 7624
Da 4:37 Now I Nebuchadnezzar **p.** and extol.... 7624
Joe 2:26 **p.** the name of the Lord your God,..... 1984
Hab 3:3 and the earth was full of his **p.**........... 8416
Zep 3:19 get them **p.** and fame in every land 8416
Zep 3:20 and a **p.** among all people of the 8416
Mt 21:16 **sucklings thou hast perfected p.**? *136*
Lu 18:43 when they saw it, gave **p.** unto God..... *136*
Lu 19:37 rejoice and **p.** God with a loud voice..... *134*
Joh 9:24 said unto him, Give God the **p.**: we.... *1391*
Joh 12:43 For they loved the **p.** of men more...... *1391*
Joh 12:43 of men more than the **p.** of God. *1391*
Ro 2:29 whose **p.** is not of men, but of God. ... *1868*
Ro 13:3 and thou shalt have **p.** of the same: *1868*
Ro 15:11 again, **P.** the Lord, all ye Gentiles; *134*
1Co 4:5 shall every man have **p.** of God. *1868*
1Co 11:2 Now I **p.** you, brethren, that ye.......... *1867*
1Co 11:17 I **p.** you, not that ye come together.... *1867*
1Co 11:22 shall I **p.** you in this? I **p.** you not...... *1867*
2Co 8:18 brother, whose **p.** is in the gospel....... *1868*
Eph 1:6 To the **p.** of the glory of his grace, ... 1868
Eph 1:12 to the **p.** of his glory, who first.......... *1868*
Eph 1:14 possession, unto the **p.** of his glory. ... *1868*
Php 1:11 Christ, unto the glory and **p.** of God. .. *1868*
Php 4:8 if there be any **p.**, think on these....... *1868*
Heb 2:12 the church will I sing **p.** unto thee. *5214*
Heb 13:15 let us offer the sacrifice of **p.** to God.... *133*
1Pe 1:7 be found unto **p.** and honour and........ *1868*
1Pe 2:14 and for the **p.** of them that do well. *1868*
1Pe 4:11 whom be **p.** and dominion for ever *1391*
Re 19:5 **P.** our God, all ye his servants, ... *134*

PRAISED

Jg 16:24 people saw him, they **p.** their god: 1984
2Sa 14:25 none to be so much **p.** as Absalom..... 1984
2Sa 22:4 on the Lord, who is worthy to be **p.**:.. 1984
1Ch 16:25 is the Lord, and greatly to be **p.**: 1984
1Ch 16:36 people said, Amen, and **p.** the Lord.... 1984
1Ch 23:5 four thousand **p.** the Lord with the 1984
2Ch 5:13 **p.** the Lord, saying, For he is good; ... 1984
2Ch 7:3 and worshipped, and **p.** the Lord,....... 3034
2Ch 7:6 when David **p.** by their ministry;......... 1984
2Ch 30:21 Levites and the priests **p.** the Lord 1984
Ezr 3:11 great shout, when they **p.** the Lord, ... 1984
Ne 5:13 said, Amen, and **p.** the Lord. 1984
Ps 18:3 the Lord, who is worthy to be **p.**: 1984
Ps 48:1 greatly to be **p.** in the city of our....... 1984
Ps 72:15 continually;...daily shall he be **p.**......... 1288
Ps 96:4 Lord is great, and greatly to be **p.**: 1984
Ps 113:3 same the Lord's name is to be **p.**....... 1984
Ps 145:3 is the Lord, and greatly to be **p.**; 1984
Pr 31:30 feareth the Lord, she shall be **p.**. 1984
Ec 4:2 I **p.** the dead which are already.......... 7623
Ca 6:9 the concubines, and they **p.** her. 1984
Isa 64:11 house, where our fathers **p.** thee, is... 1984
Da 4:34 I **p.** and honoured him that liveth 7624
Da 5:4 drank wine, and **p.** the gods of gold, ... 7624
Da 5:23 thou hast **p.** the gods of silver, and 7624
Lu 1:64 loosed, and he spake, and **p.** God....... *2127*

PRAISES

Ex 15:11 fearful in **p.**, doing wonders? 8416
2Sa 22:50 and I will sing **p.** unto thy name..............
2Ch 29:30 And they sang **p.** with gladness,......... 1984
Ps 9:11 Sing **p.** to the Lord, which.......................
Ps 18:49 heathen,...sing **p.** unto thy name. ....
Ps 22:3 that inhabitest the **p.** of Israel........... 8416
Ps 27:6 yea, I will sing **p.** unto the Lord..............
Ps 47:6 Sing **p.** to God, sing **p.**: ....
Ps 47:6 sing **p.** unto our King, sing **p.**..................
Ps 47:7 sing ye **p.** with understanding. ....
Ps 56:12 O God: I will render **p.** unto thee....... 8426
Ps 68:4 unto God, sing **p.** to his name: ....
Ps 68:32 the earth; O sing **p.** unto the Lord; ....
Ps 75:9 I will sing **p.** to the God of Jacob..............
Ps 78:4 **p.** of the Lord, and his strength, ... 8416
Ps 92:1 to sing **p.** unto thy name, O most............
Ps 108:3 I will sing **p.** unto thee among the ....
Ps 135:3 Lord is good: sing **p.** unto his name; ....
Ps 144:9 ten strings will I sing **p.** unto thee............
Ps 146:2 I will sing **p.** unto my God while I ....
Ps 147:1 it is good to sing **p.** unto our God; ....
Ps 149:3 sing **p.** unto him with the timbrel..............
Ps 149:6 the high **p.** of God be in their mouth, ...
Isa 60:6 shew forth the **p.** of the Lord........... 8416
Isa 63:7 and the **p.** of the Lord, according........ 8416
Ac 16:25 prayed, and sang **p.** unto God:................
1Pe 2:9 shew forth the **p.** of him who hath....... *703*

PRAISETH

Pr 31:28 her husband also, and he **p.** her. 1984

PRAISING

2Ch 5:13 heard in **p.** and thanking the Lord;...... 1984
2Ch 23:12 the people running and **p.** the king,...... 1984
Ezr 3:11 **p.** and giving thanks unto the Lord; 1984
Ps 84:4 thy house: they will be still **p.** thee..... 1984

Lu 2:13 heavenly host, **p.** God, and saying, *134*
Lu 2:20 glorifying and **p.** God for all the *134*
Lu 24:53 in the temple, **p.** and blessing God. *134*
Ac 2:47 **P.** God, and having favour with all *134*
Ac 3:8 walking, and leaping, and **p.** God. *134*
Ac 3:9 people saw him walking and **p.** God: *134*

PRANSING See also PRANSINGS.
Na 3:2 the **p.** horses, and of the jumping 1725

PRANSINGS
Jg 5:22 broken by the means of the **p.**, 1726
Jg 5:22 the **p.** of their mighty ones. 1726

PRATING
Pr 10:8 but a **p.** fool shall fall. 8193
Pr 10:10 sorrow: but a **p.** fool shall fall. 8193
3Jo 10 **p.** against us with malicious *5396*

PRAY See also PRAYED; PRAYETH; PRAYING.
Ge 12:13 Say, I **p.** thee, thou art my sister: 4994
Ge 13:8 Let there be no strife, I **p.** thee, 4994
Ge 13:9 separate thyself, I **p.** thee, from me: 4994
Ge 16:2 I **p.** thee, go in unto my maid; it 4994
Ge 18:3 pass not away, I **p.** thee, from thy 4994
Ge 18:4 a little water, I **p.** you, be fetched, 4994
Ge 19:2 now, my lords, turn in, I **p.** you, 4994
Ge 19:7 said, I **p.** you, brethren, do not so 4994
Ge 19:8 let me, I **p.** you, bring them out 4994
Ge 20:7 he shall **p.** for thee, and thou shalt 6419
Ge 23:13 if thou wilt give it, I **p.** thee, hear 3863
Ge 24:2 Put, I **p.** thee, thy hand under my 4994
Ge 24:12 I **p.** thee, send me good speed this 4994
Ge 24:14 Let down thy pitcher, I **p.** thee, that 4994
Ge 24:17 Let me, I **p.** thee, drink a little water 4994
Ge 24:23 daughter art thou? tell me, I **p.** thee: 4994
Ge 24:43 Give me, I **p.** thee, a little water of 4994
Ge 24:45 unto her. Let me drink, I **p.** thee 4994
Ge 25:30 said to Jacob, Feed me, I **p.** thee, 4994
Ge 27:3 take, I **p.** thee, thy weapons, thy 4994
Ge 27:19 I **p.** thee, sit and eat of my venison, 4994
Ge 27:21 Come near, I **p.** thee, that I may 4994
Ge 30:14 Give me, I **p.** thee, of thy son's 4994
Ge 30:27 I **p.** thee, if I have found favour in 4994
Ge 32:11 Deliver me, I **p.** thee, from the hand 4994
Ge 32:29 said, Tell me, I **p.** thee, thy name 4994
Ge 33:10 Jacob said, Nay, I **p.** thee, if now I 4994
Ge 33:11 Take, I **p.** thee, my blessing that is 4994
Ge 33:14 Let my lord, I **p.** thee, pass over 4994
Ge 34:8 I **p.** you give her him to wife 4994
Ge 37:6 Hear, I **p.** you, this dream which I 4994
Ge 37:14 Go, I **p.** thee, see whether it be well 4994
Ge 37:16 tell me, I **p.** thee, where they feed 4994
Ge 38:16 Go to, I **p.** thee, let me come in unto 4994
Ge 38:25 Discern, I **p.** thee, whose are these, 4994
Ge 40:8 to God? tell me them, I **p.** you. 4994
Ge 40:14 shew kindness, I **p.** thee, unto me, 4994
Ge 44:18 let thy servant, I **p.** thee, speak a 4994
Ge 44:33 I **p.** thee, let thy servant abide 4994
Ge 45:4 brethren, Come near to me, I **p.** you. 4994
Ge 47:4 we **p.** thee, let thy servants dwell in 4994
Ge 47:29 put, I **p.** thee, thy hand under my 4994
Ge 47:29 bury me not, I **p.** thee, in Egypt: 4994
Ge 48:9 Bring them, I **p.** thee, unto me, and 4994
Ge 50:4 speak, I **p.** you, in the ears of 4994
Ge 50:5 let me go up, I **p.** thee, and bury my 4994
Ge 50:17 Forgive, I **p.** thee now, the trespass 577
Ge 50:17 we **p.** thee, forgive the trespass of 4994
Ex 4:13 O my Lord, send, I **p.** thee, by 4994
Ex 4:18 Let me go, I **p.** thee, and return 4994
Ex 5:3 let us go, we **p.** thee, three days' 4994
Ex 10:17 forgive, I **p.** thee, my sin only this 4994
Ex 32:32 blot me, I **p.** thee, out of thy book 4994
Ex 33:13 therefore, I **p.** thee, if I have found 4994
Ex 34:9 let my Lord, I **p.** thee, go among us; 4994
Nu 10:31 he said, Leave us not, I **p.** thee; 4994
Nu 11:15 kill me, I **p.** thee, out of hand, if I 4994
Nu 16:8 Hear, I **p.** you, ye sons of Levi: 4994
Nu 16:26 Depart, I **p.** you, from the tents of 4994
Nu 20:17 Let us pass, I **p.** thee, through thy 4994
Nu 21:7 **p.** unto the Lord, that he take 6419
Nu 22:6 therefore, I **p.** thee, curse me this 4994
Nu 22:16 Let nothing, I **p.** thee, hinder thee 4994
Nu 22:17 therefore, I **p.** thee, curse me this 4994
Nu 22:19 I **p.** you, tarry ye also here this 4994
Nu 23:13 him, Come, I **p.** thee, with me unto 4994
Nu 23:27 Come, I **p.** thee, I will bring thee 4994
De 3:25 I **p.** thee, let me go over, and see the 4994
Jos 2:12 I **p.** you, swear unto me by the Lord, 4994
Jos 7:19 give, I **p.** thee, glory to the Lord 4994
Jg 1:24 Shew us, we **p.** thee, the entrance 4994
Jg 4:19 Give me, I **p.** thee, a little water to 4994
Jg 6:18 Depart not hence, I **p.** thee, until I 4994
Jg 6:39 let me prove, I **p.** thee, but this 4994
Jg 8:5 Give, I **p.** you, loaves of bread unto 4994
Jg 9:2 Speak, I **p.** you, in the ears of all the 4994
Jg 9:38 go out, I **p.** now, and fight with 4994
Jg 10:15 deliver us only, we **p.** thee, this day 4994
Jg 11:17 Let me, I **p.** thee, pass through thy 4994
Jg 11:19 Let us pass, we **p.** thee, through thy 4994
Jg 13:4 beware, I **p.** thee, and drink not wine 4994
Jg 13:15 I **p.** thee, let us detain thee, until 4994
Jg 15:2 take her, I **p.** thee, instead of her. 4994
Jg 16:6 Tell me, I **p.** thee, wherein thy great 4994
Jg 16:10 now tell me, I **p.** thee, wherewith 4994
Jg 16:28 Lord God, remember me, I **p.** thee, 4994
Jg 16:28 strengthen me, I **p.** thee, only this 4994
Jg 18:5 Ask counsel, we **p.** thee, of God, 4994
Jg 19:6 Be content, I **p.** thee, and tarry all 4994
Jg 19:8 said, Comfort thine heart, I **p.** thee. 4994
Jg 19:9 evening, I **p.** you tarry all night: 4994
Jg 19:11 Come, I **p.** thee, and let us turn in 4994
Jg 19:23 nay, I **p.** you, do not so wickedly; 4994
Ru 2:7 I **p.** you, let me glean and gather 4994
1Sa 2:36 Put me, I **p.** thee, into one of the 4994
1Sa 3:17 I **p.** thee hide it not from me: God 4994
1Sa 7:5 I will **p.** for you unto the Lord. 6419
1Sa 9:18 Tell me, I **p.** thee, where the seer's 4994
1Sa 10:15 Tell me, I **p.** thee, what Samuel 4994
1Sa 12:19 **P.** for thy servants unto the Lord 6419
1Sa 12:23 the Lord in ceasing to **p.** for you: 6419
1Sa 14:29 see, I **p.** you, how mine eyes have 4994
1Sa 15:25 I **p.** thee, pardon my sin, and turn 4994
1Sa 15:30 honour me now, I **p.** thee, before 4994
1Sa 16:22 Let David, I **p.** thee, stand before 4994
1Sa 19:2 now therefore, I **p.** thee, take heed 4994
1Sa 20:29 Let me go, I **p.** thee; for our family 4994
1Sa 20:29 let me get away, I **p.** thee, and see 4994
1Sa 22:3 my mother, I **p.** thee, come forth, 4994
1Sa 23:22 Go, I **p.** you, prepare yet, and know 4994
1Sa 25:8 give, I **p.** thee, whatsoever cometh 4994
1Sa 25:24 let thine handmaid, I **p.** thee, speak 4994
1Sa 25:25 Let not my lord, I **p.** thee, regard 4994
1Sa 25:28 I **p.** thee, forgive the trespass of 4994
1Sa 26:8 let me smite him, I **p.** thee, with the 4994
1Sa 26:11 I **p.** thee, take thou now the spear 4994
1Sa 26:19 I **p.** thee, let my lord the king hear 4994
1Sa 28:8 said, I **p.** thee, divine unto me by the 4994
1Sa 28:22 I **p.** thee, hearken thou also unto 4994
1Sa 30:7 I **p.** thee, bring me hither the ephod. 4994
2Sa 1:4 went the matter? I **p.** thee, tell me. 4994
2Sa 1:9 Stand, I **p.** thee, upon me, and slay 4994
2Sa 7:27 in his heart to **p.** this prayer unto 6419
2Sa 13:5 him, I **p.** thee, let my sister Tamar 4994
2Sa 13:6 I **p.** thee, let Tamar my sister come, 4994
2Sa 13:13 I **p.** thee, speak unto the king; for 4994
2Sa 13:26 I **p.** thee, let my brother Amnon go 4994
2Sa 14:2 I **p.** thee, feign thyself to be a 4994
2Sa 14:11 I **p.** thee, let the king remember the 4994
2Sa 14:12 Let thine handmaid, I **p.** thee, 4994
2Sa 14:18 Hide not from me, I **p.** thee, the 4994
2Sa 15:7 I **p.** thee, let me go and pay my vow, 4994
2Sa 15:31 O Lord, I **p.** thee, turn the counsel 4994
2Sa 16:9 go over, I **p.** thee, and take off his 4994
2Sa 18:22 let me, I **p.** thee, also run after 4994
2Sa 19:37 Let thy servant, I **p.** thee, turn back 4994
2Sa 20:16 say, I **p.** you, unto Joab, Come near 4994
2Sa 24:17 let thine hand, I **p.** thee, be against 4994
1Ki 1:12 let me, I **p.** thee, give thee counsel, 4994
1Ki 2:17 I **p.** thee, unto Solomon the king, 4994
1Ki 2:20 of thee; I **p.** thee, say me not nay.
1Ki 8:26 let thy word, I **p.** thee, be verified, 4994
1Ki 8:30 they shall **p.** toward this place: 6419
1Ki 8:33 confess thy name, and **p.**, and make 6419
1Ki 8:35 if they **p.** toward this place, and 6419
1Ki 8:42 when he shall come and **p.** toward 6419
1Ki 8:44 and shall **p.** unto the Lord toward 6419
1Ki 8:48 **p.** unto thee toward their land, which 6419
1Ki 13:6 **p.** for me, that my hand may be 6419
1Ki 14:2 wife, Arise, I **p.** thee, and disguise 4994
1Ki 17:10 Fetch me, I **p.** thee, a little water in 4994
1Ki 17:11 Bring me, I **p.** thee, a morsel of 4994
1Ki 17:21 I **p.** thee, let this child's soul come 4994
1Ki 19:20 Let me, I **p.** thee, kiss my father 4994
1Ki 20:7 I **p.** you, and see how this man 4994
1Ki 20:31 let us, I **p.** thee, put sackcloth on 4994
1Ki 20:32 Ben-hadad saith, I **p.** thee, let me 4994
1KI 20:35 Smite me, I **p.** thee. And the man 4994
1Ki 20:37 Smite me, I **p.** thee. And the man 4994
1Ki 22:5 Enquire, I **p.** thee, at the word of 4994
1Ki 22:13 let thy word, I **p.** thee, be like the 4994
2Ki 1:13 O man of God, I **p.** thee, let my life, 4994
2Ki 2:2 unto Elisha, Tarry here, I **p.** thee; 4994
2Ki 2:4 him, Elisha, tarry here, I **p.** thee; 4994
2Ki 2:6 said unto him, Tarry, I **p.** thee, 4994
2Ki 2:9 And Elisha said, I **p.** thee, let a 4994
2Ki 2:16 let them go, we **p.** thee, and seek thy 4994
2Ki 2:19 said unto Elisha, Behold, I **p.** thee, 4994
2Ki 4:10 chamber, I **p.** thee, on the wall; 4994
2Ki 4:22 Send me, I **p.** thee, one of the young 4994
2Ki 4:26 Run now, I **p.** thee, to meet her, and 4994
2Ki 5:7 wherefore consider, I **p.** you, and 4994
2Ki 5:15 I **p.** thee, take a blessing of thy 4994
2Ki 5:17 I **p.** thee, be given to thy servant 4994
2Ki 5:22 them, I **p.** thee, a talent of silver, 4994
2Ki 6:2 Let us go, we **p.** thee, unto Jordan, 4994
2Ki 6:3 Be content, I **p.** thee, and go with 4994
2Ki 6:17 said, Lord, I **p.** thee, open his eyes, 4994
2Ki 6:18 Smite this people, I **p.** thee, with 4994
2Ki 7:13 Let some take, I **p.** thee, five of the 4994
2Ki 8:4 Tell me, I **p.** thee, all the great 4994
2Ki 18:23 therefore, I **p.** thee, give pledges 4994
2Ki 18:26 Speak, I **p.** thee, to thy servants in 4994
1Ch 17:25 hath found in his heart to **p.** 6419
1Ch 21:17 let thine hand, I **p.** thee, O Lord 4994
2Ch 6:24 **p.** and make supplication before 6419
2Ch 6:26 **p.** toward this place, and confess 6419
2Ch 6:32 if they come and **p.** in this house; 6419
2Ch 6:34 they **p.** unto thee toward this city
2Ch 6:37 turn and **p.** unto thee in the land 2603
2Ch 6:38 **p.** toward their land, which thou 6419
2Ch 7:14 humble themselves, and **p.**, and seek 6419
2Ch 18:4 Enquire, I **p.** thee, at the word of 4994
2Ch 18:12 let thy word therefore, I **p.** thee, be 4994
Ezr 6:10 **p.** for the life of the king, and of 6739
Ne 1:6 I **p.** before thee now, day and 6419
Ne 1:11 prosper, I **p.** thee, thy servant this 4994
Ne 5:10 I **p.** you, let us leave off this usury 4994
Ne 5:11 Restore, I **p.** you, to them, even this 4994
Job 4:7 Remember, I **p.** thee, whoever 4994
Job 6:29 Return, I **p.** you, let it not be 4994
Job 8:8 enquire, I **p.** thee, of the former age, 4994
Job 21:15 should we have, if we **p.** unto him? 6293
Job 22:22 Receive, I **p.** thee, the law from his 4994
Job 32:21 Let me not, I **p.** you, accept any 4994
Job 33:1 Job, I **p.** thee, hear my speeches, and 4994
Job 33:26 He shall **p.** unto God, and he will 6279
Job 42:8 my servant Job shall **p.** for you: 6419
Ps 5:2 and my God: for unto thee will I **p.** 6419
Ps 32:6 this shall every one that is godly **p.** 6419
Ps 55:17 and morning, and at noon will I **p.** 7878
Ps 119:76 Let, I **p.** thee, thy merciful kindness 4994
Ps 122:6 **P.** for the peace of Jerusalem: they 7592
Isa 5:3 of Judah, judge, I **p.** you, betwixt 4994
Isa 16:12 shall come to his sanctuary to **p.**; 6419
Isa 29:11 Read this, I **p.** thee: and he saith, 4994
Isa 29:12 saying, Read this, I **p.** thee: 4994
Isa 36:8 give pledges, I **p.** thee, to my master 4994
Isa 36:11 Speak, I **p.** thee, unto thy servants 4994
Isa 45:20 and **p.** unto a god that cannot save. 6419
Jer 7:16 **p.** not thou for this people, neither 6419
Jer 11:14 **p.** not thou for this people, neither 6419
Jer 14:11 **P.** not for this people for their good. 6419
Jer 21:2 Enquire, I **p.** thee, of the Lord for 4994
Jer 29:7 and **p.** unto the Lord for it: for in 6419
Jer 29:12 ye shall go and **p.** unto me, and I 6419
Jer 32:8 Buy my field, I **p.** thee, that is in 4994
Jer 37:3 **P.** now unto the Lord our God for 6419
Jer 37:20 hear now, I **p.** thee, O my lord the 4994
Jer 37:20 let my supplication, I **p.** thee, be 4994
Jer 40:15 Let me go, I **p.** thee, and I will slay
Jer 42:2 **p.** for us unto the Lord thy God, 6419
Jer 42:4 I will **p.** unto the Lord your God 6419
Jer 42:20 **P.** for us unto the Lord our God; 6419
La 1:18 hear, I **p.** you, all people, and 4994
Eze 33:30 Come, I **p.** you, and hear what is the 4994
Jon 1:8 Tell us, we **p.** thee, for whose cause 4994
Jon 4:2 said, I **p.** thee, O Lord, was not this 577
Mic 3:1 Hear, I **p.** you, O heads of Jacob, 4994
Mic 3:9 Hear this, I **p.** you, ye heads of the 4994
Hag 2:15 now, I **p.** you, consider from this 4994
Zec 7:2 their men, to **p.** before the Lord, 2470

Zec 8:21 us go speedily to **p.** before the Lord,.. 2470
Zec 8:22 Jerusalem, and...**p.** before the Lord. ... 2470
Mal 1:9 now, I **p.** you, beseech God that........ 4994
Mt 5:44 **p.** for them which despitefully use . *4336*
Mt 6:5 to **p.** standing in the synagogues ... *4336*
Mt 6:6 **p.** to thy Father which is in secret; *4336*
Mt 6:7 ye **p.**, use not vain repetitions, ... *4336*
Mt 6:9 After this manner therefore **p.** ye: ..*4336*
Mt 9:38 **P.** ye therefore the Lord of the *1189*
Mt 14:23 up into a mountain apart to **p.**: *4336*
Mt 19:13 put his hands on them and **p.**: *4336*
Mt 24:20 **p.** ye that your flight be not in the .*4336*
Mt 26:36 ye here, while I go and **p.** yonder.. *4336*
Mt 26:41 Watch and **p.**, that ye enter not *4336*
Mt 26:53 that I cannot now **p.** to my Father, *3870*
Mk 5:17 they began to **p.** him to depart out..... *3870*
Mk 5:23 I **p.** thee, come and lay thy hands on........
Mk 6:46 he departed into a mountain to **p.**....... *4336*
Mk 11:24 ye desire, when ye **p.**, believe *4336*
Mk 13:18 **p.** ye that your flight be not in the .*4336*
Mk 13:33 watch and **p.**: for ye know not *4336*
Mk 14:32 Sit ye here, while I shall **p.**. *4336*
Mk 14:38 Watch ye and **p.**, lest ye enter into .*4336*
Lu 6:12 he went out into a mountain to **p.**, ... *4336*
Lu 6:28 **p.** for them which despitefully use . *4336*
Lu 9:28 and went up into a mountain to **p.**. *4336*
Lu 10:2 **p.** ye therefore the Lord of the...... *1189*
Lu 11:1 unto him, Lord, teach us to **p.**,........... *4336*
Lu 11:2 When ye **p.**, say, Our Father.......... *4336*
Lu 14:18 see it: I **p.** thee have me excused... *2065*
Lu 14:19 them: I **p.** thee have me excused. .. *2065*
Lu 16:27 I **p.** thee therefore, father, that *2065*
Lu 18:1 men ought always to **p.**, and not......... *4336*
Lu 18:10 went up into the temple to **p.**;....... *4336*
Lu 21:36 ye therefore, and **p.** always, that ... *1189*
Lu 22:40 **P.** that ye enter not into.............. *4336*
Lu 22:46 **p.**, lest ye enter into temptation.... *4336*
Joh 14:16 I will **p.** the Father, and he shall .. *2065*
Joh 16:26 that I will **p.** the Father for you: .. *2065*
Joh 17:9 I **p.** for them: I **p.** not for the *2065*
Joh 17:15 I **p.** not that thou shouldest take...... *2065*
Joh 17:20 Neither **p.** I for these alone, but.... *2065*
Ac 8:22 this thy wickedness, and **p.** God, ... *1189*
Ac 8:24 **P.** ye to the Lord for me, that *1189*
Ac 8:34 I **p.** thee, of whom speaketh the *1189*
Ac 10:9 went up upon the housetop to **p.**.......... *4336*
Ac 24:4 I **p.** thee that thou wouldest hear....... *3870*
Ac 27:34 I **p.** you to take some meat: for......... *3870*
Ro 8:26 we should **p.** for as we ought: *4336*
1Co 11:13 comely that a woman **p.** unto God *4336*
1Co 14:13 tongue **p.** that he may interpret. *4336*
1Co 14:14 if I **p.** in an unknown tongue, my *4336*
1Co 14:15 it then? I will **p.** with the spirit, ... *4336*
1Co 14:15 will **p.** with the understanding also: *4336*
2Co 5:20 we **p.** you in Christ's stead, be ye...... *1189*
2Co 13:7 Now **p.** to God that ye do no evil;...... *2172*
Php 1:9 And this I **p.**, that your love may......... *4336*
Col 1:9 do not cease to **p.** for you, and to...... *4336*
1Th 5:17 **P.** without ceasing. *4336*
1Th 5:23 I **p.** God your whole spirit and soul...........
1Th 5:25 Brethren, **p.** for us............................ *4336*
2Th 1:11 we **p.** always for you, that our God *4336*
2Th 3:1 brethren, **p.**for us, that the word *4336*
1Ti 2:8 therefore that men **p.** every where, ... *4336*
2Ti 4:16 I **p.** God that it may not be laid to............
Heb 13:18 **P.** for us: for we trust we have......... *4336*
Jas 5:13 among you afflicted? let him **p.**. *4336*
Jas 5:14 let them **p.** over him, anointing.......... *4336*
Jas 5:16 **p.** one for another, that ye may *2172*
1Jo 5:16 I do not say that he shall **p.** for it. *2065*

PRAYED

Ge 20:17 So Abraham **p.** unto God: and 6419
Nu 11:2 when Moses **p.** unto the Lord, ... 6419
Nu 21:7 us. And Moses **p.** for the people......... 6419
De 9:20 I **p.** for Aaron also the same time....... 6419
De 9:26 I **p.** therefore unto the Lord, and 6419
1Sa 1:10 **p.** unto the Lord, and wept sore. 6419
1Sa 1:27 For this child I **p.**; and the Lord 6419
1Sa 2:1 Hannah **p.**, and said, My heart........... 6419
1Sa 8:6 us. And Samuel **p.** unto the Lord. 6419
2Ki 4:33 them twain, and **p.** unto the Lord........ 6419
2Ki 6:17 Elisha **p.**, and said, Lord, I pray 6419
2Ki 6:18 Elisha **p.** unto the Lord, and said, ... 6419
2Ki 19:15 Hezekiah **p.** before the Lord, and........ 6419
2Ki 19:20 That which thou hast **p.** to me........... 6419
2Ki 20:2 to the wall, and **p.** unto the Lord, ... 6419
2Ch 30:18 But Hezekiah **p.** for them, saying, ... 6419
2Ch 32:20 of Amoz, **p.** and cried to heaven. 6419
2Ch 32:24 the death, and **p.** unto the Lord: 6419
2Ch 33:13 **p.** unto him: and he was intreated 6419
Ezr 10:1 Now when Ezra had **p.**, and when....... 6419
Ne 1:4 and **p.** before the God of heaven......... 6419
Ne 2:4 So I **p.** to the God of heaven............. 6419
Job 42:10 Job, when he **p.** for his friends: 6419
Isa 37:15 Hezekiah **p.** unto the Lord, saying,...... 6419
Isa 37:21 Whereas thou hast **p.** to me............. 6419
Isa 38:2 the wall, and **p.** unto the Lord, ... 6419
Jer 32:16 Neriah, I **p.** unto the Lord, saying, ... 6419
Da 6:10 **p.**, and gave thanks before his........... 6739
Da 9:4 And I **p.** unto the Lord my God, ... 6419
Jon 2:1 Jonah **p.** unto the Lord his God.......... 6419
Jon 4:2 And he **p.** unto the Lord, and said, ... 6419
Mt 26:39 fell on his face, and **p.**, saying, ... *4336*
Mt 26:42 away the second time, and **p.**, ... *4336*
Mt 26:44 **p.** the third time, saying the same...... *4336*
Mk 1:35 a solitary place, and there **p.**............ *4336*
Mk 5:18 **p.** him that he might be with him. *3870*
Mk 14:35 and **p.** that, if it were possible, ... *4336*
Mk 14:39 went away, and **p.**, and spake the *4336*
Lu 5:3 **p.** him that he would thrust out a....... *2065*
Lu 5:16 himself into the wilderness, and **p.**...... *4336*
Lu 9:29 And as he **p.**, the fashion of his *4336*
Lu 18:11 stood and **p.** thus with himself, ... *4336*
Lu 22:32 **p.** for thee, that thy faith fail not: .*1189*
Lu 22:41 east, and kneeled down and **p.**,.......... *4336*
Lu 22:44 in an agony he **p.** more earnestly: *4336*
Joh 4:31 his disciples **p.** him, saying,............... *2065*
Ac 1:24 And they **p.**, and said, Thou, Lord, ... *4336*
Ac 4:31 And when they had **p.**, the place......... *1189*
Ac 6:6 when they had **p.**, they laid their........ *4336*
Ac 8:15 **p.** for them, that they might receive ... *4336*
Ac 9:40 forth, and kneeled down, and **p.**;......... *4336*
Ac 10:2 to the people, and **p.** to God alway..... *1189*
Ac 10:30 the ninth hour I **p.** in my house, ... *4336*
Ac 10:48 **p.** they him to tarry certain days......... *2065*
Ac 13:3 when they had fasted and **p.**, and....... *4336*
Ac 14:23 **p.** with fasting, they commended......... *4336*
Ac 16:9 man of Macedonia, and **p.** him, ... *3870*
Ac 16:25 Paul and Silas **p.**, and sang................ *4336*
Ac 20:36 kneeled down, and **p.** with them all..... *4336*
Ac 21:5 kneeled down on the shore, and **p.**....... *4336*
Ac 22:17 while I **p.** in the temple, I was in a..... *4336*
Ac 23:18 **p.** me to bring this young man........... *2065*
Ac 28:8 Paul entered in, and **p.**, and laid......... *4336*
Jas 5:17 he **p.** earnestly that it might not......... *4336*
Jas 5:18 he **p.** again, and the heaven gave *4336*

PRAYER See also PRAYERS.

2Sa 7:27 heart to pray this **p.** unto thee............ 8605
1Ki 8:28 thou respect unto the **p.** of thy.......... 8605
1Ki 8:28 hearken unto the cry and to the **p.**, ... 8605
1Ki 8:29 **p.** which thy servant shall make 8605
1Ki 8:38 **p.** and supplication soever be made..... 8605
1Ki 8:45 hear thou in heaven their **p.** and 8605
1Ki 8:49 Then hear thou their **p.** and their 8605
1Ki 8:54 made an end of praying all this **p.**........ 8605
1Ki 9:3 him, I have heard thy **p.** and thy......... 8605
2Ki 19:4 lift up thy **p.** for the remnant that....... 8605
2Ki 20:5 I have heard thy **p.**, I have seen.......... 8605
2Ch 6:19 Have respect therefore to the **p.**......... 8605
2Ch 6:19 to the **p.** which thy servant prayeth.... 8605
2Ch 6:20 to hearken unto the **p.** which thy 8605
2Ch 6:29 **p.** or what supplication soever 8605
2Ch 6:35 hear thou from the heavens their **p.**..... 8605
2Ch 6:39 their **p.** and their supplications, ... 8605
2Ch 6:40 attent unto the **p.** that is made in........ 8605
2Ch 7:12 I have heard thy **p.**, and have............ 8605
2Ch 7:15 unto the **p.** that is made in this.......... 8605
2Ch 30:27 and their **p.** came up to his holy......... 8605
2Ch 33:18 Manasseh, and his **p.** unto his God, ... 8605
2Ch 33:19 His **p.** also, and how God was........... 8605
Ne 1:6 hear the **p.** of thy servant, which 8605
Ne 1:11 attentive to the **p.** of thy servant, ... 8605
Ne 1:11 and to the **p.** of thy servants, who 8605
Ne 4:9 Nevertheless we made our **p.** unto 6419
Ne 11:17 begin the thanksgiving in **p.**: and........ 8605
Job 15:4 and restrainest **p.** before God............ 7878
Job 16:17 mine hands: also my **p.** is pure. 8605
Job 22:27 Thou shalt make thy **p.** unto him,........ 6279
Ps 4:1 mercy upon me, and hear my **p.**. 8605
Ps 5:3 will I direct my **p.** unto thee, and............
Ps 6:9 the Lord will receive my **p.**.................. 8605
Ps 17:*title* A **p.** of David............................... 8605
Ps 17:1 give ear unto my **p.**, that goeth 8605
Ps 35:13 **p.** returned into mine own bosom. 8605
Ps 39:12 Hear my **p.**, O Lord, and give ear...... 8605
Ps 42:8 **p.** unto the God of my life................. 8605
Ps 54:2 Hear my **p.**, O God; give ear to the ... 8605
Ps 55:1 Give ear to my **p.**, O God; and hide ... 8605
Ps 61:1 my cry, O God; attend unto my **p.**. 8605
Ps 64:1 Hear my voice, O God, in my **p.**......... 7879
Ps 65:2 O thou that hearest **p.**, unto thee......... 8605
Ps 66:19 attended to the voice of my **p.**............ 8605
Ps 66:20 which hath not turned away my **p.**,...... 8605
Ps 69:13 for me, my **p.** is unto thee, O Lord, ... 8605
Ps 72:15 **p.** also shall be made for him............. 6419
Ps 80:4 against the **p.** of thy people? 8605
Ps 84:8 O Lord God of hosts, hear my **p.**: 8605
Ps 86:*title* A **p.** of David. 8605
Ps 86:6 Give ear, O Lord, unto my **p.**; 8605
Ps 88:2 Let my **p.** come before thee: incline ... 8605
Ps 88:13 morning shall my **p.** prevent thee. 8605
Ps 90:*title* A **p.** of Moses the man of God. 8605
Ps 102:1 Hear my **p.**, O Lord, and let my.......... 8605
Ps 102:17 will regard the **p.** of the destitute, ... 8605
Ps 102:17 and not despise their **p.**..................... 8605
Ps 109:4 but I give myself unto **p.**. 8605
Ps 109:7 and let his **p.** become sin.................. 8605
Ps 141:2 Let my **p.** be set forth before thee..... 8605
Ps 141:5 yet my **p.** also shall be in their 8605
Ps 142:*title* David; A **P.** when he was in 8605
Ps 143:1 Hear my **p.**, O Lord, give ear to my... 8605
Pr 15:8 the **p.** of the upright is his delight. 8605
Pr 15:29 he heareth the **p.** of the righteous. 8605
Pr 28:9 his **p.** shall be an abomination. 8605
Isa 26:16 poured out a **p.** when...chastening 3908
Isa 37:4 thy **p.** for the remnant that is left. 8605
Isa 38:5 I have heard thy **p.**, I have seen......... 8605
Isa 56:7 them joyful in my house of **p.**............ 8605
Isa 56:7 house shall be called an house of **p.**..... 8605
Jer 7:16 neither lift up cry nor **p.** for them, ... 8605
Jer 11:14 neither lift up a cry or **p.** for them: 8605
La 3:8 and shout, he shutteth out my **p.**. 8605
La 3:44 that our **p.** should not pass through. ... 8605
Da 9:3 seek by **p.** and supplications, with 8605
Da 9:13 we not our **p.** before the Lord our 2470
Da 9:17 God, hear the **p.** of thy servant, ... 8605
Da 9:21 whiles I was speaking in **p.**, even........ 8605
Jon 2:7 my **p.** came in unto thee, into thine..... 8605
Hab 3:1 A **p.** of Habakkuk the prophet 8605
Mt 17:21 not out but by **p.** and fasting. *4335*
Mt 21:13 shall be called the house of **p.**; but .*4335*
Mt 21:22 whatsoever ye shall ask in **p.**, ... *4335*
Mt 23:14 and for a pretence make long **p.**: *4336*
Mk 9:29 by nothing, but by **p.** and fasting...*4335*
Mk 11:17 of all nations the house of **p.**?........ *4335*
Lu 1:13 not, Zacharias: for thy **p.** is heard; *1162*
Lu 6:12 continued all night in **p.** to God. *4335*
Lu 19:46 My house is the house of **p.**: but *4335*
Lu 22:45 when he rose up from **p.**, and was *4335*
Ac 1:14 one accord in **p.** and supplication, ... *4335*
Ac 3:1 the hour of **p.**, being the ninth hour.... *4335*
Ac 6:4 will give ourselves continually to **p.**,.... *4335*
Ac 10:31 And said, Cornelius, thy **p.** is heard,.... *4335*
Ac 12:5 but **p.** was made without ceasing of *4335*
Ac 16:13 where **p.** was wont to be made;.......... *4335*
Ac 16:16 as we went to **p.**, a certain damsel...... *4335*
Ro 10:1 desire and **p.** to God for Israel is, ... *1162*
Ro 12:12 continuing instant in **p.**; *4335*
1Co 7:5 give yourselves to fasting and **p.**; *4335*
2Co 1:11 also helping together by **p.** for us, ... *1162*
2Co 9:14 by their **p.** for you, which long after ... *1162*
Eph 6:18 Praying always with all **p.** and........... *4335*
Php 1:4 Always in every **p.** of mine for you..... *1162*
Php 1:19 to my salvation through your **p.**, ... *1162*
Php 4:6 every thing by **p.** and supplication....... *4335*
Col 4:2 Continue in **p.**, and watch in the *4335*
1Ti 4:5 sanctified by...word of God and **p.**....... *1783*
Jas 5:15 the **p.** of faith shall save the sick,........ *2171*
Jas 5:16 fervent **p.** of a righteous man *1162*
1Pe 4:7 therefore sober, and watch unto **p.**. *4335*

PRAYERS

Ps 72:20 **p.** of David the son of Jesse are......... 8605
Isa 1:15 when ye make many **p.**, I will not 8605
Mk 12:40 and for a pretence make long **p.**. *4336*
Lu 2:37 with fastings and **p.** night and day....... *1162*
Lu 5:33 of John fast often, and make **p.**, ... *1162*
Lu 20:47 and for a shew make long **p.**.......... *4336*
Ac 2:42 and in breaking of bread, and in **p.**. *4335*

Ac 10:4 Thy p. and thine alms are come up *4335*
Ro 1:9 mention of you always in my p.; *4335*
Ro 15:30 with me in your p. to God for me; *4335*
Eph 1:16 making mention of you in my p.; *4335*
Col 4:12 labouring fervently for you in p., *4335*
1Th 1:2 making mention of you in our p.; *4335*
1Ti 2:1 supplications, p., intercessions, and *4335*
1Ti 5:5 continueth in supplications and p. *4335*
2Ti 1:3 have remembrance of thee in my p. *1162*
Phm 4 mention of thee always in my p., *4335*
Phm 22 through your p. I shall be given *4335*
Heb 5:7 he had offered up p....supplications *1162*
1Pe 3:7 life; that your p. be not hindered *4335*
1Pe 3:12 and his ears are open unto their p. *1162*
Re 5:8 odours, which are the p. of saints. *4335*
Re 8:3 offer it with the p. of all saints upon *4335*
Re 8:4 came with the p. of the saints, *4335*

PRAYEST
Mt 6:5 **when thou p., thou shalt not be as** *4336*
Mt 6:6 **when thou p., enter into thy closet.** *4336*

PRAYETH
1Ki 8:28 thy servant p. before thee to day: 6419
2Ch 6:19 which thy servant p. before thee: 6419
2Ch 6:20 thy servant p. toward this place. 6419
Isa 44:17 and worshippeth it, and p. unto it, 6419
Ac 9:11 **Saul, of Tarsus: for, behold, he p.,** *4336*
1Co 11:5 every woman that p. or prophesieth *4336*
1Co 14:14 my spirit p., but my understanding *4336*

PRAYING
1Sa 1:12 she continued p. before the Lord, 6419
1Sa 1:26 stood by thee here, p. unto the Lord. 6419
1Ki 8:54 Solomon had made an end of p. all 6419
2Ch 7:1 Solomon had made an end of p., 6419
Da 6:11 and found Daniel p. and making 1156
Da 9:20 And whiles I was speaking, and p., 6419
Mk 11:25 **when ye stand p., forgive, if ye** *4336*
Lu 1:10 people were p. without at the time *4336*
Lu 3:21 Jesus also being baptized, and p., *4336*
Lu 9:18 it came to pass, as he was alone p., *4336*
Lu 11:1 as he was p. in a certain place, *4336*
Ac 11:5 I was in the city of Joppa p.: and in *4336*
Ac 12:12 many were gathered together p.. *4336*
1Co 11:4 Every man p. or prophesying, *4336*
2Co 8:4 P. us with much intreaty that we *1189*
Eph 6:18 P. always with all prayer and *4336*
Col 1:3 Lord Jesus Christ, p. always for you, *4336*
Col 4:3 p. also for us, that God would open *4336*
1Th 3:10 Night and day p. exceedingly that *1189*
Jude 20 holy faith, p. in the Holy Ghost, *4336*

PREACH
See also PREACHED; PREACHEST; PREACHETH; PREACHING.
Ne 6:7 prophets to p. of thee at Jerusalem, 7121
Isa 61:1 anointed me to p. good tidings 1319
Jon 3:2 p. unto it the preaching that I bid 7121
Mt 4:17 From that time Jesus began to p., *2784*
Mt 10:7 **ye go, p., saying, The kingdom of** *2784*
Mt 10:27 **ear, that p. ye upon the housetops.** *2784*
Mt 11:1 to teach and to p. in their cities. *2784*
Mk 1:4 p. the baptism of repentance for the *2784*
Mk 1:38 **towns, that I may p. there also:** *2784*
Mk 3:14 that he might send them forth to p., *2784*
Mk 16:15 **and p. the gospel to every creature.** *2784*
Lu 4:18 **me to p. the gospel to the poor;** *2097*
Lu 4:18 **to p. deliverance to the captives,** *2784*
Lu 4:19 **p. the acceptable year of the Lord.** *2784*
Lu 4:43 **I must p. the kingdom of God to** *2097*
Lu 9:2 he sent them to p. the kingdom of *2784*
Lu 9:60 **thou and p. the kingdom of God** *1229*
Ac 5:42 not to teach and p. Jesus Christ. *2097*
Ac 10:42 he commanded us to p. unto the *2784*
Ac 14:15 and p. unto you that ye should turn *2097*
Ac 15:21 hath in every city them that p. him, *2784*
Ac 16:6 Holy Ghost to p. the word in Asia, *2980*
Ac 16:10 us for to p. the gospel unto them. *2097*
Ac 17:3 this Jesus, whom I p. unto you, is *2605*
Ro 1:15 I am ready to p. the gospel to you *2097*
Ro 10:8 is, the word of faith, which we p.; *2784*
Ro 10:15 shall they p., except they be sent? *2784*
Ro 10:15 of them that p. the gospel of peace, *2097*
Ro 15:20 so have I strived to p. the gospel, *2097*
1Co 1:17 not to baptize, but to p. the gospel: *2097*
1Co 1:23 But we p. Christ crucified, unto the *2784*
1Co 9:14 they which p. the gospel should *2605*
1Co 9:16 For though I p. the gospel, I have *2097*
1Co 9:16 woe is unto me, if I p. not the gospel! *2097*
1Co 9:18 when I p. the gospel, I may make *2097*
1Co 15:11 they, so we p., and so ye believed. *2784*
2Co 2:12 I came to Troas to p. Christ's gospel,
2Co 4:5 For we p. not ourselves, but Christ *2784*
2Co 10:16 p. the gospel in the regions beyond *2097*
Ga 1:8 p. any other gospel unto you than *2097*
Ga 1:9 man p. any other gospel unto you *2097*
Ga 1:16 I might p. him among the heathen; *2097*
Ga 2:2 which I p. among the Gentiles, *2784*
Ga 5:11 if I yet p. circumcision, why do I *2784*
Eph 3:8 I should p. among the Gentiles the *2097*
Php 1:15 Some indeed p. Christ even of envy *2784*
Php 1:16 The one p. Christ of contention, *2605*
Col 1:28 we p., warning every man, Whom *2605*
2Ti 4:2 P. the word; be instant in season, *2784*
Re 14:6 to p. unto them that dwell on the *2097*

PREACHED
Ps 40:9 have p. righteousness in the great 1319
Mt 11:5 **poor have the gospel p. to them,** *2097*
Mt 24:14 **be p. in all the world for a witness** *2784*
Mt 26:13 **this gospel shall be p. in the whole** *2784*
Mk 1:7 And p., saying, There cometh one *2784*
Mk 1:39 And he p. in their synagogues *2784*
Mk 2:2 and he p. the word unto them. *2980*
Mk 6:12 and p. that men should repent. *2784*
Mk 14:9 **this gospel shall be p. throughout** *2784*
Mk 16:20 they went forth, and p. every where, *2784*
Lu 3:18 exhortation p. he unto the people. *2097*
Lu 4:44 And he p. in the synagogues of *2784*
Lu 7:22 **raised, to the poor the gospel is p.** *2097*
Lu 16:16 **time the kingdom of God is p.,** *2097*
Lu 20:1 in the temple, and p. the gospel, *2097*
Lu 24:47 **should be p. in his name among** *2784*
Ac 3:20 which before was p. unto you: *4296*
Ac 4:2 p. through Jesus the resurrection *2605*
Ac 8:5 Samaria, and p. Christ unto them. *2784*
Ac 8:25 testified and p. the word of the *2980*
Ac 8:25 p. the gospel in many villages of *2097*
Ac 8:35 scripture, and p. unto him Jesus. *2097*
Ac 8:40 he p. in all the cities, till he came *2097*
Ac 9:20 he p. Christ in the synagogues, *2784*
Ac 9:27 how he had p. boldly at Damascus *3954*
Ac 10:37 after the baptism which John p.; *2784*
Ac 13:5 they p. the word of God in the *2605*
Ac 13:24 John had first p. before his coming *4296*
Ac 13:38 p. unto you the forgiveness of sins: *2605*
Ac 13:42 be p. to them the next sabbath. *2980*
Ac 14:7 And there they p. the gospel. *2097*
Ac 14:21 they had p. the gospel to that city, *2097*
Ac 14:25 they had p. the word in Perga, *2980*
Ac 15:36 where we have p. the word of the *2605*
Ac 17:13 that the word of God was p. of Paul *2605*
Ac 17:18 because he p. unto them Jesus, *2907*
Ac 20:7 Paul p. unto them, ready to depart *1256*
Ro 15:19 have fully p. the gospel of Christ. *4137*
1Co 9:27 when I have p. to others, I myself *2784*
1Co 15:1 you the gospel which I p. unto you, *2097*
1Co 15:2 keep in memory what I p. unto you, *2097*
1Co 15:12 if Christ be p. that he rose from the *2784*
2Co 1:19 who was p. among you by us, even *2784*
2Co 11:4 Jesus, whom we have not p., *2784*
2Co 11:7 I have p. to you the gospel of God *2097*
Ga 1:8 that which we have p. unto you, *2097*
Ga 1:11 the gospel which was p. of me is not *2097*
Ga 3:8 p. before the gospel unto Abraham, *4283*
Ga 4:13 I p. the gospel unto you at the *2097*
Eph 2:17 came and p. peace to you which *2097*
Php 1:18 pretence, or in truth, Christ is p.; *2605*
Col 1:23 which was p. to every creature *2784*
1Th 2:9 we p. unto you the gospel of God. *2784*
1Ti 3:16 p. unto the Gentiles, believed on in *2784*
Heb 4:2 For unto us was the gospel p., as *2097*
Heb 4:2 but the word p. did not profit them, *189*
Heb 4:6 and they to whom it was first p. *2097*
1Pe 1:12 them that have p. the gospel unto *2097*
1Pe 1:25 which by the gospel is p. unto you. *2097*
1Pe 3:19 and p. unto the spirits in prison; *2784*
1Pe 4:6 for this cause was the gospel p. *2097*

PREACHER
Ec *general title* Ecclesiastes; Or, The P.
Ec 1:1 words of the P., the son of David 6953
Ec 1:2 Vanity of vanities, saith the P., 6953
Ec 1:12 I the P. was king over Israel in 6953
Ec 7:27 this have I found, saith the p., 6953
Ec 12:8 Vanity of vanities, saith the p.; all 6953
Ec 12:9 because the p. was wise, he still 6953
Ec 12:10 p. sought to find out acceptable 6953
Ro 10:14 how shall they hear without a p.? *2784*
1Ti 2:7 I am ordained a p., and an apostle, *2783*
2Ti 1:11 I am appointed a p., and an apostle, *2783*
2Pe 2:5 eighth person, a p. of righteousness, *2783*

PREACHEST
Ro 2:21 that p. a man should not steal, *2784*

PREACHETH
Ac 19:13 you by Jesus whom Paul p.. *2784*
2Co 11:4 if he that cometh p. another Jesus, *2784*
Ga 1:23 now p. the faith which once he *2097*

PREACHING
Jon 3:2 unto it the p. that I bid thee. 7150
Mt 3:1 p. in the wilderness of Judaea, *2784*
Mt 4:23 and p. the gospel of the kingdom, *2784*
Mt 9:35 and p. the gospel of the kingdom, *2784*
Mt 12:41 **they repented at the p. of Jonas;** *2782*
Mk 1:14 p. the gospel of the kingdom of *2784*
Lu 3:3 p. the baptism of repentance for *2784*
Lu 8:1 p. and shewing the glad tidings of *2784*
Lu 9:6 p. the gospel, and healing every *2097*
Lu 11:32 **they repented at the p. of Jonas;** *2782*
Ac 8:4 went every where p. the word. *2097*
Ac 8:12 believed Philip p. the things *2097*
Ac 10:36 Israel, p. peace by Jesus Christ: *2097*
Ac 11:19 p. the word to none but unto the *2980*
Ac 11:20 the Grecians, p. the Lord Jesus. *2097*
Ac 15:35 and p. the word of the Lord, with *2097*
Ac 20:9 as Paul was long p., he sunk down *1256*
Ac 20:25 have gone p. the kingdom of God, *2784*
Ac 28:31 P. the kingdom of God, and *2784*
Ro 16:25 gospel, and the p. of Jesus Christ, *2782*
1Co 1:18 For the p. of the cross is to them *3056*
1Co 1:21 by the foolishness of p. to save *2782*
1Co 2:4 my p. was not with enticing words *2782*
1Co 15:14 be not risen, then is our p. vain, *2782*
2Co 10:14 to you also in p. the gospel of Christ: *2782*
2Ti 4:17 me the p. might be fully known, *2782*
Tit 1:3 manifested his word through p., *2782*

PRECEPT
See also PRECEPTS.
Isa 28:10 p. must be upon p., p. upon p.; 6673
Isa 28:13 unto them p. upon p., p. upon p.; 6673
Isa 29:13 me is taught by the p. of men: 4687
Mk 10:5 **your heart he wrote you this p.** *1785*
Heb 9:19 Moses had spoken every p. to all *1785*

PRECEPTS
Ne 9:14 and commandedst them p., 4687
Ps 119:4 commanded us to keep thy p. 6490
Ps 119:15 I will meditate in thy p., and have 6490
Ps 119:27 to understand the way of thy p.: 6490
Ps 119:40 I have longed after thy p.: quicken 6490
Ps 119:45 walk at liberty: for I seek thy p.. 6490
Ps 119:56 This I had, because I kept thy p.. 6490
Ps 119:63 thee, and of them that keep thy p. 6490
Ps 119:69 keep thy p. with my whole heart. 6490
Ps 119:78 cause: but I will meditate in thy p.. 6490
Ps 119:87 earth; but I forsook not thy p. 6490
Ps 119:93 I will never forget thy p.: for with 6490
Ps 119:94 save me; for I have sought thy p.. 6490
Ps 119:100 the ancients, because I keep thy p.. 6490
Ps 119:104 thy p. I get understanding: 6490
Ps 119:110 for me: yet I erred not from thy p.. 6490
Ps 119:128 I esteem all thy p. concerning all 6490
Ps 119:134 of man: so will I keep thy p.. 6490
Ps 119:141 despised: yet do not I forget thy p.. 6490
Ps 119:159 Consider how I love thy p.: 6490
Ps 119:168 kept thy p. and thy testimonies: 6490
Ps 119:173 help me; for I have chosen thy p.. 6490
Jer 35:18 and kept all his p., and done 4687
Da 9:5 even by departing from thy p. and 4687

PRECIOUS
Ge 24:53 and to her mother p. things. 4030
De 33:13 for the p. things of heaven, for 4022
De 33:14 p. fruits brought forth by the sun, 4022
De 33:14 p. things put forth by the moon, 4022
De 33:15 for the p. things of the lasting hills, 4022
De 33:16 for the p. things of the earth and 4022
1Sa 3:1 of the Lord was p. in those days; 3368
1Sa 26:21 my soul was p. in thine eyes this 3365
2Sa 12:30 a talent of gold with the p. stones: 3368
1Ki 10:2 and very much gold, and p. stones: 3368

1Ki 10:10 very great store, and **p.** stones: 3368
1Ki 10:11 plenty of almug trees, and **p.** stones. 3368
2Ki 1:13 thy servants, be **p.** in thy sight. 3365
2Ki 1:14 let my life now be **p.** in thy sight. 3365
2Ki 20:13 all the house of his **p.** things, 5238
2Ki 20:13 the spices, and the **p.** ointment, 2896
1Ch 20:2 and there were **p.** stones in it; 3368
1Ch 29:2 all manner of **p.** stones, and marble 3368
1Ch 29:8 they with whom **p.** stones were found
2Ch 3:6 garnished the house with **p.** stones 3368
2Ch 9:1 gold in abundance, and **p.** stones: 3368
2Ch 9:9 great abundance, and **p.** stones: 3368
2Ch 9:10 brought algum trees and **p.** stones. 3368
2Ch 20:25 the dead bodies, and **p.** jewels, 2530
2Ch 21:3 and of gold, and of **p.** things, with 4030
2Ch 32:27 and for gold, and for **p.** stones, 3368
Ezr 1:6 with beasts, and with **p.** things, 4030
Ezr 8:27 vessels of fine copper, **p.** as gold. 2530
Job 28:10 and his eyes seeth every **p.** thing. 3366
Job 28:16 gold of Ophir, with the **p.** onyx, 3368
Ps 49:8 the redemption of their soul is **p.**, 3365
Ps 72:14 and **p.** shall their blood be in his 3365
Ps 116:15 **P.** in the sight of the Lord is the 3368
Ps 126:6 and weepeth, bearing **p.** seed, 4901
Ps 133:2 It is like the **p.** ointment upon the 2896
Ps 139:17 How **p.** also are thy thoughts 3365
Pr 1:13 We shall find all **p.** substance, we 3368
Pr 3:15 She is more **p.** than rubies: and all 3368
Pr 6:26 adulteress will hunt for the **p.** life. 3368
Pr 12:27 substance of a diligent man is **p.**. 3368
Pr 17:8 A gift is as a **p.** stone in the eyes 2580
Pr 20:15 lips of knowledge are a **p.** jewel. 3366
Pr 24:4 with all **p.** and pleasant riches. 3368
Ec 7:1 name is better than **p.** ointment; 2896
Isa 13:12 a man more **p.** than fine gold; 3365
Isa 28:16 a tried stone, a **p.** corner stone, 3368
Isa 39:2 them the house of his **p.** things, 5238
Isa 39:2 the spices, and the **p.** ointment, 2896
Isa 43:4 Since thou wast **p.** in my sight, 3365
Jer 15:19 take forth the **p.** from the vile, 3368
Jer 20:5 and all the **p.** things thereof, and 3366
La 4:2 The **p.** sons of Zion, comparable 3368
Eze 22:25 taken the treasure and **p.** things; 3366
Eze 27:20 Dedan...thy merchant in **p.** clothes 2667
Eze 27:22 and with all **p.** stones, and gold 3368
Eze 28:13 every **p.** stone was thy covering, 3368
Da 11:8 **p.** vessels of silver and of gold; 2532
Da 11:38 and silver, and with **p.** stones, 3368
Da 11:43 over all the **p.** things of Egypt: 2530
Mt 26:7 alabaster box of very **p.** ointment, *927*
Mk 14:3 of ointment of spikenard very **p.**; *4185*
1Co 3:12 silver, **p.** stones, wood, hay, *5093*
Jas 5:7 waiteth for the **p.** fruit of the earth, *5093*
1Pe 1:7 more **p.** than of gold that perisheth, *5093*
1Pe 1:19 But with the **p.** blood of Christ, as *5093*
1Pe 2:4 of men, but chosen of God, and **p.**, *1784*
1Pe 2:6 Sion a chief corner stone, elect, **p.**: *1784*
1Pe 2:7 therefore which believe he is **p.**: *5092*
2Pe 1:1 that have obtained the **p.** faith *2472*
2Pe 1:4 exceeding great and **p.** promises *5093*
Re 17:4 decked with gold and **p.** stones and *5093*
Re 18:12 silver, and **p.** stones, and of pearls, *5093*
Re 18:12 all manner vessels of most **p.** wood, *5093*
Re 18:16 decked with gold, and **p.** stones, and *5093*
Re 21:11 light was like unto a stone most **p.** *5093*
Re 21:19 with all manner of **p.** stones. *5093*

PREDESTINATE See also PREDESTINATED.
Ro 8:29 also did **p.** to be conformed to the *4309*
Ro 8:30 whom he did **p.**, them he also *4309*

PREDESTINATED
Eph 1:5 Having **p.** us unto the adoption *4309*
Eph 1:11 being **p.** according to the purpose *4309*

PREEMINENCE
Ec 3:19 a man hath no **p.** above a beast: 4195
Col 1:18 all things he might have the **p.** *4409*
3Jo 9 loveth to have the **p.** among them, *5383*

PREFER See also PREFERRED; PREFERRING.
Ps 137:6 If I **p.** not Jerusalem above my 5927

PREFERRED
Es 2:9 he **p.** her and her maids unto the 8138
Da 6:3 this Daniel was **p.** above the 5330
Joh 1:15 cometh after me is **p.** before me: *1096*
Joh 1:27 coming after me is **p.** before me, *1096*
Joh 1:30 a man which is **p.** before me: *1096*

PREFERRING
Ro 12:10 love; in honour **p.** one another; *4285*
1Ti 5:21 without **p.** one before another, *4299*

PREMEDITATE
Mk 13:11 **ye shall speak, neither do ye p** *3191*

PREPARATION See also PREPARATIONS.
1Ch 22:5 will therefore now make **p.** for it. 3559
Na 2:3 flaming torches in the day of his **p.**, 3559
Mt 27:62 that followed the day of the **p.**, *3904*
Mk 15:42 was come, because it was the **p.**, *3904*
Lu 23:54 And that day was the **p.**, and the *3904*
Joh 19:14 And it was the **p.** of the passover, *3904*
Joh 19:31 because it was the **p.**, that the *3904*
Joh 19:42 because of the Jews' **p.** day; *3904*
Eph 6:15 with the **p.** of the gospel of peace; *2091*

PREPARATIONS
Pr 16:1 The **p.** of the heart in man, and 4633

PREPARE See also PREPARED; PREPAREST; PREPARETH; PREPARING.
Ex 15:2 God, and I will **p.** him an habitation; 4633
Ex 16:5 they shall **p.** that which they bring 3559
Nu 15:5 a drink offering shalt thou **p.** with 6213
Nu 15:6 thou shalt **p.** for a meat offering 6213
Nu 15:12 to the number that ye shall **p.**, so 6213
Nu 23:1 **p.** me here seven oxen and seven 3559
Nu 23:29 and **p.** me here seven bullocks and 3559
De 19:3 Thou shalt **p.** thee a way, and 3559
Jos 1:11 people, saying, **P.** you victuals; 3559
Jos 22:26 Let us now **p.** to build us an altar, 6213
1Sa 7:3 **p.** your hearts unto the Lord, and 3559
1Sa 23:22 I pray you, **p.** ye, and know and 3559
1Ki 18:44 Ahab, **P.** thy chariot, and get thee 631
1Ch 9:32 shewbread, to **p.** it every sabbath. 3559
1Ch 29:18 and **p.** their heart unto thee: and 3559
2Ch 2:9 to **p.** me timber in abundance: 3559
2Ch 31:11 to **p.** chambers in the house of the 3559
2Ch 35:4 **p.** yourselves by the houses of your 3559
2Ch 35:6 yourselves, and **p.** your brethren, 3559
Es 5:8 banquet that I shall **p.** for them, 6213
Job 8:8 **p.** thyself to the search of their 3559
Job 11:13 If thou **p.** thine heart, and stretch 3559
Job 27:16 dust, and **p.** raiment as the clay; 3559
Job 27:17 He may **p.** it, but the just shall put 3559
Ps 10:17 thou wilt **p.** their heart, thou wilt 3559
Ps 59:4 **p.** themselves without my fault: 3559
Ps 61:7 O **p.** mercy and truth, which may 4487
Ps 107:36 they may **p.** a city for habitation; 3559
Pr 24:27 **P.** thy work without, and make it 3559
Pr 30:25 they **p.** their meat in the summer; 3559
Isa 14:21 **P.** slaughter for his children for 3559
Isa 21:5 **p.** the table, watch in the 6186
Isa 40:3 **P.** ye the way of the Lord, make 6437
Isa 40:20 to **p.** a graven image, that shall 3559
Isa 57:14 ye up, **p.** the way, take up the 6437
Isa 62:10 **p.** ye the way of the people; cast 6437
Isa 65:11 that **p.** a table for that troop, and 6186
Jer 6:4 **P.** ye war against her; arise, and 6942
Jer 12:3 **p.** them for the day of slaughter. 6942
Jer 22:7 I will **p.** destroyers against thee, 6942
Jer 46:14 Stand fast, and **p.** thee; for the 3559
Jer 51:12 the watchmen, **p.** the ambushes: 3559
Jer 51:27 **p.** the nations against her, call 6942
Jer 51:28 **P.** against her the nations with the 6942
Eze 4:15 thou shalt **p.** thy bread therewith. 6213
Eze 12:3 man, **p.** thee stuff for removing, 6213
Eze 35:6 I will **p.** thee unto blood, and blood 6213
Eze 38:7 and **p.** for thyself, thou, and all thy 3559
Eze 43:25 thou **p.** every day a goat for a sin 6213
Eze 43:25 they shall also **p.** a young bullock, 3559
Eze 45:17 he shall **p.** the sin offering, and the 3559
Eze 45:22 day shall the prince **p.** for himself 3559
Eze 45:23 **p.** a burnt offering to the Lord, 3559
Eze 45:24 shall **p.** a meat offering of an ephah 3559
Eze 46:2 priests shall **p.** his burnt offering 3559
Eze 46:7 And he shall **p.** a meat offering, an 3559
Eze 46:12 shall **p.** a voluntary burnt offering 3559
Eze 46:12 he shall **p.** his burnt offering and 3559
Eze 46:13 Thou shalt daily **p.** a burnt offering 3559
Eze 46:13 thou shalt **p.** it every morning. 3559
Eze 46:14 thou shalt **p.** a meat offering for it 3559
Eze 46:15 Thus shall they **p.** the lamb, and 3559
Joe 3:9 **P.** war, wake up the mighty men, 6942
Am 4:12 thee, **p.** to meet thy God, O Israel. 3559
Mic 3:5 they even **p.** war against him. 6942
Mal 3:1 and he shall **p.** the way before me: 6437
Mt 3:3 **P.** ye the way of the Lord, make *2090*
Mt 11:10 **which shall p. thy way before thee** *2680*
Mt 26:17 **p.** for thee to eat the passover? *2090*
Mk 1:2 which shall **p.** thy way before thee. *2680*
Mk 1:3 **P.** ye the way of the Lord, make *2090*
Mk 14:12 Where wilt thou that we go and **p.** *2090*
Lu 1:76 face of the Lord to **p.** his ways; *2090*
Lu 3:4 **P.** ye the way of the Lord, make *2090*
Lu 7:27 **which shall p. thy way before thee** *2680*
Lu 22:8 **Go and p. us the passover, that we** *2090*
Lu 22:9 him, Where wilt thou that we **p.**? *2090*
Joh 14:2 **told you. I go to p. a place for you** *2090*
Joh 14:3 **And if I go and p. a place for you,** *2090*
1Co 14:8 who shall **p.** himself to the battle? *3903*
Phm 22 **p.** me also a lodging: for I trust *2090*

PREPARED See also PREPAREDST; UNPREPARED.
Ge 24:31 I have **p.** the house, and room for 6437
Ge 27:17 and the bread, which she had **p.**, 6213
Ex 12:39 neither had they **p.** for themselves 6213
Ex 23:20 into the place which I have **p.** 3559
Nu 21:27 the city of Sihon be built and **p.**: 3559
Nu 23:4 unto him, I have **p.** seven altars, 6186
Jos 4:4 he had **p.** of the children of Israel, 3559
Jos 4:13 forty thousand **p.** for war passed 2502
2Sa 15:1 Absalom **p.** him chariots and 6213
1Ki 1:5 he **p.** him chariots and horsemen, 6213
1Ki 5:18 so they **p.** timber and stones to 3559
1Ki 6:19 the oracle he **p.** in the house within, 3559
2Ki 6:23 he **p.** great provision for them: 3739
1Ch 12:39 for their brethren had **p.** for them. 3559
1Ch 15:1 and **p.** a place for the ark of God, 3559
1Ch 15:3 his place, which he had **p.** for it. 3559
1Ch 15:12 unto the place that I have **p.** for it. 3559
1Ch 22:3 And David **p.** iron in abundance for 3559
1Ch 22:5 So David **p.** abundantly before his 3559
1Ch 22:14 I have **p.** for the house of the Lord 3559
1Ch 22:14 timber also and stone have I **p.**; 3559
1Ch 29:2 Now I have **p.** with all my might for 3559
1Ch 29:3 all that I have **p.** for the holy house, 3559
1Ch 29:16 we have **p.** to build thee an house 3559
2Ch 1:4 the place which David had **p.** for it: 3559
2Ch 3:1 in the place that David had **p.** in 3559
2Ch 8:16 Now all the work of Solomon was **p.** 3559
2Ch 12:14 he **p.** not his heart to seek the Lord. 3559
2Ch 16:14 spices **p.** by the apothecaries' art: 7543
2Ch 17:18 thousand ready **p.** for the war. 2502
2Ch 19:3 hast **p.** thine heart to seek God. 3559
2Ch 20:33 people had not **p.** their hearts unto 3559
2Ch 26:14 Uzziah **p.** for them throughout all 3559
2Ch 27:6 **p.** his ways before the Lord his God. 3559
2Ch 29:19 his transgression, have we **p.** and 3559
2Ch 29:36 people, that God had **p.** the people: 3559
2Ch 31:11 of the Lord; and they **p.** them, 3559
2Ch 35:10 the service was **p.**, and the priests 3559
2Ch 35:14 the Levites **p.** for themselves, 3559
2Ch 35:15 brethren the Levites **p.** for them. 3559
2Ch 35:16 So all the service of the Lord was **p.** 3559
2Ch 35:20 this when Josiah had **p.** the temple, 3559
Ezr 7:10 Ezra had **p.** his heart to seek the law. 3559
Ne 5:18 was **p.** for me daily was one ox 6213
Ne 5:18 also the fowls were **p.** for me, and 6213
Ne 8:10 unto them for whom nothing is **p.**: 3559
Ne 13:5 had **p.** for him a great chamber, 6213
Es 5:4 the banquet that I have **p.** for him. 6213
Es 5:5 to the banquet that Esther had **p.** 6213
Es 5:12 banquet that she had **p.** but myself; 6213
Es 6:4 the gallows that he had **p.** for him. 3559
Es 6:14 the banquet that Esther had **p.** 6213
Es 7:10 the gallows that he had **p.** for 3559
Job 28:27 it; he **p.** it, yea, and searched it out. 3559
Job 29:7 city, when I **p.** my seat in the street! 3559
Ps 7:13 also **p.** for him the instruments 3559
Ps 9:7 he hath **p.** his throne for judgment. 3559
Ps 57:6 They have **p.** a net for my steps; 3559
Ps 68:10 God, hast **p.** of thy goodness for 3559
Ps 74:16 thou hast **p.** the light and the sun. 3559
Ps 103:19 hath **p.** his throne in the heavens; 3559
Pr 8:27 When he **p.** the heavens, I was 3559
Pr 19:29 Judgments are **p.** for scorners, and 3559
Pr 21:31 The horse is **p.** against the day of 3559
Isa 30:33 of old; yea, for the king it is **p.**; 3559
Isa 64:4 **p.** for him that waiteth for him. 6213
Eze 23:41 bed, and a table **p.** before it, 6186
Eze 28:13 thy pipes was **p.** in thee in the day 3559
Eze 38:7 Be thou **p.**, and prepare for thyself, 3559
Da 2:9 have **p.** lying and corrupt words 2164

Ho 2:8 and gold, which they **p.** for Baal......... 6213
Ho 6:3 going forth is **p.** as the morning; 3559
Jon 1:17 **p.** a great fish to swallow up 4487
Jon 4:6 And the Lord God **p.** a gourd, and 4487
Jon 4:7 God **p.** a worm when the morning 4487
Jon 4:8 that God **p.** a vehement east wind; 4487
Na 2:5 and the defence shall be **p.**. 3559
Zep 1:7 the Lord hath **p.** a sacrifice, he hath ... 3559
Mt 20:23 **for whom it is p. of my Father.** *2090*
Mt 22:4 **Behold, I have p. my dinner: my**... *2090*
Mt 25:34 **inherit the kingdom p. for you**...... *2090*
Mt 25:41 **p. for the devil and his angels:**...... *2090*
Mk 10:40 **be given to them for whom it is p.**. *2090*
Mk 14:15 **upper room furnished and p.:** *2092*
Lu 1:17 ready a people **p.** for the Lord........... *2680*
Lu 2:31 **p.** before the face of all people; *2090*
Lu 12:47 **his lord's will, and p. not himself,**. *2090*
Lu 23:56 and **p.** spices and ointments; *2090*
Lu 24:1 the spices which they had **p.**, and........ *2090*
Ro 9:23 which he had afore **p.** unto glory, ... *4282*
1Co 2:9 hath **p.** for them that love him........... *2090*
2Ti 2:21 use, and **p.** unto every good work...... *2090*
Heb 10:5 not, but a body hast thou **p.** me: *2675*
Heb 11:7 **p.** an ark to the saving of his house; ... *2680*
Heb 11:16 God: for he hath **p.** for them a city..... *2090*
Re 8:6 trumpets **p.** themselves to sound........ *2090*
Re 9:7 like unto horses **p.** unto battle; *2090*
Re 9:15 which were **p.** for an hour, and a *2090*
Re 12:6 where she hath a place **p.** of God, ... *2090*
Re 16:12 the kings of the east might be **p.**. *2090*
Re 21:2 **p.** as a bride adorned for her............. *2090*

PREPAREDST
Ps 80:9 Thou **p.** room before it, and didst...... 6437

PREPAREST
Nu 15:8 thou **p.** a bullock for a burnt............. 6213
Ps 23:5 Thou **p.** a table before me in the........ 6186
Ps 65:9 thou **p.** them corn, when thou 3559

PREPARETH
2Ch 30:19 That **p.** his heart to seek God, the 3559
Job 15:35 vanity, and their belly **p.** deceit.......... 3559
Ps 147:8 who **p.** rain for the earth, who........... 3559

PREPARING
Ne 13:7 in **p.** him a chamber in the courts....... 6213
1Pe 3:20 while the ark was a **p.**, wherein *2680*

PRESBYTERY
1Ti 4:14 laying on of the hands of the **p.**. *4244*

PRESCRIBED
Isa 10:1 grievousness which they have **p.**; 3789

PRESCRIBING
Ezr 7:22 and salt without **p.** how much. 3792

PRESENCE
Ge 3:8 from the **p.** of the Lord God 6440
Ge 4:16 Cain went out from the **p.** of the........ 6440
Ge 16:12 dwell in the **p.** of all his brethren. 6440
Ge 23:11 in the **p.** of the sons of my people...... 5869
Ge 23:18 in the **p.** of the children of Heth,........ 5869
Ge 25:18 died in the **p.** of all his brethren......... 6440
Ge 27:30 out from the **p.** of Isaac his father, ... 6440
Ge 41:46 went out from the **p.** of Pharaoh, ... 6440
Ge 45:3 for they were troubled at his **p.**. 6440
Ge 47:15 for why should we die in thy **p.**? 5048
Ex 10:11 driven out from Pharaoh's **p.**.............. 5869
Ex 33:14 My **p.** shall go with thee, and I.......... 6440
Ex 33:15 If thy **p.** go not with me, carry us...... 6440
Ex 35:20 departed from the **p.** of Moses. 6440
Le 22:3 soul shall be cut off from my **p.**: 6440
Nu 20:6 Moses and Aaron went from the **p.** 6440
De 25:9 unto him in the **p.** of the elders, ... 5869
Jos 4:11 the priests, in the **p.** of the people. 6440
Jos 8:32 in the **p.** of the children of Israel. 6440
1Sa 18:11 David avoided out of his **p.** twice. 6440
1Sa 19:7 he was in his **p.**, as in times past. 6440
1Sa 19:10 he slipped away out of Saul's **p.**, ... 6440
1Sa 21:15 to play the mad man in my **p.**? 5921
2Sa 16:19 I not serve in the **p.** of his son? 6440
2Sa 16:19 as I have served in thy father's **p.**, ... 6440
2Sa 16:19 so will I be in thy **p.**......................... 6440
2Sa 24:4 went out from the **p.** of the king, to ... 6440
1Ki 1:28 And she came into the king's **p.**, ... 6440
1Ki 8:22 in the **p.** of all the congregation 5048
1Ki 12:2 fled from the **p.** of king Solomon, ... 6440
1Ki 21:13 against Naboth in the **p.** of the 5048
2Ki 3:14 that I regard the **p.** of Jehoshaphat 6440
2Ki 5:27 his **p.** a leper as white as snow.......... 6440
2Ki 13:23 cast he them from his **p.** as yet. 6440
2Ki 24:20 he had cast them out from his **p.**, ... 6440
2Ki 25:19 of them that were in the king's **p.**, ... 6440
1Ch 16:27 Glory and honour are in his **p.**: 6440
1Ch 16:33 wood sing out at the **p.** of the Lord, ... 6440
1Ch 24:31 Aaron in the **p.** of David the king, ... 6440
2Ch 6:12 the **p.** of all the congregation of 5048
2Ch 9:23 earth sought the **p.** of Solomon, ... 6440
2Ch 10:2 from the **p.** of Solomon the king,........ 6440
2Ch 20:9 and in thy **p.**, (for thy name is in 6440
2Ch 34:4 down the altars of Baalim in his **p.**;...... 6440
Ne 2:1 not been beforetime sad in his **p.**. 6440
Es 1:10 in the **p.** of Ahasuerus the king.......... 6440
Es 8:15 went out from the **p.** of the king........ 6440
Job 1:12 went forth from the **p.** of the Lord. 6440
Job 2:7 Satan forth from the **p.** of the Lord. ... 6440
Job 23:15 Therefore am I troubled at his **p.** 6440
Ps 9:3 they shall fall and perish at thy **p.**....... 6440
Ps 16:11 of life: in thy **p.** is fulness of joy; 6440
Ps 17:2 sentence come forth from thy **p.**; 6440
Ps 23:5 me in the **p.** of mine enemies: 5048
Ps 31:20 hide them in the secret of thy **p.**.......... 6440
Ps 51:11 Cast me not away from thy **p.**; and 6440
Ps 68:2 the wicked perish at the **p.** of God. 6440
Ps 68:8 also dropped at the **p.** of God: 6440
Ps 68:8 itself was moved at the **p.** of God, ... 6440
Ps 95:2 before his **p.** with thanksgiving,.......... 6440
Ps 97:5 like wax at the **p.** of the Lord,........... 6440
Ps 97:5 **p.** of the Lord of the whole earth. 6440
Ps 100:2 come before his **p.** with singing.......... 6440
Ps 114:7 thou earth, at the **p.** of the Lord,....... 6440
Ps 114:7 at the **p.** of the God of Jacob;............ 6440
Ps 116:14 Lord now in the **p.** of all his people. ... 5048
Ps 116:18 now in the **p.** of all his people,........... 5048
Ps 139:7 whither shall I flee from thy **p.**? 6440
Ps 140:13 the upright shall dwell in thy **p.**.......... 6440
Pr 14:7 Go from the **p.** of a foolish man, ... 5048
Pr 17:18 surety in the **p.** of his friend............. 6440
Pr 25:6 forth thyself in the **p.** of the king, ... 6440
Pr 25:7 be put lower in the **p.** of the prince 6440
Isa 1:7 strangers devour it in your **p.**, and 5048
Isa 19:1 of Egypt shall be moved at his **p.**, ... 6440
Isa 63:9 and the angel of his **p.** saved them: 6440
Isa 64:1 mountains might flow...at thy **p.**,........ 6440
Isa 64:2 the nations may tremble at thy **p.**!...... 6440
Isa 64:3 mountains flowed down at thy **p.**. 6440
Jer 4:26 broken down at the **p.** of the Lord, ... 6440
Jer 5:22 will ye not tremble at my **p.**, which 6440
Jer 23:39 fathers, and cast you out of my **p.**: 6440
Jer 28:1 the **p.** of the priests and of all the 5869
Jer 28:5 Hananiah in the **p.** of the priests, ... 5869
Jer 28:5 and in the **p.** of all the people that...... 5869
Jer 28:11 spake in the **p.** of all the people, ... 5869
Jer 32:12 and in the **p.** of the witnesses that 5869
Jer 52:3 he had cast them out from his **p.**, ... 6440
Eze 38:20 of the earth, shall shake at my **p.**, ... 6440
Da 2:27 answered in the **p.** of the king, ... 6925
Jon 1:3 Tarshish from the **p.** of the Lord,....... 6440
Jon 1:3 Tarshish from the **p.** of the Lord......... 6440
Jon 1:10 he fled from the **p.** of the Lord, ... 6440
Na 1:5 and the earth is burned at his **p.**, ... 6440
Zep 1:7 thy peace at the **p.** of the Lord God: .. 6440
Lu 1:19 that stand in the **p.** of God;............... *1799*
Lu 13:26 **have eaten and drunk in thy p.,**.... *1799*
Lu 14:10 **in the p. of them that sit at meat**.. *1799*
Lu 15:10 **there is joy in the p. of the angels** *1799*
Joh 20:30 did Jesus in the **p.** of his disciples,...... *1799*
Ac 3:13 and denied him in the **p.** of Pilate, ... *4383*
Ac 3:16 soundness in the **p.** of you all............. *561*
Ac 3:19 come from the **p.** of the Lord; *4383*
Ac 5:41 departed from the **p.** of the council, ... *4383*
Ac 27:35 thanks to God in the **p.** of them......... *1799*
1Co 1:29 That no flesh should glory in his **p.**..... *1799*
2Co 10:1 who in **p.** am base among you, ... *4383*
2Co 10:10 but his bodily **p.** is weak, and his *3952*
Php 2:12 always obeyed, not as in my **p.** only, .. *3952*
1Th 2:17 from you for a short time in **p.**, ... *4383*
1Th 2:19 in the **p.** of our Lord Jesus Christ *1715*
2Th 1:9 from the **p.** of the Lord, and from...... *4383*
Heb 9:24 to appear in the **p.** of God for us: *4383*
Jude 24 faultless before the **p.** of his glory *2714*
Re 14:10 in the **p.** of the holy angels, and in *1799*
Re 14:10 angels, and in the **p.** of the Lamb: *1799*

PRESENT See also PRESENTED; PRESENTING; PRESENTS.
Ge 32:13 came to his hand a **p.** for Esau.......... 4503
Ge 32:18 it is a **p.** sent unto my lord Esau:........ 4503
Ge 32:20 I will appease him with the **p.** that...... 4503
Ge 32:21 So went the **p.** over before him: and... 4503
Ge 33:10 then receive my **p.** at my hand: for 4503
Ge 43:11 carry down the man a **p.**, a little 4503
Ge 43:15 the men took that **p.**, and they took ... 4503
Ge 43:25 made ready the **p.** against Joseph........ 4503
Ge 43:26 brought him the **p.** which was in 4503
Ex 34:2 Sinai, and **p.** thyself there to me 5324
Le 14:11 **p.** the man that is to be made 5975
Le 16:7 goats, and **p.** them before the Lord 5975
Le 27:8 shall **p.** himself before the priest, ... 5975
Le 27:11 shall **p.** the beast before the priest: 5975
Nu 3:6 **p.** them before Aaron the priest,........ 5975
De 31:14 **p.** yourselves in the tabernacle of....... 3320
Jg 3:15 sent a **p.** unto Eglon the king of......... 4503
Jg 3:17 he brought the **p.** unto Eglon king 4503
Jg 3:18 he had made an end to offer the **p.**,..... 4503
Jg 3:18 away the people that bare the **p.**. 4503
Jg 6:18 bring forth my **p.**, and set it before 4503
1Sa 9:7 is not a **p.** to bring to the man of....... 8670
1Sa 10:19 **p.** yourselves before the Lord by 3320
1Sa 13:15 the people that were **p.** with him, ... 4672
1Sa 13:16 the people that were **p.** with him, ... 4672
1Sa 21:3 in mine hand, or what there is **p.**. 4672
1Sa 30:26 a **p.** for you of the spoil of the.......... 1293
2Sa 20:4 three days, and be thou here **p.**. 5975
1Ki 9:16 a **p.** unto his daughter, Solomon's........ 7964
1Ki 10:25 they brought every man his **p.**,........... 4503
1Ki 15:19 unto thee a **p.** of silver and gold; 7810
1Ki 20:27 were numbered, and were all **p.**,........ 3557
2Ki 8:8 Take a **p.** in thine hand, and go, ... 4503
2Ki 8:9 took a **p.** with him, even of every 4503
2Ki 16:8 it for a **p.** to the king of Assyria. 7810
2Ki 17:4 no **p.** to the king of Assyria, as he 4503
2Ki 18:31 an agreement with me by a **p.**,........... 1293
2Ki 20:12 letters and a **p.** unto Hezekiah: 4503
1Ch 29:17 joy thy people, which are **p.** here, ... 4672
2Ch 5:11 all the priests...**p.** were sanctified,...... 4672
2Ch 9:24 they brought every man his **p.**,........... 4503
2Ch 29:29 all that were **p.** with him bowed......... 4672
2Ch 30:21 that were **p.** at Jerusalem kept the 4672
2Ch 31:1 all Israel that were **p.** went out to...... 4672
2Ch 34:32 all that were **p.** in Jerusalem and........ 4672
2Ch 34:33 all that were **p.** in Israel to serve, ... 4672
2Ch 35:7 for all that were **p.**, to the number..... 4672
2Ch 35:17 that were **p.** kept the passover at 4672
2Ch 35:18 all Judah and Israel that were **p.**,........ 4672
Ezr 8:25 all Israel there **p.**, had offered: 4672
Es 1:5 the people that were **p.** in Shushan..... 4672
Es 4:16 all the Jews that are **p.** in Shushan, ... 4672
Job 1:6 to **p.** themselves before the Lord, ... 3320
Job 2:1 to **p.** themselves before the Lord, ... 3320
Job 2:1 them to **p.** himself before the Lord..... 3320
Ps 46:1 strength, a very **p.** help in trouble...... 4672
Isa 18:7 the **p.** be brought unto the Lord of..... 7862
Isa 36:16 an agreement with me by a **p.**,.......... 1293
Isa 39:1 sent letters and a **p.** to Hezekiah: 4503
Jer 36:7 **p.** their supplication before the........... 5307
Jer 42:9 ye sent me to **p.** your supplication....... 5307
Eze 27:15 for a **p.** horns of ivory and ebony......... 814
Da 9:18 **p.** our supplications before thee 5307
Ho 10:6 Assyria for a **p.** to king Jareb: 4503
Lu 2:22 Jerusalem, to **p.** him to the Lord;....... *3936*
Lu 5:17 of the Lord was **p.** to heal them..............
Lu 13:1 There were **p.** at that season some *3918*
Lu 18:30 **receive manifold more in this p.,**.........
Joh 14:25 **unto you, being yet p. with you** ... *3306*
Ac 10:33 are we all here **p.** before God, to....... *3918*
Ac 21:18 James; and all the elders were **p.**. *3854*
Ac 25:24 all men which are here **p.** with us, ... *4810*
Ac 28:2 because of the **p.** rain, and because *2186*
Ro 7:18 for to will is **p.** with me; but how....... *3873*
Ro 7:21 would do good, evil is **p.** with me....... *3873*
Ro 8:18 sufferings of this **p.** time are not........ *3568*
Ro 8:38 nor things **p.**, nor things to come, ... *1764*
Ro 11:5 then at this **p.** time also there is a...... *3568*
Ro 12:1 ye **p.** your bodies a living sacrifice, ... *3936*
1Co 3:22 or things **p.**, or things to come; *1764*
1Co 4:11 unto this **p.** hour we both hunger,........ *737*
1Co 5:3 as absent in body, but **p.** in spirit,....... *3918*
1Co 5:3 have judged...as though I were **p.**, ... *3918*
1Co 7:26 that this is good for the **p.** distress,.... *1764*
1Co 15:6 greater part remain unto this **p.**,.......... *737*
2Co 4:14 by Jesus, and shall **p.** us with you. *3936*
2Co 5:8 body, and to be **p.** with the Lord. *1736*
2Co 5:9 that, whether **p.** or absent, we may.... *1736*

2Co 10:2 when I am **p.** with that confidence,..... *3918*
2Co 10:11 we be also in deed when we are **p.**.... *3918*
2Co 11:2 I may **p.** you as a chaste virgin to...... *3936*
2Co 11:9 And when I was **p.** with you, and....... *3918*
2Co 13:2 as if I were **p.**, the second time;........ *3918*
2Co 13:10 being **p.** I should use sharpness, ... *3918*
Ga 1:4 deliver us from this **p.** evil world,....... *1764*
Ga 4:18 not only when I am **p.** with you. *3918*
Ga 4:20 I desire to be **p.** with you now, and.... *3918*
Eph 5:27 **p.** it to himself a glorious church,....... *3936*
Col 1:22 **p.** you holy and unblameable and........ *3936*
Col 1:28 may **p.** every man perfect in Christ.... *3936*
2Ti 4:10 me, having loved this **p.** world,.......... *3568*
Tit 2:12 and godly, in this **p.** world;.............. *3568*
Heb 9:9 was a figure for the time then **p.**,........ *1764*
Heb 12:11 no chastening for the **p.** seemeth....... *3918*
2Pe 1:12 and be established in the **p.** truth....... *3918*
Jude 24 and to **p.** your faultless before the...... *2476*

PRESENTED
Ge 46:29 Goshen, and **p.** himself unto him;....... 7200
Ge 47:2 men, and **p.** them unto Pharaoh. 3322
Le 2:8 when it is **p.** unto the priest, he 7126
Le 7:35 **p.** them to minister unto the Lord...... 7126
Le 9:12 sons **p.** unto him the blood,............... 4672
Le 9:13 they **p.** the burnt offering unto him,.... 4672
Le 9:18 sons **p.** unto him the blood,............... 4672
Le 16:10 be the scapegoat, shall be **p.** alive...... 5975
De 31:14 **p.** themselves in the tabernacle of...... 3320
Jos 24:1 and they **p.** themselves before God..... 3320
Jg 6:19 unto him under the oak, and **p.** it........ 5066
Jg 20:2 **p.** themselves in the assembly of......... 3320
1Sa 17:16 evening, and **p.** himself forty days...... 3320
Jer 38:26 I **p.** my supplication before the 5307
Eze 20:28 they **p.** the provocation of their.......... 5414
Mt 2:11 treasures, they **p.** unto him gifts;....... *4374*
Ac 9:41 saints and widows, **p.** her alive.......... *3936*
Ac 23:33 governor, **p.** Paul also before him....... *3936*

PRESENTING
Da 9:20 **p.** my supplication before the Lord..... 5307

PRESENTLY
1Sa 2:16 Let them not fail to burn the fat **p.**,..... 3117
Pr 12:16 A fool's wrath is **p.** known: but a....... 3117
Mt 21:19 And **p.** the fig tree withered away....... *3916*
Mt 26:53 **shall p. give me more than twelve**.. *3936*
Php 2:23 Him therefore I hope to send **p.**,....... *1824*

PRESENTS
1Sa 10:27 him, and brought him no **p.**............... 4503
1Ki 4:21 brought **p.**, and served Solomon........... 4503
2Ki 17:3 his servant, and gave him **p.**............... 4503
2Ch 17:5 Judah brought to Jehoshaphat **p.**;.......... 4503
2Ch 17:11 brought Jehoshaphat **p.**, and.................. 4503
2Ch 32:23 and **p.** to Hezekiah king of Judah:....... 4030
Ps 68:29 shall kings bring **p.** unto thee. 7862
Ps 72:10 and of the isles shall bring **p.**:............ 4503
Ps 76:11 bring **p.** unto him that ought to be...... 7862
Mic 1:14 thou give **p.** to Moresheth-gath:......... 7964

PRESERVE See also PRESERVED; PRESERVEST; PRESERVETH.
Ge 19:32, 34 we may **p.** seed of our father........ 2421
Ge 45:5 did send me before you to **p.** life......... 4241
Ge 45:7 to **p.** you a posterity in the earth,...... 7760
De 6:24 that he might **p.** us alive, as it is........ 2421
Ps 12:7 **p.** them from this generation for 5341
Ps 16:1 **P.** me, O God: for in thee do I put.... 8104
Ps 25:21 integrity and uprightness **p.** me;......... 5341
Ps 32:7 thou shalt **p.** me from trouble;........... 5341
Ps 40:11 and thy truth continually **p.** me. 5341
Ps 41:2 The Lord will **p.** him, and keep.......... 8104
Ps 61:7 and truth, which may **p.** him. 5341
Ps 64:1 **p.** my life from fear of the enemy........ 5341
Ps 79:11 **p.** thou those that are appointed to...... 3498
Ps 86:2 **P.** my soul; for I am holy: O thou...... 8104
Ps 121:7 The Lord shall **p.** thee from all evil:.... 8104
Ps 121:7 he shall **p.** thy soul.......................... 8104
Ps 121:8 Lord shall **p.** thy going out and thy..... 8104
Ps 140:1 man: **p.** me from the violent man;........ 5341
Ps 140:4 wicked: **p.** me from the violent man;... 5341
Pr 2:11 Discretion shall **p.** thee,.................... 8104
Pr 4:6 her not, and she shall **p.** thee:........... 8104
Pr 14:3 the lips of the wise shall **p.** them........ 8104
Pr 20:28 Mercy and truth **p.** the king: and....... 5341
Pr 22:12 The eyes of the Lord **p.** knowledge,... 5341
Isa 31:5 it; and passing over he will **p.** it......... 4422
Isa 49:8 and I will **p.** thee, and give thee 5341
Jer 49:11 children, I will **p.** them alive;............. 2421
Lu 17:33 **shall lose his life shall p. it.** *2225*
2Ti 4:18 **p.** me unto his heavenly kingdom: *4982*

PRESERVED
Ge 32:30 God face to face, and my life is **p.**....... 5337
Jos 24:17 **p.** us in all the way wherein we......... 8104
1Sa 30:23 who hath **p.** us, and delivered the 8104
2Sa 8:6,14 **p.** David whithersoever he................ 3467
1Ch 18:6, 13 **p.** David whithersoever he went. ... 3467
Job 10:12 thy visitation hath **p.** my spirit........... 8104
Job 29:2 as in the days when God **p.** me; 8104
Ps 37:28 they are **p.** for ever: but the seed...... 8104
Isa 49:6 and to restore the **p.** of Israel: 5336
Ho 12:13 Egypt, and by a prophet was he **p.**..... 8104
Mt 9:17 **into new bottles, and both are p.**... *4933*
Lu 5:38 **into new bottles; and both are p.**.... *4933*
1Th 5:23 be **p.** blameless unto the coming......... *5083*
Jude 1 and **p.** in Jesus Christ, and called: *5083*

PRESERVER
Job 7:20 I do unto thee, O thou **p.** of men?...... 5341

PRESERVEST
Ne 9:6 is therein, and thou **p.** them all;........ 2421
Ps 36:6 O Lord, thou **p.** man and beast.......... 3467

PRESERVETH
Job 36:6 He **p.** not the life of the wicked: 2421
Ps 31:23 for the Lord **p.** the faithful, and 5341
Ps 97:10 he **p.** the souls of his saints; he......... 8104
Ps 116:6 the Lord **p.** the simple: I was........... 8104
Ps 145:20 The Lord **p.** all them that love him:.... 8104
Ps 146:9 The Lord **p.** the strangers; he........... 8104
Pr 2:8 and **p.** the way of his saints. 8104
Pr 16:17 he that keepeth his way **p.** his soul..... 8104

PRESIDENTS
Da 6:2 And over these three **p.**; of whom...... 5632
Da 6:3 preferred above the **p.** and princes,.... 5632
Da 6:4 the **p.** and princes sought to find........ 5632
Da 6:6 these **p.** and princes assembled.......... 5632
Da 6:7 All the **p.** of the kingdom, the........... 5632

PRESS See also PRESSED; PRESSES; PRESSETH; PRESSFAT; OPPRESS; WINEPRESS.
Joe 3:13 for the **p.** is full, the fats overflow;..... 1660
Hag 2:16 draw out fifty vessels out of the **p.**,.... 6333
Mk 2:4 not come nigh unto him for the **p.**,..... *3793*
Mk 5:27 came in the **p.** behind, and touched..... *3793*
Mk 5:30 him, turned him about in the **p.**, ... *3793*
Lu 8:19 could not come at him for the **p.**....... *3793*
Lu 8:45 multitude throng thee and **p.** thee, ... *598*
Lu 19:3 could not for the **p.**, because he.......... *3793*
Php 3:14 I **p.** toward the mark for the prize...... *1377*

PRESSED See also OPPRESSED.
Ge 19:3 And he **p.** upon them greatly; and...... 6484
Ge 19:9 they **p.** sore upon the man, even 6484
Ge 40:11 and **p.** them into Pharaoh's cup,......... 7818
Jg 16:16 she **p.** him daily with her words,........ 6693
2Sa 13:25 he **p.** him: howbeit he would not........ 6555
2Sa 13:27 But Absalom **p.** him, that he let......... 6555
Es 8:14 **p.** on by the king's commandment. 1765
Eze 23:3 there were their beasts **p.**, and.......... 4600
Am 2:13 Behold, I am **p.** under you, as a 5781
Am 2:13 as a cart is **p.** that is full of sheaves. .. 5781
Mk 3:10 they **p.** upon him for to touch him,...... *1968*
Lu 5:1 people **p.** upon him to hear the.......... *1945*
Lu 6:38 **measure, p. down, and shaken** *4085*
Ac 18:5 Paul was **p.** in the spirit, and............ *4912*
2Co 1:8 that we were **p.** out of measure, ... *916*

PRESSES See also WINEPRESSES.
Ne 13:15 treading wine **p.** on the sabbath, ... 1660
Pr 3:10 **p.** shall burst out with new wine. 3342
Isa 16:10 shall tread out no wine in their **p.**;........ 3342

PRESSETH See also OPPRESSETH.
Ps 38:2 in me, and thy hand **p.** me sore. 5181
Lu 16:16 **preached, and every man p. into it**...*971*

PRESSFAT
Hag 2:16 one came to the **p.** for to draw.......... 3342

PRESUME See also PRESUMED.
De 18:20 shall **p.** to speak a word in my.......... 2102
Es 7:5 that durst **p.** in his heart to do so?...... 4390

PRESUMED
Nu 14:44 they **p.** to go up unto the hill top: 6075

PRESUMPTUOUS
Ps 19:13 thy servant also from **p.** sins;........... 2086
2Pe 2:10 **P.** are they, selfwilled, they are........ *5113*

PRESUMPTUOUSLY
Ex 21:14 man come **p.** upon his neighbour, ... 2102
Nu 15:30 But the soul that doeth ought **p.**,....... 3027
De 1:43 and went **p.** up into the hill,............. 2102
De 17:12 And the man that will do **p.**, and........ 2087
De 17:13 and fear, and do no more **p.**.............. 2102
De 18:22 the prophet hath spoken it **p.**: 2087

PRETENCE
Mt 23:14 **and for a p. make long prayer;**...... *4392*
Mk 12:40 **for a p. make long prayers: these**.. *4392*
Php 1:18 whether in **p.**, or in truth, Christ is.... *4392*

PRETORIUM See PRAETORIUM.

PREVAIL See also PREVAILED; PREVAILEST; PREVAILETH.
Ge 7:20 cubits upward did the waters **p.**;........ 1396
Nu 22:6 peradventure I shall **p.**, that we.......... 3201
Jg 16:5 what means we may **p.** against him,.... 3201
1Sa 2:9 for by strength shall no man **p.**......... 1396
1Sa 17:9 but if I **p.** against him, and kill him, ... 3201
1Sa 26:25 great things, and also shalt still **p.**...... 3201
1Ki 22:22 shalt persuade him, and **p.** also:.......... 3201
2Ch 14:11 God; let not man **p.** against thee........ 6113
2Ch 18:21 entice him, and thou shalt also **p.**:....... 3201
Es 6:13 thou shalt not **p.** against him, but........ 3201
Job 15:24 they shall **p.** against him, as a king..... 8630
Job 18:9 the robber shall **p.** against him........... 2388
Ps 9:19 Arise, O Lord; let not man **p.**: let....... 5810
Ps 12:4 With our tongue will we **p.**; our......... 1396
Ps 65:3 Iniquities **p.** against me: as for our 1396
Ec 4:12 if one **p.** against him, two shall 8630
Isa 7:1 it, but could not **p.** against it. 3898
Isa 16:12 to pray; but he shall not **p.**.............. 3201
Isa 42:13 he shall **p.** against his enemies........... 1396
Isa 47:12 to profit, if so be thou mayest **p.** 6206
Jer 1:19 but they shall not **p.** against thee; 3201
Jer 5:22 themselves, yet can they not **p.**;......... 3201
Jer 15:20 they shall not **p.** against thee: for I..... 3201
Jer 20:10 enticed, and we shall **p.** against him,.... 3201
Jer 20:11 stumble, and they shall not **p.**............ 3201
Da 11:7 deal against them, and shall **p.**........... 2388
Mt 16:18 **gates of hell shall not p. against**... *2729*
Mt 27:24 Pilate saw...he could **p.** nothing, ... *5623*
Joh 12:19 Preceive ye how ye **p.** nothing? *5623*

PREVAILED
Ge 7:18 the waters **p.**, and were increased...... 1396
Ge 7:19 the waters **p.** exceedingly upon the...... 1396
Ge 7:24 And the waters **p.** upon the earth....... 1396
Ge 30:8 with my sister, and I have **p.** 3201
Ge 32:25 he saw that he **p.** not against him,....... 3201
Ge 32:28 with God and with men, and has **p.**.. 3201
Ge 47:20 because the famine **p.** over them:....... 2388
Ge 49:26 blessings of thy father have **p.**.......... 1396
Ex 17:11 held up his hand, that Israel **p.**.......... 1396
Ex 17:11 he let down his hand, Amalek **p.**........ 1396
Jg 1:35 the hand of the house of Joseph **p.**,.... 3513
Jg 3:10 **p.** against Chushan-rishathaim. 5810
Jg 4:24 and **p.** against Jabin the king of......... 7186
Jg 6:2 hand of Midian **p.** against Israel:......... 5810
1Sa 17:50 So David **p.** over the Philistine 2388
2Sa 11:23 Surely the men **p.** against us,............ 1396
2Sa 24:4 the king's word **p.** against Joab, ... 2388
1Ki 16:22 the people that followed Omri **p.**........ 2388
2Ki 25:3 the famine **p.** in the city, and there..... 2388
1Ch 5:2 For Judah **p.** above his brethren,........ 1396
1Ch 21:4 the king's word **p.** against Joab. 2388
2Ch 8:3 to Hamath-zobah, and **p.** against it...... 2388
2Ch 13:18 children of Judah **p.**, because they........ 553
2Ch 27:5 Ammonites, and **p.** against them. 2388
Ps 13:5 enemy say, I have **p.** against him;....... 3201
Ps 129:2 yet they have not **p.** against me.......... 3201
Jer 20:7 art stronger than I, and hast **p.**:.......... 3201
Jer 38:22 thee on, and have **p.** against thee:....... 3201
La 1:16 desolate, because the enemy **p.**........... 1396
Da 7:21 the saints, and **p.** against them; 3202
Ho 12:4 had power over the angel, and **p.**........ 3201
Ob 7 deceived thee, and **p.** against thee;....... 3201
Lu 23:23 them and of the chief priests **p.**.......... *2729*
Ac 19:16 **p.** against them, so that they fled........ *2480*
Ac 19:20 grew the word of God, and **p.**........... *2480*
Re 5:5 David hath **p.** to open the book,......... *3528*
Re 12:8 **p.** not; neither was their place........... *2480*

PREVAILEST
Job 14:20 Thou **p.** for ever against him,............ 8630

PREVAILETH
La 1:13 my bones, and it **p.** against them: 7287

PREVENT See also PREVENTED; PREVENTEST.
Job 3:12 Why did the knees **p.** me? or why....... 6923
Ps 59:10 The God of my mercy shall **p.** me:...... 6923
Ps 79:8 thy tender mercies speedily **p.** us;...... 6923
Ps 88:13 morning shall my prayer **p.** thee.......... 6923
Ps 119:148 Mine eyes **p.** the night watches, ... 6923
Am 9:10 evil shall not overtake nor **p.** us.......... 6923
1Th 4:15 shall not **p.** them which are asleep........ *5348*

PREVENTED
2Sa 22:6 about; the snares of death **p.** me;........ 6923
2Sa 22:19 **p.** me in the day of my calamity:......... 6923
Job 30:27 not: the days of affliction **p.** me. 6923
Job 41:11 Who hath **p.** me, that I should........... 6923
Ps 18:5 about: the snares of death **p.** me......... 6923
Ps 18:18 They **p.** me in the day of my............. 6923
Ps 119:147 I **p.** the dawning of the morning,......... 6923
Isa 21:14 **p.** with their bread him that fled......... 6923
Mt 17:25 come into the house, Jesus **p.** him,...... *4399*

PREVENTEST
Ps 21:3 thou **p.** him with the blessings............ 6923

PREY
Ge 49:9 from the **p.**, my son, thou art gone 2964
Ge 49:27 morning he shall devour the **p.**, ... 5706
Nu 14:3 and our children should be a **p.**? 957
Nu 14:31 ones, which ye said should be a **p.**,....... 957
Nu 23:24 not lie down until he eat of the **p.**, ... 2964
Nu 31:11 took all the spoil, and all the **p.**,......... 4455
Nu 31:12 brought the captives, and the **p.**,......... 4455
Nu 31:26 Take the sum of the **p.** that was........ 4455
Nu 31:27 And divide the **p.** into two parts;......... 4455
Nu 31:32 the **p.** which the men of war had......... 957
De 1:39 ones, which ye said should be a **p.**,....... 957
De 2:35 we took for a **p.** unto ourselves,.......... 962
De 3:7 cities, we took for a **p.** to ourselves, ... 962
Jos 8:2 ye take for a **p.** unto yourselves:......... 962
Jos 8:27 Israel took for a **p.** unto themselves,..... 962
Jos 11:14 Israel took for a **p.** unto themselves; 962
Jg 5:30 have they not divided the **p.**; to......... 7998
Jg 5:30 to Sisera a **p.** of divers colours, ... 7998
Jg 5:30 **p.** of divers colours of needlework,....... 7998
Jg 8:24, 25 every man the earrings of his **p.**.... 7998
2Ki 21:14 they shall become a **p.** and a spoil........ 957
Ne 4:4 for a **p.** in the land of captivity: 961
Es 3:13 to take the spoil of them for a **p.**......... 962
Es 8:11 to take the spoil of them for a **p.**......... 962
Es 9:15 on the **p.** they laid not their hand......... 961
Es 9:16 they laid not their hands on the **p.**, ... 961
Job 4:11 old lion perisheth for lack of **p.**, ... 2964
Job 9:26 as the eagle that hasteth to the **p.** 400
Job 24:5 work; rising betimes for a **p.**: 2964
Job 38:39 Wilt thou hunt the **p.** for the lion? 2964
Job 39:29 thence she seeketh the **p.**, and her 400
Ps 17:12 as a lion that is greedy of his **p.**,......... 2963
Ps 76:4 excellent than the mountains of **p.**. 2964
Ps 104:21 The young lions roar after their **p.**,...... 2964
Ps 124:6 not given us as a **p.** to their teeth........ 2964
Pr 23:28 She also lieth in wait as for a **p.**,........ 2863
Isa 5:29 lay hold of the **p.**, and shall carry 2964
Isa 10:2 that widows may be their **p.**, and 7998
Isa 10:6 to take the **p.**, and to tread them 957
Isa 31:4 the young lion roaring on his **p.**, ... 2964
Isa 33:23 is the **p.** of a great spoil divided; 5706
Isa 33:23 spoil divided; the lame take the **p.** 957
Isa 42:22 they are for a **p.**, and none................. 957
Isa 49:24 the **p.** be taken from the mighty, ... 4455
Isa 49:25 **p.** of the terrible shall be delivered: 4455
Isa 59:15 from evil maketh himself a **p.** 7997
Jer 21:9 his life shall be unto him for a **p.**........ 7998
Jer 30:16 **p.** upon thee will I give for a **p.**........... 962
Jer 38:2 he shall have his life for a **p.**, and....... 7998
Jer 39:18 thy life shall be for a **p.** unto thee: 7998
Jer 45:5 life will I give unto thee for a **p.** in 7998
Eze 7:21 the hands of the strangers for a **p.**,....... 957
Eze 19:3 and it learned to catch the **p.**;............ 2964
Eze 19:6 lion, and learned to catch the **p.**,......... 2964
Eze 22:25 like a roaring lion ravening the **p.**; 2964
Eze 22:27 like wolves ravening the **p.**, to shed...... 2964
Eze 26:12 and make a **p.** of thy merchandise:........ 962
Eze 29:19 and take her spoil, and take her **p.**;....... 957
Eze 34:8 because my flock became a **p.**, and....... 957
Eze 34:22 and they shall no more be a **p.**;.......... 957
Eze 34:28 shall no more be a **p.** to the heathen, ... 957
Eze 36:4 became a **p.** and derision to the.......... 957
Eze 36:5 minds, to cast it out for a **p.**............... 957
Eze 38:12 To take a spoil, and to take a **p.**;......... 957
Eze 38:13 gathered thy company to take a **p.**?...... 957
Da 11:24 he shall scatter among them the **p.**, ... 961
Am 3:4 in the forest, when he hath no **p.**?....... 2964
Na 2:12 filled his holes with **p.**, and his dens.... 2964
Na 2:13 I will cut off thy **p.** from the earth,..... 2964
Na 3:1 robbery; the **p.** departeth not;........... 2964
Zep 3:8 the day that I rise up to the **p.**.......... 5706

PRICE See also PRICES; PRISED.
Le 25:16 thou shalt increase the **p.** thereof,...... 4736
Le 25:16 thou shalt diminish the **p.** of it: 4736
Le 25:50 **p.** of his sale shall be according.......... 3701
Le 25:51 give again the **p.** of his redemption...........
Le 25:52 him again the **p.** of his redemption............
De 23:18 the **p.** of a dog, into the house of....... 4242
2Sa 24:24 I will surely buy it of thee at a **p.**........ 4242
1Ki 10:28 received the linen yarn at a **p.**........... 4242
1Ch 21:22 shalt grant it me for the full **p.**.......... 3701
1Ch 21:24 I will verily buy it for the full **p.**.......... 3701
2Ch 1:16 received the linen yarn at a **p.**. 4242
Job 28:13 Man knoweth not the **p.** thereof;........ 6187
Job 28:15 be weighed for the **p.** thereof. 4242
Job 28:18 the **p.** of wisdom is above rubies......... 4901
Ps 44:12 increase thy wealth by their **p.**. 4242
Pr 17:16 a **p.** in the hand of a fool to get 4242
Pr 27:26 the goats are the **p.** of the field. 4242
Pr 31:10 for her **p.** is far above rubies............. 4377
Isa 45:13 my captives, not for **p.** nor reward, ... 4242
Isa 55:1 without money and without **p.**............ 4242
Jer 15:13 will I give to the spoil without **p.**,........ 4242
Zec 11:12 If you think good, give me my **p.**; 7939
Zec 11:12 for my **p.** thirty pieces of silver. 7939
Zec 11:13 a goodly **p.** that I was prised at of........ 3365
Mt 13:46 **had found one pearl of great p.**, ... *4186*
Mt 27:6 because it is the **p.** of blood............. *5092*
Mt 27:9 the **p.** of him that was valued, ... *5092*
Ac 5:2 kept back part of the **p.**, his wife *5092*
Ac 5:3 keep back part of the **p.** of the land?... *5092*
Ac 19:19 and they counted the **p.** of them, ... *5092*
1Co 6:20 For ye are brought with a **p.**............... *5092*
1Co 7:23 Ye are bought with a **p.**; be not ye..... *5092*
1Pe 3:4 is in the sight of God of great **p.**........ *4185*

PRICED See PRISED.

PRICES
Ac 4:34 **p.** of the things that were sold,.......... *5092*

PRICKED
Ps 73:21 grieved, and I was **p.** in my reins....... 8150
Ac 2:37 they were **p.** in their heart, and.......... *2669*

PRICKING
Eze 28:24 shall be no more a **p.** brier unto.......... 3992

PRICKS
Nu 33:55 be **p.** in your eyes, and thorns........... 7899
Ac 9:5 **for thee to kick against the p**........ *2759*
Ac 26:14 **for thee to kick against the p**........ *2759*

PRIDE
Le 26:19 I will break the **p.** of your power; 1347
1Sa 17:28 I know thy **p.**, and the.................... 2087
2Ch 32:26 humbled himself for the **p.** of his........ 1363
Job 33:17 purpose, and hide **p.** from man. 1466
Job 35:12 because of the **p.** of evil men. 1347
Job 41:15 His scales are his **p.**, shut up 1346
Job 41:34 a king over all the children of **p.**. 7830
Ps 10:2 wicked in his **p.** doth persecute........... 1346
Ps 10:4 through the **p.** of his countenance,...... 1363
Ps 31:20 thy presence from the **p.** of man: 7407
Ps 36:11 the foot of **p.** come against me, ... 1346
Ps 59:12 them even be taken in their **p.**: 1347
Ps 73:6 **p.** compasseth them about as a........... 1346
Pr 8:13 **p.**, and arrogancy, and the evil 1344
Pr 11:2 **p.** cometh, then cometh shame: 2087
Pr 13:10 Only by **p.** cometh contention: but...... 2087
Pr 14:3 mouth of the foolish is a rod of **p.**: 1346
Pr 16:18 **P.** goeth before destruction, and........ 1347
Pr 29:23 man's **p.** shall bring him low: but....... 1346
Isa 9:9 in the **p.** and stoutness of heart, ... 1346
Isa 16:6 We have heard of the **p.** of Moab;....... 1347
Isa 16:6 even of his haughtiness, and his **p.**, ... 1347
Isa 23:9 it, to stain the **p.** of all glory, ... 1347
Isa 25:11 he shall bring down their **p.**............... 1346
Isa 28:1 Woe to the crown of **p.**, to the.......... 1348
Isa 28:3 The crown of **p.**, the drunkards of...... 1348
Jer 13:9 will I mar the **p.** of Judah,................. 1347
Jer 13:9 and the great **p.** of Jerusalem. 1347
Jer 13:17 weep in secret places for your **p.**; 1466
Jer 48:29 We have heard the **p.** of Moab, (he 1347
Jer 48:29 and his arrogancy, and his **p.**,............ 1347
Jer 49:16 thee, and the **p.** of thine heart,.......... 2087
Eze 7:10 hath blossomed, **p.** hath budded. 2087
Eze 16:49 Sodom, **p.**, fulness of bread, and......... 1347
Eze 16:56 thy mouth in the day of thy **p.**,........... 1347
Eze 30:6 and the **p.** of her power shall come..... 1347
Da 4:37 those that walk in **p.** he is able.......... 1466
Da 5:20 his mind hardened in **p.**, he was......... 2103
Ho 5:5 the **p.** of Israel doth testify to his....... 1347
Ho 7:10 the **p.** of Israel testifieth to his 1347
Ob 3 **p.** of thine heart hath deceived 2087
Zep 2:10 This shall they have for their **p.**,......... 1347
Zep 3:11 them that rejoice in thy **p.**, and........ 1346
Zec 9:6 cut off the **p.** of the Philistines.......... 1347
Zec 10:11 the **p.** of Assyria shall be brought....... 1347
Zec 11:3 for the **p.** of Jordan is spoiled. 1347
Mk 7:22 **eye, blasphemy, p., foolishness:** *5243*
1Ti 3:6 being lifted up with **p.** he fall into *5187*
1Jo 2:16 lust of the eyes, and the **p.** of life,....... *212*

PRIEST See also PRIESTHOOD; PRIEST'S; PRIESTS.
Ge 14:18 was the **p.** of the most high God......... 3548
Ge 41:45 daughter of Poti-pheran **p.** of On......... 3548
Ge 41:50 of Poti-pherah **p.** of On bare unto....... 3548
Ge 46:20 of Poti-pherah **p.** of On bare unto....... 3548
Ex 2:16 **p.** of Midian had seven daughters: 3548
Ex 3:1 father in law, the **p.** of Midian: 3548
Ex 18:1 Jethro, the **p.** of Midian, Moses' 3548
Ex 29:30 that son that is **p.** in his stead 3548
Ex 31:10 holy garments for Aaron the **p.**,.......... 3548
Ex 35:19 holy garments for Aaron the **p.**,.......... 3548
Ex 38:21 Ithamar, son to Aaron the **p.**............. 3548
Ex 39:41 holy garments for Aaron the **p.**,.......... 3548
Le 1:7 Aaron the **p.** shall put fire upon the 3548
Le 1:9 the **p.** shall burn all on the altar, ... 3548
Le 1:12 **p.** shall lay them in order on the 3548
Le 1:13 **p.** shall bring it all, and burn it............ 3548
Le 1:15 the **p.** shall bring it unto the altar, ... 3548
Le 1:17 the **p.** shall burn it upon the altar,....... 3548
Le 2:2 **p.** shall burn the memorial of it........... 3548
Le 2:8 when it is presented unto the **p.**,......... 3548
Le 2:9 **p.** shall take from the meat offering.... 3548
Le 2:16 the **p.** shall burn the memorial of it, ... 3548
Le 3:11 the **p.** shall burn it upon the altar: 3548
Le 3:16 **p.** shall burn them upon the altar:....... 3548
Le 4:3 **p.** that is anointed do sin according...... 3548
Le 4:5 **p.** that is anointed shall take of the..... 3548
Le 4:6 **p.** shall dip his finger in the blood,...... 3548
Le 4:7 **p.** shall put some of the blood upon 3548
Le 4:10 **p.** shall burn them upon the altar........ 3548
Le 4:16 **p.** that is anointed shall bring of......... 3548
Le 4:17 **p.** shall dip his finger in some of 3548
Le 4:20 the **p.** shall make an atonement for..... 3548
Le 4:25 the **p.** shall take of the blood of the 3548
Le 4:26 **p.** shall make an atonement for him 3548
Le 4:30 **p.** shall take of the blood thereof........ 3548
Le 4:31 **p.** shall make an atonement for him, ... 3548
Le 4:34 **p.** shall take of the blood of the sin..... 3548
Le 4:35 **p.** shall burn them upon the altar,....... 3548
Le 4:35 **p.** shall make an atonement for his 3548
Le 5:6 **p.** shall make an atonement for him 3548
Le 5:8 shall bring them unto the **p.**, who........ 3548
Le 5:10 **p.** shall make an atonement for him 3548
Le 5:12 Then shall he bring it to the **p.**, and ... 3548
Le 5:12 the **p.** shall take his handful of it, ... 3548
Le 5:13 **p.** shall make an atonement for him 3548
Le 5:16 thereto, and give it unto the **p.**:.......... 3548
Le 5:16 **p.** shall make an atonement for him 3548
Le 5:18 for a trespass offering, unto the **p.**: 3548
Le 5:18 **p.** shall make an atonement for him 3548
Le 6:6 for a trespass offering, unto the **p.**: 3548
Le 6:7 **p.** shall make an atonement for him 3548
Le 6:10 **p.** shall put on his linen garment, ... 3548
Le 6:12 the **p.** shall burn wood on it every...... 3548
Le 6:22 the **p.** of his sons that is anointed....... 3548
Le 6:23 offering for the **p.** shall be wholly 3548
Le 6:26 The **p.** that offereth it for sin shall...... 3548
Le 7:5 **p.** shall burn them upon the altar........ 3548
Le 7:7 the **p.** that maketh atonement............ 3548
Le 7:8 **p.** that offereth any man's burnt......... 3548
Le 7:8 **p.** shall have to himself the skin......... 3548

Le 7:31 **p.** shall burn the fat upon the altar: 3548
Le 7:32 ye give unto the **p.** for an heave 3548
Le 7:34 unto Aaron the **p.** and unto his sons 3548
Le 12:6 of the congregation, unto the **p.**: 3548
Le 12:8 **p.** shall make an atonement for her, 3548
Le 13:2 shall be brought unto Aaron the **p.**, 3548
Le 13:3 **p.** shall look on the plague in the 3548
Le 13:3 **p.** shall look on him and pronounce 3548
Le 13:4 **p.** shall shut up him that hath the 3548
Le 13:5 **p.** shall look on him the seventh 3548
Le 13:5 **p.** shall shut him up seven days 3548
Le 13:6 the **p.** shall look on him again the 3548
Le 13:6 the **p.** shall pronounce him clean: 3548
Le 13:7 that he hath been seen of the **p.** for 3548
Le 13:7 he shall be seen of the **p.** again: 3548
Le 13:8 if the **p.** see that, behold, the scab 3548
Le 13:8 **p.** shall pronounce him unclean: 3548
Le 13:9 he shall be brought unto the **p.**; 3548
Le 13:10 And the **p.** shall see him: and, 3548
Le 13:11 **p.** shall pronounce him unclean, 3548
Le 13:12 foot wheresoever the **p.** looketh; 3548
Le 13:12 Then the **p.** shall consider: and 3548
Le 13:15 the **p.** shall see the raw flesh, and 3548
Le 13:16 white, he shall come unto the **p.**; 3548
Le 13:17 And the **p.** shall see him: and, 3548
Le 13:17 the **p.** shall pronounce him clean 3548
Le 13:19 reddish, and it be shewed to the **p.**; 3548
Le 13:20 when the **p.** seeth it, behold, it be 3548
Le 13:20 **p.** shall pronounce him unclean: 3548
Le 13:21 if the **p.** look on it, and, behold, 3548
Le 13:21 **p.** shall shut him up seven days: 3548
Le 13:22 the **p.** shall pronounce him unclean: 3548
Le 13:23 the **p.** shall pronounce him clean. 3548
Le 13:25 the **p.** shall look upon it: and, 3548
Le 13:25 **p.** shall pronounce him unclean: 3548
Le 13:26 if the **p.** look on it, and, behold, 3548
Le 13:26 **p.** shall shut him up seven days: 3548
Le 13:27 **p.** shall look upon him the seventh 3548
Le 13:27 **p.** shall pronounce him unclean: 3548
Le 13:28 the **p.** shall pronounce him clean: 3548
Le 13:30 the **p.** shall see the plague: and, 3548
Le 13:30 **p.** shall pronounce him unclean: 3548
Le 13:31 **p.** look upon the plague of the scall, 3548
Le 13:31 **p.** shall shut up him that hath the 3548
Le 13:32 the **p.** shall look on the plague: 3548
Le 13:33 **p.** shall shut up him that hath the 3548
Le 13:34 day the **p.** shall look on the scall: 3548
Le 13:34 the **p.** shall pronounce him clean: 3548
Le 13:36 **p.** shall look on him: and, behold, 3548
Le 13:36 **p.** shall not seek for yellow hair; 3548
Le 13:37 the **p.** shall pronounce him clean. 3548
Le 13:39 Then the **p.** shall look: and, behold, 3548
Le 13:43 **p.** shall look upon it: and, behold, 3548
Le 13:44 the **p.** shall pronounce him utterly 3548
Le 13:49 and shall be shewed unto the **p.**: 3548
Le 13:50 the **p.** shall look upon the plague, 3548
Le 13:53 if the **p.** shall look, and, behold, the 3548
Le 13:54 **p.** shall command that they wash 3548
Le 13:55 And the **p.** shall look on the plague, 3548
Le 13:56 And if the **p.** look, and, behold, the 3548
Le 14:2 He shall be brought unto the **p.**: 3548
Le 14:3 **p.** shall go forth out of the camp; 3548
Le 14:3 **p.** shall look, and, behold, if the 3548
Le 14:4 the **p.** command to take for him 3548
Le 14:5 **p.** shall command that one of the 3548
Le 14:11 the **p.** that maketh him clean shall 3548
Le 14:12 the **p.** shall take one he lamb, and 3548
Le 14:14 the **p.** shall take some of the blood 3548
Le 14:14 **p.** shall put it upon the tip of the 3548
Le 14:15 **p.** shall take some of the log of oil, 3548
Le 14:16 the **p.** shall dip his right finger in 3548
Le 14:17 the **p.** put upon the tip of the right 3548
Le 14:18 the **p.** shall make an atonement for 3548
Le 14:19 **p.** shall offer the sin offering, and 3548
Le 14:20 the **p.** shall offer the burnt offering 3548
Le 14:20 **p.** shall make an atonement for him, 3548
Le 14:23 day for his cleansing unto the **p.**, 3548
Le 14:24 the **p.** shall take the lamb of the 3548
Le 14:24 the **p.** shall wave them for a wave 3548
Le 14:25 the **p.** shall take some of the blood 3548
Le 14:26 **p.** shall pour of the oil into the palm 3548
Le 14:27 the **p.** shall sprinkle with his right 3548
Le 14:28 the **p.** shall put of the oil that is in 3548
Le 14:31 **p.** shall make an atonement for him 3548
Le 14:35 shall come and tell the **p.**, saying, 3548
Le 14:36 the **p.** shall command that they 3548
Le 14:36 before the **p.** go into it to see the 3548
Le 14:36 the **p.** shall go in to see the house: 3548
Le 14:38 the **p.** shall go out of the house to 3548
Le 14:39 the **p.** shall come again the seventh 3548
Le 14:40 the **p.** shall command that they 3548
Le 14:44 the **p.** shall come and look, and, 3548
Le 14:48 if the **p.** shall come in, and look 3548
Le 14:48 **p.** shall pronounce the house clean, 3548
Le 15:14 and give them unto the **p.**: 3548
Le 15:15 the **p.** shall offer them, the one for 3548
Le 15:15 **p.** shall make an atonement for him 3548
Le 15:29 pigeons, and bring them unto the **p.**, 3548
Le 15:30 the **p.** shall offer the one for a sin 3548
Le 15:30 the **p.** shall make an atonement 3548
Le 16:30 shall the **p.** make an atonement for
Le 16:32 the **p.**, whom he shall anoint, and 3548
Le 17:5 unto the **p.**, and offer them for 3548
Le 17:6 And the **p.** shall sprinkle the blood 3548
Le 19:22 **p.** shall make an atonement for him 3548
Le 21:9 daughter of any **p.**, if she profane 3548
Le 21:10 the high **p.** among his brethren, 3548
Le 21:21 blemish of the seed of Aaron the **p.** 3548
Le 22:10 a sojourner of the **p.**, or an hired 3548
Le 22:11 if the **p.** buy any soul with his 3548
Le 22:14 it unto the **p.** with the holy thing 3548
Le 23:10 first fruits of...harvest unto the **p.** 3548
Le 23:11 the sabbath the **p.** shall wave it. 3548
Le 23:20 the **p.** shall wave them with the 3548
Le 23:20 shall be holy to the Lord for the **p.** 3548
Le 27:8 shall present himself before the **p.**, 3548
Le 27:8 the **p.** shall value him; according 3548
Le 27:8 that vowed shall the **p.** value him. 3548
Le 27:11 present the beast before the **p.**: 3548
Le 27:12 the **p.** shall value it, whether it be 3548
Le 27:12 who art the **p.**, so shall it be. 3548
Le 27:14 the **p.** shall estimate it, whether it 3548
Le 27:14 the **p.** shall estimate it, so shall it 3548
Le 27:18, 23 the **p.** shall reckon unto him the 3548
Nu 3:6 present them before Aaron the **p.**, 3548
Nu 3:32 Eleazar the son of Aaron the **p.** 3548
Nu 4:16 of Eleazar the son of Aaron the **p.** 3548
Nu 28:33 Ithamar the son of Aaron the **p.** 3548
Nu 5:8 even to the **p.**; beside the ram of 3548
Nu 5:9 which they bring unto the **p.**; shall 3548
Nu 5:10 whatsoever any man giveth the **p.**, 3548
Nu 5:15 the man bring his wife unto the **p.**, 3548
Nu 5:16 the **p.** shall bring her near, and set 3548
Nu 5:17 the **p.** shall take holy water in an 3548
Nu 5:17 and of the dust...the **p.** shall take, 3548
Nu 5:18 the **p.** shall set the woman before 3548
Nu 5:18 **p.** shall have in his hand the bitter 3548
Nu 5:19 the **p.** shall charge her by an oath, 3548
Nu 5:21 **p.** shall charge the woman with an 3548
Nu 5:21 the **p.** shall say unto the woman, 3548
Nu 5:23 the **p.** shall write these curses in a 3548
Nu 5:25 **p.** shall take the jealousy offering 3548
Nu 5:26 the **p.** shall take an handful of the 3548
Nu 5:30 **p.** shall execute upon her all this 3548
Nu 6:10 or two young pigeons, to the **p.**, to 3548
Nu 6:11 the **p.** shall offer the one for a sin 3548
Nu 6:16 **p.** shall bring them before the Lord, 3548
Nu 6:17 **p.** shall offer also his meat offering, 3548
Nu 6:19 **p.** shall take the sodden shoulder 3548
Nu 6:20 the **p.** shall wave them for a wave 3548
Nu 6:20 this is holy for the **p.**, with the wave 3548
Nu 7:8 of Ithamar the son of Aaron the **p.** 3548
Nu 15:25 **p.** shall make an atonement for all 3548
Nu 15:28 **p.** shall make an atonement for the 3548
Nu 16:37 Eleazar the son of Aaron the **p.**, 3548
Nu 16:39 Eleazar the **p.** took the brasen 3548
Nu 18:28 heave offering to Aaron the **p.** 3548
Nu 19:3 shall give her unto Eleazar the **p.**, 3548
Nu 19:4 And Eleazar the **p.** shall take of her 3548
Nu 19:6 the **p.** shall take cedar wood, and 3548
Nu 19:7 Then the **p.** shall wash his clothes, 3548
Nu 19:7 **p.** shall be unclean until the even. 3548
Nu 25:7 the son of Aaron the **p.**, saw it, he 3548
Nu 25:11 son of Aaron the **p.**, hath turned 3548
Nu 26:1 Eleazar the son of Aaron the **p.**, 3548
Nu 26:3 and Eleazar the **p.** spake with them 3548
Nu 26:63 by Moses and Eleazar the **p.**, who 3548
Nu 26:64 Moses and Aaron the **p.** numbered, 3548
Nu 27:2 Moses, and before Eleazar the **p.**, 3548
Nu 27:19 And set him before Eleazar the **p.**, 3548
Nu 27:21 he shall stand before Eleazar the **p.**, 3548
Nu 27:22 and set him before Eleazar the **p.**, 3548
Nu 31:6 Phinehas the son of Eleazar the **p.**, 3548
Nu 31:12 unto Moses, and Eleazar the **p.**, and 3548
Nu 31:13 Moses, and Eleazar the **p.**, and all 3548
Nu 31:21 Eleazar the **p.** said unto the men of 3548
Nu 31:26 and Eleazar the **p.**, and the chief 3548
Nu 31:29 give it unto Eleazar the **p.**, for an 3548
Nu 31:31 and Eleazar the **p.** did as the Lord 3548
Nu 31:41 unto Eleazar the **p.**, as the Lord 3548
Nu 31:51, 54 and Eleazar the **p.** took the gold 3548
Nu 32:2 unto Moses, and to Eleazar the **p.**, 3548
Nu 32:28 Moses commanded Eleazar the **p.**, 3548
Nu 33:38 the **p.** went up into mount Hor at 3548
Nu 34:17 Eleazar the **p.**, and Joshua the son 3548
Nu 35:25 in it unto the death of the high **p.**, 3548
Nu 35:28 until the death of the high **p.**: 3548
Nu 35:28 after the death of the high **p.** the 3548
Nu 35:32 the land, until the death of the **p.** 3548
De 17:12 will not hearken unto the **p.** that 3548
De 18:3 shall give unto the **p.** the shoulder, 3548
De 20:2 **p.** shall approach and speak unto 3548
De 26:3 thou shalt go unto the **p.** that shall 3548
De 26:4 **p.** shall take the basket out of thine 3548
Jos 14:1 which Eleazar the **p.**, and Joshua 3548
Jos 17:4 came near before Eleazar the **p.**, 3548
Jos 19:51 which Eleazar the **p.**, and Joshua 3548
Jos 20:6 until the death of the high **p.** that 3548
Jos 21:1 the Levites unto Eleazar the **p.**, 3548
Jos 21:4 the children of Aaron the **p.**, which 3548
Jos 21:13 gave to the children of Aaron the **p.** 3548
Jos 22:13 Phinehas the son of Eleazar the **p.**, 3548
Jos 22:30 And when Phinehas the **p.**, and the 3548
Jos 22:31 the son of Eleazar the **p.** said unto 3548
Jos 22:32 Phinehas the son of Eleazar the **p.**, 3548
Jg 17:5 one of his sons, who became his **p.** 3548
Jg 17:10 and be unto me a father and a **p.**, 3548
Jg 17:12 the young man became his **p.**, and 3548
Jg 17:13 seeing I have a Levite to my **p.** 3548
Jg 18:4 and hath hired me, and I am his **p.** 3548
Jg 18:6 **p.** said unto them, Go in peace: 3548
Jg 18:17 **p.** stood in the entering of the gate 3548
Jg 18:18 said the **p.** unto them, What do ye? 3548
Jg 18:19 us, and be to us a father and a **p.** 3548
Jg 18:19 for thee to be a **p.** unto the house of 3548
Jg 18:19 be a **p.** unto a tribe and a family in 3548
Jg 18:24 my gods which I made, and the **p.**, 3548
Jg 18:27 had made, and the **p.** which he had, 3548
1Sa 1:9 Now Eli the **p.** sat upon a seat by a 3548
1Sa 2:11 unto the Lord before Eli the **p.** 3548
1Sa 2:14 the fleshhook brought up the **p.** took 3548
1Sa 2:15 Give flesh to roast for the **p.**; for 3548
1Sa 2:28 all the tribes of Israel to be my **p.**, 3548
1Sa 2:35 And I will raise me up a faithful **p.**, 3548
1Sa 14:3 son of Eli, the Lord's **p.** in Shiloh, 3548
1Sa 14:19 while Saul talked unto the **p.**, that 3548
1Sa 14:19 Saul said unto the **p.**, Withdraw 3548
1Sa 14:36 Then said the **p.**, Let us draw near 3548
1Sa 21:1 David to Nob to Ahimelech the **p.**: 3548
1Sa 21:2 David said unto Ahimelech the **p.**, 3548
1Sa 21:4 the **p.** answered David, and said, 3548
1Sa 21:5 David answered the **p.**, and said 3548
1Sa 21:6 So the **p.** gave him hallowed bread: 3548
1Sa 21:9 the **p.** said, The sword of Goliath 3548
1Sa 22:11 king sent to call Ahimelech the **p.**, 3548
1Sa 23:9 he said to Abiathar the **p.**, Bring 3548
1Sa 30:7 And David said to Abiathar the **p.**, 3548
2Sa 15:27 king said also unto Zadok the **p.**, 3548
1Ki 1:7 and with Abiathar the **p.**: and 3548
1Ki 1:8 But Zadok the **p.**, and Benaiah the 3548
1Ki 1:19 of the king, and Abiathar the **p.**, 3548
1Ki 1:25 of the host, and Abiathar the **p.**; 3548
1Ki 1:26 me thy servant, and Zadok the **p.**, 3548
1Ki 1:32 David said, Call me Zadok the **p.**, 3548
1Ki 1:34 let Zadok the **p.** and Nathan the 3548
1Ki 1:38 So Zadok the **p.**, and Nathan the 3548
1Ki 1:39 Zadok the **p.** took an horn of oil out 3548
1Ki 1:42 the son of Abiathar the **p.** came: 3548
1Ki 1:44 with him Zadok the **p.**, and Nathan 3548
1Ki 1:45 And Zadok the **p.** and Nathan the 3548
1Ki 2:22 for him, and for Abiathar the **p.**, 3548
1Ki 2:26 unto Abiathar the **p.** said the king, 3548
1Ki 2:27 thrust out Abiathar from being **p.** 3548
1Ki 2:35 Zadok the **p.** did the king put in the 3548
1Ki 4:2 Azariah the son of Zadok the **p.**, 3548
2Ki 11:9 that Jehoiada the **p.** commanded: 3548
2Ki 11:9 and came to Jehoiada the **p.** 3548
2Ki 11:10 did the **p.** give king David's spears 3548

2Ki	11:15	Jehoiada the **p.** commanded the	3548
2Ki	11:15	**p.** had said, Let her not be slain in	3548
2Ki	11:18	slew Mattan the **p.** of Baal before	3548
2Ki	11:18	**p.** appointed officers over the house	3548
2Ki	12:2	Jehoiada the **p.** instructed him	3548
2Ki	12:7	Jehoash called for Jehoiada the **p.**,	3548
2Ki	12:9	Jehoiada the **p.** took a chest, and	3548
2Ki	12:10	scribe and the high **p.** came up,	3548
2Ki	16:10	the **p.** the fashion of the altar,	3548
2Ki	16:11	And Urijah the **p.** built an altar	3548
2Ki	16:11	Urijah the **p.** made it against king	3548
2Ki	16:15	Ahaz commanded Urijah the **p.**,	3548
2Ki	16:16	Thus did Urijah the **p.**, according	3548
2Ki	22:4	Go up to Hilkiah the high **p.**, that	3548
2Ki	22:8	And Hilkiah the high **p.** said unto	3548
2Ki	22:10	the **p.** hath delivered me a book	3548
2Ki	22:12	king commanded Hilkiah the **p.**,	3548
2Ki	22:14	So Hilkiah the **p.**, and Ahikam, and	3548
2Ki	23:4	commanded Hilkiah the high **p.**,	3548
2Ki	23:24	the book that Hilkiah the **p.** found	3548
2Ki	25:18	the guard took Seraiah the chief **p.**,	3548
2Ki	25:18	Zephaniah the second **p.**, and the	3548
1Ch	16:39	Zadok the **p.**, and his brethren the	3548
1Ch	24:6	the princes, and Zadok the **p.**, and	3548
1Ch	27:5	the son of Jehoiada, a chief **p.**:	3548
1Ch	29:22	chief governor, and Zadok to be **p.**	3548
2Ch	13:9	be a **p.** of them that are no gods	3548
2Ch	15:3	without a teaching **p.**, and without	3548
2Ch	19:11	Amariah the chief **p.** is over you in	3548
2Ch	22:11	the wife of Jehoiada the **p.**, (for she	3548
2Ch	23:8	Jehoiada the **p.** had commanded,	3548
2Ch	23:8	Jehoiada the **p.** dismissed not the	3548
2Ch	23:9	Jehoiada the **p.** delivered to the	3548
2Ch	23:14	Jehoiada the **p.** brought out the	3548
2Ch	23:14	For the **p.** said, Slay her not in the	3548
2Ch	23:17	slew Mattan the **p.** of Baal before	3548
2Ch	24:2	all the days of Jehoiada the **p.**	3548
2Ch	24:20	the son of Jehoiada the **p.**, which	3548
2Ch	24:25	of the sons of Jehoiada the **p.**,	3548
2Ch	26:17	Azariah the **p.** went in after him,	3548
2Ch	26:20	And Azariah the chief **p.**, and all	3548
2Ch	31:10	Azariah the chief **p.** of the house of	3548
2Ch	34:9	they came to Hilkiah the high **p.**,	3548
2Ch	34:14	Hilkiah the **p.** found a book of the	3548
2Ch	34:18	the **p.** hath given me a book	3548
Ezr	2:63	till there stood up a **p.** with Urim	3548
Ezr	7:5	the son of Aaron the chief **p.**:	3548
Ezr	7:11	Artaxerxes gave unto Ezra the **p.**,	3548
Ezr	7:12	unto Ezra the **p.**, a scribe of the	3549
Ezr	7:21	whatsoever Ezra the **p.**, the scribe	3548
Ezr	8:33	Meremoth the son of Uriah the **p.**;	3548
Ezr	10:10	Ezra the **p.** stood up, and said unto	3548
Ezr	10:16	Ezra the **p.**, with certain chief of	3548
Ne	3:1	high **p.** rose up with his brethren	3548
Ne	3:20	the house of Eliashib the high **p.**	3548
Ne	7:65	till there stood up a **p.** with Urim	3548
Ne	8:2	Ezra the **p.** brought the law before	3548
Ne	8:9	and Ezra the **p.** the scribe, and the	3548
Ne	10:38	**p.** the son of Aaron shall be with	3548
Ne	12:26	and of Ezra the **p.**, the scribe	3548
Ne	13:4	before this, Eliashib the **p.**, having	3548
Ne	13:13	the treasuries, Shelemiah the **p.**,	3548
Ne	13:28	the son of Eliashib the high **p.**, was	3548
Ps	110:4	art a **p.** for ever after the order of	3548
Isa	8:2	witnesses to record, Uriah the **p.**,	3548
Isa	24:2	as with the people, so with the **p.**;	3548
Isa	28:7	the **p.** and the prophet have erred	3548
Jer	6:13	from the prophet even unto the **p.**	3548
Jer	8:10	from the prophet even unto the **p.**	3548
Jer	14:18	and the **p.** go about into a land	3548
Jer	18:18	the law shall not perish from the **p.**,	3548
Jer	20:1	Pashur the son of Immer the **p.**,	3548
Jer	21:1	the son of Maaseiah the **p.**, saying,	3548
Jer	23:11	both prophet and **p.** are profane;	3548
Jer	23:33	the prophet, or a **p.**, shall ask thee,	3548
Jer	23:34	the **p.**, and the people, that shall	3548
Jer	29:25	son of Maaseiah the **p.**, and to all	3548
Jer	29:26	The Lord hath made thee **p.** in the	3548
Jer	29:26	in the stead of Jehoiada the **p.**,	3548
Jer	29:29	Zephaniah the **p.** read this letter in	3548
Jer	37:3	the son of Maaseiah the **p.** to the	3548
Jer	52:24	the guard took Seraiah the chief **p.**,	3548
Jer	52:24	and Zephaniah the second **p.**, and	3548
La	2:6	of his anger the king and the **p.**	3548
La	2:20	the **p.** and the prophet be slain in	3548
Eze	1:3	came expressly unto Ezekiel the **p.**,	3548
Eze	7:26	the law shall perish from the **p.**,	3548
Eze	44:13	to do the office of a **p.** unto me,	3547
Eze	44:21	Neither shall any **p.** drink wine,	3548
Eze	44:22	or a widow that had a **p.** before	3548
Eze	44:30	unto the **p.** the first of your dough,	3548
Eze	45:19	**p.** shall take of the blood of the sin	3548
Ho	4:4	are as they that strive with the **p.**	3548
Ho	4:6	that thou shalt be no **p.** to me:	3547
Ho	4:9	there shall be, like people, like **p.**:	3548
Am	7:10	the **p.** of Beth-el sent to Jeroboam	3548
Hag	1:1,	12,14 son of Josedech, the high **p.**,	3548
Hag	2:2	the son of Josedech, the high **p.**,	3548
Hag	2:4	son of Josedech, the high **p.**;	3548
Zec	3:1	he shewed me Joshua the high **p.**	3548
Zec	3:8	Hear now, O Joshua the high **p.**,	3548
Zec	6:11	the son of Josedech, the high **p.**;	3548
Zec	6:13	he shall be a **p.** upon his throne:	3548
Mt	8:4	**shew thyself to the p., and offer**	*2409*
Mt	26:3	unto the palace of the high **p.**, who	*749*
Mt	26:57	him away to Caiaphas the high **p.**,	*749*
Mt	26:62	And the high **p.** arose, and said unto	*749*
Mt	26:63	the high **p.** answered and said unto	*749*
Mt	26:65	Then the high **p.** rent his clothes,	*749*
Mk	1:44	**shew thyself to the p., and offer**	*2409*
Mk	2:26	**in the days of Abiathar the high p.,**	*749*
Mk	14:47	smote a servant of the high **p.**, and	*749*
Mk	14:53	they led Jesus away to the high **p.**:	*749*
Mk	14:54	even into the palace of the high **p.**:	*749*
Mk	14:60	the high **p.** stood up in the midst,	*749*
Mk	14:61	Again the high **p.** asked him, and	*749*
Mk	14:63	Then the high **p.** rent his clothes,	*749*
Mk	14:66	one of the maids of the high **p.**:	*749*
Lu	1:5	a certain **p.** named Zacharias, of	*2409*
Lu	5:14	**shew thyself to the p., and offer**	*2409*
Lu	10:31	**there came down a certain p. that**	*2409*
Lu	22:50	smote the servant of the high **p.**,	*749*
Joh	11:49	being the high **p.** that same year,	*749*
Joh	11:51	but being high **p.** that year, he	*749*
Joh	18:13	was the high **p.** that same year.	*749*
Joh	18:15	disciple was known unto the high **p.**,	*749*
Joh	18:15	Jesus into the palace of the high **p.**	*749*
Joh	18:16	which was known unto the high **p.**,	*749*
Joh	18:19	The high **p.** then asked Jesus of his	*749*
Joh	18:22	Answerest thou the high **p.** so?	*749*
Joh	18:24	him bound unto Caiaphas the high **p.**	*749*
Joh	18:26	One of the servants of the high **p.**,	*749*
Ac	4:6	Annas the high **p.**, and Caiaphas.	*749*
Ac	4:6	were of the kindred of the high **p.**,	*748*
Ac	5:17	Then the high **p.** rose up, and all	*749*
Ac	5:21	But the high **p.** came, and they that	*749*
Ac	5:24	the high **p.** and the captain of the	*749*
Ac	5:27	council: and the high **p.** asked them,	*749*
Ac	7:1	Then said the high **p.**, Are these	*749*
Ac	9:1	of the Lord, went unto the high **p.**,	*749*
Ac	14:13	Then the **p.** of Jupiter, Which was	*2409*
Ac	22:5	the high **p.** doth bear me witness,	*749*
Ac	23:2	the high **p.** Ananias commanded	*749*
Ac	23:4	said, Revilest thou God's high **p.**?	*749*
Ac	23:5	brethren, that he was the high **p.**:	*749*
Ac	24:1	Ananias the high **p.** descended with	*749*
Ac	25:2	high **p.** and the chief of the Jews	*749*
Heb	2:17	a merciful and faithful high **p.** in	*749*
Heb	3:1	and High **P.** of our profession,	*749*
Heb	4:14	then that we have a great high **p.**,	*749*
Heb	4:15	For we have not an high **p.** which	*749*
Heb	5:1	every high **p.** taken from among	*749*
Heb	5:5	not himself to be made an high **p.**;	*749*
Heb	5:6	Thou art a **p.** forever after the	*2409*
Heb	5:10	of God an high **p.** after the order of	*749*
Heb	6:20	made an high **p.** for ever after the	*749*
Heb	7:1	**p.** of the most high God, who met	*2409*
Heb	7:3	of God; abideth a **p.** continually	*2409*
Heb	7:11	**p.** should rise after the order of	*2409*
Heb	7:15	of Melchisedec...ariseth another **p.**,	*2409*
Heb	7:17	Thou art a **p.** for ever after the	*2409*
Heb	7:20	not without an oath he was made **p.**:	*2409*
Heb	7:21	Thou art a **p.** for ever after the	*2409*
Heb	7:26	such an high **p.** became us, who is	*749*
Heb	8:1	We have such an high **p.**, who is set	*749*
Heb	8:3	For every high **p.** is ordained to	*749*
Heb	8:4	on earth, he should not be a **p.**,	*2409*
Heb	9:7	went the high **p.** alone once every	*749*
Heb	9:11	But Christ being come an high **p.** of	*749*
Heb	9:25	high **p.** entereth into the holy place	*749*
Heb	10:11	**p.** standeth daily ministering and	*2409*
Heb	10:21	an high **p.** over the house of God;	*2409*
Heb	13:11	sanctuary by the high **p.** for sin,	*749*

PRIESTHOOD

Ex	40:15	shall surely be an everlasting **p.**	3550
Nu	16:10	with thee: and seek ye the **p.** also?	3550
Nu	18:1	shall bear the iniquity of your **p.**	3550
Nu	25:13	the covenant of an everlasting **p.**;	3550
Jos	18:7	**p.** of the Lord is their inheritance:	3550
Ezr	2:62	they, as polluted, put from the **p.**	3550
Ne	7:64	they, as polluted, put from the **p.**	3550
Ne	13:29	because they have defiled the **p.**,	3550
Ne	13:29	and the covenant of the **p.**, and of	3550
Heb	7:5	who receive the office of the **p.**,	*2405*
Heb	7:11	perfection were by the Levitical **p.**,	*2420*
Heb	7:12	For the **p.** being changed, there is	*2420*
Heb	7:14	Moses spake nothing concerning **p.**	*2420*
Heb	7:24	ever, hath an unchangeable **p.**	*2420*
1Pe	2:5	up a spiritual house, an holy **p.**,	*2406*
1Pe	2:9	a chosen generation, a royal **p.**,	*2406*

PRIEST'S

Ex	28:1	minister unto me in the **p.** office,	3547
Ex	28:3,	4 minister unto me in the **p.** office	3547
Ex	28:41	minister unto me in the **p.** office.	3547
Ex	29:1	minister unto me in the **p.** office:	3547
Ex	29:9	the **p.** office shall be theirs for a	3550
Ex	29:44	to minister to me in the **p.** office	3547
Ex	30:30	minister unto me in the **p.** office.	3547
Ex	31:10	sons, to minister in the **p.** office,	3547
Ex	35:19	sons, to minister in the **p.** office.	3547
Ex	39:41	garments, to minister in the **p.** office.	3547
Ex	40:13	minister unto me in the **p.** office.	3547
Ex	40:15	minister unto me in the **p.** office:	3547
Le	5:13	the remnant shall be the **p.**, as a	3548
Le	7:9	pan, shall be the **p.** that offereth it.	3548
Le	7:14	shall be the **p.** that sprinkleth the	3548
Le	7:35	unto the Lord in the **p.** office;	3547
Le	14:13	for as the sin offering is the **p.**, so	3548
Le	14:18,	29 oil that is in the **p.** hand he shall	3548
Le	16:32	to minister in the **p.** office in his	3547
Le	22:12	the **p.** daughter also be married	3548
Le	22:13	if the **p.** daughter be a widow, or	3548
Le	27:21	possession thereof shall be the **p.**	3548
Nu	3:3	to minister in the **p.** office.	3547
Nu	3:4	Ithamar ministered in the **p.** office	3547
Nu	3:10	they shall wait on their **p.** office:	3550
Nu	18:7	with thee shall keep your **p.** office	3550
Nu	18:7	I have given your **p.** office unto you	3550
De	10:6	his son ministered in the **p.** office	3547
De	18:3	be the **p.** due from the people,	3548
Jg	18:20	And the **p.** heart was glad, and he	3548
1Sa	2:13	the **p.** custom with the people was	3548
1Sa	2:13	the **p.** servant came, while the flesh	3548
1Sa	2:15	**p.** servant came, and said to the	3548
1Sa	2:36	into one of the **p.** offices, that I	3550
1Ch	6:10	that executed the **p.** office in the	3547
1Ch	24:2	and Ithamar executed the **p.** office	3547
2Ch	11:14	from executing the **p.** office unto	3547
2Ch	24:11	and the high **p.** officer came and	3548
Eze	44:30	of your oblations, shall be the **p.**:	3548
Mal	2:7	the **p.** lips should keep knowledge,	3548
Mt	26:51	struck a servant of the high **p.**,	*749*
Mt	26:58	him afar off unto the high **p.** palace,	*749*
Lu	1:8	executed the **p.** office before God	*2407*
Lu	1:9	to the custom of the **p.** office,	*2405*
Lu	22:54	brought him into the high **p.** house	*749*
Joh	18:10	it, and smote the high **p.** servant,	*749*

PRIESTS See also PRIESTS'.

Ge	47:22	the land of the **p.** bought he not;	3548
Ge	47:22	the **p.** had a portion assigned them	3548
Ge	47:26	except the land of the **p.** only,	3548
Ex	19:6	shall be unto me a kingdom of **p.**,	3548
Ex	19:22	let the **p.** also, which come near	3548
Ex	19:24	the **p.** and the people break through	3548
Le	1:5	the **p.**, Aaron's sons, shall bring	3548
Le	1:8	And the **p.**, Aaron's sons, shall lay	3548
Le	1:11	the **p.**, Aaron's sons, shall sprinkle	3548
Le	2:2	bring it to Aaron's sons the **p.**:	3548
Le	3:2	Aaron's sons the **p.** shall sprinkle	3548
Le	6:29	the males among the **p.** shall eat	3548
Le	7:6	Every male among the **p.** shall eat	3548
Le	13:2	or unto one of his sons the **p.**:	3548
Le	16:33	shall make an atonement for the **p.**,	3548
Le	21:1	Speak unto the **p.** the sons of Aaron,	3548
Nu	3:3	Aaron, the **p.** which were anointed,	3548
Nu	10:8	sons of Aaron, the **p.**, shall blow	3548
De	17:9	shalt come unto the **p.** the Levites,	3548
De	17:18	which is before the **p.** the Levites:	3548
De	18:1	The **p.** the Levites, and all the	3548

De 19:17 before the **p.** and the judges, which.... 3548
De 21:5 **p.** the sons of Levi shall come near; ... 3548
De 24:8 the **p.** the Levites shall teach you:...... 3548
De 27:9 Moses and the **p.** the Levites spake ... 3548
De 31:9 it unto the **p.** the sons of Levi,.......... 3548
Jos 3:3 and the **p.** the Levites bearing it,....... 3548
Jos 3:6 Joshua spake unto the **p.**, saying,....... 3548
Jos 3:8 command the **p.** that bear the ark...... 3548
Jos 3:13 feet of the **p.** that bear the ark of...... 3548
Jos 3:14 **p.** bearing the ark of the covenant...... 3548
Jos 3:15 feet of the **p.** that bare the ark were .. 3548
Jos 3:17 **p.** that bare the ark of the covenant.... 3548
Jos 4:9 the feet of the **p.** which bare the ark .. 3548
Jos 4:10 For the **p.** which bare the ark stood.... 3548
Jos 4:11 of the Lord passed over, and the **p.**,... 3548
Jos 4:16 Command the **p.** that bear the ark...... 3548
Jos 4:17 Joshua therefore commanded the **p.**, ... 3548
Jos 4:18 **p.** that bare the ark of the covenant.... 3548
Jos 6:4 **p.** shall bear before the ark seven...... 3548
Jos 6:4 the **p.** shall blow with the trumpets..... 3548
Jos 6:6 Joshua the son of Nun called the **p.**, ... 3548
Jos 6:6 let seven **p.** bear seven trumpets of.... 3548
Jos 6:8 seven **p.** bearing the seven trumpets... 3548
Jos 6:9 the **p.** that blew with the trumpets, ... 3548
Jos 6:9 **p.** going on, and blowing with the....... 3548
Jos 6:12 the **p.** took up the ark of the Lord. 3548
Jos 6:13 seven **p.** bearing seven trumpets.............
Jos 6:13 **p.** going on, and blowing with the....... 3548
Jos 6:16 the **p.** blew with the trumpets, ... 3548
Jos 6:20 shouted when the **p.** blew with the...... 3548
Jos 8:33 that side before the **p.** the Levites, ... 3548
Jos 21:19 of the children of Aaron, the **p.**,......... 3548
Jg 18:30 his sons were **p.** to the tribe of Dan... 3548
1Sa 1:3 the **p.** of the Lord, were there. 3548
1Sa 5:5 neither the **p.** of Dagon, nor any........ 3548
1Sa 6:2 Philistines called for the **p.** and the..... 3548
1Sa 22:11 house, the **p.** that were in Nob:......... 3548
1Sa 22:17 Turn, and slay the **p.** of the Lord;...... 3548
1Sa 22:17 hand to fall upon the **p.** of the Lord. ... 3548
1Sa 22:18 Turn thou, and fall upon the **p.**. 3548
1Sa 22:18 turned, and he fell upon the **p.**, ... 3548
1Sa 22:19 Nob, the city of the **p.**, smote he....... 3548
1Sa 22:21 that Saul had slain the Lord's **p.**........ 3548
2Sa 8:17 the son of Abiathar, were the **p.**; 3548
2Sa 15:35 thee Zadok and Abiathar the **p.**?......... 3548
2Sa 15:35 it to Zadok and Abiathar the **p.**. 3548
2Sa 17:15 unto Zadok and to Abiathar the **p.**, ... 3548
2Sa 19:11 to Zadok and to Abiathar the **p.**, ... 3548
2Sa 20:25 and Zadok and Abiathar were the **p.**..... 3548
1Ki 4:4 and Zadok and Abiathar were the **p.**..... 3548
1Ki 8:3 came, and the **p.** took up the ark. 3548
1Ki 8:4 did the **p.** and the Levites bring up.... 3548
1Ki 8:6 the **p.** brought in the ark of the 3548
1Ki 8:10 **p.** were come out of the holy place,.... 3548
1Ki 8:11 the **p.** could not stand to minister....... 3548
1Ki 12:31 made **p.** of the lowest of the people,... 3548
1Ki 12:32 in Beth-el the **p.** of the high places..... 3548
1Ki 13:2 he offer the **p.** of the high places 3548
1Ki 13:33 lowest of the people **p.** of the high..... 3548
1Ki 13:33 one of the **p.** of the high places. 3548
2Ki 10:11 men, and his kinfolks, and his **p.**, ... 3548
2Ki 10:19 Baal, all his servants, and all his **p.**;..... 3548
2Ki 12:4 And Jehoash said to the **p.**, All the..... 3548
2Ki 12:5 Let the **p.** take it to them, every....... 3548
2Ki 12:6 **p.** had not repaired the breaches of.... 3548
2Ki 12:7 the priest, and the other **p.**, and........ 3548
2Ki 12:8 **p.** consented to receive no more........ 3548
2Ki 12:9 **p.** that kept the door put therein........ 3548
2Ki 17:27 Carry thither one of the **p.** whom....... 3548
2Ki 17:28 Then one of the **p.** whom they had..... 3548
2Ki 17:32 of them **p.** of the high places,............ 3548
2Ki 19:2 the elders of the **p.**, covered with...... 3548
2Ki 23:2 the **p.**, and the prophets, and all........ 3548
2Ki 23:4 **p.** of the second order, and the 3548
2Ki 23:5 put down the idolatrous **p.**, whom ....
2Ki 23:8 the **p.** out of the cities of Judah, ... 3548
2Ki 23:8 where the **p.** had burned incense,....... 3548
2Ki 23:9 **p.** of the high places came not up....... 3548
2Ki 23:20 And he slew all the **p.** of the high...... 3548
1Ch 9:2 **p.**, Levites, and the Nethinims........... 3548
1Ch 9:10 And of the **p.**; Jedaiah, and 3548
1Ch 9:30 sons of the **p.** made the ointment....... 3548
1Ch 13:2 **p.** and Levites which are in their........ 3548
1Ch 15:11 for Zadok and Abiathar the **p.**,............ 3548
1Ch 15:14 the **p.** and the Levites sanctified 3548
1Ch 15:24 the **p.**, did blow with the trumpets..... 3548
1Ch 16:6 and Jahaziel the **p.** with trumpets 3548
1Ch 16:39 the priest, and his brethren the **p.**,...... 3548
1Ch 18:16 the son of Abiathar, were the **p.**;........ 3548
1Ch 23:2 Israel, with the **p.** and the Levites...... 3548
1Ch 24:6, 31 the chief of the fathers of the **p.**.... 3548
1Ch 28:13, 21 courses of the **p.** and the Levites,.. 3548
2Ch 4:6 the sea was for the **p.** to wash in....... 3548
2Ch 4:9 he made the court of the **p.**, and......... 3548
2Ch 5:5 the **p.** and the Levites bring up........... 3548
2Ch 5:7 the **p.** brought in the ark of the 3548
2Ch 5:11 **p.** were come out of the holy place:.... 3548
2Ch 5:11 **p.** that were present were sanctified, .. 3548
2Ch 5:12 them an hundred and twenty **p.** 3548
2Ch 5:14 **p.** could not stand to minister by........ 3548
2Ch 6:41 thy **p.**, O Lord God, be clothed with... 3548
2Ch 7:2 **p.** could not enter into the house 3548
2Ch 7:6 the **p.** waited on their offices: the....... 3548
2Ch 7:6 **p.** sounded trumpets before them,....... 3548
2Ch 8:14 courses of the **p.** to their service, ... 3548
2Ch 8:14 and minister before the **p.**, as........... 3548
2Ch 8:15 of the king unto the **p.** and Levites..... 3548
2Ch 11:13 the **p.** and the Levites that were........ 3548
2Ch 11:15 he ordained him **p.** for the high.......... 3548
2Ch 13:9 ye not cast out the **p.** of the Lord, ... 3548
2Ch 13:9 made you **p.** after the manner of........ 3548
2Ch 13:10 the **p.**, which minister unto the.......... 3548
2Ch 13:12 his **p.** with sounding trumpets to........ 3548
2Ch 13:14 and the **p.** sounded with the.............. 3548
2Ch 17:8 them Elishama and Jehoram, **p.**.......... 3548
2Ch 19:8 set of the Levites, and of the **p.**, ... 3548
2Ch 23:4 of the **p.** and of the Levites, shall....... 3548
2Ch 23:6 save the **p.**, and they that minister..... 3548
2Ch 23:18 by the hand of the **p.** the Levites,...... 3548
2Ch 24:5 together the **p.** and the Levites, ... 3548
2Ch 26:17 fourscore **p.** of the Lord, that............ 3548
2Ch 26:18 to the **p.** the sons of Aaron, that........ 3548
2Ch 26:19 while he was wroth with the **p.**,.......... 3548
2Ch 26:19 before the **p.** in the house of the........ 3548
2Ch 26:20 all the **p.**, looked upon him, and,........ 3548
2Ch 29:4 brought in the **p.** and the Levites, ... 3548
2Ch 29:16 **p.** went into the inner part of the....... 3548
2Ch 29:21 the **p.** the sons of Aaron to offer........ 3548
2Ch 29:22 the **p.** received the blood, and........... 3548
2Ch 29:24 the **p.** killed them, and they made 3548
2Ch 29:26 and the **p.** with the trumpets............. 3548
2Ch 29:34 the **p.** were too few, so that they 3548
2Ch 29:34 other **p.** had sanctified themselves: 3548
2Ch 29:34 to sanctify themselves than the **p.**. 3548
2Ch 30:3 because the **p.** had not sanctified........ 3548
2Ch 30:15 **p.** and the Levites were ashamed,...... 3548
2Ch 30:16 the **p.** sprinkled the blood, which........ 3548
2Ch 30:21 the **p.** praised the Lord day by day,.... 3548
2Ch 30:24 a great number of **p.** sanctified 3548
2Ch 30:25 with the **p.** and the Levites, and all 3548
2Ch 30:27 **p.** the Levites arose and blessed........ 3548
2Ch 31:2 appointed the courses of the **p.**.......... 3548
2Ch 31:2 **p.** and Levites for burnt offerings....... 3548
2Ch 31:4 to give the portion of the **p.** and 3548
2Ch 31:9 Hezekiah questioned with the **p.**.......... 3548
2Ch 31:15 in the cities of the **p.**, in their set 3548
2Ch 31:17 the genealogy of the **p.** by the............ 3548
2Ch 31:19 the sons of Aaron the **p.**, which......... 3548
2Ch 31:19 to all the males among the **p.**, and to.. 3548
2Ch 34:5 burnt the bones of the **p.** upon 3548
2Ch 34:30 the **p.**, and the Levites, and all the...... 3548
2Ch 35:2 he set the **p.** in their charges, and...... 3548
2Ch 35:8 willingly unto the people, to the **p.**, ... 3548
2Ch 35:8 gave unto the **p.** for the passover....... 3548
2Ch 35:10 and the **p.** stood in their place, ... 3548
2Ch 35:11 **p.** sprinkled the blood from their........ 3548
2Ch 35:14 for themselves, and for the **p.**: 3548
2Ch 35:14 the **p.** the sons of Aaron were........... 3548
2Ch 35:14 and for the **p.** the sons of Aaron. 3548
2Ch 35:18 the **p.**, and the Levites, and all.......... 3548
2Ch 36:14 the chief of the **p.**, and the people,..... 3548
Ezr 1:5 and the **p.**, and the Levites, with 3548
Ezr 2:36 The **p.**: the children of Jedaiah,.......... 3548
Ezr 2:61 And of the children of the **p.**: the....... 3548
Ezr 2:70 So the **p.**, and the Levites, and 3548
Ezr 3:2 his brethren the **p.**, and Zerubbabel.... 3548
Ezr 3:8 remnant of their brethren the **p.** 3548
Ezr 3:10 set the **p.** in their apparel with 3548
Ezr 3:12 many of the **p.** and Levites and.......... 3548
Ezr 6:9 to the appointment of the **p.** which..... 3549
Ezr 6:16 of Israel, the **p.**, and the Levites,........ 3549
Ezr 6:18 they set the **p.** in their divisions,........ 3549
Ezr 6:20 **p.** and the Levites were purified 3548
Ezr 6:20 for their brethren the **p.**, and for........ 3548
Ezr 7:7 children of Israel, and of the **p.**,......... 3548
Ezr 7:13 of his **p.** and Levites, in my realm,..... 3549
Ezr 7:16 of the **p.**, offering willingly for the 3549
Ezr 7:24 touching any of the **p.** and Levites,..... 3549
Ezr 8:15 I viewed the people, and the **p.**, ... 3548
Ezr 8:24 twelve of the chief of the **p.**,............. 3548
Ezr 8:29 them before the chief of the **p.** and..... 3548
Ezr 8:30 So took the **p.** and the Levites the..... 3548
Ezr 9:1 The people of Israel, and the **p.**,........ 3548
Ezr 9:7 have we, our kings, and our **p.**,......... 3548
Ezr 10:5 arose Ezra, and made the chief **p.**,..... 3548
Ezr 10:18 among the sons of the **p.** there were .. 3548
Ne 2:16 told it to the Jews, nor to the **p.**,...... 3548
Ne 3:1 rose up with his brethren the **p.**, ... 3548
Ne 3:22 after him repaired the **p.**, the men...... 3548
Ne 3:28 above the horse gate repaired the **p.**,.. 3548
Ne 5:12 Then I called the **p.**, and took an....... 3548
Ne 7:39 The **p.**: the children of Jedaiah, of..... 3548
Ne 7:63 And of the **p.**: the children of........... 3548
Ne 7:73 So the **p.**, and the Levites, and the 3548
Ne 8:13 the **p.**, and the Levites, unto Ezra...... 3548
Ne 9:32 on our princes, and on our **p.**, and 3548
Ne 9:34 our **p.**, nor our fathers, kept thy........ 3548
Ne 9:38 Levites, and **p.**, seal unto it. 3548
Ne 10:8 Shemaiah: these were the **p.**............ 3548
Ne 10:28 the **p.**, the Levites, the porters, the.... 3548
Ne 10:34 we cast the lots among the **p.**, the..... 3548
Ne 10:36 **p.** that minister in the house of.......... 3548
Ne 10:37 unto the **p.**, to the chambers of the.... 3548
Ne 10:39 and the **p.** that minister, and the....... 3548
Ne 11:3 Israel, the **p.**, and the Levites, and..... 3548
Ne 11:10 Of the **p.**: Jedaiah the son of............ 3548
Ne 11:20 **p.**, and the Levites, were in all the..... 3548
Ne 12:1 these are the **p.**, and the Levites....... 3548
Ne 12:7 These were the chief of the **p.** and..... 3548
Ne 12:12 the days of Joiakim were **p.**, the 3548
Ne 12:22 also the **p.**, to the reign of Darius 3548
Ne 12:30 And the **p.** and the Levites purified..... 3548
Ne 12:41 And the **p.**; Eliakim, Maaseiah, ... 3548
Ne 12:44 of the law for the **p.** and Levites:....... 3548
Ne 12:44 for Judah rejoiced for the **p.** and........ 3548
Ne 13:5 porters; and the offerings of the **p.**..... 3548
Ne 13:30 appointed the wards of the **p.** and 3548
Ps 78:64 Their **p.** fell by the sword; and.......... 3548
Ps 99:6 Moses and Aaron among his **p.**, and... 3548
Ps 132:9 **p.** be clothed with righteousness; 3548
Ps 132:16 also clothe her **p.** with salvation: 3548
Isa 37:2 elders of the **p.** covered with 3548
Isa 61:6 shall be named the **P.** of the Lord:..... 3548
Isa 66:21 take of them for **p.** and for Levites,.... 3548
Jer 1:1 of the **p.** that were in Anathoth in...... 3548
Jer 1:18 against the **p.** thereof, and against...... 3548
Jer 2:8 The **p.** said not, Where is the Lord?... 3548
Jer 2:26 and their **p.**, and their prophets, ... 3548
Jer 4:9 the **p.** shall be astonished, and the...... 3548
Jer 5:31 the **p.** bear rule by their means; 3548
Jer 8:1 the bones of the **p.**, and the bones..... 3548
Jer 13:13 and the **p.**, and the prophets, and....... 3548
Jer 19:1 and of the ancients of the **p.**;............ 3548
Jer 26:7,8 the **p.** and the prophets and all 3548
Jer 26:11 Then spake the **p.** and the prophets.... 3548
Jer 26:16 unto the **p.** and to the prophets; 3548
Jer 27:16 I spake to the **p.** and to all this.......... 3548
Jer 28:1 in the presence of the **p.** and of all..... 3548
Jer 28:5 Hananiah in the presence of the **p.**, ... 3548
Jer 29:1 to the **p.**, and to the prophets, and..... 3548
Jer 29:25 the priest, and to all the **p.**, saying, ... 3548
Jer 31:14 the soul of the **p.** with fatness, ... 3548
Jer 32:32 their **p.**, and their prophets, and 3548
Jer 33:18 Neither shall the **p.** the Levites 3548
Jer 33:21 and with the Levites the **p.**, my.......... 3548
Jer 34:19 the eunuchs, and the **p.**, and all......... 3548
Jer 48:7 forth into captivity with his **p.** and...... 3548
Jer 49:3 his **p.** and his princes together........... 3548
La 1:4 **p.** sigh, her virgins are afflicted,......... 3548
La 1:19 my **p.** and mine elders gave up the..... 3548
La 4:13 the iniquities of her **p.**, that have 3548
La 4:16 respected not the persons of the **p.**, ... 3548
Eze 22:26 Her **p.** have violated my law, and....... 3548
Eze 40:45 is for the **p.**, the keepers of the......... 3548
Eze 40:46 is toward the north is for the **p.**,........ 3548
Eze 42:13 the **p.** that approach unto the Lord..... 3548
Eze 42:14 When the **p.** enter therein, then......... 3548
Eze 43:19 shalt give to the **p.** the Levites.......... 3548

Eze 43:24 the **p.** shall cast salt upon them, ... 3548
Eze 43:27 **p.** shall make your burnt offerings 3548
Eze 44:15 But the **p.** the Levites, the sons of....... 3548
Eze 44:31 **p.** shall not eat of any thing that is 3548
Eze 45:4 of the land shall be for the **p.** the....... 3548
Eze 46:2 **p.** shall prepare his burnt offering....... 3548
Eze 46:19 into the holy chambers of the **p.**, ... 3548
Eze 46:20 **p.** shall boil the trespass offering........ 3548
Eze 48:10 even for the **p.**, shall be this holy........ 3548
Eze 48:11 be for the **p.** that are sanctified of...... 3548
Eze 48:13 over against the border of the **p.**......... 3548
Ho 5:1 Hear ye this, O **p.**; and hearken, ye ... 3548
Ho 6:9 so the company of **p.** murder in the.... 3548
Ho 10:5 the **p.** thereof that rejoiced on it, ... 3649
Joe 1:9 the **p.**, the Lord's ministers, mourn. ... 3548
Joe 1:13 yourselves, and lament, ye **p.**:............ 3548
Joe 2:17 Let the **p.**, the ministers of the 3548
Mic 3:11 **p.** thereof teach for hire, and the 3548
Zep 1:4 of the Chemarims with the **p.**;........... 3548
Zep 3:4 her **p.** have polluted the sanctuary,...... 3548
Hag 2:11 Ask now the **p.** concerning the law,.... 3548
Hag 2:12 And the **p.** answered and said, No..... 3548
Hag 2:13 **p.** answered and said, It shall be........ 3548
Zec 7:3 unto the **p.** which were in the house... 3548
Zec 7:5 to the **p.**, saying, When ye fasted........ 3548
Mal 1:6 you, O **p.**, that despise my name. 3548
Mal 2:1 O ye **p.**, this commandment is for 3548
Mt 2:4 gathered all the chief **p.** and scribes *749*
Mt 12:4 **were with him, but only for the p.?** *2409*
Mt 12:5 **the p. in the temple profane the** *2409*
Mt 16:21 the elders and chief **p.** and scribes, ... *749*
Mt 20:18 **shall be betrayed unto the chief p**... *749*
Mt 21:15 when the chief **p.** and scribes saw........ *749*
Mt 21:23 chief **p.** and the elders of the people..... *749*
Mt 21:45 chief **p.** and Pharisees had heard.......... *749*
Mt 26:3 assembled together the chief **p.**,.......... *749*
Mt 26:14 Iscariot, went unto the chief **p.**, ... *749*
Mt 26:47 the chief **p.** and elders of the people..... *749*
Mt 26:59 Now the chief **p.**, and elders, and......... *749*
Mt 27:1 the chief **p.** and elders of the people..... *749*
Mt 27:3 of silver to the chief **p.** and elders, ... *749*
Mt 27:6 the chief **p.** took the silver pieces, ... *749*
Mt 27:12 accused of the chief **p.** and elders, ... *749*
Mt 27:20 chief **p.** and elders persuaded the......... *749*
Mt 27:41 also the chief **p.** mocking him, with *749*
Mt 27:62 the chief **p.** and Pharisees came *749*
Mt 28:11 and shewed unto the chief **p.** all the..... *749*
Mk 2:26 **is not lawful to eat but for the p.**,..*2409*
Mk 8:31 of the chief **p.**, and scribes, and be *749*
Mk 10:33 **shall be delivered unto the chief p.**, .*749*
Mk 11:18 the scribes and chief **p.** heard it, ... *749*
Mk 11:27 there come to him the chief **p.**, and *749*
Mk 14:1 the chief **p.** and the scribes sought....... *749*
Mk 14:10 went unto the chief **p.** to betray.......... *749*
Mk 14:43 from the chief **p.** and the scribes *749*
Mk 14:53 him were assembled all the chief **p.**...... *749*
Mk 14:55 And the chief **p.** and all the council....... *749*
Mk 15:1 the chief **p.** held a consultation with...... *749*
Mk 15:3 the chief **p.** accused him of many......... *749*
Mk 15:10 the chief **p.** had delivered him for *749*
Mk 15:11 But the chief **p.** moved the people, ... *749*
Mk 15:31 also the chief **p.** mocking said............. *749*
Lu 3:2 and Caiaphas being the high **p.**, the...... *749*
Lu 6:4 **lawful to eat but for the p. alone?**. *2409*
Lu 9:22 **rejected of the elders and chief p**.... *749*
Lu 17:14 **Go shew yourselves unto the p**...... *2409*
Lu 19:47 But the chief **p.** and the scribes........... *749*
Lu 20:1 the chief **p.** and the scribes came......... *749*
Lu 20:19 the chief **p.** and the scribes the same ... *749*
Lu 22:2 the chief **p.** and scribes sought how....... *749*
Lu 22:4 with the chief **p.** and captains, how *749*
Lu 22:52 Then Jesus said unto the chief **p.**,......... *749*
Lu 22:66 the chief **p.** and the scribes came......... *749*
Lu 23:4 Then said Pilate to the chief **p.** and....... *749*
Lu 23:10 the chief **p.** and scribes stood and......... *749*
Lu 23:13 together the chief **p.** and the rulers...... *749*
Lu 23:23 voices...of the chief **p.** prevailed. *749*
Lu 24:20 chief **p.** and our rulers delivered.......... *749*
Joh 1:19 the Jews sent **p.** and Levites from...... *2409*
Joh 7:32 the Pharisees and the chief **p.** sent *749*
Joh 7:45 came the officers to the chief **p.** and..... *749*
Joh 11:47 Then gathered the chief **p.** and the *749*
Joh 11:57 both the chief **p.** and the Pharisees...... *749*
Joh 12:10 But the chief **p.** consulted that they...... *749*
Joh 18:3 from the chief **p.** and Pharisees, ... *749*
Joh 18:35 Thine own nation and the chief **p.**......... *749*
Joh 19:6 the chief **p.** therefore and officers........ *749*
Joh 19:15 The chief **p.** answered, We have no..... *749*
Joh 19:21 the chief **p.** of the Jews to Pilate, ... *749*
Ac 4:1 spake unto the people, the **p.**, and *2409*
Ac 4:23 the chief **p.** and elders had said........... *749*
Ac 5:24 and the chief **p.** heard these things,...... *749*
Ac 6:7 the **p.** were obedient to the faith........ *2409*
Ac 9:14 authority from the chief **p.** to bind........ *749*
Ac 9:21 bring them bound unto the chief **p.**? *749*
Ac 19:14 a Jew, and chief of the **p.**, which did *749*
Ac 22:30 and commanded the chief **p.** and all....... *749*
Ac 23:14 they came to the chief **p.** and elders,.... *749*
Ac 25:15 chief **p.** and the elders of the Jews....... *749*
Ac 26:10 received authority from the chief **p.**;...... *749*
Ac 26:12 and commission from the chief **p.**,......... *749*
Heb 7:21 **p.** were made without an oath; *2409*
Heb 7:23 they truly were many **p.**, because *2409*
Heb 7:27 needeth not daily, as those high **p.**,...... *749*
Heb 7:28 men high **p.** which have infirmity; *749*
Heb 8:4 that there are **p.** that offer gifts......... *2409*
Heb 9:6 the **p.** went always into the first *2409*
Re 1:6 made us kings and **p.** unto god *2409*
Re 5:10 us unto our God kings and **p.**: and...... *2409*
Re 20:6 they shall be **p.** of God and of........... *2409*

PRIESTS'
Jos 4:3 place where the **p.** feet stood firm,..... 3548
Jos 4:18 the soles of the **p.** feet were lifted 3548
2Ki 12:16 house of the Lord: it was the **p.**. 3548
Ezr 2:69 and one hundred **p.** garments. 3548
Ne 7:70 hundred and thirty **p.** garments............ 3548
Ne 7:72 threescore and seven **p.** garments. 3548
Ne 12:35 of the **p.** sons with trumpets: 3548

PRINCE See also PRINCE'S; PRINCES; PRINCESS.
Ge 23:6 thou art a mighty **p.** among us:.......... 5387
Ge 32:28 as a **p.** hast thou power with God and.......
Ge 34:2 **p.** of the country, saw her, he........... 5387
Ex 2:14 thee a **p.** and a judge over us?........... 8269
Nu 7:11 their offering, each **p.** on his day,....... 5387
Nu 7:18 the son of Zuar, **p.** of Issachar,.......... 5387
Nu 7:24 **p.** of the children of Zebulun, did........ 5387
Nu 7:30 **p.** of the children of Reuben, did........ 5387
Nu 7:36 **p.** of the children of Simeon, did 5387
Nu 7:42 **p.** of the children of Gad, offered: 5387
Nu 7:48 **p.** of the children of Ephraim,............ 5387
Nu 7:54 **p.** of the children of Manasseh:.......... 5387
Nu 7:60 **p.** of the children of Benjamin,........... 5387
Nu 7:66 **p.** of the children of Dan, offered: 5387
Nu 7:72 **p.** of the children of Asher, offered:.... 5387
Nu 7:78 **p.** of the children of Naphtali, ... 5387
Nu 16:13 thou make thyself altogether a **p.** 8323
Nu 17:6 him a rod apiece, for each **p.** one,...... 5387
Nu 25:14 a **p.** of a chief house among the......... 5387
Nu 25:18 the daughter of a **p.** of Midian, ... 5387
Nu 34:18 ye shall take one **p.** of every tribe,..... 5387
Nu 34:22 the **p.** of the tribe of the children of.... 5387
Nu 34:23 the **p.** of the children of Joseph, for.... 5387
Nu 34:24, 25,26,27,28 the **p.** of the tribe of....... 5387
Jos 22:14 of each chief house a **p.** throughout 5387
2Sa 3:38 **p.** and a great man fallen this day....... 8269
1Ki 11:34 make him **p.** all the days of his.......... 5387
1Ki 14:7 and made thee **p.** over my people 5057
1Ki 16:2 and made thee **p.** over my people 5057
1Ch 2:10 **p.** of the children of Judah;.............. 5387
1Ch 5:6 he was **p.** of the Reubenites............... 5387
Ezr 1:8 unto Sheshbazzar, the **p.** of Judah....... 5387
Job 21:28 say, Where is the house of the **p.**?..... 5081
Job 31:37 as a **p.** would I go near unto him. 5057
Pr 14:28 people is the destruction of the **p.**....... 7333
Pr 17:7 fool: much less do lying lips a **p.**.......... 5081
Pr 19:6 will intreat the favour of the **p.**: 5081
Pr 25:7 put lower in the presence of the **p.**...... 5081
Pr 25:15 forbearing is a **p.** persuaded, ... 7101
Pr 28:16 **p.** that wanteth understanding............ 5057
Isa 9:6 everlasting Father,...**P.** of Peace.......... 8269
Jer 51:59 And this Seraiah was a quiet **p.**.......... 8269
Eze 7:27 the **p.** shall be clothed with............... 5387
Eze 12:10 This burden concerneth the **p.** in......... 5387
Eze 12:12 **p.** that is among them shall bear 5387
Eze 21:25 profane wicked **p.** of Israel, whose 5387
Eze 28:2 of man, say unto the **p.** of Tyrus, ... 5057
Eze 30:13 no more a **p.** in the land of Egypt: 5387
Eze 34:24 servant David a **p.** among them; 5387
Eze 37:25 my servant David shall be their **p.**....... 5387
Eze 38:2 the chief **p.** of Meshech and Tubal,...... 5387
Eze 38:3 the chief **p.** of Meshech and Tubal:..... 5387
Eze 39:1 chief **p.** of Meshech and Tubal: 5387
Eze 44:3 It is for the **p.**: the **p.**, he shall sit 5387
Eze 45:7 a portion shall be for the **p.** on the..... 5387
Eze 45:16 this oblation for the **p.** in Israel.......... 5387
Eze 45:22 shall the **p.** prepare for himself and..... 5387
Eze 46:2 the **p.** shall enter by the way of the.... 5387
Eze 46:4 offering that the **p.** shall offer unto 5387
Eze 46:8 when the **p.** shall enter, he shall go..... 5387
Eze 46:10 **p.** in the midst of them, when they..... 5387
Eze 46:12 the **p.** shall prepare a voluntary.......... 5387
Eze 46:16 **p.** give a gift unto any of his sons, ... 5387
Eze 46:17 after it shall return to the **p.**: but 5387
Eze 46:18 the **p.** shalt not take of the people's.... 5387
Eze 48:21 And the residue shall be for the **p.**, ... 5387
Eze 48:21 over against the portions for the **p.**:.... 5387
Eze 48:22 of Benjamin, shall be for the **p.**......... 5387
Da 1:7 the **p.** of the eunuchs gave names: 8269
Da 1:8 requested of the **p.** of the eunuchs..... 8269
Da 1:9 love with the **p.** of the eunuchs.......... 8269
Da 1:10 **p.** of the eunuchs said unto Daniel,..... 8269
Da 1:11 whom the **p.** of the eunuchs had set... 8269
Da 1:18 **p.** of the eunuchs brought them in....... 8269
Da 8:11 himself even to the **p.** of the host, ... 8269
Da 8:25 stand up against the **P.** of princes; 8269
Da 9:25 unto the Messiah the **P.** shall be........ 5057
Da 9:26 people of the **p.** that shall come......... 5057
Da 10:13 the **p.** of the kingdom of Persia.......... 8269
Da 10:20 return to fight with the **p.** of Persia: ... 8269
Da 10:20 lo, the **p.** of Grecia shall come........... 8269
Da 10:21 these things, but Michael your **p.**. 8269
Da 11:18 a **p.** for his own behalf shall cause...... 7101
Da 11:22 yea, also the **p.** of the covenant. 5057
Da 12:1 **p.** which standeth for the children....... 8269
Ho 3:4 without a king, and without a **p.**,......... 8269
Mic 7:3 **p.** asketh, and the judge asketh for..... 8269
Mt 9:34 devils through the **p.** of the devils........ *758*
Mt 12:24 by Beelzebub the **p.** of the devils......... *758*
Mk 3:22 by the **p.** of the devils casteth he out ... *758*
Joh 12:31 **shall p. of this world be cast out**. ... *758*
Joh 14:30 **the p. of this world cometh, hath**.... *758*
Joh 16:11 **the p. of this world is judged**.......... *758*
Ac 3:15 killed the **P.** of life, whom God hath..... *747*
Ac 5:31 right hand to be a **P.** and a Saviour,..... *747*
Eph 2:2 to the **p.** of the power of the air,........ *758*
Re 1:5 and the **p.** of the kings of the earth...... *758*

PRINCE'S
Ca 7:1 thy feet with shoes, O **p.** daughter! 5081
Eze 45:17 the **p.** part to give burnt offerings, ... 5387
Eze 48:22 in the midst of that which is the **p.**, ... 5387

PRINCES
Ge 12:15 The **p.** also of Pharaoh saw her, ... 8269
Ge 17:20 twelve **p.** shall he beget, and I will...... 5387
Ge 25:16 twelve **p.** according to their nations. ... 5387
Nu 1:16 **p.** of the tribes of their fathers, ... 5387
Nu 1:44 the **p.** of Israel, being twelve men:...... 5387
Nu 7:2 the **p.** of Israel, heads of the house 5387
Nu 7:2 who were the **p.** of the tribes, and...... 5387
Nu 7:3 a wagon for two of the **p.**, and for...... 5387
Nu 7:10 the **p.** offered for dedicating of the 5387
Nu 7:10 the **p.** offered their offering before...... 5387
Nu 7:84 it was anointed, by the **p.** of Israel: 5387
Nu 10:4 then the **p.**, which are heads of the 5387
Nu 16:2 and fifty **p.** of the assembly, famous.... 5387
Nu 17:2 of all their **p.** according to the house... 5387
Nu 17:6 of their **p.** gave him a rod apiece,....... 5387
Nu 21:18 The **p.** digged the well, the nobles 8269
Nu 22:8 the **p.** of Moab abode with Balaam...... 8269
Nu 22:13 said unto the **p.** of Balak, Get you....... 8269
Nu 22:14 **p.** of Moab rose up, and they went..... 8269
Nu 22:15 Balak sent yet again **p.**, more, and..... 8269
Nu 22:21 ass, and went with the **p.** of Moab. 8269
Nu 22:35 Balaam went with the **p.** of Balak....... 8269
Nu 22:40 and to the **p.** that were with him......... 8269
Nu 23:6 sacrifice, he, and all the **p.** of Moab.... 8269
Nu 23:17 and the **p.** of Moab with him. 8269
Nu 27:2 the **p.** and all the congregation,.......... 5387
Nu 31:13 all the **p.** of the congregation, went 5387
Nu 32:2 unto the **p.** of the congregation,......... 5387
Nu 36:1 before Moses, and before the **p.**, ... 5387
Jos 9:15 **p.** of the congregation sware unto 5387
Jos 9:18 **p.** of the congregation had sworn 5387
Jos 9:18 murmured against their **p.**................. 5387
Jos 9:19 **p.** said unto all the congregation,........ 5387
Jos 9:21 **p.** said unto them, Let them live; 5387
Jos 9:21 as the **p.** had promised them. 5387
Jos 13:21 Moses smote with the **p.** of Midian,.... 5387

Jos 17:4 the son of Nun, and before the **p.**, ... 5387
Jos 22:14 And with him ten **p.**, of each chief...... 5387
Jos 22:30 **p.** of the congregation and heads of 5387
Jos 22:32 the **p.**, returned from the children 5387
Jg 5:3 O ye kings; give ear, O ye **p.**; I, ... 7336
Jg 5:15 **p.** of Issachar were with Deborah;...... 8269
Jg 7:25 two **p.** of the Midianites, Oreb and...... 8269
Jg 8:3 into your hands the **p.** of Midian, ... 8269
Jg 8:6 And the **p.** of Succoth said, Are the.... 8269
Jg 8:14 unto him the **p.** of Succoth, and 8269
Jg 10:18 **p.** of Gilead said one to another, ... 8269
1Sa 2:8 to set them among **p.**, and to make 5081
1Sa 18:30 Then the **p.** of the Philistines went...... 8269
1Sa 29:3 Then said the **p.** of the Philistines, ... 8269
1Sa 29:3 said unto the **p.** of the Philistines, ... 8269
1Sa 29:4 the **p.** of the Philistines were wroth.... 8269
1Sa 29:4 **p.** of the Philistines said unto him,...... 8269
1Sa 29:9 the **p.** of the Philistines have said, ... 8269
2Sa 10:3 **p.** of the children of Ammon said........ 8269
2Sa 19:6 regardest neither **p.** nor servants: 8269
1Ki 4:2 these were the **p.** which he had; 8269
1Ki 9:22 his **p.**, and his captains, and rulers...... 8269
1Ki 20:14 men of the **p.** of the provinces........... 8269
1Ki 20:15 numbered the young men of the **p.**...... 8269
1Ki 20:17 **p.** of the provinces went out first; 8269
1Ki 20:19 **p.** of the provinces came out of the 8269
2Ki 11:14 **p.** and the trumpeters by the king, ... 8269
2Ki 24:12 and his **p.**, and his officers: and the 8269
2Ki 24:14 all the **p.**, and all the mighty men....... 8269
1Ch 4:38 mentioned by their names were **p.**...... 5387
1Ch 7:40 men of valour, chief of the **p.** 5387
1Ch 19:3 **p.** of the children of Ammon said........ 8269
1Ch 22:17 also commanded all the **p.** of Israel..... 8269
1Ch 23:2 together all the **p.** of Israel, with........ 8269
1Ch 24:6 them before the king, and the **p.**,........ 8269
1Ch 27:22 were the **p.** of the tribes of Israel. 8269
1Ch 28:1 David assembled all the **p.** of Israel, ... 8269
1Ch 28:1 **p.** of the tribes, and the captains of 8269
1Ch 28:21 also the **p.** and all the people will be ... 8269
1Ch 29:6 **p.** of the tribes of Israel, and the 8269
1Ch 29:24 And all the **p.**, and the mighty men,.... 8269
2Ch 12:5 Rehoboam, and to the **p.** of Judah, ... 8269
2Ch 12:6 **p.** of Israel and the king humbled 8269
2Ch 17:7 he sent to his **p.**, even to Ben-hail, ... 8269
2Ch 21:4 and divers also of the **p.** of Israel. 8269
2Ch 21:9 Jehoram went forth with his **p.**, ... 8269
2Ch 22:8 and found the **p.** of Judah, and the...... 8269
2Ch 23:13 **p.** and the trumpets by the king:........ 8269
2Ch 24:10 the **p.** and all the people rejoiced,....... 8269
2Ch 24:17 came the **p.** of Judah, and made......... 8269
2Ch 24:23 destroyed all the **p.** of the people....... 8269
2Ch 28:14 and the spoil before the **p.** and all 8269
2Ch 28:21 the house of the king, and of the **p.**,... 8269
2Ch 29:30 **p.** commanded the Levites to sing...... 8269
2Ch 30:2 king had taken counsel, and his **p.**, ... 8269
2Ch 30:6 and his **p.** throughout all Israel and..... 8269
2Ch 30:12 of the king and of the **p.**, by the 8269
2Ch 30:24 the **p.** gave to the congregation a........ 8269
2Ch 31:8 when Hezekiah and the **p.** came and ... 8269
2Ch 32:3 He took counsel with his **p.** and his 8269
2Ch 32:31 ambassadors of the **p.** of Babylon, ... 8269
2Ch 35:8 **p.** gave willingly unto the people, ... 8269
2Ch 36:18 treasures of the king, and of his **p.**; 8269
Ezr 7:28 and before all the king's mighty **p.**...... 8269
Ezr 8:20 David and the **p.** had appointed for 8269
Ezr 9:1 things were done, the **p.** came to me,.. 8269
Ezr 9:2 the hand of the **p.** and rulers hath 8269
Ezr 10:8 according to the counsel of the **p.**........ 8269
Ne 9:32 on our kings, on our **p.**, and on our 8269
Ne 9:34 Neither have our kings, our **p.**, our 8269
Ne 9:38 our **p.**, Levites, and priests, seal......... 8269
Ne 12:31 Then I brought up the **p.** of Judah...... 8269
Ne 12:32 and half of the **p.** of Judah,............... 8269
Es 1:3 made a feast unto all his **p.** and his..... 8269
Es 1:3 the nobles and **p.** of the provinces, ... 8269
Es 1:11 the people and the **p.** her beauty:....... 8269
Es 1:14 the seven **p.** of Persia and Media, ... 8269
Es 1:16 before the king and the **p.**, Vashti 8269
Es 1:16 king only, but also to all the **p.**, ... 8269
Es 1:18 say this day unto all the king's **p.**, ... 8269
Es 1:21 saying pleased the king and the **p.**; 8269
Es 2:18 made a great feast unto all his **p.** 8269
Es 3:1 set his seat above all the **p.** that 8269
Es 5:11 advanced him above the **p.** and 8269
Es 6:9 of one of the king's most noble **p.**, ... 8269
Job 3:15 Or with **p.** that had gold, who filled 8269
Job 12:19 He leadeth **p.** away spoiled, and......... 3548
Job 12:21 poureth contempt upon **p.**, and 5081
Job 29:9 The **p.** refrained talking, and laid........ 8269
Job 34:18 wicked? and to **p.**, Ye are ungodly? 5081
Job 34:19 accepteth not the persons of **p.**,......... 8269
Ps 45:16 mayest make **p.** in all the earth.......... 8269
Ps 47:9 The **p.** of the people are gathered 5081
Ps 68:27 the **p.** of Judah and their council, ... 8269
Ps 68:27 the **p.** of Zebulun, and the **p.** of......... 8269
Ps 68:31 **P.** shall come out of Egypt; 2831
Ps 76:12 He shall cut off the spirit of **p.**:........... 5057
Ps 82:7 men, and fall like one of the **p.**. 8269
Ps 83:11 yea, all their **p.** as Zebah, and as 5257
Ps 105:22 To gind his **p.** at his pleasure; 8269
Ps 107:40 He poureth contempt upon **p.**, ... 5081
Ps 113:8 That he may set him with **p.**, ... 5081
Ps 113:8 even with the **p.** of his people. 5081
Ps 118:9 than to put confidence in **p.**.............. 5081
Ps 119:23 **P.** also did sit and speak against 8269
Ps 119:161 **P.** have persecuted me without a....... 8269
Ps 146:3 Put not your trust in **p.**, nor in the..... 5081
Ps 148:11 **p.**, and all judges of the earth: 8269
Pr 8:15 kings reign, and **p.** decree justice. 7336
Pr 8:16 By me **p.** rule, and nobles, even 8269
Pr 17:26 good, nor to strike **p.** for equity,........ 5081
Pr 19:10 for a servant to have rule over **p.**. 8269
Pr 28:2 of a land many are the **p.** thereof: 8269
Pr 31:4 wine; nor for **p.** strong drink: 7336
Ec 10:7 **p.** walking as servants upon the 8269
Ec 10:16 and thy **p.** eat in the morning! 8269
Ec 10:17 and thy **p.** eat in due season, for........ 8269
Isa 1:23 Thy **p.** are rebellious, and................. 8269
Isa 3:4 I will give children to be their **p.**, ... 8269
Isa 3:14 of his people, and the **p.** thereof: 8269
Isa 10:8 Are not my **p.** altogether kings?......... 8269
Isa 19:11 **p.** of Zoan are fools, the counsel 8269
Isa 19:13 The **p.** of Zoan are become fools,........ 8269
Isa 19:13 **p.** of Noph are deceived; they have 8269
Isa 21:5 arise, ye **p.**, and anoint the shield....... 8269
Isa 23:8 whose merchants are **p.**, whose......... 8269
Isa 30:4 For this **p.** were at Zoan, and his 8269
Isa 31:9 his **p.** shall be afraid of the ensign, ... 8269
Isa 32:1 and **p.** shall rule in judgment. 8269
Isa 34:12 and all her **p.** shall be nothing............ 8269
Isa 40:23 bringeth the **p.** to nothing; he........... 7336
Isa 41:25 come upon **p.** as upon morter, ... 5461
Isa 43:28 profaned the **p.** of the sanctuary,........ 8269
Isa 49:7 **p.** also shall worship, because of 8269
Jer 1:18 against the **p.** thereof, against the 8269
Jer 2:26 they, their kings, their **p.**, and their.... 8269
Jer 4:9 perish, and the heart of the **p.**;.......... 8269
Jer 8:1 the bones of his **p.**, and the bones...... 8269
Jer 17:25 **p.** sitting upon the throne of David, ... 8269
Jer 17:25 and their **p.**, the men of Judah, ... 8269
Jer 24:1 the **p.** of Judah, with the carpenters.... 8269
Jer 24:8 the king of Judah, and his **p.**,............ 8269
Jer 25:18 kings thereof, and the **p.** thereof, ... 8269
Jer 25:19 and his servants, and his **p.**, and all.... 8269
Jer 26:10 the **p.** of Judah heard these things, ... 8269
Jer 26:11 and the prophets unto the **p.** and to.... 8269
Jer 26:12 spake Jeremiah unto all the **p.** and...... 8269
Jer 26:16 Then said the **p.** and all the people..... 8269
Jer 26:21 men, and all the **p.**, heard his words, .. 8269
Jer 29:2 **p.** of Judah and Jerusalem, and the 8269
Jer 32:32 their kings, their **p.**, their priests, ... 8269
Jer 34:10 Now when all the **p.** and all the 8269
Jer 34:19 The **p.** of Judah and the **p.** of........... 8269
Jer 34:21 king of Judah and his **p.** will I give...... 8269
Jer 35:4 was by the chamber of the **p.**, which .. 8269
Jer 36:12 all the **p.** sat there, even Elishama 8269
Jer 36:12 son of Hananiah, and all the **p.**.......... 8269
Jer 36:14 all the **p.** sent Jehudi the son of......... 8269
Jer 36:19 Then said the **p.** unto Baruch, Go, ... 8269
Jer 36:21 the **p.** which stood beside the king. 8269
Jer 37:14 and brought him to the **p.**................. 8269
Jer 37:15 the **p.** were wroth with Jeremiah,....... 8269
Jer 38:4 the **p.** said unto the king, We........... 8269
Jer 38:17 unto the king of Babylon's **p.**,............ 8269
Jer 38:18, 22 forth to the king of Babylon's **p.**, ... 8269
Jer 38:22 forth to the king of Babylon's **p.**,......... 8269
Jer 38:25 if the **p.** hear that I have talked 8269
Jer 38:27 came all the **p.** unto Jeremiah, and...... 8269
Jer 39:3 **p.** of the king of Babylon came in, ... 8269
Jer 39:3 residue of the **p.** of the king of 8269
Jer 39:13 and all the king of Babylon's **p.**; 7227
Jer 41:1 the **p.** of the king, even ten men........ 7227
Jer 44:17 our fathers, our kings, and our **p.**,...... 8269
Jer 44:21 fathers, your kings, and your **p.**, ... 8269
Jer 48:7 captivity with his priests and his **p.**...... 8269
Jer 49:3 and his priests and his **p.** together...... 8269
Jer 49:38 from thence the king and the **p.**, ... 8269
Jer 50:35 of Babylon, and upon her **p.**, and 8269
Jer 51:57 And I will make drunk her **p.**, and...... 8269
Jer 52:10 also all the **p.** of Judah in Riblah. 8269
La 1:6 her **p.** are become like harts that....... 8269
La 2:2 the kingdom and the **p.** thereof............ 8269
La 2:9 her **p.** are among the Gentiles: the..... 8269
La 5:12 **P.** are hanged up by their hand:......... 8269
Eze 11:1 son of Benaiah, **p.** of the people......... 8269
Eze 17:12 the king thereof, and the **p.** thereof, ... 8269
Eze 19:1 a lamentation for the **p.** of Israel, ... 5387
Eze 21:12 shall be upon all the **p.** of Israel: 5387
Eze 22:6 Behold, the **p.** of Israel, every one....... 5387
Eze 22:27 Her **p.** in the midst thereof are like 8269
Eze 23:15 heads, all of them **p.** to look to,......... 7991
Eze 26:16 all the **p.** of the sea shall come 5387
Eze 27:21 all the **p.** of Kedar, they occupied........ 5387
Eze 32:29 is Edom, her kings, and all her **p.**, ... 5387
Eze 32:30 There be the **p.** of the north, all of..... 5257
Eze 39:18 the blood of the **p.** of the earth,......... 5387
Eze 45:8 my **p.** shall no more oppress my 5387
Eze 45:9 Let it suffice you, O **p.** of Israel: 5387
Da 1:3 of the king's seed, and of the **p.**; 6579
Da 3:2 king sent to gather together the **p.**, ... 324
Da 3:3 Then the **p.**, the governors, and.......... 324
Da 3:27 the **p.**, governors, and captains, ... 324
Da 5:2 that the king, and his **p.**, his wives, ... 7261
Da 5:3 and the king, and his **p.**, his wives, ... 7261
Da 6:1 an hundred and twenty **p.**, which......... 324
Da 6:2 **p.** might give accounts unto them, ... 324
Da 6:3 above the presidents and **p.**,............... 324
Da 6:4 the presidents and **p.** sought to find 324
Da 6:6 these presidents and **p.** assembled 324
Da 6:7 the governors, and the **p.**, the 324
Da 8:25 stand up against the Prince of **p.**; 8269
Da 9:6 our kings, our **p.**, and our fathers,...... 8269
Da 9:8 to our kings, to our **p.**, and to our 8269
Da 10:13 Michael, one of the chief **p.**, came....... 8269
Da 11:5 shall be strong, and one of his **p.**; 8269
Da 11:8 their **p.**, and with their precious......... 5257
Ho 5:10 **p.** of Judah were like them that.......... 8269
Ho 7:3 and the **p.** with their lies. 8269
Ho 7:5 the **p.** have made him sick with 8269
Ho 7:16 their **p.** shall fall by the sword for 8269
Ho 8:4 have made **p.**, and I knew it not: 8269
Ho 8:10 for the burden of the king of **p.** 8269
Ho 9:15 no more: all their **p.** are revolters. 8269
Ho 13:10 thou saidst, Give me a king and **p.**? 8269
Am 1:15 captivity, he and his **p.** together,......... 8269
Am 2:3 slay all the **p.** thereof with him, ... 8269
Mic 3:1 and ye **p.** of the house of Israel; 7101
Mic 3:9 **p.** of the house...Israel, that abhor 7101
Hab 1:10 the **p.** shall be a scorn unto them: 7336
Zep 1:8 will punish the **p.**, and the king's........ 8269
Zep 3:3 **p.** within her are roaring lions;............ 8269
Mt 2:6 not the least among the **p.** of Juda; *2232*
Mt 20:25 **that the p. of the Gentiles exercise** .. *758*
1Co 2:6 nor the **p.** of this world, that *758*
1Co 2:8 none of the **p.** of this world knew: *758*

PRINCESS See also PRINCESSES.
La 1:1 and **p.** among the provinces, how....... 8282

PRINCESSES
1Ki 11:3 he had seven hundred wives, **p.**,......... 8282

PRINCIPAL
Ex 30:23 thou also unto thee **p.** spices,............ 7218
Le 6:5 restore it in the **p.**, and shall add 7218
Nu 5:7 his trespass with the **p.** thereof, ... 7218
1Ki 4:5 the son of Nathan was **p.** officer, ... 3548
2Ki 25:19 the **p.** scribe of the host, which 8269
1Ch 24:6 one **p.** household being taken for 1
1Ch 24:31 the **p.** fathers over against their......... 7218
Ne 11:17 **p.** to begin the thanksgiving in 7218
Pr 4:7 Wisdom is the **p.** thing; therefore 7225
Isa 16:8 have broken down the **p.** plants 8291
Isa 28:25 and cast in the **p.** wheat and the 7795
Jer 25:34 in the ashes, ye **p.** of the flock:............ 117
Jer 25:35 nor the **p.** of the flock to escape.......... 117
Jer 25:36 an howling of the **p.** of the flock, ... 117
Jer 52:25 and the **p.** scribe of the host who....... 8269
Mic 5:5 shepherds, and eight **p.** men. 5257
Ac 25:23 and **p.** men of the city, *3588,2596,1851,5607*

PRINCIPALITIES
Jer 13:18 your **p.** shall come down, even 4761

Ro 8:38 nor **p.**, nor powers, nor things........... *746*
Eph 3:10 now unto the **p.** and powers in........... *746*
Eph 6:12 but against **p.**, against powers,........... *746*
Col 1:16 or dominions, or **p.**, or powers:........... *746*
Col 2:15 And having spoiled **p.** and powers,....... *746*
Tit 3:1 mind to be subject to **p.** and powers,.... *746*

PRINCIPALITY See also PRINCIPALITIES.
Eph 1:21 Far above all **p.**, and power, and......... *746*
Col 2:10 is the head of all **p.** and power:........... *746*

PRINCIPLES
Heb 5:12 the first **p.** of the oracles of God;........ *4747*
Heb 6:1 leaving the **p.** of the doctrine of........... *746*

PRINT See also PRINTED.
Le 19:28 dead, nor **p.** any marks upon you:...... 5414
Job 13:27 a **p.** upon the heels of my feet........... 2707
Joh 20:25 in his hands the **p.** of the nails,......... *5179*
Joh 20:25 my finger into the **p.** of the nails,....... *5179*

PRINTED
Job 19:23 oh that they were **p.** in a book!......... 2710

PRISCA (pris'-cah) See also PRISCILLA.
2Ti 4:19 Salute **P.** and Aquila, and the........... *4251*

PRISCILLA (pris-sil'-lah) See also PRISCA.
Ac 18:2 come from Italy, with his wife **P.**;...... *4252*
Ac 18:18 and with him **P.** and Aquila;............. *4252*
Ac 18:26 when Aquila and **P.** had heard,............ *4252*
Ro 16:3 Greet **P.** and Aquila my helpers......... *4252*
1Co 16:19 Aquila and **P.** salute you much........... *4252*

PRISED
Zec 11:13 price that I was **p.** at of them........... 3365

PRISON See also IMPRISONED; PRISONS.
Ge 39:20 and put him into the **p.**, a.......... 1004,5470
Ge 39:20 and he was there in the **p.**......... 1004,5470
Ge 39:21 sight of the keeper of the **p.**...... 1004,5470
Ge 39:22 the keeper of the **p.** committed... 1004,5470
Ge 39:22 prisoners that were in the **p.**;..... 1004,5470
Ge 39:23 keeper of the **p.** looked not to.... 1004,5470
Ge 40:3 into the **p.**, the place where....... 1004,5470
Ge 40:5 which were bound in the **p.**......... 1004,5470
Ge 42:16 ye shall be kept in **p.**, that your..............
Ge 42:19 be bound in the house of your **p.**:...... 4929
Jg 16:21 and he did grind in the **p.** house.......... 631
Jg 16:25 for Samson out of the **p.** house;.......... 631
1Ki 22:27 Put this fellow in the **p.**, and....... 1004,3608
2Ki 17:4 him up, and bound him in **p.**....... 1004,3608
2Ki 25:27 king of Judah out of **p.**;............. 1004,3608
2Ki 25:29 And changed his **p.** garments:..... 1004,3608
2Ch 16:10 seer, and put him in a **p.** house;........ 4115
2Ch 18:26 Put this fellow in the **p.**, and...... 1004,3608
Ne 3:25 that was by the court of the **p.**........... 4307
Ne 12:39 and they stood still in the **p.** gate....... 4307
Ps 142:7 Bring my soul out of **p.**, that I........... 4525
Ec 4:14 out of **p.** he cometh to reign,....... 1004,612
Isa 24:22 and shall be shut up in the **p.**,........... 4525
Isa 42:7 bring out the prisoners from the **p.**,...... 4525
Isa 42:7 in darkness out of the **p.** house.......... 3608
Isa 42:22 and they are hid in **p.** houses:........... 3608
Isa 53:8 He was taken from **p.** and from......... 6115
Isa 61:1 opening of the **p.** to them that are....... 6495
Jer 29:26 thou shouldest put him in **p.** and........ 4115
Jer 32:2 was shut up in the court of the **p.**,....... 4307
Jer 32:8 came to me in the court of the **p.**...... 4307
Jer 32:12 Jews that sat in the court of the **p.**..... 4307
Jer 33:1 yet shut up in the court of the **p.**,....... 4307
Jer 37:4 they had not put him into **p.**....... 1004,3608
Jer 37:15 in **p.** in the house of Jonathan.............. 612
Jer 37:15 for they had made that the **p.**............ 3608
Jer 37:18 that ye have put me in **p.**?.................. 3608
Jer 37:21 Jeremiah into the court of the **p.**,........ 4307
Jer 37:21 remained in the court of the **p.**.......... 4307
Jer 38:6 that was in the court of the **p.**: and.... 4307
Jer 38:13 remained in the court of the **p.**.......... 4307
Jer 38:28 abode in the court of the **p.** until........ 4307
Jer 39:14 Jeremiah out of the court of the **p.**,.... 4307
Jer 39:15 was shut up in the court of the **p.**,....... 4307
Jer 52:11 in **p.** till the day of his death...... 1004,6486
Jer 52:31 brought him forth out of **p.**,.............. 3608
Jer 52:33 And changed his **p.** garments:............ 3608
Mt 4:12 heard that John was cast into **p.**,........ *3860*
Mt 5:25 **officer, and thou be cast into p.**..... *5438*
Mt 11:2 John had heard in the **p.** the works..... *1201*
Mt 14:3 put him in **p.** for Herodias' sake,........ *5438*
Mt 14:10 sent, and beheaded John in the **p.**..... *5438*
Mt 18:30 **went and cast him into p., till he**.. *5438*
Mt 25:36 **I was in p., and ye came unto me.** .*5438*
Mt 25:39 **when saw we thee sick, or in p.,**... *5438*
Mt 25:43 **sick, and in p., and ye visited me**.. *5438*
Mt 25:44 **or sick, or in p., and did not**......... *5438*
Mk 1:14 after that John was put in **p.**,............. *3860*
Mk 6:17 bound him in **p.** for Herodias' sake,.... *5438*
Mk 6:27 went and beheaded him in the **p.**,....... *5438*
Lu 3:20 all, that he shut up John in **p.**............ *5438*
Lu 12:58 **and the officer cast thee into p.**.... *5438*
Lu 22:33 ready to go with thee, both into **p.**,.... *5438*
Lu 23:19 and for murder, was cast into **p.**.)...... *5438*
Lu 23:25 and murder was cast into **p.**,............. *5438*
Joh 3:24 For John was not yet cast into **p.**....... *5438*
Ac 5:18 and put them in the common **p.**........... *5084*
Ac 5:19 Lord by night opened the **p.** doors,.... *5438*
Ac 5:21 to the **p.** to have them brought.......... *1201*
Ac 5:22 and found them not in the **p.**,............ *5438*
Ac 5:23 The **p.** truly found we shut with.......... *1201*
Ac 5:25 the men whom ye put in **p.** are......... *5438*
Ac 8:3 women committed them to **p.**............ *5438*
Ac 12:4 he put him in **p.**, and delivered.......... *5438*
Ac 12:5 Peter therefore was kept in **p.**:.......... *5438*
Ac 12:6 keepers before the door kept the **p.**,.. *5438*
Ac 12:7 and a light shined in the **p.**: and he..... *3612*
Ac 12:17 had brought him out of the **p.**............ *5438*
Ac 16:23 they cast them into **p.**, charging.......... *5438*
Ac 16:24 thrust them into the inner **p.**, and...... *5438*
Ac 16:26 foundations...the **p.** were shaken:....... *1201*
Ac 16:27 keeper of the **p.** awaking out of......... *1200*
Ac 16:27 and seeing the **p.** doors open, he....... *5438*
Ac 16:36 keeper of the **p.** told this saying to..... *1200*
Ac 16:37 Romans, and have cast us into **p.**;...... *5438*
Ac 16:40 And they went out of the **p.**, and....... *5438*
Ac 26:10 of the saints did I shut up in **p.**,......... *5438*
1Pe 3:19 preached unto the spirits in **p.**;........... *5438*
Re 2:10 **devil cast some of you into p.**,...... *5438*
Re 20:7 Satan shall be loosed out of his **p.**,..... *5438*

PRISONER See also FELLOWPRISONER; PRISONERS.
Ps 79:11 the sighing of the **p.** come before........ 616
Ps 102:20 To hear the groaning of the **p.**;........... 615
Mt 27:15 to release unto the people a **p.**,......... *1198*
Mt 27:16 they had then a notable **p.**, called....... *1198*
Mk 15:6 he released unto them one **p.**,........... *1198*
Ac 23:18 Paul the **p.** called me unto him, and.... *1198*
Ac 25:27 to me unreasonable to send a **p.**,....... *1198*
Ac 28:17 was I delivered **p.** from Jerusalem...... *1198*
Eph 3:1 Paul, the **p.** of Jesus Christ for you.... *1198*
Eph 4:1 I therefore, the **p.** of the Lord,.......... *1198*
2Ti 1:8 of our Lord, nor of me his **p.**:........... *1198*
Phm 1 Paul, a **p.** of Jesus Christ, and.......... *1198*
Phm 9 and now also a **p.** of Jesus Christ....... *1198*

PRISONERS See also FELLOWPRISONERS.
Ge 39:20 where the king's **p.** were bound:......... 615
Ge 39:22 all the **p.** that were in the prison;........ 615
Nu 21:1 Israel, and took some of them **p.**...... 7628
Job 3:18 There the **p.** rest together; they......... 615
Ps 69:33 the poor, and despiseth not his **p.**........ 615
Ps 146:7 hungry. The Lord looseth the **p.**:........... 631
Isa 10:4 they shall bow down under the **p.**,....... 616
Isa 14:17 that opened not the house of his **p.**?..... 615
Isa 20:4 Assyria lead away...Egyptians **p.**,....... 7628
Isa 24:22 as **p.** are gathered in the pit, and......... 616
Isa 42:7 to bring out the **p.** from the prison,...... 616
Isa 49:9 That thou mayest say to the **p.**, Go..... 631
La 3:34 his feet all the **p.** of the earth,........... 615
Zec 9:11 have sent forth thy **p.** out of the pit..... 615
Zec 9:12 to the strong hold, ye **p.** of hope:......... 615
Ac 16:25 unto God: and the **p.** heard them....... *1198*
Ac 16:27 supposing that the **p.** had been fled..... *1198*
Ac 27:1 delivered Paul and certain other **p.**..... *1202*
Ac 27:42 soldiers' counsel was to kill the **p.**,..... *1202*
Ac 28:16 delivered the **p.** to the captain of........ *1198*

PRISON-HOUSE See PRISON and HOUSE.

PRISONS
Lu 21:12 **up to the synagogues, and into p.**,. *5438*
Ac 22:4 delivering into **p.** both men and.......... *5438*
2Co 11:23 in **p.** more frequent, in deaths oft....... *5438*

PRIVATE See also PRIVY.
2Pe 1:20 is of any **p.** interpretation................ *2398*

PRIVATELY See also PRIVILY.
Mt 24:3 disciples came unto him **p.**,........ *2596,2398*
Mk 6:32 into a desert place by ship **p.**..... *2596,2398*
Mk 9:28 his disciples asked him **p.**, Why.. *2596,2398*
Mk 13:3 John and Andrew asked him **p.**,.. *2596,2398*
Lu 9:10 aside **p.** into a desert place........ *2596,2398*
Lu 10:23 said **p.**, **Blessed are the eyes**... *2596,2398*
Ac 23:19 and went with him aside **p.**, and.. *2596,2398*
Ga 2:2 and put to them which were of... *2596,2398*

PRIVILY See also PRIVATELY.
Jg 9:31 messengers unto Abimelech **p.**,.......... 8649
1Sa 24:4 cut off the skirt of Saul's robe **p.**........ 3909
Ps 10:8 his eyes are **p.** set against the poor.... 6845
Ps 11:2 **p.** shoot at the upright in heart........... 652
Ps 31:4 net that they have laid **p.** for me:....... 2934
Ps 64:5 they commune of laying snares **p.**;...... 2934
Ps 101:5 Whoso **p.** slandereth his neighbour,...... 5643
Ps 142:3 have they **p.** laid a snare for me.......... 2934
Pr 1:11 let us lurk **p.** for the innocent without......
Pr 1:18 blood; they lurk **p.** for their own lives.......
Mt 1:19 was minded to put her away **p.**.......... *2977*
Mt 2:7 when he had **p.** called the wise men,.. *2977*
Ac 16:37 and now do they thrust us out **p.**?...... *2977*
Ga 2:4 came in **p.** to spy out our liberty........ *3922*
2Pe 2:1 who **p.** shall bring in damnable.......... *3918*

PRIVY See also PRIVATE.
De 23:1 or hath his **p.** member cut off,........... 8212
1Ki 2:44 which thine heart is **p.** to, that.......... 3045
Eze 21:14 entereth into their **p.** chambers.......... 2314
Ac 5:2 price, his wife also being **p.** to it,....... *4894*

PRIZE See also PRISED.
1Co 9:24 run all, but one receiveth the **p.**?....... *1017*
Php 3:14 mark for the **p.** of the high calling...... *1017*

PROBATE See REPROBATE.

PROCEED See also PROCEEDED; PROCEEDETH; PROCEEDING.
Ex 25:35 that **p.** out of the candlestick............ 3318
Jos 6:10 any word **p.** out of your mouth,......... 3318
2Sa 7:12 which shall **p.** out of thy bowels,......... 3318
Job 40:5 yea, twice; but I will **p.** no further...... 3254
Isa 29:14 I will **p.** to do a marvellous work........ 3254
Isa 51:4 for a law shall **p.** from me, and I......... 3318
Jer 9:3 for they **p.** from evil to evil, and........ 3318
Jer 30:19 out of them shall **p.** thanksgiving........ 3318
Jer 30:21 shall **p.** from the midst of them;.......... 3318
Hab 1:7 their dignity shall **p.** of themselves...... 3318
Mt 15:18 **things which p. out of the mouth**.. *1607*
Mt 15:19 **out of the heart p. evil thoughts,**... *1831*
Mk 7:21 **the heart of men, p. evil thoughts,** .*1607*
Eph 4:29 communication **p.** out...your mouth,.... *1607*
2Ti 3:9 they shall **p.** no further: for their....... *4298*

PROCEEDED
Nu 30:12 then whatsoever **p.** out of her lips...... 4161
Nu 32:24 which hath **p.** out of your mouth......... 3318
Jg 11:36 which hath **p.** out of thy mouth;......... 3318
Job 36:1 Elihu also **p.**, and said,...................... 3254
Lu 4:22 words which **p.** out of his mouth........ *1607*
Joh 8:42 **for I p. forth and came from God;**.. *1831*
Ac 12:3 he **p.** further to take Peter also.......... *4369*
Re 4:5 out of the throne **p.** lightnings........... *1607*
Re 19:21 which sword **p.** out of his mouth:....... *1607*

PROCEEDETH
Ge 24:50 The thing **p.** from the Lord: we......... 3318
Nu 30:2 to all that **p.** out of his mouth............ 3318
De 8:3 word that **p.** out of the mouth of........ 4161
1Sa 24:13 Wickedness **p.** from the wicked:.......... 3318
Ec 10:5 as an error which **p.** from the ruler:.... 3318
La 3:38 most High **p.** not evil and good?.......... 3318
Hab 1:4 therefore wrong judgment **p.**............. 3318
Mt 4:4 **word that p. out of the mouth of**... *1607*
Joh 15:26 **truth, which p. from the Father,**... *1607*
Jas 3:10 mouth **p.** blessing and cursing............ *1831*
Re 11:5 fire **p.** out of their mouth, and.......... *1607*

PROCEEDING
Re 22:1 crystal, **p.** out of the throne of God.... *1607*

PROCESS
Ge 4:3 And in **p.** of time it came to pass,...... 7093
Ge 38:12 **p.** of time the daughter of Shuah........ 7235
Ex 2:23 it came to pass in **p.** of time, that...... 7227
Jg 11:4 it came to pass in **p.** of time, that............
2Ch 21:19 it came to pass, that in **p.** of time,...........

PROCHORUS (prok'-o-rus)
Ac 6:5 Philip, and **P.**, and Nicanor, and.......... *4402*

PROCLAIM See also PROCLAIMED; PROCLAIMETH; PROCLAIMING.
Ex 33:19 and I will **p.** the name of the Lord 7121
Le 23:2 ye shall **p.** to be holy convocations, 7121
Le 23:4 which ye shall **p.** in their seasons. 7121
Le 23:21 And ye shall **p.** on the selfsame day, 7121
Le 23:37 ye shall **p.** to be holy convocations, 7121
Le 25:10 **p.** liberty throughout all the land 7121
De 20:10 against it, then **p.** peace unto it. 7121
Jg 7:3 **p.** in the ears of the people, saying, 7121
1Ki 21:9 **P.** a fast, and set Naboth on high 7121
2Ki 10:20 **P.** a solemn assembly for Baal. 6942
Ne 8:15 publish and **p.** in all their cities, 5674
Es 6:9 of the city, and **p.** before him, 7121
Pr 20:6 will **p.** every one his own goodness: 7121
Isa 61:1 to **p.** liberty to the captives, and 7121
Isa 61:2 **p.** the acceptable year of the Lord, 7121
Jer 3:12 Go and **p.** these words toward the 7121
Jer 7:2 **p.** there this word, and say, Hear 7121
Jer 11:6 **P.** all these words in the cities of 7121
Jer 19:2 **p.** there the words that I shall tell 7121
Jer 34:8 Jerusalem, to **p.** liberty unto them; 7121
Jer 34:17 I **p.** a liberty for you, saith the Lord, 7121
Joe 3:9 **P.** ye this among the Gentiles; 7121
Am 4:5 **p.** and publish the free offerings: 7121

PROCLAIMED
Ex 34:5 there, and **p.** the name of the Lord. 7121
Ex 34:6 Lord passed by before him, and **p.**, 7121
Ex 36:6 it to be **p.** throughout the camp, 5674
1Ki 21:12 They **p.** a fast, and set Naboth on 7121
2Ki 10:20 assembly for Baal. And they **p.** it. 7121
2Ki 23:16 man of God **p.**, who **p.** these words. 7121
2Ki 23:17 **p.** these things that thou hast done 7121
2Ch 20:3 and **p.** a fast throughout all Judah. 7121
Ezr 8:21 Then I **p.** a fast there, at the river 7121
Es 6:11 **p.** before him, Thus shall it be done 7121
Isa 62:11 the Lord hath **p.** unto the end of 8085
Jer 36:9 that they **p.** a fast before the Lord 7121
Jon 3:5 and **p.** a fast, and put on sackcloth, 7121
Jon 3:7 he caused it to be **p.** and published 2199
Lu 12:3 **shall be p. upon the housetops** *2784*

PROCLAIMETH
Pr 12:23 the heart of fools **p.** foolishness. 7121

PROCLAIMING
Jer 34:15 in **p.** liberty every man to his 7121
Jer 34:17 **p.** liberty, every one to his brother, 7121
Re 5:2 strong angel **p.** with a loud voice, *2784*

PROCLAMATION
Ex 32:5 and Aaron made **p.**, and said, To 7121
1Ki 15:22 king Asa made a **p.** throughout 8085
1Ki 22:36 went a **p.** throughout the host 7440
2Ch 24:9 they made a **p.** through Judah 6963
2Ch 30:5 make **p.** throughout all 5674,6963
2Ch 36:22 he made a **p.** throughout all 5674,6963
Ezr 1:1 he made a **p.** throughout all his 5674,6963
Ezr 10:7 they made **p.** throughout 5674,6963
Da 5:29 and made a **p.** concerning him, 3745

PROCURE See also PROCURED; PROCURETH.
Jer 26:19 we **p.** great evil against our souls. 6213
Jer 33:9 all the prosperity that I **p.** unto it. 6213

PROCURED
Jer 2:17 Hast thou not **p.** this unto thyself, 6213
Jer 4:18 way and thy doings have **p.** these 6213

PROCURETH
Pr 11:27 diligently seeketh good **p.** favour: 1245

PRODUCE
Isa 41:21 **P.** your cause, saith the Lord; 7126

PROFANE See also PROFANED; PROFANETH; PROFANING.
Le 18:21 shalt thou **p.** the name of thy God: 2490
Le 19:12 shalt thou **p.** the name of thy God: 2490
Le 20:3 sanctuary, and to **p.** my holy name. 2490
Le 21:4 among his people, to **p.** himself. 2490
Le 21:6 and not **p.** the name of their God: 2490
Le 21:7 take a wife that is a whore, or **p.**; 2491
Le 21:9 **p.** herself by playing the whore, 2490
Le 21:12 nor **p.** the sanctuary of his God; 2490
Le 21:14 widow, or a divorced woman, or **p.**, 2491
Le 21:15 he **p.** his seed among his people: 2490
Le 21:23 that he **p.** not my sanctuaries: for 2490
Le 22:2 that they **p.** not my holy name in 2490
Le 22:9 it, and die therefore, if they **p.** it: 2490
Le 22:15 they shall not **p.** the holy things of 2490
Le 22:32 Neither shall ye **p.** my holy name; 2490
Ne 13:17 that ye do, and **p.** the sabbath day? 2490
Jer 23:11 both prophet and priest are **p.**; 2610
Eze 21:25 thou, **p.** wicked prince of Israel, 2491
Eze 22:26 between the holy and **p.**, neither 2455
Eze 23:39 day into my sanctuary to **p.** it; 2490
Eze 24:21 Behold, I will **p.** my sanctuary, 2490
Eze 28:16 cast thee as **p.** out of the mountain 2490
Eze 42:20 the sanctuary and the **p.** place. 2455
Eze 44:23 difference between the holy and **p.**, 2455
Eze 48:15 shall be a **p.** place for the city, for 2455
Am 2:7 same maid, to **p.** my holy name: 2490
Mt 12:5 **priests in the temple p. the sabbath,** *953*
Ac 24:6 hath gone about to **p.** the temple: *953*
1Ti 1:9 and for sinners, for unholy and **p.**, *952*
1Ti 4:7 But refuse **p.** and old wives' fables, *952*
1Ti 6:20 avoiding **p.** and vain babblings, and *952*
2Ti 2:16 But shun **p.** and vain babblings: *952*
Heb 12:16 be any fornicator, or **p.** person, *952*

PROFANED
Le 19:8 hath **p.** the hallowed thing of the 2490
Ps 89:39 thou hast **p.** his crown by casting 2490
Isa 43:28 I have **p.** the princes of the 2490
Eze 22:8 things, and hast **p.** my sabbaths. 2490
Eze 22:26 law, and have **p.** mine holy things: 2490
Eze 22:26 sabbaths, and I am **p.** among them. 2490
Eze 23:38 day, and have **p.** my sabbaths. 2490
Eze 25:3 my sanctuary, when it was **p.**; 2490
Eze 36:20 they went, they **p.** my holy name, 2490
Eze 36:21 Israel had **p.** among the heathen, 2490
Eze 36:22 ye have **p.** among the heathen, 2490
Eze 36:23 which was **p.** among the heathen, 2490
Eze 36:23 ye have **p.** in the midst of them; 2490
Mal 1:12 But ye have **p.** it, in that ye say, 2490
Mal 2:11 hath **p.** the holiness of the Lord 2490

PROFANENESS
Jer 23:15 the prophets of Jerusalem is **p.** 2613

PROFANETH
Le 21:9 the whore, she **p.** her father: she 2490

PROFANING
Ne 13:18 upon Israel by **p.** the sabbath. 2490
Mal 2:10 by **p.** the covenant of our fathers? 2490

PROFESS See also PROFESSED; PROFESSING.
De 26:3 him, I **p.** this day unto the Lord 5046
Mt 7:23 **then will I p. unto them, I never** *3670*
Tit 1:16 They **p.** that they know God; but *3670*

PROFESSED
2Co 9:13 for your **p.** subjection unto the *3671*
1Ti 6:12 hast **p.** a good profession before *3670*

PROFESSING
Ro 1:22 **P.** themselves to be wise, they *5335*
1Ti 2:10 becometh women **p.** godliness) *1861*
1Ti 6:21 some **p.** have erred concerning the *1861*

PROFESSION
1Ti 6:12 good **p.** before many witnesses. *3671*
Heb 3:1 Apostle and High Priest of our **p.**, *3671*
Heb 4:14 Son of God, let us hold fast our **p.** *3671*
Heb 10:23 Let us hold fast the **p.** of our faith *3671*

PROFIT See also PROFITABLE; PROFITED; PROFITETH; PROFITING.
Ge 25:32 what **p.** shall this birthright do to me?
Ge 37:26 What **p.** is it if we slay our brother, 1215
1Sa 12:21 which cannot **p.** nor deliver; for 3276
Es 3:8 for the king's **p.** to suffer them. 7737
Job 21:15 what **p.** should we have, if we 3276
Job 30:2 the strength of their hands **p.** me,
Job 35:3 and, What **p.** shall I have, if I be 3276
Job 35:8 righteousness may **p.** the son of man.
Ps 30:9 What **p.** is there in my blood, when 1215
Pr 10:2 of wickedness **p.** nothing: but 3276
Pr 11:4 Riches **p.** not in the day of wrath: 3276
Pr 14:23 In all labour there is **p.**: but the 4195
Ec 1:3 What **p.** hath a man of all his 3504
Ec 2:11 and there was no **p.** under the sun. 3504
Ec 3:9 What **p.** hath he that worketh in 3504
Ec 5:9 the **p.** of the earth is for all: the 3504
Ec 5:16 and what **p.** hath he that hath 3504
Ec 7:11 is **p.** to them that see the sun. 3148
Isa 30:5 a people that could not **p.** them, 3276
Isa 30:5 nor be an help nor **p.**, but a shame, 3276
Isa 30:6 to a people that shall not **p.** them. 3276
Isa 44:9 their delectable things shall not **p.**; 3276
Isa 47:12 if so be thou shalt be able to **p.**, if 3276
Isa 48:17 thy God which teacheth thee to **p.**, 3276
Isa 57:12 works; for they shall not **p.** thee. 3276
Jer 2:8 walked after things that do not **p.** 3276
Jer 2:11 glory for that which doth not **p.** 3276
Jer 7:8 trust in lying words, that cannot **p.** 3276
Jer 12:13 themselves to pain, but shall not **p.**: 3276
Jer 16:19 and things wherein there is no **p.** 3276
Jer 23:31 they shall not **p.** this people at all, 3276
Mal 3:14 what **p.** is it that we have kept his 1215
Mk 8:36 **For what shall it p. a man, if he** *5623*
Ro 3:1 what **p.** is there of circumcision? *5622*
1Co 7:35 And this I speak for your own **p.**; *4851*
1Co 10:33 things, not seeking ming own **p.**, *4851*
1Co 10:33 **p.** of many, that they may be saved. *4851*
1Co 12:7 is given to every man to **p.** withal. *4851*
1Co 14:6 what shall I **p.** you, except I shall *5623*
Ga 5:2 Christ shall **p.** you nothing. *5623*
2Ti 2:14 strive not about words to no **p.**, *5539*
Heb 4:2 word preached did not **p.** them, *5623*
Heb 12:10 he for our **p.**, that we might be *4851*
Jas 2:14 What doth it **p.**, my brethren, *3786*
Jas 2:16 to the body; what doth it **p.**? *3786*

PROFITABLE See also UNPROFITABLE.
Job 22:2 Can a man be **p.** unto God, as he 5532
Job 22:2 is wise may be **p.** unto himself? 5532
Ec 10:10 but wisdom is **p.** to direct. 3504
Isa 44:10 image that is **p.** for nothing? 3276
Jer 13:7 was marred, it was **p.** for nothing. 6743
Mt 5:29, 30 **it is p. for thee that one of thy** *4851*
Ac 20:20 back nothing that was **p.** unto you, *4851*
1Ti 4:8 godliness is **p.** unto all things, *5624*
2Ti 3:16 and is **p.** for doctrine, for reproof, *5624*
2Ti 4:11 for he is **p.** to me for the ministry. *2173*
Tit 3:8 things are good and **p.** unto men. *5624*
Phm 11 but now **p.** to thee and to me: *2173*

PROFITED
Job 33:27 which was right, and it **p.** me not; 7737
Mt 15:5 **thou mightest be p. by me;** *5623*
Mt 16:26 **For what is a man p., if he shall** *5623*
Mk 7:11 **thou mightest be p. by me; he** *5623*
Ga 1:14 And **p.** in the Jews' religion above *4298*
Heb 13:9 **p.** them that have been occupied *5623*

PROFITETH
Job 34:9 It **p.** a man nothing that he 5532
Hab 2:18 What **p.** the graven image that the 3276
Joh 6:63 **the flesh p. nothing: the words** *5623*
Ro 2:25 circumcision verily **p.**, if thou keep *5623*
1Co 13:3 have not charity, it **p.** me nothing. *5623*
1Ti 4:8 For bodily exercise **p.** little: *5624,2076*

PROFITING
1Ti 4:15 that thy **p.** may appear to all. *4297*

PROFOUND
Ho 5:2 revolters are **p.** to make slaughter, 6009

PROGENITORS
Ge 49:26 blessings of my **p.** unto the utmost 2029

PROGNOSTICATORS
Isa 47:13 stargazers, the monthly **p.**, stand 3045

PROLONG See also PROLONGED; PROLONGETH.
De 4:26 shall not **p.** your days upon it, but 748
De 4:40 mayest **p.** thy days upon the earth, 748
De 5:33 ye may **p.** your days in the land 748
De 11:9 ye may **p.** your days in the land, 748
De 17:20 he may **p.** his days in his kingdom, 748
De 22:7 and that thou mayest **p.** thy days. 748
De 30:18 shall not **p.** your days upon the land, 748
De 32:47 ye shall **p.** your days in the land, 748
Job 6:11 mine end, that I should **p.** my life? 748
Job 15:29 neither shall he **p.** the perfection 5186
Ps 61:6 Thou wilt **p.** the king's life: and 3254
Pr 28:16 covetousness shall **p.** his days. 748
Ec 8:13 neither shall he **p.** his days, which 748
Isa 53:10 seed, he shall **p.** his days, and the 748

PROLONGED
De 5:16 that thy days may be **p.**, and that 748
De 6:2 life; and that thy days may be **p.** 748
Pr 28:2 the state thereof shall be **p.** 748
Ec 8:12 his days be **p.**, yet surely I know 748
Isa 13:22 come, and her days shall not be **p.** 4900
Eze 12:22 The days are **p.**, and every vision 748
Eze 12:25 it shall be no more **p.**: for in your 4900

Eze 12:28 shall none of my words be **p.** any....... 4900
Da 7:12 lives were **p.** for a season and..... 754,3052

PROLONGETH
Pr 10:27 The fear of the Lord **p.** days: but....... 3254
Ec 7:15 a wicked man that **p.** his life in........... 748

PROMISE See also PROMISED; PROMISES; PROMISING.
Nu 14:34 and ye shall know my breach of **p.**....... 748
1Ki 8:56 failed one word of all his good **p.**,....... 1697
2Ch 1:9 let thy **p.** unto David my father be..... 1697
Ne 5:12 should do according to this **p.**............ 1697
Ne 5:13 performeth not this **p.**, even thus....... 1697
Ne 5:13 the people did according to this **p.**...... 1697
Ps 77:8 doth his **p.** fail for evermore?............ 562
Ps 105:42 he remembered his holy **p.**, and........... 1697
Lu 24:49 **the p. of my Father upon you:** *1860*
Ac 1:4 **but wait for the p. of the Father,** .. *1860*
Ac 2:33 Father, the **p.** of the Holy Ghost,....... *1860*
Ac 2:39 For the **p.** is unto you, and to your.... *1860*
Ac 7:17 when the time of the **p.** drew nigh, ... *1860*
Ac 13:23 according to his **p.**, raised unto.......... *1860*
Ac 13:32 **p.** which was made unto the fathers,... *1860*
Ac 23:21 ready, looking for a **p.** from thee........ *1860*
Ac 26:6 for the hope of the **p.** made of God *1860*
Ac 26:7 Unto which **p.** our twelve tribes,..............
Ro 4:13 For the **p.**, that he should be the....... *1860*
Ro 4:14 and the **p.** made of none effect:......... *1860*
Ro 4:16 the end of the **p.** might be sure to all.. *1860*
Ro 4:20 He staggered not at the **p.** of God...... *1860*
Ro 9:8 children of the **p.** are counted for....... *1860*
Ro 9:9 this is the word of **p.**, At this time..... *1860*
Ga 3:14 the **p.** of the Spirit through faith.......... *1860*
Ga 3:17 should make the **p.** of none effect........ *1860*
Ga 3:18 be of the law, it is no more of **p.**: *1860*
Ga 3:18 but God gave it to Abraham by **p.**........ *1860*
Ga 3:19 come to whom the **p.** was made; *1861*
Ga 3:22 that the **p.** by faith of Jesus Christ...... *1860*
Ga 3:29 and heirs according to the **p.**............. *1860*
Ga 4:23 he of the freewoman was by **p.**........... *1860*
Ga 4:28 as Isaac was, are the children of **p.**... *1860*
Eph 1:13 sealed with that holy Spirit of **p.**, ... *1860*
Eph 2:12 from the covenants of **p.**, having........ *1860*
Eph 3:6 partakers of his **p.** in Christ by the..... *1860*
Eph 6:2 is the first commandment with **p.**; *1860*
1Ti 4:8 having **p.** of the life that now is, ... *1860*
2Ti 1:1 the **p.** of life which is in Christ........... *1860*
Heb 4:1 a **p.** being left us of entering into....... *1860*
Heb 6:13 when God made **p.** to Abraham,.......... *1861*
Heb 6:15 endured, he obtained the **p.**............... *1860*
Heb 6:17 to shew unto the heirs of **p.** the *1860*
Heb 9:15 the **p.** of eternal inheritance. *1860*
Heb 10:36 of God, ye might receive the **p.**........... *1860*
Heb 11:9 faith he sojourned in the land of **p.**, ... *1860*
Heb 11:9 the heirs with him of the same **p.**....... *1860*
Heb 11:39 through faith, received not the **p.**....... *1860*
2Pe 2:19 While they **p.** them liberty, they *1861*
2Pe 3:4 Where is the **p.** of his coming? *1860*
2Pe 3:9 is not slack concerning his **p.**,............ *1860*
2Pe 3:13 according to his **p.**, look for new........ *1862*
1Jo 2:25 the **p.** that he hath promised us, ... *1860*

PROMISED See also PROMISEDST.
Ex 12:25 according as he hath **p.**, that ye........ 1696
Nu 14:40 place which the Lord hath **p.**................ 559
De 1:11 and bless you, as he hath **p.** you!)....... 1696
De 6:3 Lord God of thy fathers hath **p.**.......... 1696
De 9:28 into the land which he **p.** them, ... 1696
De 10:9 as the Lord thy God **p.** him. 1696
De 12:20 thy border, as he hath **p.** thee, and 1696
De 15:6 God blesseth thee, as he **p.** thee: 1696
De 19:8 land which he **p.** to give unto thy....... 1696
De 23:23 thou hast **p.** with thy mouth. 1696
De 26:18 peculiar people, as he hath **p.** thee, ... 1696
De 27:3 God of thy fathers hath **p.** thee.......... 1696
Jos 9:21 as the princes had **p.** them............... 1696
Jos 22:4 unto your brethren, as he **p.** them:..... 1696
Jos 23:5 Lord your God hath **p.** unto you. 1696
Jos 23:10 fighteth for you, as he hath **p.** you. 1696
Jos 23:15 the Lord your God **p.** you; which....... 1696
2Sa 7:28 **p.** this goodness unto thy servant:...... 1696
1Ki 2:24 hath made me an house, as he **p.**,...... 1696
1Ki 5:12 Solomon wisdom, as he **p.** him: 1696
1Ki 8:20 throne of Israel, as the Lord **p.**, ... 1696
1Ki 8:56 Israel, according to all that he **p.**........ 1696
1Ki 8:56 which he **p.** by the hand of Moses...... 1696
1Ki 9:5 as I **p.** to David thy father, saying, ... 1696
2Ki 8:19 as he **p.** him to give him alway a......... 559
2Ch 17:26 **p.** this goodness unto thy servant:...... 1696
2Ch 6:10 throne of Israel, as the Lord **p.**, ... 1696
2Ch 6:15 that which thou hast **p.** him; and......... 1696
2Ch 6:16 which thou hast **p.** him, saying,.......... 1696
2Ch 21:7 as he **p.** to give a light to him and 559
Ne 9:23 which thou hadst **p.** to their fathers,..... 559
Es 4:7 money that Haman had **p.** to pay......... 559
Jer 32:42 all the good that I have **p.** them.......... 1696
Jer 33:14 that good thing which I have **p.**........... 1696
Mt 14:7 he **p.** with an oath to give her........... *3670*
Mk 14:11 glad, and **p.** to give him money.......... *1861*
Lu 1:72 perform the mercy **p.** to our fathers, ...
Lu 22:6 he **p.**, and sought opportunity to *1843*
Ac 7:5 yet he **p.** that he would give it...him... *1861*
Ro 1:2 he had **p.** afore by his prophets *4279*
Ro 4:21 what he had **p.**, he was able also *1861*
Tit 1:2 God, that cannot lie, **p.** before the...... *1861*
Heb 10:23 wavering; (...he is faithful that **p.**;) *1861*
Heb 11:11 judged him faithful who had **p.**........... *1861*
Heb 12:26 now he hath **p.**, saying, Yet once....... *1861*
Jas 1:12 Lord hath **p.** to them that love him...... *1861*
Jas 2:5 kingdom which he hath **p.** to them...... *1861*
1Jo 2:25 promise that he hath **p.** us, even........ *1861*

PROMISEDST
1Ki 8:24 David my father that thou **p.** him: 1696
1Ki 8:25 David my father that thou **p.** him, ... 1696
Ne 9:15 **p.** them that they should go in to......... 559

PROMISES
Ro 9:4 and the service of God, and the **p.**; ... *1860*
Ro 15:8 the **p.** made unto the fathers:............ *1860*
2Co 1:20 For all the **p.** of God in him are yea, .. *1860*
2Co 7:1 Having therefore these **p.**, dearly *1860*
Ga 3:16 and his seed were the **p.** made........... *1860*
Ga 3:21 the law then against the **p.** of God? *1860*
Heb 6:12 faith and patience inherit the **p.**.......... *1860*
Heb 7:6 and blessed him that had the **p.**......... *1860*
Heb 8:6 was established upon better **p.**........... *1860*
Heb 11:13 faith, not having received the **p.**,......... *1860*
Heb 11:17 he that had received the **p.** offered..... *1860*
Heb 11:33 obtained **p.**, stopped the mouths of..... *1860*
2Pe 1:4 exceeding great and precious **p.**: *1862*

PROMISING
Eze 13:22 his wicked way, by **p.** him life: 2421

PROMOTE See also PROMOTED.
Nu 22:17 I will **p.** thee unto very great 3513
Nu 22:37 able indeed to **p.** thee to honour?........ 3513
Nu 24:11 to **p.** thee unto great honour; but....... 3513
Es 3:1 did king Ahasuerus **p.** Haman............ 1431
Pr 4:8 Exalt her, and she shall **p.** thee: 7311

PROMOTED
Jg 9:9,11, 13 go to be **p.** over the trees?........... 5128
Es 5:11 wherein the king had **p.** him,............. 1431
Da 3:30 Then the king **p.** Shadrach,............... 6744

PROMOTION
Ps 75:6 **p.** cometh neither from the east,......... 7311
Pr 3:35 but shame shall be the **p.** of fools....... 7311

PRONOUNCE See also PRONOUNCED; PRONOUNCING.
Le 5:4 that a man shall **p.** with an oath,.......... 981
Le 13:3 look on him, and **p.** him unclean..............
Le 13:6 the skin, the priest shall **p.** him clean: ....
Le 13:8 then the priest shall **p.** him unclean:..........
Le 13:11 and the priest shall **p.** him unclean,..........
Le 13:13 he shall **p.** him clean that hath the............
Le 13:15 raw flesh, and **p.** him to be unclean: ....
Le 13:17 then the priest shall **p.** him clean...............
Le 13:20 the priest shall **p.** unclean: it is a...............
Le 13:22 then the priest shall **p.** him unclean:...........
Le 13:23 and the priest shall **p.** him clean...............
Le 13:25 the priest shall **p.** him unclean: ....
Le 13:27 then the priest shall **p.** him unclean:...........
Le 13:28 and the priest shall **p.** him clean; for.........
Le 13:30 then the priest shall **p.** him unclean:...........
Le 13:34 then the priest shall **p.** him clean:.............
Le 13:37 and the priest shall **p.** him clean...............
Le 13:44 priest shall **p.** him utterly unclean;............
Le 13:59 to **p.** it clean, or to **p.** it unclean. ....
Le 14:7 and shall **p.** him clean, and shall let............
Le 14:48 the priest shall **p.** the house clean, ...
Jg 12:6 he could not frame to **p.** it right......... 1696

PRONOUNCED
Ne 6:12 he **p.** this prophecy against me: 1696
Jer 11:17 hath **p.** evil against thee, for the 1696
Jer 16:10 **p.** all this great evil against us?.......... 1696
Jer 18:8 nation, against whom I have **p.**, ... 1696
Jer 19:15 the evil that I have **p.** against it, ... 1696
Jer 25:13 words which I have **p.** against it,......... 1696
Jer 26:13 evil that he hath **p.** against you. 1696
Jer 26:19 evil which he had **p.** against them? 1696
Jer 34:5 for I have **p.** the word, saith the........ 1696
Jer 35:17 evil that I have **p.** against them:......... 1696
Jer 36:7 Lord hath **p.** against this people. 1696
Jer 36:18 He **p.** all these words unto me 7126
Jer 36:31 evil that I have **p.** against them;......... 1691
Jer 40:2 hath **p.** this evil upon this place.......... 1691

PRONOUNCING
Le 5:4 swear, **p.** with his lips to do evil,......... 981

PROOF See also PROOFS; REPROOF.
2Co 2:9 that I might know the **p.** of you, ... *1382*
2Co 8:24 **p.** of your love, and of our boasting.... *1732*
2Co 13:3 a **p.** of Christ speaking in me,............ *1382*
Php 2:22 But ye know the **p.** of him, that,......... *1382*
2Ti 4:5 make full **p.** of thy ministry.............. *4135*

PROOFS See also REPROOFS.
Ac 1:3 his passion by many infallible **p.**, ... *5039*

PROPER
1Ch 29:3 I have of mine own **p.** good, of.......... 5459
Ac 1:19 field is called in their **p.** tongue,......... *2398*
1Co 7:7 every man hath his **p.** gift of God,....... *2398*
Heb 11:23 they saw he was a **p.** child; *791*

PROPHECIES
1Co 13:8 whether there be **p.**, they shall.......... *4394*
1Ti 1:18 the **p.** which went before on thee,...... *4394*

PROPHECY See also PROPHECIES.
2Ch 9:29 in the **p.** of Ahijah the Shilonite,......... 5016
2Ch 15:8 and the **p.** of Oded the prophet,.......... 5016
Ne 6:12 he pronounced this **p.** against me: 5016
Pr 30:1 the son of Jakeh, even the **p.**: 4853
Pr 31:1 the **p.** that his mother taught him....... 4853
Da 9:24 to seal up the vision and **p.**, and 5030
Mt 13:14 **them is fulfilled the p. of Esaias,** .. *4394*
Ro 12:6 that is given to us, whether **p.**, ... *4394*
1Co 12:10 working of miracles; to another **p.**; *4394*
1Co 13:2 though I have the gift of **p.**, and *4394*
1Ti 4:14 in thee, which was given thee by **p.**,.... *4394*
2Pe 1:19 have also a more sure word of **p.**;...... *4397*
2Pe 1:20 that no **p.** of the scripture is of any *4394*
2Pe 1:21 For the **p.** came not in old time by..... *4394*
Re 1:3 they that hear the words of this **p.**, ... *4394*
Re 11:6 it rain not in the days of their **p.**: *4394*
Re 19:10 testimony of Jesus is the spirit of **p.**.. *4394*
Re 22:7 the sayings of the **p.** of this book. *4394*
Re 22:10 the sayings of the **p.** of this book: *4394*
Re 22:18 the words of the **p.** of this book,......... *4394*
Re 22:19 the words of the book of this **p.**,......... *4394*

PROPHESIED
Nu 11:25 spirit rested upon them, they **p.**, ... 5012
Nu 11:26 tabernacle: and they **p.** in the camp. ... 5012
1Sa 10:10 upon him, and he **p.** among them. 5012
1Sa 10:11 he **p.** among the prophets, that the..... 5012
1Sa 18:10 and he **p.** in the midst of the house: ... 5012
1Sa 19:20 of Saul, and they also **p.**.................. 5012
1Sa 19:21 messengers, and they **p.** likewise........ 5012
1Sa 19:21 the third time, and they **p.** also.......... 5012
1Sa 19:23 he went on, and **p.**, until he came....... 5012
1Sa 19:24 **p.** before Samuel in like manner, ... 5012
1Ki 18:29 and they **p.** until the time of the 5012
1Ki 22:10 all the prophets **p.** before them........... 5012
1Ki 22:12 all the prophets **p.** so, saying, Go....... 5012
1Ch 25:2 **p.** according to the order of the......... 5012
1Ch 25:3 also **p.** with a harp, to give thanks...... 5012
2Ch 18:7 for he never **p.** good unto me, but 5012
2Ch 18:9 all the prophets **p.** before them........... 5012
2Ch 18:11 And all the prophets **p.** so, saying, ... 5012
2Ch 20:37 **p.** Eliezer...against Jehoshaphat,......... 5012
Ezr 5:1 **p.** unto the Jews that were in............ 5013
Jer 2:8 and the prophets **p.** by Baal, and........ 5012
Jer 20:1 that Jeremiah **p.** these things............ 5012
Jer 20:6 friends, to whom thou hast **p.** lies. 5012
Jer 23:13 they **p.** in Baal, and caused my.......... 5012
Jer 23:21 not spoken to them, yet they **p.**. 5012
Jer 25:13 hath **p.** against all the nations. 5012
Jer 26:9 thou **p.** in the name of the lord, ... 5012
Jer 26:11 for he hath **p.** against this city, as 5012
Jer 26:18 Micah the Morasthite **p.** in the days.... 5012
Jer 26:20 man that **p.** in the name of the Lord, .. 5012

Jer 26:20 who **p.** against this city and against..... 5012
Jer 28:6 thy words which thou hast **p.**, ... 5012
Jer 28:8 old **p.** both against many countries,..... 5012
Jer 29:31 that Shemaiah hath **p.** unto you,......... 5012
Jer 37:19 your prophets which **p.** unto you,....... 5012
Eze 11:13 to pass, when I **p.**, that Pelatiah 5012
Eze 37:7 So I **p.** as I was commanded: 5012
Eze 37:7 and as I **p.**, there was a noise, and...... 5012
Eze 37:10 So I **p.** as he commanded me, and...... 5012
Eze 38:17 which **p.** in those days many years 5012
Zec 13:4 one of his vision, when he hath **p.**;..... 5012
Mt 7:22 **Lord, have we not p. in thy name?** *4395*
Mt 11:13 **prophets and the law p. until John** *4395*
Mk 7:6 **Well hath Esaias p. of you** *4395*
Lu 1:67 the Holy Ghost, and **p.**, saying, ... *4395*
Joh 11:51 he **p.** that Jesus should die for that..... *4395*
Ac 19:6 and they spake with tongues, and **p.**.. *4395*
1Co 14:5 with tongues, but rather that ye **p.**:.... *4395*
1Pe 1:10 who **p.** of the grace that should *4395*
Jude 14 Adam, **p.** of these, saying, Behold, ... *4395*

PROPHESIETH

Jer 28:9 The prophet which **p.** of peace, ... 5012
Eze 12:27 he **p.** of the times that are far off....... 5012
Zec 13:3 thrust him through when he **p.**. 5012
1Co 11:5 or **p.** with her head uncovered........... *4395*
1Co 14:3 But he that **p.** speaketh unto men *4395*
1Co 14:4 but he that **p.** edifieth the church. *4395*
1Co 14:5 greater is he that **p.** than he that *4395*

PROPHESY See also PROPHESIED; PROPHESIETH; PROPHESYING.

Nu 11:27 and Medad do **p.** in the camp. 5012
1Sa 10:5 before them; and they shall **p.**: 5012
1Sa 10:6 thou shalt **p.** with them, and shalt 5012
1Ki 22:8 he doth not **p.** good concerning me,.... 5012
1Ki 22:18 would **p.** no good concerning me, ... 5012
1Ch 25:1 who should **p.** with harps, with.......... 5012
2Ch 18:17 he would not **p.** good unto me, but..... 5012
Isa 30:10 **P.** not unto us right things, speak 2372
Isa 30:10 unto us smooth things, **p.** deceits:...... 2372
Jer 5:31 The prophets **p.** falsely, and the......... 5012
Jer 11:21 **P.** not in the name of the Lord,......... 5012
Jer 14:14 The prophets **p.** lies in my name:....... 5012
Jer 14:14 they **p.** unto you a false vision and 5012
Jer 14:15 the prophets that **p.** in my name, ... 5012
Jer 14:16 the people to whom they **p.** shall be ... 5012
Jer 19:14 whither the Lord had sent him to **p.**; .. 5012
Jer 23:16 words of the prophets that **p.** unto 5012
Jer 23:25 said, that **p.** lies in my name, ... 5012
Jer 23:26 heart of the prophets that **p.** lies? 5012
Jer 23:32 against them that **p.** false dreams, ... 5012
Jer 25:30 **p.** thou against them all these........... 5012
Jer 26:12 sent me to **p.** against this house 5012
Jer 27:10 For they **p.** a lie unto you, to remove . 5012
Jer 27:14 Babylon: for they **p.** a lie unto you. 5012
Jer 27:15 Lord, yet they **p.** a lie in my name; 5012
Jer 27:15 and the prophets that **p.** unto you. 5012
Jer 27:16 of your prophets that **p.** unto you,...... 5012
Jer 27:16 Babylon: for they **p.** a lie unto you. 5012
Jer 29:9 **p.** falsely unto you in my name: 5012
Jer 29:21 **p.** a lie unto you in my name;........... 5012
Jer 32:3 Wherefore dost thou **p.**, and say, ... 5012
Eze 4:7 and thou shalt **p.** against it............... 5012
Eze 6:2 of Israel, and **p.** against them, ... 5012
Eze 11:4 **p.** against them, **p.**, O son of man...... 5012
Eze 13:2 **p.** against the prophets of Israel......... 5012
Eze 13:2 the prophets of Israel that **p.**,............ 5012
Eze 13:2 unto them that **p.** out of their own 5012
Eze 13:16 the prophets of Israel which **p.** 5012
Eze 13:17 daughters of thy people, which **p.**....... 5012
Eze 13:17 heart; and **p.** thou against them, ... 5012
Eze 20:46 **p.** against the forest of the south 5012
Eze 21:2 and **p.** against the land of Israel, ... 5012
Eze 21:9 Son of man, **p.**, and say, Thus saith.... 5012
Eze 21:14 son of man, **p.**, and smite, thine 5012
Eze 21:28 son of man, **p.** and say, Thus saith..... 5012
Eze 25:2 Ammonites, and **p.** against them; 5012
Eze 28:21 against Zidon, and **p.** against it,......... 5012
Eze 29:2 king of Egypt, and **p.** against him, ... 5012
Eze 30:2 Son of man, **p.** and say, Thus saith..... 5012
Eze 34:2 **p.** against the shepherds of Israel, ... 5012
Eze 34:2 **p.**, and say unto them, Thus saith...... 5012
Eze 35:2 mount Seir, and **p.** against it, ... 5012
Eze 36:1 **p.** unto the mountains of Israel, ... 5012
Eze 36:3 Therefore **p.** and say, Thus saith 5012
Eze 36:6 **P.** therefore concerning the land of..... 5012
Eze 37:4 **P.** upon these bones, and say unto..... 5012
Eze 37:9 **P.** unto the wind, **p.**, son of man, ... 5012
Eze 37:12 Therefore **p.** and say unto them,........ 5012
Eze 38:2 and Tubal, and **p.** against him, ... 5012
Eze 38:14 son of man, **p.** and say unto Gog, ... 5012
Eze 39:1 thou son of man, **p.** against Gog, ... 5012
Joe 2:28 sons and your daughters shall **p.**, ... 5012
Am 2:12 the prophets, saying, **P.** not............. 5012
Am 3:8 God hath spoken, who can but **p.**?...... 5012
Am 7:12 and there eat bread, and **p.** there:...... 5012
Am 7:13 **p.** not again any more at Beth-el: 5012
Am 7:15 me, Go, **p.** unto my people Israel....... 5012
Am 7:16 Thou sayest, **P.** not against Israel, ... 5012
Mic 2:6 **P.** ye not, say they to them that........ 5197
Mic 2:6 say they to them that **p.**: they shall.... 5197
Mic 2:6 they shall not **p.** to them, that they 5197
Mic 2:11 I will **p.** unto thee of wine and of 5197
Zec 13:3 that when any shall yet **p.**, then......... 5197
Mt 15:7 **well did Esaias p. of you, saying,**.. *4395*
Mt 26:68 **P.** unto us, thou Christ, Who is he..... *4395*
Mk 14:65 him, and to say unto him, **P.**:............ *4395*
Lu 22:64 **P.**, who is it that smote thee? *4395*
Ac 2:17 sons and your daughters shall **p.**, ... *4395*
Ac 2:18 of my Spirit; and they shall **p.**: *4395*
Ac 21:9 daughters, virgins, which did **p.**. *4395*
Ro 12:6 let us **p.** according to the proportion ....
1Co 13:9 we know in part, and we **p.** in part..... *4395*
1Co 14:1 gifts, but rather that ye may **p.**.......... *4395*
1Co 14:24 if all **p.**, and there come in one that.... *4395*
1Co 14:31 For ye may all **p.** one by one, that..... *4395*
1Co 14:39 covet to **p.**, and forbid not to speak.... *4395*
Re 10:11 Thou must **p.** again before many........ *4395*
Re 11:3 shall **p.** a thousand two hundred......... *4395*

PROPHESYING See also PROPHESYINGS.

1Sa 10:13 when he had made an end of **p.**, ... 5012
1Sa 19:20 the company of the prohets **p.**, ... 5012
Ezr 6:14 prospered through the **p.** of Haggai..... 5017
1Co 11:4 Every man praying or **p.**, having *4395*
1Co 14:6 or by knowledge, or by **p.**, or by *4394*
1Co 14:22 but **p.** serveth not for them that *4394*

PROPHESYINGS

1Th 5:20 Despise not **p.**................................ *4394*

PROPHET See also PROPHETESS; PROPHET'S; PROPHETS.

Ge 20:7 for he is a **p.**, and he shall pray for 5030
Ex 7:1 Aaron thy brother shall be thy **p.**. 5030
Nu 12:6 If there be a **p.** among you, I the....... 5030
De 13:1 If there arise among you a **p.**, or a...... 5030
De 13:3 hearken unto the words of that **p.**, ... 5030
De 13:5 that **p.**, or that dreamer of dreams, ... 5030
De 18:15 thy God will raise up unto thee a **P.** ... 5030
De 18:18 I will raise them up a **P.** from 5030
De 18:20 But the **p.**, which shall presume to 5030
De 18:20 of other gods, even that **p.** shall die.... 5030
De 18:22 When a **p.** speaketh in the name of..... 5030
De 18:22 **p.** hath spoken it presumptuously: 5030
De 34:10 arose not a **p.** since in Israel like 5030
Jg 6:8 Lord sent a **p.** unto the children of....... 5030
1Sa 3:20 established to be a **p.** of the Lord. 5030
1Sa 9:9 a **P.** was before time called a Seer.) 5030
1Sa 22:5 **p.** Gad said unto David, Abide not....... 5030
2Sa 7:2 the king said unto Nathan the **p.**, ... 5030
2Sa 12:25 sent by the hand of Nathan the **p.**: 5030
2Sa 24:11 of the Lord came unto the **p.** Gad, ... 5030
1Ki 1:8 Nathan the **p.**, and Shimei, and Rei,.... 5030
1Ki 1:10 Nathan the **p.**, and Benaiah, and 5030
1Ki 1:22 the king, Nathan the **p.** also came 5030
1Ki 1:23 king, saying, Behold Nathan the **p.**. 5030
1Ki 1:32 the priest, and Nathan the **p.**, and...... 5030
1Ki 1:34 Nathan the **p.** anoint him there 5030
1Ki 1:38, 44 and Nathan the **p.**, and Benaiah 5030
1Ki 1:45 Nathan the **p.** have anointed him........ 5030
1Ki 11:29 **p.** Ahijah the Shilonite found him......... 5030
1Ki 13:11 there dwelt an old **p.** in Beth-el; 5030
1Ki 13:18 him, I am a **p.** also as thou art; 5030
1Ki 13:20 unto the **p.** that brought him back: 5030
1Ki 13:23 the **p.** whom he had brought back. 5030
1Ki 13:25 in the city where the old **p.** dwelt. 5030
1Ki 13:26 when the **p.** that brought him back 5030
1Ki 13:29 the **p.** took up the carcase of the 5030
1Ki 13:29 and the old **p.** came to the city, to 5030
1Ki 14:2 there is Ahijah the **p.**, which told 5030
1Ki 14:18 hand of his servant Ahijah the **p.**......... 5030
1Ki 16:7 by the hand of the **p.** Jehu the son 5030
1Ki 16:12 against Baasha by Jehu the **p.**,........... 5030
1Ki 18:22 I only, remain a **p.** of the Lord; 5030
1Ki 18:36 Elijah the **p.** came near, and said,....... 5030
1Ki 19:16 thou anoint to be **p.** in thy room. 5030
1Ki 20:13 there came a **p.** unto Ahab king of...... 5030
1Ki 20:22 the **p.** came to the king of Israel, ... 5030
1Ki 20:38 So the **p.** departed, and waited for 5030
1Ki 22:7 Is there not here a **p.** of the Lord...... 5030
2Ki 3:11 Is there not here a **p.** of the Lord, ... 5030
2Ki 5:3 were with the **p.** that is in Samaria!.... 5030
2Ki 5:8 know that there is a **p.** in Israel......... 5030
2Ki 5:13 if the **p.** had bid thee do some great ... 5030
2Ki 6:12 but Elisha, the **p.** that is in Israel, ... 5030
2Ki 9:1 the **p.** called one of the children of 5030
2Ki 9:4 even the young man the **p.**, went to ... 5030
2Ki 14:25 Jonah the son of Amittai, the **p.**, ... 5030
2Ki 19:2 to Isaiah the **p.** the son of Amoz. 5030
2Ki 20:1 the **p.** Isaiah the son of Amoz came.... 5030
2Ki 20:11 Isaiah the **p.** cried unto the Lord: 5030
2Ki 20:14 Then came Isaiah the **p.** unto king...... 5030
2Ki 23:18 of the **p.** that came out of Samaria...... 5030
1Ch 17:1 David said to Nathan the **p.**, Lo, I...... 5030
1Ch 29:29 and in the book of Nathan the **p.**, ... 5030
2Ch 9:29 in the book of Nathan the **p.**, and....... 5030
2Ch 12:5 came Shemaiah the **p.** to Rehoboam,... 5030
2Ch 12:15 in the book of Shemaiah the **p.**, and.... 5030
2Ch 13:22 written in the story of the **p.** Iddo. 5030
2Ch 15:8 and the prophecy of Oded the **p.**, ... 5030
2Ch 18:6 Is there not here a **p.** of the Lord...... 5030
2Ch 21:12 a writing to him from Elijah the **p.**,..... 5030
2Ch 25:15 he sent unto him a **p.**, which said....... 5030
2Ch 25:16 Then the **p.** forbare, and said, I......... 5030
2Ch 26:22 did Isaiah the **p.**, the son of Amoz,..... 5030
2Ch 28:9 a **p.** of the Lord was there, whose 5030
2Ch 29:25 the king's seer, and Nathan the **p.**: 5030
2Ch 32:20 **p.** Isaiah the son of Amoz, prayed 5030
2Ch 32:32 written in the vision of Isaiah the **p.**,... 5030
2Ch 35:18 from the days of Samuel the **p.**; 5030
2Ch 36:12 Jeremiah the **p.** speaking from the...... 5030
Ezr 5:1 Haggai the **p.**, and Zechariah the........ 5029
Ezr 6:14 the prophesying of Haggai the **p.**......... 5029
Ps 51:*title* Nathan the **p.** came unto him, ... 5030
Ps 74:9 there is no more any **p.**: neither is 5030
Isa *general* *title* The Book Of The **P.** Isaiah. ....
Isa 3:2 man of war, the judge, and the **p.**, ... 5030
Isa 9:15 the **p.** that teacheth lies, he is the...... 5030
Isa 28:7 the priest and the **p.** have erred 5030
Isa 37:2 unto Isaiah the **p.** the son of Amoz..... 5030
Isa 38:1 Isaiah the **p.** the son of Amoz came.... 5030
Isa 39:3 Isaiah the **p.** unto king Hezekiah, ... 5030
Jer *general* *title* The Book Of The **P.** Jeremiah. ....
Jer 1:5 ordained thee a **p.** unto the nations..... 5030
Jer 6:13 from the **p.** even unto the priest 5030
Jer 8:10 from the **p.** even unto the priest 5030
Jer 14:18 both the **p.** and the priest go about..... 5030
Jer 18:18 the wise, nor the word from the **p.**. ... 5030
Jer 20:2 Pashur smote Jeremiah the **p.**, and..... 5030
Jer 23:11 both **p.** and priest are profane; yea, ... 5030
Jer 23:28 The **p.** that hath a dream, let him 5030
Jer 23:33 or the **p.**, or a priest shall ask thee, ... 5030
Jer 23:34 And as for the **p.**, and the priest, ... 5030
Jer 23:37 Thus shalt thou say to the **p.**, What.... 5030
Jer 25:2 Jeremiah the **p.** spake unto all the 5030
Jer 28:1 Hananiah the son of Azar the **p.**, ... 5030
Jer 28:5 **p.** Jeremiah said unto...**p.** Hananiah..... 5030
Jer 28:6 Even the **p.** Jeremiah said, Amen: 5030
Jer 28:9 The **p.** which prophesieth of peace, ... 5030
Jer 28:9 the word of the **p.** shall come to 5030
Jer 28:9 then shall the **p.** be known, that......... 5030
Jer 28:10 Hananiah the **p.** took the yoke 5030
Jer 28:10 from off the **p.** Jeremiah's neck, ... 5030
Jer 28:11 And the **p.** Jeremiah went his way....... 5030
Jer 28:12 Lord came unto Jeremiah the **p.**, ...
Jer 28:12 the **p.** had broken the yoke 5030
Jer 28:12 off the neck of the **p.** Jeremiah, ... 5030
Jer 28:15 **p.** Jeremiah unto Hananiah the **p.**, ... 5030
Jer 28:17 So Hananiah the **p.** died the same 5030
Jer 29:1 that Jeremiah the **p.** sent from............ 5030
Jer 29:26 is mad, and maketh himself a **p.**, ... 5012
Jer 29:27 which maketh himself a **p.** to you?...... 5012
Jer 29:29 in the ears of Jeremiah the **p.**............ 5030
Jer 32:2 Jeremiah the **p.** was shut up in the..... 5030
Jer 34:6 Jeremiah the **p.** spake all these 5030
Jer 36:8 Jeremiah the **p.** commanded him,......... 5030
Jer 36:26 the scribe and Jeremiah the **p.**: 5030
Jer 37:2 which he spake by the **p.** Jeremiah. 5030
Jer 37:3 the priest to the **p.** Jeremiah, ... 5030
Jer 37:6 of the Lord unto the **p.** Jeremiah,....... 5030

Jer 37:13 he took Jeremiah the **p.**, saying, 5030
Jer 38:9 they have done to Jeremiah the **p.**, 5030
Jer 38:10 take up Jeremiah the **p.** out of the 5030
Jer 38:14 took Jeremiah the **p.** unto him into 5030
Jer 42:2 And said unto Jeremiah the **p.**, Let, 5030
Jer 42:4 Jeremiah the **p.** said unto them, I 5030
Jer 43:6 and Jeremiah the **p.**, and Baruch 5030
Jer 45:1 that Jeremiah the **p.** spake unto 5030
Jer 46:1 Lord which came to Jeremiah the **p.** 5030
Jer 46:13 the Lord spake to Jeremiah the **p.**, 5030
Jer 47:1 Lord that came to Jeremiah the **p.** 5030
Jer 49:34 came to Jeremiah the **p.** against 5030
Jer 50:1 the Chaldeans by Jeremiah the **p.** 5030
Jer 51:59 which Jeremiah the **p.** commanded 5030
La 2:20 the priest and the **p.** be slain in the 5030
Eze *general* *title* The Book Of The **P.** Ezekiel.
Eze 2:5 there hath been a **p.** among them 5030
Eze 7:26 shall they seek a vision of the **p.**; 5030
Eze 14:4 his face, and cometh to the **p.**; 5030
Eze 14:7 cometh to a **p.** to enquire of him 5030
Eze 14:9 And if the **p.** be deceived when he 5030
Eze 14:9 I the Lord have deceived that **p.**, 5030
Eze 14:10 the punishment of the **p.** shall be 5030
Eze 33:33 that a **p.** hath been among them 5030
Da 9:2 the Lord came to Jeremiah the **p.**, 5030
Ho 4:5 **p.** also shall fall with thee in the 5030
Ho 9:7 the **p.** is a fool, the spiritual man 5030
Ho 9:8 the **p.** is a snare of a fowler in all 5030
Ho 12:13 by a **p.** the Lord brought Israel out 5030
Ho 12:13 and by a **p.** was he preserved. 5030
Am 7:14 I was no **p.**, neither was I a 5030
Mic 2:11 shall even be the **p.** of this people. 5197
Hab 1:1 which Habakkuk the **p.** did see. 5030
Hab 3:1 A prayer of Habakkuk the **p.** upon 5030
Hag 1:1 word of the Lord by Haggai the **p.** 5030
Hag 1:3 word of the Lord by Haggai the **p.**, 5030
Hag 1:12 and the words of Haggai the **p.**, 5030
Hag 2:1 word of the Lord by the **p.** Haggai, 5030
Hag 2:10 word of the Lord by Haggai the **p.**, 5030
Zec 1:1,7 Berechiah, the son of Iddo the **p.**, 5030
Zec 13:5 shall say, I am no **p.**, I am an 5030
Mal 4:5 Behold, I will send you Elijah the **p.** 5030
Mt 1:22 was spoken of the Lord by the **p.**, *4396*
Mt 2:5 for thus it is written by the **p.**, *4396*
Mt 2:15 was spoken of the Lord by the **p.**, *4396*
Mt 2:17 which was spoken by Jeremy the **p.**, *4396*
Mt 3:3 that was spoken of by the **p.** Esaias, *4396*
Mt 4:14 spoken by Esaias the **p.**, saying, *4396*
Mt 8:17 which was spoken by Esaias the **p.**, *4396*
Mt 10:41 **a p. in the name of a p. shall** *4396*
Mt 11:9 **what went ye out for to see? A p.?** *4396*
Mt 11:9 **say unto you, and more than a p.** *4396*
Mt 12:17 which was spoken by Esaias the **p.**, *4396*
Mt 12:39 **to it, but the sign of the p. Jonas:** *4396*
Mt 13:35 which was spoken by the **p.**, *4396*
Mt 13:57 **A p. is not without honour, save** *4396*
Mt 14:5 because they counted him as a **p.** *4396*
Mt 16:4 **it, but the sign of the p. Jonas.** *4396*
Mt 21:4 which was spoken by the **p.**, *4396*
Mt 21:11 This is Jesus the **p.** of Nazareth of *4396*
Mt 21:26 people; for all hold John as a **p.** *4396*
Mt 21:46 because they took him for a **p.** *4396*
Mt 24:15 **spoken of by Daniel the p., stand** *4396*
Mt 27:9 which was spoken by Jeremy the **p.**, *4396*
Mt 27:35 which was spoken by the **p.**, They *4396*
Mk 6:4 A **p.** is not without honour, but in *4396*
Mk 6:15 others said, That it is a **p.**, or as one *4396*
Mk 11:32 John, that he was a **p.** indeed. *4396*
Mk 13:14 spoken of by Daniel the **p.**, *4396*
Lu 1:76 be called the **p.** of the Highest: *4396*
Lu 3:4 book of the words of Esaias the **p.**, *4396*
Lu 4:17 unto him the book of the **p.** Esaias. *4396*
Lu 4:24 **No p. is accepted in his own** *4396*
Lu 4:27 **Israel in the time of Eliseus the p.;** *4396*
Lu 7:16 a great **p.** is risen up among us; *4396*
Lu 7:26 **what went ye out for to see? A p.?** *4396*
Lu 7:26 **you, and much more than a p.** *4396*
Lu 7:28 **a greater p. than John the Baptist:** *4396*
Lu 7:39 This man, if he were a **p.**, would *4396*
Lu 11:29 **it, but the sign of Jonas the p.** *4396*
Lu 13:33 **that a p. perish out of Jerusalem.** *4396*
Lu 20:6 be persuaded that John was a **p.** *4396*
Lu 24:19 which was a **p.** mighty in deed and *4396*
Joh 1:21 Art thou that **p.**? And he answered, *4396*
Joh 1:23 of the Lord, as said the **p.** Esaias. *4396*
Joh 1:25 Christ, nor Elias, neither that **p.**? *4396*
Joh 4:19 Sir, I perceive that thou art a **p.** *4396*
Joh 4:44 that a **p.** hath no honour in his own *4396*
Joh 6:14 **p.** that should come into the world. *4396*
Joh 7:40 said, Of a truth this is the **P.** *4396*
Joh 7:52 look: for out of Galilee ariseth no **p.** *4396*
Joh 9:17 thine eyes? He said, He is a **p.** *4396*
Joh 12:38 of Esaias the **p.** might be fulfilled, *4396*
Ac 2:16 which was spoken by the **p.** Joel; *4396*
Ac 2:30 being a **p.**, and knowing that God *4396*
Ac 3:22 A **p.** shall the Lord your God raise *4396*
Ac 3:23 soul, which will not hear that **p.**, *4396*
Ac 7:37 A **p.** shall the Lord your God raise *4396*
Ac 7:48 made with hands; as saith the **p.**, *4396*
Ac 8:28 in his chariot road Esaias the **p.** *4396*
Ac 8:30 and heard him read the **p.** Esaias, *4396*
Ac 8:34 of whom speaketh the **p.** this? of *4396*
Ac 13:6 sorcerer, a false **p.**, a Jew, whose *5578*
Ac 13:20 fifty years, until Samuel the **p.** *4396*
Ac 21:10 Judaea a certain **p.**, named Agabus. *4396*
Ac 28:25 the Holy Ghost by Esaias the **p.** *4396*
1Co 14:37 If any man think himself to be a **p.**, *4396*
Tit 1:12 even a **p.** of their own, said, The *4396*
2Pe 2:16 voice forbad the madness of the **p.** *4396*
Re 16:13 out of the mouth of the false **p.** *5578*
Re 19:20 the false **p.** that wrought miracles *5578*
Re 20:10 where the beast and the false **p.** are, *5578*

PROPHETESS

Ex 15:20 Miriam the **p.**, the sister of Aaron, 5031
Jg 4:4 Deborah, a **p.**, the wife of Lapidoth, 5031
2Ki 22:14 went unto Huldah the **p.**, the wife 5031
2Ch 34:22 appointed, went to Huldah the **p.**, 5031
Ne 6:14 and on the **p.** Noadiah, and the rest 5031
Isa 8:3 And I went unto the **p.**; and she 5031
Lu 2:36 was one Anna, a **p.**, the daughter *4398*
Re 2:20 **Jezebel, which calleth herself a p.,** *4398*

PROPHET'S

Am 7:14 neither was I a **p.** son; but I was a 5030
Mt 10:41 **prophet shall receive a p. reward;** *4396*

PROPHETS

Nu 11:29 that all the Lord's people were **p.**, 5030
1Sa 10:5 meet a company of **p.** coming down 5030
1Sa 10:10 behold, a company of **p.** met him; 5030
1Sa 10:11 he prophesied among the **p.**, then 5030
1Sa 10:11 Kish? Is Saul also among the **p.**? 5030
1Sa 10:12 proverb, Is Saul also among the **p.**? 5030
1Sa 19:20 they saw the company of the **p.** 5030
1Sa 19:24 they say, Is Saul also among the **p.**? 5030
1Sa 28:6 by dreams, nor by Urim, nor by **p.** 5030
1Sa 28:15 more, neither by **p.**, nor by dreams: 5030
1Ki 18:4 Jezebel cut off the **p.** of the Lord, 5030
1Ki 18:4 Obadiah took an hundred **p.**, and 5030
1Ki 18:13 Jezebel slew the **p.** of the Lord, 5030
1Ki 18:13 an hundred men of the Lord's **p.** 5030
1Ki 18:19 **p.** of Baal four hundred and fifty, 5030
1Ki 18:19 the **p.** of the groves four hundred, 5030
1Ki 18:20 gathered the **p.** together unto 5030
1Ki 18:22 Baal's **p.** are four hundred and fifty 5030
1Ki 18:25 said unto the **p.** of Baal, Choose 5030
1Ki 18:40 unto them, Take the **p.** of Baal; let 5030
1Ki 19:1 how he had slain all the **p.** with the 5030
1Ki 19:10, 14 and slain thy **p.** with the sword; 5030
1Ki 20:35 man of the sons of the **p.** said unto 5030
1Ki 20:41 discerned him that he was of the **p.** 5030
1Ki 22:6 of Israel gathered the **p.** together, 5030
1Ki 22:10 all the **p.** prophesied before them. 5030
1Ki 22:12 all the **p.** prophesied so, saying, Go 5030
1Ki 22:13 the **p.** declare good unto the king 5030
1Ki 22:22 lying spirit in…mouth of all his **p.** 5030
1Ki 22:23 in the mouth of all these thy **p.**, 5030
2Ki 2:3 sons of the **p.** that were at Beth-el 5030
2Ki 2:5 sons of the **p.** that were at Jericho 5030
2Ki 2:7 fifty men of the sons of the **p.** went, 5030
2Ki 2:15 And when the sons of the **p.** which 5030
2Ki 3:13 get thee to the **p.** of thy father, 5030
2Ki 3:13 to the **p.** of thy mother. And the 5030
2Ki 4:1 of the wives of the sons of the **p.** 5030
2Ki 4:38 sons of the **p.** were sitting before 5030
2Ki 4:38 seethe pottage for the sons of the **p.** 5030
2Ki 5:22 young men of the sons of the **p.**: 5030
2Ki 6:1 the sons of the **p.** said unto Elisha, 5030
2Ki 9:1 called one of the children of the **p.**, 5030
2Ki 9:7 the blood of my servants the **p.**, 5030
2Ki 10:19 call unto me all the **p.** of Baal, all 5030
2Ki 17:13 against Judah, by all the **p.**, and 5030
2Ki 17:13 I sent to you by my servants the **p.** 5030
2Ki 17:23 had said by all his servants the **p.** 5030
2Ki 21:10 Lord spake by his servants the **p.**, 5030
2Ki 23:2 the priests, and the **p.**, and all the 5030
2Ki 24:2 he spake by his servants the **p.** 5030
1Ch 16:22 anointed, and do my **p.** no harm. 5030
2Ch 18:5 together of **p.** four hundred men, 5030
2Ch 18:9 all the **p.** prophesied before them. 5030
2Ch 18:11 all the **p.** prophesied so, saying, Go 5030
2Ch 18:12 the **p.** declare good to the king 5030
2Ch 18:21 lying spirit in…mouth of all his **p.** 5030
2Ch 18:22 spirit in the mouth of these thy **p.**, 5030
2Ch 20:20 believe his **p.**, so shall ye prosper. 5030
2Ch 24:19 Yet he sent **p.** to them, to bring 5030
2Ch 29:25 commandment of the Lord by…**p.** 5030
2Ch 36:16 his words, and misused his **p.**, 5030
Ezr 5:1 Then the **p.**, Haggai the prophet, 5029
Ezr 5:2 were the **p.** of God helping them, 5029
Ezr 9:11 commanded by thy servants the **p.**, 5030
Ne 6:7 hast also appointed **p.** to preach 5030
Ne 6:14 the rest of the **p.**, that would have 5030
Ne 9:26 slew thy **p.** which testified against 5030
Ne 9:30 against them by thy spirit in thy **p.** 5030
Ne 9:32 and on our priests, and on our **p.**, 5030
Ps 105:15 anointed, and do my **p.** no harm. 5030
Isa 29:10 the **p.** and your rulers, the seers 5030
Isa 30:10 to the **p.**, Prophesy not unto us 2374
Jer 2:8 the **p.** prophesied by Baal, and 5030
Jer 2:26 and their priests, and their **p.**, 5030
Jer 2:30 own sword hath devoured your **p.**, 5030
Jer 4:9 astonished, and the **p.** shall wonder. 5030
Jer 5:13 And the **p.** shall become wind, and 5030
Jer 5:31 The **p.** prophesy falsely, and the 5030
Jer 7:25 unto you all my servants the **p.**, 5030
Jer 8:1 the bones of the **p.**, and the bones 5030
Jer 13:13 the priests, and the **p.**, and all the 5030
Jer 14:13 the **p.** say unto them, Ye shall not 5030
Jer 14:14 The **p.** prophesy lies in my name: 5030
Jer 14:15 **p.** that prophesy in my name, and 5030
Jer 14:15 famine shall those **p.** be consumed. 5030
Jer 23:9 me is broken because of the **p.**; 5030
Jer 23:13 seen folly in the **p.** of Samaria; 5030
Jer 23:14 seen also in the **p.** of Jerusalem 5030
Jer 23:15 Lord of hosts concerning the **p.** 5030
Jer 23:15 the **p.** of Jerusalem is profaneness 5030
Jer 23:16 not unto the words of the **p.** that 5030
Jer 23:21 I have not sent these **p.**, yet they 5030
Jer 23:25 I have heard what the **p.** said, that 5030
Jer 23:26 this be in the heart of the **p.** that 5030
Jer 23:26 **p.** of the deceit of their own heart; 5030
Jer 23:30, 31 I am against the **p.**, saith the 5030
Jer 25:4 unto you all his servants the **p.**, 5030
Jer 26:5 the words of my servants the **p.**, 5030
Jer 26:7, 8 So the priests and the **p.** and all 5030
Jer 26:11 Then spake the priests and the **p.** 5030
Jer 26:16 people unto the priests and to the **p.**; 5030
Jer 27:9 hearken not ye to your **p.**, nor to 5030
Jer 27:14 not unto the words of the **p.** that 5030
Jer 27:15 and the **p.** that prophesy unto you. 5030
Jer 27:16 of your **p.** that prophesy unto you, 5030
Jer 27:18 But if they be **p.**, and if the word 5030
Jer 28:8 The **p.** that have been before me 5030
Jer 29:1 and to the priests, and to the **p.**, and 5030
Jer 29:8 Let not your **p.** and your diviners, 5030
Jer 29:15 hath raised us up **p.** in Babylon; 5030
Jer 29:19 unto them by my servants the **p.**, 5030
Jer 32:32 and their **p.**, and the men of Judah, 5030
Jer 35:15 unto you all my servants the **p.**, 5030
Jer 37:19 Where are now your **p.** which 5030
Jer 44:4 unto you all my servants the **p.**, 5030
La 2:9 her **p.** also find no vision from the 5030
La 2:14 Thy **p.** have seen vain and foolish 5030
La 4:13 For the sins of her **p.**, and the 5030
Eze 13:2 prophesy against the **p.** of Israel 5030
Eze 13:3 Woe unto the foolsih **p.** that follow 5030
Eze 13:4 **p.** are like the foxes in the deserts. 5030
Eze 13:9 be upon the **p.** that see vanity, 5030
Eze 13:16 the **p.** of Israel which prophesy 5030
Eze 22:25 conspiracy of her **p.** in the midst 5030
Eze 22:28 her **p.** have daubed them with 5030
Eze 38:17 time by my servants the **p.** of Israel, 5030
Da 9:6 hearkened unto thy servants the **p.**, 5030
Da 9:10 set before us by his servants the **p.** 5030
Ho 6:5 have I hewed them by the **p.**; 5030
Ho 12:10 I have also spoken by the **p.**, and I 5030
Ho 12:10 by the ministry of the **p.** 5030

Am 2:11 And I raised up of your sons for **p.**,..... 5030
Am 2:12 and commanded the **p.**, saying,.......... 5030
Am 3:7 his secret unto his servants the **p.**....... 5030
Mic 3:5 the **p.** that make my people err, ... 5030
Mic 3:6 the sun shall go down over the **p.**, ... 5030
Mic 3:11 the **p.** thereof divine for money:......... 5030
Zep 3:4 Her **p.** are light and treacherous 5030
Zec 1:4 whom the former **p.** have cried,.......... 5030
Zec 1:5 and the **p.**, do they live for ever?........ 5030
Zec 1:6 I commanded my servants the **p.**, ... 5030
Zec 7:3 and to the **p.**, saying, Should I weep... 5030
Zec 7:7 Lord hath cried by the former **p.**,........ 5030
Zec 7:12 sent in his spirit by the former **p.**:....... 5030
Zec 8:9 these words by the mouth of the **p.**,.... 5030
Zec 13:2 cause the **p.** and the unclean spirit...... 5030
Zec 13:4 the **p.** shall be ashamed every one...... 5030
Mt 2:23 which was spoken by the **p.**,............ *4396*
Mt 5:12 **so persecuted they the p. which**..... *4396*
Mt 5:17 **come to destroy the law, or the p.:**. *4396*
Mt 7:12 **for this is the law and the p.**. *4396*
Mt 7:15 **Beward of false p., which come to** .*5578*
Mt 11:13 **For all the p. and the law**............ *4396*
Mt 13:17 **that many p. and righteous men**.... *4396*
Mt 16:14 others, Jeremias, or one of the **p.**. *4396*
Mt 22:40 **hand all the law and the p.**........... *4396*
Mt 23:29 **ye build the tombs of the p., and**... *4396*
Mt 23:30 **with them in the blood of the p.**.... *4396*
Mt 23:31 **of them which killed the p.**.......... *4396*
Mt 23:34 **behold, I send unto you p., and**..... *4396*
Mt 23:37 **that killest the p., and stonest** *4396*
Mt 24:11 **And many false p. shall rise, and**.. *5578*
Mt 24:24 **and false p., and shall shew great** . *5578*
Mt 26:56 **of the p. might be fulfilled**........... *4396*
Mk 1:2 As it is written in the **p.**, Behold,....... *4396*
Mk 6:15 it is a prophet, or as one of the **p.**. *4396*
Mk 8:28 Elias; and others, One of the **p.**......... *4396*
Mk 13:22 **false Christs and false p. shall rise,***5578*
Lu 1:70 spake by the mouth of his holy **p.**, ... *4396*
Lu 6:23 **did their fathers unto the p.**......... *4396*
Lu 6:26 **so did their fathers to the false p.**. *5573*
Lu 9:8 one of the old **p.** was risen again........ *4396*
Lu 9:19 one of the old **p.** is risen again, ... *4396*
Lu 10:24 **many p. and kings have desired**..... *4396*
Lu 11:47 **ye build the sepulchres of the p.,**.... *4396*
Lu 11:49 **I will send them p. and apostles,**... *4396*
Lu 11:50 **That the blood of all the p., which**. *4396*
Lu 13:28 **all the p., in the kingdom of God,**. *4396*
Lu 13:34 **Jerusalem, which killeth the p.**..... *4396*
Lu 16:16 **law and the p. were until John:**..... *4396*
Lu 16:29 **him, They have Moses and the p.;**.. *4396*
Lu 16:31 **If they hear not Moses and the p.,** . *4396*
Lu 18:31 **things that are written by the p.** *4396*
Lu 24:25 **believe all that the p. have spoken;** *4396*
Lu 24:27 beginning at Moses and all the **p.**, ... *4396*
Lu 24:44 **in the law of Moses, and in the p.,**. *4396*
Joh 1:45 law, and the **p.**, did write, Jesus of..... *4396*
Joh 6:45 **It is written in the p., And they**.... *4396*
Joh 8:52 Abraham is dead, and the **p.**; and........ *4396*
Joh 8:53 and the **p.** are dead: whom makest..... *4396*
Ac 3:18 shewed by the mouth of all his **p.**,....... *4396*
Ac 3:21 by the mouth of all his holy **p.**........... *4396*
Ac 3:24 and all the **p.** from Samuel and *4396*
Ac 3:25 Ye are the children of the **p.**, and of... *4396*
Ac 7:42 it is written in the book of the **p.**, ... *4396*
Ac 7:52 Which of the **p.** have not your.......... *4396*
Ac 10:43 To him give all the **p.** witness, that.... *4396*
Ac 11:27 days came **p.** from Jerusalem unto...... *4396*
Ac 13:1 Antioch certain **p.** and teachers;......... *4396*
Ac 13:15 the reading of the law and the **p.** *4396*
Ac 13:27 nor yet the voices of the **p.** which....... *4396*
Ac 13:40 you, which is spoken of in the **p.**; *4396*
Ac 15:15 to this agree the words of the **p.**; *4396*
Ac 15:32 being **p.** also themselves, exhorted..... *4396*
Ac 24:14 written in the law and in the **p.**.......... *4396*
Ac 26:22 which the **p.** and Moses did say......... *4396*
Ac 26:27 Agrippa, believest thou the **p.**? *4396*
Ac 28:23 and out of the **p.**, from morning till..... *4396*
Ro 1:2 by his **p.** in the holy scriptures,) *4396*
Ro 3:21 witnessed by the law and the **p.**;........ *4396*
Ro 11:3 Lord, they have killed thy **p.**, and *4396*
Ro 16:26 the scriptures of the **p.**, according...... *4397*
1Co 12:28 apostles, secondarily **p.**, thirdly......... *4396*
1Co 12:29 are all **p.**? are all teachers? are all....... *4396*
1Co 14:29 Let the **p.** speak two or three, and..... *4396*
1Co 14:32 spirits of the **p.** are subject to the **p.**. . *4396*
Eph 2:20 foundation of the apostles and **p.**, ... *4396*
Eph 3:5 holy apostles and **p.** by the Spirit; *4396*
Eph 4:11 gave some, apostles; and some, **p.**..... *4396*
1Th 2:15 the Lord Jesus, and their own **p.**,........ *4396*
Heb 1:1 past unto the fathers by the **p.**, ... *4396*
Heb 11:32 also, and Samuel, and of the **p.**:......... *4396*
Jas 5:10 the **p.**, who have spoken in the.......... *4396*
1Pe 1:10 salvation the **p.** have enquired *4396*
2Pe 2:1 there were false **p.** also among........... *5578*
2Pe 3:2 were spoken before by the holy **p.**, ... *4396*
1Jo 4:1 many false **p.** are gone out into........... *5578*
Re 10:7 declared to his servants the **p.**........... *4396*
Re 11:10 these two **p.** tormented them that...... *4396*
Re 11:18 reward unto thy servants the **p.**,......... *4396*
Re 16:6 shed the blood of saints and **p.**, and.... *4396*
Re 18:20 heaven, and ye holy apostles and **p.**..... *4396*
Re 18:24 was found the blood of **p.**, and of........ *4396*
Re 22:6 Lord God of the holy **p.**, sent his....... *4396*
Re 22:9 and of thy brethren the **p.**, and.......... *4396*

PROPITIATION

Ro 3:25 a **p.** through faith in his blood,.......... *2435*
1Jo 2:2 he is the **p.** for our sins: and not *2434*
1Jo 4:10 his Son to be the **p.** for our sins. *2434*

PROPORTION

1Ki 7:36 according to the **p.** of every one, ... 4626
Job 41:12 nor his power, nor his comely **p.**.......... 6187
Ro 12:6 according to the **p.** of faith; *356*

PROSELYTE See also PROSELYTES.

Mt 23:15 **sea and land to make one p., and**.. *4339*
Ac 6:5 and Nicolas a **p.** of Antioch: *4339*

PROSELYTES

Ac 2:10 strangers of Rome, Jews and **p.**, ... *4339*
Ac 13:43 and religious **p.** followed Paul and....... *4339*

PROSPECT

Eze 40:44 and their **p.** was toward the south:..... 6440
Eze 40:44 having the **p.** toward the north. 6440
Eze 40:45 whose **p.** is toward the south, ... 6440
Eze 40:46 whose **p.** is toward the north 6440
Eze 42:15 gate whose **p.** is toward the east, ... 6440
Eze 43:4 gate whose **p.** is toward the east. 6440

PROSPER See also PROSPERED; PROSPERETH.

Ge 24:40 angel with thee,and **p.** thy way;......... 6743
Ge 24:42 if now thou do **p.** my way which I...... 6743
Ge 39:3 made all that he did to **p.** in his 6743
Ge 39:23 he did, the Lord made it to **p.**........... 6743
Nu 14:41 of the Lord? but it shall not **p.**........... 6743
De 28:29 and thou shalt not **p.** in thy ways: 6743
De 29:9 that ye may **p.** in all that ye do........... 7919
Jos 1:7 **p.** whithersoever thou goest............ 7919
1Ki 2:3 mayest **p.** in all that thou doest,.......... 7919
1Ki 22:12 Go up to Ramoth-gilead, and **p.** 6743
1Ki 22:15 Go, and **p.**, for the Lord shall............ 6743
1Ch 22:11 **p.** thou, and build the house of the..... 6743
1Ch 22:13 Then shalt thou **p.**, if thou takest 6743
2Ch 13:12 of your fathers; for ye shall not **p.**........ 6743
2Ch 18:11 Go up to Ramoth-gilead, and **p.**: 6743
2Ch 18:14 Go ye up, and **p.**, and they shall be.... 6743
2Ch 20:20 believe his prophets, so shall ye **p.**...... 6743
2Ch 24:20 that ye cannot **p.**? because ye have 6743
2Ch 26:5 the Lord, God made him to **p.**........... 6743
Ne 1:11 and **p.**, I pray thee,thy servant this 6743
Ne 2:20 The God of heaven, he will **p.** us;....... 6743
Job 12:6 The tabernacles of robbers **p.**, and...... 7951
Ps 1:3 and whatsoever he doeth shall **p.**. 6743
Ps 73:12 the ungodly, who **p.** in the world;........ 7951
Ps 122:6 they shall **p.** that love thee. 7951
Pr 28:13 covereth his sins shall not **p.**............. 6743
Ec 11:6 knowest not whether shall **p.**,............ 3787
Isa 53:10 of the Lord shall **p.** in his hand. 6743
Isa 54:17 that is formed against thee shall **p.**; 6743
Isa 55:11 **p.** in the thing whereto I sent it.......... 6743
Jer 2:37 and thou shalt not **p.** in them............. 6743
Jer 5:28 cause of the fatherless, yet they **p.**;..... 6743
Jer 10:21 therefore they shall not **p.**, and all...... 7919
Jer 12:1 doth the way of the wicked **p.**?........... 6743
Jer 20:11 for they shall not **p.**: their................. 7919
Jer 22:30 man that shall not **p.** in his days:........ 6743
Jer 22:30 for no man of his seed shall **p.**,.......... 6743
Jer 23:5 a King shall reign and **p.**, and............ 7919
Jer 32:5 the Chaldeans, ye shall not **p.**............ 6743
La 1:5 are the chief, her enemies **p.**; 7951
Eze 16:13 and thou didst **p.** into a kingdom. 6743
Eze 17:9 Shall it **p.**? shall he not pull up.......... 6743
Eze 17:10 being planted, shall it **p.**? shall it 6743
Eze 17:15 Shall he **p.**? shall he escape that......... 6743
Da 8:24 shall **p.**, and practise, and shall.......... 6743
Da 8:25 shall cause craft to **p.** in his hand: 6743
Da 11:27 it shall not **p.**: for yet the end shall...... 6743
Da 11:36 shall **p.** till the indignation be............ 6743
3Jo 2 thou mayest **p.** and be in health, ... *2137*

PROSPERED

Ge 24:56 seeing the Lord hath **p.** my way; 6743
Jg 4:24 hand of the children of Israel **p.**, ... 1980
2Sa 11:7 people did, and how the war **p.**........... 7965
2Ki 18:7 and he **p.** whithersoever he went 7919
1Ch 29:23 of David his father, and **p.**: 6743
2Ch 14:7 every side. So they built and **p.** 6743
2Ch 31:21 he did it with all his heart, and **p.**........ 6743
2Ch 32:30 And Hezekiah **p.** in all his works. 6743
Ezr 6:14 they **p.** through the prophesying......... 6744
Job 9:4 himself against him, and hath **p.**?......... 7999
Da 6:28 Daniel **p.** in the reign of Darius,......... 6744
Da 8:12 ground; and it practised, and **p.** 6743
1Co 16:2 him in store, as God hath **p.** him,....... *2137*

PROSPERETH

Ezr 5:8 fast on, and **p.** in their hands............ 6744
Ps 37:7 because of him who **p.** in his way,....... 6743
Pr 17:8 whithersoever it turneth, it **p.**. 7919
3Jo 2 be in health, even as thy soul **p.**. *2137*

PROSPERITY

De 23:6 not seek their peace nor their **p.**......... 2896
1Sa 25:6 shall ye say to him that liveth in **p.**,..........
1Ki 10:7 and **p.** exceedeth the fame which 2896
Job 15:21 in **p.** the destroyer shall come 7965
Job 36:11 they shall spend their days in **p.**,......... 2896
Ps 30:6 in my **p.** I said, I shall never be......... 7961
Ps 35:27 pleasure in the **p.** of his servant.......... 7965
Ps 73:3 when I saw the **p.** of the wicked......... 7965
Ps 118:25 Lord, I beseech thee, send now **p.**....... 6743
Ps 122:7 walls, and **p.** within thy palaces.......... 7962
Pr 1:32 the **p.** of fools shall destroy them. 7962
Ec 7:14 In the day of **p.** be joyful, but in 2896
Jer 22:21 I spake unto thee in thy **p.**; but 7962
Jer 33:9 all the **p.** that I procure unto it. 7965
La 3:17 far off from peace: I forgat **p.**............ 2896
Zec 1:17 My cities through **p.** shall yet be........ 2896
Zec 7:7 was inhabited and in **p.**, and............. 7961

PROSPEROUS

Ge 24:21 had made his journey **p.** or not 6743
Ge 39:2 Joseph, and he was a **p.** man;............ 6743
Jos 1:8 then thou shalt make thy way **p.**, ... 6743
Jg 18:5 our way which we go shall be **p.**........ 6743
Job 8:6 habitation of thy righteousness **p.**. 7999
Isa 48:15 him, and he shall make his way **p.**...... 6743
Zec 8:12 For the seed shall be **p.**; the vine 7965
Ro 1:10 I might have a **p.** journey by the........ *2137*

PROSPEROUSLY

2Ch 7:11 in his own house, he **p.** effected. 6743
Ps 45:4 majesty ride **p.** because of truth......... 6743

PROSTITUTE

Le 19:29 Do not **p.** thy daughter, to cause 2490

PROTECTION

De 32:38 up and help you, and be your **p.**. 5643

PROTEST See also PROTESTED; PROTESTING.

Ge 43:3 The man did solemnly **p.** unto us, ... 5749
1Sa 8:9 howbeit yet **p.** solemnly unto them,.... 5749
1Co 15:31 I **p.** by your rejoicing which I have..... *3513*

PROTESTED

1Ki 2:42 by the Lord,and **p.** unto thee, ... 5749
Jer 11:7 I earnestly **p.** unto your fathers in...... 5749
Zec 3:6 angel of the Lord **p.** unto Joshua, ... 5749

PROTESTING

Jer 11:7 rising early and **p.**, saying, Obey 5749

PROUD

Job 9:13 the **p.** helpers do stoop under him...... 7293
Job 26:12 he smiteth through the **p.**................ 7293
Job 38:11 here shall thy **p.** waves be stayed?..... 1347
Job 40:11 and behold every one that is **p.**,.......... 1343
Job 40:12 Look on every one that is **p.**, and 1343
Ps 12:3 tongue that speaketh **p.** things:.......... 1419
Ps 31:23 plentifully rewarded the **p.** doer. 1346
Ps 40:4 respecteth not the **p.**, nor such as....... 7295
Ps 86:14 the **p.** are risen against me, and......... 2086
Ps 94:2 earth: render a reward to the **p.**........ 1343
Ps 101:5 look and a **p.** heart will not I suffer..... 7342
Ps 119:21 rebuked the **p.** that are cursed, ... 2086
Ps 119:51 **p.** have had me greatly in derision:..... 2086

Ps 119:69 **p.** have forged a lie against me: but..... 2086
Ps 119:78 Let the **p.** be ashamed; for they 2086
Ps 119:85 The **p.** have digged pits for me,......... 2086
Ps 119:122 good: let not the **p.** oppress me......... 2086
Ps 123:4 and with the contempt of the **p.**......... 1349
Ps 124:5 **p.** waters had gone over our soul....... 2121
Ps 138:6 but the **p.** he knoweth afar off.......... 1364
Ps 140:5 **p.** have hid a snare for me, and......... 1343
Pr 6:17 A **p.** look, a lying tongue, and............ 7311
Pr 15:25 will destroy the house of the **p.**: 1343
Pr 16:5 Every one that is **p.** in heart is an...... 1362
Pr 16:19 to divide the spoil with the **p.**............ 1343
Pr 21:4 high look, and a **p.** heart, and the...... 7342
Pr 21:24 **P.** and haughty scorner is his............ 2086
Pr 21:24 name, who dealeth in **p.** wrath............ 2087
Pr 28:25 He that is of a **p.** heart stirreth up..... 7342
Ec 7:8 is better than the **p.** in spirit............ 1362
Isa 2:12 upon every one that is **p.** and lofty, ... 1343
Isa 13:11 the arrogancy of the **p.** to cease, ... 2086
Isa 16:6 the ride of Moab; he is very **p.**:......... 1341
Jer 13:15 hear me, and give ear; be not **p.**:....... 1341
Jer 43:2 and all the **p.** men, saying unto.......... 2086
Jer 48:29 of Moab, (he is exceeding **p.**)............ 1343
Jer 50:29 hath been **p.** against the Lord,........... 2102
Jer 50:31 am against thee, O thou most **p.**,......... 2087
Jer 50:32 the most **p.** shall stumble and fall, ... 2087
Hab 2:5 he is a **p.** man, neither keepeth......... 3093
Mal 3:15 now we call the **p.** happy; yea, ... 2086
Mal 4:1 all the **p.**, yea, and all that do............ 2086
Lu 1:51 the **p.** in the imagination of their *5244*
Ro 1:30 of God, despiteful, **p.**, boasters,......... *5244*
1Ti 6:4 He is **p.**, knowing nothing, but............ *5187*
2Ti 3:2 **p.**, blasphemers, disobedient to............ *5244*
Jas 4:6 God resisteth the **p.**, but giveth......... *5244*
1Pe 5:5 God resisteth the **p.**, and giveth......... *5244*

PROUDLY
Ex 18:11 the thing wherein they dealt **p.**........... 2102
1Sa 2:3 Talk no more so exceeding **p.**;let........ 1364
Ne 9:10 that they dealt **p.** against them. 2102
Ne 9:16 But they and our fathers dealt **p.**, ... 2102
Ne 9:29 yet they dealt **p.**, and hearkened........ 2102
Ps 17:10 with their mouth they speak **p.**........... 1348
Ps 31:18 which speak grievous things **p.** 1346
Isa 3:5 the child shall behave himself **p.**.......... 7292
Ob 12 spoken **p.** in the day of distress. 1431

PROVE See also PROVED; PROVETH; PROVING; APPROVE; REPROVE.
Ex 16:4 that I may **p.** them, whether they 5254
Ex 20:20 Fear not: for God is come to **p.** you, .. 5254
De 8:2 to humble thee, and to **p.** thee, to...... 5254
De 8:16 thee, and that he might **p.** thee, ... 5254
De 33:8 whom thou didst **p.** at Massah, ... 5254
Jg 2:22 through them I may **p.** Israel,............ 5254
Jg 3:1 to **p.** Israel by them, even as many 5254
Jg 3:4 they were to **p.** Israel by them, to 5254
Jg 6:39 let me **p.**, I pray thee, but this once.... 5254
1Ki 10:1 came to **p.** him with hard questions. ... 5254
2Ch 9:1 to **p.** Solomon with hard questions 5254
Job 9:20 perfect, it shall also **p.** me perverse.........
Ps 26:2 Examine me, O Lord, and **p.** me;....... 5254
Ec 2:1 Go to now, I will **p.** thee with mirth, .. 5254
Da 1:12 **P.** thy servants, I beseech thee, ten.... 5254
Mal 3:10 **p.** me now herewith, saith the Lord 974
Lu 14:19 **yoke of oxen, and I go to p. them:** *1381*
Joh 6:6 And this he said to **p.** him: for he *3985*
Ac 24:13 Neither can they **p.** the things *3936*
Ac 25:7 Paul, which they could not **p.**............. *584*
Ro 12:2 that ye may **p.** what is that good,....... *1381*
2Co 8:8 and to **p.** the sincerity of your love....... *1381*
2Co 13:5 be in the faith; **p.** your own selves. *1381*
Ga 6:4 But let every man **p.** his own work, ... *1381*
1Th 5:21 **P.** all things; hold fast that which....... *1381*

PROVED See also APPROVED; REPROVED.
Ge 42:15 Hereby ye shall be **p.**: By the life....... 974
Ge 42:16 prison, that your words may be **p.**, ... 974
Ex 15:25 ordinance, and there he **p.** them, ... 5254
1Sa 17:39 assayed to go; for he had not **p.** it. 5254
1Sa 17:39 with these; for I have not **p.** them...... 5254
Ps 17:3 Thou hast **p.** mine heart; thou hast 974
Ps 66:10 thou, O God, hast **p.** us: thou hast 974
Ps 81:7 I **p.** thee at the waters of Meribah....... 974
Ps 95:9 me, **p.** me, and saw my work. 974
Ec 7:23 All this have I **p.** by wisdom: I 5254
Da 1:14 this matter, and **p.** them ten days. 5254
Ro 3:9 we have before **p.** both Jews and *4256*
2Co 8:22 **p.** diligent in many things, but *1381*
1Ti 3:10 let these also first be **p.**; then let....... *1381*
Heb 3:9 your fathers tempted me, **p.** me, ... *1381*

PROVENDER
Ge 24:25 have both straw and **p.** enough, ... 4554
Ge 24:32 gave straw and **p.** for the camels, ... 4554
Ge 42:27 opened his sack to give his ass **p.** in.... 4554
Ge 43:24 feet; and he gave their asses **p.**......... 4554
Jg 19:19 is both straw and **p.** for our asses; 4554
Jg 19:21 house, and gave **p.** unto the asses:..... 1101
Isa 30:24 ear the ground shall eat clean **p.**, ... 1098

PROVERB See also PROVERBS.
De 28:37 become an astonishment, a **p.**,........... 4912
1Sa 10:12 Therefore it became a **p.**, Is Saul....... 4912
1Sa 24:13 As saith the **p.** of the ancients, ... 4912
1Ki 9:7 Israel shall be a **p.** and a byword......... 4912
2Ch 7:20 to be a **p.** and a byword among all...... 4912
Ps 69:11 and I became a **p.** to them................ 4912
Pr 1:6 To understand a **p.**, and the............... 4912
Isa 14:4 take up this **p.** against the king of 4912
Jer 24:9 to be a reproach and a **p.**, a taunt 4912
Eze 12:22 that **p.** that ye have in the land of 4912
Eze 12:23 I will make this **p.** to cease, and they.. 4912
Eze 12:23 no more use it as a **p.** in Israel;......... 4911
Eze 14:8 and will make him a sign and a **p.**,...... 4912
Eze 16:44 shall use this **p.** against thee, ... 4911
Eze 18:2 ye use this **p.** concerning the land 4911
Eze 18:3 any more to use this **p.** in Israel. 4911
Hab 2:6 and a taunting **p.** against him, ... 2420
Lu 4:23 **Ye will surely say unto me this p.,** *3850*
Joh 16:29 thou plainly, and speakest no **p.** *3942*
2Pe 2:22 unto them according to the true **p.**, ... *3942*

PROVERBS
Nu 21:27 Wherefore they that speak in **p.**......... 4911
1Ki 4:32 And he spake three thousand **p.**:........ 4912
Pr *general title* The **P.**.................................. 4912
Pr 1:1 The **p.** of Solomon the son of David,... 4912
Pr 10:1 The **p.** of Solomon. A wise son.......... 4912
Pr 25:1 These are also **p.** of Solomon, which... 4912
Ec 12:9 out, and set in order many **p.**............ 4912
Eze 16:44 every one that useth **p.** shall use 4911
Joh 16:25 **have I spoken unto you in p.:** *3942*
Joh 16:25 **no more speak unto you in p.,** *3942*

PROVETH See also APPROVETH; REPROVETH.
De 13:3 for the Lord your God **p.** you, to 5254

PROVIDE See also PROVIDED; PROVIDETH; PROVIDING.
Ge 22:8 God will **p.** himself a lamb for a 7200
Ge 30:60 shall I **p.** for mine own house also?...... 6213
Ex 18:21 **p.** out of all the people able men, ... 2372
1Sa 16:17 **P.** me now a man that can play 7200
2Ch 2:7 whom David my father did **p.**. 3559
Ps 78:20 can he **p.** flesh for his people? 3559
Mt 10:9 **P. neither gold, nor silver, nor......** *2532*
Lu 12:33 **p. yourselves bags which wax not..** *4160*
Ac 23:24 And **p.** them beasts, that they may..... *3936*
Ro 12:17 **P.** things honest in the sight of.......... *4306*
1Ti 5:8 But if any **p.** not for his own, and *4306*

PROVIDED
De 33:21 And he **p.** the first part for himself, ... 7200
1Sa 16:1 have **p.** me a king among his sons. 7200
2Sa 19:32 he had **p.** the king of sustenance.............
1Ki 4:7 which **p.** victuals for the king and his ....
1Ki 4:27 **p.** victual for king Solomon, and...............
2Ch 32:29 he **p.** him cities, and possessions......... 6213
Ps 65:9 corn, when thou hast so **p.** for it........ 3559
Lu 12:20 **things be, which thou hast p.?**....... *2090*
Heb 11:40 God having **p.** some better thing......... *4265*

PROVIDENCE
Ac 24:2 done unto this nation by thy **p.**, ... *4307*

PROVIDETH
Job 38:41 Who **p.** for the raven his food? 3559
Pr 6:8 **P.** her meat in the summer, and......... 3559

PROVIDING
2Co 8:21 **P.** for honest things, not only in *4306*

PROVINCE See also PROVINCES.
Ezr 2:1 the children of the **p.** that went up 4082
Ezr 5:8 that we went into the **p.** of Judea, ... 4083
Ezr 6:2 that is in the **p.** of the Medes,........... 4082
Ezr 7:16 canst find in all the **p.** of Babylon, ... 4082
Ne 1:3 The remnant that are left...in the **p.** ... 4082
Ne 7:6 These are the children of the **p.**,......... 4082
Ne 11:3 are the chief of the **p.** that dwelt in 4082
Es 1:22 into every **p.** according to the............ 4082
Es 3:12 governors that were over every **p.**, ... 4082
Es 3:12 rulers of every people of every **p.** 4082
Es 3:14 commandment...given in every **p.**........ 4082
Es 4:3 And in every **p.**, withersoever the......... 4082
Es 8:9 unto every **p.** according to the............ 4082
Es 8:11 the power of the people and **p.** that.... 4082
Es 8:13 commandment...given in every **p.**........ 4082
Es 8:17 And in every **p.**, and in every city, ... 4082
Es 9:28 family, every **p.**, and every city; 4082
Ec 5:8 of judgment and justice in a **p.**, ... 4082
Da 2:48 ruler over the whole **p.** of Babylon, ... 4083
Da 2:49 over the affairs of the **p.** of Babylon:... 4083
Da 3:1 plain of Dura, in the **p.** of Babylon...... 4083
Da 3:12 over the affairs of the **p.** of Babylon,... 4083
Da 3:30 Abed-nego, in the **p.** of Babylon......... 4082
Da 8:2 the palace, which is the **p.** of Elam; 4082
Da 11:24 upon the fattest places of the **p.**;......... 4082
Ac 23:34 letter, he asked of what **p.** he was. *1885*
Ac 25:1 when Festus was come into the **p.**, ... *1885*

PROVINCES
1Ki 20:14 young men of the princes of the **p.**.... 4082
1Ki 20:15 young men of the princes of the **p.**, ... 4082
1Ki 20:17 princes of the **p.** went out first; 4082
1Ki 20:19 of the princes of the **p.** came out 4082
Ezr 4:15 and hurtful unto kings and **p.**, ... 4083
Es 1:1 hundred and seven and twenty **p.**;)...... 4082
Es 1:3 the nobles and princes of the **p.**, ... 4082
Es 1:16 in all the **p.** of the king Ahasuerus...... 4082
Es 1:22 he sent letters into all the king's **p.**, ... 4082
Es 2:3 in all the **p.** of his kingdom, that 4082
Es 2:18 and he made a release to the **p.**, and.. 4082
Es 3:8 people in all the **p.** of thy kingdom;...... 4082
Es 3:13 sent by posts into all the king's **p.**, ... 4082
Es 4:11 the people of the king's **p.**, do know, .. 4082
Es 8:5 Jews which are in all the king's **p.**: 4082
Es 8:9 and rulers of the **p.** which are from 4082
Es 8:9 hundred twenty and seven **p.**, unto...... 4082
Es 8:12 day in all the **p.** of king Ahasuerus,..... 4082
Es 9:2 all the **p.** of the king Ahasuerus, ... 4082
Es 9:3 And all the rulers of the **p.**, and the.... 4082
Es 9:4 went out throughout all the **p.**: 4082
Es 9:12 done in the rest of the king's **p.**? 4082
Es 9:16 Jews that were in the king's **p.**........... 4082
Es 9:20 in all the **p.** of the king Ahasuerus,..... 4082
Es 9:30 and seven **p.** of the kingdom of............ 4082
Ec 2:8 treasure of kings and of the **p.**:............ 4082
La 1:1 nations, and princess among the **p.**, ... 4082
Eze 19:8 him on every side from the **p.**, ... 4082
Da 3:2 the rulers of the **p.**, to come to the.... 4082
Da 3:3 and all the rulers of the **p.**, were 4082

PROVING See also APPROVING.
Ac 9:22 **p.** that this is very Christ. *4822*
Eph 5:10 **P.** what is acceptable unto...Lord....... *1381*

PROVISION
Ge 42:25 and to give them **p.** for the way:.......... 6720
Ge 45:21 and gave them **p.** for the way........... 6720
Jos 9:5 of their **p.** was dry and mouldy. 6718
Jos 9:12 our bread we took hot for our **p.** 6679
1Ki 4:7 man his month in a year made **p.**. 3557
1Ki 4:22 Solomon's **p.** for one day was.......... 3899
2Ki 6:23 he prepared great **p.** for them: 3740
1Ch 29:19 for the which I have made **p.**............ 3559
Ps 132:15 I will abundantly bless her **p.**: I........ 6718
Da 1:5 them a daily **p.** of the king's meat, ... 1697
Ro 13:14 and make not **p.** for the flesh, to......... *4307*

PROVOCATION See also PROVOCATIONS.
1KI 15:30 Israel sin, by his **p.** wherewith he 3708
1KI 21:22 for the **p.** wherewith thou hast 3708
Job 17:2 not mine eye continue in their **p.**? 4784
Ps 95:8 not your heart, as in the **p.**, and........ 4808
Eze 20:28 presented the **p.** of their offering:........ 3708
Heb 3:8 not your hearts, as in the **p.**, in........ *3894*
Heb 3:15 harden not your hearts, as in the **p.**,... *3894*

PROVOCATIONS
2Ki 23:26 of all the **p.** that Manasseh had.......... 3708
Ne 9:18 Egypt, and had wrought great **p.**;....... 5007
Ne 9:26 to thee, and they wrought great **p.**.... 5007
Jer 32:31 For this city hath been to me as a **p.**... 5921

PROVOKE See also PROVOKED; PROVOKETH; PROVOKING.
Ex 23:21 and obey his voice, **p.** him not;.......... 4843
Nu 14:11 How long will this people **p.** me?........ 5006
De 4:25 Lord thy God, to **p.** him to anger:............

De 9:18 of the Lord, to **p.** him to anger
De 31:20 gods, and serve them, and **p.** me, 5006
De 31:29 to **p.** him to anger through the
De 32:21 I will **p.** them to anger with a
1Ki 14:9 molten images, to **p.** me to anger,
1Ki 16:2 to **p.** me to anger with their sins;
1Ki 16:26 sin, to **p.** the Lord God of Israel to anger
1Ki 16:33 to **p.** the Lord God of Israel to anger
2Ki 17:11 things to **p.** the Lord to anger:
2Ki 17:17 of the Lord, to **p.** him to anger.
2Ki 21:6 of the Lord, to **p.** him to anger.
2Ki 22:17 they might **p.** me to anger with all
2Ki 23:19 had made to **p.** the Lord to anger,
2Ch 33:6 of the Lord, to **p.** him to anger.
2Ch 34:25 that they might **p.** me to anger
Job 12:6 and they that **p.** God are secure; 7264
Ps 78:40 did they **p.** him in the wilderness, 4784
Isa 3:8 Lord, to **p.** the eyes of his glory. 4784
Jer 7:18 that they may **p.** me to anger.
Jer 7:19 Do they **p.** me to anger? saith the
Jer 7:19 not **p.** themselves to the confusion of
Jer 11:17 **p.** me to anger in offering incense
Jer 25:6 **p.** me not to anger with the works
Jer 25:7 ye might **p.** me to anger with the
Jer 32:29 unto other gods, to **p.** me to anger.
Jer 32:32 they have done to **p.** me to anger.
Jer 44:3 have committed to **p.** me to anger,
Jer 44:8 **p.** me unto wrath with the works
Eze 8:17 have returned to **p.** me to anger:
Eze 16:26 thy whoredoms, to **p.** me to anger.
Lu 11:53 to **p.** him to speak of many things: *653*
Ro 10:19 saith, I will **p.** you to jealousy by *3863*
Ro 11:11 Gentiles, for to **p.** them to jealousy. *3863*
Ro 11:14 any means I may **p.** to emulation. *3863*
1Co 10:22 Do we **p.** the Lord to jealousy? are *3863*
Eph 6:4 **p.** not your children to wrath: *3949*
Col 3:21 **p.** not your children to anger, *2042*
Heb 3:16 when they had heard, did **p.**: *3893*
Heb 10:24 to **p.** unto love and to good works: *3948*

PROVOKED See also PROVOKEDST; PROVOKETH.
Nu 14:23 any of them that **p.** me see it: 5006
Nu 16:30 that these men have **p.** the Lord. 5006
De 9:8 in Horeb ye **p.** the Lord to wrath,
De 9:22 ye **p.** the Lord to wrath.
De 32:16 **p.** him to jealousy with strange 3707
De 32:16 abominations **p.** they him to anger.
De 32:21 **p.** me to anger with their vanities:
Jg 2:12 them, and **p.** the Lord to anger.
1Sa 1:6 And her adversary also **p.** her sore, 3707
1Sa 1:7 so she **p.** her; therefore she wept; 3707
1Ki 14:22 they **p.** him to jealousy with their sins
1Ki 15:30 **p.** the Lord God of Israel to anger.
1Ki 21:22 thou hast **p.** me to anger,
1Ki 22:53 **p.** to anger the Lord God of Israel,
2Ki 21:15 have **p.** me to anger, since the day
2Ki 23:26 that Manasseh had **p.** him withal. 3707
1Ch 21:1 and **p.** David to number Israel. 5496
2Ch 28:25 and **p.** to anger the Lord God of his
Ezr 5:12 **p.** the God of heaven unto wrath, 7265
Ne 4:5 have **p.** thee to anger before the
Ps 78:56 tempted and **p.** the most high 4784
Ps 78:58 **p.** him to anger with their high
Ps 106:7 but **p.** him at the sea, even at the 4784
Ps 106:29 they **p.** him to anger with their
Ps 106:33 Because they **p.** his spirit, so that 4784
Ps 106:43 but they **p.** him with their counsel, 4784
Isa 1:4 have **p.** the Holy One of Israel 5006
Jer 8:19 **p.** me to anger with their graven
Jer 32:30 Israel have only **p.** me to anger
Ho 12:14 Ephraim **p.** him to anger most
Zec 8:14 when your fathers **p.** me to wrath,
1Co 13:5 is not easily **p.**, thinketh no evil; *3947*
2Co 9:2 and your zeal hath **p.** very many. *2042*

PROVOKEDST
De 9:7 thou **p.** the Lord thy God to wrath

PROVOKETH
Pr 20:2 whoso **p.** him to anger sinneth 5674
Isa 65:3 A people that **p.** me to anger
Eze 8:3 of jealousy, which **p.** to jealousy.

PROVOKING
De 32:19 because of the **p.** of his sons, and 3707
1Ki 14:15 their groves, **p.** the Lord anger.
1Ki 16:7 in **p.** him to anger with the work of
1Ki 16:13 **p.** the Lord God of Israel to anger.
Ps 78:17 by **p.** themost High in the 4784
Ga 5:26 **p.** one another, envying one *4292*

PRUDENCE
2Ch 2:12 a wise son, endued with **p.** and 7922
Pr 8:12 I wisdom dwell with **p.**, and find 6195
Eph 1:8 toward us in all wisdom and **p.**; *5428*

PRUDENT
1Sa 16:18 a man of war, and **p.** in matters, 995
Pr 12:16 but a **p.** man covereth shame. 6175
Pr 12:23 A **p.** man concealeth knowledge: 6175
Pr 13:16 **p.** man dealeth with knowledge: 6175
Pr 14:8 wisdom of the **p.** is to understand 6175
Pr 14:15 but the **p.** man looketh well to his 6175
Pr 14:18 the **p.** are crowned with knowledge. 6175
Pr 15:5 he that regardeth reproof is **p.** 6191
Pr 16:21 wise in heart shall be called **p.**: 995
Pr 18:15 heart of the **p.** getteth knowledge; 995
Pr 19:14 and a **p.** wife is from the Lord. 7919
Pr 22:3 A **p.** man foreseeth the evil, and 6175
Pr 27:12 A **p.** man foreseeth the evil, and 6175
Isa 3:2 and the **p.**, and the ancient, 7080
Isa 5:21 eyes, and **p.** in their own sight! 995
Isa 10:13 for I am **p.**: and I have removed 995
Isa 29:14 the understanding of their **p.** men 995
Jer 49:7 is counsel perished from the **p.**? is 995
Ho 14:9 **p.**, and he shall know them? for the 995
Am 5:13 **p.** shall keepsilence in that time; 7919
Mt 11:25 **these things from the wise and p.**, *4908*
Lu 10:21 **these things from the wise and p.**, *4908*
Ac 13:7 country, Sergius Paulus, a **p.** man; *4908*
1Co 1:19 the understanding of the **p.**. *4908*

PRUDENTLY
Isa 52:13 my servant shall deal **p.**, he shall 7919

PRUNE See also PRUNED; PRUNING.
Le 25:3 years thou shalt **p.** thy vineyard, 2168
Le 25:4 sow thy field, nor **p.** thy vineyard. 2168

PRUNED
Isa 5:6 it shall not be **p.**, nor digged; 2167

PRUNING See also PRUNINGHOOKS.
Isa 18:5 cut off the sprigs with **p.** hooks, 4211

PRUNINGHOOKS See also PRUNING and HOOKS.
Isa 2:4 and their spears into **p.**: 4211
Joe 3:10 swords, and your **p.** into spears: 4211
Mic 4:3 and their spears into **p.**: 4211

PSALM See also PSALMS.
1Ch 16:7 David delivered first this **p.** to thank
Ps 3:*title* A **P.** of David, when he fled from 4210
Ps 4:*title* on Neginoth, A **P.** of David. 4210
Ps 5:*title* upon Nehiloth, A **P.** of David. 4210
Ps 6:*title* upon Sheminith, A **P.** of David. 4210
Ps 8:*title* upon Gittith, A **P.** of David. 4210
Ps 9:*title* upon Muth-labben, A **P.** of David. 4210
Ps 11:*title* chief Musician, A **P.** of David.
Ps 12:*title* upon Sheminith, A **P.** of David. 4210
Ps 13:*title* chief Musician, A **P.** of David. 4210
Ps 14:*title* chief Musician, A **P.** of David.
Ps 15:*title* A **P.** of David. 4210
Ps 18:*title* A **P.** of David, the servant of the 4210
Ps 19:*title* chief Musician, A **P.** of David. 4210
Ps 20:*title* chief Musician, A **P.** of David. 4210
Ps 21:*title* chief Musician, A **P.** of David. 4210
Ps 22:*title* Aijeleth Shahar, A **P.** of David. 4210
Ps 23:*title* A **P.** of David. 4210
Ps 24:*title* A **P.** of David. 4210
Ps 25:*title* A **P.** of David.
Ps 26:*title* A **P.** of David.
Ps 27:*title* A **P.** of David.
Ps 28:*title* A **P.** of David.
Ps 29:*title* A **P.** of David. 4210
Ps 30:*title* A **P.** and Song at the dedication 4210
Ps 31:*title* the chief Musician, A **P.** of David. 4210
Ps 32:*title* A **P.** of David, Maschil,
Ps 34:*title* A **P.** of David, when he changed
Ps 35:*title* A **P.** of David.
Ps 36:*title* A **P.** of David the servant of the
Ps 37:*title* A **P.** of David.
Ps 38:*title* A **P.** of David, to bring to 4210
Ps 39:*title* even to Jeduthun, A **P.** of David. 4210
Ps 40:*title* chief Musician, A **P.** of David. 4210
Ps 41:*title* chief Musician, A **P.** of David. 4210
Ps 47:*title* A **P.** for the sons of Korah. 4210
Ps 48:*title* and **P.** for the sons of Korah. 4210
Ps 49:*title* A **P.** for the sons of Korah. 4210
Ps 50:*title* A **P.** of Asaph. 4210
Ps 51:*title* A **P.** of David, when Nathan the 4210
Ps 52:*title* A **P.** of David, when Doeg the
Ps 53:*title* Mahalath, Maschil, A **P.** of David.
Ps 54:*title* A **P.** of David, when the Ziphims
Ps 55:*title* Maschil, A **P.** of David.
Ps 61:*title* upon Neginah, A **P.** of David.
Ps 62:*title* to Jeduthun, A **P.** of David. 4210
Ps 63:*title* A **P.** of David, when he was in 4210
Ps 64:*title* chief Musician, A **P.** of David. 4210
Ps 65:*title* A **P.** and Song of David. 4210
Ps 66:*title* the chief Musician, A Song or **P.**. 4210
Ps 67:*title* on Neginoth, A **P.** or Song. 4210
Ps 68:*title* Musician, A **P.** or Song of David. 4210
Ps 69:*title* Shoshannim, A **P.** of David.
Ps 70:*title* A **P.** of David, to bring to
Ps 72:*title* A **P.** for Solomon. 4210
Ps 73:*title* A **P.** of Asaph. 4210
Ps 75:*title* A **P.** or Song of Asaph. 4210
Ps 76:*title* Neginoth, A **P.** or Song of Asaph. 4210
Ps 77:*title* to Jeduthun, A **P.** of Asaph. 4210
Ps 79:*title* A **P.** of Asaph. 4210
Ps 80:*title* A **P.** of Asaph. 4210
Ps 81:*title* upon Gittith, A **P.** of Asaph.
Ps 81:2 Take a **P.**, and bring hither the 2172
Ps 82:*title* A **P.** of Asaph. 4210
Ps 83:*title* A Song or **P.** of Asaph. 4210
Ps 84:*title* A **P.** for the sons of Korah. 4210
Ps 85:*title* A **P.** for the sons of Korah. 4210
Ps 87:*title* A **P.** or Song for the sons of 4210
Ps 88:*title* A Song or **P.** for the sons of 4210
Ps 92:*title* A **P.** or Song for the sabbath day. 4210
Ps 98:*title* A **P.**. 4210
Ps 98:5 the harp, and the voice of a **p.**. 2172
Ps 100:*title* A **P.** of praise. 4210
Ps 101:*title* A **P.** of David. 4210
Ps 103:*title* A **P.** of David.
Ps 108:*title* A Song or **P.** of David. 4210
Ps 109:*title* chief Musician, A **P.** of David. 4210
Ps 110:*title* A **P.** of David. 4210
Ps 138:*title* A **P.** of David.
Ps 139:*title* chief Musician, A **P.** of David. 4210
Ps 140:*title* chief Musician, A **P.** of David. 4210
Ps 141:*title* A **P.** of David. 4210
Ps 143:*title* A **P.** of David. 4210
Ps 144:*title* A **P.** of David.
Ps 145:*title* David's **P.** of praise.
Ac 13:33 it is also written in the second **p.**, *5568*
Ac 13:35 Wherefore he saith also in another **p.**,
1Co 14:26 every one of you hath a **p.**, hath a *5568*

PSALMIST
2Sa 23:1 Jacob, and the sweet **p.** of Israel, 2158

PSALMS
1Ch 16:9 Sing unto him, sing **p.** unto him, 2167
Ps *general title* The Book Of **P.** 8416
Ps 95:2 a joyful noise unto him with **p.**. 2158
Ps 105:2 Sing unto him, sing **p.** unto him: 2167
Lu 20:42 **himself saith in the book of P.** *5568*
Lu 24:44 **and in the p., concerning me.** *5568*
Ac 1:20 it is written in the book of **P.**, Let *5568*
Eph 5:19 Speaking to yourselves in **p.** and *5568*
Col 3:16 admonishing one another in **p.** and *5568*
Jas 5:13 Is any merry? let him sing **p.**. *5567*

PSALTERIES
2Sa 6:5 even on harps, and on **p.**, and on 5035
1Ki 10:12 harps also and **p.** for singers: there 5035
1Ch 13:8 and with harps, and with **p.**, and 5035
1Ch 15:16 musick, **p.** and harp and cymbals, 5035
1Ch 15:20 and Benaiah, with **p.** on Alamoth; 5035
1Ch 15:28 making a noise with **p.** and harps. 5035
1Ch 16:5 and Jeiel with **p.** and with harps; 3627
1Ch 25:1 prophesy with harps, with **p.**, 5035
1Ch 25:6 with cymbals, **p.**, and harps, for 5035
2Ch 5:12 having cymbals and **p.** and harps, 5035
2Ch 9:11 and harps and **p.** for singers: and 5035
2Ch 20:28 they came to Jerusalem with **p.** and 5035
2Ch 29:25 with **p.**, and with harps, according 5035
Ne 12:27 with cymbals, **p.**, and with harps. 5035

PSALTERY See also PSALTERIES.
1Sa 10:5 from the high place with a **p.**, 5035
Ps 33:2 sing unto him with the **p.** and an 5035
Ps 57:8 awake, **p.** and harp: I myself will 5035
Ps 71:22 also praise thee with the **p.**, even 3627
Ps 81:2 the pleasant harp with the **p.** 5035

Ps 92:3 of ten strings, and upon the **p.**; 5035
Ps 108:2 Awake, **p.** and harp: I myself will........ 5035
Ps 144:9 upon a **p.** and an instrument of ten..... 5035
Ps 150:3 praise him with the **p.** and harp. 5035
Da 3:5 **p.**, dulcimer, and all kinds of............ 6460
Da 3:7 **p.**, and all kinds of musick, ... 6460
Da 3:10, 15 **p.**, and dulcimer, and all kinds....... 6460

PTOLEMAIS (tol-e-ma'-is) See also ACCHO.
Ac 21:7 from Tyre, we came to **P.**, and........ *4424*

PUA (pu'ah) See also PUAH.
Nu 26:23 of **P.**, the family of the Punites:......... 6312

PUAH (pu'-ah) See also PHUVAH; PUA; PUNITES.
Ex 1:15 and the name of the other **P.**: 6326
Jg 10:1 Tola the son of **P.**, the son of.......... 6312
1Ch 7:1 sons of Issachar were, Tola, and **P.**.... 6312

PUBLIC See PUBLICK.

PUBLICAN See also PUBLICANS.
Mt 10:3 Thomas, and Matthew the **p.**; *5057*
Mt 18:17 **thee as an heathen man and a p.**...... *5057*
Lu 5:27 and saw a **p.**, named Levi, sitting....... *5057*
Lu 18:10 **one a Pharisee, and the other a p.**.. *5057*
Lu 18:11 **adulterers, or even as this p.**......... *5057*
Lu 18:13 **And the p., standing afar off,**........ *5057*

PUBLICANS
Mt 5:46 **ye? do not even the p. the same?**... *5057*
Mt 5:47 **others? do not even the p. so?**....... *5057*
Mt 9:10 many **p.** and sinners came and sat...... *5057*
Mt 9:11 Why eateth your Master with **p.** and... *5057*
Mt 11:19 **a friend of p. and sinners.** *5057*
Mt 21:31 **That the p. and the harlots go into.** *5057*
Mt 21:32 **p. and the harlots believed him:**..... *5057*
Mk 2:15 house, many **p.** and sinners sat also.... *5057*
Mk 2:16 saw him eat with **p.** and sinners,........ *5057*
Mk 2:16 and drinketh with **p.** and sinners?....... *5057*
Lu 3:12 Then came also **p.** to be baptized,...... *5057*
Lu 5:29 there was a great company of **p.**......... *5057*
Lu 5:30 eat and drink with **p.** and sinners?...... *5057*
Lu 7:29 the **p.**, justified God, being baptized.... *5057*
Lu 7:34 **a friend of p. and sinners!** *5057*
Lu 15:1 Then drew near unto him all the **p.** *5057*
Lu 19:2 which was the chief among the **p.**,...... *754*

PUBLICK
Mt 1:19 willing to make her a **p.** example,....... *3856*

PUBLICKLY
Ac 18:28 convinced the Jews, and that **p.**,........ *1219*
Ac 20:20 shewed you, and have taught you **p.**,.. *1219*

PUBLISH See also PUBLISHED; PUBLISHETH.
De 32:3 I will **p.** the name of the Lord: 7121
1Sa 31:9 to **p.** it in the house of their idols,...... 1319
2Sa 1:20 **p.** it not in the streets of Askelon; 1319
Ne 8:15 **p.** and proclaim in all their cities,........ 8085
Ps 26:7 That I may **p.** with the voice of........... 8085
Jer 4:5 and **p.** in Jerusalem; and say, Blow...... 8085
Jer 4:16 behold, **p.** against Jerusalem, that....... 8085
Jer 5:20 house of Jacob, and **p.** it in Judah, ... 8085
Jer 31:7 **p.** ye, praise ye, and say, O Lord, ... 8085
Jer 46:14 Declare ye in Egypt,...**p.** in Migdol,.... 8085
Jer 46:14 and **p.** in Noph and in Tahpanhes: 8085
Jer 50:2 ye among the nations, and **p.**, ... 8085
Jer 50:2 up a standard; **p.**, and conceal not: 8085
Am 3:9 **P.** in the palaces at Ashdod, and in...... 8085
Am 4:5 proclaim and **p.** the free offerings: 8085
Mk 1:45 went out, and began to **p.** it much,..... *2784*
Mk 5:20 began to **p.** in Decapolis how great..... *2784*

PUBLISHED
Es 1:20 be **p.** throughout all his empire, ... 8085
Es 1:22 that it should be **p.** according to......... 1696
Es 3:14 province was **p.** unto all people,......... 1540
Es 8:13 province was **p.** unto all people, ... 1540
Ps 68:11 the company of those that **p.** it.......... 1319
Jon 3:7 **p.** through Nineveh by the decree........ 559
Mk 7:36 the more a great deal they **p.** it;........ *2784*
Mk 13:10 **must first be p. among all nations.**. *2784*
Lu 8:39 and **p.** throughout the whole city......... *2784*
Ac 10:37 which was **p.** throughout all Judaea, ... *1096*
Ac 13:49 And the word of the Lord was **p.**......... *1308*

PUBLISHETH
Isa 52:7 good tidings, that **p.** peace;............... 8085
Isa 52:7 tidings of good, that **p.** salvation;........ 8085
Jer 4:15 **p.** affliction from mount Ephraim. 8085
Na 1:15 good tidings, that **p.** peace!.............. 8085

PUBLIUS (pub'-le-us)
Ac 28:7 of the island, whose name was **P.**; *4196*
Ac 28:8 the father of **P.** lay sick of a fever...... *4196*

PUDENS (pu'-denz)
2Ti 4:21 Eubulus greeteth thee, and **P.**,.......... *4227*

PUFFED
1Co 4:6 that no one of you be **p.** up for one.... *5448*
1Co 4:18 Now some are **p.** up, as though I....... *5448*
1Co 4:19 the speech of them which are **p.** up,... *5448*
1Co 5:2 ye are **p.** up, and have not rather....... *5448*
1Co 13:4 vaunteth not itself, is not **p.** up,......... *5448*
Col 2:18 vainly **p.** up by his fleshly mind, ... *5448*

PUFFETH
Ps 10:5 for all his enemies, he **p.** at them....... 6315
Ps 12:5 in safety from him that **p.** at him........ 6315
1Co 8:1 Knowledge **p.** up, but charity *5448*

PUHITES (pu'-hites)
1Ch 2:53 the Ithrites, and the **P.**, and the 6336

PUL (pul)
2Ki 15:19 And **P.** the king of Assyria came........ 6322
2Ki 15:19 gave **P.** a thousand talents of............ 6322
1Ch 5:26 stirred up the spirit of **P.** king of 6322
Isa 66:19 nations, to Tarshish, **P.**, and Lud, ... 6322

PULL See also PULLED; PULLING.
1Ki 13:4 he could not **p.** it in again to him........ 7725
Ps 31:4 **P.** me out of the net that they........... 3318
Isa 22:19 thy state shall he **p.** thee down.......... 2040
Jer 1:10 to root out, and to **p.** down, and to 5422
Jer 12:3 **p.** them out like sheep for the........... 5423
Jer 18:7 and to **p.** down, and to destroy it;...... 5422
Jer 24:6 them, and not **p.** them down; 2040
Jer 42:10 build you, and not **p.** you down,......... 2040
Eze 17:9 shall he not **p.** up the roots.............. 5423
Mic 2:8 **p.** off the robe with the garment........ 6584
Mt 7:4 **p. out the mote out of thine eye;**... *1544*
Lu 6:42 **p. out the mote that is in thine**...... *1544*
Lu 6:42 **to p. out the mote that is in thy**.... *1544*
Lu 12:18 **I will p. down my barns, and**........ *2507*
Lu 14:5 **p. him out on the sabbath day?**...... *385*

PULLED
Ge 8:9 **p.** her in unto him into the ark. 4026
Ge 19:10 and **p.** Lot into the house to them, ... 935
Ezr 6:11 timber be **p.** down from his house,..... 5256
La 3:11 my ways, and **p.** me in pieces: 6582
Am 9:15 no more be **p.** up out of their land..... 5428
Zec 7:11 and **p.** away the shoulder, and........... 5414
Ac 23:10 Paul should have been **p.** in pieces *1288*

PULLING
2Co 10:4 to the **p.** down of strong holds;)......... *2506*
Jude 23 with fear, **p.** them out of the fire;....... *726*

PULPIT
Ne 8:4 the scribe stood upon a **p.** of wood,.... 4026

PULSE
2Sa 17:28 beans, and lentiles, and parched **p.**, ...
Da 1:12 and let them give us **p.** to eat, and..... 2235
Da 1:16 should drink; and gave them **p.**.......... 2235

PUNISH See also PUNISHED.
Le 26:18 I will **p.** you seven times more for...... 3256
Le 26:24 **p.** you yet seven times for your......... 5221
Pr 17:26 Also to **p.** the just is not good, nor...... 6064
Isa 10:12 will **p.** the fruit of the stout heart....... 6485
Isa 13:11 I will **p.** the world for their evil, and... 6485
Isa 24:21 shall **p.** the host of the high ones 6485
Isa 26:21 to **p.** the inhabitants of the earth........ 6485
Isa 27:1 **p.** leviathan the piercing serpent,........ 6485
Jer 9:25 that I will **p.** all them which are 6485
Jer 11:22 of hosts, Behold, I will **p.** them: 6485
Jer 13:21 thou say when he shall **p.** thee?......... 6485
Jer 21:14 I will **p.** you according to the fruit...... 6485
Jer 23:34 I will even **p.** that man and his.......... 6485
Jer 25:12 that I will **p.** the king of Babylon,....... 6485
Jer 27:8 that nation will I **p.**, saith the Lord, ... 6485
Jer 29:32 I will **p.** Shemaiah the Nehelamite,...... 6485
Jer 30:20 and I will **p.** all that oppress them. 6485
Jer 36:31 I will **p.** him and his seed and his 6485
Jer 44:13 I will **p.** them that dwell in the land.... 6485
Jer 44:29 I will **p.** you in this place, that ye....... 6485
Jer 46:25 I will **p.** the multitude of No, and 6485
Jer 50:18 I will **p.** the king of Babylon and 6485
Jer 51:44 And I will **p.** Bel in Babylon, and........ 6485
Ho 4:9 I will **p.** them for their ways, and........ 6485
Ho 4:14 I will not **p.** your daughters when....... 6485
Ho 12:2 will **p.** Jacob according to his ways;..... 6485
Am 3:2 I will **p.** you for all your iniquities....... 6485
Zep 1:8 I will **p.** the princes, and the king's..... 6485
Zep 1:9 day also will I **p.** all those that leap..... 6485
Zep 1:12 **p.** the men that are settled on their.... 6485
Zec 8:14 As I thought to **p.** you, when your 7489
Ac 4:21 how they might **p.** them, because....... *2849*

PUNISHED See also UNPUNISHED.
Ex 21:20 his hand; he shall be surely **p.**. 5358
Ex 21:21 a day or two, he shall not be **p.**: 5358
Ex 21:22 he shall be surely **p.**, according as...... 6064
Ezr 9:13 hast **p.** us less than our iniquities 2820
Job 31:11 it is an iniquity to be **p.** by the judges. ......
Job 31:28 were an iniquity to be **p.** by the judge: ......
Pr 21:11 When the scorner is **p.**, the simple..... 6064
Pr 22:3 but the simple pass on, and are **p.**...... 6064
Pr 27:12 but the simple pass on, and are **p.**...... 6064
Jer 44:13 as I have **p.** Jerusalem, by the........... 6485
Jer 50:18 as I have **p.** the king of Assyria. 6485
Zep 3:7 not be cut off, howsoever I **p.** them: .. 6485
Zec 10:3 the shepherds, and I **p.** the goats:...... 6485
Ac 22:5 unto Jerusalem, for to be **p.**, ... *5097*
Ac 26:11 I **p.** them oft in every synagogue, ... 5097
2Th 1:9 **p.**...everlasting destruction......... *1349,5099*
2Pe 2:9 unto the day of judgment to be **p.**: *2849*

PUNISHMENT See also PUNISHMENTS.
Ge 4:13 My **p.** is greater than I can bear. 5771
Le 26:41, 43 accept of the **p.** of their iniquity:.... 5771
1Sa 28:10 there shall no **p.** happen to thee for.... 5771
Job 31:3 strange **p.** to the workers of iniquity?.........
Pr 19:19 man of great wrath shall suffer **p.**:...... 6066
La 3:39 a man for the **p.** of his sins?............ 2399
La 4:6 **p.** of the iniquity of the daughter........ 5771
La 4:6 than the **p.** of the sin of Sodom, ... 2403
La 4:22 **p.** of thine iniquity...accomplished, ... 5771
Eze 14:10 shall bear the **p.** of their iniquity: 5771
Eze 14:10 the **p.** of the prophet shall be even..... 5771
Eze 14:10 as the **p.** of him that seeketh unto...... 5771
Am 1:3,6, 9,11,13 I will not turn away the **p.** ....
Am 2:1,4,6 will not turn away the **p.** thereof; ....
Zec 14:19 This shall be the **p.** of Egypt, and 2403
Zec 14:19 the **p.** of all nations that come not...... 2403
Mt 25:46 **shall go away into everlasting p.**... *2851*
2Co 2:6 Sufficient to such a man is this **p.**,...... *2009*
Heb 10:29 Of how much sorer **p.**, suppose ye,.... *5098*
1Pe 2:14 sent by him for the **p.** of evildoers, ... *1557*

PUNISHMENTS
Job 19:29 bringeth the **p.** of the sword, ... 5771
Ps 149:7 upon the heathen, and **p.** upon the 5771

PUNITES (pu'-nites)
Nu 26:23 of Pua, the family of the **P.**:.............. 6324

PUNON (pu'-non)
Nu 33:42 Zalmonah, and pitched in **P.**. 6325
Nu 33:43 they departed from **P.**, and pitched..... 6325

PUR (pur) See also PURIM.
Es 3:7 they cast **P.**, that is, the lot,............. 6332
Es 9:24 and had cast **P.**, that is, the lot, to..... 6332
Es 9:26 days Purim after the name of **P.**. 6332

PURCHASE See also PURCHASED.
Ge 49:32 The **p.** of the field and of the cave 4735
Le 25:33 if a man **p.** of the Levites, then the 1350
Jer 32:11 So I took the evidence of the **p.**, ... 4736
Jer 32:12 I gave the evidence of the **p.** unto...... 4736
Jer 32:12 that subscribed the book of the **p.**, ... 4736
Jer 32:14 evidences, this evidence of the **p.**,...... 4736
Jer 32:16 the evidence of the **p.** unto Baruch..... 4736
1Ti 3:13 **p.** to themselves a good degree, ... *4046*

PURCHASED
Ge 25:10 Abraham **p.** of the sons of Heth: 7069
Ex 15:16 pass over, which thou hast **p.**............ 7069
Ru 4:10 of Mahlon, have I **p.** to be my wife, ... 7069
Ps 74:2 which thou hast **p.** of old; the rod of... 7069
Ps 78:54 which his right hand had **p.**............. 7069
Ac 1:18 man **p.** a field with the reward of....... *2932*
Ac 8:20 gift of God may be **p.** with money. *2932*
Ac 20:28 he hath **p.** with his own blood........... *4046*
Eph 1:14 redemption of the **p.** possession, ... *4047*

PURE See also PURER.
Ex 25:11 thou shalt overlay it with **p.** gold, ... 2889
Ex 25:17 shalt make a mercy seat of **p.** gold: 2889
Ex 25:24 thou shalt overlay it with **p.** gold, ... 2889

Ex 25:29 of **p.** gold shalt thou make them........ 2889
Ex 25:31 shalt make a candlestick of **p.** gold:..... 2889
Ex 25:36 shall be one beaten work of **p.** gold. ... 2889
Ex 25:38 thereof, shall be of **p.** gold.............. 2889
Ex 25:39 a talent of **p.** gold shall he make it,..... 2889
Ex 27:20 **p.** oil olive beaten for the light,.......... 2134
Ex 28:14 two chains of **p.** gold at the ends; 2889
Ex 28:22 ends of wreathen work of **p.** gold....... 2889
Ex 28:36 thou shalt make a plate of **p.** gold,....... 2889
Ex 30:3 shalt overlay it with **p.** gold, the top ... 2889
Ex 30:23 of **p.** myrrh five hundred shekels,....... 1865
Ex 30:34 sweet spices with **p.** frankincense:...... 2134
Ex 30:35 tempered together, **p.** and holy:......... 2889
Ex 31:8 and the **p.** candlestick with all his....... 2889
Ex 37:2 he overlaid it with **p.** gold within........ 2889
Ex 37:6 he made the mercy seat of **p.** gold: 2889
Ex 37:11 And he overlaid it with **p.** gold, and.... 2889
Ex 37:16 covers to cover withal, of **p.** gold....... 2889
Ex 37:17 made the candlestick of **p.** gold: of 2889
Ex 37:22 it was one beaten work of **p.** gold. 2889
Ex 37:23 and his snuffdishes, of **p.** gold........... 2889
Ex 37:24 Of a talent of **p.** gold made he it, ... 2889
Ex 37:26 he overlaid it with **p.** gold, both the.... 2889
Ex 37:29 and the **p.** incense of sweet spices, ... 2889
Ex 39:15 ends, of wreathen work of **p.** gold...... 2889
Ex 39:25 they made bells of **p.** gold, and put..... 2889
Ex 39:30 plate of the holy crown of **p.** gold,...... 2889
Ex 39:37 The **p.** candlestick, with the lamps...... 2889
Le 24:2 bring unto thee **p.** oil olive beaten 2134
Le 24:4 the lamps upon the **p.** candlestick....... 2888
Le 24:6 upon the **p.** table before the Lord....... 2888
Le 24:7 **p.** frankincense upon each row,.......... 2134
De 32:14 drink the **p.** blood of the grape. 2561
2Sa 22:27 the **p.** thou wilt shew thyself **p.**; 1305
1Ki 5:11 and twenty measures of **p.** oil:............ 3795
1Ki 6:20 he overlaid it with **p.** gold; and so 5462
1Ki 6:21 the house within with **p.** gold; 5462
1Ki 7:49 candlesticks of **p.** gold, five on the...... 5462
1Ki 7:50 spoons, and the censers of **p.** gold; 5462
1Ki 10:21 forest of Lebanon were of **p.** gold; 5462
1Ch 28:17 Also **p.** gold for the fleshhooks, ... 2889
2Ch 3:4 he overlaid it within with **p.** gold. 2889
2Ch 4:20 before the oracle, of **p.** gold;............ 5462
2Ch 4:22 spoons, and the censers, of **p.** gold: ... 5462
2Ch 9:17 ivory, and overlaid it with **p.** gold....... 2889
2Ch 9:20 forest of Lebanon were of **p.** gold: 5462
2Ch 13:11 they in order upon the **p.** table; 2889
Ezr 6:20 all of them wre **p.**, and killed the 2889
Job 4:17 a man be more **p.** than his Maker? 2891
Job 8:6 If thou wert **p.** and upright; surely...... 2134
Job 11:4 thou hast said, My doctrine is **p.**,........ 2134
Job 16:17 in mine hands: also my prayer is **p.** ... 2134
Job 25:5 the stars are not **p.** in his sight.......... 2141
Job 28:19 shall it be valued with **p.** gold........... 2889
Ps 12:6 words of the Lord are **p.** words:......... 2889
Ps 18:26 the **p.** thou wilt shew thyself **p.**; 1305
Ps 19:8 commandment of the Lord is **p.**, ... 1249
Ps 21:3 settest a crown of **p.** gold on his......... 6337
Ps 24:4 hath clean hands, and a **p.** heart;......... 1249
Ps 119:140 Thy word is very **p.**: therefore 6884
Pr 15:26 the words of the **p.** are pleasant 2889
Pr 20:9 heart clean, I am **p.** from my sin? 2891
Pr 20:11 whether his work be **p.**, and 2134
Pr 21:8 but as for the **p.**, his work is right. 2134
Pr 30:5 Every word of God is **p.**: he is a 6884
Pr 30:12 a generation that are **p.** in their 2889
Da 7:9 hair of his head like the **p.** wool: 5343
Mic 6:11 Shall I count them **p.** with the 2135
Zep 3:9 turn to the people a **p.** language,........ 1305
Mal 1:11 unto my name, and a **p.** offering: 2889
Mt 5:8 **Blessed are the p. in heart: for**..... *2513*
Ac 20:26 I am **p.** from the blood of all men....... *2513*
Ro 14:20 All things indeed are **p.**; but it is........ *2513*
Php 4:8 are just, whatsoever things are **p.**. *53*
1Ti 1:5 is charity out of a **p.** heart, and of...... *2513*
1Ti 3:9 of the faith in a **p.** conscience............ *2513*
1Ti 5:22 of other men's sins: keep thyself **p.**. *53*
2Ti 1:3 my forefathers with **p.** conscience,...... *2513*
2Ti 2:22 call on the Lord out of a **p.** heart. *2513*
Tit 1:15 Unto the **p.** all things are **p.**: but *2513*
Tit 1:15 and unbelieving is nothing **p.**; *2513*
Heb 10:22 our bodies washed with **p.** water......... *2513*
Jas 1:27 **P.** religion and undefiled before.......... *2513*
Jas 3:17 wisdom that is from above is first **p.**,..... *53*
1Pe 1:22 love one another with a **p.** heart *2513*
2Pe 3:1 I stir up your **p.** minds by way *1506*
1Jo 3:3 purifieth himself, even as he is **p.**.......... *53*
Re 15:6 clothed in **p.** and white linen, and....... *2513*
Re 21:18 and the city was **p.** gold, like unto....... *2513*
Re 21:21 street of the city was **p.** gold, as it..... *2513*
Re 22:1 he shewed me a **p.** river of water *2513*

PURELY
Isa 1:25 and **p.** purge away the dross, and....... 1252

PURENESS
Job 22:30 delivered by the **p.** of thine hands. 1252
Pr 22:11 He that loveth **p.** of heart, for the...... 2890
2Co 6:6 By **p.**, by knowledge, by *54*

PURER
La 4:7 Her Nazarites were **p.** than snow,...... 2141
Hab 1:13 art of **p.** eyes than to behold evil, ... 2889

PURGE See also PURGED; PURGETH; PURGING; PURIFY.
2Ch 34:3 year he began to **p.** Judah and.......... 2891
Ps 51:7 **P.** me with hyssop, and I shall be 2398
Ps 65:3 thou shalt **p.** them away. 3722
Ps 79:9 deliver us, and **p.** away our sins,........ 3722
Isa 1:25 and purely **p.** away thy dross, and...... 6884
Eze 20:38 **p.** out from among you the rebels, ... 1305
Eze 43:20 thus shalt thou cleanse and **p.** it......... 3722
Eze 43:26 Seven days shall they **p.** the altar....... 3722
Da 11:35 to **p.**, and to make them white, ... 1305
Mal 3:3 and **p.** them as gold and silver,.......... 2212
Mt 3:12 he will thoroughly **p.** his floor,........... *1245*
Lu 3:17 he will thoroughly **p.** his floor, ... *1245*
1Co 5:7 **P.** out therefore the old leven, ... *1571*
2Ti 2:21 If a man therefore **p.** himself from...... *1571*
Heb 9:14 **p.** your conscience from dead............ *2511*

PURGED
1Sa 3:14 shall not be **p.** with sacrifice nor 3722
2Ch 34:8 when he had **p.** the land, and the....... 2891
Pr 16:6 mercy and truth iniquity is **p.**: 3722
Isa 4:4 have **p.** the blood of Jerusalem.......... 1740
Isa 6:7 is taken away, and thy sin **p.**............ 3722
Isa 22:14 iniquity shall not be **p.** from you.......... 3722
Isa 27:9 shall the iniquity of Jacob be **p.**; 3722
Eze 24:13 lewdness: because I have **p.** thee,...... 2891
Eze 24:13 not **p.**, thou shalt not be **p.** from....... 2891
Heb 1:3 had by himself **p.** our sins.......... *4160,2512*
Heb 9:22 are by the law **p.** with blood;............ *2511*
Heb 10:2 worshippers once **p.** should have........ *2508*
2Pe 1:9 that he was **p.** from his old sins. *2512*

PURGETH
Joh 15:2 **he p. it, that it may bring forth**.... *2508*

PURGING
Mr 7:19 **into the draught, p. all meats?**.... *2511*

PURIFICATION See also PURIFICATIONS.
Nu 19:9 of separation: it is a **p.** for sin. 2403
Nu 19:17 of the burnt heifer of **p.** for sin, ... 2403
2Ch 30:19 to the **p.** of the sanctuary. 2893
Ne 12:45 their God, and the ward of the **p.**,....... 2893
Es 2:3 their things for **p.** be given them:........ 8562
Es 2:9 speedily gave her her things for **p.**, ... 8562
Lu 2:22 And when the days of her **p.**............. *2512*
Ac 21:26 accomplishment of the days of **p.**,.......... *49*

PURIFICATIONS
Es 2:12 days of their **p.** accomplished,........... 4795

PURIFIED
Le 8:15 with his finger, and **p.** the altar,.......... 2398
Nu 8:21 And the Levites were **p.**, and they..... 2398
Nu 31:23 nevertheless it shall be **p.** with the..... 2398
2Sa 11:4 she was **p.** from her uncleanness:....... 6942
Ezr 6:20 priests and the Levites were **p.** 2891
Ne 12:30 and the Levites **p.** themselves, ... 2891
Ne 12:30 **p.** the people, and the gates, and....... 2891
Ps 12:6 furnace of earth, **p.** seven times......... 2212
Da 12:10 Many shall be **p.**, and made 1305
Ac 24:18 Asia found me **p.** in the temple, ... *48*
Heb 9:23 heavens should be **p.** with these; *2511*
1Pe 1:22 ye have **p.** your souls in obeying.......... *48*

PURIFIER
Mal 3:3 sit as a refiner and **p.** of silver:.......... 2891

PURIFIETH
Nu 19:13 and **p.** not himself, defileth the 2398
1Jo 3:3 hath this hope in him **p.** himself, ... *48*

PURIFY See also PURGE; PURIFIED; PURIFIETH; PURIFYING.
Nu 19:12 **p.** himself with it on the third day, ... 2398
Nu 19:12 if he **p.** not himself the third day,....... 2398
Nu 19:19 the seventh day he shall **p.** himself, ... 2398
Nu 19:20 unclean, and shall not **p.** himself,........ 2398
Nu 31:19 **p.** both yurselves and your.............. 2398
Nu 31:20 **p.** all your raiment, and all that is....... 2398
Job 41:25 of breakings they **p.** themselves. 2398
Isa 66:17 and **p.** themselves in the gardens 2891
Eze 43:26 shall they purge the altar and **p.** it;..... 2891
Mal 3:3 and he shall **p.** the sons of Levi, ... 2891
Joh 11:55 the passover, to **p.** themselves. *48*
Ac 21:24 take, and **p.** thyself with them, ... *48*
Tit 2:14 **p.** unto himself a peculiar people, ... *2511*
Jas 4:8 **p.** your hearts, ye double minded. *48*

PURIFYING
Le 12:4 blood of her **p.** three and thirty.......... 2893
Le 12:4 the days of her **p.** be fulfilled............ 2892
Le 12:5 blood of her **p.** three score and.......... 2893
Le 12:6 the days of her **p.** are fulfilled,........... 2892
Nu 8:7 Sprinkle water of **p.** upon them,.......... 2403
1Ch 23:28 and in the **p.** of all holy things, ... 2893
Es 2:12 things for the **p.** of the women;) 8562
Joh 2:6 manner of the **p.** of the Jews,............ *2512*
Joh 3:25 disciples and the Jews about **p.**.......... *2512*
Ac 15:9 them, **p.** their hearts by faith. *2511*
Ac 21:26 the next day **p.** himself with them *48*
Heb 9:13 sanctifieth to the **p.** of the flesh: *2514*

PURIM (pu'-rim) See also PUR.
Es 9:26 called these days **P.** after the........... 6332
Es 9:28 these days of **P.** should not fail.......... 6332
Es 9:29 confirm this second letter of **P.**.......... 6332
Es 9:31 To confirm these days of **P.** in 6332
Es 9:32 confirmed these matters of **P.**; 6332

PURITY
1Ti 4:12 charity, in spirit, in faith, in **p.**. *47*
1Ti 5:2 the younger as sisters, with all **p.**. *47*

PURLOINING
Tit 2:10 Not **p.**, but shewing all good *3557*

PURPLE
Ex 25:4 And blue, and **p.**, and scarlet, and........ 713
Ex 26:1 and blue, and **p.**, and scarlet: 713
Ex 26:31 shalt make a vail of blue, and **p.**. 713
Ex 26:36 door of the tent, of blue, and **p.**, ... 713
Ex 27:16 of twenty cubits, of blue, and **p.**, ... 713
Ex 28:5 gold, and blue,and **p.**, and scarlet,........ 713
Ex 28:6 ephod of gold, of blue, and of **p.**,......... 713
Ex 28:8 even of gold, of blue, and **p.**, and 713
Ex 28:15 make it; of gold, of blue, and of **p.**,........ 713
Ex 28:33 pomegranates of blue, and of **p.**,.......... 713
Ex 35:6 And blue, and **p.**, and scarlet, and........ 713
Ex 35:23 with whom was found blue, and **p.**, ... 713
Ex 35:25 had spun, both of blue, and of **p.**, ... 713
Ex 35:35 in blue, and in **p.**, in scarlet, and 713
Ex 36:8 twined linen, and blue, and **p.**, and....... 713
Ex 36:35 he made a vail of blue, and **p.**, and 713
Ex 36:37 tabernacle door of blue, and **p.**, and 713
Ex 38:18 was needlework, of blue, and **p.**, ... 713
Ex 38:23 an embroiderer in blue, and in **p.**, ... 713
Ex 39:1 of the blue, and **p.**, and scarlet, and..... 713
Ex 39:2 and **p.**, and scarlet, and fine twined...... 713
Ex 39:3 work it in the blue, and in the **p.**, ... 713
Ex 39:5 of gold, blue, and **p.**, and scarlet, ... 713
Ex 39:8 and **p.**, and scarlet, and fine twined...... 713
Ex 39:24 robe pomegranates of blue, and **p.**, ... 713
Ex 39:29 fine twined linen, and blue, and **p.**........ 713
Nu 4:13 and spread a **p.** cloth thereon:............ 713
Jg 8:26 **p.** raiment that was on the kings of...... 713
2Ch 2:7 and in iron, and in **p.**, and crimson, ... 710
2Ch 2:14 in **p.**, in blue, and in fine linen,............ 713
2Ch 3:14 vail of blue, and **p.**, and crimson, ... 713
Es 1:6 with cords of fine linen and **p.** to 713
Es 8:15 a garment of fine linen and **p.**:............. 713
Pr 31:22 tapestry; her clothing is silk and **p.**. 713
Ca 3:10 the covering of it of **p.**, the midst 713
Ca 7:5 and the hair of their head like **p.**;......... 713
Jer 10:9 blue and **p.** is their clothing: they......... 713
Eze 27:7 blue and **p.** from the isles of Elishah..... 713
Eze 27:16 emeralds, **p.**, and broidered work, ... 713
Mk 15:17 they clothed him with **p.**, and *4209*
Mk 15:20 they took off the **p.** from him, and........ *4209*
Lu 16:19 **was clothed in p. and fine linen,**... *4209*
Joh 19:2 and they put on him a **p.** robe, ... *4210*
Joh 19:5 crown of thorns, and the **p.** robe......... *4210*
Ac 16:14 Lydia, a seller of **p.**, of the city of...... *4211*
Re 17:4 arrayed in **p.** and scarlet colour,......... *4209*

Re 18:12 and fine linen, and **p.**, and silk, ... *4209*
Re 18:16 was clothed in fine linen, and **p.**, ... *4210*

PURPOSE See also PURPOSED; PURPOSES; PURPOSETH; PURPOSING.
Ru 2:16 of the handfuls of **p.** for her, and........ 7997
1Ki 5:5 I **p.** to build an house unto the 559
2Ch 28:10 ye **p.** to keep under the children.......... 559
Ezr 4:5 against them, to frustrate their **p.**,....... 6098
Ne 8:4 which they had made for the **p.**; 1697
Job 33:17 may withdraw man from his **p.**........... 4639
Pr 20:18 **p.** is established by counsel: and 4284
Ec 3:1 to every **p.** under the heaven: 2656
Ec 3:17 a time there for every **p.** and for 2656
Ec 8:6 Because to every **p.** there is time 2656
Isa 1:11 To what **p.** is the multitude of your ....
Isa 14:26 is the **p.** that is purposed upon 6098
Isa 30:7 shall help in vain, and to no **p.**: 7385
Jer 6:20 To what **p.** cometh there to me incense ....
Jer 26:3 which I **p.** to do unto them because.... 2803
Jer 36:3 evil which I **p.** to do unto them;.......... 2803
Jer 49:30 hath conceived a **p.** against you.......... 4284
Jer 51:29 **p.** of the Lord shall be performed....... 4284
Da 6:17 that the **p.** might not be changed........ 6640
Mt 26:8 saying, To what **p.** is this waste? ....
Ac 11:23 with **p.** of heart they would cleave...... *4286*
Ac 26:16 **have appeared unto thee for this p.**, ...
Ac 27:13 that they had obtained their **p.**,........... *4286*
Ac 27:43 Paul, kept them from their **p.**; *1013*
Ro 8:28 are the called according to his **p.**......... *4286*
Ro 9:11 the **p.** of God according to election..... *4286*
Ro 9:17 Even for this same **p.** have I raised ....
2Co 1:17 lightness? or the things that I **p.**, ... *1011*
2Co 1:17 do I **p.** according to the flesh, that *1011*
Eph 1:11 **p.** of him who worketh all things *4286*
Eph 3:11 the eternal **p.** which he purposed *4286*
Eph 6:22 I have sent unto you for the same **p.**, ...
Col 4:8 I have sent unto you for the same **p.**, ...
2Ti 1:9 but according to his own **p.** and *4286*
2Ti 3:10 doctrine, manner of life, **p.**, faith, ... *4286*
1Jo 3:8 For this **p.** the Son...was manifested, ...

PURPOSED
2Ch 32:2 that he was **p.** to fight against 6440
Ps 17:3 I am **p.** that my mouth shall not.......... 2161
Ps 140:4 have **p.** to overthrow my goings.......... 2803
Isa 14:24 as I have **p.**, so shall it stand: 3289
Isa 14:26 that is **p.** upon the whole earth: 3289
Isa 14:27 For the Lord of hosts hath **p.**, and 3289
Isa 19:12 Lord of hosts hath **p.** upon Egypt....... 3289
Isa 23:9 The Lord of hosts hath **p.** it, to......... 3289
Isa 46:11 pass; I have **p.** it, I will also do it. 3335
Jer 4:28 I have **p.** it, and will not repent, ... 2161
Jer 49:20 hath **p.** against the inhabitants............ 2803
Jer 50:45 that he hath **p.** against the land of...... 2803
La 2:8 The Lord hath **p.** to destroy the 2803
Da 1:8 Daniel **p.** in his heart that he............. 7760
Ac 19:21 Paul **p.** in the spirit, when he had....... *5087*
Ac 20:3 he **p.** to return through............ *1096,1106*
Ro 1:13 oftentimes I **p.** to come unto you, ... *4388*
Eph 1:9 which he hath **p.** in himself: *4388*
Eph 3:11 which he **p.** in Christ Jesus our......... *4160*

PURPOSES
Job 17:11 my **p.** are broken off, even the.......... 2154
Pr 15:22 Without counsel **p.** are...................... 4284
Isa 19:10 shall be broken in the **p.** thereof, ... 8356
Jer 49:20 and his **p.**, that he hath purposed 4284
Jer 50:45 and his **p.**, that he hath purposed 4284

PURPOSETH
2Co 9:7 according as he **p.** in his heart, ... *4255*

PURPOSING
Ge 27:42 doth comfort himself, **p.** to kill thee. ....

PURSE See also PURSES.
Pr 1:14 among us; let us all have one **p.**: 3599
Mk 6:8 no bread, no money in their **p.**: *2223*
Lu 10:4 **Carry neither p., nor scrip, nor** *905*
Lu 22:35 **I sent you without p., and scrip,**...... *905*
Lu 22:36 **he that hath a p., let him take it,**... *905*

PURSES
Mt 10:9 **nor silver, nor brass in your p.,**...... *2223*

PURSUE See also ENSUE; PURSUED; PURSUETH; PURSUING.
Ge 35:5 did not **p.** after the sons of Jacob. 7291
Ex 15:9 The enemy said, I will **p.**, I will......... 7291
De 19:6 avenger of the blood **p.** the slayer. 7291
De 28:22 they shall **p.** thee until thou perish...... 7291
De 28:45 shall **p.** thee, and overtake thee, ... 7291
Jos 2:5 **p.** after them quickly; for ye shall....... 7291
Jos 8:16 called together to **p.** after them: 7291
Jos 10:19 **p.** after your enemies, and smite........ 7291
Jos 20:5 the avenger of blood **p.** after him, ... 7291
1Sa 24:14 after whom dost thou **p.**? after a........ 7291
1Sa 25:29 Yet a man is risen to **p.** thee, and...... 7291
1Sa 26:18 my lord thus **p.** after his servant?....... 7291
1Sa 30:8 Shall I **p.** after this troop? shall I........ 7291
1Sa 30:8 **P.**: for thou shalt surely overtake....... 7291
2Sa 17:1 I will arise and **p.** after David this 7291
2Sa 20:6 lord's servants, and **p.** after him,....... 7291
2Sa 20:7, 13 **p.** after Sheba the son of Bichri. 7291
2Sa 24:13 thine enemies, while they **p.** thee? 7291
Job 13:25 and wilt thou **p.** the dry stubble?........ 7291
Job 30:15 they **p.** my soul as the land: and........ 7291
Ps 34:14 and do good seek peace, and **p.** it. 7291
Isa 30:16 shall they that **p.** you be swift. 7291
Jer 48:2 Madmen; the sword shall **p.** thee. 3212
Eze 35:6 blood, and blood shall **p.** thee: 7291
Eze 35:6 blood, even blood shall **p.** thee: 7291
Ho 8:3 is good: the enemy shall **p.** him. 7291
Am 1:11 did **p.** his brother with the sword, ... 7291
Na 1:8 and darkness shall **p.** his enemies. 7291

PURSUED
Ge 14:14 eighteen, and **p.** them unto Dan. 7291
Ge 14:15 and **p.** them unto Hobah, which 7291
Ge 31:23 **p.** after him seven days' journey; 7291
Ge 31:36 thou hast so hotly **p.** after me?.......... 1814
Ex 14:8 he **p.** after the children of Israel:....... 7291
Ex 14:9 But the Egyptians **p.** after them,........ 7291
Ex 14:23 And the Egyptians **p.**, and went in...... 7291
De 11:4 overflow them as they **p.** after you,.... 7291
Jos 2:7 the men **p.** after them the way to 7291
Jos 2:7 they which **p.** after them were gone ... 7291
Jos 8:16 and they **p.** after Joshua, and were..... 7291
Jos 8:17 the city open, and **p.** after Israel. 7291
Jos 24:6 the Egyptians **p.** after your fathers..... 7291
Jg 1:6 they **p.** after him, and caught him,...... 7291
Jg 4:16 Barak **p.** after the chariots, and 7291
Jg 4:22 as Barak **p.** Sisera, Jael came out 7291
Jg 7:23 and **p.** after the Midianites................ 7291
Jg 7:25 and **p.** Midian, and brought the 7291
Jg 8:12 he **p.** after them, and took the two..... 7291
Jg 20:45 **p.** hard after them unto Gidom, ... 1692
1Sa 7:11 and **p.** the Philistines, and smote........ 7291
1Sa 17:52 shouted, and **p.** the Philistines, ... 7291
1Sa 23:25 he **p.** after David in the wilderness..... 7291
1Sa 30:10 David **p.**, he and four hundred............ 7291
2Sa 2:19 And Asahel **p.** after Abnor; and in 7291
2Sa 2:24 also and Abishai **p.** after Abner: 7291
2Sa 2:28 and **p.** after Israel no more, neither 7291
2Sa 20:10 Abishai his brother **p.** after Sheba....... 7291
2Sa 22:38 I have **p.** mine enemies, and 7291
1Ki 20:20 Syrians fled; and Israel **p.** them: 7291
2Ki 25:5 of the Chaldees **p.** after the king, ... 7291
2Ch 13:19 Abijah **p.** after Jeroboam, and took...... 7291
2Ch 14:13 were with him **p.** them unto Gerar: ... 7291
Ps 18:37 I have **p.** mine enemies, and 7291
Isa 41:3 He **p.** them, and passed safely;.......... 7291
Jer 39:5 the Chaldeans' army **p.** after them, ... 7291
Jer 52:8 the Chaldeans **p.** after the king, ... 7291
La 4:19 they **p.** us upon the mountains, ... 1814

PURSUER See also PURSUERS.
La 1:6 without strength before the **p.** 7291

PURSUERS
Jos 2:16 mountain, lest the **p.** meet you; 7291
Jos 2:16 days, until the **p.** be returned: 7291
Jos 2:22 days, until the **p.** were returned:......... 7291
Jos 2:22 **p.** sought them throughout all the........ 7291
Jos 8:20 turned back upon the **p.** 7291

PURSUETH
Le 26:17 ye shall flee when none **p.** you. 7291
Le 26:36 and they shall fall when none **p.** 7291
Le 26:37 were before a sword, when none **p.**..... 7291
Pr 11:19 tendeth to life: so he that **p.** evil....... 7291
Pr 11:19 **p.** it to his own death. ....
Pr 13:21 Evil **p.** sinners: but to the................. 7291
Pr 19:7 he **p.** them with words, yet they........ 7291
Pr 28:1 The wicked flee when no man **p.**......... 7291

PURSUING
Jg 8:4 were with him, faint, yet **p.** them....... 7291
Jg 8:5 I am **p.** after Zebah and Zalmunna, ... 7291
1Sa 23:28 Saul returned from **p.** after David, ... 7291
2Sa 3:22 David and Joab came from **p.** a troop, ...
2Sa 18:16 returned from **p.** after Israel: 7291
1Ki 18:27 he is talking, or he is **p.**, or he is....... 7873
1Ki 22:33 that they turned back from **p.** him........ 310
2Ch 18:32 turned back again from **p.** him............ 310

PURTENANCE See also PERTAIN.
Ex 12:9 his legs, and with the **p.** thereof. 7130

PUSH See PUSHED; PUSHING.
Ex 21:29 ox were wont to **p.** with his horn....... 5056
Ex 21:32 ox shall **p.** a manservant or a 5055
Ex 21:36 ox hath used to **p.** in time past, ... 5056
De 33:17 **p.** the people together to the ends 5055
1Ki 22:11 these shalt thou **p.** the Syrians, ... 5055
2Ch 18:10 **p.** Syria until they be consumed. 5055
Job 30:12 they **p.** away my feet, and they 7971
Ps 44:5 thee will we **p.** down our enemies: 5055
Da 11:40 the king of the south **p.** at him: 5055

PUSHED
Eze 34:21 **p.** all the diseased with your............. 5055

PUSHING
Da 8:4 I saw the ram **p.** westward, and 5055

PUT See also PUTTEST; PUTTETH; PUTTING.
Ge 2:8 there he **p.** the man who he had 7760
Ge 2:15 **p.** him into the garden of Eden to 3240
Ge 3:15 I will **p.** enmity between thee and 7896
Ge 3:22 lest he **p.** forth his hand, and take...... 7971
Ge 8:9 he **p.** forth his hand, and took her, ... 7971
Ge 19:10 But the men **p.** forth their hand, ... 7971
Ge 24:2 **P.**, I pray thee, thy hand under 7760
Ge 24:9 the servant **p.** his hand under the....... 7760
Ge 24:47 I **p.** the earring upon her face, and..... 7760
Ge 26:11 his wife shall surely be **p.** to death. ....
Ge 27:15 **p.** them upon Jacob her younger 3847
Ge 27:16 she **p.** the skins of the kids of the...... 3847
Ge 28:11 and **p.** them for his pillows, and......... 7760
Ge 28:18 stone that he had **p.** for his pillows,.... 7760
Ge 28:20 bread to eat, and raiment to **p.** on,..... 3847
Ge 29:3 **p.** the stone again upon the well's 7725
Ge 30:40 he **p.** his own flocks by themselves,.... 7896
Ge 30:40 **p.** them not unto Laban's cattle.......... 7896
Ge 30:42 were feeble, he **p.** them not in: 7760
Ge 31:34 **p.** them in the camel's furniture, ... 7760
Ge 32:16 **p.** a space betwixt drove and drove. ... 7760
Ge 33:2 And he **p.** the handmaids and their 7760
Ge 35:2 **P.** away the strange gods that are...... 5493
Ge 37:34 **p.** sackcloth upon his loins, and......... 7760
Ge 38:14 she **p.** her widow's garments off 5493
Ge 38:19 and **p.** on the garments of her............ 3847
Ge 38:28 that the one **p.** out his hand: and 5414
Ge 39:4 all that he had he **p.** into his hand. 5414
Ge 39:20 him, and **p.** him into the prison,.......... 5414
Ge 40:3 he **p.** them in ward in the house of...... 5414
Ge 40:15 should **p.** me into the dungeon............ 7760
Ge 41:10 **p.** me in ward in the captain of the..... 5414
Ge 41:42 and **p.** it upon Joseph's hand, and....... 5414
Ge 41:42 and **p.** a gold chain about his neck; 7760
Ge 42:17 he **p.** them altogether into ward 622
Ge 43:22 who **p.** out money in our sacks........... 7760
Ge 44:1 **p.** every man's money in his sack's..... 7760
Ge 44:2 **p.** my cup, the silver cup, in the......... 7760
Ge 46:4 shall **p.** his hand upon thine eyes........ 7896
Ge 47:29 **p.**, I pray thee, thy hand under my...... 7760
Ge 48:16 **p.** thy right hand upon his head.......... 7760
Ge 50:26 and he was **p.** in a coffin in Egypt. 3455
Ex 2:3 pitch, and **p.** the child therein;........... 7760
Ex 3:5 **p.** off thy shoes from off thy feet, ... 5394
Ex 3:22 ye shall **p.** them upon your sons, ... 7760
Ex 4:4 **P.** forth thine hand, and take it by...... 7971
Ex 4:4 he **p.** forth his hand, and caught it, ... 7971
Ex 4:6 **P.** now thine hand into thy bosom........ 935
Ex 4:6 he **p.** his hand into his bosom: and....... 935
Ex 4:7 **P.** thine hand into thy bosom 7725
Ex 4:7 **p.** his hand into his bosom again;........ 7725
Ex 4:15 him, and **p.** words in his mouth:......... 7760
Ex 4:21 which I have **p.** in thine hand:........... 7760
Ex 5:21 to **p.** a sword in their hand to slay...... 5414
Ex 8:23 **p.** a division between my people 7760
Ex 11:7 doth **p.** a difference between the............
Ex 12:15 shall **p.** away leaven out of your......... 7673
Ex 15:26 I will **p.** none of these diseases......... 7760
Ex 16:33 and **p.** an omer full of manna............. 5414

Book	Ref.	Context	No.
Ex	17:12	took a stone, and **p.** it under him,	7760
Ex	17:14	utterly **p.** out the remembrance	4229
Ex	19:12	the mount shall be surely **p.** to death:	
Ex	21:12	that he die, shall be surely **p.** to death.	
Ex	21:15	his mother, shall be surely **p.** to death.	
Ex	21:16	hand, he shall surely be **p.** to death.	
Ex	21:17	his mother, shall surely be **p.** to death.	
Ex	21:29	and his owner also shall be **p.** to death.	
Ex	22:5	and shall **p.** in his beast, and shall	7971
Ex	22:8	whether he have **p.** his hand unto	7971
Ex	22:11	not **p.** his hand unto his neighbour's	7971
Ex	22:19	a beast shall surely be **p.** to death.	
Ex	23:1	**p.** not thine hand with the wicked	7896
Ex	24:6	of the blood, and **p.** it in basons;	7760
Ex	25:12	and **p.** them in the four corners	5414
Ex	25:14	shalt **p.** the staves into the rings	935
Ex	25:16	shalt **p.** into the ark the testimony	5414
Ex	25:21	**p.** the mercy seat above upon the	5414
Ex	25:21	the ark thou shalt **p.** the testimony	5414
Ex	25:26	**p.** the rings in the four corners that	5414
Ex	26:11	and **p.** the taches into the loops,	935
Ex	26:34	**p.** the mercy seat upon the ark of	5414
Ex	26:35	shalt **p.** the table on the north side.	5414
Ex	27:5	**p.** it under the compass of the altar	5414
Ex	27:7	the staves shall be **p.** into the rings,	935
Ex	28:12	shalt **p.** the two stones upon the	7760
Ex	28:23	**p.** the two rings on the two ends	5414
Ex	28:24	shalt **p.** the two wreathen chains	5414
Ex	28:25	**p.** them on the shoulderpieces of the	5414
Ex	28:26	shalt **p.** them upon the two ends	7760
Ex	28:27	**p.** them on the two sides of the	5414
Ex	28:30	**p.** in the breastplate of judgment	5414
Ex	28:37	thou shalt **p.** it on a blue lace, that	7760
Ex	28:41	**p.** them upon Aaron thy brother,	3847
Ex	29:3	shalt **p.** them into one basket,	5414
Ex	29:5	**p.** upon Aaron the coat, and the	3847
Ex	29:6	shalt **p.** the mitre upon his head,	7760
Ex	29:6	**p.** the holy crown upon the mitre.	5414
Ex	29:8	his sons, and **p.** coats upon them.	3847
Ex	29:9	sons, and **p.** the bonnets on them:	2280
Ex	29:10	**p.** their hands upon the head of	5564
Ex	29:12	**p.** it upon the horns of the altar	5414
Ex	29:15	**p.** their hands upon the head of	5564
Ex	29:17	**p.** them unto his pieces, and unto	5414
Ex	29:19	**p.** their hands upon the head of	5564
Ex	29:20	**p.** it upon the tip of the right ear	5414
Ex	29:24	shalt **p.** all in the hands of Aaron,	7760
Ex	29:30	stead shall **p.** them on seven days,	3847
Ex	30:6	**p.** it before the vail that is by the	5414
Ex	30:18	**p.** it between the tabernacle of the	5414
Ex	30:18	and thou shalt **p.** water therein.	5414
Ex	30:36	**p.** of it before the testimony in the	5414
Ex	31:6	are wise hearted I have **p.** wisdom,	5414
Ex	31:14	defileth it shall surely be **p.** to death:	
Ex	31:15	day, he shall surely be **p.** to death.	
Ex	32:27	**P.** every man his sword by his	7760
Ex	33:4	man did **p.** on him his ornaments	7896
Ex	33:5	now **p.** off thy ornaments from	3381
Ex	33:22	I will **p.** thee in a clift of the rock,	7760
Ex	34:33	with them, he **p.** a vail on his face	5414
Ex	34:35	and Moses **p.** the vail upon his face	7725
Ex	35:2	work therein shall be **p.** to death.	
Ex	35:34	hath **p.** in his heart that he may	5414
Ex	36:1	in whom the Lord **p.** wisdom and	5414
Ex	36:2	heart the Lord had **p.** wisdom,	5414
Ex	37:5	he **p.** the staves into the rings by	935
Ex	37:13	**p.** the rings upon the four corners	5414
Ex	38:7	he **p.** the staves into the rings on	935
Ex	39:7	he **p.** them on the shoulders of the	7760
Ex	39:16	**p.** the two rings in the two ends of	5414
Ex	39:17	they **p.** the two wreathen chains of	5414
Ex	39:18	**p.** them on the shoulderpieces of	5414
Ex	39:19	**p.** them on the two ends of the	7760
Ex	39:20	and **p.** them on the two sides of the	5414
Ex	39:25	gold, and **p.** the bells between the	5414
Ex	40:3	**p.** therein the ark of the testimony,	7760
Ex	40:5	**p.** the hanging of the door to the	7760
Ex	40:7	altar, and shalt **p.** water therein.	5414
Ex	40:13	**p.** upon Aaron the holy garments,	3847
Ex	40:18	**p.** in the bars thereof, and reared	5414
Ex	40:19	**p.** the covering of the tent above	7760
Ex	40:20	and **p.** the testimony into the ark,	5114
Ex	40:20	and **p.** the mercy seat above upon	5114
Ex	40:22	he **p.** the table in the tent of the	5114
Ex	40:24	he **p.** the candlestick in the tent of	7760
Ex	40:26	**p.** the golden altar in the tent of the	7760
Ex	40:29	he **p.** the altar of burnt offering by	7760
Ex	40:30	**p.** water there, to wash withal	5414
Le	1:4	he shall **p.** his hand upon the head	5564
Le	1:7	priest shall **p.** fire upon the altar,	5414
Le	2:1	it, and **p.** frankincense thereon:	5414
Le	2:15	thou shalt **p.** oil upon it, and lay	5414
Le	4:7,18	**p.** some of the blood upon the	5414
Le	4:25,	30,34 **p.** it upon the horns of the	5414
Le	5:11	offering; he shall **p.** no oil upon it,	7760
Le	5:11	he **p.** any frankincense thereon:	5414
Le	6:10	shall **p.** on his linen garment,	3847
Le	6:10	breeches shall he **p.** upon his	3847
Le	6:10	he shall **p.** them beside the altar.	7760
Le	6:11	And he shall **p.** off his garments,	6584
Le	6:11	and **p.** on other garments, and	3847
Le	6:12	in it; it shall not be **p.** out: and	3518
Le	8:7	And he **p.** upon him the coat, and	5414
Le	8:7	and **p.** the ephod upon him, and he	5414
Le	8:8	he **p.** the breastplate upon him:	7760
Le	8:8	**p.** in the breastplate the Urim and	5414
Le	8:9	he **p.** the mitre upon his head;	7760
Le	8:9	forefront, did he **p.** the golden	7760
Le	8:13	sons, and **p.** coats upon them, and	3847
Le	8:13	girdles,...**p.** bonnets upon them;	2280
Le	8:15	**p.** it upon the horns of the altar	5414
Le	8:23	**p.** it upon the tip of Aaron's right	5414
Le	8:24	**p.** of the blood upon the tip of	5414
Le	8:26	one wafer, and **p.** them on the fat,	7760
Le	8:27	And he **p.** all upon Aaron's hands,	5414
Le	9:9	**p.** it upon the horns of the altar,	5414
Le	9:20	**p.** the fat upon the beasts, and he	7760
Le	10:1	his censer, and **p.** fire therein,	5414
Le	10:1	and **p.** incense thereon, and	7760
Le	10:10	**p.** difference between holy and	
Le	11:32	it must be **p.** into water, and it	935
Le	11:38	if any water be **p.** upon the seed,	5414
Le	13:45	**p.** a covering upon his upper lip,	
Le	14:14	**p.** it upon the tip of the right ear	5414
Le	14:17	**p.** upon the tip of the right ear	5414
Le	14:25	**p.** it upon the tip of the right ear	5414
Le	14:28	shall **p.** of the oil that is in his	5414
Le	14:29	shall **p.** upon the head of him that	5414
Le	14:34	**p.** the plague of leprosy in a house	5414
Le	14:42	**p.** them in the place of those stones;	935
Le	15:19	she shall be **p.** apart seven days:	5079
Le	16:4	He shall **p.** on the holy linen coat,	3847
Le	16:4	flesh in water, and so **p.** them on	3847
Le	16:13	shall **p.** the incense upon the fire	5414
Le	16:18	**p.** it upon the horns of the altar	5414
Le	16:23	shall **p.** off the linen garments,	6584
Le	16:23	which he **p.** on when he went into	3847
Le	16:24	and **p.** on his garments, and come	3847
Le	16:32	and shall **p.** on the linen clothes,	3847
Le	18:19	is **p.** apart for her uncleanness	5079
Le	19:14	**p.** a stumblingblock before the	5414
Le	19:20	they shall not be **p.** to death,	
Le	20:2	he shall surely be **p.** to death: the	
Le	20:9	shall be surely **p.** to death: he hath	
Le	20:10	adulteress shall surely be **p.** to death.	
Le	20:11	of them shall surely be **p.** to death;	
Le	20:12	of them shall surely be **p.** to death:	
Le	20:13	they shall surely be **p.** to death;	
Le	20:15	beast, he shall surely be **p.** to death:	
Le	20:16	they shall surely be **p.** to death; their	
Le	20:25	**p.** difference between clean beasts	
Le	20:27	is a wizard, shall surely be **p.** to death:	
Le	21:7	woman **p.** away from her husband:	1644
Le	21:10	consecrated to **p.** on the garments,	3847
Le	22:14	**p.** the fifth part thereof unto it,	3254
Le	24:7	**p.** pure frankincense upon each	5414
Le	24:12	And they **p.** him in ward, that the	3240
Le	24:16	he shall surely be **p.** to death, and all	
Le	24:16	name of the Lord, shall be **p.** to death.	
Le	24:17	any man shall surely be **p.** to death.	
Le	24:21	killeth a man, he shall be **p.** to death.	
Le	26:8	of you shall **p.** ten thousand to flight:	
Le	27:29	redeemed; but shall surely be **p.** to	
Nu	1:51	that cometh nigh shall be **p.** to death.	
Nu	3:10,	38 cometh nigh shall be **p.** to death.	
Nu	4:6	shall **p.** thereon the covering of	5414
Nu	4:6	and shall **p.** in the staves thereof	7760
Nu	4:7	**p.** thereon the dishes, and the	5414
Nu	4:8	and shall **p.** in the staves thereof	7760
Nu	4:10	they shall **p.** it, and all the vessels	5414
Nu	4:10	skins, and shall **p.** it upon a bar.	5414
Nu	4:11	and shall **p.** to the staves thereof:	7725
Nu	4:12	**p.** them in a cloth of blue, and	5414
Nu	4:12	skins, and shall **p.** them on a bar:	5414
Nu	4:14	they shall **p.** upon it all the vessels	5414
Nu	4:14	skins, and **p.** to the staves of it.	7760
Nu	5:2	**p.** out of the camp every leper,	7971
Nu	5:3	male and female shall ye **p.** out,	7971
Nu	5:3	without the camp shall ye **p.** them;	7971
Nu	5:4	and p. them out without the camp:	7971
Nu	5:15	it, nor **p.** frankincense thereon;	5414
Nu	5:17	take, and **p.** it into the water:	5414
Nu	5:18	**p.** the offering of memorial in her	5414
Nu	6:18	**p.** it in the fire which is under the	5414
Nu	6:19	**p.** them upon the hands of the	5414
Nu	6:27	they shall **p.** my name upon the	7760
Nu	8:10	**p.** their hands upon the Levites:	5564
Nu	11:17	thee, and will **p.** it upon them;	7760
Nu	11:29	the Lord would **p.** his spirit upon	5414
Nu	15:34	they **p.** him in ward, because it	3240
Nu	15:35	The man shall be surely **p.** to death:	
Nu	15:38	**p.** upon the fringe of the borders	5414
Nu	16:7	And **p.** fire therein,	5414
Nu	16:7	**p.** incense in them before the	7760
Nu	16:14	thou **p.** out the eyes of these men?	5365
Nu	16:17	his censer, and **p.** incense in them,	5414
Nu	16:18	his censer, and **p.** fire in them,	5414
Nu	16:46	Take a censer, and **p.** fire therein	5414
Nu	16:46	off the altar, and **p.** on incense,	7760
Nu	16:47	and he **p.** on incense, and made an	5414
Nu	18:7	that cometh nigh shall be **p.** to death.	
Nu	19:17	running water shall be **p.** thereto	5414
Nu	20:26,	28 and **p.** them upon Eleazar his	3847
Nu	21:9	of brass, and **p.** it upon a pole, and	7760
Nu	23:5	Lord **p.** a word in Baalam's mouth,	7760
Nu	23:12	the Lord hath **p.** in my mouth?	7760
Nu	23:16	and **p.** a word in his mouth, and	7760
Nu	27:20	shalt **p.** some of thine honour upon	5414
Nu	35:16,	17, 18 shall surely be **p.** to death.	
Nu	35:21	smote him shall surely be **p.** to death;	
Nu	35:30	shall be **p.** to death by the mouth of	
Nu	35:31	but he shall be surely **p.** to death.	
Nu	36:3	shall be **p.** to the inheritance of	3254
Nu	36:4	their inheritance be **p.** unto the	3254
De	2:25	I begin to **p.** the dread of thee	5414
De	7:15	will **p.** none of the evil diseases of	7760
De	7:22	thy God will **p.** out those nations	5394
De	10:2	and thou shalt **p.** them in the ark.	7760
De	10:5	**p.** the tables in the ark which I had	7760
De	11:29	shalt **p.** the blessing upon mount	5414
De	12:5	your tribes to **p.** his name there,	7760
De	12:7	in all that ye **p.** your hand unto,	4916
De	12:21	hath chosen to **p.** his name there	7760
De	13:5	of dreams shall be **p.** to death;	
De	13:5	**p.** the evil away from the midst of	1197
De	13:9	be first upon him to **p.** him to death,	
De	16:9	beginnest to **p.** the sickle to the corn.	
De	17:6	that is worthy of death be **p.** to death;	
De	17:6	witness he shall not be **p.** to death,	
De	17:7	be first upon him to **p.** him to death,	
De	17:7	**p.** the evil away from among you.	1197
De	17:12	shalt **p.** away the evil from Israel.	1197
De	18:18	will **p.** my words in his mouth;	5414
De	19:13	**p.** away the guilt of innocent	1197
De	19:19	**p.** the evil away from among you.	1197
De	21:9	**p.** away the guilt of innocent blood	1197
De	21:13	**p.** the raiment of her captivity	5493
De	21:21	**p.** evil away from among you;	1197
De	21:22	he be to be **p.** to death, and thou hang	
De	22:5	a man **p.** on a woman's garment:	3847
De	22:19	may not **p.** her away all his days.	7971
De	22:21	**p.** evil away from among you.	1197
De	22:22	thou **p.** away evil from Israel.	1197
De	22:24	shalt **p.** away evil from among you.	1197
De	22:29	may not **p.** her away all his days.	7971
De	23:24	thou shalt not **p.** any in thy vessel.	5414
De	24:7	**p.** evil away from among you.	1197
De	24:16	fathers shall not be **p.** to death for the	
De	24:16	children be **p.** to death for the fathers:	
De	24:16	shall be **p.** to death for his own sin.	
De	25:6	his name be not **p.** out of Israel.	4229
De	26:2	shalt **p.** it in a basket, and shalt	7760
De	28:14	**p.** a yoke of iron upon the neck	5414
De	30:7	thy God will **p.** all these curses	5414
De	31:19	**p.** it in their mouths, that this	7760
De	31:26	law, and **p.** it in the side of the ark	7760
De	32:30	two **p.** ten thousand to flight, except	7760
De	33:10	they shall **p.** incense before thee,	7760

De 33:14 precious things **p.** forth by the.......... 1645
Jos 1:18 him, he shall be **p.** to death: ....
Jos 6:24 they **p.** into the treasury of the.......... 5414
Jos 7:6 and **p.** dust upon their heads. 5927
Jos 7:11 **p.** it even among their own stuff. 7760
Jos 10:24 **p.** your feet upon the necks of.......... 7760
Jos 10:24 **p.** their feet upon the necks of 7760
Jos 17:13 they **p.** the Canaanites to tribute;....... 5414
Jos 24:7 he **p.** darkness between you and........ 7760
Jos 24:14 and **p.** away the gods which your 5493
Jos 24:23 **p.** away, said he, the strange gods 5493
Jg 1:28 they **p.** the Canaanites to tribute,....... 7760
Jg 3:21 And Ehud **p.** forth his left hand,......... 7971
Jg 5:26 She **p.** her hand to the nail, and her ... 7971
Jg 6:19 flour: the flesh he **p.** in a basket, ... 7760
Jg 6:19 he **p.** the broth in a pot, and............ 7760
Jg 6:21 angel of the Lord **p.** forth the end...... 7971
Jg 6:31 be **p.** to death whilst it is yet morning:......
Jg 6:37 **p.** a fleece of wool in the floor; and 3322
Jg 7:16 **p.** a trumpet in every man's hand,...... 5414
Jg 8:27 **p.** it in his city, even in Ophrah: 3322
Jg 9:15 and **p.** your trust in my shadow; ....
Jg 9:26 of Shechem **p.** their confidence in him. ......
Jg 9:49 and **p.** them to the hold, and set........ 7760
Jg 10:16 **p.** away the strange gods from 5493
Jg 12:3 I **p.** my life in my hands, and............ 7760
Jg 14:12 I will now **p.** forth a riddle unto 2330
Jg 14:13 **P.** forth thy riddle, that we may 2330
Jg 14:16 **p.** forth a riddle unto the children....... 2330
Jg 15:4 and **p.** a firebrand in the midst........... 7760
Jg 15:15 and **p.** forth his hand, and took it, ... 7971
Jg 16:3 **p.** them upon his shoulders, and......... 7760
Jg 16:21 took him, and **p.** out his eyes, and 5365
Jg 18:7 **p.** them to shame in any thing; 3637
Jg 18:21 **p.** the little ones and the cattle 7760
Jg 20:13 Gibeah, that we may **p.** them to death, ...
Jg 20:13 and **p.** away evil from Israel. 1197
Jg 20:20 Israel **p.** themselves in array to fight.........
Jg 20:22 **p.** themselves in array the first day. ....
Jg 20:30 **p.** themselves in array against Gibeah,.......
Jg 20:33 **p.** themselves in array at Baal-tamar: ....
Jg 21:5 saying, He shall surely be **p.** to death. ......
Ru 3:3 and **p.** thy raiment upon thee, ... 7760
1Sa 1:14 **p.** away thy wine from thee. 5493
1Sa 2:36 **P.** me, I pray thee, into one of the 5596
1Sa 4:2 Philistines **p.** themselves in array, ...
1Sa 6:8 **p.** the jewels of gold, which ye.......... 7760
1Sa 6:15 and **p.** them on the great stone:.......... 7760
1Sa 7:3 then **p.** away the strange gods and 5493
1Sa 7:4 did **p.** away Baalim and Ashtaroth,...... 5493
1Sa 8:16 asses, and **p.** them to his work.......... 6213
1Sa 11:11 **p.** the people in three companies;........ 7760
1Sa 11:12 men, that we may **p.** them to death.........
1Sa 11:13 not a man be **p.** to death this day:...........
1Sa 14:26 no man **p.** his hand to his mouth: 5381
1Sa 14:27 he **p.** forth the end of the rod that 7971
1Sa 14:27 and **p.** his hand to his mouth; and....... 7725
1Sa 17:21 Philistines had **p.** the battle in array,.........
1Sa 17:38 **p.** an helmet of brass upon his........... 5414
1Sa 17:39 them. And David **p.** them off him. 5493
1Sa 17:40 **p.** them in a shepherd's bag which...... 7760
1Sa 17:49 And David **p.** his hand in his bag,....... 7971
1Sa 17:54 but he **p.** his armour in his tent. 7760
1Sa 19:5 For he did **p.** his life in his hand, ... 7760
1Sa 19:13 **p.** a pillow of goat's hair for his.......... 7760
1Sa 21:6 to **p.** hot bread in the day when it...... 7760
1Sa 22:17 king would not **p.** forth their hand 7971
1Sa 24:10 will not **p.** forth mine hand against...... 7971
1Sa 28:3 **p.** away those that had familiar 5493
1Sa 28:8 himself, and **p.** on other raiment, ... 3847
1Sa 28:21 I have **p.** my life in my hand, and....... 7760
1Sa 31:10 they **p.** his armour in the house of...... 7760
2Sa 1:24 who **p.** on ornaments of gold upon....... 5927
2Sa 3:34 bound, nor thy feet **p.** into fetters, ... 5056
2Sa 6:6 Uzzah **p.** forth his hand to the ark...... 7971
2Sa 7:15 Saul, whom I **p.** away before thee. 5493
2Sa 8:2 two lines measured he to **p.** to death, ...
2Sa 8:6 David **p.** garrisons in Syria of 7760
2Sa 8:14 And he **p.** garrisons in Edom;............ 7760
2Sa 8:14 all Edom **p.** he garrisons, and all 7760
2Sa 10:8 **p.** the battle in array at the entering ....
2Sa 10:9 **p.** them in array against the Syrians:........
2Sa 10:10 that he might **p.** them in array.................
2Sa 12:13 Lord also hath **p.** away thy sin;.......... 5674
2Sa 12:31 therein, and **p.** them under saws, ... 7760
2Sa 13:17 **P.** now this woman out from me, ... 7971
2Sa 13:19 Tamar **p.** ashes on her head, and....... 3947
2Sa 14:2 and **p.** on now mourning apparel,........ 3847
2Sa 14:3 Joab **p.** the words in her mouth. 7760
2Sa 14:19 he **p.** all these words in the mouth 7760
2Sa 15:5 he **p.** forth his hand, and took him,..... 7971
2Sa 17:23 **p.** his household in order, and hanged ....
2Sa 18:12 would I not **p.** forth mine hand 7971
2Sa 19:21 not Shimei be **p.** to death for this,...........
2Sa 19:22 there any man be **p.** to death this day.......
2Sa 20:3 **p.** them in ward, and fed them, ... 5414
2Sa 20:8 Joab's garment that he had **p.** on........ 3830
2Sa 21:9 were **p.** to death in the days of harvest, ...
1Ki 2:5 **p.** the blood of war upon his girdle 5414
1Ki 2:8 not **p.** thee to death with the sword..........
1Ki 2:24 Adonijah shall be **p.** to death this day. ....
1Ki 2:26 will not at this time **p.** thee to death, ...
1Ki 2:35 the king **p.** Benaiah the son of............ 5414
1Ki 2:35 priest did the king **p.** in the room of ... 5414
1Ki 5:3 **p.** them under the soles of his feet. 5414
1Ki 7:39 he **p.** five bases on the right side 5414
1Ki 7:51 **p.** among the treasures of the house... 5414
1Ki 8:9 which Moses **p.** there at Horeb, ... 3240
1Ki 9:3 built, to **p.** my name there for ever; ... 7760
1Ki 10:17 **p.** them in the house of the forest...... 5414
1Ki 10:24 which God had **p.** in his heart............ 5414
1Ki 11:36 chosen me to **p.** my name there. 7760
1Ki 12:4 heavy yoke which he **p.** upon us, ... 5414
1Ki 12:9 thy father did **p.** upon us lighter? 5414
1Ki 12:29 Beth-el, and the other **p.** he in Dan. ... 5414
1Ki 13:4 **p.** forth his hand from the altar, ... 7971
1Ki 13:4 hand, which he **p.** forth against 7971
1Ki 14:21 of Israel, to **p.** his name there. 7760
1Ki 18:23, 23 on wood, and **p.** no fire under: 7760
1Ki 18:25 of your gods, but **p.** no fire under. 7760
1Ki 18:33 And he **p.** the wood in order, and 6186
1Ki 18:42 and **p.** his face between his knees, ... 7760
1Ki 20:6 they shall **p.** it in their hand, and........ 7760
1Ki 20:24 and **p.** captains in their rooms:........... 7760
1Ki 20:31 pray thee, **p.** sackcloth on our loins, ... 7760
1Ki 20:32 loins, and **p.** ropes on their heads,............
1Ki 21:27 and **p.** sackcloth upon his flesh,.......... 7760
1Ki 22:10 throne, having **p.** on their robes,......... 3847
1Ki 22:23 hath **p.** a lying spirit in the mouth........ 5414
1Ki 22:27 **P.** this fellow in the prison, and......... 7760
1Ki 22:30 battle; but **p.** thou on thy robes. 3847
2Ki 2:20 a new curse, and **p.** salt therein........ 7760
2Ki 3:2 he **p.** away the image of Baal that 5493
2Ki 3:21 all that were able to **p.** on armour, ... 2296
2Ki 4:34 and **p.** his mouth upon his mouth,....... 7760
2Ki 6:7 he **p.** out his hand, and took it........... 7971
2Ki 9:13 and **p.** it under him on the top of 7760
2Ki 10:7 and **p.** their heads in baskets, and...... 7760
2Ki 11:12 king's son, and **p.** the crown upon...... 5414
2Ki 12:9 **p.** therein all the money that was....... 5414
2Ki 12:10 **p.** up in bags, and told the money 6695
2Ki 13:16 **P.** thine hand upon the bow. 7392
2Ki 13:16 And he **p.** his hand upon it: and 7760
2Ki 13:16 Elisha **p.** his hands upon the king's 7760
2Ki 14:6 not be **p.** to death for the children,..... 4191
2Ki 14:6 be **p.** to death for the fathers; 4191
2Ki 14:6 shall be **p.** to death for his own sin: 4191
2Ki 14:12 was **p.** to the worse before Israel;...........
2Ki 16:14 **p.** it on the north side of the altar. 5414
2Ki 16:17 **p.** it upon a pavement of stones......... 5414
2Ki 17:29 **p.** them in the houses of the high....... 3240
2Ki 18:11 **p.** them in Halah and in Habor 5148
2Ki 18:24 **p.** thy trust on Egypt for chariots and ....
2Ki 19:28 I will **p.** my hook in thy nose, and...... 7760
2Ki 21:4 In Jerusalem will I **p.** my name. 7760
2Ki 21:7 Israel, will I **p.** my name for ever:...... 7760
2Ki 23:5 he **p.** down the idolatrous priests, ... 7673
2Ki 23:24 did Josiah **p.** away, that he might 1197
2Ki 23:33 **p.** him in bands at Riblah in the...............
2Ki 23:33 **p.** the land to a tribute of an hundred........
2Ki 25:7 **p.** out the eyes of Zedekiah, and......... 5786
1Ch 5:20 because they **p.** their trust in him.............
1Ch 10:10 **p.** his armour in the house of their 7760
1Ch 11:19 men that have **p.** their lives in jeopardy?....
1Ch 12:15 and they **p.** to flight all them of the 7760
1Ch 13:9 Uzza **p.** forth his hand to hold the 7971
1Ch 13:10 because he **p.** his hand to the ark:....... 7971
1Ch 18:6 **p.** garrisons in Syria-damascus;.......... 7760
1Ch 18:13 And he **p.** garrisons in Edom; and 7760
1Ch 19:9 and **p.** the battle in array before the ....
1Ch 19:10 **p.** them in array against the Syrians.........
1Ch 19:16 they were **p.** to the worse before Israel, ...
1Ch 19:17 when David had **p.** the battle in array.......
1Ch 19:19 saw that they were **p.** to the worse..........
1Ch 21:27 and he **p.** up his sword again into 7725
1Ch 27:24 was the number **p.** in the account....... 5927
2Ch 1:5 he **p.** before the tabernacle of the 7760
2Ch 2:14 device which shall be **p.** to him, ... 5414
2Ch 3:16 **p.** them on the heads of the pillars; 5414
2Ch 3:16 and **p.** them on the chains................. 5414
2Ch 4:6 and **p.** five on the right hand, and....... 5414
2Ch 5:1 **p.** he among the treasures of the 5414
2Ch 5:10 two tables which Moses **p.** therein 5414
2Ch 6:11 in it have I **p.** the ark, wherein is....... 7760
2Ch 6:20 thou wouldest **p.** thy name there;....... 7760
2Ch 6:24 thy people Israel be **p.** to the worse ....
2Ch 9:16 And the king **p.** them in the house 5414
2Ch 9:23 wisdom...God had **p.** in his heart......... 5414
2Ch 10:4 his heavy yoke that he **p.** upon us, ... 5414
2Ch 10:9 yoke that thy father did **p.** upon us? ... 5414
2Ch 10:11 father **p.** a heavy yoke upon you, ... 6006
2Ch 10:11 you, I will **p.** more to your yoke: 3254
2Ch 11:11 holds, and **p.** captains in them, ... 5414
2Ch 11:12 several city he **p.** shields and spears, ...
2Ch 12:13 of Israel, to **p.** his name there. 7760
2Ch 15:8 **p.** away the abominable idols out 5674
2Ch 15:13 God of Israel should be **p.** to death,..........
2Ch 16:10 and **p.** him in a prison house; for......... 5414
2Ch 17:19 whom the king **p.** in the fences.......... 5414
2Ch 18:22 hath **p.** a lying spirit in the mouth........ 5414
2Ch 18:26 **P.** this fellow in the prison, and......... 7760
2Ch 18:29 battle; but **p.** thou on thy robes. 3847
2Ch 22:11 and **p.** him and his nurse in a 5414
2Ch 23:7 the house, he shall be **p.** to death: ....
2Ch 23:11 son, and **p.** upon him the crown, ... 5414
2Ch 25:22 was **p.** to the worse before Israel,............
2Ch 29:7 and **p.** out the lamps, and have not..... 3518
2Ch 33:7 Israel, will I **p.** my name for ever:...... 7760
2Ch 33:14 **p.** captains of war in all the fenced 7760
2Ch 34:10 **p.** it in the hand of the workmen......... 5414
2Ch 35:3 **P.** the holy ark in the house which..... 5414
2Ch 35:24 **p.** him in the second chariot that........ 7392
2Ch 36:3 Egypt **p.** him down at Jerusalem, ... 5493
2Ch 36:7 **p.** them in his temple at Babylon. 5414
2Ch 36:22 his kingdom, and **p.** it also in writing, ...
Ezr 1:1 his kingdom, and **p.** it also in writing, ...
Ezr 1:7 **p.** them in the house of his gods;....... 5414
Ezr 2:62 as polluted, **p.** from the priesthood. ....
Ezr 6:12 shall **p.** to their hand to alter and 7972
Ezr 7:27 **p.** such a thing as this in the king's..... 5414
Ezr 10:3 our God to **p.** away all the wives, ... 3318
Ezr 10:19 they would **p.** away their wives;......... 3318
Ne 2:12 **p.** in my heart to do at Jerusalem:...... 5414
Ne 3:5 **p.** not their necks to the work of......... 935
Ne 4:23 me, none of us **p.** off our clothes, ... 6584
Ne 4:23 every one **p.** them off for washing...... 7973
Ne 6:14 that would have **p.** me in fear. ....
Ne 6:19 Tobiah sent letters to **p.** me in fear. ....
Ne 7:5 And my God **p.** into mine heart to...... 5414
Ne 7:64 as polluted, **p.** from the priesthood. ....
Es 4:1 and **p.** on sackcloth with ashes,.......... 3847
Es 4:11 is one law of his to **p.** him to death, ...
Es 5:1 Esther **p.** on her royal apparel,.......... 3847
Es 8:3 to **p.** away the mischief of Haman......... 5674
Es 9:1 decree drew near to be **p.** in execution, ...
Job 1:11 But **p.** forth thine hand now, and........ 7971
Job 1:12 himself **p.** not forth thine hand........... 7971
Job 2:5 But **p.** forth thine hand now, and......... 7971
Job 4:18 Behold, he **p.** no trust in his servants; ......
Job 11:14 be in thine hand, **p.** it far away, ...
Job 13:14 and **p.** my life in mine hand?............. 7760
Job 17:3 now, **p.** me in a surety with thee; ....
Job 18:5 light of the wicked shall be **p.** out,...... 1846
Job 18:6 his candle shall be **p.** out with him. 1846
Job 19:13 hath **p.** my brethren far from me,.............
Job 21:17 is the candle of the wicked **p.** out!...... 1846
Job 22:23 **p.** away iniquity far from thy ....
Job 23:6 but he would **p.** strength in me........... 7760
Job 27:17 but the just shall **p.** it on, and the 3847
Job 29:14 I **p.** on righteousness, and it............. 3847
Job 38:36 **p.** wisdom in the inward parts? 7896
Job 41:2 thou **p.** an hook into his nose? 7760
Ps 2:12 are all they that **p.** their trust in him.........
Ps 4:5 and **p.** your trust in the Lord....................
Ps 4:7 Thou hast **p.** gladness in my heart,..... 5414
Ps 5:11 that **p.** their trust in thee rejoice: ....
Ps 7:1 Lord my God, in thee do I **p.** my trust:.....
Ps 8:6 hast **p.** all things under his feet:.......... 7896
Ps 9:5 thou hast **p.** out their name for.......... 4229
Ps 9:10 thy name will **p.** their trust in thee: ....
Ps 9:20 **P.** them in fear, O Lord: that the....... 7896

Ps 11:1 In the Lord **p.** my trust: how say ye ......
Ps 16:1 O God: for in thee do I **p.** my trust. ....
Ps 17:7 them which **p.** their trust in thee from.......
Ps 18:22 not **p.** away his statutes from me. 5493
Ps 25:20 be ashamed; for I **p.** my trust in thee. ......
Ps 27:9 **p.** not thy servant away in anger:....... 5186
Ps 30:11 thou hast **p.** off my sackcloth, and...... 6605
Ps 31:1 In thee, O Lord, do I **p.** my trust; let.......
Ps 31:18 Let the lying lips be **p.** to silence; ....
Ps 35:4 and **p.** to shame that seek after my ....
Ps 36:7 **p.** their trust under the shadow of thy.......
Ps 40:3 hath **p.** a new song in my mouth, ... 5414
Ps 40:14 and **p.** to shame that wish me evil. ....
Ps 44:7 hast **p.** them to shame that hated us. ....
Ps 44:9 thou hast cast off, and **p.** us to shame:......
Ps 53:5 thou hast **p.** them to shame, because........
Ps 55:20 He hath **p.** forth his hands against 7971
Ps 56:4 his word, in God I have **p.** my trust;..........
Ps 56:8 **p.** thou my tears into thy bottle: 5414
Ps 56:11 In God have I **p.** my trust: I will not........
Ps 70:2 backward, and **p.** to confusion,.................
Ps 71:1 In thee, O Lord, do I **p.** my trust: ....
Ps 71:1 trust; let me never be **p.** to confusion. ......
Ps 73:28 I have **p.** my trust in the Lord God, ... 7896
Ps 78:66 **p.** them to a perpetual reproach. 5414
Ps 83:17 yea, let them be **p.** to shame, and...........
Ps 88:8 hast **p.** away mine acquaintance.......... 7368
Ps 88:18 and friend, hast thou **p.** far from me, .. 7368
Ps 118:8 the Lord than to **p.** confidence in man. ......
Ps 118:9 Lord than to **p.** confidence in princes. ....
Ps 119:31 O Lord, **p.** me not to shame. ....
Ps 125:3 the righteous **p.** forth their hands....... 7971
Ps 146:3 **P.** not your trust in princes, nor in...........
Pr 4:24 **P.** away from thee a froward............ 5493
Pr 4:24 and perverse lips **p.** far from thee. 7368
Pr 8:1 understanding **p.** forth her voice? 5414
Pr 13:9 lamp of the wicked shall be **p.** out. 1846
Pr 20:20 shall be **p.** out in obscure darkness. 1846
Pr 23:2 And **p.** a knife to thy throat, if thou.... 7760
Pr 24:20 of the wicked shall be **p.** out. 1846
Pr 25:6 **P.** not forth thyself in the................ 1921
Pr 25:7 shouldest be **p.** lower in the presence ....
Pr 25:8 thy neighbour hath **p.** thee to shame. ....
Pr 25:10 he that heareth it **p.** thee to shame, ...
Pr 30:5 unto them that **p.** their trust in him. ....
Ec 3:14 nothing can be **p.** to it, nor any 3254
Ec 10:10 then must he **p.** to more strength: 1396
Ec 11:10 and **p.** away evil from thy flesh: 5674
Ca 5:3 I have **p.** off my coat; how shall I......... 6584
Ca 5:3 my coat; how shall I **p.** it on?............ 3847
Ca 5:4 beloved **p.** in his hand by the hole...... 7971
Isa 1:16 **p.** away the evil of your doings.......... 5493
Isa 5:20 **p.** darkness for light, and light for 7760
Isa 5:20 that **p.** bitter for sweet, and sweet....... 7760
Isa 10:13 **p.** down the inhabitants like a............ 3381
Isa 11:8 **p.** his hand on the cockatrice' den. 1911
Isa 20:2 and **p.** off thy shoe from thy foot. 2502
Isa 36:9 **p.** thy trust on Egypt for chariots and ....
Isa 37:29 will I **p.** my hook in thy nose, and...... 7760
Isa 42:1 I have **p.** my spirit upon him: he......... 5414
Isa 43:26 **P.** me in remembrance: let us plead ....
Isa 47:11 thou shalt not be able to **p.** it off:....... 3722
Isa 50:1 divorcement, whom I have **p.** away? ... 7971
Isa 50:1 transgressions is your mother **p.**......... 7971
Isa 51:9 **p.** on strength, O arm of the Lord;..... 3847
Isa 51:16 I have **p.** my words in thy mouth, ... 7760
Isa 51:23 **p.** it into the hand of them that.......... 7760
Isa 52:1 awake; **p.** on thy strength, O Zion;..... 3847
Isa 52:1 **p.** on thy beautiful garments, O 3847
Isa 53:10 he hath **p.** him to grief: when thou ....
Isa 54:4 for thou shalt not be **p.** to shame: ....
Isa 59:17 For he **p.** on righteousness as a......... 3847
Isa 59:17 he **p.** on the garments of vengeance ... 3847
Isa 59:21 which I have **p.** in thy mouth,............ 7760
Isa 63:11 that **p.** his holy Spirit within him?....... 7760
Jer 1:9 Then the Lord **p.** forth his hand,........ 7971
Jer 1:9 I have **p.** my words in thy mouth. 5414
Jer 3:1 If a man **p.** away his wife, and she 7971
Jer 3:8 I had **p.** her away, and given her 7971
Jer 3:19 How shall I **p.** thee among the........... 7896
Jer 4:1 **p.** away thine abominations out of....... 5493
Jer 7:21 **P.** your burnt offerings unto your....... 5595
Jer 8:14 the Lord our God hath **p.** us to silence,.....
Jer 12:13 they have **p.** themselves to pain, but.........
Jer 13:1 girdle, and **p.** it upon thy loins,.......... 7760
Jer 13:1 thy loins, and **p.** it not in water. 7760
Jer 13:2 of the Lord, and **p.** it on my loins. 7760
Jer 18:21 and let their men be **p.** to death; 2026
Jer 20:2 and **p.** him in the stocks that were 5414
Jer 26:15 that if ye **p.** me to death, ye shall ....
Jer 26:19 and all Judah **p.** him at all to death? ....
Jer 26:21 the king sought to **p.** him to death............
Jer 26:24 hand of the people to **p.** him to death........
Jer 27:2 yokes, and **p.** them upon thy neck,..... 5414
Jer 27:8 not **p.** their neck under the yoke of.... 5414
Jer 28:14 **p.** a yoke of iron upon the neck of...... 5414
Jer 29:26 thou shouldest **p.** him in prison, ... 5414
Jer 31:33 will **p.** my law in their inward parts,.... 5414
Jer 32:14 **p.** them in an earthen vessel, that...... 5414
Jer 32:40 I will **p.** my fear in their hearts,......... 5414
Jer 37:4 for they had not **p.** him into prison. 5414
Jer 37:15 **p.** him in prison in the house of......... 5414
Jer 37:18 that ye have **p.** me in prison?............ 5414
Jer 38:4 thee, let this man be **p.** to death: ....
Jer 38:7 had **p.** Jeremiah in the dungeon;.......... 5414
Jer 38:12 **P.** now these old cast clouts and........ 7760
Jer 38:15 wilt thou not surely **p.** me to death? ....
Jer 38:16 I will not **p.** thee to death, neither will......
Jer 38:25 us, and we will not **p.** thee to death;..........
Jer 39:7 Moreover he **p.** out Zedekiah's 5786
Jer 39:18 because thou hast **p.** thy trust in me,........
Jer 40:10 and **p.** them in your vessels, and........ 7760
Jer 43:3 that they might **p.** us to death, and...........
Jer 46:4 spears, and **p.** on the brigandines. 3847
Jer 47:6 **p.** up thyself into thy scabbard, ... 622
Jer 50:14 **P.** yourselves in array against.................
Jer 50:42 every one **p.** in array, like a man to..........
Jer 52:11 he **p.** out the eyes of Zedekiah; 5786
Jer 52:11 **p.** him in prison till the day of his....... 5411
Jer 52:27 **p.** them to death in Riblah in the land........
Eze 3:25 they shall **p.** bands upon thee, ... 5414
Eze 4:9 and **p.** them in one vessel, and.......... 5414
Eze 8:3 **p.** forth the form of an hand, and 7971
Eze 8:17 they **p.** the branch to their nose......... 7971
Eze 10:7 **p.** it into the hands of him that 5414
Eze 11:19 I will **p.** a new spirit within you; 5414
Eze 14:3 and **p.** the stumblingblock of their....... 5414
Eze 16:11 I **p.** bracelets upon thy hands, and....... 5414
Eze 16:12 I **p.** a jewel on thy forehead, and 5414
Eze 16:14 which I had **p.** upon thee,................. 7760
Eze 17:2 Son of man, **p.** forth a riddle, and....... 2330
Eze 19:9 they **p.** him in ward in chains, and....... 5414
Eze 22:26 **p.** no difference between the holy and.......
Eze 23:42 **p.** bracelets upon their hands, and...... 5414
Eze 24:17 **p.** on thy shoes upon thy feet, and..... 7760
Eze 26:16 **p.** off their broidered garments: 6584
Eze 29:4 I will **p.** hooks in thy jaws, and I......... 5414
Eze 30:13 will **p.** a fear in the land of Egypt. 5414
Eze 30:21 to **p.** a roller to bind it, to make it 7760
Eze 30:24 and **p.** my sword in his hand: but....... 5414
Eze 30:25 **p.** my sword into the hand of the 5414
Eze 32:7 when I shall **p.** thee out, I will........... 3518
Eze 32:25 **p.** in the midst of them that be.......... 5414
Eze 36:26 a new spirit will I **p.** within you: 5414
Eze 36:27 I will **p.** my spirit within you, and....... 5414
Eze 37:6 **p.** breath in you, and ye shall live;...... 5414
Eze 37:14 shall **p.** my spirit in you, and ye......... 5414
Eze 37:19 and will **p.** them with him, even......... 5414
Eze 38:4 back, and **p.** hooks into thy jaws, ... 5414
Eze 42:14 and shall **p.** on other garments,.......... 3847
Eze 43:9 let them **p.** away their whoredom, ... 7368
Eze 43:20 and **p.** it on the four horns of it, ... 5414
Eze 44:19 they shall **p.** off their garments 6584
Eze 44:19 they shall **p.** on other garments; 3847
Eze 44:22 a widow, nor her that is **p.** away:....... 1644
Eze 45:19 **p.** it upon the posts of the house, ... 5414
Da 5:19 and whom he would he **p.** down.......... 8214
Da 5:29 and **p.** a chain of gold about his neck,........
Ho 2:2 therefore **p.** away her whoredoms 5493
Joe 3:13 **P.** ye in the sickle, for the harvest..... 7971
Am 6:3 Ye that **p.** far away the evil day, and.........
Jon 3:5 a fast, and **p.** on sackcloth, from........ 3847
Mic 2:12 will **p.** them together as the sheep 7760
Mic 7:5 **p.** ye not confidence in a guide: ....
Zep 3:19 where they have been **p.** to shame. ....
Hag 1:6 wages to **p.** it into a bag with holes. ....
Mt 1:19 was minded to **p.** her away privily........ *630*
Mt 5:15 **candle, and p. it under a bushel,** ... *5087*
Mt 5:31 **Whosoever shall p. away his wife,**... *630*
Mt 5:32 **whosoever shall p. away his wife,** ... *630*
Mt 6:25 **for your body, what ye shall p. on.**..*1749*
Mt 8:3 And Jesus **p.** forth his hand, and *1614*
Mt 9:16 **which is p. in to fill it up taketh**.........
Mt 9:17 **men p. new wine into old bottles:**... *906*
Mt 9:17 **they p. new wine into new bottles,**.. *906*
Mt 9:25 when the people were **p.** forth, he *1544*
Mt 10:21 **and cause them to be p. to death**... *2289*
Mt 12:18 I will **p.** my spirit upon him, and *5087*
Mt 13:24, 31 parable **p.** he forth unto them,....... *3908*
Mt 14:3 **p.** him in prison for Herodias' sake, ... *5087*
Mt 14:5 he would have **p.** him to death, ... *615*
Mt 19:3 for a man to **p.** away his wife for......... *630*
Mt 19:6 **together, let not man p. asunder.** .. *5562*
Mt 19:7 divorcement, and to **p.** her away? *630*
Mt 19:8 **suffered you to p. away your wives:**.*630*
Mt 19:9 **Whosoever shall p. away his wife,**.. *630*
Mt 19:9 **marrieth her which is p. away doth**.*630*
Mt 19:13 he should **p.** his hands on them,......... *2007*
Mt 21:7 and **p.** on them their clothes, and....... *2007*
Mt 22:34 had **p.** the Sadducees to silence, ...
Mt 25:27 **p. my money to the exchangers,** *906*
Mt 26:52 **P. up again thy sword into his** *654*
Mt 26:59 against Jesus, to **p.** him to death;....... *2289*
Mt 27:1 against Jesus, to **p.** him to death:........ *2289*
Mt 27:6 for to **p.** them into the treasury,.......... *906*
Mt 27:28 him, and **p.** on him a scarlet robe......... *4060*
Mt 27:29 thorns, they **p.** it upon his head, ... *2007*
Mt 27:31 and **p.** his own raiment on him,.......... *1746*
Mt 27:48 **p.** it on a reed, and gave him to........ *4060*
Mk 1:14 after that John was **p.** in prison,......... *3860*
Mk 1:41 compassion, **p.** forth his hand, ... *1614*
Mk 2:22 **wine must be p. into new bottles.** ... *906*
Mk 4:21 **brought to be p. under a bushel,** ... *5087*
Mk 5:40 But when he had **p.** them all out, ... *1544*
Mk 6:9 sandals; and not **p.** on two coats. *1746*
Mk 7:32 beseech him to **p.** his hand upon *2007*
Mk 7:33 **p.** his fingers into his ears, and he *906*
Mk 8:23 **p.** his hands upon him, he asked *2007*
Mk 8:25 **p.** his hands again upon his eyes, ... *2007*
Mk 10:2 for a man to **p.** away his wife? *630*
Mk 10:4 divorcement, and to **p.** her away. *630*
Mk 10:9 **together, let not man p. asunder.** . *5562*
Mk 10:11 **shall p. away his wife, and marry**... *630*
Mk 10:12 **woman shall p. away her husband,** . *630*
Mk 10:16 **p.** his hands upon them, and............. *5087*
Mk 13:12 **shall cause them to be p. to death**..*2289*
Mk 14:1 him by craft, and **p.** him to death......... *615*
Mk 14:55 against Jesus to **p.** him to death;........ *2289*
Mk 15:17 thorns, and **p.** it about his head, ... *4060*
Mk 15:20 **p.** his own clothes on him, and led *1746*
Mk 15:36 full of vinegar, and **p.** it on a reed, ... *4060*
Lu 1:52 He hath **p.** down the mighty from....... *2507*
Lu 5:13 he **p.** forth his hand, and touched *1614*
Lu 5:38 **new wine must be p. into new**........ *906*
Lu 8:54 **p.** them all out, and took her by *1544*
Lu 9:62 **having p. his hand to the plough,**.. *1911*
Lu 12:22 **for the body, what ye shall p. on**... *1746*
Lu 14:7 And he **p.** forth a parable to those...... *3004*
Lu 15:22 **the best robe, and p. it on him;** ... *1746*
Lu 15:22 **p. a ring on his hand, and shoes** ... *1325*
Lu 16:4 **I am p. out of the stewardship,**..... *3179*
Lu 16:18 **that is p. away from her husband**... *630*
Lu 18:33 **scourge him, and p. him to death:**.. *615*
Lu 21:16 **shall they cause to be p. to death.**. *2289*
Lu 23:32 led with him to be **p.** to death.......... *337*
Joh 5:7 troubled, to **p.** me into the pool:.......... *906*
Joh 9:15 He **p.** clay upon mine eyes, and I....... *2007*
Joh 9:22 he should be **p.** out of the synagogue. ....
Joh 11:53 together for to **p.** him to death........... *615*
Joh 12:6 bag, and bare what was **p.** therein. *906*
Joh 12:10 might **p.** Lazarus also to death; *615*
Joh 12:42 should be **p.** out of the synagogue: *1096*
Joh 13:2 now **p.** into the heart of Judas............ *906*
Joh 16:2 **shall p. you out of the synagogues:***4160*
Joh 18:11 **P. up thy sword into the sheath:**.... *906*
Joh 18:31 for us to **p.** any man to death: *615*
Joh 19:2 of thorns, and **p.** it on his head,......... *2007*
Joh 19:2 and they **p.** on him a purple robe, ... *4016*
Joh 19:19 a title, and **p.** it on the cross............ *5087*
Joh 19:29 vinegar, and **p.** it upon hyssop, ... *4060*
Joh 19:29 and **p.** it to his mouth..................... *4374*
Joh 20:25 **p.** my finger into the print of the *906*
Ac 1:7 **Father hath p. in his own power.**.. *5087*
Ac 4:3 **p.** them in hold unto the next day: *5087*
Ac 5:18 and **p.** them in the common prison........ *5087*
Ac 5:25 the men whom ye **p.** in prison are...... *5087*
Ac 5:34 **p.** the apostles forth a little space;...... *4160*
Ac 7:33 **P.** off thy shoes from thy feet: *3089*
Ac 9:40 But Peter **p.** them all forth, and......... *1544*

Ac 12:4 him, he **p.** him in prison, *5087*
Ac 12:19 that they should be **p.** to death. *520*
Ac 13:46 seeing ye **p.** it from you, and judge *683*
Ac 15:9 **p.** no difference between us and *1252*
Ac 15:10 to **p.** a yoke upon the neck of the *2007*
Ac 26:10 when they were **p.** to death, I gave *337*
Ac 27:6 into Italy; and he **p.** us therein. *1688*
Ro 13:12 let us **p.** on the armour of light. *1746*
Ro 13:14 But **p.** ye on the Lord Jesus Christ, *1746*
Ro 14:13 that no man **p.** a stumblingblock *5087*
1Co 5:13 **p.** away from among yourselves *1808*
1Co 7:11 not the husband **p.** away his wife. *863*
1Co 7:12 with him, let him not **p.** her away. *863*
1Co 13:11 a man, I **p.** away childish things. *2673*
1Co 15:24 he shall have **p.** down all rule and *2673*
1Co 15:25 hath **p.** all enemies under his feet. *5087*
1Co 15:27 hath **p.** all things under his feet. *5293*
1Co 15:27 saith all things are **p.** under him, *5293*
1Co 15:27 which did **p.** all things under him. *5293*
1Co 15:28 subject unto him that **p.** all things *5293*
1Co 15:53 corruptible must **p.**...incorruption, *1746*
1Co 15:53 this mortal must **p.** on immortality. *1746*
1Co 15:54 shall have **p.** on incorruption, and *1746*
1Co 15:54 mortal shall have **p.** on immortality, *1746*
2Co 3:13 which **p.** a vail over his face, that *5087*
2Co 8:16 which **p.** the same earnest care *1325*
Ga 3:27 into Christ have **p.** on Christ. *1746*
Eph 1:22 hath **p.** all things under his feet, *5293*
Eph 4:22 That ye **p.** off concerning the former *659*
Eph 4:24 that ye **p.** on the new man, which *1746*
Eph 4:31 evil speaking, be **p.** away from you, *142*
Eph 6:11 **P.** on the whole armour of God, *1746*
Col 3:8 also **p.** off all these; anger, wrath, *659*
Col 3:9 **p.** off the old man with his deeds; *554*
Col 3:10 have **p.** on the new man, which is *1746*
Col 3:12 **P.** on therefore, as the elect of God, *1746*
Col 3:14 above all these things **p.** on charity,
1Th 2:4 to be **p.** in trust with the gospel, *4160*
1Ti 1:19 having **p.** away concerning faith *683*
1Ti 4:6 **p.** the brethren in remembrance *5294*
2Ti 1:6 I **p.** thee in remembrance that *363*
2Ti 2:14 things **p.** them in remembrance, *5279*
Tit 3:1 **P.** them in mind to be subject to *5279*
Phm 18 ought, **p.** that on mine account; *1677*
Heb 2:5 **p.** in subjection the world to come, *5293*
Heb 2:8 **p.** all things in subjection under his *5293*
Heb 2:8 he **p.** all in subjection under him, *5293*
Heb 2:8 nothing that is not **p.** under him. *506*
Heb 2:8 not yet all things **p.** under him. *5293*
Heb 2:13 again, I will **p.** my trust in him. *3982*
Heb 6:6 and **p.** him to an open shame. *3856*
Heb 8:10 I will **p.** my laws into their mind, *1325*
Heb 9:26 to **p.** away sin by the sacrifice of *115*
Heb 10:16 I will **p.** my laws into their hearts, *1325*
Jas 3:3 we **p.** bits in the horses' mouths, *906*
1Pe 2:15 may **p.** to silence the ignorance of *5392*
1Pe 3:18 being **p.** to death in the flesh, but *2289*
2Pe 1:12 to **p.** you always in remembrance *5279*
2Pe 1:14 I must **p.** off this my tabernacle, *595*
Jude 5 therefore **p.** you in remembrance, *5279*
Re 2:24 **p.** upon you none other burden: *906*
Re 11:9 dead bodies to be **p.** in graves. *5087*
Re 17:17 **p.** in their hearts to fulfil his will, *1325*

PUT (put) See also PHUT.
1Ch 1:8 sons of Ham; Cush,...Mizraim, **P.**, 6316
Na 3:9 **P.** and Lubim were they helpers. 6316

PUTEOLI (pu-te'-o-li)
Ac 28:13 and we came the next day to **P.** *4223*

PUTIEL (pu'-te-el)
Ex 6:25 one of the daughters of **P.** to wife; 6317

PUTRIFYING
Isa 1:6 wounds, and bruises, and **p.** sores: 2961

PUTTEST
Nu 24:21 and thou **p.** thy nest in a rock. 7760
De 12:18 all that thou **p.** thine hands unto. 4916
De 15:10 in all that thou **p.** thine hand unto. 4916
2Ki 18:14 which thou **p.** on me will I bear. 5414
Job 13:27 Thou **p.** my feet also in the stocks, 7760
Ps 119:119 Thou **p.** away all the wicked of 7673
Hab 2:15 that **p.** thy bottle to him, and 5596

PUTTETH
Ex 30:33 **p.** any of it upon a stranger, shall 5414
Nu 22:8 word that God **p.** in thy mouth, 7760
De 25:11 and **p.** forth her hand, and taketh 7971
De 27:15 and **p.** it in a secret place. 7760
1Ki 20:11 boast himself as he that **p.** it off. 6605
Job 15:15 Behold, he **p.** no trust in his saints;
Job 28:9 **p.** forth his hand upon the rock; 7971
Job 33:11 He **p.** my feet in the stocks, he 7760
Ps 15:5 He that **p.** not out his money to 5414
Ps 75:7 he **p.** down one, and setteth up 8213
Pr 28:25 he that **p.** his trust in the Lord shall be
Pr 29:25 whoso **p.** his trust in the Lord shall be
Ca 2:13 fig tree **p.** forth her green figs, 2590
Isa 57:13 he that **p.** his trust in me shall
Jer 43:12 as a shepherd **p.** on his garment; 5844
La 3:29 He **p.** his mouth in the dust; if so 5414
Eze 14:4, 7 **p.** the stumblingblock of his 7760
Mic 3:5 he that **p.** not into their mouths, 5414
Mt 9:16 **p. a piece of new cloth unto an old** *1911*
Mt 24:32 **is yet tender, and p. forth leaves,** *1631*
Mk 2:22 **man p. new wine into old bottles:** *906*
Mk 4:29 **immediately he p. in the sickle,** *649*
Mk 13:28 **is yet tender, and p. forth leaves,** *1631*
Lu 5:36 **p. a piece of a new garment upon** *1911*
Lu 5:37 **man p. new wine into old bottles;** *906*
Lu 8:16 **with a vessel, or p. it under a bed:** *5087*
Lu 11:33 **a candle, p. it in a secret place,** *5087*
Lu 16:18 **Whosoever p. away his wife, and** *630*
Joh 10:4 **when he p. forth his own sheep,** *1544*

PUTTING
Ge 21:14 **p.** it on her shoulder, and the 7760
Le 16:21 **p.** them...the head of the goat, 5414
Jg 7:6 lapped, **p.** their hand to their mouth,
Isa 58:9 **p.** forth of the finger, and speaking 7971
Mal 2:16 Israel, saith that he hateth **p.** away: 7971
Ac 9:12 **coming in,...p. his hand on him,** *2007*
Ac 9:17 **p.** his hands on him said, Brother *2007*
Ac 19:33 the Jews **p.** him forward. And *4261*
Ro 15:15 as **p.** you in mind, because of the *1878*
Eph 4:25 Wherefore **p.** away lying, speak *659*
Col 2:11 **p.** off the body of the sins of the *555*
1Th 5:8 **p.** on the breastplate of faith and *1746*
1Ti 1:12 faithful, **p.** me into the ministry; *5087*
2Ti 1:6 in thee by the **p.** on of my hands. *1936*
1Pe 3:3 of gold, or of **p.** on of apparel; *1745*
1Pe 3:21 the **p.** away of the filth of the flesh, *595*
2Pe 1:13 you up by **p.** you in remembrance; *5279*

PYGARG
De 14:5 the wild goat, and the **p.**, and the 1787

Q.

QUAILS
Ex 16:13 pass, that at even the **q.** came up, 7958
Nu 11:31 brought **q.** from the sea, and let 7958
Nu 11:32 next day, and they gathered the **q.** 7958
Ps 105:40 people asked, and he brought **q.**, 7958

QUAKE See also EARTHQUAKE; QUAKED; QUAKING.
Joe 2:10 The earth shall **q.** before them; 7264
Na 1:5 The mountains **q.** at him, and the 7493
Mt 27:51 and the earth did **q.**, and the rocks *4579*
Heb 12:21 said, I exceedingly fear and **q.**:) *1790*

QUAKED
Ex 19:18 and the whole mount **q.** greatly. 2729
1Sa 14:15 also trembled, and the earth **q.**: 7264

QUAKING
Eze 12:18 Son of man, eat thy bread with **q.**, 7494
Da 10:7 but a great **q.** fell upon them, so 2731

QUANTITY
Isa 22:24 and the issue, all vessels of small **q.**

QUARREL
Le 26:25 avenge the **q.** of my covenant: 5359
2Ki 5:7 see how he seeketh a **q.** against me. 579
Mk 6:19 Herodias had a **q.** against him, *1758*
Col 3:13 if any man have a **q.** against any: *3437*

QUARRIES
Jg 3:19 from the **q.** that were by Gilgal, 6456
Jg 3:26 and passed beyond the **q.**, and 6456

QUARTER See also QUARTERS.
Ge 19:4 all the people from every **q.**: 7098
Nu 34:3 **q.** shall be from the wilderness 6285
Jos 15:5 north **q.** was from the bay of the sea 6285
Jos 18:14 of Judah: this was the west **q.** 6285
Jos 18:15 the south **q.** was from the end of 6285
Isa 47:15 shall wander every one to his **q.**; 5676
Isa 56:11 every one for his gain, from his **q.** 7098
Mk 1:45 they came to him from every **q.** *3836*

QUARTERS
Ex 13:7 leaven seen with thee in all thy **q.** 1366
De 22:12 upon the four **q.** of thy vesture, 3671
1Ch 9:24 In four **q.** were the porters, 7307
Jer 49:36 winds from the four **q.** of heaven, 7098
Eze 38:6 of Togarmah of the north **q.**, 3411
Ac 9:32 as Peter passed throughout all **q.**,
Ac 16:3 the Jews which were in those **q.**: *5117*
Ac 28:7 In the same **q.** were possessions *5117*
Re 20:8 are in the four **q.** of the earth, *1137*

QUARTUS (quar'-tus)
Ro 16:23 saluteth you, and **Q.** a brother. *2890*

QUATERNIONS
Ac 12:4 delivered him to four **q.** of soldiers *5069*

QUEEN See also QUEENS.
1Ki 10:1 the **q.** of Sheba heard of the fame 4436
1Ki 10:4 when the **q.** of Sheba had seen all 4436
1Ki 10:10 which the **q.** of Sheba gave to king 4436
1Ki 10:13 unto the **q.** of Sheba all her desire, 4436
1Ki 11:19 wife, the sister of Tahpenes the **q.** 1377
1Ki 15:13 even her he removed from being **q.**, 1377
2Ki 10:13 the king and the children of the **q.** 1377
2Ch 9:1 **q.** of Sheba heard of the fame of 4436
2Ch 9:3 **q.** of Sheba had seen the wisdom of 4436
2Ch 9:9 the **q.** of Sheba gave king Solomon. 4436
2Ch 9:12 Solomon gave to the **q.** of Sheba all 4436
2Ch 15:16 he removed her from being **q.**, 1377
Ne 2:6 me, (the **q.** also sitting by him,) 7694
Es 1:9 Vashti the **q.** made a feast for the 4436
Es 1:11 bring Vashti the **q.** before the king 4436
Es 1:12 the **q.** Vashti refused to come at the 4436
Es 1:15 do unto the **q.** Vashti according to 4436
Es 1:16 Vashti the **q.** hath not done wrong 4436
Es 1:17 deed of the **q.** shall come abroad 4436
Es 1:17 Vashti the **q.** to be brought in. 4436
Es 1:18 have heard of the deed of the **q.** 4436
Es 2:4 which pleaseth the king be **q.** 4427
Es 2:17 and made her **q.** instead of Vashti. 4427
Es 2:22 who told it unto Esther the **q.**; 4436
Es 4:4 was the **q.** exceedingly grieved; 4436
Es 5:2 Esther the **q.** standing in the court, 4436
Es 5:3 her, What wilt thou, **q.** Esther? 4436
Es 5:12 the **q.** did let no man come in with 4436
Es 7:1 came to banquet with Esther the **q.** 4436
Es 7:2 What is thy petition, **q.** Esther? 4436
Es 7:3 Esther the **q.** answered and said, 4436
Es 7:5 said unto Esther the **q.**, Who is he, 4436
Es 7:6 afraid before the king and the **q.** 4436
Es 7:7 request for his life to Esther the **q.**; 4436
Es 7:8 Will he force the **q.** also before me. 4436
Es 8:1 Jews' enemy unto Esther the **q.** 4436
Es 8:7 Ahasuerus said unto Esther the **q.**, 4436
Es 9:12 the king said unto Esther the **q.**, 4436
Es 9:29 Then Esther the **q.**, the daughter of 4436
Es 9:31 Esther the **q.** had enjoined them, 4436
Ps 45:9 right hand did stand the **q.** in gold 7694
Jer 7:18 to make cakes to the **q.** of heaven, 4446
Jer 13:18 Say unto the king and to the **q.**, 1377

Jer 29:2 king, and the q., and the eunuchs,...... 1377
Jer 44:17 incense unto the q. of heaven,.......... 4446
Jer 44:18 to burn incense to the q. of heaven, ... 4446
Jer 44:19 burned incense to the q. of heaven, ... 4446
Jer 44:25 to burn incense to the q. of heaven, ... 4446
Da 5:10 the q. by reason of the words of........ 4433
Da 5:10 the q. spake and said, O king, live 4433
Mt 12:42 **The q. of the south shall rise up in**..*938*
Lu 11:31 **The q. of the south shall rise up in**..*938*
Ac 8:27 under Candace q. of the Ethiopians, ... *938*
Re 18:7 for she saith in her heart, I sit a q.,..... *938*

QUEENS
Ca 6:8 are threescore q., and fourscore 4436
Ca 6:9 yea, the q. and the concubines, and.... 4436
Isa 49:23 and their q. thy nursing mothers: 8282

QUENCH See also QUENCHED; UNQUENCHABLE.
2Sa 14:7 they shall q. my coal which is left,...... 3518
2Sa 21:17 that thou q. not the light of Israel. 3518
Ps 104:11 the wild asses q. their thirst. 7665
Ca 8:7 Many waters cannot q. love, ... 3518
Isa 1:31 together, and none shall q. them........ 3518
Isa 42:3 the smoking flax shall he not q.: 3518
Jer 4:4 fire, and burn that none can q. it,....... 3518
Jer 21:12 fire, and burn that none can q. it,....... 3518
Am 5:6 there be none to q. it in Beth-el. 3518
Mt 12:20 and smoking flax shall he not q., ... *4570*
Eph 6:16 q. all the fiery darts of the wicked...... *4570*
1Th 5:19 Q. not the Spirit. *4570*

QUENCHED
Nu 11:2 unto the Lord, the fire was q.. 8257
2Ki 22:17 this place, and shall not be q.. 3518
2Ch 34:25 this place, and shall not be q.. 3518
Ps 118:12 they are q. as the fire of thorns:........ 1846
Isa 34:10 It shall not be q. night nor day; 3518
Isa 43:17 they are extinct, they are q. as tow.... 3518
Isa 66:24 die, neither shall their fire be q.;.......... 3518
Jer 7:20 it shall burn, and shall not be q.......... 3518
Jer 17:27 of Jerusalem, and it shall not be q. 3518
Eze 20:47 the flaming flame shall not be q.,......... 3518
Eze 20:48 have kindled it: it shall not be q......... 3518
Mk 9:43 **into the fire that never shall be q.** .. *762*
Mk 9:44 **dieth not, and the fire is not q.**....... *4570*
Mk 9:45 **into the fire that never shall be q.** .. *762*
Mk 9:46 **dieth not, and the fire is not q.**...... *4570*
Mk 9:48 **dieth not, and the fire is not q.**...... *4570*
Heb 11:34 Q. the violence of fire, escaped the *4570*

QUESTION See also QUESTIONED; QUESTIONING; QUESTIONS.
Mt 22:35 which was a lawyer, asked him a q.,.........
Mk 8:11 began to q. with him, seeking of........ *4802*
Mk 9:16 the scribes, **What q. ye with them?**..*4802*
Mk 11:29 **I will also ask of you one q., and**.. *3056*
Mk 12:34 man after that durst ask him any q.: ....
Lu 20:40 they durst not ask him any q. at all. ....
Joh 3:25 there arose a q. between some of...... *2214*
Ac 15:2 apostles and elders about this q.. .... *2213*
Ac 18:15 if it be a q. of words and names, ... *2213*
Ac 19:40 we are in danger to be called in q. *1458*
Ac 23:6 of the dead I am called in q.............. *2919*
Ac 24:21 I am called in q. by you this day. *2919*
1Co 10:25 asking no q. for conscience sake: ....
1Co 10:27 asking no q. for conscience sake. ....

QUESTIONED
2Ch 31:9 Hezekiah q. with the priests and........ 1875
Mk 1:27 that they q. among themselves, ... *4802*
Lu 23:9 he q. with him in many words; *1905*

QUESTIONING
Mk 9:10 q. one with another what the *4802*
Mk 9:14 them, and the scribes q. with them. ... *4802*

QUESTIONS
1Ki 10:1 came to prove him with hard q.......... 2420
1Ki 10:3 And Solomon told her all her q. 1697
2Ch 9:1 to prove Solomon with hard q. at....... 2420
2Ch 9:2 And Solomon told her all her q.: 1697
Mt 22:46 that day forth ask him any more q...........
Lu 2:46 hearing them, and asking them q........ *1905*
Ac 23:29 to be accused of q. of their law. *2213*
Ac 25:19 But had certain q. against him of........ *2213*
Ac 25:20 I doubted of such manner of q.,......... *2214*
Ac 26:3 to be expert in all customs and q. *2213*
1Ti 1:4 genealogies, which minister q., ... *2214*
1Ti 6:4 about q. and strifes of words,............ *2214*
2Ti 2:23 But foolish and unlearned q. avoid, ... *2214*
Tit 3:9 avoid foolish q., and genealogies,........ *2214*

QUICK See also ALIVE; LIVING; QUICKSANDS.
Le 13:10 there be q. raw flesh in the rising; 4241
Le 13:24 q. flesh that burneth have a white 4241
Nu 16:30 and they go down q. into the pit; 2416
Ps 55:15 and let them go down q. into hell: 2416
Ps 124:3 they had swallowed us up q., when 2416
Isa 11:3 shall make him of q. understanding ....
Ac 10:42 to be the Judge of q. and dead. *2198*
2Ti 4:1 shall judge he q. and the dead at......... *2198*
Heb 4:12 the word of God is q., and powerful, .. *2198*
1Pe 4:5 ready to judge the q. and the dead. *2198*

QUICKEN See also QUICKENED; QUICKENETH; QUICKENING.
Ps 71:20 sore troubles, shalt q. me again, ... 2421
Ps 80:18 q. us, and we will call upon thy 2421
Ps 119:25 q. thou me according to thy word....... 2421
Ps 119:37 vanity; and q. thou me in thy way. 2421
Ps 119:40 q. me in thy righteousness................ 2421
Ps 119:88 Q. me after thy lovingkindness; so 2421
Ps 119:107 q. me, O Lord, according unto thy 2421
Ps 119:149 q. me according to thy judgment. 2421
Ps 119:154 me: q. me according to thy word. 2421
Ps 119:156 q. me according to thy judgments....... 2421
Ps 119:159 q. me, O Lord, according to thy 2421
Ps 143:11 Q. me, O Lord, for thy name's sake;.. 2421
Ro 8:11 also q. your mortal bodies by his........ *2227*

QUICKENED
Ps 119:50 affliction: for thy word hath q. me. 2421
Ps 119:93 for with them thou hast q. me. 2421
1Co 15:36 that which thou sowest is not q., ... *2227*
Eph 2:1 you hath he q., who were dead................
Eph 2:5 hath q. us together with Christ, ... *4806*
Col 2:13 flesh, hath he q. together with him, ... *4806*
1Pe 3:18 in the flesh, but q. by the Spirit: *2227*

QUICKENETH
Joh 5:21 **raiseth up the dead, and q. them;**.. *2227*
Joh 5:21 **even so the Son q. whom he will.**.. *2227*
Joh 6:63 **It is the spirit that q.; the flesh** *2227*
Ro 4:17 even God, who q. the dead, and........ *2227*
1Ti 6:13 the sight of God, who q. all things,..... *2227*

QUICKENING
1Co 15:45 last Adam was made a q. spirit. *2227*

QUICKLY
Ge 18:6 Make ready q. three measures of....... 4116
Ge 27:20 is it that thou hast found it so q.,....... 4116
Ex 32:8 turned aside q. out of the way.......... 4118
Nu 16:46 go q. unto the congregation, and......... 4120
De 9:3 them out, and destroy them q., ... 4118
De 9:12 get thee down q. from hence; 4118
De 9:12 they are q. turned aside out of the..... 4118
De 9:16 had turned aside q. out of the way..... 4118
De 11:17 lest ye perish q. from off the good 4120
De 28:20 and until thou perish q.; because........ 4118
Jos 2:5 pursue after them q.; for ye shall....... 4118
Jos 8:19 the ambush arose q. out of their 4120
Jos 10:6 come up to us q., and save us, and.... 4120
Jos 23:16 ye shall perish q. from off the good 4120
Jg 2:17 they turned q. out of the way............ 4118
1Sa 20:19 then thou shalt go down q., and......... 3966
2Sa 17:16 Now therefore send q., and tell 4120
2Sa 17:18 they went both of them away q., ... 4120
2Sa 17:21 Arise, and pass q. over the water: 4120
2Ki 1:11 hath the king said, Come down q. 4120
2Ch 18:8 Fetch q. Micaiah the son of Imla. 4116
Ec 4:12 a threefold cord in not q. broken........ 4120
Mt 5:25 **Agree with thine adversary q.**,...... *5035*
Mt 28:7 And go q., and tell his disciples *5035*
Mt 28:8 departed q. from the sepulchre *5035*
Mk 16:8 they went out q., and fled from the *5035*
Lu 14:21 **Go out q. into the streets and**...... *5030*
Lu 16:6 **and sit down q., and write fifty**..... *5030*
Joh 11:29 she arose q., and came unto him........ *5035*
Joh 13:27 unto him, **That thou doest, do q.**..... *5032*
Ac 12:7 him up, saying, Arise up q......... *1722,5034*
Ac 22:18 **get thee q. out of Jerusalem:** .. *1722,5034*
Re 2:5 **or else I will come unto thee q.**,.... *5035*
Re 2:16 **or else I will come unto thee q.**,.... *5035*
Re 3:11 **Behold, I come q.: hold that fast**... *5035*
Re 11:14 behold, the third woe cometh q.. .... *5035*
Re 22:7 **Behold, I come q.**: blessed is he...... *5035*
Re 22:12 **I come q.; and my reward is with**.. *5035*
Re 22:20 saith, **Surely I come q.**. Amen......... *5035*

QUICKSANDS
Ac 27:17 lest they should fall into the q., ... *4950*

QUIET See also DISQUIET; QUIETED; QUIETETH.
Jg 16:2 were q. all the night, saying, In......... 2790
Jg 18:7 of the Zidonians, q. and secure; 8252
Jg 18:27 a people that were at q. and secure:... 8252
2Ki 11:20 rejoiced, and the city was in q.: 8252
1Ch 4:40 the land was wide, and q., and 8252
2Ch 14:1 his days the land was q. ten years...... 8252
2Ch 14:5 the kingdom was q. before him.......... 8252
2Ch 20:30 the realm of Jehoshaphat was q.:........ 8252
2Ch 23:21 the city was q., after that they had..... 8252
Job 3:13 should I have lain still and been q.,..... 8252
Job 3:26 had I rest, neither was I q.;.............. 5117
Job 21:23 being wholly at ease and q................ 7961
Ps 35:20 them that are q. in the land. 7282
Ps 107:30 are they glad because they be q.;........ 8367
Pr 1:33 and shall be q. from fear of evil. 7599
Ec 9:17 of wise men are heard in q. more 5183
Isa 7:4 Take heed, and be q.; fear not, ... 8252
Isa 14:7 whole earth is at rest, and is q.: 8252
Isa 32:18 dwellings, and in q. resting places; 7600
Isa 33:20 shall see Jerusalem a q. habitation, ... 7600
Jer 30:10 shall be in rest, and be q., and 7599
Jer 47:6 how long will it be ere thou be q.? 8252
Jer 47:7 How can it be q., seeing the Lord...... 8252
Jer 49:23 sorrow on the sea; it cannot be q......... 8252
Jer 51:59 And this Seraiah was a q. prince. 4496
Eze 16:42 be q., and will be no more angry. 8252
Na 1:12 Though they be q., and likewise 8003
Ac 19:36 ye ought to be q., and to do *2687*
1Th 4:11 that ye study to be q., and to do *2270*
1Ti 2:2 may lead a q. and peaceable life......... *2263*
1Pe 3:4 ornament of a meek and q. spirit,....... *2272*

QUIETED
Ps 131:2 I have behaved and q. myself, ... 1826
Zec 6:8 have q. my spirit in the north............ 5117

QUIETETH
Job 37:17 he q. the earth by the south wind?..... 8252

QUIETLY
2Sa 3:27 in the gate to speak with him q., ... 7987
La 3:26 q. wait for the salvation of the Lord..........

QUIETNESS
Jg 8:28 the country was in q. forty years 8252
1Ch 22:9 will give peace and q. unto Israel....... 8253
Job 20:20 he shall not feel q. in his belly, ... 7961
Job 34:29 When he giveth q., who then can....... 8252
Pr 17:1 is a dry morsel, and q. therewith, ... 7962
Ec 4:6 Better is an handful with q., than....... 5183
Isa 30:15 in q. and in confidence shall be 8252
Isa 32:17 q. and assurance for ever. 8252
Ac 24:2 that by thee we enjoy great q., ... *1515*
2Th 3:12 that with q. they work, and eat *2271*

QUIT See also ACQUIT.
Ex 21:19 shall he that smote him be q............ 5352
Ex 21:28 the owner of the ox shall be q............ 5355
Jos 2:20 then we will be q. of thine oath 5355
1Sa 4:9 and q. yourselves like men,............... 1961
1Sa 4:9 q. yourselves like men, and fight..............
1Co 16:13 faith, q. you like men, be strong.......... *407*

QUITE
Ge 31:15 and hath q. devoured also our money........
Ex 23:24 and q. break down their images. ....
Nu 17:10 q. take away their murmurings 3615
Nu 33:52 q. plucked down all their high places: ....
2Sa 3:24 hast sent him away, and he is q. gone? .....
Job 6:13 and is wisdom driven q. from me?...... 5080
Hab 3:9 Thy bow was made q. naked,............ 6181

QUIVER See also QUIVERED.
Ge 27:3 thy weapons, thy q. and thy bow, ... 8522
Job 39:23 The q. rattleth against him, the........... 827
Ps 127:5 Happy is the man that hath his q........ 827
Isa 22:6 Elam bare the q. with chariot of......... 827
Isa 49:2 shaft; in his q. hath he hid me;........... 827
Jer 5:16 Their q. is as an open sepulchre,......... 827
La 3:13 of his q. to enter into my reins. 827

QUIVERED
Hab 3:16 trembled; my lips q. at the voice:....... 6750

R.

RAAMAH (ra'-a-mah)
Ge 10:7 and Havilah, and Sabtah, and **R.**,........ 7484
Ge 10:7 the sons of **R.**; Sheba, and Dedan...... 7484
1Ch 1:9 and Havilah, and Sabta, and **R.**, ... 7484
1Ch 1:9 the sons of **R.**; Sheba, and Dedan...... 7484
Eze 27:22 The merchants of Sheba and **R.**,........ 7484

RAAMIAH (ra-a-mi'-ah)
Ne 7:7 Azariah, **R.**, Nahamani, Mordecai, ... 7485

RAAMSES (ra-am'-seze) See also RAMESES.
Ex 1:11 treasure cities, Pithom, and **R.**......... 7486

RAB See RAB-MAG, RAB-SARIS; RAB-SHAKEH.

RABBAH (rab'-bah) See also RABBATH.
Jos 13:25 unto Aroer that is before **R.**; 7237
Jos 15:60 which is Kirjath-jearim, and **R.**;.......... 7237
2Sa 11:1 children of Ammon,...besieged **R.**........ 7237
2Sa 12:26 And Joab fought against **R.** of the....... 7237
2Sa 12:27 I have fought against **R.**, and have 7237
2Sa 12:29 went to **R.**, and fought against it,...... 7237
2Sa 17:27 that Shobi the son of Nahash of **R.**...... 7237
1Ch 20:1 Ammon, and came and besieged **R.**.... 7237
1Ch 20:1 Joab smote **R.**, and destroyed it......... 7237
Jer 49:2 an alarm of war to be heard in **R.** 7237
Jer 49:3 cry ye daughters of **R.**, gird you......... 7237
Eze 25:5 I will make **R.** a stable for camels, ... 7237
Am 1:14 will kindle a fire in the wall of **R.**, ... 7237

RABBATH (rab'-bath) See also RABBAH.
De 3:11 in **R.** of the children of Ammon? 7237
Eze 21:20 that the sword may come to **R.** 7237

RABBI (rab'-bi) See also RABBONI.
Mt 23:7 **and to be called of men, R., R.**..... *4461*
Mt 23:8 **But be not ye called R.: for one is**. *4461*
Joh 1:38 They said unto him, **R.**, (which is *4461*
Joh 1:49 him, **R.**, thou art the Son of God; *4461*
Joh 3:2 **R.**, we know...thou art a teacher *4461*
Joh 3:26 **R.**, he that was with thee beyond *4461*
Joh 6:25 **R.**, when camest thou hither?........... *4461*

RABBIM See BATH-RABBIM.

RABBITH (rab'-bith)
Jos 19:20 And **R.**, and Kishion, and Abez,......... 7245

RABBONI (rab-bo'-ni) See also RABBI.
Joh 20:16 herself, and saith unto him, **R.**; *4462*

RAB-MAG (rab'-mag)
Jer 39:3 Rab-saris, Nergal-sharezer, **R.**,.......... 7248
Jer 39:13 **R.**, and all the king of Babylon's 7248

RAB-SARIS (rab'-sa-ris)
2Ki 18:17 of Assyria sent Tartan and **R.** 7249
Jer 39:3 **R.**, Nergal-sharezer, Rab-mag, ... 7249
Jer 39:13 **R.**, and Nergal-sharezer, Rab-mag,..... 7249

RAB-SHAKEH (rab'-sha-keh) See also RABSHAKEH.
2Ki 18:17 and **R.** from Lachish to king.............. 7262
2Ki 18:19 **R.** said unto them, Speak ye now....... 7262
2Ki 18:26 unto **R.**, Speak, I pray thee, to thy 7262
2Ki 18:27 **R.** said unto them, Hath my master.... 7262
2Ki 18:28 Then **R.** stood and cried with a loud... 7262
2Ki 18:37 and told him the words of **R.**............. 7262
2Ki 19:4 God will hear all the words of **R.**, ... 7262
2Ki 19:8 So **R.** returned, and found the king..... 7262

RABSHAKEH (rab'-sha-keh) See also RAB-SHAKEH.
Isa 36:2 **R.** from Lachish to Jerusalem 7262
Isa 36:4 **R.** said unto them, Say ye now to...... 7262
Isa 36:11 **R.**, Speak, I pray thee, unto thy........ 7262
Isa 36:12 **R.** said, Hath my master sent me 7262
Isa 36:13 **R.** stood, and cried with a loud......... 7262
Isa 36:22 rent, and told him the words of **R.**..... 7262
Isa 37:4 thy God will hear the words of **R.**, ... 7262
Isa 37:8 So **R.** returned, and found the king..... 7262

RACA (ra'-cah)
Mt 5:22 **shall say to his brother, R., shall**.. *4469*

RACE
Ps 19:5 as a strong man to run a **r.**.............. 734
Ec 9:11 the **r.** is not to the swift, nor the....... 4793
1Co 9:24 they which run in a **r.** run all, but *4712*
Heb 12:1 patience the **r.** that is set before us,...... *73*

RACHAB (ra'-kah) See also RAHAB.
Mt 1:5 Salmon begat Booz of **R.**; and *4477*

RACHAL (ra'-kal)
1Sa 30:29 And to them which were in **R.**, ... 7403

RACHEL (ra'-chel) See also RACHEL'S; RAHEL.
Ge 29:6 **R.** his daughter cometh with the........ 7354
Ge 29:9 **R.** came with her father's sheep: 7354
Ge 29:10 Jacob saw **R.** the daughter of Laban.... 7354
Ge 29:11 Jacob kissed **R.**, and lifted up his 7354
Ge 29:12 And Jacob told **R.** that he was her...... 7354
Ge 29:16 the name of the younger was **R.**....... 7354
Ge 29:17 **R.** was beautiful and well favoured...... 7354
Ge 29:18 And Jacob loved **R.**; and said, I 7354
Ge 29:18 will serve thee seven years for **R.**...... 7354
Ge 29:20 Jacob served seven years for **R.**; 7354
Ge 29:25 did I not serve with thee for **R.**? 7354
Ge 29:28 gave him **R.** his daughter to wife 7354
Ge 29:29 And Laban gave to **R.** his daughter..... 7354
Ge 29:30 he went in also unto **R.**, and he......... 7354
Ge 29:30 he loved also **R.** more than Leah, ... 7354
Ge 29:31 her womb: but **R.** was barren. 7354
Ge 30:1 when **R.** saw that she bare Jacob 7354
Ge 30:1 **R.** envied her sister; and said unto..... 7354
Ge 30:2 Jacob's anger...kindled against **R.**: 7354
Ge 30:6 **R.** said, God hath judged me, and...... 7354
Ge 30:8 And **R.** said, With great wrestlings...... 7354
Ge 30:14 **R.** said to Leah, Give me, I pray 7354
Ge 30:15 And **R.** said, Therefore he shall lie..... 7354
Ge 30:22 And God remembered **R.**, and God 7354
Ge 30:25 pass, when **R.** had borne Joseph, ... 7354
Ge 31:4 Jacob sent and called **R.** and Leah...... 7354
Ge 31:14 **R.** and Leah answered and said 7354
Ge 31:19 and **R.** had stolen the images that 7354
Ge 31:32 knew not that **R.** had stolen them. 7354
Ge 31:34 Now **R.** had taken the images, and..... 7354
Ge 33:1 children unto Leah, and unto **R.**,........ 7354
Ge 33:2 and **R.** and Joseph hindermost. 7354
Ge 33:7 after came Joseph near and **R.**,.......... 7354
Ge 35:16 and **R.** travailed, and she had hard 7354
Ge 35:19 **R.** dies, and was buried in the way..... 7354
Ge 35:24 sons of **R.**; Joseph, and Benjamin: 7354
Ge 46:19 The sons of **R.**, Jacob's wife; 7354
Ge 46:22 These are the sons of **R.**, which......... 7354
Ge 46:25 Laban gave unto **R.** his daughter,....... 7354
Ge 48:7 **R.** died by me in the land of Canaan... 7354
Ru 4:11 thine house like **R.** and like Leah, ... 7354
Mt 2:18 **R.** weeping for her children, and........ *4478*

RACHEL'S (ra'-chelz)
Ge 30:7 Bilhah **R.** maid conceived again, ... 7354
Ge 31:33 tent, and entered into **R.** tent. 7354
Ge 35:20 that is the pillar of **R.** grave unto 7354
Ge 35:25 the sons of Bilhah, **R.** handmaid;........ 7354
1Sa 10:2 shalt find two men by **R.** sepulchre..... 7354

RADDAI (rad'-dahee)
1Ch 2:14 Nethaneel the fourth, **R.** the fifth, ... 7288

RAFTERS
Ca 1:17 house are cedar, and our **r.** of fir. 7351

RAG See RAGGED; RAGS.

RAGAU (ra'-gaw) See also REU.
Lu 3:35 Saruch, which was the son of **R.**,....... *4466*

RAGE See also OUTRAGEOUS; RAGED; RAGETH; RAGING.
2Ki 5:12 he turned and went away in a **r.**. 2534
2Ki 19:27 coming in, and thy **r.** against me. 7264
2Ki 19:28 Because thy **r.** against me and thy...... 7264
2Ch 16:10 for he was in a **r.** with him because...... 2197
2Ch 28:9 slain them in a **r.** that reacheth 2197
Job 39:24 the ground with fierceness and **r.**: 7267
Job 40:11 Cast abroad the **r.** of thy wrath: 5678
Ps 2:1 Why do the heathen **r.**, and the 7283
Ps 7:6 because of the **r.** of mine enemies: 5678
Pr 6:34 For jealousy is the **r.** of a man: 2534
Pr 29:9 whether he **r.** or laugh, there is.......... 7264
Isa 37:28 coming in, and thy **r.** against me. 7264
Isa 37:29 Because thy **r.** against me, and thy..... 7264
Jer 46:9 ye horses; and **r.**, ye chariots;........... 1984
Da 3:13 Nebuchadnezzar in his **r.** and............. 7266
Ho 7:16 sword for the **r.** of their tongue: 2195
Na 2:4 The chariots shall **r.** in the streets,..... 1984
Ac 4:25 Why did the heathen **r.**, and the *5433*

RAGED
Ps 46:6 The heathen **r.**, the kingdoms............ 1993

RAGETH
Pr 14:16 but the fool **r.**, and is confident.......... 5674

RAGGED
Isa 2:21 into the tops of the **r.** rocks, for fear ....

RAGING
Ps 89:9 Thou rulest the **r.** of the sea:............ 1348
Pr 20:1 is a mocker, strong drink is **r.**: 1993
Jon 1:15 and the sea ceased from her **r.**. 2197
Lu 8:24 the wind and the **r.** of the water: *2830*
Jude 13 **R.** waves of the sea, foaming out.......... *66*

RAGS
Pr 23:21 shall clothe a man with **r.**. 7168
Isa 64:6 righteousnesses are as filthy **r.**;........... 899
Jer 38:11 old cast clouts and old rotten **r.**, ... 4418
Jer 38:12 and rotten **r.** under thine armholes 4418

RAGUEL (ra-gu'-el)
Nu 10:29 unto Hobab, the son of **R.** the.......... 7467

RAHAB (ra'-hab) See also RACHAB.
Jos 2:1 into an harlot's house, named **R.**,....... 7343
Jos 2:3 the king of Jericho sent unto **R.**,......... 7343
Jos 6:17 only **R.** the harlot shall live, she 7343
Jos 6:23 spies went in, and brought out **R.**, ... 7343
Jos 6:25 Joshua saved **R.** the harlot alive,......... 7343
Ps 87:4 make mention of **R.** and Babylon........ 7294
Ps 89:10 Thou hast broken **R.** in pieces, as...... 7294
Isa 51:9 Art thou not it that hath cut **R.**, ... 7294
Heb 11:31 By faith the harlot **R.** perished *4460*
Jas 2:25 was not **R.** the harlot justified by *4460*

RAHAM (ra'-ham)
1Ch 2:44 And Shema begat **R.**, the father of..... 7357

RAHEL (ra'-hel) See RACHEL.
Jer 31:15 **R.** weeping for her children.............. 7354

RAIL See also RAILED; RAILING.
2Ch 32:17 also letters to **r.** on the Lord God...... 2778

RAILED
1Sa 25:14 our master; and he **r.** on them. 5860
Mk 15:29 And they that passed by **r.** on him,...... *987*
Lu 23:39 which were hanged **r.** on him,............. *987*

RAILER
1Co 5:11 idolater, or a **r.**, or a drunkard, ... *3060*

RAILING See also RAILINGS.
1Pe 3:9 rendering evil for evil, or **r.** for **r.**: *3059*
2Pe 2:11 bring not **r.** accusation against............. *989*
Jude 9 bring against him a **r.** accusation, ... *988*

RAILINGS
1Ti 6:4 whereof cometh envy, strife, **r.**, evil *988*

RAIMENT
Ge 24:53 of gold, and **r.**, and gave them to 899
Ge 27:15 goodly **r.** of her eldest son Esau,......... 899
Ge 27:27 and he smelled the smell of his **r.**, ... 899
Ge 28:20 me bread to eat, and **r.** to put on, ... 899
Ge 41:14 changed his **r.**, and came in unto......... 8071
Ge 45:22 he gave each man changes of **r.**;........ 8071
Ge 45:22 of silver, and five changes of **r.**.......... 8071
Ex 3:22 of silver, and jewels of gold, and **r.**:..... 8071
Ex 12:35 of silver, and jewels of gold, and **r.**:..... 8071
Ex 21:10 her food, her **r.**, and her duty of......... 3682
Ex 22:9 for ass, for sheep, for **r.**, or for any ... 8008
Ex 22:26 take thy neighbour's **r.** to pledge,........ 8008
Ex 22:27 only, it is his **r.** for his skin:.............. 8071
Le 11:32 it be any vessel of wood, or **r.**, or....... 899
Nu 31:20 purify all your **r.**, and all that is.......... 899
De 8:4 Thy **r.** waxed not old upon thee,......... 8071
De 10:18 stranger, in giving him food and **r.**...... 8071
De 21:13 the **r.** of her captivity from off her,..... 8071
De 22:3 and so shalt thou do with his **r.**; 8071
De 24:13 that he may sleep in his own **r.**, ... 8008
De 24:17 nor take a widow's **r.** to pledge: 899
Jos 22:8 with iron, and with very much **r.**:....... 8008

Jg	3:16	under his r. upon his right thigh........	4055
Jg	8:26	purple r. that was on the kings of........	899
Ru	3:3	thee, and put thy r. upon thee,..........	8071
1Sa	28:8	and put on other r., and he went,........	899
2Ki	5:5	pieces of gold, and ten changes of r.. ...	899
2Ki	7:8	gold, and r., and went and hid it;.........	899
2Ch	9:24	vessels of gold, and r., harness, ...	8008
Es	4:4	and she sent r. to clothe Mordecai, ...	899
Job	27:16	dust, and prepare r. as the clay;	4403
Ps	45:14	unto the king in r. of needlework:	7553
Isa	14:19	as the r. of those that are slain,.........	3830
Isa	63:3	and I will stain all my r..	4403
Eze	16:13	thy r. was of fine linen, and silk,........	4403
Zec	3:4	will clothe thee with change of r..	4254
Mt	3:4	John had his r. of camel's hair, ...	*1742*
Mt	6:25	**than meat, and the body than r.?**··	*1742*
Mt	6:28	**And why take ye thought for r.?**··	*1742*
Mt	11:8	**to see? A man clothed in soft r.?**···	*2440*
Mt	17:2	his r. was white as the light.............	*2440*
Mt	27:31	put his own r. on him, and led him.....	*2440*
Mt	28:3	and his r. white as snow:	*1742*
Mk	9:3	his r. became shining, exceeding	*2440*
Lu	7:25	**to see? A man clothed in soft r.?**···	*2440*
Lu	9:29	his r. was white and glistering.	*2441*
Lu	10:30	**thieves, which stripped him of his r.,**···	
Lu	12:23	**meat, and the body is more than r**	*1742*
Lu	23:34	they parted his r., and cast lots.	*2440*
Joh	19:24	They parted my r. among them, ...	*2440*
Ac	18:6	he shook is r., and said unto them, ...	*2440*
Ac	22:20	kept the r. of them that slew him.......	*2440*
1Ti	6:8	And having food and r. let us be	*4629*
Jas	2:2	come in also a poor man in vile r.;	*2066*
Re	3:5	**same shall be clothed in white r.;**···	*2440*
Re	3:18	**and white r., that thou mayest be**···	*2440*
Re	4:4	elders sitting, clothed in white r.;......	*2440*

RAIN See also RAINBOW; RAINED.

Ge	2:5	not caused it to r. upon the earth,......	4305
Ge	7:4	I will cause it to r. upon the earth......	4305
Ge	7:12	the r. was upon the earth forty..........	1653
Ge	8:2	the r. from heaven was restrained;.....	1653
Ex	9:18	cause it to r. a very grievous hail,......	4305
Ex	9:33	r. was not poured upon the earth.......	4306
Ex	9:34	when Pharaoh saw that the r. and	4306
Ex	16:4	will r. bread from heaven for you;......	4305
Le	26:4	I will give you r. in due season,..........	1653
De	11:11	drinketh water of the r. of heaven:.....	4306
De	11:14	I will give you the r. of your land.......	4306
De	11:14	in his due season, the first r. and.......	4456
De	11:14	and the latter r., that thou mayest......	3138
De	11:17	up the heaven, that there be no r., ...	4306
De	28:12	the r. unto thy land in his season, ...	4306
De	28:24	make the r. of thy land powder and....	4306
De	32:2	My doctrine shall drop as the r., my...	4306
De	32:2	the small r. upon the tender herb,......	8164
1Sa	12:17	and he shall send thunder and r.;	4306
1Sa	12:18	the Lord sent thunder and r. that.......	4306
2Sa	1:21	neither let there be r., upon you,........	4306
2Sa	23:4	the earth by clear shining after r.........	4306
1Ki	8:35	is shut up, and there is no r.,............	4306
1Ki	8:36	and give r. upon thy land, which	4306
1Ki	17:1	shall not be dew nor r. these years, ...	4306
1Ki	17:7	there had been no r. in the land.........	1653
1Ki	17:14	the Lord sendeth r. upon the earth.....	1653
1Ki	18:1	and I will send r. upon the earth.........	1653
1Ki	18:41	is a sound of abundance of r.,............	1653
1Ki	18:44	thee down, that the r. stop thee not...	1653
1Ki	18:45	and wind, and there was a great r......	1653
2Ki	3:17	see wind, neither shall ye see r.;	1653
2Ch	6:26	is shut up, and there is no r.,............	4306
2Ch	6:27	send r. upon thy land, which thou	4306
2Ch	7:13	shut up heaven that there be no r., ...	4306
Ezr	10:9	of this matter, and for the great r..	1653
Ezr	10:13	it is a time of much r., and we are......	1653
Job	5:10	Who giveth r. upon the earth, and.......	4306
Job	20:23	r. it upon him while he is eating..........	4305
Job	28:26	When he made a decree for the r.,......	4306
Job	29:23	they waited for me as for the r.;........	4306
Job	29:23	mouth wide as for the latter r..	4456
Job	36:27	they pour down r. according to the.....	4306
Job	37:6	to the small r., and to the great r.	1653
Job	38:26	To cause it to r. on the earth,...........	4305
Job	38:28	Hath the r. a father? or who hath.......	4306
Ps	11:6	Upon the wicked he shall r. snares, ...	4305
Ps	68:9	didst nd a plentiful r., whereby..........	1653
Ps	72:6	come down like r. upon the mown.......	4306
Ps	84:6	a well; the r. also filleth the pools.	4175
Ps	105:32	He gave them hail for r., and	1653
Ps	135:7	he maketh lightnings for the r.;..........	4306
Ps	147:8	who prepareth r. for the earth,..........	4306
Pr	16:15	favour is as a cloud of the latter r..	4456
Pr	25:14	is like clouds and wind without r..	1653
Pr	25:23	The north wind driveth away r.: so....	1653
Pr	26:1	and as r. in harvest, so honour is.......	4306
Pr	28:3	sweeping r. which leaveth no food.......	4306
Ec	11:3	If the clouds be full of r., they...........	1653
Ec	12:2	nor the clouds return after the r.	1653
Ca	2:11	is past, the r. is over and gone;..........	1653
Isa	4:6	a covert from storm and from r..	4306
Isa	5:6	the clouds that they r. no	4305
Isa	5:6	clouds that they...no r. upon it.	4306
Isa	30:23	shall he give the r. of thy seed,.........	4306
Isa	44:14	an ash, and the r. doth nourish it.	1653
Isa	55:10	For as the r. cometh down, and the ...	1653
Jer	3:3	and there hath been no latter r.;........	4456
Jer	5:24	the Lord our God, that giveth r.,.........	1653
Jer	10:13	he maketh lightnings with r., and	4306
Jer	14:4	for there was no r. in the earth, ...	1653
Jer	14:22	of the Gentiles that can cause r.?	1653
Jer	51:16	he maketh lightnings with r., and	4306
Eze	1:28	is in the cloud in the day of r., ...	1653
Eze	38:22	I will r. upon him, and upon his	4305
Eze	38:22	an overflowing r., and great	1653
Ho	6:3	and he shall come unto us as the r., ...	1653
Ho	6:3	as the latter and former r. unto the....	3384
Ho	10:12	and r. righteousness upon you............	3384
Joe	2:23	you the former r. moderately, ...	4175
Joe	2:23	cause to come down for you the r.,....	1653
Joe	2:23	down for you...the former r.,............	4175
Joe	2:23	the latter r. in the first month.	4456
Am	4:7	have withholden the r. from you, ...	1653
Am	4:7	I caused it to r. upon one city,..........	4305
Am	4:7	it not to r. upon another city:............	4305
Zec	10:1	Ask ye of the Lord r. in the time of...	4306
Zec	10:1	of the latter r.; so the Lord shall	4456
Zec	10:1	and give them showers of r., to.........	4306
Zec	14:17	even upon them shall be no r..	4306
Zec	14:18	not up, and come not, that have no r.;......	
Mt	5:45	**sendeth r. on the just and on the**··	*1026*
Mt	7:25,	27 **And the r. descended, and the**···	*1028*
Ac	14:17	and gave us r. from heaven, and........	*5205*
Ac	28:2	because of the present r., and...........	*5205*
Heb	6:7	the earth which drinketh in the r.........	*5205*
Jas	5:7	he receive the early and latter r.........	*5205*
Jas	5:17	earnestly that it might not r.:	*1026*
Jas	5:18	again, and the heaven gave r.,...........	*5205*
Re	11:6	it r. not in the days of their.......	*1026,5205*

RAINBOW

Re	4:3	was a r. round about the throne,.........	*2463*
Re	10:1	a r. was upon his head, and his	*2463*

RAINED

Ge	19:24	r. upon Sodom and Gomorrah............	4305
Ex	9:23	r. hail upon the land of Egypt............	4305
Ps	78:24	r. down manna upon them to eat,.......	4305
Ps	78:27	He r. flesh also upon them as dust, ...	4305
Eze	22:24	r. upon in the day of indignation.........	1656
Am	4:7	one piece was r. upon, and the..........	4305
Am	4:7	whereupon it r. not withered..............	4305
Lu	17:29	**r. fire and brimstone from heaven,**·	*1026*
Jas	5:17	r. not on the earth for the space of....	*1026*

RAINY

Pr	27:15	r. day and contentious woman are	5464

RAISE See also RAISED; RAISETH; RAISING.

Ge	38:8	her, and r. up seed to thy brother......	6965
Ex	23:1	Thou shalt not r. a false report;.........	5375
De	18:15	God will r. up unto thee a Prophet.....	6965
De	18:18	I will r. them up a Prophet from........	6965
De	25:7	to r. up unto his brother a name........	6965
Jos	8:29	r. thereon a great heap of stones, ...	6965
Ru	4:5,	10 r. up the name of the dead upon....	6965
1Sa	2:35	will r. me up a faithful priest, that......	6965
2Sa	12:11	I will r. up evil against thee out of......	6965
2Sa	12:17	him, to r. him up from the earth:	6965
1Ki	14:14	Lord shall r. him up a king over..........	6965
1Ch	17:11	that I will r. up thy seed after thee, ...	6965
Job	3:8	ready to r. up their mourning............	5782
Job	19:12	and r. up their way against me, ...	5549
Job	30:12	they r. up against me the ways of......	5549
Ps	41:10	merciful unto me, and r. me up, ...	6965
Isa	15:5	shall r. up a cry of destruction...........	5782
Isa	29:3	and I will r. forts against thee.	6965
Isa	44:26	and I will r. up the decayed places	6965
Isa	49:6	servant to r. up the tribes of Jacob,....	6965
Isa	58:12	thou shalt r. up the foundation...........	6965
Isa	61:4	shall r. up the former desolations, ...	6965
Jer	23:5	r. unto David a righteous Branch,........	6965
Jer	30:9	king, whom I will r. up unto them.	6965
Jer	50:9	I will r. and cause to come up	5782
Jer	50:32	fall, and none shall r. him up:	6965
Jer	51:1	I will r. up against Babylon, and.........	5782
Eze	23:22	will r. up thy lovers against thee, ...	5782
Eze	34:29	I will r. up for them a plant of...........	6965
Ho	6:2	in the third day he will r. us up, and...	6965
Joe	3:7	I will r. them out of the place.............	5782
Am	5:2	land; there is none to r. her up.	6965
Am	6:14	I will r. up against you a nation,.........	6965
Am	9:11	day will I r. up the tabernacle of........	6965
Am	9:11	I will r. up his ruins, and I will	6965
Mic	5:5	we r. against him seven shepherds, ...	6965
Hab	1:3	that r. up strife and contention.	5375
Hab	1:6	lo, I r. up the Chaldeans, that	6965
Zec	11:16	will r. up a shepherd in the land,.........	6965
Mt	3:9	to r. up children unto Abraham.	*1453*
Mt	10:8	**cleanse the lepers, r. the dead,**···	*1453*
Mt	22:24	and r. up seed unto his brother..........	*450*
Mk	12:19	and r. up seed unto his brother...........	*1817*
Lu	3:8	to r. up children unto Abraham.	*1453*
Lu	20:28	and r. up seed unto his brother.	*1817*
Joh	2:19	**and in three days I will r. it up**···	*1453*
Joh	6:39	**r. it up again at the last day**·	*450*
Joh	6:40,	44,54 **will r. him up at the last day**·	*450*
Ac	2:30	r. up Christ to sit on his throne;	*450*
Ac	3:22	shall the Lord your God r. up unto	*450*
Ac	7:37	shall the Lord your God r. up unto	*450*
Ac	26:8	you, that God should r. the dead?	*1453*
1Co	6:14	will also r. up us by his own power. ...	*1825*
2Co	4:14	Jesus shall r. up us also by Jesus, ...	*1453*
Heb	11:19	that God was able to r. him up,..........	*1453*
Jas	5:15	sick, and the Lord shall r. him up;......	*1453*

RAISED

Ex	9:16	for this cause have I r. thee up, ...	5975
Jos	5:7	whom he r. up in their stead,............	6965
Jos	7:26	r. over him a great heap of stones	6965
Jg	2:16	Nevertheless the Lord r. up judges, ...	6965
Jg	2:18	when the Lord r. them up judges,......	6965
Jg	3:9	r. up a deliverer to the children of.......	6965
Jg	3:15	the Lord r. them up a deliverer,.........	6965
2Sa	23:1	the man who was r. up on high, ...	6965
1Ki	5:13	Solomon r. a levy out of all Israel;......	5927
1Ki	9:15	the levy which king Solomon r.;	5927
2Ch	32:5	and r. it up to the towers, and	5927
2Ch	33:14	and r. it up a very great height,.........	1361
Ezr	1:5	all them whose spirit God had r., ...	5782
Job	14:12	awake, nor be r. out of their sleep.....	5782
Ca	8:5	I r. thee up under the apple tree:	5782
Isa	14:9	r. up from their thrones all the...........	6965
Isa	23:13	they r. up the palaces thereof;...........	6209
Isa	41:2	Who r. up the righteous man from.......	5782
Isa	41:25	have r. up one from the north, and.....	5782
Isa	45:13	I have r. him up in righteousness, ...	5782
Jer	6:22	a great nation shall be r. from the	5782
Jer	25:32	a great whirlwind shall be r. from.......	5782
Jer	29:15	The Lord hath r. us up prophets........	6965
Jer	50:41	many kings shall be r. up from	5782
Jer	51:11	the Lord hath r. up the spirit of..........	5782
Da	7:5	and it r. up itself on one side, ...	6966
Am	2:11	I r. up of your sons for prophets,........	6965
Zec	2:13	is r. up out of his holy habitation........	5782
Zec	9:13	and r. up thy sons, O Zion, against.....	5782
Mt	1:24	Joseph being r. from sleep did as	*1326*
Mt	11:5	**the deaf hear, the dead are r. up,**··	*1453*
Mt	16:21	and be r. again the third day.	*1453*
Mt	17:23	**the third day he shall be r. again**·	*1453*
Lu	1:69	r. up an horn of salvation for us.........	*1453*
Lu	7:22	**the deaf hear, the dead are r., to**··	*1453*
Lu	9:22	**be slain, and be r. the third day**···	*1453*
Lu	20:37	**Now that the dead are r., even**·····	*1453*
Joh	12:1	dead, whom he r. from the dead.	*1453*
Joh	12:9	whom he had r. from the dead.	*1453*
Joh	12:17	r. him from the dead, bare record.	*1453*
Ac	2:24	Whom God hath r. up, having	*450*
Ac	2:32	This Jesus hath God r. up, whereof......	*450*
Ac	3:15	whom God hath r. from the dead;	*1453*
Ac	3:26	God, having r. up his Son Jesus, ...	*450*
Ac	4:10	whom God r. from the dead, even......	*1453*
Ac	5:30	God of our fathers r. up Jesus,..........	*1453*
Ac	10:40	Him God r. up the third day, and.......	*1453*

Ac 12:7 **r.** him up, saying, Arise up quickly. ... *1453*
Ac 13:22 he **r.** up unto them David to be *1453*
Ac 13:23 **r.** unto Israel a Saviour, Jesus: *1453*
Ac 13:30 But God **r.** him from the dead: *1453*
Ac 13:33 in that he hath **r.** up Jesus again; *450*
Ac 13:34 that he **r.** him up from the dead, ... *450*
Ac 13:37 he, whom God **r.** again, saw no *1453*
Ac 13:50 **r.** persecution against Paul and *1892*
Ac 17:31 that he hath **r.** him from the dead. *450*
Ro 4:24 believe on him that **r.** up Jesus *1453*
Ro 4:25 was **r.** again for our justification, ... *1453*
Ro 6:4 as Christ was **r.** up from the dead *1453*
Ro 6:9 Christ being **r.** from the dead dieth..... *1453*
Ro 7:4 to him who is **r.** from the dead, ... *1453*
Ro 8:11 him that **r.** up Jesus from the dead *1453*
Ro 8:11 he that **r.** up Christ from the dead...... *1453*
Ro 9:17 same purpose have I **r.** thee up, ... *1825*
Ro 10:9 God hath **r.** him from the dead, ... *1453*
1Co 6:14 God hath both **r.** up the Lord, and *1453*
1Co 15:15 of God that he **r.** up Christ: *1453*
1Co 15:15 whom he **r.** not up, if so be that the... *1453*
1Co 15:16 dead rise not, then is not Christ **r.**: *1453*
1Co 15:17 Christ be not **r.**, your faith is vain; *1453*
1Co 15:35 will say, How are the dead **r.** up? *1453*
1Co 15:42 corruption, it is **r.** in incorruption: *1453*
1Co 15:43 sown in dishonour, it is **r.** in glory:..... *1453*
1Co 15:43 sown in weakness; it is **r.** in power: ... *1453*
1Co 15:44 body; it is **r.** a spiritual body. *1453*
1Co 15:52 dead shall be **r.** incorruptible, and....... *1453*
2Co 4:14 that he which **r.** up the Lord *1453*
Ga 1:1 Father, who **r.** him from the dead;) *1453*
Eph 1:20 when he **r.** him from the dead, and..... *1453*
Eph 2:6 hath **r.** us up together, and made *4891*
Col 2:12 who hath **r.** him from the dead. *1453*
1Th 1:10 whom he **r.** from the dead, even....... *1453*
2Ti 2:8 seed of David was **r.** from the dead.... *1453*
Heb 11:35 received their dead **r.** to life again:....... *386*
1Pe 1:21 God, that **r.** him up from the dead,..... *1453*

RAISER
Da 11:20 up in his estate a **r.** of taxes 5674

RAISETH
1Sa 2:8 He **r.** up the poor out of the dust,...... 6965
Job 41:25 When he **r.** up himself, the 7613
Ps 107:25 and **r.** the stormy wind, which........... 5975
Ps 113:7 **r.** up the poor out of the dust,.......... 6965
Ps 145:14 **r.** up all those that be bowed down..... 2210
Ps 146:8 **r.** them that are bowed down: 2210
Joh 5:21 **For as the Father r. up the dead,**.. *1453*
2Co 1:9 but in God which **r.** the dead:............ *1453*

RAISING
Ho 7:4 from **r.** after he hath kneaded............ 5872
Ac 24:12 neither **r.** up the people, ... *4160,1999*

RAISINS
1Sa 25:18 an hundred clusters of **r.**, and two.......... 6778
1Sa 30:12 cake of figs, and two clusters of **r.**: 6778
2Sa 16:1 an hundred bunches of **r.**, and an 6778
1Ch 12:40 cakes of figs, and bunches of **r.**, and... 6778

RAKEM (ra'-kem)
1Ch 7:16 and his sons were Ulam and **R.**. 7552

RAKKATH (rah'-kath)
Jos 19:35 Hammath, **R.**, and Chinnereth, ... 7557

RAKKON (rak'-kon)
Jos 19:46 And Me-jarkon, and **R.**, with the........ 7542

RAM See also RAM; RAM'S; RAMS.
Ge 15:9 and a **r.** of three years old, and a 352
Ge 22:13 **r.** caught in a thicket by his horns:....... 352
Ge 22:13 Abraham went and took the **r.**, and...... 352
Ex 29:15 Thou shalt also take one **r.**; and 352
Ex 29:15 their hands upon the head of the **r.**. 352
Ex 29:16 And thou shalt slay the **r.**, and thou 352
Ex 29:17 thou shalt cut the **r.** in pieces, and...... 352
Ex 29:18 burn the whole **r.** upon the altar: 352
Ex 29:19 And thou shalt take the other **r.**; 352
Ex 29:19 their hands upon the head of the **r.**. 352
Ex 29:20 Then shalt thou kill the **r.**, and take 352
Ex 29:22 thou shalt take of the **r.** the fat and...... 352
Ex 29:22 for it is a **r.** of consecration: 352
Ex 29:26 of the **r.** of Aaron's consecration,.......... 352
Ex 29:27 of the **r.** of the consecration, even of.... 352
Ex 29:31 shalt take the **r.** of the consecration, ... 352
Ex 29:32 his sons shall eat the flesh of the **r.**, ... 352
Le 5:15 unto the Lord a **r.** without blemish....... 352
Le 5:16 wih the **r.** of the trespass offering,....... 352
Le 5:18 he shall bring a **r.** without blemish 352
Le 6:6 **r.** without blemish out of the flock, ... 352
Le 8:18 the **r.** for the burnt offering:.............. 352
Le 8:18 their hands upon the head of the **r.**. 352
Le 8:20 And he cut the **r.** into pieces; and....... 352
Le 8:21 burnt the whole **r.** upon the altar: 352
Le 8:22 the other **r.**, the **r.** of consecration: 352
Le 8:22 their hands upon the head of the **r.**. 352
Le 8:29 the **r.** of consecration it was Moses' 352
Le 9:2 a **r.** for a brunt offering, without.......... 352
Le 9:4 bullock and a **r.** for peace offerings,...... 352
Le 9:18 bullock and the **r.** for a sacrifice of...... 352
Le 9:19 the fat of the bullock and of the **r.**, ... 352
Le 16:3 and a **r.** for a burnt offering. 352
Le 16:5 and one **r.** for a burnt offering. 352
Le 19:21 even a **r.** for a trespass offering. 352
Le 19:22 with the **r.** of the trespass offering........ 352
Nu 5:8 the **r.** of the atonement, whereby an 352
Nu 6:14 one **r.** without blemish for peace.......... 352
Nu 6:17 he shall offer the **r.** for a sacrifice of 352
Nu 6:19 take the sodden shoulder of the **r.**, ... 352
Nu 7:15, 21,27,33,39,45,51,57,63,69,75,81
One young bullock, one **r.**, one 352
Nu 15:6 Or for a **r.**, thou shalt prepare for a 352
Nu 15:11 or for one **r.**, or for a lamb, or a kid. ... 352
Nu 23:2 on every altar a bullock and a **r.**. 352
Nu 23:4 upon every altar a bullock and a **r.**........ 352
Nu 23:14, 30 a bullock and a **r.** on every altar...... 352
Nu 28:11 two young bullocks, and one **r.**,.......... 352
Nu 28:12 mingled with oil, for one **r.**;................ 352
Nu 28:14 the third part of an hin unto a **r.**,......... 352
Nu 28:19 two young bullocks, and one **r.**, and..... 352
Nu 28:20 bullock, and two tenth deals for a **r.**;.... 352
Nu 28:27 two young bullocks, one **r.**, seven.......... 352
Nu 28:28 bullock, two tenth deals unto one **r.**, ... 352
Nu 29:2 one young bullock, one **r.**, and seven.... 352
Nu 29:3 bullock, and two tenth deals for a **r.**,.... 352
Nu 29:8 one young bullock, one **r.**, and seven.... 352
Nu 29:9 and two tenth deals to one **r.**,............. 352
Nu 29:14 two tenth deals to each **r.** of the two ... 352
Nu 29:36 one bullock, one **r.**, seven lambs of...... 352
Nu 29:37 offerings for the bullock, for the **r.**,...... 352
Ezr 10:19 a **r.** of the flock for their trespass. 352
Eze 43:23 a **r.** out of the flock without blemish,.... 352
Eze 43:25 and a **r.** out of the flock, without 352
Eze 45:24 and an ephah for a **r.**, and an hin of 352
Eze 46:4 blemish, and a **r.** without blemish......... 352
Eze 46:5 offering shall be an ephah for a **r.**, ... 352
Eze 46:6 blemish, and six lambs, and a **r.**: 352
Eze 46:7 an ephah for a **r.**, and for the lambs 352
Eze 46:11 an ephah to a **r.**, and to the lambs 352
Da 8:3 the river a **r.** which had two horns:...... 352
Da 8:4 I saw the **r.** pushing westward, and...... 352
Da 8:6 came to the **r.** that had two horns, ... 352
Da 8:7 I saw him come close unto the **r.**, ... 352
Da 8:7 and smote the **r.**, and brake his two...... 352
Da 8:7 and there was no power in the **r.** to...... 352
Da 8:7 could deliver the **r.** out of his hand........ 352
Da 8:20 The **r.** which thou sawest having 352

RAM (ram)
Ru 4:19 Hezron begat **R.**, and **R.** begat........... 7410
1Ch 2:9 Jerahmeel, and **R.**, and Chelubai. 7410
1Ch 2:10 And **R.** begat Amminadab; and........... 7410
1Ch 2:25 of Hezron were, **R.** the firstborn,....... 7410
1Ch 2:27 And the sons of **R.** the firstborn 7410
Job 32:2 the Buzite, of the kindred of **R.**: 7410

RAMA (ra'-mah) See also RAMAH.
Mt 2:18 In **R.** was there a voice heard, ... *4471*

RAMAH (ra'-mah) See also RAMA; RAMATH.
Jos 18:25 Gibeon, and **R.**, and Beeroth,............ 7414
Jos 19:29 And then the coast turneth to **R.**, ... 7414
Jos 19:36 And Adamah, and **R.**, and Hazor, ... 7414
Jg 4:5 between **R.** and Beth-el in mount....... 7414
Jg 19:13 lodge all night, in Gibeah, or in **R.**....... 7414
1Sa 1:19 and came to their house to **R.**: and 7414
1Sa 2:11 Elkanah went to **R.** to his house. 7414
1Sa 7:17 And his return was to **R.**; for there.... 7414
1Sa 8:4 and came to Samuel unto **R.**, ... 7414
1Sa 15:34 Then Samuel went to **R.**; and Saul 7414
1Sa 16:13 So Samuel rose up, and went to **R.**. 7414
1Sa 19:18 came to Samuel to **R.**, and told him.... 7414
1Sa 19:19 Behold, David is at Naioth in **R.**. 7414
1Sa 19:22 Then went he also to **R.**, and came.... 7414
1Sa 19:22 Behold, they be at Naioth in **R.**. 7414
1Sa 19:23 he went thither to Naioth in **R.**: and... 7414
1Sa 19:23 until he came to Naioth in **R.**. 7414
1Sa 20:1 David fled from Naioth in **R.**, and........ 7414
1Sa 22:6 abode in Gibeah under a tree in **R.**,.... 7414
1Sa 25:1 and buried him in his house at **R.**......... 7414
1Sa 28:3 buried him in **R.**, even in his own 7414
1Ki 15:17 up against Judah, and built **R.**,........... 7414
1Ki 15:21 that he left off building of **R.**, and........ 7414
1Ki 15:22 and they took away the stones of **R.**,... 7414
2Ki 8:29 the Syrians had given him at **R.**, ... 7414
2Ch 16:1 up against Judah, and built **R.**, to 7414
2Ch 16:5 he left off building of **R.**, and let his.... 7414
2Ch 16:6 they carried away the stones of **R.**,.... 7414
2Ch 22:6 wounds which were given him at **R.**, .. 7414
Ezr 2:26 The children of **R.** and Gaba, six........ 7414
Ne 7:30 men of **R.**, and Gaba, six hundred 7414
Ne 11:33 Hazor, **R.**, Gittaim, ... 7414
Isa 10:29 **R.** is afraid; Gibeah of Saul is fled. 7414
Jer 31:15 the Lord; A voice was heard in **R.**, ... 7414
Jer 40:1 the guard had let him go from **R.**, ... 7414
Ho 5:8 in Gibeah, and the trumpet in **R.**:........ 7414

RAMATH (ra'-math) See also RAMAH; RAMATHAIM-ZOPHIM; RAMATHITE; RAMATH-LEHI; RAMATH-MIZPEH; RAMOTH-GILEAD.
Jos 19:8 to Baalath-beer, **R.** of the south.......... 7418

RAMATHAIM-ZOPHIM (ram-a-tha''-im-zo'-fim)
1Sa 1:1 there was a certain man of **R.**, of....... 7436

RAMATHITE (ra'-math-ite)
1Ch 27:27 the vineyards was Shimei the **R.**:....... 7435

RAMATH-LEHI (ra''-math-le'-hi)
Jg 15:17 his hand, and called that place **R.**. 7437

RAMATH-MIZPEH (ra''-math-miz'-peh)
Jos 13:26 And from Heshbon unto **R.**, and 7434

RAMESES (ram'-e-seze) See also RAAMSES.
Ge 47:11 best of the land, in the land of **R.**, ... 7486
Ex 12:37 journeyed from **R.** to Succoth,........... 7486
Nu 33:3 And they departed from **R.** in the 7486
Nu 33:5 children of Israel removed from **R.**, ... 7486

RAMIAH (ra-mi'-ah)
Ezr 10:25 sons of Parosh; **R.**, and Jeziah,.......... 7422

RAMOTH (ra'-moth) See also JARMUTH; RAMAH; RAMOTH-GILEAD; REMETH.
De 4:43 and **R.** in Gilead, of the Gadites;........ 7216
Jos 20:8 **R.** in Gilead out of the tribe of Gad, ... 7216
Jos 21:38 **R.** in Gilead with her suburbs, to be... 7216
1Sa 30:27 to them which were in south **R.**,....... 7418
1Ki 22:3 Know ye that **R.** in Gilead is ours, ... 7216
1Ch 6:73 And **R.** with her suburbs, and Anem... 7216
1Ch 6:80 **R.** in Gilead with her suburbs, and 7216
Ezr 10:29 Adaiah, Jashub, and Sheal, and **R.**. 3406

RAMOTH-GILEAD (ra''-moth-ghil'-e-ad)
1Ki 4:13 The son of Geber, in **R.**; to him 7433
1Ki 22:4 thou go with me to battle to **R.**? 7433
1Ki 22:6 Shall I go against **R.** to battle, or 7433
1Ki 22:12 saying, Go up to **R.**, and prosper: 7433
1Ki 22:15 shall we go against **R.** to battle, or...... 7433
1Ki 22:20 that he may go up and fall at **R.**? 7433
1Ki 22:29 the king of Judah went up to **R.**.......... 7433
2Ki 8:28 against Hazael king of Syria in **R.**;...... 7433
2Ki 9:1 of oil in thine hand, and go to **R.**: 7433
2Ki 9:4 young man the prophet, went to **R.**..... 7433
2Ki 9:14 (Now Joram had kept **R.**, he and all.... 7433
2Ch 18:2 him to go up with him to **R.**............ 7433
2Ch 18:3 Judah, Wilt thou go with me to **R.**? 7433
2Ch 18:5 Shall we go to **R.** to battle, or shall.... 7433
2Ch 18:11 saying, Go up to **R.**, and prosper: 7433
2Ch 18:14 shall we go to **R.** to battle, or shall 7433
2Ch 18:19 that he may go up and fall at **R.**? 7433
2Ch 18:28 the king of Judah went up to **R.**......... 7433
2Ch 22:5 against Hazael king of Syria at **R.**: 7433

RAMPART
La 2:8 the **r.** and the wall to lament; 2426
Na 3:8 whose **r.** was the sea, and her wall 2426

RAM'S
Jos 6:5 make a long blast with the **r.** horn, ... 3104

RAMS See also RAMS'.
Ge 31:10 **r.** which leaped upon the cattle 6260
Ge 31:12 **r.** which leap upon the cattle 6260
Ge 31:38 and the **r.** of the flock have I not......... 352
Ge 32:14 two hundred ewes, and twenty **r.**, ... 352

Ex 29:1 and two **r.** without blemish, 352
Ex 29:3 with the bullock, and the two **r.** 352
Ex 35:23 red skins of **r.**, and badgers' skins, 352
Le 8:2 for the sin offering, and two **r.**, 352
Le 23:18 and one young bullock, and two **r.** 352
Nu 7:17, 23,29,35,41,47,53,59,65,71,77,83
five **r.**, five he goats, five lambs of
Nu 7:87 were twelve bullocks, the **r.** twelve, 352
Nu 7:88 and four bullocks, the **r.** sixty, 352
Nu 23:1 me here seven oxen and seven **r.** 352
Nu 23:29 here seven bullocks and seven **r.** 352
Nu 29:13 thirteen young bullocks, two **r.**, and 352
Nu 29:14 deals to each ram of the two **r.**, 352
Nu 29:17 offer twelve young bullocks, two **r.**, 352
Nu 29:18 offerings for the bullocks, for the **r.**, 352
Nu 29:20 third day eleven bullocks, two **r.**, 352
Nu 29:21 offerings for the bullocks, for the **r.**, 352
Nu 29:23 the fourth day ten bullocks, two **r.**, 352
Nu 29:24 offerings for the bullocks, for the **r.**, 352
Nu 29:26 the fifth day nine bullocks, two **r.**, 352
Nu 29:27 offerings for the bullocks, for the **r.**, 352
Nu 29:29 eight bullocks, two **r.**, and fourteen 352
Nu 29:30 offerings for the bullocks, for the **r.**, 352
Nu 29:32 seven bullocks, two **r.**, and fourteen 352
Nu 29:33 offerings for the bullocks, for the **r.**, 352
De 32:14 and **r.** of the breed of Bashan, and 352
1Sa 15:22 and to hearken than the fat of **r.** 352
2Ki 3:4 an hundred thousand **r.**, with the 352
1Ch 15:26 offered seven bullocks and seven **r.**, 352
1Ch 29:21 a thousand bullocks, a thousand **r.**, 352
2Ch 13:9 with a young bullock and seven **r.**, 352
2Ch 17:11 thousand and seven hundred **r.**, 352
2Ch 29:21 brought seven bullocks, and seven **r.**, 352
2Ch 29:22 when they had killed the **r.**, they 352
2Ch 29:32 an hundred **r.**, and two hundred 352
Ezr 6:9 of, both young bullocks, and **r.**, 1798
Ezr 6:17 two hundred **r.**, four hundred 1798
Ezr 7:17 with this money bullocks, **r.**, 1798
Ezr 8:35 ninety and six **r.**, seventy and 352
Job 42:8 now seven bullocks and seven **r.**, 352
Ps 66:15 of fatlings, with the incense of **r.**; 352
Ps 114:4 The mountains skipped like **r.**, and 352
Ps 114:6 mountains, that ye skipped like **r.**; 352
Isa 1:11 am full of the burnt offerings of **r.**, 352
Isa 34:6 with the fat of the kidneys of **r.**: 352
Isa 60:7 the **r.** of Nebaioth shall minister 352
Jer 51:40 slaughter, like **r.** with he goats 352
Eze 4:2 set battering **r.** against it round 3733
Eze 21:22 battering **r.** against the gates, 3733
Eze 27:21 occupied with thee in lambs, and **r.**, 352
Eze 34:17 between the **r.** and the he goats 352
Eze 39:18 of **r.**, of lambs, and of goats, of 352
Eze 45:23 and seven **r.** without blemish daily 352
Mic 6:7 be pleased with thousands of **r.**, 352

RAMS'

Ex 25:5 And **r.** skins dyed red, and badgers' 352
Ex 26:14 for the tent of **r.** skins dyed red, 352
Ex 35:7 And **r.** skins dyed red, and badgers' 352
Ex 36:19 for the tent of **r.** skins dyed red, 352
Ex 39:34 the covering of **r.** skins dyed red, 352
Jos 6:4 ark seven trumpets of **r.** horns: 3104
Jos 6:6 bear seven trumpets of **r.** horns 3104
Jos 6:8 the seven trumpets of **r.** horns 3104
Jos 6:13 bearing seven trumpets of **r.** horns 3104

RAN See also OVERRAN.

Ge 18:2 he **r.** to meet them from the tent 7323
Ge 18:7 Abraham **r.** unto the herd, and 7323
Ge 24:17 And the servants **r.** to meet her, 7323
Ge 24:20 and **r.** again unto the well to draw 7323
Ge 24:28 the damsel **r.**, and told them of her 7323
Ge 24:29 Laban **r.** out unto the man, unto 7323
Ge 29:12 son: and she **r.** and told her father. 7323
Ge 29:13 son, that he **r.** to meet him, and 7323
Ge 33:4 Esau **r.** to meet him, and embraced 7323
Ex 9:23 the fire **r.** along upon the ground; 1980
Nu 11:27 there **r.** a young man, and told 7323
Nu 16:47 and **r.** into the midst of the 7323
Jos 7:22 and they **r.** unto the tent; and, 7323
Jos 8:19 they **r.** as soon as he had stretched 7323
Jg 7:21 and all the host **r.**, and cried, and 7323
Jg 9:21 And Jotham **r.** away, and fled, and 5127
Jg 9:44 other companies **r.** upon all the 6584
Jg 13:10 the woman made haste, and **r.**, 7323
1Sa 3:5 And he **r.** unto Eli, and said, Here 7323
1Sa 4:12 And there **r.** a man of Benjamin 7323
1Sa 10:23 they **r.** and fetched him thence: and 7323
1Sa 17:22 and **r.** into the army, and came and 7323
1Sa 17:48 and **r.** toward the army to meet the 7323
1Sa 17:51 Therefore David **r.**, and stood upon 7323
1Sa 20:36 And as the lad **r.**, he shot an arrow 7323
2Sa 18:21 bowed himself unto Joab, and **r.** 7323
2Sa 18:23 Ahimaaz **r.** by the way of the plain, 7323
1Ki 2:39 of the servants of Shimei **r.** away 1272
1Ki 18:35 the water **r.** round about the altar; 7323
1Ki 18:46 **r.** before Ahab to the entrance of 7323
1Ki 19:20 left the oxen, and **r.** after Elijah, 7323
1Ki 22:35 the blood **r.** out of the wound into 3332
2Ch 32:4 the brook that **r.** through the 7857
Ps 77:2 my sore **r.** in the night, and 5064
Ps 105:41 **r.** in the dry places like a river. 1980
Ps 133:2 that **r.** down upon the beard, even 3331
Jer 23:21 sent these prophets, yet they **r.**: 7323
Eze 1:14 living creatures **r.** and returned 7519
Eze 47:2 **r.** out waters on the right side 6379
Da 8:6 **r.** unto him in the fury of his 7323
Mt 8:32 swine **r.** violently down a steep *3729*
Mt 27:48 straightway one of them **r.**, and *5143*
Mk 5:6 afar off, he **r.** and worshipped him, *5143*
Mk 5:13 **r.** violently down a steep place *3729*
Mk 6:33 **r.** afoot thither out of all cities, *4936*
Mk 6:55 And **r.** through the whole region *4063*
Mk 15:36 one **r.** and filled a spunge full of *5143*
Lu 8:33 herd **r.** violently down a steep *3729*
Lu 15:20 **r., and fell on his neck, and kissed.** *5143*
Lu 19:4 he **r.** before, and climbed up into *4390*
Lu 24:12 Peter, and **r.** unto the sepulchre; *5143*
Joh 20:4 So they **r.** both together: and the *5143*
Ac 3:11 people **r.** together unto them in *4936*
Ac 7:57 and **r.** upon him with one accord, *3729*
Ac 8:30 And Philip **r.** thither to him, and *4370*
Ac 12:14 the gate for gladness, but **r.** in, *1532*
Ac 14:14 **r.** in among the people, crying out, *1530*
Ac 21:30 and the people **r.** together: and *4890*
Ac 21:32 centurions, and **r.** down unto them: *2701*
Ac 27:41 they **r.** the ship aground; and the *2027*
Jude 11 and **r.** greedily after the error of *1632*

RANG

1Sa 4:5 shout, so that the earth **r.** again 1949
1Ki 1:45 rejoicing, so that the city **r.** again 1949

RANGE See also RANGING; RANGES.

Job 39:8 The **r.** of the mountains is his 3491

RANGES

Le 11:35 whether it be oven, or **r.** for pots, 3600
2Ki 11:8 he that cometh without the **r.**, let 7713
2Ki 11:15 Have her forth without the **r.**: and 7713
2Ch 23:14 Have her forth of the **r.**: and 7713

RANGING

Pr 28:15 As a roaring lion, and a **r.** bear; 8264

RANK See also RANKS.

Ge 41:5 up upon one stalk, **r.** and good. 1277
Ge 41:7 devoured the seven **r.** and full ears 1277
Nu 2:16 they shall set forth in the second **r.**
Nu 2:24 they shall go forward in the third **r.**
1Ch 12:33 thousand, which could keep **r.**: 5737
1Ch 12:38 men of war, that could keep **r.**, 4634

RANKS

1Ki 7:4,5 was against light in three **r.** 6471
Joe 2:7 and they shall not break their **r.**: 734
Mk 6:40 And they sat down in **r.**, by *4237*

RANSOM See also RANSOMED.

Ex 21:30 the **r.** of his life whatsoever is 6306
Ex 30:12 give every man a **r.** for his soul 3724
Job 33:24 down to the pit: I have found a **r.** 3724
Job 36:18 then a great **r.** cannot deliver thee. 3724
Ps 49:7 nor give to God a **r.** for him: 3724
Pr 6:35 He will not regard any **r.**; neither 3724
Pr 13:8 The **r.** of a man's life are his riches: 3724
Pr 21:18 The wicked shall be a **r.** for the 3724
Isa 43:3 I gave Egypt for thy **r.**, Ethiopia 3724
Ho 13:14 I will **r.** them from the poweof 6299
Mt 20:28 **and to give his life a r. for many.** *3083*
Mk 10:45 **and to give his life a r. for many.** *3083*
1Ti 2:6 Who gave himself a **r.** for all, to be *487*

RANSOMED

Isa 35:10 the **r.** of the Lord shall return, 6299
Isa 51:10 sea a way for the **r.** to pass over? 1350
Jer 31:11 **r.** him from the hand of him that 1350

RAPHA (ra'-fah) See also BETH-RAPHA; REPHAIAH.

1Ch 8:2 Nohah the fourth, and **R.** the fifth. 7498
1Ch 8:37 **R.** was his son, Eleasah his son, 7498

RAPHU (ra'-fu)

Nu 13:9 of Benjamin, Palti the son of **R.** 7505

RARE

Da 2:11 a **r.** thing that the king requireth, 3358

RASE

Ps 137:7 **R.** it, **r.** it, even to the foundation 6168

RASH

Ec 5:2 Be not **r.** with thy mouth, and let 926
Isa 32:4 **r.** shall understand knowledge, 4116

RASHLY

Ac 19:36 to be quiet, and to do nothing **r.** *4312*

RASOR

Nu 6:5 shall no **r.** come upon his head: 8593
Jg 13:5 and no **r.** shall come on his head: 4177
Jg 16:17 hath not come a **r.** upon mine head; 4177
1Sa 1:11 shall no **r.** come upon his head. 4177
Ps 52:2 like a sharp **r.**, working deceitfully. 8593
Isa 7:20 Lord shave with a **r.** that is hired, 8593
Eze 5:1 take thee a barber's **r.**, and cause it 8593

RATE

Ex 16:4 and gather a certain **r.** every day, 1697
1Ki 10:25 horses, and mules, a **r.** year by year. 1697
2Ki 25:30 of the king, a daily **r.** for every day, 1697
2Ch 8:13 Even after a certain **r.** every day, 1697
2Ch 9:24 horses, and mules, a **r.** year by year. 1697

RATHER

Jos 22:24 have not **r.** done it for fear of this
2Sa 10:3 hath not David **r.** sent his servants
2Ki 5:13 how much **r.** then, when he saith to
Job 7:15 strangling, and death **r.** than my life,
Job 32:2 he justified himself **r.** than God.
Job 36:21 hast thou chosen **r.** than affliction.
Ps 52:3 lying **r.** than to speak righteousness.
Ps 84:10 I had **r.** be a doorkeeper in the 977
Pr 8:10 and knowledge **r.** than choice gold. 408
Pr 16:16 understanding **r.** to be chosen than
Pr 17:12 a man, **r.** than a fool in his folly. 408
Pr 22:1 A good name is **r.** to be chosen than
Pr 22:1 loving favour **r.** than silver and gold.
Jer 8:3 And death shall be chosen **r.** than life
Mt 10:6 **But go r. to the lost sheep of the** *3123*
Mt 10:28 **r. fear him which is able to** *3123*
Mt 18:8 **r. than having two hands or two** *2228*
Mt 18:9 **r. than having two eyes to be cast.** *2228*
Mt 25:9 **go ye r. to them that sell, and buy** *3123*
Mt 27:24 but that **r.** a tumult was made, he *3123*
Mk 5:26 nothing bettered, but **r.** grew worse, *3123*
Mk 15:11 should **r.** release Barabbas unto *3123*
Lu 10:20 **but r. rejoice, because your names** *3123*
Lu 11:28 **Yea r., blessed are they that hear.** *3304*
Lu 11:41 **r. give alms of such things as ye** *4133*
Lu 12:31 **But r. seek ye the kingdom of** *4133*
Lu 12:51 **I tell you, Nay; but r. division:** *2228*
Lu 17:8 **And will not r. say unto him, Make**
Lu 18:14 **to his house justified r. than the other:**
Joh 3:19 **men loved darkness r. than light,** *3123*
Ac 5:29 We ought to obey God **r.** than men. *3123*
Ro 3:8 And not **r.**, (as we be slanderously
Ro 8:34 died, yea **r.**, that is risen again, *3123*
Ro 11:11 **r.** through their fall salvation is come
Ro 12:19 but **r.** give place unto wrath: for
Ro 14:13 but judge this **r.**, that no man put *3123*
1Co 5:2 puffed up, and have not **r.** mourned, *3123*
1Co 6:7 Why do ye not **r.** take wrong? why *3123*
1Co 6:7 **r.** suffer yourselves to be defrauded? *3123*
1Co 7:21 thou mayest be made free, use it **r.** *3123*
1Co 9:12 this power over you, are not we **r.**? *3123*
1Co 14:1 gifts, but **r.** that ye may prophesy. *3123*
1Co 14:5 tongues, but **r.** that ye prophesied: *3123*
1Co 14:19 I had **r.** speak five words with my *2309*
2Co 2:7 ye ought **r.** to forgive him, and *3123*
2Co 3:8 of the spirit be **r.** glorious? *3123*
2Co 5:8 **r.** to be absent from the body, and *3123*
2Co 12:9 will I **r.** glory in my infirmities, *3123*
Ga 4:9 known God, or **r.** are known of God, *3123*
Eph 4:28 but **r.** let him labour, working with *3123*
Eph 5:4 convenient: but **r.** giving of thanks *3123*
Eph 5:11 of darkness, but **r.** reprove them. *3123*
Php 1:12 fallen out **r.** unto the furtherance of *3123*

1Ti 1:4 **r.** than godly edifying which is in *3123*
1Ti 4:7 exercise thyself **r.** unto godliness.
1Ti 6:2 but **r.** do them service, because *3123*
Phm 9 Yet for love's sake I **r.** beseech thee, *3123*
Heb 11:25 Choosing **r.** to suffer affliction with *3123*
Heb 12:9 **r.** to be in subjection unto the Father *3123*
Heb 12:13 of the way; but let it **r.** be healed. *3123*
Heb 13:19 But I beseech you the **r.** to do this, *4056*
2Pe 1:10 Wherefore the **r.**, brethren, give *3123*

RATTLETH
Job 39:23 The quiver **r.** against him, the 7439

RATTLING
Na 3:2 the noise of the **r.** of the wheels, 7494

RAVEN See also RAVENING; RAVENS; RAVIN.
Ge 8:7 And he sent forth a **r.**, which went 6158
Le 11:15 Every **r.** after his kind; 6158
De 14:14 And every **r.** after his kind, 6158
Job 38:41 Who provideth for the **r.** his food? 6158
Ca 5:11 locks are bushy, and black as a **r.** 6158
Isa 34:11 owl also and the **r.** shall dwell in it: 6158

RAVENS
1Ki 17:4 the **r.** to feed thee there. 6158
1Ki 17:6 the **r.** brought him bread and flesh 6158
Ps 147:9 food, and to the young **r.** which cry. 6158
Pr 30:17 the **r.** of the valley shall pick it out, 6158
Lu 12:24 **Consider the r.: for thy neither** *2876*

RAVENING
Ps 22:13 mouths, as a **r.** and a roaring lion. 2963
Eze 22:25 like a roaring lion **r.** the prey; they 2963
Eze 22:27 are like wolves **r.** the prey, to shed 2963
Mt 7:15 **but inwardly they are r. wolves.** *727*
Lu 11:39 **part is full of r. and wickedness.** *724*

RAVENOUS
Isa 35:9 there, nor any **r.** beast shall go up 6530
Isa 46:11 Calling a **r.** bird from the east, the 5861
Eze 39:4 give thee unto the **r.** birds of every 5861

RAVIN See also RAVENING.
Ge 49:27 Benjamin shall **r.** as a wolf: in the 2963
Na 2:12 with prey, and his dens with **r.** 2966

RAVISHED
Pr 5:19 be thou **r.** always with her love. 7686
Pr 5:20 son, be **r.** with a strange woman, 7686
Ca 4:9 Thou hast **r.** my heart, my sister, 3823
Ca 4:9 thou hast **r.** my heart with one of 3823
Isa 13:16 shall be spoiled, and their wives **r.** 7693
La 5:11 They **r.** the women in Zion, and 6031
Zec 14:2 houses rifled, and the women **r.**; 7693

RAW
Ex 12:9 Eat not of it **r.**, nor sodden at all 4995
Le 13:10 be quick **r.** flesh in the rising; 2416
Le 13:14 But when **r.** flesh appeareth in him, 2416
Le 13:15 the priest shall see the **r.** flesh, and 2416
Le 13:15 for the **r.** flesh is unclean: it is a 2416
Le 13:16 Or if the **r.** flesh turn again, and be 2416
1Sa 2:15 have sodden flesh of thee, but **r.** 2416

RAZE See RASE.

RAZOR See RASOR.

REACH See also REACHED; REACHETH; REACHING.
Ge 11:4 tower, whose top may **r.** unto heaven;
Ex 26:28 boards shall **r.** from end to end. 1272
Ex 28:42 even unto the thighs shall they **r.** 1961
Le 26:5 threshing shall **r.** unto the vintage, 5381
Le 26:5 vintage shall **r.** unto…sowing time: 5381
Nu 34:11 shall **r.** unto the side of the sea of 4229
Nu 35:4 shall **r.** from the wall of the city and
Job 20:6 and his head **r.** unto the clouds; 5060
Isa 8:8 over, he shall **r.** even to the neck; 5060
Isa 30:28 overflowing stream, shall **r.** to the 2673
Jer 48:32 they **r.** even to the sea of Jazer: the 5060
Zec 14:5 the mountains shall **r.** unto Azal: 5060
Joh 20:27 **R. hither thy finger, and behold** *5342*
Joh 20:27 **r. hither thy hand, and thrust it** *5342*
2Co 10:13 us, a measure to **r.** even unto you. *2185*

REACHED
Ge 28:12 and the top of it **r.** to heaven: and 5060
Jos 19:11 Maralah, and **r.** to Dabbasheth, 6293
Jos 19:11 **r.** to the river…before Jokneam; 6293
Ru 2:14 and he **r.** her parched corn, and 6642
Da 4:11 the height thereof **r.** unto heaven, 4291
Da 4:20 whose height **r.** unto the heaven, 4291
2Co 10:14 as though we **r.** not unto you: for *2185*
Re 18:5 For her sins have **r.** unto heaven, *190*

REACHETH
Nu 21:30 unto Nophah, which **r.** unto Medeba.
Jos 19:22 And the coast **r.** to Tabor, and 6293
Jos 19:26 and **r.** to Carmel westward, and to 6293
Jos 19:27 and **r.** to Zebulun, and to the valley 6293
Jos 19:34 and **r.** to Zebulun on the south side, 6293
Jos 19:34 and **r.** to Asher on the west side, 6293
2Ch 28:9 in a rage that **r.** up unto heaven. 5060
Ps 36:5 thy faithfulness **r.** unto the clouds.
Ps 108:4 and thy truth **r.** unto the clouds.
Pr 31:20 **r.** forth her hands to the needy. 7971
Jer 4:10 the sword **r.** unto the soul. 5060
Jer 4:18 because it **r.** unto thine heart. 5060
Jer 51:9 for her judgment **r.** unto heaven, 5060
Da 4:22 is grown, and **r.** unto heaven, 4291

REACHING
2Ch 3:11 cubits, **r.** to the wall of the house: 5060
2Ch 3:11 **r.** to the wind of the other cherub. 5060
2Ch 3:12 cubits, **r.** to the wall of the house: 5060
Php 3:13 **r.** forth unto those things which *1901*

READ See READEST; READETH; READING.
Ex 24:7 **r.** in the audience of the people: 7121
De 17:19 **r.** therein all the days of his life: 7121
De 31:11 shalt **r.** this law before all Israel 7121
Jos 8:34 he **r.** all the words of the law, 7121
Jos 8:35 which Joshua **r.** not before all the 7121
2Ki 5:7 the king of Israel had **r.** the letter, 7121
2Ki 19:14 hand of the messengers, and **r.** it: 7121
2Ki 22:8 the book of Shaphan, and he **r.** it. 7121
2Ki 22:10 And Shaphan **r.** it before the king. 7121
2Ki 22:16 which the king of Judah hath **r.**: 7121
2Ki 23:2 he **r.** in their ears all the words of 7121
2Ch 34:18 And Shaphan **r.** it before the king. 7121
2Ch 34:24 have **r.** before the king of Judah: 7121
2Ch 34:30 he **r.** in their ears all the words of 7121
Ezr 4:18 hath been plainly **r.** before me. 7123
Ezr 4:23 Artaxerxes' letter was **r.** before 7123
Ne 8:3 And he **r.** therein before the street 7121
Ne 8:8 they **r.** in the book in the law of God 7121
Ne 8:18 he **r.** in the book of the law of God. 7121
Ne 9:3 **r.** in the book of the law of the Lord 7121
Ne 13:1 day they **r.** in the book of Moses 7121
Es 6:1 and they were **r.** before the king. 7121
Isa 29:11, 12 **R.** this, I pray thee: and he saith, 7121
Isa 34:16 out of the book of the Lord, and **r.**: 7121
Isa 37:14 hand of the messengers, and **r.** it: 7121
Jer 29:29 Zephaniah the priest **r.** this letter 7121
Jer 36:6 Therefore go thou, and **r.** in the roll, 7121
Jer 36:6 shalt **r.** them in the ears of all Judah 7121
Jer 36:10 **r.** Baruch in the book the words of 7121
Jer 36:13 when Baruch **r.** the book in the ears 7121
Jer 36:14 roll wherein thou hast **r.** in the ears 7121
Jer 36:15 Sit down now, and **r.** it in our ears. 7121
Jer 36:15 ears. So Baruch **r.** it in their ears. 7121
Jer 36:21 Jehudi **r.** it in the ears of the king, 7121
Jer 36:23 Jehudi had **r.** three or four leaves, 7121
Jer 51:61 see, and shalt **r.** all these words; 7121
Da 5:7 Whosoever shall **r.** this writing, 7123
Da 5:8 but they could not **r.** the writing, 7123
Da 5:15 that they should **r.** this writing, 7123
Da 5:16 now if thou canst **r.** the writing, and 7123
Da 5:17 I will **r.** the writing unto the king, 7123
Mt 12:3 **Have ye not r. what David did,** *314*
Mt 12:5 **Or have ye not r. in the law, how** *314*
Mt 19:4 **Have ye not r., that he which made** *314*
Mt 21:16 **have ye never r., Out of the mouth** *314*
Mt 21:42 **Did ye never r. in the scriptures,** *314*
Mt 22:31 **have ye not r. that which was** *314*
Mk 2:25 **Have ye never r. what David did,** *314*
Mk 12:10 **And have ye not r. this scripture;** *314*
Mk 12:26 **ye not r. in the book of Moses,** *314*
Lu 4:16 sabbath day, and stood up for to **r.** *314*
Lu 6:3 **Have ye not r. so much as this,** *314*
Joh 19:20 This title then **r.** many of the Jews: *314*
Ac 8:28 in his chariot **r.** Esaias the prophet. *314*
Ac 8:30 heard him **r.** the prophet Esaias, *314*
Ac 8:32 the scripture which he **r.** was this, *314*
Ac 13:27 prophets which are **r.** every sabbath *314*
Ac 15:21 being **r.** in the synagogues every *314*
Ac 15:31 when they had **r.**, they rejoiced *314*
Ac 23:34 when the governor had **r.** the letter, *314*
2Co 1:13 than what ye **r.** or acknowledge; *314*
2Co 3:2 our hearts, known and **r.** of all men: *314*
2Co 3:15 even unto this day, when Moses is **r.**, *314*
Eph 3:4 when ye **r.**, ye may understand my *314*
Col 4:16 when this epistle is **r.** among you, *314*
Col 4:16 that it be **r.** also in the church of the *314*
Col 4:16 **r.** the epistle from Laodicea. *314*
1Th 5:27 be **r.** unto all the holy brethren. *314*
Re 5:4 worthy to open and to **r.** the book, *314*

READEST
Lu 10:26 **is written in the law? how r. thou?** *314*
Ac 8:30 Understandest thou what thou **r.**? *314*

READETH
Hab 2:2 tables, that he may run that **r.** it. 7121
Mt 24:15 **(whoso r., let him understand:)** *314*
Mk 13:14 **(let him that r. understand,) then** *314*
Re 1:3 Blessed is he that **r.**, and they that *314*

READINESS
Ac 17:11 received the word with all **r.** of *4288*
2Co 8:11 that as there was a **r.** to will, so *4288*
2Co 10:6 a **r.** to revenge all disobedience, *2092*

READING
Ne 8:8 caused them to understand the **r.** 4744
Jer 36:8 **r.** in the book…words of the Lord 7121
Jer 51:63 hast made an end of **r.** this book, 7121
Ac 13:15 the **r.** of the law of the prophets *320*
2Co 3:14 away in the **r.** of the old testament; *320*
1Ti 4:13 Till I come, give attendance to **r.**, *320*

READY See also ALREADY.
Ge 18:6 Make **r.** quickly three measures 4116
Ge 43:16 men home, and slay, and make **r.**; 3559
Ge 43:25 made **r.** the present against Joseph 3559
Ge 46:29 And Joseph made **r.** his chariot, 631
Ex 14:6 he made **r.** his chariot, and took 631
Ex 17:4 they be almost **r.** to stone me. 5750
Ex 19:11 And be **r.** against the third day: 3559
Ex 19:15 people. Be **r.** against the third day: 3559
Ex 34:2 And be **r.** in the morning, and come 3559
Nu 32:17 But we ourselves will go **r.** armed 2363
De 1:41 ye were **r.** to go up into the hill. 1951
De 26:5 Syrian **r.** to perish was my father,
Jos 8:4 far from the city, but be ye all **r.**: 3559
Jg 6:19 Gideon went in, and made **r.** a kid,
Jg 13:15 we shall have made **r.** a kid for thee.
1Sa 25:18 and five sheep **r.** dressed, and five
2Sa 15:15 thy servants are **r.** to do whatsoever
2Sa 18:22 that thou hast no tidings **r.**? 4672
1Ki 6:7 was built on stone made **r.** before 8003
2Ki 9:21 And Joram said, Make **r.** 631
2Ki 9:21 And his chariot was made **r.** 631
1Ch 12:23 bands that were **r.** armed to the war,
1Ch 12:24 eight hundred, **r.** armed to the war.
1Ch 28:2 and had made **r.** for the building: 3559
2Ch 17:18 thousand **r.** prepared for the war.
2Ch 35:14 they made **r.** for themselves, 3559
Ezr 7:6 a **r.** scribe in the law of Moses, 4106
Ne 9:17 but thou art a God **r.** to pardon,
Es 3:14 they should be **r.** against that day. 6264
Es 8:13 Jews should be **r.** against that day 6264
Job 3:8 are **r.** to raise up their mourning. 6264
Job 12:5 He that is **r.** to slip with his feet 3559
Job 15:23 day of darkness is **r.** at his hand. 3559
Job 15:24 him, as a king **r.** to the battle. 6264
Job 15:28 which are **r.** to become heaps. 6257
Job 17:1 are extinct, the graves are **r.** for me.
Job 18:12 destruction shall be **r.** at his side. 3559
Job 29:13 blessing of him that was **r.** to perish
Job 32:19 it is **r.** to burst like new bottles.
Ps 7:12 hath bent his bow, and made it **r.** 3559
Ps 11:2 make **r.** their arrow upon the string, 3559
Ps 21:12 thou shalt make **r.** thine arrows 3559
Ps 38:17 I am **r.** to halt, and my sorrow is 3559
Ps 45:1 tongue is the pen of a **r.** writer. 4106
Ps 86:5 Lord, art good, and **r.** to forgive;
Ps 88:15 and **r.** to die from my youth up:
Pr 24:11 and those that are **r.** to be slain; 4131
Pr 31:6 drink unto him that is **r.** to perish, 4131
Ec 5:1 be more **r.** to hear, than to give 7138
Isa 27:13 **r.** to perish in the land of Assyria,
Isa 30:13 shall be to you as a breach **r.** to fall,
Isa 32:4 shall be **r.** to speak plainly. 4116
Isa 38:20 The Lord was **r.** to save me: therefore
Isa 41:7 saying, It is **r.** for the sodering: 2896
Isa 51:13 as if he were **r.** to destroy? and 3559
Eze 7:14 the trumpet, even to make all **r.**; 3559
Da 3:15 if ye be **r.** that at what time ye 6263

Ho 7:6 made **r.** their heart like an oven, 7126
Mt 22:4 **are killed, and all things are r.:** 2092
Mt 22:8 **The wedding is r., but they which** 2092
Mt 24:44 **Therefore be ye also r.: for in** 2092
Mt 25:10 **they that were r. went in with** 2092
Mt 26:19 and they made **r.** the passover. 2090
Mk 14:15 **prepared: there make r. for us** 2090
Mk 14:16 and they made **r.** the passover. 2090
Mk 14:38 **spirit truly is r., but the flesh** 4289
Lu 1:17 **r.** a people prepared for the Lord 2090
Lu 7:2 unto him, was sick, and **r.** to die 3195
Lu 9:52 Samaritans, to make **r.** for him. 2090
Lu 12:40 **Be ye therefore r. also: for the** 2092
Lu 14:17 **Come; for all things are now r** 2092
Lu 17:8 **Make r. wherewith I may sup,** 2090
Lu 22:12 **room furnished: there make r..** 2090
Lu 22:13 and they made **r.** the passover. 2090
Lu 22:33 Lord, I am **r.** to go with thee, both 2092
Joh 7:6 **come: but your time is alway r..** 2092
Ac 10:10 they made **r.**, he fell into a trance. 3903
Ac 20:7 **r.** to depart on the morrow; and 3195
Ac 21:13 I am **r.** not to be bound only, but 2093
Ac 23:15 he come near, are **r.** to kill him. 2092
Ac 23:21 now are they **r.**, looking for a 2092
Ac 23:23 Make **r.** two hundred soldiers to 2090
Ro 1:15 am **r.** to preach the gospel to you 4289
2Co 8:19 and declaration of your **r.** mind: 4288
2Co 9:2 Achaia was **r.** a year ago; and 3903
2Co 9:3 that, as I said, ye may be **r.**: 3903
2Co 9:5 that the same might be **r.**, as a 2092
2Co 10:16 line of things made **r.** to our hand. 2092
2Co 12:14 third time I am **r.** to come to you; 2093
1Ti 6:18 in good works, **r.** to distribute, 2130
2Ti 4:6 For I am now **r.** to be offered, and 4689
Tit 3:1 to be **r.** to every good work, 2092
Heb 8:13 waxeth old is **r.** to vanish away 1451
1Pe 1:5 **r.** to be revealed in the last time 2092
1Pe 3:15 and be **r.** always to give an answer 2092
1Pe 4:5 **r.** to judge the quick and the dead. 2093
1Pe 5:2 for filthy lucre, but of a **r.** mind; 4289
Re 3:2 **which remain, that are r. to die:** 3195
Re 12:4 the woman...**r.** to be delivered, 3195
Re 19:7 and his wife hath made herself **r.**. 2090

REAIA (re-ah'-yah) See also HAROEH; REAIAH.
1Ch 5:5 Micah his son, **R.** his son, Baal his 7211

REAIAH (re-ah'-yah) See also REAIA.
1Ch 4:2 And **R.** the son of Shobal begat 7211
Ezr 2:47 of Gahar, the children of **R.**, 7211
Ne 7:50 The children of **R.**, the children of 7211

REALM
2Ch 20:30 the **r.** of Jehoshaphat was quiet: 4438
Ezr 7:13 his priests and Levites, in my **r.**, 4437
Ezr 7:23 wrath against the **r.** of the king 4437
Da 1:20 astrologers that were in all his **r.**. 4438
Da 6:3 to set him over the whole **r.**. 4437
Da 9:1 king over the **r.** of the Chaldeans; 4438
Da 11:2 stir up all against the **r.** of Grecia 4438

REAP See also REAPED; REAPEST; REAPETH; REAPING.
Le 19:9 ye **r.** the harvest of your land, 7114
Le 19:9 shalt not wholly **r.** the corners of
Le 23:10 and shall **r.** the harvest thereof, 7114
Le 23:22 ye **r.** the harvest of your land, 7114
Le 25:5 of thy harvest thou shalt not **r.**, 7114
Le 25:11 neither **r.** that which groweth of 7114
Ru 2:9 eyes be on the field that they do **r.**, 7114
1Sa 8:12 his ground, and to **r.** his harvest, 7114
2Ki 19:29 in the third year sow ye, and **r.**, 7114
Job 4:8 and sow wickedness, **r.** the same. 7114
Job 24:6 **r.** every one his corn in the field: 7114
Ps 126:5 that sow in tears shall **r.** in joy. 7114
Pr 22:8 soweth iniquity shall **r.** vanity: 7114
Ec 11:4 regardeth the clouds shall not **r.** 7114
Isa 37:30 in the third year sow ye, and **r.**, 7114
Jer 12:13 sown wheat, but shall **r.** thorns: 7114
Ho 8:7 and they shall **r.** the whirlwind: 7114
Ho 10:12 in righteousness, **r.** in mercy; 7114
Mic 6:15 shalt sow, but thou shalt not **r.**; 7114
Mt 6:26 **neither do they r., nor gather** 2325
Mt 25:26 **I r. where I sowed not, and gather** 2325
Lu 12:24 **ravens: for they neither sow nor r** 2325
Joh 4:38 **to r. that whereon ye bestowed no** 2325
1Co 9:11 if we shall **r.** your carnal things? 2325
2Co 9:6 sparingly shall **r.** also sparingly; 2325
2Co 9:6 bountifully shall **r.**...bountifully. 2325
Ga 6:7 man soweth, that shall he also **r.** 2325
Ga 6:8 shall of the flesh **r.** corruption; 2325
Ga 6:8 of the Spirit **r.** life everlasting. 2325
Ga 6:9 for in due season we shall **r.**, if we 2325
Re 14:15 Thrust in thy sickle, and **r.**: for 2325
Re 14:15 for the time is come for thee to **r.**; 2325

REAPED
Ho 10:13 wickedness, ye have **r.** iniquity; 7114
Jas 5:4 who have **r.** down your fields, 270
Jas 5:4 the cries of them which have **r.** 2325
Re 14:16 the earth; and the earth was **r.** 2325

REAPER See also REAPERS.
Am 9:13 the plowman shall overtake the **r.**, 7114

REAPERS
Ru 2:3 gleaned in the field after the **r.**: 7114
Ru 2:4 said unto the **r.**, the Lord be with 7114
Ru 2:5 his servant that was set over the **r.**, 7114
Ru 2:6 the servant that was set over the **r.**, 7114
Ru 2:7 after the **r.** among the sheaves: 7114
Ru 2:14 And she sat beside the **r.**: and he 7114
2Ki 4:18 he went out to his father to the **r.** 7114
Mt 13:30 **I will say to the r., Gather ye** 2327
Mt 13:39 **world; and the r. are the angels** 2327

REAPEST
Le 23:22 corners of thy field when thou **r.**, 7114
Lu 19:21 **and r. that thou didst not sow** 2325

REAPETH
Isa 17:5 and **r.** the ears with his arm; 7114
Joh 4:36 **he that r. receiveth wages, and** 2325
Joh 4:36 **he that r. may rejoice together** 2325
Joh 4:37 **true, One soweth, and another r** 2325

REAPING
1Sa 6:13 were **r.** their wheat harvest in the 7114
Mt 25:24 **r. where thou hast not sown, and** 2325
Lu 19:22 **down, and r. that I did not sow:** 2325

REAR See also REARED; REREWARD.
Ex 26:30 thou shalt **r.** up the tabernacle 6965
Le 26:1 neither **r.** you up a standing image, 6965
2Sa 24:18 Go up, **r.** an altar unto the Lord in 6965
Joh 2:20 wilt thou **r.** it up in three days? 1453

REARED
Ex 40:17 that the tabernacle was **r.** up. 6965
Ex 40:18 Moses **r.** up the tabernacle, and 6965
Ex 40:18 bars thereof, and **r.** up his pillars. 6965
Ex 40:33 And he **r.** up the court round about 6965
Nu 9:15 day that the tabernacle was **r.** up 6965
2Sa 18:18 and **r.** up for himself a pillar, 5324
1Ki 16:32 And he **r.** up an altar for Baal in 6965
2Ki 21:3 and he **r.** up altars for Baal, and 6965
2Ch 3:17 And he **r.** up the pillars before the 6965
2Ch 33:3 and he **r.** up altars for Baalim, and 6965

REASON See also REASONABLE; REASONED; REASONING; REASONS.
Ge 41:31 in the land by **r.** of that famine 6440
Ge 47:13 Canaan fainted by **r.** of the famine. 6440
Ex 2:23 Israel sighed by **r.** of the bondage, 4480
Ex 2:23 up unto God by **r.** of the bondage, 4480
Ex 3:7 cry by **r.** of their taskmasters; 6440
Ex 8:24 corrupted by **r.** of the swarm of flies 6440
Nu 9:10 shall be unclean by **r.** of a dead body,
Nu 18:8 I given them by **r.** of the anointing,
Nu 18:32 And ye shall bear no sin by **r.** of 5921
De 5:5 for ye were afraid by **r.** of the fire, 6440
De 23:10 that is not clean by **r.** of uncleanness
Jos 9:13 old by **r.** of the very long journey
Jg 2:18 by **r.** of them that oppressed them
1Sa 12:7 may **r.** with you before the Lord 8199
1Ki 9:15 this is the **r.** of the levy which 1697
1Ki 14:4 for his eyes were set by **r.** of his age.
2Ch 5:14 stand to minister by **r.** of the 6440
2Ch 20:15 by **r.** of this great multitude; 6440
2Ch 21:15 fall out by **r.** of the sickness day 4480
2Ch 21:19 fell out by **r.** of his sickness: 5973
Job 6:16 which are blackish by **r.** of the ice, 4480
Job 9:14 choose out my words to **r.** with him?
Job 13:3 and I desire to **r.** with God. 3198
Job 15:3 Should he **r.** with unprofitable talk? 3198
Job 17:7 Mine eye also is dim by **r.** of sorrow,
Job 31:23 and by **r.** of his highness I could not
Job 35:9 By **r.** of the multitude of oppressions
Job 35:9 cry out by **r.** of the arm of the mighty.
Job 37:19 our speech by **r.** of darkness. 6440
Job 41:25 by **r.** of breakings...purify themselves
Ps 38:8 have roared by **r.** of the disquietness
Ps 44:16 by **r.** of the enemy and avenger. 6440
Ps 78:65 man that shouteth by **r.** of wine.
Ps 88:9 eye mourneth by **r.** of affliction: 4480
Ps 90:10 if by **r.** of strength they be fourscore
Ps 102:5 By **r.** of the voice of my groaning my
Pr 20:4 will not plow by **r.** of the cold;
Pr 26:16 seven men that can render a **r.** 2940
Ec 7:25 out wisdom, and the **r.** of things, 2808
Isa 1:18 Come now, and let us **r.** together, 3198
Isa 49:19 too narrow by **r.** of the inhabitants,
Eze 19:10 full of branches by **r.** of many waters.
Eze 21:12 terrors by **r.** of the sword shall be 413
Eze 26:10 By **r.** of the abundance of his horses
Eze 27:12, 16 thy merchant by **r.** of the multitude
Eze 28:17 wisdom by **r.** of thy brightness: 5921
Da 4:36 time my **r.** returned unto me; 4486
Da 5:10 by **r.** of the words of the king and 6903
Da 8:12 daily sacrifice by **r.** of transgression,
Jon 2:2 I cried by **r.** of mine affliction unto the
Mic 2:12 noise by **r.** of the multitude of men.
Mt 16:8 **why r. ye among yourselves,** 1260
Mk 2:8 **Why r. ye these things in your** 1260
Mk 8:17 **Why r. ye, because ye have no** 1260
Lu 5:21 and the Pharisees began to **r.**, 1260
Lu 5:22 them, **What r. ye in your hearts?** 1260
Joh 6:18 sea arose by **r.** of a great wind that
Joh 12:11 by **r.** of him many of the Jews 1223
Ac 6:2 It is not **r.** that we should leave the 701
Ac 18:14 **r.** would that I should bear with 3056
Ro 8:20 by **r.** of him who hath subjected 1223
2Co 3:10 by **r.** of the glory that excelleth. 1752
Heb 5:3 by **r.** hereof he ought, as for the 1223
Heb 5:14 who by **r.** of use have their senses 1223
Heb 7:23 suffered to continue by **r.** of death:
1Pe 3:15 a **r.** of the hope that is in you with 3056
2Pe 2:2 by **r.** of whom the way of truth 1223
Re 8:13 earth by **r.** of the other voices of 1537
Re 9:2 by **r.** of the smoke of the pit. 1537
Re 18:19 in the sea by **r.** of her costliness! 1537

REASONABLE See also UNREASONABLE.
Ro 12:1 unto God, which is your **r.** service. 3050

REASONED
Mt 16:7 they **r.** among themselves, saying, 1260
Mt 21:25 they **r.** among themselves, saying, 1260
Mk 2:8 that they so **r.** among themselves, 1260
Mk 8:16 they **r.** among themselves, saying, 1260
Mk 11:31 they **r.** with themselves, saying, If 3049
Lu 20:5 they **r.** with themselves, saying, If 4817
Lu 20:14 **they r. among themselves, saying,** 1260
Lu 24:15 they communed together and **r.**, 4802
Ac 17:2 **r.** with them out of the scriptures, 1256
Ac 18:4 **r.** in the synagogue every sabbath, 1256
Ac 18:19 synagogue, and **r.** with the Jews. 1256
Ac 24:25 And as he **r.** of righteousness, 1256

REASONING
Job 13:6 Hear now my **r.**, and hearken to 8433
Mk 2:6 sitting there, and **r.** in their hearts, 1260
Mk 12:28 having heard them **r.** together, 4802
Lu 9:46 Then there arose a **r.** among them, 1261
Ac 28:29 had great **r.** among themselves. 4803

REASONS
Job 32:11 I gave ear to your **r.**, whilst ye 8394
Isa 41:21 bring forth your strong **r.**, saith the

REBA (Re'-bah)
Nu 31:8 Hur, and **R.**, five kings of Midian: 7254
Jos 13:21 and **R.**, which were dukes of Sihon, 7254

REBECCA (re-bek'-kah) See also REBEKAH.
Ro 9:10 **R.** also had conceived by one, even 4479

REBEKAH (re-bek'-kah) See also REBECCA; REBEKAH'S.
Ge 22:23 Bethuel begat **R.**: these eight 7259
Ge 24:15 **R.** came out, who was born to 7259
Ge 24:29 **R.** had a brother, and his name was 7259
Ge 24:30 he heard the words of **R.** his sister, 7259
Ge 24:45 **R.** came forth with her pitcher on 7259
Ge 24:51 **R.** is before thee, take her, and go, 7259
Ge 24:53 and raiment, and gave them to **R.**: 7259
Ge 24:58 they called **R.**, and said unto her, 7259
Ge 24:59 they sent away **R.** their sister, and 7259
Ge 24:60 they blessed **R.**, and said unto her, 7259
Ge 24:61 **R.** arose, and her damsels, and they 7259
Ge 24:61 servant took **R.**, and went his way. 7259

Ge 24:64 **R.** lifted up her eyes, and when she... 7259
Ge 24:67 took **R.**, and she became his wife;...... 7259
Ge 25:20 years old when he took **R.** to wife, ... 7259
Ge 25:21 of him, and **R.** his wife conceived....... 7259
Ge 25:28 of his venison: but **R.** loved Jacob......... 7259
Ge 26:7 of the place should kill me for **R.**; 7259
Ge 26:8 was sporting with **R.** his wife............ 7259
Ge 26:35 grief of mind unto Isaac and to **R.**.. 7259
Ge 27:5 **R.** heard when Isaac spake to Esau..... 7259
Ge 27:6 And **R.** spake unto Jacob her son, ... 7259
Ge 27:11 Jacob said to **R.** his mother, Behold,... 7259
Ge 27:15 And **R.** took goodly raiment of her...... 7259
Ge 27:42 Esau her elder son were told to **R.** 7259
Ge 27:46 **R.** said to Isaac, I am weary of my 7259
Ge 28:5 the Syrian, the brother of **R.**,............ 7259
Ge 49:31 they buried Isaac and **R.** his wife; 7259

REBEKAH'S (re-bek'-kahz)
Ge 29:12 brother, and that he was **R.** son: 7259
Ge 35:8 But Deborah **R.** nurse died, and 7259

REBEL See also REBELLED; REBELLEST; REBELS.
Nu 14:9 Only **r.** not ye against the Lord, ... 4775
Jos 1:18 doth **r.** against thy commandment,...... 4784
Jos 22:16 **r.** this day against the Lord? 4775
Jos 22:18 seeing ye **r.** to day against the Lord, .. 4775
Jos 22:19 but **r.** not against the Lord, nor......... 4775
Jos 22:19 against the Lord, nor **r.** against us,..... 4775
Jos 22:29 God forbid that we should **r.** against ... 4775
1Sa 12:14 not **r.** against the commandment 4784
1Sa 12:15 but **r.** against the commandment 4784
Ne 2:19 ye do? will ye **r.** against the king? 4775
Ne 6:6 that thou and the Jews think to **r.**: 4775
Job 24:13 of those that **r.** against the light;........ 4775
Isa 1:20 But if ye refuse and **r.**, ye shall be...... 4784
Ho 7:14 and wine, and they **r.** against me. 5493

REBELLED
Ge 14:4 and in the thirteenth year they **r.** 4775
Nu 20:24 because ye **r.** against my word at........ 4784
Nu 27:14 ye **r.** against my commandment in...... 4784
De 1:26, 43 but **r.** against the commandment.... 4784
De 9:23 ye **r.** against the commandment of...... 4784
1Ki 12:19 So Israel **r.** against the house of 6586
2Ki 1:1 Then Moab **r.** against Israel after........ 6586
2Ki 3:5 Moab **r.** against the king of Israel....... 6586
2Ki 3:7 king of Moab hath **r.** against me:......... 6586
2Ki 18:7 he **r.** against the king of Assyria, ... 4775
2Ki 24:1 then he turned and **r.** against him........ 4775
2Ki 24:20 Zedekiah **r.** against the king of........... 4775
2Ch 10:19 And Israel **r.** against the house of....... 6856
2Ch 13:6 up, and hath **r.** against his lord. 4775
2Ch 36:13 **r.** against king Nebuchadnezzar, ... 4775
Ne 9:26 disobedient, and **r.** against thee,......... 4775
Ps 5:10 for they have **r.** against thee. 4784
Ps 105:28 and they **r.** not against his word......... 4784
Ps 107:11 they **r.** against the words of God,........ 4784
Isa 1:2 and they have **r.** against me. 6586
Isa 63:10 they **r.**, and vexed his holy Spirit: 4784
Jer 52:3 Zedekiah **r.** against the king of........... 4775
La 1:18 **r.** against his commandment: 4784
La 1:20 for I have grievously **r.**: abroad.......... 4784
La 3:42 We have transgressed and have **r.**:...... 4784
Eze 2:3 nation that hath **r.** against me:.......... 4775
Eze 17:15 he **r.** against him in sending his.......... 4775
Eze 20:8 they **r.** against me, and would not 4784
Eze 20:13 **r.** against me in the wilderness: 4784
Eze 20:21 the children **r.** against me: they 4784
Da 9:5 have **r.**, even by departing from......... 4775
Da 9:9 though we have **r.** against him; 4775
Ho 13:16 for she hath **r.** against her God:......... 4784

REBELLEST
2Ki 18:20 trust, that thou **r.** against me?........... 4775
Isa 36:5 trust, that thou **r.** against me?........... 4775

REBELLION
De 31:27 I know thy **r.**, and thy stiff neck: 4805
Jos 22:22 if it be in **r.**, of if in transgression 4777
1Sa 15:23 For **r.** is as the sin of witchcraft, ... 4805
Ezr 4:19 **r.** and sedition have been made........... 4776
Ne 9:17 in their **r.** appointed a captain to 4805
Job 34:37 For he addeth **r.** unto his sin, he 6588
Pr 17:11 An evil man seeketh only **r.**: 4805
Jer 28:16 hast taught **r.** against the Lord. 5627
Jer 29:32 he hath taught **r.** against the Lord. 5627

REBELLIOUS
De 9:7 ye have been **r.** against the Lord. 4784
De 9:24 Ye have been **r.** against the Lord....... 4784
De 21:18 a man have a stubborn and **r.** son, ... 4784
De 21:20 This our son is stubborn and **r.**, he 4784
De 31:27 ye have been **r.** against the Lord; 4784
1Sa 20:30 son of the perverse **r.** woman, do 4780
Ezr 4:12 building for **r.** and the bad city,......... 4779
Ezr 4:15 and know that this city is a **r.** city, ... 4779
Ps 66:7 let not the **r.** exalt themselves........... 5637
Ps 68:6 but the **r.** dwell in a dry land............ 5637
Ps 68:18 yea, for the **r.** also, that the Lord 5637
Ps 78:8 a stubborn and **r.** generation; a.......... 4784
Isa 1:23 princes are **r.**, and companions of......... 5637
Isa 30:1 Woe to the **r.** children, saith the 5637
Isa 30:9 this is a **r.** people, lying children, ... 4805
Isa 50:5 I was not **r.**, neither turned away....... 4784
Isa 65:2 hands all the day unto a **r.** people,...... 5637
Jer 4:17 she hath been **r.** against me, saith...... 4784
Jer 5:23 hath a revolting and a **r.** heart; 4784
Eze 2:3 to a **r.** nation that hath rebelled 4775
Eze 2:5 (for they are a **r.** house,) yet shall...... 4805
Eze 2:6 looks, though they be a **r.** house........ 4805
Eze 2:7 will forbear: for they are most **r.**........ 4805
Eze 2:8 Be not thou **r.** like that **r.** house;....... 4805
Eze 3:9 looks, though they be a **r.** house........ 4805
Eze 3:26 a reprover: for they are a **r.** house,.... 4805
Eze 3:27 forbear: for they are a **r.** house. 4805
Eze 12:2 dwellest in the midst of a **r.** house, ... 4805
Eze 12:2 hear not: for they are a **r.** house......... 4805
Eze 12:3 consider, though they be a **r.** house.... 4805
Eze 12:9 the house of Israel, the **r.** house,....... 4805
Eze 12:25 O **r.** house, will I say the word, and... 4805
Eze 17:12 Say now to the **r.** house, Know ye...... 4805
Eze 24:3 utter a parable unto the **r.** house,...... 4805
Eze 44:6 thou shalt say to the **r.**, even to the... 4805

REBELS
Nu 17:10 kept for a token against the **r.**;......... 4805
Nu 20:10 Hear now, ye **r.**; must we fetch......... 4784
Eze 20:38 purge out from among you the **r.**, ... 4775

REBUKE See also REBUKED; REBUKES; REBUKETH; REBUKING; UNREBUKABLE.
Le 19:17 in any wise **r.** thy neighbour, and....... 3198
De 28:20 upon thee cursing, vexation and **r.**,...... 4045
Ru 2:16 may glean them, and **r.** her not. 1605
2Ki 19:3 day is a day of trouble, and of **r.**,....... 8433
1Ch 12:17 our fathers look thereon, and **r.** it. 3198
Ps 6:1 O Lord, **r.** me not in thine anger, ... 3198
Ps 18:15 were discovered at thy **r.**, O Lord,...... 1606
Ps 38:1 O Lord, **r.** me not in thy wrath: 3198
Ps 68:30 **R.** the company of spearmen, the....... 1605
Ps 76:6 At thy **r.**, O God of Jacob, both the.... 1606
Ps 80:16 perish at the **r.** of thy countenance..... 1606
Ps 104:7 At thy **r.** they fled; at the voice of 1606
Pr 9:8 **r.** a wise man, and he will love 3198
Pr 13:1 but a scorner heareth not **r.**............. 1606
Pr 13:8 riches: but the poor heareth not **r.**. 1606
Pr 24:25 them that **r.** him shall be delight, ... 3198
Pr 27:5 Open **r.** is better than secret love......... 8433
Ec 7:5 is better to hear the **r.** of the wise,..... 1606
Isa 2:4 and shall **r.** many people:................. 3198
Isa 17:13 God shall **r.** them, and they shall........ 1605
Isa 25:8 **r.** of his people shall he take away...... 2781
Isa 30:17 shall flee at the **r.** of one; at the 1606
Isa 30:17 at the **r.** of five shall ye flee: till ye 1606
Isa 37:3 day is a day of trouble, and of **r.**,........ 8433
Isa 50:2 behold, at my **r.** I dry up the sea, I.... 1606
Isa 51:20 fury of the Lord, the **r.** of thy God..... 1606
Isa 54:9 be wroth with thee, nor **r.** thee. 1605
Isa 66:15 fury, and his **r.** with flames of fire........ 1606
Jer 15:15 for thy sake I have suffered **r.**............ 2781
Ho 5:9 shall be desolate in the day of **r.** 8433
Mic 4:3 and **r.** strong nations afar off; 3198
Zec 3:2 The Lord **r.** thee, O Satan; even 1605
Zec 3:2 hath chosen Jerusalem **r.** thee: 1605
Mal 3:11 **r.** the devourer for your sakes, and.... 1605
Mt 16:22 took him, and began to **r.** him, ... *2008*
Mk 8:32 took him, and began to **r.** him. *2008*
Lu 17:3 **trespass against thee, r. him; and**.. *2008*
Lu 19:39 unto him, Master, **r.** thy disciples........ *2008*
Php 2:15 the sons of God, without **r.**, in the....... *298*
1Ti 5:1 **R.** not an elder, but intreat him as *1969*
1Ti 5:20 Them that sin **r.** before all, that......... *1651*
2Ti 4:2 **r.**, exhort with all longsuffering *2008*
Tit 1:13 Wherefore **r.** them sharply, that......... *1651*
Tit 2:15 exhort, and **r.** with all authority. *1651*
Jude 9 but said, The Lord **r.** thee. *2008*
Re 3:19 **many as I love, I r. and chasten:**... *1651*

REBUKED
Ge 31:42 my hands, and **r.** thee yesternight...... 3198
Ge 37:10 and his father **r.** him, and said......... 1605
Ne 5:7 and I **r.** the nobles, and the rulers,..... 7378
Ps 9:5 Thou hast **r.** the heathen, thou 1605
Ps 106:9 He **r.** the Red sea also, and it was..... 1605
Ps 119:21 hast **r.** the proud that are cursed, ... 1605
Mt 8:26 and **r.** the winds and the sea; and *2008*
Mt 17:18 And Jesus **r.** the devil; and he *2008*
Mt 19:13 pray: and the disciples **r.** them. *2008*
Mt 20:31 the multitude **r.** them, because they.... *2008*
Mk 1:25 And Jesus **r.** him, saying, **Hold thy** ... *2008*
Mk 4:39 he arose, and **r.** the wind, and said...... *2008*
Mk 8:33 he **r.** Peter, saying, **Get thee behind** .*2008*
Mk 9:25 he **r.** the foul spirit, saying unto.......... *2008*
Mk 10:13 his disciples **r.** those that brought....... *2008*
Lu 4:35 And Jesus **r.** him, saying, **Hold thy** ... *2008*
Lu 4:39 and **r.** the fever; and it left her:......... *2008*
Lu 8:24 he arose, and **r.** the wind and the *2008*
Lu 9:42 Jesus **r.** the unclean spirit, and *2008*
Lu 9:55 he turned, and **r.** them, and said,......... *2008*
Lu 18:15 his disciples saw it, they **r.** them........ *2008*
Lu 18:39 they which went before **r.** him,........... *2008*
Lu 23:40 But the other answering **r.** him,......... *2008*
Heb 12:5 nor faint when thou art **r.** of him:....... *1651*
2Pe 2:16 But was **r.** for his iniquity: the.... *2192,1649*

REBUKER
Ho 5:2 I have been a **r.** of them all. 4148

REBUKES
Ps 39:11 When thou with **r.** dost correct.......... 8433
Eze 5:15 and in fury and in furious **r.**............... 8433
Eze 25:17 upon them with furious **r.**; and.......... 8433

REBUKETH
Pr 9:7 he that **r.** a wicked man getteth......... 3198
Pr 28:23 He that **r.** a man afterwards shall....... 3198
Am 5:10 They hate him that **r.** in the gate, ... 3198
Na 1:4 He **r.** the sea, and maketh it dry,......... 1605

REBUKING
2Sa 22:16 discovered, at the **r.** of the Lord,....... 1606
Lu 4:41 he **r.** them suffered them not to......... *2008*

RECAH (re'-kah)
1Ch 4:12 These are the men of **R.**.................. 7397

RECALL
La 3:21 This I **r.** to my mind, therefore 7725

RECEIPT
Mt 9:9 Matthew, sitting at...**r.** of custom:...... *5058*
Mk 2:14 Alphaeus sitting at the **r.** of custom, ... *5058*
Lu 5:27 Levi, sitting at the **r.** of custom: *5058*

RECEIVE See also RECEIVED; RECEIVETH; RECEIVING.
Ge 4:11 mouth to **r.** thy brother's blood.......... 3947
Ge 33:10 then **r.** my present at my hand: 3947
Ge 38:20 to **r.** his pledge from the woman's 3947
Ex 27:3 make his pans to **r.** his ashes, ... 1878
Ex 29:25 thou shalt **r.** them of their hands, ... 3947
Nu 18:28 ye **r.** of the children of Israel;............ 3947
De 9:9 the mount to **r.** the tables of stone, ... 3947
De 33:3 every one shall **r.** of thy words.......... 5375
1Sa 10:4 which thou shalt **r.** of their hands. 3947
2Sa 18:12 **r.** a thousand shekels of silver in......... 8254
1Ki 5:9 there, and thou shalt **r.** them: 5375
1Ki 8:64 too little to **r.** the burnt offerings, ... 3557
2Ki 5:16 whom I stand, I will **r.** none.............. 3947
2Ki 5:26 to **r.** money, and to **r.** garments, ... 3947
2Ki 12:7 **r.** no more money of your 3947
2Ki 12:8 to **r.** no more money of the people, ... 3947
2Ch 7:7 not able to **r.** the burnt offerings, ... 3557
Job 2:10 we **r.** good at the hand of God, ... 6901
Job 2:10 of God, and shall we not **r.** evil? 6901
Job 22:22 **R.**, I pray thee, the law from his 3947
Job 27:13 they shall **r.** of the Almighty.............. 3947
Ps 6:9 the Lord will **r.** my prayer. 3947
Ps 24:5 **r.** the blessing from the Lord, ... 5375
Ps 49:15 of the grave: for he shall **r.** me.......... 3947
Ps 73:24 and afterward **r.** me to glory. 3947
Ps 75:2 When I shall **r.** the congregation I 3947
Pr 1:3 To **r.** the instruction of wisdom,......... 3947
Pr 2:1 My son, if thou wilt **r.** my words. 3947
Pr 4:10 Hear, O my son, and **r.** my sayings;... 3947
Pr 8:10 **R.** my instruction, and not silver; 3947
Pr 10:8 The wise...will **r.** commandments: 3947
Pr 19:20 Hear counsel, and **r.** instruction, ... 6901
Isa 57:6 Should I **r.** comfort in these? 5162

Jer 5:3 they have refused to **r.** correction: 3947
Jer 9:20 your ear **r.** the word of his mouth, 3947
Jer 17:23 might not hear, nor **r.** instruction. 3947
Jer 32:33 have not hearkened to **r.** instruction 3947
Jer 35:13 Will ye not **r.** instruction to hearken 3947
Eze 3:10 speak unto thee **r.** in thine heart, 3947
Eze 16:61 when thou shalt **r.** thy sisters, thine 3947
Eze 36:30 shall **r.** no more reproach of famine 3947
Da 2:6 ye shall **r.** of me gifts and rewards 6902
Ho 10:6 Ephraim shall **r.** shame, and 3947
Ho 14:2 all iniquity, and **r.** us graciously: 3947
Mic 1:11 he shall **r.** of you his standing. 3947
Zep 3:7 fear me, thou wilt **r.** instruction; 3947
Mal 3:10 shall not be room enough to **r.** it
Mt 10:14 **whosoever shall not r. you, nor** *1209*
Mt 10:41 **shall r. a prophet's reward; and** *2983*
Mt 10:41 **shall r. a righteous man's reward** *2983*
Mt 11:5 **blind r. their sight, and the lame** *308*
Mt 11:14 **if ye will r. it, this is Elias, which** *1209*
Mt 18:5 **whoso shall r. one such little child** *1209*
Mt 19:11 **All men cannot r. this saying, save** *5562*
Mt 19:12 **that is able to r. it, let him r. it** *5562*
Mt 19:29 **shall r. an hundredfold, and shall** *2983*
Mt 20:7 **is right, that shall ye r.** *2983*
Mt 21:22 **in prayer, believing, ye shall r.** *2983*
Mt 21:34 **that they might r. the fruits of it** *2983*
Mt 23:14 **ye shall r. the greater damnation** *2983*
Mk 2:2 there was no room to **r.** them, *5562*
Mk 4:16 **immediately r. it with gladness;** *2983*
Mk 4:20 **such as hear the word, and r. it,** *3858*
Mk 6:11 **whosoever shall not r. you, nor** *1209*
Mk 9:37 **shall r. one of such children in** *1209*
Mk 9:37 **whosoever shall r. me, receiveth** *1209*
Mk 10:15 **shall not r. the kingdom of God** *1209*
Mk 10:30 **he shall r. an hundredfold now** *2983*
Mk 10:51 Lord, that I might **r.** my sight. *308*
Mk 11:24 **ye pray, believe that ye r. them,** *2983*
Mk 12:2 **he might r. from the husbandmen** *2983*
Mk 12:40 **these shall r. greater damnation** *2983*
Lu 6:34 **to them of whom ye hope to r.,** *618*
Lu 6:34 **lend to sinners, to r. as much** *618*
Lu 8:13 **they hear, r. the word with joy;** *1209*
Lu 9:5 **whosoever will not r. you, when** *1209*
Lu 9:48 **shall r. this child in my name** *1209*
Lu 9:48 **whosoever shall r. me receiveth** *1209*
Lu 9:53 they did not **r.** him, because his *1209*
Lu 10:8 **city ye enter, and they r. you, eat** *1209*
Lu 10:10 **they r. you not, go your ways out** *1209*
Lu 16:4 **they may r. me into their houses** *1209*
Lu 16:9 **they may r. you into everlasting** *1209*
Lu 18:17 **shall not r. the kingdom of God as** *1209*
Lu 18:30 **not r. manifold more in this** *618*
Lu 18:41 said, Lord, that I may **r.** my sight. *308*
Lu 18:42 Jesus said unto him, **R. thy sight:** *308*
Lu 19:12 **to r. for himself a kingdom, and** *2983*
Lu 20:47 **same shall r. greater damnation** *2983*
Lu 23:41 for we **r.** the due reward of our *618*
Joh 3:11 **seen; and ye r. not our witness.** *2983*
Joh 3:27 A man can **r.** nothing, except it be *2983*
Joh 5:34 **But I r. not testimony from man:** *2983*
Joh 5:41 **I r. not honour from men.** *2983*
Joh 5:43 **Father's name, and ye r. me not:** *2983*
Joh 5:43 **in his own name, him ye will r.** *2983*
Joh 5:44 **which r. honour one of another,** *2983*
Joh 7:23 **the sabbath day r. circumcision,** *2983*
Joh 7:39 they that believe on him should **r.** *2983*
Joh 14:3 **again, and r. you unto myself;** *3880*
Joh 14:17 **whom the world cannot r.** *2983*
Joh 16:14 **for he shall r. of mine, and shall** *2983*
Joh 16:24 **ask, and ye shall r., that your joy** *2983*
Joh 20:22 unto them, **R.** ye the Holy Ghost: *2983*
Ac 1:8 **But ye shall r. power, after that** *2983*
Ac 2:38 shall **r.** the gift of the Holy Ghost. *2983*
Ac 3:5 expecting to **r.** something of them. *2983*
Ac 3:21 Whom the heaven must **r.** until *1209*
Ac 7:59 and saying, Lord Jesus, **r.** my spirit. *1209*
Ac 8:15 that they might **r.** the Holy Ghost: *2983*
Ac 8:19 hands, he may **r.** the Holy Ghost. *2983*
Ac 9:12 **on him, that he might r. his sight** *308*
Ac 9:17 that thou mightest **r.** thy sight, and *308*
Ac 10:43 in him shall **r.** remission of sins. *2983*
Ac 16:21 which are not lawful for us to **r.**, *3858*
Ac 18:27 exhorting the disciples to **r.** him: *588*
Ac 20:35 **is more blessed to give than to r.** *2983*
Ac 22:13 unto me, Brother Saul, **r.** thy sight. *308*
Ac 22:18 **r. thy testimony concerning me** *3858*
Ac 26:18 **they may r. forgiveness of sins,** *2983*
Ro 5:17 they which **r.** abundance of grace *2983*
Ro 13:2 shall **r.** to themselves damnation. *2983*
Ro 14:1 that is weak in the faith **r.** ye, *4355*
Ro 15:7 **r.** ye one another, as Christ also *4355*
Ro 16:2 That ye **r.** her in the Lord, as *4327*
1Co 3:8 man shall **r.** his own reward *2983*
1Co 3:14 thereupon, he shall **r.** a reward. *2983*
1Co 4:7 hast thou that thou didst not **r.**? *2983*
1Co 4:7 thou didst **r.** it, why dost thou glory, *2983*
1Co 14:5 that the church may **r.** edifying. *2983*
2Co 5:10 **r.** the things done in his body, *2865*
2Co 6:1 ye **r.** not the grace of God in vain. *1209*
2Co 6:17 unclean thing; and I will **r.** you, *1523*
2Co 7:2 **R.** us; we have wronged no man, *5562*
2Co 7:9 might **r.** damage by us in nothing. *2210*
2Co 8:4 intreaty that we would **r.** the gift, *1209*
2Co 11:4 of if ye **r.** another spirit, which ye *2983*
2Co 11:16 as a fool **r.** me, that I may boast *1209*
Ga 3:14 might **r.** the promise of the Spirit *2983*
Ga 4:5 we might **r.** the adoption of sons. *618*
Eph 6:8 the same shall he **r.** of the Lord, *2983*
Php 2:29 **R.** him therefore in the Lord with *4327*
Col 3:24 **r.** the reward of the inheritance: *618*
Col 3:25 **r.** for the wrong which he hath *2865*
Col 4:10 if he come unto you, **r.** him;) *1209*
1Ti 5:19 an elder **r.** not an accusation, but *3858*
Phm 12 thou therefore **r.** him, that is, *4355*
Phm 15 that thou shouldest **r.** him for ever; *568*
Phm 17 a partner, **r.** him as myself. *4355*
Heb 7:5 who **r.** the office of the priesthood, *2983*
Heb 7:8 And here men that die **r.** tithes; *2983*
Heb 9:15 might **r.** the promise of eternal *2983*
Heb 10:36 of God, ye might **r.** the promise. *2865*
Heb 11:8 should after **r.** for an inheritance, *2983*
Jas 1:7 he shall **r.** any thing of the Lord. *2983*
Jas 1:12 is tried, he shall **r.** the crown of life, *2983*
Jas 1:21 **r.** with meekness the engrafted *1209*
Jas 3:1 shall **r.** the greater condemnation. *2983*
Jas 4:3 Ye ask, and **r.** not, because ye ask *2983*
Jas 5:7 until he **r.** the early and latter rain. *2983*
1Pe 5:4 **r.** a crown of glory that fadeth not *2865*
2Pe 2:13 **r.** the reward of unrighteousness, *2865*
1Jo 3:22 whatsoever we ask, we **r.** of him, *2983*
1Jo 5:9 If we **r.** the witness of men, the *2983*
2Jo 8 but that we **r.** a full reward. *618*
2Jo 10 **r.** him not into your house, neither *2983*
3Jo 8 We therefore ought to **r.** such, that *618*
3Jo 10 doth he himself **r.** the brethren, *1926*
Re 4:11 to **r.** glory and honour and power: *2983*
Re 5:12 Lamb that was slain to **r.** power, *2983*
Re 13:16 to **r.** a mark in their right hand, *1325*
Re 14:9 **r.** his mark in his forehead, or in *2983*
Re 17:12 but **r.** power as kings one hour with *2983*
Re 18:4 and that ye **r.** not of her plagues. *2983*

RECEIVED See also RECEIVEDST.

Ge 26:12 land, and **r.** in the same year an 4672
Ex 32:4 And he **r.** them at their hand, and 3947
Ex 36:3 they **r.** of Moses all the offering, 3947
Nu 12:14 after that let her be **r.** in again. 622
Nu 23:20 I have **r.** commandment to bless: 3947
Nu 34:14 fathers, have **r.** their inheritance; 3947
Nu 34:14 have **r.** their inheritance: 3947
Nu 34:15 half tribe have **r.** their inheritance. 3947
Nu 36:3,4 the tribe whereunto they are **r.**: 1961
Jos 13:8 Gadites have **r.** their inheritance, 3947
Jos 18:2 had not yet **r.** their inheritance. 2505
Jos 18:7 have **r.** their inheritance beyond 3947
Jg 13:23 would not have **r.** a burnt offering 3947
1Sa 12:3 of whose hand have I **r.** any bribe 3947
1Sa 25:35 So David **r.** of her hand that which 3947
1Ki 10:28 merchants **r.** the linen yarn at a 3947
2Ki 19:14 Hezekiah **r.** the letter of the hand 3947
1Ch 12:18 David **r.** them, and made them 6901
2Ch 1:16 merchants **r.** the linen yarn at a 3947
2Ch 4:5 **r.** and held three thousand baths. 2388
2Ch 29:22 and the priests **r.** the blood, and 6901
2Ch 30:16 they **r.** at the hand of the Levites
Es 4:4 from him: but he **r.** it not. 6901
Job 4:12 and mine ear **r.** a little thereof. 3947
Ps 68:18 thou hast **r.** gifts for men; yea, for 3947
Pr 24:32 looked upon it, and **r.** instruction. 3947
Isa 37:14 And Hezekiah **r.** the letter from the 3947
Isa 40:2 for she hath **r.** of the Lord's hand 3947
Jer 2:30 children; they **r.** no correction: 3947
Eze 18:17 hath not **r.** usury nor increase, 3947
Zep 3:2 she **r.** not correction; she trusted 3947
Mt 10:8 **freely ye have r., freely give.** *2983*
Mt 13:19 **he which r. seed by the way side** *4687*
Mt 13:20 **that r. the seed into stony places,** *4687*
Mt 13:22 **also that r. seed among the thorns** *4687*
Mt 13:23 **that r. seed into the good ground** *4687*
Mt 17:24 they that **r.** tribute money came to *2983*
Mt 20:9 **hour, they r. every man a penny** *2983*
Mt 20:10 **that they should have r. more;** *2983*
Mt 20:10 **likewise r. every man a penny** *2983*
Mt 20:11 **And when they had r. it, they** *2983*
Mt 20:34 and immediately their eyes **r.** sight, *308*
Mt 25:16 **he that had r. the five talents** *2983*
Mt 25:17 **And likewise he that had r. two,**
Mt 25:18 **But he that had r. one went and** *2983*
Mt 25:20 **so he that had r. five talents came** *2983*
Mt 25:22 **also that had r. two talents came** *2983*
Mt 25:24 **which had r. the one talent came** *2983*
Mt 25:27 **have r. mine own with usury.** *2865*
Mk 7:4 which they have **r.** to hold, as the *3880*
Mk 10:52 And immediately he **r.** his sight, *308*
Mk 15:23 with myrrh: but he **r.** it not. *2983*
Mk 16:19 he was **r.** up into heaven, and sat on *353*
Lu 6:24 **for ye have r. your consolation** *568*
Lu 8:40 returned, the people gladly **r.** him: *588*
Lu 9:11 he **r.** them, and spake unto them *1209*
Lu 9:51 was come that he should be **r.** up, *354*
Lu 10:38 Martha **r.** him into her house. *5264*
Lu 15:27 **he hath r. him safe and sound.** *618*
Lu 18:43 And immediately he **r.** his sight, *308*
Lu 19:6 came down, and **r.** him joyfully. *5264*
Lu 19:15 **returned, having r. the kingdom,** *2983*
Joh 1:11 his own, and his own **r.** him not. *3880*
Joh 1:12 as many as **r.** him, to them gave *2983*
Joh 1:16 And of his fulness have all we **r.**, *2983*
Joh 3:33 He that hath **r.** his testimony hath *2983*
Joh 4:45 the Galilaeans **r.** him, having seen *1209*
Joh 6:21 they willingly **r.** him into the ship: *2983*
Joh 9:11 I went and washed, and I **r.** sight. *308*
Joh 9:15 asked him how he had **r.** his sight. *308*
Joh 9:18 he had been blind, and **r.** his sight, *308*
Joh 9:18 parents of him that had **r.** his sight. *308*
Joh 10:18 **This commandment have I r. of** *2983*
Joh 13:30 He then having **r.** the sop went *2983*
Joh 17:8 **they have r. them, and have known** *2983*
Joh 18:3 then, having **r.** a band of men and *2983*
Joh 19:30 Jesus therefore had **r.** the vinegar, *2983*
Ac 1:9 a cloud **r.** him out of their sight. *5274*
Ac 2:33 and having **r.** of the Father the *2983*
Ac 2:41 gladly **r.** his word were baptized: *588*
Ac 3:7 feet and ancle bones **r.** strength. *4732*
Ac 7:38 **r.** the lively oracles to give unto us: *1209*
Ac 7:53 **r.** the law by the disposition of *2983*
Ac 8:14 Samaria had **r.** the word of God, *1209*
Ac 8:17 them, and they **r.** the Holy Ghost, *2983*
Ac 9:18 he **r.** sight forthwith, and arose, *308*
Ac 9:19 And when he had **r.** meat, he was *2983*
Ac 10:16 vessel was **r.** up again into heaven. *353*
Ac 10:47 **r.** the Holy Ghost as well as we? *2983*
Ac 11:1 Gentiles had also **r.** the word of *1209*
Ac 15:4 they were **r.** of the church, and of *588*
Ac 16:24 Who, having **r.** such a charge, *2983*
Ac 17:7 Whom Jason hath **r.**: and these *5264*
Ac 17:11 they **r.** the word with all readiness *1209*
Ac 19:2 Have ye **r.** the Holy Ghost since ye *2983*
Ac 20:24 which I have **r.** of the Lord Jesus, *2983*
Ac 21:17 the brethren **r.** us gladly. *1209*
Ac 22:5 from whom also I **r.** letters unto *1209*
Ac 26:10 **r.** authority from the chief priests; *2983*
Ac 28:2 fire, and **r.** us every one, because *4355*
Ac 28:7 who **r.** us, and lodges us three days. *324*
Ac 28:21 We neither **r.** letters out of Judaea *1209*
Ac 28:30 and **r.** all that came unto him, *588*
Ro 1:5 we have **r.** grace and apostleship, *2983*
Ro 4:11 And he **r.** the sign of circumcision, *2983*
Ro 5:11 we have now **r.** the atonement. *2983*
Ro 8:15 ye have not **r.** the spirit of bondage *2983*
Ro 8:15 ye have **r.** the Spirit of adoption, *2983*
Ro 14:3 that eateth: for God hath **r.** him. *4355*
Ro 15:7 as Christ also **r.** us to the glory of *4355*
1Co 2:12 Now we have **r.**, not the spirit of *2983*
1Co 4:7 glory, as if thou hadst not **r.** it? *2983*
1Co 11:23 I have **r.** of the Lord that which *3880*
1Co 15:1 which also ye have **r.**, and wherein *3880*
1Co 15:3 you first of all that which I also **r.**, *3880*
2Co 4:1 as we have **r.** mercy, we faint not; *1653*
2Co 7:15 with fear and trembling ye **r.** him. *1209*
2Co 11:4 which ye have not **r.**, or another *29838*

2Co 11:24 times **r.** I forty stripes save one. *29838*
Ga 1:9 unto you than that ye have **r.**, *3880*
Ga 1:12 For I neither **r.** it of man, neither *3880*
Ga 3:2 **R.** ye the Spirit by the works of *2983*
Ga 4:14 but **r.** me as an angel of God, even *1209*
Php 4:9 ye have both learned, and **r.**, and *3880*
Php 4:18 having **r.** of Epaphroditus the *1209*
Col 2:6 ye have therefore **r.** Christ Jesus *3880*
Col 4:10 whom ye **r.** commandments: if *2983*
Col 4:17 which thou hast **r.** in the Lord, *3880*
1Th 1:6 **r.** the word in much affliction, *1209*
1Th 2:13 when ye **r.** the word of God which *3880*
1Th 2:13 ye **r.** it not as the word of men, *1209*
1Th 4:1 as ye have **r.** of us how ye ought *3880*
2Th 2:10 they **r.** not the love of the truth, *1209*
2Th 3:6 the tradition which he **r.** of us. *3880*
1Ti 3:16 on in the world, **r.** up into glory. *353*
1Ti 4:3 which God hath created to be **r.** *3336*
1Ti 4:4 if it be **r.** with thanksgiving: *2983*
Heb 2:2 **r.** a just recompense of reward; *2983*
Heb 7:6 from them **r.** tithes of Abraham, *1183*
Heb 7:11 (for under it the people **r.** the law,) *3549*
Heb 10:26 **r.** the knowledge of the truth, *2983*
Heb 11:11 Sara herself **r.** strength to conceive *2983*
Heb 11:13 not having **r.** the promises, but *2983*
Heb 11:17 he that had **r.** the promises offered *324*
Heb 11:19 whence also he **r.** him in a figure. *2865*
Heb 11:31 she had **r.** the spies with peace. *1209*
Heb 11:35 Women **r.** their dead raised to life *2983*
Heb 11:39 through faith, **r.** not the promise: *2865*
Jas 2:25 when she had **r.** the messengers, *5264*
1Pe 1:18 vain conversation **r.** by tradition
1Pe 4:10 As every man hath **r.** the gift, even *2983*
2Pe 1:17 he **r.** from God the Father honour *2983*
1Jo 2:27 anointing which ye have **r.** of him *2983*
2Jo 4 we have **r.** a commandment from *2983*
Re 2:27 **shivers: even as I r. of my Father.** *2983*
Re 3:3 **how thou hast r. and heard, and** *2983*
Re 17:12 which have **r.** no kingdom as yet; *2983*
Re 19:20 that had **r.** the mark of the beast, *2983*
Re 20:4 **r.** his mark upon their foreheads, *2983*

RECEIVEDST
Lu 16:5 **in thy lifetime r. thy good things,** *618*

RECEIVER
Isa 33:18 is the scribe? where is the **r.**? 8254

RECEIVETH
Jg 19:18 is no man that **r.** me to house 622
Job 35:7 him? or what **r.** he of thine hand? 3947
Pr 21:11 wise is instructed, he **r.** knowledge. 3947
Pr 29:4 but he that **r.** gifts overthroweth it.
Jer 7:28 Lord their God, nor **r.** correction: 3947
Mal 2:13 or **r.** it with good will at your hand. 3947
Mt 7:8 **For every one that asketh r.; and** *2983*
Mt 10:40 **He that r. you r. me, and he** *1209*
Mt 10:40 **that r. me r. him that sent me.** *1209*
Mt 10:41 **He that r. a prophet in the name** *2983*
Mt 10:41 **he that r. a righteous man in the** *2983*
Mt 13:20 **the word, and anon with joy r. it;** *2983*
Mt 18:5 **such little child in my name r. me.** *1209*
Mk 9:37 **little children in my name, r. me:** *1209*
Mk 9:37 **shall receive me, r. not me, but** *1209*
Lu 9:48 **this child in my name r. me:** *1209*
Lu 9:48 **receive me r. him that sent me:** *1209*
Lu 11:10 **every one that asketh r.; and he** *2983*
Lu 15:2 This man **r.** sinners, and eateth *4327*
Joh 3:32 and no man **r.** his testimony. *2983*
Joh 4:36 **And he that reapeth r. wages, and** *2983*
Joh 12:48 **r. not my words, hath one that** *2983*
Joh 13:20 **that r. whomsoever I send r. me;** *2983*
Joh 13:20 **he that r. me r. him that sent me** *2983*
1Co 2:14 the natural man **r.** not the things *1209*
1Co 9:24 race run all, but one **r.** the prize? *2983*
Heb 6:7 it is dressed, **r.** blessing from God: *3335*
Heb 7:8 but there he **r.** them, of whom it is
Heb 7:9 Levi also, who **r.** tithes, payed *2983*
Heb 12:6 scourgeth every son whom he **r.** *3858*
3Jo 9 among them, **r.** us not. *1926*
Re 2:17 **man knoweth saving he that r. it.** *2983*
Re 14:11 whosoever **r.** the mark of his name. *2983*

RECEIVING
2Ki 5:20 not **r.** at his hands that which he 3947
Ac 17:15 **r.** a commandment unto Silas and *2983*
Ro 1:27 **r.** in themselves that recompence *618*
Ro 11:15 what shall the **r.** of them be, but *4356*
Php 4:15 me as concerning giving and **r.**, *3028*
Heb 12:28 Wherefore we **r.** a kingdom which *3880*
1Pe 1:9 **R.** the end of your faith, even the *2865*

RECHAB (re'-kab) See also RECHABITES.
2Sa 4:2 and the name of the other **R.**, 7394
2Sa 4:5 sons of Rimmon...**R.** and Baanah, 7394
2Sa 4:6 **R.** and Baanah his brother escaped. 7394
2Sa 4:9 **R.** and Baanah his brother, the 7394
2Ki 10:15 the son of **R.** coming to meet him: 7394
2Ki 10:23 went, and Jehonadab the son of **R.**, 7394
1Ch 2:55 the father of the house of **R.** 7394
Ne 3:14 repaired Malchiah the son of **R.**, 7394
Jer 35:6 of **R.** our father commanded us, 7394
Jer 35:8 the voice of Jonadab the son of **R.** 7394
Jer 35:14 words of Jonadab the son of **R.**, 7394
Jer 35:16 the son of **R.** have performed the 7394
Jer 35:19 the son of **R.** shall not want a man 7394

RECHABITES (rek'-ab-ites)
Jer 35:2 Go unto the house of the **R.**, and 7397
Jer 35:3 and the whole house of the **R.**; 7397
Jer 35:5 house of the **R.** pots full of wine, 7397
Jer 35:18 said unto the house of the **R.**, 7397

RECHOKIM See JONATH-ELEM-RECHOKIM.

RECKON See also RECKONED; RECKONETH; RECKONING.
Le 25:50 he shall **r.** with him that bought 2803
Le 27:18 priest shall **r.** unto him the money 2803
Le 27:23 priest shall **r.** unto him the worth 2803
Nu 4:32 name ye shall **r.** the instruments 6485
Eze 44:26 they shall **r.** unto him seven days. 5608
Mt 18:24 **And when he had begun to r., one** *4868*
Ro 6:11 **r.** ye also yourselves to be dead *3049*
Ro 8:18 For I **r.** that the sufferings of this *3049*

RECKONED
Nu 18:27 offering shall be **r.** unto you, 2803
Nu 23:9 shall not be **r.** among the nations. 2803
2Sa 4:2 Beeroth also was **r.** to Benjamin: 2803
2Ki 12:15 they **r.** not with the men, into 2803
1Ch 5:1 and the genealogy is not to be **r.** 3187
1Ch 5:7 of their generations was **r.**, were 3187
1Ch 5:17 All these were **r.** by genealogies in 3187
1Ch 7:5 **r.** in all by their genealogies 3187
1Ch 7:7 and were **r.** by their genealogies 3187
1Ch 9:1 all Israel were **r.** by genealogies; 3187
1Ch 9:22 These were **r.** by their genealogy in 3187
2Ch 31:19 to all that were **r.** by genealogies 3187
Ezr 2:62 those that were **r.** by genealogy, 3187
Ezr 8:3 and with him were **r.** by genealogy 3187
Ne 7:5 that they might be **r.** by genealogy. 3187
Ne 7:64 those that were **r.** by genealogy, 3187
Ps 40:5 cannot be **r.** up in order unto thee:
Isa 38:13 I **r.** till morning, that, as a lion, 7737
Lu 22:37 **was r. among the transgressors:** *3049*
Ro 4:4 is the reward not **r.** of grace, but *3049*
Ro 4:9 say that faith was **r.** to Abraham *3049*
Ro 4:10 How was it then **r.**? when he was *3049*

RECKONETH
Mt 25:19 **cometh, and r. with them.** *4868,3056*

RECKONING
2Ki 22:7 there was no **r.** made with them 2803
1Ch 23:11 they were in one **r.**, according to 6486

RECOMMENDED
Ac 14:26 had been **r.** to the grace of God *3860*
Ac 15:40 being **r.** by the brethren unto the *3860*

RECOMPENCE See also RECOMPENCES; RECOMPENSE.
De 32:35 me belongeth vengeance, and **r.**; 8005
Job 15:31 vanity: for vanity shall be his **r.** 8545
Pr 12:14 the **r.** of a man's hands shall be 1576
Isa 35:4 vengeance, even God with a **r.**; he 1576
Isa 59:18 his adversaries, **r.** to his enemies; 1576
Isa 59:18 to the islands he will repay **r.** 1576
Isa 66:6 that rendereth **r.** to his enemies. 1576
Jer 51:6 he will render unto her a **r.** 1576
La 3:64 Render unto them a **r.**, O Lord, 1576
Ho 9:7 the days of **r.** are come; Israel 7966
Joe 3:4 will ye render me a **r.**? and if ye 1576
Joe 3:4 return your **r.** upon your own head; 1576
Lu 14:12 **thee again, and a r. be made thee** *468*
Ro 1:27 **r.** of their error which was meet. *489*
Ro 11:9 stumblingblock,...a **r.** unto them: *468*
2Co 6:13 Now for a **r.** in the same, (I speak *489*
Heb 2:2 received a just **r.** of reward; *3405*
Heb 10:35 which hath great **r.** of reward. *3405*
Heb 11:26 respect unto the **r.** of the reward. *3405*

RECOMPENCES
Isa 34:8 year of **r.** for the controversy of 7966
Jer 51:56 for the Lord God of **r.** shall surely 1578

RECOMPENSE See also RECOMPENCE; RECOMPENSED; RECOMPENSEST; RECOMPENSING.
Nu 5:7 he shall **r.** his trespass with the 7725
Nu 5:8 if the man have no kinsman to **r.** 7725
Ru 2:12 The Lord **r.** thy work, and a full 7999
2Sa 19:36 king **r.** it me with such a reward? 1580
Job 34:33 he will **r.** it, whether thou refuse, 7999
Pr 20:22 Say not thou, I will **r.** evil; but 7999
Isa 65:6 but will **r.**, even **r.** into their bosom, 7999
Jer 16:18 And first I will **r.** their iniquity 7999
Jer 25:14 **r.** them according to their deeds, 7999
Jer 50:29 **r.** her according to her work; 7999
Eze 7:3 and will **r.** upon thee all thine 5414
Eze 7:4 I will **r.** thy ways upon thee, and 5414
Eze 7:8 and will **r.** thee for all thine 5414
Eze 7:9 I will **r.** thee according to thy ways 5414
Eze 9:10 will **r.** their way upon their head. 5414
Eze 11:21 **r.** their way upon their own heads, 5414
Eze 16:43 will **r.** thy way upon thine 5414
Eze 17:19 even it will I **r.** upon his own head. 5414
Eze 23:49 they shall **r.** your lewdness upon 5414
Ho 12:2 to his doings will he **r.** him. 7725
Joe 3:4 if ye **r.** me, swiftly and speedily 1580
Lu 14:14 **they cannot r. thee: for thou shalt** *467*
Ro 12:17 **R.** to no man evil for evil. Provide *591*
2Th 1:6 with God to **r.** tribulation to them *467*
Heb 10:30 unto me, I will **r.**, saith the Lord. *467*

RECOMPENSED
Nu 5:8 the trespass be **r.** unto the Lord, 7725
2Sa 22:21 of my hands hath he **r.** me 7725
2Sa 22:25 Lord hath **r.** me according to my 7725
Ps 18:20 of my hands hath he **r.** me 7725
Ps 18:24 the Lord **r.** me according to my 7725
Pr 11:31 righteous shall be **r.** in the earth: 7999
Jer 18:20 Shall evil be **r.** for good? for they 7999
Eze 22:31 way have I **r.** upon their heads, 5414
Lu 14:14 **thou shalt be r. at the resurrection** *467*
Ro 11:35 and it shall be **r.** unto him again? *467*

RECOMPENSEST
Jer 32:18 and **r.** the iniquity of the fathers 7999

RECOMPENSING
2Ch 6:23 by **r.** his way upon his own head 5414

RECONCILE See also RECONCILED; RECONCILING.
Le 6:30 to **r.** withal in the holy place, 3722
1Sa 29:4 he **r.** himself unto his master? 7521
Eze 45:20 simple: so shall ye **r.** the house. 3722
Eph 2:16 **r.** both unto God in one body by the *604*
Col 1:20 him to **r.** all things unto himself; *604*

RECONCILED
Mt 5:24 **first be r. to thy brother, and** *1259*
Ro 5:10 **r.** to God by the death of his Son, *2644*
Ro 5:10 much more, being **r.**, we shall be *2644*
1Co 7:11 unmarried, or be **r.** to her husband: *2644*
2Co 5:18 of God, who hath **r.** us to himself by *2644*
2Co 5:20 in Christ's stead, be ye **r.** to God. *2644*
Col 1:21 wicked works, yet now hath he **r.** *604*

RECONCILIATION
Le 8:15 sanctified it, to make **r.** upon it. 3722
2Ch 29:24 made **r.** with their blood upon the 2398
Eze 45:15 offerings, to make **r.** for them, 3722
Eze 45:17 to make **r.** for the house of Israel. 3722
Da 9:24 and to make **r.** for iniquity, and to 3722
2Co 5:18 hath given to us the ministry of **r.**; *2643*
2Co 5:19 committed unto us the word of **r.** *2643*
Heb 2:17 make **r.** for the sins of the people. *2433*

RECONCILING
Le 16:20 made an end of **r.** the holy place, 3722
Ro 11:15 of them be the **r.** of the world, *2643*
2Co 5:19 Christ, **r.** the world unto himself, *2644*

RECORD See also RECORDED; RECORDS.
Ex 20:24 where I **r.** my name I will come 2142
De 30:19 heaven and earth to **r.** this day 5749
De 31:28 heaven and earth to **r.** against 5749
1Ch 16:4 and to **r.**, and to thank and praise 2142
Ezr 6:2 and therein was a **r.** thus written: 1799
Job 16:19 in heaven, and my **r.** is on high. 7717

Isa 8:2 unto me faithful witnesses to **r.**, 5749
Joh 1:19 And this is the **r.** of John, when *3141*
Joh 1:32 John bare **r.**, saying, I saw the *3140*
Joh 1:34 bare **r.** that this is the Son of God *3140*
Joh 8:13 him, Thou bearest **r.** of thyself; *3140*
Joh 8:13 of thyself; thy **r.** is not true. *3141*
Joh 8:14 **Though I bear r. of myself, yet** *3140*
Joh 8:14 **of myself, yet my r. is true: for** *3141*
Joh 12:17 raised him from the dead, bare **r.** *3140*
Joh 19:35 And he that saw it bare **r.**, and *3140*
Joh 19:35 his **r.** is true: and he knoweth *3141*
Ac 20:26 I take you to **r.** this day, that I am *3143*
Ro 10:2 bear them **r.** that they have a zeal *3140*
2Co 1:23 I call God for a **r.** upon my soul, *3144*
2Co 8:3 I bear **r.**, yea, and beyond their *3140*
Ga 4:15 for I bear you **r.**, that, if it had *3140*
Php 1:8 For God is my **r.**, how greatly I *3144*
Col 4:13 For I bear him **r.**, that he hath a *3140*
1Jo 5:7 are three that bear **r.** in heaven, *3140*
1Jo 5:10 the **r.** that God gave of his Son. *3141*
1Jo 5:11 this is the **r.**, that God hath given *3141*
3Jo 12 itself: yea, and we also bear **r.**; *3140*
3Jo 12 and ye know that our **r.** is true. *3141*
Re 1:2 Who bare **r.** of the word of God, *3140*

RECORDED
Ne 12:22 were **r.** chief of the fathers: also 3789

RECORDER
2Sa 8:16 the son of Ahilud was **r.**; 2142
2Sa 20:24 the son of Ahilud was **r.**: 2142
1Ki 4:3 the son of Ahilud, the **r.** 2142
2Ki 18:18 and Joah the son of Asaph the **r.** 2142
2Ki 18:37 and Joah the son of Asaph the **r.**, 2142
1Ch 18:15 Jehoshaphat the son of Ahilud, **r.** 2142
2Ch 34:8 and Joah the son of Joahaz the **r.**, 2142
Isa 36:3 and Joah, Asaph's son, the **r.** 2142
Isa 36:22 and Joah, the son of Asaph, the **r.**, 2142

RECORDS
Ezr 4:15 may be made in the book of the **r.** 1799
Ezr 4:15 thou find in the book of the **r.**, 1799
Es 6:1 the book of **r.** of the chronicles; 2146

RECOUNT
Na 2:5 He shall **r.** his worthies: they 2142

RECOVER See also RECOVERED; RECOVERING.
Jg 11:26 did ye not **r.** them within that 5337
1Sa 30:8 them, and without fail **r.** all. 5337
2Sa 8:3 went to **r.** his border at the river 7725
2Ki 1:2 whether I shall **r.** of this disease. 2421
2Ki 5:3 for he would **r.** him of his leprosy. 622
2Ki 5:6 thou mayest **r.** him of his leprosy. 622
2Ki 5:7 unto me to **r.** a man of his leprosy? 622
2Ki 5:11 hand over the place, and **r.** the leper. 622
2Ki 8:8,9 saying, Shall I **r.** of this disease? 2421
2Ki 8:10 him, Thou mayest certainly **r.**: 2421
2Ki 8:14 me that thou shouldest surely **r.** 2421
2Ch 13:20 Neither did Jeroboam **r.** strength 6113
2Ch 14:13 that they could not **r.** themselves; 4241
Ps 39:13 spare me, that I may **r.** strength, 1082
Isa 11:11 to **r.** the remnant of his people, 7069
Isa 38:16 so wilt thou **r.** me, and make me to 2492
Isa 38:21 upon the boil, and he shall **r.** 2421
Ho 2:9 will **r.** my wool and my flax given 5337
Mk 16:18 **on the sick, and they shall r.** *2192,2573*
2Ti 2:26 may **r.** themselves out of the snare *366*

RECOVERED
1Sa 30:18 **r.** all that the Amalekites had 5337
1Sa 30:19 had taken to them: David **r.** all. 7725
1Sa 30:22 ought of the spoil that we have **r.**, 5337
2Ki 13:25 him, and **r.** the cities of Israel. 7725
2Ki 14:28 how he **r.** Damascus, and Hamath, 7725
2Ki 16:6 time Rezin king of Syria **r.** Elath 7725
2Ki 20:7 and laid it on the boil and he **r.** 2421
Isa 38:9 sick, and was **r.** of his sickness: 2421
Isa 39:1 that he had been sick, and was **r.** 2388
Jer 8:22 of the daughter of my people **r.**? 5927
Jer 41:16 whom he had **r.** from Ishmael the 7725

RECOVERING
Lu 4:18 **r. of sight to the blind, to set at** *309*

RED See also RED; REDDISH.
Ge 25:25 And the first came out **r.**, all over 132
Ge 25:30 thee, with that same **r.** pottage; 122
Ge 49:12 His eyes shall be **r.** with wine, and 2447
Ex 25:5 rams' skins dyed **r.**, and badgers' 119
Ex 26:14 for the tent of rams' skins dyed **r.**, 119
Ex 35:7 rams' skins dyed **r.**, and badgers' 119
Ex 35:23 **r.** skins of rams, and badgers' skins, 119
Ex 36:19 for the tent of rams' skins dyed **r.**, 119
Ex 39:34 the covering of rams' skins dyed **r.**, 119
Nu 19:2 bring thee a **r.** heifer without spot, 122
2Ki 3:22 on the other side as **r.** as blood: 122
Es 1:6 upon a pavement of **r.**, and blue, 923
Ps 75:8 there is a cup, and the wine is **r.**; 923
Pr 23:31 thou upon the wine when it is **r.**, 119
Isa 1:18 though they be **r.** like crimson, 119
Isa 27:2 unto her, A vineyard of **r.** wine. 2561
Isa 63:2 art thou **r.** in thine apparel, and 122
Na 2:3 of his mighty men is made **r.**, 119
Zec 1:8 behold a man riding upon a **r.** horse, 122
Zec 1:8 behind him were there **r.** horses, 122
Zec 6:2 In the first chariot were **r.** horses; 122
Mt 16:2 **be fair weather: for the sky is r** *4449*
Mt 16:3 **day: for the sky is r. and lowring** *4449*
Re 6:4 out another horse that was **r.**: *4450*
Re 12:3 behold a great **r.** dragon, having *4450*

RED See also RED.
Ex 10:19 and cast them into the **R.** sea; 5488
Ex 13:18 way the wilderness of the **R.** sea: 5488
Ex 15:4 also are drowned in the **R.** sea. 5488
Ex 15:22 brought Israel from the **R.** sea, 5488
Ex 23:31 will set thy bounds from the **R.** sea 5488
Nu 14:25 wilderness by the way of the **R.** sea. 5488
Nu 21:4 mount Hor by the way of the **R.** sea, 5488
Nu 21:14 What he did in the **R.** sea, and 5492
Nu 33:10 Elim, and encamped by the **R.** sea. 5488
Nu 33:11 And they removed from the **R.** sea, 5488
De 1:1 the plain over against the **R.** sea, 5489
De 1:40 wilderness by…way of the **R.** sea. 5488
De 2:1 wilderness by the way of the **R.** sea, 5488
De 11:4 the water of the **R.** sea to overflow 5488
Jos 2:10 dried up the water of the **R.** sea 5488
Jos 4:23 Lord your God did to the **R.** sea, 5488
Jos 24:6 and horsemen unto the **R.** sea. 5488
Jg 11:16 the wilderness unto the **R.** sea, 5488
1Ki 9:26 on the shore of the **R.** sea, in the 5488
Ne 9:9 heardest their cry by the **R.** sea; 5488
Ps 106:7 him at the sea, even at the **R.** sea, 5488
Ps 106:9 He rebuked the **R.** sea also, and it 5488
Ps 106:22 and terrible things by the **R.** sea. 5488
Ps 136:13 which divided the **R.** sea into parts: 5488
Ps 136:15 Pharaoh and his host in the **R.** sea: 5488
Jer 49:21 noise…was heard in the **R.** sea. 5488
Ac 7:36 land of Egypt, and in the **R.** sea, *2281*
Heb 11:29 passed through the **R.** sea as by dry *2281*

REDDISH See also RED.
Le 13:19 spot, white, and somewhat **r.**, 125
Le 13:24 bright spot, somewhat **r.**, or white; 125
Le 13:42 a white **r.** sore; it is a leprosy 125
Le 13:43 if the rising of the sore be white **r.** 125
Le 13:49 be greenish or **r.** in the garment, 125
Le 14:37 with hollow strakes, greenish or **r.**, 125

REDEEM See also REDEEMED; REDEEMETH; REDEEMING.
Ex 6:6 **r.** you with a stretched out arm, 1350
Ex 13:13 firstling of an ass thou shalt **r.** 6299
Ex 13:13 if thou wilt not **r.** it, then thou shalt 6299
Ex 13:13 firstborn of man…shalt thou **r.** 6299
Ex 13:15 all the firstborn of my children I **r.** 6299
Ex 34:20 firstling of an ass thou shalt **r.** 6299
Ex 34:20 if thou **r.** him not, then shalt thou 6299
Ex 34:20 firstborn of thy sons thou shalt **r.** 6299
Le 25:25 and if any of his kin come to **r.** it, 1350
Le 25:25 he **r.** that which his brother sold. 1350
Le 25:26 And if the man have none to **r.** it, 1350
Le 25:26 and himself be able to **r.** it; 1353
Le 25:29 he may **r.** it within a whole year 1353
Le 25:29 within a full year may he **r.** it. 1353
Le 25:32 may the Levites **r.** at any time. 1353
Le 25:48 one of his brethren may **r.** him: 1350
Le 25:49 or his uncle's son, may **r.** him, 1350
Le 25:49 unto him of his family may **r.** him; 1350
Le 25:49 or if he be able, he may **r.** himself. 1353
Le 27:13 But if he will at all **r.** it, then he 1350
Le 27:15 that sanctified it will **r.** his house, 1350
Le 27:19 that sanctified the field will…**r.** it, 1350
Le 27:20 And if he will not **r.** the field, or if 1350
Le 27:27 he shall **r.** it according to thine 6299
Le 27:31 will at all **r.** ought of his tithes, 1350
Nu 18:15 firstborn of man shalt thou…**r.**, 6299
Nu 18:15 of unclean beasts shalt thou **r.** 6299
Nu 18:16 from a month old shalt thou **r.**, 6299
Nu 18:17 firstling of a goat, thou shalt not **r.**; 6299
Ru 4:4 If thou wilt **r.** it, **r.** it: but 1350
Ru 4:4 if thou wilt not **r.** it, then tell me, 1350
Ru 4:4 there is none to **r.** it beside thee; 1350
Ru 4:4 after thee. And he said, I will **r.** it 1350
Ru 4:6 I cannot **r.** it for myself, lest I mar 1350
Ru 4:6 **r.** thou my right to thyself; 1350
Ru 4:6 for I cannot **r.** it. 1350
2Sa 7:23 whom God went to **r.** for a people 6299
1Ch 17:21 God went to **r.** to be his own people, 6299
Ne 5:5 neither is it in our power to **r.** them;
Job 5:20 famine he shall **r.** thee from death: 6299
Job 6:23 **R.** me from the hand of the mighty? 6299
Ps 25:22 **R.** Israel, O God, out of all his 6299
Ps 26:11 **r.** me, and be merciful unto me. 6299
Ps 44:26 and **r.** us for thy mercies' sake. 6299
Ps 49:7 can by any means **r.** his brother, 6299
Ps 49:15 God will **r.** my soul from the power 6299
Ps 69:18 Draw nigh unto my soul, and **r.** it: 1350
Ps 72:14 He shall **r.** their soul from deceit 1350
Ps 130:8 **r.** Israel from all his iniquities. 6299
Isa 50:2 shortened at all, that it cannot **r.**? 6304
Jer 15:21 I will **r.** thee out of the hand of 6299
Ho 13:14 grave; I will **r.** them from death: 1350
Mic 4:10 shall **r.** thee from the hand of thine 1350
Ga 4:5 To **r.** them that were under the *1805*
Tit 2:14 he might **r.** us from all iniquity *3084*

REDEEMED See also REDEEMEDST.
Ge 48:16 Angel which **r.** me from all evil, 1350
Ex 15:13 led forth the people…thou hast **r.**: 1350
Ex 21:8 then shall he let her be **r.**: 6299
Le 19:20 not at all **r.**, nor freedom given her; 6299
Le 25:30 **r.** within the space of a full year, 1350
Le 25:31 they may be **r.**, and they shall go 1353
Le 25:48 After that he is sold he may be **r.** 1353
Le 25:54 And if he be not **r.** in these years, 1350
Le 27:20 man, it shall not be **r.** any more. 1350
Le 27:27 if it be not **r.**, then it shall be sold 1350
Le 27:28 devoted thing,…shall be sold or **r.**: 1350
Le 27:29 None devoted,…shall be **r.**; 6299
Le 27:33 shall be holy; it shall not be **r.** 1350
Nu 3:46 And for those that are to be **r.** of 6302
Nu 3:48 the odd number of them is to be **r.**, 6302
Nu 3:49 them that were **r.** by the Levites: 6306
Nu 3:51 the money of them that were **r.** 6306
Nu 18:16 that are to be **r.** from a month old 6299
De 7:8 **r.** you out of the house of bondmen, 6299
De 9:26 thou hast **r.** through thy greatness, 6299
De 13:5 **r.** you out of the house of bondage, 6299
De 15:15 and the Lord thy God **r.** thee: 6299
De 21:8 people Israel, whom thou hast **r.**, 6299
De 24:18 the Lord thy God **r.** thee thence: 6299
2Sa 4:9 hath **r.** my soul out of all adversity, 6299
1Ki 1:29 hath **r.** my soul out of all distress, 6299
1Ch 17:21 whom thou hast **r.** out of Egypt? 6299
Ne 1:10 thou hast **r.** by thy great power, 6299
Ne 5:8 have **r.** our brethren the Jews, 7069
Ps 31:5 hast **r.** me, O Lord God of truth. 6299
Ps 71:23 and my soul, which thou hast **r.** 6299
Ps 74:2 inheritance, which thou hast **r.**; 1350
Ps 77:15 hast with thine arm **r.** thy people, 1350
Ps 106:10 **r.** them from the hand of the enemy. 1350
Ps 107:2 Let the **r.** of the Lord say so, whom 1350
Ps 107:2 hath **r.** from the hand of the enemy; 1350
Ps 136:24 And hath **r.** us from our enemies: 6561
Isa 1:27 Zion shall be **r.** with judgment, 6299
Isa 29:22 saith the Lord, who **r.** Abraham, 6299
Isa 35:9 there; but the **r.** shall walk there: 1350
Isa 43:1 Fear not: for I have **r.** thee, I have 1350
Isa 44:22 return unto me; for I have **r.** thee. 1350
Isa 44:23 for the Lord hath **r.** Jacob, and 1350
Isa 48:20 The Lord hath **r.** his servant Jacob. 1350
Isa 51:11 the **r.** of the Lord shall return, 6299
Isa 52:3 and ye shall be **r.** without money. 1350
Isa 52:9 his people, he hath **r.** Jerusalem. 1350
Isa 62:12 The holy people, The **r.** of the Lord: 1350
Isa 63:4 and the year of my **r.** is come. 1350
Isa 63:9 his love and in his pity he **r.** them; 1350
Jer 31:11 For the Lord hath **r.** Jacob, and 6299
La 3:58 of my soul; thou hast **r.** my life. 1350
Ho 7:13 though I have **r.** them, yet they 6299
Mic 6:4 **r.** thee out of the house of servants; 6299
Zec 10:8 for I have **r.** them: and they shall 6299

Lu 1:68 hath visited and **r.** his people,..... *4160,3085*
Lu 24:21 he which should have **r.** Israel: *3084*
Ga 3:13 Christ hath **r.** us from the curse *1805*
1Pe 1:18 not **r.** with corruptible things,............ *3084*
Re 5:9 and hast **r.** us to God by thy blood........ *59*
Re 14:3 which were **r.** from the earth. *59*
Re 14:4 These were **r.** from among men,.......... *59*

REDEEMEDST
2Sa 7:23 which thou **r.** to thee from Egypt,...... 6299

REDEEMER
Job 19:25 I know that my **r.** liveth, and that 1350
Ps 19:14 O Lord, my strength, and my **r.**. 1350
Ps 78:35 rock, and the high God their **r.**......... 1350
Pr 23:11 For their **r.** is mighty; he shall.......... 1350
Isa 41:14 saith the Lord, and thy **r.**, the Holy.... 1350
Isa 43:14 Thus saith the Lord, your **r.**, the....... 1350
Isa 44:6 Israel, and his **r.** the Lord of hosts;.... 1350
Isa 44:24 Thus saith the Lord, thy **r.**, and he 1350
Isa 47:4 As for our **r.**, the Lord of hosts is his..1350
Isa 48:17 Thus saith the Lord, thy **R.**, the........ 1350
Isa 49:7 the **R.** of Israel, and his Holy One,..... 1350
Isa 49:26 Lord am thy Saviour and thy **R.**,......... 1350
Isa 54:5 and thy **R.** the Holy One of Israel; 1350
Isa 54:8 on thee, saith the Lord thy **R.**............ 1350
Isa 59:20 And the **R.** shall come to Zion,and...... 1350
Isa 60:16 Lord am thy Saviour and thy **R.**,......... 1350
Isa 63:16 thou, O Lord, art our father, our **r.**;... 1350
Jer 50:34 Their **R.** is strong; The Lord of......... 1350

REDEEMETH
Ps 34:22 Lord **r.** the soul of his servants: 6299
Ps 103:4 Who **r.** thy life from destruction;........ 1350

REDEEMING
Ru 4:7 concerning **r.** and concerning............ 1353
Eph 5:16 **R.** the time, because the days are...... *1805*
Col 4:5 them that are without, **r.** the time...... *1805*

REDEMPTION
Le 25:24 ye shall grant a **r.** for the land........... 1353
Le 25:51 shall give again the price of his **r.**....... 1353
Le 25:52 give him again the price of his **r.**........ 1353
Nu 3:49 Moses took the **r.** money of them...... 6306
Ps 49:8 (For the **r.** of their soul is precious,..... 6306
Ps 111:9 He sent **r.** unto his people: he........... 6304
Ps 130:7 mercy, and with him is plenteous **r.**.... 6304
Jer 32:7 the right of **r.** is thine to buy it.......... 1353
Jer 32:8 the **r.** is thine; buy it for thyself......... 1353
Lu 2:38 that looked for **r.** in Jerusalem. *3085*
Lu 21:28 **heads; for your r. draweth nigh**...... *629*
Ro 3:24 through the **r.** that is in Christ Jesus: ... *629*
Ro 8:23 adoption, to wit, the **r.** of our body...... *629*
1Co 1:30 and sanctification, and **r.**: *629*
Eph 1:7 whom we have **r.** through his blood,..... *629*
Eph 1:14 the **r.** of the purchased possession, ... *629*
Eph 4:30 ye are sealed unto the day of **r.**.......... *629*
Col 1:14 whom we have **r.** through his blood,..... *629*
Heb 9:12 having obtained eternal **r.** for us......... *3085*
Heb 9:15 for the **r.** of the transgressions that...... *629*

REDNESS
Pr 23:29 cause? who hath **r.** of eyes?............. 2498

REDOUND
2Co 4:15 of many **r.** to the glory of God. *4052*

RED-SEA See RED and SEA.

REED See also REEDS.
1Ki 14:15 as a **r.** is shaken in the water;.......... 7070
2Ki 18:21 upon the staff of this bruised **r.**,........ 7070
Job 40:21 shady trees, in the covert of the **r.**,.... 7070
Isa 36:6 in the staff of this broken **r.**, on.......... 7070
Isa 42:3 A bruised **r.** shall he not break, and.... 7070
Eze 29:6 a staff of **r.** to the house of Israel. 7070
Eze 40:3 in his hand, and a measuring **r.**; 7070
Eze 40:5 a measuring **r.** of six cubits long 7070
Eze 40:5 the breadth of the building, one **r.**; 7070
Eze 40:5 and the height, one **r.**.......................... 7070
Eze 40:6 of the gate, which was one **r.** broad;... 7070
Eze 40:6 the gate, which was one **r.** broad. 7070
Eze 40:7 was one **r.** long, and one **r.** broad; 7070
Eze 40:7 porch of the gate within was one **r.**. ... 7070
Eze 40:8 the porch of the gate within, one **r.**..... 7070
Eze 41:8 were a full **r.** of six great cubits......... 7070
Eze 42:16 east side with the measuring **r.**,......... 7070
Eze 42:16, 17 the measuring **r.** round about, ... 7070
Eze 42:18 reeds, with the measuring **r.**. 7070
Eze 42:19 reeds with the measuring **r.**, ... 7070

Mt 11:7 **to see? A r. shaken with the wind?** .*2563*
Mt 12:20 A bruised **r.** shall he not break, and... *2563*
Mt 27:29 head, and a **r.** in his right hand: *2563*
Mt 27:30 took the **r.**, and smote him on the...... *2563*
Mt 27:48 it with vinegar, and put it on a **r.**, ... *2563*
Mk 15:19 smote him on the head with a **r.**, ... *2563*
Mk 15:36 full of vinegar, and put it on a **r.**, ... *2563*
Lu 7:24 **to see? A r. shaken with the wind?** .*2563*
Re 11:1 was given me a **r.** like unto a rod:........ *2563*
Re 21:15 talked with me had a golden **r.** to........ *2563*
Re 21:16 he measured the city with the **r.**,........ *2563*

REEDS
Isa 19:6 up: the **r.** and flags shall wither. 7070
Isa 19:7 The paper **r.** by the brooks, by the ....
Isa 35:7 shall be grass with **r.** and rushes........ 7070
Jer 51:32 the **r.** they have burned with fire, ... 98
Eze 42:16 measuring reed, five hundred **r.**, ... 7070
Eze 42:17 the north side, five hundred **r.**,.......... 7070
Eze 42:18 the south side, five hundred **r.**,.......... 7070
Eze 42:19 side, and measured five hundred **r.**...... 7070
Eze 42:20 round about, five hundred **r.** long, ...
Eze 45:1 length of five and twenty thousand **r.**, ...
Eze 48:8 five and twenty thousand **r.** in breadth,......

REEL
Ps 107:27 They **r.** to and fro, and stagger 2287
Isa 24:20 earth shall **r.** to and fro like a............ 5128

REELAIAH (re-el-ah'-yah)
Ezr 2:2 Seraiah, **R.**, Mordecai, Bilshan,.......... 7480

REFINE See also REFINED.
Zec 13:9 will **r.** them as silver is refined, ... 6884

REFINED
1Ch 28:18 for the altar of incense **r.** gold 2212
1Ch 29:4 seven thousand talents of **r.** silver, ... 2212
Isa 25:6 of wines on the lees well **r.**................ 2212
Isa 48:10 I have **r.** thee, but not with silver; 6884
Zec 13:9 and will refine them as silver is **r.**, ... 6884

REFINER See also REFINER'S.
Mal 3:3 he shall sit as a **r.** and purifier of 6884

REFINER'S
Mal 3:2 for he is like a **r.** fire, and like.......... 6884

REFORMATION
Heb 9:10 on them until the time of **r.**............... *1357*

REFORMED
Le 26:23 if ye will not be **r.** by me by these 3256

REFRAIN See also REFRAINED; REFRAINETH.
Ge 45:1 Joseph could not **r.** himself before........ 662
Job 7:11 I will not **r.** my mouth; I will............ 2820
Pr 1:15 them; **r.** thy foot from their path:........ 4513
Ec 3:5 and a time to **r.** from embracing;.......... 7368
Isa 48:9 for my praise will I **r.** for thee,.......... 2413
Isa 64:12 Wilt thou **r.** thyself for these things,..... 662
Jer 31:16 **R.** thy voice from weeping, and......... 4513
Ac 5:38 **R.** from these men, and let them......... 868
1Pe 3:10 let him **r.** his tongue from evil, ... *3973*

REFRAINED
Ge 43:31 **r.** himself, and said, Set on bread. 662
Es 5:10 Nevertheless Haman **r.** himself:........... 662
Job 29:9 The princes **r.** talking, and laid 6113
Ps 40:9 I have not **r.** my lips, O Lord, thou 3607
Ps 119:101 **r.** my feet from every evil way,......... 3601
Isa 42:14 I have been still, and **r.** myself:........... 662
Jer 14:10 they have not **r.** their feet, ... 2820

REFRAINETH
Pr 10:19 sin: but he that **r.** his lips is wise. 2820

REFRESH See also REFRESHED; REFRESHETH; REFRESHING.
1Ki 13:7 home with me, and **r.** thyself, ... 5582
Ac 27:3 unto his friends to **r.** himself. *1958,5177*
Phm 20 the Lord: **r.** my bowels in the Lord...... *373*

REFRESHED
Ex 23:12 and the stranger, may be **r.**. 5314
Ex 31:17 seventh day he rested, and was **r.**....... 5314
1Sa 16:23 so Saul was **r.**, and was well, and 7304
2Sa 16:14 weary, and **r.** themselves there. 5314
Job 32:20 I will speak, that I may be **r.**:............ 7304
Ro 15:32 of God, and may with you be **r.**.......... *4875*
1Co 16:18 they have **r.** my spirit and yours:......... *373*
2Co 7:13 because his spirit was **r.** by you all. *373*
2Ti 1:16 he oft **r.** me, and was not ashamed...... *404*
Phm 7 bowels of the saints are **r.** by thee,...... *373*

REFRESHETH
Pr 25:13 for he **r.** the soul of his masters. 7725

REFRESHING
Isa 28:12 weary to rest; and this is the **r.**:........ 4774
Ac 3:19 the times of **r.** shall come from *403*

REFUGE
Nu 35:6 there shall be six cities for **r.**, ... 4733
Nu 35:11 you cities to be cities of **r.** for you; 4733
Nu 35:12 shall be unto you cities for **r.** from 4733
Nu 35:13 give six cities shall ye have for **r.**........ 4733
Nu 35:14 Canaan, which shall be cities of **r.**. 4733
Nu 35:15 These six cities shall be a **r.**, both...... 4733
Nu 35:25 shall restore him to the city of his **r.**,.. 4733
Nu 35:26 out the border of the city of his **r.**,...... 4733
Nu 35:27 the borders of the city of his **r.**, ... 4733
Nu 35:28 remained in the city of his **r.** until 4733
Nu 35:32 him that is fled to the city of his **r.**,.... 4733
De 33:27 The eternal God is thy **r.**, and........... 4585
Jos 20:2 Appoint out for you cities of **r.**, ... 4733
Jos 20:3 your **r.** from the avenger of blood. 4733
Jos 21:13, 21,27,32,38 city of **r.** for the slayer; ... 4733
2Sa 22:3 my high tower, and my **r.**, my........... 4498
1Ch 6:57 Hebron, the city of **r.**, and Libnah 4733
1Ch 6:67 gave unto them, of the cities of **r.**, ... 4733
Ps 9:9 also will be a **r.** for the oppressed, ... 4869
Ps 9:9 oppressed, a **r.** in times of trouble...... 4869
Ps 14:6 poor, because the Lord is his **r.**.......... 4268
Ps 46:1 God is our **r.** and strength, a very...... 4268
Ps 46:7, 11 us; the God of Jacob is our **r.**......... 4869
Ps 48:3 is known in her palaces for a **r.**. 4869
Ps 57:1 of thy wings will I make my **r.**,........... 2620
Ps 59:16 and **r.** in the day of my trouble............ 4498
Ps 62:7 my strength, and my **r.**, is in God. 4268
Ps 62:8 before him: God is a **r.** for us............ 4268
Ps 71:7 many; but thou art my strong **r.**. 4268
Ps 91:2 Lord, He is my **r.** and my fortress: 4268
Ps 91:9 hast made the Lord, which is my **r.**,... 4268
Ps 94:22 and my God is the rock of my **r.**......... 4268
Ps 104:18 high hills are a **r.** for the wild goats; ... 4268
Ps 142:4 **r.** failed me; no man cared for........... 4498
Ps 142:5 Thou art my **r.** and my portion in........ 4268
Pr 14:26 his children shall have a place of **r.**. 4268
Isa 4:6 for a place of **r.**, and for a covert........ 4268
Isa 25:4 a **r.** from the storm, a shadow from.... 4268
Isa 28:15 for we have made lies our **r.**, and 4268
Isa 28:17 hail shall sweep away the **r.** of lies, ... 4268
Jer 16:19 and my **r.** in the day of affliction, ... 4498
Heb 6:18 have fled for **r.** to lay hold upon the.... *2703*

REFUSE See also REFUSED; REFUSETH.
Ex 4:23 if thou **r.** to let him go, behold, I 3985
Ex 8:2 if thou **r.** to let them go, behold, I 3986
Ex 9:2 if thou **r.** to let them go, and wilt...... 3986
Ex 10:3 long wilt thou **r.** to humble thyself...... 3985
Ex 10:4 if thou **r.** to let my people go, ... 3986
Ex 16:28 **r.** ye to keep my commandments 3985
Ex 22:17 utterly **r.** to give her unto him,.......... 3985
1Sa 15:9 every thing that was vile and **r.**, ... 4549
Job 34:33 whether thou **r.**, or whether thou....... 3988
Pr 8:33 and be wise, and **r.** it not. 6544
Pr 21:7 because they **r.** to do judgment.......... 3985
Pr 21:25 him; for his hands **r.** to labour. 3985
Isa 1:20 But if ye **r.** and rebel, ye shall be 3985
Isa 7:15 that he may know to **r.** the evil, ... 3988
Isa 7:16 the child shall know to **r.** the evil, ... 3988
Jer 8:5 hold fast deceit, they **r.** to return........ 3985
Jer 9:6 through deceit they **r.** to know me, ... 3985
Jer 13:10 people, which **r.** to hear my words, ... 3987
Jer 25:28 **r.** to take the cup at thine hand to...... 3985
Jer 38:21 But if thou **r.** to go forth, this is 3986
La 3:45 and **r.** in the midst of the people. 3973
Am 8:6 yea, and sell the **r.** of the wheat?........ 4651
Ac 25:11 worthy of death, I **r.** not to die:.......... *3868*
1Ti 4:7 **r.** profane and old wives' fables,......... *3868*
1Ti 5:11 But the younger widows **r.**: for.......... *3868*
Heb 12:25 that ye **r.** not him that speaketh......... *3868*

REFUSED See also REFUSEDST.
Ge 37:35 but he **r.** to be comforted; and he 3985
Ge 39:8 he **r.**, and said unto his master's.......... 3985
Ge 48:19 his father **r.**, and said, I know it, ... 3985
Nu 20:21 Edom **r.** to give Israel passage 3985
1Sa 8:19 the people **r.** to obey the voice of 3985
1Sa 16:7 stature; because I have **r.** him: 3988
1Sa 28:23 But he **r.**, and said, I will not eat. 3985
2Sa 2:23 Howbeit he **r.** to turn aside:............... 3985

2Sa 13:9 out before him; but he **r.** to eat. 3985
1Ki 20:35 thee. And the man **r.** to smite him. 3985
1Ki 21:15 which he **r.** to give thee for money: 3985
2Ki 5:16 he urged him to take it; but he **r.** 3985
Ne 9:17 **r.** to obey, neither were mindful of 3985
Es 1:12 Vashti **r.** to come at the king's 3985
Job 6:7 things that my soul **r.** to touch are 3985
Ps 77:2 not: my soul **r.** to be comforted. 3985
Ps 78:10 of God, and **r.** to walk in his law; 3985
Ps 78:67 he **r.** the tabernacle of Joseph, 3988
Ps 118:22 The stone which the builders **r.** is 3988
Pr 1:24 Because I have called, and ye **r.**; 3985
Isa 54:6 wife of youth, when thou wast **r.**, 3988
Jer 5:3 they have **r.** to receive correction: 3985
Jer 5:3 a rock; they have **r.** to return. 3985
Jer 11:10 which **r.** to hear my words; and 3985
Jer 31:15 **r.** to be comforted for her children, 3985
Jer 50:33 them fast; they **r.** to let them go. 3985
Eze 5:6 they have **r.** my judgments and 3988
Ho 11:5 king, because they **r.** to return. 3985
Zec 7:11 But they **r.** to hearken, and pulled 3985
Ac 7:35 Moses whom they **r.**, saying, Who *720*
1Ti 4:4 God is good, and nothing to be **r.**, *579*
Heb 11:24 **r.** to be called the son of Pharaoh's *720*
Heb 12:25 escaped not who **r.** him that speak *3868*

REFUSEDST
Jer 3:3 forehead, thou **r.** to be ashamed. 3985

REFUSETH
Ex 7:14 hardened, he **r.** to let the people go. 3985
Nu 22:13 the Lord **r.** to give me leave to go 3985
Nu 22:14 said, Baalam **r.** to come with us. 3985
De 25:7 My husband's brother **r.** to raise up 3985
Pr 10:17 but he that **r.** reproof erreth. 5800
Pr 13:18 shall be to him that **r.** instruction: 6544
Pr 15:32 He that **r.** instruction despiseth 6544
Isa 8:6 people **r.** the waters of Shiloah 3988
Jer 15:18 incurable, which **r.** to be healed? 3985

REGARD See also REGARDED; REGARDEST; REGARDETH; REGARDING.
Ge 45:20 Also **r.** not your stuff; 5869,2347,5921
Ex 5:9 and let them not **r.** vain words. 8159
Le 19:31 **R.** not them that have familiar 6437
De 28:50 shall not **r.** the person of the old, 5375
1Sa 4:20 answered not, neither did she **r.** it. 3820
1Sa 25:25 I pray thee, **r.** this man of Belial, 3820
2Sa 13:20 is thy brother; **r.** not this thing. 3820
2Ki 3:14 I **r.** the presence of Jehoshaphat 5375
Job 3:4 let not God **r.** it from above, 1875
Job 35:13 neither will the Almighty **r.** it. 7789
Job 36:21 Take heed, **r.** not iniquity: for 6437
Ps 28:5 they **r.** not the works of the Lord, 995
Ps 31:6 hated them that **r.** lying vanities: 8104
Ps 66:18 If I **r.** iniquity in my heart, the 7200
Ps 94:7 neither shall the God of Jacob **r.** it. 995
Ps 102:17 will **r.** the prayer of the destitute, 6437
Pr 5:2 That thou mayest **r.** discretion, 8104
Pr 6:35 He will not **r.** any ransom; 5375,6440
Ec 8:2 that in **r.** of the oath of God. 5921,1700
Isa 5:12 they **r.** not the work of the Lord, 5027
Isa 13:17 which shall not **r.** silver; and as 2803
La 4:16 he will no more **r.** them: they 5027
Da 11:37 shall he **r.** the God of his fathers, 995
Da 11:37 desire of women, nor **r.** any god: 995
Am 5:22 will I **r.** the peace offerings of 5027
Hab 1:5 and **r.**, and wonder marvellously: 5027
Mal 1:9 means: will he **r.** your persons? 5375
Lu 18:4 **I fear not God, nor r. man;** *1788*
Ac 8:11 to him they had **r.**, because that *4337*
Ro 14:6 day, to the Lord he doth not **r.** it. *5426*

REGARDED
Ex 9:21 that **r.** not the word of the Lord 3820
1Ki 18:29 nor any to answer, nor any that **r.** 7182
1Ch 17:17 **r.** me according to the estate of a 7200
Ps 106:44 Nevertheless he **r.** their affliction, 7200
Pr 1:24 out my hand, and no man **r.**; 7181
Da 3:12 men, O king, have not **r.** thee: 7761,2942
Lu 1:48 he hath **r.** the low estate of his *1914*
Lu 18:2 **feared not God, neither r. man:** *1788*
Heb 8:9 and I **r.** them not, saith the Lord. *272*

REGARDEST
2Sa 19:6 thou **r.** neither princes nor servants:
Job 30:20 I stand up, and thou **r.** me not. 995
Mt 22:16 for thou **r.** not the person of men. *991*
Mk 12:14 for thou **r.** not the person of men, *991*

REGARDETH
De 10:17 **r.** not persons, nor taketh reward; 5375
Job 34:19 nor **r.** the rich more than the poor? 5234
Job 39:7 **r.** he the crying of the driver. 8085
Pr 12:10 man **r.** the life of his beast: 3045
Pr 13:18 that **r.** reproof shall be honoured. 8104
Pr 15:5 but he that **r.** reproof is prudent. 8104
Pr 29:7 but the wicked **r.** not to know it. 995
Ec 5:8 that is higher than the highest **r.**; 8104
Ec 11:4 that **r.** the clouds shall not reap. 7200
Isa 33:8 despised the cities, he **r.** no man. 2803
Da 6:13 of Judah, **r.** not thee, O king, 7761,2942
Mal 2:13 he **r.** not the offering any more, 6437
Ro 14:6 **r.** the day, **r.** it unto the Lord; *5426*
Ro 14:6 he that **r.** not the day, to the Lord *5426*

REGARDING
Job 4:20 perish for ever without any **r.** it. 7760
Php 2:30 nigh unto death, not **r.** his life, *3851*

REGEM (re'-ghem) See also REGEM-MELECH.
1Ch 2:47 sons of Jahdai; **R.**, and Jotham, 7276

REGEM-MELECH (re''-ghem-me'-lek)
Zec 7:2 Sherezer and **R.**, and their men, 7278

REGENERATION
Mt 19:28 **the r. when the Son of man shall** *3824*
Tit 3:5 he saved us, by the washing of **r.**, *3824*

REGION See also REGIONS.
De 3:4 all the **r.** of Argob, the kingdom of 2256
De 3:13 the **r.** of Argob, with all Bashan, 2256
1Ki 4:11 of Abinadab, in all the **r.** of Dor; 5299
1Ki 4:13 **r.** of Argob, which is in Bashan, 2256
1Ki 4:24 over all the **r.** on this side the river,
Mt 3:5 and all the **r.** round about Jordan, *4066*
Mt 4:16 sat in the **r.** and shadow of death *5561*
Mk 1:28 all the **r.** round about Galilee. *4066*
Mk 6:55 through that whole **r.** round about, *4066*
Lu 3:1 and of the **r.** of Trachonitis, and *5561*
Lu 4:14 through all the **r.** round about. *4066*
Lu 7:17 throughout all the **r.** round about. *4066*
Ac 13:49 published throughout all the **r.** *5561*
Ac 14:6 unto the **r.** that lieth round about: *4066*
Ac 16:6 Phrygia and the **r.** of Galatia, and *5561*

REGIONS
Ac 8:1 throughout the **r.** of Judaea and *5561*
2Co 10:16 preach the gospel in the **r.** beyond
2Co 11:10 this boasting in the **r.** of Achaia. *2825*
Ga 1:21 I came into the **r.** of Syria and *2825*

REGISTER
Ezr 2:62 sought their **r.** among those that 3791
Ne 7:5 I found a **r.** of the genealogy of 5612
Ne 7:64 sought their **r.** among those that 3791

REHABIAH (re-hab-i'-ah)
1Ch 23:17 sons of Eliezer were, **R.** the chief. 7345
1Ch 23:17 but the sons of **R.** were very many. 7345
1Ch 24:21 Concerning **R.**: of the sons of **R.**, 7345
1Ch 26:25 **R.** his son, and Jeshaiah his son, 7345

REHEARSE See also REHEARSED.
Ex 17:14 and **r.** it in the ears of Joshua: 7760
Jg 5:11 shall they **r.** the righteous acts of 8567

REHEARSED
1Sa 8:21 he **r.** them in the ears of the Lord. 1696
1Sa 17:31 spake, they **r.** them before Saul: 5046
Ac 11:4 But Peter **r.** the matter from the *756*
Ac 14:27 they **r.** all that God had done with *312*

REHOB (re'-hob) See also BETH-REHOB.
Nu 13:21 from the wilderness of Zin unto **R.**, 7340
Jos 19:28 Hebron, and **R.**, and Hammon, and 7340
Jos 19:30 Ummah also, and Aphek, and **R.** 7340
Jos 21:31 suburbs, and **R.** with her suburbs; 7340
Jg 1:31 of Helbah, nor of Aphik, nor of **R.** 7340
2Sa 8:3 also Hadadezer, the son of **R.**, king 7340
2Sa 8:12 spoil of Hadadezer, the son of **R.**, 7340
2Sa 10:8 Syrians of Zobah, and of **R.**, and 7340
1Ch 6:75 suburbs, and **R.** with her suburbs: 7340
Ne 10:11 Micha, **R.**, Hashabiah, 7340

REHOBOAM (re-ho-bo'-am) See also ROBOAM.
1Ki 11:43 **R.** his son reigned in his stead. 7346
1Ki 12:1 **R.** went to Shechem: for all Israel 7346
1Ki 12:3 of Israel came, and spake unto **R.**, 7346
1Ki 12:6 king **R.** consulted with the old men, 7346
1Ki 12:12 the people came to **R.** the third day, 7346
1Ki 12:17 of Judah, **R.** reigned over them. 7346
1Ki 12:18 king **R.** sent Adoram, who was over 7346
1Ki 12:18 king **R.** made speed to get him up 7346
1Ki 12:21 when **R.** was come to Jerusalem, 7346
1Ki 12:21 to bring the kingdom again to **R.** 7346
1Ki 12:23 Speak unto **R.**, the son of Solomon, 7346
1Ki 12:27 lord, even unto **R.** king of Judah, 7346
1Ki 12:27 and go again to **R.** king of Judah. 7346
1Ki 14:21 **R.** the son of Solomon reigned in 7346
1Ki 14:21 **R.** was forty and one years old when 7346
1Ki 14:25 to pass in the fifth year of king **R.**, 7346
1Ki 14:27 king **R.** made in their stead brasen 7346
1Ki 14:29 Now the rest of the acts of **R.**, and 7346
1Ki 14:30 was war between **R.** and Jeroboam 7346
1Ki 14:31 And **R.** slept with his fathers, and 7346
1Ki 15:6 was war between **R.** and Jeroboam 7346
1Ch 3:10 Solomon's son was **R.**, Abia his son, 7346
2Ch 9:31 and **R.** his son reigned in his stead. 7346
2Ch 10:1 And **R.** went to Shechem: for to 7346
2Ch 10:3 all Israel came and spake to **R.**, 7346
2Ch 10:6 **R.** took counsel with the old men 7346
2Ch 10:12 and all the people came to **R.** on 7346
2Ch 10:13 **R.** forsook the counsel of the old 7346
2Ch 10:17 of Judah, **R.** reigned over them. 7346
2Ch 10:18 **R.** sent Hadoram that was over the 7346
2Ch 10:18 **R.** made speed to get him up to his 7346
2Ch 11:1 when **R.** was come to Jerusalem, 7346
2Ch 11:1 bring the kingdom again to **R.** 7346
2Ch 11:3 Speak unto **R.** the son of Solomon, 7346
2Ch 11:5 **R.** dwelt in Jerusalem, and built 7346
2Ch 11:17 made **R.** the son of Solomon strong, 7346
2Ch 11:18 **R.** took him Mahalath the daughter 7346
2Ch 11:21 **R.** loved Maachah the daughter of 7346
2Ch 11:22 **R.** made Abijah the son of Maachah 7346
2Ch 12:1 **R.** had established the kingdom, 7346
2Ch 12:2 that in the fifth year of king **R.** 7346
2Ch 12:5 came Shemaiah the prophet to **R.**, 7346
2Ch 12:10 king **R.** made shields of brass, and 7346
2Ch 12:13 So king **R.** strengthened himself in 7346
2Ch 12:13 for **R.** was one and forty years old 7346
2Ch 12:15 Now the acts of **R.**, first and last, 7346
2Ch 12:15 wars between **R.** and Jeroboam 7346
2Ch 12:16 **R.** slept with his fathers, and was 7346
2Ch 13:7 strengthened themselves against **R.** 7346
2Ch 13:7 **R.** was young and tenderhearted, 7346

REHOBOTH (re'-ho-both)
Ge 10:11 Nineveh, and the city **R.**, and 7344
Ge 26:22 and he called the name of it **R.**; 7344
Ge 36:37 Saul of **R.** by the river reigned in 7344
1Ch 1:48 Shaul of **R.** by the river reigned in 7344

REHUM (re'-hum) See also NEHUM.
Ezr 2:2 Mizpar, Bigvai, **R.**, Baanah. 7348
Ezr 4:8 **R.** the chancellor and Shimshai 7348
Ezr 4:9 Then wrote **R.** the chancellor, and 7348
Ezr 4:17 an answer unto **R.** the chancellor, 7348
Ezr 4:23 letter was read before **R.**, and 7348
Ne 3:17 the Levites, **R.** the son of Bani. 7348
Ne 10:25 **R.**, Hashabnah, Maaseiah, 7348
Ne 12:3 Shechaniah, **R.**, Meremoth, 7348

REI (re'-i)
1Ki 1:8 the prophet, and Shimei, and **R.**, 7472

REIGN See also REIGNED; REIGNEST; REIGNETH; REIGNING.
Ge 37:8 him, Shalt thou indeed **r.** over us? 4427
Ex 15:18 The Lord shall **r.** for ever and ever. 4427
Le 26:17 that hate you shall **r.** over you; 7287
De 15:6 thou shalt **r.** over many nations, 4910
De 15:6 but they shall not **r.** over thee. 4910
Jg 9:2 threescore and ten persons, **r.** over 4910
Jg 9:2 you, or that one **r.** over you? 4910
Jg 9:8 the olive tree, **R.** thou over us. 4427
Jg 9:10 fig tree, Come thou, and **r.** over us. 4427
Jg 9:12 the vine, Come thou, and **r.** over us. 4427
Jg 9:14 bramble, Come thou, and **r.** over us. 4427
1Sa 8:7 me, that I should not **r.** over them. 4427
1Sa 8:9 of the king that shall **r.** over them. 4427
1Sa 8:11 of the king that shall **r.** over you: 4427
1Sa 9:17 this same shall **r.** over my people. 6113
1Sa 11:12 that said, Shall Saul **r.** over us? 4427
1Sa 12:12 Nay; but a king shall **r.** over us: 4427
2Sa 2:10 forty years old when he began to **r.** 4427
2Sa 3:21 **r.** over all that thine heart desireth. 4427
2Sa 5:4 thirty years old when he began to **r.**, 4427
1Ki 1:11 not heard that Adonijah...doth **r.**, 4427
1Ki 1:13 Solomon thy son shall **r.** after me, 4427

1Ki 1:13 throne? why then doth Adonijah **r.**? 4427
1Ki 1:17 Solomon thy son shall **r.** after me,....... 4427
1Ki 1:24 Adonijah shall **r.** after me, and he....... 4427
1Ki 1:30 Solomon thy son shall **r.** after me,...... 4427
1Ki 2:15 their faces on me, that I should **r.**....... 4427
1Ki 6:1 year of Solomon's **r.** over Israel,........ 4427
1Ki 11:37 **r.** according to all that thy soul.......... 4427
1Ki 14:21 one years old when he began to **r.**, ... 4427
1Ki 15:25 And Nadab...began to **r.** over Israel.... 4427
1Ki 15:33 began Baasha...to **r.** over all Israel..... 4427
1Ki 16:8 began Elah...to **r.** over Israel in......... 4427
1Ki 16:11 came to pass, when he began to **r.**,..... 4427
1Ki 16:15 did Zimri **r.** seven days in Tirzah......... 4427
1Ki 16:23 began Omri to **r.** over Israel, twelve... 4427
1Ki 16:29 began Ahab...to **r.** over Israel: 4427
1Ki 22:41 Jehoshaphat...to **r.** over Judah 4427
1Ki 22:42 five years old when he began to **r.**; 4427
1Ki 22:51 Ahaziah...began to **r.** over Israel......... 4427
2Ki 3:1 Jehoram...began to **r.** over Israel 4427
2Ki 8:16 Jehoram the son...began to **r.**............. 4427
2Ki 8:17 old was he when he began to **r.**;........ 4427
2Ki 8:25 did Ahaziah...begin to **r.**.................... 4427
2Ki 8:26 was Ahaziah when he began to **r.**;...... 4427
2Ki 9:29 began Ahaziah to **r.** over Judah. 4427
2Ki 11:3 And Athaliah did **r.** over the land....... 4427
2Ki 11:21 was Jehoash when he began to **r.**......... 4427
2Ki 12:1 year of Jehu Jehoash began to **r.**; 4427
2Ki 13:1 son of Jehu began to **r.** over Israel..... 4427
2Ki 13:10 began Jehoash...to **r.** over Israel in..... 4427
2Ki 14:2 five years old when he began to **r.**, ... 4427
2Ki 14:23 Jeroboam...began to **r.** in Samaria,...... 4427
2Ki 15:1 son of Amaziah king of Judah to **r.**...... 4427
2Ki 15:2 old was he when he began to **r.**,......... 4427
2Ki 15:8 did Zachariah...**r.** over Israel in.......... 4427
2Ki 15:13 Shallum...son of Jabesh began to **r.**.... 4427
2Ki 15:17 the son of Gadi to **r.** over Israel, ... 4427
2Ki 15:23 Pekahiah...began to **r.** over Israel....... 4427
2Ki 15:27 Pekah...began to **r.** over Israel.......... 4427
2Ki 15:32 son of Uzziah king of Judah to **r.**........ 4427
2Ki 15:33 old was he when he began to **r.**,......... 4427
2Ki 16:1 Ahaz...son of Jotham...began to **r.**....... 4427
2Ki 16:2 old was Ahaz when he began to **r.**,...... 4427
2Ki 17:1 began Hoshea...to **r.** in Samaria 4427
2Ki 18:1 that Hezekiah...began to **r.**, ... 4427
2Ki 18:2 old was he when he began to **r.**;........ 4427
2Ki 21:1 twelve years old...he began to **r.**, ... 4427
2Ki 21:19 two years old when he began to **r.**, ... 4427
2Ki 22:1 eight years old when he began to **r.**,.... 4427
2Ki 23:31 years old when he began to **r.**;.......... 4427
2Ki 23:33 that he might not **r.** in Jerusalem;........ 4427
2Ki 23:36 five years old when he began to **r.**; 4427
2Ki 24:8 years old when he began to **r.**,.......... 4427
2Ki 24:12 him in the eighth year of his **r.**.......... 4427
2Ki 24:18 one years old when he began to **r.**, ... 4427
2Ki 25:1 to pass in the ninth year of his **r.**,....... 4427
2Ki 25:27 in the year that he began to **r.** did....... 4427
1Ch 4:31 their cities unto the **r.** of David......... 4427
1Ch 26:31 the fortieth year of the **r.** of David 4438
1Ch 29:30 With all his **r.** and his might, and........ 4438
2Ch 1:8 hast made me to **r.** in his stead. 4427
2Ch 3:2 month, in the fourth year of his **r.**...... 4438
2Ch 12:13 years old when he began to **r.**,.......... 4427
2Ch 13:1 began Abijah to **r.** over Judah. 4427
2Ch 15:10 the fifteenth year of the **r.** of Asa....... 4438
2Ch 15:19 and thirtieth year of the **r.** of Asa....... 4438
2Ch 16:1 and thirtieth year of the **r.** of Asa....... 4438
2Ch 16:12 the thirty and ninth year of his **r.**....... 4438
2Ch 16:13 the one and fortieth year of his **r.**. 4427
2Ch 17:7 third year of his **r.** he sent to his....... 4427
2Ch 20:31 five years old when he began to **r.**, ... 4427
2Ch 21:5 two years old when he began to **r.**, ... 4427
2Ch 21:20 old was he when he began to **r.**,........ 4427
2Ch 22:2 was Ahaziah when he began to **r.**,...... 4427
2Ch 23:3 Behold, the king's son shall **r.**, as....... 4427
2Ch 24:1 seven years old when he began to **r.**, ..4427
2Ch 25:1 five years old when he began to **r.**, ... 4427
2Ch 26:3 was Uzziah when he began to **r.**, ... 4427
2Ch 27:1 five years old when he began to **r.**, ... 4427
2Ch 27:8 years old when he began to **r.**,.......... 4427
2Ch 28:1 years old when he began to **r.**,.......... 4427
2Ch 29:1 Hezekiah began to **r.** when he was..... 4427
2Ch 29:3 He in the first year of his **r.**, in the 4427
2Ch 29:19 king Ahaz in his **r.** did cast away........ 4438
2Ch 33:1 years old when he began to **r.**,.......... 4427
2Ch 33:21 years old when he began to **r.**,.......... 4427
2Ch 34:1 eight years old when he began to **r.**,... 4427
2Ch 34:3 in the eighth year of his **r.**, while....... 4427
2Ch 34:8 the eighteenth year of his **r.**, when..... 4427
2Ch 35:19 eighteenth year of the **r.** of Josiah...... 4438
2Ch 36:2 years old when he began to **r.**,.......... 4427
2Ch 36:5 five years old when he began to **r.**, ... 4427
2Ch 36:9 eight years old when he began to **r.**,... 4427
2Ch 36:11 years old when he began to **r.**,.......... 4427
2Ch 36:20 the **r.** of the kingdom of Persia:......... 4427
Ezr 4:5 the **r.** of Darius king of Persia, ... 4438
Ezr 4:6 And in the **r.** of Ahasuerus, in the...... 4438
Ezr 4:6 in the beginning of his **r.**, wrote......... 4438
Ezr 4:24 the second year of the **r.** of Darius..... 4437
Ezr 6:15 in the sixth year of the **r.** of Darius.... 4437
Ezr 7:1 in the **r.** of Artaxerxes king of.......... 4438
Ezr 8:1 in the **r.** of Artaxerxes the king.......... 4438
Ne 12:22 to the **r.** of Darius the Persian.......... 4438
Es 1:3 In the third year of his **r.**, he made 4427
Es 2:16 in the seventh year of his **r.**.............. 4438
Job 34:30 That the hypocrite **r.** not, lest the...... 4427
Ps 146:10 The Lord shall **r.** for ever, even thy.... 4427
Pr 8:15 By me kings **r.**, and princes decree 4427
Ec 4:14 For out of prison he cometh to **r.**;...... 4427
Isa 24:23 the Lord of hosts shall **r.** in mount..... 4427
Isa 32:1 a king shall **r.** in righteousness,.......... 4427
Jer 1:2 in the thirteenth year of his **r.**.......... 4427
Jer 22:15 Shalt thou **r.**, because thou closest..... 4427
Jer 23:5 and a King shall **r.** and prosper, ... 4427
Jer 26:1 beginning of the **r.** of Jehoiakim.......... 4468
Jer 27:1 beginning of the **r.** of Jehoiakim.......... 4467
Jer 28:1 the beginning of the **r.** of Zedekiah..... 4467
Jer 33:21 have a son to **r.** upon his throne; 4427
Jer 49:34 the **r.** of Zedekiah king of Judah, ... 4438
Jer 51:59 in the fourth year of his **r.**................ 4427
Jer 52:1 years old when he began to **r.**,.......... 4427
Jer 52:4 to pass in the ninth year of his **r.**,...... 4427
Jer 52:31 in the first year of his **r.** lifted up....... 4438
Da 1:1 third year of the **r.** of Jehoiakim......... 4438
Da 2:1 year of the **r.** of Nebuchadnezzar 4438
Da 6:28 this Daniel prospered in the **r.** of 4437
Da 6:28 and in the **r.** of Cyrus the Persian. 4437
Da 8:1 year of the **r.** of king Belshazzar 4438
Da 9:2 In the first year of his **r.** I Daniel....... 4427
Mic 4:7 shall **r.** over them in mount Zion 4427
Mt 2:22 that Archelaus did **r.** in Judaea in......... *936*
Lu 1:33 **r.** over the house of Jacob for ever;..... *936*
Lu 3:1 year of the **r.** of Tiberius Caesar......... *2231*
Lu 19:14 **not have this man to r. over us**....... *936*
Lu 19:27 **not that I should r. over them,** *936*
Ro 5:17 shall **r.** in life by one, Jesus Christ.)..... *936*
Ro 5:21 grace **r.** through righteousness unto *936*
Ro 6:12 Let not sin...**r.** in your mortal body,..... *936*
Ro 15:12 shall rise to **r.** over the Gentiles;......... *757*
1Co 4:8 us: and I would to God ye did **r.**, ... *936*
1Co 4:8 that we also might **r.** with you........... *4821*
1Co 15:25 For he must **r.**, till he hath put all *936*
2Ti 2:12 suffer, we shall also **r.** with him: *4821*
Re 5:10 and we shall **r.** on the earth................ *936*
Re 11:15 and he shall **r.** for ever and ever. *936*
Re 20:6 shall **r.** with him a thousand years........ *936*
Re 22:5 and they shall **r.** for ever and ever....... *936*

REIGNED

Ge 36:31 kings that **r.** in the land of Edom,....... 4427
Ge 36:31 before there **r.** any king over the 4427
Ge 36:32 Bela the son of Beor **r.** in Edom: 4427
Ge 36:33 and Jobab...**r.** in his stead................ 4427
Ge 36:34 and Husham...**r.** in his stead. 4427
Ge 36:35 and Hadad...**r.** in his stead:.............. 4427
Ge 36:36 Samlah of Masrekah **r.** in his stead. 4427
Ge 36:37 died, and Saul...**r.** in his stead. 4427
Ge 36:38 the son of Achbor **r.** in his stead........ 4427
Ge 36:39 died, and Hadar **r.** in his stead:.......... 4427
Jos 12:5 And **r.** in mount Hermon, and in 4910
Jos 13:10 Amorites, which **r.** in Heshbon, ... 4427
Jos 13:12 which **r.** in Ashtaroth and in Edrei, ... 4427
Jos 13:21 the Amorites, which **r.** in Heshbon, ... 4427
Jg 4:2 king of Canaan, that **r.** in Hazor; 4427
Jg 9:22 Abimelech had **r.** three years over...... 7786
1Sa 13:1 Saul **r.** one year; and when he had 4427
1Sa 13:1 he had **r.** two years over Israel, ... 4427
2Sa 2:10 reign over Israel, and **r.** two years. 4427
2Sa 5:4 to reign, and he **r.** forty years. 4427
2Sa 5:5 he **r.** over Judah seven years and....... 4427
2Sa 5:5 he **r.** thirty and three years over......... 4427
2Sa 8:15 And David **r.** over all Israel; and 4427
2Sa 10:1 and Hanun his son **r.** in his stead. 4427
2Sa 16:8 Saul, in whose stead thou hast **r.**; 4427
1Ki 2:11 that David **r.** over Israel were forty.... 4427
1Ki 2:11 seven years **r.** he in Hebron, and....... 4427
1Ki 2:11 and three years **r.** he in Jerusalem....... 4427
1Ki 4:21 And Solomon **r.** over all kingdoms 4910
1Ki 11:24 dwelt therein, and **r.** in Damascus. 4427
1Ki 11:25 abhorred Israel, and **r.** over Syria....... 4427
1Ki 11:42 Solomon **r.** in Jerusalem over all......... 4427
1Ki 11:43 Rehoboam his son **r.** in his stead........ 4427
1Ki 12:17 of Judah, Rehoboam **r.** over them....... 4427
1Ki 14:19 how he warred, and how he **r.**, ... 4427
1Ki 14:20 the days which Jeroboam **r.** were 4427
1Ki 14:20 and Nadab his son **r.** in his stead. 4427
1Ki 14:21 And Rehoboam...**r.** in Judah.............. 4427
1Ki 14:21 he **r.** seventeen years in Jerusalem,.... 4427
1Ki 14:31 And Abijam his son **r.** in his stead. 4427
1Ki 15:1 son of Nebat **r.** Abijam over Judah...... 4427
1Ki 15:2 Three years **r.** he in Jerusalem. 4427
1Ki 15:8 and Asa his son **r.** in his stead........... 4427
1Ki 15:9 king of Israel **r.** Asa over Judah. 4427
1Ki 15:10 and one years **r.** he in Jerusalem......... 4427
1Ki 15:24 Jehoshaphat his son **r.** in his stead...... 4427
1Ki 15:25 Judah, and **r.** over Israel two years..... 4427
1Ki 15:28 slay him, and **r.** in his stead............. 4427
1Ki 15:29 it came to pass, when he **r.**, that he... 4427
1Ki 16:6 and Elah his son **r.** in his stead.......... 4427
1Ki 16:10 king of Judah, and **r.** in his stead........ 4427
1Ki 16:22 so Tibni died, and Omri **r.**. 4427
1Ki 16:23 years: six years **r.** he in Tirzah.......... 4427
1Ki 16:28 and Ahab his son **r.** in his stead. 4427
1Ki 16:29 Ahab the son of Omri **r.** over Israel.... 4427
1Ki 22:40 Ahaziah his son **r.** in his stead. 4427
1Ki 22:42 and he **r.** twenty and five years in...... 4427
1Ki 22:50 Jehoram his son **r.** in his stead. 4427
1Ki 22:51 Judah, and **r.** two years over Israel..... 4427
2Ki 1:17 And Jehoram **r.** in his stead in the...... 4427
2Ki 3:1 king of Judah, and **r.** twelve years. 4427
2Ki 3:27 that should have **r.** in his stead, ... 4427
2Ki 8:15 he died; and Hazael **r.** in his stead...... 4427
2Ki 8:17 and he **r.** eight years in Jerusalem. 4427
2Ki 8:24 and Ahaziah his son **r.** in his stead...... 4427
2Ki 8:26 and he **r.** one year in Jerusalem. ....
2Ki 10:35 Jehoahaz his son **r.** in his stead.......... 4427
2Ki 10:36 the time that Jehu **r.** over Israel 4427
2Ki 12:1 and forty years **r.** he in Jerusalem. 4427
2Ki 12:21 Amaziah his son **r.** in his stead. 4427
2Ki 13:1 in Samaria, and **r.** seventeen years. ....
2Ki 13:9 and Joash his son **r.** in his stead 4427
2Ki 13:10 in Samaria, and **r.** sixteen years. ....
2Ki 13:24 Ben-hadad his son **r.** in his stead........ 4427
2Ki 14:1 **r.** Amaziah the son of Joash king......... 4427
2Ki 14:2 and **r.** twenty and nine years in 4427
2Ki 14:16 Jeroboam his son **r.** in his stead. 4427
2Ki 14:23 Samaria, and **r.** forty and one years. ....
2Ki 14:29 Zachariah his son **r.** in his stead......... 4427
2Ki 15:2 and he **r.** two and fifty years in.......... 4427
2Ki 15:7 and Jotham his son **r.** in his stead....... 4427
2Ki 15:10 and slew him, and **r.** in his stead......... 4427
2Ki 15:13 and he **r.** a full month in Samaria........ 4427
2Ki 15:14 and slew him, and **r.** in his stead......... 4427
2Ki 15:17 Israel, and **r.** ten years in Samaria. ....
2Ki 15:22 Pekahiah his son **r.** in his stead........... 4427
2Ki 15:23 Israel in Samaria, and **r.** two years. ....
2Ki 15:25 he killed him, and **r.** in his room. 4427
2Ki 15:27 in Samaria, and **r.** twenty years. ....
2Ki 15:30 and slew him, and **r.** in his stead,....... 4427
2Ki 15:33 he **r.** sixteen years in Jerusalem........... 4427
2Ki 15:38 and Ahaz his son **r.** in his stead. 4427
2Ki 16:2 and **r.** sixteen years in Jerusalem, ... 4427
2Ki 16:20 Hezekiah his son **r.** in his stead. 4427
2Ki 18:2 and he **r.** twenty and nine years in 4427
2Ki 19:37 Esarhaddon his son **r.** in his stead........ 4427
2Ki 20:21 Manasseh his son **r.** in his stead. 4427
2Ki 21:1 **r.** fifty and five years in Jerusalem...... 4427
2Ki 21:18 and Amon his son **r.** in his stead......... 4427
2Ki 21:19 and he **r.** two years in Jerusalem........ 4427
2Ki 21:26 and Josiah his son **r.** in his stead......... 4427
2Ki 22:1 and he **r.** thirty and one years in........ 4427
2Ki 23:31 he **r.** three months in Jerusalem.......... 4427
2Ki 23:36 he **r.** eleven years in Jerusalem.......... 4427
2Ki 24:6 Jehoiachin his son **r.** in his stead. 4427
2Ki 24:8 he **r.** in Jerusalem three months.......... 4427
2Ki 24:18 he **r.** eleven years in Jerusalem............ 4427
1Ch 1:43 kings that **r.** in the land of Edom......... 4427
1Ch 1:43 before any king **r.** over the children.... 4427
1Ch 1:44 Jobab the son...**r.** in his stead............. 4427
1Ch 1:45 Husham...**r.** in his stead. 4427

1Ch 1:46 Hadad the son...**r.** in his stead. 4427
1Ch 1:47 Samlah of Masrekah **r.** in his stead. 4427
1Ch 1:48 Shaul of Rehoboth...**r.** in his stead. 4427
1Ch 1:49 the son of Achbor **r.** in his stead. 4427
1Ch 1:50 was dead, Hadad **r.** in his stead: 4427
1Ch 3:4 he **r.** seven years and six months: 4427
1Ch 3:4 he **r.** thirty and three years 4427
1Ch 18:14 So David **r.** over all Israel, and 4427
1Ch 19:1 died, and his son **r.** in his stead. 4427
1Ch 29:26 David the son...**r.** over all Israel. 4427
1Ch 29:27 he **r.** over Israel was forty years; 4427
1Ch 29:27 seven years **r.** he in Hebron, and 4427
1Ch 29:27 and three years **r.** he in Jerusalem. 4427
1Ch 29:28 and Solomon his son **r.** in his stead. 4427
2Ch 1:13 congregation, and **r.** over Israel. 4427
2Ch 9:26 And he **r.** over all the kings from 4910
2Ch 9:30 Solomon **r.** in Jerusalem over all 4427
2Ch 9:31 Rehoboam his son **r.** in his stead. 4427
2Ch 10:17 of Judah, Rehoboam **r.** over them. 4427
2Ch 12:13 himself in Jerusalem, and **r.**: for 4427
2Ch 12:13 he **r.** seventeen years in Jerusalem, 4427
2Ch 12:16 and Abijah his son **r.** in his stead. 4427
2Ch 13:2 He **r.** three years in Jerusalem. 4427
2Ch 14:1 and Asa his son **r.** in his stead. 4427
2Ch 17:1 Jehoshaphat his son **r.** in his stead, 4427
2Ch 20:31 And Jehoshaphat **r.** over Judah: he 4427
2Ch 20:31 he **r.** twenty and five years in 4427
2Ch 21:1 Jehoram his son **r.** in his stead. 4427
2Ch 21:5 and he **r.** eight years in Jerusalem. 4427
2Ch 21:20 and he **r.** in Jerusalem eight years, 4427
2Ch 22:1 son of Jehoram king of Judah **r.** 4427
2Ch 22:2 and he **r.** one year in Jerusalem. 4427
2Ch 22:12 and Athaliah **r.** over the land. 4427
2Ch 24:1 and he **r.** forty years in Jerusalem. 4427
2Ch 24:27 Amaziah his son **r.** in his stead. 4427
2Ch 25:1 and he **r.** twenty and nine years in 4427
2Ch 26:3 **r.** fifty and two years in Jerusalem. 4427
2Ch 26:23 and Jotham his son **r.** in his stead. 4427
2Ch 27:1 he **r.** sixteen years in Jerusalem. 4427
2Ch 27:8 and **r.** sixteen years in Jerusalem. 4427
2Ch 27:9 and Ahaz his son **r.** in his stead. 4427
2Ch 28:1 he **r.** sixteen years in Jerusalem: 4427
2Ch 28:27 Hezekiah his son **r.** in his stead. 4427
2Ch 29:1 and he **r.** nine and twenty years in 4427
2Ch 32:33 Manassah his son **r.** in his stead. 4427
2Ch 33:1 and he **r.** fifty and five years in 4427
2Ch 33:20 and Amon his son **r.** in his stead. 4427
2Ch 33:21 and **r.** two years in Jerusalem. 4427
2Ch 34:1 he **r.** in Jerusalem one and thirty 4427
2Ch 36:2 he **r.** three months in Jerusalem. 4427
2Ch 36:5 he **r.** eleven years in Jerusalem: 4427
2Ch 36:8 Jehoiachin his son **r.** in his stead. 4427
2Ch 36:9 he **r.** three months and ten days in 4427
2Ch 36:11 and **r.** eleven years in Jerusalem. 4427
Es 1:1 (this is Ahasuerus which **r.**, from 4427
Isa 37:38 Esar-haddon his son **r.** in his stead. 4427
Jer 22:11 **r.** instead of Josiah his father, 4427
Jer 37:1 Zedekiah...**r.** instead of Coniah 4427
Jer 52:1 he **r.** eleven years in Jerusalem. 4427
Ro 5:14 death **r.** from Adam to Moses, even *936*
Ro 5:17 one man's offence death **r.** by one; *936*
Ro 5:21 as sin hath **r.** unto death, even so *936*
1Co 4:8 ye have **r.** as kings without us: *936*
Re 11:17 thee thy great power, and hast **r.** *936*
Re 20:4 and **r.** with Christ a thousand years. *936*

REIGNEST
1Ch 29:12 come of thee, and thou **r.** over all; 4910

REIGNETH
1Sa 12:14 and also the king that **r.** over you 4427
2Sa 15:10 shall say, Absalom **r.** in Hebron. 4427
1Ki 1:18 now, behold, Adonijah **r.**; and now, 4427
1Ch 16:31 among the nations, The Lord **r.** 4427
Ps 47:8 God **r.** over the heathen: God 4427
Ps 93:1 The Lord **r.**, he is clothed with 4427
Ps 96:10 the heathen that the Lord **r.**: 4427
Ps 97:1 The Lord **r.**; let the earth rejoice; 4427
Ps 99:1 The Lord **r.**; let the people 4427
Pr 30:22 For a servant when he **r.**; and a 4427
Isa 52:7 that saith unto Zion, Thy God **r.**! 4427
Re 17:18 which **r.** over the kings of the *2192,932*
Re 19:6 for the Lord God omnipotent **r.** *936*

REIGNING
1Sa 16:1 rejected him from **r.** over Israel? 4427

REINS
Job 16:13 he cleaveth my **r.** asunder, and 3629
Job 19:27 my **r.** be consumed within me. 3629
Ps 7:9 God trieth the hearts and **r.** 3629
Ps 16:7 my **r.** also instruct me in the night 3629
Ps 26:2 prove me; try my **r.** and my heart. 3629
Ps 73:21 grieved, and I was pricked in my **r.** 3629
Ps 139:13 For thou hast possessed my **r.**: 3629
Pr 23:16 my **r.** shall rejoice, when thy lips 3629
Isa 11:5 faithfulness the girdle of his **r.** 2504
Jer 11:20 that triest the **r.** and the heart, 3629
Jer 12:2 their mouth, and far from their **r.** 3629
Jer 17:10 Lord search the heart, I try the **r.**, 3629
Jer 20:12 and seest the **r.** and the heart, let 3629
La 3:13 of his quiver to enter into my **r.** 3629
Re 2:23 **which searcheth the r. and hearts:** *3510*

REJECT See also REJECTED; REJECTETH.
Ho 4:6 I will also **r.** thee, and thou shalt 3988
Mk 6:26 sat with him, he would not **r.** her. *114*
Mk 7:9 **well ye r. the commandment of** *114*
Tit 3:10 first and second admonition **r.**; *3868*

REJECTED
1Sa 8:7 they have not **r.** thee, but they 3988
1Sa 8:7 they have **r.** me, that I should not 3988
1Sa 10:19 And ye have this day **r.** your God, 3988
1Sa 15:23 thou hast **r.** the word of the Lord, 3988
1Sa 15:23 hath also **r.** thee from being king 3988
1Sa 15:26 thou hast **r.** the word of the Lord, 3988
1Sa 15:26 Lord hath **r.** thee from being king 3988
1Sa 16:1 **r.** him from reigning over Israel? 3988
2Ki 17:15 And they **r.** his statutes, and his 3988
2Ki 17:20 the Lord **r.** all the seed of Israel, 3988
Isa 53:3 He is despised and **r.** of men; a 2310
Jer 2:37 the Lord hath **r.** thy confidences, 3988
Jer 6:19 my words, not to my law, but **r.** it. 3988
Jer 6:30 because the Lord hath **r.** them. 3988
Jer 7:29 the Lord hath **r.** and forsaken the 3988
Jer 8:9 they have **r.** the word of the Lord; 3988
Jer 14:19 Hast thou utterly **r.** Judah? hath 3988
La 5:22 thou hast utterly **r.** us; thou art 3988
Ho 4:6 because thou hast **r.** knowledge, I 3988
Mt 21:42 **The stone which the builders r.,** *593*
Mk 8:31 and be **r.** of the elders, and of the *593*
Mk 12:10 **The stone which the builders r. is** *593*
Lu 7:30 and lawyers **r.** the counsel of God *114*
Lu 9:22 **be r. of the elders and chief priests** *593*
Lu 17:25 **things, and be r. of this generation** *593*
Lu 20:17 **The stone which the builders r.,** *593*
Ga 4:14 in my flesh ye despised not, nor **r.**; *1609*
Heb 6:8 beareth thorns and briers is **r.**, *96*
Heb 12:17 inherited the blessing, he was **r.**: *593*

REJECTETH
Joh 12:48 **He that r. me, and receiveth not** *114*

REJOICE See also REJOICED; REJOICEST; REJOICETH; REJOICING.
Le 23:40 shall **r.** before the Lord your God. 8055
De 12:7 shall **r.** in all that ye put your hand 8055
De 12:12 shall **r.** before the Lord your God, 8055
De 12:18 shalt **r.** before the Lord your God 8055
De 14:26 and thou shalt **r.**, thou, and thine 8055
De 16:11 shalt **r.** before the Lord thy God, 8055
De 16:14 thou shalt **r.** in thy feast, thou, and 8055
De 16:15 therefore thou shalt surely **r.** 8055
De 26:11 thou shalt **r.** in every good thing 8056
De 27:7 and **r.** before the Lord thy God. 8055
De 28:63 Lord will **r.** over you to destroy 7797
De 30:9 will again **r.** over thee for good, 7797
De 32:43 **R.**, O ye nations, with his people; 7442
De 33:18 **R.**, Zebulun, in thy going out; 8055
Jg 9:19 this day, then **r.** ye in Abimelech, 8055
Jg 9:19 and let him also **r.** in you: 8055
Jg 16:23 unto Dagon their god, and to **r.**: 8057
1Sa 2:1 because I **r.** in thy salvation. 8055
1Sa 19:5 thou sawest it, and didst **r.**; 8055
2Sa 1:20 the daughters of the Philistines **r.**, 8055
1Ch 16:10 heart of them **r.** that seek the Lord. 8055
1Ch 16:31 be glad, and let the earth **r.**: 1523
1Ch 16:32 let the fields **r.**, and all that is 5970
2Ch 6:41 and let thy saints **r.** in goodness. 8055
2Ch 20:27 made them to **r.** over their enemies, 8055
Ne 12:43 had made them **r.** with great joy: 8055
Job 3:22 Which **r.** exceedingly, and are glad, 8055
Job 20:18 be, and he shall not **r.** therein. 5965
Job 21:12 and **r.** at the sound of the organ. 8055
Ps 2:11 with fear, and **r.** with trembling. 1523
Ps 5:11 that put their trust in thee **r.**: 8055
Ps 9:2 I will be glad and **r.** in thee: I will 5970
Ps 9:14 of Zion: I will **r.** in thy salvation. 1523
Ps 13:4 trouble me **r.** when I am moved. 1523
Ps 13:5 my heart shall **r.** in thy salvation. 1523
Ps 14:7 Jacob shall **r.**, and Israel shall be 1523
Ps 20:5 We will **r.** in thy salvation, and in 7442
Ps 21:1 salvation how greatly shall he **r.**! 1523
Ps 30:1 not made my foes to **r.** over me. 8055
Ps 31:7 I will be glad and **r.** in thy mercy: 8055
Ps 32:11 Be glad in the Lord, and **r.**, ye 1524
Ps 33:1 **R.** in the Lord, O ye righteous: 7442
Ps 33:21 For our heart shall **r.** in him, 8055
Ps 35:9 Lord: it shall **r.** in his salvation. 7797
Ps 35:19 enemies wrongfully **r.** over me: 8055
Ps 35:24 and let them not **r.** over me. 8055
Ps 35:26 together that **r.** at mine hurt: 8055
Ps 38:16 otherwise they should **r.** over me: 8056
Ps 40:16 Let all those that seek thee **r.** 7797
Ps 48:11 Let mount Zion **r.**, let the 8055
Ps 51:8 bones...thou hast broken may **r.** 1523
Ps 53:6 Jacob shall **r.**, and Israel shall be 1523
Ps 58:10 righteous shall **r.** when he seeth 8055
Ps 60:6 I will **r.**, I will divide Shechem, 5937
Ps 63:7 the shadow of thy wings will I **r.** 7442
Ps 63:11 But the king shall **r.** in God; 8055
Ps 65:8 outgoings of the morning...to **r.** 7442
Ps 65:12 the little hills **r.** on every side. 1524
Ps 66:6 on foot: there did we **r.** in him. 8055
Ps 68:3 be glad; let them **r.** before God: 5970
Ps 68:3 yea, let them exceedingly **r.** 7797
Ps 68:4 name Jah, and **r.** before him. 5937
Ps 70:4 Let all those that seek thee **r.** and 7797
Ps 71:23 My lips shall greatly **r.** when I sing. 7442
Ps 85:6 that thy people may **r.** in thee? 8055
Ps 86:4 **R.** the soul of thy servant: for unto 8055
Ps 89:12 and Hermon shall **r.** in thy name. 7442
Ps 89:16 thy name shall they **r.** all the day: 1523
Ps 89:42 hast made all his enemies to **r.** 8055
Ps 90:14 we may **r.** and be glad all our days. 7442
Ps 96:11 Let the heavens **r.**, and let the 8056
Ps 96:12 shall all the trees of the wood **r.** 7442
Ps 97:1 Lord reigneth; let the earth **r.**; 1523
Ps 97:12 **R.** in the Lord, ye righteous; and 8055
Ps 98:4 make a loud noise, and **r.**, and 7442
Ps 104:31 the Lord shall **r.** in his works. 8055
Ps 105:3 heart of them **r.** that seek the Lord. 8055
Ps 106:5 may **r.** in the gladness of thy nation, 8055
Ps 107:42 The righteous shall see it, and **r.**: 8055
Ps 108:7 I will **r.**, I will divide Shechem, 5937
Ps 109:28 ashamed; but let thy servant **r.** 8055
Ps 118:24 made; we will **r.** and be glad in it. 1523
Ps 119:162 I **r.** at thy word, as one that 7797
Ps 149:2 Israel **r.** in him that made him: 8055
Pr 2:14 Who **r.** to do evil, and delight 8056
Pr 5:18 and **r.** with the wife of thy youth. 8055
Pr 23:15 wise, my heart shall **r.**, even mine. 8055
Pr 23:16 Yea, my reins shall **r.**, when thy 5937
Pr 23:24 father of the righteous shall...**r.** 1523
Pr 23:25 and she that bare thee shall **r.** 1523
Pr 24:17 **R.** not when thine enemy falleth, 8055
Pr 27:9 Ointment and perfume **r.** the heart: 8055
Pr 28:12 When righteous men do **r.**, there 5970
Pr 29:2 are in authority, the people **r.**: 8055
Pr 29:6 but the righteous doth sing and **r.** 8055
Pr 31:25 and she shall **r.** in time to come. 7832
Ec 3:12 but for a man to **r.**, and to do good 8055
Ec 3:22 a man should **r.** in his own works; 8055
Ec 4:16 that come after shall not **r.** in him. 8055
Ec 5:19 his portion, and to **r.** in his labour; 8055
Ec 11:8 live many years, and **r.** in them all; 8055
Ec 11:9 **R.**, O young man, in thy youth; 8055
Ca 1:4 we will be glad and **r.** in thee, we 8055
Isa 8:6 **r.** in Rezin and Remaliah's son; 4885
Isa 9:3 men **r.** when they divide the spoil. 1523
Isa 13:3 even them that **r.** in my highness. 5947
Isa 14:8 Yea, the fir trees **r.** at thee, and 8055
Isa 14:29 **R.** not thou, whole Palestina, 8055
Isa 23:12 Thou shalt no more **r.**, O thou 5937
Isa 24:8 the noise of them that **r.** endeth, 5947
Isa 25:9 will be glad and **r.** in his salvation. 8055
Isa 29:19 poor among men shall **r.** in the 1523
Isa 35:1 and the desert shall **r.**, and blossom. 1523
Isa 35:2 and **r.** even with joy and singing: 1523
Isa 41:16 thou shalt **r.** in the Lord, and shalt 1523
Isa 61:7 they shall **r.** in their portion: 7442
Isa 61:10 I will greatly **r.** in the Lord, my 7797
Isa 62:5 bride, so shall thy God **r.** over thee. 7797

Isa 65:13 my servants shall **r.**, but ye shall 8055
Isa 65:18 But be ye glad and **r.** for ever in 1523
Isa 65:19 And I will **r.** in Jerusalem, and joy 1523
Isa 66:10 **R.** ye with Jerusalem, and be glad...... 8055
Isa 66:10 **r.** for joy with her, all ye that........... 7797
Isa 66:14 your heart shall **r.**, and your bones..... 7797
Jer 31:13 shall the virgin **r.** in the dance, ... 8057
Jer 31:13 make them **r.** from their sorrow......... 8057
Jer 32:41 I will **r.** over them to do them good,... 7797
Jer 51:39 them drunken, that they may **r.**, ... 5937
La 2:17 caused thine enemy to **r.** over thee, ... 8055
La 4:21 **R.** and be glad, O daughter of........... 7797
Eze 7:12 let not the buyer **r.**, nor the seller 8055
Eze 35:15 As thou didst **r.** at the inheritance 8057
Ho 9:1 **R.** not, O Israel, for joy, as other 8055
Joe 2:21 Fear not, O land; be glad and **r.**: 8055
Joe 2:23 Zion, and **r.** in the Lord your God: 8055
Am 6:13 Ye which **r.** in a thing of nought,........ 8055
Mic 7:8 **R.** not against me, O mine enemy: 8056
Hab 1:15 therefore they **r.** and are glad........... 8055
Hab 3:18 Yet I will **r.** in the Lord, I will joy 5937
Zep 3:11 of thee them that **r.** in thy pride, ... 5947
Zep 3:14 be glad and **r.** with all the heart, O..... 5937
Zep 3:17 save, he will **r.** over thee with joy;..... 7797
Zec 2:10 Sing and **r.**, O daughter of Zion: 8055
Zec 4:10 for they shall **r.**, and shall see the 8055
Zec 9:9 **R.** greatly, O daughter of Zion;.......... 1523
Zec 10:7 heart shall **r.** as through wine: 8055
Zec 10:7 their heart shall **r.** in the Lord. 1523
Mt 5:12 **R., and be exceeding glad: for**...... *5463*
Lu 1:14 and many shall **r.** at his birth............. *5463*
Lu 6:23 **R. ye in that day, and leap for**...... *5463*
Lu 10:20 **Notwithstanding in this r. not,**...... *5463*
Lu 10:20 **but rather r., because your names**..*5463*
Lu 15:6 **R. with me; for I have found my**... *4796*
Lu 15:9 **R. with me; for I have found the**... *4796*
Lu 19:37 began to **r.** and praise God with a *5463*
Joh 4:36 **he that reapeth may r. together.** ... *5463*
Joh 5:35 **willing for a season to r. in his**........ *21*
Joh 14:28 **If ye loved me, ye would r.,**.......... *5463*
Joh 16:20 **lament, but the world shall r.:**...... *5463*
Joh 16:22 **again, and your heart shall r.,** *5463*
Ac 2:26 Therefore did my heart **r.**, and *2165*
Ro 5:2 and **r.** in hope of the glory of God...... *2744*
Ro 12:15 **R.** with them that do **r.**, and weep..... *5463*
Ro 15:10 **R.**, ye Gentiles, with his people......... *2165*
1Co 7:30 and they that **r.**, as though they......... *5463*
1Co 12:26 all the members **r.** with it................. *4796*
2Co 2:3 from them of whom I ought to **r.**; *5463*
2Co 7:9 I **r.**, not that ye were made sorry, ... *5463*
2Co 7:16 I **r.** therefore that I have confidence ... *5463*
Ga 4:27 **R.**, thou barren that bearest not; *2165*
Php 1:18 I therein do **r.**, yea, and will **r.**.......... *5463*
Php 2:16 that I may **r.** in the day of Christ, ... *2745*
Php 2:17 faith, I joy, and **r.** with you all........... *4796*
Php 2:18 cause also do ye joy, and **r.** with me.... *4796*
Php 2:28 when ye see him again, ye may **r.**,...... *5463*
Php 3:1 Finally, my brethren, **r.** in the Lord..... *5463*
Php 3:3 the spirit, and **r.** in Christ Jesus,........ *2744*
Php 4:4 **R.** in the Lord alway: *5463*
Php 4:4 and again I say, **R.**.............................. *5463*
Col 1:24 Who now **r.** in my sufferings for *5463*
1Th 5:16 **R.** evermore.. *5463*
Jas 1:9 Let the brother of low degree **r.**......... *2744*
Jas 4:16 But now ye **r.** in your boastings:........ *2744*
1Pe 1:6 Wherein ye greatly **r.**, though now *21*
1Pe 1:8 ye **r.** with joy unspeakable and full......... *21*
1Pe 4:13 **r.**, inasmuch as ye are partakers *5463*
Re 11:10 upon the earth shall **r.** over them, ... *5463*
Re 12:12 **r.**, ye heavens, and ye that dwell....... *2165*
Re 18:20 **R.** over her, thou heaven, and ye *2165*
Re 19:7 Let us be glad and **r.**, and give............ *21*

REJOICED

Ex 18:9 And Jethro **r.** for all the goodness 2302
De 28:63 Lord **r.** over you to do you good,....... 7797
De 30:9 for good, as he **r.** over thy fathers: 7797
Jg 19:3 saw him, he **r.** to meet him. 8055
1Sa 6:13 and saw the ark, and **r.** to see it....... 8055
1Sa 11:15 and all the men of Israel **r.** greatly. 8055
1Ki 1:40 with pipes, and **r.** with great joy, ... 8056
1Ki 5:7 words of Solomon,...he **r.** greatly....... 8055
2Ki 11:14 and all the people of the land **r.**, ... 8056
2Ki 11:20 And all the people of the land **r.**,....... 8055
1Ch 29:9 the people **r.**, for that they offered 8055
1Ch 29:9 David...also **r.** with great joy............ 8055
2Ch 15:15 And all Judah **r.** at the oath: for 8055
2Ch 23:13 and all the people of the land **r.**, ... 8056
2Ch 23:21 And all the people of the land **r.**:........ 8055
2Ch 24:10 the princes and all the people **r.**......... 8055
2Ch 29:36 And Hezekiah **r.**, and all the people, ... 8055
2Ch 30:25 Israel, and that dwelt in Judah, **r.**....... 8055
Ne 12:43 offered great sacrifices, and **r.**: 8055
Ne 12:43 the wives also and the children **r.**:...... 8055
Ne 12:44 for Judah **r.** for the priests and 8057
Es 8:15 city of Shushan **r.** and was glad.......... 6670
Job 31:25 I **r.** because my wealth was great,...... 8055
Job 31:29 If I **r.** at the destruction of him.......... 8055
Ps 35:15 But in mine adversity they **r.**, and...... 8055
Ps 97:8 and the daughters of Judah **r.** 1523
Ps 119:14 **r.** in the way of thy testimonies, ... 7797
Ec 2:10 for my heart **r.** in all my labour:......... 8055
Jer 15:17 assembly of the mockers, nor **r.**; 5937
Jer 50:11 Because ye were glad, because ye **r.**,..5937
Eze 25:6 **r.** in heart with all thy despite 8055
Ho 10:5 the priests thereof that **r.** on it, ... 1523
Ob 12 thou have **r.** over the children of......... 8055
Mt 2:10 they **r.** with exceeding great joy.......... *5463*
Lu 1:47 my spirit hath **r.** in God my Saviour....... *21*
Lu 1:58 upon her; and they **r.** with her. *4796*
Lu 10:21 In that hour Jesus **r.** in spirit,................ *21*
Lu 13:17 people **r.** for all the glorious things *5463*
Joh 8:56 **father Abraham r. to see my day:**..... *21*
Ac 7:41 **r.** in the works of their own hands. *2165*
Ac 15:31 read, they **r.** for the consolation......... *5463*
Ac 16:34 he set meat before them, and **r.**, ... *21*
1Co 7:30 that rejoice, as though they **r.** not; *5463*
2Co 7:7 toward me; so that I **r.** the more. *5463*
Php 4:10 But I **r.** in the Lord greatly, that....... *5463*
2Jo 4 I **r.** greatly that I found of thy........... *5463*
3Jo 3 For I **r.** greatly, when the brethren *5463*

REJOICEST

Jer 11:15 when thou doest evil, then thou **r.**....... 5937

REJOICETH

1Sa 2:1 and said, My heart **r.** in the Lord,...... 5970
Job 39:21 the valley, and **r.** in his strength: 7797
Ps 16:9 my heart is glad, and my glory **r.**: 1523
Ps 19:5 **r.** as a strong man to run a race. 7797
Ps 28:7 therefore my heart greatly **r.**;............ 5937
Pr 11:10 with the righteous, the city **r.**:............ 5970
Pr 13:9 The light of the righteous **r.**: but........ 8055
Pr 15:30 The light of the eyes **r.** the heart:...... 8055
Pr 29:3 Whoso loveth wisdom **r.** his father:..... 8055
Isa 5:14 he that **r.**, shall descend into it. 5938
Isa 62:5 the bridegroom **r.** over the bride,........ 4885
Isa 64:5 meetest him that **r.** and worketh........ 7797
Eze 35:14 When the whole earth **r.**, I will.......... 8055
Mt 18:13 **he r. more of that sheep, than of**.. *5463*
Joh 3:29 **r.**...because of the bridegroom's........ *5463*
1Co 13:6 **R.** not in iniquity,............................ *5463*
1Co 13:6 but **r.** in the truth;............................ *4796*
Jas 2:13 and mercy **r.** against judgment. *2620*

REJOICING

1Ki 1:45 they are come up from thence **r.**,......... 8056
2Ch 23:18 with **r.** and with singing, as it was...... 8057
Job 8:21 laughing, and thy lips with **r.**. 8643
Ps 19:8 of the Lord are right, **r.** the heart: 8055
Ps 45:15 and **r.** shall they be brought; 1524
Ps 107:22 and declare his works with **r.**. 7440
Ps 118:15 The voice of **r.** and salvation is in....... 7440
Ps 119:111 for they are the **r.** of my heart. 8342
Ps 126:6 doubtless come again with **r.**, ... 7440
Pr 8:30 his delight, **r.** always before him; 7832
Pr 8:31 **R.** in the habitable part of his............ 7832
Isa 65:18 I create Jerusalem a **r.**, and her......... 1525
Jer 15:16 me the joy and **r.** of mine heart: 8057
Hab 3:14 their **r.** was as to devour the poor...... 5951
Zep 2:15 is the **r.** city that dwelt carelessly, ... 5947
Lu 15:5 **he layeth it on his shoulders, r.**. ... *5463*
Ac 5:41 **r.** that they were counted worthy to... *5463*
Ac 8:39 more: and he went on his way **r.**. *5463*
Ro 12:12 **R.** in hope; patient in tribulation;........ *5463*
1Co 15:31 by your **r.** which I have in Christ *2746*
2Co 1:12 For our **r.** is this, the testimony of..... *2746*
2Co 1:14 that we are your **r.**, even as ye also... *2745*
2Co 6:10 As sorrowful, yet always **r.**; as.......... *5463*
Ga 6:4 shall he have **r.** in himself alone,.......... *275*
Php 1:26 your **r.** may be more abundant in......... *275*
1Th 2:19 is our hope, or joy, or crown of **r.**? *2746*
Heb 3:6 **r.** of the hope firm unto the end. *2745*
Jas 4:16 your boastings: all such **r.** is evil. *2746*

REKEM (re'-kem)

Nu 31:8 were slain; namely, Evi, and **R.**,........ 7552
Jos 13:21 the princes of Midian, Evi, and **R.**,...... 7552
Jos 18:27 And **R.**, and Irpeel, and Taralah,...... 7552
1Ch 2:43 and Tappuah, and **R.**, and Shema. 7552
1Ch 2:44 Jorkoam: and **R.** begat Shemmai. 7552

RELEASE See also RELEASED.

De 15:1 seven years thou shalt make a **r.**. 8059
De 15:2 And this is the manner of the **r.**:........ 8059
De 15:2 unto his neighbour shall **r.** it;............ 8058
De 15:2 because it is called the Lord's **r.**. 8059
De 15:3 thy brother thine hand shall **r.**; 8058
De 15:9 year, the year of **r.**, is at hand; 8059
De 31:10 in the solemnity of the year of **r.**, ... 8059
Es 2:18 and he made a **r.** to the provinces,...... 2010
Mt 27:15 to **r.** unto the people a prisoner,......... *630*
Mt 27:17 will ye that I **r.** unto you? Barabbas, ... *630*
Mt 27:21 the twain will ye that I **r.** unto you? *630*
Mk 15:9 I **r.** unto you the King of the Jews?...... *630*
Mk 15:11 rather **r.** Barabbas unto them............. *630*
Lu 23:16 therefore chastise him, and **r.** him........ *630*
Lu 23:17 must **r.** one unto them at the feast.) *630*
Lu 23:18 this man, and **r.** unto us Barabbas:....... *630*
Lu 23:20 Pilate therefore, willing to **r.** Jesus, ... *630*
Joh 18:39 **r.** unto you one at the passover: *630*
Joh 18:39 I **r.** unto you the King of the Jews?....... *630*
Joh 19:10 thee, and have power to **r.** thee?........ *630*
Joh 19:12 thenceforth Pilate sought to **r.** him:...... *630*

RELEASED

Mt 27:26 Then **r.** he Barabbas unto them:.......... *630*
Mk 15:6 feast he **r.** unto them one prisoner,...... *630*
Mk 15:15 the people, **r.** Barabbas unto them, ... *630*
Lu 23:25 And he **r.** unto them him that for......... *630*

RELIED

2Ch 13:18 they **r.** upon the Lord God of their..... 8172
2Ch 16:7 thou hast **r.** on the king of Syria, ... 8172
2Ch 16:7 and not **r.** on the Lord thy God, ... 8172

RELIEF

Ac 11:29 to send **r.** unto the brethren.............. *1248*

RELIEVE See also RELIEVED; RELIEVETH.

Le 25:35 then thou shalt **r.** him: yea,............... 2388
Isa 1:17 seek judgment, **r.** the oppressed,......... 833
La 1:11 things for meat to **r.** the soul: 7725
La 1:16 comforter that should **r.** my soul is..... 7725
La 1:19 sought their meat to **r.** their souls. 7725
1Ti 5:16 let them **r.** them, and let not the *1884*
1Ti 5:16 that it may **r.** them that are widows.... *1884*

RELIEVED

1Ti 5:10 feet, if she have **r.** the afflicted,......... *1884*

RELIEVETH

Ps 146:9 he **r.** the fatherless and widow:.......... 5749

RELIGION

Ac 26:5 sect of our **r.** I lived a Pharisee. *2356*
Ga 1:13 in time past in the Jews' **r.**, how........ *2454*
Ga 1:14 profited in the Jews' **r.** above many *2454*
Jas 1:26 own heart, this man's **r.** is vain.......... *2356*
Jas 1:27 Pure **r.** and undefiled before God *2356*

RELIGIOUS

Ac 13:43 many of the Jews and **r.** proselytes..... *4576*
Jas 1:26 any man among you seem to be **r.**, ... *2357*

RELY See also RELIED.

2Ch 16:8 because thou didst **r.** on the Lord, ... 8172

REMAIN See also REMAINED; REMAINEST; REMAINETH; REMAINING.

Ge 38:11 **R.** a widow at thy father's house,....... 3427
Ex 8:9 that they may **r.** in the river only?....... 7604
Ex 8:11 they shall **r.** in the river only............. 7604
Ex 12:10 nothing of it **r.** until the morning; 3498
Ex 23:18 shall the fat of my sacrifice **r.**............ 3885
Ex 29:34 of the bread, **r.** unto the morning,...... 3498
Le 19:6 ought **r.** until the third day, it shall..... 3498
Le 25:28 **r.** in the hand of him that...bought...... 1961
Le 25:52 **r.** but few years unto the year of....... 7604
Le 27:18 according to the years that **r.**, ... 3498
Nu 33:55 those which ye let **r.** of them shall 3498
De 2:34 of every city, we left none to **r.**:......... 8300
De 16:4 **r.** all night until the morning............. 3885
De 19:20 which **r.** shall hear, and fear, and....... 7604
De 21:13 and shall **r.** in thine house, and.......... 3427
De 21:23 His body shall not **r.** all night............ 3885

Jos 1:14 shall **r.** in the land which Moses......... 3427
Jos 2:11 **r.** any more courage in any man,........ 6965
Jos 8:22 they let none of them **r.** or escape. 8300
Jos 10:27 mouth, which **r.** until this very day. ....
Jos 10:28 that were therein; he let none **r.**:....... 8300
Jos 10:30 were therein; he let none **r.** in it;....... 8300
Jos 23:4 you by lot these nations that **r.**,......... 7604
Jos 23:7 nations, these that **r.** among you;....... 7604
Jos 23:12 even these that **r.** among you, and..... 7604
Jg 5:17 and why did Dan **r.** in ships?............ 1481
Jg 21:7, 16 do for wives for them that **r.**,....... 3498
1Sa 20:19 hand, and shalt **r.** by the stone Ezel. .. 3427
1Ki 11:16 (For six months did Joab **r.** there....... 3427
1Ki 18:22 I only, **r.** a prophet of the Lord;........ 3498
2Ki 7:13 thee, five of the horses that **r.**,........ 7604
Ezr 9:15 for we **r.** yet escaped, as it is this...... 7604
Job 21:32 grave, and shall **r.** in the tomb........... 8245
Job 27:15 that **r.** of him shall be buried in.......... 8300
Job 37:8 go into dens, and **r.** in their places. 7931
Ps 55:7 far off, and **r.** in the wilderness........... 3885
Pr 2:21 land, and the perfect shall **r.** in it. 3498
Pr 21:16 **r.** in the congregation of the dead....... 5117
Isa 10:32 yet shall he **r.** at Nob that day: he 5975
Isa 32:16 righteousness **r.** in the fruitful........... 3427
Isa 44:13 man; that it may **r.** in the house. 3427
Isa 65:4 Which **r.** among the graves, and.......... 3427
Isa 66:22 I will make, shall **r.** before me,.......... 5975
Isa 66:22 shall your seed and your name **r.**. 5975
Jer 8:3 residue...that **r.** of this evil family,...... 7604
Jer 8:3 **r.** in all the places whither I have....... 7604
Jer 17:25 and this city shall **r.** for ever............ 3427
Jer 24:8 of Jerusalem, that **r.** in this land,........ 7604
Jer 27:11 will I let **r.** still in their own land,....... 3241
Jer 27:19 of the vessels that **r.** in this city,........ 3498
Jer 27:21 the vessels that **r.** in the house of....... 3498
Jer 30:18 palace shall **r.** after that manner......... 3427
Jer 38:4 the men of war that **r.** in this city, ... 7604
Jer 42:17 none of them shall **r.** or escape.......... 8300
Jer 44:7 Judah, to leave you none to **r.**;.......... 7611
Jer 44:14 shall escape or **r.**, that they should..... 8300
Jer 51:62 that none shall **r.** in it, neither........... 3427
Eze 7:11 none of them shall **r.**, nor of their ....
Eze 17:21 and they that **r.** shall be scattered...... 7604
Eze 31:13 all the fowls of the heaven **r.**,........... 7931
Eze 32:4 all the fowls of the heaven to **r.**.......... 7931
Eze 39:14 that **r.** upon the face of the earth, ... 3498
Am 6:9 if there **r.** ten men in one house, ... 3498
Ob 14 that did **r.** in the day of distress......... 8300
Zec 5:4 shall **r.** in the midst of his house, ... 3885
Zec 12:14 All the families that **r.**, every 7604
Lu 10:7 **And in the same house r., eating**... *3306*
Joh 6:12 **Gather up the fragments that r.,**... *4052*
Joh 15:11 **that my joy might r. in you, and**... *3306*
Joh 15:16 **and that your fruit should r.**.......... *3306*
Joh 19:31 bodies should not **r.** upon the cross *3306*
1Co 7:11 if she depart, let her **r.** unmarried, ... *3306*
1Co 15:6 the greater part **r.** unto this present, .. *3306*
1Th 4:15 and **r.** unto the coming of the Lord..... *4035*
1Th 4:17 are alive and **r.** shall be caught up...... *4035*
Heb 12:27 which cannot be shaken may **r.**.......... *3306*
1Jo 2:24 from the beginning shall **r.** in you, ... *3306*
Re 3:2 **strengthen the things which r.,**..... *3062*

REMAINDER
Ex 29:34 thou shalt burn the **r.** with fire: 3498
Le 6:16 the **r.** thereof shall Aaron and his....... 3498
Le 7:16 also the **r.** of it shall be eaten:.......... 3498
Le 7:17 the **r.** of the flesh of the sacrifice......... 3498
2Sa 14:7 name nor **r.** upon the earth.............. 7611
Ps 76:10 the **r.** of wrath shalt thou restrain. 7611

REMAINED
Ge 7:23 Noah only **r.** alive, and they that........ 7604
Ge 14:10 they that **r.** fled to the mountain. 7604
Ex 8:31 from his people; there **r.** not one. 7604
Ex 10:15 there **r.** not any green thing in 3498
Ex 10:19 **r.** not one locust in all the coasts 7604
Ex 14:28 there **r.** not so much as one of them... 7604
Nu 11:26 **r.** two of the men in the camp,......... 7604
Nu 35:28 have **r.** in the city of his refuge 3427
Nu 36:12 their inheritance **r.** in the tribe.......... 1961
De 3:11 only Og king of Bashan **r.** of the........ 7604
De 4:25 ye shall have **r.** long in the land, ... 3462
Jos 10:20 the rest which **r.** of them entered 8277
Jos 11:22 in Gath, an in Ashdod, there **r.**.......... 7604
Jos 13:12 who **r.** of the remnant of the giants: ... 7604
Jos 18:2 **r.** among the children of Israel.......... 3498
Jos 21:20 which **r.** of the children of Kohath, ... 3498
Jos 21:26 of the children of Kohath that **r.**.......... 3498
Jg 7:3 and there **r.** ten thousand. 7604
1Sa 11:11 they which **r.** were scattered, so that.. 7604
1Sa 23:14 **r.** in a mountain in the wilderness....... 3427
1Sa 24:3 his men **r.** in the sides of the cave. 3427
2Sa 13:20 Tamar **r.** desolate in her brother........ 3427
1Ki 22:46 which **r.** in the days of his father........ 7604
2Ki 10:11 Jehu slew all that **r.** of the house of.... 7604
2Ki 10:17 he slew all that **r.** unto Ahab in.......... 7604
2Ki 13:6 there **r.** the grove also in Samaria.) 5975
2Ki 24:14 none **r.**, save the poorest sort of 7604
2Ki 25:22 as for the people that **r.** in the land 7604
1Ch 13:14 ark of God **r.** with the family of 3427
Ec 2:9 also my wisdom **r.** with me................ 5975
Jer 34:7 cities **r.** of the cities of Judah............ 7604
Jer 37:10 there **r.** but wounded men among......... 7604
Jer 37:16 Jeremiah had **r.** there many days;....... 3427
Jer 37:21 Thus Jeremiah **r.** in the court of the ... 3427
Jer 38:13 and Jeremiah **r.** in the court of the 3427
Jer 39:9 of the people that **r.** in the city,......... 7604
Jer 39:9 with the rest of the people that **r.**...... 7604
Jer 41:10 all the people that **r.** in Mizpah, ... 7604
Jer 48:11 therefore his taste **r.** in him, and........ 5975
Jer 51:30 fight, they have **r.** in their holds:........ 3427
Jer 52:15 of the people that **r.** in the city,......... 7604
La 2:22 Lord's anger none escaped nor **r.**:...... 8300
Eze 3:15 **r.** there astonished among them......... 3427
Da 10:8 and there **r.** no strength in me: 7604
Da 10:13 I **r.** there with the kings of Persia. 3498
Da 10:17 there **r.** no strength in me, ... 5975
Mt 11:23 **it would have r. until this day**....... *3306*
Mt 14:20 fragments that **r.** twelve baskets........ *4052*
Lu 1:22 unto them, and **r.** speechless............ *1265*
Lu 9:17 that **r.** to them twelve baskets........... *4052*
Joh 6:13 which **r.** over and above unto them..... *4052*
Ac 5:4 Whiles it **r.**, was it not thine own?....... *3306*
Ac 27:41 stuck fast, and **r.** unmovable, but *3306*

REMAINEST
La 5:19 Thou, O Lord, **r.** for ever; thy 3427
Heb 1:11 They shall perish; but thou **r.**;........... *1265*

REMAINETH
Ge 8:22 While the earth **r.**, seedtime and........ 3117
Ex 10:5 which **r.** unto you from the hail,......... 7604
Ex 12:10 which **r.** of it until the morning 3498
Ex 16:23 that which **r.** over lay up for you........ 5736
Ex 26:12 the remnant that **r.** of the curtains...... 5736
Ex 26:12 the half curtain that **r.**, shall hang....... 5736
Ex 26:13 **r.** in the length of the curtains of 5736
Le 8:32 And that which **r.** of the flesh and 3498
Le 10:12 Take the meat offering that **r.** of......... 3498
Le 16:16 that **r.** among them in the midst......... 7931
Nu 24:19 shall destroy him that **r.** of...city........ 8300
Jos 8:29 heap of stones, that **r.** unto this day. ....
Jos 13:1 there **r.** yet very much land to be 7604
Jos 13:2 This is the land that yet **r.**: all the...... 7604
Jg 5:13 made him that **r.** have dominion 8300
1Sa 6:18 which stone **r.** unto this day in the ....
1Sa 16:11 There **r.** yet the youngest, and,......... 7604
1Ch 17:1 the covenant of the Lord **r.** under ....
Ezr 1:4 whosoever **r.** in any place where........ 7604
Job 19:4 erred, mine error **r.** with myself. 3885
Job 21:34 your answers there **r.** falsehood?........ 7604
Job 41:22 In his neck **r.** strength, and.............. 3885
Isa 4:3 he that **r.** in Jerusalem, shall be 3498
Jer 38:2 He that **r.** in this city shall die by....... 3427
Jer 47:4 and Zidon every helper that **r.**: 8300
Eze 6:12 he that **r.** and is besieged shall die 7604
Hag 2:5 so my spirit **r.** among you: fear ye 5975
Zec 9:7 he that **r.**, even he, shall be for......... 7604
Joh 9:41 **say, We see; therefore your sin r.**... *3306*
1Co 7:29 it **r.**, that both they that have..... *3588,3063*
2Co 3:11 more than which **r.** is glorious. *3306*
2Co 3:14 for until this day **r.** the same vail *3306*
2Co 9:9 poor: his righteousness **r.** for ever. *3306*
Heb 4:6 it **r.** that some must enter therein,....... *620*
Heb 4:9 **r.** therefore a rest to the people of *620*
Heb 10:26 there **r.** no more sacrifice for sins,....... *620*
1Jo 3:9 his seed **r.** in him: and he cannot *3306*

REMAINING
Nu 9:22 upon the tabernacle, **r.** thereon,......... 7931
De 3:3 him until none was left to him **r.**. 8300
Jos 10:33 until he had left him none **r.**.............. 8300
Jos 10:37 he left none **r.**, according to all that.... 8300
Jos 10:39 he left none **r.**: as he had done to...... 8300
Jos 10:40 left none **r.**, but utterly destroyed 8300
Jos 11:8 them, until they left them none **r.**. 8300
Jos 21:40 **r.** of the families of the Levites,......... 3498
2Sa 21:5 **r.** in any the coasts of Israel, ... 3320
2Ki 10:11 priests, until he left him none **r.**.......... 8300
1Ch 9:33 who **r.** in the chambers were free: ....
Job 18:19 people, nor any **r.** in his dwellings. 8300
Ob 18 not be any **r.** of the house of Esau; 8300
Joh 1:33 Spirit descending, and **r.** on him,........ *3306*

REMALIAH (rem-a-li'-ah) See also REMALIAH'S.
2Ki 15:25 Pekah the son of **R.**, a captain of....... 7425
2Ki 15:27 Pekah the son of **R.** began to reign 7425
2Ki 15:30 against Pekah the son of **R.**, and......... 7425
2Ki 15:32 Pekah the son of **R.** king of Israel...... 7425
2Ki 15:37 of Syria, and Pekah the son of **R.**. 7425
2Ki 16:1 year of Pekah the son of **R.**,............. 7425
2Ki 16:5 and Pekah son of **R.** king of Israel...... 7425
2Ch 28:6 Pekah the son of **R.** slew in Judah...... 7425
Isa 7:1 Pekah the son of **R.**, king of Israel,.... 7425
Isa 7:4 with Syria, and of the son of **R.**.......... 7425
Isa 7:5 Syria, Ephraim, and the son of **R.**, ... 7425

REMALIAH'S (rem-a-li'-ahs)
Isa 7:9 and the head of Samaria is **R.** son. 7425
Isa 8:6 and rejoice in Rezin and **R.** son; 7425

REMEDY
2Ch 36:16 his people, till there was no **r.**............ 4832
Pr 6:15 shall he be broken without **r.**............. 4832
Pr 29:1 be destroyed, and that without **r.** 4832

REMEMBER See also REMEMBERED; REMEMBEREST; REMEMBERETH; REMEMBERING.
Ge 9:15 And I will **r.** my covenant, which........ 2142
Ge 9:16 I may **r.** the everlasting covenant 2142
Ge 40:23 did not the chief butler **r.** Joseph,....... 2142
Ge 41:9 saying, I do **r.** my faults this day:....... 2142
Ex 13:3 **R.** this day, in which ye came out...... 2142
Ex 20:8 **R.** the sabbath day, to keep it holy..... 2142
Ex 32:13 **R.** Abraham, Isaac, and Israel, thy 2142
Le 26:42 will I **r.** my covenant with Jacob,........ 2142
Le 26:42 covenant with Abraham will I **r.**; 2142
Le 26:42 and I will **r.** the land....................... 2142
Le 26:45 will for their sakes **r.** the covenant 2142
Nu 11:5 We **r.** the fish, which we did eat in..... 2142
Nu 15:39 and **r.** all the commandments of the.... 2142
Nu 15:40 That ye may **r.**, and do all my.......... 2142
De 5:15 And **r.** that thou wast a servant in...... 2142
De 7:18 but shalt well **r.** what the Lord thy..... 2142
De 8:2 And thou shalt **r.** all the way which 2142
De 8:18 thou shalt **r.** the Lord thy God: for 2142
De 9:7 **R.**, and forget not, how thou 2142
De 9:27 **R.** thy servants, Abraham, Isaac, ... 2142
De 15:15 shalt **r.** that thou wast a bondman........ 2142
De 16:3 thou mayest **r.** the day when thou 2142
De 16:12 shalt **r.** that thou wast a bondman....... 2142
De 24:9 **R.** what the Lord thy God did unto 2142
De 24:18 shalt **r.** that thou wast 2142
De 24:22 shalt **r.** that thou wast 2142
De 25:17 **R.** what Amalek did unto thee by 2142
De 32:7 **R.** the days of old, consider the 2142
Jos 1:13 **R.** the word which Moses the............ 2142
Jg 9:2 **r.** also that I am your bone and......... 2142
Jg 16:28 **r.** me, I pray thee, and strengthen...... 2142
1Sa 1:11 and **r.** me, and not forget thine 2142
1Sa 15:2 I **r.** that which Amalek did to............ 6485
1Sa 25:31 my lord, then **r.** thine handmaid. 2142
2Sa 14:11 let the king **r.** the Lord thy God, ... 2142
2Sa 19:19 neither do thou **r.** that which thy........ 2142
2Ki 9:25 **r.** how that, when I and thou rode....... 2142
2Ki 20:3 **r.** now how I have walked before........ 2142
1Ch 16:12 **R.** his marvellous works that he......... 2142
2Ch 6:42 **r.** the mercies of David thy servant. ... 2142
Ne 1:8 **R.**, I beseech thee, the word that...... 2142
Ne 4:14 **r.** the Lord, which is great and.......... 2142
Ne 13:14 **R.** me, O my God, concerning this,.... 2142
Ne 13:22 **R.** me, O my God, concerning this...... 2142
Ne 13:29 **R.** them, O my God, because they..... 2142
Ne 13:31 **R.** me, O my God, for good............. 2142
Job 4:7 **R.**, I pray thee, who ever perished, ... 2142
Job 7:7 Or **r.** that my life is wind: mine eye.... 2142
Job 10:9 **R.**, I beseech thee, that thou hast...... 2142
Job 11:16 and **r.** it as waters that pass away:..... 2142
Job 14:13 appoint me a set time, and **r.** me! 2142
Job 21:6 Even when I **r.** I am afraid, and......... 2142
Job 36:24 **R.** that thou magnify his work, ... 2142
Job 41:8 upon him, **r.** the battle, do no more.... 2142
Ps 20:3 **R.** all thy offerings, and accept thy..... 2142
Ps 20:7 **r.** the name of the Lord our God. 2142

Ps 22:27 All the ends of the world shall **r.**......... 2142
Ps 25:6 **R.**, O Lord, thy tender mercies and ... 2142
Ps 25:7 **R.** not the sins of my youth, nor......... 2142
Ps 25:7 **r.** thou me for thy goodness' sake,..... 2142
Ps 42:4 When I **r.** these things, I pour out...... 2142
Ps 42:6 I **r.** thee from the land of Jordan,....... 2142
Ps 63:6 When I **r.** thee upon my bed, and...... 2142
Ps 74:2 **R.** thy congregation, which thou......... 2142
Ps 74:18 **R.** this, that the enemy hath.......... 2142
Ps 74:22 **r.** how the foolish man reproacheth..... 2142
Ps 77:10 I will **r.** the years of the right hand..... 2142
Ps 77:11 I will **r.** the works of the Lord:.......... 2142
Ps 77:11 surely I will **r.** thy wonders of old...... 2142
Ps 79:8 **r.** not against us former iniquities:...... 2142
Ps 89:47 **R.** how short my time is: wherefore... 2142
Ps 89:50 **R.**, Lord, the reproach of thy........... 2142
Ps 103:18 to those that **r.** his commandments..... 2142
Ps 105:5 **R.** his marvellous works that he......... 2142
Ps 106:4 **R.** me, O Lord, with the favour that... 2142
Ps 119:49 **R.** the word unto thy servant, upon.... 2142
Ps 132:1 **r.** David, and all his afflictions:........... 2142
Ps 137:6 If I do not **r.** thee, let my tongue....... 2142
Ps 137:7 **R.**, O Lord, the children of Edom...... 2142
Ps 143:5 I **r.** the days of old; I meditate on...... 2142
Pr 31:7 poverty, and **r.** his misery no more. ... 2142
Ec 5:20 not much **r.** the days of his life;......... 2142
Ec 11:8 yet let him **r.** the days of darkness;.... 2142
Ec 12:1 **R.** now thy Creator in the days of....... 2142
Ca 1:4 we will **r.** thy love more than wine:.... 2142
Isa 38:3 **R.** now, O Lord, I beseech thee,....... 2142
Isa 43:18 **R.** ye not the former things, neither... 2142
Isa 43:25 own sake, and will not **r.** thy sins....... 2142
Isa 44:21 **R.** these, O Jacob and Israel; for....... 2142
Isa 46:8 **R.** this, and shew yourselves men:..... 2142
Isa 46:9 **R.** the former things of old: for I....... 2142
Isa 47:7 neither didst **r.** the latter end of it...... 2142
Isa 54:4 and shalt not **r.** the reproach of thy.... 2142
Isa 64:5 those that **r.** thee in thy ways:.......... 2142
Isa 64:9 O Lord, neither **r.** iniquity for ever:.... 2142
Jer 2:2 I **r.** thee, the kindness of thy............ 2142
Jer 3:16 to mind: neither shall they **r.** it;......... 2142
Jer 14:10 he will now **r.** their iniquity, and........ 2142
Jer 14:21 **r.**, break not thy covenant with us...... 2142
Jer 15:15 **r.** me, and visit me, and revenge....... 2142
Jer 17:2 Whilst their children **r.** their altars...... 2142
Jer 18:20 **R.** that I stood before thee to speak... 2142
Jer 31:20 him, I do earnestly **r.** him still:.......... 2142
Jer 31:34 and I will **r.** their sin no more.......... 2142
Jer 44:21 did not the Lord **r.** them, and came.... 2142
Jer 51:50 **r.** the Lord afar off, and let.............. 2142
La 5:1 **R.**, O Lord, what is come upon us:.... 2142
Eze 6:9 you shall **r.** me among the nations...... 2142
Eze 16:60 Nevertheless I will **r.** my covenant...... 2142
Eze 16:61 shalt **r.** thy ways, and be ashamed...... 2142
Eze 16:63 thou mayest **r.**, and be confounded,.... 2142
Eze 20:43 And there shall ye **r.** your ways,........ 2142
Eze 23:27 unto them, nor **r.** Egypt any more....... 2142
Eze 36:31 Then shall ye **r.** your own evil ways,.. 2142
Ho 7:2 that I **r.** all their wickedness:............ 2142
Ho 8:13 now will he **r.** their iniquity, and........ 2142
Ho 9:9 therefore he will **r.** their iniquity,....... 2142
Mic 6:5 **r.** now what Balak king of Moab........ 2142
Hab 3:2 make known; in wrath **r.** mercy......... 2142
Zec 10:9 they shall **r.** me in far countries;....... 2142
Mal 4:4 **R.** ye the law of Moses my servant,... 2142
Mt 16:9 **neither r. the five loaves of the**..... *3421*
Mt 27:63 Sir, we **r.** that that deceiver said,....... *3415*
Mk 8:18 **hear ye not? and do ye not r.?**....... *3421*
Lu 1:72 and to **r.** his holy covenant;............. *3415*
Lu 16:25 **Son, r. that thou in thy lifetime**.... *3415*
Lu 17:32 **R. Lot's wife**............................. *3421*
Lu 23:42 **r.** me when thou comest into thy....... *3415*
Lu 24:6 **r.** how he spake unto you when he..... *3415*
Joh 15:20 **R. the word that I said unto you**.... *3421*
Joh 16:4 **ye may r. that I told you of them**.. *3421*
Ac 20:31 **r.**, that by the space of three years.... *3421*
Ac 20:35 to **r.** the words of the Lord Jesus,...... *3421*
1Co 11:2 that ye **r.** me in all things, and.......... *3415*
Ga 2:10 would that we should **r.** the poor;...... *3421*
Eph 2:11 Wherefore **r.**, that ye being in time.... *3421*
Col 4:18 **R.** my bonds. Grace be with you....... *3421*
1Th 2:9 For ye **r.**, brethren, our labour and.... *3421*
2Th 2:5 **R.** ye not, that, when I was yet with... *3421*
2Ti 2:8 **R.** that Jesus Christ of the seed of.... *3421*
Heb 8:12 their iniquities will I **r.** no more......... *3415*
Heb 10:17 sins and iniquities will I **r.** no more..... *3415*
Heb 13:3 **R.** them that are in bonds, as........... *3403*
Heb 13:7 **R.** them which have the rule over...... *3421*
3Jo 10 will **r.** his deeds which he doeth,........ *5279*
Jude 17 **r.** ye the words which were spoken.... *3415*
Re 2:5 **R. therefore from whence thou**..... *3421*
Re 3:3 **R. therefore how thou hast**.......... *3421*

REMEMBERED

Ge 8:1 And God **r.** Noah, and every living..... 2142
Ge 19:29 that God **r.** Abraham, and sent Lot..... 2142
Ge 30:22 And God **r.** Rachel, and God............ 2142
Ge 42:9 And Joseph **r.** the dreams which he.... 2142
Ex 2:24 God **r.** his covenant with Abraham,..... 2142
Ex 6:5 and I have **r.** my covenant.............. 2142
Nu 10:9 shall be **r.** before the Lord your God, ..2142
Jg 8:34 children of Israel **r.** not the Lord........ 2142
1Sa 1:19 Hannah his wife; and the Lord **r.**......... 2142
2Ch 24:22 Joash the King **r.** not the kindness...... 2142
Es 2:1 **r.** Vashti, and what she had done,...... 2142
Es 9:28 these days should be **r.** and kept........ 2142
Job 24:20 he shall be no more **r.**; and.............. 2142
Ps 45:17 name to be **r.** in all generations:........ 2142
Ps 77:3 I **r.** God, and was troubled: I............ 2142
Ps 78:35 they **r.** that God was their rock,........ 2142
Ps 78:39 For he **r.** that they were but flesh;..... 2142
Ps 78:42 They **r.** not his hand, nor the day...... 2142
Ps 98:3 He hath **r.** his mercy and his truth..... 2142
Ps 105:8 He hath **r.** his covenant for ever,....... 2142
Ps 105:42 For he **r.** his holy promise, and......... 2142
Ps 106:7 **r.** not the multitude of thy mercies;.... 2142
Ps 106:45 And he **r.** for them his covenant,....... 2142
Ps 109:14 Let the iniquity of his fathers be **r.**...... 2142
Ps 109:16 that he **r.** not to shew mercy, but...... 2142
Ps 111:4 made his wonderful works to be **r.**..... 2143
Ps 119:52 I **r.** thy judgments of old, O Lord;....... 2142
Ps 119:55 I have **r.** thy name, O Lord, in the..... 2142
Ps 136:23 Who **r.** us in our low estate: for his.... 2142
Ps 137:1 yea, we wept, when we **r.** Zion......... 2142
Ec 9:15 yet no man **r.** that same poor man..... 2142
Isa 23:16 many songs, that thou mayest be **r.**.... 2142
Isa 57:11 thou hast lied, and hast not **r.** me,..... 2142
Isa 63:11 Then he **r.** the days of old, Moses,.... 2142
Isa 65:17 and the former shall not be **r.**, nor..... 2142
Jer 11:19 that his name may be no more **r.**....... 2142
La 1:7 Jerusalem **r.** in the days of her.......... 2142
La 2:1 **r.** not his footstool in the day of his.... 2142
Eze 3:20 which he hath done shall not be **r.**;..... 2142
Eze 16:22, 43 hast not **r.** the days of thy youth, .. 2142
Eze 21:24 ye have made your iniquity to be **r.**,... 2142
Eze 21:32 thou shalt be no more **r.**: for I the..... 2142
Eze 25:10 that the Ammonites may not be **r.**...... 2142
Eze 33:13 his righteousnesses shall not be **r.**;..... 2142
Ho 2:17 shall no more be **r.** by their name...... 2142
Am 1:9 and **r.** not the brotherly covenant:...... 2142
Jon 2:7 soul fainted within me I **r.** the Lord:... 2142
Zec 13:2 land, and they shall no more be **r.**...... 2142
Mt 26:75 And Peter **r.** the word of Jesus,......... *3415*
Lu 22:61 And Peter **r.** the word of the Lord,.... *5279*
Lu 24:8 And they **r.** his words,..................... *3415*
Joh 2:17 his disciples **r.** that it was written,...... *3415*
Joh 2:22 his disciples **r.** that he had said this.... *3415*
Joh 12:16 then **r.** they that these things were.... *3415*
Ac 11:16 Then **r.** I the word of the Lord, how.. *3415*
Re 18:5 and God hath **r.** her iniquities........... *3421*

REMEMBEREST

Ps 88:5 the grave, whom thou **r.** no more:..... 2142
Mt 5:23 **and there r. that thy brother**......... *3415*

REMEMBERETH

Ps 9:12 inquisition for blood, he **r.** them:........ 2142
Ps 103:14 our frame; he **r.** that we are dust....... 2142
La 1:9 she **r.** not her last end; therefore....... 2142
Joh 16:21 **child, she r. no more the anguish,**. *3421*
2Co 7:15 he **r.** the obedience of you all, how...... *363*

REMEMBERING

La 3:19 **R.** mine affliction and my misery,....... 2142
1Th 1:3 **R.** without ceasing your work of........ *3421*

REMEMBRANCE See also REMEMBRANCES.

Ex 17:14 utterly put out the **r.** of Amalek......... 2143
Nu 5:15 memorial, bringing iniquity to **r.**......... 2142
De 25:19 shalt blot out the **r.** of Amalek.......... 2143
De 32:26 I would make the **r.** of them to cease ..2143
2Sa 18:18 have no son to keep my name in **r.**.... 2142
1Ki 17:18 come unto me to call my sin to **r.**,..... 2142
Job 18:17 His **r.** shall perish from the earth,...... 2143
Ps 6:5 For in death there is no **r.** of thee:..... 2143
Ps 30:4 thanks at the **r.** of his holiness.......... 2143
Ps 34:16 to cut off the **r.** of them from the....... 2143
Ps 38:*title* A Psalm of David, to bring to **r.**........ 2142
Ps 70:*title* A Psalm of David, to bring to **r.**........ 2142
Ps 77:6 I call to **r.** my song in the night:........ 2142
Ps 83:4 name of Israel may be no more in **r.**... 2142
Ps 97:12 thanks at the **r.** of his holiness.......... 2143
Ps 102:12 and thy **r.** unto all generations........... 2143
Ps 112:6 righteous shall be in everlasting **r.**...... 2143
Ec 1:11 There is no **r.** of former things;......... 2146
Ec 1:11 any **r.** of things that are to come........ 2146
Ec 2:16 there is no **r.** of the wise more than... 2146
Isa 26:8 thy name, and to the **r.** of thee......... 2143
Isa 43:26 Put me in **r.**: let us plead together:.... 2142
Isa 57:8 the posts hast thou set up thy **r.**:....... 2146
La 3:20 My soul hath them still in **r.**,............. 2142
Eze 21:23 but he will call to **r.** the iniquity,........ 2142
Eze 21:24 because,...that ye are come to **r.**,...... 2142
Eze 23:19 calling to **r.** the days of her youth,..... 2142
Eze 23:21 thou calledst to **r.** the lewdness of...... 6485
Eze 29:16 which bringeth their iniquity to **r.**,...... 2142
Mal 3:16 a book of **r.** was written before......... 2146
Mk 11:21 Peter calling to **r.** saith unto him,........ *364*
Lu 1:54 servant Israel, in **r.** of his mercy;....... *3415*
Lu 22:19 **given for you: this do in r. of me**.... *364*
Joh 14:26 **and bring all things to your r.**,..... *5279*
Ac 10:31 and thine arms are had in **r.** in the..... *3415*
1Co 4:17 shall bring you into **r.** of my ways........ *363*
1Co 11:24 **broken for you: this do in r. of me**. .*364*
1Co 11:25 **as oft as ye drink it, in r. of me**..... *364*
Php 1:3 thank...God upon every **r.** of you,...... *3417*
1Th 3:6 that ye have good **r.** of us always,...... *3417*
1Ti 4:6 the brethren in **r.** of these things,...... *5294*
2Ti 1:3 I have **r.** of thee in my prayers.......... *3417*
2Ti 1:5 I call to **r.** the unfeigned faith............ *5280*
2Ti 1:6 I put thee in **r.** that thou stir up.......... *363*
2Ti 2:14 Of these things put them in **r.**,......... *5279*
Heb 10:3 there is a **r.** again made of sins........... *364*
Heb 10:32 But call to **r.** the former days, in......... *363*
2Pe 1:12 you always in **r.** of these things,........ *5179*
2Pe 1:13 stir you up by putting you in **r.**;......... *5280*
2Pe 1:15 to have these things always in **r.**......... *3418*
2Pe 3:1 up your pure minds by way of **r.**......... *5280*
Jude 5 I will therefore put you in **r.**,............. *5179*
Re 16:19 Babylon came in **r.** before God,......... *3415*

REMEMBRANCES

Job 13:12 Your **r.** are like unto ashes, your....... 2146

REMETH (re'-meth) See also RAMOTH; JARMUTH.

Jos 19:21 And **R.**, and En-gannim, and............ 7432

REMISSION

Mt 26:28 **is shed for many for the r. of sins**. . *859*
Mk 1:4 of repentance for the **r.** of sins........... *859*
Lu 1:77 his people by the **r.** of their sins,........ *859*
Lu 3:3 of repentance for the **r.** of sins;.......... *859*
Lu 24:47 **and r. of sins should be preached**.... *859*
Ac 2:38 of Jesus Christ for the **r.** of sins,......... *859*
Ac 10:43 in him shall receive **r.** of sins............. *859*
Ro 3:25 for the **r.** of sins that are past,.......... *3929*
Heb 9:22 without shedding of blood is no **r.**....... *859*
Heb 10:18 Now where **r.** of these is, there is no... *859*

REMIT See also REMITTED.

Joh 20:23 **Whose soever sins ye r., they are**.... *863*

REMITTED

Joh 20:23 **ye remit, they are r. unto them;**..... *863*

REMMON (rem'-mon) See also REMMON-METHOAR; RIMMON.

Jos 19:7 **R.**, and Ether, and Ashan; four.......... 7417

REMMON-METHOAR (rem''-mon-meth'-o-ar)

Jos 19:13 and goeth out to **R.** to Neah;............ 7417

REMNANT

Ex 26:12 **r.** that remaineth of the curtains......... 5629
Le 2:3 **r.** of the meat offering shall be.......... 3498
Le 5:13 the **r.** shall be the priest's, as a meat........
Le 14:18 **r.** of the oil that is in the priest's....... 3498
De 3:11 remained of the **r.** of giants;.............. 3499
De 28:54 **r.** of his children which he shall.......... 3499
Jos 12:4 which was of the **r.** of the giants,....... 3499
Jos 13:12 remained of the **r.** of the giants:....... 3499
Jos 23:12 cleave unto the **r.** of these nations,..... 3499
2Sa 21:2 but of the **r.** of the Amorites; and...... 3499
1Ki 12:23 to the **r.** of the people, saying,.......... 3499
1Ki 14:10 the **r.** of the house of Jeroboam,.......... 310
1Ki 22:46 the **r.** of the sodomites, which........... 3499
2Ki 19:4 lift up thy prayer for the **r.** that......... 7611

2Ki 19:30 **r.** that is escaped of the house of....... 7604
2Ki 19:31 of Jerusalem shall go forth a **r.**,......... 7611
2Ki 21:14 forsake the **r.** of mine inheritance,...... 7611
2Ki 25:11 with the **r.** of the multitude, did......... 3499
1Ch 6:70 of the **r.** of the sons of Kohath.......... 3498
2Ch 30:6 and he will return to the **r.** of you,..... 7604
2Ch 34:9 and of all the **r.** of Israel, and of........ 7611
Ezr 3:8 **r.** of their brethren the priests............ 7605
Ezr 9:8 our God, to leave us a **r.** to escape, ...
Ezr 9:14 should be no **r.** nor escaping?............ 7611
Ne 1:3 **r.** that are left of the captivity........... 7604
Job 22:20 the **r.** of them the fire consumeth......... 3499
Isa 1:9 had left unto us a very small **r.**,......... 8300
Isa 10:20 in that day, that the **r.** of Israel,......... 7605
Isa 10:21 The **r.** shall return, even the **r.** of........ 7605
Isa 10:22 sea, yet a **r.** of them shall return:...... 7605
Isa 11:11 time to recover the **r.** of his people,... 7605
Isa 11:16 an highway for the **r.** of his people,.... 7605
Isa 14:22 the name, and **r.**, and son, and.......... 7605
Isa 14:30 famine, and he shall slay thy **r.**.......... 7611
Isa 15:9 Moab, and upon the **r.** of the land....... 7611
Isa 16:14 **r.** shall be very small and feeble.......... 7605
Isa 17:3 from Damascus, and the **r.** of Syria:... 7605
Isa 37:4 lift up thy prayer for the **r.** that is...... 7611
Isa 37:31 **r.** that is escaped of the house of....... 7604
Isa 37:32 of Jerusalem shall go forth a **r.**,.......... 7611
Isa 46:3 and all the **r.** of the house of Israel,.... 7611
Jer 6:9 glean the **r.** of Israel as a vine:.......... 7611
Jer 11:23 there shall be no **r.** of them: for......... 7611
Jer 15:11 Verily it shall be well with thy **r.**;........ 8293
Jer 23:3 will gather the **r.** of my flock out......... 7611
Jer 25:20 and Ekron, and the **r.** of Ashdod,........ 7611
Jer 31:7 save thy people, the **r.** of Israel.......... 7611
Jer 39:9 captive...the **r.** of the people that....... 3499
Jer 40:11 of Babylon had left a **r.** of Judah,........ 7611
Jer 40:15 and the **r.** in Judah perish?................ 7611
Jer 41:16 the **r.** of the people whom he had...... 7611
Jer 42:2 Lord thy God, even for all this **r.**;...... 7611
Jer 42:15 word of the Lord, ye **r.** of Judah;....... 7611
Jer 42:19 concerning you, O ye **r.** of Judah;....... 7611
Jer 43:5 took all the **r.** of Judah, that were...... 7611
Jer 44:12 I will take the **r.** of Judah, that.......... 7611
Jer 44:14 none of the **r.** of Judah, which are...... 7611
Jer 44:28 all the **r.** of Judah, that are gone........ 7611
Jer 47:4 the **r.** of the country of Caphtor.......... 7611
Jer 47:5 cut off with the **r.** of their valley:........ 7611
Eze 5:10 whole **r.** of thee will I scatter into...... 7611
Eze 6:8 Yet will I leave a **r.**, that ye may........ 3498
Eze 11:13 make a full end of the **r.** of Israel?..... 7611
Eze 14:22 therein shall be left a **r.** that shall...... 6413
Eze 23:25 thy **r.** shall fall by the sword: they....... 319
Eze 25:16 and destroy the **r.** of the sea coast..... 7611
Joe 2:32 in the **r.** whom the Lord shall call........ 8300
Am 1:8 **r.** of the Philistines shall perish,......... 7611
Am 5:15 be gracious unto the **r.** of Joseph........ 7611
Am 9:12 they may possess the **r.** of Edom,....... 7611
Mic 2:12 will surely gather the **r.** of Israel;....... 7611
Mic 4:7 I will make her that halted a **r.**,......... 7611
Mic 5:3 **r.** of his brethren shall return............ 3499
Mic 5:7 **r.** of Jacob shall be in the midst......... 7611
Mic 5:8 the **r.** of Jacob shall be among the...... 7611
Mic 7:18 of the **r.** of his heritage?.................. 7611
Hab 2:8 all the **r.** of the people shall spoil....... 3499
Zep 1:4 I will cut off the **r.** of Baal from......... 7605
Zep 2:7 for the **r.** of the house of Judah;........ 7611
Zep 2:9 the **r.** of my people shall possess....... 3499
Zep 3:13 **r.** of Israel shall not do iniquity,.......... 7611
Hag 1:12 with all the **r.** of the people, obeyed... 7611
Hag 1:14 spirit of all the **r.** of the people;......... 7611
Zec 8:6 in the eyes of the **r.** of this people...... 7611
Zec 8:12 the **r.** of this people to possess all...... 7611
Mt 22:6 **And the r. took his servants, and**.. *3062*
Ro 9:27 of the sea, a **r.** shall be saved:.......... *2640*
Ro 11:5 is a **r.** according to the election of...... *3005*
Re 11:13 the **r.** were affrighted, and gave........ *3062*
Re 12:17 make war with the **r.** of her seed,....... *3062*
Re 19:21 the **r.** were slain with the sword of..... *3062*

REMOVE See also REMOVED, REMOVETH; REMOVING.
Ge 48:17 to **r.** it from Ephraim's head unto....... 5493
Nu 36:7 of Israel **r.** from tribe to tribe:........... 5437
Nu 36:9 the inheritance **r.** from one tribe........ 5437
De 19:14 not **r.** thy neighbour's landmark,......... 5253
Jos 3:3 then ye shall **r.** from your place,......... 5265
Jg 9:29 hand! then would I **r.** Abimelech.......... 5493
2Sa 6:10 So David would not **r.** the ark of........ 5493
2Ki 23:27 will **r.** Judah also out of my sight,....... 5493
2Ki 24:3 to **r.** them out of his sight, for the..... 5493
2Ch 33:8 will I any more **r.** the foot of Israel.... 5493
Job 24:2 Some **r.** the landmarks; they............ 5472
Job 27:5 not **r.** mine integrity from me........... 5493
Ps 36:11 not the hand of the wicked **r.** me........ 5110
Ps 39:10 **R.** thy stroke away from me: I.......... 5493
Ps 119:22 **R.** from me reproach...contempt;....... 1556
Ps 119:29 **R.** from me the way of lying: and....... 5493
Pr 4:27 nor to the left: **r.** thy foot from evil.... 5493
Pr 5:8 **R.** thy way far from her, and come.... 7368
Pr 22:28 **R.** not the ancient landmark,............ 5253
Pr 23:10 **R.** not the old landmark; and............ 5253
Pr 30:8 **R.** far from me vanity and lies:.......... 7368
Ec 11:10 **r.** sorrow from thy heart, and put...... 5493
Isa 13:13 the earth shall **r.** out of her place,...... 7493
Isa 46:7 from his place shall he not **r.**:........... 4185
Jer 4:1 my sight, then shalt thou not **r.**......... 5110
Jer 27:10 you, to **r.** you far from your land;...... 7368
Jer 32:31 should **r.** it from before my face......... 5493
Jer 50:3 they shall **r.**, they shall depart,......... 5110
Jer 50:8 **R.** out of the midst of Babylon, and.... 5110
Eze 12:3 **r.** by day in their sight; and thou........ 1540
Eze 12:3 **r.** from thy place to another place...... 1540
Eze 12:11 they shall **r.** and go into captivity....... 1473
Eze 21:26 **R.** the diadem, and take off the......... 5493
Eze 45:9 **r.** violence and spoil, and execute....... 5493
Ho 5:10 were like them that **r.** the bound:........ 5253
Joe 2:20 **r.** far off from you the northern......... 7368
Joe 3:6 **r.** them far from their border............ 7368
Mic 2:3 which ye shall not **r.** your necks;........ 4185
Zec 3:9 I will **r.** the iniquity of that land in...... 4185
Zec 14:4 mountain shall **r.** toward the north,..... 4185
Mt 17:20 **R. hence to yonder place; and it**.... *3327*
Mt 17:20 **to yonder place; and it shall r.**;..... *3327*
Lu 22:42 **be willing, r. this cup from me**:...... *3911*
1Co 13:2 faith, so that I could **r.** mountains,...... *3179*
Re 2:5 **r. thy candlestick out of his**.......... *2795*

REMOVED
Ge 8:13 Noah **r.** the covering of the ark,......... 5493
Ge 12:8 he **r.** from thence unto a mountain...... 6275
Ge 13:18 Then Abram **r.** his tent, and came....... 167
Ge 26:22 he **r.** from thence, and digged........... 6275
Ge 30:35 he **r.** that day the he goats that.......... 5493
Ge 47:21 he **r.** them to cities from one end....... 5674
Ex 8:31 and he **r.** the swarms of flies from...... 5493
Ex 14:19 angel **r.**...and went behind them;......... 5265
Ex 20:18 when the people saw it, they **r.**,......... 5128
Nu 12:16 the people **r.** from Hazeroth, and....... 5265
Nu 21:12, 13 From thence they **r.**, and pitched... 5265
Nu 33:5 children of Israel **r.** from Rameses,..... 5265
Nu 33:7 they **r.** from Etham, and turned.......... 5265
Nu 33:9 they **r.** from Marah, and came unto..... 5265
Nu 33:10 they **r.** from Elim, and encamped........ 5265
Nu 33:11 And they **r.** from the Red sea, and..... 5265
Nu 33:14 they **r.** from Alush, and encamped....... 5265
Nu 33:16 they **r.** from the desert of Sinai,......... 5265
Nu 33:21 they **r.** from Libnah, and pitched........ 5265
Nu 33:24 they **r.** from mount Shapher, and........ 5265
Nu 33:25 they **r.** from Haradah, and pitched....... 5265
Nu 33:26 And they **r.** from Makheloth, and........ 5265
Nu 33:28 they **r.** from Tarah, and pitched in....... 5265
Nu 33:32 And they **r.** from Bene-jaakan, and...... 5265
Nu 33:34 And they **r.** from Jotbathah, and......... 5265
Nu 33:36 And they **r.** from Ezion-gaber, and..... 5265
Nu 33:37 they **r.** from Kadesh, and pitched........ 5265
Nu 33:46 And they **r.** from Dibon-gad, and......... 5265
Nu 33:47 they **r.** from Almon-diblathaim,........... 5265
De 28:25 be **r.** into all the kingdoms of the....... 2189
Jos 3:1 they **r.** from Shittim, and came to...... 5265
Jos 3:14 when the people **r.** from their tents,... 5265
1Sa 6:3 why his hand is not **r.** from you.......... 5493
1Sa 18:13 Saul **r.** him from him, and made......... 5493
2Sa 20:12 he **r.** Amasa out of the highway.......... 5437
2Sa 20:13 he was **r.** out of the highway,............ 3014
1Ki 15:12 **r.** all the idols that his fathers........... 5493
1Ki 15:13 even her he **r.** from being queen,......... 5493
1Ki 15:14 But the high places were not **r.**:......... 5493
2Ki 15:4 Save that...high places were not **r.**:...... 5493
2Ki 15:35 Howbeit...high places were not **r.**:...... 5493
2Ki 16:17 and **r.** the laver from off them;........... 5493
2Ki 17:18 and **r.** them out of his sight: there....... 5493
2Ki 17:23 the Lord **r.** Israel out of his sight,...... 5493
2Ki 17:26 The nations which thou hast **r.**,........... 1540
2Ki 18:4 He **r.** the high places, and brake.......... 5493
2Ki 23:27 as I have **r.** Israel, and will cast off.... 5493
1Ch 8:6 and they **r.** them to Manahath:.......... 1540
1Ch 8:7 and Ahiah, and Gera, he **r.** them,........ 1540
2Ch 15:16 king, he **r.** her from being queen,......... 5493
2Ch 35:12 And they **r.** the burnt offerings,......... 5493
Job 14:18 and the rock is **r.** out of his place....... 6275
Job 18:4 shall the rock be **r.** out of his place?... 6275
Job 19:10 mine hope hath he **r.** like a tree.......... 5265
Job 36:16 would he have **r.** thee out of the......... 5496
Ps 46:2 we fear, though the earth be **r.**,......... 4171
Ps 81:6 I **r.** his shoulder from the burden:...... 5493
Ps 103:12 far hath he **r.** our transgressions......... 7368
Ps 104:5 that it should not be **r.** for ever.......... 4131
Ps 125:1 as mount Zion, which cannot be **r.**,...... 4131
Pr 10:30 The righteous shall never be **r.**:.......... 4131
Isa 6:12 the Lord have **r.** men far away,........... 7368
Isa 10:13 I have **r.** the bounds of the people,..... 5493
Isa 10:31 Madmenah is **r.**; the inhabitants.......... 5074
Isa 22:25 fastened in the sure place be **r.**,......... 4185
Isa 24:20 and shall be **r.** like a cottage; and....... 5110
Isa 26:15 **r.** it far unto all the ends of the.......... 7368
Isa 29:13 but have **r.** their heart far from me,..... 7368
Isa 30:20 yet shall not thy teachers be **r.**........... 3670
Isa 33:20 the stakes thereof shall ever be **r.**,........ 5265
Isa 38:12 **r.** from me as a shepherd's tent:.......... 1556
Isa 54:10 shall depart, and the hills be **r.**;......... 4131
Isa 54:10 the covenant of my peace be **r.**,.......... 4131
Jer 15:4 them to be **r.** into all kingdoms of....... 2189
Jer 24:9 them to be **r.** into all the kingdoms...... 2189
Jer 29:18 them to be **r.** to all the kingdoms....... 2189
Jer 34:17 you to be **r.** into all the kingdoms....... 2189
La 1:8 sinned; therefore she is **r.**................ 5206
La 3:17 hast **r.** my soul far off from peace:..... 2186
Eze 7:19 streets, and their gold shall be **r.**........ 5079
Eze 23:46 give them to be **r.** and spoiled........... 2189
Eze 36:17 the uncleanness of a **r.** woman............ 5079
Am 6:7 stretched themselves shall be **r.**........... 5493
Mic 2:4 how hath he **r.** it from me!................ 4185
Mic 7:11 in that day shall the decree be far **r.**..........
Mt 21:21 **Be thou r., and be thou cast into**.... *142*
Mk 11:23 **Be thou r., and be thou cast into**.... *142*
Ac 7:4 was dead, he **r.** him into this land,...... *3351*
Ac 13:22 when he had **r.** him, he raised up........ *3179*
Ga 1:6 I marvel that ye are so soon **r.**........... *3346*

REMOVETH
De 27:17 that **r.** his neighbour's landmark.......... 5253
Job 9:5 **r.** the mountains, and they know......... 6275
Job 12:20 **r.** away the speech of the trusty,......... 5493
Ec 10:9 Whoso **r.** stones shall be hurt............ 5265
Da 2:21 he **r.** kings, and setteth up kings:........ 5709

REMOVING
Ge 30:32 **r.** from thence all the speckled........... 5493
Isa 49:21 a captive, and **r.** to and fro? and......... 5493
Eze 12:3 of man, prepare thee stuff for **r.**,......... 1473
Eze 12:4 day in their sight, as stuff for **r.**.......... 1473
Heb 12:27 **r.** of those things that are shaken,....... *3331*

REMPHAN (rem'-fan)
Ac 7:43 the star of your god **R.**, figures.......... *4481*

REND See also RENDING; RENT.
Ex 39:23 about the hole, that it should not **r.**..........
Le 10:6 neither **r.** your clothes; lest ye........... 6533
Le 13:56 he shall **r.** it out of the garment,......... 7167
Le 21:10 his head, nor **r.** his clothes;............... 6533
2Sa 3:31 **R.** your clothes, and gird you with...... 7167
1Ki 11:11 surely **r.** the kingdom from thee,......... 7167
1Ki 11:12 will **r.** it out of the hand of thy son..... 7167
1Ki 11:13 I will not **r.** away all the kingdom;....... 7167
1Ki 11:31 **r.** the kingdom out of the hand of........ 7167
2Ch 34:27 and didst **r.** thy clothes, and weep....... 7167
Ec 3:7 A time to **r.**, and a time to sew; a...... 7167
Isa 64:1 that thou wouldest **r.** the heavens,...... 7167
Eze 13:11 fall; and a stormy wind shall **r.** it......... 1234
Eze 13:13 **r.** it with a stormy wind in my fury;.... 1234
Eze 29:7 break, and **r.** all their shoulder:.......... 1234
Ho 13:8 and will **r.** the caul of their heart,....... 7167
Joe 2:13 And **r.** your heart, and not your......... 7167
Mt 7:6 **feet, and turn again and r. you**..... *4486*
Joh 19:24 Let us not **r.** it, but cast lots for it,..... *4977*

RENDER See also RENDERED; RENDEREST; RENDERETH; RENDERING.
Nu 18:9 which thy shall **r.** unto me, shall........ 7725
De 32:41 will **r.** vengeance to mine enemies,....... 7725
De 32:43 **r.** vengeance to his adversaries,.......... 7725
Jg 9:57 did God **r.** upon their heads: and......... 7725
1Sa 26:23 **r.** to every man his righteousness....... 7725
2Ch 6:30 **r.** unto every man according unto........ 5415

Job 33:26 **r.** unto man his righteousness........... 7725
Job 34:11 work of a man shall he **r.** unto him,.... 7999
Ps 28:4 hands; **r.** to them their desert.......... 7725
Ps 38:20 They also that **r.** evil for good are...... 7999
Ps 56:12 God: I will **r.** praises unto thee.......... 7999
Ps 79:12 **r.** unto our neighbours sevenfold........ 7725
Ps 94:2 earth: **r.** a reward to the proud.......... 7725
Ps 116:12 What shall I **r.** unto the Lord for......... 7725
Pr 24:12 not he **r.** to every man according to.... 7725
Pr 24:29 **r.** to the man according to his work.... 7725
Pr 26:16 seven men that can **r.** a reason.......... 7725
Isa 66:15 to **r.** his anger with fury, and his.......... 7725
Jer 51:6 he will **r.** unto her a recompence........ 7999
Jer 51:24 I will **r.** unto Babylon and to all.......... 7999
La 3:64 **R.** unto them a recompence, O.......... 7725
Ho 14:2 so will we **r.** the valves of our lips. 7999
Joe 3:4 will ye **r.** me a recompence? and if..... 7999
Zec 9:12 that I will **r.** double unto thee;........... 7725
Mt 21:41 **r.** him the fruits in their seasons.......... *591*
Mt 22:21 **R. therefore unto Caesar the** *591*
Mk 12:17 **R. to Caesar the things that are** *591*
Lu 20:25 **R. therefore unto Caesar the** *591*
Ro 2:6 will **r.** to every man according to his *591*
Ro 13:7 **R.** therefore to all their dues:............. *591*
1Co 7:3 Let the husband **r.** unto the wife due..... *591*
1Th 3:9 what thanks can we **r.** to God again..... *467*
1Th 5:15 that none **r.** evil for evil unto any *591*

RENDERED
Jg 9:56 **r.** the wickedness of Abimelech,.......... 7725
2Ki 3:4 and **r.** unto the king of Israel an.......... 7725
2Ch 32:25 Hezekiah **r.** not again according to...... 7725
Pr 12:14 man's hands shall be **r.** unto him. 7725

RENDEREST
Ps 62:12 **r.** to every man according to his 7999

RENDERETH
Isa 66:6 that **r.** recompence to his enemies...... 7999

RENDERING
1Pe 3:9 Not **r.** evil for evil, or railing for.......... *591*

RENDING
Ps 7:2 my soul like a lion, **r.** it in pieces, ... 6561

RENEW See also RENEWED; RENEWEST; RENEWING.
1Sa 11:14 Gilgal, and **r.** the kingdom there......... 2318
Ps 51:10 and **r.** a right spirit within me............ 2318
Isa 40:31 the Lord shall **r.** their strength; 2498
Isa 41:1 and let the people **r.** their strength: 2498
La 5:21 be turned; **r.** our days as of old. 2318
Heb 6:6 to **r.** them again unto repentance: *340*

RENEWED
2Ch 15:8 and **r.** the altar of the Lord, that.......... 2318
Job 29:20 and my bow was **r.** in my hand........... 2498
Ps 103:5 thy youth is **r.** like the eagle's............ 2318
2Co 4:16 the inward man is **r.** day by day. *341*
Eph 4:23 be **r.** in the spirit of your mind;............ *365*
Col 3:10 which is **r.** in knowledge after the......... *341*

RENEWEST
Job 10:17 Thou **r.** thy witnesses against me,....... 2318
Ps 104:30 and thou **r.** the face of the earth. 2318

RENEWING
Ro 12:2 transformed by the **r.** of your mind, ... *342*
Tit 3:5 regeneration,...**r.** of the Holy Ghost; *342*

RENOUNCED
2Co 4:2 But have **r.** the hidden things of.......... *550*

RENOWN See also RENOWNED.
Ge 6:4 men which were of old, men of **r.** 8034
Nu 16:2 in the congregation, men of **r.** 8034
Eze 16:14 thy **r.** went forth among...heathen....... 8034
Eze 16:15 the harlot because of thy **r.**, and.......... 8034
Eze 34:29 I will raise up for them a plant of **r.**,... 8034
Eze 39:13 it shall be to them a **r.** the day that.... 8034
Da 9:15 hast gotten thee **r.**, as at this day; 8034

RENOWNED
Nu 1:16 were the **r.** of the congregation, ... 7121
Isa 14:20 seed of evildoers shall never be **r.**....... 7121
Eze 23:23 and rulers great lords and **r.**, all......... 7121
Eze 26:17 the **r.** city, which wast strong in......... 1984

RENT See also RENTEST.
Ge 37:29 in the pit; and he **r.** his clothes........... 7167
Ge 37:33 is without doubt **r.** in pieces.............. 2963
Ge 37:34 And Jacob **r.** his clothes, and put........ 7167
Ge 44:13 they **r.** their clothes, and laded.......... 7167
Ex 28:32 of an habergeon, that it be not **r.**....... 7167
Le 13:45 his clothes shall be **r.**, and his 6533
Nu 14:6 searched the land, **r.** their clothes: 7167
Jos 7:6 Joshua **r.** his clothes, and fell to the.... 7167
Jos 9:4 and wine bottles, old, and **r.**, and........ 1234
Jos 9:13 were new; and behold, they be **r.**: 1234
Jg 11:35 he saw her, that he **r.** his clothes,....... 7167
Jg 14:6 him, and he **r.** him as he would 8156
Jg 14:6 as he would have **r.** a kid, and he 8156
1Sa 4:12 the same day with his clothes **r.**, ... 7167
1Sa 15:27 the skirt of his mantle, and it **r.**......... 7167
1Sa 15:28 The Lord hath **r.** the kingdom of......... 7167
1Sa 28:17 Lord hath **r.** the kingdom out of.......... 7167
2Sa 1:2 camp from Saul with his clothes **r.**,...... 7167
2Sa 1:11 hold on his clothes, and **r.** them;........ 7167
2Sa 13:19 **r.** her garment of divers colours......... 7167
2Sa 13:31 stood by with their clothes **r.**. 7167
2Sa 15:32 came to meet him with his coat **r.**,..... 7167
1Ki 1:40 earth **r.** with the sound of them. 1234
1Ki 11:30 on him, and **r.** it in twelve pieces: 7167
1Ki 13:3 the altar shall be **r.**, and the ashes 7167
1Ki 13:5 the altar also was **r.**, and the ashes 7167
1Ki 14:8 And **r.** the kingdom away from the 7167
1Ki 19:11 and strong wind **r.** the mountains, ... 6561
1Ki 21:27 those words, that he **r.** his clothes, ... 7167
2Ki 2:12 clothes, and **r.** them in two pieces...... 7167
2Ki 5:7 the letter, that he **r.** his clothes, ... 7167
2Ki 5:8 the king of Israel had **r.** his clothes,.... 7167
2Ki 5:8 Wherefore hast thou **r.** thy clothes?.... 7167
2Ki 6:30 the woman, that he **r.** his clothes; 7167
2Ki 11:14 Athaliah **r.** her clothes, and cried,....... 7167
2Ki 17:21 **r.** Israel from the house of David; 7167
2Ki 18:37 to Hezekiah with their clothes **r.**, ... 7167
2Ki 19:1 heard it, that he **r.** his clothes, ... 7167
2Ki 22:11 of the law, that he **r.** his clothes. 7167
2Ki 22:19 hast **r.** thy clothes, and wept before ... 7167
2Ch 23:13 Then Athaliah **r.** her clothes, and 7167
2Ch 34:19 of the law, that he **r.** his clothes. 7167
Ezr 9:3 I **r.** my garment and my mantle, ... 7167
Ezr 9:5 and having **r.** my garment and my 7167
Es 4:1 Mordecai **r.** his clothes, and put on...... 7167
Job 1:20 Then Job arose, and **r.** his mantle, ... 7167
Job 2:12 they **r.** every one his mantle, and........ 7167
Job 26:8 the cloud is not **r.** under them. 1234
Isa 3:24 and instead of a girdle a **r.**; and 5364
Isa 36:22 to Hezekiah with their clothes **r.**, ... 7167
Isa 37:1 heard it, that he **r.** his clothes, ... 7167
Jer 36:24 not afraid, nor **r.** their garments,........ 7167
Jer 41:5 beards shaven, and their clothes **r.**,.... 7167
Eze 30:16 and No shall be **r.** asunder, and 1234
Mt 9:16 **garment, and the r. is made** *4978*
Mt 26:65 Then the high priest **r.** his clothes,..... *1284*
Mt 27:51 veil of the temple was **r.** in twain....... *4977*
Mt 27:51 earth did quake, and the rocks **r.**; *4977*
Mk 2:21 **the old, and the r. is made worse**.... *4978*
Mk 9:26 the spirit cried, and **r.** him sore, ... *4682*
Mk 14:63 Then the high priest **r.** his clothes,..... *1284*
Mk 15:38 veil of the temple was **r.** in twain....... *4977*
Lu 5:36 **then both the new maketh a r.,** *4977*
Lu 23:45 the veil of the temple was **r.** in the *4977*
Ac 14:14 they **r.** their clothes, and ran in *1284*
Ac 16:22 the magistrates **r.** off their clothes,..... *4048*

RENTEST
Jer 4:30 thou **r.** thy face with painting,............ 7167

REPAIR See also REPAIRED; REPAIRING.
2Ki 12:5 then **r.** the breaches of the house,...... 2388
2Ki 12:7 Why **r.** ye not the breaches of the...... 2388
2Ki 12:8 to **r.** the breaches of the house.......... 2388
2Ki 12:12 hewed stone to **r.** the breaches of...... 2388
2Ki 12:12 was laid out for the house to **r.** it....... 2393
2Ki 22:5 to **r.** the breaches of the house,......... 2388
2Ki 22:6 and hewn stone to **r.** the house. 2388
2Ch 24:4 Joash was minded to **r.** the house....... 2318
2Ch 24:5 money to **r.** the house of your God 2388
2Ch 24:12 and carpenters to **r.** the house of....... 2318
2Ch 34:8 to **r.** the house of the Lord his 2388
2Ch 34:10 Lord, to **r.** and amend the house: 918
Ezr 9:9 and to **r.** the desolations thereof, ... 5975
Isa 61:4 and they shall **r.** the waste cities,........ 2318

REPAIRED
Jg 21:23 **r.** the cities, and dwelt in them........... 1129
1Ki 11:27 and **r.** the breaches of the city of....... 5462
1Ki 18:30 **r.** the altar of the Lord that was 7495
2Ki 12:6 not **r.** the breaches of the house. 2388
2Ki 12:14 **r.** therewith the house of the Lord. 2388
1Ch 11:8 and Joab **r.** the rest of the city. 2421
2Ch 29:3 house of the Lord, and **r.** them.......... 2388
2Ch 32:5 **r.** Millo in the city of David, and......... 2388
2Ch 33:16 he **r.** the altar of the Lord, and.......... 1129
Ne 3:4 next unto them **r.** Meremoth the........ 2388
Ne 3:4 next unto them **r.** Meshullam the 2388
Ne 3:4 next unto them **r.** Zadok the son of...... 2388
Ne 3:5 next unto them the Tekoites **r.**;.......... 2388
Ne 3:6 the old gate **r.** Jehoida the son of....... 2388
Ne 3:7 them **r.** Melatiah the Gibeonite, ... 2388
Ne 3:8 next unto him **r.** Uzziel the son of...... 2388
Ne 3:8 Next unto him also **r.** Hananiah the..... 2388
Ne 3:9 next unto them **r.** Rephaiah the son..... 2388
Ne 3:10 next unto them **r.** Jedaiah the son 2388
Ne 3:10 next unto him **r.** Hattush the son of.... 2388
Ne 3:11 **r.** the other piece, and the tower of.... 2388
Ne 3:12 next unto him **r.** Shallum the son 2388
Ne 3:13 The valley gate **r.** Hanun, and the 2388
Ne 3:14 the dung gate **r.** Malchiah the son 2388
Ne 3:15 gate of the fountain **r.** Shallun the....... 2388
Ne 3:16 After him **r.** Nehemiah the son of....... 2388
Ne 3:17 after him **r.** the Levites, Rehum the ... 2388
Ne 3:17 Next unto him **r.** Hashabiah, the 2388
Ne 3:18 After him **r.** their brethren, Bavai........ 2388
Ne 3:19 And next to him **r.** Ezer the son of 2388
Ne 3:20 Zabbai earnestly **r.** the other piece, ... 2388
Ne 3:21 After him **r.** Meremoth the son of...... 2388
Ne 3:22 after him **r.** the priests, the men of 2388
Ne 3:23 After him **r.** Benjamin and Hashub...... 2388
Ne 3:23 After him **r.** Azariah the son of.......... 2388
Ne 3:24 After him **r.** Binnui the son of............ 2388
Ne 3:27 them the Tekoites **r.** another piece,.... 2388
Ne 3:28 above the horse gate **r.** the priests,.... 2388
Ne 3:29 After them **r.** Zadok the son of.......... 2388
Ne 3:29 After him **r.** also Shemaiah the son...... 2388
Ne 3:30 After him **r.** Hananiah the son of........ 2388
Ne 3:30 After him **r.** Meshullam the son of...... 2388
Ne 3:31 After him **r.** Malchiah the 2388
Ne 3:32 the sheep gate **r.** the goldsmiths 2388

REPAIRER
Isa 58:12 The **r.** of the breach, The restorer..... 1448

REPAIRING
2Ch 24:27 and the **r.** of the house of God, ... 3247

REPAY See also REPAYED; REPAYETH.
De 7:10 him, he will **r.** him to his face........... 7999
Job 21:31 shall **r.** him what he hath done? 7999
Job 41:11 prevented me, that I should **r.** him?.... 7999
Isa 59:18 accordingly he will **r.**, fury to his......... 7999
Isa 59:18 the islands he will **r.** recompence. 7999
Lu 10:35 **when I come again, I will r. thee** *591*
Ro 12:19 is mine; I will **r.**, saith the Lord. *467*
Phm 19 with mine own hand, I will **r.** it: *661*

REPAYED
Pr 13:21 to the righteous good shall be **r.**. 7999

REPAYETH
De 7:10 **r.** them that hate him to their............ 7999

REPEATETH
Pr 17:9 he that **r.** a matter separateth 8138

REPENT See also REPENTED; REPENTEST; REPENTETH; REPENTING.
Ex 13:17 the people **r.** when they see war,........ 5162
Ex 32:12 **r.** of this evil against thy people.......... 5162
Nu 23:19 the son of man, that he should **r.** 5162
De 32:36 and **r.** himself for his servants, ... 5162
1Sa 15:29 Strength of Israel will not lie nor **r.** 5162
1Sa 15:29 he is not a man, that he should **r.**. 5162
1Ki 8:47 and **r.**, and make supplication 7725
Job 42:6 myself, and **r.** in dust and ashes......... 5162
Ps 90:13 it **r.** thee concerning thy servants........ 5162
Ps 110:4 Lord hath sworn, and will not **r.**, ... 5162
Ps 135:14 **r.** himself concerning his servants........ 5162
Jer 4:28 I have purposed it, and will not **r.** 5162
Jer 18:8 **r.** of the evil that I thought to do....... 5162
Jer 18:10 my voice, then I will **r.** of the good, ... 5162
Jer 26:3 that I may **r.** me of the evil, which..... 5162
Jer 26:13 and the Lord will **r.** him of the evil...... 5162
Jer 42:10 I **r.** me of the evil that I have done 5162
Eze 14:6 **R.**, and turn...from your idols;........... 7725
Eze 18:30 **R.**, and turn yourselves from all......... 7725
Eze 24:14 will I spare, neither will I **r.**;.............. 5162
Joe 2:14 knoweth if he will return and **r.**, ... 5162
Jon 3:9 Who can tell if God will turn and **r.**,..... 5162
Mt 3:2 **R.** ye: for the kingdom of heaven....... *3340*

Mt 4:17 R.: for the kingdom of heaven *3340*
Mk 1:15 r. ye, and believe the gospel *3340*
Mk 6:12 and preached that men should r. *3340*
Lu 13:3,5 except ye r., ye shall all likewise *3340*
Lu 16:30 them from the dead, they will r. *3340*
Lu 17:3 him; and if he r., forgive him. *3340*
Lu 17:4 I r.; thou shalt forgive him. *3340*
Ac 2:38 R., and be baptized every one of you *3340*
Ac 3:19 R. ye therefore, and be converted, *3340*
Ac 8:22 R. therefore of this thy wickedness, *3340*
Ac 17:30 all men every where to r.: *3340*
Ac 26:20 that they should r. and turn to God, *3340*
2Co 7:8 I do not r., though I did r.: for I *3338*
Heb 7:21 The Lord sware and will not r., *3338*
Re 2:5 whence thou art fallen, and r., *3340*
Re 2:5 out of his place, except thou r. *3340*
Re 2:16 R.; or else I will come unto thee *3340*
Re 2:21 her space to r. of her fornication: *3340*
Re 2:22 except they r. of their deeds *3340*
Re 3:3 and heard, and hold fast, and r. *3340*
Re 3:19 be zealous therefore, and r. *3340*

REPENTANCE
Ho 13:14 r. shall be hid from mine eyes. 5164
Mt 3:8 Bring forth...fruits meet for r.: *3341*
Mt 3:11 baptize you with water unto r. *3341*
Mt 9:13 the righteous, but sinners to r. *3341*
Mk 1:4 and preach the baptism of r. for the *3341*
Mk 2:17 the righteous, but sinners to r. *3341*
Lu 3:3 preaching the baptism of r. for the *3341*
Lu 3:8 Bring forth...fruits worthy of r., *3341*
Lu 5:32 the righteous, but sinners to r. *3341*
Lu 15:7 just persons, which need no r. *3341*
Lu 24:47 And that r. and remission of sins *3341*
Ac 5:31 to give r. to Israel, and forgiveness *3341*
Ac 11:18 to the Gentiles granted r. unto life. *3341*
Ac 13:24 the baptism of r. to all the people *3341*
Ac 19:4 baptized with the baptism of r., *3341*
Ac 20:21 r. toward God, and faith toward *3341*
Ac 26:20 to God, and do works meet for r. *3341*
Ro 2:4 goodness of God leadeth thee to r.? *3341*
Ro 11:29 and calling of God are without r. *278*
2Co 7:9 sorry, but that ye sorrowed to r. *3341*
2Co 7:10 For godly sorrow worketh r. to *3341*
2Ti 2:25 God peradventure will give them r. *3341*
Heb 6:1 laying again the foundation of r. *3341*
Heb 6:6 to renew them again unto r.; *3341*
Heb 12:17 for he found no place of r., though *3341*
2Pe 3:9 but that all should come to r. *3341*

REPENTED
Ge 6:6 r. the Lord that he had made man 5162
Ex 32:14 Lord r. of the evil which he thought 5162
Jg 2:18 for it r. the Lord because of their 5162
Jg 21:6 children of Israel r....for Benjamin 5162
Jg 21:15 the people r. them for Benjamin, 5162
1Sa 15:35 Lord r. that he had made Saul king 5162
2Sa 24:16 the Lord r. him of the evil, and said 5162
1Ch 21:15 beheld, and he r. him of the evil, 5162
Ps 106:45 r. according to the multitude of his 5162
Jer 8:6 no man r. him of his wickedness, 5162
Jer 20:16 the Lord overthrew, and r. not: 5162
Jer 26:19 the Lord r. him of the evil which 5162
Jer 31:19 Surely after that I was turned, I r.; 5162
Am 7:3 Lord r. for this: It shall not be, 5162
Am 7:6 Lord r. for this: This also shall not 5162
Jon 3:10 God r. of the evil, that he had said 5162
Zec 8:14 saith the Lord of hosts, and I r. not: 5162
Mt 11:20 were done, because they r. not: *3340*
Mt 11:21 have r. long ago in sackcloth *3340*
Mt 12:41 they r. at the preaching of Jonas; *3340*
Mt 21:29 but afterward he r., and went. *3338*
Mt 21:32 ye had seen it, r. not afterward, *3338*
Mt 27:3 that he was condemned, r. himself, *3338*
Lu 10:13 they had a great while ago r., *3340*
Lu 11:32 they r. at the preaching of Jonas; *3340*
2Co 7:10 worketh repentance...not to be r. of: *278*
2Co 12:21 and have not r. of the uncleanness *3340*
Re 2:21 of her fornication; and she r. not. *3340*
Re 9:20 r. not of the works of their hands, *3340*
Re 9:21 Neither r. they of their murders *3340*
Re 16:9 and they r. not to give him glory. *3340*
Re 16:11 sores, and r. not of their deeds. *3340*

REPENTEST
Jon 4:2 kindness, and r. thee of the evil. 5162

REPENTETH
Ge 6:7 it r. me that I have made them. 5162
1Sa 15:11 It r. me that I have set up Saul to 5162
Joe 2:13 kindness, and r. him of the evil. 5162
Lu 15:7 in heaven over one sinner that r., *3340*
Lu 15:10 angels...over one sinner that r. *3340*

REPENTING See also REPENTINGS.
Jer 15:6 destroy thee; I am weary with r. 5162

REPENTINGS
Ho 11:8 me, my r. are kindled together. 5150

REPETITIONS
Mt 6:7 But when ye pray, use not vain r., *945*

REPHAEL (re'-fa-el)
1Ch 26:7 sons of Shemaiah; Othni, and R., 7501

REPHAH (re'-fah)
1Ch 7:25 And R. was his son, also Resheph, 7506

REPHAIAH (ref-a-i'-ah) See also RAPHA; RHESA.
1Ch 3:21 the sons of R., the sons of Arnan, 7509
1Ch 4:42 and Neariah, and R., and Uzziel, 7509
1Ch 7:2 sons of Tola; Uzzi, and R., and 7509
1Ch 9:43 Moza begat Binea; and R. his son, 7509
Ne 3:9 them repaired R. the son of Hur, 7509

REPHAIM (re-fa'-im) See also REPHAIMS.
2Sa 5:18, 22 themselves in the valley of R. 7497
2Sa 23:13 pitched in the valley of R. 7497
1Ch 11:15 encamped in the valley of R. 7497
1Ch 14:9 themselves in the valley of R. 7497
Isa 17:5 gathereth ears in the valley of R. 7497

REPHAIMS (re-fa'-ims) See also REPHAIM.
Ge 14:5 and smote the R. in Ashteroth 7497
Ge 15:20 and the Perizzites, and the R., 7497

REPHIDIM (ref'-i-dim)
Ex 17:1 of the Lord, and pitched in R.: 7508
Ex 17:8 and fought with Israel in R. 7508
Ex 19:2 For they were departed from R., 7508
Nu 33:14 and encamped at R., where was no 7508
Nu 33:15 And they departed from R., and 7508

REPLENISH See also REPLENISHED.
Ge 1:28 and multiply, and r. the earth, and 4390
Ge 9:1 and multiply, and r. the earth. 4390

REPLENISHED
Isa 2:6 because they be r. from the east, 4390
Isa 23:2 that pass over the sea, have r. 4390
Jer 31:25 and I have r. every sorrowful soul. 4390
Eze 26:2 I shall be r., now she is laid waste: 4390
Eze 27:25 wast r., and made very glorious 4390

REPLIEST
Ro 9:20 who art thou that r. against God? *470*

REPORT See also REPORTED.
Ge 37:2 brought unto his father their evil r. 1681
Ex 23:1 Thou shalt not raise a false r. 8088
Nu 13:32 brought up an evil r. of the land 1681
Nu 14:37 bring up the evil r. upon the land, 1681
De 2:25 who shall hear r. of thee, and shall 8088
1Sa 2:24 for it is no good r. that I hear: 8052
1Ki 10:6 was a true r. that I heard in mine 1697
2Ch 9:5 was a true r. which I heard in mine 1697
Ne 6:13 might have matter for an evil r., 8034
Pr 15:30 a good r. maketh the bones fat. 8052
Isa 23:5 As at the r. concerning Egypt, 8088
Isa 23:5 be sorely pained at the r. of Tyre. 8088
Isa 28:19 a vexation...to understand the r. 8052
Isa 53:1 Who hath believed our r.? and to 8052
Jer 20:10 R., say they, and we will r. it. All 5046
Jer 50:43 king of Babylon hath heard the r. 8088
Joh 12:38 Lord, who hath believed our r.? *189*
Ac 6:3 among you seven men of honest r., *3140*
Ac 10:22 and of good r. among all the nation *3140*
Ac 22:12 having a good r. of all the Jews *3140*
Ro 10:16 Lord, who hath believed our r.? *189*
1Co 14:25 and r. that God is in you of a truth. *518*
2Co 6:8 By honour and dishonour, by evil r. *1426*
2Co 6:8 and good r.: as deceivers, by evil r. *2162*
Php 4:8 whatsoever things are of good r.; *2163*
1Ti 3:7 he must have a good r. of them *3141*
Heb 11:2 it the elders obtained a good r. *3140*
Heb 11:39 obtained a good r. through faith, *3140*
3Jo 12 Demetrius hath good r. of all men, *3140*

REPORTED
Ne 6:6 It is r. among the heathen, and 8085
Ne 6:7 and now shall it be r. to the king 8085
Ne 6:19 they r. his good deeds before me, 559
Es 1:17 in their eyes, when it shall be r., 559
Eze 9:11 inkhorn by his side, r. the matter, 7725
Mt 28:15 commonly r. among the Jews is *1310*
Ac 4:23 and r. all that the chief priests and *518*
Ac 16:2 was well r. of by the brethren *3140*
Ro 3:8 (as we be slanderously r., and as *987*
1Co 5:1 It is r. commonly that there is *191*
1Ti 5:10 Well r. of for good works; if she *3140*
1Pe 1:12 which are now r. unto you by them *312*

REPROACH See also REPROACHED; REPROACHES; REPROACHEST; REPROACHETH; REPROACHFULLY.
Ge 30:23 said, God hath taken away my r. 2781
Ge 34:14 for that were a r. unto us: 2781
Jos 5:9 have I rolled away the r. of Egypt 2781
Ru 2:15 among the sheaves, and r. her not: 3637
1Sa 11:2 and lay it for a r. upon all Israel. 2781
1Sa 17:26 and taketh away the r. from Israel? 2781
1Sa 25:39 hath pleaded the cause of my r. 2781
2Ki 19:4 hath sent to r. the living God; 2778
2Ki 19:16 hath sent him to r. the living God. 2778
Ne 1:3 are in great affliction and r.: 2781
Ne 2:17 Jerusalem, that we be no more a r. 2781
Ne 4:4 turn their r. upon their own head, 2781
Ne 5:9 the r. of the heathen our enemies? 2781
Ne 6:13 evil report, that they might r. me. 2778
Job 19:5 me, and plead against me my r. 2781
Job 20:3 I have heard the check of my r., 3639
Job 27:6 my heart shall not r. me so long 2778
Ps 15:3 up a r. against his neighbour. 2781
Ps 22:6 a r. of men, and despised of the 2781
Ps 31:11 I was a r. among all mine enemies, 2781
Ps 39:8 make me not the r. of the foolish. 2781
Ps 42:10 in my bones, mine enemies r. me; 2778
Ps 44:13 makest us a r. to our neighbours, 2781
Ps 57:3 and save me from the r. of him 2778
Ps 69:7 for thy sake I have borne r.; 2781
Ps 69:10 soul with fasting, that was to my r. 2781
Ps 69:19 Thou hast known my r., and my 2781
Ps 69:20 R. hath broken my heart; and I 2781
Ps 71:13 be covered with r. and dishonour 2781
Ps 74:10 how long shall the adversary r.? 2778
Ps 78:66 he put them to a perpetual r. 2781
Ps 79:4 are become a r. to our neighbours, 2781
Ps 79:12 sevenfold into their bosom their r., 2781
Ps 89:41 him: he is a r. to his neighbours. 2781
Ps 89:50 Remember,...the r. of thy servants; 2781
Ps 89:50 bosom the r. of all the mighty people;
Ps 102:8 Mine enemies r. me all the day; 2778
Ps 109:25 I became also a r. unto them: 2781
Ps 119:22 Remove from me r. and contempt; 2781
Ps 119:39 Turn away my r. which I fear: for 2781
Pr 6:33 his r. shall not be wiped away. 2781
Pr 14:34 but sin is a r. to any people. 2617
Pr 18:3 contempt, and with ignominy r. 2781
Pr 19:26 causeth shame, and bringeth r. 2659
Pr 22:10 yea, strife and r. shall cease. 7036
Isa 4:1 by thy name, to take away our r. 2781
Isa 30:5 profit, but a shame, and also a r. 2781
Isa 37:4 hath sent to r. the living God, and 2778
Isa 37:17 hath sent to r. the living God. 2778
Isa 51:7 fear ye not the r. of men, neither 2781
Isa 54:4 remember the r. of thy widowhood 2781
Jer 6:10 word of the Lord is unto them a r.; 2781
Jer 20:8 the word of the Lord was made a r. 2781
Jer 23:40 bring an everlasting r. upon you, 2781
Jer 24:9 be a r. and a proverb, a taunt and 2781
Jer 29:18 an hissing, and a r., among all the 2781
Jer 31:19 I did bear the r. of my youth. 2781
Jer 42:18 astonishment, and a curse, and a r.; 2781
Jer 44:8 a r. among all the nations of the 2781
Jer 44:12 astonishment, and a curse, and a r. 2781
Jer 49:13 shall become a desolation, a r., a 2781
Jer 51:51 because we have heard r.: shame 2781
La 3:30 smiteth him: he is filled full with r. 2781
La 3:61 Thou hast heard their r., O Lord, 2781
La 5:1 us: consider, and behold our r. 2781
Eze 5:14 a r. among the nations that are 2781
Eze 5:15 So it shall be a r. and a taunt, an 2781
Eze 16:57 of thy r. of the daughters of Syria, 2781
Eze 21:28 Ammonites, and concerning their r.; 2781
Eze 22:4 I made thee a r. unto the heathen, 2781
Eze 36:15 bear the r. of the people any more, 2781
Eze 36:30 shall receive no more r. of famine 2781
Da 9:16 become a r. to all that are about us. 2781
Da 11:18 cause the r. offered by him to cease; 2781
Da 11:18 without his own r. he shall cause it. 2781

Ho 12:14 his **r.** shall his Lord return unto........ 2781
Joe 2:17 give not thine heritage to **r.**, that....... 2781
Joe 2:19 make you a **r.** among the heathen: 2781
Mic 6:16 ye shall bear the **r.** of my people. 2781
Zep 2:8 I have heard the **r.** of Moab, and 2781
Zep 3:18 to whom the **r.** of it was a burden...... 2781
Lu 1:25 to take away my **r.** among men. *3681*
Lu 6:22 **and shall r. you, and cast out** *3679*
2Co 11:21 I speak as concerning **r.**, as though...... *819*
1Ti 3:7 fall into **r.** and...snare of the devil. *3680*
1Ti 4:10 we both labour and suffer **r.**, ... *3679*
Heb 11:26 Esteeming the **r.** of Christ greater........ *3680*
Heb 13:13 without the camp, bearing his **r.**......... *3680*

REPROACHED
2Ki 19:22 hast thou **r.** and blasphemed? 2778
2Ki 19:23 messengers thou hast **r.** the Lord, ... 2778
Job 19:3 These ten times have ye **r.** me: ye 3637
Ps 55:12 it was not an enemy that **r.** me; 2778
Ps 69:9 reproaches of them that **r.** thee are 2778
Ps 74:18 this, that the enemy hath **r.**, O Lord,.. 2778
Ps 79:12 wherewith they have **r.** thee, O Lord.. 2778
Ps 89:51 Wherewith thine enemies have **r.**, ... 2778
Ps 89:51 they have **r.** the footsteps of thine...... 2778
Isa 37:23 hast thou **r.** and blasphemed? 2778
Isa 37:24 thy servants hast thou **r.** the Lord,..... 2778
Zep 2:8 whereby they have **r.** my people, ... 2778
Zep 2:10 have **r.** and magnified themselves 2778
Ro 15:3 reproaches of them that **r.** thee *3679*
1Pe 4:14 If ye be **r.** for the name of Christ,....... *3679*

REPROACHES
Ps 69:9 the **r.** of them that reproached thee.... 2781
Isa 43:28 Jacob to the curse, and Israel to **r.**.... 1421
Ro 15:3 The **r.** of them that reproached thee... *3679*
2Co 12:10 take pleasure in infirmities, in **r.**,....... *5196*
Heb 10:33 both by **r.** and afflictions; and *3680*

REPROACHEST
Lu 11:45 Master, thus saying thou **r.** us also..... *5195*

REPROACHETH
Nu 15:30 a stranger, the same **r.** the Lord;....... 1442
Ps 44:16 For the voice of him that **r.** and......... 2778
Ps 74:22 how the foolish man **r.** thee daily. 2781
Ps 119:42 to answer him that **r.** me: for........... 2778
Pr 14:31 oppresseth the poor **r.** his Maker:...... 2778
Pr 17:5 mocketh the poor **r.** his Maker: 2778
Pr 27:11 that I may answer him that **r.** me........ 2778

REPROACHFULLY
Job 16:10 smitten me upon the cheek **r.**;........... 2781
1Ti 5:14 to the adversary to speak **r.**....... *5484,3059*

REPROBATE See also REPROBATES.
Jer 6:30 **R.** silver shall men call them, ... 3988
Ro 1:28 God gave them over to a **r.** mind, ... *96*
2Ti 3:8 minds, **r.** concerning the faith. *96*
Tit 1:16 and unto every good work **r.**............... *96*

REPROBATES
2Co 13:5 Christ is in you, except ye be **r.**?.......... *96*
2Co 13:6 ye shall know that we are not **r.**. *96*
2Co 13:7 which is honest, though we be as **r.**. *96*

REPROOF See also REPROOFS.
Job 26:11 and are astonished at his **r.**............... 1606
Pr 1:23 Turn you at my **r.**: behold, I will........ 8433
Pr 1:25 counsel, and would none of my **r.**........ 8433
Pr 1:30 my counsel: they despised all my **r.**.... 8433
Pr 5:12 and my heart despised **r.**;.................. 8433
Pr 10:17 but he that refuseth **r.** erreth. 8433
Pr 12:1 but he that hateth **r.** is brutish........... 8433
Pr 13:18 that regardeth **r.** shall be honoured..... 8433
Pr 15:5 but he that regardeth **r.** is prudent. 8433
Pr 15:10 way: and he that hateth **r.** shall die..... 8433
Pr 15:31 The ear that heareth the **r.** of life 8433
Pr 15:32 heareth **r.** getteth understanding. 8433
Pr 17:10 A **r.** entereth more into a wise 1606
Pr 29:15 The rod and **r.** give wisdom: but......... 8433
2Ti 3:16 for doctrine, for **r.**, for correction,....... *1650*

REPROOFS
Ps 38:14 and in whose mouth are no **r.**............ 8433
Pr 6:23 **r.** of instruction are the way of life: 8433

REPROVE See also REPROVED; REPROVETH; UNREPROVABLE.
2Ki 19:4 will **r.** the words which the Lord........ 3198
Job 6:25 but what doth your arguing **r.**? 3198
Job 6:26 Do ye imagine to **r.** words, and the.... 3198
Job 13:10 He will surely **r.** you, if ye do 3198
Job 22:4 Will he **r.** thee for fear of thee? will.... 3198
Ps 50:8 I will not **r.** thee for thy sacrifices...... 3198
Ps 50:21 I will **r.** thee, and set them in order ... 3198
Ps 141:5 and let him **r.** me; it shall be an......... 3198
Pr 9:8 **R.** not a scorner, lest he hate thee:.... 3198
Pr 19:25 and **r.** one that hath understanding,.... 3198
Pr 30:6 lest he **r.** thee, and thou be found a.... 3198
Isa 11:3 **r.** after the hearing of his ears:.......... 3198
Isa 11:4 **r.** with equity for the meek of the...... 3198
Isa 37:4 will **r.** the words which the Lord......... 3198
Jer 2:19 and thy backslidings shall **r.** thee:....... 3198
Ho 4:4 let no man strive, nor **r.** another:....... 3198
Joh 16:8 **come, he will r. the world of sin.**,..*1651*
Eph 5:11 of darkness, but rather **r.** them.......... *1651*
2Ti 4:2 **r.**, rebuke, exhort with all................ *1651*

REPROVED
Ge 20:16 with all other: thus she was **r.**.......... 3198
Ge 21:25 Abraham **r.** Abimelech because 3198
1Ch 16:21 yea, he **r.** kings for their sakes,......... 3198
Ps 105:14 yea, he **r.** kings for their sakes;......... 3198
Pr 29:1 being often **r.** hardeneth his neck, ... 8433
Jer 29:27 why hast thou not **r.** Jeremiah 1605
Hab 2:1 what I shall answer when I am **r.**........ 8433
Lu 3:19 being **r.** by him for Herodias his......... *1651*
Joh 3:20 **light, lest his deeds should be r.**..... *1651*
Eph 5:13 that are **r.** are made manifest by........ *1651*

REPROVER
Pr 25:12 is a wise **r.** upon an obedient ear. 3198
Eze 3:26 dumb, and shalt not be to them a **r.** ... 3198

REPROVETH
Job 40:2 he that **r.** God, let him answer it. 3198
Pr 9:7 He that **r.** a scorner getteth to.......... 3256
Pr 15:12 scorner loveth not one that **r.** him: 3198
Isa 29:21 a snare for him that **r.** in the gate, ... 3198

REPUTATION
Ec 10:1 is in **r.** for wisdom and honour.......... 3368
Ac 5:34 had in **r.** among all the people, ... *5093*
Ga 2:2 privately to them which were of **r.**, ... *1380*
Php 2:7 But made himself of no **r.**, and *2758*
Php 2:29 gladness; and hold such in **r.**............. *1784*

REPUTED
Job 18:3 as beasts, and **r.** vile in your sight? ....
Da 4:35 of the earth are **r.** as nothing: 2804

REQUEST See also REQUESTED; REQUESTS.
Jg 8:24 them, I would desire a **r.** of you, ... 7596
2Sa 14:15 perform the **r.** of his handmaid.......... 1697
2Sa 14:22 hath fulfilled the **r.** of his servant........ 1697
Ezr 7:6 the king granted him all his **r.**,........... 1246
Ne 2:4 me, For what dost thou make **r.**?........ 1245
Es 4:8 make **r.** before him for her people...... 1245
Es 5:3 queen Esther? and what is thy **r.**?...... 1246
Es 5:6 and what is thy **r.**? even to the half.... 1246
Es 5:7 and said, My petition and my **r.** is;..... 1246
Es 5:8 my petition, and to perform my **r.**, ... 1246
Es 7:2 and what is thy **r.**? and it shall be 1246
Es 7:3 petition, and my people at my **r.**: 1246
Es 7:7 Haman stood up to make **r.** for his 1245
Es 9:12 what is thy **r.** further? and it shall 1246
Job 6:8 Oh that I might have my **r.**; and 7596
Ps 21:2 not withholden the **r.** of his lips.......... 782
Ps 106:15 he gave them their **r.**; but sent.......... 7596
Ro 1:10 Making **r.**, if by any means now at *1189*
Php 1:4 for you all making **r.** with joy,............ *1162*

REQUESTED
Jg 8:26 of the golden earrings that he **r.** 7592
1Ki 19:4 he **r.** for himself that he might die;..... 7592
1Ch 4:10 God granted him that which he **r.**........ 7592
Da 1:8 he **r.** the prince of the eunuchs.......... 1245
Da 2:49 Then Daniel **r.** of the king, and he...... 1156

REQUESTS
Php 4:6 let your **r.** be made known unto God.... *155*

REQUIRE See also REQUIRED; REQUIREST; REQUIRETH; REQUIRING.
Ge 9:5 your blood of your lives will I **r.**;........ 1875
Ge 9:5 the hand of every beast will I **r.** it,..... 1875
Ge 9:5 brother will I **r.** the life of man. 1875
Ge 31:39 of it; of my hand didst thou **r.** it, ... 1245
Ge 43:9 of my hand shalt thou **r.** him: if I 1245
De 10:12 doth the Lord thy God **r.** of thee, ... 7592
De 18:19 in my name, I will **r.** it of him. 1875
De 23:21 thy God will surely **r.** it of thee; 1875
Jos 22:23 thereon, let the Lord himself **r.** it;...... 1245
1Sa 20:16 the Lord even **r.** it at the hand of 1245
2Sa 3:13 but one thing I **r.** of thee, that is, ... 7592
2Sa 4:11 now **r.** his blood of your hand, and 1245
2Sa 19:38 whatsoever thou shalt **r.** of me,........... 977
1Ki 8:59 at all times, as the matter shall **r.**: 3117
1Ch 21:3 then doth my lord **r.** this thing? 1245
2Ch 24:22 The Lord look upon it, and **r.** it. 1875
Ezr 7:21 the God of heaven, shall **r.** of you, ... 7593
Ezr 8:22 ashamed to **r.** of the king a band........ 7592
Ne 5:12 them, and will **r.** nothing of them; 1245
Ps 10:13 in his heart, Thou wilt not **r.** it. 1875
Eze 3:18, 20 blood will I **r.** at thine hand.......... 1245
Eze 20:40 there will I **r.** your offerings, and 1875
Eze 33:6 blood will I **r.** at the watchman's 1875
Eze 33:8 his blood will I **r.** at thine hand. 1245
Eze 34:10 I will **r.** my flock at their hand, ... 1875
Mic 6:8 and what doth the Lord **r.** of thee, ... 1875
1Co 1:22 the Jews **r.** a sign, and the Greeks *154*
1Co 7:36 and need so **r.**, let him do what he..... *1096*

REQUIRED
Ge 42:22 behold, also his blood is **r.**. 1875
Ex 12:36 lent unto them such things as they **r.**........
1Sa 21:8 the king's business **r.** haste............... 1961
2Sa 12:20 when he **r.**, they set bread before...... 7592
1Ch 16:37 continually, as every day's work **r.** 3117
2Ch 8:14 priests, as the duty of every day **r.** 3117
2Ch 24:6 hast thou not **r.** of the Levites to...... 1875
Ezr 3:4 as the duty of every day **r.**;.............. 3117
Ne 5:18 **r.** not I the bread of the governor, ... 1245
Es 2:15 she **r.** nothing but what Hegai the 1245
Ps 40:6 and sin offering hast thou not **r.**......... 7592
Ps 137:3 us away captive **r.** of us a song; 7592
Ps 137:3 they that wasted us **r.** of us mirth, ...
Pr 30:7 Two things have I **r.** of thee; deny..... 7592
Isa 1:12 who hath **r.** this at your hand, to 1245
Lu 11:50 **world, may be r. this generation;** .. *1567*
Lu 11:51 **It shall be r. of this generation.**..... *1567*
Lu 12:20 **night thy soul shall be r. of thee:** *523*
Lu 12:48 **is given, of him shall be much r.**.... *2212*
Lu 19:23 **have r. mine own with usury?**....... *4238*
Lu 23:24 that it should be as they **r.**................. *155*
1Co 4:2 Moreover it is **r.** in stewards, that *2212*

REQUIREST
Ru 3:11 I will do to thee all that thou **r.**........... 559

REQUIRETH
Ec 3:15 and God **r.** that which is past. 1245
Da 2:11 it is a rare thing that the king **r.**, ... 7593

REQUIRING
Lu 23:23 voice, **r.** that he might be crucified....... *154*

REQUITE See also REQUITED; REQUITING.
Ge 50:15 and will certainly **r.** us all the evil....... 7725
De 32:6 Do ye thus **r.** the Lord, O foolish....... 1580
2Sa 2:6 and I will also **r.** you this kindness,..... 6213
2Sa 16:12 the Lord will **r.** me good for his......... 7725
2Ki 9:26 I will **r.** thee in this plat, saith the...... 7999
Ps 10:14 and spite, to **r.** it with thy hand: 5414
Ps 41:10 raise me up, that I may **r.** them......... 7999
Jer 51:56 God of recompences shall surely **r.**..... 7999
1Ti 5:4 at home, and to **r.** their parents:.... *287,591*

REQUITED
Jg 1:7 as I have done, so God hath **r.** me..... 7999
1Sa 25:21 and he hath **r.** me evil for good. 7725

REQUITING
2Ch 6:23 by **r.** the wicked, by recompensing..... 7725

REREWARD
Nu 10:25 which was the **r.** of all the camps 622
Jos 6:9 and the **r.** came after the ark, the........ 622
Jos 6:13 but the **r.** came after the ark of the 622
1Sa 29:2 passed on in the **r.** with Achish.......... 314
Isa 52:12 the God of Israel will be your **r.**. 622
Isa 58:8 the glory of the Lord shall be thy **r.**..... 622

RESCUE See also RESCUED; RESCUETH.
De 28:31 thou shalt have none to **r.** them......... 3467
Ps 35:17 look on? **r.** my soul from their........... 7725
Ho 5:14 take away, and none shall **r.** him. 5337

RESCUED
1Sa 14:45 So the people **r.** Jonathan, that he 6299
1Sa 30:18 away: and David **r.** his two wives....... 5337
Ac 23:27 came I with an army, and **r.** him, ... *1807*

RESCUETH
Da 6:27 He delivereth and **r.**, and he 5338

RESEMBLANCE
Zec 5:6 is their **r.** through all the earth. 5869

RESEMBLE See also RESEMBLED.
Lu 13:18 **like? and whereunto shall I r. it?** .. *3666*

RESEMBLED
Jg 8:18 each one **r.** the children of a king....... 8389

RESEN (re'-zen)
Ge 10:12 **R.** between Nineveh and Calah:......... 7449

RESERVE See also RESERVED; RESERVETH.
Jer 3:5 Will he **r.** his anger for ever? will....... 5201
Jer 50:20 for I will pardon them whom I **r.**........ 7604
2Pe 2:9 to **r.** the unjust unto the day of.......... *5083*

RESERVED
Ge 27:36 thou not **r.** a blessing for me?............ 680
Nu 18:9 most holy things, **r.** from the fire: ....
Jg 21:22 we **r.** not to each man his wife.......... 3947
Ru 2:18 gave to her that she had **r.** after........ 3498
2Sa 8:4 **r.** of them for an hundred chariots......... 3498
1Ch 18:4 but **r.** of them an hundred chariots. 3498
Job 21:30 is **r.** to the day of destruction? 2820
Job 38:23 Which I have **r.** against the time of..... 2820
Ac 25:21 be **r.** unto the hearing of Augustus, ... *5083*
Ro 11:4 I have **r.** to myself seven thousand..... *2641*
1Pe 1:4 not away, **r.** in heaven for you,.......... *5083*
2Pe 2:4 darkness, to be **r.** unto judgment; *5083*
2Pe 2:17 the mist of darkness is **r.** for ever...... *5083*
2Pe 3:7 **r.** unto fire against the day of............ *5083*
Jude 6 hath **r.** in everlasting chains under....... *5083*
Jude 13 to whom is **r.** the blackness of........... *5083*

RESERVETH
Jer 5:24 **r.** unto us the appointed weeks of....... 8104
Na 1:2 and he **r.** wrath for his enemies. 5201

RESH
Ps 119:153 *title* [ר] **R.**..

RESHEPH (re'-shef)
1Ch 7:25 Rephah was his son, also **R.**, and....... 7566

RESIDUE
Ex 10:5 eat the **r.** of that which is escaped,..... 3499
1Ch 6:66 And the **r.** of the families of the sons........
Ne 11:20 the **r.** of Israel, of the priests, and..... 7605
Isa 21:17 the **r.** of the number of archers, the ... 7605
Isa 28:5 of beauty, unto the **r.** of his people,.... 7605
Isa 38:10 am deprived of the **r.** of my years....... 3499
Isa 44:17 the **r.** thereof he maketh a god,.......... 7611
Isa 44:19 the **r.** thereof an abomination? 3499
Jer 8:3 **r.** of them that remain of this evil....... 7611
Jer 15:9 the **r.** of them will I deliver to the...... 7611
Jer 24:8 the **r.** of Jerusalem, that remain in...... 7611
Jer 27:19 the **r.** of the vessels that remain in..... 3499
Jer 29:1 Jerusalem unto the **r.** of the elders..... 3499
Jer 39:3 the **r.** of the princes of the king of 7611
Jer 41:10 all the **r.** of the people that were 7611
Jer 52:15 **r.** of the people that remained in........ 3499
Eze 9:8 wilt thou destroy all the **r.** of Israel.... 7611
Eze 23:25 thy **r.** shall be devoured by the fire...... 319
Eze 34:18 your feet the **r.** of your pastures? 3499
Eze 34:18 ye must foul the **r.** with your feet?..... 3498
Eze 36:3 unto the **r.** of the heathen,................ 7611
Eze 36:4 derision to the **r.** of the heathen 7611
Eze 36:5 against the **r.** of the heathen, and........ 7611
Eze 48:18 And the **r.** in length over against......... 3498
Eze 48:21 And the **r.** shall be for the prince, ... 3498
Da 7:7 stamped the **r.** with the feet of it: 7606
Da 7:19 and stamped the **r.** with his feet; 7606
Zep 2:9 **r.** of my people shall spoil them, ... 7611
Hag 2:2 and to the **r.** of the people, saying,...... 7611
Zec 8:11 be unto the **r.** of this people as in...... 7611
Zec 14:2 **r.** of the people shall not be cut off..... 3499
Mal 2:15 Yet had he the **r.** of the spirit............ 7605
Mk 16:13 they went and told it unto the **r.**: *3062*
Ac 15:17 **r.** of the men might seek after the *2645*

RESIST See also RESISTED; RESISTETH.
Zec 3:1 at his right hand to **r.** him................ 7853
Mt 5:39 **I say unto you, That ye r. not evil** .. *436*
Lu 21:15 **shall not be able to gainsay nor r.** .. *436*
Ac 6:10 were not able to **r.** the wisdom and...... *436*
Ac 7:51 ears, ye do always **r.** the Holy Ghost: .. *496*
Ro 13:2 and they that **r.** shall receive to.......... *436*
2Ti 3:8 Moses, so do these also **r.** the truth: ... *436*
Jas 4:7 **R.** the devil, and he will flee from......... *436*
Jas 5:6 the just; and he doth not **r.** you. *498*
1Pe 5:9 Whom **r.** stedfast in the faith, ... *436*

RESISTED
Ro 9:19 find fault? For who hath **r.** his will?...... *436*
Heb 12:4 Ye have not yet **r.** unto blood, ... *478*

RESISTETH
Ro 13:2 Whosoever therefore **r.** the power, ... *498*
Ro 13:2 **r.** the ordinance of God: and they........ *436*
Jas 4:6 God **r.** the proud, but giveth grace....... *498*
1Pe 5:5 God **r.** the proud, and giveth grace *498*

RESOLVED
Lu 16:4 **I am r. what to do, that, when I**... *1097*

RESORT See also RESORTED.
Ne 4:20 trumpet, **r.** ye thither unto us: 6908
Ps 71:3 whereunto I may continually **r.**.......... 935
Mk 10:1 and the people **r.** unto him again, ... *4848*
Joh 18:20 **whither the Jews always r.;** *4905*

RESORTED
2Ch 11:13 **r.** to him out of all their coasts. 3320
Mk 2:13 and all the multitude **r.** unto him, ... *2064*
Joh 10:41 many **r.** unto him, and said, John........ *2064*
Joh 18:2 Jesus ofttimes **r.** thither with his *4863*
Ac 16:13 unto the women which **r.** thither. *4905*

RESPECT See also RESPECTED; RESPECTETH.
Ge 4:4 And the Lord had **r.** unto Abel 8159
Ge 4:5 and to his offering he had not **r.**.......... 8159
Ex 2:25 Israel, and God had **r.** unto them. 3045
Le 19:15 not **r.** the person of the poor,............ 5375
Le 26:9 For I will have **r.** unto you, and........... 6437
Nu 16:15 Lord, **R.** not thou their offering: 6437
De 1:17 shall not **r.** persons in judgment; 5234
De 16:19 thou shalt not **r.** persons, neither 5234
2Sa 14:14 neither doth God **r.** any person: 5375
1Ki 8:28 have thou **r.** unto the prayer of............ 6437
2Ki 13:23 had **r.** unto them, because of his........ 6437
2Ch 6:19 Have **r.** therefore to the prayer of...... 6437
2Ch 19:7 Lord our God, nor **r.** of persons, ... 4856
Ps 74:20 Have **r.** unto the covenant: for 5027
Ps 119:6 have **r.** unto all thy commandments..... 5027
Ps 119:15 precepts, and have **r.** unto thy ways. .. 5027
Ps 119:117 **r.** unto thy statutes continually......... 8159
Ps 138:6 yet hath he **r.** unto the lowly:............ 7200
Pr 24:23 have **r.** of persons in judgment. 5234
Pr 28:21 To have **r.** of persons is not good: 5234
Isa 17:7 have **r.** to the Holy One of Israel. 7200
Isa 17:8 **r.** that which his fingers have made, ... 7200
Isa 22:11 **r.** unto him that fashioned it long........ 7200
Ro 2:11 there is no **r.** of persons with God. *4382*
2Co 3:10 glorious had no glory in this **r.**,........... *3313*
Eph 6:9 is there **r.** of persons with him. *3382*
Php 4:11 Not that I speak in **r.** of want: for....... *2596*
Col 2:16 or in **r.** of an holy day, or of the *3313*
Col 3:25 and there is no **r.** of persons............. *4382*
Heb 11:26 had **r.** unto the recompence of the....... *578*
Jas 2:1 Lord of glory, with **r.** of persons.......... *4382*
Jas 2:3 **r.** to him that weareth the gay........... *1914*
Jas 2:9 But if ye have **r.** to persons, ye.......... *4380*
1Pe 1:17 who without **r.** of persons judgeth........ *678*

RESPECTED
La 4:16 **r.** not the persons of the priests, ... 5375

RESPECTER
Ac 10:34 that God is no **r.** of persons:............. *4381*

RESPECTETH
Job 37:24 **r.** not any that are wise of heart. 7200
Ps 40:4 and **r.** not the proud, nor such as....... 6437

RESPITE
Ex 8:15 Pharaoh saw that there was **r.**........... 7309
1Sa 11:3 Give us seven days **r.**, that we........... 7503

REST See also RESTED; RESTETH; RESTING; RESTS.
Ge 8:9 dove found no **r.** for the sole of her.... 4494
Ge 18:4 and **r.** yourselves under the tree. 8172
Ge 30:36 Jacob fed the **r.** of Laban's flocks. 3498
Ge 49:15 he saw that **r.** was good, and the....... 4496
Ex 5:5 make them **r.** from their burdens. 7673
Ex 16:23 is the **r.** of the holy sabbath unto 7677
Ex 23:11 thou shalt let it **r.** and lie still; 8058
Ex 23:12 on the seventh day thou shalt **r.** 7673
Ex 23:12 thine ox and thine ass may **r.**, and....... 5117
Ex 28:10 names of the **r.** on the other stone, ... 3498
Ex 31:15 the seventh is the sabbath of **r.**, ... 7677
Ex 33:14 with thee, and I will give thee **r.**......... 5117
Ex 34:21 on the seventh day thou shalt **r.** 7673
Ex 34:21 time and in harvest thou shalt **r.** 7673
Ex 35:2 day, a sabbath of **r.** to the Lord:......... 7677
Le 5:9 **r.** of the blood shall be wrung out 7604
Le 14:17 **r.** of the oil that is in his hand........... 3499
Le 14:29 **r.** of the oil that is in the priest's 3498
Le 16:31 shall be a sabbath of **r.** unto you, ... 7677
Le 23:3 seventh day is the sabbath of **r.**,......... 7677
Le 23:32 shall be unto you a sabbath of **r.**, ... 7677
Le 25:4 be a sabbath of **r.** unto the land, ... 7677
Le 25:5 for it is a year of **r.** unto the land....... 7677
Le 26:34 then shall the land **r.**, and enjoy......... 7673
Le 26:35 long as it lieth desolate it shall **r.**; 7673
Le 26:35 it did not **r.** in your sabbaths, when.... 7673
Nu 31:8 beside the **r.** of them that were slain; ....
Nu 31:32 **r.** of the prey which the men of......... 3499
De 3:13 the **r.** of Gilead, and all Bashan,.......... 3499
De 3:20 have given **r.** unto your brethren,....... 5117
De 5:14 maidservant may **r.** as well as thou..... 5117
De 12:9 ye are not as yet come to the **r.**........ 4496
De 12:10 he giveth you **r.** from all your............ 5117
De 25:19 God hath given thee **r.** from all.......... 5117
De 28:65 shall the sole of thy foot have **r.**: 4494
Jos 1:13 Lord your God hath given you **r.**,......... 5117
Jos 1:15 Lord have given your brethren **r.**, ... 5117
Jos 3:13 shall **r.** in the waters of Jordan, ... 5117
Jos 10:20 the **r.** which remained of them............ 8300
Jos 13:27 the **r.** of the kingdom of Sihon........... 3499
Jos 14:15 And the land had **r.** from war. 8252
Jos 17:2 the **r.** of the children of Manasseh...... 3498
Jos 17:6 the **r.** of Manasseh's sons had the...... 3498
Jos 21:5 the **r.** of the children of Kohath 3498
Jos 21:34 the **r.** of the Levites, out of the.......... 3498
Jos 21:44 Lord gave them **r.** round about,.......... 5117
Jos 22:4 hath given **r.** unto your brethren, ... 5117
Jos 23:1 the Lord had given **r.** unto Israel 5117
Jg 3:11 And the land had **r.** forty years........... 8252
Jg 3:30 the land had **r.** fourscore years. 8252
Jg 5:31 And the land had **r.** forty years.......... 8252
Jg 7:6 the **r.** of the people bowed down.......... 3499
Jg 7:8 he sent all the **r.** of Israel every man........
Ru 1:9 grant you that ye may find **r.**,.............. 4496
Ru 3:1 shall I not seek **r.** for thee, that.......... 4494
Ru 3:18 the man will not be in **r.**, until he....... 8252
1Sa 13:2 the **r.** of the people he sent every....... 3499
1Sa 15:15 the **r.** we have utterly destroyed......... 3498
2Sa 3:29 Let it **r.** on the head of Joab, and......... 2342
2Sa 7:1 the Lord had given him **r.** round 5117
2Sa 7:11 thee to **r.** from all thine enemies. 5117
2Sa 10:10 the **r.** of the people he delivered......... 3499
2Sa 12:28 gather the **r.** of the people together,... 3499
2Sa 21:10 the birds of the air to **r.** on them 5117
1Ki 5:4 the Lord my God hath given me **r.**....... 5117
1Ki 8:56 that hath given **r.** unto his people....... 4496
1Ki 11:41 the **r.** of the acts of Solomon, and...... 3499
1Ki 14:19 the **r.** of the acts of Jeroboam, how.... 3499
1Ki 14:29 the **r.** of the acts of Rehoboam, and.... 3499
1Ki 15:7 Now the **r.** of the acts of Abijam,....... 3499
1Ki 15:23 The **r.** of all the acts of Asa, and 3499
1Ki 15:31 Now the **r.** of the acts of Nadab, ... 3499
1Ki 16:5 Now the **r.** of the acts of Baasha, ... 3499
1Ki 16:14 Now the **r.** of the acts of Elah, and.... 3499
1Ki 16:20 Now the **r.** of the acts of Zimri,......... 3499
1Ki 16:27 Now the **r.** of the acts of Omri.......... 3499
1Ki 20:30 But the **r.** fled to Aphek, into the....... 3498
1Ki 22:39 Now the **r.** of the acts of Ahab, ... 3499
1Ki 22:45 the **r.** of the acts of Jehoshaphat, ... 3499
2Ki 1:18 Now the **r.** of the acts of Ahaziah....... 3499
2Ki 2:15 spirit of Elijah doth **r.** on Elisha. 5117
2Ki 4:7 thou and thy children of the **r.**........... 3498
2Ki 8:23 And the **r.** of the acts of Joram,......... 3499
2Ki 10:34 Now the **r.** of the acts of Jehu, and.... 3499
2Ki 12:19 And the **r.** of the acts of Joash, and.... 3499
2Ki 13:8 Now the **r.** of the acts of Jehoahaz, ... 3499
2Ki 13:12 And the **r.** of the acts of Joash, and.... 3499
2Ki 14:15 the **r.** of the acts of Jehoash which..... 3499
2Ki 14:18 the **r.** of the acts of Amaziah, are....... 3499
2Ki 14:28 the **r.** of the acts of Jeroboam, and..... 3499
2Ki 15:6 And the **r.** of the acts of Azariah,....... 3499
2Ki 15:11 And the **r.** of the acts of Zachariah, ... 3499
2Ki 15:15 the **r.** of the acts of Shallum, and 3499
2Ki 15:21 And the **r.** of the acts of Menahem,.... 3499
2Ki 15:26 And the **r.** of the acts of Pekahiah,..... 3499
2Ki 15:31 the **r.** of the acts of Pekah, and all 3499
2Ki 15:36 Now the **r.** of the acts of Jotham,....... 3499
2Ki 16:19 the **r.** of the acts of Ahaz which he..... 3499
2Ki 20:20 And the **r.** of the acts of Hezekiah,..... 3499
2Ki 21:17 the **r.** of the acts of Manasseh, and 3499

2Ki 21:25 the **r.** of the acts of Amon which he ... 3499
2Ki 23:28 the **r.** of the acts of Josiah, and all..... 3499
2Ki 24:5 the **r.** of the acts of Jehoiakim, and..... 3499
2Ki 25:11 **r.** of the people that were left in........ 3499
1Ch 4:43 smote the **r.** of the Amalekites 7611
1Ch 6:31 Lord, after that the ark had **r.**.......... 4494
1Ch 6:77 **r.** of the children of Merari were........ 3498
1Ch 11:8 Joab repaired the **r.** of the city. 7605
1Ch 12:38 **r.** also of Israel were of one heart...... 7611
1Ch 16:41 and the **r.** that were chosen, who....... 7605
1Ch 19:11 **r.** of the people he delivered unto 3499
1Ch 22:9 to thee, who shall be a man of **r.**; 4496
1Ch 22:9 give him **r.** from all his enemies, ... 5117
1Ch 22:18 he not given you **r.** on every side?..... 5117
1Ch 23:25 hath given **r.** unto his people, that...... 5117
1Ch 24:20 **r.** of the sons of Levi were these:...... 3498
1Ch 28:2 build an house of **r.** for the ark of 4496
2Ch 9:29 Now the **r.** of the acts of Solomon,...... 7605
2Ch 13:22 And the **r.** of the acts of Abijah, ... 3499
2Ch 14:6 for the land had **r.**, and he had no...... 8252
2Ch 14:6 because the Lord had given him **r.**. 5117
2Ch 14:7 he hath given us **r.** on every side....... 5117
2Ch 14:11 for we **r.** on thee, and in thy............ 8172
2Ch 15:15 Lord gave them **r.** round about.......... 5117
2Ch 20:30 his God gave him **r.** round about........ 5117
2Ch 20:34 the **r.** of the acts of Jehoshaphat, ... 3499
2Ch 24:14 they brought the **r.** of the money 7605
2Ch 25:26 Now the **r.** of the acts of Amaziah,...... 3499
2Ch 26:22 the **r.** of the acts of Uzziah, first........ 3499
2Ch 27:7 the **r.** of the acts of Jotham, and........ 3499
2Ch 28:26 **r.** of his acts and of all his ways,........ 3499
2Ch 32:32 the **r.** of the acts of Hezekiah,........... 3499
2Ch 33:18 the **r.** of the acts of Manasseh, and 3499
2Ch 35:26 the **r.** of the acts of Josiah, and 3499
2Ch 36:8 the **r.** of the acts of Jehoiakim, ... 3499
Ezr 4:3 the **r.** of the chief of the fathers......... 7605
Ezr 4:7 and the **r.** of their companions, ... 7605
Ezr 4:9 and the **r.** of their companions; 7606
Ezr 4:10 **r.** of the nations whom the great......... 7606
Ezr 4:10 **r.** that are on this side the river, ... 7606
Ezr 4:17 **r.** of their companions that dwell........ 7606
Ezr 4:17 and unto the **r.** beyond the river, ... 7606
Ezr 6:16 **r.** of the children of the captivity, ... 7606
Ezr 7:18 the **r.** of the silver and the gold, ... 7606
Ne 2:16 nor to the **r.** that did the work. 3499
Ne 4:14, 19 to the **r.** of the people,................ 3499
Ne 6:1 and the **r.** of our enemies, heard........ 3499
Ne 6:14 and the **r.** of the prophets, that 3499
Ne 7:72 which the **r.** of the people gave 7611
Ne 9:28 But after they had **r.**, they did evil..... 5117
Ne 10:28 the **r.** of the people, the priests, ... 7605
Ne 11:1 the **r.** of the people also cast lots, to .. 7605
Es 9:12 in the **r.** of the king's provinces?........ 7605
Es 9:16 and had **r.** from their enemies, ... 5118
Job 3:13 have slept: then had I been at **r.**,........ 5117
Job 3:17 and there the weary be at **r.**............. 5117
Job 3:18 There the prisoners **r.** together; 7599
Job 3:26 was not in safety, neither had I **r.**, ... 8252
Job 11:18 thou shalt take thy **r.** in safety........... 7901
Job 14:6 Turn from him, that he may **r.**, ... 2308
Job 17:16 when our **r.** together is in the dust..... 5183
Job 30:17 season: and my sinews take no **r.**. 7901
Ps 16:9 my flesh also shall **r.** in hope............ 7931
Ps 17:14 leave the **r.** of their substance to 3499
Ps 37:7 **R.** in the Lord, and wait patiently....... 1826
Ps 38:3 neither is there any **r.** in my bones..... 7965
Ps 55:6 then would I fly away, and be at **r.**...... 7931
Ps 94:13 **r.** from the days of adversity,............ 8252
Ps 95:11 they should not enter into my **r.**. 4496
Ps 116:7 Return unto thy **r.**, O my soul; for..... 4496
Ps 125:3 the rod of the wicked shall not **r.** 5117
Ps 132:8 Arise, O Lord, into thy **r.**; thou,........ 4496
Ps 132:14 This is my **r.** for ever: here will I...... 4496
Pr 6:35 neither will he **r.** content, though thou.......
Pr 29:9 he rage or laugh, there is no **r.**. 5183
Pr 29:17 thy son, and he shall give thee **r.**: 5117
Ec 2:23 his heart taketh not **r.** in the night............
Ec 6:5 this hath more **r.** than the other......... 5183
Ca 1:7 makest thy flock to **r.** at noon: 7257
Isa 7:19 shall **r.** all of them in the desolate 5117
Isa 10:19 the **r.** of the trees of his forest........... 7605
Isa 11:2 spirit of the Lord shall **r.** upon............ 5117
Isa 11:10 seek: and his **r.** shall be glorious. 4496
Isa 14:3 shall give thee **r.** from thy sorrow,....... 5117
Isa 14:7 whole earth is at **r.**, and is quiet: 5117
Isa 18:4 I will take my **r.**, and I will................ 8252
Isa 23:12 there also shalt thou have no **r.**. 5117
Isa 25:10 shall the hand of the Lord **r.**, ... 5117
Isa 28:12 said, This is the **r.** wherewith............ 4496
Isa 28:12 ye may cause the weary to **r.**;............. 5117
Isa 30:15 returning and **r.** shall ye be saved; 5183
Isa 34:14 screech owl also shall **r.** there, ... 7280
Isa 34:14 and find for herself a place of **r.**. 4494
Isa 51:4 my judgment to **r.** for a light of 7280
Isa 57:2 they shall **r.** in their beds, each 5117
Isa 57:20 troubled sea, when it cannot **r.**, ... 8252
Isa 62:1 for Jerusalem's sake I will not **r.**, ... 8252
Isa 62:7 give him no **r.**, till he establish, ... 1824
Isa 63:14 Spirit of the Lord caused him to **r.**: 5117
Isa 66:1 and where is the place of my **r.**?........ 4496
Jer 6:16 and ye shall find **r.** for your souls....... 4771
Jer 30:10 shall return, and shall be in **r.**,........... 8252
Jer 31:2 when I went to cause him to **r.**. 7280
Jer 39:9 the **r.** of the people that remained. 3499
Jer 45:3 in my sighing, and I find no **r.**. 4496
Jer 46:27 return, and be in **r.** and at ease, ... 8252
Jer 47:6 into thy scabbard, **r.**, and be still........ 7280
Jer 50:34 that he may give **r.** to the land, ... 7280
Jer 52:15 and the **r.** of the multitude................. 3499
La 1:3 the heathen, she findeth no **r.**: 4494
La 2:18 day and night: give thyself no **r.**;........ 6314
La 5:5 we labour, and have no **r.**.................. 5117
Eze 5:13 cause my fury to **r.** upon them, ... 5117
Eze 16:42 make my fury toward thee to **r.**,.......... 5117
Eze 21:17 and I will cause my fury to **r.**: 5117
Eze 24:13 caused my fury to **r.** upon thee........... 5117
Eze 38:11 I will go to them that are at **r.**,........... 8252
Eze 44:30 the blessing to **r.** in thine house.......... 5117
Eze 45:8 **r.** of the land shall they give to the...........
Eze 48:23 As for the **r.** of the tribes, from the ... 3499
Da 2:18 the **r.** of the wise men of Babylon. 7606
Da 4:4 Nebuchadnezzar was at **r.** in mine 7954
Da 7:12 As concerning the **r.** of the beasts,..... 7606
Da 12:13 thou shalt **r.**, and stand in thy lot 5117
Mic 2:10 depart; for this is not your **r.**: 4496
Hab 3:16 I might **r.** in the day of trouble: 5117
Zep 3:17 he will **r.** in his love, he will joy......... 2790
Zec 1:11 the earth sitteth still, and is at **r.**. 8252
Zec 9:1 Damascus shall be the **r.** thereof:........ 4496
Zec 11:9 let the **r.** eat every one the flesh 7604
Mt 11:28 **heavy laden, and I will give you r.**...*373*
Mt 11:29 **ye shall find r. unto your souls**...... *372*
Mt 12:43 **seeking r., and finding none**........... *372*
Mt 26:45 **Sleep on now, and take your r.**:....... *373*
Mt 27:49 The **r.** said, Let be, let us see *3062*
Mk 6:31 **into a desert place, and r. a while**:.. *373*
Mk 14:41 **Sleep on now, and take your r.**:....... *373*
Lu 10:6 **there, your peace shall r. upon it**: ..*1879*
Lu 11:24 **through dry places, seeking r.**; *372*
Lu 12:26 **why take ye thought for the r.?**..... *3062*
Lu 24:9 unto the eleven, and to all the **r.**........ *3062*
Joh 11:13 had spoken of taking of **r.** in sleep...... *2838*
Ac 2:26 also my flesh shall **r.** in hope:............ *2681*
Ac 2:37 Peter and to the **r.** of the apostles, ... *3062*
Ac 5:13 of the **r.** durst no man join himself...... *3062*
Ac 7:49 or what is the place of my **r.**? *2663*
Ac 9:31 had the churches **r.** throughout *1515*
Ac 27:44 And the **r.**, some on boards, and......... *3062*
Ro 11:7 obtained it, and the **r.** were blinded *3062*
1Co 7:12 But to the **r.** speak I, not the Lord: *3062*
1Co 11:34 **r.** will I set in order when I come. *3062*
2Co 2:13 I had no **r.** in my spirit, because I *425*
2Co 7:5 Macedonia, our flesh had no **r.**,........... *425*
2Co 12:9 power of Christ may **r.** upon me. *1981*
2Th 1:7 to you who are troubled **r.** with us,...... *425*
Heb 3:11 They shall not enter into my **r.**.)........ *2663*
Heb 3:18 they should not enter into his **r.**,......... *2663*
Heb 4:1 being left us of entering into his **r.**, ... *2663*
Heb 4:3 which have believed do enter into **r.**, .. *2663*
Heb 4:3 if they shall enter into my **r.**:............. *2663*
Heb 4:4 God did **r.** the seventh day from *2664*
Heb 4:5 If they shall enter into my **r.**.............. *2663*
Heb 4:8 For if Jesus had given them **r.**, ... *2664*
Heb 4:9 therefore a **r.** to the people of God..... *4520*
Heb 4:10 For he that is entered into his **r.**,........ *2663*
Heb 4:11 labour therefore to enter into that **r.**,.. *2663*
1Pe 4:2 live the **r.** of his time in the flesh....... *1954*
Re 2:24 **I say, and unto the r. in Thyatira**, .*3062*
Re 4:8 and they **r.** not day and night,...... *2192,372*
Re 6:11 should **r.** yet for a little season,............ *373*
Re 9:20 **r.** of the men which were not killed *3062*
Re 14:11 and they have no **r.** day nor night, ... *372*
Re 14:13 that they may **r.** from their labours; *373*
Re 20:5 the **r.** of the dead lived not again *3062*

RESTED
Ge 2:2 he **r.** on the seventh day from all 7673
Ge 2:3 that in it he had **r.** from all his work ... 7673
Ge 8:4 the ark **r.** in the seventh month, ... 5117
Ex 10:14 and **r.** in all the coasts of Egypt: 5117
Ex 16:30 the people **r.** on the seventh day........ 7673
Ex 20:11 in them is, and **r.** the seventh day:...... 5117
Ex 31:17 and on the seventh day he **r.**, and....... 7673
Nu 9:18 tabernacle they **r.** in their tents. 2583
Nu 9:23 of the Lord they **r.** in the tents, ... 2583
Nu 10:12 the cloud **r.** in the wilderness of......... 7931
Nu 10:36 when it **r.**, he said, Return, O Lord,.... 5117
Nu 11:25 when the spirit **r.** upon them, they....... 5117
Nu 11:26 Medad: and the spirit **r.** upon them; ... 5117
Jos 11:23 tribes. And the land **r.** from war. 8252
1Ki 6:10 they **r.** on the house with timber of...... 270
2Ch 32:8 **r.** themselves upon the words of......... 5564
Es 9:17 fourteenth day of the same **r.** they, ... 5118
Es 9:18 fifteenth day of the same they **r.**, ... 5118
Es 9:22 the Jews **r.** from their enemies, ... 5117
Job 30:27 My bowels boiled, and **r.** not: the 1826
Lu 23:56 and **r.** the sabbath day according *2270*

RESTEST
Ro 2:17 art called a Jew, and **r.** in the law, ... *1879*

RESTETH
Job 24:23 him to be in safety, whereon he **r.**; 8172
Pr 14:33 Wisdom **r.** in the heart of him that 5117
Ec 7:9 for anger **r.** in the bosom of fools........ 5117
1Pe 4:14 spirit of glory and of God **r.** upon *373*

RESTING See also RESTINGPLACE.
Nu 10:33 to search out a **r.** place for them........ 4496
2Ch 6:41 O Lord God, into thy **r.** place, thou,..... 5118
Pr 24:15 righteous; spoil not his **r.** place; 7258
Isa 32:18 dwellings, and in quiet **r.** places; 4496

RESTINGPLACE See also RESTING and PLACE.
Jer 50:6 hill, they have forgotten their **r.**......... 7258

RESTITUTION
Ex 22:3 he should make full **r.**; if he have 7999
Ex 22:5 his own vineyard, shall he make **r.**. 7999
Ex 22:6 kindled...fire shall surely make **r.**. 7999
Ex 22:12 he shall make **r.** unto the owner 7999
Job 20:18 to his substance shall the **r.** be, ... 8545
Ac 3:21 until the times of **r.** of all things, ... *605*

RESTORE See also RESTORED; RESTORETH.
Ge 20:7 **r.** the man his wife; for he is a.......... 7725
Ge 20:7 if thou **r.** her not, know thou that....... 7725
Ge 40:13 head, and **r.** thee unto thy place: 7725
Ge 42:25 **r.** every man's money into his sack,.... 7725
Ex 22:1 he shall **r.** five oxen for an ox, and...... 7999
Ex 22:4 ass, or sheep; he shall **r.** double. 7999
Le 6:4 **r.** that which he took violently 7725
Le 6:5 he shall even **r.** it in the principal, ... 7999
Le 24:21 that killeth a beast, he shall **r.** it: 7999
Le 25:27 **r.** the overplus unto the man to.......... 7725
Le 25:28 But if he be not able to **r.** it to him, ... 7725
Nu 35:25 **r.** him to the city of his refuge, ... 7725
De 22:2 and thou shalt **r.** it to him again. 7725
Jg 11:13 **r.** those lands again peaceably............ 7725
Jg 17:3 now therefore I will **r.** it unto thee. 7725
1Sa 12:3 eyes therewith? and I will **r.** it you..... 7725
2Sa 9:7 will **r.** thee all the land of Saul thy....... 7725
2Sa 12:6 And he shall **r.** the lamb fourfold, ... 7999
2Sa 16:3 **r.** me the kingdom of my father. 7725
1Ki 20:34 took from thy father, I will **r.**; 7725
2Ki 8:6 **R.** all that was hers, and all the......... 7725
Ne 5:11 **R.**, I pray you, to them, even this 7725
Ne 5:12 Then said they, We will **r.** them, ... 7725
Job 20:10 and his hands shall **r.** their goods. 7725
Job 20:18 which he laboured for shall he **r.**,........ 7725
Ps 51:12 **R.** unto me the joy of thy................... 7725
Pr 6:31 he be found, he shall **r.** sevenfold;...... 7999
Isa 1:26 I will **r.** thy judges as at the first, ... 7725
Isa 42:22 for a spoil, and none saith, **R.**. 7725
Isa 49:6 and to **r.** the preserved of Israel: 7725
Isa 57:18 **r.** comforts unto him and to his.......... 7999
Jer 27:22 them up, and **r.** them to this place. 7725
Jer 30:17 For I will **r.** health unto thee, and 5927
Eze 33:15 If the wicked **r.** the pledge, give 7725
Da 9:5 to **r.** and to build Jerusalem unto......... 7725
Joe 2:25 I will **r.** to you the years that the....... 7999
Mt 17:11 **shall first come, and r. all things**.... *600*
Lu 19:8 false accusation, I **r.** him fourfold. *591*
Ac 1:6 **r.** again the kingdom to Israel?............ *600*
Ga 6:1 **r.** such an one in the spirit of............ *2675*

RESTORED
Ge 20:14 and **r.** him Sarah his wife................ 7725
Ge 40:21 And he **r.** the chief butler unto his...... 7725
Ge 41:13 me he **r.** unto mine office, and him..... 7725
Ge 42:28 My money is **r.**; and, lo, it is even..... 7725
De 28:31 and shall not be **r.** to thee: thy.......... 7725
Jg 17:3 had **r.** the eleven hundred shekels...... 7725
Jg 17:4 he **r.** the money unto his mother;....... 7725
1Sa 7:14 taken from Israel were **r.** to Israel, ... 7725
1Ki 13:6 that my hand may be **r.** me again. 7725
1Ki 13:6 the king's hand was **r.** him again, ... 7725
2Ki 8:1 whose son he had **r.** to life, ... 2421
2Ki 8:5 how he had **r.** a dead body to life,....... 2421
2Ki 8:5 woman, whose son he had **r.** to life, ... 2421
2Ki 8:5 is her son, whom Elisha **r.** to life. 2421
2Ki 14:22 He built Elath, and **r.** it to Judah, ... 7725
2Ki 14:25 He **r.** the coast of Israel from the 7725
2Ch 8:2 which Huram had **r.** to Solomon, ... 5414
2Ch 26:2 He built Eloth, and **r.** it to Judah,....... 7725
Ezr 6:5 be **r.**, and brought again unto the....... 8421
Ps 69:4 I **r.** that which I took not away. 7725
Eze 18:7 but hath **r.** to the debtor his pledge, ... 7725
Eze 18:12 hath not **r.** the pledge, and hath......... 7725
Mt 12:13 it was **r.** whole, like as the other......... *600*
Mk 3:5 his hand was **r.** whole as the other. *600*
Mk 8:25 and he was **r.**, and saw every man......... *600*
Lu 6:10 his hand was **r.** whole as the other. *600*
Heb 13:19 that I may be **r.** to you the sooner....... *600*

RESTORER
Ru 4:15 shall be unto thee a **r.** of thy life,....... 7725
Isa 58:12 breach, The **r.** of paths to dwell in. 7725

RESTORETH
Ps 23:3 He **r.** my soul: he leadeth me in........ 7725
Mk 9:12 **cometh first, and r. all things;**....... *600*

RESTRAIN See also RESTRAINED; RESTRAINEST.
Job 15:8 dost thou **r.** wisdom to thyself?.......... 1639
Ps 76:10 remainder of wrath shalt thou **r.**.......... 2296

RESTRAINED
Ge 8:2 and the rain from heaven was **r.**; 3607
Ge 11:6 now nothing will be **r.** from them, ... 1219
Ge 16:2 the Lord hath **r.** me from bearing:...... 6113
Ex 36:6 the people were **r.** from bringing........ 3607
1Sa 3:13 vile, and he **r.** them not. 3543
Isa 63:15 mercies toward me? are they **r.**? 662
Eze 31:15 and I **r.** the floods thereof, and.......... 4513
Ac 14:18 sayings scarce **r.** they the people, ... *2664*

RESTRAINEST
Job 15:4 off fear, and **r.** prayer before God. 1639

RESTRAINT
1Sa 14:6 there is no **r.** to the Lord to save 4622

RESTS
1Ki 6:6 he made narrowed **r.** round about,............

RESURRECTION
Mt 22:23 which say that there is no **r.**, and........ *386*
Mt 22:28 in the **r.** whose wife shall she be of...... *386*
Mt 22:30 **For in the r. they neither marry,**.... *386*
Mt 22:31 **But as touching the r. of the dead,**. *386*
Mt 27:53 came out the graves after his **r.**,......... *1454*
Mk 12:18 Sadducees, which say there is no **r.**; *386*
Mk 12:23 In the **r.** therefore, when they shall...... *386*
Lu 14:14 **be recompensed at the r. of the** *386*
Lu 20:27 which deny that there is any **r.**; *386*
Lu 20:33 in the **r.** whose wife of them is she? *386*
Lu 20:35 **world, and the r. from the dead,**...... *386*
Lu 20:36 **God, being the children of the r.**..... *386*
Joh 5:29 **have done good, unto the r. of life;**.. *386*
Joh 5:29 **done evil, unto the r. of damnation.**. *386*
Joh 11:24 rise again in the **r.** at the last day.......... *386*
Joh 11:25 unto her, **I am the r., and the life:**... *386*
Ac 1:22 to be a witness with us of his **r.**.......... *386*
Ac 2:31 this before spake of the **r.** of Christ, ... *386*
Ac 4:2 through Jesus the **r.** from the dead. *386*
Ac 4:33 witness of the **r.** of the Lord Jesus: *386*
Ac 17:18 preached unto them Jesus, and...**r.**......... *386*
Ac 17:32 when they heard of the **r.** of the dead, . *386*
Ac 23:6 of the hope and **r.** of the dead I am *386*
Ac 23:8 Sadducees say that there is no **r.**,........ *386*
Ac 24:15 that there shall be a **r.** of the dead,...... *386*
Ac 24:21 Touching the **r.** of the dead I am.......... *386*
Ro 1:4 of holiness, by the **r.** from the dead: *386*
Ro 6:5 be also in the likeness of his **r.**............ *386*
1Co 15:12 you that there is no **r.** of the dead?...... *386*
1Co 15:13 But if there be no **r.** of the dead, then.. *386*
1Co 15:21 by man came also the **r.** of the dead. ... *386*
1Co 15:42 So also is the **r.** of the dead. It is........ *386*
Php 3:10 know him, and the power of his **r.**,...... *386*
Php 3:11 attain unto the **r.** of the dead............ *1815*
2Ti 2:18 saying that the **r.** is past already;......... *386*
Heb 6:2 of **r.** of the dead, and of eternal........... *386*
Heb 11:35 that they might obtain a better **r.**.......... *386*
1Pe 1:3 lively hope by the **r.** of Jesus Christ..... *386*
1Pe 3:21 God,) by the **r.** of Jesus Christ:.......... *386*
Re 20:5 were finished. This is the first **r.**......... *386*
Re 20:6 is he that hath part in the first **r.**......... *386*

RETAIN See also RETAINED; RETAINETH.
Job 2:9 Dost thou still **r.** thine integrity? 2388
Pr 4:4 Let thine heart **r.** my words: keep 8551
Pr 11:16 honour: and strong men **r.** riches, ... 8551
Ec 8:8 over the spirit to **r.** the spirit; 3607
Da 11:6 shall not **r.** the power of the arm; 6113
Joh 20:23 **whose soever sins ye r., they are**... *2902*
Ro 1:28 like to **r.** God in their knowledge,....... *2192*

RETAINED
Jg 7:8 and **r.** those three hundred men:........ 2388
Jg 19:4 the damsel's father, **r.** him; and......... 2388
Da 10:8 corruption, and I **r.** no strength, ... 6113
Da 10:16 upon me, and I have **r.** no strength. ... 6113
Joh 20:23 **soever sins ye retain, they are r.**.. *2902*
Phm 13 Whom I would have **r.** with me,......... *2722*

RETAINETH
Pr 3:18 and happy is every one that **r.** her. 8551
Pr 11:16 A gracious woman **r.** honour: and....... 8551
Mic 7:18 he **r.** not his anger for ever, ... 2388

RETIRE See also RETIRED.
2Sa 11:15 and **r.** ye from him, that he may be.... 7725
Jer 4:6 **r.**, stay not: for I will bring.............. 5756

RETIRED
Jg 20:39 the men of Israel **r.** in the battle, ... 2015
2Sa 20:22 they **r.** from the city, every man........ 6327

RETURN See also RETURNED; RETURNETH; RETURNING.
Ge 3:19 bread, till thou **r.** unto the ground; 7725
Ge 3:19 art, and unto dust shalt thou **r.**.......... 7725
Ge 14:17 after his **r.** from the slaughter of........ 7725
Ge 16:9 **R.** to thy mistress, and submit 7725
Ge 18:10 said, I will certainly **r.** unto thee 7725
Ge 18:14 time appointed I will **r.** unto thee, ... 7725
Ge 31:3 **R.** unto the land of thy fathers, and.... 7725
Ge 31:13 **r.** unto the land of thy kindred........... 7725
Ge 32:9 **R.** unto thy country, and to thy 7725
Ex 4:18 **r.** unto my brethren which are in 7725
Ex 4:19 in Midian, Go, **r.** into Egypt:............. 7725
Ex 4:21 When thou goest to **r.** into Egypt,...... 7725
Ex 13:17 they see war, and they **r.** to Egypt: ... 7725
Le 25:10 **r.** every man unto his possession, ... 7725
Le 25:10 shall **r.** every man unto his family....... 7725
Le 25:13 **r.** every man unto his possession. 7725
Le 25:27 that he may **r.** unto his possession. 7725
Le 25:28 he shall **r.** unto his possession. 7725
Le 25:41 and shall **r.** unto his own family,......... 7725
Le 25:41 of his fathers shall he **r.**.................. 7725
Le 27:24 the field shall **r.** unto him of whom..... 7725
Nu 10:36 said, **R.**, O Lord, unto the many......... 7725
Nu 14:3 not better for us to **r.** into Egypt?...... 7725
Nu 14:4 captain, and let us **r.** into Egypt......... 7725
Nu 23:5 **R.** unto Balak, and thus thou shalt...... 7725
Nu 32:18 We will not **r.** unto our houses, ... 7725
Nu 32:22 then afterward ye shall **r.**, and be........ 7725
Nu 35:28 slayer shall **r.** into the land of his 7725
De 3:20 **r.** every man unto his possession, ... 7725
De 17:16 nor cause the people to **r.** to Egypt, ... 7725
De 17:16 henceforth **r.** no more that way. 7725
De 20:5 let him go and **r.** to his house,........... 7725
De 20:6 let him also go and **r.** unto his........... 7725
De 20:7, 8 him go and **r.** unto his house, ... 7725
De 30:2 shalt **r.** unto the Lord thy God, and.... 7725
De 30:3 will **r.** and gather thee from all the 7725
De 30:8 thou shalt **r.** and obey the voice of...... 7725
Jos 1:15 **r.** unto the land of your possession, ... 7725
Jos 20:6 then shall the slayer **r.**, and come 7725
Jos 22:4 therefore now **r.** ye, and get you 6437
Jos 22:8 **R.** with much riches unto your 7725
Jg 7:3 let him **r.** and depart early from......... 7725
Jg 11:31 I **r.** in peace from the children........... 7725
Ru 1:6 might **r.** from the country of Moab: 7725
Ru 1:7 way to **r.** unto the land of Judah......... 7725
Ru 1:8 Go, **r.** each to her mother's house:..... 7725
Ru 1:10 will **r.** with thee unto thy people. 7725
Ru 1:15 gods: **r.** thou after thy sister in law. ... 7725
Ru 1:16 or to **r.** from following after thee:........ 7725
1Sa 6:3 any wise **r.** him a trespass offering: 7725
1Sa 6:4 offering which we shall **r.** to him?....... 7725
1Sa 6:8 ye **r.** him for a trespass offering,........ 7725
1Sa 7:3 If ye do **r.** unto the Lord with all 7725
1Sa 7:17 And his **r.** was to Ramah; for 8666
1Sa 9:5 with him, Come, and let us **r.**; 7725
1Sa 15:26 unto Saul, I will not **r.** with thee: 7725
1Sa 26:21 **r.**, my son David: for I will no........... 7725
1Sa 29:4 Make this fellow **r.**, that he may 7725
1Sa 29:7 Wherefore now **r.**, and go in peace,.... 7725
1Sa 29:11 to **r.** into the land of the Philistines..... 7725
2Sa 2:26 **r.** from following their brethren? 7725
2Sa 3:16 Then said Abner unto him, Go, **r.**. 7725
2Sa 10:5 your beards be grown, and then **r.**. 7725
2Sa 12:23 him, but he shall not **r.** to me........... 7725
2Sa 15:19 **r.** to thy place, and abide with the...... 7725
2Sa 15:20 **r.** thou, and take back thy brethren: ... 7725
2Sa 15:27 **r.** into the city in peace, and your 7725
2Sa 15:34 if thou **r.** to the city, and say unto...... 7725
2Sa 19:14 **R.** thou, and all thy servants. 7725
2Sa 24:13 I shall **r.** to him that sent me. 7725
1Ki 2:32 **r.** his blood upon his own head, ... 7725
1Ki 2:33 blood...**r.** upon the head of Joab, ... 7725
1Ki 2:44 **r.** thy wickedness upon thine own 7725
1Ki 8:48 **r.** unto thee with all their heart,......... 7725
1Ki 12:24 **r.** every man to his house; for this..... 7725
1Ki 12:26 kingdom **r.** to the house of David: 7725
1Ki 13:16 I may not **r.** with thee, nor go in 7725
1Ki 19:15 **r.** on thy way to the wilderness of....... 7725
1Ki 20:22 **r.** of the year the king of Syria 8666
1Ki 20:26 came to pass at the **r.** of the year,..... 8666
1Ki 22:17 **r.** every man to his house in peace..... 7725
1Ki 22:28 If thou **r.** at all in peace, the Lord...... 7725
2Ki 18:14 I have offended; **r.** from me: that....... 7725
2Ki 19:7 and shall **r.** to his own land; and I...... 7725
2Ki 19:33 he came, by the same shall he **r.**, ... 7725
2Ki 20:10 shadow **r.** backward ten degrees. 7725
1Ch 19:5 your beards be grown, and then **r.**. 7725
2Ch 6:24 shall **r.** and confess thy name, and...... 7725
2Ch 6:38 they **r.** to thee with all their heart....... 7725
2Ch 10:6 give ye me to **r.** answer to this 7725
2Ch 10:9 we may **r.** answer to this people, ... 7725
2Ch 11:4 **r.** every man to his house: for this..... 7725
2Ch 18:16 let them **r.**...every man to his house... 7725
2Ch 18:26 of affliction, until I **r.** in peace........... 7725
2Ch 18:27 If thou certainly **r.** in peace, then....... 7725
2Ch 30:6 he will **r.** to the remnant of you, ... 7725
2Ch 30:9 face from you, if ye **r.** unto him. 7725
Ne 2:6 be? and when wilt thou **r.**?................ 7725
Ne 4:12 From all places whence ye shall **r.**...... 7725
Ne 9:17 a captain to **r.** to their bondage:......... 7725
Es 4:15 Esther bade them **r.** Mordecai this 7725
Es 9:25 Jews, should **r.** upon his own head, ... 7725
Job 1:21 and naked shall I **r.** thither: the 7725
Job 6:29 **R.**, I pray you, let it not be iniquity;... 7725
Job 6:29 yea, **r.** again, my righteousness is 7725
Job 7:10 He shall **r.** no more to his house,....... 7725
Job 10:21 Before I go whence I shall not **r.**, ... 7725
Job 15:22 believeth not that he shall **r.** out of..... 7725
Job 16:22 go the way whence I shall not **r.**......... 7725
Job 17:10 for you all, do ye **r.**, and come now:... 7725
Job 22:23 If thou **r.** to the Almighty, thou 7725
Job 33:25 shall **r.** to the days of his youth: 7725
Job 36:10 that they **r.** from iniquity. 7725
Job 39:4 go forth, and **r.** not unto them........... 7725
Ps 6:4 **R.**, O Lord, deliver my soul: oh 7725
Ps 6:10 them **r.** and be ashamed suddenly....... 7725
Ps 7:7 sakes therefore **r.** thou on high.......... 7725
Ps 7:16 His mischief shall **r.** upon his own 7725
Ps 59:6 They **r.** at evening: they make a........ 7725
Ps 59:14 And at evening let them **r.**; and......... 7725
Ps 73:10 Therefore his people **r.** hither:........... 7725
Ps 74:21 let not the oppressed **r.** ashamed: 7725
Ps 80:14 **R.**, we beseech thee, O God of......... 7725
Ps 90:3 and sayest, **R.**, ye children of men...... 7725
Ps 90:13 **R.**, O Lord, how long? and let it........ 7725
Ps 94:15 shall **r.** unto righteousness: and.......... 7725
Ps 104:29 they die, and **r.** to their dust............ 7725
Ps 116:7 **R.** unto thy rest, O my soul; for........ 7725
Pr 2:19 None that go unto her **r.** again, ... 7725
Pr 26:27 rolleth a stone, it will **r.** upon him. 7725
Ec 1:7 rivers come, thither they **r.** again. 7725

Ec 5:15 shall he **r.** to go as he came, and....... 7725
Ec 12:2 nor the clouds **r.** after the rain: 7725
Ec 12:7 the dust **r.** to the earth as it was: 7725
Ec 12:7 shall **r.** unto God who gave it. 7725
Ca 6:13 **R.**, **r.**, O Shulamite; 7725
Ca 6:13 **r.**, **r.**, that we may look upon thee. 7725
Isa 6:13 it shall be a tenth, and it shall **r.**, ... 7725
Isa 10:21 The remnant shall **r.**, even the 7725
Isa 10:22 yet a remnant of them shall **r.**: 7725
Isa 19:22 and they shall **r.** even to the Lord, ... 7725
Isa 21:12 will enquire, enquire ye: **r.**, come....... 7725
Isa 35:10 the ransomed of the Lord shall **r.**, ... 7725
Isa 37:7 a rumour, and **r.** to his own land; 7725
Isa 37:34 he came, by the same shall he **r.**, ... 7725
Isa 44:22 **r.** unto me; for I have redeemed........ 7725
Isa 45:23 in righteousness, and shall not **r.**,....... 7725
Isa 51:11 the redeemed of the Lord shall **r.**,....... 7725
Isa 55:7 and let him **r.** unto the Lord, and....... 7725
Isa 55:11 it shall not **r.** unto me void, but it 7725
Isa 63:17 **R.** for thy servants' sake, the tribes ... 7725
Jer 3:1 man's, shall he **r.** unto her again? 7725
Jer 3:1 **r.** again unto me, saith the Lord. 7725
Jer 3:12 **R.**, thou backsliding Israel, saith 7725
Jer 3:22 **R.**, ye backsliding children, and I 7725
Jer 4:1 If thou wilt **r.**, O Israel, saith the....... 7725
Jer 4:1 Lord, **r.** unto me: and if thou wilt....... 7725
Jer 5:3 than a rock; they have refused to **r.**. .. 7725
Jer 8:4 shall he turn away, and not **r.**? 7725
Jer 8:5 hold fast deceit, they refuse to **r.**....... 7725
Jer 12:15 I have plucked them out I will **r.**, ... 7725
Jer 15:7 since they **r.** not from their ways. 7725
Jer 15:19 If thou **r.**, then will I bring thee 7725
Jer 15:19 my mouth: let them **r.** unto thee; 7725
Jer 15:19 but **r.** not thou unto them. 7725
Jer 18:11 **r.** ye now every one from his evil 7725
Jer 22:10 for he shall **r.** no more, nor see his 7725
Jer 22:11 He shall not **r.** thither any more:........ 7725
Jer 22:27 land whereunto they desire to **r.**, ... 7725
Jer 22:27 thither shall they not **r.** 7725
Jer 23:14 none doth **r.** from his wickedness: 7725
Jer 23:20 The anger of the Lord shall not **r.**,..... 7725
Jer 24:7 **r.** unto me with their whole heart....... 7725
Jer 29:10 in causing you to **r.** to this place. 7725
Jer 30:3 I will cause them to **r.** to the land 7725
Jer 30:10 Jacob shall **r.**, and shall be in rest,...... 7725
Jer 30:24 fierce anger of the Lord shall not **r.**,... 7725
Jer 31:8 a great company shall **r.** thither. 7725
Jer 32:44 for I will cause their captivity to **r.**, ... 7725
Jer 33:7 and the captivity of Israel to **r.**, ... 7725
Jer 33:11 cause to **r.** the captivity of the land, ... 7725
Jer 33:26 for I will cause their captivity to **r.**, ... 7725
Jer 34:11 whom they had let go free, to **r.**,....... 7725
Jer 34:16 set at liberty at their pleasure, to **r.**, .. 7725
Jer 34:22 and cause them to **r.** to this city; 7725
Jer 35:15 **R.** ye now every man from his evil..... 7725
Jer 36:3 may **r.** every man from his evil way;... 7725
Jer 36:7 will **r.** every one from his evil way, ... 7725
Jer 37:7 shall **r.** to Egypt into their own land.... 7725
Jer 37:20 not to **r.** to the house of Jonathan 7725
Jer 38:26 cause me to **r.** to Jonathan's house, ... 7725
Jer 42:12 cause you to **r.** to your own land. 7725
Jer 44:14 should **r.** into the land of Judah, ... 7725
Jer 44:14 have a desire to **r.** to dwell there:...... 7725
Jer 44:14 shall **r.** but such as shall escape. 7725
Jer 44:28 shall **r.** out of the land of Egypt 7725
Jer 46:27 and Jacob shall **r.**, and be in rest........ 7725
Jer 50:9 expert man; none shall **r.** in vain. 7725
Eze 7:13 the seller shall not **r.** to that which..... 7725
Eze 7:13 multitude...which shall not **r.**; 7725
Eze 13:22 should not **r.** from his wicked way, ... 7725
Eze 16:55, 55 shall **r.** to their former estate, ... 7725
Eze 16:55 shall **r.** to your former estate. 7725
Eze 18:23 not that he should **r.** from his ways, ... 7725
Eze 21:5 sheath: it shall not **r.** any more. 7725
Eze 21:30 Shall I cause it to **r.** into his sheath? ... 7725
Eze 29:14 to **r.** into the land of Pathros, ... 7725
Eze 35:9 and thy cities shall not **r.** 3427
Eze 46:9 shall not **r.** by the way of the gate 7725
Eze 46:17 after it shall **r.** to the prince: but....... 7725
Eze 47:6 me to **r.** to the brink of the river. 7725
Da 10:20 now will I **r.** to the fight with the....... 7725
Da 11:9 and shall **r.** into his own land. 7725
Da 11:10 then shall he **r.**, and be stirred up, ... 7725
Da 11:13 For the king of the north shall **r.**,....... 7725
Da 11:28 **r.** into his land with great riches; 7725
Da 11:28 do exploits, and **r.** to his own land..... 7725
Da 11:29 At the time appointed he shall **r.**, ... 7725
Da 11:30 he shall be grieved, and **r.**, and 7725
Da 11:30 shall even **r.**, and have intelligence 7725
Ho 2:7 I will go and **r.** to my first husband;.... 7725
Ho 2:9 Therefore will I **r.**, and take away...... 7725
Ho 3:5 shall the children of Israel **r.**, and....... 7725
Ho 5:15 I will go and **r.** to my place, till they... 7725
Ho 6:1 Come, and let us **r.** unto the Lord:..... 7725
Ho 7:10 do not **r.** to the Lord their God, ... 7725
Ho 7:16 They **r.**, but not to the most High:..... 7725
Ho 8:13 their sins: they shall **r.** to Egypt. 7725
Ho 9:3 but Ephraim shall **r.** to Egypt, and...... 7725
Ho 11:5 shall not **r.** into the land of Egypt, ... 7725
Ho 11:5 his king, because they refused to **r.**.... 7725
Ho 11:9 I will not **r.** to destroy Ephraim: 7725
Ho 12:14 reproach shall his Lord **r.** unto him. 7725
Ho 14:1 O Israel, **r.** unto the Lord thy God; 7725
Ho 14:7 dwell under his shadow shall **r.**; 7725
Joe 2:14 knoweth if he will **r.** and repent, ... 7725
Joe 3:4 speedily will I **r.** your recompence...... 7725
Joe 3:7 and will **r.** your recompence upon........ 7725
Ob 15 thy reward shall **r.** upon thine own 7725
Mic 1:7 they shall **r.** to the hire of an harlot.... 7725
Mic 5:3 the remnant of his brethren shall **r.** 7725
Mal 1:4 **r.** and build the desolate places; 7725
Mal 3:7 **R.** unto me, and I will **r.** unto you, ... 7725
Mal 3:7 But ye said, Wherein shall we **r.**? 7725
Mal 3:18 Then shall ye **r.**, and discern 7725
Mt 2:12 that they should not **r.** to Herod, ... *844*
Mt 10:13 **worthy, let your peace r. to you.** ... *1994*
Mt 12:44 **will r. into my house from whence.** *1994*
Mt 24:18 **him which is in the field r. back...** *1994*
Lu 8:39 **R. to thine own house, and shew...** *5290*
Lu 11:24 **r. unto my house whence I came...** *5290*
Lu 12:36 **when he will r. from the wedding;** .. *360*
Lu 17:31 **field, let him likewise not r. back.** .*1994*
Lu 19:12 **to receive...a kingdom, and to r.** .. *5290*
Ac 13:34 now no more to **r.** to corruption, ... *5290*
Ac 15:16 After this I will **r.**, and will build.......... *390*
Ac 18:21 but I will **r.** again unto you, if God....... *344*
Ac 20:3 purposed to **r.** through Macedonia. *5290*

RETURNED

Ge 8:3 the waters **r.** from off the earth......... 7725
Ge 8:9 and she **r.** unto him into the ark, ... 7725
Ge 8:12 dove; which **r.** not again unto him 7725
Ge 14:7 they **r.**, and came to En-mishpat, ... 7725
Ge 18:33 and Abraham **r.** unto his place. 7725
Ge 21:32 **r.** into the land of the Philistines. 7725
Ge 22:19 So Abraham **r.** unto his young men,.... 7725
Ge 31:55 departed, and **r.** unto his place. 7725
Ge 32:6 the messengers **r.** to Jacob, saying, ... 7725
Ge 33:16 So Esau **r.** that day on his way unto ... 7725
Ge 37:29 And Reuben **r.** unto the pit; and, ... 7725
Ge 37:30 he **r.** unto his brethren, and said, ... 7725
Ge 38:22 he **r.** to Judah, and said, I cannot 7725
Ge 42:24 **r.** to them again, and communed 7725
Ge 43:10 now we had **r.** this second time. 7725
Ge 43:18 the money that was **r.** in our sacks..... 7725
Ge 44:13 every man his ass, and **r.** to the city. ..7725
Ge 50:14 And Joseph **r.** into Egypt, he, and 7725
Ex 4:18 And Moses went and **r.** to Jethro his .. 7725
Ex 4:20 ass, and he **r.** to the land of Egypt:.... 7725
Ex 5:22 And Moses **r.** unto the Lord, and....... 7725
Ex 14:27 and the sea **r.** to his strength when.... 7725
Ex 14:28 And the waters **r.**, and covered the 7725
Ex 19:8 Moses **r.** the words of the people 7725
Ex 32:31 And Moses **r.** unto the Lord, and....... 7725
Ex 34:31 all the rulers of the congregation **r.**...... 7725
Le 22:13 and is **r.** unto her father's house, as ... 7725
Nu 13:25 they **r.** from searching of the land 7725
Nu 14:36 sent to search the land, who **r.**,.......... 7725
Nu 16:50 Aaron **r.** unto Moses unto the door 7725
Nu 23:6 he **r.** unto him, and, lo, he stood 7725
Nu 24:25 up, and went and **r.** to his place:........ 7725
De 1:45 And ye **r.** and wept before the Lord; .. 7725
Jos 2:16 three days, until the pursuers be **r.**: ... 7725
Jos 2:22 days, until the pursuers were **r.**:........ 7725
Jos 2:23 So the two men **r.**, and descended 7725
Jos 4:18 waters of Jordan **r.** unto their place 7725
Jos 6:14 the city once, and **r.** into the camp: 7725
Jos 7:3 And they **r.** to Joshua, and said.......... 7725
Jos 8:24 that all the Israelites **r.** unto Ai, ... 7725
Jos 10:15 And Joshua **r.**, and all Israel with 7725
Jos 10:21 And all the people **r.** to the camp 7725
Jos 10:38, 43 Joshua **r.**, and all Israel with 7725
Jos 22:9 and the half tribe of Manasseh **r.**,........ 7725
Jos 22:32 **r.** from the children of Reuben, and.... 7725
Jg 2:19 they **r.**, and corrupted themselves...... 7725
Jg 5:29 her, yea, she **r.** answer to herself, ... 7725
Jg 7:3 **r.** of the people twenty and two......... 7725
Jg 7:15 **r.** into the host of Israel, and said, ... 7725
Jg 8:13 the son of Joash **r.** from battle........... 7725
Jg 11:39 that she **r.** unto her father, who did.... 7725
Jg 14:8 And after a time he **r.** to take her, ... 7725
Jg 21:23 went and **r.** unto their inheritance,..... 7725
Ru 1:22 So Naomi **r.**,...Ruth the Moabitess, ... 7725
Ru 1:22 **r.** out of the country of Moab:........... 7725
1Sa 1:19 worshipped before the Lord, and **r.**, ... 7725
1Sa 6:16 it, they **r.** to Ekron the same day....... 7725
1Sa 6:17 Philistines **r.** for a trespass offering..... 7725
1Sa 17:15 David went and **r.** from Saul to feed ... 7725
1Sa 17:53 **r.** from chasing after...Philistines, ... 7725
1Sa 17:57 **r.** from the slaughter of...Philistine, ... 7725
1Sa 18:6 **r.** from the slaughter of...Philistine, ... 7725
1Sa 23:28 Saul **r.** from pursuing after David, ... 7725
1Sa 24:1 **r.** from following the Philistines,......... 7725
1Sa 25:39 hath **r.** the wickedness of Nabal 7725
1Sa 26:25 on his way, and Saul **r.** to his place. ... 7725
1Sa 27:9 apparel, and **r.**, and came to Achish.... 7725
2Sa 1:1 David was **r.** from the slaughter of...... 7725
2Sa 1:22 and the sword of Saul **r.** not empty. ... 7725
2Sa 2:30 And Joab **r.** from following Abner: 7725
2Sa 3:16 unto him, Go, return. And he **r.**. 7725
2Sa 3:27 when Abner was **r.** to Hebron, Joab.... 7725
2Sa 6:20 David **r.** to bless his household. 7725
2Sa 8:13 he **r.** from smiting of the Syrians........ 7725
2Sa 10:14 So Joab **r.** from the children of 7725
2Sa 11:4 and she **r.** unto her house................. 7725
2Sa 12:31 all the people **r.** unto Jerusalem. 7725
2Sa 14:24 So Absalom **r.** to his own house,......... 5437
2Sa 16:8 hath **r.** upon thee all the blood of 7725
2Sa 17:3 whom thou seekest is as if all **r.**: 7725
2Sa 17:20 not find them, they **r.** to Jerusalem..... 7725
2Sa 18:16 the people **r.** from pursuing after........ 7725
2Sa 19:15 So the king **r.**, and came to Jordan. 7725
2Sa 19:39 him; and he **r.** unto his own place. 7725
2Sa 20:22 Joab **r.** to Jerusalem unto the king. 7725
2Sa 23:10 people **r.** after him only to spoil. 7725
1Ki 12:24 **r.** to depart, according to the word..... 7725
1Ki 13:10 **r.** not by the way that he came to...... 7725
1Ki 13:33 Jeroboam **r.** not from his evil way, ... 7725
1Ki 19:21 And he **r.** back from him, and took...... 7725
2Ki 2:25 and from thence he **r.** to Samaria. 7725
2Ki 3:27 from him, and **r.** to their own land...... 7725
2Ki 4:35 he **r.**, and walked in the house 7725
2Ki 5:15 And he **r.** to the man of God, he and.. 7725
2Ki 7:15 And the messengers **r.**, and told the... 7725
2Ki 8:3 that the woman **r.** out of the land........ 7725
2Ki 9:15 king Joram was **r.** to be healed in....... 7725
2Ki 14:14 and hostages, and **r.** to Samaria. 7725
2Ki 19:8 Rab-shakeh **r.**, and found the king 7725
2Ki 19:36 and went and **r.**, and dwelt at........... 7725
2Ki 23:20 upon them, and **r.** to Jerusalem.......... 7725
1Ch 16:43 and David **r.** to bless his house. 5437
1Ch 20:3 and all the people **r.** to Jerusalem. 7725
2Ch 10:2 it, that Jeroboam **r.** out of Egypt........ 7725
2Ch 11:4 **r.** from going against Jeroboam. 7725
2Ch 14:15 in abundance, and **r.** to Jerusalem....... 7725
2Ch 19:1 Jehoshaphat the king of Judah **r.**......... 7725
2Ch 19:8 when they **r.** to Jerusalem. 7725
2Ch 20:27 Then they **r.**, every man of Judah 7725
2Ch 22:6 And he **r.** to be healed in Jezreel 7725
2Ch 25:10 and they **r.** home in great anger......... 7725
2Ch 25:24 hostages also, and **r.** to Samaria......... 7725
2Ch 28:15 brethren: then they **r.** to Samaria. 7725
2Ch 31:1 Then all the children of Israel **r.**,......... 7725
2Ch 32:21 he **r.** with shame of face to his own.... 7725
2Ch 34:7 land of Israel, he **r.** to Jerusalem. 7725
2Ch 34:9 Benjamin;...they **r.** to Jerusalem......... 7725
Ezr 5:5 and then they **r.** answer by letter....... 8421
Ezr 5:11 thus they **r.** us answer, saying, We 8421
Ne 2:15 the gate of the valley, and so **r.**. 7725
Ne 4:15 we **r.** all of us to the wall, every one.. 7725
Ne 9:28 yet when they **r.**, and cried unto........ 7725
Es 2:14 the morrow she **r.** into the second 7725
Es 7:8 the king **r.** out of the palace garden 7725
Ps 35:13 my prayer **r.** into mine own bosom. 7725
Ps 60:*title* when Joab **r.**, and smote of Edom 7725
Ps 78:34 **r.** and enquired early after God......... 7725
Ec 4:1 So I **r.**, and considered all the 7725
Ec 4:7 Then I **r.**, and I saw vanity under 7725
Ec 9:11 I **r.**, and saw under the sun, that 7725
Isa 37:8 So Rabshakeh **r.**, and found the 7725

Isa 37:37 went and **r.**, and dwelt at Nineveh...... 7725
Isa 38:8 So the sun **r.** ten degrees, by which... 7725
Jer 3:7 Turn thou unto me. But she **r.** not..... 7725
Jer 14:3 they **r.** with their vessels empty; 7725
Jer 40:12 Even all the Jews **r.** out of all places... 7725
Jer 41:14 from Mizpah cast about and **r.**, ... 7725
Jer 43:5 that were **r.** from all nations,............ 7725
Eze 1:14 And the living creatures ran and **r.** 7725
Eze 8:17 have **r.** to provoke me to anger: 7725
Eze 47:7 Now when I had **r.**, behold, at the 7725
Da 4:34 mine understanding **r.** unto me, ... 7725
Da 4:36 same time my reason **r.** unto me; 7725
Da 4:36 honour and brightness **r.** unto me;...... 7725
Ho 6:11 I **r.** the captivity of my people........... 7725
Am 4:6,8, 9,10,11 have ye not **r.** unto me, ... 7725
Zec 1:6 and they **r.** and said, Like as the........ 7725
Zec 1:16 I am **r.** to Jerusalem with mercies: 7725
Zec 7:14 that no man passed through nor **r.**:..... 7725
Zec 8:3 I am **r.** unto Zion, and will dwell in..... 7725
Mt 21:18 as he **r.** into the city, he hungered. *1877*
Mk 14:40 when he **r.**, he found them asleep *5290*
Lu 1:56 months, and **r.** to her own house. *5290*
Lu 2:20 the shepherds **r.**, glorifying and.......... *1994*
Lu 2:39 they **r.** into Galilee, to their own........ *5290*
Lu 2:43 as they **r.**, the child Jesus tarried *5290*
Lu 4:1 of the Holy Ghost **r.** from Jordan, ... *5290*
Lu 4:14 Jesus **r.** in the power of the Spirit...... *5290*
Lu 8:37 up into the ship, and **r.** back again...... *5290*
Lu 8:40 to pass, that, when Jesus was **r.**, ... *5290*
Lu 9:10 the apostles, when they were **r.**, ... *5290*
Lu 10:17 And the seventh **r.** again with joy,...... *5290*
Lu 17:18 **found that r. to give glory to God,** .*5290*
Lu 19:15 **came to pass, that when he was r.,** .*1880*
Lu 23:48 done, smote their breasts, and **r.**. *5290*
Lu 23:56 And they **r.**, and prepared spices *5290*
Lu 24:9 **r.** from the sepulchre, and told all *5290*
Lu 24:33 the same hour, and **r.** to Jerusalem,.... *5290*
Lu 24:52 and **r.** to Jerusalem with great joy: *5290*
Ac 1:12 Then **r.** they unto Jerusalem from *5290*
Ac 5:22 not in the prison, they **r.**, and told,...... *390*
Ac 8:25 **r.** to Jerusalem, and preached the....... *5290*
Ac 12:25 and Saul **r.** from Jerusalem, when....... *5290*
Ac 13:13 John departing from them **r.** to *5290*
Ac 14:21 they **r.** again to Lystra, and to........... *5290*
Ac 21:6 took ship; and they **r.** home again. *5290*
Ac 23:32 to go with him, and **r.** to the castle: ... *5290*
Ga 1:17 and **r.** again unto Damascus. *5290*
Heb 11:15 have had opportunity to have **r.**........... *344*
1Pe 2:25 but are now **r.** unto the Shepherd *1994*

RETURNETH
Ps 146:4 goeth forth, he **r.** to his earth; 7725
Pr 26:11 As a dog **r.** to his vomit,.................. 7725
Pr 26:11 so a fool **r.** to his folly. 8138
Ec 1:6 the wind **r.** again according to his....... 7725
Isa 55:10 from haven, and **r.** not thither, ... 7725
Eze 35:7 that passeth out and him that **r.**.......... 7725
Zec 9:8 by, and because of him that **r.**........... 7725

RETURNING
Isa 30:15 In **r.** and rest shall ye be saved; 7729
Lu 7:10 **r.** to the house, found the servant...... *5290*
Ac 8:28 Was **r.**, and sitting in his chariot *5290*
Heb 7:1 **r.** from the slaughter of the kings,...... *5290*

REU (re'-u) See also RAGAU.
Ge 11:18 lived thirty years, and begat **R.** 7466
Ge 11:19 Peleg lived after he begat **R.** two....... 7466
Ge 11:20 And **R.** lived two and thirty years, ... 7466
Ge 11:21 **R.** lived after he begat Serug two 7466
1Ch 1:25 Eber, Peleg, **R.**,.............................. 7466

REUBEN (ru'-ben) See also REUBENITE.
Ge 29:32 a son, and she called his name **R.** 7205
Ge 30:14 And **R.** went in the days of wheat...... 7205
Ge 35:22 that **R.** went and lay with Bilhah........ 7205
Ge 35:23 sons of Leah; **R.**, Jacob's firstborn,..... 7205
Ge 37:21 **R.** heard it, and he delivered him....... 7205
Ge 37:22 **R.** said unto them, Shed no blood, ... 7205
Ge 37:29 And **R.** returned unto the pit; and, ... 7205
Ge 42:22 **R.** answered them, saying, Spake I 7205
Ge 42:37 **R.** spake unto his father, saying, ... 7205
Ge 46:8 Jacob and his sons: **R.**, Jacob's 7205
Ge 46:9 the sons of **R.**; Hanoch, and Phallu,..... 7205
Ge 48:5 as **R.** and Simeon, they shall be......... 7205
Ge 49:3 **R.**, thou art my firstborn, my............ 7205
Ex 1:2 **R.**, Simeon, Levi, and Judah, ... 7205
Ex 6:14 sons of **R.** the firstborn of Israel;....... 7205
Ex 6:14 Carmi: these be the families of **R.**...... 7205
Nu 1:5 the tribe of **R.**; Elizur the son of........ 7205
Nu 1:20 the children of **R.**, Israel's eldest 7205
Nu 1:21 tribe of **R.**, were forty and six........... 7205
Nu 2:10 be the standard of the camp of **R.**....... 7205
Nu 2:10 captain of the children of **R.** shall 7205
Nu 2:16 were numbered in the camp of **R.** 7205
Nu 7:30 prince of the children of **R.**, did 7205
Nu 10:18 the standard of the camp of **R.** set 7205
Nu 13:4 tribe of **R.**, Shammua the son of........ 7205
Nu 16:1 son of Peleth, sons of **R.**, took men: .. 7205
Nu 26:5 **R.**, the eldest son of Israel; 7205
Nu 26:5 children of **R.**; Hanoch, of whom........ 7205
Nu 32:1 Now the children of **R.** and the.......... 7205
Nu 32:2 the children of **R.** came and spake...... 7205
Nu 32:6 to the children of **R.**, Shall your......... 7205
Nu 32:25 children of **R.** spake unto Moses, ... 7205
Nu 32:29 children of **R.** will pass with your....... 7205
Nu 32:31 the children of **R.** answered, saying, ... 7205
Nu 32:33 of Gad and to the children of **R.**, ... 7205
Nu 32:37 the children of **R.** built Heshbon,........ 7205
Nu 34:14 For the tribe of the children of **R.**....... 7206
De 11:6 the sons of Eliab, the son of **R.**: 7205
De 27:13 **R.**, Gad, and Asher, and Zebulun, ... 7205
De 33:6 Let **R.** live, and not die; and let not ... 7205
Jos 4:12 And the children of **R.**, and the 7205
Jos 13:15 unto the tribe of the children of **R.** 7205
Jos 13:23 border of the children of **R.** was 7205
Jos 13:23 the inheritance of the children of **R.**.... 7205
Jos 15:6 to the stone of Bohan the son of **R.** ... 7205
Jos 18:7 and Gad, and **R.**, and half the tribe..... 7205
Jos 18:17 to the stone of Bohan the son of **R.**, .. 7205
Jos 20:8 upon the plain out of the tribe of **R.**, .. 7205
Jos 21:7 families had out of the tribe of **R.**,....... 7205
Jos 21:36 out of the tribe of **R.**, Bezer with 7205
Jos 22:9 children of **R.** and the children........... 7205
Jos 22:10, 11 children of **R.** and the children....... 7205
Jos 22:13 Israel sent unto the children of **R.**, ... 7205
Jos 22:15 they came unto the children of **R.**, ... 7205
Jos 22:21 Then the children of **R.** and the......... 7205
Jos 22:25 ye children of **R.** and children of 7205
Jos 22:30 the words that the children of **R.** 7205
Jos 22:31 priest said unto the children of **R.**, ... 7205
Jos 22:32 returned from the children of **R.**, ... 7205
Jos 22:33 the children of **R.** and Gad dwelt........ 7205
Jos 22:34 the children of **R.** and the children....... 7205
Jg 5:15, 16 divisions of **R.** there were great 7205
1Ch 2:1 are the sons of Israel; **R.**, Simeon,..... 7205
1Ch 5:1 the sons of **R.** the firstborn of Israel,.. 7205
1Ch 5:3 I say, of **R.** the firstborn of Israel 7205
1Ch 5:18 The sons of **R.**, and the Gadites, ... 7205
1Ch 6:63 their families, out of the tribe of **R.**, ... 7205
1Ch 6:78 given them out of the tribe of **R.**, ... 7205
Eze 48:6 unto the west side, a portion for **R.**..... 7205
Eze 48:7 And by the border of **R.**, from the 7205
Eze 48:31 one gate of **R.**, one gate of Judah,...... 7205
Re 7:5 of **R.** were sealed twelve thousand..... *4502*

REUBENITE (ru'-ben-ite) See also REUBENITES.
1Ch 11:42 Adina the son of Shiza the **R.**, a 7206

REUBENITES (ru'-ben-ites)
Nu 26:7 These are the families of the **R.** 7206
De 3:12 cities thereof, gave I unto the **R.** 7206
De 3:16 unto the **R.** and unto the Gadites 7206
De 4:43 in the plain country, of the **R.**; and..... 7206
De 29:8 it for an inheritance unto the **R.**,......... 7206
Jos 1:12 And to the **R.**, and to the Gadites,...... 7206
Jos 12:6 it for a possession unto the **R.**, and.... 7206
Jos 13:8 With whom the **R.** and the Gadites..... 7206
Jos 22:1 Then Joshua called the **R.**, and the..... 7206
2Ki 10:33 the Gadites, and the **R.**, and the........ 7206
1Ch 5:6 captive: he was prince of the **R.**. 7206
1Ch 5:26 he carried them away, even the **R.**,.... 7206
1Ch 11:42 a captain of the **R.**, and thirty with..... 7206
1Ch 12:37 the other side of Jordan, of the **R.**, ... 7206
1Ch 26:32 king David made rulers over the **R.**,... 7206
1Ch 27:16 the ruler of the **R.** was Eliezer the..... 7206

REUEL (re-u'-el) See also DEUEL; JETHRO; RAGUEL.
Ge 36:4 Eliphaz; and Bashemath bare **R.**;........ 7467
Ge 36:10 **R.** the son of Bashemath the wife of... 7467
Ge 36:13 these are the sons of **R.**; Nahath, ... 7467
Ge 36:17 these are the sons of **R.** Esau's son; .. 7467
Ge 36:17 these are the dukes that came of **R.**.... 7467
Ex 2:18 when they came to **R.** their father,..... 7467
Nu 2:14 shall be Eliasaph the son of **R.**. 7467
1Ch 1:35 The sons of Esau; Eliphaz, **R.**, and 7467
1Ch 1:37 The sons of **R.**; Nahath, Zerah, ... 7467
1Ch 9:8 the son of **R.**, the son of Ibnijah: 7467

REUMAH (re-u'-mah)
Ge 22:24 his concubine, whose name was **R.**,.... 7208

REVEAL See also REVEALED; REVEALETH.
Job 20:27 The heaven shall **r.** his iniquity; 1540
Jer 33:6 will **r.** unto them the abundance of..... 1540
Da 2:47 seeing thou couldest **r.** this secret...... 1541
Mt 11:27 **to whomsoever the Son will r. him.** .*601*
Lu 10:22 **he to whom the Son will r. him**...... *601*
Ga 1:16 To **r.** his Son in me, that I might......... *601*
Php 3:15 God shall **r.** even this unto you. *601*

REVEALED
De 29:29 those things which are **r.** belong 1540
1Sa 3:7 word of the Lord yet **r.** unto him. 1540
1Sa 3:21 for the Lord **r.** himself to Samuel......... 1540
2Sa 7:27 hast **r.** to thy servant, saying, I will.... 1540
Isa 22:14 it was **r.** in mine ears by the Lord...... 1540
Isa 23:1 the land of Chittim it is **r.** to them...... 1540
Isa 40:5 the glory of the Lord shall be **r.**,......... 1540
Isa 53:1 to whom is the arm of the Lord **r.**? 1540
Isa 56:1 and my righteousness to be **r.**............ 1540
Jer 11:20 for unto thee have I **r.** my cause.......... 1540
Da 2:19 was the secret **r.** unto Daniel in a 1541
Da 2:30 is not **r.** to me for any wisdom 1541
Da 10:1 Persia a thing was **r.** unto Daniel, ... 1540
Mt 10:26 **covered, that shall not be r.; and**.... *601*
Mt 11:25 **and hast r. them unto babes**............ *601*
Mt 16:17 **and blood hath not r. it unto thee,**.. *601*
Lu 2:26 **r.** unto him by the Holy Ghost,........... *5537*
Lu 2:35 thoughts of many hearts may be **r.**........ *601*
Lu 10:21 **and hast r. them unto babes:** *601*
Lu 12:2 **covered, that shall not be r.;** *601*
Lu 17:30 **the day when the Son of man is r.**...*601*
Joh 12:38 hath the arm of the Lord been **r.**? *601*
Ro 1:17 righteousness of God **r.** from faith........ *601*
Ro 1:18 the wrath of God is **r.** from heaven...... *601*
Ro 8:18 the glory which shall be **r.** in us. *601*
1Co 2:10 hath **r.** them unto us by his Spirit: *601*
1Co 3:13 it, because it shall be **r.** by fire; *601*
1Co 14:30 If any being be **r.** to another that........ *601*
Ga 3:23 faith which should afterwards be **r.**....... *601*
Eph 3:5 as it is now **r.** unto his holy apostles *601*
2Th 1:7 when the Lord Jesus shall be **r.** from.... *602*
2Th 2:3 and that man of sin be **r.**, the son........ *601*
2Th 2:6 that he might be **r.** in his time. *601*
2Th 2:8 then shall that Wicked be **r.**, whom...... *601*
1Pe 1:5 ready to be **r.** in the last time............ *601*
1Pe 1:12 Unto whom it was **r.**, that not unto...... *601*
1Pe 4:13 when his glory shall be **r.**, ye may *602*
1Pe 5:1 of the glory that shall be **r.**:............... *601*

REVEALER
Da 2:47 and a **r.** of secrets, seeing thou 1541

REVEALETH
Pr 11:13 A talebearer **r.** secrets: but he 1540
Pr 20:19 about as a talebearer **r.** secrets: 1540
Da 2:22 He **r.** the deep and secret things:....... 1541
Da 2:28 is a God in heaven that **r.** secrets, ... 1541
Da 2:29 he that **r.** secrets maketh known to 1541
Am 3:7 he **r.** his secret unto his servants........ 1540

REVELATION See also REVELATIONS.
Ro 2:5 and **r.** of the righteous judgment of...... *602*
Ro 16:25 according to the **r.** of the mystery, ... *602*
1Co 14:6 I shall speak to you either by **r.**, or *602*
1Co 14:26 doctrine, hath a tongue, hath a **r.**, ... *602*
Ga 1:12 it, but by the **r.** of Jesus Christ. *602*
Ga 2:2 And I went up by **r.**, and.................. *602*
Eph 1:17 unto you the spirit of wisdom and **r.**...... *602*
Eph 3:3 How that by **r.** he made known unto *602*
1Pe 1:13 unto you at the **r.** of Jesus Christ; *602*
Re *general title* The **R.** Of S [St.] John The.......... *602*
Re 1:1 The **R.** of Jesus Christ, which God *602*

REVELATIONS
2Co 12:1 come to visions and **r.** of the Lord....... *602*
2Co 12:7 through the abundance of the **r.**,.......... *602*

REVELLINGS
Ga 5:21 drunkenness, **r.**, and such like: *2970*
1Pe 4:3 **r.**, banquetings, and abominable *2970*

REVENGE See also REVENGED; REVENGES; REVENGETH; REVENGING.
Jer 15:15 me, and **r.** me of my persecutors;...... 5358
Jer 20:10 and we shall take our **r.** on him. 5360

Eze 25:15 the Philistines hath dealt by **r.**, 5360
2Co 7:11 desire, yea, what zeal, yea, what **r.**! *1557*
2Co 10:6 readiness to **r.** all disobedience, *1556*

REVENGED
Eze 25:12 and **r.** himself upon them; 5358

REVENGER See also REVENGERS.
Nu 35:19 The **r.** of blood himself shall slay 1350
Nu 35:21 **r.** of blood shall slay the murderer, 1350
Nu 35:24 between the slayer and...**r.** of blood 1350
Nu 35:25 out of the hand of the **r.** of blood, 1350
Nu 35:27 the **r.** of blood find him without 1350
Nu 35:27 and the **r.** of blood kill the slayer; 1350
Ro 13:4 a **r.** to execute wrath upon him *1558*

REVENGERS
2Sa 14:11 suffer the **r.** of blood to destroy 1350

REVENGES
De 32:42 beginning of **r.** upon the enemy 6546

REVENGETH
Na 1:2 God is jealous, and the Lord **r.**; 5358
Na 1:2 the Lord **r.**, and is furious; the 5358

REVENGING
Ps 79:10 **r.** of the blood of thy servants 5360

REVENUE See also REVENUES.
Ezr 4:13 shalt endamage the **r.** of the kings. 674
Pr 8:19 gold; and my **r.** than choice silver 8393
Isa 23:3 the harvest of the river is her **r.**; 8393

REVENUES
Pr 15:6 in the **r.** of the wicked is trouble 8393
Pr 16:8 than great **r.** without right. 8393
Jer 12:13 shall be ashamed of your **r.** because 8393

REVERENCE See also REVERENCED.
Le 19:30 sabbaths, and **r.** my sanctuary: 3372
Le 26:2 my sabbaths, and **r.** my sanctuary: 3372
2Sa 9:6 he fell on his face, and did **r.** 7812
1Ki 1:31 and did **r.** to the king, and said, 7812
Es 3:2 Mordecai bowed not, nor did him **r.** 7812
Es 3:5 Mordecai bowed not, nor did him **r.**, 7812
Ps 89:7 to be had in **r.** of all them that 3372
Mt 21:37 **son, saying, They will r. my son** *1788*
Mk 12:6 **them, saying, They will r. my son** *1788*
Lu 20:13 **they will r. him when they see** *1788*
Eph 5:33 wife see that she **r.** her husband *5399*
Heb 12:9 us, and we gave them **r.**: *1788*
Heb 12:28 acceptably with **r.** and godly fear: *127*

REVERENCED
Es 3:2 king's gate, bowed, and **r.** Haman: 7812

REVEREND
Ps 111:9 ever: holy and **r.** is his name 3372

REVERSE
Nu 23:20 hath blessed; and I cannot **r.** it. 7725
Es 8:5 to **r.** the letters devised by Haman 7725
Es 8:8 the king's ring, may no man **r.** 7725

REVILE See also REVILED; REVILEST; REVILINGS.
Ex 22:28 Thou shalt not **r.** the gods, nor 7043
Mt 5:11 **are ye, when men shall r. you,** *3679*

REVILED
Mt 27:39 And they that passed by **r.** him, *987*
Mk 15:32 were crucified with him **r.** him. *3679*
Joh 9:28 Then they **r.** him, and said, Thou *3058*
1Co 4:12 being **r.**, we bless; being *3058*
1Pe 2:23 Who, when he was **r.**,...not again; *3058*
1Pe 2:23 Who when he was...,**r.** not again; *486*

REVILERS
1Co 6:10 nor **r.**, nor extortioners, shall *3060*

REVILEST
Ac 23:4 said, **R.** thou God's high priest? *3058*

REVILINGS
Isa 51:7 neither be ye afraid of their **r.** 1421
Zep 2:8 the **r.** of the children of Ammon, 1421

REVIVE See also REVIVED; REVIVING.
Ne 4:2 **r.** the stones out of the heaps of 2421
Ps 85:6 Wilt thou not **r.** us again: that thy 2421
Ps 138:7 midst of trouble, thou wilt **r.** me: 2421
Isa 57:15 to **r.** the spirit of the humble, and 2421
Isa 57:15 **r.** the heart of the contrite ones. 2421
Ho 6:2 after two days will he **r.** us: in the 2421
Ho 14:7 They shall **r.** as the corn, and grow 2421
Hab 3:2 **r.** thy work in the midst of the 2421

REVIVED
Ge 45:27 the spirit of Jacob their father **r.** 2421
Jg 15:19 his spirit came again, and he **r.** 2421
1Ki 17:22 came into him again, and he **r.** 2421
2Ki 13:21 touched the bones of Elisha, he **r.**, 2421
Ro 7:9 the commandment came, sin **r.**, *326*
Ro 14:9 Christ both died, and rose, and **r.**, *326*

REVIVING
Ezr 9:8 give us a little **r.** in our bondage. 4241
Ezr 9:9 to give us a **r.**, to set up the house 4241

REVOLT See also REVOLTED; REVOLTING.
2Ch 21:10 did Libnah **r.** from under his hand; 6586
Isa 1:5 more? ye will **r.** more and more: 5627
Isa 59:13 God, speaking oppression and **r.**, 5627

REVOLTED
2Ki 8:20 Edom **r.** from under the hand of 6586
2Ki 8:22 Yet Edom **r.** from under the hand 6586
2Ki 8:22 Then Libnah **r.** at the same time. 6586
2Ch 21:8 In his days the Edomites **r.** from 6586
2Ch 21:10 So the Edomites **r.** from under the 6586
Isa 31:6 children of Israel have deeply **r.** 5627
Jer 5:23 heart: they are **r.** and gone. 5493

REVOLTERS
Jer 6:28 They are all grievous **r.**, walking 5637
Ho 5:2 the **r.** are profound to make a 7846
Ho 9:15 no more: all their princes are **r.** 5637

REVOLTING
Jer 5:23 hath a **r.** and a rebellious heart; 5637

REWARD See also REWARDED; REWARDETH; REWARDS.
Ge 15:1 shield, and thy exceeding great **r.** 7939
Nu 18:31 **r.** for your service in the tabernacle 7939
De 10:17 not persons, nor taketh **r.** 7810
De 27:25 **r.** to slay an innocent person: 7810
De 32:41 and will **r.** them that hate me. 7999
Ru 2:12 a full **r.** be given thee of the Lord 4909
1Sa 24:19 Lord **r.** thee good for that thou 7999
2Sa 3:39 the Lord shall **r.** the doer of evil 7999
2Sa 4:10 have given him a **r.** for his tidings: 1309
2Sa 19:36 recompense it me with such a **r.**? 1578
1Ki 13:7 thyself, and I will give thee a **r.** 4991
2Ch 20:11 Behold, I say, how they **r.** us, to 1580
Job 6:22 a **r.** for me of your substance? 7809
Job 7:2 hireling looketh for the **r.** of his work:
Ps 15:5 taketh **r.** against the innocent. 7810
Ps 19:11 keeping of them there is great **r.** 6118
Ps 40:15 them be desolate for a **r.** of their 6118
Ps 54:5 shall **r.** evil unto mine enemies: 7725
Ps 58:11 there is a **r.** for the righteous: 6529
Ps 70:3 for a **r.** of their shame that say, 6118
Ps 91:8 and see the **r.** of the wicked. 8011
Ps 94:2 earth: render a **r.** to the proud. 1576
Ps 109:20 this be the **r.** of mine adversaries 6468
Ps 127:3 the fruit of the womb is his **r.** 7939
Pr 11:18 righteousness shall be a sure **r.** 7938
Pr 21:14 a **r.** in the bosom strong wrath. 7810
Pr 24:14 then there shall be a **r.**, and thy 319
Pr 24:20 shall be no **r.** to the evil man; 319
Pr 25:22 head, and the Lord shall **r.** thee. 7999
Ec 4:9 have a good **r.** for their labour. 7939
Ec 9:5 neither have they any more a **r.**; 7939
Isa 3:11 **r.** of his hands shall be given him. 1576
Isa 5:23 Which justify the wicked for **r.**, 7810
Isa 40:10 behold, his **r.** is with him, and his 7939
Isa 45:13 not for price nor **r.**, saith the Lord 7810
Isa 62:11 his **r.** is with him, and his work 7939
Jer 40:5 guard gave him victuals and a **r.**, 4864
Eze 16:34 and in that thou givest a **r.**, 868
Eze 16:34 and no **r.** is given unto thee, 868
Ho 4:9 ways, and **r.** them their doings. 7725
Ho 9:1 loved a **r.** upon every cornfloor. 868
Ob 15 thy **r.** shall return upon thine own 1576
Mic 3:11 heads thereof judge for **r.**, and 7810
Mic 7:3 and the judge asketh for a **r.**; 7966
Mt 5:12 **for great is your r. in heaven: for** *3408*
Mt 5:46 **which love you, what r. have ye?** *3408*
Mt 6:1 **ye have no r. of your Father** *3408*
Mt 6:2 **I say unto you, They have their r.** *3408*
Mt 6:4 **secret himself shall r. thee openly.** *591*
Mt 6:5 **say unto you, They have their r.** *3408*
Mt 6:6 **seeth in secret shall r. thee openly.** *591*
Mt 6:16 **I say unto you, They have their r.** *3408*
Mt 6:18 **seeth in secret, shall r. thee.** *591*
Mt 10:41 **shall receive a prophet's r.; and** *3408*
Mt 10:41 **shall receive a righteous man's r.** *3408*
Mt 10:42 **he shall in no wise lose his r.** *3408*
Mt 16:27 **he shall r. every man according** *591*
Mk 9:41 **unto you, he shall not lose his r.** *3408*
Lu 6:23 **behold, your r. is great in heaven:** *3408*
Lu 6:35 **your r. shall be great, and ye** *3408*
Lu 23:41 we receive the due **r.** of our deeds: *514*
Ac 1:18 a field with the **r.** of iniquity; *3408*
Ro 4:4 worketh is the **r.** not reckoned of *3408*
1Co 3:8 every man shall receive his own **r.** *3408*
1Co 3:14 thereupon, he shall receive a **r.** *3408*
1Co 9:17 do this thing willingly, I have a **r.** *3408*
1Co 9:18 What is my **r.** then? Verily that, *3408*
Col 2:18 Let no man beguile you of your **r.** *2603*
Col 3:24 receive the **r.** of the inheritance: *469*
1Ti 5:18 The labourer is worthy of his **r.** *3408*
2Ti 4:14 the Lord **r.** him according to his *591*
Heb 2:2 received a just recompence of **r.**; *3405*
Heb 10:35 hath a great recompence of **r.** *3405*
Heb 11:26 unto the recompence of the **r.** *3405*
2Pe 2:13 receive the **r.** of the unrighteousness, *3408*
2Jo 8 but that we receive a full **r.** *3408*
Jude 11 after the error of Balaam for **r.**, *3408*
Re 11:18 shouldest give **r.** unto thy servants *3408*
Re 18:6 **R.** her even as she rewarded you, *591*
Re 22:12 **my r. is with me, to give every** *3408*

REWARDED
Ge 44:4 Wherefore have ye **r.** evil for good? 7999
1Sa 24:17 thou hast **r.** me good, whereas 1580
1Sa 24:17 whereas I have **r.** thee evil. 1580
2Sa 22:21 The Lord **r.** me according to my 1580
2Ch 15:7 weak: for your work shall be **r.** 7939
Ps 7:4 I have **r.** evil unto him that was 1580
Ps 18:20 The Lord **r.** me according to my 1580
Ps 35:12 They **r.** me evil for good to the 7999
Ps 103:10 **r.** us according to our iniquities 1580
Ps 109:5 And they have **r.** me evil for good, 7760
Pr 13:13 the commandment shall be **r.** 7999
Isa 3:9 they have **r.** evil unto themselves 1580
Jer 31:16 for thy work shall be **r.**, saith the 7939
Re 18:6 Reward her even as she **r.** you, *591*

REWARDER
Heb 11:6 a **r.** of them that diligently seek *3406*

REWARDETH
Job 21:19 he **r.** him, and he shall know it, 7999
Ps 31:23 and plentifully **r.** the proud doer. 7999
Ps 137:8 **r.** thee as thou hast served us. 7999
Pr 17:13 Whoso **r.** evil for good, evil shall 7725
Pr 26:10 formed all things both **r.** the fool, 7936
Pr 26:10 the fool, and **r.** transgressors. 7936

REWARDS
Nu 22:7 the **r.** of divination in their hand;
Isa 1:23 gifts, and followeth after **r.** 8021
Da 2:6 ye shall receive of me gifts and **r.** 5023
Da 5:17 thyself, and give thy **r.** to another; 5023
Ho 2:12 These are my **r.** that my lovers 866

REZEPH (re'-zef)
2Ki 19:12 as Gozan, and Haran, and **R.**, and 7530
Isa 37:12 as Gozan, and Haran, and **R.**, and 7530

REZIA (re-zi'-ah)
1Ch 7:39 Ulla; Arah, and Haniel, and **R.** 7525

REZIN (re'-zin)
2Ki 15:37 against Judah, **R.**...king of Syria, 7526
2Ki 16:5 Then **R.** king of Syria and Pekah 7526
2Ki 16:6 At that time **R.** king of Syria 7526
2Ki 16:9 people...captive to Kir, and slew **R.** 7526
Ezr 2:48 The children of **R.**, the children of 7526
Ne 7:50 of Reaiah, the children of **R.**, the 7526
Isa 7:1 that **R.** the king of Syria and Pekah 7526
Isa 7:4 the fierce anger of **R.** with Syria, 7526
Isa 7:8 and the head of Damascus is **R.**; 7526
Isa 8:6 rejoice in **R.** and Remaliah's son: 7526
Isa 9:11 shall set up the adversaries of **R.** 7526

REZON (re'-zon)
1Ki 11:23 adversary, **R.** the son of Eliadah, 7331

RHEGIUM (re'-je-um)
Ac 28:13 fetched a compass, and came to **R.** *4484*

RHESA (re'-sah) See also REPHAIAH.
Lu 3:27 which was the son of **R.**, which *4488*

RHODA (ro'-dah)
Ac 12:13 damsel came to hearken, named **R.** *4498*

RHODES (rodes)
Ac 21:1 and the day following unto R., *4499*

RIB See also RIBBAND; RIBS.
Ge 2:22 And the r.,…made he a woman, 6763
2Sa 2:23 spear smote him under the fifth r.,
2Sa 3:27 smote him there under the fifth r.,
2Sa 4:6 they smote him under the fifth r.
2Sa 20:10 smote him therewith in the fifth r.,

RIBAI (rib'-ahee)
2Sa 23:29 Ittai the son of R. out of Gibeah 7380
1Ch 11:31 Ithai the son of R. of Gibeah, that 7380

RIBBAND
Nu 15:38 fringe of the borders of r. of blue: 6616

RIBBON See RIBBAND.

RIBLAH (rib'-lah)
Nu 34:11 go down from Shepham to R., 7247
2Ki 23:33 put him in bands at R. in the land 7247
2Ki 25:6 up to the king of Babylon to R.; 7247
2Ki 25:20 them to the king of Babylon to R.: 7247
2Ki 25:21 and slew them at R. in the land of 7247
Jer 39:5 to R. in the land of Hamath, where 7247
Jer 39:6 slew the sons of Zedekiah in R. 7247
Jer 52:9 to R. in the land of Hamath; 7247
Jer 52:10 slew…the princes of Judah in R. 7247
Jer 52:26 them to the king of Babylon to R. 7247
Jer 52:27 and put them to death in R. in the 7247

RIBS
Ge 2:21 took one of his r., and closed up 6763
Da 7:5 it had three r. in the mouth of it 5967

RICH See also ENRICH; RICHER; RICHES.
Ge 13:2 And Abram was very r. in cattle, 3513
Ge 14:23 shouldest say, I…made Abram r.: 6238
Ex 30:15 The r. shall not give more, and 6223
Le 25:47 a sojourner or stranger wax r. 5381
Ru 3:10 young men, whether poor or r. 6223
1Sa 2:7 Lord maketh poor, and maketh r.: 6238
2Sa 12:1 the one r., and the other poor. 6223
2Sa 12:2 r. man had exceeding many flocks 6223
2Sa 12:4 came a traveller unto the r. man, 6223
Job 15:29 He shall not be r., neither shall 6238
Job 27:19 The r. man shall lie down, but he 6223
Job 34:19 nor regardeth the r. more than 7771
Ps 45:12 r. among the people shall intreat 6223
Ps 49:2 low and high, r. and poor, together. 6223
Ps 49:16 thou afraid when one is made r. 6238
Pr 10:4 the hand of the diligent maketh r. 6238
Pr 10:15 r. man's wealth is his strong city: 6223
Pr 10:22 blessing of the Lord, it maketh r., 6238
Pr 13:7 There is that maketh himself r., 6238
Pr 14:20 but the r. hath many friends. 6223
Pr 18:11 r. man's wealth is his strong city, 6223
Pr 18:23 but the r. answereth roughly. 6223
Pr 21:17 loveth wine and oil shall not be r. 6238
Pr 22:2 The r. and poor meet together: 6223
Pr 22:7 The r. ruleth over the poor, and 6223
Pr 22:16 he that giveth to the r., shall surely 6223
Pr 23:4 Labour not to be r.: cease from 6238
Pr 28:6 is perverse…though he be r. 6223
Pr 28:11 r. man is wise in his own conceit: 6223
Pr 28:20 he that maketh haste to be r. shall 6238
Pr 28:22 hasteth to be r. hath an evil eye, 1952
Ec 5:12 abundance of the r. will not suffer 6223
Ec 10:6 dignity, and the r. sit in low place. 6223
Ec 10:20 curse not the r. in thy bedchamber: 6223
Isa 53:9 wicked, and with the r. in his death; 6223
Jer 5:27 are become great, and waxen r. 6238
Jer 9:23 not the r. man glory in his riches: 6223
Eze 27:24 in chests of r. apparel, bound with
Ho 12:8 Ephraim said, Yet I am become r., 6238
Mic 6:12 the r. men…are full of violence, 6223
Zec 11:5 Blessed be the Lord; for I am r. 6238
Mt 19:23 **a r. man shall hardly enter into** *4145*
Mt 19:24 **than for a r. man to enter into the.** *4145*
Mt 27:57 there came a r. man of Arimathaea, *4145*
Mk 10:25 **than for a r. man to enter into the.** *4145*
Mk 12:41 many that were r. cast in much. *4145*
Lu 1:53 the r. he hath sent empty away. *4147*
Lu 6:24 **But woe unto you that are r.!** *4145*
Lu 12:16 **The ground of a certain r. man** *4145*
Lu 12:21 **himself, and is not r. toward God.** *4147*
Lu 14:12 **kinsmen, nor thy r. neighbours;** *4145*
Lu 16:1, **19 There was a certain r. man,** *4145*
Lu 16:21 **which fell from the r. man's table:** *4145*
Lu 16:22 **r. man also died, and was buried;** *4145*
Lu 18:23 very sorrowful: for he was very r. *4145*
Lu 18:25 **than for a r. man to enter into the.** *4145*
Lu 19:2 among the publicans, and he was r. *4145*
Lu 21:1 saw the r. men casting their gifts *4145*
Ro 10:12 is r. unto all that call upon him. *4147*
1Co 4:8 Now ye are full, now ye are r., ye *4147*
2Co 6:10 as poor, yet making many r.; *4148*
2Co 8:9 though he was r., yet for your *4145*
2Co 8:9 through his poverty might be r. *4147*
Eph 2:4 God, who is r. in mercy, for his *4145*
1Ti 6:9 that will be r. fall into temptation *4147*
1Ti 6:17 Charge them that are r. in this *4145*
1Ti 6:18 that they be r. in good works, *4147*
Jas 1:10 But the r., in that he is made low: *4145*
Jas 1:11 So also shall the r. man fade away. *4145*
Jas 2:5 the poor of this world r. in faith, *4145*
Jas 2:6 Do not r. men oppress you, and *4145*
Jas 5:1 Go to now, ye r. men, weep and *4145*
Re 2:9 **and poverty, (but thou art r.)** *4145*
Re 3:17 **Because thou sayest, I am r., and** *4145*
Re 3:18 **in the fire, that thou mayest be r.;** *4147*
Re 6:15 the r. men, and the chief captains, *4145*
Re 13:16 great, r. and poor, free and bond, *4145*
Re 18:3 merchants of the earth…waxed r. *4147*
Re 18:15 things, which were made r. by her, *4147*
Re 18:19 were made r. all that had ships *4147*

RICHER
Da 11:2 fourth shall be far r. than they all: 6238

RICHES
Ge 31:16 the r. which God hath taken from 6239
Ge 36:7 their r. were more than that they 7399
Jos 22:8 Return with much r. unto your 5233
1Sa 17:25 king will enrich him with great r., 6239
1Ki 3:11 neither hast asked r. for thyself, 6239
1Ki 3:13 hast not asked, both r., and honour: 6239
1Ki 10:23 exceeded…kings of the earth for r. 6239
1Ch 29:12 Both r. and honour come of thee, 6239
1Ch 29:28 old age, full of days, r., and honour: 6239
2Ch 1:11 not asked r., wealth, or honour, 6239
2Ch 1:12 I will give thee r., and wealth, and 6239
2Ch 9:22 passed…the kings of the earth in r. 6239
2Ch 17:5 he had r. and honour in abundance. 6239
2Ch 18:1 Jehoshaphat had r. and honour in 6239
2Ch 20:25 both r. with the dead bodies, and 7399
2Ch 32:27 Hezekiah had exceeding much r. 6239
Es 1:4 the r. of his glorious kingdom and 6239
Es 5:11 told them of the glory of his r., and 6239
Job 20:15 He hath swallowed down r., and 2428
Job 36:19 Will he esteem thy r.? no, not gold, 7769
Ps 37:16 better than the r. of many wicked. 1995
Ps 39:6 he heapeth up r., and knoweth not who
Ps 49:6 boast…in the multitude of their r.; 6239
Ps 52:7 trusted in the abundance of his r., 6239
Ps 62:10 if r. increase, set not your heart 2428
Ps 73:12 in the world; they increase in r. 2428
Ps 104:24 them all: the earth is full of thy r. 7075
Ps 112:3 and r. shall be in his house: 6239
Ps 119:14 testimonies, as much as in all r. 1952
Pr 3:16 in her left hand r. and honour. 6239
Pr 8:18 R. and honour are with me; yea, 6239
Pr 8:18 yea, durable r. and righteousness. 1952
Pr 11:4 R. profit not in the day of wrath: 1952
Pr 11:16 honour: and strong men retain r. 6239
Pr 11:28 He that trusteth in his r. shall fall: 6239
Pr 13:7 himself poor, yet hath great r. 1952
Pr 13:8 ransom of a man's life are his r. 6239
Pr 14:24 The crown of the wise is their r.; 6239
Pr 19:14 House and r. are the inheritance 1952
Pr 22:1 rather to be chosen than great r., 6239
Pr 22:4 and the fear of the Lord are r., 6239
Pr 22:16 oppresseth the poor to increase his r.,
Pr 23:5 r. certainly make themselves wings:
Pr 24:4 with all precious and pleasant r. 1952
Pr 27:24 For r. are not for ever: and doth 2633
Pr 30:8 give me neither poverty nor r.; 6239
Ec 4:8 neither is his eye satisfied with r.: 6239
Ec 5:13 r. kept for the owners thereof to 6239
Ec 5:14 But those r. perish by evil travail: 6239
Ec 5:19 whom God hath given r. and wealth, 6239
Ec 6:2 A man to whom God hath given r., 6239
Ec 9:11 nor yet r. to men of understanding, 6239
Isa 8:4 r. of Damascus and the spoil of 2428
Isa 10:14 found as a nest the r. of the people: 2428
Isa 30:6 carry their r. upon the shoulders of 2428
Isa 45:3 and hidden r. of secret places, 4301
Isa 61:6 ye shall eat the r. of the Gentiles, 2428
Jer 9:23 not the rich man glory in his r.: 6239
Jer 17:11 he that getteth r., and not by right, 6239
Jer 48:36 r.…he hath gotten are perished. 3502
Eze 26:12 they shall make a spoil of thy r., 2428
Eze 27:12 of the multitude of all kind of r.; 1952
Eze 27:18 making, for the multitude of all r.; 1952
Eze 27:27 r., and thy fairs, thy merchandise, 1952
Eze 27:33 earth with the multitude of thy r. 1952
Eze 28:4 thou hast gotten thee r., and hast 2428
Eze 28:5 traffick hast thou increased thy r., 2428
Eze 28:5 heart is lifted up because of thy r.: 2428
Da 11:2 through his r. he shall stir up all 6239
Da 11:13 a great army and with much r. 7399
Da 11:24 them the prey, and spoil, and r.: 7399
Da 11:28 return into his land with great r.; 7399
Mt 13:22 **world, and the deceitfulness of r.,** *4149*
Mk 4:19 **world, and the deceitfulness of r.,** *4149*
Mk 10:23 **they that have r. enter into the** *5536*
Mk 10:24 **that trust in r. to enter into the** *5536*
Lu 8:14 **are choked with cares and r. and** *4149*
Lu 16:11 **commit to your trust the true r.?**
Lu 18:24 **they that have r. enter into the** *5536*
Ro 2:4 Or despisest thou the r. of his *4149*
Ro 9:23 make known the r. of his glory on *4149*
Ro 11:12 fall of them to be r. of the world, *4149*
Ro 11:12 diminishing of them the r. of the *4149*
Ro 11:33 depth of the r. both of the wisdom *4149*
2Co 8:2 unto the r. of their liberality. *4149*
Eph 1:7 according to the r. of his grace; *4149*
Eph 1:18 r. of the glory of his inheritance in *4149*
Eph 2:7 shew the exceeding r. of his grace *4149*
Eph 3:8 the unsearchable r. of Christ; *4149*
Eph 3:16 according to the r. of his glory, to *4149*
Php 4:19 to his r. in glory by Christ Jesus. *4149*
Col 1:27 the r. of the glory of this mystery *4149*
Col 2:2 unto all r. of the full assurance of *4149*
1Ti 6:17 nor trust in uncertain r., but in the *4149*
Heb 11:26 reproach of Christ greater r. *4149*
Jas 5:2 Your r. are corrupted, and your *4149*
Re 5:12 was slain to receive power, and r., *4149*
Re 18:17 hour so great r. is come to nought. *4149*

RICHLY
Col 3:16 the word of Christ dwell in you r. *4146*
1Ti 6:17 who giveth us r. all things to enjoy; *4146*

RID
Ge 37:22 he might r. him out of their hands, 5337
Ex 6:6 I will r. you out of their bondage, 5337
Le 26:6 will r. evil beasts out of the land, 7673
Ps 82:4 needy: r. them out of the hand of 5337
Ps 144:7 r. me, and deliver me out of great 6475
Ps 144:11 R. me, and deliver me from the 6475

RIDDANCE
Le 23:22 not make clean r. of the corners 3615
Zep 1:18 for he shall make even a speedy r. 3617

RIDDEN
Nu 22:30 ass, upon which thou hast r. ever 7392

RIDDLE
Jg 14:12 I will now put forth a r. unto you: 2420
Jg 14:13 Put forth thy r., that we may hear 2420
Jg 14:14 not in three days expound the r. 2420
Jg 14:15 that he may declare unto us the r., 2420
Jg 14:16 thou hast put forth a r. unto the 2420
Jg 14:17 she told the r. to the children of her 2420
Jg 14:18 heifer, ye had not found out my r. 2420
Jg 14:19 unto them which expounded the r. 2420
Eze 17:2 Son of man, put forth a r., and 2420

RIDE See also RIDDEN; RIDETH; RIDING; RODE.
Ge 41:43 he made him to r. in the second 7392
De 32:13 He made him r. on the high places 7392
Jg 5:10 Speak, ye that r. on white asses, ye 7392
2Sa 16:2 be for the king's household to r. on; 7392
2Sa 19:26 me an ass, that I may r. thereon, 7392
1Ki 1:33 cause Solomon my son to r. upon 7392
1Ki 1:38 Solomon to r. upon king David's 7392
1Ki 1:44 caused him to r. upon the king's 7392
2Ki 10:16 So they made him r. in his chariot. 7392
Job 30:22 thou causest me to r. upon it, and 7392
Ps 45:4 And in thy majesty r. prosperously 7392
Ps 66:12 caused men to r. over our heads; 7392
Isa 30:16 We will r. upon the swift; therefore 7392
Isa 58:14 and I will cause thee to r. upon the 7392

Jer 6:23 they **r.** upon horses, set in array........ 7392
Jer 50:42 they shall **r.** upon horses, every one... 7392
Ho 10:11 I will make Ephraim to **r.**; Judah 7392
Ho 14:3 save us; we will not **r.** upon horses: ... 7392
Hab 3:8 thou didst **r.** upon thine horses and..... 7392
Hag 2:22 chariots, and those that **r.** in them;..... 7392

RIDER See also RIDERS.
Ge 49:17 so that this **r.** shall fall backward........ 7392
Ex 15:1, 21 horse and his **r.** hath he thrown..... 7392
Job 39:18 she scorneth the horse and his **r.**........ 7392
Jer 51:21 break in pieces the horse and his **r.**; ... 7392
Jer 51:21 in pieces the chariot and his **r.**;.......... 7392
Zec 12:4 and his **r.** with madness: and I........... 7392

RIDERS
2Ki 18:23 on thy part to set **r.** upon them. 7392
Es 8:10 **r.** on mules, camels, and young 7392
Isa 36:8 on thy part to set **r.** upon them. 7392
Hag 2:22 and their **r.** shall come down, ... 7392
Zec 10:5 **r.** on horses shall be confounded. 7392

RIDETH
Le 15:9 what saddle soever he **r.** upon that..... 7392
De 33:26 who **r.** upon the heaven in thy help, ... 7392
Es 6:8 and the horse that the king **r.** upon, ... 7392
Ps 68:4 **r.** upon the heavens by his name........ 7392
Ps 68:33 **r.** upon the heavens of heavens, ... 7392
Isa 19:1 the Lord **r.** upon a swift cloud, and..... 7392
Am 2:15 he that **r.** the horse deliver himself..... 7392

RIDGES
Ps 65:10 Thou waterest the **r.** thereof............ 8525

RIDING
Nu 22:22 Now he was **r.** upon his ass, and 7392
2Ki 4:24 slack not thy **r.** for me, except I bid... 7392
Jer 17:25 **r.** in chariots and on horses, they,...... 7392
Jer 22:4 **r.** in chariots and on horses, he, and... 7392
Eze 23:6 men, horsemen **r.** upon horses. 7392
Eze 23:12 horsemen **r.** upon horses, all of them.. 7392
Eze 23:23 all of them **r.** upon horses................ 7392
Eze 38:15 all of them **r.** upon horses, a great 7392
Zec 1:8 behold a man **r.** upon a red horse,...... 7392
Zec 9:9 lowly, and **r.** upon an ass, and........... 7392

RIE
Ex 9:32 wheat and the **r.** were not smitten: 3698
Isa 28:25 barley and the **r.** in their place? 3698

RIFLED
Zec 14:2 shall be taken, and the houses **r.**,........ 8155

RIGHT See also ARIGHT; UPRIGHT.
Ge 13:9 left hand, then I will go to the **r.**;....... 3231
Ge 13:9 if thou depart to the **r.** hand, then...... 3225
Ge 18:25 the Judge of all the earth do **r.**? 4941
Ge 24:48 which had led me in the **r.** way to 571
Ge 24:49 that I may turn to the **r.** hand, or 3225
Ge 48:13 Ephraim in his **r.** hand toward 3225
Ge 48:13 left hand toward Israel's **r.** hand,........ 3225
Ge 48:14 Israel stretched out his **r.** hand,......... 3225
Ge 48:17 **r.** hand upon the head of Ephraim, ... 3225
Ge 48:18 put thy **r.** hand upon his head........... 3225
Ex 14:22, 29 wall unto them on their **r.** hand, ... 3225
Ex 15:6 Thy **r.** hand, O Lord, is become 3225
Ex 15:6 thy **r.** hand, O Lord, hath dashed........ 3225
Ex 15:12 Thou stretchedst out thy **r.** hand,....... 3225
Ex 15:26 do that which is **r.** in his sight, ... 3477
Ex 29:20 upon the tip of the **r.** ear of Aaron, ...
Ex 29:20 the tip of the **r.** ear of his sons,......... 3233
Ex 29:20 upon the thumb of their **r.** hand, ... 3233
Ex 29:20 upon the great toe of their **r.** foot, ... 3233
Ex 29:22 is upon them, and the **r.** shoulder;...... 3233
Le 7:32 **r.** shoulder shall ye give unto the 3225
Le 7:33 have the **r.** shoulder for his part. 3225
Le 8:23 it upon the tip of Aaron's **r.** ear, ... 3233
Le 8:23 upon the thumb of his **r.** hand, ... 3233
Le 8:23 upon the great toe of his **r.** foot......... 3233
Le 8:24 blood upon the tip of their **r.** ear,....... 3233
Le 8:24 upon the thumbs of their **r.** hands, ... 3233
Le 8:24 upon the great toes of their **r.** feet: 3233
Le 8:25 and their fat, and the **r.** shoulder:....... 3225
Le 8:26 the fat, and upon the **r.** shoulder:....... 3225
Le 9:21 the **r.** shoulder Aaron waved for 3225
Le 14:14 put it upon the tip of the **r.** ear.......... 3233
Le 14:14 and upon the thumb of his **r.** hand,........ 3233
Le 14:14 and upon the great toe of his **r.** foot: .. 3233
Le 14:16 dip his **r.** finger in the oil that is in..... 3233
Le 14:17 priest put upon the tip of the **r.** ear.... 3233
Le 14:17 and upon the thumb of his **r.** hand,..... 3233
Le 14:17 and upon the great toe of his **r.** foot, .. 3233
Le 14:25 it upon the tip of the **r.** ear of him 3233
Le 14:25 and upon the thumb of the **r.** hand, ... 3233
Le 14:25 and upon the great toe of his **r.** foot: .. 3233
Le 14:27 shall sprinkle with his **r.** finger.......... 3233
Le 14:28 upon the tip of the **r.** ear of him 3233
Le 14:28 and upon the thumb of his **r.** hand,..... 3233
Le 14:28 and upon the great toe of his **r.** foot, .. 3233
Nu 18:18 and as the **r.** shoulder are thine. 3225
Nu 20:17 will not turn to the **r.** hand nor to 3225
Nu 22:26 either to the **r.** hand or to the left...... 3225
Nu 27:7 daughters of Zelophehad speak **r.**: 3651
De 2:27 neither turn unto the **r.** hand nor 3225
De 5:32 aside to the **r.** hand or to the left........ 3225
De 6:18 do that which is **r.** and good in the 3477
De 12:8 whatsoever is **r.** in his own eyes........ 3477
De 12:25 do that which is **r.** in the sight of....... 3477
De 12:28 that which is good and **r.** in the 3477
De 13:18 to do that which is **r.** in the eyes of.... 3477
De 17:11 thee, to the **r.** hand, nor to the left. ... 3225
De 17:20 to the **r.** hand, or to the left: 3225
De 21:9 which is **r.** in the sight of the Lord..... 3477
De 21:17 the **r.** of the firstborn is his.............. 4941
De 28:14 day, to the **r.** hand, or to the left,....... 3225
De 32:4 without iniquity, just and **r.** is he........ 3477
De 33:2 from his **r.** hand went a fiery law 3225
Jos 1:7 turn not from it to the **r.** hand or to ... 3225
Jos 3:16 people passed over **r.** against Jericho. ....
Jos 9:25 seemeth good and **r.** unto thee to 3477
Jos 17:7 border went along on the **r.** hand 3225
Jos 23:6 not aside therefrom to the **r.** hand...... 3225
Jg 3:16 under his raiment upon his **r.** thigh..... 3225
Jg 3:21 took the dagger from his **r.** thigh, ... 3225
Jg 5:26 **r.** hand to the workmen's hammer:..... 3225
Jg 7:20 trumpets in their **r.** hands to blow...... 3225
Jg 12:6 could not frame to pronounce it **r.**........ 3651
Jg 16:29 one with his **r.** hand, and of the......... 3225
Jg 17:6 every man did that which was **r.** 3477
Jg 21:25 every man did that which was **r.** in...... 3477
Ru 4:6 redeem thou my **r.** to thyself; for I..... 1353
1Sa 6:12 turned not aside to the **r.** hand or 3225
1Sa 11:2 I may thrust out all your **r.** eyes, ... 3225
1Sa 12:23 teach you the good and the **r.** way: 3477
2Sa 2:19 he turned not to the **r.** hand nor 3225
2Sa 2:21 Turn thee aside to thy **r.** hand or to.... 3225
2Sa 14:19 none can turn to the **r.** hand or to........ 3231
2Sa 15:3 See, thy matters are good and **r.**; 5228
2Sa 16:6 mighty men were on his **r.** hand 3225
2Sa 19:28 What **r.** therefore have I yet to cry 6666
2Sa 19:43 we have also more **r.** in David than ye: .....
2Sa 20:9 beard with the **r.** hand to kiss him....... 3225
2Sa 24:5 **r.** side of the city that lieth in the 3225
1Ki 2:19 mother: and she sat on his **r.** hand. 3225
1Ki 6:8 was in the **r.** side of the house: 3233
1Ki 7:21 he set up the **r.** pillar, and called........ 3233
1Ki 7:39 bases on the **r.** side of the house, ... 3225
1Ki 7:39 the sea on the **r.** side of the house..... 3233
1Ki 7:49 five on the **r.** side, and five on the 3225
1Ki 11:33 do that which is **r.** in mine eyes,........ 3477
1Ki 11:38 and do that is **r.** in my sight, to......... 3477
1Ki 14:8 to do that only which is **r.** in mine...... 3477
1Ki 15:5 David did that which was **r.** in the...... 3477
1Ki 15:11 Asa did that which was **r.** in the 3477
1Ki 22:19 standing by him on his **r.** hand and 3225
1Ki 22:43 that which was **r.** in the eyes of......... 3477
2Ki 10:15 Is thine heart **r.**, as my heart is.......... 3477
2Ki 10:30 executing that which is **r.** in mine....... 3477
2Ki 11:11 from the **r.** corner of the temple to 3233
2Ki 12:2 Jehoash did that which was **r.** in......... 3477
2Ki 12:9 it beside the altar, on the **r.** side........ 3225
2Ki 14:3 did that which was **r.** in the sight 3477
2Ki 15:3, 34 that which was **r.** in the sight........ 3477
2Ki 16:2 did not that which was **r.** in the 3477
2Ki 17:9 things that were not **r.** against the...... 3651
2Ki 18:3 did that which was **r.** in the sight....... 3477
2Ki 22:2 And that which was **r.** in the sight...... 3477
2Ki 22:2 turned not aside to the **r.** hand or 3225
2Ki 23:13 were on the **r.** hand of the mount 3225
1Ch 6:39 Asaph, who stood on his **r.** hand, ... 3225
1Ch 12:2 could use both the **r.** hand and 3231
1Ch 13:4 the thing was **r.** in the eyes of all....... 3477
2Ch 3:17 one on the **r.** hand, and the other 3225
2Ch 3:17 of that on the **r.** hand Jachin,............ 3227
2Ch 4:6 lavers, and put five on the **r.** hand,..... 3225
2Ch 4:7 five on the **r.** hand, and five on the 3225
2Ch 4:8 five on the **r.** side, and five on the 3225
2Ch 4:10 set the sea on the **r.** side of the 3233
2Ch 14:2 did that which was good and **r.** in....... 3477
2Ch 18:18 of heaven standing on his **r.** hand....... 3225
2Ch 20:32 that which was **r.** in the sight of 3477
2Ch 23:10 from the **r.** side of the temple to........ 3233
2Ch 24:2 Joash did that which was **r.** in the 3477
2Ch 25:2 did that which was **r.** in the sight of.... 3477
2Ch 26:4 did that which was **r.** in the sight of.... 3477
2Ch 27:2 did that which was **r.** in the sight of.... 3477
2Ch 28:1 he did not that which was **r.** in the..... 3477
2Ch 29:2 did that which was **r.** in the sight of.... 3477
2Ch 31:20 that which was good and **r.** and 3477
2Ch 34:2 did that which was **r.** in the sight of.... 3477
2Ch 34:2 declined neither to the **r.** hand,.......... 3225
Ezr 8:21 God, to seek of him a **r.** way for us, .. 3477
Ne 2:20 but ye have no portion, nor **r.**, nor..... 6666
Ne 8:4 and Maaseiah, on his **r.** hand;............ 3225
Ne 9:13 and gavest them **r.** judgments,............ 3477
Ne 9:33 for thou hast done **r.**, but we have....... 571
Ne 12:31 one went on the **r.** hand upon the 3225
Es 8:5 the thing seem **r.** before the king,...... 3787
Job 6:25 How forcible are **r.** words! but 3476
Job 23:9 he hideth himself on the **r.** hand,........ 3225
Job 30:12 Upon my **r.** hand rise the youth;........ 3225
Job 33:27 and perverted that which was **r.**,........ 3477
Job 34:6 Should I lie against my **r.**? my........... 4941
Job 34:17 Shall even he that hateth **r.** govern? ... 4941
Job 34:23 will not lay upon man more than **r.**; ....
Job 35:2 Thinkest thou this to be **r.**, that.......... 4941
Job 36:6 wicked: but giveth **r.** to the poor. 4941
Job 40:14 thine own **r.** hand can save thee. 3225
Job 42:7 spoken of me the thing that is **r.**,....... 3559
Job 42:8 spoken of me the thing which is **r.**, ... 3559
Ps 9:4 maintained my **r.** and my cause;.......... 4941
Ps 9:4 satest in the throne judging **r.** 6664
Ps 16:8 he is at my **r.** hand, I shall not 3225
Ps 16:11 at thy **r.** hand there are pleasures 3225
Ps 17:1 Hear the **r.**, O Lord, attend unto 6664
Ps 17:7 O thou that savest by thy **r.** hand 3225
Ps 18:35 and thy **r.** hand hath holden me up, ... 3225
Ps 19:8 The statutes of the Lord are **r.**,......... 3477
Ps 20:6 the saving strength of his **r.** hand....... 3225
Ps 21:8 thy **r.** hand shall find out those that 3225
Ps 26:10 and their **r.** hand is full of bribes........ 3225
Ps 33:4 For the word of the Lord is **r.**; and.... 3477
Ps 44:3 but thy **r.** hand, and thine arm,.......... 3225
Ps 45:4 thy **r.** hand shall teach thee terrible 3225
Ps 45:6 of thy kingdom is a **r.** sceptre. 4334
Ps 45:9 thy **r.** hand did stand the queen 3225
Ps 46:5 shall help her, and that **r.** early.......... 6437
Ps 48:10 **r.** hand is full of righteousness.......... 3225
Ps 51:10 and renew a **r.** spirit within me.......... 3559
Ps 60:5 save with thy **r.** hand, and hear 3225
Ps 63:8 thee: thy **r.** hand upholdeth me........... 3225
Ps 73:23 thou hast holden me by my **r.** hand. ... 3225
Ps 74:11 thou thy hand, even thy **r.** hand? 3225
Ps 77:10 of the **r.** hand of the most High. 3225
Ps 78:37 their heart was not **r.** with him,......... 3559
Ps 78:54 which his **r.** hand had purchased......... 3225
Ps 80:15 which thy **r.** hand hath planted,.......... 3225
Ps 80:17 be upon the man of thy **r.** hand, ... 3225
Ps 89:13 thy hand, and high is thy **r.** hand........ 3225
Ps 89:25 sea, and his **r.** hand in the rivers. 3225
Ps 89:42 up the **r.** hand of his adversaries; 3225
Ps 91:7 and ten thousand at thy **r.** hand; 3225
Ps 98:1 his **r.** hand, and his holy arm, hath 3225
Ps 107:7 he led them forth by the **r.** way,......... 3477
Ps 108:6 save with thy **r.** hand, and answer...... 3225
Ps 109:6 and let Satan stand at his **r.** hand. 3225
Ps 109:31 stand at the **r.** hand of the poor, ... 3225
Ps 110:1 Sit thou at my **r.** hand, until I make.... 3225
Ps 110:5 The Lord at thy **r.** hand shall strike.... 3225
Ps 118:15 **r.** hand of the Lord doeth valiantly...... 3225
Ps 118:16 The **r.** hand of the Lord is exalted:..... 3225
Ps 118:16 **r.** hand of the Lord doeth valiantly...... 3225
Ps 119:75 Lord, that thy judgments are **r.**, ... 6664
Ps 119:128 esteem all thy precepts...to be **r.**;...... 3474
Ps 121:5 Lord is thy shade upon thy **r.** hand...... 3225
Ps 137:5 let my **r.** hand forget her cunning........ 3225
Ps 138:7 and thy **r.** hand shall save me............ 3225
Ps 139:10 and thy **r.** hand shall hold me. 3225
Ps 139:14 and that my soul knoweth **r.** well 3966
Ps 140:12 the afflicted, and the **r.** of the poor...... 4941
Ps 142:4 I looked on my **r.** hand, and beheld, ... 3225
Ps 144:8, 11 hand is a **r.** hand of falsehood. ... 3225

Pr 3:16 Length of days is in her **r.** hand; 3225
Pr 4:11 I have led thee in **r.** paths. 3476
Pr 4:25 Let thine eyes look **r.** on, and let 5227
Pr 4:27 Turn not to the **r.** hand nor to the 3225
Pr 8:6 opening of my lips...be **r.** things 4339
Pr 8:9 **r.** to them that find knowledge 3477
Pr 9:15 passengers...go **r.** on their ways: 3474
Pr 12:5 thoughts of the righteous are **r.**: 4941
Pr 12:15 way of a fool is **r.** in his own eyes: 3477
Pr 14:12 There is a way which seemeth **r.** 3477
Pr 16:8 than great revenues without **r.** 4941
Pr 16:13 they love him that speaketh **r.** 3477
Pr 16:25 There is a way that seemeth **r.** 3477
Pr 20:11 work be pure, and whether it be **r.** 3477
Pr 21:2 Every way of a man is **r.** in his own 3477
Pr 21:8 but as for the pure, his work is **r.** 3477
Pr 23:16 when thy lips speak **r.** things 4339
Pr 24:26 his lips that giveth a **r.** answer. 5228
Pr 27:16 and the ointment of his **r.** hand, 3225
Ec 4:4 all travail, and every **r.** work, 3788
Ec 10:2 wise man's heart is at his **r.** hand; 3225
Ca 2:6 and his **r.** hand doth embrace me. 3225
Ca 8:3 and his **r.** hand should embrace me. 3225
Isa 9:20 And he shall snatch on the **r.** hand, 3225
Isa 10:2 to take away the **r.** from the poor 4941
Isa 30:10 Prophesy not unto us **r.** things, 5229
Isa 30:21 when ye turn to the **r.** hand, and 541
Isa 32:7 even when the needy speaketh **r.** 4941
Isa 41:10 the **r.** hand of my righteousness 3225
Isa 41:13 Lord thy God will hold thy **r.** hand, 3225
Isa 44:20 Is there not a lie in my **r.** hand? 3225
Isa 45:1 Cyrus, whose **r.** hand I have holden, 3225
Isa 45:19 I declare things that are **r.** 4339
Isa 48:13 **r.** hand...spanned the heavens: 3225
Isa 54:3 shalt break forth on the **r.** hand 3225
Isa 62:8 Lord hath sworn by his **r.** hand, 3225
Isa 63:12 led them by the **r.** hand of Moses 3225
Jer 2:21 thee a noble vine, wholly a **r.** seed: 571
Jer 5:28 **r.** of the needy do they not judge 4941
Jer 17:11 he that getteth riches, and not by **r.**, 4941
Jer 17:16 which came out of my lips was **r.** 5227
Jer 22:24 were the signet upon my **r.** hand, 3225
Jer 23:10 is evil, and their force is not **r.**
Jer 32:7 **r.** of redemption is thine to buy it. 4941
Jer 32:8 for the **r.** of inheritance is thine, 4941
Jer 34:15 and had done **r.** in my sight, in 3477
Jer 49:5 be driven out every man **r.** forth; 6440
La 2:3 he hath drawn back his **r.** hand 3225
La 2:4 with his **r.** hand as an adversary, 3225
La 3:35 To turn aside the **r.** of a man 4941
Eze 1:10 the face of a lion, on the **r.** side: 3225
Eze 4:6 them, lie again on thy **r.** side, 3227
Eze 10:3 the cherubims stood on the **r.** side 3225
Eze 16:46 sister, that dwelleth at thy **r.** hand, 3225
Eze 18:5 and do that which is lawful and **r.**, 6666
Eze 18:19 done that which is lawful and **r.**, 6666
Eze 18:21 and do that which is lawful and **r.**, 6666
Eze 18:27 doeth that which is lawful and **r.**, 6666
Eze 21:16 way or other, either on the **r.** hand, 3231
Eze 21:22 At his **r.** hand was the divination 3225
Eze 21:27 until he come whose **r.** it is; 4941
Eze 33:14 and do that which is lawful and **r.**; 6666
Eze 33:16 done that which is lawful and **r.**; 6666
Eze 33:19 and do that which is lawful and **r.**, 6666
Eze 39:3 arrows to fall out of thy **r.** hand. 3225
Eze 47:1 from the **r.** side of the house, 3233
Eze 47:2 there ran out waters on the **r.** side 3233
Da 12:7 held up his **r.** hand and his left 3225
Ho 14:9 for the ways of the Lord are **r.**, 3477
Am 3:10 they know not to do **r.**, saith the 5229
Am 5:12 the poor in the gate from their **r.**,
Jon 4:11 discern between their **r.** hand and 3225
Hab 2:16 cup of the Lord's **r.** hand shall be 3225
Zec 3:1 and Satan standing at his **r.** hand 3225
Zec 4:3 one upon the **r.** side of the bowl, 3225
Zec 4:11 upon the **r.** side of the candlestick 3225
Zec 11:17 upon his arm and upon his **r.** eye: 3225
Zec 11:17 his **r.** eye shall be utterly darkened 3225
Zec 12:6 on the **r.** hand and on the left: 3225
Mal 3:5 turn aside the stranger from his **r.**,
Mt 5:29 **if thy r. eye offend thee, pluck it** *1188*
Mt 5:30 **thy r. hand offend thee, cut it off,** *1188*
Mt 5:39 **shall smite thee on thy r. cheek,** *1188*
Mt 6:3 **hand know what thy r. hand** *1188*
Mt 20:4 **whatsoever is r. I will give you,** *1342*
Mt 20:7 **and whatsoever is r., that shall ye** *1342*
Mt 20:21 may sit, the one on thy **r.** hand, *1188*
Mt 20:23 **but to sit on my r. hand, and on** *1188*
Mt 22:44 **Sit thou on my r. hand, till I make** *1188*
Mt 25:33 **shall set the sheep on his r. hand,** *1188*
Mt 25:34 **King say unto them on his r. hand,** *1188*
Mt 26:64 **sitting on the r. hand of power,** *1188*
Mt 27:29 his head, and a reed in his **r.** hand: *1188*
Mt 27:38 one on the **r.** hand, and another on *1188*
Mk 5:15 and clothed, and in his **r.** mind: *4993*
Mk 10:37 we may sit, one on thy **r.** hand, *1188*
Mk 10:40 **But to sit on my r. hand and on** *1188*
Mk 12:36 **Sit thou on my r. hand, till I make** *1188*
Mk 14:62 **sitting on the r. hand of power,** *1188*
Mk 15:27 one on his **r.** hand, and the other *1188*
Mk 16:5 a young man sitting on the **r.** side, *1188*
Mk 16:19 and sat on the **r.** hand of God. *1188*
Lu 1:11 standing on the **r.** side of the altar *1188*
Lu 6:6 a man whose **r.** hand was withered. *1188*
Lu 8:35 Jesus, clothed, and in his **r.** mind: *4993*
Lu 10:28 unto him, **Thou hast answered r.** *3723*
Lu 12:57 **yourselves judge ye not what is r.?** *1342*
Lu 20:42 **my Lord, Sit thou on my r. hand,** *1188*
Lu 22:50 high priest, and cut off his **r.** ear *1188*
Lu 22:69 **the r. hand of the power of God** *1188*
Lu 23:33 one on the **r.** hand, and the other *1188*
Joh 18:10 servant, and cut off his **r.** ear. *1188*
Joh 21:6 **the net on the r. side of the ship,** *1188*
Ac 2:25 my face, for he is on my **r.** hand, *1188*
Ac 2:33 being by the **r.** hand of God exalted, *1188*
Ac 2:34 my Lord, Sit thou on my **r.** hand, *1188*
Ac 3:7 And he took him by the **r.** hand, *1188*
Ac 4:19 Whether it be **r.** in the sight of *1342*
Ac 5:31 hath God exalted with his **r.** hand *1188*
Ac 7:55 standing on the **r.** hand of God, *1188*
Ac 7:56 standing on the **r.** hand of God. *1188*
Ac 8:21 thy heart is not **r.** in the sight of *2117*
Ac 13:10 to pervert the **r.** ways of the Lord? *2117*
Ro 8:34 who is even at the **r.** hand of God, *1188*
2Co 6:7 righteousness on the **r.** hand and on *1188*
Ga 2:9 gave...the **r.** hands of fellowship; *1188*
Eph 1:20 and set him at his own **r.** hand in *1188*
Eph 6:1 parents in the Lord: for this is **r.** *1342*
Col 3:1 sitteth on the **r.** hand of God. *1188*
Heb 1:3 the **r.** hand of the Majesty on high; *1188*
Heb 1:13 he at any time, Sit on my **r.** hand, *1188*
Heb 8:1 is set on the **r.** hand of the throne of *1188*
Heb 10:12 sat down on the **r.** hand of God; *1188*
Heb 12:2 at the **r.** hand of the throne of God. *1188*
Heb 13:10 whereof they have no **r.** to eat *1849*
1Pe 3:22 and is on the **r.** hand of God; *1188*
2Pe 2:15 Which have forsaken the **r.** way, *2117*
Re 1:16 he had in his **r.** hand seven stars: *1188*
Re 1:17 And he laid his **r.** hand upon me, *1188*
Re 1:20 **which thou sawest in my r. hand,** *1188*
Re 2:1 **the seven stars in his r. hand,** *1188*
Re 5:1 I saw in the **r.** hand of him that sat *1188*
Re 5:7 took the book out of the **r.** hand of *1188*
Re 10:2 and he set his **r.** foot upon the sea, *1188*
Re 13:16 to receive a mark in their **r.** hand, *1188*
Re 22:14 they may have **r.** to the tree of life, *1849*

RIGHTEOUS See also UNRIGHTEOUS.

Ge 7:1 thee have I seen **r.** before me in 6662
Ge 18:23 Wilt thou also destroy the **r.** with 6662
Ge 18:24 Peradventure there be fifty **r.** 6662
Ge 18:24 place for the fifty **r.** that are therein? 6662
Ge 18:25 to slay the **r.** with the wicked: and 6662
Ge 18:25 that the **r.** should be as the wicked, 6662
Ge 18:26 If I find in Sodom fifty **r.** within the 6662
Ge 18:28 there shall lack five of the fifty **r.**: 6662
Ge 20:4 Lord, wilt thou slay also a **r.** nation? 6662
Ge 38:26 She hath been more **r.** than I; 6663
Ex 9:27 Lord is **r.**, and I and my people 6662
Ex 23:7 the innocent and **r.** slay thou not: 6662
Ex 23:8 and perverteth the words of the **r.** 6662
Nu 23:10 Let me die the death of the **r.**, and 3477
De 4:8 judgments so **r.** as all this law, 6662
De 16:19 wise, and pervert the words of the **r.** 6662
De 25:1 then they shall justify the **r.**, and 6662
Jg 5:11 rehearse the **r.** acts of the Lord, 6666
Jg 5:11 the **r.** acts toward the inhabitants 6666
1Sa 12:7 all the **r.** acts of the Lord, which he 6666
1Sa 24:17 to David, Thou art more **r.** than I: 6662
2Sa 4:11 wicked men have slain a **r.** person 6662
1Ki 2:32 who fell upon two men more **r.** and 6662
1Ki 8:32 and justifying the **r.**, to give him 6662
2Ki 10:9 and said to all the people, Ye be **r.** 6662
2Ch 6:23 and by justifying the **r.**, by giving 6662
2Ch 12:6 and they said, The Lord is **r.** 6662
Ezr 9:15 O Lord God of Israel, thou art **r.** 6662
Ne 9:8 performed thy words; for thou art **r.** 6662
Job 4:7 or where were the **r.** cut off? 6662
Job 9:15 though I were **r.**, yet would I not 6663
Job 10:15 if I be **r.**, yet will I not lift up my 6663
Job 15:14 of a woman, that he should be **r.**? 6663
Job 17:9 The **r.** also shall hold on his way, 6662
Job 22:3 to the Almighty, that thou art **r.**? 6663
Job 22:19 The **r.** see it, and are glad: and 6662
Job 23:7 the **r.** might dispute with him; 3477
Job 32:1 because he was **r.** in his own eyes. 6662
Job 34:5 For Job hath said, I am **r.**: and 6663
Job 35:7 If thou be **r.**, what givest thou him? 6663
Job 36:7 withdraweth not...eyes from the **r.**: 6662
Job 40:8 me, that thou mayest be **r.**? 6663
Ps 1:5 in the congregation of the **r.** 6662
Ps 1:6 the Lord knoweth the way of the **r.**: 6662
Ps 5:12 For thou, Lord, wilt bless the **r.**; 6662
Ps 7:9 for the **r.** God trieth the hearts and 6662
Ps 7:11 God judgeth the **r.**, and God is 6662
Ps 11:3 be destroyed, what can the **r.** do? 6662
Ps 11:5 The Lord trieth the **r.**: but the 6662
Ps 11:7 the **r.** Lord loveth righteousness; 6662
Ps 14:5 God is in the generation of the **r.** 6662
Ps 19:9 Lord are true and **r.** altogether. 6663
Ps 31:18 and contemptuously against the **r.** 6662
Ps 32:11 glad in the Lord, and rejoice, ye **r.** 6662
Ps 33:1 Rejoice in the Lord, O ye **r.**: for 6662
Ps 34:15 eyes of the Lord are upon the **r.**, 6662
Ps 34:17 The **r.** cry, and the Lord heareth,
Ps 34:19 Many are the afflictions of the **r.** 6662
Ps 34:21 that hate the **r.** shall be desolate. 6662
Ps 35:27 be glad, that favour my **r.** cause: 6664
Ps 37:16 little that a **r.** man hath is better 6662
Ps 37:17 but the Lord upholdeth the **r.** 6662
Ps 37:21 the **r.** sheweth mercy, and giveth 6662
Ps 37:25 yet have I not seen the **r.** forsaken, 6662
Ps 37:29 The **r.** shall inherit the land, and 6662
Ps 37:30 mouth of the **r.** speaketh wisdom, 6662
Ps 37:32 The wicked watcheth the **r.**, and 6662
Ps 37:39 But the salvation of the **r.** is of the 6662
Ps 52:6 The **r.** also shall see, and fear, and 6662
Ps 55:22 never suffer the **r.** to be moved. 6662
Ps 58:10 The **r.** shall rejoice when he seeth 6662
Ps 58:11 Verily there is a reward for the **r.**: 6662
Ps 64:10 The **r.** shall be glad in the Lord, 6662
Ps 68:3 let the **r.** be glad; let them rejoice 6662
Ps 69:28 and not be written with the **r.** 6662
Ps 72:7 In his days shall the **r.** flourish; 6662
Ps 75:10 horns of the **r.** shall be exalted. 6662
Ps 92:12 The **r.** shall flourish like the palm 6662
Ps 94:21 together against the soul of the **r.**, 6662
Ps 97:11 Light is sown for the **r.**, and 6662
Ps 97:12 Rejoice in the Lord, ye **r.**; and give 6662
Ps 107:42 The **r.** shall see it, and rejoice: 3477
Ps 112:4 and full of compassion, and **r.** 6662
Ps 112:6 the **r.** shall be in everlasting 6662
Ps 116:5 Gracious is the Lord, and **r.**; yea, 6662
Ps 118:15 is in the tabernacles of the **r.**: 6662
Ps 118:20 Lord, into which the **r.** shall enter. 6662
Ps 119:7 have learned thy **r.** judgments. 6664
Ps 119:62 thee because of thy **r.** judgments. 6664
Ps 119:106 that I will keep thy **r.** judgments. 6664
Ps 119:137 **R.** art thou, O Lord, and upright 6662
Ps 119:138 that thou hast commanded are **r.** 6664
Ps 119:160 thy **r.** judgments endureth for ever. 6664
Ps 119:164 thee because of thy **r.** judgments. 6664
Ps 125:3 not rest upon the lot of the **r.**; 6662
Ps 125:3 lest the **r.** put forth their hands 6662
Ps 129:4 Lord is **r.**: he hath cut asunder 6662
Ps 140:13 **r.** shall give thanks unto thy name: 6662
Ps 141:5 Let the **r.** smite me; it shall be a 6662
Ps 142:7 the **r.** shall compass me about; for 6662
Ps 145:17 The Lord is **r.** in all his ways, and 6662
Ps 146:8 bowed down: the Lord loveth the **r.**: 6662
Pr 2:7 layeth up sound wisdom for the **r.**: 3477
Pr 2:20 men, and keep the paths of the **r.** 6662
Pr 3:32 Lord: but his secret is with the **r.** 3477
Pr 10:3 suffer the soul of the **r.** to famish: 6662
Pr 10:11 mouth of a **r.** man is a well of life: 6662
Pr 10:16 labour of the **r.** tendeth to life: 6662
Pr 10:21 The lips of the **r.** feed many: but 6662
Pr 10:24 the desire of the **r.** shall be granted. 6662
Pr 10:25 the **r.** is an everlasting foundation. 6662
Pr 10:28 hope of the **r.** shall be gladness: 6662

Pr 10:30 The **r.** shall never be removed: but 6662
Pr 10:32 The lips of the **r.** know what is 6662
Pr 11:8 The **r.** is delivered out of trouble, 6662
Pr 11:10 When it goeth well with the **r.**, the 6662
Pr 11:21 seed of the **r.** shall be delivered 6662
Pr 11:23 The desire of the **r.** is only good: 6662
Pr 11:28 the **r.** shall flourish as a branch 6662
Pr 11:30 The fruit of the **r.** is a tree of life; 6662
Pr 11:31 the **r.** shall be recompensed in the 6662
Pr 12:3 root of the **r.** shall not be moved 6662
Pr 12:5 The thoughts of the **r.** are right: 6662
Pr 12:7 but the house of the **r.** shall stand 6662
Pr 12:10 A **r.** man regardeth the life of his 6662
Pr 12:12 but the root of the **r.** yieldeth fruit 6662
Pr 12:26 The **r.** is more excellent than his 6662
Pr 13:5 A **r.** man hateth lying: but a 6662
Pr 13:9 The light of the **r.** rejoiceth: but 6662
Pr 13:21 but to the **r.** good shall be repayed 6662
Pr 13:25 The **r.** eateth to the satisfying of 6662
Pr 14:9 but among the **r.** there is favour 3477
Pr 14:19 the wicked at the gates of the **r.**. 6662
Pr 14:32 but the **r.** hath hope in his death 6662
Pr 15:6 house of the **r.** is much treasure: 6662
Pr 15:19 the way of the **r.** is made plain 3477
Pr 15:28 heart of the **r.** studieth to answer: 6662
Pr 15:29 but he heareth the prayer of the **r.** 6662
Pr 16:13 **R.** lips are the delight of kings; 6664
Pr 18:5 to overthrow the **r.** in judgment 6662
Pr 18:10 the **r.** runneth into it, and is safe 6662
Pr 21:12 The **r.** man wisely considereth the 6662
Pr 21:18 wicked shall be a ransom for the **r.**, 6662
Pr 21:26 but the **r.** giveth and spareth not 6662
Pr 23:24 The father of the **r.** shall greatly 6662
Pr 24:15 man, against the dwelling of the **r.**; 6662
Pr 24:24 saith unto the wicked, Thou art **r.**; 6662
Pr 25:26 A **r.** man falling down before the 6662
Pr 28:1 but the **r.** are bold as a lion 6662
Pr 28:10 Whoso causeth the **r.** to go astray 3477
Pr 28:12 When **r.** men do rejoice, there is 6662
Pr 28:28 when they perish, the **r.** increase 6662
Pr 29:2 When the **r.** are in authority, the 6662
Pr 29:6 but the **r.** doth sing and rejoice 6662
Pr 29:7 **r.** considereth the cause of the poor: 6662
Pr 29:16 but the **r.** shall see their fall 6662
Ec 3:17 God shall judge the **r.** and the 6662
Ec 7:16 Be not **r.** over much; neither make 6662
Ec 8:14 according to the work of the **r.**: 6662
Ec 9:1 that the **r.**, and the wise, and their 6662
Ec 9:2 there is one event to the **r.**, and to 6662
Isa 3:10 Say ye to the **r.**, that it shall be well 6662
Isa 5:23 away the righteousness of the **r.** 6662
Isa 24:16 we heard songs, even glory to the **r.**. 6662
Isa 26:2 **r.** nation which keepeth the truth 6662
Isa 41:2 Who raised up the **r.** man from the 6664
Isa 41:26 that we may say, He is **r.**? yea, 6662
Isa 53:11 shall my **r.** servant justify many; 6662
Isa 57:1 **r.** perisheth, and no man layeth 6662
Isa 57:1 the **r.** is taken away from the evil 6662
Isa 60:21 Thy people also shall be all **r.**: they 6662
Jer 12:1 **R.** art thou, O Lord, when I plead 6662
Jer 20:12 O Lord of hosts, that triest the **r.**, 6662
Jer 23:5 will raise unto David a **r.** Branch, 6662
La 1:18 Lord is **r.**; for I have rebelled 6662
Eze 3:20 When a **r.** man doth turn from his 6662
Eze 3:21 if thou warn the **r.** man, that the 6662
Eze 3:21 that the **r.** sin not, and he doth not 6662
Eze 13:22 have made the heart of the **r.** sad, 6662
Eze 16:52 they are more **r.** than thou: yea, 6663
Eze 18:20 the righteousness of the **r.** shall be 6662
Eze 18:24 when the **r.** turneth away from his 6662
Eze 18:26 When a **r.** man turneth away from 6662
Eze 21:3 off from thee the **r.** and the wicked 6662
Eze 21:4 off from thee the **r.** and the wicked, 6662
Eze 23:45 the **r.** men, they shall judge them 6662
Eze 33:12 righteousness of the **r.** shall not 6662
Eze 33:12 neither shall the **r.** be able to live 6662
Eze 33:13 When I shall say to the **r.**, that he 6662
Eze 33:18 **r.** turneth from his righteousness, 6662
Da 9:14 Lord our God is **r.** in all his works 6662
Am 2:6 because they sold the **r.** for silver, 6662
Hab 1:4 wicked doth compass about the **r.**; 6662
Hab 1:13 the man that is more **r.** than he? 6662
Mal 3:18 between the **r.** and the wicked, 6662
Mt 9:13 **for I am not come to call the r.,** *1342*
Mt 10:41 **a r. man in the name of a r. man** *1342*
Mt 10:41 **shall receive a r. man's reward** *1342*
Mt 13:17 **r. men have desired to see those** *1342*
Mt 13:43 **shall the r. shine forth as the sun** *1342*
Mt 23:28 **also outwardly appear r. unto men,** *1342*
Mt 23:29 **garnish the sepulchres of the r.** *1342*
Mt 23:35 **the r. blood shed upon the earth,** *1342*
Mt 23:35 **blood of r. Abel unto the blood of** *1342*
Mt 25:37 **Then shall the r. answer him,** *1342*
Mt 25:46 **but the r. into life eternal** *1342*
Mk 2:17 **I came not to call the r., but** *1342*
Lu 1:6 And they were both **r.** before God, *1342*
Lu 5:32 **I came not to call the r., but** *1342*
Lu 18:9 in themselves that they were **r.**, *1342*
Lu 23:47 saying, certainly this was a **r.** man *1342*
Joh 7:24 **appearance, but judge r. judgment.** *1342*
Joh 17:25 **O r. Father, the world hath not** *1342*
Ro 2:5 and revelation of the **r.** judgment of *1341*
Ro 3:10 There is none **r.**, no, not one: *1342*
Ro 5:7 scarcely for a **r.** man will one die: *1342*
Ro 5:19 of one shall many be made **r.** *1342*
2Th 1:5 token of the **r.** judgment of God, *1342*
2Th 1:6 Seeing it is a **r.** thing with God to *1342*
1Ti 1:9 the law is not made for a **r.** man, *1342*
2Ti 4:8 which the Lord, the **r.** judge, shall *1342*
Heb 11:4 he obtained witness that he was **r.**, *1342*
Jas 5:16 prayer of a **r.** man availeth much *1342*
1Pe 3:12 the eyes of the Lord are over the **r.**, *1342*
1Pe 4:18 if the **r.** scarcely be saved, where *1342*
2Pe 2:8 that **r.** man dwelleth among them, *1342*
2Pe 2:8 vexed his **r.** soul from day to day *1342*
1Jo 2:1 the Father, Jesus Christ the **r.**: *1342*
1Jo 2:29 If ye know that he is **r.**, ye know *1342*
1Jo 3:7 righteousness is **r.**, even as he is **r.** *1342*
1Jo 3:12 were evil, and his brother's **r.** *1342*
Re 16:5 Thou art **r.**, O Lord, which art, and *1342*
Re 16:7 true and **r.** are thy judgments *1342*
Re 19:2 For true and **r.** are his judgments: *1342*
Re 22:11 be filthy still: and he that is **r.**, *1342*
Re 22:11 let him be **r.** still: and he that is *1344*

RIGHTEOUSLY See also UNRIGHTEOUSLY.

De 1:16 judge **r.** between every man and 6664
Ps 67:4 for thou shalt judge the people **r.**, 4334
Ps 96:10 he shall judge the people **r.** 4339
Pr 31:9 Open thy mouth, judge **r.**, and 6664
Isa 33:15 He that walketh **r.**, and speaketh 6666
Jer 11:20 O Lord of hosts, that judges **r.**, 6664
Tit 2:12 we should live soberly, **r.**, and *1346*
1Pe 2:23 himself to him that judgeth **r.**: *1346*

RIGHTEOUSNESS See also RIGHTEOUSNESS'; RIGHTEOUSNESSES; UNRIGHTEOUSNESS.

Ge 15:6 and he counted it to him for **r.** 6666
Ge 30:33 shall my **r.** answer for me in time 6666
Le 19:15 but in **r.** shalt thou judge thy 6664
De 6:25 it shall be our **r.**, if we observe 6666
De 9:4 For my **r.** the Lord hath brought 6666
De 9:5 Not for thy **r.**, or for the 6666
De 9:6 good land to possess it for thy **r.**; 6666
De 24:13 it shall be **r.** unto thee before the 6666
De 33:19 they shall offer sacrifices of **r.** 6664
1Sa 26:23 Lord render to every man his **r.** 6666
2Sa 22:21 rewarded me according to my **r.** 6666
2Sa 22:25 recompensed me according to my **r.**; 6666
1Ki 3:6 before thee in truth, and in **r.**, and 6666
1Ki 8:32 to give him according to his **r.** 6666
2Ch 6:23 by giving him according to his **r.** 6666
Job 6:29 yea, return again, my **r.** is in it 6664
Job 8:6 the habitation of thy **r.** prosperous 6664
Job 27:6 My **r.** I hold fast, and will not let it 6666
Job 29:14 I put on **r.**, and it clothed me: my 6664
Job 33:26 for he will render unto man his **r.** 6666
Job 35:2 saidst, My **r.** is more than God's? 6664
Job 35:8 thy **r.** may profit the son of man 6666
Job 36:3 and will ascribe **r.** to my Maker 6664
Ps 4:1 me when I call, O God of my **r.**: 6664
Ps 4:5 Offer the sacrifices of **r.**, and put 6664
Ps 5:8 Lead me, O Lord, in thy **r.** because 6666
Ps 7:8 me, O Lord, according to my **r.**, 6664
Ps 7:17 praise the Lord according to his **r.** 6664
Ps 9:8 And he shall judge the world in **r.**, 6664
Ps 11:7 For the righteous Lord loveth **r.**; 6666
Ps 15:2 walketh uprightly, and worketh **r.**, 6664
Ps 17:15 for me, I will behold thy face in **r.** 6664
Ps 18:20 rewarded me according to my **r.**; 6664
Ps 18:24 recompensed me according to my **r.**, 6664
Ps 22:31 shall declare his **r.** unto a people 6666
Ps 23:3 he leadeth me in the paths of **r.** 6664
Ps 24:5 **r.** from the God of his salvation 6666
Ps 31:1 be ashamed: deliver me in thy **r.** 6666
Ps 33:5 He loveth **r.** and judgment: the 6666
Ps 35:24 my God, according to thy **r.**; 6664
Ps 35:28 my tongue shall speak of thy **r.** 6664
Ps 36:6 Thy **r.** is like the great mountains; 6666
Ps 36:10 and thy **r.** to the upright in heart 6666
Ps 37:6 bring forth thy **r.** as the light, 6664
Ps 40:9 I have preached **r.** in the great 6664
Ps 40:10 not hid thy **r.** within my heart; 6666
Ps 45:4 of truth and meekness and **r.**; 6664
Ps 45:7 lovest **r.**, and hatest wickedness: 6664
Ps 48:10 earth: thy right hand is full of **r.** 6664
Ps 50:6 the heavens shall declare his **r.** 6664
Ps 51:14 tongue shall sing aloud of thy **r.** 6666
Ps 51:19 pleased with the sacrifices of **r.**, 6664
Ps 52:3 and lying rather than to speak **r.** 6664
Ps 58:1 Do ye...speak **r.**, O congregation? 6664
Ps 65:5 things in **r.** wilt thou answer us, 6664
Ps 69:27 and let them not come into thy **r.** 6666
Ps 71:2 Deliver me in thy **r.**, and cause me 6666
Ps 71:15 My mouth shall shew forth thy **r.** 6666
Ps 71:16 I will make mention of thy **r.**, even 6666
Ps 71:19 Thy **r.** also, O God, is very high, 6666
Ps 71:24 My tongue also shall talk of thy **r.** 6666
Ps 72:1 and thy **r.** unto the king's son 6666
Ps 72:2 He shall judge thy people with **r.**, 6664
Ps 72:3 people, and the little hills, by **r.** 6666
Ps 85:10 **r.** and peace have kissed each 6664
Ps 85:11 **r.** shall look down from heaven 6664
Ps 85:13 **R.** shall go before him; and shall 6664
Ps 88:12 thy **r.** in the land of forgetfulness? 6666
Ps 89:16 and in thy **r.** shall they be exalted 6666
Ps 94:15 But judgment shall return unto **r.** 6664
Ps 96:13 he shall judge the world with **r.**, 6664
Ps 97:2 **r.** and judgment are the habitation 6664
Ps 97:6 The heavens declare his **r.**, and 6664
Ps 98:2 his **r.** hath he openly shewed in 6666
Ps 98:9 with **r.** shall he judge the world, 6664
Ps 99:4 thou executest judgment and **r.** in 6666
Ps 103:6 Lord executeth **r.** and judgment 6666
Ps 103:17 and his **r.** unto children's children; 6666
Ps 106:3 and he that doeth **r.** at all times 6666
Ps 106:31 counted unto him for **r.** unto all 6666
Ps 111:3 and his **r.** endureth for ever 6666
Ps 112:3 house: and his **r.** endureth for ever. 6666
Ps 112:9 the poor; his **r.** endureth for ever; 6666
Ps 118:19 Open to me the gates of **r.**: but 6664
Ps 119:40 precepts: quicken me in thy **r.** 6666
Ps 119:123 and for the word of thy **r.** 6664
Ps 119:142 Thy **r.** is an everlasting 6666
Ps 119:142 is an everlasting **r.**, and thy law 6664
Ps 119:144 **r.** of my testimonies is everlasting: 6664
Ps 119:172 for all thy commandments are **r.** 6664
Ps 132:9 let thy priests be clothed with **r.**; 6664
Ps 143:1 answer me, and in thy **r.** 6666
Ps 145:7 goodness, and shall sing of thy **r.** 6666
Pr 2:9 Then shalt thou understand **r.**, 6664
Pr 8:8 the words of my mouth are in **r.**; 6664
Pr 8:18 me; yea, durable riches and **r.** 6666
Pr 8:20 I lead in the way of **r.**, in the 6666
Pr 10:2 but **r.** delivereth from death 6666
Pr 11:4 but **r.** delivereth from death 6666
Pr 11:5 **r.** of the perfect shall direct his 6666
Pr 11:6 **r.** of the upright shall deliver them: 6666
Pr 11:18 to him that soweth **r.** shall be a 6666
Pr 11:19 As **r.** tendeth to life: so he that 6666
Pr 12:17 speaketh truth sheweth forth **r.**: 6664
Pr 12:28 In the way of **r.** is life; and in the 6666
Pr 13:6 **R.** keepeth him that is upright in 6666
Pr 14:34 **R.** exalteth a nation: but sin is a 6666
Pr 15:9 loveth him that followeth after **r.** 6666
Pr 16:8 Better is a little with **r.** than great 6666
Pr 16:12 for the throne is established by **r.** 6666
Pr 16:31 if it be found in the way of **r.** 6666
Pr 21:21 that followeth after **r.** and mercy 6666
Pr 21:21 mercy findeth life, **r.**, and honour 6666
Pr 25:5 throne shall be established in **r.** 6664
Ec 3:16 the place of **r.**, that iniquity was 6664
Ec 7:15 just man that perisheth in his **r.**, 6664
Isa 1:21 **r.** lodged in it; but now murderers 6664
Isa 1:26 The city of **r.**, the faithful city 6664
Isa 1:27 judgment,...her converts with **r.** 6666
Isa 5:7 oppression; for **r.**, but behold a cry 6666
Isa 5:16 is holy shall be sanctified in **r.** 6666
Isa 5:23 take away the **r.** of the righteous 6666
Isa 10:22 decreed shall overflow with **r.** 6666

Isa 11:4 with r. shall he judge the poor, 6664
Isa 11:5 r. shall be the girdle of his loins, 6664
Isa 16:5 seeking judgment, and hasting r. 6664
Isa 26:9 inhabitants of the world...learn r. 6664
Isa 26:10 wicked, yet will he not learn r.: 6664
Isa 28:17 to the line, and r. to the plummet: 6666
Isa 32:1 Behold, a king shall reign in r., 6664
Isa 32:16 and r. remain in the fruitful field 6666
Isa 32:17 And the work of r. shall be peace; 6666
Isa 32:17 and the effect of r. quietness and 6666
Isa 33:5 filled Zion with judgment and r. 6666
Isa 41:10 thee with the right hand of my r. 6664
Isa 42:6 I the Lord have called thee in r., 6664
Isa 45:8 and let the skies pour down r.: 6664
Isa 45:8 and let r. spring up together; 6666
Isa 45:13 I have raised him up in r., and I 6664
Isa 45:19 I the Lord speak r., I declare 6664
Isa 45:23 word...gone out of my mouth in r., 6666
Isa 45:24 in the Lord have I r. and strength: 6666
Isa 46:12 stouthearted, that are far from r. 6666
Isa 46:13 I bring near my r.; it shall not be 6666
Isa 48:1 Israel, but not in truth, nor in r. 6666
Isa 48:18 and thy r. as the waves of the sea: 6666
Isa 51:1 ye that follow after r., ye that 6664
Isa 51:5 My r. is near; my salvation is 6664
Isa 51:6 and my r. shall not be abolished 6666
Isa 51:7 Hearken unto me, ye that know r., 6664
Isa 51:8 but my r. shall be for ever, and 6666
Isa 54:14 In r. shalt thou be established: 6666
Isa 54:17 their r. is of me, saith the Lord 6666
Isa 56:1 to come, and my r. to be revealed. 6666
Isa 57:12 I will declare thy r., and thy works; 6666
Isa 58:2 my ways, as a nation that did r., 6666
Isa 58:8 and thy r. shall go before thee; 6664
Isa 59:16 him; and his r., it sustained him 6666
Isa 59:17 For he put on r. as a breastplate, 6666
Isa 60:17 officers peace, and thine exactors r. 6666
Isa 61:3 they might be called trees of r., 6664
Isa 61:10 covered me with the robe of r., 6666
Isa 61:11 so the Lord God will cause r. and 6666
Isa 62:1 r. thereof go forth as brightness, 6664
Isa 62:2 And the Gentiles shall see thy r., 6664
Isa 63:1 I that speak in r., mighty to save. 6666
Isa 64:5 him that rejoiceth and worketh r., 6664
Jer 4:2 in truth, in judgment, and in r.; 6666
Jer 9:24 lovingkindness, judgment, and r., 6666
Jer 22:3 Execute ye judgment and r., and 6666
Jer 23:6 he shall be called, The Lord Our R. 6664
Jer 33:15 Branch of r. to grow up unto David; 6666
Jer 33:15 execute judgment and r. in the 6666
Jer 33:16 shall be called, The Lord our r. 6664
Jer 51:10 Lord hath brought forth our r. 6666
Eze 3:20 man doth turn from his r., and 6664
Eze 3:20 his r. which he hath done shall 6666
Eze 14:14 but their own souls by their r., 6666
Eze 14:20 deliver their own souls by their r. 6666
Eze 18:20 the r. of the righteous shall be upon 6666
Eze 18:22 in his r....he hath done he shall live. 6666
Eze 18:24 righteous turneth away from his r., 6666
Eze 18:24 All his r. that he hath done shall 6666
Eze 18:26 righteous man turneth...from his r., 6666
Eze 33:12 r. of the righteous shall not deliver 6666
Eze 33:12 righteous be able to live for his r. in
Eze 33:13 if he trust to his own r., and 6666
Eze 33:18 the righteous turneth from his r., 6666
Da 4:27 and break off thy sins by r., and 6665
Da 9:7 O Lord, r. belongeth unto thee, 6666
Da 9:16 O Lord, according to all thy r., I 6666
Da 9:24 to bring in everlasting r., and to 6664
Da 12:3 that turn many to r. as the stars 6663
Ho 2:19 I will betroth thee unto me in r., 6664
Ho 10:12 Sow to yourselves in r., reap in 6666
Ho 10:12 till he come and reign r. upon you. 6664
Am 5:7 and leave off r. in the earth, 6666
Am 5:24 waters, and r. as a mighty stream. 6666
Am 6:12 and the fruit of r. into hemlock: 6666
Mic 6:5 ye may know the r. of the Lord 6666
Mic 7:9 the light, and I shall behold his r. 6666
Zep 2:3 seek r., seek meekness: it may be 6664
Zec 8:8 be their God, in truth and in r. 6666
Mal 3:3 offer unto the Lord an offering in r. 6666
Mal 4:2 Sun of r. arise with healing in his 6666
Mt 3:15 **it becometh us to fulfil all r.** *1343*
Mt 5:6 **do hunger and thirst after r.:** *1343*
Mt 5:20 **say unto you, That except your r.** *1343*
Mt 5:20 **shall exceed the r. of the scribes** *1343*
Mt 6:33 **the kingdom of God, and his r.;** *1343*
Mt 21:32 **came unto you in the way of r.,** *1343*
Lu 1:75 In holiness and r. before him, all *1343*
Joh 16:8 **reprove the world of sin, and of r.,** *1343*
Joh 16:10 **Of r., because I go to my Father,** *1343*
Ac 10:35 he feareth him, and worketh r., is *1343*
Ac 13:10 of the devil, thou enemy of all r., *1343*
Ac 17:31 which he will judge the world in r. *1343*
Ac 24:25 as he reasoned of r., temperance, *1343*
Ro 1:17 therein is the r. of God revealed *1343*
Ro 2:26 keep the r. of the law, shall not *1345*
Ro 3:5 commend the r. of God, what shall *1343*
Ro 3:21 But now r. of God without the law *1343*
Ro 3:22 Even the r. of God which is by faith *1343*
Ro 3:25 to declare his r. for the remission *1343*
Ro 3:26 To declare, I say, at this time his r.: *1343*
Ro 4:3 and it was counted unto him for r. *1343*
Ro 4:5 ungodly, his faith is counted for r. *1343*
Ro 4:6 man, unto whom God imputeth r. *1343*
Ro 4:9 was reckoned to Abraham for r. *1343*
Ro 4:11 a seal of the r. of the faith which *1343*
Ro 4:11 that r. might be imputed unto them *1343*
Ro 4:13 the law, but through the r. of faith. *1343*
Ro 4:22 it was imputed to him for r. *1343*
Ro 5:17 receive abundance...of the gift of r. *1343*
Ro 5:18 by the r. of one the free gift came *1345*
Ro 5:21 so might grace reign through r. *1343*
Ro 6:13 as instruments of r. unto God *1343*
Ro 6:16 unto death, or of obedience unto r.? *1343*
Ro 6:18 sin, ye became the servants of r. *1343*
Ro 6:19 yield your members servants to r. *1343*
Ro 6:20 servants of sin, ye were free from r. *1343*
Ro 8:4 the r. of the law might be fulfilled *1345*
Ro 8:10 but the Spirit is life because of r. *1343*
Ro 9:28 the work, and cut it short in r.: *1343*
Ro 9:30 followed not after r.,...attained to r., *1343*
Ro 9:30 even the r. which is of faith. *1343*
Ro 9:31 which followed after the law of r., *1343*
Ro 9:31 hath not attained to the law of r. *1343*
Ro 10:3 For they being ignorant of God's r., *1343*
Ro 10:3 going about to establish their own r., *1343*
Ro 10:3 not submitted...unto the r. of God. *1343*
Ro 10:4 Christ is the end of the law for r. *1343*
Ro 10:5 describeth the r. which is of the law, *1343*
Ro 10:6 But the r. which is of faith speaketh *1343*
Ro 10:10 the heart man believeth unto r.; *1343*
Ro 14:17 r., and peace, and joy in the Holy *1343*
1Co 1:30 is made unto us wisdom, and r., *1343*
1Co 15:34 Awake to r., and sin not; for *1346*
2Co 3:9 ministration of r. exceed in glory. *1343*
2Co 5:21 might be made the r. of God in him. *1343*
2Co 6:7 the armour of r. on the right hand *1343*
2Co 6:14 for what fellowship hath r. with *1343*
2Co 9:9 the poor: his r. remaineth for ever. *1343*
2Co 9:10 and increase the fruits of your r.; *1343*
2Co 11:15 transformed as the ministers of r.; *1343*
Ga 2:21 if r. come by the law, then Christ *1343*
Ga 3:6 and it was accounted to him for r. *1343*
Ga 3:21 r. should have been by the law. *1343*
Ga 5:5 wait for the hope of r. by faith. *1343*
Eph 4:24 is created in r. and true holiness. *1343*
Eph 5:9 is in all goodness and r. and truth;) *1343*
Eph 6:14 and having on the breastplate of r. *1343*
Php 1:11 Being filled with the fruits of r., *1343*
Php 3:6 touching the r. which is in the law, *1343*
Php 3:9 not having mine own r., which is of *1343*
Php 3:9 the r. which is of God by faith: *1343*
1Ti 6:11 and follow after r., godliness, faith, *1343*
2Ti 2:22 but follow r., faith, charity, peace, *1343*
2Ti 3:16 for correction, for instruction in r.: *1343*
2Ti 4:8 there is laid up for me a crown of r., *1343*
Tit 3:5 Not by works of r. which we have *1343*
Heb 1:8 a sceptre of r. is the sceptre of thy *2118*
Heb 1:9 hast loved r., and hated iniquity; *1343*
Heb 5:13 milk is unskilful in the word of r.: *1343*
Heb 7:2 being by interpretation King of r., *1343*
Heb 11:7 heir of the r. which is by faith. *1343*
Heb 11:33 wrought r., obtained promises, *1343*
Heb 12:11 it yieldeth the peaceable fruit of r. *1343*
Jas 1:20 of man worketh not the r. of God. *1343*
Jas 2:23 and it was imputed unto him for r.: *1343*
Jas 3:18 And the fruit of r. is sown in peace *1343*
1Pe 2:24 dead to sins, should live unto r.: *1343*
2Pe 1:1 the r. of God and our Saviour Jesus *1343*
2Pe 2:5 the eighth person, a preacher of r., *1343*
2Pe 2:21 not to have known the way of r., *1343*
2Pe 3:13 a new earth, wherein dwelleth r. *1343*
1Jo 2:29 every one that doeth r. is born of *1343*
1Jo 3:7 he that doeth r. is righteous, even *1343*
1Jo 3:10 whosoever doeth not r. is not of God, *1343*
Re 19:8 for the fine linen is the r. of saints. *1345*
Re 19:11 in r. he doth judge and make war. *1343*

RIGHTEOUSNESS'

Ps 143:11 for thy r. sake bring my soul out 6666
Isa 42:21 is well pleased for his r. sake; 6664
Mt 5:10 **which are persecuted for r. sake:** *1343*
1Pe 3:14 But and if ye suffer for r. sake, *1343*

RIGHTEOUSNESSES

Isa 64:6 and all our r. are as filthy rags; 6666
Eze 33:13 all his r. shall not be remembered; 6666
Da 9:18 supplications before thee for our r., 6666

RIGHTLY See also UPRIGHTLY.

Ge 27:36 he said, Is not he r. named Jacob? 3588
Lu 7:43 said unto him, **Thou hast r. judged** *3723*
Lu 20:21 that thou sayest and teachest r., *3723*
2Ti 2:15 ashamed, r. dividing the word of truth.

RIGOUR

Ex 1:13 children of Israel to serve with r.: 6531
Ex 1:14 they made them serve, was with r. 6531
Le 25:43 Thou shalt not rule over him with r.; 6531
Le 25:46 not rule one over another with r. 6531
Le 25:53 other shall not rule with r. over him 6531

RIMMON (rim'-mon) See also EN-RIMMON; GATH-RIMMON; RIMMON-PAREZ.

Jos 15:32 and Shilhim, and Ain, and R.: 7417
Jg 20:45 the wilderness unto the rock of R.: 7417
Jg 20:47 to the wilderness unto the rock R., 7417
Jg 20:47 abode in the rock R. four months. 7417
Jg 21:13 Benjamin that were in the rock R., 7417
2Sa 4:2 the sons of R. a Beerothite, of the 7417
2Sa 4:5, 9 the sons of R. the Beerothite, 7417
2Ki 5:18 master goeth into the house of R. 7417
2Ki 5:18 I bow myself in the house of R.: 7417
2Ki 5:18 bow down myself in the house of R., 7417
1Ch 4:32 villages were, Etam, and Ain, R., 7417
1Ch 6:77 R. with her suburbs, Tabor with 7417
Zec 14:10 Geba to R. south of Jerusalem: 7417

RIMMON-PAREZ (rim''-mon-pa'-rez)

Nu 33:19 from Rithmah, and pitched at R. 7428
Nu 33:20 And they departed from R., and 7428

RING See also EARRING; RANG; RINGLEADER; RINGS; RINGSTRAKED.

Ge 41:42 Pharaoh took off his r. from his 2885
Ex 26:24 above the head of it unto one r.: 2885
Ex 36:29 at the head thereof, to one r.: 2885
Es 3:10 the king took his r. from his hand, 2885
Es 3:12 and sealed with the king's r. 2885
Es 8:2 And the king took off his r., which 2885
Es 8:8 name, and seal it with the king's r.: 2885
Es 8:8 name, and sealed with the king's r., 2885
Es 8:10 and sealed it with the king's r., and 2885
Lu 15:22 **put a r. on his hand, and shoes on** *1146*
Jas 2:2 assembly a man with a gold r., *5554*

RINGLEADER

Ac 24:5 a r. of the sect of the Nazarenes: 4414

RINGS See also EARRINGS.

Ex 25:12 shalt cast four r. of gold for it, 2885
Ex 25:12 two r. shall be in the one side of it, 2885
Ex 25:12 and two r. in the other side of it. 2885
Ex 25:14 thou shalt put the staves into the r. 2885
Ex 25:15 staves shall be in the r. of the ark: 2885
Ex 25:26 shalt make for it four r. of gold, 2885
Ex 25:26 and put the r. in the four corners 2885
Ex 25:27 against the border shall the r. be 2885
Ex 26:29 make their r. of gold for places for 2885
Ex 27:4 four brasen r. in the four corners 2885
Ex 27:7 the staves shall be put into the r., 2885
Ex 28:23 upon the breastplate two r. of gold, 2885
Ex 28:23 shalt put the two r. on the two ends 2885
Ex 28:24 wreathen chains of gold in the two r. 2885
Ex 28:26 And thou shalt make two r. of gold, 2885
Ex 28:27 two other r. of gold thou shalt make, 2885
Ex 28:28 shall bind the breastplate by the r. 2885
Ex 28:28 unto the r. of the ephod with a lace 2885
Ex 30:4 two golden r. shalt thou make to it 2885
Ex 35:22 bracelets, and earrings, and r., and 2885
Ex 36:34 made their r. of gold to be places 2885
Ex 37:3 And he cast for it four r. of gold, to 2885

Ex 37:3 even two **r.** upon the one side of it, ... 2885
Ex 37:3 and two **r.** upon the other side of it.... 2885
Ex 37:5 he put the staves into the **r.** by the.... 2885
Ex 37:13 And he cast for it four **r.** of gold,....... 2885
Ex 37:13 put the **r.** upon the four corners 2885
Ex 37:14 Over against the border were the **r.**, .. 2885
Ex 37:27 he made two **r.** of gold for it under 2885
Ex 38:5 he cast four **r.** for the four ends of..... 2885
Ex 38:7 he put the staves into the **r.** on the.... 2885
Ex 39:16 two ouches of gold, and two gold **r.**:... 2885
Ex 39:16 and put the two **r.** in the two ends of . 2885
Ex 39:17 wreathen chains of gold in the two **r.**.. 2885
Ex 39:19 they made two **r.** of gold, and put 2885
Ex 39:20 And they made two other golden **r.**, ... 2885
Ex 39:21 did bind the breastplate by his **r.**........ 2885
Ex 39:21 unto the **r.** of the ephod with a lace.... 2885
Nu 31:50 chains, and bracelets, **r.**, earrings,...... 2885
Es 1:6 to silver **r.** and pillars of marble: 1550
Ca 5:14 His hands are as gold **r.** set with 1550
Isa 3:21 The **r.**, and nose jewels, ... 2885
Eze 1:18 As for their **r.**, they were so high 1354
Eze 1:18 and their **r.** were full of eyes round 1354

RINGSTRAKED
Ge 30:35 he goats that were **r.** and spotted, ... 6124
Ge 30:39 brought forth cattle **r.**, speckled,........ 6124
Ge 30:40 the faces of the flocks toward the **r.**, .. 6124
Ge 31:8 said thus, The **r.** shall be thy hire; 6124
Ge 31:8 then bare all the cattle **r.**................. 6124
Ge 31:10 leaped upon the cattle were **r.**, ... 6124
Ge 31:12 which leap upon the cattle are **r.**, ... 6124

RINNAH (rin'-nah)
1Ch 4:20 of Shimon were, Amnon, and **R.**, ... 7441

RINSED
Le 6:28 be both scoured, and **r.** in water. 7857
Le 15:11 and hath not **r.** his hands in water, ... 7857
Le 15:12 vessel of wood shall be **r.** in water. 7857

RIOT See also RIOTING.
Tit 1:6 faithful children not accused of **r.** *810*
1Pe 4:4 with them to the same excess of **r.**,..... *810*
2Pe 2:13 count it pleasure to **r.** in the day........ *5172*

RIOTING
Ro 13:13 not in **r.** and drunkenness, not in *2970*

RIOTOUS
Pr 23:20 among **r.** eaters of flesh: 2151
Pr 28:7 is a companion of **r.** men shameth 2151
Lu 15:13 **wasted his substance with r. living.** *.811*

RIP See also RIPPED.
2Ki 8:12 and **r.** up their women with child........ 1234

RIPE See also FIRSTRIPE; UNRIPE.
Ge 40:10 clusters...brought forth **r.** grapes:....... 1310
Ex 22:29 delay to offer the first of thy **r.** fruits,.......
Nu 18:13 And whatsoever is first **r.** in the 1001
Jer 24:2 figs, even like the figs that are first **r.**:......
Joe 3:13 in the sickle, for the harvest is **r.**:...... 1310
Re 14:15 for the harvest of the earth is **r.**. *3583*
Re 14:18 earth; for her grapes are fully **r.**.......... *187*

RIPENING
Isa 18:5 the sour grape is **r.** in the flower, ... 1580

RIPHATH (ri'-fath)
Ge 10:3 sons of Gomer; Ashkenaz, and **R.**, ... 7384
1Ch 1:6 sons of Gomer; Ashchenaz, and **R.**,.... 7384

RIPPED
2Ki 15:16 the women...with child he **r.** up. 1234
Ho 13:16 women with child shall be **r.** up. 1234
Am 1:13 have **r.** up the women with child of..... 1234

RISE See also ARISE; RISEN; RISEST; RISETH; RISING; ROSE.
Ge 19:2 and ye shall **r.** up early, and go on 7925
Ge 31:35 that I cannot **r.** up before thee; 6965
Ex 8:20 **R.** up early in the morning, and 7925
Ex 9:13 **R.** up early in the morning, and 7925
Ex 12:31 **R.** up, and get you forth from 6965
Ex 21:19 If he **r.** again, and walk abroad 6965
Le 19:32 shalt **r.** up before the hoary head, ... 6965
Nu 10:35 **R.** up, Lord, and let thine enemies..... 6965
Nu 22:20 call thee, **r.** up, and go with them; 6965
Nu 23:18 **R.** up, Balak, and hear; hearken 6965
Nu 23:24 people shall **r.** up as a great lion, ... 6965
Nu 24:17 a Sceptre shall **r.** out of Israel, and..... 6965
De 2:13 Now **r.** up, said I, and get you over ... 6965
De 2:24 **R.** ye up, take your journey, and 6965
De 19:11 wait for him, and **r.** up against him, ... 6965
De 19:15 One witness shall not **r.** up against..... 6965
De 19:16 false witness **r.** up against any man..... 6965
De 28:7 thine enemies that **r.** up against 6965
De 29:22 your children that shall **r.** up after 6965
De 31:16 and this people will **r.** up, and go a..... 6965
De 32:38 let them **r.** up and help you, and be.... 6965
De 33:11 loins of them that **r.** against him,........ 6965
De 33:11 hate him, and they **r.** not again. 6965
Jos 8:7 ye shall **r.** up from the ambush, and.... 6965
Jos 18:4 they shall **r.**, and go through the........ 6965
Jg 8:21 said, **R.** thou, and fall upon us: 6965
Jg 9:33 **r.** early, and set upon the city: 7925
Jg 20:38 make a great flame with smoke **r.** 5927
1Sa 22:13 he should **r.** against me, to lie in......... 6965
1Sa 24:7 suffered them not to **r.** against Saul. ... 6965
1Sa 29:10 **r.** up early in the morning with thy..... 7925
2Sa 12:21 dead, thou didst **r.** and eat bread. 6965
2Sa 18:32 that **r.** against thee to do thee hurt,.... 6965
2Ki 16:7 of Israel, which **r.** up against me. 6965
Ne 2:18 they said, Let us **r.** up and build. 6965
Job 20:27 the earth shall **r.** up against him. 6965
Job 30:12 Upon my right hand **r.** the youth;....... 6965
Ps 3:1 many are they that **r.** up against me. .. 6965
Ps 17:7 from those that **r.** up against them. 6965
Ps 18:38 them that they were not able to **r.**: 6965
Ps 18:48 above those that **r.** up against me: 6965
Ps 27:3 though war should **r.** against me, ... 6965
Ps 35:11 False witnesses did **r.** up; they laid..... 6965
Ps 36:12 down, and shall not be able to **r.**........ 6965
Ps 41:8 that he lieth he shall **r.** up no more. ... 6965
Ps 44:5 them under that **r.** up against us. 6965
Ps 59:1 from them that **r.** up against me. 6965
Ps 74:23 tumult of those that **r.** up against 6965
Ps 92:11 of the wicked that **r.** up against me. ... 6965
Ps 94:16 **r.** up for me against the evildoers? 6965
Ps 119:62 At midnight I will **r.** to give thanks..... 6965
Ps 127:2 It is vain for you to **r.** up early, to 6965
Ps 139:21 not I grieved with those that **r.** up 8618
Ps 140:10 pits, that they **r.** not up again............ 6965
Pr 24:22 their calamity shall **r.** suddenly;.......... 6965
Pr 28:12 but when the wicked **r.**, a man is....... 6965
Pr 28:28 When the wicked **r.**, men hide........... 6965
Ec 10:4 spirit of the ruler **r.** up against........... 5927
Ec 12:4 shall **r.** up at the voice of the bird, ... 6965
Ca 2:10 **R.** up, my love, my fair one, and....... 6965
Ca 3:2 I will **r.** now, and go about the city..... 6965
Isa 5:11 Woe unto them that **r.** up early in...... 7925
Isa 14:21 that they do not **r.**, nor possess the ... 6965
Isa 14:22 I will **r.** up against them, saith the...... 6965
Isa 24:20 and it shall fall, and not **r.** again. 6965
Isa 26:14 they are deceased, they shall not **r.**:... 6965
Isa 28:21 the Lord shall **r.** up as in mount......... 6965
Isa 32:9 **R.** up, ye women that are at ease; 6965
Isa 33:10 Now will I **r.**, saith the Lord; now...... 6965
Isa 43:17 lie down together, they shall not **r.**:.... 6965
Isa 54:17 tongue that shall **r.** against thee in...... 6965
Isa 58:10 then shall thy light **r.** in obscurity, ... 2224
Jer 25:27 and spue, and fall, and **r.** no more, ... 6965
Jer 37:10 they **r.** up every man in his tent, ... 6965
Jer 47:2 waters **r.** up out of the north, and...... 5927
Jer 49:14 against her, and **r.** up to the battle. 6965
Jer 51:1 of them that **r.** up against me, ... 6965
Jer 51:64 shall not **r.** from the evil that I will..... 6965
La 1:14 from whom I am not able to **r.** up. 6965
Da 7:24 another shall **r.** after them; and.......... 6966
Am 5:2 is fallen; she shall no more **r.**: she...... 6965
Am 7:9 **r.** against the house of Jeroboam........ 6965
Am 8:8 and it shall **r.** up wholly as a flood; 5927
Am 8:14 shall fall, and never **r.** up again. 6965
Am 9:5 it shall **r.** up wholly like a flood; 5927
Ob 1 let us **r.** up against her in battle......... 6965
Na 1:9 affliction shall not **r.** up the second 6965
Hab 2:7 Shall they not **r.** up suddenly that....... 6965
Zep 3:8 the day that I **r.** up to the prey: for.... 6965
Zec 14:13 shall **r.** up against the hand of his...... 5927
Mt 5:45 **he maketh his sun to r. on the evil**..*393*
Mt 10:21 **and the children shall r. up against***1881*
Mt 12:41 **men of Nineveh shall r. in judgment***450*
Mt 12:42 **south shall r. up in the judgment**.. *1453*
Mt 20:19 **and the third day he shall r. again**. *450*
Mt 24:7 **For nation shall r. against nation**,.*1453*
Mt 24:11 **And many false prophets shall r.**,.. *1453*
Mt 26:46 **R., let us be going: behold, he is at***1453*
Mt 27:63 After three days I will **r.** again.......... *1453*
Mk 3:26 **And if Satan r. up against himself**,. *450*
Mk 4:27 **should sleep, and r. night and day**,.*1453*
Mk 8:31 and after three days **r.** again.............. *450*
Mk 9:31 **be killed, he shall r. the third day**. ..*450*
Mk 10:34 **and the third day he shall r. again**.. *450*
Mk 10:49 Be of good comfort, **r.**; he calleth *1453*
Mk 12:23 when they shall **r.**, whose wife............ *450*
Mk 12:25 **when they shall r. from the dead**,...... *450*
Mk 12:26 **as touching the dead, that they r.**: .*1453*
Mk 13:8 **For nation shall r. against nation**, .*1453*
Mk 13:12 **shall r. up against their parents**,... *1881*
Mk 13:22 **Christs and false prophets shall r.**,.*1453*
Mk 14:42 **R. up, let us go; lo, he that** *1453*
Lu 5:23 **thee; or to say, R. up and walk?**... *1453*
Lu 6:8 **R. up, and stand forth in the**............. *1453*
Lu 11:7 **in bed; I cannot r. and give thee**..... *450*
Lu 11:8 **Though he will not r. and give**...... *1453*
Lu 11:8 **he will r. and give him as many as**. *450*
Lu 11:31 **queen of the south shall r. up in**... *1453*
Lu 11:32 **Nineve shall r. up in the judgment**.. *450*
Lu 12:54 **ye see a cloud r. out of the west**,.... *393*
Lu 18:33 **and the third day he shall r. again**.. *450*
Lu 21:10 **Nation shall r. against nation**,...... *1453*
Lu 22:46 **r. and pray, lest ye enter into**......... *450*
Lu 24:7 crucified, and the third day **r.** again. *450*
Lu 24:46 **to r. from the dead the third day**:... *450*
Joh 5:8 unto him, **R.**, take up thy bed, and.... *1453*
Joh 11:23 her, **Thy brother shall r. again**....... *450*
Joh 11:24 I know that he shall **r.** again in the....... *450*
Joh 20:9 he must **r.** again from the dead. *450*
Ac 3:6 name of Jesus...of Nazareth **r.** up....... *1453*
Ac 10:13 to him, **R.**, Peter; kill, and eat........... *450*
Ac 26:16 **r., and stand upon thy feet; for I**.... *450*
Ac 26:23 first that should **r.** from the dead, ... *386*
Ro 15:12 shall **r.** to reign over the Gentiles; *450*
1Co 15:15 up, if so be that the dead **r.** not......... *1453*
1Co 15:16 if the dead **r.** not,...is not Christ........ *1453*
1Co 15:29 the dead, if the dead **r.** not at all? *1453*
1Co 15:32 advantageth it me, if the dead **r.** *1453*
1Th 4:16 the dead in Christ shall **r.** first: *450*
Heb 7:11 that another priest should **r.** after *450*
Re 11:1 **R.**, and measure the temple of *1453*
Re 13:1 saw a beast **r.** up out of the sea, ... *305*

RISEN See also ARISEN.
Ge 19:23 The sun was **r.** upon the earth 3318
Ex 22:3 If the sun be **r.** upon him, there 2224
Nu 32:14 ye are **r.** up in your fathers' stead, ... 6965
Jg 9:18 ye are **r.** up against my father's 6965
Ru 2:15 when she was **r.** up to glean, Boaz..... 6965
1Sa 25:29 Yet a man is **r.** to pursue thee, and.... 6965
2Sa 14:7 the whole family is **r.** against thine 6965
1Ki 8:20 I am **r.** up in the room of David my.... 6965
2Ki 6:15 the servant...of God was **r.** early, ... 6965
2Ch 6:10 am **r.** up in the room of David my...... 6965
2Ch 13:6 Solomon the son of David, is **r.** up, ... 6965
2Ch 21:4 Jehoram was **r.** up to the kingdom...... 6965
Ps 20:8 but we are **r.**, and stand upright. 6965
Ps 27:12 witnesses are **r.** up against me, ... 6965
Ps 54:3 strangers are **r.** up against me,.......... 6965
Ps 86:14 the proud are **r.** against me, and........ 6965
Isa 60:1 glory of the Lord is **r.** upon thee........ 2224
Eze 7:11 Violence is **r.** up into a rod of........... 6965
Eze 47:5 for the waters were **r.**, waters to....... 1342
Mic 2:8 my people is **r.** up as an enemy: 6965
Mt 11:11 **hath not r. a greater than John**..... *1453*
Mt 14:2 Baptist; he is **r.** from the dead; *1453*
Mt 17:9 **the Son of man be r. again from**.... *450*
Mt 26:32 **But after I am r. again, I will go** . *1453*
Mt 27:64 the people, He is **r.** from the dead: *1453*
Mt 28:6 He is not here: for he is **r.**, as he...... *1453*
Mt 28:7 his disciples that he is **r.** from the...... *1453*
Mk 6:14 John the Baptist was **r.** from the........ *1453*
Mk 6:16 beheaded: he is **r.** from the dead. *1453*
Mk 9:9 Son of man were **r.** from the dead....... *450*
Mk 14:28 **after that I am r., I will go before**.*1453*
Mk 16:6 he is **r.**; he is not here: behold the..... *1453*
Mk 16:9 Jesus was **r.** early the first day of........ *450*
Mk 16:14 had seen him after he was **r.**............. *1453*
Lu 7:16 a great prophet is **r.** up among us; *1453*
Lu 9:7 that John was **r.** from the dead; *1453*
Lu 9:8 of the old prophets was **r.** again. *450*
Lu 9:19 one of the old prophets is **r.** again. *450*
Lu 13:25 **the master of the house is r. up**,... *1453*
Lu 24:6 He is not here, but is **r.**: remember ... *1453*
Lu 24:34 The Lord is **r.** indeed, and hath......... *1453*
Joh 2:22 therefore he was **r.** from the dead,...... *1453*
Joh 21:14 after that he was **r.** from the dead...... *1453*

Ac 17:3 suffered,...**r.** again from the dead;........ *450*
Ro 8:34 died, yea rather, that is **r.** again,........ *1453*
1Co 15:13 of the dead, then is Christ not **r.**:....... *1453*
1Co 15:14 And if Christ be not **r.**, then is our..... *1453*
1Co 15:20 But now is Christ **r.** from the dead,.... *1453*
Col 2:12 **r.** with him through the faith of.......... *4891*
Col 3:1 If ye then be **r.** with Christ, seek....... *4891*
Jas 1:11 sun is...**r.** with a burning heat,............ *393*

RISEST
De 6:7 liest down, and when thou **r.** up........ 6965
De 11:19 liest down, and when thou **r.** up......... 6965

RISETH See also ARISETH.
De 22:26 a man **r.** against his neighbour,.......... 6965
Jos 6:26 **r.** up and buildeth this city Jericho: 6965
2Sa 23:4 when the sun **r.**, even a morning 2224
Job 9:7 commandeth the sun, and it **r.** not;..... 2224
Job 14:12 So man lieth down, and **r.** not: 6965
Job 24:22 he **r.** up, and no man is sure of life. ... 6965
Job 27:7 he that **r.** up against me as the.......... 6965
Job 31:14 then shall I do when God **r.** up?......... 6965
Pr 24:16 falleth seven times, and **r.** up again:.... 6965
Pr 31:15 She **r.** also while it is yet night, and ... 6965
Isa 47:11 shalt not know from whence it **r.**: 7837
Jer 46:8 Egypt **r.** up like a flood, and his......... 5927
Mic 7:6 daughter **r.** up against her mother, ... 6965
Joh 13:4 He **r.** from supper, and laid aside *1453*

RISING See also ARISING; SUNRISING; UPRISING.
Le 13:2 have in the skin of his flesh a **r.**,........ 7613
Le 13:10 if the **r.** be white in the skin, and....... 7613
Le 13:10 there be quick raw flesh in the **r.**;....... 7613
Le 13:19 place of the boil there be a white **r.**,... 7613
Le 13:28 it is a **r.** of the burning, and the......... 7613
Le 13:43 the **r.** of the sore be white reddish..... 7613
Le 14:56 for a **r.**, and for a scab, and for a....... 7613
Nu 2:3 east side toward the **r.** of the sun...... 4217
Jos 12:1 Jordan toward the **r.** of the sun,......... 4217
2Ch 36:15 **r.** up betimes, and sending;.............. 7925
Ne 4:21 spears from the **r.** of the morning...... 5927
Job 16:8 my leanness **r.** up in me beareth........ 6965
Job 24:5 their work; **r.** betimes for a prey: 7836
Job 24:14 murderer **r.** with the light killeth......... 6965
Ps 50:1 the earth from the **r.** of the sun.......... 4217
Ps 113:3 From the **r.** of the sun unto the......... 4217
Pr 27:14 **r.** early in the morning, it shall be...... 7925
Pr 30:31 against whom there is no **r.** up........... 510
Isa 41:25 from the **r.** of the sun shall he call...... 4217
Isa 45:6 may know from the **r.** of the sun, ... 4217
Isa 59:19 and his glory from the **r.** of the sun.... 4217
Isa 60:3 kings to the brightness of thy **r.**.......... 2225
Jer 7:13 **r.** up early and speaking, but ye......... 7925
Jer 7:25 **r.** up early and sending them:............ 7925
Jer 11:7 **r.** early and protesting, saying, ... 7925
Jer 25:3 unto you, **r.** early and speaking;......... 7925
Jer 25:4 the prophets, **r.** early and sending...... 7925
Jer 26:5 both **r.** up early, and sending them, ... 7925
Jer 29:19 **r.** up early and sending them;............ 7925
Jer 32:33 **r.** up early and teaching them, yet...... 7925
Jer 35:14 unto you, **r.** early and speaking;......... 7925
Jer 35:15 **r.** up early and sending them,............ 7925
Jer 44:4 the prophets, **r.** early and sending...... 7925
La 3:63 sitting down, and their **r.** up;............ 7012
Mal 1:11 from the **r.** of the sun even unto........ 4217
Mk 1:35 **r.** up a great while before day, he....... *450*
Mk 9:10 the **r.** from the dead should mean........ *305*
Mk 16:2 the sepulchre at the **r.** of the sun........ *393*
Lu 2:34 and **r.** again of many in Israel;............ *386*

RISSAH (ris'-sah)
Nu 33:21 from Libnah, and pitched at **R.**. 7446
Nu 33:22 And they journeyed from **R.**, and....... 7446

RITES
Nu 9:3 according to all the **r.** of it, and 2708

RITHMAH (rith'-mah)
Nu 33:18 Hazeroth, and pitched in **R.**. 7575
Nu 33:19 And they departed from **R.**, and 7575

RIVER See also RIVER'S; RIVERS.
Ge 2:10 a **r.** went out of Eden to water the..... 5104
Ge 2:13 the name of the second **r.** is Gihon:..... 5104
Ge 2:14 name of the third **r.** is Hiddekel: 5104
Ge 2:14 And the fourth **r.** is Euphrates........... 5104
Ge 15:18 I given this land, the **r.** of Egypt........ 5104
Ge 15:18 unto the great **r.**, the **r.** Euphrates:..... 5104
Ge 31:21 he rose up, and passed over the **r.**,..... 5104
Ge 36:37 Saul of Rehoboth by the **r.** reigned..... 5104
Ge 41:1 and, behold, he stood by the **r.**.......... 2975
Ge 41:2 came up out of the **r.** seven...kine...... 2975
Ge 41:3 came up after them out of the **r.**,....... 2975
Ge 41:3 other kine upon the brink of the **r.**....... 2975
Ge 41:17 I stood upon the bank of the **r.**:......... 2975
Ge 41:18 came up out of the **r.** seven kine, ... 2975
Ex 1:22 Every son...ye shall cast into the **r.**,... 2975
Ex 2:5 came down to wash herself at the **r.**;.. 2975
Ex 4:9 shalt take of the water of the **r.**,........ 2975
Ex 4:9 water...thou takest out of the **r.** 2975
Ex 7:17 upon the waters which are in the **r.**,... 2975
Ex 7:18 the fish that is in the **r.** shall die, ... 2975
Ex 7:18 and the **r.** shall stink; and the............ 2975
Ex 7:18 lothe to drink of the water of the **r.**..... 2975
Ex 7:20 smote the waters that were in the **r.**, ..2975
Ex 7:20 all the waters that were in the **r.**, ... 2975
Ex 7:21 And the fish that was in the **r.** died; ... 2975
Ex 7:21 and the **r.** stank, and the Egyptians.... 2975
Ex 7:21 could not drink...the water of the **r.**;... 2975
Ex 7:24 digged round about the **r.** for water.... 2975
Ex 7:24 could not drink...the water of the **r.**.... 2975
Ex 7:25 that the Lord had smitten the **r.**. 2975
Ex 8:3 And the **r.** shall bring forth frogs........ 2975
Ex 8:9 they may remain in the **r.** only? 2975
Ex 8:11 they shall remain in the **r.** only. 2975
Ex 17:5 rod, wherewith thou smotest the **r.**, ... 2975
Ex 23:31 and from the desert unto the **r.**: 5104
Nu 22:5 by the **r.** of the land of the children.... 5104
Nu 34:5 from Azmon unto the **r.** of Egypt, ... 5158
De 1:7 unto the great **r.**, the **r.** Euphrates..... 5104
De 2:24 and pass over the **r.** Arnon:.............. 5158
De 2:36 is by the brink of the **r.** of Arnon,...... 5158
De 2:36 and from the city that is by the **r.**,..... 5158
De 2:37 nor unto any place of the **r.** Jabbok,.... 5158
De 3:8 from the **r.** of Arnon unto mount........ 5158
De 3:12 Aroer, which is by the **r.** Arnon,......... 5158
De 3:16 from Gilead even unto the **r.** Arnon.... 5158
De 3:16 the border even unto the **r.** Jabbok,.... 5158
De 4:48 is by the bank of the **r.** Arnon,.......... 5158
De 11:24 from the **r.**, the **r.** Euphrates, even.... 5104
Jos 1:4 unto the great **r.**, the **r.** Euphrates,.... 5104
Jos 12:1 from the **r.** Arnon unto mount 5158
Jos 12:2 is upon the bank of the **r.** Arnon,........ 5158
Jos 12:2 and from the middle of the **r.**, and...... 5158
Jos 12:2 even unto the **r.** Jabbok, which is........ 5158
Jos 13:9 is upon the bank of the **r.** Arnon, ... 5158
Jos 13:9 city that is in the midst of the **r.**, ... 5158
Jos 13:16 that is on the bank of the **r.** Arnon,.... 5158
Jos 13:16 city that is in the midst of the **r.**, ... 5158
Jos 15:4 and went out unto the **r.** of Egypt;..... 5158
Jos 15:7 which is on the south side of the **r.**..... 5158
Jos 15:47 the **r.** of Egypt, and the great sea,..... 5158
Jos 16:8 westward unto the **r.** Kanah;............ 5158
Jos 17:9 the **r.** Kanah, southward of the **r.**: 5158
Jos 17:9 was on the north side of the **r.**,......... 5158
Jos 19:11 to the **r.** that is before Jokneam; 5158
Jg 4:7 will draw...to the **r.** Kishon Sisera,..... 5158
Jg 4:13 Harosheth...unto the **r.** of Kishon......... 5158
Jg 5:21 The **r.** of Kishon swept them away,..... 5158
Jg 5:21 that ancient **r.**, the **r.** Kishon. 5158
2Sa 8:3 his border at the **r.** Euphrates. 5104
2Sa 10:16 Syrians that were beyond the **r.**:........ 5104
2Sa 17:13 city, and...will draw it into the **r.**, ... 5158
2Sa 24:5 lieth in the midst of the **r.** of Gad,...... 5158
1Ki 4:21 from the **r.** unto the land of the......... 5104
1Ki 4:24 all the region on this side of the **r.**, ... 5104
1Ki 4:24 over all the kings on this side the **r.**: .. 5104
1Ki 8:65 of Hamath unto the **r.** of Egypt,......... 5158
1Ki 14:15 shall scatter them beyond the **r.**,......... 5104
2Ki 10:33 Aroer, which is by the **r.** Arnon,......... 5158
2Ki 17:6 and in Habor by the **r.** of Gozan, ... 5104
2Ki 18:11 and in Habor by the **r.** of Gozan, ... 5104
2Ki 23:29 king of Assyria to the **r.** Euphrates:.... 5104
2Ki 24:7 had taken from the **r.** of Egypt........... 5158
2Ki 24:7 unto the **r.** Euphrates all that 5158
1Ch 1:48 Shaul of Rehoboth by the **r.** 5104
1Ch 5:9 wilderness from the **r.** Euphrates: 5104
1Ch 5:26 and Hara, and to the **r.** Gozan,.......... 5104
1Ch 18:3 his dominion by the **r.** Euphrates........ 5104
1Ch 19:16 Syrians that were beyond the **r.**:........ 5104
2Ch 7:8 of Hamath unto the **r.** of Egypt.......... 5158
2Ch 9:26 from the **r.** even unto the land of....... 5104
Ezr 4:10 rest that are on this side the **r.**, ... 5103
Ezr 4:11 servants the men on this side the **r.**, .. 5103
Ezr 4:16 have no portion of this side the **r.**. 5103
Ezr 4:17 and unto the rest beyond the **r.**, ... 5103
Ezr 4:20 over all countries beyond the **r.**; 5103
Ezr 5:3, 6 governor on this side the **r.**,........... 5103
Ezr 5:6 Apharsachites,...on this side the **r.**, ... 5103
Ezr 6:6 Tatnai, governor beyond the **r.**, ... 5103
Ezr 6:6 Apharsachites,...beyond the **r.**,.......... 5103
Ezr 6:8 even of the tribute beyond the **r.**, ... 5103
Ezr 6:13 Tatnai, governor on this side the **r.**, ... 5103
Ezr 7:21 treasurers which are beyond the **r.**,.... 5103
Ezr 7:25 the people that are beyond the **r.**,...... 5103
Ezr 8:15 to the **r.** that runneth to Ahava;......... 5104
Ezr 8:21 a fast there, at the **r.** of Ahava, ... 5104
Ezr 8:31 we departed from the **r.** of Ahava 5104
Ezr 8:36 to the governors on this side the **r.**: ... 5104
Ne 2:7, 9 to the governors beyond the **r.**, ... 5104
Ne 3:7 of the governor on this side the **r.**....... 5104
Job 40:23 drinketh up a **r.**, and hasteth not:........ 5104
Ps 36:8 drink of the **r.** of thy pleasures. 5158
Ps 46:4 There is a **r.**, the streams whereof..... 5104
Ps 65:9 enrichest it with the **r.** of God, ... 6388
Ps 72:8 and from the **r.** unto the ends of........ 5104
Ps 80:11 sea, and her branches unto the **r.**........ 5104
Ps 105:41 they ran in the dry places like a **r.**. 5104
Isa 7:20 namely, by them beyond the **r.**,.......... 5104
Isa 8:7 up upon them the waters of the **r.**,..... 5104
Isa 11:15 shall he shake his hand over the **r.**, ... 5104
Isa 19:5 the **r.** shall be wasted and dried up..... 5104
Isa 23:3 seed of Sihor, the harvest of the **r.**, ... 2975
Isa 23:10 Pass through thy land as a **r.**, O 2975
Isa 27:12 channel of the **r.** unto the stream....... 5104
Isa 48:18 then had thy peace been as a **r.**,........ 5104
Isa 66:12 I will extend peace to her like a **r.**, ... 5104
Jer 2:18 to drink the waters of the **r.**? 5104
Jer 17:8 spreadeth out her roots by the **r.**, ... 3105
Jer 46:2 which was by the **r.** Euphrates in........ 5104
Jer 46:6 the north by the **r.** Euphrates............ 5104
Jer 46:10 north country by the **r.** Euphrates. 5104
La 2:18 let tears run down like a **r.** day 5158
Eze 1:1 the captives by the **r.** of Chebar, ... 5104
Eze 1:3 of the Chaldeans by the **r.** Chebar;..... 5104
Eze 3:15 that dwelt by the **r.** of Chebar, and 5104
Eze 3:23 which I saw by the **r.** of Chebar: 5104
Eze 10:15 that I saw by the **r.** of Chebar............ 5104
Eze 10:20 God of Israel by the **r.** of Chebar;...... 5104
Eze 10:22 faces. . .I saw by the **r.** of Chebar 5104
Eze 29:3 My **r.** is mine own, and I have 2975
Eze 29:9 The **r.** is mine, and I have made it. 2975
Eze 43:3 vision...I saw by the **r.** Chebar; 5104
Eze 47:5 was a **r.** that I could not pass over:.... 5158
Eze 47:5 a **r.** that could not be passed over....... 5158
Eze 47:6 me to return to the brink of the **r.**. 5158
Eze 47:7 bank of the **r.** were very many trees .. 5158
Eze 47:9 shall live whither the **r.** cometh.......... 5158
Eze 47:12 by the **r.** upon the bank thereof, on.... 5158
Eze 47:19 in Kadesh, the **r.** to the great sea....... 5158
Eze 48:28 and to the **r.** toward the great sea...... 5158
Da 8:2 vision, and I was by the **r.** of Ulai....... 180
Da 8:3 there stood before the **r.** a ram.......... 180
Da 8:6 I had seen standing before the **r.**,........ 180
Da 10:4 as I was by the side of the great **r.**, ... 5104
Da 12:5 on this side of the bank of the **r.**,....... 2975
Da 12:5 on that side of the bank of the **r.**. 2975
Da 12:6, 7 was upon the waters of the **r.**,......... 2975
Am 6:14 unto the **r.** of the wilderness............ 5158
Mic 7:12 from the fortress even to the **r.**,......... 5104
Zec 9:10 from the **r.** even to the ends of the.... 5104
Zec 10:11 all the deeps of the **r.** shall dry up:..... 2975
Mk 1:5 baptized of him in the **r.** of Jordan, ... *4215*
Ac 16:13 we went out of the city by a **r.** side, .. *4215*
Re 9:14 bound in the great **r.** Euphrates. *4215*
Re 16:12 vial upon the great **r.** Euphrates;........ *4215*
Re 22:1 shewed me a pure **r.** of water of life,.. *4215*
Re 22:2 of it, and on either side of the **r.**,....... *4215*

RIVER'S
Ex 2:3 laid it in the flags by the **r.** brink........ 2975
Ex 2:5 maidens walked...by the **r.** side; 2975
Ex 7:15 thou shalt stand by the **r.** brink.......... 2975
Nu 24:6 forth, as gardens by the **r.** side, ... 5104

RIVERS
Ex 7:19 upon their streams, upon their **r.**, ... 2975
Ex 8:5 over the **r.**, and over the ponds,......... 2975
Le 11:9 waters, in the seas, and in the **r.**,....... 5158
Le 11:10 scales in the seas, and in the **r.**, ... 5158
De 10:7 to Jotbath, a land of **r.** of waters. 5158
2Ki 5:12 and Pharpar, **r.** of Damascus, ... 5104
2Ki 19:24 up all the **r.** of besieged places. 2975

Job 20:17 He shall not see the **r.**, the floods, ... 6390
Job 28:10 cutteth out **r.** among the rocks; 2975
Job 29:6 the rock poured me out **r.** of oil; 6388
Ps 1:3 a tree planted by the **r.** of water, ... 6388
Ps 74:15 flood: thou driedst up mighty **r.** 5104
Ps 78:16 caused waters to run down like **r.** 5104
Ps 78:44 had turned their **r.** into blood; 2975
Ps 89:25 sea, and his right hand in the **r.** 5104
Ps 107:33 He turneth **r.** into a wilderness, ... 5104
Ps 119:136 **R.** of waters run down mine 6388
Ps 137:1 By the **r.** of Babylon, there we sat 5104
Pr 5:16 and **r.** of waters in the streets. 6388
Pr 21:1 hand of the Lord, as the **r.** of water: .. 6388
Ec 1:7 All the **r.** run into the sea; yet the 5158
Ec 1:7 the place from whence the **r.** come, ... 5158
Ca 5:12 eyes of doves by the **r.** of waters, ... 650
Isa 7:18 uttermost part of the **r.** of Egypt, ... 2975
Isa 18:1 which is beyond the **r.** of Ethiopia: 5104
Isa 18:2 whose land the **r.** have spoiled! 5104
Isa 18:7 whose land the **r.** have spoiled, to 5104
Isa 19:6 And they shall turn the **r.** far away; 5104
Isa 30:25 **r.** and streams of waters in the 6388
Isa 32:2 as **r.** of water in a dry place, ... 6388
Isa 33:21 a place of broad **r.** and streams; 5103
Isa 37:25 all the **r.** of the besieged places. 2975
Isa 41:18 I will open **r.** in high places, and 5103
Isa 42:15 and I will make the **r.** islands, and 5103
Isa 43:2 and through the **r.**, they shall not 5103
Isa 43:19 the wilderness, and **r.** in the desert. ... 5103
Isa 43:20 the wilderness, and **r.** in the desert, ... 5103
Isa 44:27 Be dry, and I will dry up thy **r.**: 5103
Isa 47:2 uncover the thigh, pass over the **r.** 5103
Isa 50:2 the sea, I make the **r.** a wilderness: ... 5103
Jer 31:9 them to walk by the **r.** of waters 5158
Jer 46:7 whose waters are moved as the **r.**? 5104
Jer 46:8 his waters are moved like the **r.**; 5104
La 3:48 runneth down with **r.** of water 6388
Eze 6:3 hills, to the **r.**, and to the valleys; 650
Eze 29:3 that lieth in the midst of his **r.**, ... 2975
Eze 29:4 will cause the fish of thy **r.** to stick 2975
Eze 29:4 thee up out of the midst of thy **r.**, ... 2975
Eze 29:4 and all the fish of thy **r.** shall stick 2975
Eze 29:5 thee and all the fish of thy **r.**: 2975
Eze 29:10 am against thee, and against thy **r.**, ... 2975
Eze 30:12 And I will make the **r.** dry, and sell 2975
Eze 31:4 **r.** running round about his plants, ... 5104
Eze 31:4 little **r.** unto all the trees. 8585
Eze 31:12 are broken by all the **r.** of the land; 650
Eze 32:2 and thou camest forth with thy **r.**, ... 5104
Eze 32:2 with thy feet, and fouledst their **r.** 5104
Eze 32:6 and the **r.** shall be full of thee. 650
Eze 32:14 and cause their **r.** to run like oil, ... 5104
Eze 34:13 the mountains of Israel by the **r.**, ... 650
Eze 35:8 and in all thy **r.**, shall they fall that 650
Eze 36:4, 6 hills, to the **r.**, and to the valleys, ... 650
Eze 47:9 whithersoever the **r.** shall come, ... 5158
Joe 1:20 for the **r.** of waters are dried up, ... 650
Joe 3:18 **r.** of Judah shall flow with waters, ... 650
Mic 6:7 or with ten thousands of **r.** of oil? 5158
Na 1:4 it dry, and drieth up all the **r.**: 5104
Na 2:6 The gates of the **r.** shall be opened, ... 5104
Na 3:8 No, that was situate among the **r.**, ... 2975
Hab 3:8 the Lord displeased against the **r.**? 5104
Hab 3:8 was thine anger against the **r.**? was 5104
Hab 3:9 Thou didst cleave the earth with **r.** 5104
Zep 3:10 From beyond the **r.** of Ethiopia my 5104
Joh 7:38 **belly shall flow r. of living water.** ..*4215*
Re 8:10 it fell upon the third part of the **r.**, ... *4215*
Re 16:4 poured out his vial upon the **r.** and *4215*

RIZPAH (riz'-pah)
2Sa 3:7 a concubine, whose name was **R.**, ... 7532
2Sa 21:8 the king took the two sons of **R.** 7532
2Sa 21:10 And **R.** the daughter of Aiah took 7532
2Sa 21:11 told David what **R.**...had done. 7532

ROAD
1Sa 27:10 Whither have ye made a **r.** to-day? 6584

ROAR See also ROARED; ROARETH; ROARING; UPROAR.
1Ch 16:32 Let the sea **r.**, and the fulness 7481
Ps 46:3 waters thereof **r.** and be troubled, ... 1993
Ps 74:4 Thine enemies **r.** in the midst of 7580
Ps 96:11 let the sea **r.**, and the fulness 7481
Ps 98:7 Let the sea **r.**, and the fulness 7481
Ps 104:21 The young lions **r.** after their prey, ... 7580
Isa 5:29 lion, they shall **r.** like young lions: 7580
Isa 5:29 yea, they shall **r.**, and lay hold of 5098
Isa 5:30 that day they shall **r.** against them 5098
Isa 42:13 a man of war: he shall cry, yea, **r.**; 6873
Isa 59:11 We **r.** all like bears, and mourn 1993
Jer 5:22 though they **r.**, yet can they not 1993
Jer 25:30 The Lord shall **r.** from on high, ... 7580
Jer 25:30 mightily **r.** upon his habitation; 7580
Jer 31:35 the sea when the waves thereof **r.**; 1993
Jer 50:42 their voice shall **r.** like the sea, and 1993
Jer 51:38 They shall **r.** together like lions: 7580
Jer 51:55 her waves do **r.** like great waters, ... 1993
Ho 11:10 the Lord: he shall **r.** like a lion: 7580
Ho 11:10 when he shall **r.**, then the children 7580
Joe 3:16 The Lord also shall **r.** out of Zion, ... 7580
Am 1:2 he said, The Lord will **r.** from Zion, ... 7580
Am 3:4 Will a lion **r.** in the forest, when he 7580

ROARED
Jg 14:5 a young lion **r.** against him. 7580
Ps 38:8 **r.** by reason of the disquietness of 7580
Isa 51:15 divided the sea, whose waves **r.**: 1993
Jer 2:15 The young lions **r.** upon him, and 7580
Am 3:8 The lion hath **r.**, who will not fear? 7580

ROARETH
Job 37:4 After it a voice **r.**: he thundereth 7580
Jer 6:23 mercy; their voice **r.** like the sea; 1993
Re 10:3 a loud voice, as when a lion **r.**: *3455*

ROARING See also ROARINGS.
Job 4:10 The **r.** of the lion, and the voice of 7581
Ps 22:1 me, and from the words of my **r.**? 7581
Ps 22:13 as a ravening and a **r.** lion. 7580
Ps 32:3 my bones waxed old through my **r.** 7581
Pr 19:12 king's wrath is as the **r.** of a lion; 5099
Pr 20:2 fear of a king is as the **r.** of a lion: 5099
Pr 28:15 As a **r.** lion, and a ranging bear; 5098
Isa 5:29 Their **r.** shall be like a lion, they 7581
Isa 5:30 shall roar...like the **r.** of the sea: 5100
Isa 31:4 and the young lion **r.** on his prey, ... 1897
Eze 19:7 thereof, by the noise of his **r.** 7581
Eze 22:25 like a **r.** lion ravening the prey; 7580
Zep 3:3 princes within her are **r.** lions; 7580
Zec 11:3 a voice of the **r.** of young lions; 7581
Lu 21:25 **the sea and the waves r.**; *2278*
1Pe 5:8 devil, as a **r.** lion, walketh about, ... *5612*

ROARINGS
Job 3:24 **r.** are poured out like the waters. 7581

ROAST See also ROASTED; ROASTETH.
Ex 12:8 the flesh in that night, **r.** with fire, ... 6748
Ex 12:9 at all with water, but **r.** with fire; 6748
De 16:7 And thou shalt **r.** and eat it in the 1310
1Sa 2:15 Give flesh to **r.** for the priest; for 6740
Isa 44:16 He roasteth **r.**, and is satisfied: 6748

ROASTED
2Ch 35:13 And they **r.** the passover with fire 1310
Isa 44:19 I have **r.** flesh, and eaten it: and 6740
Jer 29:22 whom the king of Babylon **r.** in the 7033

ROASTETH
Pr 12:27 slothful man **r.** not that which he 2760
Isa 44:16 he **r.** roast, and is satisfied: yea, ... 6740

ROB See also ROBBED; ROBBETH.
Le 19:13 thy neighbour, neither **r.** him: 1497
Le 26:22 which shall **r.** you of your children, ... 7921
1Sa 23:1 and they **r.** the threshingfloors. 8154
Pr 22:22 **R.** not the poor, because he is 1497
Isa 10:2 that they may **r.** the fatherless! 962
Isa 17:14 us, and the lot of them that **r.** us. 962
Eze 39:10 and **r.** those that robbed them, saith 962
Mal 3:8 Will a man **r.** God? Yet ye have 6906

ROBBED
Jg 9:25 they **r.** all that came along that 1497
2Sa 17:8 as a bear **r.** of her whelps in the 7909
Ps 119:61 bands of the wicked have **r.** me: 5749
Pr 17:12 Let a bear **r.** of her whelps meet a 7909
Isa 10:13 and have **r.** their treasures, and I 8154
Isa 42:22 But this is a people **r.** and spoiled; 962
Jer 50:37 her treasures; and they shall be **r.**, ... 962
Eze 33:15 pledge, give again that he had **r.**, ... 1500
Eze 39:10 rob those that **r.** them, saith the 962
Mal 3:8 man rob God? Yet ye have **r.** me. 6906
Mal 3:8 ye say, Wherein have we **r.** thee? 6906
Mal 3:9 for ye have **r.** me, even this whole 6906
2Co 11:8 I **r.** other churches, taking wages *4813*

ROBBER See also ROBBERS.
Job 5:5 **r.** swalloweth up their substance. 6782
Job 18:9 the **r.** shall prevail against him. 6782
Eze 18:10 If he beget a son that is a **r.**, a 6530
Joh 10:1 **way, the same is a thief and a r.** *3027*
Joh 18:40 Barabbas. Now Barabbas was a **r.** *3027*

ROBBERS
Job 12:6 The tabernacles of **r.** prosper, and 7703
Isa 42:24 for a spoil, and Israel to the **r.**? 962
Jer 7:11 become a den of **r.** in your eyes? 6530
Eze 7:22 for the **r.** shall enter into it, and 6530
Da 11:14 the **r.** of thy people shall exalt 6530
Ho 6:9 And as troops of **r.** wait for a man, ...
Ho 7:1 and the troop of **r.** spoileth without ....
Ob 5 thieves came to thee, if **r.** by night, ... 7703
Joh 10:8 **came before me are thieves and r.** ..*3027*
Ac 19:37 which are neither **r.** of churches, ... *2417*
2Co 11:26 in perils of waters, in perils of **r.**, ... *3027*

ROBBERY
Ps 62:10 and become not vain in **r.**: if 1498
Pr 21:7 The **r.** of the wicked shall destroy 7701
Isa 61:8 I hate **r.** for burnt offering; and 1498
Eze 22:29 used oppression, and exercised **r.**, ... 1498
Am 3:10 violence and **r.** in their palaces. 7701
Na 3:1 city! it is all full of lies and **r.**; the 6563
Php 2:6 it not **r.** to be equal with God: *725*

ROBBETH
Pr 28:24 Whoso **r.** his father or his mother, ... 1497

ROBE See also ROBES; WARDROBE.
Ex 28:4 and a **r.**, and a broidered coat, ... 4598
Ex 28:31 make the **r.** of the ephod all of blue. ... 4598
Ex 28:34 upon the hem of the **r.** round about. ... 4598
Ex 29:5 the coat, and the **r.** of the ephod, ... 4598
Ex 39:22 the **r.** of the ephod of woven work, ... 4598
Ex 39:23 was an hole in the midst of the **r.**, ... 4598
Ex 39:24 they made upon the hems of the **r.** 4598
Ex 39:25 upon the hem of the **r.**, round 4598
Ex 39:26 round about the hem of the **r.** to 4598
Le 8:7 clothed him with the **r.**, and put 4598
1Sa 18:4 Jonathan stripped himself of the **r.** 4598
1Sa 24:4 cut off the skirt of Saul's **r.** privily. 4598
1Sa 24:11 see the skirt of thy **r.** in my hand: 4598
1Sa 24:11 in that I cut off the skirt of thy **r.**, ... 4598
1Ch 15:27 David was clothed with a **r.** of fine 4598
Job 29:14 my judgment was as a **r.** and a 4598
Isa 22:21 And I will clothe him with thy **r.** 3801
Isa 61:10 me with the **r.** of righteousness, ... 4598
Jon 3:6 and he laid his **r.** from him, and 155
Mic 2:8 ye pull off the **r.** with the garment 145
Mt 27:28 him, and put on him a scarlet **r.** *5511*
Mt 27:31 they took the **r.** off from him, and *5511*
Lu 15:22 **Bring forth the best r., and put it** ..*4749*
Lu 23:11 and arrayed him in a gorgeous **r.**, ... *2066*
Joh 19:2 and they put on him a purple **r.**, ... *2440*
Joh 19:5 crown of thorns, and the purple **r.** *2440*

ROBES
2Sa 13:18 for with such **r.** were the king's 4598
1Ki 22:10 his throne, having put on their **r.**, ... 899
1Ki 22:30 the battle; but put thou on thy **r.** 899
2Ch 18:9 on his throne, clothed in their **r.**, ... 899
2Ch 18:29 the battle; but put thou on thy **r.** 899
Eze 26:16 thrones, and lay away their **r.**, ... 4598
Lu 20:46 **which desire to walk in long r.** *4749*
Re 6:11 white **r.** were given unto every one *4749*
Re 7:9 clothed with white **r.**, and palms in *4749*
Re 7:13 these which are arrayed in white **r.**? ... *4749*
Re 7:14 have washed their **r.**, and made *4749*

ROBOAM (ro-bo'-am) See also REHOBOAM.
Mt 1:7 Solomon began **R.**; and **R.** begat *4497*

ROCK See also ROCKS.
Ex 17:6 thee there upon the **r.** in Horeb; 6697
Ex 17:6 and thou shall smite the **r.**, and 6697
Ex 33:21 me, and thou shalt stand upon a **r.** 6697
Ex 33:22 I will put thee in a clift of a **r.**, and 6697
Nu 20:8 ye unto the **r.** before their eyes; 5553
Nu 20:8 forth to them water out of the **r.**, ... 5553
Nu 20:10 congregation together before the **r.**, ... 5553
Nu 20:10 we fetch you water out of this **r.**? 5553
Nu 20:11 with his rod he smote the **r.** twice: 5553
Nu 24:21 and thou puttest thy nest in a **r.** 5553
De 8:15 forth water out of the **r.** of flint; 6697
De 32:4 He is the **R.**, his work is perfect: 6697
De 32:13 him to suck honey out of the **r.**, ... 5553
De 32:13 and oil out of the flinty **r.**; 6697
De 32:15 esteemed the **R.** of his salvation. 6697

De 32:18 Of the **R.** that begat thee thou art...... 6697
De 32:30 except their **R.** and sold them, and..... 6697
De 32:31 For their **r.** is not as our **R.**, even..... 6697
De 32:37 gods, their **r.** in whom they trusted, ... 6697
Jg 1:36 from the **r.**, and upward.................. 5553
Jg 6:20 cakes, and lay them upon this **r.**, ... 5553
Jg 6:21 there rose up fire out of the **r.**, ... 6697
Jg 6:26 thy God upon the top of this **r.**,......... 4581
Jg 7:25 they slew Oreb upon the **r.** Oreb,...... 6697
Jg 13:19 offered it upon a **r.** unto the Lord: 6697
Jg 15:8 dwelt in the top of the **r.** Etam.......... 5553
Jg 15:11 went to the top of the **r.** Etam, ... 5553
Jg 15:13 and brought him up from the **r.**.......... 5553
Jg 20:45 wilderness unto the **r.** of Rimmon:....... 5553
Jg 20:47 wilderness unto the **r.** Rimmon, ... 5553
Jg 20:47 and abode in the **r.** Rimmon four......... 5553
Jg 21:13 that were in the **r.** Rimmon, and........ 5553
1Sa 2:2 is there any **r.** like our God. 6697
1Sa 14:4 was a sharp **r.** on the one side, ... 5553
1Sa 14:4 and a sharp **r.** on the other side:......... 5553
1Sa 23:25 wherefore he came down into a **r.**,..... 5553
2Sa 21:10 and spread it for her upon the **r.**,....... 6697
2Sa 22:2 said, The Lord is my **r.**, and my........ 5553
2Sa 22:3 The God of my **r.**; in him, will I......... 6697
2Sa 22:32 and who is a **r.**, save our God?......... 6697
2Sa 22:47 Lord liveth; and blessed be my **r.**;...... 6697
2Sa 22:47 the God of the **r.** of my salvation. 6697
2Sa 23:3 said, the **R.** of Israel spake to me, ... 6697
1Ch 11:15 went down to the **r.** to David, into..... 6697
2Ch 25:12 them unto the top of the **r.**, and 5553
2Ch 25:12 them down from the top of the **r.**,...... 5553
Ne 9:15 them out of the **r.** for their thirst,....... 5553
Job 14:18 the **r.** is removed out of his place....... 6697
Job 18:4 the **r.** be removed out of his place? 6697
Job 19:24 iron pen and lead in the **r.** for ever!.... 6697
Job 24:8 embrace the **r.** for want of a shelter. .. 6697
Job 28:9 putteth forth his hand upon the **r.**;...... 2496
Job 29:6 the **r.** poured me out rivers of oil;...... 6697
Job 39:1 wild goats of the **r.** bring forth? 5553
Job 39:28 dwelleth and abideth on the **r.**, ... 5553
Job 39:28 upon the crag of the **r.**, and the......... 5553
Ps 18:2 The Lord is my **r.**, and my fortress,..... 5553
Ps 18:31 Lord? or who is a **r.** save our God?.... 6697
Ps 18:46 Lord liveth; and blessed be my **r.**;...... 6697
Ps 27:5 me; he shall set me up upon a **r.**. 6697
Ps 28:1 Unto thee will I cry, O Lord my **r.**;.... 6697
Ps 31:2 be thou my strong **r.**, for an house...... 6697
Ps 31:3 thou art my **r.** and my fortress;......... 5553
Ps 40:2 clay, and set my feet upon a **r.**,......... 5553
Ps 42:9 I will say unto God my **r.**, Why hast.... 5553
Ps 61:2 lead me to the **r.** that is higher.......... 6697
Ps 62:2 He only is my **r.** and my salvation;..... 6697
Ps 62:6 He only is my **r.** and my salvation: 6697
Ps 62:7 the **r.** of my strength, and my........... 6697
Ps 71:3 thou art my **r.** and my fortress. 5553
Ps 78:16 brought streams also out of the **r.**,..... 5553
Ps 78:20 he smote the **r.**, that the waters........ 6697
Ps 78:35 remembered that God was their **r.**,.... 6697
Ps 81:16 with honey out of the **r.** should I........ 6697
Ps 89:26 God, and the **r.** of my salvation. 6697
Ps 92:15 he is my **r.**, and there is no............. 6697
Ps 94:22 And my God is the **r.** of my refuge. ... 6697
Ps 95:1 noise to the **r.** of our salvation.......... 6697
Ps 105:41 He opened the **r.**, and the waters 6697
Ps 114:8 turned the **r.** into a standing water, ... 6697
Pr 30:19 the way of a serpent upon a **r.**; 6697
Ca 2:14 that are in the clefts of the **r.**, in 5553
Isa 2:10 Enter into the **r.**, and hide thee 6697
Isa 8:14 stumbling and for a **r.** of offence 6697
Isa 10:26 slaughter of Midian at...**r.** of Oreb:..... 6697
Isa 17:10 mindful of the **r.** of thy strength,........ 6697
Isa 22:16 an habitation for himself in a **r.**?......... 5553
Isa 32:2 shadow of a great **r.** in a weary land... 5553
Isa 42:11 let the inhabitants of the **r.** sing, ... 5553
Isa 48:21 the waters to flow out of the **r.** for..... 6697
Isa 48:21 he clave the **r.** also, and the waters.... 6697
Isa 51:1 unto the **r.** whence ye are hewn, ... 6697
Jer 5:3 made their faces harder than a **r.**; 5553
Jer 13:4 and hide it there in a hole of the **r.**...... 5553
Jer 18:14 snow...from the **r.** of the field? 6697
Jer 21:13 of the valley, and **r.** of the plain, ... 6697
Jer 23:29 hammer that breaketh the **r.** in............ 5553
Jer 48:28 the cities, and dwell in the **r.**, and....... 5553
Jer 49:16 that dwellest in the clefts of the **r.**, ... 5553
Eze 24:7 her; she set it upon the top of a **r.**;..... 5553
Eze 24:8 set her blood upon the top of a **r.**, ... 5553
Eze 26:4 and make thee like the top of **r.**......... 5553
Eze 26:14 will make thee like the top of a **r.**: 5553
Am 6:12 Shall horses run upon the **r.**? will....... 5553
Ob 3 that dwellest in the clefts of the **r.**, ... 5553
Mt 7:24 **which built his house upon a r.**..... *4073*
Mt 7:25 **not: for it was founded upon a r.** .. *4073*
Mt 16:18 **this r. I will build my church;**....... *4073*
Mt 27:60 which he had hewn out in the **r.**: *4073*
Mk 15:46 sepulchre...was hewn out of a **r.**,....... *4073*
Lu 6:48 **and laid the foundation on a r.**...... *4073*
Lu 6:48 **it: for it was founded upon a r.**..... *4073*
Lu 8:6 **And some fell upon a r.; and as** *4073*
Lu 8:13 **They on the r. are they, which,**..... *4073*
Ro 9:33 a stumblingstone and **r.** of offence: *4073*
1Co 10:4 they drank of that spiritual **R.** that....... *4073*
1Co 10:4 them: and that **R.** was Christ. *4073*
1Pe 2:8 a **r.** of offence, even to them which.... *4073*

ROCKS

Nu 23:9 from the top of the **r.** I see him,........ 6697
1Sa 13:6 caves, and in thickets, and in **r.**, ... 5553
1Sa 24:2 men upon the **r.** of the wild goats. 6697
1Ki 19:11 brake in pieces the **r.** before the........ 5553
Job 28:10 cutteth out rivers among the **r.**;......... 6697
Job 30:6 caves of the earth, and in the **r.**. 3710
Ps 78:15 He clave the **r.** in the wilderness, ... 6697
Ps 104:18 goats; and the **r.** for the conies.......... 5553
Pr 30:26 make they their houses in the **r.**: 5553
Isa 2:19 shall go into the holes of the **r.**,........ 6697
Isa 2:21 To go into the clefts of the **r.**, and..... 6697
Isa 2:21 and into the tops of the ragged **r.**,...... 5553
Isa 7:19 valleys, and in the holes of the **r.**, ... 5553
Isa 33:16 shall be the munitions of **r.**: 5553
Isa 57:5 valleys under the clifts of the **r.**?......... 5553
Jer 4:29 and climb up upon the **r.**: every......... 3710
Jer 16:16 hill, and out of the holes of the **r.**........ 5553
Jer 51:25 and roll thee down from the **r.**,.......... 5553
Na 1:6 the **r.** are thrown down by him........... 6697
Mt 27:51 earth did quake, and the **r.** rent;........ *4073*
Ac 27:29 we should have fallen upon **r.**, ... *5138,5117*
Re 6:15 and in the **r.** of the mountains; *4073*
Re 6:16 And said to the mountains and **r.**,....... *4073*

ROD See also RODS.

Ex 4:2 in thine hand? And he said, A **r.** 4294
Ex 4:4 it, and it became a **r.** in his hand:....... 4294
Ex 4:17 shalt take this **r.** in thine hand, ... 4294
Ex 4:20 and Moses took the **r.** of God in his ... 4294
Ex 7:9 Take thy **r.**, and cast it before........... 4294
Ex 7:10 and Aaron cast down his **r.** before....... 4294
Ex 7:12 they cast down every man his **r.**,....... 4294
Ex 7:12 Aaron's **r.** swallowed up their rods. 4294
Ex 7:15 **r.** which was turned to a serpent 4294
Ex 7:17 smite with the **r.**...in mine hand......... 4294
Ex 7:19 Say unto Aaron, Take thy **r.**, and........ 4294
Ex 7:20 he lifted up the **r.**, and smote the....... 4294
Ex 8:5 Stretch forth thine hand with thy **r.** 4294
Ex 8:16 Stretch out thy **r.**, and smite the........ 4294
Ex 8:17 stretched out his hand with his **r.**,...... 4294
Ex 9:23 stretched...his **r.** toward heaven:......... 4294
Ex 10:13 stretched forth his **r.** over the land....... 4294
Ex 14:16 but lift thou up thy **r.**, and stretch...... 4294
Ex 17:5 and thy **r.**, wherewith thou smotest.... 4294
Ex 17:9 with the **r.** of God in mine hand.......... 4294
Ex 21:20 his servant, or his maid, with a **r.**, ... 7626
Le 27:32 of whatsoever passeth under the **r.**,..... 7626
Nu 17:2 and take of every one of them a **r.**..... 4294
Nu 17:2 thou every man's name upon his **r.**..... 4294
Nu 17:3 Aaron's name upon the **r.** of Levi:...... 4294
Nu 17:3 for one **r.** shall be for the head of 4294
Nu 17:5 the man's **r.**, whom I shall choose, ... 4294
Nu 17:6 their princes gave him a **r.** apiece,...... 4294
Nu 17:6 **r.** of Aaron was among their rods........ 4294
Nu 17:8 **r.** of Aaron for the house of Levi 4294
Nu 17:9 looked, and took every man his **r.**....... 4294
Nu 17:10 Bring Aaron's **r.** again before the 4294
Nu 20:8 Take the **r.**, and gather thou the........ 4294
Nu 20:9 Moses took the **r.** from before the 4294
Nu 20:11 with his **r.** he smote the rock twice: ... 4294
1Sa 14:27 end of the **r.** that was in his hand,...... 4294
1Sa 14:43 end of the **r.** that was in mine hand, ... 4294
2Sa 7:14 chasten him with the **r.** of man, ... 7626
Job 9:34 Let him take his **r.** away from me, ... 7626
Job 21:9 neither is the **r.** of God upon them. 7626
Ps 2:9 shalt break them with a **r.** of iron;...... 7626
Ps 23:4 **r.** and thy staff they comfort me. 7626
Ps 74:2 the **r.** of thine inheritance, which........ 7626
Ps 89:32 their transgression with the **r.**, ... 7626
Ps 110:2 the **r.** of thy strength out of Zion: 4294
Ps 125:3 the **r.** of the wicked shall not rest...... 7626
Pr 10:13 a **r.** is for the back of him that is 7626
Pr 13:24 that spareth his **r.** hateth his son:....... 7626
Pr 14:3 mouth of...foolish is a **r.** of pride:....... 2415
Pr 22:8 and the **r.** of his anger shall fail......... 7626
Pr 22:15 **r.** of correction shall drive it far 7626
Pr 23:13 for if thou beatest him with the **r.**, ... 7626
Pr 23:14 Thou shalt beat him with the **r.**, ... 7626
Pr 26:3 the ass, and a **r.** for the fool's back. ... 7626
Pr 29:15 The **r.** and reproof give wisdom: 7626
Isa 9:4 shoulder, the **r.** of his oppressor, ... 7626
Isa 10:5 the **r.** of mine anger, and the staff...... 7626
Isa 10:15 **r.** should shake itself against them...... 7626
Isa 10:24 he shall smite thee with a **r.**, and....... 7626
Isa 10:26 and as his **r.** was upon the sea, so..... 4294
Isa 11:1 forth a **r.** out of the stem of Jesse,...... 2415
Isa 11:4 smite the earth with the **r.** of his 7626
Isa 14:29 **r.** of him that smote thee is broken: ... 7626
Isa 28:27 a staff, and the cummin with a **r.**. 7626
Isa 30:31 beaten down, which smote with a **r.**. .. 7626
Jer 1:11 I said, I see a **r.** of an almond tree..... 4731
Jer 10:16 Israel is the **r.** of his inheritance: 7626
Jer 48:17 staff broken, and the beautiful **r.**! 4731
Jer 51:19 Israel is the **r.** of his inheritance: 7626
La 3:1 seen affliction by the **r.** of his wrath.... 7626
Eze 7:10 the **r.** hath blossomed, pride hath....... 4294
Eze 7:11 is risen up into a **r.** of wickedness: 4294
Eze 19:14 is gone out of a **r.** of her branches, ... 4294
Eze 19:14 hath no strong **r.** to be a sceptre 4294
Eze 20:37 cause you to pass under the **r.**, ... 7626
Eze 21:10 it contemneth the **r.** of my son, as 7626
Eze 21:13 if the sword comtemn even the **r.**?..... 7626
Mic 5:1 smite the judge of Israel with a **r.** 7626
Mic 6:9 hear ye the **r.**, and who hath............. 4294
Mic 7:14 Feed thy people with thy **r.**, the 7626
1Co 4:21 shall I come unto you with a **r.**, or..... *4464*
Heb 9:4 Aaron's **r.** that budded, and the *4464*
Re 2:27 **shall rule them with a r. of iron;** .. *4464*
Re 11:1 was given me a reed like unto a **r.**: ... *4464*
Re 12:5 to rule all nations with a **r.** of iron: *4464*
Re 19:15 he shall rule them with a **r.** of iron: *4464*

RODANIM See DODANIM.

RODE

Ge 24:61 and they **r.** upon the camels, and 7392
Jg 10:4 had thirty sons that **r.** on thirty ass 7392
Jg 12:14 that **r.** on threescore and ten ass 7392
1Sa 25:20 And it was so, as she **r.** on the ass, ... 7392
1Sa 25:42 and arose, and **r.** upon an ass,........... 7392
1Sa 30:17 young men, which **r.** upon camels,....... 7392
2Sa 18:9 Absalom **r.** upon a mule, and the........ 7392
2Sa 22:11 he **r.** upon a cherub, and did fly:........ 7392
1Ki 13:13 him the ass: and he **r.** thereon, ... 7392
1Ki 18:45 And Ahab **r.**, and went to Jezreel........ 7392
2Ki 9:16 So Jehu **r.** in a chariot, and went to.... 7392
2Ki 9:25 I and thou **r.** together after Ahab 7392
Ne 2:12 me, save the beast that I **r.** upon....... 7392
Es 8:14 the posts that **r.** upon mules and........ 7392
Ps 18:10 he **r.** upon a cherub, and did fly: 7392

RODS

Ge 30:37 Jacob took him **r.** of green poplar, ... 4731
Ge 30:37 white appear which was in the **r.**......... 4731
Ge 30:38 he set the **r.** which he had pilled........ 4731
Ge 30:39 the flocks conceived before the **r.**,....... 4731
Ge 30:41 Jacob laid the **r.** before the eyes of..... 4731
Ge 30:41 they might conceive among the **r.**........ 4731
Ex 7:12 Aaron's rod swallowed up their **r.**........ 4294
Nu 17:2 house of their fathers, twelve **r.**:......... 4294
Nu 17:6 fathers' houses, even twelve **r.**:......... 4294
Nu 17:6 rod of Aaron was among their **r.**. 4294
Nu 17:7 laid up the **r.** before the Lord in 4294
Nu 17:9 Moses brought out all the **r.** from 4294
Eze 19:11 strong **r.** for the sceptres of them 4294
Eze 19:12 her strong **r.** were broken and........... 4294
2Co 11:25 Thrice was I beaten with **r.**, once *4463*

ROE See also ROEBUCK; ROES.

2Sa 2:18 was as light of foot as a wild **r.**.......... 6643
Pr 5:19 the loving hind and pleasant **r.**; 3280
Pr 6:5 Deliver thyself as a **r.** from the.......... 6643
Ca 2:9 beloved is like a **r.** or a young hart:..... 6643
Ca 2:17 be thou like a **r.** or a young hart 6643
Ca 8:14 thou like to a **r.** or to a young hart..... 6643
Isa 13:14 And it shall be as the chased **r.**, ... 6643

ROEBUCK See also ROEBUCKS.
De 12:15 as of the **r.**, and as of the hart. 6643
De 12:22 as the **r.** and the hart is eaten, so 6643
De 14:5 The hart, and the **r.**, and the 6643
De 15:22 it alike, as the **r.**, and as the hart 6643

ROEBUCKS
1Ki 4:23 harts, and **r.**, and fallowdeer, 6643

ROES
1Ch 12:8 were as swift as the **r.** upon the 6643
Ca 2:7 by the **r.**, and by the hinds of the 6643
Ca 3:5 by the **r.**, and by the hinds of the 6643
Ca 4:5 like two young **r.** that are twins, 6646
Ca 7:3 like two young **r.** that are twins. 6646

ROGEL See EN-ROGEL.

ROGELIM (ro'-ghel-im)
2Sa 17:27 and Barzillai the Gileadite of **R.**, 7274
2Sa 19:31 the Gileadite came down from **R.**, 7274

ROHGAH (ro'-gah)
1Ch 7:34 the sons of Shamer; Ahi, and **R.**, 7303

ROI See LAHAI-ROI.

ROLL See also ROLLED; ROLLETH; ROLLING; ROLLS.
Ge 29:8 and till they **r.** the stone from the 1556
Jos 10:18 **R.** great stones upon the mouth of 1556
1Sa 14:33 **r.** a great stone unto me this day. 1556
Ezr 6:2 in the province of the Medes, a **r.**, 4040
Isa 8:1 Take thee a great **r.**, and write in 1549
Jer 36:2 Take thee a **r.** of a book, and write 4039
Jer 36:4 unto him, upon a **r.** of a book, 4039
Jer 36:6 and read in the **r.**, which thou hast 4039
Jer 36:14 Take in thine hand the **r.** wherein 4039
Jer 36:14 Baruch...took the **r.** in his hand, 4039
Jer 36:20 they laid up the **r.** in the chamber 4039
Jer 36:21 king sent Jehudi to fetch the **r.** 4039
Jer 36:23 until all the **r.** was consumed in 4039
Jer 36:25 king that he would not burn the **r.** 4039
Jer 36:27 that the king had burned the **r.**, 4039
Jer 36:28 Take thee again another **r.**, and 4039
Jer 36:28 words that were in the first **r.**, 4039
Jer 36:29 Thou hast burned this **r.**, saying, 4039
Jer 36:32 Then took Jeremiah another **r.**, 4039
Jer 51:25 and **r.** thee down from the rocks, 1556
Eze 2:9 and, lo, a **r.** of a book was therein; 4040
Eze 3:1 eat this **r.**, and go speak unto the 4040
Eze 3:2 and he caused me to eat that **r.** 4040
Eze 3:3 fill thy bowels with this **r.** that I 4040
Mic 1:10 of Aphrah **r.** thyself in the dust 6428
Zec 5:1 and looked, and behold a flying **r.** 4040
Zec 5:2 I see a flying **r.**; the length thereof 4040
Mk 16:3 Who shall **r.** us away the stone *617*

ROLLED
Ge 29:3 they **r.** the stone from the well's 1556
Ge 29:10 **r.** the stone from the well's mouth, 1556
Jos 5:9 I **r.** away the reproach of Egypt 1556
Job 30:14 they **r.** themselves upon me 1556
Isa 9:5 noise, and garments **r.** in blood; 1556
Isa 34:4 the heavens shall be **r.** together as 1556
Mt 27:60 and he **r.** a great stone to the door *4351*
Mt 28:2 came and **r.** back the stone from *617*
Mk 15:46 and **r.** a stone unto the door of the *4351*
Mk 16:4 saw that the stone was **r.** away: *617*
Lu 24:2 stone **r.** away from the sepulchre *617*
Re 6:14 as a scroll when it is **r.** together; *1507*

ROLLER
Eze 30:21 to put a **r.** to bind it, to make it 2848

ROLLETH
Pr 26:27 he that **r.** a stone, it will return 1556

ROLLING
Isa 17:13 a **r.** thing before the whirlwind 1534

ROLLS
Ezr 6:1 was made in the house of the **r.**, 5609

ROMAMTI-EZER (romam''-ti-e'-zur)
1Ch 25:4 Giddalti, and **R.**, Joshbekashah, 7320
1Ch 25:31 The four and twentieth to **R.**, he, 7320

ROMAN (ro'-mun) See also ROMANS.
Ac 22:25 you to scourge a man that is a **R.**, *4514*
Ac 22:26 thou doest: for this man is a **R.** *4514*
Ac 22:27 Tell me, art thou a **R.**? He said, *4514*
Ac 22:29 after he knew that he was a **R.**, and *4514*
Ac 23:27 having understood that he was a **R.** *4514*

ROMANS (ro'-muns)
Joh 11:48 **R.** shall come and take away both *4514*
Ac 16:21 neither to observe, being **R.** *4514*
Ac 16:37 us openly uncondemned, being **R.**, *4514*
Ac 16:38 when they heard that they were **R.** *4514*
Ac 25:16 not the manner of the **R.** to deliver *4514*
Ac 28:17 Jerusalem into the hands of the **R.** *4514*
Ro *general* *title* Of Paul The Apostle To The **R.** *4514*
Ro *subscr.* Written to the **R.** from *4514*

ROME (rome) See also ROMAN.
Ac 2:10 and strangers of **R.**, Jews and *4516*
Ac 18:2 all Jews to depart from **R.**:) and *4516*
Ac 19:21 have been there, I must also see **R.** *4516*
Ac 23:11 **must thou bear witness also at R.** *4516*
Ac 28:14 days: and so we went toward **R.** *4516*
Ac 28:16 And when we came to **R.**, the *4516*
Ro 1:7 To all that be in **R.**, beloved of God, *4516*
Ro 1:15 gospel to you that are at **R.** also. *4516*
Ga *subscr.* the Galatians written from **R.** *4516*
Eph *subscr.* from **R.** unto the Ephesians *4516*
Php *subscr.* to the Philippians from **R.** by *4516*
Col *subscr.* Written from **R.** to the *4516*
2Ti 1:17 when he was in **R.**, he sought me *4516*
2Ti *subscr.* was written from **R.**, when *4516*
Phm *subscr.* Written from **R.** to Philemon, *4516*

ROOF See also ROOFS.
Ge 19:8 they under the shadow of my **r.** 6982
De 22:8 shalt make a battlement for thy **r.**, 1406
Jos 2:6 them up to the **r.** of the house, and 1406
Jos 2:6 she had laid in order upon the **r.** 1406
Jos 2:8 she came up unto them upon the **r.**; 1406
Jg 16:27 upon the **r.** about three thousand 1406
2Sa 11:2 upon the **r.** of the king's house: 1406
2Sa 11:2 and from the **r.** he saw a woman 1406
2Sa 18:24 the watchman went up to the **r.** 1406
Ne 8:16 every one upon the **r.** of his house, 1406
Job 29:10 cleaved to the **r.** of their mouth. 2441
Ps 137:6 cleave to the **r.** of my mouth; if I 2441
Ca 7:9 **r.** of thy mouth like the best wine 2441
La 4:4 cleaveth to the **r.** of his mouth for 2441
Eze 3:26 cleave to the **r.** of thy mouth, 2441
Eze 40:13 **r.** of one little chamber to the **r.** of 1406
Mt 8:8 thou shouldest come under my **r.** *4721*
Mk 2:4 uncovered the **r.** where he was: *4721*
Lu 7:6 thou shouldest enter under my **r.** *4721*

ROOFS
Jer 19:13 upon whose **r.** they have burned 1406
Jer 32:29 upon whose **r.** they have offered 1406

ROOM See also ROOMS.
Ge 24:23 is there **r.** in thy father's house 4725
Ge 24:25 straw...enough, and **r.** to lodge in. 4725
Ge 24:31 the house, and **r.** for the camels. 4725
Ge 26:22 now the Lord hath made **r.** for us, 7337
2Sa 19:13 me continually in the **r.** of Joab. 8478
1Ki 2:35 of Jehoiada in his **r.** over the host: 8478
1Ki 2:35 the king put in the **r.** of Abiathar. 8478
1Ki 5:1 him king in the **r.** of his father: 8478
1Ki 5:5 I will set upon thy throne in thy **r.**, 8478
1Ki 8:20 I am risen up in the **r.** of David my 8478
1Ki 19:16 thou anoint to be prophet in thy **r.** 8478
2Ki 15:25 he killed him, and reigned in his **r.** 8478
2Ki 23:34 king in the **r.** of Josiah his father, 8478
2Ch 6:10 for I am risen up in the **r.** of David 8478
2Ch 26:1 king in the **r.** of his father Amaziah. 8478
Ps 31:8 thou hast set my feet in a large **r.** 4800
Ps 80:9 Thou preparedst **r.** before it, and
Pr 18:16 A man's gift maketh **r.** for him, 7337
Mal 3:10 shall not be **r.** enough to receive it.
Mt 2:22 Judaea in the **r.** of his father Herod, *473*
Mk 2:2 there was no **r.** to receive them, *5562*
Mk 14:15 **shew you a large upper r. furnished** *508*
Lu 2:7 there was no **r.** for them in the *5117*
Lu 12:17 **no r. where to bestow my fruits?**
Lu 14:8 **sit not down in the highest r.** *4411*
Lu 14:9 **with shame to take the lowest r.** *5117*
Lu 14:10 **sit down in the lowest r.; that** *5117*
Lu 14:22 **commanded, and yet there is r.** *5117*
Lu 22:12 **you a large upper r. furnished:**
Ac 1:13 in, they went up into an upper **r.**, *5253*
Ac 24:27 Porcius Festus came into Felix' **r.**: *1240*
1Co 14:16 occupieth the **r.** of the unlearned *5117*

ROOMS
Ge 16:14 **r.** shalt thou make in the ark, and 7064
1Ki 20:24 place, and put captains in their **r.**: 8478
1Ch 4:41 unto this day, and dwelt in their **r.** 8478
Mt 23:6 **love the uppermost r. at feasts,** *4411*
Mk 12:39 **and the uppermost r. at feasts:** *4411*
Lu 14:7 how they chose out the chief **r.**; *4411*
Lu 20:46 **synagogues,...the chief r. at feasts;** *4411*

ROOT See also ROOTED; ROOTS.
De 29:18 among you a **r.** that beareth gall 8328
Jg 5:14 there a **r.** of them against Amalek; 8328
1Ki 14:15 **r.** up Israel out of this good land, 5428
2Ki 19:30 of Judah shall yet again take **r.** 8328
Job 5:3 I have seen the foolish taking **r.** 8327
Job 14:8 the **r.** thereof wax old in the earth, 8328
Job 19:28 the **r.** of the matter is found in me? 8328
Job 29:19 **r.** was spread out by the waters, 8328
Job 31:12 and would **r.** out all mine increase. 8327
Ps 52:5 and **r.** thee out of the land of the 8327
Ps 80:9 didst cause it to take deep **r.**, and it 8327
Pr 12:3 **r.** of the righteous shall not be 8328
Pr 12:12 **r.** of the righteous yieldeth fruit. 8328
Isa 5:24 so their **r.** shall be as rottenness, 8328
Isa 11:10 that day there shall be a **r.** of Jesse, 8328
Isa 14:29 out of the serpent's **r.** shall come 8328
Isa 14:30 I will kill thy **r.** with famine, and he 8328
Isa 27:6 that come of Jacob to take **r.** 8327
Isa 37:31 house of Judah shall again take **r.** 8328
Isa 40:24 their stock shall not take **r.** in the 8327
Isa 53:2 and as a **r.** out of a dry ground: 8328
Jer 1:10 to **r.** out, and to pull down, and to 5428
Jer 12:2 yea, they have taken **r.**: they grow, 8327
Eze 31:7 for his **r.** was by great waters. 8328
Ho 9:16 their **r.** is dried up, they shall bear 8328
Mal 4:1 leave them neither **r.** nor branch. 8328
Mt 3:10 ax is laid unto the **r.** of the trees: *4491*
Mt 13:6 **and because they had no r., they** *4491*
Mt 13:21 **Yet hath he not r. in himself, but** *4491*
Mt 13:29 **ye r. up also the wheat with them.** *1610*
Mk 4:6 **because it had no r., it withered** *4491*
Mk 4:17 **And have no r. in themselves, and.** *4491*
Lu 3:9 axe is laid unto the **r.** of the trees: *4491*
Lu 8:13 **these have no r., which for a while** *4491*
Lu 17:6 **Be thou plucked up by the r., and.** *1610*
Ro 11:16 and if the **r.** be holy, so are the *4491*
Ro 11:17 of the **r.** and fatness of the olive *4491*
Ro 11:18 bearest not the **r.**, but the **r.** thee *4491*
Ro 15:12 There shall be a **r.** of Jesse, and he *4491*
1Ti 6:10 love of money is the **r.** of all evil: *4491*
Heb 12:15 lest any **r.** of bitterness springing *4491*
Re 5:5 the tribe of Juda, the **R.** of David, *4491*
Re 22:16 **the r. and the offspring of David,** *4491*

ROOTED
De 29:28 the Lord **r.** them out of their land 5428
Job 18:14 His confidence shall be **r.** out of his 5423
Job 31:8 eat: yea, let my offspring be **r.** out. 8327
Pr 2:22 transgressors shall be **r.** out of it. 5255
Zep 2:4 day, and Ekron shall be **r.** up. 6131
Mt 15:13 **hath not planted, shall be r. up.** *1610*
Eph 3:17 ye, being **r.** and grounded in love, *4492*
Col 2:7 **R.** and built up in him, and *4492*

ROOTS
2Ch 7:20 will I pluck them up by the **r.** out 5428
Job 8:17 His **r.** are wrapped about the heap, 8328
Job 18:16 His **r.** shall be dried up beneath, 8328
Job 28:9 overturneth the mountains by the **r.** 8328
Job 30:4 and juniper **r.** for their meat. 8328
Isa 11:1 a Branch shall grow out of his **r.** 8328
Jer 17:8 spreadeth out her **r.** by the river, 8328
Eze 17:6 and the **r.** thereof were under him: 8328
Eze 17:7 vine did bend her **r.** toward him, 8328
Eze 17:9 shall he not pull up the **r.** thereof, 8328
Eze 17:9 to pluck it up by the **r.** thereof. 8328
Da 4:15 the stump of his **r.** in the earth, 8330
Da 4:23 leave the stump of the **r.** thereof in 8330
Da 4:26 to leave the stump of the tree **r.**; 8330
Da 7:8 first horns plucked up by the **r.**: 6132
Da 11:7 out of a branch of her **r.** shall one 8328
Ho 14:5 and cast forth his **r.** as Lebanon. 8328
Am 2:9 from above, and his **r.** from beneath. 8328
Mk 11:20 the fig tree dried up from the **r.** *4491*
Jude 12 twice dead, plucked up by the **r.**; *1610*

ROPE See also ROPES.
Isa 5:18 and sin as it were with a cart **r.** 5688

ROPES
Jg 16:11 If they bind me fast with new **r.** 5688

Jg 16:12 Delilah therefore took new **r.**, and 5688
2Sa 17:13 shall all Israel bring **r.** to that city, 2256
1Ki 20:31 on our loins, and **r.** upon our heads, 2256
1Ki 20:32 loins, and put **r.** on their heads, 2256
Ac 27:32 soldiers cut off the **r.** of the boat, *4979*

ROSE See also AROSE.
Ge 4:8 **r.** up against Abel his brother, 6965
Ge 18:16 And the men **r.** up from thence, 6965
Ge 19:1 Lot seeing them **r.** up to meet them; 6965
Ge 20:8 Abimelech **r.** early in the morning, 7925
Ge 21:14 Abraham **r.** up early in the morning, 7925
Ge 21:32 then Abimelech **r.** up, and Phichol 6965
Ge 22:3 And Abraham **r.** up early in the 7925
Ge 22:3 and **r.** up, and went unto the place 6965
Ge 22:19 they **r.** up and went together to 6965
Ge 24:54 and they **r.** up in the morning, and 6965
Ge 25:34 drink and **r.** up, and went his way: 6965
Ge 26:31 they **r.** up betimes in the morning, 7925
Ge 28:18 Jacob **r.** up early in the morning, 7925
Ge 31:17 Then Jacob **r.** up, and set his sons 6965
Ge 31:21 he **r.** up, and passed over the river, 6965
Ge 31:55 early in the morning Laban **r.** up, 7925
Ge 32:22 he **r.** up that night, and took his 6965
Ge 32:31 over Penuel the sun **r.** upon him, 2224
Ge 37:35 daughters **r.** up to comfort him; 6965
Ge 43:15 and **r.** up, and went down to Egypt, 6965
Ge 46:5 And Jacob **r.** up from Beer-sheba: 6965
Ex 10:23 neither **r.** any from his place for 6965
Ex 12:30 And Pharaoh **r.** up in the night, he, 6965
Ex 15:7 hast overthrown them that **r.** up 6965
Ex 24:4 and **r.** up early in the morning, 7925
Ex 24:13 And Moses **r.** up, and his minister 6965
Ex 32:6 And they **r.** up early on the morrow, 7925
Ex 32:6 eat and to drink, and **r.** up to play 6965
Ex 33:8 that all the people **r.** up, and stood 6965
Ex 33:10 the people **r.** up and worshipped, 6965
Ex 34:4 Moses **r.** up early in the morning, 7925
Nu 14:40 And they **r.** up early in the morning, 7925
Nu 16:2 And they **r.** up before Moses, with 6965
Nu 16:25 Moses **r.** up and went unto Dathan 6965
Nu 22:13 And Balaam **r.** up in the morning, 6965
Nu 22:14 And the princes of Moab **r.** up, and 6965
Nu 22:21 And Balaam **r.** up in the morning, 6965
Nu 24:25 And Balaam **r.** up, and went and 6965
Nu 25:7 **r.** up from among the congregation, 6965
De 33:2 and **r.** up from Seir unto them; 2224
Jos 3:1 Joshua **r.** early in the morning; 7925
Jos 3:16 the waters...**r.** up upon an heap 6965
Jos 6:12 Joshua **r.** early in the morning, 7925
Jos 6:15 they **r.** early about the dawning of 7925
Jos 7:16 Joshua **r.** up early in the morning, 7925
Jos 8:10 Joshua **r.** up early in the morning, 7925
Jos 8:14 that they hasted and **r.** up early, 7925
Jg 6:21 and there **r.** up fire out of the rock, 5927
Jg 6:38 for he **r.** up early on the morrow, 7925
Jg 7:1 Gideon,...**r.** up early, and pitched 7925
Jg 9:34 And Abimelech **r.** up, and all the 6965
Jg 9:35 and Abimelech **r.** up, and the people 6965
Jg 9:43 he **r.** up against them, and smote 6965
Jg 19:5 morning, that he **r.** up to depart: 6965
Jg 19:7, 9 when the man **r.** up to depart, 6965
Jg 19:10 but he **r.** up and departed, and came 6965
Jg 19:27 And her lord **r.** up in the morning, 6965
Jg 19:28 the man **r.** up, and gat him unto his 6965
Jg 20:5 the men of Gibeah **r.** against me, 6965
Jg 20:19 the children of Israel **r.** up in the 6965
Jg 20:33 men of Israel **r.** up out of their place, 6965
Jg 21:4 the people **r.** early, and built there 7925
Ru 3:14 she **r.** up before one could know 6965
1Sa 1:9 Hannah **r.** up after they had eaten 6965
1Sa 1:19 they **r.** up in the morning early, 7925
1Sa 15:12 when Samuel **r.** early to meet Saul 7925
1Sa 16:13 Samuel **r.** up, and went to Ramah. 6965
1Sa 17:20 David **r.** up early in the morning, 7925
1Sa 24:7 But Saul **r.** up out of the cave, and 6965
1Sa 28:25 Then they **r.** up, and went away 6965
1Sa 29:11 So David...**r.** up early to depart 7925
2Sa 15:2 And Absalom **r.** up early, and stood 7925
2Sa 18:31 of all them that **r.** up against thee. 6965
2Sa 22:40 them that **r.** up...hast thou subdued 6965
2Sa 22:49 above them that **r.** up against me: 6965
1Ki 1:49 and **r.** up, and went every man his 6965
1Ki 2:19 And the king **r.** up to meet her, and 6965
1Ki 3:21 I **r.** in the morning to give my child 6965
1Ki 21:16 **r.** up to go down to the vineyard 6965
2Ki 3:22 they **r.** up early in the morning, 7925
2Ki 3:24 **r.** up and smote the Moabites, so 6965
2Ki 7:5 And they **r.** up in the twilight, to 6965
2Ki 8:21 **r.** by night, and smote the Edomites 6965
2Ch 20:20 And they **r.** early in the morning, 7925
2Ch 21:9 **r.** up...and smote the Edomites 6965
2Ch 26:19 leprosy even **r.** up in his forehead 2224
2Ch 28:15 men...expressed by name **r.** up, 6965
2Ch 29:20 Then Hezekiah the king **r.** early, 7925
Ezr 1:5 Then **r.** up the chief of the fathers 6965
Ezr 5:2 Then **r.** up Zerubbabel the son of 6965
Ezr 10:6 Ezra **r.** up from before the house 6965
Ne 3:1 Then Eliashib the high priest **r.** up 6965
Ne 4:14 And I looked, and **r.** up, and said 6965
Job 1:5 and **r.** up early in the morning, 7925
Ps 18:39 subdued under me those that **r.** up 6965
Ps 124:2 our side, when men **r.** up against us: 6965
Ca 2:1 I am the **r.** of Sharon, and the lily 2261
Ca 5:5 I **r.** up to open to my beloved; 6965
Isa 35:1 rejoice, and blossom as the **r.** 2261
Jer 26:17 Then **r.** up certain of the elders 6965
La 3:62 lips of those that **r.** up against me, 6965
Da 3:24 was astonied, and **r.** up in haste, 6965
Da 8:27 I **r.** up, and did the king's business; 6965
Jon 1:3 Jonah **r.** up to flee unto Tarshish 6965
Jon 4:7 when the morning **r.** the next day, 5927
Zep 3:7 they **r.** early, and corrupted all 7925
Mk 10:50 garment, **r.**, and came to Jesus. *450*
Lu 4:29 **r.** up, and thrust him out of the city, *450*
Lu 5:25 immediately he **r.** up before them, *450*
Lu 5:28 he left all, **r.** up, and followed him. *450*
Lu 16:31 **though one r. from the dead** *450*
Lu 22:45 And when he **r.** up from prayer, and *450*
Lu 24:33 And they **r.** up the same hour, and *450*
Joh 11:31 that she **r.** up hastily and went out, *450*
Ac 5:17 Then the high priest **r.** up, and all *450*
Ac 5:36 For before these days **r.** up Theudas, *450*
Ac 5:37 After this man **r.** up Judas of *450*
Ac 10:41 with him after he **r.** from the dead. *450*
Ac 14:20 him, he **r.** up, and came into the city: *450*
Ac 15:5 **r.** up certain of the sect of the *1817*
Ac 15:7 Peter **r.** up, and said unto them, *450*
Ac 16:22 **r.** up together against them: and *4911*
Ac 26:30 the king **r.** up, and the governor, *450*
Ro 14:9 this end Christ both died, and **r.**, *450*
1Co 10:7 to eat and drink, and **r.** up to play. *450*
1Co 15:4 and that he **r.** again the third day *1453*
1Co 15:12 preached that he **r.** from the dead, *1453*
2Co 5:15 which died for them, and **r.** again. *1453*
1Th 4:14 that Jesus died and **r.** again, even *450*
Re 19:3 her smoke **r.** up for ever and ever. 305

ROSH (rosh)
Ge 46:21 and **R.**, Muppim, and Huppim, 7220

ROT See also ROTTEN.
Nu 5:21 doth make thy thigh to **r.**, and thy 5307
Nu 5:22 belly to swell, and thy thigh to **r.**: 5307
Nu 5:27 shall swell, and her thigh shall **r.**: 5307
Pr 10:7 the name of the wicked shall **r.** 7537
Isa 40:20 chooseth a tree that will not **r.**; he 7537

ROTTEN
Job 13:28 he, as a **r.** thing, consumeth, as a 7538
Job 41:27 iron as straw,...brass as **r.** wood. 7539
Jer 38:11 old cast clouts and old **r.** rags, 4418
Jer 38:12 old cast clouts and **r.** rags under 4418
Joe 1:17 The seed is **r.** under their clods, 5685

ROTTENNESS
Pr 12:4 ashamed is as **r.** in his bones 7538
Pr 14:30 flesh: but envy the **r.** of the bones. 7538
Isa 5:24 so their root shall be as **r.**, and 4716
Ho 5:12 and to the house of Judah as **r.** 7538
Hab 3:16 **r.** entered into my bones, and I 7538

ROUGH
De 21:4 down the heifer unto a **r.** valley, 386
Isa 27:8 he stayeth his **r.** wind in the day 7186
Isa 40:4 straight, and the **r.** places plain: 7406
Jer 51:27 to come up as the **r.** caterpillers. 5569
Da 8:21 the **r.** goat is the king of Grecia: 8163
Zec 13:4 wear a **r.** garment to deceive: 8181
Lu 3:5 the **r.** ways shall be made smooth; *5138*

ROUGHLY
Ge 42:7 them, and spake **r.** unto them; 7186
Ge 42:30 spake **r.** to us, and took us for spies 7186
1Sa 20:10 what if thy father answer thee **r.**? 7186
1KI 12:13 the king answered the people **r.**, 7186
2Ch 10:13 And the king answered them **r.**; 7186
Pr 18:23 but the rich answereth **r.** 5794

ROUND
Ge 19:4 compassed the house **r.**, both old 5921
Ge 23:17 that were in all the borders **r.** 5439
Ge 35:5 the cities that were **r.** about them, 5439
Ge 37:7 your sheaves stood **r.** about, and 5437
Ge 41:48 which was **r.** about every city, 5439
Ex 7:24 Egyptians digged **r.** about the river 5439
Ex 16:13 the dew lay **r.** about the host. 5439
Ex 16:14 there lay a small **r.** thing, as 2636
Ex 19:12 bounds unto the people **r.** about, 5439
Ex 25:11 upon it a crown of gold **r.** about. 5439
Ex 25:24 thereto a crown of gold **r.** about. 5439
Ex 25:25 border of an hand breadth **r.** about, 5439
Ex 25:25 crown to the border thereof **r.** 5439
Ex 27:17 All the pillars **r.** about the court 5439
Ex 28:32 woven work **r.** about the hole of it, 5439
Ex 28:33 scarlet, **r.** about the hem thereof; 5439
Ex 28:33 of gold between them **r.** about: 5439
Ex 28:34 upon the hem of the robe **r.** about 5439
Ex 29:16 sprinkle it **r.** about upon the altar. 5439
Ex 29:20 the blood upon the altar **r.** about. 5439
Ex 30:3 the sides thereof **r.** about, and the 5439
Ex 30:3 unto it a crown of gold **r.** about 5439
Ex 37:2 made a crown of gold to it **r.** about. 5439
Ex 37:11 thereunto a crown of gold **r.** about. 5439
Ex 37:12 border of an handbreadth **r.** about; 5439
Ex 37:12 for the border thereof **r.** about. 5439
Ex 37:26 the sides thereof **r.** about, and the 5439
Ex 37:26 unto it a crown of gold **r.** about. 5439
Ex 38:16 the hangings of the court **r.** about 5439
Ex 38:20 and of the court **r.** about, were of 5439
Ex 38:31 the sockets of the court **r.** about, 5439
Ex 38:31 all the pins of the court **r.** about. 5439
Ex 39:23 with a band **r.** about the hole, that 5439
Ex 39:25 of the robe, **r.** about between the 5439
Ex 39:26 **r.** about the hem of the robe to 5439
Ex 40:8 thou shalt set up the court **r.** about, 5439
Ex 40:33 the court **r.** about the tabernacle 5439
Le 1:5 and sprinkle the blood **r.** about 5439
Le 1:11 shall sprinkle his blood **r.** about 5439
Le 3:2 the blood upon the altar **r.** about. 5439
Le 3:8 the blood thereof **r.** about upon the 5439
Le 3:13 the blood thereof upon the altar **r.** 5439
Le 7:2 he sprinkle **r.** about upon the altar. 5439
Le 8:15 upon the horns of the altar **r.** about 5439
Le 8:19, 24 the blood upon the altar **r.** about 5439
Le 9:12 sprinkled **r.** about upon the altar. 5439
Le 9:18 sprinkled upon the altar **r.** about, 5439
Le 14:41 house to be scraped within **r.** about, 5439
Le 16:18 upon the horns of the altar **r.** about. 5439
Le 19:27 not **r.** the corners of your heads, 5362
Le 25:31 which have no wall **r.** about them 5439
Le 25:44 the heathen that are **r.** about you; 5439
Nu 1:50 encamp **r.** about the tabernacle. 5439
Nu 1:53 the Levites shall pitch **r.** about the 5439
Nu 3:26 and by the altar **r.** about, and the 5439
Nu 3:37 the pillars of the court **r.** about, 5439
Nu 4:26 which is...by the altar **r.** about, 5439
Nu 4:32 the pillars of the court **r.** about, 5439
Nu 11:24 set them **r.** about the tabernacle. 5439
Nu 11:31 the other side, **r.** about the camp, 5439
Nu 11:32 for themselves **r.** about the camp. 5439
Nu 16:34 all Israel that were **r.** about them 5439
Nu 22:4 lick up all that are **r.** about us, as 5439
Nu 32:33 the cities of the country **r.** about. 5439
Nu 34:12 with the coasts thereof **r.** about. 5439
Nu 35:2 suburbs for the cities **r.** about 5439
Nu 35:4 a thousand cubits **r.** about. 5439
De 6:14 the people which are **r.** about you; 5439
De 12:10 from all your enemies **r.** about, 5439
De 13:7 the people which are **r.** about you, 5439
De 21:2 which are **r.** about him that is slain: 5439
De 25:19 from all thine enemies **r.** about, 5439
Jos 6:3 war, and go **r.** about the city once. 5362
Jos 7:9 and shall environ us **r.**, and cut 5921
Jos 15:12 of the children of Judah **r.** about 5439
Jos 18:20 by the coasts thereof **r.** about, 5439
Jos 19:8 the villages...**r.** about these cities 5439
Jos 21:11 with the suburbs thereof **r.** about it. 5439
Jos 21:42 with their suburbs **r.** about them: 5439
Jos 21:44 the Lord gave them rest **r.** about, 5439
Jos 23:1 from all their enemies **r.** about, 5439
Jg 2:12 the people that were **r.** about them, 5439
Jg 2:14 the hands of their enemies **r.** about, 5439

Jg 7:21 man in his place **r.** about the camp: 5439
Jg 19:22 of Belial, beset the house **r.** about, 5437
Jg 20:5 beset the house **r.** about upon me 5437
Jg 20:29 set liers in wait **r.** about Gibeah. 5439
Jg 20:43 inclosed the Benjamites **r.** about, 3803
1Sa 14:21 camp from the country **r.** about, 5439
1Sa 23:26 compassed David and his men **r.** about
1Sa 26:5 the people pitched **r.** about him 5439
1Sa 26:7 and the people lay **r.** about him 5439
1Sa 31:9 the land of the Philistines **r.** about, 5439
2Sa 5:9 And David built **r.** about from Millo 5439
2Sa 7:1 rest **r.** about from all his enemies; 5439
2Sa 22:12 darkness pavilions **r.** about him, 5439
1Ki 3:1 and the wall of Jerusalem **r.** about. 5439
1Ki 4:24 had peace on all sides **r.** about him. 5439
1Ki 4:31 fame was in all nations **r.** about 5439
1Ki 6:5 house he built chambers **r.** about, 5439
1Ki 6:5 the walls of the house **r.** about, 5439
1Ki 6:5 and he made chambers **r.** about: 5439
1Ki 6:6 he made narrowed rests **r.** about, 5439
1Ki 6:29 walls of the house **r.** about with 4524
1Ki 7:12 the great court **r.** about was with 5439
1Ki 7:18 and two rows **r.** about upon the one 5439
1Ki 7:20 hundred in rows **r.** about upon the 5439
1Ki 7:23 it was **r.** all about, and his 5696
1Ki 7:23 thirty cubits did compass it **r.** 5439
1Ki 7:24 under the brim of it **r.** about there 5439
1Ki 7:24 cubit, compassing the sea **r.** about: 5439
1Ki 7:31 the mouth thereof was **r.** after the 5696
1Ki 7:31 their borders, foursquare, not **r.**. 5696
1Ki 7:35 a **r.** compass of half a cubit high: 5696
1Ki 7:36 every one, and additions **r.** about. 5439
1Ki 10:19 top of the throne was **r.** behind: 5696
1Ki 18:35 the water ran **r.** about the altar; 5439
2Ki 6:17 and chariots of fire **r.** about Elisha. 5439
2Ki 11:8 ye shall compass the king **r.** about, 5439
2Ki 11:11 in his hand, **r.** about the king, 5439
2Ki 17:15 heathen that were **r.** about them, 5439
2Ki 23:5 in the places **r.** about Jerusalem; 4524
2Ki 25:1 they built forts against it **r.** about. 5439
2Ki 25:4 were against the city **r.** about:) and 5439
2Ki 25:10 the walls of Jerusalem **r.** about. 5439
2Ki 25:17 upon the chapiter **r.** about, all of 5439
1Ch 4:33 their villages that were **r.** about 5439
1Ch 6:55 and the suburbs thereof **r.** about it. 5439
1Ch 9:27 lodged **r.** about the house of God, 5439
1Ch 10:9 the land of the Philistines **r.** about, 5439
1Ch 11:8 the city **r.** about, even from Millo **r.** 5439
1Ch 22:9 rest from all his enemies **r.** about: 5439
1Ch 28:12 of all the chambers **r.** about, of the 5439
2Ch 4:2 from brim to brim, **r.** in compass, 5696
2Ch 4:2 of thirty cubits did compass it **r.** 5439
2Ch 4:3 which did compass it **r.** about: ten 5439
2Ch 4:3 cubit, compassing the sea **r.** about 5439
2Ch 14:14 smote all the cities **r.** about Gerar; 5439
2Ch 15:15 the Lord gave them rest **r.** about. 5439
2Ch 17:10 lands that were **r.** about Judah, 5439
2Ch 20:30 for his God gave him rest **r.** about. 5439
2Ch 23:7 shall compass the king **r.** about, 5439
2Ch 23:10 the temple, by the king **r.** about. 5439
2Ch 34:6 with their mattocks **r.** about. 5439
Ne 12:28 plain country **r.** about Jerusalem, 5439
Ne 12:29 them villages **r.** about Jerusalem. 5439
Job 10:8 fashioned me together **r.** about; 5439
Job 16:13 His archers compass me **r.** about, 5437
Job 19:12 encamp **r.** about my tabernacle. 5439
Job 22:10 snares are **r.** about thee, and 5439
Job 37:12 turned **r.** about by his counsels: 4524
Job 41:14 his teeth are terrible **r.** about. 5439
Ps 3:6 themselves against me **r.** about. 5439
Ps 18:11 his pavilion **r.** about him were 5439
Ps 22:12 bulls of Bashan have beset me **r.**. 3803
Ps 27:6 above mine enemies **r.** about me: 5439
Ps 34:7 encampeth **r.** about them that fear 5439
Ps 44:13 to them that are **r.** about us. 5439
Ps 48:12 about Zion, and go **r.** about her: 5362
Ps 50:3 be very tempestuous **r.** about him. 5439
Ps 59:6, 14 dog, and go **r.** about the city. 5437
Ps 76:11 be **r.** about him bring presents 5439
Ps 78:28 camp, **r.** about their habitations. 5439
Ps 79:3 like water **r.** about Jerusalem; 5439
Ps 79:4 to them that are **r.** about us. 5439
Ps 88:17 **r.** about me daily like water; 5437
Ps 89:8 to thy faithfulness **r.** about thee? 5439
Ps 97:2 and darkness are **r.** about him: 5439
Ps 97:3 burneth up his enemies **r.** about. 5439
Ps 125:2 mountains are **r.** about Jerusalem, 5439
Ps 125:2 so the Lord is **r.** about his people 5439
Ps 128:3 like olive plants **r.** about thy table. 5439
Ca 7:2 navel is like a **r.** goblet, which 5469
Isa 3:18 and their **r.** tires like the moon, 7720
Isa 15:8 gone **r.** about the borders of Moab; 5362
Isa 29:3 I will camp against thee **r.** about, 1754
Isa 42:25 it hath set him on fire **r.** about, 5439
Isa 49:18 Lift up thine eyes **r.** about, and 5439
Isa 60:4 Lift up thine eyes **r.** about, and see: 5439
Jer 1:15 against all the walls thereof **r.** about, 5439
Jer 4:17 are they against her **r.** about; 5439
Jer 6:3 their tents against her **r.** about; 5439
Jer 12:9 the birds **r.** about are against her; 5439
Jer 21:14 shall devour all things **r.** about it. 5439
Jer 25:9 against all these nations **r.** about, 5439
Jer 46:5 for fear was **r.** about, saith the 5439
Jer 46:14 sword shall devour **r.** about thee. 5439
Jer 50:14 in array against Babylon **r.** about: 5439
Jer 50:15 Shout against her **r.** about: she 5439
Jer 50:29 the bow, camp against it **r.** about; 5439
Jer 50:32 it shall devour all **r.** about him. 5439
Jer 51:2 they shall be against her **r.** about. 5439
Jer 52:4 and built forts against it **r.** about. 5439
Jer 52:7 Chaldeans were by the city **r.** about:). 5439
Jer 52:14 all the walls of Jerusalem **r.** about. 5439
Jer 52:22 upon the chapiters **r.** about, all 5439
Jer 52:23 network were an hundred **r.** about. 5439
La 1:17 adversaries should be **r.** about him: 5439
La 2:3 fire, which devoureth **r.** about. 5439
La 2:22 a solemn day my terrors **r.** about, 5439
Eze 1:18 full of eyes **r.** about them four. 5439
Eze 1:27 the appearance of fire **r.** about 5439
Eze 1:27 and it had brightness **r.** about. 5439
Eze 1:28 of the brightness **r.** about. 5439
Eze 4:2 battering rams against it **r.** about. 5439
Eze 5:5 and countries that are **r.** about her. 5439
Eze 5:6 the countries that are **r.** about her: 5439
Eze 5:7 the nations that are **r.** about you, 5439
Eze 5:7 the nations that are **r.** about you; 5439
Eze 5:12 fall by the sword **r.** about thee; 5439
Eze 5:14, 15 nations that are **r.** about thee, 5439
Eze 6:5 your bones **r.** about your altars. 5439
Eze 6:13 their idols **r.** about their altars, 5439
Eze 8:10 pourtrayed upon the wall **r.** about. 5439
Eze 10:12 wheels, were full of eyes **r.** about, 5439
Eze 11:12 the heathen that are **r.** about you. 5439
Eze 16:37 gather them **r.** about against thee, 5439
Eze 16:57 Syria, and all that are **r.** about her, 5439
Eze 16:57 which despise thee **r.** about. 5439
Eze 23:24 and shield and helmet **r.** about: 5439
Eze 27:11 army were upon thy walls **r.** about, 5439
Eze 27:11 shields upon thy walls **r.** about; 5439
Eze 28:24 thorn of all that are **r.** about them, 5439
Eze 28:26 that despise them **r.** about them; 5439
Eze 31:4 rivers running **r.** about his plants, 5439
Eze 32:23 her company is **r.** about her grave: 5439
Eze 32:24 her multitude **r.** about her grave, 5439
Eze 32:25, 26 her graves are **r.** about him: 5439
Eze 34:26 and the places **r.** about my hill a 5439
Eze 36:4 the residue…that are **r.** about; 5439
Eze 36:36 the heathen that are left **r.** about 5439
Eze 37:2 me to pass by them **r.** about: and, 5439
Eze 40:5 the outside of the house **r.** about, 5439
Eze 40:14 post of the court **r.** about the gate. 5439
Eze 40:16 posts within the gate **r.** about, 5439
Eze 40:16 windows were **r.** about inward: 5439
Eze 40:17 pavement…for the court **r.** about: 5439
Eze 40:25 and in the arches thereof **r.** about, 5439
Eze 40:29 and in the arches thereof **r.** about: 5439
Eze 40:30 the arches **r.** about were five and 5439
Eze 40:33 and in the arches thereof **r.** about: 5439
Eze 40:36 and the windows to it **r.** about: 5439
Eze 40:43 and hand broad, fastened **r.** about: 5439
Eze 41:5 **r.** about the house on every side. 5439
Eze 41:6 for the side chambers **r.** about, 5439
Eze 41:7 still upward **r.** about the house: 5439
Eze 41:8 the height of the house **r.** about: 5439
Eze 41:10 twenty cubits **r.** about the house 5439
Eze 41:11 was left was five cubits **r.** about 5439
Eze 41:12 was five cubits thick **r.** about, and 5439
Eze 41:16 galleries **r.** about on their three 5439
Eze 41:16 door, cieled with wood **r.** about, 5439
Eze 41:17 by all the wall **r.** about within and 5439
Eze 41:19 through all the house **r.** about. 5439
Eze 42:15 the east, and measured it **r.** about. 5439
Eze 42:16, 17 the measuring reed **r.** about. 5439
Eze 42:20 it had a wall **r.** about, five hundred 5439
Eze 43:12 the whole limit thereof **r.** about. 5439
Eze 43:13 by the edge thereof **r.** about shall 5439
Eze 43:20 and upon the border **r.** about: 5439
Eze 45:1 in all the borders thereof **r.** about. 5439
Eze 45:2 in breadth, square **r.** about; and 5439
Eze 45:2 and fifty cubits **r.** about for the 5439
Eze 46:23 a row of building **r.** about in them, 5439
Eze 46:23 **r.** about them four, and it was 5439
Eze 46:23 places under the rows **r.** about. 5439
Eze 48:35 It was **r.** about eighteen thousand. 5439
Joe 3:11 gather yourselves together **r.** about: 5439
Joe 3:12 to judge all the heathen **r.** about. 5439
Am 3:11 shall be even **r.** about the land; 5439
Jon 2:5 the depth closed me **r.** about, the 5437
Na 3:8 that had the waters **r.** about it, 5439
Zec 2:5 be unto her a wall of fire **r.** about, 5439
Zec 7:7 and the cities thereof **r.** about her, 5439
Zec 12:2 unto all the people **r.** about, when 5439
Zec 12:6 shall devour all the people **r.** about, 5439
Zec 14:14 wealth of all the heathen **r.** about 5439
Mt 3:5 all the region **r.** about Jordan, *4066*
Mt 14:35 out into all that country **r.** about, *4066*
Mt 21:33 **vineyard, and hedged it r. about,**
Mk 1:28 all the region **r.** about Galilee. *4066*
Mk 3:5 had looked **r.** about on them with *4017*
Mk 3:34 he looked **r.** about on them which *2943*
Mk 5:32 he looked **r.** about to see her that *4017*
Mk 6:6 And he went **r.** about the villages, *2943*
Mk 6:36 may go into the country **r.** about, *2943*
Mk 6:55 that whole region **r.** about, and *4066*
Mk 9:8 when they had looked **r.** about, *4017*
Mk 10:23 Jesus looked **r.** about, and saith *4017*
Mk 11:11 looked **r.** about upon all things, *4017*
Lu 1:65 on all that dwelt **r.** about them: *4039*
Lu 2:9 glory of the Lord shone **r.** about *4034*
Lu 4:14 through all the region **r.** about. *4066*
Lu 4:37 every place of the country **r.** about. *4066*
Lu 6:10 looking **r.** about upon them all, he
Lu 7:17 throughout all the region **r.** about. *4066*
Lu 8:37 country of the Gadarenes **r.** about *4066*
Lu 9:12 the towns and country **r.** about, *2943*
Lu 19:43 **compass thee r., and keep thee in.** *4033*
Joh 10:24 Then came the Jews **r.** about him, *2944*
Ac 5:16 the cities **r.** about unto Jerusalem, *4038*
Ac 9:3 there shined **r.** about him a light *4015*
Ac 14:6 the region that lieth **r.** about: *4066*
Ac 14:20 the disciples stood **r.** about him, *2944*
Ac 22:6 heaven a great light **r.** about me. *4015*
Ac 25:7 from Jerusalem stood **r.** about, *4026*
Ac 26:13 of the sun, shining **r.** about me *4034*
Ro 15:19 and **r.** about unto Illyricum, I *2943*
Heb 9:4 overlaid **r.** about with gold, *3840*
Re 4:3 was a rainbow **r.** about the throne, *2943*
Re 4:4 **r.** about the throne were four and *2943*
Re 4:6 and **r.** about the throne, were four *2943*
Re 5:11 many angels **r.** about the throne *2943*
Re 7:11 angels stood **r.** about the throne, *2943*

ROUSE
Ge 49:9 an old lion; who shall **r.** him up? 6965

ROVERS
1Ch 12:21 David against the band of the **r.**

ROW See also ROWED; ROWING; ROWS.
Ex 28:17 the first **r.** shall be a sardius, a 2905
Ex 28:17 carbuncle: this shall be the first **r.**. 2905
Ex 28:18 the second **r.** shall be an emerald, a 2905
Ex 28:19 the third **r.** a ligure, an agate, and 2905
Ex 28:20 the fourth **r.** a beryl, and an onyx, 2905
Ex 39:10 the first **r.** was a sardius, topaz, 2905
Ex 39:10 a carbuncle: this was the first **r.**. 2905
Ex 39:11 second **r.**, and emerald, a sapphire, 2905
Ex 39:12 the third **r.**, a ligure, an agate, and 2905
Ex 39:13 the fourth **r.**, a beryl, an onyx, and 2905
Le 24:6 set them in two rows, six on a **r.**, 4635
Le 24:7 put pure frankincense upon each **r.**, 4635
1Ki 6:36 stone, and a **r.** of cedar beams. 2905
1Ki 7:3 on forty five pillars, fifteen in a **r.**. 2905
1Ki 7:12 stones, and a **r.** of cedar beams, 2905
Ezr 6:4 stones, and a **r.** of good timber: 5073
Eze 46:23 there was a **r.** of building round 2905

ROWED
Jon 1:13 men **r.** hard to bring it to the land; 2864
Joh 6:19 they had **r.** about five and twenty *1643*

ROWERS
Eze 27:26 Thy **r.** have brought thee into 7751

ROWING
Mk 6:48 And he saw them toiling in **r.**; for *1643*

ROWS
Ex 28:17 of stones, even four **r.** of stones: 2905
Ex 39:10 And they set in it four **r.** of stones: 2905
Le 24:6 And thou shalt set them in two **r.**, 4634
1Ki 6:36 court with three **r.** of hewed stone, 2905
1Ki 7:2 upon four **r.** of cedar pillars, with 2905
1Ki 7:4 And there were windows in three **r.**, 2905
1Ki 7:12 was with three **r.** of hewed stones, 2905
1Ki 7:18 two **r.** round about upon the one 2905
1Ki 7:20 were two hundred in **r.** round about 2905
1Ki 7:24 the knops were cast in two **r.**, when 2905
1Ki 7:42 **r.** of pomegranates for one network, 2905
2Ch 4:3 Two **r.** of oxen were cast, when it 2905
2Ch 4:13 **r.** of pomegranates on each wreath, 2905
Ezr 6:4 With three **r.** of great stones, and 5073
Ca 1:10 are comely with **r.** of jewels, 8447
Eze 46:23 with boiling places under the **r.** 2918

ROYAL
Ge 49:20 fat, and he shall yield **r.** dainties 4428
Jos 10:2 great city, as one of the **r.** cities, 4467
1Sa 27:5 thy servant dwell in the **r.** city with 4467
2Sa 12:26 of Ammon, and took the **r.** city 4410
1Ki 10:13 Solomon gave her of his **r.** bounty 4428
2Ki 11:1 arose and destroyed all the seed **r.** 4467
2Ki 25:25 the son of Elishama, the seed **r.**, 4410
1Ch 29:25 such **r.** majesty as had not been 4438
2Ch 22:10 the seed **r.** of the house of Judah. 4467
Es 1:7 **r.** wine in abundance, according 4438
Es 1:9 feast for the women in the **r.** house 4438
Es 1:11 before the king with the crown **r.**, 4438
Es 1:19 go a **r.** commandment from him, 4438
Es 1:19 king give her **r.** estate unto another 4438
Es 2:16 king Ahasuerus into his house **r.** 4438
Es 2:17 he set the **r.** crown upon her head, 4438
Es 5:1 Esther put on her **r.** apparel, and 4438
Es 5:1 upon his **r.** throne in the **r.** house, 4438
Es 6:8 Let the **r.** apparel be brought 4438
Es 6:8 crown **r.** which is set upon his head: 4438
Es 8:15 in **r.** apparel of blue and white, 4438
Isa 62:3 **r.** diadem in the hand of thy God. 4410
Jer 41:1 the son of Elishama, of the seed **r.**, 4410
Jer 43:10 spread his **r.** pavilion over them. 8237
Da 6:7 together to establish a **r.** statute, 4430
Ac 12:21 Herod, arrayed in **r.** apparel, sat *937*
Jas 2:8 If ye fulfil the **r.** law according to *937*
1Pe 2:9 a **r.** priesthood, an holy nation, a *934*

RUBBING
Lu 6:1 did eat, **r.** them in their hands *5597*

RUBBISH
Ne 4:2 heaps of the **r.** which are burned? 6083
Ne 4:10 is decayed, and there is much **r.**; 6083

RUBIES
Job 28:18 the price of wisdom is above **r.** 6443
Pr 3:15 She is more precious than **r.**: and 6443
Pr 8:11 For wisdom is better than **r.**; and 6443
Pr 20:15 There is gold, and a multitude of **r.** 6443
Pr 31:10 woman? for her price is far above **r.** 6443
La 4:7 were more ruddy in body than **r.**, 6443

RUDDER
Ac 27:40 the sea, and loosed the **r.** bands, *4079*

RUDDY
1Sa 16:12 Now he was **r.**, and withal of a 132
1Sa 17:42 for he was but a youth, and **r.**, and 132
Ca 5:10 My beloved is white and **r.**, the 122
La 4:7 were more **r.** in body than rubies, 119

RUDE
2Co 11:6 But though I be **r.** in speech, yet *2399*

RUDIMENTS
Col 2:8 after the **r.** of the world, and not *4747*
Col 2:20 be dead...from the **r.** of the world, *4747*

RUE
Lu 11:42 **for ye tithe mint and r. and all** *4076*

RUFUS (ru'-fus)
Mk 15:21 the father of Alexander and **R.**, *4504*
Ro 16:13 Salute **R.** chosen in the Lord, and *4504*

RUHAMAH (ru-ha'-mah) See also LO-RUHAMAH.
Ho 2:1 Ammi; and to your sisters, **R.** 7355

RUIN See also RUINED; RUINS.
2Ch 28:23 But they were the **r.** of him, and 3782
Ps 89:40 hast brought his strong holds to **r.** 4288
Pr 24:22 who knoweth the **r.** of them both? 6365
Pr 26:28 and a flattering mouth worketh **r.** 4072
Isa 3:6 and let this **r.** be under thy hand: 4384
Isa 23:13 thereof; and he brought it to **r.** 4654
Isa 25:2 city an heap; of a defenced city a **r.** 4654
Eze 18:30 so iniquity shall not be your **r.** 4383
Eze 27:27 midst of the seas in...day of thy **r.** 4658
Eze 31:13 Upon his **r.** shall all the fowls of the 4658
Lu 6:49 **and the r. of that house was great** *4485*

RUINED
Isa 3:8 For Jerusalem is **r.**, and Judah is 3782
Eze 36:35 and **r.** cities are become fenced, 2040
Eze 36:36 that I the Lord build the **r.** places, 2040

RUINOUS
2Ki 19:25 waste fenced cities into **r.** heaps. 5327
Isa 17:1 a city, and it shall be a **r.** heap. 4654
Isa 37:26 waste defenced cities into **r.** heaps. 5327

RUINS
Eze 21:15 faint, and their **r.** be multiplied: 4383
Am 9:11 and I will raise up his **r.**, and I will 2034
Ac 15:16 I will build again the **r.** thereof, *2679*

RULE See also RULED; RULEST; RULETH; RULING; UNRULY.
Ge 1:16 the greater light to **r.** the day, 4475
Ge 1:16 and the lesser light to **r.** the night: 4475
Ge 1:18 to **r.** over the day and over the 4910
Ge 3:16 husband, and he shall **r.** over thee. 4910
Ge 4:7 desire, and thou shalt **r.** over him. 4910
Le 25:43 shalt not **r.** over him with rigour; 7287
Le 25:46 **r.** one over another with rigour 7287
Le 25:53 shall not **r.** with rigour over him in 7287
Jg 8:22 **R.** thou over us, both thou, and 4910
Jg 8:23 unto them, I will not **r.** over you, 4910
Jg 8:23 neither shall my son **r.** over you: 4910
Jg 8:23 you: the Lord shall **r.** over you. 4910
1Ki 9:23 which bare **r.** over the people that 7287
1Ki 22:31 captains that had **r.** over over his chariots,
2Ch 8:10 fifty, that bare **r.** over the people. 7287
Ne 5:15 servants bare **r.** over the people: 7980
Es 1:22 should bare **r.** in his own house, 8323
Es 9:1 Jews had **r.** over them that hated 7980
Ps 110:2 **r.** thou in the midst of thine 7287
Ps 136:8 The sun to **r.** by day: for his 4475
Ps 136:9 The moon and stars to **r.** by night: 4475
Pr 8:16 By me princes **r.**, and nobles, 8323
Pr 12:24 hand of the diligent shall bare **r.**: 4910
Pr 17:2 servant shall have **r.** over a son that 4910
Pr 19:10 a servant to have **r.** over princes. 4910
Pr 25:28 hath no **r.** over his own spirit is 4623
Pr 29:2 but when the wicked beareth **r.**, 4910
Ec 2:19 he have **r.** over all my labour 7980
Isa 3:4 and babes shall **r.** over them. 4910
Isa 3:12 oppressors,...women **r.** over them. 4910
Isa 14:2 they shall **r.** over their oppressors 7287
Isa 19:4 a fierce king shall **r.** over them, 4910
Isa 28:14 **r.** this people which is in Jerusalem 4910
Isa 32:1 and princes shall **r.** in judgment 8323
Isa 40:10 and his arm shall **r.** for him: 4910
Isa 41:2 him, and made him **r.** over king? 7287
Isa 44:13 carpenter stretcheth out his **r.**; 6957
Isa 52:5 **r.** over them make them to howl, 4910
Isa 63:19 thou never barest **r.** over them; 4910
Jer 5:31 priests bare **r.** by their means; 7287
Eze 19:11 the sceptres of them that bare **r.**, 4910
Eze 19:14 no strong rod to be a sceptre to **r.** 4910
Eze 20:33 poured out, will I **r.** over you: 4427
Eze 29:15 shall no more **r.** over the nations. 7287
Da 2:39 shall bare **r.** over all the earth. 7981
Da 4:26 known that the heavens do **r.** 7990
Da 11:3 that shall **r.** with great dominion, 4910
Da 11:39 shall cause them to **r.** over many, 4910
Joe 2:17 the heathen should **r.** over them: 4910
Zec 6:13 shall sit and **r.** upon his throne; 4910
Mt 2:6 that shall **r.** my people Israel. *4165*
Mk 10:42 **accounted to r. over the Gentiles** *757*
1Co 15:24 he shall have put down all **r.**, *746*
2Co 10:13 the **r.** which God hath distributed *2583*
2Co 10:15 you according to our **r.** abundantly, *2583*
Ga 6:16 many as walk according to this **r.**, *2583*
Php 3:16 let us walk by the same **r.**, let us *2583*
Col 3:15 the peace of God **r.** in your hearts, *1018*
1Ti 3:5 know not how to **r.** his own house, *4291*
1Ti 5:17 the elders that **r.** well be counted *4291*
Heb 13:7 them which have the **r.** over you, *2233*
Heb 13:17 Obey them that have...**r.** over you, *2233*
Heb 13:24 Salute all...that have...**r.** over you, *2233*
Re 2:27 **shall r. them with a rod of iron;** *4165*
Re 12:5 **r.** all nations with a rod of iron: *4165*
Re 19:15 he shall **r.** them with a rod of iron: *4165*

RULED
Ge 24:2 house, that **r.** over all that he had, 4910
Ge 41:40 word shall all my people be **r.**: 5401
Jos 12:2 and **r.** from Aroer, which is upon 4910
Ru 1:1 in the days when the judges **r.**, 8199
1Ki 5:16 which **r.** over the people that 7287
1Ch 26:6 that **r.** throughout the house of 4474
Ezr 4:20 which have **r.** over all countries 7990
Ps 106:41 that hated them **r.** over them. 4910
Isa 14:6 he that **r.** the nations in anger, is 7287
La 5:8 Servants have **r.** over us: there is 4910
Eze 34:4 and with cruelty have ye **r.** them. 7287
Da 5:21 God **r.** in the kingdom of men, 7990
Da 11:4 to his dominion which he **r.** 4910

RULER See also RULER'S; RULERS.
Ge 41:43 he made him **r.** over all the land of
Ge 43:16 he said to the **r.** of his house, 834,5921
Ge 45:8 a **r.** throughout all the land of 4910
Ex 22:28 nor curse the **r.** of thy people. 5387
Le 4:22 When a **r.** hath sinned, and done 5387
Nu 13:2 a man, every one a **r.** among them. 5387
Jg 9:30 Zebul the **r.** of the city heard the 8269
1Sa 25:30 appointed thee **r.** over Israel; 5057
2Sa 6:21 me **r.** over the people of the Lord, 5057
2Sa 7:8 the sheep, to be **r.** over my people, 5057
2Sa 20:26 Jairite was a chief **r.** about David.
1Ki 1:35 appointed him to be **r.** over Israel 5057
1Ki 11:28 made him **r.** over all the charge 6485
2Ki 25:22 them he made Gedaliah...**r.**, 6485
1Ch 5:2 and of him came the chief **r.**; but 5057
1Ch 9:11 the **r.** of the house of God; 5057
1Ch 9:20 Phinehas..was the **r.** over them in 5057
1Ch 11:2 shalt be **r.** over my people Israel. 5057
1Ch 17:7 be **r.** over my people Israel: 5057
1Ch 26:24 Shebuel...was **r.** of the treasures. 5057
1Ch 27:4 his course was Mikloth also the **r.** 5057
1Ch 27:16 **r.** of the Reubenites was Eliezer the 5057
1Ch 28:4 he hath chosen Judah to be the **r.**; 5057
2Ch 6:5 to be a **r.** over my people Israel: 5057
2Ch 7:18 fail thee a man to be **r.** in Israel. 4910
2Ch 11:22 to be **r.** among his brethren: for 5057
2Ch 19:11 the **r.** of the house of Judah, for 5057
2Ch 26:11 the scribe and Maaseiah the **r.**, 7860
2Ch 31:12 which Cononiah the Levite was **r.**, 5057
2Ch 31:13 Azariah the **r.** of the house of God. 5057
Ne 3:9 **r.** of the half part of Jerusalem. 8269
Ne 3:12 **r.** of the half part of Jerusalem, he 8269
Ne 3:14 the **r.** of part of Beth-haccerem; 8269
Ne 3:15 Col-hozeh, the **r.** of part of Mizpah; 8269
Ne 3:16 the **r.** of the half part of Beth-zur, 8269
Ne 3:17 the **r.** of the half part of Keilah, 8269
Ne 3:18 the **r.** of the half part of Keilah. 8269
Ne 3:19 son of Jeshua, the **r.** of Mizpah, 8269
Ne 7:2 and Hananiah the **r.** of the palace, 8269
Ne 11:11 was the **r.** of the house of God. 5057
Ps 68:27 is little Benjamin with their **r.**, 7287
Ps 105:20 the **r.** of the people, and let him 4910
Ps 105:21 house, and **r.** of all his substance: 4910
Pr 6:7 having no guide, overseer, or **r.**, 4910
Pr 23:1 When thou sittest to eat with a **r.**, 4910
Pr 28:15 is a wicked **r.** over the poor people. 4910
Pr 29:12 If a **r.** hearken to lies, all his 4910
Ec 10:4 the spirit of the **r.** rise up against 4910
Ec 10:5 which proceedeth from the **r.** 7989
Isa 3:6 be thou our **r.**, and let this ruin 7101
Isa 3:7 make me not a **r.** of the people. 7101
Isa 16:1 Send ye the lamb to the **r.** of the 4910
Jer 51:46 violence in the land, **r.** against **r.** 4910
Da 2:10 there is no king, lord, no **r.**, that 7990
Da 2:38 hath made thee **r.** over them all. 7981
Da 2:48 him **r.** over the whole province of 7981
Da 5:7,16 be the third **r.** in the kingdom. 7981
Da 5:29 be the third **r.** in the kingdom. 7990
Mic 5:2 unto me that is to be **r.** in Israel; 4910
Hab 1:14 things, that have no **r.** over them? 4910
Mt 9:18 came a certain **r.**, and worshipped *758*

Mt 24:45 **hath made r. over his household,** *2525*
Mt 24:47 **make him r. over all his goods.** *2525*
Mt 25:21, 23 **make thee r. over many things:** *2525*
Mk 5:35 from the **r.** of the synagogue's *752*
Mk 5:36 saith unto the **r.** of the synagogue, *752*
Mk 5:38 house of the **r.** of the synagogue, *752*
Lu 8:41 and he was a **r.** of the synagogue: *758*
Lu 8:49 the **r.** of the synagogue's house, *752*
Lu 12:42 **shall make r. over his household,** *2525*
Lu 12:44 **make him r. over all that he hath.** *2525*
Lu 13:14 the **r.** of the synagogue answered *752*
Lu 18:18 And a certain **r.** asked him, saying, *758*
Joh 2:9 When the **r.** of the feast had tasted *755*
Joh 3:1 named Nicodemus, a **r.** of the Jews: *758*
Ac 7:27 made thee a **r.** and a judge over us? *758*
Ac 7:35 Who made thee a **r.** and a judge? *758*
Ac 7:35 God send to be a **r.** and a deliverer *758*
Ac 18:8, 17 the chief **r.** of the synagogue, *752*
Ac 23:5 speak evil of the **r.** of thy people. *758*

RULER'S
Pr 29:26 Many seek the **r.** favour; but every 4910
Mt 9:23 when Jesus came into the **r.** house, *758*

RULERS
Ge 47:6 then make them **r.** over my cattle. 8269
Ex 16:22 the **r.** of the congregation came 5387
Ex 18:21 **r.** of thousands, and **r.** of hundreds, 8269
Ex 18:21 **r.** of fifties, and **r.** of tens: 8269
Ex 18:25 **r.** of thousands, **r.** of hundreds, 8269
Ex 18:25 **r.** of fifties, and **r.** of tens. 8269
Ex 34:31 the **r.** of the congregation returned 5387
Ex 35:27 And the **r.** brought onyx stones, 5387
De 1:13 and I will make them **r.** over you. 7218
Jg 15:11 that the Philistines are **r.** over us? 4910
2Sa 8:18 and David's sons were chief **r.**
1Ki 9:22 captains, and **r.** of his chariots, 8269
2Ki 10:1 to Samaria, unto the **r.** of Jezreel, 8269
2Ki 11:4 and fetched the **r.** over hundreds, 8269
2Ki 11:19 And he took the **r.** over hundreds, 8269
1Ch 21:2 to Joab and to the the **r.** of the people, 8269
1Ch 26:32 David made **r.** over...Reubenites, 6485
1Ch 27:31 these were the **r.** of the substance 8269
1Ch 29:6 with the **r.** of the king's work, 8269
2Ch 29:20 and gathered the **r.** of the city, and 8269
2Ch 35:8 Jethiel, **r.** of the house of God, 5057
Ezr 9:2 **r.** hath been chief in this trespass 5461
Ezr 10:14 **r.** of all the congregation stand, 8269
Ne 2:16 the **r.** knew not whither I went, 5461
Ne 2:16 nor to the nobles, nor to the **r.**, nor 5461
Ne 4:14 said unto the nobles, and to the **r.**, 5461
Ne 4:16 the **r.** were behind all the house of 8269
Ne 4:19 unto the nobles, and to the **r.**, and 5461
Ne 5:7 I rebuked the nobles, and the **r.**, 5461
Ne 5:17 hundred and fifty of the Jews and **r.**, 5461
Ne 7:5 together the nobles, and the **r.**, and 5461
Ne 11:1 And the **r.** of the people dwelt 8269
Ne 12:40 I, and the half of the **r.** with me: 5461
Ne 13:11 Then contended I with the **r.**, and 5461
Es 3:12 to the **r.** of every people of every 8269
Es 8:9 deputies and **r.** of the provinces 8269
Es 9:3 And all the **r.** of the provinces, and 8269
Ps 2:2 and the **r.** take counsel together, 7336
Isa 1:10 word of the Lord, ye **r.** of Sodom; 7101
Isa 14:5 wicked, and the sceptre of the **r.**. 4910
Isa 22:3 All thy **r.** are fled together, they 7101
Isa 29:10 prophets, and your **r.**, the seers 7218
Isa 49:7 abhorreth, to a servant of **r.**, 4910
Jer 33:26 to be **r.** over the seed of Abraham, 4910
Jer 51:23 I break in pieces captains and **r.** 5461
Jer 51:28 all the **r.** thereof, and all the land 5461
Jer 51:57 and her **r.**, and her mighty men: 5461
Eze 23:6 clothed with blue, captains and **r.**. 5461
Eze 23:12 and **r.** clothed most gorgeously, 5461
Eze 23:23 captains and **r.**, great lords and 5461
Da 3:2 and all the **r.** of the provinces, to 7984
Da 3:3 and all the **r.** of the provinces, were 7984
Ho 4:18 her **r.** with shame do love, Give ye. 4043
Mk 5:22 one of the **r.** of the synagogue, *752*
Mk 13:9 **before r. and kings for my sake,** *2232*
Lu 21:12 **kings and r. for my name's sake.** *2232*
Lu 23:13 priests and the **r.** and the people, *758*
Lu 23:35 the **r.** also with them derided him, *758*
Lu 24:20 chief priests and our **r.** delivered *758*
Joh 7:26 Do the **r.** know indeed that this is *758*
Joh 7:48 of the **r.** or of the Pharisees believed *758*
Joh 12:42 among the chief **r.**...many believed *758*
Ac 3:17 ye did it, as did also your **r.**. *758*
Ac 4:5 their **r.**, and elders, and scribes, *758*
Ac 4:8 Ye **r.** of the people, and elders of *758*
Ac 4:26 and the **r.** were gathered together *758*
Ac 13:15 the **r.** of the synagogue sent unto *752*
Ac 13:27 dwell at Jerusalem, and their **r.**, *758*
Ac 14:5 also of the Jews with their **r.**, to use *758*
Ac 16:19 into the marketplace unto the **r.**, *758*
Ac 17:6 brethren unto the **r.** of the city, *4173*
Ac 17:8 the people and the **r.** of the city, *4173*
Ro 13:3 **r.** are not a terror to good works, *758*
Eph 6:12 against the **r.** of the darkness of *2888*

RULEST
2Ch 20:6 **r.** not thou over all the kingdoms 4910
Ps 89:9 Thou **r.** the raging of the sea: when 4910

RULETH
2Sa 23:3 He that **r.** over men must be just, 4910
Ps 59:13 let them know that God **r.** in Jacob 4910
Ps 66:7 He **r.** by his power for ever; his 4910
Ps 103:19 and his kingdom **r.** over all 4910
Pr 16:32 he that **r.** his spirit than he that 4910
Pr 22:7 The rich **r.** over the poor, and the 4910
Ec 8:9 wherein one man **r.** over another 7980
Ec 9:17 the cry of him that **r.** among fools. 4910
Da 4:17, 25,32 that the most High **r.** in the 7980
Ho 11:12 but Judah yet **r.** with God, and is 7300
Ro 12:8 he that **r.**, with diligence; he that *4291*
1Ti 3:4 One that **r.** well his own house, *4291*

RULING
2Sa 23:3 must be just, **r.** in the fear of God. 4910
Jer 22:30 David, and **r.** any more in Judah. 4910
1Ti 3:12 **r.** their children and their own *4291*

RUMAH (ru'-mah) See also ARUMAH.
2Ki 23:36 the daughter of Padaiah of **R.**. 7316

RUMBLING
Jer 47:3 at the **r.** of his wheels, the fathers 1995

RUMOUR See also RUMOURS.
2Ki 19:7 and he shall hear a **r.**, and shall 8052
Isa 37:7 he shall hear a **r.**, and return to 8052
Jer 49:14 I have heard a **r.** from the Lord, 8052
Jer 51:46 fear for the **r.** that shall be heard 8052
Jer 51:46 a **r.** shall both come one year, and 8052
Jer 51:46 in another year shall come a **r.**, and 8052
Eze 7:26 mischief, and **r.** shall be upon **r.**; 8052
Ob 1 We have heard a **r.** from the Lord, 8052
Lu 7:17 And this **r.** of him went forth *3056*

RUMOURS
Mt 24:6 **shall hear of wars and r. of wars:** *189*
Mk 13:7 **shall hear of wars and r. of wars,** *189*

RUMP
Ex 29:22 take of the ram the fat and the **r.**, 451
Le 3:9 the fat thereof, and the whole **r.**, it 451
Le 7:3 the **r.**, and the fat that covereth the 451
Le 8:25 And he took the fat, and the **r.**, and 451
Le 9:19 the bullock and of the ram, the **r.**, 451

RUN See also RAN; RUNNEST; RUNNETH; RUNNING; OUTRUN.
Ge 49:22 whose branches **r.** over the wall: 6805
Le 15:3 whether his flesh **r.** with his issue, 7325
Le 15:25 or if it **r.** beyond the time of her 2100
Je 18:25 lest angry fellows **r.** upon thee, 6293
1Sa 8:11 some shall **r.** before his chariots 7323
1Sa 17:17 and **r.** to the camp to thy brethren; 7323
1Sa 20:6 that he might **r.** to Beth-lehem his 7323
1Sa 20:36 **R.**, find out now the arrows which 7323
2Sa 15:1 and fifty men to **r.** before him. 7323
2Sa 18:19 Let me now **r.**, and bear the king 7323
2Sa 18:22 me, I pray thee, also **r.** after Cushi. 7323
2Sa 18:22 Wherefore wilt thou **r.**, my son, 7323
2Sa 18:23 But howsoever, said he, let me **r.** 7323
2Sa 18:23 And he said unto him, **R.** Then 7323
2Sa 22:30 by thee I have **r.** through a troop: 7323
1Ki 1:5 and fifty men to **r.** before him. 7323
2Ki 4:22 that I may **r.** to the man of God, 7323
2Ki 4:26 **R.** now, I pray thee, to meet her, 7323
2Ki 5:20 **r.** after him, and take somewhat 7323
2Ch 16:9 the eyes of the Lord **r.** to and from 7751
Ps 18:29 by thee I have **r.** through a troop; 7323
Ps 19:5 rejoiceth as a strong man to **r.** a 7323
Ps 58:7 as waters which **r.** continually: 1980
Ps 59:4 They **r.** and prepare themselves 7323
Ps 78:16 waters to **r.** down like rivers. 3381
Ps 104:10 valleys, which **r.** among the hills. 1980
Ps 119:32 **r.** the way of thy commandments, 7323
Ps 119:136 of waters **r.** down mine eyes, 3381
Pr 1:16 For their feet **r.** to evil, and make 7323
Ec 1:7 All the rivers **r.** into the sea; yet 1980
Ca 1:4 Draw me, we will **r.** after thee: 7323
Isa 33:4 of locusts shall he **r.** upon them. 8264
Isa 40:31 they shall **r.**, and not be weary; 7323
Isa 55:5 that knew not thee shall **r.** unto thee 7323
Isa 59:7 Their feet **r.** to evil, and they make 7323
Jer 5:1 **R.**...to and fro through the streets 7751
Jer 9:18 our eyes may **r.** down with tears, 3381
Jer 12:5 If thou hast **r.** with the footmen, 7323
Jer 13:17 weep sore, and mine eye **r.** down with tears, 3381
Jer 14:17 Let mine eyes **r.** down with tears 3381
Jer 49:3 and **r.** to and fro by the hedges; 7751
Jer 49:19 I will suddenly make him **r.** away 7323
Jer 50:44 I will make them suddenly **r.** away 7323
Jer 51:31 One post shall **r.** to meet another, 7323
Le 2:18 let tears **r.** down like a river day 3381
Eze 24:16 neither shall thy tears **r.** down. 935
Eze 32:14 and cause their rivers to **r.** like oil, 3212
Da 12:4 many shall **r.** to and fro, and 7751
Joe 2:4 and as horsemen, so shall they **r.** 7323
Joe 2:7 They shall **r.** like mighty men; they 7323
Joe 2:9 They shall **r.** to and fro in the city; 8264
Joe 2:9 they shall **r.** upon the wall, they 7323
Am 5:24 let judgment **r.** down as waters, 1556
Am 6:12 Shall horse **r.** upon the rock? 7323
Am 8:12 shall **r.** to and fro to seek the word 7751
Na 2:4 they shall **r.** like the lightnings. 7323
Hab 2:2 that he may **r.** that readeth it. 7323
Hag 1:9 ye **r.** every man unto his own house. 7323
Zec 2:4 **R.**, speak to this young man, saying, 7323
Zec 4:10 **r.** to and fro through the whole 7751
Mt 28:8 did **r.** to bring his disciples word. *5143*
1Co 9:24 that they which **r.** in a race **r.** all, *5143*
1Co 9:24 prize? So **r.**, that ye may obtain. *5143*
1Co 9:26 therefore so **r.**, not as uncertainly; *5143*
Ga 2:2 means I should **r.**, or had **r.**, in vain. *5143*
Ga 5:7 Ye did **r.** well; who did hinder you *5143*
Php 2:16 that I have not **r.** in vain, neither *5143*
Heb 12:1 let us **r.** with patience the race that *5143*
1Pe 4:4 strange that ye **r.** not with them to *4936*

RUNNER See FORERUNNER.

RUNNEST
Pr 4:12 and when thou **r.**, thou shalt not 7323

RUNNETH
Ezr 8:15 to the river that **r.** to Ahava; 935
Job 15:26 He **r.** upon him, even on his neck, 7323
Job 16:14 breach, he **r.** upon me like a giant. 7323
Ps 23:5 my head with oil; my cup **r.** over. 7310
Ps 147:15 earth: his word **r.** very swiftly. 7323
Pr 18:10 the righteous **r.** into it, and is safe. 7323
La 1:16 eye, mine eye **r.** down with water, 3381
La 3:48 Mine eye **r.** down with rivers of 3381
Mt 9:17 **bottles break, and the wine r. out,** *1632*
Joh 20:2 Then she **r.**, and cometh to Simon *5143*
Ro 9:16 him that willeth, nor of him that **r.**, *5143*

RUNNING See also OVERRUNNING.
Le 14:5 in an earthen vessel over **r.** water: 2416
Le 14:6 that was killed over the **r.** water: 2416
Le 14:50 in an earthen vessel over **r.** water: 2416
Le 14:51 the slain bird, and in the **r.** water, 2416
Le 14:52 of the bird, and with the **r.** water, 2416
Le 15:2 hath a **r.** issue out of his flesh, 2100
Le 15:13 and bathe his flesh in **r.** water, and 2416
Le 22:4 is a leper, or hath a **r.** issue; 2100
Nu 19:17 **r.** water shall be put thereto in a 2416
2Sa 18:24 looked, and behold a man **r.** alone. 7323
2Sa 18:26 the watchman saw another man **r.**: 7323
2Sa 18:26 said, Behold another man **r.** alone. 7323
2Sa 18:27 the **r.** of the foremost is like 4794
2Sa 18:27 the **r.** of Ahimaaz the son of Zadok. 4794
2Ki 5:21 Naaman saw him **r.** after him, he 7323
2Ch 23:12 noise of the people **r.** and praising 7323
Pr 5:15 **r.** waters out of thine own well. 5140
Pr 6:18 feet that be swift in **r.** to mischief, 7323
Isa 33:4 as the **r.** to and fro of locusts shall 4944
Eze 31:4 rivers **r.** round about his plants, 1980
Mk 9:15 amazed, and **r.** to him saluted him. *4370*
Mk 9:25 that the people came **r.** together, *1998*
Mk 10:17 there came one **r.**, and kneeled to *4370*
Lu 6:38 **and shaken together, and r. over,** *5240*
Ac 27:16 And **r.** under a certain island *5295*
Re 9:9 of many horses **r.** to battle. *5143*

RUSH See also BULRUSH; RUSHED; RUSHES; RUSHETH; RUSHING.
Job 8:11 Can the **r.** grow up without mire? 1573
Isa 9:14 Israel head and tail, branch and **r.**, 100
Isa 17:13 nations shall **r.** like the rushing of 7582
Isa 19:15 head or tail, branch or **r.**, may do. 100

RUSHED
Jg 9:44 Abimelech...**r.** forward, and stood 6584
Jg 20:37 in wait hasted, and **r.** upon Gibeah; 6584
Ac 19:29 they **r.** with one accord into the *3729*

RUSHES See also BULRUSHES.
Isa 35:7 shall be grass with reeds and **r.** 1573

RUSHETH
Jer 8:6 as the horse **r.** into the battle 7857

RUSHING
Isa 17:12 and to the **r.** of nations, that make 7588
Isa 17:12 of nations, that make a **r.** like the 7582
Isa 17:12 like the **r.** of mighty waters! 7588
Isa 17:13 rush like the **r.** of many waters: 7588
Jer 47:3 at the **r.** of his chariots, and at the 7494
Eze 3:12 behind me a voice of a great **r.**, 7494
Eze 3:13 them, and a noise of a great **r.** 7494
Ac 2:2 from heaven as of a **r.** mighty wind, *5342*

RUST
Mt 6:19 **where moth and r. doth corrupt,** *1035*
Mt 6:20 **neither moth nor r. doth corrupt,** *1035*
Jas 5:3 the **r.** of them shall be a witness *2447*

RUTH (rooth)
Ru 1:4 and the name of the other **R.**: 7327
Ru 1:14 in law; but **R.** clave unto her 7327
Ru 1:16 **R.** said, Intreat me not to leave 7327
Ru 1:22 returned, and **R.** the Moabitess, 7327
Ru 2:2 **R.** the Moabitess said unto Naomi, 7327
Ru 2:8 then said Boaz unto **R.**, Hearest 7327
Ru 2:21 **R.** the Moabitess said, He said unto 7327
Ru 2:22 Naomi said unto **R.** her daughter 7327
Ru 3:9 answered, I am **R.** thine handmaid 7327
Ru 4:5 must buy it also of **R.** the Moabitess, 7327
Ru 4:10 **R.** the Moabitess,...wife of Mahlon, 7327
Ru 4:13 Boaz took **R.**, and she was his wife: 7327
Mt 1:5 and Booz begat Obed of **R.**; and *4503*

RYE See RIE.

S.

S. [for **St.** or **Saint**]
Mt *general title* According To **S.** [St.] Matthew 40
Mk *general title* According To **S.** [St.] Mark 40
Lu *general title* According To **S.** [St.] Luke 40
Joh *general title* According To **S.** [St.] John 40
Re *general title* Revelation Of **S.** [St.] John 40

SABACHTHANI (sa-bak'-tha-ni)
Mt 27:46 loud voice, saying, **Eli, Eli, lama s.?** *4518*
Mk 15:34 voice, saying, **Eloi, Eloi, lama s.?** *4518*

SABAOTH (sab'-a-oth)
Ro 9:29 Except the Lord of **S.** had left us a *4519*
Jas 5:4 into the ears of the Lord of **s.** *4519*

SABAS See BARSABAS.

SABBATH See also SABBATHS.
Ex 16:23 rest of the holy **s.** unto the Lord: 7676
Ex 16:25 for to day is a **s.** unto the Lord: 7676
Ex 16:26 on the seventh day, which is the **s.**, 7676
Ex 16:29 that the Lord hath given you the **s.**, 7676
Ex 20:8 Remember the **s.** day, to keep it holy. 7676
Ex 20:10 seventh day is the **s.** of the Lord thy 7676
Ex 20:11 the Lord blessed the **s.** day, and 7676
Ex 31:14 Ye shall keep the **s.** therefore; for it 7676
Ex 31:15 but in the seventh is the **s.** of rest, 7676
Ex 31:15 whosoever doeth any work in the **s.** 7676
Ex 31:16 shall keep the **s.**, to observe the **s.** 7676
Ex 35:2 an holy day, a **s.** of rest to the Lord: 7676
Ex 35:3 kindle no fire...upon the **s.** day. 7676
Le 16:31 It shall be a **s.** of rest unto you, and 7676
Le 23:3 but the seventh day is the **s.** of rest, 7676
Le 23:3 **s.** of the Lord in all your dwellings. 7676
Le 23:11 morrow after the **s.** the priest shall 7676
Le 23:15 you from the morrow after the **s.**, 7676
Le 23:16 unto the morrow after the seventh **s.** 7676
Le 23:24 shall ye have a **s.**, a memorial of 7677
Le 23:32 It shall be unto you a **s.** of rest, 7676
Le 23:32 unto even, shall ye celebrate you **s.** 7676
Le 23:39 on the first day shall be a **s.**, and 7677
Le 23:39 on the eighth day shall be a **s.** 7677
Le 24:8 Every **s.** he shall set it in order 7676
Le 25:2 then shall the land keep a **s.** unto 7676
Le 25:4 shall be a **s.** of rest unto the land, 7676
Le 25:4 a **s.** for the Lord: thou shalt neither 7676
Le 25:6 **s.** of the land shall be meat for you; 7676
Nu 15:32 gathered sticks upon the **s.** day 7676
Nu 28:9 And on the **s.** day two lambs of the 7676
Nu 28:10 is the burnt offering of every **s.**, 7676
De 5:12 Keep the **s.** day to sanctify it, as the 7676
De 5:14 seventh day is the **s.** of the Lord 7676
De 5:15 commanded thee to keep the **s.** day 7676
2Ki 4:23 it is neither new moon, nor **s.** 7676
2Ki 11:5 part of you that enter in on the **s.** 7676
2Ki 11:7 of all you that go forth on the **s.**, 7676
2Ki 11:9 men that were to come in on the **s.**, 7676
2Ki 11:9 them that should go out on the **s.**, 7676
2Ki 16:18 covert for the **s.** that they had built 7676
1Ch 9:32 shewbread, to prepare it every **s.** 7676
2Ch 23:4 third part of you entering on the **s.**, 7676
2Ch 23:8 men that were to come in on the **s.**, 7676
2Ch 23:8 them that were to go out on the **s.**: 7676
2Ch 36:21 as she lay desolate she kept **s.**, 7673
Ne 9:14 And madest known...thy holy **s.**, 7676
Ne 10:31 ware or any victuals on the **s.** day 7676
Ne 10:31 would not buy it of them on the **s.**, 7676
Ne 13:15 treading wine presses on the **s.**, 7676
Ne 13:15 brought into Jerusalem on the **s.** 7676
Ne 13:16 sold on the **s.** unto the children of 7676
Ne 13:17 that ye do, and profane the **s.** day? 7676
Ne 13:18 more wrath...by profaning the **s.** 7676
Ne 13:19 began to be dark before the **s.**, 7676
Ne 13:19 not be opened till after the **s.**: 7676
Ne 13:19 burden be brought in on the **s.** day. 7676
Ne 13:21 forth came they no more on the **s.** day. 7676
Ne 13:22 keep the gates, to sanctify the **s.** day. 7676
Ps 92:*title* A Psalm or Song for the **s.** day 7676
Isa 56:2,6 keepeth the **s.** from polluting it. 7676
Isa 58:13 thou turn away thy foot from the **s.**, 7676
Isa 58:13 and call the **s.** a delight, the holy of 7676
Isa 66:23 another, and from one **s.** to another, 7676
Jer 17:21 and bear no burden on the **s.** day, 7676
Jer 17:22 burden out of your houses on the **s.** 7676
Jer 17:22 hallow...the **s.** day, as I commanded 7676
Jer 17:24 the gates of this city on the **s.** day, 7676
Jer 17:24 but hallow the **s.** day, to do no work 7676
Jer 17:27 hearken unto me to hallow the **s.** 7676
Jer 17:27 gates of Jerusalem on the **s.** day; 7676
Eze 46:1 but on the **s.** it shall be opened, and 7676
Eze 46:4 shall offer unto the Lord in the **s.** 7676
Eze 46:12 offerings, as he did on the **s.** day: 7676
Am 8:5 and the **s.**, that we may set forth 7676
Mt 12:1 Jesus went on the **s.** day through *4521*
Mt 12:2 is not lawful to do upon the **s.** day: *4521*
Mt 12:5 **how that on the s. days the priests** *4521*
Mt 12:5 **in the temple profane the s., and** *4521*
Mt 12:8 **of man is Lord even of the s. day.** *4521*
Mt 12:10 Is it lawful to heal on the **s.** days? *4521*
Mt 12:11 **if it fall into a pit on the s. day,** *4521*
Mt 12:12 **is lawful to do well on the s. days.** *4521*
Mt 24:20 **the winter, neither on the s. day:** *4521*
Mt 28:1 In the end of the **s.**, as it began to *4521*
Mk 1:21 **s.** day he entered...the synagogue, *4521*
Mk 2:23 through the corn fields on the **s.** *4521*
Mk 2:24 on the **s.**...that which is not lawful? *4521*
Mk 2:27 **The s. was made for man, and not** *4521*
Mk 2:27 **for man, and not man for the s.:** *4521*
Mk 2:28 **Son of man is Lord also of the s.** *4521*
Mk 3:2 he would heal him on the **s.** day; *4521*
Mk 3:4 **it lawful to do good on the s. days,** *4521*
Mk 6:2 And when the **s.** day come, *4521*
Mk 15:42 that is, the day before the **s.**, *4315*
Mk 16:1 And when the **s.** was past, Mary *4521*
Lu 4:16 into the synagogue on the **s.** day, *4521*
Lu 4:31 and taught them on the **s.** days. *4521*
Lu 6:1 pass on the second **s.** after the first, *4521*
Lu 6:2 is not lawful to do on the **s.** days? *4521*
Lu 6:5 **Son of man is Lord also of the s.** *4521*
Lu 6:6 it came to pass also on another **s.**, *4521*
Lu 6:7 whether he would heal on the **s.** *4521*
Lu 6:9 **lawful on the s. days to do good,** *4521*
Lu 13:10 in one of the synagogues on the **s.** *4521*
Lu 13:14 that Jesus had healed on the **s.** day, *4521*
Lu 13:14 and be healed, and not on the **s.** day. *4521*
Lu 13:15 **one of you on the s. loose his ox** *4521*
Lu 13:16 **from this bond on the s. day?** *4521*
Lu 14:1 Pharisees to eat bread on the **s.** day, *4521*
Lu 14:3 **Is it lawful to heal on the s. day?** *4521*
Lu 14:5 **straightway pull him out on the s.** *4521*
Lu 23:54 the preparation, and the **s.** drew on. *4521*
Lu 23:56 and rested the **s.** day according to *4521*
Joh 5:9 and on the same day was the **s.** *4521*
Joh 5:10 It is the **s.** day: it is not lawful for *4521*
Joh 5:16 had done these things on the **s.** day. *4521*
Joh 5:18 he not only had broken the **s.**, but *4521*
Joh 7:22 **ye on the s. day circumcise a man.** *4521*
Joh 7:23 **on the s. day receive circumcision,** *4521*
Joh 7:23 **every whit whole on the s. day?** *4521*
Joh 9:14 **s.** day when Jesus made the clay, *4521*
Joh 9:16 because he keepeth not the **s.** day. *4521*
Joh 19:31 remain upon the cross on the **s.** day, *4521*
Joh 19:31 (for that **s.** day was an high day,) *4521*
Ac 1:12 from Jerusalem a **s.** day's journey. *4521*
Ac 13:14 into the synagogue on the **s.** day, *4521*
Ac 13:27 prophets which are read every **s.** *4521*
Ac 13:42 be preached to them the next **s.** *4521*
Ac 13:44 next **s.** day came almost the whole *4521*
Ac 15:21 read in the synagogues every **s.** day. *4521*
Ac 16:13 on the **s.** we went out of the city by *4521*
Ac 17:2 three **s.** days reasoned with them *4521*
Ac 18:4 reasoned in the synagogue every **s.**, *4521*
Col 2:16 of the new moon, or of the **s.** days: *4521*

SABBATH-DAY See SABBATH and DAY.

SABBATHS
Ex 31:13 Verily my **s.** ye shall keep: for it 7676
Le 19:3 and his father, and keep my **s.**: 7676
Le 19:30 Ye shall keep my **s.**, and reverence 7676
Le 23:15 offering; seven **s.** shall be complete: 7676
Le 23:38 Beside the **s.** of the Lord, and beside 7676
Le 25:8 thou shalt number seven **s.** of years 7676
Le 25:8 the space of the seven **s.** of years 7676
Le 26:2 Ye shall keep my **s.**, and reverence 7676
Le 26:34 Then shall the land enjoy her **s.**, 7676
Le 26:34 shall the land rest, and enjoy her **s.** 7676
Le 26:35 because it did not rest in your **s.** 7676
Le 26:43 left of them, and shall enjoy her **s.**, 7676
1Ch 23:31 sacrifices unto the Lord in the **s.**, 7676
2Ch 2:4 on the **s.**, and on the new moons, 7676
2Ch 8:13 on the **s.**, and on the new moons, 7676
2Ch 31:3 and the burnt offerings for the **s.**, 7676
2Ch 36:21 until the land had enjoyed her **s.**: 7676
Ne 10:33 of the **s.**, of the new moons, for the 7676
Isa 1:13 the new moons and **s.**, the calling 7676
Isa 56:4 unto the eunuchs that keep my **s.**, 7676
La 1:7 saw her, and did mock at her **s.** 4868
La 2:6 feasts and **s.** to be forgotten in 7676
Eze 20:12 Moreover also I gave them my **s.**, 7676
Eze 20:13 and my **s.** they greatly polluted: 7676
Eze 20:16 in my statutes, but polluted my **s.**: 7676
Eze 20:20 And hallow my **s.**; and they shall be 7676
Eze 20:21 they polluted my **s.**: then I said, 7676
Eze 20:24 statues, and had polluted my **s.**, 7676
Eze 22:8 things, and hast profaned my **s.** 7676
Eze 22:26 and have hid their eyes from my **s.**, 7676
Eze 23:38 same day, and have profaned my **s.** 7676
Eze 44:24 and they shall hallow my **s.** 7676
Eze 45:17 and in the new moons, and in the **s.**, 7676
Eze 46:3 in the **s.** and in the new moons. 7676
Ho 2:11 her new moons, and her **s.**, and all 7676

SABEANS (sab-e'-uns)
Job 1:15 And the **S.** fell upon them, and 7614
Isa 45:14 and of the **S.**, men of stature, 5436
Eze 23:42 brought **S.** from the wilderness, 5433
Joe 3:8 and they shall sell them to the **S.**, 7615

SABTA (sab'-tah) See also SABTAH.
1Ch 1:9 Seba, and Havilah, and **S.**, and 5454

SABTAH (sab'-tah) See also SABTA.
Ge 10:7 Seba, and Havilah, and S., and 5454

SABTECHA (sab'-te-kah) See also SABTECHA.
1Ch 1:9 Sabta, and Raamah, and S. 5455

SABTECHAH (sab'-te-kah) See also SABTECHA.
Ge 10:7 Sabtah, and Raamah, and S. 5455

SACAR (sa'-kar) See also SHARAR.
1Ch 11:35 Ahiam the son of S. the Hararite, 7940
1Ch 26:4 Joah the third, and S. the fourth, 7940

SACK See also SACKBUT; SACKCLOTH; SACK'S; SACKS.
Ge 42:25 every man's money into his s., 8242
Ge 42:27 as one of them opened his s. to give 8242
Ge 42:28 restored; and, lo, it is even in my s.: 572
Ge 42:35 bundle of money was in his s.: 8242
Ge 43:21 money was in the mouth of his s., 572
Ge 44:11 down every man his s. to the ground, 572
Ge 44:11 and opened every man his s. 572
Ge 44:12 the cup was found in Benjamin's s. 572
Le 11:32 of wood, or raiment, or skin, or s., 8242

SACKBUT
Da 3:5,7, 10,15 of the cornet, flute, harp, s., 5443

SACKCLOTH See also SACKCLOTHES.
Ge 37:34 clothes, put s. upon his loins, and 8242
2Sa 3:31 your clothes, and gird you with s., 8242
2Sa 21:10 Rizpah the daughter of Aiah took s., 8242
1Ki 20:31 us, I pray thee, put s. on our loins, 8242
1Ki 20:32 So they girded s. on their loins, 8242
1Ki 21:27 clothes, and put s. upon his flesh, 8242
1Ki 21:27 and fasted, and lay in s., and went 8242
2Ki 6:30 he had s. within upon his flesh 8242
2Ki 19:1 clothes, and covered himself with s., 8242
2Ki 19:2 elders of the priests, covered with s., 8242
1Ch 21:16 of Israel, who were clothed in s., 8242
Es 4:1 clothes, and put on s. with ashes, 8242
Es 4:2 into the king's gate clothed with s. 8242
Es 4:3 and many lay in s. and ashes 8242
Es 4:4 and to take away his s. from him: 8242
Job 16:15 I have sewed s. upon my skin, and 8242
Ps 30:11 thou hast put off my s., and girded 8242
Ps 35:13 they were sick, my clothing was s. 8242
Ps 69:11 I made s. also my garment; and I 8242
Isa 3:24 of a stomacher a girding of s.; 8242
Isa 15:3 they shall gird themselves with s.: 8242
Isa 20:2 and loose the s. from off thy loins, 8242
Isa 22:12 to baldness, and to girding with s.: 8242
Isa 32:11 you bare, and gird s. upon your loins.
Isa 37:1 and covered himself with s., and 8242
Isa 37:2 elders of the priests covered with s., 8242
Isa 50:3 and I make s. their covering 8242
Isa 58:5 to spread s. and ashes under him? 8242
Jer 4:8 gird you with s., lament and howl: 8242
Jer 6:26 gird thee with s., and wallow thyself 8242
Jer 48:37 be cuttings, and upon the loins s. 8242
Jer 49:3 of Rabbah, gird you with s.; lament, 8242
La 2:10 they have girded themselves with s. 8242
Eze 7:18 shall also gird themselves with s., 8242
Eze 27:31 bald for thee, and gird them with s., 8242
Da 9:3 with fasting, and s., and ashes: 8242
Joe 1:8 Lament like a virgin girded with s. 8242
Joe 1:13 come, lie all night in s., ye ministers 8242
Am 8:10 and I will bring up s. upon all loins, 8242
Jon 3:5 proclaimed a fast, and put on s., 8242
Jon 3:6 and covered him with s., and sat in 8242
Jon 3:8 man and beast be covered with s., 8242
Mt 11:21 **repented long ago in s. and ashes** *4526*
Lu 10:13 **repented, sitting in s. and ashes** *4526*
Re 6:12 the sun became black as s. of hair, *4526*
Re 11:3 and threescore days, clothed in s. *4526*

SACKCLOTHES
Ne 9:1 with fasting, and with s., and 8242

SACK'S
Ge 42:27 for, behold, it was in his s. mouth. 572
Ge 44:1 every man's money in his s. mouth. 572
Ge 44:2 cup, in the s. mouth of the youngest, 572

SACKS See also SACKS'.
Ge 42:25 Joseph commanded to fill their s. 3672
Ge 42:35 to pass as they emptied their s., 8242
Ge 43:12 the money...in the mouth of your s., 572
Ge 43:18 money that was returned in our s. 572
Ge 43:21 that we opened our s., and, behold, 572
Ge 43:22 tell who put our money in our s. 572
Ge 43:23 hath given you treasure in your s. 572
Ge 44:1 saying, Fill the men's s. with food, 572
Jos 9:4 and took old s. upon their asses, 8242

SACKS'
Ge 44:8 which we found in our s. mouths, 572

SACRIFICE See also SACRIFICED; SACRIFICES; SACRIFICETH; SACRIFICING.
Ge 31:54 Jacob offered s. upon the mount, 2077
Ex 3:18 we may s. to the Lord our God. 2076
Ex 5:3 and s. unto the Lord our God; lest 2076
Ex 5:8 Let us go and s. to our God 2076
Ex 5:17 Let us go and do s. to the Lord 2076
Ex 8:8 go, they may do s. unto the Lord 2076
Ex 8:25 Go ye, s. to your God in the land. 2076
Ex 8:26 we shall s. the abomination of the 2076
Ex 8:26 shall we s. the abomination of the 2076
Ex 8:27 and s. to the Lord our God, as he 2076
Ex 8:28 ye may s. to the Lord your God in 2076
Ex 8:29 the people go to s. to the Lord 2076
Ex 10:25 we may s. unto the Lord our God. 2077
Ex 12:27 It is the s. of the Lord's passover, 2077
Ex 13:15 I s. to the Lord all that openeth 2076
Ex 20:24 s. thereon thy burnt offerings, 2076
Ex 23:18 not offer the blood of my s. with 2077
Ex 23:18 shall the fat of my s. remain until 2282
Ex 29:28 of the s. of their peace offerings, 2077
Ex 30:9 incense thereon, nor burnt s., nor
Ex 34:15 and do s. unto their gods, and 2076
Ex 34:15 call thee, and thou eat of his s.; 2077
Ex 34:25 the blood of my s. with leaven; 2077
Ex 34:25 the s. of the feast of the passover be 2077
Le 1:3 offering be a burnt s., of the herd,
Le 1:9 to be a burnt s., an offering made
Le 1:10 or of the goats, for a burnt s.; he
Le 1:13 it is a burnt s., an offering made
Le 1:14 if the burnt s. for his offering to
Le 1:17 it is a burnt s., an offering made by
Le 3:1 oblation be a s. of peace offering, 2077
Le 3:3 offer of the s. of the peace offering 2077
Le 3:5 it on the altar upon the burnt s.,
Le 3:6 offering for a s. of peace offering 2077
Le 3:9 offer of the s. of the peace offering 2077
Le 4:10 bullock of the s. of peace offerings: 2077
Le 4:26 the fat of the s. of peace offerings: 2077
Le 4:31 from off the s. of peace offerings; 2077
Le 4:35 from the s. of the peace offerings; 2077
Le 7:11 law of the s. of peace offerings, 2077
Le 7:12 offer with the s. of thanksgiving 2077
Le 7:13 bread with the s. of thanksgiving 2077
Le 7:15 the flesh of the s. of his peace 2077
Le 7:16 if the s. of his offering be a vow, 2077
Le 7:16 same day that he offereth his s. 2077
Le 7:17 the remainder of the flesh of the s. 2077
Le 7:18 flesh of the s. of his peace offerings 2077
Le 7:20, 21 flesh of the s. of peace offerings, 2077
Le 7:29 offereth the s. of his peace offerings 2077
Le 7:29 of the s. of his peace offerings. 2077
Le 7:37 of the s. of the peace offerings; 2077
Le 8:21 a burnt s. for a sweet savour,
Le 9:4 offerings, to s. before the Lord; 2076
Le 9:17 beside the burnt s. of the morning.
Le 9:18 the ram for a s. of peace offerings, 2077
Le 17:8 offereth a burnt offering or s., 2077
Le 19:5 if ye offer a s. of peace offerings 2077
Le 22:21 offereth a s. of peace offerings unto 2077
Le 22:29 ye will offer a s. of thanksgiving 2077
Le 23:19 ye shall s. one kid of the goats 6213
Le 23:19 year for a s. of peace offerings. 2077
Le 23:37 a meat offering, a s., and drink 2077
Le 27:11 they do not offer a s. unto the Lord, 7133
Nu 6:17 the ram for a s. of peace offerings 2077
Nu 6:18 it in the fire which is under the s. 2077
Nu 7:17, 23,29,35,41,47,53,59,65,71,77,83
for a s. of peace offerings, two 2077
Nu 7:88 all oxen for the s. of the peace 2077
Nu 15:3 or a s. in performing a vow, or in 2077
Nu 15:5 with the burnt offering or s., for 2077
Nu 15:8 or for a s. in performing a vow, or 2077
Nu 15:25 s. made by fire unto the Lord, and
Nu 23:6 he stood by his burnt s., he, and
Nu 28:6 a s. made by fire unto the Lord.
Nu 28:8 thou shalt offer it, a s. made by fire,
Nu 28:13 a s. made by fire unto the Lord.
Nu 28:19 ye shall offer a s. made by fire for a
Nu 28:24 the meat of the s. made by fire, of
Nu 29:6 a s. made by fire unto the Lord.
Nu 29:13, 36 a s. made by fire, of a sweet
De 15:21 shalt not s. it unto the Lord thy 2076
De 16:2 shalt therefore s. the passover 2076
De 16:5 Thou mayest not s. the passover 2076
De 16:6 thou shalt s. the passover at even, 2076
De 17:1 shalt not s. unto the Lord thy God 2076
De 18:3 people, from them that offer a s., 2077
De 33:10 whole burnt s. upon thine altar.
Jos 22:26 not for burnt offering, nor for s. 2077
Jg 6:26 offer a burnt s. with the wood of
Jg 16:23 a great s. unto Dagon their god, 2077
1Sa 1:3 to s. unto the Lord of hosts in 2076
1Sa 1:21 offer unto the Lord the yearly s., 2077
1Sa 2:13 that, when any man offered s., the 2077
1Sa 2:19 her husband to offer the yearly s. 2077
1Sa 2:29 Wherefore kick ye at my s. and at 2077
1Sa 3:14 shall not be purged with s. nor 2077
1Sa 9:12 s. of the people to day in the high 2077
1Sa 9:13 come, because he doth bless the s.; 2077
1Sa 10:8 to s. sacrifices of peace offerings: 2076
1Sa 15:15 oxen, to s. unto the Lord thy God; 2076
1Sa 15:21 s. unto the Lord thy God in Gilgal. 2076
1Sa 15:22 to obey is better than s., and to 2077
1Sa 16:2 say, I am come to s. to the Lord. 2076
1Sa 16:3 call Jesse to the s., and I will 2077
1Sa 16:5 I am come to s. unto the Lord: 2076
1Sa 16:5 and come with me to the s. 2077
1Sa 16:5 sons, and called them to the s. 2077
1Sa 20:6 there is a yearly s. there for all the 2077
1Sa 20:29 our family hath a s. in the city; 2077
2Sa 24:22 here be oxen for burnt s., and
1Ki 3:4 king went to Gibeon to s. there; 2076
1Ki 8:62 him, offered s. before the Lord 2077
1Ki 8:63 And Solomon offered a s. of peace 2077
1Ki 12:27 this people go up to do s. in the 2077
1Ki 18:29 the offering of the evening s., 4503
1Ki 18:33 and pour it on the burnt s., and
1Ki 18:36 of the offering of the evening s., 4503
1Ki 18:38 fell, and consumed the burnt s.,
2Ki 5:17 neither burnt offering nor s. unto 2077
2Ki 10:19 I have a great s. to do to Baal; 2077
2Ki 14:4 as yet the people did s. and burnt 2076
2Ki 16:15 offering, and the king's burnt s.,
2Ki 16:15 and all the blood of the s. 2077
2Ki 17:35 nor serve them, nor s. to them: 2076
2Ki 17:36 worship, and to him shall ye do s. 2076
2Ch 2:6 save only to burn s. before him?
2Ch 7:5 And king Solomon offered a s. of 2077
2Ch 7:12 place to myself for an house of s. 2077
2Ch 11:16 to s. unto the Lord God of their 2076
2Ch 28:23 will I s. to them, that they may 2076
2Ch 33:17 people did s....in the high places, 2076
Ezr 4:2 we do s. unto him since the days of 2076
Ezr 9:4 I sat astonied until...evening s. 4503
Ezr 9:5 at the evening s. I arose up from 4503
Ne 4:2 will they s.? will they make an 2076
Ps 20:3 offerings, and accept thy burnt s.;
Ps 40:6 S. and offering thou didst not 2077
Ps 50:5 made a covenant with me by s. 2077
Ps 51:16 For thou desirest not s.; else 2077
Ps 54:6 I will freely s. unto thee: I will 2076
Ps 107:22 And let them s. the sacrifices of 2076
Ps 116:17 offer to thee...s. of thanksgiving, 2077
Ps 118:27 bind the s. with cords, even unto 2282
Ps 141:2 up of my hands as the evening s. 4503
Pr 15:8 s. of the wicked is an abomination 2077
Pr 21:3 acceptable to the Lord than s. 2077
Pr 21:27 s. of the wicked is abomination: 2077
Ec 5:1 hear, than to give the s. of fools: 2077
Isa 19:21 day, and shall do s. and oblation; 2077
Isa 34:6 the Lord hath a s. in Bozrah, and 2077
Isa 57:7 thither wentest thou up to offer s. 2077
Jer 33:11 that shall bring the s. of praise
Jer 33:18 offerings, and to do s. continually. 2077
Jer 46:10 the Lord God of hosts hath a s. in 2077
Eze 39:17 yourselves on every side to my s. 2077
Eze 39:17 that I do s. for you, even a great 2076
Eze 39:17 s. upon the mountains of Israel, 2077
Eze 39:19 s. which I have sacrificed for you. 2076
Eze 40:42 slew the burnt offering and the s. 2077
Eze 44:11 offering and the s. for the people, 2077
Eze 46:24 house shall boil the s. of the people. 2077
Da 8:11 by him the daily s. was taken away,
Da 8:12 daily s. by reason of transgression,
Da 8:13 the vision concerning the daily s.,
Da 9:27 s. and the oblation to cease, 2077
Da 11:31 and shall take away the daily s.,

Da 12:11 the daily s. shall be taken away,
Ho 3:4 and without a s., and without an 2077
Ho 4:13 s. upon the tops of the mountains, 2076
Ho 4:14 whores, and they s. with harlots: 2076
Ho 6:6 for I desired mercy, and not s.; 2077
Ho 8:13 They s. flesh for the sacrifices of 2076
Ho 12:11 vanity: they s. bullocks in Gilgal; 2076
Ho 13:2 the men that s. kiss the calves. 2076
Am 4:5 a s. of thanksgiving with leaven,
Jon 1:16 and offered a s. unto the Lord, 2077
Jon 2:9 will s. unto thee with the voice of 2076
Hab 1:16 Therefore they s. unto their net, 2076
Zep 1:7 for the Lord hath prepared a s., 2077
Zep 1:8 pass in the day of the Lord's s., 2077
Zec 14:21 they that s. shall come and take 2076
Mal 1:8 And if ye offer the blind for s., is it 2076
Mt 9:13 **I will have mercy, and not s.: for** *2378*
Mt 12:7 **I will have mercy, and not s., ye** *2378*
Mk 9:49 **every s. shall be salted with salt** *2378*
Lu 2:24 And to offer a s. according to that *2378*
Ac 7:41 and offered s. unto the idol, and *2378*
Ac 14:13 and would have done s. with the *2380*
Ac 14:18 they had not done s. unto them. *2380*
Ro 12:1 ye present your bodies a living s., *2378*
1Co 8:4 that are offered in s. unto idols, *1494*
1Co 10:19 is offered in s. to idols is any thing? *1494*
1Co 10:20 the things which the Gentiles s., *2380*
1Co 10:20 they s. to devils, and not to God: *2380*
1Co 10:28 This is offered in s. unto idols, eat *1494*
Eph 5:2 for us an offering and a s. to God *2378*
Php 2:17 the s. and service of your faith, *2378*
Php 4:18 s. acceptable, wellpleasing to God *2378*
Heb 7:27 to offer up s., first for his own sins, *2378*
Heb 9:26 to put away sin by the s. of himself. *2378*
Heb 10:5 S. and offering thou wouldest not, *2378*
Heb 10:8 S. and offering and burnt offerings *2378*
Heb 10:12 after he had offered one s. for sins *2378*
Heb 10:26 remaineth no more s. for sins, *2378*
Heb 11:4 God a more excellent s. than Cain, *2378*
Heb 13:15 let us offer the s. of praise to God *2378*

SACRIFICED See also SACRIFICEDST.
Ex 24:5 s. peace offerings of oxen unto the 2076
Ex 32:8 it, and have s. thereunto, and said, 2076
De 32:17 They s. unto devils, not to God; to 2076
Jos 8:31 the Lord, and s. peace offerings 2076
Jg 2:5 and they s. there unto the Lord. 2076
1Sa 2:15 said to the man that s., Give flesh 2076
1Sa 6:15 s. sacrifices the same day unto the 2076
1Sa 11:15 and there they s. sacrifices of peace 2076
2Sa 6:13 six paces, he s. oxen and fatlings. 2076
1Ki 3:2 Only the people s. in high places, 2076
1Ki 3:3 only he s. and burnt incense in high 2076
1Ki 11:8 incense and s. unto their gods. 2076
2Ki 12:3 the people still s. and burnt incense 2076
2Ki 15:4 the people s. and burnt incense still 2076
2Ki 15:35 the people s. and burned incense 2076
2Ki 16:4 he s. and burnt incense in the high 2076
2Ki 17:32 which s. for them in the houses of 6213
1Ch 21:28 the Jebusite, then he s. there. 2076
1Ch 29:21 they s. sacrifices unto the Lord, and 2076
2Ch 5:6 s. sheep and oxen, which could not 2076
2Ch 28:4 He s. also and burnt incense in the 2076
2Ch 28:23 he s. unto the gods of Damascus, 2076
2Ch 33:16 and s. thereon peace offerings and 2076
2Ch 33:22 Amon s. unto all the carved images 2076
2Ch 34:4 graves of them that...s. unto them. 2076
Ps 106:37 s. their sons and their daughters 2076
Ps 106:38 they s. unto the idols of Canaan: 2076
Eze 16:20 thou s. unto them to be devoured. 2076
Eze 39:19 sacrifice which I have s. for you. 2076
Ho 11:2 they s. unto Baalim, and burned 2076
1Co 5:7 Christ our passover is s. for us: *2380*
Re 2:14 **to eat things s. unto idols, and to** *1494*
Re 2:20 **and to eat things s. unto idols** *1494*

SACRIFICEDST
De 16:4 which thou s. the first day at even, 2076

SACRIFICES
Ge 46:1 and offered s. unto the God of his 2077
Ex 10:25 give us also s. and burnt offerings, 2077
Ex 18:12 a burnt offering and s. for God: 2077
Le 7:32 of the s. of your peace offerings. 2077
Le 7:34 off the s. of their peace offerings, 2077
Le 10:13 of the s. of the Lord made by fire:
Le 10:14 out of the s. of peace offerings of 2077
Le 17:5 children of Israel may bring their s., 2077
Le 17:7 no more offer their s. unto devils, 2077
Nu 10:10 over the s. of your peace offerings; 2077
Nu 25:2 the people unto the s. of their gods: 2077
Nu 28:2 my bread for my s. made by fire,
De 12:6 and your s., and your tithes, and 2077
De 12:11 your burnt offerings, and your s., 2077
De 12:27 the blood of thy s. shall be poured 2077
De 32:38 Which did eat the fat of their s., and 2077
De 33:19 they shall offer s. of righteousness: 2077
Jos 13:14 s. of the Lord...of Israel made by fire
Jos 22:27 with our s., and with our peace 2077
Jos 22:28 not for burnt offerings, nor for s.: 2077
Jos 22:29 for meat offerings, or for s., beside 2077
1Sa 6:15 sacrificed s. the same day unto the 2077
1Sa 10:8 to sacrifice s. of peace offerings: 2077
1Sa 11:15 they sacrificed s. of peace offerings 2077
1Sa 15:22 delight in burnt offerings and s., as 2077
2Sa 15:12 even from Giloh, while he offered s. 2077
2Ki 10:24 they went in to offer s. and burnt 2077
1Ch 16:1 they offered burnt s. and peace
1Ch 23:31 to offer all burnt s. unto the Lord
1Ch 29:21 they sacrificed s. unto the Lord, 2077
1Ch 29:21 and s. in abundance for all Israel: 2077
2Ch 7:1 the burnt offerings and the s.; and 2077
2Ch 7:4 people offered s. before the Lord. 2077
2Ch 13:11 every evening burnt s. and sweet
2Ch 29:31 bring s. and thank offerings into 2077
2Ch 29:31 the congregation brought in s. and 2077
Ezr 6:3 the place where they offered s., 1685
Ezr 6:10 they may offer s. of sweet savours
Ne 12:43 that day they offered great s., 2077
Ps 4:5 Offer the s. of righteousness, and 2077
Ps 27:6 I offer in his tabernacle s. of joy; 2077
Ps 50:8 I will not reprove thee for thy s. or 2077
Ps 51:17 The s. of God are a broken spirit: 2077
Ps 51:19 with the s. of righteousness, with 2077
Ps 66:15 unto thee burnt s. of fatlings, with
Ps 106:28 and ate the s. of the dead. 2077
Ps 107:22 sacrifice the s. of thanksgiving, and 2077
Pr 17:1 than an house full of s. with strife. 2077
Isa 1:11 the multitude of your s. unto me? 2077
Isa 29:1 ye year to year; let them kill s. 2282
Isa 43:23 hast thou honoured me with thy s. 2077
Isa 43:24 thou filled me with the fat of thy s. 2077
Isa 56:7 s. shall be accepted upon mine 2077
Jer 6:20 nor your s. sweet unto me. 2077
Jer 7:21 your burnt offerings unto your s., 2077
Jer 7:22 concerning burnt offerings or s. 2077
Jer 17:26 bringing burnt offerings, and s., and 2077
Jer 17:26 incense, and bringing s. of praise,
Eze 20:28 and they offered there their s., 2077
Eze 40:41 tables, whereupon they slew their s.
Ho 4:19 be ashamed because of their s. 2077
Ho 8:13 flesh for the s. of mine offerings, 2077
Ho 9:4 their s. shall be unto them as the 2077
Am 4:4 and bring your s. every morning, 2077
Am 5:25 ye offered unto me s. and offerings 2077
Mk 12:33 all whole burnt offerings and s. *2378*
Lu 13:1 Pilate had mingled with their s. *2378*
Ac 7:42 offered to me slain beasts and s. *2378*
1Co 10:18 which eat of the s. partakers of the *2378*
Heb 5:1 may offer both gifts and s. for sins: *2378*
Heb 8:3 is ordained to offer gifts and s.: *2378*
Heb 9:9 were offered both gifts and s., that *2378*
Heb 9:23 with better s. than these. *2378*
Heb 10:1 can never with those s. which they *2378*
Heb 10:3 in those s. there is a remembrance
Heb 10:6 In burnt offerings and s. for sin thou
Heb 10:11 offering oftentimes the same s., *2378*
Heb 13:16 with such s. God is well pleased. *2378*
1Pe 2:5 to offer up spiritual s., acceptable *2378*

SACRIFICETH
Ex 22:20 He that s. unto any god, save unto 2076
Ec 9:2 him that s., and to him that s. not: 2076
Isa 65:3 s. in gardens, and burneth incense 2076
Isa 66:3 he that s. a lamb, as if he cut off a 2076
Mal 1:14 s. unto the Lord a corrupt thing: 2076

SACRIFICING
1Ki 8:5 s. sheep and oxen, that could not 2076
1Ki 12:32 s. unto the calves that he had made: 2076

SACRILEGE
Ro 2:22 idols, dost thou commit s.? *2416*

SAD
Ge 40:6 them, and, behold, they were s. 2196
1Sa 1:18 and her countenance was no more s.
1Ki 21:5 Why is thy spirit so s., that thou 5620
Ne 2:1 been beforetime s. in his presence. 7451
Ne 2:2 Why is thy countenance s., seeing 7451
Ne 2:3 should not my countenance be s., 7489
Eze 13:22 made the heart of the righteous s., 3512
Eze 13:22 whom I have not made s.; and 3510
Mt 6:16 **hypocrites, of a s. countenance:** *4659*
Mk 10:22 he was s. at that saying, and went *4768*
Lu 24:17 **to another, as ye walk, and are s.?** *4659*

SADDLE See also SADDLED.
Le 15:9 what s. soever he rideth upon that 4817
2Sa 19:26 I will s. me an ass, that I may ride 2280
1Ki 13:13 said unto his sons, S. me the ass. 2280
1Ki 13:27 to his sons, saying, S. me the ass. 2280

SADDLED
Ge 22:3 in the morning, and s. his ass, 2280
Nu 22:21 in the morning, and s. his ass, 2280
Jg 19:10 there were with him two asses s., 2280
2Sa 16:1 met him, with a couple of asses s., 2280
2Sa 17:23 he s. his ass, and arose, and gat him 2280
1Ki 2:40 And Shimei arose, and s. his ass, 2280
1Ki 13:13 So they s. him the ass: and he rode 2280
1Ki 13:23 that he s. for him the ass, to wit, 2280
1Ki 13:27 Saddle me the ass. And they s. him 2280
2Ki 4:24 Then she s. an ass, and said to her 2280

SADDUCEES (sad'-du-sees)
Mt 3:7 saw many of the Pharisees and S. *4523*
Mt 16:1 Pharisees also with the S. came, *4523*
Mt 16:6 **leaven of the Pharisees and...S.** *4523*
Mt 16:11 **leaven of the Pharisees and...S.?** *4523*
Mt 16:12 doctrine of the Pharisees and...S. *4523*
Mt 22:23 The same day came to him the S., *4523*
Mt 22:34 that he had put the S. to silence, *4523*
Mk 12:18 Then come unto him the S., which *4523*
Lu 20:27 Then came to him certain of the S., *4523*
Ac 4:1 captain of the temple, and the S., *4523*
Ac 5:17 (which is the sect of the S.,) and *4523*
Ac 23:6 perceived that the one part were S., *4523*
Ac 23:7 between the Pharisees and the S. *4523*
Ac 23:8 S. say that there is no resurrection, *4523*

SADLY
Ge 40:7 Wherefore look ye sc s. to day? 7451

SADNESS
Ec 7:3 by the s. of the countenance the 7455

SADOC (sa'-dok)
Mt 1:14 begat S.; and S. begat Achim; *4524*

SAFE See also SAFEGUARD.
1Sa 12:11 on every side, and ye dwelled s. 983
2Sa 18:29, 32 Is the young man Absalom s.? 7965
Job 21:9 Their houses are s. from fear, 7965
Ps 29:25 his trust in the Lord shall be s. 7682
Ps 119:117 Hold...me up, and I shall be s.: 3467
Pr 18:10 runneth into it, and is safe. 7682
Isa 5:29 prey, and shall carry it away s., 6403
Eze 34:27 and they shall be s. in their land, 983
Lu 15:27 **he hath received him s. and sound.** *5198*
Ac 23:24 and bring him s. unto Felix the *1295*
Ac 27:44 pass, that they escaped all s. to land *1295*
Php 3:1 is not grievous, but for you it is s. *809*

SAFEGUARD
1Sa 22:23 but with me thou shalt be in s. 4931

SAFELY
Le 26:5 the full, and dwell in your land s. 983
1Ki 4:25 And Judah and Israel dwelt s., every 983
Ps 78:53 he led them on s. so that they feared 983
Pr 1:33 hearkeneth unto me shall dwell s., 983
Pr 3:23 Then shalt thou walk in thy way s., 983
Pr 31:11 of her husband doth s. trust in her,
Isa 41:3 He pursued them, and passed s.; 7965
Jer 23:6 be saved, and Israel shall dwell s.: 983
Jer 32:37 and I will cause them to dwell s.: 983
Jer 33:16 saved, and Jerusalem shall dwell s.: 983
Eze 28:26 And they shall dwell s. therein, and 983
Eze 34:25 they shall dwell s. in the wilderness, 983
Eze 34:28 they shall dwell s., and none shall 983
Eze 38:8 and they shall dwell s. all of them. 983
Eze 38:11 them that are at rest, that dwell s., 983
Eze 38:14 my people of Israel dwelleth s., 983
Eze 39:26 when they dwelt s. in their land, 983
Ho 2:18 and will make them to lie down s. 983

Zec 14:11 but Jerusalem shall be **s.** inhabited........ 983
Mk 14:44 take him, and lead him away **s.**............ *806*
Ac 16:23 charging the jailor to keep them **s.**........ *806*

SAFETY
Le 25:18 and ye shall dwell in the land in **s.**....... 983
Le 25:19 eat your fill, and dwell therein in **s.**....... 983
De 12:10 round about, so that ye dwell in **s.**;....... 983
De 33:12 beloved of the Lord shall dwell in **s.**....... 983
De 33:28 Israel then shall dwell in **s.** alone:....... 983
Job 3:26 I was not in **s.**, neither had I rest,..... 7951
Job 5:4 His children are far from **s.**, and........ 3468
Job 5:11 which mourn may be exalted to **s.**...... 3468
Job 11:18 and thou shalt take thy rest in **s.**......... 983
Job 24:23 Though it be given him to in **s.**,.......... 983
Ps 4:8 Lord, only makest me dwell in **s.**.......... 983
Ps 12:5 set him in **s.** from him that puffeth..... 3468
Ps 33:17 An horse is a vain thing for **s.**:.......... 8668
Pr 11:14 multitude of counsellers there is **s.**..... 8668
Pr 21:31 day of battle: but **s.** is of the Lord...... 8668
Pr 24:6 multitude of counsellers there is **s.**..... 8668
Isa 14:30 and the needy shall lie down in **s.**......... 983
Ac 5:23 prison...found we shut with all **s.**,........ *803*
1Th 5:3 when they shall say, Peace and **s.**;........ *803*

SAFFRON
Ca 4:14 Spikenard and **s.**; calamus and........... 3750

SAID See also SAIDEST.
Ge 1:3 And God **s.**, Let there be light: and..... 559
Ge 1:6 God **s.**, Let there be a firmament in..... 559
Ge 1:9 God **s.**, Let the waters under the........ 559
Ge 1:11 God **s.**, Let the earth bring forth........ 559
Ge 1:14 God **s.**, Let there be lights in the........ 559
Ge 1:20 God **s.**, Let the waters bring forth....... 559
Ge 1:24 God **s.**, Let the earth bring forth......... 559
Ge 1:26 And God **s.**, Let us make man in our.... 559
Ge 1:28 God **s.** unto them, Be fruitful, and....... 559
Ge 1:29 God **s.**, Behold, I have given you........ 559
Ge 2:18 God **s.**, It is not good that the man........ 559
Ge 2:23 Adam **s.**, This is now bone of my........ 559
Ge 3:1 And he **s.** unto the woman, Yea,......... 559
Ge 3:1 hath God **s.**, Ye shall not eat of every.. 559
Ge 3:2 And the woman **s.** unto the serpent,..... 559
Ge 3:3 God hath **s.**, Ye shall not eat of it,....... 559
Ge 3:4 And the serpent **s.** unto the woman,..... 559
Ge 3:9 and **s.** unto him, Where art thou?........ 559
Ge 3:10 And he **s.**, I heard thy voice in the...... 559
Ge 3:11 And he **s.**, Who told thee that thou...... 559
Ge 3:12 And the man **s.**, The woman whom....... 559
Ge 3:13 the Lord God **s.** unto the woman,........ 559
Ge 3:13 the woman **s.**, The serpent beguiled..... 559
Ge 3:14 the Lord God **s.** unto the serpent,....... 559
Ge 3:16 Unto the woman he **s.**, I will greatly.... 559
Ge 3:17 And unto Adam he **s.**, Because thou..... 559
Ge 3:22 the Lord God **s.**, Behold, the man....... 559
Ge 4:1 and **s.**, I have gotten a man from the.... 559
Ge 4:6 And the Lord **s.** unto Cain, Why art..... 559
Ge 4:9 And the Lord **s.** unto Cain, Where is..... 559
Ge 4:9 thy brother? And he **s.**, I know not:..... 559
Ge 4:10 And he **s.**, What hast thou done?......... 559
Ge 4:13 Cain **s.**...My punishment is greater....... 559
Ge 4:15 And the Lord **s.** unto him, Therefore..... 559
Ge 4:23 And Lamech **s.** unto his wives, Adah.... 559
Ge 4:25 For God, **s.** she, hath appointed me..........
Ge 6:3 And the Lord **s.**, My spirit shall not..... 559
Ge 6:7 And the Lord **s.**, I will destroy man..... 559
Ge 6:13 And God **s.** unto Noah, The end of all.. 559
Ge 7:1 the Lord **s.** unto Noah, Come thou....... 559
Ge 8:21 Lord **s.** in his heart, I will not again..... 559
Ge 9:1 and **s.** unto them, Be fruitful, and........ 559
Ge 9:12 And God **s.**, This is the token of the..... 559
Ge 9:17 God **s.** unto Noah, This is the token..... 559
Ge 9:25 he **s.**, Cursed be Canaan; a servant...... 559
Ge 9:26 he **s.**, Blessed be the...God of Shem,... 559
Ge 10:9 it is **s.**, Even as Nimrod the mighty...... 559
Ge 11:3 they **s.** one to another, Go to, let us.... 559
Ge 11:4 they **s.**, Go to, let us build us a city..... 559
Ge 11:6 Lord **s.**, Behold, the people is one,...... 559
Ge 12:1 Lord had **s.** unto Abram, Get thee....... 559
Ge 12:7 and **s.**, Unto thy seed will I give this.... 559
Ge 12:11 that he **s.** unto Sarai his wife, Behold... 559
Ge 12:18 Pharoah called Abram, and **s.**, What..... 559
Ge 13:8 Abram **s.** unto Lot, Let there be no...... 559
Ge 13:14 Lord **s.** unto Abram, after that Lot....... 559
Ge 14:19 and **s.**, Blessed be Abram of the.......... 559
Ge 14:21 the king of Sodom **s.** unto Abram,........ 559
Ge 14:22 And Abram **s.** to the king of Sodom,.... 559
Ge 15:2 Abram **s.**, Lord God, What wilt thou.... 559
Ge 15:3 Abram **s.**, Behold, to me thou hast...... 559
Ge 15:5 and **s.**, Look now toward heaven, and... 559
Ge 15:5 he **s.** unto him, So shall thy seed be..... 559
Ge 15:7 he **s.** unto him, I am the Lord that....... 559
Ge 15:8 he **s.**, Lord God, Whereby shall I........ 559
Ge 15:9 he **s.** unto him, Take me an heifer....... 559
Ge 15:13 he **s.** unto Abram, Know of a surety.... 559
Ge 16:2 Sarai **s.** unto Abram, Behold now,........ 559
Ge 16:5 Sarai **s.** unto Abram, My wrong be...... 559
Ge 16:6 Abram **s.** unto Sarai, Behold, thy......... 559
Ge 16:8 he **s.**, Hagar, Sarai's maid, whence....... 559
Ge 16:8 And she **s.**, I flee from the face of my.. 559
Ge 16:9, 10,11 angel of the Lord **s.** unto her,..... 559
Ge 16:13 for she **s.**, Have I also here looked...... 559
Ge 17:1 **s.** unto him, I am the Almighty God;.... 559
Ge 17:9 God **s.** unto Abraham, Thou shalt........ 559
Ge 17:15 God **s.** unto Abraham, As for Sarai....... 559
Ge 17:17 laughed, and **s.** in his heart, Shall a..... 559
Ge 17:18 And Abraham **s.** unto God, O that........ 559
Ge 17:19 And God **s.**, Sarah thy wife shall bear... 559
Ge 17:23 day, as God had **s.** unto him............. 1696
Ge 18:3 And **s.**, My Lord, if now I have found... 559
Ge 18:5 And they **s.**, So do, as thou hast **s.**.... 1696
Ge 18:6 into the tent unto Sarah, and **s.**,......... 559
Ge 18:9 they **s.** unto him, Where is Sarah......... 559
Ge 18:9 And he **s.**, Behold, in the tent............ 559
Ge 18:10 And he **s.**, I will certainly return.......... 559
Ge 18:13 And the Lord **s.** unto Abraham,........... 559
Ge 18:15 he **s.**, Nay; but thou didst laugh......... 559
Ge 18:17 And the Lord **s.**, Shall I hide from........ 559
Ge 18:20 And the Lord **s.**, Because the cry of.... 559
Ge 18:23 Abraham drew near, and **s.**, Wilt......... 559
Ge 18:26 the Lord **s.**, If I find in Sodom fifty...... 559
Ge 18:27 Abraham answered and **s.**, Behold....... 559
Ge 18:28 And he **s.**, If I find there forty and....... 559
Ge 18:29 and **s.**, Peradventure there shall be...... 559
Ge 18:29 And he **s.**, I will not do it for forty's..... 559
Ge 18:30 he **s.** unto him, Oh let not the Lord..... 559
Ge 18:30 And he **s.**, I will not do it, if I find....... 559
Ge 18:31 And he **s.**, Behold now, I have taken.... 559
Ge 18:31 And he **s.**, I will not destroy it for....... 559
Ge 18:32 he **s.**, Oh let not the Lord be angry,.... 559
Ge 18:32 And he **s.**, I will not destroy it for....... 559
Ge 19:2 he **s.**, Behold now, my lords, turn in,... 559
Ge 19:2 they **s.**, Nay; but we will abide in........ 559
Ge 19:5 called unto Lot, and **s.** unto him,........ 559
Ge 19:7 And **s.**, I pray you, brethren, do not.... 559
Ge 19:9 **s.**, Stand back. And they **s.** again,........ 559
Ge 19:12 And the men **s.** unto Lot, Hast thou..... 559
Ge 19:14 and **s.**, Up, get you out of this place;... 559
Ge 19:17 he **s.**, Escape for thy life; look not....... 559
Ge 19:18 And Lot **s.** unto them, Oh, not so,....... 559
Ge 19:21 And he **s.** unto him, See, I have.......... 559
Ge 19:31, 34 the firstborn **s.** unto the younger,.... 559
Ge 20:2 Abraham **s.** of Sarah his wife, She is.... 559
Ge 20:3 a dream by night, and **s.** to him,......... 559
Ge 20:4 and he **s.**, Lord, wilt thou slay also a.... 559
Ge 20:5 **S.** he not unto me, She is my sister?... 559
Ge 20:5 even she herself **s.**, He is my brother:.. 559
Ge 20:6 God **s.** unto him in a dream, Yea,........ 559
Ge 20:9 **s.** unto him, What hast thou done....... 559
Ge 20:10 Abimelech **s.** unto Abraham, What........ 559
Ge 20:11 And Abraham **s.**, Because I thought,.... 559
Ge 20:13 I **s.** unto her, This is thy kindness....... 559
Ge 20:15 Abimelech **s.**, Behold, my land is........ 559
Ge 20:16 And unto Sarah he **s.**, Behold, I have... 559
Ge 21:1 the Lord visited Sarah as he had **s.**,..... 559
Ge 21:6 And Sarah **s.**, God hath made me to..... 559
Ge 21:7 she **s.**, [559] Who would have **s.** unto..4448
Ge 21:10 Wherefore she **s.** unto Abraham,......... 559
Ge 21:12 God **s.** unto Abraham, Let it not be...... 559
Ge 21:12 in all that Sarah hath **s.** unto thee,....... 559
Ge 21:16 for she **s.**, Let me not see the death.... 559
Ge 21:17 and **s.** unto her, What aileth thee,........ 559
Ge 21:24 And Abraham **s.**, I will swear............. 559
Ge 21:26 Abimelech **s.**, I wot not who hath........ 559
Ge 21:29 Abimelech **s.** unto Abraham, What........ 559
Ge 21:30 he **s.**, For these seven ewe lambs....... 559
Ge 22:1 tempt Abraham, and **s.** unto him,.......... 559
Ge 22:1 and he **s.**, Behold, here I am............. 559
Ge 22:2 he **s.**, Take now thy son, thine only...... 559
Ge 22:5 And Abraham **s.** unto his young.......... 559
Ge 22:7 unto Abraham his father, and **s.**, My.... 559
Ge 22:7 and he **s.**, Here am I, my son,............ 559
Ge 22:7 he **s.**, Behold the fire and the wood:.... 559
Ge 22:8 And Abraham **s.**, My son, God will...... 559
Ge 22:11 **s.**, Abraham,...and he **s.**, Here am I..... 559
Ge 22:12 he **s.**, Lay not thine hand upon the....... 559
Ge 22:14 as it is **s.** to this day, In the mount...... 559
Ge 22:16 And **s.**, By myself have I sworn,......... 559
Ge 24:2 Abraham **s.** unto his eldest servant....... 559
Ge 24:5 servant **s.** unto him, Peradventure....... 559
Ge 24:6 Abraham **s.** unto him, Beware thou...... 559
Ge 24:12 And he **s.**, O Lord God of my master... 559
Ge 24:17 the servant ran to meet her, and **s.**,...... 559
Ge 24:18 And she **s.**, Drink, my lord: and she..... 559
Ge 24:19 she **s.**, I will draw water for thy.......... 559
Ge 24:23 And **s.**, Whose daughter art thou?........ 559
Ge 24:24 she **s.** unto him, I am the daughter...... 559
Ge 24:25 She **s.** moreover unto him, We have..... 559
Ge 24:27 he **s.**, Blessed be the Lord God of....... 559
Ge 24:31 he **s.**, Come in, thou blessed of the...... 559
Ge 24:33 he **s.**, I will not eat, until I have told.... 559
Ge 24:33 mine errand, And he **s.**, Speak on........ 559
Ge 24:34 And he **s.**, I am Abraham's servant...... 559
Ge 24:39 I **s.** unto my master, Peradventure....... 559
Ge 24:40 And he **s.** unto me, The Lord, before... 559
Ge 24:42 and **s.**, O Lord God of my master........ 559
Ge 24:45 and I **s.** unto her, Let me drink, I........ 559
Ge 24:46 and **s.**, Drink, and I will give thy......... 559
Ge 24:47 and **s.**, Whose daughter art thou?......... 559
Ge 24:47 she **s.**, The daughter of Bethuel,......... 559
Ge 24:50 Laban and Bethuel answered and **s.**,...... 559
Ge 24:54 and he **s.**, Send me away unto my....... 559
Ge 24:55 her brother and her mother **s.**, Let...... 559
Ge 24:56 he **s.** unto them, Hinder me not,.......... 559
Ge 24:57 and they **s.**, We will call the damsel,.... 559
Ge 24:58 **s.** unto her, Wilt thou go with this....... 559
Ge 24:58 And she **s.**, I will go........................ 559
Ge 24:60 blessed Rebekah, and **s.** unto her,....... 559
Ge 24:65 she had **s.** unto the servant, What...... 559
Ge 24:65 the servant had **s.**, It is my master:...... 559
Ge 25:22 she **s.**, If it be so, why am I thus?....... 559
Ge 25:23 the Lord **s.** unto her, Two nations....... 559
Ge 25:30 Esau **s.** to Jacob, Feed me, I pray....... 559
Ge 25:31 And Jacob **s.**, Sell me this day thy....... 559
Ge 25:32 Esau **s.**, Behold, I am at the point....... 559
Ge 25:33 And Jacob **s.**, Swear to me this day;..... 559
Ge 26:2 Lord appeared unto him, and **s.**, Go,.... 559
Ge 26:7 he **s.**, She is my sister: for he feared... 559
Ge 26:7 **s.** he, the men of the place should....... 559
Ge 26:9 And Abimelech called Isaac, and **s.**,...... 559
Ge 26:9 And Isaac **s.** unto him, Because I **s.**,.... 559
Ge 26:10 And Abimelech **s.**, What is this thou..... 559
Ge 26:16 Abimelech **s.** unto Isaac, Go from........ 559
Ge 26:22 he **s.**, For now the Lord hath made...... 559
Ge 26:24 and **s.**, I am the God of Abraham........ 559
Ge 26:27 And Isaac **s.** unto them, Wherefore...... 559
Ge 26:28 And they **s.**, We saw certainly that...... 559
Ge 26:28 and we **s.**, Let there be now an oath.... 559
Ge 26:32 **s.** unto him, We have found water........ 559
Ge 27:1 eldest son, and **s.** unto him, My son:.... 559
Ge 27:1 he **s.** unto him, Behold, here am I....... 559
Ge 27:2 he **s.**, Behold now, I am old, I know.... 559
Ge 27:11 And Jacob **s.** to Rebekah his mother,.... 559
Ge 27:13 his mother **s.** unto him, Upon me be.... 559
Ge 27:18 unto his father, and **s.**, My father:...... 559
Ge 27:18 and he **s.**, Here am I; who art thou,..... 559
Ge 27:19 And Jacob **s.** unto his father, I am........ 559
Ge 27:20 And Isaac **s.** unto his son, How is it..... 559
Ge 27:20 And he **s.**, Because the Lord thy God... 559
Ge 27:21 And Isaac **s.** unto Jacob, Come near,.... 559
Ge 27:22 **s.**, The voice is Jacob's voice, but........ 559
Ge 27:24 he **s.**, Art thou my very son Esau?...... 559
Ge 27:24 my very son Esau? And he **s.**, I am...... 559
Ge 27:25 he **s.**, Bring it near to me, and I will.... 559
Ge 27:26 his father Isaac **s.** unto him, Come....... 559
Ge 27:27 **s.**, See, the smell of my son is as the... 559
Ge 27:31 and **s.** unto his father, Let my father.... 559
Ge 27:32 Isaac his father **s.** unto him, Who......... 559
Ge 27:32 he **s.**, I am thy son, thy firstborn........ 559
Ge 27:33 trembled very exceedingly, and **s.**,....... 559
Ge 27:34 **s.** unto his father, Bless me, even....... 559
Ge 27:35 And he **s.**, Thy brother came with....... 559
Ge 27:36 And he **s.**, Is not he rightly named....... 559
Ge 27:36 and he **s.**, hast thou not reserved a...... 559
Ge 27:37 Isaac answered and **s.** unto Esau,........ 559
Ge 27:38 Esau **s.** unto his father, Hast thou........ 559
Ge 27:39 Isaac his father answered and **s.**.......... 559
Ge 27:41 Esau **s.** in his heart, The days of......... 559
Ge 27:42 and **s.** unto him, Behold, thy brother.... 559

Ge 27:46 Rebekah **s.** to Isaac, I am weary of...... 559
Ge 28:1 **s.** unto him, Thou shalt not take a....... 559
Ge 28:13 **s.**, I am the Lord God of Abraham....... 559
Ge 28:16 and he **s.**, Surely the Lord is in this..... 559
Ge 28:17 and **s.**, How dreadful is this place! 559
Ge 29:4 Jacob **s.** unto them, My brethren, ... 559
Ge 29:4 And they **s.**, Of Haran are we............ 559
Ge 29:5 he **s.** unto them, Know ye Laban the.... 559
Ge 29:5 And they **s.**, We know him............... 559
Ge 29:6 And he **s.** unto them, Is he well?......... 559
Ge 29:6 And they **s.**, He is well: and, behold,.... 559
Ge 29:7 he **s.**, Lo, it is yet high day, neither..... 559
Ge 29:8 And they **s.**, We cannot, until all the 559
Ge 29:14 Laban **s.** to him, Surely thou art my...... 559
Ge 29:15 Laban **s.** unto Jacob, Because thou....... 559
Ge 29:18 and **s.**, I will serve thee seven years.... 559
Ge 29:19 Laban **s.**, It is better that I give her..... 559
Ge 29:21 Jacob **s.** unto Laban, Give me my........ 559
Ge 29:25 he **s.** to Laban, What is this thou......... 559
Ge 29:26 Laban **s.**, It must not be so done in 559
Ge 29:32 she **s.**, Surely the Lord hath looked...... 559
Ge 29:33 and **s.**, Because the Lord hath heard.... 559
Ge 29:34 **s.**, Now this time will my husband 559
Ge 29:35 she **s.**, Now will I praise the Lord: 559
Ge 30:1 **s.** unto Jacob, Give me children, or...... 559
Ge 30:2 and he **s.**, Am I in God's stead, who 559
Ge 30:3 she **s.**, Behold my maid Bilhah, go....... 559
Ge 30:6 Rachel **s.**, God hath judged me, and..... 559
Ge 30:8 Rachel **s.**, With great wrestlings......... 559
Ge 30:11 Leah **s.**, A troop cometh: and she......... 559
Ge 30:13 And Leah **s.**, Happy am I, for the........ 559
Ge 30:14 Rachel **s.** to Leah, Give me, I pray...... 559
Ge 30:15 she **s.** unto her, Is it a small matter..... 559
Ge 30:15 And Rachel **s.**, Therefore he shall lie.... 559
Ge 30:16 and **s.**, Thou must come in unto me; 559
Ge 30:18 And Leah **s.**, God hath given me my 559
Ge 30:20 Leah **s.**, God hath endued me with a.... 559
Ge 30:23 and **s.**, God hath taken away my......... 559
Ge 30:24 and **s.**, The Lord shall add to me......... 559
Ge 30:25 that Jacob **s.** unto Laban, Send me....... 559
Ge 30:27 And Laban **s.** unto him, I pray thee,..... 559
Ge 30:28 And he **s.**, Appoint me thy wages,....... 559
Ge 30:29 he **s.** unto him, Thou knowest how I.... 559
Ge 30:31 And he **s.**, What shall I give thee?....... 559
Ge 30:31 Jacob **s.**, Thou shalt not give me 559
Ge 30:34 Laban **s.**, Behold, I would it might....... 559
Ge 31:3 the Lord **s.** unto Jacob, Return unto..... 559
Ge 31:5 **s.** unto them, I see your father's......... 559
Ge 31:8 If he **s.** thus, The speckled shall be...... 559
Ge 31:8 if he **s.** thus, The ringstraked shall...... 559
Ge 31:11 saying, Jacob: And I **s.**, Here am I...... 559
Ge 31:12 And he **s.**, Lift up now thine eyes,....... 559
Ge 31:14 **s.** unto him, Is there yet any portion..... 559
Ge 31:16 whatsoever God hath **s.** unto thee,....... 559
Ge 31:24 **s.** unto him, Take heed that thou......... 559
Ge 31:26 Laban **s.** to Jacob, What hast thou........ 559
Ge 31:31 Jacob answered and **s.** to Laban,.......... 559
Ge 31:31 for I **s.**, Peradventure thou wouldest 559
Ge 31:35 And she **s.** to her father, Let it not...... 559
Ge 31:36 and Jacob answered and **s.** to Laban,.... 559
Ge 31:43 Laban answered and **s.** unto Jacob,....... 559
Ge 31:46 Jacob **s.** unto his brethren, Gather 559
Ge 31:48 And Laban **s.**, This heap is a witness..... 559
Ge 31:49 he **s.**, The Lord watch between me........ 559
Ge 31:51 Laban **s.** to Jacob, Behold this heap,..... 559
Ge 32:2 Jacob saw them, he **s.**, This is God's.... 559
Ge 32:8 **s.**, If Esau come to the one company,... 559
Ge 32:9 And Jacob, **s.**, O God of my father........ 559
Ge 32:16 **s.** unto his servant, Pass over............ 559
Ge 32:20 he **s.**, I will appease him with the 559
Ge 32:26 And he **s.**, Let me go, for the day........ 559
Ge 32:26 he **s.**, I will not let thee go, except...... 559
Ge 32:27 he **s.** unto him, What is thy name?........ 559
Ge 32:27 is thy name? And he **s.**, Jacob............ 559
Ge 32:28 he **s.**, Thy name shall be called no 559
Ge 32:29 **s.**, Tell me, I pray thee, thy name......... 559
Ge 32:29 he **s.**, Wherefore is it that thou dost..... 559
Ge 33:5 and **s.**, Who are those with thee? 559
Ge 33:5 he **s.**, The children which God hath...... 559
Ge 33:8 he **s.**, What meanest thou by all this..... 559
Ge 33:8 he **s.**, These are to find grace in the 559
Ge 33:9 Esau **s.**, I have enough, my brother; 559
Ge 33:10 And Jacob **s.**, Nay, I pray thee, if now.. 559
Ge 33:12 and he **s.**, Let us take our journey, ... 559
Ge 33:13 And he **s.** unto him, My lord knoweth... 559
Ge 33:15 Esau **s.**, Let me now leave with thee ... 559
Ge 33:15 And he **s.**, What needeth it? let me...... 559
Ge 34:11 Shechem **s.** unto her father and unto 559
Ge 34:13 **s.**, because he had defiled Dinah 1696
Ge 34:14 And they **s.** unto them, We cannot........ 559
Ge 34:30 And Jacob **s.** to Simeon and Levi, ... 559
Ge 34:31 And they **s.**, Should he deal with our.... 559
Ge 35:1 And God **s.** unto Jacob, Arise, go up 559
Ge 35:2 Then Jacob **s.** unto his household,........ 559
Ge 35:10 God **s.** unto him, Thy name is Jacob:.... 559
Ge 35:11 And God **s.** unto him, I am God 559
Ge 35:17 the midwife **s.** unto her, Fear not; 559
Ge 37:6 And he **s.** unto hem, Hear, I pray........ 559
Ge 37:8 his brethren **s.** to him, Shalt thou 559
Ge 37:9 **s.**, Behold, I have dreamed a dream..... 559
Ge 37:10 his father rebuked him, and **s.**............ 559
Ge 37:13 And Israel **s.** unto Joseph, Do not......... 559
Ge 37:13 them. And he **s.** to him, Here am I...... 559
Ge 37:14 And he **s.** to him, Go, I pray thee, ... 559
Ge 37:16 he **s.**, I seek my brethren: tell me, I.... 559
Ge 37:17 And the man **s.**, They are departed....... 559
Ge 37:19 And they **s.** one to another, Behold,..... 559
Ge 37:21 hands; and **s.**, Let us not kill him......... 559
Ge 37:22 And Reuben **s.** unto them, Shed no....... 559
Ge 37:26 Judah **s.** unto his brethren, What 559
Ge 37:30 brethren, and **s.**, The child is not;........ 559
Ge 37:32 father; and **s.**, This have we found:....... 559
Ge 37:33 And he knew it, and **s.**, It is my son's.. 559
Ge 37:35 and he **s.**, For I will go down into the... 559
Ge 38:8 And Judah **s.** unto Onan, Go in unto..... 559
Ge 38:11 **s.** Judah to Tamar his daughter in 559
Ge 38:11 for he **s.**, Lest peradventure he die...... 559
Ge 38:16 **s.**, Go to, I pray thee, let me come in.. 559
Ge 38:16 And she **s.**, What wilt thou give me, ... 559
Ge 38:17 he **s.**, I will send thee a kid from the.... 559
Ge 38:17 she **s.**, Wilt thou give me a pledge,...... 559
Ge 38:18 he **s.**, What pledge shall I give thee?.... 559
Ge 38:18 And she **s.**, Thy signet, and thy 559
Ge 38:21 And they **s.**, There was no harlot 559
Ge 38:22 to Judah, and **s.**, I cannot find her;....... 559
Ge 38:22 men of the place **s.**, that there was...... 559
Ge 38:23 Judah **s.**, Let her take it to her, lest..... 559
Ge 38:24 And Judah **s.**, Bring her forth, and....... 559
Ge 38:25 she **s.**, Discern, I pray thee, whose 559
Ge 38:26 Judah acknowledged them, and **s.**,........ 559
Ge 38:29 and she **s.**, How hast thou broken......... 559
Ge 39:7 Joseph; and she **s.**, Lie with me. 559
Ge 39:8 refused, and **s.** unto his master's wife,.. 559
Ge 40:8 they **s.** unto him, We have dreamed..... 559
Ge 40:8 And Joseph **s.** unto them, Do not......... 559
Ge 40:9 and **s.** to him, In my dream, behold,..... 559
Ge 40:12 And Joseph **s.** unto him, This is the 559
Ge 40:16 he **s.** unto Joseph, I also was in my...... 559
Ge 40:18 Joseph answered and **s.**, This is the 559
Ge 41:15 And Pharaoh **s.** unto Joseph, I have....... 559
Ge 41:17 Pharaoh **s.** unto Joseph, In my.......... 1696
Ge 41:25 Joseph **s.** unto Pharaoh, The dream....... 559
Ge 41:38 Pharaoh **s.** unto his servants, Can we... 559
Ge 41:39 Pharaoh **s.** unto Joseph, Forasmuch...... 559
Ge 41:41 Pharaoh **s.** unto Joseph, See, I have...... 559
Ge 41:44 And Pharaoh **s.** unto Joseph, I am........ 559
Ge 41:51 God, **s.** he, hath made me forget all..........
Ge 41:54 come, according as Joseph had **s.**.......... 559
Ge 41:55 Pharaoh **s.** unto all the Egyptians,........ 559
Ge 42:1 Jacob **s.** unto his sons, Why do ye 559
Ge 42:2 And he **s.**, Behold, I have heard that.... 559
Ge 42:4 for he **s.**, Lest peradventure mischief.... 559
Ge 42:7 he **s.** unto them, Whence come ye?...... 559
Ge 42:7 they **s.**, From the land of Canaan to..... 559
Ge 42:9 **s.** unto them, Ye are spies; to see......... 559
Ge 42:10 they **s.** unto him, Nay, my lord, but..... 559
Ge 42:12 he **s.** unto them, Nay, but to see the ... 559
Ge 42:13 And they **s.**, Thy servants are twelve... 559
Ge 42:14 Joseph **s.** unto them, That is it that...... 559
Ge 42:18 Joseph **s.** unto them the third day,....... 559
Ge 42:21 they **s.** one to another, We are verily,.. 559
Ge 42:28 he **s.** unto his brethren, My money is... 559
Ge 42:31 we **s.** unto him, We are true men;........ 559
Ge 42:33 **s.** unto us, Hereby shall I know that...... 559
Ge 42:36 Jacob their father **s.** unto them, Me...... 559
Ge 42:38 he **s.**, My son shall not go down with... 559
Ge 43:2 father **s.** unto them, Go again, buy....... 559
Ge 43:5 man **s.** unto us, Ye shall not see my..... 559
Ge 43:6 Israel **s.**, Wherefore dealt ye so ill....... 559
Ge 43:7 they **s.**, The man asked us straitly of.... 559
Ge 43:8 And Judah **s.** unto Israel his father,....... 559
Ge 43:11 father Israel **s.** unto them, If it must 559
Ge 43:16 he **s.** to the ruler of his house, Bring.... 559
Ge 43:18 they **s.**, Because of the money that...... 559
Ge 43:20 And **s.**, O sir, we came indeed down.... 559
Ge 43:23 And he **s.**, Peace be to you, fear not:... 559
Ge 43:27 welfare, and **s.**, Is your father well,...... 559
Ge 43:29 and **s.**, Is this your younger brother, ... 559
Ge 43:29 he **s.**, God be gracious unto thee, my... 559
Ge 43:31 and refrained himself, and **s.**, Set on..... 559
Ge 44:4 far off, Joseph **s.** unto his steward,....... 559
Ge 44:7 they **s.** unto him. Wherefore saith........ 559
Ge 44:10 he **s.**, Now also let it be according........ 559
Ge 44:15 Joseph **s.** unto them, What deed is....... 559
Ge 44:16 Judah **s.**, What shall we say unto my 559
Ge 44:17 he **s.**, God forbid that I should do so: ... 559
Ge 44:18 and **s.**, Oh my lord, let thy servant, ... 559
Ge 44:20 And we **s.** unto my lord, We have a...... 559
Ge 44:22 we **s.** unto my lord, The lad cannot...... 559
Ge 44:25 our father **s.**, Go again, and buy us a.... 559
Ge 44:26 And we **s.**, We cannot go down: if....... 559
Ge 44:27 my father **s.** unto us, Ye know that....... 559
Ge 44:28 and I **s.**, Surely he is torn in pieces;..... 559
Ge 45:3 Joseph **s.** unto his brethren, I am......... 559
Ge 45:4 Joseph **s.** unto his brethren, Come....... 559
Ge 45:4 And he **s.**, I am Joseph your brother, ... 559
Ge 45:17 Pharaoh **s.** unto Joseph, Say unto........ 559
Ge 45:24 he **s.** unto them, See that ye fall not 559
Ge 45:27 words of Joseph, which he had **s.**....... 1697
Ge 45:28 Israel **s.**, It is enough; Joseph my 559
Ge 46:2 **s.**, Jacob, Jacob. And he **s.**, Here am.... 559
Ge 46:3 And he **s.**, I am God, the God of thy.... 559
Ge 46:30 Israel **s.** unto Joseph, Now let me......... 559
Ge 46:31 And Joseph **s.** unto his brethren, and.... 559
Ge 47:1 and **s.**, My father and my brethren,...... 559
Ge 47:3 Pharaoh **s.** unto his brethren, What...... 559
Ge 47:3 **s.** unto Pharaoh, Thy servants are 559
Ge 47:4 They **s.** moreover unto Pharaoh, For...... 559
Ge 47:8 Pharaoh **s.** unto Jacob, How old art...... 559
Ge 47:9 Jacob **s.** unto Pharaoh, The days of....... 559
Ge 47:15 unto Joseph, and **s.**, Give us bread:....... 559
Ge 47:16 Joseph **s.**, Give your cattle; and I 559
Ge 47:18 **s.** unto him, We will not hide it 559
Ge 47:23 Joseph **s.** unto the people, Behold,........ 559
Ge 47:25 they **s.**, Thou hast saved our lives: 559
Ge 47:29 and **s.** unto him, If now I have found.... 559
Ge 47:30 in their buryingplace. And he **s.**,.......... 559
Ge 47:30 I will do as thou hast **s.**.................. 1697
Ge 47:31 And he **s.**, Swear unto me. And he...... 559
Ge 48:2 one told Jacob, and **s.**, Behold, thy....... 559
Ge 48:3 And Jacob **s.** unto Joseph, God............ 559
Ge 48:4 **s.** unto me, Behold, I will make thee..... 559
Ge 48:8 Joseph's sons, and **s.**, Who are these? .. 559
Ge 48:9 Joseph **s.** unto his father, They are 559
Ge 48:9 he **s.**, Bring them, I pray thee, unto...... 559
Ge 48:11 And Israel **s.** unto Joseph, I had not..... 559
Ge 48:15 blessed Joseph, and **s.**, God, before 559
Ge 48:18 Joseph **s.** unto his father, Not so, my... 559
Ge 48:19 his father refused, and **s.**, I know it, ... 559
Ge 48:21 Israel **s.** unto Joseph, Behold, I die: 559
Ge 49:1 **s.**, Gather yourselves together, that..... 559
Ge 49:29 he charged them, and **s.** unto them, ... 559
Ge 50:6 And Pharaoh **s.**, Go up, and bury thy ... 559
Ge 50:11 **s.**, This is a grievous mourning 559
Ge 50:15 they **s.**, Joseph will peradventure......... 559
Ge 50:18 they **s.**, Behold, we be thy servants..... 559
Ge 50:19 And Joseph **s.** unto them, Fear not: 559
Ge 50:24 Joseph **s.** unto his brethren, I die:........ 559
Ex 1:9 he **s.** unto his people, Behold, the........ 559
Ex 1:16 And he **s.**, When ye do the office of..... 559
Ex 1:18 and **s.** unto them, Why have ye done.... 559
Ex 1:19 midwives **s.** unto Pharaoh, Because....... 559
Ex 2:6 and **s.**, This is one of the Hebrews'...... 559
Ex 2:7 **s.** his sister to Pharaoh's daughter, ... 559
Ex 2:8 Pharaoh's daughter **s.** to her, Go. 559
Ex 2:9 And Pharaoh daughter **s.** unto her,....... 559
Ex 2:10 she **s.**, Because I drew him out of the .. 559
Ex 2:13 and he **s.** to him that did the wrong, ... 559
Ex 2:14 he **s.**, Who made thee a prince and....... 559
Ex 2:14 Moses feared, and **s.**, Surely this......... 559
Ex 2:18 he **s.**, How is it that ye are come so 559
Ex 2:19 they **s.**, An Egyptian delivered us 559
Ex 2:20 he **s.** unto his daughters, And where 559
Ex 2:22 he **s.**, I have been a stranger in a........ 559
Ex 3:3 And Moses **s.**, I will not turn aside, ... 559
Ex 3:4 and **s.**, Moses, Moses. And he **s.**,........ 559
Ex 3:5 And he **s.**, Draw not nigh hither: 559
Ex 3:6 he **s.**, I am the God of thy father,........ 559
Ex 3:7 And the Lord **s.**, I have surely seen..... 559
Ex 3:11 And Moses **s.** unto God, Who am I,..... 559
Ex 3:12 And he **s.**, Certainly I will be with 559

Ex 3:13 And Moses s. unto God, Behold,......... 559
Ex 3:14 And God s. unto Moses, I Am That I.... 559
Ex 3:14 and he s., Thus shalt thou say unto...... 559
Ex 3:15 God s. moreover unto Moses, Thus..... 559
Ex 3:17 And I have s., I will bring you up........ 559
Ex 4:1 Moses answered and s., But, behold,... 559
Ex 4:2 the Lord s. unto him, What is that....... 559
Ex 4:2 in thine hand? And he s., A rod........... 559
Ex 4:3 And he s., Cast it on the ground.......... 559
Ex 4:4 Lord s. unto Moses, Put forth thine..... 559
Ex 4:6 Lord s. furthermore unto him, Put....... 559
Ex 4:7 he s., Put thine hand into thy bosom.... 559
Ex 4:10 Moses s. unto the Lord, O my Lord,... 559
Ex 4:11 Lord s. unto him, Who hath made........ 559
Ex 4:13 and he s., O my Lord, send, I pray..... 559
Ex 4:14 and he s., Is not Aaron the Levite....... 559
Ex 4:18 and s. unto him, Let me go, I pray...... 559
Ex 4:18 And Jethro s. to Moses, Go in peace.... 559
Ex 4:19 Lord s. unto Moses in Midian, Go,...... 559
Ex 4:21 Lord s. unto Moses, When thou goest.. 559
Ex 4:25 and s., Surely a bloody husband art...... 559
Ex 4:26 she s., A bloody husband thou art,....... 559
Ex 4:27 And the Lord s. to Aaron, Go into the.. 559
Ex 5:2 And Pharaoh s., Who is the Lord,......... 559
Ex 5:3 And they s., The God of the Hebrews.. 559
Ex 5:4 And the king of Egypt s. unto them,.... 559
Ex 5:5 And Pharaoh s., Behold, the people...... 559
Ex 5:17 But he s., Ye are idle, ye are idle:....... 559
Ex 5:19 after it was s., ye shall not minish....... 559
Ex 5:21 they s. unto them, The Lord look........ 559
Ex 5:22 returned unto the Lord, and s., Lord,... 559
Ex 6:1 Lord s. unto Moses, Now shalt thou.... 559
Ex 6:2 and s. unto him, I am the Lord:.......... 559
Ex 6:26 to whom the Lord s., Bring out the..... 559
Ex 6:30 Moses s. before the Lord, Behold, I..... 559
Ex 7:1 Lord s. unto Moses, See, I have made. 559
Ex 7:13 not unto them; as the Lord had s........ 1696
Ex 7:14 the Lord s. unto Moses, Pharaoh's....... 559
Ex 7:22 not unto them; as the Lord had s........ 1696
Ex 8:8 and s., Intreat the Lord, that he.......... 559
Ex 8:9 Moses s. unto Pharaoh, Glory over...... 559
Ex 8:10 And he s., To morrow........................ 559
Ex 8:10 he s., Be it according to thy word:...... 559
Ex 8:15 not unto them; as the Lord had s........ 1696
Ex 8:16 the Lord s. unto Moses, Say unto........ 559
Ex 8:19 the magicians s. unto Pharaoh,........... 1696
Ex 8:19 not unto them; as the Lord had s........ 1696
Ex 8:20 the Lord s. unto Moses, Rise up.......... 559
Ex 8:25 and s., Go ye, sacrifice to your God..... 559
Ex 8:26 And Moses s., It is not meet so to do;. 559
Ex 8:28 And Pharaoh s., I will let you go,........ 559
Ex 8:29 And Moses s., Behold, I go out from.... 559
Ex 9:1 the Lord s. unto Moses, Go in unto..... 559
Ex 9:8 Lord s. unto Moses and unto Aaron,..... 559
Ex 9:13 And the Lord s. unto Moses, Rise up... 559
Ex 9:22 the Lord s. unto Moses, Stretch out.... 559
Ex 9:27 and said unto them, I have sinned........ 559
Ex 9:29 And Moses s. unto him, As soon as I... 559
Ex 10:1 the Lord s. unto Moses, Go in unto..... 559
Ex 10:3 and s. unto him, Thus saith the Lord.... 559
Ex 10:7 And Pharaoh's servants s. unto him,..... 559
Ex 10:8 he s. unto them, Go, serve the Lord.... 559
Ex 10:9 Moses s., We will go with our young.... 559
Ex 10:10 he s. unto them, Let the Lord be so.... 559
Ex 10:12 the Lord s. unto Moses, Stretch out.... 559
Ex 10:16 and he s., I have sinned against the..... 559
Ex 10:21 the Lord s. unto Moses, Stretch out.... 559
Ex 10:24 and s., Go ye, serve the Lord;........... 559
Ex 10:25 Moses s., Thou must give us also........ 559
Ex 10:28 Pharaoh s. unto him, Get thee from..... 559
Ex 10:29 Moses s., Thou hast spoken well,........ 559
Ex 11:1 Lord s. unto Moses, Yet will I bring..... 559
Ex 11:4 And Moses s., Thus saith the Lord,..... 559
Ex 11:9 Lord s. unto Moses, Pharaoh shall...... 559
Ex 12:21 and s. unto them, Draw out and take.... 559
Ex 12:31 and s., Rise up, and get you forth........ 559
Ex 12:31 go, serve the Lord, as ye have s........ 1696
Ex 12:32 flocks and your herds, as ye have s.,.. 1696
Ex 12:33 for they s., We be all dead men.......... 559
Ex 12:43 the Lord s. unto Moses and Aaron,...... 559
Ex 13:3 Moses s. unto the people, Remember... 559
Ex 13:17 for God s., Lest peradventure the........ 559
Ex 14:5 And they s., Why have we done this,... 559
Ex 14:11 they s. unto Moses, Because there...... 559
Ex 14:13 And Moses s. unto the people, Fear..... 559
Ex 14:15 the Lord s. unto Moses, Wherefore..... 559
Ex 14:25 so that the Egyptians s., Let us flee..... 559
Ex 14:26 the Lord s. unto Moses, Stretch out.... 559
Ex 15:9 The enemy s., I will pursue, I will....... 559
Ex 15:26 And s., If thou will diligently hearken.... 559
Ex 16:3 the children of Israel s. unto them,...... 559
Ex 16:4 Then s. the Lord unto Moses, Behold,..559
Ex 16:6 And Moses and Aaron s. unto all the.... 559
Ex 16:8 And Moses s., This shall be, when...... 559
Ex 16:15 they s. one to another, It is manna:..... 559
Ex 16:15 And Moses s. unto them, This is the.... 559
Ex 16:19 and Moses s., Let no man leave of it... 559
Ex 16:23 he s. unto them, This is that which...... 559
Ex 16:23 the Lord hath s., To morrow is the.... 1696
Ex 16:25 and Moses s., Eat that to day; for....... 559
Ex 16:28 the Lord s. unto Moses, How long....... 559
Ex 16:32 Moses s., This is the thing which........ 559
Ex 16:33 Moses s. unto Aaron, Take a pot,....... 559
Ex 17:2 and s., Give us water that we may...... 559
Ex 17:2 And Moses s. unto them, Why chide.... 559
Ex 17:3 murmured against Moses, and s.,........ 559
Ex 17:5 the Lord s. unto Moses, Go on before.. 559
Ex 17:9 Moses s. unto Joshua, Choose us........ 559
Ex 17:10 Joshua did as Moses had s. to him,...... 559
Ex 17:14 Lord s. unto Moses, Write this for a.... 559
Ex 17:16 he s., Because the Lord hath sworn...... 559
Ex 18:3 for he s., I have been an alien in a....... 559
Ex 18:4 God of my father, s. he, was mine help,....
Ex 18:6 s. unto Moses, I thy father in law........ 559
Ex 18:10 And Jethro s., Blessed be the Lord,..... 559
Ex 18:14 he s., What is this thing that thou........ 559
Ex 18:15 And Moses s. unto his father in law,.... 559
Ex 18:17 And Moses' father in law s. unto him,... 559
Ex 18:24 in law, and did all that he had s........... 559
Ex 19:8 people answered together, and s., All... 559
Ex 19:9 the Lord s. unto Moses, Lo, I come.... 559
Ex 19:10 the Lord s. unto Moses, Go unto the... 559
Ex 19:15 And he s. unto the people, Be ready.... 559
Ex 19:21 the Lord s. unto Moses, Go down,...... 559
Ex 19:23 Moses s. unto the Lord, The people.... 559
Ex 19:24 the Lord s. unto him, Away, get thee... 559
Ex 20:19 And they s. unto Moses, Speak thou.... 559
Ex 20:20 Moses s. unto the people, Fear not:..... 559
Ex 20:22 Lord s. unto Moses, Thus thou shalt.... 559
Ex 23:13 in all things that I have s. unto you...... 559
Ex 24:1 he s. unto Moses, Come up unto the.... 559
Ex 24:3 answered with one voice, and s., All.... 559
Ex 24:3 which the Lord hath s. will we do....... 1696
Ex 24:7 the people: and they s., All that the..... 559
Ex 24:7 that the Lord hath s. will we do,........ 1696
Ex 24:8 and s., Behold the blood of the........... 559
Ex 24:12 Lord s. unto Moses, Come up to me.... 559
Ex 24:14 he s. unto the elders, Tarry ye here.... 559
Ex 30:34 Lord s. unto Moses, Take unto thee.... 559
Ex 32:1 and s. unto him, Up, make us gods,..... 559
Ex 32:2 And Aaron s. unto them, Break off...... 559
Ex 32:4 they s., These be thy gods, O Israel,... 559
Ex 32:5 Aaron made proclamation, and s.,........ 559
Ex 32:7 Lord s. unto Moses, Go, get thee...... 1696
Ex 32:8 and s., These by thy gods, O Israel,.... 559
Ex 32:9 the Lord s. unto Moses, I have seen.... 559
Ex 32:11 and s., Lord, why doth thy wrath........ 559
Ex 32:17 he s. unto Moses, There is a noise of.. 559
Ex 32:18 And he s., It is not the voice of them... 559
Ex 32:21 And Moses s. unto Aaron, What did..... 559
Ex 32:22 And Aaron s., Let not the anger of...... 559
Ex 32:23 For they s. unto me, Make us gods,.... 559
Ex 32:24 I s. unto them, Whosoever hath any..... 559
Ex 32:26 and s., Who is on the Lord's side?...... 559
Ex 32:27 he s. unto them, Thus saith the Lord... 559
Ex 32:29 Moses had s., Consecrate yourselves... 559
Ex 32:30 Moses s. unto the people, Ye have...... 559
Ex 32:31 and s., Oh, this people have sinned...... 559
Ex 32:33 the Lord s. unto Moses, Whosoever..... 559
Ex 33:1 the Lord s. unto Moses, Depart,........ 1696
Ex 33:5 Lord had s. unto Moses, Say unto....... 559
Ex 33:12 Moses s. unto the Lord, See, thou...... 559
Ex 33:12 thou hast s., I know thee by name,...... 559
Ex 33:14 And he s., My presence shall go with... 559
Ex 33:15 and he s. unto him, If thy presence...... 559
Ex 33:17 Lord s. unto Moses, I will do this........ 559
Ex 33:18 he s., I beseech thee, shew me thy..... 559
Ex 33:19 he s., I will make all my goodness....... 559
Ex 33:20 he s., Thou canst not see my face:...... 559
Ex 33:21 the Lord s., Behold, there is a place.... 559
Ex 34:1 Lord s. unto Moses, Hew thee two..... 559
Ex 34:9 And he s., If now I have found grace.... 559
Ex 34:10 he s., Behold, I make a covenant:........ 559
Ex 34:27 Lord s. unto Moses, Write thou these.. 559
Ex 35:1 s. unto them, These are the words...... 559
Ex 35:30 Moses s. unto the children of Israel,.... 559
Le 8:5 Moses s. unto the congregation,........... 559
Le 8:31 Moses s. unto Aaron, and to his sons,.. 559
Le 9:2 he s. unto Aaron, Take thee a young.... 559
Le 9:6 And Moses s., This is the thing.......... 559
Le 9:7 And Moses s. unto Aaron, Go unto...... 559
Le 10:3 Then Moses s. unto Aaron, This is it... 559
Le 10:4 and s. unto them, Come near, carry..... 559
Le 10:5 out of the camp; as Moses had s........ 1696
Le 10:6 And Moses s. unto Aaron, and unto..... 559
Le 10:19 Aaron s. unto Moses, Behold, this...... 1696
Le 16:2 Lord s. unto Moses, Speak unto.......... 559
Le 17:12 I s. unto the children of Israel, No....... 559
Le 17:14 I s. unto the children of Israel, Ye........ 559
Le 20:24 I have s. unto you, Ye shall inherit....... 559
Le 21:1 Lord s. unto moses, Speak unto the..... 559
Nu 3:40 Lord s. unto Moses, Number all the..... 559
Nu 7:11 the Lord s. unto Moses, They shall...... 559
Nu 9:7 men s. unto him, We are defiled by...... 559
Nu 9:8 Moses s. unto them, Stand still, and..... 559
Nu 10:29 Moses s. unto Hobab, the son of......... 559
Nu 10:29 unto the place of which the Lord s.,..... 559
Nu 10:30 he s. unto him, I will not go; but I....... 559
Nu 10:31 he s., Leave us not, I pray thee;......... 559
Nu 10:35 Moses s., Rise up, Lord, and let......... 559
Nu 10:36 when it rested, he s., Return, O Lord,. 559
Nu 11:4 and s., Who shall give us flesh to........ 559
Nu 11:11 Moses s. unto the Lord, Wherefore..... 559
Nu 11:16 Lord s. unto Moses, Gather unto me.... 559
Nu 11:21 Moses s., The people, among whom.... 559
Nu 11:21 thou hast s., I will give them flesh,...... 559
Nu 11:23 Lord s. unto Moses, Is the Lord's........ 559
Nu 11:27 s., Eldad and Medad do prophesy........ 559
Nu 11:28 and s., My lord Moses, forbid them...... 559
Nu 11:29 Moses s. unto him, Enviest thou for..... 559
Nu 12:2 And they s., Hath the Lord indeed....... 559
Nu 12:6 he s., Hear now my words: If there...... 559
Nu 12:11 Aaron s. unto Moses, Alas, my lord,.... 559
Nu 12:14 Lord s. unto Moses, If her father........ 559
Nu 13:17 s. unto them, Get you up this way........ 559
Nu 13:27 s., We came unto the land whither....... 559
Nu 13:30 s., Let us go up at once, and possess... 559
Nu 13:31 men that went up with him s., We be... 559
Nu 14:2 whole congregation s. unto them,......... 559
Nu 14:4 they s. one to another, Let us make.... 559
Nu 14:11 Lord s. unto Moses, How long will...... 559
Nu 14:13 Moses s. unto the Lord, Then the...... 559
Nu 14:20 Lord s., I have pardoned according...... 559
Nu 14:31 ones, which ye s. should be a prey,..... 559
Nu 14:35 I the Lord have s., I will surely do..... 1696
Nu 14:41 Moses s., Wherefore now do ye.......... 559
Nu 15:35 Lord s. unto Moses, The man shall...... 559
Nu 16:3 and against Aaron, and s. unto them,.... 559
Nu 16:8 Moses s. unto Korah, Hear, I pray...... 559
Nu 16:12 which s., We will not come up:........... 559
Nu 16:15 s. unto the Lord, Respect not thou...... 559
Nu 16:16 Moses s. unto Korah, Be thou and....... 559
Nu 16:22 fell upon their faces, and s., O God,..... 559
Nu 16:28 Moses s., Hereby ye shall know that.... 559
Nu 16:34 for they s., Lest the earth swallow...... 559
Nu 16:40 as the Lord s. to him by the hand...... 1696
Nu 16:46 And Moses s. unto Aaron, Take a....... 559
Nu 17:10 Lord s. unto Moses, Bring Aaron's...... 559
Nu 18:1 Lord s. unto Aaron, Thou and thy........ 559
Nu 18:24 I have s. unto them, Among the.......... 559
Nu 20:10 s. unto them, Hear now, ye rebels;...... 559
Nu 20:18 Edom s. unto him, Thou shalt not........ 559
Nu 20:19 children of Israel s. unto him, We........ 559
Nu 20:20 he s., Thou shalt not go through.......... 559
Nu 21:2 vowed a vow unto the Lord, and s.,..... 559
Nu 21:7 people came to Moses, and s., We...... 559
Nu 21:8 Lord s. unto Moses, Make thee a........ 559
Nu 21:14 it is s. in the book of the wars of......... 559
Nu 21:34 Lord s. unto Moses, Fear him not:...... 559
Nu 22:4 Moab s. unto the elders of Midian,....... 559
Nu 22:8 he s. unto them, Lodge here this......... 559
Nu 22:9 And God came unto Balaam, and s.,...... 559
Nu 22:10 Balaam s. unto God, Balak the son....... 559
Nu 22:12 God s. unto Balaam, Thou shalt not..... 559
Nu 22:13 s. unto the princes of Balak, Get......... 559
Nu 22:14 went unto Balak, and s., Balaam.......... 559
Nu 22:16 they came to Balaam, and s. to him,.... 559
Nu 22:18 answered and s. unto the servants....... 559
Nu 22:20 Balaam at night, and s. unto him,......... 559
Nu 22:28 she s. unto Balaam, What have I......... 559
Nu 22:29 Balaam s. unto the ass, Because.......... 559

Book	Ref	Context	No.
Nu	22:30	the ass **s.** unto Balaam, Am not I	559
Nu	22:30	do so unto thee? And he **s.**, Nay.	559
Nu	22:32	the angel of the Lord **s.** unto him, ...	559
Nu	22:34	Balaam **s.** unto the angel of the	559
Nu	22:35	angel of the Lord **s.** unto Balaam, ...	559
Nu	22:37	Balak **s.** unto Balaam, Did I not..........	559
Nu	22:38	And Balaam **s.** unto Balak, Lo, I am.....	559
Nu	23:1	Balaam **s.** unto Balak, Build me	559
Nu	23:3	Balaam **s.** unto Balak, Stand by thy......	559
Nu	23:4	and he **s.** unto him, I have prepared.....	559
Nu	23:5	**s.**, Return unto Balak, and thus...........	559
Nu	23:7	And he took up his parable, and **s.**, ...	559
Nu	23:11	Balak **s.** unto Balaam, What hast..........	559
Nu	23:12	and he answered and **s.**, Must I not.....	559
Nu	23:13	Balak **s.** unto him, Come, I pray.........	559
Nu	23:15	he **s.** unto Balak, Stand here by my	559
Nu	23:16	**s.**, Go again unto Balak, and say..........	559
Nu	23:17	Balak **s.** unto him, What hath the.........	559
Nu	23:18	and **s.**, Rise up, Balak, and hear;	559
Nu	23:19	hath he **s.**, and shall he not do it?	559
Nu	23:23	it shall be **s.** of Jacob and of Israel, ...	559
Nu	23:25	Balak **s.** unto Balaam, Neither curse.....	559
Nu	23:26	Balaam answered and **s.** unto Balak, ...	559
Nu	23:27	Balak **s.** unto Balaam, Come, I pray	559
Nu	23:29	Balaam **s.** unto Balak, Build me	559
Nu	23:30	Balak did as Balaam had **s.**, and...........	559
Nu	24:3	And he took up his parable and **s.**, ...	559
Nu	24:3	Balaam the son of Beor hath **s.**, ...	5002
Nu	24:3	man whose eyes are open hath **s.**:.......	5002
Nu	24:4	He hath **s.**, which heard the words	5002
Nu	24:10	Balak **s.** unto Balaam, I called thee.......	559
Nu	24:12	Balaam **s.** unto Balak, Spake I not........	559
Nu	24:15	he took up his parable, and **s.**, ...	559
Nu	24:15	Balaam the son of Beor hath **s.**, ...	5002
Nu	24:15	man whose eyes are open hath **s.**:......	5002
Nu	24:16	hath **s.**, which heard the words of	5002
Nu	24:20	and **s.**, Amalek was the first of the	559
Nu	24:21	**s.**, Strong is the dwellingplace, and	559
Nu	24:23	**s.**, Alas, Who shall live when God........	559
Nu	25:4	And the Lord **s.** unto Moses, Take	559
Nu	25:5	Moses **s.** unto the judges of Israel, ...	559
Nu	26:65	For the Lord had **s.** of them, They	559
Nu	27:12	Lord **s.** unto Moses, Get thee up	559
Nu	27:18	the Lord **s.** unto Moses Take thee	559
Nu	31:15	Moses **s.** unto them, Have ye saved.....	559
Nu	31:21	the priest **s.** unto the men of war	559
Nu	31:49	they **s.** unto Moses, Thy servants........	559
Nu	32:5	**s.** they, if we have found grace in........	559
Nu	32:6	Moses **s.** unto the children of Gad	559
Nu	32:16	**s.**, We will build sheepfolds here..........	559
Nu	32:20	Moses **s.** unto them, If ye will do	559
Nu	32:29	Moses **s.** unto them, If the children......	559
Nu	32:31	Lord hath **s.** unto thy servants, so......	1696
Nu	36:2	they **s.**, The Lord commanded my	559
Nu	36:5	the sons of Joseph hath **s.** well.	1696
De	1:14	ye answered me, and **s.**, The thing......	559
De	1:20	I **s.** unto you, Ye are come unto the......	559
De	1:21	of thy fathers hath **s.** unto thee;.........	1696
De	1:22	and **s.**, We will send men before us,.....	559
De	1:25	**s.**, It is a good land which the Lord......	559
De	1:27	**s.**, Because the Lord hated us, he	559
De	1:29	I **s.** unto you, Dread not, neither.........	559
De	1:39	ones, which ye **s.** should be a prey, ...	559
De	1:41	**s.** unto me, We have sinned against	559
De	1:42	Lord **s.** unto me, Say unto them, Go....	559
De	2:9	Lord **s.** unto me, Distress not the........	559
De	2:13	rise up, **s.** I, and get you over the............	
De	2:31	Lord **s.** unto me, Behold, I have..........	559
De	3:2	Lord **s.** unto me, Fear him not: for......	559
De	3:26	Lord **s.** unto me, Let it suffice thee;	559
De	4:10	when the Lord **s.** unto me, Gather.......	559
De	5:1	**s.** unto them, Hear, O Israel, the	559
De	5:24	And ye **s.**, Behold, the Lord our God ...	559
De	5:28	Lord **s.** unto me, I have heard the	559
De	5:28	have well **s.** all that they have spoken.	
De	9:3	as the Lord hath **s.** unto thee.	1696
De	9:12	Lord **s.** unto me, Arise, get thee	559
De	9:25	Lord had **s.** he would destroy you.	559
De	9:26	and **s.**, O Lord God, destroy not thy	559
De	10:1	**s.** unto me, Hew the two tables of.......	559
De	10:11	Lord **s.** unto me, Arise, take thy	559
De	11:25	tread upon, as he hath **s.** unto you.	1696
De	17:16	as the Lord hath **s.** unto you, ye	559
De	18:2	as he hath **s.** unto them.	1696
De	18:17	Lord **s.** unto me, They have well.........	559
De	29:2	**s.** unto them, Ye have seen all that......	559
De	29:13	as he hath **s.** unto thee, and as he......	1696
De	31:2	he **s.** unto them, I am an hundred........	559
De	31:2	also the Lord hath **s.** unto me, ...	559
De	31:3	before thee, as the Lord hath **s.**	1696
De	31:7	**s.** unto him in the sight of all Israel, ...	559
De	31:14, 16	the Lord **s.** unto Moses, Behold, ...	559
De	31:23	the son of Nun a charge, and **s.**, Be.....	559
De	32:20	he **s.**, I will hide my face from them, ...	559
De	32:26	I **s.**, I would scatter them into............	559
De	32:46	he **s.** unto them, Set your hearts	559
De	33:2	he **s.**, The Lord came from Sinai, ...	559
De	33:7	**s.**, Hear, Lord, the voice of Judah, ...	559
De	33:8	And of Levi he **s.**, Let thy Thummin	559
De	33:9	Who **s.** unto his father and to his.........	559
De	33:12	of Benjamin he **s.**, The beloved of........	559
De	33:13	of Joseph he **s.**, Blessed of the Lord	559
De	33:18	of Zebulun he **s.**, Rejoice, Zebulun, ...	559
De	33:20	And of Gad he **s.**, Blessed be he that ...	559
De	33:22	of Dan he **s.**, Dan is a lion's whelp:	559
De	33:23	And of Naphtali he **s.**, O Naphtali, ...	559
De	33:24	of Asher he **s.**, Let Asher be blessed ...	559
De	34:4	Lord **s.** unto him, This is the land........	559
Jos	1:3	unto you, as I **s.** unto Moses............	1696
Jos	2:4	**s.** thus, There came men unto me, ...	559
Jos	2:9	she **s.** unto the men, I know that........	559
Jos	2:16	she **s.** unto them, Get you to the	559
Jos	2:17	And the men **s.** unto her, We will be....	559
Jos	2:21	she **s.**, According unto your words, ...	559
Jos	2:24	they **s.** unto Joshua, Truly the Lord	559
Jos	3:5	Joshua **s.** unto the people, Sanctify.......	559
Jos	3:7	Lord **s.** unto Joshua, This day will........	559
Jos	3:9	Joshua **s.** unto the children of Israel,.....	559
Jos	3:10	Joshua **s.**, Hereby ye shall know..........	559
Jos	4:5	Joshua **s.** unto them, Pass over...........	559
Jos	5:2	that time the Lord **s.** unto Joshua, ...	559
Jos	5:9	Lord **s.** unto Joshua, This day have	559
Jos	5:13	**s.** unto him, Art thou for us, or for	559
Jos	5:14	he **s.**, Nay; but as captain of the..........	559
Jos	5:14	did worship, and **s.** unto him, what.......	559
Jos	5:15	captain of the Lord's host **s.** unto.........	559
Jos	6:2	Lord **s.** unto Joshua, See, I have	559
Jos	6:6	called the priests, and **s.** unto them,.....	559
Jos	6:7	he **s.** unto the people, Pass on, and	559
Jos	6:16	Joshua **s.** unto the people, Shout;........	559
Jos	6:22	Joshua had **s.** unto the two men	559
Jos	7:3	returned to Joshua, and **s.** unto him,.....	559
Jos	7:7	And Joshua **s.**, Alas, O Lord God,........	559
Jos	7:10	Lord **s.** unto Joshua, Get thee up;........	559
Jos	7:19	Joshua **s.** unto Achan, My son, give, ...	559
Jos	7:20	**s.**, Indeed I have sinned against...........	559
Jos	7:25	Joshua **s.**, Why hast thou troubled........	559
Jos	8:1	the Lord **s.** unto Joshua, Fear not, ...	559
Jos	8:18	Lord **s.** unto Joshua, Stretch out.........	559
Jos	9:6	and **s.** unto him, and to the men of	559
Jos	9:7	men of Israel **s.** unto the Hivites, ...	559
Jos	9:8	**s.** unto Joshua, We are thy servants.	559
Jos	9:8	Joshua **s.** unto them, Who art ye?	559
Jos	9:9	they **s.** unto him, From a very far.........	559
Jos	9:19	princes **s.** unto all the congregation, ...	559
Jos	9:21	the princes **s.** unto them, Let them......	559
Jos	9:24	And they answered Joshua, and **s.**,........	559
Jos	10:8	Lord **s.** unto Joshua, Fear them not:.....	559
Jos	10:12	**s.** in the sight of Israel, Sun, stand	559
Jos	10:18	Joshua **s.**, Roll great stones upon.........	559
Jos	10:22	**s.** Joshua, Open the mouth of the	559
Jos	10:24	**s.** unto the captains of the men of........	559
Jos	10:25	Joshua **s.** unto them, Fear not, nor	559
Jos	11:6	Lord **s.** unto Joshua, Be not afraid	559
Jos	11:23	to all that the Lord **s.** unto Moses;	1696
Jos	13:1	the Lord **s.** unto him, Thou art old.......	559
Jos	13:14, 33	inheritance, as he **s.** unto them......	1696
Jos	14:6	Caleb...the Kenezite **s.** unto him, ...	559
Jos	14:6	thing that the Lord **s.** unto Moses	1696
Jos	14:10	as he **s.**, these forty and five years, ...	1696
Jos	14:12	to drive them out, as the Lord **s.**	1696
Jos	15:16	**s.**, He that smiteth Kirjath-sepher, ...	559
Jos	15:18	Caleb **s.** unto her, What wouldest	559
Jos	17:16	children of Joseph **s.**, The hill is not	559
Jos	18:3	Joshua **s.** unto the children of Israel,.....	559
Jos	22:2	**s.** unto them, Ye have kept all that	559
Jos	22:21	**s.** unto the heads of the thousands	1696
Jos	22:26	we **s.**, Let us now prepare to build	559
Jos	22:28	**s.** we, that it shall be, when they	559
Jos	22:31	the priest **s.** unto the children of..........	559
Jos	23:2	**s.** unto them, I am old and stricken......	559
Jos	24:2	Joshua **s.** unto all the people, Thus.......	559
Jos	24:16	people answered and **s.**, God forbid......	559
Jos	24:19	And Joshua **s.** unto the people, Ye	559
Jos	24:21	people **s.** unto Joshua, Nay; but we	559
Jos	24:22	Joshua **s.** unto the people, Ye are	559
Jos	24:22	And they **s.**, We are witnesses............	559
Jos	24:23	put away, **s.** he, the strange gods............	
Jos	24:24	people **s.** unto Joshua, the Lord...........	559
Jos	24:27	And Joshua **s.** unto all the people, ...	559
Jg	1:2	And the Lord **s.**, Judah shall go up:	559
Jg	1:3	Judah **s.** unto Simeon his brother, ...	559
Jg	1:7	Adoni-bezek **s.**, Threescore and ten	559
Jg	1:12	And Caleb **s.**, He that smiteth.............	559
Jg	1:14	Caleb **s.** unto her, What wilt thou?	559
Jg	1:15	she **s.** unto him, Give me a blessing:	559
Jg	1:20	Hebron unto Caleb, as Moses **s.**:	1696
Jg	1:24	they **s.** unto him, Shew us, we pray.....	559
Jg	2:1	**s.**, I made you to go up out of Egypt, ..	559
Jg	2:1	I **s.**, I will never break my covenant	559
Jg	2:3	Wherefore I also **s.**, I will not drive......	559
Jg	2:15	them for evil, as the Lord had **s.**,.......	1696
Jg	2:20	and he **s.**, Because that this people	559
Jg	3:19	**s.**, I have a secret errand unto thee, ...	559
Jg	3:19	thee, O king: who **s.**, Keep silence.	559
Jg	3:20	and Ehud **s.**, I have a message from.....	559
Jg	3:24	they **s.**, Surely he covereth his feet......	559
Jg	3:28	he **s.** unto them, Follow after me:........	559
Jg	4:6	**s.** unto him, Hath not the Lord God	559
Jg	4:8	Barak **s.** unto her, If thou wilt go	559
Jg	4:9	she **s.**, I will surely go with thee:	559
Jg	4:14	Deborah **s.** unto Barak, Up; for this	559
Jg	4:18	**s.** unto him, Turn in, my lord, turn......	559
Jg	4:19	he **s.** unto her, Give me, I pray thee,...	559
Jg	4:20	he **s.** unto her, Stand in the door of	559
Jg	4:22	**s.** unto him, Come, and I will shew......	559
Jg	5:23	ye Meroz, **s.** the angel of the Lord, ...	559
Jg	6:8	which **s.** unto them, Thus saith the	559
Jg	6:10	I **s.** unto you, I am the Lord your........	559
Jg	6:12	**s.** unto him, The Lord is with thee, ...	559
Jg	6:13	Gideon **s.** unto him, Oh my Lord, if	559
Jg	6:14	**s.**, Go in this thy might, and thou	559
Jg	6:15	and he **s.** unto him, Oh my Lord, ...	559
Jg	6:16	the Lord **s.** unto him, Surely I will.......	559
Jg	6:17	he **s.** unto him, If now I have found	559
Jg	6:18	he **s.**, I will tarry until thou come	559
Jg	6:20	the angel of God **s.** unto him, Take.......	559
Jg	6:22	Gideon **s.**, Alas, O Lord God! for	559
Jg	6:23	the Lord **s.** unto him, Peace be unto	559
Jg	6:25	that the Lord **s.** unto him, Take thy......	559
Jg	6:27	did as the Lord had **s.** unto him:	1696
Jg	6:29	they **s.** one to another, Who hath	559
Jg	6:29	they **s.**, Gideon the son of Joash..........	559
Jg	6:30	the men of the city **s.** unto Joash, ...	559
Jg	6:31	Joash **s.** unto all that stood against	559
Jg	6:36	Gideon **s.** unto God, If thou wilt	559
Jg	6:36	by mine hand, as thou hast **s.**, ...	1696
Jg	6:37	by mine hand, as thou hast **s.**	1696
Jg	6:39	Gideon **s.** unto God, Let not thine	559
Jg	7:2, 4	Lord **s.** unto Gideon, The people	559
Jg	7:5	the Lord **s.** unto Gideon, Every one	559
Jg	7:7	the Lord **s.** unto Gideon, By the..........	559
Jg	7:9	that the Lord **s.** unto him, Arise, ...	559
Jg	7:13	**s.**, Behold, I dreamed a dream, and, ...	559
Jg	7:14	his fellow answered and **s.**, This is.......	559
Jg	7:15	the host of Israel, and **s.**, Arise;	559
Jg	7:17	he **s.** unto them, Look on me, and.......	559
Jg	8:1	the men of Ephraim **s.** unto him, ...	559
Jg	8:2	he **s.** unto them, What have I done	559
Jg	8:3	toward him, when he had **s.** that.	1696
Jg	8:5	he **s.** unto the men of Succoth, ...	559
Jg	8:6	princes of Succoth **s.**, Are the hands	559
Jg	8:7	Gideon **s.**, Therefore when the Lord	559
Jg	8:15	**s.**, Behold Zebah and Zalmunna, ...	559
Jg	8:18	**s.** he unto Zebah and Zalmunna, ...	559
Jg	8:19	he **s.**, They were my brethren, even	559
Jg	8:20	he **s.** unto Jether his firstborn, Up, ...	559
Jg	8:21	Zebah and Zalmunna **s.**, Rise thou, ...	559
Jg	8:22	the men of Israel **s.** unto Gideon, ...	559
Jg	8:23	Gideon **s.** unto them, I will not rule.......	559
Jg	8:24	Gideon **s.** unto them, I would desire.....	559
Jg	9:3	Abimelech; for they **s.**, He is our.........	559
Jg	9:7	**s.** unto them, Hearken unto me, ye......	559
Jg	9:8	**s.** unto the olive tree, Reign thou	559
Jg	9:9	olive tree **s.** unto them, Should I	559
Jg	9:10	trees **s.** to the fig tree, Come thou, ...	559
Jg	9:11	the fig tree **s.** unto them, Should I.......	559
Jg	9:12	**s.** the trees unto the vine, Come.........	559
Jg	9:13	vine **s.** unto them, Should I leave.........	559

Jg 9:14 **s.** all the trees unto the bramble, ... 559
Jg 9:15 And the bramble **s.** unto the trees, ... 559
Jg 9:28 Gaal the son of Ebed **s.**, Who is 559
Jg 9:29 **s.** to Abimelech, Increase the army, ... 559
Jg 9:36 he **s.** to Zebul, Behold, there come 559
Jg 9:36 Zebul **s.** unto him, Thou seest the 559
Jg 9:37 Gaal spake again and **s.**, See there 559
Jg 9:38 **s.** Zebul unto him, Where is now 559
Jg 9:48 **s.** unto the people that were with 559
Jg 9:54 **s.** unto him, Draw thy sword, and 559
Jg 10:11 Lord **s.** unto the children of Israel, ... 559
Jg 10:15 children of Israel **s.** unto the Lord, ... 559
Jg 10:18 princes of Gilead **s.** one to another, ... 559
Jg 11:2 **s.** unto him, Thou shalt not inherit 559
Jg 11:6 they **s.** unto Jephthah, Come, and be 559
Jg 11:7 And Jephthah **s.** unto the elders of 559
Jg 11:8 elders of Gilead **s.** unto Jephthah, ... 559
Jg 11:9 And Jephthah **s.** unto the elders of 559
Jg 11:10 elders of Gilead **s.** unto Jephthah, ... 559
Jg 11:15 **s.** unto him, Thus saith Jephthah, ... 559
Jg 11:19 Israel **s.** unto him, Let us pass, we 559
Jg 11:30 and **s.**, If thou shalt without fail 559
Jg 11:35 clothes, and **s.**, Alas, my daughter! 559
Jg 11:36 she **s.** unto him, My father, if thou 559
Jg 11:37 And she **s.** unto her father, Let this 559
Jg 11:38 And he **s.**, Go. And he sent her away... 559
Jg 12:1 and **s.** unto Jephthah, Wherefore 559
Jg 12:2 Jephthah **s.** unto them, I and my 559
Jg 12:4 because they **s.**, ye Gileadites are 559
Jg 12:5 Ephraimites which were escaped **s.**, ... 559
Jg 12:5 men of Gilead **s.** unto him, Art thou 559
Jg 12:5 thou an Ephraimite? If he **s.**, Nay; 559
Jg 12:6 Then **s.** they unto him, Say now 559
Jg 12:6 he **s.** Sibboleth: for he could not 559
Jg 13:3 **s.** unto her, Behold now, thou art 559
Jg 13:7 he **s.** unto me, Behold, thou shalt 559
Jg 13:8 **s.**, O my Lord, let the man of God 559
Jg 13:10 **s.** unto him, Behold, the man hath 559
Jg 13:11 **s.** unto him, Art thou the man that 559
Jg 13:11 unto the woman, And he **s.**, I am. 559
Jg 13:12 Manoah **s.**, Now let thy words come 559
Jg 13:13 angel of the Lord **s.** unto Manoah, ... 559
Jg 13:13 I **s.** unto the woman let her beware. 559
Jg 13:15 Manoah **s.** unto the angel of the 559
Jg 13:16 angel of the Lord **s.** unto Manoah, ... 559
Jg 13:17 Manoah **s.** unto the angel of the 559
Jg 13:18 the angel of the Lord **s.** unto him, ... 559
Jg 13:22 Manoah **s.** unto his wife, We shall 559
Jg 13:23 his wife **s.** unto him, If the Lord 559
Jg 14:2 and **s.**, I have seen a woman in 559
Jg 14:3 father and his mother **s.** unto him, ... 559
Jg 14:3 Samson **s.** unto his father, Get her 559
Jg 14:12 Samson **s.** unto them, I will now 559
Jg 14:13 **s.** unto him, Put forth thy riddle, ... 559
Jg 14:14 he **s.** unto them, Out of the eater 559
Jg 14:15 **s.** unto Samson's wife, Entice thy 559
Jg 14:16 and **s.**, Thou dost but hate me, and 559
Jg 14:16 And he **s.** unto her, Behold, I have 559
Jg 14:18 the men of the city **s.** unto him on 559
Jg 14:18 **s.** unto them, If ye had not plowed 559
Jg 15:1 he **s.**, I will go in to my wife into the ... 559
Jg 15:2 And her father **s.**, I verily thought 559
Jg 15:3 Samson **s.** concerning them, Now 559
Jg 15:6 the Philistines **s.**, Who hath done 559
Jg 15:7 Samson **s.** unto them, Though ye 559
Jg 15:10 the men of Judah **s.**, Why are ye 559
Jg 15:11 and **s.** to Samson, Knowest thou not 559
Jg 15:11 he **s.** unto them, As they did unto 559
Jg 15:12 they **s.** unto him, We are come down ... 559
Jg 15:12 Samson said unto them, Swear unto 559
Jg 15:16 Samson **s.**, With the jawbone of an 559
Jg 15:18 called on the Lord, and **s.**, Thou hast ... 559
Jg 16:5 and **s.** unto her, Entice him, and see 559
Jg 16:6 And Delilah **s.** to Samson, Tell me, I 559
Jg 16:7 Samson **s.** unto her, If they bind 559
Jg 16:9 she **s.** unto him, The Philistines be 559
Jg 16:10 Delilah **s.** unto Samson, Behold, ... 559
Jg 16:11 he **s.** unto her, If they bind me fast 559
Jg 16:12 and **s.** unto him, The Philistines be 559
Jg 16:13 Delilah **s.** unto Samson, Hitherto 559
Jg 16:13 And he **s.** unto her, If thou weavest 559
Jg 16:14 **s.** unto him, The Philistines be upon 559
Jg 16:15 she **s.** unto him, How canst thou 559
Jg 16:17 her all his heart, and **s.** unto her, ... 559
Jg 16:20 she **s.**, The Philistines be upon thee, ... 559
Jg 16:20 awoke out of his sleep, and **s.**, I will 559
Jg 16:23, 24 they **s.**, Our god hath delivered 559
Jg 16:25 that they **s.**, Call for Samson, that he ... 559
Jg 16:26 Samson **s.** unto the lad that held 559
Jg 16:28 and **s.**, O Lord God, remember me, ... 559
Jg 16:30 And Samson **s.**, Let me die with the 559
Jg 17:2 he **s.** unto his mother, The eleven 559
Jg 17:2 his mother **s.**, Blessed be thou of 559
Jg 17:3 his mother **s.**, I had wholly 559
Jg 17:9 Micah **s.** unto him, Whence comest 559
Jg 17:9 he **s.** unto him, I am a Levite of 559
Jg 17:10 Micah **s.** unto him, Dwell with me, ... 559
Jg 17:13 Then **s.** Micah, Now know I that the 559
Jg 18:2 **s.** unto them, Go, search the land: 559
Jg 18:3 and **s.** unto him, Who brought thee 559
Jg 18:4 he **s.** unto them, Thus and thus 559
Jg 18:5 they **s.** unto him, Ask counsel, we 559
Jg 18:6 priest **s.** unto them, Go in peace: 559
Jg 18:8 brethren **s.** unto them, What say 559
Jg 18:9 they **s.**, Arise, that we may go up 559
Jg 18:14 **s.** unto their brethren, Do ye know 559
Jg 18:18 **s.** the priest unto them, What do 559
Jg 18:19 they **s.** unto him, Hold thy peace, ... 559
Jg 18:23 and **s.** unto Micah, What aileth thee, ... 559
Jg 18:24 he **s.**, Ye have taken away my gods 559
Jg 18:25 children of Dan **s.** unto him, Let 559
Jg 19:5 damsel's father **s.** said unto his son 559
Jg 19:6 the damsel's father had **s.** unto the 559
Jg 19:8 damsel's father **s.**, Comfort thine 559
Jg 19:9 the damsel's father, **s.** unto him, ... 559
Jg 19:11 servant **s.** unto his master, Come, I 559
Jg 19:12 his master **s.** unto him, We will not 559
Jg 19:13 he **s.** unto his servant, Come, and let ... 559
Jg 19:17 the old man **s.**, Whither goest thou? 559
Jg 19:18 And he **s.** unto him, We are passing 559
Jg 19:20 the old man **s.**, Peace be with thee; 559
Jg 19:23 and **s.** unto them, Nay, my brethren, ... 559
Jg 19:28 he **s.** unto her, Up, and let us be 559
Jg 19:30 **s.**, There was no such deed done 559
Jg 20:3 Then **s.** the children of Israel, Tell 559
Jg 20:4 slain, answered and **s.**, I came into 559
Jg 20:18 and **s.**, Which of us shall go up first 559
Jg 20:18 the Lord **s.**, Judah shall go up first. 559
Jg 20:23 And the Lord **s.**, Go up against him. 559
Jg 20:28 Lord **s.**, Go up; for to morrow I will 559
Jg 20:32 of Benjamin **s.**, They are smitten 559
Jg 20:32 children of Israel **s.**, Let us flee, and 559
Jg 20:39 **s.**, Surely they are smitten down 559
Jg 21:3 **s.**, O Lord God of Israel, why is this 559
Jg 21:5 children of Israel **s.**, Who is there 559
Jg 21:6 **s.**, There is one tribe cut off from 559
Jg 21:8 And they **s.**, What one is there of the... 559
Jg 21:16 the elders of the congregation **s.**, ... 559
Jg 21:17 **s.**, There must be an inheritance 559
Jg 21:19 they **s.**, Behold, there is a feast of 559
Ru 1:8 Naomi **s.** unto her two daughters 559
Ru 1:10 **s.** unto her, Surely we will return 559
Ru 1:11 And Naomi **s.**, Turn again, my 559
Ru 1:15 she **s.**, Behold, thy sister in law is 559
Ru 1:16 Ruth **s.**, Intreat me not to leave 559
Ru 1:19 them, and they **s.**, Is this Naomi? 559
Ru 1:20 And she **s.** unto them, Call me not 559
Ru 2:2 Ruth the Moabitess **s.** unto Naomi, ... 559
Ru 2:2 she **s.** unto her, Go, my daughter. 559
Ru 2:4 **s.** unto the reapers, The Lord be 559
Ru 2:5 Then **s.** Boaz unto his servant that 559
Ru 2:6 over the reapers answered and **s.**, ... 559
Ru 2:7 she **s.**, I pray you, let me glean and 559
Ru 2:8 **s.** Boaz unto Ruth, Hearest thou 559
Ru 2:10 and **s.** unto him, Why have I found 559
Ru 2:11 Boaz answered and **s.** unto her, It 559
Ru 2:13 she **s.**, Let me find favour in thy 559
Ru 2:14 Boaz **s.** unto her, At mealtime come 559
Ru 2:19 And her mother in law **s.** unto her, ... 559
Ru 2:19 **s.**, The man's name with whom I 559
Ru 2:20 Naomi **s.** unto her daughter in law, ... 559
Ru 2:20 And Naomi **s.** unto her, The man is 559
Ru 2:21 Ruth...**s.**, He **s.** unto me also, ... 559
Ru 2:22 Naomi **s.** unto Ruth her daughter 559
Ru 3:1 Then Naomi her mother in law **s.** 559
Ru 3:5 she **s.** unto her, All that thou sayest 559
Ru 3:9 And he **s.**, Who art thou? And she 559
Ru 3:10 he **s.**, Blessed be thou of the Lord, ... 559
Ru 3:14 he **s.**, Let it not be known that a 559
Ru 3:15 he **s.**, Bring the vail that thou hast 559
Ru 3:16 she **s.**, Who art thou, my daughter? 559
Ru 3:17 she **s.**, These six measures of barley 559
Ru 3:17 he **s.** to me, Go not empty unto thy 559
Ru 3:18 **s.** she, Sit still, my daughter, until 559
Ru 4:1 unto whom he **s.**, Ho, such a one! 559
Ru 4:2 the city, and **s.**, Sit ye down here 559
Ru 4:3 he **s.** unto the kinsman, Naomi, that 559
Ru 4:4 thee. And he **s.**, I will redeem it. 559
Ru 4:5 Then **s.** Boaz, What day thou buyest 559
Ru 4:6 kinsman **s.**, I cannot redeem it for 559
Ru 4:8 the kinsman **s.** unto Boaz, Buy it 559
Ru 4:9 Boaz **s.** unto the elders, and unto all 559
Ru 4:11 and the elders, **s.**, We are witnesses 559
Ru 4:14 woman **s.** unto Naomi, Blessed be 559
1Sa 1:8 **s.** Elkanah her husband to her, ... 559
1Sa 1:11 she vowed a vow, and **s.**, O Lord of 559
1Sa 1:14 Eli **s.** unto her, How long wilt thou 559
1Sa 1:15 Hannah answered and **s.**, No, my 559
1Sa 1:17 Eli answered and **s.**, Go in peace: 559
1Sa 1:18 And she **s.**, Let thine handmaid find 559
1Sa 1:22 she **s.** unto her husband, I will not 559
1Sa 1:23 Elkanah her husband **s.** unto her, ... 559
1Sa 1:26 And she **s.**, Oh my lord, as thy soul 559
1Sa 2:1 Hannah prayed, and **s.**, My heart 559
1Sa 2:15 **s.** to the man that sacrificed, Give 559
1Sa 2:16 if any man **s.** unto him, Let them 559
1Sa 2:20 **s.**, The Lord give thee seed of this 559
1Sa 2:23 he **s.** unto them, Why do ye such 559
1Sa 2:27 of God unto Eli, and **s.** unto him, ... 559
1Sa 2:30 I **s.** indeed that thy house, and the 559
1Sa 3:5 he ran unto Eli, and **s.**, Here am I; 559
1Sa 3:5 he **s.**, I called not; lie down again. 559
1Sa 3:6, 8 went to Eli, and **s.**, Here am I; 559
1Sa 3:9 Therefore Eli **s.** unto Samuel, Go, ... 559
1Sa 3:11 the Lord **s.** to Samuel, Behold, I 559
1Sa 3:16 called Samuel, and **s.**, Samuel, my 559
1Sa 3:17 he **s.**, What is the thing that the 559
1Sa 3:17 that the Lord hath **s.** unto thee? 1696
1Sa 3:17 all the things that he **s.** unto thee 1696
1Sa 3:18 And he **s.**, It is the Lord: let him 559
1Sa 4:3 the elders of Israel **s.**, Wherefore 559
1Sa 4:6 they **s.**, What meaneth the noise of 559
1Sa 4:7 they **s.**, God is come into the camp 559
1Sa 4:7 And they **s.**, Woe unto us! for there 559
1Sa 4:14 he **s.**, What meaneth the noise of 559
1Sa 4:16 the man **s.** unto Eli, I am he that 559
1Sa 4:16 he **s.**, What is there done, my son? 559
1Sa 4:17 the messenger answered and **s.**, ... 559
1Sa 4:20 that stood by her **s.** unto her, ... 1696
1Sa 4:22 she **s.**, The glory is departed from 559
1Sa 5:7 they **s.**, The ark of the God of Israel 559
1Sa 5:8 and **s.**, What shall we do with the 559
1Sa 5:11 **s.**, Send away the ark of the God of 559
1Sa 6:3 they **s.**, If ye send away the ark of 559
1Sa 6:4 **s.** they, What shall be the trespass 559
1Sa 6:20 the men of Beth-shemesh **s.**, Who is 559
1Sa 7:5 And Samuel **s.**, Gather all Israel to 559
1Sa 7:6 and **s.** there, We have sinned against 559
1Sa 7:8 the children of Israel **s.** to Samuel, ... 559
1Sa 8:5 **s.** unto him, Behold, thou art old, ... 559
1Sa 8:6 they **s.**, Give us a king to judge us. 559
1Sa 8:7 Lord **s.** unto Samuel, Hearken unto 559
1Sa 8:11 he **s.**, This will be the manner of the 559
1Sa 8:19 they **s.**, Nay; but we will have a king ... 559
1Sa 8:22 the Lord **s.** to Samuel, Hearken unto 559
1Sa 8:22 Samuel **s.** unto the men of Israel, Go ... 559
1Sa 9:3 Kish **s.** to Saul his son, Take now 559
1Sa 9:5 **s.** to his servant that was with him, ... 559
1Sa 9:6 **s.** unto him, Behold now, there is in 559
1Sa 9:7 **s.** Saul to his servant, But, behold, ... 559
1Sa 9:8 servant answered Saul again, and **s.**, ... 559
1Sa 9:10 **s.** [559] Saul to his servant, Well **s.**; ... 1697
1Sa 9:11 and **s.** unto them, Is the seer here? 559
1Sa 9:12 they answered them, and **s.**, He is; 559
1Sa 9:17 Lord **s.** unto him, Behold the man 6030
1Sa 9:18 **s.**, Tell me, I pray thee, where the 559
1Sa 9:19 Samuel answered Saul, and **s.**, I am 559
1Sa 9:21 and **s.**, Am not I a Benjamite, of the 559
1Sa 9:23 Samuel **s.** unto the cook, Bring the 559
1Sa 9:23 of which I **s.** unto thee, Set it by thee. ..559
1Sa 9:24 Samuel **s.**, Behold that which is left! 559
1Sa 9:24 hath it been kept for thee since I **s.**, ... 559
1Sa 9:27 Samuel **s.** to Saul, Bid the servant 559
1Sa 10:1 and **s.**, Is it not because the Lord 559
1Sa 10:11 then the people **s.** one to another, ... 559
1Sa 10:12 and **s.**, But who is their father? 559
1Sa 10:14 Saul's uncle **s.** unto him and to his 559
1Sa 10:14 And he **s.**, To seek the asses: and 559

Book	Ref	Context	No.
1Sa	10:15	And Saul's uncle **s.**, Tell me, I pray	559
1Sa	10:15	pray thee, What Samuel **s.** unto you.	559
1Sa	10:16	Saul **s.** unto his uncle, He told us	559
1Sa	10:18	**s.** unto the children of Israel, Thus	559
1Sa	10:19	ye have **s.** unto him, Nay, but set a	559
1Sa	10:24	Samuel **s.** to all the people, See ye	559
1Sa	10:24	shouted, and **s.**, God save the king.	559
1Sa	10:27	children of Belial **s.**, How shall this	559
1Sa	11:1	the men of Jabesh **s.** unto Nahash,	559
1Sa	11:3	elders of Jabesh **s.** unto him, Give	559
1Sa	11:5	and Saul **s.**, What aileth the people	559
1Sa	11:9	**s.** unto the messengers that came,	559
1Sa	11:10	the men of Jabesh **s.**, To morrow we	559
1Sa	11:12	And the people **s.** unto Samuel, Who	559
1Sa	11:12	Who is he that **s.**, Shall Saul reign	559
1Sa	11:13	and Saul **s.**, There shall not a man	559
1Sa	11:14	**s.** Samuel to the people, Come, and	559
1Sa	12:1	Samuel **s.** unto all Israel, Behold, I	559
1Sa	12:1	your voice in all that ye **s.** unto me,	559
1Sa	12:4	they **s.**, Thou hast not defrauded	559
1Sa	12:5	And he **s.** unto them, The Lord is	559
1Sa	12:6	Samuel **s.** unto the people, It is the	559
1Sa	12:10	the Lord, and **s.**, We have sinned,	559
1Sa	12:12	ye **s.** unto me, Nay; but a king shall	559
1Sa	12:19	all the people **s.** unto Samuel, Pray	559
1Sa	12:20	Samuel **s.** unto the people, Fear not:	559
1Sa	13:9	And Saul **s.**, Bring hither a burnt	559
1Sa	13:11	Samuel **s.**, What hast thou done?	559
1Sa	13:11	And Saul **s.**, Because I saw that the	559
1Sa	13:12	Therefore **s.** I, The Philistines will	559
1Sa	13:13	Samuel **s.** to Saul, Thou hast done	559
1Sa	13:19	Philistines **s.**, Lest the Hebrews	559
1Sa	14:1	son of Saul **s.** unto the young man	559
1Sa	14:6	And Jonathan **s.** to the young man	559
1Sa	14:7	And his armourbearer **s.** unto him,	559
1Sa	14:8	Then **s.** Jonathan, Behold, we will	559
1Sa	14:11	Philistines **s.**, Behold, the Hebrews	559
1Sa	14:12	and **s.**, Come up to us, and we will	559
1Sa	14:12	Jonathan **s.** unto his armourbearer,	559
1Sa	14:17	Then **s.** Saul unto the people that	559
1Sa	14:18	Saul **s.** unto Ahiah, Bring hither the	559
1Sa	14:19	Saul **s.** unto the priest, Withdraw	559
1Sa	14:28	answered one of the people, and **s.**,	559
1Sa	14:29	Then **s.** Jonathan, My father hath	559
1Sa	14:33	he **s.**, Ye have transgressed: roll	559
1Sa	14:34	Saul **s.**, Disperse yourselves among	559
1Sa	14:36	Saul **s.**, Let us go down after the	559
1Sa	14:36	they **s.**, Do whatsoever seemeth good	559
1Sa	14:36	Then **s.** the priest, Let us draw near	559
1Sa	14:38	And Saul **s.**, Draw ye near hither,	559
1Sa	14:40	Then **s.** he unto all Israel, Be ye on	559
1Sa	14:40	the people **s.** unto Saul, Do what	559
1Sa	14:41	Therefore Saul **s.** unto the Lord God	559
1Sa	14:42	And Saul **s.**, Cast lots between me	559
1Sa	14:43	Then Saul **s.** to Jonathan, Tell me	559
1Sa	14:43	and **s.**, I did but taste a little honey	559
1Sa	14:45	And the people **s.** unto Saul, Shall	559
1Sa	15:1	Samuel also **s.** unto Saul, The Lord	559
1Sa	15:6	And Saul **s.** unto the Kenites, Go,	559
1Sa	15:13	Saul **s.** unto him, Blessed be thou of	559
1Sa	15:14	Samuel **s.**, What meaneth then this	559
1Sa	15:15	Saul **s.**, They have brought them	559
1Sa	15:16	Then Samuel **s.** unto Saul, Stay, and	559
1Sa	15:16	the Lord hath **s.** to me this night.	1696
1Sa	15:16	And he **s.** unto him, Say on.	559
1Sa	15:17	Samuel **s.**, When thou wast little in	559
1Sa	15:18	Lord sent thee on a journey, and **s.**,	559
1Sa	15:20	Saul **s.** unto Samuel, Yea, I have	559
1Sa	15:22	Samuel **s.**, Hath the Lord as great	559
1Sa	15:24	Saul **s.** unto Samuel, I have sinned:	559
1Sa	15:26	And Samuel **s.** unto Saul, I will not	559
1Sa	15:28	and Samuel **s.** unto him, The Lord	559
1Sa	15:30	he **s.**, I have sinned: yet honour	559
1Sa	15:32	Then **s.** Samuel, Bring ye hither to	559
1Sa	15:32	And Agag **s.**, Surely the bitterness of	559
1Sa	15:33	Samuel **s.**, As thy sword hath made	559
1Sa	16:1	And the Lord **s.** unto Samuel, How	559
1Sa	16:2	Samuel **s.**, How can I go? if Saul	559
1Sa	16:2	And the Lord **s.**, Take an heifer with	559
1Sa	16:4	and **s.**, Comest thou peaceably?	559
1Sa	16:5	And he **s.**, Peaceably: I am come to	559
1Sa	16:6	and **s.**, Surely the Lord's anointed is	559
1Sa	16:7	But the Lord **s.** unto Samuel, Look	559
1Sa	16:8,	9 **s.**, Neither hath the Lord chosen	559
1Sa	16:10	And Samuel **s.** unto Jesse, The Lord	559
1Sa	16:11	Samuel **s.** unto Jesse, Are here all	559
1Sa	16:11	And he **s.**, There remaineth yet the	559
1Sa	16:11	And Samuel **s.** unto Jesse, Send and	559
1Sa	16:12	and the Lord **s.**, Arise, anoint him:	559
1Sa	16:15	And Saul's servants **s.** unto him,	559
1Sa	16:17	Saul **s.** unto his servants, Provide	559
1Sa	16:18	and **s.**, Behold, I have seen a son of	559
1Sa	16:19	**s.**, Send me David thy son, which is	559
1Sa	17:8	and **s.** unto them, Why are ye come	559
1Sa	17:10	the Philistine **s.**, I defy the armies	559
1Sa	17:17	Jesse **s.** unto David his son, Take	559
1Sa	17:25	the men of Israel **s.**, Have ye seen	559
1Sa	17:28	and he **s.**, Why camest thou down	559
1Sa	17:29	David **s.**, What have I now done?	559
1Sa	17:32	And David **s.** to Saul, Let no man's	559
1Sa	17:33	Saul **s.** to David, Thou art not able	559
1Sa	17:34	David **s.** unto Saul, Thy servant kept	559
1Sa	17:37	David **s.** moreover, The Lord that	559
1Sa	17:37	And Saul **s.** unto David, Go, and the	559
1Sa	17:39	David **s.** unto Saul, I cannot go with	559
1Sa	17:43	the Philistine **s.** unto David, Am I a	559
1Sa	17:44	Philistine **s.** to David, Come to me,	559
1Sa	17:45	Then **s.** David to the Philistine,	559
1Sa	17:55	he **s.** unto Abner, the captain of the	559
1Sa	17:55	And Abner **s.**, As thy soul liveth, O	559
1Sa	17:56	the king **s.**, Enquire thou whose	559
1Sa	17:58	Saul **s.** to him, Whose son art thou,	559
1Sa	18:7	**s.**, Saul hath slain his thousands,	559
1Sa	18:8	and he **s.**, They have ascribed unto	559
1Sa	18:11	for he **s.**, I will smite David even to	559
1Sa	18:17	Saul **s.** to David, Behold my elder	559
1Sa	18:17	Saul **s.**, Let not mine hand be upon	559
1Sa	18:18	And David **s.** unto Saul, Who am I?	559
1Sa	18:21	Saul **s.**, I will give him her, that she	559
1Sa	18:21	Saul **s.** to David, Thou shalt this day	559
1Sa	18:23	David **s.**, Seemeth it to you a light	559
1Sa	18:25	Saul **s.**, Thus shall ye say to David,	559
1Sa	19:4	and **s.** unto him, Let not the king sin	559
1Sa	19:14	to take David, she **s.**, He is sick.	559
1Sa	19:17	And Saul **s.** unto Michal, Why hast	559
1Sa	19:17	answered Saul, He **s.** unto me, Let	559
1Sa	19:22	**s.**, Where are Samuel and David?	559
1Sa	19:22	one **s.**, Behold, they be at Naioth in	559
1Sa	20:1	and **s.** before Jonathan, What have I	559
1Sa	20:2	And he **s.** unto him, God forbid;	559
1Sa	20:3	David sware moreover, and **s.**, Thy	559
1Sa	20:4	**s.** Jonathan unto David, Whatsoever	559
1Sa	20:5	**s.** unto Jonathan, Behold, to morrow	559
1Sa	20:9	Jonathan **s.**, Far be it from thee: for	559
1Sa	20:10	**s.** David to Jonathan, Who shall tell	559
1Sa	20:11	Jonathan **s.** unto David, Come, and	559
1Sa	20:12	Jonathan **s.** unto David, O Lord God	559
1Sa	20:18	Jonathan **s.** to David, To morrow is	559
1Sa	20:27	and Saul **s.** unto Jonathan his son,	559
1Sa	20:29	And he **s.**, Let me go, I pray thee;	559
1Sa	20:30	and he **s.** unto him, Thou son of the	559
1Sa	20:32	Saul his father, and **s.** unto him,	559
1Sa	20:36	he **s.** unto his lad, Run, find out now	559
1Sa	20:37	Jonathan cried after the lad, and **s.**,	559
1Sa	20:40	**s.** unto him, Go, carry them to the	559
1Sa	20:42	Jonathan **s.** to David, Go in peace,	559
1Sa	21:1	and **s.** unto him, Why art thou alone,	559
1Sa	21:2	David **s.** unto Ahimelech the priest,	559
1Sa	21:2	hath **s.** unto me, Let no man know	559
1Sa	21:4	the priest answered David, and **s.**,	559
1Sa	21:5	David answered the priest, and **s.**	559
1Sa	21:8	And David **s.** unto Ahimelech, And is	559
1Sa	21:9	the priest **s.**, The sword of Goliath	559
1Sa	21:9	David **s.**, There is none like that;	559
1Sa	21:11	the servants of Achish **s.** unto him,	559
1Sa	21:14	Then **s.** Achish unto his servants,	559
1Sa	22:3	he **s.** unto the king of Moab, Let my	559
1Sa	22:5	And the prophet Gad **s.** unto David,	559
1Sa	22:7	Then Saul **s.** unto his servants that	559
1Sa	22:9	**s.**, I saw the son of Jesse coming to	559
1Sa	22:12	And Saul **s.**, Hear now, thou son of	559
1Sa	22:13	And Saul **s.** unto him, Why have ye	559
1Sa	22:14	answered the king, and **s.**, And who	559
1Sa	22:16	the king **s.**, Thou shalt surely die,	559
1Sa	22:17	king **s.** unto the footmen that stood	559
1Sa	22:18	the king **s.** to Doeg, Turn thou, and	559
1Sa	22:22	David **s.** unto Abiathar, I knew it	559
1Sa	23:2	Lord **s.** unto David, Go, and smite	559
1Sa	23:3	David's men **s.** unto him, Behold, we	559
1Sa	23:4	Lord answered him and **s.**, Arise, go	559
1Sa	23:7	And Saul **s.**, God hath delivered him	559
1Sa	23:9	he **s.** to Abiathar the priest, Bring	559
1Sa	23:10	**s.** David, O Lord God of Israel, thy	559
1Sa	23:11	And the Lord **s.**, He will come down.	559
1Sa	23:12	**s.** David, Will the men of Keilah	559
1Sa	23:12	Lord **s.**, They will deliver thee up.	559
1Sa	23:17	And he **s.** unto him, Fear not: for	559
1Sa	23:21	Saul **s.**, Blessed be ye of the Lord;	559
1Sa	24:4	And the men of David **s.** unto him,	559
1Sa	24:4	day of which the Lord **s.** unto thee;	559
1Sa	24:6	And he **s.** unto his men, The Lord	559
1Sa	24:9	And David **s.** to Saul, Wherefore	559
1Sa	24:10	I **s.**, I will not put forth mine hand	559
1Sa	24:16	Saul **s.**, Is this thy voice, my son	559
1Sa	24:17	And he **s.** to David, Thou art more	559
1Sa	25:5	and David **s.** unto the young men,	559
1Sa	25:10	and **s.**, Who is David? and who is the	559
1Sa	25:13	David **s.** unto his men, Gird ye on	559
1Sa	25:19	And she **s.** unto her servants, Go on	559
1Sa	25:21	Now David had **s.**, Surely in vain	559
1Sa	25:24	fell at his feet, and **s.**, Upon me, my	559
1Sa	25:32	And David **s.** to Abigail, Blessed be	559
1Sa	25:35	**s.** unto her, Go up in peace to thine	559
1Sa	25:39	he **s.**, Blessed be the Lord, that hath	559
1Sa	25:41	on her face to the earth, and **s.**,	559
1Sa	26:6	answered David and **s.** to Ahimelech	559
1Sa	26:6	Abishai **s.**, I will go down with thee	559
1Sa	26:8	Then **s.** Abishai to David, God hath	559
1Sa	26:9	And David **s.** to Abishai, Destroy	559
1Sa	26:10	David **s.** furthermore, As the Lord	559
1Sa	26:14	Then Abner answered and **s.**, Who	559
1Sa	26:15	And David **s.** to Abner, Art not thou	559
1Sa	26:17	**s.**, Is this thy voice, my son David?	559
1Sa	26:17	David **s.**, It is my voice, my lord, O	559
1Sa	26:18	he **s.**, Wherefore doth my lord thus	559
1Sa	26:21	Then **s.** Saul, I have sinned: return,	559
1Sa	26:22	David answered and **s.**, Behold the	559
1Sa	26:25	Saul **s.** to David, Blessed be thou,	559
1Sa	27:1	And David **s.** in his heart, I shall	559
1Sa	27:5	David **s.** unto Achish, If I have now	559
1Sa	27:10	Achish **s.**, Whither have ye made a	559
1Sa	27:10	And David **s.**, Against the south of	559
1Sa	28:1	And Achish **s.** unto David, Know thou	559
1Sa	28:2	And David **s.** to Achish, Surely thou	559
1Sa	28:2	And Achish **s.** to David, Therefore	559
1Sa	28:7	Then **s.** Saul unto his servants, Seek	559
1Sa	28:7	And his servants **s.** to him, Behold,	559
1Sa	28:8	he **s.**, I pray thee, divine unto me	559
1Sa	28:9	And the woman **s.** unto him, Behold,	559
1Sa	28:11	**s.** the woman, Whom shall I bring	559
1Sa	28:11	And he **s.**, Bring me up Samuel.	559
1Sa	28:13	the king **s.** unto her, Be not afraid:	559
1Sa	28:13	the woman **s.** unto Saul, I saw gods	559
1Sa	28:14	he **s.** unto her, What form is he of?	559
1Sa	28:14	And she **s.**, an old man cometh up;	559
1Sa	28:15	And Samuel **s.** to Saul, Why hast	559
1Sa	28:16	Then **s.** Samuel, Wherefore then	559
1Sa	28:21	**s.** unto him, Behold, thine handmaid	559
1Sa	28:23	he refused, and **s.**, I will not eat	559
1Sa	29:3	**s.** the princes of the Philistines,	559
1Sa	29:3	**s.** unto the princes of the Philistines,	559
1Sa	29:4	princes of the Philistines **s.** unto	559
1Sa	29:6	Achish called David, and **s.** unto	559
1Sa	29:8	And David **s.** unto Achish, But what	559
1Sa	29:9	Achish answered and **s.** to David, I	559
1Sa	29:9	the princes of the Philistines have **s.**,	559
1Sa	30:7	And David **s.** to Abiathar the priest,	559
1Sa	30:13	And David **s.** unto him, To whom	559
1Sa	30:13	he **s.**, I am a young man of Egypt,	559
1Sa	30:15	David **s.** to him, Canst thou bring	559
1Sa	30:15	he **s.**, Swear unto me by God, that	559
1Sa	30:20	cattle, and **s.**, This is David's spoil.	559
1Sa	30:22	**s.**, Because they went not with us,	559
1Sa	30:23	Then **s.** David, Ye shall not do so,	559
1Sa	31:4	Then **s.** Saul unto his armourbearer,	559
2Sa	1:3	And David **s.** unto him, From whence	559
2Sa	1:3	he **s.** unto him, Out of the camp of	559
2Sa	1:4	David **s.** unto him, How went the	559
2Sa	1:5	David **s.** unto the young man that	559
2Sa	1:6	And the young man that told him **s.**,	559
2Sa	1:8	And he **s.** unto me, Who art thou?	559
2Sa	1:9	He **s.** unto me again, Stand, I pray	559
2Sa	1:13	David **s.** unto the young man that	559
2Sa	1:14	David **s.** unto him, How wast thou	559
2Sa	1:15	and **s.**, Go near, and fall upon him.	559
2Sa	1:16	And David **s.** unto him, thy blood	559
2Sa	2:1	And the Lord **s.** unto him, Go up.	559
2Sa	2:1	David **s.**, Whither shall I go up?	559
2Sa	2:1	And he **s.**, Unto Hebron.	559
2Sa	2:5	and said unto them, Blessed be ye	559

2Sa 2:14 And Abner **s.** to Joab, Let the young.... 559
2Sa 2:14 us. And Joab **s.**, Let them arise........... 559
2Sa 2:20 him, and **s.**, Art thou Asahel?............. 559
2Sa 2:21 Abner **s.** to him, Turn thee aside.......... 559
2Sa 2:22 And Abner **s.** again to Asahel, Turn 559
2Sa 2:26 **s.**, Shall the sword devour for ever?..... 559
2Sa 2:27 And Joab **s.**, As God liveth, unless....... 559
2Sa 3:7 And Ish-bosheth **s.** to Abner,.............. 559
2Sa 3:8 and **s.**, Am I a dog's head, which......... 559
2Sa 3:13 he **s.**, Well; I will make a league.......... 559
2Sa 3:16 Then **s.** Abner unto him, Go, return..... 559
2Sa 3:21 Abner **s.** unto David, I will arise.......... 559
2Sa 3:24 Joab came to the king, and **s.**,............. 559
2Sa 3:28 he **s.**, I and my kingdom are.............. 559
2Sa 3:31 And David **s.** to Joab, and to all the....... 559
2Sa 3:33 and **s.**, Died Abner as a fool dieth? 559
2Sa 3:38 And the king **s.** unto his servants,......... 559
2Sa 4:8 **s.** to the king, Behold the head of........ 559
2Sa 4:9 and **s.** unto them, As the Lord liveth, ... 559
2Sa 5:2 and the Lord **s.** to thee, Thou shalt...... 559
2Sa 5:8 David **s.** on that day, Whosoever......... 559
2Sa 5:8 Wherefore they **s.**, The blind and......... 559
2Sa 5:19 And the Lord **s.** unto David, Go up:..... 559
2Sa 5:20 and David smote them there, and **s.**,.... 559
2Sa 5:23 Lord, he **s.**, Thou shalt not go up;....... 559
2Sa 6:9 **s.**, How shall the ark of the Lord......... 559
2Sa 6:20 and **s.**, How glorious was the king 559
2Sa 6:21 David **s.** unto Michal, It was before...... 559
2Sa 7:2 king **s.** unto Nathan the prophet, ... 559
2Sa 7:3 Nathan **s.** to the king, Go, do all 559
2Sa 7:18 and he **s.**, Who am I, O Lord God?...... 559
2Sa 7:25 it for ever, and do as thou hast **s.**......... 169
2Sa 9:1 David **s.**, Is there...any that is left......... 55
2Sa 9:2 the king **s.** unto him, Art thou Ziba? 55
2Sa 9:2 And he **s.**, Thy servant is he................ 55
2Sa 9:3 king **s.**, Is there not yet any of the 559
2Sa 9:3 And Ziba **s.** unto the king, Jonathan...... 559
2Sa 9:4 the king **s.** unto him, Where is he? 559
2Sa 9:4 Ziba **s.** unto the king, Behold, he is...... 559
2Sa 9:6 David **s.**, Mephibosheth. And he.......... 559
2Sa 9:7 And David **s.** unto him, Fear not: 559
2Sa 9:8 himself, and **s.**, What is thy servant, ... 559
2Sa 9:9 **s.** unto him, I have given unto thy 559
2Sa 9:11 **s.** Ziba unto the king, According to....... 559
2Sa 9:11 Mephibosheth, **s.** the king, he shall...........
2Sa 10:2 **s.** David, I will shew kindness unto 559
2Sa 10:3 **s.** unto Hanun their lord, Thinkest 559
2Sa 10:5 the king **s.**, Tarry at Jericho until......... 559
2Sa 10:11 he **s.**, If the Syrians be too strong for... 559
2Sa 11:3 And one **s.**, Is not this Bath-sheba, ... 559
2Sa 11:5 told David, and **s.**, I am with child. 559
2Sa 11:8 Davd **s.** to Uriah, Go down to thy........ 559
2Sa 11:10 David **s.** unto Uriah, Camest thou........ 559
2Sa 11:11 Uriah **s.** unto David, the ark, and......... 559
2Sa 11:12 David **s.** to Uriah, Tarry here to-day.... 559
2Sa 11:23 messenger **s.** unto David, Surely the.... 559
2Sa 11:25 Then David **s.** unto the messenger,...... 559
2Sa 12:1 **s.** unto him, There were two men in.... 559
2Sa 12:5 he **s.** to Nathan, As the Lord liveth,..... 559
2Sa 12:7 Nathan **s.** to David, Thou art the......... 559
2Sa 12:13 David **s.** unto Nathan, I have sinned..... 559
2Sa 12:13 And Nathan **s.** unto David, The Lord..... 559
2Sa 12:18 they **s.**, Behold, while the child was 559
2Sa 12:19 David **s.** unto his servants, Is the 559
2Sa 12:19 child dead? And they **s.**, He is dead. 559
2Sa 12:21 Then **s.** his servants unto him, What.... 559
2Sa 12:22 he **s.**, While the child was yet alive, ... 559
2Sa 12:22 for I **s.**, Who can tell whether God....... 559
2Sa 12:27 **s.**, I have fought against Rabbah, ... 559
2Sa 13:4 he **s.** unto him, Why art thou, being..... 559
2Sa 13:4 Amnon **s.** unto him, I love Tamar, ... 559
2Sa 13:5 Jonadab **s.** unto him, Lay thee down..... 559
2Sa 13:6 Amnon **s.** unto the king, I pray thee,.... 559
2Sa 13:9 Amnon **s.**, Have out all men from me. .. 559
2Sa 13:10 Amnon **s.** unto Tamar, Bring the 559
2Sa 13:11 **s.** unto her, Come lie with me, my 559
2Sa 13:15 Amnon **s.** unto her, Arise, be gone. 559
2Sa 13:16 she **s.** unto him, There is no cause: 559
2Sa 13:17 **s.**, Put now this woman out from me,... 559
2Sa 13:20 Absalom her brother **s.** unto her,......... 559
2Sa 13:24 and **s.**, Behold now, thy servant hath.... 559
2Sa 13:25 king **s.** to Absalom, Nay, my son,........ 559
2Sa 13:26 Then **s.** Absalom, If not, I pray thee, ... 559
2Sa 13:26 the king **s.** unto him, Why should he 559
2Sa 13:32 **s.**, Let not my lord suppose that they... 559
2Sa 13:35 Jonadab **s.** unto the king, Behold,......... 559
2Sa 13:35 come: as thy servant **s.**, so it is......... 1697
2Sa 14:2 **s.** unto her, I pray thee, feign thyself... 559
2Sa 14:4 did obeisance, and **s.**, Help, O king. 559
2Sa 14:5 king **s.** unto her, What aileth thee?....... 559
2Sa 14:7 they **s.**, Deliver him that smote his 559
2Sa 14:8 the king **s.** unto the woman, Go to....... 559
2Sa 14:9 woman of Tekoah **s.** unto the king, ... 559
2Sa 14:10 the king **s.**, Whosoever saith ought 559
2Sa 14:11 Then **s.** she, I pray thee, let the 559
2Sa 14:11 he **s.**, As the Lord liveth, there shall.... 559
2Sa 14:12 the woman **s.**, Let thine handmaid, I 559
2Sa 14:12 my lord the king, And he **s.**, Say on..... 559
2Sa 14:13 the woman **s.**, Wherefore then hast...... 559
2Sa 14:15 thy handmaid **s.**, I will now speak 559
2Sa 14:17 thine handmaid **s.**, The word of my...... 559
2Sa 14:18 the king answered and **s.** unto the 559
2Sa 14:18 the woman **s.**, Let my lord the king..... 559
2Sa 14:19 the king **s.**, Is not the hand of Joab 559
2Sa 14:19 the woman answered and **s.**, As thy..... 559
2Sa 14:21 the king **s.** unto Joab, Behold now,....... 559
2Sa 14:22 and Joab **s.**, To day thy servant........... 559
2Sa 14:24 the king **s.**, Let him turn to his own..... 559
2Sa 14:30 he **s.** unto his servants, See, Joab's...... 559
2Sa 14:31 **s.** unto him, Wherefore have thy 559
2Sa 15:2 him, and **s.**, Of what city art thou?....... 559
2Sa 15:2 And he **s.**, Thy servant is of one of...... 559
2Sa 15:3 And Absalom **s.** unto him, See, thy...... 559
2Sa 15:4 Absalom **s.** moreover, Oh that I were.... 559
2Sa 15:7 Absalom **s.** unto the king, I pray.......... 559
2Sa 15:9 the king **s.** unto him, Go in peace. 559
2Sa 15:14 And David **s.** unto all his servants........ 559
2Sa 15:15 the king's servants **s.** unto the king,..... 559
2Sa 15:19 Then **s.** the king to Ittai the Gittite,..... 559
2Sa 15:21 And Ittai answered the king, and **s.**,..... 559
2Sa 15:22 David **s.** to Ittai, Go and pass over. 559
2Sa 15:25 king **s.** unto Zadok, Carry back the 559
2Sa 15:27 king **s.** also unto Zadok the priest, ... 559
2Sa 15:31 David **s.**, O Lord, I pray thee, turn...... 559
2Sa 15:33 Unto whom David **s.**, If thou passest.... 559
2Sa 16:2 the king **s.** unto Ziba, What meanest..... 559
2Sa 16:2 Ziba **s.**, The asses be for the king's...... 559
2Sa 16:3 king **s.**, And where is thy master's....... 559
2Sa 16:3 Ziba **s.** unto the king, Behold, he......... 559
2Sa 16:3 for he **s.**, To day shall the house of...... 559
2Sa 16:4 **s.** the king to Ziba, Behold, thine are.... 559
2Sa 16:4 And Ziba **s.**, I humbly beseech thee...... 559
2Sa 16:7 And thus **s.** Shimei when he cursed,..... 559
2Sa 16:9 Then **s.** Abishai the son of Zeruiah...... 559
2Sa 16:10 king **s.**, What have I to do with you, ... 559
2Sa 16:10 Lord hath **s.** unto him, Curse David. 559
2Sa 16:11 David **s.** to Abishai, and to all his......... 559
2Sa 16:16 Hushai **s.** unto Absalom, God save......... 559
2Sa 16:17 And Absalom **s.** to Hushai, Is this thy... 559
2Sa 16:18 Hushai **s.** unto Absalom, Nay; but........ 559
2Sa 16:20 Then **s.** Absalom to Ahithophel, Give.... 559
2Sa 16:21 Ahithophel **s.** unto Absalom, Go in 559
2Sa 17:1 Ahithophel **s.** unto Absalom, Let me..... 559
2Sa 17:5 Then **s.** Absalom, Call now Hushai 559
2Sa 17:7 And Hushai **s.** unto Absalom, The........ 559
2Sa 17:8 **s.** Hushai, Thou knowest thy father...... 559
2Sa 17:14 Absalom and all the men of Israel **s.**,.... 559
2Sa 17:15 **s.** Hushai unto Zadok and...Abiathar 559
2Sa 17:20 they **s.**, Where is Ahimaaz and............ 559
2Sa 17:20 woman **s.** unto them, They be gone 559
2Sa 17:21 and **s.** unto David, Arise, and pass....... 559
2Sa 17:29 for they **s.**, The people is hungry,........ 559
2Sa 18:2 king **s.** unto the people, I will surely..... 559
2Sa 18:4 king **s.** unto them, What seemeth 559
2Sa 18:10 and **s.**,...I saw Absalom hanged in......... 559
2Sa 18:11 And Joab **s.** unto the man that told....... 559
2Sa 18:12 And the man **s.** unto Joab, Though I..... 559
2Sa 18:14 Then **s.** Joab, I may not tarry thus........ 559
2Sa 18:18 for he **s.**, I have no son to keep my..... 559
2Sa 18:19 Then **s.** Ahimaaz the son of Zadok, ... 559
2Sa 18:20 And Joab **s.** unto him, Thou shalt not.... 559
2Sa 18:21 **s.** Joab to Cushi, Go tell the king......... 559
2Sa 18:22 Then **s.** Ahimaaz the son of Zadok yet.. 559
2Sa 18:22 Joab **s.**, Wherefore wilt thou run,......... 559
2Sa 18:23 But howsoever, **s.** he, let me run............
2Sa 18:23 And he **s.** unto him, Run. Then.......... 559
2Sa 18:25 the king **s.**, If he be alone, there is...... 559
2Sa 18:26 and **s.**, Behold another man running...... 559
2Sa 18:26 the king **s.**, he also bringeth tidings...... 559
2Sa 18:27 And the watchman **s.**, Me thinketh....... 559
2Sa 18:27 the king **s.**, He is a good man, and 559
2Sa 18:28 and **s.** unto the king, All is well. 559
2Sa 18:28 and **s.**, Blessed be the Lord thy God,... 559
2Sa 18:29 king **s.**, Is the young man Absalom....... 559
2Sa 18:30 And the king **s.** unto him, Turn aside,.... 559
2Sa 18:31 Cushi **s.**, Tidings, my lord the king: 559
2Sa 18:32 king **s.** unto Cushi, Is the young man.... 559
2Sa 18:33 went, thus he **s.**, O my son Absalom,... 559
2Sa 19:5 to the king, and **s.**, Thou hast shamed.. 559
2Sa 19:19 And **s.** unto the king, Let not my lord .. 559
2Sa 19:21 the son of Zeruiah answered and **s.**, ... 559
2Sa 19:22 David **s.**, What have I to do with you, .. 559
2Sa 19:23 Therefore the king **s.** unto Shimei, ... 559
2Sa 19:25 king **s.** unto him, Wherefore wentest..... 559
2Sa 19:26 for thy servant **s.**, I will saddle me....... 559
2Sa 19:29 the king **s.** unto him, Why speakest...... 559
2Sa 19:29 I have **s.**, Thou and Ziba divide the 559
2Sa 19:30 And Mephibosheth **s.** unto the king, ... 559
2Sa 19:33 And the king **s.** unto Barzillai, Come..... 559
2Sa 19:34 Barzillai **s.** unto the king, How long...... 559
2Sa 19:41 and **s.** unto the king, Why have our........ 559
2Sa 19:43 and **s.**, We have ten parts in the king, .. 559
2Sa 20:1 and **s.**, We have no part in David,......... 559
2Sa 20:4 **s.** the king to Amasa, Assemble me 559
2Sa 20:6 David **s.** to Abishai, Now shall Sheba.... 559
2Sa 20:9 Joab **s.** to Amasa, Art thou in health,.... 559
2Sa 20:11 and **s.**, he that favoureth Joab, and....... 559
2Sa 20:17 her, the woman **s.**, Art thou Joab?........ 559
2Sa 20:17 she **s.** unto him, Hear the words of...... 559
2Sa 20:20 And Joab answered and **s.**, Far be it,.... 559
2Sa 20:21 woman **s.** unto Joab, Behold his head.... 559
2Sa 21:2 the Gibeonites, and **s.** unto them; 559
2Sa 21:3 David **s.** unto the Gibeonites, What...... 559
2Sa 21:4 Gibeonites **s.** unto him, We will have.... 559
2Sa 21:4 he **s.**, What ye shall say, that will I....... 559
2Sa 21:6 And the king **s.**, I will give them. 559
2Sa 22:2 And he **s.**, The Lord is my rock, and ... 559
2Sa 23:1 David the son of Jesse **s.**, and the...... 5002
2Sa 23:1 and the sweet psalmist of Israel, **s.**,..... 5002
2Sa 23:3 The God of Israel **s.**, the Rock of........ 559
2Sa 23:15 David longed, and **s.**, Oh that one......... 559
2Sa 23:17 And he **s.**, Be it far from me, O Lord,.. 559
2Sa 24:2 For the king **s.** to Joab the captain of.... 559
2Sa 24:3 Joab **s.** unto the king, Now the Lord 559
2Sa 24:10 David **s.** unto the Lord, I have sinned... 559
2Sa 24:13 and **s.** unto him, Shall seven years of.... 559
2Sa 24:14 David **s.** unto Gad, I am in a great....... 559
2Sa 24:16 and **s.** to the angel that destroyed........ 559
2Sa 24:17 and **s.**, Lo, I have sinned, and I have ... 559
2Sa 24:18 and **s.** unto him, Go up, rear an altar.... 559
2Sa 24:21 Araunah **s.**, Wherefore is my lord 559
2Sa 24:21 David **s.**, To buy the threshingfloor...... 559
2Sa 24:22 Araunah **s.** unto David, Let my lord 559
2Sa 24:23 Araunah **s.** unto the king, The Lord 559
2Sa 24:24 And the king **s.** unto Araunah, Nay; 559
1Ki 1:2 Wherefore his servants **s.** unto him,...... 559
1Ki 1:16 the king **s.**, What wouldest thou?......... 559
1Ki 1:17 And she **s.** unto him, My lord, thou 559
1Ki 1:24 And Nathan **s.**, My lord, O king, hast... 559
1Ki 1:24 hast thou **s.**, Adonijah shall reign 559
1Ki 1:28 king David answered and **s.**, Call me 559
1Ki 1:29 the king sware, and **s.**, As the Lord..... 559
1Ki 1:31 and **s.**, Let my lord king David live 559
1Ki 1:32 king David **s.**, Call me Zadok the 559
1Ki 1:33 king also **s.** unto them,, Take with....... 559
1Ki 1:36 answered the king, and **s.**, Amen:........ 559
1Ki 1:39 people **s.**, God save king Solomon......... 559
1Ki 1:41 he **s.**, Wherefore is this noise of the..... 559
1Ki 1:42 Adonijah **s.** unto him, Come in; for....... 559
1Ki 1:43 Joanathan...**s.** to Adonijah, Verily our.... 559
1Ki 1:48 thus **s.** the king, Blessed be the Lord... 559
1Ki 1:52 Solomon **s.**, If he will shew himself a.... 559
1Ki 1:53 and Solomon **s.** unto him, Go to thine... 559
1Ki 2:4 there shall not fail thee (**s.** he) a man ... 559
1Ki 2:13 and she **s.**, Comest thou peaceably? 559
1Ki 2:13 And he **s.**, Peaceably......................... 559
1Ki 2:14 He **s.** moreover, I have somewhat to.... 559
1Ki 2:14 say unto thee. And she **s.**, Say on. 559
1Ki 2:15 he **s.**, Thou knowest...the kingdom 559
1Ki 2:16 not. And she **s.** unto him, Say on. 559
1Ki 2:17 And he **s.**, Speak, I pray thee, unto 559
1Ki 2:18 Bath-sheba **s.**, Well; I will speak for..... 559
1Ki 2:20 she **s.**, I desire one small petition 559
1Ki 2:20 king **s.** unto her, Ask on, my mother:... 559
1Ki 2:21 she **s.**, Let Abishag the Shunammite..... 559
1Ki 2:22 answered and **s.** unto his mother, ... 559
1Ki 2:26 unto Abiathar the priest **s.** the king, ... 559
1Ki 2:30 and **s.** unto him, Thus saith the king,.... 559
1Ki 2:30 And he **s.**, Nay; but I will die here....... 559
1Ki 2:30 Thus **s.** Joab,...thus he answered....... 1696

1Ki 2:31 And the king **s.** unto him, 559
1Ki 2:31 Do as he hath **s.**, and fall upon him, 1696
1Ki 2:36 and **s.** unto him, Build thee an 559
1Ki 2:38 Shimei **s.** unto the king, The saying 559
1Ki 2:38 as my lord the king hath **s.**, so will 1696
1Ki 2:42 and **s.** unto him, Did I not make thee 559
1Ki 2:44 The king **s.** moreover to Shimei, 559
1Ki 3:5 God **s.**, Ask what I shall give thee. 559
1Ki 3:6 Solomon **s.**, Thou hast shewed unto 559
1Ki 3:11 God **s.** unto him, Because thou hast 559
1Ki 3:17 one woman **s.**, O my lord, I and this 559
1Ki 3:22 other woman **s.**, Nay; but the living 559
1Ki 3:22 this **s.**, No; but the dead is thy son, 559
1Ki 3:23 Then **s.** the king, The one saith, 559
1Ki 3:24 And the king **s.**, Bring me a sword. 559
1Ki 3:25 the king **s.**, Divide the living child 559
1Ki 3:26 and she **s.**, O my lord, give her the 559
1Ki 3:26 But the other **s.**, Let it be neither 559
1Ki 3:27 king answered and **s.**, Give her the 559
1Ki 5:7 and **s.**, Blessed be the Lord this day, 559
1Ki 8:12 Lord **s.** that he would dwell in the 559
1Ki 8:15 he **s.**, Blessed be the Lord God of 559
1Ki 8:18 the Lord **s.** unto David my father, 559
1Ki 8:23 he **s.**, Lord God of Israel, there is no 559
1Ki 8:29 place of which thou hast **s.**, My name 559
1Ki 9:3 the Lord **s.** unto him, I have heard 559
1Ki 9:13 he **s.**, What cities are these which 559
1Ki 10:6 And she **s.** to the king, It was a true 559
1Ki 11:2 Lord **s.** unto the children of Israel, 559
1Ki 11:11 Wherefore the Lord **s.** unto Solomon, 559
1Ki 11:21 Hadad **s.** to Pharaoh, Let me 559
1Ki 11:22 Pharaoh **s.** unto him, But what hast 559
1Ki 11:31 he **s.** to Jeroboam, Take thee ten 559
1Ki 12:5 And he **s.** unto them, Depart yet for 559
1Ki 12:6 and **s.**, How do ye advise that I may 559
1Ki 12:9 And he **s.** unto them, What counsel 559
1Ki 12:26 And Jeroboam **s.** in his heart, Now 559
1Ki 12:28 And **s.** unto them, It is too much for 559
1Ki 13:2 and **s.**, O altar, altar, thus saith the 559
1Ki 13:6 and **s.** unto the man of God, Intreat 559
1Ki 13:7 the king **s.** unto the man of God, 1696
1Ki 13:8 the man of God **s.** unto the king, If 559
1Ki 13:12 their father **s.** unto them, What 1696
1Ki 13:13 And he **s.** unto his sons, Saddle me 559
1Ki 13:14 he **s.** unto him, Art thou the man of 559
1Ki 13:14 camest from Judah? And he **s.**, I am 559
1Ki 13:15 Then he **s.** unto him, Come home 559
1Ki 13:16 he **s.**, I may not return with thee, 559
1Ki 13:17 For it was **s.** to me by the word of 1697
1Ki 13:18 He **s.** unto him, I am a prophet also 559
1Ki 13:26 he **s.**, It is the man of God, who was 559
1Ki 14:2 And Jeroboam **s.** to his wife, Arise, 559
1Ki 14:5 the Lord **s.** unto Ahijah, Behold, the 559
1Ki 14:6 that he **s.**, come in, thou wife of 559
1Ki 17:1 **s.** unto Ahab, As the Lord God of 559
1Ki 17:10 and **s.**, Fetch me, I pray thee, a little 559
1Ki 17:11 **s.**, Bring me, I pray thee, a morsel of 559
1Ki 17:12 she **s.**, As the Lord thy God liveth, 559
1Ki 17:13 and Elijah **s.** unto her, Fear not; go 559
1Ki 17:13 go and do as thou hast **s.**: but make 559
1Ki 17:18 And she **s.** unto Elijah, What have I 559
1Ki 17:19 And he **s.** unto her, Give me thy son. 559
1Ki 17:20 And he cried unto the Lord, and **s.**, 559
1Ki 17:21 **s.**, O Lord my God, I pray thee, let 559
1Ki 17:23 and Elijah **s.**, See, thy son liveth. 559
1Ki 17:24 the woman **s.** to Elijah, Now by this 559
1Ki 18:5 And Ahab **s.** unto Obadiah, Go into 559
1Ki 18:7 and **s.**, Art thou that my lord Elijah? 559
1Ki 18:9 And he **s.**, What have I sinned, that 559
1Ki 18:10 and when they **s.**, He is not there; he 559
1Ki 18:15 And Elijah **s.**, As the Lord of hosts 559
1Ki 18:17 Ahab **s.** unto him, Art thou he that 559
1Ki 18:21 **s.**, How long halt ye between two 559
1Ki 18:22 then **s.** Elijah unto the people, I, 559
1Ki 18:24 all the people answered and **s.**, It is 559
1Ki 18:25 Elijah **s.** unto the prophets of Baal, 559
1Ki 18:27 Elijah mocked them, and **s.**, Cry 559
1Ki 18:30 Elijah **s.** unto all the people, Come 559
1Ki 18:33 and **s.**, Fill four barrels with water, 559
1Ki 18:34 And he **s.**, Do it the second time. 559
1Ki 18:34 And he **s.**, Do it the third time. And 559
1Ki 18:36 and **s.**, Lord God of Abraham, Isaac, 559
1Ki 18:39 they **s.**, The Lord, he is the God; the 559
1Ki 18:40 And Elijah **s.** unto them, Take the 559
1Ki 18:41 Elijah **s.** unto Ahab, Get thee up, eat 559
1Ki 18:43 **s.** to his servant, Go up now, look 559
1Ki 18:43 and looked, and **s.**, There is nothing 559
1Ki 18:43 And he **s.**, Go again seven times. 559
1Ki 18:44 he **s.**, Behold, there ariseth a little 559
1Ki 18:44 And he **s.**, Go up, say unto Ahab, 559
1Ki 19:4 **s.**, It is enough; now, O Lord, take 559
1Ki 19:5 him, and **s.** unto him, Arise and eat 559
1Ki 19:7 touched him, and **s.**, Arise and eat; 559
1Ki 19:9 and he **s.** unto him, What doest thou 559
1Ki 19:10 he **s.**, I have been very jealous for 559
1Ki 19:11 And he **s.**, Go forth, and stand upon 559
1Ki 19:13 and **s.**, What doest thou here, Elijah? 559
1Ki 19:14 he **s.**, I have been very jealous for 559
1Ki 19:15 Lord **s.** unto him, Go, return on thy 559
1Ki 19:20 ran after Elijah, and **s.**, Let me, I 559
1Ki 19:20 And he **s.** unto him, Go back again: 559
1Ki 20:2 **s.** unto him, Thou saith Ben-hadad, 559
1Ki 20:4 of Israel answered and **s.**, My lord, 559
1Ki 20:5 and **s.**, Thus speaketh Ben-hadad, 559
1Ki 20:7 **s.**, Mark, I pray you, and see how 559
1Ki 20:8 all the people **s.** unto him, Hearken 559
1Ki 20:9 Wherefore he **s.** unto the messengers 559
1Ki 20:10 and **s.**, The gods do so unto me, and 559
1Ki 20:11 of Israel answered and **s.**, Tell him, 559
1Ki 20:12 that he **s.** unto his servants, Set 559
1Ki 20:14 And Ahab **s.**, By whom? And he **s.**, 559
1Ki 20:14 he **s.**, Who shall order the battle? 559
1Ki 20:18 he **s.**, Whether they be come out for 559
1Ki 20:22 **s.** unto him, Go, strengthen thyself, 559
1Ki 20:23 servants of the king of Syria **s.** unto 559
1Ki 20:28 unto the king of Israel, and **s.**, Thus
1Ki 20:28 Syrians have **s.**, The Lord is God of 559
1Ki 20:31 servants **s.** unto him, Behold now, 559
1Ki 20:32 **s.**, Thy servant Ben-hadad saith, 559
1Ki 20:32 And he **s.**, Is he yet alive? he is my 559
1Ki 20:33 and they **s.**, Thy brother Ben-hadad. 559
1Ki 20:33 Then he **s.**, Go ye, bring him. Then 559
1Ki 20:34 Ben-hadad **s.** unto him, The cities, 559
1Ki 20:34 Then **s.** Ahab, I will send thee away
1Ki 20:35 the sons of the prophets **s.** unto his 559
1Ki 20:36 **s.** he unto him, Because thou hast 559
1Ki 20:37 man, and **s.**, Smite me, I pray thee. 559
1Ki 20:39 he **s.**, Thy servant went out into the 559
1Ki 20:39 me, and **s.**, Keep this man: if by any 559
1Ki 20:40 king of Israel **s.** unto him, So shall 559
1Ki 20:42 he **s.** unto him, Thus saith the Lord, 559
1Ki 21:3 Naboth **s.** to Ahab, The Lord forbid 559
1Ki 21:4 for he had **s.**, I will not give thee the 559
1Ki 21:5 **s.** unto him, Why is thy spirit so 1696
1Ki 21:6 he **s.** unto her, Because I spake 1696
1Ki 21:6 **s.** unto him, Give me thy vineyard 559
1Ki 21:7 Jezebel his wife **s.** unto him, Dost 559
1Ki 21:15 that Jezebel **s.** to Ahab, Arise, take 559
1Ki 21:20 Ahab **s.** to Elijah, Hast thou found 559
1Ki 22:3 king of Israel **s.** unto his servants, 559
1Ki 22:4 he **s.** unto Jehoshaphat, Wilt thou go 559
1Ki 22:4 Jehoshaphat **s.** to the king of Israel, 559
1Ki 22:5 And Jehoshaphat **s.** unto the king of 559
1Ki 22:6 and **s.** unto them, Shall I go against 559
1Ki 22:6 they **s.**, Go up; for the Lord shall 559
1Ki 22:7 Jehoshaphat **s.**, Is there not here a 559
1Ki 22:8 king of Israel **s.** unto Jehoshaphat, 559
1Ki 22:8 Jehoshaphat **s.**, Let not the king say 559
1Ki 22:9 and **s.**, Hasten hither Micaiah the 559
1Ki 22:11 and he **s.**, Thus saith the Lord, With 559
1Ki 22:14 And Micaiah **s.**, As the Lord liveth, 559
1Ki 22:15 And the king **s.** unto him, Micaiah, 559
1Ki 22:16 king **s.** unto him, How many times 559
1Ki 22:17 And he **s.**, I saw all Israel scattered 559
1Ki 22:17 the Lord **s.**, These have no master: 559
1Ki 22:18 king of Israel **s.** unto Jehoshaphat, 559
1Ki 22:19 he **s.**, Hear thou therefore the word 559
1Ki 22:20 Lord **s.**, Who shall persuade Ahab, 559
1Ki 22:20 one **s.** on this manner, and another 559
1Ki 22:20 and another **s.** on that manner 559
1Ki 22:21 Lord, and **s.**, I will persuade him. 559
1Ki 22:22 the Lord **s.** unto him, Wherewith? 559
1Ki 22:22 And he **s.**, I will go forth, and I will 559
1Ki 22:22 And he **s.**, Thou shalt persuade him, 559
1Ki 22:24 and **s.**, Which way went the Spirit of 559
1Ki 22:25 And Micaiah **s.**, Behold, thou shalt 559
1Ki 22:26 the king of Israel **s.**, Take Micaiah, 559
1Ki 22:28 And Micaiah **s.**, If thou return at all 559
1Ki 22:28 he **s.**, Hearken, O people, every one 559
1Ki 22:30 king of Israel **s.** unto Jehoshaphat, 559
1Ki 22:32 that they **s.**, Surely it is the king of 559
1Ki 22:34 he **s.** unto the driver of his chariot, 559
1Ki 22:49 Then **s.** Ahaziah the son of Ahab 559
2Ki 1:2 and **s.** unto them, Go, enquire of 559
2Ki 1:3 the angel of the Lord **s.** to Elijah 1696
2Ki 1:5 he **s.** unto them, Why are ye now 559
2Ki 1:6 And they **s.** unto him, There came a 559
2Ki 1:6 and **s.** unto us, Go, turn again unto 559
2Ki 1:7 he **s.** unto them, What manner of 1696
2Ki 1:8 And he **s.**, It is Elijah the Tishbite. 559
2Ki 1:9 God, the king hath **s.**, Come down. 1696
2Ki 1:10 And Elijah answered and **s.** to the 1696
2Ki 1:11 And he answered and **s.** unto him, 1696
2Ki 1:11 thus hath the king **s.**, Come down 559
2Ki 1:12 Elijah answered and **s.** unto them, 1696
2Ki 1:13 besought him, and **s.** unto him, O 1696
2Ki 1:15 the angel of the Lord **s.** unto Elijah, 1696
2Ki 1:16 And he **s.** unto him, Thus saith the 1696
2Ki 2:2 Elijah **s.** unto Elisha, Tarry here, I 559
2Ki 2:2 And Elisha **s.** unto him, As the Lord 559
2Ki 2:3 and **s.** unto him, Knowest thou that 559
2Ki 2:3 he **s.**, Yea, I know it; hold ye your 559
2Ki 2:4 Elijah **s.** unto him, Elisha, tarry 559
2Ki 2:4 And he **s.**, As the Lord liveth, and as 559
2Ki 2:5 and **s.** unto him, Knowest thou that 559
2Ki 2:6 And Elijah **s.** unto him, Tarry, I pray 559
2Ki 2:6 he **s.**, As the Lord liveth, and as thy 559
2Ki 2:9 that Elijah **s.** unto Elisha, Ask what 559
2Ki 2:9 Elisha **s.**, I pray thee, let a double 559
2Ki 2:10 And he **s.**, Thou hast asked a hard 559
2Ki 2:14 smote the waters, and **s.**, Where is 559
2Ki 2:15 they **s.**, The spirit of Elijah doth rest 559
2Ki 2:16 And they **s.** unto him, Behold now, 559
2Ki 2:16 valley. And he **s.**, Ye shall not send. 559
2Ki 2:17 till he was ashamed, he **s.**, Send 559
2Ki 2:18 he **s.** unto them, Did I not say unto 559
2Ki 2:19 the men of the city **s.** unto Elisha, 559
2Ki 2:20 And he **s.**, Bring me a new cruse, 559
2Ki 2:21 and **s.**, Thus saith the Lord, I have 559
2Ki 2:23 **s.** unto him, Go up, thou bald head; 559
2Ki 3:7 And he **s.**, I will go up: I am as thou 559
2Ki 3:8 he **s.**, Which way shall we go up? 559
2Ki 3:10 the king of Israel **s.**, Alas! that the 559
2Ki 3:11 Jehoshaphat **s.**, Is there not here a 559
2Ki 3:11 and **s.**, Here is Elisha the son of 559
2Ki 3:12 And Jehoshaphat **s.**, The word of the 559
2Ki 3:13 Elisha **s.** unto the king of Israel, 559
2Ki 3:13 the king of Israel **s.** unto him, Nay: 559
2Ki 3:14 And Elisha **s.**, As the Lord of hosts 559
2Ki 3:16 he **s.**, Thus saith the Lord, Make 559
2Ki 3:23 And they **s.**, This is blood: the kings 559
2Ki 4:2 Elisha **s.** unto her, What shall I do 559
2Ki 4:2 she **s.**, Thine handmaid hath not 559
2Ki 4:3 Then he **s.**, Go, borrow thee vessls 559
2Ki 4:6 she **s.** unto her son, Bring me yet a 559
2Ki 4:6 he **s.** unto her, There is not a vessel 559
2Ki 4:7 And he **s.**, Go, sell the oil, and pay 559
2Ki 4:9 she **s.** unto her husband, Behold 559
2Ki 4:12 And he **s.** to Gehazi his servant, Call 559
2Ki 4:13 he **s.** unto him, Say now unto her, 559
2Ki 4:14 he **s.**, What then is to be done for 559
2Ki 4:15 he **s.**, Call her. And when he had 559
2Ki 4:16 he **s.**, About this season, according 559
2Ki 4:16 she **s.**, Nay, my lord, thou man of 559
2Ki 4:17 season that Elisha had **s.** unto her, 1696
2Ki 4:19 he **s.** unto his father, My head, my 559
2Ki 4:19 And he **s.** to a lad, Carry him to his 559
2Ki 4:22 **s.**, Send me, I pray thee, one of the 559
2Ki 4:23 he **s.**, Wherefore wilt thou go to him 559
2Ki 4:23 And she **s.**, It shall be well 559
2Ki 4:24 and **s.** to her servant, Drive, and go 559
2Ki 4:25 he **s.** to Gehazi his servant, Behold, 559
2Ki 4:27 the man of God **s.**, Let her alone; 559
2Ki 4:28 she **s.**, Did I desire a son of my lord? 559
2Ki 4:29 he **s.** to Gehazi, Gird up thy loins, 559
2Ki 4:30 mother of the child **s.**, As the Lord 559
2Ki 4:36 Gehazi, and **s.**, Call this Shunammite. 559
2Ki 4:36 unto him, he **s.**, Take up thy son 559
2Ki 4:38 he **s.** unto his servant, Set on the 559
2Ki 4:40 and **s.**, O thou man of God, there is 559
2Ki 4:41 But he **s.**, Then bring meal. And he 559
2Ki 4:41 he **s.**, Pour out for the people, that 559
2Ki 4:42 he **s.**, Give unto the people, that they 559
2Ki 4:43 his servitor **s.**, What, should I set 559
2Ki 4:43 He **s.** again, Give the people, that 559
2Ki 5:3 she **s.** unto her mistress, Would God 559
2Ki 5:4 thus **s.** the maid that is of the land 1696
2Ki 5:5 king of Syria **s.**, Go to, go, and I 559

2Ki 5:7 **s.**, Am I God, to kill and to make........ 559
2Ki 5:11 away, and **s.**, Behold, I thought,.......... 559
2Ki 5:13 **s.**, My father, if the prophet had bid..... 559
2Ki 5:15 and he **s.**, Behold, now I know that....... 559
2Ki 5:16 But he **s.**, As the Lord liveth, before.... 559
2Ki 5:17 Naaman **s.**, Shall there not then, I 559
2Ki 5:19 And he **s.** unto him, Go in peace. 559
2Ki 5:20 servant of Elisha, the man of God, **s.**, .. 559
2Ki 5:21 to meet him, and **s.**, Is all well? 559
2Ki 5:22 And he **s.**, All is well. My master........ 559
2Ki 5:23 Naaman **s.**, Be content, take two......... 559
2Ki 5:25 Elisha **s.** unto him, Whence comest...... 559
2Ki 5:25 he **s.**, Thy servant went no whither. 559
2Ki 5:26 he **s.** unto him, Went not mine heart.... 559
2Ki 6:1 sons of the prophets **s.** unto Elisha, ... 559
2Ki 6:3 And one **s.**, Be content, I pray thee, ... 559
2Ki 6:5 he cried, and **s.**, Alas, master! for it..... 559
2Ki 6:6 the man of God **s.**, Where fell it?......... 559
2Ki 6:7 Therefore **s.** he, Take it up to thee,..... 559
2Ki 6:11 **s.** unto them, Will ye not shew me 559
2Ki 6:12 one of his servants **s.**, None, my lord,.. 559
2Ki 6:13 he **s.**, Go and spy where he is, that..... 559
2Ki 6:15 his servant **s.** unto him, Alas, my 559
2Ki 6:17 Elisha prayed, and **s.**, Lord, I pray....... 559
2Ki 6:18 **s.**, Smite this people, I pray thee,........ 559
2Ki 6:19 Elisha **s.** unto them, This is not the 559
2Ki 6:20 that Elisha **s.**, Lord, open the eyes 559
2Ki 6:21 the king of Israel **s.** unto Elisha,.......... 559
2Ki 6:27 he **s.**, If the Lord do not help thee,....... 559
2Ki 6:28 king **s.** unto her, What aileth thee?....... 559
2Ki 6:28 This woman **s.** unto me, Give thy........ 559
2Ki 6:29 I **s.** unto her on the next day, Give....... 559
2Ki 6:31 Then he **s.**, God do so and more also... 559
2Ki 6:32 he **s.** to the elders, See ye how this..... 559
2Ki 6:33 he **s.**, Behold, this evil is of the Lord; .. 559
2Ki 7:1 Then Elisha **s.**, Hear ye the word of 559
2Ki 7:2 answered the man of God, and **s.**, ... 559
2Ki 7:2 he **s.**, Behold, thou shalt see it with..... 559
2Ki 7:3 they **s.** one to another, Why sit we...... 559
2Ki 7:6 they **s.** one to another, Lo, the king..... 559
2Ki 7:9 Then they **s.** one to another, We do..... 559
2Ki 7:12 **s.** unto his servants, I will now shew.... 559
2Ki 7:13 one of his servants answered and **s.**,.... 559
2Ki 7:17 he died, as the man of God had **s.**,...... 1696
2Ki 7:19 answered the man of God, and **s.**, ... 559
2Ki 7:19 he **s.**, Behold, thou shalt see it with..... 559
2Ki 8:5 Gehazi **s.**, My lord, O king, this is....... 559
2Ki 8:8 And the king **s.** unto Hazael, Take a..... 559
2Ki 8:9 **s.**, Thy son Ben-hadad king of Syria..... 559
2Ki 8:10 And Elisha **s.** unto him, Go, say unto ... 559
2Ki 8:12 Hazael **s.**, Why weepeth my lord?......... 559
2Ki 8:13 Hazael **s.**, But what, is thy servant...... 559
2Ki 8:14 who **s.** to him, What **s.** Elisha to 559
2Ki 9:1 and **s.** unto him, Gird up thy loins,....... 559
2Ki 9:5 he **s.**, I have an errand to thee,.......... 559
2Ki 9:5 And Jehu **s.**, Unto which of all us? 559
2Ki 9:5 And he **s.**, To thee, O captain............ 559
2Ki 9:6 **s.** unto him, Thus saith the Lord......... 559
2Ki 9:11 and one **s.** unto him, Is all well? 559
2Ki 9:11 he **s.** unto them, Ye know the man, ... 559
2Ki 9:12 And they **s.**, It is false; tell us now. 559
2Ki 9:12 he **s.**, Thus and thus spake he to me,.... 559
2Ki 9:15 Jehu **s.**, If it be your minds, then let 559
2Ki 9:17 as he came, and **s.**, I see a company.... 559
2Ki 9:17 And Joram **s.**, Take an horseman, ... 559
2Ki 9:18 **s.**, Thus saith the king, Is it peace? 559
2Ki 9:18 Jehu **s.**, What hast thou to do with....... 559
2Ki 9:19 **s.**, Thus saith the king, Is it peace? 559
2Ki 9:21 Joram **s.**, Make ready. And his........... 559
2Ki 9:22 Jehu, that he **s.**, Is it peace, Jehu?....... 559
2Ki 9:23 **s.** to Ahaziah, There is treachery, O 559
2Ki 9:25 **s.** Jehu to Bidkar his captain, Take....... 559
2Ki 9:27 **s.**, Smite him also in the chariot. 559
2Ki 9:31 she **s.**, Had Zimri peace, who slew....... 559
2Ki 9:32 window, and **s.**, Who is on my side?..... 559
2Ki 9:33 he **s.**, Throw her down. So they......... 559
2Ki 9:34 **s.**, Go, see now this cursed woman,..... 559
2Ki 9:36 he **s.**, This is the word of the Lord, ... 559
2Ki 10:4 and **s.**, Behold, two kings stood not 559
2Ki 10:8 he **s.**, Lay ye them in two heaps at...... 559
2Ki 10:9 **s.** to all the people, Ye be righteous:.... 559
2Ki 10:13 king of Judah, and **s.**, Who are ye?....... 559
2Ki 10:14 he **s.**, Take them alive. And they......... 559
2Ki 10:15 **s.** to him, Is thine heart right, as......... 559
2Ki 10:16 he **s.**, Come with me, and see my 559
2Ki 10:18 **s.** unto them, Ahab served Baal a 559
2Ki 10:20 Jehu **s.**, Proclaim a solemn assembly..... 559
2Ki 10:22 **s.** unto him that was over the vestry,... 559
2Ki 10:23 **s.** unto the worshippers of Baal, ... 559
2Ki 10:24 **s.**, If any of the men whom I have....... 559
2Ki 10:25 that Jehu **s.** to the guard and to the 559
2Ki 10:30 Lord **s.** unto Jehu, Because thou.......... 559
2Ki 11:12 hands, and **s.**, God save the king......... 559
2Ki 11:15 **s.** unto them, Have her forth without.... 559
2Ki 11:15 priest had **s.**, Let her not be slain........ 559
2Ki 12:4 Jehoash **s.** to the priests, All the 559
2Ki 12:7 **s.** unto them, Why repair ye not the 559
2Ki 13:14 and **s.**, O my father, my father! the 559
2Ki 13:15 Elisha **s.** unto him, Take bow and........ 559
2Ki 13:16 he **s.** to the king of Israel, Put thine..... 559
2Ki 13:17 he **s.**, Open the window eastward......... 559
2Ki 13:17 opened it. Then Elisha **s.**, Shoot.......... 559
2Ki 13:17 And he **s.**, The arrow of the Lord's...... 559
2Ki 13:18 he **s.**, Take the arrows. And he took.... 559
2Ki 13:18 he **s.** unto the king of Israel, Smite...... 559
2Ki 13:19 and **s.**, Thou shouldest have smitten...... 559
2Ki 14:27 **s.** not that he would blot out the........ 1696
2Ki 17:12 the Lord had **s.** unto them, Ye shall 559
2Ki 17:23 **s.**...all his servants the prophets. 1696
2Ki 18:19 Rab-shakeh **s.** unto them, Speak.......... 559
2Ki 18:22 hath **s.** to Judah and Jerusalem, Ye........ 559
2Ki 18:25 The Lord **s.** to me, Go up against........ 559
2Ki 18:26 Then **s.** Eliakim the son of Hilkiah,....... 559
2Ki 18:27 Rab-shakeh **s.** unto them, hath my....... 559
2Ki 19:3 And they **s.** unto him, Thus saith......... 559
2Ki 19:6 And Isaiah **s.** unto them, Thus shall...... 559
2Ki 19:15 and **s.**, O Lord God of Israel, which..... 559
2Ki 19:23 and hast **s.**, With the multitude of........ 559
2Ki 20:1 **s.** unto him, Thus saith the Lord, ... 559
2Ki 20:7 And Isaiah **s.**, Take a lump of figs......... 559
2Ki 20:8 Hezekiah **s.** unto Isaiah, What shall 559
2Ki 20:9 Isaiah **s.**, This sign shalt thou have....... 559
2Ki 20:14 **s.** unto him, What **s.** these men? 559
2Ki 20:14 Hezekiah **s.**, They are come from a...... 559
2Ki 20:15 he **s.**, What have they seen in thine 559
2Ki 20:16 Isaiah **s.** unto Hezekiah, Hear the 559
2Ki 20:19 Then **s.** Hezekiah unto Isaiah, Good 559
2Ki 20:19 And he **s.**, Is it not good, if peace 559
2Ki 21:4 of which the Lord **s.**, In Jerusalem....... 559
2Ki 21:7 of which the Lord **s.** to David, and........ 559
2Ki 22:8 the high priest **s.** unto Shaphan the 559
2Ki 22:9 **s.**, Thy servants have gathered the...... 559
2Ki 22:15 And she **s.** unto them, Thus saith........ 559
2Ki 23:17 he **s.**, What title is that that I see? 559
2Ki 23:18 he **s.**, Let him alone; let no man.......... 559
2Ki 23:27 the Lord **s.**, I will remove Judah.......... 559
2Ki 23:27 which, I **s.**, My name shall be there. 559
2Ki 24:13 of the Lord, as the Lord had **s.**. 1696
2Ki 25:24 **s.** unto them, Fear not to be the 559
1Ch 10:4 Then **s.** Saul to his armourbearer,......... 559
1Ch 11:2 the Lord thy God **s.** unto thee, Thou.... 559
1Ch 11:5 inhabitants of Jebus **s.** to David,.......... 559
1Ch 11:6 David **s.**, Whosoever smiteth the......... 559
1Ch 11:17 David longed, and **s.**, Oh that one......... 559
1Ch 11:19 **s.**, My God forbid it me, that I should.. 559
1Ch 12:17 answered and **s.** unto them, If ye be 559
1Ch 12:18 and he **s.**, Thine are we, David, and on.....
1Ch 13:2 David **s.** unto all the congregation........ 559
1Ch 13:4 congregation **s.** that they would do....... 559
1Ch 14:10 the Lord **s.** unto him, Go up; for I....... 559
1Ch 14:11 Then David **s.**, God hath broken in 559
1Ch 14:14 God **s.** unto him, Go not up after.......... 559
1Ch 15:2 Then David **s.**, None ought to carry..... 559
1Ch 15:12 **s.** unto them, Ye are the chief of the.... 559
1Ch 16:36 all the people **s.**, Amen, and praised..... 559
1Ch 17:1 that David **s.** to Nathan the prophet, ... 559
1Ch 17:2 Then Nathan **s.** unto David, Do all....... 559
1Ch 17:16 David...**s.**, Who am I, O Lord God,....... 559
1Ch 17:23 for ever, and do as thou hast **s.**.......... 1696
1Ch 19:2 David **s.**, I will shew kindness unto 559
1Ch 19:3 the children of Ammon **s.** to Hanun, ... 559
1Ch 19:5 the king **s.**, Tarry at Jericho until.......... 559
1Ch 19:12 he **s.**, If the Syrians be too strong 559
1Ch 21:2 David **s.** to Joab and to the rulers 559
1Ch 21:8 David **s.** unto God, I have sinned.......... 559
1Ch 21:11 Gad came to David, and **s.** unto him,..... 559
1Ch 21:13 David **s.** unto Gad, I am in a great........ 559
1Ch 21:15 **s.** to the angel that destroyed, It is...... 559
1Ch 21:17 David **s.** unto God, Is it not I that 559
1Ch 21:22 David **s.** to Ornan, Grant me the 559
1Ch 21:22 Ornan **s.** unto David, Take it to thee,... 559
1Ch 21:24 And king David **s.** to Ornan, Nay;........ 559
1Ch 22:1 David **s.**, This is the house of the........ 559
1Ch 22:5 David **s.**, Solomon my son is young...... 559
1Ch 22:7 David **s.** to Solomon, My son, as for 559
1Ch 22:11 thy God, as he hath **s.** of thee........... 1696
1Ch 23:5 instruments which I made, **s.** David, ...
1Ch 23:25 David **s.**, The Lord God of Israel.......... 559
1Ch 27:23 Lord had **s.** he would increase Israel 559
1Ch 28:2 and **s.**, Hear me, my brethren, and...... 559
1Ch 28:3 God **s.** unto me, Thou shalt not build.... 559
1Ch 28:6 he **s.** unto me, Solomon thy son, he..... 559
1Ch 28:19 All this, **s.** David, the Lord made me ....
1Ch 28:20 David **s.** to Solomon...Be strong.......... 559
1Ch 29:1 David...**s.** unto all the congregation, ... 559
1Ch 29:10 David **s.**, Blessed be thou, Lord God.... 559
1Ch 29:20 And David **s.** to all the congregation, ... 559
2Ch 1:7 and **s.** unto him, Ask what I shall......... 559
2Ch 1:8 Solomon **s.** unto God, Thou hast........... 559
2Ch 1:11 God **s.** to Solomon, Because this was ... 559
2Ch 2:12 Huram **s.** moreover, Blessed be the..... 559
2Ch 6:1 Then **s.** Solomon, The Lord hath......... 559
2Ch 6:1 Lord hath **s.** that he would dwell 559
2Ch 6:4 he **s.**, Blessed be the Lord God of......... 559
2Ch 6:8 But the Lord **s.** to David my father,..... 559
2Ch 6:14 And **s.**, O Lord God of Israel, there..... 559
2Ch 6:20 hast **s.**...thou wouldest put thy name.... 559
2Ch 7:12 and **s.** unto him, I have heard thy........ 559
2Ch 8:11 for he **s.**, My wife shall not dwell in..... 559
2Ch 9:5 And she **s.** to the king, It was a true.... 559
2Ch 10:5 he **s.** unto them, Come again unto 559
2Ch 10:9 he **s.** unto them, What advice give 559
2Ch 12:5 and **s.** unto them, Thus saith the 559
2Ch 12:6 and they **s.**, The Lord is righteous. 559
2Ch 13:4 and **s.**, Hear me, thou Jeroboam, and ... 559
2Ch 14:7 he **s.** unto Judah, Let us build these 559
2Ch 14:11 and **s.**, Lord, it is nothing with thee 559
2Ch 15:2 and **s.** unto him, Hear ye me, Asa, ... 559
2Ch 16:7 and **s.** unto him, Because thou hast...... 559
2Ch 18:3 And Ahab...**s.** unto Jehoshaphat........... 559
2Ch 18:4 And Jehoshaphat **s.** unto the king of 559
2Ch 18:5 and **s.** unto them, Shall we go to 559
2Ch 18:5 they **s.**, Go up; for God will deliver...... 559
2Ch 18:6 Jehoshaphat **s.**, Is there not here a 559
2Ch 18:7 king of Israel **s.** unto Jehoshaphat,......... 559
2Ch 18:7 Jehoshaphat **s.**, Let not the king say..... 559
2Ch 18:8 and **s.**, Fetch quickly Micaiah the.......... 559
2Ch 18:10 and **s.**, Thus saith the Lord, With......... 559
2Ch 18:13 Micaiah **s.**, As the Lord liveth, even..... 559
2Ch 18:14 king **s.** unto him, Micaiah, shall we....... 559
2Ch 18:14 And he **s.**, Go ye up, and prosper,........ 559
2Ch 18:15 king **s.** unto him, How many times......... 559
2Ch 18:16 he **s.**, I did see all Israel scattered....... 559
2Ch 18:16 the Lord **s.**, These have no master; 559
2Ch 18:17 the king of Israel **s.** to Jehoshaphat, ... 559
2Ch 18:18 Again he **s.**, Therefore hear the word... 559
2Ch 18:19 the Lord **s.**, Who shall entice Ahab 559
2Ch 18:20 the Lord, and **s.** I will entice him.......... 559
2Ch 18:20 the Lord **s.** unto him, Wherewith?......... 559
2Ch 18:21 he **s.**, I will go out, and be a lying 559
2Ch 18:21 the Lord **s.**, Thou shalt entice him, ... 559
2Ch 18:23 and **s.**, Which way went the Spirit........ 559
2Ch 18:24 Micaiah **s.**, Behold, thou shalt see........ 559
2Ch 18:25 king of Israel **s.**, Take ye Micaiah, ... 559
2Ch 18:27 Micaiah **s.**, If thou certainly return 559
2Ch 18:27 And he **s.**, Hearken, all ye people......... 559
2Ch 18:29 king of Israel **s.** unto Jehoshaphat,........ 559
2Ch 18:31 that they **s.**, It is the king of Israel. 559
2Ch 18:33 therefore he **s.** to his chariot man, ... 559
2Ch 19:2 **s.** to king Jehoshaphat, Shouldest......... 559
2Ch 19:6 And **s.** to the judges, Take heed what .. 559
2Ch 20:6 And **s.**, O Lord God of our fathers,...... 559
2Ch 20:15 he **s.**, Hearken ye, all Judah, and ye...... 559
2Ch 20:20 Jehoshaphat stood and **s.**, Hear me, ... 559
2Ch 22:9 **s.** they, he is the son of Jehoshaphat, ... 559
2Ch 23:3 he **s.** unto them, Behold, the king's...... 559
2Ch 23:3 Lord hath **s.** of the sons of David....... 1696
2Ch 23:11 him, and **s.**, God save the king............ 559
2Ch 23:13 Athaliah rent her clothes, and **s.**,......... 559
2Ch 23:14 and **s.** unto them, Have her forth of..... 559
2Ch 23:14 priest **s.**, Slay her not in the house 559
2Ch 24:5 and **s.** to them, Go out unto the cities .. 559
2Ch 24:6 and **s.** unto him, Why hast thou not....... 559
2Ch 24:20 and **s.** unto them, Thus saith God,........ 559
2Ch 24:22 died, he **s.**, The Lord look upon it, ... 559
2Ch 25:9 Amaziah **s.** to the man of God, But...... 559
2Ch 25:15 a prophet, which **s.** unto him, Why...... 559
2Ch 25:16 the king **s.** unto him, Art thou made...... 559
2Ch 25:16 the prophet forbare, and **s.**, I know...... 559
2Ch 26:18 and **s.** unto him, It appertaineth not...... 559
2Ch 26:23 for they **s.**, He is a leper: and............ 559

2Ch 28:9 and **s.** unto them, Behold, because....... 559
2Ch 28:13 And **s.** unto them, Ye shall not bring.... 559
2Ch 28:23 he **s.**, Because the gods of the kings.... 559
2Ch 29:5 **s.** unto them, Hear me, ye Levites, ... 559
2Ch 29:18 and **s.**, We have cleansed all the......... 559
2Ch 29:31 Hezekiah answered and **s.**, Now ye...... 559
2Ch 31:10 Azariah . . . answered him, and **s.** 559
2Ch 33:4 Lord had **s.**, In Jerusalem shall my....... 559
2Ch 33:7 God had **s.** to David and to Solomon..... 559
2Ch 34:15 Hilkiah answered and **s.** to Shaphan....... 559
2Ch 35:3 And **s.** unto the Levites that taught...... 559
2Ch 35:23 the king **s.** to his servants, Have me.... 559
Ezr 2:63 Tirshatha **s.** unto them, that they......... 559
Ezr 4:2 and **s.** unto them, Let us build with...... 559
Ezr 4:3 **s.** unto them, Ye have nothing to do..... 559
Ezr 5:3 and **s.** thus unto them, Who hath.......... 560
Ezr 5:4 **s.** we unto them after this manner, ... 560
Ezr 5:9 **s.** unto them thus, Who commanded..... 560
Ezr 5:15 And **s.** unto him, Take these vessels, ... 560
Ezr 8:28 I **s.** unto them, Ye are holy unto 559
Ezr 9:6 And **s.**, O my God, I am ashamed......... 559
Ezr 10:2 answered and **s.** unto Ezra, We have.... 559
Ezr 10:10 **s.** unto them, Ye have transgressed 559
Ezr 10:12 the congregation answered and **s.** 559
Ezr 10:12 As thou hast **s.**, so must we do........ 1697
Ne 1:3 they **s.** unto me, The remnant that 559
Ne 1:5 And **s.**, I beseech thee, O Lord God 559
Ne 2:2 the king **s.** unto me, Why is thy.......... 559
Ne 2:3 **s.** unto the king, Let the king live......... 559
Ne 2:4 king **s.** unto me, For what dost thou 559
Ne 2:5 I **s.** unto the king, If it please the........ 559
Ne 2:6 the king **s.** unto me, (the queen also 559
Ne 2:7 I **s.** unto the king, If it please the........ 559
Ne 2:17 **s.** I unto them, Ye see the distress...... 559
Ne 2:18 they **s.**, Let us rise up and build......... 559
Ne 2:19 **s.**, What is this thing that ye do?......... 559
Ne 2:20 **s.** unto them, The God of heaven, ... 559
Ne 4:2 and **s.**, What do these feeble Jews?...... 559
Ne 4:3 he **s.**, Even that which they build,........ 559
Ne 4:10 And Judah **s.**, The strength of the........ 559
Ne 4:11 adversaries **s.**, They shall not know,..... 559
Ne 4:12 they **s.** unto us ten times, From all...... 559
Ne 4:14, 19 **s.** unto the nobles, and to...rulers,... 559
Ne 4:22 the same time **s.** I unto the people,...... 559
Ne 5:2 For there were that **s.**, We, our sons,.. 559
Ne 5:3 were that **s.**, We have mortgaged........ 559
Ne 5:4 were also that **s.**, We have borrowed ... 559
Ne 5:7 and **s.** unto them, Ye exact usury, ... 559
Ne 5:8 I **s.** unto them, We after our ability...... 559
Ne 5:9 Also I **s.**, It is not good that ye do;...... 559
Ne 5:12 Then **s.** they, We will restore them,..... 559
Ne 5:13 I shook my lap, and **s.**, So God shake... 559
Ne 5:13 And all the congregation **s.**, Amen,........ 559
Ne 6:10 he **s.**, Let us meet together in the....... 559
Ne 6:11 I **s.**, Should such a man as I flee? 559
Ne 7:3 I **s.** unto them, Let not the gates of..... 559
Ne 7:65 And the Tirshatha **s.** unto them, ... 559
Ne 8:9 **s.** unto all the people, This day is 559
Ne 8:10 he **s.** unto them, Go your way, eat 559
Ne 9:5 **s.**, Stand up and bless the Lord your..... 559
Ne 9:18 and **s.**, This is thy God that brought..... 559
Ne 13:11 and **s.**, Why is the house of God 559
Ne 13:17 and **s.** unto them, What evil thing is 559
Ne 13:21 and **s.** unto them, Why lodge ye.......... 559
Es 1:13 Then the king **s.** to the wise men, ... 559
Es 2:2 Then **s.** the king's servants that 559
Es 3:3 **s.** unto Mordecai, Why transgressest.... 559
Es 3:8 Haman **s.** unto king Ahasuerus, ... 559
Es 3:11 king **s.** unto Haman, The silver is 559
Es 5:3 **s.** the king unto her, What wilt thou, ... 559
Es 5:5 king **s.**, Cause Haman to make haste, ... 559
Es 5:5 that he may do as Esther hath **s.**. 1697
Es 5:6 king **s.** unto Esther at the banquet 559
Es 5:7 answered Esther, and **s.**, My petition.... 559
Es 5:8 do to morrow as the king hath **s.** 1697
Es 5:12 Haman **s.** moreover, Yea, Esther......... 559
Es 5:14 **s.** Zeresh his wife and all his friends..... 559
Es 6:3 kings **s.**, What honour and dignity 559
Es 6:3 **s.** the king's servants that ministered.... 559
Es 6:4 And the king **s.**, Who is in the court? ... 559
Es 6:5 king's servants **s.** unto him, Behold, ... 559
Es 6:5 And the king **s.**, Let him come in. 559
Es 6:6 king **s.** unto him, What shall be done 559
Es 6:10 the king **s.** to Haman, Make haste, ... 559
Es 6:10 as thou hast **s.**, and do even so to...... 1696
Es 6:13 **s.** his wise men and Zeresh his wife 559
Es 7:2 And the king **s.** again unto Esther........ 559
Es 7:3 Esther the queen answered and **s.**, ... 559
Es 7:5 king Ahasuerus answered and **s.**.......... 559
Es 7:6 And Esther **s.**, The adversary and 559
Es 7:8 **s.** the king, Will he force the queen...... 559
Es 7:9 chamberlains, **s.** before the king, ... 559
Es 7:9 the king **s.**, hang him thereon. 559
Es 8:5 And **s.**, If it please the king, and it....... 559
Es 8:7 king Ahasuerus **s.** unto Esther the 559
Es 9:12 the king **s.** unto Esther the queen, ... 559
Es 9:13 Then **s.** Esther, If it please the king,.... 559
Job 1:5 Job **s.**, It may be that my sons have...... 559
Job 1:7 Lord **s.** unto Satan, Whence comest 559
Job 1:7 Satan answered the Lord, and **s.**, ... 559
Job 1:8 the Lord **s.** unto Satan, Hast thou........ 559
Job 1:9 **s.**, Doth Job fear God for nought?........ 559
Job 1:12 the Lord **s.** unto Satan, Behold, all....... 559
Job 1:14 and **s.**, The oxen were plowing, and...... 559
Job 1:16 and **s.**, The fire of God is fallen from.... 559
Job 1:17 **s.**, The Chaldeans made out three........ 559
Job 1:18 and **s.**, Thy sons and thy daughters....... 559
Job 1:21 **s.**, Naked came I out of my mother's.... 559
Job 2:2 Lord **s.** unto Satan, From whence 559
Job 2:2 Satan answered the Lord, and **s.**, ... 559
Job 2:3 the Lord **s.** unto Satan, Hast thou........ 559
Job 2:4 the Lord, and **s.**, Skin for skin, yea,..... 559
Job 2:6 And the Lord **s.** unto Satan, Behold, ... 559
Job 2:9 **s.** his wife unto him, Dost thou still...... 559
Job 2:10 But he **s.** unto her, Thou speakest....... 559
Job 3:2 And Job spake, and **s.**, ... 559
Job 3:3 the night in which it was **s.**, There....... 559
Job 4:1 the Temanite answered and **s.**........... 559
Job 6:1 But Job answered and **s.**,.................. 559
Job 8:1 answered Bildad the Shuhite, and **s.**, ... 559
Job 9:1 Then Job answered and **s.**,................ 559
Job 9:22 This is one thing, therefore I **s.** it,....... 559
Job 11:1 Zophar the Naamathite, and **s.**............ 559
Job 11:4 thou hast **s.**, My doctrine is pure,........ 559
Job 12:1 And Job answered and **s.**,.................. 559
Job 15:1 Eliphaz the Temanite, and **s.**,............. 559
Job 16:1 Then Job answered and **s.**,................ 559
Job 17:14 I have **s.** to corruption, Thou art........ 7121
Job 18:1 answered Bildad...Shuhite, and **s.**,......... 559
Job 19:1 Then Job answered and **s.**,................. 559
Job 20:1 Zophar the Naamathite, and **s.**,........... 559
Job 21:1 But Job answered and **s.**,................... 559
Job 22:1 the Temanite answered and **s.**,........... 559
Job 22:17 Which **s.** unto God, Depart from us:..... 559
Job 23:1 Then Job answered and **s.**, ... 559
Job 25:1 answered Bildad the Shuhite, and **s.**, ... 559
Job 26:1 But Job answered and **s.**, ... 559
Job 27:1 Job continued his parable, and **s.**,......... 559
Job 28:28 unto man he **s.**, Behold, the fear of...... 559
Job 29:1 Job continued his parable, and **s.**,......... 559
Job 29:18 Then I **s.**, I shall die in my nest, and.... 559
Job 31:24 or have **s.** to the fine gold, Thou art 559
Job 31:31 If the men of my tabernacle **s.** not, ... 559
Job 32:6 the Buzite answered and **s.**, I am 559
Job 32:7 I **s.**, Days should speak, and.............. 559
Job 32:10 I **s.**, Hearken to me; I also will shew.... 559
Job 32:17 I **s.**, I will answer also my part, I............
Job 34:1 Furthermore Elihu answered and **s.**,.......... 559
Job 34:5 For Job hath **s.**, I am righteous: and..... 559
Job 34:9 For he hath **s.**, It profiteth a man 559
Job 34:31 Surely it is meet to be **s.** unto God, ... 559
Job 35:1 Elihu spake moreover, and **s.**,............ 559
Job 36:1 Elihu also proceeded, and **s.**, ... 559
Job 38:1 Job out of the whirlwind, and **s.**,.......... 559
Job 38:11 **s.**, Hitherto shalt thou come, but no...... 559
Job 40:1 the Lord answered Job, and **s.**, ... 559
Job 40:3 Then Job answered the Lord, and **s.**,.... 559
Job 40:6 Job out of the whirlwind, and **s.**,.......... 559
Job 42:1 Then Job answered the Lord, and **s.**,.... 559
Job 42:7 Lord **s.** to Eliphaz the Temanite, ... 559
Ps 2:7 Lord hath **s.** unto me, Thou art my........ 559
Ps 10:6 **s.** in his heart, I shall not be moved: 559
Ps 10:11 **s.** in his heart, God hath forgotten; 559
Ps 10:13 hath **s.** in his heart, Thou wilt not........ 559
Ps 12:4 **s.**, With our tongue will we prevail;...... 559
Ps 14:1 The fool hath **s.** in his heart, There...... 559
Ps 16:2 **s.** unto the Lord, Thou art my Lord: 559
Ps 18:*title* from the hand of Saul: And he **s.**,.......... 559
Ps 27:8 heart **s.** unto thee, Thy face, Lord,...... 559
Ps 30:6 I **s.**, I shall never be moved................ 559
Ps 31:14 O Lord: I **s.**, Thou art my God. 559
Ps 31:22 I **s.** in my haste, I am cut off from........ 559
Ps 32:5 I **s.**, I will confess my transgressions.... 559
Ps 35:21 **s.**, Aha, aha, our eye hath seen it........ 559
Ps 38:16 I **s.**, Hear me, lest otherwise they....... 559
Ps 39:1 I **s.**, I will take heed to my ways, ... 559
Ps 40:7 Then **s.** I, Lo, I come: in the volume ... 559
Ps 41:4 I **s.**, Lord, be merciful unto me: heal.... 559
Ps 52:*title* **s.** unto him, David is come to the........ 559
Ps 53:1 The fool hath **s.** in his heart, There...... 559
Ps 54:*title* and **s.** to Saul, Doth not David hide...... 559
Ps 55:6 And I **s.**, Oh that I had wings like a 559
Ps 68:22 The Lord **s.**, I will bring again from...... 559
Ps 74:8 **s.** in their hearts, Let us destroy......... 559
Ps 75:4 I **s.** unto the fools, Deal not............... 559
Ps 77:10 And I **s.**, This is my infirmity; but I 559
Ps 78:19 they **s.**, Can God furnish a table in....... 559
Ps 82:6 I have **s.**, Ye are gods; and all of......... 559
Ps 83:4 They have **s.**, Come, and let us cut 559
Ps 83:12 who **s.**, Let us take to ourselves the 559
Ps 87:5 of Zion it shall be **s.**, This and that....... 559
Ps 89:2 I have **s.**, Mercy shall be built up for.... 559
Ps 94:18 When I **s.**, My foot slippeth; thy.......... 559
Ps 95:10 **s.**, It is a people that do err in their..... 559
Ps 102:24 I **s.**, O my God, take me not away in... 559
Ps 106:23 he **s.** that he would destroy them, ... 559
Ps 110:1 Lord **s.** unto my Lord, Sit thou at 5002
Ps 116:11 I **s.** in my haste, All men are liars........ 559
Ps 119:57 I have **s.** that I would keep thy 559
Ps 122:1 I was glad when they **s.** unto me,........ 559
Ps 126:2 then **s.** they among the heathen, The ... 559
Ps 137:7 who **s.**, Rase it, rase it, even to the..... 559
Ps 140:6 I **s.** unto the Lord, Thou art my God:... 559
Ps 142:5 I **s.**, Thou art my refuge and my 559
Pr 4:4 taught me also, and **s.** unto me, ... 559
Pr 7:13 with an impudent face **s.** unto him,....... 559
Pr 25:7 better it is that it be **s.** unto thee, ... 559
Ec 1:10 any thing whereof it may be **s.**,........... 559
Ec 2:1 I **s.** in mine heart, Go to now, I will..... 559
Ec 2:2 I **s.** of laughter, It is mad: and of........ 559
Ec 2:15 **s.** I in my heart, As it happeneth......... 559
Ec 2:15 I **s.** in my heart, that this also is........ 1696
Ec 3:17 I **s.** in mine heart, God shall judge 559
Ec 3:18 I **s.** in mine heart concerning the 559
Ec 7:23 I **s.**, I will be wise; but it was far 559
Ec 8:14 I **s.** that this also is vanity................. 559
Ec 9:16 Then **s.** I, Wisdom is better than......... 559
Ca 2:10 My beloved spake, and **s.** unto me,....... 559
Ca 3:3 to whom I **s.**, Saw ye him whom my.........
Ca 7:8 I **s.**, I will go up to the palm tree, I...... 559
Isa 5:9 In mine ears **s.** the Lord of hosts, Of a .....
Isa 6:3 **s.**, Holy, holy, holy, is the Lord of....... 559
Isa 6:5 **s.** I, Woe is me! for I am undone; 559
Isa 6:7 **s.**, Lo, this hath touched thy lips; 559
Isa 6:8 Then **s.** I, Here am I; send me. 559
Isa 6:9 and he **s.**, Go, and tell this people, ... 559
Isa 6:11 Then **s.** I, Lord, how long? And he 559
Isa 7:3 **s.** the Lord unto Isaiah, Go forth now... 559
Isa 7:12 But Ahaz **s.**, I will not ask, neither 559
Isa 7:13 And he **s.**, Hear ye now, O house of.... 559
Isa 8:1 Moreover the Lord **s.** unto me, Take.... 559
Isa 8:3 **s.** the Lord to me, Call his name 559
Isa 14:13 thou hast **s.** in thine heart, I will......... 559
Isa 18:4 For so the Lord **s.** unto me, I will 559
Isa 20:3 And the Lord **s.**, Like as my servant.... 559
Isa 21:6 For thus hath the Lord **s.** unto me,....... 559
Isa 21:9 And he answered and **s.**, Babylon is 559
Isa 21:12 watchman **s.**, The morning cometh,...... 559
Isa 21:16 For thus hath the Lord **s.** unto me,....... 559
Isa 22:4 **s.** I, Look away from me; I will weep... 559
Isa 23:12 he **s.**, Thou shalt no more rejoice, O.... 559
Isa 24:16 But I **s.**, My leanness, my leanness,..... 559
Isa 25:9 it shall be **s.** in that day, Lo, this........ 559
Isa 28:12 To whom he **s.**, This is the rest......... 559
Isa 28:15 Because ye have **s.**, We have made 559
Isa 29:13 Wherefore the Lord **s.**, Forasmuch....... 559
Isa 30:16 But ye **s.**, No; for we will flee upon 559
Isa 32:5 nor the churl **s.** to be bountiful. 559
Isa 36:4 Rabshakeh **s.** unto them, Say ye now ... 559
Isa 36:7 and **s.** to Judah and to Jerusalem,......... 559
Isa 36:10 the Lord **s.** unto me, Go up against...... 559
Isa 36:11 Then **s.** Eliakim and Shebna and 559
Isa 36:12 But Rabshakeh **s.**, Hath my master...... 559
Isa 36:13 **s.**, Hear ye the words of the great....... 559
Isa 37:3 And they **s.** unto him, Thus saith........ 559
Isa 37:6 Isaiah **s.** unto them, Thus shall ye........ 559
Isa 37:24 and hast **s.**, By the multitude of my 559
Isa 38:1 **s.** unto him, Thus saith the Lord, ... 559
Isa 38:3 and **s.**, Remember now, O Lord, I....... 559
Isa 38:10 I **s.** in the cutting off of my days, I...... 559
Isa 38:11 I **s.**, I shall not see the Lord, even 559

Isa 38:21 Isaiah had **s.**, Let them take a lump 559
Isa 38:22 Hezekiah also had **s.**, What is the 559
Isa 39:3 **s.** unto him, What **s.** these men? 559
Isa 39:3 Hezekiah **s.**, They had come from a 559
Isa 39:4 Then **s.** he, What have they seen in 559
Isa 39:5 Then **s.** Isaiah to Hezekiah, Hear 559
Isa 39:8 Then **s.** Hezekiah to Isaiah, Good is 559
Isa 39:8 He **s.** moreover, For there shall be 559
Isa 40:6 The voice **s.**, Cry. And he **s.**, What 559
Isa 41:6 every one **s.** to his brother, Be of 559
Isa 41:9 **s.** unto thee, Thou art my servant; 559
Isa 45:19 I **s.** not unto the seed of Jacob, Seek.... 559
Isa 47:10 thou hast **s.**, None seeth me. Thy 559
Isa 47:10 thou hast **s.** in thine heart, I am, ... 559
Isa 49:3 **s.** unto me, Thou art my servant, O....... 559
Isa 49:4 Then I **s.**, I have laboured in vain, I..... 559
Isa 49:6 he **s.**, It is a light thing that thou 559
Isa 49:14 But Zion **s.**, The Lord hath forsaken..... 559
Isa 51:23 which have **s.** to my soul, Bow down,... 559
Isa 63:8 he **s.**, Surely they are my people, ... 559
Isa 65:1 I **s.**, Behold me, behold me, unto a....... 559
Isa 66:5 sake, **s.**, Let the Lord be glorified: 559
Jer 1:6 Then **s.** I, Ah, Lord God! behold, I...... 559
Jer 1:7 the Lord **s.** unto me, Say not, I am...... 559
Jer 1:9 the Lord **s.** unto me, Behold, I have 559
Jer 1:11 I **s.**, I see a rod of an almond tree. 559
Jer 1:12 **s.** the Lord unto me, Thou hast well 559
Jer 1:13 I **s.**, I see a seething pot; and the........ 559
Jer 1:14 Then the Lord **s.** to me, Out of the 559
Jer 2:6 Neither **s.** they, Where is the Lord...... 559
Jer 2:8 priests **s.** not, Where is the Lord? 559
Jer 3:6 Lord **s.** also unto me in the days of...... 559
Jer 3:7 I **s.** after she had done all these 559
Jer 3:11 Lord **s.** unto me, The backsliding......... 559
Jer 3:19 But I **s.**, How shall I put thee among.... 559
Jer 3:19 I **s.**, Thou shalt call me, My father;...... 559
Jer 4:10 Then **s.** I, Ah, Lord God! surely.......... 559
Jer 4:11 time shall it be **s.** to this people.......... 559
Jer 4:27 Lord **s.**, The whole land shall be.......... 559
Jer 5:4 Therefore I **s.**, Surely these are 559
Jer 5:12 belied the Lord, and **s.**, It is not he; 559
Jer 6:6 the Lord of hosts **s.**, Hew ye down...... 559
Jer 6:16 they **s.**, We will not walk therein. 559
Jer 6:17 But they **s.**, We will not hearken 559
Jer 10:19 but I **s.**, Truly this is a grief, and I...... 559
Jer 11:5 answered I, and **s.**, So be it, O Lord.... 559
Jer 11:6 Lord **s.** unto me, Proclaim all these...... 559
Jer 11:9 the Lord **s.** unto me, A conspiracy....... 559
Jer 12:4 they **s.**, He shall not see our last......... 559
Jer 13:6 the Lord **s.** unto me, Arise, go to........ 559
Jer 14:11 **s.** the Lord unto me, Pray not for........ 559
Jer 14:13 Then **s.** I, Ah, Lord God! behold, ... 559
Jer 14:14 the Lord **s.** unto me, The prophets 559
Jer 15:1 **s.** the Lord unto me, Though Moses 559
Jer 15:11 Lord **s.**, Verily it shall be well with 559
Jer 16:14 shall no more be **s.**, The Lord liveth, ... 559
Jer 17:19 **s.** the Lord unto me, Go, and stand 559
Jer 18:10 wherewith I **s.** I would benefit them. 559
Jer 18:12 And they **s.**, There is no hope: but 559
Jer 18:18 Then **s.** they, Come, and let us........... 559
Jer 19:14 house; and **s.** to all the people,............ 559
Jer 20:3 **s.** Jeremiah unto him, The Lord........... 559
Jer 20:9 Then I **s.**, I will not make mention....... 559
Jer 21:3 **s.** Jeremiah unto them, Thus shall........ 559
Jer 23:17 Lord hath **s.**, Ye shall have peace;...... 1696
Jer 23:25 I have heard what the prophets **s.**,........ 559
Jer 24:3 **s.** the Lord unto me, What seest.......... 559
Jer 24:3 And I **s.**, Figs; the good figs, very....... 559
Jer 25:5 They **s.**, Turn ye again now every........ 559
Jer 26:16 Then **s.** the princes and all the people... 559
Jer 28:5 Then the prophet Jeremiah **s.** unto....... 559
Jer 28:6 Even the prophet Jeremiah **s.**,............ 559
Jer 28:15 Then **s.** the prophet Jeremiah unto....... 559
Jer 29:15 ye have **s.**, The Lord hath raised us..... 559
Jer 32:6 Jeremiah **s.**, The word of the Lord....... 559
Jer 32:8 **s.** unto me, Buy my field, I pray 559
Jer 32:25 thou hast **s.** unto me, O Lord God, ... 559
Jer 35:5 and I **s.** unto them, Drink ye wine. 559
Jer 35:6 But they **s.**, We will drink no wine: 559
Jer 35:11 that we **s.**, Come, and let us go to 559
Jer 35:18 Jeremiah **s.** unto the house of the 559
Jer 36:15 And they **s.** unto him, Sit down now,.... 559
Jer 36:16 **s.** unto Baruch, We will surely tell 559
Jer 36:19 Then **s.** the princes unto Baruch,........... 559
Jer 37:14 Then **s.** Jeremiah, It is false; I fall........ 559
Jer 37:17 **s.**, Is there any word from the Lord? ... 559
Jer 37:17 Lord? And Jeremiah **s.**, There is:......... 559
Jer 37:17 for, **s.** he, thou shalt be delivered........ 559
Jer 37:18 Jeremiah **s.** unto king Zedekiah, ... 559
Jer 38:4 the princes **s.** unto the king, We.......... 559
Jer 38:5 Then Zedekiah the king **s.**, Behold, ... 559
Jer 38:12 Ebed-melech...**s.** unto Jeremiah, ... 559
Jer 38:14 and the king **s.** unto Jeremiah, I 559
Jer 38:15 Then Jeremiah **s.** unto Zedekiah, If....... 559
Jer 38:17 Then **s.** Jeremiah unto Zedekiah,........... 559
Jer 38:19 Zedekiah the king **s.** unto Jeremiah,...... 559
Jer 38:20 But Jeremiah **s.**, They shall not 559
Jer 38:24 Then **s.** Zedekiah unto Jeremiah,.......... 559
Jer 38:25 what thou hast **s.** unto the king,.......... 1696
Jer 38:25 also what the king **s.** unto thee: 1696
Jer 40:2 took Jeremiah, and **s.** unto him,............ 559
Jer 40:3 and done according as he hath **s.**......... 1696
Jer 40:5 he **s.**, Go back also to Gedaliah the...........
Jer 40:14 **s.** unto him, Dost thou certainly 559
Jer 40:16 the son of Ahikam **s.** unto 559
Jer 41:6 he **s.** unto them, Come to Gedaliah 559
Jer 41:8 among them that **s.** unto Ishmael, ... 559
Jer 42:2 **s.** unto Jeremiah the prophet, Let, ... 559
Jer 42:4 Jeremiah the prophet **s.** unto them, ... 559
Jer 42:5 Then they **s.** to Jeremiah, The Lord..... 559
Jer 42:9 **s.** unto them, Thus saith the Lord. 559
Jer 42:19 The Lord hath **s.** concerning you,....... 1696
Jer 44:20, 24 Jeremiah **s.** unto all the people, ... 559
Jer 46:16 they **s.**, Arise, and let us go against 559
Jer 50:7 their adversaries **s.**, We offend not,...... 559
Jer 51:61 Jeremiah **s.** to Seraiah, When thou 559
La 3:18 And I **s.**, My strength and my hope 559
La 3:54 mine head; then I **s.**, I am cut off. 559
La 4:15 they **s.** among the heathen, They......... 559
La 4:20 of whom we **s.**, Under his shadow 559
Eze 2:1 he **s.** unto me, Son of man, stand 559
Eze 2:3 he **s.** unto me, Son of man, I send....... 559
Eze 3:1 Moreover he **s.** unto me, Son of man, .. 559
Eze 3:3 **s.** unto me, Son of man, cause thy...... 559
Eze 3:4 And he **s.** unto me, Son of man, go,...... 559
Eze 3:10 Moreover he **s.** unto me, Son of man, .. 559
Eze 3:22 he **s.** unto me, Arise, go forth into....... 559
Eze 3:24 me, and **s.** unto me, Go, shut thyself ... 559
Eze 4:13 And the Lord **s.**, even thus shall the 559
Eze 4:14 Then **s.** I, Ah Lord God! behold, my.... 559
Eze 4:15 Then he **s.** unto me, Lo, I have 559
Eze 4:16 Moreover he **s.** unto me, Son of man, .. 559
Eze 6:10 I have not **s.** in vain that I would 1696
Eze 8:5 **s.** he unto me, Son of man, lift up 559
Eze 8:6 He **s.** furthermore unto me, Son of 559
Eze 8:8 Then **s.** he unto me, Son of man, ... 559
Eze 8:9 he **s.** unto me, Go in, and behold the ... 559
Eze 8:12 Then **s.** he unto me, son of man,......... 559
Eze 8:13 He **s.** also unto me, Turn thee yet........ 559
Eze 8:15 **s.** he unto me, Hast thou seen this, ... 559
Eze 8:17 he **s.** unto me, Hast thou seen this, ... 559
Eze 9:4 Lord **s.** unto him, Go through the 559
Eze 9:5 to the others he **s.** in mine hearing, ... 559
Eze 9:7 he **s.** unto them, Defile the house,....... 559
Eze 9:8 face, and cried, and **s.**, Ah Lord God!... 559
Eze 9:9 Then **s.** he unto me, The iniquity of..... 559
Eze 10:2 and **s.**, Go in between the wheels, ... 559
Eze 11:2 Then **s.** he unto me, Son of man, ... 559
Eze 11:5 fell upon me, and **s.** unto me, Speak;.... 559
Eze 11:5 Thus have ye **s.**, O house of Israel: 559
Eze 11:13 a loud voice, and **s.**, Ah Lord God! 559
Eze 11:15 inhabitants of Jerusalem have **s.**, ... 559
Eze 12:9 the rebellious house, **s.** unto thee, ... 559
Eze 13:12 shall it not be **s.** unto you, Where........ 559
Eze 16:6, 6 I **s.** unto thee when thou wast in 559
Eze 20:7 **s.** I unto them, Cast ye away every 559
Eze 20:8 then I **s.**, I will pour out my fury......... 559
Eze 20:13 then I **s.**, I would pour out my fury...... 559
Eze 20:18 But I **s.** unto their children in the 559
Eze 20:21 then I **s.**, I would pour out my fury...... 559
Eze 20:29 Then I **s.** unto them, What is the 559
Eze 20:49 Then **s.** I, Ah Lord God! they say of.... 559
Eze 21:17 fury to rest: I the Lord have **s.** it....... 1696
Eze 23:36 Lord **s.** moreover unto me; Son of....... 559
Eze 23:43 Then **s.** I unto her that was old in 559
Eze 24:19 the people **s.** unto me, Wilt thou 559
Eze 26:2 Tyrus hath **s.** against Jerusalem, ... 559
Eze 27:3 thou hast **s.**, I am of perfect beauty. 559
Eze 28:2 thou hast **s.**, I am a God, I sit in the.... 559
Eze 29:3 hath **s.**, My river is mine own, and 559
Eze 29:9 he hath **s.**, The river is mine, and I 559
Eze 35:10 Because thou hast **s.**, These two......... 559
Eze 36:2 the enemy hath **s.** against you, Aha,..... 559
Eze 36:20 when they **s.** to them, These are the ... 559
Eze 37:3 And he **s.** unto me, Son of man, can 559
Eze 37:4 Again he **s.** unto me, Prophesy upon 559
Eze 37:9 Then **s.** he unto me, Prophesy unto 559
Eze 37:11 Then he **s.** unto me, Son of man, ... 559
Eze 40:4 the man **s.** unto me, Son of man, ... 1696
Eze 40:45 he **s.** unto me, This chamber, whose .. 1696
Eze 41:4 and he **s.** unto me, This is the most...... 559
Eze 41:22 he **s.** unto me, This is the table 1696
Eze 42:13 Then **s.** he unto me, The north........... 559
Eze 43:7 And he **s.** unto me, Son of man, the..... 559
Eze 43:18 And he **s.** unto me, Son of man, thus ... 559
Eze 44:2 Then **s.** the Lord unto me; This gate..... 559
Eze 44:5 the Lord **s.** unto me, Son of man,........ 559
Eze 46:20 Then **s.** he unto me, This is the place .. 559
Eze 46:24 **s.** he unto me, These are the places 559
Eze 47:6 And he **s.** unto me, Son of man, hast ... 559
Eze 47:8 **s.** he unto me, These waters issue 559
Da 1:10 prince of the eunuchs **s.** unto Daniel, ... 559
Da 1:11 Then **s.** Daniel to Melzar, whom the 559
Da 1:18 king had **s.** he should bring them 559
Da 2:3 king **s.** unto them, I have dreamed....... 559
Da 2:5 the king answered and **s.** to the 560
Da 2:7 They answered again and **s.**, Let......... 560
Da 2:8 The king answered and **s.**, I know 560
Da 2:10 and **s.**, There is not a man upon the..... 560
Da 2:15 and **s.** to Arioch the king's captain,........ 560
Da 2:20 Daniel answered and **s.**, Blessed be....... 560
Da 2:24 he went and **s.** thus unto him;............ 560
Da 2:25 and **s.** thus unto him, I have found a 560
Da 2:26 The king answered and **s.** to Daniel,..... 560
Da 2:27 and **s.**, The secret which the king........ 560
Da 2:47 king answered unto Daniel, and **s.**,........ 560
Da 3:9 and **s.** to the king, Nebuchadnezzar, ... 560
Da 3:14 Nebuchadnezzar spake and **s.** unto 560
Da 3:16 **s.** to the king, O Nebuchadnezzar, ... 560
Da 3:24 spake, and **s.** unto his counsellors, ... 560
Da 3:24 They answered and **s.** unto the king, ... 560
Da 3:25 He answered and **s.**, Lo, I see four....... 560
Da 3:26 and **s.**, Shadrach, Meshach, and........... 560
Da 3:28 Nebuchadnezzar spake, and **s.**,............. 560
Da 4:14 cried aloud, and **s.** thus, Hew down...... 560
Da 4:19 king spake, and **s.**, Belteshazzar, ... 560
Da 4:19 Belteshazzar answered and **s.**, My 560
Da 4:30 The king spake and **s.**, Is not this........ 560
Da 5:7 and **s.** to the wise men of Babylon, ... 560
Da 5:10 the queen spake and **s.**, O king, live...... 560
Da 5:13 king spake and **s.** unto Daniel, Art 560
Da 5:17 Then Daniel answered and **s.** before..... 560
Da 6:5 Then **s.** these men, We shall not 560
Da 6:6 and **s.** thus unto him, King Darius........ 560
Da 6:12 The king answered and **s.**, the 560
Da 6:13 answered they and **s.** before the.......... 560
Da 6:15 and **s.** unto the king, Know, O king,..... 560
Da 6:16 spake and **s.** unto Daniel, Thy God 560
Da 6:20 spake and **s.** to Daniel, O Daniel,......... 560
Da 6:21 Then **s.** Daniel unto the king, O......... 4449
Da 7:2 Daniel spake and **s.**, I saw in my 560
Da 7:5 they **s.** thus unto it, Arise, devour 560
Da 7:23 Thus he **s.**, The fourth beast shall 560
Da 8:13 saint **s.** unto that certain saint 559
Da 8:14 he **s.** unto me, Unto two thousand 559
Da 8:16 and **s.**, Gabriel, make this man to 559
Da 8:17 but he **s.** unto me, Understand, O 559
Da 8:19 And he **s.**, Behold, I will make thee 559
Da 9:4 **s.**, O Lord, the great and dreadful 559
Da 9:22 **s.**, O Daniel, I am now come forth to ... 559
Da 10:11 And he **s.** unto me, O Daniel, a man 559
Da 10:12 **s.** he unto me, Fear not, Daniel: for..... 559
Da 10:16 **s.** unto him that stood before me,......... 559
Da 10:19 **s.**, O man greatly beloved, fear not:..... 559
Da 10:19 and **s.**, Let my Lord speak; for 559
Da 10:20 **s.** he, Knowest thou wherefore I.......... 559
Da 12:6 one **s.** to the man clothed in linen, ... 559
Da 12:8 then **s.** I, O my Lord, what shall be 559
Da 12:9 And he **s.**, Go thy way, Daniel: for 559
Ho 1:2 Lord **s.** to Hosea, Go, take unto thee.... 559
Ho 1:4 the Lord **s.** unto him, Call his name 559
Ho 1:6 And God **s.** unto him, Call her name..... 559
Ho 1:9 **s.** God, Call his name Lo-ammi:........... 559
Ho 1:10 where it was **s.** unto them, Ye are....... 559
Ho 1:10 there it shall be **s.** unto them, Ye 559
Ho 2:5 she **s.**, I will go after my lovers, that ... 559
Ho 2:12 she hath **s.**, These are my rewards 559
Ho 3:1 Then **s.** the Lord unto me, Go yet, ... 559
Ho 3:3 And I **s.** unto her, Thou shalt abide...... 559

Ho 12:8 Ephraim s., Yet I am become rich,....... 559
Joe 2:32 be deliverance, as the Lord hath s., ... 559
Am 1:2 he s., The Lord will roar from Zion,..... 559
Am 7:2 then I s., O Lord God, forgive, I......... 559
Am 7:5 Then s. I, O Lord God, cease, I 559
Am 7:8 Lord s. unto me, Amos, what seest..... 559
Am 7:8 seest thou? And I s., A plumbline. 559
Am 7:8 Then s. the Lord, Behold, I will set..... 559
Am 7:12 Also Amaziah s. unto Amos, O thou..... 559
Am 7:14 and s. to Amaziah, I was no prophet, ... 559
Am 7:15 the Lord s. unto me, Go, prophesy,..... 559
Am 8:2 And he s., Amos, what seest thou?...... 559
Am 8:2 And I s., A basket of summer fruit. 559
Am 8:2 s. the Lord unto me, The end is 559
Am 9:1 he s., Smite the lintel of the door,....... 559
Jon 1:6 s. unto him, What meanest thou, O...... 559
Jon 1:7 And they s. every one to his fellow,..... 559
Jon 1:8 Then s. they unto him, Tell us, we...... 559
Jon 1:9 he s. unto them, I am an Hebrew;....... 559
Jon 1:10 s. unto him, Why hast thou done......... 559
Jon 1:11 Then s. they unto him, What shall 559
Jon 1:12 he s. unto them, Take me up, and....... 559
Jon 1:14 and s., We beseech thee, O Lord, we .. 559
Jon 2:2 And s., I cried by reason of mine 559
Jon 2:4 Then I s., I am cast out of thy sight; ... 559
Jon 3:4 and he cried, and s., Yet forty days, ... 559
Jon 3:10 he had s., that he would do unto........ 1696
Jon 4:2 and s., I pray thee, O Lord, was not.... 559
Jon 4:4 Then s. the lord, Doest thou well to 559
Jon 4:8 and s., It is better for me to die than ... 559
Jon 4:9 God s. to Jonah, Doest thou well......... 559
Jon 4:9 he s., I do well to be angry, even........ 559
Jon 4:10 Then s. the Lord, Thou hast had......... 559
Mic 3:1 And I s., Hear, I pray you, O heads..... 559
Mic 7:10 shall cover her which s. unto me, ... 559
Hab 2:2 Lord answered me, and s., Write 559
Zep 2:15 that s. in her heart, I am, and there..... 559
Zep 3:7 I s., Surely thou wilt fear me, thou...... 559
Zep 3:16 that day it shall be s. to Jerusalem,...... 559
Hag 2:12 And the priests answered and s., No.... 559
Hag 2:13 Then s. Haggai, If one that is 559
Hag 2:13 priests answered and s., It shall be 559
Hag 2:14 Haggai, and s., So is this people,......... 559
Zec 1:6 they returned and s., Like as the......... 559
Zec 1:9 Then s. I, O my lord, what are........... 559
Zec 1:9 angel that talked with me s. unto......... 559
Zec 1:10 the myrtle trees answered and s.,......... 559
Zec 1:11 stood among the myrtle trees, and s., .. 559
Zec 1:12 angel of the Lord answered and s., ... 559
Zec 1:14 that communed with me s. unto me,..... 559
Zec 1:19 I s. unto the angel that talked with....... 559
Zec 1:21 Then s. I, What come these to do?...... 559
Zec 2:2 Then s. I, Whither goest thou? And..... 559
Zec 2:2 And he s. unto me, To measure.......... 559
Zec 2:4 And s. unto him, Run, speak to this..... 559
Zec 3:2 And the Lord s. unto Satan, The......... 559
Zec 3:4 And unto him he s., Behold, I have...... 559
Zec 3:5 And I s., Let them set a fair mitre....... 559
Zec 4:2 And s. unto me, What seest thou?....... 559
Zec 4:2 And I s., I have looked, and behold...... 559
Zec 4:5 with me answered and s. unto me,....... 559
Zec 4:5 these be? And I s., No, my lord.......... 559
Zec 4:11 Then answered I, and s. unto him,....... 559
Zec 4:12 I answered again, and s. unto him,....... 559
Zec 4:13 he answered me and s., Knowest........ 559
Zec 4:13 these be? And I s., No, my lord.......... 559
Zec 4:14 Then s. he, These are the two............ 559
Zec 5:2 he s. unto me, What seest thou? 559
Zec 5:3 s. he unto me, This is the curse.......... 559
Zec 5:5 s. unto me, Lift up now thine eyes, ... 559
Zec 5:6 And I s., What is it? And he s., ... 559
Zec 5:6 He s. moreover, This is their............. 559
Zec 5:8 And he s., This is wickedness. And...... 559
Zec 5:10 s. I to the angel that talked with......... 559
Zec 5:11 And he s. unto me, To build it an......... 559
Zec 6:4 I answered and s. unto the angel......... 559
Zec 6:5 the angel answered and s. unto me, ... 559
Zec 6:7 and he s., Get you hence, walk to 559
Zec 11:9 Then s. I, I will not feed you: that....... 559
Zec 11:12 And I s. unto them, if ye think good,.... 559
Zec 11:13 the Lord s. unto me, Cast it unto........ 559
Zec 11:15 And the Lord s. unto me, Take unto.... 559
Mal 1:13 Ye s. also, Wherein shall we return? 559
Mal 3:7 But ye s., Wherein shall we return? 559
Mal 3:14 Ye have s., It is vain to serve God: 559
Mt 2:5 they s. unto him, In Bethlehem of...... 2036
Mt 2:8 and s., Go and search diligently 2036

Mt 3:7 he s. unto them, O generation of 2036
Mt 3:15 s. unto him, Suffer it to be so now:. 2036
Mt 4:3 he s., If thou be the Son of God, ... 2036
Mt 4:4 Jesus answered and s., It is written,. 2036
Mt 4:7 Jesus s. unto him, It is written........ 5346
Mt 5:21, 27 it was s. by them of old time,... 2046
Mt 5:31 It hath been s., Whosoever shall ... 2046
Mt 5:33 it hath been s. by them of old....... 2046
Mt 5:38 it hath been s., An eye for an eye, 2046
Mt 5:43 it hath been s., Thou shalt love..... 2046
Mt 8:8 centurion answered and s., Lord, I..... 5346
Mt 8:10 s. to them that followed, Verily I...... 4483
Mt 8:13 Jesus s. unto the centurion, Go thy ... 4483
Mt 8:19 s. unto him, Master, I will follow 4483
Mt 8:21 another of his disciples s. unto him, ... 4483
Mt 8:22 But Jesus s. unto him, Follow me;.... 4483
Mt 8:32 And he s. unto them, Go. And when .. 4483
Mt 9:2 s. unto the sick of the palsy; Son, ... 4483
Mt 9:3 of the scribes s. within themselves, ... 4483
Mt 9:4 Jesus knowing their thoughts s.,........ 4483
Mt 9:11 s. unto his disciples, Why eateth........ 4483
Mt 9:12 he s. unto them, They that be whole 4483
Mt 9:15 Jesus s. unto them, Can the children 4483
Mt 9:21 For she s. within herself, If I may...... 3004
Mt 9:22 s., Daughter be of good comfort;... 2036
Mt 9:24 He s. unto them, Give place: for...... 3004
Mt 9:28 this? They s. unto him, Yea, Lord. 3004
Mt 9:34 Pharisees s., He casteth out devils..... 3004
Mt 11:3 And s. unto him, Art thou he that 2036
Mt 11:4 s. unto them, Go and shew John...... 2036
Mt 11:25 s., I thank thee, O Father, Lord ... 2036
Mt 12:2 Pharisees saw it, they s. unto him,..... 2036
Mt 12:3 he s. unto them, Have ye not read... 2036
Mt 12:11 he s. unto them, What man shall 2036
Mt 12:23 and s., Is not this the son of David? ... 3004
Mt 12:24 they s., This fellow doth not cast....... 2036
Mt 12:25 and s. unto them, Every kingdom.... 2036
Mt 12:39 answered and s. unto them, An evil... 2036
Mt 12:47 one s. unto him, Behold, thy mother.... 2036
Mt 12:48 s. unto him that told him, Who is...... 2036
Mt 12:49 and s., Behold my mother and my.. 2036
Mt 13:10 and s. unto him, Why speakest thou ... 2036
Mt 13:11 s. unto them, Because it is given 2063
Mt 13:27 s. unto him, Sir, didst not thou..... 2063
Mt 13:28 He s. unto them, An enemy hath... 2063
Mt 13:28 The servants s. unto him, Wilt...... 5346
Mt 13:29 he s., Nay; lest while ye gather..... 5346
Mt 13:37 and s. unto them, He that soweth.... 2036
Mt 13:52 s. he unto them, Therefore every...... 2036
Mt 13:54 and s., Whence hath this man this...... 3004
Mt 13:57 s. unto them, A prophet is not........ 2036
Mt 14:2 s. unto his servant, This is John.......... 2036
Mt 14:4 John s. unto him, It is not lawful........ 3004
Mt 14:8 s., Give me here John Baptist's 5346
Mt 14:16 Jesus s. unto them, They need not... 2036
Mt 14:18 He s., Bring them hither to me. 2036
Mt 14:28 Peter...s., Lord, if it be thou, bid....... 2036
Mt 14:29 And he s., Come. And when Peter 2036
Mt 14:31 and s. unto him, O thou of little...... 3004
Mt 15:3 and s. unto them, Why do ye also.... 2036
Mt 15:10 s. unto them, Hear, and understand .2036
Mt 15:12 disciples, and s. unto him, Knowest.... 2036
Mt 15:13 he answered and s., Every plant,..... 2036
Mt 15:15 answered Peter and s. unto him,........ 2036
Mt 15:16 Jesus s., Are ye also yet without..... 2036
Mt 15:24 answered and s., I am not sent but.. 2036
Mt 15:26 and s., It is not meet to take the ... 2036
Mt 15:27 she s., Truth, Lord: yet the dogs....... 2036
Mt 15:28 answered and s. unto her, O woman, .2036
Mt 15:32 and s., I have compassion on the ... 2036
Mt 15:34 And they s., Seven, and a few little.... 2036
Mt 16:2 s. unto them, When it is evening,.. 2036
Mt 16:6 Jesus s. unto them, Take heed and... 2036
Mt 16:8 he s. unto them, O ye of little faith,.2036
Mt 16:14 they s., Some say that thou art John... 2036
Mt 16:16 Peter answered and s., Thou art........ 2036
Mt 16:17 Jesus...s. unto him, Blessed art thou,2036
Mt 16:23 and s. unto Peter, Get thee behind... 2036
Mt 16:24 s. Jesus unto his disciples, If any...... 2036
Mt 17:4 and s. unto Jesus, Lord, it is good...... 2036
Mt 17:5 a voice out of the cloud, which s.,...... 3004
Mt 17:7 and s., Arise, and be not afraid...... 2036
Mt 17:11 Jesus...s. unto them, Elias truly 2036
Mt 17:17 Jesus answered and s., O faithless.... 2036
Mt 17:19 s., Why could not we cast him out? 2036
Mt 17:20 And Jesus s. unto them, Because...... 2036
Mt 17:22 Jesus s. unto them, The Son of man 2036

Mt 17:24 and s., Doth not your master pay....... 2036
Mt 18:3 s., Verily I say unto you, Except... 2036
Mt 18:21 Peter to him, and s., Lord, how oft.... 2036
Mt 18:32 him, s. unto him, O thou wicked... 3004
Mt 19:4 and s. unto them, Have ye not read, .2036
Mt 19:5 s., For this cause shall a man....... 2036
Mt 19:11 But he s. unto them, All men cannot.2036
Mt 19:14 But Jesus s., Suffer little children, ..2036
Mt 19:16 one came and s. unto him, Good........ 2036
Mt 19:17 s. unto him, Why callest thou me.... 2036
Mt 19:18 Jesus s., Thou shalt do no murder,. 2036
Mt 19:21 Jesus s. unto him, If thou wilt be 5346
Mt 19:23 s. Jesus unto his disciples, Verily...... 2036
Mt 19:26 and s. unto them, With men this is.. 2036
Mt 19:27 answered Peter and s. unto him,........ 2036
Mt 19:28 Jesus s. unto them, Verily I say....... 2036
Mt 20:4 and s. unto them; Go ye also into ..2036
Mt 20:13 s., Friend, I do thee no wrong: 2036
Mt 20:17 apart in the way, and s. unto them, ... 2036
Mt 20:21 And he s. unto her, What wilt thou?.2036
Mt 20:22 Jesus answered and s., Ye know not. 2036
Mt 20:25 Jesus called them unto him, and s.,..... 2036
Mt 20:32 stood still, and called them, and s.,..... 2036
Mt 21:11 the multitude s., This is Jesus the...... 3004
Mt 21:13 And s. unto them, It is written, My...3004
Mt 21:16 s. unto him, Hearest thou what.......... 2036
Mt 21:19 and s. unto it, Let no fruit grow on..3004
Mt 21:21 Jesus answered and s. unto them, ... 2036
Mt 21:23 and s., By what authority doest 3004
Mt 21:24 Jesus...s. unto them, I also will ask..2036
Mt 21:27 Jesus, and s., We cannot tell. 2036
Mt 21:27 he s. unto them, Neither tell I you.. 5346
Mt 21:28 and s., Son, go work to day in my. 2036
Mt 21:29 He answered and s., I will not 2036
Mt 21:30 came to second, and s. likewise..... 2036
Mt 21:30 And he answered and s., I go, sir:. 2036
Mt 21:38 they s. among themselves, This is ..2036
Mt 22:1 them again by parables, and s.,.......... 3004
Mt 22:13 s. the king to the servants, Bind... 2036
Mt 22:18 s., Why tempt ye me, ye.............. 2036
Mt 22:24 Moses s., If a man die, having no 2036
Mt 22:29 Jesus...s. unto them, Ye do err, ... 2036
Mt 22:37 Jesus s. unto him, Thou shalt love... 2036
Mt 22:44 Lord s. unto my Lord, Sit thou on .2036
Mt 24:2 Jesus s. unto them, See ye not all 2036
Mt 24:4 Jesus...s. unto them, Take heed 2036
Mt 25:8 foolish s. unto the wise, Give us.... 2036
Mt 25:12 s., Verily I say unto you, I know .. 2036
Mt 25:21 His lord s. unto him, Well done,... 5346
Mt 25:22 s., Lord, thou deliveredst unto 2036
Mt 25:23 His lord s. unto him, Well done,... 5346
Mt 25:24 s., Lord, I knew thee that thou..... 2036
Mt 25:26 lord...s. unto him, Thou wicked... 2036
Mt 26:1 saying, he s. unto his disciples,.......... 2036
Mt 26:5 But they s., Not on the feast day,....... 3004
Mt 26:10 he s. unto them, Why trouble ye 2036
Mt 26:15 s. unto them, What will ye give me, ... 2036
Mt 26:18 he s., Go into the city to such a.... 2036
Mt 26:21 as they did eat, he s., Verily I say.... 2036
Mt 26:23 answered and s., He that dippeth 2036
Mt 26:25 Then Judas...answered and s.,........... 2036
Mt 26:25 Master, is it I? He s. unto him, ... 3004
Mt 26:25 unto him, Thou hast s.................. 2036
Mt 26:26 and s., Take, eat; this is my body.. 2036
Mt 26:33 Peter...s. unto him, Though all men.... 2036
Mt 26:34 Jesus s. unto him, Verily I say 5346
Mt 26:35 Peter s. unto him, Though I...die....... 3004
Mt 26:35 Likewise also s. all the disciples. 2036
Mt 26:49 and s., Hail, master; and kissed 2036
Mt 26:50 And Jesus s. unto him, Friend,.......... 2036
Mt 26:52 s. Jesus unto him, Put up again....... 3004
Mt 26:55 hour s. Jesus to the multitudes, ... 2036
Mt 26:61 And s., This fellow.......................... 2036
Mt 26:61 This fellow s., I am able to.............. 5346
Mt 26:62 and s. unto him, Answerest thou....... 2036
Mt 26:63 high priest...s. unto him, I adjure 2036
Mt 26:64 Jesus saith unto him, Thou hast s..... 2036
Mt 26:66 and s., He is guilty of death. 2036
Mt 26:71 maid saw him, and s. unto them.......... 3004
Mt 26:73 and s. to Peter, Surely thou also......... 2036
Mt 26:75 word of Jesus, which s. unto him, ... 2046
Mt 27:4 And they s., What is that to us? 2036
Mt 27:6 took the silver pieces, and s., it is....... 2036
Mt 27:11 Jesus s. unto him, Thou sayest. 5346
Mt 27:13 s. Pilate unto him, Hearest thou.......... 3004
Mt 27:17 Pilate s. unto them, Whom will ye...... 2036
Mt 27:21 governor...s. unto them, Whether 2036

Mt 27:21 unto you? They s., Barabbas. 2036
Mt 27:23 the governor s., Why, what evil 5346
Mt 27:25 and s., His blood be on us, and on 2036
Mt 27:41 with the scribes and elders, s., 3004
Mt 27:43 for he s., I am the Son of God. 2036
Mt 27:47 s., This man calleth for Elias. 3004
Mt 27:49 The rest s., Let be, let us see 3004
Mt 27:63 we remember that that deceiver s., 2036
Mt 27:65 Pilate s. unto them, Ye have a 5346
Mt 28:5 angel...s. unto the women, Fear not 2036
Mt 28:6 is not here: for he is risen, as he s. 2036
Mt 28:10 Then s. Jesus unto them, Be not 3004
Mk 1:17 Jesus s. unto them, Come ye after 2036
Mk 1:37 they s. unto him, All men seek for 3004
Mk 1:38 he s. unto them, Let us go into the 3004
Mk 2:5 he s. unto the sick of the palsy, Son, 3004
Mk 2:8 he s. unto them, Why reason ye 2036
Mk 2:14 and s. unto him, Follow me. And 3004
Mk 2:16 they s. unto his disciples, How is it 3004
Mk 2:19 And Jesus s. Can the children 2036
Mk 2:24 the Pharisees s. unto him, Behold, 3004
Mk 2:25 he s. unto them, Have ye never 3004
Mk 2:27 s. unto them, The sabbath was 3004
Mk 3:21 for they s., He is beside himself. 3004
Mk 3:22 scribes...s., He hath Beelzebub, 3004
Mk 3:23 and s. unto them in parables, How 3004
Mk 3:30 Because they s., He hath an unclean 3004
Mk 3:32 s. unto him, Behold, thy mother 2036
Mk 3:34 and s., Behold my mother and my 3004
Mk 4:2 and s. unto them in his doctrine, 3004
Mk 4:9 he s. unto them, He that hath ears 3004
Mk 4:11 s. unto them, Unto you it is given 3004
Mk 4:13 he s. unto them, Know ye not this 3004
Mk 4:21 s. unto them, Is a candle brought 3004
Mk 4:24 he s. unto them, Take heed what 3004
Mk 4:26 he s., So is the kingdom of God, 3004
Mk 4:30 he s., Whereunto shall we liken 3004
Mk 4:39 and s. unto the sea, Peace, be still 2036
Mk 4:40 s. unto them, Why are ye so 2036
Mk 4:41 s. one to another, What manner of 3004
Mk 5:7 and s., What have I to do with 2036
Mk 5:8 s. unto him, Come out of the man, 3004
Mk 5:28 For she s., If I may touch but his 3004
Mk 5:30 and s., Who touched my clothes? 3004
Mk 5:31 disciples s. unto him, Thou seest 3004
Mk 5:34 he s. unto her, Daughter, thy faith 2036
Mk 5:35 certain which s., Thy daughter is 3004
Mk 5:41 and s. unto her, Talitha cumi; 3004
Mk 6:4 Jesus s. unto them, A prophet is not 3004
Mk 6:10 s. unto them, In what place soever 3004
Mk 6:14 s., That John the Baptist was risen 3004
Mk 6:15 Others s., That it is Elias. And 3004
Mk 6:15 And others s., That it is a prophet, 3004
Mk 6:16 he s., It is John, whom I beheaded: 2036
Mk 6:18 John had s. unto Herod, It is not 3004
Mk 6:22 the daughter of the s. Herodias 846
Mk 6:22 king s. unto the damsel, Ask of me 2036
Mk 6:24 and s. unto her mother, What shall I 2036
Mk 6:24 she s., The head of John the Baptist 2036
Mk 6:31 s. unto them, Come ye yourselves 2036
Mk 6:35 and s., This is a desert place, and 3004
Mk 6:37 and s. unto them, Give ye them to 2036
Mk 7:6 and s. unto them, Well hath Esaias 2036
Mk 7:9 he s. unto them, Full well ye reject 3004
Mk 7:10 For Moses s., honour thy father 2036
Mk 7:14 he s. unto them, Hearken unto me 3004
Mk 7:20 s., That which cometh out of the 3004
Mk 7:27 Jesus s. unto her, Let the children 2036
Mk 7:28 and s. unto him, Yes, Lord: yet the 3004
Mk 7:29 s. unto her, For this saying go thy 2036
Mk 8:5 loaves have ye? And they s., Seven 2036
Mk 8:20 took ye up? and they s., Seven. 2036
Mk 8:21 he s. unto them, How is it that ye 3004
Mk 8:24 and s., I see men as trees, walking. 3004
Mk 8:34 he s. unto them, Whosoever will 2036
Mk 9:1 he s. unto them,...there be some 3004
Mk 9:5 and s. to Jesus, Master, it is good 3004
Mk 9:17 and s., Master, I have brought 2036
Mk 9:21 unto him? And he s., Of a child. 2036
Mk 9:23 Jesus s. unto him, If thou canst 2036
Mk 9:24 and s. with tears, Lord, I believe; 3004
Mk 9:26 insomuch that many s., He is dead. 3004
Mk 9:29 And he s. unto them, This kind 2036
Mk 9:31 and s. unto them, The Son of man 3004
Mk 9:36 him in his arms, he s. unto them, 2036
Mk 9:39 But Jesus s., Forbid him not: for 2036
Mk 10:3 and s. unto them, What did Moses 2036
Mk 10:4 And they s., Moses suffered to write 2036
Mk 10:5 Jesus answered and s. unto them, 2036
Mk 10:14 and s. unto them, Suffer the little 2036
Mk 10:18 Jesus s. unto him, Why callest thou 2036
Mk 10:20 and s. unto him, Master, all these 2036
Mk 10:21 s. unto him, One thing thou lackest 2036
Mk 10:29 And Jesus answered and s., Verily 2036
Mk 10:36 And he s. unto them, What would 2036
Mk 10:37 They s. unto him, Grant unto us 2036
Mk 10:38 But Jesus s. unto them, Ye know 2036
Mk 10:39 And they s. unto him, We can. 2036
Mk 10:39 And Jesus s. unto them, Ye shall 2036
Mk 10:51 Jesus answered and s. unto him, 3004
Mk 10:51 The blind man s. unto him, Lord, 2036
Mk 10:52 And Jesus s. unto him, Go thy way: 2036
Mk 11:5 them that stood there s. unto them, 3004
Mk 11:6 s. unto them even as Jesus had 2036
Mk 11:14 Jesus answered and s. unto it, No 2036
Mk 11:29 Jesus answered and s. unto them, 2036
Mk 11:33 they answered and s. unto Jesus, 3004
Mk 12:7 husbandmen s. among themselves, 2036
Mk 12:15 s. unto them, Why tempt ye me? 2036
Mk 12:16 And they s. unto him, Caesar's. 2036
Mk 12:17, 24 Jesus answering s. unto them, 2036
Mk 12:32 scribe s. unto him, Well, Master, 2036
Mk 12:32 thou hast s. the truth: for there is 2036
Mk 12:34 he s. unto him, Thou art not far 2036
Mk 12:35 Jesus answered and s., while he 3004
Mk 12:36 David...s. by the Holy Ghost, The 2036
Mk 12:36 Lord s. to my Lord, Sit thou on 2036
Mk 12:38 And he s. unto them in his doctrine, 3004
Mk 13:2 Jesus answering s. unto him, Seest 2036
Mk 14:2 But they s., Not on the feast day, 3004
Mk 14:4 and s., Why was this waste of the 3004
Mk 14:6 And Jesus s., Let her alone; why 2036
Mk 14:12 his disciples s. unto him, Where 3004
Mk 14:16 and found as he had s. unto them: 2036
Mk 14:18 Jesus s., Verily I say unto you, 2036
Mk 14:19 one, Is it I? and another s., Is it I?
Mk 14:20 he answered and s. unto them, It 2036
Mk 14:22 gave to them, and s., Take, eat: 2036
Mk 14:24 he s. unto them, This is my blood 2036
Mk 14:29 But Peter s. unto him, Although 5346
Mk 14:31 wise. Likewise also s. they all. 3004
Mk 14:36 And he s., Abba, Father, all things 3004
Mk 14:48 Jesus answered and s. unto them, 2036
Mk 14:61 s. unto him, Art thou the Christ, 3004
Mk 14:62 And Jesus, I am: and ye shall 2036
Mk 14:67 and s., And thou also wast with 3004
Mk 14:70 they that stood by s. again to Peter, 3004
Mk 14:72 the word that Jesus s. unto him, 2036
Mk 15:2 he answering s. unto him, Thou 2036
Mk 15:12 s. again unto them, What will ye 2036
Mk 15:14 Pilate s. unto them, Why, what evil 3004
Mk 15:31 chief priests mocking s. among 3004
Mk 15:35 heard it, s., Behold, he calleth Elias 3004
Mk 15:39 he s., Truly this man was the Son 2036
Mk 16:3 s. among themselves, Who shall 3004
Mk 16:7 ye see him, as he s. unto you. 2036
Mk 16:8 neither s. they any thing to any 2036
Mk 16:15 he s. unto them, Go ye into all the 2036
Lu 1:13 the angel s. unto him, Fear not, 2036
Lu 1:18 And Zacharias s. unto the angel, 2036
Lu 1:19 angel...s. unto him, I am Gabriel, 2036
Lu 1:28 angel came in unto her, and s., Hail, 2036
Lu 1:30 And the angel s. unto her, Fear not, 2036
Lu 1:34 s. Mary unto the angel, How shall 2036
Lu 1:35 angel...s. unto her, The Holy Ghost 2036
Lu 1:38 Mary s., Behold the handmaid of 2036
Lu 1:42 s., Blessed art thou among women, 2036
Lu 1:46 Mary s., My soul doth magnify the 2036
Lu 1:60 his mother answered and s., Not so; 2036
Lu 1:61 they s. unto her, There is none of 2036
Lu 2:10 the angel s. unto them, Fear not: 2036
Lu 2:15 shepherds s. one to another, Let us 2036
Lu 2:24 which is s. in the law of the Lord, 2046
Lu 2:28 his arms, and blessed God, and s., 2036
Lu 2:34 s. unto Mary his mother, Behold, 2036
Lu 2:48 his mother s. unto him, Son, why 2036
Lu 2:49 he s. unto them, How is it that ye 2036
Lu 3:7 Then s. he to the multitude that 3004
Lu 3:12 s. unto him, Master, what shall we 2036
Lu 3:13 he s. unto them, Exact no more 2036
Lu 3:14 he s. unto them, Do violence to no 2036
Lu 3:22 voice came from heaven, which s., 3004
Lu 4:3 the devil s. unto him, If thou be the 2036
Lu 4:6 the devil s. unto him, All this power 2036
Lu 4:8 Jesus answered and s. unto him, 2036
Lu 4:9 s. unto him, If thou be the Son of 2036
Lu 4:12 Jesus answering s. unto him, It is 2036
Lu 4:12 It is s., Thou shalt not tempt the 2046
Lu 4:22 they s., Is not this Joseph's son? 3004
Lu 4:23 he s. unto them, Ye will surely say 2036
Lu 4:24 And he s., Verily I say unto you, 2036
Lu 4:43 he s. unto them, I must preach the 2036
Lu 5:4 he s. unto Simon, Launch out into 2036
Lu 5:5 And Simon answering s. unto him, 2036
Lu 5:10 And Jesus s. unto Simon, Fear not; 2036
Lu 5:20 he s. unto him, Man, thy sins are 2036
Lu 5:22 s. unto them, What reason ye in 2036
Lu 5:24 (he s. unto the sick of the palsy,) I 2036
Lu 5:27 and he s. unto him, Follow me. 2036
Lu 5:31 And Jesus answering s. unto them, 2036
Lu 5:33 s. unto him, Why do the disciples 2036
Lu 5:34 he s. unto them, Can ye make the 2036
Lu 6:2 Pharisees s. unto them, Why do ye 2036
Lu 6:3 Jesus answering them s., Have ye 2036
Lu 6:5 he s. unto them, That the Son of 3004
Lu 6:8 and s. to the man which had the 2036
Lu 6:9 s. Jesus unto them, I will ask you 2036
Lu 6:10 he s. unto the man, Stretch forth 2036
Lu 6:20 and s., Blessed be ye poor: for 3004
Lu 7:9 s. unto the people that followed 2036
Lu 7:13 on her, and s. unto her, Weep not. 2036
Lu 7:14 he s., Young man, I say unto thee, 2036
Lu 7:20 they s., John Baptist hath sent us 2036
Lu 7:22 Jesus answering s. unto them, Go 2036
Lu 7:31 the Lord s., Whereunto then shall 2036
Lu 7:40 And Jesus answering s. unto him, 2036
Lu 7:43 Simon answered and s., I suppose 2036
Lu 7:43 he s. unto him, Thou hast rightly 2036
Lu 7:44 and s. unto Simon, Seest thou this 5346
Lu 7:48 s. unto her, Thy sins are forgiven 2036
Lu 7:50 he s. to the woman, Thy faith hath 2036
Lu 8:8 when he had s. these things, he 3004
Lu 8:10 And he s., Unto you it is given to 2036
Lu 8:20 was told him by certain which s., 3004
Lu 8:21 and s. unto them, My mother and 2036
Lu 8:22 and he s. unto them, Let us go over 2036
Lu 8:25 s. unto them, Where is your faith? 2036
Lu 8:28 and with a loud voice s., What have 2036
Lu 8:30 And he s., Legion: because many 2036
Lu 8:45 And Jesus s., Who touched me? 2036
Lu 8:45 they that were with him s., Master, 2036
Lu 8:46 Jesus s., Somebody hath touched 2036
Lu 8:48 he s. unto her, Daughter, be of good 2036
Lu 8:52 he s., Weep not; she is not dead, 2036
Lu 9:3 And he s. unto them, Take nothing 2036
Lu 9:7 because that is was s. of some, that 3004
Lu 9:9 Herod s., John have I beheaded: 2036
Lu 9:12 came the twelve, and s. unto him, 2036
Lu 9:13 But he s. unto them, Give ye them 2036
Lu 9:13 And they s., We have no more but 2036
Lu 9:14 he s. to his disciples, Make them 2036
Lu 9:19 answering s., John the Baptist; 2036
Lu 9:20 He s. unto them, But whom say ye 2036
Lu 9:20 Peter answering s., The Christ of 2036
Lu 9:23 And he s. to them all, If any man 3004
Lu 9:33 Peter s. unto Jesus, Master, it is 2036
Lu 9:33 for Elias: not knowing what he s. 3004
Lu 9:41 Jesus answering s., O faithless 2036
Lu 9:43 Jesus did, he s. unto his disciples, 2036
Lu 9:48 And s. unto them, Whosoever shall 2036
Lu 9:49 John answered and s., Master, we 2036
Lu 9:50 Jesus s. unto him, Forbid him not: 2036
Lu 9:54 they s., Lord, wilt thou that we 2036
Lu 9:55 s., Ye know not what manner of 2036
Lu 9:57 a certain man s. unto him, Lord, I 2036
Lu 9:58 And Jesus s. unto him, Foxes have 2036
Lu 9:59 And he s. unto another, Follow me 2036
Lu 9:59 But he s., Lord, suffer me first to 2036
Lu 9:60 Jesus s. unto him, Let the dead 2036
Lu 9:61 another also s., Lord, I will follow 2036
Lu 9:62 Jesus s. unto him, No man, having 2036
Lu 10:2 Therefore s. he unto them, The 3004
Lu 10:18 he s. unto them, I beheld Satan 2036
Lu 10:21 s., I thank thee, O Father, Lord 2036
Lu 10:23 s. privately, Blessed are the eyes 2036
Lu 10:26 He s. unto him, What is written in 2036
Lu 10:27 he answering s., Thou shalt love 2036
Lu 10:28 And he s. unto him, Thou hast 2036
Lu 10:29 to justify himself, s. unto Jesus, 2036
Lu 10:30 Jesus answering s., A certain man 2036
Lu 10:35 s. unto him, Take care of him; 2036

Book	Ref	Context	No.
Lu	10:37	And he s., He that shewed mercy on	2036
Lu	10:37	Then s. Jesus unto him, Go, and	2036
Lu	10:40	came to him, and s., Lord, dost thou	2036
Lu	10:41	And Jesus answered and s. unto her,	2036
Lu	11:1	one of his disciples s. unto him,	2036
Lu	11:2	he s. unto them, When ye pray, say.	2036
Lu	11:5	And he s. unto them, Which of you	2036
Lu	11:15	But some of them s., he casteth out	2036
Lu	11:17	s. unto them, Every kingdom	2036
Lu	11:27	s. unto him, Blessed is the womb	2036
Lu	11:28	But he s., Yea rather, blessed are	2036
Lu	11:39	And the Lord s. unto him, Now do	2036
Lu	11:45	lawyers, and s. unto him, Master,	3004
Lu	11:46	And he s., Woe unto you also, ye	2036
Lu	11:49	also s. the wisdom of God, I will	2036
Lu	11:53	as he s. these things unto them,	3004
Lu	12:13	one of the company s. unto him,	2036
Lu	12:14	he s. unto him, Man, who made me.	2036
Lu	12:15	And he s. unto them, Take heed,	2036
Lu	12:18	he s., This will I do: I will pull	2036
Lu	12:20	God s. unto him, Thou fool, this	2036
Lu	12:22	he s. unto his disciples, Therefore	2036
Lu	12:41	Peter s. unto him, Lord, speakest	2036
Lu	12:42	And the Lord s., Who then is that	2036
Lu	12:54	he s. also to the people, When ye	3004
Lu	13:2	And Jesus answering s. unto them,	2036
Lu	13:7	Then s. he unto the dresser of his.	2036
Lu	13:8	s. unto him, Lord, let it alone	3004
Lu	13:12	and s. unto her, Woman, thou art	2036
Lu	13:14	s. unto the people, There are six	3004
Lu	13:15	s., Thou hypocrite, doth not each	2036
Lu	13:17	when he had s. these things, all	3004
Lu	13:18	s. he, Unto what is the kingdom	3004
Lu	13:20	And again he s., Whereunto shall	2036
Lu	13:23	s. one unto him, Lord, are there few	2036
Lu	13:23	that be saved? And he s. unto them,	2036
Lu	13:32	he s. unto them, Go ye, and tell	2036
Lu	14:12	s. he also to him that bade him,	3004
Lu	14:15	he s. unto him, Blessed is he that	2036
Lu	14:16	s. he unto him, A certain man made	2036
Lu	14:18	s. unto him, I have bought a piece	2036
Lu	14:19	another s., I have bought five yoke	2036
Lu	14:20	another s., I have married a wife,	2036
Lu	14:21	s. to his servant, Go out quickly	2036
Lu	14:22	servant s., Lord, it is done as	2036
Lu	14:23	lord s. unto the servant, Go out	2036
Lu	14:25	and he turned, and s. unto them,	2036
Lu	15:11	he s., A certain man had two sons:	2036
Lu	15:12	younger of them s. to his father,	2036
Lu	15:17	he s., How many hired servants	2036
Lu	15:21	son s. unto him, Father, I have	2036
Lu	15:22	father s. to his servants, Bring	2036
Lu	15:27	he s. unto him, Thy brother is	2036
Lu	15:29	s. to his father, Lo, these many	2036
Lu	15:31	he s. unto him, Son, thou art ever	2036
Lu	16:1	s. also unto his disciples, There	3004
Lu	16:2	s. unto him, How is it that I hear	2036
Lu	16:3	steward s. within himself, What	2036
Lu	16:5	s. unto the first, How much owest	3004
Lu	16:6	he s., An hundred measures of oil.	2036
Lu	16:6	And he s. unto him, Take thy bill,	2036
Lu	16:7	Then s. he to another, And how	2036
Lu	16:7	And he s., An hundred measures of	2036
Lu	16:7	he s. unto him, Take thy bill, and.	3004
Lu	16:15	s. unto them, Ye are they which	2036
Lu	16:24	he cried and s., Father Abraham,	2036
Lu	16:25	But Abraham s., Son, remember	2036
Lu	16:27	s., I pray thee therefore, father,	2036
Lu	16:30	And he s., Nay, father Abraham:	2036
Lu	16:31	he s. unto him, If they hear not	2036
Lu	17:1	Then s. he unto the disciples, It is	2036
Lu	17:5	apostles s. unto the Lord, Increase	2036
Lu	17:6	Lord s., If ye had faith as a grain	2036
Lu	17:13	s., Jesus, Master, have mercy on	3004
Lu	17:14	s. unto them, Go shew yourselves	2036
Lu	17:17	Jesus answering s., Were there not	2036
Lu	17:19	he s. unto him, Arise, Go thy way:	2036
Lu	17:20	come, he answered them and s.,	2036
Lu	17:22	And he s. unto the disciples, The	2036
Lu	17:37	they answered and s. unto him,	3004
Lu	17:37	he s. unto them, Wheresoever the	2036
Lu	18:4	afterward he s. within himself,	2036
Lu	18:6	the Lord s., Hear what the unjust	2036
Lu	18:16	s., Suffer little children to come	2036
Lu	18:19	Jesus s. unto him, Why callest thou	2036
Lu	18:21	he s., All these have I kept from my	2036
Lu	18:22	he s. unto him, Yet lackest thou one	2036
Lu	18:24	he s., How hardly shall they that	2036
Lu	18:26	they that heard it s., Who then can	2036
Lu	18:27	s., The things which are	2036
Lu	18:28	then Peter s., Lo, we have left all,	2036
Lu	18:29	And he s. unto them, Verily I say	2036
Lu	18:31	s. unto them, Behold, we go up to	2036
Lu	18:41	And he s., Lord, that I may receive	2036
Lu	18:42	And Jesus s. unto him, Receive thy	2036
Lu	19:5	and s. unto him, Zacchaeus, make	2036
Lu	19:8	and s. unto the Lord; Behold, Lord,	2036
Lu	19:9	and Jesus s. unto him, This day is	2036
Lu	19:12	he s. therefore, A certain nobleman	2036
Lu	19:13	s. unto them, Occupy till I come	2036
Lu	19:17	he s. unto him, Well, thou good	2036
Lu	19:19	he s. likewise to him, Be thou	2036
Lu	19:24	he s. unto them that stood by,	2036
Lu	19:25	they s. unto him, Lord, he hath	2036
Lu	19:32	found even as he had s. unto them.	2036
Lu	19:33	the owners thereof s. unto them,	2036
Lu	19:34	And they s., The Lord hath need of	2036
Lu	19:39	the multitude s. unto him, Master,	2036
Lu	19:40	he answered and s. unto them, I tell	2036
Lu	20:3	he answered and s. unto them, I will	2036
Lu	20:8	Jesus s. unto them, Neither tell	2036
Lu	20:13	Then s. the lord of the vineyard,	2036
Lu	20:16	when they heard it, they s., God	2036
Lu	20:17	s., What is this then that is	2036
Lu	20:23	s. unto them, Why tempt ye me?	2036
Lu	20:24	it? They answered and s., Caesar's	2036
Lu	20:25	he s. unto them, Render therefore	2036
Lu	20:34	Jesus answering s. unto them, The	2036
Lu	20:39	certain of the scribes answering s.,	2036
Lu	20:39	Master, thou hast well s.	2036
Lu	20:41	And he s. unto them, How say they	2036
Lu	20:42	Lord s. unto my Lord, Sit thou	2036
Lu	20:45	the people he s. unto his disciples,	2036
Lu	21:3	he s., Of a truth I say unto you,	2036
Lu	21:5	with goodly stones and gifts, he s.,	2036
Lu	21:8	And he s., Take heed that ye be	2036
Lu	21:10	Then s. he unto them, Nation	3004
Lu	22:9	And they s. unto him, Where wilt	2036
Lu	22:10	And he s. unto them, Behold, when	2036
Lu	22:13	and found as he had s. unto them:	2046
Lu	22:15	And he s. unto them, With desire	2036
Lu	22:17	the cup, and gave thanks, and s.,	2036
Lu	22:25	And he s. unto them, The kings of	2036
Lu	22:31	And the Lord s., Simon, Simon,	2036
Lu	22:33	he s. unto him, Lord, I am ready	2036
Lu	22:34	And he s., I tell thee, Peter, the	3004
Lu	22:35	And he s. unto them, When I sent	2036
Lu	22:35	any thing? And they s., Nothing.	2036
Lu	22:36	Then s. he unto them, But now, he	2036
Lu	22:38	And they s., Lord, behold, here are	2036
Lu	22:38	And he s. unto them, It is enough	2036
Lu	22:40	he s. unto them, Pray that ye enter	2036
Lu	22:46	And s. unto them, Why sleep ye?	2036
Lu	22:48	But Jesus s. unto him, Judas,	2036
Lu	22:49	they s. unto him, Lord, shall we	2036
Lu	22:51	Jesus answered and s., Suffer ye	2036
Lu	22:52	Jesus s. unto the chief priests, and	2036
Lu	22:56	s., This man was also with him.	2036
Lu	22:58	and s., Thou art also of them.	5346
Lu	22:58	And Peter s., Man, I am not.	2036
Lu	22:60	And Peter s., Man, I know not what	2036
Lu	22:61	how he had s. unto him, Before the	2036
Lu	22:67	And he s. unto them, If I tell you	2036
Lu	22:70	s. they all, Art thou then the Son	5346
Lu	22:70	he s. unto them, Ye say that I am	2036
Lu	22:71	they s., What need we any further	2036
Lu	23:3	he answered him and s., Thou	5346
Lu	23:4	Then s. Pilate to the chief priests	2036
Lu	23:14	S. unto them, Ye have brought this	2036
Lu	23:22	And he s. unto them the third time,	2036
Lu	23:28	s., Daughters of Jerusalem, weep	2036
Lu	23:34	Then s. Jesus, Father, forgive	3004
Lu	23:42	he s. unto Jesus, Lord, remember	3004
Lu	23:43	Jesus s. unto him, Verily I say	2036
Lu	23:46	had cried with a loud voice, he s.,	2036
Lu	23:46	having s. thus, he gave up the ghost	2036
Lu	24:5	they s. unto them, Why seek ye the	2036
Lu	24:17	he s. unto them, What manner of	2036
Lu	24:18	Cleopas, answering s. unto him, Art	2036
Lu	24:19	And he s. unto them, What things?	2036
Lu	24:19	they s. unto him, concerning Jesus	2036
Lu	24:23	angels, which s. that he was alive	3004
Lu	24:24	it even so as the women had s.:	2036
Lu	24:25	he s. unto them, O fools, and slow	2036
Lu	24:32	they s. one to another, Did not our	2036
Lu	24:38	s. unto them, Why are ye troubled?	2036
Lu	24:41	he s. unto them, Have ye here any	2036
Lu	24:44	he s. unto them, These are the	2036
Lu	24:46	s. unto them, Thus it is written,	2036
Joh	1:22	s. they unto him, Who art thou?	2036
Joh	1:23	He s., I am the voice of one crying	5346
Joh	1:23	the Lord, as s. the prophet Esaias	2036
Joh	1:25	s. unto him, Why baptizest thou	2036
Joh	1:30	This is he of whom I s., After me	2036
Joh	1:33	the same s. unto me, Upon whom	2036
Joh	1:38	They s. unto him, Rabbi, (which is	2036
Joh	1:42	he s., Thou art Simon the son of	2036
Joh	1:46	Nathanael s. unto him, Can there	2036
Joh	1:48,	50 Jesus answered and s. unto him	2036
Joh	1:50	Because I s. unto thee, I saw thee.	2036
Joh	2:16	And s. unto them that sold doves,	2036
Joh	2:18	answered the Jews and s. unto him,	2036
Joh	2:19	Jesus answered and s. unto them,	2036
Joh	2:20	Then s. the Jews, Forty and six	2036
Joh	2:22	that he had s. this unto them;	3004
Joh	2:22	and the word which Jesus had s.	2036
Joh	3:2	s. unto him, Rabbi, we know that	2036
Joh	3:3	Jesus answered and s. unto him,	2036
Joh	3:7	s. unto thee, Ye must be born	2036
Joh	3:9	Nicodemus answered and s. unto	2036
Joh	3:10	Jesus answered and s. unto him,	2036
Joh	3:26	came unto John, and s. unto him,	2036
Joh	3:27	John answered and s., A man can	2036
Joh	3:28	that I s., I am not the Christ, but	2036
Joh	4:10,	13 Jesus answered and s. unto her,	2036
Joh	4:17	The woman answered and s., I	2036
Joh	4:17	Jesus s. unto her, Thou hast well	3004
Joh	4:17	Thou hast well s., I have no	2036
Joh	4:27	yet no man s., What seekest thou?	2036
Joh	4:32	But he s. unto them, I have meat	2036
Joh	4:33	s. the disciples one to another,	3004
Joh	4:42	s. unto the woman, Now we believe,	3004
Joh	4:48	Then s. Jesus unto him, Except ye	2036
Joh	4:52	they s. unto him, Yesterday at the	2036
Joh	4:53	in the which Jesus s. unto him, Thy	2036
Joh	5:10	The Jews therefore s. unto him	3004
Joh	5:11	the same s. unto me, Take up thy	2036
Joh	5:12	that which s. unto thee, Take up	2036
Joh	5:14	s. unto him,...thou art made whole	2036
Joh	5:18	s. also that God was his Father,	3004
Joh	5:19	answered Jesus and s. unto them,	2036
Joh	6:6	And this he s. to prove him: for he	3004
Joh	6:10	Jesus s., Make the men sit down	2036
Joh	6:12	he s. unto his disciples, Gather up	3004
Joh	6:14	s., This is of a truth that prophet	3004
Joh	6:25	they s. unto him, Rabbi, when	2036
Joh	6:26	Jesus answered them and s., Verily,	2036
Joh	6:28	s. they unto him, What shall we do,	2036
Joh	6:29	Jesus answered and s. unto them,	2036
Joh	6:30	s. therefore unto him, What sign	2036
Joh	6:32	Then Jesus s. unto them, Verily,	2036
Joh	6:34	s. they unto him, Lord, evermore	2036
Joh	6:35	Jesus s. unto them, I am the bread	2036
Joh	6:36	I s. unto you, That ye also have	2036
Joh	6:41	because he s., I am the bread which	2036
Joh	6:42	they s., Is not this Jesus, the son	3004
Joh	6:43	s. unto them, Murmur not among	2036
Joh	6:53	Jesus s. unto them, Verily, verily, I	2036
Joh	6:59	These things s. he in the synagogue,	2036
Joh	6:60	had heard this, s., This is an hard	2036
Joh	6:61	s. unto them, Doth this offend you?	2036
Joh	6:65	And he s.,...that no man can come	3004
Joh	6:65	Therefore s. I unto you, that no	2046
Joh	6:67	s. Jesus unto the twelve, Will ye	2036
Joh	7:3	His brethren therefore s. unto him,	2036
Joh	7:6	Then Jesus s. unto them, My time	3004
Joh	7:9	he had s. these words unto them,	2036
Joh	7:11	at the feast, and s., Where is he?	3004
Joh	7:12	him: for some s., He is a good man:	3004
Joh	7:12	others s., Nay; but he deceiveth the	3004
Joh	7:16	s., My doctrine is not mine, but	2036
Joh	7:20	The people...s., Thou hast a devil:	2036
Joh	7:21	s. unto them, I have done one work,	2036
Joh	7:25	Then s. some of them of Jerusalem,	3004
Joh	7:31	and s., When Christ cometh, will he	3004
Joh	7:33	s. Jesus unto them, Yet a little	2036
Joh	7:35	s. the Jews among themselves,	2036
Joh	7:36	manner of saying is this that he s.,	2036

Joh 7:38 as the scripture hath s., out of...... 2036
Joh 7:40 s., Of a truth this is the Prophet........ 3004
Joh 7:41 Others s., This is the Christ. But........ 3004
Joh 7:41 some s., Shall Christ come out of....... 3004
Joh 7:42 scripture s., That Christ cometh 2036
Joh 7:45 and they s. unto them, Why have ye... 2036
Joh 7:52 and s. unto him, Art thou also of........ 2036
Joh 8:6 This they s., tempting him, that......... 3004
Joh 8:7 up himself, and s. unto them, ... 2036
Joh 8:10 he s. unto her, Woman, where are.. 2036
Joh 8:11 She s., No man, Lord. And............... 2036
Joh 8:11 Jesus s... Neither do I condemn....... 2036
Joh 8:13 Pharisees therefore s. unto him, ... 2036
Joh 8:14 s. unto them, Though I bear record. 2036
Joh 8:19 s. they unto him, Where is thy.......... 3004
Joh 8:21 s. Jesus again unto them, I go my....... 2036
Joh 8:22 s. the Jews, Will he kill himsf?........... 3004
Joh 8:23 s. unto them, Ye are from beneath;. 2036
Joh 8:24 I s. therefore unto you, that ye...... 2036
Joh 8:25 s. they unto him, Who art thou? 3004
Joh 8:25 Even the same that I s. unto you.. 2980
Joh 8:28 s. Jesus unto them, When ye have..... 2036
Joh 8:31 Then s. Jesus to those Jews which 3004
Joh 8:39 and s. unto him, Abraham is our 2036
Joh 8:41 s. they to him, We be not born of...... 2036
Joh 8:42 Jesus s. unto them, If God were........ 2036
Joh 8:48 s. unto him, Say we not well that....... 2036
Joh 8:52 s. the Jews unto him, Now we know... 2036
Joh 8:57 s. the Jews unto him, Thou art not...... 2036
Joh 8:58 Jesus s. unto them, Verily, verily, I 2036
Joh 9:7 s. unto him, Go, wash in the pool.... 2036
Joh 9:8 s., Is not this he that sat and........... 3004
Joh 9:9 Some s., This is he: others............... 3004
Joh 9:9 others s., He is like him:.........................
Joh 9:9 He is like him: but he s., I am he. 3004
Joh 9:10 s. they unto him, How were thine....... 3004
Joh 9:11 and s., A man that is called Jesus....... 2036
Joh 9:11 and s. unto me, Go to the pool of 2036
Joh 9:12 Then s. they unto him, Where is he?.. 2036
Joh 9:12 Where is he? He s., I know not......... 3004
Joh 9:15 He s. unto them, He put clay upon..... 2036
Joh 9:16 s. some of the Pharisees, This man..... 3004
Joh 9:16 Others s., How can a man that is a..... 3004
Joh 9:17 eyes? He s., He is a prophet............. 2036
Joh 9:20 s., We know that this is our son. 2036
Joh 9:23 Therefore s. his parents, He is of 2036
Joh 9:24 s. unto him, Give God the praise: 2036
Joh 9:25 and s., Whether he be a sinner or........ 2036
Joh 9:26 s. they to him again, What did he....... 2036
Joh 9:28 him, and s., Thou art his disciple; 2036
Joh 9:30 man answered and s. unto them,......... 2036
Joh 9:34 They...s. unto him, Thou wast 2036
Joh 9:35 s. unto him, Dost thou believe on..... 2036
Joh 9:36 answered and s., Who is he, Lord, ... 2036
Joh 9:37 Jesus s. unto him, Thou hast both..... 2036
Joh 9:38 And he s., Lord, I believe, And he..... 5346
Joh 9:39 Jesus s., For judgment I am come.. 2036
Joh 9:40 and s. unto him, Are we blind also?.... 2036
Joh 9:41 Jesus s. unto them, If ye were.......... 2036
Joh 10:7 s. Jesus unto them again, Verily,...... 2036
Joh 10:20 many of them s., He hath a devil, ... 3004
Joh 10:21 Others s., These are not the words.... 3004
Joh 10:24 s. unto him, How long dost thou 3004
Joh 10:26 not of my sheep, as I s. unto you...2036
Joh 10:34 in you law, I s., Ye are gods?....... 2036
Joh 10:36 because I s., I am the Son of God?.2036
Joh 10:41 him, and s., John did no miracle:........ 3004
Joh 11:4 he s., This sickness is not unto........ 2036
Joh 11:11 These things s. he: and after that....... 2036
Joh 11:12 s. his disciples, Lord, if he sleep, he.... 2036
Joh 11:14 s. Jesus unto them plainly, Lazarus..... 2036
Joh 11:16 Then s. Thomas, which is called 2036
Joh 11:21 s. Martha unto Jesus, Lord, if thou..... 2036
Joh 11:25 s. unto her, I am the resurrection,.. 2036
Joh 11:28 she had so s., she went her way,........ 2036
Joh 11:34 And s., Where have ye laid him?.... 2036
Joh 11:34 s. unto him, Lord, come and see......... 3004
Joh 11:36 s. the Jews, Behold how he loved 3004
Joh 11:37 some of them s., Could not this......... 2036
Joh 11:39 Jesus s., Take ye away the stone....... 3004
Joh 11:40 S. I not unto thee, that, if thou.... 2036
Joh 11:41 s., Father, I thank thee that thou..2036
Joh 11:42 the people which stand by I s. it,.. 2036
Joh 11:47 a council, and s., What do we? for....... 3004
Joh 11:49 s. unto them, Ye know nothing at........ 2036
Joh 12:6 This he s., not that he cared for the... 2036
Joh 12:7 s. Jesus, Let her alone: against...... 2036
Joh 12:19 Pharisees...s. among themselves, ... 2036
Joh 12:29 and heard it, s. that it thundered:....... 3004
Joh 12:29 others s., An angel spake to him........ 3004
Joh 12:30 Jesus...s., This voice came not......... 2036
Joh 12:33 This he s., signifying what death........ 3004
Joh 12:35 Jesus s. unto them, Yet a little........ 2036
Joh 12:39 because that Esaias s. again, ... 2036
Joh 12:41 These things s. Esaias, when he........ 2036
Joh 12:44 cried and s., He that believeth........ 2036
Joh 12:50 as the Father s. unto me, so I.......... 2046
Joh 13:7 Jesus...s. unto him, What I do......... 2036
Joh 13:11 therefore s. he, Ye are not all clean.... 2036
Joh 13:12 s. unto them, Know ye what I have. 2036
Joh 13:21 When Jesus had thus s., he was......... 2036
Joh 13:21 and testified, and s., Verily, verily,... 2036
Joh 13:27 s. Jesus unto him, That thou........... 3004
Joh 13:29 Jesus had s. unto him, Buy those........ 3004
Joh 13:31 Jesus s., Now is the Son of man..... 3004
Joh 13:33 and as I s. unto the Jews, Whither 2036
Joh 13:36 Simon Peter s. unto him, Lord, ... 3004
Joh 13:37 Peter s. unto him, Lord, why............ 3004
Joh 14:23 Jesus...s. unto him, If a man love..... 2036
Joh 14:26 Whatsoever I have s. unto you...... 2036
Joh 14:28 Ye have heard how I s. unto you... 2036
Joh 14:28 because I s., I go unto the Father: 2036
Joh 15:20 the word that I s. unto you, The... 2036
Joh 16:4 I s. not unto you at the beginning, 2036
Joh 16:6 I have s. these things unto you,.... 2980
Joh 16:15 therefore s. I, that he shall take... 2036
Joh 16:17 s. some of his disciples among........... 2036
Joh 16:18 They s. therefore, What is this.......... 3004
Joh 16:19 and s. unto them, Do ye enquire...... 2036
Joh 16:19 I s., A little while, and ye shall..... 2036
Joh 16:29 His disciples s. unto him, Lo, now...... 3004
Joh 17:1 eyes to heaven, and s., Father, the.. 2036
Joh 18:4 and s. unto them, Whom seek ye?..... 2036
Joh 18:6 then as he had s. unto them, I am...... 2036
Joh 18:7 ye? and they s., Jesus of Nazareth. 2036
Joh 18:11 s. Jesus unto Peter, Put up thy....... 2036
Joh 18:20 and in secret have I s. nothing...... 2980
Joh 18:21 heard me, what I have s. unto....... 2980
Joh 18:21 behold, they know what I s............ 2036
Joh 18:25 They s. therefore unto him, Art not.... 2036
Joh 18:25 He denied it, and s., I am not. 2036
Joh 18:29 and s., What accusation bring ye........ 2036
Joh 18:30 They...s. unto him, If he were not..... 2036
Joh 18:31 s. Pilate unto them, Take ye him, ... 2036
Joh 18:31 Jews...s. unto him, It is not lawful...... 2036
Joh 18:33 s. unto him, Art thou the King of....... 2036
Joh 18:37 s. unto him, Art thou a king then?...... 2036
Joh 18:38 when he had s. this, he went out....... 2036
Joh 19:3 And s., Hail, King of the Jews!.......... 3004
Joh 19:21 s. the chief priests of the Jews to....... 3004
Joh 19:21 that he s., I am king of the Jews....... 2036
Joh 19:24 s. therefore among themselves, Let.... 2036
Joh 19:30 the vinegar, he s., It is finished:...... 2036
Joh 20:14 she had thus s., she turned herself..... 2036
Joh 20:20 he had so s., he shewed unto them.... 2036
Joh 20:21 s. Jesus to them again, Peace be........ 2036
Joh 20:22 he had s. this, he breathed on them.... 2036
Joh 20:25 other disciples...s. unto him, We........ 3004
Joh 20:25 he s. unto them, Except I shall see 2036
Joh 20:26 midst, and s., Peace be unto you..... 2036
Joh 20:28 Thomas...s. unto him, My Lord......... 2036
Joh 21:6 and he s. unto them, Cast the net.... 2036
Joh 21:17 s. unto him the third time, Lovest...... 2036
Joh 21:17 he s. unto him, Lord, thou knowest.... 2036
Joh 21:20 s., Lord, which is he that betrayeth.... 2036
Joh 21:23 yet Jesus s. not unto him, He shall..... 2036
Ac 1:7 he s. unto them, It is not for you.... 2036
Ac 1:11 Which also s., Ye men of Galilee, ... 2036
Ac 1:15 in the midst of the disciples, and s.,..... 2036
Ac 1:24 and s., Thou, Lord, which knowest..... 2036
Ac 2:13 Others mocking s., These men are..... 3004
Ac 2:14 and s. unto them, Ye men of Judaea, ... 669
Ac 2:34 The Lord s. unto my Lord, Sit thou.... 2036
Ac 2:37 s. unto Peter and to the rest of the.... 2036
Ac 2:38 Peter s. unto them, Repent, and be.... 5346
Ac 3:4 him with John s., Look on us............ 2036
Ac 3:6 Peter s., Silver and gold have I none;. 2036
Ac 3:22 Moses truly s. unto the fathers, A...... 2036
Ac 4:8 Peter,...s. unto them, Ye rulers of..... 2036
Ac 4:19 s. unto them, Whether it be right....... 2036
Ac 4:23 priests and elders had s. unto them. ... 2036
Ac 4:24 s., Lord, thou art God, which hast 2036
Ac 4:25 mouth of thy servant David hast s.,.... 2036
Ac 4:32 neither s. any of them that ought 3004
Ac 5:3 Peter s., Ananias, why hath Satan...... 2036
Ac 5:8 and she s., Yea, for so much........... 2036
Ac 5:9 Peter s. unto her, How is it that ye.... 2036
Ac 5:19 and brought them forth, and s., ... 2036
Ac 5:29 and s., We ought to obey God rather.. 2036
Ac 5:35 And s. unto them, Ye men of Israel,... 2036
Ac 6:2 s., It is not reason that we should...... 2036
Ac 6:11 men, which s., We have heard him...... 3004
Ac 6:13 set up false witnesses, which s., ... 3004
Ac 7:1 Then s. the high priest, Are these...... 2036
Ac 7:2 he s., Men, brethren, and fathers,...... 5346
Ac 7:3 s. unto him, Get thee out of thy 2036
Ac 7:7 be in bondage will I judge, s. God: 2036
Ac 7:33 then s. the Lord to him, Put off thy..... 2036
Ac 7:37 which s. unto the children of Israel, ... 2036
Ac 7:56 And s., Behold, I see the heavens...... 2036
Ac 7:60 when he had s. this, he fell asleep...... 2036
Ac 8:20 But Peter s. unto him, Thy money 2036
Ac 8:24 Simon, and s., Pray ye to the Lord 2036
Ac 8:29 the Spirit s. unto Philip, Go near, ... 2036
Ac 8:30 s., Understandest thou what thou....... 2036
Ac 8:31 and he s., How can I, except some 2036
Ac 8:34 s., I pray thee, of whom speaketh....... 2036
Ac 8:36 the eunuch s., See, here is water;...... 5346
Ac 8:37 Philip s., If thou believest with all....... 2036
Ac 8:37 And he answered and s., I believe...... 2036
Ac 9:5 And he s., Who art thou, Lord?.......... 2036
Ac 9:5 the Lord s., I am Jesus whom thou 2036
Ac 9:6 and astonished s., Lord, what wilt....... 2036
Ac 9:6 the Lord s. unto him, Arise, and go.. 2036
Ac 9:10 s. the Lord in a vision, Ananias....... 2036
Ac 9:10 and he s., Behold, I am here, Lord. ... 2036
Ac 9:11 the Lord s. unto him, Arise, and go........
Ac 9:15 the Lord s. unto him, Go thy way:... 2036
Ac 9:17 his hands on him s., Brother Saul,...... 2036
Ac 9:21 heard him were amazed, and s.;......... 3004
Ac 9:34 Peter s. unto him, AEneas, Jesus....... 2036
Ac 9:40 him to the body s., Tabitha, arise........ 2036
Ac 10:4 was afraid, and s., What is it, Lord? ... 2036
Ac 10:4 s. unto him, Thy prayers and thine..... 2036
Ac 10:14 Peter s., Not so, Lord; for I have...... 2036
Ac 10:19 Spirit s. unto him, Behold, three 2036
Ac 10:21 s., Behold, I am he whom ye seek: 2036
Ac 10:22 And they s., Cornelius the centurion,.. 2036
Ac 10:28 he s. unto them, Ye know how that.... 5346
Ac 10:30 Cornelius s., Four days ago I was 5346
Ac 10:31 s., Cornelius, thy prayer is heard,...... 5346
Ac 10:34 s., Of a truth I perceive that God....... 2036
Ac 11:8 But I s., Not so, Lord: for nothing..... 2036
Ac 11:13 s. unto him, Send men to Joppa, ... 2036
Ac 11:16 he s., John indeed baptized with.... 3004
Ac 12:8 the angel s. unto him, Gird thyself,..... 2036
Ac 12:11 he s., Now I know of a surety, that.... 2036
Ac 12:15 And they s. unto her, Thou art mad. .. 2036
Ac 12:15 so. Then s. they, It is his angel......... 3004
Ac 12:17 he s., Go shew these things unto........ 2036
Ac 13:2 the Holy Ghost s., Separate me......... 2036
Ac 13:10 And s., O full of all subtilty and all...... 2036
Ac 13:16 beckoning with his hand s., Men of..... 2036
Ac 13:22 and s., I have found David the son 2036
Ac 13:25 he s., Whom think ye that I am?........ 3004
Ac 13:34 s. on this wise, I will give you the...... 5346
Ac 13:46 s., it was necessary that the word....... 2036
Ac 14:10 S. with a loud voice, Stand upright..... 2036
Ac 15:1 and s., Except ye be circumcised after ......
Ac 15:7 Peter rose up, and s. unto them, ... 2036
Ac 15:36 Paul s. unto Barnabas, Let us go 2036
Ac 16:18 and s. to the spirit, I command thee ... 2036
Ac 16:30 and s., Sirs, what must I do to be....... 5346
Ac 16:31 they s., Believe on the Lord Jesus 2036
Ac 16:37 But Paul s. unto them, They have....... 5346
Ac 17:18 some s., What will this babbler say? ... 3004
Ac 17:22 s., ye men of Athens, I perceive........ 5346
Ac 17:28 s., For we are also his offspring......... 2046
Ac 17:32 others s., We will hear thee again 2036
Ac 18:6 s. unto them. Your blood be upon 2036
Ac 18:14 Gallio s. unto the Jews, If it were a.... 2036
Ac 19:2 He s. unto them. Have ye received 2036
Ac 19:2 And they s. unto him, We have not 2036
Ac 19:3 he s. unto them, Unto what then 2036
Ac 19:3 And they s., Unto John's baptism. 2036
Ac 19:4 s. Paul, John verily baptized with........ 2036
Ac 19:15 evil spirit...s., Jesus I know, and........ 2036
Ac 19:25 s., Sirs, ye know that by this craft 2036
Ac 19:35 s., Ye men of Ephesus, what man...... 5346
Ac 20:10 him s., Trouble not yourselves; 2036

Ac 20:18 he **s.** unto them, ye know, from the ... *2036*
Ac 20:35 words of the Lord Jesus, how he **s.**,... *2036*
Ac 21:4 who **s.** to Paul through the Spirit,........ *3004*
Ac 21:11 **s.**, Thus saith the Holy Ghost, So....... *2036*
Ac 21:20 **s.** unto him, Thou seest, brother,....... *2036*
Ac 21:37 he **s.** unto the chief captain, May I..... *3004*
Ac 21:37 Who **s.**, Canst thou speak Greek? *5346*
Ac 21:39 Paul **s.**, I am a man which am a......... *2036*
Ac 22:8 And he **s.** unto me, I am Jesus of.... *2036*
Ac 22:10 And I **s.**, What shall I do, Lord? *2036*
Ac 22:10 the Lord **s.** unto me, Arise, and go... *2036*
Ac 22:13 **s.** unto me, Brother Saul, receive........ *2036*
Ac 22:14 he **s.**, The God of our fathers hath..... *2036*
Ac 22:19 And I **s.**, Lord, they know that I......... *2036*
Ac 22:21 he **s.** unto me, Depart: for I will........ *2036*
Ac 22:22 **s.**, Away with such a fellow from *3004*
Ac 22:25 Paul **s.** unto the centurion that........... *2036*
Ac 22:27 captain came, and **s.** unto him,........... *2036*
Ac 22:27 art thou a Roman? He **s.**, Yea. *5346*
Ac 22:28 And Paul **s.**, But I was free born. *5346*
Ac 23:1 earnestly beholding the council, **s.**, ... *2036*
Ac 23:3 Then **s.** Paul unto him, God shall *2036*
Ac 23:4 **s.**, Revilest thou God's high priest?..... *2036*
Ac 23:5 **s.** Paul, I wist not, brethren, that....... *5346*
Ac 23:7 when he had so **s.**, there arose a *2980*
Ac 23:11 and **s.**, Be of good cheer, Paul: for..*2036*
Ac 23:14 and **s.**, We have bound ourselves *2036*
Ac 23:17 **s.**, Bring this young man unto the *5346*
Ac 23:18 and **s.**, Paul the prisoner called me..... *5346*
Ac 23:20 And he **s.**, The Jews have agreed....... *2036*
Ac 23:35 I will hear thee, **s.** he, when thine...... *5346*
Ac 24:22 **s.**, When Lysias the chief captain *2036*
Ac 25:5 Let them therefore, **s.** he, which........ *5346*
Ac 25:9 Paul, and **s.**, Wilt thou go up to *2036*
Ac 25:10 Then **s.** Paul, I stand at Caesar's *2036*
Ac 25:22 Agrippa **s.** unto Festus, I would.......... *5346*
Ac 25:22 To morrow, **s.** he, thou shalt hear...... *5346*
Ac 25:24 And Festus **s.**, King Agrippa, and....... *5346*
Ac 26:1 Agrippa **s.** unto Paul, Thou art........... *5346*
Ac 26:15 And I **s.**, Who art thou, Lord? *2036*
Ac 26:15 And he **s.**, I am Jesus whom thou... *2036*
Ac 26:24 Festus **s.** with a loud voice, Paul,....... *5346*
Ac 26:25 he **s.**, I am not mad, most noble *5346*
Ac 26:28 Then Agrippa **s.** unto Paul, Almost *5346*
Ac 26:29 Paul **s.**, I would to God, that not........ *2036*
Ac 26:32 **s.** Agrippa unto Festus, This man....... *5346*
Ac 27:10 **s.** unto them, Sirs, I perceive that...... *3004*
Ac 27:21 in the midst of them, and **s.**, Sirs,...... *2036*
Ac 27:31 Paul **s.** to the centurion and to the *2036*
Ac 28:4 **s.** among themselves, No doubt *3004*
Ac 28:6 minds and **s.** that he was a god.......... *3004*
Ac 28:17 he **s.** unto them, Men and brethren, ... *3004*
Ac 28:21 And they **s.** unto him, We neither *2036*
Ac 28:29 he had **s.** these words, the Jews *2036*
Ro 7:7 law had **s.**, Thou shalt not covet. *3004*
Ro 9:12 **s.** unto her, The elder shall serve *4483*
Ro 9:26 **s.** unto them, Ye are not my people;... *4483*
Ro 9:29 Esaias **s.** before, Except the Lord...... *4280*
1Co 11:24 he brake it, and **s.**, Take, eat:......... *2036*
2Co 6:16 as God hath **s.**, I will dwell in them, ... *2036*
2Co 7:3 **s.** before, that ye are in our hearts..... *4280*
2Co 9:3 that, as I **s.**, ye may be ready: *3004*
2Co 12:9 And he **s.** unto me, My grace is......... *2046*
Ga 1:9 As we **s.** before, so say I now........... *4280*
Ga 2:14 I **s.** unto Peter before them all, If *2036*
Tit 1:12 **s.**, The Cretians are alway liars, ... *2036*
Heb 1:5 the angels **s.** he at any time, Thou *2036*
Heb 1:13 angels **s.** he at any time, Sit on my *2046*
Heb 3:10 and **s.**, They do alway err in their *2036*
Heb 3:15 While it is **s.**, To day if ye will hear.... *3004*
Heb 4:3 as he **s.**, As I have sworn in my........ *2046*
Heb 4:7 as it is **s.**, To day if ye will hear his*2046*
Heb 5:5 he that **s.** unto him, Thou art my *2980*
Heb 7:21 that **s.** unto him, The Lord sware....... *3004*
Heb 10:7 then **s.** I, Lo, I come (in the *2036*
Heb 10:8 Above when he **s.**, Sacrifice and......... *3004*
Heb 10:9 Then **s.** he, Lo, I come to do thy......... *2046*
Heb 10:15 us: for after that he had **s.** before, ... *4280*
Heb 10:30 **s.**, Vengeance belongeth unto me, ... *2036*
Heb 11:18 it was **s.**, That in Isaac shall thy *2980*
Heb 12:21 Moses **s.**, I exceedingly fear and......... *2036*
Heb 13:5 he hath **s.**, I will never leave thee, ... *2046*
Jas 2:11 that **s.**, Do not commit adultery, ... *2036*
Jas 2:11 **s.** also, Do not kill. Now if thou......... *2036*
Jude 9 but **s.**, The Lord rebuke thee. *2036*
Re 4:1 which **s.**, Come up hither, and I......... *3004*
Re 5:14 **s.** And the four beasts **s.**, Amen. *3004*
Re 6:11 and it was **s.** unto them, that they...... *4483*
Re 6:16 **s.** to the mountains and rocks, ... *3004*
Re 7:14 I **s.** unto him, Sir, thou knowest. *2046*
Re 7:14 he **s.** to me, These are they which..... *2036*
Re 10:8 **s.**, Go and take the little book *3004*
Re 10:9 and **s.** unto him, Give me the little *3004*
Re 10:9 **s.** unto me, Take it, and eat it up; *3004*
Re 10:11 **s.** unto me, Thou must prophesy........ *3004*
Re 17:7 angel **s.** unto me, Wherefore didst...... *2036*
Re 19:3 And again they **s.**, Alleluia................ *2046*
Re 19:10 he **s.** unto me, See thou do it not: *3004*
Re 21:5 he that sat upon the throne **s.**, ... *2036*
Re 21:5 And he **s.** unto me, Write: for *3004*
Re 21:6 And he **s.** unto me, It is done. I *2036*
Re 22:6 he **s.** unto me, These sayings are....... *2036*

SAIDST

Ge 12:19 Why **s.** thou, She is my sister? so 559
Ge 26:9 and how **s.** thou, She is my sister? 559
Ge 32:9 the Lord which **s.** unto me, Return 559
Ge 32:12 thou **s.**, I will surely do thee good, ... 559
Ge 44:21 thou **s.** unto thy servants, Bring.......... 559
Ge 44:23 thou **s.** unto thy servants, Except 559
Ex 32:13 **s.** unto them, I will multiply your 1696
Jg 9:38 thy mouth, wherewith thou **s.**, ... 559
1Ki 2:42 and thou **s.** unto me, The word that..... 559
Job 35:2 that thou **s.**, My righteousness is......... 559
Job 35:3 For thou **s.**, What advantage will 559
Ps 27:8 When thou **s.**, Seek ye my face; my..... 559
Ps 89:19 **s.**, I have laid help upon one that is...... 559
Isa 47:7 thou **s.**, I shall be a lady for ever:........ 559
Isa 57:10 yet **s.** thou not, There is no hope: 559
Jer 2:20 thou **s.**, I will not transgress; when...... 559
Jer 2:25 thou **s.**, There is no hope: no; for I 559
Jer 22:21 but thou **s.**, I will not hear. 559
La 3:57 called upon thee: thou **s.**, Fear not....... 559
Eze 25:3 Because thou **s.**, Aha, against my 559
Ho 13:10 whom thou **s.**, Give me a king and....... 559
Joh 4:18 husband: in that **s.** thou truly....... *2046*

SAIL See also MAINSAIL; SAILED; SAILING.

Isa 33:23 they could not spread the **s.**.............. 5251
Eze 27:7 thou spreadest forth to be thy **s.**;........ 5251
Ac 20:3 as he was about to **s.** into Syria, ... *321*
Ac 20:16 For Paul had determined to **s.** by....... *3896*
Ac 27:1 that we should **s.** into Italy, they *636*
Ac 27:2 to **s.** by the coasts of Asia; one *4126*
Ac 27:17 strake **s.**, and so were driven............ *4632*
Ac 27:24 thee all them that **s.** with thee........... *4126*

SAILED

Lu 8:23 But as they **s.** he fell asleep: and *4126*
Ac 13:4 and from thence they **s.** to Cyprus....... *636*
Ac 14:26 thence **s.** to Antioch, from whence....... *636*
Ac 15:39 took Mark, and **s.** unto Cyprus; *1602*
Ac 18:18 brethren, and **s.** thence into Syria,...... *1602*
Ac 18:21 God will. And he **s.** from Ephesus........ *321*
Ac 20:6 we **s.** away from Philippi after the *1602*
Ac 20:13 before to ship, and **s.** unto Assos,........ *321*
Ac 20:15 we **s.** thence, and came the next *636*
Ac 21:3 on the left hand, and **s.** into Syria,...... *4126*
Ac 27:4 we **s.** under Cyprus, because the *5284*
Ac 27:5 we had **s.** over the sea of Cilicia *1277*
Ac 27:7 when we had **s.** slowly many days,..... *1020*
Ac 27:7 we **s.** under Crete, over against.......... *5284*
Ac 27:13 thence, they **s.** close by Crete........... *3881*

SAILING

Ac 21:2 a ship **s.** over unto Phenicia, we *1276*
Ac 27:6 a ship of Alexandria **s.** into Italy;........ *4126*
Ac 27:9 and when **s.** was now dangerous *4144*

SAILORS

Re 18:17 **s.**, and as many as trade by sea,........ *3492*

SAINT See also SAINTS.

Ps 106:16 and Aaron the **s.** of the Lord............ 6918
Da 8:13 Then I heard one **s.** speaking, ... 6918
Da 8:13 and another **s.** said unto that 6918
Da 8:13 said unto that certain **s.** which spake, ...
Php 4:21 Salute every **s.** in Christ Jesus............. *40*

SAINTS See also SAINTS'.

De 33:2 came with ten thousands of **s.** 6944
De 33:3 all his **s.** are in thy hand: and 6918
1Sa 2:9 He will keep the feet of his **s.**, ... 2623
2Ch 6:41 and let thy **s.** rejoice in goodness. 2623
Job 5:1 to which of the **s.** wilt thou turn? 6918
Job 15:15 he putteth no trust in his **s.**; yea,....... 6918
Ps 16:3 But to the **s.** that are in the earth, ... 6918
Ps 30:4 Sing unto the Lord, O ye **s.** of his,..... 2623
Ps 31:23 O love the Lord, all ye his **s.**: for....... 2623
Ps 34:9 O fear the Lord, ye his **s.**: for........... 6918
Ps 37:28 and forsaketh not his **s.**; they are....... 2623
Ps 50:5 Gather my **s.** together unto me;......... 2623
Ps 52:9 name; for it is good before thy **s.**. 2623
Ps 79:2 the flesh of thy **s.** unto the beasts...... 2623
Ps 85:8 peace unto his people, and to his **s.**: ... 2623
Ps 89:5 also in the congregation of the **s.**........ 6918
Ps 89:7 be feared in the assembly of the **s.**,..... 6918
Ps 97:10 he preserveth the souls of his **s.**; 2623
Ps 116:15 of the Lord is the death of his **s.**........ 2623
Ps 132:9 and let thy **s.** shout for joy................ 2623
Ps 132:16 and her **s.** shall shout aloud for joy. 2623
Ps 145:10 Lord; and thy **s.** shall bless thee. 2623
Ps 148:14 his people, the praise of all his **s.**; 2623
Ps 149:1 praise in the congregation of **s.**. 2623
Ps 149:5 Let the **s.** be joyful in glory: let 2623
Ps 149:9 this honour have all his **s.**. Praise....... 2623
Pr 2:8 and preserveth the way of his **s.**.......... 2623
Da 7:18 the **s.** of the most High shall take....... 6922
Da 7:21 same horn made war with the **s.**,....... 6922
Da 7:22 judgment was given to the **s.** of the.... 6922
Da 7:22 that the **s.** possessed the kingdom...... 6922
Da 7:25 wear out the **s.** of the most High, ... 6922
Da 7:27 people of the **s.** of the most High, ... 6922
Ho 11:12 God, and is faithful with the **s.**.......... 6918
Zec 14:5 shall come, and all the **s.** with thee..... 6918
Mt 27:52 bodies of the **s.** which slept arose,......... *40*
Ac 9:13 much evil he hath done to thy **s.** at *40*
Ac 9:32 also to the **s.** which dwelt at Lydda. *40*
Ac 9:41 he had called the **s.** and widows,........... *40*
Ac 26:10 many of the **s.** did I shut up in prison,.... *40*
Ro 1:7 Rome, beloved of God, called to be **s.**:... *40*
Ro 3:27 he maketh intercession for the **s.** *40*
Ro 12:13 Distributing to the necessity of **s.**; *40*
Ro 15:25 Jerusalem to minister unto the **s.** *40*
Ro 15:26 the poor **s.** which are at Jerusalem. *40*
Ro 15:31 Jerusalem may be accepted of the **s.**; *40*
Ro 16:2 her in the Lord, as becometh **s.**,........... *40*
Ro 16:15 and all the **s.** which are with them. *40*
1Co 1:2 in Christ Jesus, called to be **s.**, ... *40*
1Co 6:1 the unjust, and not before the **s.**? *40*
1Co 6:2 that the **s.** shall judge the world?........... *40*
1Co 14:33 of peace, as in all churches of the **s.**. *40*
1Co 16:1 concerning the collection for the **s.**, ... *40*
1Co 16:15 addicted...to the ministry of the **s.**,)....... *40*
2Co 1:1 all the **s.** which are in all Achaia: *40*
2Co 8:4 fellowship of...ministering to the **s.**. *40*
2Co 9:1 as touching the ministering to the **s.**, ... *40*
2Co 9:12 not only supplieth the want of the **s.**, ... *40*
2Co 13:13 All the **s.** salute you. *40*
Eph 1:1 to the **s.** which are at Ephesus, and....... *40*
Eph 1:15 Lord Jesus, and love unto all the **s.**, ... *40*
Eph 1:18 the glory of his inheritance in the **s.**,...... *40*
Eph 2:19 fellowcitizens with the **s.**, and of the *40*
Eph 3:8 who am less than the least of all **s.**,....... *40*
Eph 3:18 to comprehend with all **s.** what is the..... *40*
Eph 4:12 For the perfecting of the **s.**, for the....... *40*
Eph 5:3 named among you, as becometh **s.**; *40*
Eph 6:18 and supplication for all **s.**; *40*
Php 1:1 to all the **s.** in Christ Jesus which are..... *40*
Php 4:22 All the **s.** salute you, chiefly they *40*
Col 1:2 To the **s.** and faithful brethren in.......... *40*
Col 1:4 the love which ye have to all the **s.**, ... *40*
Col 1:12 of the inheritance of the **s.** in light: *40*
Col 1:26 but now is made manifest to his **s.**: *40*
1Th 3:13 the coming of...Christ with all his **s.**....... *40*
2Th 1:10 he shall come to be glorified in his **s.**, ... *40*
Phm 5 the Lord Jesus, and toward all **s.**;.......... *40*
Phm 7 the bowels of the **s.** are refreshed by..... *40*
Heb 6:10 in that ye have ministered to the **s.**, ... *40*
Heb 13:24 have the rule over you, and all the **s.**...... *40*
Jude 3 faith...once delivered unto the **s.**. *40*
Jude 14 cometh with ten thousands of his **s.**, ... *40*
Re 5:8 odours, which are the prayers of **s.**. *40*
Re 8:3 offer it with the prayers of all **s.**............ *40*
Re 8:4 came with the prayers of the **s.**, ... *40*
Re 11:18 servants the prophets, and to the **s.**, ... *40*
Re 13:7 unto him to make war with the **s.**,......... *40*
Re 13:10 the patience and the faith of the **s.**. *40*
Re 14:12 Here is the patience of the **s.**: here....... *40*
Re 15:3 true are thy ways, thou King of **s.**.......... *40*
Re 16:6 shed the blood of **s.** and prophets,......... *40*
Re 17:6 drunken with the blood of the **s.**, ... *40*

Re 18:24 the blood of prophets, and of **s**., and...... *40*
Re 19:8 fine linen is the righteousness of **s**......... *40*
Re 20:9 and compassed the camp of the **s**......... *40*

SAINTS'
1Ti 5:10 if she have washed the **s**. feet, if she..... *40*

SAITH
Ge 22:16 myself have I sworn, **s**. the Lord, ... 5002
Ge 32:4 Thy servant Jacob **s**. thus, I have........ 559
Ge 41:55 unto Joseph; what he **s**. to you, do. 559
Ge 44:7 Wherefore **s**. my lord these words? 1696
Ge 45:9 Thus **s**. thy son Joseph, God hath........ 559
Ex 4:22 Thus **s**. the Lord, Israel is my son,...... 559
Ex 5:1 **s**. the Lord God of Israel, Let my......... 559
Ex 5:10 **s**. Pharaoh, I will not give you straw. ... 559
Ex 7:17 **s**. the Lord, In this thou shalt know 559
Ex 8:1, 20 **s**. the Lord, Let my people go,....... 559
Ex 9:1, 13 **s**. the Lord God of the Hebrews, ... 559
Ex 10:3 **s**. the Lord God of the Hebrews,......... 559
Ex 11:4 **s**. the Lord, About midnight will I........ 559
Ex 32:27 **s**. the Lord God of Israel, Put every 559
Nu 14:28 As truly as I live, **s**. the Lord, as ye 559
Nu 20:14 **s**. thy brother Israel, Thou knowest 559
Nu 22:16 Thus **s**. Balak the son of Zippor, Let.... 559
Nu 24:13 but what the Lord **s**., that will I......... 1696
Nu 32:27 the Lord to battle, as my lord **s**......... 1696
Jos 5:14 What **s**. my lord unto his servant?...... 1696
Jos 7:13 **s**. the Lord God of Israel, There is...... 559
Jos 22:16 Thus **s**. the whole congregation of........ 559
Jos 24:2 Thus **s**. the Lord God of Israel, Your 559
Jg 6:8 **s**. the Lord God of Israel, I brought 559
Jg 11:15 **s**. Jephthah, Israel took not away......... 559
1Sa 2:27 **s**. the Lord, Did I plainly appear.......... 559
1Sa 2:30 Wherefore...Lord God of Israel **s**., ... 5002
1Sa 2:30 now the Lord **s**., Be it far from me; ... 5002
1Sa 9:6 all that he **s**. cometh...to pass: 1696
1Sa 10:18 **s**. the Lord God of Israel, I brought..... 559
1Sa 15:2 **s**. the Lord of hosts, I remember 559
1Sa 20:3 he **s**., Let not Jonathan know this, ... 559
1Sa 24:13 As **s**. the proverb of the ancients,........ 559
2Sa 7:5 Thus **s**. the Lord, Shalt thou build......... 559
2Sa 7:8 **s**. the Lord of hosts, I took thee 559
2Sa 12:7 Thus **s**. the Lord...I anointed thee 559
2Sa 12:11 **s**. the Lord, Behold, I will raise up 559
2Sa 14:10 Whosoever **s**. ought unto thee, ... 1696
2Sa 17:5 and let us hear likewise what he **s**...... 6310
2Sa 24:12 Thus **s**. the Lord, I offer thee three ... 1696
1Ki 2:30 him, Thus **s**. the king, Come forth. 559
1Ki 3:23 one **s**., This is my son that liveth, ... 559
1Ki 3:23 and the other **s**., Nay; but thy son is.... 559
1Ki 11:31 thus **s**. the Lord, the God of Israel, ... 559
1Ki 12:24 Thus **s**. the Lord, Ye shall not go up,... 559
1Ki 13:2 said, O altar, altar, thus **s**. the Lord;.... 559
1Ki 13:21 Thus **s**. the Lord, Forasmuch as.......... 559
1Ki 14:7 Thus **s**. the Lord God of Israel,........... 559
1Ki 17:14 For thus **s**. the Lord God of Israel. 559
1Ki 20:2 said unto him, Thus **s**. Ben-hadad, ... 559
1Ki 20:13 Thus **s**. the Lord, Hast thou seen all.... 559
1Ki 20:14 Thus **s**. the Lord, Even by the young... 559
1Ki 20:28 **s**. the Lord, Because the Syrians.......... 559
1Ki 20:32 Thy servant Ben-hadad **s**., I pray......... 559
1Ki 20:42 **s**. the Lord, Because thou hast let go... 559
1Ki 21:19 Thus **s**. the Lord, Hast thou killed, ... 559
1Ki 21:19 **s**. the Lord, In the place where dogs.... 559
1Ki 22:11 **s**. the Lord, With these shalt thou 559
1Ki 22:14 what the Lord **s**. unto me, that will...... 559
1Ki 22:27 Thus **s**. the king, Put this fellow in 559
2Ki 1:4 **s**. the Lord, Thou shalt not come 559
2Ki 1:6 Thus **s**. the Lord, Is it not because...... 559
2Ki 1:16 **s**. the Lord, Forasmuch as thou........... 559
2Ki 2:21 **s**. the Lord, I have healed these.......... 559
2Ki 3:16 **s**. the Lord, Make this valley full of...... 559
2Ki 3:17 **s**. the Lord, Ye shall not see wind, ... 559
2Ki 4:43 for thus **s**. the Lord, They shall eat,...... 559
2Ki 5:13 he **s**. to thee, Wash, and be clean? 559
2Ki 7:1 **s**. the Lord, To morrow about this....... 559
2Ki 9:3 **s**. the Lord, I have anointed thee......... 559
2Ki 9:6 **s**. the Lord...I have anointed thee........ 559
2Ki 9:12 **s**. the Lord, I have anointed thee......... 559
2Ki 9:18, 19 Thus **s**. the king, Is it peace? 559
2Ki 9:26 the blood of his sons, **s**. the Lord; 559
2Ki 9:26 requite...in this plat, **s**. the Lord. 5002
2Ki 18:19 Thus **s**. the great king, the king of....... 559
2Ki 18:29 Thus **s**. the king, Let not Hezekiah...... 559
2Ki 18:31 thus **s**. the king of Assyria, Make an 559
2Ki 19:3 Thus **s**. Hezekiah, This day is a day..... 559
2Ki 19:6 Thus **s**. the Lord, Be not afraid of 559
2Ki 19:20 Thus **s**. the Lord God of Israel, That.... 559
2Ki 19:32 **s**. the Lord concerning the king........... 559
2Ki 19:33 come into this city, **s**. the Lord.......... 5002
2Ki 20:1 Thus **s**. the Lord, Set thine house 559
2Ki 20:5 Thus **s**. the Lord, the God of David 559
2Ki 20:17 nothing shall be left, **s**. the Lord.......... 559
2Ki 21:12 **s**. the Lord God of Israel, Behold, ... 559
2Ki 22:15 **s**. the Lord God of Israel, Tell the....... 559
2Ki 22:16 **s**. the Lord, Behold, I will bring evil..... 559
2Ki 22:18 Thus **s**. the Lord God of Israel, As...... 559
2Ki 22:19 also have heard thee, **s**. the Lord....... 5002
1Ch 17:4 Thus **s**. the Lord, Thou shalt not.......... 559
1Ch 17:7 **s**. the Lord of hosts, I took thee 559
1Ch 21:10 **s**. the Lord, I offer thee three things:... 559
1Ch 21:11 him, Thus **s**. the Lord, Choose thee...... 559
2Ch 11:4 Thus **s**. the Lord, Ye shall not go up,... 559
2Ch 12:5 **s**. the Lord, Ye have forsaken me,........ 559
2Ch 18:10 **s**. the Lord, With these thou shalt 559
2Ch 18:13 what my God **s**., that will I speak. 559
2Ch 18:26 Thus **s**. the king, Put this fellow in 559
2Ch 20:15 **s**. the Lord unto you, Be not afraid...... 559
2Ch 21:12 **s**. the Lord God of David thy father, ... 559
2Ch 24:20 Thus **s**. God, Why transgress ye the.... 559
2Ch 32:10 **s**. Sennacherib king of Assyria,............ 559
2Ch 34:23 Thus **s**. the Lord God of Israel, Tell..... 559
2Ch 34:24 Thus **s**. the Lord,...I will bring evil 559
2Ch 34:26 Thus **s**. the Lord God of Israel............ 559
2Ch 34:27 even heard thee also, **s**. the Lord....... 5002
2Ch 36:23 Thus **s**. Cyrus king of Persia, All......... 559
Ezr 1:2 Thus **s**. Cyrus king of Persia, The 559
Ne 6:6 and Gashmu **s**. it, that thou and the 559
Job 28:14 The depth **s**., It is not in me: and........ 559
Job 28:14 and the sea **s**., It is not in me............ 559
Job 33:24 and **s**., Deliver him from going............ 559
Job 35:10 But none **s**., Where is God my maker,.. 559
Job 37:6 For he **s**. to the snow, Be thou on....... 559
Job 39:25 He **s**. among the trumpets, Ha, ha;...... 559
Ps 12:5 needy, now will I arise, **s**. the Lord; 559
Ps 36:1 The transgression of the wicked **s**...... 5002
Ps 50:16 unto the wicked God **s**., What hast...... 559
Pr 9:4, 16 understanding, she **s**. to him, ... 559
Pr 20:14 is naught, it is naught, **s**. the buyer:..... 559
Pr 22:13 The slothful man **s**., There is a lion...... 559
Pr 23:7 Eat and drink, **s**. he to thee; but his..... 559
Pr 24:24 He that **s**. unto the wicked, Thou 559
Pr 26:13 The slothful man **s**., There is a lion...... 559
Pr 26:19 neighbour, and **s**., Am not I in sport? ... 559
Pr 28:24 and **s**., It is not transgression; 559
Pr 30:16 the fire that **s**. not, It is enough. 559
Pr 30:20 and **s**., I have done no wickedness. 559
Ec 1:2 Vanity of vanities, **s**. the Preacher, ... 559
Ec 4:8 neither **s**. he, For whom do I labour, ...
Ec 7:27 this have I found, **s**. the preacher, ... 559
Ec 10:3 he **s**. to every one that he is a fool. 559
Ec 12:8 Vanity of vanities, **s**. the preacher;....... 559
Isa 1:11 sacrifices unto me? **s**. the Lord: 559
Isa 1:18 let us reason together, **s**. the Lord: 559
Isa 1:24 **s**. the Lord, the Lord of hosts,.......... 5002
Isa 3:15 the poor? **s**. the Lord God of hosts..... 5002
Isa 3:16 Moreover the Lord **s**., Because the...... 559
Isa 7:7 **s**. the Lord God, It shall not stand, ... 559
Isa 10:8 For he **s**., Are not my princes............ 559
Isa 10:13 he **s**., By the strength of my hand, ... 559
Isa 10:24 thus **s**. the Lord God of hosts, O......... 559
Isa 14:22 against them, **s**. the Lord of hosts,..... 5002
Isa 14:22 and son, and nephew, **s**. the Lord. 5002
Isa 14:23 destruction, **s**. the Lord of hosts, ... 5002
Isa 17:3 the glory...of Israel, **s**. the Lord 5002
Isa 17:6 thereof, **s**. the Lord God of Israel. 5002
Isa 19:4 shall rule over them, **s**. the Lord,........ 5002
Isa 22:14 ye die, **s**. the Lord God of hosts, ... 559
Isa 22:15 **s**. the Lord God of hosts, Go, get 559
Isa 22:25 In that day, **s**. the Lord of hosts, ... 5002
Isa 28:16 **s**. the Lord God,...I lay in Zion 559
Isa 29:11 and he **s**., I cannot; for it is sealed:...... 559
Isa 29:12 thee: and he **s**., I am not learned......... 559
Isa 29:22 thus **s**. the Lord, who redeemed.......... 559
Isa 30:1 rebellious children, **s**. the Lord, ... 5002
Isa 30:12 **s**. the Holy One of Israel, Because....... 559
Isa 30:15 **s**. the Lord God, the Holy One of........ 559
Isa 31:9 afraid of the ensign, **s**. the Lord,........ 5002
Isa 33:10 Now will I rise, **s**. the Lord; now 559
Isa 36:4 Thus **s**. the great king, the king of....... 559
Isa 36:14 Thus **s**. the king, Let not Hezekiah...... 559
Isa 36:16 thus **s**. the king of Assyria, Make an 559
Isa 37:3 Thus **s**. Hezekiah, This day is a day..... 559
Isa 37:6 Thus **s**. the Lord, Be not afraid of 559
Isa 37:21 **s**. the Lord God of Israel, Whereas...... 559
Isa 37:33 thus **s**. the Lord concerning the king 559
Isa 37:34 not come into this city, **s**. the Lord. ... 5002
Isa 38:1 Thus **s**. the Lord, Set thine house in.... 559
Isa 38:5 say to Hezekiah, Thus **s**. the Lord,...... 559
Isa 39:6 nothing shall be left, **s**. the Lord.......... 559
Isa 40:1 comfort ye my people, **s**. your God...... 559
Isa 40:25 or shall I be equal? **s**. the Holy One. 559
Isa 41:14 I will help thee, **s**. the Lord, and........ 5002
Isa 41:21 Produce your cause, **s**. the Lord;......... 559
Isa 41:21 strong reasons, **s**. the King of Jacob..... 559
Isa 42:5 **s**. God the Lord, he that created the.... 559
Isa 42:22 for a spoil, and none **s**., Restore.......... 559
Isa 43:1 thus **s**. the Lord that created thee, ... 559
Isa 43:10 Ye are my witnesses, **s**. the Lord, ... 5002
Isa 43:12 ye are my witnesses, **s**. the Lord,...... 5002
Isa 43:14 Thus **s**. the Lord, your redeemer, ... 559
Isa 43:16 **s**. the Lord, which maketh a way in 559
Isa 44:2 Thus **s**. the Lord that made thee, ... 559
Isa 44:6 Thus **s**. the Lord the king of Israel, ... 559
Isa 44:16 **s**., Aha, I am warm, I have seen the.... 559
Isa 44:17 **s**., Deliver me; for thou art my god. 559
Isa 44:24 Thus **s**. the Lord, thy redeemer, ... 559
Isa 44:26 that **s**. to Jerusalem, Thou shalt be 559
Isa 44:27 That **s**. to the deep, Be dry, and I....... 559
Isa 44:28 That **s**. of Cyrus, He is my shepherd,... 559
Isa 45:1 Thus **s**. the Lord to his anointed,......... 559
Isa 45:10 Woe...him that **s**. unto his father, ... 559
Isa 45:11 Thus **s**. the Lord, the Holy One of........ 559
Isa 45:13 nor reward, **s**. the Lord of hosts. 559
Isa 45:14 Thus **s**. the Lord, The labour of.......... 559
Isa 45:18 thus **s**. the Lord that created the.......... 559
Isa 48:17 Thus **s**. the Lord, thy Redeemer, ... 559
Isa 48:22 There is no peace, **s**. the Lord, unto..... 559
Isa 49:5 **s**. the Lord that formed me from......... 559
Isa 49:7 Thus **s**. the Lord, the Redeemer of...... 559
Isa 49:8 Thus **s**. the Lord, In an acceptable....... 559
Isa 49:18 As I live, **s**. the Lord, thou shalt........ 5002
Isa 49:22 Thus **s**. the Lord God, Behold, I 559
Isa 49:25 thus **s**. the Lord, Even the captives 559
Isa 50:1 Thus **s**. the Lord, Where is the bill...... 559
Isa 51:22 thus **s**. thy Lord the Lord, and thy....... 559
Isa 52:3 For thus **s**. the Lord, Ye have sold 559
Isa 52:4 For thus **s**. the Lord God, My people... 559
Isa 52:5 what have I here, **s**. the Lord, ... 5002
Isa 52:5 make them to howl, **s**. the Lord;........ 5002
Isa 52:7 that **s**. unto Zion, Thy God reigneth! 559
Isa 54:1 of the married wife, **s**. the Lord. 559
Isa 54:6 when thou wast refused, **s**. thy God..... 559
Isa 54:8 on thee, **s**. the Lord thy Redeemer...... 559
Isa 54:10 **s**. the Lord that hath mercy on thee..... 559
Isa 54:17 righteousness is of me, **s**. the Lord. ... 5002
Isa 55:8 are your ways my ways, **s**. the Lord... 5002
Isa 56:1 **s**. the Lord, Keep ye judgment, ... 559
Isa 56:4 thus **s**. the Lord unto the eunuchs 559
Isa 56:8 gathereth the outcasts of Israel **s**., ... 5002
Isa 57:15 For thus **s**. the high and lofty One 559
Isa 57:19 to him that is near, **s**. the Lord;......... 559
Isa 57:21 no peace, **s**. my God, to the wicked..... 559
Isa 59:20 from transgression...**s**. the Lord......... 5002
Isa 59:21 covenant with them, **s**. the Lord;......... 559
Isa 59:21 mouth of thy seed's seed, **s**. the Lord, .. 559
Isa 65:7 of your fathers together, **s**. the Lord, ... 559
Isa 65:8 Thus **s**. the Lord, As the new wine is .. 559
Isa 65:8 cluster, and one **s**., Destroy it not; 559
Isa 65:13 thus **s**. the Lord God, Behold, my 559
Isa 65:25 all my holy mountain, **s**. the Lord. 559
Isa 66:1 Thus **s**. the Lord, The heaven is my 559
Isa 66:2 things have been **s**. the Lord:............ 5002
Isa 66:9 cause to bring forth? **s**. the Lord: 559
Isa 66:9 and shut the womb? **s**. thy God........... 559
Isa 66:12 **s**. the Lord,...I will extend peace to..... 559
Isa 66:17 consumed together, **s**. the Lord. 5002
Isa 66:20 mountain Jerusalem, **s**. the Lord, ... 559
Isa 66:21 priests and for Levites, **s**. the Lord...... 559
Isa 66:22 remain before me, **s**. the Lord,.......... 5002
Isa 66:23 to worship before me, **s**. the Lord. 559
Jer 1:8 thee to deliver thee, **s**. the Lord......... 5002
Jer 1:15 kingdoms of the north, **s**. the Lord; 5002
Jer 1:19 thee, **s**. the Lord, to deliver thee. 5002
Jer 2:2 Thus **s**. the Lord; I remember thee,..... 559
Jer 2:3 shall come upon them, **s**. the Lord. 5002
Jer 2:5 **s**. the Lord, What iniquity have 559
Jer 2:9 yet plead with you, **s**. the Lord,......... 5002
Jer 2:12 be ye very desolate, **s**. the Lord......... 5002
Jer 2:19 my fear is not in thee, **s**. the Lord 5002
Jer 2:22 marked before me, **s**. the Lord God.... 5002

Jer 2:29 all have transgressed...s. the Lord...... 5002
Jer 3:1 yet return again to me, s. the Lord. ... 5002
Jer 3:10 heart, but feignedly, s. the Lord. 5002
Jer 3:12 thou backsliding Israel, s. the Lord;..... 5002
Jer 3:12 for I am merciful, s. the Lord, and I... 5002
Jer 3:13 not obeyed my voice, s. the Lord....... 5002
Jer 3:14 backsliding children, s. the Lord;........ 5002
Jer 3:16 s. the Lord, they shall say no more, ... 5002
Jer 3:20 me, O house of Israel, s. the Lord..... 5002
Jer 4:1 wilt return, O Israel, s. the Lord, ... 5002
Jer 4:3 For thus s. the Lord to the men of...... 559
Jer 4:9 to pass at that day, s. the Lord, ... 5002
Jer 4:17 rebellious against me, s. the Lord....... 5002
Jer 5:9 visit for these things? s. the Lord:...... 5002
Jer 5:11 dealt...treacherously...s. the Lord. 5002
Jer 5:14 s. the Lord God of hosts, Because....... 559
Jer 5:15 far, O house of Israel, s. the Lord:..... 5002
Jer 5:18 s. the Lord, I will not make a full....... 5002
Jer 5:22 Fear ye not me? s. the Lord: will....... 5002
Jer 5:29 visit for these things? s. the Lord:...... 5002
Jer 6:9 s. the Lord of hosts, They shall 559
Jer 6:12 inhabitants of the land, s. the Lord. 5002
Jer 6:15 shall be cast down, s. the Lord. 559
Jer 6:16 Thus s. the Lord, Stand ye in the....... 559
Jer 6:21 thus s. the Lord, Behold, I will lay....... 559
Jer 6:22 Thus s. the Lord, Behold, a people...... 559
Jer 7:3 Thus s. the Lord of hosts, the God...... 559
Jer 7:11 even I have seen it, s. the Lord. 5002
Jer 7:13 done all these works, s. the Lord,...... 5002
Jer 7:19 provoke me to anger? s. the Lord:..... 5002
Jer 7:20 thus s. the Lord God; Behold, mine..... 559
Jer 7:21 s. the Lord of hosts, the God of.......... 559
Jer 7:30 done evil in my sight, s. the Lord: 5002
Jer 7:32 behold, the days come, s. the Lord, ... 5002
Jer 8:1 At that time, s. the Lord, they shall ... 5002
Jer 8:3 I have driven them, s. the Lord of 5002
Jer 8:4 Thus s. the Lord; Shall they fall, ... 559
Jer 8:12 they shall be cast down, s. the Lord..... 559
Jer 8:13 surely consume them, s. the Lord:..... 5002
Jer 8:17 and they shall bite you, s. the Lord. ... 5002
Jer 9:3 and they know not me, s. the Lord. ... 5002
Jer 9:6 refuse to know me, s. the Lord. 5002
Jer 9:7 thus s. the Lord of hosts, Behold, ... 559
Jer 9:9 them for these things? s. the Lord: 5002
Jer 9:13 the Lord s., Because they have........... 559
Jer 9:15 thus s. the Lord of hosts, the God of... 559
Jer 9:17 Thus s. the Lord of hosts, Consider..... 559
Jer 9:22 s. the Lord, Even the carcases.......... 5002
Jer 9:23 Thus s. the Lord, Let not the wise...... 559
Jer 9:24 these things I delight, s. the Lord. 5002
Jer 9:25 the days come, s. the Lord, that I...... 5002
Jer 10:2 Thus s. the Lord, Learn not the.......... 559
Jer 10:18 thus s. the Lord, Behold, I will sling 559
Jer 11:3 s. the Lord God of Israel; Cursed be.... 559
Jer 11:11 s. the Lord, Behold, I will bring evil.... 559
Jer 11:21 s. the Lord of the men of Anathoth,..... 559
Jer 11:22 thus s. the Lord of hosts, Behold, I...... 559
Jer 12:14 Thus s. the Lord against all mine......... 559
Jer 12:17 destroy that nation, s. the Lord. 5002
Jer 13:1 Thus s. the Lord unto me, Go and....... 559
Jer 13:9 s. the Lord, After this manner will....... 559
Jer 13:11 whole house of Judah, s. the Lord;..... 5002
Jer 13:12 s. the Lord God of Israel, Every 559
Jer 13:13 s. the Lord, Behold, I will fill all the..... 559
Jer 13:14 and the sons together, s. the Lord:..... 5002
Jer 13:25 thy measures from me, s. the Lord; ... 5002
Jer 14:10 Thus s. the Lord unto this people,....... 559
Jer 14:15 s. the Lord concerning the prophets..... 559
Jer 15:2 s. the Lord; Such as are for death,...... 559
Jer 15:3 over them four kinds, s. the Lord: 5002
Jer 15:6 Thou hast forsaken me, s. the Lord,... 5002
Jer 15:9 before their enemies, s. the Lord....... 5002
Jer 15:19 Therefore thus s. the Lord, If thou...... 559
Jer 15:20 and to deliver thee, s. the Lord.......... 5002
Jer 16:3 s. the Lord concerning the sons and...... 559
Jer 16:5 s. the Lord, Enter not into the house... 559
Jer 16:5 from this people, s. the Lord,............ 5002
Jer 16:9 thus s. the Lord of hosts, the God....... 559
Jer 16:11 and have forsaken me, s. the Lord, ... 5002
Jer 16:14 s. the Lord, that it shall no more 5002
Jer 16:16 send for many fishers, s. the Lord,..... 5002
Jer 17:5 Thus s. the Lord; Cursed be the......... 559
Jer 17:21 Thus s. the Lord; Take heed to 559
Jer 17:24 hearken unto me, s. the Lord, to......... 5002
Jer 18:6 with you as this potter? s. the Lord.... 5002
Jer 18:11 s. the Lord; Behold, I frame evil 559
Jer 18:13 Therefore thus s. the Lord; Ask ye...... 559
Jer 19:1 s. the Lord, Go and get a potter's 559
Jer 19:3 Thus s. the Lord of hosts, the God...... 559
Jer 19:6 days come, s. the Lord, that this....... 5002
Jer 19:11 Thus s. the Lord of hosts; Even.......... 559
Jer 19:12 I do unto this place, s. the Lord, ... 5002
Jer 19:15 Thus s. the Lord of hosts, the God...... 559
Jer 20:4 s. the Lord, Behold, I will make.......... 559
Jer 21:4 s. the Lord God of Israel; Behold, I..... 559
Jer 21:7 s. the Lord, I will deliver Zedekiah..... 5002
Jer 21:8 s. the Lord; Behold, I set before.......... 559
Jer 21:10 evil, and not for good, s. the Lord:..... 5002
Jer 21:12 s. the Lord; Execute judgment in......... 559
Jer 21:13 and rock of the plain, s. the Lord;...... 5002
Jer 21:14 fruit of your doings, s. the Lord:........ 5002
Jer 22:1 s. the Lord; Go down to the house...... 559
Jer 22:3 s. the Lord; Execute ye judgment......... 559
Jer 22:5 I swear by myself, s. the Lord, ... 5002
Jer 22:6 thus s. the Lord unto the king's 559
Jer 22:11 thus s. the Lord touching Shallum........ 559
Jer 22:14 s., I will build me a wide house and 559
Jer 22:16 not this to know me? s. the Lord. 5002
Jer 22:18 s. the Lord concerning Jehoiakim 559
Jer 22:24 s. the Lord, though Coniah the........... 5002
Jer 22:30 Thus s. the Lord, Write ye this man 559
Jer 23:1 sheep of my pasture! s. the Lord. 5002
Jer 23:2 s. the Lord God of Israel against 559
Jer 23:2 evil of your doings, s. the Lord.......... 5002
Jer 23:4 shall they be lacking, s. the Lord. 5002
Jer 23:5 Behold, the days come, s. the Lord,... 5002
Jer 23:7 days come, s. the Lord, that they...... 5002
Jer 23:11 their wickedness, s. the Lord............ 5002
Jer 23:12 year of their visitation, s. the Lord. 5002
Jer 23:15 s. the Lord of hosts concerning the...... 559
Jer 23:16 Thus s. the Lord of hosts, Hearken 559
Jer 23:23 Am I a God at hand, s. the Lord,....... 5002
Jer 23:24 I shall not see him? s. the Lord. 5002
Jer 23:24 I fill heaven and earth? s. the Lord. 5002
Jer 23:28 the chaff to the wheat? s. the Lord..... 5002
Jer 23:29 my word like as a fire? s. the Lord;.... 5002
Jer 23:30, 31 against the prophets, s. the Lord, .. 5002
Jer 23:31 use their tongues, and say, He s......... 5002
Jer 23:32 prophesy false dreams, s. the Lord,.... 5002
Jer 23:32 profit this people at all, s. the Lord. ... 5002
Jer 23:33 I will even forsake you, s. the Lord.... 5002
Jer 23:38 thus s. the Lord; Because ye say 559
Jer 24:5 Thus s. the Lord, the God of Israel; 559
Jer 24:8 surely thus s. the Lord, So will I......... 559
Jer 25:7 hearkened unto me, s. the Lord;........ 5002
Jer 25:8 thus s. the Lord of hosts; Because....... 559
Jer 25:9 families of the north, s. the Lord,...... 5002
Jer 25:12 and that nation, s. the Lord, for......... 5002
Jer 25:15 s. the Lord God of Israel unto me; 559
Jer 25:27 Thus s. the Lord of hosts, the God of.. 559
Jer 25:28 Thus s. the Lord of hosts; Ye shall...... 559
Jer 25:29 of the earth, s. the Lord of hosts. 5002
Jer 25:31 wicked to the sword, s. the Lord. 5002
Jer 25:32 s. the Lord of hosts, Behold, evil 559
Jer 26:2 s. the Lord; Stand in the court of the... 559
Jer 26:4 s. the Lord; If ye will not hearken 559
Jer 26:18 s. the Lord of hosts; Zion shall be 559
Jer 27:2 s. the Lord to me; Make thee bonds.... 559
Jer 27:4 Thus s. the Lord of hosts, the God...... 559
Jer 27:8 nation will I punish, s. the Lord, ... 5002
Jer 27:11 still in their own land, s. the Lord; 5002
Jer 27:15 I have not sent them, s. the Lord, ... 5002
Jer 27:16 Thus s. the Lord: Hearken not to......... 559
Jer 27:19 thus s. the Lord of hosts concerning..... 559
Jer 27:21 thus s. the Lord of hosts, the God of... 559
Jer 27:22 day that I visit them, s. the Lord;...... 5002
Jer 28:4 that went into Babylon, s. the Lord: 5002
Jer 28:11 s. the Lord; Even so will I break......... 559
Jer 28:13 Thus s. the Lord; Thou hast broken..... 559
Jer 28:14 thus s. the Lord of hosts, the God of.... 559
Jer 28:16 thus s. the Lord; Behold, I will cast..... 559
Jer 29:4 Thus s. the Lord of hosts, the God of.. 559
Jer 29:8 thus s. the Lord of hosts, the God of... 559
Jer 29:9 I have not sent them, s. the Lord. 5002
Jer 29:10 For thus s. the Lord, That after.......... 559
Jer 29:11 I think toward you, s. the Lord,......... 5002
Jer 29:14 will be found of you, s. the Lord:...... 5002
Jer 29:14 I have driven you, s. the Lord; and 5002
Jer 29:16 that thus s. the Lord of the king......... 559
Jer 29:17 Thus s. the Lord of hosts; Behold, ... 559
Jer 29:19 to my words, s. the Lord, which........ 5002
Jer 29:19 but ye would not hear, s. the Lord. 5002
Jer 29:21 Thus s. the Lord of hosts, the God...... 559
Jer 29:23 and am a witness, s. the Lord. 5002
Jer 29:31 s. the Lord concerning Shemaiah 559
Jer 29:32 thus s. the Lord; Behold, I will 559
Jer 29:32 will do for my people, s. the Lord; 5002
Jer 30:3 For, lo, the days come, s. the Lord,... 5002
Jer 30:3 Israel and Judah, s. the Lord:.............. 559
Jer 30:5 thus s. the Lord; We have heard a....... 559
Jer 30:8 in that day, s. the Lord of hosts, ... 5002
Jer 30:10 O my servant Jacob, s. the Lord;....... 5002
Jer 30:11 I am with thee, s. the Lord, to save... 5002
Jer 30:12 For thus s. the Lord, Thy bruise is 5002
Jer 30:17 heal thee of thy wounds, s. the Lord; ....
Jer 30:18 Thus s. the Lord; Behold, I will 559
Jer 30:21 approach unto me? s. the Lord. 5002
Jer 31:1 time, s. the Lord, will I be the God.... 5002
Jer 31:2 Thus s. the Lord, the people which...... 559
Jer 31:7 For thus s. the Lord; Sing with........... 559
Jer 31:14 with my goodness, s. the Lord. 5002
Jer 31:15 s. the Lord; A voice was heard in........ 559
Jer 31:16 s. the Lord; Refrain thy voice from...... 559
Jer 31:16 work...be rewarded, s. the Lord; 5002
Jer 31:17 is hope in thine end, s. the Lord. 5002
Jer 31:20 have mercy upon him, s. the Lord. 5002
Jer 31:23 s. the Lord of hosts, the God of.......... 559
Jer 31:27 the days come, s. the Lord, that I...... 5002
Jer 31:28 to build, and to plant, s. the Lord....... 5002
Jer 31:31 the days come, s. the Lord, that I....... 5002
Jer 31:32 an husband unto them, s. the Lord: 5002
Jer 31:33 s. the Lord, I will put my law in 5002
Jer 31:34 the greatest of them, s. the Lord:...... 5002
Jer 31:35 s. the Lord, which giveth the sun 559
Jer 31:36 depart from...me, s. the Lord,........... 5002
Jer 31:37 s. the Lord; If heaven above can 559
Jer 31:37 that they have done, s. the Lord........ 5002
Jer 31:38 Behold, the days come, s. the Lord,... 5002
Jer 32:3 s. the Lord,...I will give this city 559
Jer 32:5 be until I visit him, s. the Lord: 5002
Jer 32:14, 15 s. the Lord of hosts, the God of...... 559
Jer 32:28 s. the Lord;...I will give this city......... 559
Jer 32:30 work of their hands, s. the Lord. 5002
Jer 32:36 thus s. the Lord, the God of Israel, ... 559
Jer 32:42 thus s. the Lord; Like as I have.......... 559
Jer 32:44 captivity to return, s. the Lord. 5002
Jer 33:2 s. the Lord the maker thereof, the....... 559
Jer 33:4 thus s. the Lord, the God of Israel, ... 559
Jer 33:10 Thus s. the Lord; Again there shall....... 559
Jer 33:11 the land, as at the first, s. the Lord..... 559
Jer 33:12 Thus s. the Lord of hosts; Again in...... 559
Jer 33:13 him that telleth them, s. the Lord........ 559
Jer 33:14 the days come, s. the Lord, that I...... 5002
Jer 33:17 thus s. the Lord; David shall never 559
Jer 33:20 Thus s. the Lord; If ye can break 559
Jer 33:25 Thus s. the Lord; If my covenant 559
Jer 34:2 Thus s. the Lord, the God of Israel; 559
Jer 34:2 s. the Lord;...I will give this city 559
Jer 34:4 Thus s. the Lord of thee, Thou shalt..... 559
Jer 34:5 pronounced the word, s. the Lord. 5002
Jer 34:13 Thus s. the Lord, the God of Israel; 559
Jer 34:17 s. the Lord; Ye have not hearkened 559
Jer 34:17 a liberty for you, s. the Lord, to........ 5002
Jer 34:22 I will command s. the Lord, and......... 5002
Jer 35:13 Thus s. the Lord of hosts, the God....... 559
Jer 35:13 hearken to my words, s. the Lord...... 5002
Jer 35:17 thus s. the Lord God of hosts, the....... 559
Jer 35:18 Thus s. the Lord of hosts, the God....... 559
Jer 35:19 thus s. the Lord of hosts, the God....... 559
Jer 36:29 Thus s. the Lord; Thou hast burned..... 559
Jer 36:30 thus s. the Lord of Jehoiakim king.......... 559
Jer 37:7 Thus s. the Lord, the God of Israel; 559
Jer 37:9 s. the Lord; Deceive not yourselves,.... 559
Jer 38:2 Thus s. the Lord, He that remaineth.... 559
Jer 38:3 Thus s. the Lord, This city shall........... 559
Jer 38:17 Thus s. the Lord, the God of hosts,..... 559
Jer 39:16 Thus s. the Lord of hosts, the God...... 559
Jer 39:17 deliver...in that day, s. the Lord: 5002
Jer 39:18 put thy trust in me, s. the Lord........ 5002
Jer 42:9 Thus s. the Lord, the God of Israel, ... 559
Jer 42:11 be not afraid of him, s. the Lord: 5002
Jer 42:15, 18 s. the Lord of hosts, the God of...... 559
Jer 43:10 s. the Lord of hosts, the God of.......... 559
Jer 44:2 s. the Lord of hosts, the God of.......... 559
Jer 44:7 thus s. the Lord, the God of hosts,...... 559
Jer 44:11 thus s. the Lord of hosts, the God of... 559
Jer 44:25 s. the Lord of hosts, the God of.......... 559
Jer 44:26 sworn by my great name, s. the Lord,.. 559
Jer 44:29 be a sign unto you, s. the Lord, ... 5002
Jer 44:30 s. the Lord; Behold, I will give........... 559
Jer 45:2 Thus s. the Lord, the God of Israel, ... 559

Jer 45:4 The Lord **s.** thus; Behold, that............ 559
Jer 45:5 evil upon all flesh, **s.** the Lord: 5002
Jer 46:5 fear was round about, **s.** the Lord....... 5002
Jer 46:8 he **s.**, I will go up, and will cover.......... 559
Jer 46:18 As I live, **s.** the King, whose name..... 5002
Jer 46:23 cut down her forest, **s.** the Lord,....... 5002
Jer 46:25 the God of Israel, **s.**; Behold, I 559
Jer 46:26 as in the days of old, **s.** the Lord. 5002
Jer 46:28 Fear not, O Jacob...**s.** the Lord: 5002
Jer 47:2 **s.** the Lord; Behold, waters rise............ 559
Jer 48:1 Against Moab...**s.** the Lord of hosts, ... 559
Jer 48:12 the days come, **s.** the Lord, that........ 5002
Jer 48:15 **s.** the King, whose name is the 5002
Jer 48:25 and his arm is broken, **s.** the Lord. 5002
Jer 48:30 I know his wrath, **s.** the Lord; but 5002
Jer 48:35 cause to cease in Moab, **s.** the Lord, .. 5002
Jer 48:38 wherein is no pleasure, **s.** the Lord. ... 5002
Jer 48:40 For thus **s.** the Lord; Behold, he......... 559
Jer 48:43 inhabitant of Moab, **s.** the Lord........... 5002
Jer 48:44 year of their visitation, **s.** the Lord. 5002
Jer 48:47 Moab in the latter days, **s.** the Lord. .. 5002
Jer 49:1 **s.** the Lord; Hath Israel no sons? 559
Jer 49:2 days come, **s.** the Lord, that I will....... 559
Jer 49:2 that were his heirs, **s.** the Lord. 5002
Jer 49:5 thee, **s.** the Lord God of hosts, ... 5002
Jer 49:6 children of Ammon, **s.** the Lord. 5002
Jer 49:7 **s.** the Lord of hosts; Is wisdom no 559
Jer 49:12 **s.** the Lord; Behold, they whose 559
Jer 49:13 have sworn by myself, **s.** the Lord, ... 5002
Jer 49:16 down from thence, **s.** the Lord. 5002
Jer 49:18 **s.** the Lord, no man shall abide 559
Jer 49:26 cut off in that day, **s.** the Lord of....... 5002
Jer 49:28 thus **s.** the Lord; Arise ye, go up 559
Jer 49:30 inhabitants of Hazor, **s.** the Lord;....... 5002
Jer 49:31 dwelleth without care, **s.** the Lord,...... 5002
Jer 49:32 from all sides thereof, **s.** the Lord. 5002
Jer 49:35 thus **s.** the Lord of hosts; Behold, ... 559
Jer 49:37 even my fierce anger, **s.** the Lord;..... 5002
Jer 49:38 king and the princes, **s.** the Lord. 5002
Jer 49:39 the captivity of Elam, **s.** the Lord....... 5002
Jer 50:4 **s.** the Lord, the children of Israel....... 5002
Jer 50:10 spoil her...be satisfied, **s.** the Lord..... 5002
Jer 50:18 thus **s.** the Lord of hosts, the God....... 559
Jer 50:20 **s.** the Lord, the iniquity of Israel........ 5002
Jer 50:21 destroy after them **s.** the Lord, ... 5002
Jer 50:30 be cut off in that day, **s.** the Lord. 5002
Jer 50:31 proud, **s.** the Lord God of hosts:........ 5002
Jer 50:33 Thus **s.** the Lord of hosts; The........... 559
Jer 50:35 is upon the Chaldeans, **s.** the Lord, ... 5002
Jer 50:40 neighbour cities...**s.** the Lord;............ 5002
Jer 51:1 **s.** the Lord: Behold, I will raise........... 559
Jer 51:24 in Zion in your sight, **s.** the Lord. 5002
Jer 51:25 O destroying mountain, **s.** the Lord, ... 5002
Jer 51:26 be desolate for ever, **s.** the Lord. 5002
Jer 51:33 thus **s.** the Lord of hosts, the God....... 559
Jer 51:36 **s.** the Lord; Behold, I will plead 559
Jer 51:39 sleep, and not wake, **s.** the Lord........ 5002
Jer 51:48 unto her from the north, **s.** the Lord... 5002
Jer 51:52 days come, **s.** the Lord, that I will 5002
Jer 51:53 spoilers come unto her, **s.** the Lord.... 5002
Jer 51:57 not wake, **s.** the King, whose name.... 5002
Jer 51:58 Thus **s.** the Lord of hosts; The 559
La 3:24 Lord is my portion, **s.** my soul;............ 559
La 3:37 Who is he that **s.**, and it cometh to..... 559
Eze 2:4 unto them, Thus **s.** the Lord God. 559
Eze 3:11 tell them, Thus **s.** the Lord God;.......... 559
Eze 3:27 unto them, Thus **s.** the Lord God; 559
Eze 5:5 **s.** the Lord God; This is Jerusalem: 559
Eze 5:7 thus **s.** the Lord God; Because ye 559
Eze 5:8 **s.** the Lord God; Behold, I, even I, ... 559
Eze 5:11 as I live, **s.** the Lord God; Surely,...... 5002
Eze 6:3 **s.** the Lord God to the mountains, ... 559
Eze 6:11 **s.** the Lord God; Smite with thine........ 559
Eze 7:2 **s.** the Lord God unto the land of 559
Eze 7:5 **s.** the Lord God; An evil, an only 559
Eze 11:5 **s.** the Lord; Thus have ye said, O 559
Eze 11:7 Therefore thus **s.** the Lord God; 559
Eze 11:8 sword upon you, **s.** the Lord God....... 5002
Eze 11:16, 17 say, Thus **s.** the Lord God;............ 559
Eze 11:21 upon their own heads, **s.** the Lord..... 5002
Eze 12:10 Thus **s.** the Lord God; This burden...... 559
Eze 12:19 **s.** the Lord God of the inhabitants........ 559
Eze 12:23 **s.** the Lord God; I will make this.......... 559
Eze 12:25 will perform it, **s.** the Lord God.......... 5002
Eze 12:28 Thus **s.** the Lord God; There shall........ 559
Eze 12:28 shall be done, **s.** the Lord God 5002
Eze 13:3 **s.** the Lord God; Woe unto the 559
Eze 13:6 divination, saying, The Lord **s.**:.......... 5002
Eze 13:7 The Lord **s.** it; albeit I have not........... 5002
Eze 13:8 **s.** the Lord God; Because ye have 559
Eze 13:8 am against you, **s.** the Lord God. 5002
Eze 13:13 thu **s.** the Lord God; I will even.......... 559
Eze 13:16 there is no peace, **s.** the Lord God..... 5002
Eze 13:18 And say, Thus **s.** the Lord God;.......... 559
Eze 13:20 Wherefore thus **s.** the Lord God;.......... 559
Eze 14:4 unto them, Thus **s.** the Lord God; 559
Eze 14:6 **s.** the Lord God; Repent, and turn........ 559
Eze 14:11 may be their God, **s.** the Lord God. ... 5002
Eze 14:14 righteousness, **s.** the Lord God.......... 5002
Eze 14:16, 18, 20 as I live, **s.** the Lord God,........ 5002
Eze 14:21 **s.** the Lord God; How much more 559
Eze 14:23 I have done in it, **s.** the Lord God...... 5002
Eze 15:6 **s.** the Lord God; As the vine tree 559
Eze 15:8 committed a trespass, **s.** the Lord...... 5002
Eze 16:3 **s.** the Lord God unto Jerusalem;.......... 559
Eze 16:8 a covenant with thee, **s.** the Lord....... 5002
Eze 16:14 had put upon thee, **s.** the Lord God.... 5002
Eze 16:19 and thus it was, **s.** the Lord God. 5002
Eze 16:23 woe unto thee! **s.** the Lord God;)....... 5002
Eze 16:30 weak is thine heart, **s.** the Lord......... 5002
Eze 16:36 Thus **s.** the Lord God; Because thy 559
Eze 16:43 way upon thine head, **s.** the Lord...... 5002
Eze 16:48 **s.** the Lord God, Sodom thy sister 5002
Eze 16:58 thine abominations, **s.** the Lord.......... 5002
Eze 16:59 thus **s.** the Lord God; I will even......... 559
Eze 16:63 that thou hast done, **s.** the Lord 5002
Eze 17:3 **s.** the Lord God; A great eagle with..... 559
Eze 17:9 **s.** the Lord God; Shall it prosper?........ 559
Eze 17:16 As I live, **s.** the Lord God, Surely...... 5002
Eze 17:19 thus **s.**, the Lord God; As I live, ... 559
Eze 17:22 Thus **s.** the Lord God; I will also.......... 559
Eze 18:3 As I live, **s.** the Lord God, Ye shall.... 5002
Eze 18:9 he shall surely live, **s.** the Lord God... 5002
Eze 18:23 wicked should die? **s.** the Lord God: ... 5002
Eze 18:29 Yet **s.** the house of Israel, The way 559
Eze 18:30 to his ways **s.**, the Lord God............. 5002
Eze 18:32 of him that dieth, **s.** the Lord God:..... 5002
Eze 20:3 Thus **s.** the Lord God; Are ye come 559
Eze 20:3 As I live, **s.** the Lord God, I will......... 5002
Eze 20:5 Thus **s.** the Lord God; In the day........ 559
Eze 20:27 say unto them, Thus **s.** the Lord......... 559
Eze 20:30 **s.** the Lord God; Are ye polluted......... 559
Eze 20:31 As I live, **s.** the Lord God, I will....... 5002
Eze 20:33 As I live **s.** the Lord God, surely 5002
Eze 20:36 I plead with you, **s.** the Lord God, ... 5002
Eze 20:39 thus **s.** the Lord God; Go ye, serve..... 559
Eze 20:40 **s.** the Lord God, there shall all.......... 5002
Eze 20:44 ye house of Israel, **s.** the Lord God.... 5002
Eze 20:47 Thus **s.** the Lord God; Behold, I......... 559
Eze 21:3 land of Israel, Thus **s.** the Lord;.......... 559
Eze 21:7 brought to pass, **s.** the Lord God. 5002
Eze 21:9 prophesy,...say, Thus **s.** the Lord;....... 559
Eze 21:13 shall be no more, **s.** the Lord God...... 5002
Eze 21:24 thus **s.** the Lord God; Because ye 559
Eze 21:26 Thus **s.** the Lord God; Remove the...... 559
Eze 21:28 Thus **s.** the Lord God concerning......... 559
Eze 22:3 **s.** the Lord God, The city sheddeth 559
Eze 22:12 forgotten me, **s.** the Lord God............ 5002
Eze 22:19 thus **s.** the Lord God; Because ye 559
Eze 22:28 **s.** the Lord God, when the Lord.......... 559
Eze 22:31 upon their heads, **s.** the Lord God...... 5002
Eze 23:22 Aholibah, thus **s.** the Lord God; 559
Eze 23:28 For thus **s.** the Lord God; Behold, I..... 559
Eze 23:32 Thus **s.** the Lord God; Thou shalt......... 559
Eze 23:34 I have spoken it, **s.** the Lord God........ 559
Eze 23:35 thus **s.** the Lord God; Because thou..... 559
Eze 23:46 thus **s.** the Lord God; I will bring......... 559
Eze 24:3 Thus **s.** the Lord God; Set on a pot, ... 559
Eze 24:6, 9 thus **s.** the Lord God; Woe to the...... 559
Eze 24:14 they judge thee, **s.** the Lord God. 5002
Eze 24:21 Thus **s.** the Lord God; Behold, I 559
Eze 25:3 Thus **s.** the Lord God; Because........... 559
Eze 25:6 For thus **s.** the Lord God; Because...... 559
Eze 25:8, 12 Thus **s.** the Lord God; Because 559
Eze 25:13 thus **s.** the Lord God; I will also........... 559
Eze 25:14 my vengeance, **s.** the Lord God. 5002
Eze 25:15 Thus **s.** the Lord God; Because the 559
Eze 25:16 thus **s.** the Lord God; Behold, I will..... 559
Eze 26:3 thus **s.** the Lord God; Behold, I am 559
Eze 26:5 I have spoken it, **s.** the Lord God: 5002
Eze 26:7 thus **s.** the Lord God; Behold, I will..... 559
Eze 26:14 have spoken it, **s.** the Lord God. 5002
Eze 26:15 **s.** the Lord God to Tyrus; Shall not 559
Eze 26:19 thus **s.** the Lord God; When I shall...... 559
Eze 26:21 be found again, **s.** the Lord God......... 5001
Eze 27:3 **s.** the Lord God; O Tyrus, thou 559
Eze 28:2 **s.** the Lord God; Because thine heart... 559
Eze 28:6 **s.** the Lord God; Because thou hast..... 559
Eze 28:10 I have spoken it, **s.** the Lord God. 5002
Eze 28:12 **s.** the Lord God; Thou sealest up 559
Eze 28:22 say, Thus **s.** the Lord God; Behold, ... 559
Eze 28:25 **s.** the Lord God; When I shall have...... 559
Eze 29:3 Thus **s.** the Lord God; Behold, I am 559
Eze 29:8 thus **s.** the Lord God; Behold, I will..... 559
Eze 29:13 thus **s.** the Lord God; At the end of..... 559
Eze 29:19 thus **s.** the Lord God; Behold, I will..... 559
Eze 29:20 wrought for me, **s.** the Lord God. 5002
Eze 30:2 **s.** the Lord God; Howl ye, Woe 559
Eze 30:6 **s.** the Lord; They also that uphold....... 559
Eze 30:6 it by the sword, **s.** the Lord God. 5002
Eze 30:10, 13 **s.** the Lord God; I will also 559
Eze 30:22 thus **s.** the Lord God; Behold, I am 559
Eze 31:10 **s.** the Lord God; because thou hast...... 559
Eze 31:15 **s.** the Lord God; In the day when........ 559
Eze 31:18 all his multitude, **s.** the Lord God. 5002
Eze 32:3 **s.** the Lord God; I will therefore 559
Eze 32:8 upon thy land, **s.** the Lord God......... 5002
Eze 32:11 **s.** the Lord God; The sword of the 559
Eze 32:14 to run like oil, **s.** the Lord God.......... 5002
Eze 32:16 all her multitude, **s.** the Lord God. 5002
Eze 32:31 slain by the sword, **s.** the Lord God. .. 5002
Eze 32:32 all his multitude, **s.** the Lord God...... 5002
Eze 33:11 **s.** the Lord God, I have no pleasure ... 5002
Eze 33:25 Thus **s.** the Lord God; Ye eat with 559
Eze 33:27 Thus **s.** the Lord God; As I live, ... 559
Eze 34:2 **s.** the Lord God unto the shepherds;.... 559
Eze 34:8 **s.** the Lord God, surely because 5002
Eze 34:10 Thus **s.** the Lord God; Behold, I am 559
Eze 34:11 **s.** the Lord God; Behold, I, even I, ... 559
Eze 34:15 them to lie down, **s.** the Lord God. 5002
Eze 34:17 O my flock, thus **s.** the Lord God;....... 559
Eze 34:20 thus **s.** the Lord God unto them; 559
Eze 34:30 are my people, **s.** the Lord God.......... 5002
Eze 34:31 I am your God, **s.** the Lord God. 5002
Eze 35:3 **s.** the Lord God; Behold, O mount....... 559
Eze 35:6 **s.** the Lord God, I will prepare.......... 5002
Eze 35:11 **s.** the Lord, God, I will even do 5002
Eze 35:14 Thus **s.** the Lord God; When the.......... 559
Eze 36:2 **s.** the Lord God; Because the enemy ... 559
Eze 36:3 Thus **s.** the Lord God; Because they.... 559
Eze 36:4 **s.** the Lord God to the mountains, ... 559
Eze 36:5 thus **s.** the Lord God; Surely in the...... 559
Eze 36:6 Thus **s.** the Lord God; Behold, I 559
Eze 36:7 thus **s.** the Lord God; I have lifted....... 559
Eze 36:13 **s.** the Lord God; Because they say...... 559
Eze 36:14 nations any more, **s.** the Lord God. 5002
Eze 36:15 to fall any more, **s.** the Lord God....... 5002
Eze 36:22 Thus **s.** the Lord God; I do not this..... 559
Eze 36:23 I am the Lord, **s.** the Lord God, ... 5002
Eze 36:32 **s.** the Lord God, be it known unto 5002
Eze 36:33 Thus **s.** the Lord God; In the day........ 559
Eze 36:37 Thus **s.** the Lord God; I will yet for..... 559
Eze 37:5 **s.** the Lord God unto these bones;....... 559
Eze 37:9 Thus **s.** the Lord God; Come from....... 559
Eze 37:12 Thus **s.** the Lord God; Behold, O my... 559
Eze 37:14 it, and performed it, **s.** the Lord. 5002
Eze 37:19, 21 Thus **s.** the Lord God; Behold, I..... 559
Eze 38:3 Thus **s.** the Lord God; Behold, I am 559
Eze 38:10 Thus **s.** the Lord God; It shall also 559
Eze 38:14 Thus **s.** the Lord God; In that day 559
Eze 38:17 **s.** the Lord God; Art thou he of.......... 559
Eze 38:18 the land of Israel, **s.** the Lord God, ... 5002
Eze 38:21 my mountains, **s.** the Lord God: 5002
Eze 39:1 Thus **s.** the Lord God; Behold, I am 559
Eze 39:5 I have spoken it, **s.** the Lord God. 5002
Eze 39:8 and it is done, **s.** the Lord God;......... 5002
Eze 39:10 that robbed them, **s.** the Lord God..... 5002
Eze 39:13 I shall be e glorified, **s.** the Lord God. .5002
Eze 39:17 thus **s.** the Lord God; Speak unto........ 559
Eze 39:20 all men of war, **s.** the Lord God......... 5002
Eze 39:25 **s.** the Lord God; Now will I bring........ 559
Eze 39:29 house of Israel, **s.** the Lord God. 5002
Eze 43:18 Son of man, thus **s.** the Lord God;....... 559
Eze 43:19 unto me, **s.** the Lord God, a young 5002
Eze 43:27 I will accept you, **s.** the Lord God..... 5002
Eze 44:6 Thus **s.** the Lord God; O ye house 559
Eze 44:9 Thus **s.** the Lord God; No stranger,..... 559
Eze 44:12 against them, **s.** the Lord God, ... 5002

Book	Ref	Context	No.
Eze	44:15	fat and the blood, s. the Lord God:	5002
Eze	44:27	his sin offering, s. the Lord God.	5002
Eze	45:9	s. the Lord God; Let it suffice you, ...	5002
Eze	45:9	from my people, s. the Lord God.	559
Eze	45:15	reconciliation for them, s. the Lord.....	5002
Eze	45:18	Thus s. the Lord God; In the first	559
Eze	46:1	s. the Lord God; The gate of the	559
Eze	46:16	s. the Lord God; If the prince give	559
Eze	47:13	s. the Lord God; This shall be the	559
Eze	47:23	his inheritance, s. the Lord God.........	5002
Eze	48:29	are their portions, s. the Lord God.....	5002
Ho	2:13	lovers, and forgat me, s. the Lord......	5002
Ho	2:16	it shall be at that day, s. the Lord, ...	5002
Ho	2:21	I will hear, s. the Lord, I will hear	5002
Ho	11:11	them in their houses, s. the Lord.......	5002
Joe	2:12	Therefore also now, s. the Lord, ...	5002
Am	1:3	Thus s. the Lord; For three	559
Am	1:5	into captivity unto Kir, s. the Lord.......	559
Am	1:6	Thus s. the Lord; For three	559
Am	1:8	shall perish, s. the Lord God.	559
Am	1:9,	11,13 Thus s. the Lord; For three	559
Am	1:15	his princes together, s. the Lord.	559
Am	2:1	Thus s. the Lord; For three	559
Am	2:3	the princes...with him, s. the Lord.......	559
Am	2:4,	6 Thus s. the Lord; For three..............	559
Am	2:11	ye children of Israel? s. the Lord.	5002
Am	2:16	away naked in that day, s. the Lord....	5002
Am	3:10	know not to do right, s. the Lord, ...	5002
Am	3:11	thus s. the Lord God; An adversary	559
Am	3:12	s. the Lord; As the shepherd taketh.....	559
Am	3:13	s. the Lord God, the God of hosts, ...	5001
Am	3:15	shall have an end, s. the Lord.	5001
Am	4:3	them into the palace, s. the Lord.	5001
Am	4:5	ye children of Israel, s. the Lord........	5001
Am	4:6,	8,9,10,11 unto me, s. the Lord...........	5001
Am	5:3	For thus s. the Lord God; The city......	559
Am	5:4	thus s. the Lord unto the house of.......	559
Am	5:16	the Lord, s. thus; Wailing shall be........	559
Am	5:17	will pass through thee, s. the Lord.......	559
Am	5:27	beyond Damascus, s. the Lord, ...	559
Am	6:8	s. the Lord the God of hosts, I..........	5002
Am	6:14	Israel, s. the Lord the God of hosts;...	5002
Am	7:3	this: It shall not be, s. the Lord.	559
Am	7:6	also shall not be, s. the Lord God........	559
Am	7:11	For thus Amos s., Jeroboam shall	559
Am	7:17	thus s. the Lord; Thy wife shall be	559
Am	8:3	howlings in that day, s. the Lord........	5002
Am	8:9	s. the Lord God, that I will cause.......	5002
Am	8:11	s. the Lord God, that I will send a	5002
Am	9:7	O children of Israel? s. the Lord.	5002
Am	9:8	the house of Jacob, s. the Lord..........	5002
Am	9:12	name, s. the Lord that doeth this.......	5002
Am	9:13	come, s. the Lord, that the plowman ..	5002
Am	9:15	given them, s. the Lord thy God.	559
Ob	1	s. the Lord God concerning Edom;.......	559
Ob	3	that s. in his heart, Who shall bring......	559
Ob	4	will I bring thee down, s. the Lord.	5002
Ob	8	Shall I not in that day, s. the Lord, ...	5002
Mic	2:3	Therefore thus s. the Lord; Behold, ...	559
Mic	3:5	Thus s. the Lord concerning the..........	559
Mic	4:6	s. the Lord, will I assemble her	5002
Mic	5:10	to pass in that day, s. the Lord, ...	5002
Mic	6:1	Hear ye now what the Lord s.;	559
Na	1:12	s. the Lord: Though they be quiet, ...	559
Na	2:13	against thee, s. the Lord of hosts,......	5002
Na	3:5	against thee, s. the Lord of hosts;......	5002
Hab	2:19	Woe unto him that s. to the wood,.......	559
Zep	1:2	from off the land, s. the Lord............	5002
Zep	1:3	man from off the land, s. the Lord......	5002
Zep	1:10	to pass in that day, s. the Lord, ...	5002
Zep	2:9	as I live, s. the Lord of hosts, the......	5002
Zep	3:8	wait ye upon me, s. the Lord, until	5002
Zep	3:20	back your captivity...s. the Lord.	559
Hag	1:5,7	thus s. the Lord of hosts; Consider......	559
Hag	1:8	it, and I will be glorified, s. the Lord....	559
Hag	1:9	Why? s. the Lord of hosts. Because ...	5002
Hag	1:13	saying, I am with you, s. the Lord.	5002
Hag	2:4	strong, O Zerubbabel, s. the Lord;	5002
Hag	2:4	ye people of the land, s. the Lord, ...	5002
Hag	2:4	I am with you, s. the Lord of hosts: ...	5002
Hag	2:6	thus s. the Lord of hosts; Yet once,.....	559
Hag	2:7	fill this house with glory, s. the Lord....	559
Hag	2:8	gold is mine, s. the Lord of hosts.......	5002
Hag	2:9	of the former, s. the Lord of hosts:.....	5002
Hag	2:9	I give peace, s. the Lord of hosts........	559
Hag	2:11	Thus s. the Lord of hosts: Ask now.....	559
Hag	2:14	this nation before me, s. the Lord;.....	5002
Hag	2:17	yet ye turned not to me, s. the Lord..	5002
Hag	2:23	day, s. the Lord of hosts, will I take...	5002
Hag	2:23	s. the Lord, and will make thee as	5002
Hag	2:23	chosen thee, s. the Lord of hosts........	5002
Zec	1:3	Thus s. the Lord of hosts; Turn..........	559
Zec	1:3	ye unto me, s. the Lord of hosts, ...	5002
Zec	1:3	unto you, s. the Lord of hosts............	559
Zec	1:4	Thus s. the Lord of hosts; Turn ye......	559
Zec	1:4	nor hearken unto me, s. the Lord.	5002
Zec	1:14	s. the Lord of hosts; I am jealous.......	5002
Zec	1:16	thus s. the Lord; I am returned to.......	559
Zec	1:16	be built in it, s. the Lord of hosts, ...	5002
Zec	1:17	Thus s. the Lord of hosts; My cities	559
Zec	2:5	s. the Lord, will be unto her a wall.....	5002
Zec	2:6	the land of the north, s. the Lord:.......	5002
Zec	2:6	winds of the heaven, s. the Lord........	5002
Zec	2:8	s. the Lord of hosts; After the glory	559
Zec	2:10	in the midst of thee, s. the Lord........	5002
Zec	3:7	s. the Lord of hosts; If thou wilt	559
Zec	3:9	the graving...s. the Lord of hosts........	5002
Zec	3:10	s. the Lord of hosts, shall ye call	5002
Zec	4:6	by my spirit, s. the Lord of hosts.	559
Zec	5:4	bring it forth, s. the Lord of hosts,.....	5002
Zec	7:13	not hear, s. the Lord of hosts:...........	559
Zec	8:2	s. the Lord of hosts; I was jealous.......	559
Zec	8:3	s. the Lord; I am returned unto	559
Zec	8:4	s. the Lord of hosts; There shall	559
Zec	8:6	Thus s. the Lord of hosts; If it be	559
Zec	8:6	mine eyes? s. the Lord of hosts.........	5002
Zec	8:7	s. the Lord of hosts; Behold, I will	559
Zec	8:9	Thus s. the Lord of hosts; Let your.....	559
Zec	8:11	former days, s. the Lord of hosts.......	5002
Zec	8:14	s. the Lord of hosts; As I thought	559
Zec	8:14	provoked me to wrath, s. the Lord	559
Zec	8:17	are things that I hate, s. the Lord.	5002
Zec	8:19	Thus s. the Lord of hosts; The fast	559
Zec	8:20	Thus s. the Lord of hosts; It shall	559
Zec	8:23	s. the Lord of hosts; In those days	559
Zec	10:12	down in his name, s. the Lord.	5002
Zec	11:4	s. the Lord my God; Feed the flock.....	559
Zec	11:6	inhabitants of...land, s. the Lord:........	5002
Zec	12:1	s. the Lord, which stretcheth forth.....	5002
Zec	12:4	day, s. the Lord, I will smite every	5002
Zec	13:2	in that day, s. the Lord of hosts, ...	5002
Zec	13:7	is my fellow, s. the Lord of hosts:......	5002
Zec	13:8	s. the Lord, two parts therein shall.....	5002
Mal	1:2	I have loved you, s. the Lord. Yet	5002
Mal	1:2	Esau Jacob's brother? s. the Lord:	559
Mal	1:4	Edom s., We are impoverished, but	559
Mal	1:4	thus s. the Lord of hosts, They shall....	559
Mal	1:6	s. the Lord of hosts unto you, O	559
Mal	1:8	thy person? s. the Lord of hosts..........	559
Mal	1:9	he regard your persons? s. the Lord	559
Mal	1:10	no pleasure in you, s. the Lord of........	559
Mal	1:11	among the heathen, s. the Lord of........	559
Mal	1:13	ye have snuffed at it, s. the Lord	559
Mal	1:13	this of your hand? s. the Lord.............	559
Mal	1:14	a great King, s. the Lord of hosts,........	559
Mal	2:2	give glory unto my name, s. the Lord...	559
Mal	2:4	might be with Levi, s. the Lord of.......	559
Mal	2:8	covenant of Levi, s. the Lord of..........	559
Mal	2:16	s. that he hateth putting away:............	559
Mal	2:16	his garment, s. the Lord of hosts.........	559
Mal	3:1	he shall come, s. the Lord of hosts.	559
Mal	3:5	fear not me, s. the Lord of hosts.........	559
Mal	3:7	I will return unto you, s. the Lord	559
Mal	3:10	prove me now herewith, s. the Lord	559
Mal	3:11	the time in the field, s. the Lord of......	559
Mal	3:12	be a delightsome land, s. the Lord	559
Mal	3:13	been stout against me, s. the Lord.......	559
Mal	3:17	shall be mine, s. the Lord of hosts,......	559
Mal	4:1	burn them up, s. the Lord of hosts, ...	559
Mal	4:3	I shall do this, s. the Lord of hosts.	559
Mt	4:6	s. unto him, If thou be the Son of	*3004*
Mt	4:9	And s. unto him, All these things	*3004*
Mt	4:10	s. Jesus unto him, Get thee hence, ...	*3004*
Mt	4:19	And he s. unto them, Follow me, ...	*3004*
Mt	7:21	Not every one that s. unto me,.......	*3004*
Mt	8:4	Jesus s. unto him, See thou tell	*3004*
Mt	8:7	Jesus s. unto him, I will come and ...	*3004*
Mt	8:20	Jesus s. unto him, The foxes have	*3004*
Mt	8:26	And he s. unto them, Why are ye.....	*3004*
Mt	9:6	(then s. he to the sick of the palsy,)...	*3004*
Mt	9:9	and he s. unto him, Follow me..........	*3004*
Mt	9:28	Jesus s. unto them, Believe ye that ..	*3004*
Mt	9:37	Then s. he unto his disciples, The......	*3004*
Mt	12:13	s. he to the man, Stretch forth........	*3004*
Mt	12:44	Then he s., I will return into my...	*3004*
Mt	13:14	s., By hearing ye shall hear,..........	*3004*
Mt	13:51	Jesus s. unto them, Have ye	*3004*
Mt	15:34	And Jesus s. unto them, How many..	*3004*
Mt	16:15	He s. unto them, But whom say ye..	*3004*
Mt	17:25	He s., Yes. And when he was come ...	*3004*
Mt	17:26	Peter s. unto him, Of strangers.	*3004*
Mt	17:26	Jesus s. unto him, Then are the.......	*5346*
Mt	18:22	Jesus s. unto him, I say not unto.....	*3004*
Mt	19:8	He s. unto them, Moses because of..	*3004*
Mt	19:18	He s. unto him, Which? Jesus said,.....	*3004*
Mt	19:20	The young man s. unto him, All.........	*3004*
Mt	20:6	s. unto them, Why stand ye here...	*3004*
Mt	20:7	s. unto them, Go ye also into the..	*3004*
Mt	20:8	lord of the vineyard s. unto his.......	*3004*
Mt	20:21	She s. unto him, Grant that these	*3004*
Mt	20:23	he s. unto them, Ye shall drink.......	*3004*
Mt	21:16	Jesus s. unto them, Yea; have ye	*3004*
Mt	21:31	Jesus s. unto them, Verily I say.......	*3004*
Mt	21:42	Jesus s. unto them, Did ye never......	*3004*
Mt	22:8	Then s. he to his servants, The	*3004*
Mt	22:12	s. unto him, Friend, how camest...	*3004*
Mt	22:20	he s. unto them, Whose is this	*3004*
Mt	22:21	Then s. he unto them, Render..........	*3004*
Mt	22:43	He s. unto them, How then doth	*3004*
Mt	26:18	The master s., My time is at hand..	*3004*
Mt	26:31	s. Jesus unto them, All ye shall be...	*3004*
Mt	26:36	s. unto the disciples, Sit ye here,......	*3004*
Mt	26:38	Then s. he unto them, My soul is.....	*3004*
Mt	26:40	s. unto Peter, What, could ye not ...	*3004*
Mt	26:45	s. unto them, Sleep on now, and.....	*3004*
Mt	26:64	Jesus s. unto him, Thou hast said: ...	*3004*
Mt	27:22	Pilate s. unto them, What shall I........	*3004*
Mk	1:41	s. unto him, I will; be thou clean....	*3004*
Mk	1:44	s. unto him, See thou say nothing...	*3004*
Mk	2:10	(he s. to the sick of the palsy,).........	*3004*
Mk	2:17	Jesus heard it, he s. unto them,.........	*3004*
Mk	3:3	he s. unto the man which had the.......	*3004*
Mk	3:4	he s. unto them, Is it lawful to do...	*3004*
Mk	3:5	s. unto the man, Stretch forth thine .	*3004*
Mk	4:35	he s. unto them, Let us pass over....	*3004*
Mk	5:19	s. unto him, Go home to thy friends,	*3004*
Mk	5:36	s. unto the ruler of the synagogue,.....	*3004*
Mk	5:39	he s. unto them, What make ye.......	*3004*
Mk	6:38	He s. unto them, How many loaves .	*3004*
Mk	6:50	s. unto them, Be of good cheer: it...	*3004*
Mk	7:18	And he s. unto them, Are ye so........	*3004*
Mk	7:34	s. unto him, Ephphatha, that is,.......	*3004*
Mk	8:1	his disciples unto him, and s. unto......	*3004*
Mk	8:12	s., Why doth this generation seek ..	*3004*
Mk	8:17	he s. unto them, Why reason ye, ...	*3004*
Mk	8:29	he s. unto them, But whom say ye ..	*3004*
Mk	8:29	Peter answereth and s. unto him,.......	*3004*
Mk	9:19	and s., O faithless generation, how .	*3004*
Mk	9:35	called the twelve, and s. unto them, ...	*3004*
Mk	10:11	s. unto them, Whosoever shall put ..	*3004*
Mk	10:23	s. unto his disciples, How hardly......	*3004*
Mk	10:24	answereth again, and s. unto them,.....	*3004*
Mk	10:27	Jesus looking upon them s., With......	*3004*
Mk	10:42	s. unto them, Ye know that they......	*3004*
Mk	11:2	s. unto them, Go your way into the..	*3004*
Mk	11:21	s. unto him, Master, behold, the........	*3004*
Mk	11:22	s. unto them, Have faith in God......	*3004*
Mk	11:23	things which he s. shall come to ...	*3004*
Mk	11:23	he shall have whatsoever he s........	*3004*
Mk	11:33	And Jesus answering s. unto them,.....	*3004*
Mk	12:16	And he s. unto them, Whose is this..	*3004*
Mk	12:43	him his disciples, and s. unto them, ...	*3004*
Mk	13:1	one of his disciples s. unto him	*3004*
Mk	14:13	s. unto them, Go ye into the city, ...	*3004*
Mk	14:14	s., Where is the guestchamber,......	*3004*
Mk	14:27	Jesus s. unto them, All ye shall be...	*3004*
Mk	14:30	And Jesus s. unto him, Verily I say ..	*3004*
Mk	14:32	he s. to his disciples, Sit ye here,.....	*3004*
Mk	14:34	s. unto them, My soul is exceeding..	*3004*
Mk	14:37	s. unto Peter, Simon, sleepest thou?.	*3004*
Mk	14:41	and s. unto them, Sleep on now,......	*3004*
Mk	14:45	and s., Master, master: and kissed.....	*3004*
Mk	14:63	and s., What need we any further	*3004*
Mk	15:28	the scripture was fulfilled, which s., ...	*3004*
Mk	16:6	he s. unto them, Be not affrighted:.....	*3004*
Lu	3:11	and s. unto them, He that hath two....	*3004*
Lu	5:39	new: for he s., This old is better...	*3004*
Lu	7:40	thee. And he s., Master, say on.........	*5346*
Lu	11:24	he s., I will return unto my house..	*3004*
Lu	16:29	Abraham s. unto him, They have...	*3004*
Lu	18:6	Hear what the unjust judge s........	*3004*

Lu 19:22 s. unto him, Out of thine own....... 3004
Lu 20:42 And David himself s. in the book .. 3004
Lu 22:11 The Master s. unto thee, Where is. 3004
Lu 24:36 and s. unto them, Peace be unto...... 3004
Joh 1:21 Art thou Elias? And he s., I am not.... 3004
Joh 1:29 s., Behold the Lamb of God, which..... 3004
Joh 1:36 he s., Behold the Lamb of God!......... 3004
Joh 1:38 and s. unto them, What seek ye?..... 3004
Joh 1:39 He s. unto them, Come and see........ 3004
Joh 1:41 and s. unto him, We have found the.... 3004
Joh 1:43 Philip, s. unto him, Follow me......... 3004
Joh 1:45 and s. unto him, We have found him, .. 3004
Joh 1:46 Philip, s. unto him, Come and see...... 3004
Joh 1:47 and s. of him, Behold an Israelite ... 3004
Joh 1:48 Nathanael s. unto him, Whence.......... 3004
Joh 1:49 Nathanael answered and s. unto......... 3004
Joh 1:51 he s. unto him, Verily, verily, I say. 3004
Joh 2:3 the mother of Jesus s. unto him,........ 3004
Joh 2:4 Jesus s. unto her, Woman, what...... 3004
Joh 2:5 His mother s. unto the servants,......... 3004
Joh 2:5 Whatsoever, he s. unto you, do it...... 3004
Joh 2:7 Jesus s. unto them, Fill the............ 3004
Joh 2:8 he s. unto them, Draw out now, and.3004
Joh 2:10 And s. unto him, Every man at the..... 3004
Joh 3:4 Nicodemus s. unto him, How can a...... 3004
Joh 4:7 Jesus s. unto her, Give me to drink. .3004
Joh 4:9 s. the woman of Samaria unto him,..... 3004
Joh 4:10 who it is that s. to thee, Give me .. 3004
Joh 4:11 The woman s. unto him, Sir, thou...... 3004
Joh 4:15 woman s. unto him, Sir, give me......... 3004
Joh 4:16 Jesus s. unto her, Go, call thy......... 3004
Joh 4:19 woman s. unto him, Sir, I perceive..... 3004
Joh 4:21 Jesus s. unto her, Woman, believe... 3004
Joh 4:25 woman s. unto him, I know that.......... 3004
Joh 4:26 Jesus s. unto her, I that speak unto..3004
Joh 4:28 way into the city, and s. to the men, .. 3004
Joh 4:34 Jesus s. unto them, My meat is to.... 3004
Joh 4:49 nobleman s. unto him, Sir, come........ 3004
Joh 4:50 Jesus s. unto him, Go thy way; thy.. 3004
Joh 5:6 he s. unto him, Wilt thou be made .. 3004
Joh 5:8 Jesus s. unto him, Rise, take up thy..3004
Joh 6:5 he s. unto Philip, Whence shall we... 3004
Joh 6:8 Simon Peter's brother, s. unto him,.... 3004
Joh 6:20 But he s. unto them, It is I; be not.. 3004
Joh 6:42 then that he s., I came down from..... 3004
Joh 7:50 Nicodemus s. unto them, (he that....... 3004
Joh 8:22 because he s., Whither I go, ye......... 3004
Joh 8:25 Jesus s. unto them, Even the same... 3004
Joh 8:39 Jesus s. unto them, If ye were......... 3004
Joh 11:7 after that s. he to his disciples, Let.... 3004
Joh 11:11 and after that he s. unto them, Our ... 3004
Joh 11:23 Jesus s. unto her, Thy brother......... 3004
Joh 11:24 Martha s. unto him, I know that he 3004
Joh 11:27 She s. unto him, Yea, Lord: I........... 3004
Joh 11:39 s. unto him, Lord, by this time he...... 3004
Joh 11:40 Jesus s. unto her, Said I not unto.... 3004
Joh 11:44 Jesus s. unto them, Loose him, and . 3004
Joh 12:4 Then s. one of his disciples, Judas...... 3004
Joh 13:6 Peter s. unto him, Lord, dost thou...... 3004
Joh 13:8 Peter s. unto him, Thou shalt never ... 3004
Joh 13:9 Simon Peter s. unto him, Lord, not 3004
Joh 13:10 Jesus s. to him, He that is washed... 3004
Joh 13:25 breast s. unto him, Lord, who is it?.... 3004
Joh 14:5 Thomas s. unto him, Lord, we 3004
Joh 14:6 Jesus s. unto him, I am the way,...... 3004
Joh 14:8 Philip s. unto him, Lord, shew us....... 3004
Joh 14:9 Jesus s. unto him, Have I been so 3004
Joh 14:22 Judas s. unto him, not Iscariot, ... 3004
Joh 16:17 What is this that he s. unto us, A 3004
Joh 16:18 What is this that he s., A little........... 3004
Joh 16:18 while? we cannot tell what he s. 2980
Joh 18:5 Jesus s. unto them, I am he. And 3004
Joh 18:17 s. the damsel that kept the door 3004
Joh 18:17 man's disciples? He s., I am not......... 3004
Joh 18:26 s., Did not I see thee in the garden.... 3004
Joh 18:38 Pilate s. unto him, What is truth?....... 3004
Joh 18:38 s. unto them, I find in him no fault 3004
Joh 19:4 s. unto them, Behold, I bring him........ 3004
Joh 19:5 Pilate s. unto them, Behold the man! .. 3004
Joh 19:6 Pilate s. unto them, Take ye him, ... 3004
Joh 19:9 s. unto Jesus, Whence art thou?......... 3004
Joh 19:10 s. Pilate unto him, Speakest thou 3004
Joh 19:14 he s. unto the Jews, Behold your 3004
Joh 19:15 Pilate s. unto them, Shall I crucify...... 3004
Joh 19:24 which s., They parted my raiment...... 3004
Joh 19:26 s. unto his mother, Woman, behold.. 3004
Joh 19:27 s. he to the disciples, Behold thy 3004
Joh 19:28 scripture might be fulfilled, s., I......... 3004
Joh 19:35 and he knoweth that he s. true, that.... 3004
Joh 19:37 scripture s., They shall look on him.... 3004
Joh 20:2 and s. unto them, They have taken..... 3004
Joh 20:13 She s. unto them, Because they......... 3004
Joh 20:15 s. unto her, Woman, why weepest... 3004
Joh 20:15 s. unto him, Sir, if thou have borne 3004
Joh 20:16 Jesus s. unto her, Mary. She............ 3004
Joh 20:16 and s. unto him, Rabboni; which is 3004
Joh 20:17 Jesus s. unto her, Touch me not;..... 3004
Joh 20:19 s. unto them, Peace be unto you..... 3004
Joh 20:22 s. unto them, Receive ye the Holy... 3004
Joh 20:27 s. he to Thomas, Reach hither thy .. 3004
Joh 20:29 Jesus s. unto him, Thomas, because. 3004
Joh 21:3 Simon Peter s. unto them, I go a....... 3004
Joh 21:5 Jesus s. unto them, Children, have... 3004
Joh 21:7 loved s. unto Peter, It is the Lord...... 3004
Joh 21:10 Jesus s. unto them, Bring of the....... 3004
Joh 21:12 Jesus s. unto them, Come and dine. ..3004
Joh 21:15 Jesus s. to Simon Peter, Simon, son ..3004
Joh 21:15 He s. unto him, Yea, Lord; thou 3004
Joh 21:15 He s. unto him, Feed my lambs....... 3004
Joh 21:16 He s. to him again the second time,.... 3004
Joh 21:16 He s. unto him, Yea, Lord; thou 3004
Joh 21:16 He s. unto him, Feed my sheep....... 3004
Joh 21:17 He s. unto him the third time, ... 3004
Joh 21:17 Jesus s. unto him, Feed my sheep. ... 3004
Joh 21:19 this, he s. unto him, Follow me. 3004
Joh 21:21 s. to Jesus, Lord, and what shall........ 3004
Joh 21:22 Jesus s. unto him, If I will that he... 3004
Ac 1:4 Which, s. he, ye have heard of me......
Ac 2:17 to pass in the last days, s. God, ... 3004
Ac 2:34 he s. himself, The Lord said unto....... 3004
Ac 7:48 with hands; as s. the prophet, ... 3004
Ac 7:49 house will ye build me? s. the Lord: ... 3004
Ac 12:8 he s. unto him, Cast thy garment....... 3004
Ac 13:35 he s. also in another psalm, Thou....... 3004
Ac 15:17 s. the Lord, who doeth all these 3004
Ac 21:11 Thus s. the Holy Ghost, So shall........ 3004
Ac 22:2 kept the more silence: and he s.,)...... 5346
Ro 3:19 that what things soever the law s.,..... 3004
Ro 3:19 s. to them who are under the law: 2980
Ro 4:3 what s. the Scripture? Abraham 3004
Ro 9:15 he s. to Moses, I will have mercy on.. 3004
Ro 9:17 For the scripture s. unto Pharaoh,...... 3004
Ro 9:25 he s. also in Osee, I will call them..... 3004
Ro 10:8 But what s. it? The word is nigh........ 3004
Ro 10:11 For the scripture s., Whosoever 3004
Ro 10:16 Esaias s., Lord, who hath believed..... 3004
Ro 10:19 First Moses s., I will provoke you to .. 3004
Ro 10:20 Esaias is very bold, and s., I was....... 3004
Ro 10:21 to Israel he s., All day long I have 3004
Ro 11:2 ye not what the scripture s. of Elias?.. 3004
Ro 11:4 But what s. the answer of God unto ... 3004
Ro 11:9 David s., Let their table be made a 3004
Ro 12:19 is mine; I will repay, s. the Lord......... 3004
Ro 14:11 As I live, s. the Lord, every knee...... 3004
Ro 15:10 again he s., Rejoice, ye Gentiles, ... 3004
Ro 15:12 Esaias s., There shall be a root of...... 3004
1Co 1:12 every one of you s., I am of Paul;...... 3004
1Co 3:4 For while one s., I am of Paul; and 3004
1Co 6:16 for two, s. he, shall be one flesh........ 5346
1Co 9:8 or s. not the law the same also? 3004
1Co 9:10 Or s. he it altogether for our sakes? ... 3004
1Co 14:21 will they not hear me, s. the Lord...... 3004
1Co 14:34 under obedience, as also s. the law...... 3004
1Co 15:27 But when he s. all things are put 2036
2Co 6:2 (For he s., I have heard thee in a 3004
2Co 6:17 and be ye separate, s. the Lord, and .. 3004
2Co 6:18 daughters, s. the Lord Almighty......... 3004
Ga 3:16 He s. not, And to seeds, as of many;.. 3004
Ga 4:30 Nevertheless what s. the scripture?.... 3004
Eph 4:8 Wherefore he s., When he ascended.... 3004
Eph 5:14 Wherefore he s., Awake thou that...... 3004
1Ti 5:18 For the scripture s., Thou shalt not.... 3004
Heb 1:6 he s., And let all the angels of God 3004
Heb 1:7 of the angels he s., Who maketh his ... 3004
Heb 1:8 But unto the Son he s., Thy throne, O......
Heb 3:7 (as the Holy Ghost s., To day if ye 3004
Heb 5:6 s. also in another place, Thou art a..... 3004
Heb 8:5 for, See, s. he, that thou make all...... 5346
Heb 8:8 For finding fault with them, he s., ... 3004
Heb 8:8 days come, s. the Lord, when I will..... 3004
Heb 8:9 I regarded them not, s. the Lord......... 3004
Heb 8:10 Israel after those days, s. the Lord;.... 3004
Heb 8:13 In that he s., A new covenant, he 3004
Heb 10:5 he s., Sacrifice and offering thou 3004
Heb 10:16 s. the Lord, I will put my laws into 3004
Heb 10:30 me, I will recompense, s. the Lord..... 3004
Jas 2:23 the scripture was fulfilled which s.,..... 3004
Jas 4:5 the scripture s. in vain, The spirit 3004
Jas 4:6 Wherefore he s., God resisteth the..... 3004
1Jo 2:4 He that s., I know him, and keepeth... 3004
1Jo 2:6 He that s. he abideth in him ought...... 3004
1Jo 2:9 He that s. he is in the light, and 3004
Re 1:8 s. the Lord, which is, and which was, ..3004
Re 2:1 s. he that holdeth the seven stars.. 3004
Re 2:7 him hear what the Spirit s. unto... 3004
Re 2:8 things s. the first and the last,....... 3004
Re 2:11 him hear what the Spirit s. unto... 3004
Re 2:12 These things s. he which hath the..3004
Re 2:17 him hear what the Spirit s. unto... 3004
Re 2:18 These things s. the Son of God,...... 3004
Re 2:29 him hear what the Spirit s. unto... 3004
Re 3:1 s. he that hath the seven Spirits.... 3004
Re 3:6 him hear what the Spirit s. unto... 3004
Re 3:7 These things s. he that is holy, he..3004
Re 3:13 him hear what the Spirit s. unto... 3004
Re 3:14 These things s. the Amen, the....... 3004
Re 3:22 him hear what the Spirit s. unto... 3004
Re 5:5 of the elders s. unto me, Weep not: ... 3004
Re 14:13 Yea, s. the Spirit, that they may rest.. 3004
Re 17:15 he s. unto me, The waters which....... 3004
Re 18:7 for she s. in her heart, I sit a queen,.. 3004
Re 19:9 he s. unto me, Write, Blessed are...... 3004
Re 19:9 he s. unto me, These are the true 3004
Re 22:9 s. he unto me, See thou do it not: 3004
Re 22:10 he s. unto me, Seal not the sayings.... 3004
Re 22:20 He which testifieth these things s.,..... 3004

SAKE See also SAKES.

Ge 3:17 cursed is the ground for thy s.; 5668
Ge 8:21 the ground any more for man's s.;...... 5668
Ge 12:13 it may be well with me for thy s.; 5668
Ge 12:16 he entreated Abram well for her s...... 5668
Ge 18:29 he said, I will not do it for forty's s.. .. 5668
Ge 18:31 I will not destroy it for twenty's s.. 5668
Ge 18:32 I will not destroy it for ten's s........... 5668
Ge 20:11 they will slay me for my wife's s........ 1697
Ge 26:24 seed for my servant Abraham's s.. 5668
Ge 30:27 Lord hath blessed me for thy s........ 1558
Ge 39:5 Egyptian's house for Joseph's s.;........ 1558
Ex 18:8 and to the Egyptians for Israel's s.,...... 182
Ex 21:26 let him go free for his eye's s............ 8478
Ex 21:27 shall let him go free for his tooth's s....8478
Nu 11:29 said unto him, Enviest thou for my s.? ....
Nu 25:11 zealous for my s. among them, ... 7068
Nu 25:18 day of the plague for Peor's s........... 1697
1Sa 12:22 his people for his great name's s.:....... 5668
1Sa 23:10 to destroy the city for my s.. 5668
2Sa 5:12 kingdom for his people Israel's s.. 5668
2Sa 7:21 For thy word's s., and according to 5668
2Sa 9:1 him kindness for Jonathan's s.? 5668
2Sa 9:7 for Jonathan thy father's s.,............... 5668
2Sa 18:5 gently for my s. with the young man,........
1Ki 8:41 of a far country for thy name's s.;...... 4616
1Ki 11:12 not do it for David thy father's s.:....... 4616
1Ki 11:13 thy son for David my servant's s.,...... 4616
1Ki 11:13 Jerusalem's s. which I have chosen..... 4616
1Ki 11:32 one tribe for my servant David's s.,..... 4616
1Ki 11:32 for Jerusalem's s., the city which I 4616
1Ki 11:34 of his life for David my servant's s., ... 4616
1Ki 15:4 for David's s. did the Lord his God..... 4616
2Ki 8:19 Judah for David his servant's s.,.......... 4616
2Ki 19:34 this city, to save it, for mine own s.,.. 4616
2Ki 19:34 and for my servant David's s............. 4616
2Ki 20:6 defend this city for mine own s.,.......... 4616
2Ki 20:6 and for my servant David's s............. 4616
1Ch 17:19 Lord, for thy servants s. and.............. 5668
2Ch 6:32 far country for thy great name's s. 4616
Ne 9:31 for thy great mercies' s. thou didst...........
Job 19:17 for the children's s. of my own body. ....
Ps 6:4 oh save me for thy mercies' s............ 4616
Ps 23:3 of righteousness for his name's s.......... 4616
Ps 25:7 me for thy goodness s., O Lord.......... 4616
Ps 25:11 For thy name's s., O Lord, pardon..... 4616
Ps 31:3 for thy name's s. lead me, and........... 4616
Ps 31:16 servant: save me for thy mercies' s.. ....
Ps 44:22 for thy s. are we killed all the day............
Ps 44:26 redeem us for thy mercies' s............. 4616
Ps 69:6 God of hosts, be ashamed for my s. ....
Ps 69:6 seek thee be confounded for my s., ...
Ps 69:7 for thy s. I have borne reproach 5921

Ps 79:9 away our sins, for thy name's **s.** 4616
Ps 106:8 he saved them for his name's **s.**, ... 4616
Ps 109:21 God the Lord, for thy name's **s.** 4616
Ps 115:1 for thy mercy, and for thy truth's **s.**. ....
Ps 132:10 servant David's **s.** turn not away 5668
Ps 143:11 me, O Lord, for thy name's **s.** ....
Ps 143:11 righteousness' **s.** bring my soul out ....
Isa 37:35 this city to save it for mine own **s.**, ...
Isa 37:35 and for my servant David's **s.**; 4616
Isa 42:21 pleased for his righteousness' **s.**; 4616
Isa 43:14 For your **s.** I have sent to Babylon, ... 4616
Isa 43:25 thy transgressions for mine own **s.**, ... 4616
Isa 45:4 For Jacob my servant's **s.** and 4616
Isa 48:9 name's **s.** will I defer mine anger, ... 4616
Isa 48:11 mine own **s.**, even for mine own **s.**, ... 4616
Isa 54:15 against thee shall fall for thy **s.** 5921
Isa 62:1 and for Jerusalem's **s.** I will not 4616
Isa 62:1 Zion's **s.** will I not hold my peace, ... 4616
Isa 63:17 Return for thy servants' **s.**, the 4616
Isa 66:5 that cast you out for my name's **s.** 4616
Jer 14:7 us, do thou it for thy name's **s.**: 4616
Jer 14:21 Do not abhor us, for thy name's **s.**, ... 4616
Jer 15:15 for thy **s.** I have suffered rebuke. ....
Eze 20:9, 14 I wrought for my name's **s.**, ... 4616
Eze 20:22 and wrought for my name's **s.**, that 4616
Eze 20:44 wrought with you for my name's **s.** 4616
Eze 36:22 but for mine holy name's **s.**, which ....
Da 9:17 that is desolate, for the Lord's **s.**. 4616
Da 9:19 not, for thine own **s.**, O my God: 4616
Jon 1:12 for my **s.** this great tempest is 7945
Mic 3:12 shall Zion for your **s.** be plowed as 1558
Mt 5:10 persecuted for righteousness' **s.** *1752*
Mt 5:11 evil against you falsely, for my **s.** ... *1752*
Mt 10:18 governors and kings for my **s.**, for .*1752*
Mt 10:22 hated of all men for my name's **s.** ....
Mt 10:39 that loseth his life for my **s.** shall ..*1752*
Mt 14:3 put him in prison for Herodias' **s.**, ...
Mt 14:9 nevertheless for the oath's **s.**, and ....
Mt 16:25 will lose his life for my **s.** shall *1752*
Mt 19:12 for the kingdom of heaven's **s.**. ....
Mt 19:29 or lands, for my name's **s.**, shall ... *1752*
Mt 24:9 of all nations for my name's **s.** ....
Mt 24:22 the elect's **s.** those days shall be ....
Mk 4:17 persecution ariseth for the word's **s.**, ...
Mk 6:17 him in prison for Herodias' **s.**, ...
Mk 6:26 yet for his oath's **s.**, and for their ....
Mk 8:35 shall lose his life for my **s.** and *1752*
Mk 10:29 lands, for my **s.**, and the gospel's, ..*1752*
Mk 13:9 before rulers and kings for my **s.**, . *1752*
Mk 13:13 hated of all men for my name's **s.** ....
Mk 13:20 for the elect's **s.**, whom he hath ....
Lu 6:22 as evil, for the Son of man's **s.** *1752*
Lu 9:24 will lose his life for my **s.**, the *1752*
Lu 18:29 for the kingdom of God's **s.** *1752*
Lu 21:12 kings and rulers for my name's **s.** . *1752*
Lu 21:17 hated of all men for my name's **s.** ....
Joh 12:9 they came not for Jesus' **s.** only, ...
Joh 13:37 I will lay down my life for thy **s.**. ....
Joh 13:38 thou lay down thy life for my **s.**? ....
Joh 14:11 believe me for the very works' **s.**. ....
Joh 15:21 they do unto you for my name's **s.**, ...
Ac 9:16 he must suffer for my name's **s.** ....
Ac 26:7 For which hope's **s.**, king Agrippa, ...
Ro 4:23 was not written for his **s.** alone, ...
Ro 8:36 For thy **s.** we are killed all the day *1752*
Ro 13:5 wrath, but also for conscience **s.**. ....
Ro 15:30 for the Lord Jesus Christ's **s.**, and ....
1Co 4:10 We are fools for Christ's **s.**, but ye ....
1Co 9:23 this I do for the gospel's **s.**, that I ....
1Co 10:25, 27 no question for conscience **s.**: ....
1Co 10:28 eat not for his **s.** that shewed it, ...
1Co 10:28 for conscience **s.**: for the earth ....
2Co 4:5 your servants for Jesus' **s.** ....
2Co 4:11 delivered unto death for Jesus' **s.**, ...
2Co 12:10 in distresses for Christ's **s.**: for ....
Eph 4:32 for Christ's **s.** hath forgiven you. *1722*
Php 1:29 him, but also to suffer for his **s.**; ....
Col 1:24 Christ in my flesh for his body's **s.**, ...
Col 3:6 For which things's **s.** the wrath of ....
1Th 1:5 we were among you for your **s.** ....
1Th 5:13 highly in love for their work's **s.** ....
1Ti 5:23 a little wine for thy stomach's **s.** ....
Tit 1:11 they ought not, for filthy lucre's **s.** ....
Phm 9 Yet for love's **s.** I rather beseech ....
1Pe 2:13 ordinance of man for the Lord's **s.**: ....
1Pe 3:14 if ye suffer for righteousness' **s.**, ...
1Jo 2:12 are forgiven you for his name's **s.** ....
2Jo 2 For the truth's **s.**, which dwelleth ....
3Jo 7 for his name's **s.** they went forth, ...
Re 2:3 and for my name's **s.** hast laboured, ...

SAKES
Ge 18:26 will spare all the place for their **s.** 5668
Le 26:45 for their **s.** remember the covenant ....
De 1:37 was angry with me for your **s.**, ... 1558
De 3:26 was wroth with me for your **s.**, ... 6616
De 4:21 was angry with me for your **s.**, ... 1697
Jg 21:22 Be favourable unto them for our **s.** ....
Ru 1:13 it grieveth me much for your **s.** that ....
1Ch 16:21 he reproved kings for their **s.**, ... 5921
Ps 7:7 for their **s.** therefore return thou 5921
Ps 105:14 yea, he reproved kings for their **s.**, ... 5921
Ps 106:32 it went ill with Moses for their **s.** 5668
Ps 122:8 my brethren and companions' **s.**, ... 6616
Isa 65:8 so will I do for my servants' **s.**, that ... 6616
Eze 36:22 I do not this for your **s.**, O house of ... 6616
Eze 36:32 Not for your **s.** do I this, saith the 6616
Da 2:30 for their **s.** that shall make known 1701
Mal 3:11 I will rebuke the devourer for your **s.**, ...
Mk 6:26 and for their **s.** which sat with him, ...
Joh 11:15 glad for your **s.** that I was not there, ..
Joh 12:30 because of me, but for your **s.** ....
Joh 17:19 And for their **s.** I sanctify myself, ...
Ro 11:28 they are enemies for your **s.**: ....
Ro 11:28 are beloved for the fathers' **s.** ....
1Co 4:6 and to Apollos for your **s.**; ....
1Co 9:10 saith he it altogether for our **s.**? ....
1Co 9:10 For our **s.**, no doubt, this is ....
2Co 2:10 for your **s.** forgave I it in the ....
2Co 4:15 all things are for your **s.**, that ....
2Co 8:9 yet for your **s.** he became poor, ...
1Th 3:9 joy for your **s.** before our God; ....
2Ti 2:10 endure all things for the elect's **s.**, ...

SALA (sa'-lah) See also SALAH.
Lu 3:35 of Heber, which was the son of **S.**, ... *4527*

SALAH (sa'-lah) See also SALA.
Ge 10:24 Arphaxad begat **S.**; and **S.** begat 7974
Ge 11:12 five and thirty years, and begat **S.**: 7974
Ge 11:13 Arphaxad lived after he begat **S.** 7974
Ge 11:14 **S.** lived thirty years, and begat 7974
Ge 11:15 **S.** lived after he begat Eber four 7974

SALAMIS (sal'-a-mis)
Ac 13:5 And when they were at **S.**, they *4529*

SALATHIEL (sa-la'-the-el) See also SHEALTIEL.
1Ch 3:17 sons of Jeconiah; Assir, **S.** his 7597
Mt 1:12 to Babylon, Jechonias begat **S.**; *4528*
Mt 1:12 and **S.** begat Zorobabel; *4528*
Lu 3:27 which was the son of **S.**, which *4528*

SALCAH (sal'-kah) See also SALCHAH.
Jos 12:5 in mount Hermon, and in **S.**, ... 5548
Jos 13:11 Hermon, and all Bashan unto **S.**; 5548
1Ch 5:11 in the land of Bashan unto **S.**: 5548

SALCHAH (sal'-kah) See also SALCAH.
De 3:10 all Bashan, unto **S.** and Edrei, ... 5548

SALE
Le 25:27 count the years of the **s.** thereof, ... 4465
Le 25:50 price of his **s.** shall be according 4465
De 18:8 cometh of the **s.** of his patrimony. 4465

SALEM (sa'-lem) See also JERUSALEM.
Ge 14:18 Melchizedek king of **S.** brought 8004
Ps 76:2 In **S.** also in his tabernacle, and his 8004
Heb 7:1 For this Melchisedec king of **S.**, ... *4532*
Heb 7:2 after that also King of **S.**, which is, ... *4532*

SALIM (sa'-lim)
Joh 3:23 was baptizing in Aenon near to **S.**, ... *4530*

SALLAI (sal'-lahee) See also SALLU.
Ne 11:8 And after him Gabbai, **S.**, nine 5543
Ne 12:20 Of **S.**, Kallai; of Amok, Eber; 5543

SALLU (sal'-lu) See also SALLAI.
1Ch 9:7 **S.** the son of Meshullam, the son 5543
Ne 11:7 **S.** the son of Meshullam, the son 5543
Ne 12:7 **S.**, Amok, Hilkiah, Jedaiah. These 5543

SALMA (sal'-mah) See also SALMON; ZALMA.
1Ch 2:11 begat **S.**, and **S.** begat Boaz, ... 8007
1Ch 2:51 **S.** the father of Beth-lehem, ... 8007
1Ch 2:54 The sons of **S.**; Beth-lehem, and 8007

SALMON (sal'-mon) See also SALMA.
Ru 4:20 Nahshon, and Nahson begat **S.**, ... 8009
Ru 4:21 And **S.** begat Boaz, and Boaz 8012
Ps 68:14 in it, it was white as snow in **S.** 6756
Mt 1:4 Naasson; and Naasson begat **S.**; *4533*
Mt 1:5 **S.** begat Booz of Rachab; and Booz *4533*
Lu 3:32 of Booz, which was the son of **S.**, ... *4533*

SALMONE (sal-mo'-ne)
Ac 27:7 under Crete, over against **S.**; *4534*

SALOME (sa-lo'-me)
Mk 15:40 the less and of Joses, and **S.**; *4539*
Mk 16:1 Mary the mother of James, and **S.**, ... *4539*

SALT See also SALTED; SALTPITS.
Ge 14:3 vale of Siddim, which is the **s.** sea 4417
Ge 19:26 him, and she became a pillar of **s.**. 4417
Le 2:13 offering shalt thou season with **s.**. 4417
Le 2:13 the **s.** of the covenant of thy God 4417
Le 2:13 thine offerings thou shalt offer **s.** 4417
Nu 18:19 it is a covenant of **s.** for ever before ... 4417
Nu 34:3 coast of the **s.** sea eastward: 4417
Nu 34:12 out of it shall be at the **s.** sea: 4417
De 3:17 the sea of the plain, even the **s.** sea, .. 4417
De 29:23 land thereof is brimstone, and **s.**, ... 4417
Jos 3:16 the sea of the plain, even the **s.** sea, .. 4417
Jos 12:3 the sea of the plain, even the **s.** sea .. 4417
Jos 15:2 was from the shore of the **s.** sea, ... 4417
Jos 15:5 And the east border was the **s.** sea, ... 4417
Jos 15:62 and the city of **S.**, and En-gedi; 5898
Jos 18:19 were at the north bay of the **s.** sea 4417
Jg 9:45 down the city, and sowed it with **s.**. ... 4417
2Sa 8:13 of the Syrians in the valley of **s.**, ... 4417
2Ki 2:20 Bring me a new cruse, and put **s.** 4417
2Ki 2:21 the waters, and cast the **s.** in there, ... 4417
2Ki 14:7 He slew of Edom in the valley of **s.** 4417
1Ch 18:12 slew...Edomites in the valley of **s.** 4417
2Ch 13:5 and to his sons by a covenant of **s.**? ... 4417
2Ch 25:11 went to the valley of **s.**, and smote 4417
Ezr 6:9 wheat, **s.**, wine, and oil, according 4416
Ezr 7:22 **s.** without prescribing how much. 4416
Job 6:6 is unsavoury be eaten without **s.**? 4417
Ps 60:*title* smote of Edom in the valley of **s.** 4417
Jer 17:6 in a **s.** land and not inhabited. 4420
Eze 43:24 priests shall cast **s.** upon them, ... 4417
Eze 47:11 be healed; they shall be given to **s.** 4417
Mt 5:13 Ye are the **s.** of the earth: but if *217*
Mt 5:13 but if the **s.** have lost his savour, ... *217*
Mk 9:49 sacrifice shall be salted with **s.** *251*
Mk 9:50 **S.** is good: but if the **s.** have lost *217*
Mk 9:50 Have **s.** in yourselves, and have *217*
Lu 14:34 **S.** is good: but if the **s.** have lost *217*
Col 4:6 alway with grace, seasoned with **s.**, ... *217*
Jas 3:12 both yield **s.** water and fresh. *252*

SALTED
Eze 16:4 not **s.** at all, nor swaddled at all. 4414
Mt 5:13 savour, wherewith shall it be **s.**? *233*
Mk 9:49 For every one shall be **s.** with fire, ... *233*
Mk 9:49 every sacrifice shall be **s.** with salt. .*233*

SALTNESS
Mk 9:50 but if the salt have lost his **s.**, . *1096,358*

SALTPITS
Zep 2:9 the breeding of nettles, and **s.**, and 4417

SALT-SEA See SALT and SEA.

SALU (sa'-lu)
Ne 25:14 was Zimri, the son of **S.**, a prince 5543

SALUTATION See also SALUTATIONS.
Lu 1:29 what manner of **s.** this should be. *783*
Lu 1:41 when Elisabeth heard the **s.** of Mary, ... *783*
Lu 1:44 voice of thy **s.** sounded in mine ears, ... *783*
1Co 16:21 **s.** of me Paul with mine own hand. *783*
Col 4:18 The **s.** by the hand of me Paul. *783*
2Th 3:17 The **s.** of Paul with mine own hand, ... *783*

SALUTATIONS
Mk 12:38 and love **s.** in the marketplaces, ... *783*

SALUTE See also SALUTED; SALUTETH.
1Sa 10:4 And they will **s.** thee, and give 7965
1Sa 13:10 to meet him, that he might **s.** him. 1288
1Sa 25:14 of the wilderness to **s.** our master; 1288
2Sa 8:10 son unto king David, to **s.** him, ... 7592,7965
2Ki 4:29 if thou meet any man, **s.** him not; 1288
2Ki 4:29 and if any **s.** thee, answer him not. 1288
2Ki 10:13 to **s.** the children of the king and 7965
Mt 5:47 And if ye **s.** your brethren only, ... *782*
Mt 10:12 when ye come into an house, **s.** it ... *782*

Mk 15:18 began to s. him, Hail, King of the........ 782
Lu 10:4 **shoes: and s. no man by the way.** ... 782
Ac 25:13 came unto Caesarea to s. Festus......... 782
Ro 16:5 S. my wellbeloved Epaenetus, who 782
Ro 16:7 S. Andronicus and Junia, my 782
Ro 16:9 S. Urbane, our helper in Christ,.......... 782
Ro 16:10 S. Apelles approved in Christ.............. 782
Ro 16:10 S. them which are of Aristobulus' 782
Ro 16:11 S. Herodion my kinsman. Greet 782
Ro 16:12 S. Tryphena and Tryphosa, who.......... 782
Ro 16:12 S. the beloved Persis, which............... 782
Ro 16:13 S. Rufus chosen in the Lord, and.......... 782
Ro 16:14 S. Asyncritus, Phlegon, Hermas, ... 782
Ro 16:15 S. Philologus, and Julia, Nereus, ... 782
Ro 16:16 S. one another with an holy kiss........... 782
Ro 16:16 The churches of Christ s. you............. 782
Ro 16:21 and Sosipater, my kinsmen, s. you........ 782
Ro 16:22 who wrote this epistle, s. you in the 782
1Co 16:19 The churches of Asia s. you. 782
1Co 16:19 Aquila and Priscilla s. you much in 782
2Co 13:13 All the saints s. you............................ 782
Php 4:21 S. every saint in Christ Jesus............. 782
Php 4:22 All the saints s. you, chiefly they......... 782
Col 4:15 S. the brethren...in Laodicea, ... 782
2Ti 4:19 S. Prisca and Aquila, and the 782
Tit 3:15 All that are with me s. thee. Greet...... 782
Phm 23 There s. thee Epaphras, my............... 782
Heb 13:24 S. all them that have the rule over....... 782
Heb 13:24 all the saints. They of Italy s. you........ 782
3Jo 14 Peace be to thee. Our friends s. thee... 782

SALUTED
Jg 18:15 house of Micah, and s. him. 7592,7965
1Sa 17:22 and came and s. his brethren...... 7592,7965
1Sa 30:21 near to the people, he s. them. .. 7592,7965
2Ki 10:15 he s. him, and said to him, Is thine 1288
Mk 9:15 amazed, and running to him s. him........ 782
Lu 1:40 house of Zacharias, and s. Elisabeth. 782
Ac 18:22 and gone up, and s. the church, he 782
Ac 21:7 and s. the brethren, and abode with 782
Ac 21:19 when he had s. them, he declared......... 782

SALUTETH
Ro 16:23 and of the whole church, s. you........... 782
Ro 16:23 the chamberlain of the city s. you, ... 782
Col 4:10 Aristarchus...s. you, and Marcus, ... 782
Col 4:12 Epaphras, who is one of you,...s. you,.. 782
1Pe 5:13 church that is at Babylon, s....you;....... 782

SALVATION
Ge 49:18 I have waited for thy s., O Lord. 3444
Ex 14:13 still, and see the s. of the Lord, ... 3444
Ex 15:2 and song, and he is become my s.:........ 3444
De 32:15 lightly esteemed the Rock of his s.. 3444
1Sa 2:1 enemies; because I rejoice in thy s........ 3444
1Sa 11:13 Lord hath wrought s. in Israel. 8668
1Sa 14:45 wrought this great s. in Israel? 3444
1Sa 19:5 Lord wrought a great s. for all............ 8668
2Sa 22:3 my shield, and the horn of my s.,......... 3468
2Sa 22:36 also given me the shield of thy s.: 3468
2Sa 22:47 be the God of the rock of my s.. 3468
2Sa 22:51 He is the tower of s. for his king: 3444
2Sa 23:5 this is all my s., and all my desire, ... 3468
1Ch 16:23 shew forth from day to day his s.......... 3444
1Ch 16:35 Save us, O God of our s. and.............. 3468
2Ch 6:41 thy priests,...be clothed with s., ... 8668
2Ch 20:17 see the s. of the Lord with you, ... 3444
Job 13:16 He also shall be my s.: for an............ 3444
Ps 3:8 S. belongeth unto the Lord: thy.......... 3444
Ps 9:14 of Zion: I will rejoice in thy s............. 3444
Ps 13:5 my heart shall rejoice in thy s............. 3444
Ps 14:7 Oh that the s. of Israel were come..... 3444
Ps 18:2 buckler, and the horn of my s.,.......... 3468
Ps 18:35 also given me the shield of thy s.: 3468
Ps 18:46 and let the God of my s. be exalted..... 3468
Ps 20:5 We will rejoice in thy s., and in the 3444
Ps 21:1 and in thy s. how...shall he rejoice! 3444
Ps 21:5 His glory is great in thy s.: honour..... 3444
Ps 24:5 righteousness from...God of his s........ 3468
Ps 25:5 for thou art the God of my s.;........... 3468
Ps 27:1 Lord is my light and my s.; whom...... 3468
Ps 27:9 neither forsake me, O God of my s. 3468
Ps 35:3 me: say unto my soul, I am thy s.,..... 3444
Ps 35:9 the Lord: it shall rejoice in his s......... 3444
Ps 37:39 s. of the righteous is of the Lord: 8668
Ps 38:22 haste to help me, O Lord my s. 8668
Ps 40:10 declared thy faithfulness and thy s.: 8668
Ps 40:16 let such as love...s. say continually, ... 8668
Ps 50:23 aright will I shew the s. of God. 3468
Ps 51:12 Restore unto me the joy of thy s.; 3468
Ps 51:14 O God, thou God of my s.:................ 8668
Ps 53:6 Oh that the s. of Israel were come..... 3444
Ps 62:1 upon God: from him cometh my s.. 3444
Ps 62:2, 6 He only is my rock and s.; he......... 3444
Ps 62:7 In God is my s. and my glory:........... 3468
Ps 65:5 thou answer us, O God of our s.;....... 3468
Ps 68:19 benefits, even the God of our s.. 3444
Ps 68:20 that is our God is the God of s.; 4190
Ps 69:13 hear me, in the truth of thy s........... 3468
Ps 69:29 let thy s., O God, set me up on high. ..3444
Ps 70:4 let such as love...s. say continually, ... 3444
Ps 71:15 thy righteousness and thy s. all.......... 8668
Ps 74:12 working s. in the midst of the............ 3444
Ps 78:22 in God, and trusted not in his s.: 3444
Ps 79:9 Help us, O God of our s., for the....... 3468
Ps 85:4 Turn us, O God of our s., and cause .. 3468
Ps 85:7 mercy, O Lord, and grant us thy s.. ... 3468
Ps 85:9 his s. is nigh them that fear him;........ 3468
Ps 88:1 O Lord God of my s., I have cried..... 3444
Ps 89:26 my God, and the rock of my s........... 3444
Ps 91:16 I satisfy him, and shew him my s...... 3444
Ps 95:1 joyful noise to the rock of our s........ 3468
Ps 96:2 shew forth his s. from day to day...... 3444
Ps 98:2 The Lord hath made known his s.: 3444
Ps 98:3 earth have seen the s. of our God. 3444
Ps 106:4 thy people: O visit me with thy s.; 3444
Ps 116:13 I will take the cup of s., and call......... 3444
Ps 118:14 and song, and is become my s.. 3444
Ps 118:15 The voice of rejoicing and s. is in....... 3444
Ps 118:21 heard me, and art become my s.......... 3444
Ps 119:41 O Lord, even thy s., according to 8668
Ps 119:81 My soul fainteth for thy s.: but I......... 8668
Ps 119:123 Mine eyes fail for thy s., and for......... 3444
Ps 119:155 S. is far from the wicked: for they 3444
Ps 119:166 Lord, I have hoped for thy s., and....... 3444
Ps 119:174 I have longed for thy s., O Lord; 3444
Ps 132:16 also clothe her priests with s.:.......... 3468
Ps 140:7 the Lord, the strength of my s., ... 3444
Ps 144:10 It is he that giveth s. unto kings: 8668
Ps 149:4 he will beautify the meek with s.......... 3444
Isa 12:2 Behold, God is my s.; I will trust, ... 3444
Isa 12:2 my song; he also is become my s. 3444
Isa 12:3 ye draw water out of the wells of s.... 3444
Isa 17:10 hast forgotten the God of thy s.,......... 3468
Isa 25:9 will be glad and rejoice in his s.. 3444
Isa 26:1 s. will God appoint for walls and......... 3444
Isa 33:2 our s. also in the time of trouble......... 3444
Isa 33:6 of thy times, and strength of s.:.......... 3444
Isa 45:8 and let them bring forth s., and let....... 3468
Isa 45:17 in the Lord with an everlasting s.:........ 8668
Isa 46:13 be far off, and my s. shall not tarry: ... 8668
Isa 46:13 I will place s. in Zion for Israel my 8668
Isa 49:6 my s. unto the end of the earth. 3444
Isa 49:8 in a day of s. have I helped thee: 3444
Isa 51:5 my s. is gone forth, and mine arms 3468
Isa 51:6 but my s. shall be for ever, and my..... 3444
Isa 51:8 and my s. from generation to 3444
Isa 52:7 tidings of good, that publisheth s.;...... 3444
Isa 52:10 earth shall see the s. of our God......... 3444
Isa 56:1 for my s. is near to come, and my 3444
Isa 59:11 for s., but it is far off from us. 3444
Isa 59:16 his arm brought s. unto him; and......... 3467
Isa 59:17 and an helmet of s. upon his head; 3444
Isa 60:18 but thou shalt call thy walls S., and 3444
Isa 61:10 me with the garments of s., ... 3468
Isa 62:1 s. thereof as a lamp that burneth......... 3444
Isa 62:11 of Zion, Behold, thy s. cometh;........... 3468
Isa 63:5 mine own arm brought s. unto me; 3467
Jer 3:23 Truly in vain is s. hoped for from the........
Jer 3:23 Lord our God is the s. of Israel. 8668
La 3:26 quietly wait for the s. of the Lord. 8668
Jon 2:9 I have vowed. S. is of the Lord. 3444
Mic 7:7 I will wait for the God of my s.:......... 3468
Hab 3:8 thine horses and thy chariots of s.?..... 3444
Hab 3:13 forth for the s. of thy people,............ 3468
Hab 3:13 even for s. with thine anointed;.......... 3468
Hab 3:18 Lord, I will joy in the God of my s..... 3468
Zec 9:9 he is just, and having s.; lowly,.......... 3467
Lu 1:69 hath raised up an horn of s. for us...... 4991
Lu 1:77 knowledge of s. unto his people by 4991
Lu 2:30 For mine eyes have seen thy s.,.......... 4991
Lu 3:6 And all flesh shall see the s. of God..... 4992
Lu 19:9 **This day is s. come to this house,**. 4991
Joh 4:22 **we worship: for s. is of the Jews** .. 4991
Ac 4:12 Neither is there s. in any other: for.... 4991
Ac 13:26 to you is the word of this s. sent. 4991
Ac 13:47 be for s. unto the ends of the earth..... 4991
Ac 16:17 which shew unto us the way of s.. 4991
Ac 28:28 s. of God is sent unto the Gentiles, ... 4992
Ro 1:16 power of God unto s. to every one..... 4991
Ro 10:10 mouth confession is made unto s.. 4991
Ro 11:11 fall s. is come unto the Gentiles, ... 4991
Ro 13:11 s. nearer than when we believed. 4991
2Co 1:6 it is for your consolation and s., ... 4991
2Co 1:6 it is for your consolation and s.. 4991
2Co 6:2 in the day of s. have I succoured 4991
2Co 6:2 time: behold, now is the day of s..) 4991
2Co 7:10 sorrow worketh repentance to s........ 4991
Eph 1:13 of truth, the gospel of your s.: 4991
Eph 6:17 And take the helmet of s., and the 4992
Php 1:19 turn to my s. through your prayer, ... 4991
Php 1:28 but to you of s., and that of God....... 4991
Php 2:12 work out your own s. with fear and.... 4991
1Th 5:8 and for an helmet, the hope of s.. 4991
1Th 5:9 but to obtain s. by our Lord Jesus...... 4991
2Th 2:13 you to s. through sanctification of....... 4991
2Ti 2:10 also obtain the s. which is in Christ 4991
2Ti 3:15 are able to make thee wise unto s...... 4991
Tit 2:11 the grace of God that bringeth s. 4992
Heb 1:14 for them who shall be heirs of s.? 4991
Heb 2:3 we escape, if we neglect so great s.;.. 4991
Heb 2:10 make the captain of their s. perfect..... 4991
Heb 5:9 author of eternal s. unto all them 4991
Heb 6:9 you, and things that accompany s., ... 4991
Heb 9:28 the second time without sin unto s.. .. 4991
1Pe 1:5 power of God through faith unto s....... 4991
1Pe 1:9 your faith, even the s. of your souls. .. 4991
1Pe 1:10 Of which s. the prophets have 4991
2Pe 3:15 the longsuffering of our Lord is s.; 4991
Jude 3 to write unto you of the common s.,... 4991
Re 7:10 S. to our God which sitteth upon 4991
Re 12:10 Now is come s., and strength, and 4991
Re 19:1 saying, Alleluia; S., and glory, ... 4991

SAMARIA (sa-ma'-re-ah) See also SAMARITAN.
1Ki 13:32 places which are in the cities of S., ... 8111
1Ki 16:24 he bought the hill S. of Shemer for...... 8111
1Ki 16:24 of Shemer, owner of the hill, S., ... 8111
1Ki 16:28 his fathers, and was buried in S.: 8111
1Ki 16:29 Ahab...reigned over Israel in S. 8111
1Ki 16:32 of Baal, which he had built in S.......... 8111
1Ki 18:2 And there was a sore famine in S....... 8111
1Ki 20:1 and he went up and besieged S.,......... 8111
1Ki 20:10 if the dust of S. shall suffice for 8111
1Ki 20:17 There are men come out of S.. 8111
1Ki 20:34 Damascus, as my father made in S.. ... 8111
1Ki 20:43 and displeased, and came to S.. 8111
1Ki 21:1 by the palace of Ahab king of S.. 8111
1Ki 21:18 Ahab king of Israel, which is in S.: 8111
1Ki 22:10 in the entrance of the gate of S.; 8111
1Ki 22:37 king died, and was brought to S.;......... 8111
1Ki 22:37 and they buried the king in S.. 8111
1Ki 22:38 washed the chariot in the pool of S.;.... 8111
1Ki 22:51 began to reign over Israel in S. the 8111
2Ki 1:2 his upper chamber that was in S., ... 8111
2Ki 1:3 the messengers of the king of S.,........ 8111
2Ki 2:25 and from thence he returned to S....... 8111
2Ki 3:1 began to reign over Israel in S. the 8111
2Ki 3:6 king Jehoram went out of S. the 8111
2Ki 5:3 were with the prophet that is in S.! 8111
2Ki 6:19 ye seek. But he led them to S.. 8111
2Ki 6:20 pass, when they were come into S., ... 8111
2Ki 6:20 behold, they were in the midst of S. 8111
2Ki 6:24 host, and went up, and besieged S.. ... 8111
2Ki 6:25 And there was a great famine in S.:.... 8111
2Ki 7:1 barley for a shekel, in the gate of S.. . 8111
2Ki 7:18 about this time in the gate of S.:........ 8111
2Ki 10:1 And Ahab had seventy sons in S.. 8111
2Ki 10:1 Jehu wrote letters, and sent to S., ... 8111
2Ki 10:12 arose and departed, and came to S..... 8111
2Ki 10:17 And when he came to S., he slew...... 8111
2Ki 10:17 all that remained unto Ahab in S., ... 8111
2Ki 10:35 father: and they buried him in S........ 8111
2Ki 10:36 that Jehu reigned over Israel in S........ 8111
2Ki 13:1 began to reign over Israel in S., ... 8111
2Ki 13:6 there remained the grove also in S..).. 8111
2Ki 13:9 fathers; and they buried him in S.: 8111
2Ki 13:10 Jehoahaz to reign over Israel in S.,...... 8111
2Ki 13:13 Joash was buried in S. with the.......... 8111
2Ki 14:14 and hostages, and returned to S......... 8111
2Ki 14:16 was buried in S. with the kings of...... 8111
2Ki 14:23 king of Israel began to reign in S., ... 8111

2Ki 15:8 of Jeroboam reign over Israel in S...... 8111
2Ki 15:13 and he reigned a full month in S......... 8111
2Ki 15:14 up from Tirzah, and came to S.,........ 8111
2Ki 15:14 Shallum the son of Jabesh in S.,........ 8111
2Ki 15:17 Israel, and reigned ten years in S....... 8111
2Ki 15:23 began to reign over Israel in S., ... 8111
2Ki 15:25 smote him in S., in the palace 8111
2Ki 15:27 began to reign over Israel in S., ... 8111
2Ki 17:1 the son of Elah to reign in S. over 8111
2Ki 17:5 and went up to S., and besieged it 8111
2Ki 17:6 the king of Assyria took S., and......... 8111
2Ki 17:24 and placed them in the cities of S....... 8111
2Ki 17:24 and they possessed S., and dwelt in ... 8111
2Ki 17:26 and placed in the cities of S., know 8111
2Ki 17:28 whom they had carried...from S.......... 8111
2Ki 18:9 king of Assyria came up against S., ... 8111
2Ki 18:10 king of Israel, S. was taken............... 8111
2Ki 18:34 they delivered S. out of mine hand?.... 8111
2Ki 21:13 over Jerusalem the line of S., and 8111
2Ki 23:18 of the prophet that came out of S........ 8111
2Ki 23:19 places that were in the cities of S., ... 8111
2Ch 18:2 years he went down to Ahab to S. 8111
2Ch 18:9 at the entering in of the gate of S.; 8111
2Ch 22:9 caught him, (for he was hid in S.,) 8111
2Ch 25:13 Judah, from S....unto Beth-horon,....... 8111
2Ch 25:24 hostages also, and returned to S......... 8111
2Ch 28:8 them, and brought the spoil to S........ 8111
2Ch 28:9 out before the host that came to S., ... 8111
2Ch 28:15 brethren: then they returned to S. 8111
Ezr 4:10 and set in the cities of S., and the...... 8115
Ezr 4:17 their companions that dwell in S.,....... 8115
Ne 4:2 his brethren and the army of S.,........ 8111
Isa 7:9 And the head of Ephraim is S., and 8111
Isa 7:9 the head of S. is Remaliah's son.......... 8111
Isa 8:4 the spoil of S. shall be taken away...... 8111
Isa 9:9 Ephraim and the inhabitant of S., ... 8111
Isa 10:9 as Arpad? is not S. as Damascus? 8111
Isa 10:10 excel them of Jerusalem and of S.; 8111
Isa 10:11 I have done unto S. and her idols,....... 8111
Isa 36:19 they delivered S. out of my hand? 8111
Jer 23:13 seen folly in the prophets of S.;......... 8111
Jer 31:5 vines upon the mountains of S.: 8111
Jer 41:5 and from S., even fourscore men, ... 8111
Eze 16:46 thine elder sister is S., she and her.... 8111
Eze 16:51 Neither hath S. committed half of....... 8111
Eze 16:53 captivity of S. and her daughters, ... 8111
Eze 16:55 S. and her daughters shall return 8111
Eze 23:4 S. is Aholah, and Jerusalem............... 8111
Eze 23:33 with the cup of thy sister S............... 8111
Ho 7:1 and the wickedness of S.: for they 8111
Ho 8:5 Thy calf, O S., hath cast thee off; 8111
Ho 8:6 calf of S. shall be broken in pieces...... 8111
Ho 10:5 inhabitants of S. shall fear because...... 8111
Ho 10:7 As for S., her king is cut off as the 8111
Ho 13:16 S. shall become desolate; for she 8111
Am 3:9 upon the mountains of S., and 8111
Am 3:12 Israel be taken out that dwell in S...... 8111
Am 4:1 that are in the mountain of S.,.......... 8111
Am 6:1 and trust in the mountain of S., ... 8111
Am 8:14 that sware by the sin of S., and say, .. 8111
Ob 19 of Ephraim, and the fields of S.: 8111
Mic 1:1 saw concerning S. and Jerusalem......... 8111
Mic 1:5 transgression of Jacob? is it not S.? 8111
Mic 1:6 will make S. as an heap of the field, ... 8111
Lu 17:11 he passed through the midst of S....... 4540
Joh 4:4 And he must needs go through S. 4540
Joh 4:5 cometh he to a city of S., which 4540
Joh 4:7 a woman of S. to draw water: 4540
Joh 4:9 saith the woman of S. unto him, ... 4540
Joh 4:9 of me, which am a woman of S.? 4540
Ac 1:8 and in S., and unto the uttermost . 4540
Ac 8:1 the regions of Judaea and S., except... 4540
Ac 8:5 Philip went down to the city of S., ... 4540
Ac 8:9 and bewitched the people of S., ... 4540
Ac 8:14 S. had received the word of God,....... 4540
Ac 9:31 all Judaea and Galilee and S., and 4540
Ac 15:3 passed through Phenice and S., ... 4540

SAMARITAN (sa-mar'-i-tun) See also SAMARITANS.
Lu 10:33 But a certain S., as he journeyed, ..4541
Lu 17:16 him thanks: and he was a S. 4541
Joh 8:48 Say we not well that thou art a S.,..... 4541

SAMARITANS (sa-mar'-i-tuns)
2Ki 17:29 places which the S. had made,........... 8118
Mt 10:5 into any city of the S. enter...not:. 4541
Lu 9:52 and entered into a village of the S., ... 4541
Joh 4:9 Jews have no dealings with the S.) 4541
Joh 4:39 many of the S. of that city believed 4541
Joh 4:40 when the S. were come unto him,...... 4541
Ac 8:25 gospel in many villages of the S. 4541

SAME See also SELFSAME.
Ge 2:13 the s. is it that compasseth the.......... 1931
Ge 5:29 This s. shall comfort us concerning ....
Ge 6:4 the s. became mighty men which........ 1992
Ge 7:11 the s. day were all the fountains 2088
Ge 10:12 and Calah: the s. is a great city. 1931
Ge 14:8 the king of Bela (the s. is Zoar;) 1931
Ge 15:18 s. day the Lord made a covenant 1931
Ge 19:37 the s. is the father of the Moabites..... 1931
Ge 19:38 the s. is the father of the children 1931
Ge 21:8 feast the s. day...Isaac was weaned. ....
Ge 23:2 the s. as Hebron in the land of 1931
Ge 23:19 Mamre: the s. is Hebron in the 1931
Ge 24:14 let the s. be she that thou hast...............
Ge 24:44 let the s. be the woman whom the Lord....
Ge 25:30 thee, with that s. red pottage; 2088
Ge 26:12 and received in the s. year an............ 1931
Ge 26:24 appeared unto him the s. night,.......... 1931
Ge 26:32 And it came to pass the s. day, ...
Ge 32:13 And he lodged there that s. night; 1931
Ge 41:48 about every city, laid he up in the s..........
Ge 44:6 he spake unto them these s. words. ....
Ge 48:7 of Ephrath; the s. is Beth-lehem. 1931
Ex 5:6 Pharaoh commanded the s. day the..... 1931
Ex 12:6 Fourteenth day of the s. month:......... 2088
Ex 19:1 s. day came they into ... wilderness.... 2088
Ex 12:6 fourteenth day of the s. month:.......... 2088
Ex 25:31 and his flowers, shall be of the s. ....
Ex 25:35, 35,35, under two branches of the s.,.........
Ex 25:36 and their branches shall be of the s.:.........
Ex 27:2 his horns shall be of the s.: and thou.........
Ex 28:8 which is upon it, shall be of the s., ...
Ex 30:2 the horns thereof shall be of the s. ....
Ex 37:17 knops, and his flowers, were of the s.:.....
Ex 37:21, 21,21 under two branches of the s.,..........
Ex 37:22 and their branches were of the s.: ....
Ex 37:25 of it; the horns thereof were of the s. ......
Ex 38:2 of it; the horns thereof were of the s.: .....
Ex 39:5 ephod, that was upon it, was of the s., ...
Le 7:15 be eaten the s. day that it is offered; ....
Le 7:16 be eaten the s. day that he offereth ....
Le 19:6 be eaten the s. day ye offer it, and on ......
Le 22:30 the s. day it shall be eaten up; ye 1931
Le 23:6 fifteenth day of the s. month is the..... 2088
Le 23:28 ye shall do no work in that s. day: 6106
Le 23:29 shall not be afflicted in that s. day, ... 6106
Le 23:30 doeth any work in that s. day,........... 6106
Le 23:30 s. soul will I destroy from among 6106
Nu 4:8 cover the s. with a covering of............ 853
Nu 6:11 shall hallow his head that s. day. 1931
Nu 9:13 s. soul shall be cut off from among 1931
Nu 10:32 do unto us, the s. will we do unto thee. ....
Nu 15:30 the s. reproacheth the Lord; and......... 1931
Nu 32:10 anger was kindled the s. time, and 1931
De 9:20 I prayed for Aaron also the s. time. 1931
De 14:28 tithe of thine increase the s. year,....... 1931
De 27:11 Moses charged the people the s. day, ..1931
De 31:22 Moses...wrote this song the s. day,.... 1931
Jos 6:15 the city after the s. manner seven....... 2088
Jos 11:16 of Israel, and the valley of the s.;..........
Jos 15:8 the Jebusite; the s. is Jerusalem:........ 1931
Jg 6:25 it came to pass the s. night, that the .. 1931
Jg 7:4 with thee, the s. shall go with thee;.... 1931
Jg 7:4 not go with thee, the s. shall not go. .. 1931
Jg 7:9 it came to pass the s. night, that........ 1931
1Sa 4:12 came to Shiloh the s. day with his...... 1931
1Sa 6:15 sacrificed sacrifices the s. day unto..... 1931
1Sa 6:16 they returned to Ekron the s. day. 1931
1Sa 9:17 this s. shall reign over my people......... 2088
1Sa 10:12 one of the s. place answered and said, ...
1Sa 14:35 the s. was the first altar that he built ....
1Sa 17:23 and spake according to the s. words: 428
1Sa 17:30 and spake after the s. manner: 2088
1Sa 31:6 all his men, that s. day together.......... 1931
2Sa 2:23 there, and died in the s. place: 8478
2Sa 5:7 of Zion: the s. is the city of David...... 1931
2Sa 23:7 burned with fire in the s. place. ....
2Sa 23:8 the s. was Adino the Eznite: he......... 1931
1Ki 7:35 and the borders thereof were of the s. ......
1Ki 8:64 The s. day did the king hallow the...... 1931
1Ki 13:3 he gave a sign the s. day, saying, ... 1931
1Ki 13:9 again by the s. way that thou camest. ....
2Ki 3:6 went out of Samaria the s. time, ... 1931
2Ki 8:22 Libnah revolted at the s. time........... 1931
2Ki 19:29 year that which springeth of the s.; ....
2Ki 19:33 that he came, by the s. shall he return, ...
1Ch 1:27 Abram; the s. is Abraham................ 1931
1Ch 4:33 that were round about the s. cities, ...
1Ch 16:17 confirmed the s. to Jacob for a law, ...
1Ch 17:3 And it came to pass the s. night, ... 1931
2Ch 7:8 the s. time Solomon kept the feast 1931
2Ch 13:9 s. may be a priest of them that are no ......
2Ch 15:11 offered unto the Lord the s. time, ... 1931
2Ch 16:10 some of the people the s. time. 1931
2Ch 18:7 always evil: the s. is Micaiah the........ 1931
2Ch 20:26 therefore the name of the s. place...... 1931
2Ch 21:10 s. time also did Libnah revolt from 1931
2Ch 27:5 of Ammon gave him the s. year an..... 1931
2Ch 32:12 Hath not the s. Hezekiah taken.......... 1931
2Ch 32:30 This s. Hezekiah also stopped the 1931
2Ch 34:28 and upon the inhabitants of the s.............
2Ch 35:16 service...was prepared the s. day,...... 1931
Ezr 4:15 sedition within the s. of old time: 1459
Ezr 5:3 At the s. time came to them Tatnai, ...
Ezr 5:13 s. king Cyrus made a decree to build ....
Ezr 5:16 Then came the s. Sheshbazzar,.......... 1791
Ezr 6:3 the s. Cyrus the king made a decree.........
Ezr 10:23 and Kelaiah, (the s. is Kelita,) 1933
Ne 4:22 the s. time said I unto the people,...... 1931
Ne 6:4 answered...after the s. manner. 2088
Ne 10:37 that the s. Levites might have the...... 1992
Es 9:1 Adar, on the thirteenth day of the s., ...
Es 9:17 fourteenth day of the s. rested they, ...
Es 9:18 the fifteenth day of the s. they rested, ...
Es 9:21 and the fifteenth day of the s., yearly, ...
Job 4:8 and sow wickedness, reap the s. ....
Job 13:2 What ye know, the s. do I know also: ....
Ps 68:23 the tongue of thy dogs in the s. ....
Ps 75:8 and he poureth out the s.: but the...... 2088
Ps 102:27 But thou art the s., and thy years 1931
Ps 105:10 confirmed the s. unto Jacob for a law, ...
Ps 113:3 the sun unto the going down of the s. ....
Pr 28:24 s. is the companion of a destroyer...... 1931
Ec 9:15 man remembered that s. poor man. 1931
Isa 7:20 In the s. day shall the Lord shave 1931
Isa 20:2 At the s. time spake the Lord 1931
Isa 37:30 year that which springeth of the s............
Isa 37:34 he came, by the s. shall he return, ...
Jer 27:8 will not serve the s. Nebuchadnezzar ....
Jer 28:1 And it came to pass the s. year, in..... 1931
Jer 28:17 the prophet died the s. year in the 1931
Jer 31:1 At the s. time, saith the Lord, will 1931
Jer 39:10 vineyards and fields at the s. time. 1931
Eze 3:18 the s. wicked man shall die in his 1931
Eze 10:16 the s. wheels also turned not from 1992
Eze 10:22 s. faces which I saw by the river of.... 1992
Eze 21:26 the crown: this shall not be the s.: 2063
Eze 23:38 defiled my sanctuary in the s. day, ... 1931
Eze 23:39 came the s. day into my sanctuary...... 1931
Eze 24:2 of the day, even of this s. day: 6106
Eze 24:2 against Jerusalem this s. day. 6106
Eze 38:10 at the s. time shall things come 1931
Eze 38:18 the s. time when Gog shall come 1931
Eze 44:3 and shall go out by the way of the s. ......
Da 3:6 the s. hour be cast into the midst of.........
Da 3:15 be cast the s. hour into the midst of.........
Da 4:33 s. hour was the thing fulfilled upon...........
Da 4:36 the s. time my reason returned unto.........
Da 5:5 s. hour came forth fingers of a man's ....
Da 5:12 were found in the s. Daniel, whom ....
Da 7:21 s. horn made war with the saints, ... 1797
Da 12:1 was a nation even to that s. time: 1931
Am 2:7 his father will go in unto the s. maid, ...
Zep 1:9 s. day also will I punish all those........ 1931
Zec 6:10 and come thou the s. day, and go into..1931
Mal 1:11 even unto the going down of the s...........
Mt 3:4 s. John had his raiment of camel's 846
Mt 5:19 the s. shall be called great in the .. 3778
Mt 5:46 do not even the publicans the s.? 846
Mt 10:19 that s. hour what ye shall speak. .. 1565
Mt 12:50 the s. is my brother, and sister, ... 846
Mt 13:1 s. day went Jesus out of the house, ... 1565
Mt 13:20 the s. is he that heareth the word, .3778
Mt 15:22 woman...came out of the s. coasts,..... 1565
Mt 18:1 the s. time came the disciples unto 1565
Mt 18:4 the s. is greatest in the kingdom ... 3778
Mt 18:28 the s. servant went out, and found .1565
Mt 21:42 s. is become the head of the.......... 3778

Mt	22:23	s. day came to him the Sadducees,	1565
Mt	24:13	unto the end, the s. shall be saved.	3778
Mt	25:16	talents went and traded with the s.,	846
Mt	26:23	in the dish, the s. shall betray me.	3778
Mt	26:44	the third time, saying the s. words.	846
Mt	26:48	Whomsoever I...kiss, that s. is he:	846
Mt	26:55	In that s. hour said Jesus to the	1565
Mt	27:44	with him, cast the s. in his teeth.	846
Mk	3:35	s. is my brother, and my sister,	3778
Mk	4:35	s. day, when the even was come,	1565
Mk	8:35	the gospel's, the s. shall save it.	3778
Mk	9:35	to be first, the s. shall be last of all,	
Mk	10:10	asked him again of the s. matter.	846
Mk	13:13	unto the end, the s. shall be saved.	3778
Mk	14:39	and prayed, and spake the s. words.	846
Mk	14:44	Whomsoever I...kiss, that s. is he;	846
Lu	2:8	were in the s. country shepherds	846
Lu	2:25	the s. man was just and devout,	3778
Lu	6:33	ye? for sinners also do even the s.	846
Lu	6:38	s. measure that ye mete withal it	846
Lu	7:21	that s. hour he cured many of their	846
Lu	7:47	little is forgiven, the s. loveth little.	
Lu	9:24	for my sake, the s. shall save it.	3778
Lu	9:48	among you all, the s. shall be	3778
Lu	10:7	And in the s. house remain, eating	846
Lu	10:10	ways out into the streets of the s.,	846
Lu	12:12	the s. hour what ye ought to say.	846
Lu	13:31	The s. day there came certain of the	846
Lu	16:1	s. was accused unto him that he	3778
Lu	17:29	s. day that Lot went out of Sodom it	
Lu	20:17	s. is become...head of the corner?	3778
Lu	20:19	s. hour sought to lay hands on him:	846
Lu	20:47	s....receive greater damnation.	3778
Lu	23:12	And the s. day Pilate and Herod	846
Lu	23:40	thou art in the s. condemnation?	846
Lu	23:51	(The s. had not consented to the	3778
Lu	24:13	went that s. day to a village called	846
Lu	24:33	And they rose up the s. hour, and	846
Joh	1:2	s. was in the beginning with God.	3778
Joh	1:7	The s. came for a witness, to bear	3778
Joh	1:33	s. said unto me, Upon whom thou	1565
Joh	1:33	s. is he which baptizeth with the	3778
Joh	3:2	The s. came to Jesus by night, and	3778
Joh	3:26	the s. baptizeth, and all men come	3778
Joh	4:53	knew that it was at the s. hour,	1565
Joh	5:9	and on the s. day was the sabbath.	1565
Joh	5:11	s. said unto me, Take up thy bed,	1565
Joh	5:36	s. works that I do, bear witness	846
Joh	7:18	s. is true, and no unrighteousness	3778
Joh	8:25	Even the s. that I said unto you,	3748
Joh	10:1	way, the s. is a thief and a robber.	1565
Joh	11:6	abode two days still in the s. place	
Joh	11:49	being the high priest that s. year,	1565
Joh	12:21	s. came therefore to Philip, which	3778
Joh	12:48	s. shall judge him in the last day.	1565
Joh	15:5	the s. bringeth forth much fruit:	3778
Joh	18:13	was the high priest that s. year.	1565
Joh	20:19	s. day at evening, being the first	1565
Ac	1:11	s. Jesus, which is taken up from	3778
Ac	1:22	s. day that he was taken up from us,	
Ac	2:36	that God hath made that s. Jesus,	5126
Ac	2:41	s. day there were added unto them	1565
Ac	7:19	s. dealt subtilly with our kindred,	3778
Ac	7:35	s. did God send to be a ruler and a	5126
Ac	8:9	beforetime in the s. city used sorcery,	
Ac	8:35	and began at the s. scripture, and	5026
Ac	12:6	the s. night Peter was sleeping	1565
Ac	13:33	hath fulfilled the s. unto us their	5026
Ac	14:9	The s. heard Paul speak: who	3778
Ac	15:27	also tell you the s. things by mouth.	846
Ac	16:17	s. followed Paul and us, and cried,	3778
Ac	16:18	her. And he came out the s. hour.	846
Ac	16:33	took them the s. hour of the night,	1565
Ac	18:3	because he was of the s. craft, he	3673
Ac	19:23	s. time there arose no small stir	1565
Ac	21:9	the s. man had four daughters,	5129
Ac	22:13	the s. hour I looked up upon him.	846
Ac	24:20	Or else let these s. here say, if	3778
Ac	28:7	s. quarters were possessions of	1565
Ro	1:32	not only do the s., but have pleasure	846
Ro	2:1	that judgest doest the s. things.	846
Ro	2:3	and doest the s., that thou shalt	846
Ro	8:20	who hath subjected the s. in hope,	
Ro	9:17	s. purpose have I raised thee up,	846
Ro	9:21	the s. lump to make one vessel unto	846
Ro	10:12	for the s. Lord over all is rich unto	846
Ro	12:4	all members have not the s. office:	846
Ro	12:16	Be of the s. mind one toward another	846
Ro	13:3	and thou shalt have praise of the s.:	846
1Co	1:10	that ye all speak the s. thing, and	846
1Co	1:10	the s. mind and in the s. judgment.	846
1Co	7:20	every man abide in the s. calling	5026
1Co	8:3	love God, the s. is known of him.	5778
1Co	9:8	or saith not the law the s. also?	5023
1Co	10:3	did all eat the s. spiritual meat;	846
1Co	10:4	did all drink the s. spiritual drink:	846
1Co	11:23	s. night in which he was betrayed	846
1Co	11:25	s. manner also he took the cup,	5615
1Co	12:4	diversities of gifts, but the s. Spirit.	846
1Co	12:5	of administrations, but the s. Lord.	846
1Co	12:6	it is the s. God which worketh all	846
1Co	12:8	word of knowledge by the s. Spirit;	846
1Co	12:9	To another faith by the s. Spirit; to	846
1Co	12:9	the gifts of healing by the s. Spirit;	846
1Co	12:25	have the s. care one for another.	846
1Co	15:39	All flesh is not the s. flesh: but	846
2Co	1:6	in the enduring of the s. sufferings	846
2Co	2:2	the s. which is made sorry by me?	
2Co	2:3	And I wrote this s. unto you, lest,	846
2Co	3:14	day remaineth the s. vail untaken	846
2Co	3:18	are changed into the s. image from	846
2Co	4:13	We having the s. spirit of faith,	846
2Co	6:13	Now for a recompence in the s., (I	846
2Co	7:8	the s. epistle hath made you sorry,	1565
2Co	8:6	also finish in you the s. grace also.	846
2Co	8:16	put the s. earnest care into the	846
2Co	8:19	by us to the glory of the s. Lord,	3778
2Co	9:4	in this s. confident boasting.	5026
2Co	9:5	that the s. might be ready, as a	5026
2Co	12:18	walked we not in the s. spirit?	846
2Co	12:18	walked we not in the s. steps?	846
Ga	2:8	s. was mighty in me toward the	2532
Ga	2:10	the s. which I also was forward	846,5124
Ga	3:7	the s. are the children of Abraham.	3778
Eph	3:6	be fellowheirs, and of the s. body,	4954
Eph	4:10	is the s. also that ascended up	846
Eph	6:8	the s. shall he receive of the Lord,	3778
Eph	6:9	ye masters, do the s. things unto	846
Eph	6:22	sent unto you for the s. purpose,	846
Php	1:30	Having the s. conflict which ye saw	846
Php	2:2	ye be likeminded, having the s. love	846
Php	2:18	For the s. cause also do ye joy, and	846
Php	3:1	To write the s. things to you, to me	846
Php	3:16	let us walk by the s. rule, let us	846
Php	3:16	rule, let us mind the s. thing.	846
Php	4:2	they be of the s. mind in the Lord.	846
Col	4:2	watch in the s. with thanksgiving;	846
Col	4:8	sent unto you for the s. purpose,	846
2Ti	2:2	s. commit thou to faithful men,	5023
Heb	1:12	but thou art the s., and thy years	846
Heb	2:14	himself likewise took part of the s.;	846
Heb	4:11	fall after the s. example of unbelief.	846
Heb	6:11	one of you do shew the s. diligence	846
Heb	10:11	offering oftentimes the s. sacrifices,	846
Heb	11:9	the heirs with him of the s. promise:	
Heb	13:8	Jesus Christ the s. yesterday, and	846
Jas	3:2	in word, the s. is a perfect man,	3778
Jas	3:10	Out of the s. mouth proceedeth	846
Jas	3:11	the s. place sweet water and bitter?	846
1Pe	2:7	s. is made the head of the corner,	3778
1Pe	4:1	likewise with the s. mind: for he	846
1Pe	4:4	with them to the s. excess of riot,	846
1Pe	4:10	so minister the s. one to another,	846
1Pe	5:9	the s. afflictions are accomplished	846
2Pe	2:19	the s. is he brought in bondage.	3778
2Pe	3:7	by the s. word are kept in store,	846
1Jo	2:23	Son, the s. hath not the Father:	3761
1Jo	2:27	as the s. anointing teacheth you	846
Re	3:5	the s. shall be clothed in white	3778
Re	11:13	s. hour was...a great earthquake,	1565
Re	14:10	The s. shall drink of the wine of	846

SAMECH (saw'mek)

Ps	119:113	*title* [ס] S.	

SAMGAR-NEBO (sam''-gar-ne'-bo)

Jer	39:3	Nergal-sharezer, S., Sarsechim,	5562

SAMLAH (sam'-lah)

Ge	36:36	S. of Masrekah reigned in his	8072
Ge	36:37	S. died, and Saul of Rehoboth by	8072
1Ch	1:47	S. of Masrekah reigned in his	8072
1Ch	1:48	S. was dead, Shaul of Rehoboth	8072

SAMOS (sa'-mos)

Ac	20:15	and the next day we arrived at S.,	4544

SAMOTHRACIA (sam-o-thra'-she-ah)

Ac	16:11	came with a straight course to S.,	4543

SAMSON (sam'-sun) See also SAMSON'S.

Jg	13:24	a son, and called his name S.:	8123
Jg	14:1	And S. went down to Timnath, and	8123
Jg	14:3	S. said unto his father, Get her for	8123
Jg	14:5	Then went S. down, and his father	8123
Jg	14:7	woman; and she pleased S. well,	8123
Jg	14:10	and S. made there a feast; for so	8123
Jg	14:12	S. said unto them, I will now put	8123
Jg	15:1	that S. visited his wife with a kid;	8123
Jg	15:3	And S. said concerning them,	8123
Jg	15:4	S. went and caught three hundred	8123
Jg	15:6	S., the son in law of the Timnite,	8123
Jg	15:7	S. said unto them, Though ye have	8123
Jg	15:10	To bind S. are we come up, to do	8123
Jg	15:11	said to S., Knowest thou not that	8123
Jg	15:12	S. said unto them, Sware unto me,	8123
Jg	15:16	S. said, With the jawbone of an ass,	8123
Jg	16:1	Then went S. to Gaza, and saw	8123
Jg	16:2	Gazites, saying, S. is come hither.	8123
Jg	16:3	And S. lay till midnight, and arose	8123
Jg	16:6	And Delilah said to S., Tell me, I	8123
Jg	16:7	S. said unto her, If they bind me	8123
Jg	16:9	The Philistines be upon thee, S.	8123
Jg	16:10	And Delilah said unto S., Behold,	8123
Jg	16:12	The Philistines be upon thee, S.	8123
Jg	16:13	And Delilah said unto S., Hitherto	8123
Jg	16:14, 20	The Philistines be upon thee, S.	8123
Jg	16:23	delivered S. our enemy into our	8123
Jg	16:25	Call for S., that he may make us	8123
Jg	16:25	they called for S. out of the prison	8123
Jg	16:26	S. said unto the lad that held him	8123
Jg	16:27	that beheld while S. made sport.	8123
Jg	16:28	S. called unto the Lord, and said,	8123
Jg	16:29	And S. took hold of the two middle	8123
Jg	16:30	And S. said, Let me die with the	8123
Heb	11:32	Barak, and of S., and of Jephthae;	4546

SAMSON'S (sam'-suns)

Jg	14:15	they said unto S. wife, Entice thy	8123
Jg	14:16	S. wife wept before him, and said,	8123
Jg	14:20	S. wife was given to his companion,	8123

SAMUEL (sam'-u-el) See also SHEMUEL.

1Sa	*general*	*title* The First Book Of S.	8050
1Sa	1:20	a son, and called his name S.,	8050
1Sa	2:18	But S. ministered before the Lord,	8050
1Sa	2:21	the child S. grew before the Lord.	8050
1Sa	2:26	the child S. grew on, and was in	8050
1Sa	3:1	child S. ministered unto the Lord	8050
1Sa	3:3	was, and S. was laid down to sleep:	8050
1Sa	3:4	That the Lord called S.: and he	8050
1Sa	3:6	And the Lord called yet again, S..	8050
1Sa	3:6	S. arose and went to Eli, and said,	8050
1Sa	3:7	Now S. did not yet know the Lord,	8050
1Sa	3:8	the Lord called S. again the third	8050
1Sa	3:9	Eli said unto S., Go, lie down: and	8050
1Sa	3:9	S. went and lay down in his place	8050
1Sa	3:10	and called as at other times, S., S.	8050
1Sa	3:10	Then S. answered, Speak; for thy	8050
1Sa	3:11	the Lord said to S., Behold, I will	8050
1Sa	3:15	And S. lay until the morning, and	8050
1Sa	3:15	S. feared to show Eli the vision.	8050
1Sa	3:16	Eli called S., and said, S., my son.	8050
1Sa	3:18	S. told him every whit, and hid	8050
1Sa	3:19	S. grew, and the Lord was with	8050
1Sa	3:20	knew that S. was established to be	8050
1Sa	3:21	for the Lord revealed himself to S.	8050
1Sa	4:1	the word of S. came to all Israel.	8050
1Sa	7:3	S. spake unto all the house of	8050
1Sa	7:5	And S. said, Gather all Israel to	8050
1Sa	7:6	S. judged the children of Israel in	8050
1Sa	7:8	the children of Israel said to S.,	8050
1Sa	7:9	And S. took a sucking lamb, and	8050
1Sa	7:9	S. cried unto the Lord for Israel;	8050
1Sa	7:10	as S. was offering up the burnt	8050
1Sa	7:12	Then S. took a stone, and set it	8050
1Sa	7:13	the Philistines all the days of S..	8050
1Sa	7:15	S. judged Israel all the days of his	8050
1Sa	8:1	when S. was old, that he made his	8050
1Sa	8:4	and came to S. unto Ramah,	8050
1Sa	8:6	But the thing displeased S., when	8050
1Sa	8:6	us. And S. prayed unto the Lord.	8050
1Sa	8:7	the Lord said unto S., Hearken	8050
1Sa	8:10	S. told all the words of the Lord	8050
1Sa	8:19	refused to obey the voice of S.;	8050

1Sa 8:21 And S. heard all the words of the ... 8050
1Sa 8:22 the Lord said to S., Hearken unto ... 8050
1Sa 8:22 And S. said unto the men of Israel, ... 8050
1Sa 9:14 behold, S. came out against them; ... 8050
1Sa 9:15 Now the Lord had told S. in his ear ... 8050
1Sa 9:17 when S. saw Saul, the Lord said ... 8050
1Sa 9:18 Saul drew near to S. in the gate, ... 8050
1Sa 9:19 S. answered Saul,...I am the seer: ... 8050
1Sa 9:22 And S. took Saul and his servant, ... 8050
1Sa 9:23 And S. said unto the cook, Bring ... 8050
1Sa 9:24 S. said, Behold that which is left! ...
1Sa 9:24 So Saul did eat with S. that day ... 8050
1Sa 9:25 S. communed with Saul upon the top ...
1Sa 9:26 S. called Saul to the top of the ... 8050
1Sa 9:26 went out both of them, he and S., ... 8050
1Sa 9:27 S. said to Saul, Bid the servant pass ... 8050
1Sa 10:1 S. took a vial of oil, and poured it ... 8050
1Sa 10:9 had turned his back to go from S., ... 8050
1Sa 10:14 they were no where, we came to S. ... 8050
1Sa 10:15 Tell me,...what S. said unto you ... 8050
1Sa 10:16 of the kingdom, whereof S. spake, ... 8050
1Sa 10:17 And S. called the people together ... 8050
1Sa 10:20 when S. had caused all the tribes of ... 8050
1Sa 10:24 S. said to all the people, See ye him ... 8050
1Sa 10:25 S. told the people the manner of ... 8050
1Sa 10:25 And S. sent all the people away, ... 8050
1Sa 11:7 not forth after Saul and after S., ... 8050
1Sa 11:12 the people said unto S., Who is he ... 8050
1Sa 11:14 Then said S. to the people, Come, ... 8050
1Sa 12:1 And S. said unto all Israel, Behold, ... 8050
1Sa 12:6 S. said unto...people, It is the Lord ... 8050
1Sa 12:11 Lord sent...Jephthah, and S., and ... 8050
1Sa 12:18 So S. called unto the Lord; and the ... 8050
1Sa 12:18 greatly feared the Lord and S. ... 8050
1Sa 12:19 people said unto S., Pray for thy ... 8050
1Sa 12:20 S. said unto the people, Fear not: ... 8050
1Sa 13:8 the set time that S. had appointed: ... 8050
1Sa 13:8 but S. came not to Gilgal; and the ... 8050
1Sa 13:10 S. came; and Saul went out to meet ... 8050
1Sa 13:11 And S. said, What hast thou done? ... 8050
1Sa 13:13 And S. said to Saul, Thou hast done ... 8050
1Sa 13:15 And S. arose, and gat him up from ... 8050
1Sa 15:1 S....said unto Saul, The Lord sent ... 8050
1Sa 15:10 came the word of the Lord unto S., ... 8050
1Sa 15:11 And it grieved S.; and he cried unto ... 8050
1Sa 15:12 when S. rose early to meet Saul in ... 8050
1Sa 15:12 it was told S., saying, Saul came ... 8050
1Sa 15:13 And S. came to Saul: and Saul said ... 8050
1Sa 15:14 S. said, What meaneth then this ... 8050
1Sa 15:16 S. said unto Saul, Stay, and I will ... 8050
1Sa 15:17 And S. said, When thou wast little ... 8050
1Sa 15:20 And Saul said unto S., Yea, I have ... 8050
1Sa 15:22 And S. said, Hath the Lord as great ... 8050
1Sa 15:24 Saul said unto S., I have sinned: ... 8050
1Sa 15:26 S. said unto Saul, I will not return ... 8050
1Sa 15:27 And as S. turned about to go away, ... 8050
1Sa 15:28 And S. said...The Lord hath rent ... 8050
1Sa 15:31 So S. turned again after Saul; and ... 8050
1Sa 15:32 Then said S., Bring ye hither to me ... 8050
1Sa 15:33 S. said, As thy sword hath made ... 8050
1Sa 15:33 S. hewed Agag in pieces before the ... 8050
1Sa 15:34 Then S. went to Ramah; and Saul; ... 8050
1Sa 15:35 S. came no more to see Saul until ... 8050
1Sa 15:35 nevertheless S. mourned for Saul: ... 8050
1Sa 16:1 the Lord said unto S., How long ... 8050
1Sa 16:2 And S. said, How can I go? if Saul ... 8050
1Sa 16:4 S. did that which the Lord spake, ... 8050
1Sa 16:7 Lord said unto S., Look not on his ... 8050
1Sa 16:8 and made him pass before S. ... 8050
1Sa 16:10 seven of his sons to pass before S. ... 8050
1Sa 16:10 S. said unto Jesse, The Lord hath ... 8050
1Sa 16:11 S. said unto Jesse, Are here all thy ... 8050
1Sa 16:11 S. said unto Jesse, Send and fetch ... 8050
1Sa 16:13 Then S. took the horn of oil, and ... 8050
1Sa 16:13 So S. rose up, and went to Ramah ... 8050
1Sa 19:18 escaped, and came to S. to Ramah, ... 8050
1Sa 19:18 he and S. went and dwelt in Naioth ... 8050
1Sa 19:20 S. standing as appointed over them, ... 8050
1Sa 19:22 and said, Where are S. and David? ... 8050
1Sa 19:24 and prophesied before S. in like ... 8050
1Sa 25:1 And S. died; and all the Israelites ... 8050
1Sa 28:3 Now S. was dead, and all Israel had ... 8050
1Sa 28:11 thee? And he said, Bring me up S. ... 8050
1Sa 28:12 when the woman saw S., she cried ... 8050
1Sa 28:14 And Saul perceived that it was S., ... 8050
1Sa 28:15 And S. said to Saul, Why hast thou ... 8050
1Sa 28:16 Then said S., Wherefore then dost ... 8050
1Sa 28:20 afraid, because of the words of S.: ... 8050
2Sa *general title* The Second Book Of S. ... 8050
1Ch 6:28 the sons of S.; the firstborn Vashni, ... 8050
1Ch 9:22 David and S. the seer did ordain ... 8050
1Ch 11:3 to the word of the Lord by S. ... 8050
1Ch 26:28 And all that S. the seer, and Saul ... 8050
1Ch 29:29 written in the book of S. the seer, ... 8050
2Ch 35:18 from the days of S. the prophet; ... 8050
Ps 99:6 and S. among them that call upon ... 8050
Jer 15:1 Though Moses and S. stood before ... 8050
Ac 3:24 Yea, and all the prophets from S. ... *4545*
Ac 13:20 and fifty years, until S. the prophet. ... *4545*
Heb 11:32 of David also, and S., and of the ... *4545*

SANBALLAT (san-bal'-lat)
Ne 2:10 When S. the Horonite, and Tobiah ... 5571
Ne 2:19 when S. the Horonite, and Tobiah ... 5571
Ne 4:1 when S. heard that we builded the ... 5571
Ne 4:7 to pass, that when S., and Tobiah, ... 5571
Ne 6:1 came to pass, when S., and Tobiah, ... 5571
Ne 6:2 That S. and Geshem sent unto me, ... 5571
Ne 6:5 Then sent S. his servant unto me ... 5571
Ne 6:12 for Tobiah and S. had hired him ... 5571
Ne 6:14 God, think thou upon Tobiah and S. ... 5571
Ne 13:28 was so in law to S. the Horonite: ... 5571

SANCTIFICATION
1Co 1:30 righteousness,...s., and redemption: ... *38*
1Th 4:3 this is the will of God, even your s., ... *38*
1Th 4:4 possess his vessel in s. and honour; ... *38*
2Th 2:13 to salvation through s. of the Spirit ... *38*
1Pe 1:2 Father, through s. of the Spirit, unto ... *38*

SANCTIFIED
Ge 2:3 blessed the seventh day, and s. it: ... 6942
Ex 19:14 unto the people, and s. the people; ... 6942
Ex 29:43 tabernacle shall be s. by my glory. ... 6942
Le 8:10 all that was therein, and s. them ... 6942
Le 8:15 at the bottom of the altar, and s. it, ... 6942
Le 8:30 and s. Aaron, and his garments, ... 6942
Le 10:3 I will be s. in them that come nigh ... 6942
Le 27:15 if he that s. it will redeem his house, ... 6942
Le 27:19 if he that s. the field will in any wise ... 6942
Nu 7:1 and had anointed it, and s. it, and ... 6942
Nu 7:1 had anointed them, and s. them; ... 6942
Nu 8:17 land of Egypt I s. them for myself ... 6942
Nu 20:13 the Lord, and he was s. in them ... 6942
De 32:51 because ye s. me not in the midst ... 6942
1Sa 7:1 s. Eleazar his son to keep the ark ... 6942
1Sa 16:5 And he s. Jesse and his sons, and ... 6942
1Sa 21:5 it were s. this day in the the vessel ... 6942
1Ch 15:14 priests and...Levites s. themselves ... 6942
2Ch 5:11 priests that were present were s., ... 6942
2Ch 7:16 have I chosen and s. this house, ... 6942
2Ch 7:20 house, which I have s. for my name, ... 6942
2Ch 29:15 their brethren, and s. themselves, ... 6942
2Ch 29:17 so they s. the house of the Lord in ... 6942
2Ch 29:19 vessels,...have we prepared and s., ... 6942
2Ch 29:34 the other priests had s. themselves: ... 6942
2Ch 30:3 had not s. themselves sufficiently, ... 6942
2Ch 30:8 sanctuary, which he hath s. for ever: ... 6942
2Ch 30:15 were ashamed, and s. themselves, ... 6942
2Ch 30:17 the congregation that were not s. ... 6942
2Ch 30:24 number of priests s. themselves ... 6942
2Ch 31:18 they s. themselves in holiness: ... 6942
Ne 3:1 they s. it, and set up the doors of it; ... 6942
Ne 3:1 unto the tower of Meah they s. it, ... 6942
Ne 12:47 they s. holy things unto the Levites; ... 6942
Ne 12:47 s. them unto the children of Aaron. ... 6942
Job 1:5 about that Job sent and s. them, and ... 6942
Isa 5:16 is holy shall be s. in righteousness ... 6942
Isa 13:3 I have commanded my s. ones, I ... 6942
Jer 1:5 camest...out of the womb I s. thee, ... 6942
Eze 20:41 will be s. in you before the heathen ... 6942
Eze 28:22 in her, and shall be s. in her ... 6942
Eze 28:25 be s....in the sight of the heathen, ... 6942
Eze 36:23 shall be s. in you before their eyes ... 6942
Eze 38:16 when I shall be s. in thee, O Gog, ... 6942
Eze 39:27 am s. in them in the sight of many ... 6942
Eze 48:11 the priests that are s. of the sons of ... 6942
Joh 10:36 **whom the Father hath s., and sent** ... *37*
Joh 17:19 **also might be s. through the truth** ... *37*
Ac 20:32 among all them which are s. ... *37*
Ac 26:18 **among them which are s. by faith** ... *37*
Ro 15:16 being s. by the Holy Ghost ... *37*
1Co 1:2 to them that are s. in Christ Jesus, ... *37*
1Co 6:11 but ye are washed, but ye are s., but ... *37*
1Co 7:14 unbelieving husband is s. by the wife, ... *37*
1Co 7:14 unbelieving wife is s. by the husband: ... *37*
1Ti 4:5 For it is s. by the word of God and ... *37*
2Ti 2:21 s., and meet for the master's use, and ... *37*
Heb 2:11 that sanctifieth and they who are s. ... *37*
Heb 10:10 By the which will we are s. through ... *37*
Heb 10:14 perfected for ever them that are s. ... *37*
Heb 10:29 of the covenant, wherewith he was s., ... *37*
Jude 1 them that are s. by God the Father, ... *37*

SANCTIFIETH
Mt 23:17 **gold, or the temple that s. the gold?** ... *37*
Mt 23:19 **gift, or the altar that s. the gift?** ... *37*
Heb 2:11 that s. and they who are sanctified ... *37*
Heb 9:13 s. to the purifying of the flesh: ... *37*

SANCTIFY See also SANCTIFIED; SANCTIFIETH.
Ex 13:2 S. unto me all the firstborn, ... 6942
Ex 19:10 and s. them to day and to morrow, ... 6942
Ex 19:22 let the priests...s. themselves, ... 6942
Ex 19:23 bounds about the mount, and s. it. ... 6942
Ex 28:41 and consecrate them, and s. them, ... 6942
Ex 29:27 s. the breast of the wave offering, ... 6942
Ex 29:33 made, to consecrate and to s. them: ... 6942
Ex 29:36 it, and thou shalt anoint it, to s. it. ... 6942
Ex 29:37 atonement for the altar, and s. it; ... 6942
Ex 29:44 And I will s. the tabernacle of the ... 6942
Ex 29:44 I will s. also both Aaron and his sons, ... 6942
Ex 30:29 And thou shalt s. them, that they ... 6942
Ex 31:13 that I am the Lord that doth s. you. ... 6942
Ex 40:10 and all his vessels, and s. the altar: ... 6942
Ex 40:11 shall anoint the laver...and s. it ... 6942
Ex 40:13 and anoint him, and s. him; ... 6942
Le 8:11 the laver and his foot, to s. them ... 6942
Le 8:12 head, and anointed him, to s. him ... 6942
Le 11:44 ye shall therefore s. yourselves, ... 6942
Le 20:7 S. yourselves therefore, and be ye ... 6942
Le 20:8 them: I am the Lord which s. you. ... 6942
Le 21:8 Thou shalt s. him therefore; for he ... 6942
Le 21:8 I the Lord, which s. you, am holy. ... 6942
Le 21:15 his people: for I the Lord do s. him ... 6942
Le 21:23 for I the Lord do s. them ... 6942
Le 22:9 profane it: I the Lord do s. them ... 6942
Le 22:16 things: for I the Lord do s. them ... 6942
Le 27:14 when a man shall s. his house to ... 6942
Le 27:16 a man shall s. unto the Lord some ... 6942
Le 27:17 If he s. his field from the year of ... 6942
Le 27:18 if he s. his field after the jubile, ... 6942
Le 27:22 if a man s. unto the Lord a field ... 6942
Le 27:26 Lord's firstling, no man shall s. it; ... 6942
Nu 11:18 S. yourselves against to morrow, ... 6942
Nu 20:12 s. me in the eyes of the children of ... 6942
Nu 27:14 s. me at the water before their eyes: ... 6942
De 5:12 Keep the sabbath day to s. it, as the ... 6942
De 15:19 shalt s. unto the Lord thy God: ... 6942
Jos 3:5 said unto the people, S. yourselves: ... 6942
Jos 7:13 Up, s. the people, and say, ... 6942
Jos 7:13 S. yourselves against to morrow: ... 6942
1Sa 16:5 s. yourselves, and come with me to ... 6942
1Ch 15:12 s. yourselves, both ye and your ... 6942
1Ch 23:13 he should s. the most holy things, ... 6942
2Ch 29:5 me, ye Levites, s. now yourselves, ... 6942
2Ch 29:5 and s. the house of the Lord God of ... 6942
2Ch 29:17 first day of the first month to s., ... 6942
2Ch 29:34 upright in heart to s. themselves ... 6942
2Ch 30:17 not clean, to s. them unto the Lord ... 6942
2Ch 35:6 kill the passover, and s. yourselves, ... 6942
Ne 13:22 the gates, to s. the sabbath day ... 6942
Isa 8:13 S. the Lord of hosts himself; and ... 6942
Isa 29:23 of him, they shall s. my name, ... 6942
Isa 29:23 and s. the Holy One of Jacob, and ... 6942
Isa 66:17 They that s. themselves, and purify ... 6942
Eze 20:12 that I am the Lord that s. them ... 6942
Eze 36:23 And I will s. my great name, which ... 6942
Eze 37:28 know that I the Lord do s. Israel, ... 6942
Eze 38:23 I magnify myself, and s. myself; ... 6942
Eze 44:19 shall not s. the people with their ... 6942
Eze 46:20 the utter court, to s. the people ... 6942
Joe 1:14 S. ye a fast, call a solemn assembly, ... 6942
Joe 2:15 s. a fast, call a solemn assembly: ... 6942
Joe 2:16 s. the congregation, assemble the ... 6942
Joh 17:17 **S. them through thy truth: thy** ... *37*
Joh 17:19 **for their sakes I s. myself, that they** ... *37*
Eph 5:26 he might s. and cleanse it with the ... *37*
1Th 5:23 the very God of peace s. you wholly; ... *37*
Heb 13:12 he might s. the people with his own ... *37*
1Pe 3:15 But s. the Lord God in your hearts: ... *37*

SANCTUARIES
Le 21:23 that he profane not my s.: for I......... 4720
Le 26:31 and bring your s. unto desolation,....... 4720
Jer 51:51 strangers are come into the s. of....... 4720
Eze 28:18 Thou hast defiled thy s. by the.......... 4720
Am 7:9 the s. of Israel shall be laid waste;..... 4720

SANCTUARY See also SANCTUARIES.
Ex 15:17 S., O Lord, which thy hands have...... 4720
Ex 25:8 let them make me a s.; that I may..... 4720
Ex 30:13 shekel after the shekel of the s.:........ 6944
Ex 30:24 after the shekel of the s., and of........ 6944
Ex 36:1 of work for the service of the s.,........ 6944
Ex 36:3 the work of the service of the s.,....... 6944
Ex 36:4 that wrought all the work of the s.,.... 6944
Ex 36:6 work for the offering of the s........... 6944
Ex 38:24 shekels, after the shekel of the s......... 6944
Ex 38:25 shekels, after the shekel of the s.:..... 6944
Ex 38:26 shekel, after the shekel of the s.,....... 6944
Ex 38:27 were cast the sockets of the s., and... 6944
Le 4:6 the Lord, before the vail of the s....... 6944
Le 5:15 of silver, after the shekel of the s.,..... 6944
Le 10:4 from before the s. out of the camp..... 6944
Le 12:4 nor come into the s., until the........... 4720
Le 16:33 make an atonement for the holy s.,...... 4720
Le 19:30 my sabbaths, and reverence my s.:..... 4720
Le 20:3 to defile my s., and to profane my...... 4720
Le 21:12 Neither shall he go out of the s.,....... 4720
Le 21:12 nor profane the s. of his God; for....... 4720
Le 26:2 my sabbaths, and reverence my s.:..... 4720
Le 27:3 silver, after the shekel of the s.......... 6944
Le 27:25 according to the shekel of the s.:....... 6944
Nu 3:28 keeping the charge of the s................ 6944
Nu 3:31 vessels of the s. wherewith they........ 6944
Nu 3:32 them that keep the charge of the s...... 6944
Nu 3:38 keeping the charge of the s. for.......... 4720
Nu 3:47 shekel of the s. shalt thou take.......... 6944
Nu 3:50 shekels, after the shekel of the s.:..... 6944
Nu 4:12 wherewith they minister in the s.,...... 6944
Nu 4:15 made an end of covering the s.,......... 6944
Nu 4:15 and all the vessels of the s., as the.... 6944
Nu 4:16 and of all that therein is, in the s.,.... 6944
Nu 7:9 the service of the s. belonging unto.... 6944
Nu 7:13, 19,25,31,37,43,49,55,61,67,73,79,85
shekels, after the shekel of the s.;...........
Nu 7:86 apiece, after the shekel of the s.:....... 6944
Nu 8:19 of Israel come nigh unto the s............ 6944
Nu 10:21 set forward, bearing the s.: and......... 4720
Nu 18:1 shall bear the iniquity of the s.:........ 4720
Nu 18:3 not come nigh the vessels of the s..... 6944
Nu 18:5 ye shall keep the charge of the s.,....... 6944
Nu 18:16 shekels, after the shekel of the s.,..... 6944
Nu 19:20 hath defiled the s. of the Lord:.......... 4720
Jos 24:26 oak, that was by the s. of the Lord.... 4720
1Ch 9:29 and all the instruments of the s.,........ 6944
1Ch 22:19 build ye the s. of the Lord God,......... 4720
1Ch 24:5 for the governors of the s., and......... 6944
1Ch 28:10 thee to build an house for the s.:....... 4720
2Ch 20:8 built thee a s. therein for thy name,..... 4720
2Ch 26:18 go out of the s.; for thou hast........... 4720
2Ch 29:21 kingdom, for the s., and for Judah...... 4720
2Ch 30:8 unto the Lord, and enter into his s.,... 4720
2Ch 30:19 to the purification of the s................ 6944
2Ch 36:17 the sword in the house of their s.,...... 4720
Ne 10:39 where are the vessels of the s., and... 4720
Ps 20:2 Send thee help from the s., and......... 6944
Ps 63:2 so as I have seen thee in the s........... 6944
Ps 68:24 of my God, my King, in the s............. 6944
Ps 73:17 Until I went into the s. of God;......... 4720
Ps 74:3 hath done wickedly in the s............... 6944
Ps 74:7 They have cast fire into thy s., they... 4720
Ps 77:13 Thy way, O God, is in the s.: who is.. 6944
Ps 78:54 them to the border of his s., even...... 6944
Ps 78:69 built his s. like high palaces, like....... 4720
Ps 96:6 strength and beauty are in his s......... 4720
Ps 102:19 down from the height of his s.;.......... 6944
Ps 114:2 Judah was his s., and Israel his......... 6944
Ps 134:2 Lift up your hands in the s., and........ 6944
Ps 150:1 Praise God in his s.: praise him......... 6944
Isa 8:14 he shall be for a s.; but for a stone.... 4720
Isa 16:12 that he shall come to his s. to pray;.... 4720
Isa 43:28 profaned the princes of the s.,........... 6944
Isa 60:13 to beautify the place of my s.;........... 4720
Isa 63:18 adversaries...trodden down thy s........ 4720
Jer 17:12 beginning is the place of our s........... 4720
La 1:10 the heathen entered into her s.,.......... 4720
La 2:7 he hath abhorred his s., he hath......... 4720
La 2:20 prophet be slain in...s. of the Lord?.... 4720
La 4:1 stones of the s. are poured out in...... 6944
Eze 5:11 because thou hast defiled my s........... 4720
Eze 8:6 that I should go far off from my s.?.... 4720
Eze 9:6 is the mark; and begin at my s........... 4720
Eze 11:16 yet will I be to them as a little s. in.... 4720
Eze 11:38 have defiled my s. in the same day..... 4720
Eze 23:39 same day into my s. to profane it;...... 4720
Eze 24:21 Behold, I will profane my s., the........ 4720
Eze 25:3 thou saidst, Aha, against my s.,......... 4720
Eze 37:26 will set my s. in the midst of them..... 4720
Eze 37:28 my s. shall be in the midst of them..... 4720
Eze 41:21 squared, and the face of the s.;.......... 6944
Eze 41:23 temple and the s. had two doors........ 6944
Eze 42:20 make a separation between the s........ 6944
Eze 43:21 place of the house, without the s........ 4720
Eze 44:1 the gate of the outward s. which........ 4720
Eze 44:5 with every going forth of the s........... 4720
Eze 44:7 have brought into my s. strangers,...........
Eze 44:7 to be in my s., to pollute it, even....... 4720
Eze 44:8 set keepers of my charge in my s....... 4720
Eze 44:9 in flesh, shall enter into my s.,........... 4720
Eze 44:11 they shall be ministers in my s.,........ 4720
Eze 44:15 kept the charge of my s. when the..... 4720
Eze 44:16 They shall enter into my s., and........ 4720
Eze 44:27 the day that he goeth into the s.,....... 6944
Eze 44:27 inner court, to minister in the s.,....... 6944
Eze 45:2 for the s. five hundred in length......... 6944
Eze 45:3 the s. and the most holy place........... 4720
Eze 45:4 the priests the ministers of the s.,...... 4720
Eze 45:4 houses, and an holy place for the s..... 4720
Eze 45:18 without blemish, and cleanse the s.:.... 4720
Eze 47:12 waters they issued out of the s.:......... 4720
Eze 48:8 the s. shall be in the midst of it.......... 4720
Eze 48:10 s. of the Lord shall be in the midst..... 4720
Eze 48:21 s. of the house shall be in the midst... 4720
Da 8:11 the place of his s. was cast down....... 4720
Da 8:13 to give both the s. and the host to..... 6944
Da 8:14 days; then shall the s. be cleansed...... 6944
Da 9:17 cause thy face to shine upon thy s...... 4720
Da 9:26 shall destroy the city and the s.;......... 6944
Da 11:31 shall pollute the s. of strength, and..... 4720
Zep 3:4 her priests have polluted the s.,.......... 6944
Heb 8:2 A minister of the s., and of the true...... *39*
Heb 9:1 of divine service, and a worldly s......... *39*
Heb 9:2 shewbread; which is called the s.......... *39*
Heb 13:11 whose blood is brought into the s.......... *39*

SAND See also QUICKSANDS.
Ge 22:17 s. which is upon the sea shore;.......... 2344
Ge 32:12 make thy seed as the s. of the sea,.... 2344
Ge 41:49 gathered corn as the s. of the sea,..... 2344
Ex 2:12 the Egyptian, and hid him in the s..... 2344
De 33:19 seas, and of treasures hid in the s..... 2344
Jos 11:4 as the s. that is upon the sea shore.... 2344
Jg 7:12 the s. by the sea side for multitude.... 2344
1Sa 13:5 as the s. which is on the sea shore..... 2344
2Sa 17:11 as the s. that is by the sea for........... 2344
1Ki 4:20 many, as the s. which is by the sea..... 2344
1Ki 4:29 as the s. that is on the sea shore........ 2344
Job 6:3 be heavier than the s. of the sea:....... 2344
Job 29:18 I shall multiply my days as the s........ 2344
Ps 78:27 fowls like as the s. of the sea:............ 2344
Ps 139:18 are more in number than the s.:......... 2344
Pr 27:3 stone is heavy, and the s. weighty;..... 2344
Isa 10:22 people Israel be as the s. of the sea,.. 2344
Isa 48:19 Thy seed also had been as the s.,......... 2344
Jer 5:22 have placed the s. for the bound of..... 2344
Jer 15:8 to me above the s. of the seas:........... 2344
Jer 33:22 neither the s. of the sea measured:.... 2344
Ho 1:10 Israel shall be as the s. of the sea,..... 2344
Hab 1:9 shall gather the captivity as the s...... 2344
Mt 7:26 which built his house upon the s.:.. *285*
Ro 9:27 of Israel be as the s. of the sea,.......... *285*
Heb 11:12 as the s. which is by the sea shore...... *285*
Re 13:1 And I stood upon the s. of the sea,...... *285*
Re 20:8 the number...is as the s. of the sea...... *285*

SANDALS
Mk 6:9 But be shod with s.; and not put........ *4547*
Ac 12:8 Gird thyself, and bind on thy s........... *4547*

SANG
Ex 15:1 Then s. Moses and the children of........ 7891
Nu 21:17 Then Israel s. this song, Spring up,.... 7891
Jg 5:1 Then s. Deborah and Barak the.......... 7891
1Sa 29:5 Is not this David, of whom they s...... 6030
2Ch 29:28 the singers s., and the trumpeters...... 7891
2Ch 29:30 they s. praises with gladness, and..........
Ezr 3:11 And they s. together by course in....... 6030
Ne 12:42 the singers s. loud, with Jezrahiah...... 7891
Job 38:7 the morning stars s. together, and...... 7442
Ps 7:*title* David, which he s. unto the Lord,....... 7891
Ps 106:12 they his words; they s. his praise........ 7891
Ac 16:25 prayed, and s. praises unto God:......... *5214*

SANK
Ex 15:5 they s. into the bottom as a stone....... 3381
Ex 15:10 s. as lead in the mighty waters.......... 6749

SANSANNAH (san-san'-nah) See also KIRJATH-SANNAH.
Jos 15:31 Ziklag, and Madmannah, and S.,.......... 5578

SAP
Ps 104:16 The trees of the Lord are full of s.;..........

SAPH (saf) See also SIPHAI.
2Sa 21:18 Sibbechai the Hushathite slew S.,........ 5593

SAPHIR (sa'-fur)
Mic 1:11 ye away, thou inhabitant of S.,........... 8208

SAPPHIRA (saf-fi'-rah)
Ac 5:1 named Ananias, with S. his wife,......... *4551*

SAPPHIRE See also SAPPHIRES.
Ex 24:10 were a paved work of a s. stone,........ 5601
Ex 28:18 row shall be an emerald, a s., and....... 5601
Ex 39:11 the second row, an emerald, a s.,....... 5601
Job 28:16 with the precious onyx, or the s......... 5601
La 4:7 rubies, their polishing was of s.:.......... 5601
Eze 1:26 as the appearance of a s. stone:.......... 5601
Eze 10:1 over them as it were a s. stone, as...... 5601
Eze 28:13 and the jasper, the s., the emerald,...... 5601
Re 21:19 was jasper; the second, s.; the........... *4552*

SAPPHIRES
Job 28:6 stones of it are the place of s.: and.... 5601
Ca 5:14 is as bright ivory overlaid with s........ 5601
Isa 54:11 and lay thy foundations with s........... 5601

SARA (sa'-rah) See also SARAH.
Heb 11:11 S. herself received strength to........... *4564*
1Pe 3:6 as s. obeyed Abraham, calling him....... *4564*

SARAH (sa'-rah) See also SARA; SARAH'S; SARAI; SERAH.
Ge 17:15 Sarai, but S. shall her name be........... 8283
Ge 17:17 shall S., that is ninety years old,......... 8283
Ge 17:19 S. thy wife shall bare thee a son......... 8283
Ge 17:21 which S. shall bare unto thee at......... 8283
Ge 18:6 hastened into the tent unto S., and..... 8283
Ge 18:9 unto him, Where is S. thy wife?......... 8283
Ge 18:10 lo, S. thy wife shall have a son........... 8283
Ge 18:10 S. heard it in the tent door, which...... 8283
Ge 18:11 Abraham and S. were old and well...... 8283
Ge 18:11 with S. after the manner of women...... 8283
Ge 18:12 S. laughed within herself, saying,........ 8283
Ge 18:13 Wherefore did S. laugh, saying,.......... 8283
Ge 18:14 of life, and S. shall have a son........... 8283
Ge 18:15 S. denied, saying, I laughed not;......... 8283
Ge 20:2 Abraham said of S. his wife, She is..... 8283
Ge 20:2 king of Gerar sent, and took S........... 8283
Ge 20:14 and restored him S. his wife.............. 8283
Ge 20:16 and unto S. he said, Behold, I have.... 8283
Ge 20:18 because of S. Abraham's wife............. 8283
Ge 21:1 the Lord visited S. as he had said,...... 8283
Ge 21:1 Lord did unto S. as he had spoken..... 8283
Ge 21:2 S. conceived, and bare Abraham a....... 8283
Ge 21:3 him, whom S. bare to him, Isaac........ 8283
Ge 21:6 And S. said, God hath made me to...... 8283
Ge 21:7 S. should have given children suck?.... 8283
Ge 21:9 And S. saw the son of Hagar the........ 8283
Ge 21:12 in all that S. hath said unto thee,....... 8283
Ge 23:1 S. was an hundred and seven and....... 8283
Ge 23:1 were the years of the life of S........... 8283
Ge 23:2 S. died in Kirjath-arba; the same......... 8283
Ge 23:2 and Abraham came to mourn for S.,... 8283
Ge 23:19 Abraham buried S. his wife in the....... 8283
Ge 24:36 S. my master's wife bare a son to...... 8283
Ge 25:10 Abraham buried, and S. his wife........ 8283
Ge 49:31 buried Abraham and S. his wife;......... 8283
Nu 26:46 of the daughter of Asher was S.......... 8294
Isa 51:2 father, and unto S. that bare you:...... 8283
Ro 9:9 I come, and S. shall have a son......... *4564*

SARAH'S (sa'-rahs)
Ge 24:67 her into his mother s. tent, and......... 8283
Ge 25:12 S. handmaid, bare unto Abraham:....... 8283
Ro 4:19 yet the deadness of S. womb:........... *4564*

SARAI (sa'-rahee) See also SARAH; SARAI'S.
Ge 11:29 the name of Abram's wife was **S.**; 8297
Ge 11:30 **S.** was barren; she had no child. 8297
Ge 11:31 and **S.** his daughter in law, his son 8297
Ge 12:5 Abram took **S.** his wife, and Lot 8297
Ge 12:11 he said unto **S.** his wife, Behold 8297
Ge 12:17 with great plagues because of **S.** 8297
Ge 16:1 Now **S.** Abram's wife bare him no 8297
Ge 16:2 **S.** said unto Abram, Behold now, 8297
Ge 16:2 Abram hearkened to the voice of **S.** 8297
Ge 16:3 **S.** Abram's wife took Hagar her 8297
Ge 16:5 **S.** said unto Abram, My wrong be 8297
Ge 16:6 Abram said unto **S.**, Behold, thy 8297
Ge 16:6 when **S.** dealt hardly with her, she 8297
Ge 16:8 from the face of my mistress **S.** 8297
Ge 17:15 As for **S.** thy wife, thou shalt not 8297
Ge 17:15 thou shalt not call her name **S.**, but 8297

SARAI'S (sa'-rahees)
Ge 16:8 he said, Hagar, **S.** maid, whence 8297

SARAPH (sa'-raf)
1Ch 4:22 **S.**, who had the dominion in Moab, 8315

SARDINE
Re 4:3 upon like a jasper and a **s.** stone: *4555*

SARDIS (sar'-dis)
Re 1:11 and unto Thyatira, and unto **S.**, *4554*
Re 3:1 angel of the church in **S.** write *4554*
Re 3:4 Thou hast a few names even in **S.** *4554*

SARDITES (sar'-dites)
Nu 26:26 of Sered, the family of the **S.**: of 5625

SARDIUS (sar'-de-us)
Ex 28:17 the first row shall be a **s.**, a topaz, 124
Ex 39:10 the first row was a **s.**, a topaz, and 124
Eze 28:13 thy covering, the **s.**, and the diamond, 124
Re 21:20 The fifth, sardonyx; the sixth, **s.**; *4556*

SARDONYX (sar'-do-nix)
Re 21:20 The fifth, **s.**; the sixth, sardius; *4557*

SAREPTA (sa-rep'-tah) See also ZAREPHATH.
Lu 4:26 save unto **S.**, a city of Sidon, unto *4558*

SARGON (sar'-gon)
Isa 20:1 **S.** the king of Assyria sent him,) 5623

SARID (sa'-rid)
Jos 19:10 of their inheritance was unto **S.**: 8301
Jos 19:12 And turned from **s.** eastward 8301

SARON (sa'-ron) See also SHARON.
Ac 9:35 all that dwelt at Lydda and **S.** saw *4565*

SARSECHIM (sar'-se-kim)
Jer 39:3 Nergal-sharezer, Samgar-nebo, **S.**, 8310

SARUCH (sa'-ruk) See also SERUG.
Lu 3:35 Which was the son of **S.**, which *4562*

SAT See also SATEST.
Ge 18:1 he **s.** in the tent door in the heat 3427
Ge 19:1 and Lot **s.** in the gate of Sodom: 3427
Ge 21:16 and **s.** her down over against him a 3427
Ge 21:16 And she **s.** over against him, and 3427
Ge 31:34 the images,...and **s.** upon them. 3427
Ge 37:25 And they **s.** down to eat bread: and 3427
Ge 38:14 and **s.** in an open place, which is by 3427
Ge 43:33 they **s.** before him, the firstborn 3427
Ge 48:2 himself, and **s.** upon the bed. 3427
Ex 2:15 Midian: and he **s.** down by a well. 3427
Ex 12:29 of Pharaoh that **s.** on his throne 3427
Ex 16:3 when we **s.** by the flesh pots, and 3427
Ex 17:12 put it under him, and he **s.** thereon; 3427
Ex 18:13 that Moses **s.** to judge the people: 3427
Ex 32:6 people **s.** down to eat and to drink, 3427
Le 15:6 whereon he **s.** that hath the issue 3427
Le 15:22 toucheth any thing that she **s.** upon 3427
De 33:3 and they **s.** down at thy feet; 8497
Jg 6:11 and **s.** under an oak which was in 3427
Jg 13:9 the woman as she **s.** in the field: 3427
Jg 19:6 And they **s.** down, and did eat and 3427
Jg 19:15 **s.** him down in a street of the city: 3427
Jg 20:26 wept, and **s.** there before the Lord, 3427
Ru 2:14 And she **s.** beside the reapers: and 3427
Ru 4:1 to the gate, and **s.** him down there: 3427
Ru 4:1 And he turned aside, and **s.** down. 3427
Ru 4:2 ye down here. And they **s.** down. 3427
1Sa 1:9 Eli the priest **s.** upon a seat by a 3427
1Sa 4:13 Eli **s.** upon a seat by the wayside 3427
1Sa 19:9 as he **s.** in his house with his javelin 3427
1Sa 20:24 the king **s.** him down to eat meat. 3427
1Sa 20:25 king **s.** upon his seat, as at other 3427
1Sa 20:25 Abner **s.** by Saul's side, and David's 3427
1Sa 28:23 from the earth, and **s.** upon the bed. 3427
2Sa 2:13 they **s.** down, the one on the one side 3427
2Sa 7:1 pass, when the king **s.** in his house, 3427
2Sa 7:18 David in, and **s.** before the Lord, 3427
2Sa 18:24 And David **s.** between the two gates: 3427
2Sa 19:8 the king arose, and **s.** in the gate. 3427
2Sa 23:8 The Tachmonite that **s.** in the seat, 3427
1Ki 2:12 **s.** Solomon upon the throne of David 3427
1Ki 2:19 and **s.** down on his throne, and 3427
1Ki 2:19 and she **s.** on his right hand. 3427
1Ki 13:20 came to pass, as they **s.** at the table, 3427
1Ki 16:11 reign, as soon as he **s.** on his throne, 3427
1Ki 19:4 and **s.** down under a juniper tree: 3427
1Ki 21:13 children of Belial, and **s.** before him: 3427
1Ki 22:10 king of Judah **s.** each on his throne, 3427
2Ki 1:9 behold, he **s.** on the top of an hill. 3427
2Ki 4:20 mother, he **s.** on her knees till noon, 3427
2Ki 6:32 But Elisha **s.** in his house, and the 3427
2Ki 6:32 house, and the elders **s.** with him; 3427
2Ki 11:19 he **s.** on the throne of the kings. 3427
2Ki 13:13 and Jeroboam **s.** upon his throne: 3427
1Ch 17:1 to pass, as David **s.** in his house, 3427
1Ch 17:16 king came and **s.** before the Lord, 3427
1Ch 29:23 Solomon **s.** on the throne of the Lord. 3427
2Ch 18:9 **s.** either of them on his throne, 3427
2Ch 18:9 and they **s.** in a void place at the 3427
Ezr 9:3 of my beard, and **s.** down astonied. 3427
Ezr 9:4 and I **s.** astonied until the evening 3427
Ezr 10:9 **s.** in the street of the house of God. 3427
Ezr 10:16 **s.** down in the first day of the tenth. 3427
Ne 1:4 I **s.** down and wept, and mourned 3427
Ne 8:17 booth, and **s.** under the booths: 3427
Es 1:2 king Ahasuerus **s.** on the throne 3427
Es 1:14 which **s.** the first in the kingdom;) 3427
Es 2:19 then Mordecai **s.** in the king's gate. 3427
Es 2:21 while Mordecai **s.** in the king's gate, 3427
Es 3:15 king and Haman **s.** down to drink; 3427
Es 5:1 the king **s.** upon his royal throne 3427
Job 2:8 and he **s.** down among the ashes. 3427
Job 2:13 **s.** down with him upon the ground. 3427
Job 29:25 I chose out their way, and **s.** chief, 3427
Ps 26:4 I have not **s.** with vain persons, 3427
Ps 137:1 rivers of Babylon, there we **s.** down, 3427
Ca 2:3 I **s.** down under his shadow with 3427
Jer 3:2 In the ways hast thou **s.** for them, 3427
Jer 15:17 I **s.** not in the assembly of the 3427
Jer 15:17 I **s.** alone because of thy hand: for 3427
Jer 26:10 **s.** down in the entry of the new gate 3427
Jer 32:12 and, lo, all the princes **s.** there, 3427
Jer 36:12 and, lo, all the princes **s.** there, 3427
Jer 36:22 Now the king **s.** in the winterhouse 3427
Jer 39:3 came in, and **s.** in the middle gate, 3427
Eze 3:15 of Chebar, and I **s.** where they **s.**, 3427
Eze 8:1 of the month, as I **s.** in mine house, 3427
Eze 8:1 the elders of Judah **s.** before me, 3427
Eze 8:14 **s.** women weeping for Tammuz. 3427
Eze 14:1 elders...unto me, and **s.** before me. 3427
Eze 20:1 elders of Israel...and **s.** before me. 3427
Da 2:49 but Daniel **s.** in the gate of the king.
Jon 3:6 with sackcloth, and **s.** in ashes. 3427
Jon 4:5 and **s.** on the east side of the city, 3427
Jon 4:5 booth, and **s.** under it in the shadow, 3427
Mt 4:16 The people which **s.** in darkness *2521*
Mt 4:16 which **s.** in the region and shadow *2521*
Mt 9:10 as Jesus **s.** at meat in the house, *345*
Mt 9:10 and **s.** down with him and his *4873*
Mt 13:1 the house, and **s.** by the sea side. *2521*
Mt 13:2 that he went into a ship, and **s.**; *2521*
Mt 13:48 they drew to shore, and **s.** down, *2523*
Mt 14:9 them which **s.** with him at meat, *4873*
Mt 15:29 a mountain, and **s.** down there. *2521*
Mt 24:3 as he **s.** upon the mount of Olives, *2521*
Mt 26:7 it on his head, as he **s.** at meat. *345*
Mt 26:20 come, he **s.** down with the twelve. *345*
Mt 26:55 I **s.** daily with you teaching in the *2516*
Mt 26:58 went in, and **s.** with the servants, *2521*
Mt 26:69 Now Peter **s.** without in the palace: *2521*
Mt 28:2 stone from the door, and **s.** upon it. *2521*
Mk 2:15 as Jesus **s.** at meat in his house, *2621*
Mk 2:15 sinners **s.** also together with Jesus *4873*
Mk 3:32 And the multitude **s.** about him, *2521*
Mk 3:34 looked...on them which **s.** about him, *2521*
Mk 4:1 into a ship, and **s.** in the sea; *2521*
Mk 6:22 Herod and them that **s.** with him, *4873*
Mk 6:26 for their sakes which **s.** with him, *4873*
Mk 6:40 they **s.** down in ranks, by hundreds, *377*
Mk 9:35 he **s.** down, and called the twelve, *2523*
Mk 10:46 **s.** by the highway side begging. *2521*
Mk 11:2 colt tied, whereon never man **s.** *2523*
Mk 11:7 on him; and he **s.** upon him. *2523*
Mk 12:41 Jesus **s.** over against the treasury, *2523*
Mk 13:3 as he **s.** upon the mount of Olives *2521*
Mk 14:3 as he **s.** at meat,...came a woman *2621*
Mk 14:18 as they **s.** and did eat, Jesus said, *345*
Mk 14:54 and he **s.** with the servants, and *4775*
Mk 16:14 unto the eleven as they **s.** at meat, *345*
Mk 16:19 and **s.** on the right hand of God. *2523*
Lu 4:20 again to the minister, and **s.** down. *2523*
Lu 5:3 **s.** down, and taught the people out *2523*
Lu 5:29 of others that **s.** down with them. *2621*
Lu 7:15 he that was dead **s.** up, and began *339*
Lu 7:36 house, and **s.** down to meat. *347*
Lu 7:37 knew that Jesus **s.** at meat in the *345*
Lu 7:49 And they that **s.** at meat with him *4873*
Lu 10:39 Mary which also **s.** at Jesus' feet, *3869*
Lu 11:37 he went in, and **s.** down to meat. *377*
Lu 14:15 one of them that **s.** at meat with *4873*
Lu 18:35 blind man **s.** by the way side *2521*
Lu 19:30 tied, whereon never yet man **s.** *2523*
Lu 22:14 the hour was come he **s.** down, and *377*
Lu 22:55 Peter **s.** down among them. *2521*
Lu 22:56 maid beheld him as he **s.** by the *2521*
Lu 24:30 as he **s.** at meat with them, he took *2625*
Joh 4:6 his journey, **s.** thus on the well: *2516*
Joh 6:3 and there he **s.** with his disciples. *2521*
Joh 6:10 So the men **s.** down, in number *377*
Joh 8:2 and he **s.** down, and taught them. *2523*
Joh 9:8 Is not this he that **s.** and begged? *2521*
Joh 11:20 him: but Mary **s.** still in the house. *2516*
Joh 12:2 them that **s.** at the table with him. *4873*
Joh 12:14 had found a young ass, **s.** thereon; *2523*
Joh 19:13 **s.** down in the judgment seat in a *2523*
Ac 2:3 of fire, and it **s.** upon each of them. *2523*
Ac 3:10 it was he which **s.** for alms at the *2521*
Ac 6:15 all that **s.** in the council, looking *2516*
Ac 9:40 and when she saw Peter, she **s.** up. *399*
Ac 12:21 **s.** upon his throne, and made an *2523*
Ac 13:14 on the sabbath day, and **s.** down. *2523*
Ac 14:8 there **s.** a certain man at Lystra, *2521*
Ac 16:13 and we **s.** down, and spake unto *2523*
Ac 20:9 And there **s.** in a window a certain *2521*
Ac 25:17 I **s.** on the judgment seat, and *2523*
Ac 26:30 Bernice,...they that **s.** with them: *4775*
1Co 10:7 people **s.** down to eat and drink, *2523*
Heb 1:3 **s.** down on the right hand of the *2523*
Heb 10:12 **s.** down on the right hand of God; *2523*
Re 4:2 heaven, and one **s.** on the throne. *2521*
Re 4:3 he that **s.** was to look upon like a *2521*
Re 4:9 thanks to him that **s.** on the throne, *2521*
Re 4:10 before him that **s.** on the throne, *2521*
Re 5:1 hand of him that **s.** on the throne *2521*
Re 5:7 hand of him that **s.** upon the throne. *2521*
Re 6:2 he that **s.** on him had a bow; and a *2521*
Re 6:4 was given to him that **s.** thereon to *2521*
Re 6:5 **s.** on him had a pair of balances *2521*
Re 6:8 his name that **s.** on him was Death, *2521*
Re 9:17 and them that **s.** on them, having *2521*
Re 11:16 which **s.** before God on their seats, *2521*
Re 14:14 one **s.** like unto the Son of man, *2521*
Re 14:15 voice to him that **s.** on the cloud, *2521*
Re 14:16 **s.** on the cloud thrust in his sickle *2521*
Re 19:4 God that **s.** on the throne, saying, *2521*
Re 19:11 **s.** upon him was called Faithful *2521*
Re 19:19 against him that **s.** on the horse, *2521*
Re 19:21 sword of him that **s.** upon the horse, *2521*
Re 20:4 thrones, and they **s.** upon them, *2523*
Re 20:11 white throne, and him that **s.** on *2521*
Re 21:5 he that **s.** upon the throne said, *2521*

SATAN (sa'-tun) See also SATAN'S.
1Ch 21:1 **S.** stood up against Israel, and 7854
Job 1:6 and **S.** came also among them. 7854
Job 1:7 Lord said unto **S.**, Whence comest 7854
Job 1:7 **S.** answered the Lord, and said, 7854
Job 1:8 the Lord said unto **S.**, Hast thou 7854
Job 1:9 **S.** answered the Lord, and said, 7854
Job 1:12 Lord said unto **S.**, Behold, all that 7854
Job 1:12 **S.** went forth from the presence of 7854
Job 2:1 and **S.** came also among them to 7854

Job 2:2 Lord said unto S., From whence........ 7854
Job 2:2 S. answered the Lord, and said, ... 7854
Job 2:3 the Lord said unto S., Hast thou........ 7854
Job 2:4 S. answered the Lord, and said, ... 7854
Job 2:6 Lord said unto S., Behold, he is in..... 7854
Job 2:7 went S. forth from the presence of..... 7854
Ps 109:6 and let S. stand at his right hand........ 7854
Zec 3:1 S. standing at his right hand to.......... 7854
Zec 3:2 the Lord said unto S., The Lord.......... 7854
Zec 3:2 Lord rebuke thee, O S.; even the...... 7854
Mt 4:10 unto him, **Get thee hence, S.**:.......... *4567*
Mt 12:26 **if S. cast out S., he is divided**....... *4567*
Mt 16:23 **Get thee behind me, S.: thou art**... *4567*
Mk 1:13 forty days, tempted of S.; and was..... *4567*
Mk 3:23 parables, **How can S. cast out S.?**... *4567*
Mk 3:26 **S. rise up against himself, and be**.. *4567*
Mk 4:15 **S. cometh immediately, and**.......... *4567*
Mk 8:33 saying, **Get thee behind me, S.**........ *4567*
Lu 4:8 unto him, **Get thee behind me, S.**.... *4567*
Lu 10:18 **I beheld S. as lightning fall from**.. *4567*
Lu 11:18 **S. also be divided against himself,**.. *4567*
Lu 13:16 **of Abraham, whom S. hath bound,**. *4567*
Lu 22:3 Then entered S. into Judas *4567*
Lu 22:31 **S. hath desired to have you, that**... *4567*
Joh 13:27 after the sop S. entered into him. *4567*
Ac 5:3 why hath S. filled thine heart to lie..... *4567*
Ac 26:18 **from the power of S. unto God,**..... *4567*
Ro 16:20 bruise S. under your feet shortly........ *4567*
1Co 5:5 To deliver such an one unto S............. *4567*
1Co 7:5 that S. tempt you not for your........... *4567*
2Co 2:11 S. should get an advantage of us: *4567*
2Co 11:14 S. himself is transformed into an........ *4567*
2Co 12:7 the messenger of S. to buffet me,...... *4567*
1Th 2:18 and again; but S. hindered us. *4567*
2Th 2:9 is after the working of S. with all....... *4567*
1Ti 1:20 whom I have delivered unto S., ... *4567*
1Ti 5:15 are already turned aside after S. *4567*
Re 2:9 **not, but are the synagogue of S.** ... *4567*
Re 2:13 **among you, where S. dwelleth**....... *4567*
Re 2:24 **have not known the depths of S.,**... *4567*
Re 3:9 **make them of the synagogue of S.,** *4567*
Re 12:9 serpent, called the Devil, and S., ... *4567*
Re 20:2 serpent, which is the Devil, and S.,..... *4567*
Re 20:7 S. shall be loosed out of his prison, ... *4567*

SATAN'S (sa'-tuns)
Re 2:13 **dwellest, even where S. seat is:**..... *4567*

SATEST
Ps 9:4 s. in the throne judging right. 3427
Eze 23:41 s. upon a stately bed, and a table....... 3427

SATIATE See also SATIATED; UNSATIABLE.
Jer 31:14 and I will s. the soul of the priests 7301
Jer 46:10 and it shall be s. and made drunk....... 7646

SATIATED
Jer 31:25 I have s. the weary soul, and I.......... 7301

SATISFACTION
Nu 35:31 no s. for the life of a murderer, ... 3724
Nu 35:32 no s. for him that is fled to the city.... 3724

SATISFIED
Ex 15:9 my lust shall be s. upon them; I......... 4390
Le 26:26 and ye shall eat, and not be s............ 7646
De 14:29 shall come, and shall eat and be s.;...... 7646
De 33:23 O Naphtali, s. with favour, and.......... 7649
Job 19:22 God, and are not s. with my flesh?..... 7646
Job 27:14 offspring shall not be s. with bread. 7646
Job 31:31 had of his flesh! we cannot be s......... 7646
Ps 17:15 I shall be s., when I awake, with 7646
Ps 22:26 The meek shall eat and be s.: they..... 7646
Ps 36:8 They shall be abundantly s. with 7301
Ps 37:19 days of famine they shall be s............ 7646
Ps 59:15 meat, and grudge if they be not s........ 7646
Ps 63:5 My soul shall be s. as with marrow 7646
Ps 65:4 we shall be s. with the goodness of.... 7646
Ps 81:16 of the rock should I have s. thee........ 7649
Ps 104:13 earth is s. with the fruit of thy.......... 7646
Ps 105:40 s. them with the bread of heaven........ 7649
Pr 12:11 He that tilleth his land shall be s. 7646
Pr 12:14 A man shall be s. with good by the..... 7646
Pr 14:14 a good man shall be s. from himself. ....
Pr 18:20 A man's belly shall be s. with the....... 7646
Pr 19:23 he that hath it shall abide s.; he......... 7649
Pr 20:13 and thou shalt be s. with bread. 7646
Pr 27:20 so the eyes of man are never s. 7646
Pr 30:15 are three things that are never s.,....... 7646
Ec 1:8 the eye is not s. with seeing, nor....... 7646
Ec 4:8 neither is his eye s. with riches; 7646
Ec 5:10 He that loveth silver shall not be s. 7646
Isa 9:20 left hand, and they shall not be s........ 7646
Isa 44:16 flesh; he roasteth roast, and is s. 7646
Isa 53:11 travail of his soul, and shall be s. 7646
Isa 66:11 suck, and be s. with the breasts 7646
Jer 31:14 and my people shall be s. with my...... 7646
Jer 50:10 all that spoil her shall be s., saith...... 7646
Jer 50:19 and his soul shall be s. upon mount..... 7646
La 5:6 the Assyrians, to be s. with bread...... 7646
Eze 16:28 them, and yet couldest not be s......... 7646
Eze 16:29 and yet thou wast not s. herewith. 7646
Joe 2:19 oil, and ye shall be s. therewith: 7646
Joe 2:26 ye shall eat in plenty, and be s., ... 7646
Am 4:8 drink water; but they were not s........ 7646
Mic 6:14 Thou shalt eat, but not be s.; and...... 7646
Hab 2:5 and is as death, and cannot be s., ... 7646

SATISFIEST
Ps 145:16 s. the desire of every living thing. 7646

SATISFIETH
Ps 103:5 s. thy mouth with good things; 7646
Ps 107:9 he s. the longing soul, and filleth........ 7646
Isa 55:2 your labour for that which s. not?....... 7654

SATISFY See also SATISFIED; SATISFIEST; SASTISFIETH; SATISFYING.
Job 38:27 s. the desolate and waste ground; 7646
Ps 90:14 O s. us early with thy mercy; that...... 7646
Ps 91:16 With long life will I s. him, and.......... 7646
Ps 132:15 I will s. her poor with bread............. 7646
Pr 5:19 let her breasts s. thee at all times; 7301
Pr 6:30 if he steal to s. his soul when he........ 4390
Isa 58:10 hungry, and s. the afflicted soul; 7646
Isa 58:11 s. thy soul in drought, and make 7646
Eze 7:19 they shall not s. their souls, ... 7646
Mk 8:4 can a man s. these men with bread..... *5526*

SATISFYING
Pr 13:25 eateth to the s. of his soul: but.......... 7648
Col 2:23 any honour to the s. of the flesh. *4140*

SATYR (sa'-tur) See also SATYRS.
Isa 34:14 and the s. shall cry to his fellow;........ 8163

SATYRS (sa'-turs)
Isa 13:21 there, and s. shall dance there........... 8163

SAUL (sawl) See also PAUL; SAUL'S; SHAUL.
Ge 36:37 and S. of Rehoboth by the river......... 7586
Ge 36:38 And S. died, and Baal-hanan the......... 7586
1Sa 9:2 he had a son, whose name was S.,..... 7586
1Sa 9:3 Kish said to S. his son, Take now...... 7586
1Sa 9:5 S. said to his servant that was with.... 7586
1Sa 9:7 said S. to his servant, But, behold,..... 7586
1Sa 9:8 the servant answered S. again, and..... 7586
1Sa 9:10 said S. to his servant, Well said;........ 7586
1Sa 9:15 told Samuel...a day before S. came,.... 7586
1Sa 9:17 when Samuel saw S., the Lord said.... 7586
1Sa 9:18 S. drew near to Samuel in the gate, ... 7586
1Sa 9:19 Samuel answered S., and said, I am.... 7586
1Sa 9:21 S. answered and said, Am not I a 7586
1Sa 9:22 Samuel took S. and his servant, ... 7586
1Sa 9:24 was upon it, and set it before S.......... 7586
1Sa 9:24 So S. did eat with Samuel that day. 7586
1Sa 9:25 communed with S. upon the top of..... 7586
1Sa 9:26 Samuel called S. to the top of the 7586
1Sa 9:26 S. arose, and they went out both of.... 7586
1Sa 9:27 Samuel said to S., Bid the servant...... 7586
1Sa 10:11, 12 Is S. also among the prophets?...... 7586
1Sa 10:16 S. said unto his uncle, He told us....... 7586
1Sa 10:21 and S. the son of Kish was taken:...... 7586
1Sa 10:26 S. also went home to Gibeah; and...... 7586
1Sa 11:4 the messengers to Gibeah of S., ... 7586
1Sa 11:5 S. came after the herd out of the....... 7586
1Sa 11:5 S. said, What aileth the people that 7586
1Sa 11:6 And the Spirit of God came upon S..... 7586
1Sa 11:7 cometh not forth after S. and after 7586
1Sa 11:11 that S. put the people in three........... 7586
1Sa 11:12 he that said, Shall S. reign over us?.... 7586
1Sa 11:13 S. said, There shalt not a man be 7586
1Sa 11:15 made S. king before the Lord in 7586
1Sa 11:15 there S. and all the men of Israel....... 7586
1Sa 13:1 S. reigned one year; and when he....... 7586
1Sa 13:2 S. chose him three thousand men....... 7586
1Sa 13:2 two thousand were with S. in............ 7586
1Sa 13:3 S. blew the trumpet throughout all 7586
1Sa 13:4 S. had smitten a garrison of the......... 7586
1Sa 13:4 called together after S. to Gilgal......... 7586
1Sa 13:7 As for S., he was yet in Gilgal, and.... 7586
1Sa 13:9 And S. said, Bring hither a burnt 7586
1Sa 13:10 and S. went out to meet him, that...... 7586
1Sa 13:11 And S. said, Because I saw that the ... 7586
1Sa 13:13 Samuel said to S., Thou hast done 7586
1Sa 13:15 S. numbered the people that were...... 7586
1Sa 13:16 S., and Jonathan his son, and the 7586
1Sa 13:22 of the people that were with S. and.... 7586
1Sa 13:22 with S. and with Jonathan his son....... 7586
1Sa 14:1 that Jonathan the son of S. said 7586
1Sa 14:2 S. tarried in the uttermost part of...... 7586
1Sa 14:16 the watchmen of S. in Gibeah of 7586
1Sa 14:17 said S. unto the people that were........ 7586
1Sa 14:18 S. said unto Ahiah, Bring hither......... 7586
1Sa 14:19 while S. talked unto the priest, that.... 7586
1Sa 14:19 S. said unto the priest, Withdraw....... 7586
1Sa 14:20 And S. and all the people that were.... 7586
1Sa 14:21 Israelites that were with S. and........ 7586
1Sa 14:24 S. had adjured the people, saying, ... 7586
1Sa 14:33 Then they told S., saying, Behold, ... 7586
1Sa 14:34 S. said, Disperse yourselves among.... 7586
1Sa 14:35 S. built an altar unto the Lord: the..... 7586
1Sa 14:36 S. said, Let us go down after the....... 7586
1Sa 14:37 S. asked counsel of God, Shall I go 7586
1Sa 14:38 S. said, Draw ye near hither, all the... 7586
1Sa 14:40 the people said unto S., Do what 7586
1Sa 14:41 S. said unto the Lord God of Israel, ... 7586
1Sa 14:41 S. and Jonathan were taken: but 7586
1Sa 14:42 And S. said, Cast lots between me...... 7586
1Sa 14:43 S. said to Jonathan, Tell me what....... 7586
1Sa 14:44 S. answered, God do so and more....... 7586
1Sa 14:45 people said unto S., Shall Jonathan..... 7586
1Sa 14:46 Then S. went up from following......... 7586
1Sa 14:47 S. took the kingdom over Israel,........ 7586
1Sa 14:49 the sons of S. were Jonathan, and...... 7586
1Sa 14:51 And Kish was the father of S.; and..... 7586
1Sa 14:52 the Philistines all the days of S. 7586
1Sa 14:52 when S. saw any strong man, or any .. 7586
1Sa 15:1 Samuel also said unto S., The Lord 7586
1Sa 15:4 S. gathered the people together, ... 7586
1Sa 15:5 S. came to a city of Amalek, and........ 7586
1Sa 15:6 And S. said unto the Kenites, Go,....... 7586
1Sa 15:7 And S. smote the Amalekites from..... 7586
1Sa 15:9 S. and the people spared Agag, and.... 7586
1Sa 15:11 repenteth me that I have set up S...... 7586
1Sa 15:12 Samuel rose early to meet S. in......... 7586
1Sa 15:12 Samuel, saying, S. came to Carmel,.... 7586
1Sa 15:13 Samuel came to S.: and S. said 7586
1Sa 15:15 S. said, They have brought them 7586
1Sa 15:16 Samuel said unto S., Stay, and I 7586
1Sa 15:20 S. said unto Samuel, Yea, I have........ 7586
1Sa 15:24 S. said unto Samuel, I have sinned: 7586
1Sa 15:26 And Samuel said unto S., I will not..... 7586
1Sa 15:31 So Samuel turned again after S.; 7586
1Sa 15:31 and S. worshipped the Lord. 7586
1Sa 15:34 and S. went up to his house............. 7586
1Sa 15:34 up to his house to Gibeah of S. 7586
1Sa 15:35 And Samuel came no more to see S. .. 7586
1Sa 15:35 Samuel mourned for S.: and the......... 7586
1Sa 15:35 repented that he had made S. king..... 7586
1Sa 16:1 How long wilt thou mourn for S., ... 7586
1Sa 16:2 I go? if S. hear it, he will kill me. 7586
1Sa 16:14 Spirit of the Lord departed from S.,..... 7586
1Sa 16:17 S. said unto his servants, Provide 7586
1Sa 16:19 S. sent messengers unto Jesse, and.... 7586
1Sa 16:20 sent them by David his son unto S. 7586
1Sa 16:21 And David came to S., and stood 7586
1Sa 16:22 S. sent to Jesse, saying, Let David,.... 7586
1Sa 16:23 evil spirit from God was upon S., ... 7586
1Sa 16:23 so S. was refreshed, and was well,..... 7586
1Sa 17:2 And S. and the men of Israel were...... 7586
1Sa 17:8 a Philistine, and ye servants to S.?...... 7586
1Sa 17:11 When S. and all Israel heard those 7586
1Sa 17:12 for an old man in the days of S.......... 7586
1Sa 17:13 sons of Jesse went and followed S...... 7586
1Sa 17:14 and the three eldest followed S.......... 7586
1Sa 17:15 David went and returned from S. 7586
1Sa 17:19 S., and they, and all the men of......... 7586
1Sa 17:31 they rehearsed them before S.: 7586
1Sa 17:32 And David said to S., Let no man's 7586
1Sa 17:33 S. said to David, Thou art not able...... 7586
1Sa 17:34 David said unto S., Thy servant.......... 7586
1Sa 17:37 S. said unto David, Go, and the......... 7586
1Sa 17:38 S. armed David with his armour,........ 7586
1Sa 17:39 And David said unto S., I cannot go.... 7586
1Sa 17:55 S. saw David go forth against the....... 7586
1Sa 17:57 S. with the head of the Philistine........ 7586

Book	Ref	Context	No.
1Sa	17:58	**S.** said unto him, Whose son art	7586
1Sa	18:1	made an end of speaking unto **S.**,	7586
1Sa	18:2	**S.** took him that day, and would let	7586
1Sa	18:5	David went...whithersoever **S.** sent	7586
1Sa	18:5	**S.** set him over the men of war,	7586
1Sa	18:6	singing...dancing, to meet king **S.**,	7586
1Sa	18:7	said, **S.** has slain his thousands,	7586
1Sa	18:8	**S.** was very wroth, and the saying	7586
1Sa	18:9	**S.** eyed David from that day and	7586
1Sa	18:10	evil spirit from God came upon **S.**,	7586
1Sa	18:11	**S.** cast the javelin; for he said, I	7586
1Sa	18:12	**S.** was afraid of David, because the	7586
1Sa	18:12	him, and was departed from **S.**,	7586
1Sa	18:13	**S.** removed him from him, and	7586
1Sa	18:15	**S.** saw that he behaved himself very	7586
1Sa	18:17	**S.** said to David, Behold my elder	7586
1Sa	18:17	**S.** said, Let not my hand be upon	7586
1Sa	18:18	And David said unto **S.**, Who am I?	7586
1Sa	18:20	they told **S.**, and the thing pleased	7586
1Sa	18:21	**S.** said, I will give him her, that she	7586
1Sa	18:21	**S.** said to David, Thou shalt this	7586
1Sa	18:22	And **S.** commanded his servants,	7586
1Sa	18:24	the servants of **S.** told him, saying,	7586
1Sa	18:25	**S.** said, Thus shall ye say to David,	7586
1Sa	18:25	**S.** thought to make David fall by	7586
1Sa	18:27	**S.** gave him Michal his daughter to	7586
1Sa	18:28	**S.** saw and knew that the Lord was	7586
1Sa	18:29	**S.** was yet the more afraid of David;	7586
1Sa	18:29	and **S.** became David's enemy	7586
1Sa	18:30	wisely than all the servants of **S.**;	7586
1Sa	19:1	**S.** spake to Jonathan his son, and	7586
1Sa	19:2	**S.** my father seeketh to kill thee:	7586
1Sa	19:4	spake good of David unto **S.** his	7586
1Sa	19:6	**S.** hearkened unto the voice of	7586
1Sa	19:6	**S.** sware, As the Lord liveth, he	7586
1Sa	19:7	Jonathan brought David to **S.**, and	7586
1Sa	19:9	spirit from the Lord was upon **S.**,	7586
1Sa	19:10	**S.** sought to smite David even to	7586
1Sa	19:11	**S.**...sent messengers unto David's	7586
1Sa	19:14	**S.** sent messengers to take David,	7586
1Sa	19:15	**S.** sent the messengers again to	7586
1Sa	19:17	**S.** said unto Michal, Why hast thou	7586
1Sa	19:17	Michal answered **S.**, He said unto	7586
1Sa	19:18	and told him all that **S.** had done to	7586
1Sa	19:19	And it was told **S.**, saying, Behold,	7586
1Sa	19:20	**S.** sent messengers to take David:	7586
1Sa	19:20	was upon the messengers of **S.**,	7586
1Sa	19:21	told **S.**, he sent other messengers,	7586
1Sa	19:21	**S.** sent messengers...the third	7586
1Sa	19:24	Is **S.** also among the prophets?	7586
1Sa	20:26	**S.** spake not any thing that day:	7586
1Sa	20:27	and **S.** said unto Jonathan his son,	7586
1Sa	20:28	And Jonathan answered **S.**, David	7586
1Sa	20:32	Jonathan answered **S.** his father,	7586
1Sa	20:33	**S.** cast a javelin at him to smite	7586
1Sa	21:7	a certain man of the servants of **S.**	7586
1Sa	21:7	of the herdmen that belonged to **S.**	7586
1Sa	21:10	and fled that day for fear of **S.**, and	7586
1Sa	21:11	**S.** hath slain his thousands, and	7586
1Sa	22:6	**S.** heard that David was discovered,	7586
1Sa	22:6	**S.** abode in Gibeah under a tree in	7586
1Sa	22:7	**S.** said unto his servants that stood	7586
1Sa	22:9	was set over the servants of **S.**, and	7586
1Sa	22:12	And **S.** said, Hear now, thou son of	7586
1Sa	22:13	And **S.** said unto him, Why have ye	7586
1Sa	22:21	that **S.** had slain the Lord's priests.	7586
1Sa	22:22	there, that he would surely tell **S.**:	7586
1Sa	23:7	told **S.** that David was come to	7586
1Sa	23:7	**S.** said, God hath delivered him	7586
1Sa	23:8	**S.** called all the people...to war,	7586
1Sa	23:9	that **S.** secretly practised mischief	7586
1Sa	23:10	that **S.** seeketh to come to Keilah,	7586
1Sa	23:11	will **S.** come down, as thy servant	7586
1Sa	23:12	and my men into the hand of **S.**?	7586
1Sa	23:13	told **S.** that David was escaped	7586
1Sa	23:14	**S.** sought him every day, but God	7586
1Sa	23:15	that **S.** was come...to seek his life:	7586
1Sa	23:17	hand of **S.** my father shall not find	7586
1Sa	23:17	that also **S.** my father knoweth.	7586
1Sa	23:19	Then came up the Ziphites to **S.** to	7586
1Sa	23:21	**S.** said, Blessed be ye of the Lord;	7586
1Sa	23:24	arose, and went to Ziph before **S.**:	7586
1Sa	23:25	**S.**...and his men went to seek him.	7586
1Sa	23:25	when **S.** heard that, he pursued	7586
1Sa	23:26	And **S.** went on this side of the	7586
1Sa	23:26	haste to get away for fear of **S.**;	7586
1Sa	23:26	**S.** and his men compassed David	7586
1Sa	23:27	there came a messenger unto **S.**,	7586
1Sa	23:28	**S.** returned from pursuing after	7586
1Sa	24:1	**S.** was returned from following the	7586
1Sa	24:2	**S.** took three thousand chosen men	7586
1Sa	24:3	and **S.** went in to cover his feet:	7586
1Sa	24:7	suffered them not to rise against **S.**.	7586
1Sa	24:7	But **S.** rose up out of the cave, and	7586
1Sa	24:8	cried after **S.**, saying, My lord the	7586
1Sa	24:8	when **S.** looked behind him, David	7586
1Sa	24:9	And David said to **S.**, Wherefore	7586
1Sa	24:16	of speaking these words unto **S.**,	7586
1Sa	24:16	**S.** said, Is this thy voice, my son	7586
1Sa	24:16	**S.** lifted up his voice, and wept.	7586
1Sa	24:22	sware unto **S.**. And **S.** went home;	7586
1Sa	25:44	**S.** had given Michal his daughter,	7586
1Sa	26:1	Ziphites came unto **S.** to Gibeah,	7586
1Sa	26:2	**S.** arose, and went down to the	7586
1Sa	26:3	**S.** pitched in the hill of Hachilah,	7586
1Sa	26:3	saw that **S.** came after him in the	7586
1Sa	26:4	understood that **S.** was come in	7586
1Sa	26:5	to the place where **S.** had pitched:	7586
1Sa	26:5	and David beheld...where **S.** lay,	7586
1Sa	26:5	**S.** lay in the trench, and the people	7586
1Sa	26:6	go down with me to **S.** to the camp?	7586
1Sa	26:7	**S.** lay sleeping within the trench,	7586
1Sa	26:17	**S.** knew David's voice, and said, Is	7586
1Sa	26:21	Then said **S.**, I have sinned:	7586
1Sa	26:25	**S.** said to David, Blessed be thou,	7586
1Sa	26:25	way, and **S.** returned to his place.	7586
1Sa	27:1	perish one day by the hand of **S.**:	7586
1Sa	27:1	**S.** shall despair of me, to seek me	7586
1Sa	27:4	was told **S.** that David was fled to	7586
1Sa	28:3	And **S.** had put away those that had	7586
1Sa	28:4	and **S.** gathered all Israel together,	7586
1Sa	28:5	**S.** saw the host of the Philistines,	7586
1Sa	28:6	**S.** enquired of the Lord, the Lord	7586
1Sa	28:7	Then said **S.** unto his servants,	7586
1Sa	28:8	**S.** disguised himself, and put on	7586
1Sa	28:9	thou knowest what **S.** hath done,	7586
1Sa	28:10	**S.** sware to her by the Lord, saying,	7586
1Sa	28:12	the woman spake to **S.**, saying,	7586
1Sa	28:12	thou deceived me? for thou art **S.**.	7586
1Sa	28:13	woman said unto **S.**, I saw gods	7586
1Sa	28:14	**S.** perceived that it was Samuel,	7586
1Sa	28:15	Samuel said to **S.**, Why hast thou	7586
1Sa	28:15	**S.** answered, I am sore distressed;	7586
1Sa	28:20	**S.** fell straightway all along on the	7586
1Sa	28:21	the woman came unto **S.**, and saw	7586
1Sa	28:25	And she brought it before **S.**, and	7586
1Sa	29:3	Is not this David, the servant of **S.**	7586
1Sa	29:5	**S.** slew his thousands, and David	7586
1Sa	31:2	Philistines followed hard upon **S.**	7586
1Sa	31:3	the battle went sore against **S.**,	7586
1Sa	31:4	said **S.** unto his armourbearer,	7586
1Sa	31:4	**S.** took a sword, and fell upon it.	7586
1Sa	31:5	armourbearer saw...**S.** was dead,	7586
1Sa	31:6	So **S.** died, and his three sons, and	7586
1Sa	31:7	and that **S.** and his sons were dead,	7586
1Sa	31:8	found **S.** and his three sons fallen	7586
1Sa	31:11	the Philistines had done to **S.**;	7586
1Sa	31:12	took the body of **S.** and the bodies	7586
2Sa	1:1	came to pass after the death of **S.**,	7586
2Sa	1:2	a man came out of the camp from **S.**	7586
2Sa	1:4	**S.** and Jonathan his son are dead	7586
2Sa	1:5	**S.** and Jonathan his son be dead?	7586
2Sa	1:6	behold, **S.** leaned upon his spear;	7586
2Sa	1:12	fasted until even, for **S.**, and for	7586
2Sa	1:17	with this lamentation over **S.** and	7586
2Sa	1:21	is vilely cast away, the shield of **S.**,	7586
2Sa	1:22	sword of **S.** returned not empty.	7586
2Sa	1:23	**S.** and Jonathan were lovely and	7586
2Sa	1:24	daughters of Israel, weep over **S.**,	7586
2Sa	2:4	were they that buried **S.**.	7586
2Sa	2:5	shewed this kindness...unto **S.**,	7586
2Sa	2:7	for your master **S.** is dead, and also	7586
2Sa	2:8	took Ish-bosheth the son of **S.**,	7586
2Sa	2:12	servants of Ish-bosheth...son of **S.**,	7586
2Sa	2:15	pertained to Ish-bosheth...son of **S.**,	7586
2Sa	3:1	long war between the house of **S.**	7586
2Sa	3:1	the house of **S.** waxed weaker and	7586
2Sa	3:6	was war between the house of **S.**	7586
2Sa	3:6	himself strong for the house of **S.**.	7586
2Sa	3:7	**S.** had a concubine, whose name	7586
2Sa	3:8	kindness...unto the house of **S.**	7586
2Sa	3:10	the kingdom from the house of **S.**,	7586
2Sa	4:4	tidings came of **S.** and Jonathan	7586
2Sa	4:8	head of Ish-bosheth the son of **S.**	7586
2Sa	4:8	avenged my lord...this day of **S.**,	7586
2Sa	4:10	told me, saying, Behold, **S.** is dead,	7586
2Sa	5:2	past, when **S.** was king over us,	7586
2Sa	6:20	the daughter of **S.** came out to meet	7586
2Sa	6:23	the daughter of **S.** had no child	7586
2Sa	7:15	as I took it from **S.**, whom I put	7586
2Sa	9:1	any that is left of the house of **S.**,	7586
2Sa	9:2	was of the house of **S.** a servant	7586
2Sa	9:3	there not yet any of the house of **S.**,	7586
2Sa	9:6	the son of Jonathan, the son of **S.**,	7586
2Sa	9:7	restore thee all the land of **S.** thy	7586
2Sa	9:9	master's son all that pertained to **S.**	7586
2Sa	12:7	delivered thee out of the hand of **S.**;	7586
2Sa	16:5	man of the family of the house of **S.**,	7586
2Sa	16:8	all the blood of the house of **S.**,	7586
2Sa	19:17	Ziba the servant of the house of **S.**,	7586
2Sa	19:24	Mephibosheth son of **S.** came	7586
2Sa	21:1	It is for **S.**, and for his bloody house	7586
2Sa	21:2	**S.** sought to slay them in his zeal	7586
2Sa	21:4	will have no silver nor gold of **S.**,	7586
2Sa	21:6	will hang them up in Gibeah of **S.**,	7586
2Sa	21:7	the son of Jonathan the son of **S.**,	7586
2Sa	21:7	David and Jonathan the son of **S.**	7586
2Sa	21:8	two sons...whom she bare unto **S.**,	7586
2Sa	21:8	sons of Michal the daughter of **S.**,	7586
2Sa	21:11	what Rizpah...the concubine of **S.**,	7586
2Sa	21:12	David went and took the bones of **S.**	7586
2Sa	21:12	Philistines had slain **S.** in Gilboa:	7586
2Sa	21:13	up from thence the bones of **S.** and	7586
2Sa	21:14	bones of **S.** and Jonathan his son	7586
2Sa	22:1	enemies, and out of the hand of **S.**	7586
1Ch	5:10	in the days of **S.** they made war	7586
1Ch	8:33	Ner begat Kish, and Kish begat **S.**,	7586
1Ch	8:33	and **S.** begat Jonathan, and	7586
1Ch	9:39	Ner begat Kish; and Kish begat **S.**;	7586
1Ch	9:39	and **S.** begat Jonathan, and	7586
1Ch	10:2	Philistines followed hard after **S.**,	7586
1Ch	10:2	and Malchi-shua, the sons of **S.**.	7586
1Ch	10:3	And the battle went sore against **S.**,	7586
1Ch	10:4	Then said **S.** to his armourbearer,	7586
1Ch	10:4	So **S.** took a sword, and fell upon it.	7586
1Ch	10:5	his armourbearer saw that **S.** was	7586
1Ch	10:6	So **S.** died, and his three sons, and	7586
1Ch	10:7	and that **S.** and his sons were dead,	7586
1Ch	10:8	they found **S.** and his sons fallen	7586
1Ch	10:11	that the Philistines had done to **S.**,	7586
1Ch	10:12	men, and took away the body of **S.**,	7586
1Ch	10:13	So **S.** died for his transgression	7586
1Ch	11:2	time past, even when **S.** was king,	7586
1Ch	12:1	kept himself close because of **S.**	7586
1Ch	12:19	came with the Philistines against **S.**	7586
1Ch	12:19	He will fall to his master **S.** to the	7586
1Ch	12:23	to turn the kingdom of **S.** to him,	7586
1Ch	12:29	of Benjamin, the kindred of **S.**,	7586
1Ch	12:29	kept the ward of the house of **S.**	7586
1Ch	13:3	enquired not at it in the days of **S.**	7586
1Ch	15:29	Michal the daughter of **S.** looking	7586
1Ch	26:28	the seer, and **S.** the son of Kish,	7586
Ps	18:*title*	enemies, and from the hand of **S.**	7586
Ps	52:*title*	the Edomite came and told **S.**,	7586
Ps	54:*title*	the Ziphims came and said to **S.**,	7586
Ps	57:*title*	when he fled from **S.** in the cave.	7586
Ps	59:*title*	when **S.** sent, and they watched	7586
Isa	10:29	is afraid; Gibeah of **S.** is fled.	7586
Ac	7:58	man's feet, whose name was **S.**.	*4569*
Ac	8:1	**S.** was consenting unto his death.	*4569*
Ac	8:3	As for **S.**, he made havock of the	*4569*
Ac	9:1	**S.**, yet breathing out threatenings	*4569*
Ac	9:4	**S., S., why persecutest thou me?**	*4569*
Ac	9:8	And **S.** arose from the earth; and	*4569*
Ac	9:11	**house of Judas for one called S.,**	*4569*
Ac	9:17	Brother **S.**, the Lord, even Jesus,	*4569*
Ac	9:19	**S.** certain days with the disciples.	*4569*
Ac	9:22	**S.** increased the more in strength,	*4569*
Ac	9:24	their laying await was known of **S.**	*4569*
Ac	9:26	when **S.** was come to Jerusalem,	*4569*
Ac	11:25	Barnabas to Tarsus, for to seek **S.**	*4569*
Ac	11:30	by the hands of Barnabas and **S.**	*4569*
Ac	12:25	and **S.** returned from Jerusalem,	*4569*
Ac	13:1	up with Herod the tetrarch, and **S.**	*4569*
Ac	13:2	Separate me Barnabas and **S.** for	*4569*
Ac	13:7	who called for Barnabas and **S.**,	*4569*
Ac	13:9	Then **S.**, (who also is called Paul,)	*4569*
Ac	13:21	gave unto them **S.** the son of Cis,	*4569*

Ac 22:7 **S., S., why persecutest thou me?** ... *4569*
Ac 22:13 me, Brother **S.**, receive thy sight........ *4569*
Ac 26:14 **S., S., why persecutest thou me?** ... *4569*

SAUL'S (sawls)

1Sa 9:3 asses of Kish **S.** father were lost, ... 7586
1Sa 10:14 **S.** uncle said unto him and to his........ 7586
1Sa 10:15 **S.** uncle said, Tell me, I pray thee, ... 7586
1Sa 14:50 the name of **S.** wife was Ahinoam,...... 7586
1Sa 14:50 was Abner, the son of Ner, **S.** uncle... 7586
1Sa 16:15 **S.** servants said unto him, Behold 7586
1Sa 18:5 and also in the sight of **S.** servants..... 7586
1Sa 18:10 and there was a javelin in **S.** hand. 7586
1Sa 18:19 **S.** daughter should have been given 7586
1Sa 18:20 Michal **S.** daughter loved David:......... 7586
1Sa 18:23 **S.** servants spake those words in....... 7586
1Sa 18:28 that Michal **S.** daughter loved him. 7586
1Sa 19:2 Jonathan **S.** son delighted much in 7586
1Sa 19:10 he slipped away out of **S.** presence,.... 7586
1Sa 20:25 and Abner sat by **S.** side, and........... 7586
1Sa 20:30 Then **S.** anger was kindled against....... 7586
1Sa 23:16 Jonathan **S.** son arose, and went to..... 7586
1Sa 24:4 and cut off the skirt of **S.** robe 7586
1Sa 24:5 because he had cut off **S.** skirt. 7586
1Sa 26:12 the cruse of water from **S.** bolster;...... 7586
1Sa 31:2 and Melchi-shua, **S.** sons................. 7586
2Sa 2:8 But Abner...captain of **S.** host, ... 7586
2Sa 2:10 Ish-bosheth **S.** son was forty years...... 7586
2Sa 3:13 thou first bring Michal **S.** daughter,..... 7586
2Sa 3:14 messengers to Ish-bosheth **S.** son, ... 7586
2Sa 4:1 **S.** son heard that Abner was dead...... 7586
2Sa 4:2 And **S.** son had two men that were 7586
2Sa 4:4 Jonathan, **S.** son, had a son...lame...... 7586
2Sa 6:16 Michal **S.** daughter looked through...... 7586
2Sa 9:9 the king called to Ziba, **S.** servant, ... 7586
1Ch 12:2 even of **S.** brethren of Benjamin.......... 7586

SAVE See also SAVED; SAVEST; SAVETH; SAVING.

Ge 12:12 kill me, but they will **s.** thee alive....... 2421
Ge 14:24 **S.** only that which the young men 1107
Ge 39:6 **s.** the bread which he did eat....... 3588,518
Ge 45:7 and to **s.** your lives by a great.......... 2421
Ge 50:20 is this day, to **s.** much people alive..... 2421
Ex 1:22 and every daughter ye shall **s.** alive. ... 2421
Ex 12:16 **s.** that which every man must eat, ... 389
Ex 22:20 any god, **s.** unto the Lord only, ... 1115
Nu 14:30 **s.** Caleb the son of Jephunneh, ... 3588,518
Nu 26:65 **s.** Caleb the son of Jephunneh,...... 3588,518
Nu 32:12 **S.** Caleb the son of Jephunneh 3588,518
De 1:36 **S.** Caleb the son of Jephunneh;.......... 2108
De 15:4 **S.** when there shall be no poor............ 657
De 20:4 against your enemies, to **s.** you. 3467
De 20:16 **s.** alive nothing that breatheth:.......... 2421
De 22:27 cried, and there was none to **s.** her. ... 3467
De 28:29 evermore, and no man shall **s.** thee. ... 3467
Jos 2:13 that ye will **s.** alive my father, ... 2421
Jos 10:6 come up to us quickly, and **s.** us,........ 3467
Jos 11:13 burned none of them, **s.** Hazor 2108
Jos 11:19 **s.** the Hivites the inhabitants of.......... 1115
Jos 14:4 in the land, **s.** cities to dwell in, ... 3588,518
Jos 22:22 the Lord, (**s.** us not this day,) 3467
Jg 6:14 shalt **s.** Israel from the hand of the..... 3467
Jg 6:15 Lord, wherewith shall I **s.** Israel?........ 3467
Jg 6:31 ye plead for Baal? will ye **s.** him?........ 3467
Jg 6:36, 37 thou wilt **s.** Israel by mine hand,..... 3467
Jg 7:7 men that lapped will I **s.** you, and....... 3467
Jg 7:14 else **s.** the sword of Gideon......... 1115,518
1Sa 4:3 it may **s.** us out of the hand of our..... 3467
1Sa 7:8 that he will **s.** us out of the hand of..... 3467
1Sa 9:16 he may **s.** my people out of the hand .. 3467
1Sa 10:24 shouted, and said, God **s.** the king...... 2421
1Sa 10:27 said, How shall this man **s.** us?.......... 3467
1Sa 11:3 and then, if there be no man to **s.** us,..3467
1Sa 14:6 is no restraint to the Lord to **s.** by..... 3467
1Sa 19:11 If thou **s.** not thy life to night, ... 4422
1Sa 21:9 for there is no other **s.** that here. 2108
1Sa 23:2 smite...Philistines, and **s.** Keilah......... 3467
1Sa 30:17 **s.** four hundred young men,......... 3588,518
1Sa 30:22 **s.** to every man his wife and his... 3588,518
2Sa 3:18 servant David I will **s.** my people 3467
2Sa 12:3 nothing, **s.** one little ewe lamb, ... 3588,518
2Sa 16:16 God **s.** the king, God **s.** the king........ 2421
2Sa 22:28 the afflicted people thou wilt **s.**: 3467
2Sa 22:32 For who is God, **s.** the Lord? and 1107
2Sa 22:32 and who is a rock, **s.** our God?.......... 1107
2Sa 22:42 looked, but there was none to **s.**;....... 3467
1Ki 1:12 thou mayest **s.** thine own life, and....... 4422
1Ki 1:25 and say, God **s.** king Adonijah........... 2421
1Ki 1:34 and say, God **s.** king Solomon............ 2421
1Ki 1:39 people said, God **s.** king Solomon. 2421
1Ki 3:18 the house, **s.** we two in the house...... 2108
1Ki 8:9 the ark **s.** the two tables of stone,...... 7535
1Ki 15:5 **s.** only in the matter of Uriah the............
1Ki 18:5 to **s.** the horses and mules alive,........ 2421
1Ki 20:31 peradventure he will **s.** thy life.......... 2421
1Ki 22:31 **s.** only with the king of Israel. 3588,518
2Ki 4:2 in the house, **s.** a pot of oil 3588,518
2Ki 7:4 if they **s.** us alive, we shall live;......... 2421
2Ki 11:12 hands, and said, God **s.** the king. 2421
2Ki 15:4 **S.** that the high places were not 7535
2Ki 16:7 **s.** me out of the hand of the king....... 3467
2Ki 19:19 **s.** thou us out of his hand, that all....... 3467
2Ki 19:34 I will defend this city, to **s.** it, for 3467
2Ki 21:17 left him, **s.** Jehoahaz, the 3588,518
2Ki 24:14 **s.** the poorest sort of the people of 2108
1Ch 16:35 ye, **S.** us, O God of our salvation,...... 3467
2Ch 2:6 **s.** only to burn sacrifice before him? 518
2Ch 5:10 nothing in the ark **s.** the two tables 7535
2Ch 18:30 **s.** only with the king of Israel. 3588,518
2Ch 23:6 house of the Lord, **s.** the priests, . 3588,518
2Ch 23:11 him, and said, God **s.** the king........... 2421
Ne 2:12 **s.** the beast that I rode upon. 3588,518
Ne 6:11 go into the temple to **s.** his life?......... 2425
Job 2:6 he is in thine hand; but **s.** his life. 8104
Job 20:20 not **s.** of that which he desired. 4422
Job 22:29 and he shall **s.** the humble person....... 3467
Job 40:14 thine own right hand can **s.** thee. 3467
Ps 3:7 **s.** me, O my God: for thou hast......... 3467
Ps 6:4 soul: oh **s.** me for thy mercies' sake. .. 3467
Ps 7:1 **s.** me from all them that persecute 3467
Ps 18:27 thou wilt **s.** the afflicted people; but.... 3467
Ps 18:31 For who is God **s.** the Lord?............ 1107
Ps 18:31 or who is a rock **s.** our God?............ 2108
Ps 18:41 but there was none to **s.** them:.......... 3467
Ps 20:9 **S.**, Lord: let the king hear us when.... 3467
Ps 22:21 **S.** me from the lion's mouth: for........ 3467
Ps 28:9 **S.** thy people, and bless thine........... 3467
Ps 31:2 for an house of defence to **s.** me........ 3467
Ps 31:16 **s.** me for thy mercies' sake.............. 3467
Ps 37:40 them from the wicked, and **s.** them, ... 3467
Ps 44:3 neither did their own arm **s.** them: 3467
Ps 44:6 bow, neither shall my sword **s.** me. 3467
Ps 54:1 **S.** me, O God, by thy name, and....... 3467
Ps 55:16 upon God; and the Lord shall **s.** me.... 3467
Ps 57:3 and **s.** me from the reproach of him.... 3467
Ps 59:2 and **s.** me from bloody men.............. 3467
Ps 60:5 **s.** with thy right hand, and hear......... 3467
Ps 69:1 **S.** me, O God; for the waters are...... 3467
Ps 69:35 For God will **s.** Zion, and will build..... 3467
Ps 71:2 thine ear unto me, and **s.** me. 3467
Ps 71:3 hast given commandment to **s.** me;....... 3467
Ps 72:4 he shall **s.** the children of the needy,... 3467
Ps 72:13 and shall **s.** the souls of the needy,..... 3467
Ps 76:9 to **s.** all the meek of the earth........... 3467
Ps 80:2 thy strength, and come and **s.** us. 3444
Ps 86:2 **s.** thy servant that trusteth in............ 3467
Ps 86:16 and **s.** the son of thine handmaid. 3467
Ps 106:47 **S.** us, O Lord our God, and gather..... 3467
Ps 108:6 **s.** with thy right hand, and answer...... 3467
Ps 109:26 O **s.** me according to thy mercy:........ 3467
Ps 109:31 to **s.** him from those that condemn..... 3467
Ps 118:25 **S.** now, I beseech thee, O Lord: 3467
Ps 119:94 I am thine, **s.** me; for I have............ 3467
Ps 119:146 cried unto thee; **s.** me, and I shall...... 3467
Ps 138:7 and thy right hand shall **s.** me........... 3467
Ps 145:19 hear their cry, and will **s.** them.......... 3467
Pr 20:22 on the Lord, and he shall **s.** thee. 3467
Isa 25:9 waited for him, and he will **s.** us: 3467
Isa 33:22 the Lord is our king; he will **s.** us. 3467
Isa 35:4 your God...will come and **s.** you.......... 3467
Isa 37:20 Lord our God, **s.** us from his hand, ... 3467
Isa 37:35 For I will defend this city to **s.** it 3467
Isa 38:20 The Lord was ready to **s.** me:............ 3467
Isa 45:20 and pray unto a god that cannot **s.**....... 3467
Isa 46:7 nor **s.** him out of his trouble............. 3467
Isa 47:13 **s.** thee from these things that shall..... 3467
Isa 47:15 to his quarter; none shall **s.** thee........ 3467
Isa 49:25 with thee, and I will **s.** thy children..... 3467
Isa 59:1 is not shortened, that it cannot **s.**;....... 3467
Isa 63:1 in righteousness, mighty to **s.**............ 3467
Jer 2:27 they will say, Arise, and **s.** us. 3467
Jer 2:28 **s.** thee in the time of thy trouble: 3467
Jer 11:12 shall not **s.** them at all in the time...... 3467
Jer 14:9 as a mighty man that cannot **s.**?......... 3467
Jer 15:20 for I am with thee to **s.** thee and to.... 3467
Jer 17:14 **s.** me, and I shall be saved: for thou.... 3467
Jer 30:10 for, lo, I will **s.** thee from afar, and 3467
Jer 30:11 with thee, saith the Lord, to **s.** thee: .. 3467
Jer 31:7 **s.** thy people, the remnant of Israel. ... 3467
Jer 42:11 for I am with you to **s.** you, and to..... 3467
Jer 46:27 I will **s.** thee from afar off, and thy..... 3467
Jer 48:6 Flee, **s.** your lives, and be like the 4422
La 4:17 for a nation that could not **s.** us. 3467
Eze 3:18 from his wicked way, to **s.** his life; 2421
Eze 13:18 will ye **s.** the souls alive that come 2421
Eze 13:19 to **s.** the souls alive that should not 2421
Eze 18:27 and right, he shall **s.** his soul alive...... 2421
Eze 34:22 Therefore will I **s.** my flock, and 3467
Eze 36:29 I will also **s.** you from all your........... 3467
Eze 37:23 but I will **s.** them out of all their 3467
Da 6:7 **s.** of thee, O king, he shall be cast..... 3861
Da 6:12 **s.** of thee, O king, shall be cast......... 3861
Ho 1:7 will **s.** them by the Lord their God, ... 3467
Ho 1:7 and will not **s.** them by bow, nor by 3467
Ho 13:10 that may **s.** thee in all thy cities?........ 3467
Ho 14:3 Asshur shall not **s.** us: we will not...... 3467
Hab 1:2 of violence, and thou wilt not **s.**!........ 3467
Zep 3:17 he will **s.**, he will rejoice over thee...... 3467
Zep 3:19 and I will **s.** her that halteth, and 3467
Zec 8:7 I will **s.** my people from the east........ 3467
Zec 8:13 so will I **s.** you, and ye shall be a....... 3467
Zec 9:16 the Lord their God shall **s.** them in..... 3467
Zec 10:6 I will **s.** the house of Joseph, and I..... 3467
Zec 12:7 Lord also shall **s.** the tents of Judah.... 3467
Mt 1:21 shall **s.** his people from their sins. *4982*
Mt 8:25 him, saying, Lord, **s.** us: we perish. ... *4982*
Mt 11:27 **any man the Father, s. the Son,**.... *1508*
Mt 13:57 **honour, s. in his own country, and**.*1508*
Mt 14:30 sink, he cried, saying, Lord, **s.** me. *4982*
Mt 16:25 **whosoever will s. his life shall** *4982*
Mt 17:8 they saw no man, **s.** Jesus only.......... *1508*
Mt 18:11 **is come to s. that which was lost**..*4982*
Mt 19:11 **saying, s. they to whom it is given**.. *235*
Mt 27:40 buildest it in three days, **s.** thyself...... *4982*
Mt 27:42 saved others; himself he cannot **s.**...... *4982*
Mt 27:49 whether Elias will come to **s.** him....... *4982*
Mk 3:4 **or to do evil? to s. life, or to kill?** . *4982*
Mk 5:37 no man to follow him, **s.** Peter, and.... *1508*
Mk 6:5 **s.** that he laid his hands upon a few.... *1508*
Mk 6:8 for their journey, **s.** a staff only; *1508*
Mk 8:35 **whosoever will s. his life shall** *4982*
Mk 8:35 **the gospel's, the same shall s. it**.... *4982*
Mk 9:8 saw no man any more, **s.** Jesus only..... *235*
Mk 15:30 **S.** thyself, and come down from......... *4982*
Mk 15:31 saved others; himself he cannot **s.**...... *4982*
Lu 4:26 **s. unto Sarepta, a city of Sidon,**.... *1508*
Lu 6:9 **do evil? to s. life, or to destroy it?**..*4982*
Lu 8:51 suffered no man to go in, **s.** Peter,..... *1508*
Lu 9:24 **whosoever will s. his life shall** *4982*
Lu 9:24 **for my sake, the same shall s. it**.. *4982*
Lu 9:56 **destroy men's lives, but to s.**.......... *4982*
Lu 17:18 **give glory to God, s. this stranger**..*1508*
Lu 17:33 **seek to s. his life shall lose it;** *4982*
Lu 18:19 **none is good, s. one, that is, God**.. *1508*
Lu 19:10 **seek and to s. that which was lost**..*4982*
Lu 23:35 let him **s.** himself, if he be Christ, ... *4982*
Lu 23:37 be the king of the Jews, **s.** thyself....... *4982*
Lu 23:39 If thou be Christ, **s.** thyself and us. *4982*
Joh 6:22 **s.** that one whereinto his disciples *1508*
Joh 6:46 **s. he which is of God, he hath** *1508*
Joh 12:27 **Father, s. me from this hour:** *4982*
Joh 12:47 **the world, but to s. the world**......... *4982*
Joh 13:10 **needeth not s. to wash his feet,** *2228*
Ac 2:40 **S.** yourselves from this untoward *4982*
Ac 20:23 **S.** that the Holy Ghost witnesseth...... *4133*
Ac 21:25 **s.** only that they keep themselves *1508*
Ac 27:43 the centurion, willing to **s.** Paul,........ *1295*
Ro 11:14 flesh, and might **s.** some of them. *4982*
1Co 1:21 preaching to **s.** them that believe........ *4982*
1Co 2:2 **s.** Jesus Christ, and him crucified. *1508*
1Co 2:11 **s.** the spirit of man which is in him?..... *1508*
1Co 7:16 whether thou shalt **s.** thy husband?..... *4982*
1Co 7:16 whether thou shalt **s.** thy wife?.......... *4982*
1Co 9:22 that I might by all means **s.** some....... *4982*
2Co 11:24 received I forty stripes **s.** one. *3844*
Ga 1:19 none, **s.** James the Lord's brother. *1508*
Ga 6:14 **s.** in the cross of our Lord Jesus......... *1508*
1Ti 1:15 came into the world to **s.** sinners; *4982*
1Ti 4:16 thou shalt both **s.** thyself, and them.... *4982*
Heb 5:7 that was able to **s.** him from death, ... *4982*
Heb 7:25 also to **s.** them to the uttermost *4982*
Jas 1:21 word, which is able to **s.** your souls.... *4982*

Jas 2:14 have not works? can faith s. him?....... *4982*
Jas 4:12 who is able to s. and to destroy: who ..*4982*
Jas 5:15 the prayer of faith shall s. the sick,..... *4982*
Jas 5:20 his way shall s. a soul from death,...... *4982*
1Pe 3:21 even baptism doth also now s. us....... *4982*
Jude 23 others s. with fear, pulling them......... *4982*
Re 13:17 or sell, s. he that had the mark, ... *1508*

SAVED
Ge 47:25 Thou hast s. our lives: let us find............
Ex 1:17 but s. the men children alive. 2421
Ex 1:18 and have s. the men children alive?..... 2421
Ex 14:30 the Lord s. Israel that day out of....... 3467
Nu 10:9 ye shall be s. from your enemies........ 3467
Nu 22:33 I had slain thee, and s. her alive. 2421
Nu 31:15 Have ye s. all the women alive?......... 2421
De 33:29 O people s. by the Lord, the shield.... 3467
Jos 6:25 Joshua s. Rahab the harlot alive, ... 2421
Jg 7:2 saying, Mine own hand hath s. me...... 3467
Jg 8:19 if ye had s. them alive I would not..... 2421
Jg 21:14 them wives which they had s. alive..... 2421
1Sa 10:19 s. you out of all your adversities........ 3467
1Sa 14:23 So the Lord s. Israel that day: and...... 3467
1Sa 23:5 David s. the inhabitants of Keilah. 3467
1Sa 27:11 David s. neither man nor woman........ 2421
2Sa 19:5 which this day have s. thy life, ... 4422
2Sa 19:9 king s. us out of the hand of our........ 5337
2Sa 22:4 shall I be s. from mine enemies. 3467
2Ki 6:10 and s. himself there, not once nor........ 8104
2Ki 14:27 s. them by the hand of Jeroboam......... 3467
1Ch 11:14 s. them by a great deliverance............ 3467
2Ch 32:22 Thus the Lord s. Hezekiah and the...... 3467
Ne 9:27 who s. them out of the hand of their... 3467
Ps 18:3 shall I be s. from mine enemies. 3467
Ps 33:16 is no king s. by the multitude of......... 3467
Ps 34:6 and s. him out of all his troubles, ... 3467
Ps 44:7 thou hast s. us from our enemies, ... 3467
Ps 80:3 face to shine; and we shall be s.. 3467
Ps 80:7, 19 to shine; and we shall be s.. 3467
Ps 106:8 he s. them for his name's sake, ... 3467
Ps 106:10 he s. them from the hand of him........ 3467
Ps 107:13 he s. them out of their distresses....... 3467
Pr 28:18 walketh uprightly shall be s.: but........ 3467
Isa 30:15 returning and rest shall ye be s.;........ 3467
Isa 43:12 I have declared, and have s., and....... 3467
Isa 45:17 But Israel shall be s. in the Lord........ 3467
Isa 45:22 Look unto me, and be ye s., all the..... 3467
Isa 63:9 the angel of his presence s. them:...... 3467
Isa 64:5 is continuance, and we shall be s........ 3467
Jer 4:14 wickedness, that thou mayest be s.. ... 3467
Jer 8:20 summer is ended, and we are not s.... 3467
Jer 17:14 save me, and I shall be s.: for thou.... 3467
Jer 23:6 In his days Judah shall be s., and 3467
Jer 30:7 trouble; but he shall be s. out of it. 3467
Jer 33:16 In those days shall Judah be s.,.......... 3467
Mt 10:22 **endureth to the end shall be s.........** *4982*
Mt 19:25 amazed, saying, Who then can be s.?... *4982*
Mt 24:13 **unto the end, the same shall be s..** *4982*
Mt 24:22 **there should no flesh be s.: but.....** *4982*
Mt 27:42 He s. others; himself he cannot *4982*
Mk 10:26 themselves, Who then can be s.? *4982*
Mk 13:13 unto the end, the same shall be s......... *4982*
Mk 13:20 **those days, no flesh should be s.....** *4982*
Mk 15:31 He s. others; himself he cannot *4982*
Mk 16:16 **and is baptized shall be s.;............** *4982*
Lu 1:71 we should be s. from our enemies,..... *4991*
Lu 7:50 **Thy faith hath s. thee; go in.........** *4982*
Lu 8:12 **lest they should believe and be s...** *4982*
Lu 13:23 him, Lord, are there few that be s.?... *4982*
Lu 18:26 heard it said, Who then can be s.?...... *4982*
Lu 18:42 **thy sight: thy faith hath s. thee....** *4982*
Lu 23:35 He s. others; let him save himself,..... *4982*
Joh 3:17 **the world through him might be s..** *4982*
Joh 5:34 **things I say, that ye might be s....** *4982*
Joh 10:9 **if any man enter in, he shall be s.,.** *4982*
Ac 2:21 on the name of the Lord shall be s.. ... *4982*
Ac 2:47 church daily such as should be s......... *4982*
Ac 4:12 among men, whereby we must be s..... *4982*
Ac 11:14 thou and all thy house shall be s.. ...... *4982*
Ac 15:1 manner of Moses, ye cannot be s....... *4982*
Ac 15:11 the grace of...Christ we shall be s.,.... *4982*
Ac 16:30 said, Sirs, what must I do to be s.?.... *4982*
Ac 16:31 thou shalt be s., and thy house........... *4982*
Ac 27:20 all hope that we should be s. was....... *4982*
Ac 27:31 abide in the ship, ye cannot be s........ *4982*
Ro 5:9 shall be s. from wrath through him. *4982*
Ro 5:10 reconciled, we shall be s. by his life.... *4982*
Ro 8:24 For we are s. by hope: but hope........ *4982*
Ro 9:27 of the sea, a remnant shall be s......... *4982*
Ro 10:1 Israel is, that they might be s............ *4991*
Ro 10:9 from the dead, thou shalt be s............ *4982*
Ro 10:13 the name of the Lord shall be s.. .... *4982*
Ro 11:26 And so all Israel shall be s.: as it *4982*
1Co 1:18 unto us which are s. it is the power.... *4982*
1Co 3:15 but he himself shall be s.; yet so........ *4982*
1Co 5:5 the spirit may be s. in the day of *4982*
1Co 10:33 profit of many, that they may be s...... *4982*
1Co 15:2 By which also ye are s., if ye keep..... *4982*
2Co 2:15 in them that are s., and in them.......... *4982*
Eph 2:5 with Christ, (by grace ye are s.;) *4982*
Eph 2:8 by grace are ye s. through faith; *4982*
1Th 2:16 the Gentiles that they might be s., ... *4982*
2Th 2:10 of the truth, that they might be s., ... *4982*
1Ti 2:4 Who will have all men to be s., and.... *4982*
1Ti 2:15 she shall be s. in childbearing, if......... *4982*
2Ti 1:9 Who hath s. us, and called us with *4982*
Tit 3:5 but according to his mercy he s. us, ... *4982*
1Pe 3:20 is, eight souls were s. by water.......... *1295*
1Pe 4:18 And if the righteous scarcely be s.,..... *4982*
2Pe 2:5 but s. Noah the eighth person, a........ *5442*
Jude 5 s. the people out of the land of.......... *4982*
Re 21:24 which are s. shall walk in the light...... *4982*

SAVEST
2Sa 22:3 saviour; thou s. me from violence....... 3467
Job 26:2 how s. thou the arm that hath no....... 3467
Ps 17:7 O thou that s. by thy right hand......... 3467

SAVETH
1Sa 14:39 the Lord liveth, which s. Israel, ... 3467
1Sa 17:47 Lord s. not with sword and spear:....... 3467
Job 5:15 he s. the poor from the sword, from.... 3467
Ps 7:10 God, which s. the upright in heart. 3467
Ps 20:6 I that the Lord s. his anointed; 3467
Ps 34:18 s. such as be of a contrite spirit......... 3467
Ps 107:19 he s. them out of their distresses....... 3467

SAVING
Ge 19:19 hast shewed unto me in s. my life;..... 2421
Ne 4:23 s. that every one put them off for............
Ps 20:6 the s. strength of his right hand......... 3468
Ps 28:8 the s. strength of his anointed. 3444
Ps 67:2 the s. health among all nations........... 3444
Ec 5:11 s. the beholding of them with their...... 518
Am 9:8 s. that I will not utterly destroy........... 657
Mt 5:32 **s. for the cause of fornication,......** *3924*
Lu 4:27 **cleansed, s. Naaman the Syrian. ...** *1508*
Heb 10:39 that believe to the s. of the soul. *4047*
Heb 11:7 an ark to the s. of his house; by *4991*
Re 2:17 **knoweth s. he that receiveth it......** *1508*

SAVIOUR See also SAVIOURS.
2Sa 22:3 tower, and my refuge, my s.;............ 3467
2Ki 13:5 (And the Lord gave Israel a s., so...... 3467
Ps 106:21 They forgat God their s., which had.... 3467
Isa 19:20 he shall send them a s., and a great.... 3467
Isa 43:3 God, the Holy One of Israel, thy S.... 3467
Isa 43:11 Lord; and beside me there is no s...... 3467
Isa 45:15 thyself, O God of Israel, the S.. 3467
Isa 45:21 a just God and a S.; there is none....... 3467
Isa 49:26 know that I the Lord am thy S. and.... 3467
Isa 60:16 know that I the Lord am thy S. and.... 3467
Isa 63:8 that will not lie: so he was their S..... 3467
Jer 14:8 the s. thereof in time of trouble, ... 3467
Ho 13:4 me: for there is no s. beside me. 3467
Lu 1:47 spirit hath rejoiced in God my S........ *4990*
Lu 2:11 this day in the city of David a S.,....... *4990*
Joh 4:42 the Christ, the S. of the world. *4990*
Ac 5:31 right hand to be a Prince and a S.,..... *4990*
Ac 13:23 his promise raised unto Israel a S.,..... *4990*
Eph 5:23 church: and he is the s. of the body.... *4990*
Php 3:20 we look for the S., the Lord Jesus *4990*
1Ti 1:1 the commandment of God our S.,....... *4990*
1Ti 2:3 acceptable in the sight of...our S.;...... *4990*
1Ti 4:10 God, who is the S. of all men,........... *4990*
2Ti 1:10 appearing of our S. Jesus Christ,........ *4990*
Tit 1:3 the commandment of God our S.;........ *4990*
Tit 1:4 and the Lord Jesus Christ our S......... *4990*
Tit 2:10 the doctrine of God our S. in all......... *4990*
Tit 2:13 great God and our S. Jesus Christ,..... *4990*
Tit 3:4 and love of God our S. toward man *4990*
Tit 3:6 through Jesus Christ our S.;............. *4990*
2Pe 1:1 righteousness of God and our S. *4990*
2Pe 1:11 kingdom of our Lord and S. Jesus *4990*
2Pe 2:20 the knowledge of the Lord and S. *4990*
2Pe 3:2 us the apostles of the Lord and S....... *4990*
2Pe 3:18 the knowledge of our Lord and S. *4990*
1Jo 4:14 Father sent the Son to be the S. of.... *4990*
Jude 25 To the only wise God our S., be........ *4990*

SAVIOURS
Ne 9:27 mercies thou gavest them s., who...... 3467
Ob 21 s. shall come up on mount Zion to...... 3467

SAVOUR See also SAVOUREST; SAVOURS.
Ge 8:21 And the Lord smelled a sweet s.;....... 7381
Ex 5:21 ye have made our s. to be abhorred ... 7381
Ex 29:18 it is a sweet s., an offering made by ... 7381
Ex 29:25 for a sweet s. before the Lord:.......... 7381
Ex 29:41 for a sweet s., an offering made by 7381
Le 1:9, 13,17 of a sweet s. unto the Lord. 7381
Le 2:2 by fire, of a sweet s. unto the Lord:... 7381
Le 2:9 by fire, of a sweet s. unto the Lord.... 7381
Le 2:12 be burnt on the altar for a sweet s.. ... 7381
Le 3:5 by fire, of a sweet s. unto the Lord.... 7381
Le 3:16 offering made by fire for a sweet s.: ... 7381
Le 4:31 altar for a sweet s. unto the Lord; 7381
Le 6:15 burn it upon the altar for a sweet s., .. 7381
Le 6:21 offer for a sweet s. unto the Lord. 7381
Le 8:21 was a burnt sacrifice for a sweet s., .. 7381
Le 8:28 were consecrations for a sweet s.: 7381
Le 17:6 the fat for a sweet s. unto the Lord.... 7381
Le 23:13 by fire unto the Lord for a sweet s.:... 7381
Le 23:18 by fire, of sweet s. unto the Lord. 7381
Le 26:31 smell the s. of your sweet odours. 7381
Nu 15:3 to make a sweet s. unto the Lord, ... 7381
Nu 15:7 wine, for a sweet s. unto the Lord. 7381
Nu 15:10, 13 fire, of a sweet s. unto the Lord.... 7381
Nu 15:14 by fire, of a sweet s. unto the Lord;... 7381
Nu 15:24 for a sweet s. unto the Lord, with....... 7381
Nu 18:17 by fire, for a sweet s. unto the Lord... 7381
Nu 28:2 made by fire, for a sweet s. unto me, . 7381
Nu 28:6 in mount Sinai for a sweet s.,........... 7381
Nu 28:8 by fire, of a sweet s. unto the Lord.... 7381
Nu 28:13 for a burnt offering of a sweet s., a.... 7381
Nu 28:24 by fire, of a sweet s. unto the Lord:... 7381
Nu 28:27 offering for a sweet s. unto the Lord; ..7381
Nu 29:2 offering for a sweet s. unto the Lord; ..7381
Nu 29:6 for a sweet s., a sacrifice made by 7381
Nu 29:8 offering unto the Lord for a sweet s.; ..7381
Nu 29:13 by fire, of a sweet s. unto the Lord;... 7381
Nu 29:36 by fire, of a sweet s. unto the Lord:... 7381
Ec 10:1 apothecary to send...a stinking s.: 7381
Ca 1:3 of the s. of thy good ointments.......... 7381
Eze 6:13 did offer sweet s. to all their idols. 7381
Eze 16:19 set it before them for a sweet s.:....... 7381
Eze 20:28 there also they made their sweet s.,... 7381
Eze 20:41 I will accept you with your sweet s.,... 7381
Joe 2:20 and his ill s. shall come up,.............. 6709
Mt 5:13 **but if the salt have lost his s., ...** *3471*
Lu 14:34 **but if the salt have lost his s., ...** *3471*
2Co 2:14 manifest the s. of his knowledge *3744*
2Co 2:15 are unto God a sweet s. of Christ, ... *2175*
2Co 2:16 we are the s. of death unto death;...... *3744*
2Co 2:16 to the other the s. of life unto life. *3744*
Eph 5:2 to God for a sweetsmelling s............. *3744*

SAVOUREST
Mt 16:23 **s. not the things that be of God, ...** *5426*
Mk 8:33 **s. not the things that be of God, ...** *5426*

SAVOURS
Ezr 6:10 sweet s. unto the God of heaven,........ 5208

SAVOURY See also UNSAVOURY.
Ge 27:4 make me s. meat, such as I love,........ 4303
Ge 27:7 me venison, and make me s. meat,..... 4303
Ge 27:9 I will make...s. meat for thy father, ... 4303
Ge 27:14 his mother made s. meat, such as 4303
Ge 27:17 she gave the s. meat and the bread, ... 4303
Ge 27:31 And he also had made s. meat, and 4303

SAW See also FORESAW; SAWED; SAWEST; SAWN; SAWS.
Ge 1:4 God s. the light, that it was good:...... 7200
Ge 1:10, 12,18,21,25 God s. that it was good. .. 7200
Ge 1:31 God s. every thing that he had made, ..7200
Ge 3:6 woman s. that the tree was good 7200
Ge 6:2 the sons of God s. the daughters of.... 7200
Ge 6:5 God s. that the wickedness of man..... 7200
Ge 9:22 s. the nakedness of his father,........... 7200
Ge 9:23 they s. not their father's nakedness. ... 7200
Ge 12:15 The princes also of Pharaoh s. her, ... 7200
Ge 16:4,5 she s. that she had conceived,........... 7200
Ge 18:2 and when he s. them, he ran to meet ..7200
Ge 21:9 And Sarah s. the son of Hagar the...... 7200
Ge 21:19 her eyes, and she s. a well of water:.. 7200

Book	Ref	Context	No.
Ge	22:4	up his eyes, and **s.** the place afar off	7200
Ge	24:30	when he **s.** the earring and bracelets	7200
Ge	24:63	and he lifted up his eyes, and **s.**,	7200
Ge	24:64	when she **s.** Isaac, she lighted off	7200
Ge	26:8	looked out at a window, and **s.**, and	7200
Ge	26:28	We **s.** certainly...the Lord was with	7200
Ge	28:6	When Esau **s.** that Isaac had blessed	7200
Ge	29:10	when Jacob **s.** Rachel the daughter	7200
Ge	29:31	the Lord **s.** that Leah was hated,	7200
Ge	30:1	Rachel **s.** that she bare Jacob no	7200
Ge	30:9	Leah **s.** that she had left bearing,	7200
Ge	31:10	up mine eyes, and **s.** in a dream,	7200
Ge	32:2	And when Jacob **s.** them, he said,	7200
Ge	32:25	he **s.** that he prevailed not against	7200
Ge	33:5	and **s.** the women and the children;	7200
Ge	34:2	Shechem...**s.** her, he took her, and	7200
Ge	37:4	**s.** that their father loved him more	7200
Ge	37:18	And when they **s.** him afar off, even	7200
Ge	38:2	Judah **s.**...a daughter of a certain	7200
Ge	38:14	for she **s.** that Shelah was grown,	7200
Ge	38:15	When Judah **s.** her, he thought her	7200
Ge	39:3	his master **s.** that the Lord was with	7200
Ge	39:13	she **s.** that he had left his garment	7200
Ge	40:16	chief baker **s.** that the interpretation	7200
Ge	41:19	as I never **s.** in all the land of Egypt	7200
Ge	41:22	And I **s.** in my dream, and, behold,	7200
Ge	42:1	when Jacob **s.** that there was corn	7200
Ge	42:7	And Joseph **s.** his brethren, and he	7200
Ge	42:21	in that we **s.** the anguish of his soul,	7200
Ge	42:35	their father **s.** the bundles of money,	7200
Ge	43:16	when Joseph **s.** Benjamin with them,	7200
Ge	43:29	eyes, and **s.** his brother Benjamin,	7200
Ge	44:28	in pieces; and I **s.** him not since:	7200
Ge	45:27	he **s.** the wagons which Joseph had	7200
Ge	48:17	when Joseph **s.** that his father laid	7200
Ge	49:15	And he **s.** that rest was good, and	7200
Ge	50:11	**s.** the mourning in the floor of Atad,	7200
Ge	50:15	**s.** that their father was dead, they	7200
Ge	50:23	And Joseph **s.** Ephraim's children	7200
Ex	2:2	when she **s.** him that he was a goodly	7200
Ex	2:5	when she **s.** the ark among the flags,	7200
Ex	2:6	she had opened it, she **s.** the child:	7200
Ex	2:12	when he **s.** that there was no man,	7200
Ex	3:4	Lord **s.** that he turned aside to see,	7200
Ex	8:15	Pharaoh **s.** that there was respite,	7200
Ex	9:34	when Pharaoh **s.** that the rain and	7200
Ex	10:23	They **s.** not one another, neither	7200
Ex	14:30	and Israel **s.** the Egyptians dead	7200
Ex	14:31	And Israel **s.** that great work which	7200
Ex	16:15	when the children of Israel **s.** it,	7200
Ex	18:14	And when Moses' father in law **s.** all	7200
Ex	20:18	all the people **s.** the thunderings,	7200
Ex	20:18	when the people **s.** it, they removed,	7200
Ex	24:10	And they **s.** the God of Israel: and	7200
Ex	24:11	they **s.** God, and did eat and drink	2372
Ex	32:1	the people **s.** that Moses delayed	7200
Ex	32:5	when Aaron **s.** it, he built an altar	7200
Ex	32:19	that he **s.** the calf, and the dancing:	7200
Ex	32:25	Moses **s.** that the people were naked;	7200
Ex	33:10	all the people **s.** the cloudy pillar	7200
Ex	34:30	all the children of Israel **s.** Moses,	7200
Ex	34:35	children of Israel **s.**...face of Moses,	7200
Le	9:24	when all the people **s.**, they shouted,	7200
Nu	13:28	we **s.** the children of Anak there.	7200
Nu	13:32	people that we **s.** in it are men of a	7200
Nu	13:33	we **s.** the giants, the sons of Anak,	7200
Nu	20:29	congregation **s.**...Aaron was dead,	7200
Nu	22:2	Balak...**s.** all that Israel had done	7200
Nu	22:23	And the ass **s.** the angel of the Lord	7200
Nu	22:25,	27 the ass **s.** the angel of the Lord,	7200
Nu	22:31	and he **s.** the angel of the Lord	7200
Nu	22:33	And the ass **s.** me, and turned from	7200
Nu	24:1	Balaam **s.** that it pleased the Lord	7200
Nu	24:2	and he **s.** Israel abiding in his tents	7200
Nu	24:4,	16 **s.** the vision of the Almighty,	2372
Nu	25:7	the son of Aaron the priest, **s.** it,	7200
Nu	32:1	and when they **s.** the land of Jazer,	7200
Nu	32:9	valley of Eshcol, and **s.** the land,	7200
De	1:19	terrible wilderness, which ye **s.** by	7200
De	4:12	of the words, but **s.** no similitude;	7200
De	4:15	for ye **s.** no manner of similitude on	7200
De	7:19	temptations which thine eyes **s.**,	7200
De	32:19	when the Lord **s.** it, he abhorred	7200
Jos	7:21	I **s.** among the spoils a goodly	7200
Jos	8:14	when the king of Ai **s.** it, that they	7200
Jos	8:20	they **s.**, and, behold, the smoke of	7200
Jos	8:21	Israel **s.** that the ambush had taken	7200
Jg	1:24	the spies **s.** a man come forth out of	7200
Jg	3:24	when they **s.** that, behold, the doors	7200
Jg	9:36	when Gaal **s.** the people, he said to	7200
Jg	9:55	the men of Israel **s.** that Abimelech	7200
Jg	11:35	when he **s.** her, that he rent his	7200
Jg	12:3	when I **s.** that ye delivered me not,	7200
Jg	14:1	and **s.** a woman in Timnath of the	7200
Jg	14:11	when they **s.** him, that they brought	7200
Jg	16:1	to Gaza, and **s.** there an harlot, and	7200
Jg	16:18	when Delilah **s.** that he had told all	7200
Jg	16:24	And when the people **s.** him, they	7200
Jg	18:7	**s.** the people that were therein, how	7200
Jg	18:26	Micah **s.** that they were too strong	7200
Jg	19:3	the father of the damsel **s.** him, he	7200
Jg	19:17	he **s.** a wayfaring man in the street	7200
Jg	19:30	all that **s.** it said, There was no	7200
Jg	20:36	of Benjamin **s.**...they were smitten:	7200
Jg	20:41	**s.** that evil was come upon them.	7200
Ru	1:18	**s.** that she was stedfastly minded	7200
Ru	2:18	mother in law **s.** what she...gleaned:	7200
1Sa	5:7	the men of Ashdod **s.** that it was so,	7200
1Sa	6:13	lifted up their eyes, and **s.** the ark,	7200
1Sa	9:17	And when Samuel **s.** Saul, the Lord	7200
1Sa	10:11	that knew him beforetime **s.** that,	7200
1Sa	10:14	when we **s.** that they were no where,	7200
1Sa	12:12	when ye **s.** that Nahash the king of	7200
1Sa	13:6	men of Israel **s.** that they were in a	7200
1Sa	13:11	I **s.** that the people were scattered	7200
1Sa	14:52	and when Saul **s.** any strong man,	7200
1Sa	17:24	when they **s.** the man, fled from	7200
1Sa	17:42	Philistine looked about,...**s.** David,	7200
1Sa	17:51	Philistines **s.** their champion was	7200
1Sa	17:55	Saul **s.** David go forth against the	7200
1Sa	18:15	Saul **s.** that he behaved himself	7200
1Sa	18:28	Saul **s.** and knew that the Lord was	7200
1Sa	19:20	they **s.** the company of the prophets	7200
1Sa	22:9	**s.** the son of Jesse coming to Nob,	7200
1Sa	23:15	David **s.** that Saul was come out to	7200
1Sa	25:23	when Abigail **s.** David, she hasted,	7200
1Sa	25:25	I thine handmaid **s.** not the young	7200
1Sa	26:3	he **s.** that Saul came after him into	7200
1Sa	26:12	no man **s.** it, or knew it, neither	7200
1Sa	28:5	Saul **s.** the host of the Philistines,	7200
1Sa	28:12	when the woman **s.** Samuel, she	7200
1Sa	28:13	I **s.** gods ascending out of the	7200
1Sa	28:21	and **s.** that he was sore troubled,	7200
1Sa	31:5	armourbearer **s.**...Saul was dead,	7200
1Sa	31:7	**s.** that the men of Israel fled, and	7200
2Sa	1:7	he looked behind him, he **s.** me,	7200
2Sa	6:16	**s.** king David leaping and dancing	7200
2Sa	10:6	**s.** that they stank before David,	7200
2Sa	10:9	Joab **s.** that the front of the battle	7200
2Sa	10:14	Ammon **s.**...the Syrians were fled,	7200
2Sa	10:15	Syrians **s.** that they were smitten	7200
2Sa	10:19	servants to Hadarezer **s.** that they	7200
2Sa	11:2	he **s.** a woman washing herself;	7200
2Sa	12:19	when David **s.** that his servants	7200
2Sa	14:24,	28 and **s.** not the king's face	7200
2Sa	17:18	Nevertheless a lad **s.** them, and told	7200
2Sa	17:23	**s.** that his counsel was not followed,	7200
2Sa	18:10	a certain man **s.** it, and told Joab,	7200
2Sa	18:10	I **s.** Absalom hanged in an oak.	7200
2Sa	18:26	watchman **s.** another man running:	7200
2Sa	18:29	I **s.** a great tumult, but I knew not	7200
2Sa	20:12	when the man **s.** that all the people	7200
2Sa	20:12	**s.** that every one that came by him	7200
2Sa	24:17	**s.** the angel that smote the people,	7200
2Sa	24:20	**s.** the king and his servants coming	7200
1Ki	3:28	**s.** that the wisdom of God was in	7200
1Ki	12:16	Israel **s.** that the king hearkened	7200
1Ki	13:25	and **s.** the carcase cast in the way,	7200
1Ki	16:18	Zimri **s.** that the city was taken,	7200
1Ki	18:17	when Ahab **s.** Elijah, that Ahab	7200
1Ki	18:39	when all the people **s.** it, they fell	7200
1Ki	19:3	when he **s.** that, he arose, and went	7200
1Ki	22:17	I **s.** all Israel scattered upon the	7200
1Ki	22:19	I **s.** the Lord sitting on his throne,	7200
1Ki	22:32	the captains of the chariots **s.**	7200
2Ki	2:12	And Elisha **s.** it, and he cried, My	7200
2Ki	2:12	he **s.** him no more: and he took	7200
2Ki	2:15	were to view at Jericho **s.** him,	7200
2Ki	3:22	**s.** the water on the other side as red	7200
2Ki	3:26	of Moab **s.** that the battle was too	7200
2Ki	4:25	when the man of God **s.** her afar off,	7200
2Ki	5:21	Naaman **s.** him running after him,	7200
2Ki	6:17	eyes of the young man; and he **s.**:	7200
2Ki	6:20	Lord opened their eyes, and they **s.**;	7200
2Ki	6:21	said unto Elisha, when he **s.** them,	7200
2Ki	9:22	when Joram **s.** Jehu, that he said,	7200
2Ki	9:27	Ahaziah the king of Judah **s.** this,	7200
2Ki	11:1	**s.** that her son was dead, she arose	7200
2Ki	12:10	they **s.** that there was much money	7200
2Ki	13:4	for he **s.** the oppression of Israel,	7200
2Ki	14:26	the Lord **s.** the affliction of Israel,	7200
2Ki	16:10	**s.** an altar that was at Damascus:	7200
2Ki	16:12	Damascus, the king **s.** the altar:	7200
1Ch	10:5	armourbearer **s.**...Saul was dead,	7200
1Ch	10:7	were in the valley **s.** that they fled,	7200
1Ch	15:29	window **s.** king David dancing and	7200
1Ch	19:6	the children of Ammon **s.** that they	7200
1Ch	19:10	Now when Joab **s.** that the battle	7200
1Ch	19:15	Ammon **s.**...the Syrians were fled,	7200
1Ch	19:16	Syrians **s.** that they were put to the	7200
1Ch	19:19	servants of Hadarezer **s.** that they	7200
1Ch	21:16	and **s.** the angel of the Lord stand	7200
1Ch	21:20	Ornan turned back, and **s.** the angel;	7200
1Ch	21:21	Ornan, Ornan looked and **s.** David,	7200
1Ch	21:28	when David **s.** that the Lord had	7200
2Ch	7:3	children of Israel **s.** how the fire	7200
2Ch	10:16	**s.** that the king would not hearken	7200
2Ch	12:7	the lord **s.** that they humbled	7200
2Ch	15:9	**s.** that the Lord his God was with	7200
2Ch	18:18	**s.** the Lord sitting upon his throne,	7200
2Ch	18:31	of the chariots **s.** Jehoshaphat,	7200
2Ch	22:10	Ahaziah **s.** that her son was dead,	7200
2Ch	24:11	they **s.** that there was much money,	7200
2Ch	25:21	they **s.** one another in the face,	7200
2Ch	31:8	the princes came and **s.** the heaps,	7200
2Ch	32:2	Hezekiah **s.** that Sennacherib was	7200
Ne	6:16	heathen that were about us **s.** these	7200
Ne	13:15	days **s.** I in Judah some treading	7200
Ne	13:23	**s.** I Jews that had married wives of	7200
Es	1:14	**s.** the king's face, and which sat	7200
Es	3:5	Haman **s.** that Mordecai bowed not,	7200
Es	5:2	when the king **s.** Esther the queen	7200
Es	5:9	Haman **s.** Mordecai in the king's	7200
Es	7:7	**s.** that there was evil determined	7200
Job	2:13	**s.** that his grief was very great.	7200
Job	3:16	as infants which never **s.** light	7200
Job	20:9	eye...which **s.** him shall see him	7805
Job	29:8	The young men **s.** me, and hid	7200
Job	29:11	when the eye **s.** me, it gave witness	7200
Job	31:21	when I **s.** my help in the gate:	7200
Job	32:5	Elihu **s.** that there was no answer	7200
Job	42:16	**s.** his sons, and his sons' sons, even	7200
Ps	48:5	They **s.** it, and so they marvelled;	7200
Ps	73:3	I **s.** the prosperity of the wicked.	7200
Ps	77:16	**s.** thee, O God, the waters **s.** thee;	7200
Ps	95:9	me, proved me, and **s.** my work.	7200
Ps	97:4	world: the earth **s.**, and trembled.	7200
Ps	114:3	The sea **s.** it, and fled: Jordan was	7200
Pr	24:32	Then I **s.**, and considered it well:	2372
Ec	2:13	I **s.** that wisdom excelleth folly, as	7200
Ec	2:24	This also I **s.**, that it was from the	7200
Ec	3:16	I **s.** under the sun the place of	7200
Ec	4:7	and I **s.** vanity under the sun.	7200
Ec	8:10	And so I **s.** the wicked buried, who	7200
Ec	9:11	I returned, and **s.** under the sun,	7200
Ca	3:3	**S.** ye him whom my soul loveth?	7200
Ca	6:9	daughters **s.** her, and blessed her;	7200
Isa	1:1	which he **s.** concerning Judah and	2372
Isa	2:1	son of Amoz **s.** concerning Judah	2372
Isa	6:1	I **s.** also the Lord sitting upon a	7200
Isa	10:15	the **s.** magnify itself against him	4883
Isa	21:7	he **s.** a chariot with a couple of	7200
Isa	41:5	The isles **s.** it, and feared; the ends	7200
Isa	59:15	the Lord **s.** it, and it displeased him	7200
Isa	59:16	And he **s.** that there was no man,	7200
Jer	3:7	her treacherous sister Judah **s.** it	7200
Jer	3:8	And I **s.**, when for all the causes	7200
Jer	39:4	Zedekiah the king of Judah **s.** them,	7200
Jer	41:13	people...with Ishmael **s.** Johanan	7200
Jer	44:17	and were well, and **s.** no evil.	7200
La	1:7	adversaries **s.** her, and did mock at	7200
Eze	1:1	opened, and I **s.** visions of God.	7200
Eze	1:27	And I **s.** as the colour of amber, as	7200
Eze	1:27	**s.** as it were the appearance of fire,	7200
Eze	1:28	when I **s.** it, I fell upon my face, and	7200
Eze	3:23	which I **s.** by the river of Chebar:	7200
Eze	8:4	to the vision that I **s.** in the plain.	7200
Eze	8:10	I went in and **s.**; and behold every	7200

Eze 10:15 that I s. by the river of Chebar 7200
Eze 10:20 creature that I s. under the God of 7200
Eze 10:22 which I s. by the river of Chebar, 7200
Eze 11:1 I s. Jaazaniah the son of Azur, and 7200
Eze 16:6 s. thee polluted in thine own blood, 7200
Eze 16:50 I took them away as I s. good 7200
Eze 19:5 when she s. that she had waited, and 7200
Eze 20:28 then they s. every high hill, and all 7200
Eze 23:11 when her sister Aholibah s. this, 7200
Eze 23:13 Then I s. that she was defiled, that 7200
Eze 23:14 when she s. men pourtrayed upon 7200
Eze 23:16 as soon as she s. them with her eyes,
Eze 41:8 I s. also the height of the house 7200
Eze 43:3 appearance of the vision which I s., 7200
Eze 43:3 even according to the vision that I s. 7200
Eze 43:3 like the vision that I s. by the river 7200
Da 3:27 s. these men, upon whose bodies 2370
Da 4:5 I s. a dream which made me afraid, 2370
Da 4:10 I s., and behold a tree in the midst 2370
Da 4:13 I s. in the visions of my head upon 2370
Da 4:23 whereas the king s. a watcher and 2370
Da 5:5 s. the part of the hand that wrote. 2370
Da 7:2 and said, I s. in my vision by night, 2370
Da 7:7 After this I s. in the night visions, 2370
Da 7:13 I s. in the night visions, and, 2370
Da 8:2 And I s. in a vision; and it came to 7200
Da 8:2 when I s., that I was at Shushan 7200
Da 8:2 and I s. in a vision, and I was by 7200
Da 8:3 Then I lifted up mine eyes, and s., 7200
Da 8:4 I s. the ram pushing westward, and 7200
Da 8:7 I s. him come close unto the ram, 7200
Da 10:7 And I Daniel alone s. the vision: 7200
Da 10:7 men...with me s. not the vision; 7200
Da 10:8 left alone, and s. this great vision, 7200
Ho 5:13 When Ephraim s. his sickness, and 7200
Ho 5:13 and Judah s. his wound, then went
Ho 9:10 I s. your fathers as the firstripe in 7200
Ho 9:13 Ephraim, as I s. Tyrus, is planted 7200
Am 1:1 which he s. concerning Israel in 2372
Am 9:1 I s. the Lord standing upon the 7200
Jon 3:10 And God s. their works, that they 7200
Mic 1:1 which he s. concerning Samaria 2372
Hab 3:7 I s....tents of Cushan in affliction: 7200
Hab 3:10 The mountains s. thee, and they 7200
Hag 2:3 that s. this house in her first glory? 7200
Zec 1:8 I s. by night, and behold a man 7200
Zec 1:18 Then lifted I up mine eyes, and s., 7200
Mt 2:9 the star, which they s. in the east, 1492
Mt 2:10 When they s. the star, they rejoiced 1492
Mt 2:11 s. the young child with Mary his 2147
Mt 2:16 when he s. that he was mocked of 1492
Mt 3:7 when he s. many of the Pharisees 1492
Mt 3:16 he s. the Spirit of God descending 1492
Mt 4:16 which sat in darkness s. great light; 1492
Mt 4:18 s. two brethren, Simon called Peter, 1492
Mt 4:21 thence, he s. other two brethren, 1492
Mt 8:14 he s. his wife's mother laid, and 1492
Mt 8:18 Now when Jesus s. great multitudes 1492
Mt 8:34 when they s. him, they besought 1492
Mt 9:8 But when the multitudes s. it, they 1492
Mt 9:9 he s. a man, named Matthew, 1492
Mt 9:11 when the Pharisees s. it, they said 1492
Mt 9:22 when he s. her, he said, **Daughter,** 1492
Mt 9:23 and s. the minstrels and the people 1492
Mt 9:36 But when he s. the multitudes, he 1492
Mt 12:2 But when the Pharisees s. it, they 1492
Mt 12:22 blind and dumb both spake and s. 991
Mt 14:14 forth, and s. a great multitude, 1492
Mt 14:26 disciples s. him walking on the sea, 1492
Mt 14:30 when he s. the wind boisterous, he 991
Mt 15:31 when they s. the dumb to speak, 991
Mt 17:8 they s. no man, save Jesus only 1492
Mt 18:31 **fellowservants s. what was done,** 1492
Mt 20:3 **and s. others standing idle in the** 1492
Mt 21:15 scribes s. the wonderful things that 1492
Mt 21:19 when he s. a fig tree in the way, he 1492
Mt 21:20 the disciples s. it, they marvelled, 1492
Mt 21:38 **when the husbandmen s. the son,** 1492
Mt 22:11 **s. there a man which had not on a** 1492
Mt 25:37 **Lord, when s. we thee an hungred,** 1492
Mt 25:38 **When s. we thee a stranger, and** 1492
Mt 25:39 **when s. we thee sick, or in prison,** 1492
Mt 25:44 **Lord, when s. we thee an hungred,** 1492
Mt 26:8 But when his disciples s. it, they 1492
Mt 26:71 another maid s. him, and said unto 1492
Mt 27:3 when he s. that he was condemned, 1492
Mt 27:24 When Pilate s. that he could prevail 1492
Mt 27:54 s. the earthquake, and those 1492
Mt 28:17 when they s. him, they worshipped 1492
Mk 1:10 he s. the heavens opened, and the 1492
Mk 1:16 he s. Simon and Andrew his brother 1492
Mk 1:19 he s. James the son of Zebedee, and 1492
Mk 2:5 When Jesus s. their faith, he said 1492
Mk 2:12 We never s. it on this fashion 1492
Mk 2:14 he s. Levi the son of Alphaeus 1492
Mk 2:16 Pharisees s. him eat with publicans 1492
Mk 3:11 unclean spirits, when they s. him, 2334
Mk 5:6 when he s. Jesus afar off, he ran 1492
Mk 5:16 And they that s. it told them how it 1492
Mk 5:22 when he s. him, he fell at his feet, 1492
Mk 6:33 And the people s. them departing, 1492
Mk 6:34 when he came out, s. much people 1492
Mk 6:48 And he s. them toiling in rowing; 1492
Mk 6:49 they s. him walking upon the sea, 1492
Mk 6:50 they all s. him, and were troubled. 1492
Mk 7:2 they s. some of his disciples eat 1492
Mk 8:23 him, he asked him if he s. ought 991
Mk 8:25 restored, and s. every man clearly 1689
Mk 9:8 s. no man any more, save Jesus 1492
Mk 9:14 he s. a great multitude about them, 1492
Mk 9:20 when he s. him, straightway the 1492
Mk 9:25 When Jesus s. that the people came 1492
Mk 9:38 we s. one casting out devils in thy 1492
Mk 10:14 But when Jesus s. it, he was much 1492
Mk 11:20 they s. the fig tree dried up from the 1492
Mk 12:34 s. that he answered discreetly, he 1492
Mk 14:67 when she s. Peter warming himself, 1492
Mk 14:69 a maid s. him again, and began to 1492
Mk 15:39 s. that he so cried out, and gave up 1492
Mk 16:4 s. that the stone was rolled away: 2334
Mk 16:5 s. a young man sitting on the right 1492
Lu 1:12 And when Zacharias s. him, he was 1492
Lu 1:29 when she s. him, she was troubled 1492
Lu 2:48 And when they s. him, they were 1492
Lu 5:2 s. two ships standing by the lake: 1492
Lu 5:8 When Simon Peter s. it, he fell down 1492
Lu 5:20 when he s. their faith, he said unto 1492
Lu 5:27 s. a publican, named Levi, sitting 2300
Lu 7:13 And when the Lord s. her, he had 1492
Lu 7:39 Pharisee which had bidden him s. it, 1492
Lu 8:28 When he s. Jesus, he cried out, and 1492
Lu 8:34 When they that fed them s. what 1492
Lu 8:36 They also which s. it told them by 1492
Lu 8:47 the woman s. that she was not hid, 1492
Lu 9:32 they were awake, they s. his glory, 1492
Lu 9:49 we s. one casting out devils in thy 1492
Lu 9:54 disciples James and John s. this, 1492
Lu 10:31 **when he s. him, he passed by on** 1492
Lu 10:33 **when he s. him, he had compassion** 1492
Lu 11:38 And when the Pharisee s. it, he 1492
Lu 13:12 when Jesus s. her, he called her to 1492
Lu 15:20 **father s. him, and had compassion,** 1492
Lu 17:14 And when he s. them, he said unto 1492
Lu 17:15 when he s. that he was healed, 1492
Lu 18:15 but when his disciples s. it, they 1492
Lu 18:24 Jesus s....he was very sorrowful, 1492
Lu 18:43 all the people, when they s. it, gave 1492
Lu 19:5 he looked up, and s. him, and said 1492
Lu 19:7 when they s. it, they all murmured, 1492
Lu 20:14 **when the husbandmen s. him, they** 1492
Lu 21:1 s. the rich men casting their gifts 1492
Lu 21:2 s. also a certain poor widow casting 1492
Lu 22:49 they which were about him s. what 1492
Lu 22:58 after a little while another s. him, 1492
Lu 23:8 And when Herod s. Jesus, he was 1492
Lu 23:47 the centurion s. what was done, 1492
Lu 24:24 had said: but him they s. not 1492
Joh 1:32 I s. the Spirit descending from 2300
Joh 1:34 I s., and bare record that this is 3708
Joh 1:38 turned, and s. them following, and 2300
Joh 1:39 They came and s. where he dwelt, 1492
Joh 1:47 Jesus s. Nathanael coming to him, 1492
Joh 1:48 **wast under the fig tree, I s. thee** 1492
Joh 1:50 **thee, I s. thee under the fig tree,** 1492
Joh 2:23 they s. the miracles which he did. 2334
Joh 5:6 When Jesus s. him lie, and knew 1492
Joh 6:2 they s. his miracles which he did 3708
Joh 6:5 s. a great company come unto him, 2300
Joh 6:22 s. that there was none other boat 1492
Joh 6:24 people...s. that Jesus was not there, 1492
Joh 6:26 **me, not because ye s. the miracles,** 1492
Joh 8:10 and s. none but the woman, he said 2300
Joh 8:56 **my day: and he s. it, and was glad.** 1492
Joh 9:1 s. a man which was blind from his 1492
Joh 11:31 when they s. Mary, that she rose up, 1492
Joh 11:32 come where Jesus was, and s. him, 1492
Joh 11:33 Jesus therefore s. her weeping, 1492
Joh 12:41 said Esaias, when he s. his glory, 1492
Joh 19:6 chief priests...and officers s. him, 1492
Joh 19:26 When Jesus therefore s. his mother, 1492
Joh 19:33 and s. that he was dead already, 1492
Joh 19:35 And he that s. it bare record, and 3708
Joh 20:5 in, s. the linen clothes lying, yet 991
Joh 20:8 sepulchre, and he s., and believed. 1492
Joh 20:14 s. Jesus standing, and knew not 2334
Joh 20:20 glad, when they s. the Lord 1492
Joh 21:9 land, they s. a fire of coals there, 991
Ac 3:9 all the people s. him walking and 1492
Ac 3:12 when Peter s. it, he answered unto 1492
Ac 4:13 s. the boldness of Peter and John, 2334
Ac 6:15 s. his face as it had been the face 1492
Ac 7:31 When Moses s. it, he wondered at 1492
Ac 7:55 and s. the glory of God, and Jesus 1492
Ac 8:18 Simon s. that through laying on of 2300
Ac 8:39 that the eunuch s. him no more: 1492
Ac 9:8 eyes were opened, he s. no man: 991
Ac 9:35 dwelt at Lydda and Saron s. him, 1492
Ac 9:40 and when she s. Peter, she sat up. 1492
Ac 10:3 He s. in a vision evidently about 1492
Ac 10:11 s. heaven opened, and a certain 2334
Ac 11:5 in a trance I s. a vision, A certain 1492
Ac 11:6 s. fourfooted beasts of the earth, 1492
Ac 12:3 because he s. it pleased the Jews, 1492
Ac 12:9 angel; but thought he s. a vision. 991
Ac 12:16 had opened the door, and s. him, 1492
Ac 13:12 deputy, when he s. what was done, 1492
Ac 13:36 unto his fathers, and s. corruption: 1492
Ac 13:37 God raised again, s. no corruption. 1492
Ac 13:45 when the Jews s. the multitudes, 1492
Ac 14:11 the people s. what Paul had done, 1492
Ac 16:19 her masters s. that the hope of their 1492
Ac 17:16 when he s. the city wholly given 2334
Ac 21:27 when they s. him in the temple, 2300
Ac 21:32 when they s. the chief captain and 1492
Ac 22:9 were with me s. indeed the light, 2300
Ac 22:18 And s. him saying unto me, **Make** 1492
Ac 26:13 I s. in the way a light from heaven, 1492
Ac 28:4 barbarians s. the venomous beast 1492
Ac 28:6 and s. no harm come to him, they 2334
Ac 28:15 whom when Paul s., he thanked 1492
Ga 1:19 other of the apostles s. I none, save 1492
Ga 2:7 when they s. that the gospel of the 1492
Ga 2:14 I s. that they walked not uprightly 1492
Php 1:30 the same conflict which ye s. in me, 1492
Heb 3:9 me, and s. my works forty years. 1492
Heb 11:23 they s. he was a proper child; and 1492
Re 1:2 Christ, and of all things that he s. 1492
Re 1:12 I s. seven golden candlesticks; 1492
Re 1:17 when I s. him, I fell at his feet as 1492
Re 4:4 I s. four and twenty elders sitting, 1492
Re 5:1 s. in the right hand of him that sat 1492
Re 5:2 s. a strong angel proclaiming with 1492
Re 6:1 I s. when the Lamb opened one of 1492
Re 6:2 And I s., and behold a white horse: 1492
Re 6:9 s. under the altar the souls of them 1492
Re 7:1 s. four angels standing on the four 1492
Re 7:2 I s. another angel ascending from 1492
Re 8:2 I s. the seven angels which stood 1492
Re 9:1 I s. a star fall from heaven unto the 1492
Re 9:17 thus I s. the horses in the vision, 1492
Re 10:1 s. another mighty angel come down 1492
Re 10:5 angel which I s. stand upon the sea 1492
Re 11:11 fear fell upon them which s. them 2334
Re 12:13 dragon s. that he was cast unto 1492
Re 13:1 and s. a beast rise up out of the sea, 1492
Re 13:2 which I s. was like unto a leopard, 1492
Re 13:3 And I s. one of his heads as it were 1492
Re 14:6 s. another angel fly in the midst of 1492
Re 15:1 I s. another sign in heaven, great 1492
Re 15:2 s. as it were a sea of glass mingled 1492
Re 16:13 I s. three unclean spirits like frogs 1492
Re 17:3 and I s. a woman sit upon a scarlet 1492
Re 17:6 I s. the woman drunken with the 1492
Re 17:6 and when I s. her, I wondered with 1492
Re 18:1 these things I s. another angel come 1492
Re 18:18 they s. the smoke of her burning, 3708
Re 19:11 I s. heaven opened, and behold a 1492
Re 19:17 I s. an angel standing in the sun; 1492
Re 19:19 I s. the beast, and the kings of the 1492
Re 20:1 And I s. an angel come down from 1492
Re 20:4 s. thrones, and they sat upon them, 1492

Re	20:4	and I **s.** the souls of them that were.........	
Re	20:11	I **s.** a great white throne, and him......	*1492*
Re	20:12	And I **s.** the dead, small and great,.....	*1492*
Re	21:1	I **s.** a new heaven and a new earth:....	*1492*
Re	21:2	And I John **s.** the holy city, new	*1492*
Re	21:22	I **s.** no temple therein: for the Lord....	*1492*
Re	22:8	I John **s.** these things, and heard.........	*991*

SAWED

1Ki	7:9	**s.** with saws, within and without, ...	1641

SAWEST

Ge	20:10	What **s.** thou, that thou hast done	7200
1Sa	19:5	Israel: thou **s.** it, and didst rejoice:.....	7200
1Sa	28:13	Be not afraid: for what **s.** thou?	7200
2Sa	18:11	behold, thou **s.** him, and why didst	7200
Ps	50:18	When thou **s.** a thief, then thou	7200
Isa	57:8	lovedst their bed where thou **s.** it.......	2372
Da	2:31	king, **s.**, and behold a great image........	2370
Da	2:34	Thou **s.** till that a stone was cut out ...	2370
Da	2:41	whereas thou **s.** the feet and toes, ...	2370
Da	2:41	as thou **s.** the iron mixed with miry	2370
Da	2:43	thou **s.** iron mixed with miry clay, ...	2370
Da	2:45	thou **s.** that the stone was cut of the ..	2370
Da	4:20	The tree that thou **s.**, which grew,......	2370
Da	8:20	The ram which thou **s.** having two........	7200
Re	1:20	of the seven stars which thou **s.**....	*1492*
Re	1:20	candlesticks which thou **s.** are the.	*1492*
Re	17:8	The beast that thou **s.** was, and is......	*1492*
Re	17:12	the ten horns which thou **s.** are ten....	*1492*
Re	17:15	The waters which thou **s.**, where.......	*1492*
Re	17:16	the ten horns which thou **s.** upon.......	*1492*
Re	17:18	woman which thou **s.** is that great......	*1492*

SAWN

Heb	11:37	were stoned, they were **s.** asunder,....	*4249*

SAWS

2Sa	12:31	and put them under **s.**, and under.......	4050
1Ki	7:9	sawed with **s.**, within and without,......	4050
1Ch	20:3	cut them with **s.**, and with harrows.....	4050

SAY See also GAINSAY; SAID; SAITH; SAYING.

Ge	12:12	that they shall **s.**, This is his wife:	559
Ge	12:13	**S.**, I pray thee, thou art my sister:......	559
Ge	14:23	thou...**s.**, I have made Abram rich:.......	559
Ge	20:13	come, **s.** of me, He is my brother........	559
Ge	24:14	damsel to whom I shall **s.**, Let down....	559
Ge	24:14	she shall **s.**, Drink, and I will give........	559
Ge	24:43	and I **s.** to her, Give me, I pray thee, ..	559
Ge	24:44	And she **s.** to me, Both drink thou,......	559
Ge	26:7	for he feared to **s.**, She is my wife;......	559
Ge	32:18	Then thou shalt **s.**, They be thy..........	559
Ge	32:20	**s.** ye...Behold, thy servant Jacob.........	559
Ge	34:11	what ye shall **s.** unto me I will give......	559
Ge	34:12	according as ye shall **s.** unto me:	559
Ge	37:17	I heard them **s.**, Let us go to Dothan. ..	559
Ge	37:20	and we will **s.**, Some evil beast hath.....	559
Ge	41:15	I have heard **s.** of thee, that thou	559
Ge	43:7	he would **s.**, Bring your brother down? ..	559
Ge	44:4	**s.** unto them, Wherefore have ye.........	559
Ge	44:16	said, What shall we **s.** unto my lord?	559
Ge	45:9	and **s.** unto him, Thus saith thy son	559
Ge	45:17	**S.** unto thy brethren, This do ye;	559
Ge	46:31	and shew Pharaoh, and **s.** unto him, ...	559
Ge	46:33	shall **s.**, What is your occupation?	559
Ge	46:34	That ye shall **s.**, Thy servants' trade....	559
Ge	50:17	So shall ye **s.** unto Joseph, Forgive, ...	559
Ex	3:13	and shall **s.** unto them, The God of......	559
Ex	3:13	and they shall **s.** to me, What is his	559
Ex	3:13	name? what shall I **s.** unto them?.........	559
Ex	3:14,	15 thou **s.** unto the children of Israel, ...	559
Ex	3:16	**s.** unto them, The Lord God of your	559
Ex	3:18	ye shall **s.** unto him, The Lord God......	559
Ex	4:1	for they will **s.**, The Lord hath not.......	559
Ex	4:12	and teach thee what thou shalt **s.**.......	1696
Ex	4:22	thou shalt **s.** unto Pharaoh, Thus	559
Ex	4:23	I **s.** unto thee, Let my son go, that......	559
Ex	5:16	and they **s.** to us, Make brick: and,......	559
Ex	5:17	ye **s.**, Let us go and do sacrifice to......	559
Ex	6:6	**s.** unto the children of Israel, I am.......	559
Ex	6:29	of Egypt all that I **s.** unto thee.	1696
Ex	7:9	then thou shalt **s.** unto Aaron, Take.....	559
Ex	7:16	thou shalt **s.** unto him, The Lord..........	559
Ex	7:19	**S.** unto Aaron, Take thy rod, and........	559
Ex	8:1	Go unto Pharaoh, and **s.** unto him,.......	559
Ex	8:5	**S.** unto Aaron, Stretch forth thine........	559
Ex	8:16	**S.** unto Aaron, Stretch out thy rod,.......	559
Ex	8:20	**s.** unto him, Thus saith the Lord, ...	559
Ex	9:13	before Pharaoh, and **s.** unto him, ...	559
Ex	12:26	your children shall **s.** unto you,...........	559
Ex	12:27	ye shall **s.**, It is the sacrifice of the......	559
Ex	13:14	thou shalt **s.** unto him, By strength......	559
Ex	14:3	Pharaoh will **s.** of the children of..........	559
Ex	16:9	**S.** unto all the congregation of the	559
Ex	19:3	shalt thou **s.** to the house of Jacob, ...	559
Ex	20:22	shalt **s.** unto the children of Israel,.......	559
Ex	21:5	if the servant shall plainly **s.**, I love.....	559
Ex	32:12	and **s.**, For mischief did he bring	559
Ex	33:5	**S.** unto the children of Israel, Ye are....	559
Le	1:2	and **s.** unto them, If any man of you.....	559
Le	15:2	and **s.** unto them, When any man.........	559
Le	17:2	and **s.** unto them; This is the thing	559
Le	17:8	shalt **s.** unto them, Whatsoever man......	559
Le	18:2	and **s.** unto them, I am the Lord your...	559
Le	19:2	and **s.** unto them, Ye shall be holy:	559
Le	20:2	thou shalt **s.** to the children of Israel, ...	559
Le	21:1	and **s.** unto them, There shall none	559
Le	22:3	**S.** unto them, Whosoever he be of.......	559
Le	22:18	and **s.** unto them, Whatsoever he be	559
Le	23:2	and **s.**...Concerning the feasts of..........	559
Le	23:10	and **s.** unto them, When ye be come	559
Le	25:2	and **s.** unto them, When ye come into...	559
Le	25:20	And if ye shall **s.**, What shall we eat.....	559
Le	27:2	and **s.**...When a man shall make a........	559
Nu	5:12	**s.** unto them, If any man's wife go.......	559
Nu	5:19	and **s.** unto the woman, If no man........	559
Nu	5:21	the priest shall say unto the woman,......	559
Nu	5:22	the woman shall **s.**, Amen, amen.	559
Nu	6:2	and **s.** unto them, When either man.......	559
Nu	8:2	and **s.** unto him, When thou lightest	559
Nu	11:12	shouldest **s.** unto me, Carry them........	559
Nu	11:18	**s.** thou unto the people, Sanctify..........	559
Nu	14:28	**S.** unto them, As truly as I live,..........	559
Nu	15:2	and **s.** unto them, When ye be come	559
Nu	15:18	and **s.** unto them, When ye come into...	559
Nu	18:26	and **s.** unto them, When ye take of	559
Nu	18:30	**s.** unto them, When ye have heaved.....	559
Nu	21:27	that speak in proverbs **s.**, Come into....	559
Nu	22:19	the Lord will **s.** unto me more...........	1696
Nu	22:20	word which I shall **s.** unto thee, ...	1696
Nu	22:38	any power at all to **s.** any thing?	1696
Nu	23:16	Go again unto Balak, and **s.** thus........	1696
Nu	25:12	Wherefore **s.**, Behold, I give unto........	559
Nu	28:2	and **s.** unto them, My offering, and......	559
Nu	28:3	**s.** unto them, This is the offering........	559
Nu	33:51	**s.** unto them, When ye are passed.......	559
Nu	34:2	and **s.** unto them, When ye come into...	559
Nu	35:10	**s.** unto them, When ye be come over...	559
De	1:42	**S.** unto them, Go not up, neither.........	559
De	4:6	and **s.**, Surely this great nation is a......	559
De	5:27	all that the Lord our God shall **s.**:	559
De	5:30	Go **s.** to them, Get you into your tents.	559
De	6:21	thou shalt **s.** unto thy son, We were.....	559
De	7:17	shalt **s.** in thine heart, These nations....	559
De	8:17	And thou **s.** in thine heart, My power....	559
De	9:2	and of whom thou hast heard **s.**, Who	
De	9:28	**s.**, Because the Lord was not able.......	559
De	12:20	and thou shalt **s.**, I will eat flesh,.........	559
De	13:12	thou shalt hear **s.** in one of thy cities, ...	
De	15:16	if he **s.** unto thee, I will not go...........	559
De	17:14	shalt **s.**, I will set a king over me, ...	559
De	18:21	**s.** in thine heart, How shall we know....	559
De	20:3	shall **s.** unto them, Hear, O Israel,.......	559
De	20:8	and they shall **s.**, What man is there.....	559
De	21:7	and **s.**, Our hands have not shed this....	559
De	21:20	shall **s.** unto the elders of his city, ...	559
De	22:14	and **s.**, I took this woman, and when....	559
De	22:16	father shall **s.** unto the elders, I gave ...	559
De	25:7	**s.**, My husband's brother refuseth to....	559
De	25:8	to it, and **s.**, I like not to take her;	559
De	25:9	answer and **s.**, So shall it be done.......	559
De	26:3	and **s.** unto him, I profess this day.......	559
De	26:5	**s.** before the Lord thy God, A Syrian ...	559
De	26:13	shalt **s.** before the Lord thy God, ...	559
De	27:14	and **s.** unto all the men of Israel with....	559
De	27:15	people shall answer and **s.**, Amen.	559
De	27:16,	17,18,19,20,21,22,23,24,25,26	
		And all the people shall **s.**, Amen.........	559
De	28:67	morning thou shalt **s.**, Would God........	559
De	28:67	and at even thou shalt **s.**, Would God ...	559
De	29:22	shall **s.**, when they see the plagues......	559
De	29:24	Even all nations shall **s.**, Wherefore......	559
De	29:25	shall **s.**, Because they have forsaken.....	559
De	30:12,	13 thou shouldest **s.**, Who shall go.......	559
De	31:17	**s.** in that day, Are not these evils........	559
De	32:27	lest they should **s.**, Our hand is high, ...	559
De	32:37	he shall **s.**, Where are their gods,........	559
De	32:40	hand to heaven, and **s.**, I live for ever. ..	559
De	33:27	thee; and shall **s.**, Destroy them..........	559
Jos	7:8	O Lord, what shall I **s.**, when Israel.....	559
Jos	7:13	and **s.**, Sanctify yourselves against	559
Jos	8:6	for they will **s.**, They flee before us, ...	559
Jos	9:11	**s.** unto them, We are your servants:	559
Jos	22:11	And the children of Israel heard **s.**, ...	559
Jos	22:27	children may not **s.** to our children.......	559
Jos	22:28	when they should so **s.** to us or to.......	559
Jos	22:28	we may **s.** again, Behold the pattern.....	559
Jg	4:20	enquire of thee, and **s.**, Is there any	559
Jg	4:20	man here? that thou shalt **s.**, No.	559
Jg	7:4	of whom I **s.** unto thee, This shall go ...	559
Jg	7:4	of whomsoever I **s.**...This shall not	559
Jg	7:11	And thou shalt hear what they **s.**;.......	1696
Jg	7:18	and **s.**, The sword of the Lord, and.......	559
Jg	9:54	that men **s.** not of me, A woman slew ..	559
Jg	12:6	they unto him, **S.** now Shibboleth:	559
Jg	16:15	How canst thou **s.**, I love thee, when...	559
Jg	18:8	brethren said unto them, What **s.** ye? ...	559
Jg	18:24	and what is this that ye **s.** unto me, ...	559
Jg	21:22	we will **s.** unto them, Be favourable	559
Ru	1:12	If I should **s.**, I have hope, if I...........	559
1Sa	2:36	and shall **s.**, Put me, I pray thee, into ..	559
1Sa	3:9	that thou shalt **s.**, Speak, Lord; for	559
1Sa	8:7	people in all that they **s.** unto thee:	559
1Sa	10:2	and they will **s.** unto thee, The asses ...	559
1Sa	11:9	**s.** unto the men of Jabesh-gilead, ...	559
1Sa	13:4	Israel heard **s.** that Saul had smitten.....	559
1Sa	14:9	If they **s.** thus unto us, Tarry until.......	559
1Sa	14:10	if they **s.** thus, Come up unto us;	559
1Sa	14:34	and **s.** unto them, Bring me hither	559
1Sa	15:16	And he said unto him, **S.** on.............	1696
1Sa	16:2	and **s.**, I am come to sacrifice to the	559
1Sa	18:22	and **s.**, Behold, the king hath delight.....	559
1Sa	18:25	Thus shall ye **s.** to David, The king......	559
1Sa	19:24	Wherefore they **s.**, Is Saul also among..	559
1Sa	20:6	then **s.**, David earnestly asked leave.....	559
1Sa	20:7	If he **s.** thus, It is well; thy servant......	559
1Sa	20:21	If I expressly **s.** unto the lad, Behold,...	559
1Sa	20:22	But if I **s.** thus unto the young man,.....	559
1Sa	25:6	**s.** to him that liveth in prosperity,........	559
2Sa	7:8	thou **s.** unto my servant David, ...	559
2Sa	7:20	And what can David **s.** more unto.......	1696
2Sa	11:20	and he **s.** unto thee, Wherefore...........	559
2Sa	11:21	then **s.** thou, Thy servant Uriah the	559
2Sa	11:25	thou **s.** unto Joab, Let not this thing.....	559
2Sa	13:5	**s.** unto him, I pray thee, let my sister..	559
2Sa	13:28	when I **s.** unto you, Smite Amnon;.......	559
2Sa	14:12	lord the king. And he said, **S.** on.	1696
2Sa	14:32	to **s.**, Wherefore am I come from	559
2Sa	15:10	then ye shall **s.**, Absalom reigneth........	559
2Sa	15:26	But if he thus **s.**, I have no delight.......	559
2Sa	15:34	and **s.** unto Absalom, I will be thy........	559
2Sa	16:10	Who shall then **s.**, Wherefore hast	559
2Sa	17:9	whosoever heareth it will **s.**, There......	559
2Sa	19:2	the people heard **s.** that day how the....	559
2Sa	19:13	And **s.** ye to Amasa, Art thou not of....	559
2Sa	20:16	**s.**, I pray you, unto Joab, Come near....	559
2Sa	21:4	What ye shall **s.**, that will I do for........	559
2Sa	24:1	moved David against them to **s.**, Go,.....	559
2Sa	24:12	Go and **s.** unto David, Thus saith.........	559
1Ki	1:13	**s.** unto him, Didst not thou, my lord, ...	559
1Ki	1:25	him, and **s.**, God save king Adonijah.....	559
1Ki	1:34	and **s.**, God save king Solomon............	559
1Ki	1:36	God of my lord the king **s.** so too........	559
1Ki	2:14	I have somewhat to **s.** unto thee.........	1697
1Ki	2:14	unto thee. And she said, **S.** on..........	1696
1Ki	2:16	not. And she said unto him, **S.** on.	1696
1Ki	2:17	king, (for he will not **s.** thee nay,)......	7725
1Ki	2:20	thee; I pray thee, **s.** me not nay.	7725
1Ki	2:20	mother: for I will not **s.** thee nay.	7725
1Ki	9:8	they shall **s.**, Why hath the Lord........	7725
1Ki	12:10	thus shalt thou **s.** unto them, My	1696
1Ki	13:22	of the which the Lord did **s.** to thee, ..	1696
1Ki	14:5	thus shalt thou **s.** unto her: for it.......	1696
1Ki	16:16	people that were encamped heard **s.**,....	559
1Ki	18:44	Go up, **s.** unto Ahab, Prepare thy........	559
1Ki	22:8	said, Let not the king **s.** so.	559
1Ki	22:27	And **s.**, Thus saith the king, Put this....	559
2Ki	1:3	**s.** unto them, Is it not because..........	1696
2Ki	1:6	**s.** unto him, Thus saith the Lord,........	1696
2Ki	2:18	them, Did I not **s.** unto you, Go not? ...	559

2Ki 4:13 S. now unto her, Behold, thou hast...... 559
2Ki 4:26 and s. unto her, Is it well with thee?.... 559
2Ki 4:28 did I not s., Do not deceive me?......... 559
2Ki 7:4 If we s., We will enter into the city, ... 559
2Ki 7:13 behold, I s., they are even as all the.........
2Ki 8:10 him, Go, s. unto him, Thou mayest...... 559
2Ki 9:3 and s., Thus saith the Lord, I have...... 559
2Ki 9:17 them, and let him s., Is it peace? 559
2Ki 9:37 they shall not s., This is Jezebel.......... 559
2Ki 18:22 But if ye s. unto me, We trust in the ... 559
2Ki 19:6 Thus shall ye s. to your master, Thus .. 559
2Ki 19:9 when he heard s. of Tirhakah king 559
2Ki 22:18 thus shall ye s. to him, Thus saith 559
1Ch 5:3 sons, I s., of Reuben the firstborn of........
1Ch 16:31 and let men s. among the nations,......... 559
1Ch 16:35 And s. ye, Save us, O God of our 559
1Ch 17:7 shalt thou s. unto my servant David, ... 559
1Ch 21:18 Lord commanded Gad to s. to David, ... 559
2Ch 7:21 that he shall s., Why hath the Lord...... 559
2Ch 10:10 thus shalt thou s. unto them, My......... 559
2Ch 18:7 said, Let not the king s. so. 559
2Ch 18:15 thou s. nothing but the truth to me 559
2Ch 18:26 And s., Thus saith the king, Put this 559
2Ch 20:11 Behold, I s., how they reward us, to ....
2Ch 20:21 and to s., Praise the Lord; for his........ 559
2Ch 34:26 so shall ye s. unto him, Thus saith....... 559
Ezr 8:17 what they should s. unto Iddo,........... 1696
Ezr 9:10 God, what shall we s. after this? 559
Ne 7:7 I s., of the men of the people of Israel......
Ne 9:8 to give it, I s., to his seed, and hast.........
Es 1:18 s. this day unto all the king's 559
Job 6:22 Did I s., Bring unto me? or, Give a 559
Job 7:4 I lie down, I s., When shall I arise, ... 559
Job 7:13 I s., My bed shall comfort me, my....... 559
Job 9:12 will s. unto him, What doest thou? 559
Job 9:20 if I s., I am perfect, it shall also prove ......
Job 9:27 If I s., I will forget my complaint, ... 559
Job 10:2 s. unto God, Do not condemn me; 559
Job 19:28 ye should s., Why persecute we him, ... 559
Job 20:7 they which have seen him shall s., ... 559
Job 21:14 they s. unto God, Depart from us; 559
Job 21:28 For ye s., Where is the house of the.... 559
Job 22:29 thou shalt s., There is lifting up;......... 559
Job 23:5 understand what he would s. unto......... 559
Job 28:22 Destruction and death s., We have....... 559
Job 32:11 whilst ye searched out what to s........ 4405
Job 32:13 Lest ye should s., We have found......... 559
Job 33:27 men, and if any s., I have sinned, ... 559
Job 33:32 If thou hast anything to s., answer 4405
Job 34:18 Is it fit to s. to a king, Thou art.......... 559
Job 36:23 or who can s., Thou hast wrought 559
Job 37:19 Teach us what we shall s. unto him;..... 559
Job 38:35 go, and s. unto thee, Here we are?....... 559
Ps 3:2 Many there be which s. of my soul, ... 559
Ps 4:6 There be many that s., Who will 559
Ps 11:1 how s. ye to my soul, Flee as a bird to .559
Ps 13:4 Lest mine enemy s., I have prevailed ... 559
Ps 27:14 thine heart: wait, I s., on the Lord. ....
Ps 35:3 s. unto my soul, I am thy salvation. 559
Ps 35:10 All my bones shall s., Lord, who is 559
Ps 35:25 Let them not s. in their hearts, Ah, ... 559
Ps 35:25 let them not s., We have swallowed..... 559
Ps 35:27 yea, let them s. continually, Let the..... 559
Ps 40:15 shame that s. unto me; Aha, aha. 559
Ps 40:16 as love thy salvation s. continually, ... 559
Ps 41:8 An evil disease, s. they, cleaveth fast........
Ps 42:3 they continually s. unto me, Where 559
Ps 42:9 I will s. unto God my rock, Why hast ... 559
Ps 42:10 while they s. daily unto me, Where 559
Ps 58:11 So that a man shall s., Verily there 559
Ps 59:7 their lips: for who, s. they, doth hear? ......
Ps 64:5 they s., Who shall see them? 559
Ps 66:3 S. unto God, How terrible art thou 559
Ps 70:3 a reward of their shame that s., Aha, ... 559
Ps 70:4 as love thy salvation s. continually, ... 559
Ps 73:11 And they s., How doth God know? 559
Ps 73:15 If I s., I will speak thus; behold, I 559
Ps 79:10 Wherefore should the heathen s.,......... 559
Ps 91:2 I will s. of the Lord, He is my refuge ... 559
Ps 94:7 Yet they s., The Lord shall not see,..... 559
Ps 96:10 S. among the heathen that the Lord..... 559
Ps 106:48 and let all the people s., Amen............ 559
Ps 107:2 Let the redeemed of the Lord s. so, ... 559
Ps 115:2 Wherefore should the heathen s.,......... 559
Ps 118:2 Let Israel now s., that his mercy......... 559
Ps 118:3 Let the house of Aaron now s., that..... 559
Ps 118:4 Let them now that fear the Lord s.,..... 559

Ps 122:8 I will now s., Peace be within thee..... 1696
Ps 124:1 was on our side, now may Israel s.;..... 559
Ps 129:1 from my youth, may Israel now s.: 559
Ps 129:8 Neither do they which go by s., The 559
Ps 130:6 I s., more than they that watch for the......
Ps 139:11 If I s., Surely the darkness shall.......... 559
Pr 1:11 If they s., Come with us, let us lay...... 559
Pr 3:28 S. not unto thy neighbour, Go, and...... 559
Pr 5:12 s., How have I hated instruction,.......... 559
Pr 7:4 S. unto wisdom, Thou art my sister; 559
Pr 20:9 Who can s., I have made my heart....... 559
Pr 20:22 S. not thou, I will recompense evil;...... 559
Pr 23:35 They have stricken me, shalt thou s. ....
Pr 24:29 S. not, I will do so to him as he hath ... 559
Pr 30:9 deny thee, and s., Who is the Lord? 559
Pr 30:15 yea, four things s. not, It is enough: 559
Ec 5:6 neither s. thou before the angel,.......... 559
Ec 6:3 I s., that an untimely birth is better 559
Ec 7:10 S. not thou, What is the cause that...... 559
Ec 8:4 who may s. unto him, What doest........ 559
Ec 12:1 nigh, when thou shalt s., I have no 559
Isa 2:3 many people shall go and s., Come 559
Isa 3:10 S. ye to the righteous, that it shall...... 559
Isa 5:19 That s., Let him make speed, and 559
Isa 7:4 And s. unto him, Take heed, and be...... 559
Isa 8:12 S. ye not, A confederacy, to all them ... 559
Isa 8:12 them to whom this people shall s., A.... 559
Isa 8:19 when they shall s. unto you, Seek........ 559
Isa 9:9 that s. in the pride and stoutness of..... 559
Isa 12:1 in that day thou shalt s., O Lord, ... 559
Isa 12:4 that day shall ye s., Praise the Lord, ... 559
Isa 14:4 s., How hath the oppressor ceased! 559
Isa 14:10 they shall speak and s. unto thee, ... 559
Isa 19:11 how s. ye unto Pharaoh, I am the son .. 559
Isa 20:6 of this isle shall s. in that day,............ 559
Isa 22:15 which is over the house, and s.,.......... 559
Isa 29:15 dark, and they s., Who seeth us? 559
Isa 29:16 the work s. of him that made it, ... 559
Isa 29:16 thing framed s. of him that framed 559
Isa 30:10 Which s. to the seers, See not; and 559
Isa 30:22 thou shalt s. unto it, Get thee hence. ... 559
Isa 33:24 inhabitant shall not s., I am sick: 559
Isa 35:4 S. to them that are of a fearful........... 559
Isa 36:4 S. ye now to Hezekiah, Thus saith....... 559
Isa 36:5 I s., sayest thou,...I have counsel........ 559
Isa 36:7 thou s. to me, We trust in the Lord..... 559
Isa 37:6 Thus shall ye s. unto your master,....... 559
Isa 37:9 heard s. concerning Tirhakah king........ 559
Isa 38:5 Go, and s. to Hezekiah, Thus saith 559
Isa 38:15 What shall I s.? he hath both............ 1696
Isa 40:9 s. unto the cities of Judah, Behold........ 559
Isa 41:26 that we may s., He is righteous? 559
Isa 41:27 The first shall s. to Zion, Behold, ...
Isa 42:17 s. to the molten images, Ye are our 559
Isa 43:6 I will s. to the north, Give up; and....... 559
Isa 43:9 or let them hear, and s., It is truth. 559
Isa 44:5 One shall s., I am the Lord's; and........ 559
Isa 44:19 knowledge nor understanding to s., ... 559
Isa 44:20 nor s., Is there not a lie in my right..... 559
Isa 45:9 the clay s. to him that fashioneth it, ... 559
Isa 45:24 shall one s., in the Lord have I 559
Isa 48:5 shouldest s., Mine idol hath done......... 559
Isa 48:7 thou...s., Behold, I knew them............ 559
Isa 48:20 s. ye. The Lord hath redeemed his 559
Isa 49:9 thou mayest s. to the prisoners, Go..... 559
Isa 49:20 s. again in thine ears, The place is....... 559
Isa 49:21 Then shalt thou s. in thine heart,......... 559
Isa 51:16 s. unto Zion, Thou art my people.......... 559
Isa 56:3 enuch s., Behold, I am a dry tree. 559
Isa 56:12 Come ye, s. they, I will fetch wine,..........
Isa 57:14 And shall s., Cast ye up, cast ye up, ... 559
Isa 58:3 we fasted, s. they, and thou seest not? .....
Isa 58:9 cry, and he shall s., Here I am............ 559
Isa 62:11 world, S. ye to the daughter of Zion,.... 559
Isa 65:5 Which s., Stand by thyself, come not.... 559
Jer 1:7 said unto me, s. not, I am a child: 559
Jer 2:23 canst thou s., I am not polluted, I........ 559
Jer 2:27 time of their trouble they will s.,.......... 559
Jer 2:31 wherefore s. my people, We are.......... 559
Jer 3:1 They s., If a man put away his wife, ... 559
Jer 3:12 and s., Return, thou backsliding........... 559
Jer 3:16 s. no more, The ark of the covenant 559
Jer 4:5 s., Blow ye the trumpet in the land:..... 559
Jer 4:5 and s., Assemble yourselves, and let.... 559
Jer 5:2 though they s., The Lord liveth;.......... 559
Jer 5:15 understandest what they s................ 1696
Jer 5:19 shall come to pass, when ye shall s.,.... 559

Jer 5:24 Neither s. they in their heart, Let us.... 559
Jer 7:2 s., Hear the word of the Lord, all ye.... 559
Jer 7:10 s., We are delivered to do all these....... 559
Jer 7:28 shalt s. unto them, This is a nation 559
Jer 8:4 Moreover thou shalt s. unto them,........ 559
Jer 8:8 How do ye s., We are wise, and the 559
Jer 10:11 Thus shall ye s. unto them, The.......... 560
Jer 11:3 And s. thou unto them, Thus saith....... 559
Jer 13:12 they shall s. unto thee, Do we not....... 559
Jer 13:13 Then shalt thou s. unto them, Thus 559
Jer 13:18 S. unto the king and to the queen,....... 559
Jer 13:21 thou s. when he shall punish thee?....... 559
Jer 13:22 if thou s. in thine heart, Wherefore 559
Jer 14:13 the prophets s. unto them, Ye shall...... 559
Jer 14:15 yet they s., Sword and famine shall....... 559
Jer 14:17 thou shalt s. this word unto them; 559
Jer 15:2 if they s. unto thee, Whither shall........ 559
Jer 16:10 they shall s. unto thee, Wherefore 559
Jer 16:11 shalt thou s. unto them, Because......... 559
Jer 16:19 and shall s., Surely our fathers have...... 559
Jer 17:15 they s. unto me, Where is the word..... 559
Jer 17:20 s. unto them, Hear ye the word of....... 559
Jer 19:3 And s., Hear ye the word of the Lord, . 559
Jer 19:11 shalt s. unto them, Thus saith the....... 559
Jer 20:10 Report, s. they, and we will report it. ....
Jer 21:3 them, Thus shall ye s. to Zedekiah:...... 559
Jer 21:8 And unto this people thou shalt s.,....... 559
Jer 21:11 s., Hear ye the word of the Lord;...........
Jer 21:13 which s., Who shall come down........... 559
Jer 22:2 And s., Hear the word of the Lord, O .. 559
Jer 22:8 shall s. every man to his neighbour, ... 559
Jer 23:7 shall no more s., The Lord liveth,........ 559
Jer 23:17 s. still unto them that despise me, ... 559
Jer 23:17 s....No evil shall come upon you........ 559
Jer 23:31 use their tongues, and s., He saith. ....
Jer 23:33 then s. unto them, What burden?......... 559
Jer 23:34 shall s., The burden of the Lord, ... 559
Jer 23:35 ye s. every one to his neighbour, ... 559
Jer 23:37 Thus shalt thou s. to the prophet,........ 559
Jer 23:38 since ye s., The burden of the Lord;.... 559
Jer 23:38 Because ye s. this word, The burden ... 559
Jer 23:38 shall not s., The burden of the Lord;.... 559
Jer 25:27 Therefore thou shalt s. unto them,........ 559
Jer 25:28 then shalt thou s. unto them, Thus 559
Jer 25:30 s. unto them, The Lord shall roar........ 559
Jer 26:4 And thou shalt s. unto them, Thus....... 559
Jer 27:4 them to s. unto their masters, Thus..... 559
Jer 27:4 Thus shall ye s. unto your masters; 559
Jer 31:7 ye, and s., O Lord, save thy people,..... 559
Jer 31:10 and s., He that scattered Israel will...... 559
Jer 31:29 In those days they shall s. no more,..... 559
Jer 32:3 and s., Thus saith the Lord, Behold, ... 559
Jer 32:36 concerning this city, whereof ye s., ... 559
Jer 32:43 whereof ye s., It is desolate without..... 559
Jer 33:10 which ye s. shall be desolate without.... 559
Jer 33:11 voice of them that shall s., Praise........ 559
Jer 36:29 shalt s. to Jehoiakim king of Judah,....... 559
Jer 37:7 shall ye s. to the king of Judah,........... 559
Jer 38:22 those women shall s., Thy friends........ 559
Jer 38:25 s. unto thee, Declare unto us now 559
Jer 38:26 thou shalt s. unto them, I presented..... 559
Jer 39:12 him even as he shall s. unto thee. 1696
Jer 42:13 But if ye s., We will not dwell in......... 559
Jer 42:20 all that the Lord our God shall s.,......... 559
Jer 43:2 not sent thee to s., Go not into Egypt.. 559
Jer 43:10 s. unto them, Thus saith the Lord 559
Jer 45:3 Thou didst s., Woe is me now! for....... 559
Jer 45:4 Thus shalt thou s. unto him, The......... 559
Jer 46:14 s. ye, Stand fast, and prepare thee; 559
Jer 48:14 How s. ye, We are mighty and strong .. 559
Jer 48:17 s., How is the strong staff broken,....... 559
Jer 48:19 that escapeth, and s., What is done? 559
Jer 50:2 conceal not: s., Babylon is taken,........ 559
Jer 51:35 shall the inhabitant of Zion s.; and........ 559
Jer 51:35 of Chaldea, shall Jerusalem s............... 559
Jer 51:62 Then shalt thou s., O Lord, thou.......... 559
Jer 51:64 thou shalt s., Thus shall Babylon 559
La 2:12 They s. to their mothers, Where is....... 559
La 2:16 they s., We have swallowed her up:..... 559
Eze 2:4 thou shalt s. unto them, Thus saith...... 559
Eze 2:8 of man, hear what I s. unto thee;....... 1696
Eze 3:18 When I s. unto the wicked, Thou......... 559
Eze 3:27 thou shalt s. unto them, Thus saith...... 559
Eze 6:3 s., Ye mountains of Israel, hear the...... 559
Eze 6:11 s., Alas for all the evil abominations 559
Eze 8:12 for they s., The Lord seeth us not;...... 559
Eze 9:9 they s., The Lord hath forsaken the..... 559

Eze 11:3 Which s., It is not near; let us build 559
Eze 11:16, 17 Therefore s., Thus saith the Lord.... 559
Eze 12:10 S. thou unto them, Thus saith the 559
Eze 12:11 S., I am your sign: like as I have......... 559
Eze 12:19 s. unto the people of the land, Thus 559
Eze 12:23 but s. unto them, The days are at....... 1696
Eze 12:25 I s. the word, and will perform it, ... 1696
Eze 12:27 house of Israel s., The vision that........ 559
Eze 12:28 Therefore s. unto them, Thus saith...... 559
Eze 13:2 and s. thou unto them that prophesy 559
Eze 13:7 whereas ye s., The Lord saith it; 559
Eze 13:11 S. unto them which daub it with 559
Eze 13:15 s. unto you, The wall is no more, ... 559
Eze 13:18 s., Thus saith the Lord God; Woe to.... 559
Eze 14:4 s. unto them, Thus saith the Lord 559
Eze 14:6 s. unto the house of Israel, Thus.......... 559
Eze 14:17 and s., Sword, go through the land; 559
Eze 16:3 s., Thus saith the Lord God unto......... 559
Eze 17:3 And s., Thus saith the Lord God; A..... 559
Eze 17:9 S. thou, Thus saith the Lord God; 559
Eze 17:12 S. now to the rebellious house, Know... 559
Eze 18:19 Yet s. ye, Why? doth not the son 559
Eze 18:25 Yet ye s., The way of the Lord is not .. 559
Eze 19:2 s., What is thy mother? A lioness: 559
Eze 20:3 the elders of Israel, and s. unto them, .. 559
Eze 20:5, 27 s. unto them, Thus saith the Lord ... 559
Eze 20:30 s. unto the house of Israel, Thus......... 559
Eze 20:32 ye s., We will be as the heathen, as..... 559
Eze 20:47 s. to the forest of the south, Hear the.. 559
Eze 20:49 they s. of me, Doth he not speak 559
Eze 21:3 s. to the land of Israel, Thus saith 559
Eze 21:7 when they s. unto thee, Wherefore 559
Eze 21:9 and s., Thus saith the Lord; 559
Eze 21:9 S., A sword, a sword is sharpened, ... 559
Eze 21:24 I s., that ye are come to remembrance,.....
Eze 21:28 and s., Thus saith the Lord God......... 559
Eze 21:28 even s. thou, The sword, the sword........ 559
Eze 22:3 s. thou, Thus saith the Lord God,......... 559
Eze 22:24 s. unto her, Thou art the land that....... 559
Eze 24:3 s. unto them, Thus saith the Lord 559
Eze 25:3 s. unto the Ammonites, Hear the......... 559
Eze 25:8 Because that Moab and Seir do s.,........ 559
Eze 26:17 s. to thee, How art thou destroyed, ... 559
Eze 27:3 And s. unto Tyrus, O thou that art 559
Eze 28:2 s. unto the prince of Tyrus, Thus 559
Eze 28:9 yet s. before him that slayeth thee, ... 559
Eze 28:12 the king of Tyrus, and s. unto him, ... 559
Eze 28:22 and s., Thus saith the Lord God,.......... 559
Eze 29:3 and s., Thus saith the Lord God;......... 559
Eze 30:2 and s., Thus saith the Lord God;......... 559
Eze 32:2 s. unto him, Thou art like a young....... 559
Eze 33:2 and s. unto them, When I bring the...... 559
Eze 33:8 When I s. unto the wicked, O wicked ... 559
Eze 33:11 S. unto them, As I live, saith the 559
Eze 33:12 s. unto the children of thy people,......... 559
Eze 33:13 When I shall s. to the righteous,.......... 559
Eze 33:14 I s. unto the wicked, Thou shalt.......... 559
Eze 33:17 Yet the children of thy people s., The... 559
Eze 33:20 Yet ye s., The way of the Lord is not .. 559
Eze 33:25 Wherefore s. unto them, Thus saith..... 559
Eze 33:27 S. thou thus unto them, Thus saith....... 559
Eze 34:2 s. unto them, Thus saith the Lord 559
Eze 35:3 s. unto it, Thus saith the Lord God;..... 559
Eze 36:1 s., Ye mountains of Israel, hear the...... 559
Eze 36:3 prophesy and s., Thus saith the........... 559
Eze 36:6 s. unto the mountains, and to the 559
Eze 36:13 s. unto you, Thou land devourest up 559
Eze 36:22 s. unto the house of Israel, Thus......... 559
Eze 36:35 And they shall s., This land that was.... 559
Eze 37:4 s. unto them, O ye dry bones, hear 559
Eze 37:9 and s. to the wind, Thus saith the 559
Eze 37:11 they s., Our bones are dried, and our... 559
Eze 37:12 s. unto them, Thus saith the Lord 559
Eze 37:19 S. unto them, Thus saith the Lord 1696
Eze 37:21 s. unto them, Thus saith the Lord...... 1696
Eze 38:3 And s., Thus saith the Lord God; 559
Eze 38:11 And thou shalt s., I will go up to the.... 559
Eze 38:13 s. unto thee, Art thou come to take..... 559
Eze 38:14 prophesy and s. unto God, Thus.......... 559
Eze 39:1 prophesy against Gog, and s., Thus....... 559
Eze 44:5 all that I s. unto thee concerning......... 1696
Eze 44:6 thou shalt s. to the rebellious, even...... 559
Da 4:35 or s. unto him, What doest thou?......... 560
Da 5:11 king, I s., thy father made master of.........
Ho 2:1 S. ye unto your brethren, Ammi;......... 559
Ho 2:7 shall she s., I will go and return to 559
Ho 2:23 I will s. to them which were not my..... 559
Ho 2:23 and they shall s., Thou art my God....... 559
Ho 10:3 now they shall s., We have no king, ... 559
Ho 10:8 shall s. to the mountains, Cover us; 559
Ho 13:2 they s. of them, Let the men that........ 559
Ho 14:2 s. unto him, Take away all iniquity, ... 559
Ho 14:3 will we s. any more to the work of 559
Ho 14:8 Ephraim shall s., What have I to do..........
Joe 2:17 and let them s., Spare thy people, O.... 559
Joe 2:17 should they s. among the people,........ 559
Joe 2:19 Lord will answer and s. unto his.......... 559
Joe 3:10 spears: let the weak s., I am strong..... 559
Am 3:9 s., Assemble yourselves upon the........ 559
Am 4:1 s. to their masters, Bring, and let us.... 559
Am 5:16 s. in all the highways, Alas! alas!......... 559
Am 6:10 s. unto him that is by the sides of......... 559
Am 6:10 any with thee? and he shall s., No. 559
Am 6:10 Then shall he s., Hold thy tongue: 559
Am 6:13 which s., Have we not taken to us....... 559
Am 8:14 and s., Thy god, O Dan, liveth; and..... 559
Am 9:10 which s., The evil shall not overtake 559
Mic 2:4 and s., We be utterly spoiled: he......... 559
Mic 2:6 ye not, s. they to them that prophesy: ......
Mic 3:11 and s., Is not the Lord among us? 559
Mic 4:2 s., Come, and let us go up to the........ 559
Mic 4:11 thee, that s., Let her be defiled, and.... 559
Na 3:7 thee, and s., Nineveh is laid waste:.... 559
Hab 2:1 to see what he will s. unto me, ... 1696
Hab 2:6 against him, and s., Woe to him 559
Zep 1:12 s. in their heart, The Lord will not....... 559
Hag 1:2 This people s., The time is not come, .. 559
Zec 1:3 s. thou unto them, Thus saith the........ 559
Zec 11:5 they that sell them s., Blessed be the... 559
Zec 12:5 governors of Judah shall s. in their...... 559
Zec 13:3 s. unto him, Thou shalt not live;.......... 559
Zec 13:5 he shall s., I am no prophet, I am an.... 559
Zec 13:6 s. unto him, What are these wounds..... 559
Zec 13:9 hear them: I will s., It is my people: 559
Zec 13:9 they shall s., The Lord is my God. 559
Mal 1:2 Yet ye s., Wherein hast thou loved 559
Mal 1:5 and ye shall s., The Lord will be 559
Mal 1:6 ye s., Wherein have we despised thy.... 559
Mal 1:7 and ye s., Wherein have we polluted 559
Mal 1:7 In that ye s., The table of the Lord 559
Mal 1:12 But ye have profaned it, in that ye s., .. 559
Mal 2:14 Yet ye s., Wherefore? Because the...... 559
Mal 2:17 Yet ye s., Wherein have we wearied 559
Mal 2:17 When ye s., Every one that doeth 559
Mal 3:8 But ye s., Wherein have we robbed 559
Mal 3:13 ye s., What have we spoken so much... 559
Mt 3:9 think not to s. within yourselves, ... 3004
Mt 3:9 I s. unto you, that God is able of 3004
Mt 4:17 and to s., **Repent: for the kingdom** .. 3004
Mt 5:11 **s. all manner of evil against you** ... 2036
Mt 5:18 **I s. unto you, Till heaven and** 3004
Mt 5:20 **I s. unto you, That except your** 3004
Mt 5:22 **But I s. unto you, That whosoever** . 3004
Mt 5:22 **whosoever shall s. to his brother,** .. 2036
Mt 5:22 **but whosoever shall s., Thou fool,** .. 2036
Mt 5:26 **I s. unto thee, Thou shalt by no** 3004
Mt 5:28, 32 **I s. unto you, That whosoever** ... 3004
Mt 5:34 **I s. unto you, Swear not at all;** 3004
Mt 5:39 **I s. unto you, That ye resist not** 3004
Mt 5:44 **I s. unto you, Love your enemies,** .. 3004
Mt 6:2, 5, 16 **I s. unto you, They have their** .. 3004
Mt 6:25 **I s. unto you, Take no thought for** . 3004
Mt 6:29 **I s. unto you, That even Solomon** .. 3004
Mt 7:4 **Or how wilt thou s. to thy brother,** 2046
Mt 7:22 **Many will s. to me in that day,** 2046
Mt 8:9 I s. to this man, Go, and he goeth; 3004
Mt 8:10 **I s. unto you, I have not found so** .. 3004
Mt 8:11 **I s. unto you, That many shall** 3004
Mt 9:5 **easier, to s., Thy sins be forgiven** .. 2036
Mt 9:5 **thee; or to s., Arise, and walk?** 2036
Mt 10:15 **I s....It shall be more tolerable** 3004
Mt 10:23 **I s. unto you, Ye shall not have** 3004
Mt 10:42 **I s. unto you, he shall in no wise** .. 3004
Mt 11:7 to s. unto the multitudes concerning.... 3004
Mt 11:9 **yea, I s. unto you, and more than** . 3004
Mt 11:11 **s. unto you, Among them that are** . 3004
Mt 11:18 **and they s., He hath a devil** 3004
Mt 11:19 **they s., Behold a man gluttonous,** .. 3004
Mt 11:22 **I s....It shall be more tolerable** 3004
Mt 11:24 **I s....it shall be more tolerable** 3004
Mt 12:6 **But I s. unto you, That in this** 3004
Mt 12:31 **I s. unto you, All manner of sin** 3004
Mt 12:36 **s. unto you, That every idle word** .. 3004
Mt 13:17 **s. unto you, That many prophets** ... 3004
Mt 13:30 **I will s. to the reapers, Gather** 2046
Mt 13:51 They s. unto him, Yea, Lord............. 3004
Mt 14:17 s. unto him, We have...five loaves,...... 3004
Mt 15:5 **But ye s., Whosoever shall** 3004
Mt 15:5 **s. to his father or his mother** 2036
Mt 15:33 his disciples s. unto him, Whence 3004
Mt 16:2 **it is evening, ye s., It will be fair** .. 3004
Mt 16:13 **men s. that I the Son of man am?** .. 3004
Mt 16:14 Some s. that thou art John the.................
Mt 16:15 them, **But whom s. ye that I am?** ... 3004
Mt 16:18 **I s. also...That thou art Peter,** 3004
Mt 16:28 **Verily I s....There be some** 3004
Mt 17:10 Why then s. the scribes that Elias 3004
Mt 17:12 **I s. unto you, That Elias is come** . 3004
Mt 17:20 **verily I s. unto you, If ye have** 3004
Mt 17:20 **ye shall s. unto this mountain,** 2046
Mt 18:3 **I s....Except ye be converted,** 3004
Mt 18:10 **for I s. unto you, That in heaven** .. 3004
Mt 18:13 **I s. unto you, he rejoiceth more** 3004
Mt 18:18 **I s....Whatsoever ye shall bind on** . 3004
Mt 18:19 **I s. unto you, That if two of you** ... 3004
Mt 18:22 **s. not unto thee, Until seven times:** 3004
Mt 19:7 They s. unto him, Why did Moses 3004
Mt 19:9 **I s. unto you, Whosoever shall put** . 3004
Mt 19:10 His disciples s. unto him, If the case... 3004
Mt 19:23 **Verily I s. unto you, That a rich** ... 3004
Mt 19:24 **again I s....It is easier for a camel** . 3004
Mt 19:28 **I s....That ye which have followed** .. 3004
Mt 20:7 **They s. unto him, Because no** 3004
Mt 20:22 They s. unto him, We are able. 3004
Mt 20:33 s. unto him, Lord, that our eyes 3004
Mt 21:3 **And if any man s. ought unto** 2036
Mt 21:3 **ye shall s., The Lord hath need** 2046
Mt 21:16 him, Hearest thou what these s.? 3004
Mt 21:21 **I s. unto you, If ye have faith** 3004
Mt 21:21 **if ye shall s. unto this mountain,** .. 2036
Mt 21:25 If we shall s., From heaven;.............. 2036
Mt 21:25 he will s. unto us, Why did ye not...... 2046
Mt 21:26 But if we shall s., Of men; we fear..... 2036
Mt 21:31 They s. unto him, The first. Jesus....... 3004
Mt 21:31 **I s. unto you, That the publicans** .. 3004
Mt 21:41 They s. unto him, He will miserably.... 3004
Mt 21:43 **s. I unto you, The kingdom of** 3004
Mt 22:21 They s. unto him, Caesar's. Then 3004
Mt 22:23 which s....there is no resurrection, ... 3004
Mt 22:42 They s. unto him, The son of David. .. 3004
Mt 23:3 **works: for they s., and do not** 3004
Mt 23:16 **blind guides, which s., Whosoever** . 3004
Mt 23:30 **s., If we had been in the days** 3004
Mt 23:36 **I s. unto you, All these things** 3004
Mt 23:39 **I s. unto you, Ye shall not see me** . 3004
Mt 23:39 **till ye shall s., Blessed is he that** .. 2036
Mt 24:2 **I s....There shall not be left one** 3004
Mt 24:23 **if any man shall s....Lo, here is** 2036
Mt 24:26 **shall s....Behold, he is in the** 2036
Mt 24:34 **I s. unto you, This generation** 3004
Mt 24:47 **s....That he shall make him ruler** .. 3004
Mt 24:48 **evil servant shall s. in his heart,** ... 2036
Mt 25:12 **I s. unto you, I know you not.** 3004
Mt 25:34 **King s. unto them on his right** 2046
Mt 25:40 **King shall answer and s. unto** 2046
Mt 25:40 **Verily I s. unto you, Inasmuch as** .. 3004
Mt 25:41 **he s. also unto them on the left** 2046
Mt 25:45 **Verily I s. unto you, Inasmuch as** . 3004
Mt 26:13 **Verily I s. unto you, Wheresoever** . 3004
Mt 26:18 **and s. unto him, The Master saith,** 2036
Mt 26:21 **I s. unto you, that one of you** 3004
Mt 26:22 them to s. unto him, Lord is it I?....... 3004
Mt 26:29 **I s. unto you, I will not drink** 3004
Mt 26:34 **I s. unto thee, That this night,** 5346
Mt 26:64 **I s. unto you, Hereafter shall ye** ... 3004
Mt 27:22 They all s....Let him be crucified........ 3004
Mt 27:33 that is to s., a place of a skull, ... 3004
Mt 27:46 that is to s., My God, my God, why.........
Mt 27:64 and s. unto the people, He is risen..... 2036
Mt 28:13 S. ye, His disciples came by night, ... 2036
Mk 1:44 **See thou s. nothing to any man:** ... 2036
Mk 2:9 **s. to the sick of the palsy, Thy** 2036
Mk 2:9 **to s., Arise, and take up thy bed,** .. 2036
Mk 2:11 **I s. unto thee, Arise, and take up** . 3004
Mk 2:18 come and s....Why do the disciples..... 3004
Mk 3:28 **Verily I s. unto you, All sins shall** . 3004
Mk 4:38 and s. unto him, Master, carest thou .. 3004
Mk 5:41 Damsel, I s. unto thee, arise............ 3004

Mk 6:11 I s....It shall be more tolerable...... 3004
Mk 6:37 And they s....Shall we go and buy...... 3004
Mk 6:38 knew, they s., Five, and two fishes..... 3004
Mk 7:2 that is to s., with unwashen, hands,.... 3004
Mk 7:11 But ye s., If a man shall............. 3004
Mk 7:11 shall s. to his father or mother,.... 2036
Mk 7:11 It is Corban, that is to s., a gift.........
Mk 8:12 I s. unto you, There shall no sign.. 3004
Mk 8:19 ye up? They s. unto him, Twelve...... 3004
Mk 8:27 them, Whom do men s. that I am?. 3004
Mk 8:28 John the Baptist: but some s.. Elias;.........
Mk 8:29 them, But whom s. ye that I am?... 3004
Mk 9:1 I s. unto you, That there be some.. 3004
Mk 9:6 For he wist not what to s.; for....... 2980
Mk 9:11 Why s. the scribes that Elias must..... 3004
Mk 9:13 I s. unto you, That Elias is indeed. 3004
Mk 9:41 I s. unto you, he shall not lose..... 3004
Mk 10:15 I s. unto you, Whosoever shall...... 3004
Mk 10:28 Peter began to s....Lo, we have left... 3004
Mk 10:29 Verily I s. unto you, There is no... 3004
Mk 10:47 and s., Jesus, thou son of David,........ 3004
Mk 11:3 man s. unto you, Why do ye this?.. 2036
Mk 11:3 s. ye that the Lord hath need of.... 2036
Mk 11:23 I s. unto you, That whosoever....... 3004
Mk 11:23 shall s. unto this mountain, Be...... 2036
Mk 11:24 I s. unto you, What things soever.. 3004
Mk 11:28 And s. unto him, By what authority.... 3004
Mk 11:31 If we shall s., From heaven:............. 2036
Mk 11:31 he will s., Why...did ye not believe..... 2046
Mk 11:32 But if we shall s., Of men; they......... 2036
Mk 12:14 they s. unto him, Master, we know.... 3004
Mk 12:18 which s. there is no resurrection;....... 3004
Mk 12:35 How s. the scribes that Christ is.... 3004
Mk 12:43 Verily I s. unto you, That this...... 3004
Mk 13:5 began to s., Take heed that no man. 3004
Mk 13:21 if any man shall s. to you, Lo,...... 2036
Mk 13:30 Verily I s....that this generation.... 3004
Mk 13:37 what I s. unto you I s. unto all,.... 3004
Mk 14:9 Verily I s. unto you, Wheresoever. 3004
Mk 14:14 s. ye to the goodman of the house,. 2036
Mk 14:18 Verily I s. unto you, One of you..... 3004
Mk 14:19 to s. unto him one by one, Is it I?...... 3004
Mk 14:25 I s. unto you, I will drink no more. 3004
Mk 14:30 I s. unto thee, That this day,........ 3004
Mk 14:58 We heard him s., I will destroy this.... 3004
Mk 14:65 him, and to s. unto him, Prophesy:..... 3004
Mk 14:69 began to s....This is one of them........ 3004
Lu 3:8 begin not to s. within yourselves,....... 3004
Lu 3:8 for I s. unto you, That God is able..... 3004
Lu 4:21 he began to s. unto them, This day... 3004
Lu 4:23 surely s. unto me this proverb,....... 2046
Lu 4:24 Verily I s. unto you, No prophet.... 3004
Lu 5:23 easier, to s., Thy sins be forgiven.. 2036
Lu 5:23 thee; or to s., Rise up and walk?... 2036
Lu 5:24 I s. unto thee, Arise, and take up.. 3004
Lu 6:27 But I s. unto you which hear.......... 3004
Lu 6:42 how canst thou s. to thy brother,.. 3004
Lu 6:46 and do not the things which I s.?... 3004
Lu 7:7 but s. in a word, and my servant....... 2036
Lu 7:8 I s. unto one, Go, and he goeth;........ 3004
Lu 7:9 I s. unto you, I have not found so.. 3004
Lu 7:14 Young man, I s. unto thee, Arise... 3004
Lu 7:26 Yea, I s. unto you, and much....... 3004
Lu 7:28 s. unto you, Among those that are. 3004
Lu 7:33 wine; and ye s., He hath a devil.... 3004
Lu 7:34 ye s., Behold a gluttonous man,...... 3004
Lu 7:40 I have somewhat to s. unto thee.... 2036
Lu 7:40 thee. And he saith, Master, s. on...... 2036
Lu 7:47 I s. unto thee, Her sins, which are. 3004
Lu 7:49 s. within themselves, Who is this....... 3004
Lu 9:18 Whom s. the people that I am?...... 3004
Lu 9:19 John the Baptist;...some s., Elias;...... 2036
Lu 9:19 others s.,...one of the old prophets..........
Lu 9:20 But whom s. ye that I am? Peter... 3004
Lu 10:5 first s., Peace be to this house...... 3004
Lu 10:9 s. unto them, The kingdom of God. 3004
Lu 10:10 the streets of the same, and s.,..... 2036
Lu 10:12 s....that it shall be more tolerable. 3004
Lu 11:2 ye pray, s., Our Father which....... 3004
Lu 11:5 s. unto him, Friend, lend me three. 2036
Lu 11:7 answer and s., Trouble me not:...... 2036
Lu 11:8 I s. unto you, Though he will not. 3004
Lu 11:9 I s. unto you, Ask, and it shall be. 3004
Lu 11:18 because ye s. that I cast out devils. 3004
Lu 11:29 to s., This is an evil generation:.... 3004
Lu 11:51 I s. unto you, It shall be required. 3004
Lu 12:1 he began to s. unto his disciples......... 3004
Lu 12:4 I s. unto you my friends, Be not... 3004
Lu 12:5 hell; yea, I s. unto you, Fear him.. 3004
Lu 12:8 I s....Whosoever shall confess........ 3004
Lu 12:11 shall answer, or what ye shall s.... 2036
Lu 12:12 same hour what ye ought to s....... 2036
Lu 12:19 And I will s. to my soul, Soul,...... 2046
Lu 12:22 I s. unto you, Take no thought..... 3004
Lu 12:27 I s. unto you, that Solomon in all. 3004
Lu 12:37 I s. unto you, that he shall gird.... 3004
Lu 12:44 I s....that he will make him ruler.. 3004
Lu 12:45 and if that servant s. in his heart,.. 2036
Lu 12:54 ye s., There cometh a shower;....... 3004
Lu 12:55 wind blow, ye s., There will be....... 3004
Lu 13:24 for many, I s....will seek to enter.. 3004
Lu 13:25 and s. unto you, I know you not.. 2046
Lu 13:26 ye begin to s., We have eaten........ 3004
Lu 13:27 shall s., I tell you, I know you...... 2046
Lu 13:35 s. unto you, Ye shall not see me,... 3004
Lu 13:35 when ye shall s., Blessed is he...... 2036
Lu 14:9 s. to thee, Give this man place;..... 2046
Lu 14:10 he may s. unto thee, Friend, go.... 2036
Lu 14:17 to s. to them that were bidden,..... 2036
Lu 14:24 I s. unto you, That none of those.. 3004
Lu 15:7 I s. unto you, that likewise joy.... 3004
Lu 15:10 I s. unto you, there is joy in the.... 3004
Lu 15:18 will s. unto him, Father, I have.... 2046
Lu 16:9 I s. unto you, Make to yourselves. 3004
Lu 17:6 ye might s. unto this sycamine..... 3004
Lu 17:7 will s. unto him by and by, when.. 2046
Lu 17:8 will not rather s. unto him, Make.. 2046
Lu 17:10 s., We are unprofitable servants:... 3004
Lu 17:21 Neither shall they s., Lo here! or,.. 2046
Lu 17:23 they shall s. to you, See here; or,.. 2046
Lu 18:17 Verily I s. unto you, Whosoever.... 3004
Lu 18:29 Verily I s. unto you, There is no... 3004
Lu 19:26 s. unto you, That unto every one... 3004
Lu 19:31 shall ye s. unto him, Because....... 2046
Lu 20:5 If we shall s., From heaven;............ 2036
Lu 20:5 he will s., Why then believed ye........ 2046
Lu 20:6 if we s., Of men; all the people......... 2036
Lu 20:41 How s. they that Christ is David's. 2036
Lu 21:3 Of a truth I s. unto you, that this. 3004
Lu 21:32 I s. unto you, This generation....... 3004
Lu 22:11 ye shall s. unto the goodman of.... 2046
Lu 22:16 For I s. unto you, I will not any... 3004
Lu 22:18 For I s. unto you, I will not drink. 3004
Lu 22:37 For I s. unto you, that this that is. 3004
Lu 22:70 said unto them, Ye s. that I am....... 3004
Lu 23:29 in the which they shall s., Blessed. 2046
Lu 23:30 they begin to s. to the mountains,. 3004
Lu 23:43 Verily I s. unto thee, To day shalt. 3004
Joh 1:38 (which is to s., being interpreted,....... 3004
Joh 1:51 I s. unto you, Hereafter ye shall.... 3004
Joh 3:3,5 verily, I s. unto thee, Except a...... 3004
Joh 3:11 Verily, verily, I s. unto thee, We... 3004
Joh 4:20 and ye s., that in Jerusalem is the...... 3004
Joh 4:35 S. not ye, There are yet four......... 3004
Joh 4:35 I s. unto you, Lift up your............ 3004
Joh 5:19 verily, I s. unto you, The Son can. 3004
Joh 5:24 I s. unto you, He that heareth my.. 3004
Joh 5:25 I s. unto you, The hour is coming,. 3004
Joh 5:34 these things I s., that ye might be.. 3004
Joh 6:26 verily, I s. unto you, Ye seek me,.. 3004
Joh 6:32 I s. unto you, Moses gave you not. 3004
Joh 6:47 I s. unto you, He that believeth.... 3004
Joh 6:53 I s. unto you, Except ye eat the.... 3004
Joh 7:26 and they s. nothing unto him. Do....... 3004
Joh 8:4 s. unto him, Master, this woman......... 3004
Joh 8:26 things to s. and to judge of you:... 2980
Joh 8:34 verily, I s. unto you, Whosoever.... 3004
Joh 8:46 if I s. the truth, why do ye not..... 3004
Joh 8:48 S. we not well that thou art a......... 3004
Joh 8:51 I s. unto you, If a man keep my... 3004
Joh 8:54 whom ye s., that he is your God:.. 3004
Joh 8:55 if I should s., I know him not,...... 3004
Joh 8:58 s. unto you, Before Abraham was,. 3004
Joh 9:17 They s. unto the blind man again,......... 3004
Joh 9:19 your son, who ye s. was born blind?.... 3004
Joh 9:41 but now ye s., We see; therefore... 3004
Joh 10:1 verily, I s. unto you, He that......... 3004
Joh 10:7 I s. unto you, I am the door of..... 3004
Joh 10:36 S. ye of him, whom the Father..... 3004
Joh 11:8 His disciples s. unto him, Master,...... 3004
Joh 12:24 I s. unto you, Except a corn......... 3004
Joh 12:27 what shall I s.? Father, save me.... 2036
Joh 12:49 should s., and what I should......... 2036
Joh 13:13 Master and Lord: and ye s. well;... 3004
Joh 13:16 I s. unto you, The servant is not... 3004
Joh 13:20 I s. unto you, He that receiveth.... 3004
Joh 13:21 I s. unto you, that one of you....... 3004
Joh 13:33 cannot come; so now I s. to you.... 3004
Joh 13:38 I s. unto thee, The cock shall not.. 3004
Joh 14:12 I s. unto you, He that believeth.... 3004
Joh 16:12 yet many things to s. unto you,.... 3004
Joh 16:20 I s. unto you, That ye shall weep.. 3004
Joh 16:23 I s. unto you, Whatsoever ye......... 3004
Joh 16:26 I s. not unto you, that I will pray. 3004
Joh 20:13 s. unto her, Woman, why weepest..... 3004
Joh 20:16 Rabboni; which is to s., Master.......... 3004
Joh 20:17 s. unto them, I ascend unto my..... 2036
Joh 21:3 They s. unto him, We also go with...... 3004
Joh 21:18 I s. unto thee, When thou wast..... 3004
Ac 1:19 Aceldama, that is to s., The field of..........
Ac 3:22 whatsoever he shall s. unto you.......... 2980
Ac 4:14 they could s. nothing against it.......... 471
Ac 5:38 now I s. unto you, Refrain from.......... 3004
Ac 6:14 For we have heard him s., that.......... 3004
Ac 10:37 That word, I s., ye know which was.........
Ac 13:15 exhortation for the people, s. on........ 3004
Ac 17:18 said, What will this babbler s.?........... 3004
Ac 21:23 therefore this that we s. to thee:........ 3004
Ac 23:8 s. that there is no resurrection,.......... 3004
Ac 23:18 hath something to s. unto thee.......... 2980
Ac 23:30 to s. before thee what they had.......... 3004
Ac 24:20 else let these same here s., if they..... 2036
Ac 26:22 which...Moses did s. should come:...... 2980
Ac 28:26 and s., Hearing ye shall hear,............ 2036
Ro 3:5 of God, what shall we s.? Is God....... 2046
Ro 3:8 as some affirm that we s.,) Let us...... 3004
Ro 3:26 I s., at this time his righteousness:...........
Ro 4:1 s. then that Abraham our father,......... 2046
Ro 4:9 we s. that faith was reckoned to......... 3004
Ro 6:1 What shall we s. then? Shall we......... 2046
Ro 7:7 What shall we s. then? Is the law....... 2046
Ro 8:31 shall we then s. to these things?......... 2046
Ro 9:1 I s. the truth in Christ, I lie not,......... 3004
Ro 9:14 What shall we s. then? Is there......... 2046
Ro 9:19 Thou wilt s. then unto me, Why......... 2046
Ro 9:20 Shall the thing formed s. to him......... 2046
Ro 9:30 What shall we s. then? That the......... 2046
Ro 10:6 S. not in thine heart, Who shall.......... 2036
Ro 10:18 I s., Have they not heard? Yes.......... 3004
Ro 10:19 But I s., Did not Israel know? Yes...... 3004
Ro 11:1 I s. then, Hath God cast away his...... 2046
Ro 11:11 I s. then, Have they stumbled that...... 2046
Ro 11:19 Thou wilt s. then, The branches......... 2046
Ro 12:3 For I s., through the grace given......... 3004
Ro 15:8 s. that Jesus Christ was a minister...... 3004
1Co 1:12 Now this I s., that every one of you... 3004
1Co 1:15 s. that I had baptized in mine............ 2036
1Co 7:8 I s. therefore to the unmarried.......... 3004
1Co 7:26 I s., that it is good for a man so to be......
1Co 7:29 I s., brethren, the time is short:......... 5346
1Co 9:8 S. I these things as a man? or........... 2980
1Co 10:15 to wise men; judge ye what I s.......... 5346
1Co 10:19 What s. I then? that the idol is any..... 5346
1Co 10:20 But I s., that the things which the............
1Co 10:28 But if any man s. unto you, This........ 2036
1Co 10:29 Conscience, I s., not thine own,......... 3004
1Co 11:22 What shall I s. to you? shall I............ 2036
1Co 12:3 no man can s....Jesus is the Lord,....... 2036
1Co 12:15 If the foot shall s., Because I am........ 2036
1Co 12:16 if the ear shall s., Because I am......... 2036
1Co 12:21 the eye cannot s. unto the hand, I...... 2036
1Co 14:16 s. Amen at thy giving of thanks,......... 2046
1Co 14:23 will they not s. that ye are mad?......... 2046
1Co 15:12 how s. some among you that there...... 3004
1Co 15:35 But some man will s., How are the..... 2046
1Co 15:50 Now this I s., brethren, that flesh...... 5346
2Co 5:8 We are confident, I s., and willing..........
2Co 9:4 we (that we s. not, ye) should be........ 3004
2Co 9:6 thus I s., He which soweth sparingly,.........
2Co 10:10 For his letters, s. they, are weighty... 5346
2Co 11:16 I s. again, Let no man think me a....... 3004
2Co 12:6 for I will s. the truth: but now I.......... 2046
Ga 1:9 so s. I...again, If any man preach....... 3004
Ga 3:17 this I s., that the covenant that.......... 3004
Ga 4:1 Now I s., That the heir, as long as...... 3004
Ga 5:2 I Paul s. unto you, that if ye be.......... 3004
Ga 5:16 I s. then, Walk in the Spirit, and ye.... 3004
Eph 4:17 This I s....and testify in the Lord,....... 3004
Php 4:4 alway: and again I s., Rejoice............ 2046
Col 1:20 by him, I s., whether they be things.........

Col 2:4 And this I s., lest any man should...... 3004
Col 4:17 s. to Archippus, Take heed to the...... 2036
1Th 4:15 this we s. unto you by the word........ 3004
1Th 5:3 For when they shall s., Peace and........ 3004
1Ti 1:7 understanding neither what they s.. 3004
2Ti 2:7 Consider what I s.; and the Lord....... 3004
Tit 2:8 having no evil thing to s. of you......... 3004
Phm 19 I do not s. to thee how thou owest 3004
Phm 21 thou wilt also do more than I s.......... 3004
Heb 5:11 whom we have many things to s., ... 3056
Heb 7:9 And as I may so s., Levi also,.... 2031,2036
Heb 9:11 that is to s., not of this building; ....
Heb 10:20 through the veil, that is to s., his flesh;.....
Heb 11:14 they that s. such things declare.......... 3004
Heb 11:32 what shall I more s.? for the time 3004
Heb 13:6 So that we may boldly s., The Lord.... 3004
Jas 1:13 Let no man s. when he is tempted, ... 3004
Jas 2:3 and s. unto him, Sit thou here in a..... 2036
Jas 2:3 s. to the poor, Stand thou there, or.... 2036
Jas 2:14 though a man s. he hath faith, and...... 3004
Jas 2:16 one of you s. unto them, Depart 2036
Jas 2:18 a man may s., Thou hast faith, ... 2046
Jas 4:13 Go to now, ye that s., To day or....... 3004
Jas 4:15 that ye ought to s., If the Lord will, ... 3004
1Jo 1:6 If we s. that we have fellowship......... 2036
1Jo 1:8 If we s. that we have no sin, we........ 2036
1Jo 1:10 If we s. that we have not sinned,....... 2036
1Jo 4:20 If a man s., I love God, and hateth..... 2036
1Jo 5:16 do not s. that he shall pray for it........ 3004
Re 2:2 **them which s. they are apostles,** ... 5335
Re 2:9 **of them which s. they are Jews,** 3004
Re 2:24 **unto you I s., and unto the rest** 3004
Re 3:9 **which s. they are Jews, and are** 3004
Re 6:3 the second beast s., Come and see....... 3004
Re 6:5 the third beast s., Come and see. 3004
Re 6:6 in the midst of the four beasts s., ... 3004
Re 6:7 the fourth beast s., Come and see........ 3004
Re 16:5 heard the angel of the waters s.,......... 3004
Re 16:7 heard another out of the altar s.,........ 3004
Re 22:17 the Spirit and the bride s., Come. 3004
Re 22:17 And let him that heareth s., Come...... 2036

SAYERS See GAINSAYERS; SOOTHSAYERS.

SAYEST

Ex 33:12 s. unto me, Bring up this people:......... 559
Nu 22:17 I will do whatsoever thou s. unto.......... 559
Ru 3:5 All that thou s. unto me I will do. 559
1Ki 18:11, 14 And now thou s., Go, tell thy lord, .. 559
2Ki 18:20 Thou s.,...I have counsel and.............. 559
2Ch 25:19 Thou s., Lo, thou hast smitten the....... 559
Ne 5:12 of them; so will we do as thou s. 559
Ne 6:8 are no such things done as thou s.,....... 559
Job 22:13 And thou s., How doth God know? 559
Job 35:14 thou s. thou shalt not see him, yet....... 559
Ps 90:3 and s., Return, ye children of men......... 559
Pr 24:12 If thou s., Behold, we knew it not; 559
Isa 36:5 I say, s. thou, (but they are but vain.........
Isa 40:27 Why s. thou, O Jacob,...speakest,........ 559
Isa 47:8 that s. in thine heart, I am, and none ... 559
Jer 2:35 Yet thou s., Because I am innocent, ... 559
Jer 2:35 because thou s., I have not sinned. 559
Am 7:16 Thou s., Prophesy not against Israel,..... 559
Mt 26:70 saying, I know not what thou s.......... 3004
Mt 27:11 And Jesus said unto him, **Thou s.**...... 3004
Mk 5:31 thee, and s. thou, Who touched me?... 3004
Mk 14:68 neither understand I what thou s...... 3004
Mk 15:2 answering said unto him, **Thou s. it**... 3004
Lu 8:45 and s. thou, Who touched me?........... 2036
Lu 20:21 that thou s. and teachest rightly,........ 3004
Lu 22:60 said, Man, I know not what thou s.. ... 3004
Lu 23:3 answered him and said, **Thou s. it**..... 3004
Joh 1:22 sent us. What s. thou of thyself?......... 3004
Joh 8:5 should be stoned: but what s. thou?.... 3004
Joh 8:33 how s. thou, Ye shall be made free? ... 3004
Joh 8:52 thou s., If a man keep my saying, ... 3004
Joh 9:17 What s. thou of him, that he hath....... 3004
Joh 12:34 how s. thou, The Son of man must..... 3004
Joh 14:9 **how s. thou then, Shew us the** 3004
Joh 18:34 **S. thou this thing of thyself**.......... 3004
Joh 18:37 **Thou s. that I am a king**............. 3004
Ro 2:22 that s. a man should not commit 3004
1Co 14:16 he understandeth not what thou s.? 3004
Re 3:17 **thou s., I am rich, and increased**... 3004

SAYING See also GAINSAYING; SAYINGS; SOOTHSAYING.

Ge 1:22 God blessed them, s., Be fruitful, ... 559
Ge 2:16 s., Of every tree of the garden thou..... 559
Ge 3:17 s., Thou shalt not eat of it: cursed....... 559
Ge 5:29 called his name Noah, s., This same..... 559
Ge 8:15 And God spake unto Noah, s.,............ 559
Ge 9:8 Noah, and to his sons with him, s.,...... 559
Ge 15:1 s., Fear not, Abram: I am thy shield, ... 559
Ge 15:4 him, s., This shall not be thine heir;..... 559
Ge 15:18 s., Unto thy seed have I given this 559
Ge 17:3 face: and God talked with him, s.,........ 559
Ge 18:12 Sarah laughed within herself, s.,......... 559
Ge 18:13 Wherefore did Sarah laugh, s., Shall..... 559
Ge 18:15 Sarah denied, s., I laughed not; for...... 559
Ge 19:15 Lot, s., Arise, take thy wife, and thy ... 559
Ge 21:22 spake unto Abraham, s., God is with.... 559
Ge 22:20 that it was told Abraham, s., Behold,.... 559
Ge 23:3 and spake unto the sons of Heth, s.,.... 559
Ge 23:5 answered Abraham, s. unto him,.......... 559
Ge 23:8 he communed with them, s., If it be..... 559
Ge 23:10 went in at the gate of his city, s.,........ 559
Ge 23:13 s., But if thou wilt give it, I pray........ 559
Ge 23:14 answered Abraham, s. unto him,.......... 559
Ge 24:7 and that sware unto me, s., Unto thy... 559
Ge 24:30 the words of Rebekah his sister, s.,..... 559
Ge 24:37 my master made me swear, s., Thou ... 559
Ge 26:11 Abimelech charged all his people, s., ... 559
Ge 26:20 herdmen, s., The water is ours: and 559
Ge 27:6 spake unto Jacob her son, s., Behold,... 559
Ge 27:6 speak unto Esau thy brother, s.. 559
Ge 28:6 s., Thou shalt not take a wife of the..... 559
Ge 28:20 Jacob vowed a vow, s., If God will be... 559
Ge 31:1 heard the words of Laban's sons, s., ... 559
Ge 31:11 spake unto me in a dream, s., Jacob: ....
Ge 31:29 spake unto me yesternight, s., Take..... 559
Ge 32:4 he commanded them, s., Thus shall..... 559
Ge 32:6 the messengers returned to Jacob, s.,.... 559
Ge 32:17 commanded the foremost, s., When...... 559
Ge 32:17 and asketh thee, s., Whose art thou?.... 559
Ge 32:19 s., On this manner shall ye speak........ 559
Ge 34:4 s., Get me this damsel to wife. 559
Ge 34:8 with them, s., The soul of my son...... 559
Ge 34:20 with the men of their city, s., ... 559
Ge 37:11 but his father observed the s............ 1697
Ge 37:15 asked him, s., What seekest thou?....... 559
Ge 38:13 Tamar, s., Behold thy father in law...... 559
Ge 38:21 s., Where is the harlot, that was......... 559
Ge 38:24 s., Tamar thy daughter in law hath....... 559
Ge 38:25 s., By the man, whose these are, am... 559
Ge 38:28 thread, s., This came out first............. 559
Ge 39:12 him by his garment, s., Lie with me:.... 559
Ge 39:14 and spake unto them, s., See, he hath.. 559
Ge 39:17 s., The Hebrew servant, which thou..... 559
Ge 39:19 unto him, s., After this manner did 559
Ge 40:7 s., Wherefore look ye so sadly to day? ..559
Ge 41:9 s., I do remember my faults this day: ... 559
Ge 41:16 Pharaoh, s., It is not in me: God......... 559
Ge 42:14 I spake unto you, s., Ye are spies: 559
Ge 42:22 them, s., Spake I not unto you, s., Do . 559
Ge 42:28 s. one to another, What is this that...... 559
Ge 42:29 told him all that befell unto them; s.,..... 559
Ge 42:37 Reuben spake unto his father, s.,......... 559
Ge 43:3 Judah spake unto him, s., The man...... 559
Ge 43:3 protest unto us, s., Ye shall not see..... 559
Ge 43:7 kindred, s., Is your father yet alive?..... 559
Ge 44:1 s., Fill the men's sacks with food, as..... 559
Ge 44:19 My lord asked his servants, s., Have.... 559
Ge 44:32 unto my father, s., If I bring him not.... 559
Ge 45:16 s., Joseph's brethren are come: and 559
Ge 45:26 told him, s., Joseph is yet alive, and..... 559
Ge 47:5 unto Joseph, s., Thy father and thy...... 559
Ge 48:20 day, s., In thee shall Israel bless, ... 559
Ge 48:20 s., God make thee as Ephraim and as... 559
Ge 50:4 s., If now I have found grace in........... 559
Ge 50:4 pray you, in the ears of Pharaoh, s., ... 559
Ge 50:5 My father made me swear, s., Lo, I 559
Ge 50:16 sent a messenger unto Joseph, s., ... 559
Ge 50:16 did command before he died, s.,.......... 559
Ge 50:25 s., God will surely visit you, and ye 559
Ex 1:22 his people, s., Every son that is born... 559
Ex 3:16 unto me, s., I have surely visited you,.. 559
Ex 5:6 of the people, and their officers, s.,...... 559
Ex 5:8 s., Let us go and sacrifice to our God... 559
Ex 5:10 s., Thus saith Pharaoh, I will not.......... 559
Ex 5:13 taskmasters hasted them, s., Fulfil....... 559
Ex 5:15 cried unto Pharaoh, s., Wherefore......... 559
Ex 6:10 And the Lord spake unto Moses, s., ... 559
Ex 6:12 And Moses spake before the Lord, s.,.. 559
Ex 6:29 spake unto Moses, s., I am the Lord:... 559
Ex 7:8 unto Moses and unto Aaron, s., ... 559
Ex 7:9 unto you, s., Shew a miracle for you: ... 559
Ex 7:16 s., Let my people go, that they may 559
Ex 9:5 s., To morrow the Lord shall do this.... 559
Ex 11:8 themselves unto me, s., Get thee out,.. 559
Ex 12:1 and Aaron in the land of Egypt, s., ... 559
Ex 12:3 s., In the tenth day of this month........ 559
Ex 13:1 And the Lord spake unto Moses, s.,...... 559
Ex 13:8 shew thy son in that day, s., This is 559
Ex 13:14 in time to come, s., What is this?........ 559
Ex 13:19 Israel, s., God will surely visit you;...... 559
Ex 14:1 And the Lord spake unto Moses, s., ... 559
Ex 14:12 we did tell thee in Egypt, s., Let us..... 559
Ex 15:1 and spake, s., I will sing unto the........ 559
Ex 15:24 Moses, s., What shall we drink?.......... 559
Ex 16:11 And the Lord spake unto Moses, s., ... 559
Ex 16:12 them, s., At even ye shall eat flesh,..... 559
Ex 17:4 Moses cried unto the Lord, s., What.... 559
Ex 17:7 s., Is the Lord among us, or not?......... 559
Ex 19:3 s., Thus shalt thou say to the house..... 559
Ex 19:12 s., Take heed to yourselves, that ye 559
Ex 19:23 s., Set bounds about the mount, and 559
Ex 20:1 And God spake all these words, s.,...... 559
Ex 25:1 And the Lord spake unto Moses, s., ... 559
Ex 30:11, 17,22 the Lord spake unto Moses, s., .. 559
Ex 30:31 speak unto the children of Israel, s.,..... 559
Ex 31:1, 12 the Lord spake unto Moses, s., ... 559
Ex 31:13 s., Verily my sabbaths ye shall keep:.... 559
Ex 33:1 Jacob, s., Unto thy seed will I give it: .. 559
Ex 35:4 of Israel, s., This is the thing which...... 559
Ex 35:4 thing which the Lord commanded, s., ... 559
Ex 36:5 spake unto Moses, s., The people 559
Ex 36:6 s., Let neither man nor woman make ... 559
Ex 40:1 And the Lord spake unto Moses, s., ... 559
Le 1:1 tabernacle of the congregation, s.,........ 559
Le 4:1 And the Lord spake unto Moses, s., ... 559
Le 4:2 Israel, s., If a soul shall sin through 559
Le 5:14 And the Lord spake unto Moses, s., ... 559
Le 6:1,8 the Lord spake unto Moses, s.,............ 559
Le 6:9 Command Aaron and his sons, s., ... 559
Le 6:19, 24 the Lord spake unto Moses, s., ... 559
Le 6:25 s., This is the law of the sin offering: ... 559
Le 7:22 And the Lord spake unto Moses, s., ... 559
Le 7:23 s., Ye shall eat no manner of fat, of 559
Le 7:28 And the Lord spake unto Moses, s., ... 559
Le 7:29 of Israel, s., He that offereth the......... 559
Le 8:1 And the Lord spake unto Moses, s., ... 559
Le 8:31 s., Aaron and his sons shall eat it. 559
Le 9:3 s., Take ye a kid of the goats for a....... 559
Le 10:3 s., I will be sanctified in them that....... 559
Le 10:8 And the Lord spake unto Aaron, s., ... 559
Le 10:16 of Aaron which were left alive, s., ... 559
Le 11:1 Moses and to Aaron, s. unto them, ... 559
Le 11:2 s., These are the beasts which ye 559
Le 12:1 And the Lord spake unto Moses, s., ... 559
Le 12:2 s., If a woman have conceived seed, ... 559
Le 13:1 Lord spake unto Moses and Aaron, s.,.. 559
Le 14:1 And the Lord spake unto Moses, s., ... 559
Le 14:33 spake unto Moses and unto Aaron, s.,... 559
Le 14:35 tell the priest, s., It seemeth to me..... 559
Le 15:1 spake unto Moses and to Aaron, s.,..... 559
Le 17:1 And the Lord spake unto Moses, s., ... 559
Le 17:2 which the Lord hath commanded, s., ... 559
Le 18:1 And the Lord spake unto Moses, s., ... 559
Le 19:1 And the Lord spake unto Moses, s., ... 559
Le 20:1 And the Lord spake unto Moses, s., ... 559
Le 21:16 And the Lord spake unto Moses, s., ... 559
Le 21:17 Speak unto Aaron, s., Whosoever he..... 559
Le 22:1, 17,26 the Lord spake unto Moses, s., .. 559
Le 23:1, 9, 23 the Lord spake unto Moses, s.,... 559
Le 23:24 s., In the seventh month, in the first.... 559
Le 23:26, 33 the Lord spake unto Moses, s., ... 559
Le 23:34 s., The fifteenth day of this seventh...... 559
Le 24:1, 13 the Lord spake unto Moses, s., ... 559
Le 24:15 s., Whosoever curseth his God shall..... 559
Le 25:1 spake unto Moses in mount Sinai, s.,.... 559
Le 27:1 And the Lord spake unto Moses, s., ... 559
Nu 1:1 come out of the land of Egypt, s., ... 559
Nu 1:48 the Lord had spoken unto Moses, s., ... 559
Nu 2:1 spake unto Moses and unto Aaron, s., .. 559
Nu 3:5, 11 the Lord spake unto Moses, s., ... 559
Nu 3:14 Moses in the wilderness of Sinai, s., ... 559
Nu 3:44 And the Lord spake unto Moses, s., ... 559
Nu 4:1, 17 unto Moses and unto Aaron, s., ... 559
Nu 4:21 And the Lord spake unto Moses, s., ... 559
Nu 5:1, 5,11 the Lord spake unto Moses, s.,.... 559
Nu 6:1, 22 the Lord spake unto Moses, s., ... 559
Nu 6:23 s., On this wise ye shall bless............ 559

Nu 6:23 ye shall bless...Israel, **s.** unto them...... 559
Nu 7:4 And the Lord spake unto Moses, **s.**, ... 559
Nu 8:1, 5,23 the Lord spake unto Moses, **s.**, ... 559
Nu 9:1 come out of the land of Egypt, **s.**, ... 559
Nu 9:9 And the Lord spake unto Moses, **s.**, ... 559
Nu 9:10 **s.**, If any man of you or of your 559
Nu 10:1 And the Lord spake unto Moses, **s.**, ... 559
Nu 11:13 **s.**, Give us flesh, that we may eat. 559
Nu 11:18 **s.**, Who shall give us flesh to eat?........ 559
Nu 11:20 **s.**, Why came we forth out of Egypt? ... 559
Nu 12:13 **s.**, Heal her now, O God, I beseech..... 559
Nu 13:1 And the Lord spake unto Moses, **s.**, ... 559
Nu 13:32 **s.**, The land, through which we have 559
Nu 14:7 **s.**, The land, which we passed 559
Nu 14:15 heard the fame of thee will speak, **s.**, ... 559
Nu 14:17 according as thou hast spoken, **s.**,........ 559
Nu 14:26 spake unto Moses and unto Aaron, **s.**, .. 559
Nu 14:40 **s.**, Lo, we be here, and will go up....... 559
Nu 15:1, 17,37 Lord spake unto Moses, **s.**,........ 559
Nu 16:5 **s.**, Even to morrow the Lord will 559
Nu 16:20 spake unto Moses and unto Aaron, **s.**, .. 559
Nu 16:23 And the Lord spake unto Moses, **s.**, ... 559
Nu 16:24 **s.**, Get you up from about the............. 559
Nu 16:26 **s.**, Depart, I pray you, from the tents .. 559
Nu 16:36 And the Lord spake unto Moses, **s.**, ... 559
Nu 16:41 **s.**, Ye have killed the people of the...... 559
Nu 16:44 And the Lord spake unto Moses, **s.**, ... 559
Nu 17:1 And the Lord spake unto Moses, **s.**, ... 559
Nu 17:12 Moses, **s.**, Behold, we die, we perish,.. 559
Nu 18:25 And the Lord spake unto Moses, **s.**, ... 559
Nu 19:1 spake unto Moses and unto Aaron, **s.**, .. 559
Nu 19:2 **s.**, Speak unto the children of Israel, ... 559
Nu 20:3 **s.**, Would God that we had died when... 559
Nu 20:7 And the Lord spake unto Moses, **s.**, ... 559
Nu 20:23 by the coast of the land of Edom, **s.**,.... 559
Nu 21:21 unto Sihon king of the Amorites, **s.**, ... 559
Nu 22:5 **s.**, Behold, there is a people come....... 559
Nu 22:10 king of Moab, hath sent unto me, **s.**, ...
Nu 23:7 **s.**, Come, curse me Jacob, and come, ...
Nu 23:26 **s.**, All that the Lord speaketh, that 559
Nu 24:12 which thou sentest unto me, **s.**, ... 559
Nu 25:10, 16 the Lord spake unto Moses, **s.**, ... 559
Nu 26:1 and unto Eleazar...the priest, **s.**, ... 559
Nu 26:3 of Moab by Jordan near Jericho, **s.**, ... 559
Nu 26:52 And the Lord spake unto Moses, **s.**, ... 559
Nu 27:2 tabernacle of the congregation, **s.**,........ 559
Nu 27:6 And the Lord spake unto Moses, **s.**, ... 559
Nu 27:8 **s.**, If a man die, and have no son,........ 559
Nu 27:15 And Moses spake unto the Lord, **s.**, ... 559
Nu 28:1 And the Lord spake unto Moses, **s.**, ... 559
Nu 30:1 **s.**, This is the thing which the............ 559
Nu 31:1 And the Lord spake unto Moses, **s.**, ... 559
Nu 31:3 **s.**, Arm some of yourselves unto the.... 559
Nu 31:25 And the Lord spake unto Moses, **s.**, ... 559
Nu 32:2 the princes of the congregation, **s.**, ... 559
Nu 32:10 the same time, and he sware, **s.**,......... 559
Nu 32:25 of Reuben spake unto Moses, **s.**, Thy... 559
Nu 32:31 children of Reuben answered, **s.**, As..... 559
Nu 33:50 of Moab by Jordan near Jericho, **s.**,...... 559
Nu 34:1 And the Lord spake unto Moses, **s.**, ... 559
Nu 34:13 children of Israel, **s.**, This is the.......... 559
Nu 34:16 And the Lord spake unto Moses, **s.**, ... 559
Nu 35:1 of Moab by Jordan near Jericho, **s.**,...... 559
Nu 35:9 And the Lord spake unto Moses, **s.**, ... 559
Nu 36:5 word of the Lord, **s.**, The tribe of 559
Nu 36:6 **s.**, Let them marry to whom they........ 559
De 1:5 began Moses to declare this law, **s.**,..... 559
De 1:6 **s.**, Ye have dwelt long enough in this ... 559
De 1:9 **s.**, I am not able to bear you myself..... 559
De 1:16 **s.**, Hear the causes between your........ 559
De 1:23 the **s.** pleased me well: and I took...... 1697
De 1:28 **s.**, The people is greater and taller 559
De 1:34 words, and was wroth, and sware, **s.**, .. 559
De 1:37 **s.**, Thou also shalt not go in thither...... 559
De 2:2 And the Lord spake unto me, **s.**, ... 559
De 2:4 **s.**, Ye are to pass through the coast..... 559
De 2:17 That the Lord spake unto me, **s.**, ... 559
De 2:26 of Heshbon with words of peace, **s.**,...... 559
De 3:18 **s.**, The Lord your God hath given........ 559
De 3:21 **s.**, Thine eyes have seen all that 559
De 3:23 I besought the Lord at that time, **s.**, ... 559
De 5:5 and went not up into the mount;) **s.**, ... 559
De 6:20 **s.**, What mean the testimonies, and...... 559
De 9:4 **s.**, For my righteousness the Lord....... 559
De 9:13 me, **s.**, I have seen this people, and,.... 559
De 9:23 **s.**, Go up and possess the land which ... 559
De 12:30 **s.**, How did these nations serve their ... 559

De 13:2 **s.**, Let us go after other gods, which.... 559
De 13:6 **s.**, Let us go and serve other gods, ... 559
De 13:12 hath given thee to dwell there, **s.**, ... 559
De 13:13 **s.**, Let us go and serve other gods, ... 559
De 15:9 **s.**, The seventh year, the year of........ 559
De 15:11 **s.**, Thou shalt open thine hand wide 559
De 18:16 **s.**, Let me not hear again the voice...... 559
De 19:7 **s.**, Thou shalt separate three cities 559
De 20:5 **s.**, What man...hath built a new........... 559
De 22:17 **s.**, I found not thy daughter a maid; 559
De 27:1 **s.**, Keep all the commandments.......... 559
De 27:9 **s.**, Take heed, and hearken, O Israel;... 559
De 27:11 charged the people the same day, **s.**,.... 559
De 29:19 **s.**, I shall have peace, though I walk..... 559
De 31:10 **s.**, At the end of every seven years, ... 559
De 31:25 ark of the covenant of the Lord, **s.**, ... 559
De 32:48 unto Moses that selfsame day, **s.**,........ 559
De 34:4 **s.**, I will give it unto thy seed: I have... 559
Jos 1:1 the son of Nun, Moses' minister, **s.**, ... 559
Jos 1:10 Joshua commanded the officers...**s.**,...... 559
Jos 1:11 **s.**, Prepare you victuals; for within....... 559
Jos 1:12 tribe of Manasseh, spake Joshua, **s.**,..... 559
Jos 1:13 **s.**, The Lord your God hath given........ 559
Jos 1:16 **s.**, all that thou commandest us we 559
Jos 2:1 **s.**, Go view the land, even Jericho. 559
Jos 2:2 **s.**, Behold, there came men in hither.... 559
Jos 2:3 **s.**, Bring forth the men that are come... 559
Jos 3:3 **s.**, When ye see the ark of the........... 559
Jos 3:6 **s.**, Take up the ark of the covenant, ... 559
Jos 3:8 **s.**, When ye are come to the brink of.... 559
Jos 4:1 that the Lord spake unto Joshua, **s.**,...... 559
Jos 4:3 **s.**, Take you hence out of the midst..... 559
Jos 4:6 **s.**, What mean ye by these stones?...... 559
Jos 4:15 And the Lord spake unto Joshua, **s.**,...... 559
Jos 4:17 priests, **s.**, Come ye up out of Jordan. .. 559
Jos 4:21 **s.**, When your children shall ask 559
Jos 4:21 come, **s.**, What mean these stones? 559
Jos 4:22 **s.**, Israel came over this Jordan on....... 559
Jos 6:10 **s.**, Ye shall not shout, nor make any 559
Jos 6:26 **s.**, Cursed be the man before the 559
Jos 7:2 them, **s.**, Go up and view the country... 559
Jos 8:4 them, **s.**, Behold, ye shall lie in wait..... 559
Jos 9:11 **s.**, Take victuals with you for the 559
Jos 9:22 **s.**, Wherefore have ye beguiled us, ... 559
Jos 9:22 **s.**, We are very far from you; when 559
Jos 10:3 and unto Debir king of Eglon, **s.**, ... 559
Jos 10:6 **s.**, Slack not thy hand from thy 559
Jos 10:17 **s.**, The five kings are found hid in a 559
Jos 14:9 **s.**, Surely the land whereon thy feet...... 559
Jos 17:4 **s.**, The Lord commanded Moses to...... 559
Jos 17:14 **s.**, Why hast thou given me but one..... 559
Jos 17:17 **s.**, Thou art a great people, and hast.... 559
Jos 18:8 **s.**, Go and walk through the land, ... 559
Jos 20:1 The Lord also spake unto Joshua, **s.**...... 559
Jos 20:2 **s.**, Appoint out for you cities of.......... 559
Jos 21:2 **s.**, The Lord commanded by the hand... 559
Jos 22:8 **s.**, Return with much riches unto......... 559
Jos 22:15 Gilead, and they spake with them, **s.**,... 559
Jos 22:24 **s.**, In time to come your children.......... 559
Jos 22:24 **s.**, What have ye to do with the 559
Jg 1:1 **s.**, Who shall go up for us against 559
Jg 4:6 **s.**, Go and draw toward mount Tabor,.......
Jg 5:1 the son of Abinoam on that day, **s.**,...... 559
Jg 6:13 **s.**, Did not the Lord bring us up from... 559
Jg 6:32 **s.**, Let Baal plead against him, ... 559
Jg 7:2 **s.**, Mine own hand hath saved me........ 559
Jg 7:3 **s.**, Whosoever is fearful and afraid, ... 559
Jg 7:24 **s.**, Come down against...Midianites, ... 559
Jg 8:9 **s.**, When I come again in peace, I will .. 559
Jg 8:15 **s.**, Are the hands of Zebah and............ 559
Jg 9:1 the house of his mother's father, **s.**...... 559
Jg 9:31 **s.**, Behold, Gaal the son of Ebed and.... 559
Jg 10:10 **s.**, We have sinned against thee, both... 559
Jg 11:12 **s.**, What hast thou to do with me, ... 559
Jg 11:17 **s.**, Let me, I pray thee, pass through... 559
Jg 13:6 **s.**, A man of God came unto me, and ... 559
Jg 15:13 **s.**, No; but we will bind thee fast,........ 559
Jg 16:2 Gazites, **s.**, Samson is come hither....... 559
Jg 16:2 **s.**, In the morning, when it is day,....... 559
Jg 16:18 **s.**, Come up this once, for he hath....... 559
Jg 19:22 **s.**, Bring forth the man that came 559
Jg 20:8 **s.**, We will not any of us go to his 559
Jg 20:12 **s.**, What wickedness is this that is 559
Jg 20:23 **s.**, Shall I go up again to battle........... 559
Jg 20:28 **s.**, Shall I yet again go out to battle 559
Jg 21:1 **s.**, There shall not any of us give his.... 559
Jg 21:5 **s.**, He shall surely be put to death. 559

Jg 21:10 **s.**, Go and smite the inhabitants 559
Jg 21:18 **s.**, Cursed be he that giveth a wife to... 559
Jg 21:20 **s.**, Go...lie in wait in the vineyards; 559
Ru 2:15 **s.**, Let her glean even among the 559
Ru 4:4 **s.**, Buy it before the inhabitants, and.... 559
Ru 4:17 **s.**, There is a son born to Naomi; and .. 559
1Sa 1:20 **s.**, Because I have asked him of the ....
1Sa 4:21 **s.**, The glory is departed from 559
1Sa 5:10 **s.**, They have brought about the ark..... 559
1Sa 6:2 **s.**, What shall we do to the ark of the .. 559
1Sa 6:21 **s.**, The Philistines have brought........... 559
1Sa 7:3 **s.**, If ye do return unto the Lord 559
1Sa 7:12 **s.**, Hitherto hath the Lord helped us..... 559
1Sa 9:15 Lord had told Samuel in his ear...**s.**,..... 559
1Sa 9:26 **s.**, Up, that I may send thee away........ 559
1Sa 10:2 you, **s.**, What shall I do for my son?..... 559
1Sa 11:7 **s.**, Whosoever cometh not forth after ... 559
1Sa 13:3 the land, **s.**, Let the Hebrews hear. 559
1Sa 14:24, 28 **s.**, Cursed be the man that............ 559
1Sa 14:33 told Saul, **s.**, Behold, the people sin 559
1Sa 15:10 word of the Lord unto Samuel, **s.**, ... 559
1Sa 15:12 Samuel, **s.**, Saul came to Carmel, ... 559
1Sa 16:22 **s.**, Let David,...stand before me;......... 559
1Sa 17:26 **s.**, What shall be done to the man........ 559
1Sa 17:27 **s.**, So shall it be done to the man 559
1Sa 18:8 wroth, and the **s.** displeased him; 1697
1Sa 18:22 **s.**, Commune with David secretly, ...
1Sa 18:24 **s.**, On this manner spake David........... 559
1Sa 19:2 **s.**, Saul my father seeketh to kill 559
1Sa 19:11 **s.**, If thou save not thy life to night,........ 559
1Sa 19:15 **s.**, Bring him up to me in the bed,....... 559
1Sa 19:19 **s.**,...David is at Naioth in Ramah. 559
1Sa 20:16 **s.**, Let the Lord even require it at...........
1Sa 20:21 send a lad, **s.**, Go, find out the arrows......
1Sa 20:42 **s.**, The Lord be between me and.......... 559
1Sa 21:11 **s.**, Saul hath slain his thousands,.......... 559
1Sa 23:1 **s.**,...the Philistines fight against 559
1Sa 23:2 David enquired of the Lord, **s.**, Shall.... 559
1Sa 23:19 **s.**, Doth not David hide himself with..... 559
1Sa 23:27 unto Saul, **s.**, Haste thee, and come;.... 559
1Sa 24:1 **s.**, Behold, David is in the wilderness... 559
1Sa 24:8 cried after Saul, **s.**, My lord the king.... 559
1Sa 24:9 **s.**, Behold, David seeketh thy hurt? 559
1Sa 25:14 Nabal's wife, **s.**, Behold, David sent..... 559
1Sa 25:40 unto her, **s.**, David sent us unto thee, .. 559
1Sa 26:1 **s.**, Doth not David hide himself in........ 559
1Sa 26:6 **s.**, Who will go down with me to 559
1Sa 26:14 Ner, **s.**, Answerest thou not, Abner?.... 559
1Sa 26:19 the Lord, **s.**, Go, serve other gods. 559
1Sa 27:11 Gath, **s.**, Lest they should tell on us, ... 559
1Sa 27:11 **s.**, So did David, and so will be his 559
1Sa 27:12 **s.**, He hath made his people Israel 559
1Sa 28:10 **s.**, As the Lord liveth, there shall no..... 559
1Sa 28:12 **s.**, Why hast thou deceived me? for 559
1Sa 29:5 **s.**, Saul slew his thousands, and 559
1Sa 30:8 **s.**, Shall I pursue after this troop?........ 559
1Sa 30:26 **s.**, Behold a present for you of the 559
2Sa 1:16 **s.**, I have slain the Lord's anointed....... 559
2Sa 2:1 enquired of the Lord, **s.**, Shall I go 559
2Sa 2:4 **s.**, That the men of Jabesh-gilead........ 559
2Sa 3:12 on his behalf, **s.**, Whose is the land?..... 559
2Sa 3:12 **s.** also, Make thy league with me, ... 559
2Sa 3:14 Saul's son, **s.**, Deliver me my wife....... 559
2Sa 3:17 **s.**, Ye sought for David in times 559
2Sa 3:18 **s.**, By the hand of my servant David 559
2Sa 3:23 told Joab, **s.**, Abner the son of Ner 559
2Sa 3:35 David sware, **s.**, So do God to me,...... 559
2Sa 4:10 told me, **s.**, Behold, Saul is dead, ... 559
2Sa 5:1 **s.**,...we are thy bone and thy flesh........ 559
2Sa 5:6 **s.**, Except thou take away the blind...... 559
2Sa 5:19 **s.**, Shall I go up to the Philistines?....... 559
2Sa 6:12 **s.**, The Lord hath blessed the house 559
2Sa 7:4 of the Lord came unto Nathan, **s.**, ... 559
2Sa 7:7 **s.**, Why build ye not me an house of.... 559
2Sa 7:26 **s.**, The Lord of hosts is the God 559
2Sa 7:27 **s.**, I will build thee an house:............. 559
2Sa 11:6 Joab, **s.**, Send me Uriah the Hittite. 559
2Sa 11:10 **s.**, Uriah went not down unto his......... 559
2Sa 11:15 **s.**, Set ye Uriah in the forefront 559
2Sa 11:19 **s.**, When thou hast made an end of...... 559
2Sa 13:7 **s.**, Go not to thy brother Amnon's 559
2Sa 13:28 **s.**, Mark ye now when Amnon's 559
2Sa 13:30 **s.**, Absalom hath slain all the king's 559
2Sa 14:32 I sent unto thee, **s.**, Come hither, ... 559
2Sa 15:8 **s.**, If the Lord shall bring me again 559
2Sa 15:10 **s.**, As soon as ye hear the sound of..... 559
2Sa 15:13 **s.**, The hearts of the men of Israel 559

Book	Ref	Context	No.
2Sa	15:31	David, **s.**, Ahithophel is among the	559
2Sa	17:4	the **s.** pleased Absalom well, and	1697
2Sa	17:6	**s.**, Ahithophel hath spoken after	559
2Sa	17:6	shall we do after his **s.**? if not;	1697
2Sa	17:16	**s.**, Lodge not this night in the	559
2Sa	18:5	**s.**, Deal gently for my sake with the	559
2Sa	18:12	**s.**, Beware that none touch the	559
2Sa	19:8	**s.**,...the king doth sit in the gate.	559
2Sa	19:9	**s.**, The king saved us out of the	559
2Sa	19:11	**s.**, Speak unto the elders of Judah,	559
2Sa	19:11	**s.**, Why are ye the last to bring the	559
2Sa	20:18	**s.**, They were wont to speak in old	559
2Sa	20:18	**s.**, They shall surely ask counsel at	559
2Sa	21:17	**s.**, Thou shalt go no more out with	559
2Sa	24:11	the prophet Gad, David's seer, **s.**,	559
2Sa	24:19	David, according to the **s.** of Gad,	1697
1Ki	1:5	exalted himself, **s.**, I will be king:	559
1Ki	1:6	time in **s.**, Why hast thou done so?	559
1Ki	1:11	**s.**, Hast thou not heard that	559
1Ki	1:13	**s.**, Assuredly Solomon thy son shall	559
1Ki	1:17	**s.**, Assuredly Solomon thy son shall	559
1Ki	1:23	**s.**, Behold Nathan the prophet	559
1Ki	1:30	**s.**, Assuredly Solomon thy son shall	559
1Ki	1:47	**s.**, God make the name of Solomon	559
1Ki	1:51	**s.**,...Adonijah feareth king Solomon:	559
1Ki	1:51	**s.**, Let king Solomon swear unto me	559
1Ki	2:1	and he charged Solomon his son, **s.**,	559
1Ki	2:4	**s.**, If thy children take heed to their	559
1Ki	2:8	**s.**, I will not put thee to death	559
1Ki	2:23	king Solomon sware by the Lord, **s.**,	559
1Ki	2:29	of Jehoiada, **s.**, Go, fall upon him.	559
1Ki	2:30	**s.**, Thus said Joab, and thus he	559
1Ki	2:38	said unto the king, The **s.** is good:	1697
1Ki	2:39	**s.**, Behold, thy servants be in Gath.	559
1Ki	2:42	**s.**, Know for a certain, on the day	559
1Ki	5:2	And Solomon sent to Hiram, **s.**,	559
1Ki	5:5	**s.**, Thy son, whom I will set upon	559
1Ki	5:8	**s.**, I have considered the things	559
1Ki	6:11	of the Lord came to Solomon, **s.**,	559
1Ki	8:15	hath with his hand fulfilled it, **s.**,	559
1Ki	8:25	**s.**, There shall not fail thee a man	559
1Ki	8:47	**s.**, We have sinned, and have done	559
1Ki	8:55	of Israel with a loud voice, **s.**,	559
1Ki	9:5	**s.**, There shall not fail thee a man	559
1Ki	12:3	came, and spake unto Rehoboam, **s.**,	559
1Ki	12:7	**s.**, If thou wilt be a servant unto	559
1Ki	12:9	**s.**, Make the yoke which thy father	559
1Ki	12:10	**s.**, Thus shalt thou speak unto this	559
1Ki	12:10	**s.**, Thy father made our yoke heavy,	559
1Ki	12:12	**s.**, Come to me again the third day.	559
1Ki	12:14	**s.**, my father made your yoke heavy,	559
1Ki	12:15	that he might perform his **s.**,	1697
1Ki	12:16	**s.**, What portion have we in David?	559
1Ki	12:22	unto Shemaiah the man of God, **s.**,	559
1Ki	12:23	and to the remnant of the people, **s.**,	559
1Ki	13:3	**s.**, This is the sign which the Lord	559
1Ki	13:4	Jeroboam heard the **s.** of the man	1697
1Ki	13:4	from the altar, **s.**, Lay hold on him.	559
1Ki	13:9	**s.**, Eat no bread, nor drink water,	559
1Ki	13:18	**s.**, Bring him back with thee into	559
1Ki	13:21	Judah, **s.**, Thus saith the Lord,	559
1Ki	13:27	to his sons, **s.**, Saddle me the ass.	559
1Ki	13:30	over him, **s.**, Alas, my brother	
1Ki	13:31	**s.**, When I am dead, then bury me	559
1Ki	13:32	the **s.** which he cried by the word	1697
1Ki	15:18	Syria, that dwelt at Damascus, **s.**,	559
1Ki	15:29	according unto the **s.** of the Lord,	1697
1Ki	16:1	son of Hanani against Baasha, **s.**,	559
1Ki	17:2,8	of the Lord came unto him, **s.**,	559
1Ki	17:15	did according to the **s.** of Elijah:	1697
1Ki	18:1	**s.**, Go, shew thyself unto Ahab;	559
1Ki	18:26	until noon, **s.**, O Baal, hear us.	559
1Ki	18:31	came, **s.**, Israel shall be thy name;	559
1Ki	19:2	**s.**, So let the gods do to me, and	559
1Ki	20:4	according to thy **s.**, I am thine,	1697
1Ki	20:5	**s.**, Although I have sent unto thee,	559
1Ki	20:5	**s.**. Thou shalt deliver me thy	559
1Ki	20:13	**s.**, Thus saith the Lord, Hast thou	559
1Ki	20:17	**s.**, There are men come out of	559
1Ki	21:2	**s.**, Give me thy vineyard, that I may	559
1Ki	21:9	**s.**, Proclaim a fast, and set Naboth	559
1Ki	21:10	**s.**, Thou didst blaspheme God and	559
1Ki	21:13	**s.**, Naboth did blaspheme God	
1Ki	21:14	sent to Jezebel, **s.**, Naboth is stoned,	559
1Ki	21:17	Lord came to Elijah the Tishbite, **s.**,	559
1Ki	21:19	**s.**, Thus saith the Lord, Hast	559
1Ki	21:19	**s.**, Thus saith the Lord, In the	559
1Ki	21:23	**s.**, The dogs shall eat Jezebel by	559
1Ki	21:28	Lord came to Elijah the Tishbite, **s.**,	559
1Ki	22:12	**s.**, Go up to Ramoth-gilead, and	559
1Ki	22:13	**s.**, Behold now, the words of the	559
1Ki	22:31	**s.**, Fight neither with small nor	559
1Ki	22:36	**s.**, Every man to his city, and every	559
2Ki	2:22	according to the **s.** of Elisha which	1697
2Ki	3:7	**s.**, The king of Moab hath rebelled	559
2Ki	4:1	**s.**, Thy servant my husband is dead;	559
2Ki	4:31	told him, **s.**, The child is not awaked.	559
2Ki	5:4	**s.**, Thus and thus said the maid	559
2Ki	5:6	**s.**, Now when this letter is come	559
2Ki	5:8	**s.**, Wherefore hast thou rent thy	559
2Ki	5:10	**s.**, Go and wash in Jordan seven	559
2Ki	5:14	to the **s.** of the man of God: and	1697
2Ki	5:22	**s.**,...even now there be come to	559
2Ki	6:8	**s.**, In such and such a place shall be	559
2Ki	6:9	**s.**, Beware that thou pass not	559
2Ki	6:13	told him, **s.**, Behold he is in Dothan.	559
2Ki	6:26	unto him, **s.**, Help, my lord, O king.	559
2Ki	7:10	**s.**, We came to the camp of the	559
2Ki	7:12	**s.**, When they come out of the city,	559
2Ki	7:14	host of the Syrians, **s.**, Go and see.	559
2Ki	7:18	**s.**, Two measures of barley for a	559
2Ki	8:1	**s.**, Arise, and go thou and thine	559
2Ki	8:2	after the **s.** of the man of God:	1697
2Ki	8:4	**s.**, Tell me, I pray thee, all the	559
2Ki	8:6	**s.**, Restore all that was hers, and all	559
2Ki	8:7	**s.**, The man of God is come hither	559
2Ki	8:8,	9 **s.**, Shall I recover of this disease?	559
2Ki	9:12	**s.**, Thus saith the Lord, I have	559
2Ki	9:13	blew with trumpets, **s.**, Jehu is king.	559
2Ki	9:18	**s.**, The messenger came to them,	559
2Ki	9:20	**s.**, He came even unto them, and	559
2Ki	9:36	**s.**, In the portion of Jezreel shall	559
2Ki	10:1	that brought up Ahab's children, **s.**,	559
2Ki	10:5	sent to Jehu, **s.**, We are thy servants,	559
2Ki	10:6	**s.**, If ye be mine, and if ye will	559
2Ki	10:8	**s.**, They have brought the heads of	559
2Ki	10:17	according to the **s.** of the Lord,	1697
2Ki	11:5	**s.**, This is the thing that ye shall	559
2Ki	14:6	**s.**, The fathers shall not be put to	559
2Ki	14:8	**s.**, Come, let us look one another in	559
2Ki	14:9	Judah, **s.**, The thistle that was in	559
2Ki	14:9	**s.**, Give thy daughter to my son to	559
2Ki	15:12	**s.**, Thy sons shall sit on the throne of	559
2Ki	16:7	**s.**, I am thy servant and thy son:	559
2Ki	16:15	**s.**, Upon the great altar burn	559
2Ki	17:13	**s.**, Turn ye from your evil ways,	559
2Ki	17:26	**s.**, The nations which thou hast	559
2Ki	17:27	**s.**, Carry thither one of the priests	559
2Ki	17:35	**s.**, Ye shall not fear other gods, nor	559
2Ki	18:14	**s.**, I have offended; return from me	559
2Ki	18:28	**s.**, Hear the word of the great king,	559
2Ki	18:30	**s.**, The Lord will surely deliver us,	559
2Ki	18:32	you, **s.**, The Lord will deliver us.	559
2Ki	18:36	commandment...**s.**, Answer him not.	559
2Ki	19:9	messengers again unto Hezekiah, **s.**,	559
2Ki	19:10	**s.**, Let not thy God in whom thou	559
2Ki	19:10	**s.**, Jerusalem shall not be delivered	559
2Ki	19:20	**s.**, Thus saith the Lord God of Israel,	559
2Ki	20:2	wall, and prayed unto the Lord, **s.**,	559
2Ki	20:4	word of the Lord came to him, **s.**,	559
2Ki	21:10	by his servants the prophets, **s.**,	559
2Ki	22:3	scribe, to the house of the Lord, **s.**,	559
2Ki	22:10	**s.**, Hilkiah the priest hath delivered	559
2Ki	22:12	Asahiah a servant of the king's, **s.**,	559
2Ki	23:21	**s.**, Keep the passover unto the Lord	559
1Ch	4:9	**s.**, Because I bare him with sorrow.	559
1Ch	4:10	Jabez called on the God of Israel, **s.**,	559
1Ch	11:1	**s.**, Behold, we are thy bone and thy	559
1Ch	12:19	**s.**, He will fall to his master Saul to	559
1Ch	13:12	**s.**, How shall I bring the ark of God	559
1Ch	14:10	David enquired of God, **s.**, Shall I go	559
1Ch	16:18	**S.**, Unto thee will I give the land of	559
1Ch	16:22	**S.**, Touch not mine anointed, and do	
1Ch	17:3	the word of God came to Nathan, **s.**,	559
1Ch	17:6	**s.**, Why have ye not built me an	559
1Ch	17:24	**s.**, The Lord of hosts is the God of	559
1Ch	21:9	spake unto Gad, David's seer, **s.**,	559
1Ch	21:10	Go and tell David, **s.** Thus saith the	559
1Ch	21:19	David went up at the **s.** of Gad,	1697
1Ch	22:8	**s.**, Thou hast shed blood abundantly,	559
1Ch	22:17	of Israel to help Solomon his son, **s.**,	
2Ch	2:3	**s.**, As thou didst deal with David my	559
2Ch	5:13	praised the Lord, **s.**, For he is good:	
2Ch	6:4	his mouth to my father David, **s.**,	559
2Ch	6:16	**s.**, There shall not fail thee a man	559
2Ch	6:37	**s.**, We have sinned, we have done	559
2Ch	7:3	praised the Lord, **s.**, For he is good;	
2Ch	7:18	**s.**, There shall not fail thee a man	559
2Ch	10:3	came and spake to Rehoboam, **s.**,	559
2Ch	10:6	**s.**, What counsel give ye me to return	559
2Ch	10:7	**s.**, If thou be kind to this people,	559
2Ch	10:9	**s.**, Ease somewhat the yoke that thy	559
2Ch	10:10	**s.**, Thus shalt thou answer the people	559
2Ch	10:10	**s.**, Thy father made our yoke heavy,	559
2Ch	10:12	**s.**, Come again to me on the third	559
2Ch	10:14	**s.**, My father made your yoke heavy,	559
2Ch	10:16	**s.**, What portion have we in David?	559
2Ch	11:2	to Shemaiah the man of God, **s.**,	559
2Ch	11:3	all Israel in Judah and Benjamin, **s.**,	559
2Ch	12:7	**s.**, They have humbled themselves;	559
2Ch	16:2	of Syria, that dwelt at Damascus, **s.**,	559
2Ch	18:11	**s.**, Go up to Ramoth-gilead, and	559
2Ch	18:12	**s.**, Behold, the words of the prophets	559
2Ch	18:19	And one spake **s.** after this manner,	559
2Ch	18:19	and another **s.** after that manner.	559
2Ch	18:30	**s.**, Fight ye not with small or great,	559
2Ch	19:9	**s.**, Thus shall ye do in the fear of the	559
2Ch	20:2	**s.**, There cometh a great multitude	559
2Ch	20:8	a sanctuary therein for thy name, **s.**,	559
2Ch	20:37	**s.**, Because thou hast joined thyself	559
2Ch	21:12	**s.**, Thus saith the Lord God of David	559
2Ch	25:4	**s.**, The fathers shall not die for the	559
2Ch	25:7	**s.**, O king, let not the army of Israel	559
2Ch	25:17	**s.**, Come, let us see one another in	559
2Ch	25:18	**s.**, The thistle that was in Lebanon	559
2Ch	25:18	**s.**, Give thy daughter to my son to	559
2Ch	30:6	**s.**, Ye children of Israel, turn again	559
2Ch	30:18	**s.**, The good Lord pardon every one	559
2Ch	32:4	**s.**, Why should the kings of Assyria	559
2Ch	32:6	and spake comfortably to them, **s.**,	559
2Ch	32:9	all Judah that were at Jerusalem, **s.**,	559
2Ch	32:11	**s.**, The Lord our God shall deliver	559
2Ch	32:12	**s.**, Ye shall worship before one altar,	559
2Ch	32:17	**s.**, As the gods of the nations of other	559
2Ch	34:16	**s.**, All that was committed to thy	559
2Ch	34:18	**s.**, Hilkiah the priest hath given me	559
2Ch	34:20	Asaiah a servant of the king's, **s.**,	559
2Ch	35:21	**s.**, What have I to do with thee, thou	559
2Ch	36:22	and put it also in writing, **s.**,	559
Ezr	1:1	and put it also in writing, **s.**,	559
Ezr	5:11	**s.**, We are the servants of the God	560
Ezr	8:22	**s.**, The hand of our God is upon all	559
Ezr	9:1	**s.**, The people of Israel, and the	559
Ezr	9:11	**s.**, The land, unto which ye go to	559
Ne	1:8	**s.**, If ye transgress, I will scatter you	559
Ne	6:2	**s.**, Come, let us meet together in	559
Ne	6:3	**s.**, I am doing a great work, so that	559
Ne	6:7	**s.**, There is a king in Judah: and	559
Ne	6:8	**s.**, There are no such things done	559
Ne	6:9	**s.**, Their hands shall be weakened	559
Ne	8:11	**s.**, Hold your peace, for the day is	559
Ne	8:15	**s.**, Go forth unto the mount, and	559
Ne	13:25	**s.**, Ye shall not give your daughters	
Es	1:21	the **s.** pleased the king and the	1697
Job	4:16	was silence, and I heard a voice, **s.**,	
Job	8:18	deny him, **s.**, I have not seen thee.	
Job	15:23	abroad for bread, **s.**, Where is it?	
Job	24:15	twilight, **s.**, No eye shall see me:	559
Job	33:8	I have heard the voice of thy words, **s.**,	
Ps	2:2	the Lord, and against his anointed, **s.**,	
Ps	22:7	out the lip, they shake the head, **s.**,	
Ps	49:4	open my dark **s.** upon the harp.	2420
Ps	71:11	**S.**, God hath forsaken him:	559
Ps	105:11	**S.**, Unto thee will I give the land of	559
Ps	105:15	**S.**, Touch not mine anointed, and do	
Ps	119:82	**s.**, When wilt thou comfort me?	559
Ps	137:3	**s.**, Sing us one of the songs of Zion.	
Pr	1:21	in the city she uttereth her words, **s.**,	
Ec	1:16	**s.**, Lo, I am come to great estate,	559
Ca	5:2	**s.**, Open to me, my sister, my love,	
Isa	3:6	**s.**, Thou hast clothing, be thou our	
Isa	3:7	swear, **s.**, I will not be an healer;	559
Isa	4:1	**s.**, We will eat our own bread, and	559
Isa	6:8	**s.**, Whom shall I send, and who will	559
Isa	7:2	**s.**, Syria is confederate with	559
Isa	7:5	taken evil counsel against thee, **s.**,	559
Isa	7:10	the Lord spake again unto Ahaz, **s.**,	559
Isa	8:5	Lord spake also unto me again, **s.**,	559

Isa 8:11 not walk in the way of this people, **s.**, 559
Isa 14:8 **s.**, Since thou art laid down, no feller
Isa 14:16 **s.**, Is this the man that made the earth
Isa 14:24 **s.**, Surely as I have thought, so 559
Isa 16:14 **s.**, Within three years, as the years 559
Isa 18:2 **s.**, Go, ye swift messengers, to a nation
Isa 19:25 **s.**, Blessed be Egypt my people, 559
Isa 20:2 **s.**, Go and loose the sackcloth from 559
Isa 23:4 **s.**, I travail not, nor bring forth 559
Isa 29:11, 12 learned, **s.**, Read this, I pray thee: 559
Isa 30:21 **s.**, This is the way, walk ye in it, 559
Isa 36:15 **s.**, The Lord will surely deliver us: 559
Isa 36:18 you, **s.**, The Lord will deliver us. 559
Isa 36:21 commandment...**s.**, Answer him not. 559
Isa 37:9 he sent messengers to Hezekiah, **s.**, 559
Isa 37:10 **s.**, Let not thy God in whom thou 559
Isa 37:10 **s.**, Jerusalem shall not be given into 559
Isa 37:15 Hezekiah prayed unto the Lord, **s.**, 559
Isa 37:21 **s.**, Thus saith the Lord God of 559
Isa 38:4 the word of the Lord to Isaiah, **s.**, 559
Isa 41:7 **s.**, It is ready for the sodering: and 559
Isa 41:13 **s.** unto thee, Fear not; I will help 559
Isa 44:28 even **s.**, to Jerusalem, Thou shalt be 559
Isa 45:14 **s.**, Surely God is in thee; and there
Isa 46:10 **s.**, My counsel shall stand, and I 559
Isa 56:3 **s.**, The Lord hath utterly separated 559
Isa 63:11 **s.**, Where is he that brought them up
Jer 1:4 word of the Lord came unto me, **s.**, 559
Jer 1:11 me, **s.**, Jeremiah, What seest thou? 559
Jer 1:13 second time, **s.**, What seest thou? 559
Jer 2:1 the word of the Lord came to me, **s.**, 559
Jer 2:2 **s.**, Thus saith the Lord; I remember 559
Jer 2:27 **S.** to a stock, Thou art my father; 559
Jer 4:10 **s.**, Ye shall have peace; whereas the 559
Jer 4:31 **s.**, Woe is me now! for my soul is
Jer 5:20 Jacob, and publish it in Judah, **s.**, 559
Jer 6:14 **s.**, Peace, peace; when there is no 559
Jer 6:17 **s.**, Hearken to the sound of the
Jer 7:1 came to Jeremiah from the Lord, **s.**, 559
Jer 7:4 **s.**, The temple of the Lord, The 559
Jer 7:23 **s.**, Obey my voice, and I will be your 559
Jer 8:6 wickedness, **s.**, What have I done? 559
Jer 8:11 **s.**, Peace, peace; when there is no 559
Jer 11:1 came to Jeremiah from the Lord, **s.**, 559
Jer 11:4 **s.**, Obey my voice, and do them, 559
Jer 11:6 **s.**, Hear ye...words of this covenant, 559
Jer 11:7 and protesting, **s.**, Obey my voice, 559
Jer 11:19 **s.**, Let us destroy the tree with the
Jer 11:21 **s.**, Prophesy not in the name of the 559
Jer 13:3 came unto me the second time, **s.**, 559
Jer 13:8 word of the Lord came unto me, **s.**, 559
Jer 16:1 of the Lord came also unto me, **s.**,
Jer 18:1 came to Jeremiah from the Lord, **s.**, 559
Jer 18:5 word of the Lord came to me, **s.**, 559
Jer 18:11 Jerusalem, **s.**, Thus saith the Lord; 559
Jer 20:10 **s.**, Peradventure he will be enticed,
Jer 20:15 **s.**, A man child is born unto thee; 559
Jer 21:1 the son of Maaseiah the priest, **s.**, 559
Jer 22:18 **s.**, Ah my brother! or, Ah sister!
Jer 22:18 **s.**, Ah lord! or, Ah his glory!
Jer 23:25 **s.**, I have dreamed, I have dreamed. 559
Jer 23:33 **s.**, What is the burden of the Lord? 559
Jer 23:38 **s.**, Ye shall not say, The burden of 559
Jer 24:4 word of the Lord came unto me, **s.**, 559
Jer 25:2 all the inhabitants of Jerusalem, **s.**, 559
Jer 26:1 came this from the Lord, **s.**, 559
Jer 26:8 took him, **s.**, Thou shalt surely die. 559
Jer 26:9 **s.**, This house shall be like Shiloh, 559
Jer 26:11 **s.**, This man is worthy to die; for 559
Jer 26:12 **s.**, The Lord sent me to prophesy 559
Jer 26:17 to all the assembly of the people, **s.**, 559
Jer 26:18 **s.**, Thus saith the Lord of hosts; 559
Jer 27:1 unto Jeremiah from the Lord, **s.**, 559
Jer 27:9 **s.**, Ye shall not serve the king of 559
Jer 27:12 **s.**, Bring your necks under the yoke 559
Jer 27:14 **s.**, Ye shall not serve the king of 559
Jer 27:16 people, **s.**, Thus saith the Lord; 559
Jer 27:16 you, **s.**,...the vessels of the Lord's 559
Jer 28:1 the priests and of all the people, **s.**, 559
Jer 28:2 **s.**, I have broken the yoke of the 559
Jer 28:11 the people, **s.**, Thus saith the Lord; 559
Jer 28:12 the neck of the prophet Jeremiah, **s.**, 559
Jer 28:13 Go and tell Hananiah, **s.**, Thus 559
Jer 29:3 Nebuchadnezzar king of Babylon,) **s.**, 559
Jer 29:22 **s.**,...Lord make thee like Zedekiah 559
Jer 29:24 to Shemaiah the Nehelamite, **s.**, 559
Jer 29:25 **s.**, Because thou hast sent letters 559
Jer 29:25 priest, and to all the priests, **s.**, 559
Jer 29:28 Babylon, **s.**, This captivity is long: 559
Jer 29:30 word of the Lord unto Jeremiah, **s.**, 559
Jer 29:31 **s.**, Thus saith the Lord concerning 559
Jer 30:1 came to Jeremiah from the Lord, **s.**, 559
Jer 30:2 **s.**, Write thee all the words that I 559
Jer 30:17 Outcast, **s.**, This is Zion, whom no man
Jer 31:3 me, **s.**, Yea, I have loved thee with an
Jer 31:34 his brother, **s.**, Know the Lord: 559
Jer 32:3 **s.**, Wherefore dost thou prophesy, 559
Jer 32:6 word of the Lord came unto me, **s.**, 559
Jer 32:7 **s.**, Buy thee my field that is in 559
Jer 32:13 I charged Baruch before them, **s.**, 559
Jer 32:16 Neriah, I prayed unto the Lord, **s.**, 559
Jer 32:26 word of the Lord unto Jeremiah, **s.**, 559
Jer 33:1 shut up in the court of the prison, **s.**, 559
Jer 33:19 of the Lord came unto Jeremiah, **s.**, 559
Jer 33:23 of the Lord came to Jeremiah, **s.**, 559
Jer 33:24 **s.**, The two families which the Lord 559
Jer 34:1 and against all the cities thereof, **s.**, 559
Jer 34:5 **s.**, Ah lord! for I have pronounced
Jer 34:12 to Jeremiah from the Lord, **s.**, 559
Jer 34:13 out of the house of bondmen, **s.**, 559
Jer 35:1 the son of Josiah king of Judah, **s.**, 559
Jer 35:6 **s.**, Ye shall drink no wine, neither 559
Jer 35:12 word of the Lord unto Jeremiah, **s.**, 559
Jer 35:15 **s.**, Return ye now every man from 559
Jer 36:1 unto Jeremiah from the Lord, **s.**, 559
Jer 36:5 **s.**, I am shut up; I cannot go into 559
Jer 36:14 **s.**, Take in thine hand the roll 559
Jer 36:17 they asked Baruch, **s.**, Tell us now, 559
Jer 36:27 wrote at the mouth of Jeremiah, **s.**, 559
Jer 36:29 **s.**, Why hast thou written therein, 559
Jer 36:29 **s.**, The king of Babylon shall 559
Jer 37:3 **s.**, Pray now unto the Lord our 559
Jer 37:6 Lord unto the prophet Jeremiah, **s.**, 559
Jer 37:9 **s.**, The Chaldeans shall surely 559
Jer 37:13 prophet, **s.**, Thou fallest away to the 559
Jer 37:19 **s.**, The king of Babylon shall not 559
Jer 38:1 had spoken unto all the people, **s.**, 559
Jer 38:8 house, and spake to the king, **s.**, 559
Jer 38:10 **s.**, Take from hence thirty men with 559
Jer 38:16 **s.**, As the Lord liveth, that made 559
Jer 39:11 the captain of the guard, **s.**, 559
Jer 39:15 shut up in the court of the prison, **s.**, 559
Jer 39:16 **s.**, Thus saith the Lord of hosts, 559
Jer 40:9 **s.**, Fear not to serve the Chaldeans: 559
Jer 40:15 **s.**, Let me go, I pray thee, and I 559
Jer 42:14 **S.**, No; but we will go into the land 559
Jer 42:20 **s.**, Pray for us unto the Lord our 559
Jer 43:2 **s.** unto Jeremiah, Thou speakest 559
Jer 43:8 unto Jeremiah in Tahpanhes, **s.**, 559
Jer 44:1 and in the country of Pathros, **s.**, 559
Jer 44:4 **s.**, Oh, do not this abominable thing 559
Jer 44:15 in Pathros, answered Jeremiah, **s.**, 559
Jer 44:20 which had given him that answer, **s.**, 559
Jer 44:25 **s.**; Ye and your wives have both 559
Jer 44:25 **s.**, We will surely perform our vows 559
Jer 44:26 of Egypt, **s.**, The Lord God liveth 559
Jer 45:1 the son of Josiah king of Judah, **s.**, 559
Jer 48:39 shall howl, **s.**, How is it broken down!
Jer 49:4 **s.**, Who shall come unto me?
Jer 49:14 **s.**, Gather ye together, and come
Jer 49:34 of Zedekiah king of Judah, **s.**, 559
Jer 50:5 **s.**, Come, and let us join ourselves
Jer 51:14 **s.**, Surely I will fill thee with men, as
La 2:15 **s.**, Is this the city that men call The
Eze 3:12 **s.**, Blessed be the glory of the Lord
Eze 3:16 word of the Lord came unto me, **s.**, 559
Eze 6:1 word of the Lord came unto me, **s.**, 559
Eze 7:1 word of the Lord came unto me, **s.**, 559
Eze 9:1 **s.**, Cause them that have charge 559
Eze 9:11 **s.**, I have done as thou...commanded 559
Eze 10:6 **s.**, Take fire from between the 559
Eze 11:14 word of the Lord came unto me, **s.**, 559
Eze 12:1 of the Lord also came unto me, **s.**, 559
Eze 12:8 the word of the Lord unto me, **s.**, 559
Eze 12:17 the word of the Lord came to me, **s.**, 559
Eze 12:21 word of the Lord came unto me, **s.**, 559
Eze 12:22 **s.**, The days are prolonged, and 559
Eze 12:26 the word of the Lord came to me, **s.**, 559
Eze 13:1 word of the Lord came unto me, **s.**, 559
Eze 13:6 lying divination, **s.**, The Lord saith: 559
Eze 13:10 have seduced my people, **s.**, Peace; 559
Eze 14:2 word of the Lord came unto me, **s.**, 559
Eze 14:12 of the Lord came again to me, **s.**, 559
Eze 15:1 word of the Lord came unto me, **s.**, 559
Eze 16:1 word of the Lord came unto me, **s.**, 559
Eze 16:44 **s.**, As...the mother, so...her daughter. 559
Eze 17:1, 11 of the Lord came unto me, **s.**, 559
Eze 18:1 of the Lord came unto me again, **s.**, 559
Eze 18:2 **s.**, The fathers have eaten sour 559
Eze 20:2 the word of the Lord unto me, **s.**, 559
Eze 20:5 them, **s.**, I am the Lord your God; 559
Eze 20:45 word of the Lord came unto me, **s.**, 559
Eze 21:1, 8 word of the Lord came unto me, **s.**, 559
Eze 21:18 of the Lord came unto me again, **s.**, 559
Eze 22:1, 17,23 of the Lord came unto me, **s.**, 559
Eze 22:28 **s.**, Thus saith the Lord God, when 559
Eze 23:1 the Lord came again unto me, **s.**, 559
Eze 24:1, 15,20 of the Lord came unto me, **s.**, 559
Eze 25:1 of the Lord came again unto me, **s.**, 559
Eze 26:1 word of the Lord came unto me, **s.**, 559
Eze 27:1 of the Lord came again unto me, **s.**, 559
Eze 27:32 **s.**, What city is like Tyrus, like the
Eze 28:1 of the Lord came again unto me, **s.**, 559
Eze 28:11, 20 of the Lord came unto me, **s.**, 559
Eze 29:1, 17 of the Lord came unto me, **s.**, 559
Eze 30:1 the Lord came again unto me, **s.**, 559
Eze 30:20 word of the Lord came unto me, **s.**, 559
Eze 31:1 word of the Lord came unto me, **s.**, 559
Eze 32:1, 17 of the Lord came unto me, **s.**, 559
Eze 33:1 word of the Lord came unto me, **s.**, 559
Eze 33:10 **s.**, If our transgressions and our 559
Eze 33:21 unto me, **s.**, The city is smitten. 559
Eze 33:23 word of the Lord came unto me, **s.**, 559
Eze 33:24 speak, **s.**, Abraham was one, and he 559
Eze 33:30 **s.**, Come, I pray you, and hear what 559
Eze 34:1 word of the Lord came unto me, **s.**, 559
Eze 35:1 word of the Lord came unto me, **s.**, 559
Eze 35:12 **s.**, They are laid desolate, they are 559
Eze 36:16 word of the Lord came unto me, **s.**, 559
Eze 37:15 of the Lord came again unto me, **s.**, 559
Eze 37:18 **s.**, Wilt thou not shew us what thou 559
Eze 38:1 word of the Lord came unto me, **s.**, 559
Da 4:8 and before him I told the dream, **s.**,
Da 4:23 **s.**, Hew the tree down, and destroy 560
Da 4:31 **s.**, O king Nebuchadnezzar, to thee
Am 2:12 the prophets, **s.**, Prophesy not. 559
Am 3:1 up from the land of Egypt, **s.** 559
Am 7:10 **s.**, Amos hath conspired against the 559
Am 8:5 **S.**, When will the new moon be gone, 559
Jon 1:1 unto Jonah the son of Amittai, **s.**, 559
Jon 3:1 unto Jonah the second time, **s.**, 559
Jon 3:7 **s.**, Let neither man nor beast, herd 559
Jon 4:2 was not this my **s.**, when I was 1697
Mic 2:11 **s.**, I will prophesy unto thee of wine
Hag 1:1 son of Josedech, the high priest, **s.**, 559
Hag 1:2 **s.**, This people say, The time is not 559
Hag 1:3 the Lord by Haggai the prophet, **s.**, 559
Hag 1:13 **s.**, I am with you, saith the Lord. 559
Hag 2:1 the Lord by the prophet Haggai, **s.**, 559
Hag 2:2 and to the residue of the people, **s.**, 559
Hag 2:10 the Lord by Haggai the prophet, **s.**, 559
Hag 2:11 the priests concerning the law, **s.**, 559
Hag 2:20 and twentieth day of the month, **s.**, 559
Hag 2:21 **s.**, I will shake the heavens and the 559
Zec 1:1 the son of Iddo the prophet, **s.**, The 559
Zec 1:4 **s.**, Thus saith the Lord of hosts; 559
Zec 1:7 the son of Iddo the prophet, **s.**, 559
Zec 1:14 Cry thou, **s.**, Thus saith the Lord of 559
Zec 1:17 Cry yet, **s.**, Thus saith the Lord of 559
Zec 1:21 **s.**, These are the horns which have 559
Zec 2:4 **s.**, Jerusalem shall be inhabited as 559
Zec 3:4 **s.**, Take away the filthy garments 559
Zec 3:6 the Lord protested unto Joshua, **s.**, 559
Zec 4:4 me, **s.**, What are these, my lord? 559
Zec 4:6 **s.**, This is the word of the Lord unto 559
Zec 4:6 **s.**, not by might, nor by power, but 559
Zec 4:8 word of the Lord came unto me, **s.**, 559
Zec 6:8 **s.**,...these that go toward the north 559
Zec 6:9 word of the Lord came unto me, **s.**, 559
Zec 6:12 **s.**, Thus speaketh the Lord of hosts, 559
Zec 6:12 **s.**, Behold the man whose name is 559
Zec 7:3 **s.**, Should I weep in the fifth month, 559
Zec 7:4 of the Lord of hosts unto me, **s.**, 559
Zec 7:5 **s.**, When ye fasted and mourned in 559
Zec 7:8 of the Lord came unto Zechariah, **s.**, 559
Zec 7:9 **s.**, Execute true judgment, and shew 559
Zec 8:1 the Lord of hosts came to me, **s.**, 559
Zec 8:18 the Lord of hosts came unto me, **s.**, 559
Zec 8:21 **s.**, Let us go speedily to pray before 559
Zec 8:23 **s.**, We will go with you: for we have 559
Mt 1:20 **s.**, Joseph, thou son of David, fear *3004*

Mt 1:22 of the Lord by the prophet, s., 3004
Mt 2:2 S., Where is he that is born King 3004
Mt 2:13 s., Arise, and take the young child 3004
Mt 2:15 s., Out of Egypt have I called my 3004
Mt 2:17 spoken by Jeremy the prophet, s., 3004
Mt 2:20 S., Arise, and take the young child 3004
Mt 3:2 And s., Repent ye: for the kingdom 3004
Mt 3:3 s., The voice of one crying in the 3004
Mt 3:14 s., I have need to be baptized of 3004
Mt 3:17 s., This is my beloved Son, in whom 3004
Mt 4:14 spoken by Esaias the prophet, s., 3004
Mt 5:2 his mouth, and taught them, s., 3004
Mt 6:31 no thought, s., What shall we eat? 3004
Mt 8:2 s., Lord, if thou wilt, thou canst 3004
Mt 8:3 him, s., I will; be thou clean 3004
Mt 8:6 s., Lord, my servant lieth at home 3004
Mt 8:17 s., Himself took our infirmities, and 3004
Mt 8:25 him, s., Lord, save us: we perish 3004
Mt 8:27 s., What manner of man is this, that 3004
Mt 8:29 s., What have we to do with thee, 3004
Mt 8:31 s., If thou cast us out, suffer us to 3004
Mt 9:14 s., Why do we and the Pharisees 3004
Mt 9:18 s., My daughter is even now dead: 3004
Mt 9:27 s., Thou son of David, have mercy 3004
Mt 9:29 s., According to your faith be it 3004
Mt 9:30 them, s., See that no man know it. 3004
Mt 9:33 s., It was never so seen in Israel. 3004
Mt 10:5 s., Go not into the way of 3004
Mt 10:7 as ye go, preach, s. the kingdom
Mt 11:17 s., We have piped unto you, and 3004
Mt 12:10 s., Is it lawful to heal on…sabbath 3004
Mt 12:17 spoken by Esaias the prophet, s., 3004
Mt 12:38 s., Master, we would see a sign from 3004
Mt 13:3 s., Behold, a sower went forth to 3004
Mt 13:24 them s., The kingdom of heaven is 3004
Mt 13:31 s., The kingdom of heaven is like 3004
Mt 13:35 s., I open my mouth in parables; 3004
Mt 13:36 s., Declare unto us the parable of 3004
Mt 14:15 s., This is a desert place, and the 3004
Mt 14:26 s., It is a spirit; and they cried out 3004
Mt 14:27 s., Be of good cheer; it is I; be 3004
Mt 14:30 to sink, he cried, s., Lord, save me 3004
Mt 14:33 s., Of a truth thou art the Son of 3004
Mt 15:1 and Pharisees,…of Jerusalem, s., 3004
Mt 15:4 s., Honour thy father and mother: 3004
Mt 15:7 did Esaias prophesy of you, s., 3004
Mt 15:12 offended, after they heard this s.? 3056
Mt 15:22 s., Have mercy on me, O Lord, 3004
Mt 15:23 s., Send her away; for she crieth 3004
Mt 15:25 worshipped him, s., Lord, help me. 3004
Mt 16:7 s., It is because we have taken no 3004
Mt 16:13 s., Whom do men say that I the 3004
Mt 16:22 him, s., Be it far from thee, Lord: 3004
Mt 17:9 s., Tell the vision to no man, until 3004
Mt 17:10 s., Why then say the scribes that 3004
Mt 17:14 man, kneeling down to him, and s., 3004
Mt 17:25 s., What thinkest thou, Simon? 3004
Mt 18:1 Jesus, s., Who is the greatest in the 3004
Mt 18:26 s., Lord, have patience with me, 3004
Mt 18:28 s., Pay me that thou owest. 3004
Mt 18:29 s., Have patience with me, and I 3004
Mt 19:3 tempting him, and s. unto him, Is 3004
Mt 19:11 All men cannot receive this s., 3056
Mt 19:22 when the young man heard that s., 3056
Mt 19:25 s., Who then can be saved? 3004
Mt 20:12 S., These last have wrought but 3004
Mt 20:30, 31 s., Have mercy on us, O Lord, 3004
Mt 21:2 S. unto them, Go into the village 3004
Mt 21:4 was spoken by the prophet, s., 3004
Mt 21:9 s., Hosanna to the son of David: 3004
Mt 21:10 the city was moved, s., Who is this? 3004
Mt 21:15 s., Hosanna to the son of David; 3004
Mt 21:20 s., How soon is the fig tree 3004
Mt 21:25 s., If we shall say, From heaven; he 3004
Mt 21:37 son, s., They will reverence my 3004
Mt 22:4 s., Tell them which are bidden. 3004
Mt 22:16 s., Master, we know that thou art 3004
Mt 22:24 S., Master, Moses said, If a man 3004
Mt 22:31 was spoken unto you by God, s., 3004
Mt 22:35 a question, tempting him, and s., 3004
Mt 22:42 S., What think ye of Christ? 3004
Mt 22:43 David in spirit call him Lord, s., 3004
Mt 23:2 S., The scribes and the Pharisees 3004
Mt 24:3 s., Tell us, when shall these things 3004
Mt 24:5 come in my name, s., I am Christ; 3004
Mt 25:9 s., Not so; lest there be not 3004
Mt 25:11 virgins, s., Lord, Lord, open to us 3004
Mt 25:20 and brought other five talents, s., 3004
Mt 25:37, 44 s., Lord, when saw we thee an 3004
Mt 25:45 s., Verily I say unto you, 3004
Mt 26:8 s., To what purpose is this waste? 3004
Mt 26:17 s. unto him, Where wilt thou that 3004
Mt 26:27 it to them, s., Drink ye all of it; 3004
Mt 26:39 s., O my Father, if it be possible, 3004
Mt 26:42 s., O my Father, if this cup 3004
Mt 26:44 the third time, s. the same words. 2036
Mt 26:48 s., Whomsoever I shall kiss, that 3004
Mt 26:65 s., He hath spoken blasphemy; 3004
Mt 26:68 S., Prophesy unto us, thou Christ, 3004
Mt 26:69 s., Thou also wast with Jesus of 3004
Mt 26:70 s., I know not what thou sayest 3004
Mt 26:74 and to swear, s., I know not the man.
Mt 27:4 S., I have sinned in that I have 3004
Mt 27:9 s., And they took the thirty pieces 3004
Mt 27:11 s., Art thou the King of the Jews? 3004
Mt 27:19 s., Have thou nothing to do with 3004
Mt 27:23 the more, s., Let him be crucified. 3004
Mt 27:24 s., I am innocent of the blood of 3004
Mt 27:29 him, s., Hail, King of the Jews! 3004
Mt 27:40 And s., Thou that destroyest the 3004
Mt 27:46 s., Eli, Eli, lama sabachthani? 3004
Mt 27:54 s., Truly this was the Son of God. 3004
Mt 27:63 S., Sir, we remember that that 3004
Mt 28:9 behold, Jesus met them, s., All hail. 3004
Mt 28:13 S., Say ye, His disciples came by 3004
Mt 28:15 and this s. is commonly reported 3056
Mt 28:18 s., All power is given unto me in 3004
Mk 1:7 s., There cometh one mightier than 3004
Mk 1:11 heaven, s., Thou art my beloved Son,
Mk 1:15 s., The time is fulfilled, and the 3004
Mk 1:24 S., Let us alone; what have we to 3004
Mk 1:25 s., Hold thy peace, and come out 3004
Mk 1:27 themselves, s., What thing is this? 3004
Mk 1:40 and s. unto him, If thou wilt, thou 3004
Mk 2:12 s., We never saw it on this fashion 3004
Mk 3:11 cried, s., Thou art the Son of God. 3004
Mk 3:33 s., Who is my mother, or my 3004
Mk 5:9 answered, s., My name is Legion: 3004
Mk 5:12 s., Send us into the swine, that we 3004
Mk 5:23 s., My little daughter lieth at the 3004
Mk 6:2 s., From whence hath this man 3004
Mk 6:25 s., I will that thou give me by and 3004
Mk 7:29 unto her, For this s. go thy way; 3056
Mk 7:37 s., He hath done all things well: 3004
Mk 8:15 he charged them, s., Take heed, 3004
Mk 8:16 s., It is because we have no bread. 3004
Mk 8:26 s., Neither go into the town, nor 3004
Mk 8:27 s. unto them, Whom do men say 3004
Mk 8:32 And he spake that s. openly. And 3056
Mk 8:33 s., Get thee behind me, Satan: 3004
Mk 9:7 s., This is my beloved Son: hear 3004
Mk 9:10 they kept that s. with themselves, 3056
Mk 9:11 s., Why say the scribes that Elias 3004
Mk 9:25 s. unto him, Thou dumb and deaf 3004
Mk 9:32 But they understood not that s. 4487
Mk 9:38 s., Master, we saw one casting out 3004
Mk 10:22 he was sad at that s., and went 3056
Mk 10:26 s. among themselves, Who then 3004
Mk 10:33 S., Behold, we go up to Jerusalem
Mk 10:35 s., Master, we would that thou 3004
Mk 10:49 s. unto him, Be of good comfort, 3004
Mk 11:9 s., Hosanna; Blessed is he that 3004
Mk 11:17 s. unto them, Is it not written, My 3004
Mk 11:31 s., If we shall say, From heaven; 3004
Mk 12:6 s., They will reverence my son. 3004
Mk 12:18 and they asked him, s., 3004
Mk 12:26 s., I am the God of Abraham, and 3004
Mk 13:6 s., I am Christ; and shall deceive 3004
Mk 14:44 s., Whomsoever I shall kiss, that 3004
Mk 14:57 bare false witness against him, s., 3004
Mk 14:60 s., Answerest thou nothing? what 3004
Mk 14:68 he denied, s., I know not, neither 3004
Mk 14:71 s., I know not this man of whom ye
Mk 15:4 again, s., Answerest thou nothing? 3004
Mk 15:9 s., Will ye that I release unto you 3004
Mk 15:29 and s., Ah, thou that destroyest the 3004
Mk 15:34 s., Eloi, Eloi, lama sabachthani? 3004
Mk 15:36 gave him to drink, s., Let alone; 3004
Lu 1:24 and hid herself five months, s., 3004
Lu 1:29 him, she was troubled at his s., 3056
Lu 1:63 and wrote, s., His name is John. 3004
Lu 1:66 s., What manner of child shall this 3004
Lu 1:67 the Holy Ghost, and prophesied, s., 3004
Lu 2:13 heavenly host praising God, and s., 3004
Lu 2:17 abroad the s. which was told 4487
Lu 2:50 the s. which he spake unto them. 4487
Lu 3:4 s., The voice of one crying in the 3004
Lu 3:10 him, s., What shall we do then? 3004
Lu 3:14 him, s., And what shall we do? 3004
Lu 3:16 John answered, s. unto them all, 3004
Lu 4:4 s., It is written, That man shall 3004
Lu 4:34 S., Let us alone; what have we to 3004
Lu 4:35 rebuked him, s., Hold thy peace, 3004
Lu 4:36 themselves, s., What a word is this! 3004
Lu 4:41 s., Thou art Christ the Son of God. 3004
Lu 5:8 s., Depart from me; for I am a 3004
Lu 5:12 s., Lord, if thou wilt, thou canst 3004
Lu 5:13 him, s., I will: be thou clean 2036
Lu 5:21 s., Who is this which speaketh 3004
Lu 5:26 s., We have seen strange things to 3004
Lu 5:30 s., Why do ye eat and drink, with 3004
Lu 7:4 s., That he was worthy for whom 3004
Lu 7:6 s. unto him, Lord, trouble not 3004
Lu 7:16 s., That a great prophet is risen up 3004
Lu 7:19, 20 s., Art thou he that should 3004
Lu 7:32 s., We have piped unto you, and 3004
Lu 7:39 s., This man, if he were a prophet, 3004
Lu 8:9 s., What might this parable be? 3004
Lu 8:24 him, s., Master, master, we perish 3004
Lu 8:25 s. one to another, What manner of 3004
Lu 8:30 s., What is thy name? And he 3004
Lu 8:38 him: but Jesus sent him away, s., 3004
Lu 8:49 s. to him, Thy daughter is dead; 3004
Lu 8:50 s., Fear not: believe only, and 3004
Lu 8:54 hand, and called, s., Maid, arise. 3004
Lu 9:18 s., Whom say the people that I 3004
Lu 9:22 S., The Son of man must suffer 2036
Lu 9:35 s., This is my beloved Son: hear 3004
Lu 9:38 s., Master, I beseech thee, look 3004
Lu 9:45 But they understood not this s., 4487
Lu 9:45 they feared to ask him of that s. 4487
Lu 10:17 s., Lord, even the devils are subject 3004
Lu 10:25 s.,…what shall I do to inherit 3004
Lu 11:45 thus s. thou reproachest us also. 3004
Lu 12:16 s., The ground of a certain rich 3004
Lu 12:17 And he thought within himself, s., 3004
Lu 13:25 s., Lord, Lord, open unto us; and 3004
Lu 13:31 s. unto him, Get thee out, and 3004
Lu 14:3 s., Is it lawful to heal on the 3004
Lu 14:5 s., Which of you shall have an ass 2036
Lu 14:7 the chief rooms; s. unto them, 3004
Lu 14:30 S., This man began to build, and 3004
Lu 15:2 s., This man receiveth sinners, and 3004
Lu 15:3 spake this parable unto them, s. 3004
Lu 15:6 s. unto them, Rejoice with me; 3004
Lu 15:9 s., Rejoice with me; for I have 3004
Lu 17:4 s., I repent; thou shalt forgive 3004
Lu 18:2 S., There was in a city a judge, 3004
Lu 18:3 s., Avenge me of mine adversary. 3004
Lu 18:13 s., God be merciful to me a sinner. 3004
Lu 18:18 s., Good Master, what shall I do to 3004
Lu 18:34 this s. was hid from them, neither 4487
Lu 18:38 cried, s., Jesus, thou son of David 3004
Lu 18:41 S., What wilt thou that I shall do 3004
Lu 19:7 s., That he was gone to be guest 3004
Lu 19:14 s., We will not have this man to 3004
Lu 19:16, 18 s., Lord, thy pound hath gained 3004
Lu 19:20 s., Lord, behold, here is thy pound, 3004
Lu 19:30 S., Go ye into the village over 2036
Lu 19:38 S., Blessed be the King that 3004
Lu 19:42 S., If thou hadst known, even 3004
Lu 19:46 S. unto them, It is written, My 3004
Lu 20:2 s., Tell us, by what authority doest 3004
Lu 20:5 s., If we shall say, From heaven; 3004
Lu 20:14 s., This is the heir: come, let us 3004
Lu 20:21 s., Master, we know…thou sayest 3004
Lu 20:28 S., Master, Moses wrote unto us, 3004
Lu 21:7 s., Master…when shall these things 3004
Lu 21:8 s., I am Christ; and the time 3004
Lu 22:8 s. Go and prepare us the passover, 2036
Lu 22:19 s., This is my body which is given 3004
Lu 22:20 s., This cup is the new testament 3004
Lu 22:42 S., Father, if thou be willing, 3004
Lu 22:57 him, s., Woman, I know him not. 3004
Lu 22:59 s., Of a truth this fellow also was 3004
Lu 22:64 s., Prophesy, who is it that smote 3004
Lu 22:66 and led him into their council, s., 3004
Lu 23:2 s., We found this fellow perverting 3004
Lu 23:2 s. that he himself is Christ a King. 3004
Lu 23:3 s., Art thou the King of the Jews? 3004
Lu 23:5 fierce, s., He stirreth up the people, 3004

Lu	23:18	**s.**, Away with this man, and release	*3004*
Lu	23:21	cried, **s.**, Crucify him, crucify him	*3004*
Lu	23:35	**s.**, He saved others; let him save	*3004*
Lu	23:37	**s.**, If thou be the king of the Jews,	*3004*
Lu	23:39	**s.**, If thou be Christ, save thyself	*3004*
Lu	23:40	**s.**, Dost not thou fear God, seeing	*3004*
Lu	23:47	**s.**, Certainly this was a righteous	*3004*
Lu	24:7	**S.**, The Son of man must be	*3004*
Lu	24:23	**s.**, that they had also seen a vision	*3004*
Lu	24:29	constrained him, **s.**, Abide with us:	*3004*
Lu	24:34	**S.**, The Lord is risen indeed, and	*3004*
Joh	1:15	**s.**, This was he of whom I spake,	*3004*
Joh	1:26	**s.**, I baptize with water: but there	*3004*
Joh	1:32	**s.**, I saw the Spirit descending	*3004*
Joh	4:31	prayed him, **s.**, Master, eat.	*3004*
Joh	4:37	**herein is that s. true, One soweth,**	*3056*
Joh	4:39	on him for the **s.** of the woman,	*3056*
Joh	4:42	we believe, not because of thy **s.**:	*2981*
Joh	4:51	and told him, **s.**, Thy son liveth.	*3004*
Joh	6:52	**s.**, How can this man give us his	*3004*
Joh	6:60	This is an hard **s.**; who can hear it?	*3056*
Joh	7:15	**s.**, How knoweth this man letters,	*3004*
Joh	7:28	**s.**, **Ye both know me, and ye know**	*3004*
Joh	7:36	manner of **s.** is this that he said,	*3056*
Joh	7:37	**s.**, **if any man thirst, let him come**	*3004*
Joh	7:40	when they heard this **s.**, said, Of a	*3056*
Joh	8:12	**s.**, **I am the light of the world: he**	*3004*
Joh	8:51	**If a man keep my s., he shall**	*3056*
Joh	8:52	If a man keep my **s.** he	
Joh	8:55	**but I know him, and keep his s.,**	*3056*
Joh	9:2	**s.**, Master, who did sin, this man,	*3004*
Joh	9:19	**s.**, Is this your son, who ye say was	*3004*
Joh	10:33	**s.**, For a good work we stone thee	*3004*
Joh	11:3	**s.**, Lord,...he whom thou lovest is	*3004*
Joh	11:28	**s.**, The Master is come, and calleth	*2036*
Joh	11:31	**s.**, She goeth unto the grave to	*3004*
Joh	11:32	**s.** unto him, Lord, if thou hadst	*3004*
Joh	12:21	him, **s.**, Sir, we would see Jesus.	*3004*
Joh	12:23	**s.**, **The hour is come, that the Son**	*3004*
Joh	12:28	**s.**, I have both glorified it, and will	
Joh	12:38	That the **s.** of Esaias the prophet	*3056*
Joh	15:20	**if they have kept my s., they will**	*3056*
Joh	18:9	That the **s.** might be fulfilled,	*3056*
Joh	18:22	**s.**, Answerest thou the high priest	*2036*
Joh	18:32	**s.** of Jesus might be fulfilled,	*3056*
Joh	18:40	**s.**, Not this man, but Barabbas.	*3004*
Joh	19:6	out, **s.**, Crucify him, crucify him	*3004*
Joh	19:8	Pilate therefore heard that **s.**, he	*3056*
Joh	19:12	**s.**, If thou let this man go, thou	*3004*
Joh	19:13	Pilate therefore heard that **s.**, he	*3056*
Joh	21:23	this **s.** abroad among the brethren,	*3056*
Ac	1:6	**s.**, Lord, wilt thou at this time	*3004*
Ac	2:7	**s.** one to another, Behold, are not	*3004*
Ac	2:12	**s.** one to another, What meaneth	*3004*
Ac	2:40	**s.**, Save yourselves from this	*3004*
Ac	3:25	**s.**, unto Abraham, And in thy seed	*3004*
Ac	4:16	**S.**, What shall we do to these men?	*3004*
Ac	5:23	**S.**, The prison truly found we shut	*3004*
Ac	5:25	**s.**, Behold, the men whom ye put	*3004*
Ac	5:28	**S.**, Did not we straitly command	*3004*
Ac	6:5	**s.**, pleased the whole multitude:	*3056*
Ac	7:26	**s.**, Sirs, ye are brethren; why do	*2036*
Ac	7:27	**s.**, Who made thee a ruler and a	*2036*
Ac	7:29	Then fled Moses at this **s.**, and	*3056*
Ac	7:32	**S.**, I am the God of thy fathers, the	
Ac	7:35	**s.**, Who made thee a ruler and a	*2036*
Ac	7:40	**S.** unto Aaron, Make us gods to go	*2036*
Ac	7:59	**s.**, Lord Jesus, receive my spirit.	*3007*
Ac	8:10	**s.**, This man is the great power of	*3007*
Ac	8:19	**S.**, Give me also this power, that on	*3007*
Ac	8:26	**s.**, Arise and go toward the south	*3007*
Ac	9:4	a voice **s.** unto him, **Saul, Saul, why**	*3007*
Ac	10:3	him, and **s.** unto him, Cornelius.	*2036*
Ac	10:26	Peter took him up, **s.**, Stand up;	*3004*
Ac	11:3	**S.**, Thou wentest in to men	*3004*
Ac	11:4	expounded it by order unto them, **s.**,	*3004*
Ac	11:7	I heard a voice **s.** unto me, Arise,	*3004*
Ac	11:18	**s.**, Then hath God also to the	*3004*
Ac	12:7	raised him up, **s.**, Rise up quickly	*3004*
Ac	12:22	**s.**, It is the voice of a god, and not	
Ac	13:15	**s.**, Ye men and brethren, if ye have	*3004*
Ac	13:47	**s.**, I have set thee to be a light of the	
Ac	14:11	**s.** in the speech of Lycaonia, The	*3004*
Ac	14:15	**s.**, Sirs, why do ye these things?	*3004*
Ac	15:5	**s.**,...it was needful to circumcise	*3004*
Ac	15:13	**s.**, Men and brethren, hearken unto	*3004*
Ac	15:24	**s.**, Ye must be circumcised, and	*3004*
Ac	16:9	**s.**, Come over into Macedonia, and	*3004*
Ac	16:15	**s.**, If ye have judged me to be	*3004*
Ac	16:17	**s.**, These men are the servants of	*3004*
Ac	16:20	**s.**, These men, being Jews, do	*2036*
Ac	16:28	**s.**, Do thyself no harm: for we	*3004*
Ac	16:35	serjeants, **s.**, Let those men go.	*3004*
Ac	16:36	of the prison told this **s.** to Paul,	*3056*
Ac	17:7	**s.** that there is another king, one	*3004*
Ac	17:19	**s.**, May we know what this new	*3004*
Ac	18:13	**S.**, This fellow persuadeth men to	*3004*
Ac	18:21	**s.**, I must by all means keep this	*2036*
Ac	19:4	**s.** unto the people, that they should	*3004*
Ac	19:13	**s.**, We adjure you by Jesus whom	*3004*
Ac	19:21	**s.**, After I have been there, I must	*2036*
Ac	19:26	**s.** that they be no gods, which are	*3004*
Ac	19:28	**s.**, Great is Diana of the Ephesians	*3004*
Ac	20:23	**s.** that the bonds and afflictions	*3004*
Ac	21:14	**s.**, The will of the Lord be done.	*2036*
Ac	21:21	**s.**...they ought not to circumcise	*3004*
Ac	21:40	unto them in the Hebrew tongue, **s.**,	*3004*
Ac	22:7	heard a voice **s.** unto me, **Saul, Saul,**	*3004*
Ac	22:18	saw him **s.** unto me, Make haste,	*3004*
Ac	22:26	**s.**, Take heed what thou doest:	*3004*
Ac	23:9	**s.**, We find no evil in this man:	*3004*
Ac	23:12	**s.** that they would neither eat nor	*3004*
Ac	23:23	**s.**, Make ready two hundred	*2036*
Ac	24:2	**s.**, Seeing that by thee we enjoy	*3004*
Ac	24:9	**s.** that these things were so.	*5335*
Ac	25:14	**s.**, There is a certain man left in	*3004*
Ac	26:14	**s.** in the Hebrew tongue, **Saul, Saul,**	*3004*
Ac	26:22	**s.** none other things than those	*3004*
Ac	26:31	**s.**, This man doeth nothing worthy	*3004*
Ac	27:24	**S.**, Fear not, Paul; thou must be	*3004*
Ac	27:33	**s.**, This day is the fourteenth day	*3004*
Ac	28:26	**S.**, Go unto this people, and say,	*3004*
Ro	4:7	**S.**, Blessed are they whose iniquities	
Ro	11:2	intercession...against Israel, **s.**,	*3004*
Ro	13:9	is briefly comprehended in this **s.**,	*3056*
1Co	11:25	**s.**, **This cup is the new testament**	*3004*
1Co	15:54	then shall be brought to pass the **s.**	*3056*
Ga	3:8	**s.**, in thee shall all nations be blessed	
1Ti	1:15	This is a faithful **s.**, and worthy of	*3056*
1Ti	3:1	This is a true **s.**, If a man desire the	*3056*
1Ti	4:9	This is a faithful **s.** and worthy of	*3056*
2Ti	2:11	It is a faithful **s.**: For if we be dead	*3056*
2Ti	2:18	**s.** that the resurrection is past	*3004*
Tit	3:8	This is a faithful **s.**, and these	*3056*
Heb	2:6	**s.**, What is man, that thou art	*3004*
Heb	2:12	**S.**, I will declare thy name unto my	*3004*
Heb	4:7	**s.** in David, To day, after so long a	*3004*
Heb	6:14	**S.**, Surely blessing I will bless thee	*3004*
Heb	8:11	man his brother, **s.**, Know the Lord:	*3004*
Heb	9:20	**S.**, this is the blood of the testament	*3004*
Heb	12:26	**s.**,...I shake not the earth only,	*3004*
2Pe	3:4	And **s.**, Where is the promise of his	*3004*
Jude	14	**s.**, Behold, the Lord cometh with	*3004*
Re	1:11	**S.**, **I am Alpha and Omega, the**	*3004*
Re	1:17	hand upon me, **s.** unto me, **Fear not;**	*3004*
Re	4:8	day and night, **s.**, Holy, holy, holy,	*3004*
Re	4:10	their crowns before the throne, **s.**,	*3004*
Re	5:9	a new song, **s.**, Thou art worthy	*3004*
Re	5:12	**S.** with a loud voice, Worthy is the	*3004*
Re	5:13	heard I **s.**, Blessing, and honour,	*3004*
Re	6:1	of the four beasts **s.**, Come and see.	*3004*
Re	6:10	**s.**, How long, O Lord, holy and true,	*3004*
Re	7:3	**S.**, Hurt not the earth, neither the	*3004*
Re	7:10	**s.**, Salvation to our God which	*3004*
Re	7:12	**S.**, Amen: Blessing, and glory, and	*3004*
Re	7:13	**s.** unto me, What are these which	*3004*
Re	8:13	**s.** with a loud voice, Woe, woe, woe,	*3004*
Re	9:14	**S.** to the sixth angel which had the	*3004*
Re	10:4	voice from heaven **s.** unto me, Seal	*3004*
Re	11:1	**s.**, Rise, and measure the temple of	*3004*
Re	11:12	**s.** unto them, Come up hither	*3004*
Re	11:15	**s.**, The kingdoms of this world are	*3004*
Re	11:17	**S.**, We give thee thanks, O Lord God.	*3004*
Re	12:10	**s.** in heaven, Now is come salvation,	*3004*
Re	13:4	**s.**, Who is like unto the beast? who	*3004*
Re	13:14	**s.** to them that dwell on the earth,	*3004*
Re	14:7	**S.** with a loud voice, Fear God, and	*3004*
Re	14:8	**s.**, Babylon is fallen, is fallen, that	*3004*
Re	14:9	**s.** with a loud voice, If any man	*3004*
Re	14:13	**s.** unto me, Write, Blessed are the	*3004*
Re	14:18	**s.**, Thrust in thy sharp sickle, and	*3004*
Re	15:3	**s.**, Great and marvellous are thy	*3004*
Re	16:1	**s.** to the seven angels, Go your ways,	*3004*
Re	16:17	from the throne, **s.**, It is done.	*3004*
Re	17:1	with me, **s.** unto me, Come hither;	*3004*
Re	18:2	**s.**, Babylon the great is fallen, is	*3004*
Re	18:4	**s.**, Come out of her, my people, that	*3004*
Re	18:10	**s.**, Alas, alas that great city Babylon,	*3004*
Re	18:16	And **s.**, alas, alas that great city,	*3004*
Re	18:18	**s.**, What city is like unto this great	*3004*
Re	18:19	**s.**, Alas, alas that great city,	*3004*
Re	18:21	**s.**, Thus...shall that great city be	*3004*
Re	19:1	much people in heaven, **s.**, Alleluia;	*3004*
Re	19:4	on the throne, **s.**, Amen; Alleluia	*3004*
Re	19:5	throne, **s.**, Praise our God, all ye his	*3004*
Re	19:6	of mighty thunderings, **s.**, Alleluia:	*3004*
Re	19:17	**s.** to all the fowls that fly in the	*3004*
Re	21:3	**s.**, Behold, the tabernacle of God is	*3004*
Re	21:9	**s.**, Come hither, I will shew thee the	*3004*

SAYINGS

Nu	14:39	Moses told these **s.** unto all the	1697
Jg	13:17	that when thy **s.** come to pass we	1697
1Sa	25:12	and came and told him all those **s.**	1697
2Ch	13:22	Abijah, and his ways, and his **s.**,	1697
2Ch	33:19	written among the **s.** of the seers	1697
Ps	49:13	their posterity approve their **s.**	6310
Ps	78:2	parable: I will utter dark **s.** of old:	2420
Pr	1:6	words of the wise, and their dark **s.**	2420
Pr	4:10	Hear, O my son, and receive my **s.**;	561
Pr	4:20	words; incline thine ear unto my **s.**	561
Mt	7:24	**whosoever heareth these s. of**	*3056*
Mt	7:26	**one that heareth these s. of mine,**	*3056*
Mt	7:28	when Jesus had ended these **s.**, the	*3056*
Mt	19:1	when Jesus had finished these **s.**,	*3056*
Mt	26:1	when Jesus...finished all these **s.**,	*3056*
Lu	1:65	all these **s.** were noised abroad	*4487*
Lu	2:51	but his mother kept all these **s.** in	*4487*
Lu	6:47	**heareth my s., and doeth them,**	*3056*
Lu	7:1	ended all his **s.** in the audience of	*4487*
Lu	9:28	about an eight days after these **s.**,	*3056*
Lu	9:44	**Let these s. sink...into your ears:**	*3056*
Joh	10:19	again among the Jews for these **s.**	*3056*
Joh	14:24	**loveth me not keepeth not my s.**	*3056*
Ac	14:18	with these **s.** scarce restrained	*3004*
Ac	19:28	when they heard these **s.**, they were	
Ro	3:4	mightest be justified in thy **s.**,	*3056*
Re	19:9	me, These are the true **s.** of God.	*3056*
Re	22:6	me, These **s.** are faithful and true:	*3056*
Re	22:7	that keepeth the **s.** of the prophecy	*3056*
Re	22:9	them which keep the **s.** of this book:	*3056*
Re	22:10	Seal not the **s.** of the prophecy of	*3056*

SCAB See also SCABBED.

Le	13:2	a rising, a **s.**, or bright spot, and it	5597
Le	13:6	pronounce him clean: it is but a **s.**	4556
Le	13:7	**s.** spread much abroad in the skin,	4556
Le	13:8	behold, the **s.** spreadeth in the skin,	4556
Le	14:56	and for a **s.**, and for a bright spot:	5597
De	28:27	and with the **s.**, and with the itch,	1618
Isa	3:17	will smite with a **s.** the crown of	5596

SCABBARD

Jer	47:6	put up thyself into thy **s.**, rest, and	8593

SCABBED

Le	21:20	or **s.**, or hath his stones broken;	3217
Le	22:22	scurvy, or **s.**, ye shall not offer these	3217

SCAFFOLD

2Ch	6:13	Solomon had made a brasen **s.**, of	3595

SCALES

Le	11:9	whatsoever hath fins and **s.** in the	7193
Le	11:10	that have not fins and **s.** in the seas,	7193
Le	11:12	Whatsoever hath no fins nor **s.** in	7193
De	14:9	all that have fins and **s.** shall ye eat:	7193
De	14:10	hath not fins and **s.** ye may not eat;	7193
Job	41:15	His **s.** are his pride, shut up	650,4043
Isa	40:12	and weighed the mountains in **s.**,	6425
Eze	29:4	cause the fish...to stick unto thy **s.**,	7193
Eze	29:4	all the fish...shall stick unto thy **s.**	7193
Ac	9:18	fell from his eyes as it had been **s.**:	*3013*

SCALETH

Pr	21:22	wise man **s.** the city of the mighty,	5927

SCALL

Le	13:30	it is a dry **s.**, even a leprosy upon	5424
Le	13:31	priest look on the plague of the **s.**,	5424
Le	13:31	shall shut up him that hath...the **s.**	5424
Le	13:32	and behold, if the **s.** spread not,	5424

Le 13:32 the **s.** be not in sight deeper than....... 5424
Le 13:33 but the **s.** shall he not shave; 5424
Le 13:33 shall shut up him that hath the **s.** 5424
Le 13:34 day the priest shall look on the **s.**....... 5424
Le 13:34 if the **s.** be not spread in the skin,...... 5424
Le 13:35 if the **s.** spread much in the skin........ 5424
Le 13:36 if the **s.** be spread in the skin,.......... 5424
Le 13:37 But if the **s.** be in his sight at a stay,.. 5424
Le 13:37 the **s.** is healed, he is clean: and........ 5424
Le 14:54 manner of plague of leprosy, and **s.**, ... 5424

SCALP
Ps 68:21 hairy **s.** of such an one as goeth......... 6936

SCANT
Mic 6:10 the **s.** measure that is abominable? 7332

SCAPEGOAT
Le 16:8 Lord, and the other lot for the **s.**....... 5799
Le 16:10 on which the lot fell to be the **s.**, ... 5799
Le 16:10 him go for a **s.** into the wilderness. 5799
Le 16:26 goat for the **s.** shall wash his............ 5799

SCARCE See also SCARCELY.
Ge 27:30 Jacob was yet **s.** gone out from the...........
Ac 14:18 **s.** restrained they the people, ... *3433*
Ac 27:7 **s.** were come over against Cnidus, ... *3433*

SCARCELY See also SCARCE.
Ro 5:7 **s.** for a righteous man will one die:..... *3433*
1Pe 4:18 if the righteous **s.** be saved, where..... *3433*

SCARCENESS
De 8:9 thou shalt eat bread without **s.**,.......... 4544

SCAREST
Job 7:14 Then thou **s.** me with dreams,.......... 2865

SCARLET
Ge 38:28 bound upon his hand a **s.** thread,........ 8144
Ge 38:30 had the **s.** thread upon his hand: 8144
Ex 25:4 purple, and **s.**, and fine linen, ... 8144,8438
Ex 26:1 and blue, and purple, and **s.** 8144,8438
Ex 26:31 vail of blue, and purple, and **s.**,... 8144,8438
Ex 26:36 of blue, and purple, and **s.**, and... 8144,8438
Ex 27:16 of blue, and purple, and **s.**, and... 8144,8438
Ex 28:5 purple, and **s.**, and fine linen. 8144,8438
Ex 28:6 of blue, and of purple, of **s.**, and..8144,8438
Ex 28:8 gold, of blue, and purple, and **s.**,..8144,8438
Ex 28:15, 33 blue, and of purple, and of **s.**, .8144,8438
Ex 35:6 And blue, and purple, and **s.**, ... 8144,8438
Ex 35:23 found blue, and purple, and **s.**,.... 8144,8438
Ex 35:25 of blue, and of purple, and of **s.**, ..8144,8438
Ex 35:35 in blue, and in purple, in **s.**, and.. 8144,8438
Ex 36:8 and blue, and purple, and **s.**: 8144,8438
Ex 36:35 vial of blue, and purple, and **s.**,... 8144,8438
Ex 36:37 door of blue, and purple, and **s.**, . 8144,8438
Ex 38:18 of blue, and purple, and **s.**, and... 8144,8438
Ex 38:23 purple, and in **s.**, and fine linen... 8144,8438
Ex 39:1 of the blue, and purple, and **s.**,... 8144,8438
Ex 39:2 gold, blue, and purple, and **s.**, ... 8144,8438
Ex 39:3 in the purple, and in the **s.**, ... 8144,8438
Ex 39:5, 8 gold, blue, and purple, and **s.**,... 8144,8438
Ex 39:24 of blue, and purple, and **s.**, and... 8144,8438
Ex 39:29 purple, and **s.**, of needlework; 8144,8438
Le 14:4 cedar wood, and **s.**, and hyssop: ..8144,8438
Le 14:6 and the cedar wood, and the **s.**,... 8144,8438
Le 14:49 cedar wood, and **s.**, and hyssop: ..8144,8438
Le 14:51 and the hyssop, and the **s.**, and .. 8144,8438
Le 14:52 with the hyssop, and with the **s.** . 8144,8438
Nu 4:8 spread upon them a cloth of **s.**,... 8144,8438
Nu 19:6 cedarwood, and hyssop, and **s.**, .. 8144,8438
Jos 2:18 shalt bind this line of **s.** thread in 8144
Jos 2:21 bound the **s.** line in the window. 8144
2Sa 1:24 over Saul, who clothed you in **s.**, ... 8144
Pr 31:21 household are clothed with **s.**. 8144
Ca 4:3 Thy lips are like a thread of **s.**,.......... 8144
Isa 1:18 though your sins be as **s.**, they.......... 8144
La 4:5 they that were brought up in **s.** 8144
Da 5:7 shall be clothed with **s.**, and have 711
Da 5:16 thou shalt be clothed with **s.**, and 711
Da 5:29 they clothed Daniel with **s.**, and put 711
Na 2:3 red, the valiant men are in **s.**: 8529
Mt 27:28 him, and put on him a **s.** robe............ *2847*
Heb 9:19 water, and **s.** wool, and hyssop,......... *2847*
Re 17:3 woman sit upon a **s.** coloured beast, ... *2847*
Re 17:4 arrayed in purple and **s.** colour,......... *2847*
Re 18:12 and purple, and silk, and **s.**, and all..... *2847*
Re 18:16 in fine linen, and purple, and **s.**, ... *2847*

SCARLET-COLOURED See SCARLET and COLOURED.

SCATTER See also SCATTERED; SCATTERETH; SCATTERING.
Ge 11:9 did the Lord **s.** them abroad upon....... 6327
Ge 49:7 in Jacob, and **s.** them in Israel. 6327
Le 26:33 I will **s.** you among the heathen, ... 2210
Nu 16:37 and **s.** thou the fire yonder; for.......... 2219
De 4:27 shall **s.** you among the nations, ... 6327
De 28:64 Lord shall **s.** thee among all people, ... 6327
De 32:26 said, I would **s.** them into corners, ... 6284
1Ki 14:15 and shall **s.** them beyond the river,..... 2219
Ne 1:8 **s.** you abroad among the nations: 6327
Ps 59:11 **s.** them by thy power; and bring 5128
Ps 68:30 **s.** thou the people that delight in 967
Ps 106:27 and to **s.** them in the lands. 2219
Ps 144:6 Cast forth lightning, and **s.** them: 6327
Isa 28:25 the fitches, and **s.** the cummin, ... 2236
Isa 41:16 and the whirlwind shall **s.** them: 6327
Jer 9:16 **s.** them also among the heathen, ... 6327
Jer 13:24 will I **s.** them as the stubble that........ 6327
Jer 18:17 I will **s.** them as with an east wind 6327
Jer 23:1 that destroy and **s.** the sheep of my.... 6327
Jer 49:32 I will **s.** into all winds them that......... 2219
Jer 49:36 will **s.** them toward all those winds; 2219
Eze 5:2 third part thou shalt **s.** in the wind;..... 2219
Eze 5:10 remnant...will I **s.** into all the winds.... 2219
Eze 5:12 and I will **s.** a third part into all the 2219
Eze 6:5 **s.** your bones...about your altars. 2219
Eze 10:2 coals...and **s.** them over the city. 2236
Eze 12:14 I will **s.** toward every wind all that 2219
Eze 12:15 shall **s.** them among the nations, ... 6327
Eze 20:23 would **s.** them among the heathen, ... 6327
Eze 22:15 I will **s.** thee among the heathen, ... 6327
Eze 29:12 I will **s.** the Egyptians among the 6327
Eze 30:23, 26 will **s.** the Egyptians among the 6327
Da 4:14 off his leaves, and **s.** his fruit: 921
Da 11:24 he shall **s.** among them the prey, ... 967
Da 12:7 to **s.** the power of the holy people,..... 5310
Hab 3:14 came out as a whirlwind to **s.** me: 6327
Zec 1:21 over the land of Judah to **s.** it............ 2219

SCATTERED
Ge 11:4 we be **s.** abroad upon the face of 6327
Ge 11:8 So the Lord **s.** them abroad from 6327
Ex 5:12 people were **s.** abroad throughout....... 6327
Nu 10:35 Lord, and let thine enemies be **s.**;...... 6327
De 30:3 the Lord thy God hath **s.** thee. 6327
1Sa 11:11 that they which remained were **s.**,...... 6327
1Sa 13:8 and the people were **s.** from him. 6327
1Sa 13:11 that the people were **s.** from me, ... 5310
2Sa 18:8 the battle was there **s.** over the......... 6327
2Sa 22:15 he sent out arrows, and **s.** them; 6327
1Ki 22:17 I saw all Israel **s.** upon the hills, as..... 6327
2Ki 25:5 and all his army were **s.** from him. 6327
2Ch 18:16 all Israel **s.** upon the mountains,.......... 6327
Es 3:8 is a certain people **s.** abroad and 6340
Job 4:11 stout lion's whelps are **s.** abroad. 6504
Job 18:15 brimstone shall be **s.** upon his........... 2219
Ps 18:14 sent out his arrows, and **s.** them;........ 6327
Ps 44:11 and hast **s.** us among the heathen....... 2219
Ps 53:5 God hath **s.** the bones of him that 6340
Ps 60:1 hast cast us off, thou hast **s.** us, ... 6555
Ps 68:1 God arise, let his enemies be **s.**.......... 6327
Ps 68:14 When the Almighty **s.** kings in it, ... 6566
Ps 89:10 thou hast **s.** thine enemies with.......... 6340
Ps 92:9 the workers of iniquity shall be **s.**....... 6504
Ps 141:7 Our bones are **s.** at the grave's 6340
Isa 18:2 to a nation **s.** and peeled, to a 4900
Isa 18:7 present...of a people **s.** and peeled, ... 4900
Isa 33:3 up of thy self the nations were **s.**........ 5310
Jer 3:13 hast **s.** thy ways to the strangers 6340
Jer 10:21 and all their flocks shall be **s.**............. 6327
Jer 23:2 Ye have **s.** my flock, and driven......... 6327
Jer 30:11 all nations whither I have **s.** thee,....... 6327
Jer 31:10 He that **s.** Israel will gather him,........ 2219
Jer 40:15 gathered unto thee should be **s.**, ... 6327
Jer 50:17 Israel is a **s.** sheep; the lions have...... 6340
Jer 52:8 and all his army was **s.** from him. 6327
Eze 6:8 shall be **s.** through the countries. 2219
Eze 11:16 have **s.** them among the countries, ... 6327
Eze 11:17 the countries where ye have been **s.**,.. 6327
Eze 17:21 shall be **s.** toward all winds: 6566
Eze 20:34 of the countries wherein ye are **s.**, ... 6327
Eze 20:41 countries wherein ye have been **s.**;..... 6327
Eze 28:25 the people among whom they are **s.**;... 6327
Eze 29:13 the people whither they were **s.**:........ 6327
Eze 34:5 And they were **s.**, because there is 6327
Eze 34:5 of the field, when they were **s.**. 6327
Eze 34:6 was **s.** upon all the face of the earth, .. 6327
Eze 34:12 he is among his sheep that are **s.**....... 6566
Eze 34:12 all places where they have been **s.** 6327
Eze 34:21 horns, till ye have **s.** them abroad; 6327
Eze 36:19 And I **s.** them among the heathen,...... 6327
Eze 46:18 **s.** every man from his possession. 6327
Joe 3:2 they have **s.** among the nations,......... 6327
Na 3:18 people is **s.** upon the mountains, ... 6340
Hab 3:6 the everlasting mountains were **s.**,....... 6327
Zec 1:19, 21 the horns which have **s.** Judah, ... 2219
Zec 7:14 I **s.** them with a whirlwind among............
Zec 13:7 and the sheep shall be **s.**: and I 6327
Mt 9:36 were **s.** abroad, as sheep having *4496*
Mt 26:31 **of the flock shall be s. abroad.**......... *1287*
Mk 14:27 **shepherd, and the sheep shall be s.**.*1287*
Lu 1:51 **s.** the proud in the imagination of....... *1287*
Joh 11:52 children of God that were **s.** abroad. ... *1287*
Joh 16:32 **is now come, that ye shall be s.,**... *4650*
Ac 5:36 were **s.**, and brought to nought. *1262*
Ac 8:1 they were all **s.** abroad throughout...... *1289*
Ac 8:4 they that were **s.** abroad went........... *1289*
Ac 11:19 they which were **s.** abroad upon the.... *1289*
Jas 1:1 twelve tribes which are **s.** abroad, ... *1290*
1Pe 1:1 strangers **s.** throughout Pontus, ... *1290*

SCATTERETH
Job 37:11 cloud: he **s.** his bright cloud: 6327
Job 38:24 **s.** the east wind upon the earth? 6327
Ps 147:16 he **s.** the hoarfrost like ashes. 6340
Pr 11:24 There is that **s.**, and yet increaseth; ... 6340
Pr 20:8 **s.** away all evil with his eyes. 2219
Pr 20:26 A wise king **s.** the wicked, and.......... 2219
Isa 24:1 **s.** abroad the inhabitants thereof. 6327
Mt 12:30 **gathereth not with me s. abroad.**... *4650*
Lu 11:23 **he that gathereth not with me s.**... *4650*
Joh 10:12 **catcheth them, and s. the sheep.** ... *4650*

SCATTERING
Isa 30:30 **s.**, and tempest, and hailstones. 5311

SCENT
Job 14:9 through the **s.** of water it will bud. 7381
Jer 48:11 in him, and his **s.** is not changed. 7381
Ho 14:7 **s.** thereof shall be as the wine of 2143

SCEPTRE See also SCEPTRES.
Ge 49:10 **s.** shall not depart from Judah, ... 7626
Nu 24:17 and a **S.** shall rise out of Israel, ... 7626
Es 4:11 king shall hold out the golden **s.**,......... 8275
Es 5:2 held out to Esther the golden **s.**......... 8275
Es 5:2 near, and touched the top of the **s.**...... 8275
Es 8:4 out the golden **s.** toward Esther.......... 8275
Ps 45:6 and ever: the **s.** of thy kingdom 7626
Ps 45:6 of thy kingdom is a right **s.**.................. 7626
Isa 14:5 the wicked, and the **s.** of the rulers. ... 7626
Eze 19:14 she hath no strong rod to be a **s.** to ... 7626
Am 1:5 him that holdeth the **s.** from the.......... 7626
Am 1:8 that holdeth the **s.** from Ashkelon,...... 7626
Zec 10:11 the **s.** of Egypt shall depart away. 7626
Heb 1:8 a **s.** of righteousness is the **s.** of........ *4464*

SCEPTRES
Eze 19:11 she had strong rods for the **s.** of.......... 7626

SCEVA (see'-vah)
Ac 19:14 there were seven sons of one **S.**,....... *4630*

SCHIN (sheen)
Ps 119:161 *title* [ש] **S.**...

SCHISM
1Co 12:25 there should be no **s.** in the body;...... *4978*

SCHOLAR
1Ch 25:8 the great, the teacher as the **s.**. 8527
Mal 2:12 the master and the **s.**, out of the 6030

SCHOOL See also SCHOOLMASTER.
Ac 19:9 daily in the **s.** of one Tyrannus. *4981*

SCHOOLMASTER
Ga 3:24 law was our **s.** to bring us unto *3807*
Ga 3:25 we are no longer under a **s.**.............. *3807*

SCIENCE
Da 1:4 knowledge, and understanding **s.**, ... 4093
1Ti 6:20 oppositions of **s.** falsely so called: *1108*

SCOFF
Hab 1:10 And they shall **s.** at the kings, ... 7046

SCOFFERS
2Pe 3:3 shall come in the last days **s.**,............ *1703*

SCORCH See also SCORCHED.
Re 16:8 unto him to s. men with fire *2739*

SCORCHED
Mt 13:6 the sun was up, they were s.; *2739*
Mk 4:6 when the sun was up, it was s.; *2739*
Re 16:9 And men were s. with great heat, *2739*

SCORE See FOURSCORE; SIXSCORE; THREESCORE.

SCORN See also SCORNEST; SCORNETH; SCORNFUL; SCORNING.
2Ki 19:21 thee, and laughed thee to s.;
2Ch 30:10 but they laughed them to s., and
Ne 2:19 heard it, they laughed us to s.,
Es 3:6 s. to lay hands on Mordecai alone; 959
Job 12:4 the just upright man is laughed to s.
Job 16:20 My friends s. me: but mine eye 3887
Job 22:19 and the innocent laugh them to s.
Ps 22:7 they that see me laugh me to s.:
Ps 44:13 a s. and a derision to them that 3933
Ps 79:4 a s. and derision to them that are 3933
Isa 37:22 thee, and laughed thee to s.;
Eze 23:32 thou shalt be laughed to s. and
Hab 1:10 princes shall be a s. unto them: 4890
Mt 9:24 sleepeth...they laughed him to s. *2606*
Mk 5:40 And they laughed him to s.. But *2606*
Lu 8:53 they laughed him to s., knowing *2606*

SCORNER See also SCORNERS.
Pr 9:7 he that reproveth a s. getteth to 3887
Pr 9:8 Reprove not a s., lest he hate thee: 3887
Pr 13:1 but a s. heareth not rebuke 3887
Pr 14:6 A s. seeketh wisdom, and findeth 3887
Pr 15:12 a s. loveth not one that reproveth 3887
Pr 19:25 Smite a s., and the simple will 3887
Pr 21:11 When the s. is punished, the simple 3887
Pr 21:24 Proud and haughty s. is his name. 3887
Pr 22:10 Cast out the s., and contention 3887
Pr 24:9 the s. is an abomination to men. 3887
Isa 29:20 the s. is consumed, and all that 3887

SCORNERS
Pr 1:22 the s. delight in their scorning, 3887
Pr 3:34 Surely he scorneth the s.: but he 3887
Pr 19:29 Judgments are prepared for s., 3887
Ho 7:5 he stretched out his hand with s. 3945

SCORNEST
Pr 9:12 if thou s., thou alone shalt bear 3887
Eze 16:31 as an harlot, in that thou s. hire; 7046

SCORNETH
Job 39:7 He s. the multitude of the city, 7832
Job 39:18 high, she s. the horse and his rider. 7832
Pr 3:34 Surely he s. the scorners: but he 3887
Pr 19:28 An ungodly witness s. judgment: 3887

SCORNFUL
Ps 1:1 nor sitteth in the seat of the s. 3887
Pr 29:8 S. men bring a city into a snare: 3944
Isa 28:14 the word of the Lord, ye s. men, 3944

SCORNING
Job 34:7 who drinketh up s. like water? 3933
Ps 123:4 the s. of those that are at ease, 3933
Pr 1:22 the scorners delight in their s., 3944

SCORPION See also SCORPIONS.
Lu 11:12 ask an egg, will he offer him a s.? *4651*
Re 9:5 torment was as the torment of a s., *4651*

SCORPIONS
De 8:15 were fiery serpents, and s., and 6137
1Ki 12:11, 14 but I will chastise you with s. 6137
2Ch 10:11, 14 but I will chastise you with s. 6137
Eze 2:6 thee, and thou dost dwell among s. 6137
Lu 10:19 power to tread on serpents and s., *4651*
Re 9:3 as the s. of the earth have power *4651*
Re 9:10 And they had tails like unto s., and *4651*

SCOURED
Le 6:28 pot, it shall be both s., and rinsed 4838

SCOURGE See also SCOURGED; SCOURGES; SCOURGETH; SCOURGING.
Job 5:21 be hid from the s. of the tongue: 7752
Job 9:23 If the s. slay suddenly, he will 7752
Isa 10:26 the Lord of hosts shall stir up a s. 7752
Isa 28:15 overflowing s. shall pass through, 7885
Isa 28:18 overflowing s. shall pass through; 7752
Mt 10:17 will s. you in their synagogues; *3164*
Mt 20:19 to mock, and to s., and to crucify *3164*
Mt 23:34 some of them shall ye s. in your *3164*
Mk 10:34 shall s. him, and shall spit upon *3164*
Lu 18:33 they shall s. him, and put him to *3164*
Joh 2:15 he had made a s. of small cords, *5416*
Ac 22:25 Is it lawful for you to s. a man *3147*

SCOURGED
Le 19:20 she shall be s.; they shall not be 1244
Mt 27:26 and when he had s. Jesus, he *5417*
Mk 15:15 when he had s. him, to be crucified. *5417*
Joh 19:1 therefore took Jesus, and s. him. *3146*

SCOURGES
Jos 23:13 s. in your sides, and thorns in your 7850

SCOURGETH
Heb 12:6 s. every son whom he receiveth. *3146*

SCOURGING See also SCOURGINGS.
Ac 22:24 that he should be examined by s.; *3148*

SCOURGINGS
Heb 11:36 trial of cruel mockings and s., *3148*

SCOURING See OFFSCOURING.

SCRABBLED
1Sa 21:13 and s. on the doors of the gate, 8427

SCRAPE See also SCRAPED.
Le 14:41 the dust that they s. off without 7096
Job 2:8 a potsherd to s. himself withal; 1623
Eze 26:4 I will also s. her dust from her, 5500

SCRAPED
Le 14:41 cause the house to be s. within 7106
Le 14:43 and after he hath s. the house, 7096

SCREECH
Isa 34:14 the s. owl also shall rest there, 3917

SCRIBE See also ASCRIBE; DESCRIBE; PRESCRIBED; SCRIBE'S; SCRIBES.
2Sa 8:17 priests; and Seraiah was the s.; 5608
2Sa 20:25 And Sheva was s.: and Zadok and 5608
2Ki 12:10 the king's s. and the high priest 5608
2Ki 18:18, 37 Shebna the s., and Joah the son 5608
2Ki 19:2 Shebna the s., and the elder of the 5608
2Ki 22:3 the son of Meshullam, the s., to the 5608
2Ki 22:8 priest said unto Shaphan the s., 5608
2Ki 22:9 Shaphan the s. came to the king, 5608
2Ki 22:10 Shaphan the s. shewed the king, 5608
2Ki 22:12 And Shaphan the s., and Asahiah a 5608
2Ki 25:19 and the principal s. of the host, 5608
1Ch 18:16 the priests; and Shavsha was s.; 5608
1Ch 24:6 Shemaiah...son of Nethaneel the s., 5608
1Ch 27:32 a counseller, a wise man, and a s. 5608
2Ch 24:11 king's s. and...high priest's officer 5608
2Ch 26:11 Jeiel the s. and Maaseiah the ruler, 5608
2Ch 34:15 Hilkiah...said to Shaphan the s., 5608
2Ch 34:18 Then Shaphan the s. told the king, 5608
2Ch 34:20 and Shaphan the s., and Asaiah a 5608
Ezr 4:8 and Shimshai the s. wrote a letter 5613
Ezr 4:9 the chancellor, and Shimshai the s., 5613
Ezr 4:17 chancellor, and to Shimshai the s., 5613
Ezr 4:23 Before Rehum, and Shimshai the s., 5613
Ezr 7:6 a ready s. in the law of Moses, 5608
Ezr 7:11 gave unto Ezra the priest, the s., 5608
Ezr 7:11 even a s. of the...commandments 5608
Ezr 7:12, 21 s. of the law of...God of heaven, 5613
Ne 8:1 and they spake unto Ezra the s. 5608
Ne 8:4 And Ezra the s. stood upon a pulpit 5608
Ne 8:9 And Ezra the priest the s., and the 5608
Ne 8:13 were gathered...unto Ezra the s., 5608
Ne 12:26 and of Ezra the priest, the s. 5608
Ne 12:36 of God, and Ezra the s. before them 5608
Ne 13:13 Shelemiah...and Zadok the s., 5608
Isa 33:18 Where is the s.? where is the 5608
Isa 36:3 Shebna the s., and Joah, Asaph's 5608
Isa 36:22 Shebna the s., and Joah, the son of 5608
Isa 37:2 and Shebna the s., and the elders of 5608
Jer 36:10 Gemariah...son of Shaphan the s., 5608
Jer 36:12 sat there, even Elishama the s., and 5608
Jer 36:20 in the chamber of Elishama the s., 5608
Jer 36:26 to take Baruch the s. and Jeremiah 5608
Jer 36:32 roll, and gave it to Baruch the s., 5608
Jer 37:15 in the house of Jonathan the s. 5608
Jer 37:20 to the house of Jonathan the s. 5608
Jer 52:25 and the principal s. of the host, who 5608
Mt 8:19 And a certain s. came, and said *1122*
Mt 13:52 every s. which is instructed unto *1122*
Mk 12:32 the s. said unto him, Well, Master, *1122*
1Co 1:20 Where is the wise? where is the s.? *1122*

SCRIBE'S
Jer 36:12 king's house, into the s. chamber: 5608
Jer 36:21 it out of Elishama the s. chamber. 5608

SCRIBES
1Ki 4:3 and Ahiah, the sons of Shisha, s.; 5608
1Ch 2:55 the families of the s. which dwelt at 5608
2Ch 34:13 and of the Levites there were s., 5608
Es 3:12 Then were the king's s. called on 5608
Es 8:9 Then were the king's s. called at 5608
Jer 8:8 he it; the pen of the s. is in vain. 5608
Mt 2:4 chief priests and s. of the people *1122*
Mt 5:20 exceed the righteousness of the s. *1122*
Mt 7:29 having authority, and not as the s. *1122*
Mt 9:3 behold, certain of the s. said within *1122*
Mt 12:38 certain of the s. and of the Pharisees *1122*
Mt 15:1 came to Jesus s. and Pharisees, *1122*
Mt 16:21 the elders and chief priests and s., *1122*
Mt 17:10 Why then say the s. that Elias must *1122*
Mt 20:18 the chief priests and unto the s., *1122*
Mt 21:15 when the chief priests and s. saw *1122*
Mt 23:2 s. and the Pharisees sit in Moses' *1122*
Mt 23:13 woe unto you, s. and Pharisees, *1122*
Mt 23:14 Woe unto you, s. and Pharisees, *1122*
Mt 23:15, 23,25,27,29 Woe unto you, s. and *1122*
Mt 23:34 prophets, and wise men, and s. *1122*
Mt 26:3 the chief priests, and the s., and the *1122*
Mt 26:57 s. and the elders were assembled *1122*
Mt 27:41 mocking him, with the s. and elders, *1122*
Mk 1:22 had authority, and not as the s. *1122*
Mk 2:6 were certain of the s. sitting there, *1122*
Mk 2:16 the s. and Pharisees saw him eat *1122*
Mk 3:22 s. which came down from Jerusalem *1122*
Mk 7:1 Pharisees, and certain of the s., *1122*
Mk 7:5 the Pharisees and s. asked him, *1122*
Mk 8:31 and of the chief priests, and s., *1122*
Mk 9:11 Why say the s. that Elias must first *1122*
Mk 9:14 and the s. questioning with them. *1122*
Mk 9:16 he asked the s., What question ye *1122*
Mk 10:33 the chief priests, and unto the s. *1122*
Mk 11:18 And the s. and chief priests heard it, *1122*
Mk 11:27 the chief priests, and the s., and the *1122*
Mk 12:28 And one of the s. came, and having *1122*
Mk 12:35 say the s. that Christ is the son *1122*
Mk 12:38 Beware of the s., which love to *1122*
Mk 14:1 chief priests and the s. sought how *1122*
Mk 14:43 from the chief priests and the s. and *1122*
Mk 14:53 priests and the elders and the s. *1122*
Mk 15:1 consultation with the elders and s. *1122*
Mk 15:31 said among themselves with the s., *1122*
Lu 5:21 s. and...Pharisees began to reason, *1122*
Lu 5:30 their s. and Pharisees murmured *1122*
Lu 6:7 the s. and Pharisees watched him, *1122*
Lu 9:22 the elders and chief priests and s., *1122*
Lu 11:44 Woe unto you, s. and Pharisees, *1122*
Lu 11:53 s. and the Pharisees began to urge *1122*
Lu 15:2 Pharisees and s. murmured, saying, *1122*
Lu 19:47 the chief priests and the s. and the *1122*
Lu 20:1 priests and the s. came upon him *1122*
Lu 20:19 chief priests and...s. the same hour *1122*
Lu 20:39 certain of the s. answering said, *1122*
Lu 20:46 Beware of the s., which desire to *1122*
Lu 22:2 the chief priests and s. sought how *1122*
Lu 22:66 priests and the s. came together, *1122*
Lu 23:10 And the chief priests and s. stood *1122*
Joh 8:3 s. and Pharisees brought unto him *1122*
Ac 4:5 that their rulers, and elders, and s., *1122*
Ac 6:12 the people, and the elders, and the s., *1122*
Ac 23:9 s. that were of the Pharisees' part *1122*

SCRIP
1Sa 17:40 bag which he had, even in a s.; 3219
Mt 10:10 Nor s. for your journey, neither *4082*
Mk 6:8 no s., no bread, no money in their *4082*
Lu 9:3 neither staves, nor s., neither *4082*
Lu 10:4 Carry neither purse, nor s., nor *4082*
Lu 22:35 sent you without purse, and s. *4082*
Lu 22:36 him take it, and likewise his s.: *4082*

SCRIPTURE See also SCRIPTURES.
Da 10:21 which is noted in the s. of truth: 3791
Mk 12:10 have ye not read this s.; The stone *1124*
Mk 15:28 the s. was fulfilled, which saith, *1124*
Lu 4:21 This day is this s. fulfilled in your *1124*
Joh 2:22 they believed the s., and the word *1124*
Joh 7:38 as the s. hath said, out of his belly *1124*
Joh 7:42 Hath not the s. said, That Christ *1124*
Joh 10:35 and the s. cannot be broken; *1124*

Joh 13:18 **that the s. may be fulfilled, He**..... 1124
Joh 17:12 **that the s. might be fulfilled**......... 1124
Joh 19:24 that the s. might be fulfilled, which..... 1124
Joh 19:28 that the s. might be fulfilled, saith, ... 1124
Joh 19:36 s. should be fulfilled, A bone of him.... 1124
Joh 19:37 again another s. saith, They shall 1124
Joh 20:9 For as yet they knew not the s., ... 1124
Ac 1:16 s. must needs have been fulfilled, ... 1124
Ac 8:32 The place of the s. which he read 1124
Ac 8:35 began at the same s., and preached.... 1124
Ro 4:3 For what saith the s.? Abraham 1124
Ro 9:17 the s. saith unto Pharaoh, Even for 1124
Ro 10:11 the s. saith, Whosoever believeth........ 1124
Ro 11:2 Wot ye not what the s. saith of Elias?..1124
Ga 3:8 the s., foreseeing that God would........ 1124
Ga 3:22 the s. hath concluded all under sin, ... 1124
Ga 4:30 Nevertheless what saith the s.? 1124
1Ti 5:18 the s. saith, Thou shalt not muzzle...... 1124
2Ti 3:16 All s. is given by inspiration of God, ... 1124
Jas 2:8 the royal law according to the s., ... 1124
Jas 2:23 And the s. was fulfilled which saith, ... 1124
Jas 4:5 ye think that the s. saith in vain,........ 1124
1Pe 2:6 Wherefore...it is contained in the s., ... 1124
2Pe 1:20 no prophecy of the s. is of...private.... 1124

SCRIPTURES
Mt 21:42 **Did ye never read in the s., The**.... 1124
Mt 22:29 **Ye do err, not knowing the s.**, ... 1124
Mt 26:54 **how then shall the s. be fulfilled**,.. 1124
Mt 26:56 **s. of the prophets might be** 1124
Mk 12:24 **err, because ye know not the s.**,.... 1124
Mk 14:49 **not: but the s. must be fulfilled**..... 1124
Lu 24:27 expounded unto them in all the s......... 1124
Lu 24:32 and while he opened to us the s.? 1124
Lu 24:45 that they might understand the s., ... 1124
Joh 5:39 **Search the s.; for in them ye** 1124
Ac 17:2 reasoned with them out of the s.,......... 1124
Ac 17:11 and searched the s. daily, whether...... 1124
Ac 18:24 eloquent man, and mighty in the s., ... 1124
Ac 18:28 shewing by the s. that Jesus was 1124
Ro 1:2 afore by his prophets in the holy s.,)... 1124
Ro 15:4 patience and comfort of the s. we....... 1124
Ro 16:26 by the s. of the prophets, according..... 1124
1Co 15:3 died for our sins according to the s.;... 1124
1Co 15:4 the third day according to the s. 1124
2Ti 3:15 child thou hast known the holy s., ... 1121
2Pe 3:16 wrest, as they do also the other s., ... 1124

SCROLL
Isa 34:4 shall be rolled together as a s............ 5612
Re 6:14 And the heaven departed as a s........... 975

SCULL See SKULL.

SCUM
Eze 24:6 to the pot whose s. is therein,........... 2457
Eze 24:6 and whose s. is not gone out of it! 2457
Eze 24:11 that the s. of it may be consumed. 2457
Eze 24:12 great s. went not forth out of her:...... 2457
Eze 24:12 her s. shall be in the fire................. 2457

SCURVY
Le 21:20 hath a blemish in his eye, or be s.,..... 1618
Le 22:22 or maimed, or having a wen, or s.,..... 1618

SCYTHIAN (sith'-e-un)
Col 3:11 Barbarian, S., bond nor free:............. 4658

SEA See also SEAFARING; SEAS.
Ge 1:26,28 dominion over the fish of the s., ... 3220
Ge 9:2 and upon all the fishes of the s.; 3220
Ge 14:3 vale of Siddim, which is the salt s......... 3220
Ge 22:17 sand which is upon the s. shore; 3220
Ge 32:12 make thy seed as the sand of the s., .. 3220
Ge 41:49 gathered corn as the sand of the s.,.... 3220
Ge 49:13 shall dwell at the haven of the s.;....... 3220
Ex 10:19 and cast them into the Red s.;........... 3220
Ex 13:18 way of the wilderness of the Red s..... 3220
Ex 14:2 between Migdol and the s., over........ 3220
Ex 14:2 before it shall ye encamp by the s.. 3220
Ex 14:9 overtook them encamping by the s., ... 3220
Ex 14:16 stretch out thine hand over the s., ... 3220
Ex 14:16 ground through the midst of the s.. 3220
Ex 14:21 stretched out his hand over the s.; 3220
Ex 14:21 s. to go back by a strong east wind 3220
Ex 14:21 and made the s. dry land, and the 3220
Ex 14:22 midst of the s. upon the dry ground:... 3220
Ex 14:23 in after them to the midst of the s.,.... 3220
Ex 14:26 Stretch out thine hand over the s., ... 3220
Ex 14:27 stretched forth his hand over the s., ... 3220
Ex 14:27 and the s. returned to his strength..... 3220
Ex 14:27 Egyptians in the midst of the s.. 3220
Ex 14:28 that came into the s. after them;........ 3220
Ex 14:29 upon dry land in the midst of the s.; ... 3220
Ex 14:30 Egyptians dead upon the s. shore....... 3220
Ex 15:1 rider hath he thrown into the s.......... 3220
Ex 15:4 his host hath he cast into the s.......... 3220
Ex 15:4 also are drowned in the Red s.. 3220
Ex 15:8 congealed in the heart of the s.......... 3220
Ex 15:10 with thy wind, the s. covered them: ... 3220
Ex 15:19 and with his horsemen into the s.,...... 3220
Ex 15:19 the waters of the s. upon them;......... 3220
Ex 15:19 on dry land in the midst of the s. 3220
Ex 15:21 rider hath he thrown into the s.. 3220
Ex 15:22 brought Israel from the Red s.,.......... 3220
Ex 20:11 the s., and all that in them is, and...... 3220
Ex 23:31 will set thy bounds from the Red s..... 3220
Ex 23:31 even unto the s. of the Philistines, ... 3220
Nu 11:22 fish of the s. be gathered together...... 3220
Nu 11:31 and brought quails from the s., and...... 3220
Nu 13:29 and the Canaanites dwell by the s.,..... 3220
Nu 14:25 wilderness by the way of the Red s.... 3220
Nu 21:4 Hor by the way of the Red s.,............ 3220
Nu 21:14 What he did in the Red s., and in the........
Nu 33:8 midst of the s. into the wilderness,..... 3220
Nu 33:10 Elim, and encamped by the Red s.. 3220
Nu 33:11 And they removed from the Red s.,..... 3220
Nu 34:3 coast of the salt s. eastward:............. 3220
Nu 34:5 goings out of it shall be at the s......... 3220
Nu 34:6 even have the great s. for a border: ... 3220
Nu 34:7 great s. ye shall point out for you....... 3220
Nu 34:11 the side of the s. of Chinnereth 3220
Nu 34:12 out of it shall be at the salt s............ 3220
De 1:1 in the plain over against the Red s.,..........
De 1:7 in the south, and by the s. side, ... 3220
De 1:40 wilderness by the way of the Red s.. .. 3220
De 2:1 wilderness by the way of the Red s., .. 3220
De 3:17 the s. of the plain, even the salt s., ... 3220
De 4:49 even unto the s. of the plain, under.... 3220
De 11:4 the Red s. to overflow them as they... 3220
De 11:24 uttermost s. shall our coast be........... 3220
De 30:13 Neither is it beyond the s., that......... 3220
De 30:13 Who shall go over the s. for us, and... 3220
De 34:2 land of Judah, unto the utmost s.,....... 3220
Jos 1:4 unto the great s. toward the going...... 3220
Jos 2:10 up the water of the Red s. for you, ... 3220
Jos 3:16 the s. of the plain, even the salt s.,.... 3220
Jos 4:23 Lord your God did to the Red s.,........ 3220
Jos 5:1 Canaanites, which were by the s., ... 3220
Jos 9:1 all the coasts of the great s. over....... 3220
Jos 11:4 the sand that is upon the s. shore...... 3220
Jos 12:3 the plain to the s. of Chinneroth on 3220
Jos 12:3 east, and unto the s. of the plain,....... 3220
Jos 12:3 plain, even the salt s. on the east,...... 3220
Jos 13:27 the edge o the s. of Chinnereth on...... 3220
Jos 15:2 was from the shore of the salt s., ... 3220
Jos 15:4 out of that coast were at the s. 3220
Jos 15:5 And the east border was the salt s., ... 3220
Jos 15:5 s. at the uttermost part of Jordan:...... 3220
Jos 15:11 out of the border were at the s.. 3220
Jos 15:12 the west border was to the great s.,... 3220
Jos 15:46 From Ekron even unto the s., all 3220
Jos 15:47 great s., and the border thereof:........ 3220
Jos 16:3 the goings out thereof are at the s.. ... 3220
Jos 16:6 toward the s. to Michmethah on......... 3220
Jos 16:8 goings out thereof were at the s. 3220
Jos 17:9 the outgoings of it were at the s. 3220
Jos 17:10 Manasseh's...the s. is his border;....... 3220
Jos 18:14 and compassed the corner of the s. 3220
Jos 18:19 were at the north bay of the salt s. 3220
Jos 19:11 their border went up toward the s.,..... 3220
Jos 19:29 at the s. from the coast to Achzib: 3220
Jos 23:4 even unto the great s. westward. 3220
Jos 24:6 of Egypt: and ye came unto the s.;..... 3220
Jos 24:6 and horsemen unto the Red s.. 3220
Jos 24:7 and brought the s. upon them, and..... 3220
Jg 5:17 Asher continued on the s. shore,........ 3220
Jg 7:12 sand by the s. side for multitude. 3220
Jg 11:16 the wilderness unto the Red s., ... 3220
1Sa 13:5 as the sand which is on the s. shore... 3220
2Sa 17:11 as the sand that is by the s. for......... 3220
2Sa 22:16 the channels of the s. appeared, the.... 3220
1Ki 4:20 as the sand which is by the s. in........ 3220
1Ki 4:29 as the sand that is on the s. shore. 3220
1Ki 5:9 down from Lebanon unto the s. 3220
1Ki 5:9 I will convey them by s. in floats........ 3220
1Ki 7:23 And he made a molten s., ten cubits... 3220
1Ki 7:24 compassing the s. round about:.......... 3220
1Ki 7:25 the s. was set above upon them,........ 3220
1Ki 7:39 he set the s. on the right side of........ 3220
1Ki 7:44 s., and twelve oxen under the s.;....... 3220
1Ki 9:26 Eloth, on the shore of the Red s.,....... 3220
1Ki 9:27 that had knowledge of the s., with....... 3220
1Ki 10:22 king had at s. a navy of Tharshish...... 3220
1Ki 18:43 Go up now, look toward the s.. And... 3220
1Ki 18:44 ariseth a little cloud out of the s.,........ 3220
2Ki 14:25 Hamath unto the s. of the plain,......... 3220
2Ki 16:17 down the s. from off the brasen......... 3220
2Ki 25:13 the brasen s. that was in the house.... 3220
2Ki 25:16 The two pillars, one s., and the 3220
1Ch 16:32 Let the s. roar, and the fulness 3220
1Ch 18:8 Solomon made the brasen s., and....... 3220
2Ch 2:16 it to thee in floats by s. to Joppa;....... 3220
2Ch 4:2 he made a molten s. of ten cubits....... 3220
2Ch 4:3 compassing the s. round about. 3220
2Ch 4:4 and the s. was set above upon them, .. 3220
2Ch 4:6 s. was for the priests to wash in......... 3220
2Ch 4:10 he set the s. on the right side of the .. 3220
2Ch 4:15 One s., and twelve oxen under it. 3220
2Ch 8:17 at the s. side in the land of Edom. 3220
2Ch 8:18 that had knowledge of the s.; and....... 3220
2Ch 20:2 beyond the s. on this side Syria; 3220
Ezr 3:7 from Lebanon to the s. of Joppa,........ 3220
Ne 9:9 heardest their cry by the Red s.; 3220
Ne 9:11 And thou didst divide the s. before..... 3220
Ne 9:11 through the midst of the s. on...dry.... 3220
Es 10:1 land, and upon the isles of the s......... 3220
Job 6:3 be heavier than the sand of the s. 3220
Job 7:12 Am I a s., or a whale, that thou......... 3220
Job 9:8 treadeth upon the waves of the s.. 3220
Job 11:9 the earth, and broader than the s.. 3220
Job 12:8 the fishes of the s. shall declare......... 3220
Job 14:11 As the waters fail from the s., and 3220
Job 26:12 He divideth the s. with his power,...... 3220
Job 28:14 and the s. saith, It is not with me. 3220
Job 36:30 and covereth the bottom of the s.. 3220
Job 38:8 Or who shut up the s. with doors,...... 3220
Job 38:16 entered into the springs of the s.?...... 3220
Job 41:31 he maketh the s. like a pot of........... 3220
Ps 8:8 the fish of the s., and whatsoever 3220
Ps 33:7 He gathereth the waters of the s. 3220
Ps 46:2 be carried into the midst of the s.; 3220
Ps 65:5 them that are afar off upon the s........ 3220
Ps 66:6 he turned the s. into dry land: they 3220
Ps 68:22 again from the depths of the s. 3220
Ps 72:8 have dominion also from s. to s. 3220
Ps 74:13 didst divide the s. by the strength: 3220
Ps 77:19 Thy way is in the s., and thy path...... 3220
Ps 78:13 He divided the s., and caused them 3220
Ps 78:27 fowls like as the sand of the s. 3220
Ps 78:53 the s. overwhelmed their enemies. 3220
Ps 80:11 sent out her boughs unto the s., ... 3220
Ps 89:9 Thou rulest the raging of the s. 3220
Ps 89:25 I will set his hand also in the s., ... 3220
Ps 93:4 than the mighty waves of the s.. 3220
Ps 95:5 The s. is his, and he made it: and...... 3220
Ps 96:11 let the s. roar, and the fulness........... 3220
Ps 98:7 let the s. roar, and the fulness........... 3220
Ps 104:25 So is this great and wide s., wherein .. 3220
Ps 106:7 him at the s., even at the Red s.. 3220
Ps 106:9 He rebuked the Red s. also, and it 3220
Ps 106:22 and terrible things by the Red s......... 3220
Ps 107:23 that go down to the s. in ships, that ... 3220
Ps 114:3 The s. saw it, and fled: Jordan was..... 3220
Ps 114:5 What ailed thee, O thou s., that......... 3220
Ps 136:13 which divided the Red s. into parts: 3220
Ps 136:15 Pharaoh and his host in the Red s...... 3220
Ps 139:9 in the uttermost parts of the s.;.......... 3220
Ps 146:6 the s., and all that therein is: 3220
Pr 8:29 When he gave to the s. his decree, ... 3220
Pr 23:34 lieth down in the midst of the s., ... 3220
Pr 30:19 way of a ship in the midst of the s.; ... 3220
Ec 1:7 into the s.; yet the s. is not full; 3220
Isa 5:30 them like the roaring of the s.: 3220
Isa 9:1 afflict her by the way of the s.,........... 3220
Isa 10:22 Israel be as the sand of the s., ... 3220
Isa 10:26 as his rod was upon the s., so shall.... 3220
Isa 11:9 the Lord, as the waters cover the s.... 3220
Isa 11:11 and from the islands of the s.. 3220
Isa 11:15 the tongue of the Egyptian s.; 3220
Isa 16:8 out, they are gone over the s............. 3220
Isa 18:2 sendeth ambassadors by the s., ... 3220

Isa 19:5 the waters shall fail from the s.,......... 3220
Isa 21:1 The burden of the desert of the s.. 3220
Isa 23:2 of Zidon, that pass over the s., have... 3220
Isa 23:4 for the s. hath spoken, even the........ 3220
Isa 23:4 even the strength of the s., saying, ... 3220
Isa 23:11 stretched out his hand over the s., ... 3220
Isa 24:14 they shall cry aloud from the s.......... 3220
Isa 24:15 God of Israel in the isles of the s.. 3220
Isa 27:1 slay the dragon that is in the s.. 3220
Isa 42:10 ye that go down to the s., and all....... 3220
Isa 43:16 which maketh a way in the s., and...... 3220
Isa 48:18 righteousness as the waves of the s.... 3220
Isa 50:2 at my rebuke I dry up the s., I.......... 3220
Isa 51:10 not it which hath dried the s., the...... 3220
Isa 51:10 made the depths of the s. a way for... 3220
Isa 51:15 Lord thy God that divided the s., ... 3220
Isa 57:20 the wicked are like the troubled s.,..... 3220
Isa 60:5 the abundance of the s. shall be......... 3220
Isa 63:11 that brought them up out of the s....... 3220
Jer 5:22 the sand for the bound of the s.......... 3220
Jer 6:23 their voice roareth like the s.; and...... 3220
Jer 25:22 the isles which are beyond the s., ... 3220
Jer 27:19 concerning the s., and concerning....... 3220
Jer 31:35 which divideth the s. when the 3220
Jer 33:22 the sand of the s. measured: so......... 3220
Jer 46:18 and as Carmel by the s., so shall he... 3220
Jer 47:7 Ashkelon, and against the s. shore? 3220
Jer 48:32 thy plants are gone over the s., they.. 3220
Jer 48:32 they reach even to the s. of Jazer: 3220
Jer 49:21 thereof was heard in the Red s.......... 3220
Jer 49:23 there is sorrow on the s.; it cannot 3220
Jer 50:42 their voice shall roar like the s.,........ 3220
Jer 51:36 I will dry up her s., and make her...... 3220
Jer 51:42 The s. is come up upon Babylon: 3220
Jer 52:17 the brasen s. that was in the house.... 3220
Jer 52:20 The two pillars, one s., and twelve..... 3220
La 2:13 for thy breach is great like the s........ 3220
La 4:3 Even the s. monsters draw out...............
Eze 25:16 destroy...remnant of the s. coast.......... 3220
Eze 26:3 s. causeth his waves to come up......... 3220
Eze 26:5 of nets in the midst of the s.: for....... 3220
Eze 26:16 all the princes of the s. shall come...... 3220
Eze 26:17 which wast strong in the s., she and.... 3220
Eze 26:18 that are in the s. shall be troubled...... 3220
Eze 27:3 art situate at the entry of the s.,......... 3220
Eze 27:9 ships of the s. with their mariners...... 3220
Eze 27:29 all the pilots of the s., shall come....... 3220
Eze 27:32 the destroyed in the midst of the s.?... 3220
Eze 38:20 So that the fishes of the s., and the.... 3220
Eze 39:11 the passengers on the east of the s. ... 3220
Eze 47:8 into the desert, and go into the s....... 3220
Eze 47:8 being brought forth into the s., ... 3220
Eze 47:10 as the fish of the great s., exceeding.. 3220
Eze 47:15 the north side fom the great s., ... 3220
Eze 47:17 And the border from the s. shall be.... 3220
Eze 47:18 from the border unto the east s......... 3220
Eze 47:19 in Kadesh, the river to the great s.. ... 3220
Eze 47:20 west side also shall be the great s...... 3220
Eze 48:28 and to the river toward the great s..... 3220
Da 7:2 heaven strove upon the great s.......... 3221
Da 7:3 great beasts came up from the s., ... 3221
Ho 1:10 Israel shall be as...sand of the s., ... 3220
Ho 4:3 fishes of the s. also shall be taken...... 3220
Joe 2:20 with his face toward the east s., and... 3220
Joe 2:20 hinder part toward the utmost s., ... 3220
Am 5:8 that calleth for the waters of the s.,..... 3220
Am 8:12 And they shall wander from s. to s., ... 3220
Am 9:3 my sight in the bottom of the s.,......... 3220
Am 9:6 that calleth for the waters of the s.,..... 3220
Jon 1:4 sent out a great wind into the s., ... 3220
Jon 1:4 was a mighty tempest in the s., so..... 3220
Jon 1:5 that were in the ship into the s., ... 3220
Jon 1:9 which hath made the s. and the dry.... 3220
Jon 1:11 that the s. may be calm unto us? 3220
Jon 1:11 unto us? for the s. wrought, and was.. 3220
Jon 1:12 up, and cast me forth into the s.; 3220
Jon 1:12 so shall the s. be calm unto.............. 3220
Jon 1:13 s. wrought, and was tempestuous....... 3220
Jon 1:15 Jonah, and cast him forth into the s. ... 3220
Jon 1:15 and the s. ceased from her raging. 3220
Mic 7:12 from s. to s., and from mountain........ 3220
Mic 7:19 their sins into the depths of the s....... 3220
Na 1:4 He rebuketh the s., and maketh it....... 3220
Na 3:8 about it, whose rampart was the s.,..... 3220
Na 3:8 and her wall was from the s.?........... 3220
Hab 1:14 makest men as the fishes of the s., ... 3220
Hab 2:14 the Lord, as the waters cover the s.... 3220
Hab 3:8 was thy wrath against the s., that 3220
Hab 3:15 walk through the s. with thine 3220
Zep 1:3 the heaven, and the fishes of the s., .. 3220
Zep 2:5 unto the inhabitants of the s. coast, ... 3220
Zep 2:6 the s. coast shall be dwellings and...... 3220
Hag 2:6 heavens, and the earth, and the s.,..... 3220
Zec 9:4 he will smite her power in the s.;....... 3220
Zec 9:10 dominion shall be from s. even to s., .. 3220
Zec 10:11 pass through the s. with affliction, ... 3220
Zec 10:11 and shall smite the waves in the s., ... 3220
Zec 14:8 half of them toward the former s.,....... 3220
Zec 14:8 half of them toward the hinder s. 3220
Mt 4:13 which is upon the s. coast, in the....... *3864*
Mt 4:15 by the way of the s., beyond Jordan, ... *2281*
Mt 4:18 Jesus, walking by the s. of Galilee, ... *2281*
Mt 4:18 brother, casting a net into the s......... *2281*
Mt 8:24 arose a great tempest in the s., ... *2281*
Mt 8:26 and rebuked the winds and the s.; *2281*
Mt 8:27 even the winds and the s. obey him!... *2281*
Mt 8:32 down a steep place into the s., and..... *2281*
Mt 13:1 of the house, and sat by the s. side.... *2281*
Mt 13:47 **a net, that was cast into the s.,**..... *2281*
Mt 14:24 ship was now in the midst of the s., ... *2281*
Mt 14:25 went unto them, walking on the s....... *2281*
Mt 14:26 disciples saw him walking on the s.,.... *2281*
Mt 15:29 came nigh unto the s. of Galilee;........ *2281*
Mt 17:27 **thou to the s., and cast an hook,**... *2281*
Mt 18:6 **drowned in the depth of the s.** *2281*
Mt 21:21 **and be thou cast into the s.** *2281*
Mt 23:15 **compass s. and land to make one**.. *2281*
Mk 1:16 as he walked by the s. of Galilee, he .. *2281*
Mk 1:16 brother casting a net into the s.......... *2281*
Mk 2:13 he went forth again by the s. side; *2281*
Mk 3:7 himself with his disciples to the s. *2281*
Mk 4:1 began again to teach by the s. side:.... *2281*
Mk 4:1 entered into a ship, and sat in the s.;.. *2281*
Mk 4:1 whole multitude was by the s. on....... *2281*
Mk 4:39 and said unto the s., **Peace, be still**.. *2281*
Mk 4:41 even the wind and the s. obey him?.... *2281*
Mk 5:1 over unto the other side of the s.,....... *2281*
Mk 5:13 down a steep place into the s., ... *2281*
Mk 5:13 thousand;) and...choked in the s......... *2281*
Mk 5:21 him: and he was nigh unto the s.. ...... *2281*
Mk 6:47 the ship was in the midst of the s., ... *2281*
Mk 6:48 unto them, walking upon the s., ... *2281*
Mk 6:49 they saw him walking upon the s.,...... *2281*
Mk 7:31 he came unto the s. of Galilee, ... *2281*
Mk 9:42 **neck, and he were cast into the s.**.. *2281*
Mk 11:23 **and be thou cast into the s.;** *2281*
Lu 6:17 from the s. coast of Tyre and Sidon,... *3882*
Lu 17:2 **his neck, and he cast into the s.,**.. *2281*
Lu 17:6 **root, and be thou planted in the s.** .. *2281*
Lu 21:25 **the s. and the waves roaring;**........ *2281*
Joh 6:1 Jesus went over the s. of Galilee,....... *2281*
Joh 6:1 Galilee, which is the s. of Tiberias...... *2281*
Joh 6:16 his disciples went down unto the s.,.... *2281*
Joh 6:17 went over the s. toward Capernaum. .. *2281*
Joh 6:18 s. arose by reason of a great wind....... *2281*
Joh 6:19 they see Jesus walking on the s., ... *2281*
Joh 6:22 stood on the other side of the s. saw.. *2281*
Joh 6:25 him on the other side of the s., ... *2281*
Joh 21:1 the disciples at the s. of Tiberias;....... *2281*
Joh 21:7 and did cast himself into the s.. .... *2281*
Ac 4:24 made heaven, and earth, and the s., ... *2281*
Ac 7:36 in the Red s., and in the wilderness.... *2281*
Ac 10:6 whose house is by the s. side:........... *2281*
Ac 10:32 one Simon a tanner by the s. side: *2281*
Ac 14:15 made heaven, and earth, and the s., ... *2281*
Ac 17:14 away Paul to go as it were to the s.... *2281*
Ac 27:5 we had sailed over the s. of Cilicia *3989*
Ac 27:30 had let down the boat into the s.,........ *2281*
Ac 27:38 and cast out the wheat into the s.. ..... *2281*
Ac 27:40 committed themselves unto the s., ... *2281*
Ac 27:43 should cast themselves first into the s., ...
Ac 28:4 though he hath escaped the s., yet..... *2281*
Ro 9:27 of Israel be as the sand of the s.,........ *2281*
1Co 10:1 cloud, and all passed through the s.; ... *2281*
1Co 10:2 Moses in the cloud and in the s.; *2281*
2Co 11:26 in perils in the s., in perils among *2281*
Heb 11:12 is by the s. shore innumerable........... *2281*
Heb 11:29 passed through the Red s. as by dry... *2281*
Jas 1:6 that wavereth is like a wave of the s... *2281*
Jas 3:7 and of things in the s., is tamed,........ *1724*
Jude 13 Raging waves of the s., foaming *2281*
Re 4:6 was a s. of glass like unto crystal: *2281*
Re 5:13 such as are in the s., and all that *2281*
Re 7:1 not blow on the earth, nor on the s., .. *2281*
Re 7:2 given to hurt the earth and the s.,....... *2281*
Re 7:3 Hurt not the earth, neither the s.,....... *2281*
Re 8:8 with fire was cast into the s.: and *2281*
Re 8:8 third part of the s. became blood;....... *2281*
Re 8:9 the creatures which were in the s., ... *2281*
Re 10:2 and he set his right foot upon the s., .. *2281*
Re 10:5 angel which I saw stand upon the s..... *2281*
Re 10:6 s., and the things which are therein, ... *2281*
Re 10:8 the angel which standeth upon the s.... *2281*
Re 12:12 inhabiters of the earth and of the s.! ... *2281*
Re 13:1 And I stood upon the sand of the s.,... *2281*
Re 13:1 and saw a beast rise up out of the s., . *2281*
Re 14:7 the s., and the fountains of waters...... *2281*
Re 15:2 were a s. of glass mingled with fire: ... *2281*
Re 15:2 stand on the s. of glass, having the..... *2281*
Re 16:3 poured out his vial upon the s.; and.... *2281*
Re 16:3 and every living soul died in the s.. .... *2281*
Re 18:17 sailors, and as many as trade by s., ... *2281*
Re 18:19 made rich all that had ships in the s.... *2281*
Re 18:21 millstone, and cast it into the s., ... *2281*
Re 20:8 of whom is as the sand of the s.. .... *2281*
Re 20:13 s. gave up the dead which were in it;.. *2281*
Re 21:1 away; and there was no more s.. .... *2281*

SEAFARING

Eze 26:17 that wast inhabited of s. men, the 3220

SEAL See also SEALED; SEALEST; SEALETH; SEALING; SEALS.

1Ki 21:8 name, and sealed them with his s., ... 2368
Ne 9:38 Levites, and priests, s. unto it........... 2856
Es 8:8 name, and s. it with the king's ring:.... 2856
Job 38:14 It is turned as clay to the s.; and....... 2368
Job 41:15 shut up together as with a close s.. 2368
Ca 8:6 Set me as a s. upon thine heart, ... 2368
Ca 8:6 as a s. upon thine arm: for love is...... 2368
Isa 8:16 s. the law among my disciples. 2856
Jer 32:44 subscribe evidences, and s. them, ... 2856
Da 9:24 to s. up the vision and prophecy, ... 2856
Da 12:4 shut up the words, and s. the book, ... 2856
Joh 3:33 hath set to his s. that God is true. *4972*
Ro 4:11 s. of the righteousness of the faith...... *4973*
1Co 9:2 s. of mine apostleship are ye in the *4973*
2Ti 2:19 of God standeth sure, having this s.,... *4973*
Re 6:3 when he had opened the second s., ... *4973*
Re 6:5 when he had opened the third s., ... *4973*
Re 6:7 when he had opened the fourth s., ... *4973*
Re 6:9 and when he had opened the fifth s.,... *4973*
Re 6:12 when he had opened the sixth s., ... *4973*
Re 7:2 east, having the s. of the living God:... *4973*
Re 8:1 when he had opened the seventh s., ... *4973*
Re 9:4 not the s. of God in their foreheads.... *4973*
Re 10:4 S. up those things which the seven..... *4972*
Re 20:3 shut him up, and set a s. upon him, ... *4972*
Re 22:10 S. not the sayings of the prophecy *4972*

SEALED

De 32:34 and s. up among my treasures?.......... 2856
1Ki 21:8 name, and s. them with his seal, ... 2856
Ne 10:1 Now those that s. were, Nehemiah,.... 2856
Es 3:12 wirtten, and s. with the king's ring. 2856
Es 8:8 name, and s. with the kings ring, ... 2856
Es 8:10 s. it with the king's ring, and sent...... 2856
Job 14:17 My transgression is s. up in a bag, ... 2856
Ca 4:12 a spring shut up, a fountain s.. 2856
Isa 29:11 as the words of a book that is s. 2856
Isa 29:11 and he saith, I cannot; for it is s. 2856
Jer 32:10 subscribed the evidence, and s. it,...... 2856
Jer 32:11 which was s. according to the law 2856
Jer 32:14 both which is s., and this evidence 2856
Da 6:17 the king s. it with his own signet, ... 2857
Da 12:9 up and s. till the time of the end. 2856
Joh 6:27 **for him hath God the Father s.**..... *4972*
Ro 15:28 this, and have s. to them this fruit,..... *4972*
2Co 1:22 Who hath also s. us, and given the *4972*
Eph 1:13 s. with that holy Spirit of promise,...... *4972*
Eph 4:30 are s. unto the day of redemption....... *4972*
Re 5:1 the backside, s. with seven seals........ *2696*
Re 7:3 we have s. the servants of our God.... *4972*
Re 7:4 the number of them which were s. *4972*
Re 7:4 there were s. an hundred and forty..... *4972*
Re 7:5 of Juda were s. twelve thousand........ *4972*
Re 7:5 Reuben were s. twelve thousand. *4972*
Re 7:5 of Gad were s. twelve thousand. *4972*
Re 7:6 of Aser were s. twelve thousand. *4972*
Re 7:6 Nepthalim were s. twelve thousand..... *4972*
Re 7:6 Manasses were s. twelve thousand. *4972*
Re 7:7 of Simeon were s. twelve thousand..... *4972*
Re 7:7 of Levi were s. twelve thousand. *4972*

Re 7:7 Issachar were **s.** twelve thousand....... *4972*
Re 7:8 Zabulon were **s.** twelve thousand........ *4972*
Re 7:8 Joseph were **s.** twelve thousand......... *4972*
Re 7:8 Benjamin were **s.** twelve thousand...... *4972*

SEALEST
Eze 28:12 Thou **s.** up the sum, full of.............. 2856

SEALETH
Job 9:7 riseth not; and **s.** up the stars........... 2856
Job 33:16 of men, and **s.** their instruction,......... 2856
Job 37:7 He **s.** up the hand of every man;......... 2856

SEALING
Mt 27:66 **s.** the stone, and setting a watch........ *4972*

SEALS
Re 5:1 the backside, sealed with seven **s.**....... *4973*
Re 5:2 book, and to loose the **s.** thereof?....... *4973*
Re 5:5 and to loose the seven **s.** thereof......... *4973*
Re 5:9 the book, and to open the **s.** thereof:.. *4973*
Re 6:1 when the Lamb opened one of the **s.**, ..*4973*

SEAM
Joh 19:23 now the coat was without **s.**, woven..... *729*

SEA-MONSTER See SEA and MONSTER.

SEARCH See also SEARCHED; SEARCHEST; SEARCHETH; SEARCHING; UNSEARCHABLE.
Le 27:33 He shall not **s.** whether it be good...... 1239
Nu 10:33 to **s.** out a resting place for them....... 8446
Nu 13:2 men, that they may **s.** the land of....... 8446
Nu 13:32 through which we have gone to **s.**........ 8446
Nu 14:7 which we passed through to **s.** it,....... 8446
Nu 14:36 which Moses sent to **s.** the land,........ 8446
Nu 14:38 the men that went to **s.** the land,........ 8446
De 1:22 and they shall **s.** us out the land,........ 2658
De 1:33 to **s.** you out a place to pitch your...... 8446
De 13:14 shalt thou enquire, and make **s.**, ... 2713
Jos 2:2 of Israel to **s.** out the country........... 2658
Jos 2:3 be come to **s.** out all the country. 2658
Jg 18:2 to spy out the land, and to **s.** it; 2713
Jg 18:2 said unto them, Go, **s.** the land:......... 2713
1Sa 23:23 that I will **s.** him out throughout......... 2664
2Sa 10:3 to **s.** the city, and to spy it out,......... 2713
1Ki 20:6 and they shall **s.** thine house, and....... 2664
2Ki 10:23 **S.**, and look that there be here.......... 2664
1Ch 19:3 servants come unto thee for to **s.**,....... 2713
Ezr 4:15 **s.** may be made in the book of the 1240
Ezr 4:19 and **s.** hath been made, and it is 1240
Ezr 5:17 be **s.** made in the king's treasure 1240
Ezr 6:1 **s.** was made in the house of the 1240
Job 8:8 thyself to the **s.** of their fathers: 2714
Job 13:9 Is it good that he should **s.** you 2713
Job 38:16 walked in the **s.** of the depth?............ 2714
Ps 44:21 Shall not God **s.** this out? for he 2713
Ps 64:6 They **s.** out iniquities; they 2664
Ps 64:6 they accomplish a diligent **s.**.............. 2665
Ps 77:6 and my spirit made diligent **s.**............. 2664
Ps 139:23 **S.** me...and know my heart:................ 2713
Pr 25:2 of kings is to **s.** out a matter.............. 2713
Pr 25:27 to **s.** their own glory is not glory.......... 2714
Ec 1:13 to seek and **s.** out by wisdom............... 8446
Ec 7:25 and to **s.**, and to seek out wisdom,..... 8446
Jer 2:34 I have not found it by secret **s.**,.......... 4290
Jer 17:10 I the Lord **s.** the heart, I try the 2713
Jer 29:13 shall **s.** for me with all your heart....... 1875
La 3:40 Let us **s.** and try our ways, and.......... 2664
Eze 34:6 none did **s.** or seek after them........... 1875
Eze 34:8 did my shepherds **s.** for my flock, ... 1875
Eze 34:11 I, will both **s.** my sheep, and seek...... 1875
Eze 39:14 end of seven months shall they **s.**........ 2713
Am 9:3 will **s.** and take them out thence; 2664
Zep 1:12 I will **s.** Jerusalem with candles,......... 2664
Mt 2:8 **s.** diligently for the young child; *1833*
Joh 5:39 **S. the scriptures; for in them ye**.... *2045*
Joh 7:52 **S.**, and look: for out of Galilee........... *2045*

SEARCHED
Ge 31:34 Laban **s.** all the tent, but found.......... 4959
Ge 31:35 he **s.**, but found not the images. 2664
Ge 31:37 whereas thou hast **s.** all my stuff,........ 4959
Ge 44:12 he **s.**, and began at the eldest, ... 2664
Nu 13:21 **s.** the land from the wilderness.......... 8446
Nu 13:32 of the land which they had **s.** unto........ 8446
Nu 14:6 were of them that **s.** the land, rent....... 8446
Nu 14:34 of the days in which ye **s.** the land, ... 8446
De 1:24 the valley of Eshcol, and **s.** it out....... 7270
Job 5:27 Lo this, we have **s.** it, so it is; 2713
Job 28:27 it; he prepared it, yea, and **s.** it out.... 2713
Job 29:16 the cause which I knew not I **s.** out.... 2713
Job 32:11 whilst ye **s.** out what to say............. 2713
Job 36:26 the number of his years be **s.** out....... 2714
Ps 139:1 O Lord, thou hast **s.** me, and........... 2713
Jer 31:37 the foundations of the earth **s.** out...... 2713
Jer 46:23 though it cannot be **s.**; because.......... 2713
Ob 6 How are the things of Esau **s.** out! 2664
Ac 17:11 **s.** the scriptures daily, whether *350*
1Pe 1:10 have enquired and **s.** diligently, ... *1830*

SEARCHEST
Job 10:6 mine iniquity, and **s.** after my sin? 1875
Pr 2:4 and **s.** for her as for hid treasures; 2664

SEARCHETH
1Ch 28:9 for the Lord **s.** all hearts, and........... 1875
Job 28:3 and **s.** out all perfection: the............. 2713
Job 39:8 and he **s.** after every green thing. 1875
Pr 18:17 his neighbour cometh and **s.** him. 2713
Pr 28:11 hath understanding **s.** him out............ 2713
Ro 8:27 And he that **s.** the hearts knoweth...... *2045*
1Co 2:10 for the Spirit **s.** all things, yea, the..... *2045*
Re 2:23 **he which s. the reins and hearts:**.. *2045*

SEARCHING See also SEARCHINGS.
Nu 13:25 they returned from **s.** of the land 8446
Job 11:7 Canst thou by **s.** find out God? 2714
Pr 20:27 **s.** all the inward parts of the belly. 2664
Isa 40:28 is no **s.** of his understanding.............. 2714
1Pe 1:11 **S.** what, or what manner of time........ *2045*

SEARCHINGS
Jg 5:16 there were great **s.** of heart............. 2714

SEARED
1Ti 4:2 conscience **s.** with a hot iron; *2743*

SEAS
Ge 1:10 of the waters called he **S.**: and 3220
Ge 1:22 and fill the waters in the **s.**, and.......... 3220
Le 11:9 and scales in the waters, in the **s.**, ... 3220
Le 11:10 have not fins and scales in the **s.**,....... 3220
De 33:19 suck of the abundance of the **s.**,.......... 3220
Ne 9:6 the **s.**, and all that is therein, and........ 3220
Ps 8:8 passeth through the paths of the **s.**...... 3220
Ps 24:2 For he hath founded it upon the **s.**, ... 3220
Ps 65:7 Which stilleth the noise of the **s.**, ... 3220
Ps 69:34 the **s.**, and every thing that moveth.... 3220
Ps 135:6 earth, in the **s.**, and all deep places. ... 3220
Isa 17:12 a noise like the noise of the **s.**; 3220
Jer 15:8 to me above the sand of the **s.**........... 3220
Eze 27:4 borders are in the midst of the **s.**,....... 3220
Eze 27:25 very glorious in the midst of the **s.**..... 3220
Eze 27:26 broken thee in the midst of the **s.**. 3220
Eze 27:27 shall fall into the midst of the **s.** in...... 3220
Eze 27:33 thy wares went forth out of the **s.**,...... 3220
Eze 27:34 thou shalt be broken by the **s.** in......... 3220
Eze 28:2 seat of God, in the midst of the **s.**;...... 3220
Eze 28:8 that are slain in the midst of the **s.**...... 3220
Eze 32:2 and thou art as a whale in the **s.**......... 3220
Da 11:45 of his palace between the **s.** in the 3220
Jon 2:3 the deep, in the midst of the **s.**; 3220
Ac 27:41 into a place where two **s.** met, ... *1337*

SEA-SHORE See SEA and SHORE.

SEA-SIDE See SEA and SIDE.

SEASON See also SEASONED; SEASONS.
Ge 40:4 and they continued a **s.** in ward. 3117
Ex 13:10 keep this ordinance in his **s.** from....... 4150
Le 2:13 offering shalt thou **s.** with salt;........... 4414
Le 26:4 I will give you rain in due **s.**, and....... 6256
Nu 9:2 the passover at his appointed **s.**.......... 4150
Nu 9:3 ye shall keep it in his appointed **s.**....... 4150
Nu 9:7 of the Lord in his appointed **s.**............ 4150
Nu 9:13 of the Lord in his appointed **s.**,........... 4150
Nu 28:2 to offer unto me in their due **s.**........... 4150
De 11:14 the rain of your land in his due **s.**,....... 6256
De 16:6 the **s.** that thou camest forth out.......... 4150
De 28:12 the rain unto thy land in his **s.**,........... 6256
Jos 24:7 dwelt in the wilderness a long **s.**. 3117
2Ki 4:16 About this **s.**, according to the........... 4150
2Ki 4:17 bare a son at that **s.** that Elisha had.... 4150
1Ch 21:29 offering, were at that **s.** in the........... 6256
2Ch 15:3 a long **s.** Israel hath been without....... 3117
Job 5:26 shock of corn cometh in in his **s.**........ 6256
Job 30:17 are pierced in me in the night **s.** ....
Job 38:32 bring forth Mazzaroth in his **s.**?........... 6256
Ps 1:3 bringeth forth his fruit in his **s.**; 6256
Ps 22:2 in the night **s.**, and am not silent..............
Ps 104:27 give them their meat in due **s.**........... 6256
Ps 145:15 givest them their meat in due **s.**. 6256
Pr 15:23 a word spoken in due **s.**, how good 6256
Ec 3:1 To every thing there is a **s.**, and a 2165
Ec 10:17 and thy princes eat in due **s.**, for 6256
Isa 50:4 know how to speak a word in **s.** to..........
Jer 5:24 the former and the latter, in his **s.**:...... 6256
Jer 33:20 not be day and night in their **s.**; 6256
Eze 34:26 the shower to come down in his **s.**; 6256
Da 7:12 their lives were prolonged for a **s.**...... 2166
Ho 2:9 and my wine in the **s.** thereof, and 4150
Mt 24:45 **to give them meat in due s.?**....... *2540*
Mk 9:50 **saltness, wherewith will ye s. it?**..... *741*
Mk 12:2 **the s. he sent to the husbandmen**.. *2540*
Lu 1:20 which shall be fulfilled in their **s.**. *2540*
Lu 4:13 he departed from him for a **s.**............. *2540*
Lu 12:42 **their portion of meat in due s.?**....... *2540*
Lu 13:1 were present at that **s.** some that *2540*
Lu 20:10 **at the s. he sent a servant to the**... *2540*
Lu 23:8 he was desirous to see him of a long **s.**, ...
Joh 5:4 down at a certain **s.** into the pool, ... *2540*
Joh 5:35 **ye were willing for a s. to rejoice**.. *5610*
Ac 13:11 blind, not seeing the sun for a **s.**......... *2540*
Ac 19:22 he himself stayed in Asia for a **s.**. *5550*
Ac 24:25 when I have a convenient **s.**, I will *2540*
2Co 7:8 sorry, though it were but for a **s.**........ *5610*
Ga 6:9 for in due **s.** we shall reap, if we......... *2540*
2Ti 4:2 Preach the word; be instant in **s.**, ... *2121*
2Ti 4:2 be instant...out of **s.**; reprove, ... *171*
Phm 15 he therefore departed for a **s.**, that..... *5610*
Heb 11:25 enjoy the pleasures of sin for a **s.**;...... *4340*
1Pe 1:6 rejoice, though now for a **s.**, if........... *3641*
Re 6:11 they should rest yet for a little **s.**,...... *5550*
Re 20:3 that he must be loosed a little **s.**....... *5550*

SEASONED
Lu 14:34 **his savour, wherewith shall it be s.?** *741*
Col 4:6 be alway with grace, **s.** with salt,......... *741*

SEASONS
Ge 1:14 let them be for signs, and for **s.**,......... 4150
Ex 18:22 them judge the people at all **s.**:.......... 6256
Ex 18:26 they judged the people at all **s.**: 6256
Le 23:4 which ye shall proclaim in their **s.**....... 4150
Ps 16:7 reins also instruct me in the night **s.**.........
Ps 104:19 He appointed the moon for **s.**:........... 4150
Da 2:21 he changeth the times and the **s.**:....... 2166
Mt 21:41 render him the fruits in their **s.**......... *2540*
Ac 1:7 **you to know the times or the s.,**... *2540*
Ac 14:17 us rain from heaven, and fruitful **s.**, ... *2540*
Ac 20:18 I have been with you at all **s.**, ... *5550*
1Th 5:1 of the times and the **s.**, brethren,........ *2540*

SEAT See also MERCYSEAT; SEATED; SEATS; SEATWARD.
Ex 25:17 shalt make a mercy **s.** or pure gold:..........
Ex 25:18 in the two ends of the mercy **s.**...............
Ex 25:19 even of the mercy **s.** shall ye make the .....
Ex 25:20 the mercy **s.** with their wings, and............
Ex 25:20 toward the mercy **s.** shall the faces..........
Ex 25:21 put the mercy **s.** above upon the ark;........
Ex 25:22 with thee from above the mercy **s.**.........
Ex 26:34 put the mercy **s.** upon the ark of the.........
Ex 30:6 before the mercy **s.** that is over the ....
Ex 31:7 and the mercy **s.** that is thereupon, ...
Ex 35:12 staves thereof, with the mercy **s.**, ...
Ex 37:6 he made the mercy **s.** of pure gold: ....
Ex 37:7 on the two ends of the mercy **s.**; ....
Ex 37:8 out of the mercy **s.** made he the ....
Ex 37:9 with their wings over the mercy **s.**, ...
Ex 39:35 the staves thereof, and the mercy **s.**, ...
Ex 40:20 and put the mercy **s.** above upon the ....
Le 16:2 within the vail before the mercy **s.**, ...
Le 16:2 in the cloud upon the mercy **s.**..................
Le 16:13 the incense may cover the mercy **s.**...........
Le 16:14 finger upon the mercy **s.** eastward;...........
Le 16:14 and before the mercy **s.** shall he ....
Le 16:15 and sprinkle it upon the mercy **s.**, ...
Le 16:15 and before the mercy **s.**: ....
Nu 7:89 unto him from off the mercy **s.** that ....
Jg 3:20 thee. And he arose out of his **s.**............. 3678
1Sa 1:9 Eli the priest sat upon a **s.** by a post .. 3678
1Sa 4:13 lo, Eli sat upon a **s.** by the wayside 3678
1Sa 4:18 he fell from off the **s.** backward by 3678
1Sa 20:18 because thy **s.** will be empty. 4186
1Sa 20:25 And the king sat upon his **s.**, as at 4186
1Sa 20:25 times, even upon a **s.** by the wall: 4186
2Sa 23:8 The Tachmonite that sat in the **s.**,....... 7674
1Ki 2:19 **s.** to be set for the king's mother;...... 3678

1Ki 10:19 either side on the place of the s., 7675
1Ch 28:11 and of the place of the mercy s.,
Es 3:1 and set his s. above all the princes 3678
Job 23:3 that I might come even to his s.! 8499
Job 29:7 I prepared my s. in the street! 4186
Ps 1:1 nor sitteth in the s. of the scornful. 4186
Pr 9:14 on a s. in the high places of the 3678
Eze 8:3 the s. of the image of jealousy, 4186
Eze 28:2 I am a God, I sit in the s. of God, 4186
Am 6:3 cause the s. of violence to come 7675
Mt 23:2 **and the Pharisees sit in Moses' s.** *2515*
Mt 27:19 he was set down on the judgment s., *968*
Joh 19:13 and sat down in the judgment s. in a *968*
Ac 18:12 and brought him to the judgment s., *968*
Ac 18:16 he drave them from the judgment s. *968*
Ac 18:17 and beat him before the judgment s. *968*
Ac 25:6 next day sitting on the judgment s. *968*
Ac 25:10 Paul, I stand at Caesar's judgment s., *968*
Ac 25:17 the morrow I sat on the judgment s., *968*
Ro 14:10 before the judgment s. of Christ. *968*
2Co 5:10 before the judgment s. of Christ; *968*
Re 2:13 **dwellest, even where Satan's s. is:** *2332*
Re 13:2 and his s., and great authority. *2332*
Re 16:10 out his vial upon the s. of the beast; *2332*

SEATED See also SET.
De 33:21 portion of the lawgiver, was he s.; 5603

SEATS
Mt 21:12 and the s. of them that sold doves, *2515*
Mt 23:6 **and the chief s. in the synagogues,** *4410*
Mk 11:15 and the s. of them that sold doves; *2515*
Mk 12:39 **the chief s. in the synagogues, and** *4410*
Lu 1:52 put down the mighty from their s., *2362*
Lu 11:43 **uppermost s. in the synagogues,** *4410*
Lu 20:46 **the highest s. in the synagogues,** *4410*
Jas 2:6 draw you before the judgment s.?
Re 4:4 throne were four and twenty s.: *2362*
Re 4:4 upon the s. I saw four and twenty *2362*
Re 11:16 which sat before God on their s., *2362*

SEATWARD
Ex 37:9 to the mercy s. were the faces of the

SEBA (se'-bah) See also SABEANS; SHEBA.
Ge 10:7 S., and Havilah, and Sabtah, and 5434
1Ch 1:9 S., and Havilah, and Sabta, and 5434
Ps 72:10 of Sheba and S. shall offer gifts. 5434
Isa 43:3 ransom, Ethiopia and S. for thee. 5434

SEBAT (se'-bat)
Zec 1:7 month, which is the month S., 7627

SECACAH (se-ca'-cah)
Jos 15:61 Beth-arabah, Middin, and S. 5527

SECHU (se'-ku)
1Sa 19:22 came to a great well that is in S. 7906

SECOND
Ge 1:8 and the morning were the s. day. 8145
Ge 2:13 the name of the s. river is Gihon: 8145
Ge 6:16 with lower, s., and third stories 8145
Ge 7:11 in the s. month, the seventeenth 8145
Ge 8:14 in the s. month, on the seven and 8145
Ge 22:15 Abraham out of heaven the s. time, 8145
Ge 30:7 again, and bare Jacob a s. son. 8145
Ge 30:12 Leah's maid bare Jacob a s. son. 8145
Ge 32:19 And so commanded he the s., and 8145
Ge 41:5 he slept and dreamed the s. time: 8145
Ge 41:43 made him to ride in the s. chariot 4932
Ge 41:52 name of the s. called he Ephraim: 8145
Ge 43:10 now we had returned this s. time.
Ge 47:18 they came unto him the s. year, 8145
Ex *general* *title* The S. Book of Moses, Called
Ex 2:13 And when he went out the s. day, 8145
Ex 16:1 on the fifteenth day of the s. month 8145
Ex 26:4 curtain, in the coupling of the s. 8145
Ex 26:5 that is in the coupling of the s.; 8145
Ex 26:10 the curtain which coupleth the s. 8145
Ex 26:20 And for the s. side of the tabernacle 8145
Ex 28:18 And the s. row shall be an emerald, 8145
Ex 36:11 curtain, in the coupling of the s. 8145
Ex 36:12 which was in the coupling of the s. 8145
Ex 36:17 the curtain which coupleth the s. 8145
Ex 39:11 the s. row, an emerald, a sapphire, 8145
Ex 40:17 in the first month in the s. year, 8145
Le 5:10 offer the s. for a burnt offering. 8145
Le 13:58 then it shall be washed the s. time, 8145
Nu 1:1 on the first day of the s. month, 8145
Nu 1:1 s. year after they were come out of 8145
Nu 1:18 on the first day of the s. month, 8145
Nu 2:16 they shall set forth in the s. rank. 8145
Nu 7:18 s. day Nethaneel the son of Zuar, 8145
Nu 9:1 in the first month of the s. year 8145
Nu 9:11 fourteenth day of the s. month at 8145
Nu 10:6 When ye blow an alarm the s. time, 8145
Nu 10:11 twentieth day of the s. month, in 8145
Nu 10:11 the s. year,...the cloud was taken 8145
Nu 29:17 on the s. day ye shall offer twelve 8145
Jos 5:2 circumcise...of Israel the s. time. 8145
Jos 6:14 s. day they compassed the city once, 8145
Jos 10:32 took it on the s. day, and smote it 8145
Jos 19:1 And the s. lot came forth to Simeon, 8145
Jg 6:25 the s. bullock of seven years old, 8145
Jg 6:26 and take the s. bullock, and offer a 8145
Jg 6:28 the s. bullock was offered upon the 8145
Jg 20:24 children of Benjamin the s. day. 8145
Jg 20:25 them out of Gibeah the s. day, and 8145
1Sa 8:2 and the name of his s., Abiah: 4932
1Sa 20:27 which was the s. day of the month, 8145
1Sa 20:34 eat no meat the s. day of the month: 8145
1Sa 26:8 I will not smite him the s. time 8138
2Sa *general* *title* The S. Book of Samuel, [ב]
2Sa *general* *title* Called, The S. Book of . . .Kings.
2Sa 3:3 And his s., Chileab, of Abigail the 4932
2Sa 14:29 when he sent again the s. time, 8145
1Ki 6:1 month Zif, which is the s. month, 8145
1Ki 9:2 appeared to Solomon the s. time, 8145
1Ki 15:25 the s. year of Asa king of Judah, 8147
1Ki 18:34 And he said, Do it the s. time. 8138
1Ki 18:34 And they did it the s. time. 8138
1Ki 19:7 angel...came again the s. time, 8145
2Ki *general* *title* The S. Book Of The Kings, [ב]
2Ki 1:17 in the s. year of Jehoram the son 8147
2Ki 9:19 Then he sent out a s. on horseback, 8145
2Ki 10:6 Then he wrote a letter the s. time 8145
2Ki 14:1 s. year of Joash son of Jehoahaz 8147
2Ki 15:32 In the s. year of Pekah the son of 8147
2Ki 19:29 in the s. year that which springeth 8145
2Ki 23:4 the priests of the s. order, and the 4932
2Ki 25:17 like unto these had the s. pillar 8145
2Ki 25:18 and Zephaniah the s. priest, and 4932
1Ch 2:13 Abinadab the s., and Shimma the 8145
1Ch 3:1 the s., Daniel, of Abigail the 8145
1Ch 3:15 s. Jehoiakim, the third Zedekiah, 8145
1Ch 7:15 the name of the s. was Zelophehad: 8145
1Ch 8:1 Ashbel the s., and Aharah the third, 8145
1Ch 8:39 Jehush the s., and Eliphelet the 8145
1Ch 12:9 Ezer the first, Obadiah the s., Eliab 8145
1Ch 15:18 their brethren of the s. degree, 4932
1Ch 23:11 was the chief, and Zizah the s.: 8145
1Ch 23:19 Amariah the s., Jahaziel the third, 8145
1Ch 23:20 Micah the first, and Jesiah the s. 8145
1Ch 24:7 forth to Jehoiarib, the s. to Jedaiah, 8145
1Ch 24:23 Jeriah the first, Amariah the s., 8145
1Ch 25:9 the s. to Gedaliah, who with his 8145
1Ch 26:2 Jediael the s., Zebadiah the third, 8145
1Ch 26:4 Jehozabad the s., Joah the third, 8145
1Ch 26:11 Hilkiah the s., Tebaliah the third, 8145
1Ch 27:4 And over the course of the s. month 8145
1Ch 29:22 made Solomon...king the s. time, 8145
2Ch *general* *title* The S. Book Of The Chronicles. [ב]
2Ch 3:2 build in the s. day of the s. month, 8145
2Ch 27:5 him, both the s. year, and the third. 8145
2Ch 30:2 keep the passover in the s. month. 8145
2Ch 30:13 unleavened bread in the s. month, 8145
2Ch 30:15 the fourteenth day of the s. month: 8145
2Ch 35:24 and put him in the s. chariot that 4932
Ezr 1:10 silver basons of a s. sort four 4932
Ezr 3:8 Now in the s. year of their coming 8145
Ezr 3:8 in the s. month, began Zerubbabel 8145
Ezr 4:24 the s. year of the reign of Darius 8648
Ne 8:13 the s. day were gathered together 8145
Ne 11:9 son of Senuah was s. over the city. 4932
Ne 11:17 and Bakbukiah the s. among his 4932
Es 2:14 she returned into the s. house of 8145
Es 2:19 were gathered together the s. time, 8145
Es 7:2 said again unto Esther on the s. day 8145
Es 9:29 to confirm this s. letter of Purim. 8145
Job 42:14 and the name of the s., Kezia; 8145
Ec 4:8 is one alone, and there is not a s.; 8145
Ec 4:15 with the s. child that shall stand 8145
Isa 11:11 shall set his hand again the s. time 8145
Isa 37:30 the s. year that which springeth of 8145
Jer 1:13 the Lord came unto me the s. time, 8145
Jer 13:3 the Lord came unto me the s. time, 8145
Jer 33:1 came unto Jeremiah the s. time, 8145
Jer 41:4 s. day after he had slain Gedaliah, 8145
Jer 52:22 s. pillar also and the pomegranates 8145
Jer 52:24 and Zephaniah the s. priest, and 4932
Eze 10:14 the s. face was the face of a man, 8145
Eze 43:22 on the s. day thou shalt offer a kid 8145
Da 2:1 in the s. year of...Nebuchadnezzar 8147
Da 7:5 another beast, a s., like to a bear, 8578
Jon 3:1 Lord came unto Jonah the s. time, 8145
Na 1:9 affliction shall not rise up the s. time.
Zep 1:10 and an howling from the s., and 4932
Hag 1:1 In the s. year of Darius the king, 8147
Hag 1:15 in the s. year of Darius the king. 8147
Hag 2:10 month, in the s. year of Darius, 8147
Zec 1:1 month, in the s. year of Darius, 8147
Zec 1:7 Sebat, in the s. year of Darius, 8147
Zec 6:2 and in the s. chariot black horses; 8145
Mt 21:30 **came to the s., and said likewise** *1208*
Mt 22:26 Likewise the s. also, and the third, *1208*
Mt 22:39 **s. is like unto it, Thou shalt love** *1208*
Mt 26:42 He went away again the s. time, *1208*
Mk 12:21 the s. took her, and died, neither *1208*
Mk 12:31 **the s. is like,...Thou shalt love** *1208*
Mk 14:72 And the s. time the cock crew. *1208*
Lu 6:1 it came to pass on the s. sabbath *1207*
Lu 12:38 **if he shall come in the s. watch,** *1208*
Lu 19:18 **s. came, saying, Lord, thy pound** *1208*
Lu 20:30 the s. took her to wife, and he died *1208*
Joh 3:4 the s. time into his mother's womb, *1208*
Joh 4:54 again the s. miracle that Jesus did, *1208*
Joh 21:16 He saith to him again the s. time, *1208*
Ac 7:13 the s. time Joseph was made known *1208*
Ac 10:15 spake unto him again the s. time, *1208*
Ac 12:10 were past the first and the s. ward, *1208*
Ac 13:33 as it is also written in the s. psalm, *1208*
1Co 15:47 the s. man is the Lord from heaven. *1208*
2Co *general* *title* The S. Epistle Of Paul The *1208*
2Co 1:15 that ye might have a s. benefit; *1208*
2Co 13:2 as if I were present, the s. time; *1208*
2Co *subscr.* s. epistle to the Corinthians. *1208*
2Th *general* *title* The S. Epistle Of Paul The *1208*
2Th *subscr.* The s. epistle to..Thessalonians *1208*
2Ti *subscr.* The s. epistle unto Timotheuse, *1208*
2Ti *general* *title* The S. Epistle Of Paul The *1208*
2Ti *subscr.* brought before Nero the s. time. *1208*
Tit 3:10 after the first and s. admonition *1208*
Heb 8:7 no place have been sought for the s. *1208*
Heb 9:3 And after the s. veil, the tabernacle *1208*
Heb 9:7 into the s. went the high priest *1208*
Heb 9:28 he appear the s. time without sin *1208*
Heb 10:9 first, that he may establish the s. *1208*
2Pe *general* *title* The S. Epistle General Of *1208*
2Pe 3:1 This s. epistle, beloved, I now write *1208*
2Jo *general* *title* The S. Epistle Of John. *1208*
Re 2:11 **shall not be hurt of the s. death** *1208*
Re 4:7 a lion, and the s. beast like a calf, *1208*
Re 6:3 and when he had opened the s. seal, *1208*
Re 6:3 I heard the s. beast say, Come and *1208*
Re 8:8 And the s. angel sounded, and as it *1208*
Re 11:14 The s. woe is past; and, behold, the *1208*
Re 16:3 And the s. angel poured out his vial *1208*
Re 20:6 on such the s. death hath no power, *1208*
Re 20:14 lake of fire. This is the s. death. *1208*
Re 21:8 brimstone: which is the s. death. *1208*
Re 21:19 was jasper; the s., sapphire; the *1208*

SECONDARILY
1Co 12:28 first apostles, s. prophets, thirdly *1208*

SECRET See also SECRETS.
Ge 49:6 soul, come not thou into their s.; 5475
De 27:15 and putteth it in a s. place. 5643
De 29:29 s. things belong unto the Lord 5641
Jg 3:19 I have a s. errand unto thee, O 5643
Jg 13:18 after my name, seeing it is s.? 6383
1Sa 5:9 had emerods in their s. parts. 8368
1Sa 19:2 and abide in a s. place, and hide 5643
Job 14:13 that thou wouldest keep me s., 5641
Job 15:8 Hast thou heard the s. of God? 5475
Job 15:11 is there any s. thing with thee? 328
Job 20:26 darkness...be hid in his s. places: 6845
Job 29:4 s. of God was upon my tabernacle; 5475
Job 40:13 and bind their faces in s. 2934
Ps 10:8 in the s. places doth he murder 4565
Ps 17:12 a young lion lurking in s. places. 4565
Ps 18:11 He made darkness his s. place; 5643
Ps 19:12 cleanse thou me from s. faults. 5641

Ps 25:14 The s. of the Lord is with them......... 5475
Ps 27:5 in the s. of his tabernacle shall he 5643
Ps 31:20 hide them in the s. of thy presence 5643
Ps 64:2 Hide me from the s. counsel of the..... 5475
Ps 64:4 may shoot in s. at the perfect:........... 4565
Ps 81:7 thee in the s. place of thunder:.......... 5643
Ps 90:8 thee, our s. sins in the light of thy 5956
Ps 91:1 dwelleth in the s. place of the most 5643
Ps 139:15 from thee, when I was made in s., ... 5643
Pr 3:32 but his s. is with the righteous. 5475
Pr 9:17 and bread eaten in s. is pleasant. 5643
Pr 21:14 A gift in s. pacifieth anger: and a........ 5643
Pr 25:9 and discover not a s. to another:........ 5475
Pr 27:5 rebuke is better than s. love. 5641
Ec 12:14 judgment, with every s. thing. 5956
Ca 2:14 in the s. places of the stairs, let......... 5643
Isa 3:17 Lord will discover their s. parts. 6596
Isa 45:3 hidden riches of s. places, that........... 4565
Isa 45:19 I have not spoken in s., in a dark....... 5643
Isa 48:16 I have not spoken in s. from the 5643
Jer 2:34 I have not found it by s. search, but ....
Jer 13:17 weep in s. places for your pride;........ 4565
Jer 23:24 Can any hide himself in s. places 4565
Jer 49:10 I have uncovered his s. places, and..... 4565
La 3:10 in wait, and as a lion in s. places........ 4565
Eze 7:22 and they shall pollute my s. place: 6845
Eze 28:3 is no s. that they can hide from 5640
Da 2:18 God of heaven concerning this s.;....... 7328
Da 2:19 s. revealed unto Daniel in a night 7328
Da 2:22 revealeth the deep and s. things:........ 5642
Da 2:27 s. which the king hath demanded......... 7328
Da 2:30 this s. is not revealed to me for......... 7328
Da 2:47 seeing thou couldest reveal this s.. 7328
Da 4:9 and no s. troubleth me, tell me the..... 7328
Am 3:7 revealeth his s. unto his servants 5475
Mt 6:4 That thine alms may be in s.: and. *2927*
Mt 6:4 and thy Father which seeth in s.... *2927*
Mt 6:6 pray to thy Father which is in s.;.. *2927*
Mt 6:6 thy Father which seeth in s. shall.. *2927*
Mt 6:18 but unto thy Father which is in s...*2927*
Mt 6:18 thy Father, which seeth in s.,....... *2927*
Mt 13:35 things which have been kept s.......... *2928*
Mt 24:26 behold, he is in the s. chambers;... *5009*
Mk 4:22 neither was any thing kept s., but .. *614*
Lu 8:17 For nothing is s., that shall not.... *2927*
Lu 11:33 a candle, putteth it in a s. place,... *2926*
Joh 7:4 no man that doeth any thing is s., ... *2927*
Joh 7:10 not openly, but as it were in s.. .... *2927*
Joh 18:20 and in s. have I said nothing. *2927*
Ro 16:25 was kept s. since the world began, ... *4601*
Eph 5:12 which are done of them in s.. .... *2931*

SECRETLY
Ge 31:27 didst thou flee away s., and steal 2244
De 13:6 entice thee s., saying, Let us go......... 5643
De 27:24 he that smiteth his neighbour s.. 5643
De 28:57 eat them for want of all things s. in 5643
Jos 2:1 out of Shittim two men to spy s.,........ 2791
1Sa 18:22 Commune with David s., and say, ... 3909
1Sa 23:9 Saul s. practised mischief against........ 2790
2Sa 12:12 For thou didst it s.: but I will do.......... 5643
2Ki 17:9 the children of Israel did s. those 2644
Job 4:12 a thing was s. brought to me............. 1589
Job 13:10 you, if ye do s. accept persons. 5643
Job 31:27 my heart hath been s. enticed, or......... 5643
Ps 10:9 He lieth in wait s. as a lion in his 4565
Ps 31:20 shalt keep them s. in a pavilion.......... 6845
Jer 37:17 king asked him s. in his house, ... 5643
Jer 38:16 the king sware s. unto Jeremiah, ... 5643
Jer 40:15 spake to Gedaliah in Mizpah s.,.......... 5643
Hab 3:14 was as to devour the poor s.............. 4565
Joh 11:28 way, and called Mary her sister s.,..... *2977*
Joh 19:38 Jesus, but s. for fear of the Jews, ... *2928*

SECRETS
De 25:11 hand, and taketh him by the s. 4016
Job 11:6 shew thee the s. of wisdom, that 8587
Ps 44:21 for he knoweth the s. of the heart...... 8587
Pr 11:13 A talebearer revealeth s.: but he......... 5475
Pr 20:19 about as a talebearer revealeth s.......... 5475
Da 2:28 a God in heaven that revealeth s., ... 7328
Da 2:29 and he that revealeth s. maketh.......... 7328
Da 2:47 lord of kings, and a revealer of s.,....... 7328
Ro 2:16 God shall judge the s. of men............ *2927*
1Co 14:25 the s. of his heart made manifest; *2927*

SECT
Ac 5:17 (which is the s. of the Sadducees,)....... *139*
Ac 15:5 up certain of the s. of the Pharisees..... *139*
Ac 24:5 ringleader of the s. of the Nazarenes; ... *139*
Ac 26:5 the most straitest s. of our religion *139*
Ac 28:22 for as concerning this s. we know........ *139*

SECUNDUS (se-cun'-dus)
Ac 20:4 Aristarchus and S.; and Gaius............ *4580*

SECURE
Jg 8:11 the host: for the host was s................ 983
Jg 18:7 of the Zidonians, quiet and s.; 982
Jg 18:10 ye shall come unto a people s., and...... 982
Jg 18:27 a people that were at quiet and s......... 982
Job 11:18 thou shalt be s., because there is 982
Job 12:6 and they that provoke God are s.; 987
Mt 28:14 will persuade him, and s. you....... *4160,275*

SECURELY
Pr 3:29 seeing he dwelleth s. by thee.............. 983
Mic 2:8 pass by s. as men averse from war...... 983

SECURITY
Ac 17:9 when they had taken s. of Jason,......... *2425*

SEDITION See also SEDITIONS.
Ezr 4:15 that they have moved s. within............ 849
Ezr 4:19 rebellion and s. have been made 849
Lu 23:19 for a certain s. made in the city, ... *4714*
Lu 23:25 for s. and murder was cast into *4714*
Ac 24:5 a mover of s. among all the Jews *4714*

SEDITIONS
Ga 5:20 emulations, wrath, strife, s., ... *1370*

SEDUCE See also SEDUCED; SEDUCETH; SEDUCING.
Mk 13:22 to s., if it were possible, even the... *635*
1Jo 2:26 you, concerning them that s. you. *4105*
Re 2:20 to teach and to s. my servants to.. *4105*

SEDUCED
2Ki 21:9 Manasseh s. them to do more evil...... 8582
Isa 19:13 they have also s. Egypt, even they..... 8582
Eze 13:10 they have s. my people, saying, ... 2937

SEDUCERS
2Ti 3:13 and s. shall wax worse and worse, ... *1114*

SEDUCETH
Pr 12:26 the way of the wicked s. them.......... 8582

SEDUCING
1Ti 4:1 giving heed to s. spirits, and *4108*

SEE See also OVERSEE; SAW; SEEING; SEEN; SEEST; SEETH.
Ge 2:19 to s. what he would call them:.......... 7200
Ge 8:8 to s. if the waters were abated.......... 7200
Ge 11:5 Lord came down to s. the city and..... 7200
Ge 12:12 when the Egyptians shall s. thee, ... 7200
Ge 18:21 and s. whether they have done 7200
Ge 19:21 unto him, S., I have accepted thee..... 2009
Ge 21:16 me not s. the death of the child. 7200
Ge 27:1 were dim, so that he could not s.,....... 7200
Ge 27:27 S., the smell of my son is as the 7200
Ge 31:5 I s. your father's countenance, that..... 7200
Ge 31:12 s., all the rams which leap upon the..... 7200
Ge 31:50 s., God is witness betwixt me and....... 7200
Ge 32:20 me, and afterward I will s. his face;.... 7200
Ge 34:1 out to s. the daughters of the land,..... 7200
Ge 37:14 s. whether it be well with thy............ 7200
Ge 37:20 s. what will become of his dreams. 7200
Ge 39:14 S., he hath brought in an Hebrew 7200
Ge 41:41 S., I have set thee over all the land.... 7200
Ge 42:9, 12 to s. the nakedness of the land...... 7200
Ge 43:3,5 Ye shall not s. my face, except.......... 7200
Ge 44:23 you, ye shall s. my face no more. 7200
Ge 44:26 for we may not s. the man's face, ... 7200
Ge 44:34 lest peradventure I s. the evil that...... 7200
Ge 45:12 behold, your eyes s., and the eyes..... 7200
Ge 45:24 S. that ye fall not out by the way............
Ge 45:28 I will go and s. him before I die. 7200
Ge 48:10 dim for age, so that he could not s.... 7200
Ge 48:11 I had not thought to s. thy face: 7200
Ex 1:16 women, and s. them upon the stools;.. 7200
Ex 3:3 turn aside, and s. this great sight, ... 7200
Ex 3:4 Lord saw that he turned aside to s., ... 7200
Ex 4:18 and s. whether they be yet alive. 7200
Ex 4:21 s. that thou do all those wonders 7200
Ex 5:19 did s. that they were in evil case, ... 7200
Ex 6:1 thou s. what I will do to Pharaoh: 7200
Ex 7:1 S., I have made thee a god to........... 7200
Ex 10:5 one cannot be able to s. the earth: 7200
Ex 10:28 heed to thyself, s. my face no more;... 7200
Ex 10:29 I will s. thy face again no more.......... 7200
Ex 12:13 when I s. the blood, I will pass over... 7200
Ex 13:17 the people repent when they s. war,... 7200
Ex 14:13 and s. the salvation of the Lord, ... 7200
Ex 14:13 s. them again no more for ever.......... 7200
Ex 16:7 ye shall s. the glory of the Lord; for... 7200
Ex 16:29 S., for that the Lord hath given you ... 7200
Ex 16:32 they may s. the bread wherewith I..... 7200
Ex 22:8 to s. whether he have put his hand...........
Ex 23:5 s. the ass of him that hateth thee....... 7200
Ex 31:2 S., I have called by name Bezaleel 7200
Ex 33:12 S., thou sayest unto me, Bring up...... 7200
Ex 33:20 he said, Thou canst not s. my face: 7200
Ex 33:20 there shall no man s. me, and live. 7200
Ex 33:23 and thou shalt s. my back parts: 7200
Ex 34:10 art shall s. the work of the Lord: 7200
Ex 35:30 S., the Lord hath called by name 7200
Le 13:8 if the priest s. that, behold, the scab... 7200
Le 13:10 And the priest shall s. him: and, ... 7200
Le 13:15 And the priest shall s. the raw flesh,... 7200
Le 13:17 And the priest shall s. him: and, ... 7200
Le 13:30 Then the priest shall s. the plague:..... 7200
Le 14:36 priest go into it to s. the plague,........ 7200
Le 14:36 priest shall go in to s. the house: 7200
Le 20:17 and s. her nakedness, and she s. his... 7200
Nu 4:20 not go in to s. when the holy things.... 7200
Nu 11:15 and let me not s. my wretchedness. ... 7200
Nu 11:23 thou shalt s. now whether my word.... 7200
Nu 13:18 And s. the land, what it is; and the..... 7200
Nu 14:23 they shall not s. the land which I........ 7200
Nu 14:23 any of them that provoked me s. it:..... 7200
Nu 22:41 that thence he might s. the utmost 7200
Nu 23:9 from the top of the rocks I s. him, ... 7200
Nu 23:13 from whence thou mayest s. them:....... 7200
Nu 23:13 thou shalt s. but the utmost part of 7200
Nu 23:13 of them, and shalt not s. them all:...... 7200
Nu 24:17 I shall s. him, but not now: I shall...... 7200
Nu 27:12 and s. the land which I have given...... 7200
Nu 32:8 from Kadesh-barnea to s. the land. 7200
Nu 32:11 shall s. the land which I swear unto.... 7200
De 1:35 evil generation s. that good land,........ 7200
De 1:36 son of Jephunneh; he shall s. it, and.... 7200
De 3:25 and s. the good land that is beyond..... 7200
De 3:28 inherit the land...thou shalt s............. 7200
De 4:28 which neither s., nor hear, nor eat, ... 7200
De 18:16 neither let me s. this great fire any 7200
De 22:1 Thou shalt not s. thy brother's ox 7200
De 22:4 Thou shalt not s. thy brother's ass 7200
De 23:14 that he s. no unclean thing in thee,..... 7200
De 28:10 s. that thou art called by the name 7200
De 28:34, 67 thine eyes which thou shalt s.. 7200
De 28:68 Thou shalt s. it no more again: and..... 7200
De 29:4 eyes to s., and ears to hear, unto 7200
De 29:22 they s. the plagues of that land, ... 7200
De 30:15 S., I have set before thee this day 7200
De 32:20 I will s. what their end shall be: for 7200
De 32:39 S. now that I, even I, am he, and...... 7200
De 32:52 thou shalt s. the land before thee; 7200
De 34:4 caused thee to s. it with thine eyes, ... 7200
Jos 3:3 ye s. the ark of the covenant of the.... 7200
Jos 6:2 S., I have given into thine hand 7200
Jos 8:1 s., I have given into thine hand the..... 7200
Jos 8:1 S. ye do. S., I have commanded you. ..7200
Jos 22:10 by Jordan, a great altar to s. to. 4758
Jg 9:37 said, S. there come people down......... 2009
Jg 14:8 aside to s. the carcase of the lion: 7200
Jg 16:5 s. wherein his great strength lieth, ... 7200
Jg 21:21 s., and, behold, if the daughters of..... 7200
1Sa 2:32 s. an enemy in my habitation, in......... 5027
1Sa 3:2 to wax dim, that he could not s.; 7200
1Sa 4:15 eyes were dim, that he could not s....... 7200
1Sa 6:9 s., if it goeth up by the way of his 7200
1Sa 6:13 saw the ark, and rejoiced to s. it........ 7200
1Sa 10:24 S. ye him whom the Lord hath 7200
1Sa 12:16 stand and s. this great thing, which...... 7200
1Sa 12:17 and s. that your wickedness is great, .. 7200
1Sa 14:17 now, and s. who is gone from us. 7200
1Sa 14:29 s., I pray you, how mine eyes have.... 7200
1Sa 14:38 s. wherein this sin hath been this 7200
1Sa 15:35 Samuel came no more to s. Saul 7200
1Sa 17:28 that thou mightest s. the battle.......... 7200
1Sa 19:3 and what I s., that I will tell thee. 7200
1Sa 19:15 the messengers again to s. David, ... 7200
1Sa 20:29 I pray thee, and s. my brethren. 7200
1Sa 21:14 servants, Lo, ye s. the man is mad: ... 7200
1Sa 23:22 and s. his place where his haunt is, ... 7200

1Sa 23:23 S. therefore, and take knowledge of.... 7200
1Sa 24:11 s., yea, s. the skirt of thy robe in my.. 7200
1Sa 24:11 and s. that there is neither evil nor..... 7200
1Sa 24:15 s., and plead my cause, and deliver 7200
1Sa 25:35 s., I have hearkened to thy voice, ... 7200
1Sa 26:16 s. where the king's spear is, and the... 7200
2Sa 3:13 Thou shalt not s. my face, except 7200
2Sa 3:13 when thou comest to s. my face. 7200
2Sa 7:2 S. now, I dwell in an house of........... 7200
2Sa 13:5 when thy father cometh to s. thee,..... 7200
2Sa 13:5 I may s. it, and eat it at her hand. 7200
2Sa 13:6 when the king was come to s. him, ... 7200
2Sa 14:24 house, and let him not s. my face....... 7200
2Sa 14:30 S., Joab's field is near mine, and he.... 7200
2Sa 14:32 let me s. the king's face; and if.......... 7200
2Sa 15:3 S., thy matters are good and right;..... 7200
2Sa 15:28 S., I will tarry in the plain of the....... 7200
2Sa 24:3 eyes of my lord the king may s. it:....... 7200
2Sa 24:13 s. what answer I shall return to him ... 7200
1Ki 9:12 came out from Tyre to s. the cities 7200
1Ki 12:16 now s. to thine own house, David. 7200
1Ki 14:4 Ahijah could not s.; for his eyes........ 7200
1Ki 17:23 and Elijah said, S., thy son liveth. 7200
1Ki 20:7 s. how this man seeketh mischief: 7200
1Ki 20:22 and mark, and s. what thou doest:...... 7200
1Ki 22:25 Behold, thou shalt s. in that day,........ 7200
2Ki 2:10 s. me when I am taken from thee, ... 7200
2Ki 3:14 not look toward thee, nor s. thee....... 7200
2Ki 3:17 not s. wind, neither shall ye s. rain;.... 7200
2Ki 5:7 s. how we seekest a quarrel............. 7200
2Ki 6:17 thee, open his eyes, that he may s...... 7200
2Ki 6:20 eyes of these men, that they may s.... 7200
2Ki 6:32 S. ye how this son of a murderer....... 7200
2Ki 7:2 thou shalt s. it with thine eyes, but 7200
2Ki 7:13 consumed:) and let us send and s....... 7200
2Ki 7:14 of the Syrians, saying, Go and s......... 7200
2Ki 7:19 shalt s. it with thine eyes, but shalt.... 7200
2Ki 8:29 Ahaziah...went down to s. Joram........ 7200
2Ki 9:16 Judah was come down to s. Joram. 7200
2Ki 9:17 he came, and said, I s. a company...... 7200
2Ki 9:34 Go, s. now this cursed woman, and..........
2Ki 10:16 me, and s. my zeal for the Lord. 7200
2Ki 19:16 open, Lord, thine eyes, and s.: and 7200
2Ki 22:20 thine eyes shall not s. all the evil 7200
2Ki 23:17 he said, What title is that that I s.? 7200
2Ki 10:16 now, David, s. to thine own house. 7200
2Ch 18:16 did s. all Israel scattered upon the...... 7200
2Ch 18:24 Behold, thou shalt s. on that day........ 7200
2Ch 20:17 and s. the salvation of the Lord with... 7200
2Ch 22:6 Ahaziah...went down to s. Jehoram..... 7200
2Ch 24:5 and s. that ye hasten the matter. ....
2Ch 25:17 let us s. one another in the face......... 7200
2Ch 29:8 to hissing, as ye s. with your eyes. 7200
2Ch 30:7 gave them up to desolation, as ye s.... 7200
2Ch 34:28 thine eyes s. all the evil that I will...... 7200
Ezr 4:14 for us to s. the king's dishonour,......... 2370
Ne 2:17 Ye s. the distress that we are in, ... 7200
Ne 4:11 They shall not know, neither s., till 7200
Ne 9:9 didst s. the affliction of our fathers 7200
Es 3:4 to s. whether Mordecai's matters 7200
Es 5:13 as I s. Mordecai the Jew sitting at....... 7200
Es 8:6 For how can I endure to s. the evil 7200
Es 8:6 to s. the destruction of my kindred?.... 7200
Job 3:9 let it s. the dawning of the day: 7200
Job 6:21 ye s. my casting down, and are 7200
Job 7:7 mine eye shall no more s. good. 7200
Job 7:8 hath seen me shall s. me no more:..... 7789
Job 9:11 he goeth by me, and I s. him not:....... 7200
Job 9:25 they flee away, they s. no good. 7200
Job 10:15 therefore s. thou mine affliction;......... 7200
Job 17:15 as for my hope, who shall s. it?......... 7789
Job 19:26 body, yet in my flesh shall I s. God: ... 2372
Job 19:27 Whom I shall s. for myself, and 2372
Job 20:9 which saw him shall s. him no more;.........
Job 20:17 He shall not s. the rivers, the........... 7200
Job 21:20 His eyes shall s. his destruction, ... 7200
Job 22:11 Or darkness, that thou canst not s.;.... 7200
Job 22:19 The righteous s. it, and are glad: 7200
Job 23:9 the right hand, that I cannot s. him:..... 7200
Job 24:1 that know him not s. his days? 2372
Job 24:15 saying, No eye shall s. me:............... 7789
Job 28:27 Then did he s. it, and declare it;........ 7200
Job 31:4 Doth not he s. my ways, and count 7200
Job 33:26 and he shall s. his face with joy: 7200
Job 33:28 pit, and his life shall s. the light. 7200
Job 34:32 That which I s. not teach thou me;..... 2372
Job 35:5 Look unto the heavens, and s.;......... 7200
Job 35:14 thou sayest thou shalt not s. him,....... 7789
Job 36:25 Every man may s. it; man may.......... 2372
Job 37:21 now men s. not the bright light.......... 7200
Ps 10:11 hideth his face; he will never s. it....... 7200
Ps 14:2 to s. if...any that did understand, ... 7200
Ps 16:10 thine Holy One to s. corruption.......... 7200
Ps 22:7 they that s. me laugh me to scorn:..... 7200
Ps 27:13 to s. the goodness of the Lord in the.. 7200
Ps 31:11 that did s. me without fled from me.... 7200
Ps 34:8 taste and s. that the Lord is good: 7200
Ps 34:12 many days, that he may s. good? 7200
Ps 36:9 life: in thy light shall we s. light......... 7200
Ps 37:34 wicked are cut off, thou shalt s. it. 7200
Ps 40:3 many shall s. it, and fear, and shall..... 7200
Ps 41:6 if he come to s. me, he speaketh....... 7200
Ps 49:9 live for ever, and not s. corruption. 7200
Ps 49:19 fathers; they shall never s. light. 7200
Ps 52:6 The righteous also shall s., and fear,.... 7200
Ps 53:2 to s. if...any that did understand, ... 7200
Ps 58:8 that they may not s. the sun. 2372
Ps 59:10 God shall let me s. my desire upon..... 7200
Ps 63:2 To s. thy power and thy glory, so as.. 7200
Ps 64:5 they say, Who shall s. them?............. 7200
Ps 64:8 all that s. them shall flee away........... 7200
Ps 66:5 Come and s. the works of God: he..... 7200
Ps 69:23 eyes be darkened, that they s. not; 7200
Ps 69:32 humble shall s. this, and be glad;........ 7200
Ps 74:9 We s. not our signs: there is no 7200
Ps 86:17 that they which hate me may s. it, ... 7200
Ps 89:48 that liveth, and shall not s. death? 7200
Ps 91:8 and s. the reward of the wicked......... 7200
Ps 92:11 s. my desire on mine enemies,............ 5027
Ps 94:7 The Lord shall not s., neither shall..... 7200
Ps 94:9 formed the eye, shall he not s.?......... 5027
Ps 97:6 and all the people s. his glory............ 7200
Ps 106:5 That I may s. the good of thy chosen,. 7200
Ps 107:24 These s. the works of the Lord, and... 7200
Ps 107:42 righteous shall s. it, and rejoice:......... 7200
Ps 112:8 he s. his desire upon his enemies....... 7200
Ps 112:10 wicked shall s. it, and be grieved; 7200
Ps 115:5 eyes have they, but they s. not: 7200
Ps 118:7 I s. my desire upon them that hate..... 7200
Ps 119:74 thee will be glad when they s. me;...... 7200
Ps 128:5 thou shalt s. the good of Jerusalem..... 7200
Ps 128:6 thou shalt s. thy children's children, ... 7200
Ps 135:16 eyes have they, but they s. not; 7200
Ps 139:16 Thine eyes did s. my substance, ... 7200
Ps 139:24 s. if there be any wicked way in me, .. 7200
Pr 24:18 Lest the Lord s. it, and it displease 7200
Pr 29:16 but the righteous shall s. their fall. 7200
Ec 1:10 it may be said, S., this is new?.......... 7200
Ec 2:3 till I might s. what was that good........ 7200
Ec 3:18 s. that they themselves are beasts...... 7200
Ec 3:22 him to s. what shall be after him?....... 7200
Ec 7:11 is profit to them that s. the sun. 7200
Ec 8:16 and to s. the business that is done 7200
Ca 2:14 let me s. thy countenance, let me 7200
Ca 6:11 of nuts to s. the fruits of the valley, ... 7200
Ca 6:11 to s. whether the vine flourished,........ 7200
Ca 6:13 What will ye s. in the Shulamite?........ 2372
Ca 7:12 let us s. if the vine flourish, ... 7200
Isa 5:19 hasten his work, that we may s. it: 7200
Isa 6:9 and s. ye indeed, but perceive not...... 7200
Isa 6:10 lest they s. with their eyes, and hear.. 7200
Isa 13:1 Isaiah the son of Amoz did s.. 2372
Isa 14:16 that s. thee shall narrowly look.......... 7200
Isa 18:3 s. ye, when he lifteth up an ensign...... 7200
Isa 26:11 hand is lifted up, they will not s......... 2372
Isa 26:11 but they shall s., and be ashamed....... 2372
Isa 29:18 the blind shall s. out of obscurity,....... 7200
Isa 30:10 Which say to the seers, S. not; 7200
Isa 30:20 but thine eyes shall s. thy teachers:..... 7200
Isa 32:3 eyes of them that s. shall not be dim, . 7200
Isa 33:17 eyes shall s. the king in his beauty: 2372
Isa 33:19 Thou shalt not s. a fierce people, ... 7200
Isa 33:20 s. Jerusalem a quiet habitation, ... 7200
Isa 35:2 they shall s. the glory of the Lord, ... 7200
Isa 37:17 open thine eyes, O Lord, and s. 7200
Isa 38:11 I said, I shall not s. the Lord, even 7200
Isa 40:5 and all flesh shall s. it together: 7200
Isa 41:20 That they may s., and know, and....... 7200
Isa 42:18 and look, ye blind, that ye may s.. 7200
Isa 44:9 they s. not, nor know; that they 7200
Isa 44:18 shut their eyes, that they cannot s.; ... 7200
Isa 48:6 Thou hast heard, s. all this; and......... 2372
Isa 49:7 Kings shall s. and arise, princes......... 7200
Isa 52:8 for they shall s. eye to eye, when...... 7200
Isa 52:10 shall s. the salvation of our God......... 7200
Isa 52:15 had not been told them shall they s.; .. 7200
Isa 53:2 when we...s. him, there is no beauty.. 7200
Isa 53:10 he shall s. his seed, he shall prolong... 7200
Isa 53:11 He shall s. of the travail of his soul,.... 7200
Isa 60:4 up thine eyes round about, and s........ 7200
Isa 60:5 Then thou shalt s., and flow....... 3372,7200
Isa 61:9 all that s. them shall acknowledge...... 7200
Isa 62:2 Gentiles shall s. thy righteousness. 7200
Isa 64:9 s., we beseech thee, we are all thy.... 5027
Isa 66:14 when ye s. this, your heart shall......... 7200
Isa 66:18 they shall come, and s. my glory......... 7200
Jer 1:10 S., I have this day set thee over the .. 7200
Jer 1:11 I said, I s. a rod of an almond tree..... 7200
Jer 1:13 And I said, I s. a seething pot; and..... 7200
Jer 2:10 over the isles of Chittim, and s.;........ 7200
Jer 2:10 and s. if there be such a thing. 7200
Jer 2:19 s. that it is an evil thing and bitter,..... 7200
Jer 2:23 s. thy way in the valley, know what..... 7200
Jer 2:31 O generation, s. ye the word of the.... 7200
Jer 3:2 and s. where thou hast not been lien... 7200
Jer 4:21 How long shall I s. the standard,........ 7200
Jer 5:1 s. now, and know, and seek in the 7200
Jer 5:12 shall we s. sword nor famine:............ 7200
Jer 5:21 which have eyes, and s. not; which..... 7200
Jer 6:16 Stand ye in the ways, and s., and....... 7200
Jer 7:12 s. what I did to it for the wickedness.. 7200
Jer 11:20 let me s. thy vengeance on them: 7200
Jer 12:4 said, He shall not s. our last end......... 7200
Jer 14:13 Ye shall not s. the sword, neither....... 7200
Jer 17:6 and shall not s. when good cometh; 7200
Jer 17:8 and shall not s. when heat cometh, ... 7200
Jer 20:12 let me s. thy vengeance on them: 7200
Jer 20:18 the womb to s. labour and sorrow, ... 7200
Jer 22:10 no more, nor s. his native country...... 7200
Jer 22:12 and shall s. this land no more. 7200
Jer 23:24 secret places that I shall not s. him? ... 7200
Jer 30:6 and s. whether a man doth travail........ 7200
Jer 30:6 do I s. every man with his hands 7200
Jer 42:14 Egypt, where we shall s. no war, ... 7200
Jer 42:18 and ye shall s. this place no more....... 7200
Jer 51:61 and shalt s., and shalt read all these ... 7200
La 1:11 s., O Lord, and consider; for I am....... 7200
La 1:12 s. if there be any sorrow like unto...... 7200
Eze 8:6 thou shalt s. greater abominations....... 7200
Eze 8:13, 15 shalt s. greater abominations......... 7200
Eze 12:2 which have eyes to s., and s. not;...... 7200
Eze 12:6 face, that thou s. not the ground:........ 7200
Eze 12:12 he s. not the ground with his eyes. 7200
Eze 12:13 shall he not s. it, though he...die........ 7200
Eze 13:9 upon the prophets that s. vanity,........ 2374
Eze 13:16 which s. visions of peace for her, ... 2374
Eze 13:23 ye shall s. no more vanity, nor 2372
Eze 14:22 s. their way and their doings: 7200
Eze 14:23 ye s. their ways and their doings:....... 7200
Eze 16:37 they may s. all thy nakedness............ 7200
Eze 20:48 flesh shall s. that I the Lord have....... 7200
Eze 21:29 Whiles they s. vanity unto thee.......... 2372
Eze 32:31 Pharaoh shall s. them, and shall 7200
Eze 33:6 the watchman s. the sword come, ... 7200
Eze 39:21 heathen shall s. my judgment that....... 7200
Da 1:10 should he s. your faces worse liking.... 7200
Da 2:8 ye s. the thing is gone from me......... 2370
Da 3:25 Lo, I s. four men loose, walking in....... 2370
Da 5:23 which s. not, nor hear, nor know: 2370
Joe 2:28 your young men shall s. visions:......... 7200
Am 6:2 Pass ye unto Calneh, and s.; and 7200
Jon 4:5 s. what would become of the city. 7200
Mic 6:9 man of wisdom shall s. thy name:........ 7200
Mic 7:10 she that is mine enemy shall s. it, ... 7200
Mic 7:16 nations shall s. and be confounded...... 7200
Hab 1:1 Habakkuk the prophet did s.............. 2372
Hab 2:1 to s. what he will say unto me,.......... 7200
Zep 3:15 thou shalt not s. evil any more. 7200
Hag 2:3 how do ye s. it now? is it not in 7200
Zec 2:2 s. what is the breadth thereof, and..... 7200
Zec 4:10 shall s. the plummet in the hand of..... 7200
Zec 5:2 And I answered, I s. a flying roll;....... 7200
Zec 5:5 s. what is this that goeth forth.......... 7200
Zec 9:5 Askelon shall s. it, and fear;............. 7200
Zec 9:5 Gaza also shall s. it, and be very.............
Zec 10:7 yea, their children shall s. it, and 7200
Mal 1:5 your eyes shall s., and ye shall say....... 7200
Mt 5:8 **in heart: for they shall s. God......** *3700*
Mt 5:16 **that they may s. your good works,** *1492*
Mt 7:5 **then shalt thou s. clearly to cast...** *1227*
Mt 8:4 unto him, **S. thou tell no man;........** *3708*

Mt 9:30 saying, **S. that no man know it** 3708
Mt 11:4 **things which ye do hear and s.** 991
Mt 11:7 **ye out into the wilderness to s.?** 2300
Mt 11:8, 9 **But what went ye out for to s.?** 1492
Mt 12:38 we would s. a sign from thee. 1492
Mt 13:13 **because they seeing s. not; and** 991
Mt 13:14 **and seeing ye shall s., and shall** 991
Mt 13:15 **they should s. with their eyes,** 1492
Mt 13:16 **blessed are your eyes, for they s.** 991
Mt 13:17 **have desired to s. those things** 1492
Mt 13:17 **those things which ye s., and have** 991
Mt 15:31 lame to walk, and the blind to s. 991
Mt 16:28 **till they s. the Son of man** 1492
Mt 22:11 **the king came in to s. the guests,** 2300
Mt 23:39 **Ye shall not s. me henceforth,** 1492
Mt 24:2 them, **S. ye not all these things?** 991
Mt 24:6 **s. that ye be not troubled: for all** 3708
Mt 24:15 **s. the abomination of desolation,** 1492
Mt 24:30 **shall s. the Son of man coming** 3700
Mt 24:33 **when ye shall s. all these things,** 1492
Mt 26:58 sat with the servants, to s. the end. 1492
Mt 26:64 **s. the Son of man sitting on the** 3700
Mt 27:4 What is that to us? s. thou to that. 3700
Mt 27:24 blood of this just person: s. ye to it. 3700
Mt 27:49 s. whether Elias will come to save 1492
Mt 28:1 the other Mary to s. the sepulchre. 2334
Mt 28:6 s. the place where the Lord lay. 1492
Mt 28:7 there shall ye s. him: lo, I have 3700
Mt 28:10 **Galilee, and there shall they s.** 3700
Mk 1:44 **S. thou say nothing to any man:** 3708
Mk 4:12 **That seeing they may s., and not** 991
Mk 5:14 to s. what it was that was done. 1492
Mk 5:15 s. him that was possessed with 2334
Mk 5:32 to s. her that had done this thing. 1492
Mk 6:38 **many loaves have ye? go and s.** 1492
Mk 8:18 **Having eyes, s. ye not? and having** 991
Mk 8:24 and said, I s. men as trees, walking. 991
Mk 12:15 **bring me a penny, that I may s.** 1492
Mk 13:1 s. what manner of stones and 2396
Mk 13:14 **s. the abomination of desolation,** 1492
Mk 13:26 **shall they s....Son of man coming** 3700
Mk 13:29 **shall s. these things come to pass,** 1492
Mk 14:62 **s. the Son of man sitting on the** 3700
Mk 15:32 cross, that we may s. and believe. 1492
Mk 15:36 s. whether Elias will come to take 1492
Mk 16:7 there shall ye s. him, as he said 3700
Lu 2:15 and s. this thing which is come to 1492
Lu 2:26 that he should not s. death, before 1492
Lu 3:6 flesh shall s. the salvation of God. 3700
Lu 6:42 **thou s. clearly to pull out the** 1227
Lu 7:22 **that the blind s., the lame walk,** 308
Lu 7:24 **out into the wilderness for to s.?** 2300
Lu 7:25, 26 **But what went ye out to s.?** 1492
Lu 8:10 **that seeing they might not s.,** 991
Lu 8:16 **they which enter in may s. light** 991
Lu 8:20 stand without, desiring to s. thee. 1492
Lu 8:35 they went out to s. what was done; 1492
Lu 9:9 things? And he desired to s. him. 1492
Lu 9:27 **till they s. the kingdom of God** 1492
Lu 10:23 **eyes which s. the things that ye s.** 991
Lu 10:24 **have desired to s. those things** 1492
Lu 10:24 **those things which ye s., and** 991
Lu 11:33 **they which come in may s. light** 991
Lu 12:54 **ye s. a cloud rise out of the west,** 1492
Lu 12:55 **when ye s. the south wind blow,**
Lu 13:28 **ye shall s. Abraham, and Issac,** 3700
Lu 13:35 **Ye shall not s., me, until** 1492
Lu 14:18 **and I must needs go and s. it:** 1492
Lu 17:22 **desire to s. one of the days of** 1492
Lu 17:22 **Son of man, and ye shall not s.** 3700
Lu 17:23 **they shall say to you, S. here;** 2400
Lu 17:23 **s. there: go not after them, nor** 2400
Lu 19:3 he sought to s. Jesus who he was; 1492
Lu 19:4 up into a sycomore tree to s. him: 1492
Lu 20:13 **reverence him when they s. him** 1492
Lu 21:20 **shall s. Jerusalem compassed** 1492
Lu 21:27 **shall they s....Son of man** 3700
Lu 21:30 **ye s. and know of your own selves** 991
Lu 21:31 **ye s. these things come to pass,** 1492
Lu 23:8 desirous to s. him of a long season, 1492
Lu 24:39 **it is I myself: handle me, and s.;** 1492
Lu 24:39 **flesh and bones, as ye s. me** 2334
Joh 1:33 thou shalt s. the Spirit descending, 1492
Joh 1:39 He saith unto them, **Come and s.** 1492
Joh 1:46 Philip saith unto him, Come and s. 1492
Joh 1:50 **shalt s. greater things than these** 3700
Joh 1:51 **Hereafter ye shall s. heaven** 3700
Joh 3:3 **he cannot s. the kingdom of God** 1492
Joh 3:36 not the Son shall not s. life; but 3700
Joh 4:29 s. a man, which told me all things 1492
Joh 4:48 **Except ye s. signs and wonders,** 1492
Joh 6:19 they s. Jesus walking on the sea, 2334
Joh 6:30 that we may s., and believe thee? 1492
Joh 6:62 **ye shall s. the Son of man ascend** 2334
Joh 7:3 thy disciples also may s. the works 2334
Joh 8:51 **my saying, he shall never s.** 2334
Joh 8:56 **Abraham rejoiced to s. my day:** 1492
Joh 9:15 mine eyes, and I washed, and do s. 991
Joh 9:19 blind? how then doth he now s.? 991
Joh 9:25 that, whereas I was blind, now I s. 991
Joh 9:39 **that they which s. not might s.; and** 991
Joh 9:39 **they which s. might be made blind.** 991
Joh 9:41 **but now ye say, We s.; therefore** 991
Joh 11:34 said unto him, Lord, come and s. 1492
Joh 11:40 **thou shouldest s. the glory of God?** 3700
Joh 12:9 that they might s. Lazarus also, 1492
Joh 12:21 him, saying, Sir, we would s. Jesus. 1492
Joh 12:40 they should not s. with their eyes, 1492
Joh 14:19 **seeth me no more; but ye s. me:** 2334
Joh 16:10 **my Father, and ye s. me no more;** 2334
Joh 16:16 **little while, and ye shall not s. me:** 2334
Joh 16:16 **a little while, and ye shall s. me,** 3700
Joh 16:17 while, and ye shall not s. me: and 2334
Joh 16:17 a little while, and ye shall s. me: 3700
Joh 16:19 **while, and ye shall not s. me: and** 2334
Joh 16:19 **a little while, and ye shall s. me?** 3700
Joh 16:22 **but I will s. you again, and your** 3700
Joh 18:26 Did not I s. thee in the garden with 1492
Joh 20:25 I shall s. in his hands the print of 1492
Ac 2:17 your young men shall s. visions, 3070
Ac 2:27 thine Holy One to s. corruption. 1492
Ac 2:31 neither his flesh did s. corruption. 1492
Ac 2:33 this, which ye now s. and hear. 991
Ac 3:16 strong, whom ye s. and know: 2334
Ac 7:56 I s. the heavens opened, and the 2334
Ac 8:36 eunuch said, S., here is water; 2400
Ac 13:35 thine Holy One to s. corruption. 1492
Ac 15:36 word of the Lord, and s. how they do.
Ac 19:21 been there, I must also s. Rome. 1492
Ac 19:26 Moreover ye s. and hear, that not 2334
Ac 20:25 of God, shall s. my face no more. 3700
Ac 20:38 they should s. his face no more. 2234
Ac 22:11 I could not s. for the glory of that 1689
Ac 22:14 his will, and s. that Just One, 1492
Ac 23:22 S. thou tell no man that thou hast
Ac 25:24 ye s. this man, about whom all the 2334
Ac 28:20 have I called for you, to s. you, and 1492
Ac 28:26 and seeing ye shall s., and not 991
Ac 28:27 lest they should s. with their eyes, 1492
Ro 1:11 I long to s. you, that I may impart 1492
Ro 7:23 I s. another law in my members, 991
Ro 8:25 But if we hope for that we s. not, 991
Ro 11:8 eyes that they should not s., and ears 991
Ro 11:10 be darkened, that they may not s., 991
Ro 15:21 he was not spoken of, they shall s.: 3700
Ro 15:24 for I trust to s. you in my journey, 2300
1Co 1:26 For ye s. your calling, brethren, 991
1Co 8:10 For if any man s. thee which hast 1492
1Co 13:12 now we s. through a glass, darkly; 991
1Co 16:7 I will not s. you now by the way; 1492
1Co 16:10 s. that he may be...without fear: 991
2Co 8:7 s. that ye abound in this grace also.
Ga 1:18 went up to Jerusalem to s. Peter, 2477
Ga 6:11 Ye s. how large a letter I have 1492
Eph 3:9 all men s. what is the fellowship 5461
Eph 5:15 S. then that ye walk circumspectly, 991
Eph 5:33 and the wife s. that she reverence her
Php 1:27 whether I come and s. you, or else 1492
Php 2:23 as I shall s. how it will go with me 542
Php 2:28 that, when ye s. him again, ye may 1492
1Th 2:17 more abundantly to s. your face 1492
1Th 3:6 always, desiring greatly to s. us, 1492
1Th 3:6 us, as we also to s. you:
1Th 3:10 praying...that we might s. your face, 1492
1Th 5:15 S. that none render evil for evil 3708
1Ti 6:16 whom no man hath seen, nor can s. 1492
2Ti 1:4 Greatly desiring to s. thee, being 1492
Heb 2:8 s. not yet all things put under him 3708
Heb 2:9 we s. Jesus, who was made a little 991
Heb 3:19 So we s. that they could not enter in 991
Heb 8:5 S., saith he, that thou make all 3708
Heb 10:25 more, as ye s. the day approaching. 991
Heb 11:5 that he should not s. death; 1492
Heb 12:14 which no man shall s. the Lord: 3700
Heb 12:25 S....ye refuse not him that speaketh 991
Heb 13:23 if he come shortly, I will s. you. 3700
Jas 2:24 Ye s. then how that by works a 3708
1Pe 1:8 in whom, though now ye s. him not, 3708
1Pe 1:22 s. that ye love one another with a
1Pe 3:10 that will love life, and s. good days. 1492
2Pe 1:9 is blind, and cannot s. afar off, 3467
1Jo 3:2 him; for we shall s. him as he is. 3700
1Jo 5:16 If any man s. his brother sin a sin 1492
3Jo 14 But I trust I shall shortly s. thee, 1492
Re 1:7 and every eye shall s. him, and 3700
Re 1:12 to s. the voice that spake with me. 991
Re 3:18 **with eyesalve, that thou mayest s.** 991
Re 6:1 the four beasts saying, Come and s. 991
Re 6:3 the second beast say, Come and s. 991
Re 6:5 the third beast say, Come and s. 991
Re 6:6 s. thou hurt not the oil and the wine.
Re 6:7 the fourth beast say, Come and S. 991
Re 9:20 which neither can s., nor hear, nor 991
Re 11:9 shall s. their dead bodies three days 991
Re 16:15 walk naked, and they s. his shame. 991
Re 18:7 no widow, and shall s. no sorrow. 1492
Re 18:9 shall s. the smoke of her burning, 991
Re 19:10 he said unto me, S. thou do it not: 3700
Re 22:4 And they shall s. his face; and his 3708
Re 22:9 saith he unto me, S. thou do it not: 3708

SEED See also SEED'S; SEEDS; SEEDTIME.

Ge 1:11 the herb yielding s., and the fruit 2233
Ge 1:11 after his kind, whose s. is in itself, 2233
Ge 1:12 and herb yielding s. after his kind, 2233
Ge 1:12 yielding fruit, whose s. was in itself, 2233
Ge 1:29 given you every herb bearing s., 2233
Ge 1:29 is the fruit of a tree yielding s.; 2233
Ge 3:15 and between thy s. and her s.; 2233
Ge 4:25 appointed me another s. instead of 2233
Ge 7:3 to keep s. alive upon the face of all 2233
Ge 9:9 with you, and with your s. after you; 2233
Ge 12:7 Unto thy s. will I give this land: 2233
Ge 13:15 will I give it, and to thy s. for ever. 2233
Ge 13:16 I will make thy s. as the dust of the 2233
Ge 13:16 then shall thy s. also be numbered 2233
Ge 15:3 Behold, to me thou hast given no s. 2233
Ge 15:5 said unto him, So shall thy s. be. 2233
Ge 15:13 thy s. shall be a stranger in a land 2233
Ge 15:18 Unto thy s. have I given this land, 2233
Ge 16:10 I will multiply thy s. exceedingly, 2233
Ge 17:7 between me and thee and thy s. 2233
Ge 17:7 unto thee, and to thy s. after thee 2233
Ge 17:8 unto thee, and to thy s. after thee, 2233
Ge 17:9 thou, and thy s. after thee in their 2233
Ge 17:10 between me and you and thy s. 2233
Ge 17:12 any stranger, which is not of thy s. 2233
Ge 17:19 covenant, and with his s. after him. 2233
Ge 19:32, 34 may preserve s. of our father. 2233
Ge 21:12 for in Isaac shall thy s. be called. 2233
Ge 21:13 make a nation, because he is thy s. 2233
Ge 22:17 I will multiply thy s. as the stars of 2233
Ge 22:17 thy s. shall possess the gate of his 2233
Ge 22:18 And in thy s. shall all the nations of 2233
Ge 24:7 Unto thy s. will I give this land; 2233
Ge 24:60 let thy s. possess the gate of those 2233
Ge 26:3 for unto thee, and unto thy s., I will 2233
Ge 26:4 make thy s. to multiply as the stars 2233
Ge 26:4 give unto thy s. all these countries; 2233
Ge 26:4 and in thy s. shall all the nations of 2233
Ge 26:24 and multiply thy s. for my servant 2233
Ge 28:4 to thee, and to thy s. with thee; 2233
Ge 28:13 to thee will I give it, and to thy s.; 2233
Ge 28:14 And thy s. shall be as the dust of 2233
Ge 28:14 and in thy s. shall all the families 2233
Ge 32:12 make thy s. as the sand of the sea, 2233
Ge 35:12 to thy s. after thee will I give the 2233
Ge 38:8 her, and raise up s. to thy brother. 2233
Ge 38:9 knew that the s. should not be his; 2233
Ge 38:9 that he should give s. to his brother. 2233
Ge 46:6 Jacob, and all his s. with him: 2233
Ge 46:7 all his s. brought he with him into 2233
Ge 47:19 give us s., that we may live, and not 2233
Ge 47:23 here is s. for you, and ye shall sow 2233
Ge 47:24 for s. of the field, and for your food, 2233
Ge 48:4 and will give this land to thy s. after 2233
Ge 48:11 lo, God hath shewed me also thy s. 2233
Ge 48:19 his s. shall become a multitude of 2233
Ex 16:31 and it was like coriander s., white; 2233
Ex 28:43 statute for ever unto him and his s. 2233
Ex 30:21 to him and to his s. throughout 2233

Ex 32:13 I will multiply your s. as the stars 2233
Ex 32:13 spoken of will I give unto your s., ... 2233
Ex 33:1 saying, Unto thy s. will I give it: 2233
Le 11:37 carcase fall upon any sowing s. 2233
Le 11:38 But if any water be put upon the s., ... 2233
Le 12:2 If a woman have conceived s., and 2233
Le 15:16 any man's s. of copulation go out........ 2233
Le 15:17 whereon is the s. of copulation, ... 2233
Le 15:18 man shall lie with s. of copulation, ... 2233
Le 15:32 him whose s. goeth from him, ... 7902, 2233
Le 18:21 any of thy s. pass through the fire...... 2233
Le 19:19 not sow thy field with mingled s. ....
Le 20:2 giveth any of his s. unto Molech; 2233
Le 20:3 he hath given of his s. unto Molech, ... 2233
Le 20:4 he giveth of his s. unto Molech, ... 2233
Le 21:15 Neither shall he profane his s. 2233
Le 21:17 saying, Whosoever he be of thy s. 2233
Le 21:21 hath a blemish of the s. of Aaron 2233
Le 22:3 Whosoever he be of all your s. 2233
Le 22:4 What man soever of the s. of Aaron ... 2233
Le 22:4 man whose s. goeth from him; 7902, 2233
Le 26:16 and ye shall sow your s. in vain, for ... 2233
Le 27:16 estimation...be according to the s. 2233
Le 27:16 homer of barley s. shall be valued 2233
Le 27:30 whether of the s. of the land, or of..... 2233
Nu 5:28 shall be free, and shall conceive s. 2233
Nu 11:7 And the manna was as coriander s. 2233
Nu 14:24 he went; and his s. shall possess it..... 2233
Nu 16:40 which is not of the s. of Aaron, ... 2233
Nu 18:19 unto thee and to thy s. with thee. 2233
Nu 20:5 it is no place of s., or of figs, or of...... 2233
Nu 24:7 and his s. shall be in many waters, ... 2233
Nu 25:13 shall have it, and his s. after him........ 2233
De 1:8 unto them and to their s. after them. .. 2233
De 4:37 he chose their s. after them, and 2233
De 10:15 and he chose their s. after them, ... 2233
De 11:9 to give unto them and to their s., ... 2233
De 11:10 where thou sowedst thy s., and 2233
De 14:22 truly tithe all the increase of thy s., ... 2233
De 22:9 fruit of thy s. which thou hast sown, ... 2233
De 28:38 carry much s. out into the field, ... 2233
De 28:46 a wonder, and upon thy s. for ever..... 2233
De 28:59 the plagues of thy s., even great........ 2233
De 30:6 thine heart, and the heart of thy s., ... 2233
De 30:19 that both thou and thy s. may live: 2233
De 31:21 out of the mouths of their s. 2233
De 34:4 saying, I will give it unto thy s. 2233
Jos 24:3 of Canaan, and multiplied his s., ... 2233
Ru 4:12 s. which the Lord shall give thee........ 2233
1Sa 2:20 The Lord give thee s. of this woman .. 2233
1Sa 8:15 he will take the tenth of your s. 2233
1Sa 20:42 between my s. and thy s. for ever. 2233
1Sa 24:21 thou wilt not cut off my s. after me, ... 2233
2Sa 4:8 king this day of Saul, and of his s.. 2233
2Sa 7:12 I will set up thy s. after thee, which ... 2233
2Sa 22:51 David, and to his s. for evermore. 2233
1Ki 2:33 and upon the head of his s. for ever: .. 2233
1Ki 2:33 but upon David, and upon his s., ... 2233
1Ki 11:14 he was of the king's s. in Edom. 2233
1Ki 11:39 I will for this afflict the s. of David, ... 2233
1Ki 18:32 would contain two measures of s.. 2233
2Ki 5:27 unto thee, and unto thy s. for ever..... 2233
2Ki 11:1 arose and destroyed all the s. royal. ... 2233
2Ki 17:20 the Lord rejected all the s. of Israel, ... 2233
2Ki 25:25 the son of Elishama, of the s. royal, ... 2233
1Ch 16:13 O ye s. of Israel his servant, ye 2233
1Ch 17:11 that I will raise up thy s. after thee, ... 2233
2Ch 20:7 gavest it to the s. of Abraham thy 2233
2Ch 22:10 arose and destroyed all the s. royal 2233
Ezr 2:59 their father's house, and their s., ... 2233
Ezr 9:2 holy s. have mingled themselves 2233
Ne 7:61 their father's house, nor their s. 2233
Ne 9:2 s. of Israel separated themselves........ 2233
Ne 9:8 to give it, I say, to his s., and hast 2233
Es 6:13 if Mordecai be of the s. of the Jews, ... 2233
Es 9:27 took upon them, and upon their s., ... 2233
Es 9:28 memorial...perish from their s. 2233
Es 9:31 for themselves and for their s., ... 2233
Es 10:3 and speaking peace to all his s. 2233
Job 5:25 know also that thy s. shall be great, ... 2233
Job 21:8 Their s. is established in their sight 2233
Job 39:12 that he will bring home thy s., and 2233
Ps 18:50 David, and to his s. for evermore. 2233
Ps 21:10 s. from among the children of men. 2233
Ps 22:23 all ye the s. of Jacob, glorify him; 2233
Ps 22:23 and fear him, all ye the s. of Israel. 2233
Ps 22:30 A s. shall serve him; it shall be.......... 2233
Ps 25:13 and his s. shall inherit the earth. 2233
Ps 37:25 forsaken, nor his s. begging bread. 2233
Ps 37:26 and lendeth; and his s. is blessed. 2233
Ps 37:28 the s. of the wicked shall be cut off. ... 2233
Ps 69:36 s. also of his servants shall inherit 2233
Ps 89:4 Thy s. will I establish for ever, and 2233
Ps 89:29 His s. also will I make to endure for ... 2233
Ps 89:36 His s. shall endure for ever, and his ... 2233
Ps 102:28 their s. shall be established before 2233
Ps 105:6 O ye s. of Abraham his servant, ye 2233
Ps 106:27 overthrow their s. also among the 2233
Ps 112:2 His s. shall be mighty upon earth; 2233
Ps 126:6 and weepeth, bearing precious s., ... 2233
Pr 11:21 but the s. of the righteous shall be 2233
Ec 11:6 In the morning sow thy s., and in....... 2233
Isa 1:4 a s. of evildoers, children that are 2233
Isa 5:10 s. of an homer shall yield an ephah. 2233
Isa 6:13 so the holy s. shall be the substance ... 2233
Isa 14:20 the s. of evildoers shall never be......... 2233
Isa 17:11 shalt thou make thy s. to flourish: 2233
Isa 23:3 by great waters the s. of Sihor, the 2233
Isa 30:23 shall he give the rain of thy s., that 2233
Isa 41:8 the s. of Abraham my friend. 2233
Isa 43:5 I will bring thy s. from the east, ... 2233
Isa 44:3 I will pour my spirit upon thy s., ... 2233
Isa 45:19 I said not unto the s. of Jacob, Seek ... 2233
Isa 45:25 In the Lord shall all the s. of Israel..... 2233
Isa 48:19 Thy s. also had been as the sand, ... 2233
Isa 53:10 he shall see his s., he shall prolong..... 2233
Isa 54:3 thy s. shall inherit the Gentiles, ... 2233
Isa 55:10 that it may give s. to the sower, ... 2233
Isa 57:3 s. of the adulterer and the whore. 2233
Isa 57:4 of transgression, a s. of falsehood, ... 2233
Isa 59:21 nor out of the mouth of thy s., ... 2233
Isa 59:21 nor of the mouth of thy seed's s., ... 2233
Isa 61:9 their s. shall be known among the 2233
Isa 61:9 the s. which the Lord hath blessed. 2233
Isa 65:9 I will bring forth a s. out of Jacob, ... 2233
Isa 65:23 are the s. of the blessed of the Lord, .. 2233
Isa 66:22 your s. and your name remain. 2233
Jer 2:21 thee a noble vine, wholly a right s. 2233
Jer 7:15 even the whole s. of Ephraim. 2233
Jer 22:28 are they cast out, he and his s., and ... 2233
Jer 22:30 for no man of his s. shall prosper, ... 2233
Jer 23:8 led the s. of the house of Israel out 2233
Jer 29:32 Shemaiah the Nehelamite,...his s. 2233
Jer 30:10 s. from the land of their captivity; 2233
Jer 31:27 s. of man, and with the s. of beast. 2233
Jer 31:36 s. of Israel also shall cease from 2233
Jer 31:37 cast off all the s. of Israel for all 2233
Jer 33:22 will I multiply the s. of David my 2233
Jer 33:26 will I cast away the s. of Jacob, ... 2233
Jer 33:26 I will not take any of his s. to be 2233
Jer 33:26 to be rulers over the s. of Abraham, ... 2233
Jer 35:7 nor sow s., nor plant vineyard, ... 2233
Jer 35:9 have we vineyard, nor field, nor s. 2233
Jer 36:31 I will punish him and his s. and his 2233
Jer 41:1 the son of Elishama, of the s. royal, ... 2233
Jer 46:27 s. from the land of their captivity; 2233
Jer 49:10 his s. is spoiled, and his brethren, ... 2233
Eze 17:5 He took also of the s. of the land, ... 2233
Eze 17:13 And hath taken of the king's s., and.... 2233
Eze 20:5 unto the s. of the house of Jacob, ... 2233
Eze 43:19 Levites that be of the s. of Zadok, ... 2233
Eze 44:22 of the s. of the house of Israel, ... 2233
Da 1:3 of the king's s., and of the princes; 2233
Da 2:43 themselves with the s. of men: 2234
Da 9:1 Ahasuerus, of the s. of the Medes, ... 2233
Joe 1:17 the s. is rotten under their clods, ... 6507
Am 9:13 of grapes him that soweth s.; 2233
Hag 2:19 Is the s. yet in the barn? yea, as 2233
Zec 8:12 for the s. shall be prosperous; the...... 2233
Mal 2:3 I will corrupt your s., and spread 2233
Mal 2:15 one? That he might seek a godly s.. ... 2233
Mt 13:19 **which received s. by the way side.. *4687***
Mt 13:20 **received the s. into stony places, ... *4687***
Mt 13:22 **that received s. among the thorns ..*4687***
Mt 13:23 **received s. into the good ground.... *4687***
Mt 13:24 **which sowed good s. in his field: ... *4690***
Mt 13:27 **not thou sow good s. in thy field? ..*4690***
Mt 13:31 **heaven is like to a grain of mustard s.,.**
Mt 13:37 **the good s. is the Son of man; *4690***
Mt 13:38 **the good s. are the children of the..*4690***
Mt 17:20 **ye have faith as a grain of mustard s., .**
Mt 22:24 and raise up s. unto his brother. *4690*
Mk 4:26 **should cast s. into the ground: *4703***
Mk 4:27 **the s. should spring and grow up,.. *4703***
Mk 4:31 **It is like a grain of mustard s., ... *4690***
Mk 12:19 and raise up s. unto his brother. *4690*
Mk 12:20 took a wife, and dying left no s. *4690*
Mk 12:21 her, and died, neither left he any s. *4690*
Mk 12:22 the seven had her, and left no s. *4690*
Lu 1:55 to Abraham, and to his s. for ever...... *4690*
Lu 8:5 **A sower went out to sow his s. *4703***
Lu 8:11 **is this: The s. is the word of God. . *4703***
Lu 13:19 **It is like a grain of mustard s., which .**
Lu 17:6 **ye had faith as a grain of mustard s.,..**
Lu 20:28 and raise up s. unto his brother. *4690*
Joh 7:42 Christ cometh of the s. of David, ... *4690*
Joh 8:33 We be Abraham's s., and were *4690*
Joh 8:37 **I know that ye are Abraham's s.; .. *4690***
Ac 3:25 in thy s. shall all the kindreds of *4690*
Ac 7:5 possession, and to his s. after him, ... *4690*
Ac 7:6 his s. should sojourn in a strange *4690*
Ac 13:23 Of this man's s. hath God according.... *4690*
Ro 1:3 which was made of the s. of David *4690*
Ro 4:13 was not to Abraham, or to his s., ... *4690*
Ro 4:16 promise might be sure to all the s. *4690*
Ro 4:18 was spoken, So shall thy s. be. *4690*
Ro 9:7 because they are the s. of Abraham, ... *4690*
Ro 9:7 but, In Isaac shall thy s. be called. *4690*
Ro 9:8 the promise are counted for the s. *4690*
Ro 9:29 the Lord of Sabaoth had left us a s., ... *4690*
Ro 11:1 an Israelite, of the s. of Abraham, ... *4690*
1Co 15:38 him, and to every s. his own body...... *4690*
2Co 9:10 he that ministereth s. to the sower..... *4690*
2Co 9:10 food, and multiply your s. sown, ... *4703*
2Co 11:22 Are they the s. of Abraham? so am *4690*
Ga 3:16 and his s. were the promises made...... *4690*
Ga 3:16 one, And to thy s., which is Christ..... *4690*
Ga 3:19 till the s. should come to whom the *4690*
Ga 3:29 Christ's, then are ye Abraham's s., ... *4690*
2Ti 2:8 Jesus Christ of the s. of David was..... *4690*
Heb 2:16 he took on him the s. of Abraham. *4690*
Heb 11:11 received strength to conceive s. *4690*
Heb 11:18 That in Isaac shall thy s. be called: *4690*
1Pe 1:23 born again, not of corruptible s.. .... *4701*
1Jo 3:9 for his s. remaineth in him: and *4690*
Re 12:17 war with the remnant of her s., ... *4690*

SEED'S
Isa 59:21 out of the mouth of thy s. seed, ... 2233

SEEDS
De 22:9 not sow thy vineyard with divers s. ....
Mt 13:4 **some s. fell by the way side, and the ...**
Mt 13:32 **which indeed is the least of all s... *4690***
Mk 4:31 **is less than all the s. that be......... *4690***
Ga 3:16 He saith not, And to s., as of many; ... *4690*

SEEDTIME
Ge 8:22 s. and harvest, and cold and heat, ... 2233

SEEING See also FORESEEING.
Ge 15:2 wilt thou give me, s. I go childless, ...
Ge 18:18 s. that Abraham shall surely become a.......
Ge 19:1 Lot s. them rose up to meet them; 7200
Ge 22:12 s. thou hast not withheld thy son,.............
Ge 24:56 s. the Lord hath prospered my way; ....
Ge 26:27 s. ye hate me, and have sent me away......
Ge 28:8 And Esau s. that the daughters of 7200
Ge 44:30 s. that his life is bound up in the lad's ......
Ex 4:11 the dumb, or the deaf, or the s., ... 6493
Ex 21:8 s. he hath dealt deceitfully with her. ....
Ex 22:10 hurt, or driven away, no man s. it: 7200
Ex 23:9 s. ye were strangers in the land of..... 3588
Le 10:17 in the holy lace, s. it is most holy, ... 3588
Nu 15:26 s. all the people were in ignorance....... 3588
Nu 16:3 you, s. all the congregation are holy, ... 3588
Nu 35:23 s. him not, and cast it upon him, ... 7200
Jos 17:14 to inherit, s. I am a great people, ...
Jos 22:18 s. ye rebel to day against the Lord, ...
Jg 13:18 thus after my name, s. it is secret? ....
Jg 17:13 s. I have a Levite to my priest. 3588
Jg 19:23 s. that this man is come into mine 310
Jg 21:7 s. we have sworn by the Lord that..........
Jg 21:16 s. the women are destroyed out of 3588
Ru 1:21 s. the Lord hath testified against me. ....
Ru 2:10 knowledge of me, s. I am a stranger? ....
1Sa 16:1 s. I have rejected him from reigning..........
1Sa 17:36 s. he hath defied the armies of the 3588
1Sa 18:23 s. that I am a poor man, and lightly ....
1Sa 24:6 him, s. he is the anointed of the Lord. ....
1Sa 25:26 s. the Lord hath withholden thee from.......
1Sa 28:16 s. the Lord is departed from thee, and......
2Sa 13:39 concerning Amnon, s. he was dead. ....

2Sa 15:20 s. I go whither I may, return thou,
2Sa 18:22 s. that thou hast no tidings ready?
2Sa 19:11 s. the speech of all Israel is come to
1Ki 1:48 this day, mine eyes even s. it 7200
1Ki 11:28 Solomon s. the young man that 7200
2Ki 10:2 s. your master's sons are with you,
1Ch 12:17 s. there is no wrong in my hands, the
2Ch 2:6 s. the heaven and heaven of heavens
Ezr 9:13 s. that thou our God hast punished 3588
Ne 2:2 countenance sad, s. thou art not sick?
Job 14:5 S. his days are determined, the 518
Job 19:28 s. the root of the matter is found in
Job 21:22 s. he judgeth those that are high.
Job 21:34 s. in your answers there remaineth
Job 24:1 s. times are not hidden from thee
Job 28:21 S. it is hid from the eyes of all living,
Ps 22:8 deliver him, s. he delighted in him.
Ps 50:17 S. thou hatest instruction, and castest
Pr 3:29 thy neighbour, s. he dwelleth securely
Pr 17:16 get wisdom, s. he hath no heart to it?
Pr 20:12 The hearing ear, and the s. eye, 7200
Ec 1:8 the eye is not satisfied with s., nor 7200
Ec 2:16 s. that which now is in the days to
Ec 6:11 S. there be many things that 3588
Isa 21:3 it; I was dismayed at the s. of it. 7200
Isa 33:15 and shutteth his eyes from s. evil; 7200
Isa 42:20 S. many things, but thou observest 7200
Isa 49:21 s. I have lost my children, and am
Jer 11:15 s. she hath wrought lewdness with
Jer 47:7 s. the Lord hath given it a charge
Eze 16:30 s., thou doest all these things, the
Eze 17:18 S. he despised the oath by breaking
Eze 21:4 S. then that I will cut off from 3282
Eze 22:28 s. vanity, and divining lies unto
Da 2:47 s. thou couldest reveal this secret. 1768
Ho 4:6 s. thou hast forgotten the law of thy
Mt 5:1 s. the multitudes, he went up into *1492*
Mt 9:2 Jesus s. their faith said unto the *1492*
Mt 13:13 **parables: because they s. see not;** *991*
Mt 13:14 **s. ye shall see, shall not perceive:** *991*
Mk 4:12 **s. they may see, and not perceive;** *991*
Mk 11:13 s. a fig tree afar off having leaves, *1492*
Lu 1:34 shall this be, s. I know not a man? *1893*
Lu 5:12 who s. Jesus fell on his face, and *1492*
Lu 8:10 **s. they might not see, and hearing** *991*
Lu 23:40 s. thou art in the...condemnation? *3754*
Joh 2:18 us, s. that thou doest these things?
Joh 9:7 therefore, and washed, and came s. *991*
Joh 21:21 Peter s. him saith to Jesus, Lord, *1492*
Ac 2:15 s. it is but the third hour of the day. *1063*
Ac 2:31 He s. this before spake of the *4275*
Ac 3:3 Who s. Peter and John about to go *1492*
Ac 7:24 And s. one of them suffer wrong, he *1492*
Ac 8:6 and s. the miracles which he did. *991*
Ac 9:7 hearing a voice, but s. no man. *2334*
Ac 13:11 blind, not s. the sun for a season. *991*
Ac 13:46 but s. ye put it from you, and judge *1894*
Ac 16:27 s. the prison doors open, he drew *1492*
Ac 17:24 s. that he is Lord of heaven and
Ac 17:25 s. he giveth to all life, and breath,
Ac 19:36 S. then that these things cannot be
Ac 24:2 S. that by thee we enjoy great
Ac 28:26 and s. ye shall see, and not perceive: *991*
Ro 3:30 S. it is one God, which shall justify *1897*
1Co 14:16 s. he understandeth not what thou *1894*
2Co 3:12 S. then that we have such hope, we
2Co 4:1 s. we have this ministry, as we have
2Co 11:18 S. that many glory after the flesh, *1893*
2Co 11:19 gladly, s. ye yourselves are wise.
Col 3:9 s. that ye have put off the old man
2Th 1:6 S. it is a righteous thing with God *1512*
Heb 4:6 S. therefore it remaineth that some *1893*
Heb 4:14 S. then that we have a great high
Heb 5:11 uttered, s. ye are dull of hearing. *1893*
Heb 6:6 s. they crucify to themselves the Son
Heb 7:25 s. he ever liveth to make intercession
Heb 8:4 s. that there are priests that offer
Heb 11:27 endured, as s. him who is invisible. *3708*
Heb 12:1 s. we also are compassed about
1Pe 1:22 S. ye have purified your souls in
2Pe 2:8 among them, in s. and hearing, *990*
2Pe 3:11 S. then that all these things shall be
2Pe 3:14 s. that ye look for such things, be
2Pe 3:17 s. ye know these things before,

SEEK See also SEEKEST; SEEKETH; SEEKING; SOUGHT.
Ge 37:16 I s. my brethren: tell me, I pray 1245
Ge 43:18 that he may s. occasion against us, 1556
Le 13:36 priest shall not s. for yellow hair; 1239
Le 19:31 neither s. after wizards, to be 1245
Nu 15:39 ye s. not after your own heart and 8446
Nu 16:10 thee: and s. ye the priesthood also? 1245
Nu 24:1 times, to s. for enchantments, 7125
De 4:29 thou shalt s. the Lord thy God, 1245
De 4:29 if thou s. him with all thy heart 1875
De 12:5 even unto his habitation shall ye s., 1875
De 22:2 thee until thy brother s. after it. 1875
De 23:6 Thou shalt not s. their peace nor 1875
Ru 3:1 shall I not s. rest for thee, that it 1245
1Sa 9:3 with thee, and arise, go s. the asses 1245
1Sa 10:2 which thou wentest to s. are found: 1245
1Sa 10:14 And he said, To s. the asses: and 1245
1Sa 16:16 to s. out a man, who is a cunning 1245
1Sa 23:15 Saul was come out to s. his life: 1245
1Sa 23:25 Saul...and his men went to s. him. 1245
1Sa 24:2 went to s. David and his men upon 1245
1Sa 25:26 they that s. evil to my lord, be as 1245
1Sa 25:29 to pursue thee, and to s. thy soul: 1245
1Sa 26:2 s. David in the wilderness of Ziph 1245
1Sa 26:20 of Israel is come out to s. a flea, as 1245
1Sa 27:1 to s. me any more in any coast of 1245
1Sa 28:7 S. me a woman that hath a 1245
2Sa 5:17 the Philistines came up to s. David; 1245
1Ki 2:40 Gath to Achish to s. his servants: 1245
1Ki 18:10 my lord hath not sent to s. thee: 1245
1Ki 19:10, 14 they s. my life, to take it away. 1245
2Ki 2:16 go, we pray thee, and s. thy master: 1245
2Ki 6:19 bring you to the man whom ye s. 1245
1Ch 4:39 valley, to s. pasture for their flocks. 1245
1Ch 14:8 the Philistines went up to s. David. 1245
1Ch 16:10 of them rejoice that s. the Lord. 1245
1Ch 16:11 S. the Lord and his strength, 1875
1Ch 16:11 strength, s. his face continually. 1245
1Ch 22:19 your soul to s. the Lord your God; 1875
1Ch 28:8 s. for all the commandments of the 1875
1Ch 28:9 if thou s. him, he will be found of 1875
2Ch 7:14 s. my face, and turn from their 1245
2Ch 11:16 set their hearts to s. the Lord God 1245
2Ch 12:14 prepared not his heart to s. the 1875
2Ch 14:4 commanded Judah to s. the Lord 1875
2Ch 15:2 if ye s. him, he will be found of you; 1875
2Ch 15:12 into a covenant to s. the Lord God 1875
2Ch 15:13 whosoever would not s. the Lord 1875
2Ch 19:3 hast prepared thine heart to s. God. 1875
2Ch 20:3 and set himself to s. the Lord, and 1875
2Ch 20:4 of Judah they came to s. the Lord. 1245
2Ch 30:19 prepareth his heart to s. God, the 1875
2Ch 31:21 the commandments, to s. his God, 1875
2Ch 34:3 began to s. after the God of David 1875
Ezr 4:2 for we s. your God, as ye do; and 1875
Ezr 6:21 land, to s. the Lord God of Israel, 1875
Ezr 7:10 his heart to s. the law of the Lord, 1875
Ezr 8:21 to s. of him a right way for us, and 1245
Ezr 8:22 upon all them for good that s. him; 1245
Ezr 9:12 nor s. their peace or their wealth 1875
Ne 2:10 to s. the welfare of the children of 1245
Job 5:8 I would s. unto God, and unto God 1875
Job 7:21 thou shalt s. me in the morning, 7836
Job 8:5 If thou wouldest s. unto God 7836
Job 20:10 children shall s. to please the poor,
Ps 4:2 love vanity, and s. after leasing? 1245
Ps 9:10 not forsaken them that s. thee. 1875
Ps 10:4 countenance, will not s. after God: 1875
Ps 10:15 s. out his wickedness till thou find 1875
Ps 14:2 that did understand, and s. God. 1875
Ps 22:26 shall praise the Lord that s. him: 1875
Ps 24:6 the generation of them that s. him, 1875
Ps 24:6 him, that s. thy face, O Jacob. 1245
Ps 27:4 of the Lord, that will I s. after; 1245
Ps 27:8 When thou saidst, S. ye my face; 1245
Ps 27:8 unto thee, Thy face, Lord, will I s. 1245
Ps 34:10 that s. the Lord shall not want 1875
Ps 34:14 do good; s. peace, and pursue it. 1245
Ps 35:4 put to shame that s. after my soul: 1245
Ps 38:12 s. after my life lay snares for me: 1245
Ps 38:12 that s. my hurt speak mischievous 1875
Ps 40:14 that s. after my soul to destroy it; 1245
Ps 40:16 Let all those that s. thee rejoice 1245
Ps 53:2 did understand, that did s. God. 1875
Ps 54:3 and oppressors s. after my soul: 1245
Ps 63:1 art my God; early will I s. thee: 7836
Ps 63:9 those that s. my soul, to destroy 1245
Ps 69:6 those that s. thee be confounded 1245
Ps 69:32 your heart shall live that s. God. 1875
Ps 70:2 confounded that s. after my soul: 1245
Ps 70:4 all those that s. thee rejoice and be 1245
Ps 71:13 and dishonour that s. my hurt. 1245
Ps 71:24 unto shame, that s. my hurt. 1245
Ps 83:16 that they may s. thy name, O Lord. 1245
Ps 104:21 prey, and s. their meat from God. 1245
Ps 105:3 of them rejoice that s. the Lord. 1245
Ps 105:4 S. the Lord, and his strength: 1875
Ps 105:4 strength: s. his face evermore. 1245
Ps 109:10 let them s. their bread also out of 1875
Ps 119:2 that s. him with the whole heart. 1875
Ps 119:45 at liberty: for I s. thy precepts. 1875
Ps 119:155 wicked: for they s. not thy statutes. 1875
Ps 119:176 s. thy servant; for I do not forget 1245
Ps 122:9 the Lord our God I will s. thy good. 1245
Pr 1:28 they shall s. me early, but they 7836
Pr 7:15 diligently to s. thy face, and I have 7836
Pr 8:17 those that s. me early shall find me. 7836
Pr 21:6 to and fro of them that s. death. 1245
Pr 23:30 they that go to s. mixed wine. 2713
Pr 23:35 shall I awake? I will s. it yet again. 1245
Pr 28:5 they that s. the Lord understand 1245
Pr 29:10 the upright: but the just s. his soul. 1245
Pr 29:26 Many s. the ruler's favour; but 1245
Ec 1:13 my heart to s. and search out by 1875
Ec 7:25 to search, and to s. out wisdom. 1245
Ec 8:17 though a man labour to s. it out, 1245
Ca 3:2 will s. him whom my soul loveth: 1245
Ca 6:1 that we may s. him with thee. 1245
Isa 1:17 s. judgment, relieve the oppressed, 1875
Isa 8:19 S. unto them that have familiar 1875
Isa 8:19 not a people s. unto their God? for 1875
Isa 9:13 them, neither do they s. the Lord 1875
Isa 11:10 to it shall the Gentiles s.: and his 1875
Isa 19:3 and they shall s. to the idols, and to 1875
Isa 26:9 within me will I s. thee early: 7836
Isa 29:15 Woe unto them that s. deep to hide
Isa 31:1 of Israel, neither s. the Lord! 1875
Isa 34:16 S. ye out of the book of the Lord, 1875
Isa 41:12 Thou shalt s. them, and shalt not 1245
Isa 41:17 When the poor and needy s. water, 1245
Isa 45:19 the seed of Jacob, S. ye me in vain: 1245
Isa 51:1 righteousness, ye that s. the Lord: 1245
Isa 55:6 S. ye the Lord while he may be 1875
Isa 58:2 Yet they s. me daily, and delight 1875
Jer 2:24 all they that s. her will not weary 1245
Jer 2:33 trimmest thou thy way to s. love? 1245
Jer 4:30 despise thee, they will s. thy life. 1245
Jer 5:1 and s. in the broad places thereof, 1245
Jer 11:21 that s. thy life, saying, Prophesy 1245
Jer 19:7 hands of them that s. their lives: 1245
Jer 19:9 and they that s. their lives, shall 1245
Jer 21:7 the hand of those that s. their life: 1245
Jer 22:25 the hand of them that s. thy life, 1245
Jer 29:7 s. the peace of the city whither I 1875
Jer 29:13 ye shall s. me, and find me, when 1245
Jer 30:14 forgotten thee; they s. thee not; 1875
Jer 34:20 the hand of them that s. their life: 1245
Jer 34:21 the hand of them that s. their life, 1245
Jer 38:16 hand of these men that s. thy life. 1245
Jer 44:30 the hand of them that s. his life; 1245
Jer 45:5 things for thyself? s. them not: 1245
Jer 46:26 hand of those that s. their lives, 1245
Jer 49:37 and before them that s. their life: 1245
Jer 50:4 shall go, and s. the Lord their God. 1245
La 1:11 All her people sigh, they s. bread; 1245
Eze 7:25 they shall s. peace, and there shall 1245
Eze 7:26 shall they s. a vision of the prophet; 1245
Eze 34:6 none did search or s. after them. 1245
Eze 34:11 search my sheep, and s. them out. 1239
Eze 34:12 so will I s. out my sheep, and will 1239
Eze 34:16 I will s. that which was lost, and 1245
Da 9:3 to s. by prayer and supplications, 1245
Ho 2:7 she shall s. them, but shall not 1245
Ho 3:5 s. the Lord their God, and David 1245
Ho 5:6 and with their herds to s. the Lord; 1245
Ho 5:15 their offence, and s. my face: in 1245
Ho 5:15 affliction they will s. me early. 7836
Ho 7:10 their God, nor s. him for all this. 1245
Ho 10:12 for it is time to s. the Lord, till he 1875
Am 5:4 Israel, S. ye me, and ye shall live: 1875
Am 5:5 But s. not Beth-el, nor enter into 1875
Am 5:6 S. the Lord, and ye shall live; lest 1875
Am 5:8 S. him that maketh the seven stars
Am 5:14 S. good, and not evil, that ye may 1875

Am 8:12 and fro to **s.** the word of the Lord,..... 1245
Na 3:7 shall I **s.** comforters for thee?........... 1245
Na 3:11 **s.** strength because of the enemy....... 1245
Zep 2:3 **S.** ye the Lord, all ye meek of the..... 1245
Zep 2:3 **s.** righteousness, **s.** meekness: it....... 1245
Zec 8:21 Lord, and to **s.** the Lord of hosts:...... 1245
Zec 8:22 shall come to **s.** the Lord of hosts...... 1245
Zec 11:16 neither shall **s.** the young one, nor..... 1245
Zec 12:9 I will **s.** to destroy all the nations....... 1245
Mal 2:7 should **s.** the law at his mouth:.......... 1245
Mal 2:15 That he might **s.** a godly seed.......... 1245
Mal 3:1 and the Lord, whom ye **s.**, shall.......... 1245
Mt 2:13 **s.** the young child to destroy him......... *2212*
Mt 6:32 **all these things do the Gentiles s.:)** *1934*
Mt 6:33 **But s. ye first the kingdom**.......... *2212*
Mt 7:7 **s., and ye shall find; knock,**.......... *2212*
Mt 28:5 ye **s.** Jesus, which was crucified.......... *2212*
Mk 1:37 said unto him, All men **s.** for thee...... *2212*
Mk 3:32 thy brethren without **s.** for thee......... *2212*
Mk 8:12 **this generation s. after a sign?**...... *1934*
Mk 16:6 Ye **s.** Jesus of Nazareth, which was.... *2212*
Lu 11:9 **s., and ye shall find; knock,**........ *2212*
Lu 11:29 **they s. a sign; and there shall no**.. *1934*
Lu 12:29 **And s. not ye what ye shall eat,**.... *2212*
Lu 12:30 **the nations of the world s. after:**... *1934*
Lu 12:31 **rather s. ye the kingdom of God:**... *2212*
Lu 13:24 **for many,...will s. to enter in,**....... *2212*
Lu 15:8 **and s. diligently till she find it?**.... *2212*
Lu 17:33 **shall s. to save his life shall**.......... *2212*
Lu 19:10 **s. and to save that which was**....... *2212*
Lu 24:5 **s.** ye the living among the dead?....... *2212*
Joh 1:38 and saith unto them, **What s. ye?**..... *2212*
Joh 5:30 **because I s. not mine own will,**..... *2212*
Joh 5:44 **s. not the honour that cometh**....... *2212*
Joh 6:26 **Ye s. me, not because ye saw**........ *2212*
Joh 7:25 not this he, whom they **s.** to kill?...... *2212*
Joh 7:34 **Ye shall s. me, and shall not**........ *2212*
Joh 7:36 Ye shall **s.** me, and shall.......................
Joh 8:21 **ye shall s. me, shall die in your**.... *2212*
Joh 8:37 **ye s. to kill me, because my**.......... *2212*
Joh 8:40 **But now ye s. to kill me, a man**.... *2212*
Joh 8:50 **And I s. not mine own glory:**......... *2212*
Joh 13:33 **Ye shall s. me: and as I said**.......... *2212*
Joh 18:4 and said unto them, **Whom s. ye?**..... *2212*
Joh 18:7 asked he them again, **Whom s. ye?**... *2212*
Joh 18:8 **if therefore ye s. me, let these**...... *2212*
Ac 10:19 him, Behold, three men **s.** thee......... *2212*
Ac 10:21 said, Behold, I am he whom ye **s.**...... *2212*
Ac 11:25 Barnabas to Tarsus, for to **s.** Saul:....... *327*
Ac 15:17 of men might **s.** after the Lord.......... *1567*
Ac 17:27 That they should **s.** the Lord, if......... *2212*
Ro 2:7 in well doing **s.** for glory and............. *2212*
Ro 11:3 am left alone, and they **s.** my life....... *2212*
1Co 1:22 and the Greeks **s.** after wisdom:......... *2212*
1Co 7:27 unto a wife? **s.** not to be loosed......... *2212*
1Co 7:27 loosed from a wife? **s.** not a wife........ *2212*
1Co 10:24 Let no man **s.** his own, but every....... *2212*
1Co 14:12 **s.** that ye may excel to the edifying..... *2212*
2Co 12:14 for I **s.** not yours, but you: for the..... *2212*
2Co 13:3 ye **s.** a proof of Christ speaking in...... *2212*
Ga 1:10 or do I **s.** to please men? for if I......... *2212*
Ga 2:17 while we **s.** to be justified by Christ,... *2212*
Php 2:21 For all **s.** their own, not the things..... *2212*
Col 3:1 **s.** those things which are above,......... *2212*
Heb 11:6 of them that diligently **s.** him............. *1567*
Heb 11:14 plainly that they **s.** a country............. *1934*
Heb 13:14 city, but we **s.** one to come............... *1934*
1Pe 3:11 let him **s.** peace, and ensue it............ *2212*
Re 9:6 in those days shall men **s.** death,......... *2212*

SEEKEST
Ge 37:15 asked him, saying, What **s.** thou?....... 1245
Jg 4:22 shew thee the man whom thou **s.**........ 1245
2Sa 17:3 the man whom thou **s.** is as if all........ 1245
2Sa 20:19 thou **s.** to destroy a city and a.......... 1245
1Ki 11:22 thou **s.** to go to thine own country?.... 1245
Pr 2:4 If thou **s.** her as silver, and.............. 1245
Jer 45:5 **s.** thou great things for thyself?......... 1245
Joh 4:27 yet no man said, What **s.** thou?.......... *2212*
Joh 20:15 **why weepest thou? whom s.**........... *2212*

SEEKETH
1Sa 19:2 Saul my father **s.** to kill thee: now...... 1245
1Sa 20:1 thy father, that he **s.** my life?........... 1245
1Sa 22:23 for he that **s.** my life **s.** thy life:......... 1245
1Sa 23:10 that Saul **s.** to come to Keilah, to........ 1245
1Sa 24:9 saying, Behold, David **s.** thy hurt?...... 1245
2Sa 16:11 forth of my bowels, **s.** my life:........... 1245
1Ki 20:7 and see how this man **s.** mischief:...... 1245
2Ki 5:7 see how he **s.** a quarrel against me...... 579
Job 39:29 From thence she **s.** the prey, and...... 2658
Ps 37:32 the righteous, and **s.** to slay him....... 1245
Pr 11:27 **s.** good procureth favour: but............ 7836
Pr 11:27 he that **s.** mischief, it shall come........ 1875
Pr 14:6 A scorner **s.** wisdom, and findeth....... 1245
Pr 15:14 hath understand **s.** knowledge:........... 1245
Pr 17:9 covereth a transgression **s.** love;........ 1245
Pr 17:11 an evil man **s.** only rebellion:............ 1245
Pr 17:19 exalteth his gate **s.** destruction.......... 1245
Pr 18:1 **s.** and intermeddleth with all............ 1245
Pr 18:15 the ear of the wise **s.** knowledge........ 1245
Pr 31:13 She **s.** wool, and flax, and................ 1875
Ec 7:28 Which yet my soul **s.**, but I find.......... 1245
Isa 40:20 **s.** unto him a cunning workman.......... 1245
Jer 5:1 executeth judgment,...**s.** the truth;..... 1245
Jer 30:17 is Zion, whom no man **s.** after........... 1875
Jer 38:4 **s.** not the welfare of this people,........ 1875
La 3:25 wait for him, to the soul that **s.** him.... 1875
Eze 14:10 punishment of him that **s.** unto.......... 1875
Eze 34:12 As a shepherd **s.** out his flock in........ 1243
Mt 7:8 **receiveth; and he that s. findeth;**... *2212*
Mt 12:39 **evil...generation s. after a sign;**..... *1934*
Mt 16:4 **wicked...generation s. after**........... *1934*
Mt 18:12 **and s. that which is gone astray?**.. *2212*
Lu 11:10 **receiveth; and he that s. findeth;**.. *2212*
Joh 4:23 **the Father s. such to worship**....... *2212*
Joh 7:4 he himself **s.** to be known openly....... *2212*
Joh 7:18 **speaketh of himself s. his glory:**.... *2212*
Joh 7:18 **he that s. his glory that sent**......... *2212*
Joh 8:50 **there is one that s. and judgeth**..... *2212*
Ro 3:11 there is none that **s.** after God.......... *1567*
Ro 11:7 not obtained that which he **s.** for;....... *1934*
1Co 13:5 itself unseemly, **s.** not her own,......... *2212*

SEEKING
Es 10:3 **s.** the wealth of his people, and......... 1875
Isa 16:5 judging, and **s.** judgment, and........... 1875
Mt 12:43 **places, s. rest, and findeth none**.... *2212*
Mt 13:45 **a merchant man, s. goodly pearls:**...*2212*
Mk 8:11 him, **s.** of him a sign from heaven,..... *2212*
Lu 2:45 back again to Jerusalem, **s.** him......... *2212*
Lu 11:24 **walketh through dry places, s.**....... *2212*
Lu 11:54 and **s.** to catch something out of his.... *2212*
Lu 13:7 **three years I come s. fruit on**......... *2212*
Joh 6:24 came to Capernaum, **s.** for Jesus......... *2212*
Ac 13:8 **s.** to turn away the deputy from the... *2212*
Ac 13:11 **s.** some to lead him by the hand......... *2212*
1Co 10:33 not **s.** mine own profit, but the.......... *2212*
1Pe 5:8 about, **s.** whom he may devour:......... *2212*

SEEM See also SEEMED; SEEMETH.
Ge 27:12 shall **s.** to him as a deceiver;...... 1961,5869
De 15:18 It shall not **s.** hard unto thee,........... 7185
De 25:3 brother should **s.** vile unto thee......... 7034
Jos 24:15 **s.** evil unto you to serve the...... 1961,5869
1Sa 24:4 as it shall **s.** good unto thee....... 1961,5869
2Sa 19:37 what shall **s.** good unto thee....... 1961,5869
2Sa 19:38 which shall **s.** good unto thee:.... 1961,5869
1Ki 21:2 if it **s.** good to thee, I will give.... 1961,5869
1Ch 13:2 If it **s.** good unto you, and that it............
Ezr 5:17 if it **s.** good to the king, let there be.........
Ezr 7:18 whatsoever shall **s.** good to thee,........ 3191
Ne 9:32 let not all the trouble **s.** little............ 4591
Es 5:4 If it **s.** good unto the king, let the...........
Es 8:5 the thing **s.** right before the king,............
Jer 40:4 If it **s.** good unto thee to come.......... 5869
Jer 40:4 but if it **s.** ill unto thee to come......... 5869
Na 2:4 they shall **s.** like torches, they.......... 4758
1Co 11:16 if any man **s.** to be contentious,......... *1380*
1Co 12:22 body, which **s.** to be more feeble,...... *1380*
2Co 10:9 I may not **s.** as if I would terrify........ *1380*
Heb 4:1 of you should **s.** to come short of it.... *1380*
Jas 1:26 man among you **s.** to be religious,...... *1380*

SEEMED
Ge 19:14 he **s.** as one that mocked unto.... 1961,5869
Ge 29:20 **s.** unto him but a few days,....... 1961,5869
2Sa 3:19 all that **s.** good to Israel, and............ 5869
2Sa 3:19 that **s.** good to the whole house of..... 5869
Ec 9:13 the sun, and it **s.** great unto me:............
Jer 18:4 as **s.** good to the potter to make it..... 5869
Jer 27:5 have given it unto whom it **s.** meet..... 5869
Mt 11:26 **for so it s. good in thy sight**.. *1096,2107*
Lu 1:3 It **s.** good to me also, having had....... *1380*
Lu 10:21 **for so it s. good in thy sight**.. *1096,2107*
Lu 24:11 words **s.** to them as idle tales, and..... *5316*
Ac 15:25 **s.** good unto us, being assembled....... *1380*
Ac 15:28 For it **s.** good to the Holy Ghost,....... *1380*
Ga 2:6 But of these who **s.** to be somewhat,.. *1380*
Ga 2:6 **s.** to be somewhat in conference........ *1380*
Ga 2:9 and John, who **s.** to be pillars........... *1380*

SEEMETH
Le 14:35 It **s.** to me there is as it were a......... 7200
Nu 16:9 **S.** it but a small thing unto you,...............
Jos 9:25 as it **s.** good and right unto thee........ 5869
Jg 10:15 us whatsoever **s.** good unto thee;....... 5869
Jg 19:24 unto them what **s.** good unto you:...... 5869
1Sa 1:23 Do what **s.** thee good; tarry until....... 5869
1Sa 3:18 let him do what **s.** him good............. 5869
1Sa 11:10 with us all that **s.** good unto you........ 5869
1Sa 14:36 Do whatsoever **s.** good unto thee....... 5869
1Sa 14:40 Do what **s.** good unto thee............... 5869
1Sa 18:23 **S.** it to you a light thing to be a......... 5869
2Sa 10:12 Lord do that which **s.** him good......... 5869
2Sa 15:26 him do to me as **s.** good unto him...... 5869
2Sa 18:4 What **s.** you best I will do................ 5869
2Sa 24:22 offer up what **s.** good unto him:......... 5869
Es 3:11 with them as it **s.** good to thee.......... 5869
Pr 14:12 a way which **s.** right unto a man,....... 6440
Pr 16:25 is a way that **s.** right unto a man,....... 6440
Pr 18:17 that is first in his own cause **s.** just;..........
Jer 26:14 do with me as **s.** good and meet........ 5869
Jer 40:4 it **s.** good and convenient for thee...... 5869
Jer 40:5 wheresoever it **s.** convenient unto...... 5869
Eze 34:18 **S.** it a small thing unto you to have..........
Lu 8:18 **even that which he s. to have**........ *1380*
Ac 17:18 He **s.** to be a setter forth of strange... *1380*
Ac 25:27 it **s.** to me unreasonable to send a...... *1380*
1Co 3:18 you **s.** to be wise in this world,......... *1380*
Heb 12:11 for the present **s.** to be joyous, but.... *1380*

SEEMLY See also UNSEEMLY.
Pr 19:10 Delight is not **s.** for a fool; much........ 5000
Pr 26:1 so honour is not **s.** for a fool............ 5000

SEEN
Ge 7:1 thee have I **s.** righteous before me..... 7200
Ge 8:5 were the tops of the mountains **s.**...... 7200
Ge 9:14 the bow shall be **s.** in the cloud:......... 7200
Ge 22:14 the mount of the Lord it shall be **s.**.... 7200
Ge 31:12 I have **s.** all that Laban doeth unto..... 7200
Ge 31:42 God hath **s.** mine affliction and the...... 7200
Ge 32:30 I have **s.** God face to face, and my..... 7200
Ge 33:10 for therefore I have **s.** thy face,......... 7200
Ge 33:10 as though I had **s.** the face of God,..... 7200
Ge 45:13 Egypt, and of all that ye have **s.**;....... 7200
Ge 46:30 let me die, since I have **s.** thy face...... 7200
Ex 3:7 I have surely **s.** the affliction of my..... 7200
Ex 3:9 and I have also **s.** the oppression........ 7200
Ex 3:16 **s.** that which is done to you in Egypt:.......
Ex 10:6 nor thy fathers' fathers have **s.**,......... 7200
Ex 13:7 no leavened bread be **s.** with thee,..... 7200
Ex 13:7 shall there be leaven **s.** with thee....... 7200
Ex 14:13 for the Egyptians whom ye have **s.**...... 7200
Ex 19:4 Ye have **s.** what I did unto the........... 7200
Ex 20:22 Ye have **s.** that I have talked with...... 7200
Ex 32:9 unto Moses, I have **s.** this people,....... 7200
Ex 33:23 parts: but my face shall not be **s.**....... 7200
Ex 34:3 any man be **s.** throughout all the......... 7200
Le 5:1 whether he hath **s.** or known of it;...... 7200
Le 13:7 that he hath been **s.** of the priest....... 7200
Le 13:7 he shall be **s.** of the priest again:....... 7200
Nu 14:14 that thou Lord art **s.** face to face,....... 7200
Nu 14:22 those men which have **s.** my glory,...... 7200
Nu 23:21 neither hath he **s.** perverseness in....... 7200
Nu 27:13 And when thou hast **s.** it, thou also.... 7200
De 1:28 we have **s.** the sons of the Anakims.... 7200
De 1:31 **s.** how that the Lord thy God bare..... 7200
De 3:21 eyes have **s.** all that the Lord your..... 7200
De 4:3 Your eyes have **s.** what the Lord did.. 7200
De 4:9 the things which thine eyes have **s.**,... 7200
De 5:24 **s.** this day that God doth talk with...... 7200
De 9:13 I have **s.** this people, and, behold,...... 7200
De 10:21 things, which thine eyes have **s.**......... 7200
De 11:2 have not **s.** the chastisement of the.... 7200
De 11:7 your eyes have **s.** all the great acts.... 7200
De 16:4 shall be no leavened bread **s.** with...... 7200
De 21:7 blood, neither have our eyes **s.** it....... 7200
De 29:2 Ye have **s.** all that the Lord did......... 7200
De 29:3 temptations...thine eyes have **s.**,........ 7200
De 29:17 And ye have **s.** their abominations,..... 7200
De 33:9 and to his mother, I have not **s.** him;.. 7200
Jos 23:3 have **s.** all that the Lord your God...... 7200

Jos 24:7 your eyes have s. what I have done.... 7200
Jg 2:7 who had s. all the great works of....... 7200
Jg 5:8 was there a shield or spear s. among.. 7200
Jg 6:22 I have s. an angel of the Lord face..... 7200
Jg 9:48 What ye have s. me do, make haste, .. 7200
Jg 13:22 surely die, because we have s. God.... 7200
Jg 14:2 I have s. a woman in Timnath of the... 7200
Jg 18:9 we have s. the land, and, behold,....... 7200
Jg 19:30 was no such deed done nor s. from 7200
1Sa 6:16 lords of the Philistines had s. it,........ 7200
1Sa 16:18 Behold, I have s. a son of Jesse the ... 7200
1Sa 17:25 Have ye s. this man that is come....... 7200
1Sa 23:22 haunt is, and who hath s. him there:... 7200
1Sa 24:10 eyes have s. how that the Lord had.... 7200
2Sa 17:17 not be s. to come into the city: 7200
2Sa 18:21 Go tell the king what thou hast s.. 7200
2Sa 22:11 was s. upon the wings of the wind...... 7200
1Ki 6:18 was cedar; there was no stone s........ 7200
1Ki 8:8 that the ends of the staves were s. 7200
1Ki 8:8 and they were not s. without: and...... 7200
1Ki 10:4 when the queen of Sheba had s. all..... 7200
1Ki 10:7 I came, and mine eyes had s. it: 7200
1Ki 10:12 trees, nor were s. unto this day......... 7200
1Ki 13:12 s. what way the man of God went,..... 7200
1Ki 20:13 thou s. all this great multitude? 7200
2Ki 9:26 s. yesterday the blood of Naboth,........ 7200
2Ki 20:5 thy prayer, I have s. thy tears:.......... 7200
2Ki 20:15 What have they s. in thine house?...... 7200
2Ki 20:15 that are in mine house have they s.: ... 7200
2Ki 23:29 at Megiddo, when he had s. him. 7200
1Ch 29:17 now have I s. with joy thy people,...... 7200
2Ch 5:9 ends of...staves were s. from the ark.. 7200
2Ch 5:9 but they were not s. without. 7200
2Ch 9:3 queen of Sheba had s. the wisdom...... 7200
2Ch 9:6 I came, and mine eyes had s. it: 7200
2Ch 9:11 none such s. before in the land of....... 7200
Ezr 3:12 men, that had s. the first house, ... 7200
Es 9:26 they had s. concerning this matter, ... 7200
Job 4:8 as I have s., they that plow iniquity, ... 7200
Job 5:3 I have s. the foolish taking root: 7200
Job 7:8 the eye of him that hath s. me........... 7210
Job 8:18 him, saying, I have not s. thee. 7200
Job 10:18 up the ghost, and no eye had s. me!... 7200
Job 13:1 mine eye hath s. all this, mine ear....... 7200
Job 15:17 that which I have s. I will declare;...... 2372
Job 20:7 they which have s. him shall say, ... 7200
Job 27:12 all ye yourselves have s. it; why........ 2372
Job 28:7 which the vulture's eye hath not s.: 7805
Job 31:19 If I have s. any perish for want of 7200
Job 33:21 consumed...that it cannot be s.; 7210
Job 33:21 bones that were not s. stick out......... 7200
Job 38:17 s. the doors of the shadow of death?... 7200
Job 38:22 hast thou s. the treasures of the hail,.. 7200
Ps 10:14 Thou hast s. it; for thou beholdest...... 7200
Ps 18:15 the channels of waters were s., ... 7200
Ps 35:21 said, Aha, aha, our eye hath s. it. 7200
Ps 35:22 This thou hast s., O Lord: keep not ... 7200
Ps 37:25 have I not s. the righteous forsaken,... 7200
Ps 37:35 I have s. the wicked in great power,... 7200
Ps 48:8 s. in the city of the Lord of hosts,...... 7200
Ps 54:7 mine eye hath s. his desire upon........ 7200
Ps 55:9 s. violence and strife in the city. 7200
Ps 63:2 as I have s. thee in the sanctuary....... 2372
Ps 68:24 They have s. thy goings, O God; 7200
Ps 90:15 the years wherein we have s. evil. 7200
Ps 98:3 have s. the salvation of our God......... 7200
Ps 119:96 I have s. an end of all perfection: 7200
Pr 25:7 the prince whom thine eyes have s...... 7200
Ec 1:14 I have s. all the works that are done... 7200
Ec 3:10 I have s. the travail, which God hath... 7200
Ec 4:3 who hath not s. the evil work that...... 7200
Ec 5:13 evil which I have s. under the sun,..... 7200
Ec 5:18 Behold that which I have s.: it is........ 7200
Ec 6:1 evil which I have s. under the sun,..... 7200
Ec 6:5 Moreover he hath not s. the sun,......... 7200
Ec 6:6 twice told, yet hath he s. no good: 7200
Ec 7:15 have I s. in the days of my vanity: 7200
Ec 8:9 All this have I s., and applied my 7200
Ec 9:13 This wisdom have I s. also under 7200
Ec 10:5 evil which I have s. under the sun,..... 7200
Ec 10:7 I have s. servants upon horses, and.... 7200
Isa 6:5 for mine eyes have s. the King, the.... 7200
Isa 9:2 in darkness have s. a great light:........ 7200
Isa 16:12 when it is s. that Moab is weary........ 7200
Isa 22:9 s. also the breaches of the city.......... 7200
Isa 38:5 heard thy prayer, I have s. thy tears: ..7200
Isa 39:4 What have they s. in thine house?...... 7200
Isa 39:4 that is in mine house have they s.:..... 7200
Isa 44:16 Aha, I am warm, I have s. the fire:..... 7200
Isa 47:3 uncovered...thy shame shall be s.:....... 7200
Isa 57:18 I have s. his ways, and will heal him:.. 7200
Isa 60:2 and his glory shall be s. upon thee...... 7200
Isa 64:4 by the ear, neither hath the eye s., ... 7200
Isa 66:8 a thing? who hath s. such things?....... 7200
Isa 66:19 my fame, neither have s. my glory; 7200
Jer 1:12 Thou hast well s.: for I will hasten 7200
Jer 3:6 s. that which backsliding Israel.......... 7200
Jer 7:11 even I have s. it, saith the Lord. 7200
Jer 12:3 hast s. me, and tried mine heart 7200
Jer 13:27 I have s. thine adulteries, and thy 7200
Jer 23:13 s. folly in the prophets of Samaria, ... 7200
Jer 23:14 s. also in the prophets of Jerusalem 7200
Jer 44:2 Ye have s. all the evil that I have....... 7200
Jer 46:5 Wherefore have I s. them dismayed.... 7200
La 1:8 they have s. her nakedness:............. 7200
La 1:10 hath s. that the heathen entered 7200
La 2:14 have s. vain and foolish things 2372
La 2:14 but have s. for thee false burdens 2372
La 2:16 for; we have found, we have s. it....... 7200
La 3:1 I am the man that hath s. affliction 7200
La 3:59 O Lord, thou hath s. my wrong: 7200
La 3:60 Thou hast s. all their vengeance......... 7200
Eze 8:12 hast thou s. what the ancients of........ 7200
Eze 8:15, 17 Hast thou s. this, O son of man? ... 7200
Eze 11:24 So the vision that I had s. went up..... 7200
Eze 13:3 own spirit, and have s. nothing! 7200
Eze 13:6 s. vanity and lying divination,............ 2372
Eze 13:7 Have ye not s. a vain vision, and 2372
Eze 13:8 ye have spoken vanity, and s. lies. 2372
Eze 47:6 me, Son of man, hast thou s. this? 7200
Da 2:26 me the dream which I have s., ... 2370
Da 4:9 visions of my dream that I have s.,...... 2370
Da 4:18 I king Nebuchadnezzar have s............ 2370
Da 8:6 I had s. standing before the river,....... 7200
Da 8:15 I, even I Daniel, had s. the vision, ... 7200
Da 9:21 Gabriel, whom I had s. in the vision.... 7200
Ho 6:10 I have s. an horrible thing in the........ 7200
Zec 9:8 for now have I s. with mine eyes. 7200
Zec 9:14 And the Lord shall be s. over them, ... 7200
Zec 10:2 and the diviners have s. a lie, and...... 2372
Mt 2:2 for we have s. his star in the east,..... *1492*
Mt 6:1 **alms before men, to be s. of them:** .*2300*
Mt 6:5 **that they may be s. of men**............ *5316*
Mt 9:33 saying, It was never so s. in Israel. *5316*
Mt 13:17 **ye see, and have not s. them;**....... *1492*
Mt 21:32 **ye, when ye had s. it, repented**...... *1492*
Mt 23:5 **works they do for to be s. of men:**. *2300*
Mk 9:1 **they have s. the kingdom of God** ... *1492*
Mk 9:9 no man what things they had s., ... *1492*
Mk 16:11 was alive, and had been s. of her, ... *2300*
Mk 16:14 believed not them which had s. him *2300*
Lu 1:22 perceived that he had s. a vision in..... *3708*
Lu 2:17 they had s. it, they made known *1492*
Lu 2:20 things that they had heard and s., ... *1492*
Lu 2:26 before he had s. the Lord's Christ...... *1492*
Lu 2:30 For mine eyes have s. thy salvation, ... *1492*
Lu 5:26 We have s. strange things to day. *1492*
Lu 7:22 **tell John what things ye have s**...... *1492*
Lu 9:36 of those things which they had s.. ...... *3708*
Lu 10:24 **ye see, and have not s. them:**........ *1492*
Lu 19:37 the mighty works that they had s.; *1492*
Lu 23:8 he hoped to have s. some miracle *1492*
Lu 24:23 they had also s. a vison of angels, ... *3708*
Lu 24:37 supposed that they had s. a spirit....... *2334*
Joh 1:18 No man hath s. God at any time; *3708*
Joh 3:11 **know, and testify that we have s.;** . *3708*
Joh 3:32 what he hath s. and heard, that he *3708*
Joh 4:45 having s. all the things that he did...... *3708*
Joh 5:37 **voice at any time, nor s. his shape**. *3708*
Joh 6:14 had s. the miracle that Jesus did, ... *1492*
Joh 6:36 **ye also have s. me, and believe**...... *3708*
Joh 6:46 **that any man hath s. the Father,** .. *3708*
Joh 6:46 **is of God, he hath s. the Father**.... *3708*
Joh 8:38 **which I have s. with my Father:** *3708*
Joh 8:38 **which ye have s. with your father**. . *3708*
Joh 8:57 old, and hast thou s. Abraham? *3708*
Joh 9:8 had s. him that he was blind,............. *2334*
Joh 9:37 **Thou hast both s. him, and it is**.... *3708*
Joh 11:45 had s. the things which Jesus did,....... *2300*
Joh 14:7 **ye know him, and have s. him.** *3708*
Joh 14:9 **that hath s. me hath s. the** *3708*
Joh 15:24 **now have they both s. hated me**.... *3708*
Joh 20:18 disciples that she had s. the Lord,...... *3708*
Joh 20:25 said unto him, We have s. the Lord.... *3708*
Joh 20:29 **because thou hast s. me, thou** *3708*
Joh 20:29 **blessed are they that have not s.,** .. *1492*
Ac 1:3 being s. of them forty days, and......... *3700*
Ac 1:11 as ye have s. him go into heaven. *2300*
Ac 4:20 which we have s. and heard. *1492*
Ac 7:34 I have s.,...the affliction of my........... *1492*
Ac 7:34 I have s. the affliction of my people, ... *1492*
Ac 7:44 to the fashion that he had s.............. *3708*
Ac 9:12 **hath s. in a vision a man named** ... *1492*
Ac 9:27 how he had s. the Lord in the way, ... *1492*
Ac 10:17 vision which he had s. should mean,.... *1492*
Ac 11:13 how he had s. an angel in his house, ... *1492*
Ac 11:23 came, and had s. the grace of God, ... *1492*
Ac 13:31 And he was s. many days of them...... *3700*
Ac 16:10 And after he had s. the vision,........... *1492*
Ac 16:40 and when they had s. the brethren, ... *1492*
Ac 21:29 (For they had s. before with him........ *4308*
Ac 22:15 of what thou hast s. and heard.......... *3708*
Ac 26:16 **of these things which thou hast s.,** .*1492*
Ro 1:20 creation of the world are clearly s., ... *2529*
Ro 8:24 but hope that is s. is not hope: for....... *991*
1Co 2:9 Eye hath not s., nor ear heard, ... *1492*
1Co 9:1 have I not s. Jesus Christ our............ *3708*
1Co 15:5 And that he was s. of Cephas,........... *3700*
1Co 15:6 he was s. of above five hundred......... *3700*
1Co 15:7 After that, he was s. of James;.......... *3700*
1Co 15:8 And last of all he was s. of me also, ... *3700*
2Co 4:18 look not at the things which are s., ... *991*
2Co 4:18 but at the things which are not s.: *991*
2Co 4:18 things which are s. are temporal; *991*
2Co 4:18 things which are not s. are eternal. *991*
Php 4:9 and heard, and s. in me, do; *1492*
Col 2:1 as have not s. my face in the flesh; *3708*
Col 2:18 those things which he hath not s., ... *3708*
1Ti 3:16 justified in the Spirit, s. of angels, ... *3700*
1Ti 6:16 whom no man hath s., nor can see: *1492*
Heb 11:1 for, the evidence of things not s.. .... *991*
Heb 11:3 things which are s. were not made........ *991*
Heb 11:7 warned of God of things not s. as yet,.. *991*
Heb 11:13 but having s. them afar off, and *1492*
Jas 5:11 and have s. the end of the Lord;......... *1492*
1Pe 1:8 Whom having not s., ye love; in.......... *1492*
1Jo 1:1 which we have s. with our eyes, ... *3708*
1Jo 1:2 and we have s. it, and bear witness, ... *3708*
1Jo 1:3 That which we have s. and heard....... *3708*
1Jo 3:6 whosoever sinneth hath not s. him,..... *3708*
1Jo 4:12 No man hath s. God at any time. *2300*
1Jo 4:14 And we have s. and do testify that..... *2300*
1Jo 4:20 not his brother whom he hath s., ... *3708*
1Jo 4:20 he love God whom he hath not s.? *3708*
3Jo 11 he that doeth evil hath not s. God. *3780*
Re 1:19 **Write the things...thou hast s.,** *1492*
Re 11:19 there was s. in his temple the ark...... *3700*
Re 22:8 And when I had heard and s., I fell...... *991*

SEER See also OVERSEER; SEER'S; SEERS.

1Sa 9:9 Come, and let us go to the s.: for...... 7200
1Sa 9:9 Prophet was beforetime called a S..)... 7200
1Sa 9:11 and said unto them, Is the s. here? 7200
1Sa 9:19 answered Saul, and said, I am the s.: .. 7200
2Sa 15:27 Zadok the priest, Art not thou a s.?.... 7200
2Sa 24:11 unto the prophet Gad, David's s.,........ 2374
1Ch 9:22 David and Samuel the s. did ordain..... 7200
1Ch 21:9 Lord spake unto Gad, David's s., ... 2374
1Ch 25:5 the sons of Heman the king's s. in...... 2374
1Ch 26:28 all that Samuel the s., and Saul......... 7200
1Ch 29:29 in the book of Samuel the s.,............ 7200
1Ch 29:29 and in the book of Gad the s., ... 2374
2Ch 9:29 and in the visions Iddo the s............. 2374
2Ch 12:15 Iddo the s. concerning genealogies? 2374
2Ch 16:7 Hanani the s. came to Asa king......... 7200
2Ch 16:10 Then Asa was wroth with the s., ... 7200
2Ch 19:2 of Hanani the s. went out to meet...... 2374
2Ch 29:25 of David, and of God the king's s., ... 2374
2Ch 29:30 of David, and of Asaph the s........... 2374
2Ch 35:15 Heman, and Jeduthun the king's s.;..... 2374
Am 7:12 O thou s., go, flee thee away into...... 2374

SEER'S

1Sa 9:18 Tell me,...where the s. house is. 7200

SEERS See also OVERSEERS.

2Ki 17:13 all the prophets, and by all the s., ... 2374
2Ch 33:18 words of the s. that spake to him....... 2374
2Ch 33:19 written among the sayings of the s.. ... 2374
Isa 29:10 your rulers, the s. hath he covered..... 2374

Isa 30:10 Which say to the **s.**, See not; and 7200
Mic 3:7 Then shall the **s.** be ashamed, and 2374

SEEST
Ge 13:15 For all the land which thou **s.**, to 7200
Ge 16:13 spake unto her, Thou God **s.** me; 7210
Ge 31:43 and all that thou **s.** is mine: and 7200
Ex 10:28 day thou **s.** my face thou shalt die, 7200
De 4:19 and when thou **s.** the sun, and the 7200
De 12:13 offerings in every place...thou **s.**: 7200
De 20:1 and **s.** horses, and chariots, and a 7200
De 21:11 **s.** among the captives a beautiful 7200
Jg 9:36 **s.** the shadow of the mountains as 7200
1Ki 21:29 **S.** thou how Ahab humbleth 7200
Job 10:4 of flesh? or **s.** thou as man seeth? 7200
Pr 22:29 **S.** thou a man diligent in his 2372
Pr 26:12 **S.** thou a man wise in his own 7200
Pr 29:20 **S.** thou a man that is hasty in his 2372
Ec 5:8 thou **s.** the oppression of the poor, 7200
Isa 58:3 fasted, say they, and thou **s.** not? 7200
Isa 58:7 when thou **s.** the naked, that thou 7200
Jer 1:11 saying, Jeremiah, what **s.** thou? 7200
Jer 1:13 second time, saying, What **s.** thou? 7200
Jer 7:17 **S.** thou not what they do in the 7200
Jer 20:12 and **s.** the reins and the heart, let 7200
Jer 24:3 unto me, What **s.** thou, Jeremiah? 7200
Jer 32:24 to pass; and, behold, thou **s.** it, 7200
Eze 8:6 Son of man, **s.** thou what they do? 7200
Eze 40:4 declare all that thou **s.** to the house 7200
Da 1:13 as thou **s.**, deal with thy servants 7200
Am 7:8 said unto me, Amos, what **s.** thou? 7200
Am 8:2 And he said, Amos, what **s.** thou? 7200
Zec 4:2 And said unto me, What **s.** thou? 7200
Zec 5:2 he said unto me, What **s.** thou? 7200
Mk 5:31 **s.** the multitude thronging thee, *991*
Mk 13:2 him, **S. thou these great buildings?** *991*
Lu 7:44 unto Simon, **S. thou this woman?** *991*
Ac 21:20 him, Thou **s.**, brother, how many *2334*
Jas 2:22 **S.** thou how faith wrought with his *991*
Re 1:11 **What thou s., write in a book, and** *991*

SEETH See also FORSEETH.
Ge 16:13 here looked after him that **s.** me? 7210
Ge 44:31 when he **s.** that the lad is not with 7200
Ex 4:14 when he **s.** thee, he will be glad in 7200
Ex 12:23 he **s.** the blood upon the lintel, and 7200
Le 13:20 when the priest **s.** it, behold, it be 7200
De 32:36 he **s.** that their power is gone, and 7200
1Sa 16:7 him: for the Lord **s.** not as man
1Sa 16:7 not as man **s.**; for man looketh 7200
2Ki 2:19 this city is pleasant, as my lord **s.**: 7200
Job 8:17 heap, and **s.** the place of stones. 2372
Job 10:4 of flesh? or seest thou as man **s.**? 7200
Job 11:11 he **s.** wickedness also; will he not 7200
Job 22:14 a covering to him, that he **s.** not; 7200
Job 28:10 his eye **s.** every precious thing. 7200
Job 28:24 and **s.** under the whole heaven; 7200
Job 34:21 of man, and he **s.** all his goings 7200
Job 42:5 the ear: but now mine eye **s.** thee 7200
Ps 37:13 for he **s.** that his day is coming 7200
Ps 49:10 he **s.** that wise men die, likewise 7200
Ps 58:10 rejoice when he **s.** the vengeance; 2372
Ec 8:16 neither day nor night **s.** sleep with 7200
Isa 21:6 let him declare what he **s.** 7200
Isa 28:4 he that looketh upon it **s.**, while it 7200
Isa 29:15 the dark, and they say, Who **s.** us? 7200
Isa 29:23 when he **s.** his children, the work 7200
Isa 47:10 thou hast said, None **s.** me. Thy 7200
Eze 8:12 The Lord **s.** us not; the Lord hath 7200
Eze 9:9 the earth, and the Lord **s.** not. 7200
Eze 12:27 vision that he **s.** is for many days 2372
Eze 18:14 **s.** all his father's sins which he 7200
Eze 33:3 **s.** the sword come upon the land, 7200
Eze 39:15 when any **s.** a man's bone, then 7200
Mt 6:4 **and thy Father which s. in secret** *991*
Mt 6:6 **thy Father which s. in secret shall** *991*
Mt 6:18 **which s. in secret, shall reward** *991*
Mk 5:38 **s.** the tumult, and them that wept *2334*
Lu 16:23 **s. Abraham afar off, and Lazarus** *3708*
Joh 1:29 John **s.** Jesus coming unto him, *991*
Joh 5:19 **but what he s. the Father do: for** *991*
Joh 6:40 **that every one which s. the Son** *2334*
Joh 9:21 means he now **s.**, we know not; or *991*
Joh 10:12 **s. the wolf coming, and leaveth** *2334*
Joh 11:9 **he s. the light of this world** *991*
Joh 12:45 **that s. me s. him that sent me** *2334*
Joh 14:17 **it s. him not, neither knoweth** *2334*
Joh 14:19 **and the world s. me no more; but** *2334*
Joh 20:1 **s.** the stone taken away from the *991*
Joh 20:6 sepulchre, and **s.** the linen clothes *2334*
Joh 20:12 **s.** two angels in white sitting, the *2334*
Joh 21:20 **s.** the disciple whom Jesus loved *991*
Ro 8:24 for what a man **s.**, why doth he *991*
2Co 12:6 me above that which he **s.** me to be, *991*
1Jo 3:17 and **s.** his brother have need. *2334*

SEETHE See also SEETHING; SOD.
Ex 16:23 to day, and **s.** that ye will **s.**; 1310
Ex 23:19 not **s.** a kid in his mother's milk. 1310
Ex 29:31 and **s.** his flesh in the holy place. 1310
Ex 34:26 not **s.** a kid in his mother's milk. 1310
De 14:21 not **s.** a kid in his mother's milk. 1310
2Ki 4:38 and **s.** pottage for the sons of the 1310
Eze 24:5 let them **s.** the bones of it therein. 1310
Zec 14:21 and take of them, and **s.** therein: 1310

SEETHED See SOD.

SEETHING
1Sa 2:13 came while the flesh was in **s.**, 1310
Job 41:20 as out of a **s.** pot or caldron. 5301
Jer 1:13 I see a **s.** pot; and the face thereof 5301

SEGUB (se'-gub)
1Ki 16:34 thereof in his youngest son **S.**, 7687
1Ch 2:21 years old; and she bare him **S.** 7687
1Ch 2:22 And **S.** begat Jair, who had three 7687

SEIR (se'-ur)
Ge 14:6 And the Horites in their mount **S.**, 8165
Ge 32:3 his brother unto the land of **S.**, the 8165
Ge 33:14 until I come unto my lord unto **S.** 8165
Ge 33:16 that day on his way unto **S.** 8165
Ge 36:8 Thus dwelt Esau in mount **S.**: Esau 8165
Ge 36:9 father of the Edomites in mount **S.**: 8165
Ge 36:20 These are the sons of **S.** the Horite, 8165
Ge 36:21 children of **S.** in the land of Edom. 8165
Ge 36:30 among their dukes in the land of **S.** 8165
Nu 24:18 **S.** also shall be a possession for his 8165
De 1:2 from Horeb by the way of mount **S.** 8165
De 1:44 as bees do, and destroyed you in **S.**, 8165
De 2:1 we compassed mount **S.** many days. 8165
De 2:4 children of Esau, which dwell in **S.**; 8165
De 2:5 I have given mount **S.** unto Esau 8165
De 2:8 children of Esau, which dwelt in **S.**, 8165
De 2:12 Horims also dwelt in **S.** beforetime; 8165
De 2:22 children of Esau, which dwelt in **S.**, 8165
De 2:29 chidren of Esau which dwelt in **S.**, 8165
De 33:2 and rose up from **S.** unto them; 8165
Jos 11:17 mount Halak, that goeth up to **S.**, 8165
Jos 12:7 mount Halak, that goeth up to **S.**; 8165
Jos 15:10 Baalah westward unto mount **S.**, 8165
Jos 24:4 and I gave unto Esau mount **S.**, to 8165
Jg 5:4 Lord, when thou wentest out of **S.**, 8165
1Ch 1:38 the sons of **S.**; Lotan, and Shobal, 8165
1Ch 4:42 five hundred men, went to mount **S.**, 8165
2Ch 20:10 of Ammon and Moab and mount **S.**, 8165
2Ch 20:22 of Ammon, Moab, and mount **S.**, 8165
2Ch 20:23 the inhabitants of mount **S.**, 8165
2Ch 20:23 an end of the inhabitants of **S.**, 8165
2Ch 25:11 of the children of **S.** ten thousand. 8165
2Ch 25:14 the gods of the children of **S.** 8165
Isa 21:11 Dumah. He calleth to me out of **S.**, 8165
Eze 25:8 Because that Moab and **S.** do say, 8165
Eze 35:2 set thy face against mount **S.**, and 8165
Eze 35:3 Behold, O mount **S.**, I am against 8165
Eze 35:7 I make mount **S.** most desolate, 8165
Eze 35:15 thou shalt be desolate, O mount **S.**, 8165

SEIRATH (se'-ur-ath)
Jg 3:26 the quarries, and escaped unto **S.** 8167

SEIZE See also SEIZED.
Jos 8:7 the ambush, and **s.** upon the city: 3423
Job 3:6 that night, let darkness **s.** upon it: 3947
Ps 55:15 Let death **s.** upon them, and let 3451
Mt 21:38 **and let us s. on his inheritance.** *2722*

SEIZED
Jer 49:24 to flee, and fear hath **s.** on her: 2388

SELA (se'-lah) See also SELAH; SELA-HAMMAHLEKOTH.
Isa 16:1 the land from **S.** to the wilderness, 5554

SELAH (se'-lah) See also JOKTHEEL; SELA.
2Ki 14:7 and took **S.** by war, and called the 5554
Ps 3:2 is no help for him in God. **S.** 5542
Ps 3:4 heard me out of his holy hill. **S.** 5542
Ps 3:8 blessing is upon thy people. **S.** 5542
Ps 4:2 vanity, and seek after leasing? **S.** 5542
Ps 4:4 upon your bed, and be still. **S.** 5542
Ps 7:5 lay mine honour in the dust. **S.** 5542
Ps 9:16 of his own hands. Higgaion. **S.** 5542
Ps 9:20 know themselves to be but men. **S.** 5542
Ps 20:3 and accept thy burnt sacrifice; **S.** 5542
Ps 21:2 the request of his lips. **S.** 5542
Ps 24:6 that seek thy face, O Jacob. **S.** 5542
Ps 24:10 hosts, he is the King of glory. **S.** 5542
Ps 32:4 into the drought of summer. **S.** 5542
Ps 32:5 forgavest the iniquity of my sin. **S.** 5542
Ps 32:7 with songs of deliverance. **S.** 5542
Ps 39:5 best state is altogether vanity. **S.** 5542
Ps 39:11 surely every man is vanity. **S.** 5542
Ps 44:8 and praise thy name for ever. **S.** 5542
Ps 46:3 shake with the swelling thereof. **S.** 5542
Ps 46:7, 11 God of Jacob is our refuge. **S.** 5542
Ps 47:4 of Jacob whom he loved. **S.** 5542
Ps 48:8 God will establish it for ever. **S.** 5542
Ps 49:13 approve their sayings. **S.** 5542
Ps 49:15 grave: for he shall receive me. **S.** 5542
Ps 50:6 for God is judge himself. **S.** 5542
Ps 52:3 than to speak righteousness. **S.** 5542
Ps 52:5 out of the land of the living. **S.** 5542
Ps 54:3 have not set God before them. **S.** 5542
Ps 55:7 and remain in the wilderness. **S.** 5542
Ps 55:19 even he that abideth of old. **S.** 5542
Ps 57:3 him that would swallow me up. **S.** 5542
Ps 57:6 they are fallen themselves. **S.** 5542
Ps 59:5 to any wicked transgressors. **S.** 5542
Ps 59:13 unto the ends of the earth. **S.** 5542
Ps 60:4 displayed because of the truth. **S.** 5542
Ps 61:4 trust in the covert of thy wings. **S.** 5542
Ps 62:4 mouth, but they curse inwardly. **S.** 5542
Ps 62:8 him: God is a refuge for us. **S.** 5542
Ps 66:4 they shall sing to thy name. **S.** 5542
Ps 66:7 the rebellious exalt themselves. **S.** 5542
Ps 66:15 I will offer bullocks with goats. **S.** 5542
Ps 67:1 cause his face to shine upon us; **S.** 5542
Ps 67:4 govern the nations upon earth. **S.** 5542
Ps 68:7 march through the wilderness; **S.** 5542
Ps 68:19 even the God of our salvation. **S.** 5542
Ps 68:32 O sing praises unto the Lord; **S.** 5542
Ps 75:3 I bear up the pillars of it. **S.** 5542
Ps 76:3 and the sword, and the battle. **S.** 5542
Ps 76:9 save all the meek of the earth. **S.** 5542
Ps 77:3 my spirit was overwhelmed. **S.** 5542
Ps 77:9 shut up his tender mercies? **S.** 5542
Ps 77:15 the sons of Jacob and Joseph. **S.** 5542
Ps 81:7 thee at the waters of Meribah. **S.** 5542
Ps 82:2 the persons of the wicked? **S.** 5542
Ps 83:8 holpen the children of Lot. **S.** 5542
Ps 84:4 they will be still praising thee. **S.** 5542
Ps 84:8 give ear, O God of Jacob. **S.** 5542
Ps 85:2 thou hast covered all their sin. **S.** 5542
Ps 87:3 spoken of thee, O city of God. **S.** 5542
Ps 87:6 that this man was born there. **S.** 5542
Ps 88:7 afflicted me with all thy waves. **S.** 5542
Ps 88:10 the dead arise and praise thee? **S.** 5542
Ps 89:4 thy throne to all generations. **S.** 5542
Ps 89:37 as a faithful witness in heaven. **S.** 5542
Ps 89:45 hast covered him with shame. **S.** 5542
Ps 89:48 from the hand of the grave? **S.** 5542
Ps 140:3 poison is under their lips. **S.** 5542
Ps 140:5 they have set gins for me. **S.** 5542
Ps 140:8 lest they exalt themselves. **S.** 5542
Ps 143:6 after thee, as a thirsty land. **S.** 5542
Hab 3:3 Holy One from mount Paran. **S.** 5542
Hab 3:9 of the tribes, even thy word. **S.** 5542
Hab 3:13 the foundation unto the neck. **S.** 5542

SELA-HAMMAHLEKOTH (se''-lah-ham-mah'-le-koth)
1Sa 23:28 therefore they called that place **S.** 5555

SELED (se'-led)
1Ch 2:30 sons of Nadab; **S.**, and Appaim: 5540
1Ch 2:30 but **S.** died without children. 5540

SELEUCIA (sel-u-si'-ah)
Ac 13:4 the Holy Ghost, departed unto **S.**; *4581*

SELF See also HERSELF; HIMSELF; ITSELF; MYSELF; SELFSAME; SELFWILL; SELVEDGE; SELVES; THYSELF.
Ex 32:13 to whom thou swarest by thine own **s.**,
Joh 5:30 **I can of mine own s. do nothing:** *1683*
Joh 17:5 **glorify thou me with thine own s.** *4572*
1Co 4:3 yea, I judge not mine own **s.** *1683*

Phm 19 owest unto me even thine own **s.**........ *4572*
1Pe 2:24 Who his own **s.** bare our sins in his...... *846*

SELFSAME
Ge 7:13 In the **s.** day entered Noah,....... 2088,6106
Ge 17:23 of their foreskin in the **s.** day,.... 2088,6106
Ge 17:26 in the **s.** day was Abraham......... 2088,6106
Ex 12:17 this **s.** day have I brought your... 2088,6106
Ex 12:41 even the **s.** day it came to pass, . 2088,6106
Ex 12:51 And it came to pass the **s.** day, .. 2088,6106
Le 23:14 **s.** day that ye have brought 2088,6106
Le 23:21 ye shall proclaim on the **s.** day,... 2088,6106
De 32:48 spake unto Moses that **s.** day,.... 2088,6106
Jos 5:11 and parched corn in the **s.** day.... 2088,6106
Eze 40:1 the **s.** day the hand of the Lord .. 2088,6106
Mt 8:13 servant was healed in the **s.** hour....... *1565*
1Co 12:11 worketh that one and the **s.** Spirit,....... *846*
2Co 5:5 wrought us for the **s.** thing is....... *846,5124*
2Co 7:11 For behold this **s.** thing, that ye *846*

SELFWILL See also SELFWILLED.
Ge 49:6 their **s.** they digged down a wall........ 7522

SELFWILLED
Tit 1:7 not **s.**, not soon angry, not given to *829*
2Pe 2:10 Presumptuous are they, **s.**, they.......... *829*

SELL See also SELLEST; SELLETH; SOLD.
Ge 25:31 said, **S.** me this day thy birthright. 4376
Ge 37:27 and let us **s.** him to the Ishmeelites, ... 4376
Ex 21:7 **s.** his daughter to be a maidservant, ... 4376
Ex 21:8 to **s.** her unto a strange nation he 4376
Ex 21:35 then they shall **s.** the live ox, and....... 4376
Ex 22:1 ox, or a sheep, and kill it, or **s.** it; 4376
Le 25:14 thou **s.** ought unto thy neighbour,........ 4376
Le 25:15 of the fruits he shall **s.** unto thee: 4376
Le 25:16 of the fruits doth he **s.** unto thee. 4376
Le 25:29 **s.** a dwelling house in a walled city, ... 4376
Le 25:47 and **s.** himself unto the stranger or...... 4376
De 2:28 Thou shalt **s.** me meat for money,...... 7666
De 14:21 thou mayest **s.** it unto an alien:.......... 4376
De 21:14 shalt not **s.** her at all for money,........ 4376
Jg 4:9 the Lord shall **s.** Sisera into the......... 4376
1Ki 21:25 did **s.** himself to work wickedness 4376
2Ki 4:7 Go, **s.** the oil, and pay thy debt, and.... 4376
Ne 5:8 and will ye even **s.** your brethren?...... 4376
Ne 10:31 victuals on the sabbath day to **s.**, ... 4376
Pr 23:23 Buy the truth, and **s.** it not; also........ 4376
Eze 30:12 **s.** the land into the hand of the.......... 4376
Eze 48:14 And they shall not **s.** of it, neither...... 4376
Joe 3:8 And I will **s.** your sons and your 4376
Joe 3:8 they shall **s.** them to the Sabeans,....... 4376
Am 8:5 be gone, that we may **s.** corn? 7666
Am 8:6 yea, and **s.** the refuse of the wheat? ... 7666
Zec 11:5 they that **s.** them say, Blessed be 4376
Mt 19:21 go and **s.** that thou hast, and give. *4453*
Mt 25:9 go ye rather to them that **s.**, and .. *4453*
Mk 10:21 **s.** whatsoever thou hast, and give.. *4453*
Lu 12:33 **S.** that ye have, and give alms; *4453*
Lu 18:22 **s.** all that thou hast, and............ *4453*
Lu 22:36 no sword, let him **s.** his garment,.. *4453*
Jas 4:13 and buy and **s.**, and get gain:............ *1710*
Re 13:17 that no man might buy or **s.**, save...... *4453*

SELLER See also SELLERS.
Isa 24:2 as with the buyer, so with the **s.**; 4376
Eze 7:12 buyer rejoice, nor the **s.** mourn: 4376
Eze 7:13 For the **s.** shall not return to that....... 4376
Ac 16:14 named Lydia, a **s.** of purple,.............. *4211*

SELLERS
Ne 13:20 merchants and **s.** of all kinds of.......... 4376

SELLEST
Ps 44:12 Thou **s.** thy people for nought, ... 4376

SELLETH
Ex 21:16 that stealeth a man, and **s.** him, ... 4376
De 24:7 merchandise of him, or **s.** him; 4376
Ru 4:3 **s.** a parcel of land, which was our 4376
Pr 11:26 upon the head of him that **s.** it.......... 7666
Pr 31:24 She maketh fine linen, and **s.** it;........ 4376
Na 3:4 **s.** nations through her whoredoms, ... 4376
Mt 13:44 goeth and **s.** all that he hath, and ..*4453*

SELVEDGE
Ex 26:4 from the **s.** in the coupling; and 7098
Ex 36:11 from the **s.** in the coupling: 7098

SELVES See also OURSELVES; THEMSELVES; YOURSELVES.
Le 11:43 Ye shall not make your **s.**................. 5315
Jos 23:11 good heed therefore unto your **s.**, ... 5315
Lu 21:30 own **s.** that summer is now nigh ... *1438*
Ac 20:30 Also of your own **s.** shall men arise,..... *846*
2Co 8:5 first gave their own **s.** to the Lord, ... *1438*
2Co 13:5 be in the faith; prove your own **s.**. *1438*
2Co 13:5 Know ye not your own **s.**, how that.... *1438*
2Ti 3:2 men shall be lovers of their own **s.**, ... *5367*
Jas 1:22 hearers only, deceiving...own **s.**. *846*

SEM (sem) See also SHEM.
Lu 3:36 which was the son of **S.**, which.......... *4590*

SEMACHIAH (sem-a-ki'-ah)
1Ch 26:7 were strong men, Elihu, and **S.**. 5565

SEMBLANCE See RESEMBLANCE.

SEMEI (sem'-e-i) See also SHEMAIAH.
Lu 3:26 which was the son of **S.** which.......... *4584*

SENAAH (sen'-a-ah) See also HASSENAAH.
Ezr 2:35 The children of **S.**, three thousand...... 5570
Ne 7:38 The children of **S.**, three thousand...... 5570

SENATE
Ac 5:21 all the **s.** of the children of Israel,....... *1087*

SENATORS
Ps 105:22 pleasure; and teach his **s.** wisdom....... 2205

SEND See also SENDEST; SENDETH; SENDING; SENT.
Ge 24:7 he shall **s.** his angel before thee,........ 7971
Ge 24:12 thee, **s.** me good speed this day, ... 7136
Ge 24:40 will **s.** his angel with thee, and.......... 7971
Ge 24:54 said, **S.** me away unto my master. 7971
Ge 24:56 **s.** me away that I may go to my 7971
Ge 27:45 then I will **s.**, and fetch thee from 7971
Ge 30:25 **s.** me away, that I may go unto 7971
Ge 37:13 come, and I will **s.** thee unto them. 7971
Ge 38:17 I will **s.** thee a kid from the flock. 7971
Ge 38:17 thou give me a pledge, till thou **s.** it? .. 7971
Ge 42:16 **S.** one of you, and let him fetch......... 7971
Ge 43:4 If thou wilt **s.** our brother with us, ... 7971
Ge 43:5 But if thou wilt not **s.** him, we will 7971
Ge 43:8 **S.** the lad with me, and we will 7971
Ge 43:14 he may **s.** away your other brother..... 7971
Ge 45:5 For God did **s.** me before you to........ 7971
Ex 3:10 I will **s.** thee unto Pharaoh, that......... 7971
Ex 4:13 he said, O my Lord, **S.**, I pray thee, .. 7971
Ex 4:13 the hand of him whom thou wilt **s.**...... 7971
Ex 7:2 that he **s.** the children of Israel out...... 7971
Ex 8:21 I will **s.** swarms of flies upon thee, ... 7971
Ex 9:14 will at this time **s.** all my plagues 7971
Ex 9:19 **S.** therefore now, and gather thy 7971
Ex 12:33 they might **s.** them out of the land...... 7971
Ex 23:20 I **s.** an Angel before thee, to keep...... 7971
Ex 23:27 I will **s.** my fear before thee, and....... 7971
Ex 23:28 And I will **s.** hornets before thee,....... 7971
Ex 33:2 And I will **s.** an angel before thee;...... 7971
Ex 33:12 know whom thou wilt **s.** with me........ 7971
Le 16:21 shall **s.** him away by the hand of a...... 7971
Le 26:22 will also **s.** wild beasts among you, ... 7971
Le 26:25 I will **s.** the pestilence among you;...... 7971
Le 26:36 I will **s.** a faintness into their.............. 935
Nu 13:2 **S.** thou men, that may search the 7971
Nu 13:2 of their fathers shall ye **s.** a man, ... 7971
Nu 22:37 earnestly **s.** unto thee to call thee?..... 7971
Nu 31:4 of Israel, shall ye **s.** to the war......... 7971
De 1:22 We will **s.** men before us, and they 7971
De 7:20 the Lord thy God will **s.** the hornet 7971
De 11:15 I will **s.** grass in thy fields for thy....... 5414
De 19:12 elders...shall **s.** and fetch him........... 7971
De 24:1 hand, and **s.** her out of his house, ... 7971
De 28:20 The Lord shall **s.** upon the cursing, ... 7971
De 28:48 which the Lord shall **s.** against thee, ... 7971
De 32:24 **s.** the teeth of beasts upon them,........ 7971
Jos 18:4 I will **s.** them, and they shall rise, ... 7971
Jg 13:8 thou didst **s.** come again unto us,........ 7971
1Sa 5:11 **S.** away the ark of the God of Israel,.. 7971
1Sa 6:2 wherewith we shall **s.** it to his place. .. 7971
1Sa 6:3 **s.** away the ark of the God of Israel. .. 7971
1Sa 6:3 **s.** it not empty; but in any wise 7971
1Sa 6:8 and **s.** it away, that it may go............ 7971
1Sa 9:16 I will **s.** thee a man out of the land..... 7971
1Sa 9:26 saying, Up, that I may **s.** thee away. .. 7971
1Sa 11:3 we may **s.** messengers unto all the...... 7971
1Sa 12:17 and he shall **s.** thunder and rain; 5414
1Sa 16:1 **s.** thee to Jesse the Beth-lehemite:...... 7971
1Sa 16:11 said unto Jesse, **S.** and fetch him: 7971
1Sa 16:19 **S.** me David thy son, which is with 7971
1Sa 20:12 I then **s.** not unto thee, and shew 7971
1Sa 20:13 will shew it thee, and **s.** thee away,.... 7971
1Sa 20:21 I will **s.** a lad, saying, Go, find out...... 7971
1Sa 20:31 now **s.** and fetch him unto me, for....... 7971
1Sa 21:2 the business whereabout I **s.** thee, ... 7971
1Sa 25:25 men of my lord, whom thou didst **s.**. .. 7971
2Sa 11:6 saying, **S.** me Uriah the Hittite. 7971
2Sa 14:32 that I may **s.** thee to the king, to....... 7971
2Sa 15:36 by them ye shall **s.** unto me every 7971
2Sa 17:16 now therefore **s.** quickly, and tell 7971
1Ki 8:44 whithersoever thou shalt **s.** them,....... 7971
1Ki 18:1 and I will **s.** rain upon the earth. 5414
1Ki 18:19 **s.**, and gather to me all Israel unto..... 7971
1Ki 20:6 Yet I will **s.** my servants unto thee..... 7971
1Ki 20:9 that thou didst **s.** for to thy servant.... 7971
1Ki 20:34 **s.** thee away with this covenant. 7971
2Ki 2:16 valley. And he said, Ye shall not **s.**...... 7971
2Ki 2:17 till he was ashamed, he said, **S.**......... 7971
2Ki 4:22 **S.** me, I pray thee, one of the young.. 7971
2Ki 5:5 **s.** a letter unto the king of Israel........ 7971
2Ki 5:7 doth **s.** unto me to recover a man 7971
2Ki 6:13 he is, that I may **s.** and fetch him....... 7971
2Ki 7:13 consumed:) and let us **s.** and see. 7971
2Ki 9:17 an horseman, and **s.** to meet them, ... 7971
2Ki 15:37 the Lord began to **s.** against Judah...... 7971
2Ki 19:7 I will **s.** a blast upon him, and he 5414
1Ch 13:2 let us **s.** abroad unto our brethren 7971
2Ch 2:3 and didst **s.** him cedars to build him.... 7971
2Ch 2:7 **S.** me now therefore a man cunning.... 7971
2Ch 2:8 **S.** me also cedar trees, fir trees, ... 7971
2Ch 2:15 of, let him **s.** unto his servants: 7971
2Ch 6:27 **s.** rain upon thy land, which thou........ 5414
2Ch 6:34 the way that thou shalt **s.** them, ... 7971
2Ch 7:13 if I **s.** pestilence among my people;...... 7971
2Ch 28:16 Ahaz **s.** unto the kings of Assyria 7971
2Ch 32:9 king of Assyria **s.** his servants to 7971
Ezr 5:17 let the king **s.** his pleasure to us 7972
Ne 2:5 thou wouldest **s.** me unto Judah, ... 7971
Ne 2:6 So it pleased the king to **s.** me; 7971
Ne 8:10 **s.** portions unto them for whom 7971
Ne 8:12 and to drink, and to **s.** portions,......... 7971
Job 21:11 They **s.** forth their little ones like....... 7971
Job 38:35 Canst thou **s.** lightnings, that they 7971
Ps 20:2 **S.** thee help from the sanctuary, ... 7971
Ps 43:3 O **s.** out thy light and thy truth:......... 7971
Ps 57:3 He shall **s.** from heaven, and save 7971
Ps 57:3 God shall **s.** forth his mercy and his.... 7971
Ps 68:9 O God, didst **s.** a plentiful rain,.......... 5130
Ps 68:33 lo, he doth **s.** out his voice, and......... 5414
Ps 110:2 shall **s.** the rod of thy strength 7971
Ps 118:25 I beseech thee, **s.** now prosperity. ....
Ps 144:7 **S.** thine hand from above; rid me, ... 7971
Pr 10:26 is the sluggard to them that **s.** him. 7971
Pr 22:21 of truth to them that **s.** unto thee? 7971
Pr 25:13 messenger to them that **s.** him: 7971
Ec 10:1 to **s.** forth a stinking savour: 5042
Isa 6:8 Whom shall I **s.**, and who will go........ 7971
Isa 6:8 Then said I, Here am I; **s.** me........... 7971
Isa 10:6 I will **s.** him against an hypocritical...... 7971
Isa 10:16 **s.** among his fat ones leanness;.......... 7971
Isa 16:1 **S.** ye the lamb to the ruler of the 7971
Isa 19:20 and he shall **s.** them a saviour, and..... 7971
Isa 32:20 **s.** forth thither the feet of the ox 7971
Isa 37:7 I will **s.** a blast upon him, and he 7971
Isa 57:9 and didst **s.** thy messengers far off, ... 7971
Isa 66:19 I will **s.** those that escape of them...... 7971
Jer 1:7 shalt go to all that I shall **s.** thee,....... 7971
Jer 2:10 and **s.** unto Kedar, and consider......... 7971
Jer 8:17 I will **s.** serents, cockatrices,............ 7971
Jer 9:16 and I will **s.** a sword after them, till.... 7971
Jer 9:17 and **s.** for cunning women, that they ... 7971
Jer 16:16 I will **s.** for many fishers, saith the 7971
Jer 16:16 and after will I **s.** for many hunters,.... 7971
Jer 24:10 I will **s.** the sword, the famine, and 7971
Jer 25:9 I will **s.** and take all the families of 7971
Jer 25:15 all the nations, to whom I **s.** thee,...... 7971
Jer 25:16 sword that I will **s.** among them......... 7971
Jer 25:27 sword which I will **s.** among you. 7971
Jer 27:3 And **s.** them to the king of Edom,...... 7971
Jer 29:17 I will **s.** upon them the sword, the...... 7971
Jer 29:31 **S.** to all them of the captivity, ... 7971
Jer 42:5 the Lord thy God shall **s.** thee to us. .. 7971
Jer 42:6 Lord our God, to whom we **s.** thee; ... 7971
Jer 43:10 I will **s.** and take Nebuchadrezzar....... 7971
Jer 48:12 that I will **s.** unto him wanderers,....... 7971
Jer 49:37 and I will **s.** the sword after them, ... 7971
Jer 51:2 And will **s.** unto Babylon fanners, ... 7971
Eze 2:3 I **s.** thee to the children of Israel,....... 7971

Eze 2:4 I do s. thee unto them; and thou........ 7971
Eze 5:16 shall s. upon them the evil arrows...... 7971
Eze 5:16 and which I will s. to destroy you:...... 7971
Eze 5:17 So will I s. upon you famine and........ 7971
Eze 7:3 and I will s. mine anger upon thee,..... 7971
Eze 14:13 and will s. famine upon it, and will...... 7971
Eze 14:19 Or if I s. a pestilence into that land, ... 7971
Eze 14:21 When I s. my four sore judgments...... 7971
Eze 28:23 For I will s. into her pestilence, and ... 7971
Eze 39:6 And I will s. a fire on Magog, and...... 7971
Ho 8:14 but I will s. a fire upon his cities,....... 7971
Joe 2:19 I will s. you corn, and wine, and oil, ... 7971
Am 1:4 s. a fire into the house of Hazael,....... 7971
Am 1:7 I will s. a fire on the wall of Gaza, ... 7971
Am 1:10 I will s. a fire on the wall of Tyrus, ... 7971
Am 1:12 But I will s. a fire upon Teman,......... 7971
Am 2:2 But I will s. a fire upon Moab, and..... 7971
Am 2:5 But I will s. a fire upon Judah, and..... 7971
Am 8:11 that I will s. a famine in the land,....... 7971
Mal 2:2 I will even s. a curse upon you, and ... 7971
Mal 3:1 Behold, I will s. my messenger,......... 7971
Mal 4:5 I will s. you Elijah the prophet.......... 7971
Mt 9:38 **s. forth labourers into his harvest**..*1544*
Mt 10:16 **I s. you forth as sheep in the midst** .*649*
Mt 10:34 **I am come to s. peace on earth:**...... *906*
Mt 10:34 **I come not to s. peace, but a sword**.*906*
Mt 11:10 **I s. my messenger before thy face,**.. *649*
Mt 12:20 he s. forth judgment unto victory. *1544*
Mt 13:41 **Son of man shall s. forth his angels,***649*
Mt 14:15 s. the multitude away, that they.......... *630*
Mt 15:23 S. her away; for she crieth after us...... *630*
Mt 15:32 **I will not s. them away fasting, lest**.*630*
Mt 21:3 **and straightway he will s. them**........ *649*
Mt 23:34 **behold, I s. unto you prophets, and**..*649*
Mt 24:31 **he shall s. his angels with a great**... *649*
Mk 1:2 I s. my messenger before thy face,...... *649*
Mk 3:14 he might s. them forth to preach, ... *649*
Mk 5:10 that he would not s. them away out...... *649*
Mk 5:12 S. us into the swine, that we may...... *3992*
Mk 6:7 to s. them forth by two and two;......... *649*
Mk 6:36 S. them away, that they may go.......... *630*
Mk 8:3 **if I s. them away fasting to their**.... *630*
Mk 11:3 **straightway he will s. him hither**.... *649*
Mk 12:13 s. unto him certain of the Pharisees..... *649*
Mk 13:27 **then shall he s. his angels, shall**..... *649*
Lu 7:27 **I s. my messenger before thy face,**.. *649*
Lu 9:12 S. the multitude away, that they.......... *630*
Lu 10:2 **s. forth labourers into his harvest**..*1544*
Lu 10:3 **s. you forth as lambs among wolves**.*649*
Lu 11:49 **I will s. them prophets and apostles,***649*
Lu 12:49 **I am come to s. fire on the earth;**... *906*
Lu 16:24 **s. Lazarus, that he may dip the tip** *3992*
Lu 16:27 **s. him to my father's house:** *3992*
Lu 20:13 **I will s. my beloved son: it may be**.*3992*
Lu 24:49 **I s. the promise of my Father upon** .*649*
Joh 13:20 **whomsoever I s. receiveth me;**....... *3992*
Joh 14:26 **whom Father will s. in my name,**.. *3992*
Joh 15:26 **I will s. unto you from the Father,** *3992*
Joh 16:7 **if I depart, I will s. him unto you**..*3992*
Joh 17:8 **have believed that thou didst s. me**..*649*
Joh 20:21 **hath sent me, even so s. I you**...... *3992*
Ac 3:20 And he shall s. Jesus Christ, which *649*
Ac 7:34 now come, I will s. thee into Egypt...... *649*
Ac 7:35 the same did God s. to be a ruler........ *649*
Ac 10:5 s. men to Joppa, and call for one........ *3992*
Ac 10:22 angel to s. for thee into his house, ... *3343*
Ac 10:32 S. therefore to Joppa, and call *3992*
Ac 11:13 S. men to Joppa, and call for Simon,..... *649*
Ac 11:29 s. relief unto the brethren which....... *3992*
Ac 15:22 s. chosen men of their own company... *3992*
Ac 15:23 and elders and brethren s. greeting..........
Ac 15:25 to s. chosen men unto you with our.... *3992*
Ac 22:21 **I will s. thee far hence unto the**.... *1821*
Ac 25:3 he would s. for him to Jerusalem,....... *3343*
Ac 25:21 be kept till I might s. him to Caesar. .. *3992*
Ac 25:25 Augustus, I...determined to s. him. *3992*
Ac 25:27 to me unreasonable to s. a prisoner, ... *3992*
Ac 26:17 **Gentiles, unto whom now I s. thee,** .*649*
1Co 16:3 will I s. to bring your liberality.......... *3992*
Php 2:19 to s. Timotheus shortly unto you,....... *3992*
Php 2:23 Him...I hope to s. presently, so......... *3992*
Php 2:25 necessary to s. to you Epaphroditus,... *3992*
2Th 2:11 God shall s. them strong delusion,...... *3992*
Tit 3:12 When I shall s. Artemas unto thee,..... *3992*
Jas 3:11 fountain s. forth at the same time....... *1032*
Re 1:11 **s. it unto the seven churches**......... *3992*
Re 11:10 and shall s. gifts one to another; *3992*

SENDEST
De 15:13 thou s. him out free from thee,.......... 7971
De 15:18 thou s. him away free from thee; 7971
Jos 1:16 whithersoever thou s. us, we will........ 7971
2Ki 1:6 thou s. to enquire of Baal-zebub......... 7971
Job 14:20 his continuance, and s. him away........ 7971
Ps 104:30 Thou s. forth thy spirit, they are........ 7971

SENDETH
De 24:3 hand, and s. her out of his house; 7971
1Ki 17:14 until the day that the Lord s. rain....... 5414
Job 5:10 and s. waters upon the fields:............. 7971
Job 12:15 he s. them out, and they overturn....... 7971
Ps 104:10 He s. the springs into the valleys, ... 7971
Ps 147:15 He s. forth his commandment upon..... 7971
Ps 147:18 He s. out his word, and melteth......... 7971
Pr 26:6 s. a message by the hand of a fool 7971
Ca 1:12 my spikenard s. forth the smell.......... 5414
Isa 18:2 That s. ambassadors by the sea, ... 7971
Mt 5:45 **and s. rain on the just and on the** . *1026*
Mk 11:1 he s. forth two of his disciples,............ *649*
Mk 14:13 And he s. forth two of his disciples, ... *649*
Lu 14:32 **he s. an ambassage, and desireth** *649*
Ac 23:26 excellent governor Felix s. greeting. ....

SENDING
2Sa 13:16 this evil in s. me away is greater 7971
2Ch 36:15 rising up betimes, and s.; because 7971
Es 9:19 and of s. portions one to another........ 4916
Es 9:22 and of s. portions one to another,........ 4916
Ps 78:49 by s. evil angels among them. 4917
Isa 7:25 it shall be for the s. forth of oxen,...... 4916
Jer 7:25 daily rising up early and s. them:........ 7971
Jer 25:4 prophets, rising early and s. them; 7971
Jer 26:5 both rising up early, and s. them,........ 7971
Jer 29:19 rising up early and s. them;................ 7971
Jer 35:15 rising up early and s. them,............... 7971
Jer 44:4 prohets, rising early and s. them,........ 7971
Eze 17:15 in s. his ambassadors into Egypt, ... 7971
Ro 8:3 God s. his own Son in the likeness..... *3992*

SENEH (se'-neh)
1Sa 14:4 and the name of the other S............. 5573

SENIR (se'-nur) See also SHENIR.
1Ch 5:23 Bashan unto Baal-hermon and S., ... 8149
Eze 27:5 thy ship boards of fir trees of S.: 8149

SENNACHERIB (sen-nak'-er-ib)
2Ki 18:13 did S. king of Assyria come up 5576
2Ki 19:16 and hear the words of S., which 5576
2Ki 19:20 thou hast prayed to me against S. 5576
2Ki 19:36 So S. king of Assyria departed,.......... 5576
2Ch 32:1 S. king of Assyria came, and............ 5576
2Ch 32:2 Hezekiah saw that S. was come,........ 5576
2Ch 32:9 this did S. king of Assyria send his..... 5576
2Ch 32:10 Thus saith S. king of Assyria,............ 5576
2Ch 32:22 the hand of S. the king of Assyria, ... 5576
Isa 36:1 that S. king of Assyria came up 5576
Isa 37:17 and hear all the words of S., which..... 5576
Isa 37:21 thou hast prayed to me against S. 5576
Isa 37:37 So S. king of Assyria departed,.......... 5576

SENSE See also SENSES.
Ne 8:8 of God distinctly, and gave the s., ... 7922

SENSES
Heb 5:14 have their s. exercised to discern *145*

SENSUAL
Jas 3:15 above but is earthly, s., devilish......... *5591*
Jude 19 s., having not the Spirit.................... *5591*

SENT See also ASSENT; CONSENT; PRESENT; SENTEST.
Ge 3:23 the Lord God s. him forth from 7971
Ge 8:7 And he s. forth a raven, which went... 7971
Ge 8:8 And he s. forth a dove from him, to ... 7971
Ge 8:10 again he s. forth the dove out of the... 7971
Ge 8:12 s. forth the dove; which returned....... 7971
Ge 12:20 and they s. him away, and his wife, ... 7971
Ge 19:13 the Lord hath s. us to destroy it........ 7971
Ge 19:29 and s. Lot out of the midst of the 7971
Ge 20:2 and Abimelech king of Gerar s., and ... 7971
Ge 21:14 the child, and s. her away: and she..... 7971
Ge 24:59 they s. away Rebekah their sister,...... 7971
Ge 25:6 s. them away from Isaac his son, ... 7971
Ge 26:27 me, and have s. me away from you?... 7971
Ge 26:29 and have s. thee away in peace:......... 7971
Ge 26:31 and Isaac s. them away, and they....... 7971
Ge 27:42 she s. and called Jacob her younger 7971
Ge 28:5 And Isaac s. away Jacob: and he 7971
Ge 28:6 and s. him away to Padan-aram,......... 7971
Ge 31:4 And Jacob s. and called Rachel and..... 7971
Ge 31:27 might have s. thee away with mirth, ... 7971
Ge 31:42 thou hadst s. me away now empty...... 7971
Ge 32:3 Jacob s. messengers before him to 7971
Ge 32:5 and I have s. to tell my lord, that I 7971
Ge 32:18 is a present s. unto my lord Esau:...... 7971
Ge 32:23 he took them, and s. them over......... 5674
Ge 32:23 brook, and s. over all that he had....... 5674
Ge 37:14 s. him out of the vale of Hebron, ... 7971
Ge 37:32 they s. the coat of many colours, ... 7971
Ge 38:20 Judah s. the kid by the hand of his 7971
Ge 38:23 I s. this kid, and thou hast not found... 7971
Ge 38:25 she s. to her father in law, saying, ... 7971
Ge 41:8 s. and called for all the magicians 7971
Ge 41:14 then Pharaoh s. and called Joseph,...... 7971
Ge 42:4 Jacob s. not with his brethren;........... 7971
Ge 43:34 he took and s. messes unto them....... 7971
Ge 44:3 was light, the men were s. away,....... 7971
Ge 45:7 God s. me before you to preserve...... 7971
Ge 45:8 it was not you that s. me hither,......... 7971
Ge 45:23 And to his father he s. after this........ 7971
Ge 45:24 So he s. his brethren away, and......... 7971
Ge 45:27 the wagons which Joseph had s. to..... 7971
Ge 46:5 the wagons which Pharaoh had s........ 7971
Ge 46:28 s. Judah before him unto Joseph,........ 7971
Ge 50:16 they s. a messenger unto Joseph,............
Ex 2:5 flags, she s. her maid to fetch it. 7971
Ex 3:12 token unto thee, that I have s. thee:... 7971
Ex 3:13 God of your fathers hath s. me.......... 7971
Ex 3:14 of Israel, I Am hath s. me unto you.... 7971
Ex 3:15 God of Jacob, hath s. me unto you: 7971
Ex 4:28 words of the Lord who had s. him,..... 7971
Ex 5:22 why is it that thou hast s. me? 7971
Ex 7:16 Lord God of the Hebrews hath s. me.. 7971
Ex 9:7 And Pharaoh s., and, behold, there..... 7971
Ex 9:23 and the Lord s. thunder and hail, ... 5414
Ex 9:27 Pharaoh s., and called for Moses........ 7971
Ex 18:2 wife, after he had s. her back,........... 7964
Ex 24:5 he s. young men of the children of..... 7971
Nu 13:3 s. them from the wilderness of.......... 7971
Nu 13:16 which Moses s. to spy out the land. ... 7971
Nu 13:17 Moses s. them to spy out the land..... 7971
Nu 14:36 which Moses s. to search the land,..... 7971
Nu 16:12 And Moses s. to call Dathan and........ 7971
Nu 16:28 shall know that the Lord hath s. me.... 7971
Nu 16:29 men; then the Lord hath not s. me..... 7971
Nu 20:14 Moses s. messengers from Kadesh....... 7971
Nu 20:16 he heard our voice, and s. an angel, ... 7971
Nu 21:6 Lord s. fiery serpents among the 7971
Nu 21:21 Israel s. messengers unto Sihon......... 7971
Nu 21:32 And Moses s. to spy out Jaazer, ... 7971
Nu 22:5 He s. messengers...unto Balaam 7971
Nu 22:10 king of Moab, hath s. unto me,.......... 7971
Nu 22:15 And Balak s. yet again princes,.......... 7971
Nu 22:40 oxen and sheep, and s. to Balaam, ... 7971
Nu 31:6 And Moses s. them to the war, a....... 7971
Nu 32:8 s. them from Kadesh-barnea to see 7971
De 2:26 s. messengers out of the wilderness ... 7971
De 9:23 Lord s. you from Kadesh-barnea, ... 7971
De 24:4 former husband, which s. her away,.... 7971
De 34:11 which the Lord s. him to do in the 7971
Jos 2:1 s. out of Shittim two men to spy........ 7971
Jos 2:3 the king of Jericho s. unto Rahab,....... 7971
Jos 2:21 And she s. them away, and they 7971
Jos 6:17 she hid the messengers that we s.. 7971
Jos 6:25 which Joshua s. to spy out Jericho. 7971
Jos 7:2 Joshua s. men from Jericho to Ai,....... 7971
Jos 7:22 So Joshua s. messengers, and they..... 7971
Jos 8:3 valour, and s. them away by night...... 7971
Jos 8:9 Joshua therefore s. them forth: 7971
Jos 10:3 king of Jerusalem s. unto Hoham........ 7971
Jos 10:6 the men of Gibeon s. unto Joshua....... 7971
Jos 11:1 that he s. to Jobab king of Madon,....... 7971
Jos 14:7 s. me from Kadesh-barnea to espy 7971
Jos 14:11 I was in the day that Moses s. me: 7971
Jos 22:6 blessed them, and s. them away: 7971
Jos 22:7 And when Joshua s. them away also.... 7971
Jos 22:13 s. unto the children of Reuben,......... 7971
Jos 24:5 I s. Moses also and Aaron, and I 7971
Jos 24:9 and s. and called Balaam the son........ 7971
Jos 24:12 And I s. the hornet before you, ... 7971
Jg 1:23 of Joseph s. to descry Beth-el. 7971
Jg 3:15 Israel s. a present unto Eglon............ 7971
Jg 3:18 he s. away the people that bare the.... 7971
Jg 4:6 she s. and called Barak the son of...... 7971

Book	Ref	Context	No.
Jg	5:15	he was **s.** on foot into the valley.	7971
Jg	6:8	Lord **s.** a prophet unto the children.	7971
Jg	6:14	the Midianites: have not I **s.** thee?	7971
Jg	6:35	he **s.** messengers throughout all	7971
Jg	6:35	he **s.** messengers unto Asher, and	7971
Jg	7:8	he **s.** all the rest of Israel every	7971
Jg	7:24	Gideon **s.** messengers throughout	7971
Jg	9:23	Then God **s.** an evil spirit between	7971
Jg	9:31	he **s.** messengers unto Abimelech	7971
Jg	11:12	Jephthah **s.** messengers unto the	7971
Jg	11:14	Jephthah **s.** messengers again unto	7971
Jg	11:17	Israel **s.** messengers unto the king	7971
Jg	11:17	they **s.** unto the king of Moab: but	7971
Jg	11:19	Israel **s.** messengers unto Sihon	7971
Jg	11:28	words of Jephthah which he **s.** him.	7971
Jg	11:38	And he **s.** her away for two months:	7971
Jg	12:9	daughters, whom he **s.** abroad,	7971
Jg	16:18	she **s.** and called for the lords of	7971
Jg	18:2	children of Dan **s.** of their family	7971
Jg	19:29	**s.** her into all the coast of Israel.	7971
Jg	20:6	**s.** her throughout all the country	7971
Jg	20:12	tribes of Israel **s.** men through all	7971
Jg	21:10	the congregation **s.** thither twelve	7971
Jg	21:13	congregation **s.** some to speak to	7971
1Sa	4:4	So the people **s.** to Shiloh, that	7971
1Sa	5:8	**s.** therefore and gathered all the	7971
1Sa	5:10	they **s.** the ark of God to Ekron	7971
1Sa	5:11	**s.** and gathered together all...lords	7971
1Sa	6:21	**s.** messengers to the inhabitants	7971
1Sa	10:25	And Samuel **s.** all the people away,	7971
1Sa	11:7	**s.** them throughout all the coasts of	7971
1Sa	12:8	then the Lord **s.** Moses and Aaron,	7971
1Sa	12:11	the Lord **s.** Jerubbaal, and Bedan,	7971
1Sa	12:18	Lord **s.** thunder and rain that day:	5414
1Sa	13:2	people he **s.** every man to his tent.	7971
1Sa	15:1	The Lord **s.** me to anoint thee to be	7971
1Sa	15:18	the Lord **s.** thee on a journey, and	7971
1Sa	15:20	gone the way which the Lord **s.** me,	7971
1Sa	16:12	he **s.**, and brought him in. Now he	7971
1Sa	16:19	Saul **s.** messengers unto Jesse, and	7971
1Sa	16:20	**s.** them by David his son unto Saul.	7971
1Sa	16:22	Saul **s.** to Jesse, saying, Let David,	7971
1Sa	17:31	before Saul: and he **s.** for him.	3947
1Sa	18:5	out whithersoever Saul **s.** him,	7971
1Sa	19:11	**s.** messengers unto David's house,	7971
1Sa	19:14	Saul **s.** messengers to take David,	7971
1Sa	19:15	Saul **s.** the messengers again to	7971
1Sa	19:17	**s.** away mine enemy, that he is	7971
1Sa	19:20	Saul **s.** messengers to take David:	7971
1Sa	19:21	told Saul, he **s.** other messengers,	7971
1Sa	19:21	Saul **s.** messengers again the third	7971
1Sa	20:22	for the Lord hath **s.** thee away.	7971
1Sa	22:11	the king **s.** to call Ahimelech the	7971
1Sa	25:5	And David **s.** out ten young men,	7971
1Sa	25:14	David **s.** messengers out of the	7971
1Sa	25:32	which **s.** thee this day to meet me:	7971
1Sa	25:39	And David **s.** and communed with	7971
1Sa	25:40	David **s.** us unto thee, to take thee	7971
1Sa	26:4	David therefore **s.** out spies, and	7971
1Sa	30:26	he **s.** of the spoil unto the elders of	7971
1Sa	31:9	**s.** into the land of the Philistines	7971
2Sa	2:5	David **s.** messengers unto the men	7971
2Sa	3:12	Abner **s.** messengers to David on	7971
2Sa	3:14	David **s.** messengers to Ish-bosheth	7971
2Sa	3:15	Ish-bosheth **s.**, and took her from	7971
2Sa	3:21	David **s.** Abner away; and he went	7971
2Sa	3:22	for he had **s.** him away, and he was	7971
2Sa	3:23	to the king, and he hath **s.** him away.	7971
2Sa	3:24	is it that thou hast **s.** him away,	7971
2Sa	3:26	he **s.** messengers after Abner,	7971
2Sa	5:11	Hiram king of Tyre **s.** messengers	7971
2Sa	8:10	Toi **s.** Joram...unto king David,	7971
2Sa	9:5	Then king David **s.**, and fetched	7971
2Sa	10:2	And David **s.** to comfort him by the	7971
2Sa	10:3	he hath **s.** comforters unto thee?	7971
2Sa	10:3	not David rather **s.** his servants	7971
2Sa	10:4	to their buttocks, and **s.** them away.	7971
2Sa	10:5	he **s.** to meet them, because the	7971
2Sa	10:6	children of Ammon **s.** and hired	7971
2Sa	10:7	when David heard of it, he **s.** Joab	7971
2Sa	10:16	Hadarezer **s.**, and brought out the	7971
2Sa	11:1	that David **s.** Joab, and his servants	7971
2Sa	11:3	And David **s.** and enquired after the	7971
2Sa	11:4	David **s.** messengers, and took her;	7971
2Sa	11:5	**s.** and told David, and said, I am	7971
2Sa	11:6	David **s.** to Joab, saying, Send me	7971
2Sa	11:6	And Joab **s.** Uriah to David.	7971
2Sa	11:14	and **s.** it by the hand of Uriah.	7971
2Sa	11:18	Then Joab **s.** and told David all the	7971
2Sa	11:22	David all that Joab had **s.** him for.	7971
2Sa	11:27	David **s.** and fetched her to his	7971
2Sa	12:1	the Lord **s.** Nathan unto David	7971
2Sa	12:25	he **s.** by the hand of Nathan the	7971
2Sa	12:27	And Joab **s.** messengers to David,	7971
2Sa	13:7	David **s.** home to Tamar, saying,	7971
2Sa	14:2	And Joab **s.** to Tekoah, and fetched	7971
2Sa	14:29	Therefore Absalom **s.** for Joab, to	7971
2Sa	14:29	when he **s.** again the second time,	7971
2Sa	14:32	I **s.** unto thee, saying, Come hither,	7971
2Sa	15:10	Absalom **s.** spies throughout all	7971
2Sa	15:12	And Absalom **s.** for Ahithophel the	7971
2Sa	18:2	David **s.** forth a third part of the	7971
2Sa	18:29	When Joab **s.** the king's servant,	7971
2Sa	19:11	And king David **s.** to Zadok and to	7971
2Sa	19:14	they **s.** this word unto the king,	7971
2Sa	22:15	he **s.** out arrows, and scattered	7971
2Sa	22:17	He **s.** from above, he took me; he	7971
2Sa	24:13	I shall return to him that **s.** me.	7971
2Sa	24:15	So the Lord **s.** a pestilence upon	5414
1Ki	1:44	the king hath **s.** with him Zadok	7971
1Ki	1:53	So king Solomon **s.**, and they	7971
1Ki	2:25	Solomon **s.** by the hand of Benaiah	7971
1Ki	2:29	Then Solomon **s.** Benaiah the son of	7971
1Ki	2:36,	42 king **s.** and called for Shimei,	7971
1Ki	5:1	Hiram king of Tyre **s.** his servants	7971
1Ki	5:2	And Solomon **s.** to Hiram, saying,	7971
1Ki	5:8	Hiram **s.** to Solomon, saying, I have	7971
1Ki	5:14	And he **s.** them to Lebanon, ten	7971
1Ki	7:13	And king Solomon **s.** and fetched	7971
1Ki	8:66	eighth day he **s.** the people away:	7971
1Ki	9:14	And Hiram **s.** to the king sixscore	7971
1Ki	9:27	Hiram **s.** in the navy his servants,	7971
1Ki	12:3	That they **s.** and called him. And	7971
1Ki	12:18	Then king Rehoboam **s.** Adoram,	7971
1Ki	12:20	they **s.** and called him unto the	7971
1Ki	14:6	am **s.** to thee with heavy tidings.	7971
1Ki	15:18	king Asa **s.** them to Ben-hadad, the	7971
1Ki	15:19	have **s.** unto thee a present of silver	7971
1Ki	15:20	**s.** the captains of the hosts which	7971
1Ki	18:10	my lord hath not **s.** to seek thee:	7971
1Ki	18:20	Ahab **s.** unto all the children of	7971
1Ki	19:2	Jezebel **s.** a messenger unto Elijah,	7971
1Ki	20:2	he **s.** messengers to Ahab king of	7971
1Ki	20:5	Although I have **s.** unto thee,	7971
1Ki	20:7	for he **s.** unto me for my wives, and	7971
1Ki	20:10	Ben-hadad **s.** unto him, and said,	7971
1Ki	20:17	Ben-hadad **s.** out, and they told	7971
1Ki	20:34	with him, and **s.** him away.	7971
1Ki	21:8	**s.** the letters unto the elders and to	7971
1Ki	21:11	did as Jezebel had **s.** unto them,	7971
1Ki	21:11	letters which she had **s.** unto them.	7971
1Ki	21:14	Then they **s.** to Jezebel, saying,	7971
2Ki	1:2	he **s.** messengers, and said unto	7971
2Ki	1:6	again unto the king that **s.** you,	7971
2Ki	1:9	the king **s.** unto him a captain of	7971
2Ki	1:11	he **s.** unto him another captain of	7971
2Ki	1:13	he **s.** again a captain of the third	7971
2Ki	1:16	thou has **s.** messengers to enquire	7971
2Ki	2:2	for the Lord hath **s.** me to Beth-el.	7971
2Ki	2:4	for the Lord hath **s.** me to Jericho.	7971
2Ki	2:6	for the Lord hath **s.** me to Jordan	7971
2Ki	2:17	They **s.** therefore fifty men; and	7971
2Ki	3:7	he went and **s.** to Jehoshaphat the	7971
2Ki	5:6	therewith **s.** Naaman my servant	7971
2Ki	5:8	his clothes, that he **s.** to the king,	7971
2Ki	5:10	Elisha **s.** a messenger unto him,	7971
2Ki	5:22	My master hath **s.** me, saying,	7971
2Ki	6:9	the man of God **s.** unto the king of	7971
2Ki	6:10	the king of Israel **s.** to the place	7971
2Ki	6:14	Therefore **s.** he thither horses, and	7971
2Ki	6:23	eaten and drunk, he **s.** them away,	7971
2Ki	6:32	the king **s.** a man from before him:	7971
2Ki	6:32	how this son of a murderer hath **s.**	7971
2Ki	7:14	king **s.** after the host of the Syrians,	7971
2Ki	8:9	king of Syria hath **s.** me to thee,	7971
2Ki	9:19	he **s.** out a second on horseback,	7971
2Ki	10:1	wrote letters, and **s.** to Samaria,	7971
2Ki	10:5	elders also,...**s.** to Jehu, saying,	7971
2Ki	10:7	baskets, and **s.** him them to Jezreel.	7971
2Ki	10:21	Jehu **s.** through all Israel: and all	7971
2Ki	11:4	Jehoiada **s.** and fetched the rulers	7971
2Ki	12:18	and **s.** it to Hazael king of Syria:	7971
2Ki	14:8	Amaziah **s.** messengers to Jehoash,	7971
2Ki	14:9	the king of Israel **s.** to Amaziah	7971
2Ki	14:9	**s.** to the cedar that was in Lebanon,	7971
2Ki	14:19	but they **s.** after him to Lachish,	7971
2Ki	16:7	So Ahaz **s.** messengers to	7971
2Ki	16:8	and **s.** it for a present to the king of	7971
2Ki	16:10	king Ahaz **s.** to Urijah the priest	7971
2Ki	16:11	king Ahaz had **s.** from Damascus:	7971
2Ki	17:4	he had **s.** messengers to So king of	7971
2Ki	17:13	which I **s.** to you by my servants	7971
2Ki	17:25	Lord **s.** lions among them, which	7971
2Ki	17:26	he hath **s.** lions among them, and,	7971
2Ki	18:14	king of Judah **s.** to the king of	7971
2Ki	18:17	the king of Assyria **s.** Tartan and	7971
2Ki	18:27	my master **s.** me to thy master, and	7971
2Ki	18:27	hath he not **s.** me to the men which	
2Ki	19:2	he **s.** Eliakim, which was over the	7971
2Ki	19:4	hath **s.** to reproach the living God;	7971
2Ki	19:9	**s.** messengers again unto Hezekiah,	7971
2Ki	19:16	**s.** him to reproach the living God.	7971
2Ki	19:20	the son of Amoz **s.** to Hezekiah,	7971
2Ki	20:12	Babylon, **s.** letters and a present	7971
2Ki	22:3	that the king **s.** Shaphan the son of	7971
2Ki	22:15	Tell the man that **s.** you to me,	7971
2Ki	22:18	which **s.** you to enquire of the Lord,	7971
2Ki	23:1	And the king **s.**, and they gathered	7971
2Ki	23:16	and **s.**, and took the bones out of	7971
2Ki	24:2	Lord **s.** against him bands of the	7971
2Ki	24:2	**s.** them against Judah to destroy it,	7971
1Ch	8:8	Moab, afterhe had **s.** them away;	7971
1Ch	10:9	**s.** into the land of the Philistines	7971
1Ch	12:19	upon advisement **s.** him away,	7971
1Ch	14:1	Hiram king of Tyre **s.** messengers	7971
1Ch	18:10	**s.** Hadoram his son to king David,	7971
1Ch	19:2	David **s.** messengers to comfort him	7971
1Ch	19:3	he hath **s.** comforters unto thee?	7971
1Ch	19:4	their buttocks, and **s.** them away.	7971
1Ch	19:5	he **s.** to meet them: for the men	7971
1Ch	19:6	**s.** a thousand talents of silver to	7971
1Ch	19:8	when David heard of it, he **s.** Joab,	7971
1Ch	19:16	they **s.** messengers, and drew forth	7971
1Ch	21:12	shall bring again to him that **s.** me.	7971
1Ch	21:14	Lord **s.** pestilence upon Israel:	5414
1Ch	21:15	God **s.** an angel unto Jerusalem to	7971
2Ch	2:3	Solomon **s.** to Huram the king of	7971
2Ch	2:11	in writing, which he **s.** to Solomon,	7971
2Ch	2:13	And now I have **s.** a cunning man,	7971
2Ch	7:10	**s.** the people away into their tents,	7971
2Ch	8:18	Huram **s.** him by the hands of his	7971
2Ch	10:3	And they **s.** and called him. So	7971
2Ch	10:18	Then king Rehoboam **s.** Hadoram	7971
2Ch	16:2	and **s.** to Ben-hadad king of Syria,	7971
2Ch	16:3	I have **s.** thee silver and gold; go,	7971
2Ch	16:4	**s.** the captains of his armies against	7971
2Ch	17:7	year of his reign he **s.** to his princes,	7971
2Ch	17:8	and with them he **s.** Levites, even	
2Ch	24:19	he **s.** prophets to them, to bring	7971
2Ch	24:23	and **s.** all the spoil of them unto the	7971
2Ch	25:13	the army which Amaziah **s.** back,	7725
2Ch	25:15	he **s.** unto him a prophet, which	7971
2Ch	25:17	**s.** to Joash, the son of Jehoahaz,	7971
2Ch	25:18	Joash king of Israel **s.** to Amaziah	7971
2Ch	25:18	**s.** to the cedar that was in Lebanon,	7971
2Ch	25:27	but they **s.** to Lachish after him,	7971
2Ch	30:1	And Hezekiah **s.** to all Israel and	7971
2Ch	32:21	the Lord **s.** an angel, which cut off	7971
2Ch	32:31	who **s.** unto him to enquire of the	7971
2Ch	34:8	he **s.** Shaphan the son of Azaliah,	7971
2Ch	34:23	Tell ye the man that **s.** you to me,	7971
2Ch	34:26	who **s.** you to enquire of the Lord,	7971
2Ch	34:29	the king **s.** and gathered together	7971
2Ch	35:21	he **s.** ambassadors to him, saying,	7971
2Ch	36:10	Nebuchadnezzar **s.**, and brought	7971
2Ch	36:15	God of their fathers **s.** to them by	7971
Ezr	4:11	copy of the letter that they **s.** unto	7972
Ezr	4:14	have we **s.** and certified the king;	7972
Ezr	4:17	**s.** the king an answer unto Rehum	7972
Ezr	4:18	The letter which ye **s.** unto us hath	7972
Ezr	5:6	the river, **s.** unto Darius the king:	7972
Ezr	5:7	They **s.** a letter unto him, wherein	7972
Ezr	6:13	that which Darius the king had **s.**,	7972
Ezr	7:14	as thou art **s.** of the king, and of	7972
Ezr	8:16	Then **s.** I for Eliezer, for Ariel, for	7971
Ezr	8:17	I **s.** them with commandment unto	6680
Ne	2:9	Now the king had **s.** captains of	7971
Ne	6:2	Sanballat and Geshem **s.** unto me,	7971
Ne	6:3	I **s.** messengers unto them, saying,	7971
Ne	6:4	they **s.** unto me four times after	7971
Ne	6:5	Then **s.** Sanballat his servant unto	7971

Ne 6:8 Then I s. unto him, saying, There...... 7971
Ne 6:12 I perceived that God had not s. him;... 7971
Ne 6:17 nobles of Judah s. many letters......... 1980
Ne 6:19 And Tobiah s. letters to put me in...... 7971
Es 1:22 For he s. letters into all the king's...... 7971
Es 3:13 letters were s. by posts into all the.... 7971
Es 4:4 she s. raiment to clothe Mordecai,...... 7971
Es 5:10 he s. and called for his friends, and..... 7971
Es 8:10 and s. letters by posts on horseback, .. 7971
Es 9:20 and s. letters unto all the Jews that.... 7971
Es 9:30 he s. the letters unto all the Jews, ... 7971
Job 1:4 s. and called for their three sisters..... 7971
Job 1:5 that Job s. and sanctified them,.......... 7971
Job 22:9 Thou hast s. widows away empty,....... 7971
Job 39:5 Who hath s. out the wild ass free? 7971
Ps 18:14 Yea, he s. out his arrows, and.......... 7971
Ps 18:16 He s. from above, he took me, he...... 7971
Ps 59:*title* when Saul s., and they watched........ 7971
Ps 77:17 the skies s. out a sound: thine......... 5414
Ps 78:25 food: he s. them meat to the full........ 7971
Ps 78:45 s. divers sorts of flies among them, ... 7971
Ps 80:11 She s. out her boughs unto the sea, ... 7971
Ps 105:17 He s. a man before them, even......... 7971
Ps 105:20 The king s. and loosed him; even....... 7971
Ps 105:26 He s. Moses his servant; and Aaron... 7971
Ps 105:28 He s. darkness, and made it dark;...... 7971
Ps 106:15 but s. leanness into their soul........... 7971
Ps 107:20 He s. his word, and healed them,....... 7971
Ps 111:9 He s. redemption unto his people: 7971
Ps 135:9 Who s. tokens and wonders into the... 7971
Pr 9:3 She hath s. forth her maidens: she..... 7971
Pr 17:11 messenger shall be s. against him....... 7971
Isa 9:8 The Lord s. a word into Jacob, and.... 7971
Isa 20:1 Sargon the king of Assyria s. him,)..... 7971
Isa 36:2 king of Assyria s. Rabshakeh from...... 7971
Isa 36:12 my master s. me to thy master......... 7971
Isa 36:12 hath he not s. me to the men that............
Isa 37:2 And he s. Eliakim, who was over....... 7971
Isa 37:4 hath s. to reproach the living God, ... 7971
Isa 37:9 it, he s. messengers to Hezekiah, ... 7971
Isa 37:17 hath s. to reproach the living God. 7971
Isa 37:21 the son of Amoz s. unto Hezekiah, ... 7971
Isa 39:1 s. letters and a present to Hezekiah:... 7971
Isa 42:19 or deaf, as my messenger that I s.?.... 7971
Isa 43:14 For your sake I have s. to Babylon,.... 7971
Isa 48:16 God, and his Spirit, hath s. me.......... 7971
Isa 55:11 prosper in the thing whereto I s. it..... 7971
Isa 61:1 s. me to bind up the brokenhearted, ... 7971
Jer 7:25 even s. unto you all my servants the... 7971
Jer 14:3 their nobles have s. their little ones.... 7971
Jer 14:14 I s. them not, neither have I............ 7971
Jer 14:15 I s. them not, yet they say, Sword..... 7971
Jer 19:14 the Lord had s. him to prophesy;....... 7971
Jer 21:1 king Zedekiah s. unto him Pashur....... 7971
Jer 23:21 I have not s. these prophets, yet....... 7971
Jer 23:32 yet I s. them not, nor commanded....... 7971
Jer 23:38 I have s. unto you, saying, Ye shall.... 7971
Jer 24:5 whom I have s. out of this place........ 7971
Jer 25:4 hath s. unto you all his servants the.... 7971
Jer 25:17 unto whom the Lord had s. me:......... 7971
Jer 26:5 the prophets, whom I s. unto you, ... 7971
Jer 26:12 The Lord s. me to prophesy against... 7971
Jer 26:15 Lord hath s. me unto you to speak..... 7971
Jer 26:22 king s. men into Egypt, namely,......... 7971
Jer 27:15 I have not s. them, saith the Lord,..... 7971
Jer 28:9 that the Lord hath truly s. him. 7971
Jer 28:15 The Lord hath not s. thee; but thou... 7971
Jer 29:1 the prophet s. from Jerusalem unto..... 7971
Jer 29:3 king of Judah s. unto Babylon to......... 7971
Jer 29:9 I have not s. them, saith the Lord...... 7971
Jer 29:19 I s. unto them by my servants the..... 7971
Jer 29:20 whom I have s. from Jerusalem to...... 7971
Jer 29:25 Because thou hast s. letters in thy..... 7971
Jer 29:28 therefore he s. unto us in Babylon,..... 7971
Jer 29:31 I s. him not, and he caused you to..... 7971
Jer 35:15 s. also unto you all my servants the.... 7971
Jer 36:14 all the princes s. Jehudi the son......... 7971
Jer 36:21 the king s. Jehudi to fetch the roll: 7971
Jer 37:3 Zedekiah the king s. Jehucal the......... 7971
Jer 37:7 s. you unto me to enquire of me;....... 7971
Jer 37:17 Zedekiah the king s., and took him..... 7971
Jer 38:14 Then Zedekiah the king s., and took... 7971
Jer 39:13 the captain of the guard s., and......... 7971
Jer 39:14 Even they s., and took Jeremiah......... 7971
Jer 40:14 s. Ishmael the son of Nethaniah to...... 7971
Jer 42:9 s. me to present your supplication...... 7971
Jer 42:20 ye s. me unto the Lord your God,...... 7971
Jer 42:21 the which he hath s. me unto you. 7971
Jer 43:1 Lord their God had s. him to them,.... 7971
Jer 43:2 Lord our God hath not s. thee to....... 7971
Jer 44:4 I s. unto you all my servants the........ 7971
Jer 49:14 ambassador is s. unto the heathen, ... 7971
La 1:13 From above hath he s. fire into my..... 7971
Eze 2:9 behold, an hand was s. unto me;........ 7971
Eze 3:5 For thou art not s. to a people of a.... 7971
Eze 3:6 Surely, had I s. thee to them, they..... 7971
Eze 13:6 and the Lord hath not s. them: and.... 7971
Eze 23:16 and s. messengers unto them into...... 7971
Eze 23:40 that ye have s. for men to come........ 7971
Eze 23:40 unto whom a messenger was s.;......... 7971
Eze 31:4 s. out her little rivers unto all the....... 7971
Da 3:2 the king s. to gather together the....... 7972
Da 3:28 the God...who hath s. his angel, ... 7972
Da 5:24 the part of the hand s. from him; 7972
Da 6:22 My God hath s. his angel, and hath.... 7972
Da 10:11 upright: for unto thee am I now s....... 7971
Ho 5:13 the Assyrian, and s. to king Jareb:...... 7971
Joe 2:25 great army which I s. among you. 7971
Am 4:10 I have s. among you the pestilence..... 7971
Am 7:10 priest of Beth-el s. to Jeroboam......... 7971
Ob 1 and an ambassador is s. among the...... 7971
Jon 1:4 the Lord s. out a great wind into....... 2904
Mic 6:4 I s. before thee Moses, Aaron, and.... 7971
Hag 1:12 as the Lord their God had s. him, ... 7971
Zec 1:10 the Lord hath s. to walk to and fro..... 7971
Zec 2:8 he s. me unto the nations which......... 7971
Zec 2:9 that the Lord of hosts hath s. me....... 7971
Zec 2:11 Lord of hosts hath s. me unto thee..... 7971
Zec 4:9 Lord of hosts hath s. me unto you...... 7971
Zec 6:15 Lord of hosts hath s. me unto you...... 7971
Zec 7:2 they had s. unto the house of God...... 7971
Zec 7:12 Lord of hosts hath s. in his spirit...... 7971
Zec 9:11 I have s. forth thy prisoners out of...... 7971
Mal 2:4 that I have s. this commandment........ 7971
Mt 2:8 And he s. them to Bethlehem, and..... *3992*
Mt 2:16 s. forth, and slew all the children......... *649*
Mt 10:5 These twelve Jesus s. forth, and *649*
Mt 10:40 **receive me receiveth him that s. me.** *649*
Mt 11:2 of Christ, he s. two of his disciples,.... *3992*
Mt 13:36 Then Jesus s. the multitude away, ... *863*
Mt 14:10 he s., and beheaded John in the......... *3992*
Mt 14:22 while he s. the multitudes away........... *630*
Mt 14:23 when he had s. the multitudes away,.... *630*
Mt 14:35 they s. out into all that country.......... *649*
Mt 15:24 **I am not s. but unto the lost sheep**.. *649*
Mt 15:39 he s. away the multitude, and took....... *630*
Mt 20:2 **a day, he s. them into his vineyard.** *649*
Mt 21:1 of Olives, then s. Jesus two disciples,.... *649*
Mt 21:34 **s. his servants to the husbandmen,** . *649*
Mt 21:36 **he s. other servants more than the**.. *649*
Mt 21:37 **last of all he s. unto them his son,** . *649*
Mt 22:3 **s. forth his servants to call them**.... *649*
Mt 22:4 **he s. forth other servants, saying,**... *649*
Mt 22:7 **s. forth his armies, and destroyed** ..*3992*
Mt 22:16 they s. out unto him their disciples....... *649*
Mt 23:37 **stonest them which are s. unto thee,***649*
Mt 27:19 his wife s. unto him, saying, Have........ *649*
Mk 1:43 him, and forthwith s. him away;......... *1544*
Mk 3:31 standing without, s. unto him,............ *649*
Mk 4:36 they had s. away the multitude,........... *863*
Mk 6:17 s. forth and laid hold upon John, ... *649*
Mk 6:27 the king s. an executioner, and............ *649*
Mk 6:45 while he s. away the people............... *628*
Mk 6:46 And when he had s. them away, he...... *657*
Mk 8:9 thousand: and he s. them away. *630*
Mk 8:26 he s. him away to his house, saying, ... *649*
Mk 9:37 **receiveth not me, him that s. me.** *649*
Mk 12:2 **he s. to the husbandmen a servant,**. *649*
Mk 12:3 **beat him, and s. him away empty.**.. *649*
Mk 12:4 **he s. unto them another servant;**.... *649*
Mk 12:4 **s. him away shamefully handled.**..... *649*
Mk 12:5 **again he s. another; and him they**.. *649*
Mk 12:6 **he s. him also last unto them.**......... *649*
Lu 1:19 am s. to speak unto thee, and to........ *649*
Lu 1:26 the angel Gabriel was s. from God....... *649*
Lu 1:53 the rich he hath s. empty away.......... *1821*
Lu 4:18 **s. me to heal the brokenhearted, to** . *649*
Lu 4:26 **unto none of them was Elias s.,**..... *3992*
Lu 4:43 **cities also: for therefore am I s.** *649*
Lu 7:3 s. unto him the elders of the Jews, ... *649*
Lu 7:6 the centurion s. friends to him, ... *3992*
Lu 7:10 they that were s., returning to the..... *3992*
Lu 7:19 of his disciples, s. them to Jesus, ...
Lu 7:20 John Baptist hath s. us unto thee,........ *649*
Lu 8:38 with him: but Jesus s. him away, ... *630*
Lu 9:2 he s. them to preach the kingdom........ *649*
Lu 9:48 **receive me receiveth him that s. me:** *649*
Lu 9:52 And s. messengers before his face: *649*
Lu 10:1 s. them two and two before his face..... *649*
Lu 10:16 **me, despiseth him that s. me.**......... *649*
Lu 13:34 **stonest them that are s. unto thee;** ..*649*
Lu 14:17 **s. his servant at supper time to say**..*649*
Lu 15:15 **s. him into his fields to feed swine.***3992*
Lu 19:14 **and s. a message after him, saying,** .*649*
Lu 19:29 of Olives, he s. two of his disciples, ... *649*
Lu 19:32 they that were s. went their way,)........ *649*
Lu 20:10 **he s. a servant to the husbandmen**.. *640*
Lu 20:10 **beat him, and s. him away empty**.. *1821*
Lu 20:11 **And again he s. another servant:**... *3992*
Lu 20:11 **shamefully...s. him away empty.**... *1821*
Lu 20:12 **And again he s. a third: and they**.. *3992*
Lu 20:20 s. forth spies, which should feign......... *649*
Lu 22:8 he s. Peter and John, saying, Go and .. *649*
Lu 22:35 **When I s. you without purse, and**... *649*
Lu 23:7 he s. him to Herod, who himself.......... *375*
Lu 23:11 robe, and s. him again to Pilate. *375*
Lu 23:15 nor yet Herod: for I s. you to him; *375*
Joh 1:6 There was a man s. from God,............ *649*
Joh 1:8 was s. to bear witness of that Light..........
Joh 1:19 Jews s. priests and Levites from.......... *649*
Joh 1:22 give an answer to them that s. us. *3992*
Joh 1:24 which were s. were of the Pharisees. ... *649*
Joh 1:33 that s. me to baptize with water, ... *3992*
Joh 3:17 **God s. not his Son into the world to***649*
Joh 3:28 Christ, but that I am s. before him....... *649*
Joh 3:34 God hath s. speaketh the words of....... *649*
Joh 4:34 **is to do the will of him that s. me,**.*3992*
Joh 4:38 **I s. you to reap that whereon ye**..... *649*
Joh 5:23 **not the Father which hath s. him.** .*3992*
Joh 5:24 **believeth on him that s. me, hath**.. *3992*
Joh 5:30 **will of the Father hath s. me.**....... *3992*
Joh 5:33 **Ye s. unto John, and he bare**.......... *649*
Joh 5:36 **of me, that the Father hath s. me**... *649*
Joh 5:37 **Father himself, which hath s. me,**. *3992*
Joh 5:38 **for whom he hath s., him ye believe***649*
Joh 6:29 **ye believe on him whom he hath s.**..*649*
Joh 6:38 **will, but the will of him s. me.** *3992*
Joh 6:39 **the Father's will which hath s. me,***3992*
Joh 6:40 **this is the will of him that s. me,**.. *3992*
Joh 6:44 **Father hath s. me draw him:**........ *3992*
Joh 6:57 **As the living Father hath s. me,**..... *649*
Joh 7:16 **is not mine, but his that s. me.**..... *3992*
Joh 7:18 **that seeketh his glory that s. him,** .*3992*
Joh 7:28 **he that s. me is true, whom know.** *3992*
Joh 7:29 **am from him, and he hath s. me.** ... *649*
Joh 7:32 chief priests s. officers to take him....... *649*
Joh 7:33 **and then I go unto him that s. me.***3992*
Joh 8:16 **but I and the Father that s. me.** ... *3992*
Joh 8:18 **Father s. me beareth witness of**.... *3992*
Joh 8:26 **he that s. me is true; and I speak**.. *3992*
Joh 8:29 **that s. me is with me: the Father**.. *3992*
Joh 8:42 **came I of myself, but he s. me.** *649*
Joh 9:4 **work the works of him that s. me,** .*3992*
Joh 9:7 (which is by interpretation, S..)......... *649*
Joh 10:36 **sanctified, and s. into the world**..... *649*
Joh 11:3 Therefore his sisters s. unto him,........ *649*
Joh 11:42 **may believe that thou hast s. me.** ... *649*
Joh 12:44 **not on me, but on him that s. me..** *3992*
Joh 12:45 **that seeth me seeth him s. me.**........ *3992*
Joh 12:49 **the Father which s. me, he gave**... *3992*
Joh 13:16 **is s. greater than he that s. him.** *652*
Joh 13:20 **me receiveth him that s. me.**......... *3992*
Joh 14:24 **mine, but Father's which s. me.**.... *3992*
Joh 15:21 **they know not him that s. me.**........ *3992*
Joh 16:5 **I go my way to him that s. me;**........ *3992*
Joh 17:3 **Jesus Christ, whom thou hast s.** *649*
Joh 17:18 **As thou hast s. me into the world,**.. *649*
Joh 17:18 **have I also s. them into the world.** ..*649*
Joh 17:21 **may believe that thou hast s. me.** ... *649*
Joh 17:23 **may know that thou hast s. me,** *649*
Joh 17:25 **have known that thou hast s. me.**... *649*
Joh 18:24 had s. him bound unto Caiaphas.......... *649*
Joh 20:21 **as my Father hath s. me, even so**... *649*
Ac 3:26 his Son Jesus, s. him to bless you,....... *649*
Ac 5:21 and s. to the prison to have them........ *649*
Ac 7:12 Egypt, he s. out our fathers first........ *1821*
Ac 7:14 Then s. Joseph,...called his father........ *649*
Ac 8:14 they s. unto them Peter and John: *649*

Ac 9:17 hath s. me, that thou mightest 649
Ac 9:30 and s. him forth to Tarsus. *1821*
Ac 9:38 they s. unto him two men, desiring *649*
Ac 10:8 unto them, he s. them to Joppa. *649*
Ac 10:17 the men which were s. from *649*
Ac 10:20 doubting nothing...I have s. them. *649*
Ac 10:21 to the men which were s. unto him *649*
Ac 10:29 gainsaying, as soon as I was s. for: *3343*
Ac 10:29 for what intent ye have s. for me?...... *3343*
Ac 10:33 Immediately therefore I s. to thee; *3992*
Ac 10:36 God s. unto the children of Israel, ... *649*
Ac 11:11 I was, s. from Caesarea unto me. *649*
Ac 11:22 and they s. forth Barnabas, that he...... *1821*
Ac 11:30 s. it to the elders by the hands of.......... *649*
Ac 12:11 that the Lord hath s. his angel, ... *1821*
Ac 13:3 hands on them, they s. them away........ *630*
Ac 13:4 being s. forth by the Holy Ghost, ... *1599*
Ac 13:15 of the synagogue s. unto them, ... *649*
Ac 13:26 you is the word of this salvation s. *649*
Ac 15:27 s. therefore Judas and Silas, who *649*
Ac 16:35 magistrates s. the serjeants, saying, ... *649*
Ac 16:36 magistrates have s. to let you go: *649*
Ac 17:10 s. away Paul and Silas by night *1599*
Ac 17:14 the brethren s. away Paul to go as *1821*
Ac 19:22 he s. into Macedonia two of them *649*
Ac 19:31 s. unto him, desiring him that he *3992*
Ac 20:17 s. to Ephesus, and called the elders *3992*
Ac 23:30 I s. straightway to thee, and gave *3992*
Ac 24:24 he s. for Paul, and heard him *3343*
Ac 24:26 wherefore he s. for him the oftener, ... *3343*
Ac 28:28 salvation...is s. unto the Gentiles, ... *649*
Ro 10:15 shall they preach, except they be s.? *649*
Ro *subscr.* s. by Phebe servant of the church ....
1Co 1:17 For Christ s. me not to baptize, but *649*
1Co 4:17 cause have I s. unto you Timotheus, ...
2Co 8:18 we have s. with him the brother, ... *4842*
2Co 8:22 we have s. with them our brother, ... *4842*
2Co 9:3 Yet have I s. the brethren, lest our *3992*
2Co 12:17 any of them whom I s. unto you? *649*
2Co 12:18 Titus, and with him I s. a brother. *4882*
Gal 4:4 God s. forth his Son, made of a *1821*
Gal 4:6 God hath s. forth the Spirit of his *1821*
Eph 6:22 Whom I have s. unto you for the *3992*
Php 2:28 s. him therefore the more carefully, ... *3992*
Php 4:16 ye s. once and again unto my *3992*
Php 4:18 the things which were s. from you, ...
Col 4:8 Whom I have s. unto you for the *3992*
1Th 3:2 And s. Timotheus, our brother, and *3992*
1Th 3:5 I s. to know your faith, lest by some *375*
2Ti 4:12 And Tychicus have I s. to Ephesus. *649*
Phm 12 Whom I have s. again: thou *628*
Heb 1:14 s. forth to minister for them who *649*
Jas 2:25 and had s. them out another way? *1524*
1Pe 1:12 Holy Ghost s. down from heaven; *649*
1Pe 2:14 unto them that are s. by him for *3992*
1Jo 4:9 God s. his only begotten Son into *649*
1Jo 4:10 and s. his Son to be the propitiation *649*
1Jo 4:14 Father s. the Son to be the Saviour *649*
Re 1:1 he s. and signified it by his angel *649*
Re 5:6 of God s. forth into all the earth. *649*
Re 22:6 God of the holy prophets s. his angel.... *649*
Re 22:16 **Jesus have s. mine angel to testify** .*3992*

SENTENCE See also SENTENCES.
De 17:9 shall shew thee the s. of judgment: 1697
De 17:10 thou shalt do according to the s., ... 1697
De 17:11 According to the s. of the law 6310
De 17:11 from the s. which they shall shew 1697
Ps 17:2 Let my s. come forth from thy 4941
Pr 16:10 divine s. is in the lips of the king: 7081
Ec 8:11 s. against an evil work is not 6599
Jer 4:12 also will I give s. against them. 4941
Lu 23:24 Pilate gave s. that it should be *1948*
Ac 15:19 my s. is, that we trouble not them, ... *2919*
2Co 1:9 we had the s. of death in ourselves, ... *610*

SENTENCES
Da 5:12 shewing of hard s., and dissolving 280
Da 8:23 understanding dark s., shall stand 2420

SENTEST
Ex 15:7 thou s. forth thy wrath, which 7971
Nu 13:27 unto the land whither thou s. us, ... 7971
Nu 24:12 messengers which thou s. unto me. 7971
1Ki 5:8 the things which thou s. to me for: 7971

SENUAH (sen'-u-ah) See also HASSENUAH.
Ne 11:9 son of S. was second over the city. 5574

SEORIM (se-o'-rim)
1Ch 24:8 third to Harim, the fourth to S., ... 8188

SEPARATE See also SEPARATED; SEPARATETH; SEPARATING.
Ge 13:9 s. thyself, I pray thee, from me: 6504
Ge 30:40 And Jacob did s. the lambs, and 6504
Ge 49:26 him that was s. from his brethren. 5139
Le 15:31 shall ye s. the children of Israel 5144
Le 22:2 s. themselves from the holy things 5144
Nu 6:2 s. themselves to vow a vow of a 6381
Nu 6:2 to s. themselves unto the Lord: 5144
Nu 6:3 He shall s. himself from wine and 5144
Nu 8:14 thou s. the Levites from among the 914
Nu 16:21 S. yourselves from among this 914
De 19:2 Thou shalt s. three cities for thee 914
De 19:7 Thou shalt s. three cities for thee. 914
De 29:21 s. him unto evil out of all the tribes 914
Jos 16:9 the s. cities for the children of 3995
1Ki 8:53 s. them from among all the people 914
Ezr 10:11 s. yourselves from the people of the 914
Jer 37:12 to s. himself thence in the midst 2505
Eze 41:12 was before the s. place at the end 1508
Eze 41:13 the s. place, and the building, with 1508
Eze 41:14 and of the s. place toward the east, ... 1508
Eze 41:15 the s. place which was behind it, ... 1508
Eze 42:1 that was over against the s. place, ... 1508
Eze 42:10 the east, over against the s. place, ... 1508
Eze 42:13 which are before the s. place, they 1508
Mt 25:32 **he shall s. them one from another,** ..*873*
Lu 6:22 **shall s. you from their company,** *873*
Ac 13:2 S. me Barnabas and Saul for the *873*
Ro 8:35 shall s. us from the love of Christ? *5562*
Ro 8:39 able to s. us from the love of God. *5562*
2Co 6:17 them, and be ye s., saith the Lord, ... *873*
Heb 7:26 undefiled, s. from sinners, and *5562*
Jude 19 These be they who s. themselves, ... *592*

SEPARATED
Ge 13:11 they s. themselves the one from 6504
Ge 13:14 after that Lot was s. from him, ... 6504
Ge 25:23 two manner of people shall be s. 6504
Ex 33:16 so shall we be s., I and thy people, ... 6395
Le 20:24 have s. you from other people 914
Le 20:25 I have s. from you as unclean. 914
Nu 16:9 God of Israel hath s. you from the 914
De 10:8 time the Lord s. the tribe of Levi, ... 914
De 32:8 when he s. the sons of Adam, he 6504
De 33:16 him that was s. from his brethren. 5139
1Ch 12:8 there s. themselves unto David into 914
1Ch 23:13 and Aaron was s., that he should 914
1Ch 25:1 s. to the service of the sons of Asaph, .. 914
2Ch 25:10 Then Amaziah s. them, to wit, the 914
Ezr 6:21 s. themselves unto them from the 6395
Ezr 8:24 Then I s. twelve of the chief of the 914
Ezr 9:1 not s. themselves from the people of 914
Ezr 10:8 himself s. from the congregation of 914
Ezr 10:16 all of them by their names, were s., ... 914
Ne 4:19 we are s. upon the wall, one far 6504
Ne 9:2 seed of Israel s. themselves from 914
Ne 10:28 all they that had s. themselves from 914
Ne 13:3 they s. from Israel all the mixed 914
Pr 18:1 desire a man, having s. himself, ... 6504
Pr 19:4 the poor is s. from his neighbour. 6504
Isa 56:3 Lord hath utterly s. me from his 914
Isa 59:2 your iniquities have s. between you 914
Ho 4:14 themselves are s. with whores, ... 6504
Ho 9:10 s. themselves unto that shame; 5144
Ac 19:9 from them, and s. the disciples, ... *873*
Ro 1:1 apostle, s. unto the gospel of God, ... *873*
Ga 1:15 who s. me from my mother's womb, ... *873*
Ga 2:12 he withdrew and s. himself, fearing *873*

SEPARATETH
Nu 6:5 which he s. himself unto the Lord, ... 5144
Nu 6:6 that he s. himself unto the Lord 5144
Pr 16:28 and a whisperer s. chief friends. 6504
Pr 17:9 repeateth a matter s. very friends. 6504
Eze 14:7 which s. himself from me, and 5144

SEPARATING
Zec 7:3 s. myself, as I have done these so 5144

SEPARATION
Le 12:2 according to the days of the s. for 5079
Le 12:5 be unclean two weeks, as in her s.: 5079
Le 15:20 she lieth upon in her s. shall be 5079
Le 15:25 many days out of the time of her s., ... 5079
Le 15:25 if it run beyond the time of her s.; 5079
Le 15:25 shall be as the days of her s.: she 5079
Le 15:26 be unto her as the bed of her s.: 5079
Le 15:26 as the uncleanness of her s. 5079
Nu 6:4 All the days of his s. shall he eat 5145
Nu 6:5 days of the vow of his s. there shall ... 5145
Nu 6:8 the days of his s. he is holy unto 5145
Nu 6:12 unto the Lord the days of his s., ... 5145
Nu 6:12 be lost, because his s. was defiled. 5145
Nu 6:13 when the days of his s. are fulfilled: 5145
Nu 6:18 shave the head of his s. at the door 5145
Nu 6:18 take the hair of the head of his s., ... 5145
Nu 6:19 after the hair of his s. is shaven: 5145
Nu 6:21 his offering unto the Lord for his s., ... 5145
Nu 6:21 he must do after the law of his s. 5145
Nu 19:9 children of Israel for a water of s.: 5079
Nu 19:13 the water of s. was not sprinkled 5079
Nu 19:20 water of s. hath not been sprinkled 5079
Nu 19:21 he that sprinkleth the water of s. 5079
Nu 19:21 he that toucheth water of s. 5079
Nu 31:23 be purified with the water of s.: 5079
Eze 42:20 to make a s. between the sanctuary 914

SEPHAR (se'-far)
Ge 10:30 as thou goest unto S. a mount of 5611

SEPHARAD (sef'-a-rad)
Ob 20 the captivity...which is in S., ... 5614

SEPHARVAIM (sef-ar-va'-im) See also SEPHARVITES.
2Ki 17:24 and from Hamath, and from S., ... 5617
2Ki 17:31 and Anammelech, the gods of S. 5617
2Ki 18:34 where are the gods of S., Hena, ... 5617
2Ki 19:13 the king of the city of S., of Hena, ... 5617
Isa 36:19 Arphad? where are the gods of S.? 5617
Isa 37:13 and the king of the city of S., Hena, ... 5617

SEPHARVITES (sef'-ar-vites)
2Ki 17:31 the S. burnt their children in fire 5616

SEPULCHRE See also SEPULCHRES.
Ge 23:6 shall withhold from thee his s., ... 6913
De 34:6 but no man knoweth of his s. 6900
Jg 8:32 and was buried in the s. of Joash 6913
1Sa 10:2 shalt find two men by Rachel's s. 6900
2Sa 2:32 buried him in the s. of his father, ... 6913
2Sa 4:12 and buried it in the s. of Abner in 6913
2Sa 17:23 was buried in the s. of his father. 6913
2Sa 21:14 Zelah, in the s. of Kish his father: 6913
1Ki 13:22 not come unto the s. of thy fathers. 6913
1Ki 13:31 s. wherein the man of God is buried; .. 6913
2Ki 9:28 him in his s. with his fathers 6900
2Ki 13:21 cast the man into the s. of Elisha: 6913
2Ki 21:26 in his s. in the garden of Uzza: 6900
2Ki 23:17 It is the s. of the man of God, ... 6913
2Ki 23:30 and buried him in his own s. 6900
Ps 5:9 their throat is an open s.; they 6913
Isa 22:16 thou hast hewed thee out a s. here, ... 6913
Isa 22:16 that heweth him out a s. on high, ... 6913
Jer 5:16 Their quiver is as an open s., they 6913
Mt 27:60 a great stone to the door of the s., ... *3419*
Mt 27:61 Mary, sitting over against the s. *5028*
Mt 27:64 s. be made sure until the third day, ... *5028*
Mt 27:66 So they went, and made the s. sure, .. *5028*
Mt 28:1 and the other Mary to see the s. *5028*
Mt 28:8 they departed quickly from the s. *3419*
Mk 15:46 laid him in a s. which was hewn *3419*
Mk 15:46 a stone unto the door of the s. *3419*
Mk 16:2 they came unto the s. at the rising *3419*
Mk 16:3 the stone from the door of the s.? *3419*
Mk 16:5 And entering into the s., they saw *3419*
Mk 16:8 out quickly, and fled from the s.; *3419*
Lu 23:53 and laid it in a s. that was hewn *3418*
Lu 23:55 beheld the s., and how his body *3419*
Lu 24:1 morning, they came unto the s., ... *3418*
Lu 24:2 the stone rolled away from the s. *3419*
Lu 24:9 returned from the s., and told all *3419*
Lu 24:12 arose Peter, and ran unto the s.; *3419*
Lu 24:22 which were early at the s.; *3419*
Lu 24:24 which were with us went to the s., ... *3419*
Joh 19:41 in the garden a new s., wherein *3419*
Joh 19:42 day; for the s. was nigh at hand. *3419*
Joh 20:1 when it was yet dark, unto the s., ... *3419*
Joh 20:1 the stone taken away from the s. *3419*
Joh 20:2 taken away the Lord out of the s., ... *3419*
Joh 20:3 other disciple, and came to the s. *3419*
Joh 20:4 outrun Peter, and came...to the s. *3419*
Joh 20:6 and went into the s., and seeth the *3419*
Joh 20:8 disciple, which came first to the s., ... *3419*
Joh 20:11 But Mary stood without at the s. *3419*
Joh 20:11 stooped down, and looked in the s., ... *3419*

Ac 2:29 his s. is with us unto this day. *3418*
Ac 7:16 and laid in the s. that Abraham *3418*
Ac 13:29 from the tree, and laid him in a s. *3419*
Ro 3:13 Their throat is an open s.; with *5028*

SEPULCHRES
Ge 23:6 in the choice of our s. bury thy 6913
2Ki 23:16 he spied the s. that were there in 6913
2Ki 23:16 and took the bones out of the s., and 6913
2Ch 16:14 And they buried him in his own s., 6913
2Ch 21:20 David, but not in the s. of the kings. 6913
2Ch 24:25 buried him not in the s. of the kings. 6913
2Ch 28:27 him not into the s. of the kings of 6913
2Ch 32:33 in the chiefest of the s. of the sons 6913
2Ch 35:24 buried in one of the s. of his fathers. 6913
Ne 2:3 the city, the place of my father's s., 6913
Ne 2:5 unto the city of my father's s., that 6913
Ne 3:16 place over against the s. of David, 6913
Mt 23:27 **ye are like unto whited s., which** *5028*
Mt 23:29 **garnish the s. of the righteous,** *3419*
Lu 11:47 **for ye build the s. of the prophets,** *3419*
Lu 11:48 **killed them, and ye build their s.** *3419*

SERAH (se'-rah) See also SARAH; TIMNATH-SERAH.
Ge 46:17 and Beriah, and S. their sister: 8294
1Ch 7:30 and Beriah, and S. their sister. 8294

SERAIAH (se-ra-i'-ah) See also SHAVSHA.
2Sa 8:17 priests; and S. was the scribe; 8304
2Ki 25:18 the guard took S. the chief priest, 8304
2Ki 25:23 and S. the son of Tanhumeth the 8304
1Ch 4:13 the sons of Kenaz; Othniel, and S.: 8304
1Ch 4:14 and S. begat Joab, the father of 8304
1Ch 4:35 the son of Josibiah, the son of S., 8304
1Ch 6:14 begat S., and S. begat Jehozadak, 8304
Ezr 2:2 Jeshua, Nehemiah, S., Reelaiah, 8304
Ezr 7:1 Ezra the son of S., the son of 8304
Ne 10:2 S., Azariah, Jeremiah, 8304
Ne 11:11 S. the son of Hilkiah, the son of 8304
Ne 12:1 and Jeshua: S., Jeremiah, Ezra, 8304
Ne 12:12 chief of the fathers: of S., Meraiah; 8304
Jer 36:26 S. the son of Azrial, and Shelemiah 8304
Jer 40:8 and S. the son of Tanhumeth, and 8304
Jer 51:59 commanded S. the son of Neriah, 8304
Jer 51:59 And this S. was a quiet prince. 8304
Jer 51:61 Jeremiah said to S., When thou 8304
Jer 52:24 the guard took S. the chief priest, 8304

SERAPHIMS (ser'-a-fims)
Isa 6:2 Above it stood the s.: each one 8314
Isa 6:6 Then flew one of the s. unto me, 8314

SERED (se'-red) See also SARDITES.
Ge 46:14 sons of Zebulun; S., and Elon, 5624
Nu 26:26 of S., the family of the Sardites: 5624

SERGIUS (sur'-je-us)
Ac 13:7 S. Paulus, a prudent man; who *4588*

SERJEANTS
Ac 16:35 the magistrates sent the s., saying, *4465*
Ac 16:38 the s. told these words unto the *4465*

SERPENT See also SERPENT'S; SERPENTS.
Ge 3:1 s. was more subtil than any beast 5175
Ge 3:2 woman said unto the s., We may eat 5175
Ge 3:4 s. said unto the woman, Ye shall not 5175
Ge 3:13 The s. beguiled me, and I did eat. 5175
Ge 3:14 Lord God said unto the s., Because 5175
Ge 49:17 Dan shall be a s. by the way, an 5175
Ex 4:3 on the ground, and it became a s.; 5175
Ex 7:9 Pharaoh, and it shall become a s. 8577
Ex 7:10 his servants, and it became a s. 8577
Ex 7:15 the rod which was turned to a s. 5175
Nu 21:8 Make thee a fiery s., and set it 8314
Nu 21:9 Moses made a s. of brass, and put 5175
Nu 21:9 that if a s. had bitten any man, 5175
Nu 21:9 when he beheld the s. of brass, he 5175
2Ki 18:4 the brasen s. that Moses had made: 5175
Job 26:13 hand hath formed the crooked s. 5175
Ps 58:4 poison is like the poison of a s.: 5175
Ps 140:3 sharpened their tongues like a s.; 5175
Pr 23:32 At the last it biteth like a s., and 5175
Pr 30:19 the way of a s. upon a rock; the way 5175
Ec 10:8 breaketh an hedge, a s. shall bite 5175
Ec 10:11 s. will bite without enchantment; 5175
Isa 14:29 his fruit shall be a fiery flying s. 8314
Isa 27:1 punish leviathan the piercing s., 5175
Isa 27:1 even leviathan that crooked s.; and 5175
Isa 30:6 lion, the viper and fiery flying s., 8314
Jer 46:22 voice thereof shall go like a s.; 5175
Am 5:19 hand on the wall, and a s. bit him. 5175
Am 9:3 sea, thence will I command the s., 5175
Mic 7:17 They shall lick the dust like a s., 5175
Mt 7:10 **ask a fish, will he give him a s.?** *3789*
Lu 11:11 **will he for a fish give him a s.?** *3789*
Joh 3:14 **as Moses lifted up the s. in the** *3789*
2Co 11:3 as the s. beguiled Eve through his *3789*
Re 12:9 old s., called the Devil, and Satan, *3789*
Re 12:14 half a time, from the face of the s. *3789*
Re 12:15 the s. cast out of his mouth water *3789*
Re 20:2 old s., which is the Devil, and Satan, *3789*

SERPENT'S
Isa 14:29 out of the s. root shall come forth 5175
Isa 65:25 and dust shall be the s. meat. 5175

SERPENTS
Ex 7:12 man his rod, and they became s.: 8577
Nu 21:6 the Lord sent fiery s. among the 5175
Nu 21:7 that he take away the s. from us. 5175
De 8:15 wilderness, wherein were fiery s., 5175
De 32:24 with the poison of s. of the dust. 2119
Jer 8:17 I will send s., cockatrices, among 5175
Mt 10:16 **be ye therefore wise as s., and** *3789*
Mt 23:33 **Ye s., ye generation of vipers, how** *3789*
Mk 16:18 **They shall take up s.; and if they** *3789*
Lu 10:19 **power to tread on s. and scorpions,** *3789*
1Co 10:9 tempted, and were destroyed of s. *3789*
Jas 3:7 of s., and of things in the sea, in *2062*
Re 9:19 for their tails were like unto s., *3789*

SERUG (se'-rug) See also SARUCH.
Ge 11:20 and thirty years, and begat S.: 8286
Ge 11:21 Reu lived after he begat S. two 8286
Ge 11:22 S. lived thirty years, and begat 8286
Ge 11:23 S. lived after he begat Nahor two 8286
1Ch 1:26 S., Nahor, Terah, 8286

SERVANT See also BONDSERVANT; MAIDSERVANT; SERVANT'S; SERVANTS; SERVITOR.
Ge 9:25 a s. of servants shall he be unto 5650
Ge 9:26, 27 Shem;...Canaan shall be his s. 5650
Ge 18:3 not away, I pray thee, from thy s.: 5650
Ge 18:5 therefore are ye come to your s. 5650
Ge 19:19 thy s. hath found grace in thy sight, 5650
Ge 24:2 Abraham said unto his eldest s. 5650
Ge 24:5 s. said unto him, Peradventure 5650
Ge 24:9 the s. put his hand under the thigh 5650
Ge 24:10 And the s. took ten camels of the 5650
Ge 24:14 that thou hast appointed for thy s. 5650
Ge 24:17 the s. ran to meet her, and said, 5650
Ge 24:34 And he said, I am Abraham's s. 5650
Ge 24:52 Abraham's s. heard their words, 5650
Ge 24:53 And the s. brought forth jewels of 5650
Ge 24:59 and Abraham's s., and his men. 5650
Ge 24:61 the s. took Rebekah, and went his 5650
Ge 24:65 she had said unto the s., What man 5650
Ge 24:65 the s. had said, It is my master: 5650
Ge 24:66 the s. told Isaac all things that 5650
Ge 26:24 thy seed for my s. Abraham's sake. 5650
Ge 32:4 Thy s. Jacob saith thus, I have 5650
Ge 32:10 thou hast shewed unto thy s.; for 5650
Ge 32:18 shalt say, They be thy s. Jacob's; 5650
Ge 33:20 Behold, thy s. Jacob is behind us. 5650
Ge 33:5 God hath graciously given thy s. 5650
Ge 33:14 I pray thee, pass over before his s.: 5650
Ge 39:17 Hebrew s., which thou hast brought 5650
Ge 39:19 After this manner did thy s. to me; 5650
Ge 41:12 s. to the captain of the guard; and 5650
Ge 43:28 Thy s. our father is in good health, 5650
Ge 44:10 whom it is found shall be my s.; 5650
Ge 44:17 the cup is found, he shall be my s.; 5650
Ge 44:18 let thy s., I pray thee, speak a word 5650
Ge 44:18 not thine anger burn against thy s.: 5650
Ge 44:24 we came up unto thy s. my father, 5650
Ge 44:27 thy s. my father said unto us, Ye 5650
Ge 44:30 when I come to thy s. my father, 5650
Ge 44:31 bring down the gray hairs of thy s. 5650
Ge 44:32 thy s. became surety for the lad 5650
Ge 44:33 let thy s. abide instead of the lad a 5650
Ge 49:15 and became a s. unto tribute. 5647
Ex 4:10 thou hast spoken unto thy s.: but 5650
Ex 12:44 every man's s. that is bought for 5650
Ex 12:45 an hired s. shall not eat thereof. 7916
Ex 14:31 the Lord, and his s. Moses. 5650
Ex 21:2 If thou buy an Hebrew s., six years 5650
Ex 21:5 If the s. shall plainly say, I love my 5650
Ex 21:20 if a man smite his s., or his maid, 5650
Ex 21:26 And if a man smite the eye of his s., 5650
Ex 33:11 but his s. Joshua, the son of Nun, 8334
Le 22:10 hired s., shall not eat of the holy 7916
Le 25:6 and for thy s., and for thy maid, 5650
Le 25:6 and for thy hired s., and for thy 7916
Le 25:40 as an hired s., and as a sojourner, 7916
Le 25:50 according to the time of an hired s. 7916
Le 25:53 a yearly hired s. shall he be with 7916
Nu 11:11 hast thou afflicted thy s.? and 5650
Nu 11:28 the son of Nun, the s. of Moses, 8334
Nu 12:7 My s. Moses is not so, who is 5650
Nu 12:8 to speak against my s. Moses? 5650
Nu 14:24 But my s. Caleb, because he had 5650
De 3:24 begun to shew thy s. thy greatness, 5650
De 5:15 thou wast a s. in the land of Egypt, 5650
De 15:17 door, and he shall be thy s. for ever. 5650
De 15:18 hath been worth a double hired s. 7916
De 23:15 not deliver unto his master the s. 5650
De 24:14 shalt not oppress an hired s. that 7916
De 34:5 So Moses the s. of the Lord died 5650
Jos 1:1 death of Moses the s. of the Lord 5650
Jos 1:2 Moses my s. is dead; now therefore 5650
Jos 1:7 Moses my s. commanded thee: 5650
Jos 1:13 which Moses the s. of the Lord 5650
Jos 1:15 which Moses the Lord's s. gave you 5650
Jos 5:14 What saith my lord unto his s.? 5650
Jos 8:31 As Moses the s. of the Lord 5650
Jos 8:33 As Moses the s. of the Lord had 5650
Jos 9:24 commanded his s. Moses to give 5650
Jos 11:12 them, as Moses the s. of the Lord 5650
Jos 11:15 the Lord commanded Moses his s., 5650
Jos 12:6 Them did Moses the s. of the Lord 5650
Jos 12:6 Moses the s. of the Lord gave it 5650
Jos 13:8 Moses the s. of the Lord gave them; 5650
Jos 14:7 Moses the s. of the Lord sent me 5650
Jos 18:7 Moses the s. of the Lord gave them. 5650
Jos 22:2 Moses...s. of the Lord commanded 5650
Jos 22:4 Moses the s. of the Lord gave you 5650
Jos 22:5 Moses the s. of the Lord charged 5650
Jos 24:29 the son of Nun, the s. of the Lord, 5650
Jg 2:8 the son of Nun, the s. of the Lord, 5650
Jg 7:10 with Phurah thy s. down to the 5288
Jg 7:11 went he down with Phurah his s. 5288
Jg 15:18 deliverance into the hand of thy s.: 5650
Jg 19:3 having his s. with him, and a 5288
Jg 19:9 he, and his concubine, and his s., 5288
Jg 19:11 the s. said unto his master, Come. 5288
Jg 19:13 he said unto his s., Come, and let 5288
Ru 2:5 Boaz unto his s. that was set over 5288
Ru 2:6 the s. that was set over the reapers 5288
1Sa 2:13 the priest's s. came, while the flesh 5288
1Sa 2:15 the priest's s. came, and said to the 5288
1Sa 3:9 Speak, Lord; for thy s. heareth. 5650
1Sa 3:10 answered, Speak; for thy s. heareth. 5650
1Sa 9:5 Saul said to his s. that was with 5288
1Sa 9:7 said Saul to his s., But, behold, if 5288
1Sa 9:8 And the s. answered Saul again, 5288
1Sa 9:10 Then said Saul to his s., Well said; 5288
1Sa 9:22 And Samuel took Saul and his s., 5288
1Sa 9:27 Saul, Bid the s. pass on before us, 5288
1Sa 10:14 uncle said unto him and to his s., 5288
1Sa 17:32 thy s. will go and fight with this 5650
1Sa 17:34 Thy s. kept his father's sheep, and 5650
1Sa 17:36 Thy s. slew both the lion and the 5650
1Sa 17:58 I am the son of thy s. Jesse the 5650
1Sa 19:4 Let not the king sin against his s., 5650
1Sa 20:7 It is well; thy s. shall have peace: 5650
1Sa 20:8 thou shalt deal kindly with thy s.; 5650
1Sa 20:8 hast brought thy s. into a covenant 5650
1Sa 22:8 hath stirred up my s. against me, 5650
1Sa 22:15 king impute any thing unto his s., 5650
1Sa 22:15 for thy s. knew nothing of all this, 5650
1Sa 23:10 s. hath certainly heard that Saul 5650
1Sa 23:11 come down, as thy s. hath heard? 5650
1Sa 23:11 of Israel I beseech thee, tell thy s. 5650
1Sa 25:39 and hath kept his s. from evil: for 5650
1Sa 25:41 handmaid be a s. to wash the feet 5650
1Sa 26:18 my lord thus pursue after his s.? 5650
1Sa 26:19 the king hear the words of his s. 5650
1Sa 27:5 why should thy s. dwell in the royal 5650
1Sa 27:12 therefore he shall be my s. for ever. 5650
1Sa 28:2 thou shalt know what thy s. can do. 5650
1Sa 29:3 Is not this David, the s. of Saul the 5650
1Sa 29:8 what hast thou found in thy s. so 5650
1Sa 30:13 man of Egypt, s. to an Amalekite; 5650
2Sa 3:18 By the hand of my s. David I will 5650

Book	Ref.	Context	No.
2Sa	7:5	Go and tell my **s.** David, Thus saith	5650
2Sa	7:8	so shalt thou say unto my **s.** David,	5650
2Sa	7:20	for thou, Lord God, knowest thy **s.**	5650
2Sa	7:21	things, to make thy **s.** know them.	5650
2Sa	7:25	thou hast spoken concerning thy **s.**,	5650
2Sa	7:26	and let the house of thy **s.** David be	5650
2Sa	7:27	of Israel, hast revealed to thy **s.**,	5650
2Sa	7:27	hath thy **s.** found in his heart to	5650
2Sa	7:28	promised this goodness unto thy **s.**:	5650
2Sa	7:29	thee to bless the house of thy **s.**,	5650
2Sa	7:29	let the house of thy **s.** be blessed	5650
2Sa	9:2	there was of the house of Saul a **s.**	5650
2Sa	9:2	Ziba? And he said, Thy **s.** is he.	5650
2Sa	9:6	and he answered, Behold thy **s.**!	5650
2Sa	9:8	What is thy **s.**, that thou shouldest	5650
2Sa	9:9	the king called to Ziba, Saul's **s.**,	5288
2Sa	9:11	commanded his **s.**, so shall thy **s.**	5650
2Sa	11:21	Thy **s.** Uriah the Hittite is dead.	5650
2Sa	11:24	and thy **s.** Uriah the Hittite is dead	5650
2Sa	13:17	called his **s.** that ministered unto	5288
2Sa	13:18	Then his **s.** brought her out, and	8334
2Sa	13:24	now, thy **s.** hath sheepshearers;	5650
2Sa	13:24	and his servants go with thy **s.**	5650
2Sa	13:35	sons come: as thy **s.** said, so it is.	5650
2Sa	14:19	thy **s.** Jacob, he bade me, and he	5650
2Sa	14:20	hath thy **s.** Joab done this thing:	5650
2Sa	14:22	To day thy **s.** knoweth that I have	5650
2Sa	14:22	hath fulfilled the request of his **s.**	5650
2Sa	15:2	Thy **s.** is of one of the tribes of	5650
2Sa	15:8	thy **s.** vowed a vow while I abode	5650
2Sa	15:21	life, even there also will thy **s.** be.	5650
2Sa	15:34	Absalom, I will be thy **s.**, O king;	5650
2Sa	15:34	have been thy father's **s.** hitherto,	5650
2Sa	15:34	so will I now also be thy **s.**: then	5650
2Sa	16:1	Ziba the **s.** of Mephibosheth met	5288
2Sa	18:29	sent the king's **s.**, and me thy **s.**,	5650
2Sa	19:17	Ziba the **s.** of the house of Saul,	5288
2Sa	19:19	remember that which thy **s.** did	5650
2Sa	19:20	thy **s.** doth know...I have sinned:	5650
2Sa	19:26	My lord, O king, my **s.** deceived me:	5650
2Sa	19:26	for thy **s.** said, I will saddle me an	5650
2Sa	19:26	to the king; because thy **s.** is lame.	5650
2Sa	19:27	he hath slandered thy **s.** unto my	5650
2Sa	19:28	didst thou set thy **s.** among them	5650
2Sa	19:35	can thy **s.** taste what I eat or what	5650
2Sa	19:35	then should thy **s.** be yet a burden	5650
2Sa	19:36	Thy **s.** will go a little way over	5650
2Sa	19:37	Let thy **s.**, I pray thee, turn back	5650
2Sa	19:37	But behold thy **s.** Chimham; let	5650
2Sa	24:10	take away the iniquity of thy **s.**;	5650
2Sa	24:21	is my lord the king come to his **s.**?	5650
1Ki	1:19	Solomon thy **s.** hath he not called.	5650
1Ki	1:26	But me, even me thy **s.**, and Zadok	5650
1Ki	1:26	thy **s.** Solomon, hath he not called.	5650
1Ki	1:27	thou hast not shewed it unto thy **s.**,	5650
1Ki	1:51	to day that he will not slay his **s.**	5650
1Ki	2:38	the king hath said, so will thy **s.** do.	5650
1Ki	3:6	shewed unto thy **s.** David my father	5650
1Ki	3:7	made thy **s.** king instead of David	5650
1Ki	3:8	thy **s.** is in the midst of thy people	5650
1Ki	3:9	Give...thy **s.** an understanding	5650
1Ki	8:24	Who hast kept with thy **s.** David	5650
1Ki	8:25	keep with thy **s.** David my father	5650
1Ki	8:26	thou spakest unto thy **s.** David my	5650
1Ki	8:28	respect unto the prayer of thy **s.**,	5650
1Ki	8:28	which thy **s.** prayeth before thee	5650
1Ki	8:29	the prayer which thy **s.** shall make	5650
1Ki	8:30	thou to the supplication of thy **s.**,	5650
1Ki	8:52	unto the supplication of thy **s.**,	5650
1Ki	8:53	spakest by the hand of Moses thy **s.**,	5650
1Ki	8:56	promised by...hand of Moses his **s.**	5650
1Ki	8:59	that he maintain the cause of his **s.**,	5650
1Ki	8:66	the Lord had done for David his **s.**,	5650
1Ki	11:11	from thee, and will give it to thy **s.**	5650
1Ki	11:26	Ephrathite of Zereda, Solomon's **s.**,	5650
1Ki	11:32	one tribe for my **s.** David's sake,	5650
1Ki	11:36	that David my **s.** may have a light	5650
1Ki	11:38	commandments, as David my **s.** did;	5650
1Ki	12:7	If thou wilt be a **s.** unto this people	5650
1Ki	14:8	thou hast not been as my **s.** David,	5650
1Ki	14:18	spake by the hand of his **s.** Ahijah	5650
1Ki	15:29	which he spake by his **s.** Ahijah the	5650
1Ki	16:9	And his **s.** Zimri, captain of half his	5650
1Ki	18:9	deliver thy **s.** into the hand of Ahab,	5650
1Ki	18:12	but I thy **s.** fear the Lord from my	5650
1Ki	18:36	that I am thy **s.**, and that I have	5650
1Ki	18:43	And said to his **s.**, Go up now,	5288
1Ki	19:3	to Judah, and left his **s.** there.	5288
1Ki	20:9	that thou didst send for to thy **s.**	5650
1Ki	20:32	Thy **s.** Ben-hadad saith, I pray thee,	5650
1Ki	20:39	Thy **s.** went out into the midst of	5650
1Ki	20:40	as thy **s.** was busy here and there,	5650
2Ki	4:1	saying, Thy **s.** my husband is dead;	5650
2Ki	4:1	that thy **s.** did fear the Lord: and	5650
2Ki	4:12	he said to Gehazi his **s.**, Call this	5288
2Ki	4:24	and said to her **s.**, Drive, and go	5288
2Ki	4:25	he said to Gehazi his **s.**, Behold,	5288
2Ki	4:38	he said unto his **s.**, Set on the great	5288
2Ki	5:6	sent Naaman my **s.** to thee, that	5650
2Ki	5:15	pray thee, take a blessing of thy **s.**	5650
2Ki	5:17	given to thy **s.** two mules' burden	5650
2Ki	5:17	thy **s.** will henceforth offer neither	5650
2Ki	5:18	this thing the Lord pardon thy **s.**,	5650
2Ki	5:18	the Lord pardon thy **s.** in this thing.	5650
2Ki	5:20	the **s.** of Elisha the man of God,	5288
2Ki	5:25	he said, thy **s.** went no whither.	5650
2Ki	6:15	the **s.** of the man of God was risen	8334
2Ki	6:15	And his **s.** said unto him, Alas, my	5288
2Ki	8:4	Gehazi the **s.** of the man of God,	5288
2Ki	8:13	said, But what, is thy **s.** a dog,	5650
2Ki	9:36	spake by his **s.** Elijah the Tishbite,	5650
2Ki	10:10	which he spake by his **s.** Elijah.	5650
2Ki	14:25	spake by the hand of his **s.** Jonah,	5650
2Ki	16:7	saying, I am thy **s.** and thy son:	5650
2Ki	17:3	and Hoshea became his **s.**, and gave	5650
2Ki	18:12	Moses...**s.** of the Lord commanded,	5650
2Ki	19:34	sake, and for my **s.** David's sake.	5650
2Ki	20:6	sake, and for my **s.** David's sake.	5650
2Ki	21:8	my **s.** Moses commanded them.	5650
2Ki	22:12	and Asahiah a **s.** of the king's.	5650
2Ki	24:1	and Jehoiakim became his **s.** three	5650
2Ki	25:8	guard, a **s.** of the king of Babylon,	5650
1Ch	2:34	And Sheshan had a **s.**, an Egyptian,	5650
1Ch	2:35	his daughter to Jarha his **s.** to wife;	5650
1Ch	6:49	all that Moses the **s.** of God had	5650
1Ch	16:13	O ye seed of Israel his **s.**, ye children	5650
1Ch	17:4	Go and tell David my **s.**, Thus saith	5650
1Ch	17:7	shalt thou say unto my **s.** David,	5650
1Ch	17:18	to thee for the honour of thy **s.**?	5650
1Ch	17:18	for thou knowest thy **s.**	5650
1Ch	17:23	concerning thy **s.** and concerning	5650
1Ch	17:24	house of David thy **s.** be established	5650
1Ch	17:25	**s.** that thou wilt build him...house:	5650
1Ch	17:25	**s.** hath found in his heart to pray	5650
1Ch	17:26	promised this goodness unto thy **s.**:	5650
1Ch	17:27	thee to bless the house of thy **s.**,	5650
1Ch	21:8	thee, do away the iniquity of thy **s.**;	5650
2Ch	1:3	Moses the **s.** of the Lord had made	5650
2Ch	6:15	which hast kept with thy **s.** David	5650
2Ch	6:16	keep with thy **s.** David my father	5650
2Ch	6:17	thou hast spoken unto thy **s.** David.	5650
2Ch	6:19	therefore to the prayer of thy **s.**,	5650
2Ch	6:19	which thy **s.** prayeth before thee:	5650
2Ch	6:20	thy **s.** prayeth toward this place.	5650
2Ch	6:21	unto the supplications of thy **s.**,	5650
2Ch	6:42	the mercies of David thy **s.**	5650
2Ch	13:6	the **s.** of Solomon the son of David,	5650
2Ch	24:6	of Moses the **s.** of the Lord, and of	5650
2Ch	24:9	that Moses the **s.** of God laid upon	5650
2Ch	32:16	God, and against his **s.** Hezekiah.	5650
2Ch	34:20	scribe, and Asaiah a **s.** of the king's,	5650
Ne	1:6	mayest hear the prayer of thy **s.**,	5650
Ne	1:7	thou commandedst thy **s.** Moses.	5650
Ne	1:8	thou commandedst thy **s.** Moses,	5650
Ne	1:11	be attentive to the prayer of thy **s.**,	5650
Ne	1:11	prosper, I pray thee, thy **s.** this day,	5650
Ne	2:5	and if thy **s.** have found favour in	5650
Ne	2:10	and Tobiah the **s.**, the Ammonite,	5650
Ne	2:19	Tobiah the **s.**, the Ammonite, and	5650
Ne	4:22	with his **s.** lodge within Jerusalem,	5288
Ne	6:5	sent Sanballat his **s.** unto me in	5288
Ne	9:14	laws, by the hand of Moses thy **s.**:	5650
Ne	10:29	was given by Moses the **s.** of God,	5650
Job	1:8	Hast thou considered my **s.** Job,	5650
Job	2:3	Hast thou considered my **s.** Job,	5650
Job	3:19	and the **s.** is free from his master.	5650
Job	7:2	a **s.** earnestly desireth the shadow,	5650
Job	19:16	I called my **s.**, and he gave me no	5650
Job	41:4	wilt thou take him for a **s.** for ever?	5650
Job	42:7	that is right, as my **s.** Job hath.	5650
Job	42:8	and go to my **s.** Job, and offer up	5650
Job	42:8	and my **s.** Job shall pray for you:	5650
Job	42:8	thing which is right, like my **s.** Job.	5650
Ps	18:*title*	of David, the **s.** of the Lord, who	5650
Ps	19:11	by them is thy **s.** warned: and in	5650
Ps	19:13	thy **s.** also from presumptuous	5650
Ps	27:9	me; put not thy **s.** away in anger:	5650
Ps	31:16	Make thy face to shine upon thy **s.**	5650
Ps	35:27	pleasure in the prosperity of his **s.**	5650
Ps	36:*title*	of David the **s.** of the Lord.	5650
Ps	69:17	And hide not thy face from thy **s.**;	5650
Ps	78:70	He chose David also his **s.**, and took	5650
Ps	86:2	save thy **s.** that trusteth in thee.	5650
Ps	86:4	Rejoice the soul of thy **s.**: for unto	5650
Ps	86:16	give thy strength unto thy **s.**, and	5650
Ps	89:3	I have sworn unto David my **s.**,	5650
Ps	89:20	I have found David my **s.**; with my	5650
Ps	89:39	made void the covenant of thy **s.**:	5650
Ps	105:6	O ye seed of Abraham his **s.**, ye	5650
Ps	105:17	even Joseph, who was sold for a **s.**	5650
Ps	105:26	He sent Moses his **s.**; and Aaron	5650
Ps	105:42	holy promise, and Abraham his **s.**	5650
Ps	109:28	be ashamed; but let thy **s.** rejoice.	5650
Ps	116:16	O Lord, truly I am thy **s.**;	5650
Ps	116:16	I am thy **s.**, and the son of thine	5650
Ps	119:17	Deal bountifully with thy **s.**, that I	5650
Ps	119:23	thy **s.** did meditate in thy statutes.	5650
Ps	119:38	Stablish thy word unto thy **s.**, who	5650
Ps	119:49	Remember the word unto thy **s.**,	5650
Ps	119:65	Thou hast dealt well with thy **s.**, O	5650
Ps	119:76	according to thy word unto thy **s.**	5650
Ps	119:84	How many are the days of thy **s.**?	5650
Ps	119:122	Be surety for thy **s.** for good: let not	5650
Ps	119:124	thy **s.** according unto thy mercy,	5650
Ps	119:125	am thy **s.**; give me understanding,	5650
Ps	119:135	Make thy face to shine upon thy **s.**;	5650
Ps	119:140	very pure: therefore thy **s.** loveth it	5650
Ps	119:176	astray like a lost sheep; seek thy **s.**;	5650
Ps	132:10	thy **s.** David's sake turn not away	5650
Ps	136:22	Even an heritage unto Israel his **s.**	5650
Ps	143:2	enter not into judgment with thy **s.**	5650
Ps	143:12	that afflict my soul: for I am thy **s.**	5650
Ps	144:10	who delivereth David his **s.** from the	5650
Pr	11:29	and the fool shall be **s.** to the wise	5650
Pr	12:9	He that is despised, and hath a **s.**,	5650
Pr	14:35	king's favour is toward a wise **s.**:	5650
Pr	17:2	A wise **s.** shall have rule over a son	5650
Pr	19:10	much less for a **s.** to have rule over	5650
Pr	22:7	and the borrower is **s.** to the lender.	5650
Pr	29:19	A **s.** will not be corrected by words:	5650
Pr	29:21	He that delicately bringeth up his **s.**	5650
Pr	30:10	Accuse not a **s.** unto his master,	5650
Pr	30:22	For a **s.** when he reigneth; and a	5650
Ec	7:21	lest thou hear thy **s.** curse thee:	5650
Isa	20:3	Like as my **s.** Isaiah hath walked	5650
Isa	22:20	I will call my **s.** Eliakim the son of	5650
Isa	24:2	as with the **s.**, so with his master;	5650
Isa	37:35	sake, and for my **s.** David's sake.	5650
Isa	41:8	But thou, Israel, art my **s.**, Jacob	5650
Isa	41:8	and said unto thee, Thou art my **s.**;	5650
Isa	42:1	Behold my **s.**, whom I uphold; mine	5650
Isa	42:19	Who is blind, but my **s.**? or deaf, as	5650
Isa	42:19	perfect, and blind as the Lord's **s.**?	5650
Isa	43:10	and my **s.** whom I have chosen:	5650
Isa	44:1	Yet now hear, O Jacob my **s.**; and	5650
Isa	44:2	Fear not, O Jacob, my **s.**; and thou,	5650
Isa	44:21	for thou art my **s.**: I have formed	5650
Isa	44:21	thou art my **s.**: O Israel, thou shalt	5650
Isa	44:26	That confirmeth the word of his **s.**,	5650
Isa	48:20	Lord hath redeemed his **s.** Jacob.	5650
Isa	49:3	Thou art my **s.**, O Israel, in whom	5650
Isa	49:5	me from the womb to be his **s.**,	5650
Isa	49:6	thing that thou shouldest be my **s.**	5650
Isa	49:7	nation abhorreth, to a **s.** of rulers,	5650
Isa	50:10	that obeyeth the voice of his **s.**, that	5650
Isa	52:13	Behold, my **s.** shall deal prudently,	5650
Isa	53:11	shall my righteous **s.** justify many;	5650
Jer	2:14	Is Israel a **s.**? is he a homeborn	5650
Jer	25:9	and...the king of Babylon, my **s.**,	5650
Jer	27:6	hand of...the king of Babylon, my **s.**;	5650
Jer	30:10	fear thou not, O my **s.** Jacob, saith	5650
Jer	33:21	covenant be broken with David my **s.**,	5650
Jer	33:22	I multiply the seed of David my **s.**,	5650
Jer	33:26	the seed of Jacob, and David my **s.**,	5650
Jer	34:16	and caused every man his **s.**, and	5650
Jer	43:10	take...the king of Babylon, my **s.**,	5650
Jer	46:27	But fear not thou, O my **s.** Jacob,	5650
Jer	46:28	Fear thou not, O Jacob my **s.**, saith	5650
Eze	28:24	land...I have given to my **s.** Jacob.	5650
Eze	34:23	shall feed them, even my **s.** David;	5650
Eze	34:24	my **s.** David a prince among them;	5650

Eze 37:24 David my s. shall be king over them; 5650
Eze 37:25 that I have given unto Jacob my s., 5650
Eze 37:25 my s. David shall be their prince 5650
Da 6:20 O Daniel, s. of the living God, is 5649
Da 9:11 in the law of Moses the s. of God, 5650
Da 9:17 O our God, hear the prayer of thy s., 5650
Da 10:17 how can the s. of this my lord talk 5650
Hag 2:23 I take thee, O Zerubbabel, my s., 5650
Zec 3:8 I will bring forth my s. the Branch 5650
Mal 1:6 son...his father, and a s. his master: 5650
Mal 4:4 Remember ye the law of Moses my s., 5650
Mt 8:6 s. lieth at home sick of the palsy, 3816
Mt 8:8 only, and my s. shall be healed. 3816
Mt 8:9 to my s., Do this, and he doeth it. 1401
Mt 8:13 his s. was sealed in the selfsame 3816
Mt 10:24 **master, nor the s. above his lord** 1401
Mt 10:25 **his master, and the s. as his lord.** 1401
Mt 12:18 Behold my s., whom I have chosen; 3816
Mt 18:26 **The s. therefore fell down, and** 1401
Mt 18:27 **the lord of that s. was moved with** 1401
Mt 18:28 **the same s. went out, and found** 1401
Mt 18:32 **O thou wicked s., I forgave thee** 1401
Mt 20:27 **chief among you, let him be s.** 1401
Mt 23:11 **greatest among you shall be s.** 1249
Mt 24:45 **Who then is a faithful and wise s.,** 1401
Mt 24:46 **Blessed is that s., whom his lord** 1401
Mt 24:48 **if that evil s. shall say in his heart,** 1401
Mt 24:50 **lord of that s. shall come in a day.** 1401
Mt 25:21 **done, thou good and faithful s.:** 1401
Mt 25:23 **Well done, good and faithful s.;** 1401
Mt 25:26 **Thou wicked and slothful s., thou** 1401
Mt 25:30 **unprofitable s. into outer darkness:** 1401
Mt 26:51 and struck a s. of the high priest's, 1401
Mk 9:35 **shall be last of all, and s. of all.** 1249
Mk 10:44 **be the chiefest, shall be s. of all,** 1401
Mk 12:2 **he sent to the husbandmen a s.,** 1401
Mk 12:4 **he sent unto them another s.;** 1401
Mk 14:47 and smote a s. of the high priest, 1401
Lu 1:54 He hath holpen his s. Israel, in 3816
Lu 1:69 for us in the house of his s. David; 3816
Lu 2:29 lettest thou thy s. depart in peace, 1401
Lu 7:2 a certain centurion's s., who was 1401
Lu 7:3 that he would come and heal his s. 1401
Lu 7:7 a word, and my s. shall be healed. 3816
Lu 7:8 to my s., Do this, and he doeth it. 1401
Lu 7:10 the s. whole that had been sick 1401
Lu 12:43 **Blessed is that s., whom his lord** 1401
Lu 12:45 **But and if that s. say in his heart,** 1401
Lu 12:46 **lord of that s. will come in a day** 1401
Lu 12:47 **that s., which knew his lord's will,** 1401
Lu 14:17 **And send his s. at supper time to** 1401
Lu 14:21 **that s. came, and shewed his lord** 1401
Lu 14:21 **angry said to his s., Go out quickly** 1401
Lu 14:22 **the s. said, Lord, it is done as thou** 1401
Lu 14:22 **lord said unto his s., Go out into** 1401
Lu 16:13 **No s. can serve two masters: for** 3610
Lu 17:7 **having a s. plowing or feeding** 1401
Lu 17:9 **Doth he thank that s. because he** 1401
Lu 19:17 **said unto him, Well, thou good s.** 1401
Lu 19:22 **will I judge thee, thou wicked s.** 1401
Lu 20:10 **he sent a s. to the husbandmen,** 1401
Lu 20:11 **And again he sent another s.:** and 1401
Lu 22:50 them smote the s. of the high priest, 1401
Joh 8:34 **committeth sin is the s. of sin.** 1401
Joh 8:35 **the s. abideth not in the house for** 1401
Joh 12:26 **I am, there shall also my s. be:** 1249
Joh 13:16 **The s. is not greater than his lord;** 1401
Joh 15:15 **s. knoweth not what his lord:** 1401
Joh 15:20 **The s. is not greater than his lord** 1401
Joh 18:10 and smote the high priest's s., and 1401
Ac 4:25 Who by the mouth of thy s. David 3816
Ro 1:1 Paul, a s. of Jesus Christ, called 1401
Ro 14:4 that judgest another man's s.? 3610
Ro 16:1 sister, which is a s. of the church 1249
Ro *subscr.* sent by Phebe s. of the church 1249
1Co 7:21 Art thou called being a s.? care 1401
1Co 7:22 being a s., is the Lord's freeman: 1401
1Co 7:22 is called, being free, is Christ's s. 1401
1Co 9:19 yet have I made myself s. unto all, 1402
Ga 1:10 I should not be the s. of Christ. 1401
Ga 4:1 a child, differeth nothing from a s., 1401
Ga 4:7 Wherefore thou art no more a s., 1401
Php 2:7 and took upon him the form of a s., 1401
Col 4:12 who is one of you, a s. of Christ, 1401
2Ti 2:24 the s. of the Lord must not strive; 1401
Tit 1:1 Paul, a s. of God, and an apostle of 1401
Phm 16 Not now as a s., but above a s., 1401
Phm *subsc.* Philemon, by Onesimus a s. 3610
Heb 3:5 faithful in all his house, as a s., 2324
Jas 1:1 James, a s. of God and of the Lord 1401
2Pe 1:1 Simon Peter, a s. and an apostle of 1401
Jude 1 Jude, the s. of Jesus Christ, and 1401
Re 1:1 it by his angel unto his s. John: 1401
Re 15:3 sing the song of Moses the s. of God, 1401

SERVANT'S

Ge 19:2 in, I pray you, into your s. house, 5650
2Sa 7:19 hast spoken also of thy s. house 5650
1Ki 11:13 to thy son for David my s. sake, 5650
1Ki 11:34 days of his life for David my s. sake, 5650
2Ki 8:19 destroy Judah for David his s. sake, 5650
1Ch 17:17 hast also spoken of thy s. house 5650
1Ch 17:19 Lord, for thy s. sake, and according 5650
Isa 45:4 For Jacob my s. sake, and Israel 5650
Joh 18:10 ear. The s. name was Malchus. 1401

SERVANTS See also SERVANTS'; MAIDSERVANTS; MENSERVANTS; WOMENSERVANTS.

Ge 9:25 a servant of s. shall he be unto his 5650
Ge 14:14 he armed his trained s., born in his
Ge 14:15 he and his s., by night, and smote 5650
Ge 20:8 Abimelech...called all his s., and told 5650
Ge 21:25 Abimelech's s. had violently taken 5650
Ge 26:14 of herds, and great store of s.: 5657
Ge 26:15 which his father's s. had digged 5650
Ge 26:19 And Issac's s. digged in the valley, 5650
Ge 26:25 and there Isaac's s. digged a well. 5650
Ge 26:32 that Isaac's s. came, and told him 5650
Ge 27:37 brethren have I given to him for s.; 5650
Ge 32:16 delivered...into the hand of his s., 5650
Ge 32:16 said unto his s., Pass over before 5650
Ge 40:20 that he made a feast unto all his s. 5650
Ge 40:20 and of the chief baker among his s. 5650
Ge 41:10 Pharaoh was wroth with his s., and 5650
Ge 41:37 Pharaoh, and in the eyes of all his s. 5650
Ge 41:38 Pharaoh said unto his s., Can we 5650
Ge 42:10 but to buy food are thy s. come. 5650
Ge 42:11 we are true men, thy s. are no spies. 5650
Ge 42:13 Thy s. are twelve brethren, the sons 5650
Ge 44:7 God forbid that thy s. should do 5650
Ge 44:9 whomsoever of thy s. it be found, 5650
Ge 44:9 found out the iniquity of thy s.: 5650
Ge 44:9 behold, we are my lord's s., both 5650
Ge 44:19 My lord asked his s., saying, Have 5650
Ge 44:21 thou saidst unto thy s., Bring him 5650
Ge 44:23 And thou saidst unto thy s., Except 5650
Ge 44:31 and thy s. shall bring down the gray 5650
Ge 45:16 it pleased Pharaoh well, and his s. 5650
Ge 47:3 Thy s. are shepherds, both we, and 5650
Ge 47:4 thy s. have no pasture for their 5650
Ge 47:4 thy s. dwell in the land of Goshen. 5650
Ge 47:19 and we and our land will be s. unto 5650
Ge 47:25 lord, and we will be Pharaoh's s. 5650
Ge 50:2 commanded his s. the physicians 5650
Ge 50:7 him went up all the s. of Pharaoh, 5650
Ge 50:17 trespass of the s. of the God of thy 5650
Ge 50:18 and they said, Behold, we be thy s. 5650
Ex 5:15 dealest thou thus with thy s.? 5650
Ex 5:16 There is no straw given unto thy s., 5650
Ex 5:16 and, behold, thy s. are beaten; but 5650
Ex 5:21 Pharaoh, and in the eyes of his s., 5650
Ex 7:10 before Pharaoh, and before his s., 5650
Ex 7:20 Pharaoh, and in the sight of his s.; 5650
Ex 8:3 bed, and into the house of thy s., 5650
Ex 8:4 thy people, and upon all thy s. 5650
Ex 8:9 I intreat for thee, and for thy s., 5650
Ex 8:11 from thy houses, and from thy s., 5650
Ex 8:21 of flies upon thee, and upon thy s., 5650
Ex 8:29, 31 from Pharaoh, from his s., and 5650
Ex 9:14 upon thine heart, and upon thy s., 5650
Ex 9:20 feared...among the s. of Pharaoh 5650
Ex 9:20 made his s. and his cattle flee into 5650
Ex 9:21 left his s. and his cattle in the field. 5650
Ex 9:30 But as for thee and thy s., I know 5650
Ex 9:34 hardened his heart, he and his s. 5650
Ex 10:1 his heart, and the heart of his s., 5650
Ex 10:6 houses, and the houses of all thy s., 5650
Ex 10:7 And Pharaoh's s. said unto him, 5650
Ex 11:3 in the sight of Pharaoh's s., and in 5650
Ex 11:8 all these thy s. shall come down 5650
Ex 12:30 up in the night, he, and all his s., 5650
Ex 14:5 the heart of Pharaoh and of his s. 5650
Ex 32:13 Abraham, Isaac, and Israel, thy s., 5650
Le 25:42 For they are my s., which I brought 5650
Le 25:55 unto me the children of Israel are s.; 5650
Le 25:55 they are my s. whom I brought 5650
Nu 22:18 and said unto the s. of Balak, 5650
Nu 22:22 ass, and his two s. were with him. 5288
Nu 31:49 Thy s. have taken the sum of the 5650
Nu 32:4 for cattle, and thy s. have cattle: 5650
Nu 32:5 let this land be given unto thy s. 5650
Nu 32:25 s. will do as my lord commandeth 5650
Nu 32:27 But thy s. will pass over, every man 5650
Nu 32:31 As the Lord hath said unto thy s., 5650
De 9:27 Remember thy s., Abraham, Isaac, 5650
De 29:2 unto Pharaoh, and unto all his s., 5650
De 32:36 and repent himself for his s., when 5650
De 32:43 he will avenge the blood of his s., 5650
De 34:11 to Pharaoh, and to all his s., and to 5650
Jos 9:8 said unto Joshua, We are thy s. 5650
Jos 9:9 a very far country thy s. are come 5650
Jos 9:11 and say unto them, We are your s. 5650
Jos 9:24 Because it was certainly told thy s., 5650
Jos 10:6 Slack not thy hand from thy s.; 5650
Jg 3:24 When he was gone out, his s. came; 5650
Jg 6:27 Then Gideon took ten men of his s., 5650
Jg 19:19 the young man which is with thy s.: 5650
1Sa 4:9 ye be not s. unto the Hebrews, as 5647
1Sa 8:14 of them, and give them to his s. 5650
1Sa 8:15 and give to his officers, and to his s. 5650
1Sa 8:17 your sheep: and ye shall be his s. 5650
1Sa 9:3 Take now one of the s. with thee, 5650
1Sa 12:19 Pray for thy s. unto the Lord thy 5650
1Sa 16:15 And Saul's s. said unto him, Behold 5650
1Sa 16:16 Let our lord now command thy s., 5650
1Sa 16:17 And Saul said unto his s., Provide 5650
1Sa 16:18 Then answered one of the s., and 5288
1Sa 17:8 I a Philistine, and ye s. to Saul? 5650
1Sa 17:9 to kill me, then will we be your s. 5650
1Sa 17:9 kill him, then shall ye be our s., 5650
1Sa 18:5 and also in the sight of Saul's s. 5650
1Sa 18:22 And Saul commanded his s., saying, 5650
1Sa 18:22 in thee, and all his s. love thee: 5650
1Sa 18:23 And Saul's s. spake those words in 5650
1Sa 18:24 And the s. of Saul told him, saying, 5650
1Sa 18:26 And when his s. told David these 5650
1Sa 18:30 more wisely than all the s. of Saul; 5650
1Sa 19:1 Jonathan his son, and to all his s., 5650
1Sa 21:2 I have appointed my s. to such 5288
1Sa 21:7 man of the s. of Saul was there 5650
1Sa 21:11 the s. of Achish said unto him, Is 5650
1Sa 21:14 Then said Achish unto his s., Lo, ye 5650
1Sa 22:6 all his s. were standing about him;) 5650
1Sa 22:7 Saul said unto his s. that stood 5650
1Sa 22:9 which was set over the s. of Saul, 5650
1Sa 22:14 faithful among all thy s. as David, 5650
1Sa 22:17 But the s. of the king would not put 5650
1Sa 24:7 So David stayed his s. with these 582
1Sa 25:8 cometh to thine hand unto thy s., 5650
1Sa 25:10 Nabal answered David's s., and 5650
1Sa 25:10 be many s. now a days that break 5650
1Sa 25:19 she said unto her s., Go on before 5288
1Sa 25:40 when the s. of David were come to 5650
1Sa 25:41 wash the feet of the s. of my lord. 5650
1Sa 28:7 Then said Saul unto his s., Seek 5650
1Sa 28:7 his s. said to him, Behold, there is 5650
1Sa 28:23 his s., together with the woman, 5650
1Sa 28:25 it before Saul, and before his s.; 5650
1Sa 29:10 in the morning with thy master's s. 5650
2Sa 2:12 and the s. of Ish-bosheth the son of 5650
2Sa 2:13 the s. of David, went out, and met 5650
2Sa 2:15 Saul, and twelve of the s. of David. 5650
2Sa 2:17 men of Israel, before the s. of David 5650
2Sa 2:30 there lacked of David's s. nineteen 5650
2Sa 2:31 But the s. of David had smitten of 5650
2Sa 3:22 the s. of David and Joab came from 5650
2Sa 3:38 king said unto his s., Know ye not 5650
2Sa 6:20 the eyes of the handmaids of his s., 5650
2Sa 8:2 so the Moabites became David's s., 5650
2Sa 8:6 the Syrians became s. to David, 5650
2Sa 8:7 shields of gold that were on the s. 5650
2Sa 8:14 they of Edom became David's s. 5650
2Sa 9:10 thy sons, and thy s., shall till the 5650
2Sa 9:10 Ziba had fifteen sons and twenty s. 5650
2Sa 9:12 Ziba were s. unto Mephibosheth 5650
2Sa 10:2 comfort him by the hand of his s. 5650
2Sa 10:2 David's s. came into the land of the 5650
2Sa 10:3 David rather sent his s. unto thee, 5650
2Sa 10:4 Hanun took David's s., and shaved 5650
2Sa 10:19 the kings that were s. to Hadarezer 5650
2Sa 11:1 sent Joab, and his s. with him, and 5650
2Sa 11:9 house with all the s. of his lord, 5650

2Sa 11:11 my lord Joab, and the **s.** of my lord, ... 5650
2Sa 11:13 to lie on his bed with the **s.** of his...... 5650
2Sa 11:17 of the people of the **s.** of David; 5650
2Sa 11:24 shot from off the wall upon thy **s.**;...... 5650
2Sa 11:24 and some of the king's **s.** be dead, ... 5650
2Sa 12:18 **s.** of David feared to tell him that....... 5650
2Sa 12:19 David saw that his **s.** whispered,........ 5650
2Sa 12:19 David said unto his **s.**, Is the child...... 5650
2Sa 12:21 Then said his **s.** unto him, What......... 5650
2Sa 13:24 thee, and his **s.** go with thy servant.... 5650
2Sa 13:28 Absalom had commanded his **s.**,.......... 5288
2Sa 13:29 **s.** of Absalom did unto Amnon as 5288
2Sa 13:31 **s.** stood by with their clothes rent...... 5650
2Sa 13:36 also and all his **s.** wept very sore. 5650
2Sa 14:30 Therefore he said unto his **s.**, See,...... 5650
2Sa 14:30 Absalom's **s.** set the field on fire. 5650
2Sa 14:31 have thy **s.** set my field on fire?......... 5650
2Sa 15:14 David said unto all his **s.** that were..... 5650
2Sa 15:15 the king's **s.** said unto the king, ... 5650
2Sa 15:15 thy **s.** are ready to do whatsoever...... 5650
2Sa 15:18 And all his **s.** passed on beside him;.... 5650
2Sa 16:6 and at all the **s.** of King David: and..... 5650
2Sa 16:11 said to Abishai, and to all his **s.**, ... 5650
2Sa 17:20 Absalom's **s.** came to the woman to.... 5650
2Sa 18:7 were slain before the **s.** of David,........ 5650
2Sa 18:9 And Absalom met the **s.** of David........ 5650
2Sa 19:5 this day the face of all thy **s.**, ... 5650
2Sa 19:6 regardest neither princes nor **s.** 5650
2Sa 19:7 and speak comfortably unto thy **s.** 5650
2Sa 19:14 king, Return thou, and all thy **s.**......... 5650
2Sa 19:17 sons and his twenty **s.** with him; 5650
2Sa 20:6 take thou thy lord's **s.**, and pursue 5650
2Sa 21:15 went down, and his **s.** with him, ... 5650
2Sa 21:22 of David, and by the hand of his **s.**. 5650
2Sa 24:20 and his **s.** coming on toward him: 5650
1Ki 1:2 Wherefore his **s.** said unto him, Let.... 5650
1Ki 1:9 all the men of Judah the king's **s.** 5650
1Ki 1:33 Take with you the **s.** of your lord,...... 5650
1Ki 1:47 the king's **s.** came to bless our lord 5650
1Ki 2:39 **s.** of Shimei ran away unto Achish...... 5650
1Ki 2:39 saying, Behold, thy **s.** be in Gath. 5650
1Ki 2:40 to Gath to Achish to seek his **s.**:......... 5650
1Ki 2:40 went, and brought his **s.** from Gath. ... 5650
1Ki 3:15 and made a feast to all his **s.** 5650
1Ki 5:1 Hiram...sent his **s.** unto Solomon;........ 5650
1Ki 5:6 my **s.** shall be with thy **s.**: and unto.... 5650
1Ki 5:6 will I give hire for thy **s.** according..... 5650
1Ki 5:9 My **s.** shall bring them down from 5650
1Ki 8:23 covenant and mercy with thy **s.** 5650
1Ki 8:32 heaven, and do, and judge thy **s.**,........ 5650
1Ki 8:36 forgive the sin of thy **s.**, and of thy 5650
1Ki 9:22 they were men of war, and his **s.**,....... 5650
1Ki 9:27 And Hiram sent in the navy his **s.**, ... 5650
1Ki 9:27 of the sea, with the **s.** of Solomon. 5650
1Ki 10:5 his table, and the sitting of his **s.**, ... 5650
1Ki 10:8 happy are these thy **s.**, which stand.... 5650
1Ki 10:13 to her own country, she and her **s.**...... 5650
1Ki 11:17 certain Edomites of his father's **s.**...... 5650
1Ki 12:7 then they will be thy **s.** for ever. 5650
1Ki 15:18 them into the hand of his **s.**: and........ 5650
1Ki 20:6 Yet I will send my **s.** unto thee to...... 5650
1Ki 20:6 house, and the houses of thy **s.**; 5650
1Ki 20:12 he said unto his **s.**, Set yourselves 5650
1Ki 20:23 the **s.** of the king of Syria said unto.... 5650
1Ki 20:31 his **s.** said unto him, Behold now,....... 5650
1Ki 22:3 the king of Israel said unto his **s.**, ... 5650
1Ki 22:49 Let my **s.** go with thy **s.** in the.......... 5650
2Ki 1:13 and the life of these fifty thy **s.**, be...... 5650
2Ki 2:16 be with thy **s.** fifty strong men; 5650
2Ki 3:11 of the king of Israel's **s.** answered...... 5650
2Ki 5:13 his **s.** came near, and spake unto 5650
2Ki 5:23 and laid them upon two of his **s.**; 5288
2Ki 6:3 I pray thee, and go with thy **s.**, ... 5650
2Ki 6:8 took counsel with his **s.**, saying,......... 5650
2Ki 6:11 and he called his **s.**, and said unto 5650
2Ki 6:12 one of his **s.** said, None, my lord, ... 5650
2Ki 7:12 in the night, and said unto his **s.**, ... 5650
2Ki 7:13 one of his **s.** answered and said, ... 5650
2Ki 9:7 I may avenge the blood of my **s.**......... 5650
2Ki 9:7 the blood of all the **s.** of the Lord....... 5650
2Ki 9:11 came forth to the **s.** of his lord: and..... 5650
2Ki 9:28 And his **s.** carried him in a chariot...... 5650
2Ki 10:5 sent to Jehu, saying, We are thy **s.**, ... 5650
2Ki 10:19 Baal, all his **s.**, and all his priests; 5647
2Ki 10:23 with you none of the **s.** of the Lord, ... 5650
2Ki 12:20 his **s.** arose, and made a conspiracy, ... 5650
2Ki 12:21 his **s.**, smote him, and he died;.......... 5650
2Ki 14:5 slew his **s.** which had slain the king 5650
2Ki 17:13 I sent to you by my **s.** the prophets. .. 5650
2Ki 17:23 had said by all his **s.** the prophets. 5650
2Ki 18:24 of the least of my master's **s.**, and 5650
2Ki 18:26 Speak,...to thy **s.** in the Syrian 5650
2Ki 19:5 So the **s.** of king Hezekiah came to..... 5650
2Ki 19:6 the **s.** of the king of Assyria have....... 5288
2Ki 21:10 Lord spake by his **s.** the prophets, ... 5650
2Ki 21:23 the **s.** of Amon conspired against........ 5650
2Ki 22:9 Thy **s.** have gathered the money........ 5650
2Ki 23:30 his **s.** carried him in a chariot dead 5650
2Ki 24:2 he spake by his **s.** the prophets. 5650
2Ki 24:10 the **s.** of Nebuchadnezzar king of........ 5650
2Ki 24:11 the city, and his **s.** did besiege it........ 5650
2Ki 24:12 he, and his mother, and his **s.**, and...... 5650
2Ki 25:24 Fear not to be the **s.** of the Chaldees:. 5650
1Ch 18:2 the Moabites became David's **s.**, ... 5650
1Ch 18:6 and the Syrians became David's **s.**,..... 5650
1Ch 18:7 shields of gold that were on the **s.**...... 5650
1Ch 18:13 all the Edomites became David's **s.**..... 5650
1Ch 19:2 the **s.** of David came into the land 5650
1Ch 19:3 are not his **s.** come unto thee for to ... 5650
1Ch 19:4 Wherefore Hanun took David's **s.**, ... 5650
1Ch 19:19 the **s.** of Hadarezer saw that they 5650
1Ch 19:19 with David, and became his **s.**: 5647
1Ch 20:8 David, and by the hand of his **s.** 5650
1Ch 21:3 king, are they not all my lord's **s.**? 5650
2Ch 2:8 that thy **s.** can skill to cut timber 5650
2Ch 2:8 behold, my **s.** shall be with thy **s.**,...... 5650
2Ch 2:10 I will give to thy **s.**, the hewers......... 5650
2Ch 2:15 spoken of, let him send unto his **s.**: 5650
2Ch 6:14 and shewest mercy unto thy **s.**, that... 5650
2Ch 6:23 and judge thy **s.**, by requiting the....... 5650
2Ch 6:27 forgive the sin of thy **s.**, and of thy 5650
2Ch 8:9 Solomon make no **s.** for his work; 5650
2Ch 8:18 sent him by the hands of his **s.**.......... 5650
2Ch 8:18 **s.** that had knowledge of the sea;....... 5650
2Ch 8:18 they went with the **s.** of Solomon 5650
2Ch 9:4 his table, and the sitting of his **s.**, ... 5650
2Ch 9:7 happy are these thy **s.**, which stand.... 5650
2Ch 9:10 And the **s.** also of Huram, and the...... 5650
2Ch 9:10 **s.** of Solomon, which brought gold...... 5650
2Ch 9:12 to her own land, she and her **s.**. 5650
2Ch 9:21 to Tarshish with the **s.** of Huram: 5650
2Ch 10:7 to them, they will be thy **s.** for ever... 5650
2Ch 12:8 Nevertheless they shall be his **s.**;........ 5650
2Ch 24:25 his own **s.** conspired against him 5650
2Ch 25:3 slew his **s.** that had killed the king...... 5650
2Ch 32:9 of Assyria send his **s.** to Jerusalem, ... 5650
2Ch 32:16 his **s.** spake yet more against the 5650
2Ch 33:24 And his **s.** conspired against him, ... 5650
2Ch 34:16 that was committed to thy **s.**, they..... 5650
2Ch 35:23 king said to his **s.**, Have me away; 5650
2Ch 35:24 His **s.** therefore took him out of the.... 5650
2Ch 36:20 where they were **s.** to him and his 5650
Ezr 2:55 The children of Solomon's **s.**: the 5650
Ezr 2:58 and the children of Solomon's **s.**, ... 5650
Ezr 2:65 Beside their **s.** and their maids, of....... 5650
Ezr 4:11 Thy **s.** the men on this side the 5649
Ezr 5:11 We are the **s.** of the God of heaven.... 5649
Ezr 9:11 commanded by thy **s.** the prohets,...... 5650
Ne 1:6 for the children of Israel thy **s.**, and.... 5650
Ne 1:10 these are thy **s.** and thy people,......... 5650
Ne 1:11 to the prayer of thy **s.**, who desire 5650
Ne 2:20 we his **s.** will arise and build: but 5650
Ne 4:16 half of my **s.** wrought in the work, ... 5288
Ne 4:23 I, nor my brethren, nor my **s.**, nor...... 5288
Ne 5:5 sons and our daughters to be **s.**, ... 5650
Ne 5:10 my **s.**, might exact of them money 5288
Ne 5:15 their **s.** bare rule over the people: 5288
Ne 5:16 my **s.** were gathered thither unto....... 5288
Ne 7:57 The children of Solomon's **s.**: the 5650
Ne 7:60 and the children of Solomon's **s.**, ... 5650
Ne 9:10 upon Pharaoh, and on all his **s.**, and.... 5650
Ne 9:36 Behold, we are **s.** this day, and for..... 5650
Ne 9:36 good thereof, behold, we are **s.** in it: .. 5650
Ne 11:3 and the children of Solomon's **s.**......... 5650
Ne 13:19 some of my **s.** set I at the gates, ... 5288
Es 1:3 unto all his princes and his **s.**;........... 5650
Es 2:2 Then said the king's **s.** that............... 5288
Es 2:18 unto all his princes and his **s.**,............ 5650
Es 3:2 all the king's **s.**, that were in the........ 5650
Es 3:3 Then the king's **s.**, which were in....... 5650
Es 4:11 All the king's **s.**, and the people of 5650
Es 5:11 above the princes and **s.** of the king.... 5650
Es 6:3 Then said the king's **s.** that............... 5288
Es 6:5 the king's **s.** said unto him, Behold, ... 5288
Job 1:15 have slain the **s.** with the edge of the.. 5288
Job 1:16 burned up the sheep, and the **s.**, and.. 5288
Job 1:17 and slain the **s.** with the edge of the... 5288
Job 4:18 Behold, he put no trust in his **s.**; 5650
Ps 34:22 Lord redeemeth the soul of his **s.**:...... 5650
Ps 69:36 The seed also of his **s.** shall inherit..... 5650
Ps 79:2 The dead bodies of thy **s.** have they ... 5650
Ps 79:10 the revenging of the blood of thy **s.** 5650
Ps 89:50 Remember,...the reproach of thy **s.**; ... 5650
Ps 90:13 let it repent thee concerning thy **s.** 5650
Ps 90:16 Let thy work appear unto thy **s.**, ... 5650
Ps 102:14 thy **s.** take pleasure in her stones,...... 5650
Ps 102:28 children of thy **s.** shall continue, ... 5650
Ps 105:25 people, to deal subtilly with his **s.**....... 5650
Ps 113:1 Praise, O ye **s.** of the Lord, praise 5650
Ps 119:91 thine ordinances: for all are thy **s.**. 5650
Ps 123:2 as the eyes of **s.** look unto the hand ... 5650
Ps 134:1 ye the Lord, all ye **s.** of the Lord,...... 5650
Ps 135:1 praise him, O ye **s.** of the Lord. 5650
Ps 135:9 upon Pharaoh, and upon all his **s.**. 5650
Ps 135:14 repent himself concerning his **s.**. 5650
Pr 29:12 to lies, all his **s.** are wicked............... 8334
Ec 2:7 I got me **s.** and maidens, and had....... 5650
Ec 2:7 and had **s.** born in my house; also............
Ec 10:7 I have seen **s.** upon horses, and......... 5650
Ec 10:7 and princes walking as **s.** upon the...... 5650
Isa 14:2 of the Lord for **s.** and handmaids:....... 5650
Isa 36:9 of the least of my master's **s.**, ... 5650
Isa 36:11 Speak,...unto thy **s.** in the Syrian 5650
Isa 37:5 **s.** of king Hezekiah came to Isaiah...... 5650
Isa 37:6 the **s.** of the king of Assyria have....... 5288
Isa 37:24 By thy **s.**...reproached the Lord,......... 5650
Isa 54:17 the heritage of the **s.** of the Lord,....... 5650
Isa 56:6 the name of the Lord, to be his **s.**,...... 5650
Isa 65:9 it, and my **s.** shall dwell there. 5650
Isa 65:13 **s.** shall eat, but ye shall be hungry: 5650
Isa 65:13 my **s.** shall drink, but ye shall be....... 5650
Isa 65:13 my **s.** shall rejoice, but ye shall be...... 5650
Isa 65:14 my **s.** shall sing for joy of heart, but ... 5650
Isa 65:15 and call his **s.** by another name: 5650
Isa 66:14 Lord shall be known toward his **s.**, ... 5650
Jer 7:25 even sent unto you all my **s.** the........ 5650
Jer 21:7 Zedekiah king of Judah, and his **s.**,....... 5650
Jer 22:2 throne of David, thou, and thy **s.**, ... 5650
Jer 22:4 and on horses, he, and his **s.**, and...... 5650
Jer 25:4 hath sent unto you all his **s.** the......... 5650
Jer 25:19 king of Egypt, and his **s.**, and his 5650
Jer 26:5 hearken to the words of my **s.** the 5650
Jer 29:19 unto them by my **s.** the prophets, ... 5650
Jer 34:11 caused the **s.** and the handmaids, ... 5650
Jer 34:11 them into subjection for **s.** and for...... 5650
Jer 34:16 unto you for **s.** and for handmaids....... 5650
Jer 35:15 I have sent also unto you all my **s.**..... 5650
Jer 36:24 nor any of his **s.** that heard all these... 5650
Jer 36:31 punish him and his seed and his **s.**....... 5650
Jer 37:2 But neither he, nor his **s.**, nor the....... 5650
Jer 37:18 against thee, or against thy **s.**, or....... 5650
Jer 44:4 Howbeit I sent unto you all my **s.** 5650
Jer 46:26 and into the hands of his **s.**: and 5650
La 5:8 **S.** have ruled over us: there is none... 5650
Eze 38:17 I have spoken in old time by my **s.**...... 5650
Eze 46:17 of his inheritance to one of his **s.**, ... 5650
Da 1:12 Prove thy **s.**, I beseech thee, ten....... 5650
Da 1:13 and as thou seest, deal with thy **s.**. 5650
Da 2:4 tell thy **s.** the dream, and we will....... 5649
Da 2:7 Let the king tell his **s.** the dream, ... 5649
Da 3:26 ye **s.** of the most high God, come 5649
Da 3:28 delivered his **s.** that trusted in him, ... 5649
Da 9:6 have we hearkened unto thy **s.** the..... 5650
Da 9:10 which he set before us by his **s.** the ... 5650
Joe 2:29 And also upon the **s.** and upon the...... 5650
Am 3:7 revealeth his secret unto his **s.** the...... 5650
Mic 6:4 redeemed thee out of...house of **s.**; 5650
Zec 1:6 I commanded my **s.** the prophets, ... 5650
Zec 2:9 they shall be a spoil to their **s.**: 5647
Mt 13:27 **the s. of the householder came and** *1401*
Mt 13:28 **s. said unto him, Wilt thou then** ... *1401*
Mt 14:2 And said unto his **s.**, This is John *3816*
Mt 18:23 **would take account of his s.** *1401*
Mt 21:34 **he sent his s. to the husbandmen,** . *1401*
Mt 21:35 **husbandmen took his s., and beat** .. *1401*
Mt 21:36 **sent other s. more than the first:** .. *1401*
Mt 22:3 **sent forth his s. to call them that**.. *1401*
Mt 22:4 **he sent forth other s., saying, Tell** . *1401*

Mt 22:6 **And the remnant took his s., and..** *1401*
Mt 22:8 **saith he to his s., The wedding is ..** *1401*
Mt 22:10 **s. went out into the highways, and.** *1401*
Mt 22:13 **said the king to the s., Bind him...** *1249*
Mt 25:14 **called his own s., and delivered.....** *1401*
Mt 25:19 **time the lord of those s. cometh,...** *1401*
Mt 26:58 and sat with the s., to see the end..... *5257*
Mk 1:20 in the ship with the hired s., ... *3411*
Mk 13:34 **and gave authority to his s., and to** *1401*
Mk 14:43 he sat with the s., and warmed.......... *5257*
Mk 14:65 s. did strike him with the palms of........ *5257*
Lu 12:37 **Blessed are those s., whom the .....** *1401*
Lu 12:38 **find them so, blessed are those s...** *1401*
Lu 15:17 **many hired s. of my father's have ..** *3407*
Lu 15:19 **son: make measure of thy hired s..** *3407*
Lu 15:22 **But the father said to his s., Bring** *1401*
Lu 15:26 **he called one of the s., and asked..** *3816*
Lu 17:10 **say, We are unprofitable s.: we.....** *1401*
Lu 19:13 **he called his ten s., and delivered..** *1401*
Lu 19:15 **he commanded these s. to be called** *1401*
Joh 2:5 His mother saith unto the s., ... *1249*
Joh 2:9 the s. which drew the water knew:)..... *1249*
Joh 4:51 going down, his s. met him, and *1401*
Joh 15:15 **Henceforth I call you not s.;.........** *1401*
Joh 18:18 the s. and officers stood there, who.... *1401*
Joh 18:26 One of the s. of the high priest,......... *1401*
Joh 18:36 **this world, then would my s. fight,** *5257*
Ac 2:18 on my s. and on my handmaidens........ *1401*
Ac 4:29 and grant unto thy s., that with all....... *1401*
Ac 10:7 he called two of his household s., and ....
Ac 16:17 are the s. of the most high God,......... *1401*
Ro 6:16 whom ye yield yourselves s. to obey,.. *1401*
Ro 6:16 his s. ye are to whom ye obey; *1401*
Ro 6:17 thanked that ye were the s. of sin, ... *1401*
Ro 6:18 ye became the s. of righteousness...... *1402*
Ro 6:19 your members s. to uncleanness *1401*
Ro 6:19 your members s. to righteousness...... *1401*
Ro 6:20 when ye were the s. of sin, ye were .. *1401*
Ro 6:22 and become s. to God, ye have your... *1402*
1Co 7:23 a price; be not ye the s. of men. *1401*
2Co 4:5 ourselves your s. for Jesus' sake......... *1401*
Eph 6:5 S., be obedient to them that are......... *1401*
Eph 6:6 but as the s. of Christ, doing the *1401*
Php 1:1 s. of Jesus Christ, to all the saints...... *1401*
Col 3:22 S., obey in all things your masters *1401*
Col 4:1 give unto your s. that which is just..... *1401*
1Ti 6:1 as many s. as are under the yoke....... *1401*
Tit 2:9 Exhort s. to be obedient unto their...... *1401*
1Pe 2:16 maliciousness, but as the s. of God..... *1401*
1Pe 2:18 S., be subject to your masters........... *3610*
2Pe 2:19 they...are the s. of corruption;........... *1401*
Re 1:1 to shew unto his s. things which *1401*
Re 2:20 **to teach and to seduce my s. to......** *1401*
Re 7:3 we have sealed the s. of our God in ... *1401*
Re 10:7 hath declared to his s. the prophets. ... *1401*
Re 11:18 reward unto thy s. the prophets,......... *1401*
Re 19:2 hath avenged the blood of his s. at *1401*
Re 19:5 Praise our God, all ye his s., and ye... *1401*
Re 22:3 in it; and his s. shall serve him: *1401*
Re 22:6 sent his angel to shew unto his s. *1401*

SERVANTS'
Ge 46:34 s. trade hath been about cattle........... 5650
Ex 8:24 of Pharaoh, and into his s. houses, ... 5650
Isa 63:17 Return, for thy s. sake, the tribes of .. 5650
Isa 65:8 so will I do for my s. sake, that I....... 5650

SERVE See also OBSERVE; PRESERVE; RESERVE; SERVED; SERVEST; SERVETH; SERVING.
Ge 15:13 is not theirs, and shall s. them;.......... 5647
Ge 15:14 that nation, whom they shall s. also, ... 5647
Ge 25:23 and the elder shall s. the younger....... 5647
Ge 27:29 Let people s. thee, and nations bow.... 5647
Ge 27:40 thou live, and shalt s. thy brother;...... 5647
Ge 29:15 thou therefore s. me for nought?......... 5647
Ge 29:18 I will s. thee seven years for Rachel ... 5647
Ge 29:25 did not I s. with thee for Rachel? 5647
Ge 29:27 s. with me yet seven other years........ 5647
Ex 1:13 children of Israel to s. with rigour: 5647
Ex 1:14 they made them s., was with rigour..... 5647
Ex 3:12 ye shall s. God upon this mountain. 5647
Ex 4:23 Let my son go, that he may s. me: 5647
Ex 7:16 they may s. me in the wilderness;....... 5647
Ex 8:1,20 people go, that they may s. me. 5647
Ex 9:1 my people go, that they may s. me. 5647
Ex 9:13 my people go, that they may s. me. 5647
Ex 10:3 my people go, that they may s. me. 5647
Ex 10:7 they may s. the Lord their God: 5647
Ex 10:8 them, Go, s. the Lord your God: 5647
Ex 10:11 ye that are men, and s. the Lord; 5647
Ex 10:24 Moses, and said, Go ye, s. the Lord;.. 5647
Ex 10:26 we take to s. the Lord our God;.......... 5647
Ex 10:26 not with what we must s. the Lord,.... 5647
Ex 12:31 and go, s. the Lord, as ye have said... 5647
Ex 14:12 that we may s. the Egyptians?........... 5647
Ex 14:12 better for us to s. the Egyptians, ... 5647
Ex 20:5 down thyself to them, nor s. them:...... 5647
Ex 21:2 servant, six years he shall s.: and 5647
Ex 21:6 aul; and he shall s. him for ever.......... 5647
Ex 23:24 down to their gods, nor s. them,......... 5647
Ex 23:25 And ye shall s. the Lord your God, ... 5647
Ex 23:33 if thou s. their gods, it will surely........ 5647
Le 25:39 compel him to s. as a bondservant:..... 5656
Le 25:40 and shall s. thee unto the year of....... 5647
Nu 4:24 families of the Gershonites, to s.,........ 5647
Nu 4:26 is made for them: so shall they s.. 5647
Nu 8:25 thereof, and shall s. no more:............ 5647
Nu 18:7 and within the vail; and ye shall s.:..... 5647
Nu 18:21 for their service which they s., even... 5647
De 4:19 to worship them, and s. them, for....... 5647
De 4:28 there ye shall s. gods, the work of..... 5647
De 5:9 thyself unto them, nor s. them: 5647
De 6:13 fear the Lord thy God, and s. him,...... 5647
De 7:4 me, that they may s. other gods: 5647
De 7:16 neither shalt thou s. their gods; 5647
De 8:19 walk after other gods, and s. them, ... 5647
De 10:12 to s. the Lord thy God with all thy..... 5647
De 10:20 him shalt thou s., and to him shalt...... 5647
De 11:13 and to s. him with all your heart 5647
De 11:16 ye turn aside, and s. other gods,......... 5647
De 12:30 How did these nations s. their gods?... 5647
De 13:2 hast not known, and let us s. them;.... 5647
De 13:4 and ye shall s. him, and cleave unto.... 5647
De 13:6, 13 Let us go and s. other gods,......... 5647
De 15:12 unto thee, and s. thee six years;......... 5647
De 20:11 unto thee, and they shall s. thee......... 5647
De 28:14 to go after other gods to s. them. 5647
De 28:36 and there shalt thou s. other gods,...... 5647
De 28:48 shalt thou s. thine enemies which....... 5647
De 28:64 and there thou shalt s. other gods,..... 5647
De 29:18 and s. the gods of these nations;......... 5647
De 30:17 worship other gods, and s. them;........ 5647
De 31:20 turn unto other gods, and s. them, ... 5647
Jos 16:10 unto this day, and s. under tribute...... 5647
Jos 22:5 and to s. him with all your heart 5647
Jos 23:7 neither s. them, nor bow yourselves... 5647
Jos 24:14 and s. him in sincerity and in truth: 5647
Jos 24:14 and in Egypt; and s. ye the Lord. 5647
Jos 24:15 it seem evil unto you to s. the Lord, .. 5647
Jos 24:15 choose you this day whom ye will s.; .. 5647
Jos 24:15 and my house, we will s. the Lord. 5647
Jos 24:16 forsake the Lord, to s. other gods;....... 5647
Jos 24:18 therefore will we also s. the Lord;...... 5647
Jos 24:19 Ye cannot s. the Lord: for he is an..... 5647
Jos 24:20 the Lord, and s. strange gods, then.... 5647
Jos 24:21 Nay; but we will s. the Lord. 5647
Jos 24:22 have chosen you the Lord, to s. him... 5647
Jos 24:24 The Lord our God will we s., and 5647
Jg 2:19 in following other gods to s. them, ... 5647
Jg 9:28 is Shechem, that we should s. him? 5647
Jg 9:28 s. the men of Hamor the father of 5647
Jg 9:28 Shechem: for why should we s. him? .. 5647
Jg 9:38 Abimelech, that we should s. him?...... 5647
1Sa 7:3 unto the Lord, and s. him only: 5647
1Sa 10:7 that thou do as occasion s. thee;........ 5647
1Sa 11:1 covenant with us,...we will s. thee. 5647
1Sa 12:10 of our enemies, and we will s. thee. ... 5647
1Sa 12:14 If ye will fear the Lord, and s. him, ... 5647
1Sa 12:20 but s. the Lord with all your heart;..... 5647
1Sa 12:24 s. him in truth with all your heart:...... 5647
1Sa 17:9 shall ye be our servants, and s. us. 5647
1Sa 26:19 the Lord, saying, Go, s. other gods.... 5647
2Sa 15:8 Jerusalem, then I will s. the Lord....... 5647
2Sa 16:19 And again, whom should I s.? 5647
2Sa 16:19 should I not s. in the presence of....... 5647
2Sa 22:44 which I knew not shall s. me.............. 5647
1Ki 9:6 go and s. other gods, and worship...... 5647
1Ki 12:4 upon us, lighter,...we will s. thee......... 5647
1Ki 12:7 and wilt s. them, and answer them. 5647
2Ki 10:18 little; but Jehu shall s. him much. 5647
2Ki 17:35 nor s. them, nor sacrifice to them: 5647
2Ki 25:24 land, and s. the king of Babylon; 5647
1Ch 28:9 s. him with a perfect heart and with.... 5647
2Ch 7:19 and shall go and s. other gods, and..... 5647
2Ch 10:4 he put upon us, and we will s. thee. ... 5647
2Ch 29:11 to stand before him, to s. him, ... 8334
2Ch 30:8 and s. the Lord your God, that the..... 5647
2Ch 33:16 commanded Judah to s. the Lord......... 5647
2Ch 34:33 all that were present in Israel to s.,.... 5647
2Ch 34:33 even to s. the Lord their God. And 5647
2Ch 35:3 s. now the Lord your God, and his..... 5647
Job 21:15 Almighty, that we should s. him?........ 5647
Job 36:11 If they obey and s. him, they shall...... 5647
Job 39:9 the unicorn be willing to s. thee, ... 5647
Ps 2:11 S. the Lord with fear, and rejoice........ 5647
Ps 18:43 whom I have not known shall s. me. ... 5647
Ps 22:30 A seed shall s. him; it shall be........... 5647
Ps 72:11 before him: all nations shall s. him. 5647
Ps 97:7 be all they that s. graven images,....... 5647
Ps 100:2 S. the Lord with gladness: come......... 5647
Ps 101:6 in a perfect way, he shall s. me. 8334
Ps 102:22 and the kingdoms, to s. the Lord. 5647
Isa 14:3 wherein thou wast made to s.,........... 5647
Isa 19:23 and the Egyptians shall s. with the 5647
Isa 43:23 caused thee to s. with an offering,...... 5647
Isa 43:24 hast made me to s. with thy sins, ... 5647
Isa 56:6 themselves to the Lord, to s. him, ... 8334
Isa 60:12 that will not s. thee shall perish; 5647
Jer 5:19 so shall ye s. strangers in a land........ 5647
Jer 11:10 went after other gods to s. them:........ 5647
Jer 13:10 walk after other gods, to s. them, ... 5647
Jer 16:13 ye s. other gods day and night;.......... 5647
Jer 17:4 will cause thee to s. thine enemies 5647
Jer 25:6 go not after other gods to s. them,..... 5647
Jer 25:11 nations shall s. the king of Babylon 5647
Jer 25:14 kings shall s. themselves of them 5647
Jer 27:6 have I given him also to s. him. 5647
Jer 27:7 And all nations shall s. him, and......... 5647
Jer 27:7 kings shall s. themselves of him. 5647
Jer 27:8 not s. the same Nebuchadnezzar 5647
Jer 27:9 Ye shall not s. the king of Babylon: 5647
Jer 27:11 of the king of Babylon, and s. him, ... 5647
Jer 27:12 and s. him and his people, and live. 5647
Jer 27:13 that will not s. the king of Babylon?.... 5647
Jer 27:14 Ye shall not s. the king of Babylon: 5647
Jer 27:17 s. the king of Babylon, and live:......... 5647
Jer 28:14 that they may s. Nebuchadnezzar 5647
Jer 28:14 and they shall s. him: and I have........ 5647
Jer 30:8 shall no more s. themselves of him:.... 5647
Jer 30:9 they shall s. the Lord their God,......... 5647
Jer 34:9 none should s. himself of them, to...... 5647
Jer 34:10 none should s. themselves of them 5647
Jer 35:15 go not after other gods to s. them,..... 5647
Jer 40:9 Fear not to s. the Chaldeans: dwell 5647
Jer 40:9 land, and s. the king of Babylon, ... 5647
Jer 40:10 s. the Chaldeans, which will 5975,6440
Jer 44:3 to s. other gods, whom they knew 5647
Eze 20:32 countries, to s. wood and stone. 8334
Eze 20:39 Go ye, s. ye every one his idols, ... 5647
Eze 20:40 all of them in the land, s. me:........... 5647
Eze 29:18 caused his army to s. a great service.. 5647
Eze 48:18 for food unto them that s. the city...... 5647
Eze 48:19 And they that s. the city shall s......... 5647
Eze 48:19 s. it out of all the tribes of Israel. 5647
Da 3:12 they s. not thy gods, nor worship....... 6399
Da 3:14 do not ye s. my gods, nor worship..... 6399
Da 3:17 God whom we s. is able to deliver 6399
Da 3:18 we will not s. thy gods, nor worship... 6399
Da 3:28 might not s. nor worship any god, ... 6399
Da 7:14 and languages, should s. him: 6399
Da 7:27 dominions shall s. and obey him. 6399
Zep 3:9 Lord, to s. him with one consent. 5647
Mal 3:14 Ye have said, It is vain to s. God: 5647
Mt 4:10 **God, and him only shalt thou s.....** *3000*
Mt 6:24 **No man can s. two masters: for ....** *1398*
Mt 6:24 **Ye cannot s. God and mammon.....** *1398*
Lu 1:74 might s. him without fear,................... *3000*
Lu 4:8 **God, and him only shalt thou s. ....** *3000*
Lu 10:40 my sister hath left me to s. alone? *1247*
Lu 12:37 **and will come forth and s. them....** *1247*
Lu 15:29 **Lo, these many years do I s. thee,..** *1398*
Lu 16:13 **No servant can s. two masters: for** *1398*
Lu 16:13 **Ye cannot s. God and mammon.....** *1398*
Lu 17:8 **sup, and gird thyself, and s. me....** *1247*
Lu 22:26 **he that is chief, as he that doth s..** *1247*
Joh 12:26 **If any man s. me, let him follow...** *1247*
Joh 12:26 **if any man s. me, him will my......** *1247*
Ac 6:2 leave the word of God, and s. tables... *1247*
Ac 7:7 come forth, and s. me in this place..... *3000*
Ac 27:23 of God, whose I am, and whom I s.,.... *3000*
Ro 1:9 whom I s. with my spirit in the.......... *3000*

Ro 6:6 hence forth we should not s. sin. *1398*
Ro 7:6 we should s. in newness of spirit,........ *1398*
Ro 7:25 mind I myself s. the law of God;........ *1398*
Ro 9:12 her, The elder shall s. the younger..... *1398*
Ro 16:18 such s. not our Lord Jesus Christ,....... *1398*
Ga 5:13 flesh, but by love s. one another........ *1398*
Col 3:24 for ye s. the Lord Christ.................. *1398*
1Th 1:9 idols to s. the living and true God; *1398*
2Ti 1:3 whom I s. from my forefathers *3000*
Heb 8:5 Who s. unto the example and *3000*
Heb 9:14 dead works to s. the living God? *3000*
Heb 12:28 we may s. God acceptably with........... *3000*
Heb 13:10 right to eat which s. the tabernacle..... *3000*
Re 7:15 s. him day and night in his temple: *3000*
Re 22:3 it; and his servants shall s. him:......... *3000*

SERVED See also OBSERVED; PRESERVED; RE- SERVED; SER- VEDST.

Ge 14:4 years they s. Chedorlaomer, and........ 5647
Ge 29:20 Jacob s. seven years for Rachel; 5647
Ge 29:30 s. with him yet seven other years. 5647
Ge 30:26 children, for whom I have s. thee,...... 5647
Ge 30:29 Thou knowest how I have s. thee, ... 5647
Ge 31:6 all my power have I s. your father...... 5647
Ge 31:41 I s. thee fourteen years for thy two.... 5647
Ge 39:4 grace in his sight, and he s. him: 8334
Ge 40:4 Joseph with them, and he s. them: 8334
De 12:2 ye shall possess s. their gods, ... 5647
De 17:3 And hath gone and s. other gods,....... 5647
De 29:26 For they went and s. other gods,....... 5647
Jos 23:16 and have gone and s. other gods,....... 5647
Jos 24:2 of Nachor: and they s. other gods. 5647
Jos 24:14, 15 the gods which your fathers s....... 5647
Jos 24:31 Israel s. the Lord all the days of........ 5647
Jg 2:7 people s. the Lord all the days of....... 5647
Jg 2:11 sight of the Lord, and s. Baalim:........ 5647
Jg 2:13 Lord, and s. Baal and Ashtaroth......... 5647
Jg 3:6 to their sons, and s. their gods........... 5647
Jg 3:7 God, and s. Baalim and the groves. 5647
Jg 3:8 Israel s. Cushan-rishathaim eight 5647
Jg 3:14 Israel s. Eglon the king of Moab 5647
Jg 8:1 him, Why hast thou s. us thus,.......... 6213
Jg 10:6 and s. Baalim, and Ashtaroth, and 5647
Jg 10:6 forsook the Lord, and s. not him........ 5647
Jg 10:10 forsaken our God, and...s. Baalim....... 5647
Jg 10:13 forsaken me, and s. other gods:........ 5647
Jg 10:16 from among them, and s. the Lord: 5647
1Sa 7:4 and Ashtaroth, and s. the Lord only.... 5647
1Sa 8:8 forsaken me, and s. other gods,......... 5647
1Sa 12:10 and have s. Baalim and Ashtaroth:...... 5647
2Sa 10:19 made peace with Israel, and s. them.. 5647
2Sa 16:19 as I have s. in thy father's presence, .. 5647
1Ki 4:21 s. Solomon all the days of his life. 5647
1Ki 9:9 have worshipped them, and s. them:... 5647
1Ki 16:31 went and s. Baal, and worshipped....... 5647
1Ki 22:53 For he s. Baal, and worshipped him,... 5647
2Ki 10:18 unto them, Ahab s. Baal a little;......... 5647
2Ki 17:12 For they s. idols, whereof the Lord.... 5647
2Ki 17:16 all the host of heaven, and s. Baal...... 5647
2Ki 17:33 the Lord, and s. their own gods,........ 5647
2Ki 17:41 Lord, and s. their graven images,....... 5647
2Ki 18:7 the king of Assyria, and s. him not...... 5647
2Ki 21:3 all the host of heaven, and s. them..... 5647
2Ki 21:21 and s. the idols that his father s.,........ 5647
1Ch 19:5 how the men were s. And he sent...... 5921
1Ch 27:1 and their officers that s. the king........ 8334
2Ch 7:22 worshipped them, and s. them: 5647
2Ch 24:18 fathers, and s. groves and idols:......... 5647
2Ch 33:3 all the host of heaven, and s. them..... 5647
2Ch 33:22 his father had made, and s. them; 5647
Ne 9:35 have not s. thee in their kingdom, ... 5647
Es 1:10 s. in the presence of Ahasuerus.......... 8334
Ps 106:36 And they s. their idols: which........... 5647
Ps 137:8 rewardeth thee as thou hast s. us. 1580
Ec 5:9 the king himself is s. by the field........ 5647
Jer 5:19 and s. strange gods in your land, so.... 5647
Jer 8:2 have loved, and whom they have s.,... 5647
Jer 16:11 after other gods, and have s. them,.... 5647
Jer 22:9 worshipped other gods, and s. them.... 5647
Jer 34:14 and when he hath s. thee six years,..... 5647
Jer 52:12 which s. the king of Babylon, ... 5975,6440
Eze 29:18 service that he had s. against it: 5647
Eze 29:20 labour wherewith he s. against it,....... 5647
Eze 34:27 of those that s. themselves of them.... 5647
Ho 12:12 Israel s. for a wife, and for a wife 5647
Lu 2:37 s. God with fastings and prayers *3000*
Joh 12:2 made him a supper; and Martha s....... *1247*
Ac 13:36 after he had s. his own generation...... *5256*
Ro 1:25 and s. the creature more than the *3000*
Php 2:22 he hath s. with me in the gospel........ *1398*

SERVEDST

De 28:47 s. not the Lord...with joyfulness,........ 5647

SERVEST See also PRESERVEST.

Da 6:16 Thy God whom thou s. continually,..... 6399
Da 6:20 thy God, whom thou s. continually,..... 6399

SERVETH See also PRESERVETH.

Nu 3:36 thereof, and all that s. thereto, ... 5656
Mal 3:17 spareth his own son that s. him. 5647
Mal 3:18 that s. God and him that s. him not. ... 5647
Lu 22:27 **that sitteth at meat, or he that s.?** .*1247*
Lu 22:27 **but I am among you as he that s.** ..*1247*
Ro 14:18 he that in these things s. Christ is...... *1398*
1Co 14:22 but prophesying s., not for them that........
Ga 3:19 Wherefore then s. the law? It was...........

SERVICE See also BONDSERVICE; EYESERVICE.

Ge 29:27 for the s. which thou shalt serve........ 5656
Ge 30:26 knowest my s. which I have done....... 5656
Ex 1:14 and in all manner of s. in the field: 5656
Ex 1:14 all their s.,...was with rigour. 5656
Ex 12:25 promised, that ye shall keep this s...... 5656
Ex 12:26 unto you, What mean ye by this s.?.... 5656
Ex 13:5 thou shalt keep this s. in this month. .. 5656
Ex 27:19 the tabernacle in all the s. thereof, ... 5656
Ex 30:16 it for the s. of the tabernacle of the.... 5656
Ex 31:10 And the cloths of s., and the holy....... 8278
Ex 35:19 The cloths of s., to do...................... 8278
Ex 35:19 to do s. in the holy place,................. 8334
Ex 35:21 and for all his s., and for the holy....... 5656
Ex 35:24 shittim wood for any work of the s.,... 5656
Ex 36:1 of work for the s. of the sanctuary, ... 5656
Ex 36:3 the work of the s. of the sanctuary,.... 5656
Ex 36:5 than enough for the s. of the work, ... 5656
Ex 38:21 for the s. of Levites, by the hand....... 5656
Ex 39:1 scarlet, they made cloths of s.,......... 8278
Ex 39:1 do s. in the holy place, and made 8334
Ex 39:40 vessels of the s. of the tabernacle, ... 5656
Ex 39:41 The cloths of s. to do 8278
Ex 39:41 to do s. in the holy place,................. 8334
Nu 3:7,8 to do the s. of the tabernacle. 5656
Nu 3:26 the cords of it for all the s. thereof..... 5656
Nu 3:31 the hanging, and all the s. thereof. 5656
Nu 4:4 shall be the s. of the sons of Kohath... 5656
Nu 4:19 and appoint them every one to his s. .. 5656
Nu 4:23 all that enter in to perform the s.,...... 5656
Nu 4:24 s. of the families of the Gershonites,... 5656
Nu 4:26 and all the instruments of their s.,...... 5656
Nu 4:27 s. of the sons of the Gershonites, ... 5656
Nu 4:27 their burdens, and in all their s.: 5656
Nu 4:28 is the s. of the families...of Gershon ... 5656
Nu 4:30 every one that entereth into the s.,.... 6635
Nu 4:31 according to all their s. in the........... 5656
Nu 4:32 instruments, and with all their s.: 5656
Nu 4:33 s. of the families...of Merari,............ 5656
Nu 4:33 according to all their s., in the.......... 5656
Nu 4:35 every one that entereth into the s.,.... 6635
Nu 4:37 that might do s. in the tabernacle 5647
Nu 4:39 every one that entereth into the s.,.... 6635
Nu 4:41 that might do s. in the tabernacle 5647
Nu 4:43 every one that entereth into the s.,.... 6635
Nu 4:47 came to do the s. of the ministry, ... 5656
Nu 4:47 s. of the burden in the tabernacle....... 5656
Nu 4:49 every one according to his s., and...... 5656
Nu 7:5 may be to do the s. of the tabernacle.. 5656
Nu 7:5 to every man according to his s.. 5656
Nu 7:7 of Gershon, according to their s.:....... 5656
Nu 7:8 of Merari, according unto their s.,...... 5656
Nu 7:9 s. of the sanctuary belonging unto 5656
Nu 8:11 they may execute the s. of the Lord... 5656
Nu 8:15 go in to do the s. of the tabernacle..... 5647
Nu 8:19 do the s. of the children of Israel 5656
Nu 8:22 went the Levites in to do their s......... 5656
Nu 8:24 wait upon the s. of the tabernacle....... 5656
Nu 8:25 cease waiting upon the s. thereof, ... 5656
Nu 8:26 keep the charge, and shall do no s....... 5656
Nu 16:9 to do the s. of the tabernacle of the.... 5656
Nu 18:4 for all the s. of the tabernacle:.......... 5656
Nu 18:6 to do the s. of the tabernacle of the.... 5656
Nu 18:7 priest's office unto you as a s. of gift: ..5656
Nu 18:21 for their s. which they serve, ... 5656
Nu 18:21 even the s. of the tabernacle of the 5656
Nu 18:23 shall do the s. of the tabernacle of...... 5656
Nu 18:31 reward for your s. in the tabernacle 5656
Jos 22:27 that we might do the s. of the Lord.... 5656
1Ki 12:4 thou the grievous s. of thy father, ... 5656
1Ch 6:31 whom David set over the s. of song ... 3027
1Ch 6:48 all manner of s. of the tabernacle 5656
1Ch 9:13 work of the s. of the house of God...... 5656
1Ch 9:19 were over the work of the s., keepers .5656
1Ch 23:24 work for the s. of the house of the..... 5656
1Ch 23:26 any vessels of it for the s. thereof...... 5656
1Ch 23:28 for the s. of the house of the Lord, ... 5656
1Ch 23:28 work of the s. of the house of God; 5656
1Ch 23:32 in the s. of the house of the Lord. 5656
1Ch 24:3 according to their offices in their s...... 5656
1Ch 24:19 the orderings of them in their s. 5656
1Ch 25:1 separated to the s. of the sons of....... 5656
1Ch 25:1 workmen according to their s. was: 5656
1Ch 25:6 harps, for the s. of the house of God, . 5656
1Ch 26:8 able men for strength for the s., ... 5656
1Ch 26:30 the Lord, and in the s. of the king...... 5656
1Ch 28:13 work of the s. of the house of the...... 5656
1Ch 28:13 the vessels of s. in the house of the ... 5656
1Ch 28:14 all instruments of all manner of s.; 5656
1Ch 28:14 all instruments of every kind of s.: 5656
1Ch 28:20 finished all the work for the s. of the .. 5656
1Ch 28:21 for all the s. of the house of God: 5656
1Ch 28:21 skilful man, for any manner of s.: 5656
1Ch 29:5 is willing to consecrate his s. this....... 3027
1Ch 29:7 gave for the s. of the house of God..... 5656
2Ch 8:14 the courses of the priests to their s.,.. 5656
2Ch 12:8 that they may know my s., and.......... 5656
2Ch 12:8 s. of the kingdoms of the countries..... 5656
2Ch 24:12 to such as did the work of the s. of.... 5656
2Ch 29:35 So the s. of the house of the Lord 5656
2Ch 31:2 every man according to his s., the...... 5656
2Ch 31:16 daily portion for their s. in their......... 5656
2Ch 31:21 began in the s. of the house of God,... 5656
2Ch 34:13 the work in any manner of s.:........... 5656
2Ch 35:2 and encouraged them to the s. of the.. 5656
2Ch 35:10 So the s. was prepared, and the 5656
2Ch 35:15 they might not depart from their s.;.... 5656
2Ch 35:16 all the s. of the Lord was prepared..... 5656
Ezr 6:18 their courses, for the s. of God, ... 5673
Ezr 7:19 given thee for the s. of the house 6402
Ezr 8:20 had appointed for the s. of the.......... 5656
Ne 10:32 the third part of a shekel for the s...... 5656
Ps 104:14 cattle, and herb for the s. of man: 5656
Jer 22:13 useth his neighbour's s. without 5647
Eze 29:18 caused his army to serve a great s..... 5656
Eze 29:18 the s. that he had served against it:.... 5656
Eze 44:14 of the house, for all the s. thereof, ... 5656
Joh 16:2 **will think that he doeth God s.** *2999*
Ro 9:4 and the s. of God, and the promises; .. *2999*
Ro 12:1 God, which is your reasonable s......... *2999*
Ro 15:31 s. which I have for Jerusalem may...... *1248*
2Co 9:12 administration of this s. not only......... *3009*
2Co 11:8 taking wages of them, to do you s...... *1248*
Ga 4:8 did s. unto them which by nature *1398*
Eph 6:7 With good will doing s., as to the....... *1398*
Php 2:17 the sacrifice and s. of your faith, ... *3009*
Php 2:30 to supply your lack of s. toward me.... *3009*
1Ti 6:2 but rather do them s., because *1398*
Heb 9:1 had also ordinances of divine s.,......... *2999*
Heb 9:6 accomplishing the s. of God.............. *2999*
Heb 9:9 make him that did the s. perfect, ... *3000*
Re 2:19 **thy works, and charity, and s.,** *1248*

SERVILE

Le 23:7,8 ye shall do no s. work therein. 5656
Le 23:21 ye shall do no s. work therein: it 5656
Le 23:25 Ye shall do no s. work therein: but..... 5656
Le 23:35, 36 ye shall do no s. work therein. 5656
Nu 28:18 do no manner of s. work therein: 5656
Nu 28:25 convocation; ye shall do no s. work. ... 5656
Nu 28:26 convocation; ye shall do no s. work: ... 5656
Nu 29:1 convocation; ye shall do no s. work: ... 5656
Nu 29:12 convocation: ye shall do no s. work, ... 5656
Nu 29:35 ye shall do no s. work therein: 5656

SERVING

Ex 14:5 we have let Israel go from s. us? 5647
De 15:18 to thee, in s. thee six years: 5647
Lu 10:40 was cumbered about much s., and...... *1248*
Ac 20:19 S. the Lord with all humility of.......... *1398*
Ac 26:7 instantly s. God day and night,........... *3000*
Ro 12:11 fervent in spirit; s. the Lord;............ *1398*
Tit 3:3 s. divers lusts and pleasures, living..... *1398*

SERVITOR
2Ki 4:43 And his **s.** said, What, should I.......... 8334

SERVITUDE
2Ch 10:4 thou somewhat the grievous **s.** of....... 5656
La 1:3 affliction, and because of great **s.**:....... 5656

SET See also BESET; SEATED; SETTEST; SETTETH; SETTING.
Ge 1:17 God **s.** them in the firmament of........ 5414
Ge 4:15 And the Lord **s.** a mark upon Cain,..... 7760
Ge 6:16 of the ark shalt thou **s.** in the side...... 7760
Ge 9:13 I do **s.** my bow in the cloud, and it..... 5414
Ge 17:21 shall bear unto thee at this **s.** time 4150
Ge 18:8 had dressed, and **s.** it before them; 5414
Ge 19:16 forth, and **s.** him without the city. 3240
Ge 21:2 **s.** time of which God had spoken........ 4150
Ge 21:28 Abraham **s.** seven ewe lambs of........ 5324
Ge 21:29 which thou hast **s.** by themselves?........ 5324
Ge 24:33 And there was **s.** meat before him...... 7760
Ge 28:11 all night, because the sun was **s.**; 935
Ge 28:12 behold a ladder **s.** up on the earth, ... 5324
Ge 28:18 pillows, and **s.** it up for a pillar, ... 7760
Ge 28:22 stone, which I have **s.** for a pillar, ... 7760
Ge 30:36 he **s.** three days' journey betwixt 7760
Ge 30:38 he **s.** the rods which he had pilled 3322
Ge 30:40 **s.** the faces of the flocks toward 5414
Ge 31:17 and **s.** his sons and his wives upon 5375
Ge 31:21 and **s.** his face toward the mount........ 7760
Ge 31:37 **s.** it here before my brethren and...... 7760
Ge 31:45 Jacob took a stone, and **s.** it up for..... 7311
Ge 35:14 Jacob **s.** up a pillar in the place 5324
Ge 35:20 Jacob **s.** a pillar upon her grave:......... 5324
Ge 41:33 and **s.** him over the land of Egypt. 7896
Ge 41:41 **s.** thee over all the land of Egypt. 5414
Ge 43:9 unto thee, and **s.** him before thee,...... 3322
Ge 43:31 himself, and said, **S.** on bread......... 7760
Ge 43:32 And they **s.** on for him by himself, ... 7760
Ge 44:21 that I may **s.** mine eyes upon him. 7760
Ge 47:7 father, and **s.** him before Pharaoh:...... 5975
Ge 48:20 he **s.** Ephraim before Manasseh. 7760
Ex 1:11 they did **s.** over them taskmasters...... 7760
Ex 4:20 his sons, and **s.** them upon an ass,...... 7392
Ex 5:14 taskmasters had **s.** over them,........... 7760
Ex 7:23 did he **s.** his heart to this also. 7896
Ex 9:5 And the Lord appointed a **s.** time,....... 4150
Ex 13:12 thou shalt **s.** apart unto the Lord all.........
Ex 19:12 thou shalt **s.** bounds unto the people.........
Ex 19:23 **S.** bounds about the mount, and..............
Ex 21:1 which thou shalt **s.** before them. 7760
Ex 23:31 **s.** thy bounds from the Red sea 7896
Ex 25:7 and stones to be **s.** in the ephod, ... 4394
Ex 25:30 shalt **s.** upon the table shewbread....... 5414
Ex 26:17 **s.** in order one against another: 7947
Ex 26:35 shalt **s.** the table without the vail,....... 7760
Ex 28:11 them to be **s.** in ouches of gold......... 4142
Ex 28:17 shalt **s.** in it settings of stones,........ 4390
Ex 28:20 be **s.** in gold in their inclosings.......... 7660
Ex 31:5 in cutting of stones, to **s.** them,......... 4390
Ex 32:22 people, that they are **s.** on mischief. ....
Ex 35:9 and stones to be **s.** for the ephod,...... 4394
Ex 35:27 and stones to be **s.**, for the ephod,...... 4394
Ex 35:33 the cutting of stones, to **s.** them, ... 4390
Ex 37:3 to be **s.** by the four corners of it;............
Ex 39:10 they **s.** in it four rows of stones:........ 4390
Ex 39:37 even with the lamps to be **s.** in order,.......
Ex 40:2 first month shalt thou **s.** up the.......... 6965
Ex 40:4 table, and **s.** in order the things ....
Ex 40:4 that are to be **s.** in order upon it;............
Ex 40:5 And thou shalt **s.** the altar of gold 5414
Ex 40:6 thou shalt **s.** the altar of the burnt...... 5414
Ex 40:7 And thou shalt **s.** the layer between.... 5414
Ex 40:8 thou shalt **s.** up the court round......... 7760
Ex 40:18 **s.** up the boards thereof, and put in.... 7760
Ex 40:20 and **s.** the staves on the ark, and put.. 7760
Ex 40:21 and **s.** up the vail of the covering, ... 7760
Ex 40:23 he **s.** the bread in order upon it......... 6186
Ex 40:28 he **s.** up the hanging at the door 7760
Ex 40:30 he **s.** the layer between the tent of..... 7760
Ex 40:33 **s.** up the hanging of the court gate. 5414
Le 17:10 even **s.** my face against that soul....... 5414
Le 20:3 I will **s.** my face against that man,...... 5414
Le 20:5 I will **s.** my face against that man, ... 7760
Le 20:6 even **s.** my face against that soul,....... 5414
Le 24:6 thou shalt **s.** them in two rows, ... 7760
Le 24:8 he shall **s.** it in order before the..............
Le 26:1 neither shall ye **s.** up any image.......... 5414
Le 26:11 I will **s.** my tabernacle among you: 5414
Le 26:17 And I will **s.** my face against you,....... 5414
Nu 1:51 pitched, the Levites shall **s.** it up: 6965
Nu 2:9 armies. These shall first **s.** forth. 5265
Nu 2:16 shall **s.** forth in the second rank......... 5265
Nu 2:17 congregation shall **s.** forward with....... 5265
Nu 2:17 encamp, so shall they **s.** forward, ... 5265
Nu 2:34 so they **s.** forward, every one after 5265
Nu 4:15 as the camp is to **s.** forward; after..... 5265
Nu 5:16 near, and **s.** her before the Lord:....... 5975
Nu 5:18, 30 **s.** the woman before the Lord, ... 5975
Nu 7:1 had fully **s.** up the tabernacle,............ 6965
Nu 8:13 thou shalt **s.** the Levites before 5975
Nu 10:17 and the sons of Merari **s.** forward, ... 5265
Nu 10:18 of the camp of Reuben **s.** forward....... 5265
Nu 10:21 And the Kohathites **s.** forward,.......... 5265
Nu 10:21 the other did **s.** up the tabernacle....... 6965
Nu 10:22 children of Ephraim **s.** forward........... 5265
Nu 10:25 of the children of Dan **s.** forward,....... 5265
Nu 10:28 their armies, when they **s.** forward. 5265
Nu 10:35 to pass, when the ark **s.** forward,....... 5265
Nu 11:24 and **s.** them round about the............. 5975
Nu 21:8 fiery serpent, and **s.** it upon a pole: 7760
Nu 21:10 the children of Israel **s.** forward, ... 5265
Nu 22:1 the children of Israel **s.** forward, ... 5265
Nu 24:1 **s.** his face toward the wilderness........ 7896
Nu 27:16 **s.** a man over the congregation, ... 6485
Nu 27:19, 22 **s.** him before Eleazar the 5975
Nu 29:39 do unto the Lord in your **s.** feasts, ... 4150
De 1:8 I have **s.** the land before you: go 5414
De 1:21 God hath **s.** the land before thee: 5414
De 4:8 law, which I **s.** before you this day?.... 5414
De 4:44 law...Moses **s.** before the children..... 7760
De 7:7 Lord did not **s.** his love upon you, ...
De 11:26 I **s.** before you this day a blessing...... 5414
De 11:32 which I **s.** before you this day. 5414
De 14:24 God shall choose to **s.** his name......... 7760
De 16:22 shalt thou **s.** thee up any image; 6965
De 17:14 I will **s.** a king over me, like as all...... 7760
De 17:15 in any wise **s.** him king over thee,...... 7760
De 17:15 brethren shalt thou **s.** king over......... 7760
De 17:15 mayest not **s.** a stranger over thee,.... 5414
De 19:14 time have **s.** in thine inheritance,........ 1379
De 26:4 **s.** it down before the altar of the........ 3240
De 26:10 shalt **s.** it before the Lord thy God, ... 3240
De 27:2 thou shalt **s.** thee up great stones, ... 6965
De 27:4 ye shall **s.** up these stones, which I.... 6965
De 28:1 God will **s.** thee on high above all...... 5414
De 28:36 king which thou shalt **s.** over thee, ... 6965
De 28:56 to **s.** the sole of her foot upon the...... 3322
De 30:1 curse, which I have **s.** before thee,..... 5414
De 30:15 I have **s.** before thee this day life...... 5414
De 30:19 I have **s.** before you life and death,..... 5414
De 32:8 he **s.** the bounds of the people........... 5324
De 32:22 **s.** on fire the foundations of the ....
De 32:46 **S.** your hearts unto all the words......... 7760
Jos 4:9 Joshua **s.** up twelve stones in the 6965
Jos 6:26 son shall he **s.** up the gates of it. 5324
Jos 8:8 that ye shall **s.** the city on fire:........... 3341
Jos 8:12 **s.** them to lie in ambush between....... 7760
Jos 8:13 when they had **s.** the people, even 7760
Jos 8:19 and hasted and **s.** the city on fire. ....
Jos 10:18 and **s.** men by it for to keep them:..... 6485
Jos 18:1 and **s.** up the tabernacle of the 7931
Jos 24:25 **s.** them a statute and an ordinance 7760
Jos 24:26 and **s.** it up there under an oak,........ 6965
Jg 1:8 the sword, and **s.** the city on fire. 7971
Jg 6:18 my present, and **s.** it before thee. 3240
Jg 7:5 him shalt thou **s.** by himself;............... 3322
Jg 7:19 they had but newly **s.** the watch: 6965
Jg 7:22 Lord **s.** every man's sword against 7760
Jg 9:25 men of Shechem **s.** liers in wait for..... 7760
Jg 9:33 rise early, and **s.** upon the city: 6584
Jg 9:49 and **s.** the hold on fire upon them;...........
Jg 15:5 when he had **s.** the brands on fire, ...
Jg 16:25 they **s.** him between the pillars.......... 5975
Jg 18:30 children of Dan **s.** up the graven 6965
Jg 18:31 **s.** them up Micah's graven image, ... 7760
Jg 20:22 **s.** their battle again in array in.................
Jg 20:29 And Israel **s.** liers in wait round......... 7760
Jg 20:36 which they had **s.** beside Gibeah. 7760
Jg 20:48 **s.** on fire all the cities that they......... 7971
Ru 2:5,6 his servant that was **s.** over the......... 5324
1Sa 2:8 to **s.** them among princes, and to....... 3427
1Sa 2:8 he hath **s.** the world upon them. 7896
1Sa 5:2 of Dagon, and **s.** it by Dagon............ 3322
1Sa 5:3 and **s.** him in his place again............. 7725
1Sa 6:18 they **s.** down the ark of the Lord: 3240
1Sa 7:12 **s.** it between Mizpeh and Shen, ... 7760
1Sa 8:12 and will **s.** them to ear his ground, ...
1Sa 9:20 days ago, **s.** not thy mind on them; 7760
1Sa 9:23 I said unto thee, **S.** it by thee. 7760
1Sa 9:24 was upon it, and **s.** it before Saul........ 7760
1Sa 9:24 is left! **s.** it before thee, and eat: 7760
1Sa 10:19 him, Nay, but **s.** a king over us. 7760
1Sa 12:13 the Lord hath **s.** a king over you........ 5414
1Sa 13:8 **s.** time that Samuel had appointed: 4150
1Sa 15:11 that I have **s.** up Saul to be king: 4427
1Sa 15:12 he **s.** him up a place, and is gone 5324
1Sa 17:2 **s.** the battle in array against the..............
1Sa 17:8 come out to **s.** your battle in array? ....
1Sa 18:5 Saul **s.** him over the men of war, ... 7760
1Sa 18:30 so that his name was much **s.** by. 3335
1Sa 22:9 was **s.** over the servants of Saul, ... 5324
1Sa 26:24 thy life was much **s.** by this day......... 1431
1Sa 26:24 much **s.** by in the eyes of the Lord,.... 1431
1Sa 28:22 **s.** a morsel of bread before thee: 7760
2Sa 3:10 to **s.** up the throne of David over....... 6965
2Sa 6:3 **s.** the ark of God upon a new cart,..... 7392
2Sa 6:17 of the Lord, and **s.** it in his place,....... 3322
2Sa 7:12 I will **s.** up thy seed after thee, ... 6965
2Sa 10:17 the Syrians **s.** themselves in array...........
2Sa 11:15 **S.** ye Uriah in the forefront of the...... 3051
2Sa 12:20 they **s.** bread before him, and he........ 7760
2Sa 12:30 stones: and it was **s.** on David's head........
2Sa 14:30 barley there; go and **s.** it on fire. ....
2Sa 14:30 servants **s.** the field on fire. ....
2Sa 14:31 thy servants **s.** my field on fire?..............
2Sa 15:24 and they **s.** down the ark of God;....... 3332
2Sa 18:1 and **s.** captains of thousands and......... 7760
2Sa 18:13 wouldest have **s.** thyself against 3320
2Sa 19:28 thou **s.** thy servant among them......... 7896
2Sa 20:5 he tarried longer than the **s.** time....... 4150
2Sa 23:23 And David **s.** him over his guard. 7760
1Ki 2:15 that all Israel **s.** their faces on me, ... 7760
1Ki 2:19 seat to be **s.** for the king's mother; 7760
1Ki 2:24 **s.** me on the throne of David my 3427
1Ki 5:5 whom I will **s.** upon thy throne in....... 5414
1Ki 6:19 to **s.** there the ark of the covenant..... 5414
1Ki 6:27 And he **s.** the cherubims within the..... 5414
1Ki 7:16 to **s.** upon the tops of the pillars: 5414
1Ki 7:21 he **s.** up the pillars in the porch of...... 6965
1Ki 7:21 and he **s.** up the right pillar, and 6965
1Ki 7:21 he **s.** up the left pillar, and called 6965
1Ki 7:25 and the sea was **s.** above upon them,........
1Ki 7:39 he **s.** the sea on the right side of 5414
1Ki 8:21 I have **s.** there a place for the ark,..... 7760
1Ki 9:6 my statutes which I have **s.** before....... 5414
1Ki 10:9 to **s.** thee on the throne of Israel: 5414
1Ki 12:29 And he **s.** the one in Beth-el, and....... 7760
1Ki 14:4 eyes were **s.** by reason of his age...... 6965
1Ki 15:4 to **s.** up his son after him, and to 6965
1Ki 16:34 and **s.** up the gates thereof in his 5324
1Ki 20:12 servants, **S.** yourselves in array.......... 7760
1Ki 20:12 they **s.** themselves in array against..... 7760
1Ki 21:9 and **s.** Naboth on high among the 3427
1Ki 21:10 **s.** two men, sons of Belial, before....... 3427
1Ki 21:12 and **s.** Naboth on high among the 3427
2Ki 4:4 shalt **s.** aside that which is full. 5265
2Ki 4:10 and let us **s.** for him there a bed,....... 7760
2Ki 4:38 **S.** on the great pot, and seethe 8239
2Ki 4:43 should I **s.** this before an hundred 5414
2Ki 4:44 So he **s.** it before them, and they....... 5414
2Ki 6:22 **s.** bread and water before them, ... 7760
2Ki 8:12 strong holds wilt thou **s.** on fire, ... 7971
2Ki 10:3 and **s.** him on his father's throne, ... 7760
2Ki 12:4 money that every man is **s.** at, ... 6187
2Ki 12:9 **s.** it beside the altar, on the right....... 5414
2Ki 12:17 and Hazael **s.** his face to go up to 7760
2Ki 17:10 **s.** them up images and groves in......... 5324
2Ki 18:23 on thy part to **s.** riders upon them...... 5414
2Ki 20:1 **S.** thine house in order; for thou ....
2Ki 21:7 he **s.** a graven image of the grove 7760
2Ki 25:19 an officer that was **s.** over the men 6496
2Ki 25:28 **s.** his throne above the throne of 5414
1Ch 6:31 David **s.** over the service of song....... 5975
1Ch 9:22 seer did ordain in their **s.** office. 530
1Ch 9:26 chief porters, were in their **s.** office, ... 530
1Ch 9:31 **s.** office over the things that were 530
1Ch 11:14 **s.** themselves in the midst of that....... 3320
1Ch 11:25 and David **s.** him over his guard......... 7760
1Ch 16:1 **s.** it in the midst of the tent that....... 3322
1Ch 19:10 that the battle was **s.** against him............

Book	Ref	Context	No.
1Ch	19:11	and they **s.** themselves in array	
1Ch	19:17	**s.** the battle in array against them.	
1Ch	20:2	in it; and it was **s.** upon David's head	
1Ch	21:18	**s.** up an altar, unto the Lord in	6965
1Ch	22:2	**s.** masons to hew wrought stones	5975
1Ch	22:19	**s.** your heart and your soul to seek	5414
1Ch	23:4	**s.** forward the work of the house	5329
1Ch	23:31	new moons, and on the **s.** feasts,	4150
1Ch	29:2	onyx stones, and stones to be **s.**,	4394
1Ch	29:3	I have **s.** my affection to the house of	
2Ch	2:18	he **s.** threescore and ten thousand	6213
2Ch	2:18	overseers to **s.** the people a work.	
2Ch	3:5	**s.** thereon palm trees and chains.	5927
2Ch	4:4	and the sea was **s.** above upon them,	
2Ch	4:7	and **s.** them in the temple, five on	5414
2Ch	4:10	he **s.** the sea on the right side of the	5414
2Ch	4:19	tables whereon the shewbread was **s.**;	
2Ch	6:10	and am **s.** on the throne of Israel,	3427
2Ch	6:13	had **s.** it in the midst of the court:	5414
2Ch	7:19	statutes…which I have **s.** before you,	5414
2Ch	9:8	in thee to **s.** thee on his throne,	5414
2Ch	11:16	as **s.** their hearts to seek the Lord	5414
2Ch	13:3	And Abijah **s.** the battle in array	631
2Ch	13:3	Jeroboam also **s.** the battle in array	
2Ch	13:11	the shewbread also **s.** they in order	
2Ch	14:10	**s.** the battle in array in the valley	
2Ch	17:2	**s.** garrisons in the land of Judah,	5414
2Ch	19:5	he **s.** judges in the land throughout	5975
2Ch	19:8	did Jehoshaphat **s.** of the Levites,	5975
2Ch	20:3	and **s.** himself to seek the Lord,	5414
2Ch	20:17	**s.** yourselves, stand ye still, and	3320
2Ch	20:22	the Lord **s.** ambushments against	5414
2Ch	23:10	And he **s.** all the people, every man	5975
2Ch	23:14	that were **s.** over the host,	6485
2Ch	23:19	And he **s.** the porters at the gates	5975
2Ch	23:20	and **s.** the king upon the throne of	3427
2Ch	24:8	and **s.** it without at the gate of the	5414
2Ch	24:13	**s.** the house of God in his state,	5975
2Ch	25:14	Seir, and **s.** them up to be his gods,	5975
2Ch	29:25	he **s.** the Levites in the house of the	5975
2Ch	29:35	house of the Lord was **s.** in order.	3559
2Ch	31:3	new moons, and for the **s.** feasts,	4150
2Ch	31:15	of the priests, in their **s.** office, to	530
2Ch	31:18	for in their **s.** office they sanctified	530
2Ch	32:6	**s.** captains of war over the people,	5414
2Ch	33:7	And he **s.** a carved image, the idol	7760
2Ch	33:19	**s.** up groves and graven images,	5975
2Ch	34:12	of the Kohathites, to **s.** it forward;	5329
2Ch	35:2	he **s.** the priests in their charges,	5975
Ezr	2:68	house of God to **s.** it up in his place:	5975
Ezr	3:3	they **s.** the altar upon his bases;	3559
Ezr	3:5	and of all the **s.** feasts of the Lord	4150
Ezr	3:8	**s.** forward the work of the house	5329
Ezr	3:9	to **s.** forward the workmen in the	5329
Ezr	3:10	they **s.** the priests in their apparel	5975
Ezr	4:10	and **s.** in the cities of Samaria,	3488
Ezr	4:12	and have **s.** up the walls thereof,	3635
Ezr	4:13	be builded, the walls **s.** up again,	3635
Ezr	4:16	again, and the walls thereof **s.** up,	3635
Ezr	5:11	king of Israel builded and **s.** up.	3635
Ezr	6:11	being **s.** up, let him be hanged	2211
Ezr	6:18	**s.** the priests in their divisions,	6966
Ezr	7:25	**s.** magistrates and judges, which	4483
Ezr	9:9	to **s.** up the house of our God, and	7311
Ne	1:9	I have chosen to **s.** my name there	7931
Ne	2:6	to send me; and I **s.** him a time.	5414
Ne	3:1	sanctified it, and **s.** up the doors of	5975
Ne	3:3,	6,13,14,15 **s.** up the doors thereof,	5975
Ne	4:9	**s.** a watch against them day and	5975
Ne	4:13	Therefore **s.** I in the lower places	5975
Ne	4:13	**s.** the people after their families	5975
Ne	5:7	**s.** a great assembly against them.	5414
Ne	6:1	**s.** up the doors upon the gates;)	5975
Ne	7:1	was built, and I had **s.** up the doors,	5975
Ne	9:37	kings whom thou hast **s.** over us	5414
Ne	10:33	the new moons, for the **s.** feasts,	4150
Ne	13:11	together,…**s.** them in their place.	5975
Ne	13:19	some of my servants **s.** I at the gates,	5975
Es	2:17	**s.** the royal crown upon her head,	7760
Es	3:1	and **s.** his seat above all the princes	7760
Es	6:8	royal which is **s.** upon his head:	5414
Es	8:2	Esther **s.** Mordecai over the house	7760
Job	5:11	To **s.** up on high those that be low;	7760
Job	6:4	terrors of God do **s.** themselves in	
Job	7:17	shouldest **s.** thine heart upon him?	7896
Job	7:20	thou **s.** me as a mark against thee,	7760
Job	9:19	who shall **s.** me a time to plead?	3259
Job	14:13	wouldest appoint me a **s.** time,	2706
Job	16:12	pieces, and **s.** me up for his mark.	6965
Job	19:8	he hath **s.** darkness in my paths.	7760
Job	30:1	have **s.** with the dogs of my flock.	7896
Job	30:13	path, they **s.** forward my calamity,	
Job	33:5	**s.** thy words in order before me,	
Job	34:14	If he **s.** his heart upon man, if he	7760
Job	34:24	and **s.** others in their stead.	5975
Job	36:16	that which should be **s.** on thy table	5183
Job	38:10	place, and **s.** bars and doors,	7760
Job	38:33	**s.** the dominion…in the earth?	7760
Ps	2:2	kings of the earth **s.** themselves,	3320
Ps	2:6	Yet have I **s.** my king upon my	5258
Ps	3:6	have **s.** themselves against me	7896
Ps	4:3	the Lord hath **s.** apart him that is	6395
Ps	8:1	**s.** thy glory above the heavens.	5414
Ps	10:8	are privily **s.** against the poor.	6845
Ps	12:5	I will **s.** him in safety from him	7896
Ps	16:8	have **s.** the Lord always before me:	7737
Ps	17:11	**s.** their eyes bowing down to the	7896
Ps	19:4	hath he **s.** a tabernacle for the sun,	7760
Ps	20:5	of our God we will **s.** up our banners:	
Ps	27:5	he shall **s.** me up upon a rock.	7311
Ps	31:8	hast **s.** my feet in a large room.	5975
Ps	40:2	clay, and **s.** my feet upon a rock,	6965
Ps	50:21	**s.** them in order before thine eyes.	
Ps	54:3	they have not **s.** God before them.	7760
Ps	57:4	even among them that are **s.** on fire,	
Ps	62:10	**s.** not your heart upon them.	7896
Ps	69:29	salvation, O God, **s.** me up on high.	
Ps	73:9	They **s.** their mouth against the	8371
Ps	73:18	didst **s.** them in slippery places:	7896
Ps	74:4	they **s.** up their ensigns for signs.	7760
Ps	74:17	hast **s.** all the borders of the earth:	5324
Ps	78:7	they might **s.** their hope in God,	7760
Ps	78:8	that **s.** not their heart aright, and	3559
Ps	85:13	shall **s.** us in the way of his steps.	7760
Ps	86:14	and have not **s.** thee before them.	7760
Ps	89:25	I will **s.** his hand also in the sea,	7760
Ps	89:42	hast **s.** up the right hand of his	7311
Ps	90:8	Thou hast **s.** our iniquities before	7896
Ps	91:14	Because he hath **s.** his love upon me,	
Ps	91:14	I will **s.** him on high, because he hath	
Ps	101:3	I will **s.** no wicked thing before	7896
Ps	102:13	to favour her, yea, the **s.** time, is come	
Ps	104:9	Thou hast **s.** a bound that they	7760
Ps	109:6	**S.** thou a wicked man over him:	6485
Ps	113:8	That he may **s.** him with princes,	3427
Ps	118:5	me, and **s.** me in a large place.	
Ps	122:5	there are **s.** thrones of judgment,	3427
Ps	132:11	thy body will I **s.** upon thy throne.	7896
Ps	140:5	wayside; they have **s.** gins for me.	7896
Ps	141:2	be **s.** forth before thee as incense;	3559
Ps	141:3	**S.** a watch, O Lord, before my	7896
Pr	1:25	have **s.** at nought all my counsel,	
Pr	8:23	I was **s.** up from everlasting, from	5258
Pr	8:27	he **s.** a compass upon the face of	2710
Pr	22:28	landmark,…thy fathers have **s.**	6213
Pr	23:5	Wilt thou **s.** thine eyes upon that	5774
Ec	3:11	he hath **s.** the world in their heart,	5414
Ec	7:14	God also hath **s.** the one over	6213
Ec	8:11	of men is fully **s.** in them to do evil.	
Ec	10:6	Folly is **s.** in great dignity, and	5414
Ec	12:9	and **s.** in order many proverbs.	
Ca	5:12	washed with milk, and fitly **s.**	3427
Ca	5:14	are as gold rings **s.** with the beryl:	4390
Ca	5:15	**s.** upon sockets of fine gold: his	3245
Ca	7:2	heap of wheat **s.** about with lilies	5473
Ca	8:6	**S.** me as a seal upon thine heart,	7760
Isa	3:24	and instead of well **s.** hair baldness;	
Isa	7:6	and **s.** a king in the midst of it, even	
Isa	9:11	Lord shall **s.** up the adversaries	7682
Isa	11:11	the Lord shall **s.** his hand again the	
Isa	11:12	**s.** up an ensign for the nations,	5375
Isa	14:1	and **s.** them in their own land: and	3240
Isa	17:10	and shalt **s.** it with strange slips:	2232
Isa	19:2	I will **s.** the Egyptians against	5526
Isa	21:6	Go, **s.** a watchman, let him declare	5975
Isa	21:8	I am **s.** in my ward whole nights:	5324
Isa	22:7	horsemen shall **s.** themselves in	7896
Isa	23:13	they **s.** up the towers thereof, they	6965
Isa	27:4	**s.** the briers and thorns against	5414
Isa	27:11	women come, and **s.** them on fire:	
Isa	36:8	thy part to **s.** riders upon them.	5414
Isa	38:1	**S.** thine house in order: for thou	
Isa	41:19	I will **s.** in the desert the fir tree,	7760
Isa	42:4	he have **s.** judgment in the earth:	7760
Isa	42:25	it hath **s.** him on fire round about,	7760
Isa	44:7	declare it,…**s.** it in order for me,	
Isa	45:20	that **s.** up the wood of their graven	5375
Isa	46:7	him, and **s.** him in his place, and	3240
Isa	49:22	**s.** up my standard to the people:	7311
Isa	50:7	have I **s.** my face like a flint, and	7760
Isa	57:7	mountain hast thou **s.** thy bed:	7760
Isa	57:8	hast thou **s.** up thy remembrance:	7760
Isa	62:6	**s.** watchmen upon thy walls, O	6485
Isa	66:19	I will **s.** a sign among them, and I	7760
Jer	1:10	this day **s.** thee over the nations	6485
Jer	1:15	they shall **s.** every one his throne	5414
Jer	4:6	**S.** up the standard toward Zion:	5375
Jer	5:26	they **s.** a trap, they catch men.	5324
Jer	6:1	Tekoa, and **s.** up a sign of fire in	5375
Jer	6:17	Also I **s.** watchmen over you,	6965
Jer	6:23	**s.** in array as men for war against	
Jer	6:27	I have **s.** thee for a tower and a	5414
Jer	7:12	where I **s.** my name at the first,	7931
Jer	7:30	they have **s.** their abominations in	7760
Jer	9:13	my law which I **s.** before them,	5414
Jer	10:20	more, and to **s.** up my curtains.	6965
Jer	11:13	ye **s.** up altars to that shameful	7760
Jer	21:8	I **s.** before you the way of life, and	5414
Jer	21:10	I have **s.** my face against this city	7760
Jer	23:4	I will **s.** up shepherds over them	6965
Jer	24:1	of figs were **s.** before the temple	3259
Jer	24:6	**s.** mine eyes upon them for good,	7760
Jer	26:4	law, which I have **s.** before you,	5414
Jer	31:21	**S.** thee up waymarks, make thee	5324
Jer	31:21	**s.** thine heart toward the highway,	7896
Jer	31:29	the children's teeth are **s.** on edge.	
Jer	31:30	grape, his teeth shall be **s.** on edge.	
Jer	32:20	**s.** signs and wonders in the land	7760
Jer	32:29	shall come and **s.** fire on this city,	
Jer	32:34	they **s.** their abominations in the	7760
Jer	34:16	had **s.** at liberty at their pleasure,	7971
Jer	35:5	I **s.** before the sons of the house	5414
Jer	38:22	Thy friends have **s.** thee on, and	5496
Jer	40:11	**s.** over them Gedaliah the son of	6485
Jer	42:15	**s.** your faces to enter into Egypt,	7760
Jer	42:17	that **s.** their faces to go into Egypt	7760
Jer	43:10	will **s.** his throne upon these stones	7760
Jer	44:10	I **s.** before you and before your	5414
Jer	44:11	I will **s.** my face against you for	7760
Jer	44:12	**s.** their faces to go into the land of	7760
Jer	49:38	And I will **s.** my throne in Elam,	7760
Jer	50:2	and publish, and **s.** up a standard;	5375
Jer	50:9	**s.** themselves in array against her;	
Jer	51:12	**S.** up the standard upon the walls	5375
Jer	51:12	**s.** up the watchmen, prepare the	6965
Jer	51:27	**S.** ye up a standard in the land,	5375
Jer	52:32	**s.** his throne above the throne of	5414
La	2:17	he hath **s.** up the horn of thine	7311
La	3:6	He hath **s.** me in dark places, as	3427
La	3:12	and **s.** me as a mark for the arrow.	5324
Eze	2:2	**s.** me upon my feet, that I heard	5975
Eze	3:24	**s.** me upon my feet, and speak with	5975
Eze	4:2	it; **s.** the camp also against it, and	5414
Eze	4:2	**s.** battering rams against it round	7760
Eze	4:3	and **s.** it for a wall of iron between	5414
Eze	4:3	**s.** thy face against it, and it shall	3559
Eze	4:7	shalt **s.** thy face toward the siege of	3559
Eze	5:5	**s.** it in the midst of the nations	7760
Eze	6:2	**s.** thy face toward the mountains	7760
Eze	7:20	his ornament, he **s.** it in majesty:	7760
Eze	7:20	have I **s.** it far from them.	5414
Eze	9:4	**s.** a mark upon the foreheads of	8427
Eze	12:6	I have **s.** thee for a sign unto the	5414
Eze	13:17	**s.** thy face against the daughters	7760
Eze	14:3	men have **s.** up their idols in their	5927
Eze	14:8	will **s.** my face against that man,	5414
Eze	15:7	And I will **s.** my face against them;	5414
Eze	15:7	when I **s.** my face against them.	7760
Eze	16:18	hast **s.** mine oil and mine incense	5414
Eze	16:19	even **s.** it before them for a sweet	5414
Eze	17:4	he **s.** it in a city of merchants.	7760
Eze	17:5	waters, and **s.** it as a willow tree.	7760
Eze	17:22	of the high cedar, and will **s.** it;	5414
Eze	18:2	the children's teeth are **s.** on edge?	
Eze	19:8	nations **s.** against him on every	5414
Eze	20:46	**s.** thy face toward the south, and	7760
Eze	21:2	**s.** thy face toward Jerusalem, and	7760
Eze	21:15	I have **s.** the point of the sword	5414
Eze	21:16	left, whithersoever thy face is **s.**	3259
Eze	22:7	thy **s.** light by father and mother:	
Eze	22:10	her that was **s.** apart for pollution.	5079

Eze 23:24 **s.** against thee buckler and shield 7760
Eze 23:24 I will **s.** judgment before them, ... 5414
Eze 23:25 I will **s.** my jealousy against thee,....... 5414
Eze 23:41 hast **s.** mine incense and mine oil. 7760
Eze 24:2 king of Babylon **s.** himself against....... 5564
Eze 24:3 **S.** on a pot, **s.** it on, and also pour..... 8239
Eze 24:7 she **s.** it upon the top of a rock;......... 7760
Eze 24:8 I have **s.** her blood upon the top of..... 5414
Eze 24:11 **s.** it empty upon the coals thereof, ... 5975
Eze 24:25 whereupon they **s.** their minds,.......... 4853
Eze 25:2 Son of man, **s.** thy face against 7760
Eze 25:4 they shall **s.** their palaces in thee, ... 3427
Eze 26:9 shall **s.** engines of war against thy 5414
Eze 26:20 **s.** thee in the low parts of the.......... 3427
Eze 26:20 **s.** glory in the land of the living; 5414
Eze 27:10 thee; they **s.** forth thy comeliness. 5414
Eze 28:2,6 **s.** thine heart as the heart of............ 5414
Eze 28:14 I have **s.** thee so: thou wast upon 5414
Eze 28:21 of man, **s.** thy face against Zidon, ... 7760
Eze 29:2 **s.** thy face against Pharaoh king......... 7760
Eze 30:8 when I have **s.** a fire in Egypt, and..... 5414
Eze 30:14 and will **s.** fire in Zoan, and will 5414
Eze 30:16 And I will **s.** fire in Egypt: Sin shall 5414
Eze 31:4 the deep **s.** him up on high with......... 7311
Eze 32:8 and **s.** darkness upon thy land,........... 5414
Eze 32:23 graves are **s.** in the sides of the pit, ... 5414
Eze 32:25 They have **s.** her a bed in the midst ... 5414
Eze 33:2 and **s.** for him their watchman: 5414
Eze 33:7 I have **s.** thee a watchman unto the 5414
Eze 34:23 And I will **s.** up one shepherd over..... 6965
Eze 35:2 **s.** thy face against mount Seir, and..... 7760
Eze 37:1 and **s.** me down in the midst of the 5117
Eze 37:26 will **s.** my sanctuary in the midst........ 5414
Eze 38:2 **s.** thy face against God, the land of..... 7760
Eze 39:9 and shall **s.** on fire and burn the......... 1197
Eze 39:15 then shall he **s.** up a sign by it,.......... 1129
Eze 39:21 **s.** my glory among the heathen,........ 5414
Eze 40:2 **s.** me upon a very high mountain,........ 5117
Eze 40:4 **s.** thine heart upon all that I shall....... 7760
Eze 44:8 ye have **s.** keepers of my charge in 7760
Da 1:11 the eunuchs had **s.** over Daniel, ... 4487
Da 2:44 God of heaven **s.** up a kingdom,......... 6966
Da 2:49 and he **s.** Shadrach, Meshach, and........ 4483
Da 3:1 he **s.** it up in the plain of Dura, in 6966
Da 3:2 Nebuchadnezzar the king had **s.** up. 6966
Da 3:3 Nebuchadnezzar the king had **s.** up; 6966
Da 3:3 that Nebuchadnezzar had **s.** up........... 6966
Da 3:5 Nebuchadnezzar the king hath **s.** up: ... 6966
Da 3:7 Nebuchadnezzar the king had **s.** up. 6966
Da 3:12 whom thou hast **s.** over the affairs...... 4483
Da 3:12 image which thou hast **s.** up. 6966
Da 3:14 golden image which I have **s.** up? 6966
Da 3:18 golden image which thou hast **s.** up...... 6966
Da 5:19 and whom he would he **s.** up; and 7313
Da 6:1 It pleased Darius to **s.** over the 6966
Da 6:3 to **s.** him over the whole realm. 6966
Da 6:14 **s.** his heart on Daniel to deliver 7761
Da 7:10 judgment was **s.**, and the books 3488
Da 8:18 he touched me, and **s.** me upright. 5975
Da 9:3 I **s.** my face unto the Lord God, to..... 5414
Da 9:10 he **s.** before us by his servants the..... 5414
Da 10:10 which **s.** me upon my knees and 5128
Da 10:12 didst **s.** thine heart to understand, ... 5414
Da 10:15 I **s.** my face toward the ground,........ 5414
Da 11:11 shall **s.** forth a great multitude; 5975
Da 11:13 shall **s.** forth a multitude greater 5975
Da 11:17 He shall also **s.** his face to enter 7760
Da 12:11 that maketh desolate **s.** up, there 5414
Ho 2:3 **s.** her as in the day that she was 3322
Ho 2:3 **s.** her like a dry land, and slay........... 7896
Ho 4:8 **s.** their heart on their iniquity, ... 5375
Ho 6:11 he hath **s.** an harvest for thee, ... 7896
Ho 8:1 **S.** the trumpet to thy mouth. He............
Ho 8:4 They have **s.** up kings, but not by............
Ho 11:8 how shall I **s.** thee as Zeboim?........... 7761
Joe 2:5 a strong people **s.** in battle array.............
Am 7:8 **s.** a plumbline in the midst of my 7760
Am 8:5 we may **s.** forth wheat, making the...... 6605
Am 9:4 **s.** mine eyes upon them for evil, ... 7760
Ob 4 thou **s.** thy nest among the stars,....... 7760
Na 3:6 and will **s.** thee as a gazingstock. 7760
Na 3:13 gates of thy land shall be **s.** wide.............
Hab 2:1 and **s.** me upon the tower, and 3320
Hab 2:9 that he may **s.** his nest on high,......... 7760
Zec 3:5 them **s.** a fair mitre upon his head. 7760
Zec 3:5 they **s.** a fair mitre upon his head, ... 7760
Zec 5:11 and **s.** there upon her own base......... 3240
Zec 6:11 **s.** them upon the head of Joshua 7760
Zec 8:10 I **s.** all men every one against his....... 7971
Mal 3:15 that work wickedness are **s.** up;......... 1129
Mt 5:1 and when he was **s.**, his disciples *2523*
Mt 5:14 **that is s. on an hill cannot be hid.** .*2749*
Mt 10:35 **to s. a man at variance against**..... *1369*
Mt 18:2 and **s.** him in the midst of them, ... *2476*
Mt 21:7 clothes, and they **s.** him thereon. *1940*
Mt 25:33 **s. the sheep on his right hand,**...... *2476*
Mt 27:19 was **s.** down on the judgment seat,...... *2521*
Mt 27:37 **s.** up over his head his accusation....... *2007*
Mk 1:32 at even, when the sun did **s.**, they *1416*
Mk 4:21 **and not to be s. on a candlestick?** ..*2007*
Mk 6:41 to his disciples to **s.** before them;....... *3908*
Mk 8:6 to his disciples to **s.** before them;....... *3908*
Mk 8:6 they did **s.** them before the people. *3908*
Mk 8:7 to **s.** them also before them. *3908*
Mk 9:12 **many things, and be s. at nought**...*1847*
Mk 9:36 and **s.** him in the midst of them: *2476*
Mk 12:1 **s. an hedge about it, and digged**.... *4060*
Lu 1:1 to **s.** forth in order a declaration of....... *392*
Lu 2:34 child is **s.** for the fall and rising.......... *2749*
Lu 4:9 **s.** him on a pinnacle of the temple, ... *2476*
Lu 4:18 **s. at liberty them that are bruised,** ..*649*
Lu 7:8 also am a man **s.** under authority,....... *5021*
Lu 9:16 disciples to **s.** before the multitude. *3908*
Lu 9:47 took a child, and **s.** him by him, ... *2476*
Lu 9:51 **s.** his face to go to Jerusalem, ... *4741*
Lu 10:8 **such things as are s. before you:** ... *3908*
Lu 10:34 **and s. him on his own beast,** *1913*
Lu 11:6 **I have nothing to s. before him?** *3908*
Lu 19:35 the colt, and they **s.** Jesus thereon. *1913*
Lu 22:55 and were **s.** down together, Peter...... *4776*
Lu 23:11 his men of war **s.** him at nought,........ *1848*
Joh 2:6 there were **s.** there six waterpots *2749*
Joh 2:10 beginning doth **s.** forth good wine;...... *5087*
Joh 3:33 hath **s.** to his seal that God is true. *4972*
Joh 6:11 disciples to them that were **s.** down; *345*
Joh 8:3 when they had **s.** her in the midst, ... *2476*
Joh 13:12 garments, and was **s.** down again,........ *377*
Joh 19:29 was **s.** a vessel full of vinegar:........... *2749*
Ac 4:7 when they had **s.** them in the midst, ... *2476*
Ac 4:11 the stone which was **s.** at nought *1848*
Ac 5:27 they **s.** them before the council;........ *2476*
Ac 6:6 Whom they **s.** before the apostles: *2476*
Ac 6:13 And **s.** up false witnesses, which........ *2476*
Ac 7:5 not so much as to **s.** his foot on: *968*
Ac 7:26 would have **s.** them at one again, ... *4900*
Ac 12:21 upon a **s.** day Herod, arrayed in......... *5002*
Ac 13:9 the Holy Ghost, **s.** his eyes on him, ... *816*
Ac 13:47 I have **s.** thee to be a light of the....... *5087*
Ac 15:16 ruins thereof, and I will **s.** it up: *461*
Ac 16:34 his house, he **s.** meat before them,...... *3908*
Ac 17:5 and **s.** all the city on an uproar, ... *2350*
Ac 18:10 **no man shall s. on thee to hurt**..... *2007*
Ac 19:27 is in danger to be **s.** at nought;.......... *2064*
Ac 21:2 we went abroad, and **s.** forth. *321*
Ac 22:30 down, and **s.** him before them. *2476*
Ac 23:24 beasts, that they may **s.** Paul on, ... *1913*
Ac 26:32 man might have been **s.** at liberty, ... *630*
Ro 3:25 hath **s.** forth to be a propitiation.......... *4388*
Ro 14:10 dost thou **s.** at nought thy brother?..... *1848*
1Co 4:9 God hath **s.** forth us the apostles......... *584*
1Co 6:4 **s.** them to judge who are least *2523*
1Co 10:27 whatsoever is **s.** before you, eat, ... *3908*
1Co 11:34 rest will I **s.** in order when I come. *1299*
1Co 12:18 But now hath God **s.** the members *5087*
1Co 12:28 And God hath **s.** some in the church, .. *5087*
Ga 3:1 Christ hath been evidently **s.** forth,..... *4270*
Eph 1:20 **s.** him at his own right hand in........... *2523*
Php 1:17 **s.** for the defence of the gospel. *2749*
Col 3:2 **S.** your affection on things above,........ *5426*
Tit 1:5 shouldest **s.** in order the things.......... *1930*
Heb 2:7 didst **s.** him over the works of thy...... *2525*
Heb 6:18 hold upon the hope **s.** before us:........ *4295*
Heb 8:1 who is **s.** on the right hand of the *2523*
Heb 12:1 the race that is **s.** before us,............ *4295*
Heb 12:2 for the joy that was **s.** before him *4295*
Heb 12:2 is **s.** down at the right hand of the...... *2523*
Heb 13:23 our brother Timothy is **s.** at liberty; *630*
Jas 3:6 nature; and it is **s.** on fire of hell......... *5394*
Jude 7 flesh, are **s.** forth for an example, ... *4295*
Re 3:8 **have s. before thee an open door,** .. *1325*
Re 3:21 **s. down with my Father in his**...... *2523*
Re 4:2 behold, a throne was **s.** in heaven, ... *2749*
Re 10:2 he **s.** his right foot upon the sea, ... *5087*
Re 20:3 him up, and **s.** a seal upon him, ... *4972*

SETH (seth) See also SHETH.
Ge 4:25 a son, and called his name **S.**: 8352
Ge 4:26 to **S.**, to him also there was born a 8352
Ge 5:3 his image; and called his name **S.**: 8352
Ge 5:4 of Adam after he had begotten **S.**......... 8352
Ge 5:6 **S.** lived an hundred and five years,..... 8352
Ge 5:7 **S.** lived after he begat Enos eight 8352
Ge 5:8 And all the days of **S.** were nine 8352
Lu 3:38 Enos, which was the son of **S.**, ... *4589*

SETHUR (se'-thur)
Nu 13:13 of Asher, **S.** the son of Michael. 5639

SETTER See also UNDERSETTERS.
Ac 17:18 to be a **s.** forth of strange gods: *2604*

SETTEST
De 23:20 in all that thou **s.** thine hand to.......... 4916
De 28:8 in all that thou **s.** thine hand unto; 4916
De 28:20 in all that thou **s.** thine hand unto 4916
Job 7:12 that thou **s.** a watch over me? 7760
Job 13:27 **s.** a print upon the heels of my feet. ....
Ps 21:3 thou **s.** a crown of pure gold on......... 7896
Ps 41:12 and **s.** me before thy face for ever. 5324

SETTETH
Nu 1:51 when the tabernacle **s.** forward, ... 5265
Nu 4:5 And when the camp **s.** forward, ... 5265
De 24:15 is poor, and **s.** his heart upon it: 5375
De 27:16 that **s.** light by his father or his.......... 7034
2Sa 22:34 and **s.** me upon my high places. 5975
Job 28:3 He **s.** an end to darkness, and........... 7760
Ps 18:33 and **s.** me upon my high places. 5975
Ps 36:4 he **s.** himself in a way that is not 3320
Ps 65:6 his strength **s.** fast the mountains;...... 3559
Ps 68:6 God **s.** the solitary in families: he 3427
Ps 75:7 down one, and **s.** up another. 7311
Ps 83:14 flame **s.** the mountains on fire;.......... 3857
Ps 107:41 **s.** he the poor on high from affliction,.........
Jer 5:26 they lay wait,as he that **s.** snares; 7918
Jer 43:3 of Neriah **s.** thee on against us, ... 5496
Eze 14:4 that **s.** up his idols in his heart,.......... 5927
Eze 14:7 and **s.** up his idols in his heart, ... 5927
Da 2:21 removeth kings, and **s.** up kings:......... 6966
Da 4:17 and **s.** up over it the basest of men. ... 6966
Mt 4:5 and **s.** him on the pinnacle of the........ *2476*
Lu 8:16 **s. it on a candlestick, that they**.... *2007*
Jas 3:6 **s.** on fire the course of nature; *5394*

SETTING See also SETTINGS.
Eze 43:8 In their **s.** of their threshold by.......... 5414
Mt 27:66 sealing the stone, and **s.** a watch........ *3326*
Lu 4:40 Now when the sun was **s.**, all they..... *1416*

SETTINGS
Ex 28:17 thou shalt set in it **s.** of stones, ... 4396

SETTLE See also SETTLED; SETTLEST.
1Ch 17:14 I will **s.** him in mine house and 5975
Eze 36:11 will **s.** you after your old estates,........ 3427
Eze 43:14 the lower **s.** shall be two cubits, ... 5835
Eze 43:14 the lesser **s.** even to the greater........ 5835
Eze 43:14 greater **s.** shall be four cubits, ... 5835
Eze 43:17 the **s.** shall be fourteen cubits long 5835
Eze 43:20 and on the four corners of the **s.**,........ 5835
Eze 45:19 upon the four corners of the **s.** of 5835
Lu 21:14 **S. it therefore in your hearts, not.** *5087*
1Pe 5:10 stablish, strengthen, **s.** you. *2311*

SETTLED
1Ki 8:13 a **s.** place for thee to abide in for 4349
2Ki 8:11 he **s.** his countenance stedfastly, ... 5975
Ps 119:89 O Lord, thy word is **s.** in heaven. 5324
Pr 8:25 Before the mountains were **s.**,........... 2883
Jer 48:11 he hath **s.** on his lees, and hath 8252
Zep 1:12 the men that are **s.** on their lees:........ 7087
Col 1:23 in the faith grounded and **s.**, and *1476*

SETTLEST
Ps 65:10 thou **s.** the furrows thereof: thou 5181

SEVEN See also SEVENFOLD; SEVENS; SEVENTEEN.
Ge 5:7 Enos eight hundred and **s.** years, ... 7651
Ge 5:25 an hundred eighty and **s.** years, ... 7651
Ge 5:26 Lamech **s.** hundred eighty and 7651
Ge 5:31 days of Lamech were **s.** hundred......... 7651
Ge 5:31 seventy and **s.** years: and he died. 7651
Ge 7:4 **s.** days, and I will cause it to rain....... 7651
Ge 7:10 it came to pass after **s.** days, that 7651

Ge 8:10, 12 And he stayed yet other **s.** days; 7651
Ge 8:12 he stayed yet other **s.** days, and 7651
Ge 8:14 **s.** and twentieth day of the month, 7651
Ge 11:21 Serug two hundred and **s.** years, 7651
Ge 21:28 Abraham set **s.** ewe lambs of the 7651
Ge 21:29 What mean these **s.** ewe lambs 7651
Ge 21:30 these **s.** ewe lambs shalt thou take 7651
Ge 23:1 Sarah was an hundred and **s.** and 7651
Ge 25:17 hundred and thirty and **s.** years: 7651
Ge 29:18 will serve thee **s.** years for Rachel 7651
Ge 29:20 Jacob served **s.** years for Rachel; 7651
Ge 29:27 serve with me yet **s.** other years. 7651
Ge 29:30 served with him yet **s.** other years. 7651
Ge 31:23 pursued after him **s.** days' journey; 7651
Ge 33:3 himself to the ground **s.** times, 7651
Ge 41:2 of the river **s.** well favoured kine 7651
Ge 41:3 **s.** other kine came up after them 7651
Ge 41:4 eat up the **s.** well favoured and fat 7651
Ge 41:5 **s.** ears of corn came up upon one 7651
Ge 41:6 **s.** thin ears and blasted with the 7651
Ge 41:7 And the **s.** thing ears devoured the
Ge 41:7 devoured the **s.** rank and full ears. 7651
Ge 41:18 came up out of the river **s.** kine, 7651
Ge 41:19 **s.** other kine came up after them, 7651
Ge 41:20 kine did eat up the first **s.** fat kine: 7651
Ge 41:22 **s.** ears came up in one stalk, full 7651
Ge 41:23 **s.** ears, withered, thin, and blasted 7651
Ge 41:24 ears devoured the **s.** good ears: 7651
Ge 41:26 The **s.** good kine are **s.** years; and 7651
Ge 41:26 and the **s.** good ears are **s.** years: 7651
Ge 41:27 the **s.** thin and ill favoured kine 7651
Ge 41:27 came up after them are **s.** years; 7651
Ge 41:27 the **s.** empty ears blasted with the 7651
Ge 41:27 east wind shall be **s.** years of famine 7651
Ge 41:29 there come **s.** years of great plenty 7651
Ge 41:30 arise after them **s.** years of famine; 7651
Ge 41:34 of Egypt in the **s.** plenteous years. 7651
Ge 41:36 land against the **s.** years of famine, 7651
Ge 41:47 in the **s.** plenteous years the earth 7651
Ge 41:48 up all the food of the **s.** years, 7651
Ge 41:53 the **s.** years of plenteousness, that 7651
Ge 41:54 **s.** years of dearth began to come, 7651
Ge 46:25 unto Jacob: all the souls were **s.**. 7651
Ge 47:28 was an hundred forty and **s.** years. 7651
Ge 50:10 a mourning for his father **s.** days. 7651
Ex 2:16 priest of Midian had **s.** daughters: 7651
Ex 6:16 an hundred thirty and **s.** years. 7651
Ex 6:20 hundred and thirty and **s.** years 7651
Ex 7:25 **s.** days were fulfilled, after that 7651
Ex 12:15 **S.** days shall ye eat unleavened 7651
Ex 12:19 **S.** days shall there be no leaven 7651
Ex 13:6 **S.** days thou shalt eat unleavened 7651
Ex 13:7 bread shall be eaten **s.** days; and 7651
Ex 22:30 **s.** days it shall be with his dam; on 7651
Ex 23:15 shalt eat unleavened bread **s.** days, 7651
Ex 25:37 shalt make the **s.** lamps thereof: 7651
Ex 29:30 his stead shall put them on **s.** days, 7651
Ex 29:35 **s.** days shalt thou consecrate them. 7651
Ex 29:37 **S.** days thou shalt make an 7651
Ex 34:18 **S.** days thou shalt eat unleavened 7651
Ex 37:23 And he made his **s.** lamps, and his 7651
Ex 38:24 and **s.** hundred and thirty shekels, 7651
Ex 38:25 thousand **s.** hundred and threescore 7651
Ex 38:28 thousand **s.** hundred seventy and 7651
Le 4:6 and sprinkle of the blood **s.** times 7651
Le 4:17 sprinkle it **s.** times before the Lord, 7651
Le 8:11 thereof upon the altar **s.** times, 7651
Le 8:33 of the congregation in **s.** days, 7651
Le 8:33 for **s.** days shall he consecrate you. 7651
Le 8:35 congregation day and night **s.** days, 7651
Le 12:2 then she shall be unclean **s.** days; 7651
Le 13:4 him that hath the plague **s.** days: 7651
Le 13:5 shall shut him up **s.** days more: 7651
Le 13:21, 26 priest shall shut him up **s.** days: 7651
Le 13:31 hath the plague of the scall **s.** days: 7651
Le 13:33 that hath the scall **s.** days more: 7651
Le 13:50 up it that hath the plague **s.** days: 7651
Le 13:54 he shall shut it up **s.** days more: 7651
Le 14:7 cleansed from the leprosy **s.** times, 7651
Le 14:8 tarry abroad out of his tent **s.** days. 7651
Le 14:16 of the oil with his fingers **s.** times 7651
Le 14:27 is in his left hand **s.** times before 7651
Le 14:38 and shut up the house **s.** days: 7651
Le 14:51 and sprinkle the house **s.** times: 7651
Le 15:13 he shall number to himself **s.** days 7651
Le 15:19 she shall be put apart **s.** days: and 7651
Le 15:24 him, he shall be unclean **s.** days; 7651
Le 15:28 she shall number to herself **s.** days, 7651
Le 16:14 of the blood with his finger **s.** times. 7651
Le 16:19 upon it with his finger **s.** times, 7651
Le 22:27 it shall be **s.** days under the dam; 7651
Le 23:6 **s.** days ye must eat unleavened 7651
Le 23:8 made by fire unto the Lord **s.** days: 7651
Le 23:15 **s.** sabbaths shall be complete: 7651
Le 23:18 **s.** lambs without blemish of the 7651
Le 23:34 feast of tabernacles for **s.** days unto 7651
Le 23:36 **S.** days ye shall offer an offering 7651
Le 23:39 keep a feast unto the Lord **s.** days: 7651
Le 23:40 before the Lord your God **s.** days. 7651
Le 23:41 keep a feast unto the Lord **s.** days 7651
Le 23:42 Ye shall dwell in booths **s.** days; all 7651
Le 25:8 shalt number **s.** sabbaths of years 7651
Le 25:8 years unto thee, **s.** times **s.** years; 7651
Le 25:8 space of the **s.** sabbaths of years 7651
Le 26:18 I will punish you **s.** times more 7651
Le 26:21 I will bring **s.** times more plagues 7651
Le 26:24 and will punish you yet **s.** times 7651
Le 26:28 chastise you **s.** times for your sins 7651
Nu 1:31 were fifty and **s.** thousand and four 7651
Nu 1:39 and two thousand and **s.** hundred. 7651
Nu 2:8 were fifty and **s.** thousand and four 7651
Nu 2:26 and two thousand and **s.** hundred. 7651
Nu 2:31 thousand and fifty and **s.** thousand 7651
Nu 3:22 numbered of them were **s.** thousand 7651
Nu 4:36 were two thousand **s.** hundred and 7651
Nu 8:2 the **s.** lamps shall give light over 7651
Nu 12:14 should she not be ashamed **s.** days? 7651
Nu 12:14 be shut out from the camp **s.** days, 7651
Nu 12:15 was shut out from the camp **s.** days: 7651
Nu 13:22 Hebron was built **s.** years before 7651
Nu 16:49 fourteen thousand and **s.** hundred, 7651
Nu 19:4 of the congregation **s.** times: 7651
Nu 19:11 any man shall be unclean **s.** days. 7651
Nu 19:14 the tent, shall be unclean **s.** days. 7651
Nu 19:16 or a grave, shall be unclean **s.** days. 7651
Nu 23:1 unto Balak, Build me here **s.** altars, 7651
Nu 23:1 me here **s.** oxen and **s.** rams. 7651
Nu 23:4 I have prepared **s.** altars, and I 7651
Nu 23:14 built **s.** altars, and offered a bullock 7651
Nu 23:29 unto Balak, Build me here **s.** altars, 7651
Nu 23:29 me here **s.** bullocks and **s.** rams. 7651
Nu 26:7 and three thousand and **s.** hundred 7651
Nu 26:34 and two thousand and **s.** hundred. 7651
Nu 26:51 a thousand **s.** hundred and thirty. 7651
Nu 28:11 **s.** lambs of the first year without 7651
Nu 28:17 **s.** days shall unleavened bread be 7651
Nu 28:19 ram, and **s.** lambs of the first year: 7651
Nu 28:21 lamb, throughout the **s.** lambs: 7651
Nu 28:24 offer daily, throughout the **s.** days, 7651
Nu 28:27 one ram, **s.** lambs of the first year; 7651
Nu 28:29 one lamb, throughout the **s.** lambs; 7651
Nu 29:2 **s.** lambs of the first year without 7651
Nu 29:4 one lamb, throughout the **s.** lambs: 7651
Nu 29:8 ram, and **s.** lambs of the first year; 7651
Nu 29:10 one lamb, throughout the **s.** lambs: 7651
Nu 29:12 keep a feast unto the Lord **s.** days: 7651
Nu 29:32 on the seventh day **s.** bullocks, two 7651
Nu 29:36 **s.** lambs of the first year without 7651
Nu 31:19 ye abide without the camp **s.** days: 7651
Nu 31:36 three hundred thousand and **s.** and 7651
Nu 31:43 thirty thousand and **s.** thousand 7651
Nu 31:52 sixteen thousand **s.** hundred and 7651
De 7:1 **s.** nations greater and mightier 7651
De 15:1 **s.** years thou shalt make a release. 7651
De 16:3 **s.** days shalt thou eat unleavened 7651
De 16:4 with thee in all thy coast **s.** days; 7651
De 16:9 **S.** weeks shalt thou number unto 7651
De 16:9 begin to number the **s.** weeks from 7651
De 16:13 the feast of tabernacles **s.** days, 7651
De 16:15 **S.** days shalt thou keep a solemn 7651
De 28:7 way, and flee before thee **s.** ways. 7651
De 28:25 them, and flee **s.** ways before them: 7651
De 31:10 At the end of every **s.** years, in the 7651
Jos 6:4 **s.** priests shall bear before the ark 7651
Jos 6:4 ye shall compass the city **s.** times, 7651
Jos 6:4 **s.** trumpets of rams' horns: and 7651
Jos 6:6 let **s.** priests bear **s.** trumpets of 7651
Jos 6:8 **s.** priests bearing the **s.** trumpets 7651
Jos 6:13 And **s.** priests bearing **s.** trumpets 7651
Jos 6:15 after the same manner **s.** times: 7651
Jos 6:15 they compassed the city **s.** times 7651
Jos 18:2 the children of Israel **s.** tribes, 7651
Jos 18:5 they shall divide it into **s.** parts: 7651
Jos 18:6 describe the land into **s.** parts, and 7651
Jos 18:9 described it by cities into **s.** parts 7651
Jg 6:1 into the hand of Midian **s.** years. 7651
Jg 6:25 the second bullock of **s.** years old, 7651
Jg 8:26 a thousand and **s.** hundred shekels 7651
Jg 12:9 And he judged Israel **s.** years. 7651
Jg 14:12 me within the **s.** days of the feast, 7651
Jg 14:17 she wept before him the **s.** days, 7651
Jg 16:7 If they bind me with **s.** green withs 7651
Jg 16:8 brought up to her **s.** green withs 7651
Jg 16:13 weavest the **s.** locks of my head 7651
Jg 16:19 to shave off the **s.** locks of his head; 7651
Jg 20:15 numbered **s.** hundred chosen men 7651
Jg 20:16 **s.** hundred chosen men lefthanded; 7651
Ru 4:15 which is better to thee than **s.** sons, 7651
1Sa 2:5 so that the barren hath born **s.**; 7651
1Sa 6:1 country of the Philistines **s.** months. 7651
1Sa 10:8 **s.** days shalt thou tarry, till I come 7651
1Sa 11:3 Give us **s.** days respite, that we 7651
1Sa 13:8 And he tarried **s.** days, according to 7651
1Sa 16:10 Jesse made **s.** of his sons to pass 7651
1Sa 31:13 a tree at Jabesh, and fasted **s.** days. 7651
2Sa 2:11 the house of Judah was **s.** years 7651
2Sa 5:5 over Judah **s.** years and six months: 7651
2Sa 8:4 chariots, and **s.** hundred horsemen, 7651
2Sa 10:18 slew the men of **s.** hundred chariots 7651
2Sa 21:6 **s.** men of his sons be delivered unto 7651
2Sa 21:9 they fell all **s.** together, and were 7651
2Sa 23:39 the Hittite: thirty and **s.** in all. 7651
2Sa 24:13 **s.** years of famine come unto thee 7651
1Ki 2:11 **s.** years reigned he in Hebron, and 7651
1Ki 6:6 and the third was **s.** cubits broad: 7651
1Ki 6:38 it. So was he **s.** years in building it. 7651
1Ki 7:17 **s.** for the one chapiter, and **s.** for the 7651
1Ki 8:65 **s.** days and **s.** days, even fourteen 7651
1Ki 11:3 he had **s.** hundred wives, princesses, 7651
1Ki 16:15 did Zimri reign **s.** days in Tirzah. 7651
1Ki 18:43 And he said, Go again **s.** times. 7651
1Ki 19:18 I have left me **s.** thousand in Israel, 7651
1Ki 20:15 children of Israel, being **s.** thousand. 7651
1Ki 20:29 one over against the other **s.** days. 7651
1Ki 20:30 fell upon twenty and **s.** thousand of 7651
2Ki 3:9 a compass of **s.** days journey: 7651
2Ki 3:26 took with him **s.** hundred men that 7651
2Ki 4:35 the child sneezed **s.** times, and the 7651
2Ki 5:10 Go and wash in Jordan **s.** times, 7651
2Ki 5:14 dipped himself **s.** times in Jordan, 7651
2Ki 8:1 also come upon the land **s.** years. 7651
2Ki 8:2 the land of the Philistines **s.** years. 7651
2Ki 8:3 it came to pass at the **s.** years' end, 7651
2Ki 11:21 **S.** years old was Jehoash when he 7651
2Ki 24:16 the men of might, even **s.** thousand, 7651
2Ki 25:27 pass in the **s.** and thirtieth year of 7651
2Ki 25:27 on the **s.** and twentieth day of the 7651
1Ch 3:4 he reigned **s.** years and six months: 7651
1Ch 3:24 and Dalaiah, and Anani, **s.**. 7651
1Ch 5:13 and Jachan, and Zia, and Heber, **s.**. 7651
1Ch 5:18 four and forty thousand **s.** hundred 7651
1Ch 7:5 fourscore and **s.** thousand. 7651
1Ch 9:13 and **s.** hundred and threescore; 7651
1Ch 9:25 to come after **s.** days from time to 7651
1Ch 10:12 oak in Jabesh, and fasted **s.** days. 7651
1Ch 12:25 war, **s.** thousand and one hundred. 7651
1Ch 12:27 three thousand and **s.** hundred; 7651
1Ch 12:34 and spear thirty and **s.** thousand. 7651
1Ch 15:26 they offered **s.** bullocks and **s.** rams. 7651
1Ch 18:4 **s.** thousand horsemen, and twenty 7651
1Ch 19:18 slew of the Syrians **s.** thousand men 7651
1Ch 26:30 a thousand and **s.** hundred, were 7651
1Ch 26:32 and **s.** hundred chief fathers, whom 7651
1Ch 29:4 **s.** thousand talents of refined silver, 7651
1Ch 29:27 **s.** years reigned he in Hebron, and 7651
2Ch 7:8 Solomon kept the feast **s.** days, 7651
2Ch 7:9 the dedication of the altar **s.** days, 7651
2Ch 7:9 and the feast **s.** days. 7651
2Ch 13:9 with a young bullock and **s.** rams, 7651
2Ch 15:11 **s.** hundred oxen and **s.** thousand 7651
2Ch 17:11 **s.** thousand and **s.** hundred rams, 7651
2Ch 17:11 and **s.** thousand and **s.** hundred 7651
2Ch 24:1 Joash was **s.** years old when he 7651
2Ch 26:13 and **s.** thousand and five hundred, 7651
2Ch 29:21 brought **s.** bullocks, and **s.** rams, 7651
2Ch 29:21 and **s.** lambs, and **s.** he goats, for a 7651
2Ch 30:21 feast of unleavened bread **s.** days 7651
2Ch 30:22 eat throughout the feast **s.** days, 7651
2Ch 30:23 took counsel to keep other **s.** days: 7651
2Ch 30:23 kept other **s.** days with gladness. 7651
2Ch 30:24 bullocks and **s.** thousand sheep; 7651

2Ch 35:17 feast of unleavened bread s. days....... 7651
Ezr 2:5 Arah, s. hundred seventy and five. 7651
Ezr 2:9 Zaccai, s. hundred and threescore....... 7651
Ezr 2:25 s. hundred and forty and three........... 7651
Ezr 2:33 Ono, s. hundred twenty and five. 7651
Ezr 2:38 thousand two hundred forty and s....... 7651
Ezr 2:65 there were s. thousand three 7651
Ezr 2:65 three hundred thirty and s. 7651
Ezr 2:66 Their horses were s. hundred thirty.... 7651
Ezr 2:67 thousand s. hundred and twenty. 7651
Ezr 6:22 unleavened bread s. days with joy: 7651
Ezr 7:14 king, and of his s. counsellors,........... 7655
Ezr 8:35 seventy and s. lambs, twelve he 7651
Ne 7:14 Zaccai, s. hundred and threescore....... 7651
Ne 7:18 six hundred threescore and s............. 7651
Ne 7:19 two thousand threescore and s........... 7651
Ne 7:29 Beeroth, s. hundred forty and three.... 7651
Ne 7:37 Ono, s. hundred twenty and one. 7651
Ne 7:41 thousand two hundred forty and s....... 7651
Ne 7:67 maidservants, of whom there were s... 7651
Ne 7:67 three hundred thirty and s.: and......... 7651
Ne 7:68 horses, s. hundred thirty and six: 7651
Ne 7:69 s. hundred and twenty asses. 7651
Ne 7:72 threescore and s. priests' garments. ... 7651
Ne 8:18 they kept the feast s. days; and on..... 7651
Es 1:1 over an hundred and s. and twenty..... 7651
Es 1:5 both unto great and small, s. days, ... 7651
Es 1:10 s. chamberlains that served in the 7651
Es 1:14 the s. princes of Persia and Media,..... 7651
Es 2:9 s. maidens, which were meet to be 7651
Es 8:9 hundred twenty and s. provinces,....... 7651
Es 9:30 hundred twenty and s. provinces....... 7651
Job 1:2 there were born unto him s. sons........ 7651
Job 1:3 also was s. thousand sheep, and......... 7651
Job 2:13 the ground s. days and s. nights, ... 7651
Job 5:19 in s. there shall no evil touch thee...... 7651
Job 42:8 you now s. bullocks and s. rams,..............
Job 42:13 also s. sons and three daughters. 7658
Ps 12:6 furnace of earth, purified s. times. 7659
Ps 119:164 S. times a day do I praise thee.......... 7651
Pr 6:16 s. are an abomination unto him: 7651
Pr 9:1 she hath hewn out her s. pillars: 7651
Pr 24:16 For a just man falleth s. times, and..... 7651
Pr 26:16 s. men that can render a reason........... 7651
Pr 26:25 are s. abominations in his heart........... 7651
Ec 11:2 Give a portion to s., and also to......... 7651
Isa 4:1 s. women shall take hold of one 7651
Isa 11:15 shall smite it in the s. streams,............ 7651
Isa 30:26 sevenfold, as the light of s. days, ... 7651
Jer 15:9 that hath borne s. languisheth: 7651
Jer 34:14 end of s. years let ye go every man ... 7651
Jer 52:25 s. men of them that were near the...... 7651
Jer 52:30 captive of the Jews s. hundred........... 7651
Jer 52:31 s. and thirtieth year of the captivity 7651
Eze 3:15 astonished among them s. days........... 7651
Eze 3:16 came to pass at the end of s. days, ... 7651
Eze 29:17 pass in the s. and twentieth year,....... 7651
Eze 39:9 shall burn them with fire s. years: 7651
Eze 39:12 s. months shall the house of Israel...... 7651
Eze 39:14 end of s. months shall they search...... 7651
Eze 40:22 they went up into it by s. steps; 7651
Eze 40:26 there were s. steps to go up to it, ... 7651
Eze 41:3 the breadth of the door, s. cubits. 7651
Eze 43:25 S. days shalt thou prepare every......... 7651
Eze 43:26 S. days shall they purge the altar 7651
Eze 44:26 they shall reckon unto him s. days...... 7651
Eze 45:21 the passover, a feast of s. days; 7651
Eze 45:23 s. days of the feast he shall prepare.... 7651
Eze 45:23 s. bullocks and s. rams without.......... 7651
Eze 45:23 without blemish daily the s. days;....... 7651
Eze 45:25 the like in the feast of the s. days, ... 7651
Da 3:19 the furnace one s. times more 7655
Da 4:16 and let s. times pass over him............ 7655
Da 4:23 field, till s. times pass over him; 7655
Da 4:25, 32 and s. times shall pass over thee, .. 7655
Da 9:25 the Prince shall be s. weeks, and....... 7651
Am 5:8 Seek him that maketh the s. stars 3598
Mic 5:5 we raise against him s. shepherds, ... 7651
Zec 3:9 upon one stone shall be s. eyes: 7651
Zec 4:2 top of it, and his s. lamps thereon, ... 7651
Zec 4:2 and s. pipes to the...lamps, which 7651
Zec 4:2 pipes to the s. lamps, which are......... 7651
Zec 4:10 hand of Zerubbabel with those s.; 7651
Mt 12:45 s. other spirits more wicked than .. *2033*
Mt 15:34 they said, S., and a few little fishes. ... *2033*
Mt 15:36 And he took the s. loaves and the *2033*
Mt 15:37 meat that was left s. baskets full. *2033*
Mt 16:10 Neither the s. loaves of the four..... *2033*
Mt 18:21 and I forgive him? till s. times?.......... *2034*
Mt 18:22 say not unto thee, Until s. times:.. *2034*
Mt 18:22 but, Until seventy times s. *2033*
Mt 22:25 Now there were with us s. brethren: .. *2033*
Mt 22:28 whose wife shall she be of the s.? *2033*
Mk 8:5 loaves have ye? And they said, S.. ... *2033*
Mk 8:6 and he took the s. loaves, and gave *2033*
Mk 8:8 meat that was left s. baskets............ *2033*
Mk 8:20 when the s. among four thousand .. *2033*
Mk 8:20 took ye up? And they said, S........... *2033*
Mk 12:20 Now there were s. brethren: and........ *2033*
Mk 12:22 And the s. had her, and left no seed.. *2033*
Mk 12:23 them? for the s. had her to wife. *2033*
Mk 16:9 out of whom he had cast s. devils. *2033*
Lu 2:36 had lived with an husband s. years...... *2033*
Lu 8:2 out of whom went s. devils. *2033*
Lu 11:26 him s. other spirits more wicked... *2033*
Lu 17:4 against thee s. times in a day, ... *2034*
Lu 17:4 and s. times in a day turn again... *2034*
Lu 20:29 There were therefore s. brethren:....... *2033*
Lu 20:31 and in like manner the s. also: and *2033*
Lu 20:33 them is she? for s. had her to wife. *2033*
Ac 6:3 among you s. men of honest report, ... *2033*
Ac 13:19 destroyed s. nations in the land of...... *2033*
Ac 19:14 there were s. sons of one Sceva, a...... *2033*
Ac 20:6 five days; where we abode s. days. *2033*
Ac 21:4 disciples, we tarried there s. days: *2033*
Ac 21:8 which was one of the s.; and abode *2033*
Ac 21:27 And when the s. days were almost *2033*
Ac 28:14 desired to tarry with them s. days:..... *2033*
Ro 11:4 to myself s. thousand men, who......... *2035*
Heb 11:30 were compassed about s. days........... *2033*
Re 1:4 John to the s. churches which are....... *2033*
Re 1:4 and from the s. Spirits which are......... *2033*
Re 1:11 the s. churches which are in Asia;. *2033*
Re 1:12 I saw s. golden candlesticks; *2033*
Re 1:13 in the midst of the s. candlesticks....... *2033*
Re 1:16 he had in his right hand s. stars: *2033*
Re 1:20 The mystery of the s. stars which. *2033*
Re 1:20 and the s. golden candlesticks....... *2033*
Re 1:20 s. stars are the angels of the s. *2033*
Re 1:20 and the s. candlesticks which thou. *2033*
Re 1:20 thou sawest are the s. churches..... *2033*
Re 2:1 he that holdeth the s. stars in his. *2033*
Re 2:1 of the s. golden candlesticks;......... *2033*
Re 3:1 s. Spirits of God, and the s. stars;. *2033*
Re 4:5 there were s. lamps of fire burning..... *2033*
Re 4:5 which are the s. Spirits of God. *2033*
Re 5:1 the backside, sealed with s. seals....... *2033*
Re 5:5 and to loose the s. seals thereof. *2033*
Re 5:6 slain, having s. horns and s. eyes, ... *2033*
Re 5:6 which are the s. Spirits of God *2033*
Re 8:2 And I saw the s. angels which stood... *2033*
Re 8:2 to them were given s. trumpets.......... *2033*
Re 8:6 s. angels which had the s. trumpets *2033*
Re 10:3 s. thunders uttered their voices. *2033*
Re 10:4 s. thunders had uttered their voices, .. *2033*
Re 10:4 which the s. thunders uttered, and *2033*
Re 11:13 were slain of men s. thousand: and..... *2033*
Re 12:3 having s. heads and ten horns, and..... *2033*
Re 12:3 and s. crowns upon his heads. *2033*
Re 13:1 having s. heads and ten horns, and..... *2033*
Re 15:1 s. angels having the s. last plagues; *2033*
Re 15:6 s. angels came out of the temple,........ *2033*
Re 15:6 having the s. plagues, clothed in......... *2033*
Re 15:7 unto the s. angels s. golden vials......... *2033*
Re 15:8 the s. plagues of the s. angels were.... *2033*
Re 16:1 saying to the s. angels, Go your *2033*
Re 17:1 the s. angels which had the s. vials,..... *2033*
Re 17:3 having s. heads and ten horns........... *2033*
Re 17:7 hath the s. heads and ten horns. *2033*
Re 17:9 The s. heads are s. mountains, on...... *2033*
Re 17:10 there are s. kings: five are fallen,....... *2033*
Re 17:11 and is of the s., and goeth into.......... *2033*
Re 21:9 came unto me one of the s. angels *2033*
Re 21:9 s. vials full of the s. last plagues, ... *2033*

SEVENFOLD
Ge 4:15 vengeance...be taken on him s........... 7659
Ge 4:24 If Cain shall be avenged s., truly........ 7659
Ge 4:24 truly Lamech seventy and s.. 7659
Ps 79:12 render unto our neighbours s. into...... 7659
Pr 6:31 if he be found, he shall restore s.;....... 7659
Isa 30:26 and the light of the sun shall be s....... 7659

SEVEN-HUNDRED See SEVEN and HUNDRED.

SEVENS
Ge 7:2 beast thou shalt take to thee by s., ... 7651
Ge 7:3 Of fowls also of the air by s., the....... 7651

SEVENTEEN
Ge 37:2 Joseph, being s. years old,......... 7651,6240
Ge 47:28 in the land of Egypt s. years: 7651,6240
Jg 8:14 even threescore and s. men. 7657,7651
1Ki 14:21 reigned s. years in Jerusalem,..... 7651,6240
2Ki 13:1 Samaria, and reigned s. years..... 7651,6240
1Ch 7:11 s. thousand and two hundred...... 7651,6240
2Ch 12:13 he reigned s. years in Jerusalem, .7651,6240
Ezr 2:39 of Harim, a thousand and s.. 7651,6240
Ne 7:42 of Harim, a thousand and s.. 7651,6240
Jer 32:9 the money, even s. shekels of...... 7651,6240

SEVENTEENTH
Ge 7:11 month, the s. day of the month,.. 7651,6240
Ge 8:4 on the s. day of the month, ... 7651,6240
1Ki 22:51 Israel in Samaria the s. year....... 7651,6240
2Ki 16:1 the s. year of Pekah the son of... 7651,6240
1Ch 24:15 The s. of Hezir, the eighteenth... 7651,6240
1Ch 25:24 The s. to Joshbekashah, he,....... 7651,6240

SEVENTH
Ge 2:2 s. day God ended his work which....... 7637
Ge 2:2 rested on the s. day from all his 7637
Ge 2:3 And God blessed the s. day, and........ 7637
Ge 8:4 the ark rested in the s. month, on...... 7637
Ex 12:15 from the first day until the s. day, ... 7637
Ex 12:16 in the s. day there shall be an holy..... 7637
Ex 13:6 s. day shall be a feast to the Lord...... 7637
Ex 16:26 but on the s. day, which is the 7637
Ex 16:27 people on the s. day for to gather, ... 7637
Ex 16:29 go out of his place on the s. day. 7637
Ex 16:30 So the people rested on the s. day. 7637
Ex 20:10 s. day is the sabbath of the Lord........ 7637
Ex 20:11 in them is, and rested the s. day:....... 7637
Ex 21:2 and in the s. he shall go out free........ 7637
Ex 23:11 s. year thou shalt let it rest and lie..... 7637
Ex 23:12 and on the s. day thou shalt rest:....... 7637
Ex 24:16 s. day he called unto Moses out of 7637
Ex 31:15 in the s. is the sabbath of rest, holy ... 7637
Ex 31:17 on the s. day he rested, and was 7637
Ex 34:21 but on the s. day thou shalt rest: 7637
Ex 35:2 s. day there shall be to you an holy 7637
Le 13:5 priest shall look on him the s. day: 7637
Le 13:6 shall look on him again the s. day:...... 7637
Le 13:27 shall look upon him the s. day: 7637
Le 13:32, 34 s. day the priest shall look on.......... 7637
Le 13:51 look on the plague on the s. day: 7637
Le 14:9 But it shall be on the s. day, that....... 7637
Le 14:39 priest shall come again the s. day,...... 7637
Le 16:29 that in the s. month, on the tenth 7637
Le 23:3 the s. day is the sabbath of rest, a..... 7637
Le 23:8 the s. day is an holy convocation:....... 7637
Le 23:16 s. sabbath shall ye number fifty......... 7637
Le 23:24 the s. month, in the first day of the...... 7637
Le 23:27 on the tenth day of this s. month 7637
Le 23:34 The fifteenth day of this s. month....... 7637
Le 23:39 in the fifteenth day of the s. month,.... 7637
Le 23:41 ye shall celebrate it in the s. month.... 7637
Le 25:4 But in the s. year shall be a sabbath ... 7637
Le 25:9 on the tenth day of the s. month,....... 7637
Le 25:20 say, What shall we eat the s. year? 7637
Nu 6:9 on the s. day shall he shave it. 7637
Nu 7:48 On the s. day Elishama the son of...... 7637
Nu 19:12 and on the s. day he shall be clean: 7637
Nu 19:12 the s. day he shall not be clean......... 7637
Nu 19:19 on the third day, and on the s. day:.... 7637
Nu 19:19 and on the s. day he shall purify 7637
Nu 28:25 on the s. day ye shall have an holy..... 7637
Nu 29:1 in the s. month, on the first day of...... 7637
Nu 29:7 on the tenth day of this s. month 7637
Nu 29:12 on the fifteenth day of the s. month.... 7637
Nu 29:32 And on the s. day seven bullocks, ... 7637
Nu 31:19 on the third day, and on the s. day..... 7637
Nu 31:24 wash your clothes on the s. day,........ 7637
De 5:14 But the s. day is the sabbath of the.... 7637
De 15:9 The s. year, the year of release, is 7637
De 15:12 s. year thou shalt let him go free 7637
De 16:8 s. day shall be a solemn assembly 7637
Jos 6:4 the s. day ye shall compass the city..... 7637
Jos 6:15 And it came to pass on the s. day, ... 7637
Jos 6:16 And it came to pass at the s. time,..... 7637
Jos 19:40 the s. lot came out for the tribe of..... 7637
Jg 14:15 And it came to pass on the s. day,...... 7637
Jg 14:17 on the s. day, that he told her,.......... 7637

Jg 14:18 s. day before the sun went down, 7637
2Sa 12:18 on the s. day, that the child died. 7637
1Ki 8:2 Ethanim, which is the s. month. 7637
1Ki 16:10, 15 in the twenty and s. year of Asa 7651
1Ki 18:44 And it came to pass at the s. time, 7637
1Ki 20:29 in the s. day the battle was joined: 7637
2Ki 11:4 s. year Jehoiada sent and fetched 7637
2Ki 12:1 the s. year of Jehu Jehoash began 7651
2Ki 13:10 In the thirty and s. year of Joash 7651
2Ki 15:1 the twenty and s. year of Jeroboam 7651
2Ki 18:9 which was the s. year of Hoshea 7651
2Ki 25:8 month, on the s. day of the month, 7651
2Ki 25:25 in the s. month, that Ishmael 7637
1Ch 2:15 Ozem the sixth, David the s.: 7637
1Ch 12:11 Attai the sixth, Eliel the s., 7637
1Ch 24:10 s. to Hakkoz, the eighth to Abijah, 7637
1Ch 25:14 The s. to Jesharelah, he, his sons, 7637
1Ch 26:3 Jehohanan the sixth, Elioenai the s. 7637
1Ch 26:5 Ammiel the sixth, Issachar the s., 7637
1Ch 27:10 The s. captain for the s. month was 7637
2Ch 5:3 feast which was in the s. month. 7637
2Ch 7:10 and twentieth day of the s. month 7637
2Ch 23:1 in the s. year Jehoiada strengthened 7637
2Ch 31:7 and finished them in the s. month 7637
Ezr 3:1 And when the s. month was come, 7637
Ezr 3:6 From the first day of the s. month 7637
Ezr 7:7 the s. year of Artaxerxes the king. 7651
Ezr 7:8 was in the s. year of the king. 7637
Ne 7:73 and when the s. month came, the 7637
Ne 8:2 upon the first day of the s. month. 7637
Ne 8:14 booths in the feast of the s. month: 7637
Ne 10:31 and that we would leave the s. year, 7637
Es 1:10 s. day, when the heart of the king 7637
Es 2:16 Tebeth, in the s. year of his reign. 7651
Jer 28:17 died the same year in the s. month. 7637
Jer 41:1 in the s. month, that Ishmael 7637
Jer 52:28 in the s. year three thousand Jews 7651
Eze 20:1 And it came to pass in the s. year, 7637
Eze 30:20 month, in the s. day of the month, 7651
Eze 45:20 shalt do the s. day of the month 7651
Eze 45:25 In the s. month, in the fifteenth day 7651
Hag 2:1 In the s. month, in the one and 7637
Zec 7:5 mourned in the fifth and s. month, 7637
Zec 8:19 the fast of the s., and the fast of the 7637
Mt 22:26 also, and the third, unto the s. *2035*
Joh 4:52 at the s. hour the fever left him. *1442*
Heb 4:4 spake...of the s. day on this wise, *1442*
Heb 4:4 rest the s. day from all his works. *1442*
Jude 14 And Enoch also, the s. from Adam, *1442*
Re 8:1 when he had opened the s. seal, *1442*
Re 10:7 the days of the voice of the s. angel, *1442*
Re 11:15 And the s. angel sounded; and *1442*
Re 16:17 And the s. angel poured out his vial *1442*
Re 21:20 the s., chrysolite; the eighth, beryl; *1442*

SEVEN-THOUSAND See SEVEN and THOUSAND.

SEVENTY
Ge 4:24 truly Lamech s. and sevenfold. 7657
Ge 5:12 And Cainan lived s. years, and begat 7657
Ge 5:31 seven hundred s. and seven years: 7657
Ge 11:26 And Terah lived s. years, and begat 7657
Ge 12:4 and Abram was s. and five years old 7657
Ex 1:5 of the lions of Jacob were s. souls: 7657
Ex 24:1 Abihu, and s. of the elders of Israel; 7657
Ex 24:9 Abihu, and s. of the elders of Israel: 7657
Ex 38:28 seven hundred s. and five shekels 7657
Ex 38:29 brass of the offering was s. talents, 7657
Nu 7:13, 19,25,31,37 bowl of s. shekels, 7657
Nu 7:43 a silver bowl of s. shekels, after 7657
Nu 7:49, 55,61,67,73,79 bowl of s. shekels, 7657
Nu 7:85 and thirty shekels, each bowl s.: 7657
Nu 11:16 me s. men of the elders of Israel, 7657
Nu 11:24 s. men of the elders of the people, 7657
Nu 11:25 him, and gave it unto the s. elders: 7657
Nu 31:32 and s. thousand and five thousand 7657
Jg 9:56 father, in slaying his s. brethren: 7657
2Sa 24:15 to Beer-sheba s. thousand men. 7657
2Ki 10:1 And Ahab had s. sons in Samaria 7657
2Ki 10:6 the king's sons, being s. persons, 7657
2Ki 10:7 the king's sons, and slew s. persons, 7657
1Ch 21:14 there fell of Israel s. thousand men 7657
Ezr 2:3 thousand an hundred s. and two. 7657
Ezr 2:4 three hundred s. and two 7657
Ezr 2:5 of Arah, seven hundred s. and five. 7657
Ezr 2:36 Jeshua, nine hundred s. and three 7657
Ezr 2:40 children of Hodaviah, s. and four. 7657
Ezr 8:7 of Athaliah, and with him s. males. 7657
Ezr 8:14 Zabbud, and with them s. males. 7657
Ezr 8:35 s. and seven lambs, twelve he goats 7657
Ne 7:8 thousand an hundred s. and two. 7657
Ne 7:9 three hundred s. and two 7657
Ne 7:39 Jeshua, nine hundred s. and three 7657
Ne 7:43 children of Hodevah, s. and four 7657
Ne 11:19 gates, were an hundred s. and two. 7657
Es 9:16 of their foes s. and five thousand, 7657
Isa 23:15 Tyre shall be forgotten s. years, 7657
Isa 23:15 end of s. years shall Tyre sing as an 7657
Isa 23:17 to pass after the end of s. years, 7657
Jer 25:11 serve the king of Babylon s. years 7657
Jer 25:12 when s. years are accomplished, 7657
Jer 29:10 after s. years be accomplished at 7657
Eze 8:11 before them s. men of the ancients 7657
Eze 41:12 toward the west was s. cubits broad; 7657
Da 9:2 that he would accomplish s. years 7657
Da 9:24 S. weeks are determined upon thy 7657
Zec 7:5 even those s. years, did ye at all fast 7657
Mt 18:22 **times: but, Until s. times seven.** *1441*
Lu 10:1 the Lord appointed other s. also, *1440*
Lu 10:17 And the s. returned again with joy, *1440*

SEVENTY-THOUSAND See SEVENTY and THOUSAND.

SEVER See also SEVERED.
Ex 8:22 s. in that day the land of Goshen, 6395
Ex 9:4 shall s. between the cattle of Israel 6395
Eze 39:14 they shall s. out men of continual 914
Mt 13:49 **s. the wicked from among the just,** *873*

SEVERAL
Nu 28:13 a s. tenth deal of flour mingled with
Nu 28:21 A s. tenth deal shalt thou offer for
Nu 28:29 A s. tenth deal unto one lamb,
Nu 29:10 A s. tenth deal for one lamb,
Nu 29:15 And a s. tenth deal to each lamb of the
2Ki 15:5 death, and dwelt in a s. house. 2669
2Ch 11:12 And in every s. city he put shields and
2Ch 26:21 death, and dwelt in a s. house, 2669
2Ch 28:25 in every s. city of Judah he made high
2Ch 31:19 suburbs of their cities, in every s. city,
Mt 25:15 **man according to his s. ability;** *2398*
Re 21:21 every s. gate was of one pearl: *303,1520*

SEVERALLY
1Co 12:11 dividing to every man s. as he will. *2398*

SEVERED
Le 20:26 and have s. you from other people, 914
De 4:41 s. three cities on this side Jordan 914
Jg 4:11 had s. himself from the Kenites, 6504

SEVERITY
Ro 11:22 Behold...the goodness and s. of God: *663*
Ro 11:22 on them which fell, s.; but toward *663*

SEW See also SEWED; SEWEST; SEWETH.
Ec 3:7 A time to rend, and a time to s.; 8609
Eze 13:18 Woe to the women that s. pillows 8609

SEWED
Ge 3:7 they s. fig leaves together, and 8609
Job 16:15 I have s. sackcloth upon my skin, 8609

SEWEST
Job 14:17 and thou s. up mine iniquity. 2950

SEWETH
Mk 2:21 **No man...s. a piece of new cloth** *1976*

SHAALABBIN (sha-al-ab'-bin) See also SHAALBIM.
Jos 19:42 And S., and Ajalon, and Jethlah, 8169

SHAALBIM (sha-al'-bim) See also SHAALABBIN; SHAALBONITE.
Jg 1:35 mount Heres in Aijalon, and in S.: 8169
1Ki 4:9 son of Dekar, in Makaz, and in S., 8169

SHAALBONITE (sha-al'-bo-nite)
2Sa 23:32 Eliahba the S., of the sons of 8170
1Ch 11:33 the Baharumite, Eliahba the S., 8170

SHAAPH (sha'-af)
1Ch 2:47 and Pelet, and Ephah, and S. 8174
1Ch 2:49 She bare also S. the father of 8174

SHAARAIM (sha-a-ra'-im) See also SHARAIM; SHARUHEN.
1Sa 17:52 fell down by the way to S., even 8189
1Ch 4:31 and at Beth-birei, and at S. 8189

SHAASHGAZ (sha-ash'-gaz)
Es 2:14 to the custody of S., the king's 8190

SHABBETHAI (shab'-be-thahee)
Ezr 10:15 and S. the Levite helped them 7678
Ne 8:7 S., Hodijah, Maaseiah, Kelita, 7678
Ne 11:16 And S. and Jozabad, of the chief of 7678

SHACHIA (sha-ki'-ah)
1Ch 8:10 And Jeuz, and S., and Mirma. 7634

SHADE See also SHADOW.
Ps 121:5 Lord is thy s. upon thy right hand. 6738

SHADOW See also OVERSHADOW; SHADE; SHADOWING; SHADOWS.
Ge 19:8 come they under the s. of my roof. 6738
Jg 9:15 come and put your trust in my s.: 6738
Jg 9:36 Thou seest the s. of the mountains 6738
2Ki 20:9 shall the s. go forward ten degrees, 6738
2Ki 20:10 for the s. to go down ten degrees: 6738
2Ki 20:10 the s. return backward ten degrees. 6738
2Ki 20:11 the s. ten degrees backward, by 6738
1Ch 29:15 our days on the earth are as a s., 6738
Job 3:5 and the s. of death stain it; let a 6757
Job 7:2 servant earnestly desireth the s., 6738
Job 8:9 our days upon earth are a s.:) 6738
Job 10:21 of darkness and the s. of death; 6757
Job 10:22 and of the s. of death, without any 6757
Job 12:22 bringeth out to light the s. of death. 6757
Job 14:2 is cut down: he fleeth also as a s., 6738
Job 16:16 on my eyelids is the s. of death; 6757
Job 17:7 and all my members are as a s. 6738
Job 24:17 is to them even as the s. of death: 6757
Job 24:17 are in the terrors of the s. of death. 6757
Job 28:3 of darkness, and the s. of death. 6757
Job 34:22 is no darkness, nor s. of death, 6757
Job 38:17 seen the doors of the s. of death? 6757
Job 40:22 trees cover him with their s.; the 6752
Ps 17:8 hide me under the s. of thy wings, 6738
Ps 23:4 the valley of the s. of death, 6757
Ps 36:7 trust under the s. of thy wings. 6738
Ps 44:19 and covered us with the s. of death. 6757
Ps 57:1 in the s. of thy wings will I make 6738
Ps 63:7 in the s. of thy wings will I rejoice. 6738
Ps 80:10 hills were covered with the s. of it, 6738
Ps 91:1 abide under the s. of the Almighty. 6738
Ps 102:11 days are like a s. that declineth; 6738
Ps 107:10 in darkness and in the s. of death, 6757
Ps 107:14 out of darkness and the s. of death, 6757
Ps 109:23 I am gone like the s. when it 6738
Ps 144:4 days are as a s. that passeth away. 6738
Ec 6:12 vain life which he spendeth as a s.? 6738
Ec 8:13 prolong his days, which are as a s.; 6738
Ca 2:3 I sat down under his s. with great 6738
Isa 4:6 tabernacle for a s. in the daytime 6738
Isa 9:2 dwell in the land of the s. of death, 6757
Isa 16:3 make thy s. as the night in the 6738
Isa 25:4 a s. from the heat, when the blast 6738
Isa 25:5 even the heat with the s. of a cloud: 6738
Isa 30:2 and to trust in the s. of Egypt! 6738
Isa 30:3 the trust in the s. of Egypt your 6738
Isa 32:2 s. of a great rock in a weary land. 6738
Isa 34:15 and hatch, and gather under her s.: 6738
Isa 38:8 bring again the s. of the degrees, 6738
Isa 49:2 in the s. of his hand hath he hid me, 6738
Isa 51:16 thee in the s. of mine hand, 6738
Jer 2:6 of drought, and of the s. of death, 6757
Jer 13:16 light, he turn it into the s. of death, 6757
Jer 48:45 fled stood under the s. of Heshbon 6738
La 4:20 Under his s. we shall live among 6738
Eze 17:23 the s. of the branches thereof shall 6738
Eze 31:6 under his s. dwelt all great nations. 6738
Eze 31:12 the earth are gone down from his s., 6738
Eze 31:17 dwelt under his s. in the midst of 6738
Da 4:12 beasts of the field had s. under it, 2927
Ho 4:13 because the s. thereof is good; 6738
Ho 14:7 dwell under his s. shall return; 6738
Am 5:8 the s. of death into the morning, 6757
Jon 4:5 sat under it in the s., till he might 6738
Jon 4:6 that it might be a s. over his head, 6738
Mt 4:16 sat in the region and s. of death *4639*
Mk 4:32 **air may lodge under the s. of it.** *4639*
Lu 1:79 in darkness and in the s. of death. *4639*
Ac 5:15 the s. of Peter passing by might *4639*
Col 2:17 Which are a s. of things to come; *4639*
Heb 8:5 example and s. of heavenly things, *4639*
Heb 10:1 the law having a s. of good things *4639*
Jas 1:17 variableness, neither s. of turning. *644*

SHADOWING
Isa 18:1 Woe to the land s. with wings, 6767

Eze 31:3 with a s. shroud, and of an high 6751
Heb 9:5 of glory s. the mercyseat; *2683*

SHADOWS
Ca 2:17 day break, and the s. flee away, 6752
Ca 4:6 the day break, and the s. flee away, 6752
Jer 6:4 s. of the evening are stretched out. 6752

SHADRACH (sha'-drak) See also HANANIAH.
Da 1:7 and to Hananiah, of S.; and to 7714
Da 2:49 set S., Meshach, and Abed-nego, 7715
Da 3:12 of the province of Babylon, S., 7715
Da 3:13 and fury commanded to bring S., 7715
Da 3:14 them, Is it true, O S., Meshach, 7715
Da 3:16 S., Meshach, and Abed-nego, 7715
Da 3:19 his visage was changed against S., 7715
Da 3:20 that were in his army to bind S., 7715
Da 3:22 slew those men that took up S., 7715
Da 3:23 S., Meshach, Abed-nego, fell down 7715
Da 3:26 said, S., Meshach, and Abed-nego, 7715
Da 3:26 Then S., Meshach, and Abed-nego, 7715
Da 3:28 Blessed be the God of S., Meshach, 7715
Da 3:29 thing amiss against the God of S., 7715
Da 3:30 the king promoted S., Meshach, and 7715

SHADY
Job 40:21 he lieth under the s. trees, in the 6628
Job 40:22 The s. trees cover him with their 6628

SHAFT
Ex 25:31 his s., and his branches, his bowls, 3409
Ex 37:17 his s., and his branch, his bowls, 3409
Nu 8:4 beaten gold, unto the s. thereof, 3409
Isa 49:2 me, and made me a polished s.; 2671

SHAGE (sha'-ghe)
1Ch 11:34 the son of S. the Hararite, 7681

SHAHAR (sha'-har) See also ZARETH-SHAHAR.
Ps 22:*title* chief Musician upon Aijeleth S., 7837

SHAHARAIM (sha-ha-ra'-im)
1Ch 8:8 S. begat children in the country 7842

SHAHAZIMAH (sha-haz'-i-mah)
Jos 19:22 coast reacheth to Tabor, and S., 7831

SHAKE See also SHAKED; SHAKEN; SHAKETH; SHAKING; SHOOK.
Jg 16:20 times before, and s. myself. 5287
Ne 5:13 So God s. out every man from his 5287
Job 4:14 which made all my bones to s. 6342
Job 15:33 s. off his unripe grape as the vine. 2554
Job 16:4 you, and s. mine head at you 5128
Ps 22:7 shoot out the lip, they s. the head, 5128
Ps 46:3 mountains s. with the swelling 7493
Ps 69:23 make their loins continually to s. 4571
Ps 72:16 fruit thereof shall s. like Lebanon: 7493
Isa 2:19, 21 ariseth to s. terribly the earth. 6206
Isa 10:15 if the rod should s. itself against 5130
Isa 10:32 he shall s. his hand against the 5130
Isa 11:15 shall he s. his hand over the river. 5130
Isa 13:2 s. the hand, that they may go into 5130
Isa 13:13 I will s. the heavens, and the 7264
Isa 14:16 to tremble, that did s. kingdoms; 7493
Isa 24:18 the foundations of the earth do s. 7493
Isa 33:9 and Carmel s. off their fruits. 5287
Isa 52:2 S. thyself from the dust; arise, and 5287
Jer 23:9 all my bones s.; I am like a 7363
Eze 26:10 thy walls shall s. at the noise of 7493
Eze 26:15 the isles s. at the sound of thy fall, 7493
Eze 27:28 suburbs shall s. at the sound of the 7493
Eze 31:16 nations to s. at the sound of his fall, 7493
Eze 38:20 of the earth, shall s. at my presence, 7493
Da 4:14 s. off his leaves, and scatter his 5426
Joe 3:16 the heavens and the earth shall s.: 7493
Am 9:1 of the door, that the posts may s.: 7493
Hag 2:6 while, and I will s. the heavens, 7493
Hag 2:7 I will s. all nations, and the desire 7493
Hag 2:21 I will s. the heavens and the earth; 7493
Zec 2:9 I will s. mine hand upon them, and 5130
Mt 10:14 **or city, s. off the dust of your feet.** *1621*
Mt 28:4 for fear of him the keepers did s., *4579*
Mk 6:11 **s. off the dust under your feet for** *1621*
Lu 6:48 **that house, and could not s. it: for** *4531*
Lu 9:5 **s. off the very dust from your feet** *660*
Heb 12:26 once more I s. not the earth only, *4579*

SHAKED See also SHAKEN; SHOOK.
Ps 109:25 upon me they s. their heads 5128

SHAKEH See RAB-SHAKEH.

SHAKEN See also SHAKED.
Le 26:36 the sound of a s. leaf chase them; 5086
1Ki 14:15 Israel, as a reed is s. in the water, 5110
2Ki 19:21 of Jerusalem hath s. her head at 5128
Ne 5:13 even thus be he s. out, and 5287
Job 16:12 by my neck, and s. me to pieces, 6327
Job 38:13 the wicked might be s. out of it? 5287
Ps 18:7 of the hills moved and were s., 1607
Isa 37:22 of Jerusalem hath s. her head at 5128
Na 2:3 the fir trees shall be terribly s. 7477
Na 3:12 if they be s., they shall even fall 5128
Mt 11:7 **to see? A reed s. with the wind?** *4531*
Mt 24:29 **powers of the heavens shall be s.:** *4531*
Mk 13:25 **that are in heaven shall be s.** *4531*
Lu 6:38 **measure, pressed down, s. together,** *4531*
Lu 7:24 **to see? A reed s. with the wind?** *4531*
Lu 21:26 **the powers of heaven shall be s.** *4531*
Ac 4:31 the place was s. where they were *4531*
Ac 16:26 foundations of the prison were s.: *4531*
2Th 2:2 That ye be not soon s. in mind, or *4531*
Heb 12:27 removing of those things that are s., *4531*
Heb 12:27 which cannot be s. may remain. *4531*
Re 6:13 when she is s. of a mighty wind. *4579*

SHAKETH
Job 9:6 s. the earth out of her place, and 7264
Ps 29:8 of the Lord s. the wilderness; 2342
Ps 29:8 Lord s. the wilderness of Kadesh. 2342
Ps 60:2 the breaches thereof; for it s. 4131
Isa 10:15 itself against him that s. it? as 5130
Isa 19:16 Lord of hosts, which he s. over it. 5130
Isa 33:15 that s. his hands from holding of 5287

SHAKING
Job 41:29 he laugheth at the s. of a spear. 7494
Ps 44:14 a s. of the head among the people. 4493
Isa 17:6 left in it, as the s. of an olive tree, 5363
Isa 19:16 the s. of the hand of the Lord of 8573
Isa 24:13 shall be as the s. of an olive tree, 5363
Isa 30:32 battles of s. will he fight with it. 8573
Eze 37:7 was a noise, and behold a s., and 7494
Eze 38:19 be a great s. in the land of Israel; 7494

SHALAL See MAHER-SHALAL-HASH-BAZ.

SHALEM (sha'-lem)
Ge 33:18 And Jacob came to S., a city of 8003

SHALIM (sha'-lim)
1Sa 9:4 passed through the land of S., 8171

SHALISHA (shal'-i-shah) See also BAAL-SHALISHA.
1Sa 9:4 passed through the land of S., 8031

SHALL See in the APPENDIX; also SHALT; SHOULD.

SHALLECHETH (shal'-le-keth)
1Ch 26:16 westward, with the gate S., by the 7996

SHALLUM (shal'-lum) See also JEHOAHAZ; MESH-ELEMIAH; SHILLEM.
2Ki 15:10 S. the son of Jabesh conspired 7967
2Ki 15:13 S. the son of Jabesh began to 7967
2Ki 15:14 and smote S. the son of Jabesh in 7967
2Ki 15:15 And the rest of the acts of S., and 7967
2Ki 22:14 the wife of S. the son of Tikvah, 7967
1Ch 2:40 Sisamai, and Sisamai begat S., 7967
1Ch 2:41 S. begat Jekamiah, and Jekamiah 7967
1Ch 3:15 the third Zedekiah, the fourth S. 7967
1Ch 4:25 S. his son, Mibsam his son, 7967
1Ch 6:12 begat Zadok, and Zadok begat S., 7967
1Ch 6:13 S. begat Hilkiah, and Hilkiah 7967
1Ch 7:13 Jezer, and S., the sons of Bilhah. 7967
1Ch 9:17 the porters were, S., and Akkub, 7967
1Ch 9:17 their brethren: S. was the chief; 7967
1Ch 9:19 And S. the son of Kore, the son of 7967
1Ch 9:31 the firstborn of S. the Korahite, 7967
2Ch 28:12 Jehizkiah the son of S., and Amasa 7967
2Ch 34:22 the wife of S. the son of Tikvath, 7967
Ezr 2:42 the children of S., the children of 7967
Ezr 7:2 The son of S., the son of Zadok, 7967
Ezr 10:24 porters: S., and Telem, and Uri. 7967
Ezr 10:42 S., Amariah, and Joseph. 7967
Ne 3:12 repaired S. the son of Halohesh, 7967
Ne 7:45 The porters: the children of S., 7967
Jer 22:11 saith the Lord touching S. the son 7967
Jer 32:7 Hanameel the son of S. thine uncle 7967
Jer 35:4 chamber of Maaseiah the son of S., 7967

SHALLUN (shal'-lun)
Ne 3:15 gate of the fountain repaired S. 7968

SHALMAI (shal'-mahee)
Ezr 2:46 the children of S., the children of 8073
Ne 7:48 of Hagaba, the children of S., 8014

SHALMAN (shal'-man) See also SHALMANESER.
Ho 10:14 as S. spoiled Beth-arbel in the day 8020

SHALMANESER (shal-man-e'-zer) See also SHALMAN.
2Ki 17:3 him came up S. king of Assyria; 8022
2Ki 18:9 that S. king of Assyria came up 8022

SHALOM See JEHOVAH-SHALOM.

SHALT See in the APPENDIX.

SHAMA (sha'-mah)
1Ch 11:44 S. and Jehiel the sons of Hothan 8091

SHAMBLES
1Co 10:25 Whatsoever is sold in the s., that *3111*

SHAME See also ASHAMED; SHAMED; SHAMEFACEDNESS; SHAMEFUL; SHAMELESSLY; SHAMETH.
Ex 32:25 made them naked unto their s. 8103
Jg 18:7 that might put them to s. in any 3637
1Sa 20:34 because his father had done him s. 3637
2Sa 13:13 whither shall I cause my s. to go? 2781
2Ch 32:21 with s. of face to his own land. 1322
Job 8:22 hate thee shall be clothed with s.; 1322
Ps 4:2 long will ye turn my glory into s.? 3639
Ps 35:4 put to s. that seek after my soul: 3637
Ps 35:26 let them be clothed with s. and 1322
Ps 40:14 and put to s. that wish me evil. 3637
Ps 40:15 for a reward of their s. that say 1322
Ps 44:7 hast put them to s. that hated us. 954
Ps 44:9 hast cast off, and put us to s.; 3637
Ps 44:15 the s. of my face hath covered me, 1322
Ps 53:5 thou hast put them to s., because 954
Ps 69:7 reproach; s. hath covered my face. 3639
Ps 69:19 known my reproach, and my s., 1322
Ps 70:3 for a reward of their s. that say, 1322
Ps 71:24 for they are brought unto s., that 2659
Ps 83:16 Fill their faces with s.; that they 7036
Ps 83:17 let them be put to s., and perish: 2659
Ps 89:45 thou hast covered him with s. 955
Ps 109:29 adversaries be clothed with s., 3639
Ps 119:31 O Lord, put me not to s. 954
Ps 132:18 His enemies will I clothe with s. 1322
Pr 3:35 s. shall be the promotion of fools. 7036
Pr 9:7 a scorner getteth to himself s. 7036
Pr 10:5 in harvest is a son that causeth s. 954
Pr 11:2 pride cometh, then cometh s.: but 7036
Pr 12:16 but a prudent man covereth s. 7036
Pr 13:5 is loathsome, and cometh to s. 2659
Pr 13:18 Poverty and s. shall be to him 7036
Pr 14:35 is against him that causeth s. 954
Pr 17:2 have rule over a son that causeth s., 954
Pr 18:13 it, it is folly and s. unto him. 3639
Pr 19:26 mother, is a son that causeth s., 954
Pr 25:8 thy neighbour hath put thee to s. 3637
Pr 25:10 he that heareth it put thee to s., 2616
Pr 29:15 himself bringeth his mother to s. 954
Isa 20:4 uncovered, to the s. of Egypt. 6172
Isa 22:18 shall be the s. of thy lord's house. 7036
Isa 30:3 strength of Pharaoh be your s., 1322
Isa 30:5 profit, but a s., and also a reproach. 1322
Isa 47:3 yea, thy s. shall be seen: 2781
Isa 50:6 not my face from s. and spitting. 3639
Isa 54:4 for thou shalt not be put to s.: 2659
Isa 54:4 shalt forget the s. of thy youth, 1322
Isa 61:7 For your s. ye shall have double; 1322
Jer 3:24 s. hath devoured the labour of our 1322
Jer 3:25 We lie down in our s., and our 1322
Jer 13:26 thy face, that thy s. may appear. 7036
Jer 20:18 days should be consumed with s.? 1322
Jer 23:40 a perpetual s., which shall not be 3640
Jer 46:12 The nations have heard of thy s., 7036
Jer 48:39 hath Moab turned the back with s.! 954
Jer 51:51 s. hath covered our faces: for 3639
Eze 7:18 and s. shall be upon all faces, and 955
Eze 16:52 bear thine own s. for thy sins that 3639
Eze 16:52 confounded also, and bear thy s., 3639
Eze 16:54 That thou mayest bear thine own s., 3639
Eze 16:63 mouth any more because of thy s., 3639
Eze 32:24, 25 yet have they borne their s. 3639
Eze 32:30 and bear their s. with them that go 3639
Eze 34:29 neither bear the s. of the heathen 3639
Eze 36:6 yet have borne the s. of the heathen: 3639
Eze 36:7 about you, they shall bear their s. 3639
Eze 36:15 bear in thee the s. of the heathen 3639

Eze 39:26 After that they have borne their **s.**, ... 3639
Eze 44:13 but they shall bear their **s.**, and 3639
Da 12:2 to **s.** and everlasting contempt. 2781
Ho 4:7 will I change their glory into **s.**. 7036
Ho 4:18 her rulers with **s.** do love, Give ye..... 7036
Ho 9:10 separated themselves…that **s.**; 1322
Ho 10:6 Ephraim shall receive **s.**, and............. 1317
Ob 10 brother Jacob **s.** shall cover thee,.......... 955
Mic 1:11 of Saphir, having thy **s.** naked:........... 1322
Mic 2:6 them, that they shall not take **s.**. 3639
Mic 7:10 **s.** shall cover her which said unto 955
Na 3:5 and the kingdoms thy **s.**. 7036
Hab 2:10 hast consulted **s.** to thy house by 1322
Hab 2:16 Thou art filled with **s.** for glory: 7036
Zep 3:5 but the unjust knoweth no **s.**. 1322
Zep 3:19 land where they have been put to **s.**. 1322
Lu 14:9 **begin with s. to take the lowest** *152*
Ac 5:41 worthy to suffer **s.** for his name. *818*
1Co 4:14 I write not these things to **s.** you, ... *1788*
1Co 6:5 I speak to your **s.**. Is it so, that......... *1791*
1Co 11:6 it be a **s.** for a woman to be shorn....... *149*
1Co 11:14 have long hair, it is a **s.** unto him? *819*
1Co 11:22 of God, and **s.** them who have not? *2617*
1Co 14:35 **s.** for women to speak in…church. *149*
1Co 15:34 of God: I speak this to your **s.**. *1791*
Eph 5:12 a **s.** even to speak of those things........ *149*
Php 3:19 and whose glory is in their **s.**, who *152*
Heb 6:6 afresh, and put him to an open **s.**.......... *3856*
Heb 12:2 endured the cross, despising the **s.**, ... *152*
Jude 13 the sea, foaming out their own **s.**;........ *152*
Re 3:18 **s. of thy nakedness do not appear;** .. *152*
Re 16:15 he walk naked, and they see his **s.**....... *808*

SHAMED See also ASHAMED.
Ge 38:23 Let her take it to her, lest we be **s.**:.... 937
2Sa 19:5 hast **s.** this day the faces of all thy 3001
Ps 14:6 Ye have **s.** the counsel of the poor, ... 954

SHAMED (sha'-med)
1Ch 8:12 and **S.** who built Ono, and Lod, ... 8106

SHAMEFACEDNESS
1Ti 2:9 apparel, with **s.** and sobriety; *127*

SHAMEFUL
Jer 11:13 have ye…altars to that **s.** thing, ... 1322
Hab 2:16 **s.** spewing shall be on thy glory, ... 7022

SHAMEFULLY
Ho 2:5 that conceived them hath done **s.**: 3001
Mk 12:4 **and sent him away s. handled**......... *821*
Lu 20:11 **him also, and entreated him s.,** *818*
1Th 2:2 and were **s.** entreated, as ye know, ... *5195*

SHAMELESSLY
2Sa 6:20 vain fellows **s.** uncovereth himself!...... 1540

SHAMER (sha'-mur) See also SHOMER.
1Ch 6:46 the son of Bani, the son of **S.**,........... 8106
1Ch 7:34 the sons of **S.**; Ahi, and Rohgah,......... 8106

SHAMETH
Pr 28:7 of riotous men **s.** his father. 3637

SHAMGAR (sham'-gar)
Jg 3:31 him was **S.** the son of Anath, ... 8044
Jg 5:6 In the days of **S.** the son of Anath,..... 8044

SHAMHUTH (sham'-huth) See also SHAMMOTH.
1Ch 27:8 fifth month was **S.** the Izrahite:.......... 8049

SHAMIR (sha'-mur)
Jo 15:48 And in the mountains, **S.**, and 8069
Jg 10:1 he dwelt in **S.** in mount Ephraim. 8069
Jg 10:2 and died, and was buried in **S.**........... 8069
1Ch 24:24 Michah: of the sons of Michah; **S.**. 8053

SHAMMA (sham'-mah) See also SHAMMAH.
1Ch 7:37 and Hod, and **S.**, and Shilshah, ... 8037

SHAMMAH (sham'-mah) See also SHAMMA; SHAMMOTH; SHIMEA; SHIMMA.
Ge 36:13 and Zerah, **S.**, and Mizzah: 8048
Ge 36:17 duke Zerah, duke **S.**, duke Mizzah:..... 8048
1Sa 16:9 Then Jesse made **S.** to pass by.......... 8048
1Sa 17:13 him Abinadab, and the third **S.**........... 8048
2Sa 23:11 after him as **S.** the son of Agee 8048
2Sa 23:25 **S.** the Harodite, Elika the Harodite,..... 8048
2Sa 23:33 **S.** the Hararite, Ahiam the son of....... 8048
1Ch 1:37 Nahath, Zerah, **S.**, and Mizzah........... 8048

SHAMMAI (sham'-mahee)
1Ch 2:28 sons of Onam were, **S.**, and Jada. 8060
1Ch 2:28 And the sons of **S.**; Nadab, and......... 8048
1Ch 2:32 the sons of Jada the brother of **S.**; 8048
1Ch 2:44 Jorkoam: and Rekem begat **S.**. 8048
1Ch 2:45 And the son of **S.** was Maon: and 8048
1Ch 4:17 and she bare Miriam, and **S.**, and......... 8048

SHAMMOTH (sham'-moth) See also SHAMMAH; SHAMHUTH.
1Ch 11:27 **S.** the Harorite, Helez the 8054

SHAMMUA (sham-mu'-ah) See also SHAMMUAH; SHEMAIH; SHIMEA.
Nu 13:4 of Reuben, **S.** the son of Zaccur......... 8051
1Ch 14:4 **S.**, and Shobab, Nathan, and 8051
Ne 11:17 and Abda the son of **S.**, the son of..... 8051
Ne 12:18 of Bilgah, **S.**; of Shemaiah,............... 8051

SHAMMUAH (sham-mu'-ah) See also SHAMMUA.
2Sa 5:14 **S.**, and Shobab, and Nathan, and........ 8051

SHAMSHERAI (sham'-she-rahee)
1Ch 8:26 **S.**, and Shehariah, and Athaliah, ... 8125

SHAN See BETH-SHAN.

SHAPE See also SHAPEN; SHAPES.
Lu 3:22 a bodily **s.** like a dove upon him, ... *1491*
Joh 5:37 **voice at any time, nor seen him s.**...*1491*

SHAPEN
Ps 51:5 I was **s.** in iniquity; and in sin........... 2342

SHAPES
Re 9:7 **s.** of the locusts were like unto.......... *3667*

SHAPHAM (sha'-fam)
1Ch 5:12 of Joel the chief, and **S.** the next,....... 8223

SAHPHAN (sha'-fan)
2Ki 22:3 the king sent **S.** the son of Azaliah, ... 8227
2Ki 22:8 high priest said unto **S.** the scribe, ... 8227
2Ki 22:9 And Hilkiah gave the book to **S.**,........ 8227
2Ki 22:9 And **S.** the scribe came to the king,...... 8227
2Ki 22:10 And **S.** the scribe shewed the king, ... 8227
2Ki 22:10 And **S.** read it before the king. 8227
2Ki 22:12 Ahikam the son of **S.**, and Achbor 8227
2Ki 22:12 and **S.** the scribe, and Asahiah a 8227
2Ki 22:14 **S.**, and Asahiah, went unto Huldah 8227
2Ki 25:22 son Ahikam, the son of **S.**, ruler. 8227
2Ch 34:8 he sent **S.** the son of Azaliah, and 8227
2Ch 34:15 answered and said to **S.** the scribe, ... 8227
2Ch 34:15 Hilkiah delivered the book to **S.**. 8227
2Ch 34:16 And **S.** carried the book to the king, ... 8227
2Ch 34:18 Then **S.** the scribe told the king,........ 8227
2Ch 34:18 And **S.** read it before the king. 8227
2Ch 34:20 Hilkiah, and Ahikam the son of **S.**,....... 8227
2Ch 34:20 the son Micah, and **S.** the scribe,....... 8227
Jer 26:24 the hand of Ahikam the son of **S.**........ 8227
Jer 29:3 By the hand of Elasah the son of **S.**,.... 8227
Jer 36:10 Gemariah the son of **S.** the scribe, ... 8227
Jer 36:11 the son of Gemariah, the son of **S.**,.... 8227
Jer 36:12 and Gemariah the son of **S.**, and......... 8227
Jer 39:14 the son of Ahikam the son of **S.**......... 8227
Jer 40:5 the son of Ahikam the son of **S.**,........ 8227
Jer 40:9 son of Ahikam the son of **S.** sware 8227
Jer 40:11 the son of Ahikam the son of **S.**;........ 8227
Jer 41:2 son of Ahikam the son of **S.** with 8227
Jer 43:6 the son of Ahikam the son of **S.**,........ 8227
Eze 8:11 stood Jaazaniah the son of **S.**, with 8227

SHAPHAT (sha'-fat)
Nu 13:5 of Simeon, **S.** the son of Hori. 8202
1Ki 19:16 son of **S.** of Abel-meholah shalt.......... 8202
1Ki 19:19 found Elisha the son of **S.**, who was ... 8202
2Ki 3:11 Here is Elisah the son of **S.**, which..... 8202
2Ki 6:31 if the head of Elisha the son of **S.** 8202
1Ch 3:22 Bariah, and Neariah, and **S.**, six......... 8202
1Ch 5:12 next, and Jaanai, and **S.** in Bashan. 8202
1Ch 27:29 in the valleys was **S.** the son of......... 8202

SHAPHER (sha'-fur)
Nu 33:23 and pitched in mount **S.**.................... 8234
Nu 33:24 And they removed from mount **S.**, ... 8234

SHARAI (sha'-rahee)
Ezr 10:40 Machnadebai, Shashai, **S.**,................. 8298

SHARAIM (sha-ra'-im) See also SHAARAIM.
Jos 15:36 **S.**, and Adithaim, and Gederah, ... 8189

SHARAR (sha'-rar) See also SARAR.
2Sa 23:33 Ahiam the son of **S.** the Hararite,....... 8325

SHARE See also PLOWSHARES.
1Sa 13:20 to sharpen every man his **s.**, and 4282

SHAREZER (sha-re'-zur) See also SHEREZER.
2Ki 19:37 and **S.** his son smote him with the...... 8272
Isa 37:38 and **S.** his son smote him with the...... 8272

SHARON (sha'-run) See also SARON; SHARONITE.
1Ch 5:16 and in all the suburbs of **S.**, upon......... 8289
1Ch 27:29 over the herds that fed in **S.** was......... 8289
Ca 2:1 I am the rose of **S.**, and the lily of 8289
Isa 33:9 **S.** is like a wilderness; and Bashan 8289
Isa 35:2 the excellency of Carmel and **S.**, ... 8289
Isa 65:10 And **S.** shall be a fold of flocks, and.... 8289

SHARONITE (sha'-run-ite)
1Ch 27:29 fed in Sharon was Shitrai the **S.**: 8290

SHARP See also SHARPER.
Ex 4:25 Then Zipporah took a **s.** stone, ... 6864
Jos 5:2 unto Joshua, Make thee **s.** knives, ... 6697
Jos 5:3 Joshua made him **s.** knives, and 6697
1Sa 14:4 was a **s.** rock on the one side,........... 8127
1Sa 14:4 and a **s.** rock on the other side: 8127
Job 41:30 **S.** stones are under him: he.............. 2303
Job 41:30 **s.** pointed things upon the mire.......... 2742
Ps 45:5 Thine arrows are **s.** in the heart 8150
Ps 52:2 mischiefs; like a **s.** rasor, working 3913
Ps 57:4 and their tongue a **s.** sword............... 2299
Ps 120:4 **S.** arrows of the mighty, with............ 8150
Pr 5:4 **s.** as a twoedged sword.................... 2299
Pr 25:18 maul, and a sword, and a **s.** arrow....... 8150
Isa 5:28 Whose arrows are **s.**, and all their...... 8150
Isa 41:15 a new **s.** threshing instrument............ 2742
Isa 49:2 made my mouth like a **s.** sword; 2299
Eze 5:1 take thee a **s.** knife, take thee a 2299
Ac 15:39 contention was so **s.** between them, ...
Re 1:16 mouth went a **s.** twoedged sword: *3691*
Re 2:12 **hath the s. sword with two edges;** . *3691*
Re 14:14 crown, and in his hand a **s.** sickle. *3691*
Re 14:17 heaven, he also having a **s.** sickle. *3691*
Re 14:18 cry to him that had the **s.** sickle,......... *3691*
Re 14:18 Thrust in thy **s.** sickle, and gather *3691*
Re 19:15 out of his mouth goeth a **s.** sword, ... *3691*

SHARPEN See also SHARPENED; SHARPENETH.
1Sa 13:20 to **s.** every man his share, and his...... 3913
1Sa 13:21 for the axes, and to **s.** the goads........ 5324

SHARPENED
Ps 140:3 They have **s.** their tongues like a 8150
Eze 21:9 A sword, a sword is **s.**, and also........ 2300
Eze 21:10 It is **s.** to make a sore slaughter; 2300
Eze 21:11 this sword is **s.**, and it is furbished, ... 2300

SHARPENETH
Job 16:9 mine enemy **s.** his eyes upon me. 3913
Pr 27:17 Iron **s.** iron; so a man **s.** the............ 2300

SHARPER
Mic 7:4 the most upright is **s.** than a thorn............
Heb 4:12 and **s.** than any two edged sword, ... *5114*

SHARPLY
Jg 8:1 And they did chide with him **s.**. 2394
Tit 1:13 Wherefore rebuke them **s.**, that *664*

SHARPNESS
2Co 13:10 lest being present I should use **s.** *664*

SHARUHEN (sha-ru'-hen) See also SHAARAIM; SHILHIM.
Jos 19:6 And Beth-lebaoth, and **S.**;................. 8287

SHASHAI (sha'-shahee)
Ezr 10:40 Machnadebai, **S.**, Sharai, ... 8343

SHASHAK (sha'-shak)
1Ch 8:14 And Ahio, **S.**, and Jeremoth, ... 8349
1Ch 8:25 and Penuel, the sons of **S.**;............... 8349

SHAUL (sha'-ul) See also SAUL; SHAULITES.
Ge 46:10 and **S.** the son of a Canaanitish.......... 7586
Ex 6:15 **S.** the son of a Canaanitish woman: 7586
Nu 26:13 of **S.**, the family of the Shaulites. 7586
1Ch 1:48 **S.** of Rehoboth by the river reigned.... 7586
1Ch 1:49 when **S.** was dead, Baal-hanan the...... 7586
1Ch 4:24 and Jamin, Jarib, Zerah, and **S.**. 7586
1Ch 6:24 son, Uzziah his son, and **S.** his son..... 7586

SHAULITES (sha'-ul-ites)
Nu 26:13 of Shaul, the family of the **S.**............ 7587

SHAVE See also SHAVED; SHAVEN.
Le 13:33 but the scall shall he not **s.**; 1548
Le 14:8 **s.** off all his hair, and was himself....... 1548
Le 14:9 **s.** all his hair off his head and his 1548
Le 14:9 even all his hair he shall **s.** off: and..... 1548
Le 21:5 they **s.** off the corner of their beard,... 1548

Nu 6:9 shall **s.** his head in the day of his 1548
Nu 6:9 on the seventh day shall he **s.** it. 1548
Nu 6:18 shall **s.** the head of his separation....... 1548
Nu 8:7 let them **s.** all their flesh, and..... 5674,8593
De 21:12 she shall **s.** her head, and pare 1548
Jg 16:19 to **s.** off the seven locks of his head;... 1548
Isa 7:20 Lord **s.** with a rasor that is hired, ... 1548
Eze 44:20 Neither shall they **s.** their heads,........ 1548
Ac 21:24 them, that they may **s.** their heads: *3587*

SHAVED See also SHAVEN.
Ge 41:14 and he **s.** himself, and changed his...... 1548
2Sa 10:4 **s.** off the one half of their beards, ... 1548
1Ch 19:4 **s.** them, and cut off their garments..... 1548
Job 1:20 **s.** his head, and fell down upon.......... 1494

SHAVEH (sha'-veh)
Ge 14:5 and the Emims in **S.** Kiriathaim,......... 7741
Ge 14:17 at the valley of **S.**, which is the 7740

SHAVEH-KIRIATHAIM See SHAVEH and KIRIATHAIM.

SHAVEN See also SHAVED.
Le 13:33 He shall be **s.**, but the scall shall....... 1548
Nu 6:19 the hair of his separation is **s.**............ 1548
Jg 16:17 if I be **s.**, then my strength will go..... 1548
Jg 16:22 hair...grow again after he was **s.**........ 1548
Jer 41:5 men, having their beards **s.**, and 1548
1Co 11:5 is even all one as if she were **s.**......... *3587*
1Co 11:6 for a woman to be shorn or **s.**, let...... *3587*

SHAVSHA (shav'-shah) See also SERIAH; SHEVA; SHISHA.
1Ch 18:16 the priests; and **S.** was scribe; 7798

SHE See in the APPENDIX; also HER.

SHEAF See also SHEAVES.
Ge 37:7 and, lo, my **s.** arose, and also stood..... 485
Ge 37:7 about, and made obeisance to my **s.**..... 485
Le 23:10 shall bring a **s.** of the firstfruits......... 6016
Le 23:11 shall wave the **s.** before the Lord,...... 6016
Le 23:12 ye wave the **s.** an he lamb without..... 6016
Le 23:15 brought the **s.** of the wave offering;.... 6016
De 24:19 and hast forgot a **s.** in the field, ... 6016
Job 24:10 take away the **s.** from the hungry,....... 6016
Zec 12:6 and like a torch of fire in a **s.**; 5995

SHEAL (she'-al)
Ez 10:29 Jashub, and **S.**, and Ramoth. 7594

SHEALTIEL (she-al'-te-el) See also SALATHIEL.
Ezr 3:2 and Zerubbabel the son of **S.**, and...... 7597
Ezr 3:8 began Zerubbabel the son of **S.**,......... 7597
Ezr 5:2 rose up Zerubbabel the son of **S.**, ... 7597
Ne 12:1 up with Zerubbabel the son of **S.**,........ 7597
Hab 1:1 unto Zerubbabel the son of **S.**,........... 7597
Hab 1:12 Then Zerubbabel the son of **S.**, and.... 7597
Hab 1:14 spirit of Zerubbabel the son of **S.**, ... 7597
Hab 2:2 now to Zerubbabel the son of **S.**, ... 7597
Hab 2:23 my servant, the son of **S.**, saith......... 7597

SHEAN See BETH-SHEAN.

SHEAR See also SHEARER; SHEARING; SHORN.
Ge 31:19 And Laban went to **s.** his sheep:........ 1494
Ge 38:13 up to Timnath to **s.** his sheep........... 1494
De 15:19 nor **s.** the firstling of thy sheep......... 1494
1Sa 25:4 that Nabal did **s.** his sheep............... 1494

SHEAR See SHEAR-JASHUB.

SHEARER See also SHEARERS.
Ac 8:32 like a lamb dumb before his **s.**, ... *2751*

SHEARERS See also SHEEPSHEARERS.
1Sa 25:7 I have heard that thou hast **s.**........... 1494
1Sa 25:11 flesh that I have killed for my **s.**, ... 1494
Isa 53:7 as a sheep before her **s.** is dumb, so .. 1494

SHEARIAH (she-a-ri'-ah)
1Ch 8:38 Ishmael, and **S.**, and Obadiah, ... 8187
1Ch 9:4 Ishmael, and **S.**, and Obadiah, ... 8187

SHEARING
1Sa 25:2 he was **s.** his sheep in Carmel. 1494
2Ki 10:12 at the **s.** house in the way, ... 1044,7462
2Ki 10:14 at the pit of the **s.** house, even......... 1044

SHEARING-HOUSE See SHEARING and HOUSE.

SHEAR-JASHUB (she''-ar-ja'-shub)
Isa 7:3 meet Ahaz, thou, and **S.** thy son,....... 7610

SHEATH
1Sa 17:51 and drew it out of his **s.** thereof,........ 8593
2Sa 20:8 upon his loins in the **s.** thereof;.......... 8593
1Ch 21:27 put his sword again into the **s.** 5084
Eze 21:3 forth my sword out of his **s.**,............ 8593
Eze 21:4 my sword go forth out of his **s.** 8593
Eze 21:5 drew forth my sword out of his **s.**:..... 8593
Eze 21:30 cause it to return into his **s.**? I will...... 8593
Joh 18:11 **Put up thy sword into the s.;**...... *2336*

SHEAVES
Ge 37:7 we were binding **s.** in the fields,.......... 485
Ge 37:7 behold, your **s.** stood round about,....... 485
Ru 2:7 after the reapers among the **s.**........... 6016
Ru 2:15 Let her glean even among the **s.**,....... 6016
Ne 13:15 bringing in **s.**, and lading asses;.......... 6194
Ps 126:6 rejoicing, bringing his **s.** with him........ 485
Ps 129:7 nor he that bindeth **s.** his bosom.......... 485
Am 2:13 a cart is pressed that is full of **s.**........ 5995
Mic 4:12 gather them as the **s.** into the floor. 5995

SHEBA (she'-bah) See also BATH-SHEBA; BEER SHEBA; SHEBAH.
Ge 10:7 sons of Raamah; **S.**, and Dedan. 7614
Ge 10:28 And Obal, and Abimael, and **S.**, ... 7614
Ge 25:3 And Jokshan begat **S.**, and Dedan....... 7614
Jos 19:2 inheritance Beer-sheba, and **S.**,.......... 7652
2Sa 20:1 man of Belial, whose name was **S.**,...... 7652
2Sa 20:2 and followed **S.** the son of Bichri:........ 7652
2Sa 20:6 **S.** the son of Bichri do us more........ 7652
2Sa 20:7 pursue after **S.** the son of Bichri........ 7652
2Sa 20:10 pursued after **S.** the son of Bichri....... 7652
2Sa 20:13 pursue after **S.** the son of Bichri........ 7652
2Sa 20:21 **S.** the son of Bichri by name,............ 7652
2Sa 20:22 the head of **S.** the son of Bichri,......... 7652
1Ki 10:1 queen of **S.** heard of the fame of......... 7614
1Ki 10:4 queen of **S.** had seen all Solomon's 7614
1Ki 10:10 queen of **S.** gave to king Solomon. 7614
1Ki 10:13 unto the queen of **S.** all her desire, ... 7614
1Ch 1:9 sons of Raamah; **S.**, and Dedan. 7614
1Ch 1:22 And Ebal, and Abimael, and **S.**, ... 7614
1Ch 1:32 sons of Jokshan; **S.**, and Dedan.......... 7614
1Ch 5:13 Meshullam; and **S.**, and Jorai,........... 7652
2Ch 9:1 queen of **S.** heard of the fame of......... 7614
2Ch 9:3 queen of **S.** had seen the wisdom....... 7614
2Ch 9:9 spice as the queen of **S.** gave king 7614
2Ch 9:12 to the queen of **S.** all her desire, ... 7614
Job 6:19 companies of **S.** waited for them. 7614
Ps 72:10 kings of **S.** and Seba shall offer.......... 7614
Ps 72:15 shall be given of the gold of **S.**:.......... 7614
Isa 60:6 all they from **S.** shall come: they........ 7614
Jer 6:20 there to me incense from **S.**, and....... 7614
Eze 27:22 The merchants of **S.**, and Raamah, ... 7614
Eze 27:23 the merchants of **S.**, Asshur, and........ 7614
Eze 38:13 **S.**, and Dedan, and the merchants...... 7614

SHEBAH (she'-bah) See also SHEBA.
Ge 26:33 and he called it **S.**: therefore the........ 7656

SHEBAM (she'-bam) See also SHIBMAH.
Nu 32:3 Elealeh, and **S.**, and Nebo, and......... 7643

SHEBANIAH (sheb-a-ni'-ah) See also SHECHANIAH.
1Ch 15:24 And **S.**, and Jehoshaphat, and........... 7645
Ne 9:4 Kadmiel, **S.**, Bunni, Sherebiah, ... 7645
Ne 9:5 Hodijah, **S.**, and Pethahiah, said, ... 7645
Ne 10:4 Hattush, **S.**, Malluch,...................... 7645
Ne 10:10 their brethren, **S.**, Hodijah, Kelita, ... 7645
Ne 10:12 Zaccur, Sherebiah, **S.**,...................... 7645
Ne 12:14 Melicu, Jonathan; of **S.**, Joseph; 7645

SHEBARIM (sheb'-a-rim)
Jos 7:5 from before the gate even unto **S.**,...... 7671

SHEBER (she'-bur)
1Ch 2:48 Caleb's concubine, bare **S.**, and.......... 7669

SHEBNA (sheb'-nah)
2Ki 18:18 **S.** the scribe, and Joah the son of 7644
2Ki 18:26 **S.**, and Joah, unto Rab-shakeh, ... 7644
2Ki 18:37 **S.** the scribe, and Joah the son of 7644
2Ki 19:2 the household, and **S.** the scribe, ... 7644
Isa 22:15 unto this treasurer, even unto **S.**, ... 7644
Isa 36:3 over the house, and **S.** the scribe,...... 7644
Isa 36:11 Then said Eliakim and **S.** and 7644
Isa 36:22 **S.** the scribe, and Joah, the son of 7644
Isa 37:2 **S.** the scribe, and the elders of the 7644

SHEBUEL (she-bu'-el) See also SHUBAEL.
1Ch 23:16 of Gershom, **S.** was the chief. 7619
1Ch 25:4 Uzziel, **S.**, and Jerimoth, ... 7619
1Ch 26:24 And **S.** the son of Gershom, the son... 7619

SHECANIAH (shek-a-ni'-ah) See also SHEBANIAH; SHECHANIAH.
1Ch 24:11 ninth to Jeshuah, the tenth to **S.**,...... 7935
2Ch 31:15 and Shemaiah, Amariah, and **S.**,......... 7935

SHECHANIAH (shek-a-ni'-ah) See also SHEBANIAH; SHECANIAH.
1Ch 3:21 sons of Obadiah, the sons of **S.**. 7935
1Ch 3:22 the sons of **S.**; Shemaiah: and the 7935
Ezr 8:3 Of the sons of **S.**, of the sons of........ 7935
Ezr 8:5 Of the sons of **S.**; the son of............ 7935
Ezr 10:2 And **S.** the son of Jehiel, one of......... 7935
Ne 3:29 also Shemaiah the son of **S.**, the 7935
Ne 6:18 son in law of **S.** the son of Arah; 7935
Ne 12:3 **S.**, Rehum, Meremoth,..................... 7935

SHECHEM (she'-kem) See also SHECHEMITES; SHECHEM'S; SICHEM; SYCHEM.
Ge 33:18 came to Shalem a city of **S.**, ... 7927
Ge 34:2 **S.** the son of Hamor the Hivite,......... 7927
Ge 34:4 **S.** spake unto his father Hamor,......... 7927
Ge 34:6 father of **S.** went out unto Jacob 7927
Ge 34:8 son **S.** longeth for you daughter: 7927
Ge 34:11 **S.** said unto her father and unto......... 7927
Ge 34:13 and the sons of Jacob answered **S.** 7927
Ge 34:18 their words pleased Hamor, and **S.**..... 7927
Ge 34:20 Hamor and **S.** his son came unto......... 7927
Ge 34:24 unto **S.** his son hearkened all that....... 7927
Ge 34:26 they slew Hamor and **S.** his son......... 7927
Ge 35:4 under the oak which was by **S.**.......... 7927
Ge 37:12 to feed their father's flock in **S.**. 7927
Ge 37:13 thy brethren feed the flock in **S.**?....... 7927
Ge 37:14 vale of Hebron, and he came to **S.**. 7927
Nu 26:31 **S.**, the family of the Shechemites: 7928
Jos 17:2 and for the children of **S.**, and for 7928
Jos 17:7 Michmethah, that lieth before **S.**; 7927
Jos 20:7 and **S.** in mount Ephraim, and 7927
Jos 21:21 gave them **S.** with her suburbs in....... 7927
Jos 24:1 all the tribes of Israel to **S.**, and 7927
Jos 24:25 to statue and an ordinance in **S.**......... 7927
Jos 24:32 up out of Egypt, buried they in **S.**,..... 7927
Jos 24:32 the father of **S.** for an hundred 7927
Jg 8:31 And his concubine that was in **S.**,....... 7927
Jg 9:1 son of Jerubbaal went to **S.** unto........ 7927
Jg 9:2 in the ears of all the men of **S.**,......... 7927
Jg 9:3 in the ears of all the men of **S.** all....... 7927
Jg 9:6 the men of **S.** gathered together, ... 7927
Jg 9:6 plain of the pillar that was in **S.**. 7927
Jg 9:7 Hearken unto me, ye men of **S.**,......... 7927
Jg 9:18 king over the men of **S.**, because........ 7927
Jg 9:20 and devour the men of **S.**, and the 7927
Jg 9:20 fire come out from the men of **S.**,........ 7927
Jg 9:23 Abimelech and the men of **S.**; and...... 7927
Jg 9:23 the men of **S.** dealt treacherously....... 7927
Jg 9:24 upon the men of **S.**, which aided 7927
Jg 9:25 And the men of **S.** set liers in wait..... 7927
Jg 9:26 his brethren, and went over to **S.**: 7927
Jg 9:26 men of **S.** put their confidence in......... 7927
Jg 9:28 Who is Abimelech, and who is **S.**, ... 7927
Jg 9:28 the men of Hamor the father of **S.**: 7927
Jg 9:31 and his brethren become to **S.**:........... 7927
Jg 9:34 they laid wait against **S.** in four........... 7927
Jg 9:39 went out before the men of **S.**, and.... 7927
Jg 9:41 that they should not dwell in **S.**. 7927
Jg 9:46 men of the tower of **S.** heard that, ... 7927
Jg 9:47 the men of the tower of **S.** were........ 7927
Jg 9:49 men of the tower of **S.** died also, ... 7927
Jg 9:57 and all the evil of the men of **S.**......... 7927
Jg 21:19 that goeth up from Beth-el to **S.**, ... 7927
1Ki 12:1 And Rehoboam went to **S.**: for all 7927
1Ki 12:1 were come to **S.** to make him king..... 7927
1Ki 12:25 Then Jerobom built **S.** in mount 7927
1Ch 6:67 **S.** in mount Ephraim with her............ 7927
1Ch 7:19 of Shemidah were, Ahain, and **S.**,....... 7928
1Ch 7:28 **S.** also and the towns thereof, ... 7927
2Ch 10:1 and Rehoboam went to **S.**: for to 7927
2Ch 10:1 **S.** were all Israel come to make......... 7927
Ps 60:6 I will divide **S.**, and mete out the 7927
Ps 108:7 I will rejoice, I will divide **S.**, and....... 7927
Jer 41:5 That there came certain from **S.**, ... 7927

SHECHEMITES (she'-kem-ites)
Nu 26:31 of Shechem, the family of the **S.** 7930

SHECHEM'S (she'-kems)
Ge 33:19 the children of Hamor, **S.** father,......... 7927
Ge 34:26 and took Dinah out of **S.** house,......... 7927

SHED See also SHEDDETH; SHEDDING.
Ge 9:6 by man shall his blood be s.: for 8210
Ge 37:22 S. no blood, but cast him into............ 8210
Ex 22:2 die, there shall no blood be s. for him. ......
Ex 22:3 him, there shall be blood s. for him: ....
Le 17:4 he hath s. blood; and that man.............. 8210
Nu 35:33 be cleansed of the blood that is s. 8210
Nu 35:33 but by the blood of him that s. it........ 8210
De 19:10 That innocent blood be not s. in......... 8210
De 21:7 Our hands have not s. this blood, ... 8210
1Sa 25:26 thee from coming to s. blood, ...
1Sa 25:31 thou hast s. blood causeless, or 8210
1Sa 25:33 me this day from coming to s. blood, ...
2Sa 20:10 s. out his bowels to the ground,.......... 8210
1Ki 2:5 and s. the blood of war in peace, ... 7760
1Ki 2:31 the innocent blood, which Joab s., ... 8210
2Ki 21:16 Manasseh s. innocent blood very......... 8210
2Ki 24:4 for the innocent blood that he s. 8210
1Ch 22:8 Thou hast s. blood abundantly, and..... 8210
1Ch 22:8 thou hast s. much blood upon the....... 8210
1Ch 28:3 a man of war, and hast s. blood. 8210
Ps 79:3 Their blood have they s. like water...... 8210
Ps 79:10 blood of thy servants which is s.......... 8210
Ps 106:38 s. innocent blood, even the blood 8210
Pr 1:16 to evil, and make haste to s. blood. 8210
Pr 6:17 and hands that s. innocent blood,........ 8210
Isa 59:7 make haste to s. innocent blood: 8210
Jer 7:6 s. not innocent blood in this place,...... 8210
Jer 22:3 s. innocent blood in this place............ 8210
Jer 22:17 and for to s. innocent blood, and........ 8210
La 4:13 s. the blood of the just in the midst 8210
Eze 16:38 wedlock and s. blood are judged;........ 8210
Eze 22:4 in thy blood that thou hast s.: and...... 8210
Eze 22:6 in thee to their power to s. blood........ 8210
Eze 22:9 are men that carry tales to s. blood: ... 8210
Eze 22:12 have they taken gifts to s. blood; 8210
Eze 22:27 ravening the prey, to s. blood, and...... 8210
Eze 23:45 manner of women that s. blood; 8210
Eze 33:25 toward your idols, and s. blood: 8210
Eze 35:5 hast s. the blood of the children......... 5064
Eze 36:18 that they had s. upon the land, ... 8210
Joe 3:19 s. innocent blood in their land............ 8210
Mt 23:35 **righteous blood s. upon the earth,** .. *1632*
Mt 26:28 **for many for the remission of sins.** *1632*
Mk 14:24 **testament, which is s. for many.** ... *1632*
Lu 11:50 **which was s. from the foundation**. *1632*
Lu 22:20 **in my blood, which is s. for you.**... *1632*
Ac 2:33 he hath s. forth this, which ye now.... *1632*
Ac 22:20 blood of thy martyr Stephen was s., ... *1632*
Ro 3:15 Their feet are swift to s. blood: *1632*
Ro 5:5 the love of God is s. abroad in our *1632*
Tit 3:6 s. on us abundantly through Jesus....... *1632*
Re 16:6 For they have s. the blood of saints..... *1632*

SHEDDER
Eze 18:10 son that is a robber, a s. of blood, ... 8210

SHEDDETH
Ge 9:6 Whoso s. man's blood, by man........... 8210
Eze 22:3 The city s. blood in the midst of it, ... 8210

SHEDDING
Heb 9:22 and without s. of blood is no.............. *130*

SHEDEUR (shed'-e-ur)
Nu 1:5 of Reuben; Elizur the son of S............ 7707
Nu 2:10 Rueben shall be Elizur the son of S.. .. 7707
Nu 7:30 the fourth day Elizur the son of S., ... 7707
Nu 7:35 the offering of Elizur the son of S.. 7707
Nu 10:18 his host was Elizur the son of S......... 7707

SHEEP See also SHEEPCOTE; SHEEPFOLD; SHEEPMASTER; SHEEP'S; SHEEPSHEARERS; SHEEPSKINS; SHEPHERD.
Ge 4:2 Abel was a keeper of s., but Cain 6629
Ge 12:16 he had s., and oxen, and he asses, ... 6629
Ge 20:14 And Abimelech took s., and oxen, ... 6629
Ge 21:27 And Abraham took s. and oxen, and.... 6629
Ge 29:2 were three flocks of s. lying by it;...... 6629
Ge 29:3 watered the s., and put the stone....... 6629
Ge 29:6 his daughter cometh with the s.. 6629
Ge 29:7 water ye the s., and go and feed......... 6629
Ge 29:8 well's mouth; then we water the s...... 6629
Ge 29:9 Rachel came with her father's s. 6629
Ge 29:10 s. of Laban his mother's brother, ... 6629
Ge 30:32 all the brown cattle among the s., ... 3775
Ge 30:33 the goats, and brown among the s.,.... 3775
Ge 30:35 and all the brown among the s., ... 3775
Ge 31:19 And Laban went to shear his s. 6629
Ge 34:28 They took their s., and their oxen, ... 6629
Ge 38:13 goeth up to Gimnath to shear his s..... 6629
Ex 9:3 upon the oxen, and upon the s........... 6629
Ex 12:5 ye shall take it out from the s., or...... 3532
Ex 20:24 offerings, thy s., and thine oxen:......... 6629
Ex 22:1 If a man shall steal an ox, or a s., ... 7716
Ex 22:1 oxen for an ox, and four s. for a 6629
Ex 22:1 for an ox, and four...for a s............... 7716
Ex 22:4 whether it be ox, or ass, or s.; he 7716
Ex 22:9 whether it be for ox, for ass, for s., ... 7716
Ex 22:10 and ass, or an ox, or a s., or any....... 7716
Ex 22:30 with thine oxen, and with thy s.......... 6629
Ex 34:19 whether ox or s., that is male. 7716
Le 1:10 of the s., or of the goats, for a.......... 3775
Le 7:23 of fat, of ox, or of s., or of goat. 3775
Le 22:19 the beeves, of the s., or of the goats...3775
Le 22:21 a freewill offering in beeves or s., ... 6629
Le 22:27 When a bullock, or a s., or a goat, ... 3775
Le 27:26 whether it be ox, or s.: it is the 7716
Nu 18:17 the firstling of a s., or the firstling...... 3775
Nu 22:40 And Balak offered oxen and s., and..... 6629
Nu 27:17 not as s. which have no shepherd....... 6629
Nu 31:28 and of the asses, and of the s............ 6629
Nu 31:32 thousand and five thousand s., ... 6629
Nu 31:36 thousand and five hundred s.: 6629
Nu 31:37 And the Lord's tribute of the s. was... 6629
Nu 31:43 seven thousand and five hundred s....... 6629
Nu 32:24 little ones, and folds for your s.; 6792
Nu 32:36 fenced cities: and folds for s.............. 6629
De 7:13 and the flocks of thy s., in the land..... 6629
De 14:4 eat: the ox, the s., and the goat, ... 3775
De 14:26 for oxen, or for s., or for wine, or 6629
De 15:19 nor shear the firstling of thy s.. 6629
De 17:1 bullock, or s., wherein is blemish, ... 7716
De 18:3 sacrifice, whether it be ox or s.; 7716
De 18:4 and the first of the fleece of thy s., ... 6629
De 22:1 brother's ox or his s. go astray, ... 7716
De 28:4, 18 kine and the flocks of thy s........... 6629
De 28:31 s. shall be given unto thine enemies,... 6629
De 28:51 of thy kine, or flocks of thy s., ... 6629
De 32:14 Butter of kine, and milk of s., with...... 6629
Jos 6:21 and s., and ass, with the edge of 7716
Jos 7:24 his asses, and his s., and his tent,...... 6629
Jg 6:4 Israel, neither s., nor ox, nor ass......... 7716
1Sa 8:17 He will take the tenth of your s. 6629
1Sa 14:32 and took s., and oxen, and calves,...... 6629
1Sa 14:34 every man his s., and slay them......... 7716
1Sa 15:3 infant and suckling, ox and s.,............ 7716
1Sa 15:9 the best of the s., and of the oxen, ... 6629
1Sa 15:14 meaneth then this bleating of the s. 6629
1Sa 15:15 the people spared the best of the s..... 6629
1Sa 15:21 people took of the spoil, s. and oxen,.. 6629
1Sa 16:11 and, behold he keepeth the s............. 6629
1Sa 16:19 David thy son, which is with the s...... 6629
1Sa 17:15 from Saul to feed his father's s. at...... 6629
1Sa 17:20 left the s. with a keeper, and took,..... 6629
1Sa 17:28 whom hast thou left those few s. 6629
1Sa 17:34 Thy servant kept his father's s., ... 6629
1Sa 22:19 and s., with the edge of the sword. 7716
1Sa 25:2 he had three thousand s., and a 6629
1Sa 25:2 he was shearing his s. in Carmel. 6629
1Sa 25:4 that Nabal did shear his s.. 6629
1Sa 25:16 we were with them keeping the s........ 6629
1Sa 25:18 of wine, and five s. ready dressed, ... 6629
1Sa 27:9 took away the s., and the oxen, and... 6629
2Sa 7:8 sheepcote, from following the s.,........ 6629
2Sa 17:29 And honey, and butter, and s., and..... 6629
2Sa 24:17 but these s., what have they done? 6629
1Ki 1:9 Adonijah slew s. and oxen and fat....... 6629
1Ki 1:19 hath slain oxen and fat cattle and s. ... 6629
1Ki 1:25 and fat cattle and s. in abundance. 6629
1Ki 4:23 an hundred s., beside harts, and 6629
1Ki 8:5 sacrificing s. and oxen, that could....... 6629
1Ki 8:63 hundred and twenty thousand s.......... 6629
1Ki 22:17 as s. that have not a shepherd:........... 6629
2Ki 5:26 and vineyards, and s., and oxen, ... 6629
1Ch 5:21 s. two hundred and fifty thousand,....... 6629
1Ch 12:40 oil, and oxen, and s. abundantly: 6629
1Ch 17:7 even from following the s., that thou... 6629
1Ch 21:17 for these s., what have they done?..... 6629
2Ch 5:6 sacrificed s. and oxen, which could 6629
2Ch 7:5 hundred and twenty thousand s. 6629
2Ch 14:15 away s. and camels in abundance,....... 6629
2Ch 15:11 oxen and seven thousand s.. 6629
2Ch 18:2 Ahab killed s. and oxen for him in 6629
2Ch 18:16 as s. that have no shepherd: and........ 6629
2Ch 29:33 oxen and three thousand s. 6629
2Ch 30:24 bullocks and seven thousand s.; 6629
2Ch 30:24 bullocks and ten thousand s.; and 6629
2Ch 31:6 brought in the tithe of oxen and s.,..... 6629
Ne 3:1 priests, and they builded the s. gate; .. 6629
Ne 3:32 corner unto the s. gate repaired......... 6629
Ne 5:18 daily was one ox and six choice s.; 6629
Ne 12:39 tower of Meah, even unto the s. gate: .6629
Job 1:3 substance...was seven thousand s., ... 6629
Job 1:16 hath burned up the s., and the........... 6629
Job 31:20 warmed with the fleece of my s.; 3532
Job 42:12 for he had fourteen thousand s.,........ 6629
Ps 8:7 all s. and oxen, yea, and the 6792
Ps 44:11 us like s. appointed for meat; 6629
Ps 44:22 are counted as s. for the slaughter. 6629
Ps 49:14 Like s. they are laid in the grave; 6629
Ps 74:1 smoke against the s. of thy pasture?... 6629
Ps 78:52 his own people to go forth like s., ... 6629
Ps 79:13 we thy people and s. of thy pasture.... 6629
Ps 95:7 his pasture, and the s. of his hand. 6629
Ps 100:3 his people, and the s. of his pasture.... 6629
Ps 119:176 I have gone astray like a lost s.; 7716
Ps 144:13 our s. may bring forth thousands 6629
Ca 4:2 Thy teeth are like a flock of s. that...........
Ca 6:6 Thy teeth are as a flock of s. which.... 7353
Isa 7:21 nourish a young cow, and two s.; 6629
Isa 13:14 and as a s. that no man taketh up: 6629
Isa 22:13 slaying oxen, and killing s., eating....... 6629
Isa 53:6 All we like s. have gone astray; we..... 6629
Isa 53:7 and as a s. before her shearers is 7353
Jer 12:3 them out like s. for the slaughter, ... 6629
Jer 23:1 and scatter the s. of my pasture! 6629
Jer 50:6 My people hath been lost s.: their...... 6629
Jer 50:17 Israel is a scattered s.; the lions 7716
Eze 34:6 My s. wandered through all the 6629
Eze 34:11 even I, will both search my s., and..... 6629
Eze 34:12 in the day that he is among his s........ 6629
Eze 34:12 so will I seek out my s., and will 6629
Ho 12:12 for a wife, and for a wife he kept s..........
Joe 1:18 the flocks of s. are made desolate. 6629
Mic 2:12 them together as the s. of Bozrah, ... 6629
Mic 5:8 a young lion among the flocks of s....... 6629
Zec 13:7 and the s. shall be scattered: and I..... 6629
Mt 9:36 abroad, as s. having no shepherd........ *4263*
Mt 10:6 **rather to the lost s. of the house**... *4263*
Mt 10:16 **send you forth as s. in the midst**... *4263*
Mt 12:11 **shall have one s., and if it fall**...... *4263*
Mt 12:12 **then is a man better than a s.?** *4263*
Mt 15:24 **but unto the lost s. of the house of** *4263*
Mt 18:12 **if a man have an hundred s., and**.. *4263*
Mt 18:13 **he rejoiceth more of that s., than**........
Mt 25:32 **divideth his s. from the goats:**....... *4263*
Mt 25:33 **shall set the s. on his right hand,**... *4263*
Mt 26:31 **s. of the flock shall be scattered**.... *4263*
Mk 6:34 were as s. not having a shepherd: *4263*
Mk 14:27 **and the s. shall be scattered**.......... *4263*
Lu 15:4 **man of you, having an hundred s.,**.*4263*
Lu 15:6 **I have found my s. which was lost.** *4263*
Joh 2:14 that sold oxen and s. and doves, ... *4263*
Joh 2:15 temple, and the s., and the oxen; *4263*
Joh 5:2 Jerusalem by the s. market a pool, ... *4262*
Joh 10:2 **the door is the shepherd of the s.**.. *4263*
Joh 10:3 **openeth; and the s. hear his voice:** *4263*
Joh 10:3 **and he calleth his own s. by name,**.*4263*
Joh 10:4 **when he putteth forth his own s.**,.. *4263*
Joh 10:4 **before them, and the s. follow him:***4263*
Joh 10:7 **unto you, I am the door of the s.**.. *4263*
Joh 10:8 **but the s. did not hear them.** *4263*
Joh 10:11 **shepherd giveth his life for the s.**...*4263*
Joh 10:12 **shepherd, whose own the s. are not,**.*4263*
Joh 10:12 **and leaveth the s., and fleeth:**....... *4263*
Joh 10:12 **them, and scattereth the s.** *4263*
Joh 10:13 **hireling, and careth not for the s.**..*4263*
Joh 10:14 **know my s., and am known of mine,**...
Joh 10:15 **and I lay down my life for the s.**... *4263*
Joh 10:16 **And other s. I have, which are not**.*4263*
Joh 10:26 **ye are not of my s., as I said unto**.*4263*
Joh 10:27 **My s. hear my voice, and I know**.. *4263*
Joh 21:16 He saith unto him, **Feed my s.**. *4263*
Joh 21:17 Jesus saith unto him, **Feed my s.**. *4263*
Ac 8:32 He was led as a s. to the slaughter; ... *4263*
Ro 8:36 accounted as s. for the slaughter. *4263*
Heb 13:20 Jesus, that great shepherd of the s., ... *4263*
1Pe 2:25 For ye were as s. going astray; but.... *4263*
Re 18:13 and beasts, and s., and horses, and.... *4263*

SHEEPCOTE See also SHEEPCOTES.
2Sa 7:8 I took thee from the s., from 5116
1Ch 17:7 I took thee from the s., even from..... 5116

SHEEPCOTES
1Sa 24:3 he came to the **s.** by the way,.... 1448,6629

SHEEPFOLD See also SHEEPFOLDS.
Joh 10:1 not by the door into the s., but.*833,4263*

SHEEPFOLDS
Nu 32:16 build **s.** here for our cattle,........ 1488,6629
Jg 5:16 Why abodest thou among the **s.**,........ 4942
Ps 78:70 and took him from the **s.**.......... 4356,6629

SHEEP-GATE See SHEEP and GATE.

SHEEP-MARKET See SHEEP and MARKET.

SHEEPMASTER
2Ki 3:4 and Mesha king of Moab was a **s.**, ... 5349

SHEEP'S
Mt 7:15 which come to you in s. clothing,.. *4263*

SHEEPSHEARERS
Ge 38:12 went...unto his **s.** to Timnath, ... 1494,6629
2Sa 13:23 Absalom had **s.** in Baal-hazor,............ 1494
2Sa 13:24 Behold now, thy servant hath **s.**;........ 1494

SHEEPSKINS
Heb 11:37 they wandered about in **s.** and.......... *3374*

SHEET See also SHEETS.
Ac 10:11 great **s.** knit at the four corners,........ *3607*
Ac 11:5 as it had been a great **s.**, let down..... *3607*

SHEETS
Jg 14:12 will give you thirty **s.** and thirty......... 5466
Jg 14:13 then shall ye give me thirty **s.** and...... 5466

SHEHARIAH (she-ha-ri'-ah)
1Ch 8:26 Shamsherai, and **S.**, and Athaliah,....... 7841

SHEKEL (she'-kul) See also SHEKELS.
Ge 24:22 golden earring of half a **s.** weight,....... 1235
Ex 30:13 half a **s.** after the **s.** of the............... 8255
Ex 30:13 sanctuary: (a **s.** is twenty gerahs:)...... 8255
Ex 30:13 an half **s.** shall be the offering of........ 8255
Ex 30:15 shall not give less than half a **s.**, ... 8255
Ex 30:24 after the **s.** of the sanctuary,............. 8255
Ex 38:24 after the **s.** of the sanctuary............. 8255
Ex 38:25 after the **s.** of the sanctuary:............ 8255
Ex 38:26 for every man, that is, half a **s.**, ... 8255
Ex 38:26 after the **s.** of the sanctuary,............. 8255
Le 5:15 after the **s.** of the sanctuary,............. 8255
Le 27:3 silver, after the **s.** of the sanctuary..... 8255
Le 27:25 according to the **s.** of the sanctuary: ... 8255
Le 27:25 twenty gerahs shall be the **s.**............. 8255
Nu 3:47 after the **s.** of the sanctuary shalt....... 8255
Nu 3:47 (the **s.** is twenty gerahs:)............... 8255
Nu 3:50 after the **s.** of the sanctuary:............. 8255
Nu 7:13, 19,25,31,37,43,49,55,61,67,73,79
after the **s.** of the sanctuary;............ 8255
Nu 7:85 after the **s.** of the sanctuary:............ 8255
Nu 7:86 apiece, after the **s.** of the sanctuary:... 8255
Nu 18:16 after the **s.** of the sanctuary,............ 8255
1Sa 9:8 the fourth part of a **s.** of silver: 8255
2Ki 7:1 of fine flour be sold for a **s.**, and........ 8255
2Ki 7:1 and two measures of barley for a **s.**,... 8255
2Ki 7:16 of fine flour was sold for a **s.**, and...... 8255
2Ki 7:16 and two measures of barley for a **s.**,... 8255
2Ki 7:18 Two measures of barley for a **s.**, ... 8255
2Ki 7:18 and a measure of fine flour for a **s.**,.... 8255
Ne 10:32 the third part of a **s.** for the sevice..... 8255
Eze 45:12 And the **s.** shall be twenty gerahs: 8255
Am 8:5 the ephah small, and the **s.** great, ... 8255

SHEKELS
Ge 23:15 worth four hundred **s.** of silver; 8255
Ge 23:16 four hundred **s.** of silver, current........ 8255
Ge 24:22 bracelets . . . of ten **s.** weight of gold; ......
Ex 21:32 unto their master thirty **s.** of silver,.... 8255
Ex 30:23 spices, of pure myrrh five hundred **s.**,.......
Ex 30:23 much, even two hundred and fifty **s.**, ...
Ex 30:23 calamus two hundred and fifty **s.**, ...
Ex 30:24 And of cassia five hundred **s.**,..................
Ex 38:24 and seven hundred and thirty **s.**, ... 8255
Ex 38:25 and threescore and fifteen **s.**, ... 8255
Ex 38:28 seven hundred seventy and five **s.**...........
Ex 38:29 two thousand and four hundred **s.**....... 8255
Le 5:15 with thy estimation by **s.** of silver,...... 8255
Le 27:3 estimation shall be fifty **s.** of silver,...... 8255
Le 27:4 thy estimation shall be thirty **s.**.......... 8255
Le 27:5 shall be of the male twenty **s.**,........... 8255
Le 27:5 and for the female ten **s.**................. 8255
Le 27:6 be of the male five **s.** of silver,.......... 8255
Le 27:6 estimation shall be three **s.** of silver.... 8255
Le 27:7 thy estimation shall be fifteen **s.**,........ 8255
Le 27:7 and for the female ten **s.**................. 8255
Le 27:16 shall be valued at fifty **s.** of silver....... 8255
Nu 3:47 even take five **s.** apiece by the poll,.... 8255
Nu 3:50 hundred and threescore and five **s.**, ...
Nu 7:13 was an hundred and thirty **s.**,.................
Nu 7:13 one silver bowl of seventy **s.**, after..... 8255
Nu 7:14 one spoon of ten **s.** of gold, full of...........
Nu 7:19 was an hundred and thirty **s.**,..................
Nu 7:19 one silver bowl of seventy **s.**, after..... 8255
Nu 7:20 One spoon of gold of ten **s.**, full of ....
Nu 7:25 was an hundred and thirty **s.**, ...
Nu 7:25 one silver bowl of seventy **s.**, after..... 8255
Nu 7:26 One golden spoon of ten **s.**, full of...........
Nu 7:31 was an hundred and thirty **s.**, ...
Nu 7:31 one silver bowl of seventy **s.**, after..... 8255
Nu 7:32 One golden spoon of ten **s.**, full of...........
Nu 7:37 was an hundred and thirty **s.**, ...
Nu 7:37 one silver bowl of seventy **s.**, after..... 8255
Nu 7:38 One golden spoon of ten **s.**, full of...........
Nu 7:43 was an hundred and thirty **s.**, ...
Nu 7:43 one silver bowl of seventy **s.**, after..... 8255
Nu 7:44 One golden spoon of ten **s.**, full of...........
Nu 7:49 was an hundred and thirty **s.**, ...
Nu 7:49 one silver bowl of seventy **s.**, after..... 8255
Nu 7:50 One golden spoon of ten **s.**, full of...........
Nu 7:55 was an hundred and thirty **s.**, ...
Nu 7:55 one silver bowl of seventy **s.**, after..... 8255
Nu 7:56 One golden spoon of ten **s.**, full of...........
Nu 7:61 was an hundred and thirty **s.**, ...
Nu 7:61 one silver bowl of seventy **s.**, after..... 8255
Nu 7:62 One golden spoon of ten **s.**, full of...........
Nu 7:67 was an hundred and thirty **s.**, ...
Nu 7:67 one silver bowl of seventy **s.**, after..... 8255
Nu 7:68 One golden spoon of ten **s.**, full of...........
Nu 7:73 was an hundred and thirty **s.**, ...
Nu 7:73 one silver bowl of seventy **s.**, after..... 8255
Nu 7:74 One golden spoon of ten **s.**, full of...........
Nu 7:79 was an hundred and thirty **s.**, ...
Nu 7:79 one silver bowl of seventy **s.**, after..... 8255
Nu 7:80 One golden spoon of ten **s.**, full of...........
Nu 7:85 weighing an hundred and thirty **s.**,...........
Nu 7:85 two thousand and four hundred **s.**,...........
Nu 7:86 full of incense, weighing ten **s.** apiece,.......
Nu 7:86 spoons was an hundred and twenty **s.**. ......
Nu 18:16 estimation, for the money of five **s.**, ... 8255
Nu 31:52 thousand seven hundred and fifty **s.** ... 8255
De 22:19 amerce him in an hundred **s.** of silver,.......
De 22:29 the damsel's father fifty **s.** of silver..........
Jos 7:21 and two hundred **s.** of silver, and....... 8255
Jos 7:21 a wedge of gold of fifty **s.** weight, ... 8255
Jg 8:26 thousand and seven hundred **s.** of gold; .....
Jg 17:2 The eleven hundred **s.** of silver that.........
Jg 17:3 had resored the eleven hundred **s.** of........
Jg 17:4 mother took two hundred **s.** of silver, ...
Jg 17:10 and I will give thee ten **s.** of silver by.......
1Sa 17:5 coat was five thousand **s.** of brass. 8255
1Sa 17:7 weighed six hundred **s.** of iron:.......... 8255
2Sa 14:26 hair of his head two hundred **s.**.......... 8255
2Sa 18:11 would have given thee ten **s.** of silver, ...
2Sa 18:12 a thousand **s.** of silver in mine hand, ...
2Sa 21:16 weighed three hundred **s.** of brass in............
2Sa 24:24 and the oxen for fifty **s.** of silver........ 8255
1Ki 10:16 hundred **s.** of gold went to one target. ......
1Ki 10:29 of Egypt for six hundred **s.** of silver,..........
2Ki 15:20 of each man fifty **s.** of silver, to.......... 8255
1Ch 21:25 for the place six hundred **s.** of gold..... 8255
2Ch 1:17 a chariot for six hundred **s.** of silver,.........
2Ch 3:9 of the nails was fifty **s.** of gold........... 8255
2Ch 9:15 hundred **s.** of beaten gold went to one.......
2Ch 9:16 hundred **s.** of gold went to one shield.........
Ne 5:15 and wine, beside forty **s.** of silver;....... 8255
Jer 32:9 money, even seventeen **s.** of silver..... 8255
Eze 4:10 shall be by weight, twenty **s.** a day:.... 8255
Eze 45:12 twenty **s.**, five and twenty **s.**,............ 8255
Eze 45:12 fifteen **s.**, shall be your maneh. 8255

SHELAH (she'-lah) See also SALAH; SHELANITES.
Ge 38:5 a son: and called his name **S.**: 7956
Ge 38:11 house, till **S.** my son be grown: 7956
Ge 38:14 for she saw that **S.** was grown, ... 7956
Ge 38:26 that I gave her not to **S.** my son........ 7956
Ge 46:12 of Judah; Er, and Onan, and **S.**, ... 7956
Nu 26:20 of **S.**, the family of the Shelanites:...... 7956
1Ch 1:18 Arphaxad begat **S.**, and **S.** begat......... 7974
1Ch 1:24 Shem, Arphaxad, **S.**, ... 7956
1Ch 2:3 of Judah; Er, and Onan, and **S.**: 7956
1Ch 4:21 The sons of **S.** the son of Judah......... 7956

SHELANITES (she'-lan-ites)
Nu 26:20 **S.**, the family of the Shelanites: 8024

SHELEMIAH (shel-e-mi'-ah) See also MESHELEMIAH; SHALLUM.
1Ch 26:14 And the Lot eastward fell to **S.**.......... 8018
Ezr 10:39 And **S.**, and Nathan, and Adaiah,........ 8018
Ezr 10:41 Azareel, and **S.**, Shemariah, ... 8018
Ne 3:30 repaired Hananiah the son of **S.**,......... 8018
Ne 13:13 over the treasuries, **S.** the priest, ... 8018
Jer 36:14 the son of **S.**, the son of Cushi, ... 8018
Jer 36:26 Azriel, and **S.** the son of Abdeel, to.... 8018
Jer 37:3 the king sent Jehucal the son of **S.** 8018
Jer 37:13 name was Irijah, the son of **S.**, ... 8018
Jer 38:1 and Jucal the son of **S.**, and Pashur 8018

SHELEPH (she'-lef)
Ge 10:26 Joktan begat Almodad, and **S.**,.......... 8026
1Ch 1:20 Joktan begat Almodad, and **S.**,.......... 8026

SHELESH (she'-lesh)
1Ch 7:35 and Imna, and **S.**, and Amal. 8028

SHELOMI (shel'-o-mi)
Nu 34:27 of Asher, Ahihud the son of **S.**. 8015

SHELOMITH (shel'-o-mith) See also SHELOMOTH.
Le 24:11 his mother's name was **S.**, the........... 8019
1Ch 3:19 and Hananiah, and **S.** their sister:........ 8019
1Ch 23:9 **S.**, and Haziel, and Haran, three. 8013
1Ch 23:18 Of the sons of Izhar; **S.** their chief. 9019
1Ch 26:25 and Zichri his son, and **S.** his son. 8013
1Ch 26:26 Which **S.** and his brethren were.......... 8013
1Ch 26:28 thing, it was under the hand of **S.**, ... 8019
2Ch 11:20 Abijah, and Attai, and Ziza, and **S.**...... 8019
Ezr 8:10 And of the sons of **S.**; the son of....... 8019

SHELOMOTH (shel'-o-moth) See also SHELOMITH.
1Ch 24:22 **S.**: of the sons of **S.**; Jahath. 8013

SHELTER
Job 24:8 embrace the rock for want of a **s.**. 4268
Ps 61:3 thou hast been a **s.** for me, and a....... 4268

SHELUMIEL (she-lu'-me-el)
Nu 1:6 **S.** the son of Zurishaddai. 8017
Ps 2:12 shall be **S.** the son of Zurishaddai. 8017
Ps 7:36 fifth day **S.** the son of Zurishaddai, ... 8017
Ps 7:41 of **S.** the son of Zurishaddai............... 8017
Ps 10:19 was **S.** the son of Zurishaddai. 8017

SHEM (shem) See also SEM.
Ge 5:32 Noah begat **S.**, Ham, and Japheth....... 8035
Ge 6:10 Noah begat three sons, **S.**, Ham, ... 8035
Ge 7:13 same day entered Noah, and **S.**, ... 8035
Ge 9:18 that went forth of the ark, were **S.**,.... 8035
Ge 9:23 **S.** and Japheth took a garment,.......... 8035
Ge 9:26 Blessed be the Lord God of **S.**; 8035
Ge 9:27 he shall dwell in the tents of **S.**; 8035
Ge 10:1 the sons of Noah; **S.**, Ham, and......... 8035
Ge 10:21 Unto **S.** also, the father of all the....... 8035
Ge 10:22 children of **S.**; Elam, and Asshur, ... 8035
Ge 10:31 the sons of **S.**, after their families, ... 8035
Ge 11:10 These are the generations of **S.**:......... 8035
Ge 11:10 **S.** was an hundred years old, and........ 8035
Ge 11:11 **S.** lived after be begat Arphaxad 8035
1Ch 1:4 Noah, **S.**, Ham, and Japheth. 8035
1Ch 1:17 The sons of **S.**; Elam, and Asshur, ... 8035
1Ch 1:24 **S.**, Arphaxad, Shelah, ... 8035

SHEMA (she'-mah) See also SHEMAIAH; SHIMHI.
Jos 15:26 Amam, and **S.**, and Moladah,............ 8087
1Ch 2:43 and Tappuah, and Rekem, and **S.**....... 8087
1Ch 2:44 And **S.** begat Raham, the father of..... 8087
1Ch 5:8 Bela the son of Azaz, the son of **S.**, ... 8087
1Ch 8:13 Beriah also, and **S.**, who were........... 8087
Ne 8:4 him stood Mattithiah, and **S.**, and....... 8087

SHEMAAH (shem'-a-ah)
1Ch 12:3 the sons of **S.** the Gebeathite; 8093

SHEMAIAH (shem-a-i'-ah) See also SHAMMUA; SHEMA; SHIMEI; SIMEI.
1Ki 12:22 word of God came unto **S.** the.......... 8098
1Ch 3:22 And the sons of Shechaniah; **S.**: 8098
1Ch 3:22 and the sons of **S.**; Hattush, and........ 8098
1Ch 4:37 the son of Shimri, the son of **S.**;........ 8098
1Ch 5:4 **S.** his son, Gog his son, Shimei his..... 8098
1Ch 9:14 **S.** the son of Hasshub, the son of..... 8098
1Ch 9:16 And Obadiah the son of **S.**, the son.... 8098

1Ch 15:8 S. the chief, and his brethren two 8098
1Ch 15:11 S., and Eliel, and Amminadab, ... 8098
1Ch 24:6 And S. the son of Nethaneel the 8098
1Ch 26:4 S. the firstborn, Jehozabad the.......... 8098
1Ch 26:6 Also unto S. his son were sons.......... 8098
1Ch 26:7 The sons of S.; Othni, and Rephael, ... 8098
2Ch 11:2 the word of the Lord came to S......... 8098
2Ch 12:5 came s. the prophet the Rehoboam,.... 8098
2Ch 12:7 the word of the Lord came to S.,....... 8098
2Ch 12:15 they not written in the book of S. 8098
2Ch 17:8 with them he sent Levites, even S., ... 8098
2Ch 29:14 sons of Jeduthun; S., and Uzziel......... 8098
2Ch 31:15 and S., Amariah, and Shecaniah, ... 8098
2Ch 35:9 also, and S. and Nethaneel, his.......... 8098
Ezr 8:13 are these, Eliphelet, Jeiel, and S., ... 8098
Ezr 8:16 sent I for Eliezer, for Ariel, for S.,..... 8098
Ezr 10:21 and Elijah, and S., and Jehiel, and 8098
Ezr 10:31 Ishijah, Malchiah, S., Shimeon, ... 8098
Ne 3:29 After him repaired also S. the son...... 8098
Ne 6:10 I came unto the house of S. the......... 8098
Ne 10:8 Bilgai, S.; these were the priests. 8098
Ne 11:15 the Levites: S. the son of Hashub, ... 8098
Ne 12:6 S., and Joiarib, Jedaiah, ... 8098
Ne 12:18 Shammua; of S., Jehonathan; 8098
Ne 12:34 Benjamin, and S., and Jeremiah,......... 8098
Ne 12:35 the son of S., the son of Mattaniah,.... 8098
Ne 12:36 And his brethren, S., and Axarael, ... 8098
Ne 12:42 And Maaseiah, and S., and Eleazar, ... 8098
Jer 26:20 the son of S. of Kirjath-jearim, ... 8098
Jer 29:24 Thus shalt thou also speak to S. 8098
Jer 29:31 Thus saith the Lord concerning S....... 8098
Jer 29:31 that S. hath prophesied unto you, ... 8098
Jer 29:32 I will punish S. the Nehelamite, ... 8098
Jer 36:12 and Delaiah the son of S., and........... 8098

SHEMARIAH (shem-a-ri'-ah)
1Ch 12:5 Bealiah, and S., and Shephathiah 8114
2Ch 11:19 Jeush, and S., and Zaham. 8114
Ezr 10:32 Benjamin, Malluch, and S.. 8114
Ezr 10:41 Azareel, and Shelemiah, S., ... 8114

SHEMEBER (shem-e'-bur)
Ge 14:2 S. king of Zeboiim, and the king......... 8038

SHEMER (she'-mur)
1Ki 16:24 bought the hill Samaria of S. for......... 8106
1Ki 16:24 after the name of S., owner of the 8106

SHEMESH See BETH-SHEMESH; EN-SHEMESH; IR-SHEMESH.

SHEMIDA (shem-i'-dah) See also SHEMIDAH.
Nu 26:32 S., the family of the Shemidaites: 8061
Jos 17:2 Hepher, and for the children of S. 8061

SHEMIDAH (shem-i'-dah) See also SHEMIDA; SHEMIDAITES.
1Ch 7:19 And the sons of S. were, Ahian, ... 8061

SHEMIDAITES (shem'-i-dah-ites)
Nu 26:32 of Shemida, the family of the S.......... 8062

SHEMINITH (shem'-i-nith)
1Ch 15:21 with harps on the S. to excel. 8067
Ps 6:*title* Musician on Neginoth upon S., ... 8067
Ps 12:*title* To the chief Musician upon S., ... 8067

SHEMIRAMOTH (she-mir'-a-moth)
1Ch 15:18 and Jaaziel, and S., and Jehiel, ... 8070
1Ch 15:20 and Aziel, and S., and Jehiel, and 8070
1Ch 16:5 to him Zachariah, Jeiel, and S., ... 8070
2Ch 17:8 Asahel, and S., and Jehonathan, ... 8070

SHEMITE See BETH-SHEMITE.

SHEMUEL (shem-u'-el) See also SAMUEL.
Nu 34:20 Simeon, S. the son of Ammihud. 8050
1Ch 6:33 the son of Joel, the son of S., ... 8050
1Ch 7:2 S., heads of their father's house,........ 8050

SHEN (shen)
1Sa 7:12 and set it between Mizpeh and S., ... 8129

SHENAZAR (she-na'-zar)
1Ch 3:18 also, and Pedaiah, and S.,................. 8137

SHENIR (she'-nur) See also SENIR; SION.
De 3:9 and the Amorites call it S.;) 8149
Ca 4:8 from the top of S. and Hermon, ... 8149

SHEPHAM (she'-fam) See also SHIPMITE.
Nu 34:10 border from Hazar-enan to S. 8221
Nu 34:11 shall go down from S. to Riblah, ... 8221

SHEPHATIAH (shef-a-ti'-ah)
2Sa 3:4 and the fifth, S. the son of Abital; 8203
1Ch 3:3 The fifth, S. of Abital: the sixth, ... 8203
1Ch 9:8 and Meshullam the son of S., the....... 8203
1Ch 12:5 Shemariah, and S. the Haruphite, ... 8203
1Ch 27:16 Simeonites, S. the son of Maachah: 8203
2Ch 21:2 and Azariah, and Michael, and S.: 8203
Ezr 2:4 The children of S., three hundred....... 8203
Ezr 2:57 The children of S., the children of...... 8203
Ezr 8:8 And of the sons of S.; Zebadiah the.... 8203
Ne 7:9 The children of S., three hundred....... 8203
Ne 7:59 The children of S., the children of...... 8203
Ne 11:4 the son of S., the son of Mahalaleel,... 8203
Jer 38:1 Then S. the son of Mattan, and......... 8203

SHEPHERD See also SHEPHERD'S; SHEPHERDS.
Ge 46:34 every s. is an abomination 7462,6629
Ge 49:24 (from thence is the s., the stone of 7462
Nu 27:17 be not as sheep which have no s........ 7462
1Ki 22:17 hills, as sheep that have not a s.: 7462
2Ch 18:16 as sheep that have no s.; and the....... 7462
Ps 23:1 The Lord is my s.; I shall not want. ... 7462
Ps 80:1 Give ear, O S. of Israel, thou that...... 7462
Ec 12:11 which are given from one s.. 7462
Isa 40:11 He shall feed his flock like a s.: he 7462
Isa 44:28 That saith of Cyrus, He is my s.,....... 7462
Isa 63:11 of the sea with the s. of the flock? 7462
Jer 31:10 and keep him, as a s. doth his flock.... 7462
Jer 43:12 as a s. putteth on his garment; 7462
Jer 49:19 and who is that s. that will stand........ 7462
Jer 50:44 and who is that s. that will stand........ 7462
Jer 51:23 in pieces...the s. and his flock; 7462
Eze 34:5 scattered, because there is no s.:........ 7462
Eze 34:8 because there was no s., neither did... 7462
Eze 34:12 As a s. seeketh out his flock in the..... 7462
Eze 34:23 And I will set up one s. over them, ... 7462
Eze 34:23 feed them, and he shall be their s.. 7462
Eze 37:24 and they all shall have one s.: they..... 7462
Am 3:12 As the s. taketh out of the mouth of... 7462
Zec 10:2 troubled, because there was no s.. 7462
Zec 11:15 yet the instruments of a foolish s.. 7462
Zec 11:16 lo, I will raise up a s. in the land,...... 7462
Zec 11:17 Woe to the idol s. that leaveth the 7473
Zec 13:7 Awake, O sword, against my s., ... 7462
Zec 13:7 smite the s., and the sheep shall be.... 7462
Mt 9:36 abroad, as sheep having no s.. .... *4166*
Mt 25:32 **a s. divideth his sheep from the**..... *4166*
Mt 26:31 **I will smite the s., and the sheep** .. *4166*
Mk 6:34 they were as sheep not having a s.:.... *4166*
Mk 14:27 **I will smite the s., and the sheep** .. *4166*
Joh 10:2 **in by the door is the s. of the sheep.** *4166*
Joh 10:11 **I am the good s.: the good s.** *4166*
Joh 10:12 **that is an hireling, and not the s.,**.. *4166*
Joh 10:14 **I am the good s., and know my**..... *4166*
Joh 10:16 **there shall be one fold, and one s.**.. *4166*
Heb 13:20 Jesus, that great s. of the sheep, ... *4166*
1Pe 2:25 returned unto the S. and Bishop of..... *4166*
1Pe 5:4 And when the chief S. shall appear,...... *750*

SHEPHERD'S
1Sa 17:40 put them in a s. bag which he had, ... 7462
Isa 38:12 is removed from me as a s. tent; 7473

SHEPHERDS See also SHEPHERDS'.
Ge 46:32 the men are s., for their trade.... 7462,6629
Ge 47:3 Thy servants are s., both we, ... 7462,6629
Ex 2:17 And the s. came and drove them......... 7462
Ex 2:19 us out of the hand of the s., and......... 7462
1Sa 25:7 now thy s. which were with us, we 7462
Isa 13:20 neither shall the s. make their fold...... 7462
Isa 31:4 when a multitude of s. is called forth... 7462
Isa 56:11 they are s. that cannot understand:..... 7462
Jer 6:3 The s. with their flocks shall come 7462
Jer 23:4 And I will set up s. over them which .. 7462
Jer 25:34 Howl, ye s., and cry; and wallow 7462
Jer 25:35 And the s. shall have no way to flee, .. 7462
Jer 3:36 A voice of the cry of the s., and an 7462
Jer 33:12 an habitation of s. causing their.......... 7462
Jer 50:6 their s. have caused them to go......... 7462
Eze 34:2 prophesy against the s. of Israel,........ 7462
Eze 34:2 saith the Lord God unto the s.; Woe... 7462
Eze 34:2 Woe be to the s. of Israel that do 7462
Eze 34:2 should not the s. feed the flocks? 7462
Eze 34:7 ye s., hear the word of the Lord;....... 7462
Eze 34:8 did my s. search for my flock, ... 7462
Eze 34:8 but the s. fed themselves, and fed....... 7462
Eze 34:9 O ye s., hear the word of the Lord; ... 7462
Eze 34:10 Behold, I am against the s.; and I 7462
Eze 34:10 neither shall the s. feed themselves 7462
Am 1:2 habitiations of the s. shall mourn, ... 7462
Mic 5:5 shall we raise against him seven s., ... 7462
Na 3:18 thy s. slumber, O king of Assyria: 7462
Zep 2:6 be dwellings and cottages for s., and... 7462
Zec 10:3 anger was kindled against the s., ... 7462
Zec 11:3 is a voice of the howling of the s.;...... 7462
Zec 11:5 and their own s. pity them not........... 7462
Zec 11:8 Three s. also I cut off in one month;... 7462
Lu 2:8 country s. abiding in the field,............ *4166*
Lu 2:15 the s. said one to another, Let us *4166*
Lu 2:18 which were told them by the s.. .... *4166*
Lu 2:20 And the s. returned, glorifying and *4166*

SHEPHERDS'
Ca 1:8 feed thy kids beside the s. tents, ... 7462

SHEPHI (she'-fi) See also SHEPHO.
1Ch 1:40 and Ebal, S., and Onam. 8195

SHEPHO (she'-fo) See also SHEPHI.
Ge 36:23 and Ebal, S., and Onam. 8195

SHEPHUPHAN (shef'-u-fan) See also SHUPHAM; SHUPPIM.
1Ch 8:5 And Gera, and S., and Huram. 8197

SHERAH (she'-rah) See also UZZEN-SHERAH.
1Ch 7:24 his daughter was S., who built........... 7609

SHERD See also POTSHERD; SHERDS; SHRED.
Isa 30:14 be found in the bursting of it a s. 2789

SHERDS See also POTSHERDS.
Eze 23:34 thou shalt break the s. thereof,.......... 2789

SHEREBIAH (sher-e-bi'-ah)
Ezr 8:18 and S., with his sons and his............ 8274
Ezr 8:24 S., Hashabiah, and ten of their 8274
Ne 8:7 and Bani, and S., Jamin, Akkub,.......... 8274
Ne 9:4 Bunni, S., Bani, and Chenani, and 8274
Ne 9:5 Bani, Hashabniah, S., Hodijah, ... 8274
Ne 10:12 Zaccur, S., Shebaniah, ... 8274
Ne 12:8 Binnui, Kadmiel, S., Judah, and.......... 8274
Ne 12:24 Hashabiah, S., and Jeshua the son 8274

SHERESH (she'-resh)
1Ch 7:16 the name of his brother was S.; 8329

SHEREZER (she-re'-zur) See also SHAREZER.
Zec 7:2 S. and Regem-melech, and their......... 8272

SHERIFFS
Da 3:2,3 the s., and all the rulers of the 8614

SHESHACH (she'-shak) See also BABYLON.
Jer 25:26 king of S. shall drink after them. 8347
Jer 51:41 How is S. taken! and how is the 8347

SHESHAI (she'-shahee)
Nu 13:22 S., and Talmai, the children of........... 8344
Jos 15:14 sons of Anak, S., and Ahiman, and..... 8344
Jg 1:10 and they slew S., and Ahiman, and..... 8344

SHESHAN (she'-shan)
1Ch 2:31 and the sons of Ishi: S.. 8348
1Ch 2:31 and the children of S.; Ahlai. 8348
1Ch 2:34 S. had no sons, but daughters, ... 8348
1Ch 2:34 And S. had a servant, an Egyptian,..... 8348
1Ch 2:35 S. gave his daughter to Jarha his........ 8348

SHESHBAZZAR (shesh-baz'-zur) See also ZERUBBABEL.
Ezr 1:8 and numbered them unto S., the........ 8339
Ezr 1:11 All these did S. bring up with them 8339
Ezr 5:14 unto one, whose name was S., whom . 8339
Ezr 5:16 Then came the same S., and laid 8339

SHETH (sheth) See also SETH.
Nu 24:17 and destroy all the children of S.. 8352
1Ch 1:1 Adam, S., Enosh, ... 8352

SHETHAR (she'-thar) See also SHETHAR-BOZNAI.
Es 1:14 Carshena, S., Admatha, Tarshish, ... 8369

SHETHAR-BOZNAI (she''-thar-boz'-nahee)
Ezr 5:3 and S., and their companions, and 8370
Ezr 5:6 and S., and his companions the.......... 8370
Ezr 6:6 S., and your companions the 8370
Ezr 6:13 S.,...their companions, according........ 8370

SHEVA (she'-vah) See also SHAVSHA.
2Sa 20:25 And S. was scribe: and Zodak and...... 7724
1Ch 2:49 S. the father of Machbenah, and 7724

SHEW See also SHEWBREAD; SHEWED; SHEWEST; SHEWETH; SHEWING.
Ge 12:1 unto a land that I will s. thee:............ 7200
Ge 20:13 thy kindness which thou shalt s.......... 6213
Ge 24:12 and s. kindness unto my master......... 6213

Ge 40:14 s. kindness, I pray thee, unto me,...... 6213
Ge 46:31 I will go up, and s. Pharaoh, and....... 5046
Ex 7:9 you, saying, S. a miracle for you:....... 5414
Ex 9:16 up, for to s. in thee my power; 7200
Ex 10:1 that I might s. these my signs 7896
Ex 13:8 thou shalt s. thy son in that day,........ 5046
Ex 14:13 which he will s. to you to day: for...... 6213
Ex 18:20 shalt s. them the way wherein.......... 3045
Ex 25:9 According to all that I s. thee,.......... 7200
Ex 33:13 s. me now thy way, that I may......... 3045
Ex 33:18 I beseech thee, s. me thy glory. 7200
Ex 33:19 will s. mercy on whom I will s. mercy.......
Nu 16:5 the Lord will s. who are his, and........ 3045
De 1:33 to s. you by what way ye should go,... 7200
De 3:24 to s. thy servants thy greatness,........ 7200
De 5:5 to s. you the word of the Lord: 5046
De 7:2 with them, nor s. mercy unto them: ....
De 13:17 of his anger, and s. thee mercy, ... 5414
De 17:9 they shall s. thee the sentence of....... 5046
De 17:10 the Lord shall choose shall s. thee;..... 5046
De 17:11 sentence which they shall s. thee, ... 5046
De 28:50 of the old, nor s. favour to the young:.......
De 32:7 ask thy father, and he will s. thee; 5046
Jos 2:12 ye will also s. kindness unto my......... 6213
Jos 5:6 he would not s. them the land, ... 7200
Jg 1:24 S. us, we pray thee, the entrance....... 7200
Jg 1:24 the city, and we will s. thee mercy..... 6213
Jg 4:22 will s. thee the man...thou seekest. 7200
Jg 6:17 s. me a sign that thou talkest with...... 6213
1Sa 3:15 Samuel feared to s. Eli the vision. 5046
1Sa 8:9 and s. them the manner of the king.... 5046
1Sa 9:6 peradventure he can s. us our way..... 5046
1Sa 9:27 I may s. thee the word of God. 8085
1Sa 10:8 and s. thee what thou shalt do. 3045
1Sa 14:12 up to us, and we will s. you a thing.... 3045
1Sa 16:3 I will s. thee what thou shalt do:........ 3045
1Sa 20:2 or small, but that he will s. it me:..... 1540
1Sa 20:12 sent not unto thee, and s. it thee;...... 1540
1Sa 20:13 then I will s. it thee, and send thee.... 1540
1Sa 20:14 s. me the kindness of the Lord, ... 6213
1Sa 22:17 he fled, and did not s. it to me. 1540
1Sa 25:8 young men, and they will s. thee........ 5046
2Sa 2:6 s. kindness and truth unto you:.......... 6213
2Sa 3:8 s. kindness this day unto the house 6213
2Sa 9:1 may s. him kindness for Jonathan's 6213
2Sa 9:3 that I may s. the kindness of God 6213
2Sa 9:7 surely s. thee kindness for Jonathan.... 6213
2Sa 10:2 I will s. kindness unto Hanun the 6213
2Sa 15:25 s. me both it, and his habitation: 7200
2Sa 22:26 merciful thou wilt s. thyself merciful,.........
2Sa 22:26 man thou wilt s. thyself upright. ....
2Sa 22:27 the pure thou wilt s. thyself pure; ....
2Sa 22:27 froward thou wilt s. thyself unsavoury. ......
1Ki 1:52 If he will s. himself a worthy man,...........
1Ki 2:2 therefore, and s. thyself a man; ....
1Ki 2:7 s. kindness unto...sons of Barzillai...... 6213
1Ki 18:1 saying Go, s. thyself unto Ahab; 7200
1Ki 18:2 Elijah went to s. himself unto Ahab...... 7200
1Ki 18:15 I will surely s. myself unto him.......... 7200
2Ki 6:11 s. me which of us is for the king........ 5046
2Ki 7:12 s. you what the Syrians have done 5046
1Ch 16:23 s....from day to day his salvation. 1319
1Ch 19:2 I will s. kindness unto Hanun the 6213
2Ch 16:9 to s. himself strong in the behalf of..........
Ezr 2:59 could not s. their father's house, ... 5046
Ne 7:61 could not s. their father's house, ... 5046
Ne 9:19 of fire by night, to s. them light, ...
Es 1:11 to s. the people...her beauty: 7200
Es 2:10 charged her...she should not s. it. 5046
Es 4:8 to s. it unto Esther, and to declare..... 7200
Job 10:2 s. me wherefore thou contendest 3045
Job 11:6 s. thee the secrets of wisdom,........... 5046
Job 15:17 I will s. thee, hear me; and that......... 2331
Job 32:6 and durst not s. you mine opinion....... 2331
Job 32:10 to me; I also will s. mine opinion........ 2331
Job 32:17 my part, I also will s. mine opinion. 2331
Job 33:23 to s. unto man his uprightness: 5046
Job 36:2 Suffer me a little, and I will s. 2331
Ps 4:6 that say, Who will s. us any good? 7200
Ps 9:1 s. forth all thy marvellous works. 5608
Ps 9:14 That I may s. forth all thy praise......... 5608
Ps 16:11 Thou wilt s. me the path of life:......... 3045
Ps 17:7 S. thy marvellous lovingkindness, ...
Ps 18:25 merciful thou wilt s. thyself merciful;.........
Ps 18:25 man thou wilt s. thyself upright; ....
Ps 18:26 the pure thou wilt s. thyself pure; ....
Ps 18:26 froward thou wilt s. thyself froward. ....
Ps 25:4 S. me thy ways, O Lord; teach me 3045
Ps 25:14 and he will s. them his covenant. 3045
Ps 39:6 every man walketh in a vain s. 6754
Ps 50:23 will I s. the salvation of god. 7200
Ps 51:15 my mouth shall s. forth thy praise. 5046
Ps 71:15 shall s. forth thy righteousness 5608
Ps 79:13 s. forth thy praise to all generations.... 5608
Ps 85:7 S. us thy mercy, O Lord, and 7200
Ps 86:17 S. me a token for good; that they 6213
Ps 88:10 Wilt thou s. wonders to the dead? 6213
Ps 91:16 him, and s. him my salvation. 7200
Ps 92:2 To s. forth thy lovingkindness in 5046
Ps 92:15 To s. that the Lord is upright: he....... 5046
Ps 94:1 vengeance belongeth, s. thyself. 3313
Ps 96:2 s....his salvation from day to day........ 1319
Ps 106:2 who can s. forth all his praise?.......... 8085
Ps 109:16 he remembered not to s. mercy,........ 6213
Pr 18:24 hath friends must s. himself friendly: ....
Isa 3:9 The s. of their countenance doth........ 1971
Isa 27:11 formed them will s. them no favour. ....
Isa 30:30 s. the lighting down of his arm,.......... 7200
Isa 41:22 and s. us what shall happen:.............. 5046
Isa 41:22 let them s. the former things, what 5046
Isa 41:23 S. the things that are to come........... 5046
Isa 43:9 this, and s. us former things? 8085
Isa 43:21 they shall s. forth my praise. 5608
Isa 44:7 shall come, let them s. unto them. 5046
Isa 46:8 Remember this, and s. yourselves men:.....
Isa 47:6 thou didst s. them no mercy; 7760
Isa 49:9 are in darkness, S. yourselves. 1540
Isa 58:1 s. my people their transgression,......... 5046
Isa 60:6 s. forth the praises of the Lord.......... 1319
Jer 16:10 shalt s. this people all these words, ... 5046
Jer 16:13 where I will not s. you favour............ 5414
Jer 18:17 I will s. them the back, and not 7200
Jer 33:3 s. thee great and mighty things,......... 5046
Jer 42:3 the Lord thy God may s. us the way .. 5046
Jer 42:12 And I will s. mercies unto you,.......... 5414
Jer 50:42 they are cruel, and will not s. mercy: ....
Jer 51:31 to s. the king of Babylon...his city...... 5046
Jer 22:2 shalt s. her all her abominations. 3045
Eze 22:2 yea, thou shalt s. her all her 3645
Eze 33:31 their mouth they s. much love, ... 6213
Eze 37:18 thou not s. us what thou meanest......... 5046
Eze 40:4 heart upon all that I shall s. thee;....... 7200
Eze 40:4 that I might s. them unto thee art 7200
Eze 43:10 s. the house to the house of Israel, ... 5046
Eze 43:11 s. them the form of the house, ... 3045
Da 2:2 for to s. the king his dreams. 5046
Da 2:4 and we will s. the interpretation. 2324
Da 2:6 But if ye s. the dream, and the.......... 2324
Da 2:6 therefore s. me the dream, and the 2324
Da 2:7 we will s. the interpretation of it. 2324
Da 2:9 that ye can s. me the interpretation 2324
Da 2:10 earth that can s. the king's matter: 2324
Da 2:11 there is none other that can s. it........ 2324
Da 2:16 s. the king the interpretation. 2324
Da 2:24 s. unto the king the interpretation. 2324
Da 2:27 the soothsayers, s. unto the king; 2324
Da 4:2 I thought it good to s. the signs......... 2324
Da 5:7 s. me the interpretation thereof, ... 2324
Da 5:12 and he will s. the interpretation. 2324
Da 5:15 they could not s. the interpretation..... 2324
Da 9:23 forth, and I am come to s. thee; 5046
Da 10:21 I will s. thee that which is noted........ 5046
Da 11:2 And now will I s. thee the truth......... 5046
Joe 2:30 I will s. wonders in the heavens......... 5414
Mic 7:15 I s. unto him marvellous things. 7200
Na 3:5 I will s. the nations thy nakedness, ... 7200
Hab 1:3 Why dost thou s. me iniquity, and 7200
Zec 1:9 unto me, I will s. thee what these be...7200
Zec 7:9 and s. mercy and compassions 6213
Mt 8:4 **thy way, s. thyself to the priest,**.... *1166*
Mt 11:4 **Go and s. John again those things**... *518*
Mt 12:18 shall s. judgment to the Gentiles.......... *518*
Mt 14:2 mighty works do s....themselves *1754*
Mt 16:1 would s. them a sign from heaven. *1925*
Mt 16:21 began Jesus to s. unto his disciples,.... *1166*
Mt 22:19 **S. me the tribute money.** And......... *1925*
Mt 24:1 s. him the buildings of the temple....... *1925*
Mt 24:24 **shall s. great signs and wonders;**... *1325*
Mk 1:44 **thy way, s. thyself to the priest,**... *1166*
Mk 6:14 mighty works do s....themselves *1754*
Mk 13:22 **and shall s. signs and wonders, to**..*1325*
Mk 14:15 **he will s. you a large upper room**.. *1166*
Lu 1:19 and to s. thee these glad tidings......... *2097*
Lu 5:14 **but go, and s. thyself to the priest,**.*1166*
Lu 6:47 **I will s. you to whom he is like:**... *5263*
Lu 8:39 **s. how great things God hath done.***1334*
Lu 17:14 **Go s. yourselves unto the priests**... *1925*
Lu 20:24 **S. me a penny. Whose image and**.. *1925*
Lu 20:47 **and for a s. make long prayers:**..... *4392*
Lu 22:12 **he shall s. you a large upper room.***1166*
Joh 5:20 **s. him greater works than these,**... *1166*
Joh 7:4 things, s. thyself to the world............ *5319*
Joh 11:57 knew where he was, he should s. it,... *3377*
Joh 14:8 s. us the Father, and it sufficeth *1166*
Joh 14:9 **sayest thou the, S. us the Father?**..*1166*
Joh 16:13 **and he will s. you things to come**.. *312*
Joh 16:14, **15 of mine, and shall s. it unto**....... *312*
Joh 16:25 **I shall s. you plainly of the Father.** *312*
Ac 1:24 s. whether of these two thou hast........ *322*
Ac 2:19 I will s. wonders in heaven above,....... *1325*
Ac 7:3 into the land which I shall s. thee. *1166*
Ac 9:16 **I will s. him how great things**....... *5263*
Ac 12:17 Go s. these things unto James, and...... *518*
Ac 16:17 s. unto us the way of salvation. *2605*
Ac 24:27 willing to s. the Jews a pleasure,........ *2698*
Ac 26:23 should s. light unto the people, ... *2605*
Ro 2:15 s. the work of the law written in......... *1731*
Ro 9:17 that I might s. my power in thee,....... *1731*
Ro 9:22 What if God, willing to s. his wrath,.... *1731*
1Co 11:26 ye do s. the Lord's death till he *2605*
1Co 12:31 s. I unto you a more excellent way..... *1166*
1Co 15:51 I s. you a mystery; We shall not........ *3004*
2Co 8:24 Wherefore s. ye to them, and before .. *1731*
Ga 6:12 desire to make a fair s. in the flesh, ... *2146*
Eph 2:7 he might s. the exceeding riches *1731*
Col 2:15 he made a s. of them openly, ... *1165*
Col 2:23 things have indeed a s. of wisdom *3056*
1Th 1:9 s. of us what manner of entering *518*
1Ti 1:16 might s. forth all longsuffering,........... *1731*
1Ti 5:4 learn first to s. piety at home, and *2151*
1Ti 6:15 Which in his times he shall s., ... *1166*
2Ti 2:15 Study to s. thyself approved unto *3936*
Heb 6:11 one of you do s. the same diligence *1731*
Heb 6:17 to s. unto the heirs of promise the *1925*
Jas 2:18 s. me thy faith without thy works,...... *1166*
Jas 2:18 I will s. thee my faith by my works. ... *1166*
Jas 3:13 let him s. out of a good conversation... *1166*
1Pe 2:9 should s. forth the praises of him *1804*
1Jo 1:2 and s. unto you that eternal life, ... *518*
Re 1:1 to s. unto his servants things which.... *1166*
Re 4:1 I will s. thee things which must be *1166*
Re 17:1 I will s. unto thee the judgment of...... *1166*
Re 21:9 I will s. thee the bride, the Lamb's..... *1166*
Re 22:6 to s. unto his servants the things *1166*

SHEWBREAD

Ex 25:30 shalt set upon the table s. 3899,6440
Ex 35:13 and all his vessels, and the s.,.... 3899,6440
Ex 39:36 the vessels thereof, and the s.;... 3899,6440
Nu 4:7 upon the table of s. they shall spread.. 6440
1Sa 21:6 was no bread there but the s., ... 3899,6440
1Ki 7:48 of gold, whereupon the s. was,... 3899,6440
1Ch 9:32 were over the s., to prepare it... 3899,4635
1Ch 23:29 Both for the s., and for the fine.. 3899,4635
1Ch 28:16 he gave gold for the tables of s.,........ 4635
2Ch 2:4 incense, and for the continual s.,........ 4635
2Ch 4:19 tables whereon the s. was set; ... 3899,6440
2Ch 13:11 the s. also set they in order....... 3899,4635
2Ch 29:18 and the s. table, with all the vessels ... 4635
Ne 10:33 For the s., and...the continual 3899,4635
Mt 12:4 **eat the s., which was not**........ *740,4286*
Mk 2:26 **eat the s., which is not lawful**..*740,4286*
Lu 6:4 **and did take and eat the s.,**..... *740,4286*
Heb 9:2 and the table, and the s.; *4286,740*

SHEWED See also SHEWEDST.

Ge 19:19 thou hast s. unto me in saving my...... 6213
Ge 24:14 hast s. kindness unto my master. 6213
Ge 32:10 which thou hast s. unto thy servant; ... 6213
Ge 39:21 with Joseph, and s. him mercy,.......... 5186
Ge 41:25 God hath s. Pharaoh what he is 5046
Ge 41:39 Forasmuch as God hath s. thee all...... 3045
Ge 48:11 lo, God hath s. me also thy seed........ 7200
Ex 15:25 and the Lord s. him a tree, which 3384
Ex 25:40 which was s. thee in the mount. 7200
Ex 26:30 which was s. thee in the mount. 7200
Ex 27:8 as it was s. thee in the mount, so...... 7200
Le 13:19 reddish, and it be s. to the priest; 7200
Le 13:49 and shall be s. unto the priest: 7200

Le 24:12 mind of the Lord might be **s.** them. 6567
Nu 8:4 patter...the Lord had **s.** Moses, ... 7200
Nu 13:26 and **s.** them the fruit of the land......... 7200
Nu 14:11 signs...I have **s.** among them? 6213
De 4:35 Unto thee it was **s.**, that thou.............. 7200
De 4:36 upon earth he **s.** thee his great fire;.... 7200
De 5:24 Lord our God hath **s.** us his glory 7200
De 6:22 the Lord **s.** signs and wonders,.......... 5414
De 34:1 Lord **s.** him all the land of Gilead, ... 7200
De 34:12 terror which Moses **s.** in the sight...... 6213
Jos 2:12 since I have **s.** you kindness, that....... 6213
Jg 1:25 when he **s.** them the entrance into 7200
Jg 4:12 And they **s.** Sisera that Barak........... 5046
Jg 8:35 **s.** they kindness to the house of 6213
Jg 8:35 to all the goodness which he had **s.** 6213
Jg 13:10 and ran, and **s.** her husband, and........ 5046
Jg 13:23 neither would he have **s.** us all 7200
Jg 16:18 for he hath **s.** me all his heart........... 5046
Ru 2:11 It hath fully been **s.** me, all that thou .. 5046
Ru 2:19 she **s.** her mother in law with whom... 5046
Ru 3:10 **s.** more kindness in the latter 3190
1Sa 11:9 messengers...**s.** it to the men of 5046
1Sa 15:6 **s.** kindness to all the children of......... 6213
1Sa 19:7 Jonathan **s.** him all those things.......... 5046
1Sa 22:21 Abiathar **s.** David...Saul had slain........ 5046
1Sa 24:18 **s.** this day how...thou hast dealt 5046
2Sa 2:5 **s.** this kindness unto your lord,.......... 6213
2Sa 10:2 as his father **s.** kindness unto me. 6213
2Sa 11:22 **s.** David all that Joab had sent him...... 5046
1Ki 1:27 hast not **s.** it unto thy servant, ... 3045
1Ki 3:6 hast **s.** unto thy servant David my....... 6213
1Ki 16:27 he did, and his might that he **s.**, ... 6213
1Ki 22:45 and his might that he **s.**, and how....... 6213
2Ki 6:6 fell it? And he **s.** him the place. 7200
2Ki 8:10 Lord hath **s.** me that he shall...die...... 7200
2Ki 8:13 Lord hath **s.** me thou shalt be king..... 7200
2Ki 11:4 Lord, and **s.** them the king's son........ 7200
2Ki 20:13 **s.** them...the house of his precious..... 7200
2Ki 20:13 nothing...that Hezekiah **s.** them not. ... 7200
2Ki 20:15 treasures that I have not **s.** them. 7200
2Ki 22:10 Shaphan the scribe **s.** the king, ... 7200
1Ch 19:2 his father **s.** kindness to me. 6213
2Ch 1:8 hast **s.** great mercy unto David my....... 6213
2Ch 7:10 the Lord had **s.** unto David, and to...... 6213
Ezr 9:8 grace hath been **s.** from the Lord.............
Es 1:4 he **s.** the riches of his glorious........... 7200
Es 2:10 Esther had not **s.** her people nor........ 5046
Es 2:20 Esther had not yet **s.** her kindred......... 5046
Es 3:6 had **s.** him the people of Mordecai: 5046
Job 6:14 pity should be **s.** from his friend;..............
Ps 31:21 he hath **s.** me his marvellous kindness.......
Ps 60:3 Thou hast **s.** thy people hard things: ....
Ps 71:18 I have **s.** thy strength unto this.......... 5046
Ps 71:20 hast **s.** me great and sore troubles, ... 7200
Ps 78:11 his wonders that he had **s.** them. 7200
Ps 98:2 righteousness hath he openly **s.** in...... 1540
Ps 105:27 They **s.** his signs among them, and..... 7760
Ps 111:6 hath **s.** his people the power of his...... 5046
Ps 118:27 is the Lord, which hath **s.** us light: ....
Ps 142:2 him; I **s.** before him my trouble. 5046
Pr 26:26 wickedness shall be **s.** before the 1540
Ec 2:19 I have **s.** myself wise under the sun..........
Isa 26:10 Let favour be **s.** to the wicked, yet...........
Isa 39:2 **s.** them the house of his precious......... 7200
Isa 39:2 dominion, that Hezekiah **s.** them not, .. 7200
Isa 39:4 treasures that I have not **s.** them. 7200
Isa 40:14 **s.**...him the way of understanding?...... 3045
Isa 43:12 have saved, and I have **s.**, when........ 8085
Isa 48:3 out of my mouth, and I **s.** them; 8085
Isa 48:5 before it came to pass I **s.** it thee: 8085
Isa 48:6 **s.** thee new things from this time, ... 8085
Jer 24:1 The Lord **s.** me, and, behold, two...... 7200
Jer 38:21 the word that the Lord hath **s.** me: 7200
Eze 11:25 the things that the Lord had **s.** me. 7200
Eze 20:11 and **s.** them my judgments, which....... 3045
Eze 22:26 neither have they **s.** difference........... 3045
Am 7:1 hath the Lord God **s.** unto me; 7200
Am 7:4 Thus hath the Lord God **s.** unto me:... 7200
Am 7:7 Thus he **s.** me: and, behold, the 7200
Am 8:1 Thus hath the Lord God **s.** unto me:... 7200
Mic 6:8 He hath **s.** thee, O man, what is 5046
Zec 1:20 the Lord **s.** me four carpenters.......... 7200
Zec 3:1 And he **s.** me Joshua the high priest ... 7200
Mt 28:11 and **s.** unto the chief priests all the *518*
Lu 1:51 He hath **s.** strength with his arm;........ *4160*
Lu 1:58 Lord had **s.** great mercy upon her; *3170*
Lu 4:5 **s.** unto him all the kingdoms of the..... *1166*
Lu 7:18 of John **s.** him of all these things.......... *518*
Lu 10:37 he said, He that **s.** mercy on him. *4160*
Lu 14:21 **came, and s. his lord these things**... *518*
Lu 20:37 **even Moses s. at the bush, when** ... *3377*
Lu 24:40 he **s.** them his hands and his *1925*
Joh 10:32 **good works have I s. you from my** .*1166*
Joh 20:20 he **s.** unto them his hands and his *1166*
Joh 21:1 Jesus **s.** himself again to the............. *5319*
Joh 21:1 and on this wise **s.** he himself............ *5319*
Joh 21:14 third time that Jesus **s.** himself to......... *5319*
Ac 1:3 To whom also he **s.** himself alive........ *3936*
Ac 3:18 **s.** by...mouth of all his prophets,........ *4293*
Ac 4:22 this miracle of healing was **s.**............. *1096*
Ac 7:26 he **s.** himself unto them as they *3700*
Ac 7:36 **s.** wonders and signs in the land *4160*
Ac 7:52 slain them which **s.** before of the......... *4293*
Ac 10:28 God hath **s.** me that I should not........ *1166*
Ac 10:40 day, and **s.** him openly;...... *1325,1717,1096*
Ac 11:13 he **s.** us how he and seen an angel....... *518*
Ac 19:18 and confessed, and **s.** their deeds. *312*
Ac 20:20 but have **s.** you, and have taught *312*
Ac 20:35 I have **s.** you all things, how that *5263*
Ac 23:22 thou hast **s.** these things to me.......... *1718*
Ac 26:20 **s.** first unto them of Damascus, and *518*
Ac 28:2 people **s.** us no little kindness:........... *3930*
Ac 28:21 came **s.** or spake any harm of thee. *518*
Ro 1:19 for God hath **s.** it unto them.............. *5319*
1Co 10:28 eat not for his sake that **s.** it, and *3377*
Heb 6:10 which ye have **s.** toward his name, ... *1731*
Heb 8:5 the pattern **s.** to thee in the mount..... *1166*
Jas 2:13 mercy, that hath **s.** no mercy; *4160*
2Pe 1:14 our Lord Jesus Christ hath **s.** me. *1213*
Re 21:10 and **s.** me that great city, the holy...... *1166*
Re 22:1 he **s.** me a pure river of water of....... *1166*
Re 22:8 the angel which **s.** me these things. *1166*

SHEWEDST

Ne 9:10 And **s.** signs and wonders upon.......... 5414
Jer 11:18 it: then thou **s.** me their doings.......... 7200

SHEWEST

2Ch 6:14 **s.** mercy unto thy servants, that walk ....
Job 10:16 thou **s.** thyself marvellous upon me...........
Jer 32:18 Thou **s.** lovingkindness unto 6213
Joh 2:18 What sign **s.** thou unto us, seeing....... *1166*
Joh 6:30 What sign **s.** thou then, that we......... *4160*

SHEWETH

Ge 41:28 about to do he **s.** unto Pharaoh. 7200
Nu 23:3 and whatsoever he **s.** me I will tell 7200
1Sa 22:8 is none that **s.** me that my son..... 1540,241
1Sa 22:8 or **s.** unto me that my son hath.... 1540,241
2Sa 22:51 and **s.** mercy to his anointed, unto....... 6213
Job 36:9 Then he **s.** them their work, and........ 5046
Job 36:33 The noise thereof **s.** concering it, ... 5046
Ps 18:50 and **s.** mercy to his anointed, to......... 6213
Ps 19:1 the firmament **s.** his handywork. 5046
Ps 19:2 night unto night **s.** knowledge. 2331
Ps 37:12 righteous **s.** mercy, and giveth...............
Ps 112:5 A good man **s.** favour, and lendeth: ....
Ps 147:19 He **s.** his word unto Jacob, his........... 5046
Pr 12:17 He that speaketh truth **s.** forth 5046
Pr 27:25 tender grass **s.** itself, and herbs 7200
Isa 41:26 there is none that **s.**, yea, there is 5046
Mt 4:8 and **s.** him all the kingdoms of the *1166*
Joh 5:20 **s. him all things that himself doeth**:.*1166*
Ro 9:16 runneth, but of God that **s.** mercy. *1653*
Ro 12:8 he that **s.** mercy, with cheerfulness. ... *1653*

SHEWING

Ex 20:6 **s.** mercy unto thousands of them........ 6213
De 5:10 **s.** mercy unto thousands of them......... 6213
Ps 78:4 **s.** to the generation to come the 5608
Ca 2:9 **s.** himself through the lattice. 6692
Da 4:27 iniquities by **s.** mercy to the poor; ....
Da 5:12 **s.** of hard sentences, and dissolving...... 263
Lu 1:80 till the day of his **s.** unto Israel........... *323*
Lu 8:1 preaching and **s.** the glad tidings..............
Ac 9:39 **s.** the coats and garments which *1925*
Ac 18:28 **s.** by the scriptures that Jesus was....... *1925*
2Th 2:4 of God, **s.** himself that he is God.......... *584*
Tit 2:7 **s.** thyself a pattern of good works: *3930*
Tit 2:7 in doctrine **s.** uncorruptness, gravity, ...
Tit 2:10 but **s.** all good fidelity; that 1731
Tit 3:2 gentle, **s.** all meekness unto all men.... *1731*

SHIBBOLETH (shib'-bo-leth) See also SIBBOLETH.

Jg 12:6 said they unto him, Say now **S.**: 7641

SHIBMAH (shib'-mah) See also SHEBAM; SIBMAH.

Nu 32:38 names being changed,) and **S.**:........... 7643

SHICRON (shi'-cron)

Jos 15:11 and the border was drawn to **S.**,........ 7942

SHIELD See also SHIELDS.

Ge 15:1 Fear not, Abram: I am thy **s.**, and...... 4043
De 33:29 by the Lord, the **s.** of thy help, ... 4043
Jg 5:8 was there a **s.** or spear seen among ... 4043
1Sa 17:7 one bearing a **s.** went before him. 6793
1Sa 17:41 man that bare the **s.** went before 6793
1Sa 17:45 and with a spear, and with a **s.**........... 3591
2Sa 1:21 **s.** of the mighty is vilely cast away,.... 4043
2Sa 1:21 the **s.** of Saul, as though he had not.... 4043
2Sa 22:3 he is my **s.**, and the horn of my......... 4043
2Sa 22:36 given me the **s.** of thy salvation: 4043
1Ki 10:17 three pound of gold went to one **s.**..... 4043
2Ki 19:32 nor come before it with **s.**, nor cast.... 4043
1Ch 12:8 that could handle **s.** and buckler, ... 6793
1Ch 12:24 The children of Judah that bare **s.**........ 6793
1Ch 12:34 with **s.** and spear thirty and seven...... 6793
2Ch 9:16 shekels of gold sent to one **s.**............ 4043
2Ch 17:17 him armed men with bow and **s.** 4043
2Ch 25:5 that could handle spear and **s.**............ 6793
Job 39:23 the glittering spear and the **s.**............ 3591
Ps 3:3 But thou, O Lord, art a **s.** for me; 4043
Ps 5:12 thou compass him as with a **s.**........... 6793
Ps 18:35 given me the **s.** of thy salvation: 4043
Ps 28:7 The Lord is my strength and my **s.**; 4043
Ps 33:20 the Lord: he is our help and our **s.**..... 4043
Ps 35:2 Take hold of **s.** and buckler, and 4043
Ps 59:11 bring them down, O Lord our **s.**. 4043
Ps 76:3 he the arrows of the bow, the **s.**,........ 4043
Ps 84:9 Behold, O God our **s.**, and look 4043
Ps 84:11 For the Lord God is a sun and **s.**........ 4043
Ps 91:4 his truth shall be thy **s.** and.............. 6793
Ps 115:9, 10,11 he is their help and their **s.**........ 4043
Ps 119:114 art my hiding place and my **s.**............ 4043
Ps 144:2 my **s.**, and he in whom I trust;.......... 4043
Pr 30:5 he is a **s.** unto them that put their...... 4043
Isa 21:5 arise, ye princes, and anoint the **s.**. 4043
Isa 22:6 and Kir uncovered the **s.**................... 4043
Jer 46:3 Order ye the buckler and **s.**, and........ 6793
Jer 46:9 the Libyans, that handle the **s.**;.......... 4043
Eze 23:24 buckler and **s.** and helmet round......... 4043
Eze 27:10 hanged the **s.** and helmet in thee;....... 4043
Eze 38:5 all the them with **s.** and helmet:......... 4043
Na 2:3 **s.** of his mighty men is made red, ... 4043
Eph 6:16 taking the **s.** of faith, wherewith......... *2375*

SHIELDS

2Sa 8:7 David took the **s.** of gold that were 7982
1Ki 10:17 three hundred **s.** of beaten gold; 4043
1Ki 14:26 took away all the **s.** of gold which....... 4043
1Ki 14:27 made in their stead brasen **s.**, and....... 4043
2Ki 11:10 give king David's spears and **s.**, ... 7982
1Ch 18:7 David took the **s.** of gold that were 7982
2Ch 9:16 three hundred **s.** made of beaten......... 4043
2Ch 11:12 every several city he puts **s.** and........ 6793
2Ch 12:9 he carried away also the **s.** of gold 4043
2Ch 12:10 king Rehoboam made **s.** of brass, ... 4043
2Ch 14:8 that bare **s.** and drew bows, two......... 4043
2Ch 23:9 spears, and bucklers, and **s.**, that....... 7982
2Ch 26:14 them throughout all the host **s.**,......... 4043
2Ch 32:5 and darts and **s.** in abundance........... 4043
2Ch 32:27 and for **s.**, and for all manner of.......... 4043
Ne 4:16 the spears, the **s.**, and the bows,........ 4043
Ps 47:9 the **s.** of the earth belong unto God: ... 4043
Ca 4:4 bucklers, all **s.** of mighty men............ 7982
Isa 37:33 nor come before it with **s.**, nor.......... 4043
Jer 51:11 bright the arrows; gather the **s.**: 7982
Eze 27:11 hanged their **s.** upon thy walls 7982
Eze 38:4 company with bucklers and **s.**, ... 4043
Eze 39:9 both the **s.** and the bucklers, the........ 4043

SHIGGAION (shig-gah'-yon) See also SHIGIONOTH.

Ps 7:*title* **S.** of David, which he sang unto......... 7692

SHIGIONOTH (shig-i'-o-noth) See also SHIGGAION.

Hab 3:1 Habakkuk the prophet upon **S.**........... 7692

SHIHON (shi'-hon)

Jos 19:19 And Haphraim, and **S.**, and 7866

SHIHOR (shi'-hor) See also SHIHOR-LIBNATH; SIHOR.

1Ch 13:5 from **S.** of Egypt even unto the 7883

SHIHOR-LIBNATH (shi''-hor-lib'-nath)

Jos 19:26 to Carmel westward, and to **S.**; 7884

SHILHI (shil'-hi)
1Ki 22:42 was Azubah the daughter of **S.**. 7977
2Ch 20:31 was Azubah the daughter of **S.**. 7977

SHILHIM (shil'-him) See also SHAARAIM; SHARUHEN.
Jos 15:32 Lebaoth, and **S.**, and Ain, and 7978

SHILLEM (shil'-lem) See also SHALLUM; SHILLEMITES.
Ge 46:24 and Guni, and Jezer, and **S.**. 8006
Nu 26:49 of **S.**, the family of the Shillemites. 8006

SHILLEMITES (shil'-lem-ites)
Nu 26:49 of Shillem, the family of the **S.**. 8016

SHILOAH (shi-lo'-ah) See also SILOAH; SILOAM.
Isa 8:6 people refuseth the waters of **S.** 7975

SHILOH (shi'-loh) See also SHILONITE; TAANATH-SHILOH.
Ge 49:10 between his feet, until **S.** come; 7886
Jos 18:1 of Israel assemble together at **S.**, 7887
Jos 18:8 lots for you before the Lord in **S.** 7887
Jos 18:9 again to Joshua to the host at **S.**. 7887
Jos 18:10 Joshua cast lots for them in **S.** 7887
Jos 19:51 an inheritance by lot in **S.** before 7887
Jos 21:2 spake unto them at **S.** in the land 7887
Jos 22:9 the children of Israel out of **S.**, 7887
Jos 22:12 together at **S.**, to go up to war 7887
Jg 18:31 that the house of God was in **S.** 7887
Jg 21:12 brought them unto the camp to **S.**, 7887
Jg 21:19 is a feast of the Lord in **S.** yearly 7887
Jg 21:21 daughters of **S.** come out to dance 7887
Jg 21:21 his wife of the daughters of **S.**, 7887
1Sa 1:3 sacrifice unto the Lord...in **S.**, 7887
1Sa 1:9 rose up after they had eaten in **S.**, 7887
1Sa 1:24 unto the house of the Lord in **S.**: 7887
1Sa 2:14 they did in **S.** unto all the Israelites 7887
1Sa 3:21 the Lord appeared again in **S.**: 7887
1Sa 3:21 revealed himself to Samuel in **S.** 7887
1Sa 4:3 the covenant of the Lord out of **S.** 7887
1Sa 4:4 So the people sent to **S.**, that they 7887
1Sa 4:12 came to **S.** the same day with his 7887
1Sa 14:3 the Lord's priest in **S.**, wearing an 7887
1Ki 2:27 concerning the house of Eli in **S.** 7887
1Ki 14:2 and get thee to **S.**: behold, there is 7887
1Ki 14:4 did so, and arose, and went to **S.**, 7887
Ps 78:60 he forsook the tabernacle of **S.**, 7887
Jer 7:12 unto my place which was in **S.**, 7887
Jer 7:14 your fathers, as I have done to **S.**. 7887
Jer 26:6 will I make this house like **S.**, and 7887
Jer 26:9 This house shall be like **S.**, and 7887
Jer 41:5 certain from Shechem, from **S.**, 7887

SHILONI (shi-lo'-ni) See also SHILONITE.
Ne 11:5 son of Zechariah, the son of **S.**. 8023

SHILONITE (shi'-lon-ite) See also SHILONI; SHILONITES.
1Ki 11:29 the **S.** found him in the way; 7888
1Ki 12:15 the Lord spake by Ahijah the **S.** 7888
1Ki 15:29 sake by his servant Ahijah the **S.**: 7888
2Ch 9:29 in the prophecy of Ahijah the **S.**, 7888
2Ch 10:15 spake by the hand of Ahijah the **S.** 7888

SHILONITES (shi'-lon-ites)
1Ch 9:5 And of the **S.**; Asaiah the firstborn, 7888

SHILSHAH (shil'-shah)
1Ch 7:37 Shamma, and **S.**, and Ithran, and 8030

SHIMEA (shim'-e-ah) See also SHAMMAH; SHAMMUA; SHAMMUAH; SHIMEAH; SHIMEATHITES; SHIMMA.
1Ch 3:5 **S.**, and Shobab, and Nathan, and 8092
1Ch 6:30 **S.** his son, Haggiah his son, Asaiah 8092
1Ch 6:39 son of Berachiah, the son of **S.**, 8092
1Ch 20:7 Jonathan the son of **S.** David's 8092

SHIMEAH (shim'-e-ah) See also SHIMEA; SHIMEAM.
2Sa 13:3 the son of **S.** David's brother: 8093
2Sa 13:32 the son of **S.** David's brother, 8093
2Sa 21:21 Jonathan the son of **S.** the 8096
1Ch 8:32 And Mikloth begat **S.** And these 8039

SHIMEAM (shim'-e-am) See also SHIMEA.
1Ch 9:38 And Mikloth begat **S.** And they 8043

SHIMEATH (shim'-e-ath)
2Ki 12:21 For Jozachar the son of **S.**, and 8100
2Ch 24:26 the son of **S.** an Ammonitess, and 8100

SHIMEATHITES (shim'-e-ath-ites)
1Ch 2:55 the Tirathites, and **S.**, and 8101

SHIMEI (shim'-e-i) See also SHEMAIAH; SHIMHI; SHIMI; SHIMITES.
Nu 3:18 by their families; Libni, and **S.** 8096
2Sa 16:5 whose name was **S.**, the son of 8096
2Sa 16:7 And thus said **S.** when he cursed, 8096
2Sa 16:13 **S.** went along on the hill's side over 8096
2Sa 19:16 **S.** the son of Gera, a Benjamite, 8096
2Sa 19:18 **S.** the son of Gera fell down before 8096
2Sa 19:21 Shall not **S.** be put to death for this, 8096
2Sa 19:23 the king said unto **S.**, Thou shalt 8096
1Ki 1:8 Nathan the prophet, and **S.**, and 8096
1Ki 2:8 hast with thee **S.** the son of Gera, 8096
1Ki 2:36 And the king sent and called for **S.**, 8096
1Ki 2:38 **S.** said unto the king, The saying 8096
1Ki 2:38 **S.** dwelt in Jerusalem many days. 8096
1Ki 2:39 two of the servants of **s.** ran away 8096
1Ki 2:39 And they told **S.**, saying, Behold, 8096
1Ki 2:40 And **S.** arose, and saddled his ass, 8096
1Ki 2:40 **S.** went, and brought his servants 8096
1Ki 2:41 was told Solomon that **S.** had gone 8096
1Ki 2:42 And the king sent and called for **S.**, 8096
1Ki 2:44 The king said moreover to **S.**, Thou 8096
1Ki 4:18 **S.** the son of Elah, in Benjamin: 8096
1Ch 3:19 Pedaiah were, Zerubbabel, and **S.**: 8096
1Ch 4:26 son, Zacchur his son, **S.** his son. 8096
1Ch 4:27 And **S.** had sixteen sons and six 8096
1Ch 5:4 his son, Gog his son, **S.** his son, 8096
1Ch 6:17 sons of Gershom; Libni, and **S.** 8096
1Ch 6:29 Libni his son, **S.** his son, Uzza his 8096
1Ch 6:42 the son of Zimmah, the son of **S.**, 8096
1Ch 23:7 Gershonites were, Laadan, and **S.**. 8096
1Ch 23:9 The sons of **S.**; Shelomith, and 8096
1Ch 23:10 And the sons of **S.** were, Jahath, 8096
1Ch 23:10 These four were he sons of **S.**. 8096
1Ch 25:17 The tenth to **S.**, he, his sons, and 8096
1Ch 27:27 over the vineyards was **S.** the 8096
2Ch 29:14 the sons of Heman; Jehiel, and **S.**: 8096
2Ch 31:12 and **S.** his brother was the next. 8096
2Ch 31:13 the hand of Cononiah and **S.** his 8096
Ezr 10:23 of the Levites; Jozabad, and **S.**, 8096
Ezr 10:33 Jeremai, Manasseh, and **S.** 8096
Ezr 10:38 And Bani, and Binnui, **S.**, 8096
Es 2:5 the son of Jair, the son of **S.**, the 8096
Zec 12:13 the family of **S.** a part, and their 8097

SHIMEON (shim'-e-on) See also SIMEON.
Ezr 10:31 Ishijah, Malchiah, Shemaiah, **S.**, 8095

SHIMHI (shim'-hi) See also SHEMA; SHIMEI.
1Ch 8:21 and Shimrath, the sons of **S.**; 8096

SHIMI (shi'-mi) See also SHIMEI; SHIMITES.
Ex 6:17 **S.**, according to their families. 8096

SHIMITES (shi'-mites)
Nu 3:21 Libnites, and the family of the **S.**: 8097

SHIMMA (shim'-mah) See also SHAMMAH.
1Ch 2:13 the second, and **S.** the third, 8092

SHIMON (shi'-mon)
1Ch 4:20 the sons of **S.** were, Amnon, and 7889

SHIMRATH (shim'-rath)
1Ch 8:21 and **S.**, the sons of Shimhi; 8119

SHIMRI (shim'-ri) See also SIMRI.
1Ch 4:37 the son of Jedaiah, the son of **S.**, 8113
1Ch 11:45 Jediael the son of **S.**, and Joha his 8113
2Ch 29:13 sons of Elizaphan; **S.**, and Jeiel: 8113

SHIMRITH (shim'-rith) See also SHOMER.
2Ch 24:26 and Jehozabad the son of **S.** a 8116

SHIMROM (shim'-rom) See also SHIMRON.
1Ch 7:1 And Puah, Jashub, and **S.**, four. 8110

SHIMRON (shim'-ron) See also SHIMROM; SHIMRONITES; SHIMRON-MERON.
Ge 46:13 and Phuvah, and Job, and **S.**. 8110
Nu 26:24 of **S.**, the family of the Shimronites. 8110
Jos 11:1 and to the king of **S.**, and to the 8110
Jos 19:15 Kattath, and Nahallal, and **S.**, and 8110

SHIMRONITES (shim'-ron-ites)
Nu 26:24 of Shimron, the family of the **S.**. 8117

SHIMRON-MERON (shim''-ron-me'-ron) See also SHIMRON.
Jos 12:20 The king of **S.**, one; the king of 8112

SHIMSHAI (shim'-shahee)
Ezr 4:8 **S.** the scribe wrote a letter 8124
Ezr 4:9 and **S.** the scribe, and the rest 8124
Ezr 4:17 to **S.** the scribe, and to the rest of 8124
Ezr 4:23 **S.** the scribe, and their companions, 8124

SHINAB (shi'-nab)
Ge 14:2 **S.** king of Admah, and Shemeber 8134

SHINAR (shi'-nar)
Ge 10:10 and Calneh, in the land of **S.**. 8152
Ge 11:2 found a plain in the land of **S.**; 8152
Ge 14:1 in the days of Amraphel king of **S.**, 8152
Ge 14:9 Amraphel king of **S.**, and Arioch 8152
Isa 11:11 and from **S.**, and from Hamath, 8152
Da 1:2 land of **S.** to the house of his god; 8152
Zec 5:11 build it an house in the land of **S.**: 8152

SHINE See also SHINED; SHINETH; SHINING; SHONE.
Nu 6:25 Lord make his face **s.** upon thee, 215
Job 3:4 neither let the light **s.** upon it. 3313
Job 10:3 **s.** upon the counsel of the wicked? 3313
Job 11:17 thou shalt **s.** forth, thou shalt be 5774
Job 18:5 the spark of his fire shall not **s.** 5050
Job 22:28 the light shall **s.** upon thy ways. 5050
Job 36:32 commandeth it not to **s.** by the cloud
Job 37:15 caused the light of his cloud to **s.**? 3313
Job 41:18 By his neesings a light doth **s.**, 1984
Job 41:32 He maketh a path to **s.** after him: 215
Ps 31:16 thy face to **s.** upon thy servant: 215
Ps 67:1 and cause his face to **s.** upon us. 215
Ps 80:1 between the cherubims, **s.** forth. 3313
Ps 80:3 and cause thy face to **s.**; and we 215
Ps 80:7, 19 cause thy face to **s.**; and we 215
Ps 104:15 oil to make his face to **s.**, and 6670
Ps 119:135 thy face to **s.** upon thy servant; 215
Ec 8:1 man's wisdom maketh his face to **s.**, 215
Isa 13:10 shall not cause her light to **s.** 5050
Isa 60:1 Arise, **s.**; for thy light is come, 215
Jer 5:28 They are waxen fat, they **s.**: yea, 6245
Da 9:17 thy face to **s.** upon thy sanctuary 215
Da 12:3 they that be wise shall **s.** as the 2094
Mt 5:16 **Let your light so s. before men,** *2989*
Mt 13:43 **Then shall the righteous s. forth** *1584*
Mt 17:2 his face did **s.** as the sun, and his *2989*
2Co 4:4 image of God, should **s.** unto them. *826*
2Co 4:6 who commanded the light to **s.** *2989*
Php 2:15 among whom ye **s.** as lights in *5316*
Re 18:23 light of candle shall **s.** no more *5316*
Re 21:23 neither of the moon, to **s.** in it: *5316*

SHINED See also SHONE.
De 33:2 he **s.** forth from mount Paran, and 3313
Job 29:3 When his candle **s.** upon my head, 1984
Job 31:26 If I beheld the sun when it **s.**, or 1984
Ps 50:2 perfection of beauty, God hath **s.** 3313
Isa 9:2 upon them hath the light **s.** 5050
Eze 43:2 and the earth **s.** with his glory. 215
Ac 9:3 **s.** round about him a light from *4015*
Ac 12:7 him, and a light **s.** in the prison: *2989*
2Co 4:6 of darkness, hath **s.** in our hearts, *2989*

SHINETH
Job 25:5 even the moon, and it **s.** not; 166
Ps 139:12 but the night **s.** as the day: the 215
Pr 4:18 **s.** more and more unto the perfect 215
Mt 24:27 **east, and s. even unto the west;** *5316*
Lu 17:24 **s. unto the other part under** *2989*
Joh 1:5 And the light **s.** in darkness; and *5316*
2Pe 1:19 unto a light that **s.** in a dark place, *5316*
1Jo 2:8 is past, and the true light now **s.** *5316*
Re 1:16 was as the sun **s.** in his strength. *5316*

SHINING
2Sa 23:4 of the earth by clear **s.** after rain. 5051
Pr 4:18 path of the just is as the **s.** light, 5051
Isa 4:5 the **s.** of the flaming fire by night: 5051
Joe 2:10 the stars shall withdraw their **s.**: 5051
Joe 3:15 the stars shall withdraw their **s.**. 5051
Hab 3:11 at the **s.** of thy glittering spear. 5051
Mk 9:3 And his raiment became **s.**, *4744*
Lu 11:36 **bright s. of a candle doth give** *796*
Lu 24:4 men stood by them in **s.** garments: *797*
Joh 5:35 **He was a burning and a s. light:** *5316*
Ac 26:13 **s.** round about me and them *4034*

SHIP See also FORESHIP; SHIPMASTER; SHIPMEN; SHIPPING; SHIPS; SHIPWRECK.
Pr 30:19 way of a **s.** in the midst of the sea; 591
Isa 33:21 oars, neither shall gallant **s.** pass 6716
Eze 27:5 made all thy **s.** boards of fir trees
Jon 1:3 he found a **s.** going to Tarshish: 591
Jon 1:4 that the **s.** was like to be broken. 591
Jon 1:5 the wares that were in the **s.** into 591
Jon 1:5 gone down into the sides of the **s.**; 5600

Mt 4:21 in a **s.** with Zebedee their father, ... *4143*
Mt 4:22 they immediately left the **s.** and *4143*
Mt 8:23 when he was entered into a **s.**, his *4143*
Mt 8:24 the **s.** was coverd with the waves: *4143*
Mt 9:1 he entered into a **s.**, and passed *4143*
Mt 13:2 so that he went into a **s.**, and sat; *4143*
Mt 14:13 he departed thence by **s.** into a *4143*
Mt 14:22 his disciples to get into a **s.**, and *4143*
Mt 14:24 **s.** was now in the midst of the sea, ... *4143*
Mt 14:29 Peter was come down out of the **s.**, ... *4143*
Mt 14:32 when they were come into the **s.**, ... *4143*
Mt 14:33 they that were in the **s.** came and *4143*
Mt 15:39 took **s.**, and came into the coasts *4143*
Mk 1:19 were in the **s.** mending their nets *4143*
Mk 1:20 left their father Zebedee in the **s.** *4143*
Mk 3:9 that a small **s.** should wait on him *4142*
Mk 4:1 so that he entered into a **s.**, and *4143*
Mk 4:36 took him even as he was in the **s.** *4143*
Mk 4:37 and the waves beat into the **s.**, so *4143*
Mk 4:38 he was in the hinder part of the **s.** ....
Mk 5:2 when he was come out of the **s.**, ... *4143*
Mk 5:18 And when he was come into the **s.**, ... *4143*
Mk 5:21 again by **s.** unto the other side, ... *4143*
Mk 6:32 into a desert place by **s.** privately *4143*
Mk 6:45 his disciples to get into the **s.**, ... *4143*
Mk 6:47 the **s.** was in the midst of the sea, ... *4143*
Mk 6:51 he went up unto them into the **s.**; *4143*
Mk 6:54 when they were come out of the **s.**, ... *4143*
Mk 8:10 straightway he entered into a **s.** *4143*
Mk 8:13 and entering into the **s.** again *4143*
Mk 8:14 had they in the **s.** with them more *4143*
Lu 5:3 and taught the people out of the **s.**, ... *4143*
Lu 5:7 which were in the other **s.**, that *4143*
Lu 8:22 that he went into a **s.** with his *4143*
Lu 8:37 and he sent up into the **s.**, and *4143*
Joh 6:17 entered into a **s.**, and went over the ... *4143*
Joh 6:19 sea, and drawing nigh unto the **s.**: *4143*
Joh 6:21 willingly received him into the **s.**: *4143*
Joh 6:21 and immediately the **s.** was at the *4143*
Joh 21:3 and entered into a **s.** immediately; *4143*
Joh 21:6 **the net on the right side of the s.**, .. *4143*
Joh 21:8 other disciples came in a little **s.**; *4142*
Ac 20:13 we went before to **s.**, and sailed *4143*
Ac 20:38 they accompanied him unto the **s.** *4143*
Ac 21:2 And finding a **s.** sailing over unto *4143*
Ac 21:3 the **s.** was to unlade her burden *4143*
Ac 21:6 leave one of another, we took **s.**; *4143*
Ac 27:2 entering into a **s.** of Adramyttium, ... *4143*
Ac 27:6 centurion found a **s.** of Alexandria *4143*
Ac 27:10 not only of the lading and **s.**, but *4143*
Ac 27:11 the master and the owner of the **s.**, ... *3490*
Ac 27:15 And when the **s.** was caught, and *4143*
Ac 27:17 used helps, undergirding the **s.**; *4143*
Ac 27:18 the next day they lightened the **s.**; ....
Ac 27:19 own hands the tackling of the **s.** *4143*
Ac 27:22 man's life among you, but of the **s.** *4143*
Ac 27:30 were about to flee out of the **s.**, ... *4143*
Ac 27:31 Except these abide in the **s.**, ye *4143*
Ac 27:37 were in all in the **s.** two hundred *4143*
Ac 27:38 they lightened the **s.**, and cast out *4143*
Ac 27:39 it were possible, to thrust in the **s.** *4143*
Ac 27:41 seas met, they ran the **s.** around; *3491*
Ac 27:44 some on broken pieces of the **s.** *4143*
Ac 28:11 we departed in a **s.** of Alexandria, ... *4143*

SHIPHI (shi'-fi)
1Ch 4:37 And Ziza the son of **S.**, the son of 8230

SHIPHMITE (shif'-mite)
1Ch 27:27 wine cellars was Zabdi the **S.**: 8225

SHIPHRAH (shif'-rah)
Ex 1:15 which the name of the one was **S.**, ... 8236

SHIPHTAN (shif'-tan)
Nu 34:24 Ephraim, Kemuel the son of **S.** 8204

SHIPMASTER
Jon 1:6 So the **S.** came to him, and 7227,2259
Re 18:17 every **s.**, and all the company in *2942*

SHIPMEN
1Ki 9:27 **s.** that had knowledge of the 582,591
Ac 27:27 **s.** deemed that they drew near to *3492*
Ac 27:30 the **s.** were about to flee out of the *3492*

SHIPPING
Joh 6:24 they also took **s.**, and came to *4143*

SHIPS
Ge 49:13 and he shall be for an haven of **s.**; 591
Nu 24:24 **s.** shall come from the coast of 6716
De 28:68 bring the into Egypt again with **s.**, ... 591
Jg 5:17 and why did Dan remain in **s.**? 591
1Ki 9:26 made a navy of **s.** in Ezion-geber, ...
1Ki 22:48 Jehoshaphat made **s.** of Tharshish 591
1Ki 22:48 the **s.** were broken at Ezion-geber. 591
1Ki 22:49 go with thy servants in the **s.** 591
2Ch 8:18 him by the hands of his servants **s.**, ... 591
2Ch 9:21 the king's **s.** went to Tarshish with 591
2Ch 9:21 the **s.** of Tarshish bringing gold, ... 591
2Ch 20:36 him to make **s.** to go to Tarshish: 591
2Ch 20:36 they made the **s.** in Ezion-gaber. 591
2Ch 20:37 the **s.** were broken, that they were 591
Job 9:26 are passed away as the swift **s.**: 591
Ps 48:7 Thou breakest the **s.** of Tarshish 591
Ps 104:26 There go the **s.**: there is that 591
Ps 107:23 They that go down to the sea in **s.**, ... 591
Pr 31:14 She is like the merchants' **s.**; she 591
Isa 2:16 And upon all the **s.** of Tarshish, ... 591
Isa 23:1 Howl, ye **s.** of Tarshish; for it is 591
Isa 23:14 Howl, ye **s.** of Tarshish: for your 591
Isa 43:14 Chaldeans, whose cry is in the **s.** 591
Isa 60:9 for me, and the **s.** of Tarshish first, ... 591
Eze 27:9 **s.** of the sea with their mariners 591
Eze 27:25 The **s.** of Tarshish did song of thee 591
Eze 27:29 shall come down from their **s.**, ... 591
Eze 30:9 messengers go forth from me in **s.** 6716
Da 11:30 **s.** of Chittim shall come against 6716
Da 11:40 with horsemen, and with many **s.**; 591
Mk 4:36 were also with him other little **s.** *4142*
Lu 5:2 saw two **s.** standing by the lake: *4143*
Lu 5:3 And he entered into one of the **s.**, ... *4143*
Lu 5:7 they came, and filled both the **s.**, ... *4143*
Lu 5:11 they had brought their **s.** to land, ... *4143*
Jas 3:4 Behold also the **s.**, which though *4143*
Re 8:9 third part of the **s.** were destroyed *4143*
Re 18:17 all the company in **s.**, and sailors, ... *4143*
Re 18:19 made rich all that had **s.** in the sea *4143*

SHIPWRECK
2Co 11:25 thrice I suffered **s.**, a night and a 3489
1Ti 1:19 Concerning faith have made **s.**: 3489

SHISHA (shi'-shah) See also SHAVSHA.
1Ki 4:3 and Ahiah, the sons of **S.**, scribes; 7894

SHISHAK (shi'-shak)
1Ki 11:40 into Egypt, unto **S.** king of Egypt, ... 7895
1Ki 14:25 **S.** king of Egypt came up against 7895
2Ch 12:2 **S.** king of Egypt came up against 7895
2Ch 12:5 together to Jerusalem because of **S.**, ... 7895
2Ch 12:5 I also left you in the hand of **S.** 7895
2Ch 12:7 upon Jerusalem by the hand of **S.** 7895
2Ch 12:9 **S.** king of Egypt came up against 7895

SHITRAI (shit'-ra-i)
1Ch 27:29 in Sharon was **S.** the Sharonite: 7861

SHITTAH (shit'-tah) See also BETH-SHITTAH; SHITTIM.
Isa 41:49 cedar, the **s.** tree, and the myrtle, ... 7848

SHITTAH-TREE See SHITTAH and TREE.

SHITTIM See also SHITTAH; SHITTIM.
Ex 25:5 and badgers' skins, and **s.** wood, ... 7848
Ex 25:10 they shall make an ark of **s.** wood: 7848
Ex 25:13 thou shalt make staves of **s.** wood, ... 7848
Ex 25:23 shalt also make a table of **s.** wood: 7848
Ex 25:28 shalt make the staves of **s.** wood, ... 7848
Ex 26:15 boards for the tabernacle of **s.** wood ... 7848
Ex 26:26 thou shalt make bars of **s.** wood; 7848
Ex 26:32 hang it upon four pillars of **s.** wood 7848
Ex 26:37 the hanging five pilars of **s.** wood, ... 7848
Ex 27:1 thou shalt make an altar of **s.** wood, ... 7848
Ex 27:6 for the altar, staves of **s.** wood, and ... 7848
Ex 30:1 of **s.** wood shalt thou make it. 7848
Ex 30:5 shalt make the staves of **s.** wood, ... 7848
Ex 35:7 and badgers' skins, and **s.** wood, ... 7848
Ex 35:24 with whom was found **s.** wood for 7848
Ex 36:20 for the tabernacle of **s.** wood, ... 7848
Ex 36:31 And he made bars of **s.** wood; five 7848
Ex 36:36 thereunto four pillars of **s.** wood, ... 7848
Ex 37:1 Bezaleel made the ark of **s.** wood: 7848
Ex 37:4 and he made staves of **s.** wood, and ... 7848
Ex 37:10 And he made the table of **s.** wood: 7848
Ex 37:15 And he made the staves of **s.** wood, ... 7848
Ex 37:25 made the incense altar of **s.** wood: 7848
Ex 37:28 And he made the staves of **s.** wood, ... 7848
Ex 38:1 altar of burnt offering of **s.** wood: 7848
Ex 38:6 And he made the staves of **s.** wood, ... 7848
De 10:3 And I made an ark of **s.** wood, and 7848

SHITTIM (shit'-tim) See also ABEL-SHITTIM.
Nu 25:1 And Israel abode in **S.**, and the 7851
Jos 2:1 son of Nun sent out of **S.** two men 7851
Jos 3:1 they removed from **S.**, and came 7851
Joe 3:18 and shall water the valley of **S.** 7851
Mic 6:5 answered him from **S.** unto Gilgal; 7851

SHITTIM-WOOD See SHITTIM and WOOD.

SHIVERS
Re 2:27 **potter shall they be broken to s.**: .. *4937*

SHIZA (shi'-zah)
1Ch 11:42 Adina the son of **S.** the Reubenite, ... 7877

SHOA (sho'-ah)
Eze 23:23 all the Chaldeans, Pekod, and **S.**, ... 7772

SHOBAB (sho'-bab)
2Sa 5:14 Shammuah, and **S.**, and Nathan, ... 7727
1Ch 2:18 sons are these; Jesher, and **S.**, ... 7727
1Ch 3:5 Shimea, and **S.**, and Nathan, and 7727
1Ch 14:4 and **S.**, Nathan, and Solomon, ... 7727

SHOBACH (sho'-bak) See also SHOPHACH.
2Sa 10:16 and **S.** the captain of the host of 7731
2Sa 10:18 smote **S.** the captain of their host, ... 7731

SHOBAI (sho'-bahee)
Ezr 2:42 the children of **S.**, in all an 7630
Ne 7:45 of Hatita, the children of **S.**, an 7630

SHOBAL (sho'-bal)
Ge 36:20 Lotan, and **S.**, and Zibeon, and 7732
Ge 36:23 And the children of **S.** were these; 7732
Ge 36:29 duke Lotan, duke **S.**, duke Zibeon, ... 7732
1Ch 1:38 the sons of Seir, and Lotan, and **S.**, ... 7732
1Ch 1:40 The sons of **S.**; Alion, and 7732
1Ch 2:50, 52 **S.** the father of Kirjath-jearim, ... 7732
1Ch 4:1 and Carmi, and Hur, and **S.** 7732
1Ch 4:2 And Reaiah the son of **S.** begat 7732

SHOBEK (sho'-bek)
Ne 10:24 Hallohesh, Pileha, **S.**, ... 7733

SHOBI (sho'-bi)
2Sa 17:27 **S.** the son of Nahash of Rabbah of 7629

SHOCHO (sho'-ko) See also SHOCHOH.
2Ch 28:18 and **S.** with the villages thereof, ... 7755

SHOCHOH (sho'-ko) See also SHOCHO; SHOCO; SOCHOH; SOCO; SOCOH.
1Sa 17:1 and were gathered together at **S.**, ... 7755
1Sa 17:1 pitched between **S.** and Azekah, ... 7755

SHOCK See also SHOCKS.
Job 5:26 **s.** of corn cometh in in his season. 1430

SHOCKS
Jg 15:5 and burnt up both the **s.**, and also 1430

SHOCO (sho'-co) See also SHOCHOH.
2Ch 11:7 Beth-zur, and **S.**, and Adullam, ... 7755

SHOD See also DRYSHOD; UNSHOD.
2Ch 28:15 arrayed them, and **s.** them, and 5274
Eze 16:10 and **s.** the with badgers' skin, and 5274
Mk 6:9 But be **s.** with sandals; and not *5265*
Eph 6:15 your feet **s.** with the preparation *5265*

SHOE See also SHOD; SHOELATCHET; SHOE'S; SHOES.
De 25:9 and loose his **s.** from off his foot, ... 5275
De 25:10 of him that hath his **s.** loosed 5275
De 29:5 **s.** is not waxen old upon thy foot. 5275
Jos 5:15 Loose thy **s.** from off thy foot; for 5275
Ru 4:7 a man plucked off his **s.**, and gave 5275
Ru 4:8 it for thee. So he drew off his **s.** 5275
Ps 60:8 over Edom will I cast out my **s.**: 5275
Ps 108:9 over Edom will I cast out my **s.**; 5275
Isa 20:2 and put off thy **s.** from thy foot 5275

SHOELATCHET
Ge 14:23 from a thread even to a **s.**, ... 8288,5275

SHOE'S
Joh 1:27 **s.** latchet I am not worthy to *5266*

SHOES
Ex 3:5 put off thy **s.** from off thy feet, ... 5275
Ex 12:11 your **s.** on your feet, and your staff 5275
De 33:25 Thy **s.** shall be iron and brass; 4515
Jos 9:5 old **s.** and clouted upon their feet, ... 5275
Jos 9:13 our **s.** are become old by reason of 5275

1Ki 2:5 and in his s. that were on his feet. 5275
Ca 7:1 How beautiful are thy feet with s., ... 5275
Isa 5:27 the latchet of their s. be broken:......... 5275
Eze 24:17 and put on thy s. upon thy feet,......... 5275
Eze 24:23 heads, and your s. upon your feet: 5275
Am 2:6 and the poor for a pair of s.; 5275
Am 8:6 and the needy for a pair of s.; 5275
Mt 3:11 whose s. I am not worthy to bear: 5266
Mt 10:10 neither two coasts, neither s., nor..5266
Mk 1:7 the latchet of whose s. I am not 5266
Lu 3:16 the latchet of whose s. I am not 5266
Lu 10:4 neither purse, nor scrip, nor s....... 5266
Lu 15:22 on his hand, and s. on his feet:...... 5266
Lu 22:35 without purse, and scrip, and s.,... 5266
Ac 7:33 Put off thy s. from thy feet: for the.... 5266
Ac 13:25 s. of his feet I am not worthy to........ 5266

SHOHAM (sho'-ham)
1Ch 24:27 Beno, and S., and Zaccur, and........... 7719

SHOMER (sho'-mur) See also SHAMER; SHIMRITH.
2Ki 12:21 and Jehozabad the son of S., his 7763
1Ch 7:32 And Heber begat Japhlet, and S., ... 7763

SHONE See also SHINED.
Ex 34:29 wist not that the skin of his face s...... 7160
Ex 34:30 behold, the skin of his face s.; and 7160
Ex 34:35 that the skin of Moses' face s.: and 7160
2Ki 3:22 and the sun s. upon the water, and..... 2224
Lu 2:9 and the glory of the Lord s. round........ 4034
Ac 22:6 s. from heaven a great light round...... 4015
Re 8:12 the day s. not for a third part of it, ... 5316

SHOOK See also SHAKED.
2Sa 6:6 took hold of it; for the oxen s. it........ 8058
2Sa 22:8 Then the earth s. and trembled;........ 1607
2Sa 22:8 foundations of heaven moved and s., ... 1607
Ne 5:13 Also I s. my lap, and said, So God 5287
Ps 18:7 Then the earth s. and trembled;......... 1607
Ps 68:8 The earth s., the heavens also........... 7493
Ps 77:18 world: the earth trembled and s......... 7493
Isa 23:11 over the sea, he s. the kingdoms: 7264
Ac 13:51 s. off the dust of their feet against...... 1621
Ac 18:6 he s. his raiment, and said unto 1621
Ac 28:5 he s. off the beast into the fire, and..... 660
Heb 12:26 Whose voice then s. the earth: but...... 4531

SHOOT See also SHOOTETH; SHOOTING; SHOT.
Ex 36:33 the middle bar to s. through the......... 1272
1Sa 20:20 s. three arrows on the side thereof,.... 3384
1Sa 20:36 find out now the arrows which I s.. 3384
2Sa 11:20 that they would s. from the wall? 3384
2Ki 13:17 Then Elisha said, S. And he shot. 3384
2Ki 19:32 into this city, nor s. an arrow there, ... 3384
1Ch 5:18 and sword, and to s. with bow,........... 1869
2Ch 26:15 s. arrows and great stones withal. 3384
Ps 11:2 privily s. at the upright in heart. 3384
Ps 22:7 they s. out the lip, they shake the...... 6362
Ps 58:7 he bendeth his bow to s. his arrows, ...
Ps 64:3 bend their bows to s. their arrows,...........
Ps 64:4 may s. in secret at the perfect:.......... 3384
Ps 64:4 suddenly do they s. at him, and 3384
Ps 64:7 God shall s. at them with an arrow;.... 3384
Ps 144:6 s. out thine arrows, and destroy 7971
Isa 37:33 into this city, nor s. an arrow there, ...
Jer 50:14 bow, s. at her, spare no arrows:......... 3034
Eze 31:14 s. up their top among the thick......... 5414
Eze 36:8 ye shall s. forth your branches, and.... 5414
Lu 21:30 When they now s. forth, ye see..... 4261

SHOOTERS
2Sa 11:24 s. shot from off the wall upon thy........ 3384

SHOOTETH
Job 8:16 his branch s. forth in his garden......... 3318
Isa 27:8 In measure, when it s. forth, thou........ 7971
Mk 4:32 s. out great branches; so that........ 4160

SHOOTING
1Ch 12:2 the left in hurling stones and s. arrows......
Am 7:1 of the s. up of the latter growth;........ 5927

SHOPHACH (sho'-fak) See also SHOBACH.
1Ch 19:16 and S. the captain of the host of 7780
1Ch 19:18 Killed S. the captain of the host......... 7780

SHOPHAN (sho'-fan) See also ZAPHON.
Nu 32:35 S., and Jaazer, and Jogbehah, ... 5855

SHORE
Ge 22:17 the sand which is upon the sea s.;...... 8193
Ex 14:30 the Egyptians dead uopn the sea s...... 8193
Jos 11:4 that is upon the sea s. in multitude,.... 8193
Jos 15:2 was from the s. of the salt sea, ... 7097
Jg 5:17 Asher continued on the sea s., ... 2348
1Sa 13:5 as the sand which is on the sea s......... 8193
1Ki 4:29 as the sand that is on the sea s.. 8193
1Ki 9:26 on the s. of the Red sea, in the......... 8193
Jer 47:7 Askelon, and against the sea s.?.......... 2348
Mt 13:2 whole multitude stood on the s.......... 123
Mt 13:48 when it was full, they drew to s.,.... 123
Mk 6:53 of Gennesaret, and drew to the s.. 4358
Joh 21:4 now come, Jesus stood on the s.: 123
Ac 21:5 and we kneeled down on the s., and..... 123
Ac 27:39 discovered a certain creek with a s., ... 123
Ac 27:40 to the wind, and made toward s.. 123
Heb 11:12 as the sand which is by the sea s.......... 5491

SHORN
Ca 4:2 a flock of sheep that are even s., ... 7094
Ac 18:18 having s. his head in Cenchrea:.......... 2751
1Co 11:6 be not covered, let her also be s.:....... 2751
1Co 11:6 it be a shame for a woman to be s. 2751

SHORT See also SHORTER.
Nu 11:23 Is the Lord's hand waxed s.?............ 7114
2Ki 10:32 days the Lord began to cut Israel s.: ....
Job 17:12 the light is s. because of darkness. 7138
Job 20:5 the triumphing of the wicked is s.,........ 7138
Ps 89:47 Remember how s. my time is:........... 2465
Ro 3:23 and come s. of the glory of God;......... 5302
Ro 9:28 and cut it s. in righteousness:............ 4932
Ro 9:28 a s. work will the Lord make upon 4932
1Co 7:29 this I say, Brethren, the time is s.: 4958
1Th 2:17 being taken from you for a s. time...... 5610
Heb 4:1 of you should seem to come s. of it. ... 5302
Re 12:12 knoweth that he hath but a s. time. 3641
Re 17:10 he must continue a s. space. 3641

SHORTENED
Ps 89:45 The days of his youth hast thou s.:..... 7114
Ps 102:23 strength in the way; he s. my days...... 7114
Pr 10:27 the years of the wicked shall be s.. 7114
Isa 50:2 Is my hand s. at all, that it cannot...... 7114
Isa 59:1 Behold, the Lord's hand is not s., ... 7114
Mt 24:22 except those days should be s.,...... 2856
Mt 24:22 elect's sake those days shall be s... 2856
Mk 13:20 that the Lord had s. those days,..... 2856
Mk 13:20 he hath chosen, he hath s. the days..2856

SHORTER
Isa 28:20 the bed is s. than that a man can 7114
Eze 42:5 Now the upper chambers were s.:....... 7114

SHORTLY
Ge 41:32 and God will s. bring it to pass. 4116
Jer 27:16 s. be brought again from Babylon: 4120
Eze 7:8 I s. pour out my fury upon thee,......... 7138
Ac 25:4 himself...depart s. thither. 1722,5034
Ro 16:20 bruise Satan under your feet s.... 1722,5034
1Co 4:19 I will come to you s., if the Lord 5030
Php 2:19 to send Timotheus s. unto you, ... 5030
Php 2:24 that I also myself shall come s.......... 5030
1Ti 3:14 thee, hoping to come unto thee s.: 5032
2Ti 4:9 thy diligence to come s. unto me:........ 5030
Heb 13:23 with whom, if he come s., I will see... 5032
2Pe 1:14 that s. I must put off this my 5031
3Jo 14 But I trust I shall s. see thee, and 2112
Re 1:1 which must s. come to pass;...... 1722,5034
Re 22:6 things which must s. be done. 1722,5034

SHOSHANNIM (sho-shan'-nim) See also SHOSHANNIM-EDUTH.
Ps 45:title To the chief Musician upon S., ... 7799
Ps 69:title To the chief Musician upon S., ... 7799

SHOSHANNIM-EDUTH (sho-shan''-nim-e'-duth)
Ps 80:title To the chief Musician upon S., ... 7802

SHOT See also BOWSHOT.
Ge 40:10 budded, and her blossoms s. forth;..... 5927
Ge 49:23 and s. at him, and hated him: 7232
Ex 19:13 surely be stoned, or s. through;......... 3384
Nu 21:30 We have s. at them; Heshbon is 3384
1Sa 20:20 thereof, as though I s. at a mark........ 7971
1Sa 20:36 ran, he s. an arrow beyond him. 3384
1Sa 20:37 the arrow which Jonathan had s.,........ 3384
2Sa 11:24 And the shooters s. from off the wall.. 3384
2Ki 13:17 Then Elisha said, Shoot. And he s. 3384
2Ch 35:23 And the archers s. at king Josiah;....... 3384
Ps 18:14 an he s. out lightnings, and............... 7232
Jer 9:8 tongue is as an arrow s. out; it........... 7819
Eze 17:6 forth branches, and s. forth sprigs. 7971
Eze 17:7 s. forth her branches toward him,........ 7971
Eze 31:5 multitude of waters,...he s. forth........ 7971
Eze 31:10 he hath s. up his top among the......... 7971

SHOULD See also SHOULDEST.
Ge 2:18 is not good that the man s. be alone; ....
Ge 4:15 Cain, lest any finding him s. kill him.........
Ge 18:25 that the righteous s. be as the wicked,.......
Ge 21:7 that Sarah s. have given children suck! ......
Ge 23:8 it be your mind that I s. bury my dead......
Ge 26:7 men of the place s. kill me for Rebekah;....
Ge 27:45 why s. I be deprived also of you both ....
Ge 29:7 is it time that the cattle s. be gathered......
Ge 29:19 than that I s. give her to another man: ......
Ge 30:38 s. conceive when they came to drink.........
Ge 33:13 and if men s. overdrive them one day, ...
Ge 34:31 S. he deal with our sister as with an.........
Ge 38:9 Onan knew that the seed s. not be his; .....
Ge 38:9 that he s. give seed to his brother...........
Ge 40:15 that they s. put me into the dungeon. ....
Ge 43:25 heard that they s. eat bread there. ....
Ge 44:7 God forbid that thy servants s. do ....
Ge 44:8 how then s. we steal out of thy lord's ....
Ge 44:17 he said, God forbid that I s. do so:..........
Ge 44:22 for if he s. leave his father, his father ....
Ge 47:15 for why s. we die in thy presence? for ......
Ge 47:26 that Pharaoh s. have the fifth part; ....
Ex 3:11 Who am I, that I s. go unto Pharaoh,.........
Ex 3:11 and that I s. bring forth the children ....
Ex 5:2 I s. obey his voice to let Israel go?..........
Ex 14:12 than that we s. die in the wilderness? ....
Ex 22:3 him; for he s. make full restitution;...........
Ex 32:12 Wherefore s. the Egyptians speak, ...
Ex 35:1 hath commanded, that ye s. do them...........
Ex 39:7 that they s. be stones for a memorial.........
Ex 39:23 about the hole, that it s. not rend.............
Le 4:13, 22 things which s. not be done, ...
Le 9:6 the Lord commanded that ye s. do: ....
Le 10:18 ye s. indeed have eaten it in the holy.........
Le 10:19 s. it have been accepted in the sight ....
Le 11:43 unclean with them, that ye s. be defiled ....
Le 20:26 from other people, that ye s. be mine. ......
Le 24:23 s. bring forth him that had cursed.............
Le 26:13 that ye s. not be their bondmen; ....
Le 27:26 beasts, which s. be the Lord's firstling, ...
Nu 7:9 that they s. bear upon their shoulders. ......
Nu 9:4 Israel, that they s. keep the passover. ......
Nu 11:13 Whence s. I have flesh to give unto all......
Nu 12:14 s. she not be ashamed seven days? ....
Nu 14:3 wives and our children s. be a prey?.........
Nu 14:31 little ones, which ye said s. be a prey, ...
Nu 15:34 not declared what s. be done to him. ....
Nu 20:4 that we and our cattle s. die there? ....
Nu 23:19 God is not a man, that he s. lie; neither....
Nu 23:19 the son of man, that he s. repent: ....
Nu 27:4 Why s. the name of our father be done .....
Nu 32:9 that they s. not go into the land which ....
Nu 35:28 Because he s. have remained in the city....
Nu 35:32 he s. come again to dwell in the land, ...
De 1:18 that time all the things which ye s. do.......
De 1:33 to shew you by what way ye s. go, and.....
De 1:39 little ones, which ye said s. be a prey, ...
De 4:5 that ye s. do so in the land whither ye ....
De 4:21 and sware that I s. not go over Jordan, ...
De 4:21 that I s. not go in unto that good land, ...
De 4:42 which s. kill his neighbour unawares,.........
De 5:25 Now therefore why s. we die? for this ......
De 17:16 to the end that he s. multiply horses:........
De 20:18 so s. ye sin against the Lord your God.......
De 25:3 if he s. exceed, and beat him above..........
De 25:3 then thy brother s. seem vile unto thee.....
De 29:18 Lest there s. be among you a man, or ......
De 29:18 lest there s. be among you a root that ......
De 32:27 adversaries s. behave themselves ....
De 32:27 and lest they s. say, Our hand is high, ...
De 32:30 How s. one chase a thousand, and two.......
Jos 8:29 that they s. take his carcase down...........
Jos 8:33 that they s. bless the people of Israel.......
Jos 9:27 day, in the place which he s. choose.........
Jos 11:20 they s. come against Israel in battle, ...
Jos 22:28 s. so say to us or to our generations.........
Jos 22:29 that we s. rebel against the Lord,.............
Jos 24:16 God forbid that we s. forsake the Lord,......
Jg 8:6 that we s. give bread unto thine army?.......
Jg 8:15 that we s. give bread unto thy men ....
Jg 9:9 S. I leave my fatness, wherewith by.........
Jg 9:11 S. I forsake my sweetness, and my..........

Jg 9:13 S. I leave my wine, which cheereth
Jg 9:28 who is Shechem, that we s. serve him?
Jg 9:28 of Shechem: for why s. we serve him?
Jg 9:38 is Abimelech, that we s. serve him?
Jg 9:41 that they s. not dwell in Shechem.
Jg 20:38 they s. make a great flame with smoke
Jg 21:3 s. be to day one tribe lacking in Israel?
Jg 21:22 them a this time, that ye s. be guilty.
Ru 1:12 If I s. say, I have hope,
Ru 1:12 if I s. have an husband also to night,
Ru 1:12 also to night, and s. also bear sons;
1Sa 2:30 thy father, s. walk before me for ever:
1Sa 8:7 me, that I s. not reign over them.
1Sa 9:6 he can shew us our way that we s. go.
1Sa 10:22 further, if the man s. yet come thither.
1Sa 12:21 for then s. ye go after vain things,
1Sa 12:23 forbid that I s. sin against the Lord
1Sa 15:21 which s. have been utterly destroyed,
1Sa 15:29 for he is not a man, that he s. repent.
1Sa 17:26 he s. defy the armies of the living God?
1Sa 18:18 that I s. be son in law to the king?
1Sa 18:19 daughter s. have been given to David,
1Sa 19:1 his servants, that they s. kill David.
1Sa 19:17 me, Let me go; why s. I kill thee?
1Sa 20:2 s. my father hide this thing from me?
1Sa 20:5 s. not fail to sit with the king at meat:
1Sa 22:13 that he s. rise against me, to lie in
1Sa 24:6 The Lord forbid that I s. do this thing
1Sa 26:11 forbid that I s. stretch forth mine hand
1Sa 27:1 that I s. speedily escape into the land
1Sa 27:5 s. thy servant dwell in the royal city
1Sa 27:11 Lest they s. tell on us, saying, So did
1Sa 29:4 for wherewith s. he reconcile himself
1Sa 29:4 s. it not be with the heads of these men?
2Sa 2:22 s. I smite thee to the ground?
2Sa 2:22 how then s. I hold up my face to Joab
2Sa 12:23 now he is dead, wherefore s. I fast?
2Sa 13:26 unto him, Why s. he go with thee?
2Sa 15:20 s. I this day make thee go up and down
2Sa 16:9 Why s. this dead dog curse my lord
2Sa 16:19 And again, whom s. I serve?
2Sa 16:19 s. I not serve in...presence of his son?
2Sa 18:12 Though I s. receive a thousand shekels
2Sa 18:13 I s. have wrought falsehood against
2Sa 19:19 that the king s. take it to his heart.
2Sa 19:22 ye s. this day be adversaires unto me?
2Sa 19:34 that I s. go up with the king unto
2Sa 19:35 s. thy servant be yet a burden unto
2Sa 19:36 why s. the king recompense it me
2Sa 19:43 advice s. not be first had in bringing
2Sa 20:20 me, that I s. swallow up or destroy.
2Sa 21:5 we s. be destroyed from remaining in
2Sa 23:17 far from me, O Lord, that I s. do this:
1Ki 1:27 who s. sit on the throne of my lord
1Ki 2:1 of David drew nigh that he s. die;
1Ki 2:15 set their faces on me, that I s. reign:
1Ki 6:6 beams s. not be fastened in the walls
1Ki 8:36 the good way wherein thy s. walk,
1Ki 11:10 that he s. not go after other gods:
1Ki 14:2 me that I s. be king over this people.
1Ki 21:3 I s. give the inheritance of my fathers
2Ki 3:27 son that s. have reigned in his stead,
2Ki 4:43 s. I set this before an hundred men?
2Ki 6:33 what s. I wait for the Lord any longer?
2Ki 7:19 the Lord s. make windows in heaven,
2Ki 8:13 a dog, that he s. do this great thing?
2Ki 11:9 them that s. go out on the sabbath,
2Ki 11:17 that they s. be the Lord's people;
2Ki 17:15 them, that they s. not do like them.
2Ki 17:28 taught them how they s. fear the Lord.
2Ki 18:35 s. deliver Jerusalem out of mine hand?
2Ki 22:19 s. become a desolation and a curse,
1Ch 9:28 they s. brng them in and out by tale.
1Ch 11:19 forbid it me, that I s. do this thing:
1Ch 16:42 for those that s. made a sound,
1Ch 21:17 on thy people, that they s. be plagued.
1Ch 21:18 David s. go up, and set up an altar
1Ch 23:13 he s. sanctify the most holy things,
1Ch 23:32 s. keep the charge of the tabernacle
1Ch 25:1 who s. prophesy with harps, with
1Ch 29:14 that we s. be able to offer so willingly
2Ch 2:6 am I then, that I s. build him an house,
2Ch 4:20 they s. burn after the manner before
2Ch 6:27 the good way, wherein they s. walk;
2Ch 15:13 Lord God of Israel s. be put to death,
2Ch 20:21 that s. praise the beauty of holiness,
2Ch 23:16 king, that they s. be the Lord's people.
2Ch 23:19 was unclean in any thing s. enter in.
2Ch 25:13 that they s. not go with him to battle,
2Ch 29:11 that ye s. minister unto him, and burn
2Ch 29:24 sin offering s. be made for all Israel.
2Ch 30:1 they s. come to the house of the Lord
2Ch 30:5 that they s. come to keep the passover
2Ch 32:4 Why s. the kings of Assyria come, and
2Ch 32:14 your God s. be able to deliver you
Ezr 2:63 they s. not eat of the most holy things,
Ezr 4:22 why s. damage grow to the hurt of the
Ezr 7:23 s. there be wrath against the realm
Ezr 8:17 told them what they s. say unto Iddo,
Ezr 8:17 that s. bring unto us ministers
Ezr 9:14 S. we...break thy commandments,
Ezr 9:14 there s. be no remnant nor escaping?
Ezr 10:5 that they s. do according to this word.
Ezr 10:7 they s. gather themselves together
Ezr 10:8 all his substance s. be forfeited, and
Ne 2:3 why s. not my countenance be sad,
Ne 5:12 they s. do according to this promise
Ne 6:3 why s. the work cease, whilst I leave
Ne 6:11 And I said, S. such a man as I flee?
Ne 6:13 that I s. be afraid, and do so, and sin,
Ne 7:65 they s. not eat of the most holy things,
Ne 8:14 children of Israel s. dwell in booths
Ne 8:15 s. publish and proclaim in all their
Ne 9:12 light in the way wherein they s. go.
Ne 9:15 that they s. go in to possess the land.
Ne 9:19 light, and the way wherein they s. go.
Ne 9:23 fathers, that they s. go in to possess it,
Ne 10:37 s. bring the firstfruits of our dough,
Ne 11:23 a certain portion s. be for the singers,
Ne 13:1 s. not come into the congregation of
Ne 13:2 Balaam against them, that he s. curse
Ne 13:19 I commanded that the gates s. be shut,
Ne 13:19 s. not be opened till after the sabbath:
Ne 13:19 there s. no burden he brought in on
Ne 13:22 that they s. cleanse themselvs, and
Ne 13:22 that they s. come and keep the gates,
Es 1:8 they s. do...to every man's pleasure.
Es 1:22 that every man s. bear rule in his own
Es 1:22 that it s. be published according to
Es 2:10 charged her that she s. not shew it.
Es 2:11 Esther did, and what s. become of her.
Es 3:14 that they s. be ready against that day.
Es 4:8 her that she s. go in unto the king,
Es 8:13 the Jews s. be ready against that day
Es 9:21 they s. keep the fourteenth day of the
Es 9:22 they s. make them days of feasting
Es 9:25 s. return upon his own head, and that
Es 9:25 his sons s. be hanged on the gallows
Es 9:27 so as it s. not fail, that they would keep
Es 9:28 these days s. be remembered and kept
Es 9:28 days of Purim s. not fail from among
Job 3:12 me? or why the breasts that I s. suck?
Job 3:13 now s. I have lain still and been quiet,
Job 3:13 still and been quiet, I s. have slept:
Job 6:10 Then s. I yet have comfort: yea, I
Job 6:11 What is my strength, and that I s. hope?
Job 6:11 is mine end, that I s. prolong my life?
Job 6:14 pity s. be shewed from his friend;
Job 8:7 yet thy latter end s. greatly increase.
Job 9:2 but how s. man be just with God?
Job 9:32 a man, as I am, that I s. answer him,
Job 9:32 we s. come together in judgment.
Job 10:19 I s. have been as though I had not
Job 10:19 I s. have been carried from the womb
Job 11:2 S. not the multitide of words be
Job 11:2 and s. a man full of talk be justified?
Job 11:3 S. they lies make men hold their peace?
Job 13:5 your peace! and it s. be your wisdom.
Job 13:9 Is it good that he s. search you out?
Job 15:2 S. a wise man utter vain knowledge,
Job 15:3 S. he reason with unprofitable talk?
Job 15:14 What is man, that he s. be clean? and
Job 15:14 of a woman, that he s. be righteous?
Job 16:5 of my lips s. asswage your grief.
Job 19:28 But ye s. say, Why persecute we him,
Job 21:4 so, why s. not my spirit be troubled?
Job 21:15 is the Almighty, that we s. serve him?
Job 21:15 what profit s. we have, if we pray unto
Job 23:7 so s. I be delivered for ever from my
Job 27:5 God forbid that I s. justify you: till I
Job 31:1 why then s. I think upon a maid?
Job 31:28 I s. have denied the God that is above.
Job 32:7 I said, Days s. speak, and
Job 32:7 multitude of years s. teach wisdom.
Job 32:13 Lest ye s. say, We have found out
Job 34:6 S. I lie against my right? my wound
Job 34:9 that he s. delight himself with God.
Job 34:10 it from God that he s. do wickedness;
Job 34:10 Almighty, that he s. commit iniquity.
Job 34:23 he s. enter into judgment with God.
Job 34:33 S. it be according to they mind? he will
Job 36:16 and that which s. be set on thy table
Job 36:16 be set on thy table s. be full of fatness.
Job 41:11 prevented me, that I s. repay him?
Ps 27:3 Thou an host s. encamp against me,
Ps 27:3 though war s. rise against me, in this
Ps 30:3 alive, that I s. not go down to the pit
Ps 38:16 lest otherwise they s. rejoice over me:
Ps 49:5 Wherefore s. I fear in the days of evil,
Ps 49:9 That he s. still live for ever, and not
Ps 69:22 which s. have been for their welfare,
Ps 73:15 I s. offend against the generation of
Ps 78:5 s. make them known to their chilren:
Ps 78:6 even the children which s. be born;
Ps 78:6 who s. arise and declare them to their
Ps 79:10 Wherefore s. the heathen say, Where
Ps 81:14 I s. soon have subdued their enemies,
Ps 81:15 haters of the Lord s. have submitted
Ps 81:15 their time s. have endured for ever.
Ps 81:16 s. have fed them also with the finest
Ps 81:16 of the rock s. I have satisfied thee
Ps 95:11 that they s. not enter into my rest.
Ps 104:5 that it s. not be removed for ever.
Ps 106:23 his wrath, lest he s. destroy them.
Ps 115:2 Wherefore s. the heathen say, Where
Ps 119:92 I s.... have perished in mine affliction.
Ps 139:18 If I s. count them, they are more in
Ps 143:8 to know the way wherein I s. walk;
Pr 8:29 waters s. not pass his commandment:
Pr 22:6 Train up a child in the way he s. go:
Pr 22:27 s. he take away thy bed from under
Ec 2:3 which they s. do under the heaven all
Ec 2:18 I s. leave it unto the man that shall
Ec 2:24 a man, than that he s. eat and drink,
Ec 2:24 that he s. make his soul enjoy good
Ec 3:13 also that every man s. eat and drink,
Ec 3:14 doeth it, that men s. fear before him.
Ec 3:22 a man s. rejoice in his own works;
Ec 5:6 wherefore s. God be angry at thy voice,
Ec 7:14 that man s. find nothing after him.
Ca 1:7 why s. I be as one that turneth aside
Ca 8:1 when I s. find thee without, I would
Ca 8:1 kiss thee; yea, I s. not be despised.
Ca 8:3 His left hand s. be under my head,
Ca 8:3 and his right hand s. embrace me.
Isa 1:5 Why s. ye be stricken any more? ye
Isa 1:9 remnant, we s. have been as Sodom,
Isa 1:9 we s. have been like unto Gomorrah.
Isa 5:2 he looked that it s. bring forth grapes,
Isa 5:4 I looked that it s. bring forth grapes,
Isa 8:11 I s. not walk in the way of this people,
Isa 8:19 s. not a people seek unto their God?
Isa 10:15 if the rod s. shake itself against them
Isa 10:15 or as if the staff s. lift up itself, as if it
Isa 36:20 Lord s. deliver Jerusalem out of my
Isa 41:7 it with nails, that it s. not be moved.
Isa 48:11 for how s. my name be polluted? and I
Isa 48:19 his name s. not have been cut off nor
Isa 49:15 she s. not have compassion on the son
Isa 50:4 that I s. know how to speak a word in
Isa 51:14 and that he s. not die in the pit, nor
Isa 51:14 in the pit, nor that his bread s. fail.
Isa 53:2 is no beauty that we s. desire him.
Isa 54:9 waters of Noah s. no more go over the
Isa 57:6 offering. S. I receive comfort in these?
Isa 57:16 for the spirit s. fail before me, and the
Isa 63:13 wilderness, that they s. not stumble?
Jer 5:17 thy sons and thy daughters s. eat:
Jer 20:18 my days s. be consumed with shame?
Jer 23:22 s. have turned them from their evil
Jer 25:29 name, and s. ye be utterly unpunished?
Jer 26:24 that they s. not give him into the hand
Jer 27:10 I s. drive you out, and ye s. perish
Jer 27:17 wherefore s. this city be laid waste?
Jer 29:26 that ye s. be officers in the house of
Jer 32:31 I s. remove it from before my face,
Jer 32:35 they s. do this abomination, to cause
Jer 33:20 and that there s. not be day and night
Jer 33:21 that he s. not have a son to reign upon
Jer 33:24 they s. be nor more a nation before
Jer 34:9 That every man s. let his manservant,

Jer 34:9 that none s. serve himself of them,
Jer 34:10 that every one s. let his manservant,
Jer 34:10 that none s. serve themselves of them
Jer 37:10 yet s. they rise up every man in his
Jer 37:21 s. commit Jeremiah into the court
Jer 37:21 they s. give him daily a piece of bread
Jer 39:14 Shaphan, that he s. carry him home:
Jer 40:15 wherefore s. he slay thee, that all the
Jer 40:15 are gathered unto thee s. be scattered,
Jer 44:14 they s. return into the land of Judah,
Jer 46:13 king of Babylon s. come and smite the
Jer 51:53 Babylon s. mount up to heaven,
Jer 51:53 and though she s. fortify the height
Jer 51:60 all the evil that s. come upon Babylon,
La 1:10 they s. not enter thy congregation.
La 1:16 comforter that s. relieve my soul is far
La 1:17 his adversaries s. be round about him:
La 3:26 It is good that a man s. both hope and
La 3:44 that our prayer s. not pass through
La 4:12 enemy s. have entered into the gates
Eze 8:6 that I s. go far off from my sanctuary?
Eze 13:19 bread, to slay the souls that s. not die,
Eze 13:19 to save the souls alive that s. not live,
Eze 13:22 he s. not return from his wicked way,
Eze 14:3 s. I be enquired of at all by them?
Eze 14:14 they s. deliver but their own souls by
Eze 18:23 any pleasure...that the wicked s. die?
Eze 18:23 not that he s. return from his ways,
Eze 19:9 his voice s. no more be heard upon the
Eze 20:9, 14 that it s. not be polluted before the
Eze 20:22 it s. not be polluted in the sight of the
Eze 20:25 judgments whereby they s. not live;
Eze 21:10 s. we then make mirth? it contemneth
Eze 22:30 s. make up the hedge, and stand in
Eze 22:30 for the land, that I s. not destroy it:
Eze 24:8 top of a rock, that it s. not be covered.
Eze 33:10 away in them, how s. we then live?
Eze 34:2 s. not the shepherds feed the flocks?
Da 1:3 he s. bring certain of the children of
Da 1:10 why s. he see your faces worse liking
Da 1:16 meat, and the wine that they s. drink;
Da 1:18 the king had said he s. bring them in,
Da 2:13 forth that the wise men s. be slain;
Da 2:18 Daniel and his fellows s. not perish
Da 2:29 bed, what s. come to pass hereafter:
Da 2:46 they s. offer oblation and sweet
Da 3:11 s. be cast into the midst of a burning
Da 3:19 they s. heat the furnace one seven
Da 5:15 that they s. read this writing, and
Da 5:29 s. be the third ruler in the kingdom.
Da 6:1 which s. be over the whole kingdom.
Da 6:2 and the king s. have no damage.
Da 6:23 they s. take Daniel up out of the den.
Da 7:14 nations, and languages, s. serve him:
Ho 10:3 Lord; what then s. a king do to us?
Ho 10:10 in my desire that I s. chastise them;
Ho 13:13 he s. not stay long in the place of the
Joe 2:17 that the heathen s. rule over them:
Joe 2:17 s. they say among the people, Where
Jon 4:11 s. not I spare Nineveh, that great city,
Mic 6:16 that I s. make thee a desolation, and
Zep 3:7 so their dwelling s. not be cut off,
Hag 1:2 time that the Lord's house s. be built.
Zec 7:3 saying, S. I weep in the fifth month,
Zec 7:7 S. ye not hear the words which the
Zec 7:11 their ears, that they s. not hear.
Zec 7:12 lest they s. hear the law, and the
Zec 8:6 s. it also be marvellous in mine eyes?
Mal 1:13 s. I accept this of your hand? saith the
Mal 2:7 the priest's lips s. keep knowledge,
Mal 2:7 and they s. seek the law at his mouth:
Mt 2:4 of them where Christ s. be born.
Mt 2:12 that they s. not return to Herod,
Mt 5:29 **that one of thy members s. perish,**
Mt 5:29 **thy whole body s. be cast into hell.**
Mt 5:30 **that one of thy members s. perish,**
Mt 5:30 **thy whole body s. be cast into hell.**
Mt 7:12 **ye would that men s. do to you,**
Mt 11:3 Art thou he that s. come, or do we
Mt 12:16 that they s. not make him known:
Mt 13:15 **any time they s. see with their eyes,**
Mt 13:15 **and s. understand with their heart,**
Mt 13:15 **s. be converted, and I s. heal them**
Mt 15:33 Whence s. we have so much bread in
Mt 16:11 **that ye s. beware of the leaven of the**
Mt 16:20 s. tell no man that he was Jesus the
Mt 17:27 **lest we s. offend them, go thou to the**
Mt 18:14 **that one of these little ones s. perish**
Mt 18:30 **into prison, till he s. pay the debt.**
Mt 18:34 **he s. pay all that was due unto him.**
Mt 19:13 he s. put his hands on them, and pray:
Mt 20:10 **that they s. have received more;**
Mt 20:31 because they s. hold their peace:
Mt 24:22 **except those days s. be shortened,**
Mt 24:22 **there s. no flesh be saved: but for the**
Mt 25:27 **coming I s. have received mine own**
Mt 26:35 Though I s. die with thee, yet will *1163*
Mt 27:20 multitude that they s. ask Barabbas,
Mk 3:9 a small ship s. wait on him because of
Mk 3:9 multitude, lest they s. throng him.
Mk 3:12 that they s. not make him known.
Mk 3:14 twelve, that they s. be with him,
Mk 4:12 **at any time they s. be converted,**
Mk 4:12 **and their sins s. be forgiven them.**
Mk 4:22 **secret, but that it s. come abroad.**
Mk 4:26 **a man s. cast seed into the ground;**
Mk 4:27 **And s. sleep, and rise night and day,**
Mk 4:27 **and the seed s. spring and grow up,**
Mk 5:43 them straitly that no man s. know it;
Mk 5:43 that something s. be given her to eat.
Mk 6:8 they s. take nothing for their journey,
Mk 6:12 and preached that men s. repent.
Mk 7:36 them that they s. tell no man:
Mk 8:30 them that they s. tell no man of him.
Mk 9:9 s. tell no man what things they had
Mk 9:10 the rising from the dead s. mean.
Mk 9:18 disciples that they s. cast him out;
Mk 9:30 would not that any man s. know it.
Mk 9:34 themselves, who s. be the greatest.
Mk 10:13 to him, that he s. touch them: and
Mk 10:32 what things s. happen unto him, *3195*
Mk 10:36 **What would ye that I s. do for you?**
Mk 10:48 him that he s. hold his peace:
Mk 10:51 **What wilt thou that I s. do unto thee?**
Mk 11:16 that any man s. carry any vessel
Mk 12:19 that his brother s. take his wife, and
Mk 13:20 **those days, no flesh s. be saved:**
Mk 14:31 If I s. die with thee, I will not *1163*
Mk 15:11 that he s. rather release Barabbas
Mk 15:24 upon them, what every man s. take.
Lu 1:29 what manner of salutation this s. be.
Lu 1:43 mother of my Lord s. come to me?
Lu 1:57 time came that she s. be delivered;
Lu 1:71 we s. be saved from our enemies, and
Lu 2:1 that all the world s. be taxed.
Lu 2:6 accomplished that she s. be delivered.
Lu 2:26 that he s. not see death, before he had
Lu 4:42 him, that he s. not depart from them.
Lu 5:7 that they s. come and help them.
Lu 6:31 **as ye would that men s. do to you,**
Lu 7:4 was worthy for whom he s. do this:
Lu 7:19, 20 Art thou he that s. come? or look
Lu 8:12 **lest they s. believe and be saved.**
Lu 8:56 they s. tell no man what was done.
Lu 9:13 except we s. go and buy meat for all
Lu 9:31 he s. accomplish at Jerusalem. *3195*
Lu 9:46 them, which of them s. be greatest.
Lu 9:51 was come that he s. be received up,
Lu 15:32 **It was meet that we s. make merry,**
Lu 17:2 **s. offend one of these littles ones**
Lu 17:6 **planted in the sea; and its s. obey**
Lu 17:20 when the kingdom of God s. come,
Lu 18:39 him, that he s. hold his peace: but
Lu 19:11 of God s. immediately appear. *3195*
Lu 19:27 **would not that I s. reign over them,**
Lu 19:40 **these s. hold their peace, the stones**
Lu 20:10 **s. give him of the fruit of the**
Lu 20:20 which s. feign themselves just men,
Lu 20:28 his brother s. take his wife, and raise
Lu 22:23 them it was that s. do this thing. *3195*
Lu 22:24 of them s. be accounted the greatest.
Lu 23:24 that it s. be as they required.
Lu 24:16 holden that they s. not know him.
Lu 24:21 he which s. have redeemed Israel: *3195*
Lu 24:47 **remission of sins s. be preached in**
Joh 1:31 that he s. be made manifest to Israel,
Joh 2:25 needed not that any s. testify of man:
Joh 3:15 **believeth in him s. not perish,**
Joh 3:16 **believeth in him s. not perish,**
Joh 3:20 **light, lest his deeds s. be reproved.**
Joh 5:23 **That all men s. honour the Son**
Joh 6:14 prophet that s. come into the world.
Joh 6:39 **he hath given me I s. lose nothing,**
Joh 6:39 **s. raise it up again at the last day**
Joh 6:64 believed not, and who s. betray him.
Joh 6:71 for he it was that s. betray him, *3195*
Joh 7:23 **the law of Moses s. not be broken;**
Joh 7:39 that believe on him s. receive: *3195*
Joh 8:5 us, that such s. be stoned:
Joh 8:19 **ye s. have known my Father also.**
Joh 8:55 **and if I s. say, I know him not, I**
Joh 9:3 **of God s. be made manifest in him.**
Joh 9:22 he s. be put out of the synagogue.
Joh 9:41 **If ye were blind, ye s. have no sin:**
Joh 11:27 of God, which s. come into the world.
Joh 11:37 even this man s. not have died?
Joh 11:50 that one man s. die for the people,
Joh 11:51 that Jesus s. die for that nation; *3195*
Joh 11:52 he s. gather together in one the
Joh 11:57 he s. shew it, that they might take
Joh 12:4 Simon's son, which s. betray him, *3195*
Joh 12:23 **the Son of man s. be glorified.**
Joh 12:33 signifying what death he s. die. *3195*
Joh 12:40 that they s. not see with their eyes,
Joh 12:40 and be converted, and I s. heal them.
Joh 12:42 they s. be put out of the synagogue:
Joh 12:46 **on me s. not abide in darkness.**
Joh 12:49 **what I s. say, and what I s. speak.**
Joh 13:1 hour was come that he s. depart out
Joh 13:11 For he knew who s. betray him;
Joh 13:15 **that ye s. do as I have done to you.**
Joh 13:24 that he s. ask who it s. be of whom
Joh 13:29 that he s. give something to the poor.
Joh 14:7 **ye s. have known my Father also:**
Joh 15:16 **that ye s. go and bring forth fruit,**
Joh 15:16 **fruit, and that your fruit s. remain;**
Joh 16:1 **unto you, that ye s. not be offended.**
Joh 16:30 needest not that any man s. ask thee:
Joh 17:2 **s. give eternal life to as many as**
Joh 18:4 all things that s. come upon him,
Joh 18:14 that one man s. die for the people.
Joh 18:28 judgment hall, lest they s. be defiled;
Joh 18:32 signifying what death he s. die. *3195*
Joh 18:36 **I s. not be delivered to the Jews:**
Joh 18:37 **I s. bear witness unto the truth.**
Joh 18:39 that I s. release unto you one at the
Joh 19:31 bodies s. not remain upon the cross on
Joh 19:36 done, that the scripture s. be fulfilled,
Joh 21:19 by what death he s. glorify God.
Joh 21:23 brethren, that that disciple s. not die:
Joh 21:25 which, if they s. be written every one,
Joh 21:25 contain the books that s. be written.
Ac 1:4 they s. not depart from Jerusalem,
Ac 2:24 not possible that he s. be holden of
Ac 2:25 right hand, that I s. not be moved:
Ac 2:47 the church daily such as s. be saved.
Ac 3:18 his prophets, that Christ s. suffer,
Ac 5:26 people, lest they s. have been stoned.
Ac 5:28 you that ye s. not teach in this name?
Ac 5:40 s. not speak in...name of Jesus,
Ac 6:2 that we s. leave the word of God, and
Ac 7:6 his seed s. sojourn in a strange land;
Ac 7:6 that they s. bring them into bondage,
Ac 7:44 he s. make it acording to the fashion
Ac 8:31 can I, except some man s. guide me?
Ac 10:17 vision which he hath seen s. mean,
Ac 10:28 that I s. not call any man common
Ac 10:47 water, that these s. not be baptized,
Ac 11:22 that he s. go as far as Antioch.
Ac 11:28 s. be great dearth throughout all *3195*
Ac 12:19 commanded...they s. be put to death.
Ac 13:28 desired they Pilate that he s. be slain.
Ac 13:46 word of God s. first have been spoken
Ac 14:15 that ye s. turn from these vanities
Ac 15:2 s. go up to Jerusalem unto the apostles
Ac 15:7 Gentiles by my mouth s. hear the word
Ac 17:27 That they s. seek the Lord, if haply
Ac 18:14 reason would that I s. bear with you:
Ac 19:4 people, that they s. believe on him
Ac 19:4 on him which s. come after him, that
Ac 19:27 great goddess Diana s. be despised,
Ac 19:27 her magnificence s. be destroyed, *3195*
Ac 20:38 that they s. see his face no more. *3195*
Ac 21:4 that he s. not go up to Jerusalem.
Ac 21:16 an old disciple, with whom we s. lodge.
Ac 21:26 an offering s. be offered for evey one
Ac 22:22 earth: for it is not fit that he s. live.
Ac 22:24 that he s. be examined by scourging;
Ac 22:29 him which s. have examined him: *3195*
Ac 23:10 Paul s. have been pulled in pieces of
Ac 23:27 and s. have been killed of them: *3195*

Ac 24:23 he **s.** forbid none of his acquaintance
Ac 24:26 that money **s.** have been given him of
Ac 25:4 that Paul **s.** be kept at Caesarea, and
Ac 26:8 **s.** it be thought a thing incredible
Ac 26:8 with you, that God **s.** riase the dead?
Ac 26:20 that they **s.** repent and turn to God,
Ac 26:22 prophets and Moses...say **s.** come: *3195*
Ac 26:23 That Christ **s.** suffer, and that he
Ac 26:23 suffer, and that he **s.** be the first that
Ac 26:23 be the first that **s.** rise from the dead,
Ac 26:23 **s.** shew light unto the people, and *3195*
Ac 27:1 determined that we **s.** sail into Italy,
Ac 27:17 lest they **s.** fall into the quicksands,
Ac 27:20 all hope that we **s.** be saved was then
Ac 27:21 ye **s.** have hearkened unto me, and *1163*
Ac 27:29 least we **s.** have fallen upon rocks,
Ac 27:42 lest any of them **s.** swim out, and
Ac 27:43 **s.** cast themselves first into the sea,
Ac 28:6 looked when he **s.** have swollen, *3195*
Ac 28:27 lest they **s.** see with their eyes, and
Ac 28:27 with their heart, and **s.** be converted,
Ac 28:27 be converted, and I **s.** heal them.
Ro 2:21 that preachest a man **s.** not steal,
Ro 2:22 sayest a man **s.** not commit adultery,
Ro 4:13 that he **s.** be the heir of the world,
Ro 6:4 so we also **s.** walk in newness of life
Ro 6:6 that henceforth we **s.** not serve sin
Ro 6:12 that ye **s.** obey it in the lusts thereof.
Ro 7:4 that ye **s.** be married to another,
Ro 7:4 that we **s.** bring forth fruit unto God.
Ro 7:6 that we **s.** serve in newness of spirit,
Ro 8:26 know not what we **s.** pray for as we
Ro 11:8 eyes that they **s.** not see, and ears
Ro 11:8 and ears that they **s.** not hear;) unto
Ro 11:11 Have they stumbled that they **s.** fall?
Ro 11:25 that ye **s.** be ignorant of this mystery,
Ro 11:25 ye **s.** be wise in your own conceits;
Ro 15:16 I **s.** be the minister of Jesus Christ to
Ro 15:20 lest I **s.** build upon another man's
1Co 1:15 **s.** say that I had baptized in mine own
1Co 1:17 the cross of Christ **s.** be made of none
1Co 1:29 That no flesh **s.** glory in his presence
1Co 2:5 your faith **s.** not stand in the wisdom
1Co 4:3 small thing that I **s.** be judged of you.
1Co 5:1 that one **s.** have his father's wife.
1Co 9:10 he that ploweth **s.** plow in hope; *3784*
1Co 9:10 in hope **s.** be partaker of his hope.
1Co 9:12 lest we **s.** hinder the gospel of Christ.
1Co 9:14 preach the gospel **s.** live of the gospel.
1Co 9:15 things, that it **s.** be so done unto me:
1Co 9:15 any man **s.** make my glorying void.
1Co 9:27 to others, I myself **s.** be a castaway.
1Co 10:1 I would not that ye **s.** be ignorant,
1Co 10:6 intent we **s.** not lust after evil things,
1Co 10:20 that ye **s.** have fellowship with devils.
1Co 11:31 judge ourselves, we **s.** not be judged.
1Co 11:32 **s.** not be condemned with the world.
1Co 12:25 there **s.** be no schism in the body;
1Co 12:25 **s.** have the same care one for another
2Co 1:9 that we **s.** not trust in ourselves, but
2Co 1:17 that with me there **s.** be yea yea, and
2Co 2:3 I **s.** have sorrow from them of whom I
2Co 2:4 not that ye **s.** be grieved, but that ye
2Co 2:7 such a one **s.** be swallowed up with
2Co 2:11 Lest Satan **s.** get an advantage of us:
2Co 4:4 the image of God, **s.** shine unto them
2Co 5:15 **s.** not henceforth live unto themselves,
2Co 8:20 no man **s.** blame us in this abundance
2Co 9:3 lest our boasting of you **s.** be in vain
2Co 9:4 **s.** be ashamed in this same confident
2Co 10:8 though I **s.** boast somewhat more of
2Co 10:8 destruction, I **s.** not be ashamed:
2Co 11:3 so your minds **s.** be corrupted from
2Co 12:6 lest any man **s.** think of me above
2Co 12:7 lest I **s.** be exalted above measure
2Co 12:7 me, lest I **s.** be exalted above measure.
2Co 13:7 evil; not that we **s.** appear approved,
2Co 13:7 that ye **s.** do that which is honest,
2Co 13:10 lest being present I **s.** use sharpness,
Ga 1:10 men, I **s.** not be the servant of Christ.
Ga 2:2 lest by any means I **s.** run, or had run,
Ga 2:9 that we **s.** go unto the heathen, and
Ga 2:10 would that we **s.** remember the poor;
Ga 3:1 that ye **s.** not obey the truth, before
Ga 3:17 it **s.** make the promise of none effect.
Ga 3:19 the seed **s.** come to whom the promise
Ga 3:21 verily righteousness **s.** have been by
Ga 3:23 the faith which **s.** afterwards be *3195*
Ga 5:7 you that ye **s.** not obey the truth?
Ga 6:12 **s.** suffer persecution for the cross of
Ga 6:14 God forbid that I **s.** glory, save in the
Eph 1:4 **s.** be holy and without blame before
Eph 1:12 **s.** be to the praise of his glory, who
Eph 2:9 Not of works, lest any man **s.** boast.
Eph 2:10 ordained that we **s.** walk in them.
Eph 3:6 That the Gentiles **s.** be fellowheirs,
Eph 3:8 I **s.** preach among the Gentiles the
Eph 5:27 it **s.** be holy and without blemish.
Php 1:12 But I would ye **s.** understand,
Php 2:10 the name of Jesus every knee **s.** bow,
Php 2:11 every tongue **s.** confess that Jesus
Php 2:27 lest I **s.** have sorrow upon sorrow.
Col 1:19 that in him **s.** all fulness dwell;
Col 2:4 lest any man **s.** beguile you with
1Th 3:3 That no man **s.** be moved by these
1Th 3:4 that we **s.** suffer tribulation; *3195*
1Th 4:3 that ye **s.** abstain from fornication:
1Th 4:4 one of you **s.** know how to possess his
1Th 5:4 that day **s.** overtake you as a thief.
1Th 5:10 or sleep, we **s.** live together with him.
2Th 2:11 delusion, that they **s.** believe a lie;
2Th 3:10 any would not work, neither **s.** he eat.
1Ti 1:16 them which **s.** hereafter believe *3195*
Tit 2:12 we **s.** live soberly, righteously, and
Tit 3:7 we **s.** be made heirs according to the
Phm 14 that thy benefit **s.** not be as it were
Heb 2:1 lest at any time we **s.** let them slip.
Heb 2:9 he by the grace of God **s.** taste death
Heb 3:18 whom sware he that they **s.** not enter
Heb 4:1 any of you **s.** seem to come short of it.
Heb 7:11 was there that another priest **s.** rise
Heb 8:4 were on earth, he **s.** not be a priest,
Heb 8:7 then **s.** no place have been sought for
Heb 9:23 of things in the heaven **s.** be purified
Heb 9:25 Nor yet that he **s.** offer himself often,
Heb 10:2 purged **s.** have no more conscience
Heb 10:4 of bulls and of goats **s.** take away sins.
Heb 11:5 translated that he **s.** not see death;
Heb 11:8 a place which he **s.** after receive *3195*
Heb 11:28 destroyed the firstborn **s.** touch them.
Heb 11:40 without us **s.** not be made perfect.
Heb 12:19 that the word **s.** not be spoken to them.
Jas 1:18 that we **s.** be a kind of firstfruits of his
1Pe 1:10 of the grace that **s.** come unto you:
1Pe 1:11 Christ, and the glory that **s.** follow.
1Pe 2:9 that ye **s.** shew forth the praises of
1Pe 2:21 example, that ye **s.** follow his steps:
1Pe 2:24 to sins, **s.** live unto righteousness:
1Pe 3:9 called, that ye **s.** inherit the blessing.
1Pe 4:2 That he no longer **s.** live the rest of
2Pe 2:6 those that after **s.** live ungodly; *3195*
2Pe 3:9 not willing that any **s.** perish, but
2Pe 3:9 but that all **s.** come to repentance.
1Jo 3:1 that we **s.** be called the sons of God:
1Jo 3:11 beginning, that we **s.** love one another.
1Jo 3:23 we **s.** believe on the name of his Son
1Jo 4:3 ye have heard that it **s.** come; and
2Jo 6 from the beginning, ye **s.** walk in it.
Jude 3 ye **s.** earnestly contend for the faith
Jude 18 they told you there **s.** be mockers
Jude 18 **s.** walk after their own ungodly lusts.
Re 6:4 earth, and that they **s.** kill one another:
Re 6:11 they **s.** rest yet for a little season,
Re 6:11 that **s.** be killed as they were, *3195*
Re 6:11 be killed as they were, **s.** be fulfilled.
Re 7:1 the wind **s.** not blow on the earth, nor
Re 8:3 that he **s.** offer it with the prayers of
Re 9:4 that they **s.** not hurt the grass of the
Re 9:5 it was given that they **s.** not kill them,
Re 9:5 that they **s.** be tormented five months:
Re 9:20 that they **s.** not worship devils, and
Re 10:6 that there **s.** be time no longer:
Re 10:7 the mystery of God **s.** be finished, as
Re 11:18 that they **s.** be judged, and that thou
Re 12:6 they **s.** feed her there a thousand two
Re 13:14 they **s.** make an image to the beast,
Re 13:15 the image of the beast **s.** both speak,
Re 13:15 the image of the beast **s.** be killed,
Re 19:8 that she **s.** be arrayed in fine linen,
Re 19:15 that with it he **s.** smite the nations:
Re 20:3 that he **s.** deceive the nations no more,
Re 20:3 till the thousand years **s.** be fulfilled:

SHOULDER See also SHOULDERPIECES; SHOULDERS.

Ge 21:14 unto Hagar, putting it on her **s.**, 7926
Ge 24:15 brother, with her pitcher upon her **s.** 7926
Ge 24:45 forth with her pitcher on her **s.**; 7926
Ge 24:46 and let down her pitcher from her **s.**,
Ge 49:15 bowed his **s.** to bear, and became 7926
Ex 29:22 is upon them, and the right **s.**; 7785
Ex 29:27 the **s.** of the heave offering, which 7785
Le 7:32 the right **s.** shall ye give unto the 7785
Le 7:33 shall have the right **s.** for his part 7785
Le 7:34 and the heave **s.** have I taken of 7785
Le 8:25 and their fat, and the right **s.**: 7785
Le 8:26 on the fat, and upon the right **s.**: 7785
Le 9:21 and the right **s.** Aaron waved 7785
Le 10:14 and heave **s.** shall ye eat in a clean 7785
Le 10:15 heave **s.** and the wave breast shall 7785
Nu 6:19 take the sodden **s.** of the ram, 2220
Nu 6:20 with the wave breast and heave **s.**: 7785
Nu 18:18 breast and as the right **s.** are thine. 7785
De 18:3 shall give unto the priest the **s.**, 2220
Jos 4:5 man of you a stone upon his **s.**, 7926
Jg 9:48 and took it, and laid it on his **s.**, 7926
1Sa 9:24 And the cook took up the **s.**, and 7785
Ne 9:29 withdrew the **s.**, and hardened 3802
Job 31:22 mine arm fall from my **s.** blade, 7929
Job 31:36 Surely I would take it upon my **s.**, 7926
Ps 81:6 I removed his **s.** from the burden: 7926
Isa 9:4 and the staff of his **s.**, the rod of his 7926
Isa 9:6 government shall be upon his **s.**: 7926
Isa 10:27 shall be taken away from off thy **s.** 7926
Isa 22:22 house of David will I lay upon his **s.**; 7926
Isa 46:7 They bear him upon the **s.**, they 3802
Eze 12:7 I bear it upon my **s.** in their sight 3802
Eze 12:12 bear upon his **s.** in the twilight, 3802
Eze 24:4 good piece, the thigh, and the **s.**; 3802
Eze 29:7 didst break, and rend all their **s.**: 3802
Eze 29:18 bald, and every **s.** was peeled: 3802
Eze 34:21 have thrust with side and with **s.**, 3802
Zec 7:11 to hearken, and pulled away the **s.**, 3802

SHOULDER-BLADE See SHOULDER and BLADE.

SHOULDERPIECES

Ex 28:7 It shall have the two **s.** thereof 3802
Ex 28:25 on the **s.** of the ephod before it. 3802
Ex 39:4 They made **s.** for it, to couple it 3802
Ex 39:18 and put them on the **s.** of the ephod, 3802

SHOULDERS

Ge 9:23 and laid it upon both their **s.**, and 7926
Ex 12:34 up in their clothes upon their **s.** 7926
Ex 28:12 stones upon the **s.** of the ephod 3802
Ex 28:12 upon his two **s.** for a memorial. 3802
Ex 39:7 he put them on the **s.** of the ephod, 3802
Nu 7:9 that they should bear upon their **s.** 3802
De 33:12 and he shall dwell between his **s.** 3802
Jg 16:3 put them upon his **s.**, and carried 3802
1Sa 9:2 from his **s.** and upward he was 7926
1Sa 10:23 the people from his **s.** and upward 7926
1Sa 17:6 a target of brass between his **s.** 3802
1Ch 15:15 bare the ark of God upon their **s.** 3802
2Ch 35:3 shall not be a burden upon your **s.**: 3802
Isa 11:14 fly upon the **s.** of the Philistines 3802
Isa 14:25 burden depart from off their **s.** 7926
Isa 30:6 riches upon the **s.** of young asses, 3802
Isa 49:22 shall be carried upon their **s.** 3802
Eze 12:6 sight shalt thou bear it upon thy **s.**, 3802
Mt 23:4 **borne, and lay them on men's s.;** *5606*
Lu 15:5 **hath found it, he layeth it on his s.,** *5606*

SHOULDEST

Ge 3:11 commanded thee that thou **s.** not eat?
Ge 14:23 lest thou **s.** say, I have made Abram
Ge 26:10 thou **s.** have brought guiltiness upon
Ge 29:15 **s.** thou therefore serve me for nought?
Nu 11:12 that thou **s.** say unto me, Carry them
De 4:19 **s.** be driven to worship them, and
De 26:18 thou **s.** keep all his commandments;
De 29:12 That thou **s.** enter into covenant
De 30:12 It is not in heaven, that thou **s.** say,
De 30:13 is it beyond the sea, that thou **s.** say,
Jg 11:23 people Israel, and **s.** thou possess it?
Ru 2:10 that thou **s.** take knowledge of me,
1Sa 20:8 why **s.** thou bring me to thy father?
2Sa 9:8 thou **s.** look upon such a dead dog
1Ki 1:20 that thou **s.** tell them who shall sit
2Ki 8:14 told me that thou **s.** surely recover.
2Ki 13:19 Thou **s.** have smitten five or six

2Ki 14:10 for why **s.** thou meddle to thy hurt,..........
2Ki 14:10 that thou **s.** fall, even thou, and ....
2Ki 19:25 thou **s.** be to lay waste fenced cities ....
1Ch 17:7 **s.** be ruler over my people Israel: ....
2Ch 19:2 **S.** thou help the ungodly, and love...........
2Ch 25:16 forbear; why **s.** thou be smitten?.............
2Ch 25:19 why **s.** thou meddle to thine hurt,............
2Ch 25:19 that thou **s.** fall, even thou, and ....
Job 7:17 is man, that thou **s.** magnify him? ....
Job 7:17 thou **s.** set thine heart upon him? ....
Job 7:18 that thou **s.** visit him every morning,.........
Job 10:3 it good unto thee that thou **s.** oppress, ...
Job 10:3 thou **s.** despise the work of thine ....
Job 38:20 thou **s.** take it to the bound thereof, ...
Job 38:20 thou **s.** know the paths to the house ....
Ps 50:16 **s.** take my covenant in thy mouth? ....
Ps 130:3 If thou, Lord, **s.** mark iniquities, O ....
Pr 5:6 Lest thou **s.** ponder the path of life,..........
Pr 25:7 than that thou **s.** be put lower in the.........
Pr 27:22 thou **s.** bray a fool in a mortar among........
Ec 5:5 Better is it that thou **s.** not vow,..............
Ec 5:5 than that thou **s.** vow and not pay. ....
Ec 7:16 wise: why **s.** thou destroy thyself?............
Ec 7:17 why **s.** thou die before thy time?..............
Ec 7:18 is good that thou **s.** take hold of this; ....
Isa 37:26 that thou **s.** be to lay waste defenced........
Isa 48:5 lest thou **s.** say, Mine idol hath done........
Isa 48:7 lest thou **s.** say, Behold, I knew them. ....
Isa 48:17 thee by the way that thou **s.** go. ....
Isa 49:6 light thing that thou **s.** be my servant........
Isa 51:12 **s.** be afraid of a man that shall die, ...
Jer 14:8 why **s.** thou be as a stranger in the ....
Jer 14:9 Why **s.** thou be as a man astonied, ...
Jer 29:26 that thou **s.** put him in prison, and in.........
Jer 49:16 **s.** make thy nest as high as the eagle,........
Ob 12 thou **s.** not have looked on the day of ....
Ob 12 neither **s.** thou have rejoiced over ....
Ob 12 neither **s.** thou have spoken proudly..........
Ob 13 Thou **s.** not have entered into the ....
Ob 13 thou **s.** not have looked on their..............
Ob 14 **s.** thou have stood in the crossway,..........
Ob 14 neither **s.** thou have delivered up.............
Mt 8:8 that thou **s.** come under my roof: ....
Mt 18:33 **S. not thou also have had compassion..**
Mk 10:35 thou **s.** do for us whatsoever we shall ....
Lu 7:6 that thou **s.** enter under my roof: ....
Joh 11:40 **believe, thou s. see the glory of God?...**
Joh 17:15 **thou s. take them out of the world,.....**
Joh 17:15 **that thou s. keep them from the evil...**
Ac 13:47 that thou **s.** be for salvation unto the.........
Ac 22:14 that thou **s.** know his will, and see............
Ac 22:14 and **s.** hear the voice of his mouth. ....
Tit 1:5 that thou **s.** set in order the things ....
Phm 15 that thou **s.** receive him for ever;.............
Re 11:18 thou **s.** give reward unto thy servants ....
Re 11:18 **s.** destroy them which destroy the............

SHOUT See also SHOUTED; SHOUTETH; SHOUTING.
Ex 32:18 voice of them that **s.** for mastery, ... 6030
Nu 23:21 the **s.** of a king is among them. 8643
Jos 6:5 the trumpet, all the people shall **s.**....... 7321
Jos 6:5 with a great **s.**; and the wall of.......... 8643
Jos 6:10 shall not **s.**, nor make any noise......... 7321
Jos 6:10 day I bid you **s.**; then shall ye **s.**........ 7321
Jos 6:16 Joshua said unto the people, **S.**; for.... 7321
Jos 6:20 the people shouted with a great **s.**,...... 8643
1Sa 4:5 all Israel shouted with a great **s.**, ... 8643
1Sa 4:6 Philistines heard the noise of the **s.**, ... 8643
1Sa 4:6 noise of this great **s.** in the camp 8643
2Ch 13:15 Then the men of Judah gave a **s.**:........ 7321
Ezr 3:11 the people shouted with a great **s.**,...... 8643
Ezr 3:13 not discern the noise of the **s.** of joy... 8643
Ezr 3:13 the people shouted with a loud **s.**, ... 8643
Ps 5:11 let them ever **s.** for joy, because........ 7442
Ps 32:11 **s.** for joy, all ye that are upright in..... 7442
Ps 35:27 Let them **s.** for joy, and be glad,........ 7442
Ps 47:1 **s.** unto God with the voice of............ 7321
Ps 47:5 God is gone up with a **s.**, the Lord...... 8643
Ps 65:13 they **s.** for joy, they also sing. 7321
Ps 132:9 and let thy saints **s.** for joy. 7442
Ps 132:16 her saints shall **s.** aloud for joy. 7442
Isa 12:6 Cry out and **s.**, thou inhabitant of 7442
Isa 42:11 **s.** from the top of the mountains. 6681
Isa 44:23 **s.**, ye lower parts of the earth: 7321
Jer 25:30 he shall give a **s.**, as they that.... 6030,1959
Jer 31:7 **s.** among the chief of the nations:........ 6670
Jer 50:15 **S.** against her round about: she 7321
Jer 51:14 they shall lift up a **s.** against thee. 1959
La 3:8 when I cry and **s.**, he shutteth out 7768
Zep 3:14 **s.**, O Israel; be glad and rejoice 7321
Zec 9:9 Zion; **s.**, O daughter of Jerusalem: 7321
Ac 12:22 And the people gave a **s.**, saying,....... *2019*
1Th 4:16 descend from heaven with a **s.**,.......... *2752*

SHOUTED
Ex 32:17 the noise of the people as they **s.**,....... 7452
Le 9:24 when all the people saw, they **s.**, ... 7442
Jos 6:20 people **s.** when the priests blew......... 7321
Jos 6:20 the people **s.** with a great shout,......... 7321
Jg 15:14 Lehi, the Philistines **s.** against him:..... 7321
1Sa 4:5 all Israel **s.** with a great shout, so 7321
1Sa 10:24 the people **s.**, and said, God save the.. 7321
1Sa 17:20 to the fight, and **s.** for the battle. 7321
1Sa 17:52 of Israel and of Judah arose, and **s.**,.... 7321
2Ch 13:15 as the men of Judah **s.**, it came to....... 7321
Ezr 3:11 all the people **s.** with a great shout,.... 7321
Ezr 3:12 voice; and many **s.** aloud for joy:........ 8643
Ezr 3:13 for the people **s.** with a loud shout, ... 7321
Job 38:7 and all the sons of God **s.** for joy? 7321

SHOUTETH
Ps 78:65 man that **s.** by reason of wine. 7442

SHOUTING See also SHOUTINGS.
2Sa 6:15 up the ark of the Lord with **s.**, ... 8643
1Ch 15:28 up the ark...of the Lord with **s.**, ... 8643
2Ch 15:14 with a loud voice, and with **s.**, and 8643
Job 39:25 thunder of the captains, and the **s.**....... 8643
Pr 11:10 when the wicked perish, there is **s.**.... 7440
Isa 16:9 for the **s.** for thy summer fruits 1959
Isa 16:10 singing, neither shall there be **s.**: 7321
Isa 16:10 made their vintage **s.** to cease. 1959
Jer 20:16 morning, and the **s.** at noontide;......... 8643
Jer 48:33 none shall tread with **s.**; 1959
Jer 48:33 their **s.** shall be no **s.**...................... 1959
Eze 21:22 to lift up the voice with **s.**,................ 8643
Am 1:14 thereof, with **s.** in the day of battle,..... 8643
Am 2:2 Moab shall die with tumult, with **s.**, ... 8643

SHOUTINGS
Zec 4:7 the headstone thereof with **s.**, ... 8663

SHOVEL See also SHOVELS.
Isa 30:24 hath been winnowed with the **s.** 7371

SHOVELS
Ex 27:3 and his **s.**, and his basons, and his...... 3257
Ex 38:3 pots, and the **s.**, and the basons, ... 3257
Nu 4:14 the fleshhooks, and the **s.**, and the 3257
1Ki 7:40 Hiram made the lavers, and the **s.**,...... 3257
1Ki 7:45 pots, and the **s.**, and the basons: 3257
2Ki 25:14 pots, and the **s.**, and the snuffers,....... 3257
2Ch 4:11 Huram made the pots, and the **s.**, ... 3257
2Ch 4:16 The pots also, and the **s.**, and the...... 3257
Jer 52:18 The caldrons also, and the **s.**, and...... 3257

SHOW See SHEW.

SHOWER See also SHOWERS.
Eze 13:11 there shall be an overflowing **s.**;........... 1653
Eze 13:13 and there shall be an overflowing **s.**..... 1653
Eze 34:26 I will cause the **s.** to come down in 1653
Lu 12:54 **ye say, There cometh a s.; and so..** *3655*

SHOWERS
De 32:2 and as the **s.** upon the grass: 7241
Job 24:8 wet with the **s.** of the mountains, ... 2230
Ps 65:10 thou makest it soft with **s.**: thou 7241
Ps 72:6 grass: as **s.** that water the earth. 7241
Jer 3:3 the **s.** have been withholden, and 7241
Jer 14:22 rain? or can the heavens give **s.**? 7241
Eze 34:26 there shall be **s.** of blessing............... 1653
Mic 5:7 the Lord, as the **s.** upon the grass, ... 7241
Zec 10:1 clouds, and give them **s.** of rain, ... 1653

SHRANK
Ge 32:32 eat not of the sinew which **s.**,............ 5384
Ge 32:32 Jacob's thigh in the sinew that **s.**......... 5384

SHRED See also SHERD.
2Ki 4:39 **s.** them into the pot of pottage: 6398

SHRINES
Ac 19:24 which made silver **s.** for Diana,.......... *3485*

SHRINK See SHRANK.

SHROUD
Eze 31:3 and with a shadowing **s.**, and of an 2793

SHRUBS
Ge 21:15 cast the child under one of the **s.**. 7880

SHUA (shu'-ah) See also BATH-SHUA; SHUAH.
1Ch 2:3 daughter of **S.** the Canaanitess.......... 7770
1Ch 7:32 and Hotham, and **S.** their sister. 7774

SHUAH (shu'-ah) See also SHUA; SHUHITE.
Ge 25:2 and Midian, and Ishbak, and **S.**. 7744
Ge 38:2 Canaanite, whose name was **S.**; 7770
Ge 38:12 daughter of **S.** Judah's wife died; 7770
1Ch 1:32 and Midian, and Ishbak, and **S.**. 7744
1Ch 4:11 the brother of **S.** begat Mehir,........... 7746

SHUAL (shu'-al) See also HAZAR-SHUAL.
1Sa 13:17 to Ophrah, unto the land of **S.**: 7777
1Ch 7:36 and Harnepher, and **S.**, and Beri, ... 7777

SHUBAEL (shu'-ba-el) See also SHEBUEL.
1Ch 24:20 Of the sons of Amram; **S.**: of the....... 2619
1Ch 25:20 thirteenth to **S.**, he, his sons, and...... 2619

SHUHAM (shu'-ham) See also HUSHIM; SHUHAMITES.
Nu 26:42 **S.**, the family of the Shuhamites......... 7748

SHUHAMITES (shu'-ham-ites)
Nu 26:42 of Shuham, the family of the **S.**.......... 7749
Nu 26:43 the families of the **S.**, according 7749

SHUHITE (shu'-hite)
Job 2:11 the Temanites, and Bildad the **S.**, ... 7747
Job 8:1 Then answered Bildad the **S.**, and...... 7747
Job 18:1 Then answered Bildad the **S.**, and...... 7747
Job 25:1 Then answered Bildad the **S.**, and...... 7747
Job 42:9 the Temanite and Bildad the **S.**.......... 7747

SHULAMITE (shu'-lam-ite)
Ca 6:13 Return, return, O **S.**; return, ... 7759
Ca 6:13 What will ye see in the **S.**? As it........ 7759

SHUMATHITES (shu'-math-ites)
1Ch 2:53 the Puhites, and the **S.**, and the 8126

SHUN See also SHUNNED.
2Ti 2:16 But **s.** profane and vain babblings: *4026*

SHUNAMMITE (shu'-nam-mite)
1Ki 1:3 and found Abishag a **S.**, and............. 7767
1Ki 1:15 Abishag the **S.** ministered unto 7767
1Ki 2:17 he give me Abishag the **S.** to wife...... 7767
1Ki 2:21 Abishag the **S.** be given to Adonijah.... 7767
1Ki 2:22 ask Abishag the **S.** for Adonijah? 7767
2Ki 4:12 to Gehazi his servant, Call this **S.**. 7767
2Ki 4:25 servant; Behold, yonder is that **S.**...... 7767
2Ki 4:36 called Gehazi, and said, Call this **S.**...... 7767

SHUNEM (shu'-nem) See also SHUNAMMITE.
Jos 19:18 Jezreel, and Chesulloth, and **S.**, ... 7766
1Sa 28:4 and came and pitched in **S.**: 7766
2Ki 4:8 on a day, that Elisha passed to **S.**, ... 7766

SHUNI (shu'-ni) See also SHUNITES.
Ge 46:16 and Haggi, **S.**, and Ezbon, Eri, ... 7764
Nu 26:15 of **S.**, the family of the Shunites:........ 7764

SHUNITES (shu'-nites)
Nu 26:15 of Shuni, the family of the **S.**:............ 7765

SHUNNED
Ac 20:27 I have not **s.** to declare unto you *5288*

SHUPHAM (shu'-fam) See also SHEPHUPHAN; SHUPHAMITES.
Nu 26:39 **S.**, the family of the Shuphamites: 8197

SHUPHAMITES (shu'-fam-ites)
Nu 26:39 Of Shupham, the family of the **S.**: 7781

SHUPPIM (shup'-pim) See also MUPPIM; SHEPHUPHAN.
1Ch 7:12 **S.** also, and Huppim, the children....... 8206
1Ch 7:15 to wife the sister of Huppim and **S.**, ... 8206
1Ch 26:16 To **S.** and Hosah the lot came forth..... 8206

SHUR (shur)
Ge 16:7 by the fountain in the way to **S.**......... 7793
Ge 20:1 dwelled between Kadesh and **S.**......... 7793
Ge 25:18 they dwelt from Havilah unto **S.**,........ 7793
Ex 15:22 went out into the wilderness of **S.**; 7793
1Sa 15:7 Havilah until thou comest to **S.**, ... 7793
1Sa 27:8 as thou goest to **S.**, even unto the 7793

SHUSHAN (shu'-shan) See also SHOSHANNIM; SHUSHAN-EDUTH.
Ne 1:1 year, as I was in **S.** the palace, ... 7800
Es 1:2 throne...which was in **S.** the palace,.... 7800
Es 1:5 the people that were present in **S.** 7800
Es 2:3 all the fair young virgins unto **S.** 7800

Es 2:5 in S. the palace...was a certain Jew, ... 7800
Es 2:8 were gathered together unto S. 7800
Es 3:15 decree was given in S. the palace....... 7800
Es 3:15 but the city S. was perplexed........... 7800
Es 4:8 of the decree that was given at S....... 7800
Es 4:16 all the Jews that are present in S., ... 7800
Es 8:14 decree was given at S. the palace. 7800
Es 8:15 the city of S. rejoiced and was glad. ... 7800
Es 9:6 in S. the palace the Jews slew and 7800
Es 9:11 the number of those...slain in S. 7800
Es 9:12 destroyed five hundred men in S........ 7800
Es 9:13 granted to the Jews which are in S..... 7800
Es 9:14 and the decree was given at S.;......... 7800
Es 9:15 the Jews that were in S. gathered...... 7800
Es 9:15 and slew three hundred men at S.;..... 7800
Es 9:18 the Jews that were at S. assembled.... 7800
Da 8:2 saw, that I was at S. in the palace, ... 7800

SHUSHAN-EDUTH (shu''-shan-e'-duth)
Ps 60:*title* To the chief Musician upon S., ... 7802

SHUT See also SHUTTETH; SHUTTING.
Ge 7:16 him: and the Lord s. him in.............. 5462
Ge 19:6 unto them, and s. the door after him,.. 5462
Ge 19:10 house to them, and s. to the door. 5462
Ex 14:3 the wilderness hath s. them in.......... 5462
Le 13:4 priest shall s. up him that hath the 5462
Le 13:5 priest shall s. him up seven days........ 5462
Le 13:11 unclean, and shall not s. him up: 5462
Le 13:21, 26 priest shall s. him up seven days:... 5462
Le 13:31, 33 priest shall s. up him that hath 5462
Le 13:50 s. up it that hath the plague seven...... 5462
Le 13:54 he shall s. it up seven days more: 5462
Le 14:38 and s. up the house seven days: 5462
Le 14:46 into the house...while that it is s........ 5462
Nu 12:14 let her be s. out from the camp 5462
Nu 12:15 Miriam was s. out from the camp 5462
De 11:17 s. up the heaven, that there be no 6113
De 15:7 nor s. thine hand from thy poor 7092
De 32:30 and the Lord had s. them up?........... 5462
De 32:36 and there is none s. up, or left. 6113
Jos 2:7 were gone out, they s. the gate......... 5462
Jos 6:1 Jericho was straitly s. up because 5462
Jg 3:23 and s. the doors of the parlour upon ... 5462
Jg 9:51 they of the city, and s. it to them, ... 5462
1Sa 1:5 but the Lord had s. up her womb......... 5462
1Sa 1:6 the Lord had s. up her womb............ 5462
1Sa 6:10 and s. up their calves at home:.......... 3607
1Sa 23:7 for he is s. in, by entering into a........ 5462
2Sa 20:3 s. up unto the day of their death, ... 6887
1Ki 8:35 When heaven is s. up, and there is..... 6113
1Ki 14:10 him that is s. up and left in Israel,...... 6113
1Ki 21:21 him that is s. up and left in Israel,...... 6113
2Ki 4:4 thou shalt s. the door upon thee 5462
2Ki 4:5 and s. the door upon her and upon 5462
2Ki 4:21 s. the door upon him, and went out. ... 5462
2Ki 4:33 and s. the door upon them twain, ... 5462
2Ki 6:32 s. the door, and hold him fast at the ... 5462
2Ki 9:8 him that is s. up and left in Israel....... 6113
2Ki 14:26 for there was not any s. up, nor any.... 6113
2Ki 17:4 the king of Assyria s. him up, and...... 6113
2Ch 6:26 When the heaven is s. up, and there... 6113
2Ch 7:13 I s. up heaven that there be no rain,... 6113
2Ch 28:24 s. up the doors of the house of the..... 5462
2Ch 29:7 have s. up the doors of the porch,...... 5462
Ne 6:10 son of Mehetabeel, who was s. up;..... 6113
Ne 6:10 let us s. the doors of the temple: 5462
Ne 7:3 let them s. the doors, and bar them:... 1479
Ne 13:19 that the gates should be s., and......... 5462
Job 3:10 s. not up the doors of my mother's..... 5462
Job 11:10 If he cut off, and s. up, or gather....... 5462
Job 38:8 Or who s. up the sea with doors,....... 5526
Job 41:15 s. up together as with a close seal...... 5462
Ps 31:8 s. me up into the hand of the enemy;.. 5462
Ps 69:15 not the pit s. her mouth upon me. 332
Ps 77:9 in anger s. up his tender mercies?....... 7092
Ps 88:8 I am s. up, and I cannot come........... 3607
Ec 12:4 the doors shall be s. in the streets, ... 5462
Ca 4:12 a spring s. up, a fountain sealed......... 5274
Isa 6:10 their ears heavy, and s. their eyes; 8173
Isa 22:22 he shall open, and none shall s.;......... 5462
Isa 22:22 and he shall s., and none shall open. ... 5462
Isa 24:10 every house is s. up, that no man 5462
Isa 24:22 and shall be s. up in the prison, ... 5462
Isa 26:20 and s. thy doors about thee:.............. 5462
Isa 44:18 for he hath s. their eyes, that they..... 2902
Isa 45:1 and the gates shall not be s.;............ 5462
Isa 52:15 kings shall s. their mouths at him: 7092
Isa 60:11 they shall not be s. day nor night; 5462
Isa 66:9 to bring forth, and s. the womb?........ 6113
Jer 13:19 cities of the south shall be s. up,........ 5462
Jer 20:9 a burning fire s. up in my bones,......... 6113
Jer 32:2 Jeremiah...was s. up in the court........ 3607
Jer 32:3 For Zedekiah...had s. him up,............ 3607
Jer 33:1 while he was yet s. up in the court..... 6113
Jer 36:5 saying, I am s. up; I cannot go.......... 6113
Jer 39:15 while he was s. up in the court of...... 6113
Eze 3:24 Go, s. thyself within thine house........ 5462
Eze 44:1 toward the east; and it was s.. 5462
Eze 44:2 This gate shall be s., it shall not be.... 5462
Eze 44:2 entered in...therefore it shall be s.. 5462
Eze 46:1 shall be s. the six working days; 5462
Eze 46:2 gate shall not be s. until...evening. 5462
Eze 46:12 going forth one shall s. the gate......... 5462
Da 6:22 and hath s. the lions' mouths, that...... 5463
Da 8:26 wherefore s. thou up the vision;......... 5640
Da 12:4 But thou, O Daniel, s. up the words, .. 5640
Mal 1:10 would s. the doors for nought? 5462
Mt 6:6 **and when thou hast s. thy door**...... *2808*
Mt 23:13 **for ye s. up the kingdom of heaven** *2808*
Mt 25:10 **the marriage: and the door was s.**..*2808*
Lu 3:20 all, that he s. up John in prison.......... *2623*
Lu 4:25 **heaven was s. up three years and** .. *2808*
Lu 11:7 **the door is now s., and my children** .*2808*
Lu 13:25 **is risen up, and hath s. to the door,** .*608*
Joh 20:19 doors were s. where the disciples *2808*
Joh 20:26 then came Jesus, the doors being s.,.... *2808*
Ac 5:23 The prison truly found we s. with....... *2808*
Ac 21:30 and forth with the doors were s.. .... *2808*
Ac 26:10 of the saints did I s. up in prison,....... *2623*
Ga 3:23 s. up unto the faith which should........ *4788*
Re 3:8 **open door, and no man can s. it:** .. *2808*
Re 11:6 These have power to s. heaven, that .. *2808*
Re 20:3 the bottomless pit, and s. him up, ... *2808*
Re 21:25 the gates of it shall not be s. at all *2808*

SHUTHALHITES (shu'-thal-hites)
Nu 26:35 Shuthelah, the family of the S.:.......... 8364

SHUTHELAH (shu'-the-lah) See also SHUTHALHITES.
Nu 26:35 of S. the family of...Shuthalhites:........ 7803
Nu 26:36 And these are the sons of S.:............ 7803
1Ch 7:20 sons of Ephraim; S., and Bered......... 7803
1Ch 7:21 And Zabad his son, and S. his son,..... 7803

SHUTTETH
Job 12:14 he s. up a man, and there can be....... 5462
Pr 16:30 He s. his eyes to devise froward......... 6095
Pr 17:28 that s. his lips is esteemed a man 331
Isa 33:15 and s. his eyes from seeing evil;......... 6105
La 3:8 and shout, he s. out my prayer.......... 5640
1Jo 3:17 s. up his bowels of compassion *2808*
Re 3:7 **he that openeth, and no man s.;**.... *2808*
Re 3:7 **and s., and no man openeth;**......... *2808*

SHUTTING
Jos 2:5 about the time of s. of the gate, ... 5462

SHUTTLE
Job 7:6 days are swifter than a weaver's s., ... 708

SIA (si'-ah) See also SIAHA.
Ne 7:47 children of S., the children of........... 5517

SIAHA (si'-a-hah) See also SIA.
Ezr 2:44 children of S., the children of........... 5517

SIBBECAI (sib'-be-cahee) See also SIBBECHAI.
1Ch 11:29 S. the Hushathite, Ilai the Ahohite,..... 5444
1Ch 27:11 was S. the Hushathite, of the sons 5444

SIBBECHAI (sib'-be-kahee) See also SIBBECAI.
2Sa 21:18 S. the Hushathite slew Saph,............ 5444
1Ch 20:4 S. the Hushathite slew Sippai, ... 5444

SIBBOLETH (sib'-bo-leth) See also SHIBBOLETH.
Jg 12:6 and he said S.: for he could not 5451

SIBMAH (sib'-mah)
Jos 13:19 S., and Zareth-shahar in the............ 7643
Isa 16:8 languish, and the vine of S.: the......... 7643
Isa 16:9 weeping of Jazer the vine of S.: 7643
Jer 48:32 O vine of S., I will weep for thee....... 7643

SIBRAIM (sib'-ra-im)
Eze 47:16 S.,which is between the border of...... 5453

SICHEM (si'-kem) See also SHECHEM; SYCHEM.
Ge 12:6 the land unto the place of S., ... 7927

SICK
Ge 48:1 Joseph, Behold, thy father is s.......... 2470
Le 15:33 of her that is s. of her flowers, and 1739
1Sa 19:14 to take David, she said, He is s.. 2470
1Sa 30:13 because three days agone I fell s........ 2470
2Sa 12:15 bare unto David, and it was very s....... 605
2Sa 13:2 that he fell s. for his sister Tamar; 2470
2Sa 13:5 on thy bed, and make thyself s. 2470
2Sa 13:6 lay down, and made himself s. 2470
1Ki 14:1 Abijah the son of Jeroboam fell s.. 2470
1Ki 14:5 of thee for her son; for he is s. 2470
1Ki 17:17 the mistress of the house, fell s.; 2470
2Ki 1:2 that was in Samaria, and was s. 2470
2Ki 8:7 the king of Syria was s.; and it 2470
2Ki 8:29 Ahab in Jezreel, because he was s.. 2470
2Ki 13:14 Elisha was fallen s. of his sickness...... 2470
2Ki 20:1 days was Hezekiah s. unto death........ 2470
2Ki 20:12 heard that Hezekiah had been s.. 2470
2Ch 22:6 Ahab at Jezreel, because he was s...... 2470
2Ch 32:24 days Hezekiah was s. to the death,...... 2470
Ne 2:2 sad, seeing thou art not s.? this......... 2470
Ps 35:13 when they were s., my clothing......... 2470
Pr 13:12 Hope deferred maketh the heart s...... 2470
Pr 23:35 shalt thou say, and I was not s.; 2470
Ca 2:5 me with apples: for I am s. of love..... 2470
Ca 5:8 that ye tell him, I am s. of love. 2470
Isa 1:5 the whole head is s., and the whole.... 2483
Isa 33:24 inhabitant shall not say, I am s.......... 2470
Isa 38:1 days was Hezekiah s. unto death........ 2470
Isa 38:9 king of Judah, when he had been s., ... 2470
Isa 39:1 he had heard that he had been s., ... 2470
Jer 14:18 them that are s. with famine! 8463
Eze 34:4 have ye healed that which was s., ... 2470
Eze 34:16 will strengthen that which was s......... 2470
Da 8:27 fainted, and was s. certain days; 2470
Ho 7:5 king the princes have made him s........ 2470
Mic 6:13 will I make thee s. in smiting thee,..... 2470
Mal 1:8 if ye offer the lame and s., is it not 2470
Mal 1:13 was torn, and the lame, and the s.; 2470
Mt 4:24 brought unto him all s. people..... *2192,2560*
Mt 8:6 servant...at home s. of the palsy, ... *3885*
Mt 8:14 wife's mother laid,...s. of a fever........ *4445*
Mt 8:16 and healed all that were s.......... *2192,2560*
Mt 9:2 brought...a man s. of the palsy, ... *3885*
Mt 9:2 faith said unto the s. of the palsy; *3885*
Mt 9:6 (then saith he to the s. of the palsy,).. *3885*
Mt 9:12 **physician, but they that are s**.. *2192,2560*
Mt 10:8 **Heal the s., cleanse the lepers,**....... *770*
Mt 14:14 toward them, and he healed their s..... *732*
Mt 25:36 **I was s., and ye visited me: I was**... *770*
Mt 25:39 **when saw we thee s., or in prison,**.. *772*
Mt 25:43 **s., and in prison, and ye visited me**..*772*
Mt 25:44 **naked, or s., or in prison, and did**... *772*
Mk 1:30 Simon's wife's mother lay s. of a........ *4445*
Mk 1:34 he healed many that were s....... *2192,2560*
Mk 2:3 him, bringing one s. of the palsy, ... *3885*
Mk 2:4 bed wherein the s. of the palsy lay..... *3885*
Mk 2:5 he said unto the s. of the palsy, **Son,**. *3885*
Mk 2:9 **easier to say to the s. of the palsy,**.*3885*
Mk 2:10 **sins,** (he saith to the s. of the palsy,). *3885*
Mk 2:17 **physician, but they that are s.**. *2192,2560*
Mk 6:5 laid his hands upon a few s. folks,........ *732*
Mk 6:13 anointed with oil many that were s.,..... *732*
Mk 6:55 in beds those that were s., ... *2192,2560*
Mk 6:56 they laid the s. in the streets, and....... *770*
Mk 16:18 **they shall lay hands on the s.,**......... *732*
Lu 4:40 all they that had any s. with divers....... *770*
Lu 5:24 (he said unto the s. of the palsy,)........ *3885*
Lu 5:31 **physician; but they that are s**... *2192,2560*
Lu 7:2 him, was s., and ready to die. *2192,2560*
Lu 7:10 the servant whole that had been s........ *770*
Lu 9:2 kingdom of God, and to heal the s.. ..... *770*
Lu 10:9 **And heal the s. that are therein,**..... *772*
Joh 4:46 whose son was s. at Capernaum. *770*
Joh 11:1 Now a certain man was s., named........ *770*
Joh 11:2 hair, whose brother Lazarus was s..).... *770*
Joh 11:3 behold, he whom thou lovest is s.......... *770*
Joh 11:6 had heard therefore that he was s.,....... *770*
Ac 5:15 they brought forth the s. into the......... *772*
Ac 5:16 bringing s. folks, and them which......... *772*
Ac 9:33 years, and was s. of the palsy. *3885*
Ac 9:37 days, that she was s., and died: *770*
Ac 19:12 brought unto the s. handkerchiefs *770*
Ac 28:8 father of Publius lay s. of a fever and.........
Php 2:26 ye had heard that he had been s.......... *770*
Php 2:27 indeed he was s. nigh unto death:........ *770*
2Ti 4:20 Trophimus have I left at Miletum s.. .... *770*

Jas 5:14 Is any s. among you? let him call... *770*
Jas 5:15 prayer of faith shall save the s.,... *2577*

SICKLE

De 16:9 beginnest to put the s. to the corn... 2770
De 23:25 not move a s. unto thy neighbour's... 2770
Jer 50:16 that handleth the s. in the time of... 4038
Joe 3:13 Put ye in the s., for the harvest is... 4038
Mk 4:29 **immediately he putteth in the s.,**... *1407*
Re 14:14 crown, and in his hand a sharp s... *1407*
Re 14:15 cloud, Thrust in thy s., and reap:... *1407*
Re 14:16 cloud thrust in his s. on the earth;... *1407*
Re 14:17 heaven, he also having a sharp s... *1407*
Re 14:18 cry to him that had the sharp s.,... *1407*
Re 14:18 Thrust in thy sharp s., and gather... *1407*
Re 14:19 angel thrust in his s. into the earth,... *1407*

SICKLY

1Co 11:30 many are weak and s. among you,... *732*

SICKNESS See also SICKNESSES.

Ex 23:25 I will take s. away from the midst... 4245
Le 20:18 lie with a woman having her s.,... 1739
De 7:15 will take away from thee all s.,... 2483
De 28:61 Also every s., and every plague,... 2483
1Ki 8:37 plague, whatsoever s. there be;... 4245
1Ki 17:17 his s. was so sore, that there was... 2483
2Ki 13:14 Now Elisha was fallen sick of his s.... 2483
2Ch 6:28 sore or whatsoever s. there be:... 4245
2Ch 21:15 shalt have great s. by disease of... 2483
2Ch 21:15 bowels fall out by reason of the s.... 2483
2Ch 21:19 bowels fell out by reason of his s.... 2483
Ps 41:3 wilt make all his bed in his s... 2483
Ec 5:17 sorrow and wrath with his s... 2483
Isa 38:9 sick, and was recovered of his s.... 2483
Isa 38:12 he will cut me off with pining s.,...
Ho 5:13 When Ephraim saw his s., and... 2483
Mt 4:23 healing all manner of s. and all... *3554*
Mt 9:35 healing every s. and every disease... *3554*
Mt 10:1 to heal all manner of s. and all... *3554*
Joh 11:4 **This s. is not unto death, but for**... *769*

SICKNESSES

De 28:59 sore s. and of long continuance... 2483
De 29:22 s. which the Lord hath laid upon... 8463
Mt 8:17 our infirmities, and bare our s... *3554*
Mk 3:15 to have power to heal s., and to... *3554*

SIDDIM (sid'-dim)

Ge 14:3 joined toether in the vale of S.,... 7708
Ge 14:8 battle with them in the vale of S.;... 7708
Ge 14:10 the vale of S. was full of slimepits;... 7708

SIDE See also ASIDE; BACKSIDE; BESIDE; INSIDE; OUTSIDE; SIDES; UPSIDE.

Ge 6:16 ark shalt thou set in the s. thereof;... 6654
Ge 38:21 harlot, that was openly by the way s.?...
Ex 2:5 walked along by the river's s.; and... 3027
Ex 12:7 strike it on the two s. posts and on...
Ex 12:22 strike the lintel and the two s. posts...
Ex 12:23 upon the lintel, and on the two s. posts,...
Ex 17:12 one s., and the other on the other s.;...
Ex 25:12 rings shall be in the one s. of it,... 6763
Ex 25:12 and two rings in the other s. of it... 6763
Ex 25:32 of the candlestick out of the one s.,... 6654
Ex 25:32 the candlestick out of the other s.:... 6654
Ex 26:13 a cubit on the one s., and a cubit on...
Ex 26:13 the other s. of that which remaineth...
Ex 26:13 on this s. and on that s., to cover...
Ex 26:18 boards on the south s. southward... 6285
Ex 26:20 the second s. of the tabernacle on... 6763
Ex 26:20 the north s. there shall be twenty... 6285
Ex 26:26 of the one s. of the tabernacle,... 6763
Ex 26:27 of the other s. of the tabernacle, and... 6763
Ex 26:27 boards of the s. of the tabernacle,... 6763
Ex 26:35 the s. of the tabernacle toward the... 6763
Ex 26:35 shalt put the table on the north s... 6763
Ex 27:9 for the south s. southward there... 6285
Ex 27:9 an hundred cubits long for one s.... 6285
Ex 27:11 likewise for the north s. in length... 6285
Ex 27:12 the west s. shall be hangings of fifty... 6285
Ex 27:13 breadth of the court on the east s.... 6285
Ex 27:14 The hangings of one s. of the gate... 3802
Ex 27:15 on the other s. shall be hangings... 3802
Ex 28:26 is in the s. of the ephod inward... 5676
Ex 32:15 on the one s. and on the other were...
Ex 32:26 said, Who is on the Lord's s.? let him...
Ex 32:27 Put every man his sword by his s.,... 3409
Ex 36:11 uttermost s. of another curtain,... 8193
Ex 36:23 boards for the south s. southward:... 6285
Ex 36:25 for the other s. of the tabernacle,... 6763
Ex 36:31 of the one s. of the tabernacle,... 6763
Ex 36:32 of the other s. of the tabernacle,... 6763
Ex 37:3 even two rings upon the one s. of it,... 6763
Ex 37:3 and two rings upon the other s. of it... 6763
Ex 37:8 One cherub on the end on this s.,...
Ex 37:8 cherub on the other end on that s....
Ex 37:18 out of the one s. thereof, and... 6654
Ex 37:18 out of the other s. thereof:... 6654
Ex 38:9 south s. southward the hangings... 6285
Ex 38:11 for the north s. the hangings were... 6285
Ex 38:12 for the west s. were hangings of... 6285
Ex 38:13 for the east s. eastward fifty cubits... 6285
Ex 38:14 hangings of the one s. of the gate... 3802
Ex 38:15 for the other s. of the court gate,... 3802
Ex 39:19 was on the s. of the ephod inward... 5676
Ex 40:22 the s. of the tabernacle northward,... 3409
Ex 40:24 the s. of the tabernacle southward... 3409
Le 1:11 shall kill it on the s. of the altar... 3409
Le 1:15 be wrung out at the s. of the altar:... 7023
Le 5:9 sin offering upon the s. of the altar;... 7023
Nu 2:3 the east s. toward the rising of the... 6924
Nu 2:10 On the south s. shall be the standard...
Nu 2:18 On the west s. shall be the standard...
Nu 2:25 camp of Dan shall be on the north s....
Nu 3:29 the s. of the tabernacle southward... 3409
Nu 3:35 the s. of the tabernacle northward... 3409
Nu 10:6 the camps that lie on the south s....
Nu 11:31 it were a day's journey on this s.,... 3541
Nu 11:31 a day's journey on the other s.,... 3541
Nu 16:27 Dathan, and Abiram, on every s.... 5439
Nu 21:13 pitched on the other s. of Arnon... 5676
Nu 22:1 Moab on this s. Jordan by Jericho... 5676
Nu 22:24 being on this s., and a wall on that s....
Nu 24:6 as gardens by the river's s., as the...
Nu 32:19 not inherit...on yonder s. Jordan,... 5676
Nu 32:19 is fallen to us on this s. Jordan... 5676
Nu 32:32 inheritance on this s. Jordan may... 5676
Nu 34:11 to Riblah, on the east s. of Ain;... 6924
Nu 34:11 unto the s. of the sea of Chinnereth... 3802
Nu 34:15 their inheritance on this s. Jordan... 5676
Nu 35:5 on the east s. two thousand cubits,... 6285
Nu 35:5 on the south s. two thousand cubits,... 6285
Nu 35:5 on the west s. two thousand cubits,... 6285
Nu 35:5 on the north s. two thousand cubits;... 6285
Nu 35:14 give three cities on this s. Jordan,... 5676
De 1:1 unto all Israel on this s. Jordan in... 5676
De 1:5 On this s. Jordan, in the land of... 5676
De 1:7 in the south,and by the sea s.,... 2348
De 3:8 land that was on this s. Jordan,... 5676
De 4:32 one s. of heaven unto the other,... 7097
De 4:41 cities on this s. Jordan toward the... 5676
De 4:46 On this s. Jordan, in the valley over... 5676
De 4:47 were on this s. Jordan toward the... 5676
De 4:49 plain on this s. Jordan eastward,... 5676
De 11:30 Are they not on the other s. Jordan,... 5676
De 31:26 in the s. of the ark of the covenant... 6654
Jos 1:14 Moses gave you on this s. Jordan;... 5676
Jos 1:15 gave you on this s. Jordan toward... 5676
Jos 2:10 that were on the other s. Jordan,... 5676
Jos 5:1 were on the s. of Jordan westward,... 5676
Jos 7:2 Beth-aven, on the east s. of Beth-el,...
Jos 7:7 and dwelt on the other s. Jordan!... 5676
Jos 8:9 Beth-el and Ai, on the west s. of Ai:...
Jos 8:11 and pitched on the north s. of Ai:...
Jos 8:12 and Ai, on the west s. of the city...
Jos 8:22 in the midst of Israel, some on this s.,...
Jos 8:22 and some on that s.: and they smote...
Jos 8:33 their judges, stood on this s. the ark...
Jos 8:33 that s. before the priests the Levites,...
Jos 9:1 which were on this s. Jordan, in... 5676
Jos 12:1 other s. Jordan toward the rising... 5676
Jos 12:7 Israel smote on this s. Jordan on... 5676
Jos 13:27 on the other s. Jordan eastward... 5676
Jos 13:32 of Moab, on the other s. Jordan, by... 5676
Jos 14:3 half tribe on the other s. Jordan:... 5676
Jos 15:3 to the south s. to Maaleh-acrabbim,...
Jos 15:3 on the south s. unto Kadesh-barnea,...
Jos 15:7 which is on the south s. of the river:...
Jos 15:8 unto the south s. of the Jebusite;... 3802
Jos 15:10 along unto the s. of mount Jearim,... 3802
Jos 15:10 which is Chesalon, on the north s.,...
Jos 15:11 unto the s. of Ekron northward:... 3802
Jos 16:5 inheritance on the east s. was...
Jos 16:6 to Michmethah on the north s.;...
Jos 17:5 which were on the other s. Jordan;... 5676
Jos 17:9 was on the north s. of the river,...
Jos 18:12 border on the north s. was from... 6285
Jos 18:12 border went up to the s. of Jericho... 3802
Jos 18:12 of Jericho on the north s., and went...
Jos 18:13 to the s. of Luz, which is Beth-el,... 3802
Jos 18:13 the south s. of the nether Beth-horon...
Jos 18:16 to the s. of Jebusi on the south,... 3802
Jos 18:18 toward the s. over against Arabah... 3802
Jos 18:19 the s. of Beth-hoglah northward:... 3802
Jos 18:20 was the border of it on the east s.... 6285
Jos 19:14 it on the north s. to Hannathon:...
Jos 19:27 toward the north s. of Beth-emek,... 6285
Jos 19:34 reacheth to Zebulun on the south s.,...
Jos 19:34 and reacheth to Asher on the west s.,...
Jos 20:8 on the other s. Jordan by Jericho... 5676
Jos 22:4 gave you on the other s. Jordan... 5676
Jos 22:7 their brethren on this s. Jordan... 5676
Jos 24:2 Your fathers dwelt on the other s.... 5676
Jos 24:3 from the other s. of the flood, and... 5676
Jos 24:8 which dwelt on the other s. Jordan;... 5676
Jos 24:14 fathers served on the other s. of... 5676
Jos 24:15 were on the other s. of the flood,... 5676
Jos 24:30 the north s. of the hill of Gaash...
Jg 2:9 on the north s. of the hill Gaash...
Jg 7:1 Midianites were on the north s....
Jg 7:12 sand by the sea s. for multitude... 8193
Jg 7:18 also on every s. of all the camp,... 5439
Jg 7:25 to Gideon on the other s. Jordan... 5676
Jg 8:34 of all their enemies on every s.:... 5439
Jg 10:8 that were on the other s. Jordan... 5676
Jg 11:18 by the east s. of the land of Moab,...
Jg 11:18 pitched on the other s. of Arnon,... 5676
Jg 19:1 on the s. of mount Ephraim, who... 3411
Jg 19:18 toward the s. of mount Ephraim;... 3411
Jg 21:19 which is on the north s. of Beth-el,...
Jg 21:19 on the east s. of the highway that...
1Sa 4:18 backward by the s. of the gate,... 3027
1Sa 6:8 in a coffer by the s. thereof; and... 6654
1Sa 12:11 hand of your enemies on every s.,... 5439
1Sa 14:1 garrison, that is on the other s.... 5676
1Sa 14:4 was a sharp rock on the one s.,... 5676
1Sa 14:4 and a sharp rock on the other s.... 5676
1Sa 14:40 he unto all Israel, Be ye on one s.,... 5676
1Sa 14:40 my son will be on the other s.... 5676
1Sa 14:47 against all his enemies on every s.,... 5439
1Sa 17:3 stood on a mountain on the one s.,...
1Sa 17:3 stood on a mountain on the other s....
1Sa 20:20 I will shoot three arrows on the s.... 6654
1Sa 20:21 the arrows are on this s. of thee,...
1Sa 20:25 and Abner sat by Saul's s., and... 6654
1Sa 23:26 went on this s. of the mountain,... 6654
1Sa 23:26 his men on that s. of the mountain:... 6654
1Sa 26:13 David went over to the other s.,... 5676
1Sa 31:7 Israel that were on the other s. of... 5676
1Sa 31:7 that were on the other s. Jordan,... 5676
2Sa 2:13 the one on the one s. of the pool,...
2Sa 2:13 the other on the other s. of the pool...
2Sa 2:16 thrust his sword in his fellow's s.;... 6654
2Sa 13:34 by the way of the hill s. behind... 6654
2Sa 16:13 Shimei went along on the hill's s.... 6763
2Sa 18:4 And the king stood by the gate s.,... 3027
2Sa 24:5 on the right s. of the city that lieth... 3225
1Ki 4:24 all the region on this s. the river,... 5676
1Ki 4:24 all the kings on this s. the river:... 5676
1Ki 5:3 which were about him on every s.,...
1Ki 5:4 hath given me rest on every s.,... 5439
1Ki 6:8 was in the right s. of the house:... 3802
1Ki 6:31 lintel and s. posts were a fifth part...
1Ki 7:7 cedar from one s. of the floor to the...
1Ki 7:30 molten, at the s. of every addition... 5676
1Ki 7:39 bases on the right s. of the house,... 3802
1Ki 7:39 and five on the left s. of the house:... 3802
1Ki 7:39 the sea on the right s. of the house... 3802
1Ki 7:49 of pure gold, five on the right s., and...
1Ki 10:19 were stays on either s. on the place of...
1Ki 10:20 twelve lions stood there on the one s....
2Ki 3:22 the water on the other s. as red... 5048
2Ki 9:32 and said, Who is on my s.?...
2Ki 12:9 it beside the altar, on the right s.... 3225
2Ki 16:14 put it on the north s. of the altar... 3409
1Ch 4:39 even unto the east s. of the valley,... 4217
1Ch 6:78 on the other s. Jordan by Jericho,... 5676
1Ch 6:78 on the east s. of Jordan, were... 4217
1Ch 12:18 Thine are we, David, and on thy s.,...
1Ch 12:37 on the other s. of Jordan, of the... 5676
1Ch 22:18 he not given you rest on every s.?... 5439
1Ch 26:30 them of Israel on this s. Jordan... 5676
2Ch 4:8 five on the right s., and five on the...

2Ch 4:10 he set the sea on the right s. of the ... 3802
2Ch 8:17 at the sea s. in the land of Edom. 8193
2Ch 9:18 stays on each s. of the sitting place, ...
2Ch 9:19 lions stood there on the one s., and.........
2Ch 11:12 having Judah and Benjamin on his s..........
2Ch 14:7 he hath given us rest on every s........ 5439
2Ch 20:2 beyond the sea on this s. Syria; ....
2Ch 23:10 from the right s. of the temple to....... 3802
2Ch 23:10 to the left s. of the temple, along by... 3802
2Ch 32:22 and guided them on every s.. 5439
2Ch 32:30 to the west s. of the city of David...........
2Ch 33:14 on the west s. of Gihon, in the valley,.......
Ezr 4:10 rest that are on this s. the river, ... 5675
Ezr 4:11 the men on this s. the river, and at.... 5675
Ezr 4:16 have no portion on this s. the river..... 5675
Ezr 5:3, 6 Tatnai, governor on this s. the........ 5675
Ezr 5:6 which were on this s. the river, ... 5675
Ezr 6:13 Tatnai, governor on this s. the river, .. 5675
Ezr 8:36 the governors on this s. the river:...... 5676
Ne 3:7 of the governor on this s. the river..... 5676
Ne 4:18 had his sword girded by his s., ... 4975
Job 1:10 about all that he hath on every s.?...... 5439
Job 18:11 shall make him afraid on every s., ... 5439
Job 18:12 destruction...be ready at his s.. 6763
Job 19:10 He hath destroyed me on every s., ... 5439
Ps 12:8 The wicked walk on every s., when.... 5439
Ps 31:13 fear was on every s.: while they........ 5439
Ps 65:12 the little hills rejoice on every s.. 2296
Ps 71:21 and comfort me on every s.. 5437
Ps 91:7 A thousand shall fall at thy s., and...... 6654
Ps 118:6 Lord is on my s.; I will not fear:............
Ps 124:1, 2 been the Lord who was on our s., ...
Ec 4:1 s. of their oppressors there was......... 3027
Isa 60:4 daughters...be nursed at thy s.. 6654
Jer 6:25 the enemy and fear is on every s...... 5439
Jer 20:10 defaming of many, fear on every s...... 5439
Jer 49:29 cry unto them, Fear is on every s...... 5439
Jer 52:23 and six pomegranates on a s.; 7307
Eze 1:10 the face of a lion, on the right s......... 3225
Eze 1:10 had the face of an ox on the left s.;.... 8040
Eze 1:23 had two, which covered on this s., ...
Eze 1:23 had two, which covered on that s............
Eze 4:4 Lie thou also upon thy left s., and...... 6654
Eze 4:6 lie again on thy right s., and thou....... 6654
Eze 4:8 turn thee from one s. to another,........ 6654
Eze 4:9 days that thou shalt lie upon thy s., ... 6654
Eze 9:2 with a writer's inkhorn by his s.......... 4975
Eze 9:3 had the writer's inkhorn by his s.; 4975
Eze 9:11 which had the inkhorn by his s.,......... 4975
Eze 10:3 cherubims stood on the right s. of..... 3225
Eze 11:23 mountain which is on the east s. of..... 6924
Eze 16:33 come unto thee on every s. for thy 5439
Eze 19:8 nations set against him on every s...... 5439
Eze 23:22 bring them against thee on every s.;... 5439
Eze 25:9 I will open the s. of Moab from the 3802
Eze 28:23 by the sword upon her on every s.;.... 5439
Eze 34:21 thrust with s. and with shoulder,........ 6654
Eze 36:3 and swallowed you up on every s., ... 5439
Eze 37:21 and will gather them on every s.,....... 5439
Eze 39:17 gather yourselves on every s. to my... 5439
Eze 40:10 on this s., and three on that s.; 6311
Eze 40:10 measure on this s. and on that s.. ....
Eze 40:12 chambers was one cubit on this s., ...
Eze 40:12 the space was one cubit on that s.............
Eze 40:12 on this s., and six cubits on that s............
Eze 40:18 pavement by the s. of the gates......... 3802
Eze 40:21 three on this s. and three on that s.; ....
Eze 40:26 on this s., and another on that s., ...
Eze 40:34, 37 thereof, on this s., and on that s...........
Eze 40:39 on this s., and two tables on that s.,.........
Eze 40:40 at the s. without, as one goeth up...... 3802
Eze 40:40 and on the other s., which was at 3802
Eze 40:41 on this s., and four tables on that s., .. 3802
Eze 40:41 by the s. of the gate; eight tables,...... 3802
Eze 40:44 was at the s. of the north gate; 3802
Eze 40:44 one at the s. of the east gate having... 3802
Eze 40:48 on this s., and five cubits on that s..........
Eze 40:48 on this s., and three cubits on that s.........
Eze 40:49 one on this s., and another on that s..........
Eze 41:1 six cubits broad on the one s.,........... 6311
Eze 41:1 six cubits broad on the other s.,.................
Eze 41:2 were five cubits on the one s., ...
Eze 41:2 and five cubits on the other s.: ....
Eze 41:5 the breadth of every s. chamber, ... 6763
Eze 41:5 round about the house on every s.. 5439
Eze 41:6 And the s. chambers were three, ... 6763
Eze 41:6 of the house for the s. chambers........ 6763
Eze 41:7 still upward to the s. chambers: 6763
Eze 41:8 the foundations of the s. chambers...... 6763
Eze 41:9 was for the s. chamber without,......... 6763
Eze 41:9 was the place of the s. chambers 6763
Eze 41:10 about the house on every s.............. 5439
Eze 41:11 the doors of the s. chambers were 6763
Eze 41:15 galleries thereof on the one s. and............
Eze 41:15 on the other s., an hundred cubits, ...
Eze 41:19 toward the palm tree on the one s.,..........
Eze 41:19 toward the palm tree on the other s. ....
Eze 41:26 palm trees on the one s. and on..............
Eze 41:26 and on the other s., on the sides of..........
Eze 41:26 upon the s. chambers of the house, ... 6763
Eze 42:9 was the entry on the east s., as 6921
Eze 42:16 east s. with the measuring reed, ... 7307
Eze 42:17 the north s., five hundred reeds,......... 7307
Eze 42:18 the south s., five hundred reeds,........ 7307
Eze 42:19 He turned about to the west s., and... 7307
Eze 45:7 shall be for the prince on the one s..........
Eze 45:7 other s. of the oblation of the holy...........
Eze 45:7 city, from the west s. westward,........ 6285
Eze 45:7 and from the east s. eastward: 6285
Eze 46:19 which was at the s. of the gate, ...
Eze 47:1 from the right s. of the house,.................
Eze 47:1 house, at the south s. of the altar...........
Eze 47:2 there ran out waters on...right s.. 3802
Eze 47:7 many trees on the one s. and on the.........
Eze 47:12 upon the bank thereof, on this s. and........
Eze 47:12 on that s., shall grow all trees for............
Eze 47:15 of the land toward the north s.,.......... 6285
Eze 47:17 Hamath. And this is the north s.. 6285
Eze 47:18 the east s. ye shall measure from....... 6285
Eze 47:18 east sea. And this is the east s.......... 6285
Eze 47:19 And the south s. southward, from 6285
Eze 47:19 And this is the south s. southward...... 6285
Eze 47:20 The west s. also shall be the great..... 6285
Eze 47:20 Hamath. This is the west s................ 6285
Eze 48:2 the border of Dan, from the east s..... 6285
Eze 48:2 the west s., a portion for Asher......... 6285
Eze 48:3 the east s. even unto the west s.,........ 6285
Eze 48:4, 5 from the east s. unto the west s., ... 6285
Eze 48:6 the east s. even unto the west s.,...... 6285
Eze 48:7, 8 from the east s. unto the west s., ... 6285
Eze 48:8 from the east s. unto the west s.:...... 6285
Eze 48:16 the north s. four thousand and five..... 6285
Eze 48:16 the south s. four thousand and five..... 6285
Eze 48:16 the east s. four thousand and five....... 6285
Eze 48:16 the west s. four thousand and five....... 6285
Eze 48:21 on the one s. and on the other of the.. 6285
Eze 48:23, 24,25,26,27 east s. unto the west s.,.. 6285
Eze 48:28 of Gad, at the south s. southward, ... 6285
Eze 48:30 out of the city on the north s., ... 6285
Eze 48:32 at the east s. four thousand and......... 6285
Eze 48:33 the south s. four thousand and five..... 6285
Eze 48:34 the west s. four thousand and five...... 6285
Da 7:5 and it raised up itself on one s.,......... 7859
Da 10:4 I was by the s. of the great river,...... 3027
Da 11:17 but she shall not stand on his s., ...
Da 12:5 on this s. of the bank of the river,..........
Da 12:5 the other on that s. of the bank of...........
Ob 11 that thou stoodest on the other s., ... 5048
Jon 4:5 and sat on the east s. of the city,....... 6924
Zec 4:3 one upon the right s. of the bowl, ...
Zec 4:3 and the other upon the left s. thereof.......
Zec 4:11 upon the right s. of the candlestick ....
Zec 4:11 and upon the left s. thereof?....................
Zec 5:3 shall be cut off as on this s. according.......
Zec 5:3 shall be cut off as on that s. according.......
Mt 8:18 to depart unto the other s................. *4008*
Mt 8:28 when he was come to the other s. *4008*
Mt 13:1 of the house, and sat by the sea s...... *3844*
Mt 13:4 **some seeds fell by the way s., and** . *3844*
Mt 13:19 **which received seed by the way s..** . *3844*
Mt 14:22 to go before him unto the other s.,........ *4008*
Mt 16:5 disciples were come to the other s., ... *4008*
Mt 20:30 blind men sitting by the way s., ... *3844*
Mk 2:13 he went forth again by the sea s.; *3844*
Mk 4:1 began again to teach by the s. *3844*
Mk 4:4 **he sowed, some fell by the way s.,** .. *3844*
Mk 4:15 **And these are they by the way s.,** ... *3844*
Mk 4:35 **Let us pass over unto the other s.** .. *4008*
Mk 5:1 over unto the other s. of the sea, ... *4008*
Mk 5:21 again by ship unto the other s., ... *4008*
Mk 6:45 the other s. before unto Bethsaida,..... *4008*
Mk 8:13 ship again departed to the other s.. .... *4008*
Mk 10:1 Judaea by the farther s. of Jordan:...... *4008*
Mk 10:46 sat by the highway s. begging........... *3844*
Mk 16:5 young man sitting on the right s.,........ *1188*
Lu 1:11 standing on the right s. of the altar..... *1188*
Lu 8:5 **he sowed, some fell by the way s..** . *3844*
Lu 8:12 **Those by the way s. are they that** . *3844*
Lu 8:22 **over unto the other s. of the lake..** *4008*
Lu 10:31 **him, he passed by on the other s..** . *492*
Lu 10:32 **him, and passed by on the other s...** *492*
Lu 18:35 man sat by the way s. begging: *3844*
Lu 19:43 **round, and keep thee in on every s..** *3840*
Joh 6:22 stood on the other s. of the sea.......... *4008*
Joh 6:25 found him on the other s. of the *4008*
Joh 19:18 other with him, on either s., one,....... *1782*
Joh 19:34 with a spear pierced his s., and *4125*
Joh 20:20 unto them his hands and his s............ *4125*
Joh 20:25 and thrust my hand into his s., I........ *4125*
Joh 20:27 **thy hand, and thrust it into my s..** *4125*
Joh 21:6 **Cast the net on the right s. of the** .. *3313*
Ac 10:6 he whose house is by the sea s. *3844*
Ac 10:32 one Simon a tanner by the sea s. *3844*
Ac 12:7 smote Peter on the s., and raised *4125*
Ac 16:13 went out of the city by a river s., ... *3844*
2Co 4:8 We are troubled on every s., yet not........
2Co 7:5 but we were troubled on every s.;...........
Re 22:2 on either s. of the river, was there..... *1782*

SIDE-CHAMBER See SIDE and CHAMBER.

SIDE-POSTS See SIDE and POSTS.

SIDES
Ex 25:14 into the rings by the s. of the ark, ... 6763
Ex 25:32 shall come out of the s. of it; 6654
Ex 26:13 hand over the s. of the tabernacle 6654
Ex 26:22 the s. of the tabernacle westward....... 3411
Ex 26:23 of the tabernacle in the two s............ 3411
Ex 26:27 tabernacle, for the two s. westward.... 3411
Ex 27:7 be upon the two s. of the altar, ... 6763
Ex 28:27 two s. of the ephod underneath,.......... 3802
Ex 30:3 and the s. thereof round about,.......... 7023
Ex 30:4 the two s. of it shalt thou make it; 6654
Ex 32:15 were written on both their s.; 5676
Ex 36:27 the s. of the tabernacle westward....... 3411
Ex 36:28 of the tabernacle in the two s............ 3411
Ex 36:32 the tabernacle for the s. westward...... 3411
Ex 37:5 into the rings by the s. of the ark, ... 6763
Ex 37:18 going out of the s. thereof; 6654
Ex 37:26 and the s. thereof round about,.......... 7023
Ex 37:27 upon the two s. thereof, to be........... 6654
Ex 38:7 the rings on the s. of the altar,.......... 6763
Ex 39:20 two s. of the ephod underneath,......... 3802
Nu 33:55 your eyes, and thorns in your s., ... 6654
Jos 23:13 and scourges in your s., and thorns 6654
Jg 2:3 they shall be as thorns in your s., ... 6654
Jg 5:30 colours of needlework on both s.,.............
1Sa 24:3 remained in the s. of the cave. 3411
1Ki 4:24 and he had peace on all s. round........ 5676
1Ki 6:16 cubits on the s. of the house,............ 3411
2Ki 19:23 mountains, to the s. of Lebanon, ... 3411
Ps 48:2 mount Zion, on the s. of the north,..... 3411
Ps 128:3 vine by the s. of thine house: 3411
Isa 14:13 congregation, in the s. of the north:.... 3411
Isa 14:15 down to hell, to the s. of the pit. 3411
Isa 37:24 mountains, to the s. of Lebanon; 3411
Isa 66:12 ye shall be borne upon her s., and...... 6654
Jer 6:22 be raised from the s. of the earth....... 3411
Jer 48:28 nest in the s. of the hole's mouth....... 5676
Jer 49:32 their calamity from all s. thereof,....... 5676
Eze 1:8 under their wings on their four s.;...... 7253
Eze 1:17 went, they went upon their four s....... 7253
Eze 10:11 went, they went upon their four s.; 7253
Eze 32:23 graves are set in the s. of the pit,...... 3411
Eze 41:2 the s. of the door were five cubits....... 3802
Eze 41:26 on the s. of the porch, and upon........ 3802
Eze 42:20 He measured it by the four s.: it........ 7307
Eze 46:19 a place on the two s. westward. 3411
Eze 48:1 for these are his s. east and west; 6285
Am 6:10 him that is by the s. of the house,....... 3411
Jon 1:5 gone down into the s. of the ship; 3411

SIDON (si'-don) See also SIDONIANS; ZIDON.
Ge 10:15 And Canaan begat S. his firstborn,...... 6721
Ge 10:19 of the Canaanites was from S., ... 6721
Mt 11:21 **had been done in Tyre and S.,**........ *4605*
Mt 11:22 **be more tolerable for Tyre and S...** *4605*
Mt 15:21 into the coasts of Tyre and S. *4605*
Mk 3:8 and they about Tyre and S., a great ... *4605*
Mk 7:24 into the borders of Tyre and S., ... *4605*
Mk 7:31 from the coasts of Tyre and S., ... *4605*
Lu 4:26 **save unto Sarepta, a city of S., unto** *4605*

Lu 6:17 from the sea coast of Tyre and S., ... *4605*
Lu 10:13 had been done in Tyre and S., ... *4605*
Lu 10:14 be more tolerable for Tyre and S. ... *4605*
Ac 12:20 displeased with them of Tyre and S. ... *4605*
Ac 27:3 And the next day we touched at S. *4605*

SIDONIANS (si-do'-ne-uns) See also ZIDONIANS.
De 3:9 Which Hermon the S. call Sirion; 6722
Jos 13:4 and Mearah that is beside the S., ... 6722
Jos 13:6 and all the S., them will I drive out 6722
Jg 3:3 and all the Canaanites, and the S., ... 6722
1Ki 5:6 skill to hew timber like unto the S., ... 6722

SIEGE See also BESIEGE.
De 20:19 down...to employ them in the s. 4692
De 28:53 in the s., and in the straitness, ... 4692
De 28:55 he hath nothing left in the s., and 4692
De 28:57 secretly in the s. and straitness, ... 4692
1Ki 15:27 and all Israel laid s. to Gibbethon. 6696
2Ch 32:9 but he himself laid s. against Lachish, ...
2Ch 32:10 ye abide in the s. in Jerusalem? 4692
Isa 29:3 and will lay s. against thee with a 6696
Jer 19:9 eat the flesh of his friend in the s. 4692
Eze 4:2 And lay s. against it, and build a 4692
Eze 4:3 and thou shalt lay s. against it. 6696
Eze 4:7 face toward the s. of Jerusalem, ... 4692
Eze 4:8 thou hast ended the days of thy s. 4692
Eze 5:2 when the days of the s. are fulfilled: ... 4692
Mic 5:1 troops: he hath laid s. against us: 4692
Na 3:14 Draw thee waters for the s., fortify 4692
Zec 12:2 shall be in the s. both against Judah 4692

SIEVE
Isa 30:28 the nations with the s. of vanity: 5299
Am 9:9 nations, like as corn is sifted in a s., ... 3531

SIFT See also SIFTED.
Isa 30:28 to s. the nations with the sieve of 5130
Am 9:9 I will s. the house of Israel among 5128
Lu 22:31 you, that he may s. you as wheat: ..*4617*

SIFTED
Am 9:9 nations, like as corn is s. in a sieve, ... 5128

SIGH See also SIGHED; SIGHEST; SIGHETH; SIGHING; SIGHS.
Isa 24:7 all the merryhearted do s. 584
La 1:4 priests s., her virgins are afflicted, ... 584
La 1:11 All her people s., they seek bread; 584
La 1:21 They have heard that I s.: there is 584
Eze 9:4 upon the foreheads of the men that s. ... 584
Eze 21:6 S. therefore, thou son of man, with 584
Eze 21:6 with bitterness s. before their eyes. 584

SIGHED
Ex 2:23 children of Israel s. by reason of 584
Mk 7:34 And looking up to heaven, he s., ... *4727*
Mk 8:12 he s. deeply in his spirit, and saith, ... *389*

SIGHEST
Eze 21:7 say unto thee, Wherefore s. thou? 584

SIGHETH
La 1:8 yea, she s., and turneth backward 584

SIGHING
Job 3:24 For my s. cometh before I eat, and 585
Ps 12:5 of the poor, for the s. of the needy, ... 603
Ps 31:10 with grief, and my years with s.: 585
Ps 79:11 the s. of the prisoner come before 603
Isa 21:2 the s. thereof have I made to cease. 585
Isa 35:10 and sorrow and s. shall flee away 585
Jer 45:3 fainted in my s., and I find no rest. 585

SIGHS
La 1:22 for my s. are many, and my heart is 585

SIGHT See also OVERSIGHT; SIGHTS.
Ge 2:9 every tree that is pleasant to the s., ... 4758
Ge 18:3 now I have found favour in thy s., ... 5869
Ge 19:19 servant hath found grace in thy s., ... 5869
Ge 21:11 was very grievous in Abraham's s. 5869
Ge 21:12 Let it not be grievous in thy s. 5869
Ge 23:4 may bury my dead out of my s.. 6440
Ge 23:8 should bury my dead out of my s.; 6440
Ge 32:5 lord,...I may find grace in thy s.. 5869
Ge 33:8 to find grace in the s. of my lord. 5869
Ge 33:10 if now I have found grace in thy s., ... 5869
Ge 33:15 me find grace in the s. of my lord. 5869
Ge 38:7 was wicked in the s. of the Lord; 5869
Ge 39:4 And Joseph found grace in his s., ... 5869
Ge 39:21 him favour in the s. of the keeper 5869
Ge 47:18 not ought left in the s. of my lord, ... 6440
Ge 47:25 us find grace in the s. of my lord, ... 5869
Ge 47:29 If now I have found grace in thy s., ... 5869
Ex 3:3 turn aside, and see this great s., ... 4758
Ex 3:21 favour in the s. of the Egyptians: 5869
Ex 4:30 did the signs in the s. of the people. ... 5869
Ex 7:20 in the river, in the s. of Pharaoh, ... 5869
Ex 7:20 and in the s. of his servants; and 5869
Ex 9:8 the heaven in the s. of Pharaoh. 5869
Ex 11:3 favour in the s. of the Egyptians. 5869
Ex 11:3 in the s. of Pharoah's servants, and 5869
Ex 11:3 and in the s. of the people. 5869
Ex 12:36 favour in the s. of the Egyptians, ... 5869
Ex 15:26 wilt do that which is right in his s., ... 5869
Ex 17:6 Moses did so in the s. of the elders. ... 5869
Ex 19:11 down in the s. of all the people upon ... 5869
Ex 24:17 the s. of the glory of the Lord 4758
Ex 33:12 hast also found grace in my s.. 5869
Ex 33:13 if I have found grace in thy s., ... 5869
Ex 33:13 that I may find grace in thy s.: and 5869
Ex 33:16 people have found grace in thy s.? 5869
Ex 33:17 for thou hast found grace in my s., ... 5869
Ex 34:9 If now I have found grace in thy s., ... 5869
Ex 40:38 in the s. of all the house of Israel, ... 5869
Le 10:19 been accepted in the s. of the Lord? ... 5869
Le 13:3 the plague in s. be deeper than the 4758
Le 13:4 in s. be not deeper than the skin, ... 4758
Le 13:5 if the plague in his s. be at a stay, ... 5869
Le 13:20 it be in s. lower than the skin, ... 4758
Le 13:25, 30 it be in s. deeper than the skin; 4758
Le 13:31 it be not in s. deeper than the skin, ... 4758
Le 13:32 be not in s. deeper than the skin; 4758
Le 13:34 nor be in s. deeper than the skin; 4758
Le 13:37 if the scall be in his s. at a stay, ... 5869
Le 14:37 which in s. are lower than the 4758
Le 20:17 be cut off in the s. of their people: 5869
Le 25:53 rule with rigour over him in thy s. 5869
Le 26:45 of Egypt in the s. of the heathen, ... 5869
Nu 3:4 in the s. of Aaron their father. 6440
Nu 11:11 have I not found favour in thy s., ... 5869
Nu 11:15 If I have found favour in thy s.; 5869
Nu 13:33 were in our own s. as grasshoppers, ... 5869
Nu 13:33 and so we were in their s.. 5869
Nu 19:5 one shall burn the heifer in his s.; 5869
Nu 20:27 Hor in the s. of all the congregation. ... 5869
Nu 25:6 woman in the s. of Moses, and in 5869
Nu 25:6 the s. of all the congregation of the 5869
Nu 27:19 and give him a charge in their s.. 5869
Nu 32:5 if we have found grace in thy s., let 5869
Nu 32:13 had done evil in the s. of the Lord, ... 5869
Nu 33:3 hand in the s. of all the Egyptians. 5869
De 4:6 wisdom...in the s. of the nations. 5869
De 4:25 shall do evil in the s. of the Lord 5869
De 4:37 brought thee out in his s. with his 6440
De 6:18 and good in the s. of the Lord: 5869
De 9:18 wickedly in the s. of the Lord, to 5869
De 12:25 which is right in the s. of the Lord. 5869
De 12:28 good and right in the s. of the Lord 5869
De 17:2 wickedness in the s. of the Lord 5869
De 21:9 which is right in the s. of the Lord. 5869
De 28:34 mad for the s. of thine eyes which 4758
De 28:67 for the s. of thine eyes which thou 4758
De 31:7 unto him in the s. of all Israel, ... 5869
De 31:29 ye will do evil in the s. of the Lord, ... 5869
De 34:12 Moses shewed in the s. of all Israel. ... 5869
Jos 3:7 magnify thee in the s. of all Israel, ... 5869
Jos 4:14 Joshua in the s. of all Israel; and 5869
Jos 10:12 and he said in the s. of Israel, Sun, ... 5869
Jos 23:5 and drive them from out of your s.; 6440
Jos 24:17 did those great signs in our s., and 5869
Jg 2:11 Israel did evil in the s. of the Lord, ... 5869
Jg 3:7 Israel did evil in the s. of the Lord, ... 5869
Jg 3:12 did evil again in the s. of the Lord: 5869
Jg 3:12 had done evil in the s. of the Lord. 5869
Jg 4:1 again did evil in the s. of the Lord, ... 5869
Jg 6:1 Israel did evil in the s. of the Lord: 5869
Jg 6:17 If now I have found grace in thy s., ... 5869
Jg 6:21 of the Lord departed out of his s.. 5869
Jg 10:6 did evil again in the s. of the Lord, ... 5869
Jg 13:1 did evil again in the s. of the Lord; 5869
Ru 2:2 him in whose s. I shall find grace. 5869
Ru 2:13 Let me find favour in thy s., my 5869
1Sa 1:18 handmaid find grace in thy s.. 5869
1Sa 12:17 ye have done in the s. of the Lord, ... 5869
1Sa 15:17 thou wast little in thine own s., ... 5869
1Sa 15:19 and didst evil in the s. of the Lord? 5869
1Sa 16:22 for he hath found favour in my s.. 5869
1Sa 18:5 was accepted in the s. of all the 5869
1Sa 18:5 also in the s. of Saul's servants. 5869
1Sa 29:6 me in the host is good in my s. 5869
1Sa 29:9 know that thou art good in my s., ... 5869
2Sa 6:22 and will be base in mine own s.: 5869
2Sa 7:9 off all thine enemies out of thy s., ... 6440
2Sa 7:19 was yet a small thing in thy s., ... 5869
2Sa 12:9 of the Lord, to do evil in his s.? 5869
2Sa 12:11 with thy wives in the s. of this sun. 5869
2Sa 13:5 dress the meat in my s., that I 5869
2Sa 13:6 make me a couple of cakes in my s., .. 5869
2Sa 13:8 made cakes in his s., and did bake 5869
2Sa 14:22 that I have found grace in thy s., ... 5869
2Sa 16:4 thee that I may find grace in thy s., ... 5869
2Sa 16:22 concubines in the s. of all Israel. 5869
2Sa 22:25 to my cleanness in his eye s. 5869
1Ki 8:25 shall not fail thee a man in my s. 6440
1Ki 9:7 my name, will I cast out of my s.; 6440
1Ki 11:6 did evil in the s. of the Lord, and 5869
1Ki 11:19 great favour in the s. of Pharaoh, ... 5869
1Ki 11:38 do that is right in my s., to keep 5869
1Ki 14:22 Judah did evil in the s. of the Lord, ... 5869
1Ki 15:26, 34 he did evil in the s. of the Lord, ... 5869
1Ki 16:7 evil...he did in the s. of the Lord, ... 5869
1Ki 16:19 in doing evil in the s. of the Lord, ... 5869
1Ki 16:30 Omri did evil in the s. of the Lord 5869
1Ki 21:20 to work evil in the s. of the Lord. 5869
1Ki 21:25 wickedness in the s. of the Lord, ... 5869
1Ki 22:52 he did evil in the s. of the Lord, and ... 5869
2Ki 1:13 thy servants, be precious in thy s. 5869
2Ki 1:14 my life now be precious in thy s.. 5869
2Ki 3:2 wrought evil in the s. of the Lord; 5869
2Ki 3:18 a light thing in the s. of the Lord: 5869
2Ki 8:18 and he did evil in the s. of the Lord. ... 5869
2Ki 8:27 and did evil in the s. of the Lord, ... 5869
2Ki 12:2 was right in the s. of the Lord all 5869
2Ki 13:2 which was evil in the s. of the Lord, ... 5869
2Ki 13:11 which was evil in the s. of the Lord; ... 5869
2Ki 14:3 was right in the s. of the Lord, ... 5869
2Ki 14:24 which was evil in the s. of the Lord: ... 5869
2Ki 15:3 was right in the s. of the Lord, ... 5869
2Ki 15:9 which was evil in the s. of the Lord, ... 5869
2Ki 15:18, 24,28 was evil in the s. of the Lord: ... 5869
2Ki 15:34 was right in the s. of the Lord: he 5869
2Ki 16:2 was right in the s. of the Lord his 5869
2Ki 17:2 which was evil in the s. of the Lord, ... 5869
2Ki 17:17 to do evil in the s. of the Lord, to 5869
2Ki 17:18 and removed them out of his s. 6440
2Ki 17:20 until he had cast them out of his s. 6440
2Ki 17:23 Lord removed Israel out of his s., ... 6440
2Ki 18:3 was right in the s. of the Lord, ... 5869
2Ki 20:3 done that which was good in thy s. 5869
2Ki 21:2 which was evil in the s. of the Lord, ... 5869
2Ki 21:6 wickedness in the s. of the Lord, ... 5869
2Ki 21:15 done that which was evil in my s., ... 5869
2Ki 21:16 which was evil in the s. of the Lord. ... 5869
2Ki 21:20 which was evil in the s. of the Lord, ... 5869
2Ki 22:2 was right in the s. of the Lord, ... 5869
2Ki 23:27 remove Judah also out of my s., ... 6440
2Ki 23:32, 37 was evil in the s. of the Lord, ... 5869
2Ki 24:3 to remove them out of his s., for 6440
2Ki 24:9, 19 was evil in the s. of the Lord, ... 5869
1Ch 2:3 was evil in the s. of the Lord; and 5869
1Ch 19:13 do that which is good in his s.. 5869
1Ch 22:8 blood upon the earth in my s. 6440
1Ch 28:8 therefore in the s. of all Israel the 5869
1Ch 29:25 exceedingly in the s. of all Israel, ... 5869
2Ch 6:16 shall not fail thee a man in my s. 6440
2Ch 7:20 will I cast out of my s., and will 6440
2Ch 20:32 was right in the s. of the Lord. 5869
2Ch 22:4 he did evil in the s. of the Lord like 5869
2Ch 24:2 was right in the s. of the Lord all 5869
2Ch 25:2 was right in the s. of the Lord, ... 5869
2Ch 26:4 was right in the s. of the Lord, ... 5869
2Ch 27:2 was right in the s. of the Lord, ... 5869
2Ch 28:1 was right in the s. of the Lord, ... 5869
2Ch 29:2 was right in the s. of the Lord, ... 5869
2Ch 32:23 magnified in the s. of all nations 5869
2Ch 33:2 which was evil in the s. of the Lord, ... 5869
2Ch 33:6 much evil in the s. of the Lord, ... 5869
2Ch 33:22 which was evil in the s. of the Lord, ... 5869
2Ch 34:2 was right in the s. of the Lord, ... 5869
2Ch 36:5 evil in the s. of the Lord his God 5869
2Ch 36:9 which was evil in the s. of the Lord. ... 5869
2Ch 36:12 evil in the s. of the Lord his God, ... 5869
Ezr 9:9 us in the s. of the kings of Persia, ... 6440

Ne 1:11 him mercy in the s. of this man. 6440
Ne 2:5 servant have found favour in thy s., 6440
Ne 8:5 book in the s. of all the people; 5869
Es 2:15 in the s. of all them that looked 5869
Es 2:17 obtained grace and favour in his s. 6440
Es 5:2 that she obtained favour in his s. 5869
Es 5:8 found favour in the s. of the king, 5869
Es 7:3 have found favour in thy s., O king, 5869
Es 8:5 and if I have found favour in his s. 5869
Job 15:15 the heavens are not clean in his s. 5869
Job 18:3 beasts, and reputed vile in your s.? 5869
Job 19:15 stranger: I am an alien in their s. 5869
Job 21:8 established in their s. with them, 6440
Job 25:5 the stars are not pure in his s. 5869
Job 34:26 wicked men in...open s. of others; 7200
Job 41:9 be cast down even at the s. of him? 4758
Ps 5:5 foolish shall not stand in thy s. 5869
Ps 9:19 the heathen be judged in thy s. 6440
Ps 10:5 are far above out of his s.: as for 5048
Ps 19:14 be acceptable in thy s., O Lord, 6440
Ps 51:4 sinned and done this evil in thy s. 5869
Ps 72:14 precious...their blood be in his s. 5869
Ps 76:7 who may stand in thy s. when once 6440
Ps 78:12 did he in the s. of their fathers, 5048
Ps 79:10 known among the heathen in our s. 5869
Ps 90:4 For a thousand years in thy s. are 5869
Ps 98:2 shewed in the s. of the heathen. 5869
Ps 101:7 telleth lies shall not tarry in my s. 5869
Ps 116:15 Precious in the s. of the Lord is the 5869
Ps 143:2 in thy s. shall no man living be 6440
Pr 1:17 net is spread in the s. of any bird 5869
Pr 3:4 understanding in the s. of God and 5869
Pr 4:3 beloved in the s. of my mother. 6440
Ec 2:26 man that is good in his s. wisdom, 6440
Ec 6:9 Better is the s. of the eyes than 4758
Ec 8:3 Be not hasty to go out of his s. 6440
Ec 11:9 heart, and in the s. of thine eyes: 4758
Isa 5:21 eyes, and prudent in their own s.! 6440
Isa 11:3 not judge after the s. of his eyes, 4758
Isa 26:17 so have we been in thy s., O Lord. 6440
Isa 38:3 done that which is good in thy s. 5869
Isa 43:4 Since thou wast precious in my s., 5869
Jer 4:1 thine abominations out of my s., 6440
Jer 7:15 And I will cast you out of my s., as 6440
Jer 7:30 of Judah have done evil in my s., 5869
Jer 15:1 cast them out of my s., and let 6440
Jer 18:10 If it do evil in my s., that it obey not 5869
Jer 18:23 neither blot...their sin from thy s., 6440
Jer 19:10 break the bottle in...s. of the men 5869
Jer 32:12 in the s. of Hanameel mine uncle's 5869
Jer 34:15 and had done right in my s., 5869
Jer 43:9 in the s. of the men of Judah; 5869
Jer 51:24 they have done in Zion in your s., 5869
Eze 4:12 that cometh out of man, in their s. 5869
Eze 5:8 of thee in the s. of the nations 5869
Eze 5:14 thee, in the s. of all that pass by 5869
Eze 10:2 the city. And he went in in my s. 5869
Eze 10:19 mounted up from the earth in my s. 5869
Eze 12:3 and remove by day in their s.; 5869
Eze 12:3 place to another place in their s. 5869
Eze 12:4 forth thy stuff by day in their s., 5869
Eze 12:4 shalt go forth at even in their s., 5869
Eze 12:5 Dig...through the wall in their s., 5869
Eze 12:6 In their s. shalt thou bear it upon 5869
Eze 12:7 bare it upon my shoulder in their s. 5869
Eze 16:41 upon thee in the s. of many women: 5869
Eze 20:9 in whose s. I made myself known 5869
Eze 20:14 in whose s. I brought them out 5869
Eze 20:22 be polluted in the s. of the heathen, 5869
Eze 20:22 in whose s. I brought them forth 5869
Eze 20:43 lothe yourselves in your own s. 6440
Eze 21:23 as a false divination in their s., 5869
Eze 22:16 in thyself in the s. of the heathen, 5869
Eze 28:18 the s. of all them that behold thee. 5869
Eze 28:25 in them in the s. of the heathen, 5869
Eze 36:31 lothe yourselves in your own s. 6440
Eze 36:34 in the s. of all that passed by. 5869
Eze 39:27 in them in the s. of many nations; 5869
Eze 43:11 and write it in their s., that they 5869
Da 4:11 and the s. thereof to the end of all 2379
Da 4:20 and the s. thereof to all the earth; 2379
Ho 2:2 her whoredoms out of her s., 6440
Ho 2:10 lewdness in the s. of her lovers, 5869
Ho 6:2 us up, and we shall live in his s. 6440
Am 9:3 though they be hid from my s. in 5869
Jon 2:4 Then I said, I am cast out of thy s.; 5869
Mal 2:17 evil is good in the s. of the Lord, 5869
Mt 11:5 **The blind receive their s., and the** *308*
Mt 11:26 **for so it seemed good in thy s.** *1715*
Mt 20:34 immediately their eyes received s., *308*
Mk 10:51 Lord, that I might receive my s. *308*
Mk 10:52 And immediately he received his s., *308*
Lu 1:15 shall be great in the s. of the Lord. *1799*
Lu 4:18 **and recovering of s. to the blind,** *309*
Lu 7:21 many that were blind he gave s. *991*
Lu 10:21 **for so it seemed good in thy s.** *1715*
Lu 15:21 **against heaven, and in thy s.,** *1799*
Lu 16:15 **is abomination in the s. of God.** *1799*
Lu 18:41 Lord, that I may receive my s. *308*
Lu 18:42 Jesus said unto him, **Receive thy s.** *308*
Lu 18:43 And immediately he received his s., *308*
Lu 23:48 that came together to that s., *2335*
Lu 24:31 him; and he vanished out of their s.
Joh 9:11 went and washed, and I received s. *308*
Joh 9:15 him how he had received his s. *308*
Joh 9:18 had been blind, and received his s., *308*
Joh 9:18 parents of him that...received his s. *308*
Ac 1:9 cloud received him out of their s. *3788*
Ac 4:19 Whether it be right in...s. of God *1799*
Ac 7:10 and wisdom in the s. of Pharaoh *1726*
Ac 7:31 saw it, he wondered at the s. *3705*
Ac 8:21 heart is not right in the s. of God. *1799*
Ac 9:9 And he was three days without s., *991*
Ac 9:12 **him, that he might receive his s.** *308*
Ac 9:17 that thou mightest receive thy s., *308*
Ac 9:18 he received s. forthwith, and arose, *308*
Ac 10:31 in remembrance in the s. of God. *1799*
Ac 22:13 me, Brother Saul, receive thy s. *308*
Ro 3:20 shall no flesh be justified in his s. *1799*
Ro 12:17 things honest in the s. of all men. *1799*
2Co 2:17 the s. of God speak we in Christ. *2714*
2Co 4:2 man's conscience in the s. of God. *1799*
2Co 5:7 (For we walk by faith, not by s.:) *1491*
2Co 7:12 care for you in the s. of God might *1799*
2Co 8:21 not only in the s. of the Lord, but *1799*
2Co 8:21 Lord, but also in the s. of men. *1799*
Ga 3:11 by the law in the s. of God, it is *3844*
Col 1:22 and unreproveable in his s.: *2714*
1Th 1:3 in the s. of God and our Father *1715*
1Ti 2:3 in the s. of God our Saviour; *1799*
1Ti 6:13 I give thee charge in the s. of God, *1799*
Heb 4:13 that is not manifest in his s. *1799*
Heb 12:21 And so terrible was the s., that *5324*
Heb 13:21 that which is wellpleasing in his s., *1799*
Jas 4:10 yourselves in the s. of the Lord, *1799*
1Pe 3:4 is in the s. of God of great price. *1799*
1Jo 3:22 things that are pleasing in his s. *1799*
Re 4:3 throne, in s. like unto an emerald. *3706*
Re 13:13 on the earth in the s. of men, *1799*
Re 13:14 power to do in the s. of the beast; *1799*

SIGHTS

Lu 21:11 **fearful s. and great signs shall** *5400*

SIGN See also ENSIGN; SIGNED; SIGNS.

Ex 4:8 hearken to the voice of the first s., 226
Ex 4:8 will believe the voice of the latter s. 226
Ex 8:23 people: to morrow shall this s. be. 226
Ex 13:9 for a s. unto thee upon thine hand, 226
Ex 31:13 for it is a s. between me and you 226
Ex 31:17 a s. between me and the children of 226
Nu 16:38 they shall be a s. unto the children 226
Nu 26:10 fifty men: and they became a s. 5251
De 6:8 bind them for a s. upon thine hand, 226
De 11:18 bind them for a s. upon your hand, 226
De 13:1 and giveth thee a s. or a wonder, 226
De 13:2 the s. or the wonder come to pass, 226
De 28:46 they shall be upon thee for a s. and 226
Jos 4:6 That this may be a s. among you, 226
Jg 6:17 me a s. that thou talkest with me. 226
Jg 20:38 there was an appointed s. between
1Sa 2:34 this shall be a s. unto thee, that 226
1Sa 14:10 hand: and this shall be a s. unto us. 226
1Ki 13:3 he gave a s. the same day, saying, 4159
1Ki 13:3 the s. which the Lord hath spoken; 4159
1Ki 13:5 according to the s. which the man of 4159
2Ki 19:29 And this shall be a s. unto thee, Ye 226
2Ki 20:8 What shall be the s. that the Lord 226
2Ki 20:9 This s. shalt thou have of the Lord. 226
2Ch 32:24 unto him, and he gave him a s. 4159
Isa 7:11 Ask thee a s. of the Lord thy God; 226
Isa 7:14 the Lord himself shall give you a s.; 226
Isa 19:20 it shall be for a s. and for a witness 226
Isa 20:3 s. and wonder upon Egypt and upon 226
Isa 37:30 this shall be a s. unto thee, Ye shall 226
Isa 38:7 this shall be a s. unto thee from the 226
Isa 38:22 What is the s. that I shall go up to 226
Isa 55:13 for an everlasting s. that shall not be 226
Isa 66:19 I will set a s. among them, and I 226
Jer 6:1 up a s. of fire in Beth-haccerem: 4864
Jer 44:29 And this shall be a s. unto you, 226
Eze 4:3 shall be a s. to the house of Israel. 226
Eze 12:6 for a s. unto the house of Israel. 4159
Eze 12:11 Say, I am your s.: like as I have 4159
Eze 14:8 will make him a s. and a proverb, 226
Eze 20:12 to be a s. between me and them, 226
Eze 20:20 shall be a s. between me and you, 226
Eze 24:24 Thus Ezekiel is unto you a s.: 4159
Eze 24:27 and thou shalt be a s. unto them; 4159
Eze 39:15 then shall he set up a s. by it, till 6725
Da 6:8 and s. the writing, that it be not 7560
Mt 12:38 we would see a s. from thee. *4592*
Mt 12:39 **generation seeketh after a s.** *4592*
Mt 12:39 **there shall no s. be given to it,** *4592*
Mt 12:39 **but the s. of the prophet Jonas:** *4592*
Mt 16:1 would shew them a s. from heaven. *4592*
Mt 16:4 **generation seeketh after a s.** *4592*
Mt 16:4 **and there...no s. be given unto it,** *4592*
Mt 16:4 **but the s. of the prophet Jonas** *4592*
Mt 24:3 what shall be the s. of thy coming, *4592*
Mt 24:30 **appear the s. of the Son of man in** *4592*
Mt 26:48 that betrayed him gave them a s., *4592*
Mk 8:11 seeking of him a s. from heaven, *4592*
Mk 8:12 **doth this generation seek after a s.?** *4592*
Mk 8:12 **no s. be given unto this generation.** *4592*
Mk 13:4 what shall be the s. when all these *4592*
Lu 2:12 And this shall be a s. unto you; Ye *4592*
Lu 2:34 and for a s. which shall be spoken *4592*
Lu 11:16 sought of him a s. from heaven. *4592*
Lu 11:29 **an evil generation: they seek a s.** *4592*
Lu 11:29 **and there shall no s. be given it,** *4592*
Lu 11:29 **but the s. of Jonas the prophet** *4592*
Lu 11:30 **Jonas was a s. unto the Ninevites,** *4592*
Lu 21:7 what s. will there be when these *4592*
Joh 2:18 him, What s. shewest thou unto us, *4592*
Joh 6:30 What s. shewest thou then, that we *4592*
Ac 28:11 whose s. was Castor and Pollux. *3902*
Ro 4:11 he received the s. of circumcision, *4592*
1Co 1:22 For the Jews require a s., and the *4592*
1Co 14:22 Wherefore tongues are for a s., *4592*
Re 15:1 I saw another s. in heaven, great *4592*

SIGNED See also ASSIGNED.

Da 6:9 king Darius s. the writing and the 7560
Da 6:10 Daniel knew that the writing was s., 7560
Da 6:12 Hast thou not s. a decree, that 7560
Da 6:13 nor the decree that thou hast s., but 7560

SIGNET See also SIGNETS.

Ge 38:18 Thy s., and thy bracelets, and thy 2368
Ge 38:25 the s., and bracelets, and staff. 2858
Ex 28:11 stone, like the engravings of a s., 2368
Ex 28:21 names, like the engravings of a s.; 2368
Ex 28:36 upon it, like the engravings of a s., 2368
Ex 39:14 names, like the engravings of a s., 2368
Ex 39:30 like to the engravings of a s., 2368
Jer 22:24 were the s. upon my right hand, 2368
Da 6:17 the king sealed it with his own s., 5824
Da 6:17 and with the s. of his lords; that the 5824
Hag 2:23 Lord, and will make thee as a s. 2368

SIGNETS

Ex 39:6 of gold, graven, as s. are graven 2368

SIGNIFICATION

1Co 14:10 and none of them is without s. *880*

SIGNIFIED

Ac 11:28 s. by the spirit that there should be *4591*
Re 1:1 s. it by his angel unto his servant *4591*

SIGNIFIETH

Heb 12:27 s. the removing of those things *1218*

SIGNIFY See also SIGNIFIED; SIGNIFIETH; SIGNIFYING.

Ac 21:26 to s. the accomplishment of the *1229*
Ac 23:15 the council s. to the chief captain *1718*
Ac 25:27 to s. the crimes laid against him *4591*
1Pe 1:11 of Christ which was in them s. *1213*

SIGNIFYING

Joh 12:33 said, s. what death he should die, *4591*
Joh 18:32 spake, s. what death he should die. *4591*

Joh 21:19 s. by what death he should glorify...... *4591*
Heb 9:8 The Holy Ghost this s., that the........ *1213*

SIGNS See also ENSIGNS.
Ge 1:14 let them be for s. and for seasons,....... 226
Ex 4:9 will not believe also these two s.,........ 226
Ex 4:17 hand, wherewith thou shalt do s.......... 226
Ex 4:28 all the s. which he had commanded...... 226
Ex 4:30 did the s. in the sight of the people...... 226
Ex 7:3 my s. and my wonders in the land of.... 226
Ex 10:1 might shew these my s. before him:..... 226
Ex 10:2 and my s. which I have done among..... 226
Nu 14:11 for all the s. which I have shewed........ 226
De 4:34 by s., and by wonders, and by war,..... 226
De 6:22 the Lord shewed s. and wonders,........ 226
De 7:19 and the s., and the wonders, and the.... 226
De 26:8 and with s., and with wonders:........... 226
De 29:3 the s. and those great miracles:........... 226
De 34:11 In all the s. and the wonders, which..... 226
Jos 24:17 which did those great s. in our sight,.... 226
1Sa 10:7 when these s. are come unto thee,...... 226
1Sa 10:9 all those s. came to pass that day........ 226
Ne 9:10 s. and wonders upon Pharaoh and....... 226
Ps 74:4 they set up their ensigns for s........... 226
Ps 74:9 We see not our s.: there is no more.... 226
Ps 78:43 How he had wrought his s. in Egypt,.... 226
Ps 105:27 shewed his s. among them.......... 1697,226
Isa 8:18 are for s. and for wonders in Israel...... 226
Jer 10:2 not dismayed at the s. of heaven;........ 226
Jer 32:20 hast set s. and wonders in the land...... 226
Jer 32:21 out of the land of Egypt with s., and.... 226
Da 4:2 I thought it good to shew the s. and..... 852
Da 4:3 How great are his s.! and how........... 852
Da 6:27 and he worketh s. and wonders in......... 852
Mt 16:3 **ye not discern the s. of the times?**. *4592*
Mt 24:24 **shall shew great s. and wonders;**... *4592*
Mk 13:22 **and shall shew s. and wonders, to**..*4592*
Mk 16:17 **And these s. shall follow them that** *4592*
Mk 16:20 and confirming the word with s.......... *4592*
Lu 1:62 they made s. to his father, how he..... *1770*
Lu 21:11 **s. shall there be from heaven**........ *4592*
Lu 21:25 **And there shall be s. in the sun,**... *4592*
Joh 4:48 **Except ye see s. and wonders, ye**... *4592*
Joh 20:30 many other s. truly did Jesus in the.... *4592*
Ac 2:19 above, and s. in the earth beneath;..... *4592*
Ac 2:22 by miracles and wonders and s.,........ *4592*
Ac 2:43 wonders and s. were done by the....... *4592*
Ac 4:30 that s. and wonders may be done by... *4592*
Ac 5:12 were many s. and wonders wrought.... *4592*
Ac 7:36 shewed wonders and s. in the land..... *4592*
Ac 8:13 mircles and s. which were done......... *4592*
Ac 14:3 granted s. and wonders to be done..... *4592*
Ro 15:19 Through mighty s. and wonders, by.... *4592*
2Co 12:12 Truly the s. of an apostle were.......... *4592*
2Co 12:12 in s., and wonders, and mighty.......... *4592*
2Th 2:9 of Satan with all power and s. and...... *4592*
Heb 2:4 witness, both with s. and wonders,..... *4592*

SIHON (si'-hon)
Nu 21:21 Israel sent messengers unto S.,......... 5511
Nu 21:23 S. would not suffer Israel to pass....... 5511
Nu 21:23 but S. gathered all his people............ 5511
Nu 21:26 For Heshbon was the city of S. the.... 5511
Nu 21:27 city of S. be built and prepared:......... 5511
Nu 21:28 a flame from the city of S.: it hath..... 5511
Nu 21:29 into captivity unto S. king of the........ 5511
Nu 21:34 him as thou didst unto S. king of......... 5511
Nu 32:33 kingdom of S. king of the Amorites,.... 5511
De 1:4 After he had slain S. the king of........ 5511
De 2:24 into thine hand S. the Amorite,.......... 5511
De 2:26 wilderness of Kedemoth unto S.......... 5511
De 2:30 S. king of Heshbon would not let us... 5511
De 2:31 have begun to give S. and his land..... 5511
De 2:32 Then S. came out against us, he........ 5511
De 3:2 as thou didst unto S. king of the........ 5511
De 3:6 as we did unto S. king of Heshbon,.... 5511
De 4:46 land of S. king of the Amorites,......... 5511
De 29:7 this place, S. the king of Heshbon,...... 5511
De 31:4 shall do unto them as he did to S....... 5511
Jos 2:10 the other side Jordan, S. and Og,....... 5511
Jos 9:10 to S. king of Heshbon, and to Og....... 5511
Jos 12:2 S. king of the Amorites, who dwelt.... 5511
Jos 12:5 the border of S. king of Heshbon......... 5511
Jos 13:10 cities of S. king of the Amorites,........ 5511
Jos 13:21 all the kingdom of S. king of the........ 5511
Jos 13:21 which were dukes of S., dwelling........ 5511
Jos 13:27 kingdom of S. king of Heshbon,......... 5511
Jg 11:19 Israel sent messengers unto S........... 5511
Jg 11:20 But S. trusted not Israel to pass....... 5511
Jg 11:20 S. gathered all his people together....... 5511
Jg 11:21 Lord God of Israel delivered S. and.... 5511
1Ki 4:19 country of S. king of the Amorites,..... 5511
Ne 9:22 So they possessed the land of S.,........ 5511
Ps 135:11 S. king of the Amorites, and Og........ 5511
Ps 136:19 S. king of the Amorites: for his......... 5511
Jer 43:45 and a flame from the midst of S.,....... 5511

SIHOR (si'-hor) See also SHIHOR.
Jos 13:3 From S., which is before Egypt,........ 7883
Isa 23:3 And by great waters the seed of S.,... 7883
Jer 2:18 Egypt, to drink the waters of S.?....... 7883

SILAS (si'-las) See also SILVANUS.
Ac 15:22 Barsabas....S., chief men among........ *4609*
Ac 15:27 have sent therefore Judas and S.,....... *4609*
Ac 15:32 Judas and S., being prophets also....... *4609*
Ac 15:34 it pleased S. to abide there still......... *4609*
Ac 15:40 And Paul chose S., and departed,....... *4609*
Ac 16:19 they caught Paul and S., and drew..... *4609*
Ac 16:25 at midnight Paul and S. prayed,......... *4609*
Ac 16:29 and fell down before Paul and S.,....... *4609*
Ac 17:4 and consorted with Paul and S.;......... *4609*
Ac 17:10 sent away Paul and S. by night......... *4609*
Ac 17:14 but S. and Timotheus abode there....... *4609*
Ac 17:15 receiving a commandment unto S....... *4609*
Ac 18:5 when S. and Timotheus were come.... *4609*

SILENCE
Jg 3:19 thee, O king: who said, Keep s.......... 2013
Job 4:16 there was s., and I heard a voice,...... 1827
Job 29:21 waited, and kept s. at my counsel...... 1826
Job 31:34 that I kept s., and went not out of..... 1826
Ps 31:18 Let the lying lips be put to s.;............. 481
Ps 32:3 When I kept s., my bones waxed....... 2790
Ps 35:22 keep not s.: O Lord, be not far.......... 2790
Ps 39:2 I was dumb with s., I held my........... 1747
Ps 50:3 shall come, and shall not keep s......... 2790
Ps 50:21 hast thou done, and I kept s.;............ 2790
Ps 83:1 Keep not thou s., O God: hold not..... 1824
Ps 94:17 my soul had almost dwelt in s............ 1745
Ps 115:17 neither any that go down into s.......... 1745
Ec 3:7 a time to keep s., and a time to.......... 2814
Isa 15:1 is laid waste, and brought to s.;......... 1820
Isa 41:1 Keep s. before me, O islands; and...... 2790
Isa 62:6 mention of the Lord, keep not s.......... 1824
Isa 65:6 I will not keep s., but will............... 2814
Jer 8:14 the Lord our God hath put us to s.,..... 1826
La 2:10 sit upon the ground, and keep s.......... 1826
La 3:28 He sitteth alone and keepeth s.,.......... 1826
Am 5:13 Therefore the prudent shall keep s..... 1826
Am 8:3 shall cast them forth with s............. 2013
Hab 2:20 temple: let all the earth keep s.......... 2013
Mt 22:34 he had put the Sadducees to s........... *5892*
Ac 15:12 Then all the multitude kept s.,........... *4601*
Ac 21:40 when there was made a great s.,........ *4602*
Ac 22:2 to them, they kept the more s........... *2271*
1Co 14:28 let him keep s. in the church; and....... *4601*
1Co 14:34 Let your women keep s. in the.......... *4601*
1Ti 2:11 Let the woman learn in s. with all...... *2771*
1Ti 2:12 over the man, but to be in s............. *2771*
1Pe 2:15 put to s. the ignorance of foolish....... *5392*
Re 8:1 there was s. in heaven about the......... *4602*

SILENT
1Sa 2:9 the wicked shall be s. in darkness;..... 1826
Ps 22:2 in the night season, and am not s....... 1747
Ps 28:1 O Lord my rock; be not s. to me:....... 2790
Ps 28:1 lest, if thou be s. to me, I become..... 2790
Ps 30:12 sing praise to thee and not be s......... 1826
Ps 31:17 and let them be s. in the grave.......... 1826
Isa 47:5 Sit thou s., and get thee into............. 1748
Jer 8:14 cities, and let us be s. there; for......... 1826
Zec 2:13 Be s., O all flesh, before the Lord:..... 2013

SILK
Pr 31:22 her clothing is s. and purple............. 8336
Eze 16:10 linen, and I covered thee with s......... 4897
Eze 16:13 raiment was of fine linen, and s.,........ 4897
Re 18:12 and purple, and s. and scarlet,........... *2596*

SILLA (sil'-lah)
2Ki 12:20 Millo, which goeth down to S........... 5538

SILLY
Job 5:2 man and envy slayeth the s. one........ 6601
Ho 7:11 Ephraim also is like a s. dove............ 6601
2Ti 3:6 lead captive s. women laden with....... *1133*

SILOAH (si-lo'-ah) See also SHILOAH; SILOAM.
Ne 3:15 the wall of the pool of S. by the......... 7975

SILOAM (si-lo'-am) See also SILOAH.
Lu 13:4 **upon whom the tower in S. fell,**.... *4611*
Joh 9:7 **him, Go, wash in the pool of S.,**.... *4611*
Joh 9:11 said unto me, Go to the pool of S.,.... *4611*

SILVANUS (sil-va'-nus) See also SILAS.
2Co 1:19 even by me and S. and Timotheus...... *4610*
1Th 1:1 Paul, and S., and Timotheus, unto...... *4610*
2Th 1:1 Paul, and S., and Timotheus, unto...... *4610*
1Pe 5:12 By S., a faithful brother unto you,...... *4610*

SILVER See also SILVERLINGS; SILVERSMITH.
Ge 13:2 was very rich in cattle, in s., and....... 3701
Ge 20:16 thy brother a thousand pieces of s...... 3701
Ge 23:15 worth four hundred shekels of s.;........ 3701
Ge 23:16 Abraham weighed to Ephron the s.,.... 3701
Ge 23:16 four hundred shekels of s., current..... 3701
Ge 24:35 given him flocks, and heards, and s.,... 3701
Ge 24:53 servants brought forth jewels of s.,..... 3701
Ge 37:28 Ishmeelites for twenty pieces of s....... 3701
Ge 44:2 the s. cup, in the sack's mouth of......... 3701
Ge 44:8 we steal out of thy lord's house s. or.. 3701
Ge 45:22 he gave three hundred pieces of s.,.... 3701
Ex 3:22 in her house, jewels of s., and........... 3701
Ex 11:2 of her neighbour, jewels of s., and...... 3701
Ex 12:35 of the Egyptians jewels of s., and........ 3701
Ex 20:23 shall not make with me gods of s.,..... 3701
Ex 21:32 their master thirty shekels of s.,......... 3701
Ex 25:3 of them; gold, and s., and brass,......... 3701
Ex 26:19 forty sockets of s. under the twenty... 3701
Ex 26:21 And their forty sockets of s.; two........ 3701
Ex 26:25 boards, and their sockets of s.,........... 3701
Ex 26:32 gold, upon the four sockets of s.......... 3701
Ex 27:10 pillars and their fillets shall be of s.,.... 3701
Ex 27:11 the pillars and their fillets of s........... 3701
Ex 27:17 the court shall be filleted with s.;........ 3701
Ex 27:17 their hooks shall be of s., and their..... 3701
Ex 31:4 to work in gold, and in s., and in......... 3701
Ex 35:5 the Lord; gold, and s., and brass,....... 3701
Ex 35:24 offer an offering of s. and brass.......... 3701
Ex 35:32 to work in gold, and in s., and in....... 3701
Ex 36:24 forty sockets of s. he made under....... 3701
Ex 36:26 And their forty sockets of s.: two........ 3701
Ex 36:30 sockets were sixteen sockets of s.,..... 3701
Ex 36:36 he cast for them four sockets of s....... 3701
Ex 38:10 pillars and their fillets were of s........ 3701
Ex 38:11, 12 pillars and their fillets of s........... 3701
Ex 38:17 the pillars and their fillets of s........... 3701
Ex 38:17 overlaying of their chapiters of s.;...... 3701
Ex 38:17 of the court were filleted with s......... 3701
Ex 38:19 their hooks of s., and the overlaying... 3701
Ex 38:19 their chapiters and their fillets of s..... 3701
Ex 38:25 the s. of them that were numbered..... 3701
Ex 38:27 the hundred talents of s. were cast..... 3701
Le 5:15 with thy estimation by shekels of s.,... 3701
Le 27:3 estimation shall be fifty shekels of s.,.. 3701
Le 27:6 be of the male five shekels of s.......... 3701
Le 27:6 for the female...three shekels of s...... 3701
Le 27:16 be valued at fifty shekels of s............ 3701
Nu 7:13 And his offering was one s. charger.... 3701
Nu 7:13 one s. bowl of seventy shekels.......... 3701
Nu 7:19 for his offering one s. charger,.......... 3701
Nu 7:19 one s. bowl of seventy shekels,.......... 3701
Nu 7:25 His offering was one s. charger,......... 3701
Nu 7:25 one s. bowl of seventy shekels,.......... 3701
Nu 7:31 His offering was one s. charger of....... 3701
Nu 7:31 one s. bowl of seventy shekels,.......... 3701
Nu 7:37 His offering was one s. charger,......... 3701
Nu 7:37 one s. bowl of seventy shekels,.......... 3701
Nu 7:43 His offering was one s. charger of....... 3701
Nu 7:43 a s. bowl of seventy shekels, after...... 3701
Nu 7:49 His offering was one s. charger.......... 3701
Nu 7:49 one s. bowl of seventy shekels,.......... 3701
Nu 7:55 His offering was one s. charge of........ 3701
Nu 7:55 one s. bowl of seventy shekels,.......... 3701
Nu 7:61 His offering was one s. charger,......... 3701
Nu 7:61 one s. bowl of seventy shekels,.......... 3701
Nu 7:67 His offering was one s. charger,......... 3701
Nu 7:67 one s. bowl of seventy shekels,.......... 3701
Nu 7:73 His offering was one s. charger,......... 3701
Nu 7:73 one s. bowl of seventy shekels,.......... 3701
Nu 7:79 His offering was one s. charger,......... 3701
Nu 7:79 one s. bowl of seventy shekels,.......... 3701
Nu 7:84 chargers of s., twelve s. bowls,.......... 3701
Nu 7:85 Each charger of s. weighing an.......... 3701

Nu	7:85	s. vessels weighed two thousand	3701
Nu	10:2	Make thee two trumpets of s.; of a	3701
Nu	22:18	give me his house full of s. and gold,	3701
Nu	24:13	give me his house full of s. and gold,	3701
Nu	31:22	Only the gold, and the s., the brass,	3701
De	7:25	thou shalt not desire the s. or gold	3701
De	8:13	thy s. and thy gold is multiplied,	3701
De	17:17	multiply to himself s. and gold.	3701
De	22:19	him in an hundred shekels of s.,	3701
De	22:29	damsel's father fifty shekels of s.,	3701
De	29:17	idols, wood, and stone, s. and gold.	3701
Jos	6:19	But all the s., and gold, and vessels	3701
Jos	6:24	only the s., and the gold, and the	3701
Jos	7:21	and two hundred shekels of s., and	3701
Jos	7:21	midst of my tent, and the s. under it.	3701
Jos	7:22	hid in his tent, and the s. under it.	3701
Jos	7:24	and the s., and the garment, and the	3701
Jos	22:8	with s., and with gold, and with	3701
Jos	24:32	for an hundred pieces of s.:	7192
Jg	9:4	him threescore and ten pieces of s.	3701
Jg	16:5	of us eleven hundred pieces of s..	3701
Jg	17:2	The eleven hundred shekels of s.	3701
Jg	17:2	mine ears, behold, the s. is with me;	3701
Jg	17:3	the eleven hundred shekels of s.	3701
Jg	17:3	dedicated the s. unto the Lord	3701
Jg	17:4	took two hundred shekels of s.,	3701
Jg	17:10	and I will give thee ten shekels of s.	3701
1Sa	2:36	and crouch to him for a piece of s.	3701
1Sa	9:8	the fourth part of a shekel of s.:	3701
2Sa	8:10	brought with him vessels of s.,	3701
2Sa	8:11	s. and gold that he had dedicated	3701
2Sa	18:11	have given thee ten shekels of s.,	3701
2Sa	18:12	receive a thousand shekels of s. in	3701
2Sa	21:4	We will have no s. nor gold of Saul,	3701
2Sa	24:24	and the oxen for fifty shekels of s..	3701
1Ki	7:51	even the s., and the gold, and the	3701
1Ki	10:21	were of pure gold; none were of s.	3701
1Ki	10:22	bringing gold, and s., ivory, and	3701
1Ki	10:25	vessels of s., and vessels of gold,	3701
1Ki	10:27	s. to be in Jerusalem as stones,	3701
1Ki	10:29	for six hundred shekels of s. and	3701
1Ki	15:15	into the house of the Lord, s., and	3701
1Ki	15:18	Asa took all the s. and the gold	3701
1Ki	15:19	unto thee a present of s. and gold;	3701
1Ki	16:24	of Shemer for the two talents of s.,	3701
1Ki	20:3	Thy s. and they gold is mine; thy	3701
1Ki	20:5	Thou shalt deliver me thy s., and	3701
1Ki	20:7	and for my s., and for my gold;	3701
1Ki	20:39	or else thou shalt pay a talent of s.	3701
2Ki	5:5	and took with him ten talents of s..	3701
2Ki	5:22	give them, I pray thee, a talent of s.,	3701
2Ki	5:23	bound two talents of s. in two bags,	3701
2Ki	6:25	was sold for fourscore pieces of s.	3701
2Ki	6:25	of dove's dung for five pieces of s..	3701
2Ki	7:8	and carried thence s., and gold, and	3701
2Ki	12:13	the house of the Lord bowls of s.,	3701
2Ki	12:13	any vessels of gold, or vessels of s.	3701
2Ki	14:14	And he took all the gold and s., and	3701
2Ki	15:19	gave Pul a thousand talents of s.,	3701
2Ki	15:20	of each man fifty shekels of s., to	3701
2Ki	16:8	Ahaz took the s. and gold that was	3701
2Ki	18:14	Judah three hundred talents of s.	3701
2Ki	18:15	Hezekiah gave him all the s. that	3701
2Ki	20:13	the s. and the gold, and the spices,	3701
2Ki	22:4	may sum the s. which is brought	3701
2Ki	23:33	tribute of an hundred talents of s.,	3701
2Ki	23:35	Jehoiakim gave the s. and the gold	3701
2Ki	23:35	he exacted the s. and the gold of the	3701
2Ki	25:15	were of gold, in gold, and of s., in s.,	3701
1Ch	18:10	all manner of vessels of gold and s.	3701
1Ch	18:11	s. and the gold that he brought	3701
1Ch	19:6	sent a thousand talents of s. to hire	3701
1Ch	22:14	a thousand thousand talents of s.:	3701
1Ch	22:16	Of the gold, the s., and the brass,	3701
1Ch	28:14	of all manner of service; s. also	
1Ch	28:14	for all instruments of s. by weight	3701
1Ch	28:15	for the candlesticks of s. by weight,	3701
1Ch	28:16	and likewise s. for the tables of s.:	3701
1Ch	28:17	for every bason; and likewise s.	
1Ch	28:17	by weight for every bason of s.:	3701
1Ch	29:2	of gold, and the s. for things of s.,	3701
1Ch	29:3	own proper good, of gold and s.,	3701
1Ch	29:4	seven thousand talents of refined s.,	3701
1Ch	29:5	of gold, and the s. for things of s.,	3701
1Ch	29:7	and of s. ten thousand talents, and	3701
2Ch	1:15	made s. and gold...as plenteous	3701
2Ch	1:17	for six hundred shekels of s., and	3701
2Ch	2:7	cunning to work in gold, and in s.,	3701
2Ch	2:14	skilful to work in gold, and in s.,	3701
2Ch	5:1	and the s., and the gold, and all the	3701
2Ch	9:14	brought gold and s. to Solomon.	3701
2Ch	9:20	were of pure gold: none were of s.;	3701
2Ch	9:21	bringing gold, and s., ivory, and	3701
2Ch	9:24	vessels of s., and vessels of gold,	3701
2Ch	9:27	made s. in Jerusalem as stones,	3701
2Ch	15:18	dedicated, s., and gold, and vessels.	3701
2Ch	16:2	Asa brought out s. and gold out of	3701
2Ch	16:3	behold, I have sent thee s. and gold;	3701
2Ch	17:11	brought...presents, and tribute s.;	3701
2Ch	21:3	father gave them great gifts of s.,	3701
2Ch	24:14	spoons, vessels of gold and s.	3701
2Ch	25:6	Israel for an hundred talents of s.	3701
2Ch	25:24	And he took all the gold and the s.,	3701
2Ch	27:5	same year an hundred talents of s.,	3701
2Ch	32:27	he made himself treasures for s.,	3701
2Ch	36:3	the land in an hundred talents of s.	3701
Ezr	1:4	men of his place help him with s.	3701
Ezr	3:6	hands with vessels of s., with gold,	3701
Ezr	3:9	of gold, a thousand chargers of s.,	3701
Ezr	3:10	s. basons of a second sort four	3701
Ezr	3:11	All the vessels of gold and of s.	3701
Ezr	2:69	and five thousand pound of s.,	3701
Ezr	5:14	And the vessels also of gold and s.	3702
Ezr	6:5	also let the golden and s. vessels	3702
Ezr	7:15	And to carry the s. and gold, which	3702
Ezr	7:16	all the s. and gold that thou canst	3702
Ezr	7:18	with the rest of the s. and the gold,	3702
Ezr	7:22	Unto an hundred talents of s., and	3702
Ezr	8:25	And weighed unto them the s.,	3701
Ezr	8:26	six hundred and fifty talents of s.,	3701
Ezr	8:26	and s. vessels an hundred talents,	3701
Ezr	8:28	the s. and the gold are a freewill	3701
Ezr	8:30	the weight of the s., and the gold,	3701
Ezr	8:33	was the s. and the gold...weighed	3701
Ne	5:15	and wine, beside forty shekels of s.;	3701
Ne	7:71	and two hundred pound of s..	3701
Ne	7:72	gold, and two thousand pound of s.,	3701
Es	1:6	to s. rings and pillars of marble:	3701
Es	1:6	the beds were of gold and s., upon	3701
Es	3:9	I will pay ten thousand talents of s.	3701
Es	3:11	s. is given to thee, the people also,	3701
Job	3:15	who filled their houses with s.:	3701
Job	22:25	and thou shalt have plenty of s..	3701
Job	27:16	Though he heap up s. as the dust,	3701
Job	27:17	and the innocent shall divide the s..	3701
Job	28:1	Surely there is a vein for the s.,	3701
Job	28:15	s. be weighed for the price thereof.	3701
Ps	12:6	as s. tried in a furnace of earth,	3701
Ps	66:10	thou hast tried us, as s. is tried.	3701
Ps	68:13	the wings of a dove covered with s.,	3701
Ps	68:30	submit himself with pieces of s.:	3701
Ps	105:37	He brought them forth also with s.	3701
Ps	115:4	Their idols are s. and gold, the work	3701
Ps	119:72	me than thousands of gold and s..	3701
Ps	135:15	idols of the heathen are s. and gold,	3701
Pr	2:4	If thou seekest her as s., and	3701
Pr	3:14	is better than the merchandise of s.,	3701
Pr	8:10	Receive my instruction, and not s.;	3701
Pr	8:19	and my revenue than choice s.	3701
Pr	10:20	tongue of the just is as choice s.:	3701
Pr	16:16	rather to be chosen than s.!	3701
Pr	17:3	fining pot is for s., and the furnace	3701
Pr	22:1	and loving favour rather than s. and	3701
Pr	25:4	Take away the dross from the s.,	3701
Pr	25:11	like apples of gold in pictures of s.	3701
Pr	26:23	a potsherd covered with s. dross.	3701
Pr	27:21	fining pot for s., and the furance	3701
Ec	2:8	I gathered me also s. and gold, and	3701
Ec	5:10	He that loveth s. shall not be	3701
Ec	5:10	shall not be satisfied with s.;	3701
Ec	12:6	Or ever the s. cord be loosed, or the	3701
Ca	1:11	borders of gold with studs of s..	3701
Ca	3:10	He made the pillars thereof of s.,	3701
Ca	8:9	will build upon her a palace of s.;	3701
Ca	8:11	was to bring a thousand pieces of s..	3701
Isa	1:22	Thy s. is become dross, thy wine	3701
Isa	2:7	Their land also is full of s. and gold,	3701
Isa	2:20	day a man shall cast his idols of s.,	3701
Isa	13:17	Medes...which shall not regard s.;	3701
Isa	30:22	covering of thy graven images of s.,	3701
Isa	31:7	man shall cast away his idols of s.,	3701
Isa	39:2	the s., and the gold, and the spices,	3701
Isa	40:19	with gold, and casteth s. chains.	3701
Isa	46:6	and weigh s. in the balance, and	3701
Isa	48:10	I have refined thee, but not with s.;	3701
Isa	60:9	their s. and their gold with them,	3701
Isa	60:17	and for iron I will bring s., and for	3701
Jer	6:30	Reprobate s. shall men call them,	3701
Jer	10:4	They deck it with s. and with gold;	3701
Jer	10:9	S. spread into plates is brought	3701
Jer	32:9	even seventeen shekels of s.	3701
Jer	52:19	gold, and that which was of s. in s.,	3701
Eze	7:19	shall cast their s. in the streets,	3701
Eze	7:19	their s. and their gold shall not be	3701
Eze	16:13	wast thou decked with gold and s.;	3701
Eze	16:17	fair jewels of my gold and of my s.,	3701
Eze	22:18	they are even the dross of s..	3701
Eze	22:20	they gather s., and brass, and iron,	3701
Eze	22:22	As s. is melted in the midst of the	3701
Eze	27:12	with s., iron, tin, and lead, they	3701
Eze	28:4	gold and s. into thy treasures:	3701
Eze	38:13	to carry away s. and gold, to take	3701
Da	2:32	gold, his breast and his arms of s.,	3702
Da	2:35	clay, the brass, the s., and the gold,	3702
Da	2:45	brass, the clay, the s., and the gold;	3702
Da	5:2	to bring the golden and s. vessels	3702
Da	5:4	praised the gods of gold, and of s.,	3702
Da	5:23	thou hast praised the gods of s.,	3702
Da	11:8	with their precious vessels of s.	3701
Da	11:38	shall he honour with gold, and s.,	3701
Da	11:43	the treasures of gold and of s., and	3701
Ho	2:8	and multiplied her s. and gold,	3701
Ho	3:2	her to me for fifteen pieces of s.,	3701
Ho	8:4	of their s. and their gold have they	3701
Ho	9:6	pleasant places for their s., nettles	3701
Ho	13:2	them molten images of their s., and	3701
Joe	3:5	ye have taken my s. and my gold,	3701
Am	2:6	they sold the righteous for s., and	3701
Am	8:6	That we may buy the poor for s.,	3701
Na	2:9	Take ye the spoil of s., take the	3701
Hab	2:19	it is laid over the gold and s., and	3701
Zep	1:11	all they that bear s. are cut off:	3701
Zep	1:18	Neither their s. nor their gold shall	3701
Hag	2:8	s. is mine, and the gold is mine,	3701
Zec	6:11	Then take s. and gold, and make	3701
Zec	9:3	heaped up s. as the dust, and fine	3701
Zec	11:12	for my price thirty pieces of s..	3701
Zec	11:13	I took the thirty pieces of s., and	3701
Zec	13:9	and will refine them as s. is refined,	3701
Zec	14:14	together, gold, and s., and apparel,	3701
Mal	3:3	sit as a refiner and purifier of s.:	3701
Mal	3:3	and purge them as gold and s.,	3701
Mt	10:9	**neither gold, nor s., nor brass in**	*696*
Mt	26:15	with him for thirty pieces of s.	*694*
Mt	27:3	the thirty pieces of s. to the chief	*694*
Mt	27:5	he cast down the pieces of s. in the	*694*
Mt	27:6	the chief priests took the s. pieces,	*694*
Mt	27:9	took the thirty pieces of s., the price	*694*
Lu	15:8	**what woman having ten pieces...s.,**	*1406*
Ac	3:6	said, S. and gold have I none; but	*694*
Ac	17:29	the Godhead is like unto gold, or s.,	*696*
Ac	19:19	found it fifty thousand pieces of s.	*694*
Ac	19:24	which make s. shrines for Diana,	*693*
Ac	20:33	I have coveted no man's s., or gold,	*694*
1Co	3:12	this foundation gold, s., precious	*696*
2Ti	2:20	not only vessels of gold and of s.,	*693*
Jas	5:3	Your gold and s. is cankered; and	*696*
1Pe	1:18	corruptible things, as s. and gold,	*694*
Re	9:20	devils, and idols of gold, and s., and	*693*
Re	18:12	The merchandise of gold, and s.,	*696*

SILVERLINGS

Isa	7:23	a thousand vines at a thousand s.,	3701

SILVERSMITH

Ac	19:24	certain man named Demetrius, a s.,	*695*

SIMEON (sim'-e-un) See also SHIMEON; SIMEONITES; SIMON.

Ge	29:33	also; and she called his name S.	8095
Ge	34:25	of the sons of Jacob, S. and Levi,	8095
Ge	34:30	And Jacob said to S. and Levi, Ye	8095
Ge	35:23	and S., and Levi, and Judah, and	8095
Ge	42:24	and took from them S., and bound	8095
Ge	42:36	Joseph is not, and S. is not, and ye	8095
Ge	43:23	And he brought S. out unto them.	8095
Ge	46:10	And the sons of S.; Jemuel, and	8095
Ge	48:5	as Reuben and S., they shall be	8095
Ge	49:5	S. and Levi are brethren;	8095
Ex	1:2	Reuben, S., Levi, and Judah,	8095
Ex	6:15	And the sons of S.; Jemuel, and	8095
Ex	6:15	woman; these are the families of S..	8095
Nu	1:6	of S.; Shelumiel the son of	8095

Nu 1:22 Of the children of **S.**, by their 8095
Nu 1:23 even of the tribe of **S.**, were fifty 8095
Nu 2:12 by him shall be the tribe of **S.**; 8095
Nu 2:12 captain of the children of **S.** shall 8095
Nu 7:36 prince of the children of **S.**, did 8095
Nu 10:19 of the tribe of the children of **S.** 8095
Nu 13:5 Of the tribe of **S.**, Shaphat the son 8095
Nu 26:12 The sons of **S.** after their families: 8095
Nu 34:20 of the tribe of the children of **S.**, 8095
De 27:12 **S.**, and Levi, and Judah, and 8095
Jos 19:1 the second lot came forth to **S.**, 8095
Jos 19:1, 8 children of **S.** according to their 8095
Jos 19:9 inheritance of the children of **S.**: 8095
Jos 19:9 children of **S.** had their inheritance 8095
Jos 21:4 and out of the tribe of **S.**, and out 8099
Jos 21:9 of the tribe of the children of **S.**, 8095
Jg 1:3 Judah said unto **S.** his brother, 8095
Jg 1:3 into thy lot. So **S.** went with him. 8095
Jg 1:17 Judah went with **S.** his brother, 8095
1Ch 2:1 Reuben, **S.**, Levi, and Judah, 8095
1Ch 4:24 The sons of **S.** were, Nemuel, and 8095
1Ch 4:42 even of the sons of S, five hundred 8095
1Ch 6:65 of the tribe of the children of **S.**, 8095
1Ch 12:25 Of the children of **S.**, mighty men 8095
2Ch 15:9 Ephraim and Manasseh...out of **S.** 8095
2Ch 34:6 and **S.**, even unto Naphtali, with 8095
Eze 48:24 west side, **S.** shall have a portion. 8095
Eze 48:25 by the border of **S.**, from the east 8095
Eze 48:33 one gate of **S.**, one gate of 8095
Lu 2:25 Jerusalem, whose name was **S.**; *4826*
Lu 2:34 And **S.** bless them, and said unto *4826*
Lu 3:30 Which was the son of **S.**, which was *4826*
Ac 13:1 and **S.** that was called Niger, and *4826*
Ac 15:14 **S.** hath declared how God at the *4826*
Re 7:7 the tribe of **S.** were sealed twelve *4826*

SIMEONITES (sim'-e-un-ites)
Nu 25:14 of a chief house among the **S.** 8099
Nu 26:14 These are the families of the **S.**, 8099
1Ch 27:16 of the **S.**, Shephatiah the son 8099

SIMILITUDE See also SIMILITUDES.
Nu 12:8 the **s.** of the Lord shall he behold: 8544
De 4:12 voice of the words, but saw no **s.**; 8544
De 4:15 ye saw no manner of **s.** on the day 8544
De 4:16 the **s.** of any figure, the likeness of 8544
2Ch 4:3 under it was the **s.** of oxen, which 1823
Ps 106:20 their glory into the **s.** of an ox 8403
Ps 144:12 polished after the **s.** of a palace: 8403
Da 10:16 **s.** of the sons of men touched my 1823
Ro 5:14 the **s.** of Adam's transgression. *3667*
Heb 7:15 the **s.** of Melchisedec there ariseth *3665*
Jas 8:9 are made after the **s.** of God. *3669*

SIMILITUDES
Ho 12:10 and used **s.**, by the ministry of the 1819

SIMON (si'-mun) See also BAR-JONA; NIGER; PETER; SIMEON; SIMON'S; ZELOTES.
Mt 4:18 **S.** called Peter, and Andrew his *4613*
Mt 10:2 The first, **S.**, who is called Peter, *4613*
Mt 10:4 **S.** the Canaanite, and Judas *4613*
Mt 13:55 and Joses, and **S.**, and Judas? *4613*
Mt 16:16 **S.** Peter answered and said, Thou *4613*
Mt 16:17 **Blessed are thou, S. Bar-jona; for** *4613*
Mt 17:25 **What thinkest thou, S.? of whom** *4613*
Mt 26:6 in the house of **S.** the leper, *4613*
Mt 27:32 a man of Cyrene, **S.** by name: him *4613*
Mk 1:16 he saw **S.** and Andrew his brother *4613*
Mk 1:29 entered into the house of **S.** and *4613*
Mk 1:36 **S.** and they that were with him *4613*
Mk 3:16 And **S.** he surnamed Peter; *4613*
Mk 3:18 Thaddaeus, and **S.** the Canaanite, *4613*
Mk 6:3 and Joses, and of Juda, and **S.**? *4613*
Mk 14:3 in the house of **S.** the leper, as he *4613*
Mk 14:37 saith unto Peter, **S., sleepest thou?** *4613*
Mk 15:21 they compel one **S.** a Cyrenian who *4613*
Lu 5:4 he said unto **S., Launch out into** *4613*
Lu 5:5 And **S.** answering said unto him, *4613*
Lu 5:8 When **S.** Peter saw it, he fell down *4613*
Lu 5:10 which were partners with **S.** *4613*
Lu 5:10 Jesus said unto **S., Fear not; from** *4613*
Lu 6:14 **S.**, (whom he also named Peter,) *4613*
Lu 6:15 of Alphaeus, and **S.** called Zelotes, *4613*
Lu 7:40 **S., I have somewhat to say unto** *4613*
Lu 7:43 **S.** answered and said, I suppose *4613*
Lu 7:44 unto **S., Seest thou this woman?** *4613*
Lu 22:31 **S., S., behold Satan hath desired** *4613*
Lu 23:26 away, they laid hold upon one **S.**, *4613*
Lu 24:34: indeed, and hath appeared to **S.** *4613*
Joh 1:40 was Andrew, **S.** Peter's brother. *4613*
Joh 1:41 He first findeth his own brother **S.** *4613*
Joh 1:42 **Thou art S. the son of Jona: thou** *4613*
Joh 6:8 Andrew, **S.** Peter's brother, saith *4613*
Joh 6:68 Then **S.** Peter answered him, Lord *4613*
Joh 6:71 of Judas Iscariot the son of **S.**; for *4613*
Joh 13:6 Then cometh he to **S.** Peter: and *4613*
Joh 13:9 **S.** Peter saith unto him, Lord, not *4613*
Joh 13:24 **S.** Peter therefore beckoned to him, *4613*
Joh 13:26 it to Judas Iscariot, the son of **S.** *4613*
Joh 13:36 **S.** Peter said unto him, Lord, *4613*
Joh 18:10 **S.** Peter having a sword drew it, *4613*
Joh 18:15 **S.** Peter followed Jesus, and so did *4613*
Joh 18:25 **S.** Peter stood and warmed himself *4613*
Joh 20:2 runneth, and cometh to **S.** Peter, *4613*
Joh 20:6 cometh **S.** Peter following him, and *4613*
Joh 21:2 There were together **S.** Peter, and *4613*
Joh 21:3 **S.** Peter saith unto them, I go a *4613*
Jon 21:7 when **S.** Peter heard that it was *4613*
Joh 21:11 **S.** Peter went up, and drew the net *4613*
Joh 21:15 Jesus saith to **S.** Peter, **S., son of** *4613*
Joh 21:16, 17 **S., son of Jonas, lovest thou me?** *4613*
Ac 1:13 **S.** Zelotes, and Judas the brother *4613*
Ac 8:9 there was a certain man, called **S.** *4613*
Ac 8:13 Then **S.** himself believed also: and *4613*
Ac 8:18 when **S.** saw that through laying *4613*
Ac 8:24 Then answered **S.**, and said, Pray *4613*
Ac 9:43 days in Joppa with one **S.** a tanner. *4613*
Ac 10:5 for one **S.**, whose surname is Peter: *4613*
Ac 10:6 He lodgeth with one **S.** a tanner, *4613*
Ac 10:18 **S.**, which was surnamed Peter, *4613*
Ac 10:32 call hither **S.**, whose surname is *4613*
Ac 10:32 in the house of one **S.** a tanner by *4613*
Ac 11:13 call for **S.**, whose surname is Peter; *4613*
2Pe 1:1 **S.** Peter, a servant and an apostle *4613*

SIMON'S (si-muns)
Mk 1:30 But **S.** wife's mother lay sick of a *4613*
Lu 4:38 and entered into **S.** house. And *4613*
Lu 4:38 **S.** wife's mother was taken with a *4613*
Lu 5:3 into one of the ships, which was **S.**, *4613*
Joh 12:4 disciples, Judas Iscariot, **S.** son, *4613*
Joh 13:2 the heart of Judas Iscariot, **S.** son, *4613*
Ac 10:17 had made enquiry for **S.** house, *4613*

SIMPLE
Ps 19:7 Lord is sure, making wise the **s.** 6612
Ps 116:6 The Lord preserveth the **s.**; I was 6612
Ps 119:130 giveth understanding unto the **s.** 6612
Pr 1:4 To give subtilty to the **s.**, to the 6612
Pr 1:22 How long, ye **s.** ones, will ye love 6612
Pr 1:32 the turning away of the **s.** shall 6612
Pr 7:7 and beheld among the **s.** ones, I 6612
Pr 8:5 O ye **s.**, understand wisdom: and, 6612
Pr 9:4 Whoso is **s.**, let him turn in hither: 6612
Pr 9:13 she is **s.**, and knoweth nothing 6615
Pr 9:16 Whoso is **s.**, let him turn in hither: 6612
Pr 14:15 The **s.** believeth every word: but 6612
Pr 14:18 **s.** inherit folly: but the prudent 6612
Pr 19:25 a scorner, and the **s.** will beware: 6612
Pr 21:11 is punished, the **s.** is made wise: 6612
Pr 22:3 the **s.** pass on, and are punished. 6612
Pr 27:12 the **s.** pass on, and are punished. 6612
Eze 45:20 that erreth, and for him that is **s.** 6612
Ro 16:18 deceive the hearts of the **s.** *172*
Ro 16:19 is good, and **s.** concerning evil. *185*

SIMPLICITY
2Sa 15:11 and they went in their **s.**, and they 8537
Pr 1:22 ye simple ones, will ye love **s.**? 6612
Ro 12:8 that giveth, let him do it with **s.**; *572*
2Co 1:12 that in **s.** and godly sincerity, not *572*
2Co 11:3 from the **s.** that is in Christ. *572*

SIMRI (sim'-ri) See also SHIMRI.
1Ch 26:10 Hosah,...had sons; **S.** the chief, 8113

SIN See also SINFUL; SINNED; SINNEST; SINNETH; SINNING; SINS.
Ge 4:7 doest not well, **s.** lieth at the door 2403
Ge 18:20 because their **s.** is very grievous; 2403
Ge 20:9 me and on my kingdom a great **s.**? 2401
Ge 31:36 what is my **s.**, that thou hast so 2403
Ge 39:9 wickedness, and **s.** against God? 2398
Ge 42:22 saying, Do not **s.** against the child; 2398
Ge 50:17 of thy brethren, and their **s.**; 2403
Ex 10:17 forgive,...my **s.** only this once. 2403
Ex 20:20 before your faces, that ye **s.** not. 2398
Ex 23:33 lest they make thee **s.** against me: 2398
Ex 29:14 the camp: it is a **s.** offering. 2403
Ex 29:36 every day a bullock for a **s.** offering 2403
Ex 30:10 of the **s.** offering of atonements: 2403
Ex 32:21 brought so great a **s.** upon them? 2401
Ex 32:30 people. Ye have sinned a great **s.** 2401
Ex 32:30 make an atonement for your **s.** 2403
Ex 32:31 this people have sinned a great **s.**, 2401
Ex 32:32 now, if thou wilt forgive their **s.**—; 2403
Ex 32:34 visit I will visit their **s.** upon them. 2403
Ex 34:7 iniquity and transgression and **s.**, 2402
Ex 34:9 pardon our iniquity and our **s.**, 2403
Le 4:2 a soul shall **s.** through ignorance 2398
Le 4:3 If the priest that is anointed do **s.** 2398
Le 4:3 according to the **s.** of the people; 819
Le 4:3 then let him bring for his **s.**, 2403
Le 4:3 unto the Lord for a **s.** offering. 2403
Le 4:8 fat of the bullock for the **s.** offering; 2403
Le 4:13 of Israel **s.** through ignorance, 7686
Le 4:14 When the **s.**, which they have 2403
Le 4:14 offer a young bullock for the **s.**, 2403
Le 4:20 with the bullock for a **s.** offering 2403
Le 4:21 a **s.** offering for the congregation. 2403
Le 4:23 if his **s.**, wherein he hath sinned, 2403
Le 4:24 before the Lord: it is a **s.** offering. 2403
Le 4:25 take of the blood of the **s.** offering 2403
Le 4:26 for him as concerning his **s.**, 2403
Le 4:27 any one of the common people **s.** 2398
Le 4:28 Or if his **s.**, which he hath sinned, 2403
Le 4:28 for his **s.** which he hath sinned. 2403
Le 4:29 upon the head of the **s.** offering, 2403
Le 4:29 slay the **s.** offering in the place of 2403
Le 4:32 if he bring a lamb for a **s.** offering, 2403
Le 4:33 upon the head of the **s.** offering. 2403
Le 4:33 slay it for a **s.** offering in the place 2403
Le 4:34 take of the blood of the **s.** offering 2403
Le 4:35 make an atonement for his **s.** that 2403
Le 5:1 if a soul **s.**, and hear the voice of 2398
Le 5:6 for his **s.** which he hath sinned, 2403
Le 5:6 a kid of the goats, for a **s.** offering; 2403
Le 5:6 for him concerning his **s.** 2403
Le 5:7 one for a **s.** offering, and the other 2403
Le 5:8 which is for the **s.** offering first, 2403
Le 5:9 the blood of the **s.** offering upon the 2403
Le 5:9 of the altar; it is a **s.** offering. 2403
Le 5:10 him for his **s.** which he hath sinned, 2403
Le 5:11 ephah of fine flour for a **s.** offering; 2403
Le 5:11 thereon: for it is a **s.** offering. 2403
Le 5:12 unto the Lord: it is a **s.** offering. 2403
Le 5:13 touching his **s.** that he hath sinned 2403
Le 5:15 **s.** through ignorance, in the holy 2398
Le 5:17 And if a soul **s.**, and commit any of 2398
Le 6:2 If a soul **s.**, and commit a trespass 2398
Le 6:17 is most holy, as is the **s.** offering, 2403
Le 6:25 This is the law of the **s.** offering: 2403
Le 6:25 shall the **s.** offering be killed before 2403
Le 6:26 that offereth it for **s.** shall eat it: 2398
Le 6:30 no **s.** offering, whereof any of the 2403
Le 7:7 As the **s.** offering is, so is the 2403
Le 7:37 and of the **s.** offering, and of the 2403
Le 8:2 and a bullock for the **s.** offering, 2403
Le 8:14 the bullock for the **s.** offering: 2403
Le 8:14 of the bullock for the **s.** offering. 2403
Le 9:2 thee a young calf for a **s.** offering, 2403
Le 9:3 a kid of the goats for a **s.** offering; 2403
Le 9:7 the altar, and offer they **s.** offering, 2403
Le 9:8 and slew the calf of the **s.** offering, 2403
Le 9:10 above the liver of the **s.** offering, 2403
Le 9:15 was the **s.** offering for the people, 2403
Le 9:15 slew it, and offered it for the **s.**, as 2403
Le 9:22 from offering of the **s.** offering, 2403
Le 10:16 sought the goat of the **s.** offering, 2403
Le 10:17 have ye not eaten the **s.** offering in 2403
Le 10:19 have they offered their **s.** offering 2403
Le 10:19 I had eaten the **s.** offering to day, 2403
Le 12:6 or a turtledove, for a **s.** offering, 2403
Le 12:8 and the other for a **s.** offering: 2403
Le 14:13 where he shall kill the **s.** offering 2403
Le 14:13 as the **s.** offering is the priest's, so 2403
Le 14:19 the priest shall offer the **s.** offering, 2403
Le 14:22 and the one shall be a **s.** offering, 2403
Le 14:31 able to get, the one for a **s.** offering, 2403
Le 15:15 the one for a **s.** offering, and the 2403
Le 15:30 shall offer the one for a **s.** offering, 2403
Le 16:3 a young bullock for the **s.** offering, 2403
Le 16:5 kids of the goats for a **s.** offering, 2403
Le 16:6 offer his bullock of the **s.** offering, 2403

Le 16:9 fell, and offer him for a **s.** offering. 2403
Le 16:11 bring the bullock of the **s.** offering, 2403
Le 16:11 kill the bullock of the **s.** offering, 2403
Le 16:15 he kill the goat of the **s.** offering, 2403
Le 16:25 fat of the **s.** offering shall he burn 2403
Le 16:27 And the bullock for the **s.** offering, 2403
Le 16:27 and the goat for the **s.** offering, 2403
Le 19:17 and not suffer **s.** upon him. 2399
Le 19:22 for his **s.** which he hath done: 2403
Le 19:22 the **s.** which he hath done shall be 2403
Le 20:20 they shall bear their **s.**; they shall 2399
Le 22:9 lest they bear **s.** for it, and die 2399
Le 23:19 kid of the goats for a **s.** offering, 2403
Le 24:15 curseth his God shall bear his **s.**. 2399
Nu 5:6 commit any **s.** that men commit, 2403
Nu 5:7 Then they shall confess their **s.** 2403
Nu 6:11 offer the one for a **s.** offering, and 2403
Nu 6:14 without blemish for a **s.** offering, 2403
Nu 6:16 shall offer his **s.** offering, and his 2403
Nu 7:16, 22,28,34,40,46,52,59,64,70,76,82
of the goats for a **s.** offering: 2403
Nu 7:87 the kids of the goats for **s.** offering 2403
Nu 8:8 shalt thou take for a **s.** offering. 2403
Nu 8:12 shalt offer the one for a **s.** offering, 2403
Nu 9:13 that man shall bear his **s.** 2399
Nu 12:11 lay not the **s.** upon us, wherein 2403
Nu 15:24 kid of the goats for a **s.** offering. 2403
Nu 15:25 their **s.** offering before the Lord, 2403
Nu 15:27 if any soul **s.** through ignorance, 2398
Nu 15:27 of the first year for a **s.** offering. 2403
Nu 16:22 shall one man **s.**, and wilt thou be 2398
Nu 18:9 and every **s.** offering of theirs, and 2403
Nu 18:22 lest they bear **s.**, and die. 2399
Nu 18:32 ye shall bear no **s.** by reason of it, 2399
Nu 19:9 separation: it is a purification for **s.** 2403
Nu 19:17 burnt heifer of purification for **s.**, 2403
Nu 27:3 but died in his own **s.**, and had no 2399
Nu 28:15 kid of the goats for a **s.** offering 2403
Nu 28:22 one goat for a **s.** offering, to make 2403
Nu 29:5 kid of the goats for a **s.** offering, 2403
Nu 29:11 kid of the goats for a **s.** offering; 2403
Nu 29:11 beside the **s.** offering of atonement, 2403
Nu 29:16, 19 kid of the goats for a **s.** offering; 2403
Nu 29:22 one goat for a **s.** offering; beside 2403
Nu 29:25 kid of the goats for a **s.** offering; 2403
Nu 29:28, 31,34,38 one goat for a **s.** offering; 2403
Nu 32:23 be sure your **s.** will find you out. 2403
De 9:21 I took your **s.**, the calf which ye had 2403
De 9:27 to their wickedness, nor to their **s.**: 2403
De 15:9 thee, and it be **s.** unto thee. 2399
De 19:15 for any iniquity, or for any **s.**, 2403
De 19:15 in any **s.** that he sinneth: at the 2399
De 20:18 so should ye **s.** against the Lord 2398
De 21:22 And if a man have committed a **s.** 2399
De 22:26 the damsel no **s.** worthy of death: 2399
De 23:21 three; and it would be **s.** in thee. 2399
De 23:22 to vow, it shall be no **s.** in thee. 2399
De 24:4 thou shalt not cause the land to **s.**, 2398
De 24:15 the Lord, and it be **s.** unto thee. 2399
De 24:16 shall be put to death for his own **s.** 2399
1Sa 2:17 the **s.** of the young men was very 2403
1Sa 2:25 If one man **s.** against another, the 2398
1Sa 2:25 but if a man **s.** against the Lord, 2398
1Sa 12:23 God forbid that I should **s.** against 2398
1Sa 14:33 people **s.** against the Lord, in that 2398
1Sa 14:34 **s.** not against the Lord in eating 2398
1Sa 14:38 see wherein this **s.** hath been this 2403
1Sa 15:23 rebellion is as the **s.** of witchcraft, 2403
1Sa 15:25 I pray thee, pardon my **s.**, and turn 2403
1Sa 19:4 Let not the king **s.** against his 2398
1Sa 19:5 wilt thou **s.** against innocent blood, 2398
1Sa 20:1 what is my **s.** before thy father, 2403
2Sa 12:13 Lord also hath put away thy **s.**; 2403
1Ki 8:34 forgive the **s.** of thy people Israel, 2403
1Ki 8:35 thy name, and turn from their **s.**, 2403
1Ki 8:36 and forgive the **s.** of thy servants, 2403
1Ki 8:46 If they **s.** against thee, (for there 2398
1Ki 12:30 And this thing became a **s.**: for 2403
1Ki 13:34 became **s.** unto...house of Jeroboam, 2403
1Ki 14:16 the sins of Jeroboam, who did **s.**, 2398
1Ki 14:16 and who made Israel to **s.** 2398
1Ki 15:26 way of his father, and in his **s.** 2403
1Ki 15:26 wherewith he made Israel to **s.** 2398
1Ki 15:30 sinned, and which he made Israel **s.**, 2398
1Ki 15:34 the way of Jeroboam, and in his **s.** 2403
1Ki 15:34 wherewith he made Israel to **s.** 2398
1Ki 16:2 hast made my people Israel to **s.**, 2398
1Ki 16:13 by which they made Israel to **s.**, 2398
1Ki 16:19 the way of Jeroboam, and in his **s.** 2403
1Ki 16:19 which he did, to make Israel to **s.** 2398
1Ki 16:26 way of Jeroboam...and in his **s.** 2403
1Ki 16:26 wherewith he made Israel to **s.**, 2398
1Ki 17:18 me to call my **s.** to remembrance, 5771
1Ki 21:22 me to anger, and made Israel to **s.**. 2398
1Ki 22:52 Jeroboam...who made Israel to **s.**: 2398
2Ki 3:3 Jeroboam...which made Israel to **s.**; 2398
2Ki 10:29 Jeroboam...who made Israel to **s.**, 2398
2Ki 10:31 Jeroboam, which made Israel to **s.** 2398
2Ki 12:16 **s.** money was not brought into the
2Ki 13:2 of Nebat, which made Israel to **s.**; 2398
2Ki 13:6 of Jeroboam, who made Israel **s.**, 2398
2Ki 13:11 Jeroboam...who made Israel **s.**: 2398
2Ki 14:6 shall be put to death for his own **s.** 2399
2Ki 14:24 Jeroboam...who made Israel to **s.**. 2398
2Ki 15:9, 18,24,28 who made Israel to **s.** 2398
2Ki 17:21 and made them **s.** [2398] a great **s.**. 2401
2Ki 21:11 and hath made Judah also to **s.** 2398
2Ki 21:16 beside his **s.** wherewith he made 2403
2Ki 21:16 wherewith he made Judah to **s.**, 2398
2Ki 21:17 he did, and his **s.** that he sinned, 2403
2Ki 23:15 Jeroboam...who made Israel to **s.**, 2398
2Ch 6:22 If a man **s.** against his neighbour, 2398
2Ch 6:25 forgive the **s.** of thy people Israel, 2403
2Ch 6:26 thy name, and turn from their **s.**, 2408
2Ch 6:27 and forgive the **s.** of thy servants 2398
2Ch 6:36 if they **s.** against thee, (for there 2398
2Ch 7:14 heaven, and will forgive their **s.**, 2403
2Ch 24:4 every man shall die for his own **s.** 2403
2Ch 29:21 for a **s.** offering for the kingdom, 2403
2Ch 29:23 for the **s.** offering for the king, 2403
2Ch 29:24 **s.** offering should be made for all 2403
Ezr 6:17 and for a **s.** offering for all Israel, 2409
Ezr 8:35 twelve he goats for a **s.** offering: 2408
Ne 4:5 and let not their **s.** be blotted out 2408
Ne 6:13 should be afraid, and do so, and **s.**, 2398
Ne 10:33 **s.** offerings to make an atonement 2403
Ne 13:26 Did not Solomon king of Israel **s.** 2398
Ne 13:26 did outlandish women cause to **s.** 2398
Job 2:10 all this did not Job **s.** with his lips. 2398
Job 5:24 thy habitation, and shalt not **s.** 2398
Job 10:6 and searchest after my **s.**? 2403
Job 10:14 If I **s.**, then thou markest me, and 2398
Job 13:23 know my transgression and my **s.** 2403
Job 14:16 dost thou not watch over my **s.**? 2403
Job 20:11 bones are full of the **s.** of his youth, 2403
Job 31:30 have I suffered my mouth to **s.** 2398
Job 34:37 he addeth rebellion unto his **s.**, 2403
Job 35:3 I have, if I be cleansed from my **s.**? 2403
Ps 4:4 Stand in awe, and **s.** not: commune 2398
Ps 32:1 is forgiven, whose **s.** is covered. 2403
Ps 32:5 I acknowledged my **s.** unto thee, 2403
Ps 32:5 thou forgavest the iniquity of my **s.** 2403
Ps 38:3 rest in my bones because of my **s.** 2403
Ps 38:18 iniquity; I will be sorry for my **s.** 2403
Ps 39:1 ways, that I **s.** not with my tongue: 2398
Ps 40:6 **s.** offering hast thou not required. 2401
Ps 51:2 and cleanse me from my **s.** 2403
Ps 51:3 and my **s.** is ever before me 2403
Ps 51:5 in **s.** did my mother conceive me. 2399
Ps 51:12 the **s.** of their mouth and the words 2403
Ps 59:3 my transgression, nor for my **s.**, 2403
Ps 85:2 thou hast covered all their **s.**. 2403
Ps 109:7 and let his prayer become **s.** 2401
Ps 109:14 and let not the **s.** of his mother be 2403
Ps 119:11 that I might not **s.** against thee. 2398
Pr 10:16 to life: the fruit of the wicked to **s.**. 2403
Pr 10:19 of words there wanteth not **s.** 6588
Pr 14:9 Fools make a mock at **s.**: but 817
Pr 14:34 but **s.** is a reproach to any people. 2403
Pr 20:9 heart clean, I am pure from my **s.**? 2403
Pr 21:4 and the plowing of the wicked, is **s.** 2403
Pr 24:9 The thought of foolishness is **s.** 2403
Ec 5:6 thy mouth to cause thy flesh to **s.** 2398
Isa 3:9 they declare their **s.** as Sodom, 2403
Isa 5:18 and **s.** as it were with a cart rope: 2402
Isa 6:7 is taken away, and thy **s.** purged. 2403
Isa 27:9 is all the fruit to take away his **s.**; 2403
Isa 30:1 spirit, that they may add **s.** to **s.**; 2403
Isa 31:7 hands have made unto you for a **s.**. 2399
Isa 53:10 make his soul an offering for **s.**. 817
Isa 53:12 he bare the **s.** of many, and made 2399
Jer 16:10 or what is our **s.** that we have 2403
Jer 16:18 their iniquity and their **s.** double; 2403
Jer 17:1 **s.** of Judah is written with a pen of 2403
Jer 17:3 spoil, and thy high places for **s.**, 2403
Jer 18:23 neither blot out their **s.** from thy 2403
Jer 31:34 I will remember their **s.** no more 2403
Jer 32:35 abomination, to cause Judah to **s.**. 2398
Jer 36:3 forgive their iniquity and their **s.**, 2403
Jer 51:5 was filled with **s.** against the Holy 817
La 4:6 the punishment of the **s.** of Sodom,
Eze 3:20 warning, he shall die in his **s.**, 2403
Eze 3:21 man, that the righteous **s.** not, 2398
Eze 3:21 and he doth not **s.**, he shall surely 2398
Eze 18:24 and in his **s.** that he hath sinned, 2403
Eze 33:14 if he turn from his **s.**, and do that 2403
Eze 40:39 burnt offering and the **s.** offering 2403
Eze 42:13 meat offering, and the **s.** offering, 2403
Eze 43:19 a young bullock for a **s.** offering 2403
Eze 43:21 the bullock also of the **s.** offering, 2403
Eze 43:22 without blemish for a **s.** offering; 2403
Eze 43:25 every day a goat for a **s.** offering: 2403
Eze 44:27 he shall offer his **s.** offering, saith 2403
Eze 44:29 meat offering, and the **s.** offering: 2403
Eze 45:17 he shall prepare the **s.** offering, and 2403
Eze 45:19 take of the blood of the **s.** offering, 2403
Eze 45:22 the land a bullock for a **s.** offering. 2403
Eze 45:23 of the goats daily for a **s.** offering. 2403
Eze 45:25 days, according to the **s.** offering, 2403
Eze 46:20 tresspass offering and the **s.** offering 2403
Da 9:20 my **s.** and the **s.** of my people, Israel.. 2403
Ho 4:8 They eat up the **s.** of my people, 2403
Ho 8:11 hath made many altars to **s.**, 2398
Ho 8:11 altars shall be unto him to **s.**, 2398
Ho 10:8 places also of Aven, the **s.** of Israel, 2403
Ho 12:8 none iniquity in me that were **s.** 2399
Ho 13:2 And now they **s.** more and more, 2398
Ho 13:12 Ephraim is bound up; his **s.** is hid. 2403
Am 8:14 that swear by the **s.** of Samaria, 819
Mic 1:13 she is the beginning of the **s.** to 2403
Mic 3:8 transgression, and to Israel his **s.** 2403
Mic 6:7 of my body for the **s.** of my soul? 2403
Zec 13:1 fountain . . . for **s.** and . . . uncleanness..2403
Mt 12:31 **All manner of s. and blasphemy** *266*
Mt 18:21 oft shall my brother **s.** against me, *264*
Joh 1:29 taketh away the **s.** of the world. *266*
Joh 5:14 **s. no more, lest a worse thing** *264*
Joh 8:7 **He that is without s. among you** *361*
Joh 8:11 **condemn thee: go, and s. no more** *264*
Joh 8:34 **committeth s. is the servant of s.,** *266*
Joh 8:46 **Which of you convinceth me of s.?** *266*
Joh 9:2 Master, who did **s.**, this man, or his *264*
Joh 9:41 **ye were blind, ye should have no s.** *266*
Joh 9:41 **We see; therefore your s. remaineth** *266*
Joh 15:22 **unto them, they had not had s.: but** *266*
Joh 15:22 **now they have no cloke for their s.** *266*
Joh 15:24 **other man did, they had not had s.** *266*
Joh 16:8 **he will reprove the world of s., and** *266*
Joh 16:9 **s., because they believe not on me** *266*
Joh 19:11 **delivered me...hath the greater s.** *266*
Ac 7:60 Lord, lay not this **s.** to their charge *266*
Ro 3:9 Gentiles, that they are all under **s.**; *266*
Ro 3:20 for by the law is the knowledge of **s.** *266*
Ro 4:8 whom the Lord will not impute **s.** *266*
Ro 5:12 by one man **s.** entered into the world, *266*
Ro 5:12 into the world, and death by **s.**; *266*
Ro 5:13 until the law **s.** was in the world: *266*
Ro 5:13 **s.** is not imputed when there is no *266*
Ro 5:20 But where **s.** abounded, grace did *266*
Ro 5:21 that as **s.** hath reigned unto death, *266*
Ro 6:1 Shall we continue in **s.**, that grace *266*
Ro 6:2 How shall we that are dead to **s.**, live *266*
Ro 6:6 the body of **s.** might be destroyed, *266*
Ro 6:6 henceforth we should not serve **s.** *266*
Ro 6:7 For he that is dead is freed from **s.** *266*
Ro 6:10 in that he died, he died unto **s.** once: *266*
Ro 6:11 ye also... to be dead indeed unto **s.**, *266*
Ro 6:12 Let not **s.** therefore reign in your *266*
Ro 6:13 of unrighteousness unto **s.**: *266*
Ro 6:14 **s.** shall not have dominion over you: *266*
Ro 6:15 shall we **s.**, because we are not under *264*
Ro 6:16 whether of **s.** unto death, or of *266*
Ro 6:17 that ye were the servants of **s.**, but *266*
Ro 6:18 Being then made free from **s.**, ye *266*
Ro 6:20 For when ye were the servants of **s.**, *266*
Ro 6:22 But now being made free from **s.**, *266*
Ro 6:23 For the wages of **s.** is death; but the *266*
Ro 7:7 Is the law **s.**? God forbid. Nay, *266*

Ro 7:7 I had not known s., but by the law: *266*
Ro 7:8 But s., taking occasion by the *266*
Ro 7:8 For without the law s. was dead. *266*
Ro 7:9 the commandment came, s. revived, *266*
Ro 7:11 For s., taking occasion by the *266*
Ro 7:13 But s., that it might appear s., *266*
Ro 7:13 that s. by the commandment might *266*
Ro 7:14 but I am carnal, sold under s.. *266*
Ro 7:17, 20 it, but s. that dwelleth in me. *266*
Ro 7:23 me into captivity to the law of s. *266*
Ro 7:25 God; but with the flesh the law of s.. *266*
Ro 8:2 me free from the law of s. and death *266*
Ro 8:3 likeness of sinful flesh, and for s., *266*
Ro 8:3 condemned s. in the flesh: *266*
Ro 8:10 you, the body is dead because of s.; *266*
Ro 14:23 for whatsoever is not of faith is s. *266*
1Co 6:18 Every s. that a man doeth is without *265*
1Co 8:12 when ye s. so against the brethren, *264*
1Co 8:12 weak conscience, ye s. against Christ. *264*
1Co 15:34 Awake to righteousness, and s. not; *264*
1Co 15:56 The sting of death is s.; and the *266*
1Co 15:56 and the strength of s. is the law. *266*
2Co 5:21 him to be s. for us, who knew no s.; *266*
Ga 2:17 is therefore Christ the minister of s.? *266*
Ga 3:22 hath concluded all under s., that *266*
Eph 4:26 Be ye angry, and s. not: let not the *264*
2Th 2:3 that man of s. be revealed, the son *266*
1Ti 5:20 Them that s. rebuke before all, *264*
Heb 3:13 through the deceitfulness of s. *266*
Heb 4:25 like as we are, yet without s. *266*
Heb 9:26 hath he appeared to put away s. *266*
Heb 9:28 appear...without s. unto salvation. *266*
Heb 10:6 burnt offerings and sacrifices for s. *266*
Heb 10:8 burnt offerings and offering for s. *266*
Heb 10:18 is, there is no more offering for s.. *266*
Heb 10:26 if we s. wilfully after that we have *264*
Heb 11:25 than to enjoy the pleasures of s. for *266*
Heb 12:1 s. which doth so easily beset us, *266*
Heb 12:4 unto blood, striving against s. *266*
Heb 13:11 sanctuary by the high priest for s., *266*
Jas 1:15 it bringeth forth s.: and s., when it *266*
Jas 2:9 respect of persons, ye commit s.. *266*
Jas 4:17 and doeth it not, to him it is s. *266*
1Pe 2:22 Who did no s., neither was guile *266*
1Pe 4:1 in the flesh hath ceased from s.; *266*
2Pe 2:14 and that cannot cease from s.; *266*
1Jo 1:7 his Son cleanseth us from all s.. *266*
1Jo 1:8 If we say that we have no s., we *266*
1Jo 2:1 write I unto you, that ye s. not. *264*
1Jo 2:1 if any man s., we have an advocate *264*
1Jo 3:4 committeth s. transgresseth also *266*
1Jo 3:4 for s. is the transgression of the law. *266*
1Jo 3:5 away our sins; and in him is no s.. *266*
1Jo 3:8 He that committeth s. is of the devil; *266*
1Jo 3:9 is born of God doth not commit s.; *266*
1Jo 3:9 he cannot s., because he is born of *264*
1Jo 5:16 if any man see his brother s. *264*
1Jo 5:16 a s. which is not unto death, he *266*
1Jo 5:16 for them that s. not unto death. *264*
1Jo 5:16 There is a s. unto death: I do not *266*
1Jo 5:17 All unrighteousness is s.: and there *266*
1Jo 5:17 and there is a s. not unto death. *266*

SIN (sin)
Ex 16:1 came unto the wilderness of S., 5512
Ex 17:1 journeyed from the wilderness of S., 5512
Nu 33:11 encamped in the wilderness of S.. 5512
Nu 33:12 journey out of the wilderness of S., 5512
Eze 30:15 and I will pour my fury upon S., 5512
Eze 30:16 S. shall have great pain, and No 5512

SINA (si'-nah) See also SINAI.
Ac 7:30 him in the wilderness of mount S. *4614*
Ac 7:38 which spake to him in the mount S., *4614*

SINAI (si'-nahee) See also HOREB; SINA.
Ex 16:1 which is between Elim and S., on 5514
Ex 19:1 came they into the wilderness of S. 5514
Ex 19:2 were come to the desert of S., and 5514
Ex 19:11 of all the people upon mount S.. 5514
Ex 19:18 And mount S. was altogether on a 5514
Ex 19:20 Lord came down upon mount S., 5514
Ex 19:23 cannot come up to mount S.: for 5514
Ex 24:16 of the Lord abode upon mount S., 5514
Ex 31:18 him upon mount S., two tables 5514
Ex 34:2 up in the morning unto mount S., 5514
Ex 34:4 and went up unto mount S., as the 5514
Ex 34:29 Moses came down from mount S. 5514
Ex 34:32 had spoken with him in mount S.. 5514
Le 7:38 commanded Moses in mount S., in 5514
Le 7:38 the Lord, in the wilderness of S. 5514
Le 25:1 spake unto Moses in mount S., 5514
Le 26:46 children of Israel in mount S. by 5514
Le 27:34 the children of Israel in mount S.. 5514
Nu 1:1 unto Moses in the wilderness of S., 5514
Nu 1:19 them in the wilderness of S.. 5514
Nu 3:1 spake with Moses in mount S. 5514
Nu 3:4 the Lord in the wilderness of S. 5514
Nu 3:14 unto Moses in the wilderness of S., 5514
Nu 9:1 unto Moses in the wilderness of S., 5514
Nu 9:5 at even in the wilderness of S.: 5514
Nu 10:12 journeys out of...wilderness of S.; 5514
Nu 26:64 of Israel in the wilderness of S.. 5514
Nu 28:6 which was ordained in mount S. 5514
Nu 33:15 and pitched in the wilderness of S.. 5514
Nu 33:16 removed from the desert of S., 5514
De 33:2 The Lord came from S., and rose 5514
Jg 5:5 even that S. from before the Lord 5514
Ne 9:13 camest down also upon mount S., 5514
Ps 68:8 even S. itself was moved at the 5514
Ps 68:17 the Lord is among them, as in S., 5514
Ga 4:24 the one from the mount S., which *4614*
Ga 4:25 this Agar is mount S. in Arabia, *4614*

SINCE See also SITH.
Ge 30:30 Lord hath blessed thee s. my coming:
Ge 44:28 in pieces; and I saw him not s.: 2008
Ge 46:30 let me die, s. I have seen thy face, 310
Ex 4:10 nor s. thou hast spoken unto thy 227
Ex 5:23 s. I came to Pharaoh to speak in 4480
Ex 9:18 in Egypt s. the foundation thereof 4480
Ex 9:24 all the land of Egypt s. it became a 227
Ex 10:6 s. the day that they were upon the 4480
Nu 22:30 hast ridden ever s. I was thine 5750
De 4:32 s. the day that God created man 4480
De 34:10 a prophet s. in Israel like unto 5750
Jos 2:12 s. I have shewed you kindness, 3588
Jos 14:10 s. the Lord spake this word unto 227
Ru 2:11 law s. the death of thine husband: 310
1Sa 8:8 works which they have done s. the day
1Sa 9:24 hath it been kept for thee s. I said,
1Sa 21:5 about these three days, s. I came out,
1Sa 29:3 him s. he fell unto me unto this day?
1Sa 29:6 s. the day of they coming unto me unto
2Sa 7:6 s. the time that I brought up the
2Sa 7:11 as s. the time that I commanded 4480
1Ki 8:16 S. the day that I brought forth my 4480
2Ki 8:6 field s. the day that she left the land.
2Ki 21:15 s. the day their fathers came forth 4480
1Ch 17:5 s. the day that I brought up Israel 4480
1Ch 17:10 s. the time that I commanded judges
2Ch 6:5 S. the day that I brought forth my 4480
2Ch 30:26 s. the time of Solomon the son of
2Ch 31:10 S. the people began to bring the
Ezr 4:2 unto him s. the days of Esar-haddon
Ezr 5:16 s. that time even until now hath 4481
Ezr 9:7 s. the days of our fathers have we been
Ne 8:17 s. the days of Jeshua the son of Nun
Ne 9:32 s. the time of the kings of Assyria
Job 20:4 s. man was placed upon earth, 4480
Job 38:12 commanded the morning s. thy days; 4480
Isa 14:8 S. thou art laid down, no feller is 227
Isa 16:13 spoken concerning Moab s. that time.
Isa 43:4 S. thou wast precious in my sight,
Isa 44:7 me, s. I appointed the ancient people?
Isa 64:4 s. the beginning of the world men
Jer 7:25 S. the day that your fathers came 4480
Jer 15:7 s. they return not from their ways 4480
Jer 20:8 For s. I spake, I cried out, I cried 1767
Jer 23:38 s. ye say. The burden of the Lord; 518
Jer 31:20 for s. I spake against him, I do 1767
Jer 44:18 s. we left off to burn incense 4480,227
Jer 48:27 for s. thou spakest of him, thou 1767
Da 12:1 as never was s. there was a nation
Hag 2:16 S. those days were, when one came
Mt 24:21 **not s. the beginning of the world** *575*
Mk 9:21 **How long is it ago s. this came** *5613*
Lu 1:70 have been s. the world began: *575*
Lu 7:45 **this woman s. the time I came in** *575*
Lu 16:16 **s. that time the kingdom of God is** *575*
Lu 24:21 third day s. these things were done *575*
Joh 9:32 S. the world began was it not *1537*
Ac 3:21 holy prophets s. the world began. *575*
Ac 19:2 the Holy Ghost s. ye believed?
Ac 24:11 but twelve days s. I went up to *575,3739*
Ro 16:25 was kept secret s. the world began,
1Co 15:21 For s. by man came death, by man *1894*
2Co 13:3 S. ye seek a proof of Christ *1893*
Col 1:4 S. we heard of your faith in Christ
Col 1:6 also in you, s. the day ye heard of it, *575*
Col 1:9 s. the day we heard it, do not cease *575*
Heb 7:28 of the oath, which was s. the law *3326*
Heb 9:26 s. the foundation of the world: *575*
2Pe 3:4 s. the fathers fell asleep, all *575,3739*
Re 16:18 such as was not s. men were *575,3739*

SINCERE
Php 1:10 ye may be s. and without offence *1506*
1Pe 2:2 desire the s. milk of the word, that *97*

SINCERELY
Jg 9:16 if ye have done truly and s., in 8549
Jg 9:19 If ye then have dealt truly and s. 8549
Php 1:16 preach Christ of contention, not s., *55*

SINCERITY
Jos 24:14 and serve him in s. and in truth: 8549
1Co 5:8 with the unleavened bread of s. and *1505*
2Co 1:12 that in simplicity and godly s., not *1505*
2Co 2:17 but as of s., but as of God, in the *1505*
2Co 8:8 and to prove the s. of your love *1103*
Eph 6:24 love our Lord Jesus Christ in s. *861*
Tit 2:7 shewing uncorruptness, gravity, s., *861*

SINEW See also SINEWS.
Ge 32:32 eat not of the s. which shrank, 1517
Ge 32:32 Jacob's thigh in the s. that shrank. 1517
Isa 48:4 and thy neck is an iron s., and thy 1517

SINEWS
Job 10:11 hast fenced me with bones and s. 1517
Job 30:17 season: and my s. take no rest. 6207
Job 40:17 the s. of his stones are wrapped 1517
Eze 37:6 and I will lay s. upon you, and will 1517
Eze 37:8 s. and the flesh came up upon them, 1517

SINFUL
Nu 32:14 an increase of s. men, to augment 2400
Isa 1:4 Ah s. nation, a people laden with 2398
Am 9:8 Lord God are upon the s. kingdom, 2401
Mk 8:38 **this adulterous and s. generation:** *268*
Lu 5:8 from me; for I am a s. man, O Lord. *268*
Lu 24:7 delivered into the hands of s. men, *268*
Ro 7:13 sin...might become exceeding s.. *268*
Ro 8:3 own Son in the likeness of s. flesh, *266*

SING See also SANG; SINGETH; SINGING; SUNG.
Ex 15:1 I will s. unto the Lord, for he hath 7891
Ex 15:21 S. ye to the Lord, for he hath 7891
Ex 32:18 the noise of them that s. do I hear. 6031
Nu 21:17 Spring up, O well: s. ye unto it: 6030
Jg 5:3 I, even I, will s. unto the Lord; 7891
Jg 5:3 will s. praise to the Lord of Israel. 2167
1Sa 21:11 s. one to another of him in dances, 6030
2Sa 22:50 I will s. praises unto thy name. 2167
1Ch 16:9 S. unto him...talk ye of all his 7891
1Ch 16:9 s. psalms unto him, talk ye of all
1Ch 16:23 S. unto the Lord, all the earth; 7891
1Ch 16:33 shall the trees of the wood s. out 7442
2Ch 20:22 they began to s. and to praise, 7440
2Ch 23:13 and such as taught to s. praise. 1984
2Ch 29:30 to s. praise unto the Lord with the 1984
Job 29:13 the widow's heart to s. for joy. 7442
Ps 7:17 will s. praise to the name of the Lord
Ps 9:2 I will s. praise to thy name, O thou
Ps 9:11 S. praises to the Lord, which
Ps 13:6 I will s. unto the Lord, because he 7891
Ps 18:49 and s. praises unto thy name.
Ps 21:13 so will we s. and praise thy power. 7891
Ps 27:6 sacrifice of joy; I will s., yea, 7891
Ps 27:6 I will s. praises unto the Lord. 2167
Ps 30:4 S. unto the Lord, O ye saints of his, 2167
Ps 30:12 that my glory may s. praise to thee. 2167
Ps 33:2 s. unto him with the psaltery and 2167
Ps 33:3 S. unto him a new song: play 7891
Ps 47:6 S. praises to God, s. praises: 2167
Ps 47:6 s. praises unto our King, s. praises. 2167
Ps 47:7 s. ye praises with understanding 2167
Ps 51:14 shall s. aloud of thy righteousness. 7442
Ps 57:7 is fixed: I will s. and give praise 7891
Ps 57:9 s. unto thee among the nations. 2167
Ps 59:16 But I will s. of thy power; yea, I 7891
Ps 59:16 I will s. aloud of thy mercy in the 7442
Ps 59:17 Unto thee, O my strength, will I s.: 2167

Ps 61:8 So will I **s.** praise unto thy name for... 2167
Ps 65:13 they shout for joy, they also **s.**. 7891
Ps 66:2 **S.** forth the honour of his name: 2167
Ps 66:4 worship thee, and ...**s.** unto thee; 2167
Ps 66:4 they shall **s.** to thy name. Selah. 2167
Ps 67:4 the nations be glad and **s.** for joy: 7442
Ps 68:4 **S.** unto God...extol him that rideth 7891
Ps 68:4 **s.** praises to his name: extol him 2167
Ps 68:32 **S.** unto God, ye kingdoms of the 7891
Ps 68:32 O **s.** praises unto the Lord; Selah: 2167
Ps 71:22 unto thee will I **s.** with the harp, 2167
Ps 71:23 greatly rejoice when I **s.** unto thee; 2167
Ps 75:9 I will **s.** praises to the God of Jacob.
Ps 81:1 **S.** aloud unto god our strength: 7442
Ps 89:1 I will **s.** of the mercies of the Lord 7891
Ps 92:1 and to **s.** praises unto thy name, O 2167
Ps 95:1 O come, let us **s.** unto the Lord: 7442
Ps 96:1 O **s.** unto the Lord a new song: 7891
Ps 96:1 **s.** unto the Lord, all the earth 7891
Ps 96:2 **S.** unto the Lord, bless his name; 7891
Ps 98:1 O **s.** unto the Lord a new song; for 7891
Ps 98:4 noise, and rejoice, and **s.** praise. 2167
Ps 98:5 **S.** unto the Lord with the harp; 2167
Ps 101:1 I will **s.** of mercy and judgment: 7891
Ps 101:1 unto thee, O Lord, will I **s.**. 2167
Ps 104:12 which **s.** among the branches 5414,6963
Ps 104:33 **s.** unto the Lord as long as I live: 7891
Ps 104:33 **s.** praise to my God while I have 2167
Ps 105:2 **S.** unto him,...talk ye of all his 7891
Ps 105:2 **s.** psalms unto him: talk ye of 2167
Ps 108:1 I will **s.** and give praise, even with 7891
Ps 108:3 I will **s.** praises unto thee among 2167
Ps 135:3 **s.** praises unto his name; for it is 2167
Ps 137:3 **S.** us one of the songs of Zion. 7891
Ps 137:4 **s.** the Lord's song in a strange 7891
Ps 138:1 the gods will I **s.** praise unto thee. 2167
Ps 138:5 shall **s.** in the ways of the Lord: 7891
Ps 144:9 I will **s.** a new song unto thee, O 7891
Ps 144:9 ten strings will I **s.** praises unto 2167
Ps 145:7 and shall **s.** of thy righteousness. 7442
Ps 146:2 I will **s.** praises unto...God while I 2167
Ps 147:1 is good to **s.** praises unto our God; 2167
Ps 147:7 **S.** unto...Lord with thanksgiving; 6030
Ps 147:7 **s.** praise upon the harp unto our 2167
Ps 149:1 **S.** unto the Lord a new song, and 7891
Ps 149:3 **s.** praises unto him with...timbrel 2167
Ps 149:5 let them **s.** aloud upon their beds. 7442
Pr 29:6 the righteous doth **s.** and rejoice. 7442
Isa 5:1 will I **s.** to my wellbeloved a song 7891
Isa 12:5 **S.** unto the Lord; for he hath 2167
Isa 23:15 years shall Tyre **s.** as an harlot. 7892
Isa 23:16 make sweet melody, **s.** many songs,
Isa 24:14 shall **s.** for the majesty of the 7442
Isa 26:19 Awake and **s.**, ye that dwell in 7442
Isa 27:2 In that day **s.** ye unto her, A 6031
Isa 35:6 and the tongue of the dumb **s.**: 7442
Isa 38:20 therefore we will **s.** my songs to 5057
Isa 42:10 **S.** unto the Lord a new song, and 7891
Isa 42:11 let the inhabitants of the rock **s.**, 7442
Isa 44:23 **S.**, O ye heavens; for the Lord 7442
Isa 49:13 **S.**, O heavens; and be joyful, O 7442
Isa 52:8 the voice together shall they **s.**: 7442
Isa 52:9 joy, **s.** together, ye waste places of 7442
Isa 54:1 **S.**, O baren, thou that didst not 7442
Isa 65:14 servants shall **s.** for joy of heart, 7442
Jer 20:13 **S.** unto the Lord, praise ye the 7891
Jer 31:7 **S.** with gladness for Jacob, and 7442
Jer 31:12 come and **s.** in the height of Zion, 7442
Jer 51:48 that is therein, shall **s.** for Babylon: 7442
Eze 27:25 ships of Tarshish did **s.** of thee in 7788
Ho 2:15 she shall **s.** there, as in the days 6030
Zep 2:14 voice shall **s.** in the windows; 7891
Zep 3:14 **S.**, O daughter of Zion; shout, O 7442
Zec 2:10 **S.** and rejoice, O daughter of Zion: 7442
Ro 15:9 Gentiles, and **s.** unto they name. *5567*
1Co 14:15 also: I will **s.** with the spirit, and *5567*
1Co 14:15 will **s.** with the understanding also. *5567*
Heb 2:12 the church will I **s.** praise unto thee *5214*
Jas 5:13 is any merry? let him **s.** psalms *5567*
Re 15:3 And they **s.** the song of Moses the *103*

SINGED
Da 3:27 nor was an hair of their head **s.**, 2761

SINGER See also SINGERS.
1Ch 6:33 Heman a **s.**, the son of Joel, the 7891
Hab 3:19 To the chief **s.** on my stringed 5329

SINGERS
1Ki 10:12 harps also and psalteries for **s.** 7891
1Ch 9:33 these are the **s.**, chief of the fathers 7891
1Ch 15:16 the **s.** with instruments of musick, 7891
1Ch 15:19 So the **s.**, Heman, Asaph, and 7891
1Ch 15:27 that bare the ark and the **s.**, and 7891
1Ch 15:27 the master of the song with the **s.** 7891
2Ch 5:12 the Levites which were the **s.**, all of 7891
2Ch 5:13 the trumpeters and **s.** were as one, 7891
2Ch 9:11 and harps and psalteries for **s.** 7891
2Ch 20:21 he appointed **s.** unto the Lord, and 7891
2Ch 23:13 the **s.** with instruments of musick, 7891
2Ch 29:28 and the **s.** sang, and the trumpets 7892
2Ch 35:15 And the **s.** the sons of Asaph were 7891
Ezr 2:41 The **s.**: the children of Asaph, an 7891
Ezr 2:70 people, and the **s.**, and the porters, 7891
Ezr 7:7 priests, and the Levites, and the **s.**, 7891
Ezr 7:24 Levites, **s.**, porters, Nethinims, 2171
Ezr 10:24 Of the **s.** also; Eliashib: and of 7891
Ne 7:1 and the **s.** and the Levites were 7891
Ne 7:44 The **s.**: the children of Asaph, an 7891
Ne 7:73 Levites, and the porters, and the **s.**, 7891
Ne 10:28 Levites, the porters, the **s.**, the 7891
Ne 10:39 minister...the porters, and the **s.**: 7891
Ne 11:22 the **s.** were over the business of the 7891
Ne 11:23 certain portion should be for the **s.**, 7891
Ne 12:28 And the sons of the **s.** gathered 7891
Ne 12:29 **s.** had builded them villages round 7891
Ne 12:42 the **s.** sang loud, with Jezrahiah. 7891
Ne 12:45 both the **s.** and the porters kept 7891
Ne 12:46 of old they were chief of the **s.**, 7891
Ne 12:47 gave the portions of the **s.** and the 7891
Ne 13:5 be given to the Levites, and the **s.**, 7891
Ne 13:10 the Levites, and the **s.**, that did the 7891
Ps 68:25 The **s.** went before, the players on 7891
Ps 87:7 As well the **s.** as the players on 7891
Ec 2:8 I gat me men **s.** and women **s.**, and 7891
Eze 40:44 the chambers of the **s.** in the inner 7891

SINGETH
Pr 25:20 so is he that **s.** songs to an heavy 7891

SINGING
1Sa 18:6 cities of Israel, **s.** and dancing, 7891
2Sa 19:35 the voice of **s.** men and **s.** women? 7891
1Ch 6:32 of the congregation with **s.**, until 7892
1Ch 13:8 with **s.**, and with harps, and with 7892
2Ch 23:18 Moses, with rejoicing and with **s.**, 7892
2Ch 30:21 **s.** with loud instruments unto the
2Ch 35:25 all the **s.** men and the **s.** women 7891
Ezr 2:65 two hundred **s.** men and **s.** women. 7891
Ne 7:67 and five **s.** men and **s.** women. 7891
Ne 12:27 with thanksgivings, and with **s.**, 7892
Ps 100:2 come before his presence with **s.**. 7445
Ps 126:2 laughter, and our tongue with **s.**: 7440
Ca 2:12 time of the **s.** of birds is come, 2158
Isa 14:7 is quiet: they break forth into **s.** 7440
Isa 16:10 the vineyards there shall be no **s.**, 7442
Isa 35:2 and rejoice even with joy and **s.** 7442
Isa 44:23 break forth into **s.**, ye mountains, 7440
Isa 48:20 with a voice of **s.** declare ye, tell 7440
Isa 49:13 break forth into **s.**, O mountains: 7440
Isa 51:11 return, and come with **s.** unto Zion; 7440
Isa 54:1 break forth into **s.**, and cry aloud, 7440
Isa 55:12 shall break forth before you into **s.**, 7440
Zep 3:17 love, he will joy over thee with **s.**. 7440
Eph 5:19 **s.** and making melody in your *103*
Col 3:16 **s.** with grace in your hearts to the *103*

SINGLE
Mt 6:22 **if therefore thine eye be s., thy** *573*
Lu 11:34 **therefore when thine eye is s., thy.** *573*

SINGLENESS
Ac 2:46 with gladness and **s.** of heart, *858*
Eph 6:5 in **s.** of your heart, as unto Christ; *572*
Col 3:22 but in **s.** of heart, fearing God: *572*

SINGULAR
Le 27:2 when a man shall make a **s.** vow, 6381

SINIM (si'-nim)
Isa 49:12 and these from the land of **S.**. 5515

SINITE (si'-nite)
Ge 10:17 Hivite, and the Arkite, and the **S.**, 5513
1Ch 1:15 Hivite, and the Arkite, and the **S.**, 5513

SINK See also SANK; SUNK.
Ps 69:2 I **s.** in deep mire, where there is 2883
Ps 69:14 out of the mire, and let me not **s.** 2883
Jer 51:64 Thus shall Babylon **s.**, and shall 8257
Mt 14:30 beginning to **s.**, he cried, saying, *2670*
Lu 5:7 the ships, so that they began to **s.** *1036*
Lu 9:44 **sayings s. down into your ears:** *5087*

SINNED
Ex 9:27 unto them, I have **s.** this time: 2398
Ex 9:34 he **s.** yet more, and hardened his 2398
Ex 10:16 I have **s.** against the Lord your God, 2398
Ex 32:30 the people, Ye have **s.** a great sin: 2398
Ex 32:31 Oh, this people have **s.** a great sin, 2398
Ex 32:33 Whosoever hath **s.** against me, him 2398
Le 4:3 bring for his sin, which he hath **s.**, 2398
Le 4:14 sin, which they have **s.** against it, is 2398
Le 4:22 When a ruler hath **s.**, and done 2398
Le 4:23 if his sin, wherein he hath **s.**, come 2398
Le 4:28 if his sin, which he hath **s.**, come to 2398
Le 4:28 for his sin which he hath **s.**. 2398
Le 5:5 that he shall confess that he hath **s.** 2398
Le 5:6 Lord for his sin which he hath **s.**, 2398
Le 5:10 for him for his sin which he hath **s.**, 2398
Le 5:11 that **s.** shall bring for his offering 2398
Le 5:13 as touching his sin that he hath **s.** 2398
Le 6:4 because he hath **s.**, and is guilty, 2398
Nu 6:11 for him, for that he **s.** by the dead, 2398
Nu 12:11 foolishly, and wherein we have **s.**. 2398
Nu 14:40 Lord hath promised: for we have **s.**. 2398
Nu 21:7 We have **s.**, for we have spoken 2398
Nu 22:34 I have **s.**; for I knew not that thou 2398
Nu 32:23 behold, ye have **s.** against the Lord: 2398
De 1:41 We have **s.** against the Lord, we 2398
De 9:16 ye had **s.** against the Lord your God, 2398
De 9:18 because of all your sins which ye **s.**, 2398
Jos 7:11 Israel hath **s.**, and they have also 2398
Jos 7:20 Indeed I have **s.** against the Lord 2398
Jg 10:10 saying, we have **s.** against thee, 2398
Jg 10:15 We have **s.**: do thou unto us 2398
Jg 11:27 I have not **s.** against thee, but thou 2398
1Sa 7:6 We have **s.** against the Lord. 2398
1Sa 12:10 unto the Lord, and said, We have **s.**, 2398
1Sa 15:24 Saul said unto Samuel, I have **s.** 2398
1Sa 15:30 Then he said, I have **s.**: yet honour 2398
1Sa 19:4 because he hath not **s.** against thee, 2398
1Sa 24:11 and I have not **s.** against thee; 2398
1Sa 26:21 Then said Saul, I have **s.**: return, 2398
2Sa 12:13 Nathan, I have **s.** against the Lord. 2398
2Sa 19:20 servant doth know that I have **s.** 2398
2Sa 24:10 I have **s.** greatly in that I have done: 2398
2Sa 24:17 Lo, I have **s.**, and I have done 2398
1Ki 8:33 because they have **s.** against thee, 2398
1Ki 8:35 because they have **s.** against thee; 2398
1Ki 8:47 saying, We have **s.**, and have done 2398
1Ki 8:50 And forgive they people that have **s.** 2398
1Ki 15:30 the sins of Jeroboam which he **s.**, 2398
1Ki 16:13 of Elah his son, by which they **s.**, 2398
1Ki 16:19 his sins which he **s.** in doing evil 2398
1Ki 18:9 What have I **s.**, that thou wouldest 2398
2Ki 17:7 Israel had **s.** against the Lord their 2398
2Ki 21:17 that he did, and his sin that he **s.**, 2398
1Ch 21:8 said unto God, I have **s.** greatly, 2398
1Ch 21:17 even I it is that have **s.** and done 2398
2Ch 6:24, 26 because they have **s.** against 2398
2Ch 6:37 We have **s.**, we have done amiss, 2398
2Ch 6:39 forgive thy people which have **s.** 2398
Ne 1:6 which we have **s.** against thee: 2398
Ne 1:6 I and my father's house have **s.**. 2398
Ne 9:29 but **s.** against thy judgments, 2398
Job 1:5 It may be that my sons have **s.**, 2398
Job 1:22 In all this Job **s.** no, nor charged 2398
Job 7:20 I have **s.**; what shall I do unto thee, 2398
Job 8:4 If thy children have **s.** against him, 2398
Job 24:19 doth the grave those which have **s.** 2398
Job 33:27 if any say, I have **s.**, and perverted 2398
Ps 41:4 my soul; for I have **s.** against thee. 2398
Ps 51:4 Against thee, thee only, have I **s.**, 2398
Ps 78:17 and they **s.** yet more against him 2398
Ps 78:32 For all this they **s.** still, and believed 2398
Ps 106:6 We have **s.** with our fathers, we 2398
Isa 42:24 Lord, he against whom we have **s.**? 2398
Isa 43:27 Thy first father hath **s.**, and thy 2398
Isa 64:5 thou art wroth; for we have **s.** 2398
Jer 2:35 because thou sayest, I have not **s.** 2398
Jer 3:25 for we have **s.** against the Lord our 2398
Jer 8:14 because we have **s.** against the Lord 2398
Jer 14:7 are many; we have **s.** against thee. 2398

Jer 14:20 favors: for we have s. against thee. 2398
Jer 33:8 whereby they have s. against me; 2398
Jer 33:8 iniquities, whereby they have s., ... 2398
Jer 40:3 because ye have s. against the Lord, .. 2398
Jer 44:23 because ye have s. against the Lord, .. 2398
Jer 50:7 they have s. against the Lord, ... 2398
Jer 50:14 for she hath s. against the Lord. 2398
La 1:8 Jerusalem hath grievously s.; 2398
La 5:7 Our fathers have s., and are not; 2398
La 5:16 head: woe unto us, that we have s.! ... 2398
Eze 18:24 and in his sin that he hath s., in......... 2398
Eze 28:16 thee with violence, and thou hast s...... 2398
Eze 37:23 dwelling places, wherein they...s., ... 2398
Da 9:5 We have s., and have committed........ 2398
Da 9:8 because we have s. against thee. 2398
Da 9:11 because we have s. against him. 2398
Da 9:15 we have s., we have done wickedly. ... 2398
Ho 4:7 increased, so they s. against me: 2398
Ho 10:9 thou hast s. from the days of Gibeah:.. 2398
Mic 7:9 Lord, because I have s. against him, ... 2398
Hab 2:10 people, and hath s. against thy soul. ... 2398
Zep 1:17 they have s. against the Lord: 2398
Mt 27:4 I have s. in that I have betrayed.......... *264*
Lu 15:18, 21 **Father, I have s. against heaven,**. *264*
Joh 9:3 **Neither hath this man s., nor his**.... *264*
Ro 2:12 For as many as have s. without law *264*
Ro 2:12 and as many as have s. in the law........ *264*
Ro 3:23 For all have s., and come short of *264*
Ro 5:12 upon all men, for that all have s. *264*
Ro 5:14 that had not s. after the similitude........ *264*
Ro 5:16 And not as it was by one that s., so..... *264*
1Co 7:28 and if thou marry, thou has not s.; *264*
1Co 7:28 if a virgin marry, she hath not s.. .... *264*
2Co 12:21 many which have s. already,............... *4258*
2Co 13:2 to them which heretofore have s., ... *4258*
Heb 3:17 was it not with them that had s., ... *264*
2Pe 2:4 God spared not the angels that s., ... *264*
1Jo 1:10 If we say that we have not s., we *264*

SINNER See also SINNERS.

Pr 11:31 much more the wicked and the s........ 2398
Pr 13:6 wickedness overthroweth the s.. 2403
Pr 13:22 the wealth of the s. is laid up for 2398
Ec 2:26 but to the s. he giveth travail, to 2398
Ec 7:26 but the s. shall be taken by her. 2398
Ec 8:12 Through a s. do evil an hundred.......... 2398
Ec 9:2 as is the good, so is the s.; and he...... 2398
Ec 9:18 but one s. destroyeth much good. 2398
Isa 65:20 the s. being an hundred years old....... 2398
Lu 7:37 woman in the city, which was a s., ... *268*
Lu 7:39 that toucheth him: for she is a s., ... *268*
Lu 15:7 **heaven over one s. that repenteth,** .. *268*
Lu 15:10 **of God over one s. that repenteth**.... *268*
Lu 18:13 **saying, God be merciful to me a s**... *268*
Lu 19:7 to be guest with a man that is a s......... *268*
Joh 9:16 man that is a s. do much miracles?........ *268*
Joh 9:24 we know that this man is a s.. .... *268*
Joh 9:25 Whether he be a s. or no, I know not: . *268*
Ro 3:7 why yet am I also judged as a s.? *268*
Jas 5:20 converteth the s. from the error of *268*
1Pe 4:18 shall the ungodly and the s. appear? *268*

SINNERS

Ge 13:13 men of Sodom were wicked and s. 2400
Nu 16:38 The censers of these s. against........... 2400
1Sa 15:18 destroy the s. the Amalekites, ... 2400
Ps 1:1 nor standeth in the way of s., nor 2400
Ps 1:5 nor s. in the congregation of the 2400
Ps 25:8 therefore will he teach s. in the way... 2400
Ps 26:9 Gather not my soul with s., nor my.... 2400
Ps 51:13 s. shall be converted unto thee. 2400
Ps 104:35 s. be consumed out of the earth,......... 2400
Pr 1:10 if s. entice thee, consent thou not. 2400
Pr 13:21 Evil pursueth s.: but to the................ 2400
Pr 23:17 Let not thine heart envy s.: but be..... 2400
Isa 1:28 of the transgressors and of the s........ 2400
Isa 13:9 and he shall destroy the s. thereof...... 2400
Isa 33:14 The s. in Zion are afraid; fearfulness... 2400
Am 9:10 All the s. of my people shall die by..... 2400
Mt 9:10 many publicans and s. came and *268*
Mt 9:11 your Master with publicans and s.?........ *268*
Mt 9:13 **the righteous, but s. to repentance**.. *268*
Mt 11:19 **a friend of publicans and s.,** *268*
Mt 26:45 is betrayed into the hands of s.. .... *268*
Mk 2:15 **publicans and s. sat also together**... *268*
Mk 2:16 **saw him eat with publicans and s.**,.. *268*
Mk 2:16 **and drinketh with publicans and s.?** *268*
Mk 2:17 **righteous, but s. to repentance.** *268*
Mk 14:41 **is betrayed into the hands of s.?** *268*
Lu 5:30 eat and drink with publicans and s.?...... *268*
Lu 5:32 **the righteous, but s. to repentance.**. *268*
Lu 6:32 **for s. also love those that love them**.. *268*
Lu 6:33 **ye? for s. also do even the same**...... *268*
Lu 6:34 **s. also lend to s., to receive as**........ *268*
Lu 7:34 **a friend of publicans and s.!**.......... *268*
Lu 13:2 **were s. above all the Galilaeans,**..... *268*
Lu 13:4 **were s. above all men that dwelt**... *3781*
Lu 15:1 publicans and s. for to hear him. *268*
Lu 15:2 This man receiveth s., and eateth *268*
Joh 9:31 we know that God heareth not s.:......... *268*
Ro 5:8 while we were yet s., Christ died for ... *268*
Ro 5:19 disobedience many were made s., ... *268*
Ga 2:15 by nature, and not s. of the Gentiles, ... *268*
Ga 2:17 we ourselves also are found s., is *268*
1Ti 1:9 for the ungodly and for s., for unholy.... *268*
1Ti 1:15 Jesus came into the world to save s.; ... *268*
Heb 7:26 undefiled, separate from s., and........... *268*
Heb 12:3 contradiction of s. against himself, ... *268*
Jas 4:8 Cleanse your hands, ye s.; and........... *268*
Jude 15 ungoldly s. have spoken against him. *268*

SINNEST

Job 35:6 If thou s., what doest thou against...... 2398

SINNETH

Nu 15:28 for the soul that s. ignorantly, ... 7683
Nu 15:28 s. by ignorance before the Lord 2398
Nu 15:29 for him that s. through ignorance,........ 6213
De 19:15 for any sin, in any sin that he s.......... 2398
1Ki 8:46 (for there is no man that s. not,).......... 2398
2Ch 6:36 (for there is no man which s. not,) 2398
Pr 8:36 s. against me wrongeth his own 2398
Pr 14:21 He that despiseth his neighbour s....... 2398
Pr 19:2 and he that hasteth with his feet s...... 2398
Pr 20:2 whoso provoketh him to anger s. 2398
Ec 7:20 earth, that doeth good, and s. not. 2398
Eze 14:13 when the land s. against me by........... 2398
Eze 18:4 mine: the soul that s., it shall die. 2398
Eze 18:20 The soul that s., it shall die. The 2398
Eze 33:12 righteousness in the day that he s. 2398
1Co 6:18 fornication s. against his own body. *264*
1Co 7:36 let him do what he will, he s. not: *264*
Tit 3:11 he that is such is subverted, and s., ... *264*
1Jo 3:6 Whosoever abideth in him s. not:......... *264*
1Jo 3:6 whosoever s. hath not seen him, ... *264*
1Jo 3:8 for the devil s. from the beginning. *264*
1Jo 5:18 whosoever is born of God s. not;.......... *264*

SINNING

Ge 20:6 for I also withheld thee from s........... 2398
Le 6:3 these that a man doeth, s. therein:...... 2398

SIN-OFFERING See SIN and OFFERING.

SINS

Le 16:16 their transgressions in all their s. 2403
Le 16:21 their transgressions in all their s., ... 2403
Le 16:30 from all your s. before the Lord.......... 2403
Le 16:34 of Israel for all their s. once a year...... 2403
Le 26:18 you seven times more for your s......... 2403
Le 26:21 upon you according to your s............. 2403
Le 26:24 you yet seven times for your s. 2403
Le 26:28 chastise you seven times for your s.... 2403
Nu 16:26 lest ye be consumed in all their s.. 2403
De 9:18 because of all your s. which ye 2403
Jos 24:19 your transgressions nor your s.......... 2403
1Sa 12:19 added unto all our s. this evil,............ 2403
1Ki 14:16 up because of the s. of Jeroboam, ... 2403
1Ki 14:22 their s. which they had committed, ... 2403
1Ki 15:3 he walked in all the s. of his father, ... 2403
1Ki 15:30 the s. of Jeroboam which he sinned,..... 2403
1Ki 16:2 provoke me to anger with their s.; 2403
1Ki 16:13 For all the s. of Baasha, and the 2403
1Ki 16:13 and the s. of Elah his son, by which ... 2403
1Ki 16:19 his s. which he sinned in doing evil 2403
1Ki 16:31 him to walk in the s. of Jeroboam........ 2403
2Ki 3:3 he cleaved unto the s. of Jeroboam..... 2403
2Ki 10:29 s. of Jeroboam the son of Nebat,......... 2399
2Ki 10:31 not from the s. of Jeroboam, ... 2403
2Ki 13:2 and followed the s. of Jeroboam 2403
2Ki 13:6 the s. of the house of Jeroboam, ... 2403
2Ki 13:11 from all the s. of Jeroboam the son..... 2403
2Ki 14:24 from all the s. of Jeroboam the son..... 2403
2Ki 15:9, 18,24,28 s. of Jeroboam the son of..... 2403
2Ki 17:22 walked in all the s. of Jeroboam 2403
2Ki 24:3 for the s. of Manasseh, according to ... 2403
2Ch 28:10 you, s. against the Lord your God? 819
2Ch 28:13 ye intend to add more to our s. 2403
2Ch 33:19 and all his s., and his trespass, and...... 2403
Ne 1:6 and confess the s. of the children of..... 2403
Ne 9:2 and stood and confessed their s.,........ 2403
Ne 9:37 hast set over us because of our s.:...... 2403
Job 13:23 many are mine iniquities and s.? 2403
Ps 19:13 servant also from presumptuous s.;...........
Ps 25:7 Remember not the s. of my youth,..... 2403
Ps 25:18 and my pain: and forgive all my s.. 2403
Ps 51:9 Hide thy face from my s., and blot 2399
Ps 69:5 and my s. are not hid from thee. 819
Ps 79:9 deliver us, and purge away our s.,....... 2403
Ps 90:8 our secret s. in the light of thy ....
Ps 103:10 hath not dealt with us after our s.; 2399
Pr 5:22 be holden with the cords of his s......... 2403
Pr 10:12 up strifes: but love covereth all s.. 6588
Pr 28:13 covereth his s. shall not prosper: 6588
Isa 1:18 though your s. be as scarlet, they 2399
Isa 38:17 hast cast all my s. behind thy back. 2399
Isa 40:2 Lord's hand double for all her s.......... 2403
Isa 43:24 hast made me to serve with thy s., ... 2403
Isa 43:25 sake, and will not remember thy s....... 2403
Isa 44:22 as a cloud, thy s.: return unto me; 2403
Isa 58:1 and the house of Jacob their s.. 2403
Isa 59:2 your s. have hid his face from you,..... 2403
Isa 59:12 thee, and our s. testify against us:...... 2403
Jer 5:25 and your s. have withholden good....... 2403
Jer 14:10 their iniquity, and visit their s.. 2403
Jer 15:13 and that for all thy s., even in all 2403
Jer 30:14 because thy s. were increased. 2403
Jer 30:15 because thy s. were increased, I 2403
Jer 50:20 the s. of Judah, and they shall not 2403
La 3:39 man for the punishment of his s.? 2399
La 4:13 For the s. of her prophets, and the 2403
La 4:22 of Edom; he will discover thy s.......... 2403
Eze 16:51 Samaria committed half of thy s.; 2403
Eze 16:52 for thy s. that thou hast committed..... 2403
Eze 18:14 that seeth all his father's s. which........ 2403
Eze 18:21 all his s. that he hath committed, ... 2403
Eze 21:24 all your doings your s. do appear;....... 2403
Eze 23:49 ye shall bear the s. of your idols: 2399
Eze 33:10 If our transgressions and our s. be 2403
Eze 33:16 of his s. that he hath committed.......... 2403
Da 4:27 break off thy s. by righteousness,........ 2408
Da 9:16 for our s., and for the iniquities 2399
Da 9:24 to make an end of s., and to make 2403
Ho 8:13 their iniquity, and visit their s.: 2403
Ho 9:9 their iniquity, he will visit their s.. 2403
Am 5:12 transgressions and your mighty s........ 2403
Mic 1:5 and for the s. of the house of Israel.... 2403
Mic 6:13 thee desolate because of thy s.. 2403
Mic 7:19 their s. into the depths of the sea. 2403
Mt 1:21 shall save his people from their s.. ...... *266*
Mt 3:6 of him in Jordan, confessing their s....... *266*
Mt 9:2 **good cheer; thy s. be forgiven thee.** .*266*
Mt 9:5 **to say, Thy s. be forgiven thee; or** .. *266*
Mt 9:6 **hath power on earth to forgive s.,**.... *266*
Mt 26:28 **for many for the remission of s.** *266*
Mk 1:4 of repentance for the remission of s.. ... *266*
Mk 1:5 river of Jordan, confessing their s.. .... *266*
Mk 2:5 palsy, **Son, thy s. be forgiven thee.** .. *266*
Mk 2:7 who can forgive s. but God only?......... *266*
Mk 2:9 **the palsy, Thy s. be forgiven thee;** .. *266*
Mk 2:10 **hath power on earth to forgive s.,**.... *266*
Mk 3:28 **s. shall be forgiven unto the sons**.... *265*
Mk 4:12 **their s. should be forgiven them.** *265*
Lu 1:77 people by the remission of their s., ... *266*
Lu 3:3 repentance for the remission of s.; *266*
Lu 5:20 him, **Man, thy s. are forgiven thee**..... *266*
Lu 5:21 Who can forgive s., but God alone? *266*
Lu 5:23 **to say, Thy s. be forgiven thee; or** .. *266*
Lu 5:24 **power upon earth to forgive s.,**........ *266*
Lu 7:47 **Her s., which are many, are**........... *266*
Lu 7:48 said unto her, **Thy s. are forgiven.** *266*
Lu 7:49 Who is this that forgiveth s. also? *266*
Lu 11:4 **forgive us our s.; for we also**.......... *266*
Lu 24:47 **remission of s. should be preached**.. *266*
Joh 8:21 **seek me, and shall die in your s.:** ... *266*
Joh 8:24 **you, that ye shall die in your s.**...... *266*
Joh 8:24 **I am he, ye shall die in your s.**...... *266*
Joh 9:34 Thou wast altogether born in s., ... *266*
Joh 20:23 **Whose soever s. ye remit, they are**.. *266*
Joh 20:23 **whose soever s. ye retain, they are**......
Ac 2:38 Jesus Christ for the remission of s., ... *266*
Ac 3:19 that your s. may be blotted out, ... *266*
Ac 5:31 to Israel, and forgiveness of s.. .... *266*

Ac 10:43 in him receive shall remission of **s.**....... *266*
Ac 13:38 unto you the forgiveness of **s.**............ *266*
Ac 22:16 be baptized, and wash away thy **s.**,...... *266*
Ac 26:18 **they may receive forgiveness of s.,**.. *266*
Ro 3:25 for the remission of **s.** that are past,.... *265*
Ro 4:7 forgiven, and whose **s.** are covered....... *266*
Ro 7:5 the motions of **s.**, which were by the.... *266*
Ro 11:27 when I shall take away their **s.**........... *266*
1Co 15:3 how that Christ died for our **s.**............ *266*
1Co 15:17 faith is vain; ye are yet in your **s.**....... *266*
Ga 1:4 who gave himself for our **s.**, that he..... *266*
Eph 1:7 the forgiveness of **s.**, according to...... *3900*
Eph 2:1 who were dead in trespasses and **s.**;.... *266*
Eph 2:5 Even when we were dead in **s.**,........ *3900*
Col 1:14 blood, even the forgiveness of **s.**......... *266*
Col 2:11 off the body of the **s.** of the flesh by.... *266*
Col 2:13 And you, being dead in your **s.**.......... *3900*
1Th 2:16 be saved, to fill up their **s.** alway:........ *266*
1Ti 5:22 be partaker of other men's **s.**:............ *266*
1Ti 5:24 Some men's **s.** are open beforehand,.... *266*
2Ti 3:6 captive silly women laden with **s.**,........ *266*
Heb 1:3 he had by himself purged our **s.**, sat..... *266*
Heb 2:17 reconciliation for the **s.** of the people.... *266*
Heb 5:1 offer both gifts and sacrifices for **s.**:..... *266*
Heb 5:3 so also for himself, to offer for **s.**........ *266*
Heb 7:27 first for his own **s.**, and then for the..... *266*
Heb 8:12 and their **s.** and their iniquities will I..... *266*
Heb 9:28 once offered to bear the **s.** of many;..... *266*
Heb 10:2 have had no more conscience of **s.**........ *266*
Heb 10:3 is a remembrance again made of **s.**........ *266*
Heb 10:4 and of goats should take away **s.**......... *266*
Heb 10:11 which can never take away **s.**:............ *266*
Heb 10:12 he had offered one sacrifice for **s.**.......... *266*
Heb 10:17 **s.** and iniquities will I remember.......... *266*
Heb 10:26 remaineth no more sacrifice for **s.**,......... *266*
Jas 5:15 if he have committed **s.**, they shall......... *266*
Jas 5:20 and shall hide a multitude of **s.**........... *266*
1Pe 2:24 own self bare our **s.** in his own body.... *266*
1Pe 2:24 that we, being dead to **s.**, should live.... *266*
1Pe 3:18 Christ also hath once suffered for **s.**,.... *266*
1Pe 4:8 shall cover the multitude of **s.**............ *266*
2Pe 1:9 that he was purged from his old **s.**........ *266*
1Jo 1:9 If we confess our **s.**, he is faithful and.. *266*
1Jo 1:9 faithful and just to forgive us our **s.**,..... *266*
1Jo 2:2 And he is the propitiation for our **s.**:...... *266*
1Jo 2:2 but also for the **s.** of the whole world........
1Jo 2:12 because your **s.** be forgiven you for...... *266*
1Jo 3:5 was manifested to take away our **s.**;...... *266*
1Jo 4:10 Son to be the propitiation for our **s.**..... *266*
Re 1:5 and washed us from our **s.** in his own.... *266*
Re 18:4 that ye be not partakers of her **s.**,........ *266*
Re 18:5 her **s.** have reached unto heaven,........ *266*

SION (si'-on) See also SHENIR; SIRION; ZION.
De 4:48 unto mount **S.**, which is Hermon......... 7865
Ps 65:1 waiteth for thee, O God, in **S.**:.......... 6726
Mt 21:5 Tell ye the daughter of **S.**, Behold,....... *4622*
Joh 12:15 Fear not, daughter of **S.**: behold,....... *4622*
Ro 9:33 I lay in **S.** a stumblingstone and......... *4622*
Ro 11:26 shall come out of **S.** the Deliverer,..... *4622*
Heb 12:22 But ye are come unto mount **S.**,......... *4622*
1Pe 2:6 I lay in **S.** a chief corner stone,......... *4622*
Re 14:1 lo, a Lamb stood on the mount **S.**,..... *4622*

SIPHMOTH (sif'-moth)
1Sa 30:28 and to them which were in **S.**,........... 8224

SIPPAI (sip'-pahee) See also SAPH.
1Ch 20:4 Sibbechai the Hushathite slew **S.**,........ 5598

SIR See also SIRS.
Ge 43:20 O **s.**, we came indeed down at the....... 113
Mt 13:27 **S., didst not thou sow good seed**.... *2962*
Mt 21:30 **and said, I go, s.; and went not**..... *2962*
Mt 27:63 **S.**, we remember that that deceiver.... *2962*
Joh 4:11 **S.**, thou hast nothing to draw with,..... *2962*
Joh 4:15 **S.**, give me this water, that I thirst.... *2962*
Joh 4:19 **S.**, I perceive...thou art a prophet...... *2962*
Joh 4:49 **S.**, come down ere my child die......... *2962*
Joh 5:7 **S.**, I have no man, when the water.... *2962*
Joh 12:21 saying, **S.**, we would see Jesus.......... *2962*
Joh 20:15 **S.**, if thou have borne him hence,....... *2962*
Re 7:14 I said unto him, **S.**, thou knowest....... *2962*

SIRAH (si'-rah)
2Sa 3:26 him again from the well of **S.**.............. 5626

SIRION (sir'-e-on) See also HERMON.
De 3:9 Hermon the Sidonians call **S.**;............ 8303
Ps 29:6 Lebanon and **S.** like a...unicorn.......... 8303

SIRS
Ac 7:26 **S.**, ye are brethren; why do ye........... *435*
Ac 14:15 saying, **S.**, why do ye these things?..... *435*
Ac 16:30 **S.**, what must I do to be saved?........ *2962*
Ac 19:25 **S.**, ye know that by this craft we........ *435*
Ac 27:10 **S.**, I perceive that this voyage will....... *435*
Ac 27:21 **S.**, ye should have hearkened unto....... *435*
Ac 27:25 Wherefore, **s.**, be of good cheer: for.... *435*

SISAMAI (sis'-a-mahee)
1Ch 2:40 Eleasah begat **S.**, and **S.** begat.......... 5581

SISERA (sis'-e-rah)
Jg 4:2 the captain of whose host was **S.**,...... 5516
Jg 4:7 **S.** the captain of Jabin's army, with..... 5516
Jg 4:9 the Lord shall sell **S.** into the hand..... 5516
Jg 4:12 And they shewed **S.** that Barak the.... 5516
Jg 4:13 And **S.** gathered together all his......... 5516
Jg 4:14 Lord hath delivered **S.** into thine........ 5516
Jg 4:15 And the Lord discomfited **S.**, and....... 5516
Jg 4:15 that **S.** lighted down off his chariot,.... 5516
Jg 4:16 host of **S.** fell upon the edge of the.... 5516
Jg 4:17 **S.** fled away on his feet to the tent.... 5516
Jg 4:18 And Jael went out to meet **S.**, and..... 5516
Jg 4:22 as Barak pursued **S.**, Jael came out.... 5516
Jg 4:22 **S.** lay dead, and the nail was in his..... 5516
Jg 5:20 in their courses fought against **S.**....... 5516
Jg 5:26 and with the hammer she smote **S.**,...... 5516
Jg 5:28 The mother of **S.** looked out at a........ 5516
Jg 5:30 to **S.** a prey of divers colours, a........ 5516
1Sa 12:9 he sold them into the hand of **S.**,........ 5516
Ezr 2:53 the children of **S.**, the children of....... 5516
Ne 7:55 the children of **S.**, the children of....... 5516
Ps 83:9 as to **S.**, as to Jabin, at the brook...... 5516

SISTER See also SISTER'S; SISTERS.
Ge 4:22 the **s.** of Tubal-cain was Naamah......... 269
Ge 12:13 Say, I pray thee, thou art my **s.**.......... 269
Ge 12:19 Why saidst thou, She is my **s.**? so I..... 269
Ge 20:2 said of Sarah his wife, She is my **s.**....... 269
Ge 20:5 Said he not unto me, She is my **s.**?...... 269
Ge 20:12 And yet indeed she is my **s.**; she is..... 269
Ge 24:30 heard the words of Rebekah his **s.**,...... 269
Ge 24:59 they sent away Rebekah their **s.**,........ 269
Ge 24:60 and said unto her, Thou art our **s.**,...... 269
Ge 25:20 the **s.** to Laban the Syrian................. 269
Ge 26:7 said, She is my **s.**: for he feared......... 269
Ge 26:9 and how saidst thou, She is my **s.**?...... 269
Ge 28:9 the **s.** of Nebajoth, to be his wife......... 269
Ge 30:1 no children, Rachel envied her **s.**;........ 269
Ge 30:8 have I wrestled with my **s.**, and I........ 269
Ge 34:13 he had defiled Dinah their **s.**:............. 269
Ge 34:14 our **s.** to one that is uncircumcised;...... 269
Ge 34:27 because they had defiled their **s.**......... 269
Ge 34:31 deal with our **s.** as with an harlot?....... 269
Ge 36:3 Ishmael's daughter, **s.** of Nebajoth........ 269
Ge 36:22 Heman; and Lotan's **s.** was Timna........ 269
Ge 46:17 Isui, and Beriah, and Serah their **s.**....... 269
Ex 2:4 And his **s.** stood afar off, to wit what.... 269
Ex 2:7 said his **s.** to Pharaoh's daughter,........ 269
Ex 6:20 Jochebed his father's **s.** to wife:......... 1733
Ex 6:23 Amminadab **s.** of Naashon, to wife;...... 269
Ex 15:20 the prophetess, the **s.** of Aaron,.......... 269
Le 18:9 nakedness of thy **s.**, the daughter......... 269
Le 18:11 begotten of thy father, she is thy **s.**..... 269
Le 18:12 the nakedness of thy father's **s.**........... 269
Le 18:13 the nakedness of thy mother's **s.**......... 269
Le 18:18 shalt thou take a wife to her **s.**,........... 269
Le 20:17 And if a man shall take his **s.**, his........ 269
Le 20:19 the nakedness of thy mother's **s.**, nor... 269
Le 20:19 of thy father's **s.**: for he uncovereth..... 269
Le 21:3 And for his **s.** a virgin, that is nigh....... 269
Nu 6:7 mother, for his brother, or for his **s.**,... 269
Nu 25:18 of a prince of Midian, their **s.**,............. 269
Nu 26:59 and Moses, and Miriam their **s.**,........... 269
De 27:22 Cursed be he that lieth with his **s.**,...... 269
Jg 15:2 nor her younger **s.** fairer than she?....... 269
Ru 1:15 thy **s.** in law is gone back unto her..... 2994
Ru 1:15 gods: return thou after thy **s.** in law... 2994
2Sa 13:1 the son of David had a fair **s.**,............ 269
2Sa 13:2 that he fell sick for his **s.** Tamar:......... 269
2Sa 13:4 Tamar, my brother Absalom's **s.**.......... 269
2Sa 13:5 let my **s.** Tamar come, and give me..... 269
2Sa 13:6 let Tamar my **s.** come, and make me..... 269
2Sa 13:11 unto her, Come lie with me, my **s.**....... 269
2Sa 13:20 thee? but hold now thy peace, my **s.**..... 269
2Sa 13:22 because he had forced his **s.** Tamar...... 269
2Sa 13:32 the day that he forced his **s.** Tamar...... 269
2Sa 17:25 Nahash, **s.** to Zeruiah Joab's mother..... 269
1Ki 11:19 him to wife the **s.** of his own wife,....... 269
1Ki 11:19 wife, the **s.** of Tahpenes the queen....... 269
1Ki 11:20 **s.** of Tahpenes bare him Genubath....... 269
2Ki 11:2 But Jehosheba,...**s.** of Ahaziah,............ 269
1Ch 1:39 Homam: and Timna was Lotan's **s.**........ 269
1Ch 3:9 the concubines, and Tamar their **s.**........ 269
1Ch 3:19 Hananiah, and Shelomith their **s.**.......... 269
1Ch 4:3 name of their **s.** was Hazelelponi:......... 269
1Ch 4:19 of his wife Hodiah the **s.** of Naham,...... 269
1Ch 7:15 took to wife the **s.** of Huppim and........ 269
1Ch 7:18 And his **s.** Hammoleketh bare Ishod,..... 269
1Ch 7:30 and Beriah, and Serah their **s.**............. 269
1Ch 7:32 and Hotham, and Shua their **s.**............ 269
2Ch 22:11 (for she was the **s.** of Ahaziah,) hid....... 269
Job 17:14 Thou art my mother, and my **s.**........... 269
Pr 7:4 Say unto wisdom, Thou art my **s.**;......... 269
Ca 4:9 Thou hast ravished my heart, my **s.**,.... 269
Ca 4:10 How fair is thy love, my **s.**, my.......... 269
Ca 4:12 A garden inclosed is my **s.**, my.......... 269
Ca 5:1 I am come into my garden, my **s.**, my.. 269
Ca 5:2 knocketh, saying, Open to me, my **s.**,.. 269
Ca 8:8 We have a little **s.**, and she hath no..... 269
Ca 8:8 what shall we do for our **s.** in the day... 269
Jer 3:7 her treacherous **s.** Judah saw it........... 269
Jer 3:8 her treacherous **s.** Judah feared not,..... 269
Jer 3:10 her treacherous **s.** Judah hath not........ 269
Jer 22:18 Ah my brother! or, Ah **s.**! they shall....... 269
Eze 16:45 and thou art the **s.** of thy sisters,........ 269
Eze 16:46 And thine elder **s.** is Samaria, she........ 269
Eze 16:46 thy younger **s.**, that dwelleth at thy...... 269
Eze 16:48 Sodom thy **s.** hath not done, she nor.... 269
Eze 16:49 was the iniquity of thy **s.** Sodom,........ 269
Eze 16:56 For thy **s.** Sodom was not mentioned.... 269
Eze 22:11 another in thee hath humbled his **s.**,..... 269
Eze 23:4 the elder, and Aholibah her **s.**............. 269
Eze 23:11 when her **s.** Aholibah saw this, she...... 269
Eze 23:11 more than her **s.** in her whoredoms...... 269
Eze 23:18 my mind was alienated from her **s.**....... 269
Eze 23:31 hast walked in the way of thy **s.**;.......... 269
Eze 23:33 with the cup of thy **s.** Samaria............ 269
Eze 44:25 or for **s.** that hath had no husband,...... 269
Mt 12:50 **the same is my brother, and s., and**.. *79*
Mk 3:35 **the same is my brother, and my s.,**.. *79*
Lu 10:39 And she had a **s.** called Mary, which...... *79*
Lu 10:40 not care that my **s.** hath left me to........ *79*
Joh 11:1 the town of Mary and her **s.** Martha...... *79*
Joh 11:5 Now Jesus loved Martha, and her **s.**,..... *79*
Joh 11:28 called Mary her **s.** secretly, saying,....... *79*
Joh 11:39 Martha, the **s.** of him that was dead,..... *79*
Joh 19:25 his mother, and his mother's **s.**,............ *79*
Ro 16:1 I commend unto you Phebe our **s.**,........ *79*
Ro 16:15 and Julia, Nereus, and his **s.**, and.......... *79*
1Co 7:15 A brother or a **s.** is not under.............. *79*
1Co 9:5 we not power to lead about a **s.**, a......... *79*
Jas 2:15 If a brother or **s.** be naked, and........... *79*
2Jo 13 The children of thy elect **s.** greet.......... *79*

SISTER-IN-LAW See SISTER and LAW.

SISTER'S
Ge 24:30 and bracelets upon his **s.** hands,.......... 269
Ge 29:13 heard the tidings of Jacob his **s.** son,.... 269
Le 20:17 he hath uncovered his **s.** nakedness;..... 269
1Ch 7:15 whose **s.** name was Maachah:) and........ 269
Eze 23:32 shalt drink of thy **s.** cup deep and........ 269
Ac 23:16 when Paul's **s.** son heard of their.......... *79*
Col 4:10 and Marcus, **s.** son to Barnabas,.......... *431*

SISTERS
Jos 2:13 and my brethren, and my **s.**, and all..... 269
1Ch 2:16 Whose **s.** were Zeruiah, and Abigail...... 269
Job 1:4 called for their three **s.** to eat and to.... 269
Job 42:11 him all his brethren, and all his **s.**,....... 269
Eze 16:45 thou art the sister of thy **s.**, which........ 269
Eze 16:51 hast justified thy **s.** in all thine............ 269
Eze 16:52 Thou also, which hast judged thy **s.**....... 269
Eze 16:52 in that thou hast justified thy **s.**,.......... 269
Eze 16:55 thy **s.**, Sodom and her daughters,......... 269
Eze 16:61 when thou shalt receive thy **s.**, thine.... 269
Ho 2:1 Ammi; and to your **s.**, Ruhamah.......... 269
Mt 13:56 And his **s.**, are they not all with us?...... *79*
Mt 19:29 **forsaken houses, or brethren, or s.,**... *79*
Mk 6:3 and are not his **s.** here with us?............ *79*
Mk 10:29 **hath left house, or brethren, or s.,**... *79*
Mk 10:30 **houses, and brethren, and s., and**..... *79*
Lu 14:26 **and children, and brethren, and s.,**... *79*

Joh 11:3 Therefore his **s.** sent unto him, *79*
1Ti 5:2 the younger as **s.**, with all purity. *79*

SIT See also SAT; SITTEST; SITTETH; SITTING.
Ge 27:19 **s.** and eat of my venison, that thy 3427
Nu 32:6 go to war, and shall ye **s.** here? 3427
Jg 5:10 ye that **s.** in judgment, and walk by 3427
Ru 3:18 **S.** still, my daughter, until thou 3427
Ru 4:1 a one! turn aside, **s.** down here. 3427
Ru 4:2 the city, and said, **S.** ye down here. 3427
1Sa 9:22 made them **s.** in the chiefest place 5414
1Sa 16:11 for we will not **s.** down till he come 5437
1Sa 20:5 fail to **s.** with the king at meat: 3427
2Sa 19:8 Behold, the king doth **s.** in the gate. 3427
1Ki 1:13 and he shall **s.** upon my throne? 3427
1Ki 1:17 and he shall **s.** upon my throne. 3427
1Ki 1:20 shall **s.** on the throne of my lord 3427
1Ki 1:24 and he shall **s.** upon my throne? 3427
1Ki 1:27 should **s.** on the throne of my lord 3427
1Ki 1:30 he shall **s.** upon my throne in my 3427
1Ki 1:35 may come and **s.** upon my throne; 3427
1Ki 1:48 hath given one to **s.** on my throne 3427
1Ki 3:6 him a son to **s.** on his throne, as it 3427
1Ki 8:20 **s.** on the throne of Israel, as the 3427
1Ki 8:25 sight to **s.** on the throne of Israel; 3427
2Ki 7:3 Why **s.** we here until we die? 3427
2Ki 7:4 and if we **s.** still here, we die also. 3427
2Ki 10:30 shall **s.** on the throne of Israel. 3427
2Ki 15:12 Thy sons shall **s.** on the throne of 3427
2Ki 18:27 me to the men which **s.** on the wall, 3427
1Ch 28:5 Solomon...to **s.** upon the throne of 3427
2Ch 6:16 to **s.** upon the throne of Israel; 3427
Ps 26:5 and will not **s.** with the wicked. 3427
Ps 69:12 They that **s.** in the gate speak 3427
Ps 107:10 Such as **s.** in darkness and in the 3427
Ps 110:1 **S.** thou at my right hand, until I 3427
Ps 119:23 Princes also did **s.** and speak 3427
Ps 127:2 you to rise up early, to **s.** up late, 3427
Ps 132:12 shall also **s.** upon thy throne for 3427
Ec 10:6 dignity, and the rich **s.** in low place. 3427
Isa 3:26 desolate shall **s.** upon the ground. 3427
Isa 14:13 I will **s.** also upon the mount of the 3427
Isa 16:5 he shall **s.** upon it in truth in the 3427
Isa 30:7 this, Their strength is to **s.** still. 7674
Isa 36:12 to the men that **s.** upon the wall, 3427
Isa 42:7 **s.** in darkness out of the prison 3427
Isa 47:1 Come down, and **s.** in the dust, O 3427
Isa 47:1 of Babylon, **s.** on the ground: 3427
Isa 47:5 **S.** thou silent, and get thee into 3427
Isa 47:8 I shall not **s.** as a widow, neither 3427
Isa 47:14 to warm at, nor fire to **s.** before it. 3427
Isa 52:2 arise, and **s.** down; O Jerusalem: 3427
Jer 8:14 Why do we **s.** still? assemble 3427
Jer 13:13 kings that **s.** upon David's throne, 3427
Jer 13:18 queen, humble yourselves, **s.** down: 3427
Jer 16:8 to **s.** with them to eat and to drink. 3427
Jer 33:17 want a man to **s.** upon the throne of 3427
Jer 36:15 **S.** down now, and read it in our 3427
Jer 36:30 have none to **s.** upon the throne of 3427
Jer 48:18 from thy glory, and **s.** in thirst; for 3427
La 1:1 How doth the city **s.** solitary, that 3427
La 2:10 the daughter of Zion **s.** upon the 3427
Eze 26:16 they shall **s.** upon the ground, and 3427
Eze 28:2 I **s.** in the seat of God, in the midst 3427
Eze 33:31 they **s.** before thee as my people, 3427
Eze 44:3 he shall **s.** in it to eat bread before 3427
Da 7:9 the Ancient of days did **s.**, whose 3488
Da 7:26 But the judgment shall **s.**, and they 3488
Joe 3:12 will I **s.** to judge all the heathen 3427
Mic 4:4 shall **s.** every man under his vine 3427
Mic 7:8 when I **s.** in darkness, the Lord 3427
Zec 3:8 and thy fellows that **s.** before thee: 3427
Zec 6:13 shall **s.** and rule upon his throne; 3427
Mal 3:3 he shall **s.** as a refiner and purifier 3427
Mt 8:11 **shall s. down with Abraham, and** *347*
Mt 14:19 multitude to **s.** down on the grass, *347*
Mt 15:35 multitude to **s.** down on the ground. *377*
Mt 19:28 **Son of man shall s. in the throne** *2523*
Mt 19:28 **ye also shall s. upon twelve** *2523*
Mt 20:21 that these my two sons may **s.**, the *2523*
Mt 20:23 **to s. on my right hand, and on** *2523*
Mt 22:44 **S. thou on my right hand, till I** *2521*
Mt 23:2 **the Pharisees s. in Moses' seat:** *2523*
Mt 25:31 **then shall he s. upon the throne** *2523*
Mt 26:36 **S. ye here, while I go and pray** *2523*
Mk 6:39 to make all **s.** down by companies *347*
Mk 8:6 people to **s.** down on the ground: *377*
Mk 10:37 Grant unto us that we may **s.**, one *2523*
Mk 10:40 **But to s. on my right hand and** *2523*
Mk 12:36 **S. thou on my right hand, till I** *2521*
Mk 14:32 **S. ye here, while I shall pray** *2523*
Lu 1:79 light to them that **s.** in darkness *2521*
Lu 9:14 **Make them s. down by fifties in** *2625*
Lu 9:15 did so, and made them all **s.** down. *347*
Lu 12:37 **and make them to s. down to** *347*
Lu 13:29 **s. down in the kingdom of God** *347*
Lu 14:8 **s. not down in the highest room;** *2625*
Lu 14:10 **go and s. down in the lowest** *377*
Lu 14:10 **of them that s. at meat with thee** *4873*
Lu 16:6 **s. down quickly, and write fifty.** *2523*
Lu 17:7 **the field, Go and s. down to meat?** *377*
Lu 20:42 **Lord, S. thou on my right hand,** *2521*
Lu 22:30 **s. on thrones judging the twelve** *2523*
Lu 22:69 **Son of man s. on the right hand** *2521*
Joh 6:10 Jesus said, **Make the men s. down.** *377*
Ac 2:30 raise up Christ to **s.** on his throne; *2523*
Ac 2:34 Lord, **S.** thou on my right hand, *2521*
Ac 8:31 he would come up and **s.** with him. *2523*
1Co 8:10 **s.** at meat in the idol's temple, *2621*
Eph 2:6 made us **s.** together in heavenly *4776*
Heb 1:18 **S.** on my right hand, until I make *2521*
Jas 2:3 him, **S.** thou here in a good place; *2521*
Jas 2:3 or **s.** here under my footstool: *2521*
Re 3:21 **grant to s. with me in my throne,** *2523*
Re 17:3 woman **s.** upon a scarlet coloured *2521*
Re 18:7 I **s.** a queen, and am no widow, and *2521*
Re 19:18 of them that **s.** on them, and the *2521*

SITH See also SINCE.
Eze 35:6 **s.** thou hast not hated blood, even 518

SITNAH (sit'-nah)
Ge 26:21 and he called the name of it **S.** 7856

SITTEST
Ex 18:14 why **s.** thou thyself alone, and all 3427
De 6:7 them when thou **s.** in thine house, 3427
De 11:19 them when thou **s.** in thine house, 3427
Ps 50:20 Thou **s.** and speakest against thy 3427
Pr 23:1 When thou **s.** to eat with a ruler, 3427
Jer 22:2 that **s.** upon the throne of David, 3427
Ac 23:3 **s.** thou to judge me after the law, *2521*

SITTETH
Ex 11:5 Pharaoh that **s.** upon his throne, 3427
Le 15:4 every thing, whereon he **s.**, shall be 3427
Le 15:6 he that **s.** on any thing whereon he 3427
Le 15:20 every thing also that she **s.** upon 3427
Le 15:23 bed, or on any thing whereon she **s.**, 3427
Le 15:26 and whatsoever she **s.** upon shall be 3427
De 17:18 when he **s.** upon the throne of his 3427
1Ki 1:46 Solomon **s.** on the throne of the 3427
Es 6:10 the Jew, that **s.** at the king's gate: 3427
Ps 1:1 nor **s.** in the seat of the scornful. 3427
Ps 2:4 that **s.** in the heavens shall laugh: 3427
Ps 10:8 He **s.** in the lurking places of the 3427
Ps 29:10 The Lord **s.** upon the flood; 3427
Ps 29:10 yea, the Lord **s.** King for ever 3427
Ps 47:8 **s.** upon the throne of his holiness. 3427
Ps 99:1 he **s.** between the cherubims; let 3427
Pr 9:14 For she **s.** at the door of her house, 3427
Pr 20:8 that **s.** in the throne of judgment 3427
Pr 31:23 when he **s.** among the elders of the 3427
Ca 1:12 While the king **s.** at his table, my
Isa 28:6 to him that **s.** in judgment, 3427
Isa 40:22 that **s.** upon the circle of the earth, 3427
Jer 17:11 As the partridge **s.** on eggs, and 1716
Jer 29:16 that **s.** upon the throne of David, 3427
La 3:28 He **s.** alone and keepeth silence, 3427
Zec 1:11 all the earth **s.** still, and is at rest. 3427
Zec 5:7 that **s.** in the midst of the ephah. 3427
Mt 23:22 **of God, and by him that s. thereon.** *2521*
Lu 14:28 **s. not down first, and counteth** *2523*
Lu 14:31 **s. not down first, and consulteth** *2523*
Lu 22:27 **is greater, he that s. at meat, or** *345*
Lu 22:27 **is not he that s. at meat? but I am** *345*
1Co 14:30 be revealed to another that **s.** by, *2521*
Col 3:1 Christ **s.** on the right hand of God. *2521*
2Th 2:4 he as God **s.** in the temple of God, *2523*
Re 5:13 unto him that **s.** upon the throne, *2521*
Re 6:16 face of him that **s.** on the throne, *2521*
Re 7:10 our God which **s.** upon the throne, *2521*
Re 7:15 he that **s.** on the throne shall dwell *2521*
Re 17:1 whore that **s.** upon many waters: *2521*
Re 17:9 mountains, on which the woman **s.** *2521*
Re 17:15 where the whore **s.**, are peoples, *2521*

SITTING See also DOWNSITTING.
De 22:6 and the dam **s.** upon the young, or 7257
Jg 3:20 and he was **s.** in a summer parlour, 3427
1Ki 10:5 table, and the **s.** of his servants, 4186
1Ki 13:14 and found him **s.** under an oak: 3427
1Ki 22:19 I saw the Lord **s.** on his throne, and 3427
2Ki 4:38 of the prophets were **s.** before him: 3427
2Ki 9:5 the captains of the host were **s.**; 3427
2Ch 9:4 table, and the **s.** of his servants, 4186
2Ch 9:18 stays on each side of the **s.** place, 3427
2Ch 18:18 I saw the Lord **s.** upon his throne, 3427
Ne 2:6 unto me, (the queen also **s.** by him,) 3427
Es 5:13 Mordecai...**s.** at the king's gate. 3427
Isa 6:1 saw also the Lord **s.** upon a throne, 3427
Jer 17:25 princes **s.** upon the throne of David, 3427
Jer 22:4 kings **s.** upon the throne of David, 3427
Jer 22:30 **s.** upon the throne of David, and 3427
Jer 38:7 then **s.** in the gate of Benjamin; 3427
La 3:63 Behold their **s.** down, and their 3427
Mt 9:9 **s.** at the receipt of custom: *2521*
Mt 11:16 **unto children s. in the markets,** *2521*
Mt 20:30 two blind men **s.** by the way side, *2521*
Mt 21:5 thee, meek, and **s.** upon an ass, *1910*
Mt 26:64 **Son of man s. on the right hand** *2521*
Mt 27:36 **s.** down they watched him there; *2521*
Mt 27:61 Mary, **s.** over against the sepulchre. *2521*
Mk 2:6 were certain of the scribes **s.** there, *2521*
Mk 2:14 Alphaeus **s.** at the receipt of custom, *2521*
Mk 5:15 had the legion, **s.**, and clothed, and *2521*
Mk 14:62 **Son of man s. on the right hand** *2521*
Mk 16:5 a young man **s.** on the right side, *2521*
Lu 2:46 **s.** in the midst of the doctors, both *2516*
Lu 5:17 and doctors of the law **s.** by, which *2521*
Lu 5:27 Levi, **s.** at the receipt of custom: *2521*
Lu 7:32 **children s. in the marketplace,** *2521*
Lu 8:35 **s.** at the feet of Jesus, clothed, and *2521*
Lu 10:13 **repented, s. in sackcloth and** *2521*
Joh 2:14 and the changers of money **s.**: *2521*
Joh 12:15 King cometh, **s.** on an ass's colt. *2521*
Joh 20:12 And seeth two angels in white **s.**, *2516*
Ac 2:2 all the house where they were **s.** *2521*
Ac 8:28 **s.** in his chariot read Esaias the *2521*
Ac 25:6 next day **s.** on the judgment seat *2523*
Re 4:4 I saw four and twenty elders **s.**, *2521*

SITTING-PLACE See SITTING and PLACE.

SITUATE
1Sa 14:5 one was **s.** northward over against 4690
Eze 27:3 that art **s.** at the entry of the sea, 3427
Na 3:8 No, that was **s.** among the rivers, 3427

SITUATION
2Ki 2:19 the **s.** of this city is pleasant, as 4186
Ps 48:2 Beautiful for **s.**, the joy of the 5131

SIVAN (si'-van)
Es 8:9 third month, that is, the month **S.**, 5510

SIX See also SIXSCORE; SIXTEEN.
Ge 7:6 Noah was **s.** hundred years old 8337
Ge 7:11 the **s.** hundredth year of Noah's life, 8337
Ge 8:13 in the **s.** hundredth and first year, 8337
Ge 16:16 Abram was fourscore and **s.** years 8337
Ge 30:20 because I have born him **s.** sons: 8337
Ge 31:41 and **s.** years for thy cattle: 8337
Ge 46:26 the souls were threescore and **s.**; 8337
Ex 12:37 **s.** hundred thousand on foot that 8337
Ex 14:7 he took **s.** hundred chosen chariots, 8337
Ex 16:26 **S.** days ye shall gather it; but on 8337
Ex 20:9 **S.** days shalt thou labour, and do 8337
Ex 20:11 **s.** days the Lord made heaven and 8337
Ex 21:2 servant, **s.** years he shall serve: 8337
Ex 23:10 **s.** years thou shalt sow thy land, 8337
Ex 23:12 **S.** days thou shalt do thy work, and 8337
Ex 24:16 and the cloud covered it **s.** days: 8337
Ex 25:32 **s.** branches shall come out of the 8337
Ex 25:33 the **s.** branches that come out of the 8337
Ex 25:35 the **s.** branches that proceed out of 8337
Ex 26:9 and **s.** curtains by themselves, and 8337
Ex 26:22 westward thou shalt make **s.** boards 8337
Ex 28:10 **S.** of their names on one stone, and 8337
Ex 28:10 **s.** names of the rest on the other 8337
Ex 31:15 **S.** days may work be done; but in 8337
Ex 31:17 **s.** days the Lord made heaven and 8337
Ex 34:21 **S.** days thou shalt work, but on the 8337
Ex 35:2 **S.** days shall work be done, but on 8337
Ex 36:16 and **s.** curtains by themselves. 8337
Ex 36:27 westward he made **s.** boards. 8337

Ex	37:18	**s.** branches going out of the sides	8337
Ex	37:19	the **s.** branches going out of the	8337
Ex	37:21	to the **s.** branches going out of it.	8337
Ex	38:26	for **s.** hundred thousand and three	8337
Le	12:5	purifying threescore and **s.** days.	8337
Le	23:3	**S.** days shall work be done: but	8337
Le	24:6	set them in two rows, **s.** on a row,	8337
Le	25:3	**S.** years thou shalt sow thy field,	8337
Le	25:3	and **s.** years thou shalt prune thy	8337
Nu	1:21	and **s.** thousand and five hundred.	8337
Nu	1:25	five thousand **s.** hundred and fifty.	8337
Nu	1:27	fourteen thousand and **s.** hundred.	8337
Nu	1:46	**s.** hundred thousand and three	8337
Nu	2:4	fourteen thousand and **s.** hundred.	8337
Nu	2:9	and **s.** thousand and four hundred,	8337
Nu	2:11	and **s.** thousand and five hundred.	8337
Nu	2:15	thousand and **s.** hundred and fifty.	8337
Nu	2:31	seven thousand and **s.** hundred.	8337
Nu	2:32	**s.** hundred thousand and three	8337
Nu	3:28	eight thousand and **s.** hundred,	8337
Nu	3:34	were **s.** thousand and two hundred.	8337
Nu	4:40	two thousand and **s.** hundred and	8337
Nu	7:3	**s.** covered wagons, and twelve oxen;	8337
Nu	11:21	are **s.** hundred thousand footmen;	8337
Nu	26:41	and five thousand and **s.** hundred.	8337
Nu	26:51	of Israel, **s.** hundred thousand and	8337
Nu	31:32	**s.** hundred thousand and seventy	8337
Nu	31:37	was **s.** hundred and threescore and	8337
Nu	31:38	beeves were thirty and **s.** thousand;	8337
Nu	31:44	And thirty and **s.** thousand beeves,	8337
Nu	35:6	there shall be **s.** cities for refuge,	8337
Nu	35:13	**s.** cities shall ye have for refuge.	8337
Nu	35:15	These **s.** cities shall be a refuge,	8337
De	5:13	**S.** days thou shalt labour, and do	8337
De	15:12	unto thee, and serve thee **s.** years;	8337
De	15:18	to thee, in serving thee **s.** years:	8337
De	16:8	**S.** days thou shalt eat unleavened	8337
Jos	6:3	once. Thus shalt thou do **s.** days.	8337
Jos	6:14	into the camp: so they did **s.** days.	8337
Jos	7:5	smote...about thirty and **s.** men:	8337
Jos	15:59,	62 **s.** cities with their villages.	8337
Jg	3:31	slew of the Philistines **s.** hundred	8337
Jg	12:7	Jephthah judged Israel **s.** years.	8337
Jg	18:11,	16 **s.** hundred men appointed with	8337
Jg	18:17	**s.** hundred men that were appointed	8337
Jg	20:15	cities twenty and **s.** thousand men	8337
Jg	20:47	**s.** hundred men turned and fled to	8337
Ru	3:15	he measured **s.** measures of barley,	8337
Ru	3:17	**s.** measures of barley gave he me;	8337
1Sa	13:5	chariots, and **s.** thousand horsemen,	8337
1Sa	13:15	with him, about **s.** hundred men.	8337
1Sa	14:2	him were about **s.** hundred men;	8337
1Sa	17:4	height was **s.** cubits and a span.	8337
1Sa	17:7	spear's head weighed **s.** hundred	8337
1Sa	23:13	men, which were about **s.** hundred,	8337
1Sa	27:2	passed over with the **s.** hundred men.	8337
1Sa	30:9	**s.** hundred men that were with	8337
2Sa	2:11	was seven years and **s.** months.	8337
2Sa	5:5	Judah seven years and **s.** months:	8337
2Sa	6:13	ark of the Lord had gone **s.** paces,	8337
2Sa	15:18	**s.** hundred men which came after	8337
2Sa	21:20	that had on every hand **s.** fingers,	8337
2Sa	21:20	and on every foot **s.** toes, four and	8337
1Ki	6:6	and the middle was **s.** cubits broad,	8337
1Ki	10:14	Solomon in one year was **s.** hundred	8337
1Ki	10:14	threescore and **s.** talents of gold,	8337
1Ki	10:16	**s.** hundred shekels of gold went to	8337
1Ki	10:19	The throne had **s.** steps, and the	8337
1Ki	10:20	and on the other upon the **s.** steps:	8337
1Ki	10:29	for **s.** hundred shekels of silver,	8337
1Ki	11:16	**s.** months did Joab remain there	8337
1Ki	16:23	**s.** years reigned he in Tirzah.	8337
2Ki	5:5	and **s.** thousand pieces of gold, and	8337
2Ki	11:3	in the house of the Lord **s.** years.	8337
2Ki	13:19	have smitten five or **s.** times;	8337
2Ki	15:8	over Israel in Samaria **s.** months.	8337
1Ch	3:4	**s.** were born unto him in Hebron;	8337
1Ch	3:4	reigned seven years and **s.** months:	8337
1Ch	3:22	and Neariah, and Shaphat, **s.**.	8337
1Ch	4:27	had sixteen sons and **s.** daughters;	8337
1Ch	7:2	twenty thousand and **s.** hundred.	8337
1Ch	7:4	for war, **s.** and thirty thousand men:	8337
1Ch	7:40	was twenty and **s.** thousand men.	8337
1Ch	8:38	And Azel had **s.** sons, whose names	8337
1Ch	9:6	brethren, **s.** hundred and ninety.	8337
1Ch	9:9	nine hundred and fifty and **s.**.	8337
1Ch	9:44	And Azel had **s.** sons, whose names	8337
1Ch	12:24	**s.** thousand and eight hundred,	8337
1Ch	12:26	Levi four thousand and **s.** hundred.	8337
1Ch	12:35	and eight thousand and **s.** hundred.	8337
1Ch	20:6	**s.** on each hand, and **s.** on each foot:	8337
1Ch	21:25	**s.** hundred shekels of gold by	8337
1Ch	23:4	and **s.** thousand were officers and	8337
1Ch	25:3	Hashabiah, and Mattithiah, **s.**,	8337
1Ch	26:17	Eastward were **s.** Levites,	8337
2Ch	1:17	a chariot for **s.** hundred shekels of	8337
2Ch	2:2	and **s.** hundred to oversee them.	8337
2Ch	2:17	three thousand and **s.** hundred.	8337
2Ch	2:18	thousand and **s.** hundred overseers	8337
2Ch	3:8	amounting to **s.** hundred talents.	8337
2Ch	9:13	Solomon in one year was **s.** hundred	8337
2Ch	9:13	threescore and **s.** talents of gold;	8337
2Ch	9:15	**s.** hundred shekels of beaten gold	8337
2Ch	9:18	there were **s.** steps to the throne,	8337
2Ch	9:19	and on the other upon the **s.** steps.	8337
2Ch	16:1	**s.** and thirtieth year of the reign	8337
2Ch	22:12	hid in the house of God **s.** years:	8337
2Ch	26:12	were two thousand and **s.** hundred.	8337
2Ch	29:33	were **s.** hundred oxen and three	8337
2Ch	35:8	and **s.** hundred small cattle, and	8337
Ezr	2:10	of Bani, **s.** hundred forty and two.	8337
Ezr	2:11	of Bebai, **s.** hundred twenty and	8337
Ezr	2:13	Adonikam, **s.** hundred sixty and **s.**.	8337
Ezr	2:14	Bigvai, two thousand fifty and **s.**.	8337
Ezr	2:22	The men of Netophah, fifty and **s.**.	8337
Ezr	2:26	Gaba, **s.** hundred twenty and one.	8337
Ezr	2:30	Magbish, an hundred fifty and **s.**.	8337
Ezr	2:35	three thousand and **s.** hundred	8337
Ezr	2:60	Nekoda, **s.** hundred fifty and two.	8337
Ezr	2:66	were seven hundred thirty and **s.**;	8337
Ezr	2:67	**s.** thousand seven hundred and	8337
Ezr	8:26	**s.** hundred and fifty talents of	8337
Ezr	8:35	for all Israel, ninety and **s.** rams,	8337
Ne	5:18	was one ox and **s.** choice sheep;	8337
Ne	7:10	of Arah, **s.** hundred fifty and two.	8337
Ne	7:15	Binnui, **s.** hundred forty and eight.	8337
Ne	7:16	of Bebai, **s.** hundred twenty and	8337
Ne	7:18	Adonikam, **s.** hundred threescore	8337
Ne	7:20	of Adin, **s.** hundred fifty and five.	8337
Ne	7:30	Gaba, **s.** hundred twenty and one.	8337
Ne	7:62	Nekoda, **s.** hundred forty and two.	8337
Ne	7:68	horses, seven hundred thirty and **s.**:	8337
Ne	7:69	**s.** thousand seven hundred and	8337
Es	2:12	to wit, **s.** months with oil of myrrh,	8337
Es	2:12	and **s.** months with sweet odours,	8337
Job	5:19	He shall deliver thee in **s.** troubles:	8337
Job	42:12	**s.** thousand camels, and a thousand.	8337
Pr	6:16	These **s.** things doth the Lord hate:	8337
Isa	6:2	seraphims: each one had **s.** wings;	8337
Jer	34:14	when he hath served thee **s.** years,	8337
Jer	52:23	were ninety and **s.** pomegranates	8337
Jer	52:30	were four thousand and **s.** hundred.	8337
Eze	9:2	**s.** men came from the way of the	8337
Eze	40:5	a measuring reed of **s.** cubits long	8337
Eze	40:12	**s.** cubits on this side, and **s.** cubits	8337
Eze	41:1	**s.** cubits broad on the one side, and	8337
Eze	41:1	**s.** cubits broad on the other side,	8337
Eze	41:3	two cubits; and the door, **s.** cubits;	8337
Eze	41:5	the wall of the house, **s.** cubits;	8337
Eze	41:8	were a full reed of **s.** great cubits.	8337
Eze	46:1	shall be shut the **s.** working days;	8337
Eze	46:4	shall be **s.** lambs without blemish,	8337
Eze	46:6	blemish, and **s.** lambs, and a ram:	8337
Da	3:1	and the breadth thereof **s.** cubits:	8353
Mt	17:1	after **s.** days Jesus taketh Peter,	*1803*
Mk	9:2	after **s.** days Jesus taketh with him	*1803*
Lu	4:25	shut up three years and **s.** months,	*1803*
Lu	13:14	are **s.** days in which men ought to	*1803*
Joh	2:6	were set there **s.** waterpots of stone,	*1803*
Joh	2:20	Forty and **s.** years was this temple	*1803*
Joh	12:1	**s.** days before the passover came to	*1803*
Ac	11:12	these **s.** brethren accompanied me,	*1803*
Ac	18:11	there a year and **s.** months,	*1803*
Jas	5:17	space of three years and **s.** months.	*1803*
Re	4:8	each of them **s.** wings about him;	*1803*
Re	13:18	is S. hundred threescore and **s.**.	*5516*
Re	14:20	thousand and **s.** hundred furlongs.	*1812*

SIX-HUNDRED See SIX and HUNDRED.

SIXSCORE

1Ki	9:14	to the king **s.** talents of gold.	3967,6242
Jon	4:11	more than **s.** thousand	8147,6240,7239

SIXTEEN

Ge	46:18	she bare unto Jacob, even **s.**	8337,6240
Ex	26:25	sockets of silver, **s.** sockets;	8337,6240
Ex	36:30	their sockets were **s.** sockets of	8337,6240
Nu	26:22	**s.** thousand and five hundred.	8337,6240
Nu	31:40	the persons were **s.** thousand;	8337,6240
Nu	31:46	And **s.** thousand persons;)	8337,6240
Nu	31:52	**s.** thousand seven hundred and	8337,6240
Jos	15:41	**s.** cities with their villages:	8337,6240
Jos	19:22	**s.** cities with their villages.	8337,6240
2Ki	13:10	Samaria, and reigned **s.** years.	8337,6240
2Ki	14:21	which was **s.** years old, and	8337,6240
2Ki	15:2	**S.** years old was he when he	8337,6240
2Ki	15:33	reigned **s.** years in Jerusalem.	8337,6240
2Ki	16:2	reigned **s.** years in Jerusalem,	8337,6240
1Ch	4:27	Shimei had **s.** sons and six	8337,6240
1Ch	24:4	of Eleazar there were **s.** chief	8337,6240
2Ch	13:21	two sons, and **s.** daughters.	8337,6240
2Ch	26:1	Uzziah, who was **s.** years old,	8337,6240
2Ch	26:3	**S.** years old was Uzziah when	8337,6240
2Ch	27:1	reigned **s.** years in Jerusalem.	8337,6240
2Ch	27:8	reigned **s.** years in Jerusalem.	8337,6240
2Ch	28:1	reigned **s.** years in Jerusalem:	8337,6240
Ac	27:37	threescore and **s.** souls.	*1440,1803*

SIXTEENTH

1Ch	24:14	to Bilgah, the **s.** to Immer,	8337,6240
1Ch	25:23	The **s.** to Hananiah, he, his	8337,6240
2Ch	29:17	in the **s.** day of the first month	8337,6240

SIXTH

Ge	1:31	and the morning were the **s.** day.	8345
Ge	30:19	again, and bare Jacob the **s.** son.	8345
Ex	16:5	on the **s.** day they shall prepare	8345
Ex	16:22	on the **s.** day they gathered twice	8345
Ex	16:29	on the **s.** day the bread of two days;	8345
Ex	26:9	shalt double the **s.** curtain in the	8345
Le	25:21	blessing upon you in the **s.** year,	8345
Nu	7:42	On the **s.** day Eliasaph the son of	8345
Nu	29:29	on the **s.** day eight bullocks, two	8345
Jos	19:32	The **s.** lot came out to the children	8345
2Sa	3:5	the **s.**, Ithream, by Eglah David's	8345
1Ki	16:8	In the twenty and **s.** year of Asa	8337
2Ki	18:10	even in the **s.** year of Hezekiah,	8337
1Ch	2:15	Ozem the **s.**, David the seventh:	8345
1Ch	3:3	**s.**, Ithream by Eglah his wife.	8345
1Ch	12:11	Attai the **s.**, Eliel the seventh,	8345
1Ch	24:9	to Malchijah, the **s.** of Mijamin,	8345
1Ch	25:13	The **s.** to Bukkiah, he, his sons, and	8345
1Ch	26:3	Elam the fifth, Jehohanan the **s.**,	8345
1Ch	26:5	Ammiel the **s.**, Issachar the	8345
1Ch	27:9	The **s.** captain for the **s.** month was	8345
Ezr	6:15	was in the **s.** year of the reign of	8353
Ne	3:30	and Hanun the **s.** son of Zalaph,	8345
Eze	4:11	by measure, the **s.** part of an hin:	8345
Eze	8:1	pass in the **s.** year, in the **s.** month,	8345
Eze	39:2	and leave but the **s.** part of thee,	8338
Eze	45:13	offer; the **s.** part of an ephah of an	8345
Eze	45:13	give the **s.** part of an ephah of an	8341
Eze	46:14	the **s.** part of an ephah, and the	8345
Hag	1:1	of Darius the king, in the **s.** month,	8345
Hag	1:15	and twentieth day of the **s.** month,	8345
Mt	20:5	**out about the s. and ninth hour,**	*1623*
Mt	27:45	the **s.** hour there was darkness	*1623*
Mk	15:33	when the **s.** hour was come, there	*1623*
Lu	1:26	the **s.** month the angel Gabriel was	*1623*
Lu	1:36	this is the **s.** month with her, who	*1623*
Lu	23:44	it was about the **s.** hour, and there	*1623*
Joh	4:6	well: and it was about the **s.** hour.	*1623*
Joh	19:14	passover, and about the **s.** hour:	*1623*
Ac	10:9	housetop to pray about the **s.** hour:	*1623*
Re	6:12	when he had opened the **s.** seal,	*1623*
Re	9:13	the **s.** angel sounded, and I heard a	*1623*
Re	9:14	Saying to the **s.** angel which had	*1623*
Re	16:12	And the **s.** angel poured out his vial	*1623*
Re	21:20	The fifth, sardonyx; the **s.**, sardius;	*1623*

SIX-THOUSAND See SIX and THOUSAND.

SIXTY See also SIXTYFOLD.

Ge	5:15	Mahalaleel lived **s.** and five years,	8346
Ge	5:18	Jared lived an hundred **s.** and two	8346
Ge	5:20	Jared were nine hundred **s.** and two	8346
Ge	5:21	And Enoch lived **s.** and five years,	8346
Ge	5:23	of Enoch were three hundred **s.** and	8346
Ge	5:27	Methuselah were nine hundred **s.**	8346
Le	27:3	from twenty years old even unto **s.**	8346
Le	27:7	if it be from **s.** years old and above;	8346

Nu 7:88 the rams s., the he goats s., 8346
Nu 7:88 the lambs of the first year s.. This 8346
Ezr 2:13 Adonikam, six hundred s. and six. 8346
Mt 13:23 **some an hundredfold, some s.,** *1835*
Mk 4:8 **some thirty, and some s., and** *1835*
Mk 4:20 **some thirtyfold, some s., and** *1835*

SIXTYFOLD
Mt 13:8 **some s., some thirtyfold.** *1835*

SIZE
Ex 36:9 the curtains were all of one s.. 4060
Ex 36:15 the eleven curtains were of one s. 4060
1Ki 6:25 were of one measure and one s.. 7095
1Ki 7:37 casting, one measure, and one s.. 7095
1Ch 23:29 for all manner of measure and s.; 4060

SKIES
2Sa 22:12 waters, and thick clouds of the s.. 7834
Ps 18:11 waters and thick clouds of the s.. 7834
Ps 77:17 out water: the s. sent out a sound: 7834
Isa 45:8 let the s. pour down righteousness: 7834
Jer 51:9 and is lifted up even to the s.. 7834

SKILFUL See also UNSKILFUL.
1Ch 5:18 and s. in war, were four and forty 3925
1Ch 15:22 about the song, because he was s. 995
1Ch 28:21 every willing s. man, for any 2451
2Ch 2:14 s. to work in gold, and in silver, in 3045
Eze 21:31 of brutish men, and s. to destroy. 2796
Da 1:4 favoured, and s. in all wisdom, 7919
Am 5:16 such as are s. of lamentation to 3045

SKILFULLY
Ps 33:3 song; play s. with a loud noise. 3190

SKILFULNESS
Ps 78:72 them by the s. of his hands. 8394

SKILL See also SKILFUL.
1Ki 5:6 can s. to hew timber like unto the 3045
2Ch 2:7 s. to grave with the cunning men 3045
2Ch 2:8 thy servants can s. to cut timber 3045
2Ch 34:12 could s. of instruments of musick. 995
Ec 9:11 nor yet favour to men of s.; but 3045
Da 1:17 and s. in all learning and wisdom: 7919
Da 9:22 to give thee s. and understanding. 7919

SKIN See also FORESKIN; SKINS.
Ex 22:27 only, it is his raiment for his s. 5785
Ex 29:14 the flesh of the bullock, and his s., 5785
Ex 34:29 wist not that the s. of his face shone 5785
Ex 34:30 behold, the s. of his face shone; 5785
Ex 34:35 that the s. of Moses' face shone: 5785
Le 4:11 And the s. of the bullock, and all 5785
Le 7:8 himself the s. of the burnt offering 5785
Le 11:32 vessel of wood, or raiment, or s., or 5785
Le 13:2 have in the s. of his flesh a rising, 5785
Le 13:2 it be in the s. of his flesh like the 5785
Le 13:3 on the plague in the s. of the flesh: 5785
Le 13:3 be deeper than the s. of his flesh, 5785
Le 13:4 spot be white in the s. of his flesh, 5785
Le 13:4 in sight be not deeper than the s., 5785
Le 13:5 and the plague spread not in the s.; 5785
Le 13:6 the plague spread not in the s., the 5785
Le 13:7 scab spread much abroad in the s., 5785
Le 13:8 the scab spreadeth in the s., then 5785
Le 13:10 if the rising be white in the s., and 5785
Le 13:11 an old leprosy in the s. of his flesh, 5785
Le 13:12 leprosy break out abroad in the s., 5785
Le 13:12 leprosy cover all the s. of him that 5785
Le 13:18 in the s. thereof, was a boil, and is 5785
Le 13:20 it be in sight lower than the s., and 5785
Le 13:21 and if it be not lower than the s., 5785
Le 13:22 if it spread much abroad in the s., 5785
Le 13:24 s. whereof there is a hot burning, 5785
Le 13:25 it be in sight deeper than the s.; 5785
Le 13:26 it be no lower than the other s., 5785
Le 13:27 it be spread much abroad in the s., 5785
Le 13:28 his place, and spread not in the s., 5785
Le 13:30 if it be in sight deeper than the s.; 5785
Le 13:31 it be not in sight deeper than the s., 5785
Le 13:32 be not in s. deeper then the s.; 5785
Le 13:34 if the scall be not spread in the s., 5785
Le 13:34 nor be in sight deeper than the s.; 5785
Le 13:35 if the scall spread much in the s. 5785
Le 13:36 if the scall be spread in the s., the 5785
Le 13:38 in the s. of their flesh bright spots, 5785
Le 13:39 bright spots in the s. of their flesh 5785
Le 13:39 spot that groweth in the s.; he is 5785
Le 13:43 appeareth in the s. of the flesh; 5785
Le 13:48 in a s., or in any thing made of s.; 5785
Le 13:49 reddish in the garment, or in the s., 5785
Le 13:49 in the woof, or in any thing of s.; 5785
Le 13:51 the warp, or in the woof, or in a s., 5785
Le 13:51 or in any work that is made of s.; 5785
Le 13:52 or any thing of s., wherein the 5785
Le 13:53 or in the woof, or in any thing of s.; 5785
Le 13:56 out of the garment, or out of the s., 5785
Le 13:57 or in the woof, or in any thing of s.; 5785
Le 13:58 or whatsoever thing of s. it be, 5785
Le 15:17 And every garment, and every s.,
Nu 19:5 burn the heifer in his sight; her s., 5785
Job 2:4 S. for s., yea, all that a man 5785
Job 7:5 my s. is broken, and become 5785
Job 10:11 hast clothed me with s. and flesh, 5785
Job 16:15 have sewed sackcloth upon my s., 1539
Job 18:13 shall devour the strength of his s. 5785
Job 19:20 My bone cleaveth to my s. and to 5785
Job 19:20 and I am escaped with the s. of my 5785
Job 19:26 though after my s. worms destroy 5785
Job 30:30 My s. is black upon me, and my 5785
Job 41:7 thou fill his s. with barbed irons? 5785
Ps 102:5 my bones cleave to my s.. 1320
Jer 13:23 Can the Ethiopian change his s., 5785
La 3:4 flesh and my s. hath he made old: 5785
La 4:8 their s. cleaveth to their bones; it 5785
La 5:10 Our s. was black like an oven 5785
Eze 16:10 and shod thee with badgers' s., and
Eze 37:6 upon you, and cover you with s., 5785
Eze 37:8 and the s. covered them above: but 5785
Mic 3:2 pluck off their s. from off them, 5785
Mic 3:3 and flay their s. from off them; and 5785
Mk 1:6 a girdle of a s. about his loins; *1193*

SKINS See also FORESKINS; GOATSKINS; SHEEPSKINS.
Ge 3:21 did the Lord God make coats of s., 5785
Ge 27:16 he put the s. of the kids of the 5785
Ex 25:5 rams' s. dyed red, and badgers' s., 5785
Ex 26:14 for the tent of rams' s. dyed red, 5785
Ex 26:14 and a covering above of badgers' s.. 5785
Ex 35:7 rams' s. dyed red, and badgers' s., 5785
Ex 35:23 and red s. of rams, and badgers' s., 5785
Ex 36:19 for the tent of rams' s. dyed red, 5785
Ex 36:19 and a covering of badgers' s. above 5785
Ex 39:34 the covering of rams's s. dyed red, 5785
Ex 39:34 the covering of badgers's s., and the 5785
Le 13:59 warp, or woof, or any thing of s., 5785
Le 16:27 they shall burn in the fire their s., 5785
Nu 4:6 thereon the covering of badgers' s., 5785
Nu 4:8 same with a covering of badgers' s., 5785
Nu 4:10 within a covering of badgers' s., 5785
Nu 4:11 it with a covering of badgers' s., 5785
Nu 4:12 them with a covering of badgers' s., 5785
Nu 4:14 upon it a covering of badgers' s., 5785
Nu 4:25 covering of the badgers' s. that is
Nu 31:20 all that is made of s., and all work 5785

SKIP See also SKIPPED; SKIPPING.
Ps 29:6 them also to s. like a calf; 7540

SKIPPED See also SKIPPEDST.
Ps 114:4 The mountains s. like rams, and 7540
Ps 114:6 mountains, that ye s. like rams; 7540

SKIPPEDST
Jer 48:27 spakest of him, thou s. for joy. 5110

SKIPPING
Ca 2:8 the mountains, s. upon the hills 7092

SKIRT See also SKIRTS.
De 22:30 wife, nor discover his father's s.. 3671
De 27:20 he uncovereth his father's s.. 3671
Ru 3:9 spread therefore thy s. over thine 3671
1Sa 15:27 laid hold upon the s. of his mantle, 3671
1Sa 24:4 cut off the s. of Saul's robe privily. 3671
1Sa 24:5 because he had cut off Saul's s.. 3671
1Sa 24:11 see the s. of thy robe in my hand: 3671
1Sa 24:11 in that I cut off the s. of thy robe, 3671
Eze 16:8 and I spread my s. over thee, and 3671
Hag 2:12 holy flesh in the s. of his garment, 3671
Hag 2:12 and with his s. do touch bread, or 3671
Zec 8:23 hold of the s. of him that is a Jew, 3671

SKIRTS
Ps 133:2 down to the s. of his garments; 6310
Jer 2:34 Also in thy s. is found the blood of 3671
Jer 13:22 iniquity are thy s. discovered, and 7757
Jer 13:26 I discover thy s. upon thy face, 7757
La 1:9 Her filthiness is in her s.; she 7757
Eze 5:3 number, and bind them in thy s.. 3671
Na 3:5 will discover thy s. upon thy face, 7757

SKULL
Jg 9:53 head, and all to brake his s.. 1538
2Ki 9:35 found no more of her than the s., 1538
Mt 27:33 that is to say, a place of a s., *2898*
Mk 15:22 being interpreted, The place of a s.. *2898*
Joh 19:17 into a place called the place of a s., *2898*

SKY See also SKIES.
De 33:26 and in his excellency on the s.. 7834
Job 37:18 thou with him spread out the s., 7834
Mt 16:2 **be fair weather: for the s. is red** *3772*
Mt 16:3 **for the s. is red and lowering** *3772*
Mt 16:3 **ye can discern the face of the s.** *3772*
Lu 12:56 **ye can discern the face of the s.** *3772*
Heb 11:12 so many as the stars of the s. in *3772*

SLACK See also SLACKED.
De 7:10 not be s. to him that hateth him, 309
De 23:21 thy God, thou shalt not s. to pay it: 309
Jos 10:6 S. not thy hand from thy servants; 7503
Jos 18:3 How long are ye s. to go to possess 7503
2Ki 4:24 s. not thy riding for me, except I 6113
Pr 10:4 poor that dealeth with a s. hand: 7423
Zep 3:16 Zion, Let not thine hands be s.. 7503
2Pe 3:9 The Lord is not s. concerning his *1019*

SLACKED
Hab 1:4 the law is s., and judgment doth 6313

SLACKNESS
2Pe 3:9 promise, as some men count s.; *1022*

SLAIN
Ge 4:23 I have s. a man to my wounding, 2026
Ge 34:27 sons of Jacob came upon the s., 2491
Le 14:51 them in the blood of the s. bird, 7819
Le 26:17 shall be s. before your enemies: 5062
Nu 11:22 flocks of the herds be s. for 7819
Nu 14:16 hath s. them in the wilderness. 7819
Nu 19:16 one that is s. with a sword in 2491
Nu 19:18 a bone, or one s., or one dead, or a 2491
Nu 22:33 surely now also I had s. thee, and 2026
Nu 23:24 and drink the blood of the s.. 2491
Nu 25:14 name of the Israelite that was s., 5221
Nu 25:14 was s. with the Midianitish woman, 5221
Nu 25:15 Midianitish woman that was s. was 5221
Nu 25:18 was s. in the day of the plague for 5221
Nu 31:8 the rest of them that were s.; 2491
Nu 31:19 and whosoever hath touched any s., 2491
De 1:4 he had s. Sihon the king of the 5221
De 21:1 be found s. in the land which the 2491
De 21:1 it be not known who hath s. him: 2491
De 21:2 are round about him that is s.: 2491
De 21:3 city which is next unto the s. man, 2491
De 21:6 that are next unto the s. man, shall 2491
De 28:31 Thine ox shall be s. before thine 2873
De 32:42 with the blood of the s. and of the 2491
Jos 11:6 deliver them up all s. before Israel: 2491
Jos 13:22 among them that were s. by them. 2491
Jg 9:18 and have s. his sons, threescore 2026
Jg 15:16 an ass have I s. a thousand men. 5221
Jg 20:4 husband of the woman that was s., 7523
Jg 20:5 night, and thought to have s. me: 2026
1Sa 4:11 Hophni and Phinehas, were s. 4191
1Sa 18:7 Saul hath s. his thousands, and 5221
1Sa 19:6 the Lord liveth, he shall not be s.. 4191
1Sa 19:11 to morrow thou shalt be s. 4191
1Sa 20:32 Wherefore shall he be s.? what 4191
1Sa 21:11 Saul hath s. his thousands, and 5221
1Sa 22:21 Saul had s. the Lord's priests. 2026
1Sa 31:1 and fell down s. in mount Gilboa. 2491
1Sa 31:8 the Philistines came to strip the s., 2491
2Sa 1:16 I have s. the Lord's anointed. 4191
2Sa 1:19 The beauty of Israel is s. upon thy 2491
2Sa 1:22 From the blood of the s., from the 2491
2Sa 1:25 thou wast s. in thine high places. 2491
2Sa 3:30 he had s. their brother Asahel at 4191
2Sa 4:11 men have s. a righteous person in 2026
2Sa 12:9 and hast s. him with the sword of 2026
2Sa 13:30 Absalom hath s. all the king's 5221
2Sa 13:32 s. all the young men the king's 4191
2Sa 18:7 people of Israel s. before the 5062
2Sa 21:12 Philistines had s. Saul in Gilboa: 5221
2Sa 21:16 sword, thought to have s. David. 5221
1Ki 1:19, 25 s. oxen and fat cattle and sheep 2076
1Ki 9:16 s. the Canaanites that dwelt in the 2026

1Ki 11:15 host was gone up to buy the **s.**, 2491
1Ki 13:26 which hath torn him, and **s.** him, 4191
1Ki 16:16 and hath also **s.** the king: 5221
1Ki 19:1 how he had **s.** all the prophets 2026
1Ki 19:10, 14 **s.** thy prophets with the sword; 2026
2Ki 3:23 the kings are surely **s.**, and they 2717
2Ki 11:2 the king's sons which were **s.**; 4191
2Ki 11:2 from Athaliah, so that he was not **s.** 4191
2Ki 11:8 within the ranges, let him be **s.**: 4191
2Ki 11:15 Let her not be **s.** in the house of the 4191
2Ki 11:16 king's house: and there was she **s.** 4191
2Ki 14:5 his servants which had **s.** the king 5221
1Ch 5:22 there fell down many **s.**, because 2491
1Ch 10:1 and fell down **s.** in mount Gilboa. 2491
1Ch 10:8 the Philistines came to strip the **s.**, 2491
1Ch 11:11 hundred **s.** by him at one time. 2491
2Ch 13:17 fell down **s.** of Israel five hundred 2491
2Ch 21:13 also hast **s.** thy brethren of thy 2026
2Ch 22:1 to the camp had **s.** all the eldest. 2026
2Ch 22:9 and when they had **s.** him, they 4191
2Ch 22:11 among the king's sons that were **s.**, 4191
2Ch 23:14 her, let him be **s.** with the sword. 4191
2Ch 23:21 they had **s.** Athaliah with the sword. 4191
2Ch 28:9 and ye have **s.** them in a rage that 2026
Es 7:4 my people, to be destroyed, to be **s.**, 2026
Es 9:11 of those that were **s.** in Shushan 2026
Es 9:12 The Jews have **s.** and destroyed 2026
Job 1:15, 17 **s.** the servants with the edge of 5221
Job 39:30 and where the **s.** are, there is she 2491
Ps 62:3 ye shall be **s.** all of you: as a 7523
Ps 88:5 like the **s.** that lie in the grave, 2491
Ps 89:10 Rahab in pieces, as one that is **s.**; 2491
Pr 7:26 strong men have been **s.** by her 2026
Pr 22:13 without, I shall be **s.** in the streets. 7523
Pr 24:11 and those that are ready to be **s.**; 2027
Isa 10:4 and they shall fall under the **s.** 2026
Isa 14:19 as the raiment of those that are **s.**, 2026
Isa 14:20 thy land, and **s.** thy people: 2026
Isa 22:2 **s.** men are not **s.** with the sword, 2491
Isa 26:21 and shall no more cover her **s.** 2026
Isa 27:7 he **s.** according to the slaughter of 2026
Isa 27:7 of them that are **s.** by him? 2026
Isa 34:3 Their **s.** also shall be cast out, and 2491
Isa 66:16 the **s.** of the Lord shall be many. 2491
Jer 9:1 the **s.** of the daughter of my people! 2491
Jer 14:18 then behold the **s.** with the sword! 2491
Jer 18:21 young men be **s.** by the sword in 5221
Jer 25:33 **s.** of the Lord shall be at that day 2491
Jer 33:5 whom I have **s.** in mine anger 5221
Jer 41:4 day after he had **s.** Gedaliah, 4191
Jer 41:9 he had **s.** because of Gedaliah, 5221
Jer 41:9 filled it with them that were **s.** 2491
Jer 41:16 **s.** Gedaliah the son of Ahikam, 5221
Jer 41:18 son of Nethaniah had **s.** Gedaliah 5221
Jer 51:4 the **s.** shall fall in the land of the 2491
Jer 51:47 her **s.** shall fall in the midst of her. 2491
Jer 51:49 hath caused the **s.** of Israel to fall, 2491
Jer 51:49 shall fall the **s.** of all the earth. 2491
La 2:20 the priest and the prophet be **s.** in 2026
La 2:21 **s.** them in the day of thine anger; 2026
La 3:43 thou hast **s.**, thou hast not pitied. 2026
La 4:9 They that be **s.** with the sword are 2491
La 4:9 than they that be **s.** with hunger: 2491
Eze 6:4 down your **s.** men before your idols. 2491
Eze 6:7 the **s.** shall fall in the midst of you, 2491
Eze 6:13 when their **s.** men shall be among 2491
Eze 9:7 house, and fill the courts with the **s.** 2491
Eze 11:6 have multiplied your **s.** in this city, 2491
Eze 11:6 filled the streets thereof with the **s.** 2491
Eze 11:7 Your **s.** whom ye have laid in the 2491
Eze 16:21 That thou hast **s.** my children, and 7819
Eze 21:14 the third time, the sword of the **s.** 2491
Eze 21:14 sword of the great men that are **s.**, 2491
Eze 21:29 upon the necks of them that are **s.**, 2491
Eze 23:39 when they had **s.** their children to 7819
Eze 26:6 the field shall be **s.** by the sword; 2026
Eze 28:8 are **s.** in the midst of the seas. 2491
Eze 30:4 when the **s.** shall fall in Egypt, and 2491
Eze 30:11 Egypt, and fill the land with the **s.** 2491
Eze 31:17 them that be **s.** with the sword; 2491
Eze 31:18 with them that be **s.** by the sword. 2491
Eze 32:20 of them that are **s.** by the sword: 2491
Eze 32:21 lie uncircumcised, **s.** by the sword. 2491
Eze 32:22 all of them **s.**, fallen by the sword: 2491
Eze 32:23, 24 all of them **s.**, fallen by the sword, 2491
Eze 32:25 set her a bed in the midst of the **s.** 2491
Eze 32:25 uncircumcised, **s.** by the sword: 2491
Eze 32:25 put in the midst of them that be **s.** 2491
Eze 32:26 uncircumcised, **s.** by the sword, 2490
Eze 32:28 them that are **s.** with the sword. 2491
Eze 32:29 by them that were **s.** by the sword: 2491
Eze 32:30 which are gone down with the **s.**; 2491
Eze 32:30 with them that be **s.** by the sword, 2491
Eze 32:31 Pharaoh and all his army **s.** by the 2491
Eze 32:32 them that are **s.** with the sword, 2491
Eze 35:8 fill his mountains with his **s.** men: 2491
Eze 35:8 they fall that are **s.** with the sword. 2491
Eze 37:9 breathe upon these **s.**, that they 2026
Da 2:13 that the wise men should be **s.**; 6992
Da 2:13 Daniel and his fellows to be **s.** 6992
Da 5:30 was...the king of the Chaldeans **s.** 6992
Da 7:11 I beheld even till the beast was **s.**, 6992
Da 11:26 and many shall fall down **s.** 2491
Ho 6:5 **s.** them by the words of my mouth: 2026
Am 4:10 young men have I **s.** with the sword, 2026
Na 3:3 and there is a multitude of **s.**, and 2491
Zep 2:12 also, ye shall be **s.** by my sword. 2491
Lu 9:22 be s., and be raised the third day *615*
Ac 2:23 wicked hands have crucified and **s.** *337*
Ac 5:36 who was **s.**; and all, as many as *337*
Ac 7:42 have ye offered to me **s.** beasts and *4968*
Ac 7:52 they have **s.** them which shewed *615*
Ac 13:28 they Pilate that he should be **s.** *337*
Ac 23:14 eat nothing until we have **s.** Paul. *615*
Eph 2:16 cross, having **s.** the enmity thereby: *615*
Heb 11:37 were **s.** with the sword: *1722,5408,599*
Re 2:13 martyr, who was s. among you, *615*
Re 5:6 stood a Lamb as it had been **s.**, *4969*
Re 5:9 thou wast **s.**, and hast redeemed *4969*
Re 5:12 Worthy is the Lamb that was **s.** to *4969*
Re 6:9 that were **s.** for the word of God, *4969*
Re 11:13 were **s.** of men seven thousand: *615*
Re 13:8 the Lamb **s.** from the foundation *4969*
Re 18:24 of all that were **s.** upon the earth. *4969*
Re 19:21 remnant were **s.** with the sword of *615*

SLANDER See also SLANDERED; SLANDEREST; SLANDERETH; SLANDERS.
Nu 14:36 by bringing up a **s.** upon the land, 1681
Ps 31:13 For I have heard the **s.** of many: 1681
Pr 10:18 and he that uttereth a **s.**, is a fool. 1681

SLANDERED
2Sa 19:27 hath **s.** thy servant unto my lord 7270

SLANDEREST
Ps 50:20 **s.** thine own mother's son. 5414,1848

SLANDERETH
Ps 101:5 Whoso privily **s.** his neighbour, 3960

SLANDEROUSLY
Ro 3:8 (as we be **s.** reported, and as some *987*

SLANDERS
Jer 6:28 revolters, walking with **s.**: 7400
Jer 9:4 every neighbour will walk with **s.** 7400

SLANDERERS
1Ti 3:11 must their wives be grave, not **s.**, *1228*

SLANG
1Sa 17:49 and took thence a stone, and **s.** it, 7049

SLAUGHTER
Ge 14:17 from the **s.** of Chedorlaomer, 5221
Jos 10:10 and slew them with a great **s.** at 4347
Jos 10:20 slaying them with a very great **s.**, 4347
Jg 11:33 the vineyards, with a very great **s.** 4347
Jg 15:8 them hip and thigh with a great **s.**: 4347
1Sa 4:10 and there was a very great **s.**; for 4347
1Sa 4:17 there hath been also a great **s.** 4046
1Sa 6:19 many of the people with a great **s.** 4347
1Sa 14:14 And that first **s.**, which Jonathan 4347
1Sa 14:30 not been now a much greater **s.** 4347
1Sa 17:57 David returned from the **s.** of the 5221
1Sa 18:6 David was returned from the **s.** of 5221
1Sa 19:8 and slew them with a great **s.**; 4347
1Sa 23:5 and smote them with a great **s.** 4347
2Sa 1:1 David was returned from the **s.** of 5221
2Sa 17:9 **s.** among the people that follow 4046
2Sa 18:7 there was there a great **s.** that day. 4046
1Ki 20:21 slew the Syrians with a great **s.** 4347
2Ch 13:17 people slew them with a great **s.** 4347
2Ch 25:14 come from the **s.** of the Edomites, 5221
2Ch 28:5 who smote him with a great **s.** 4347
Es 9:5 the sword, and **s.**, and destruction, 2027
Ps 44:22 we are counted as sheep for the **s.** 2878
Pr 7:22 as an ox goeth to the **s.**, or as a 2875
Isa 10:26 according to the **s.** of Midian at 4347
Isa 14:21 Prepare **s.** for his children for the 4293
Isa 27:7 according to the **s.** of them that 2027
Isa 30:25 of waters in the day of the great **s.**, 2027
Isa 34:2 he hath delivered them to the **s.** 2875
Isa 34:6 a great **s.** in the land of Idumea. 2875
Isa 53:7 he is brought as a lamb to the **s.**, 2875
Isa 65:12 and ye shall all bow down to the **s.** 2875
Jer 7:32 of Hinnom, but the valley of **s.** 2028
Jer 11:19 or an ox that is brought to the **s.**; 2873
Jer 12:3 pull them out like sheep for the **s.**, 2873
Jer 12:3 and prepare them for the day of **s.** 2028
Jer 19:6 of Hinnom, but The valley of **s.** 2028
Jer 25:34 for the days of your **s.** and of your 2873
Jer 48:15 young men are gone...to the **s.** 2875
Jer 50:27 let them go down to the **s.**: woe 2875
Jer 51:40 them down like lambs to the **s.**, 2873
Eze 9:2 every man a **s.** weapon in his hand; 4660
Eze 21:10 It is sharpened to make a sore **s.**; 2873
Eze 21:15 bright, it is wrapped up for the **s.** 2875
Eze 21:22 to open the mouth in the **s.**, to lift 7524
Eze 21:28 is drawn: for the **s.** it is furbished, 2875
Eze 26:15 when the **s.** is made in the midst 2027
Ho 5:2 revolters are profound to make **s.**, 7819
Ob 9 mount of Esau may be cut off by **s.** 6993
Zec 11:4 my God; Feed the flock of the **s.**; 2028
Zec 11:7 And I will feed the flock of **s.**, even 2028
Ac 8:32 He was led as a sheep to the **s.**; *4967*
Ac 9:1 **s.** against the disciples of the Lord, *5408*
Ro 8:36 are accounted as sheep for the **s.** *4967*
Heb 7:1 returning from the **s.** of the kings, *2871*
Jas 5:5 your hearts, as in a day of **s.** *4967*

SLAVE See also SLAVES.
Jer 2:14 Israel a servant? is he a homeborn **s.**?

SLAVES
Re 18:13 chariots, and **s.**, and souls of men. *4983*

SLAY See also SLAIN; SLAYETH; SLAYING; SLEW.
Ge 4:14 one that findeth me shall **s.** me. 2026
Ge 18:25 **s.** the righteous with the wicked: 4191
Ge 20:4 thou **s.** also a righteous nation? 2026
Ge 20:11 they will **s.** me for my wife's sake. 2026
Ge 22:10 and took the knife to **s.** his son. 7819
Ge 27:41 then will I **s.** my brother Jacob. 2026
Ge 34:30 together against me, and **s.** me; 5221
Ge 37:18 conspired against him to **s.** him. 4191
Ge 37:20 let us **s.** him, and cast him into 2026
Ge 37:26 What profit is it if we **s.** our brother, 2026
Ge 42:37 **S.** my two sons, if I bring him not 4191
Ge 43:16 Bring these men home, and **s.**, 2875
Ex 2:15 this thing, he sought to **s.** Moses. 2026
Ex 4:23 I will **s.** thy son, even thy firstborn. 2026
Ex 5:21 put a sword in their hand to **s.** us. 2026
Ex 21:14 his neighbour, to **s.** him with guile; 2026
Ex 23:7 innocent and righteous **s.** thou not: 2026
Ex 29:16 And thou shalt **s.** the ram, and 7819
Ex 32:12 out, to **s.** them in the mountains, 2026
Ex 32:27 **s.** every man his brother, and every 2026
Le 4:29 **s.** the sin offering in the place of 7819
Le 4:33 **s.** it for a sin offering in the place 7819
Le 14:13 he shall **s.** the lamb in the place 7819
Le 20:15 death: and ye shall **s.** the beast. 2026
Nu 19:3 one shall **s.** her before his face: 7819
Nu 25:5 **S.** ye every one his men that were 2026
Nu 35:19 himself shall **s.** the murderer: 4191
Nu 35:19 he meeteth him, he shall **s.** him. 4191
Nu 35:21 of blood shall **s.** the murderer, 4191
De 9:28 out to **s.** them in the wilderness. 4191
De 19:6 the way is long, and **s.** him; 5221
De 27:25 reward to **s.** an innocent person: 5221
Jos 13:22 children of Israel **s.** with the sword. 2026
Jg 8:19 saved them alive, I would not **s.** you. 2026
Jg 8:20 his firstborn, Up, and **s.** them. 2026
Jg 9:54 Draw thy sword, and **s.** me, that 4191
1Sa 2:25 because the Lord would **s.** them. 4191
1Sa 5:10 ark...to us, to **s.** us and our people. 4191
1Sa 5:11 that it **s.** us not, and our people: 4191
1Sa 14:34 sheep, and **s.** them here, and eat; 7819
1Sa 15:3 but **s.** both man and woman, 4191
1Sa 19:5 blood, to **s.** David without a cause? 4191
1Sa 19:11 him, and to **s.** him in the morning: 4191
1Sa 19:15 to me in the bed, that I may **s.** him. 4191
1Sa 20:8 be in me iniquity, **s.** me thyself; 4191
1Sa 20:33 determined of his father to **s.** David. 4191
1Sa 22:17 Turn, and **s.** the priests of the Lord; 4191

2Sa	1:9	Stand...upon me, and **s.** me: for	4191
2Sa	3:37	it was not of the king to **s.** Abner	4191
2Sa	21:2	Saul sought to **s.** them in his zeal	5221
1Ki	1:51	not **s.** his servant with the sword.	4191
1Ki	3:26	the living child, and in no wise **s.** it.	4191
1Ki	3:27	the living child, and in no wise **s.** it:	4191
1Ki	15:28	did Baasha **s.** him, and reigned in	4191
1Ki	17:18	to remembrance, and to **s.** my son?	4191
1Ki	18:9	into the hand of Ahab, to **s.** me?	4191
1Ki	18:12	he cannot find thee, he shall **s.** me:	2026
1Ki	18:14	Elijah is here: and he shall **s.** me	2026
1Ki	19:17	the sword of Hazael shall Jehu **s.**	4191
1Ki	19:17	the sword of Jehu shall Elisha **s.**	4191
1Ki	20:36	from me, a lion shall **s.** thee	5221
2Ki	8:12	young men wilt thou **s.** with the	2026
2Ki	10:25	the captains, Go in, and **s.** them;	5221
2Ki	17:26	**s.** them, because they know not	4191
2Ch	20:23	utterly to **s.** and destroy them:	2763
2Ch	23:14	**S.** her not in the house of the Lord,	4191
Ne	4:11	and **s.** them, and cause the work to	2026
Ne	6:10	for they will come to **s.** thee;	2026
Ne	6:10	the night will they come to **s.** thee.	2026
Es	8:11	to **s.**, and to cause to perish, all the	2026
Job	9:23	If the scourge **s.** suddenly, he will	4191
Job	13:15	Though he **s.** me, yet will I trust	6991
Job	20:16	the viper's tongue shall **s.** him.	2026
Ps	34:21	Evil shall **s.** the wicked: and they	4191
Ps	37:14	and to **s.** such as be of upright	2873
Ps	37:32	righteous, and seeketh to **s.** him.	4191
Ps	59:11	**S.** them not, lest my people forget:	2026
Ps	94:6	**s.** the widow and the stranger, and	2026
Ps	109:16	might even **s.** the broken in heart	4191
Ps	139:19	Surely thou wilt **s.** the wicked,	6991
Pr	1:32	away of the simple shall **s.** them,	2026
Isa	11:4	of his lips shall he **s.** the wicked	4191
Isa	14:30	and he shall **s.** thy remnant.	2026
Isa	27:1	he shall **s.** the dragon that is in the	2026
Isa	65:15	for the Lord God shall **s.** thee, and	4191
Jer	5:6	lion out of the forest shall **s.** them,	5221
Jer	15:3	sword to **s.**, and the dogs to tear,	2026
Jer	18:23	their counsel against me to **s.** me:	1194
Jer	20:4	and shall **s.** them with the sword	5221
Jer	29:21	he shall **s.** them before your eyes;	5221
Jer	40:14	son of Nethaniah to **s.** thee?	5221,5315
Jer	40:15	and I will **s.** Ishmael the son of	5221
Jer	40:15	wherefore should he **s.** thee, that	5221
Jer	41:8	that said unto Ishmael, **S.** us not:	4191
Jer	50:27	**S.** all her bullocks; let them go	2717
Eze	9:6	**S.** utterly old and young, both	2026
Eze	13:19	to **s.** the souls that should not die,	4191
Eze	23:47	they shall **s.** their sons and their	4191
Eze	26:8	**s.** with the sword thy daughters in	4191
Eze	26:11	he shall **s.** thy people by the sword,	4191
Eze	40:39	to **s.** thereon the burnt offering	7819
Eze	44:11	they shall **s.** the burnt offering and	7819
Da	2:14	was gone forth to **s.** the wise men	6992
Ho	2:3	a dry land, and **s.** her with thirst	4191
Ho	9:16	I **s.** even the beloved fruit of their	4191
Am	2:3	will **s.** all the princes thereof with	2026
Am	9:1	**s.** the last of them with the sword:	2026
Am	9:4	the sword, and it shall **s.** them:	2026
Hab	1:17	spare continually to **s.** the nations?	2026
Zec	11:5	Whose possessors **s.** them, and hold	2026
Lu	11:49	**and some of them they shall s**	*615*
Lu	19:27	**hither, and s. them before me**	*2695*
Joh	5:16	Jesus, and sought to **s.** him,	*615*
Ac	5:33	heart, and took counsel to **s.** them.	*337*
Ac	9:29	but they went about to **s.** him.	*337*
Ac	11:7	unto me, Arise, Peter; **s.** and eat.	*2380*
Re	9:15	year, for to **s.** the third part of men.	*615*

SLAYER See also MANSLAYER.

Nu	35:11	that the **s.** may flee thither, which	7523
Nu	35:24	between the **s.** and the revenger	5221
Nu	35:25	congregation shall deliver the **s.**	7523
Nu	35:26	But if the **s.** shall at any time come	7523
Nu	35:27	the revenger of blood kill the **s.**;	7523
Nu	35:28	**s.** shall return into the land of his	7523
De	4:42	That the **s.** might flee thither,	7523
De	19:3	that every **s.** may flee thither.	7523
De	19:4	this is the case of the **s.**, which	7523
De	19:6	avenger of the blood pursue the **s.**,	7523
Jos	20:3	That the **s.** that killeth any person	7523
Jos	20:5	they shall not deliver the **s.** up into	7523
Jos	20:6	then shall the **s.** return, and come	7523
Jos	21:13,	21,27,32,38 city of refuge for...**s.**;	7523
Eze	21:1	to give it into the hand of the **s.**	2026

SLAYETH

Ge	4:15	him, Therefore whosoever **s.** Cain,	2026
De	22:26	his neighbour, and **s.** him,	7523,5315
Job	5:2	man, and envy **s.** the silly one.	4191
Eze	28:9	before him that **s.** thee, I am God?	2026
Eze	28:9	in the hand of him that **s.** thee	2490

SLAYING

Jos	8:24	end of **s.** all the inhabitants of Ai	2026
Jos	10:20	had made an end of **s.** them with	5221
Jg	9:56	father, in **s.** his seventy brethren:	2026
1Ki	17:20	whom I sojourn, by **s.** her son?	4191
Isa	22:13	**s.** oxen, and killing sheep, eating	2026
Isa	57:5	**s.** the children in the valleys	7819
Eze	9:8	to pass, while they were **s.** them,	5221

SLEEP See also ASLEEP; SLEEPEST; SLEEPETH; SLEEPING; SLEPT.

Ge	2:21	a deep **s.** to fall upon Adam, and	3462
Ge	15:12	down, a deep **s.** fell upon Abram;	8639
Ge	28:11	and lay down in that place to **s.**	7901
Ge	28:16	And Jacob awaked out of his **s.**,	8142
Ge	31:40	and my **s.** departed from mine eyes.	8142
Ex	22:27	for his skin: wherein shall he **s.**?	7901
De	24:12	poor, shall not **s.** with his pledge:	7901
De	24:13	that he may **s.** in his own raiment,	7901
De	31:16	thou shalt **s.** with thy fathers; and	7901
Jg	16:14	And he awaked out of his **s.**, and went	8142
Jg	16:19	she made him **s.** upon her knees;	3462
Jg	16:20	he awoke out of his **s.**, and said,	8142
1Sa	3:3	was, and Samuel was laid down to **s.**;	
1Sa	26:12	a deep **s.** from the Lord was fallen	8639
2Sa	7:12	and thou shalt **s.** with thy fathers,	7901
1Ki	1:21	the king shall **s.** with his fathers,	7901
Es	6:1	that night could not the king **s.**,	8142
Job	4:13	when deep **s.** falleth on men,	8639
Job	7:21	for now shall I **s.** in the dust; and	7901
Job	14:12	awake, nor be raised out of their **s.**	8142
Job	33:15	when deep **s.** falleth upon men, in	
Ps	4:8	both lay me down in peace, and **s.**;	3462
Ps	13:3	God: lighten mine eyes, lest I **s.**	3462
Ps	13:3	lest I...the **s.** of death;	
Ps	76:5	spoiled, they have slept their **s.**	8142
Ps	76:6	and horse is cast into a dead **s.**	7290
Ps	78:65	the Lord awaked as one out of **s.**,	3463
Ps	90:5	as with a flood; they are as a **s.**	8142
Ps	121:4	Israel shall neither slumber nor **s.**	3462
Ps	127:2	for so he giveth his beloved **s.**	8142
Ps	132:4	I will not give **s.** to mine eyes, or	8142
Pr	3:24	down, and thy **s.** shall be sweet,	8142
Pr	4:16	For they **s.** not, except they have	3462
Pr	4:16	and their **s.** is taken away, unless	8142
Pr	6:4	Give not **s.** to thine eyes, nor	8142
Pr	6:9	How long wilt thou **s.**, O sluggard?	7901
Pr	6:9	when wilt thou arise out of thy **s.**?	8142
Pr	6:10	Yet a little **s.**, a little slumber, a	8142
Pr	6:10	a little folding of the hands to **s.**	7901
Pr	19:15	Slothfulness casteth into a deep **s.**;	3462
Pr	20:13	Love not **s.**, lest thou come to	8142
Pr	24:33	Yet a little **s.**, a little slumber, a	8142
Pr	24:33	a little folding of the hands to **s.**	7901
Ec	5:12	**s.** of a labouring man is sweet,	8142
Ec	5:12	of the rich will not suffer him to **s.**	3462
Ec	8:16	nor night seeth **s.** with his eyes:)	8142
Ca	5:2	I **s.**, but my heart waketh: it is the	3463
Isa	5:27	none shall slumber nor **s.**; neither	3463
Isa	29:10	out upon you the spirit of deep **s.**,	8639
Jer	31:26	and my **s.** was sweet unto me.	8142
Jer	51:39	that they may rejoice, and **s.**	3462
Jer	51:39	a perpetual **s.**, and not wake,	8142
Jer	51:57	mighty men: and they shall **s.**	3462
Jer	51:57	a perpetual **s.**, and not wake	8142
Eze	34:25	wilderness, and **s.** in the woods.	3462
Da	2:1	and his **s.** brake from him.	8142
Da	6:18	him: and his **s.** went from him.	8139
Da	8:18	I was in a deep **s.** on my face	7290
Da	10:9	then was I in a deep **s.** on my face,	7290
Da	12:2	many of them that **s.** in the dust	3463
Zec	4:1	man that is wakened out of his **s.**,	8142
Mt	1:24	Joseph being raised from **s.** did as	*5258*
Mt	26:45	**S. on now, and take your rest:**	*2518*
Mk	4:27	**And should s., and rise night and**	*2518*
Mk	14:41	**S. on now, and take your rest:**	*2518*
Lu	9:32	were with him were heavy with **s.**	*5258*
Lu	22:46	**Why s. ye? rise and pray, lest ye**	*2518*
Joh	11:11	**that I may awake him out of s**	*1852*
Joh	11:12	Lord, if he **s.**, he shall do well.	*2837*
Joh	11:13	had spoken of taking of rest in **s.**	*5258*
Ac	13:36	fell on **s.**, and was laid unto his	*2837*
Ac	16:27	of the prison awaking out of his **s.**,	*1853*
Ac	20:9	being fallen into a deep **s.**;	*5258*
Ac	20:9	he sunk down with **s.**, and fell	*5258*
Ro	13:11	it is high time to awake out of **s.**	*5258*
1Co	11:30	sickly among you, and many **s.**	*2837*
1Co	15:51	We shall not all **s.**, but we shall all	*2837*
1Th	4:14	so them also which **s.** in Jesus	*2837*
1Th	5:6	let us not **s.**, as do others; but let	*2518*
1Th	5:7	For they that **s. s.** in the night;	*2518*
1Th	5:10	for us, that, whether we wake or **s.**,	*2518*

SLEEPER

Jon	1:6	What meanest thou, O **s.**? arise,	7290

SLEEPEST

Ps	44:23	why **s.** thou, O Lord? arise, cast	3462
Pr	6:22	when thou **s.**, it shall keep thee;	7901
Mk	14:37	saith unto Peter, **Simon, s. thou?**	*2518*
Eph	5:14	Awake thou that **s.**, and arise from	*2518*

SLEEPETH

1Ki	18:27	peradventure he **s.**, and must be	3463
Pr	10:5	**s.** in harvest is a son that causeth	7290
Ho	7:6	wait: their baker **s.** all the night;	3463
Mt	9:24	**for the maid is not dead, but s**	*2518*
Mk	5:39	**the damsel is not dead, but s**	*2518*
Lu	8:52	**Weep not; she is not dead, but s**	*2518*
Joh	11:11	unto them, **Our friend Lazarus s**	*2837*

SLEEPING

1Sa	26:7	Saul lay **s.** within the trench, and	3463
Isa	56:10	**s.**, lying down, loving to slumber.	1957
Mk	13:36	**coming suddenly he find you s**	*2518*
Mk	14:37	he cometh, and findeth them **s.**,	*2518*
Lu	22:45	he found them **s.** for sorrow,	*2837*
Ac	12:6	Peter was **s.** between two soldiers,	*2837*

SLEIGHT

Eph	4:14	by the **s.** of men, and cunning	*2940*

SLEPT

Ge	2:21	to fall upon Adam, and he **s.**: and	3462
Ge	41:5	And he **s.** and dreamed the second	3462
2Sa	11:9	Uriah **s.** at the door of the king's	7901
1Ki	2:10	David **s.** with his fathers, and was	7901
1Ki	3:20	while thine handmaid **s.**, and laid	3463
1Ki	11:21	that David **s.** with his fathers, and	7901
1Ki	11:43	And Solomon **s.** with his fathers,	7901
1Ki	14:20	he **s.** with his fathers, and Nadab	7901
1Ki	14:31	And Rehoboam **s.** with his fathers,	7901
1Ki	15:8	And Abijam **s.** with his fathers; and	7901
1Ki	15:24	Asa **s.** with his fathers, and was	7901
1Ki	16:6	So Baasha **s.** with his fathers, and	7901
1Ki	16:28	So Omri **s.** with his fathers, and	7901
1Ki	19:5	he lay and **s.** under a juniper tree,	3462
1Ki	22:40	So Ahab **s.** with his fathers; and	7901
1Ki	22:50	Jehoshaphat **s.** with his fathers,	7901
2Ki	8:24	And Joram **s.** with his fathers, and	7901
2Ki	10:35	And Jehu **s.** with his fathers: and	7901
2Ki	13:9	And Jehoahaz **s.** with his fathers;	7901
2Ki	13:13	And Joash **s.** with his fathers; and	7901
2Ki	14:16	And Jehoash **s.** with his fathers,	7901
2Ki	14:22	that the king **s.** with his fathers.	7901
2Ki	14:29	And Jeroboam **s.** with his fathers,	7901
2Ki	15:7	So Azariah **s.** with his fathers; and	7901
2Ki	15:22	And Menahem **s.** with his fathers;	7901
2Ki	15:38	Jotham **s.** with his fathers, and was	7901
2Ki	16:20	Ahaz **s.** with his fathers, and was	7901
2Ki	20:21	And Hezekiah **s.** with his fathers:	7901
2Ki	21:18	And Manasseh **s.** with his fathers,	7901
2Ki	24:6	So Jehoiakim **s.** with his fathers:	7901
2Ch	9:31	Solomon **s.** with his fathers, and he	7901
2Ch	12:16	And Rehoboam **s.** with his fathers,	7901
2Ch	14:1	So Abijah **s.** with his fathers, and	7901
2Ch	16:13	Asa **s.** with his fathers, and died in	7901
2Ch	21:1	Jehoshaphat **s.** with his fathers,	7901
2Ch	26:2	that the king **s.** with his fathers.	7901
2Ch	26:23	So Uzziah **s.** with his fathers, and	7901
2Ch	27:9	Jotham **s.** with his fathers, and they	7901
2Ch	28:27	And Ahaz **s.** with his fathers, and	7901
2Ch	32:33	And Hezekiah **s.** with his fathers,	7901
2Ch	33:20	So Manasseh **s.** with his fathers, and	7901
Job	3:13	and been quiet, I should have **s.**	3462
Ps	3:5	I laid me down and **s.**; I awaked;	3462
Ps	76:5	spoiled, they have **s.** their sleep:	5123
Mt	13:25	**But while men s., his enemy**	*2518*
Mt	25:5	**tarried, they all slumbered and s**	*2518*
Mt	27:52	bodies of the saints which **s.** arose,	*2837*
Mt	28:13	and stole him away while we **s.**	*2837*
1Co	15:20	the firstfruits of them that **s.**	*2837*

SLEW See also SLEWEST.
Ge 4:8 Abel his brother, and s. him. 2026
Ge 4:25 seed instead of Abel, whom Cain s. 2026
Ge 34:25 the city boldly, and s. all the males. 2026
Ge 34:26 they s. Hamor and Shechem his son 2026
Ge 38:7 of the Lord; and the Lord s. him. 4191
Ge 38:10 the Lord: wherefore he s. him also. 4191
Ge 49:6 for in their anger they s. a man, 2026
Ex 2:12 he s. the Egyptian, and hid him in 5221
Ex 13:15 the Lord s. all the firstborn in the 2026
Le 8:15 And he s. it; and Moses took the 7819
Le 8:23 And he s. it; and Moses took of the 7819
Le 9:8 s. the calf of the sin offering, which 7819
Le 9:12 And he s. the burnt offering; and 7819
Le 9:15 s. it, and offered it for sin, as the 7819
Le 9:18 He s. also the bullock and the ram 7819
Nu 31:7 Moses; and they s. all the males. 2026
Nu 31:8 they s. the kings of Midian, beside 2026
Nu 31:8 son of Beor they s. with the sword. 2026
Jos 8:21 again, and s. the men of Ai. 5221
Jos 9:26 of Israel, that they s. them not. 2026
Jos 10:10 s. them with a great slaughter at 5221
Jos 10:11 children of Israel s. with…sword. 2026
Jos 10:26 Joshua smote them, and s. them, 4191
Jos 11:17 took, and smote them, and s. them. 4191
Jg 1:4 s. of them in Bezek ten thousand 5221
Jg 1:5 and they s. the Canaanites and the 5221
Jg 1:10 and they s. Sheshai, and Ahiman, 5221
Jg 1:17 s. the Canaanites that inhabited 5221
Jg 3:29 they s. of Moab at that time about 5221
Jg 3:31 s. of the Philistines six hundred 5221
Jg 7:25 they s. Oreb upon the rock Oreb, 2026
Jg 7:25 and Zeeb they s. at the winepress of 2026
Jg 8:17 Penuel, and s. the men of the city, 2026
Jg 8:18 were they whom ye s. at Tabor? 2026
Jg 8:21 arose, and s. Zebah and Zalmunna, 2026
Jg 9:5 s. his brethren…sons of Jerubbaal, 2026
Jg 9:24 their brother, which s. them; and 2026
Jg 9:44 were in the fields, and s. them. 5221
Jg 9:45 s. the people that was therein, 2026
Jg 9:54 say not of me, A woman s. him. 2026
Jg 12:6 s. him at the passages of Jordan: 7819
Jg 14:19 s. thirty men of them, and took 5221
Jg 15:15 and s. a thousand men therewith. 5221
Jg 16:24 our country, which s. many of us. 2491
Jg 16:30 the dead which he s. at his death 4191
Jg 16:30 than they which he s. in his life. 4191
Jg 20:45 and s. two thousand men of them. 5221
1Sa 1:25 they s. a bullock, and brought the 7819
1Sa 4:2 and they s. of the army in the field 5221
1Sa 11:11 s. the Ammonites until the heat of 5221
1Sa 14:13 and his armourbearer s. after him. 4191
1Sa 14:32 calves, and s. them on the ground: 7819
1Sa 14:34 him that night, and s. them there. 7819
1Sa 17:35 beard, and smote him, and s. him. 4191
1Sa 17:36 Thy servant s. both the lion and 5221
1Sa 17:50 smote the Philistine, and s. him; 4191
1Sa 17:51 and s. him, and cut off his head 4191
1Sa 18:27 s. of the Philistines two hundred 5221
1Sa 19:5 in his hand, and s. the Philistine, 5221
1Sa 19:8 and s. them with a great slaughter; 5221
1Sa 22:18 s. on that day fourscore and five 4191
1Sa 29:5 Saul s. his thousands, and David 5221
1Sa 30:2 they s. not any, either great or 4191
1Sa 31:2 and the Philistines s. Jonathan, 5221
2Sa 1:10 So I stood upon him, and s. him, 4191
2Sa 3:30 and Abishai his brother s. Abner, 2026
2Sa 4:7 and they smote him, and s. him, 4191
2Sa 4:10 hold of him, and s. him in Ziklag, 2026
2Sa 4:12 and they s. them, and cut off their 2026
2Sa 8:5 David s. of the Syrians two and 5221
2Sa 10:18 David s. the men of seven hundred 2126
2Sa 14:6 one smote the other, and s. him. 4191
2Sa 14:7 the life of his brother whom he s.; 2026
2Sa 18:15 and smote Absalom, and s. him 4191
2Sa 21:1 house, because he s. the Gibeonites, 4191
2Sa 21:18 Sibbechai the Hushathite s. Saph, 5221
2Sa 21:19 s. the brother of Goliath the Gittite, 5221
2Sa 21:21 the brother of David s. him. 5221
2Sa 23:8 hundred, whom he s. at one time. 2491
2Sa 23:12 defended it, and s. the Philistines: 5221
2Sa 23:18 three hundred, and s. them, and 2491
2Sa 23:20 he s. two lionlike men of Moab: 5221
2Sa 23:20 and s. a lion in the midst of a pit 5221
2Sa 23:21 And he s. an Egyptian, a goodly 2026
2Sa 23:21 and s. him with his own spear. 5221
1Ki 1:9 Adonijah s. sheep and oxen and 2076
1Ki 2:5 and unto Amasa…whom he s., 2026
1Ki 2:32 than he, and s. them with the sword, 2026
1Ki 2:34 up, and fell upon him, and s. him: 4191
1Ki 11:24 when David s. them of Zobah: 2026
1Ki 13:24 met him by the way, and s. him: 4191
1Ki 16:11 that he s. all the house of Baasha: 5221
1Ki 18:13 I did when Jezebel s. the prophets 2026
1Ki 18:40 brook Kishon, and s. them there. 7819
1Ki 19:21 took a yoke of oxen, and s. them, 2076
1Ki 20:20 And they s. every one his man: 5221
1Ki 20:21 and s. the Syrians with a great 5221
1Ki 20:29 Israel s. of the Syrians an hundred 5221
1Ki 20:36 him, a lion found him, and s. him. 5221
2Ki 9:31 Zimri peace, who s. his master? 2026
2Ki 10:7 king's sons, and s. seventy persons, 7819
2Ki 10:9 against my master, and s. him: 2026
2Ki 10:9 but who s. all these? 5221
2Ki 10:11 So Jehu s. all that remained of the 5221
2Ki 10:14 s. them at the pit of the shearing 7819
2Ki 10:17 he s. all that remained unto Ahab 5221
2Ki 11:18 and s. Mattan the priest of Baal 2026
2Ki 11:20 they s. Athaliah with the sword 4191
2Ki 12:20 and s. Joash in the house of Millo, 5221
2Ki 14:5 s. his servants which had slain the 5221
2Ki 14:6 children of…murderers he s. not: 4191
2Ki 14:7 s. of Edom in the valley of salt ten 5221
2Ki 14:19 him to Lachish, and s. him there. 4191
2Ki 15:10, 14 s. him, and reigned in his stead. 4191
2Ki 15:30 s. him, and reigned in his stead, 4191
2Ki 16:9 of it captive to Kir, and s. Rezin. 4191
2Ki 17:25 them, which s. some of them. 2026
2Ki 21:23 and s. the king in his own house. 4191
2Ki 21:24 s. all them that had conspired 5221
2Ki 23:20 he s. all the priests of the high 2076
2Ki 23:29 he s. him at Megiddo, when he had 4191
2Ki 25:7 And they s. the sons of Zedekiah 7819
2Ki 25:21 s. them at Riblah in the land. 4191
1Ch 2:3 sight of the Lord; and he s. him. 4191
1Ch 7:21 that were born in that land s., 2026
1Ch 10:2 and the Philistines s. Jonathan, 5221
1Ch 10:14 s. him, and turned the kingdom 4191
1Ch 11:14 delivered it, and s. the Philistines; 5221
1Ch 11:20 against three hundred, he s. them, 2490
1Ch 11:22 he s. two lionlike men of Moab: 5221
1Ch 11:22 s. a lion in a pit in a snowy day. 5221
1Ch 11:23 he s. an Egyptian, a man of great 5221
1Ch 11:23 and s. him with his own spear. 2026
1Ch 18:5 David s. of the Syrians two and 5221
1Ch 18:12 s. of the Edomites in the valley of 5221
1Ch 19:18 and David s. of the Syrians seven 2026
1Ch 20:4 Sibbechai the Hushathite s. Sippai, 5221
1Ch 20:5 Elhanan the son of Jair s. Lahmi 5221
1Ch 20:7 of Shimea David's brother s. him. 5221
2Ch 13:17 And Abijah and his people s. them 5221
2Ch 21:4 s. all his brethren with the sword, 2026
2Ch 22:8 ministered to Ahaziah, he s. them. 2026
2Ch 22:11 Athaliah, so that she s. him not. 4191
2Ch 23:15 the king's house, they s. her there. 4191
2Ch 23:17 and s. Mattan the priest of Baal 2026
2Ch 24:22 not the kindness…but s. his son. 2026
2Ch 24:25 and s. him on his bed, and he died: 2026
2Ch 25:3 he s. his servants that had killed 2026
2Ch 25:4 But he s. not their children, but 4191
2Ch 25:27 to Lachish after him, and s. him 4191
2Ch 28:6 s. in Judah an hundred and 2026
2Ch 28:7 s. Maaseiah the king's son, and 2026
2Ch 32:21 s. him there with the sword. 5307
2Ch 33:24 and s. him in his own house. 4191
2Ch 33:25 s. all them that had conspired 5221
2Ch 36:17 who s. their young men with the 2026
Ne 9:26 and s. thy prophets which testified 2026
Es 9:6 Jews s. and destroyed five hundred 2026
Es 9:10 the enemy of the Jews, s. they; 2026
Es 9:15 s. three hundred men at Shushan; 2026
Es 9:16 and s. of their foes seventy and five 2026
Ps 78:31 s. the fattest of them, and smote 2026
Ps 78:34 When he s. them, then they sought 2026
Ps 105:29 waters into blood, and s. their fish 4191
Ps 135:10 great nations, and s. mighty kings; 2026
Ps 136:18 And s. famous kings; for his mercy 2026
Isa 66:3 killeth an ox if he s. a man; 5221
Jer 20:17 he s. me not from the womb; or 4191
Jer 26:23 king; who s. him with the sword, 5221
Jer 39:6 Babylon s. the sons of Zedekiah 7819
Jer 39:6 Babylon s. all the nobles of Judah. 7819
Jer 41:2 s. him, whom the king of Babylon 4191
Jer 41:3 Ishmael also s. all the Jews that 5221
Jer 41:7 the son of Nethaniah s. them, and 7819
Jer 41:8 s. them not among their brethren. 4191
Jer 52:10 Babylon s. the sons of Zedekiah 7819
Jer 52:10 he s. also all the princes of Judah 7819
La 2:4 s. all that were pleasant to the eye 2026
Eze 9:7 they went forth, and s. in the city. 5221
Eze 23:10 daughters, and s. her with the sword:
Eze 40:41 whereupon they s.…sacrifices. 7819
Eze 40:42 they s. the burnt offering and the 7819
Da 3:22 the flame of the fire s. those men 6992
Da 5:19 whom he would he s.; and whom he 6992
Mt 2:16 s. all the children…in Bethlehem, *337*
Mt 21:39 **out of the vineyard, and s. him** *615*
Mt 22:6 **them spitefully, and s. them** *615*
Mt 23:35 **s. between the temple and…altar** *5407*
Lu 13:4 **tower in Siloam fell, and s. them,** *615*
Ac 5:30 raised up Jesus, whom ye s. and *1315*
Ac 10:39 whom they s. and hanged on a tree: *337*
Ac 22:20 kept the raiment of them that s. him. *337*
Ro 7:11 deceived me, and by it s. me. *615*
1Jo 3:12 wicked one, and s. his brother. *4969*
1Jo 3:12 And wherefore s. he him? Because *4969*

SLEWEST
1Sa 21:9 whom thou s. in the valley of Elah, 5221

SLIDDEN
Jer 8:5 this people of Jerusalem s. back 7725

SLIDE See also BACKSLIDING; SLIDDEN; SLIDETH.
De 32:35 their foot shall s. in due time: 4131
Ps 26:1 the Lord; therefore I shall not s. 4571
Ps 37:31 his heart; none of his steps shall s. 4571

SLIDETH
Ho 4:16 s. back as a backsliding heifer: 5637

SLIGHT See SLEIGHT.

SLIGHTLY
Jer 6:14 of the daughter of my people s., 7043
Jer 8:11 of the daughter of my people s., 7043

SLIME See also SLIMEPITS.
Ge 11:3 stone, and s. had they for morter. 2564
Ex 2:3 daubed it with s. and with pitch, 2564

SLIMEPITS
Ge 14:10 the vale of Siddim was full of s. 2564

SLING See also SLANG; SLINGS; SLINGSTONES.
Jg 20:16 could s. stones at an hair breadth, 7049
1Sa 17:40 and his s. was in his hand: and he 7050
1Sa 17:50 with a s. and with a stone, 7050
1Sa 25:29 enemies, them shall he s. out, as 7049
1Sa 25:29 as out of the middle of a s. 7050
Pr 26:8 As he that bindeth a stone in a s., 4773
Jer 10:18 s. out the inhabitants of the land 7049
Zec 9:15 devour, and subdue with s. stones; 7050

SLINGERS
2Ki 3:25 the s. went about it, and smote it. 7051

SLINGS
2Ch 26:14 and bows, and s. to cast stones. 7050

SLINGSTONES See also SLING and STONES.
Job 41:28 s. are turned with him into 68,7050

SLIP See also SLIPPED; SLIPPETH; SLIPS.
2Sa 22:37 me; so that my feet did not s. 4571
Job 12:5 He that is ready to s. with his feet 4571
Ps 17:5 thy paths, that my footsteps s. not. 4131
Ps 18:36 under me, that my feet did not s. 4571
Heb 2:1 at any time we should let them s. *3901*

SLIPPED
1Sa 19:10 he s. away out of Saul's presence, 6362
Ps 73:2 gone; my steps had well nigh s. 8210

SLIPPERY
Ps 35:6 Let their way be dark and s.: and 2519
Ps 73:18 thou didst set them in s. places: 2513
Jer 23:12 way shall be unto them as s. ways 2519

SLIPPETH
De 19:5 and the head s. from the helve, 5394
Ps 38:16 when my foot s., they magnify 4131
Ps 94:18 When I said, My foot s.; thy mercy, 4131

SLIPS
Isa 17:10 and shalt set it with strange s. 2156

SLOTHFUL
Jg 18:9 be not s. to go, and to enter to 6101
Pr 12:24 but the s. shall be under tribute. 7423
Pr 12:27 The s. man roasteth not that which 7423
Pr 15:19 way of the s. man is as an hedge 6102
Pr 18:9 He also that is s. in his work is 7503
Pr 19:24 A s. man hideth his hand in his 6102
Pr 21:25 The desire of the s. killeth him; 6102
Pr 22:13 The s. man saith, There is a lion 6102
Pr 24:30 I went by the field of the s., and by 6102
Pr 26:13 The s. man saith, There is a lion in 6102
Pr 26:14 hinges, so doth the s. upon his bed. 6102
Pr 26:15 s. hideth his hand in his bosom; 6102
Mt 25:26 Thou wicked and s. servant, thou *3636*
Ro 12:11 Not s. in business; fervent in spirit; *3636*
Heb 6:12 That ye be not s., but followers of *3576*

SLOTHFULNESS
Pr 19:15 S. casteth into a deep sleep; and 6103
Ec 10:18 By much s. the building decayeth; 6103

SLOW
Ex 4:10 s. of speech, and of a s. tongue. 3515
Ne 9:17 s. to anger, and of great kindness, 750
Ps 103:8 s. to anger, and plenteous in mercy, 750
Ps 145:8 s. to anger, and of great mercy. 750
Pr 14:29 He that is s. to wrath is of great 750
Pr 15:18 that is s. to anger appeaseth strife. 750
Pr 16:32 He that is s. to anger is better than 750
Joe 2:13 s. to anger, and of great kindness, 750
Jon 4:2 s. to anger, and of great kindness, 750
Na 1:3 The Lord is s. to anger, and great in 750
Lu 24:25 O fools, and s. of heart to believe *1021*
Tit 1:12 alway liars, evil beasts, s. bellies. *692*
Jas 1:19 to hear, s. to speak, s. to wrath; *1021*

SLOWLY
Ac 27:7 when we had sailed s. many days, *1020*

SLUGGARD
Pr 6:6 Go to the ant, thou s.; consider 6102
Pr 6:9 How long wilt thou sleep, O s.? 6102
Pr 10:26 so is the s. to them that send him. 6102
Pr 13:4 The soul of the s. desireth, and 6102
Pr 20:4 The s. will not plow by reason of 6102
Pr 26:16 The s. is wiser in his own conceit 6102

SLUICES
Isa 19:10 that make s. and ponds for fish. 7938

SLUMBER See also SLUMBERED; SLUMBERETH; SLUMBERING.
Ps 121:3 he that keepeth thee will not s. 5123
Ps 121:4 Israel shall neither s. nor sleep. 5123
Ps 132:4 to my eyes, or s. to mine eyelids, 8572
Pr 6:4 thine eyes, nor s. to thine eyelids. 8572
Pr 6:10 Yet a little sleep, a little s., a little 8572
Pr 24:33 Yet a little sleep, a little s., a little 8572
Isa 5:27 none shall s. nor sleep; neither 5123
Isa 56:10 sleeping, lying down, loving to s. 5123
Na 3:18 Thy shepherds s., O king of 5123
Ro 11:8 hath given them the spirit of s., *2659*

SLUMBERED
Mt 25:5 tarried, they all s. and slept. *3573*

SLUMBERETH
2Pe 2:3 not, and their damnation s. not. *3573*

SLUMBERINGS
Job 33:15 upon men, in s. upon the bed; 8572

SMALL See also SMALLEST.
Ge 19:11 with blindness, both s. and great: 6996
Ge 30:15 a s. matter that thou hast taken 4592
Ex 9:9 shall become s. dust in all the land
Ex 16:14 wilderness…lay a s. round thing, 1851
Ex 16:14 as s. as the hoar frost on the ground. 1851
Ex 18:22 every s. matter they shall judge: 6990
Ex 18:26 s. matter they judged themselves. 6990
Ex 30:36 thou shalt beat some of it very s., 1854
Le 16:12 full of sweet incense beaten s., 1851
Nu 16:9 it but a s. thing unto you, that 4592
Nu 16:13 s. thing that thou hast brought us 4592
Nu 32:41 and took the s. towns thereof,
De 1:17 hear the s. as well as the great; 6996
De 9:21 stamped it, and ground it very s., 3190
De 9:21 even until it was as s. as dust: 1854
De 25:13 divers weights, a great and a s. 6996
De 25:14 divers measures, a great and a s. 6996
De 32:2 as the s. rain upon the tender herb,
1Sa 5:9 men of the city, both s. and great, 6996
1Sa 20:2 will do nothing either great or s., 6996
1Sa 30:2 slew not any, either great or s., 6996
1Sa 30:19 to them, neither s. nor great, 6996
2Sa 7:19 this was yet a s. thing in thy sight, 6994
2Sa 17:13 be not one s. stone found there. 1571
2Sa 22:43 I beat them as s. as the dust of the
1Ki 2:20 I desire one s. petition of thee; 6996
1Ki 19:12 and after the fire a still s. voice. 1851
1Ki 22:31 Fight neither with s. nor great, 6996
2Ki 19:26 their inhabitants were of s. power, 7116
2Ki 23:2 all the people, both s. and great: 6996
2Ki 23:6, 15 and stamped it s. to powder, 1854
2Ki 25:26 all the people, both s. and great, 6996
1Ch 17:17 this was a s. thing in thine eyes, 6994
1Ch 25:8 ward, as well the s. as the great, 6996
1Ch 26:13 lots, as well the s. as the great, 6996
2Ch 15:13 put to death, whether s. or great, 6996
2Ch 18:30 Fight ye not with s. or great, save 6996
2Ch 24:24 came with a s. company of men, 4705
2Ch 31:15 as well to the great as to the s. 6996
2Ch 34:30 and all the people, great and s. 6996
2Ch 35:8 thousand and six hundred s. cattle,
2Ch 35:9 offerings five thousand s. cattle,
2Ch 36:18 of the house of God, great and s., 6996
Es 1:5 both unto great and s., seven days, 6996
Es 1:20 honour, both to great and s. 6996
Job 3:19 The s. and great are there; and the 6996
Job 8:7 Though thy beginning was s., yet 4705
Job 15:11 consolations of God s. with thee? 4592
Job 36:27 he maketh s. the drops of water: 1639
Job 37:6 likewise to the s. rain, and to the
Ps 18:42 did I beat them s. as the dust before
Ps 104:25 both s. and great beasts. 6996
Ps 115:13 fear the Lord, both s. and great. 6996
Ps 119:141 I am s. and despised: yet do not 6810
Pr 24:10 day of adversity, thy strength is s. 6862
Ec 2:7 possessions of great and s. cattle
Isa 1:9 left unto us a very s. remnant, 4592
Isa 7:13 Is it a s. thing for you to weary men, 4592
Isa 16:14 the remnant shall be very s. and 4213
Isa 22:24 all vessels of s. quantity, from the 6996
Isa 29:5 thy strangers shall be like s. dust, 1851
Isa 37:27 their inhabitants were of s. power, 7116
Isa 40:15 counted as the s. dust of the balance:
Isa 41:15 the mountains, and beat them s., 1854
Isa 43:23 me the s. cattle of thy burnt offerings;
Isa 54:7 For a s. moment have I forsaken 6996
Isa 60:22 and a s. one a strong nation: 6810
Jer 16:6 Both the great and the s. shall die 6996
Jer 30:19 them, and they shall not be s. 6819
Jer 44:28 Yet a s. number that escape the 4962
Jer 49:15 I will make thee s. among the 6996
Eze 16:20 of thy whoredoms a s. matter, 4592
Eze 34:18 Seemeth it a s. thing unto you to 4592
Da 11:23 become strong with a s. people. 4592
Am 7:2,5 shall Jacob arise? for he is s. 6996
Am 8:5 forth wheat, making the ephah s., 6694
Ob 2 made thee s. among the heathen: 6996
Zec 4:10 hath despised the day of s. things? 6996
Mk 3:9 that a s. ship should wait on him *4142*
Mk 8:7 And they had a few s. fishes: and *2485*
Joh 2:15 he had made a scourge of s. cords, *4979*
Joh 6:9 five barley loaves,…two s. fishes: *3795*
Ac 12:18 was no s. stir among the soldiers, *3641*
Ac 15:2 no s. dissension and disputation *3641*
Ac 19:23 arose no s. stir about that way. *3641*
Ac 19:24 no s. gain unto the craftsman; *3641*
Ac 26:22 witnessing both to s. and great, *3398*
Ac 27:20 and no s. tempest lay on us, all *3641*
1Co 4:3 with me it is a very s. thing that *1646*
Jas 3:4 turned about with a very s. helm, *1646*
Re 11:18 that fear thy name, s. and great; *3398*
Re 13:16 both s. and great, rich and poor, *3398*
Re 19:5 that fear him, both s. and great. *3398*
Re 19:18 free and bond, both s. and great. *3398*
Re 20:12 And I saw the dead, s. and great, *3398*

SMALLEST
1Sa 9:21 of the s. of the tribes of Israel? 6996
1Co 6:2 unworthy to judge the s. matters? *1646*

SMART
Pr 11:15 for a stranger shall s. for it: 7321,7451

SMELL See also SMELLED; SMELLETH; SMELLING.
Ge 27:27 he smelled the s. of his raiment, 7381
Ge 27:27 s. of my son is as the s. of a field 7381
Ex 30:38 make like unto that, to s. thereto, 7306
Le 26:31 will not s. the savour of your sweet 7306
De 4:28 see, nor hear, nor eat, nor s. 7306
Ps 45:8 All thy garments s. of myrrh, and
Ps 115:6 noses have they, but they s. not: 7306
Ca 1:12 my spikenard sendeth forth the s. 7381
Ca 2:13 the tender grape give a good s. 7381
Ca 4:10 and the s. of thine ointments than 7381
Ca 4:11 the s. of thy garments is like the 7381
Ca 4:11 garments is like the s. of Lebanon. 7381
Ca 7:8 and the s. of thy nose like apples; 7381
Ca 7:13 The mandrakes give a s., and at 7381
Isa 3:24 instead of sweet s. there shall be 1314
Da 3:27 nor the s. of fire had passed on 7382
Ho 14:6 olive tree, and his s. as Lebanon. 7381
Am 5:21 not s. in your solemn assemblies. 7306
Php 4:18 an odour of a sweet s., a sacrifice *2175*

SMELLED
Ge 8:21 And the Lord s. a sweet savour; 7306
Ge 27:27 and he s. the smell of his raiment, 7306

SMELLETH
Job 39:25 and he s. the battle afar off, the 7306

SMELLING See also SWEETSMELLING.
Ca 5:5 my fingers with sweet s. myrrh, 5674
Ca 5:13 lilies, dropping sweet s. myrrh. 5674
1Co 12:17 were hearing, where were the s.? *3750*

SMITE See also SMITEST; SMITETH; SMITING; SMITTEN; SMOTE.
Ge 8:21 neither will I again s. any more 5221
Ge 32:8 come to the one company, and s. it, 5221
Ge 32:11 him, lest he will come and s. me, 5221
Ex 3:20 s. Egypt with all my wonders which 5221
Ex 7:17 I will s. with the rod that is in mine 5221
Ex 8:2 I will s. all thy borders with frogs: 5062
Ex 8:16 and s. the dust of the land, that it 5221
Ex 9:15 I may s. thee and thy people with 5221
Ex 12:12 will s. all the firstborn in the land of 5221
Ex 12:13 you, when I s. the land of Egypt. 5221
Ex 12:23 pass through to s. the Egyptians; 5062
Ex 12:23 come in unto your houses to s. you. 5062
Ex 17:6 thou shalt s. the rock, and there 5221
Ex 21:18 and one s. another with a stone, or 5221
Ex 21:20 And if a man s. his servant, or his 5221
Ex 21:26 if a man s. the eye of his servant, 5221
Ex 21:27 he s. out his manservant's tooth, 5307
Nu 14:12 I will s. them with the pestilence, 5221
Nu 22:6 that we may s. them, and that I may 5221
Nu 24:17 and shall s. the corners of Moab, 4272
Nu 25:17 Vex the Midianites, and s. them: 5221
Nu 35:16 if he s. him with an instrument of 5221
Nu 35:17 if he s. him with throwing a stone, 5221
Nu 35:18 if he s. him with an hand weapon 5221
Nu 35:21 Or in enmity s. him with his hand, 5221
De 7:2 thou shalt s. them, and utterly 5221
De 13:15 Thou shalt surely s. the inhabitants 5221
De 19:11 and s. him mortally that he die, and 5221
De 20:13 thou shalt s. every male thereof 5221
De 28:22 shall s. thee with a consumption, 5221
De 28:27 s. thee with the botch of Egypt, 5221
De 28:28 Lord shall s. thee with madness, 5221
De 28:35 The Lord shall s. thee in the knees, 5221
De 33:11 s. through the loins of them that 4272
Jos 7:3 thousand men go up and s. Ai; 6221
Jos 10:4 help me, that we may s. Gibeon: 6221
Jos 10:19 and s. the hindmost of them;
Jos 12:6 Lord and the children of Israel s. 5221
Jos 13:12 these did Moses s., and cast them 5221
Jg 6:16 shalt s. the Midianites as one man. 5221
Jg 20:31 and they began to s. of the people, 5221
Jg 20:39 Benjamin began to s. and kill of the 5221
Jg 21:10 saying, Go and s. the inhabitants of 5221
1Sa 15:3 Now go and s. Amalek, and utterly 5221
1Sa 17:46 I will s. thee, and take thine head 5221
1Sa 18:11 I will s. David even to the wall with 5221
1Sa 19:10 Saul sought to s. David even to the 5221
1Sa 20:33 Saul cast a javelin at him to s. him: 5221
1Sa 23:2 Shall I go and s. thee Philistines? 5221
1Sa 23:2 Go, and s. the Philistines, and save 5221
1Sa 26:8 therefore let me s. him, I pray thee, 5221
1Sa 26:8 and I will not s. him the second time.
1Sa 26:10 Lord liveth, the Lord shall s. him; 5062
2Sa 2:22 should I s. thee to the ground? 5221
2Sa 5:24 to s. the host of the Philistines. 5221
2Sa 13:28 when I say unto you, S. Amnon; 5221
2Sa 15:14 and s. the city with the edge of the 5221
2Sa 17:2 flee; and I will s. the king only: 5221
2Sa 18:11 thou not s. him there to the ground? 5221

1Ki 14:15 the Lord shall s. Israel, as a reed....... 5221
1Ki 20:35 word of the Lord, S. me, I pray thee.. 5221
1Ki 20:35 And the man refused to s. him. 5221
1Ki 20:37 man, and said, S. me, I pray thee. 5221
2Ki 3:19 And ye shall s. every fenced city,....... 5221
2Ki 6:18 S. this people, I pray thee, with 5221
2Ki 6:21 shall I s. them? shall I s. them? 5221
2Ki 6:22 answered, Thou shalt not s. them: 5221
2Ki 6:22 thou s. those whom thou hast taken.... 5221
2Ki 9:7 thou shalt s. the house of Ahab thy 5221
2Ki 9:27 and said, S. him also in the chariot. 5221
2Ki 13:17 thou shalt s. the Syrians in Aphek, ... 5221
2Ki 13:18 king of Israel, S. upon the ground. 5221
2Ki 13:19 now thou shalt s. Syria but thrice. 5221
1Ch 14:15 to s. the host of the Philistines. 5221
2Ch 21:14 plague will the Lord s. thy people,...... 5062
Ps 121:6 The sun shall not s. thee by day, ... 5221
Ps 141:5 Let the righteous s. me; it shall be..... 1986
Pr 19:25 S. a scorner, and the simple will........ 5221
Isa 3:17 Lord will s. with a scab the crown...... 5596
Isa 10:24 he shall s. thee with a rod, and......... 5221
Isa 11:4 he shall s. the earth with the rod of.... 5221
Isa 11:15 and shall s. it in the seven streams,.... 5221
Isa 19:22 And the Lord shall s. Egypt: he......... 5062
Isa 19:22 he shall s. and heal it: and they 5062
Isa 49:10 shall the heat nor sun s. them: 5221
Isa 58:4 and to s. with the fist of wickedness: .. 5221
Jer 18:18 and let us s. him with the tongue, ... 5221
Jer 21:6 And I will s. the inhabitants of this 5221
Jer 21:7 he shall s. them with the edge of the .. 5221
Jer 43:11 he shall s. the land of Egypt, and....... 5221
Jer 46:13 come and s. the land of Egypt. 5221
Jer 49:28 which Nebuchadrezzar...shall s.,......... 5221
Eze 5:2 part, and s. about it with a knife: 5221
Eze 6:11 S. with thine hand, and stamp with..... 5221
Eze 9:5 after him through the city, and s. 5221
Eze 21:12 s. therefore upon thy thigh............... 5606
Eze 21:14 and s. thine hands together, and 5221
Eze 21:17 I will also s. mine hands together, ... 5221
Eze 32:15 when I shall s. all them that dwell 5221
Eze 39:3 And I will s. thy bow out of thy left.... 5221
Am 3:15 I will s. the winter house with the..... 5221
Am 6:11 and he will s. the great house with..... 5221
Am 9:1 S. the lintel of the door, that the 5221
Mic 5:1 s. the judge of Israel with a rod......... 5221
Na 2:10 the knees s. together, and much......... 6375
Zec 9:4 and he will s. her power in the sea;.... 5221
Zec 10:11 and shall s. the waves in the sea, ... 5221
Zec 11:6 they shall s. the land, and out of........ 3807
Zec 12:4 s. every horse with astonishment, ... 5221
Zec 12:4 s. every horse of the people with........ 5221
Zec 13:7 s. the shepherd, and the sheep shall ... 5221
Zec 14:12 the Lord will s. all the people that...... 5062
Zec 14:18 the Lord will s. the heathen that........ 5062
Mal 4:6 come and s. the earth with a curse...... 5221
Mt 5:39 **shall s. thee on thy right cheek,**.... *4474*
Mt 24:49 **begin to s. his fellowservants,** *5180*
Mt 26:31 **I will s. the shepherd, and the** *3960*
Mk 14:27 **I will s. the shepherd, and the** *3960*
Lu 22:49 Lord, shall we s. with the sword? *3960*
Ac 23:2 by him to s. him on the mouth. *5180*
Ac 23:3 God shall s. thee, thou whited wall: *5180*
2Co 11:20 if a man s. you on the face. *1194*
Re 11:6 to s. the earth with all plagues,.......... *3960*
Re 19:15 with it he should s. the nations: *3960*

SMITERS
Isa 50:6 I gave my back to the s., and my....... 5221

SMITEST
Ex 2:13 Wherefore s. thou thy fellow?............ 5221
Joh 18:23 **evil: but if well, why s. thou me?** .. *1194*

SMITETH
Ex 21:12 He that s. a man, so that he die, ... 5221
Ex 21:15 he that s. his father, or his mother,.... 5221
De 25:11 out of the hand of him that s. him, ... 5221
De 27:24 he that s. his neighbour secretly. 5221
Jos 15:16 He that s. Kirjath-sepher, and 5221
Jg 1:12 He that s. Kirjath-sepher, and 5221
2Sa 5:8 and s. the Jebusites, and the lame...... 5221
1Ch 11:6 Whosoever s. the Jebusites first......... 5221
Job 26:12 he s. through the proud.................... 4272
Isa 9:13 turneth not unto him that s. them,...... 5221
La 3:30 giveth his cheek to him that s. him:.... 5221
Eze 7:9 know that I am the Lord that s.......... 5221
Lu 6:29 **that s. thee on the one cheek** *5180*

SMITH See also COPPERSMITH; SMITHS.
1Sa 13:19 no s. found throughout all the........... 2796
Isa 44:12 The s. with the tongs both 2796,1270
Isa 54:16 created the s. that bloweth the.......... 2796

SMITHS
2Ki 24:14 and all the craftsmen and s.:............... 4525
2Ki 24:16 craftsmen and s. a thousand, all 4525
Jer 24:1 with the carpenters and s., from........ 4525
Jer 29:2 and the carpenters, and the s., were... 4525

SMITING
Ex 2:11 he spied an Egyptian s. an Hebrew,.... 5221
2Sa 8:13 he returned from s. of the Syrians...... 5221
1Ki 20:37 him, so that in s. he wounded him...... 5221
2Ki 3:24 they went forward s. the Moabites, ... 5221
Mic 6:13 will I make thee sick in s. thee, ... 5221

SMITTEN
Ex 7:25 that the Lord had s. the river............ 5221
Ex 9:31 And the flax and the barley was s....... 5221
Ex 9:32 the wheat and the rie were not s. 5221
Ex 22:2 breaking up, and be s. that he die, ... 5221
Nu 14:42 ye be not s. before your enemies. 5062
Nu 22:28 thou hast s. me thee three times? 5221
Nu 22:32 thou s. thine ass these three times?.... 5221
Nu 33:4 which the Lord had s. among them: 5221
De 1:42 lest ye be s. before your enemies. 5062
De 28:7 thee to be s. before thy face: they 5062
De 28:25 thee to be s. before thine enemies: 5062
Jg 1:8 s. it with the edge of the sword,......... 5221
Jg 20:32 They are s. down before us, as at...... 5062
Jg 20:36 of Benjamin saw that they were s....... 5062
Jg 20:39 Surely they are s. down before us, ... 5062
1Sa 4:2 Israel was s. before the Philistines:.... 5062
1Sa 4:3 Wherefore hath the Lord s. us to........ 5062
1Sa 4:10 Philistines fought, and Israel was s., ... 5062
1Sa 5:12 died not were s. with the emerods: 5221
1Sa 6:19 the Lord had s. many of the people 5221
1Sa 7:10 and they were s. before Israel. 5062
1Sa 13:4 that Saul had s. a garrison of the........ 5221
1Sa 30:1 s. Ziklag, and burned it with fire; 5221
2Sa 2:31 servants of David...s. of Benjamin, ... 5221
2Sa 8:9 that David had s. all the host of.......... 5221
2Sa 8:10 against Hadadezer, and s. him: 5221
2Sa 10:15, 19 that they were s. before Israel, ... 5062
2Sa 11:15 ye from him, that he may be s., ... 5221
1Ki 8:33 When thy people Israel be s. down..... 5062
1Ki 11:15 he had s. every male in Edom; 5221
2Ki 2:14 when he also had s. the waters,......... 5221
2Ki 3:23 and they have s. one another: now...... 5221
2Ki 13:19 shouldest have s. five or six times;..... 5221
2Ki 13:19 s. Syria till thou hadst consumed it: 5221
2Ki 14:10 Thou hast indeed s. Edom, and.......... 5221
1Ch 18:9 how David had s. all the host of......... 5221
1Ch 18:10 against Hadarezer, and s. him;........... 5221
2Ch 20:22 against Judah; and they were s., ... 5062
2Ch 25:16 forbear; why shouldest thou be s.? 5221
2Ch 25:19 Lo, thou hast s. the Edomites; 5221
2Ch 26:20 out, because the Lord had s. him. 5060
2Ch 28:17 Edomites had come and s. Judah, ... 5221
Job 16:10 they have s. me upon the cheek 5221
Ps 3:7 s. all mine enemies upon the cheek..... 5221
Ps 69:26 persecute him whom thou hast s.; 5221
Ps 102:4 My heart is s., and withered like......... 5221
Ps 143:3 he hath s. my life down to the........... 1792
Isa 5:25 against them, and hath s. them: 5221
Isa 24:12 and the gate is s. with destruction. 3807
Isa 27:7 Hath he s. him, as he smote those 5221
Isa 53:4 stricken, s. of God, and afflicted.......... 5221
Jer 2:30 In vain have I s. your children; 5221
Jer 14:19 why hast thou s. us, and there is no... 5221
Jer 37:10 ye had s. the whole army of the 5221
Eze 22:13 have s. mine hand at thy dishonest 5221
Eze 33:21 unto me, saying, The city is s.. 5221
Eze 40:1 year after that the city was s., in....... 5221
Ho 6:1 he hath s., and he will bind us up........ 5221
Ho 9:16 Ephraim is s., their root is dried 5221
Am 4:9 I have s. you with blasting and 5221
Ac 23:3 me to be s. contrary to the law? *5180*
Re 8:12 the third part of the sun was s., ... *4141*

SMOKE See also SMOKING.
Ge 19:28 the s. of the country went up as 7008
Ge 19:28 went up as the s. of a furnace. 7008
Ex 19:18 Sinai was altogether on a s.,............... 6225
Ex 19:18 fire: and the s. thereof ascended 6227
Ex 19:18 ascended as the s. of a furnace,.......... 6227
De 29:20 jealousy shall s. against that man, ... 6225
Jos 8:20 the s. of the city ascended up to.......... 6227
Jos 8:21 and that the s. of the city ascended, ... 6227
Jg 20:38 great flame with s. rise up out of....... 6227
Jg 20:40 up out of the city with a pillar of s.,.... 6227
2Sa 22:9 went up a s. out of his nostrils, and.... 6227
Job 41:20 Out of his nostrils goeth s., as out 6227
Ps 18:8 went up a s. out of his nostrils, and.... 6227
Ps 37:20 into s. shall they consume away. 6227
Ps 68:2 As s. is driven away, so drive them.... 6227
Ps 74:1 thine anger s. against the sheep......... 6225
Ps 102:3 my days are consumed like s., and 6227
Ps 104:32 toucheth the hills, and they s............. 6225
Ps 119:83 am become like a bottle in the s.; 7008
Ps 144:5 the mountains, and they shall s.. 6225
Pr 10:26 to the teeth, and as s. to the eyes, ... 6227
Ca 3:6 of the wilderness like pillars of s., ... 6227
Isa 4:5 assemblies, a cloud and s. by day,....... 6227
Isa 6:4 and the house was filled with s.. 6227
Isa 9:18 mount up like the lifting up of s.. 6227
Isa 14:31 there shall come from the north as s.,..6227
Isa 34:10 the s. thereof shall go up for ever: 6227
Isa 51:6 heavens shall vanish away like s.,....... 6227
Isa 65:5 These are a s. in my nose, a fire that..6227
Ho 13:3 and as the s. out of the chimney. 6227
Joe 2:30 blood, and fire, and pillars of s.......... 6227
Na 2:13 I will burn her chariots in the s.,........ 6227
Ac 2:19 blood, and fire, and vapour of s.......... *2586*
Re 8:4 And the s. of the incense, which........ *2586*
Re 9:2 and there arose a s. out of the pit,..... *2586*
Re 9:2 as the s. of a great furnace; and the ... *2586*
Re 9:2 was darkened by reason of the s.......... *2586*
Re 9:3 there came out of the s. locusts......... *2586*
Re 9:17 issued fire and s. and brimstone. *2586*
Re 9:18 killed, by the fire, and by the s.,......... *2586*
Re 14:11 the s. of their torment ascendeth *2586*
Re 15:8 filled with s. from the glory of God,.... *2586*
Re 18:9 they shall see the s. of her burning,.... *2586*
Re 18:18 when they saw the s. of her burning,.. *2586*
Re 19:3 And her s. rose up for ever and ever...*2586*

SMOKING
Ge 15:17 behold a s. furnace, and a burning 6227
Ex 20:18 the trumpet, and the mountain s. 6226
Isa 7:4 the two tails of these s. firebrands,..... 6226
Isa 42:3 the s. flax shall he not quench: 3544
Mt 12:20 and s. flax shall he not quench,.......... *5187*

SMOOTH See also SMOOTHER; SMOOTHETH.
Ge 27:11 a hairy man, and I am a s. man:......... 2509
Ge 27:16 hands, and upon the s. of his neck:...... 2513
1Sa 17:40 chose him five s. stones out of the..... 2512
Isa 30:10 speak unto us s. things, prophesy....... 2513
Isa 57:6 Among the s. stones of the stream..... 2511
Lu 3:5 the rough ways shall be made s.; *3006*

SMOOTHER
Ps 55:21 of his mouth were s. than butter,....... 2505
Pr 5:3 and her mouth is s. than oil:............. 2513

SMOOTHETH
Isa 41:7 and he that s. with the hammer 2505

SMOTE See also SMOTEST.
Ge 14:5 and s. the Rephaims in Ashteroth......... 5221
Ge 14:7 s. all the country of the Amalekites,.... 5221
Ge 14:15 by night, and s. them, and pursued..... 5221
Ge 19:11 s. the men that were at the door of.... 5221
Ge 36:35 who s. Midian in the field of Moab,..... 5221
Ex 7:20 s. the waters that were in the river,.... 5221
Ex 8:17 his rod, and s. the dust of the earth, .. 5221
Ex 9:25 the hail s. throughout the land of........ 5221
Ex 9:25 the hail s. every herb of the field, ... 5221
Ex 12:27 Egypt, when he s. the Egyptians,....... 5062
Ex 12:29 the Lord s. all the firstborn in the 5221
Ex 21:19 then shall he that s. him be quit:....... 5221
Nu 3:13 that I s. all the firstborn in the land 5221
Nu 8:17 that I s. every firstborn in the land..... 5221
Nu 11:33 Lord s. the people with a very great... 5221
Nu 14:45 and s. them, and discomfited them,..... 5221
Nu 20:11 with his rod he s. the rock twice:......... 5221
Nu 21:24 Israel s. him with the edge of the....... 5221
Nu 21:35 So they s. him, and his sons, and........ 5221
Nu 22:23 Balaam s. the ass, to turn her into 5221
Nu 22:25 the wall: and he s. her again. 5221
Nu 22:27 and he s. the ass with a staff............. 5221
Nu 24:10 and he s. his hands together: 5606
Nu 32:4 the country which the Lord s. 5221
Nu 35:21 he that s. him shall surely be put to.... 5221

De 2:33 we s. him, and his sons, and all his 5221
De 3:3 we s. him until none was left to him ... 5221
De 4:46 Moses and the children of Israel s., ... 5221
De 25:18 the way, and s. the hindmost of thee, ...
De 29:7 us unto battle, and we s. them: 5221
Jos 7:5 men of Ai s. of them about thirty 5221
Jos 7:5 and s. them in the going down: 5221
Jos 8:22 they s. them, so that they let none..... 5221
Jos 8:24 unto Ai, and s. it with the edge of..... 5221
Jos 9:18 the children of Israel s. them not, ... 5221
Jos 10:10 and s. them to Azekah, and unto........ 5221
Jos 10:26 afterward Joshua s. them, and slew..... 5221
Jos 10:28 and s. it with the edge of the sword, .. 5221
Jos 10:30 he s. it with the edge of the sword,.... 5221
Jos 10:32 and s. it with the edge of the sword, .. 5221
Jos 10:33 and Joshua s. him and his people, ... 5221
Jos 10:35, 37 s. it with the edge of the sword,.... 5221
Jos 10:39 s. them with the edge of the sword, ... 5221
Jos 10:40 Joshua s....the country of the hills, ... 5221
Jos 10:41 s. them from Kadesh-barnea even 5221
Jos 11:8 who s. them, and chased them unto.... 5221
Jos 11:8 s. them, until they left them none 5221
Jos 11:10 s. the king thereof with the sword:..... 5221
Jos 11:11 s. all the souls that were therein........ 5221
Jos 11:12 s. them with the edge of the sword, ... 5221
Jos 11:14 every man they s. with the edge of 5221
Jos 11:17 their kings he took, and s. them, ... 5221
Jos 12:1 land, which the children of Israel s.,.... 5221
Jos 12:7 Joshua and the children of Israel s. 5221
Jos 13:21 whom Moses s. with the princes of 5221
Jos 19:47 and s. it with the edge of the sword, .. 5221
Jos 20:5 he s. his neighbour unwittingly,.......... 5221
Jg 1:25 they s. the city with the edge of the... 5221
Jg 3:13 and Amalek, and went and s. Israel, ... 5221
Jg 4:21 and s. the nail into his temples, ... 8628
Jg 5:26 with the hammer she s. Sisera,.......... 1986
Jg 5:26 she s. off his head, when she had....... 4277
Jg 7:13 unto a tent, and s. it that it fell,......... 5221
Jg 8:11 Gideon went up...and s. the host: 5221
Jg 9:43 rose up against them, and s. them...... 5221
Jg 11:21 hand of Israel, and they s. them:........ 5221
Jg 11:33 And he s. them from Aroer, even 5221
Jg 12:4 and the men of Gilead s. Ephraim,...... 5221
Jg 15:8 s. them hip and thigh with a great...... 5221
Jg 18:27 s. them with the edge of the sword, ... 5221
Jg 20:35 Lord s. Benjamin before Israel:.......... 5062
Jg 20:37 s. all the city with the edge of the...... 5221
Jg 20:48 s. them with the edge of the sword, ... 5221
1Sa 4:8 are the Gods that s. the Egyptians 5221
1Sa 5:6 s. them with emerods, even Ashdod ... 5221
1Sa 5:9 s. the men of the city, both small........ 5221
1Sa 6:9 that it is not his hand that s. us; 5060
1Sa 6:19 even he s. of the people fifty thousand ......
1Sa 6:19 he s. the men of Beth-shemesh, ... 5221
1Sa 7:11 pursued the Philistines, and s. them,... 5221
1Sa 13:3 s. the garrison of the Philistines......... 5221
1Sa 14:31 And they s. the Philistines that day..... 5221
1Sa 14:48 an host, and s. the Amalekites, and.... 5221
1Sa 15:7 And Saul s. the Amalekites from........ 5221
1Sa 17:35 I went out after him, and s. him, ... 5221
1Sa 17:35 caught him by his beard, and s. him,... 5221
1Sa 17:49 and s. the Philistine in his forehead,.... 5221
1Sa 17:50 with a stone, and s. the Philistine,....... 5221
1Sa 19:10 and he s. the javelin into the wall: 5221
1Sa 22:19 s. he with the edge of the sword, ... 5221
1Sa 23:5 and s. them with a great slaughter...... 5221
1Sa 24:5 afterward, that David's heart s. him, ... 5221
1Sa 25:38 the Lord s. Nabal, that he died. 5062
1Sa 27:9 David s. the land, and left neither....... 5221
1Sa 30:17 David s. them from the twilight.......... 5221
2Sa 1:15 him. And he s. him that he died......... 5221
2Sa 2:23 spear s. him under the fifth rib, ... 5221
2Sa 3:27 and s. him there under the fifth rib, ... 5221
2Sa 4:6 and they s. him under the fifth rib: 5221
2Sa 4:7 and they s. him, and slew him, and..... 5221
2Sa 5:20 and David s. them there, and said, ... 5221
2Sa 5:25 s. the Philistines from Geba until........ 5221
2Sa 6:7 and God s. him there for his error;..... 5221
2Sa 8:1 that David s. the Philistines, and......... 5221
2Sa 8:2 he s. Moab, and measured them 5221
2Sa 8:3 David s. also Hadadezer, the son of.... 5221
2Sa 10:18 s. Shobach...captain of their host,....... 5221
2Sa 11:21 Who s. Abimelech the son of............ 5221
2Sa 14:6 the one s. the other, and slew him. 5221
2Sa 14:7 Deliver him that s. his brother, that.... 5221
2Sa 18:15 and s. Absalom, and slew him............ 5221
2Sa 20:10 he s. him therewith in the fifth rib,..... 5221
2Sa 21:17 and s. the Philistine, and killed him..... 5221
2Sa 23:10 s. the Philistines until his hand was..... 5221
2Sa 24:10 David's heart s. him after that he........ 5221
2Sa 24:17 he saw the angel that s. the people, ... 5221
1Ki 15:20 the cities of Israel, and s. Ijon, and..... 5221
1Ki 15:27 and Baasha s. him at Gibbethon, ... 5221
1Ki 15:29 he s. all the houses of Jeroboam; 5221
1Ki 16:10 Zimri went in and s. him, and killed 5221
1Ki 20:21 s. the horses and chariots, and slew ... 5221
1Ki 20:37 the man s. him, so that in smiting 5221
1Ki 22:24 near, and s. Micaiah on the cheek, ... 5221
1Ki 22:34 s. the king of Israel between the........ 5221
2Ki 2:8 his mantle,...and s. the waters,.......... 5221
2Ki 2:14 the mantle...and s. the waters, ... 5221
2Ki 3:24 rose up and s. the Moabites,.............. 5221
2Ki 3:25 the slingers went about it, and s. it. ... 5221
2Ki 6:18 s. them with blindness according........ 5221
2Ki 8:21 rose by night, and s. the Edomites..... 5221
2Ki 9:24 and s. Jehoram between his arms, ... 5221
2Ki 10:25 s. them with the edge of the sword; ... 5221
2Ki 10:32 Hazael s. them in all the coasts of...... 5221
2Ki 12:21 his servants, s. him, and he died;........ 5221
2Ki 13:18 And he s. thrice, and stayed. 5221
2Ki 15:5 And the Lord s. the king, so that he.... 5221
2Ki 15:10 s. him before the people, and slew 5221
2Ki 15:14 and s. Shallum the son of Jabesh in..... 5221
2Ki 15:16 Then Menahem s. Tiphsah, and all 5221
2Ki 15:16 not to him, therefore he s. it;............ 5221
2Ki 15:25 against him, and s. him in Samaria, ... 5221
2Ki 15:30 s. him, and slew him, and reigned 5221
2Ki 18:8 s. the Philistines, even unto Gaza,...... 5221
2Ki 19:35 s. in the camp of the Assyrians an...... 5221
2Ki 19:37 his sons s. him with the sword: 5221
2Ki 25:21 And the king of Babylon s. them, ... 5221
2Ki 25:25 ten men with him, and s. Gedaliah,..... 5221
1Ch 1:46 which s. Midian in the field of Moab,... 5221
1Ch 4:41 s. their tents, and the habitations, ... 5221
1Ch 4:43 they s. the rest of the Amalekites 5221
1Ch 13:10 kindled against Uzza, and he s. him, ... 5221
1Ch 14:11 and David s. them there.................. 5221
1Ch 14:16 s. the hosts of the Philistines from 5221
1Ch 18:1 that David s. the Philistines, and........ 5221
1Ch 18:2 And he s. Moab; and the Moabites....... 5221
1Ch 18:3 David s. Hadarezer king of Zobah........ 5221
1Ch 20:1 Joab s. Rabbah, and destroyed it. 5221
1Ch 21:7 this thing; therefore he s. Israel......... 5221
2Ch 13:15 God s. Jeroboam and all Israel........... 5062
2Ch 14:12 Lord s. the Ethiopians before Asa, ... 5062
2Ch 14:14 they s. all the cities round about 5221
2Ch 14:15 They s. also the tents of cattle, and.... 5221
2Ch 16:4 and they s. Ijon, and Dan, and........... 5221
2Ch 18:23 and s. Micaiah upon the cheek, and 5221
2Ch 18:33 s. the king of Israel between the........ 5221
2Ch 21:9 up by night, and s. the Edomites........ 5221
2Ch 21:18 the Lord s. him in his bowels with...... 5062
2Ch 22:5 and the Syrians s. Joram.................. 5221
2Ch 25:11 and s. of the children of Seir ten........ 5221
2Ch 25:13 and s. three thousand of them, and...... 5221
2Ch 28:5 and they s. him, and carried away 5221
2Ch 28:5 who s. him with a great slaughter....... 5221
2Ch 28:23 gods of Damascus, which s. him:........ 5221
Ne 13:25 s. certain of them, and plucked off....... 5221
Es 9:5 the Jews s. all their enemies with........ 5221
Job 1:19 s. the four corners of the house,........ 5060
Job 2:7 s. Job with sore boils from the........... 5221
Ps 60: *title* and s. of Edom in the valley of 5221
Ps 78:20 he s. the rock, that the waters 5221
Ps 78:31 s. down the chosen men of Israel....... 3766
Ps 78:51 And s. all the firstborn in Egypt; 5221
Ps 78:66 And he s. his enemies in the hinder.... 5221
Ps 105:33 He s. their vines also and their fig...... 5221
Ps 105:36 He s. also all the firstborn in their...... 5221
Ps 135:8 Who s. the firstborn of Egypt, both 5221
Ps 135:10 Who s. great nations, and slew 5221
Ps 136:10 him that s. Egypt in their firstborn: 5221
Ps 136:17 To him which s. great kings: for 5221
Ca 5:7 me, they s. me, they wounded me; 5221
Isa 10:20 again stay upon him that s. them;........ 5221
Isa 14:6 He who s. the people in wrath with.... 5221
Isa 14:29 rod of him that s. thee is broken:....... 5221
Isa 27:7 Hath he smitten him, as he s............. 4347
Isa 27:7 those that s. him? or is he slain......... 5221
Isa 30:31 beaten down, which s. with a rod. 5221
Isa 37:36 and s. in the camp of the Assyrians 5221
Isa 37:38 his sons s. him with the sword; 5221
Isa 41:7 the hammer him that s. the anvil,....... 1986
Isa 57:17 was I wroth, and s. him: I hid me, ... 5221
Isa 60:10 for in my wrath I s. thee, but in my ... 5221
Jer 20:2 Pashur s. Jeremiah the prophet,......... 5221
Jer 31:19 was instructed, I s. upon my thigh:..... 5606
Jer 37:15 wroth with Jeremiah, and s. him,........ 5221
Jer 41:2 s. Gedaliah the son of Ahikam the 5221
Jer 46:2 Nebuchadrezzar king of Babylon s....... 5221
Jer 47:1 before that Pharaoh s. Gaza. 5221
Jer 52:27 And the king of Babylon s. them, ... 5221
Da 2:34 s. the image upon his feet that were... 4223
Da 2:35 the stone that s. the image became 4223
Da 5:6 his knees s. one against another......... 5368
Da 8:7 and s. the ram, and brake his two...... 5221
Jon 4:7 and it s. the gourd that it withered. 5221
Hag 2:17 I s. you with blasting and with........... 5221
Mt 26:51 the high priest's, and s. off his ear....... *851*
Mt 26:67 others s. him with the palms of.......... *4474*
Mt 26:68 thou Christ, Who is he that s. thee? ... *3817*
Mt 27:30 the reed, and s. him on the head. *5180*
Mk 14:47 and s. a servant of the high priest, ... *3817*
Mk 15:19 s. him on the head with a reed, ... *5180*
Lu 18:13 **s. upon his breast, saying, God be**..*5180*
Lu 22:50 s. the servant of the high priest, ... *3960*
Lu 22:63 held Jesus mocked him,...s. him......... *1194*
Lu 22:64 Prophesy, who is it that s. thee?........ *3817*
Lu 23:48 s. their breasts, and returned. *5180*
Joh 18:10 and s. the high priest's servant, ... *3817*
Joh 19:3 they s. him with their hands....... *1325,4475*
Ac 7:24 oppressed, and s. the Egyptian: *3960*
Ac 12:7 he s. Peter on the side, and raised..... *3960*
Ac 12:23 angel of the Lord s. him, because....... *3960*

SMOTEST
Ex 17:5 rod, wherewith thou s. the river, ... 5221

SMYRNA (smir'-nah)
Re 1:11 **unto S., and unto Pergamos, and**.. *4667*
Re 2:8 **unto the angel of the church in S.**..*4668*

SNAIL
Le 11:30 and the lizard, and the s., and the...... 2546
Ps 58:8 As a s. which melteth, let every 7642

SNARE See also SNARED; SNARES.
Ex 10:7 shall this man be a s. unto us?........... 4170
Ex 23:33 it will surely be a s. unto thee............ 4170
Ex 34:12 it be for a s. in the midst of thee: 4170
De 7:16 for that will be a s. unto thee............ 4170
Jg 2:3 their gods shall be a s. unto you. 4170
Jg 8:27 thing became a s. unto Gideon,.......... 4170
1Sa 18:21 that she may be a s. to him, and........ 4170
1Sa 28:9 then layest thou a s. for my life, ... 5367
Job 18:8 feet, and he walketh upon a s............ 7639
Job 18:10 s. is laid for him in the ground,.......... 2256
Ps 69:22 Let their table become a s. before...... 6341
Ps 91:3 thee from the s. of the fowler, and..... 6341
Ps 106:36 idols: which were a s. unto them........ 4170
Ps 119:110 The wicked have laid a s. for me: 6341
Ps 124:7 bird out of the s. of the fowlers: 6341
Ps 124:7 s. is broken, and we are escaped. 6341
Ps 140:5 The proud have hid a s. for me, and... 6341
Ps 142:3 have they privily laid a s. for me........ 6341
Pr 7:23 as a bird hasteth to the s., and.......... 6341
Pr 18:7 and his lips are the s. of his soul........ 4170
Pr 20:25 It is a s. to the man who devoureth.... 4170
Pr 22:25 his ways, and get a s. to thy soul....... 4170
Pr 29:6 of an evil man there is a s.: but the.... 4170
Pr 29:8 Scornful men bring a city into a s....... 6315
Pr 29:25 The fear of man bringeth a s............. 4170
Ec 9:12 birds that are caught in the s.;........... 6341
Isa 8:14 and for a s. to the inhabitants of 4170
Isa 24:17 the pit, and the s., are upon thee,....... 6341
Isa 24:18 of the pit shall be taken in the s......... 6341
Isa 29:21 lay a s. for him that reproveth in........ 6983
Jer 48:43 the pit, and the s., shall be upon........ 6341
Jer 48:44 of the pit shall be taken in the s......... 6341
Jer 50:24 I have laid a s. for thee, and thou 3369
La 3:47 Fear and a s. is come upon us,.......... 6354
Eze 12:13 and he shall be taken in my s. 4686
Eze 17:20 him, and he shall be taken in my s., ... 4686
Ho 5:1 ye have been a s. on Mizpah, and 6341
Ho 9:8 the prophet is a s. of a fowler in all.... 6341
Am 3:5 a bird fall in a s. upon the earth,....... 6341
Am 3:5 shall one take up a s. from the 6341
Lu 21:35 **as a s. shall it come on all them** ... *3803*
Ro 11:9 Let their table be made a s., and a..... *3803*
1Co 7:35 not that I may cast a s. upon you,...... *1029*
1Ti 3:7 reproach and the s. of the devil. *3803*
1Ti 6:9 rich fall into temptation and a s., ... *3803*
2Ti 2:26 themselves out of the s. of the devil, .. *3803*

SNARED See also ENSNARED.
De 7:25 unto thee, lest thou be **s.** therein: 3369
De 12:30 thou be not **s.** by following them, ... 5367
Ps 9:16 wicked is **s.** in the work of his own 5367
Pr 6:2 **s.** with the words of thy mouth, ... 3369
Pr 12:13 wicked is **s.** by the transgression........ 4170
Ec 9:12 the sons of men **s.** in an evil time, ... 3369
Isa 8:15 be broken, and be **s.**, and be taken..... 3369
Isa 28:13 and be broken, and **s.**, and taken. 3369
Isa 42:22 they are all of them **s.** in holes, ... 6351

SNARES
Jos 23:13 shall be **s.** and traps unto you, ... 6341
2Sa 22:6 the **s.** of death prevented me; 4170
Job 22:10 Therefore **s.** are round about thee, ... 6341
Job 40:24 eyes: his nose pierceth through **s.**...... 4170
Ps 11:6 Upon the wicked he shall rain **s.**, ... 6341
Ps 18:5 the **s.** of death prevented me. 4170
Ps 38:12 seek after my life lay **s.** for me:.......... 5367
Ps 64:5 they commune of laying **s.** privily; 4170
Ps 141:9 me from the **s.** which they have......... 6341
Pr 13:14 life, to depart from the **s.** of death...... 4170
Pr 14:27 life, to depart from the **s.** of death...... 4170
Pr 22:5 Thorns and **s.** are in the way of........... 6341
Ec 7:26 whose heart is **s.** and nets, and 4685
Jer 5:26 lay wait, as he that setteth **s.**; 3353
Jer 18:22 to take me, and hid **s.** for my feet...... 6341

SNATCH
Isa 9:20 And he shall **s.** on the right hand,....... 1504

SNEEZED
2Ki 4:35 and the child **s.** seven times, and 2237

SNEEZINGS See NEESINGS.

SNORTING
Jer 8:16 The **s.** of his horses was heard.......... 5170

SNOUT
Pr 11:22 As a jewel of gold in a swine's **s.**,........ 639

SNOW
Ex 4:6 behold, his hand was leprous as **s.**...... 7950
Nu 12:10 became leprous, white as **s.**: and........ 7950
2Sa 23:20 in the midst of a pit in time of **s.**......... 7950
2Ki 5:27 his presence a leper as white as **s.**..... 7950
Job 6:16 the ice, and wherein the **s.** is hid: 7950
Job 9:30 If I wash myself with **s.** water, and...... 7950
Job 24:19 and heat consume the **s.** waters:........ 7950
Job 37:6 For he saith to the **s.**, Be thou on...... 7950
Job 38:22 entered into the treasures of the **s.**? ... 7950
Ps 51:7 me, and I shall be whiter than **s.**........ 7950
Ps 68:14 in it, it was white as **s.** in Salmon....... 7949
Ps 147:16 He giveth **s.** like wool: he.................. 7950
Ps 148:8 Fire, and hail; **s.**, and vapours; 7950
Pr 25:13 As the cold of **s.** in the time of......... 7950
Pr 26:1 As **s.** in summer, and as rain in 7950
Pr 31:21 She is not afraid of the **s.** for her 7950
Isa 1:18 scarlet, they shall be as white as **s.**; ... 7950
Isa 55:10 down, and the **s.** from heaven, and..... 7950
Jer 18:14 Will a man leave the **s.** of Lebanon..... 7950
La 4:7 Her Nazarites were purer than **s.**,...... 7950
Da 7:9 whose garment was white as **s.**, ... 8517
Mt 28:3 and his raiment white as **s.** *5510*
Mk 9:3 shining, exceeding white as **s.**............ *5510*
Re 1:14 were white like wool, as white as **s.** *5510*

SNOWY
1Ch 11:22 slew a lion in a pit in a **s.** day........... 7950

SNUFF See SNUFFDISHES; SNUFFED; SNUFFETH.

SNUFFDISHES
Ex 25:38 the **s.** thereof, shall be of pure 4289
Ex 37:23 his snuffers, and his **s.**, of pure gold. .. 4289
Nu 4:9 lamps, and his tongs, and his **s.**, ... 4289

SNUFFED
Jer 14:6 they **s.** up the winds like dragons; 7602
Mal 1:13 ye have **s.** at it, saith the Lord of....... 5301

SNUFFERS
Ex 37:23 made his seven lamps, and his **s.**, ... 4457
1Ki 7:50 the bowls, and the **s.**, and the 4212
2Ki 12:13 of the Lord bowls of silver, **s.**, ... 4212
2Ki 25:14 pots, and the shovels, and the **s.**,........ 4212
2Ch 4:22 And the **s.**, and the basons, and the.... 4212
Jer 52:18 and the **s.**, and the bowls, and the..... 4212

SNUFFETH
Jer 2:24 **s.** up the wind at her pleasure; 7602

SO See also ALSO; INSOMUCH; SOEVER.
Ge 1:7 the firmament: and it was **s.**.............. 3651
Ge 1:9 the dry land appear: and it was **s.**. 3651
Ge 1:11 itself, upon the earth: and it was **s.**. ... 3651
Ge 1:15 light upon the earth: and it was **s.**..... 3651
Ge 1:24 earth after his kind: and it was **s.**....... 3651
Ge 1:27 **S.** God created man in his own image, ...
Ge 1:30 green herb for meat: and it was **s.** 3651
Ge 3:24 **S.** he drove out the man; and he.............
Ge 6:22 God commanded him, **s.** did he. 3651
Ge 8:11 **s.** Noah knew that the waters were ....
Ge 11:8 **S.** the Lord scattered them abroad ....
Ge 12:4 **S.** Abram departed, as the Lord had ....
Ge 12:19 **s.** I might have taken her to me to ....
Ge 13:6 **s.** that they could not dwell together. ....
Ge 13:16 **s.** that if a man can number the........... 834
Ge 15:5 unto him, **S.** shall thy seed be. 3541
Ge 18:5 they said, **S.** do, as thou hast said...... 3651
Ge 19:7 pray you, brethren, do not **s.** wickedly. .....
Ge 19:11 **s.** that they wearied themselves to find......
Ge 19:18 said unto them, Oh, not **s.**, my Lord:........
Ge 20:17 **S.** Abraham prayed unto God: and............
Ge 21:6 **s.** that all that hear will laugh with me. ......
Ge 22:8 **s.** they went both of them together. ....
Ge 22:19 **s.** Abraham returned unto his young men, ..
Ge 24:46 **s.** I drank, and she made the camels drink ..
Ge 25:22 she said, If it be **s.**, why am I thus? ... 3651
Ge 27:1 old, and his eyes were dim, **s.** that he.......
Ge 27:20 is it that thou hast found it **s.** quickly, ...
Ge 27:23 Esau's hands: **s.** he blessed him. ....
Ge 28:21 **S.** that I come again to my father's...........
Ge 29:26 not be **s.** done in our country, ... 3651
Ge 29:28 And Jacob did **s.**, and fulfilled her 3651
Ge 30:33 **S.** shall my righteousness answer for ....
Ge 30:42 **s.** the feebler were Laban's, and the ....
Ge 31:21 **S.** he fled with all that he had; and he.......
Ge 31:28 hast now done foolishly in **s.** doing...........
Ge 31:36 thou hast **s.** hotly pursued after me? ....
Ge 32:19 **s.** commanded he the second, and 1571
Ge 32:21 **S.** went the present over before him:........
Ge 33:16 **S.** Esau returned that day on his way.......
Ge 34:12 Ask me never **s.** much dowry and gift, ...
Ge 35:6 **S.** Jacob came to Luz, which is in the ....
Ge 37:14 **S.** he sent him out of the vale of..............
Ge 40:7 Wherefore look ye **s.** sadly to day? ....
Ge 41:4 and fat kine. **S.** Pharaoh awoke. ....
Ge 41:13 as he interpreted to us, **s.** it was; 3651
Ge 41:21 as at the beginning. **S.** I awoke................
Ge 41:39 there is none **s.** discreet and wise as ....
Ge 41:57 the famine was **s.** sore in all lands. ....
Ge 42:20 **s.** shall your words be verified, ...
Ge 42:20 ye shall not die. And they did **s.**. 3651
Ge 42:34 **s.** will I deliver you your brother, and ....
Ge 43:6 Wherefore dealt ye **s.** ill with me, as to.....
Ge 43:11 If it must be **s.** now, do this; take...... 3651
Ge 43:34 mess was five times **s.** much as ....
Ge 44:5 ye have done evil in **s.** doing............... 834
Ge 44:17 God forbid that I should do **s.**............ 2063
Ge 45:8 **S.** now it was not you that sent me ....
Ge 45:21 And the children of Israel did **s.**......... 3651
Ge 45:24 **S.** he sent his brethren away, and ....
Ge 47:13 **s.** that the land of Egypt and all the..........
Ge 47:20 them: **s.** the land became Pharaoh's. ....
Ge 47:28 **s.** the whole age of Jacob was an...............
Ge 48:10 dim for age, **s.** that he could not see.........
Ge 48:18 Not **s.**, my father: for this is the........ 3651
Ge 49:17 **s.** that his rider shall fall backward.............
Ge 50:3 for **s.** are fulfilled the days of............ 3651
Ge 50:17 **S.** shall ye say unto Joseph, ... 3541
Ge 50:26 **S.** Joseph died, being an hundred and........
Ex 1:10 us, and **s.** get them up out of the land.......
Ex 2:18 that ye are come **s.** soon to day? ....
Ex 4:26 **S.** he let him go: then she said, A............
Ex 5:12 **S.** the people were scattered abroad ....
Ex 5:22 thou **s.** evil entreated this people? ....
Ex 6:9 Moses spake **s.** unto the children 3651
Ex 7:6 Lord commanded them, **s.** did they..... 3651
Ex 7:10 did **s.** as the Lord had commanded: 3651
Ex 7:20 And Moses and Aaron did **s.**, as the ... 3651
Ex 7:22 did **s.** with their enchantments: 3651
Ex 8:7 the magicians did **s.** with their 3651
Ex 8:17 And they did **s.**: for Aaron stretched... 3651
Ex 8:18 the magicians did **s.** with their ....
Ex 8:18 **s.** there were lice upon man, and 3651
Ex 8:24 the Lord did **s.**; and there came a 3651
Ex 8:26 Moses said, It is not meet **s.** to do;.... 3651
Ex 9:24 **S.** there was hail, and fire mingled............
Ex 10:10 Let the Lord be **s.** with you, as I....... 3651
Ex 10:11 Not **s.**: go now ye that are men,........ 3651
Ex 10:15 earth, **s.** that the land was darkened; ....
Ex 10:20 **s.** that he would not let the children..........
Ex 11:10 **s.** that he would not let the children..........
Ex 12:28 Moses and Aaron, **s.** did they........... 3651
Ex 12:36 **s.** that they lent unto them such...............
Ex 12:50 Moses and Aaron, **s.** did they............ 3651
Ex 14:4 I am the Lord. And they did **s.**.......... 3651
Ex 14:20 **s.** that the one came not near the.............
Ex 14:25 **s.** that the Egyptians said, Let us flee ....
Ex 14:28 remained not **s.** much as one of 5704
Ex 15:22 **S.** Moses brought Israel from the.............
Ex 16:17 And the children of Israel did **s.**, ... 3651
Ex 16:30 **S.** the people rested on the seventh ....
Ex 16:34 Moses, **s.** Aaron laid it up before the ....
Ex 17:6 And Moses did **s.** in the sight of 3651
Ex 17:10 **S.** Joshua did as Moses had said to...........
Ex 18:22 **s.** shall it be easier for thyself, and...........
Ex 18:23 God commanded thee **s.**, then thou...........
Ex 18:24 **S.** Moses hearkened to the voice of..........
Ex 19:16 **s.** that all the people that was in the ....
Ex 19:25 **S.** Moses went down unto the people,........
Ex 21:12 that smiteth a man, **s.** that he die,............
Ex 21:22 **s.** that her fruit depart from her, and ....
Ex 22:6 **s.** that the stacks of corn, or the...............
Ex 25:9 thereof, even **s.** shall ye make it......... 3651
Ex 25:33 **s.** in the six branches that come......... 3651
Ex 27:8 in the mount, **s.** shall they make it. 3651
Ex 28:7 and **s.** it shall be joined together...............
Ex 30:21 **S.** they shall wash their hands and............
Ex 30:23 of sweet cinnamon half **s.** much, even ....
Ex 32:21 hast brought **s.** great a sin upon...............
Ex 32:21 that thou hast brought **s.** great a sin ....
Ex 32:24 **S.** they gave it me: then I cast it into ....
Ex 33:16 **s.** shall we be separated, I and thy ....
Ex 36:6 **s.** the people were restrained from bringing.
Ex 36:13 taches: **s.** it became one tabernacle...........
Ex 37:19 **s.** throughout the six branches........... 3651
Ex 39:32 commanded Moses, **s.** did they,.......... 3651
Ex 39:42 **s.** the children of Israel made all 3651
Ex 39:43 even **s.** had they done it: and Moses... 3651
Ex 40:16 Lord commanded him, **s.** did he. 3651
Ex 40:33 gate. **S.** Moses finished the work. ....
Le 4:20 offering, **s.** shall he do with this: 3651
Le 7:7 offering is, **s.** is the trespass offering: ....
Le 8:34 **s.** the Lord hath commanded to do, to.......
Le 8:35 die not: for **s.** I am commanded: 3651
Le 8:36 **S.** Aaron and his sons did all things..........
Le 10:5 **S.** they went near, and carried them.........
Le 10:13 made by fire: for **s.** I commanded....... 3651
Le 11:32 until the even; **s.** it shall be cleansed.........
Le 14:13 the priest's, **s.** is the trespass offering:......
Le 14:21 if he be poor, and cannot get **s.** much; ......
Le 16:4 flesh in water, and **s.** put them on. ....
Le 16:16 **s.** shall he do for the tabernacle of...... 3651
Le 24:19 done, **s.** shall it be done to him;......... 3651
Le 24:20 **s.** shall it be done to him again. 3651
Le 26:15 **s.** that ye will not do all my.....................
Le 27:12 it, who art the priest, **s.** shall it be. 3651
Le 27:14 shall estimate it, **s.** shall it stand. 3651
Nu 1:19 commanded Moses, **s.** he numbered..........
Nu 1:45 **S.** were all those that were numbered.......
Nu 1:54 commanded Moses, **s.** did they. 3651
Nu 2:17 **s.** shall they set forward, every man... 3651
Nu 2:34 **s.** they pitched by their standards,...... 3651
Nu 2:34 **s.** they set forward, every one after ... 3651
Nu 4:26 made for them: **s.** shall they serve. ....
Nu 5:4 the children of Israel did **s.**, and.......... 3651
Nu 5:4 Moses, **s.** did the children of Israel..... 3651
Nu 6:21 **s.** he must do after the law of his........ 3651
Nu 8:3 And Aaron did **s.**;.............................. 3651
Nu 8:4 Moses, **s.** he made the candlestick. 3651
Nu 8:7 clothes, and **s.** make themselves clean........
Nu 8:20 **s.** did the children of Israel unto......... 3651
Nu 8:22 the Levites, **s.** did they unto them...... 3651
Nu 9:5 Moses, **s.** did the children of Israel..... 3651
Nu 9:14 the manner thereof, **s.** shall he do: 3651
Nu 9:16 **S.** it was alway: the cloud covered 3651
Nu 9:20 **s.** it was, when the cloud was a few ....
Nu 9:21 **s.** it was, when the cloud abode from........
Nu 12:7 My servant Moses is not **s.**, who is.... 3651
Nu 13:21 **S.** they went up, and searched the ....
Nu 13:33 and **s.** we were in their sight..................
Nu 14:28 in mine ears, **s.** will I do to you: 3651
Nu 15:12 prepare, **s.** shall ye do to every one ... 3602

Nu 15:14 the Lord; as ye do, **s.** he shall do. 3651
Nu 15:15 **s.** shall the stranger be before the
Nu 15:20 threshingfloor, **s.** shall ye heave it. 3651
Nu 16:27 **S.** they gat up from the tabernacle
Nu 17:11 And Moses did **s.**: as the Lord
Nu 17:11 Lord commanded him, **s.** did he. 3651
Nu 20:8 **s.** thou shalt give the congregation
Nu 21:35 **S.** they smote him, and his sons, and
Nu 22:30 was I ever wont to do **s.** great a sin
Nu 22:35 **S.** Balaam went with the princes of
Nu 25:8 **S.** the plague was stayed from the
Nu 31:5 **S.** there were delivered out of the
Nu 32:23 if ye will not do **s.**, behold, ye have 3651
Nu 32:28 **S.** concerning them Moses
Nu 32:31 unto thy servants, **s.** will we do. 3651
Nu 35:7 **S.** all the cities which ye shall give
Nu 35:16 an instrument of iron, **s.** that he die,
Nu 35:29 **S.** these things shall be for a statute of
Nu 35:33 **S.** ye shall not pollute the land
Nu 36:3 **s.** shall it be taken from the lot of our
Nu 36:4 **s.** shall their inheritance be taken
Nu 36:7 **S.** shall not the inheritance of the
Nu 36:10 Moses, **s.** did the daughters of 3651
De 1:11 you a thousand times **s.** many more
De 1:15 **S.** I took the chief of your tribes, wise
De 1:43 **S.** I spake unto you; and ye would
De 1:46 **S.** ye abode in Kadesh many days,
De 2:5 no, not **s.** much as a foot breadth;
De 2:16 **S.** it came to pass, when all the men
De 3:3 **S.** the Lord our God delivered into
De 3:21 **s.** shall the Lord do unto all the 3651
De 3:29 **S.** we abode in the valley over against
De 4:5 that we should do **s.** in the land 3651
De 4:7 For what nation is there **s.** great,
De 4:7 who hath God **s.** nigh unto them, as
De 4:8 And what nation is there **s.** great, that
De 4:8 and judgments **s.** righteous as all this
De 7:4 **s.** will the anger of the Lord be
De 7:19 **s.** shall the Lord thy God do unto 3651
De 8:5 **s.** the Lord thy God chasteneth thee.
De 8:20 before your face, **s.** shall ye perish; 3651
De 9:3 **s.** shalt thou drive them out, and
De 9:8 **s.** that the Lord was angry with you
De 9:15 **S.** I turned and came down from the
De 12:4 shall not do **s.** unto the Lord your 3651
De 12:10 round about, **s.** that ye dwell in safety;
De 12:22 is eaten, **s.** thou shalt eat them: 3651
De 12:30 gods? even **s.** will I do likewise 3651
De 12:31 shalt not do **s.** unto the Lord thy 3651
De 13:5 **S.** shalt thou put the evil away from
De 14:24 **s.** that thou art not able to carry
De 17:7 **S.** thou shalt put the evil away from
De 18:14 hath not suffered thee **s.** to do. 3651
De 19:10 inheritance, and **s.** blood be upon thee
De 19:19 **s.** shalt thou put the evil away from
De 20:18 **s.** should ye sin against the Lord your
De 21:9 **S.** shalt thou put away the guilt of
De 21:21 **s.** shalt thou put evil away from
De 22:3 **s.** shalt thou do with his raiment; 3651
De 22:5 all that do **s.** are abomination unto 428
De 22:21 **s.** shalt thou put evil away from
De 22:22 **s.** shalt thou put away evil from Israel.
De 22:24 **s.** thou shalt put away evil from
De 22:26 slayeth him, even **s.** is this matter: 3651
De 24:8 them, **s.** ye shall observe to do
De 25:9 **S.** shall it be done unto that man 3602
De 28:34 **S.** that thou shalt be mad for the
De 28:54 **S.** that the man that is tender among
De 28:55 **S.** that he will not give to any of them
De 28:63 **s.** the Lord will rejoice over you 3651
De 29:22 **S.** that the generation to come of
De 30:17 turn away, **s.** that thou wilt not hear,
De 31:17 **s.** that they will say in that day, Are
De 32:12 **S.** the Lord alone did lead him, and
De 33:25 as thy days, **s.** shall thy strength be.
De 34:5 **S.** Moses the servant of the Lord died
De 34:8 **s.** the days of weeping and mourning
Jos 1:5 was with Moses, **s.** I will be with thee:
Jos 1:17 **s.** will we hearken unto thee: 3651
Jos 2:21 According unto your words, **s.** be it. 3651
Jos 2:23 **S.** the two men returned, and
Jos 3:7 was with Moses, **s.** I will be with thee.
Jos 4:8 did **s.** as Joshua commanded, 3651
Jos 5:15 standest is holy. And Joshua did **s.** 3651
Jos 6:11 **S.** the ark of the Lord compassed the
Jos 6:14 the camp: **s.** they did six days. 3541
Jos 6:20 **S.** the people shouted when the
Jos 6:20 **s.** that the people went up into the
Jos 6:27 **S.** the Lord was with Joshua; and his
Jos 7:4 **S.** there went up thither of the people
Jos 7:16 **S.** Joshua rose up early in the morning,
Jos 7:22 **S.** Joshua sent messengers, and they
Jos 7:26 **S.** the Lord turned from...fierceness
Jos 8:3 **S.** Joshua arose, and all the people of
Jos 8:22 **s.** they were in the midst of Israel,
Jos 8:22 **s.** that they let none of them 5704
Jos 8:25 **s.** it was, that all that fell that day,
Jos 9:26 **s.** did he unto them, and delivered 3651
Jos 10:1 **s.** he had done to Ai and her king; 3651
Jos 10:7 **S.** Joshua ascended from Gilgal, he,
Jos 10:13 **S.** the sun stood still in the midst of
Jos 10:23 And they did **s.**, and brought forth 3651
Jos 10:39 **s.** he did to Debir, and to the king 3651
Jos 10:40 **S.** Joshua smote all the country of the
Jos 11:7 **S.** Joshua came, and all the people of
Jos 11:15 **s.** did Moses command Joshua, 3651
Jos 11:15 command Joshua,...**s.** did Joshua; 3651
Jos 11:16 **S.** Joshua took all that land, the hills,
Jos 11:23 **S.** Joshua took the whole land,
Jos 14:5 **s.** the children of Israel did, and 3651
Jos 14:11 even **s.** is my strength now, for war,
Jos 14:12 if **s.** be the Lord will be with me,
Jos 15:7 **s.** northward, looking toward Gilgal,
Jos 16:4 **S.** the children of Joseph, Manasseh
Jos 19:51 **S.** they made an end of dividing the
Jos 21:40 **S.** all the cities for the children of
Jos 22:6 **S.** Joshua blessed them, and sent
Jos 22:25 **s.** shall your children make our
Jos 22:28 they should **s.** say to us or to our
Jos 23:15 **s.** shall the Lord bring upon you 3651
Jos 24:10 still: **s.** I delivered you out of his hand.
Jos 24:25 **S.** Joshua made a covenant with the
Jos 24:28 **S.** Joshua let the people depart, every
Jg 1:3 thy lot. **S.** Simeon went with him.
Jg 1:7 done, **s.** God hath requited me. 3651
Jg 1:35 prevailed, **s.**...they became tributaries.
Jg 2:14 **s.** that they could not any longer
Jg 2:17 of the Lord; but they did not **s.** 3651
Jg 3:14 **S.** the children of Israel served Eglon
Jg 3:22 **s.**...he could not draw the dagger 3588
Jg 3:30 **S.** Moab subdued that day under the
Jg 4:14 **S.** Barak went down from mount
Jg 4:15 **s.** that Sisera lighted down off his
Jg 4:21 fast asleep and weary. **S.** he died.
Jg 4:23 **S.** God subdued on that day Jabin the
Jg 5:28 Why is his chariot **s.** long in coming?
Jg 5:31 **S.** let all thine enemies perish, O 3651
Jg 6:3 And **s.** it was, when Israel had sown,
Jg 6:20 pour out the broth. And he did **s.** 3651
Jg 6:27 **s.** it was, because he feared his father's
Jg 6:38 it was **s.**: for he rose up early on 3651
Jg 6:40 God did **s.** that night: for it was 3651
Jg 7:1 **s.**...the host of the Midianites were
Jg 7:5 **S.** he brought down the people unto
Jg 7:8 **S.** the people took victuals in their
Jg 7:15 it was **s.**, when Gideon heard the
Jg 7:17 be that, as I do, **s.** shall ye do 3651
Jg 7:19 **S.** Gideon, and the hundred men that
Jg 8:18 As thou art, **s.** were they; each 1992
Jg 8:21 for as the man is, **s.** is his strength.
Jg 8:28 **s.** that they lifted up their heads no
Jg 9:49 **s.** that all the men of the tower of
Jg 10:9 **s.** that Israel was sore distressed.
Jg 11:5 And it was **s.**, that when the children
Jg 11:10 if we do not **s.** according to thy 3651
Jg 11:21 **s.** Israel possessed all the land of the
Jg 11:23 **S.** now the Lord God of Israel hath
Jg 11:24 **S.** whomsoever the Lord our God
Jg 11:32 **S.** Jephthah passed over unto the
Jg 12:5 and it was **s.**, that when those
Jg 13:19 **S.** Manoah took a kid with a meat
Jg 14:10 **S.** his father went down unto the
Jg 14:10 for **s.** used the young men to do. 3651
Jg 14:15 us to take that we have? is it not **s.**?
Jg 15:11 me, **s.** have I done unto them. 3651
Jg 16:9 fire. **S.** his strength was not known.
Jg 16:16 **s.** that his soul was vexed unto death;
Jg 16:30 **S.** the dead which he slew at his
Jg 17:10 thy victuals. **S.** the Levite went in.
Jg 18:21 **S.** they turned and departed, and put
Jg 19:4 **s.** they did eat and drink, and lodged
Jg 19:21 **S.** he brought him into his house, and
Jg 19:23 nay, I pray you, do not **s.** wickedly;
Jg 19:24 this man do not **s.** vile a thing. 2063
Jg 19:25 **s.** the man took his concubine, and
Jg 19:30 And it was **s.**, that all that saw it said,
Jg 20:11 **S.** all the men of Israel were gathered
Jg 20:36 **S.** the children of Benjamin saw that
Jg 20:46 **S.** that all which fell that day of
Jg 21:14 and yet **s.** they sufficed them not. 3651
Jg 21:23 And the children of Benjamin did **s.**, 3651
Ru 1:17 Lord do **s.** to me, and more also, if 3541
Ru 1:19 **S.** they two went out until they
Ru 1:22 **S.** Naomi returned, and Ruth the
Ru 2:7 **s.** she came, and hath continued even
Ru 2:17 **S.** she gleaned in the field until even,
Ru 2:23 **S.** she kept fast by the maidens of
Ru 4:8 it for thee. **S.** he drew off his shoe
Ru 4:13 **S.** Boaz took Ruth, and she was his
1Sa 1:7 as he did **s.** year by year, when she 3651
1Sa 1:7 **s.** she provoked her; therefore she 3651
1Sa 1:9 **S.** Hannah rose up after they had
1Sa 1:18 **S.** the woman went her way, and did
1Sa 1:23 **S.** the woman abode, and gave her son
1Sa 2:3 Talk no more **s.** exceeding proudly;
1Sa 2:5 **s.** that the barren hath born seven; 5704
1Sa 2:14 **S.** they did in Shiloh unto all the 3602
1Sa 2:21 visited Hannah, **s.** that she conceived,
1Sa 3:9 **S.** Samuel went and lay down in his
1Sa 3:17 God do **s.** to thee, and more also, if 3541
1Sa 4:4 **S.** the people sent to Shiloh, that they
1Sa 4:5 shout, **s.** that the earth rang again.
1Sa 5:7 men of Ashdod saw that it was **s.**, 3651
1Sa 5:9 it was **s.**, that, after they had carried
1Sa 5:11 **S.** they sent and gathered together
1Sa 6:10 And the men did **s.**; and took two 3651
1Sa 7:13 **S.** the Philistines were subdued, and
1Sa 8:8 gods, **s.** do they also unto thee. 3651
1Sa 9:10 **S.** they went unto the city where the
1Sa 9:21 then speakest thou **s.** to me? 1697
1Sa 9:24 **S.** Saul did eat with Samuel that day.
1Sa 10:9 it was **s.**, that, when he had turned his
1Sa 11:7 **s.** shall it be done unto his oxen 3541
1Sa 11:11 it was **s.** on the morrow, that Saul
1Sa 11:11 **s.** that two of them were not left
1Sa 12:18 **S.** Samuel called unto the Lord; and
1Sa 13:22 **S.** it came to pass in the day of
1Sa 14:15 **s.** it was a very great trembling.
1Sa 14:23 **S.** the Lord saved Israel that day: and
1Sa 14:24 **S.** none of the people tasted any food.
1Sa 14:44 God do **s.** and more also: for thou 3541
1Sa 14:45 **S.** the people rescued Jonathan, that
1Sa 14:47 **S.** Saul took the kingdom over Israel,
1Sa 15:6 **S.** the Kenites departed from among
1Sa 15:31 **S.** Samuel turned again after Saul;
1Sa 15:33 **s.** shall thy mother be childless 3651
1Sa 16:13 **S.** Samuel rose up, and went to
1Sa 16:23 **s.** Saul was refreshed, and was well,
1Sa 17:27 **S.** shall it be done to the man that 3541
1Sa 17:50 **S.** David prevailed over the Philistine
1Sa 18:30 **s.** that his name was much set by
1Sa 19:12 **S.** Michal let David down through a
1Sa 19:17 Why hast thou deceived me **s.**, and 3602
1Sa 19:18 **S.** David fled, and escaped, and came
1Sa 20:2 this thing from me? it is not **s.**
1Sa 20:13 The Lord do **s.** and much more to 3541
1Sa 20:16 **S.** Jonathan made a covenant with the
1Sa 20:24 **S.** David hid himself in the field: and
1Sa 20:34 **S.** Jonathan arose from the table in
1Sa 21:6 **S.** the priest gave him hallowed bread:
1Sa 22:14 And who is **s.** faithful among all thy
1Sa 23:5 **S.** David and his men went to Keilah,
1Sa 23:5 **S.** David saved the inhabitants of
1Sa 24:7 **S.** David stayed his servants with
1Sa 25:12 **S.** David's young men turned their
1Sa 25:20 it was **s.**, as she rode on the ass, that
1Sa 25:21 **s.** that nothing was missed of all that
1Sa 25:22 **S.** and more also do God unto the 3541
1Sa 25:25 for as his name is, **s.** is he; Nabal 3651
1Sa 25:35 **S.** David received of her hand that
1Sa 26:7 **S.** David and Abishai came to the
1Sa 26:12 **S.** David took the spear and the cruse
1Sa 26:24 **s.** let my life be much set by in the 3651
1Sa 26:25 **S.** David went on his way, and Saul
1Sa 27:1 **s.** shall I escape out of his hand.
1Sa 27:11 **S.** did David, and **s.** will be his 3541
1Sa 28:23 **S.** he arose from the earth, and sat
1Sa 29:8 thy servant **s.** long as I have been with
1Sa 29:11 **S.** David and his men rose up early to
1Sa 30:3 **S.** David and his men came to the

1Sa 30:9 **S.** David went, he and the six hundred
1Sa 30:10 were **s.** faint that they could not go
1Sa 30:21 were **s.** faint that they could not follow
1Sa 30:23 Ye shall not do **s.**, my brethren, 3651
1Sa 30:24 **s.** shall his part be that tarrieth by the
1Sa 30:25 And it was **s.** from that day forward,
1Sa 31:6 **S.** Saul died, and his three sons, and
2Sa 1:2 and **s.** it was, when he came to David,
2Sa 1:10 **S.** I stood upon him, and slew him,
2Sa 2:2 **S.** David went up thither, and his two
2Sa 2:16 side; **s.** they fell down together:
2Sa 2:28 **S.** Joab blew a trumpet, and all the
2Sa 2:31 **s.** that three hundred and threescore
2Sa 3:9 **S.** do God to Abner, and more also, ... 3541
2Sa 3:9 to David, even **s.** I do to him; 3651
2Sa 3:20 **S.** Abner came to David to Hebron,
2Sa 3:30 **S.** Joab and Abishai his brother slew
2Sa 3:34 before wicked men, **s.** fellest thou.
2Sa 3:35 **S.** do God to me, and more also, if 3541
2Sa 5:3 **S.** all the elders of Israel came to the
2Sa 5:9 **S.** David dwelt in the fort, and called
2Sa 5:25 And David did **s.**, as the Lord had 3651
2Sa 6:10 **S.** David would not remove the ark of
2Sa 6:12 **S.** David went and brought up the ark
2Sa 6:13 it was **s.**, that when they that bare the
2Sa 6:15 **S.** David and all the house of Israel
2Sa 6:19 **S.** all the people departed every one to
2Sa 7:8 **s.** shalt thou say unto my servant
2Sa 7:17 **s.** did Nathan speak unto David 3651
2Sa 8:2 And **s.** the Moabites became David's
2Sa 9:11 his servant, **s.** shall thy servant do. 3651
2Sa 9:13 **S.** Mephibosheth dwelt in Jerusalem:
2Sa 10:14 **S.** Joab returned from the children of
2Sa 10:19 **S.** the Syrians feared to help the
2Sa 11:12 **S.** Uriah abode in Jerusalem that day,
2Sa 11:20 if **s.** be that the king's wrath arise,
2Sa 11:20 approached ye **s.** nigh unto the city
2Sa 11:22 **S.** the messenger went, and came and
2Sa 12:31 **S.** David and all the people returned
2Sa 13:2 And Amnon was **s.** vexed, that he fell
2Sa 13:6 **S.** Amnon lay down, and made
2Sa 13:8 **S.** Tamar went to her brother
2Sa 13:15 **s.** that the hatred wherewith he hated
2Sa 13:20 **S.** Tamar remained desolate in her
2Sa 13:35 come: as thy servant said, **s.** it is 3651
2Sa 13:38 **S.** Absalom fled, and went to Geshur,
2Sa 14:3 **S.** Joab put the words in her mouth.
2Sa 14:7 **s.** they shall quench my coal which is
2Sa 14:17 **s.** is my lord the king to discern 3651
2Sa 14:23 **S.** Joab arose and went to Geshur,
2Sa 14:24 **S.** Absalom returned to his own house,
2Sa 14:25 be **s.** much praised as Absalom for
2Sa 14:28 **S.** Absalom dwelt two full years in
2Sa 14:33 **S.** Joab came to the king, and told
2Sa 15:2 it was **s.**, that when any man that had
2Sa 15:5 it was **s.**, that when any man came
2Sa 15:6 **s.** Absalom stole the hearts of the men
2Sa 15:9 **S.** he arose, and went to Hebron.
2Sa 15:34 **s.** will I now also be thy servant:
2Sa 15:37 **S.** Hushai David's friend came into
2Sa 16:10 **s.** let him curse, because the 3588
2Sa 16:10 say, Wherefore hast thou done **s.**? 3651
2Sa 16:19 presence, **s.** will I be in thy presence 3651
2Sa 16:22 **S.** they spread Absalom a tent upon
2Sa 16:23 **s.** was...the counsel of Ahithophel 3651
2Sa 17:3 **s.** all the people shall be in peace.
2Sa 17:12 **S.** shall we come upon him in some
2Sa 17:12 shall not be left **s.** much as one. 1571
2Sa 17:26 **S.** Israel and Absalom pitched in the
2Sa 18:6 **S.** the people went out into the field
2Sa 19:13 God do **s.** to me, and more also, if 3541
2Sa 19:14 **s.** that they sent this word unto the
2Sa 19:15 **S.** the king returned, and came to
2Sa 20:2 **S.** every man of Israel went up from
2Sa 20:3 **S.** they were shut up unto the day of
2Sa 20:5 **S.** Amasa went to assemble the men
2Sa 20:10 **s.** he smote him therewith in the fifth
2Sa 20:10 **S.** Joab and Abishai his brother
2Sa 20:18 and **s.** they ended the matter. 3651
2Sa 20:21 The matter is not **s.**: but a man of 3651
2Sa 22:4 **s.** shall I be saved from mine enemies.
2Sa 22:35 **s.** that a bow of steel is broken by
2Sa 22:37 under me; **s.** that my feet did not slip.
2Sa 23:5 my house be not **s.** with God; yet 3651
2Sa 24:8 **S.** when they had gone through all
2Sa 24:13 **S.** Gad came to David, and told him,
2Sa 24:15 **S.** the Lord sent a pestilence upon
2Sa 24:24 **S.** David bought the threshingfloor
2Sa 24:25 **S.** the Lord was intreated for the
1Ki 1:3 **S.** they sought for a fair damsel
1Ki 1:6 in saying, Why hast thou done **s.**? 3602
1Ki 1:30 even **s.** will I certainly do this day. 3651
1Ki 1:36 God of my lord the king say **s.** too. 3651
1Ki 1:37 king, even **s.** be he with Solomon, 3651
1Ki 1:38 **S.** Zadok the priest, and Nathan the
1Ki 1:40 **s.** that the earth rent with the sound
1Ki 1:45 rejoicing, **s.** that the city rang again.
1Ki 1:53 **S.** king Solomon sent, and they
1Ki 2:7 for **s.** they came to me when I fled 3651
1Ki 2:10 **S.** David slept with his fathers, and
1Ki 2:23 God do **s.** to me, and more also, if 3541
1Ki 2:27 **S.** Solomon thrust out Abiathar from
1Ki 2:34 **S.** Benaiah the son of Jehoiada went
1Ki 2:38 hath said, **s.** will thy servant do. 3651
1Ki 2:46 **S.** the king commanded Benaiah the
1Ki 3:9 judge this thy **s.** great a people?
1Ki 3:12 **s.** that there was none like thee before
1Ki 3:13 **s.** that there shall not be any among
1Ki 4:1 **S.** king Solomon was king over all
1Ki 5:4 **s.** that there is neither adversary nor
1Ki 5:10 **S.** Hiram gave Solomon cedar trees
1Ki 5:18 **s.** they prepared timber and stones to
1Ki 6:7 **s.** that there was neither hammer nor
1Ki 6:9 **S.** he built the house, and finished it;
1Ki 6:14 **S.** Solomon built the house, and
1Ki 6:20 and **s.** covered the altar which was of
1Ki 6:21 **S.** Solomon overlaid the house within
1Ki 6:26 and **s.** was it of the other cherub. 3651
1Ki 6:27 **s.** that the wing of the one touched the
1Ki 6:33 **S.** also made he for the door of the 3651
1Ki 6:38 **S.** was he seven years in building it.
1Ki 7:9 **s.** on the outside toward the great
1Ki 7:18 and **s.** did he for the other chapiter. 3651
1Ki 7:22 **s.** was the work of the pillars finished.
1Ki 7:40 **S.** Hiram made an end of doing all
1Ki 7:51 **S.** was ended all the work that king
1Ki 8:11 **S.** that the priests could not stand to
1Ki 8:25 **s.** that thy children take heed 7535
1Ki 8:46 **s.** that they carry them away captives
1Ki 8:48 And **s.** return unto thee with all their
1Ki 8:54 And it was **s.**, that when Solomon had
1Ki 8:63 **S.** the king and all the children of
1Ki 9:25 the Lord. **S.** he finished the house.
1Ki 10:13 **S.** she turned and went to her own
1Ki 10:23 **S.** king Solomon exceeded all the
1Ki 10:29 and **s.** for all the kings of the Hittites,
1Ki 11:19 **s.** that he gave him to wife the sister
1Ki 12:12 **S.** Jeroboam and all the people came
1Ki 12:16 **S.** when all Israel saw that the king
1Ki 12:16 **S.** Israel departed unto their tents.
1Ki 12:19 **S.** Israel rebelled against the house
1Ki 12:32 **S.** did he in Beth-el, sacrificing 3651
1Ki 12:33 **S.** he offered upon the altar which he
1Ki 13:4 **s.** that he could not pull it in again to
1Ki 13:9 **s.** was it charged me by the word 3651
1Ki 13:10 **S.** he went another way, and returned
1Ki 13:13 **S.** they saddled him the ass: and he
1Ki 13:19 **S.** he went back with him, and did
1Ki 14:4 Jeroboam's wife did **s.**, and arose, 3651
1Ki 14:6 And it was **s.**, when Ahijah heard the
1Ki 14:28 And it was **s.**, when the king went into
1Ki 15:20 **S.** Ben-hadad hearkened unto...Asa,
1Ki 16:6 **S.** Baasha slept with his fathers, and
1Ki 16:22 **s.** Tibni died, and Omri reigned.
1Ki 16:28 **S.** Omri slept with his fathers, and
1Ki 17:5 **S.** he went and did according unto the
1Ki 17:10 **S.** he arose and went to Zarephath.
1Ki 17:17 and his sickness was **s.** sore, that 3966
1Ki 18:4 For it was **s.**, when Jezebel cut off the
1Ki 18:6 **S.** they divided the land between them
1Ki 18:12 **s.** when I come and tell Ahab, and he
1Ki 18:16, **S.** Obadiah went to meet Ahab, and
1Ki 18:20 **S.** Ahab sent unto all the children of
1Ki 18:42 **S.** Ahab went up to eat and drink.
1Ki 19:2 **S.** let the gods do to me, and more 3541
1Ki 19:13 And it was **s.**, when Elijah heard it,
1Ki 19:19 **S.** he departed thence, and found
1Ki 20:10 The gods do **s.** unto me, and more 3541
1Ki 20:19 **S.** these young men of the princes of
1Ki 20:25 unto their voice, and did **s.**, 3651
1Ki 20:29 And **s.** it was, that in the seventh day
1Ki 20:32 **S.** they girded sackcloth on their
1Ki 20:34 **S.** he made a covenant with him, and
1Ki 20:37 **s.** that in smiting he wounded him.
1Ki 20:38 **S.** the prophet departed, and waited
1Ki 20:40 him, **S.** shall thy judgment be; 3651
1Ki 21:5 Why is thy spirit **s.** sad, that thou 2088
1Ki 21:8 **S.** she wrote letters in Ahab's name,
1Ki 22:8 said, Let not the king say **s.** 3651
1Ki 22:12 prophesied **s.**, saying, Go up to 3651
1Ki 22:15 **S.** he came to the king. And the king
1Ki 22:22 prevail also: go forth, and do **s.** 3651
1Ki 22:29 **S.** the king of Israel and Jehoshaphat
1Ki 22:37 **S.** the king died, and was brought to
1Ki 22:40 **S.** Ahab slept with his fathers; and
2Ki 1:17 **S.** he died according to the word of
2Ki 2:2 thee. **S.** they went down to Beth-el.
2Ki 2:4 leave thee. **S.** they came to Jericho.
2Ki 2:8 **s.** that they two went over on dry
2Ki 2:10 from thee, it shall be **s.** unto thee; 3651
2Ki 2:10 but if not, it shall not be **s.**
2Ki 2:22 **S.** the waters were healed unto this
2Ki 3:9 **S.** the king of Israel went, and the
2Ki 3:12 **S.** the king of Israel and Jehoshaphat
2Ki 3:24 **s.** that they fled before them: but
2Ki 4:5 **S.** she went from him, and shut the
2Ki 4:8 **s.** it was, that as oft as he passed by,
2Ki 4:25 **S.** she went and came unto the man of
2Ki 4:36 **S.** he called her. And when she was
2Ki 4:40 **S.** they poured out for the men to eat.
2Ki 4:44 **S.** he set it before them, and they did
2Ki 5:8 And it was **s.**, when Elisha the man of
2Ki 5:9 **S.** Naaman came with his horses and
2Ki 5:12 **S.** he turned and went away in a rage.
2Ki 5:19 **S.** he departed from him a little way.
2Ki 5:21 **S.** Gehazi followed after Naaman.
2Ki 6:4 **S.** he went with them. And when
2Ki 6:23 **S.** the bands of Syria came no more
2Ki 6:29 **S.** we boiled my son, and did eat him:
2Ki 6:31 God do **s.** and more also to me, if 3541
2Ki 7:10 **S.** they came and called unto the
2Ki 7:16 **S.** a measure of fine flour was sold for
2Ki 7:20 And **s.** it fell out unto him: for the 3651
2Ki 8:6 **S.** the king appointed unto her a
2Ki 8:9 **S.** Hazael went to meet him, and took
2Ki 8:14 **S.** he departed from Elisha, and came
2Ki 8:15 spread it on his face, **s.** that he died:
2Ki 8:21 **S.** Joram went over to Zair, and all the
2Ki 9:4 **S.** the young man, even the young
2Ki 9:14 **S.** Jehu the son of Jehoshaphat the
2Ki 9:16 **S.** Jehu rode in a chariot, and went to
2Ki 9:18 **S.** there went one on horseback to
2Ki 9:22 **s.** long as the whoredoms of thy
2Ki 9:22 and her witchcrafts are **s.** many?
2Ki 9:27 And they did **s.** at the going up to Gur,
2Ki 9:33 **S.** they threw her down: and some of
2Ki 9:37 **s.** that they shall not say, This is
2Ki 10:11 **S.** Jehu slew all that remained of the
2Ki 10:16 **S.** they made him ride in his chariot
2Ki 10:21 **s.** that there was not a man left that
2Ki 11:2 Athaliah, **s.** that he was not slain.
2Ki 11:6 **s.** shall ye keep the watch of the
2Ki 12:6 But it was **s.**, that in the three and
2Ki 12:10 And it was **s.**, when they saw that
2Ki 13:5 a saviour, **s.** that they went out from
2Ki 13:24 **S.** Hazael king of Syria died: and
2Ki 15:5 **s.** that he was a leper unto the day of
2Ki 15:7 **S.** Azariah slept with his fathers;
2Ki 15:12 And **s.** it came to pass. 3651
2Ki 15:20 **S.** the king of Assyria turned back,
2Ki 16:7 **S.** Ahaz sent messengers to
2Ki 16:11 **s.** Urijah the priest made it 3651
2Ki 17:7 For **s.** it was, that the children of
2Ki 17:23 **S.** was Israel carried away out of
2Ki 17:25 And **s.** it was at the beginning of their
2Ki 17:32 **S.** they feared the Lord, and made
2Ki 17:41 **S.** these nations feared the Lord, and
2Ki 17:41 their fathers, **s.** do they unto this day.
2Ki 18:5 **s.** that after him was none like him
2Ki 18:21 **s.** is Pharaoh king of Egypt unto 3651
2Ki 19:5 **S.** the servants of king Hezekiah
2Ki 19:8 **S.** Rab-shakeh returned, and found
2Ki 19:36 **S.** Sennacherib king of Assyria
2Ki 22:14 **S.** Hilkiah the priest, and Ahikam,
2Ki 23:18 **S.** they let his bones alone, with the
2Ki 24:6 **S.** Jehoiakim slept with his fathers:
2Ki 25:6 **S.** they took the king, and brought
2Ki 25:21 **S.** Judah was carried away out of
1Ch 9:1 **S.** all Israel were reckoned by

1Ch 9:23 **S.** they and their children had the
1Ch 10:4 **S.** Saul took a sword, and fell upon it.
1Ch 10:6 **S.** Saul died, and his three sons, and
1Ch 10:13 **S.** Saul died for his transgression.
1Ch 11:6 **S.** Joab the son of Zeruiah went first
1Ch 11:9 **S.** David waxed greater and greater:
1Ch 13:4 said that they would do **s.**: for 3651
1Ch 13:5 **S.** David gathered all Israel together,
1Ch 13:13 **S.** David brought not the ark home to
1Ch 14:11 **S.** they came up to Baal-perazim: and
1Ch 15:14 **S.** the priests and...Levites sanctified
1Ch 15:17 **S.** the Levites appointed Heman the
1Ch 15:19 **S.** the singers, Heman, Asaph, and
1Ch 15:25 **S.** David, and the elders of Israel, and
1Ch 16:1 **S.** they brought the ark of God, and
1Ch 17:15 all this vision, **s.** did Nathan speak 3651
1Ch 16:37 **S.** he left there before the ark of the
1Ch 18:14 **S.** David reigned over all Israel, and
1Ch 19:2 **S.** the servants of David came into the
1Ch 19:7 **S.** they hired thirty and two thousand
1Ch 19:14 **S.** Joab and the people that were with
1Ch 19:17 **S.** when David had put the battle in
1Ch 20:3 **s.** dealt David with all the cities 3651
1Ch 21:3 an hundred times **s.** many more 1992
1Ch 21:11 **S.** Gad came to David, and said unto
1Ch 21:14 **S.** the Lord sent pestilence upon
1Ch 21:25 **S.** David gave to Ornan for the place
1Ch 22:5 **S.** David prepared abundantly before
1Ch 23:1 **S.** when David was old and full of
1Ch 25:7 **S.** the number of them, with their
1Ch 29:14 able to offer **s.** willingly after this sort?
2Ch 1:3 **S.** Solomon, and all the congregation
2Ch 1:10 judge this thy people, that is **s.** great?
2Ch 1:17 **s.** brought they out horses for all the
2Ch 2:3 dwell therein, even **s.** deal with me.
2Ch 5:14 **S.** that the priests could not stand to
2Ch 6:16 yet **s.** that thy children take heed to
2Ch 6:31 **s.** long as they live in the land 3605
2Ch 7:5 **s.** the king and all the people dedicated
2Ch 7:21 **s.** that he shall say, Why hath the
2Ch 8:14 for **s.** had David the man of God 3651
2Ch 8:16 **S.** the house of the Lord was
2Ch 9:12 **S.** she turned, and went away to her
2Ch 10:3 **S.** Jeroboam and all Israel came and
2Ch 10:12 **S.** Jeroboam and all the people came
2Ch 10:15 **S.** the king hearkened not unto the
2Ch 10:16 **S.** all Israel went to their tents.
2Ch 11:17 **S.** they strengthened the kingdom of
2Ch 12:9 **S.** Shishak king of Egypt came up
2Ch 12:13 **S.** king Rehoboam strengthened
2Ch 13:9 **s.**...whosoever cometh to consecrate
2Ch 13:13 **s.** they were before Judah, and the
2Ch 13:17 **s.** there fell down slain of Israel five
2Ch 14:1 **S.** Abijah slept with his fathers, and
2Ch 14:7 side. **S.** they built and prospered.
2Ch 14:12 **S.** the Lord smote the Ethiopians
2Ch 15:10 **S.** they gathered themselves together
2Ch 17:10 **s.** that they made no war against
2Ch 18:7 said, Let not the king say **s.** 3651
2Ch 18:11 And all the prophets prophesied **s.**, 3651
2Ch 18:21 also prevail: go out, and do even **s.**. 3651
2Ch 18:28 **S.** the king of Israel and Jehoshaphat
2Ch 18:29 **S.** the king of Israel disguised
2Ch 19:10 **s.** wrath come upon you, and upon
2Ch 20:6 **s.** that none is able to withstand thee?
2Ch 20:20 your God, **s.** shall ye be established;
2Ch 20:20 his prophets, **s.** shall ye prosper.
2Ch 20:25 gathering of the spoil, it was **s.** much.
2Ch 20:30 **S.** the realm of Jehoshaphat was
2Ch 21:10 **S.** the Edomites revolted from under
2Ch 21:17 **s.** that there was never a son left him,
2Ch 21:19 sickness: **s.** he died of sore diseases.
2Ch 22:1 **S.** Ahaziah the son fo Jehoram king
2Ch 22:9 **S.** the house of Ahaziah had no power
2Ch 22:11 **S.** Jehoshabeath, the daughter of the
2Ch 22:11 Athaliah, **s.** that she slew him not.
2Ch 23:8 **S.** the Levites and all Judah did
2Ch 23:15 **S.** they laid hands on her; and when
2Ch 24:13 **S.** the workmen wrought, and the
2Ch 24:24 **S.** they executed judgment against
2Ch 25:21 **S.** Joash the king of Israel went up;
2Ch 26:23 **S.** Uzziah slept with his fathers, and
2Ch 27:5 **S.** much did the children of 2063
2Ch 27:6 **S.** Jotham became mighty, because
2Ch 28:14 **S.** the armed men left the captives
2Ch 29:17 **s.** they sanctified the house of the
2Ch 29:22 **S.** they killed the bullocks, and the
2Ch 29:25 **s.** was the commandment of the Lord.
2Ch 29:34 **s.** that they could not flay all the
2Ch 29:35 **S.** the service of the house of the
2Ch 30:5 **S.** they established a decree to make
2Ch 30:6 **S.** the posts went with the letters
2Ch 30:9 **s.** that they should come again into
2Ch 30:10 **S.** the posts passed from city to city
2Ch 30:16 **S.** there was great joy in Jerusalem:
2Ch 32:4 **S.** there was gathered much people
2Ch 32:17 **s.** shall not the God of Hezekiah 3651
2Ch 32:21 **S.** he returned with shame of face to
2Ch 32:23 **s.** that he was magnified in the sight
2Ch 32:26 **s.** that the wrath of the Lord came not
2Ch 33:8 **s.** that they will take heed to do all
2Ch 33:9 **S.** Manasseh made Judah and the
2Ch 33:20 **S.** Manasseh slept with his fathers,
2Ch 34:6 **s.** did he in the cities of Mansseh,
2Ch 34:26 **s.** shall ye say unto him, Thus saith
2Ch 34:28 **S.** they brought the king word again.
2Ch 35:6 **S.** kill the passover, and sanctify
2Ch 35:10 **S.** the service was prepared, and the
2Ch 35:12 And **s.** did they with the oxen. 3651
2Ch 35:16 **S.** all the service of the Lord was
Ezr 2:70 **S.** the priests, and the Levites, and
Ezr 3:13 **S.** that the people could not discern
Ezr 4:13 and **s.** thou shalt endamage the
Ezr 4:15 **s.** shalt thou find in the book of the
Ezr 4:24 **S.** it ceased unto the second year of
Ezr 5:17 whether it be **s.**, that a decree was
Ezr 6:13 king had sent, **s.** they did speedily. 3660
Ezr 8:23 **S.** we fasted and besought our God
Ezr 8:30 **S.** took the priests and the Levites the
Ezr 9:2 **s.** that the holy seed have mingled
Ezr 9:14 **s.** that there should be no remnant
Ezr 10:12 As thou hast said, **s.** must we do. 3651
Ezr 10:16 the children of the captivity did **s.** 3651
Ne 2:4 **S.** I prayed to the God of heaven.
Ne 2:6 **S.** it pleased the king to send me; and
Ne 2:11 **S.** I came to Jerusalem, and was there
Ne 2:15 the gate of the valley, and **s.** returned.
Ne 2:18 **S.** they strengthened their hands for
Ne 4:6 **S.** built we the wall; and all the wall
Ne 4:10 **s.** that we are not able to build the
Ne 4:18 girded by his side, and **s.** builded
Ne 4:21 **S.** we laboured in the work: and half
Ne 4:23 **S.** neither I, nor my brethren, nor my
Ne 5:12 them; **s.** will we do as thou sayest. 3651
Ne 5:13 **S.** God shake out every man from 3602
Ne 5:15 **s.** did not I, because of the fear of 3651
Ne 6:3 work, **s.** that I cannot come down:
Ne 6:13 be afraid, and do **s.**, and sin, and 3651
Ne 6:15 **S.** the wall was finished in the twenty
Ne 7:73 **S.** the priests, and the Levites, and the
Ne 8:8 **S.** they read in the book in the law of
Ne 8:11 **S.** the Levites stilled all the people,
Ne 8:16 **S.** the people went forth, and brought
Ne 8:17 not the children of Israel done **s.** 3651
Ne 9:10 **S.** didst thou get thee a name, as it
Ne 9:11 **s.** that they went through the midst of
Ne 9:21 wilderness, **s.**...they lacked nothing;
Ne 9:22 **s.** they possessed the land of Sihon,
Ne 9:24 **S.** the children went in and possessed
Ne 9:25 **s.** they did eat, and were filled, and
Ne 9:28 **s.** that they had the dominion over
Ne 12:40 **S.** stood the two companies of them
Ne 12:43 **s.** that the joy of Jerusalem was heard
Ne 13:20 **S.** the merchants and sellers of all
Ne 13:21 if ye do **s.** again, I will lay hands on
Es 1:8 for **s.** the king had appointed to all 3651
Es 1:13 (for **s.** was the king's manner 3651
Es 1:17 **s.**...they shall despise their husbands
Es 2:4 pleased the king; and he did **s.**. 3651
Es 2:8 **S.** it came to pass, when the king's
Es 2:12 (for **s.** were the days of their 3651
Es 2:16 **S.** Esther was taken unto king
Es 2:17 **s.** that he set the royal crown upon her
Es 3:2 for the king had **s.** commanded 3651
Es 4:4 **S.** Esther's maids and her
Es 4:6 **S.** Hatach went forth to Mordecai
Es 4:16 **s.** will I go in unto the king, which 3651
Es 4:17 **S.** Mordecai went his way, and did
Es 5:2 it was **s.**, when the king saw Esther
Es 5:2 **S.** Esther drew near, and touched the
Es 5:5 **S.** the king and Haman came to the
Es 5:13 **s.** long as I see Mordecai the Jew 6256
Es 6:6 **S.** Haman came. And the king
Es 6:10 do even **s.** to Mordecai the Jew, 3651
Es 7:1 **S.** the king and Haman came to
Es 7:5 presume in his heart to do **s.**? 3651
Es 7:10 **S.** they hanged Haman on the gallows
Es 8:4 **S.** Esther arose, and stood before the
Es 8:14 **S.** the posts that rode upon mules and
Es 9:14 king commanded it **s.** to be done: 3651
Es 9:27 **s.** as it should not fail, that they would
Job 1:3 **s.** that this man was the greatest of
Job 1:5 And it was **s.**, when the days of their
Job 1:12 **S.** Satan went forth from the presence
Job 2:7 **S.** went Satan forth from the presence
Job 2:13 **S.** they sat down with him upon the
Job 5:12 **s.** that their hands cannot perform
Job 5:16 **S.** the poor hath hope, and iniquity
Job 5:27 Lo this, we have search it, **s.** it is ; 3651
Job 7:3 **S.** am I made to possess months of 3651
Job 7:9 **s.** he that goeth down to the grave 3651
Job 7:15 **S.** that my soul chooseth strangling,
Job 7:20 thee, **s.** that I am a burden to myself?
Job 8:13 **S.** are the paths of all that forget 3651
Job 9:2 I know it is **s.** of a truth: but how 3651
Job 9:30 and make my hands never **s.** clean;
Job 9:35 fear him; but it is not **s.** with me. 3651
Job 13:9 mocketh another, do ye **s.** mock him?
Job 14:12 **S.** man lieth down, and riseth not:
Job 21:4 and it were **s.**, why should not my
Job 23:7 **s.** should I be delivered for ever from
Job 24:19 **s.** doth the grave those which have
Job 24:25 And if it be not **s.** now, who will make
Job 27:6 reproach me **s.** long as I live. 3605
Job 32:1 **S.** these three men ceased to answer
Job 32:22 in **s.** doing my maker would soon take
Job 33:20 **S.** that his life abhorreth bread, and
Job 34:25 the night, **s.** that they are destroyed.
Job 34:28 **S.** that they cause the cry of the poor
Job 35:15 because it was not **s.**, he hath visted
Job 36:16 Even **s.** would he have removed thee
Job 41:10 None is **s.** fierce that dare stir him up:
Job 41:16 One is **s.** near to another, that no air
Job 42:7 And it was **s.**, that after the Lord had
Job 42:9 **S.** Eliphaz the Temanite and Bildad
Job 42:12 **S.** the Lord blessed the latter end of
Job 42:15 were no women found **s.** fair as the
Job 42:17 **S.** Job died, being old and full of days.
Ps 1:4 The ungodly are not **s.**: but are 3651
Ps 7:7 **S.** shall the congregation of the people
Ps 18:3 **s.** shall I be saved from mine enemies.
Ps 18:34 **s.** that a bow of steel is broken by
Ps 21:13 **s.** will we sing and praise thy power.
Ps 22:1 why art thou **s.** far from helping me,
Ps 26:6 **s.** will I compass thine altar, O Lord:
Ps 35:25 their hearts, Ah, **s.** would we have it:
Ps 37:3 **s.** shalt thou dwell in the land, and
Ps 40:12 me, **s.** that I am not able to look up;
Ps 42:1 **s.** panteth my soul after thee, O 3651
Ps 45:11 **S.** shall the king greatly desire thy
Ps 48:5 They saw it, and **s.** they marvelled; 3651
Ps 48:8 **s.** have we seen in the city of the 3651
Ps 48:10 **s.** is thy praise unto the ends of the 3651
Ps 58:5 charmers, charming never **s.** wisely.
Ps 58:11 **S.** that a man shall say, Verily there
Ps 61:8 **S.** will I sing praise unto thy name 3651
Ps 63:2 **s.** as I have seen thee in the 3651
Ps 64:8 **S.** they shall make their own tongue
Ps 65:9 when thou hast **s.** provided for it. 3651
Ps 68:2 As smoke is driven away, **s.** drive them
Ps 68:2 **s.** let the wicked perish at the presence.
Ps 72:7 **s.** long as the moon endureth. 5704
Ps 73:20 **s.**, O Lord, when thou awakest, thou
Ps 73:22 **S.** foolish was I, and ignorant: I was
Ps 77:4 I am **s.** troubled that I cannot speak.
Ps 77:13 who is **s.** great a God as our God?
Ps 78:21 **s.** a fire was kindled against Jacob,
Ps 78:29 **S.** they did eat, and were well filled:
Ps 78:53 them on safely **s.** that they feared not:
Ps 78:60 **S.** that he forsook the tabernacle of
Ps 78:72 **S.** he fed them according to the
Ps 79:13 **S.** we thy people and sheep of thy
Ps 80:12 **S.** that all they which pass by the way
Ps 80:18 **S.** will not we go back from thee:
Ps 81:12 **S.** I gave them up unto their own
Ps 83:15 **S.** persecute them with thy 3651
Ps 90:11 according to thy fear, **s.** is thy wrath.
Ps 90:12 **S.** teach us to number our days, 3651

Ps 102:4 grass; **s.** that I forget to eat my bread.
Ps 102:15 **S.** the heathen shall fear the name of
Ps 103:5 **s.** that thy youth is renewed like the
Ps 103:11 **s.** great is his mercy toward them that
Ps 103:12 **s.** far hath he removed our
Ps 103:13 **S.** the Lord pitieth them that fear him.
Ps 103:15 flower of the field, **s.** he flourisheth. ... 3652
Ps 104:25 **S.** is this great and wide sea, wherein
Ps 106:9 **s.** he led them through the depths, as
Ps 106:30 and **s.** the plague was stayed.
Ps 106:32 **s.** that it went ill with Moses for their
Ps 106:33 **S.** that he spake unadvisedly with his
Ps 107:2 Let the redeemed of the Lord say **s.**,
Ps 107:29 **s.** that the waves thereof are still.
Ps 107:30 **s.** he bringeth them unto their desired
Ps 107:38 **s.** that they are multiplied greatly;
Ps 109:17 loved cursing, **s.** let it come unto him:
Ps 109:17 in blessing, **s.** let it be far from him.
Ps 109:18 **s.** let it come into his bowels like
Ps 115:8 **s.** is every one that trusteth in them.
Ps 119:27 **s.** shall I talk of thy wondrous words.
Ps 119:42 **S.** shall I have wherewith to answer
Ps 119:44 **S.** shall I keep thy law continually
Ps 119:88 **S.** shall I keep the testimony of thy
Ps 119:134 the oppression of man: **s.** will I keep... 3602
Ps 123:2 **s.** our eyes wait upon the Lord 3651
Ps 125:2 **s.** the Lord is round about his people
Ps 127:2 for **s.** he giveth his beloved sleep. 3651
Ps 127:4 man; **s.** are children of the youth 3651
Ps 135:18 **s.** is every one that trusteth in them.
Ps 147:20 hath not dealt **s.** with any nation: 3651
Pr 1:19 **S.** are the ways of every one that is... 3651
Pr 2:2 **S.** that thou incline thine ear unto
Pr 3:4 **S.** shalt thou find favour and good
Pr 3:10 **S.** thy barns be filled with plenty,
Pr 3:22 **S.** shall they be life unto thy soul, and
Pr 6:11 **S.** shall thy poverty come as one that
Pr 6:29 **S.** he that goeth in to his 3651
Pr 7:13 **S.** she caught him, and kissed him.
Pr 10:25 passeth, **s.** is the wicked no more:
Pr 10:26 **s.** is the sluggard to them that send
Pr 11:19 **s.** he that pursueth evil pursueth it to
Pr 11:22 **s.** is a fair woman which is without
Pr 15:7 heart of the foolish doeth not **s.**. 3651
Pr 19:24 not **s.** much as bring it to his mouth.
Pr 20:30 **s.** do stripes the inward parts of the
Pr 23:7 he thinketh in his heart, **s.** is he: 3651
Pr 24:14 **S.** shall the knowledge of wisdom 3651
Pr 24:29 I will do **s.** to him as he hath done 3651
Pr 24:34 **S.** shall thy poverty come as one that ..3651
Pr 25:12 **s.** is a wise reprover upon an obedient .3651
Pr 25:13 **s.** is a faithful messenger to them that..3651
Pr 25:16 eat **s.** much as is sufficient for thee, ... 3651
Pr 25:17 he be weary of thee, and **s.** hate thee. .3651
Pr 25:20 **s.** is he that singeth songs to an heavy .3651
Pr 25:23 **s.** doth an angry countenance a 3651
Pr 25:25 **s.** is good news from a far country. 3651
Pr 25:27 **s.** for men to search their own glory is.3651
Pr 26:1 **s.** honour is not seemly for a fool. 3651
Pr 26:2 **s.** the curse causeless shall not 3651
Pr 26:7 **s.** is a parable in the mouth of fools.
Pr 26:8 **s.** is he that giveth honour to a 3651
Pr 26:9 **s.** is a parable in the mouth of fools.
Pr 26:11 vomit, **s.** a fool returneth to his folly.
Pr 26:14 **s.** doth the slothful upon his bed.
Pr 26:19 **S.** is the man that deceiveth his 3651
Pr 26:20 **s.** where there is no talebearer, the
Pr 26:21 **s.** is a contentious man to kindle
Pr 27:8 **s.** is a man that wandereth from 3651
Pr 27:9 **s.** doth the sweetness of a man's
Pr 27:17 **s.** a man sharpeneth the countenance
Pr 27:18 **s.** he that waiteth on his master shall
Pr 27:19 face, **s.** the heart of man to man. 3651
Pr 27:20 **s.** the eyes of man are never satisfied.
Pr 27:21 for gold; **s.** is a man to his praise.
Pr 28:15 **s.** is a wicked ruler over the poor
Pr 30:33 **s.** the forcing of wrath bringeth forth
Pr 31:11 **s.** that he shall have no need of spoil.
Ec 2:9 **S.** I was great, and increased more
Ec 2:15 the fool, **s.** it happeneth even to me;
Ec 3:11 **s.** that no man can find out the
Ec 3:19 the one dieth, **s.** dieth the other; 3651
Ec 3:19 **s.** that a man hath no preeminence
Ec 4:1 **S.** I returned, and considered all the
Ec 5:16 points as he came, **s.** shall he go: 3651
Ec 6:2 **s.** that he wanteth nothing for his soul
Ec 6:3 **s.** that the days of his years by many,
Ec 7:6 pot, **s.** is the laughter of the fool: 3651
Ec 8:10 And **s.** I saw the wicked buried, 3651
Ec 8:10 in the city where they had **s.** done: 3651
Ec 9:2 as is the good, **s.** is the sinner: and he
Ec 9:12 **s.** are the sons of men snared in 1992
Ec 10:1 **s.** doth a little folly him that is in
Ec 11:5 even **s.** thou knowest not the 3602
Ca 2:2 **s.** is my love among the daughters. 3651
Ca 2:3 **s.** is my beloved among the sons 3651
Ca 5:9 that thou dost **s.** charge us? 3602
Isa 5:24 **s.** their root shall be as rottenness,
Isa 6:13 **s.** the holy seed shall be the substance
Isa 10:7 Howbeit he meaneth not **s.**, 3651
Isa 10:7 neither doth his heart think **s.**; but 3651
Isa 10:11 **s.** do to Jeusalem and her idols? 3651
Isa 10:26 **s.** shall he lift it up after the manner
Isa 14:24 as I have thought. **s.** shall it come 3652
Isa 14:24 I have purposed, **s.** shall it stand: 3651
Isa 16:2 **s.** the daughters of Moab shall be at
Isa 16:6 wrath: but his lies shall not be **s.**. 3651
Isa 18:4 For **s.** the Lord said unto me, I will.... 3541
Isa 20:2 And he did **s.**, walking naked and 3651
Isa 20:4 **S.** shall the king of Assyria lead 3651
Isa 21:1 **s.** it cometh from the desert, from a
Isa 22:22 **s.** he shall open, and none shall shut;
Isa 23:1 **s.** that there is no house, no entering
Isa 23:5 **s.** shall they be sorely pained at the
Isa 24:2 with the people, **s.** with the priest;
Isa 24:2 with the servant, **s.** with his master;
Isa 24:2 with the maid, **s.** with her mistress;
Isa 24:2 as with the buyer, **s.** with the seller;
Isa 24:2 with the lender, **s.** with the borrower;
Isa 24:2 **s.** with the giver of usury to him.
Isa 26:17 **s.** have we been in thy sight, O 3651
Isa 28:8 **s.** that there is no place clean.
Isa 29:8 **s.** shall the multitude of all the 3652
Isa 30:14 **s.** that there shall not be found in the
Isa 31:4 **s.** shall the Lord of hosts come 3651
Isa 31:5 as birds flying, **s.** will the Lord of 3652
Isa 36:6 **s.** is Pharaoh king of Egypt to all 3651
Isa 37:5 **S.** the servants of king Hezekiah
Isa 37:8 **S.** Rabshakeh returned, and found the
Isa 37:37 **S.** Sennacherib king of Assyria
Isa 38:8 **S.** the sun returned ten degrees, by
Isa 38:13 **S.** will he break all my bones: 3651
Isa 38:14 crane or a swallow, **s.** did I chatter: 3651
Isa 38:16 **s.** wilt thou recover me, and make me
Isa 40:20 He that is **s.** improverished that he
Isa 41:7 **S.** the carpenter encouraged the
Isa 47:7 **s.** that thou didst not lay these 5704
Isa 47:12 if **s.** be thou shalt be able to profit,
Isa 47:12 if **s.** be thou mayest prevail.
Isa 52:14 his visage was **s.** marred more than any
Isa 52:15 **S.** shall he sprinkly many nations; 3651
Isa 53:7 dumb, **s.** he openeth not his mouth.
Isa 54:9 **s.** have I sworn that I would not be 3651
Isa 55:9 **s.** are my ways higher than your 3651
Isa 55:11 **S.** shall my word be that goeth 3651
Isa 59:19 **S.** shall they fear the name of the
Isa 60:15 **s.** that no man went through thee.
Isa 61:11 **s.** the Lord God will cause 3651
Isa 62:5 a virgin, **s.** shall thy sons marry thee:
Isa 62:5 **s.** shall thy God rejoice over thee.
Isa 63:8 will not lie: **s.** he was their Saviour.
Isa 63:14 **s.** didst thou lead thy people, to 3651
Isa 65:8 **s.** will I do for my servants' sakes, 3651
Isa 66:13 comforteth, **s.** will I comfort you; 3651
Isa 66:22 **s.** shall your seed and your name 3651
Jer 2:26 **s.** is the house of Israel ashamed; 3651
Jer 2:36 Why gaddest thou about **s.** much
Jer 3:20 **s.** have ye dealt treacherously with 3651
Jer 5:19 **s.** shall ye serve strangers in a land 3651
Jer 5:27 **s.** are their houses full of deceit: 3651
Jer 5:31 and my people love to have it **s.**: 3651
Jer 6:7 **s.** she casteth out her wickedness: 3651
Jer 9:10 **s.** that none can pass through
Jer 10:18 them, that they may find it **s.**.
Jer 11:4 **s.** shall ye be my people, and I will be
Jer 11:5 and said, **S.** be it, O Lord. 543
Jer 13:2 **S.** I got a girdle according to the
Jer 13:5 **S.** I went, and hid it by Euphrates,
Jer 13:11 **s.** have I caused to cleave unto me 3651
Jer 17:11 **s.** he that getteth riches, and not by
Jer 18:4 **s.** he made it again another vessel,
Jer 18:6 **s.** are ye in mine hand, O house of 3651
Jer 19:11 Even **s.** will I break this people 3602
Jer 21:2 if **s.** be that the Lord will deal with us
Jer 24:2 not be eaten, they were **s.** bad.
Jer 24:3 cannot be eaten, they are **s.** evil.
Jer 24:5 **s.** will I acknowledge them that 3651
Jer 24:8 cannot be eaten, they are **s.** evil;
Jer 24:8 **S.** will I give Zedekiah the king of 3651
Jer 26:3 if **s.** be they will hearken, and turn
Jer 26:7 **S.** the priests and the prophets and
Jer 28:6 Amen: the Lord do **s.**: the Lord 3651
Jer 28:11 Even **s.** will I break the yoke of 3602
Jer 28:17 **S.** Hananiah the prophet died the
Jer 29:17 cannot be eaten, they are **s.** evil.
Jer 30:7 day is great, **s.** that none is like:
Jer 31:28 **s.** will I watch over them, to build, 3651
Jer 32:8 **S.** Hanameel mine uncle's son came
Jer 32:11 **S.** I took the evidence of the
Jer 32:42 **s.** will I bring upon them all the 3651
Jer 33:22 **s.** will I multiply the seed of David 3651
Jer 33:26 **s.** that I will not take any of his seed
Jer 34:5 **s.** shall they burn odours for thee; 3651
Jer 35:11 Syrians: **s.** we dwell at Jerusalem.
Jer 36:14 **S.** Baruch the son of Neriah took the
Jer 36:15 ears. **S.** Baruch read it in their ears.
Jer 36:21 **S.** the king sent Jehudi to fetch the
Jer 37:14 **s.** Irijah took Jeremiah, and brought
Jer 38:6 mire: **s.** Jeremiah sunk in the mire.
Jer 38:11 **S.** Ebed-melech took the men with
Jer 38:12 the cords. And Jeremiah did **s.** 3651
Jer 38:13 **S.** they drew up Jeremiah with cords,
Jer 38:16 **s.** Zedekiah the king sware secretly
Jer 38:2 **s.** it shall be well unto thee, and thy
Jer 38:23 **S.** they shall brng out all thy wives
Jer 38:27 **S.** they left off speaking with him;
Jer 38:28 **S.** Jeremiah abode in the court of the
Jer 39:13 **S.** Nebuzar-adan the captain of the
Jer 39:14 home: **s.** he dwelt among the people.
Jer 40:5 **S.** the captain of the guard gave him
Jer 41:7 it was **s.**, when they came into the
Jer 41:8 **S.** he forbare, and slew them not
Jer 41:14 **S.** all the people that Ishmael had
Jer 42:17 **S.** shall it be with all the men that set
Jer 42:18 **s.** shall my fury be poured forth 3651
Jer 42:20 **s.** declare unto us, and we will do it. .. 3651
Jer 43:4 **S.** Johanan the son of Kareah, and all
Jer 43:7 **S.** they came into the land of Egypt:
Jer 44:14 **S.** that none of the remnant of Judah,
Jer 44:22 **S.** that the Lord could no longer bear,
Jer 46:18 Carmel by the sea, **s.** shall he come.
Jer 48:30 the Lord; but it shall not be **s.**; 3651
Jer 48:30 his lies shall not **s.** effect it. 3651
Jer 49:39 **s.** shall Moab be a derision and a
Jer 50:40 **s.** shall no man abide there, neither
Jer 51:8 her pain, if **s.** be she may be healed.
Jer 51:49 **s.** at Babylon shall fall the slain of all
Jer 51:60 **S.** Jeremiah wrote in a book all the
Jer 52:5 **S.** the city was besieged unto the
Jer 52:6 **s.** that there was no bread for the
Jer 52:26 **S.** Nebuzar-adan the captain of the
La 2:22 **s.** that in the day of the Lord's anger
La 3:29 the dust; if **s.** be there my be hope.
La 4:14 **s.** that men could not touch their
La 5:20 for ever, and forsake us **s.** long time?
Eze 1:18 were **s.** high that they were dreadful;
Eze 1:28 **s.** was the appearance of the 3651
Eze 3:2 **S.** I opened my mouth, and he caused
Eze 3:14 **S.** the spirit lifted me up, and took me
Eze 4:5 **s.** shalt thou bear the iniquity of the
Eze 5:15 **S.** it shall be a reproach and a taunt,
Eze 5:17 **S.** will I send upon you famine and
Eze 6:14 **S.** will I stretch out my hand upon
Eze 8:5 **S.** I lifted up mine eyes the way
Eze 8:10 **S.** I went in and saw; and behold
Eze 11:24 **S.** the vision that I had seen went up
Eze 12:7 and I did **s.** as I was commanded: 3651
Eze 12:11 done, **s.** shall it be done unto them: 3651
Eze 13:14 **S.** will I break down the wall that ye... 3651
Eze 13:14 **s.** that the foundation thereof shall 3651
Eze 14:15 **s.** that it be desolate, that no man 3651
Eze 14:17 **s.** that I cut off man and beast from it: .3651
Eze 15:6 **s.** will I give the inhabitants of 3651
Eze 16:16 shall not come, neither shall it be **s.**.
Eze 16:42 **S.** will I make my fury toward thee.
Eze 16:44 As is the mother, **s.** is her daughter.
Eze 17:6 **s.** it became a vine, and brought forth
Eze 18:4 **s.** also the soul of the son is mine:
Eze 18:30 **s.** iniquity shall not be your ruin.
Eze 19:14 **s.** that she hath no strong rod to be a
Eze 20:36 **s.** will I plead with you, saith the 3651

Eze 21:24 s. that in all your doings your sins do........
Eze 22:20 s. will I gather you in mine anger....... 3651
Eze 22:22 s. shall ye be melted in the midst....... 3651
Eze 23:18 S. she discovered her whoredoms, ...
Eze 23:27 s. that thou shalt not lift up thine ....
Eze 23:44 s. went they in unto Aholah and......... 3651
Eze 24:18 S. I spake unto the people in the ....
Eze 24:19 things are to us, that thou doest s.? ....
Eze 28:14 and I have set thee s.: thou wast upon......
Eze 31:9 s. that all the trees of Eden, thath...........
Eze 33:7 S. thou, O son of man I have set thee ......
Eze 34:12 s. will I seek out my seep, and.......... 3651
Eze 35:15 desolate, s. will I do unto thee: 3651
Eze 36:38 s. shall the waste cities be filled.......... 3651
Eze 37:7 S. I prophesied as I was commanded: ....
Eze 37:10 S. I prophesied as he commanded me, ...
Eze 37:23 s. shall they be my people, and I will........
Eze 38:20 S. that the fishes of the sea, and the ....
Eze 39:7 S. will I make my holy name known..........
Eze 39:10 S. that they shall take no wood out of.........
Eze 39:22 S. the house of Israel shall know that........
Eze 39:23 enemies; s. fell they all by the sword........
Eze 40:5 s. he measured the breadth of the...........
Eze 40:47 S. he measured the court, and hundred.....
Eze 41:4 S. he measured the length thereof,..........
Eze 41:7 s. increased from the lowest chamber.........
Eze 41:13 S. he measured the house, an hundred......
Eze 41:18 s. that a palm tree was between a...........
Eze 41:19 S. that the face of a man was toward.........
Eze 43:5 S. the spirit took my up, and brought.........
Eze 43:15 S. the altar shall be four cubits; and..........
Eze 43:27 and s. forward, the priests shall make ....
Eze 45:20 s. thou shalt do the seventh day 3651
Eze 45:20 simple: s. shall ye reconcile the house.......
Eze 47:21 S. shall ye divide this land unto you...........
Da 1:5 s. nourishing them three years, that..........
Da 1:14 S. he consented to them in this ....
Da 2:2 S. they came and stood before the ....
Da 2:15 is the decree s. hasty from the king? ....
Da 2:42 s. the kingdom shall be partly strong,........
Da 3:17 If it be s. our God whom we serve is........
Da 5:6 s. that the joints of his loins were............
Da 6:23 S. Daniel was taken up out of the den,......
Da 6:28 S. this Daniel prospered in the reign..........
Da 7:16 S. he told me, and made me know the......
Da 8:4 s. that no beasts might stand before ....
Da 8:17 S. he came near where I stood: and ....
Da 10:7 s. that they fled to hide themselves. ....
Da 11:9 S. the king of the south shall come...........
Da 11:15 S. the king of the north shall come, ...
Da 11:30 s. shall he do; he shall even return, ...
Ho 1:3 S. he went and took Gomer the ....
Ho 3:2 S. I bought her to me for fifteen pieces.....
Ho 3:3 man: s. will I also be for thee........... 1571
Ho 4:7 s. they sinned against me: 3651
Ho 6:9 s. the company of priests murder in..........
Ho 8:7 if s. be it yield, the strangers shall...........
Ho 10:15 S. shall Beth-el do unto you.............. 3602
Ho 11:2 them, s. they went from them: 3602
Ho 13:6 to their pasture, s. were they filled;..........
Ho 14:2 s. will we render the calves of our............
Joe 2:4 as horsemen, s. shall they run.......... 3651
Joe 3:17 S. shall ye know that I am the Lord..........
Am 3:12 s. shall the children of Israel be 3651
Am 4:8 S. two or three cities wandered unto ....
Am 5:9 s. that the spoiled shall come against.........
Am 5:14 and s. the Lord, the God of hosts, ... 3651
Ob 16 s. shall all the heathen drink...................
Jon 1:3 s. he paid the fare thereof, and went ....
Jon 1:4 s. that the ship was like to be broken. ......
Jon 1:6 if s. be that God will think upon us............
Jon 1:6 S. the shipmaster came to him, and..........
Jon 1:7 S. they cast lots, and the lot fell upon.......
Jon 1:12 s. shall the sea be calm unto you: for.........
Jon 1:15 S. they took up Jonah, and cast him..........
Jon 3:3 S. Jonah arose, and went unto................
Jon 3:5 S. the people of Nineveh believed God, ...
Jon 4:5 S. Jonah went out of the city, and sat ....
Jon 4:6 S. Jonah was exceeding glad of the..........
Mic 2:2 s. they oppress a man and his house,........
Mic 5:14 of thee: s. will I destroy thy cities............
Mic 7:3 mischievous desire: s. they wrap it up.......
Zep 3:6 s. that there is no man, that there............
Zep 3:7 s. their dwelling should not be cut off,.......
Hag 2:5 s. my spirit remaineth among you:............
Hag 2:14 S. is this people, and s. is this........... 3651
Hag 2:14 s. is every work of their hands;......... 3651

Zec 1:6 doings, s. hath he dealt with us. 3651
Zec 1:14 S. the angel that communed with me ....
Zec 1:21 s. that no man did lift up his head:...........
Zec 3:5 S. they set a fair mitre upon his head, ...
Zec 4:4 S. I answered and spake to the angel.........
Zec 6:7 S. they walked to and fro through the ....
Zec 7:3 as I have done these s. many years?.........
Zec 7:13 s. they cried, and I would not hear;.... 3651
Zec 8:13 s. will I save you, ... 3651
Zec 8:15 S. again have I thought in these.......... 3651
Zec 10:1 s. the Lord shall make bright clouds,..........
Zec 11:11 s. the poor of the flock that waited..... 3651
Zec 11:12 S. they weighed for my price thirty ....
Zec 14:15 And s. shall be the plague of the.......... 3651
Mal 3:13 have we spoken s. much against thee? ......
Mt 1:17 S. all the generations from................ 3767
Mt 3:15 said unto him, Suffer it to be s. ....
Mt 5:12 s. persecuted they the prophets 3779
Mt 5:16 Let your light s. shine before........ 3779
Mt 5:19 shall teach men s., he shall be...... 3779
Mt 5:47 do not even the publicans s.? 3779
Mt 6:30 if God s. clothe the grass of the.... 3779
Mt 7:12 do to you, do ye even s. to them: .. 3779
Mt 7:17 Even s. every good tree bringeth... 3779
Mt 8:10 I have not found s. great faith,..... 5118
Mt 8:13 hast believed, s. be it done unto..........
Mt 8:28 s. that no man might pass by that 5620
Mt 8:31 S. the devils besought him, saying,..... 1161
Mt 9:19 followed him, and s. did his disciples. ....
Mt 9:33 It was never s. seen in Israel............ 3779
Mt 11:26 Even s., Father: for ...it seemed....... 3779
Mt 11:26 for s. it seemed good in thy sight.. 3779
Mt 12:40 s. shall the Son of man be three..... 3779
Mt 12:45 Even s. shall it be also unto this... 3779
Mt 13:2 s. that he went into a ship, and 5620
Mt 13:27 S. the servants of the householder..1161
Mt 13:32 s. that the birds of the air come.... 5620
Mt 13:40 s. shall it be in the end of this...... 3779
Mt 13:49 S. shall it be at the end of the 3779
Mt 15:33 s. much bread in the wilderness,......... 5118
Mt 15:33 as to fill s. great a multitude? 5118
Mt 18:13 s. be that he find it, verily I say ... 1437
Mt 18:14 Even s. it is not the will of your ... 3779
Mt 18:31 S. when his fellowservants saw 1161
Mt 18:35 S. likewise shall my heavenly......... 3779
Mt 19:8 from the beginning it was not s... 3779
Mt 19:10 of the man be s. with his wife, ... 3779
Mt 19:12 born from their mother's womb:... 3779
Mt 20:8 S. shen even was come, the lord.... 1161
Mt 20:16 S. the last shall be first, and the... 3779
Mt 20:26 But it shall not be s. among you:.. 3779
Mt 20:34 S. Jesus had compassion on them,...... 1161
Mt 22:10 S. those servants went out into..... 2532
Mt 23:28 Even s. ye also outwardly appear .. 3779
Mt 24:27 s. shall also the coming of the 3779
Mt 24:33 S. likewise ye, when ye shall see... 3779
Mt 24:37, 39 s. shall also the coming of the.. 3779
Mt 24:46 whe he cometh shall find s. doing.. 3779
Mt 25:9 Not s.; lest there be not enough for3779
Mt 25:20 s. he that had received five.......... 2532
Mt 27:64 s. the last error shall be worse.......... 2532
Mt 27:66 S. they went and made the.............. 1161
Mt 28:15 S. they took the money, and did as.... 1161
Mk 2:2 not s. much as about the door: 3366
Mk 2:8 s. reasoned within themselves, ... 3779
Mk 3:20 again, s. that they could not.............. 5620
Mk 3:20 could not s. much as eat bread. 3383
Mk 4:1 s. that he entered into a ship, and...... 5620
Mk 4:17 and s. endured but for a time:..........
Mk 4:26 said, S. is the kingdom of God,........ 3779
Mk 4:32 s. that the fowls of the air may..... 5620
Mk 4:37 the ship, s. that it was now full.......... 5620
Mk 4:40 unto them, Why are ye s. fearful?... 3779
Mk 6:31 they had no leisure s. much as to......... 3761
Mk 7:18 Are ye s. without understanding.... 3779
Mk 7:36 s. much the more a great deal................
Mk 8:8 S. they did eat, and were filled: 1161
Mk 9:3 s. as no fuller on earth can white 3634
Mk 10:8 s. then they are no more twain,...... 5620
Mk 10:43 But s. shall it not be among you:.. 3779
Mk 13:29 S. ye in like manner, when ye....... 2532
Mk 14:59 neither s. did their witness agree 3779
Mk 15:5 nothing; s. that Pilate marveled............ 5620
Mk 15:15 s. Pilate, willing to content the people, ...
Mk 15:39 saw that he s. cried out, and gave...... 3779
Mk 16:19 S. then after the Lord had................ 3303
Lu 1:21 that he tarried s. long in the temple.........

Lu 1:60 Not s.; but he shall be called John. ....
Lu 2:6 s. it was, that, while they were there, ...
Lu 2:21 which was s. named of the angel.............
Lu 5:7 ships, s. that they began to sink. 5620
Lu 5:10 And s. was also James and John, ... 3668
Lu 5:15 s. much the more went there a...............
Lu 6:3 have ye not read s. much as this,.. 3761
Lu 6:10 And he did s.: and his hand was......... 3779
Lu 6:26 s. did their fathers to the....... 2596,5623
Lu 7:9 I have not found s. great faith,..... 5118
Lu 9:15 they did s., and made them all sit......... 3779
Lu 10:21 them unto babes: even s., Father; ..3488
Lu 10:21 for s. it seemed good in thy sight.. 3779
Lu 11:2 be done, as in heaven, s. in earth.. 2532
Lu 11:30 s. shall also the Son of man be to . 3779
Lu 12:21 S. is he that layeth up treasure..... 3779
Lu 12:28 If then god s. clothe the grass,...... 3779
Lu 12:38 and find them s., blessed are......... 3779
Lu 12:43 when he cometh shall find s. 3779
Lu 12:54 There cometh a shower; and s. it .. 3779
Lu 14:21 S. that servant came, and shewed.. 2532
Lu 14:33 S. likewise, whosoever he be of..... 3767
Lu 16:5 S. he called every one of his 2532
Lu 16:26 s. that they which would pass......... 3704
Lu 17:10 S. likewise ye, when ye shall have. 3779
Lu 17:24 s. shall also the Son of man be in . 3779
Lu 17:26 s. shall it be also in the days of.... 3779
Lu 18:13 not lift up s. much as his eyes...... 3761
Lu 18:39 cried s. much the more, Thou son...... 3123
Lu 20:15 S....cast him out of the vineyard,.. 2532
Lu 20:20 that s. they might deliver him unto...... 1519
Lu 21:31 S. likewise ye, when ye see these .. 3779
Lu 21:34 s. that day come upon you..................
Lu 22:26 But ye shall not be s.: but he......... 3779
Lu 24:24 found it even s. as the women had..... 3779
Joh 3:8 s. is every one that is born of the.. 3779
Joh 3:14 s. must the son of man be lifted.... 3779
Joh 3:16 For God s. loved the world, that ... 3779
Joh 4:40 S. when the Samaritans were............ 3767
Joh 4:46 S. Jesus came again into Cana of........ 3767
Joh 4:53 S. the father knew that it was at......... 3767
Joh 5:21 even s. the Son quickeneth whom.. 3779
Joh 5:26 s. hath he given to the Son to......... 3779
Joh 6:9 but what are they among s. many? 5118
Joh 6:10 S. the men sat down, in number............ 3767
Joh 6:19 S. when they had rowed about five...... 3767
Joh 6:57 s. he that eateth me, even he 2532
Joh 7:43 S. there was a division among the...... 3767
Joh 8:7 S. when they continued asking........... 1161
Joh 8:59 midst of them, and s. passed by.......... 3779
Joh 10:15 me, even s. know I the Father: ....
Joh 11:28 And when she had s. said, she 5023
Joh 12:37 done s. may miracles before them, ... 5118
Joh 12:50 Father said unto me, s. I speak..... 3779
Joh 13:12 S. after he had washed their feet, ... 3767
Joh 13:13 Lord: and ye say well; for s. I am.......
Joh 13:33 ye cannot come; s. now I say to.... 2532
Joh 14:2 if it were not s., I would have............
Joh 14:9 Have I been s. long time with........ 5118
Joh 14:31 gave me commandment, even s. I.. 3779
Joh 15:8 fruit; s. shall ye be my disciples.... 2532
Joh 15:9 loved me, s. have I loved you:....... 2504
Joh 17:18 even s. have I also sent them into the..
Joh 18:15 Jesus, and s. did another disciple: ....
Joh 18:22 Answereth thou the high priest s.? 3779
Joh 20:4 S. they ran both together: and the 1161
Joh 20:20 And when he had s. said, he shewed .. 5124
Joh 20:21 hath sent me, even s. send I you.........
Joh 21:11 and for all there were s. many, yet..... 5118
Joh 21:15 S. when they had dined, Jesus........... 3767
Ac 1:11 shall s. come in like manner as ye...... 3779
Ac 3:12 or why look ye s. earnestly on us, as........
Ac 3:18 should suffer, he hath s. fulfilled......... 3779
Ac 4:21 S. when they...further threatened....... 1161
Ac 5:8 ye sold the land for s. much?................ 5118
Ac 5:8 And she said, Yea, for s. much.......... 5118
Ac 5:32 s. is also the Holy Ghost, whom God........
Ac 7:1 high priest, Are these things s.? 3779
Ac 7:5 no, not s. much as to set his foot on:........
Ac 7:8 and s. Abraham begat Isaac, and......... 3779
Ac 7:15 S. Jacob went down into Egypt,......... 1161
Ac 7:19 s. that they cast out their young.............
Ac 7:51 as your fathers did, s. do ye. 2532
Ac 8:32 s. opened he not his mouth:.................. 3779
Ac 10:14 Peter said, Not s., Lord; for I have.... 3365
Ac 11:8 But I said, Not s., Lord: for nothing.... 3365
Ac 12:8 bind on thy sandals. And s. he did...... 3779

Ac 12:15 constantly affirmed…it was even **s.**…… 3779
Ac 13:4 **S.** they, being sent forth by the……… 3767
Ac 13:8 **s.** is his name by interpretation)……… 3779
Ac 13:47 **s.** hath the Lord commanded us,……… 3779
Ac 14:1 and **s.** spake, that a great multitude…. 3779
Ac 15:30 **S.** when they were dismissed, they…. 3767
Ac 15:39 contention was **s.** sharp between……… 5620
Ac 15:39 **s.** Barnabas took Mark, and sailed…… 5037
Ac 16:5 **s.** were the churches established in…… 3767
Ac 16:26 **s.** that the foundations of the………… 5620
Ac 17:11 whether those things were **s.**………… 3779
Ac 17:33 **S.** Paul departed from among………… 3779
Ac 19:2 have not **s.** much as heard whether…. 3761
Ac 19:10 **s.** that all they which dwelt in Asia….. 5620
Ac 19:12 **S.** that from his body were brought…. 5620
Ac 19:14 chief of the priests, which did **s.**……. 5124
Ac 19:16 **s.** they fled out of that house……… 5620
Ac 19:20 **S.** mightily grew the word of God…… 3779
Ac 19:22 **S.** he sent into Macedonia two of them……
Ac 19:27 **S.** that not only this our craft is in…………
Ac 20:11 till break of day, **s.** he departed……… 3779
Ac 20:13 for **s.** had he appointed, minding……… 3779
Ac 20:24 **s.** that I might finish my course……… 5613
Ac 20:35 **s.** labouring ye ought to support……… 3779
Ac 21:11 **S.** shall the Jews at Jerusalem bind….. 3779
Ac 21:35 **s.** it was, that he was borne of the….. 4819
Ac 22:24 wherefore they dried **s.** against………. 3779
Ac 23:7 And when he had **s.** said, there……… 5124
Ac 23:11 **s. must thou bear witness also at** .. 3779
Ac 23:18 **S.** he took him, and brought him……… 3767
Ac 23:22 **S.** the chief captain then let the……… 3767
Ac 24:9 saying that these things were **s.**……… 3779
Ac 24:14 **s.** worship I the God of my fathers,…. 3779
Ac 27:17 strake sail, and **s.** were driven………. 3779
Ac 27:44 **s.** it came to pass, that they escaped .. 3779
Ac 28:9 **S.** when this was done, others………… 3767
Ac 28:14 and **s.** we went toward Rome………… 3779
Ro 1:15 **S.**, as much as in me is, I am ready…. 3779
Ro 1:20 **s.** that they are without excuse:……… 1519
Ro 4:18 was spoken, **S.** shall thy seed be……… 3779
Ro 5:3 And not only **s.**, but we glory in……………
Ro 5:11 And not only **s.**, but we also joy in God…..
Ro 5:12 **s.** death passed upon all men, for……. 3779
Ro 5:15 the offence, **s.** also is the free gift……. 3779
Ro 5:16 was by one that sinned, **s.** is the gift: …….
Ro 5:18 even **s.** by the righteousness of one…. 3779
Ro 5:19 **s.** by the obedience of one shall……… 3779
Ro 5:21 even **s.** might grace reign through……. 3779
Ro 6:3 **s.** many of us as were baptized………. 3745
Ro 6:4 **s.** we also should walk in newneww…… 3779
Ro 6:19 even **s.** now yield your members……… 3779
Ro 7:2 to her husband **s.** long as he liveth; ……….
Ro 7:3 **S.** them if, while her husband…………. 686
Ro 7:3 **s.** that she is no adulteress, though ……….
Ro 7:25 **S.** then with the mind I myself………. 686
Ro 8:8 **S.** then they that are in the flesh…………..
Ro 8:9 if **s.** be that the Spirit of God dwell in …….
Ro 8:17 if **s.** be that we suffer with him, that……..
Ro 9:16 **S.** then it is not of him that willeth,…… 686
Ro 10:17 **S.** then faith cometh by hearing,……… 686
Ro 11:5 Even **s.** then at this present time……. 3779
Ro 11:16 root be holy, **s.** are the branches. …… 2532
Ro 11:26 And **s.** all Israel shall be saved: as it…. 3779
Ro 11:31 **s.** have these also now not believed,… 3779
Ro 12:5 **S.** we, being many, are one body……. 3779
Ro 12:20 in **s.** doing thou shalt heap coals……… 5124
Ro 14:12 **S.** then every one of us shall give……… 686
Ro 15:19 **s.** that from Jerusalem, and…………… 5620
Ro 15:20 Yea, **s.** have I strived to preach the…. 3779
1Co 1:7 **S.** that ye come behind in no gift: ……. 5620
1Co 2:11 even **s.** the things of God knoweth….. 3779
1Co 3:7 **S.** then neither is he that planteth…… 5620
1Co 3:15 shall be saved; yet **s.** as by fire. …….. 3779
1Co 4:1 Let a man **s.** account of us, as of……. 3779
1Co 5:1 not **s.** much as named among the……. 3761
1Co 5:3 him that hath **s.** done this deed,……… 3779
1Co 6:5 Is it **s.**, that there is not a wiseman…. 3779
1Co 7:17 called every one, **s.** let him walk……. 3779
1Co 7:17 And **s.** ordain I in all churches………. 3779
1Co 7:26 that it is good for a man **s.** to be. …… 3779
1Co 7:36 need **s.** require, let him do what he…. 3779
1Co 7:37 hath **s.** decreed in his heart that……… 5124
1Co 7:38 **S.** then he that giveth her in………… 5620
1Co 7:40 But she is happier if she **s.** abide,….. 3779
1Co 8:12 when ye sin **s.** against the brethren,… 3779
1Co 9:14 Even **s.** hath the Lord ordained……… 3779
1Co 9:15 that it should be **s.** done unto me:……. 3779
1Co 9:24 prize? **S.** run, that ye may obtain. …… 3779
1Co 9:26 therefore **s.** run, not as uncertainly;…. 3779
1Co 9:26 **s.** fight I, not as one that beateth……. 3779
1Co 11:12 **s.** is the man also by the woman;……. 3779
1Co 11:28 and **s.** let him eat of that bread,……… 3779
1Co 12:12 are one body: **s.** also is Christ………. 3779
1Co 13:2 **s.** that I could remove mountains,……. 5620
1Co 14:9 **S.** likewise ye, except ye utter by…… 3779
1Co 14:10 **s.** many kinds of voices in the……….. 5118
1Co 14:12 Even **s.** ye, forasmuch as ye are……. 3779
1Co 14:25 **s.** falling down on his face he will……. 3779
1Co 15:11 **s.** we preach, and **s.** ye believed. …….. 379
1Co 15:15 up, if **s.** be that the dead rise not……. 686
1Co 15:22 **s.** in Christ shall be all made alive. ….. 3779
1Co 15:42 **s.** also is the resurrection of the……. 3779
1Co 15:45 **s.** it is written, the first man Adam….. 3779
1Co 15:54 **S.** when this corruptible shall………… 1161
1Co 16:1 churches of Galatia, even **s.** do ye…… 3779
2Co 1:5 **s.** our consolation also aboundeth……. 3779
2Co 1:7 **s.** shal ye be also of the consolation…. 3779
2Co 1:10 delivered us from **s.** great a death,….. 5082
2Co 2:7 **S.** that contrariwise ye ought………… 5620
2Co 3:7 **s.** that the children of Israel could….. 5620
2Co 4:12 **S.** then death worketh in us, but……. 5620
2Co 5:3 If **s.** be that being clothed we shall ……….
2Co 7:7 me; **s.** that I rejoiced the more………. 5620
2Co 7:14 even **s.** our boasting, which I made….. 3779
2Co 8:6 **s.** he would also finish in you the ……. 3779
2Co 8:11 **s.** there may b a performance also…… 3779
2Co 9:7 purposeth in his heart, **s.** let him give; ……
2Co 10:7 is Christ's, even **s.** are we Christ's…. 3779
2Co 11:3 **s.** your minds should be corrupted……. 3779
2Co 11:9 unto you, and **s.** will I keep myself. ……….
2Co 11:22 Are they Hebrews? **s.** am I…………. 2504
2Co 11:22 Are they Israelites? **s.** am I…………. 2504
2Co 11:22 they the seed of Abraham? **s.** am I…. 2504
2Co 12:16 But be it **s.**, I did not burden you:…………
Ga 1:6 that ye are **s.** soon removed from…… 3779
Ga 1:9 we said before, **s.** say I now again,….. 2532
Ga 3:3 Are ye **s.** foolish: having begun in……. 3779
Ga 3:4 suffered **s.** many things in vain? ……… 5118
Ga 3:9 **S.** then they which be of faith are……. 5620
Ga 4:3 Even **s.** we, when we were children, .. 3779
Ga 4:29 after the Spirit, even **s.** it is now. …… 3779
Ga 4:31 **S.** then, brethren, we are not…………. 686
Ga 5:17 **s.** that ye cannot do the things………. 2443
Ga 6:2 and **s.** fulfil the law of Christ………… 3779
Eph 2:15 twain one new man, **s.** making peace; …….
Eph 4:20 But ye have not **s.** learned Christ;…… 3779
Eph 4:21 If **s.** be that ye have heard him, and… 3779
Eph 5:24 **s.** let the wives be to their own……… 3779
Eph 5:28 **S.** ought men to love their wives as…. 3779
Eph 5:33 **s.** love his wife even as himself;……… 3779
Php 1:13 **S.** that my bonds in Christ are……….. 5620
Php 1:20 **s.** now also Christ shall be magnified……..
Php 2:23 **s.** soon as I shall see how it will go…. 5613
Php 3:17 **s.** as ye have us for an ensample. …… 3779
Php 4:1 **s.** stand fast in the Lord, my dearly…. 3779
Col 2:6 Jesus the Lord, **s.** walk ye in him:…………
Col 3:13 Christ forgave you, **s.** also do ye……. 3779
1Th 1:7 **S.** that ye were ensamples to all……… 5620
1Th 1:8 **s.** that we need not to speak any……… 5620
1Th 2:4 with the gospel, even **s.** we speak;….. 3779
1Th 2:8 **S.** being affectionately desirous of…… 3779
1Th 4:1 **s.** ye would abound more and more. ……….
1Th 4:14 even **s.** them also which sleep in……… 3779
1Th 4:17 **s.** shall we ever be with the Lord……. 3779
1Th 5:2 **s.** cometh as a thief in the night……… 3779
2Th 1:4 **S.** that we ourselves glory in you……. 5620
2Th 2:4 **s.** that he as God sitteth in the………. 5620
2Th 3:17 token in every epistle: **s.** I write……… 3779
1Ti 1:4 godly edifying which is in faith: **s.** do………..
1Ti 3:11 Even **s.** must their wives be grave, …. 5615
1Ti 6:20 oppositions of science falsely **s.** called:…….
2Ti 3:8 **s.** do these also resist the truth: …….. 3779
Heb 1:4 **s.** much better than the angels,………. 5118
Heb 2:3 if we neglect **s.** reat salvation; ………. 5082
Heb 3:11 **S.** I sware in my wrath, They ………. 5613
Heb 3:19 **S.** we see that they could not enter…. 2532
Heb 4:7 To day, after **s.** long a time; as it……. 5118
Heb 5:3 **s.** also for himself, to offer for sins….. 3779
Heb 5:5 **S.** also Christ glorified not himself….. 3779
Heb 6:15 And **s.**, after he had patiently ………. 3779
Heb 7:9 And as I may **s.** say, Levi also, who… 5613
Heb 7:22 By **s.** much was Jesus made a……… 5118
Heb 9:28 **S.** Christ was once offered to bear….. 3779
Heb 10:25 **s.** much the more, as ye see the……. 5118
Heb 10:33 of them that were **s.** used…………… 3779
Heb 11:3 **s.** that things which are seen were….. 1519
Heb 11:12 **s.** many as the stars of they sky in……….
Heb 12:1 with **s.** great a cloud of witnesses,…… 5118
Heb 12:1 the sin which doth **s.** easily beset us, ……..
Heb 12:20 And if **s.** much as a beast touch the……….
Heb 12:21 And **s.** terrible was the sight, that…… 3779
Heb 13:6 **S.** that we may boldly say, The ……… 5620
Jas 1:11 **s.** also shall the rich man fade………. 3779
Jas 2:12 **S.** speak ye, and **s.** do, as they that… 3779
Jas 2:17 Even **s.** faith, if it hath not works,…… 3779
Jas 2:26 **s.** faith without works in dead also….. 3779
Jas 3:4 which though they be **s.** great, ………. 5082
Jas 3:5 **s.** the tongue is a little member, …….. 3779
Jas 3:6 **s.** is the tongue among our …………… 3779
Jas 3:10 these things ought not **s.** to be. ……… 3779
Jas 3:12 **s.** can no fountain both yield salt……. 3779
1Pe 1:15 **s.** be ye holy in all manner of………… 2532
1Pe 2:3 If **s.** be ye have tasted that the Lord………
1Pe 2:15 For **s.** is the will of god, that with….. 3779
1Pe 3:17 if the will of God be **s.**, that ye suffer …….
1Pe 4:10 **s.** minister the same one to another,………
1Pe 5:13 you; and **s.** doth Marcus my son. …………
2Pe 1:11 **s.** an entrance shall be ministered……. 3779
1Jo 2:6 him ought himself also **s.** to walk,……. 3779
1Jo 4:11 Beloved, if God **s.** loved us, we ought.. 3779
1Jo 4:17 as he is, **s.** are we in this world……… 2532
Re 1:7 because of him. Even **s.**, Amen. ……… 3483
Re 2:15 **S. hast thou also them that hold** … 3779
Re 3:16 **S. then because thou art** ………….. 3779
Re 8:12 **s.** as the third part of them was……… 2443
Re 13:13 **s.** that he maketh fire come down…… 2443
Re 16:7 Even **s.**, Lord God Almighty, true…… 3483
Re 16:18 the earth, **s.** mighty an earthquake, …. 5082
Re 16:18 an earthquake, and **s.** great…………. 3779
Re 17:3 **S.** he carried me away in the spirit….. 2532
Re 18:7 **s.** much torment and sorrow give……. 5118
Re 18:17 **s.** great riches is come to nought. …… 5118
Re 22:20 Amen, Even **s.**, come, Lord Jesus……. 3483

SO (so)
2Ki 17:4 messengers to **S.** king of Egypt, ……… 5471

SOAKED
Isa 34:7 their land shall be **s.** with blood,……… 7301

SOAP See SOPE.

SO-BE-IT See SO.

SOBER
2Co 5:13 or whether we be **s.**, it is for your….. 4993
1Th 5:6 others; but let us watch and be **s.**…… 3525
1Th 5:8 But let us, who are of the day, be **s.**, .. 3525
1Ti 3:2 husband of one wife, vigilant, **s.**,……… 4998
1Ti 3:11 wives be grave, not slanderers, **s.**,….. 3524
Tit 1:8 a lover of good men, **s.**, just, ………… 4998
Tit 2:2 That the aged men be **s.**, grave, ……… 3524
Tit 2:4 teach the young women to be **s.**. …….. 4994
Tit 2:6 likewise exhort to be **s.** minded. ……… 4993
1Pe 1:13 be **s.**, and hope to the end for the…… 3525
1Pe 4:7 be ye therefore **s.**, and watch unto….. 4993
1Pe 5:8 Be **s.**, be vigilant: because your ……… 3525

SOBERLY
Ro 12:3 but to think **s.**, according as……. 1519,4993
Tit 2:12 we should live **s.**, righteously, and…… 4996

SOBER-MINDED See SOBER and MINDED.

SOBERNESS
Ac 26:25 forth the words of truth and **s.**. ……… 4997

SOBRIETY
1Ti 2:9 with shamefacedness and **s.**; not ……. 4997
1Ti 2:15 and charity and holiness with **s.**……… 4997

SOCHO (so'-ko) See also SOCHOH.
1Ch 4:18 and Heber the father of **S.**, and ……… 7755

SOCHOH (so'-ko) See also SHOCHOH; SOCHO; SOCOH.
1Ki 4:10 to him pertained **S.**, and all the………. 7755

SOCKET See also SOCKETS.
Ex 38:27 hundred talents, a talent for a **s.**………. 134

SOCKETS
Ex 26:19 forty **s.** of silver under the twenty……. 134
Ex 26:19 two **s.** under one board for his two…… 134

Ex 26:19 and two s. under another board for 134
Ex 26:21 And their forty s. of silver; 134
Ex 26:21 two s. under one board, ... 134
Ex 26:21 and two s. under another board. 134
Ex 26:25 and their s. of silver, sixteen s.; 134
Ex 26:25 two s. under one board, ... 134
Ex 26:25 and two s. under another board. 134
Ex 26:32 be of gold, upon the four s. of silver. ... 134
Ex 26:37 shalt cast five s. of brass for them. 134
Ex 27:10 their twenty s. shall be of brass; 134
Ex 27:11 pillars and their twenty s. of brass; 134
Ex 27:12 their pillars ten, their s. ten. 134
Ex 27:14, 15 pillars three, and their s. three 134
Ex 27:16 shall be four, and their s. four. 134
Ex 27:17 be of silver, and their s. of brass. 134
Ex 27:18 twined linen, and their s. of brass. 134
Ex 35:11 his bars, his pillars, and his s., ... 134
Ex 35:17 his pillars, and their s., and the 134
Ex 36:24 forty s. of silver he made under the 134
Ex 36:24 tow s. under one board for his two 134
Ex 36:24 two s. under another board for his 134
Ex 36:26 And their forty s. of silver; 134
Ex 36:26 two s. under one board, ... 134
Ex 36:26 and two s. under another board. 134
Ex 36:30 and their s. were sixteen s. of silver, ... 134
Ex 36:30 under every board two s. 134
Ex 36:36 he cast for them four s. of silver. 134
Ex 36:38 but their five s. were of brass. 134
Ex 38:10 twenty, and their brasen s. twenty; 134
Ex 38:11 and their s. of brass twenty; 134
Ex 38:12 their pillars ten, and their s. ten; 134
Ex 38:14 pillars three, and their s. three. 134
Ex 38:15 pillars three, and their s. three. 134
Ex 38:17 the s. for the pillars were of brass; 134
Ex 38:19 were four, and their s. of brass four; 134
Ex 38:27 were cast the s. of the sanctuary, ... 134
Ex 38:27 sanctuary, and the s. of the vail; 134
Ex 38:27 hundred s. of the hundred talents, ... 134
Ex 38:30 s. to the door of the tabernacle 134
Ex 38:31 And the s. of the court round about, ... 134
Ex 38:31 and the s. of the court gate, and all 134
Ex 39:33 his bars, and his pillars, and his s., ... 134
Ex 39:40 of the court, his pillars, and his s. 134
Ex 40:18 fastened his s., and set up the boards ... 134
Nu 3:36 the pillars thereof, and the s. thereof, ... 134
Nu 3:37 their s., and their pins, and their 134
Nu 4:31 the pillars thereof, and s. thereof, ... 134
Nu 4:32 their s., and their pins, and their 134
Ca 5:15 of marble, set upon s. of fine gold: 134

SOCOH (so'-ko) See also SOCHOH.
Jos 15:35 and Adullam, S., and Azekah, ... 7755
Jos 15:48 Shamir, and Jattir, and S., ... 7755

SOD See also SEETHE; SODDEN.
Ge 25:29 And Jacob s. pottage: and Esau 2102
2Ch 35:13 other holy offerings s. they in pots, ... 1310

SODDEN
Ex 12:9 it raw, nor s. at all with water, ... 1310
Le 6:28 the earthen vessel wherein it is s. 1310
Le 6:28 and if it be s. in a brasen pot, it 1310
Nu 6:19 priest shall take the s. shoulder 1311
1Sa 2:15 he will not have s. flesh of thee, ... 1310
La 4:10 women have s. their own children: 1310

SODERING
Isa 41:7 saying, It is ready for the s.: 1694

SODI (so'-di)
Nu 13:10 Zebulun, Gaddiel the son of S. 5476

SODOM (sod'-om) See also SODOMA; SODOMITE.
Ge 10:19 goest, unto S., and Gomorrah, ... 5467
Ge 13:10 before the Lord destroyed S. and 5467
Ge 13:12 and pitched his tent toward S. 5467
Ge 13:13 men of S. were wicked and sinners 5467
Ge 14:2 made war with Bera king of S., ... 5467
Ge 14:8 there went out the king of S., and 5467
Ge 14:10 kings of S. and Gomorrah fled, ... 5467
Ge 14:11 they took all the goods of S. and 5467
Ge 14:12 brother's son, who dwelt in S., and 5467
Ge 14:17 the king of S. went out to meet 5467
Ge 14:21 And the king of S. said unto Abram, ... 5467
Ge 14:22 And Abram said to the king of S., I 5467
Ge 18:16 from thence, and looked toward S.: 5467
Ge 18:20 cry of S. and Gomorrah is great, ... 5467
Ge 18:22 from thence, and went toward S.: 5467
Ge 18:26 said, If I find in S. fifty righteous 5467
Ge 19:1 And there came two angels to S. at 5467
Ge 19:1 even; and Lot sat in the gate of S.: 5467
Ge 19:4 the men of S., compassed the house ... 5467
Ge 19:24 rained upon S. and upon Gomorrah 5467
Ge 19:28 he looked toward S. and Gomorrah, ... 5467
De 29:23 like the overthrow of S., and 5467
De 32:32 For their vine is of the vine of S., ... 5467
Isa 1:9 we should have been as S., and we 5467
Isa 1:10 word of the Lord, ye rulers of S.; 5467
Isa 3:9 and they declare their sin as S., ... 5467
Isa 13:19 as when God overthrew S. and 5467
Jer 23:14 they are all of them unto me as S., ... 5467
Jer 49:18 the overthrow of S. and Gomorrah 5467
Jer 50:40 As God overthrew S. and Gomorrah ... 5467
La 4:6 the punishment of the sin of S., ... 5467
Eze 16:46 right hand, is S. and her daughters. 5467
Eze 16:48 S. thy sister hath not done, she nor ... 5467
Eze 16:49 this was the iniquity of thy sister S., ... 5467
Eze 16:53 captivity of S. and her daughters, ... 5467
Eze 16:55 thy sisters, S. and her daughters, ... 5467
Eze 16:56 thy sister S. was not mentioned by 5467
Am 4:11 God overthrew S. and Gomorrah, ... 5467
Zep 2:9 Surely Moab shall be as S., and the 5467
Mt 10:15 **more tolerable for the land of S.** ... *4670*
Mt 11:23 **done in thee, had been done in S.,** .. *4670*
Mt 11:24 **more tolerable for the land of S.** ... *4670*
Mk 6:11 **shall be more tolerable for S. and** . *4670*
Lu 10:12 **some tolerable in that day for S.,** .. *4670*
Lu 17:29 **same day that Lot went out of S.** .. *4670*
2Pe 2:6 And turning the cities of S. and *4670*
Jude 7 Even as S. and Gomorrha, and the *4670*
Re 11:8 city, which spiritually is called S. *4670*

SODOMA (om'-o-mah) See also SODOM.
Ro 9:29 we had been as S., and been made *4670*

SODOMITE (sod'-om-ite) See also SODOMITES.
De 23:17 nor a s. of the sons of Israel. 6945

SODOMITES (sod'-om-ites)
1Ki 14:24 there were also s. in the land: 6945
1Ki 15:12 took away the s. out of the land, ... 6945
1Ki 22:46 And the remnant of the s., which 6945
2Ki 23:7 he brake down the houses of the s., ... 6945

SOEVER See also WHATSOEVER; WHENSOEVER; WHERESOEVER; WHITHERSOEVER; WHOMSOEVER; WHOSESOEVER; WHOSOEVER.
Le 15:9 what saddle s. he rideth upon that 834
Le 17:3 man s. there be of the house of Israel, ...
Le 22:4 What man s. of the seed of Aaron is a ......
De 12:32 What thing s. I command you, ... 834
2Sa 15:35 that what thing s. thou shalt hear out ... 834
2Sa 24:3 unto the people, how many s. they be, ...
1Ki 8:38 What prayer and suplication s. 834
2Ch 6:29 what prayer or what supplication s. 834
2Ch 19:10 And what cause s. shall come to you ......
Mk 3:28 **blasphemies wherewith s. they.** *3745,302*
Mk 6:10 **what place s. ye enter into an** *1437*
Mk 11:24 **What things s. ye desire, when** .*3745,302*
Joh 5:19 **what things s. he doeth, these** . *3745,302*
Joh 20:23 **Whose s. sins ye remit, they** *3745,302*
Joh 20:23 **whose s. sins ye retain, they** *3745,302*
Ro 8:19 that what things s. the law saith, ... *1437*

SOFT See also SOFTER.
Job 23:16 For God maketh my heart s., and 7401
Job 41:3 will he speak s. words unto thee? 7390
Ps 65:10 thou makest it s. with showers: 4127
Pr 15:1 A s. answer turneth away wrath: 7390
Pr 25:15 and a s. tongue braketh the bone. 7390
Mt 11:8 **A man clothed in s. raiment?** *3120*
Mt 11:8 **behold, they that wear s. clothing** . *3120*
Lu 7:25 **a man clothed in s. raiment?** *3120*

SOFTER
Ps 55:21 his words were s. than oil, yet 7401

SOFTLY
Ge 33:14 I will lead on s., according as the 328
Jg 4:21 and went s. unto him, and smote 3814
Ru 3:7 came s. and uncovered his feet, ... 3909
1Ki 21:27 and lay in sackcloth, and went s. 328
Isa 8:6 the waters of Shiloah that go s., ... 328
Isa 38:15 I shall go s. all my years in the ......
Ac 27:13 And when the south wind blew s., ... *5285*

SOIL
Eze 17:8 It was planted in a good s. by 7704

SOJOURN See also SOJOURNED; SOJOURNER; SOJOURNETH; SOJOURNING.
Ge 12:19 went down into Egypt to s. there; 1481
Ge 19:9 This one fellow came in to s., and 1481
Ge 26:3 S. in this land, and I will be with 1481
Ge 47:4 For to s. in the land are we come; 1481
Ex 12:48 when a stranger shall s. with thee, ... 1481
Le 17:8 the strangers which s. among you, ... 1481
Le 17:10, 13 the strangers that s. among you, ... 1481
Le 19:33 And if a stranger s. wth thee in 1481
Le 20:2 or of the strangers that s. in Israel, ... 1481
Le 25:45 the strangers that do s. among you, ... 1481
Nu 9:14 if a stranger shall s. among you, ... 1481
Nu 15:14 And if a stranger s. with you, or 1481
Jg 17:8 to s. where he could find a place: 1481
Jg 17:9 I go to s. where I may find a place. 1481
Ru 1:1 went to s. in the country of Moab. 1481
1Ki 17:20 evil upon the widow with whom I s., ... 1481
2Ki 8:1 and s. wheresoever thou canst s.: 1481
Ps 120:5 Woe is me, that I s. in Mesech, that .. 1481
Isa 23:7 feet shall carry her afar off to s. 1481
Isa 52:4 aforetime into Egypt to s. there; 1481
Jer 42:15 enter into Egypt, and go to s. there; .. 1481
Jer 42:17 faces to go into Egypt to s. there; 1481
Jer 42:22 whither ye desire to go and to s. 1481
Jer 43:2 say, Go not into Egypt to s. there: 1481
Jer 44:12, 14,28 the land of Egypt to s. there, ... 1481
La 4:15 They shall no more s. there. 1481
Eze 20:38 out of the country where they s. 4033
Eze 47:22 to the strangers that s. among you, ... 1481
Ac 7:6 should s. in a strange land; *1510,3941*

SOJOURNED
Ge 20:1 Kadesh and Shur, and s. in Gerar. 1481
Ge 21:23 to the land wherein thou hast s. 1481
Ge 21:34 And Abraham s. in the Philistines' 1481
Ge 32:4 I have s. with Laban, and stayed 1481
Ge 35:27 where Abraham and Isaac s. 1481
De 18:6 gates out of all Israel, where he s., ... 1481
De 26:5 Egypt, and s. there with a few, ... 1481
Jg 17:7 who was a Levite, and he s. there. 1481
Jg 19:16 and he s. in Gibeah: but the men 1481
2Ki 8:2 and s. in the land of the Philistines 1481
Ps 105:23 and Jacob s. in the land of Ham. 1481
Heb 11:9 faith he s. in the land of promise, ... *3939*

SOJOURNER See also SOJOURNERS.
Ge 23:4 I am a stranger and a s. with you: 8453
Le 22:10 a s. of the priest, or an hired 8453
Le 25:35 though he be a stranger, or a s.; 8453
Le 25:40 But as an hired servant, and as a s., ... 8453
Le 25:47 a s. or stranger wax rich by thee, ... 1616
Le 25:47 sell himself unto the stranger or s. 8453
Nu 35:15 and for the s. among them: that 8453
Ps 39:12 and a s., as all my fathers were. 8453

SOJOURNERS
Le 25:23 ye are strangers and s. with me. 8453
2Sa 4:3 and were s. there until this day.) 1481
1Ch 29:15 are strangers before thee, and s., ... 8453

SOJOURNETH
Ex 3:22 of her that s. in her house, jewels 1481
Ex 12:49 unto the stranger that s. among 1481
Le 16:29 or a stranger that s. among you: 1481
Le 17:12 any stranger that s. among you eat 1481
Le 18:26 nor any stranger that s. among you: ... 1481
Le 25:6 for thy stranger that s. with thee, ... 1481
Nu 15:15 for the stranger that s. with you, ... 1481
Nu 15:16 for the stranger that s. with you. 1481
Nu 15:26 the stranger that s. among them; 1481
Nu 15:29 the stranger that s. among them. 1481
Nu 19:10 the stranger that s. among them, ... 1481
Jos 20:9 the stranger that s. among them, ... 1481
Ezr 1:4 remaineth in any place where he s., ... 1481
Eze 14:7 or of the stranger that s. in Israel, ... 1481
Eze 47:23 that in what tribe the stranger s., ... 1481

SOJOURNING
Ex 12:40 the s. of the children of Israel, ... 4186
Jg 19:1 a certain Levite s. on the side of 1481
1Pe 1:17 the time of your s. here in fear: *3940*

SOLACE
Pr 7:18 let us s. ourselves with loves. 5965

SOLD
Ge 25:33 he s. his birthright unto Jacob. 4876
Ge 31:15 for he hath s. us, and hath quite 4876
Ge 37:28 and s. Joseph to the Ishmeelites for 4876

Ge 37:36 Midianites s. him into Egypt unto....... 4876
Ge 41:56 and s. unto the Egyptians; and.......... 7666
Ge 42:6 he it was that s. to all the people....... 7666
Ge 45:4 brother, whom ye s. into Egypt......... 4376
Ge 45:5 yourselves, that ye s. me hither:......... 4376
Ge 47:20 Egyptians s. every man his field,........ 4376
Ge 47:22 wherefore they s. not their lands........ 4376
Ex 22:3 then he shall be s. for his theft.......... 4376
Le 25:23 The land shall not be s. for ever:....... 4376
Le 25:25 hath s. away...of his possession,........ 4376
Le 25:25 redeem that which his brother s......... 4465
Le 25:27 unto the man to whom he s. it;......... 4376
Le 25:28 that which is s. shall remain in.......... 4465
Le 25:29 within a whole year after it is s.;........ 4465
Le 25:33 then the house that was s., and the.... 4465
Le 25:34 of their cities may not be s.;............ 4376
Le 25:39 waxen poor, and be s. unto thee;....... 4376
Le 25:42 they shall not be s. as bondmen......... 4376
Le 25:48 After...he is s. he may be redeemed... 4376
Le 25:50 from the year that he was s. to him.... 4376
Le 27:20 he have s. the field to another man,.... 4376
Le 27:27 be s. according to thy estimation........ 4376
Le 27:28 possession, shall be s. or redeemed:... 4376
De 15:12 Hebrew woman, be s. unto thee,....... 4376
De 28:68 ye shall be s. unto your enemies....... 4376
De 32:30 except their Rock had s. them, and.... 4376
Jg 2:14 he s. them into the hands of their...... 4376
Jg 3:8 and he s. them into the hand of......... 4376
Jg 4:2 Lord s. them into the hand of Jabin...... 4376
Jg 10:7 and he s. them into the hands of the.... 4376
1Sa 12:9 he s. them into the hand of Sisera,..... 4376
1Ki 21:20 hast s. thyself to work evil in the....... 4376
2Ki 6:25 ass's head was s. for fourscore pieces.......
2Ki 7:1 of fine flour be s. for a shekel,...............
2Ki 7:16 of fine flour was s. for a shekel,..............
2Ki 17:17 and s. themselves to do evil in the..... 4376
Ne 5:8 which were s. unto the heathen;........ 4376
Ne 5:8 or shall they be s. unto us?............... 4376
Ne 13:15 in the day wherein they s. victuals...... 4376
Ne 13:16 s. on the sabbath unto the children..... 4376
Es 7:4 For we are s., I and my people, to..... 4376
Es 7:4 if we had been s. for bondmen and..... 4376
Ps 105:17 Joseph, who was s. for a servant:...... 4376
Isa 50:1 creditors is it to whom I have s. you?. 4376
Isa 50:1 iniquites have ye s. yourselves,.......... 4376
Isa 52:3 Ye have s. yourselves for nought;...... 4376
Jer 34:14 which hath been s. unto thee;........... 4376
La 5:4 money; our wood is s. unto us..... 935,4242
Eze 7:13 shall not return to that which is s.,..... 4465
Jos 3:3 s. a girl for wine, that they might....... 4376
Jos 3:6 have ye s. unto the Grecians,............ 4376
Jos 3:7 the place whither ye have s. them,..... 4376
Am 2:6 they s. the righteous for silver, and...... 4376
Mt 10:29 **not two sparrows s. for a farthing.** *4453*
Mt 13:46 **went and s. all that he had, and....** *4097*
Mt 18:25 **his lord commanded him to be s....** *4097*
Mt 21:12 that s. and bought in the temple,........ *4453*
Mt 21:12 the seats of them that s. doves,......... *4453*
Mt 26:9 ointment might have been s. for........... *4097*
Mk 11:15 that s. and bought in the temple,........ *4453*
Mk 11:15 and the seats of them that s. doves;... *4453*
Mk 14:5 s. for more than three hundred.......... *4097*
Lu 12:6 **five sparrows s. for two farthings,..** *4453*
Lu 17:28 **they bought, they s., they planted.** *4453*
Lu 19:45 to cast out them that s. therein, and... *4453*
Joh 2:14 in the temple those that s. oxen and... *4453*
Joh 2:16 said unto them that s. doves, **Take....** *4453*
Joh 12:5 this ointment s. for three hundred...... *4097*
Ac 2:45 And s. their possessions and goods,.... *4097*
Ac 4:34 of lands or houses s. them, and......... *4458*
Ac 4:34 prices of the things that were s........ *4097*
Ac 4:37 Having land, s. it, and brought the...... *4453*
Ac 5:1 Sapphira his wife, s. a possession,...... *4453*
Ac 5:4 and after it was s., was it not in........ *4097*
Ac 5:8 whether ye s. the land for so much?..... *591*
Ac 7:9 with envy, s. Joseph into Egypt:.......... *591*
Ro 7:14 but I am carnal, s. under sin............ *4097*
1Co 10:25 Whatsoever is s. in the shambles....... *4453*
Heb 12:16 morsel of meat s. his birthright........... *591*

SOLDERING See SODERING.

SOLDIER See also SOLDIERS.
Joh 19:23 made four parts, to every s. a part;.... *4757*
Ac 10:7 a devout s. of them that waited on..... *4757*
Ac 28:16 by himself with a s. that kept him...... *4757*
2Ti 2:3 as a good s. of Jesus Christ............. *4757*
2Ti 2:4 who hath chosen him to be a s......... *4758*

SOLDIERS See also FELLOWSOLDIERS; SOLDIERS'.
1Ch 7:4 fathers, were bands of s. for war,...... 6635
1Ch 7:11 thousand and two hundred s.,.................
2ch 25:13 the s. of the army which Amaziah....... 1121
Ezr 8:22 to require of the king a band of s....... 2428
Isa 15:4 the armed s. of Moab...cry out;......... 2502
Mt 8:9 authority, having s. under me:........... *4757*
Mt 27:27 the s. of the governor took Jesus....... *4757*
Mt 27:27 unto him the whole band of s..................
Mt 28:12 they gave large money unto the s.,...... *4757*
Mk 15:16 the s. led him away into the hall,....... *4757*
Lu 3:14 the s. likewise demanded of him,........ *4754*
Lu 7:8 authority, having under me s.,........... *4757*
Lu 23:36 the s. also mocked him, coming to...... *4757*
Joh 19:2 the s. platted a crown of thorns,....... *4757*
Joh 19:23 s., when they had crucified Jesus,...... *4757*
Joh 19:24 These things therefore the s. did....... *4757*
Joh 19:32 Then came the s., and brake the........ *4757*
Joh 19:34 one of the s. with a spear pierced...... *4757*
Ac 12:4 him to four quaternions of s. to.......... *4757*
Ac 12:6 Peter was sleeping between two s.,.... *4757*
Ac 12:18 was no small stir among the s.,.......... *4757*
Ac 21:32 Who immediately took s. and............ *4757*
Ac 21:32 saw the chief captain and the s.,....... *4757*
Ac 21:35 that he was borne of the s. **for the....** *4757*
Ac 23:10 commanded the s. to go down, and..... *4753*
Ac 23:23 Make ready two hundred s. to go to.... *4757*
Ac 23:31 the s., as it was commanded them,..... *4757*
Ac 27:31 said to the centurion and to the s.,..... *4757*
Ac 27:32 Then the s. cut off the ropes of the.... *4757*

SOLDIERS'
Ac 27:42 And the s. counsel was to kill the....... *4757*

SOLE See also SOLES.
Ge 8:9 no rest for the s. of her foot,............ 3709
De 28:35 from the s. of thy foot unto the top.... 3709
De 28:56 to set the s. of her foot upon the....... 3709
De 28:65 shall the s. of thy foot have rest:....... 3709
Jos 1:3 the s. of your foot shall tread upon,.... 3709
2Sa 14:25 from the s. of his foot even to the...... 3709
2Ki 19:24 with the s. of my feet have I dried..... 3709
Job 2:7 the s. of his foot unto his crown........ 3709
Isa 1:6 s. of the foot even unto the head....... 3709
Isa 37:25 with the s. of my feet have I dried..... 3709
Eze 1:7 s. of their feet was like the s. of a..... 3709

SOLEMN
Le 23:36 it is a s. assembly; and ye shall......... 6116
Nu 10:10 gladness, and in your s. days,............ 4150
Nu 15:3 in your s. feasts, to make a sweet...... 4150
Nu 29:35 day ye shall have a s. assembly:......... 6116
De 16:8 seventh day shall be a s. assembly..... 6116
De 16:15 thou keep a s. feast unto the Lord..... 2287
2Ki 10:20 Proclaim a s. assembly for Baal......... 6116
2Ch 2:4 on the s. easts of the Lord your........ 4150
2Ch 7:9 day they made a s. assembly:........... 6116
2Ch 8:13 new moons, and on the s. feasts,....... 4150
Ne 8:18 the eighth day was a s. assembly,....... 6116
Ps 81:3 appointed, on our s. feast day........... 2282
Ps 92:3 upon the harp with a s. sound..................
Isa 1:13 it is iniquity, even the s. meeting........ 6116
La 1:4 because none come to the s. feasts:... 4150
La 2:6 Lord hath caused the s. feasts and..... 4150
La 2:7 Lord, as in the day of a s. feast......... 4150
La 2:22 called as in a s. day my terrors.......... 4150
Eze 36:38 of Jerusalem in her s. feasts; so......... 4150
Eze 46:9 before the Lord in the s. feasts,........ 4150
Ho 2:11 her sabbaths, and all her s. feasts...... 4150
Ho 9:5 What will ye do in the s. day, and...... 4150
Ho 12:9 as in the days of the s. feast............. 4150
Joe 1:14 ye a fast, call a s. assembly,.............. 6116
Joe 2:15 sanctify a fast, call a s. assembly:....... 6116
Am 5:21 not smell in your s. assemblies.......... 6116
Na 1:15 keep thy s. feasts, perform thy.......... 2282
Zep 3:18 are sorrowful for the s. assembly,...... 4150
Mal 2:3 even the dung of your s. feasts;......... 2282

SOLEMNITIES
Isa 33:20 Look upon Zion, the city of our s....... 4150
Eze 45:17 in all s. of the house of Israel:........... 4150
Eze 46:11 in the s. the meat offering shall be..... 4150

SOLEMNITY See also SOLEMNITITES.
De 31:10 in the s. of the year of release,......... 4150
Isa 30:29 the night when a holy s. is kept;........ 2282

SOLEMNLY
Ge 43:3 The man did s. protest unto us,......... 5749
1Sa 8:9 howbeit yet protest s. unto them,...... 5749

SOLES
De 11:24 s. of your feet shall tread shall be...... 3709
Jos 3:13 the s. of the feet of the priests that.... 3709
Jos 4:18 s. of the priests' feet were lifted......... 3709
1Ki 5:3 put them under the s. of his feet........ 3709
Isa 60:14 down at the s. of thy feet; and.......... 3709
Eze 43:7 and the place of the s. of my feet,...... 3709
Mal 4:3 be ashes under the s. of your feet...... 3709

SOLITARILY
Mic 7:14 which dwell s. in the wood, in he......... 910

SOLITARY
Job 3:7 Lo, let that night be s., let no........... 1565
Job 30:3 For want and famine they were s.;...... 1565
Ps 68:6 God setteth the s. in families: he....... 3173
Ps 107:4 in the wilderness in a s. way;............ 3452
Isa 35:1 s. place shall be glad for them;.......... 6723
La 1:1 How doth the city sit s., that was........ 910
Mk 1:35 out, and departed into a s. place,....... *2048*

SOLOMON (sol'-o-mun) See also JEDIDIAH; SOLOMAN'S.
2Sa 5:14 Shobab, and Nathan, and S.,............. 8010
2Sa 12:24 a son, and he called his name S.:....... 8010
1Ki 1:10 and S. his brother, he called not........ 8010
1Ki 1:11 unto Bath-sheba the mother of S.,....... 8010
1Ki 1:12 own life, and the life of thy son S....... 8010
1Ki 1:13, 17 S. thy son shall reign after me,..... 8010
1Ki 1:19 S. thy servant hath he not called........ 8010
1Ki 1:21 I and my son S. shall be counted........ 8010
1Ki 1:26 thy servant S., hath he not called....... 8010
1Ki 1:30 S. thy son shall reign after me,.......... 8010
1Ki 1:33 S. my son to ride upon mine own....... 8010
1Ki 1:34 and say, God save king S................ 8010
1Ki 1:37 even so be he with S., and make....... 8010
1Ki 1:38 and caused S. to ride upon king......... 8010
1Ki 1:39 of the tabernacle, and anointed S........ 8010
1Ki 1:39 the people said, God save king S....... 8010
1Ki 1:43 king David hath made S. king............ 8010
1Ki 1:46 also S. sitteth on the throne of the..... 8010
1Ki 1:47 name of S. better than thy name,....... 8010
1Ki 1:50 And Adonijah feared because of S.,..... 8010
1Ki 1:51 And it was told S., saying, Behold,..... 8010
1Ki 1:51 Adonijah feareth king S.: for, lo,........ 8010
1Ki 1:51 Let king S. swear unto me to day...... 8010
1Ki 1:52 S. said, If he will shew himself a........ 8010
1Ki 1:53 So king S. sent, and they brought...... 8010
1Ki 1:53 and bowed himself to king S.:............ 8010
1Ki 1:53 and S. said unto him, Go to thine....... 8010
1Ki 2:1 and he charged S. his son, saying,...... 8010
1Ki 2:12 sat S. upon the throne of David.......... 8010
1Ki 2:13 to Bath-sheba the mother of S............ 8010
1Ki 2:17 Speak, I pray thee, unto S. the king,.. 8010
1Ki 2:19 Bath-sheba...went unto king S.,.......... 8010
1Ki 2:22 king S. answered and said unto his..... 8010
1Ki 2:23 Then king S. sware by the Lord,........ 8010
1Ki 2:25 And king S. sent by the hand of......... 8010
1Ki 2:27 S. thrust out Abiathar from being........ 8010
1Ki 2:29 it was told king S. that Joab was........ 8010
1Ki 2:29 Then S. sent Benaiah the son of......... 8010
1Ki 2:41 And it was told S. that Shimei had...... 8010
1Ki 2:45 king S. shall be blessed, and the........ 8010
1Ki 2:46 was established in the hand of S........ 8010
1Ki 3:1 And S. made a affinity with Pharaoh.... 8010
1Ki 3:3 S. loved the Lord, walking in the........ 8010
1Ki 3:4 burnt offerings, did S. offer upon......... 8010
1Ki 3:5 Lord appeared t S. in a dream by........ 8010
1Ki 3:6 S. said, Thou hast shewed unto.......... 8010
1Ki 3:10 Lord, that S. had asked this thing........ 8010
1Ki 3:15 And S. awoke, and behold, it was a..... 8010
1Ki 4:1 king S. was king over all Israel.......... 8010
1Ki 4:7 And S. had twelve officers over all...... 8010
1Ki 4:11 had Taphath the daughter of S. to....... 8010
1Ki 4:15 Basmath the daughter of S. to........... 8010
1Ki 4:21 S. reigned over all kingdoms from....... 8010
1Ki 4:21 served S. all the days of his life......... 8010
1Ki 4:25 to Beer-sheba, all the days of S.......... 8010
1Ki 4:26 S. had forty thousand stalls of............ 8010
1Ki 4:27 provided victual for king S., and.......... 8010
1Ki 4:29 S. wisdom and understanding............. 8010
1Ki 4:34 all people to hear the wisdom of S.,..... 8010
1Ki 5:1 of Tyre sent his servants unto S.;....... 8010
1Ki 5:2 And S. sent to Hiram, saying,............. 8010
1Ki 5:7 when Hiram heard the words of S.,...... 8010
1Ki 5:8 Hiram sent to S., saying, I have......... 8010
1Ki 5:10 So Hiram gave S. cedar trees and....... 8010
1Ki 5:11 S. gave Hiram twenty thousand.......... 8010
1Ki 5:11 gave S. to Hiram year by year........... 8010

1Ki 5:12 the Lord gave S. wisdom, as he 8010
1Ki 5:12 was peace between Hiram and S.; 8010
1Ki 5:13 S. raised a levy out of all Israel; 8010
1Ki 5:15 And S. had threescore and ten 8010
1Ki 6:2 house which king S. built for the........ 8010
1Ki 6:11 the word of the Lord came to S.,........ 8010
1Ki 6:14 So S. built the house, and finished...... 8010
1Ki 6:21 S. overlaid the house within with........ 8010
1Ki 7:1 But s. was building his own house 8010
1Ki 7:8 S. made also an house for Pharaoh's... 8010
1Ki 7:13 king S. sent and fetched Hiram out..... 8010
1Ki 7:14 he came to king S., and wrought all.... 8010
1Ki 7:40 work that he made king S. for the...... 8010
1Ki 7:45 which Hiram made to king S. for........ 8010
1Ki 7:47 S. left all the vessels unweighed, ... 8010
1Ki 7:48 And S. made all the vessels that 8010
1Ki 7:51 all the work that king S. made for 8010
1Ki 7:51 And S. brought in the things which..... 8010
1Ki 8:1 S. assembled the elders of Israel,....... 8010
1Ki 8:1 Israel, unto king S. in Jerusalem, ... 8010
1Ki 8:2 assembled themselves unto king S...... 8010
1Ki 8:5 king s., and all the congregation of 8010
1Ki 8:12 Then spake S., The Lord said that..... 8010
1Ki 8:22 S. stood before the altar of the Lord... 8010
1Ki 8:54 S. had made an end of praying all...... 8010
1Ki 8:63 And S. offered a sacrifice of peace...... 8010
1Ki 8:65 at that time S. held a feast, and all..... 8010
1Ki 9:1 when S. had finished the building........ 8010
1Ki 9:2 appeared to S. the second time,......... 8010
1Ki 9:10 when S. had built the two houses,....... 8010
1Ki 9:11 king of Tyre had furnished S. with...... 8010
1Ki 9:11 king S. gave Hiram twenty cities......... 8010
1Ki 9:12 the cities which S. had given him; 8010
1Ki 9:15 of the levy which king S. raised; 8010
1Ki 9:17 S. built Gezer, and Beth-horon the..... 8010
1Ki 9:19 all the cities of store that S. had, ... 8010
1Ki 9:19 and that which S. desired to build....... 8010
1Ki 9:21 upon those did S. levy a tribute of....... 8010
1Ki 9:22 of Israel did S. make no bondmen: 8010
1Ki 9:24 house which S. had built for her:..............
1Ki 9:25 a year did S. offer burnt offerings....... 8010
1Ki 9:26 king S. made a navy of ships in 8010
1Ki 9:27 of the sea, with the servants of S.. 8010
1Ki 9:28 talents, and brought it to king S........ 8010
1Ki 10:1 of Sheba heard of the fame of S......... 8010
1Ki 10:2 and when she was come to S., she..... 8010
1Ki 10:3 S. told her all her questions: there 8010
1Ki 10:10 the queen of Sheba gave to king S.. ... 8010
1Ki 10:13 S. gave unto the queen of Sheba all.... 8010
1Ki 10:13 S. gave her of his royal bounty.......... 8010
1Ki 10:14 of gold that came to S. in one year..... 8010
1Ki 10:16 king S. made two hundred targets 8010
1Ki 10:21 accounted of in the days of S.. 8010
1Ki 10:23 So king S. exceeded all the kings 8010
1Ki 10:24 all the earth sought to S., to hear 8010
1Ki 10:26 S. gathered together chariots and........ 8010
1Ki 10:28 S. had horses brought out of Egypt, ... 8010
1Ki 11:1 king S. loved many strange women, ... 8010
1Ki 11:2 gods: S. clave unto these in love......... 8010
1Ki 11:4 when S. was old, that his wives......... 8010
1Ki 11:5 S. went after Ashtoreth the goddess... 8010
1Ki 11:6 S. did evil in the sight of the Lord,...... 8010
1Ki 11:7 S. build an high place for Chemosh, ... 8010
1Ki 11:9 Lord was angry with S., because 8010
1Ki 11:11 the Lord said unto S., Forasmuch 8010
1Ki 11:14 stirred up an adversary unto S.,......... 8010
1Ki 11:25 to Israel all the days of S., ... 8010
1Ki 11:27 S. built Millo, and repaired the 8010
1Ki 11:28 S. seeing the young man that he......... 8010
1Ki 11:31 the kingdom out of the hand of S., ... 8010
1Ki 11:40 S. sought...to kill Jeroboam. And........ 8010
1Ki 11:40 was in Egypt until the death of S. 8010
1Ki 11:41 And the rest of the acts of S., and..... 8010
1Ki 11:41 in the book of the acts of S.? 8010
1Ki 11:42 time that S. reigned in Jerusalem 8010
1Ki 11:43 S. slept with his fathers, and was....... 8010
1Ki 12:2 fled from the presence of king S., ... 8010
1Ki 12:6 men, that stood before S. his father.... 8010
1Ki 12:21 again to Rehoboam the son of S.......... 8010
1Ki 12:23 unto Rehoboam, the son of S., ... 8010
1Ki 14:21 Rehoboam the son of S. reigned in..... 8010
1Ki 14:26 shields of gold which S. had made. 8010
2Ki 21:7 said to David, and to S. his son, ... 8010
2Ki 23:13 S. the king of Israel had builded......... 8010
2Ki 24:13 the vessels of gold which S. king of.... 8010
2Ki 25:16 bases which S. had made for the........ 8010
1Ch 3:5 Shobab, and Nathan, and S., four, ... 8010
1Ch 6:10 temple that S. built in Jerusalem.) 8010
1Ch 6:32 S. had built the house of the Lord...... 8010
1Ch 14:4 and Shobab, Nathan, and S., ... 8010
1Ch 18:8 wherewith S. made the brasen sea, ... 8010
1Ch 22:5 S. my son is young and tender, and.... 8010
1Ch 22:6 Then he called for S. his son, and...... 8010
1Ch 22:7 David said to S., My son, as for me, .. 8010
1Ch 22:9 or his name shall be S., and I will 8010
1Ch 22:17 princes of Israel to help S. his son, ... 8010
1Ch 23:1 made S. his son king over Israel. 8010
1Ch 28:5 chosen S. my son to sit upon the....... 8010
1Ch 28:6 S. thy son, he shall build my house 8010
1Ch 28:9 S. my son, know thou the God of 8010
1Ch 28:11 Then David gave to S. his son the 8010
1Ch 28:20 David said to S. his son, Be strong 8010
1Ch 29:1 S. my son, whom alone God hath....... 8010
1Ch 29:19 give unto S. my son a perfect heart,... 8010
1Ch 29:22 they made S. the son of David king.... 8010
1Ch 29:23 S. sat on the throne of the Lord as 8010
1Ch 29:24 submitted themselves unto S. the....... 8010
1Ch 29:25 the Lord magnified S. exceedingly 8010
1Ch 29:28 and S. his son reigned in his stead. 8010
2Ch 1:1 And S....was strengthened in his........ 8010
2Ch 1:2 Then S. spake unto all Israel, to the... 8010
2Ch 1:3 So S., and all the congregation 8010
2Ch 1:5 and S. and the congregation sought...... 8010
2Ch 1:6 S. went up thither to the brasen........ 8010
2Ch 1:7 that night did God appear unto S.,...... 8010
2Ch 1:8 And S. said unto god, Thou hast........ 8010
2Ch 1:11 And God said to S., Because this 8010
2Ch 1:13 Then S. came from his journey to 8010
2Ch 1:14 And S. gathered chariots and............ 8010
2Ch 1:16 S. had horses brought out of Egypt, ... 8010
2Ch 2:1 S. determined to build an house for 8010
2Ch 2:2 And S. told out threescore and ten...... 8010
2Ch 2:3 S. sent to Huram the king of Tyre, ... 8010
2Ch 2:11 in writing, which he sent to S.,.......... 8010
2Ch 2:17 S. numbered all the strangers that...... 8010
2Ch 3:1 S. began to build the house of the...... 8010
2Ch 3:3 things wherein S. was instructed........ 8010
2Ch 4:11 that he was to make for king S. for.... 8010
2Ch 4:16 Huram his father make to king S....... 8010
2Ch 4:18 S. made all the vessels in great 8010
2Ch 4:19 S. made all the vessels that were....... 8010
2Ch 5:1 all the work that S. made for the 8010
2Ch 5:1 and S. brought in all the things that.... 8010
2Ch 5:2 S. assembled the elders of Israel,....... 8010
2Ch 5:6 king S., and all the congregation 8010
2Ch 6:1 Then said S. The Lord hath said......... 8010
2Ch 6:13 For S. had made a brasen scaffold, ... 8010
2Ch 7:1 S. had made an end of praying,.......... 8010
2Ch 7:5 S. offered a sacrifice of twenty and..... 8010
2Ch 7:7 Moreover S. hallowed the middle of.... 8010
2Ch 7:7 the brasen altar which S. had made 8010
2Ch 7:8 time S. kept the feast seven days 8010
2Ch 7:10 had shewed unto David, and to S., ... 8010
2Ch 7:11 S. finished the house of the Lord, ... 8010
2Ch 7:12 the Lord appeared to S. by night, ... 8010
2Ch 8:1 wherin S. had built the house of......... 8010
2Ch 8:2 which Huram had restored to S., ... 8010
2Ch 8:2 S. built them, and caused the 8010
2Ch 8:3 And S. went to Hamath-zobah, and..... 8010
2Ch 8:6 and all the store cities that S. had, ... 8010
2Ch 8:6 and all that S. desired to build in....... 8010
2Ch 8:8 them did S. make to pay tribute......... 8010
2Ch 8:9 of Israel did S. make no servants 8010
2Ch 8:11 And S. brought up the daughter of 8010
2Ch 8:12 S. offered burnt offerings unto the...... 8010
2Ch 8:16 work of S. was prepared unto the 8010
2Ch 8:17 Then went S. to Ezion-geber, and...... 8010
2Ch 8:18 with the servants of S. to Ophir,........ 8010
2Ch 8:18 gold, and brought them to king S.. 8010
2Ch 9:1 of Sheba heard of the fame of S.,....... 8010
2Ch 9:1 she came to prove S. with hard......... 8010
2Ch 9:1 and when she was come to S., she...... 8010
2Ch 9:2 And S. told her all her questions:....... 8010
2Ch 9:2 nothing hid from S. which he told........ 8010
2Ch 9:3 of Sheba had seen the wisdom of S., .. 8010
2Ch 9:9 as the queen of Sheba gave king S.. ... 8010
2Ch 9:10 servants of S., which brought gold...... 8010
2Ch 9:12 S. gave to the queen of Sheba all....... 8010
2Ch 9:13 weight of gold that came to S. in 8010
2Ch 9:14 brought gold and silver to S.. 8010
2Ch 9:15 king S. made two hundred targets 8010
2Ch 9:20 drinking vessels of king S. were of..... 8010
2Ch 9:20 accounted of in the days of S.. 8010
2Ch 9:22 S. passed all the kings of the earth..... 8010
2Ch 9:23 kings...sought the presence of S., ... 8010
2Ch 9:25 And S. had four thousand stalls for..... 8010
2Ch 9:28 they brought unto s. horses out of...... 8010
2Ch 9:29 Now the rest of the acts of S., first.... 8010
2Ch 9:30 S. reigned in Jerusalem over all 8010
2Ch 9:31 And S. slept with his fathers, and....... 8010
2Ch 10:2 he had fled from the presence of S..... 8010
2Ch 10:6 stood before S. his father while he 8010
2Ch 11:3 unto Rehoboam the son of S., king..... 8010
2Ch 11:17 Rehoboam the son of S. strong,......... 8010
2Ch 11:17 walked in the way of David and S........ 8010
2Ch 12:9 shields of gold which s. had made........ 8010
2Ch 13:6 the servant of S. the son of David,..... 8010
2Ch 13:7 against Rehobaom the son of S., ... 8010
2Ch 30:26 for since the time of S. the son of...... 8010
2Ch 33:7 had said to Daivd and to S. his son,.... 8010
2Ch 35:3 house which s. the son of David......... 8010
2Ch 35:4 to the writing of S. his son. 8010
Ne 12:45 commandment of David, and of S. 8010
Ne 13:26 Did not S. king of Israel sin by.......... 8010
Ps 72:*title* A Psalm for S. 8010
Ps 127:*title* A song of degrees for S.. 8010
Pr 1:1 The proverbs of S. the son of David,.. 8010
Pr 10:1 proverbs of S.. a wise son maketh 8010
Ca *general* *title* The Song of S.......................... 7892
Pr 25:1 These area also proverbs of S., which. 8010
Ca 1:5 of Kedar, as the curtains of S........... 8010
Ca 3:9 King S. made himself a chariot of........ 8010
Ca 3:11 and behold king S. with the crown...... 8010
Ca 8:11 S. had a vineyard at Baal-hamon; 8010
Ca 8:12 thou, O S., must have a thousand, ... 8010
Jer 52:20 king S. had made in the house of 8010
Mt 1:6 and David the king begat S. of her *4672*
Mt 1:7 S. begat Roboam; and Roboam *4672*
Mt 6:29 **S. in all his glory was not arrayed** .*4672*
Mt 12:42 **the earth to hear the wisdom of S.;** *4672*
Mt 12:42 **behold, a greater than S. is here.** .. *4672*
Lu 11:31 **the earth to hear he wisdom of S.;** .*4672*
Lu 11:31 **behold, a greater than S. is here.** .. *4672*
Lu 12:27 **S. in all his glory was not arrayed** .*4672*
Ac 7:47 But S. built him an house. *4672*

SOLOMON'S (sol'-o-muns)
1Ki 4:22 And S. provision for one day was....... 8010
1Ki 4:27 all that came unto king S. table,........ 8010
1Ki 4:30 S. wisdom excelled the wisodm of........ 8010
1Ki 5:16 Beside the chief of S. officers which ... 8010
1Ki 5:18 S. builders, and Hiram's builders........ 8010
1Ki 6:1 fourth year of S. reign over Israel, ... 8010
1Ki 9:1 S. desire which he was pleased to....... 8010
1Ki 9:16 present unto his daughter, S. wife...... 8010
1Ki 9:23 the officers that were over S. work, ... 8010
1Ki 10:4 of Sheba had seen all S. wisdom, ... 8010
1Ki 10:21 all king S. drinking vessels were of..... 8010
1Ki 11:26 S. servant, whose mother's name......... 8010
1Ch 3:10 S. son was Rehoboam, Abia his son,... 8010
2Ch 7:11 all that came into S. heart to make..... 8010
2Ch 8:10 were the chief of king S. officers,....... 8010
Ezr 2:55 The children of S. servants: the......... 8010
Ezr 2:58 and the children of S. servants, ... 8010
Ne 7:57 The children of S. servants: the......... 8010
Ne 7:60 and the children of S. servants, ... 8010
Ne 11:3 and the children of S. servants. 8010
Ca 1:1 The son of songs, which is S.............. 8010
Ca 3:7 Behold his bed, which is S.;.............. 8010
Joh 10:23 walked in the temple in S. porch. *4672*
Ac 3:11 them in the porch that is called S.,..... *4672*
Ac 5:12 all with one accord in S. porch............ *4672*

SOLVE See DISSOLVE; RESOLVED.

SOME See also BURDENSOME; DELIGHTSOME; LOATHSOME; NOISOME; SOMEBODY; SOMETHING; SOMETIME; SOMEWHAT; WEARISOME; WHOLESOME.
Ge 19:19 lest s. evil take me, and I die:....................
Ge 27:3 to the field, and take me s. venison;.........
Ge 30:35 and every one that had s. white in it,........
Ge 33:15 Let me . . . leave with thee s. of the folk..
Ge 37:20 slay him, and cast him into s. pit, ... 259
Ge 37:20 S. evil beast hath devoured him: ....
Ge 47:2 he took s. of his brethren, even......... 7097
Ex 16:17 did so, and gahtered, s. more, s. less. ......
Ex 16:20 but s. of them left of it until the.......... 582
Ex 16:27 went out s. of the people on the.............
Ex 30:36 thou shalt beat s. of it very small, ...
Le 4:7 the priest shall put s. of the blood............
Le 4:17 shall dip his finger in s. of the blood,.........
Le 4:18 put s. of the blood upon the horns............

Le 14:14 take s. of the blood of the trespass..........
Le 14:15 the priest shall take s. of the log of oil, ...
Le 14:25 the priest shall take s. of the blood of.......
Le 14:27 with his right finger s. of the oil that.........
Le 25:25 hath sold away s. of his possession,.........
Le 27:16 s. part of a field of his possession............
Nu 5:20 s. man have lain with thee beside............
Nu 21:1 Israel, and took s. of them prisoners.........
Nu 27:20 shalt put s. of thine honour upon him, ...
Nu 31:3 Arm s. of yourselves unto the war, ... 582
De 24:1 hath found s. uncleanness in her:........ 1697
Jos 8:22 s. on this side, and s. on that side: 428
Jg 21:13 whole congregation sent s. to speak..........
Ru 2:16 let fall also s. of the handfuls of...............
1Sa 8:11 and s. shall run before his chariots............
1Sa 13:7 s. of the Hebrews went over Jordan to......
1Sa 24:10 and s. bade me ill thee: but mine eye........
1Sa 27:5 let them give me a place in s. town...... 259
2Sa 11:17 and there fell s. of the people of the.........
2Sa 11:24 and s. of the king's servants be dead, ...
2Sa 17:9 he is hid now in s. pit, or in s. other.... 259
2Sa 17:9 s. of them be overthrown at the first,... 259
2Sa 17:12 shall we come upon him in s. place 259
1Ki 14:13 in him there is found s. good thing............
2Ki 2:16 and cast him upon s. mountain, ... 259
2Ki 2:16 mountain, or unto s. valley................ 259
2Ki 5:13 had bid thee do s. great thing..................
2Ki 7:9 light, s. mischief will come upon us:..........
2Ki 7:13 Let s. take, I pray thee, five of the..........
2Ki 9:33 s. of her blood was sprinkled on the ....
2Ki 17:25 among them which slew s. of them..........
1Ch 4:42 s. of them, even of the sons of Simeon, ...
1Ch 9:29 S. of them also were appointed to............
1Ch 9:30 And s. of the sons of the priests made......
1Ch 12:19 And there fell s. of Manasseh to David, ...
2Ch 12:7 I will grant them s. deliverance;......... 4592
2Ch 16:10 And Asa oppressed s. of the people............
2Ch 17:11 also s. of the Philistines brought...............
2Ch 20:2 there came s. that told Jehoshaphat, ...
Ezr 2:68 And s. of the chief of the fathers, when.....
Ezr 2:70 s. of the people, and the singers, and........
Ezr 7:7 there went up s. of the children of............
Ezr 10:44 s. of them had wives by whom they..........
Ne 2:12 night, I and s. few men with me; 4592
Ne 5:3 S. also there were that said, We have.......
Ne 5:5 S. of our daughters are brought unto ....
Ne 6:2 in s. one of the villages in the plain of.......
Ne 7:70 s. of the chief of the fathers gave....... 7097
Ne 7:71 S. of the chief of the fathers gave to.........
Ne 7:73 and the singers and s. of the people,..........
Ne 11:25 s. of the children of Judah dwelt at ....
Ne 12:44 s. appointed over the chambers for 582
Ne 13:15 in Judah s. treading wine presses on ....
Ne 13:19 s. of my servants set I at the gates, ...
Job 24:2 S. remove the landmarks; they ....
Ps 20:7 S. trust in chariots, and s. in 428
Ps 69:20 and I looked for s. to take pity, but ....
Pr 4:16 away, unless they cause s. to fall..............
Jer 49:9 they not leave s. gleaning grapes? ....
Eze 6:8 have s. that shall escape the sword...........
Da 8:10 it cast down s. of the host and of the........
Da 11:35 s. of them of understanding shall fall, ...
Da 12:2 shall awake, s. to everlasting life, ... 428
Da 12:2 s. to shame...everlasting contempt....... 428
Am 4:11 I have overthrown s. of you, as God.........
Ob 5 thee, would they not leave s. grapes? ....
Mt 13:4 **s. seeds fell by the way side,**... *3588,3303*
Mt 13:5 **S. fell...stony places, where**...... *3588,243*
Mt 13:7 **s. fell among thorns; and the**... *3588,243*
Mt 13:8 **forth fruit, s. an hundredfold,** .*3588,3303*
Mt 13:8 **s. sixtyfold, s. thirtyfold,**........ *3588,1161*
Mt 13:23 **forth, s....hundredfold,**............ *3588,3033*
Mt 13:24 **hundredfold, s. sixty, s. thirty**.*3588,1161*
Mt 16:14 S. say...thou art John the Baptist:*3588,3033*
Mt 16:14 s., Elias; and others, Jeremias, ... *3588,3033*
Mt 16:28 **There be a s. standing hee, which**. *5100*
Mt 19:12 **For there are s. eunuchs, which were**..
Mt 19:12 **and there are s. eunuchs, which were**..
Mt 23:34 **s. of them ye shall kill and crucify;**.....
Mt 23:34 **s. of them shall ye scourge in your**......
Mt 27:47 S. of them that stood there, when...... *5100*
Mt 28:11 s. of the watch came into the city, ... *5100*
Mt 28:17 worshipped him: but s. doubted. *3588*
Mk 2:1 entered into Capernaum after s. days; ....
Mk 4:4 **he sowed, s. fell by...way side,***3588,3303*
Mk 4:5 **s. fell on stony ground, where it**..... *243*
Mk 4:7 **and s. fell among thorns, and the**... *243*
Mk 4:8 **and brought forth, S. thrity,** *1520*
Mk 4:8 **and s. sixty, and s. an hundred.** *1520*
Mk 4:20 **and bring forth fruit, s. thrityfold,** .*1520*
Mk 4:20 **s. sixty, and s. and hundred.** *1520*
Mk 7:2 saw s. of his disciples eat bread......... *5100*
Mk 8:28 s. say, Elias; and others, One of *243*
Mk 9:1 **be s. of them that stand here,** *5100*
Mk 12:5 **many others; beating s., and**.. *3588,3303*
Mk 12:5 **others; beating...and killing s.**........ *3588*
Mk 14:4 were s. that had indignation.............. *5100*
Mk 14:65 And s. began to spit on him, and to.... *5100*
Mk 15:35 And so of them that stood by, when... *5100*
Lu 8:5 **sowed, s. fell by the way side;**.*3588,3303*
Lu 8:6 **s. fell upon a rock; and as soon** ... *2087*
Lu 8:7 **And s. fell among thorns; and the** ..*2087*
Lu 9:7 because that it was said of s., that *5100*
Lu 9:8 And of s., that Elias had appeared; *5100*
Lu 9:19 but s. say, Elias; and others say,......... *243*
Lu 9:27 **there be s. standing here, which**.... *5100*
Lu 11:15 But s. of them said, He casteth out.... *5100*
Lu 11:49 **and s. of them they shall slay and**.......
Lu 13:1 s. that told him of the Galilaeans, ... *5100*
Lu 19:39 s. of the Pharisees from among the *5100*
Lu 21:5 And as s. spake of the temple, how.... *5100*
Lu 21:16 **s. of you shall they cause to be put**.....
Lu 23:8 have seen s. miracle done by him....... *5100*
Joh 3:25 between s. of John's disciples and............
Joh 6:64 **are s. of you that believe not.** *5100*
Joh 7:12 for s. said, He is a good man: *3588,3303*
Joh 7:25 Then said s. of them of Jerusalem, ... *5100*
Joh 7:41 s. said, Shall Christ come out of........... *243*
Joh 7:44 s. of them would have taken him;........ *5100*
Joh 9:9 S. said, This is he: others said, He...... *243*
Joh 9:16 said s. of the Pharisees, this man........ *5100*
Joh 9:40 S. of the Pharisees which were with.........
Joh 10:1 **but climbeth up s. other way, the**........
Joh 11:37 s. of them said, Could not this.......... *5100*
Joh 11:46 s. of them went their ways to the *5100*
Joh 13:29 s. of them thought, because Judas *5100*
Joh 16:17 Then said s. of his disciples among ....
Ac 5:15 by might overshadow s. of them. *5100*
Ac 8:9 out that himself was s. great one: *5100*
Ac 8:31 I, except s. man should guide me?...... *5100*
Ac 8:34 this? of himself, or of s. other man?.... *5100*
Ac 11:20 s. of them were men of Cyprus and.... *5100*
Ac 13:11 seeking s. to lead him by the hand...........
Ac 15:36 And s. days after Paul said unto......... *5100*
Ac 17:4 s. of them believed, and consorted *5100*
Ac 17:18 s. said, What will this babbler say? *5100*
Ac 17:18 s., He seemeth to be a setter forth.... *3588*
Ac 17:21 to tell, or to hear s. new thing.) *5100*
Ac 17:32 the resurrection...s. mocked: *3588,3303*
Ac 18:23 after he had spent s. time there,......... *5100*
Ac 19:32 S....cried one thing, and s. another: *243*
Ac 21:34 And s. cried one thing, s. another,....... *243*
Ac 27:27 that they drew near o s. country;......... *5100*
Ac 27:34 I pray you to take s. meat: for this is........
Ac 27:36 good cheer, and they also took s. meat. ....
Ac 27:44 And the rest, s. on boards,........ *3588,3303*
Ac 27:44 on boards, and s. on broken pieces....... *1161*
Ac 28:24 s. believed the things which *3588,3303*
Ac 28:24 were spoken, and s. believed not. *3588*
Ro 1:11 impart unto you s. spiritual gift, ... *5100*
Ro 1:13 I might have s. fruit among you *5100*
Ro 3:3 For what if s. did not believe? shall *5100*
Ro 3:8 and as s. affirm that we say,) Let....... *5100*
Ro 5:7 good man s. would even dare to die.... *5100*
Ro 11:14 flesh, and might save s. of them. *5100*
Ro 11:17 if s. of the branches be broken off, ... *5100*
Ro 15:15 more boldly unto you in a s. sort,. *575,3313*
1Co 4:18 Now s. are puffed up, as though I....... *5100*
1Co 6:11 And such were s. of you: but ye are... *5100*
1Co 8:7 for s. with conscience of the idol......... *5100*
1Co 9:22 that I might by all means save s.......... *5100*
1Co 10:7 be ye idolaters, as were s. of them; ... *5100*
1Co 10:8 fornication,...s. of them committed, ... *5100*
1Co 10:9 Christ, as s. of them also tempted, ... *5100*
1Co 10:10 ye, as s. of them also murmured, ... *5100*
1Co 12:28 God hath set s. in the church, ... *3588,3303*
1Co 15:6 present, but s. are fallen asleep. *5100*
1Co 15:12 say s. among you that there is no *5100*
1Co 15:34 s. have not the knowledge of God: *5100*
1Co 15:35 s. man will say, How are the dead...... *5100*
1Co 15:37 of wheat, or of s. other grain: *5100*
2Co 3:1 or need we, as s. others, epistles of... *5100*
2Co 10:2 bold against s., which think of us........ *5100*
2Co 10:12 or compare ourselves with s. that....... *5100*
Ga 1:7 but there be s. that trouble you.......... *5100*
Eph 4:11 And he gave s., apostles; *3588,3303*
Eph 4:11 apostles; and s., prophets; and *3588*
Eph 4:11 and s., evangelists; and s., pastors..... *3588*
Php 1:15 S. indeed preach Christ even of........... *5100*
Php 1:15 and strife; and s. also of good will: *5100*
Col 3:7 the which ye also walked s. time,...... *4218*
1Th 3:5 lest by s. means the tempter have...... *3381*
2Th 3:11 are s. which walk among you............ *5100*
1Ti 1:3 s. that they teach no other doctrine, ... *5100*
1Ti 1:6 s. having swerved have turned.......... *5100*
1Ti 1:19 s. having put away concerning faith..... *5100*
1Ti 4:1 times s. shall depart from the faith, ... *5100*
1Ti 5:15 s. are already turned aside after.......... *5100*
1Ti 5:24 S. men's sins are open beforehand,...... *5100*
1Ti 5:24 and s. men they follow after.............. *5100*
1Ti 5:25 also the good works of s. are manifest ......
1Ti 6:10 which while s. coveted after, they *5100*
1Ti 6:21 s. professing have erred concerning *5100*
2Ti 2:18 and overthrow the faith of s.. .... *5100*
2Ti 2:20 and of earth; s. to honour,........ *3588,3303*
2Ti 2:20 to honour, and s. to dishonour........... *3588*
Heb 3:4 For every house is builded by s.......... *5100*
Heb 3:16 For s., when they had heard, did *5100*
Heb 4:6 it remaineth that s. must enter *5100*
Heb 10:25 together, as the manner of s. is;......... *5100*
Heb 11:40 provided s. beter thing for us, ... *5100*
Heb 13:2 thereby s. have entertained angels...... *5100*
1Pe 4:12 though s. strange thing happened ....
2Pe 3:9 as s. men count slackness; but *5100*
2Pe 3:16 s. things hard to be understood,.......... *5100*
Jude 22 s. have compassion, making *3588,3303*
Re 2:10 devil shall cast s. of you into prison, ...

SOMEBODY
Lu 8:46 Jesus said, **S. hath touched me:** *5100*
Ac 5:36 Theudas, boasting himself to be s.;...... *5100*

SOMETHING
1Sa 20:26 S. hath befallen him, he is not 4745
Mk 5:43 that s. should be given her to eat............
Lu 11:54 to catch s. out of his mouth, that *5100*
Joh 13:29 that he should give s. to the poor........ *5100*
Ac 3:5 expecting to receive s. of them.......... *5100*
Ac 23:15 s. more perfectly concerning him:............
Ac 23:18 thee, who hath s. to say unto thee. *5100*
Ga 6:3 a man think himself to be s., when *5100*

SOMETIME See also SOME and TIME; SOMETIMES.
Col 1:21 you, that were s. alienated and.......... *4218*
1Pe 3:20 Which s. were disobedient, when *4218*

SOMETIMES See also SOMETIME.
Eph 2:13 ye who s. were far off are made *4218*
Eph 5:8 For ye were s. darkness, but now...... *4218*
Tit 3:3 we ourselves also were s. foolish, ... *4218*

SOMEWHAT
Le 4:13 they have done s. against any of the ....
Le 4:22 done s. through ignorance against............
Le 4:27 while he doeth s. against any of the..........
Le 13:6 behold, if the plague be s. dark,......... 3544
Le 13:19 bright spot, white, and s. reddish, ...
Le 13:21 than the skin, but be s. dark; 3544
Le 13:24 bright spot, s. reddish, or white;............
Le 13:26 the other skin, but be s. dark;........... 3544
Le 13:28 not in the skin, but it be s. dark; 3544
Le 13:56 be s. dark after the washing of it; 3544
1Ki 2:14 I have s. to say unto thee. And ....
2Ki 5:20 run after him, and take s. of him........ 3972
2Ch 10:4 ease thou s. the grievous servitude...........
2Ch 10:9 Ease s. the yoke that thy father did..........
2Ch 10:10 but make thou it s. lighter for us;............
Lu 7:40 **Simon, I have s. to say unto thee.** *5100*
Ac 23:20 enquire s. of him more perfectly. *5100*
Ac 25:26 had, I might have s. to write............. *5100*
Ro 15:24 I be s. flled with your company.......... *3318*
2Co 5:12 that ye may have s. to answer them ....
2Co 10:8 boast s. more of our authority, ... *5100*
Ga 2:6 But of these who seemed to be s.,....... *5100*
Ga 2:6 who seemed to be s. in conference...........
Heb 8:3 that this man have s. also to offer. *5100*
Re 2:4 **Nevertheless I have s. against thee,**.....

SON See also SON'S; SONS.
Ge 4:17 after the name of his s., Enoch.......... 1121
Ge 4:25 she bare a s., and called his name...... 1121

Book	Ref	Context	No.
Ge	4:26	to him also there was born a **s.**;	1121
Ge	5:3	begat a **s.** in his own likeness, after	
Ge	5:28	and two years, and begat a **s.**:	1121
Ge	9:24	his younger **s.** had done unto him	1121
Ge	11:31	Terah took Abram his **s.**, and Lot	1121
Ge	11:31	Lot the **s.** of Haran his son's s, and	
Ge	11:31	daughter in law, his **s.** Abram's wife;	
Ge	12:5	and Lot his brother's **s.**, and all	1121
Ge	14:12	took Lot, Abram's brother's **s.**, who	1121
Ge	16:11	art with child, and shalt bear a **s.**,	1121
Ge	16:15	Hagar bare Abram a **s.**: and Abram	1121
Ge	17:16	her, and give thee a **s.** also of her:	1121
Ge	17:19	thy wife shall bear thee a **s.** indeed;	1121
Ge	17:23	And Abraham took Ishmael his **s.**,	1121
Ge	17:25	Ishmael his **s.** was thriteen years	1121
Ge	17:26	circumcised, and Ishmael his **s.**.	1121
Ge	18:10	lo, Sarah thy wife shall have a **s.**.	1121
Ge	18:14	of life, and Sarah shall have a **s.**.	1121
Ge	19:12	**s.** in law, and thy sons, and thy	1121
Ge	19:37	the firstborn bare a **s.**, and called	1121
Ge	19:38	she also bare a **s.**, and called his	1121
Ge	21:2	bare Abraham a **s.** in his old age.	1121
Ge	21:3	Abraham called the name of his **s.**	1121
Ge	21:4	Abraham circumcised his **s.** Isaac.	1121
Ge	21:5	his **s.** Isaac was born unto him.	1121
Ge	21:7	I have born him a **s.** in his old age.	1121
Ge	21:9	And Sarah saw the **s.** of Hagar the	1121
Ge	21:10	out this bondwoman and her **s.**:	1121
Ge	21:10	for the **s.** of this bondwoman shall	1121
Ge	21:10	shall not be heir with my **s.**, even	
Ge	21:11	Abraham's sight because of his **s.**.	1121
Ge	21:13	**s.** of the bondwoman will I make a	1121
Ge	21:23	with my **s.**, nor with my son's **s.**:	5220
Ge	22:2	And he said, Take now thy **s.**,	1121
Ge	22:2	thine only **s.** Isaac, whom thou	
Ge	22:3	men with him, and Isaac his **s.**,	1121
Ge	22:6	and laid it upon Isaac his **s.**; and	1121
Ge	22:7	and he said, Here am I, my **s.**	1121
Ge	22:8	My **s.**, God will provide himself a	1121
Ge	22:9	and bound Isaac his **s.**, and laid	1121
Ge	22:10	and took the knife to slay his **s.**.	1121
Ge	22:12	seeing thou hast not withheld thy **s.**,	1121
Ge	22:12	withheld…thine only **s.** from me.	
Ge	22:13	burnt offering in the stead of his **s.**.	1121
Ge	22:16	thing, and hast not withheld thy **s.**,	1121
Ge	22:16	withheld…thine only **s.**:	
Ge	23:8	for me to Ephron the **s.** of Zohar,	1121
Ge	24:3	shalt not take a wife unto my **s.** of	1121
Ge	24:4	and take a wife unto my **s.** Isaac.	1121
Ge	24:5	must I needs bring thy **s.** again	1121
Ge	24:6	that thou bring not my **s.** thither	1121
Ge	24:7	thou shalt take a wife unto my **s.**	1121
Ge	24:8	only bring not my **s.** thither again.	1121
Ge	24:15	was born to Bethuel, **s.** of Milcah,	1121
Ge	24:24	daughter of Bethuel the **s.** of Milcah,	1121
Ge	24:36	master's wife bare a **s.** to my master	1121
Ge	24:37	shalt not take a wife to my **s.** of the	1121
Ge	24:38	kindred, and take a wife unto my **s.**	1121
Ge	24:40	take a wife for my **s.** of my kindred,	1121
Ge	24:44	appointed out for my master's **s.**.	1121
Ge	24:47	daughter of Bethuel, Nahor's **s.**,	1121
Ge	24:48	brother's daughter unto his **s.**.	1121
Ge	25:6	sent them away from Isaac his **s.**,	1121
Ge	25:9	the field of Ephron the **s.** of Zohar	1121
Ge	25:11	that God blessed his **s.** Isaac;	1121
Ge	25:12	of Ishmael, Abraham's **s.**,	1121
Ge	25:19	generations of Isaac, Abraham's **s.**:	1121
Ge	27:1	he called Esau his eldest **s.**, and	1121
Ge	27:1	and said unto him, My **s.**: and he	1121
Ge	27:5	when Isaac spake to Esau his **s.**.	1121
Ge	27:6	Rebekah spake unto Jacob her **s.**,	1121
Ge	27:8	theefore, my **s.**, obey my voice	1121
Ge	27:13	Upon me by thy curse, my **s.**: only	1121
Ge	27:15	raiment of her eldest **s.** Esau,	1121
Ge	27:15	them upon Jacob her youngest **s.**:	1121
Ge	27:17	into the hand of her **s.** Jacob.	1121
Ge	27:18	Here am I; who art thou, my **s.**?	1121
Ge	27:20	Isaac said unto his **s.**, How is it	1121
Ge	27:20	thou hast found it so quickly, my **s.**?	1121
Ge	27:21	that I may feel thee, my **s.**, whether	1121
Ge	27:21	thou be my very **s.** Esau or not.	1121
Ge	27:24	he said, Art thou my very **s.** Esau?	1121
Ge	27:26	Come near now, and kiss me, my **s.**	1121
Ge	27:27	the smell of my **s.** is as the smell of	1121
Ge	27:32	I am thy **s.**, thy firstborn Esau.	1121
Ge	27:37	shall I do now unto thee, my **s.**?	1121
Ge	27:42	these words of Esau her elder **s.**	1121
Ge	27:42	and called Jacob her younger **s.**,	1121
Ge	27:43	therefore, my **s.**, obey my voice;	1121
Ge	28:5	Laban, **s.** of Bethuel the Syrian,	1121
Ge	28:9	daughter of Ishmael Abraham's **s.**,	1121
Ge	29:5	Know ye Laban the **s.** of Nahor?	1121
Ge	29:12	and that he was Rebekah's **s.**	1121
Ge	29:13	the tidings of Jacob his sister's **s.**,	1121
Ge	29:32	And Leah conceived, and bare a **s.**	1121
Ge	29:33	she conceived again, and bare a **s.**;	1121
Ge	29:33	hath therefore given me this **s.** also:	
Ge	29:34	she conceived again, and bare a **s.**;	1121
Ge	29:35	she conceived again, and bare a **s.**:	1121
Ge	90:5	conceived, and bare Jacob a **s.**	1121
Ge	90:6	my voice, and hath given me a **s.**:	1121
Ge	90:7	again, and bare Jacob a second **s.**.	1121
Ge	90:10	Zilpah Leah's maid bare Jacob a **s.**.	1121
Ge	90:12	Leah's maid bare Jacob a second **s.**.	1121
Ge	90:17	and bare Jacob the fifth **s.**	1121
Ge	90:19	again, and bare Jacob the sixth **s.**.	1121
Ge	90:23	And she conceived, and bare a **s.**;	1121
Ge	90:24	Lord shall add to me another **s.**.	1121
Ge	34:2	And when Shechem the **s.** of Hamor	1121
Ge	34:8	soul of my **s.** Shechem longeth for	1121
Ge	34:18	Hamor, and Shechem Hamor's **s.**	1121
Ge	34:20	Hamor and Shechem his **s.** came	1121
Ge	34:24	Hamor and unto Shechem his **s.**	1121
Ge	34:26	slew Hamor and Shechem his **s.**	1121
Ge	35:17	not; thou shalt have this **s.** also.	1121
Ge	36:10	Eliphaz the **s.** of Adah the wife of	1121
Ge	36:10	Reuel the **s.** of Bashemath the wife	1121
Ge	36:12	concubine to Eliphaz Esau's **s.**;	1121
Ge	36:15	of Eliphaz the firstborn **s.** of Esau;	
Ge	36:17	are the sons of Reuel Esau's **s.**;	1121
Ge	36:32	Bela the **s.** of Beor riegned in Edom:	1121
Ge	36:33	Jobab the **s.** of Zerah of Bozrah	1121
Ge	36:35	Hadad the **s.** of Bedad, who smote	1121
Ge	36:38	Baal-hanan the **s.** of Achbor reigned	1121
Ge	36:39	Baal-hanan the **s.** of Achbor died,	1121
Ge	37:3	because he was the **s.** of his old age:	1121
Ge	37:34	and mourned for his **s.** many days.	1121
Ge	37:35	go down into the grave unto my **s.**	1121
Ge	38:3	And she conceived, and bare a **s.**;	1121
Ge	38:4	she conceived again, and bare a **s.**;	1121
Ge	38:5	yet again conceived, and bare a **s.**;	1121
Ge	38:11	house, till Shelah my **s.** be grown:	1121
Ge	38:26	that I gave her not to Shelah my **s.**.	1121
Ge	42:38	My **s.** shall not go down with you;	1121
Ge	43:29	brother Benjamin, his mother's **s.**,	1121
Ge	43:29	God be gracious unto thee, my **s.**	1121
Ge	45:9	Thus saith thy **s.** Joseph, God hath	1121
Ge	45:28	enough; Joseph my **s.** is yet alive:	1121
Ge	46:10	and Shaul the **s.** of a Canaanitish	1121
Ge	47:29	die: and he called his **s.** Joseph, and	1121
Ge	48:2	Behold, thy **s.** Joseph cometh unto	1121
Ge	48:19	said, I know it, my **s.**, I know it:	1121
Ge	49:9	they prey, my **s.**, thou art gone up:	1121
Ge	50:23	also of Machir the **s.** of Manasseh	1121
Ex	1:16	if it be a **s.**, then ye shall kill him:	1121
Ex	1:22	Every **s.** that is born ye shall cast	1121
Ex	2:2	woman conceived, and bare a **s.**	1121
Ex	2:10	daughter, and he became her **s.**.	1121
Ex	2:22	she bare him a **s.**, and he called	1121
Ex	4:22	Thus saith the Lord, Israel is my **s.**,	1121
Ex	4:23	Let my **s.** go, that he may serve me:	1121
Ex	4:23	behold, I will slay thy **s.**, even thy	1121
Ex	4:25	and cut of the foreskin of her **s.**,	1121
Ex	6:15	and Shaul the **s.** of a Canaanitish	1121
Ex	6:25	Eleazar Aaron's **s.** took him one of	1121
Ex	10:2	ears of thy **s.**, and of thy son's **s.**,	1121
Ex	13:8	thou shalt shew thy **s.** in that day,	1121
Ex	13:14	be when thy **s.** asketh thee n time	1121
Ex	20:10	not do any work, thou, nor thy **s.**,	1121
Ex	21:9	if he have betrothed her unto his **s.**,	1121
Ex	21:31	Whether he have gored a **s.**, or have	1121
Ex	23:12	and the **s.** of thy handmaid, and the	1121
Ex	29:30	that **s.** that is priest in his stead	1121
Ex	31:2	Bezalel the **s.** of Uri, the **s.** of Hur,	1121
Ex	31:6	Aholiab, the **s.** of Ahisamach, of the	1121
Ex	32:29	every man upon his **s.**, and upon	1121
Ex	33:11	Joshua, the **s.** of Nun, a young man,	1121
Ex	35:30	Bezaleel the **s.** of Uri, the **s.** of Hur,	1121
Ex	35:34	Aholiab, the **s.** of Ahisamach, of the	1121
Ex	38:21	of Ithamar, **s.** to Aaron the priest.	1121
Ex	38:22	Bezaleel the **s.** of Uri, the **s.** of Hur,	1121
Ex	38:23	him was Aholiab **s.** of Ahisamach,	1121
Le	12:6	her purifying are fulfilled, for a **s.**,	1121
Le	21:2	and for his **s.**, and for his duaghter,	1121
Le	24:10	the **s.** of an Israelitish woman,	1121
Le	24:10	this **s.** of the Israelitish woman	1121
Le	24:11	Israelitish woman's **s.** blasphemed	1121
Le	25:49	Either his uncle, or his uncle's **s.**,	1121
Nu	1:5	Reuben; Elizur the **s.** of Shedeur	1121
Nu	1:6	Shelumiel the **s.** of Zurishaddai	1121
Nu	1:7	Nahshon the **s.** of Amminadab	1121
Nu	1:8	Issachar; Nethaneel the **s.** of Zuar.	1121
Nu	1:9	Of Zebulun; Eliab the **s.** of Helon.	1121
Nu	1:10	Elishama the **s.** of Ammihud:	1121
Nu	1:10	Gamaliel the **s.** of Pedahzur	1121
Nu	1:11	Benjamin; Abidan the **s.** of Gideoni.	1121
Nu	1:12	Ahiezer the **s.** of Ammishaddai.	1121
Nu	1:13	of Asher; Pagiel the **s.** of Ocran.	1121
Nu	1:14	of Gad; Eliasaph the **s.** of Deuel	1121
Nu	1:15	Of Naphtali; Ahira the **s.** of Enan.	1121
Nu	1:20	children of Reuben, Israel's elders **s.**,	
Nu	2:3	Nahshon the **s.** of Amminadab	1121
Nu	2:5	Nethanel the **s.** of Zuar shall be	1121
Nu	2:7	and Eliab the **s.** of Helon shall be	1121
Nu	2:10	shall be Elizur the **s.** of Shedeur.	1121
Nu	2:12	Be Shelumiel the **s.** of Zurishaddai.	1121
Nu	2:14	shall be Eliasaph the **s.** of Reuel	1121
Nu	2:18	Be Elishama the **s.** of Ammihud.	1121
Nu	2:20	be Gamaliel the **s.** of Pedahzur.	1121
Nu	2:22	shall be Abidan the **s.** of Gideoni.	1121
Nu	2:25	be Ahiezer the **s.** of Ammishaddai	1121
Nu	2:27	shall be Pagiel the **s.** of Ocran.	1121
Nu	2:29	shall be Ahira the **s.** of Enan.	1121
Nu	3:24	shall be Eliasaph the **s.** of Lael.	1121
Nu	3:30	shall be Elizaphan the **s.** of Uzziel	1121
Nu	3:32	Eleazar the **s.** of Aaron the priest	1121
Nu	3:35	was Zuriel the **s.** of Abihail:	1121
Nu	4:16	Eleazar the **s.** of Aaron the priest	1121
Nu	4:28,	33 Ithamar…**s.** of Aaron the priest.	1121
Nu	7:8	Ithamar the **s.** of Aaron the priest.	1121
Nu	7:12	was Nahshon the **s.** of Amminadab,	1121
Nu	7:17	of Nahshon the **s.** of Amminadab.	1121
Nu	7:18	Nethaneel the **s.** of Zuar, prince of	1121
Nu	7:23	offering of Nethaneel the **s.** of Zuar.	1121
Nu	7:24	Eliab the **s.** of Helon, prince of the	1121
Nu	7:29	the offering of Eliab the **s.** of Helon.	1121
Nu	7:30	Elizur the **s.** of Shedeur, prince of	1121
Nu	7:35	offering of Elizur the **s.** of Shedeur.	1121
Nu	7:36	Shelumiel the **s.** of Zurishaddai,	1121
Nu	7:41	of Shelumiel the **s.** of Zurishaddai.	1121
Nu	7:42	Eliasaph the **s.** of Deuel, prince of	1121
Nu	7:47	offering of Eliasaph the **s.** of Deuel.	1121
Nu	7:48	day Elishama the **s.** of Ammihud,	1121
Nu	7:53	of Elishama the **s.** of Ammihud.	1121
Nu	7:54	offered Gamaliel the **s.** of Pedahzur,	1121
Nu	7:59	of Gamaliel the **s.** of Pedahzur.	1121
Nu	7:60	Abidan the **s.** of Gideoni, prince of	1121
Nu	7:65	offering of Abidan the **s.** of Gideoni.	1121
Nu	7:66	day Ahiezer the **s.** of Ammishaddai,	1121
Nu	7:71	of Ahiezer the **s.** of Ammishaddai.	1121
Nu	7:72	Pagiel the **s.** of Ocran, prince of the	1121
Nu	7:77	offering of Pagiel the **s.** of Ocran.	1121
Nu	7:78	Ahira the **s.** of Enan, prince of	1121
Nu	7:83	the offering of Ahira the **s.** of Enan.	1121
Nu	10:14	was Nahson the **s.** of Amminadab.	1121
Nu	10:15	was Nethaneel the **s.** of Zuar.	1121
Nu	10:16	Zebulun was Eliab the **s.** of Helon.	1121
Nu	10:18	host was Elizur the **s.** of Shedeur.	1121
Nu	10:19	Shelumiel the **s.** of Zurishaddai.	1121
Nu	10:20	of Gad was Eliasaph the **s.** of Deuel.	1121
Nu	10:22	was Elishama the **s.** of Ammihud.	1121
Nu	10:23	was Gamaliel the **S.** of Pedahzur.	1121
Nu	10:24	was Abidan the **s.** of Gideoni.	1121
Nu	10:25	was Ahiezer the **s.** of Ammishaddai.	1121
Nu	10:26	of Asher was Pagiel the **s.** of Ocran.	1121
Nu	10:27	Naphtali was Ahira the **s.** of Enan.	1121
Nu	10:29	said unto Hobab, the **s.** of Raguel	1121
Nu	11:28	Joshua the **s.** of Nun, the servant of	1121
Nu	13:4	Rueben, Shammua the **s.** of Zaccur.	1121
Nu	13:5	of Simeon, Shaphat the **s.** of Hori.	1121
Nu	13:6	Judah, Caleb the **s.** of Jephunneh.	1121
Nu	13:7	of Issachar, Igal the **s.** of Joseph.	1121
Nu	13:8	of Ephraim, Oshea the **s.** of Nun.	1121
Nu	13:9	of Benjamin, Palti the **s.** of Raphu.	1121
Nu	13:10	of Zebulun, Gaddiel the **s.** of Sodi.	1121
Nu	13:11	of Manasseh, Gaddi the **s.** of Susi.	1121
Nu	13:12	of Dan, Ammiel the **s.** of Gemalli.	1121
Nu	13:13	of Asher, Sethur the **s.** of Michael.	1121
Nu	13:14	of Naphtali, Nahbi the **s.** of Vophsi.	1121
Nu	13:15	tribe of Gad, Geuel the **s.** of Machi.	1121

Nu 13:16 called Oshea...**s.** the Nun Jehoshua. 1121
Nu 14:6 and Joshua the **s.** of Nun, and 1121
Nu 14:6 and Caleb the **s.** of Jephunneh, 1121
Nu 14:30 save Caleb the **s.** of Jephunneh, 1121
Nu 14:30 and Joshua the **s.** of Nun. 1121
Nu 14:38 But Joshua the **s.** of Nun, and Caleb 1121
Nu 14:38 and Caleb the **s.** of Jephunneh, 1121
Nu 16:1 Now Korah, the **s.** of Izhar. 1121
Nu 16:1 the **s.** fo Kohath, the **s.** of Levi, and 1121
Nu 16:1 of Eliab, and On, the **s.** of Peleth, 1121
Nu 16:37 Eleazar the **s.** of Aaron the priest, 1121
Nu 20:25 Take Aaron and Eleazar his **s.**, and 1121
Nu 20:26 and put them upon Eleazar his **s.**: 1121
Nu 20:28 and put them upon Eleazar his **s.**; 1121
Nu 22:2 Balak the **s.** of Zippor saw all that 1121
Nu 22:4 Balak the **s.** of Zippor was king of 1121
Nu 22:5 Balaam the **s.** of Beor to Pethor, 1121
Nu 22:10 Balak...**s.** of Zippor, king of Moab, 1121
Nu 22:10 Thus saith Balak the **s.** of Zippor, 1121
Nu 23:18 hearken unto me, thou **s.** of Zippor: 1121
Nu 23:19 **s.** of man, that he should repent: 1121
Nu 24:3, 15 Balaam the **s.** of Beor hath said, 1121
Nu 25:7 when Phinehas, the **s.** of Eleazar, 1121
Nu 25:7 the **s.** of Aaron the priest, saw it, he 1121
Nu 25:11 Phinehas, the **s.** of Eleazar, the 1121
Nu 25:11 the **s.** of Aaron the priest, hath 1121
Nu 25:14 Zimri, the **s.** of Salu, a prince of a 1121
Nu 26:1 Eleazar the **s.** of Aaron the priest, 1121
Nu 26:5 Reuben, the eldest **s.** of Israel: the
Nu 26:33 Zelophehad the **s.** of Hepher had 1121
Nu 26:65 save Caleb the **s.** of Jephunneh, 1121
Nu 26:65 and Joshua the **s.** of Nun. 1121
Nu 27:1 of Zelophehad, the **s.** of Hepher, 1121
Nu 27:1 the **s.** of Gilead, the **s.** of Machir, 1121
Nu 27:1 the **s.** of Manasseh, of the families 1121
Nu 27:1 of Manasseh the **s.** of Joseph: 1121
Nu 27:4 his family, because he hath no **s.**? 1121
Nu 27:8 If a man die, and have no **s.**, then 1121
Nu 27:18 Take thee Joshua the **s.** of Nun, a 1121
Nu 31:6 Phinehas...**s.** o Eleazar the priest, 1121
Nu 31:8 Balaam also the **s.** of Beor they slew 1121
Nu 32:12 Save Caleb the **s.** of Jephunneh the 1121
Nu 32:12 and Joshua the **s.** of Nun: for thy 1121
Nu 32:28 Joshua the **s.** of Nun, and the chief 1121
Nu 32:33 tribe of Manasseh the **s.** of Joseph, 1121
Nu 32:39 children of Machir...**s.** of Manasseh 1121
Nu 32:40 unto Machir the **s.** of Manasseh; 1121
Nu 32:41 Jair the **s.** of Manasseh went and 1121
Nu 34:17 the priest, and Joshua the **s.** of Nun 1121
Nu 34:19 Judah, Caleb the **s.** of Jephunneh. 1121
Nu 34:20 Shemuel the **s.** of Ammihud. 1121
Nu 34:21 Benjamin, Elidad the **s.** of Chislon. 1121
Nu 34:22 of Dan, Bukki the **s.** of Jogli. 1121
Nu 34:23 Manasseh, Hanniel the **s.** of Ephod. 1121
Nu 34:24 Kemuel the **s.** of Shiphtan. 1121
Nu 34:25 Elizaphan the **s.** of Parnach. 1121
Nu 34:26 of Issachar, Paltiel the **s.** of Azzan. 1121
Nu 34:27 of Asher, Ahihud the **s.** of Shelomi. 1121
Nu 34:28 Pedahel the **s.** of Ammihud. 1121
Nu 36:1 the **s.** of Machir, the **s.** of Manasseh, 1121
Nu 36:12 sons of Manasseh the **s.** of Joseph, 1121
De 1:31 bare thee, as a man doth bear his **s.**, 1121
De 1:36 Save Caleb the **s.** of Jephunneh; he 1121
De 1:38 But Joshua the **s.** of Nun, which 1121
De 3:14 Jair the **s.** of Manasseh took all the 1121
De 5:14 not do any work, thou, nor thy **s.**, 1121
De 6:2 thou, and thy **s.**, and thy son's **s.**, 1121
De 6:20 when thy **s.** asketh thee in time to 1121
De 6:21 Then thou shalt say unto thy **s.**, We 1121
De 7:3 thou shalt not give unto his **s.**, 1121
De 7:3 nor his daughter...unto thy **s.** 1121
De 7:4 turn away thy **s.** from following me, 1121
De 8:5 as a man chasteneth his **s.**, so the 1121
De 10:6 Eleazar his **s.** ministered in the 1121
De 11:6 the sons of Eliab, the **s.** of Reuben: 1121
De 12:18 thou, and thy **s.**, and thy daughter, 1121
De 13:6 the **s.** of thy mother, or thy **s.**, or thy 1121
De 16:11, 14 and thy **s.**, and thy daughter, 1121
De 18:10 maketh his **s.** or...daughter to pass 1121
De 21:15 if the firstborn **s.** be hers that was 1121
De 21:16 may not make the **s.** of the beloved 1121
De 21:16 firstborn before the **s.** of the hated, 1121
De 21:17 acknowledge the **s.** of the hated for 1121
De 21:18 have a stubborn and rebellious **s.**, 1121
De 21:20 our **s.** is stubborn and rebellious, 1121
De 23:4 Balaam the **s.** of Beor of Pethor of 1121
De 28:56 and toward her **s.**, and toward her 1121
De 31:23 gave Joshua the **s.** of Nun a charge, 1121
De 32:44 he, and Hoshea the **s.** of Nun. 1121
De 34:9 Joshua the **s.** of Nun was full of 1121
Jos 1:1 spake unto Joshua the **s.** of Nun, 1121
Jos 2:1 And Joshua the **s.** of Nun sent out of 1121
Jos 2:23 and came to Joshua the **s.** of Nun, 1121
Jos 6:6 And Joshua the **s.** of Nun called the 1121
Jos 6:26 in his youngest **s.** shall he set up the
Jos 7:1 for Achan, the **s.** of Carmi, 1121
Jos 7:1 the **s.** of Zabdi, the **s.** of Zerah, of 1121
Jos 7:18 man; and Achan, the **s.** of Carmi, 1121
Jos 7:18 the **s.** of Zabdi, the **s.** of Zerah, of the 1121
Jos 7:19 And Joshua said unto Achan, My **s.**, 1121
Jos 7:24 took Achan the **s.** of Zerah, and the 1121
Jos 13:22 Balaam also the **s.** of Beor, the 1121
Jos 13:31 of Machir the **s.** of Manasseh, 1121
Jos 14:1 the priest, and Joshua the **s.** of Nun, 1121
Jos 14:6, 13,14 Caleb the **s.** of Jephunneh 1121
Jos 15:6 the stone of Bohan the **s.** of Reuben: 1121
Jos 15:8 by the valley of the **s.** of Hinnom 1121
Jos 15:13 unto Caleb the **s.** of Jephunneh he 1121
Jos 15:17 Othniel the **s.** of Kenaz, the brother 1121
Jos 17:2 of Manasseh the **s.** of Joseph by 1121
Jos 17:3 But Zelophehad, the **s.** of Hepher, 1121
Jos 17:3 the **s.** of Gilead, the **s.** of Machir, 1121
Jos 17:3 the **s.** of Manasseh, had no sons, but 1121
Jos 17:4 and before Joshua the **s.** of Nun, 1121
Jos 18:16 the valley of the **s.** of Hinnom, 1121
Jos 18:17 the stone of Bohan the **s.** of Reuben, 1121
Jos 19:49 Joshua the **s.** of Nun among them: 1121
Jos 19:51 the priest, and Joshua the **s.** of Nun, 1121
Jos 21:1 and unto Joshua the **s.** of Nun, and 1121
Jos 21:12 they to Caleb the **s.** of Jephunneh 1121
Jos 22:13 Phinehas...**s.** of Eleazar the priest, 1121
Jos 22:20 not Achan the **s.** of Zerah commit 1121
Jos 22:31 Phinehas the **s.** of Eleazar the priest 1121
Jos 22:32 Phinehas...**s.** of Eleazar the priest, 1121
Jos 24:9 Then Balak the **s.** of Zippor, king 1121
Jos 24:9 and called Ballam the **s.** of Beor 1121
Jos 24:29 Joshua the **s.** of Nun, the servant 1121
Jos 24:33 And Eleazar the **s.** of Aaron died; 1121
Jos 24:33 that pertained to Phinehas his **s.**, 1121
Jg 1:13 Othniel the **s.** of Kenaz, Caleb's 1121
Jg 2:8 Joshua the **s.** of Nun, the servant 1121
Jg 3:9 Othniel the **s.** of Kenaz, Caleb's 1121
Jg 3:11 and Othniel the **s.** of Kenaz died. 1121
Jg 3:15 Ehud the **s.** of Gera, a Benjamite, 1121
Jg 3:31 him was Shamgar the **s.** of Anath, 1121
Jg 4:6 called Barak the **s.** of Abinoam out 1121
Jg 4:12 Barak the **s.** of Abinoam was gone 1121
Jg 5:1 Barak the **s.** of Abinoam on that 1121
Jg 5:6 days of Shamgar the **s.** of Anath, 1121
Jg 5:12 captive, thou **s.** of Abinoam. 1121
Jg 6:11 his **s.** Gideon threshed wheat by 1121
Jg 6:29 Gideon the **s.** of Joash hath done 1121
Jg 6:30 Joash, Bring out thy **s.**, that he 1121
Jg 7:14 sword of Gideon the **s.** of Joash, 1121
Jg 8:13 Gideon the **s.** of Joash returned 1121
Jg 8:22 and thy **s.**, and thy son's **s.** also: 1121
Jg 8:23 neither shall my **s.** rule over you: 1121
Jg 8:29 Jerubbaal the **s.** of Joash went and 1121
Jg 8:31 she also bare him a **s.**, whose name 1121
Jg 8:32 Gideon the **s.** of Joash died in a 1121
Jg 9:1 Abimelech the **s.** of Jerubbaal went 1121
Jg 9:5 Jotham...youngest **s.** of Jerubbaal 1121
Jg 9:18 Abimelech,...**s.** of his maidservant, 1121
Jg 9:25 Gaal the **s.** of Ebed came with his 1121
Jg 9:28 Gaal the **s.** of Ebed said, Who is 1121
Jg 9:28 is not he the **s.** of Jerubbaal? and 1121
Jg 9:30 the words of Gaal the **s.** of Ebed, 1121
Jg 9:31 Behold, Gaal the **s.** of Ebed and his 1121
Jg 9:35 And Gaal the **s.** of Ebed went out, 1121
Jg 9:57 curse of Jotham...**s.** of Jerubbaal, 1121
Jg 10:1 Tola the **s.** of Puah, the **s.** of Dodo, 1121
Jg 11:1 and he was the **s.** of an harlot: and 1121
Jg 11:2 thou art the **s.** of strange woman. 1121
Jg 11:25 better than Balak the **s.** of Zippor, 1121
Jg 11:34 her he had neither **s.** nor daughter. 1121
Jg 12:13 after him Abdon the **s.** of Hillel, a 1121
Jg 12:15 And Abdon the **s.** of Hillel, the 1121
Jg 13:3 thou shalt conceive, and bear a **s.** 1121
Jg 13:5, 7 shalt conceive, and bear a **s.**; 1121
Jg 13:24 the woman bare a **s.**, and called 1121
Jg 15:6 Samson,...**s.** in law of the Timnite, 2860
Jg 17:2 be thou of the Lord, my **s.** 1121
Jg 17:3 the Lord from my hand for my **s.**, 1121
Jg 18:30 Jonathan, the **s.** of Gershom, 1121
Jg 18:30 the **s.** of Manasseh, he and his 1121
Jg 19:5 father said unto his **s.** in law, 2860
Jg 20:28 And Phinehas, the **s.** of Eleazar, 1121
Jg 20:28 the **s.** of Aaron, stood before it 1121
Ru 4:13 her conception, and she bare a **s.** 1121
Ru 4:17 There is a **s.** born to Naomi; and 1121
1Sa 1:1 was Elkanah, the **s.** of Jeroham, 1121
1Sa 1:1 the **s.** of Elihu, the **s.** of Tohu, 1121
1Sa 1:1 the **s.** of Zuph, an Ephrathite: 1121
1Sa 1:20 that she bare a **s.**, and called his 1121
1Sa 1:23 gave her **s.** suck until she weaned 1121
1Sa 3:6 I called not my **s.**; lie down again. 1121
1Sa 3:16 Samuel, and said, Samuel, my **s.** 1121
1Sa 4:16 said, What is there done, my **s.**? 1121
1Sa 4:20 Fear not; for thou hast born a **s.** 1121
1Sa 7:1 Eleazar his **s.** to keep the ark of 1121
1Sa 9:1 Kish, the **s.** of Abiel, the **s.** of Zeror, 1121
1Sa 9:1 **s.** of Bechorath, the **s.** of Aphiah, 1121
1Sa 9:2 he had a **s.**, whose name was Saul, 1121
1Sa 9:3 Kish said to Saul his **s.**, Take now 1121
1Sa 10:2 saying, What shall I do for my **s.**? 1121
1Sa 10:11 that is come unto the **s.** of Kish? 1121
1Sa 10:21 and Saul the **s.** of Kish was taken: 1121
1Sa 13:16 Saul, and Jonathan his **s.**, and the 1121
1Sa 13:22 Saul and with Jonathan his **s.** was 1121
1Sa 14:1 that Jonathan the **s.** of Saul said 1121
1Sa 14:3 Ahiah, the **s.** of Ahitub, I-chabod's 1121
1Sa 14:3 brother, the **s.** of Phinehas, the 1121
1Sa 14:3 the **s.** of Eli, the Lord's priest 1121
1Sa 14:39 though it be in Jonathan my **s.**, he 1121
1Sa 14:40 I and Jonathan my **s.** will be on 1121
1Sa 14:42 between me and Jonathan my **s.** 1121
1Sa 14:50 Abner, the **s.** of Ner, Saul's uncle. 1121
1Sa 14:51 father of Abner was the **s.** of Abiel, 1121
1Sa 16:18 a **s.** of Jesse the Beth-lehemite, 1121
1Sa 16:19 Send me David thy **s.**, which is 1121
1Sa 16:20 them by David his **s.** unto Saul. 1121
1Sa 17:12 David was the **s.** of that Ephrathite 1121
1Sa 17:17 Jesse said unto David his **s.**, Take 1121
1Sa 17:55 Abner, whose **s.** is this youth? And 1121
1Sa 17:56 thou whose **s.** the stripling is 1121
1Sa 17:58 Whose **s.** art thou, thou young man? 1121
1Sa 17:58 I am the **s.** of thy servant Jesse the 1121
1Sa 18:18 I should be **s.** in law to the king? 2860
1Sa 18:21 shalt this day be my **s.** in law in 2859
1Sa 18:22 therefore be the king's **s.** in law. 2859
1Sa 18:23 light thing to be a king's **s.** in law, 2859
1Sa 18:26 well to be the king's **s.** in law: 2859
1Sa 18:27 he might be the kings's **s.** in law. 2859
1Sa 19:1 Saul spake to Jonathan his **s.**, 1121
1Sa 19:2 Jonathan Saul's **s.** delighted much 1121
1Sa 20:27 and Saul said unto Jonathan his **s.**, 1121
1Sa 20:27 cometh not the **s.** of Jesse to meat, 1121
1Sa 20:30 Thou **s.** of the perverse rebellious 1121
1Sa 20:30 thou hast chosen the **s.** of Jesse 1121
1Sa 20:31 For a long as the **s.** of Jesse liveth 1121
1Sa 22:7 the **s.** of Jesse give every one of you 1121
1Sa 22:8 sheweth me that my **s.** hath made 1121
1Sa 22:8 a league with the **s.** of Jesse, 1121
1Sa 22:8 my **s.** hath stirred up my servant 1121
1Sa 22:9 I saw the **s.** of Jesse coming to Nob, 1121
1Sa 22:9 Nob, to Ahimelech the **s.** of Ahitub. 1121
1Sa 22:11 call Ahimelech...the **s.** of Ahitub, 1121
1Sa 22:12 said, Hear now, thou **s.** of Ahitub. 1121
1Sa 22:13 me, thou and the **s.** of Jesse, 1121
1Sa 22:14 as David,...the king's **s.** in law, 2860
1Sa 22:20 of Ahimelech the **s.** of Ahitub, 1121
1Sa 23:6 Abiathar the **s.** of Ahimelech fled 1121
1Sa 23:16 Jonathan Saul's **s.** arose, and went 1121
1Sa 24:16 said, Is this thy voice, my **s.** David? 1121
1Sa 25:8 thy servants, and to thy **s.** David. 1121
1Sa 25:10 David? and who is the **s.** of Jesse? 1121
1Sa 25:17 for he is such a **s.** of Belial, that a 1121
1Sa 25:44 to Phalti the **s.** of Laish, which was 1121
1Sa 26:5 Abner the **s.** of Ner, the captain of 1121
1Sa 26:6 and to Abishai the **s.** of Zeruiah, 1121
1Sa 26:14 and to Abner the **s.** of Ner, saying, 1121
1Sa 26:17 said, Is this thy voice, my **s.** David? 1121
1Sa 26:21 I have sinned: return, my **s.** David: 1121
1Sa 26:25 Blessed be thou, my **s.** David: 1121
1Sa 27:2 unto Achish, the **s.** of Maoch, king 1121
1Sa 30:7 Abiathar the priest, Ahimelech's **s.**, 1121
2Sa 1:4 Saul and Jonathan his **s.** are dead 1121
2Sa 1:5 Saul and Jonathan his **s.** be dead? 1121
2Sa 1:12 for Saul, and for Jonathan his **s.**, 1121
2Sa 1:13 I am the **s.** of a stranger, an 1121
2Sa 1:17 over Saul and over Jonathan his **s.** 1121

2Sa 2:8 But Abner the s. of Ner, captain of 1121
2Sa 2:8 took Ish-bosheth, the s. of Saul, ... 1121
2Sa 2:10 Ish-bosheth Saul's s. was forty........... 1121
2Sa 2:12 Abner...s. of Ner, and the servants 1121
2Sa 2:12 of Ish-bosheth the s. of Saul, went 1121
2Sa 2:13 And Joab the s. of Zeruiah, and the 1121
2Sa 2:15 to Ish-bosheth the s. of Saul, and....... 1121
2Sa 3:3 Absalom the s. of Maacah the............ 1121
2Sa 3:4 fourth, Adonijah the s. of Haggith;...... 1121
2Sa 3:4 fifth, Shephatiah the s. of Abital; 1121
2Sa 3:14 to Ish-bosheth Saul's s., saying, ... 1121
2Sa 3:15 even from Phaltiel the s. of Laish....... 1121
2Sa 3:23 Abner the s. of Ner came to the........ 1121
2Sa 3:25 Thou knowest Abner the s. of Ner, ... 1121
2Sa 3:28 the blood of Abner the s. of Ner: 1121
2Sa 3:37 king to slay Abner the s. of Ner. 1121
2Sa 4:1 Saul's s. heard that Abner was........... 1121
2Sa 4:2 Saul's s., had two men that were 1121
2Sa 4:4 Saul's s., had a s. that was lame 1121
2Sa 4:8 head of Ish-bosheth the s. of Saul....... 1121
2Sa 7:14 his father, and he shall be my s.. 1121
2Sa 8:3 also Hadadezer, the s. of Rehob,......... 1121
2Sa 8:10 Toi sent Joram his s. unto king.......... 1121
2Sa 8:12 spoil of Hadadezer, s. of Rehob, ... 1121
2Sa 8:16 Joab the s. of Zeruiah was over the 1121
2Sa 8:16 Jehoshaphat the s. of Ahilud was 1121
2Sa 8:17 And Zadok the s. of Ahitub, and......... 1121
2Sa 8:17 and Ahimelech, the s. of Abiathar, ... 1121
2Sa 8:18 Benaiah the s. of Jehoiada was........... 1121
2Sa 9:3 Jonathan hath yet a s., which is 1121
2Sa 9:4, 5 in Machir, the s. of Ammiel,........... 1121
2Sa 9:6 Mephibosheth, the s. of Jonathan,....... 1121
2Sa 9:6 the s. of Saul, was come unto David, .. 1121
2Sa 9:9 I have given unto thy master's s. 1121
2Sa 9:10 master's s. may have food to eat:....... 1121
2Sa 9:10 thy master's s. shall eat bread 1121
2Sa 9:12 And Mephibosheth had a young s., ... 1121
2Sa 10:1 Hanun his s. reigned in his stead........ 1121
2Sa 10:2 unto Hanun the s. of Nahash, as 1121
2Sa 11:21 Abimelech the s. of Jerubbesheth?...... 1121
2Sa 11:27 became his wife, and bare him a s. 1121
2Sa 12:24 and she bare a s., and he called his 1121
2Sa 13:1 Absalom the s. of David had a fair...... 1121
2Sa 13:1 Amnon the s. of David loved her........ 1121
2Sa 13:3 Jonadab, the s. of Shimeah David's 1121
2Sa 13:4 art thou, being the king's s., lean 1121
2Sa 13:25 Nay, my s., let us not all now go, ... 1121
2Sa 13:32 Jonadab, the s. of Shimeah David's 1121
2Sa 13:37 went to Talmai, the s. of Ammihud,.... 1121
2Sa 13:37 David mourned for his s. every day. ... 1121
2Sa 14:1 Joab the s. of Zeruiah perceived......... 1121
2Sa 14:11 any more, lest they destroy my s....... 1121
2Sa 14:11 there shall not one hair of thy s. fall ... 1121
2Sa 14:16 destroy me and my s. together.......... 1121
2Sa 15:27 two sons with you, Ahimaaz thy s., ... 1121
2Sa 15:27 and Jonathan the s. of Abiathar. 1121
2Sa 15:36 their two sons, Ahimaaz Zadok's s.,.........
2Sa 15:36 and Jonathan Abiathar's s.; ....
2Sa 16:3 said, And where is thy master's s.?..... 1121
2Sa 16:5 name was Shimei, the s. of Gera:....... 1121
2Sa 16:8 into the hand of Absalom thy s.: 1121
2Sa 16:9 Then said Abishai the s. of Zeruiah..... 1121
2Sa 16:11 Behold, my s., which came forth of 1121
2Sa 16:19 I not serve in the presence of his s.? .. 1121
2Sa 17:25 Amasa was a man's s., whose name.... 1121
2Sa 17:27 Shobi the s. of Nahash of Rabbah, ... 1121
2Sa 17:27 and Machir the s. of Ammiel of.......... 1121
2Sa 18:2 hand of Abishai the s. of Zeruiah, ... 1121
2Sa 18:12 mine hand against the king's s.: 1121
2Sa 18:18 said, I have no s. to keep my name 1121
2Sa 18:19 Then said Ahimaaz the s. of Zadok, ... 1121
2Sa 18:20 because the king's s. is dead.............. 1121
2Sa 18:22 Then said Ahimaaz the s. of Zadok 1121
2Sa 18:22 Wherefore wilt thou run, my s.,......... 1121
2Sa 18:27 running of Ahimaaz the s. of Zadok..... 1121
2Sa 18:33 said, O my s. Absalom, my s., my s.... 1121
2Sa 18:33 for thee, O Absalom, my s., my s.! 1121
2Sa 19:2 how the king was grieved for his s.. ... 1121
2Sa 19:4 with a loud voice, O my s. Absalom, ... 1121
2Sa 19:4 Absalom, O Absalom, my s., my s.! 1121
2Sa 19:16 Shimei the s. of Gera, a Benjamite, ... 1121
2Sa 19:18 Shimei the s. of Gera fell down.......... 1121
2Sa 19:21 Abishai the s. of Zeruiah answered 1121
2Sa 19:24 Mephibosheth the s. of Saul came 1121
2Sa 20:1 name was Sheba, the s. of Bichri, ... 1121
2Sa 20:1 we inheritance in the s. of Jesse: 1121
2Sa 20:2 and followed Sheba the s. of Bichri: 1121
2Sa 20:6 Sheba the s. of Bichri do us more 1121
2Sa 20:7 pursue after Sheba the s. of Bichri. 1121
2Sa 20:10 pursued after Sheba the s. of Bichri..... 1121
2Sa 20:13 pursue after Sheba the s. of Bichri. 1121
2Sa 20:21 Sheba the s. of Bichri by name, ... 1121
2Sa 20:22 the head of Sheba the s. of Bichri, ... 1121
2Sa 20:23 Benaiah the s. of Jehoiada was over.... 1121
2Sa 20:24 Jehoshaphat the s. of Ahilud was 1121
2Sa 21:7 Mephibosheth, the s. of Jonathan........ 1121
2Sa 21:7 of Jonathan the s. of Saul,................. 1121
2Sa 21:7 David and Jonathan the s. of Saul. 1121
2Sa 21:8 up for Adriel the s. of Barzillai the...... 1121
2Sa 21:12 and the bones of Jonathan his s.......... 1121
2Sa 21:13 and the bones of Jonathan his s.;........ 1121
2Sa 21:14 bones of Saul and Jonathan his s......... 1121
2Sa 21:17 Abishai the s. of Zeruiah succoured..... 1121
2Sa 21:19 Elhanan the s. of Jaare-oregim, ... 1121
2Sa 21:21 Jonathan the s. of Shimeah the........... 1121
2Sa 23:1 David the s. of Jesse said, and the 1121
2Sa 23:9 Eleazar the s. of Dodo the Ahohite, ... 1121
2Sa 23:11 was Shammah the s. of Agee the 1121
2Sa 23:18 And Abishai,...the s. of Zeruiah,......... 1121
2Sa 23:20 And Benaiah the s. of Jehoiada, the 1121
2Sa 23:20 the s. of a valiant man, of Kabzeel,..... 1121
2Sa 23:22 did Benaiah the s. of Jehoiada, ... 1121
2Sa 23:24 Elhanan the s. of Dodo of................. 1121
2Sa 23:26 Ira the s. of Ikkesh the Tekoite, ... 1121
2Sa 23:29 Heleb the s. of Baanah, a................. 1121
2Sa 23:29 Ittai the s. of Ribai out of Gibeah 1121
2Sa 23:33 Ahiam the s. of Sharar the Hararite, ... 1121
2Sa 23:34 Eliphelet the s. of Ahasbai, ... 1121
2Sa 23:34 the s. of the Maachathite,.................. 1121
2Sa 23:34 Eliam the s. of Ahithophel the 1121
2Sa 23:36 Igal the s. of Nathan of Zobah, ... 1121
2Sa 23:37 to Joab the s. of Zeruiah, and............ 1121
1Ki 1:5 Adonijah the s. of Haggith exalted 1121
1Ki 1:7 with Joab the s. of Zeruiah, and 1121
1Ki 1:8 and Benaiah the s. of Jehoiada, ... 1121
1Ki 1:11 Adonijah the s. of Haggith doth.......... 1121
1Ki 1:12 life, and the life of thy s. Solomon. 1121
1Ki 1:13, 17 Solomon thy s. shall reign after...... 1121
1Ki 1:21 I and my s. Solomon...be counted 1121
1Ki 1:26 and Benaiah the s. of Jehoiada, ... 1121
1Ki 1:30 Solomon thy s. shall reign after me, ... 1121
1Ki 1:32 and Benaiah the s. of Jehoiada. 1121
1Ki 1:33 cause Solomon my s. to ride upon....... 1121
1Ki 1:36 Benaiah the s. of Jehoiada answered..... 1121
1Ki 1:38 and Benaiah the s. of Jehoiada, ... 1121
1Ki 1:42 Jonathan...s. of Abiathar the priest...... 1121
1Ki 1:44 and Benaiah the s. of Jehoiada, ... 1121
1Ki 2:1 he charged Solomon his s., saying, ... 1121
1Ki 2:5 what Joab the s. of Zeruiah did to....... 1121
1Ki 2:5 Israel, unto Abner the s. of Ner,......... 1121
1Ki 2:5 and unto Amasa the s. of Jether,......... 1121
1Ki 2:8 with thee Shimei the s. of Gera, ... 1121
1Ki 2:13 Adonijah the s. of Haggith came to 1121
1Ki 2:22 and for Joab the s. of Zeruiah. 1121
1Ki 2:25 hand of Benaiah the s. of Jehoiada; 1121
1Ki 2:29 sent Benaiah the s. of Jehoiada, ... 1121
1Ki 2:32 Abner the s. of Ner, captain of the..... 1121
1Ki 2:32 Amasa the s. of Jether, captain of........ 1121
1Ki 2:34 Benaiah the s. of Jehoiada went up, ... 1121
1Ki 2:35 king put Benaiah the s. of Jehoiada 1121
1Ki 2:39 Achish s. of Maachach king of Gath. ... 1121
1Ki 2:46 Benaiah the s. of Jehoiada;................ 1121
1Ki 3:6 given him a s. to sit on his throne, ... 1121
1Ki 3:20 and took my s. from beside me,.......... 1121
1Ki 3:21 it was not my s., which I did bear. 1121
1Ki 3:22 living is my s.,...the dead is thy s.. 1121
1Ki 3:22 dead is thy s.,...the living is my s.. 1121
1Ki 3:23 my s....liveth, and thy s. is the dead:.. 1121
1Ki 3:23 thy s. is dead, and my s. is...living..... 1121
1Ki 3:26 for her bowels yearned upon her s., ... 1121
1Ki 4:2 Azariah the s. of Zadok the priest,...... 1121
1Ki 4:3 Jehoshaphat the s. of Ahilud, the........ 1121
1Ki 4:4 Benaiah the s. of Jehoiada was over.... 1121
1Ki 4:5 Azariah the s. of Nathan was over...... 1121
1Ki 4:5 Zabud...s. of Nathan was principal 1121
1Ki 4:6 Adoniram the s. of Abda was over....... 1121
1Ki 4:8 The s. of Hur, in mount Ephraim: 1133
1Ki 4:9 The s. of Dekar, in Makaz, and in....... 1128
1Ki 4:10 The s. of Hesed, in Aruboth; to.......... 1136
1Ki 4:11 The s. of Abinadab, in all the............. 1125
1Ki 4:12 Baana the s. of Ahilud; to him 1121
1Ki 4:13 The s. of Geber, in Ramoth-gilead;..... 1127
1Ki 4:13 towns of Jair the s. of Manasseh, ... 1121
1Ki 4:14 Ahinadab the s. of Iddo had.............. 1121
1Ki 4:16 Baanah the s. of Hushai was in.......... 1121
1Ki 4:17 Jehoshaphat the s. of Paruah, in......... 1121
1Ki 4:18 Shimei the s. of Elah, in Benjamin: 1121
1Ki 4:19 Geber the s. of Uri was in the........... 1121
1Ki 5:5 Thy s., whom I will set upon thy 1121
1Ki 5:7 hath given unto David a wise s. 1121
1Ki 7:14 He was a widow's s. of the tribe of 1121
1Ki 8:19 thy s. that shall come forth out of 1121
1Ki 11:12 rend it out of the hand of thy s......... 1121
1Ki 11:13 but will give one tribe to thy s. for..... 1121
1Ki 11:20 bare him Genubath his s., whom 1121
1Ki 11:23 adversary, Rezon the s. of Eliadah,..... 1121
1Ki 11:26 And Jeroboam the s. of Nebat, an 1121
1Ki 11:36 And unto his s. will I give one tribe, ... 1121
1Ki 11:43 and Rehoboam his s. reigned in his..... 1121
1Ki 12:2 when Jeroboam the s. of Nebat,......... 1121
1Ki 12:15 unto Jeroboam the s. of Nebat. 1121
1Ki 12:16 we inheritance in the s. of Jesse: 1121
1Ki 12:21 to Rehoboam the s. of Solomon. 1121
1Ki 12:23 unto Rehoboam, the s. of Solomon, ... 1121
1Ki 14:1 Abijah the s. of Jeroboam fell sick....... 1121
1Ki 14:5 to ask a thing of thee for her s.; 1121
1Ki 14:20 Nadab his s. reigned in his stead........ 1121
1Ki 14:21 Rehoboam...s. of Solomon reigned...... 1121
1Ki 14:31 Abijam his s. reigned in his stead. 1121
1Ki 15:1 of king Jeroboam the s. of Nebat........ 1121
1Ki 15:4 to set up his s. after him, and to........ 1121
1Ki 15:8 and Asa his s. reigned in his stead...... 1121
1Ki 15:18 Ben-hadad, the s. of Tabrimon,.......... 1121
1Ki 15:18 the s. of Hezion, king of Syria, ... 1121
1Ki 15:24 Jehoshaphat his s. reigned in his........ 1121
1Ki 15:25 Nadab the s. of Jeroboam began to..... 1121
1Ki 15:27 And Baasha the s. of Ahijah, of the..... 1121
1Ki 15:33 began Baasha the s. of Ahijah to 1121
1Ki 16:1 came to Jehu the s. of Hanani........... 1121
1Ki 16:3 house of Jeroboam the s. of Nebat...... 1121
1Ki 16:6 Elah his s. reigned in his stead. 1121
1Ki 16:7 the prophet Jehu the s. of Hanani....... 1121
1Ki 16:8 began Elah the s. of Baasha to reign... 1121
1Ki 16:13 Baasha, and the sins of Elah his s., ... 1121
1Ki 16:21 followed Tibni the s. of Ginath,.......... 1121
1Ki 16:22 that followed Tibni the s. of Ginath: 1121
1Ki 16:26 way of Jeroboam the s. of Nebat, ... 1121
1Ki 16:28 Ahab his s. reigned in his stead. 1121
1Ki 16:29 began Ahab the s. of Omri to reign..... 1121
1Ki 16:29 Ahab the s. of Omri reigned over........ 1121
1Ki 16:30 Ahab the s. of Omri did evil in the 1121
1Ki 16:31 sins of Jeroboam the s. of Nebat, ... 1121
1Ki 16:34 thereof in his youngest s. Segub,..............
1Ki 16:34 he spake by Joshua the s. of Nun....... 1121
1Ki 17:12 go in and dress it for me and my s....... 1121
1Ki 17:13 after make for thee and for thy s.. 1121
1Ki 17:17 the s. of the woman, the mistress of... 1121
1Ki 17:18 to remembrance, and to slay my s.? ... 1121
1Ki 17:19 he said unto her, Give me thy s. 1121
1Ki 17:20 whom I sojourn, by slaying her s.? 1121
1Ki 17:23 and Elijah said, See, thy s. liveth. 1121
1Ki 19:16 Jehu the s. of Nimshi shalt thou 1121
1Ki 19:16 and Elisha the s. of Shaphat of........... 1121
1Ki 19:19 found Elisha the s. of Shaphat, who 1121
1Ki 21:22 house of Jeroboam the s. of Nebat,...... 1121
1Ki 21:22 house of Baasha the s. of Ahijah, ... 1121
1Ki 22:8 one man, Micaiah the s. of Imlah,........ 1121
1Ki 22:9 hither Micaiah the s. of Imlah. 1121
1Ki 22:11 And Zedekiah the s. of Chenaanah...... 1121
1Ki 22:24 Zedekiah the s. of Chenaanah went..... 1121
1Ki 22:26 the city, and to Joash the king's s.;..... 1121
1Ki 22:40 Ahaziah his s. reigned in his stead. 1121
1Ki 22:41 Jehoshaphat the s. of Asa began to..... 1121
1Ki 22:49 said Ahaziah the s. of Ahab unto 1121
1Ki 22:50 Jehoram his s. reigned in his stead. 1121
1Ki 22:51 Ahaziah...s. of Ahab began to reign..... 1121
1Ki 22:52 way of Jeroboam the s. of Nebat, ... 1121
2Ki 1:17 of Jehoram the s. of Jehoshaphat........ 1121
2Ki 1:17 of Judah; because he had no s. 1121
2Ki 3:1 Now Jehoram the s. of Ahab began..... 1121
2Ki 3:3 sins of Jeroboam the s. of Nebat, ... 1121
2Ki 3:11 Here is Elisha the s. of Shaphat, ... 1121
2Ki 3:27 took his eldest s. that should have...... 1121
2Ki 4:6 that she said unto her s., Bring me 1121
2Ki 4:16 time of life, thou shalt embrace a s..... 1121
2Ki 4:17 and bare a s. at that season that 1121
2Ki 4:28 said, Did I desire a s. of my lord? 1121
2Ki 4:36 unto him, he said, Take up thy s........ 1121

2Ki 4:37 and took up her s., and went out. 1121
2Ki 6:28 Give thy s., that we may eat him 1121
2Ki 6:28 and we will eat my s. to morrow 1121
2Ki 6:29 So we boiled my s., and did eat him: 1121
2Ki 6:29 Give thy s. that we may eat him: 1121
2Ki 6:29 eat him: and she hath hid her son 1121
2Ki 6:31 head of Elisha the s. of Shaphat 1121
2Ki 6:32 See ye how this s. of a murderer 1121
2Ki 8:1,5 whose s. he had restored to life, 1121
2Ki 8:5 and this is her s., whom Elisha 1121
2Ki 8:9 Thy s. Ben-hadad king of Syria 1121
2Ki 8:16 Joram the s. of Ahab king of Israel, 1121
2Ki 8:16 Jehoram the s. of Jehoshaphat king 1121
2Ki 8:24 Ahaziah his s. reigned in his stead. 1121
2Ki 8:25 Joram the s. of Ahab king of Israel 1121
2Ki 8:25 Ahaziah th s. of Jehoram king of 1121
2Ki 8:27 the s. in law of the house of Ahab. 2860
2Ki 8:28 he went with Joram the s. of Ahab 1121
2Ki 8:29 Ahaziah the s. of Jehoram king of 1121
2Ki 8:29 down to see Joram the s. of Ahab 1121
2Ki 9:2 look out there Jehu the s. of 1121
2Ki 9:2 Jehoshaphat the s. of Nimshi, 1121
2Ki 9:9 house of Jeroboam the s. of Nebat, 1121
2Ki 9:9 house of Baasha the s. of Ahijah: 1121
2Ki 9:14 So Jehu the s. of Jehoshaphat the 1121
2Ki 9:14 the s. of Nimshi conspired 1121
2Ki 9:20 driving of Jehu the s. of Nimshi; 1121
2Ki 9:29 of Joram the s. of Ahab began 1121
2Ki 10:15 on Jehonadab the s. of Rechab 1121
2Ki 10:23 and Jehonadab the s. of Rechab, 1121
2Ki 10:29 sins of Jeroboam the s. of Nebat, 1121
2Ki 10:35 And Jehoahaz his s. reigned in his 1121
2Ki 11:1 Athaliah...saw that her s. was dead, 1121
2Ki 11:2 took Joash the s. of Ahaziah, and 1121
2Ki 11:4 and shewed them the king's s. 1121
2Ki 11:12 And he brought forth the king's s., 1121
2Ki 12:21 For Jozachar the s. of Shimeath, 1121
2Ki 12:21 and Jehozabad the s. of Shomer, 1121
2Ki 12:21 Amaziah his s. reigned in his stead. 1121
2Ki 13:1 of Joash the s. of Ahaziah king of 1121
2Ki 13:1 Jehoahaz the s. of Jehu began to 1121
2Ki 13:2 sins of Jeroboam the s. of Nebat, 1121
2Ki 13:3 hand of Ben-hadad the s. of Hazael, 1121
2Ki 13:9 Joash his s. reigned in his stead. 1121
2Ki 13:10 Jehoash the s. of Jehoahaz to reign 1121
2Ki 13:11 sins of Jeroboam the s. of Nebat, 1121
2Ki 13:24 and Ben-hadad his s. reigned in his 1121
2Ki 13:25 Jehoash the s. of Jehoahaz took 1121
2Ki 13:25 hand of Ben-hadad the s. of Hazael 1121
2Ki 14:1 year of Joash s. of Jehoahaz king 1121
2Ki 14:1 Amaziah the s. of Joash king of 1121
2Ki 14:8 to Jehoash, the s. of Jehoahaz 1121
2Ki 14:8 s. of Jehu, king of Israel, saying, 1121
2Ki 14:9 Give thy daughter to my s. to wife: 1121
2Ki 14:13 the s. of Jehoash the s. of Ahaziah, 1121
2Ki 14:16 Jeroboam his s. reigned in his stead. 1121
2Ki 14:17 Amaziah the s. of Joash king of 1121
2Ki 14:17 the death of Jehoash s. of Jehoahaz 1121
2Ki 14:23 Amaziah the s. of Joash king of 1121
2Ki 14:23 Jeroboam the s. of Joash king of 1121
2Ki 14:24 sins of Jeroboam the s. of Nebat, 1121
2Ki 14:25 servant Jonah, the s. of Amittai, 1121
2Ki 14:27 hand of Jeroboam the s. of Joash. 1121
2Ki 14:29 Zachariah his s. reigned in his 1121
2Ki 15:1 began Azariah s. of Amaziah king 1121
2Ki 15:5 Jotham the king's s. was over the 1121
2Ki 15:7 Jotham his s. reigned in his stead. 1121
2Ki 15:8 did Zachariah the s. of Jeroboam 1121
2Ki 15:9 sins of Jeroboam the s. of Nebat, 1121
2Ki 15:10 Shallum the s. of Jabesh conspired 1121
2Ki 15:13 Shallum the s. of Jabesh began to 1121
2Ki 15:14 Menahem the s. of Gadi went up 1121
2Ki 15:14 smote Shallum the s. of Jabesh 1121
2Ki 15:17 Menahem the s. of Gadi to reign 1121
2Ki 15:18 sins of Jeroboam the s. of Nebat, 1121
2Ki 15:22 Pekahiah his s. reigned in his 1121
2Ki 15:23 Pekahiah the s. of Menahem began 1121
2Ki 15:24 sins of Jeroboam the s. of Nebat, 1121
2Ki 15:25 But Pekah the s. of Remaliah, a 1121
2Ki 15:27 Pekah the s. of Remaliah began to 1121
2Ki 15:28 sins of Jeroboam the s. of Nebat, 1121
2Ki 15:30 Hoshea the s. of Elah made a 1121
2Ki 15:30 against Pekah the s. of Remaliah, 1121
2Ki 15:30 year of Jotham the s. of Uzziah 1121
2Ki 15:32 Pekah the s. of Remaliah king of 1121
2Ki 15:32 Jotham the s. of Uzziah king of 1121
2Ki 15:37 And Pekah the s. of Remaliah 1121
2Ki 15:38 and Ahaz his s. reigned in his stead. 1121
2Ki 16:1 year of Pekah the s. of Remaliah 1121
2Ki 16:1 Ahaz the s. of Jotham king of Judah 1121
2Ki 16:3 made his s. to pass through the fire, 1121
2Ki 16:5 Pekah s. of Remaliah king of Israel 1121
2Ki 16:7 I am thy servant and thy s.: come 1121
2Ki 16:20 Hezekiah his s. reigned in his stead. 1121
2Ki 17:1 began Hoshea the s. of Elah to reign 1121
2Ki 17:21 Jeroboam the s. of Nebat king: 1121
2Ki 18:1 of Hoshea s. of Elah king of Israel, 1121
2Ki 18:1 that Hezekiah the s. of Ahaz king 1121
2Ki 18:9 of Hoshea s. of Elah king of Israel, 1121
2Ki 18:18 to them Eliakim the s. of Hilkiah, 1121
2Ki 18:18 Joah the s. of Asaph the recorder. 1121
2Ki 18:26 Then said Eliakim the s. of Hilkiah, 1121
2Ki 18:37 came Eliakim the s. of Hilkiah, 1121
2Ki 18:37 Joah the s. of Asaph the recorder, 1121
2Ki 19:2 to Isaiah the prophet the s. of Amoz. 1121
2Ki 19:20 Isaiah the s. of Amoz sent to 1121
2Ki 19:37 Esarhaddon his s. reigned in his 1121
2Ki 20:1 prophet Isaiah the s. of Amoz came 1121
2Ki 20:12 Berodach-baladan,...s. of Baladan, 1121
2Ki 20:21 Manasseh his s. reigned in his stead. 1121
2Ki 21:6 made his s. pass through the fire, 1121
2Ki 21:7 said to David, and to Solomon his s., 1121
2Ki 21:18 Amon his s. reigned in his stead. 1121
2Ki 21:24 made Josiah his s. king in his stead. 1121
2Ki 21:26 Josiah his s. reigned in his stead. 1121
2Ki 22:3 sent Shaphan the s. of Azaliah, 1121
2Ki 22:3 the s. of Meshullam, the scribe, to 1121
2Ki 22:12 and Ahikam the s. of Shaphan, 1121
2Ki 22:12 and Achbor the s. of Michaiah, and 1121
2Ki 22:14 the wife of Shallum the s. of Tikvah, 1121
2Ki 22:14 the s. of Harhas, keeper of the 1121
2Ki 23:10 make his s. or his daughter to pass 1121
2Ki 23:15 which Jeroboam the s. of Nebat, 1121
2Ki 23:30 took Jehoahaz the s. of Josiah, 1121
2Ki 23:34 made Eliakim the s. of Josiah king 1121
2Ki 24:6 Jehoiachin his s. reigned in his 1121
2Ki 25:22 made Gedaliah the s. of Ahikam, 1121
2Ki 25:22 the s. of Shaphan, ruler. 1121
2Ki 25:23 even Ishmael the s. of Nethaniah, 1121
2Ki 25:23 and Johanan the s. of Careah, and 1121
2Ki 25:23 Seraiah the s. of Tanhumeth the 1121
2Ki 25:23 Jaazaniah the s. of a Maachathite, 1121
2Ki 25:25 that Ishmael the s. of Nethaniah, 1121
2Ki 25:25 the s. of Elishama, of the seed royal, 1121
1Ch 1:43 of Israel; Bela the s. of Beor: 1121
1Ch 1:44 Jobab the s. of Zerah of Bozrah 1121
1Ch 1:46 Hadad the s. of Bedad, which 1121
1Ch 1:49 Baal-hanan the s. of Achbor reigned 1121
1Ch 2:18 And Caleb the s. of Hezron begat 1121
1Ch 2:45 And the s. of Shammai was Maon: 1121
1Ch 2:50 the sons of Caleb the s. of Hur, 1121
1Ch 3:2 Absalom the s. of Maachah the 1121
1Ch 3:2 fourth, Adonijah the s. of Haggith: 1121
1Ch 3:10 And Solomon's s. was Rehoboam, 1121
1Ch 3:10 Abia his s., Asa his s., 1121
1Ch 3:10 Jehoshaphat his s., 1121
1Ch 3:11 Joram his s., Ahaziah his s., 1121
1Ch 3:11 Joash his s., 1121
1Ch 3:12 Amaziah his s., 1121
1Ch 3:12 Azariah his s., Jotham his s., 1121
1Ch 3:13 Ahaz his s., Hezekiah his s., 1121
1Ch 3:13 Manasseh his s., 1121
1Ch 3:14 Amon his s., Josiah his s. 1121
1Ch 3:16 Jeconiah his s., Zedekiah his s. 1121
1Ch 3:17 of Jeconiah; Assir, Salathiel his s., 1121
1Ch 4:2 And Reaiah the s. of Shobal begat 1121
1Ch 4:8 of Aharhel the s. of Harum. 1121
1Ch 4:15 sons of Caleb the s. of Jephunneh; 1121
1Ch 4:21 The sons of Shelah the s. of Judah 1121
1Ch 4:25 Shallum his s., 1121
1Ch 4:25 Mibsam his s., Mishma his s. 1121
1Ch 4:26 Hamuel his s., Zacchur his s., 1121
1Ch 4:26 Shimei his s. 1121
1Ch 4:34 and Joshah the s. of Amaziah, 1121
1Ch 4:35 Joel, and Jehu the s. of Josibiah, 1121
1Ch 4:35 the s. of Seraiah, the s. of Asiel, 1121
1Ch 4:37 Ziza the s. of Shiphi, the s. of Allon, 1121
1Ch 4:37 the s. of Jedaiah, the s. of Shimri, 1121
1Ch 4:37 the s. of Shemaiah; 1121
1Ch 5:1 the sons of Joseph the s. of Israel: 1121
1Ch 5:4 sons of Joel; Shemaiah his s., 1121
1Ch 5:4 Gog his s., Shimei his s., 1121
1Ch 5:5 Micah his s., 1121
1Ch 5:5 Reaia his s., Baal his s., 1121
1Ch 5:6 Beerah his s., whom 1121
1Ch 5:8 And Bela the s. of Azaz, 1121
1Ch 5:8 the s. of Shema, the s. of Joel, who 1121
1Ch 5:14 children of Abihail the s. of Huri, 1121
1Ch 5:14 the s. of Jaroah, the s. of Gilead, 1121
1Ch 5:14 s. of Michael, the s. of Jeshishai, 1121
1Ch 5:14 the s. of Jahdo, the s. of Buz; 1121
1Ch 5:15 Ahi the s. of Abdiel, the s. of Guni, 1121
1Ch 6:20 Of Gershom; Libni his s., 1121
1Ch 6:20 Jahath his s., Zimmah his s., 1121
1Ch 6:21 Joah his s., Iddo his s., 1121
1Ch 6:21 Zerah his s., Jeaterai his s. 1121
1Ch 6:22 sons of Kohath; Amminadab his s., 1121
1Ch 6:22 Korah his s., Assir his s., 1121
1Ch 6:23 Elkanah his s., and Ebiasaph 1121
1Ch 6:23 Ebiasaph his s., and Assir his s., 1121
1Ch 6:24 Tahath his s., Uriel his s., 1121
1Ch 6:24 Uzziah his s., and Shaul his s. 1121
1Ch 6:26 Zophai his s., and Nahath his s., 1121
1Ch 6:27 Eliab his s., Jeroham his s., 1121
1Ch 6:27 Elkanah his s. 1121
1Ch 6:29 sons of Merari; Mahli, Libni his s., 1121
1Ch 6:29 Shimei his s., Uzza his s., 1121
1Ch 6:30 Shimea his s., Haggiah his s., 1121
1Ch 6:30 Asaiah his s. 1121
1Ch 6:33 Heman a singer, the s. of Joel, 1121
1Ch 6:33 the s. of Shemuel, 1121
1Ch 6:34 s. of Elkanah, the s. of Jeroham, 1121
1Ch 6:34 the s. of Eliel, the s. of Toah, 1121
1Ch 6:35 The s. of Zuph, the s. of Elkanah. 1121
1Ch 6:35 the s. of Mahath, the s. of Amasai, 1121
1Ch 6:36 The s. of Elkanah, the s. of Joel, 1121
1Ch 6:36 s. of Azariah, the s. of Zephaniah, 1121
1Ch 6:37 The s. of Tahath, the s. of Assir, 1121
1Ch 6:37 the s. of Ebiasaph, the s. of Korah, 1121
1Ch 6:38 The s. of Izhar, the s. of Kohath, 1121
1Ch 6:38 the s. of Levi, the s. of Israel. 1121
1Ch 6:39 even Asaph the s. of Berachiah, 1121
1Ch 6:39 the s. of Shimea, 1121
1Ch 6:40 s. of Michael, the s. of Baaseiah, 1121
1Ch 6:40 of Baaseiah, the s. of Malchiah, 1121
1Ch 6:41 The s. of Ethni, the s. of Zerah, 1121
1Ch 6:41 of Zerah, the s. of Adaiah, 1121
1Ch 6:42 The s. of Ethan, the s. of Zimmah, 1121
1Ch 6:42 of Zimmah, the s. of Shimei, 1121
1Ch 6:43 The s. of Jahath, the s. of Gershom, 1121
1Ch 6:43 of Gershom, the s. of Levi. 1121
1Ch 6:44 left hand: Ethan the s. of Kishi, 1121
1Ch 6:44 the s. of Abdi, the s. of Malluch, 1121
1Ch 6:45 s. of Hashabiah, the s. of Amaziah, 1121
1Ch 6:45 of Amaziah, the s. of Hilkiah, 1121
1Ch 6:46 The s. of Amzi, the s. of Bani, the 1121
1Ch 6:46 of Bani, the s. of Shamer, 1121
1Ch 6:47 The s. of Mahli, the s. of Mushi, 1121
1Ch 6:47 the s. of Merari, the s. of Levi. 1121
1Ch 6:50 the sons of Aaron; Eleazar his s., 1121
1Ch 6:50 Phinehas his s., Abishua his s., 1121
1Ch 6:51 Bukki his s., Uzzi his s., 1121
1Ch 6:51 Zerahiah his s., 1121
1Ch 6:52 Meraioth his s., 1121
1Ch 6:52 Amariah his s., Ahitub his s., 1121
1Ch 6:53 Zadok his s., Ahimaaz his s. 1121
1Ch 6:56 gave to Caleb the s. of Jephunneh. 1121
1Ch 7:16 the wife of Machir bare a s., and 1121
1Ch 7:17 sons of Gilead, the s. of Machir, 1121
1Ch 7:17 the s. of Manasseh. 1121
1Ch 7:20 Shuthelah, and Bered his s., and 1121
1Ch 7:20 and Tahath his s., 1121
1Ch 7:20 Eladah his s., and Tahath his s., 1121
1Ch 7:21 Zabad his s., and Shuthelah his s., 1121
1Ch 7:23 she conceived, and bare a s., and he 1121
1Ch 7:25 Rephah was his s., also Resheph, 1121
1Ch 7:25 and Telah his s., and Tahan his s., 1121
1Ch 7:26 Laadan his s., Ammihud his s., 1121
1Ch 7:26 Elishama his s., 1121
1Ch 7:27 Non his s., Jehoshuah his s. 1121
1Ch 7:29 children of Joseph the s. of Israel. 1121
1Ch 8:30 his firstborn s. Abdon, and Zur, and 1121
1Ch 8:34 the s. of Jonathan was Merib-baal; 1121
1Ch 8:37 begat Binea: Rapha was his s., 1121
1Ch 8:37 Eleasah his s., Azel his s.: 1121
1Ch 9:4 Uthai the s. of Ammihud, 1121
1Ch 9:4 the s. of Omri, the s. of Imri, 1121
1Ch 9:4 s. of Bani, of the children of Pharez 1121
1Ch 9:4 children of Pharez the s. of Judah. 1121
1Ch 9:7 Sallu the s. of Meshullam, 1121
1Ch 9:7 s. of Hodaviah, the s. of Hasenuah, 1121

1Ch 9:8 And Ibneiah the **s.** of Jeroham, 1121
1Ch 9:8 Elah the **s.** of Uzzi, the **s.** of Michri, 1121
1Ch 9:8 Meshullam the **s.** of Shephathiah, 1121
1Ch 9:8 the **s.** of Reuel, the **s.** of Ibnijah; 1121
1Ch 9:11 And Azariah the **s.** of Hilkiah, 1121
1Ch 9:11 the **s.** of Meshullam, 1121
1Ch 9:11 the **s.** of Zadok, the **s.** of Meraioth, 1121
1Ch 9:11 **s.** of Ahitub, the ruler of the house 1121
1Ch 9:12 And Adaiah the **s.** of Jeroham, 1121
1Ch 9:12 **s.** of Pashur, the **s.** of Malchijah, 1121
1Ch 9:12 and Maasiai the **s.** of Adiel, 1121
1Ch 9:12 **s.** of Jahzerah, the **s.** of Meshullam, 1121
1Ch 9:12 **s.** of Meshillemith, the **s.** of Immer; 1121
1Ch 9:14 Shemaiah the **s.** of Hasshub, the 1121
1Ch 9:14 the **s.** of Azrikam, 1121
1Ch 9:14 the **s.** of Hashabiah, of the sons of 1121
1Ch 9:15 and Mattaniah the **s.** of Micah, 1121
1Ch 9:15 the **s.** of Zichri, the **s.** of Asaph; 1121
1Ch 9:16 And Obadiah the **s.** of Shemaiah, 1121
1Ch 9:16 the **s.** of Galal, the **s.** of Jeduthun, 1121
1Ch 9:16 and Berechiah the **s.** of Asa, 1121
1Ch 9:16 the **s.** of Elkanah, that dwelt in 1121
1Ch 9:19 And Shallum the **s.** of Kore, 1121
1Ch 9:19 the **s.** of Ebiasaph, the **s.** of Korah, 1121
1Ch 9:20 Phinehas the **s.** of Eleazar was the 1121
1Ch 9:21 Zechariah the **s.** of Meshelemiah 1121
1Ch 9:36 And his firstborn **s.** Abdon, then 1121
1Ch 9:40 the **s.** of Jonathan was Merib-baal: 1121
1Ch 9:43 begat Binea; and Rephaiah his **s.**, 1121
1Ch 9:43 Eleasah his **s.**, Azel his **s.** 1121
1Ch 10:14 kingdom unto David the **s.** of Jesse 1121
1Ch 11:6 So Joab the **s.** of Zeruiah went first 1121
1Ch 11:12 him was Eleazar the **s.** of Dodo, 1121
1Ch 11:22 Benaiah the **s.** of Jehoiada, the 1121
1Ch 11:22 the **s.** of a valiant man of Kabzeel, 1121
1Ch 11:24 did Benaiah the **s.** of Jehoiada, 1121
1Ch 11:26 of Joab, Elhanan the **s.** of Dodo of 1121
1Ch 11:28 Ira the **s.** of Ikkesh the Tekoite, 1121
1Ch 11:30 Heled the **s.** of Baanah the 1121
1Ch 11:31 Ithai the **s.** of Ribai of Gibeah, that 1121
1Ch 11:34 Jonathan the **s.** of Shage the 1121
1Ch 11:35 Ahiam the **s.** of Sacar the Hararite, 1121
1Ch 11:35 the Hararite, Eliphal the **s.** of Ur, 1121
1Ch 11:37 Carmelite, Naarai the **s.** of Ezbai, 1121
1Ch 11:38 Nathan, Mibhar the **s.** of Haggeri, 1121
1Ch 11:39 of Joab the **s.** of Zeruiah, 1121
1Ch 11:41 the Hittite, Zabad the **s.** of Ahlai, 1121
1Ch 11:42 Adina the **s.** of Shiza the 1121
1Ch 11:43 Hanan the **s.** of Maachah, and 1121
1Ch 11:45 Jediael the **s.** of Shimri, and Joha 1121
1Ch 12:1 close because of Saul the **s.** of Kish: 1121
1Ch 12:18 and on thy side thou **s.** of Jesse: 1121
1Ch 15:17 appointed Heman the **s.** of Joel; 1121
1Ch 15:17 brethren, Asaph the **s.** of Berechiah; 1121
1Ch 15:17 Ethan the **s.** of Kushaiah: 1121
1Ch 16:38 Obed-edom also the **s.** of Jeduthun 1121
1Ch 17:13 his father, and he shall be my **s.**: 1121
1Ch 18:10 sent Hadoram his **s.** to king David, 1121
1Ch 18:12 Abishai the **s.** of Zeruiah slew of 1121
1Ch 18:15 Joab the **s.** of Zeruiah was over the 1121
1Ch 18:15 and Jehoshaphat the **s.** of Ahilud, 1121
1Ch 18:16 And Zadok the **s.** of Ahitub, and 1121
1Ch 18:16 Abimelech the **s.** of Abiathar, were 1121
1Ch 18:17 Benaiah the **s.** of Jehoiada was 1121
1Ch 19:1 and his **s.** reigned in his stead. 1121
1Ch 19:2 unto Hanun the **s.** of Nahash, 1121
1Ch 20:5 Elhanan the **s.** of Jair slew Lahmi 1121
1Ch 20:6 he also was the **s.** of the giant. 3205
1Ch 20:7 Jonathan the **s.** of Shimea David's 1121
1Ch 22:5 said, Solomon my **s.** is younger and 1121
1Ch 22:6 Then he called for Solomon his **s.**, 1121
1Ch 22:7 David said to Solomon, My **s.**, as 1121
1Ch 22:9 a **s.** shall be born to thee, who shall 1121
1Ch 22:10 he shall be my **s.**, and I will be his 1121
1Ch 22:11 Now, my **s.**, the Lord be with thee; 1121
1Ch 22:17 of Israel to help Solomon his **s.**, 1121
1Ch 23:1 he made Solomon his **s.** king over 1121
1Ch 24:6 Shemaiah the **s.** of Nethaneel the 1121
1Ch 24:6 and Ahimelech the **s.** of Abiathar, 1121
1Ch 24:29 Kish: the **s.** of Kish was Jerahmeel. 1121
1Ch 26:1 was Meshelemiah the **s.** of Kore, of 1121
1Ch 26:6 Shemaiah his **s.** were sons born, 1121
1Ch 26:14 Then for Zechariah his **s.**, a wise 1121
1Ch 26:24 And Shebuel the **s.** of Gershom, 1121
1Ch 26:24 the **s.** of Moses, was ruler over 1121
1Ch 26:25 by Eliezer; Rehabiah his **s.**, and 1121
1Ch 26:25 Jeshaiah his **s.**, and Joram his **s.**, 1121
1Ch 26:25 Zichri his **s.**, and Shelomith his **s.** 1121
1Ch 26:28 the seer, and Saul the **s.** of Kish, 1121
1Ch 26:28 and Abner the **s.** of Ner, 1121
1Ch 26:28 and Joab the **s.** of Zeruiah, had 1121
1Ch 27:2 was Jashobeam the **s.** of Zabdiel: 1121
1Ch 27:5 was Benaiah the **s.** of Jehoiada, 1121
1Ch 27:6 his course was Ammizabad his **s.** 1121
1Ch 27:7 and Zebadiah his **s.** after him: 1121
1Ch 27:9 Ira the **s.** of Ikkesh the Tekoite: 1121
1Ch 27:16 was Eliezer the **s.** of Zichri: 1121
1Ch 27:16 Shephatiah the **s.** of Maachah: 1121
1Ch 27:17 Hashabiah the **s.** of Kemuel: 1121
1Ch 27:18 Issachar, Omri the **s.** of Michael: 1121
1Ch 27:19 Zebulun, Ishmaiah the **s.** of Obadiah: 1121
1Ch 27:19 Naphtali, Jerimoth the **s.** of Azriel: 1121
1Ch 27:20 Hoshea the **s.** of Azaziah: 1121
1Ch 27:20 Manasseh, Joel the **s.** of Pedaiah: 1121
1Ch 27:21 in Gilead, Iddo the **s.** of Zechariah: 1121
1Ch 27:21 Benjamin, Jaasiel the **s.** of Abner: 1121
1Ch 27:22 Of Dan, Azareel the **s.** of Jeroham. 1121
1Ch 27:24 Joab the **s.** of Zeruiah began to 1121
1Ch 27:25 was Azmaveth the **s.** of Adiel: 1121
1Ch 27:25 was Jehonathan the **s.** of Uzziah: 1121
1Ch 27:26 ground was Ezri the **s.** of Chelub: 1121
1Ch 27:29 was Shaphat the **s.** of Adlai: 1121
1Ch 27:32 Jehiel the **s.** of Hachmoni was with 1121
1Ch 27:34 was Jehoiada the **s.** of Benaiah, 1121
1Ch 28:5 chosen Solomon my **s.** to sit upon 1121
1Ch 28:6 Solomon thy **s.**, he shall build 1121
1Ch 28:6 for I have chosen him to be my **s.**, 1121
1Ch 28:9 Solomon my **s.**, know thou the God 1121
1Ch 28:11 gave to Solomon his **s.** the pattern 1121
1Ch 28:20 And David said to Solomon his **s.**, 1121
1Ch 29:1 Solomon my **s.**, whom alone God 1121
1Ch 29:19 unto Solomon my **s.** a perfect heart, 1121
1Ch 29:22 made Solomon the **s.** of David king 1121
1Ch 29:26 David the **s.** of Jesse reigned over 1121
1Ch 29:28 Solomon his **s.** reigned in his stead. 1121
2Ch 1:1 And Solomon the **s.** of David was 1121
2Ch 1:5 Bezaleel the **s.** of Uri, the **s.** of Hur, 1121
2Ch 2:12 given to David the king a wise **s.**, 1121
2Ch 2:14 The **s.** of a woman of the daughters 1121
2Ch 6:9 thy **s.** which shall come forth out of 1121
2Ch 9:29 against Jeroboam the **s.** of Nebat? 1121
2Ch 9:31 and Rehoboam his **s.** reigned in his 1121
2Ch 10:2 when Jeroboam the **s.** of Nebat, 1121
2Ch 10:15 to Jeroboam the **s.** of Nebat. 1121
2Ch 10:16 none inheritance in the **s.** of Jesse: 1121
2Ch 11:3 unto Rehoboam the **s.** of Solomon, 1121
2Ch 11:17 Rehoboam the **s.** of Solomon strong, 1121
2Ch 11:18 of Jerimoth the **s.** of David to wife, 1121
2Ch 11:18 daughter of Eliab the **s.** of Jesse; 1121
2Ch 11:22 Abijah the **s.** of Maachah the chief, 1121
2Ch 12:16 Abijah his **s.** reigned in his stead. 1121
2Ch 13:6 Yet Jeroboam the **s.** of Nebat, the 1121
2Ch 13:6 servant of Solomon the **s.** of David, 1121
2Ch 13:7 against Rehoboam...**s.** of Solomon, 1121
2Ch 14:1 and Asa his **s.** reigned in his stead. 1121
2Ch 15:1 came upon Azariah the **s.** of Oded: 1121
2Ch 17:1 Jehoshaphat his **s.** reigned in his 1121
2Ch 17:16 him was Amasiah the **s.** of Zichri, 1121
2Ch 18:7 the same is Micaiah the **s.** of Imla. 1121
2Ch 18:8 Fetch quickly Micaiah the **s.** of Imla. 1121
2Ch 18:10 And Zedekiah the **s.** of Chenaanah 1121
2Ch 18:23 Zedekiah the **s.** of Chenaanah came 1121
2Ch 18:25 the city, and to Joash the king's **s.**; 1121
2Ch 19:2 Jehu the **s.** of Hanani the seer went 1121
2Ch 19:11 and Zebadiah the **s.** of Ishmael, the 1121
2Ch 20:14 upon Jahaziel the **s.** of Zechariah, 1121
2Ch 20:14 the **s.** of Benaiah, the **s.** of Jeiel, the 1121
2Ch 20:14 the **s.** of Mattaniah, a Levite of the 1121
2Ch 20:34 in the book of Jehu the **s.** of Hanani, 1121
2Ch 20:37 Then Eliezer the **s.** of Dodavah of 1121
2Ch 21:1 Jehoram his **s.** reigned in his stead. 1121
2Ch 21:17 there was never a **s.** left him, save 1121
2Ch 22:1 made Ahaziah his youngest **s.** king 1121
2Ch 22:1 So Ahaziah the **s.** of Jehoram king 1121
2Ch 22:5 went with Jehoram the **s.** of Ahab 1121
2Ch 22:6 And Azariah the **s.** of Jehoram king 1121
2Ch 22:6 down to see Jehoram the **s.** of Ahab 1121
2Ch 22:7 against Jehu the **s.** of Nimshi, 1121
2Ch 22:9 they, he is the **s.** of Jehoshaphat, 1121
2Ch 22:10 Athaliah...saw that her **s.** was dead, 1121
2Ch 22:11 took Joash the **s.** of Ahaziah, and 1121
2Ch 23:1 Azariah the **s.** of Jeroham, and 1121
2Ch 23:1 and Ishmael the **s.** of Jehohanan, 1121
2Ch 23:1 and Azariah the **s.** of Obed, and 1121
2Ch 23:1 and Maaseiah the **s.** of Adaiah, and 1121
2Ch 23:1 and Elishaphat the **s.** of Zichri, 1121
2Ch 23:3 Behold, the king's **s.** shall reign, 1121
2Ch 23:11 they brought out the king's **s.**, and 1121
2Ch 24:20 Zechariah...**s.** of Jehoiada the priest, 1121
2Ch 24:22 had done to him, but slew his **s.** 1121
2Ch 24:26 Zabad the **s.** of Shimeath an 1121
2Ch 24:26 Jehozabad the **s.** of Shimrith a 1121
2Ch 24:27 Amaziah his **s.** reigned in his stead. 1121
2Ch 25:17 sent to Joash, the **s.** of Jehoahaz, 1121
2Ch 25:17 the **s.** of Jehu, king of Israel, 1121
2Ch 25:18 Give thy daughter to my **s.** to wife: 1121
2Ch 25:23 took Amaziah...the **s.** of Joash, 1121
2Ch 25:23 of Joash, the **s.** of Jehoahaz, 1121
2Ch 25:25 And Amaziah the **s.** of Joash king of 1121
2Ch 25:25 death of Joash **s.** of Jehoahaz king 1121
2Ch 26:21 Jotham his **s.** was over the king's 1121
2Ch 26:22 Isaiah the prophet, the **s.** of Amoz, 1121
2Ch 26:23 Jotham his **s.** reigned in his stead. 1121
2Ch 27:9 Ahaz his **s.** reigned in his stead. 1121
2Ch 28:3 in the valley of the **s.** of Hinnom, 1121
2Ch 28:6 Pekah the **s.** of Remaliah slew in 1121
2Ch 28:7 slew Maaseiah the king's **s.**, and 1121
2Ch 28:12 Azariah the **s.** of Johanan, 1121
2Ch 28:12 Berechiah the **s.** of Meshillemoth, 1121
2Ch 28:12 and Jehizkiah the **s.** of Shallum, 1121
2Ch 28:12 and Amasa the **s.** of Hadlai, stood 1121
2Ch 28:27 and Hezekiah his **s.** reigned in his 1121
2Ch 29:12 arose, Mahath the **s.** of Amasai, 1121
2Ch 29:12 and Joel the **s.** of Azariah, of the 1121
2Ch 29:12 sons of Merari, Kish the **s.** of Abdi, 1121
2Ch 29:12 and Azariah the **s.** of Jehalelel: 1121
2Ch 29:12 Joah the **s.** of Zimmah, 1121
2Ch 29:12 and Eden the **s.** of Joah: 1121
2Ch 30:26 time of Solomon the **s.** of David 1121
2Ch 31:14 Kore the **s.** of Imnah the Levite, the 1121
2Ch 32:20 the prophet Isaiah the **s.** of Amoz, 1121
2Ch 32:32 Isaiah the prophet, the **s.** of Amoz, 1121
2Ch 32:33 And Manasseh his **s.** reigned in his 1121
2Ch 33:6 in the valley of the **s.** of Hinnom: 1121
2Ch 33:7 said to David and to Solomon his **s.**, 1121
2Ch 33:20 Amon his **s.** reigned in his stead. 1121
2Ch 33:25 made Josiah his **s.** king in his stead. 1121
2Ch 34:8 he sent Shaphan the **s.** of Azaliah, 1121
2Ch 34:8 Joah the **s.** of Joahaz the recorder, 1121
2Ch 34:20 And Ahikam the **s.** of Shaphan, 1121
2Ch 34:20 and Abdon the **s.** of Micah, and 1121
2Ch 34:22 wife of Shallum the **s.** of Tikvath, 1121
2Ch 34:22 Tikvath, the **s.** of Hasrah, keeper of 1121
2Ch 35:3 which Solomon the **s.** of David king 1121
2Ch 35:4 to the writing of Solomon his **s.** 1121
2Ch 36:1 land took Jehoahaz the **s.** of Josiah, 1121
2Ch 36:8 and Jehoiachin his **s.** reigned in his 1121
Ezr 3:2 stood up Jeshua the **s.** of Jozadak, 1121
Ezr 3:2, 8 Zerubbabel the **s.** of Shealtiel, 1121
Ezr 3:8 and Jeshua the **s.** of Jozadak, and 1121
Ezr 5:1 and Zechariah the **s.** of Iddo, 1247
Ezr 5:2 up Zerubbabel the **s.** of Shealtiel, 1247
Ezr 5:2 and Jeshua the **s.** of Jozadak, and 1247
Ezr 6:14 and Zechariah the **s.** of Iddo. 1247
Ezr 7:1 of Persia, Ezra the **s.** of Seraiah, 1121
Ezr 7:1 the **s.** of Azariah, the **s.** of Hilkiah, 1121
Ezr 7:2 The **s.** of Shallum, the **s.** of Zadok, 1121
Ezr 7:2 of Zadok, the **s.** of Ahitub, 1121
Ezr 7:3 **s.** of Amariah, the **s.** of Azariah, 1121
Ezr 7:3 of Azariah, the **s.** of Meraioth, 1121
Ezr 7:4 The **s.** of Zerahiah, the **s.** of Uzzi, 1121
Ezr 7:4 of Uzzi, the **s.** of Bukki, 1121
Ezr 7:5 **s.** of Abishua, the **s.** of Phinehas, 1121
Ezr 7:5 the **s.** of Eleazar, **s.** of Aaron the 1121
Ezr 8:4 Elihoenai the **s.** of Zerahiah, and 1121
Ezr 8:5 the **s.** of Jahaziel, and with him 1121
Ezr 8:6 Ebed the **s.** of Jonathan, and with 1121
Ezr 8:7 Jeshaiah the **s.** of Athaliah, and 1121
Ezr 8:8 Zebadiah the **s.** of Michael, and 1121
Ezr 8:9 Obadiah the **s.** of Jehiel, and with 1121
Ezr 8:10 the **s.** of Josiphiah, and with him 1121
Ezr 8:11 Zechariah the **s.** of Bebai, and with 1121
Ezr 8:12 Johanan the **s.** of Hakkatan, and 1121
Ezr 8:18 Mahli,...**s.** of Levi, the **s.** of Israel; 1121
Ezr 8:33 hand of Meremoth the **s.** of Uriah 1121
Ezr 8:33 was Eleazar the **s.** of Phinehas; 1121
Ezr 8:33 was Jozabad the **s.** of Jeshua, and 1121
Ezr 8:33 Noadiah the **s.** of Binnui, Levites; 1121
Ezr 10:2 And Shechaniah the **s.** of Jehiel, 1121
Ezr 10:6 of Johanan the **s.** of Eliashib: 1121
Ezr 10:15 Only Jonathan the **s.** of Asahel and 1121

Book	Ref.	Context	No.
Ezr	10:15	Jahaziah the **s.** of Tikvah were	1121
Ezr	10:18	sons of Jeshua the **s.** of Jozadak,	1121
Ne	1:1	of Nehemiah the **s.** of Hachaliah.	1121
Ne	3:2	them builded Zaccur the **s.** or Imri	1121
Ne	3:4	Meremoth...**s.** of Urijah,...**s.** of Koz.	1121
Ne	3:4	Meshullam the **s.** of Berechiah,	1121
Ne	3:4	Berechiah, the **s.** of Meshezabeel.	1121
Ne	3:4	repaired Zadok the **s.** of Baana.	1121
Ne	3:6	repaired Jehoiada the **s.** of Paseah,	1121
Ne	3:6	and Meshullam the **s.** of Besodeiah;	1121
Ne	3:8	repaired Uzziel the **s.** of Harhaiah,	1121
Ne	3:8	the **s.** of one of the apothecaries,	1121
Ne	3:9	repaired Rephaiah the **s.** of Hur,	1121
Ne	3:10	Jedaiah the **s.** of Harumaph, even	1121
Ne	3:10	Hattush the **s.** of Hashabniah.	1121
Ne	3:11	Malchijah the **s.** of Harim, and	1121
Ne	3:11	Hashub the **s.** of Pahath-moab,	1121
Ne	3:12	repaired Shallum the **s.** of Halohesh,	1121
Ne	3:14	repaired Malchiah the **s.** of Rechab,	1121
Ne	3:15	repaired Shallun the **s.** of Col-hozeh,	1121
Ne	3:16	repaired Nehemiah the **s.** of Azbuk,	1121
Ne	3:17	repaired...Rehum the **s.** of Bani.	1121
Ne	3:18	brethren, Bavai the **s.** of Henadad,	1121
Ne	3:19	him repaired Ezer the **s.** of Jeshua,	1121
Ne	3:20	Baruch the **s.** of Zabbai earnestly	1121
Ne	3:21	Meremoth...**s.** of Urijah...**s.** of Koz.	1121
Ne	3:23	Azariah the **s.** of Maaseiah	1121
Ne	3:23	the **s.** of Ananiah by his house.	1121
Ne	3:24	repaired Binnui the **s.** of Henadad	1121
Ne	3:25	Palal the **s.** of Uzai, over against	1121
Ne	3:25	After him Pedaiah the **s.** of Parosh.	1121
Ne	3:29	repaired Zadok the **s.** of Immer	1121
Ne	3:29	Shemaiah the **s.** of Shechaniah,	1121
Ne	3:30	Hananiah the **s.** of Shelemiah,	1121
Ne	3:30	and Hanun the sixth **s.** of Zalaph,	1121
Ne	3:30	Meshullam the **s.** of Berechiah	1121
Ne	3:31	Malchiah the goldsmith's **s.**	1121
Ne	6:10	house of Shemaiah the **s.** of Delaiah	1121
Ne	6:10	the **s.** of Mehetabeel, who was shut	1121
Ne	6:18	he was the **s.** in law of Shechaniah	2860
Ne	6:18	of Shechaniah the **s.** of Arah;	1121
Ne	6:18	and his **s.** Johanan had taken the	1121
Ne	6:18	of Meshullam the **s.** of Berechiah.	1121
Ne	8:17	days of Jeshua the **s.** of Nun unto	1121
Ne	10:1	Nehemiah,...the **s.** of Hachaliah,	1121
Ne	10:9	Both Jeshua the **s.** of Azaniah,	1121
Ne	10:38	priest the **s.** of Aaron shall be with	1121
Ne	11:4	Judah; Athaiah the **s.** of Uzziah,	1121
Ne	11:4	**s.** of Zechariah, the **s.** of Amariah,	1121
Ne	11:4	the **s.** of Shephatiah,	1121
Ne	11:4	the **s.** of Mahalaleel,	1121
Ne	11:5	And Maaseiah the **s.** of Baruch,	1121
Ne	11:5	the **s.** of Col-hozeh,	1121
Ne	11:5	**s.** of Hazaiah, the **s.** of Adaiah,	1121
Ne	11:5	**s.** of Joiarib, the **s.** of Zechariah,	1121
Ne	11:5	of Zechariah, the **s.** of Shiloni.	1121
Ne	11:7	Sallu the **s.** of Meshullam,	1121
Ne	11:7	the **s.** of Joed, the **s.** of Pedaiah,	1121
Ne	11:7	**s.** of Kolaiah, the **s.** of Maaseiah,	1121
Ne	11:7	the **s.** of Ithiel, the **s.** of Jesaiah.	1121
Ne	11:9	And Joel the **s.** of Zichri was their	1121
Ne	11:9	Judah the **s.** of Senuah was second	1121
Ne	11:10	Jedaiah the **s.** of Joiarib, Jachin	1121
Ne	11:11	Seraiah the **s.** of Hilkiah,	1121
Ne	11:11	the **s.** of Meshullam,	1121
Ne	11:11	the **s.** of Zadok, the **s.** of Meraioth,	1121
Ne	11:11	the **s.** of Ahitub, was the ruler of	1121
Ne	11:12	and Adaiah the **s.** of Jeroham,	1121
Ne	11:12	the **s.** of Pelaliah,	1121
Ne	11:12	the **s.** of Amzi, the **s.** of Zechariah,	1121
Ne	11:12	the **s.** of Pashur, the **s.** of Malchiah,	1121
Ne	11:13	and Amashai the **s.** of Azareel,	1121
Ne	11:13	**s.** of Ahasai, the **s.** of Meshillemoth,	1121
Ne	11:13	the **s.** of Immer,	1121
Ne	11:14	Zabdiel, the **s.** of one of the great	1121
Ne	11:15	Shemaiah the **s.** of Hashub,	1121
Ne	11:15	the **s.** of Azrikam,	1121
Ne	11:15	**s.** of Hashabiah, the **s.** of Bunni;	1121
Ne	11:17	And Mattaniah the **s.** of Micha,	1121
Ne	11:17	the **s.** of Zabdi, the **s.** of Asaph, was	1121
Ne	11:17	and Abda the **s.** of Shammua,	1121
Ne	11:17	the **S.** of Galal, the **s.** of Jeduthun.	1121
Ne	11:22	was Uzzi the **s.** of Bani, the	1121
Ne	11:22	the **s.** of Hashabiah,	1121
Ne	11:22	the **s.** of Mattaniah, the **s.** of Micha.	1121
Ne	11:24	Pethahiah the **s.** of Meshezabeel, of	1121
Ne	11:24	children of Zerah the **s.** of Judah,	1121
Ne	12:1	Zerubbabel the **s.** of Shealtiel, and	1121
Ne	12:23	days of Johanan the **s.** of Eliashib.	1121
Ne	12:24	Jeshua the **s.** of Kadmiel, with their	1121
Ne	12:26	days of Joiakim the **s.** of Jeshua,	1121
Ne	12:26	the **s.** of Jozadak, and in the days	1121
Ne	12:35	Zechariah the **s.** of Jonathan,	1121
Ne	12:35	the **s.** of Shemaiah,	1121
Ne	12:35	**s.** of Mattaniah, the **s.** of Michaiah,	1121
Ne	12:35	the **s.** of Zaccur, the **s.** of Asaph:	1121
Ne	12:45	of David, and of Solomon his **s.**	1121
Ne	13:13	them was Hanan the **s.** of Zaccur,	1121
Ne	13:13	the **s.** of Mattaniah: for they were	1121
Ne	13:28	Joiada, the **s.** of Eliashib the high	1121
Ne	13:28	was **s.** in law to Sanballat the	2860
Es	2:5	name was Mordecai, the **s.** of Jair,	1121
Es	2:5	the **s.** of Shimei, the **s.** of Kish, a	1121
Es	3:1,	10 Haman the **s.** of Hammedatha	1121
Es	8:5	by Haman the **s.** of Hammedatha	1121
Es	9:10,	24 Haman the **s.** of Hammedatha,	1121
Job	18:19	shall neither have **s.** nor nephew	5209
Job	25:6	the **s.** of man, which is a worm?	1121
Job	32:2	wrath of Elihu the **s.** of Barachel	1121
Job	32:6	Elihu the **s.** of Barachel the Buzite	1121
Job	35:8	may profit the **s.** of man.	1121
Ps	2:7	hath said unto me, Thou art my **S.**;	1121
Ps	2:12	Kiss the **S.**, lest he be angry, and	1248
Ps	3:*title*	when he fled from Absalom his **s.**	1121
Ps	8:4	**s.** of man, that thou visitest him?	1121
Ps	50:20	slanderest thine own mother's **s.**	1121
Ps	72:1	righteousness unto the king's **s.**	1121
Ps	72:20	prayers of David the **s.** of Jesse are	1121
Ps	80:17	upon the **s.** of man whom thou	1121
Ps	86:16	and save the **s.** of thine handmaid	1121
Ps	89:22	nor the **s.** of wickedness afflict him.	1121
Ps	116:16	and the **s.** of thine handmaid:	1121
Ps	144:3	or the **s.** of man, that thou makest	1121
Ps	146:3	nor in the **s.** of man, in whom there	1121
Pr	1:1	of Solomon the **s.** of David, king	1121
Pr	1:8	My **s.**, hear the instruction of thy	1121
Pr	1:10	My **s.**, if sinners entice thee,	1121
Pr	1:15	My **s.**, walk not thou in the way	1121
Pr	2:1	My **s.**, if thou wilt receive my	1121
Pr	3:1	My **s.**, forget not my law; but let	1121
Pr	3:11	My **s.**, despise not the chastening	1121
Pr	3:12	even as a father the **s.** in whom he	1121
Pr	3:21	My **s.**, let not them depart from	1121
Pr	4:3	For I was my father's **s.**, tender	1121
Pr	4:10	Hear, O my **s.**, and receive my	1121
Pr	4:20	My **s.**, attend to my words; incline	1121
Pr	5:1	My **s.**, attend unto my wisdom, and	1121
Pr	5:20	why wilt thou, my **s.**, be ravished	1121
Pr	6:1	My **s.**, if thou be surety for thy	1121
Pr	6:3	Do this now, my **s.**, and deliver	1121
Pr	6:20	My **s.**, keep thy father's	1121
Pr	7:1	My **s.**, keep my words, and lay up	1121
Pr	10:1	A wise **s.** maketh a glad father:	1121
Pr	10:1	but a foolish **s.** is the heaviness of	1121
Pr	10:5	gathereth in summer is a wise **s.**:	1121
Pr	10:5	harvest is a **s.** that causeth shame.	1121
Pr	13:1	A wise **s.** heareth his father's	1121
Pr	13:24	that spareth his rod hateth his **s.**:	1121
Pr	15:20	A wise **s.** maketh a glad father: but	1121
Pr	17:2	servant shall have rule over a **s.**	1121
Pr	17:25	A foolish **s.** is a grief to his father,	1121
Pr	19:13	A foolish **s.** is the calamity of his	1121
Pr	19:18	Chasten thy **s.** while there is hope,	1121
Pr	19:26	is a **s.** that causeth shame, and	1121
Pr	19:27	Cease, my **s.**, to hear the	1121
Pr	23:15	My **s.**, if thine heart be wise, my	1121
Pr	23:19	Hear thou, my **s.**, and be wise, and	1121
Pr	23:26	My **s.**, give me thine heart, and let	1121
Pr	24:13	My **s.**, eat thou honey, because it is	1121
Pr	24:21	My **s.**, fear thou the Lord and the	1121
Pr	27:11	My **s.**, be wise, and make my heart	1121
Pr	28:7	Whoso keepeth the law is a wise **s.**:	1121
Pr	29:17	Correct thy **s.**, and he shall give	1121
Pr	29:21	shall have him become his **s.** at	4497
Pr	30:1	The words of Agur the **s.** of Jakeh,	1121
Pr	31:2	my **s.**?...what, the **s.** of my womb?	1248
Pr	31:2	and what, the **s.** of my vows?	1248
Ec	1:1	of the Preacher, the **s.** of David,	1121
Ec	5:14	and he begetteth a **s.**, and there is	1121
Ec	10:17	when thy king is the **s.** of nobles,	1121
Ec	12:12	And further, by these, my **s.**, be	1121
Isa	1:1	The vision of Isaiah the **s.** of Amoz,	1121
Isa	2:1	word that Isaiah the **s.** of Amoz	1121
Isa	7:1	the days of Ahaz the **s.** of Jotham	1121
Isa	7:1	the **s.** of Uzziah, the king of Judah,	1121
Isa	7:1	and Pekah the **s.** of Remaliah, king	1121
Isa	7:3	thou, and Shear-jashub thy **s.**, at	1121
Isa	7:4	Syria, and of the **s.** of Remaliah,	1121
Isa	7:5	Ephraim, and the **s.** of Remaliah,	1121
Isa	7:6	midst of it, even the **s.** of Tabeal:	1121
Isa	7:9	head of Samaria is Remaliah's **s.**	1121
Isa	7:14	virgin shall conceive, and bare a **s.**,	1121
Isa	8:2	Zechariah the **s.** of Jeberechiah.	1121
Isa	8:3	and she conceived, and bare a **s.**	1121
Isa	8:6	rejoice in Rezin and Remaliah's **s.**;	1121
Isa	9:6	child is born, unto us a **s.** is given:	1121
Isa	13:1	Isaiah the **s.** of Amoz did see.	1121
Isa	14:12	O Lucifer, **s.** of the morning! how	1121
Isa	14:22	and remnant, and **s.**, and nephew	5209
Isa	19:11	Pharaoh, I am the **s.** of the wise,	1121
Isa	19:11	the **s.** of ancient kings?	1121
Isa	20:2	the Lord by Isaiah the **s.** of Amoz,	1121
Isa	22:20	servant Eliakim the **s.** of Hilkiah:	1121
Isa	36:3	unto him Eliakim, Hilkiah's **s.**	1121
Isa	36:3	and Joah, Asaph's **s.**, the recorder.	1121
Isa	36:22	came Eliakim, the **s.** of Hilkiah,	1121
Isa	36:22	Joah, the **s.** of Asaph, the recorder,	1121
Isa	37:2	Isaiah the prophet the **s.** of Amoz.	1121
Isa	37:21	Isaiah the **s.** of Amoz sent unto	1121
Isa	37:38	Esar-haddon his **s.** reigned in his	1121
Isa	38:1	Isaiah the prophet the **s.** of Amoz.	1121
Isa	39:1	Merodach-baladan,...**s.** of Baladan.	1121
Isa	49:15	compassion on the **s.** of her womb?	1121
Isa	51:12	and of the **s.** of man which shall be	1121
Isa	56:2	and the **s.** of man that layeth hold	1121
Isa	56:3	Neither let the **s.** of the stranger,	1121
Jer	1:1	of Jeremiah the **s.** of Hilkiah,	1121
Jer	1:2	days of Josiah the **s.** of Amon king	1121
Jer	1:3	days of Jehoiakim the **s.** of Josiah	1121
Jer	1:3	year of Zedekiah the **s.** of Josiah	1121
Jer	6:26	thee mourning, as for an only **s.**,	3173
Jer	7:31	in the valley of the **s.** of Hinnom,	1121
Jer	7:32	nor the valley of the **s.** of Hinnom,	1121
Jer	15:4	of Manasseh the **s.** of Hezekiah	1121
Jer	19:2	unto the valley of the **s.** of Hinnom,	1121
Jer	19:6	nor The valley of the **s.** of Hinnom,	1121
Jer	20:1	Pashur the **s.** of Immer the priest,	1121
Jer	21:1	unto him Pashur the **s.** of Melchiah,	1121
Jer	21:1	and Zephaniah the **s.** of Maaseiah	1121
Jer	22:11	touching Shallum the **s.** of Josiah	1121
Jer	22:18	Jehoiakim the **s.** of Josiah king of	1121
Jer	22:24	Coniah the **s.** of Jehoiakim king of	1121
Jer	24:1	Jeconiah the **s.** of Jehoiakim king	1121
Jer	25:1	year of Jehoiakim the **s.** of Josiah	1121
Jer	25:3	year of Josiah the **s.** of Amon king	1121
Jer	26:1	reign of Jehoiakim the **s.** of Josiah	1121
Jer	26:20	Urijah the **s.** of Shemaiah of	1121
Jer	26:22	Elnathan the **s.** of Achbor, and	1121
Jer	26:24	hand of Ahikam the **s.** of Shaphan	1121
Jer	27:1	reign of Jehoiakim the **s.** of Josiah	1121
Jer	27:7	him, and his **s.**, and his son's **s.**,	1121
Jer	27:20	Jeconiah the **s.** of Jehoiakim king	1121
Jer	28:1	that Hananiah the **s.** of Azur the	1121
Jer	28:4	Jeconiah the **s.** of Jehoiakim king	1121
Jer	29:3	hand of Elasah the **s.** of Shaphan,	1121
Jer	29:3	and Gemariah the **s.** of Hilkiah,	1121
Jer	29:21	of Israel, of Ahab the **s.** of Kolaiah,	1121
Jer	29:21	of Zedekiah the **s.** of Maaseiah,	1121
Jer	29:25	Zephaniah the **s.** of Maaseiah the	1121
Jer	31:20	Is Ephraim my dear **s.**? is he a	1121
Jer	32:7	Hanameel the **s.** of Shallum thine	1121
Jer	32:8	So Hanameel mine uncle's **s.** came	1121
Jer	32:9	the field of Hanameel my uncle's **s.**,	1121
Jer	32:12	unto Baruch the **s.** of Neriah,	1121
Jer	32:12	the **s.** of Maaseiah,	1121
Jer	32:12	sight of Hanameel mine uncle's **s.**,	
Jer	32:16	unto Baruch the **s.** of Neriah,	1121
Jer	32:35	in the valley of the **s.** of Hinnom,	1121
Jer	33:21	should not have a **s.** to reign upon	1121
Jer	35:1	of Jehoiakim the **s.** of Josiah king	1121
Jer	35:3	took Jaazaniah the **s.** of Jeremiah,	1121
Jer	35:3	the **s.** of Habaziniah, and his	1121
Jer	35:4	Hanan, the **s.** of Igdaliah, a man of	1121
Jer	35:4	of Maaseiah the **s.** of Shallum, the	1121
Jer	35:6	for Jonadab the **s.** of Rechab our	1121
Jer	35:8	voice of Jonadab the **s.** of Rechab	1121
Jer	35:14	words of Jonadab the **s.** of Rechab,	1121
Jer	35:16	sons of Jonadab the **s.** of Rechab	1121

Jer 35:19 Jonadab the **s.** of Rechab shall not 1121
Jer 36:1 Jehoiakim the **s.** of Josiah king of........ 1121
Jer 36:4 called Baruch the **s.** of Neriah: and..... 1121
Jer 36:8 And Baruch the **s.** of Neriah did........ 1121
Jer 36:9 Jehoiakim the **s.** of Josiah king of........ 1121
Jer 36:10 of Gemariah the **s.** of Shaphan the...... 1121
Jer 36:11 When Michaiah the **s.** of Gemariah,..... 1121
Jer 36:11 **s.** of Shaphan, had heard out of the 1121
Jer 36:12 and Delaiah the **s.** of Shemaiah, ... 1121
Jer 36:12 and Elnathan the **s.** of Achbor,........... 1121
Jer 36:12 and Gemariah the **s.** of Shaphan, ... 1121
Jer 36:12 and Zedekiah the **s.** of Hananiah, ... 1121
Jer 36:14 sent Jehudi the **s.** of Nethaniah, ... 1121
Jer 36:14 the **s.** of Shelemiah, the **s.** of Cushi, ... 1121
Jer 36:14 Baruch the **s.** of Neriah took the roll... 1121
Jer 36:26 Jerahmeel the **s.** of Hammelech,......... 1121
Jer 36:26 and Seraiah the **s.** of Azriel, and 1121
Jer 36:26 and Shelemiah the **s.** of Abdeel, ... 1121
Jer 36:32 Baruch the scribe, the **s.** of Neriah;.... 1121
Jer 37:1 Zedekiah the **s.** of Josiah reigned......... 1121
Jer 37:1 instead of Coniah...**s.** of Jehoiakim, ... 1121
Jer 37:3 sent Jehucal the **s.** of Selemiah 1121
Jer 37:3 and Zephaniah the **s.** of Maaseiah 1121
Jer 37:13 was Irijah, the **s.** of Shelemiah, the..... 1121
Jer 37:13 the **s.** of Hananiah; and he took 1121
Jer 38:1 Then Shephatiah the **s.** of Mattan, ... 1121
Jer 38:1 and Gedaliah the **s.** of Pashur, ... 1121
Jer 38:1 and Jucal the **s.** of Shelemiah, ... 1121
Jer 38:1 and Pashur the **s.** of Malchiah, ... 1121
Jer 38:6 of Malchiah the **s.** of Hammelech,........ 1121
Jer 39:14 unto Gedaliah the **s.** of Ahikam 1121
Jer 39:14 the **s.** of Shaphan, that he should 1121
Jer 40:5 also to Gedaliah the **s.** of Ahikam 1121
Jer 40:5 the **s.** of Shaphan, whom the king........ 1121
Jer 40:6 unto Gedaliah the **s.** of Ahikam to........ 1121
Jer 40:7 made Gedaliah the **s.** of Ahikam......... 1121
Jer 40:8 even Ishmael the **s.** of Nethaniah,....... 1121
Jer 40:8 and Seraiah the **s.** of Tanhumeth, ... 1121
Jer 40:8 Jezaniah the **s.** of a Maachathite, ... 1121
Jer 40:9 And Gedaliah the **s.** of Ahikam........... 1121
Jer 40:9 the **s.** of Shaphan sware unto them..... 1121
Jer 40:11 them Gedaliah the **s.** of Ahikam 1121
Jer 40:11 the **s.** of Shaphan;............................ 1121
Jer 40:13 Johanan the **s.** of Kareah, and all........ 1121
Jer 40:14 sent Ishmael the **s.** of Nethaniah 1121
Jer 40:14 Gedaliah the **s.** of Ahikam believed 1121
Jer 40:15 Johanan the **s.** of Kareah spake to 1121
Jer 40:15 slay Ishmael the **s.** of Nethaniah,........ 1121
Jer 40:16 Gedaliah the **s.** of Ahikam said unto 1121
Jer 40:16 said unto Johanan the **s.** of Kareah,..... 1121
Jer 41:1 that Ishmael the **s.** of Nethaniah......... 1121
Jer 41:1 **s.** of Elishama, of the seed royal,........ 1121
Jer 41:1 unto Gedaliah the **s.** of Ahikam to....... 1121
Jer 41:2 arose Ishmael the **s.** of Nethaniah,....... 1121
Jer 41:2 smote Gedaliah the **s.** of Ahikam........ 1121
Jer 41:2 the **s.** of Shaphan with the sword, ... 1121
Jer 41:6 Ishmael the **s.** of Nethaniah went 1121
Jer 41:6 Come to Gedaliah the **s.** of Ahikam..... 1121
Jer 41:7 Ishmael the **s.** of Nethaniah slew........ 1121
Jer 41:9 Ishmael the **s.** of Nethaniah filled........ 1121
Jer 41:10 to Gedaliah the **s.** of Ahikam: 1121
Jer 41:10 and Ishmael the **s.** of Nethaniah 1121
Jer 41:11 when Johanan the **s.** of Kareah, and.... 1121
Jer 41:11 that Ishmael the **s.** of Nethaniah......... 1121
Jer 41:12 with Ishmael the **s.** of Nethaniah, ... 1121
Jer 41:13 saw Johanan the **s.** of Kareah, and...... 1121
Jer 41:14 went unto Johanan the **s.** of Kareah. ... 1121
Jer 41:15 But Ishmael the **s.** of Nethaniah......... 1121
Jer 41:16 took Johanan the **s.** of Kareah, and...... 1121
Jer 41:16 from Ishmael the **s.** of Nethaniah,....... 1121
Jer 41:16 had slain Gedaliah the **s.** of Ahikam,.... 1121
Jer 41:18 Ishmael the **s.** of Nethaniah had 1121
Jer 41:18 slain Gedaliah the **s.** of Ahikam, ... 1121
Jer 42:1 and Johanan the **s.** of Kareah, ... 1121
Jer 42:1 and Jezaniah the **s.** of Hoshaiah, ... 1121
Jer 42:8 called he Johanan the **s.** of Kareah, ... 1121
Jer 43:2 spake Azariah the **s.** of Hoshaiah, ... 1121
Jer 43:2 and Johanan the **s.** of Kareah, and 1121
Jer 43:3 Baruch the **s.** of Neriah setteth the..... 1121
Jer 43:4 So Johanan the **s.** of Kareah, and 1121
Jer 43:5 But Johanan the **s.** of Kareah, and 1121
Jer 43:6 with Gedaliah the **s.** of Ahikam the 1121
Jer 43:6 the **s.** of Shaphan, and Jeremiah......... 1121
Jer 43:6 and Baruch the **s.** of Neriah. 1121
Jer 45:1 spake unto Baruch the **s.** of Neriah,.... 1121
Jer 45:1 Jehoiakim the **s.** of Josiah king of........ 1121
Jer 46:2 Jehoiakim the **s.** of Josiah king of........ 1121
Jer 49:18 neither shall a **s.** of man dwell in it..... 1121
Jer 49:33 there, nor any **s.** of man dwell in it..... 1121
Jer 50:40 shall any **s.** of may dwell therein. 1121
Jer 51:43 doth any **s.** of may pass thereby. 1121
Jer 51:59 Seraiah the **s.** of Neriah,.................. 1121
Jer 51:59 the **s.** of Maaseiah, when he went...... 1121
Eze 1:3 Ezekiel the priest, the **s.** of Buzi,....... 1121
Eze 2:1 **S.** of man, stand upon thy feet, and.... 1121
Eze 2:3 **S.** of man, I send thee to the........... 1121
Eze 2:6 **s.** of man, be not afraid of them,........ 1121
Eze 2:8 **s.** of man, hear what I say unto 1121
Eze 3:1 **S.** of man, eat that thou findest; 1121
Eze 3:3 **S.** of man, cause thy belly to eat,....... 1121
Eze 3:4 **S.** of man, go, get thee unto the......... 1121
Eze 3:10 **S.** of man, all my words that I shall.... 1121
Eze 3:17 **S.** of man, I have made thee a........... 1121
Eze 3:25 O **s.** of man, behold, they shall put..... 1121
Eze 4:1 **s.** of man, take thee a tile, and lay 1121
Eze 4:16 **S.** of man, behold, I will break the 1121
Eze 5:1 **s.** of man, take thee a sharp knife, ... 1121
Eze 6:2 **S.** of man, set thy face toward the 1121
Eze 7:2 thou **s.** of man, thus saith the Lord..... 1121
Eze 8:5 **S.** of man, lift up thine eyes now 1121
Eze 8:6 **S.** of man, seest thou what they do?... 1121
Eze 8:8 **S.** of man, dig now in the wall: and 1121
Eze 8:11 stood Jaazaniah the **s.** of Shaphan, ... 1121
Eze 8:12 **S.** of man, hast thou seen what the 1121
Eze 8:15, 17 Hast thou seen this, O **s.** of man?.. 1121
Eze 11:1 I saw Jaazaniah the **s.** of Azur, ... 1121
Eze 11:1 and Pelatiah the **s.** of Benaiah,........... 1121
Eze 11:2 **S.** of man, these are the men that...... 1121
Eze 11:4 them, prophesy, O **s.** of man............ 1121
Eze 11:13 that Pelatiah the **s.** of Benaiah died..... 1121
Eze 11:15 **S.** of man, thy brethren, even thy...... 1121
Eze 12:2 **S.** of man, thou dwellest in the......... 1121
Eze 12:3 thou **s.** of man, prepare thee stuff...... 1121
Eze 12:9 **S.** of man, hath not the house of........ 1121
Eze 12:18 **S.** of man, eat thy bread with........... 1121
Eze 12:22 **S.** of man, what is that proverb that... 1121
Eze 12:27 **S.** of man, behold, they of the house .. 1121
Eze 13:2 **S.** of man, prophesy against the......... 1121
Eze 13:17 thou **s.** of man, set thy face against 1121
Eze 14:3 **S.** of man, these men have set up...... 1121
Eze 14:13 **S.** of man, when the land sinneth....... 1121
Eze 14:20 deliver neither **s.** nor daughter;......... 1121
Eze 15:2 **S.** of man, What is the vine tree........ 1121
Eze 16:2 **S.** of man, cause Jerusalem to know ... 1121
Eze 17:2 **S.** of man, put forth a riddle, and....... 1121
Eze 18:4 so also the soul of the **s.** is mine:........ 1121
Eze 18:10 If he beget a **s.** that is a robber, a 1121
Eze 18:14 Now, lo, if he beget a **s.**, that seeth... 1121
Eze 18:19 the **s.** bear the iniquity of the father? .. 1121
Eze 18:19 **s.** hath done that which is lawful 1121
Eze 18:20 **s.** shall not bear the iniquity of the 1121
Eze 18:20 father bear the iniquity of the **s.**:........ 1121
Eze 20:3 **S.** of man, speak unto the elders of.... 1121
Eze 20:4 **s.** of man, wilt thou judge them? 1121
Eze 20:27 **s.** of man, speak unto the house of...... 1121
Eze 20:46 **S.** of man, set thy face toward the 1121
Eze 21:2 **S.** of man, set thy face toward 1121
Eze 21:6 Sigh therefore, thou **s.** of man, with.... 1121
Eze 21:9 **S.** of man, prophesy, and say, Thus.... 1121
Eze 21:10 it contemneth the rod of my **s.**, as 1121
Eze 21:12 Cry and howl, **s.** of man: for it shall.... 1121
Eze 21:14 **s.** of man, prophesy, and smite.......... 1121
Eze 21:19 **s.** of man, appoint thee two ways,...... 1121
Eze 21:28 thou, **s.** of man, prophesy and say,...... 1121
Eze 22:2 Now, thou **s.** of man, wilt thou judge, .. 1121
Eze 22:18 **s.** of man, the house of Israel is to..... 1121
Eze 22:24 **S.** of man, say unto her, Thou art...... 1121
Eze 23:2 **S.** of man, there were two women. 1121
Eze 23:36 **S.** of man, wilt thou judge Aholah....... 1121
Eze 24:2 **S.** of man, write thee the name of...... 1121
Eze 24:16 **S.** of man, behold, I take away......... 1121
Eze 24:25 **s.** of man, shall it not be in the day 1121
Eze 25:2 **S.** of man, set thy face against the 1121
Eze 26:2 **S.** of man, because that Tyrus hath.... 1121
Eze 27:2 **s.** of man, take up a lamentation 1121
Eze 28:2 **S.** of man, say unto the prince of....... 1121
Eze 28:12 **S.** of man, take up a lamentation........ 1121
Eze 28:21 **S.** of man, set thy face against 1121
Eze 29:2 **S.** of man, set thy face against 1121
Eze 29:18 **S.** of man, Nebuchadrezzar king of...... 1121
Eze 30:2 **S.** of man, prophesy and say, Thus..... 1121
Eze 30:21 **S.** of man, I have broken the arm 1121
Eze 31:2 **S.** of man, speak unto Pharaoh 1121
Eze 32:2 **S.** of man, take up a lamentation........ 1121
Eze 32:18 **S.** of man, wail for the multitude........ 1121
Eze 33:2 **S.** of man, speak to the children of..... 1121
Eze 33:7 So thou, O **s.** of man, I have set thee..1121
Eze 33:10 **s.** of man, speak unto the house of 1121
Eze 33:12 **s.** of man, say unto the children of 1121
Eze 33:24 **S.** of man, they that inhabit those....... 1121
Eze 33:30 thou **s.** of man, the children of thy...... 1121
Eze 34:2 **S.** of man, prophesy against the......... 1121
Eze 35:2 **S.** of man, set thy face against 1121
Eze 36:1 Also, thou **s.** of man, prophesy unto ... 1121
Eze 36:17 **S.** of man, when the house of Israel ... 1121
Eze 37:3 me, **S.** of man, can these bones live?.. 1121
Eze 37:9 prophesy, **s.** of man, and say to the.... 1121
Eze 37:11 **S.** of man, these bones are the.......... 1121
Eze 37:16 thou **s.** of man, take thee one stick,.... 1121
Eze 38:2 **S.** of man, set thy face against Gog, ... 1121
Eze 38:14 **s.** of man, prophesy and say unto....... 1121
Eze 39:1 **s.** of man, prophesy against Gog, ... 1121
Eze 39:17 **s.** of man, thus saith the Lord God;.... 1121
Eze 40:4 **S.** of man, behold with thine eyes, ... 1121
Eze 43:7 **S.** of man, the place of my throne, ... 1121
Eze 43:10 Thou **s.** of man, shew the house to 1121
Eze 43:18 **S.** of man, thus saith the Lord........... 1121
Eze 44:5 **S.** of man, mark well, and behold....... 1121
Eze 44:25 mother, or for **s.**, or for daughter,....... 1121
Eze 47:6 me, **S.** of man, hast thou seen this?.... 1121
Da 3:25 of the fourth is like the **S.** of God. 1247
Da 5:22 And thou his **s.**, O Belshazzar, hast.... 1247
Da 7:13 one like the **S.** of man came with....... 1247
Da 8:17 unto me, Understand, O **s.** of man: 1121
Da 9:1 year of Darius the **s.** of Ahasuerus, ... 1121
Ho 1:1 came unto Hosea, the **s.** of Beeri,...... 1121
Ho 1:1 days of Jeroboam the **s.** of Joash, ... 1121
Ho 1:3 which conceived, and bare him a **s.**..... 1121
Ho 1:8 she conceived, and bare a **s.**. 1121
Ho 11:1 him and called my **s.** out of Egypt. 1121
Ho 13:13 he is an unwise **s.**; for he should........ 1121
Joe 1:1 that came to Joel the **s.** of Pethuel. 1121
Am 1:1 days of Jeroboam the **s.** of Joash........ 1121
Am 7:14 neither was I a prophet's **s.**;............. 1121
Am 8:10 make it as the mourning of an only **s.**........
Jon 1:1 came unto Jonah the **s.** of Amittai,...... 1121
Mic 6:5 Balaam the **s.** of Beor answered........... 1121
Mic 7:6 For the **s.** dishonoureth the father, ... 1121
Zep 1:1 unto Zephaniah the **s.** of Cushi,.......... 1121
Zep 1:1 **s.** of Gedaliah, the **s.** of Amariah,........ 1121
Zep 1:1 of Amariah, the **s.** of Hizkiah, in......... 1121
Zep 1:1 the days of Josiah the **s.** of Amon,..... 1121
Hag 1:1 unto Zerubbabel the **s.** of Shealtiel,..... 1121
Hag 1:1 and to Joshua the **s.** of Josedech. 1121
Hag 1:12 Then Zerubbabel the **s.** of Shealtiel,.... 1121
Hag 1:12 and Joshua the **s.** of Josedech, the...... 1121
Hag 1:14 of Zerubbabel the **s.** of Shealtiel, ... 1121
Hag 1:14 spirit of Joshua the **s.** of Josedech,...... 1121
Hag 2:2 to Zerubbabel the **s.** of Shealtiel,......... 1121
Hag 2:2 and to Joshua the **s.** of Josedech, ... 1121
Hag 2:4 be strong, O Joshua, **s.** of Josedech, ... 1121
Hag 2:23 my servant, the **s.** of Shealtiel. 1121
Zec 1:1 unto Zechariah, **s.** of Berechiah,.......... 1121
Zec 1:1 the **s.** of Iddo the prophet,................ 1121
Zec 1:7 Zechariah, the **s.** of Berechiah, ... 1121
Zec 1:7 the **s.** of Iddo the prophet,................ 1121
Zec 6:10 house of Josiah the **s.** of Zephaniah; ... 1121
Zec 6:11 head of Joshua the **s.** of Josedech. 1121
Zec 6:14 and to Hen the **s.** of Zephaniah, for 1121
Zec 12:10 as one mourneth for his only **s.**,...............
Mal 1:6 A **s.** honoureth his father, and a......... 1121
Mal 3:17 as a man spareth his own **s.** that........ 1121
Mt 1:1 of Jesus Christ, the **s.** of David,......... *5207*
Mt 1:1 of David, the **s.** of Abraham. *5207*
Mt 1:20 Joseph, thou **s.** of David, fear not to... *5207*
Mt 1:21 she shall bring forth a **s.**, and thou *5207*
Mt 1:23 child, and shall bring forth a **s.**,.......... *5207*
Mt 1:25 had brought forth her firstborn **s.**: *5207*
Mt 2:15 Out of Egypt have I called my **s.**......... *5207*
Mt 3:17 This is my beloved **S.**, in whom I....... *5207*
Mt 4:3 If thou be the **S.** of God, command..... *5207*
Mt 4:6 If thou be the **S.** of God, cast............ *5207*
Mt 4:21 James the **s.** of Zebedee, and John his.......
Mt 7:9 **his s. ask bread, will he give him..** *5207*
Mt 8:20 **S. of man hath not where to lay...** *5207*
Mt 8:29 do with thee, Jesus, thou **S.** of God? .. *5207*
Mt 9:2 **S., be of good cheer; thy sins be...** *5048*
Mt 9:6 **S. of man hath power on earth to...** *5207*
Mt 9:27 Thou **s.** of David, have mercy on us. .. *5207*
Mt 10:2 James the **s.** of Zebedee, and John his.......
Mt 10:3 James the **s.** of Alphaeus, and.................

Mt 10:23 Israel, till the S. of man be come 5207
Mt 10:37 loveth s. or daughter more than 5207
Mt 11:19 The S. of man came eating and 5207
Mt 11:27 and no man knoweth the S., but 5207
Mt 11:27 any man the Father, save the S., 5207
Mt 11:27 whomsoever the S. will reveal him. 5207
Mt 12:8 S. of man is Lord...of the sabbath. 5207
Mt 12:23 and said, Is not this the s. of David? 5207
Mt 12:32 a word against the S. of man, 5207
Mt 12:40 shall the S. of man be three days 5207
Mt 13:37 the good seed is the S. of man; 5207
Mt 13:41 The S. of man shall send forth 5207
Mt 13:55 Is not this the carpenter's s.? is not 5207
Mt 14:33 Of a truth thou art the S. of God. 5207
Mt 15:22 on me, O Lord, thou s. of David; 5207
Mt 16:13 men say that I the S. of man am? 5207
Mt 16:16 the Christ, the S. of the living God. 5207
Mt 16:27 S. of man shall come in the glory 5207
Mt 16:28 till they see the S. of man coming 5207
Mt 17:5 This is my beloved S., in whom I 5207
Mt 17:9 until the S. of man be risen again. 5207
Mt 17:12 shall...the S. of man suffer of 5207
Mt 17:15 Lord, have mercy on my s.: for he 5207
Mt 17:22 S. of man shall be betrayed into 5207
Mt 18:11 For the S. of man is come to save 5207
Mt 19:28 S. of man shall sit in the throne 5207
Mt 20:18 S. of man shall be betrayed unto 5207
Mt 20:28 S. man came not to be ministered 5207
Mt 20:30, 31 on us, O Lord, thou s. of David. 5207
Mt 21:9 saying Hosanna to the s. of David: 5207
Mt 21:15 saying, Hosanna to the s. of David; 5207
Mt 21:28 S., go work to day in my vineyard. 5043
Mt 21:37 last of all he sent unto them his s., 5207
Mt 21:37 saying, They will reverence my s. 5207
Mt 21:38 when the husbandmen saw the s., 5207
Mt 22:2 which made a marriage for his s., 5207
Mt 22:42 think ye of Christ? whose s. is he? 5207
Mt 22:42 They say unto him, The s. of David.
Mt 22:45 call him Lord, how is he his s.? 5207
Mt 23:35 blood of Zacharias s. of Barachias, 5207
Mt 24:27 also the coming of the S. of man 5207
Mt 24:30 sign of the S. of man in heaven: 5207
Mt 24:30 S. of man coming in the clouds 5207
Mt 24:37, 39 the coming of the S. of man be 5207
Mt 24:44 ye think not the S. of man cometh. 5207
Mt 25:13 wherein the S. of man cometh. 5207
Mt 25:31 S. of man shall come in his glory, 5207
Mt 26:2 the S. of man is betrayed to be 5207
Mt 26:24 S. of man goeth as it is written 5207
Mt 26:24 whom the S. of man is betrayed! 5207
Mt 26:45 S. of man is betrayed into the 5207
Mt 26:63 thou be the Christ, the S. of God. 5207
Mt 26:64 the S. of man sitting on the right 5207
Mt 27:40 If thou be the S. of God, come down 5207
Mt 27:43 for he said, I am the S. of God. 5207
Mt 27:54 Truly this was the S. of God. 5207
Mt 28:19 name of the Father, and of the S., 5207
Mk 1:1 of Jesus Christ, the S. of God; 5207
Mk 1:11 Thou art my beloved S., in whom I 5207
Mk 1:19 he saw James the s. of Zebedee, and
Mk 2:5 S., thy sins be forgiven thee. 5043
Mk 2:10 S. of man hath power on earth 5207
Mk 2:14 he saw Levi the s. of Alphaeus sitting
Mk 2:28 S. of man is Lord...of the sabbath. 5207
Mk 3:11 saying, Thou art the S. of God. 5207
Mk 3:17 And James the s. of Zebedee, and
Mk 3:18 and James the s. of Alphaeus, and
Mk 5:7 thou S. of the most high God? 5207
Mk 6:3 this the carpenter, the s. of Mary, 5207
Mk 8:31 S. of man must suffer many things, 5207
Mk 8:38 shall the S. of man be ashamed, 5207
Mk 9:7 This is my beloved S.: hear him. 5207
Mk 9:9 S. of man were risen from the dead. 5207
Mk 9:12 how it is written of the S. of man, 5207
Mk 9:17 I have brought unto thee my s., 5207
Mk 9:31 The S. of man is delivered into the 5207
Mk 10:33 S. of man shall be delivered unto 5207
Mk 10:45 the S. of man came not to be 5207
Mk 10:46 blind Bartimaeus, the s. of Timaeus, 5207
Mk 10:47 Jesus, thou s. of David, have mercy 5207
Mk 10:48 Thou s. of David, have mercy on me. 5207
Mk 12:6 Having yet therefore one s., his 5207
Mk 12:6 saying, They will reverence my s. 5207
Mk 12:35 that Christ is the s. of David? 5207
Mk 12:37 and whence is he then his s.? 5207
Mk 13:12 to death, and the father the s.; 5043
Mk 13:26 see the S. of man coming in the 5207
Mk 13:32 neither the S., but the Father. 5207
Mk 13:34 the S. of man is as a man taking
Mk 14:21 S. of man indeed goeth, as it is 5207
Mk 14:21 whom the S. of man is betrayed! 5207
Mk 14:41 S. of man is betrayed into the 5207
Mk 14:61 the Christ, the S. of the Blessed? 5207
Mk 14:62 S. of man sitting on the right 5207
Mk 15:39 Truly this man was the S. of God. 5207
Lu 1:13 wife Elisabeth shall bear thee a s., 5207
Lu 1:31 bring forth a s., and shalt call his 5207
Lu 1:32 shall be called the S. of the Highest; 5207
Lu 1:35 thee shall be called the S. of God, 5207
Lu 1:36 also conceived a s. in her old age: 5207
Lu 1:57 and she brought forth a s. 5207
Lu 2:7 she brought forth her firstborn s., 5207
Lu 2:48 S., why hast thou thus dealt with 5043
Lu 3:2 came unto John the s. of Zacharias 5207
Lu 3:22 Thou art my beloved S.; in thee 5207
Lu 3:23 (as was supposed) the s. of Joseph, 5207
Lu 3:23 which was the s. of Heli,
Lu 3:24 Which was the s. of Matthat,
Lu 3:24 which was the s. of Levi,
Lu 3:24 which was the s. of Melchi,
Lu 3:24 which was the s. of Janna,
Lu 3:24 which was the s. of Joseph,
Lu 3:25 Which was the s. of Mattathias,
Lu 3:25 which was the s. of Amos,
Lu 3:25 which was the s. of Naum,
Lu 3:25 which was the s. of Esli,
Lu 3:25 which was the s. of Nagge,
Lu 3:26 Which was the s. of Maath,
Lu 3:26 which was the s. of Mattathias,
Lu 3:26 which was the s. of Semei,
Lu 3:26 which was the s. of Joseph,
Lu 3:26 which was the s. of Juda,
Lu 3:27 Which was the s. of Joanna,
Lu 3:27 which was the s. of Rhesa,
Lu 3:27 which was the s. of Zorobabel,
Lu 3:27 which was the s. of Salathiel,
Lu 3:27 which was the s. of Neri,
Lu 3:28 Which was the s. of Melchi,
Lu 3:28 which was the s. of Addi,
Lu 3:28 which was the s. of Cosam,
Lu 3:28 which was the s. of Elmodam,
Lu 3:28 which was the s. of Er,
Lu 3:29 Which was the s. of Jose,
Lu 3:29 which was the s. of Eliezer,
Lu 3:29 which was the s. of Jorim,
Lu 3:29 which was the s. of Matthat,
Lu 3:29 which was the s. of Levi,
Lu 3:30 Which was the s. of Simeon,
Lu 3:30 which was the s. of Juda,
Lu 3:30 which was the s. of Joseph,
Lu 3:30 which was the s. of Jonan,
Lu 3:30 which was the s. of Eliakim,
Lu 3:31 Which was the s. of Melea,
Lu 3:31 which was the s. of Menan,
Lu 3:31 which was the s. of Mattatha,
Lu 3:31 which was the s. of Nathan,
Lu 3:31 which was the s. of David,
Lu 3:32 Which was the s. of Jesse,
Lu 3:32 which was the s. of Obed,
Lu 3:32 which was the s. of Booz,
Lu 3:32 which was the s. of Salmon,
Lu 3:32 which was the s. of Naasson,
Lu 3:33 Which was the s. of Aminadab,
Lu 3:33 which was the s. of Aram,
Lu 3:33 which was the s. of Esrom,
Lu 3:33 which was the s. of Phares,
Lu 3:33 which was the s. of Juda,
Lu 3:34 Which was the s. of Jacob,
Lu 3:34 which was the s. of Isaac,
Lu 3:34 which was the s. of Abraham,
Lu 3:34 which was the s. of Thara,
Lu 3:34 which was the s. of Nachor,
Lu 3:35 Which was the s. of Saruch,
Lu 3:35 which was the s. of Ragau,
Lu 3:35 which was the s. of Phalec,
Lu 3:35 which was the s. of Heber,
Lu 3:35 which was the s. of Sala,
Lu 3:36 Which was the s. of Cainan,
Lu 3:36 which was the s. of Arphaxad,
Lu 3:36 which was the s. of Sem,
Lu 3:36 which was the s. of Noe,
Lu 3:36 which was the s. of Lamech,
Lu 3:37 Which was the s. of Mathusala,
Lu 3:37 which was the s. of Enoch,
Lu 3:37 which was the s. of Jared,
Lu 3:37 which was the s. of Maleleel,
Lu 3:37 which was the s. of Cainan,
Lu 3:38 Which was the s. Enos,
Lu 3:38 which was the s. of Seth,
Lu 3:38 which was the s. of Adam,
Lu 3:38 which was the s. of God.
Lu 4:3 If thou be the S. of God, command. 5207
Lu 4:9 If thou be the S. of God, cast 5207
Lu 4:22 they said, Is not this Joseph's s.? 5207
Lu 4:41 Thou art Christ the S. of God. 5207
Lu 5:24 S. of man hath power upon earth 5207
Lu 6:5 S. of man is Lord..of the sabbath. 5207
Lu 6:15 James the s. of Alphaeus, and Simon
Lu 6:22 as evil, for the S. of man's sake. 5207
Lu 7:12 the only s. of his mother, and she 5207
Lu 7:34 The S. of man is come eating and 5207
Lu 8:28 Jesus, thou S. of God most high? 5207
Lu 9:22 S. of man must suffer many 5207
Lu 9:26 shall the S. of man be ashamed, 5207
Lu 9:35 This is my beloved S.: hear him. 5207
Lu 9:38 I beseech thee, look upon my s.: 5207
Lu 9:41 suffer you? Bring thy s. hither. 5207
Lu 9:44 S. of man shall be delivered into 5207
Lu 9:56 S. of man is not come to destroy 5207
Lu 9:58 the S. of man hath not where to 5207
Lu 10:6 and if the s. of peace be there, 5207
Lu 10:22 no man knoweth who the S. is, 5207
Lu 10:22 and who the Father is, but the S., 5207
Lu 10:22 and he to whom the S. will reveal 5207
Lu 11:11 If a s. shall ask bread of any of 5207
Lu 11:30 S. of man be to this generation. 5207
Lu 12:8 shall the S. of man also confess 5207
Lu 12:10 a word against the S. of man, 5207
Lu 12:40 S. of man cometh at an hour 5207
Lu 12:53 shall be divided against the s., 5207
Lu 12:53 and the s. against the father; the 5207
Lu 15:13 younger s. gathered all together, 5207
Lu 15:19 no more worthy to be called thy s. 5207
Lu 15:21 And the s. said unto him, Father, 5207
Lu 15:21 more worthy to be called thy s. 5207
Lu 15:24 For this my s. was dead, and is 5207
Lu 15:25 Now his elder s. was in the field: 5207
Lu 15:30 as soon as this thy s. was come 5207
Lu 15:31 S., thou art ever with me, and all 5043
Lu 16:25 S., remember that thou in thy 5043
Lu 17:22 one of the days of the S. of man, 5207
Lu 17:24 also the S. of man be in his day. 5207
Lu 17:26 also in the days of the S. of man. 5207
Lu 17:30 when the S. of man is revealed. 5207
Lu 18:8 when the S. of man cometh, shall 5207
Lu 18:31 prophets concerning the S. of man 5207
Lu 18:38, 39 s. of David, have mercy on me. 5207
Lu 19:9 as he also is a S. of Abraham. 5207
Lu 19:10 For the S. of man is come to seek 5207
Lu 20:13 I will send my beloved s.: it may 5207
Lu 20:41 say they that Christ is David's s.? 5207
Lu 20:44 him Lord, how is he then his s.? 5207
Lu 21:27 the S. of man coming in a cloud 5207
Lu 21:36 and to stand before the S. of man. 5207
Lu 22:22 And truly the S. of man goeth, as 5207
Lu 22:48 betrayest thou the S. of man with 5207
Lu 22:69 S. of man sit on the right hand 5207
Lu 22:70 all, Art thou then the S. of God? 5207
Lu 24:7 S. of man must be delivered into 5207
Joh 1:18 the only begotten S., which is in 5207
Joh 1:34 record that this is the S. of God. 5207
Joh 1:42 Thou art Simon the s. of Jona: 5207
Joh 1:45 Jesus of Nazareth, the S. of Joseph. 5207
Joh 1:49 Rabbi, thou art the S. of God; 5207
Joh 1:51 descending upon the S. of man. 5207
Joh 3:13 the S. of man which is in heaven. 5207
Joh 3:14 so must the S. of man be lifted up: 5207
Joh 3:16 that he gave his only begotten S., 5207
Joh 3:17 God sent not his S. into the world 5207
Joh 3:18 of the only begotten S. of God. 5207
Joh 3:35 The Father loveth the S., and hath 5207
Joh 3:36 He that believeth on the S. hath 5207
Joh 3:36 and he that believeth not the S. 5207
Joh 4:5 that Jacob gave to his s. Joseph. 5207
Joh 4:46 whose s. was sick at Capernaum. 5207
Joh 4:47 would come down, and heal his s.: 5207
Joh 4:50 unto him, Go thy way; thy s. liveth. 5207
Joh 4:51 told him, saying, Thy s. liveth. 3816

Joh 4:53 Jesus said unto him, Thy **s.** liveth:...... *5207*
Joh 5:19 **The S. can do nothing of himself,** . *5207*
Joh 5:19 **these also doeth the S. likewise**.... *5207*
Joh 5:20 **For the Father loveth the S., and**.. *5207*
Joh 5:21 **so the S. quickeneth whom he will**. *5207*
Joh 5:22 **all judgment unto the S.:**............. *5207*
Joh 5:23 **That all men should honour the S.,** *5207*
Joh 5:23 **He that honoureth not the S.**........ *5207*
Joh 5:25 **hear the voice of the S. of God:** *5207*
Joh 5:26 **he given to the S. to have life**...... *5207*
Joh 5:27 **also, because he is the S. of man.** ..*5207*
Joh 6:27 **which the S. of man shall give**...... *5207*
Joh 6:40 **that every one which seeth the S.,**. *5207*
Joh 6:42 Is not this Jesus, the **s.** of Joseph,...... *5207*
Joh 6:53 **ye eat the flesh of the S. of man,**.. *5207*
Joh 6:62 **shall see the S. of man ascend up**.. *5207*
Joh 6:69 art that Christ, the **S.** of the living *5207*
Joh 6:71 of Judas Iscariot the **s.** of Simon:.............
Joh 8:28 **ye have lifted up the S. of man,** *5207*
Joh 8:35 **for ever: but the S. abideth ever**.... *5207*
Joh 8:36 **S. therefore shall make you free,** .. *5207*
Joh 9:19 Is this your **s.**, who ye say was born .. *5207*
Joh 9:20 We know that this is our **s.**, and........ *5207*
Joh 9:35 **thou believe on the S. of God?** *5207*
Joh 10:36 **I said, I am the S. of God?** *5207*
Joh 11:4 **the S. of God might be glorified**.... *5207*
Joh 11:27 thou art the Christ, the **S.** of God, ... *5207*
Joh 12:4 Simon's **s.**, which should betray him,.........
Joh 12:23 **the S. of man should be glorified**. . *5207*
Joh 12:34 The **S.** of man must be lifted up?....... *5207*
Joh 12:34 lifted up? who is this **S.** of man? *5207*
Joh 13:2 Iscariot, Simon's **s.**, to betray him; ....
Joh 13:26 it to Judas Iscariot, the **s.** of Simon...........
Joh 13:31 **Now is the S. of man glorified,** *5207*
Joh 14:13 **Father may be glorified in the S.**. ..*5207*
Joh 17:1 **the hour is come; glorify thy S.,** ... *5207*
Joh 17:1 **that thy S. also may glorify thee:**.. *5207*
Joh 17:12 **is lost, but the s. of perdition;**....... *5207*
Joh 19:7 he made himself the **S.** of God. *5207*
Joh 19:26 his mother, **Woman, behold thy s.!**.. *5207*
Joh 20:31 Jesus is the Christ, the **S.** of God; *5207*
Joh 21:15 **s. of Jonas, lovest thou me more than** ..
Joh 21:16, 17 **Simon, s. of Jonas, lovest thou me?**..
Ac 1:13 James the **s.** of Alphaeus, and Simon.........
Ac 3:13 fathers...glorified his **S.** Jesus;........... *3816*
Ac 3:26 having raised up his **S.** Jesus, sent *3816*
Ac 4:36 interpreted, The **s.** of consolation,)..... *5207*
Ac 7:21 and nourished him for her own **s.**.......... *5207*
Ac 7:56 the **S.** of man standing on the right..... *5207*
Ac 8:37 that Jesus Christ is the **S.** of God....... *5207*
Ac 9:20 that he is the **S.** of God. *5207*
Ac 13:21 gave unto them Saul the **s.** of Cis,...... *5207*
Ac 13:22 I have found David the **s.** of Jesse,..... *5207*
Ac 13:33 Thou art my **S.**, this day have I.......... *5207*
Ac 16:1 Timotheus,...**s.** of a certain woman, ... *5207*
Ac 23:6 am a Pharisee, the **s.** of a Pharisee: ... *5207*
Ac 23:16 And when Paul's sister's **s.** heard of.... *5207*
Ro 1:3 has **S.** Jesus Christ our Lord,............ *5207*
Ro 1:4 declared to be the **S.** of God with *5207*
Ro 1:9 my spirit in the gospel of his **S.**, ... *5207*
Ro 5:10 reconciled...by the death of his **S.**, ... *5207*
Ro 8:3 sending his own **S.** in the likeness...... *5207*
Ro 8:29 be conformed to the image of his **S.**, .. *5207*
Ro 8:32 He that spared not his own **S.**, but...... *5207*
Ro 9:9 I come, and Sarah shall have a **s.**....... *5207*
1Co 1:9 of his **S.** Jesus Christ our Lord. *5207*
1Co 4:17 Timotheus, who is my beloved **s.**, ... *5043*
1Co 15:28 the **S.** also himself be subject unto *5207*
2Co 1:19 For the **S.** of God, Jesus Christ, ... *5207*
Ga 1:16 To reveal his **S.** in me, that I might.... *5207*
Ga 2:20 I live by the faith of the **S.** of God, ... *5207*
Ga 4:4 God sent forth his **S.**, made of a........ *5207*
Ga 4:6 the Spirit of his **S.** into your hearts,.... *5207*
Ga 4:7 art no more a servant, but a **s.**;......... *5207*
Ga 4:7 if a **s.**, then an heir of God through *5207*
Ga 4:30 Cast out the bondwoman and her **s.**..... *5207*
Ga 4:30 **s.** of the bondwoman shall not be *5207*
Ga 4:30 heir with the **s.** of the freewoman....... *5207*
Eph 4:13 of the knowledge of the **S.** of God,...... *5207*
Php 2:22 him, that, as a **s.** with the father,....... *5043*
Col 1:13 into the kingdom of his dear **S.**:......... *5207*
Col 4:10 Marcus, sister's **s.** to Barnabas, ... *431*
1Th 1:10 to wait for his **S.** from heaven, ... *5207*
2Th 2:3 be revealed, the **s.** of perdition; *5207*
1Ti 1:2 Timothy, my own **s.** in the faith: *5043*
1Ti 1:18 I commit unto thee, **s.** Timothy, ... *5043*
2Ti 1:2 To Timothy, my dearly beloved **s.**....... *5043*
2Ti 2:1 my **s.**, be strong in the grace that...... *5043*
Tit 1:4 To Titus, mine own **s.** after the......... *5043*
Phm 10 I beseech thee for my **s.** Onesimus,..... *5043*
Heb 1:2 last days spoken unto us by his **S.**,...... *5207*
Heb 1:5 Thou art my **S.**, this day have I......... *5207*
Heb 1:5 Father, and he shall be to me a **S.**?.... *5207*
Heb 1:8 unto the **S.** he saith, Thy throne, ... *5207*
Heb 2:6 the **s.** of man, that thou visitest him? .. *5207*
Heb 3:6 Christ as a **s.** over his own house; *5207*
Heb 4:14 the heavens, Jesus the **S.** of God, ... *5207*
Heb 5:5 him, Thou art my **S.**, to day have I.... *5207*
Heb 5:8 Though he were a **S.**, yet learned he.. *5207*
Heb 6:6 they crucify...the **S.** of God afresh,..... *5207*
Heb 7:3 but made like unto the **S.** of God; *5207*
Heb 7:28 maketh the **S.**, who is consecrated..... *5207*
Heb 10:29 trodden under foot the **S.** of God, ... *5207*
Heb 11:17 offered up his only begotten **s.**,................
Heb 11:24 the **s.** of Pharaoh's daughter;............ *5207*
Heb 12:5 My **s.**, despise not...the chastening..... *5207*
Heb 12:6 and scourgeth every **s.** whom he.......... *5207*
Heb 12:7 **s.** is he whom the father chasteneth.... *5207*
Jas 2:21 offered Isaac his **s.** upon the altar? *5207*
1Pe 5:13 you; and so doth Marcus my **s.**.......... *5207*
2Pe 1:17 This is my beloved **S.**, in whom I am.. *5207*
2Pe 2:15 the way of Balaam the **s.** of Bosor,...........
1Jo 1:3 and with his **S.** Jesus Christ............. *5207*
1Jo 1:7 the blood of Jesus Christ his **S.**.......... *5207*
1Jo 2:22 that denieth the Father and the **S.**....... *5207*
1Jo 2:23 Whosoever denieth the **S.**, the same... *5207*
1Jo 2:23 he that acknowledgeth the **S.** hath...........
1Jo 2:24 ye also shall continue in the **S.**,......... *5207*
1Jo 3:8 For this purpose the **S.** of God was..... *5207*
1Jo 3:23 believe on the name of his **S.** Jesus *5207*
1Jo 4:9 God sent his only begotten **S.** into...... *5207*
1Jo 4:10 his **S.** to be the propitiation for our..... *5207*
1Jo 4:14 **S.** to be the Saviour of the world. *5207*
1Jo 4:15 confess that Jesus is the **S.** of God, ... *5207*
1Jo 5:5 believeth that Jesus is the **S.** of God?.. *5207*
1Jo 5:9 which he hath testified of his **S.**. *5207*
1Jo 5:10 He that believeth on the **S.** of God...... *5207*
1Jo 5:10 the record that God gave of his **S.**. *5207*
1Jo 5:11 life, and this life is in his **S.**............. *5207*
1Jo 5:12 He that hath the **S.** hath life; and....... *5207*
1Jo 5:12 hath not the **S.** of God hath not life. ... *5207*
1Jo 5:13 on the name of the **S.** of God;........... *5207*
1Jo 5:13 on the name of the **S.** of God............ *5207*
1Jo 5:20 we know that the **S.** of God is come,.. *5207*
1Jo 5:20 is true, even in his **S.** Jesus Christ. *5207*
2Jo 3 Jesus Christ, the **S.** of the Father, ... *5207*
2Jo 9 he hath both the Father and the **S.**..... *5207*
Re 1:13 one like unto the **S.** of man,............ *5207*
Re 2:18 **These things saith the S. of God,** .. *5207*
Re 14:14 one sat like unto the **S.** of man,......... *5207*
Re 21:7 be his God, and he shall be my **s.**. *5207*

SONG See also SONGS.

Ex 15:1 of Israel this **s.** unto the Lord,........... 7892
Ex 15:2 The Lord is my strength and **s.**, ... 2176
Nu 21:17 Israel sang this **s.**, Spring up, O.......... 7892
De 31:19 therefore write ye this **s.** for you, ... 7892
De 31:19 that this **s.** may be a witness for me... 7892
De 31:21 this **s.** shall testify against them as 7892
De 31:22 Moses therefore wrote this **s.** the 7892
De 31:30 of Israel the words of this **s.**, ... 7892
De 32:44 and spake all the words of this **s.** in.... 7892
Jg 5:12 Deborah: awake, awake, utter a **s.** 7892
2Sa 22:1 unto the Lord the words of this **s.**...... 7892
1Ch 6:31 David set over the service of **s.**.......... 7892
1Ch 15:22 chief of the Levites, was for **s.**......... 4853
1Ch 15:22 he instructed about the **s.**, because..... 4853
1Ch 15:27 Chenaniah the master of the **s.** with.... 4853
1Ch 25:6 the hands of their father for **s.** in 7892
2Ch 29:27 **s.** of the Lord began also with the...... 7892
Job 30:9 And now am I their **s.**, yea, I am........ 5058
Ps 18:*title* unto the Lord...words of this **s.**........ 7892
Ps 28:7 and with my **s.** will I praise him. 7892
Ps 30:*title* A Psalm and **S.** at the dedication........ 7892
Ps 33:3 Sing unto him a new **s.**; play 7892
Ps 40:3 he hath put a new **s.** in my mouth,........ 7892
Ps 42:8 in the night his **s.** shall be with me, ... 7892
Ps 45:*title* of Korah, Maschil, A **S.** of loves. 7892
Ps 46:*title* of Korah, A **S.** upon Alamoth. 7892
Ps 48:*title* A **S.** and Psalm for the sons of.......... 7892
Ps 65:*title* A Psalm and **S.** of David. 7892
Ps 66:*title* the chief Musician, A **S.** or Psalm. 7892
Ps 67:*title* on Neginoth, A Psalm or **S.**................ 7892
Ps 68:*title* Musician, A Psalm or **S.** of David. 7892
Ps 69:12 and I was the **s.** of the drunkards....... 5058
Ps 69:30 praise the name of God with a **s.**, ... 7892
Ps 75:*title* A Psalm or **S.** of Asaph.................... 7892
Ps 76:*title* A Psalm or **S.** of Asaph.................... 7892
Ps 77:6 I call to remembrance my **s.** in the 5058
Ps 83:*title* A **S.** or Psalm of Asaph.................... 7892
Ps 87:*title* Psalm or **S.** for the sons of Korah. 7892
Ps 88:*title* **S.** or Psalm for the sons of Korah, ... 7892
Ps 92:*title* A Psalm or **S.** for the sabbath day...... 7892
Ps 96:1 O sing unto the Lord a new **s.**........... 7892
Ps 98:1 O sing unto the Lord a new **s.**; for..... 7892
Ps 108:*title* A **S.** or Psalm of David. 7892
Ps 118:14 The Lord is my strength and **s.**, ... 2176
Ps 120:*title* A **S.** of degrees. 7892
Ps 121:*title* A **S.** of degrees. 7892
Ps 122:*title* A **S.** of degrees of David. 7892
Ps 123:*title* A **S.** of degrees. 7892
Ps 124:*title* A **S.** of degrees of David. 7892
Ps 125:*title* A **S.** of degrees. 7892
Ps 126:*title* A **S.** of degrees. 7892
Ps 127:*title* A **S.** of degrees for Solomon. 7892
Ps 128:*title* A **S.** of degrees. 7892
Ps 129:*title* A **S.** of degrees. 7892
Ps 130:*title* A **S.** of degrees. 7892
Ps 131:*title* A **S.** of degrees of David. 7892
Ps 132:*title* A **S.** of degrees. 7892
Ps 133:*title* A **S.** of degrees of David. 7892
Ps 134:*title* A **S.** of degrees. 7892
Ps 137:3 captive required of us a **s.**; 1697,7892
Ps 137:4 How shall we sing the Lord's **s.** in a... 7892
Ps 144:9 I will sing a new **s.** unto thee, O........ 7892
Ps 149:1 Sing unto the Lord a new **s.**, and....... 7892
Ec 7:5 for a man to hear the **s.** of fools. 7892
Ca *general title* The **S.** Of Solomon. 7892
Ca 1:1 The **s.** of songs, which is Solomon's.... 7892
Isa 5:1 will sing to my wellbeloved a **s.** 7892
Isa 12:2 Jehovah is my strength and my **s.**;........ 2176
Isa 24:9 shall not drink wine with a **s.**;............ 7892
Isa 26:1 this **s.** be sung in the land of Judah;.... 7892
Isa 30:29 Ye shall have a **s.**, as in the night........ 7892
Isa 42:10 Sing unto the Lord a new **s.**, and....... 7892
La 3:14 my people; and their **s.** all the day...... 5058
Eze 33:32 art unto them as a very lovely **s.** 7892
Re 5:9 And they sung a new **s.**, saying, ... *5603*
Re 14:3 And they sung as it were a new **s.**;...... *5603*
Re 14:3 no man could learn that **s.** but the...... *5603*
Re 15:3 And they sing the **s.** of Moses the...... *5603*
Re 15:3 and the **s.** of the Lamb, saying, ... *5603*

SONGS

Ge 31:27 thee away with mirth, and with **s.**, ... 7892
1Ki 4:32 and his **s.** were a thousand and five. ... 7892
1Ch 25:7 instructed in the **s.** of the Lord,......... 7892
Ne 12:46 **s.** of praise and thanksgiving unto....... 7892
Job 35:10 maker, who giveth **s.** in the night;....... 2158
Ps 32:7 me about with **s.** of deliverance.......... 7438
Ps 119:54 Thy statutes have been my **s.** in........ 2158
Ps 137:3 Sing us one of the **s.** of Zion. 7892
Pr 25:20 he that singeth **s.** to an heavy heart.... 7892
Ca 1:1 The song of **s.**, which is Solomon's..... 7892
Isa 23:16 make sweet melody, sing many **s.**, ... 7892
Isa 24:16 part of the earth have we heard **s.**, ... 2158
Isa 35:10 to Zion with **s.** and everlasting........... 7440
Isa 38:20 we will sing my **s.** to the stringed 5058
Eze 26:13 cause the noise of thy **s.** to cease; 7892
Am 5:23 away from me the noise of thy **s.**;...... 7892
Am 8:3 And the **s.** of the temple shall be 7892
Am 8:10 and all your **s.** into lamentation; 7892
Eph 5:19 psalms and hymns and spiritual **s.**. *5603*
Col 3:16 psalms and hymns and spiritual **s.**....... *5603*

SON-IN-LAW See SON and LAW.

SON'S

Ge 11:31 Lot the son of Haran his **s.** son, ... 1121
Ge 16:15 Abram called his **s.** name, which 1121
Ge 21:23 with my son, nor with my **s.** son:....... 5220
Ge 24:51 let her be thy master's **s.** wife, as...... 1121
Ge 27:25 me, and I will eat of my **s.** venison,.... 1121
Ge 27:31 arise, and eat of his **s.** venison,.......... 1121
Ge 30:14 Give me,...of thy **s.** mandrakes. 1121
Ge 30:15 take away my **s.** mandrakes also?....... 1121
Ge 30:15 to thee to night for thy **s.** mandrakes...... 1121
Ge 30:16 hired thee with my **s.** mandrakes......... 1121
Ge 37:32 now whether it be thy **s.** coat or no.... 1121
Ge 37:33 knew it, and said, It is my **s.** coat; 1121
Ex 10:2 ears of thy son, and of thy **s.** son,...... 1121
Le 18:10 The nakedness of thy **s.** daughter,...... 1121

Le 18:15 she is thy **s.** wife; thou shalt not........ 1121
Le 18:17 shalt thou take her **s.** daughter, ... 1121
De 6:2 thou, and thy son, and thy **s.** son,...... 1121
Jg 8:22 and thy son, and thy **s.** son also:........ 1121
1Ki 11:35 the kingdom out of his **s.** hand,......... 1121
1Ki 21:29 in his **s.** days will I bring the evil....... 1121
Pr 30:4 his name, and what is his **s.** name,..... 1121
Jer 27:7 him, and his son, and his **s.** son,........ 1121

SONS See also SONS'.

Ge 5:4, 7,10,13,16,19,22,26,30 begat **s.** and.... 1121
Ge 6:2 the **s.** of God saw the daughters of..... 1121
Ge 6:4 the **s.** of God came in unto the.......... 1121
Ge 6:10 Noah begat three **s.**, Shem, Ham,...... 1121
Ge 6:18 come into the ark, thou, and thy **s.**,.... 1121
Ge 7:7 Noah went in, and his **s.**, and his....... 1121
Ge 7:13 Ham, and Japheth, the **s.** of Noah,...... 1121
Ge 7:13 three wives of his **s.** with them,......... 1121
Ge 8:16 ark, thou, and thy wife, and thy **s.**,.... 1121
Ge 8:18 Noah went forth, and his **s.**, and his ... 1121
Ge 9:1 God blessed Noah and his **s.**, and........ 1121
Ge 9:8 unto Noah, and to his **s.** with him,...... 1121
Ge 9:18 the **s.** of Noah, that went forth of....... 1121
Ge 9:19 These are the three **s.** of Noah: and... 1121
Ge 10:1 the generations of the **s.** of Noah;...... 1121
Ge 10:1 unto them were **s.** born after the....... 1121
Ge 10:2 The **s.** of Japheth; Gomer, and.......... 1121
Ge 10:3 the **s.** of Gomer; Ashkenaz, and......... 1121
Ge 10:4 And the **s.** of Javan; Elishah, and........ 1121
Ge 10:6 the **s.** of Ham; Cush, and Mizraim,...... 1121
Ge 10:7 the **s.** of Cush; Seba, and Havilah,...... 1121
Ge 10:7 and the **s.** of Raamah; Sheba, and....... 1121
Ge 10:20 These are the **s.** of Ham, after their... 1121
Ge 10:25 unto Eber were born two **s.**: the........ 1121
Ge 10:29 all these were the **s.** of Joktan........... 1121
Ge 10:31 These are the **s.** of Shem, after.......... 1121
Ge 10:32 are the families of the **s.** of Noah,...... 1121
Ge 11:11, 13,15,17,19,21,23,25 begat **s.** and...... 1121
Ge 19:12 son in law, and thy **s.**, and thy........... 1121
Ge 19:14 out, and spake unto his **s.** in law,....... 2860
Ge 19:14 one that mocked unto his **s.** in law...... 2860
Ge 23:3 and spake unto the **s.** of Heth,.......... 1121
Ge 23:11 the presence of the **s.** of my people.... 1121
Ge 23:16 in the audience of the **s.** of Heth,....... 1121
Ge 23:20 of a buryingplace by the **s.** of Heth..... 1121
Ge 25:3 the **s.** of Dedan were Asshurim, and.... 1121
Ge 25:4 And the **s.** of Midian; Ephah, and....... 1121
Ge 25:6 But unto the **s.** of the concubines,...... 1121
Ge 25:9 his **s.** Isaac and Ishmael buried......... 1121
Ge 25:10 purchased of the **s.** of Heth: there........ 1121
Ge 25:13 are the names of the **s.** of Ishmael,..... 1121
Ge 25:16 These are the **s.** of Ishmael, and........ 1121
Ge 27:29 thy mother's **s.** bow down to thee:...... 1121
Ge 29:34 because I have born him three **s.**:...... 1121
Ge 30:20 me, because I have born him six **s.**:... 1121
Ge 30:35 gave them into the hand of his **s.**....... 1121
Ge 31:1 he heard the word's of Laban's **s.**,...... 1121
Ge 31:17 his **s.** and his wives upon camels;....... 1121
Ge 31:28 not suffered me to kiss my **s.** and....... 1121
Ge 31:55 kissed his **s.** and his daughters,.......... 1121
Ge 32:22 womenservants, and his eleven **s.**,....... 3206
Ge 34:5 now his **s.** were with his cattle in....... 1121
Ge 34:7 **s.** of Jacob came out of the field......... 1121
Ge 34:13 **s.** of Jacob answered Shechem and...... 1121
Ge 34:25 two of the **s.** of Jacob, Simeon and...... 1121
Ge 34:27 **s.** of Jacob came upon the slain,......... 1121
Ge 35:5 did not pursue after the **s.** of Jacob..... 1121
Ge 35:22 Now the **s.** of Jacob were twelve:....... 1121
Ge 35:23 The **s.** of Leah; Reuben, Jacob's......... 1121
Ge 35:24 And the **s.** of Rachel; Joseph and........ 1121
Ge 35:25 **s.** of Bilhah, Rachel's handmaid;.......... 1121
Ge 35:26 the **s.** of Zilpah, Leah's handmaid;....... 1121
Ge 35:26 these are the **s.** of Jacob, which......... 1121
Ge 35:29 his **s.** Esau and Jacob buried him........ 1121
Ge 36:5 these are the **s.** of Esau, which were.. 1121
Ge 36:6 Esau took his wives, and his **s.**, and... 1121
Ge 36:10 These are the names of Esau's **s.**;...... 1121
Ge 36:11 **s.** of Eliphaz were Teman, Omar,....... 1121
Ge 36:12 were the **s.** of Adah Esau's wife......... 1121
Ge 36:13 are the **s.** of Reuel; Nahath, and......... 1121
Ge 36:13 the **s.** of Bashemath Esau's wife......... 1121
Ge 36:14 the **s.** of Aholibamah, the daughter...... 1121
Ge 36:15 These were dukes of the **s.** of Esau:.. 1121
Ge 36:15 **s.** of Eliphaz the firstborn son of........ 1121
Ge 36:16 Edom; these were the **s.** of Adah........ 1121
Ge 36:17 are the **s.** of Reuel Esau's son;.......... 1121
Ge 36:17 the **s.** of Bashemath Esau's wife......... 1121
Ge 36:18 the **s.** of Aholibamath Esau's wife;...... 1121
Ge 36:19 the **s.** of Esau, who is Edom, and...... 1121
Ge 36:20 These are the **s.** of Seir the Horite,.... 1121
Ge 37:2 the lad was with the **s.** of Bilhah,....... 1121
Ge 37:2 with the **s.** of Zilpah, his father's....... 1121
Ge 37:35 his **s.** and all his daughters rose up..... 1121
Ge 41:50 And unto Joseph were born two **s.**..... 1121
Ge 42:1 Jacob said unto his **s.**, Why do ye....... 1121
Ge 42:5 the **s.** of Israel came to buy corn....... 1121
Ge 42:11 We are all one man's **s.**; we are......... 1121
Ge 42:13 the **s.** of one man in the land of.......... 1121
Ge 42:32 twelve brethren, **s.** of our father;....... 1121
Ge 42:37 Slay my two **s.**, if I bring him not....... 1121
Ge 44:27 know that my wife bare me two **s.**:..........
Ge 46:5 **s.** of Israel carried Jacob their........... 1121
Ge 46:7 His **s.**, and his sons' **s.** with him,...... 1121
Ge 46:8 came into Egypt, Jacob and his **s.**:...... 1121
Ge 46:9 **s.** of Reuben; Hanoch, and Phallu,...... 1121
Ge 46:10 **s.** of Simeon; Jemuel, and Jamin,........ 1121
Ge 46:11 the **s.** of Levi; Gershon, Kohath,........ 1121
Ge 46:12 the **s.** of Judah; Er, and Onan,............ 1121
Ge 46:12 the **s.** of Pharez were Hezron and....... 1121
Ge 46:13 And the **s.** of Issachar; Tolah, and...... 1121
Ge 46:14 the **s.** of Zebulun; Sered, and Elon,.... 1121
Ge 46:15 These be the **s.** of Leah, which she..... 1121
Ge 46:15 the souls of his **s.** and his daughters... 1121
Ge 46:16 the **s.** of Gad; Ziphion, and Haggi,...... 1121
Ge 46:17 And the **s.** of Asher; Jimnah, and....... 1121
Ge 46:17 and the **s.** of Beriah; Heber, and........ 1121
Ge 46:18 These are the **s.** of Zilpah, whom....... 1121
Ge 46:19 The **s.** of Rachel Jacob's wife;............ 1121
Ge 46:21 And the **s.** of Benjamin were Belah,.... 1121
Ge 46:22 These are the **s.** of Rachel, which...... 1121
Ge 46:23 And the **s.** of Dan; Hushim............... 1121
Ge 46:24 **s.** of Naphtali; Jahzeel, and Guni,....... 1121
Ge 46:25 These are the **s.** of Bilhah, which....... 1121
Ge 46:27 the **s.** of Joseph, which were born...... 1121
Ge 48:1 and he took with him his two **s.**,........ 1121
Ge 48:5 thy two **s.**, Ephraim and Manasseh,.... 1121
Ge 48:8 Israel beheld Joseph's **s.**, and said,..... 1121
Ge 48:9 They are my **s.**, whom God hath........ 1121
Ge 49:1 Jacob called unto his **s.**, and said,....... 1121
Ge 49:2 together, and hear, ye **s.** of Jacob;...... 1121
Ge 49:33 made an end of commanding his **s.**,..... 1121
Ge 50:12 his **s.** did unto him according as he..... 1121
Ge 50:13 his **s.** carried him into the land of....... 1121
Ex 3:22 and ye shall put them upon your **s.**,.... 1121
Ex 4:20 And Moses took his wife and his **s.**,... 1121
Ex 6:14 The **s.** of Reuben the firstborn of....... 1121
Ex 6:15 And the **s.** of Simeon; Jemuel, and...... 1121
Ex 6:16 are the names of the **s.** of Levi.......... 1121
Ex 6:17 **s.** of Gershon; Libni, and Shimi,......... 1121
Ex 6:18 And the **s.** of Kohath; Amram, and..... 1121
Ex 6:19 And the **s.** of Merari; Mahali, and...... 1121
Ex 6:21 And the **s.** of Izhar; Korah, and......... 1121
Ex 6:22 And the **s.** of Uzziel; Mishael, and...... 1121
Ex 6:24 And the **s.** of Korah; Assir, and......... 1121
Ex 10:9 with our **s.** and with our daughters,.... 1121
Ex 12:24 to thee and to thy **s.** for ever........... 1121
Ex 18:3 her two **s.**; of which the name of....... 1121
Ex 18:5 came with his **s.** and his wife unto...... 1121
Ex 18:6 thy wife, and her two **s.** with her....... 1121
Ex 21:4 she have born him **s.** or daughters;..... 1121
Ex 22:29 firstborn of thy **s.** shalt thou give....... 1121
Ex 27:21 Aaron and his **s.** shall order it........... 1121
Ex 28:1 thy brother, and his **s.** with him,........ 1121
Ex 28:1 Eleazar and Ithamar, Aaron's **s.**......... 1121
Ex 28:4 for Aaron thy brother, and his **s.**,........ 1121
Ex 28:40 Aaron's **s.** thou shalt make coats,....... 1121
Ex 28:41 thy brother, and his **s.** with him;........ 1121
Ex 28:43 be upon Aaron, and upon his **s.**,.......... 1121
Ex 29:4 Aaron and his **s.** thou shalt bring........ 1121
Ex 29:8 shalt bring his **s.**, and put coats......... 1121
Ex 29:9 with girdles, Aaron and his **s.**, and...... 1121
Ex 29:9 shalt consecrate Aaron and his **s.**........ 1121
Ex 29:10, 15,19 Aaron and his **s.** shall put......... 1121
Ex 29:20 the tip of the right ear of his **s.**,.......... 1121
Ex 29:21 upon his garments, and upon his **s.**,.... 1121
Ex 29:21 upon the garments of his **s.** with........ 1121
Ex 29:21 and his garments and his **s.**, and........ 1121
Ex 29:24 Aaron, and in the hands of his **s.**......... 1121
Ex 29:27 and of that which is for his **s.**............ 1121
Ex 29:32 Aaron and his **s.** shall eat the flesh..... 1121
Ex 29:35 thou do unto Aaron, and to his **s.**,....... 1121
Ex 29:44 sanctify also both Aaron and his **s.**,..... 1121
Ex 30:19 Aaron and his **s.** shall wash their........ 1121
Ex 30:30 thou shalt anoint Aaron and his **s.**....... 1121
Ex 31:10 the garments of his **s.**, to minister...... 1121
Ex 32:2 the ears of your wives, of your **s.**,..... 1121
Ex 32:26 the **s.** of Levi gathered themselves..... 1121
Ex 34:16 take of their daughters unto thy **s.**,...... 1121
Ex 34:16 and make thy **s.** go a whoring after..... 1121
Ex 34:20 All the firstborn of thy **s.** thou.......... 1121
Ex 35:19 the garments of his **s.**, to minister....... 1121
Ex 39:27 work for Aaron, and for his **s.**,........... 1121
Ex 40:12 thou shalt bring Aaron and his **s.**........ 1121
Ex 40:14 thou shalt bring his **s.**, and clothe....... 1121
Ex 40:31 Moses and Aaron and his **s.** washed.... 1121
Le 1:5 Aaron's **s.**, shall bring the blood,........ 1121
Le 1:7 **s.** of Aaron the priest shall put fire..... 1121
Le 1:8 Aaron's **s.**, shall lay the parts, the...... 1121
Le 1:11 Aaron's **s.**, shall sprinkle his blood...... 1121
Le 2:2 And he shall bring it to Aaron's **s.**...... 1121
Le 3:2 Aaron's **s.** the priests shall sprinkle..... 1121
Le 3:5 And Aaron's **s.** shall burn it on the..... 1121
Le 3:8 Aaron's **s.** shall sprinkle the blood....... 1121
Le 3:13 and the **s.** of Aaron shall sprinkle...... 1121
Le 6:9 Command Aaron and his **s.**, saying,.... 1121
Le 6:14 the **s.** of Aaron shall offer it before..... 1121
Le 6:16 thereof shall Aaron and his **s.** eat:...... 1121
Le 6:20 the offering of Aaron and of his **s.**,..... 1121
Le 6:22 priest of his **s.** that is anointed in....... 1121
Le 6:25 Speak unto Aaron and to his **s.**,.......... 1121
Le 7:10 shall all the **s.** of Aaron have, one...... 1121
Le 7:33 He among the **s.** of Aaron, that......... 1121
Le 7:34 Aaron the priest and unto his **s.** by..... 1121
Le 7:35 of the anointing of his **s.**, out of......... 1121
Le 8:2 Take Aaron and his **s.** with him,......... 1121
Le 8:6 Moses brought Aaron and his **s.**,........ 1121
Le 8:13 Moses brought Aaron's **s.**, and put...... 1121
Le 8:14, 18,22 Aaron and his **s.** laid their......... 1121
Le 8:24 he brought Aaron's **s.**, and Moses....... 1121
Le 8:30 his garments, and upon his **s.**, and...... 1121
Le 8:30 and his **s.**, and his sons' garments...... 1121
Le 8:31 said unto Aaron and to his **s.**,............ 1121
Le 8:31 saying, Aaron and his **s.** shall eat it..... 1121
Le 8:36 So Aaron and his **s.** did all things....... 1121
Le 9:1 that Moses called Aaron and his **s.**,.... 1121
Le 9:9 the **s.** of Aaron brought the blood....... 1121
Le 9:12, 18 Aaron's **s.** presented unto him....... 1121
Le 10:1 Nadab and Abihu, the **s.** of Aaron,....... 1121
Le 10:4 the **s.** of Uzziel the uncle of Aaron,.... 1121
Le 10:6 Eleazar and unto Ithamar, his **s.**,........ 1121
Le 10:9 drink, thou, nor thy **s.** with thee,....... 1121
Le 10:12 unto Ithamar, his **s.** that were left,...... 1121
Le 10:14 thy **s.**, and thy daughters with thee:... 1121
Le 10:16 the **s.** of Aaron which were left........... 1121
Le 13:2 or unto one of his **s.** the priests:......... 1121
Le 16:1 the death of the two **s.** of Aaron,....... 1121
Le 17:2 Speak unto Aaron, and unto his **s.**,..... 1121
Le 21:1 unto the priests the **s.** of Aaron,........ 1121
Le 21:24 told it unto Aaron, and to his **s.**......... 1121
Le 22:2 Speak unto Aaron, and to his **s.**,........ 1121
Le 22:18 Speak unto Aaron, and to his **s.**,........ 1121
Le 26:29 And ye shall eat the flesh of your **s.**,.. 1121
Nu 2:14 and the captain of the **s.** of Gad......... 1121
Nu 2:18 the captain of the **s.** of Ephraim......... 1121
Nu 2:22 the captain of the **s.** of Benjamin........ 1121
Nu 3:2 are the names of the **s.** of Aaron;....... 1121
Nu 3:3 are the names of the **s.** of Aaron,....... 1121
Nu 3:9 the Levites unto Aaron and to his **s.**.... 1121
Nu 3:10 thou shalt appoint Aaron and his **s.**,.... 1121
Nu 3:17 were the **s.** of Levi by their names;.... 1121
Nu 3:18 are the names of the **s.** of Gershon.... 1121
Nu 3:19 the **s.** of Kohath by their families;...... 1121
Nu 3:20 the **s.** of Merari by their families;...... 1121
Nu 3:25 the charge of the **s.** of Gershon in...... 1121
Nu 3:29 The families of the **s.** of Kohath......... 1121
Nu 3:36 charge of the **s.** of Merari shall be...... 1121
Nu 3:38 and Aaron and his **s.**, keeping the....... 1121
Nu 3:48 redeemed, unto Aaron and to his **s.**.... 1121
Nu 3:51 redeemed unto Aaron and to his **s.**,.... 1121
Nu 4:2 Take the sum of the **s.** of Kohath....... 1121
Nu 4:2 from among the **s.** of Levi, after........ 1121
Nu 4:4 be the service of the **s.** of Kohath....... 1121
Nu 4:5 Aaron shall come, and his **s.**, and....... 1121
Nu 4:15 when Aaron and his **s.** have made...... 1121
Nu 4:15 **s.** of Kohath shall come to bear it:...... 1121
Nu 4:15 are the burden of the **s.** of Kohath..... 1121
Nu 4:19 Aaron and his **s.** shall go in, and........ 1121
Nu 4:22 also the sum of the **s.** of Gershon,..... 1121
Nu 4:27 appointment of Aaron and his **s.**......... 1121
Nu 4:27 service of the **s.** of the Gershonites,... 1121
Nu 4:28 the families of the **s.** of Gershon........ 1121

Nu 4:29 As for the **s.** of Merari, thou shalt...... 1121
Nu 4:33 of the families of the **s.** of Merari,...... 1121
Nu 4:34 numbered the **s.** of the Kohathites...... 1121
Nu 4:38 numbered of the **s.** of Gershon, ... 1121
Nu 4:41 the families of the **s.** of Gershon, ... 1121
Nu 4:42, 45 the families of the **s.** of Merari, ... 1121
Nu 6:23 Speak unto Aaron and unto his **s.**, ... 1121
Nu 7:7 he gave unto the **s.** of Gershon,......... 1121
Nu 7:8 oxen he gave unto the **s.** of Merari,.... 1121
Nu 7:9 unto the **s.** of Kohath he gave none: ... 1121
Nu 8:13 before Aaron, and before his **s.**,......... 1121
Nu 8:19 as a gift to Aaron and to his **s.** 1121
Nu 8:22 before Aaron, and before his **s.**: as..... 1121
Nu 10:8 And the **s.** of Aaron, the priests,........ 1121
Nu 10:17 **s.** of Gershon and the **s.** of Merari 1121
Nu 13:33 we saw the giants, the **s.** of Anak. 1121
Nu 16:1 and Abiram, the **s.** of Eliab, ... 1121
Nu 16:1 of Peleth, **s.** of Reuben, took men:..... 1121
Nu 16:7 too much upon you, ye **s.** of Levi....... 1121
Nu 16:8 Hear, I pray you, ye **s.** of Levi:......... 1121
Nu 16:10 all thy brethren the **s.** of Levi with..... 1121
Nu 16:12 and Abiram, the **s.** of Eliab: which...... 1121
Nu 16:27 wives, and their **s.**, and their little...... 1121
Nu 18:1 Thou and thy **s.** and thy father's 1121
Nu 18:1 **s.** with thee shall bear the iniquity...... 1121
Nu 18:2 and thy **s.** with thee shall minister...... 1121
Nu 18:7 thy **s.** with thee shall keep your......... 1121
Nu 18:8 to thy **s.**, by an ordinance for ever. 1121
Nu 18:9 most holy for thee and for thy **s.**........ 1121
Nu 18:11 to thy **s.** and to thy daughters with..... 1121
Nu 18:19 thy **s.** and thy daughters with thee, ... 1121
Nu 21:29 he hath given his **s.** that escaped,....... 1121
Nu 21:35 So they smote him, and his **s.**, and..... 1121
Nu 26:8 And the **s.** of Pallu; Eliab,................ 1121
Nu 26:9 the **s.** of Eliab; Nemuel and Dathan,.... 1121
Nu 26:12 **s.** of Simeon after their families:......... 1121
Nu 26:19 The **s.** of Judah were Er and Onan: 1121
Nu 26:20 the **s.** of Judah after their families....... 1121
Nu 26:21 the **s.** of Pharez were; of Hezron, ... 1121
Nu 26:23 **s.** of Issachar after their families: 1121
Nu 26:26 **s.** of Zebulun after their families: 1121
Nu 26:28 The **s.** of Joseph after their families 1121
Nu 26:29 Of the **s.** of Manasseh: of Machir, ... 1121
Nu 26:30 These are the **s.** of Gilead: of........... 1121
Nu 26:33 the son of Hepher had no **s.**, but 1121
Nu 26:35 **s.** of Ephraim after their families: 1121
Nu 26:36 And these are the **s.** of Shuthelah:...... 1121
Nu 26:37 the families of the **s.** of Ephraim 1121
Nu 26:37 the **s.** of Joseph after their families. 1121
Nu 26:38 **s.** of Benjamin after their families: 1121
Nu 26:40 **s.** of Bela were Ard and Naaman:....... 1121
Nu 26:41 **s.** of Benjamin after their families: 1121
Nu 26:42 the **s.** of Dan after their families:........ 1121
Nu 26:45 Of the **s.** of Beriah; of Heber, the....... 1121
Nu 26:47 are the families of the **s.** of Asher 1121
Nu 26:48 **s.** of Naphtali after their families:........ 1121
Nu 27:3 died in his own sin, and had no **s.**. 1121
Nu 36:1 of the families of the **s.** of Joseph, ... 1121
Nu 36:3 to any of the **s.** of the other tribes 1121
Nu 36:5 tribe of the **s.** of Joseph hath said....... 1121
Nu 36:11 unto their father's brothers' **s.**: 1121
Nu 36:12 the families of the **s.** of Manasseh 1121
De 1:28 we have seen the **s.** of the Anakims ... 1121
De 2:33 we smote him, and his **s.**, and all....... 1121
De 4:9 teach them thy **s.**, and thy sons' **s.**,.... 1121
De 11:6 Dathan and Abiram, the **s.** of Eliab, ... 1121
De 12:12 ye, and your **s.**, and your daughters,... 1121
De 12:31 even their **s.** and their daughters........ 1121
De 18:5 of the Lord, him and his **s.** for ever...... 1121
De 21:5 the priests the **s.** of Levi shall come ... 1121
De 21:16 maketh his **s.** to inherit that which...... 1121
De 23:17 nor a sodomite of the **s.** of Israel. 1121
De 28:32 **s.** and thy daughters shall be given..... 1121
De 28:41 Thou shalt beget **s.** and daughters,...... 1121
De 28:53 flesh of thy **s.** and of thy daughters,.... 1121
De 31:9 it unto the priests the **s.** of Levi, ... 1121
De 32:8 when he separated the **s.** of Adam,..... 1121
De 32:19 because of the provoking of his **s.**, ... 1121
Jos 7:24 wedge of gold, and his **s.**, and his 1121
Jos 15:14 drove thence the three **s.** of Anak, ... 1121
Jos 17:3 the son of Manasseh, had no **s.**, but ... 1121
Jos 17:6 had an inheritance among his **s.**:......... 1121
Jos 17:6 rest of Manasseh's **s.** had the land....... 1121
Jos 24:32 Jacob bought of the **s.** of Hamor........ 1121
Jg 1:20 expelled thence...three **s.** of Anak. 1121
Jg 3:6 gave their daughters to their **s.**,......... 1121
Jg 8:19 brethren, even the **s.** of my mother: ... 1121
Jg 8:30 Gideon had threescore and ten **s.**........ 1121
Jg 9:2 either that all the **s.** of Jerubbaal, ... 1121
Jg 9:5 his brethren the **s.** of Jerubbaal, ... 1121
Jg 9:18 have slain his **s.**, threescore and ten ... 1121
Jg 9:24 threescore and ten **s.** of Jerubbaal 1121
Jg 10:4 he had thirty **s.** that rode on thirty 1121
Jg 11:2 Gilead's wife bare him **s.**; and his 1121
Jg 11:2 wife's **s.** grew up, and they thrust 1121
Jg 12:9 had thirty **s.**, and thirty daughters, ... 1121
Jg 12:9 daughters from abroad for his **s.**.......... 1121
Jg 12:14 he had forty **s.** and thirty nephews, ... 1121
Jg 17:5 and consecrated one of his **s.**, who..... 1121
Jg 17:11 man was unto him as one of his **s.**...... 1121
Jg 18:30 he and his **s.** were priests to the........ 1121
Jg 19:22 certain **s.** of Belial, beset the house.... 1121
Ru 1:1 Moab, he, and his wife, and his two **s.**. 1121
Ru 1:2 the name of his two **s.** Mahlon and..... 1121
Ru 1:3 and she was left, and her two **s.**. 1121
Ru 1:5 left of her two **s.** and her husband...... 3206
Ru 1:11 there yet any more **s.** in my womb,.... 1121
Ru 1:12 to night, and should also bear **s.**;........ 1121
Ru 4:15 which is better to thee than seven **s.**, ..1121
1Sa 1:3 two **s.** of Eli, Hophni and Phinehas, ... 1121
1Sa 1:4 her **s.** and her daughters, portions:..... 1121
1Sa 1:8 am not I better to thee than ten **s.**?.... 1121
1Sa 2:12 Now the **s.** of Eli were **s.** of Belial; 1121
1Sa 2:21 she conceived, and bare three **s.** and .. 1121
1Sa 2:22 all that his **s.** did unto all Israel; 1121
1Sa 2:24 Nay, my **s.**; for it is no good report.... 1121
1Sa 2:29 and honourest thy **s.** above me, to 1121
1Sa 2:34 thy two **s.**, Hophni and Phinehas, ... 1121
1Sa 3:13 because his **s.** made themselves vile, .. 1121
1Sa 4:4,11 **s.** of Eli, Hophni and Phinehas, ... 1121
1Sa 4:17 two **s.** also, Hophni and Phinehas, ... 1121
1Sa 8:1 he made his **s.** judges over Israel. 1121
1Sa 8:3 his **s.** walked not in his ways, but....... 1121
1Sa 8:5 and thy **s.** walk not in thy ways: 1121
1Sa 8:11 He will take your **s.**, and appoint........ 1121
1Sa 12:2 and, behold, my **s.** are with you:........ 1121
1Sa 14:49 **s.** of Saul were Jonathan, and Ishui, ... 1121
1Sa 16:1 provided me a king among his **s.**. 1121
1Sa 16:5 And he sanctified Jesse and his **s.**,....... 1121
1Sa 16:10 Jesse made seven of his **s.** to pass 1121
1Sa 17:12 was Jesse; and he had eight **s.**:.......... 1121
1Sa 17:13 eldest **s.** of Jesse...followed Saul 1121
1Sa 17:13 names of his three **s.** that went to...... 1121
1Sa 22:20 one of the **s.** of Ahimelech the son 1121
1Sa 28:19 shalt thou and thy **s.** be with me:....... 1121
1Sa 30:3 and their **s.** and their daughters, ... 1121
1Sa 30:6 every man for his **s.** and for his 1121
1Sa 30:19 nor great, neither **s.** nor daughters, ... 1121
1Sa 31:2 hard upon Saul and upon his **s.**; 1121
1Sa 31:2 and Melchi-shua, Saul's **s.**................. 1121
1Sa 31:6 So Saul died, and his three **s.**, and 1121
1Sa 31:7 and that Saul and his **s.** were dead, ... 1121
1Sa 31:8 found Saul and his three **s.** fallen in.... 1121
1Sa 31:12 body of Saul and the bodies of his **s.**.... 1121
2Sa 2:18 there were three **s.** of Zeruiah there,.. 1121
2Sa 3:2 unto David were **s.** born in Hebron:.... 1121
2Sa 3:39 **s.** of Zeruiah be too hard for me: 1121
2Sa 4:2 the **s.** of Rimmon a Beerothite,.......... 1121
2Sa 4:5 the **s.** of Rimmon the Beerothite, ... 1121
2Sa 4:9 the **s.** of Rimmon the Beerothite, ...
2Sa 5:13 yet **s.** and daughters born to David..... 1121
2Sa 6:3 Uzzah and Ahio, the **s.** of Abinadab,.... 1121
2Sa 8:18 and David's **s.** were chief rulers. 1121
2Sa 9:10 Thou...and thy **s.**, and thy servants, ... 1121
2Sa 9:10 had fifteen **s.** and twenty servants. 1121
2Sa 9:11 at my table, as one of the king's **s.**..... 1121
2Sa 13:23 Absalom invited all the king's **s.**. 1121
2Sa 13:27 and all the king's **s.** go with him......... 1121
2Sa 13:29 Then all the king's **s.** arose, and 1121
2Sa 13:30 Absalom hath slain all the king's **s.**,...... 1121
2Sa 13:32 slain...the young men the king's **s.**;..... 1121
2Sa 13:33 think that all the king's **s.** are dead: 1121
2Sa 13:35 king, Behold, the king's **s.** come: 1121
2Sa 13:36 the king's **s.** came, and lifted up......... 1121
2Sa 14:6 thy handmaid had two **s.**, and they 1121
2Sa 14:27 Absalom there were born three **s.**. 1121
2Sa 15:27 in peace, and your two **s.** with you, ... 1121
2Sa 15:36 have there with them their two **s.**. 1121
2Sa 16:10 I to do with you, ye **s.** of Zeruiah? 1121
2Sa 19:5 lives of thy **s.** and of thy daughters,.... 1121
2Sa 19:17 fifteen **s.** and his twenty servants....... 1121
2Sa 19:22 I to do with you, ye **s.** of Zeruiah,...... 1121
2Sa 21:6 Let seven men of his **s.** be delivered .. 1121
2Sa 21:8 the king took the two **s.** of Rizpah...... 1121
2Sa 21:8 five **s.** of Michal...daughter of Saul,..... 1121
2Sa 21:16 which was of the **s.** of the giant, ... 3211
2Sa 21:18 which was of the **s.** of the giant. 3211
2Sa 23:6 the **s.** of Belial shall be all of them as........
2Sa 23:32 of the **s.** of Jashen, Jonathan,............ 1121
1Ki 1:9 called all his brethren the king's **s.**,...... 1121
1Ki 1:19 and hath called all the **s.** of the king,... 1121
1Ki 1:25 and hath called all the king's **s.**, ... 1121
1Ki 2:7 kindness unto the **s.** of Barzillai.......... 1121
1Ki 4:3 Ahiah, the **s.** of Shisha, scribes;........ 1121
1Ki 4:31 and Darda, the **s.** of Mahol: and......... 1121
1Ki 11:20 household among the **s.** of Pharaoh. 1121
1Ki 12:31 which were not of the **s.** of Levi. 1121
1Ki 13:11 and his **s.** came and told him all......... 1121
1Ki 13:12 his **s.** had seen what way the man...... 1121
1Ki 13:13 And he said unto his **s.**, saddle me...... 1121
1Ki 13:27 he spake to his **s.**, saying, Saddle....... 1121
1Ki 13:31 he spake to his **s.**, saying, When I....... 1121
1Ki 18:31 of the tribes of the **s.** of Jacob, ... 1121
1Ki 20:35 man of the **s.** of the prophets said...... 1121
1Ki 21:10 set two men, **s.** of Belial, before........ 1121
2Ki 2:3,5 the **s.** of the prophets that were 1121
2Ki 2:7 men of the **s.** of the prophets went,.... 1121
2Ki 2:15 when the **s.** of the prophets which...... 1121
2Ki 4:1 wives of the **s.** of the prophets unto ... 1121
2Ki 4:1 come to take unto him my two **s.**........ 3206
2Ki 4:4 door upon thee and upon thy **s.**, ... 1121
2Ki 4:5 the door upon her and upon her **s.**, ... 1121
2Ki 4:38 the **s.** of the prophets were sitting...... 1121
2Ki 4:38 pottage for the **s.** of the prophets....... 1121
2Ki 5:22 men of the **s.** of the prophets: give..... 1121
2Ki 6:1 **s.** of the prophets said unto Elisha,..... 1121
2Ki 9:26 of Naboth, and the blood of his **s.**,....... 1121
2Ki 10:1 Ahab had seventy **s.** in Samaria.......... 1121
2Ki 10:2 seeing your master's **s.** are with 1121
2Ki 10:3 and meetest of your master's **s.**,......... 1121
2Ki 10:6 heads of the men your master's **s.**,...... 1121
2Ki 10:6 Now the king's **s.**, being seventy......... 1121
2Ki 10:7 that they took the king's **s.**, and......... 1121
2Ki 10:8 brought the heads of the king's **s.**........ 1121
2Ki 11:2 and stole from among the king's **s.** 1121
2Ki 15:12 Thy **s.** shall sit on the throne of......... 1121
2Ki 17:17 caused their **s.** and their daughters 1121
2Ki 19:37 and Sharezer his **s.** smote him with 1121
2Ki 20:18 of thy **s.** that shall issue from thee, ... 1121
2Ki 25:7 they slew the **s.** of Zedekiah before 1121
1Ch 1:5 **s.** of Japheth; Gomer, and Magog, ... 1121
1Ch 1:6 the **s.** of Gomer; Ashchenaz, and 1121
1Ch 1:7 **s.** of Javan; Elishah, and Tarshish, ... 1121
1Ch 1:8 The **s.** of Ham; Cush, Mizraim, ... 1121
1Ch 1:9 **s.** of Cush; Seba, and Havilah, and 1121
1Ch 1:9 And the **s.** of Raamah; Sheba, and....... 1121
1Ch 1:17 **s.** of Shem; Elam, and Asshur, and...... 1121
1Ch 1:19 And unto Eber were born two **s.**......... 1121
1Ch 1:23 All these were the **s.** of Joktan. 1121
1Ch 1:28 The **s.** of Abraham; Isaac, and........... 1121
1Ch 1:31 These are the **s.** of Ishmael. 1121
1Ch 1:32 Now the **s.** of Keturah, Abraham's...... 1121
1Ch 1:32 **s.** of Jokshan; Sheba, and Dedan. 1121
1Ch 1:33 **s.** of Midian; Ephah, and Epher,.......... 1121
1Ch 1:33 All these are the **s.** of Keturah. 1121
1Ch 1:34 The **s.** of Isaac; Esau and Israel.......... 1121
1Ch 1:35 The **s.** of Esau; Eliphaz, Reuel, and..... 1121
1Ch 1:36 **s.** of Eliphaz; Teman, and Omar,......... 1121
1Ch 1:37 The **s.** of Reuel; Nahoth, Zerah, ... 1121
1Ch 1:38 **s.** of Seir; Lotan, and Shobal, and........ 1121
1Ch 1:39 the **s.** of Lotan; Hori, and Homam:..... 1121
1Ch 1:40 **s.** of Shobal; Alian, and Manahath,...... 1121
1Ch 1:40 the **s.** of Zibeon; Aiah, and Anah. 1121
1Ch 1:41 The **s.** of Anah; Dishon. And the........ 1121
1Ch 1:41 **s.** of Dishon; Amram, and Eshban, ... 1121
1Ch 1:42 The **s.** of Ezer; Bilhan, and Zavan, ... 1121
1Ch 1:42 The **s.** of Dishan; Uz, and Aran. 1121
1Ch 2:1 These are the **s.** of Israel; Reuben, ... 1121
1Ch 2:3 The **s.** of Judah; Er, and Onan,.......... 1121
1Ch 2:4 Zerah. All the **s.** of Judah were five. ... 1121
1Ch 2:5 **s.** of Pharez; Hezron, and Hamul........ 1121
1Ch 2:6 the **s.** of Zerah; Timri, and Ethan;...... 1121
1Ch 2:7 **s.** of Carmi; Achar, the troubler of..... 1121
1Ch 2:8 And the **s.** of Ethan; Azariah............ 1121
1Ch 2:9 **s.** also of Hezron, that were born........ 1121
1Ch 2:16 **s.** of Zeruiah; Abishai, and Joab,........ 1121
1Ch 2:18 her **s.** are these: Jesher, and............ 1121
1Ch 2:23 these belonged to the **s.** of Machir 1121

1Ch 2:25 the **s.** of Jerahmeel the firstborn of 1121
1Ch 2:27 And the **s.** of Ram the firstborn of 1121
1Ch 2:28 **s.** of Onam were, Shammai, and 1121
1Ch 2:28 the **s.** of Shammai; Nadab, and 1121
1Ch 2:30 **s.** of Nadab; Seled, and Appaim: 1121
1Ch 2:31 And the **s.** of Appaim; Ishi 1121
1Ch 2:31 the **s.** of Ishi; Sheshan. And the 1121
1Ch 2:32 **s.** of Jada the brother of Shammai; 1121
1Ch 2:33 **s.** of Jonathan; Peleth, and Zaza. 1121
1Ch 2:33 These were the **s.** of Jerahmeel. 1121
1Ch 2:34 Sheshan had no **s.**, but daughters. 1121
1Ch 2:42 Now the **s.** of Caleb the brother of 1121
1Ch 2:42 the **s.** of Mareshah the father of 1121
1Ch 2:43 **s.** of Hebron; Korah, and Tappuah, 1121
1Ch 2:47 **s.** of Jahdai; Regem, and Jotham, 1121
1Ch 2:50 These were the **s.** of Caleb the son 1121
1Ch 2:52 the father of Kirjath-jearim had **s.**; 1121
1Ch 2:54 The **s.** of Salma; Beth-lehem, and 1121
1Ch 3:1 Now these were the **s.** of David, 1121
1Ch 3:9 These were all the **s.** of David, 1121
1Ch 3:9 beside the **s.** of the concubines, and 1121
1Ch 3:15 the **s.** of Josiah were, the firstborn 1121
1Ch 3:16 **s.** of Jehoiakim; Jeconiah his son, 1121
1Ch 3:17 **s.** of Jeconiah; Assir, Salathiel his 1121
1Ch 3:19 the **s.** of Pedaiah were, Zerubbabel, 1121
1Ch 3:19 **s.** of Zerubbabel; Meshullam, and 1121
1Ch 3:21 the **s.** of Hananiah; Pelatiah, and 1121
1Ch 3:21 the **s.** of Rephaiah, the **s.** of Arnan, 1121
1Ch 3:21 **s.** of Obadiah, the **s.** of Shechaniah. 1121
1Ch 3:22 the **s.** of Shechaniah; Shemaiah: 1121
1Ch 3:22 **s.** of Shemaiah; Hattush, and Igeal, 1121
1Ch 3:23 the **s.** of Neariah: Elioenai, and 1121
1Ch 3:24 **s.** of Elioenai were, Hodaiah, and 1121
1Ch 4:1 **s.** of Judah; Pharez, Hezron, and 1121
1Ch 4:4 are the **s.** of Hur, the firstborn 1121
1Ch 4:6 These were the **s.** of Naarah 1121
1Ch 4:7 And the **s.** of Helah were, Zereth, 1121
1Ch 4:13 **s.** of Kenaz; Othniel, and Seraiah: 1121
1Ch 4:13 and the **s.** of Othniel; Hathath 1121
1Ch 4:15 **s.** of Caleb the son of Jephunneh; 1121
1Ch 4:15 and the **s.** of Elah, even Kenaz. 1121
1Ch 4:16 **s.** of Jehaleleel; Ziph, and Ziphah, 1121
1Ch 4:17 And the **s.** of Ezra were, Jether, and 1121
1Ch 4:18 And these are the **s.** of Bithiah the 1121
1Ch 4:19 And the **s.** of his wife Hodiah the 1121
1Ch 4:20 And the **s.** of Shimon were, Amnon, 1121
1Ch 4:20 And the **s.** of Ishi were, Zoheth, and 1121
1Ch 4:21 **s.** of Shelah the son of Judah were, 1121
1Ch 4:24 The **s.** of Simeon were, Nemuel, and 1121
1Ch 4:26 the **s.** of Mishma; Hamuel his son, 1121
1Ch 4:27 And Shimei had sixteen **s.** and six 1121
1Ch 4:42 of them, even of the **s.** of Simeon, 1121
1Ch 4:42 Rephaiah, and Uzziel, the **s.** of Ishi 1121
1Ch 5:1 **s.** of Reuben the firstborn of Israel, 1121
1Ch 5:1 the **s.** of Joseph the son of Israel: 1121
1Ch 5:3 The **s.**, of Reuben the firstborn 1121
1Ch 5:4 The **s.** of Joel; Shemaiah his son, 1121
1Ch 5:18 The **s.** of Reuben, and the Gadites, 1121
1Ch 6:1 **s.** of Levi; Gershon, Kohath, and 1121
1Ch 6:2 **s.** of Kohath; Amram, Izhar, and 1121
1Ch 6:3 **s.** also of Aaron; Nadab and Abihu, 1121
1Ch 6:16 **s.** of Levi; Gershom, Kohath, and 1121
1Ch 6:17 be the names of the **s.** of Gershom: 1121
1Ch 6:18 the **s.** of Kohath were, Amram, and 1121
1Ch 6:19 The **s.** of Merari; Mahli, and Mushi. 1121
1Ch 6:22 **s.** of Kohath; Amminadab his son, 1121
1Ch 6:25 And the **s.** of Elkanah; Amasai, and 1121
1Ch 6:26 the **s.** of Elkanah; Zophai his son, 1121
1Ch 6:28 **s.** of Samuel; the firstborn Vashni, 1121
1Ch 6:29 **s.** of Merari; Mahli, Libni his son, 1121
1Ch 6:33 Of the **s.** of the Kohathites: Heman 1121
1Ch 6:44 And their brethren the **s.** of Merari 1121
1Ch 6:49 But Aaron and his **s.** offered upon 1121
1Ch 6:50 And these are the **s.** of Aaron; 1121
1Ch 6:54 in their coasts, of the **s.** of Aaron, 1121
1Ch 6:57 to the **s.** of Aaron they gave the 1121
1Ch 6:61 And unto the **s.** of Kohath, which 1121
1Ch 6:62 to the **s.** of Gershom throughout 1121
1Ch 6:63 Unto the **s.** of Merari were given by 1121
1Ch 6:66 of the families of the **s.** of Kohath 1121
1Ch 6:70 of the remnant of the **s.** of Kohath. 1121
1Ch 6:71 Unto the **s.** of Gershom were given 1121
1Ch 7:1 Now the **s.** of Issachar were, Tola, 1121
1Ch 7:2 the **s.** of Tola; Uzzi, and Rephaiah, 1121
1Ch 7:3 And the **s.** of Uzzi; Izrahiah: and 1121
1Ch 7:3 the **s.** of Izrahiah; Michael, and 1121
1Ch 7:4 for they had many wives and **s.** 1121
1Ch 7:6 **s.** of Benjamin; Bela, and Becher, and
1Ch 7:7 And the **s.** of Bela; Ezbon, and 1121
1Ch 7:8 And the **s.** of Becher; Zemira, and 1121
1Ch 7:8 All these are the **s.** of Becher. 1121
1Ch 7:10 The **s.** also of Jediael; Bilhan: and 1121
1Ch 7:10 **s.** of Bilhan; Jeush, and Benjamin, 1121
1Ch 7:11 All these are the **s.** of Jediael, by 1121
1Ch 7:12 of Ir, and Hushim, the **s.** of Aher. 1121
1Ch 7:13 **s.** of Naphtali; Jahziel, and Guni, 1121
1Ch 7:13 and Shallum, the **s.** of Bilhah. 1121
1Ch 7:14 **s.** of Manasseh; Ashriel, whom she 1121
1Ch 7:16 and his **s.** were Ulam and Rakem. 1121
1Ch 7:17 And the **s.** of Ulam; Bedan. These 1121
1Ch 7:17 the **s.** of Gilead, the son of Machir, 1121
1Ch 7:19 the **s.** of Shemidah were, Ahian, 1121
1Ch 7:20 the **s.** of Ephraim; Shuthelah, and 1121
1Ch 7:30 The **s.** of Asher; Imnah, and Isuah, 1121
1Ch 7:31 And the **s.** of Beriah; Heber, and 1121
1Ch 7:33 And the **s.** of Japhlet; Pasach, and 1121
1Ch 7:34 And the **s.** of Shamer; Ahi, and 1121
1Ch 7:35 And the **s.** of his brother Helem; 1121
1Ch 7:36 The **s.** of Zophah; Suah, and 1121
1Ch 7:38 And the **s.** of Jether; Jephunneh, 1121
1Ch 7:39 the **s.** of Ulla; Arah, and Haniel, 1121
1Ch 8:3 And the **s.** of Bela were, Addar, and 1121
1Ch 8:6 And these are the **s.** of Ehud: these 1121
1Ch 8:10 These were his **s.**, heads of the 1121
1Ch 8:12 **s.** of Elpaal; Eber, and Misham, 1121
1Ch 8:16 Ispah, and Joha, the **s.** of Beriah. 1121
1Ch 8:18 and Jobab, the **s.** of Elpaal; 1121
1Ch 8:21 and Shimrath, the **s.** of Shimhi; 1121
1Ch 8:25 and Penuel, the **s.** of Shashak; 1121
1Ch 8:27 and Zichri, the **s.** of Jeroham. 1121
1Ch 8:35 And the **s.** of Micah were, Pithon, 1121
1Ch 8:38 And Azel had six **s.**, whose names 1121
1Ch 8:38 All these were the **s.** of Azel. 1121
1Ch 8:39 the **s.** of Eshek his brother were, 1121
1Ch 8:40 the **s.** of Ulam were mighty men of 1121
1Ch 8:40 and had many **s.**, and sons' **s.**, an 1121
1Ch 8:40 All these were of the **s.** of Benjamin. 1121
1Ch 9:5 Asaiah the firstborn, and his **s.**. 1121
1Ch 9:6 of the **s.** of Zerah; Jeuel, and their 1121
1Ch 9:7 of the **s.** of Benjamin; Sallu the 1121
1Ch 9:14 Hashabiah, of the **s.** of Merari; 1121
1Ch 9:30 of the **s.** of the priests made the 1121
1Ch 9:32 the **s.** of the Kohathites, were over 1121
1Ch 9:41 And the **s.** of Micah were, Pithon, 1121
1Ch 9:44 Azel had six **s.**, whose names are 1121
1Ch 9:44 Hanan: these were the **s.** of Azel. 1121
1Ch 10:2 hard after Saul, and after his **s.**; 1121
1Ch 10:2 and Malchi-shua, the **s.** of Saul. 1121
1Ch 10:6 So Saul died, and his three **s.**, and 1121
1Ch 10:7 and that Saul and his **s.** were dead, 1121
1Ch 10:8 they found Saul and his **s.** fallen in 1121
1Ch 10:12 of Saul, and the bodies of his **s.**, 1121
1Ch 11:34 The **s.** of Hashem the Gizonite, 1121
1Ch 11:44 Shama and Jehiel the **s.** of Hothan 1121
1Ch 11:46 and Joshaviah the **s.** of Elnaam, 1121
1Ch 12:3 the **s.** of Shemaah the Gibeathite; 1121
1Ch 12:3 and Pelet, the **s.** of Azmaveth; 1121
1Ch 12:7 the **s.** of Jeroham of Gedor. 1121
1Ch 12:14 These were of the **s.** of Gad, 1121
1Ch 14:3 David begat more **s.** and daughters. 1121
1Ch 15:5 Of the **s.** of Kohath; Uriel the chief, 1121
1Ch 15:6 the **s.** of Merari; Asaiah the chief, 1121
1Ch 15:7 the **s.** of Gershom; Joel the chief, 1121
1Ch 15:8 Of the **s.** of Elizaphan; Shemaiah 1121
1Ch 15:9 Of the **s.** of Hebron; Eliel the chief, 1121
1Ch 15:10 Of the **s.** of Uzziel; Amminadab the 1121
1Ch 15:17 of the **s.** of Merari their brethren, 1121
1Ch 16:42 the **s.** of Jeduthun were porters. 1121
1Ch 17:11 after thee, which shall be of thy **s.**; 1121
1Ch 18:17 **s.** of David were chief about the 1121
1Ch 21:20 four **s.** with him hid themselves. 1121
1Ch 23:6 into courses among the **s.** of Levi, 1121
1Ch 23:8 **s.** of Laadan; the chief was Jehiel, 1121
1Ch 23:9 **s.** of Shimei; Shelomith, and Haziel, 1121
1Ch 23:10 **s.** of Shimei were, Jahath, Zina, and 1121
1Ch 23:10 These four were the **s.** of Shimei. 1121
1Ch 23:11 Jeush and Beriah had not many **s.**; 1121
1Ch 23:12 The **s.** of Kohath; Amram, Izhar, 1121
1Ch 23:13 The **s.** of Amram; Aaron and Moses: 1121
1Ch 23:13 holy things, he and his **s.** for ever, 1121
1Ch 23:14 **s.** were named of the tribe of Levi 1121
1Ch 23:15 The **s.** of Moses were, Gershom, and 1121
1Ch 23:16 Of the **s.** of Gershom, Shebuel was 1121
1Ch 23:17 the **s.** of Eliezer were, Rehabiah the 1121
1Ch 23:17 And Eliezer had none other **s.**; but 1121
1Ch 23:17 the **s.** of Rehabiah were very many. 1121
1Ch 23:18 the **s.** of Izhar; Shelomith the chief. 1121
1Ch 23:19 the **s.** of Hebron; Jeriah the first, 1121
1Ch 23:20 Of the **s.** of Uzziel; Micah the first 1121
1Ch 23:21 The **s.** of Merari; Mahli, and Mushi. 1121
1Ch 23:21 The **s.** of Mahli; Eleazar, and Kish. 1121
1Ch 23:22 Eleazar died, and had no **s.**, but 1121
1Ch 23:22 brethren the **s.** of Kish took them. 1121
1Ch 23:23 The **s.** of Mushi; Mahli, and Eder, 1121
1Ch 23:24 These were the **s.** of Levi after the 1121
1Ch 23:28 to wait on the **s.** of Aaron for the 1121
1Ch 23:32 the charge of the **s.** of Aaron their 1121
1Ch 24:1 are the divisions of the **s.** of Aaron. 1121
1Ch 24:1 The **s.** of Aaron; Nadab, and Abihu, 1121
1Ch 24:3 both Zadok of the **s.** of Eleazar, and 1121
1Ch 24:3 and Ahimelech of the **s.** of Ithamar, 1121
1Ch 24:4 men found of the **s.** of Eleazar 1121
1Ch 24:4 than of the **s.** of Ithamar; and thus 1121
1Ch 24:4 Among the **s.** of Eleazar there were 1121
1Ch 24:4 and eight among the **s.** of Ithamar 1121
1Ch 24:5 of God, were of the **s.** of Eleazar, 1121
1Ch 24:5 and of the **s.** of Ithamar. 1121
1Ch 24:20 And the rest of the **s.** of Levi were 1121
1Ch 24:20 Of the **s.** of Amram; Shubael: of 1121
1Ch 24:20 of the **s.** of Shubael; Jehdeiah. 1121
1Ch 24:21 of the **s.** of Rehabiah, the first was 1121
1Ch 24:22 of the **s.** of Shelomoth; Jahath. 1121
1Ch 24:23 the **s.** of Hebron; Jeriah the first, 1121
1Ch 24:24 Of the **s.** of Uzziel; Michah: 1121
1Ch 24:24 of the **s.** of Michah; Shamir. 1121
1Ch 24:25 of the **s.** of Isshiah; Zechariah. 1121
1Ch 24:26 **s.** of Merari were Mahli and Mushi: 1121
1Ch 24:26 Mushi: the **s.** of Jaaziah; Beno. 1121
1Ch 24:27 The **s.** of Merari by Jaaziah; Beno, 1121
1Ch 24:28 Mahli came Eleazar, who had no **s.** 1121
1Ch 24:30 **s.** also of Mushi; Mahli, and Eder, 1121
1Ch 24:30 were the **s.** of the Levites after the 1121
1Ch 24:31 their brethren the **s.** of Aaron. 1121
1Ch 25:1 of the **s.** of Asaph, and of Heman, 1121
1Ch 25:2 the **s.** of Asaph; Zaccur, and Joseph, 1121
1Ch 25:2 the **s.** of Asaph under the hands of 1121
1Ch 25:3 the **s.** of Jeduthun; Gedaliah, and 1121
1Ch 25:4 **s.** of Heman; Bukkiah, Mattaniah, 1121
1Ch 25:5 All these were the **s.** of Heman the 1121
1Ch 25:5 God gave to Heman fourteen **s.** and 1121
1Ch 25:9 who with his brethren and **s.** were 1121
1Ch 25:10 Zaccur, he, his **s.**, and his brethren, 1121
1Ch 25:11 to Izri, he, his **s.**, and his brethren, 1121
1Ch 25:12 to Nethaniah, he, his **s.**, and his 1121
1Ch 25:13 to Bukkiah, he, his **s.**, and his 1121
1Ch 25:14 to Jesharelah, he, his **s.**, and his 1121
1Ch 25:15 to Jeshaiah, he, his **s.**, and his 1121
1Ch 25:16 to Mattaniah, he, his **s.**, and his 1121
1Ch 25:17 Shimei, he, his **s.**, and his brethren, 1121
1Ch 25:18 Azareel, he, his **s.**, and his brethren, 1121
1Ch 25:19 to Hashabiah, he, his **s.**, and his 1121
1Ch 25:20 Shubael, he, his **s.**, and his brethren, 1121
1Ch 25:21 to Mattithiah, he, his **s.**, and his 1121
1Ch 25:22 to Jeremoth, he, his **s.**, and his 1121
1Ch 25:23 to Hananiah, he, his **s.**, and his 1121
1Ch 25:24 Joshbekashah, he, his **s.**, and his 1121
1Ch 25:25 Hanani, he, his **s.**, and his brethren, 1121
1Ch 25:26 to Mallothi, he, his **s.**, and his 1121
1Ch 25:27 to Eliathah, he, his **s.**, and his 1121
1Ch 25:28 Hothir, he, his **s.**, and his brethren, 1121
1Ch 25:29 to Giddalti, he, his **s.**, and his 1121
1Ch 25:30 to Mahazioth, he, his **s.**, and his 1121
1Ch 25:31 Romamti-ezer, he, his **s.**, and his 1121
1Ch 26:1 the son of Kore, of the **s.** of Asaph. 1121
1Ch 26:2 And the **s.** of Meshelemiah were, 1121
1Ch 26:4 Moreover the **s.** of Obed-edom were, 1121
1Ch 26:6 unto Shemaiah his son were **s.** born, 1121
1Ch 26:7 The **s.** of Shemaiah; Othni, and 1121
1Ch 26:8 All these of the **s.** of Obed-edom: 1121
1Ch 26:8 they and their **s.** and their brethren, 1121
1Ch 26:9 Meshelemiah had **s.** and brethren, 1121
1Ch 26:10 of the children of Merari, had **s.**; 1121
1Ch 26:11 all the **s.** and brethren of Hosah 1121
1Ch 26:15 and to his **s.** the house of Asuppim. 1121
1Ch 26:19 of the porters among the **s.** of Kore, 1121
1Ch 26:19 and among the **s.** of Merari. 1121
1Ch 26:21 As concerning the **s.** of Laadan; 1121
1Ch 26:21 the **s.** of the Gershonite Laadan, 1121
1Ch 26:22 The **s.** of Jehieli; Zetham, and Joel. 1121
1Ch 26:29 Chenaniah and his **s.** were for the 1121

1Ch 27:32 Hachmoni was with the king's **s.**: 1121
1Ch 28:1 possession of the king, and of his **s.**,.... 1121
1Ch 28:4 among the **s.** of my father he liked..... 1121
1Ch 28:5 And of all my **s.**, (for the Lord hath.... 1121
1Ch 28:5 hath given me many **s.**,) he hath........ 1121
1Ch 29:24 and all the **s.** likewise of king David, ... 1121
2Ch 5:12 with their **s.** and their brethren,......... 1121
2Ch 11:14 Jeroboam and his **s.** had cast them...... 1121
2Ch 11:21 and begat twenty and eight **s.**, and..... 1121
2Ch 13:5 to him and to his **s.** by a covenant...... 1121
2Ch 13:8 Lord in the hand of the **s.** of David;.... 1121
2Ch 13:9 the **s.** of Aaron, and the Levites, ... 1121
2Ch 13:10 unto the Lord, are the **s.** of Aaron, ... 1121
2Ch 13:21 and begat twenty and two **s.**, and....... 1121
2Ch 20:14 a Levite of the **s.** of Asaph, ... 1121
2Ch 21:2 had brethren the **s.** of Jehoshaphat,..... 1121
2Ch 21:2 these were the **s.** of Jehoshaphat........ 1121
2Ch 21:7 a light to him and to his **s.** for ever. ... 1121
2Ch 21:17 in the king's house, and his **s.** also. 1121
2Ch 21:17 Jehoahaz, the youngest of his **s.**......... 1121
2Ch 22:8 the **s.** of the brethren of Ahaziah,....... 1121
2Ch 22:11 among the king's **s.** that were slain, ... 1121
2Ch 23:3 Lord hath said of the **s.** of David........ 1121
2Ch 23:11 Jehoiada and his **s.** anointed him,........ 1121
2Ch 24:3 and he begat **s.** and daughters. 1121
2Ch 24:7 for the **s.** of Athaliah, that wicked....... 1121
2Ch 24:25 for the blood of the **s.** of Jehoiada....... 1121
2Ch 24:27 Now concerning his **s.**, and the.......... 1121
2Ch 26:18 but to the priests the **s.** of Aaron,...... 1121
2Ch 28:8 women, **s.**, and daughters, and took.... 1121
2Ch 29:9 our **s.** and our daughters and our 1121
2Ch 29:11 My **s.**, be not now negligent: for the... 1121
2Ch 29:12 Azariah, of the **s.** of the Kohathites: ... 1121
2Ch 29:12 of the **s.** of Merari, Kish the son of.... 1121
2Ch 29:13 And of the **s.** of Elizaphan; Shimri, ... 1121
2Ch 29:13 and of the **s.** of Asaph; Zechariah, ... 1121
2Ch 29:14 And of the **s.** of Heman; Jehiel, and.... 1121
2Ch 29:14 of the **s.** of Jeduthun; Shemaiah,......... 1121
2Ch 29:21 the **s.** of Aaron to offer them on the ... 1121
2Ch 31:18 their wives, and their **s.**, and their....... 1121
2Ch 31:19 Also of the **s.** of Aaron the priests,..... 1121
2Ch 32:33 of the sepulchres of the **s.** of David: ... 1121
2Ch 34:12 the Levites, of the **s.** of Merari; 1121
2Ch 34:12 of the **s.** of the Kohathites, ... 1121
2Ch 35:14 priests the **s.** of Aaron were busied.... 1121
2Ch 35:14 and for the priests the **s.** of Aaron...... 1121
2Ch 35:15 the singers the **s.** of Asaph were in 1121
2Ch 36:20 servants to him and his **s.** until.......... 1121
Ezr 3:9 stood Jeshua with his **s.** and his 1121
Ezr 3:9 Kadmiel and his **s.**, the **s.** of Judah, ... 1121
Ezr 3:9 the **s.** of Henadad, with their **s.** and.... 1121
Ezr 3:10 and the Levites the **s.** of Asaph with... 1121
Ezr 6:10 the life of the king, and of his **s.**. 1123
Ezr 7:23 the realm of the king and his **s.**? 1123
Ezr 8:2 Of the **s.** of Phinehas; Gershom: 1121
Ezr 8:2 of the **s.** of Ithamar; Daniel: of the 1121
Ezr 8:2 Daniel: of the **s.** of David; Hattush. 1121
Ezr 8:3 Of the **s.** of Shechaniah, of the 1121
Ezr 8:3 of the **s.** of Pharosh; Zachariah: 1121
Ezr 8:4 **s.** of Pahath-moab; Elihoenai............ 1121
Ezr 8:5 Of the **s.** of Shechaniah; the son of..... 1121
Ezr 8:6 Of the **s.** also of Adin; Ebed the son... 1121
Ezr 8:7 And of the **s.** of Elam; Jeshaiah the..... 1121
Ezr 8:8 of the **s.** of Shephatiah; Zebadiah........ 1121
Ezr 8:9 Of the **s.** of Joab; Obadiah the son...... 1121
Ezr 8:10 And of the **s.** of Shelomith; the son 1121
Ezr 8:11 And of the **s.** of Bebai; Zechariah 1121
Ezr 8:12 And of the **s.** of Azgad; Johanan the.... 1121
Ezr 8:13 of the last **s.** of Adonikam, whose...... 1121
Ezr 8:14 Of the **s.** also of Bigvai; Uthai, and...... 1121
Ezr 8:15 found there none of the **s.** of Levi. 1121
Ezr 8:18 of the **s.** of Mahli, the son of Levi, ... 1121
Ezr 8:18 his **s.** and his brethren, eighteen; 1121
Ezr 8:19 him Jeshaiah of the **s.** of Merari, ... 1121
Ezr 8:19 his brethren and their **s.**, twenty;........ 1121
Ezr 9:2 for themselves, and for their **s.**:......... 1121
Ezr 9:12 not your daughters unto their **s.**,........ 1121
Ezr 9:12 take their daughters unto your **s.**, ... 1121
Ezr 10:2 one of the **s.** of Elam, answered and... 1121
Ezr 10:18 among the **s.** of the priests there 1121
Ezr 10:18 of the **s.** of Jeshua the son of........... 1121
Ezr 10:20 of the **s.** of Immer; Hanani, and......... 1121
Ezr 10:21 of the **s.** of Harim; Maaseiah, and....... 1121
Ezr 10:22 And of the **s.** of Pashur; Elioenai,....... 1121
Ezr 10:25 of the **s.** of Parosh; Ramiah, and........ 1121
Ezr 10:26 And of the **s.** of Elam; Mattaniah,....... 1121
Ezr 10:27 And of the **s.** of Zattu; Elioenai, ... 1121

Ezr 10:28 Of the **s.** also of Bebai; Jehohanan, ... 1121
Ezr 10:29 And of the **s.** of Bani; Meshullam, ... 1121
Ezr 10:30 of the **s.** of Pahath-moab; Adna, ... 1121
Ezr 10:31 And of the **s.** of Harim; Eliezer,......... 1121
Ezr 10:33 Of the **s.** of Hashum; Mattenai,.......... 1121
Ezr 10:34 Of the **s.** of Bani; Maadai, Amram, ... 1121
Ezr 10:43 Of the **s.** of Nebo; Jeiel, Mattithiah, ... 1121
Ne 3:3 gate did the **s.** of Hassenaah build, ... 1121
Ne 4:14 and fight for your brethren, your **s.**, ... 1121
Ne 5:2 We, our **s.**, and our daughters, are..... 1121
Ne 5:5 we bring into bondage our **s.** and 1121
Ne 10:9 Binnui of the **s.** of Henadad,.............. 1121
Ne 10:28 their **s.**, and their daughters, every..... 1121
Ne 10:30 nor take their daughters for our **s.**:..... 1121
Ne 10:36 Also the firstborn of our **s.**, and of 1121
Ne 11:6 All the **s.** of Perez that dwelt at......... 1121
Ne 11:7 these are the **s.** of Benjamin; Sallu 1121
Ne 11:22 Of the **s.** of Asaph, the singers were .. 1121
Ne 12:23 The **s.** of Levi, the chief of the.......... 1121
Ne 12:28 And the **s.** of the singers gathered...... 1121
Ne 12:35 of the priests' **s.** with trumpets; 1121
Ne 13:25 give your daughters unto their **s.**,........ 1121
Ne 13:25 take their daughters unto your **s.**, ... 1121
Ne 13:28 one of the **s.** of Joiada, the son of 1121
Ne 13:10 The ten **s.** of Haman the son of, ... 1121
Es 9:12 palace, and the ten **s.** of Haman;......... 1121
Es 9:13 let Haman's ten **s.** be hanged upon 1121
Es 9:14 and they hanged Haman's ten **s.**.......... 1121
Es 9:25 he and his **s.** should be hanged on...... 1121
Job 1:2 him seven **s.** and three daughters. 1121
Job 1:4 his **s.** went and feasted in their.......... 1121
Job 1:5 It may be that my **s.** have sinned, ... 1121
Job 1:6 when the **s.** of God came to present ... 1121
Job 1:13 when his **s.** and his daughters were 1121
Job 1:18 Thy **s.** and thy daughters were.......... 1121
Job 2:1 when the **s.** of God came to present ... 1121
Job 14:21 His **s.** came to honour, and he........... 1121
Job 38:7 all the **s.** of God shouted for joy? 1121
Job 38:32 thou guide Arcturus with his **s.**?......... 1121
Job 42:13 also seven **s.** and three daughters....... 1121
Job 42:16 saw his **s.**, and his sons' **s.**, even....... 1121
Ps 4:2 O ye **s.** of men, how long will ye 1121
Ps 31:19 trust in thee before the **s.** of men 1121
Ps 33:13 he beholdeth all the **s.** of men. 1121
Ps 42:*title* Maschil, for the **s.** of Korah. 1121
Ps 44:*title* Musician for the **s.** of Korah, ... 1121
Ps 45:*title* Shoshannim, for the **s.** of Korah, ... 1121
Ps 46:*title* chief Musician for the **s.** of Korah,...... 1121
Ps 47:*title* A Psalm for the **s.** of Korah. 1121
Ps 48:*title* and Psalm for the **s.** of Korah............ 1121
Ps 49:*title* A Psalm for the **s.** of Korah. 1121
Ps 57:4 even the **s.** of men, whose teeth are... 1121
Ps 58:1 judge uprightly, O ye **s.** of men? 1121
Ps 77:15 people, the **s.** of Jacob and Joseph...... 1121
Ps 84:*title* A Psalm for the **s.** of Korah. 1121
Ps 85:*title* A Psalm for the **s.** of Korah. 1121
Ps 87:*title* Psalm or Song for the **s.** of Korah. 1121
Ps 88:*title* Psalm for the **s.** of Korah, to the 1121
Ps 89:6 who among the **s.** of the mighty can ... 1121
Ps 106:37 they sacrificed their **s.** and their........ 1121
Ps 106:38 even the blood of their **s.** and of 1121
Ps 144:12 That our **s.** may be as plants grown.... 1121
Ps 145:12 To make known to the **s.** of men 1121
Pr 8:4 and my voice is to the **s.** of man. 1121
Pr 8:31 delights were with the **s.** of men. 1121
Ec 1:13 hath God given to the **s.** of man to..... 1121
Ec 2:3 was that good for the **s.** of men, ... 1121
Ec 2:8 and the delights of the **s.** of men,....... 1121
Ec 3:10 God hath given to the **s.** of men 1121
Ec 3:18 concerning...estate of the **s.** of men, ... 1121
Ec 3:19 that which befalleth the **s.** of men....... 1121
Ec 8:11 heart of the **s.** of men is fully set in.... 1121
Ec 9:3 heart of the **s.** of men is full of evil,.... 1121
Ec 9:12 so are the **s.** of men snared in an........ 1121
Ca 2:3 so is my beloved among the **s.**. 1121
Isa 37:38 Adrammelech and Sharezer his **s.**........ 1121
Isa 39:7 thy **s.** that shall issue from thee, ... 1121
Isa 43:6 bring my **s.** from far, and my............ 1121
Isa 45:11 things to come concerning my **s.**, ... 1121
Isa 49:22 shall bring thy **s.** in their arms, ... 1121
Isa 51:18 none to guide her among all the **s.**...... 1121
Isa 51:18 taketh her by the hand of all the **s.**...... 1121
Isa 51:20 Thy **s.** have fainted, they lie at the..... 1121
Isa 52:14 his form more than the **s.** of men:....... 1121
Isa 56:5 and a name better than of **s.** and....... 1121
Isa 56:6 Also the **s.** of the stranger, that......... 1121
Isa 57:3 ye **s.** of the sorceress, the seed of..... 1121

Isa 60:4 thy **s.** shall come from far, and thy..... 1121
Isa 60:9 to bring thy **s.** from far, their silver.... 1121
Isa 60:10 the **s.** of strangers shall build up 1121
Isa 60:14 **s.** also of them that afflicted thee 1121
Isa 61:5 the **s.** of the alien shall be your.......... 1121
Isa 62:5 virgin, so shall thy **s.** marry thee:....... 1121
Isa 62:8 **s.** of the stranger shall not drink 1121
Jer 3:24 herds, their **s.** and their daughters...... 1121
Jer 5:17 **s.** and thy daughters should eat:......... 1121
Jer 6:21 fathers and...**s.** together shall fall....... 1121
Jer 7:31 burn their **s.** and their daughters in..... 1121
Jer 11:22 **s.** and their daughters shall die by 1121
Jer 13:14 the fathers and the **s.** together, ... 1121
Jer 14:16 nor their **s.**, nor their daughters:........ 1121
Jer 16:2 shalt thou have **s.** or daughters in....... 1121
Jer 16:3 saith the Lord concerning the **s.**.......... 1121
Jer 19:5 to burn their **s.** with fire for burnt 1121
Jer 19:9 them to eat the flesh of their **s.** and.... 1121
Jer 29:6 wives, and beget **s.** and daughters;..... 1121
Jer 29:6 and take wives for your **s.**, and give ... 1121
Jer 29:6 they may bear **s.** and daughters, ... 1121
Jer 32:19 upon all the ways of the **s.** of men...... 1121
Jer 32:35 their **s.** and their daughters to pass..... 1121
Jer 35:3 his brethren, and all his **s.**, and the..... 1121
Jer 35:4 the chamber of the **s.** of Hanan, the.... 1121
Jer 35:5 I set before the **s.** of the house of....... 1121
Jer 35:6 neither ye, nor your **s.** for ever: 1121
Jer 35:8 wives, our **s.**, nor our daughters, ... 1121
Jer 35:14 commanded his **s.** not to drink wine, ... 1121
Jer 35:16 Because the **s.** of Jonadab the son 1121
Jer 39:6 of Babylon slew the **s.** of Zedekiah 1121
Jer 40:8 and Jonathan the **s.** of Kareah,........... 1121
Jer 40:8 the **s.** of Ephai the Netophathite,......... 1121
Jer 48:46 for thy **s.** are taken captives, and 1121
Jer 49:1 Hath Israel no **s.**? hath he no heir? 1121
Jer 52:10 of Babylon slew the **s.** of Zedekiah 1121
La 4:2 precious **s.** of Zion, comparable to 1121
Eze 5:10 the fathers shall eat the **s.** in the........ 1121
Eze 5:10 and the **s.** shall eat their fathers;....... 1121
Eze 14:16 deliver neither **s.** nor daughters; 1121
Eze 14:18 deliver neither **s.** nor daughters, ... 1121
Eze 14:22 forth, both **s.** and daughters: 1121
Eze 16:20 thou hast taken thy **s.** and thy........... 1121
Eze 20:31 your **s.** to pass through the fire, ... 1121
Eze 23:4 and they bare **s.** and daughters. 1121
Eze 23:10 they took her **s.** and her daughters, ... 1121
Eze 23:25 shall take thy **s.** and thy daughters; 1121
Eze 23:37 have also caused their **s.**, whom......... 1121
Eze 23:47 they shall slay their **s.** and their......... 1121
Eze 24:21 your **s.** and your daughters whom....... 1121
Eze 24:25 minds, their **s.** and their daughters, ... 1121
Eze 40:46 altar: these are the **s.** of Zadok.......... 1121
Eze 40:46 among the **s.** of Levi which come 1121
Eze 44:15 priests the Levites, the **s.** of Zadok, ... 1121
Eze 46:16 prince give a gift unto any of his **s.**.... 1121
Eze 46:18 he shall give his **s.** inheritance out...... 1121
Eze 48:11 are sanctified of the **s.** of Zadok; 1121
Da 5:21 he was driven from the **s.** of men,...... 1123
Da 10:16 like the similitude of the **s.** of men...... 1121
Da 11:10 But his **s.** shall be stirred up, and....... 1121
Ho 1:10 Ye are the **s.** of the living God. 1121
Joe 1:12 withered away from the **s.** of men 1121
Joe 2:28 your **s.** and your daughters shall......... 1121
Joe 3:8 will sell your **s.** and your daughters..... 1121
Am 2:11 I raised up of your **s.** for prophets,..... 1121
Am 7:17 thy **s.** and thy daughters shall fall 1121
Mic 5:7 man, nor waiteth for the **s.** of men 1121
Zec 9:13 and raised up thy **s.**, O Zion............... 1121
Zec 9:13 against thy **s.**, O Greece, and made.... 1121
Mal 3:3 and he shall purify the **s.** of Levi. 1121
Mal 3:6 ye **s.** of Jacob are not consumed 1121
Mt 20:20 of Zebedee's children with her **s.**......... *5207*
Mt 20:21 Grant that these my two **s.** may sit, ... *5207*
Mt 21:28 **A certain man had two s.; and he..** ***5043***
Mt 26:37 Peter and the two **s.** of Zebedee *5207*
Mk 3:17 which is, The **s.** of thunder: *5207*
Mk 3:28 **be forgiven unto the s. of men** *5207*
Mk 10:35 James and John, the **s.** of Zebedee,..... *5207*
Lu 5:10 James, and John the **s.** of Zebedee,...... *5207*
Lu 11:19 **whom do your s. cast them out?**.... *5207*
Lu 15:11 he said, **A certain man had two s.:** ..*5207*
Joh 1:12 he power to become the **s.** of God *5043*
Joh 21:2 the **s.** of Zebedee, and two other ....
Ac 2:17 your **s.** and your daughters shall......... *5207*
Ac 7:16 sum of money of the **s.** of Emmor *5207*
Ac 7:29 of Madian, where he begat two **s.** *5207*
Ac 19:14 there were seven **s.** of one Sceva, ... *5207*

Ro 8:14 Spirit of God, they are the s. of God. *5207*
Ro 8:19 the manifestation of the s. of God *5207*
1Co 4:14 but as my beloved s. I warn you *5043*
2Co 6:18 ye shall be my s. and daughters, *5207*
Ga 4:5 might receive the adoption of s. *5206*
Ga 4:6 because ye are s., God hath sent *5207*
Ga 4:22 Abraham had two s., the one by a *5207*
Eph 3:5 not made known unto the s. of men *5207*
Php 2:15 the s. of God, without rebuke, *5043*
Heb 2:10 in bringing many s. unto glory, *5207*
Heb 7:5 they that are of the s. of Levi, who *5207*
Heb 11:21 blessed both the s. of Joseph; and *5207*
Heb 12:7 God dealeth with you as with s.; *5207*
Heb 12:8 then are ye bastards, and not s. *5207*
1Jo 3:1 we should be called the s. of God: *5043*
1Jo 3:2 Beloved, now are we the s. of God, *5043*

SONS'
Ge 6:18 wife, and thy s. wives with thee. 1121
Ge 7:7 his wife, and his s. wives with him, 1121
Ge 8:16 sons, and thy s. wives with thee. 1121
Ge 8:18 his wife, and his s. wives with him: 1121
Ge 46:7 His sons, and his s. sons with him, 1121
Ge 46:7 his daughters, and his s. daughters, 1121
Ge 46:26 besides Jacob's s. wives, all the 1121
Ex 29:21 sons, and his s. garments with him. 1121
Ex 29:28 it shall be Aaron's and his s. by a 1121
Ex 29:29 of Aaron shall be his s. after him 1121
Ex 39:41 and his s. garments, to minister in 1121
Le 2:3,10 shall be Aaron's and his s.: 1121
Le 7:31 breast shall be Aaron's and his s. 1121
Le 8:27 hands, and upon his s. hands, 1121
Le 8:30 and upon his s. garments with him; 1121
Le 8:30 sons, and his s. garments with him. 1121
Le 10:13 it is thy due, and thy s. due, of the 1121
Le 10:14 for they be thy due, and thy s. due, 1121
Le 10:15 shall be thine, and thy s. with thee, 1121
Le 24:9 and it shall be Aaron's and his s.; 1121
De 4:9 them thy sons, and thy s. sons; 1121
1Ch 8:40 and s. sons, an hundred and fifty 1121
Job 42:16 his s. sons, even four generations. 1121
Eze 46:16 inheritance thereof shall be his s.; 1121
Eze 46:17 but his inheritance shall be his s. 1121

SOON See also SOONER.
Ge 18:33 as s. as he had left communing 834
Ge 27:30 as s. as Isaac had made an end of 834
Ge 44:3 As s. as the morning was light, the
Ex 2:18 How is it that ye are come so s. 4116
Ex 9:29 As s. as I am gone out of the city, I
Ex 32:19 as s. as he came nigh unto the camp, 834
De 4:26 ye shall s. utterly perish from off 4116
Jos 2:7 as s. as they which pursued after 834
Jos 2:11 And as s. as we had heard these
Jos 3:13 as s. as the soles of the feet of the
Jos 8:19 as s. as he had stretched out his hand:
Jos 8:29 and as s. as the sun was down, Joshua
Jg 8:33 to pass, as s. as Gideon was dead. 834
Jg 9:33 as s. as the sun is up, thou shalt rise
1Sa 9:13 As s. as ye be come into the city, ye
1Sa 13:10 that as s. as he had made an end of
1Sa 20:41 And as s. as the lad was gone, David
1Sa 29:10 and as s. as ye be up early in the
2Sa 6:18 And as s. as David had made an end
2Sa 13:36 as s. as he had made an end of
2Sa 15:10 As s. as ye hear the sound of the
2Sa 22:45 as s. as they hear, they shall be
1Ki 16:11 as s. as he sat on his throne, that he
1Ki 18:12 pass, as s. as I am gone up from thee
1Ki 20:36 as s. as thou art departed from me.
1Ki 20:36 as s. as he was departed from him,
2Ki 10:2 Now as s. as this letter cometh to you,
2Ki 10:25 as s. as he had made an end of offering
2Ki 14:5 as s. as the kingdom was confirmed 834
2Ch 31:5 as s. as the commandment came
Job 32:22 my maker would s. take me away. 4592
Ps 18:44 s. as they hear of me, they shall obey
Ps 37:2 shall s. be cut down like the grass, 4120
Ps 58:3 go astray as s. as they be born,
Ps 68:31 Ethiopia shall s. stretch out her 7323
Ps 81:14 s. have subdued their enemies, 4592
Ps 90:10 for it is s. cut off, and we fly away. 2440
Ps 106:13 They s. forgat his works; they 4116
Pr 14:17 that is s. angry dealeth foolishly: 7116
Isa 66:8 s. as Zion travailed, she brought 1571
Eze 23:16 s. as she saw them with her eyes, 4758
Mt 21:20 How s. is the fig tree withered *3916*
Mk 1:42 And as s. as he had spoken,
Mk 5:36 As s. as Jesus heard the word that *2112*
Mk 11:2 **and as s. as ye be entered into it,** *2112*
Mk 14:45 And as s. as he was come, he goeth
Lu 1:23 s. as the days of his ministration
Lu 1:44 as s. as the voice of thy salutation
Lu 8:6 **s. as it was sprung up, it withered**
Lu 15:30 **as s. as this thy son was come,** *3753*
Lu 22:66 And as s. as it was day, the elders
Lu 23:7 And as s. as he knew that he belonged
Joh 11:20 as s. as she heard that Jesus was
Joh 11:29 As s. as she heard that, she arose
Joh 16:21 **but as s. as she is delivered of the** *3752*
Joh 18:6 As s. then as he had said unto
Joh 21:9 As s. then as they were come to
Ac 10:29 gainsaying, as s. as I was sent for:
Ac 12:18 as s. as it was day, there was no *1096*
Ga 1:6 ye are so s. removed from him *5030*
Php 2:23 so s. as I shall see how it will go
2Th 2:2 That ye be not s. shaken in mind. *5030*
Tit 1:7 not s. angry, not given to wine, no *3711*
Re 10:10 as s. as I had eaten it, my belly *3753*
Re 12:4 for to devour her child as s. as it *3752*

SOONER
Heb 13:19 I may be restored to you the s. *5032*
Jas 1:11 sun is no s. risen with a burning heat,

SOOTH See FORSOOTH; SOOTHSAYER.

SOOTHSAYER See also SOOTHSAYERS.
Jos 13:22 Balaam also the son of Beor, the s., 7080

SOOTHSAYERS
Isa 2:6 and are s. like the Philistines, and 6049
Da 2:27 the s., shew unto the king; 1505
Da 4:7 the Chaldeans, and the s.: and I 1505
Da 5:7 the Chaldeans, and the s. 1505
Da 5:11 astrologers, Chaldeans, and s. 1505
Mic 5:12 and thou shalt have no more s. 6049

SOOTHSAYING
Ac 16:16 her masters much gain by s. *3132*

SOP
Joh 13:26 **He it is, to whom I shall give a s.,** *5596*
Joh 13:26 when he had dipped the s., he gave *5596*
Joh 13:27 after the s. Satan entered into him. *5596*
Joh 13:30 He then having received the s. *5596*

SOPATER (so'-pa-tur) See also SOSIPATER.
Ac 20:4 accompanied him into Asia S. of *4986*

SOPE
Jer 2:22 and take thee much s., yet thine 1287
Mal 3:2 refiner's fire, and like fullers' s.: 1287

SOPHERETH (so-fe'-reth)
Ezr 2:55 of Sotai, the children of S., the *5618*
Ne 7:57 of Sotai, the children of S., the *5618*

SORCERER See also SORCERERS; SORCERESS.
Ac 13:6 they found a certain s., a false *3097*
Ac 13:8 But Elymas the s. (for so is his *3097*

SORCERERS
Ex 7:11 called the wise men and the s. 3784
Jer 27:9 nor to your s., which speak unto 3786
Da 2:2 and the s., and the Chaldeans, for 3784
Mal 3:5 be a swift witness against the s., 3784
Re 21:8 and whoremongers, and s., and *5332*
Re 22:15 For without are dogs, and s., and *5333*

SORCERESS
Isa 57:3 near hither, ye sons of the s., 6049

SORCERIES
Isa 47:9 for the multitude of thy s., and 3785
Isa 47:12 and with the multitude of thy s., 3785
Ac 8:11 he had bewitched them with s. *3095*
Re 9:21 of their murders, nor of their s., *5331*
Re 18:23 by thy s. were all nations deceived. *5331*

SORCERY See also SORCERIES.
Ac 8:9 beforetime in the same city used s., *3096*

SORE See also SORER; SORES.
Ge 19:9 and they pressed s. upon the man, 3966
Ge 20:8 ears: and the men were s. afraid. 3966
Ge 31:30 thou s. longedst after thy father's
Ge 34:25 when they were s., that two of 3510
Ge 41:56 the famine waxed s. in the land of 2388
Ge 41:57 the famine was so s. in all lands. 2388
Ge 43:1 And the famine was s. in the land. 3515
Ge 47:4 famine is s. in the land of Canaan: 3515
Ge 47:13 the famine was very s., so that the 3515
Ge 50:10 a great and very s. lamentation: 3515
Ex 14:10 them; and they were s. afraid: 3966
Le 13:42 bald forehead, a white reddish s., 5061
Le 13:43 rising of the s. be white reddish 5061
Nu 22:3 Moab was s. afraid of the people, 3966
De 6:22 signs and wonders, great and s. 7451
De 28:35 a s. botch that cannot be healed, 7451
De 28:59 and s. sicknesses, and of long 7451
Jos 9:24 we were s. afraid of our lives 3966
Jg 10:9 so that Israel was s. distressed 3966
Jg 14:17 her, because she lay s. upon him:
Jg 15:18 And he was s. athirst, and called 3966
Jg 20:34 all Israel, and the battle was s. 3513
Jg 21:2 up their voices, and wept s.: 1065,1419
1Sa 1:6 adversary also provoked her s., 3708
1Sa 1:10 prayed unto the Lord, and wept s.
1Sa 5:7 his hand is s. upon us, and upon 7185
1Sa 14:52 was s. war against the Philistines 2389
1Sa 17:24 fled from him, and were s. afraid 3966
1Sa 21:12 was s. afraid of Achish the king of 3966
1Sa 28:15 Saul answered, I am s. distressed; 3966
1Sa 28:20 on the earth, and was s. afraid, 3966
1Sa 28:21 and saw that he was s. troubled, 3966
1Sa 31:3 the battle went s. against Saul, 3513
1Sa 31:3 he was s. wounded of the archers. 3966
1Sa 31:4 would not; for he was s. afraid. 3966
2Sa 2:17 there was a very s. battle that day; 7188
2Sa 13:36 and all his servants wept very s. 1419
1Ki 17:17 and his sickness was so s., that 2389
1Ki 18:2 there was a s. famine in Samaria. 2389
2Ki 3:26 that the battle was too s. for him, 2388
2Ki 6:11 king of Syria was s. troubled for this
2Ki 20:3 thy sight. And Hezekiah wept s. 1419
1Ch 10:3 the battle went s. against Saul, 3513
1Ch 10:4 would not; for he was s. afraid. 3966
2Ch 6:28 whatsoever s. or whatsoever 5061
2Ch 6:29 one shall know his own s. and his 5061
2Ch 21:19 so he died of s. diseases. And his 7451
2Ch 28:19 and transgressed s. against the Lord.
2Ch 35:23 me away; for I am s. wounded. 3966
Ezr 10:1 for the people wept very s.
Ne 2:2 of heart. Then I was very s. afraid, 7235
Ne 13:8 it grieved me s.: therefore I cast 3966
Job 2:7 smote Job with s. boils from the 7451
Job 5:18 For he maketh s., and bindeth up: 3510
Ps 2:5 and vex them in his s. displeasure.
Ps 6:3 My soul is also s. vexed: but thou, 3966
Ps 6:10 enemies be ashamed and s. vexed; 3966
Ps 38:2 in me, and thy hand presseth me s.
Ps 38:8 I am feeble and s. broken: I 5704,3966
Ps 38:11 friends stand aloof from my s.; 5061
Ps 44:19 s. broken us in the place of dragons,
Ps 55:4 My heart is s. pained within me: and
Ps 71:20 shewed me great and s. troubles, 7451
Ps 77:2 my s. ran in the night, and ceased 3027
Ps 118:13 Thou hast thrust s. at me that I might
Ps 118:18 The Lord hath chastened me s.: but
Ec 1:13 this s. travail hath God given to 7451
Ec 4:8 is also vanity, yea, it is a s. travail. 7451
Ec 5:13 a s. evil which I have seen under 2470
Ec 5:16 this also is a s. evil, that in all 2470
Isa 27:1 his s. and great and strong sword 7186
Isa 38:3 sight. And Hezekiah wept s. 1419
Isa 59:11 like bears, and mourn s. like doves:
Isa 64:9 Be not wroth very s., O Lord, 3966
Isa 64:12 thy peace, and afflict us very s.? 3966
Jer 13:17 and mine eye shall weep s., and run
Jer 22:10 but weep s. for him that goeth away:
Jer 50:12 mother shall be s. confounded; 3966
Jer 52:6 the famine was s. in the city, so 2388
La 1:2 She weepeth s. in the night, and her
La 3:52 Mine enemies chased me s., like a
Eze 14:21 I send my four s. judgments upon 7451
Eze 21:10 sharpened to make a s. slaughter;
Eze 27:35 and their kings shall be s. afraid, 8178
Da 6:14 was s. displeased with himself, 7690
Mic 2:10 you, even with a s. destruction. 4834
Zec 1:2 s. displeased with your fathers.
Zec 1:15 very s. displeased with the heathen
Mt 17:6 on their face, and were s. afraid *4970*
Mt 17:15 for he is lunatick, and s. vexed: *2560*
Mt 21:15 of David; they were s. displeased, *23*
Mk 6:51 were s. amazed in themselves *3029*
Mk 9:6 to say; for they were s. afraid. *1630*
Mk 9:26 the spirit cried, and rent him s., *4183*

Mk 14:33 began to be **s.** amazed, and to be *1568*
Lu 2:9 them: and they were **s.** afraid *3173*
Ac 20:37 they all wept **s.**, and fell on Paul's *2425*
Re 16:2 fell a noisome and grievous **s.** upon *1668*

SOREK (so'-rek)
Jg 16:4 loved a woman in the valley of **S.**, 7796

SORELY
Ge 49:23 The archers have **s.** grieved him, 4843
Isa 23:5 they be **s.** pained at the report of Tyre.

SORER
Heb 10:29 Of how much **s.** punishment, *5501*

SORES
Isa 1:6 and bruises, and putrifying **s.** 4347
Lu 16:20 **was laid at his gate, full of s..** *1669*
Lu 16:21 **the dogs came and licked his s..** *1668*
Re 16:11 because of their pains and their **s.**, *1668*

SORROW See also SORROWED; SORROWETH; SORROWFUL; SORROWING; SORROWS.
Ge 3:16 said, I will greatly multiply thy **s.** 6093
Ge 3:16 in **s.** shalt thou bring forth 6089
Ge 3:17 in **s.** shalt thou eat of it all the 6093
Ge 42:38 my gray hairs with **s.** to the grave 3015
Ge 44:29 my gray hairs with **s.** to the grave 7451
Ge 44:31 our father with **s.** to the grave 3015
Ex 15:14 **s.**...take hold on the inhabitants 2427
Le 26:16 the eyes, and cause **s.** of heart: 1727
De 28:65 failing of eyes, and **s.** of mind: 1671
1Ch 4:9 Because I bare him with **s.**. 6090
Ne 2:2 this is nothing else but **s.** of heart. 7455
Es 9:22 turned unto them from **s.** to joy, 3015
Job 3:10 womb, nor hid **s.** from mine eyes. 5999
Job 6:10 yea, I would harden myself in **s.** 2427
Job 17:7 eye also is dim by reason of **s.**, 3708
Job 41:22 **s.** is turned into joy before him. 1670
Ps 13:2 soul, having **s.** in my heart daily? 3015
Ps 38:17 my **s.** is continually before me. 4341
Ps 39:2 from good; and my **s.** was stirred. 3511
Ps 55:10 mischief...and **s.** are in the midst 5999
Ps 90:10 yet is their strength labour and **s.**; 205
Ps 107:39 oppression, affliction, and **s.**. 3015
Ps 116:3 upon me: I found trouble and **s.**. 3015
Pr 10:10 winketh with the eye causeth **s.** 6094
Pr 10:22 rich, and he addeth no **s.** with it. 6089
Pr 15:13 but by **s.** of the heart the spirit is 6094
Pr 17:21 begetteth a fool doeth it to his **s.** 8424
Pr 23:29 Who hath woe? who hath **s.**? who 17
Ec 1:18 knowledge increaseth **s.** 4341
Ec 5:17 **s.** and wrath with his sickness. 3708
Ec 7:3 **S.** is better than laughter: for by 3708
Ec 11:10 Therefore remove **s.** from thy heart, 3708
Isa 5:30 the land, behold darkness and **s.**, 6862
Isa 14:3 shall give thee rest from thy **s.**, 6090
Isa 17:11 day of grief and of desperate **s.** 3511
Isa 29:2 there shall be heaviness and **s.** 592
Isa 35:10 and **s.** and sighing shall flee away. 3015
Isa 50:11 mine hand; ye shall lie down in **s.** 4620
Isa 51:11 **s.** and mourning shall flee away. 3015
Isa 65:14 but ye shall cry for **s.** of heart, and 3511
Jer 8:18 I would comfort myself against **s.**, 3015
Jer 20:18 of the womb to see labour and **s.**, 3015
Jer 30:15 **s.** is incurable for the multitude 4341
Jer 31:12 they shall not **s.** any more at all. 1669
Jer 31:13 make them rejoice from their **s.**. 3015
Jer 45:3 Lord hath added grief to my **s.**; 4341
Jer 49:23 there is **s.** on the sea; it cannot be 1674
Jer 51:29 And the land shall tremble and **s.** 2342
La 1:12 if there be any **s.** like unto my **s.**, 4341
La 1:18 you, all people, and behold my **s.** 4341
La 3:65 Give them **s.** of heart, thy curse 4044
Eze 23:33 be filled with drunkenness and **s.**, 3015
Ho 8:10 they shall **s.** a little for the burden 2490
Lu 22:45 he found them sleeping for **s.**, *3077*
Joh 16:6 **unto you, s. hath filled your heart** *3077*
Joh 16:20 **your s. shall be turned into joy.** *3077*
Joh 16:21 **when she is in travail hath s.,** *3077*
Joh 16:22 **ye now therefore have s.: but I** *3077*
Ro 9:2 and continual **s.** in my heart. *3601*
2Co 2:3 **s.** from them of whom I ought to *3077*
2Co 2:7 be swallowed up with overmuch **s.** *3077*
2Co 7:10 For godly **s.** worketh repentance to *3077*
2Co 7:10 the **s.** of the world worketh death. *3077*
Php 2:27 also, lest I should have **s.** upon **s.**. *3077*
1Th 4:13 that ye **s.** not, even as others which *3076*
Re 18:7 so much torment and **s.** give her: *3997*
Re 18:7 am no widow, and shall see no **s.**. *3997*
Re 21:4 neither **s.**, nor crying, neither shall *3997*

SORROWED
2Co 7:9 sorry, but that ye **s.** to repentance: *3076*
2Co 7:11 thing, that ye **s.** after a godly sort, *3076*

SORROWETH
1Sa 10:2 **s.** for you, saying, What shall I 1672

SORROWFUL
1Sa 1:15 lord, I am a woman of a **s.** spirit: 7186
Job 6:7 refused to touch are as my **s.** meat. 1741
Ps 69:29 But I am poor and **s.**: let thy 3510
Pr 14:13 Even in laughter the heart is **s.**; 3510
Jer 31:25 I have replenished every **s.** soul. 1669
Zep 3:18 are **s.** for the solemn assembly, 3013
Zec 9:5 also shall see it, and be very **s.**, 2342
Mt 19:22 that saying, he went away **s.**: for *3076*
Mt 26:22 they were exceeding **s.**, and began *3076*
Mt 26:37 and began to be **s.** and very heavy. *3076*
Mt 26:38 **My soul is exceeding s., even unto** *4036*
Mk 14:19 And they began to be **s.**, and to say *3076*
Mk 14:34 **My soul is exceeding s. unto death** *4036*
Lu 18:23 when he heard this, he was very **s.** *4036*
Lu 18:24 when Jesus saw that he was very **s.**, *4036*
Joh 16:20 **ye shall be s., but your sorrow** *3076*
2Co 6:10 As **s.**, yet alway rejoicing; as poor, *3076*
Php 2:28 and that I may be the less **s.**. *253*

SORROWING
Lu 2:48 father and I have sought thee **s.** *3600*
Ac 20:38 **S.** most of all for the words which *3600*

SORROWS
Ex 3:7 taskmasters; for I know their **s.**; 4341
2Sa 22:6 **s.** of hell compassed me about; 2256
Job 9:28 I am afraid of all my **s.**, I know 6094
Job 21:17 God distributeth **s.** in his anger. 2256
Job 39:3 young ones, they cast out their **s.**. 2256
Ps 16:4 Their **s.** shall be multiplied that 6094
Ps 18:4 The **s.** of death compassed me, 2256
Ps 18:5 **s.** of hell compassed me about: 2256
Ps 32:10 Many **s.** shall be to the wicked: but 4341
Ps 116:3 The **s.** of death compassed me, 2256
Ps 127:2 sit up late, to eat the bread of **s.**: 6089
Ec 2:23 all his days are **s.**, and his travail 4341
Isa 13:8 and **s.** shall take hold of them; 2256
Isa 53:3 a man of **s.**, and acquainted with 4341
Isa 53:4 our griefs, and carried our **s.** 4341
Jer 13:21 shall not **s.** take thee, as a woman 2256
Jer 49:24 anguish and **s.** have taken her, as a 2256
Da 10:16 vision my **s.** are turned upon me, 6735
Ho 13:13 The **s.** of a travailing woman shall 2256
Mt 24:8 **All these are the beginning of s.** *5604*
Mk 13:8 **these are the beginnings of s.** *5604*
1Ti 6:10 themselves through with many **s.** *3601*

SORRY
1Sa 22:8 is none of you that is **s.** for me, 2470
Ne 8:10 neither be ye **s.**; for the joy of the 6087
Ps 38:18 iniquity; I will be **s.** for my sin. 1672
Isa 51:19 thee; who shall be **s.** for thee? 5110
Mt 14:9 And the king was **s.**: nevertheless *3076*
Mt 17:23 **again. And they were exceeding s.** *3076*
Mt 18:31 **what was done, they were very s.,** *3076*
Mk 6:26 And the king was exceeding **s.** *4036*
2Co 2:2 For if I make you **s.**, who is he *3076*
2Co 2:2 the same which is made **s.** by me? *3076*
2Co 7:8 though I made you **s.** with a letter, *3076*
2Co 7:8 the same epistle hath made you **s.**, *3076*
2Co 7:9 rejoice, not that ye were made **s.**, *3076*
2Co 7:9 were made **s.** after a godly manner, *3076*

SORT See also CONSORTED; RESORT; SORTS.
Ge 6:19 two of every **s.** shall thou bring into
Ge 6:20 two of every **s.** shall come unto thee,
Ge 7:14 his kind, every bird of every **s.** 3671
2Ki 24:14 save the poorest **s.** of the people
1Ch 24:5 were divided by lot, one **s.** with another;
1Ch 29:14 able to offer so willingly after this **s.**?
2Ch 30:5 long time in such **s.** as it was written.
Ezr 1:10 silver basons of a second **s.** four
Ezr 4:8 to Artaxerxes the king in this **s.** 3660
Ne 6:4 unto me four times after this **s.**; 1697
Eze 23:42 men of the common **s.** were brought 120
Eze 39:4 unto the ravenous birds of every **s.**, 3671
Eze 44:30 of every **s.** of your oblations, shall be
Da 1:10 children which are of your **s.**? 1524
Da 3:29 God that can deliver after this **s.**.
Ac 17:5 certain lewd fellows of the baser **s.**,
Ro 15:15 more boldly unto you in some **s.**, *3313*
1Co 3:13 every man's work of what **s.** it is. *3697*
2Co 7:11 that ye sorrowed after a godly **s.**, what
2Ti 3:6 For of this **s.** are they which creep into
3Jo 6 on their journey after a godly **s.**, *516*

SORTS
De 22:11 shalt not wear a garment of divers **s.**,
Ne 5:18 in ten days store of all **s.** of wine;
Ps 78:45 He sent divers **s.** of flies among them,
Ps 105:31 spake, and there came divers **s.** of flies,
Ec 2:8 musical instruments, and that of all **s.**.
Eze 27:24 thy merchants in all **s.** of things, 4360
Eze 38:4 clothed with all **s.** of armour, 4358

SOSIPATER (so-sip'-a-tur) See also SOPATER.
Ro 16:21 and **S.**, my kinsmen, salute you. *4989*

SOSTHENES (sos'-the-neze)
Ac 18:17 Greeks took **S.**, the chief ruler *4988*
1Co 1:1 will of God, and **S.** our brother, *4988*

SOTAI (so'-tahee)
Ezr 2:55 the children of **S.**, the children of 5479
Ne 7:57 the children of **S.**, the children of 5479

SOTTISH
Jer 4:22 they are **s.** children, and they 5530

SOUGHT See also BESOUGHT.
Ge 43:30 and he **s.** where to weep: and he 1245
Ex 2:15 this thing, he **s.** to slay Moses 1245
Ex 4:19 the men are dead which **s.** thy life. 1245
Ex 4:24 Lord met him, and **s.** to kill him. 1245
Ex 33:7 every one which **s.** the Lord went 1245
Le 10:16 Moses diligently **s.** the goat of the 1875
Nu 35:23 his enemy, neither **s.** his harm: 1245
De 13:10 he hath **s.** to thrust thee away from 1245
Jos 2:22 the pursuers **s.** them throughout 1245
Jg 14:4 that he **s.** an occasion against the 1245
Jg 18:1 the Danites **s.** them an inheritance 1245
1Sa 10:21 when they **s.** him, he could not be 1245
1Sa 13:14 Lord hath **s.** him a man after his 1245
1Sa 14:4 by which Jonathan **s.** to go over 1245
1Sa 19:10 Saul **s.** to smite David even to the 1245
1Sa 23:14 And Saul **s.** him every day, but God 1245
1Sa 27:4 and he **s.** no more again for him. 1245
2Sa 3:17 Ye **s.** for David in times past to be 1245
2Sa 4:8 Saul thine enemy, which **s.** thy life; 1245
2Sa 17:20 they had **s.** and could not find them, 1245
2Sa 21:2 and Saul **s.** to slay them in his zeal 1245
1Ki 1:2 Let there be **s.** for my lord the king 1245
1Ki 1:3 So they **s.** for a fair damsel 1245
1Ki 10:24 And all the earth **s.** to Solomon, 1245
1Ki 11:40 Solomon **s.**...to kill Jeroboam. 1245
2Ki 2:17 **s.** three days, but found him not. 1245
1Ch 15:13 we **s.** him not after the due order. 1875
1Ch 26:31 the reign of David they were **s.** for, 1875
2Ch 1:5 and the congregation **s.** unto it. 1875
2Ch 9:23 earth **s.** the presence of Solomon, 1245
2Ch 14:7 we have **s.** the Lord our God, 1875
2Ch 14:7 we have **s.** him, and he hath given 1875
2Ch 15:4 and **s.** him, he was found of them. 1245
2Ch 15:15 and **s.** him with their whole desire; 1245
2Ch 16:12 his disease he **s.** not to the Lord, 1875
2Ch 17:3 David, and **s.** not unto Baalim; 1875
2Ch 17:4 **s.** to the Lord God of his father, 1875
2Ch 22:9 he **s.** Ahaziah: and they caught 1245
2Ch 22:9 who **s.** the Lord with all his heart. 1875
2Ch 25:15 **s.** after the gods of the people, 1875
2Ch 25:20 they **s.** after the gods of Edom. 1875
2Ch 26:5 he **s.** God in the days of Zechariah, 1875
2Ch 26:5 as long as he **s.** the Lord, God made 1875
Ezr 2:62 These **s.** their register among 1245
Ne 7:64 These **s.** their register among those 1245
Ne 12:27 they **s.** the Levites out of all their 1245
Es 2:2 fair young virgins **s.** for the king: 1245
Es 2:21 **s.** to lay hand on...king Ahasuerus. 1245
Es 3:6 Haman **s.** to destroy all the Jews 1245
Es 6:2 **s.** to lay hand on...king Ahasuerus. 1245
Es 9:2 lay hand on such as **s.** their hurt: 1245
Ps 34:4 I **s.** the Lord, and he heard me, 1875
Ps 37:36 I **s.** him, but he could not be found. 1245
Ps 77:2 day of my trouble I **s.** the Lord: 1875
Ps 78:34 he slew them, then they **s.** him: 1875
Ps 86:14 violent men have **s.** after my soul; 1245
Ps 111:2 **s.** out of all...that have pleasure 1875
Ps 119:10 my whole heart have I **s.** thee: 1875

Ps 119:94 save me; for I have s. thy precepts.... 1875
Ec 2:3 I s. in mine heart to give myself........ 8446
Ec 7:29 they have s. out many inventions. 1245
Ec 12:9 and s. out, and set in order many........ 2713
Ec 12:10 s. to find out acceptable words: 1245
Ca 3:1 bed I s. him whom my soul loveth:..... 1245
Ca 3:1 I s. him, but I found him not............ 1245
Ca 5:6 I s. him, but I could not find him:....... 1245
Isa 62:12 called, S. out, A city not forsaken. 1875
Isa 65:1 I am s. of them that asked not for...... 1875
Isa 65:1 am found of them that s. me not:....... 1245
Isa 65:10 in, for my people that have s. me........ 1875
Jer 8:2 whom they have s., and whom they.... 1875
Jer 10:21 brutish, and have not s. the Lord: 1875
Jer 26:21 the king s. to put him to death: 1245
Jer 44:30 his enemy, and that s. his life............ 1245
Jer 50:20 iniquity of Israel shall be s. for,.......... 1245
La 1:19 while they s. their meat to relieve...... 1245
Eze 22:30 And I s. for a man among them, ... 1245
Eze 26:21 though thou be s. for, yet shalt.......... 1245
Eze 34:4 neither have ye s. that which was 1245
Da 2:13 they s. Daniel and his fellows to......... 1158
Da 4:36 and my lords s. unto me; and I was.... 1158
Da 6:4 s. to find occasion against Daniel........ 1158
Da 8:15 the vision, and s. for the meaning....... 1245
Ob 6 how are his hidden things s. up!......... 1156
Zep 1:6 those that have not s. the Lord. 1245
Zec 6:7 and s. to go that they might walk....... 1245
Mt 2:20 which s. the young child's life............ 2212
Mt 21:46 when they s. to lay hands on him, ... 2212
Mt 26:16 he s. opportunity to betray him.......... 2212
Mt 26:59 s. false witness against Jesus, to........ 2212
Mk 11:18 and s. how they might destroy him:.... 2212
Mk 12:12 And they s. to lay hold on him, but 2212
Mk 14:1 scribes s. how they might take him...... 2212
Mk 14:11 he s. how he might conveniently 2212
Mk 14:55 council s. for witness against Jesus 2212
Lu 2:44 they s. him among their kinsfolk.......... 327
Lu 2:48 and I have s. thee sorrowing............. 2212
Lu 2:49 unto them, How is it that ye s. me? .2212
Lu 4:42 the people s. him, and came unto....... 2212
Lu 5:18 and they s. means to bring him in, ... 2212
Lu 6:19 whole multitude s. to touch him: 2212
Lu 11:16 him, s. of him a sign from heaven. 2212
Lu 13:6 and he came and s. fruit thereon,.. 2212
Lu 19:3 And he s. to see Jesus who he was; ... 2212
Lu 19:47 of the people s. to destroy him,.......... 2212
Lu 20:19 same hour s. to lay hands on him;...... 2212
Lu 22:2 scribes s. how they might kill him; 2212
Lu 22:6 s. opportunity to betray him unto 2212
Joh 5:16 persecute Jesus, and s. to slay him,.... 2212
Joh 5:18 the Jews s. the more to kill him,......... 2212
Joh 7:1 because the Jews s. to kill him. 2212
Joh 7:11 Then the Jews s. him at the feast, ... 2212
Joh 7:30 Then they s. to take him: but no 2212
Joh 10:39 they s. again to take him: but he......... 2212
Joh 11:8 the Jews of late s. to stone thee; 2212
Joh 11:56 Then s. they for Jesus, and spake 2212
Joh 19:12 thenceforth Pilate s. to release him:.... 2212
Ac 12:19 And when Herod had s. for him, ... 1934
Ac 17:5 s. to bring them out to the people......... 2212
Ro 9:32 Because they s. it not by faith, but..... 2212
Ro 10:20 I was found of them that s. me not;.... 2212
1Th 2:6 Nor of men s. we glory, neither of..... 2212
2Ti 1:17 he s. me out very diligently, and........ 2212
Heb 8:7 then should no place have been s. 2212
Heb 12:17 though he s. it carefully with tears...... 1567

SOUL See also SOUL'S; SOULS.
Ge 2:7 life; and man became a living s.......... 5315
Ge 12:13 and my s. shall live because of thee.... 5315
Ge 17:14 that s. shall be cut off from his.......... 5315
Ge 19:20 a little one?) and my s. shall live. 5315
Ge 27:4 my s. may bless thee before I die. 5315
Ge 27:19 venison, that thy s. may bless me. 5315
Ge 27:25 venison, that my s. may bless thee..... 5315
Ge 27:31 venison, that thy s. may bless me. 5315
Ge 34:3 And his s. clave unto Dinah the 5315
Ge 34:8 The s. of my son Shechem longeth..... 5315
Ge 35:18 as her s. was in departing, (for she 5315
Ge 42:21 that we saw the anguish of his s., ... 5315
Ge 49:6 O my s., come not thou into their...... 5315
Ex 12:15 that s. shall be cut off from Israel....... 5315
Ex 12:19 even that s. shall be cut off from the .. 5315
Ex 30:12 give every man a ransom for his s...... 5315
Ex 31:14 that s. shall be cut off from among..... 5315
Le 4:2 If a s. shall sin through ignorance....... 5315
Le 5:1 And if a s. sin, and hear the voice...... 5315
Le 5:2 Or if a s. touch any unclean thing,...... 5315
Le 5:4 Or if a s. swear, pronouncing with...... 5315
Le 5:15 If a s. commit a trespass, and sin....... 5315
Le 5:17 And if a s. sin, and commit any of...... 5315
Le 6:2 If a s. sin, and commit a trespass....... 5315
Le 7:18 the s. that eateth of it shall bear his ... 5315
Le 7:20 the s. that eateth of the flesh of the ... 5315
Le 7:20 even that s. shall be cut off from........ 5315
Le 7:21 the s. that shall touch any unclean 5315
Le 7:21 even that s. shall be cut off from his... 5315
Le 7:25 the s. that eateth it shall be cut off..... 5315
Le 7:27 Whatsoever s. it be that eateth any 5315
Le 7:27 even that s. shall be cut off from his... 5315
Le 17:10 will even set my face against that s. ... 5315
Le 17:11 maketh an atonement for the s.. 5315
Le 17:12 No s. of you shall eat blood, neither ... 5315
Le 17:15 every s. that eateth that which died.... 5315
Le 19:8 that s. shall be cut off from among 5315
Le 20:6 the s. that turneth after such as......... 5315
Le 20:6 even set my face against that s.,........ 5315
Le 22:3 that s. shall be cut off from my.......... 5315
Le 22:6 The s. which hath touched any such..... 5315
Le 22:11 But if the priest buy any s. with his.... 5315
Le 23:29 whatsoever s. it be that shall not be ... 5315
Le 23:30 whatsoever s. it be that doeth any...... 5315
Le 23:30 same s. will I destroy from among....... 5315
Le 26:11 and my s. shall not abhor you............ 5315
Le 26:15 or if your s. abhor my judgments, ... 5315
Le 26:30 idols, and my s. shall abhor you. 5315
Le 26:43 their s. abhorred my statutes. 5315
Nu 9:13 same s. shall be cut off from among.... 5315
Nu 11:6 But now our s. is dried away: there.... 5315
Nu 15:27 if any s. sin through ignorance, ... 5315
Nu 15:28 make an atonement for the s. that...... 5315
Nu 15:30 But the s. that doeth ought.............. 5315
Nu 15:30 that s. shall be cut off from among 5315
Nu 15:31 that s. shall utterly be cut off; 5315
Nu 19:13 that s. shall be cut off from Israel:...... 5315
Nu 19:20 that s. shall be cut off from among 5315
Nu 19:22 s. that toucheth it shall be unclean...... 5315
Nu 21:4 and the s. of the people was much 5315
Nu 21:5 and our s. loatheth this light bread...... 5315
Nu 30:2 an oath to bind his s. with a bond;...... 5315
Nu 30:4 wherewith she hath bound her s.,........ 5315
Nu 30:4 wherewith she hath bound her s......... 5315
Nu 30:5 wherewith she hath bound her s.,........ 5315
Nu 30:6 lips, wherewith she bound her s.;........ 5315
Nu 30:7 bonds wherewith she bound her s....... 5315
Nu 30:8 lips, wherewith she bound her s.,....... 5315
Nu 30:10 bound her s. by a bond with an oath; .. 5315
Nu 30:11 bond wherewith she bound her s........ 5315
Nu 30:12 or concerning the bond of her s., ... 5315
Nu 30:13 every binding oath to afflict the s., ... 5315
Nu 31:28 one s. of five hundred, both of the 5315
De 4:9 and keep thy s. diligently, lest thou 5315
De 4:29 with all thy heart and with all thy s..... 5315
De 6:5 all thine heart, and with all thy s., ... 5315
De 10:12 with all thy heart and with all thy s.,... 5315
De 11:13 all your heart and with all your s., ... 5315
De 11:18 words in your heart and in your s.,..... 5315
De 12:15 whatsoever thy s. lusteth after, ... 5315
De 12:20 because thy s. longeth to eat flesh;..... 5315
De 12:20, 21 whatsoever thy s. lusteth after. 5315
De 13:3 all you heart and with all your s.. 5315
De 13:6 friend, which is as thine own s.,......... 5315
De 14:26 for whatsoever thy s. lusteth after,..... 5315
De 14:26 or for whatsoever thy s. desireth: 5315
De 26:16 all thine heart, and with all thy s.. 5315
De 30:2 all thine heart, and with all thy s.; 5315
De 30:6 all thine heart, and with all thy s., ... 5315
De 30:10 all thine heart, and with all thy s.. 5315
Jos 22:5 all your heart and with all your s........ 5315
Jg 5:21 O my s., thou hast trodden down....... 5315
Jg 10:16 his s. was grieved for the misery of.... 5315
Jg 16:16 so that his s. was vexed unto death; ... 5315
1Sa 1:10 And she was in bitterness of s., and.... 5315
1Sa 1:15 poured out my s. before the Lord. 5315
1Sa 1:26 as thy s. liveth, my lord, I am the...... 5315
1Sa 2:16 take as much as thy s. desireth; 5315
1Sa 17:55 As thy s. liveth, O king, I cannot......... 5315
1Sa 18:1 that the s. of Jonathan was knit.......... 5315
1Sa 18:1 was knit with the s. of David,........... 5315
1Sa 18:1 Jonathan loved him as his own s......... 5315
1Sa 18:3 because he loved him as his own s. ... 5315
1Sa 20:3 as thy s. liveth, there is but a step..... 5315
1Sa 20:4 Whatsoever thy s. desireth, I will....... 5315
1Sa 20:17 he loved him as he loved his own s.. .. 5315
1Sa 23:20 according to all the desire of thy s....... 5315
1Sa 24:11 yet thou huntest my s. to take it......... 5315
1Sa 25:26 and as thy s. liveth, seeing the Lord... 5315
1Sa 25:29 to pursue thee, and to seek thy s.:...... 5315
1Sa 25:29 s. of my lord shall be bound in the 5315
1Sa 26:21 my s. was precious in thine eyes........ 5315
1Sa 30:6 the s. of all the people was grieved, ... 5315
2Sa 4:9 who hath redeemed my s. out of all.... 5315
2Sa 5:8 blind, that are hated of David's s.,....... 5315
2Sa 11:11 as thy s. liveth, I will not do this 5315
2Sa 13:39 the s. of king David longed to go forth......
2Sa 14:19 As thy s. liveth, my lord the king,....... 5315
1Ki 1:29 redeemed my s. out of all distress,..... 5315
1Ki 2:4 all their heart and with all their s.,....... 5315
1Ki 8:48 all their heart, and with all their s.,..... 5315
1Ki 11:37 according to all that thy s. desireth,.... 5315
1Ki 17:21 let this child's s. come into him.......... 5315
1Ki 17:22 the s. of the child came into him, ... 5315
2Ki 2:2, 4,6 Lord liveth, and as thy s. liveth, ... 5315
2Ki 4:27 for her s. is vexed within her: 5315
2Ki 4:30 Lord liveth, and as thy s. liveth, ... 5315
2Ki 23:3 with all their heart and all their s.,....... 5315
2Ki 23:25 all his heart, and with all his s., ... 5315
1Ch 22:19 set your heart and your s. to seek 5315
2Ch 6:38 all their heart and with all their s........ 5315
2Ch 15:12 all their heart and with all their s.;...... 5315
2Ch 34:31 all his heart, and with all his s., ... 5315
Job 3:20 and life unto the bitter in s.;............. 5315
Job 6:7 things that my s. refused to touch...... 5315
Job 7:11 complain in the bitterness of my s.. 5315
Job 7:15 So that my s. chooseth strangling,...... 5315
Job 9:21 yet would I not know my s.: 5315
Job 10:1 My s. is weary of my life; I will......... 5315
Job 10:1 speak in the bitterness of my s.......... 5315
Job 12:10 hand is the s. of every living thing,..... 5315
Job 14:22 and his s. within him shall mourn....... 5315
Job 16:4 if your s. were in my soul's stead, I ... 5315
Job 19:2 How long will ye vex my s., and........ 5315
Job 21:25 dieth in the bitterness of his s., and.... 5315
Job 23:13 and what his s. desireth, even that..... 5315
Job 24:12 the s. of the wounded crieth out: 5315
Job 27:2 Almighty, who hath vexed my s.; 5315
Job 27:8 when God taketh away his s.? 5315
Job 30:15 they pursue my s. as the wind:.......... 5082
Job 30:16 now my s. is poured out upon me; 5315
Job 30:25 was not my s. grieved for the poor? ... 5315
Job 31:30 to sin by wishing a curse to his s.. 5315
Job 33:18 keepeth back his s. from the pit,........ 5315
Job 33:20 bread, and his s. dainty meat............. 5315
Job 33:22 his s. draweth near unto the grave, ... 5315
Job 33:28 He will deliver his s. from going......... 5315
Job 33:30 To bring back his s. from the pit,........ 5315
Ps 3:2 Many there be which say of my s.,...... 5315
Ps 6:3 My s. is also sore vexed: but thou, ... 5315
Ps 6:4 Return, O Lord, deliver my s.: O....... 5315
Ps 7:2 Lest he tear my s. like a lion, ... 5315
Ps 7:5 Let the enemy persecute my s., ... 5315
Ps 11:1 how say ye to my s., Flee as a bird ... 5315
Ps 11:5 that loveth violence his s. hateth. 5315
Ps 13:2 long shall I take counsel in my s., ... 5315
Ps 16:2 O my s., thou hast said unto the Lord,......
Ps 16:10 thou wilt not leave my s. in hell; 5315
Ps 17:13 deliver my s. from the wicked, ... 5315
Ps 19:7 Lord is perfect, converting the s........ 5315
Ps 22:20 Deliver my s. from the sword; my...... 5315
Ps 22:29 and none can keep alive his own s..... 5315
Ps 23:3 He restoreth my s.: he leadeth me..... 5315
Ps 24:4 not lifted up his s. unto vanity, ... 5315
Ps 25:1 thee, O Lord, do I lift up my s.. 5315
Ps 25:13 His s. shall dwell at ease; and his....... 5315
Ps 25:20 O keep my s., and deliver me: let...... 5315
Ps 26:9 Gather not my s. with sinners, nor...... 5315
Ps 30:3 brought up my s. from the grave:....... 5315
Ps 31:7 hast known my s. in adversities; 5315
Ps 31:9 with grief, yea, my s. and my belly...... 5315
Ps 33:19 To deliver their s. from death, and..... 5315
Ps 33:20 Our s. waiteth for the Lord: he is 5315
Ps 34:2 My s. shall make her boast in the 5315
Ps 34:22 The Lord redeemeth the s. of his....... 5315
Ps 35:3 say unto my s., I am thy salvation...... 5315
Ps 35:4 put to shame that seek after my s...... 5315
Ps 35:7 cause they have digged for my s.. 5315
Ps 35:9 my s. shall be joyful in the Lord:........ 5315
Ps 35:12 evil for good to the spoiling of my s.... 5315
Ps 35:13 I humbled my s. wth fasting; and 5315

Ps 35:17 rescue my s. from...destructions, 5315
Ps 40:14 that seek after my s. to destroy it; 5315
Ps 41:4 heal my s.; for I have sinned 5315
Ps 42:1 so panteth my s. after thee, O God. 5315
Ps 42:2 My s. thirsteth for God, for the 5315
Ps 42:4 things, I pour out my s. in me: 5315
Ps 42:5 Why art thou cast down, O my s.? 5315
Ps 42:6 God, my s. is cast down within me: 5315
Ps 42:11 Why art thou cast down, O my s.? 5315
Ps 43:5 Why art thou cast down, O my s.? 5315
Ps 44:25 For our s. is bowed down to the 5315
Ps 49:8 redemption of their s. is precious, 5315
Ps 49:15 But God will redeem my s. from the 5315
Ps 49:18 while he lived he blessed his s. 5315
Ps 54:3 and oppressors seek after my s. 5315
Ps 54:4 is with them that uphold my s.. 5315
Ps 55:18 He hath delivered my s. in peace 5315
Ps 56:6 my steps, when they wait for my s. 5315
Ps 56:13 hast delivered my s. from death: 5315
Ps 57:1 for my s. trusteth in thee: yea, in 5315
Ps 57:4 My s. is among lions: and I lie even 5315
Ps 57:6 for my steps; my s. is bowed down: 5315
Ps 59:3 For, lo, they lie in wait for my s. 5315
Ps 62:1 Truly my s. waiteth upon God: 5315
Ps 62:5 my s., wait thou only upon God; 5315
Ps 63:1 my s. thirsteth for thee, my flesh 5315
Ps 63:5 My s. shall be satisfied as with 5315
Ps 63:8 My s. followeth hard after thee: 5315
Ps 63:9 those that seek my s., to destroy 5315
Ps 66:9 Which holdeth our s. in life, and 5315
Ps 66:16 declare what he hath done for my s.. 5315
Ps 69:1 the waters are come in unto my s.. 5315
Ps 69:10 and chastened my s. with fasting, 5315
Ps 69:18 Draw nigh unto my s., and redeem 5315
Ps 70:2 confounded that seek after my s. 5315
Ps 71:10 they that lay wait for my s. take 5315
Ps 71:13 that are adversaries to my s.; 5315
Ps 71:23 my s., which thou hast redeemed. 5315
Ps 72:14 shall redeem their s. from deceit 5315
Ps 74:19 deliver not the s. of thy turtledove 5315
Ps 77:2 my s. refused to be comforted. 5315
Ps 78:50 he spared not their s. from death, 5315
Ps 84:2 My s. longeth, yea, even fainteth 5315
Ps 86:2 Preserve my s.; for I am holy: O 5315
Ps 86:4 Rejoice the s. of thy servant: for 5315
Ps 86:4 unto thee, O Lord, do I lift up my s.. 5315
Ps 86:13 delivered my s. from the lowest 5315
Ps 86:14 violent men...sought after my s.; and.. 5315
Ps 88:3 For my s. is full of troubles: and 5315
Ps 88:14 Lord, why castest thou off my s.? 5315
Ps 89:48 shall he deliver his s. from the hand 5315
Ps 94:17 my s. had almost dwelt in silence. 5315
Ps 94:19 thy comforts delight my s. 5315
Ps 94:21 against the s. of the righteous, 5315
Ps 103:1 Bless the Lord, O my s.: and all 5315
Ps 103:2 Bless the Lord, O my s., and forget 5315
Ps 103:22 dominion: bless the Lord, O my s.. 5315
Ps 104:1 Bless the Lord, O my s.. O Lord 5315
Ps 104:35 Bless thou the Lord, O my s. 5315
Ps 106:15 but sent leanness into their s. 5315
Ps 107:5 and thirsty, their s. fainted in them. 5315
Ps 107:9 For he satisfieth the longing s., and 5315
Ps 107:9 filleth the hungry s. with goodness. 5315
Ps 107:18 s. abhorreth all manner of meat; 5315
Ps 107:26 their s. is melted because of trouble. 5315
Ps 109:20 them that speak evil against my s. 5315
Ps 109:31 him from those that condemn his s. 5315
Ps 116:4 Lord, I beseech thee, deliver my s.. 5315
Ps 116:7 Return unto thy rest, O my s.; for 5315
Ps 116:8 hast delivered my s. from death, 5315
Ps 119:20 My s. breaketh for the longing that 5315
Ps 119:25 My s. cleaveth unto the dust: 5315
Ps 119:28 My s. melteth for heaviness: 5315
Ps 119:81 My s. fainteth for thy salvation: 5315
Ps 119:109 My s. is continually in my hand: 5315
Ps 119:129 therefore doth my s. keep them. 5315
Ps 119:167 My s. hath kept thy testimonies; 5315
Ps 119:175 Let my s. live, and it shall praise 5315
Ps 120:2 Deliver my s., O Lord, from lying 5315
Ps 120:6 My s. hath long dwelt with him 5315
Ps 121:7 all evil: he shall preserve thy s.. 5315
Ps 123:4 Our s. is exceedingly filled with the 5315
Ps 124:4 us, the stream had gone over our s. 5315
Ps 124:5 proud waters had gone over our s.. 5315
Ps 124:7 Our s. is escaped as a bird out of 5315
Ps 130:5 I wait for the Lord, my s. doth wait, 5315
Ps 130:6 My s. waiteth for the Lord more 5315
Ps 131:2 my s. is even as a weaned child. 5315
Ps 138:3 me with strength in my s. 5315
Ps 139:14 and that my s. knoweth right well. 5315
Ps 141:8 my trust; leave not my s. destitute. 5315
Ps 142:4 failed me; no man cared for my s.. 5315
Ps 142:7 Bring my s. out of prison, that I 5315
Ps 143:3 the enemy hath persecuted my s.; 5315
Ps 143:6 my s. thirsteth after thee, as a 5315
Ps 143:8 walk; for I lift up my s. unto thee. 5315
Ps 143:11 sake bring my s. out of trouble. 5315
Ps 143:12 destroy all them that afflict my s. 5315
Ps 146:1 Lord. Praise the Lord, O my s.. 5315
Pr 2:10 knowledge is pleasant unto thy s.; 5315
Pr 3:22 So shall they be life unto thy s., 5315
Pr 6:30 a thief, if he steal to satisfy his s. 5315
Pr 6:32 that doeth it destroyeth his own s.. 5315
Pr 8:36 against me wrongeth his own s. 5315
Pr 10:3 not suffer the s. of the righteous to 5315
Pr 11:17 man doeth good to his own s. 5315
Pr 11:25 The liberal s. shall be made fat: 5315
Pr 13:2 the s. of the transgressors shall eat 5315
Pr 13:4 The s. of the sluggard desireth, and 5315
Pr 13:4 s. of the diligent shall be made fat. 5315
Pr 13:19 accomplished is sweet to the s. 5315
Pr 13:25 eateth to the satisfying of his s. 5315
Pr 15:32 instruction despiseth his own s. 5315
Pr 16:17 keepeth his way preserveth his s. 5315
Pr 16:24 as an honeycomb, sweet to the s., 5315
Pr 18:7 and his lips are the snare of his s. 5315
Pr 19:2 that the s. be without knowledge, 5315
Pr 19:8 getteth wisdom loveth his own s.: 5315
Pr 19:15 and an idle s. shall suffer hunger. 5315
Pr 19:16 commandment keepeth his own s.; 5315
Pr 19:18 let not thy s. spare for his crying. 5315
Pr 20:2 anger sinneth against his own s. 5315
Pr 21:10 The s. of the wicked desireth evil: 5315
Pr 21:23 tongue keepeth his s. from troubles. 5315
Pr 22:5 he that doth keep his s. shall be far 5315
Pr 22:23 spoil the s. of those that spoiled 5315
Pr 22:25 his ways, and get a snare to thy s. 5315
Pr 23:14 and shalt deliver his s. from hell 5315
Pr 24:12 he that keepeth thy s., doth not he 5315
Pr 24:14 knowledge of wisdom be unto thy s. 5315
Pr 25:13 he refresheth the s. of his masters. 5315
Pr 25:25 As cold waters to a thirsty s., so is 5315
Pr 27:7 The full s. loatheth an honeycomb; 5315
Pr 27:7 to the hungry s. every bitter thing 5315
Pr 29:10 upright: but the just seek his s. 5315
Pr 29:17 he shall give delight unto thy s.. 5315
Pr 29:24 with a thief hateth his own s. 5315
Ec 2:24 he should make his s. enjoy good 5315
Ec 4:8 labour, and bereave my s. of good? 5315
Ec 6:2 he wanteth nothing for his s. of all 5315
Ec 6:3 and his s. be not filled with good, 5315
Ec 7:28 Which yet my s. seeketh, but I find 5315
Ca 1:7 Tell me, O thou whom my s. loveth, 5315
Ca 3:1 I sought him whom my s. loveth: 5315
Ca 3:2 I will seek him whom my s. loveth: 5315
Ca 3:3 Saw ye him whom my s. loveth? 5315
Ca 3:4 I found him whom my s. loveth: 5315
Ca 5:6 gone: my s. failed when he spake: 5315
Ca 6:12 my s. made me like the chariots of 5315
Isa 1:14 your appointed feasts my s. hateth: 5315
Isa 3:9 Woe unto their s.! for they have 5315
Isa 10:18 his fruitful field, both s. and body: 5315
Isa 26:8 the desire of our s. is to thy name, 5315
Isa 26:9 With my s. have I desired thee in 5315
Isa 29:8 he awaketh, and his s. is empty: 5315
Isa 29:8 he is faint, and his s. hath appetite: 5315
Isa 32:6 to make empty the s. of the hungry, 5315
Isa 38:15 my years in the bitterness of my s.. 5315
Isa 38:17 thou hast in love to my s. delivered 5315
Isa 42:1 elect, in whom my s. delighteth; 5315
Isa 44:20 aside, that he cannot deliver his s., 5315
Isa 51:23 which have said to thy s., Bow down, 5315
Isa 53:10 thou shalt make his s. an offering 5315
Isa 53:11 He shall see of the travail of his s., 5315
Isa 53:12 hath poured out his s. unto death: 5315
Isa 55:2 let your s. delight itself in fatness. 5315
Isa 55:3 me: hear, and your s. shall live; 5315
Isa 58:3 wherefore have we afflicted our s., 5315
Isa 58:5 a day for a man to afflict his s.? is it 5315
Isa 58:10 thou draw out thy s. to the hungry, 5315
Isa 58:10 hungry, and satisfy the afflicted s.; 5315
Isa 58:11 and satisfy thy s. in drought, and 5315
Isa 61:10 my s. shall be joyful in my God; 5315
Isa 66:3 s. delighteth in their abominations. 5315
Jer 4:10 the sword reacheth unto the s.. 5315
Jer 4:19 O my s., the sound of the trumpet, 5315
Jer 4:31 s. is wearied because of murderers. 5315
Jer 5:9, 29 s. be avenged on such a nation 5315
Jer 6:8 lest my s. depart from thee; lest 5315
Jer 9:9 shall not my s. be avenged on such 5315
Jer 12:7 the dearly beloved of my s. into the 5315
Jer 13:17 my s. shall weep in secret places 5315
Jer 14:19 Judah? hath thy s. lothed Zion? 5315
Jer 18:20 for they have digged a pit for my s. 5315
Jer 20:13 he hath delivered the s. of the poor 5315
Jer 31:12 and their s. shall be as a watered 5315
Jer 31:14 I will satiate the s. of the priests 5315
Jer 31:25 I have satiated the weary s., and I 5315
Jer 31:25 replenished every sorrowful s.. 5315
Jer 32:41 whole heart and with my whole s.. 5315
Jer 38:16 Lord liveth, that made us this s., 5315
Jer 38:17 then thy s. shall live, and this city 5315
Jer 38:20 well unto thee, and thy s. shall live. 5315
Jer 50:19 his s. shall be satisfied upon mount 5315
Jer 51:6 and deliver every man his s.: be 5315
Jer 51:45 deliver ye every man his s. from 5315
La 1:11 things for meat to relieve the s.: 5315
La 1:16 comforter that should relieve my s. 5315
La 2:12 when their s. was poured out into 5315
La 3:17 thou hast removed my s. far off 5315
La 3:20 My s. hath them...in remembrance, 5315
La 3:24 Lord is my portion, saith my s.; 5315
La 3:25 for him, to the s. that seeketh him, 5315
La 3:58 hast pleaded the causes of my s.; 5315
Eze 3:19 but thou hast delivered thy s.. 5315
Eze 3:21 also thou hast delivered thy s.. 5315
Eze 4:14 my s. hath not been polluted: 5315
Eze 18:4 are mine; as the s. of thine father, 5315
Eze 18:4 so also the s. of the son is mine: 5315
Eze 18:4 the s. that sinneth, it shall die. 5315
Eze 18:20 The s. that sinneth, it shall die. 5315
Eze 18:27 and right, he shall save his s. alive. 5315
Eze 24:21 and that which your s. pitieth; 5315
Eze 33:5 taketh warning shall deliver his s. 5315
Eze 33:9 but thou hast delivered thy s.. 5315
Ho 9:4 bread for their s. shall not come 5315
Jon 2:5 me about, even to the s.: the 5315
Jon 2:7 When my s. fainted within me I 5315
Mic 6:7 of my body for the sin of my s.? 5315
Mic 7:1 my s. desired the firstripe fruit, 5315
Hab 2:4 his s. which is lifted up is not 5315
Hab 2:10 and hast sinned against thy s.. 5315
Zec 11:8 one month; and my s. lothed them, 5315
Zec 11:8 and their s. also abhorred me. 5315
Mt 10:28 **but are not able to kill the s.** *5590*
Mt 10:28 **to destroy both s. and body in hell** *5590*
Mt 12:18 in whom my s. is well pleased: *5590*
Mt 16:26 **whole world, and lose his own s.?** *5590*
Mt 16:26 **a man give in exchange for his s.?** *5590*
Mt 22:37 **all thy heart, and with all thy s.,** *5590*
Mt 26:38 **My s. is exceeding sorrowful, even** *5590*
Mk 8:36 **whole world, and lose his own s.?** *5590*
Mk 8:37 **a man give in exchange for his s.?** *5590*
Mk 12:30 **all thy heart, and with all thy s.,** *5590*
Mk 12:33 understanding, and with all the s., *5590*
Mk 14:34 **My s. is exceeding sorrowful unto** *5590*
Lu 1:46 said, My s. doth magnify the Lord, *5590*
Lu 2:35 shall pierce through thy own s. *5590*
Lu 10:27 all thy heart, and with all thy s., *5590*
Lu 12:19 **say to my s., S., thou hast much** *5590*
Lu 12:20 **this night thy s. shall be required** *5590*
Joh 12:27 **Now is my s. troubled; and what** *5590*
Ac 2:27 thou wilt not leave my s. in hell, *5590*
Ac 2:31 that his s. was not left in hell, *5590*
Ac 2:43 And fear came upon every s.: and *5590*
Ac 3:23 every s., which will not hear that *5590*
Ac 4:32 were of one heart and of one s. *5590*
Ro 2:9 every s. of man that doeth evil; *5590*
Ro 13:1 Let every s. be subject unto the *5590*
1Co 15:45 man Adam was made a living s.; *5590*
2Co 1:23 call God for a record upon my s., *5590*
1Th 5:23 your whole spirit and s. and body *5590*
Heb 4:12 dividing asunder of s. and spirit, *5590*
Heb 6:19 we have as an anchor of the s., *5590*
Heb 10:38 my s. shall have no pleasure in *5590*
Heb 10:39 that believe to the saving of the s.. *5590*
Jas 5:20 his way shall save a s. from death, *5590*
1Pe 2:11 lusts, which war against the s.; *5590*
2Pe 2:8 vexed his righteous s. from day to *5590*
3Jo 2 in health, even as thy s. prospereth. *5590*

Re 16:3 and every living s. died in the sea. *5590*
Re 18:14 fruits that thy s. lusted after are *5590*

SOUL'S
Job 16:4 if your soul were in my s. stead,........ 5315

SOULS
Ge 12:5 and the s. that they had gotten in....... 5315
Ge 46:15 the s. of his sons and his daughters.... 5315
Ge 46:18 bare unto Jacob, even sixteen s.......... 5315
Ge 46:22 to Jacob: all the s. were fourteen. 5315
Ge 46:25 unto Jacob: all the s. were seven. 5315
Ge 46:26 All the s. that came with Jacob 5315
Ge 46:26 all the s. were threescore and six;...... 5315
Ge 46:27 born him in Egypt, were two s. 5315
Ge 46:27 all the s. of the house of Jacob, ... 5315
Ex 1:5 all the s. that came out of the loins...... 5315
Ex 1:5 the loins of Jacob were seventy s....... 5315
Ex 12:4 according to the number of the s.;...... 5315
Ex 30:15, 16 make an atonement for your s..... 5315
Le 16:29 ye shall afflict your s., and do no........ 5315
Le 16:31 ye shall afflict your s., by a statute 5315
Le 17:11 to make an atonement for your s....... 5315
Le 18:29 the s. that commit them shall be 5315
Le 20:25 make your s. abominable by beast, ... 5315
Le 23:27 ye shall afflict your s., and offer an..... 5315
Le 23:32 of rest, and ye shall afflict your s. 5315
Nu 16:38 these sinners against their own s.,....... 5315
Nu 29:7 ye shall afflict your s.: ye shall not 5315
Nu 30:9 they have bound their s., shall........... 5315
Nu 31:50 to make an atonement for our s. 5315
Jos 10:28, 30 and all the s. that were therein;...... 5315
Jos 10:32 and all the s. that were therein,......... 5315
Jos 10:35 and all the s. that were therein he....... 5315
Jos 10:37 and all the s. that were therein;......... 5315
Jos 10:37 and all the s. that were therein. 5315
Jos 10:39 all the s. that were therein; he left...... 5315
Jos 11:11 smote all the s. that were therein....... 5315
Jos 23:14 all your hearts and in all your s.,........ 5315
1Sa 25:29 the s. of thine enemies, them shall..... 5315
Ps 72:13 and shall save the s. of the needy. 5315
Ps 97:10 preserveth the s. of his saints; he 5315
Pr 11:30 life; and he that winneth s. is wise. 5315
Pr 14:25 A true witness delivereth s.: but a 5315
Isa 57:16 and the s. which I have made. 5397
Jer 2:34 the blood of the s. of the poor........... 5315
Jer 6:16 and ye shall find rest for your s. 5315
Jer 26:19 procure great evil against our s......... 5315
Jer 44:7 ye this great evil against your s., ... 5315
La 1:19 sought their meat to relieve their s..... 5315
Eze 7:19 they shall not satisfy their s., ... 5315
Eze 13:18 the head of every stature to hunt s.!... 5315
Eze 13:18 Will ye hunt the s. of my people, ... 5315
Eze 13:18 will ye save the s. alive that come....... 5315
Eze 13:19 to slay the s. that should not die, ... 5315
Eze 13:19 to save the s. alive that should not..... 5315
Eze 13:20 there hunt the s. to make them fly,.... 5315
Eze 13:20 your arms, and will let the s. go, ... 5315
Eze 13:20 s. that ye hunt to make them fly. 5315
Eze 14:14 they should deliver but their own s..... 5315
Eze 14:20 they shall but deliver their own s. 5315
Eze 18:4 Behold, all s. are mine; as the soul....... 5315
Eze 22:25 they have devoured s.; they have....... 5315
Eze 22:27 to shed blood, and to destroy s., to.... 5315
Mt 11:29 **and ye shall find rest unto your s...** *5590*
Lu 21:19 **your patience possess ye your s.....** *5590*
Ac 2:41 unto them about three thousand s........ *5590*
Ac 7:14 kindred, threescore and fifteen s.. ...... *5590*
Ac 14:22 Confirming the s. of the disciples,....... *5590*
Ac 15:24 with words, subverting your s., ... *5590*
Ac 27:37 hundred threescore and sixteen s.. ..... *5590*
1Th 2:8 of God only, but also our own s., ... *5590*
Heb 13:17 for they watch for your s., as they...... *5590*
Jas 1:21 word, which is able to save your s.. ... *5590*
1Pe 1:9 faith, even the salvation of your s........ *5590*
1Pe 1:22 have purified your s. in obeying the *5590*
1Pe 2:25 Shepherd and Bishop of your s. *5590*
1Pe 3:20 is, eight s. were saved by water. *5590*
1Pe 4:19 commit the keeping of their s. to *5590*
2Pe 2:14 from sin; beguiling unstable s............ *5590*
Re 6:9 under the altar the s. of them that:.... *5590*
Re 18:13 chariots, and slaves, and s. of men. *5590*
Re 20:4 the s. of them that were beheaded *5590*

SOUND See also SOUNDED; SOUNDETH; SOUNDING; SOUNDS.
Ex 28:35 and his s. shall be heard when he....... 6963
Le 25:9 trumpet of the jubile to s. on the 5674
Le 25:9 the trumpet s. throughout all your...... 5674
Le 26:36 the s. of a shaken leaf shall chase....... 6963
Nu 10:7 blow, but ye shall not s. an alarm....... 7321
Jos 6:5 when ye hear the s. of the trumpet, ... 6963
Jos 6:20 people heard the s. of the trumpet, ... 6963
2Sa 5:24 the s. of a going in the tops of the 6963
2Sa 6:15 and with the s. of the trumpet. 6963
2Sa 15:10 as ye hear the s. of the trumpet, ... 6963
1Ki 1:40 the earth rent with the s. of them. 6963
1Ki 1:41 Joab heard the s. of the trumpet, ... 6963
1Ki 14:6 when Ahijah heard the s. of her feet, .. 6963
1Ki 18:41 there is a s. of abundance of rain. 6963
2Ki 6:32 s. of his master's feet behind him?...... 6963
1Ch 14:15 hear a s. of going in the tops of the.... 6963
1Ch 15:19 to s. with cymbals of brass; 8085
1Ch 15:28 and with s. of the cornet, and with..... 6963
1Ch 16:5 but Asaph made a s. with cymbals;..... 8085
1Ch 16:42 for those that should make a s.,......... 8085
2Ch 5:13 one s. to be heard in praising and....... 6963
Ne 4:20 ye hear the s. of the trumpet, ... 6963
Job 15:21 A dreadful s. is in his ears: in........... 6963
Job 21:12 and rejoice at the s. of the organ. 6963
Job 37:2 the s. that goeth out of his mouth. 1899
Job 39:24 he that it is the s. of the trumpet....... 6963
Ps 47:5 the Lord with the s. of a trumpet....... 6963
Ps 77:17 out water: the skies sent out a s........ 6963
Ps 89:15 the people that know the joyful s........ 8643
Ps 92:3 upon the harp with a solemn s........... 1902
Ps 98:6 With trumpets and s. of cornet 6963
Ps 119:80 Let my heart be s. in thy statutes;..... 8549
Ps 150:3 him with the s. of the trumpet:.......... 8629
Pr 2:7 He layeth up s. wisdom for the.......... 8454
Pr 3:21 keep s. wisdom and discretion: 8454
Pr 8:14 Counsel is mine, and s. wisdom: I...... 8454
Pr 14:30 A s. heart is the life of the flesh: 4832
Ec 12:4 when the s. of the grinding is low, ... 6963
Isa 16:11 my bowels shall s. like an harp for...... 1993
Jer 4:19 the s. of the trumpet, the alarm of 6963
Jer 4:21 and hear the s. of the trumpet? 6963
Jer 6:17 Hearken to the s. of the trumpet. 6963
Jer 8:16 trembled at the s. of the neighing....... 6963
Jer 25:10 s. of the millstones, and the light 6963
Jer 42:14 nor hear the s. of the trumpet, ... 6963
Jer 48:36 mine heart shall s. for Moab like 1993
Jer 48:36 mine heart shall s. like pipes for......... 1993
Jer 50:22 A s. of battle is in the land, and of 6963
Jer 51:54 A s. of a cry cometh from Babylon, ... 6963
Eze 10:5 the s. of the cherubims' wings was...... 6963
Eze 26:13 the s. of thy harps shall be no more ... 6963
Eze 26:15 the isles shake at the s. of thy fall,..... 6963
Eze 27:28 shake at the s. of the cry of thy......... 6963
Eze 31:16 nations to shake at the s. of his fall, ... 6963
Eze 33:4 whosoever heareth the s. of the.......... 6963
Eze 33:5 He heard the s. of the trumpet, and ... 6963
Da 3:5 ye hear the s. of the cornet, flute, ... 7032
Da 3:7 people heard the s. of the cornet, ... 7032
Da 3:10 that shall hear the s. of the cornet,..... 7032
Da 3:15 ye hear the s. of the cornet, flute, ... 7032
Joe 2:1 s. an alarm in my holy mountain:........ 7321
Am 2:2 and with the s. of the trumpet: 6963
Am 6:5 That chant to the s. of the viol, and.... 6310
Mt 6:2 **do not s. a trumpet before thee,....** *4537*
Mt 24:31 **with a great s. of a trumpet,..........** *5456*
Lu 15:27 **he hath received him safe and s....** *5198*
Joh 3:8 **thou hearest the s. thereof, but.....** *5456*
Ac 2:2 there came a s. from heaven as of...... *2279*
Ro 10:18 their s. went into all the earth, ... *5353*
1Co 14:7 even things without life giving s., ... *5456*
1Co 14:8 if the trumpet give an uncertain s.,...... *5456*
1Co 15:52 the trumpet shall s., and the dead *4537*
1Ti 1:10 that is contrary to s. doctrine; *5198*
2Ti 1:7 and of love, and of a s. mind. *4995*
2Ti 1:13 Hold fast the form of s. words,.......... *5198*
2Ti 4:3 they will not endure s. doctrine;......... *5198*
Tit 1:9 he may be able by s. doctrine both..... *5198*
Tit 1:13 that they may be s. in the faith;......... *5198*
Tit 2:1 things which become s. doctrine:......... *5198*
Tit 2:2 s. in faith, in charity, in patience. *5198*
Tit 2:8 S. speech, that cannot be *5199*
Heb 12:19 And the s. of a trumpet, and the........ *2279*
Re 1:15 his voice as the s. of many waters...... *5456*
Re 8:6 angels...prepared themselves to s.!..... *4537*
Re 8:13 the three angels, which are yet to s.!.. *4537*
Re 9:9 and the s. of their wings was as the ... *5456*
Re 9:9 as the s. of chariots of many horses.... *5456*
Re 10:7 angel, when he shall begin to s., ... *4537*
Re 18:22 s. of a millstone shall be heard no *5456*

SOUNDED
Ex 19:19 when the voice of the trumpet s. 1961
1Sa 20:12 when I have s. my father about 2713
2Ch 7:6 priests s. trumpets before them, ... 2690
2Ch 13:14 the priests s. with the trumpet, ... 2690
2Ch 23:13 rejoiced, and s. with trumpets 8628
2Ch 29:28 sang, and the trumpeters s. 2690
Ne 4:18 he that s. the trumpet was by me. 8628
Lu 1:44 of thy salutation s. in mine ears, ... *1096*
Ac 27:28 s., and found it twenty fathoms:......... *1001*
Ac 27:28 they s. again, and found it fifteen *1001*
1Th 1:8 you s. out the word of the Lord.......... *1837*
Re 8:7 The first angel s., and there............. *4537*
Re 8:8 the second angel s., and as it were...... *4537*
Re 8:10 the third angel s., and there fell a *4537*
Re 8:12 the fourth angel s., and the third........ *4537*
Re 9:1 the fifth angel s., and I saw a star...... *4537*
Re 9:13 the sixth angel s., and I heard a......... *4537*
Re 11:15 And the seventh angel s.; and there.... *4537*

SOUNDETH
Ex 19:13 when the trumpet s. long, they shall.........

SOUNDING
1Ch 15:16 harps and cymbals, s., by lifting 8085
2Ch 5:12 twenty priests s. with trumpets:) 2690
2Ch 13:12 with s. trumpets to cry alarm 8643
Ps 150:5 him upon the high s. cymbals. 8643
Isa 63:15 the s. of thy bowels and of thy 1995
Eze 7:7 not the s. again of the mountains........ 1906
1Co 13:1 I am become as s. brass, or a *2278*

SOUNDNESS
Ps 38:3 no s. in my flesh because of thine 4974
Ps 38:7 and there is no s. in my flesh. 4974
Isa 1:6 unto the head there is no s. in it;....... 4974
Ac 3:16 him hath given him this perfect s........ *3647*

SOUNDS
1Co 14:7 they give a distinction in the s., ... *5353*

SOUR
Isa 18:5 and the s. grape is ripening in the 1155
Jer 31:29 The fathers have eaten a s. grape, ... 1155
Jer 31:30 every man that eateth the s. grape,.... 1155
Eze 18:2 The fathers have eaten s. grapes, ... 1155
Ho 4:18 Their drink is s.: they have.............. 5493

SOUTH See also SOUTHWARD.
Ge 12:9 going on still toward the s................ 5045
Ge 13:1 had, and Lot with him, into the s.. 5045
Ge 13:3 journey from the s....to Beth-el, ... 5045
Ge 20:1 from thence toward the s. country,..... 5045
Ge 24:62 for he dwelt in the s. country. 5045
Ge 28:14 east, and to the north, and to the s.... 5045
Ex 26:18 boards on the s. side southward......... 5045
Ex 26:35 of the tabernacle toward the s. 8486
Ex 27:9 s. side southward there shall be 5045
Ex 36:23 boards for the s. side southward: 5045
Ex 38:9 s. side southward the hangings of....... 5045
Nu 2:10 the s. side shall be the standard......... 8486
Nu 10:6 camps that lie on the s. side shall....... 8486
Nu 13:22 And they ascended by the s., and....... 5045
Nu 13:29 Amalekites dwell in...the s.:.............. 5045
Nu 21:1 Canaanite, which dwelt in the s.,......... 5045
Nu 33:40 which dwelt in the s. in the land of..... 5045
Nu 34:3 your s. quarter shall be from the......... 5045
Nu 34:3 your s. border shall be the outmost 5045
Nu 34:4 turn from the s. to the ascent of 5045
Nu 34:4 be from the s. to Kadesh-barnea, ... 5045
Nu 35:5 on the s. side two thousand cubits,...... 5045
De 1:7 in the vale, and in the s., and by the .. 5045
De 33:23 possess thou the west and the s.. 1864
De 34:3 the s., and the plain of the valley of.... 5045
Jos 10:40 country of the hills, and of the s., ... 5045
Jos 11:2 and of the plains s. of Chinneroth, ... 5045
Jos 11:16 all the s. country, and all the land....... 5045
Jos 12:3 the s., under Ashdoth-pisgah: 8486
Jos 12:8 wilderness, and in the s. country;....... 5045
Jos 13:4 From the s., all the land of the......... 8486
Jos 15:1 the uttermost part of the s. coast....... 5045
Jos 15:2 their s. border was from the shore 5045
Jos 15:3 to the s. side to Maaleh-acrabbim,....... 5045
Jos 15:3 on the s. side unto Kadesh-barnea, ... 5045
Jos 15:4 the sea: this shall be your s. coast. 5045
Jos 15:7 which is on the s. side of the river: 5045
Jos 15:8 unto the s. side of the Jebusite; 5045
Jos 15:19 for thou hast given me a s. land;......... 5045
Jos 18:5 shall abide in their coast on the s., ... 5045

Jos 18:13 hill that lieth on the s. side of the 5045
Jos 18:15 the s. quarter was from the end of 5045
Jos 18:16 to the side of Jebusi on the s., and 5045
Jos 18:19 the salt sea at the s. end of Jordan: 5045
Jos 18:19 of Jordan: this was the s. coast 5045
Jos 19:8 to Baalath-beer, Ramath of the s. 5045
Jos 19:34 reacheth to Zebulun on the s. side, 5045
Jg 1:9 in the mountain, and in the s., and 5045
Jg 1:15 for thou hast given me a s. land; 5045
Jg 1:16 which lieth in the s. of Arad; 5045
Jg 21:19 Shechem, and on the s. of Lebonah. 5045
1Sa 20:41 arose out of a place toward the s., 5045
1Sa 23:19 which is on the s. of Jeshimon? 3225
1Sa 23:24 in the plain on the s. of Jeshimon. 3225
1Sa 27:10 said, Against the s. of Judah, and 5045
1Sa 27:10 against the s. of the Jerahmeelites, 5045
1Sa 27:10 and against the s. of the Kenites. 5045
1Sa 30:1 the Amalekites had invaded the s., 5045
1Sa 30:14 upon the s. of the Cherethites, 5045
1Sa 30:14 to Judah, and upon the s. of Caleb; 5045
1Sa 30:27 to them which were in s. Ramoth, 5045
2Sa 24:7 they went out to the s. of Judah, 5045
1Ki 7:25 and three looking toward the s., 5045
1Ki 7:39 house eastward over against the s. 5045
1Ch 9:24 toward the east, west, north, and s. 5045
2Ch 4:4 and three looking toward the s., 5045
2Ch 4:10 of the east end, over against the s. 5045
2Ch 28:18 low country, and of the s. of Judah, 5045
Job 9:9 and the chambers of the s. 8486
Job 37:9 Out of the s. cometh...whirlwind: 2315
Job 37:17 quieteth the earth by the s. wind? 1864
Job 39:26 stretch her wings toward the s.? 8486
Ps 75:6 from the west, nor from the s. 4057
Ps 78:26 power he brought in the s. wind. 8486
Ps 89:12 north and the s. thou hast created 3225
Ps 107:3 from the north, and from the s. 3220
Ps 126:4 O Lord, as the streams in the s. 5045
Ec 1:6 The wind goeth toward the s., 1864
Ec 11:3 and if the tree fall toward the s., 1864
Ca 4:16 O north wind; and come, thou s.; 8486
Isa 21:1 As whirlwinds in the s. pass 5045
Isa 30:6 The burden of the beasts of the s. 5045
Isa 43:6 up; and to the s., Keep not back: 8486
Jer 13:19 The cities of the s. shall be shut 5045
Jer 17:26 the mountains, and from the s., 5045
Jer 32:44 valley, and in the cities of the s. 5045
Jer 33:13 the vale, and in the cities of the s., 5045
Eze 20:46 man, set thy face toward the s., 8486
Eze 20:46 and drop thy word toward the s., 1864
Eze 20:46 against the forest of the s. field; 5045
Eze 20:47 say to the forest of the s., Hear the 5045
Eze 20:47 all faces from the s. to the north 5045
Eze 21:4 all flesh from the s. to the north: 5045
Eze 40:2 was as the frame of a city on the s. 5045
Eze 40:24 that he brought me toward the s., 1864
Eze 40:24 and behold a gate toward the s. 1864
Eze 40:27 in the inner court toward the s. 1864
Eze 40:27 from gate to gate toward the s. 1864
Eze 40:28 to the inner court by the s. gate: 1864
Eze 40:28 he measured the s. gate according 1864
Eze 40:44 their prospect was toward the s. 1864
Eze 40:45 whose prospect is toward the s., 1864
Eze 41:11 and another door toward the s. 1864
Eze 42:12 chambers that were toward the s. 1864
Eze 42:13 chambers and the s. chambers, 1864
Eze 42:18 measured the s. side, five hundred 1864
Eze 46:9 go out by the way of the s. gate; 5045
Eze 46:9 entereth by the way of the s. gate 5045
Eze 47:1 the house, at the s. side of the altar. 5045
Eze 47:19 And the s. side southward, from 5045
Eze 47:19 And this is the s. side southward. 8486
Eze 48:10 and toward the s. five and twenty 5045
Eze 48:16 the s. side four thousand and five 5045
Eze 48:17 and toward the s. two hundred and 5045
Eze 48:28 of Gad, at the s. side southward, 5045
Eze 48:33 at the s. side four thousand and 5045
Da 8:9 toward the s., and toward the east, 5045
Da 11:5 the king of the s. shall be strong, 5045
Da 11:6 for the king's daughter of the s. 5045
Da 11:9 So the king of the s. shall come 5045
Da 11:11 the king of the s. shall be moved 5045
Da 11:14 stand up against the king of the s. 5045
Da 11:15 arms of the s. shall not withstand, 5045
Da 11:25 courage against the king of the s. 5045
Da 11:25 king of the s. shall be stirred up to 5045
Da 11:29 return, and come toward the s.; 5045
Da 11:40 shall the king of the s. push at 5045
Ob 19 And they of the s. shall possess the 5045
Ob 20 shall possess the cities of the s. 5045
Zec 6:6 go forth toward the s. country. 8486
Zec 7:7 inhabited the s. and the plain? 5045
Zec 9:14 shall go with whirlwinds of the s. 8486
Zec 14:4 north, and half of it toward the s. 5045
Zec 14:10 Geba to Rimmon s. of Jerusalem: 5045
Mt 12:42 **queen of the s. shall rise up in** *3558*
Lu 11:31 **queen of the s. shall rise up in** *3558*
Lu 12:55 **when ye see the s. wind blow,** *3558*
Lu 13:29 **from the s., and shall sit down** *3558*
Ac 8:26 Arise, and go toward the s. unto *3314*
Ac 27:12 toward the s. west and north west. *3047*
Ac 27:13 And when the s. wind blew softly, *3558*
Ac 28:13 and after one day the s. wind blew, *3558*
Re 21:13 three gates; on the s. three gates; *3558*

SOUTH-COUNTRY See SOUTH and COUNTRY.

SOUTH-QUARTER See SOUTH and QUARTER.

SOUTH-SIDE See SOUTH and SIDE.

SOUTHWARD
Ge 13:14 s., and eastward, and westward: 5045
Ex 26:18 twenty boards on the south side s. 8486
Ex 27:9 south side s. there shall be hangings 8486
Ex 36:23 twenty boards for the south side s. 8486
Ex 38:9 on the south side s. the hangings 8486
Ex 40:24 the south side of the tabernacle s. 5045
Nu 3:29 on the side of the tabernacle s. 8486
Nu 13:17 Get you up this way s., and go up 5045
De 3:27 northward, and s., and eastward, 8486
Jos 15:1 the wilderness of Zin s. was the 8486
Jos 15:2 sea, from the bay that looketh s. 5045
Jos 15:21 Judah toward the coast of Edom s. 5045
Jos 17:9 unto the river Kanah, s. of the river: 5045
Jos 17:10 S. it was Ephraim's, and northward 5045
Jos 18:13 side of Luz, which is Beth-el, s.; 5045
Jos 18:14 compassed the corner of the sea s., 5045
Jos 18:14 hill that lieth before Beth-horon s.; 5045
1Sa 14:5 the other s. over against Gibeah. 5045
1Ch 26:15 To Obed-edom s.; and to his sons 5045
1Ch 26:17 northward four a day, s. four a day, 5045
Eze 47:19 And the south side s., from Tamar 5045
Eze 47:19 sea. And this is the south side s. 5045
Eze 48:28 border of Gad, at the south side s., 5045
Da 8:4 westward, and northward, and s.; 5045

SOUTH-WEST See SOUTH and WEST.

SOUTH-WIND See SOUTH and WIND.

SOW See also SOWED; SOWEST; SOWETH; SOWING; SOWN.
Ge 47:23 for you, and ye shall s. the land. 2232
Ex 23:10 six years thou shalt s. thy land, 2232
Le 19:19 shalt not s. thy field with mingled 2232
Le 25:3 Six years thou shalt s. thy field, 2232
Le 25:4 thou shalt neither s. thy field, nor 2232
Le 25:11 ye shall not s., neither reap that 2232
Le 25:20 we shall not s., nor gather in our 2232
Le 25:22 And ye shall s. the eight year, and 2232
Le 26:16 and ye shall s. your seed in vain, 2232
De 22:9 shalt not s. thy vineyard with divers 2232
2Ki 19:29 in the third year s. ye, and reap, 2232
Job 4:8 plow iniquity, and s. wickedness, 2232
Job 31:8 Then let me s., and let another eat; 2232
Ps 107:37 s. the fields, and plant vineyards, 2232
Ps 126:5 that s.; in tears shall reap in joy. 2232
Ec 11:4 observeth the wind shall not s.; 2232
Ec 11:6 In the morning s. thy seed, and in 2232
Isa 28:24 the plowman plow all day to s.? 2232
Isa 30:23 seed, that thou shalt s. the ground 2232
Isa 32:20 Blessed are ye that s. beside all 2232
Isa 37:30 in the third year s. ye, and reap, 2232
Jer 4:3 ground, and s. not among thorns. 2232
Jer 31:27 that I will s. the house of Israel and 2232
Jer 35:7 shall ye build house, nor s. seed, 2232
Ho 2:23 I will s. her unto me in the earth; 2232
Ho 10:12 S. to yourselves in righteousness, 2232
Mic 6:15 Thou shalt s., but thou shalt not 2232
Zec 10:9 I will s. them among the people: 2232
Mt 6:26 **fowls of the air: for they s. not,** *4687*
Mt 13:3 **Behold, a sower went forth to s.;** *4687*
Mt 13:27 **Sir, didst thou not s. good seed in.** *4687*
Mk 4:3 **there went out a sower to s.** *4687*
Lu 8:5 **A sower went out to s. his seed:** *4687*
Lu 12:24 **for they neither s. nor reap;** *4687*
Lu 19:21 **and reapest that thou didst not s.** *4687*
Lu 19:22 **and reaping that I did not s.:** *4687*
2Pe 2:22 and the s. that was washed to her *5300*

SOWED See also SOWEDST.
Ge 26:12 Then Isaac s. in that land, and 2232
Jg 9:45 down the city, and s. it with salt. 2232
Mt 13:4 **when he s., some seeds fell by** *4687*
Mt 13:24 **unto a man which s. good seed in** *4687*
Mt 13:25 **and s. tares among the wheat,** *4687*
Mt 13:31 **a man took, and s. in his field:** *4687*
Mt 13:39 **enemy that s. them is the devil;** *4687*
Mt 25:26 **knewest that I reap where I s. not,** *4687*
Mk 4:4 **he s., some fell by the way side,** *4687*
Lu 8:5 **he s., some fell by the way side;** *4687*

SOWEDST
De 11:10 where thou s. thy seed, and 2232

SOWER
Isa 55:10 that it may give seed to the s., 2232
Jer 50:16 Cut off the s. from Babylon, and 2232
Mt 13:3 **Behold, a s. went forth to sow;** *4687*
Mt 13:18 **Hear ye...the parable of the s.** *4687*
Mk 4:3 **Behold, there went out a s. to** *4687*
Mk 4:14 **The s. soweth the word.** *4687*
Lu 8:5 **A s. went out to sow his seed: and** *4687*
2Co 9:10 he that ministereth seed to the s. *4687*

SOWEST
1Co 15:36 which thou s. is not quickened, *4687*
1Co 15:37 And that which thou s., *4687*
1Co 15:37 thou s. not that body that shall be *4687*

SOWETH
Pr 6:14 continually; he s. discord. 7971
Pr 6:19 that s. discord among brethren. 7971
Pr 11:18 but to him that s. righteousness 2232
Pr 16:28 A froward man s. strife: and a 7971
Pr 22:8 He that s. iniquity shall reap 2232
Am 9:13 treader of grapes him that s. seed; 4900
Mt 13:37 **that s. the good seed is the Son** *4687*
Mk 4:14 **The sower s. the word.** *4687*
Joh 4:36 **that both he that s. and he that** *4687*
Joh 4:37 **true, One s., and another reapeth.** *4687*
2Co 9:6 He which s. sparingly shall reap *4687*
2Co 9:6 he which s. bountifully shall reap *4687*
Ga 6:7 whatsoever a man s., that shall he *4687*
Ga 6:8 For he that s. to his flesh shall of *4687*
Ga 6:8 but he that s. to the Spirit shall of *4687*

SOWING
Le 11:37 their carcase fall upon any s. seed 2221
Le 26:5 shall reach unto the s. time: 2233

SOWING-TIME See SOWING and TIME.

SOWN
Ex 23:16 which thou hast s. in the field: 2232
Le 11:37 any sowing seed which is to be s., 2232
De 21:4 which is neither eared nor s., 2232
De 22:9 fruit of thy seed which thou hast s., 2232
De 29:23 and burning, that it is not s., nor 2232
Jg 6:3 And so it was when Israel had s., 2232
Ps 97:11 Light is s. for the righteous, and 2232
Isa 19:7 every thing s. by the brooks, shall 4218
Isa 40:24 yea, they shall not be s.: yea, 2232
Isa 61:11 things that are s. in it to spring 2221
Jer 2:2 in a land that was not s. 2232
Jer 12:13 They have s. wheat, but shall reap 2232
Eze 36:9 you, and ye shall be tilled and s. 2232
Ho 8:7 For they have s. the wind, and they 2232
Na 1:14 that no more of thy name be s. 2232
Hab 1:6 Ye have s. much, and bring in 2232
Mt 13:19 **that which was s. in his heart** *4687*
Mt 25:24 **reaping where thou hast not s.,** *4687*
Mk 4:15 **way side, where the word is s.;** *4687*
Mk 4:15 **word that was s. in their hearts.** *4687*
Mk 4:16 **which are s. on stony ground** *4687*
Mk 4:18 **they which are s. among thorns;** *4687*
Mk 4:20 **they which are s. on good ground;** *4687*
Mk 4:31 **when it is s. in the earth, is less** *4687*
Mk 4:32 **when it is s., it groweth up, and** *4687*
1Co 9:11 have s. unto you spiritual things, *4687*
1Co 15:42 It is s. in corruption; it is raised in *4687*
1Co 15:43 It is s. in dishonour; it is raised in *4687*
1Co 15:43 it is s. in weakness; it is raised in *4687*
1Co 15:44 It is s. a natural body; it is raised *4687*
2Co 9:10 multiply your seed s., and increase
Jas 3:18 fruit of righteousness is s. in peace *4687*

SPACE
Ge 29:14 abode with him the s. of a month. 3117
Ge 32:16 put a s. betwixt drove and drove. 7305
Le 25:8 the s. of the seven sabbaths of 3117
Le 25:30 within the s. of a full year, then 4390
De 2:14 And the s. in which we came from 3117
Jos 3:4 shall be a s. between you and it, 7350
1Sa 26:13 a great s. being between them: 4725
Ezr 9:8 a little s. grace hath been shewed 7281
Jer 28:11 within the s. of two full years. 5750
Eze 40:12 s. also before the little chambers 1366
Eze 40:12 the s. was one cubit on that side: 1366
Lu 22:59 And about the s. of one hour after *1339*
Ac 5:7 it was about the s. of three hours *1292*
Ac 5:34 to put the apostles forth a little s.; *1024*
Ac 7:42 by the s. of forty years in the
Ac 13:20 the s. of four hundred and fifty years,
Ac 13:21 of Benjamin, but the s. of forty years.
Ac 15:33 after they had tarried there a s., *5550*
Ac 19:8 boldly for the s. of three months, *1909*
Ac 19:10 continued by the s. of two years; *1909*
Ac 19:34 about the s. of two hours cried out, *1909*
Ac 20:31 the s. of three years I ceased not *4158*
Jas 5:17 the s. of three years and six months.
Re 2:21 **And I gave her s. to repent of her** *5550*
Re 8:1 in heaven about the s. of half an hour.
Re 14:20 s. of a thousand and six hundred *575*
Re 17:10 cometh, he must continue a short s.

SPAIN (spane)
Ro 15:24 I take my journey into S., I will *4681*
Ro 15:28 fruit, I will come by you into S. *4681*

SPAKE See also SPAKEST.
Ge 8:15 And God s. unto Noah, saying, 1696
Ge 9:8 And God s. unto Noah, and to his 559
Ge 16:13 name of the Lord that s. unto her, 1696
Ge 18:29 And he s. unto him yet again, and 1696
Ge 19:14 out, and s. unto his sons in law, 1696
Ge 21:22 chief captain...s. unto Abraham, 559
Ge 22:7 Isaac s. unto Abraham his father, 559
Ge 23:3 s. unto the sons of Heth, saying, 1696
Ge 23:13 he s. unto Ephron in the audience 1696
Ge 24:7 which s. unto me, and that sware 1696
Ge 24:30 Thus s. the man unto me; that he 1696
Ge 27:5 when Isaac s. to Esau his son. 1696
Ge 27:6 Rebekah s. unto Jacob her son, 559
Ge 29:9 And while he yet s. with them, 1696
Ge 31:11 angel of God s. unto me in a dream, 559
Ge 31:29 the God of your father s. unto me 559
Ge 34:3 and s. kindly unto the damsel. 1696
Ge 34:4 And Shechem s. unto his father 559
Ge 35:15 the place where God s. with him, 1696
Ge 39:10 as she s. to Joseph day by day, 1696
Ge 39:14 house, and s. unto them, saying, 559
Ge 39:17 And she s. unto him according to 1696
Ge 39:19 of his wife, which she s. unto him, 1696
Ge 41:9 s. the chief butler unto Pharaoh, 1696
Ge 42:7 them, and s. roughly unto them; 1696
Ge 42:14 That is it that I s. unto you, saying, 1696
Ge 42:22 S. I not unto you, saying, Do not 559
Ge 42:23 he s. unto them by an interpreter.
Ge 42:30 lord of the land, s. roughly to us, 1696
Ge 42:37 Reuben s. unto his father, saying, 559
Ge 43:3 And Judah s. unto him, saying, The 559
Ge 43:27 well, the old man of whom ye s.? 559
Ge 43:29 brother, of whom ye s. unto me? 559
Ge 44:6 and he s. unto them these same 1696
Ge 46:2 God s. unto Israel in the visions of 559
Ge 47:5 Pharaoh s. unto Joseph, saying, Thy 559
Ge 49:28 it that their fathers s. unto them, 1696
Ge 50:4 were past, Joseph s. unto the house 1696
Ge 50:17 And Joseph wept when they s. unto 1696
Ge 50:21 them, and s. kindly unto them. 1696
Ex 1:15 s. to the Hebrew midwives, 559
Ex 4:30 Aaron s. all the words which the 1696
Ex 5:10 and they s. to the people, saying, 559
Ex 6:2 And God s. unto Moses, and said 1696
Ex 6:9 And Moses s. so unto the children 1696
Ex 6:10 And the Lord s. unto Moses, saying, 1696
Ex 6:12 And Moses s. before the Lord, 1696
Ex 6:13 Lord s. unto Moses and unto Aaron, 1696
Ex 6:27 These are they which s. to Pharaoh 1696
Ex 6:28 day when the Lord s. unto Moses 1696
Ex 6:29 That the Lord s. unto Moses, saying, 1696
Ex 7:7 old, when they s. unto Pharaoh. 1696
Ex 7:8 Lord s. unto Moses and unto Aaron, 559
Ex 7:19 Lord s. unto Moses, Say unto Aaron, 559
Ex 8:1 And the Lord s. unto Moses, Go unto 559
Ex 8:5 Lord s. unto Moses, Say unto Aaron, 559
Ex 12:1 the Lord s. unto Moses and Aaron 559
Ex 13:1 the Lord s. unto Moses, saying, 1696
Ex 14:1 And the Lord s. unto Moses, saying, 1696
Ex 15:1 this song unto the Lord, and s., 559
Ex 16:9 Moses s. unto Aaron, Say unto all 559
Ex 16:10 Aaron s. unto the...congregation 1696
Ex 16:11 And the Lord s. unto Moses, saying, 1696
Ex 19:19 Moses s., and God answered him by 1696
Ex 19:25 unto the people, and s. unto them. 559
Ex 20:1 And God s. all these words, saying, 1696
Ex 25:1 And the Lord s. unto Moses, saying, 1696
Ex 30:11, 17 the Lord s. unto Moses, saying, 1696
Ex 30:22 Moreover the Lord s. unto Moses, 1696
Ex 31:1 And the Lord s. unto Moses, saying, 1696
Ex 31:12 And the Lord s. unto Moses, saying, 559
Ex 33:11 Lord s. unto Moses face to face, 1696
Ex 34:34 and s. unto the children of Israel 1696
Ex 35:4 Moses s. unto all the congregation 559
Ex 36:5 And they s. unto Moses, saying, The 559
Ex 40:1 the Lord s. unto Moses, saying, 1696
Le 1:1 s. unto him out of the tabernacle of 1696
Le 4:1 And the Lord s. unto Moses, saying, 1696
Le 5:14 And the Lord s. unto Moses, saying 1696
Le 6:1, 8,19,24 Lord s. unto Moses, saying, 1696
Le 7:22, 28 the Lord s. unto Moses, saying, 1696
Le 8:1 And the Lord s. unto Moses, saying, 1696
Le 10:3 This is it that the Lord s., saying, I 1696
Le 10:8 And the Lord s. unto Aaron, saying, 1696
Le 10:12 And Moses s. unto Aaron, and unto 1696
Le 11:1 Lord s. unto Moses and to Aaron, 1696
Le 12:1 And the Lord s. unto Moses, saying, 1696
Le 13:1 the Lord s. unto Moses and Aaron, 1696
Le 14:1 And the Lord s. unto Moses, saying 1696
Le 14:33 Lord s. unto Moses and unto Aaron, 1696
Le 15:1 Lord s. unto Moses and to Aaron, 1696
Le 16:1 Lord s. unto Moses after the death 1696
Le 17:1 And the Lord s. unto Moses, saying, 1696
Le 18:1 And the Lord s. unto Moses, saying, 1696
Le 19:1 And the Lord s. unto Moses, saying, 1696
Le 20:1 And the Lord s. unto Moses, saying, 1696
Le 21:16 And the Lord s. unto Moses, saying, 1696
Le 22:1, 17,26 Lord s. unto Moses, saying, 1696
Le 23:1, 9,23,26,33 Lord s. unto Moses, 1696
Le 24:1, 13 the Lord s. unto Moses, saying, 1696
Le 24:23 Moses s. to the children of Israel, 1696
Le 25:1 Lord s. unto Moses in mount Sinai, 1696
Le 27:1 And the Lord s. unto Moses, saying, 1696
Nu 1:1 And the Lord s. unto Moses in the 1696
Nu 2:1 Lord s. unto Moses and unto Aaron, 1696
Nu 3:1 Lord s. with Moses in mount Sinai. 1696
Nu 3:5, 11 the Lord s. unto Moses, saying, 1696
Nu 3:14 And the Lord s. unto Moses in the 1696
Nu 3:44 And the Lord s. unto Moses, saying, 1696
Nu 4:1, 17 Lord s. unto Moses and...Aaron, 1696
Nu 4:21 And the Lord s. unto Moses, saying, 1696
Nu 5:1 And the Lord s. unto Moses, saying, 1696
Nu 5:4 As the Lord s. unto Moses, so did 1696
Nu 5:5, 11 the Lord s. unto Moses, saying, 1696
Nu 6:1, 22 the Lord s. unto Moses, saying, 1696
Nu 7:4 And the Lord s. unto Moses, saying, 559
Nu 7:89 cherubims: and he s. unto him. 1696
Nu 8:1, 5, 23 Lord s. unto Moses, saying, 1696
Nu 9:1 And the Lord s. unto Moses in the 1696
Nu 9:4 And Moses s. unto the children of 1696
Nu 9:9 And the Lord s. unto Moses, saying, 1696
Nu 10:1 And the Lord s. unto Moses, saying, 1696
Nu 11:25 down in a cloud, and s. unto him, 1696
Nu 12:1 Miriam and Aaron s. against Moses 1696
Nu 12:4 the Lord s. suddenly unto Moses, 559
Nu 13:1 the Lord s. unto Moses, saying, 1696
Nu 14:7 they s. unto all the company of the 559
Nu 14:26 Lord s. unto Moses and...Aaron, 1696
Nu 15:1, 17 And the Lord s. unto Moses, 1696
Nu 15:37 And the Lord s. unto Moses, saying, 559
Nu 16:5 he s. unto Korah and unto all his 1696
Nu 16:20 Lord s. unto Moses and unto Aaron, 1696
Nu 16:23 And the Lord s. unto Moses, saying, 1696
Nu 16:26 And he s. unto the congregation, 1696
Nu 16:36, 44 the Lord s. unto Moses, saying, 1696
Nu 17:1 And the Lord s. unto Moses, saying, 1696
Nu 17:6 And Moses s. unto the children of 1696
Nu 17:12 children of Israel s. unto Moses, 559
Nu 18:8 And the Lord s. unto Aaron, 1696
Nu 18:20 And the Lord s. unto Aaron, 559
Nu 18:25 the Lord s. unto Moses, saying, 1696
Nu 19:1 Lord s. unto Moses and unto Aaron, 1696
Nu 20:3 people chode with Moses, and s., 559
Nu 20:7 the Lord s. unto Moses, saying, 1696
Nu 20:12 Lord s. unto Moses and Aaron, 559
Nu 20:23 the Lord s. unto Moses and Aaron 559
Nu 21:5 And the people s. against God, 1696
Nu 21:16 whereof the Lord s. unto Moses, 559
Nu 22:7 and s. unto him the words of Balak 1696
Nu 24:12 S. I not also to thy messengers 1696
Nu 25:10, 16 the Lord s. unto Moses, saying, 1696
Nu 26:1 Lord s. unto Moses and...Eleazar 559
Nu 26:3 Moses and Eleazar the priest s. 1696
Nu 26:52 And the Lord s. unto Moses, saying, 1696
Nu 27:6 And the Lord s. unto Moses, saying, 559
Nu 27:15 Moses s. unto the Lord, saying, 1696
Nu 28:1 And the Lord s. unto Moses, saying, 1696
Nu 30:1 And Moses s. unto the heads of the 1696
Nu 31:1 And the Lord s. unto Moses, saying, 1696
Nu 31:3 And Moses s. unto the people, 1696
Nu 31:25 And the Lord s. unto Moses, saying, 559
Nu 32:2 Reuben came and s. unto Moses, 559
Nu 32:25 children of Reuben s. unto Moses, 559
Nu 33:50 Lord s. unto Moses in the plains 1696
Nu 34:1, 16 the Lord s. unto Moses, saying, 1696
Nu 35:1 Lord s. unto Moses in the plains 1696
Nu 35:9 And the Lord s. unto Moses, saying, 1696
Nu 36:1 came near, and s. before Moses, 1696
De 1:1 which Moses s. unto all Israel 1696
De 1:3 Moses s. unto the children of Israel, 1696
De 1:6 Lord our God s. unto us in Horeb, 1696
De 1:9 I s. unto you at that time, saying, I 559
De 1:43 So I s. unto you; and ye would not 1696
De 2:1 Red sea, as the Lord s. unto me: 1696
De 2:2 And the Lord s. unto me, saying, 559
De 2:17 That the Lord s. unto me, saying, 1696
De 4:12 Lord s. unto you out of the midst 1696
De 4:15 that the Lord s. unto you in Horeb 1696
De 4:45 Moses s. unto the children of Israel, 1696
De 5:22 the Lord s. unto all your assembly 1696
De 5:28 of your words, when ye s. unto me; 1696
De 9:10 the Lord s. with you in the mount 1696
De 9:13 Futhermore the Lord s. unto me, 559
De 10:4 the Lord s. unto you in the mount 1696
De 13:2 to pass, whereof he s. unto thee, 1696
De 27:9 the Levites s. unto all Israel, saying, 1696
De 28:68 by the way whereof I s. unto thee, 559
De 31:1 Moses went and s. these words 1696
De 31:30 And Moses s. in the ears of all the 1696
De 32:44 and s. all the words of this song 1696
De 32:48 Lord s. unto Moses that selfsame 1696
Jos 1:1 the Lord s. unto Joshua the son of 559
Jos 1:12 the tribe of Manasseh, s. Joshua, 559
Jos 3:6 Joshua s. unto the priests, saying, 559
Jos 4:1 that the Lord s. unto Joshua, saying, 559
Jos 4:8 as the Lord s. unto Joshua, 1696
Jos 4:12 of Israel, as Moses s. unto them: 1696
Jos 4:15 the Lord s. unto Joshua, saying, 559
Jos 4:21 And he s. unto the children of Israel, 559
Jos 7:2 and s. unto them, saying, Go up and 559
Jos 9:11 inhabitants of our country s. to us, 559
Jos 9:22 them, and he s. unto them, saying, 1696
Jos 10:12 Then s. Joshua to the Lord in the 1696
Jos 14:10 the Lord s. this word unto Moses, 1696
Jos 14:12 whereof the Lord s. in that day; 1696
Jos 17:14 children of Joseph s. unto Joshua, 1696
Jos 17:17 Joshua s. unto the house of Joseph, 559
Jos 20:1 Lord also s. unto Joshua, saying, 1696
Jos 20:2 I s. unto you by the hand of Moses: 1696
Jos 21:2 they s. unto them at Shiloh in the 1696
Jos 22:8 he s. unto them, saying, Return 559
Jos 22:15 and they s. with them, saying, 1696
Jos 22:30 and the children of Manasseh s., 1696
Jos 23:14 things which the Lord your God s. 1696
Jos 24:27 the words of the Lord which he s. 1696
Jg 2:4 the angel of the Lord s. these words 1696
Jg 8:8 Penuel, and s. unto them likewise: 1696
Jg 8:9 he s. also unto the men of Penuel, 559
Jg 9:3 his mother's brethren s. of him in 1696
Jg 9:37 Gaal s. again and said, See there 1696
Jg 15:13 And they s. unto him, saying, No; 559
Jg 19:22 and s. to the master of the house, 559
Ru 4:1 kinsman of whom Boaz s. came 1696
1Sa 1:13 Now Hannah, she s. in her heart; 1696
1Sa 7:3 And Samuel s. unto all the house of 559
1Sa 9:9 went to enquire of God, thus he s., 559

1Sa 9:17 the man whom I **s.** to thee of! this....... 559
1Sa 10:16 the kingdom, whereof Samuel **s.**, he..... 559
1Sa 16:4 Samuel did that which the Lord **s.**, ... 1696
1Sa 17:23 **s.** according to the same words:......... 1696
1Sa 17:26 David **s.** to the men that stood by........ 559
1Sa 17:28 heard when he **s.** unto the men; 1696
1Sa 17:30 and **s.** after the same manner:............. 559
1Sa 17:31 words were heard which David **s.**,...... 1696
1Sa 18:23 Saul's servants **s.** those words in the .. 1696
1Sa 18:24 saying, On this manner **s.** David......... 1696
1Sa 19:1 And Saul **s.** to Jonathan his son, and ... 1696
1Sa 19:4 And Jonathan **s.** good of David unto 1696
1Sa 20:26 Saul **s.** not any thing that day: for 1696
1Sa 25:9 **s.** to Nabal according to all those......... 1696
1Sa 25:40 they **s.** unto her, saying, David sent ... 1696
1Sa 28:12 and the woman **s.** to Saul, saying,........ 559
1Sa 28:17 hath done to him, as he **s.** by me:...... 1696
1Sa 30:6 for the people **s.** of stoning him,.......... 559
2Sa 3:19 And Abner also **s.** in the ears of 1696
2Sa 5:1 **s.**, saying, Behold, we are thy bone 559
2Sa 5:6 which **s.** unto David, saying, Except..... 559
2Sa 7:7 **s.** I a word with any of the tribes....... 1696
2Sa 12:18 child was yet alive, we **s.** unto him,.... 1696
2Sa 13:22 And Absalom **s.** unto his brother........ 1696
2Sa 14:4 the woman of Tekoah **s.** to the king, ... 559
2Sa 17:6 Absalom **s.** unto him, saying, ... 559
2Sa 20:18 Then she **s.**, saying, They were wont... 559
2Sa 22:1 David **s.** unto the Lord the words....... 1696
2Sa 23:2 The Spirit of the Lord **s.** by me, and .. 1696
2Sa 23:3 the Rock of Israel **s.** to me, He that ... 1696
2Sa 24:17 David **s.** unto the Lord when he saw.... 559
1Ki 1:11 Nathan **s.** unto Bath-sheba the 559
1Ki 1:42 while he yet **s.**, behold, Jonathan........ 1696
1Ki 2:4 word which he **s.** concerning me, ... 1696
1Ki 2:27 he **s.** concerning the house of Eli in.... 1696
1Ki 3:22 son. Thus they **s.** before the king....... 1696
1Ki 3:26 Then **s.** the woman whose the living..... 559
1Ki 4:32 he **s.** three thousand proverbs: 1696
1Ki 4:33 he **s.** of trees, from the cedar tree 1696
1Ki 4:33 he **s.** also of beasts, and of fowl, and .. 1696
1Ki 5:5 the Lord **s.** unto David my father, ... 1696
1Ki 6:12 which I **s.** unto David thy father:........ 1696
1Ki 8:12 Then **s.** Solomon, The Lord said.......... 559
1Ki 8:15 **s.** with his mouth unto David............ 1696
1Ki 8:20 hath performed his word that he **s.**,.... 1696
1Ki 12:3 Israel came, and **s.** unto Rehoboam,.... 1696
1Ki 12:7 they **s.** unto him, saying, If thou 1696
1Ki 12:10 grown up with him **s.** unto him, ... 1696
1Ki 12:10 unto this people that **s.** unto thee,...... 1696
1Ki 12:14 **s.** to them after the counsel of the 1696
1Ki 12:15 which the Lord **s.** by Ahijah the 1696
1Ki 13:18 an angel **s.** unto me by the word of 1696
1Ki 13:26 of the Lord, which he **s.** unto him. 1696
1Ki 13:27 he **s.** to his sons, saying, Saddle me ... 1696
1Ki 13:31 him, that he **s.** to his sons, saying, ... 559
1Ki 14:18 he **s.** by the hand of his servant......... 1696
1Ki 15:29 which he **s.** by his servant Ahijah 1696
1Ki 16:12 which he **s.** against Baasha by Jehu..... 1696
1Ki 16:34 which he **s.** by Joshua the son of........ 1696
1Ki 17:16 of the Lord, which he **s.** by Elijah. 1696
1Ki 20:28 God, and **s.** unto the king of Israel,...... 559
1Ki 21:2 Ahab **s.** unto Naboth, saying, Give...... 1696
1Ki 21:6 I **s.** unto Naboth the Jezreelite, and 1696
1Ki 21:23 of Jezebel also **s.** the Lord, saying,..... 1696
1Ki 22:13 gone to call Micaiah **s.** unto him,........ 1696
1Ki 22:38 the word of the Lord which he **s.**....... 1696
2Ki 1:9 he **s.** unto him, Thou man of God,...... 1696
2Ki 2:22 to the saying of Elisha which he **s.**..... 1696
2Ki 5:13 **s.** unto him, and said, My father, if..... 1696
2Ki 7:17 who **s.** when the king came down....... 1696
2Ki 8:1 Then **s.** Elisha unto the woman,......... 1696
2Ki 9:12 Thus and thus **s.** he to me, saying, ... 559
2Ki 9:36 which he **s.** by his servant Elijah 1696
2Ki 10:10 the Lord **s.** concerning the house of.... 1696
2Ki 10:10 which he **s.** by his servant Elijah. 1696
2Ki 10:17 of the Lord, which he **s.** to Elijah. 1696
2Ki 14:25 he **s.** by the hand of his servant......... 1696
2Ki 15:12 of the Lord which he **s.** unto Jehu, ... 1696
2Ki 17:26 they **s.** to the king of Assyria,............ 559
2Ki 18:28 in the Jews' language, and **s.**, ... 1696
2Ki 21:10 And the Lord **s.** by his servants the.... 1696
2Ki 22:19 heardest what I **s.** against this place,... 1696
2Ki 24:2 he **s.** by his servants the prophets...... 1696
2Ki 25:28 And he **s.** kindly to him, and set his.... 1696
1Ch 15:16 David **s.** to the chief of the Levites...... 559
1Ch 17:6 **s.** I a word to any of the judges of..... 1696
1Ch 21:9 And the Lord **s.** unto Gad, David's..... 1696
1Ch 21:19 which he **s.** in the name of the Lord. .. 1696
2Ch 1:2 Then Solomon **s.** unto all Israel, to....... 559
2Ch 6:4 that which he **s.** with his mouth 1696
2Ch 10:3 all Israel came and **s.** to Rehoboam,.... 1696
2Ch 10:7 they **s.** unto him, saying, If thou be.... 1696
2Ch 10:10 brought up with him **s.** unto him, ... 1696
2Ch 10:10 answer the people that **s.** unto thee, ... 1696
2Ch 10:15 which he **s.** by the hand of Ahijah....... 1696
2Ch 18:12 that went to call Micaiah **s.** to him,..... 1696
2Ch 18:19 one **s.** saying after this manner,........... 559
2Ch 30:22 Hezekiah **s.** comfortably unto all........... 1696
2Ch 32:6 **s.** comfortably to them, saying,.......... 1696
2Ch 32:16 his servants **s.** yet more against the.... 1696
2Ch 32:19 **s.** against the God of Jerusalem,......... 1696
2Ch 32:24 he **s.** unto him, and he gave him a 559
2Ch 33:10 And the Lord **s.** to Manasseh, and...... 1696
2Ch 33:18 words of the seers that **s.** to him in.... 1696
2Ch 34:22 and they **s.** to her to that effect.......... 1696
2Ch 35:25 the singing women **s.** of Josiah in......... 559
Ne 4:2 he **s.** before his brethren and the......... 559
Ne 8:1 and they **s.** unto Ezra the scribe to 559
Ne 13:24 their children **s.** half in the speech...... 1696
Es 3:4 pass, when they **s.** daily unto him, ... 559
Es 4:10 Again Esther **s.** unto Hatach, and......... 559
Es 8:3 And Esther **s.** yet again before the..... 1696
Job 2:13 and none **s.** a word unto him: for 1696
Job 3:2 And Job **s.**, and said, ... 6030
Job 19:18 I arose, and they **s.** against me.......... 1696
Job 29:22 After my words they **s.** not again; and.......
Job 32:16 (for they **s.** not, but stood still, and 1696
Job 35:1 Elihu **s.** moreover, and said,.............. 6030
Ps 18:*title* who **s.** unto the Lord the words.......... 1696
Ps 33:9 For he **s.**, and it was done; he 559
Ps 39:3 burned: then **s.** I with my tongue, ... 1696
Ps 78:19 Yea, they **s.** against God; they said,.... 1696
Ps 99:7 He **s.** unto them in the cloudy pillar: ... 1696
Ps 105:31 He **s.**, and there came divers sorts 559
Ps 105:34 He **s.**, and the locusts came, and......... 559
Ps 106:33 so that he **s.** unadvisedly with his 981
Pr 30:1 the man **s.** unto Ithiel, even unto 5002
Ca 2:10 My beloved **s.**, and said unto me,........ 6030
Ca 5:6 gone: my soul failed when he **s.**.......... 1696
Isa 7:10 Lord **s.** again unto Ahaz, saying, ... 1696
Isa 8:5 The Lord **s.** also unto me again, ... 1696
Isa 8:11 For the Lord **s.** thus to me with a 559
Isa 20:2 At the same time **s.** the Lord by........ 1696
Isa 65:12 when I **s.**, ye did not hear; but did..... 1696
Isa 66:4 when I **s.**, they did not hear: but 1696
Jer 7:13 I **s.** unto you, rising up early and 1696
Jer 7:22 For I **s.** not unto your fathers, nor 1696
Jer 8:6 and heard, but they **s.** not aright:....... 1696
Jer 14:14 them, neither **s.** unto them: 1696
Jer 19:5 which I commanded not, nor **s.** it, ... 1696
Jer 20:8 For since I **s.**, I cried out, I cried 1696
Jer 22:21 I **s.** unto thee in thy prosperity; but.... 1696
Jer 25:2 the prophet **s.** unto all the people of ... 1696
Jer 26:11 **s.** the priests and the prophets unto..... 559
Jer 26:12 **s.** Jeremiah unto all the princes 559
Jer 26:17 **s.** to all the assembly of the people, ... 559
Jer 26:18 **s.** to all the people of Judah, saying,..... 559
Jer 27:12 I **s.** also to Zedekiah king of Judah...... 1696
Jer 27:16 Also I **s.** to the priests and to all........ 1696
Jer 28:1 **s.** unto me in the house of the Lord,.... 559
Jer 28:11 And Hananiah **s.** in the presence of...... 559
Jer 30:4 that the Lord **s.** concerning Israel...... 1696
Jer 31:20 for since I **s.** against him, I do.......... 1696
Jer 34:6 Jeremiah the prophet **s.** all these........ 1696
Jer 36:2 nations, from the day I **s.** unto thee,... 1696
Jer 37:2 he **s.** by the prophet Jeremiah. 1696
Jer 38:8 the king's house, and **s.** to the king, ... 1696
Jer 40:15 the son of Kareah **s.** to Gedaliah in...... 559
Jer 43:2 **s.** Azariah the son of Hoshaiah, and...... 559
Jer 45:1 that Jeremiah the prophet **s.** unto........ 1696
Jer 46:13 word that the Lord **s.** to Jeremiah 1696
Jer 50:1 that the Lord **s.** against Babylon......... 1696
Jer 51:12 done that which he **s.** against the 1696
Jer 52:32 And **s.** kindly unto him, and set his..... 1696
Eze 1:28 and I heard a voice of one that **s.**...... 1696
Eze 2:2 spirit entered into me when he **s.**....... 1696
Eze 2:2 that I heard him that **s.** unto me. 1696
Eze 3:24 me upon my feet, and **s.** with me,...... 1696
Eze 10:2 he **s.** unto the man clothed with 559
Eze 11:25 I **s.** unto them of the captivity........... 1696
Eze 24:18 So I **s.** unto the people in the........... 1696
Da 1:3 And the king **s.** unto Ashpenaz the....... 559
Da 2:4 Then **s.** the Chaldeans to the king...... 1696
Da 3:9 They **s.** and said to the king............. 6032
Da 3:14 Nebuchadnezzar **s.** and said unto 6032
Da 3:19 therefore he **s.**, and commanded 6032
Da 3:24 rose up in haste, and **s.**, and said....... 6032
Da 3:26 **s.**, and said, Shadrach, Meshach,......... 6032
Da 3:28 Then Nebuchadnezzar **s.**, and said. 6032
Da 4:19 The king **s.**, and said, Belteshazzar,.... 6032
Da 4:30 The king **s.**, and said, Is not this........ 6032
Da 5:7 king **s.**, and said to the wise men....... 6032
Da 5:10 and the queen **s.** and said, O king, ... 6032
Da 5:13 the king **s.** and said unto Daniel, ... 6032
Da 6:12 and **s.** before the king concerning......... 560
Da 6:16 the king **s.** and said unto Daniel, ... 6032
Da 6:20 and the king **s.** and said to Daniel,...... 6032
Da 7:2 Daniel **s.** and said, I saw in my.......... 6032
Da 7:11 the great words which the horn **s.**....... 4449
Da 7:20 a mouth that **s.** very great things, ... 4449
Da 8:13 unto that certain saint which **s.**, ... 1696
Da 9:6 which **s.** in thy name to our kings,...... 1696
Da 9:12 which he **s.** against us, and against..... 1696
Da 10:16 then I opened my mouth, and **s.**, ... 1696
Ho 12:4 in Beth-el, and there he **s.** with us; 1696
Ho 13:1 When Ephraim **s.** trembling, he.......... 1696
Jon 2:10 And the Lord **s.** unto the fish, and....... 559
Hag 1:13 **s.** Haggai the Lord's messenger........... 559
Zec 1:21 he **s.**, saying, These are the horns....... 559
Zec 3:4 And he answered and **s.** unto those...... 559
Zec 4:4 So I answered and **s.** to the angel........ 559
Zec 4:6 Then he answered and **s.** unto me, ... 559
Zec 6:8 he upon me, and **s.** unto me,............. 1696
Mal 3:16 the Lord **s.** often one to another: 1696
Mt 9:18 While he **s.** these things unto them,.... *2980*
Mt 9:33 the devil was cast out, the dumb **s.** *2980*
Mt 12:22 blind and dumb both **s.** and saw. *2980*
Mt 13:3 he **s.** many things...in parables,......... *2980*
Mt 13:33 Another parable **s.** he unto them; *2980*
Mt 13:34 these things **s.** Jesus...in parables;...... *2980*
Mt 13:34 and without a parable **s.** he not.......... *2980*
Mt 14:27 straightway Jesus **s.** unto them, ... *2980*
Mt 16:11 **s. it not to you concerning bread,**.. *2036*
Mt 17:5 While he yet **s.**, behold, a bright *2980*
Mt 17:13 **s.** unto them of John the Baptist. *2036*
Mt 21:45 they perceived that he **s.** of them....... *3004*
Mt 22:1 **s.** unto them again by parables,.......... *2036*
Mt 23:1 Then **s.** Jesus to the multitude,........... *2980*
Mt 26:47 And while he yet **s.**, lo, Judas, one..... *2980*
Mt 28:18 And Jesus came and **s.** unto them,...... *2980*
Mk 3:9 he **s.** to his disciples, that a small....... *2036*
Mk 4:33 many such parables **s.** he the word..... *2980*
Mk 4:34 But without a parable **s.** he not.......... *2980*
Mk 5:35 While he yet **s.**, there came from........ *2980*
Mk 7:35 tongue was loosed, and he **s.** plain...... *2980*
Mk 8:32 And he **s.** that saying openly. And....... *2980*
Mk 9:18 and I **s.** to thy disciples that they *2036*
Mk 12:26 **how in the bush God s. unto him,**.. *2036*
Mk 14:31 But he **s.** the more vehemently,......... *3004*
Mk 14:39 prayed, and **s.** the same words. *2036*
Mk 14:43 while he yet **s.**, cometh Judas, one..... *2980*
Lu 1:42 And she **s.** out with a loud voice,......... *400*
Lu 1:55 As he **s.** to our fathers, to Abraham, .. *2980*
Lu 1:64 and his tongue loosed, and he **s.**, ... *2980*
Lu 1:70 A he **s.** by the mouth of his holy........ *2980*
Lu 2:38 **s.** of him to all them that looked *2980*
Lu 2:50 the saying which he **s.** unto them. *2980*
Lu 4:36 amazed, and **s.** among themselves, ... *4814*
Lu 5:36 he **s.** also a parable unto them; *3004*
Lu 6:39 And he **s.** a parable unto them,.......... *2036*
Lu 7:39 he **s.** within himself, saying, This *2036*
Lu 8:4 out of every city, he **s.** by a parable: .. *2036*
Lu 8:49 While he yet **s.**, there cometh one...... *2980*
Lu 9:11 and **s.** unto them of the kingdom........ *2980*
Lu 9:31 **s.** of his decease which he should....... *3004*
Lu 9:34 While he thus **s.**, there came a.......... *3004*
Lu 11:14 devil was gone out, the dumb **s.**; *2980*
Lu 11:27 as he **s.** these things, a certain.......... *3004*
Lu 11:37 And as he **s.**, a certain Pharisee.......... *2980*
Lu 12:16 he **s.** a parable unto them, saying,...... *2036*
Lu 13:6 He **s.** also this parable; **A certain**..... *3004*
Lu 14:3 **s.** unto the lawyers and Pharisees, ... *2036*
Lu 15:3 And he **s.** this parable unto them,....... *2036*
Lu 18:1 he **s.** a parable unto them to this........ *3004*
Lu 18:9 he **s.** this parable unto certain............ *2036*
Lu 19:11 he added and **s.** a parable, because..... *2036*
Lu 20:2 And **s.** unto him, saying, Tell us, ... *2036*
Lu 21:5 And as some **s.** of the temple, how *3004*
Lu 21:29 he **s.** to them a parable; **Behold**........ *2036*
Lu 22:47 And while he yet **s.**, behold a............ *2980*
Lu 22:60 while he yet **s.**, the cock crew........... *2980*

Lu 22:65 blasphemously s. they against him. *3004*
Lu 23:20 to release Jesus, s. again to them....... *4377*
Lu 24:6 remember how he s. unto you........... *2980*
Lu 24:36 And as they thus s., Jesus himself....... *2980*
Lu 24:44 **are the words which I s. unto** *2980*
Joh 1:15 This was he of whom I s., He that..... *2036*
Joh 2:21 he s. of the temple of his body. *3004*
Joh 6:71 He s. of Judas Iscariot the son of....... *3004*
Joh 7:13 Howbeit no man s. openly of him *2980*
Joh 7:39 (But this s. he of the Spirit, which...... *2036*
Joh 7:46 Never man s. like this man. *2980*
Joh 8:12 Then s. Jesus again unto them,.......... *2980*
Joh 8:20 words s. Jesus in the treasury,.......... *2980*
Joh 8:27 that he s. to them of the Father. *3004*
Joh 8:30 As he s. these words, many............... *2980*
Joh 9:22 These words s. his parents,............... *2036*
Joh 9:29 We know that God s. unto Moses: *2980*
Joh 10:6 This parable s. Jesus unto them: *2036*
Joh 10:6 what things they were which he s. *2980*
Joh 10:41 things that John s. of this man........... *2036*
Joh 11:13 Howbeit Jesus s. of his death: *2046*
Joh 11:51 And this s. he not of himself: *2036*
Joh 11:56 and s. among themselves, as they *3004*
Joh 12:29 others said, An angel s. to him. *2980*
Joh 12:36 These things s. Jesus, and................ *2980*
Joh 12:38 might be fulfilled, which he s., ... *2036*
Joh 12:41 he saw his glory, and s. of him. *2980*
Joh 13:22 another, doubting of whom he s......... *3004*
Joh 13:24 who it should be of whom he s.......... *3004*
Joh 13:28 knew for what intent he s. this *2036*
Joh 17:1 These words s. Jesus, and lifted *2980*
Joh 18:9 might be fulfilled, which he s., ... *2036*
Joh 18:16 and s. unto her that kept the door,..... *2036*
Joh 18:20 **I s. openly to the world; I ever**...... *2980*
Joh 18:32 he s., signifying what death he........... *2036*
Joh 21:19 s. he, signifying by what death he *2036*
Ac 1:16 David s. before concerning Judas,....... *4277*
Ac 2:31 s. of the resurrection of Christ, ... *2980*
Ac 4:1 And as they s. unto the people, ... *2980*
Ac 4:31 s. the word of God with boldness........ *2980*
Ac 6:10 wisdom and...spirit by which he s....... *2980*
Ac 7:6 And God s. on this wise, That his....... *2980*
Ac 7:38 angel which s. to him in the mount...... *2980*
Ac 8:6 unto those things which Philip s., ... *3004*
Ac 8:26 angel of the Lord s. unto Philip,......... *2980*
Ac 9:29 s. boldly in the name of the Lord *2980*
Ac 10:7 the angel which s. unto Cornelius *2980*
Ac 10:15 voice s. unto him again the second............
Ac 10:44 While Peter yet s. these words,.......... *2980*
Ac 11:20 s. unto the Grecians, preaching the..... *2980*
Ac 13:45 s. against those things which were....... *483*
Ac 14:1 and so s., that a great multitude *2980*
Ac 16:13 s. unto the women which resorted........ *2980*
Ac 16:32 s. unto him the word of the Lord, ... *2980*
Ac 18:9 s. the Lord to Paul in the night by *2036*
Ac 18:25 s. and taught diligently the things *2980*
Ac 19:6 and s. with tongues, and prophesied.... *2980*
Ac 19:8 s. boldly for the space of three *2980*
Ac 19:9 but s. evil of that way before the *2551*
Ac 20:38 of all for the words which he s., ... *2046*
Ac 21:40 he s. unto them in the Hebrew........... *4377*
Ac 22:2 he s. in the Hebrew tongue to them, .. *4377*
Ac 22:9 heard not the voice of him that s........ *2980*
Ac 26:24 And as he thus s. for himself, ... *626*
Ac 28:19 But when the Jews s. against it, ... *483*
Ac 28:21 shewed or s. any harm of thee. *2980*
Ac 28:25 Well s. the Holy Ghost by Esaias *2980*
1Co 13:11 When I was a child, I s. as a child,...... *2980*
1Co 14:5 I would that ye all s. with tongues,...... *2980*
2Co 7:14 as we s. all things to you in truth,...... *2980*
Ga 4:15 Where is then the blessedness ye s. of? ....
Heb 1:1 s. in time past unto the fathers.......... *2980*
Heb 4:4 For he s. in a certain place of the *2046*
Heb 7:14 of which tribe Moses s. nothing.......... *2980*
Heb 12:25 refused him that s. on earth, who....... *5537*
2Pe 1:21 men of God s. as they were moved..... *2980*
Re 1:12 And I turned to see the voice that s.... *2980*
Re 10:8 from heaven s. unto me again,............ *2980*
Re 13:11 like a lamb, and he s. as a dragon. *2980*

SPAKEST
Jg 13:11 the man that s. unto the woman? 1696
Jg 17:2 cursedst, and s. of also in mine ears,..... 559
1Sa 28:21 thy words which thou s. unto me. 1696
1Ki 8:24 thou s. also with thy mouth, and........ 1696
1Ki 8:26 thou s. unto thy servant David my...... 1696
1Ki 8:53 as thou s. by the hand of Moses thy... 1696
2Ch 6:15 s. with thy mouth, and hast fulfilled 1696
Ne 9:13 and s. with them from heaven, and...... 1696
Ps 89:19 Then thou s. in vision to thy holy....... 1696
Jer 48:27 for since thou s. of him, thou 1697

SPAN See also SPANNED.
Ex 28:16 a s. shall be the length thereof, ... 2239
Ex 28:16 a s. shall be the breadth thereof......... 2239
Ex 39:9 a s. was the length thereof, and a 2239
Ex 39:9 and a s. the breadth thereof, being..... 2239
1Sa 17:4 whose height was six cubits and a s..... 2239
Isa 40:12 and meted out heaven with the s.,...... 2239
La 2:20 fruit, and children of a s. long? 2949
Eze 43:13 thereof round about shall be a s. 2239

SPANNED
Isa 48:13 right hand hath s. the heavens:.......... 2946

SPARE See also SPARED; SPARETH; SPARING.
Ge 18:24 also destroy and not s. the place........ 5375
Ge 18:26 will s. all the place for their sakes. 5375
De 13:8 eye pity him, neither shalt thou s., ... 2550
De 29:20 The Lord will not s. him, but then....... 5545
1Sa 15:3 that they have, and s. them not;.......... 2550
Ne 13:22 s. me according to the greatness........ 2347
Job 6:10 let him not s.; for I have not............ 2550
Job 16:13 my reins asunder, and doth not s.; 2550
Job 20:13 Though he s. it, and forsake it not; 2550
Job 27:22 shall cast upon him, and not s.:.......... 2550
Job 30:10 me, and s. not to spit in my face. 2820
Ps 39:13 O s. me, that I may recover 8159
Ps 72:13 He shall s. the poor and needy, ... 2347
Pr 6:34 will not s. in the day of vengeance...... 2550
Pr 19:18 let not thy soul s. for his crying......... 5375
Isa 9:19 fire: no man shall s. his brother. 2550
Isa 13:18 their eye shall not s. children. 2347
Isa 30:14 broken in pieces; he shall not s.......... 2550
Isa 54:2 s. not, lengthen thy cords, and.......... 2820
Isa 58:1 Cry aloud, s. not, lift up thy voice....... 2820
Jer 13:14 I will not pity, nor s., nor have.......... 2347
Jer 21:7 he shall not s. them, neither have 2347
Jer 50:14 bow, shoot at her, s. no arrows:......... 2550
Jer 51:3 s. ye not her young men; destroy 2550
Eze 5:11 neither shall mine eye s., neither 2347
Eze 7:4 mine eye shall not s. thee, neither...... 2347
Eze 7:9 And mine eye shall not s., neither 2347
Eze 8:18 mine eye shall not s., neither will I..... 2347
Eze 9:5 let not your eye s., neither have ye.... 2347
Eze 9:10 mine eye shall not s., neither will I..... 2347
Eze 24:14 I will not go back, neither will I s.,..... 2347
Joe 2:17 S. thy people, O Lord, and give not ... 2347
Jon 4:11 should not I s. Nineveh, that great 2347
Hab 1:17 and not s. continually to slay the 2550
Mal 3:17 I will s. them, as a man spareth........ 2550
Lu 15:17 **have bread enough and to s.,** *4052*
Ro 11:21 take heed lest he also s. not thee....... *5339*
1Co 7:28 trouble in the flesh: but I s. you. *5339*
2Co 1:23 to s. you I came not as yet unto *5339*
2Co 13:2 that, if I come again, I will not s. *5339*

SPARED
1Sa 15:9 But Saul and the people s. Agag, ... 2550
1Sa 15:15 people s. the best of the sheep and 2550
1Sa 24:10 but mine eye s. thee; and I said,........ 2347
2Sa 12:4 he s. to take of his own flock and....... 2550
2Sa 21:7 But the king s. Mephibosheth, the...... 2550
2Ki 5:20 my master hath s. Naaman this.......... 2820
Ps 78:50 he s. not their soul from death, ... 2820
Eze 20:17 mine eye s. them from destroying....... 2347
Ro 8:32 He that s. not his own Son, but.......... *5339*
Ro 11:21 if God s. not the natural branches,....... *5339*
2Pe 2:4 if God s. not the angels that sinned, ... *5339*
2Pe 2:5 And s. not the old world, but saved.... *5339*

SPARETH
Pr 13:24 He that s. his rod hateth his son:........ 2820
Pr 17:27 that hath knowledge s. his words: 2820
Pr 21:26 but the righteous giveth and s. not. 2820
Mal 3:17 man s. his own son that serveth 2550

SPARING
Ac 20:29 wolves enter...not s. the flock. *5339*

SPARINGLY
2Co 9:6 which soweth s. shall reap also s.;....... *5340*

SPARK See also SPARKS.
Job 18:5 the s. of his fire shall not shine.......... 7632
Isa 1:31 as tow, and the maker of it as a s., ... 5213

SPARKLED
Eze 1:7 s. like the colour of burnished........... 5340

SPARKS
Job 5:7 trouble, as the s. fly upward. 1121,7565
Job 41:19 lamps, and s. of fire leap out. 3590
Isa 50:11 compass yourselves about with s........ 2131
Isa 50:11 and in the s. that ye have kindled....... 2131

SPARROW See also SPARROWS.
Ps 84:3 Yea, the s. hath found an house, ... 6833
Ps 102:7 am as a s. alone upon the house 6833

SPARROWS
Mt 10:29 **Are not two s. sold for a farthing?** *4765*
Mt 10:31 **ye are of more value than many s.** *4765*
Lu 12:6 **not five s. sold for two farthings,..** *4765*
Lu 12:7 **ye are of more value than many s..** *4765*

SPAT See also SPITTED.
Joh 9:6 he s. on the ground, and made *4429*

SPEAK See also SPAKE; SPEAKEST; SPEAKETH; SPEAKING; SPOKEN; UNSPEAKABLE.
Ge 18:27 taken upon me to s. unto the Lord, ... 1696
Ge 18:30 not the Lord be angry, and I will s..... 1696
Ge 18:31 taken upon me to s. unto the Lord: 1696
Ge 18:32 and I will s. yet but this once: 1696
Ge 24:33 mine errand. And he said, S. on. 1696
Ge 24:50 we cannot s. unto thee bad or good..... 1696
Ge 27:6 I heard thy father s. unto Esau thy..... 1696
Ge 31:24 Take heed that thou s. not to Jacob.... 1696
Ge 31:29 thou heed that thou s. not to Jacob..... 1696
Ge 32:4 Thus shall ye s. unto my lord Esau; 559
Ge 32:19 this manner shall ye s. unto Esau, ... 1696
Ge 37:4 could not s. peaceably unto him. 1696
Ge 44:16 say unto my lord? what shall we s.?.... 1696
Ge 44:18 thee, s. a word in my lord's ears, ... 1696
Ge 50:4 s.,...in the ears of Pharaoh, saying, ... 1696
Ex 4:14 brother? I know that he can s. well. ... 1696
Ex 4:15 And thou shalt s. unto him, and put.... 1696
Ex 5:23 came to Pharaoh to s. in thy name, ... 1696
Ex 6:11 s. unto Pharaoh king of Egypt, that 1696
Ex 6:29 s. thou unto Pharaoh king of Egypt..... 1696
Ex 7:2 shalt s. all that I command thee: 1696
Ex 7:2 thy brother shall s. unto Pharaoh,....... 1696
Ex 7:9 When Pharaoh shall s. unto you, ... 1696
Ex 11:2 S. now in the ears of the people, ... 1696
Ex 12:3 S. ye unto all the congregation of........ 1696
Ex 14:2 S. unto the children of Israel, that...... 1696
Ex 14:15 s. unto the children of Israel, that 1696
Ex 16:12 s. unto them, saying, At even ye 1696
Ex 19:6 shalt s. unto the children of Israel. 1696
Ex 19:9 may hear when I s. with thee, and 1696
Ex 20:19 said unto Moses, S. thou with us, ... 1696
Ex 20:19 let not God s. with us, lest we die. 1696
Ex 23:2 neither shalt thou s. in a cause to....... 6030
Ex 23:22 obey his voice, and do all that I s.;..... 1696
Ex 25:2 S. unto the children of Israel, that...... 1696
Ex 28:3 s. unto all that are wise hearted,........ 1696
Ex 29:42 will meet you, to s. there unto thee.... 1696
Ex 30:31 shalt s. unto the children of Israel, ... 1696
Ex 31:13 S. thou...unto the children of Israel, ... 1696
Ex 32:12 Wherefore should the Egyptians s., ... 559
Ex 34:34 in before the Lord to s. with him, ... 1696
Ex 34:35 until he went in to s. with him. 1696
Le 1:2 S. unto the children of Israel, and 1696
Le 4:2 S. unto the children of Israel,............... 1696
Le 6:25 S. unto Aaron and to his sons, ... 1696
Le 7:23, 29 S. unto the children of Israel............ 1696
Le 9:3 the children of Israel thou shalt s., ... 1696
Le 11:2 S. unto the children of Israel, ... 1696
Le 12:2 S. unto the children of Israel, ... 1696
Le 15:2 S. unto the children of Israel, and 1696
Le 16:2 S. unto Aaron thy brother, that he 1696
Le 17:2 S. unto Aaron, and unto his sons, ... 1696
Le 18:2 S. unto the children of Israel, and 1696
Le 19:2 S. unto all the congregation of the...... 1696
Le 21:1 S. unto the priests the sons of........... 559
Le 21:17 S. unto Aaron, saying, Whosoever...... 1696
Le 22:2 S. unto Aaron and to his sons, that 1696
Le 22:18 S. unto Aaron, and to his sons, and.... 1696
Le 23:2, 10,24,34 S. unto...children of Israel, ... 1696
Le 24:15 shalt s. unto the children of Israel, ... 1696
Le 25:2 S. unto the children of Israel, and 1696
Le 27:2 S. unto the children of Israel, and 1696
Nu 5:6, 12 S. unto the children of Israel,........ 1696
Nu 6:2 S. unto the children of Israel, and 1696
Nu 6:23 S. unto Aaron and unto his sons, ... 1696

Nu 7:89 Moses was gone...to **s.** with him,....... 1696
Nu 8:2 **S.** unto Aaron, and say unto him,....... 1696
Nu 9:10 **S.** unto the children of Israel,........... 1696
Nu 12:6 and will **s.** unto him in a dream......... 1696
Nu 12:8 With him will I **s.** mouth to mouth,..... 1696
Nu 12:8 afraid to **s.** against my servant........... 1696
Nu 14:15 have heard the fame of thee will **s.**,..... 559
Nu 15:2, 18,38 **S.** unto...children of Israel,....... 1696
Nu 16:24 **S.** unto the congregation, saying,....... 1696
Nu 16:37 **S.** unto Eleazar the son of Aaron......... 559
Nu 17:2 **S.** unto the children of Israel, and...... 1696
Nu 18:26 Thus **s.** unto the Levites, and say...... 1696
Nu 19:2 **S.** unto the children of Israel, that...... 1696
Nu 20:8 **s.** ye unto the rock before their eyes;. 1696
Nu 21:27 they that **s.** in proverbs say, Come..........
Nu 22:8 as the Lord shall **s.** unto me:............ 1696
Nu 22:35 I...**s.** unto thee, that thou shalt **s.**....... 1696
Nu 22:38 putteth in my mouth, that shall I **s.**...... 1696
Nu 23:5 unto Balak, and thus thou shalt **s.**........ 1696
Nu 23:12 to **s.** that which the Lord hath put...... 1696
Nu 24:13 what the Lord saith, that will I **s.**?...... 1696
Nu 27:7 daughters of Zelophehad **s.** right:........ 1696
Nu 27:8 shalt **s.** unto the children of Israel,..... 1696
Nu 33:51 **S.** unto the children of Israel, and...... 1696
Nu 35:10 **S.** unto the children of Israel, and...... 1696
De 3:26 **s.** no more unto me of this matter...... 1696
De 5:1 judgments which I **s.** in your ears....... 1696
De 5:27 **s.** thou unto us all that the Lord........ 1696
De 5:27 the Lord our God shall **s.** unto thee;... 1696
De 5:31 **s.** unto thee all the commandments,.... 1696
De 9:4 **S.** not thou in thine heart, after........... 559
De 11:2 for I **s.** not with your children which.........
De 18:18 **s.** unto them all that I...command....... 1696
De 18:19 words which he shall **s.** in my name,... 1696
De 18:20 presume to **s.** a word in my name,..... 1696
De 18:20 I have not commanded him to **s.**,....... 1696
De 18:20 shall **s.** in the name of other gods,...... 1696
De 20:2 approach and **s.** unto the people,........ 1696
De 20:5 the officers shall **s.** unto the people,.... 1696
De 20:8 the officers shall **s.** further unto the.... 1696
De 25:8 city shall call him, and **s.** unto him:..... 1696
De 26:5 shalt **s.** and say before the Lord......... 6030
De 27:14 And the Levites shall **s.**, and say........ 6030
De 31:28 I may **s.** these words in their ears,..... 1696
De 32:1 Give ear, O ye heavens, and I will **s.**;...1696
Jos 4:10 Lord commanded Joshua to **s.** unto..... 1696
Jos 20:2 **S.** to the children of Israel, saying,..... 1696
Jos 22:24 children might **s.** unto our children,...... 559
Jg 5:10 **S.**, ye that ride on white asses,......... 7878
Jg 6:39 me, and I will **s.** but this once:.......... 1696
Jg 9:2 **S.**, I pray you, in the ears of all the... 1696
Jg 19:3 to **s.** friendly unto her, and to bring.... 1696
Jg 19:30 it, take advice, and **s.** your minds....... 1696
Jg 21:13 to **s.** to the children of Benjamin........ 1696
1Sa 3:9 **S.**, Lord; for thy servant heareth....... 1696
1Sa 3:10 **S.**; for thy servant heareth................ 1696
1Sa 25:17 Belial, that a man cannot **s.** to him..... 1696
1Sa 25:24 handmaid,...**s.** in thine audience,......... 1696
2Sa 3:19 went also to **s.** in the ears of David.... 1696
2Sa 3:27 in the gate to **s.** with him quietly,....... 1696
2Sa 7:17 vision, so did Nathan **s.** unto David..... 1696
2Sa 13:13 Now...I pray thee, **s.** unto the king;... 1696
2Sa 14:3 and **s.** on this manner unto him......... 1696
2Sa 14:12 **s.** one word unto my lord the king...... 1696
2Sa 14:13 the king doth **s.** this thing as one....... 1696
2Sa 14:15 to **s.** of this thing unto my lord the..... 1696
2Sa 14:15 said, I will now **s.** unto the king;........ 1696
2Sa 14:18 said, Let my lord the king now **s.**........ 1696
2Sa 17:6 do after his saying? if not; **s.** thou...... 1696
2Sa 19:7 **s.** comfortably unto thy servants:....... 1696
2Sa 19:10 why **s.** ye not a word of bringing........ 2790
2Sa 19:11 **S.** unto the elders of Judah,............ 1696
2Sa 20:16 Come near...that I may **s.** with thee... 1696
2Sa 20:18 They were wont to **s.** in old time,...... 1696
1Ki 2:17 said, **S.**, I pray thee, unto Solomon...... 559
1Ki 2:18 I will **s.** for thee unto the king.......... 1696
1Ki 2:19 to **s.** unto him for Adonijah............... 1696
1Ki 12:7 and **s.** good words to them, then........ 1696
1Ki 12:10 Thus shalt thou **s.** unto this people....... 559
1Ki 12:23 **S.** unto Rehoboam, the son of............ 559
1Ki 21:19, 19 And thou shalt **s.** unto him,........... 1696
1Ki 22:13 of them, and **s.** that which is good...... 1696
1Ki 22:14 Lord saith unto me, that will I **s.**...... 1696
1Ki 22:24 Spirit...from me to **s.** unto thee?........ 1696
2Ki 18:19 **S.** ye now to Hezekiah, Thus saith....... 559
2Ki 18:26 **S.**,...to thy servants in the Syrian...... 1696
2Ki 18:27 and to thee, to **s.** these words?......... 1696
2Ki 19:10 Thus shall ye **s.** to Hezekiah king........ 559
1Ch 17:15 so did Nathan **s.** unto David............ 1696
1Ch 17:18 What can David **s.** more to thee for the.....
2Ch 10:7 them, and **s.** good words to them,...... 1696
2Ch 11:3 **S.** unto Rehoboam the son of............. 559
2Ch 18:12 one of theirs, and **s.** thou good......... 1696
2Ch 18:13 what my God saith, that will I **s.**........ 1696
2Ch 18:23 Spirit...from me to **s.** unto thee?........ 1696
2Ch 32:17 God of Israel, and to **s.** against him...... 559
Ne 13:24 could not **s.** in the Jews' language,...... 1696
Es 5:14 to morrow **s.** thou unto the king......... 559
Es 6:4 to **s.** unto the king to hang Mordecai.... 559
Job 7:11 will **s.** in the anguish of my spirit;....... 1696
Job 8:2 How long wilt thou **s.** these.............. 4448
Job 9:19 If I **s.** of strength, lo, he is strong: and.....
Job 9:35 Then would I **s.**, and not fear him;..... 1696
Job 10:1 I will **s.** in the bitterness of my soul.... 1696
Job 11:5 But oh that God would **s.**, and open.... 1696
Job 12:8 **s.** to the earth, and it shall teach........ 7878
Job 13:3 Surely I would **s.** to the Almighty,...... 1696
Job 13:7 Will ye **s.** wickedly for God? and......... 1696
Job 13:13 peace, let me alone, that I may **s.**,..... 1696
Job 13:22 or let me **s.**, and answer thou me...... 1696
Job 16:4 I also could **s.** as ye do: if your soul... 1696
Job 16:6 Though I **s.**, my grief is not.............. 1696
Job 18:2 mark, and afterwards we will **s.**........ 1696
Job 21:3 Suffer me that I may **s.**; and after...... 1696
Job 27:4 My lips shall not **s.** wickedness, nor.... 1696
Job 32:7 Days should **s.**, and multitude of........ 1696
Job 32:20 I will **s.**, that I may be refreshed:....... 1696
Job 33:31 me: hold thy peace, and I will **s.**........ 1696
Job 33:32 me: **s.**, for I desire to justify thee...... 1696
Job 34:33 I: therefore **s.** what thou knowest...... 1696
Job 36:2 I have yet to **s.** on God's behalf......... 4405
Job 37:20 Shall it be told him that I **s.**?........... 1696
Job 37:20 if a man **s.**,...he shall be swallowed...... 559
Job 41:3 will he **s.** soft words unto thee?......... 1696
Job 42:4 Hear, I beseech thee, and I will **s.**...... 1696
Ps 2:5 shall he **s.** unto them in his wrath,...... 1696
Ps 5:6 shalt destroy them that **s.** leasing:...... 1696
Ps 12:2 They **s.** vanity every one with his...... 1696
Ps 12:2 and with a double heart do they **s.**...... 1696
Ps 17:10 with their mouth they **s.** proudly......... 1696
Ps 28:3 which **s.** peace to their neighbours,..... 1696
Ps 29:9 doth every one **s.** of his glory............ 559
Ps 31:18 which **s.** grievous things proudly......... 1696
Ps 35:20 For they **s.** not peace: but they......... 1696
Ps 35:28 shall **s.** of thy righteousness and......... 1897
Ps 38:12 that seek my hurt **s.** mischievous....... 1696
Ps 40:5 if I would declare and **s.** of them,....... 1696
Ps 41:5 Mine enemies **s.** evil of me, When....... 559
Ps 45:1 I **s.** of the things which I have made..... 559
Ps 49:3 My mouth shall **s.** of wisdom; and...... 1696
Ps 50:7 Hear, O my people, and I will **s.**; O.... 1696
Ps 52:3 rather than to **s.** righteousness......... 1696
Ps 58:1 Do ye indeed **s.** righteousness, O......... 1696
Ps 59:12 cursing and lying which they **s.**.......... 5608
Ps 63:11 mouth of them that **s.** lies shall be...... 1696
Ps 69:12 that sit in the gate **s.** against me;....... 7878
Ps 71:10 For mine enemies **s.** against me;......... 559
Ps 73:8 They are corrupt, and **s.** wickedly...... 1696
Ps 73:8 oppression: they **s.** loftily.................. 1696
Ps 73:15 If I say, I will **s.** thus; behold, I......... 5608
Ps 75:5 on high: **s.** not with a stiff neck......... 1696
Ps 77:4 I am so troubled that I cannot **s.**........ 1696
Ps 85:8 will hear what God the Lord will **s.**...... 1696
Ps 85:8 he will **s.** peace unto his people,........ 1696
Ps 94:4 shall they utter and **s.** hard things?..... 1696
Ps 109:20 them that **s.** evil against my soul........ 1696
Ps 115:5 They have mouths, but they **s.** not:.... 1696
Ps 115:7 **s.** they through their throat............ 1897
Ps 119:23 Princes...did sit and **s.** against me:..... 1696
Ps 119:46 I will **s.** of thy testimonies also......... 1696
Ps 119:172 My tongue shall **s.** of thy word:......... 6030
Ps 120:7 but when I **s.**, they are for war......... 1696
Ps 127:5 but they shall **s.** with the enemies...... 1696
Ps 135:16 They have mouths, but they **s.** not;.... 1696
Ps 139:20 For they **s.** against thee wickedly,........ 559
Ps 145:5 I will **s.** of the glorious honour of....... 7878
Ps 145:6 men shall **s.** of the might of thy........... 559
Ps 145:11 They shall **s.** of the glory of thy.......... 559
Ps 145:21 My mouth shall **s.** the praise of the.... 1696
Pr 8:6 for I will **s.** of excellent things;.......... 1696
Pr 8:7 For my mouth shall **s.** truth; and........ 1897
Pr 23:9 **S.** not in the ears of a fool: for he...... 1696
Pr 23:16 when thy lips **s.** right things............. 1696
Ec 3:7 to keep silence, and a time to **s.**;....... 1696
Ca 7:9 lips of those that are asleep to **s.**....... 1680
Isa 8:10 **s.** the word, and it shall not stand:..... 1696
Isa 8:20 they **s.** not according to this word,....... 559
Isa 14:10 they shall **s.** and say unto thee,......... 6030
Isa 19:18 Egypt **s.** the language of Canaan,....... 1696
Isa 28:11 another tongue will he **s.** to this......... 1696
Isa 29:4 and shalt **s.** out of the ground, and.... 1696
Isa 30:10 **s.** unto us smooth things, prophesy..... 1696
Isa 32:4 the stammerers shall be ready to **s.**.... 1696
Isa 32:6 the vile person will **s.** villany, and........ 1696
Isa 36:11 **S.**, I pray thee, unto thy servants...... 1696
Isa 36:11 **s.** not to us in the Jews' language,...... 1696
Isa 36:12 and to thee to **s.** these words?......... 1696
Isa 37:10 Thus shall ye **s.** to Hezekiah king........ 559
Isa 40:2 **S.** ye comfortably to Jerusalem,......... 1696
Isa 41:1 them come near; then let them **s.**...... 1696
Isa 45:19 I the Lord **s.** righteousness, I............ 1696
Isa 50:4 know how to **s.** a word in season....... 5790
Isa 52:6 that day that I am he that doth **s.**....... 1696
Isa 56:3 hath joined himself to the Lord, **s.**,...... 559
Isa 59:4 they trust in vanity, and **s.** lies;......... 1696
Isa 63:1 I that **s.** in righteousness, mighty....... 1696
Jer 1:6 Ah, Lord God! behold, I cannot **s.**...... 1696
Jer 1:7 I command thee thou shalt **s.**............ 1696
Jer 1:17 **s.** unto them all that I command.......... 1696
Jer 5:5 great men, and will **s.** unto them;......... 1696
Jer 5:14 Because ye **s.** this word, behold, I..... 1696
Jer 6:10 To whom shall I **s.**, and give............ 1696
Jer 7:27 shalt **s.** all these words unto them;.... 1696
Jer 9:5 neighbour, and will not **s.** the truth:.... 1696
Jer 9:5 have taught their tongue to **s.** lies,..... 1696
Jer 9:22 **S.**, Thus saith the Lord, Even the...... 1696
Jer 10:5 as the palm tree, but **s.** not: they....... 1696
Jer 11:2 and **s.** unto the men of Judah, and...... 1696
Jer 12:6 though they **s.** fair words unto thee.... 1696
Jer 13:12 thou shalt **s.** unto them this word;...... 559
Jer 18:7, 9 I shall **s.** concerning a nation,.......... 1696
Jer 18:11 go to, **s.** to the men of Judah, and....... 559
Jer 18:20 before thee to **s.** good for them,........ 1696
Jer 20:9 him, nor **s.** any more in his name....... 1696
Jer 22:1 of Judah, and **s.** there this word,........ 1696
Jer 23:16 they **s.** a vision of their own heart,..... 1696
Jer 23:28 word, let him **s.** my word faithfully..... 1696
Jer 26:2 and **s.** unto all the cities of Judah,....... 1696
Jer 26:2 I command thee to **s.** unto them;....... 1696
Jer 26:8 commanded him to **s.** unto all the....... 1696
Jer 26:15 **s.** all these words in your ears.......... 1696
Jer 27:9 your sorcerers, which **s.** unto you,....... 559
Jer 27:14 of the prophets that **s.** unto you,......... 559
Jer 28:7 this word that I **s.** in thine ears,........ 1696
Jer 29:24 shalt thou also **s.** to Shemaiah the........ 559
Jer 32:4 shall **s.** with him mouth to mouth,...... 1696
Jer 34:2 Go and **s.** to Zedekiah king of............ 559
Jer 34:3 he shall **s.** with thee mouth to........... 1696
Jer 35:2 the Rechabites, and **s.** unto them,...... 1696
Jer 38:20 of the Lord, which I **s.** unto thee:...... 1696
Jer 39:16 Go and **s.** to Ebed-melech the............ 559
Eze 2:1 thy feet, and I will **s.** unto thee......... 1696
Eze 2:7 thou shalt **s.** my words unto them,..... 1696
Eze 3:1 and go **s.** unto the house of Israel...... 1696
Eze 3:4 and **s.** with my words unto them......... 1696
Eze 3:10 all my words that I shall **s.** unto......... 1696
Eze 3:11 and **s.** unto them, and tell them,........ 1696
Eze 3:27 when I **s.** with thee, I will open thy.... 1696
Eze 11:5 upon me, and said unto me, **S.**;........... 559
Eze 12:25 For I am the Lord: I will **s.**, and......... 1696
Eze 12:25 word that I shall **s.** shall come to....... 1696
Eze 14:4 Therefore **s.** unto them, and say......... 1696
Eze 17:2 and **s.** a parable unto the house of...... 4911
Eze 20:3 man, **s.** unto the elders of Israel,....... 1696
Eze 20:27 man, **s.** unto the house of Israel,........ 1696
Eze 20:49 of me, Doth he not **s.** parables?......... 4911
Eze 24:21 **S.** unto the house of Israel, Thus........ 559
Eze 24:27 and thou shalt **s.**, and be no more...... 1696
Eze 29:3 **S.**, and say, Thus saith the Lord........ 1696
Eze 31:2 **s.** unto Pharaoh king of Egypt,............ 559
Eze 32:21 strong among the mighty shall **s.**......... 1696

Eze 33:2 s. to the children of thy people, and.... 1696
Eze 33:8 dost not s. to warn the wicked from... 1696
Eze 33:10 man, s. unto the house of Israel; 559
Eze 33:10 ye s., saying, If our transgressions....... 559
Eze 33:24 those wastes of the land of Israel s., ... 559
Eze 33:30 s. one to another, every one to his..... 1696
Eze 37:18 of thy people shall s. unto thee, ... 559
Eze 39:17 S. unto every feathered fowl, and........ 559
Da 2:9 and corrupt words to s. before me, ... 560
Da 3:29 which s. any thing amiss against 560
Da 7:25 he shall s. great words against........... 4449
Da 10:11 understand the words that I s........... 1696
Da 10:19 said, Let my lord s.; for thou hast...... 1696
Da 11:27 and they shall s. lies at one table; 1696
Da 11:36 shall s. marvellous things against........ 1696
Ho 2:14 and s. comfortably unto her............... 1696
Hab 2:3 but at the end it shall s., and not 6315
Zep 3:13 shall not do iniquity, nor s. lies; 1696
Hag 2:2 S. now to Zerubbabel the son of.......... 559
Hag 2:21 S. to Zerubbabel, governor of 559
Zec 2:4 Run, s. to this young man, saying, ... 1696
Zec 6:12 And s. unto him, saying, Thus 559
Zec 7:3 to s. unto the priests which were 559
Zec 7:5 S. unto all the people of the land, ... 559
Zec 8:16 S. ye every man the truth to his........ 1696
Zec 9:10 he shall s. peace unto the heathen:..... 1696
Mt 8:8 s. the word only, and my servant......... *2036*
Mt 10:19 **thought how or what ye shall s.**..... *2980*
Mt 10:19 **that same hour what ye shall s.**.... *2980*
Mt 10:20 **For it is not ye that s., but the**..... *2980*
Mt 10:27 **in darkness, that s. ye in light:**..... *2036*
Mt 12:34 **can ye, being evil, s. good things?**.. *2980*
Mt 12:36 **every idle word that men shall s.**,.. *2980*
Mt 12:46 without, desiring to s. with him.......... *2980*
Mt 12:47 without, desiring to s. with thee......... *2980*
Mt 13:13 **Therefore s. I to them in parables:**. *2980*
Mt 15:31 when they saw the dumb to s., the *2980*
Mk 1:34 and suffered not the devils to s.,....... *2980*
Mk 2:7 doth this man thus s. blasphemies? *2980*
Mk 7:37 the deaf to hear, and the dumb to s.... *2980*
Mk 9:39 **that can lightly s. evil of me**......... *2551*
Mk 12:1 began to s. unto them by parables...... *3004*
Mk 13:11 **beforehand what ye shall s.**,......... *2980*
Mk 13:11 **given you in that hour, that s. ye:**.. *2980*
Mk 13:11 **it is not ye that s., but the Holy** ... *2980*
Mk 14:71 know not this man of whom ye s........ *3004*
Mk 16:17 **they shall s. with new tongues;**...... *2980*
Lu 1:19 and am sent to s. unto thee, and to.... *2980*
Lu 1:20 shalt be dumb, and not able to s., ... *2980*
Lu 1:22 out, he could not s. unto them:.......... *2980*
Lu 4:41 them suffered them not to s.............. *2980*
Lu 6:26 **when all men shall s. well of you!**. *2036*
Lu 7:15 was dead sat up, and began to s.. ...... *2980*
Lu 7:24 s. unto...people concerning John,........ *3004*
Lu 11:53 provoke him to s. of many things:........ *653*
Lu 12:10 **s. a word against the Son of man**,. *2046*
Lu 12:13 Master, s. to my brother, that he *2036*
Lu 20:9 he to s. to the people this parable; *3004*
Joh 1:37 the two disciples heard him s., and..... *2980*
Joh 1:40 One of the two which heard John s., ...
Joh 3:11 **s. that we do know, and testify**..... *2980*
Joh 4:26 **unto her, I that s. unto thee am he**.. *2980*
Joh 6:63 **the words that I s. unto you, they**. *2980*
Joh 7:17 **of God, or whether I s. of myself**. .. *2980*
Joh 8:26 **and I s. to the world those things**.. *3004*
Joh 8:28 **hath taught me, I s. these things**. . *2980*
Joh 8:38 **I s. that which I have seen with**.... *2980*
Joh 9:21 ask him: he shall s. for himself. *2980*
Joh 12:49 **I should say, and what I should s.**.. *2980*
Joh 12:50 **whatsoever I s. therefore, even as** .. *2980*
Joh 12:50 **the Father said unto me, so I s.**.... *2980*
Joh 13:18 **I s. not of you all: I know whom I**. *3004*
Joh 14:10 **the words that I s. unto you**.......... *2980*
Joh 14:10 **I s. not of myself: but the Father**.. *2980*
Joh 16:13 **for he shall not s. of himself; but**.. *2980*
Joh 16:13 **he shall hear, that shall he s.**: *2980*
Joh 16:25 **no more s. unto you in proverbs**,... *2980*
Joh 17:13 **these things I s. in the world**,........ *2980*
Ac 2:4 they began to s. with other tongues,.... *2980*
Ac 2:6 heard them s. in his own language...... *2980*
Ac 2:7 are not all these which s. Galilaeans? .. *2980*
Ac 2:11 we do hear them s. in our tongues...... *2980*
Ac 2:29 let me freely s....of the patriarch........ *2036*
Ac 4:17 they s. henceforth to no man in *2980*
Ac 4:18 commanded them not to s. at all *5350*
Ac 4:20 s. the things which we have seen....... *2980*
Ac 4:29 all boldness they may s. thy word, ... *2980*
Ac 5:20 Go, stand and s. in the temple to the.. *2980*
Ac 5:40 should not s. in the name of Jesus,..... *2980*
Ac 6:11 heard him s. blasphemous words *2980*
Ac 6:13 man ceaseth not to s. blasphemous *2980*
Ac 10:32 when he cometh, shall s. unto thee..... *2980*
Ac 10:46 they heard them s. with tongues, ... *2980*
Ac 11:15 as I began to s., the Holy Ghost fell... *2980*
Ac 14:9 the same heard Paul s.: who............ *2980*
Ac 18:9 **Be not afraid, but s., and hold**...... *2980*
Ac 18:26 began to s. boldly in the synagogue: ....
Ac 21:37 chief captain, May I s. unto thee?....... *2036*
Ac 21:37 Who said, Canst thou s. Greek?......... *1097*
Ac 21:39 suffer me to s. unto the people.......... *2980*
Ac 23:5 shalt not s. evil of the ruler of thy...... *2046*
Ac 24:10 had beckoned unto him to s., ... *3004*
Ac 26:1 Thou art permitted to s. for thyself. ... *3004*
Ac 26:25 but s. forth the words of truth and....... *669*
Ac 26:26 things, before whom...I s. freely: *2980*
Ac 28:20 you, to see you, and to s. with you: ... *4354*
Ro 3:5 taketh vengeance? (I s. as a man) *3004*
Ro 6:19 I s. after the manner of men *3004*
Ro 7:1 (for I s. to them that know the law,)... *2980*
Ro 11:13 For I s. to you Gentiles, inasmuch...... *3004*
Ro 15:18 I will not dare to s. of any of those *2980*
1Co 1:10 that ye all s. the same thing, and *3004*
1Co 2:6 we s. wisdom among them that........... *2980*
1Co 2:7 But we s. the wisdom of God in a....... *2980*
1Co 2:13 Which things also we s., not in the..... *2980*
1Co 3:1 not s. unto you as unto spiritual,........ *2980*
1Co 6:5 I s. to your shame. Is it so, that........ *3004*
1Co 7:6 I s. this by permission, and not of....... *3004*
1Co 7:12 But to the rest s. I, not the Lord:....... *3004*
1Co 7:35 And this I s. for your own profit; *3004*
1Co 10:15 I s. as to wise men; judge ye what I... *3004*
1Co 12:30 do all s. with tongues? do all............ *2980*
1Co 13:1 I s. with the tongues of men and of.... *2980*
1Co 14:6 except I shall s. to you either by........ *2980*
1Co 14:9 spoken? for ye shall s. into the air...... *2980*
1Co 14:18 I s. with tongues more than ye all: *2980*
1Co 14:19 I had rather s. five words with my *2980*
1Co 14:21 other lips will I s. unto this people;..... *2980*
1Co 14:23 one place, and all s. with tongues,...... *2980*
1Co 14:27 any man s. in an unknown tongue,...... *2980*
1Co 14:28 let him s. to himself, and to God........ *2980*
1Co 14:29 Let the prophets s. two or three,........ *2980*
1Co 14:34 it is not permitted unto them to s.;..... *2980*
1Co 14:35 is a shame for women to s. in the...... *2980*
1Co 14:39 and forbid not to s. with tongues........ *2980*
1Co 15:34 of God: I s. this to your shame.......... *3004*
2Co 2:17 in the sight of God s. we in Christ. *2980*
2Co 4:13 we also believe, and therefore s.;....... *2980*
2Co 6:13 (I s. as unto my children,) be ye also.. *3004*
2Co 7:3 I s. not this to condemn you: for I *3004*
2Co 8:8 I s. not by commandment, but by........ *3004*
2Co 11:17 That which I s., I s. it not after the.... *2980*
2Co 11:21 I s. as concerning reproach, as *3004*
2Co 11:21 bold, (I s. foolishly,) I am bold also..... *3004*
2Co 11:23 Christ? (I s. as a fool) I am more; *2980*
2Co 12:19 we s. before God in Christ: but we *2980*
Ga 3:15 I s. after the manner of men; *3004*
Eph 4:25 s. every man truth with his............... *2980*
Eph 5:12 a shame even to s. of those things *3004*
Eph 5:32 but I s. concerning Christ and the *3004*
Eph 6:20 that therein I may s. boldly, as I ought......
Eph 6:20 boldly, as I ought to s.................... *2980*
Php 1:14 are much more bold to s. the word..... *2980*
Php 4:11 Not that I s. in respect of want: *3004*
Col 4:3 to s. the mystery of Christ, for.......... *2980*
Col 4:4 make it manifest, as I ought to s........ *2980*
1Th 1:8 so that we need not to s. any thing. ... *2980*
1Th 2:2 bold in our God to s. unto you the *2980*
1Th 2:4 trust with the gospel, even so we s.; .. *2980*
1Th 2:16 Forbidding us to s. to the Gentiles *2980*
1Ti 2:7 s. the truth in Christ, and lie not;)...... *3004*
1Ti 5:14 to the adversary to s. reproachfully...........
Tit 2:1 s. thou the things which become *2980*
Tit 2:15 These things s., and exhort, and........ *2980*
Tit 3:2 To s. evil of no man, to be no *987*
Heb 2:5 the world to come, whereof we s....... *2980*
Heb 6:9 salvation, though we thus s.............. *2980*
Heb 9:5 we cannot now s. particularly. *3004*
Jas 1:19 to hear, slow to s., slow to wrath: *2980*
Jas 2:12 So s. ye, and so do, as they that *2980*
Jas 4:11 S. not evil one of another, ... *2635*
1Pe 2:12 they s. against you as evildoers, ... *2635*
1Pe 3:10 and his lips that they s. no guile:........ *2980*
1Pe 3:16 whereas they s. evil of you, as of....... *2635*
1Pe 4:11 If any man s., let him *2980*
1Pe 4:11 him s. as the oracles of God;............ *2980*
2Pe 2:10 are not afraid to s. evil of dignities....... *987*
2Pe 2:12 s. evil of the things that they.............. *987*
2Pe 2:18 when they s. great swelling words...... *5350*
1Jo 4:5 therefore s. they of the world, and..... *2980*
2Jo 12 s. face to face, that our joy may be.... *2980*
3Jo 14 thee, and we shall s. face to face. *2980*
Jude 8 dominion, and s. evil of dignities. *987*
Jude 10 these s. evil of those things which *987*
Re 2:24 **the depths of Satan, as they s.**;..... *3004*
Re 13:15 image of the beast should both s., ... *2980*

SPEAKER

Ps 140:11 not an evil s. be established......... 376,3956
Ac 14:12 because he was the chief s............... *3056*

SPEAKEST

1Sa 9:21 wherefore then s. thou so to me?........ 1696
2Sa 19:29 him, Why s. thou any more of thy...... 1696
2Ki 6:12 words...thou s. in thy bedchamber...... 1696
Job 2:10 Thou s. as one of the foolish women... 1696
Ps 50:20 sittest and s. against thy brother;....... 1696
Ps 51:4 mightest be justified when thou s., ... 1696
Isa 40:27 Why sayest thou, O Jacob, and s., O .. 1696
Jer 40:16 for thou s. falsely of Ishmael. 1696
Jer 43:2 unto Jeremiah, Thou s. falsely: 1696
Eze 3:18 nor s. to warn the wicked from his..... 1696
Zec 13:3 thou s. lies in the name of the Lord:.... 1696
Mt 13:10 Why s....unto them in parables?......... *2980*
Lu 12:41 Lord, s. thou this parable unto us,...... *3004*
Joh 16:29 unto him, Lo, now s. thou plainly, ... *2980*
Joh 16:29 thou plainly, and s. no proverb........... *3004*
Joh 19:10 unto him, S. thou not unto me? *2980*
Ac 17:19 new doctrine, whereof thou s., is?...... *2980*

SPEAKETH

Ge 45:12 is my mouth that s. unto you,........... 1696
Ex 33:11 to face, as a man s. unto his friend..... 1696
Nu 23:26 All that the Lord s., that I must do? ... 1696
De 18:22 When a prophet s. in the name of 1696
1Ki 20:5 said, Thus s. Ben-hadad, saying,.......... 559
Job 2:10 as one of the foolish women s.. 1696
Job 17:5 He that s. flattery to his friends, ... 5046
Job 33:14 God s. once, yea twice, yet man........ 1696
Ps 12:3 the tongue that s. proud things: 1696
Ps 15:2 and s. the truth in his heart. 1696
Ps 37:30 mouth of the righteous s. wisdom,...... 1897
Ps 41:6 if he come to see me, he s. vanity: 1696
Ps 144:8 Whose mouth s. vanity, and their....... 1696
Ps 144:11 children, whose mouth s. vanity, ... 1696
Pr 2:12 the man that s. froward things;.......... 1696
Pr 6:13 he s. with his feet, he teacheth.......... 4448
Pr 6:19 A false witness that s. lies, and he 6315
Pr 10:32 mouth of the wicked s. frowardness..........
Pr 12:17 He that s. truth showeth forth........... 6315
Pr 12:18 s. like the piercings of a sword:........... 981
Pr 14:25 but a deceitful witness s. lies............ 6315
Pr 16:13 and they love him that s. right........... 1696
Pr 19:5 he that s. lies shall not escape........... 6315
Pr 19:9 and he that s. lies shall perish. 6315
Pr 21:28 man that heareth s. constantly. 1696
Pr 26:25 When he s. fair, believe him not: 6963
Isa 9:17 and every mouth s. folly.................. 1696
Isa 32:7 words, even when the needy s. right. ..1696
Isa 33:15 righteously, and s. uprightly; 1696
Jer 9:8 as an arrow shot out; it s. deceit: 1696
Jer 9:8 one s. peaceably to his neighbour........ 1696
Jer 10:1 word which the Lord s. unto you, ... 1696
Jer 28:2 Thus s. the Lord of hosts, the God...... 559
Jer 29:25 Thus s. the Lord of hosts, the God...... 559
Jer 30:2 Thus s. the Lord God of Israel,........... 559
Eze 10:5 of the Almighty God when he s.......... 1696
Am 5:10 they abhor him that s. uprightly. 1696
Hag 1:2 Thus s. the Lord of hosts, saying, ... 559
Zec 6:12 Thus s. the Lord of hosts, saying, ... 559
Zec 7:9 Thus s. the Lord of hosts, saying, ... 559
Mt 10:20 **of your Father which s. in you**. *2980*
Mt 12:32 **whosoever s. a word against the**.... *2036*
Mt 12:32 **whosoever s. against the Holy**....... *2036*
Mt 12:34 **out...of the heart the mouth s.** *2980*
Lu 5:21 Who is this which s. blasphemies? *2980*
Lu 6:45 **of the heart his mouth s.**.............. *2980*
Joh 3:31 earth is earthly, and s. of the earth: ... *2980*
Joh 3:34 God hath sent s. the words of God:.... *2980*
Joh 7:18 **He that s. of himself seeketh his**... *2980*

Joh 7:26 But, lo, he **s.** boldly, and they say...... *2980*
Joh 8:44 **When he s. a lie, he s. of his own:** *2980*
Joh 19:12 himself a king **s.** against Caesar.......... *483*
Ac 2:25 For David **s.** concerning him, I *3004*
Ac 8:34 thee, of whom **s.** the prophet this? *3004*
Ro 10:6 which is of faith **s.** on this wise,......... *3004*
1Co 14:2 he that **s.** in an unknown tongue *2980*
1Co 14:2 **s.** not unto men, but unto God: for..... *2980*
1Co 14:2 in the spirit he **s.** mysteries. *2980*
1Co 14:3 he that prophesieth **s.** unto men........... *2980*
1Co 14:4 **s.** in an unknown tongue edifieth *2980*
1Co 14:5 than he that **s.** with tongues,............. *2980*
1Co 14:11 be unto him that **s.** a barbarian, ... *2980*
1Co 14:11 and he that **s.** shall be a barbarian *2980*
1Co 14:13 let him that **s.** in an unknown *2980*
1Ti 4:1 the Spirit **s.** expressly, that in the *3004*
Heb 11:4 and by it he being dead yet **s.**. *2980*
Heb 12:5 which **s.** unto you as unto children,..... *1256*
Heb 12:24 that **s.** better things than that of *2980*
Heb 12:25 See that ye refuse not him that **s.**. *2980*
Heb 12:25 away from him that **s.** from heaven:.........
Jas 4:11 He that **s.** evil of his brother, and *2635*
Jas 4:11 **s.** evil of the law, and judgeth the *2635*
Jude 16 mouth **s.** great swelling words, ... *2980*

SPEAKING See also SPEAKINGS.
Ge 24:15 to pass, before he had done **s.**,.......... 1696
Ge 24:45 before I had done **s.** in mine heart,..... 1696
Ex 34:33 till Moses had done **s.** with them,....... 1696
Nu 7:89 heard the voice of one **s.** unto him 1696
Nu 16:31 made an end of **s.** all these words, ... 1696
De 4:33 God **s.** out of the midst of the fire,..... 1696
De 5:26 God **s.** out of the midst of the fire,..... 1696
De 11:19 **s.** of them when thou sittest in.......... 1696
De 20:9 made an end of **s.** unto the people,..... 1696
De 32:45 Moses made an end of **s.** all these........ 1696
Jg 15:17 when he had made an end of **s.**, ... 1696
Ru 1:18 with her, then she left **s.** unto her...... 1696
1Sa 18:1 had made an end of **s.** unto Saul, ... 1696
1Sa 24:16 an end of **s.** these words unto Saul,..... 1696
2Sa 13:36 soon as he had made an end of **s.**, ... 1696
2Ch 36:12 the prophet **s.** from the mouth of the........
Es 10:3 people, and **s.** peace to all his seed..... 1696
Job 1:16, 17,18 While he was yet **s.**, there 1696
Job 4:2 who can withhold himself from **s.**? 4405
Job 32:15 answered no more: they left off **s.**....... 4405
Ps 34:13 evil, and thy lips from **s.** guile. 1696
Ps 58:3 as soon as they be born, **s.** lies. 1696
Isa 58:9 forth of the finger, and **s.** vanity;........ 1696
Isa 58:13 pleasure, nor **s.** thine own words: 1696
Isa 59:13 **s.** oppression and revolt, conceiving.... 1696
Isa 65:24 while they are yet **s.**, I will hear. 1696
Jer 7:13 rising up early and **s.**, but ye heard 1696
Jer 25:3 rising early and **s.**; but ye have.......... 1696
Jer 26:7 heard Jeremiah **s.** these words in 1696
Jer 26:8 Jeremiah had made an end of **s.** all 1696
Jer 35:14 unto you, rising early and **s.**; but........ 1696
Jer 38:4 people, in **s.** such words unto them: ... 1696
Jer 38:27 So they left off **s.** with him; for the 2790
Jer 43:1 had made an end of **s.** unto all the...... 1696
Eze 43:6 I heard him **s.** unto me out of the 1696
Da 7:8 man, and a mouth **s.** great things. 4449
Da 8:13 Then I heard one saint **s.**, and........... 1696
Da 8:18 Now as he was **s.** with me, I was in... 1696
Da 9:20 And whiles I was **s.**, and praying,....... 1696
Da 9:21 whiles I was **s.** in prayer, even the..... 1696
Mt 6:7 **shall be heard for their much s.**.... *4180*
Lu 5:4 Now when he had left **s.**, he said *2980*
Ac 1:3 **s.** of the things pertaining to the *3004*
Ac 7:44 **s.** unto Moses, that he should *2980*
Ac 13:43 who, **s.** to them, persuaded them....... *4354*
Ac 14:3 abode thy **s.** boldly in the Lord, ...
Ac 20:30 **s.** perverse things, to draw away *2980*
Ac 26:14 I heard a voice **s.** unto me, and *2980*
1Co 12:3 that no man **s.** by the Spirit of God *2980*
1Co 14:6 I come unto you **s.** with tongues, ... *2980*
2Co 13:3 ye seek a proof of Christ **s.** in me,..... *2980*
Eph 4:15 **s.** the truth in love, may grow up *226*
Eph 4:31 and evil **s.**, be put away from you, ... *988*
Eph 5:19 **S.** to yourselves in psalms and........... *2980*
1Ti 4:2 **S.** lies in hypocrisy; having their *5573*
1Ti 5:13 **s.** things which they ought not. *2980*
1Pe 4:4 same excess of riot, **s.** evil of you: *987*
2Pe 2:16 the dumb ass **s.** with man's voice *5350*
2Pe 3:16 epistles, **s.** in them of these things; *2980*
Re 13:5 him a mouth **s.** great things and......... *2980*

SPEAKINGS
1Pe 2:1 and envies, and all evil **s.**,................. *2636*

SPEAR See also SPEARMEN; SPEAR'S; SPEARS.
Jos 8:18 Stretch out the **s.** that is in thy.......... 3591
Jos 8:18 Joshua stretched out the **s.** that 3591
Jos 8:26 wherewith he stretched out the **s.**, ... 3591
Jg 5:8 a shield or **s.** seen among forty.......... 7420
1Sa 13:22 neither sword nor **s.** found in the 2595
1Sa 17:7 staff of his **s.** was like a weaver's....... 2595
1Sa 17:45 to me with a sword, and with a **s.**, ... 2595
1Sa 17:47 Lord saveth not with sword and **s.** 2595
1Sa 21:8 here under thine hand **s.** or sword? 2595
1Sa 22:6 having his **s.** in his hand, and all........ 2595
1Sa 26:7 his **s.** stuck in the ground at his......... 2595
1Sa 26:8 with the **s.** even to the earth at......... 2595
1Sa 26:11 now the **s.** that is at his bolster, ... 2595
1Sa 26:12 So David took the **s.** and the cruse..... 2595
1Sa 26:16 now see where the king's **s.** is, and.... 2595
1Sa 26:22 and said, Behold the king's **s.**! and...... 2595
2Sa 1:6 behold, Saul leaned upon his **s.**; 2595
2Sa 2:23 end of the **s.** smote him under the...... 2595
2Sa 2:23 that the **s.** came out behind him;........ 2595
2Sa 21:16 **s.** weighed three hundred shekels....... 7013
2Sa 21:19 of whose **s.** was like a weaver's......... 2595
2Sa 23:7 with iron and the staff of a **s.**; and...... 2595
2Sa 23:8 lift up his **s.** against eight hundred, ...
2Sa 23:18 up his **s.** against three hundred, ... 2595
2Sa 23:21 the Egyptian had a **s.** in his hand;....... 2595
2Sa 23:21 the **s.** out of the Egyptian's hand,....... 2595
2Sa 23:21 hand, and slew him with his own **s.**. ... 2595
1Ch 11:11 up his **s.** against three hundred 2595
1Ch 11:20 up his **s.** against three hundred, ... 2595
1Ch 11:23 was a **s.** like a weaver's beam; and..... 2595
1Ch 11:23 the **s.** out of the Egyptian's hand,....... 2595
1Ch 11:23 hand, and slew him with his own **s.**. ... 2595
1Ch 12:24 of Judah that bare shield and **s.**.......... 7420
1Ch 12:34 them with shield and **s.** thirty and....... 2595
1Ch 20:5 whose **s.** staff was like a weaver's...... 2595
2Ch 25:5 that could handle **s.** and shield. 7420
Job 39:23 the glittering **s.** and the shield. 2595
Job 41:26 the **s.**, the dart, nor the habergeon..... 2595
Job 41:29 he laugheth at the shaking of a **s.**....... 3591
Ps 35:3 Draw out also the **s.**, and stop the 2595
Ps 46:9 bow, and cutteth the **s.** in sunder;...... 2595
Jer 6:23 They shall lay hold on bow and **s.**;...... 3591
Na 3:3 bright sword and the glittering **s.**......... 2595
Hab 3:11 at the shining of thy glittering **s.**. 2595
Joh 19:34 soldiers with a **s.** pierced his side,...... *3057*

SPEARMEN
Ps 68:30 Rebuke the company of **s.**, the 7070
Ac 23:23 **s.** two hundred, at the third hour *1187*

SPEAR'S
1Sa 17:7 his **s.** head weighed six hundred......... 2595

SPEARS
1Sa 13:19 Hebrews make them swords or **s.**....... 2595
2Ki 11:10 give king David's **s.** and shields,......... 2595
2Ch 11:12 several city he put shields and **s.**,....... 7420
2Ch 14:8 of men that bare targets and **s.**, ... 7420
2Ch 23:9 to the captains of hundreds **s.**,........... 2595
2Ch 26:14 all the host shields, and **s.**, and.......... 7420
Ne 4:13 their swords, their **s.**, and their 7420
Ne 4:16 half of them held both the **s.**, and....... 7420
Ne 4:21 half of them held the **s.** from the........ 7420
Job 41:7 irons? or his head with fish **s.**? 6767
Ps 57:4 whose teeth are **s.** and arrows,........... 2595
Isa 2:4 and their **s.** into pruninghooks:........... 2595
Jer 46:4 furbish the **s.**, and put on the 7420
Eze 39:9 and the handstaves, and the **s.**, and.... 7420
Joe 3:10 and your pruninghooks into **s.**............ 7420
Mic 4:3 and their **s.** into pruninghooks:........... 2595

SPECIAL
De 7:6 to be a **s.** people unto himself,........... 5459
Ac 19:11 God wrought **s.** miracles *3756,3858,5177*

SPECIALLY See also ESPECIALLY.
De 4:10 **S.** the day that thou stoodest before.........
Ac 25:26 and **s.** before thee, O king Agrippa, ... *3122*
1Ti 4:10 of all men, **s.** of those that believe....... *3122*
1Ti 5:8 and **s.** for those of his own house,...... *3122*
Tit 1:10 **s.** they of the circumcision: *3122*
Phm 16 servant, a brother beloved, **s.** to me,.. *3122*

SPECKLED
Ge 30:32 thence all the **s.** and spotted cattle, ... 5348
Ge 30:32 the spotted and **s.** among the goats: ... 5348
Ge 30:33 not **s.** and spotted among the goats, ... 5348
Ge 30:35 she goats that were **s.** and spotted, ... 5348
Ge 30:39 cattle ringstraked, **s.**, and spotted....... 5348
Ge 31:8 said thus, The **s.** shall be thy wages; .. 5348
Ge 31:8 wages; then all the cattle bare **s.**......... 5348
Ge 31:10 were ringstraked, **s.**, and grisled. 5348
Ge 31:12 are ringstraked, **s.**, and grisled: 5348
Jer 12:9 heritage is unto me as a **s.** bird, ... 6641
Zec 1:8 there red horses, **s.**, and white.......... 8320

SPECTACLE
1Co 4:9 we are made a **s.** unto the world,....... *2302*

SPED
Jg 5:30 Have they not **s.**? have they not 4672

SPEECH See also SPEECHES; SPEECHLESS.
Ge 4:23 of Lamech, hearken unto my **s.**........... 565
Ge 11:1 was of one language, and of one **s.**..... 1697
Ge 11:7 not understand one another's **s.**. 8193
Ex 4:10 but I am slow of **s.**, and of a slow 6310
De 22:14 give occasions of **s.** against her, ... 1697
De 22:17 given occasions of **s.** against her, ... 1697
De 32:2 my **s.** shall distil as the dew, as the 565
2Sa 14:20 To fetch about this form of **s.** hath 1697
2Sa 19:11 **s.** of all Israel is come to the king, ... 1697
1Ki 3:10 **s.** pleased the Lord, that Solomon 1697
2Ch 32:18 with a loud voice in the Jews' **s.**,......... 3066
Ne 13:24 spake half in the **s.** of Ashdod, and..... 3066
Job 12:20 removeth away the **s.** of the trusty,..... 8193
Job 13:17 Hear diligently my **s.**, and my........... 4405
Job 21:2 Hear diligently my **s.**, and let this be... 4405
Job 24:25 and make my **s.** nothing worth? 4405
Job 29:22 and my **s.** dropped upon them. 4405
Job 37:19 we cannot order our **s.** by reason of ....
Ps 17:6 thine ear to me, and hear my **s.**. 565
Ps 19:2 Day unto day uttereth **s.**, and night...... 562
Ps 19:3 There is no **s.** nor language, where...... 562
Pr 7:21 With her much fair **s.** she caused 3948
Pr 17:7 Excellent **s.** becometh not a fool: 8193
Ca 4:3 of scarlet, and thy **s.** is comely: 4057
Isa 28:23 my voice; hearken, and hear my **s.**. 565
Isa 29:4 thy **s.** shall be low out of the dust,....... 565
Isa 29:4 thy **s.** shall whisper out of the dust. 565
Isa 32:9 daughters; give ear unto my **s.**............ 565
Isa 33:19 a people of a deeper **s.** than thou....... 8193
Jer 31:23 use this **s.** in the land of Judah,.......... 1697
Eze 1:24 the voice of **s.**, as the noise of an 1999
Eze 3:5 not sent to a people of a strange **s.** 8193
Eze 3:6 to many a people of a strange **s.** and... 8193
Hab 3:2 O Lord, I have heard thy **s.**, and 8088
Mt 26:73 them; for thy **s.** bewrayeth thee......... *2981*
Mk 7:32 and had an impediment in his **s.**; *3424*
Mk 14:70 and thy **s.** agreeth thereto. *2981*
Joh 8:43 **Why do ye not understand my s.?**.. *2981*
Ac 14:11 saying in the **s.** of Lycaonia,.............. *3072*
Ac 20:7 continued his **s.** until midnight........... *3056*
1Co 2:1 with excellency of **s.** or of wisdom,..... *3056*
1Co 2:4 my **s.** and my preaching was not *3056*
1Co 4:19 not the **s.** of them which are puffed *3056*
2Co 3:12 hope, we use great plainness of **s.**...........
2Co 7:4 Great is my boldness of **s.** toward ....
2Co 10:10 is weak, and his **s.** contemptible.......... *3056*
2Co 11:6 But though I be rude in **s.**, yet not..... *3056*
Col 4:6 Let your **s.** be always with grace, ... *3056*
Tit 2:8 Sound **s.**, that cannot be condemned; .. *3056*

SPEECHES
Nu 12:8 apparently, and not in dark **s.**; 2420
Job 6:26 and the **s.** of one that is desperate, ... 561
Job 15:3 **s.** wherewith he can do no good? 4405
Job 32:14 will I answer him with your **s.**............. 561
Job 33:1 Job, I pray thee, hear my **s.**, and 4405
Ro 16:18 fair **s.** deceive the hearts of the *2129*
Jude 15 hard **s.** which ungodly sinners have..........

SPEECHLESS
Mt 22:12 **wedding garment? And he was s.**... *5392*
Lu 1:22 unto them, and remained **s.**............... *2974*
Ac 9:7 which journeyed with him stood **s.**,..... *1769*

SPEED See also SPED.
Ge 24:12 send me good **s.** this day, and shew ... 7136
1Sa 20:38 the lad, Make **s.**, haste, stay not........ 4120
2Sa 15:14 make **s.** to depart, lest he overtake 4116
1Ki 12:18 Rehoboam made **s.** to get him up to........ 553
2Ch 10:18 Rehoboam made **s.** to get him up to..... 553
Ezr 6:12 a decree; let it be done with **s.**. 629

Isa 5:19 Let him make **s.**, and hasten his 4116
Isa 5:26 they shall come with **s.** swiftly: 4120
Ac 17:15 for to come to him with all **s.**, *5613,5033*
2Jo 10 house, neither bid him God **s.** *5463*
2Jo 11 For he that biddeth him God **s.** is *5463*

SPEEDILY
Ge 44:11 they **s.** took down every man his 4116
1Sa 27:1 I should **s.** escape into the land of 4422
2Sa 17:16 the wilderness, but **s.** pass over; 5674
2Ch 35:13 divided them **s.** among all the people.
Ezr 6:13 the king had sent, so they did **s.**. 629
Ezr 7:17 thou mayest buy **s.** with this money 629
Ezr 7:21 shall require of you, it be done **s.**, 629
Ezr 7:26 judgment be executed **s.** upon him, 629
Es 2:9 and he **s.** gave her her things for 926
Ps 31:2 thine ear to me; deliver me **s.**: 4120
Ps 69:17 for I am in trouble: hear me **s.**. 4118
Ps 79:8 thy tender mercies **s.** prevent us: 4118
Ps 102:2 in the day when I call answer me **s.** 4118
Ps 143:7 Hear me **s.**, O Lord: my spirit 4118
Ec 8:11 an evil work is not executed **s.**, 4120
Isa 58:8 thine health shall spring forth **s.** 4120
Joe 3:4 **s.** will I return your recompence 4120
Zec 8:21 us go **s.** to pray before the Lord, 1980
Lu 18:8 **that he will avenge them s.** *1722,5034*

SPEEDY
Zep 1:18 a **s.** riddance of all them that dwell 926

SPEND See also SPENDEST; SPENDETH; SPENT.
De 32:23 I will **s.** mine arrows upon them. 3615
Job 21:13 they **s.** their days in wealth, 1086,3615
Job 36:11 shall **s.** their days in prosperity, 3615
Ps 90:9 we **s.** our years as a tale that is 3615
Isa 55:2 do ye **s.** money for that which is 8254
Ac 20:16 he would not **s.** the time in Asia: *5551*
2Co 12:15 I will very gladly **s.** and be spent *1159*

SPENDEST
Lu 10:35 **whatsoever thou s. more, when I** *4325*

SPENDETH
Pr 21:20 wise; but a foolish man **s.** it up. 1104
Pr 29:3 with harlots **s.** his substance. 6
Ec 6:12 vain life which he **s.** as a shadow? 6213

SPENT
Ge 21:15 And the water was **s.** in the bottle, 3615
Ge 47:18 my lord, how that our money is **s.**; 8552
Le 26:20 your strength shall be **s.** in vain: 8552
Jg 19:11 were by Jebus, the day was far **s.**; 7286
1Sa 9:7 for the bread is **s.** in our vessels, 235
Job 7:6 shuttle, and are **s.** without hope. 3615
Ps 31:10 For my life is **s.** with grief, and 3615
Isa 49:4 I have **s.** my strength for nought, 3615
Jer 37:21 all the bread in the city were **s.**. 8552
Mk 5:26 had **s.** all that she had, and was *1159*
Mk 6:35 when the day was now far **s.**, his
Lu 8:43 which had **s.** all her living upon *4321*
Lu 15:14 **when he had s. all, there arose a** *1159*
Lu 24:29 evening, and the day is far **s.**. *2827*
Ac 17:21 there **s.** their time in nothing else, *2119*
Ac 18:23 after he had **s.** some time there, *4160*
Ac 27:9 Now when much time was **s.**, and *1230*
Ro 13:12 The night is far **s.**, the day is at *4298*
2Co 12:15 gladly spend and be **s.** for you; *1550*

SPEWING See also SPUE.
Hab 2:16 shameful **s.** shall be on thy glory. 7022

SPICE See also SPICED; SPICES.
Ex 35:28 **s.**, and oil for the light, and for 1314
1Ki 10:15 of the traffick of the **s.** merchants, 7402
2Ch 9:9 there any such **s.** as the queen of 1314
Ca 5:1 gathered my myrrh with my **s.**; 1313
Eze 24:10 consume the flesh, and **s.** it well, 7543

SPICED
Ca 8:2 cause thee to drink of **s.** wine of 7544

SPICE-MERCHANTS See SPICE and MERCHANTS.

SPICERY
Ge 37:25 bearing **s.** and balm and myrrh, 5219

SPICES
Ge 43:11 **s.**, and myrrh, nuts, and almonds: 5219
Ex 25:6 **s.** for anointing oil, and for sweet 1314
Ex 30:23 also unto thee principal **s.**, of pure 1314
Ex 30:34 Take unto thee sweet **s.**, stacte, 5561
Ex 30:34 sweet **s.** with pure frankincense: 5561
Ex 35:8 **s.** for anointing oil, and for the 1314
Ex 37:29 and the pure incense of sweet **s.**, 5561
1Ki 10:2 with camels that bare **s.**, and very 1314
1Ki 10:10 of gold, and of **s.** very great store, 1314
1Ki 10:10 no more such abundance of **s.** as 1314
1Ki 10:25 garments, and armour, and **s.**, and 1314
2Ki 20:13 gold, and the **s.**, and the precious 1314
1Ch 9:29 and the frankincense, and the **s.** 1314
1Ch 9:30 priests made the ointment of the **s.**. 1314
2Ch 9:1 and camels that bare **s.**, and gold in 1314
2Ch 9:9 of gold, and of **s.** great abundance, 1314
2Ch 9:24 raiment, harness, and **s.**, horses, 1314
2Ch 16:14 sweet odours and divers kinds of **s.**
2Ch 32:27 precious stones, and for **s.**, and 1314
Ca 4:10 smell of thine ointments than all **s.**! 1314
Ca 4:14 and aloes, with all the chief **s.**: 1314
Ca 4:16 that the **s.** thereof may flow out. 1314
Ca 5:13 His cheeks are as a bed of **s.**, as 1314
Ca 6:2 into his garden, to the beds of **s.**. 1314
Ca 8:14 hart upon the mountains of **s.**. 1314
Isa 39:2 and the gold, and the **s.**, and the 1314
Eze 27:22 in thy fairs with chief of all **s.**, 1314
Mk 16:1 and Salome, had bought sweet **s.**, *759*
Lu 23:56 and prepared **s.** and ointments; *759*
Lu 24:1 bringing the **s.** which they had *759*
Joh 19:40 wound it in linen clothes with the **s.**, *759*

SPIDER See also SPIDER'S.
Pr 30:28 The **s.** taketh hold with her hands, 8079

SPIDER'S
Job 8:14 and whose trust shall be a **s.** web. 5908
Isa 59:5 eggs, and weave the **s.** web: 5908

SPIED See also ESPIED.
Ex 2:11 And he **s.** an Egyptian smiting an 7200
Jos 6:22 men that had **s.** out the country, 7270
2Ki 9:17 he **s.** the company of Jehu as he 7200
2Ki 13:21 that, behold, they **s.** a band of men; 7200
2Ki 23:16 he **s.** the sepulchres that were there 7200
2Ki 23:24 abominations that were **s.** in the 7200

SPIES
Ge 42:9 and said unto them, Ye are **s.**; 7270
Ge 42:11 true men, thy servants are no **s.**. 7270
Ge 42:14 spake unto you, saying, Ye are **s.** 7270
Ge 42:16 the life of Pharaoh surely ye are **s.** **7270**
Ge 42:30 and took us for s. of the country. 7270
Ge 42:31 We are true men; we are no **s.** 7270
Ge 42:34 I know that ye are no **s.**, but that 7270
Nu 21:1 Israel came by the way of the **s.**; 871
Jos 6:23 young men that were **s.** went in, 7270
Jg 1:24 the **s.** saw a man come forth out of 8104
1Sa 26:4 David therefore sent out **s.**, and 7270
2Sa 15:10 Absalom sent **s.** throughout all the 7270
Lu 20:20 watched him, and sent forth **s.**, *1455*
Heb 11:31 when she had received the **s.** with *2685*

SPIKENARD
Ca 1:12 my **s.** sendeth forth the smell 5373
Ca 4:13 pleasant fruits; camphire, with **s.**, 5373
Ca 4:14 **S.** and saffron; calamus and 5373
Mk 14:3 box of ointment of **s.** very *3487,4101*
Joh 12:3 Mary a pound of ointment of **s.** *3487,4101*

SPILLED See also SPILT.
Ge 38:9 that he **s.** it on the ground, lest 7843
Mk 2:22 **the bottles, and the wine is s.,** *1632*
Lu 5:37 **will burst the bottles, and be s.,** *1632*

SPILT See also SPILLED.
2Sa 14:14 and are as water **s.** on the ground, 5064

SPIN See also SPUN.
Ex 35:25 that were wise hearted did **s.** 2901
Mt 6:28 **they toil not, neither do they s.** *3514*
Lu 12:27 **grow: they toil not, they s. not;** *3514*

SPINDLE
Pr 31:19 She layeth her hands to the **s.**, 3601

SPIRIT See also SPIRITS.
Ge 1:2 **S.** of God moved upon the face of 7307
Ge 6:3 My **s.** shall not always strive with 7307
Ge 41:8 morning that his **s.** was troubled; 7307
Ge 41:38 is, a man in whom the **S.** of God is? 7307
Ge 45:27 the **s.** of Jacob their father revived: 7307
Ex 6:9 not unto Moses for anguish of **s.**, 7307
Ex 28:3 I have filled with the **s.** of wisdom, 7307
Ex 31:3 I have filled him with the **s.** of God, 7307
Ex 35:21 one whom his **s.** made willing, 7307
Ex 35:31 hath filled him with the **s.** of God, 7307
Le 20:27 or woman that hath a familiar **s.**, 178
Nu 5:14, 14 **s.** of jealousy came upon him, 7307
Nu 5:30 the **s.** of jealousy cometh upon him, 7307
Nu 11:17 take of the **s.** which is upon thee, 7307
Nu 11:25 took of the **s.** that was upon him, 7307
Nu 11:25 when the **s.** rested upon them, they 7307
Nu 11:26 and the **s.** rested upon them; and 7307
Nu 11:29 Lord would put his **s.** upon them! 7307
Nu 14:24 he had another **s.** with him, and 7307
Nu 24:2 and the **s.** of God came upon him. 7307
Nu 27:18 of Nun, a man in whom is the **s.**, 7307
De 2:30 the Lord thy God hardened his **s.**, 7307
De 34:9 of Nun was full of the **s.** of wisdom; 7307
Jos 5:1 was there **s.** in them any more, 7307
Jg 3:10 the **S.** of the Lord came upon him, 7307
Jg 6:34 **S.** of the Lord came upon Gideon, 7307
Jg 9:23 Then God sent an evil **s.** between 7307
Jg 11:29 Then the **S.** of the Lord came upon 7307
Jg 13:25 **S.** of the Lord began to move him 7307
Jg 14:6 **S.** of the Lord came mightily upon 7307
Jg 14:19 the **S.** of the Lord came upon him, 7307
Jg 15:14 the **S.** of the Lord came mightily upon 7307
Jg 15:19 his **s.** came again, and he revived: 7307
1Sa 1:15 I am a woman of a sorrowful **s.** 7307
1Sa 10:6 **S.** of the Lord will come upon thee, 7307
1Sa 10:10 and the **S.** of God came upon him, 7307
1Sa 11:6 And the **S.** of God came upon Saul 7307
1Sa 16:13 **S.** of the Lord came upon David 7307
1Sa 16:14 **S.** of the Lord departed from Saul, 7307
1Sa 16:14 evil **s.** from the Lord troubled him. 7307
1Sa 16:15 an evil **s.** from God troubleth thee. 7307
1Sa 16:16 the evil **s.** from God is upon thee, 7307
1Sa 16:23 the evil **s.** from God was upon Saul, 7307
1Sa 16:23 and the evil **s.** departed from him. 7307
1Sa 18:10 evil **s.** from God came upon Saul, 7307
1Sa 19:9 evil **s.** from the Lord was upon Saul, 7307
1Sa 19:20 **S.** of God was upon the messengers 7307
1Sa 19:23 the **S.** of God was upon him also, 7307
1Sa 28:7 a woman that hath a familiar **s.**, 178
1Sa 28:7 is a woman that hath a familiar **s.**, 178
1Sa 28:8 divine unto me by the familiar **s.**, 178
1Sa 30:12 eaten, his **s.** came again to him: 7307
2Sa 23:2 The **S.** of the Lord spake by me, 7307
1Ki 10:5 Lord; there was no more **s.** in her. 7307
1Ki 18:12 the **S.** of the Lord shall carry thee 7307
1Ki 21:5 Why is thy **s.** so sad, that thou 7307
1Ki 22:21 And there came forth a **s.**, and stood 7307
1Ki 22:22 I will be a lying **s.** in the mouth of 7307
1Ki 22:23 hath put a lying **s.** in the mouth of 7307
1Ki 22:24 Which way went the **S.** of the Lord 7307
2Ki 2:9 double portion of thy **s.** be upon me 7307
2Ki 2:15 The **s.** of Elijah doth rest on Elisha 7307
2Ki 2:16 **S.** of the Lord hath taken him up, 7307
1Ch 5:26 up the **s.** of Pul king of Assyria, 7307
1Ch 5:26 and the **s.** of Tilgath-pilneser king 7307
1Ch 10:13 of one that had a familiar **s.**, 178
1Ch 12:18 Then the **s.** came upon Amasai, 7307
1Ch 28:12 pattern of all that he had by the **s.**, 7307
2Ch 9:4 Lord; there was no more **s.** in her. 7307
2Ch 15:1 the **S.** of God came upon Azariah 7307
2Ch 18:20 Then there came out a **s.**, and stood 7307
2Ch 18:21 be a lying **s.** in the mouth of all his 7307
2Ch 18:22 hath put a lying **s.** in the mouth of 7307
2Ch 18:23 Which way went the **S.** of the Lord 7307
2Ch 20:14 came the **S.** of the Lord in the midst 7307
2Ch 21:16 Jehoram the **s.** of the Philistines, 7307
2Ch 24:20 the **S.** of God came upon Zechariah 7307
2Ch 33:6 and dealt with a familiar **s.**, and 178
2Ch 36:22 up the **s.** of Cyrus king of Persia, 7307
Ezr 1:1 up the **s.** of Cyrus king of Persia, 7307
Ezr 1:5 all them whose **s.** God had raised, 7307
Ne 9:20 gavest also thy good **s.** to instruct 7307
Ne 9:30 testifiedst against them by thy **s.** in 7307
Job 4:15 Then a **s.** passed before my face; 7307
Job 6:4 poison whereof drinketh up my **s.** 7307
Job 7:11 I will speak in the anguish of my **s.**; 7307
Job 10:12 visitation hath preserved my **s.**. 7307
Job 15:13 that turnest thy **s.** against God, 7307
Job 20:3 and the **s.** of my understanding 7307
Job 21:4 why should not my **s.** be troubled? 7307
Job 26:4 and whose **s.** came from thee? 5397
Job 26:13 By his **s.** he hath garnished the 7307
Job 27:3 and the **s.** of God is in my nostrils; 7307
Job 32:8 But there is a **s.** in man: and the 7307
Job 32:18 the **s.** within me constraineth me. 7307
Job 33:4 The **S.** of God hath made me, and 7307

Job 34:14 if he gather unto himself his s. and..... 7307
Ps 31:5 Into thine hand I commit my s.:........ 7307
Ps 32:2 and in whose s. there is no guile........ 7307
Ps 34:18 saveth such as be of a contrite s......... 7307
Ps 51:10 and renew a right s. within me. 7307
Ps 51:11 and take not thy holy s. from me. 7307
Ps 51:12 and uphold me with thy free s.......... 7307
Ps 51:17 sacrifices of God are a broken s......... 7307
Ps 76:12 He shall cut off the s. of princes: 7307
Ps 77:3 and my s. was overwhelmed. 7307
Ps 77:6 and my s. made diligent search. 7307
Ps 78:8 whose s. was not stedfast with God.... 7307
Ps 104:30 Thou sendest forth thy s., they are.... 7307
Ps 106:33 Because they provoked his s., so....... 7307
Ps 139:7 Whither shall I go from thy s.? or...... 7307
Ps 142:3 When my s. was overwhelmed........... 7307
Ps 143:4 is my s. overwhelmed within me; 7307
Ps 143:7 speedily, O Lord: my s. faileth: 7307
Ps 143:10 thou art my God: thy s. is good;........ 7307
Pr 1:23 I will pour out my s. unto you, I........ 7307
Pr 11:13 he that is of a faithful s. concealeth..... 7307
Pr 14:29 he that is hasty of s. exalteth folly...... 7307
Pr 15:4 perverseness...is a breach in the s.. ... 7307
Pr 15:13 sorrow of the heart the s. is broken. .. 7307
Pr 16:18 and an haughty s. before a fall. 7307
Pr 16:19 be of an humble s. with the lowly,....... 7307
Pr 16:32 and he that ruleth his s. than he 7307
Pr 17:22 but a broken s. drieth the bones. 7307
Pr 17:27 understanding is of an excellent s.. 7307
Pr 18:14 The s. of a man will sustain his.......... 7307
Pr 18:14 but a wounded s. who can bear? 7307
Pr 20:27 The s. of man is the candle of the...... 5397
Pr 25:28 that hath no rule over his own s. 7307
Pr 29:23 shall uphold the humble in s............ 7307
Ec 1:14 all is vanity and vexation of s............. 7307
Ec 1:17 that this also is vexation of s.. 7307
Ec 2:11 all was vanity and vexation of s.,........ 7307
Ec 2:17 all is vanity and vexation of s............ 7307
Ec 2:26 also is vanity and vexation of s.. 7307
Ec 3:21 the s. of man that goeth upward, ... 7307
Ec 3:21 s. of the beast that goeth downward... 7307
Ec 4:4 is also vanity and vexation of s.. 7307
Ec 4:6 full with travail and vexation of s.. 7307
Ec 4:16 also is vanity and vexation of s.. 7307
Ec 6:9 is also vanity and vexation of s.. 7307
Ec 7:8 and the patient in s. is better 7307
Ec 7:8 is better than the proud in s............. 7307
Ec 7:9 Be not hasty in thy s. to be angry:..... 7307
Ec 8:8 power over the s. to retain the s.; 7307
Ec 10:4 If the s. of the ruler rise up against.... 7307
Ec 11:5 knowest not...the way of the s., ... 7307
Ec 12:7 and the s. shall return unto God......... 7307
Isa 4:4 midst thereof by the s. of judgment, ... 7307
Isa 4:4 judgment, and by the s. of burning. 7307
Isa 11:2 s. of the Lord shall rest upon him, ... 7307
Isa 11:2 the s. of wisdom and understanding, ... 7307
Isa 11:2 the s. of counsel and might, ... 7307
Isa 11:2 the s. of knowledge and of the fear..... 7307
Isa 19:3 s. of Egypt shall fail in the midst........ 7307
Isa 19:14 Lord hath mingled a perverse s.......... 7307
Isa 26:9 with my s. within me will I seek 7307
Isa 28:6 a s. of judgment to him that sitteth..... 7307
Isa 29:4 be, as of one that hath a familiar s., ... 178
Isa 29:10 out upon you the s. of deep sleep, ... 7307
Isa 29:24 They also that erred in s. shall 7307
Isa 30:1 with a covering, but not of my s., ... 7307
Isa 31:3 and their horses flesh, and not s........ 7307
Isa 32:15 Until the s. be poured upon us from... 7307
Isa 34:16 and his s. it hath gathered them......... 7307
Isa 38:16 all these things is the life of my s....... 7307
Isa 40:7 the s. of the Lord bloweth upon it: 7307
Isa 40:13 hath directed the S. of the Lord,........ 7307
Isa 42:1 I have put my s. upon him: he shall.... 7307
Isa 42:5 and s. to them that walk therein: 7307
Isa 44:3 I will pour my s. upon thy seed, ... 7307
Isa 48:16 Lord God, and his S., hath sent me.... 7307
Isa 54:6 a woman forsaken and grieved in s., ... 7307
Isa 57:15 that is of a contrite and humble s., ... 7307
Isa 57:15 to revive the s. of the humble and...... 7307
Isa 57:16 for the s. should fail before me, and.... 7307
Isa 59:19 S. of the Lord...lift up a standard....... 7307
Isa 59:21 My s. that is upon thee, and my......... 7307
Isa 61:1 The S. of the Lord God is upon me;... 7307
Isa 61:3 of praise for the s. of heaviness; 7307
Isa 63:10 rebelled, and vexed his holy S.: 7307
Isa 63:11 he that put his holy S. within him? 7307
Isa 63:14 S. of the Lord caused him to rest: 7307
Isa 65:14 and shall howl for vexation of s......... 7307
Isa 66:2 him that is poor and of a contrite s.,... 7307
Jer 51:11 up the s. of the kings of the Medes:... 7307
Eze 1:12 whither the s. was to go, they went; .. 7307
Eze 1:20 Whithersoever the s. was to go 7307
Eze 1:20 went, thither was their s. to go; 7307
Eze 1:20, 21 s. of the living creature was in 7307
Eze 2:2 s. entered into me when he spake...... 7307
Eze 3:12 Then the s. took me up, and I heard .. 7307
Eze 3:14 So the s. lifted me up, and took me... 7307
Eze 3:14 in bitterness, in the heat of my s.; 7307
Eze 3:24 Then the s. entered into me, and....... 7307
Eze 8:3 s. lifted me up between the earth....... 7307
Eze 10:17 the s. of the living creature was in 7307
Eze 11:1 Moreover the s. lifted me up, and...... 7307
Eze 11:5 the S. of the Lord fell upon me, ... 7307
Eze 11:19 and I will put a new s. within you;...... 7307
Eze 11:24 Afterwards the s. took me up, and..... 7307
Eze 11:24 brought me...by the S. of God into...... 7307
Eze 13:3 prophets, that follow their own s.,...... 7307
Eze 18:31 make you a new heart and a new s..... 7307
Eze 21:7 be feeble, and every s. shall faint, ... 7307
Eze 36:26 and a new s. will I put within you:...... 7307
Eze 36:27 And I will put my s. within you,......... 7307
Eze 37:1 carried me out in the s. of the Lord,... 7307
Eze 37:14 And shall put my s. in you, and ye 7307
Eze 39:29 poured out my s. upon the house of.... 7307
Eze 43:5 So the s. took me up, and brought 7307
Da 2:1 wherewith his s. was troubled, ... 7307
Da 2:3 s. was troubled to know the dream..... 7307
Da 4:8 in whom is the s. of the holy gods:..... 7308
Da 4:9 the s. of the holy gods is in thee,....... 7308
Da 4:18 for the s. of the holy gods is in thee. .. 7308
Da 5:11 in whom is the s. of the holy gods;..... 7308
Da 5:12 Forasmuch as an excellent s., and...... 7308
Da 5:14 that the s. of the gods is in thee. 7308
Da 6:3 because an excellent s. was in him; 7308
Da 7:15 I Daniel was grieved in my s. in the ... 7308
Ho 4:12 s. of whoredoms hath caused them...... 7307
Ho 5:4 s. of whoredoms is in the midst of...... 7307
Joe 2:28 I will pour out my s. upon all flesh; 7307
Joe 2:29 in those days will I pour out my s.. 7307
Mic 2:7 is the s. of the Lord straitened?......... 7307
Mic 2:11 If a man walking in the s. and........... 7307
Mic 3:8 full of power by the s. of the Lord, ... 7307
Hag 1:14 stirred up the s. of Zerubbabel the 7307
Hag 1:14 s. of Joshua the son of Josedech,........ 7307
Hag 1:14 s. of all the remnant of the people; 7307
Hag 2:5 so my s. remaineth among you: 7307
Zec 4:6 might, nor by power, but by my s.,.... 7307
Zec 6:8 quieted my s. in the north country...... 7307
Zec 7:12 the Lord of hosts hath sent in his s. ... 7307
Zec 12:1 formeth the s. of man within him........ 7307
Zec 12:10 the s. of grace and of supplications: ... 7307
Zec 13:2 prophets and the unclean s. to pass... 7307
Mal 2:15 Yet had he the residue of the s......... 7307
Mal 2:15 Therefore take heed to your s........... 7307
Mal 2:16 therefore take heed to your s.,......... 7307
Mt 3:16 he saw the S. of God descending....... 4151
Mt 4:1 led up of the s. into the wilderness..... 4151
Mt 5:3 **Blessed are the poor in s.: for**....... 4151
Mt 10:20 **S. of your Father which speaketh** ..4151
Mt 12:18 I will put my s. upon him, and he....... 4151
Mt 12:28 **I cast out devils by the S. of God,**. 4151
Mt 12:43 **When the unclean s. is gone out**... 4151
Mt 14:26 were troubled, saying, It is a s.; 5326
Mt 22:43 **doth David in s. call him Lord,**..... 4151
Mt 26:41 **the s. indeed is willing, but the**..... 4151
Mk 1:10 and the S. like a dove descending....... 4151
Mk 1:12 immediately the s. driveth him........... 4151
Mk 1:23 a man with an unclean s.; and he 4151
Mk 1:26 when the unclean s. had torn him, ... 4151
Mk 2:8 Jesus perceived in his s. that they...... 4151
Mk 3:30 they said, He hath an unclean s.. 4151
Mk 5:2 tombs a man with an unclean s., ... 4151
Mk 5:8 **out of the man, thou unclean s.**.... 4151
Mk 6:49 they supposed it had been a s., ... 5326
Mk 7:25 daughter had an unclean s.,............... 4151
Mk 8:12 And he sighed deeply in his s., and..... 4151
Mk 9:17 thee my son, which hath a dumb s.; ... 4151
Mk 9:20 him, straightway the s. tare him;........ 4151
Mk 9:25 he rebuked the foul s., saying unto...... 4151
Mk 9:25 **Thou dumb and deaf s., I charge**... 4151
Mk 9:26 And the s. cried, and rent him sore, ...
Mk 14:38 **The s. truly is ready, but the flesh** .4151
Lu 1:17 him in the s. and power of Elias,........ 4151
Lu 1:47 And my s. hath rejoiced in God my..... 4151
Lu 1:80 child grew, and waxed strong in s., ... 4151
Lu 2:27 came by the S. into the temple:......... 4151
Lu 2:40 child grew, and waxed strong in s., ... 4151
Lu 4:1 led by the S. into the wilderness,....... 4151
Lu 4:14 in the power of the S. into Galilee:..... 4151
Lu 4:18 **The S. of the Lord is upon me,** 4151
Lu 4:33 which had a s. of an unclean devil,...... 4151
Lu 8:29 unclean s. to come out of the man...... 4151
Lu 8:55 her s. came again, and she arose 4151
Lu 9:39 And, lo, a s. taketh him, and he......... 4151
Lu 9:42 And Jesus rebuked the unclean s., ... 4151
Lu 9:55 **not what manner of s. ye are of**.... 4151
Lu 10:21 In that hour Jesus rejoiced in s., ... 4151
Lu 11:13 **Father give the Holy S. to them**.... 4151
Lu 11:24 **When the unclean s. is gone out** ... 4151
Lu 13:11 woman which had a s. of infirmity...... 4151
Lu 23:46 **into thy hands I commend my s.**... 4151
Lu 24:37 supposed that they had seen a s.. 4151
Lu 24:39 **for a s. hath not flesh and bones,**.. 4151
Joh 1:32 I saw the S. descending from............ 4151
Joh 1:33 thou shalt see the S. descending, ... 4151
Joh 3:5 **be born of water and of the S.,** 4151
Joh 3:6 **that which is born of the S. is s.**... 4151
Joh 3:8 **is every one that is born of the S.**. .4151
Joh 3:34 God giveth not the S. by measure....... 4151
Joh 4:23 **shall worship the Father in s. and.** 4151
Joh 4:24 **God is a S.: and they that worship** .4151
Joh 4:24 **him must worship him in s. and**.... 4151
Joh 6:63 **It is the s. that quickeneth; the**..... 4151
Joh 6:63 **you, they are s., and they are life.** .4151
Joh 7:39 (But this spake he of the S., which..... 4151
Joh 11:33 her, he groaned in the s., and was..... 4151
Joh 13:21 thus said, he was troubled in s., ... 4151
Joh 14:17 **Even the S. of truth; whom the**..... 4151
Joh 15:26 **the S. of truth, which proceedeth**.. 4151
Joh 16:13 **when he, the S. of truth, is come,**. 4151
Ac 2:4 as the S. gave them utterance........... 4151
Ac 2:17 God, I will pour out of my S. upon..... 4151
Ac 2:18 pour out in those days of my S.;........ 4151
Ac 5:9 to tempt the S. of the Lord? 4151
Ac 6:10 the wisdom and the s. by which he..... 4151
Ac 7:59 saying, Lord Jesus, receive my s........ 4151
Ac 8:29 Then the S. said unto Philip, Go 4151
Ac 8:39 S. of the Lord caught away Philip,...... 4151
Ac 10:19 S. said unto him, Behold, three 4151
Ac 11:12 And the S. bade me go with them, ... 4151
Ac 11:28 and signified by the s. that there........ 4151
Ac 16:7 but the S. suffered them not............. 4151
Ac 16:16 with a s. of divination met us,........... 4151
Ac 16:18 grieved, turned and said to the s.,....... 4151
Ac 17:16 his s. was stirred in him, when he...... 4151
Ac 18:5 Paul was pressed in the s., and 4151
Ac 18:25 being fervent in the s., he spake........ 4151
Ac 19:15 And the evil s. answered and said, ... 4151
Ac 19:16 the man in whom the evil s. was........ 4151
Ac 19:21 Paul purposed in the s., when he 4151
Ac 20:22 go bound in the s. unto Jerusalem, ... 4151
Ac 21:4 who said to Paul through the S., ... 4151
Ac 23:8 resurrection, neither angel, nor s. 4151
Ac 23:9 but if a s. or an angel hath spoken...... 4151
Ro 1:4 according to the s. of holiness, by 4151
Ro 1:9 I serve with my s. in the gospel of...... 4151
Ro 2:29 in the s., and not in the letter; 4151
Ro 7:6 we should serve in newness of s.,........ 4151
Ro 8:1 not after the flesh, but after the S...... 4151
Ro 8:2 the law of the S. of life in Christ........ 4151
Ro 8:4 not after the flesh, but after the S...... 4151
Ro 8:5 after the S. the things of the S.......... 4151
Ro 8:9 are not in the flesh, but in the S.,....... 4151
Ro 8:9 be that the S. of God dwell in you...... 4151
Ro 8:9 any man have not the S. of Christ, ... 4151
Ro 8:10 S. is life because of righteousness. 4151
Ro 8:11 the S. of him that raised up Jesus 4151
Ro 8:11 by his S. that dwelleth in you. 4151
Ro 8:13 if ye through the S. do mortify the..... 4151
Ro 8:14 many as are led by the S. of God,...... 4151
Ro 8:15 have not received the s. of bondage.... 4151
Ro 8:15 have received the S. of adoption, ... 4151
Ro 8:16 S. itself beareth witness with our 4151
Ro 8:16 beareth witness with our s., that........ 4151
Ro 8:23 which have the firstfruits of the S.,..... 4151
Ro 8:26 Likewise the S. also helpeth our 4151
Ro 8:26 S. itself maketh intercession for us..... 4151
Ro 8:27 knoweth what is the mind of the S., ... 4151
Ro 11:8 hath given them the s. of slumber, ... 4151
Ro 12:11 fervent in s.; serving the Lord;.......... 4151
Ro 15:19 by the power of the S. of God;.......... 4151

Ro 15:30 and for the love of the **S.**, that ye...... *4151*
1Co 2:4 but in demonstration of the **S.** and...... *4151*
1Co 2:10 revealed them unto us by his **S.**:........ *4151*
1Co 2:10 for the **S.** searcheth all things, yea, ... *4151*
1Co 2:11 save the **s.** of man which is in him? *4151*
1Co 2:11 knoweth no man, but the **S.** of God.... *4151*
1Co 2:12 received, not the **s.** of the world, ... *4151*
1Co 2:12 world, but the **s.** which is of God; *4151*
1Co 2:14 not the things of the **S.** of God: *4151*
1Co 3:16 that the **S.** of God dwelleth in you? *4151*
1Co 4:21 in love, and in the **s.** of meekness?..... *4151*
1Co 5:3 absent in body, but present in **s.**,....... *4151*
1Co 5:4 my **s.**, with the power of our Lord *4151*
1Co 5:5 that the **s.** may be saved in the day.... *4151*
1Co 6:11 Jesus, and by the **S.** of our God......... *4151*
1Co 6:17 is joined unto the Lord is one **s.** *4151*
1Co 6:20 and in your **s.**, which are God's. *4151*
1Co 7:34 may be holy both in body and in **s.** *4151*
1Co 7:40 also that I have the **S.** of God. *4151*
1Co 12:3 no man speaking by the **S.** of God....... *4151*
1Co 12:4 diversities of gifts, but the same **S.**. ... *4151*
1Co 12:7 of the **S.** is given to every man to...... *4151*
1Co 12:8 one is given by the **S.** the word of..... *4151*
1Co 12:8 word of knowledge by the same **S.**;.... *4151*
1Co 12:9 To another faith by the same **S.**;........ *4151*
1Co 12:9 the gifts of healing by the same **S.**; *4151*
1Co 12:11 that one and the selfsame **S.**, ... *4151*
1Co 12:13 by one **S.** are we all baptized into *4151*
1Co 12:13 been all made to drink into one **S.**...... *4151*
1Co 14:2 in the **s.** he speaketh mysteries. *4151*
1Co 14:14 an unknown tongue, my **s.** prayeth, ... *4151*
1Co 14:15 I will pray with the **s.**, and I will........ *4151*
1Co 14:15 I will sing with the **s.**, and I will........ *4151*
1Co 14:16 when thou shalt bless with the **S.**,....... *4151*
1Co 15:45 Adam was made a quickening **s.**.......... *4151*
1Co 16:18 For they have refreshed my **s.** and...... *4151*
2Co 1:22 and given the earnest of the **S.** in *4151*
2Co 2:13 I had no rest in my **s.**, because I *4151*
2Co 3:3 but with the **S.** of the living God; *4151*
2Co 3:6 not of the letter, but of the **s.**: for....... *4151*
2Co 3:6 letter killeth, but the **s.** giveth life. *4151*
2Co 3:8 the ministration of the **s.** be rather *4151*
2Co 3:17 Now the Lord is that **S.**: and where ... *4151*
2Co 3:17 where the **S.** of the Lord is, there is .. *4151*
2Co 3:18 glory, even as by the **S.** of the Lord... *4151*
2Co 4:13 We having the same **s.** of faith,.......... *4151*
2Co 5:5 given unto us the earnest of the **S.**..... *4151*
2Co 7:1 all filthiness of the flesh and **s.**,.......... *4151*
2Co 7:13 because his **s.** was refreshed by you... *4151*
2Co 11:4 or if ye receive another **s.**, which ye... *4151*
2Co 12:18 walked we not in the same **s.**?........... *4151*
Ga 3:2 Received ye the **S.** by the works of.... *4151*
Ga 3:3 having begun in the **S.**, are ye now *4151*
Ga 3:5 that ministereth to you the **S.**, and..... *4151*
Ga 3:14 might receive the promise of the **S.**..... *4151*
Ga 4:6 sent forth the **S.** of his Son into......... *4151*
Ga 4:29 him that was born after the **S.**,.......... *4151*
Ga 5:5 we through the **S.** wait for the hope ... *4151*
Ga 5:16 Walk in the **S.**, and ye shall not *4151*
Ga 5:17 For the flesh lusteth against the **S.**,.... *4151*
Ga 5:17 and the **S.** against the flesh: and *4151*
Ga 5:18 But if ye be led of the **S.**, ye are not.. *4151*
Ga 5:22 fruit of the **S.** is love, joy, peace,....... *4151*
Ga 5:25 If we live in the **S.**, let us also walk ... *4151*
Ga 5:25 let us also walk in the **S.**.................. *4151*
Ga 6:1 such an one in the **s.** of meekness;..... *4151*
Ga 6:8 soweth to the **S.** shall of the **S.** reap .. *4151*
Ga 6:18 Lord Jesus Christ be with your **s.**....... *4151*
Eph 1:13 sealed with that holy **S.** of promise,.... *4151*
Eph 1:17 may give unto you the **s.** of wisdom.... *4151*
Eph 2:2 the **s.** that now worketh in the *4151*
Eph 2:18 access by one **S.** unto the Father......... *4151*
Eph 2:22 habitation of God through the **S.**.. ...... *4151*
Eph 3:5 apostles and prophets by the **S.**; *4151*
Eph 3:16 strengthened with might by his **S.** *4151*
Eph 4:3 to keep the unity of the **S.** in the....... *4151*
Eph 4:4 There is one body, and one **S.**, ... *4151*
Eph 4:23 be renewed in the **s.** of your mind;..... *4151*
Eph 4:30 And grieve not the holy **S.** of God,..... *4151*
Eph 5:9 (For the fruit of the **S.** is in all *4151*
Eph 5:18 excess; but be filled with the **S.**;......... *4151*
Eph 6:17 the sword of the **S.**, which is the *4151*
Eph 6:18 prayer and supplication in the **S.**, ... *4151*
Php 1:19 supply of the **S.** of Jesus Christ, ... *4151*
Php 1:27 that ye stand fast in one **s.**, with......... *4151*
Php 2:1 of love, if any fellowship of the **S.**, ... *4151*
Php 3:3 which worship God in the **s.**, and *4151*
Col 1:8 unto us your love in the **S.**. *4151*
Col 2:5 yet am I with you in the **s.**, joying...... *4151*
1Th 4:8 hath also given unto us his holy **S.**. *4151*
1Th 5:19 Quench not the **S.**............................ *4151*
1Th 5:23 your whole **s.** and soul and body be.... *4151*
2Th 2:2 neither by **s.**, nor by word, nor by *4151*
2Th 2:8 consume with the **s.** of his mouth, ... *4151*
2Th 2:13 through sanctification of the **S.**........... *4151*
1Ti 3:16 justified in the **S.**, seen of angels,....... *4151*
1Ti 4:1 Now the **S.** speaketh expressly, ... *4151*
1Ti 4:12 in charity, in **s.**, in faith, in purity....... *4151*
2Ti 1:7 hath not given us the **s.** of fear;......... *4151*
2Ti 4:22 Lord Jesus Christ be with thy **s.**. *4151*
Phm 25 Lord Jesus Christ be with your **s.**........ *4151*
Heb 4:12 the dividing asunder of soul and **s.**,..... *4151*
Heb 9:14 who through the eternal **s.** offered....... *4151*
Heb 10:29 done despite unto the **S.** of grace? *4151*
Jas 2:26 as the body without the **s.** is dead, ... *4151*
Jas 4:5 The **s.** that dwelleth in us lusteth....... *4151*
1Pe 1:2 through sanctification of the **S.**,.......... *4151*
1Pe 1:11 **S.** of Christ which was in them did *4151*
1Pe 1:22 obeying the truth through the **S.** *4151*
1Pe 3:4 ornament of a meek and quiet **s.**, ... *4151*
1Pe 3:18 the flesh, but quickened by the **S.** *4151*
1Pe 4:6 but live according to God in the **s.**...... *4151*
1Pe 4:14 **s.** of glory and of God resteth upon *4151*
1Jo 3:24 by the **S.** which he hath given us. *4151*
1Jo 4:1 Beloved, believe not every **s.**, but...... *4151*
1Jo 4:2 Hereby know ye the **S.** of God: *4151*
1Jo 4:2 Every **s.** that confesseth that Jesus..... *4151*
1Jo 4:3 every **s.** that confesseth not that........ *4151*
1Jo 4:3 this is that **s.** of antichrist, whereof..........
1Jo 4:6 the **s.** of truth, and the **s.** of error...... *4151*
1Jo 4:13 because he hath given us of his **S.**...... *4151*
1Jo 5:6 it is the **S.** that beareth witness, ... *4151*
1Jo 5:6 witness, because the **S.** is truth. *4151*
1Jo 5:8 **s.**, and the water, and the blood: *4151*
Jude 19 sensual, having not the **S.**................. *4151*
Re 1:10 I was in the **S.** on the Lord's day, ... *4151*
Re 2:7, 11, 17 **S. saith unto the churches**;.. *4151*
Re 2:29 **the S. saith unto the churches**. *4151*
Re 3:6, 13, 22 **S. saith unto the churches**... *4151*
Re 4:2 And immediately I was in the **s.**:........ *4151*
Re 11:11 the **S.** of life from God entered into.... *4151*
Re 14:13 Yea, saith the **S.**, that they may *4151*
Re 17:3 So he carried me away in the **s.**......... *4151*
Re 18:2 devils, and the hold of every foul **s.**,... *4151*
Re 19:10 of Jesus is the **s.** of prophecy. *4151*
Re 21:10 And he carried me away in the **s.** to... *4151*
Re 22:17 the **S.** and the bride say, Come. *4151*

SPIRITS
Le 19:31 Regard not...that have familiar **s.**,........ 178
Le 20:6 turneth after such as have familiar **s.**, ... 178
Nu 16:22 God, the God of the **s.** of all flesh, ... 7307
Nu 27:16 Lord, the God of the **s.** of all flesh, ... 7307
De 18:11 or a consulter with familiar **s.**, or......... 178
1Sa 28:3 put away those that had familiar **s.**, ... 178
1Sa 28:9 cut off those that have familiar **s.**, ... 178
2Ki 21:6 dealt with familiar **s.** and wizards: 178
2Ki 23:24 Moreover...workers with familiar **s.**,..... 178
Ps 104:4 Who maketh his angels **s.**; his 7307
Pr 16:2 eyes; but the Lord weigheth the **s.**...... 7307
Isa 8:19 Seek...them that have familiar **s.**,......... 178
Isa 19:3 and to them that have familiar **s.**,......... 178
Zec 6:5 are the four **s.** of the heavens, ... 7307
Mt 8:16 he cast out the **s.** with his word,......... *4151*
Mt 10:1 gave them power against unclean **s.**... *4151*
Mt 12:45 **seven other s. more wicked than** ... *4151*
Mk 1:27 commandeth he even the unclean **s.**,... *4151*
Mk 3:11 unclean **s.**, when they saw him, fell *4151*
Mk 5:13 And the unclean **s.** went out, and....... *4151*
Mk 6:7 gave them power over unclean **s.**; *4151*
Lu 4:36 he commandeth the unclean **s.**.......... *4151*
Lu 6:18 that were vexed with unclean **s.**......... *4151*
Lu 7:21 and plagues, and of evil **s.**; and.......... *4151*
Lu 8:2 which had been healed of evil **s.**......... *4151*
Lu 10:20 **that the s. are subject unto you**; ... *4151*
Lu 11:26 **seven other s. more wicked than** ... *4151*
Ac 5:16 which were vexed with unclean **s.** *4151*
Ac 8:7 unclean **s.**, crying with loud voice, ... *4151*
Ac 19:12 and the evil **s.** went out of them. *4151*
Ac 19:13 call over them which had evil **s.** *4151*
1Co 12:10 to another discerning of **s.**; to............ *4151*
1Co 14:32 **s.** of the prophets are subject to the ... *4151*
1Ti 4:1 giving heed to seducing **s.**, and.......... *4151*
Heb 1:7 Who maketh his angels **s.**, and his...... *4151*
Heb 1:14 Are they not all ministering **s.**, sent.... *4151*
Heb 12:9 in subjection unto the Father of **s.**, ... *4151*
Heb 12:23 to the **s.** of just men made perfect,..... *4151*
1Pe 3:19 and preached unto the **s.** in prison;..... *4151*
1Jo 4:1 try the **s.** whether they are of God: *4151*
Re 1:4 the seven **S.** which are before his *4151*
Re 3:1 **he that hath the seven S. of God**,.. *4151*
Re 4:5 which are the seven **S.** of God. *4151*
Re 5:6 which are the seven **S.** of God sent.... *4151*
Re 16:13 three unclean **s.** like frogs come out.... *4151*
Re 16:14 they are the **s.** of devils, working....... *4151*

SPIRITUAL
Ho 9:7 is a fool, the **s.** man is mad,............. 7307
Ro 1:11 may impart unto you some **s.** gift, ... *4152*
Ro 7:14 For we know that the law is **s.**: but.... *4152*
Ro 15:27 made partakers of their **s.** things, ... *4152*
1Co 2:13 comparing **s.** things with **s.** *4152*
1Co 2:15 But he that is **s.** judgeth all things, ... *4152*
1Co 3:1 not speak unto you as unto **s.**,........... *4152*
1Co 9:11 If we have sown unto you **s.** things, ... *4152*
1Co 10:3 And did all eat the same **s.** meat;....... *4152*
1Co 10:4 And did all drink the same **s.** drink: *4152*
1Co 10:4 drank of that **s.** Rock that followed *4152*
1Co 12:1 Now concerning **s.** gifts, brethren, I.... *4152*
1Co 14:1 after charity, and desire **s.** gifts, ... *4152*
1Co 14:12 as ye are zealous of **s.** gifts, seek *4151*
1Co 14:37 himself to be a prophet, or **s.**,........... *4152*
1Co 15:44 natural body; it is raised a **s.** body..... *4152*
1Co 15:44 natural body, and there is a **s.** body.... *4152*
1Co 15:46 that was not first which is **s.**, but....... *4152*
1Co 15:46 and afterward that which is **s.**............ *4152*
Ga 6:1 ye which are **s.**, restore such an one .. *4152*
Eph 1:3 blessed us with all **s.** blessings in *4152*
Eph 5:19 in psalms and hymns and **s.** songs, ... *4152*
Eph 6:12 against **s.** wickedness in high............. *4152*
Col 1:9 all wisdom and **s.** understanding; *4152*
Col 3:16 in psalms and hymns and **s.** songs, ... *4152*
1Pe 2:5 stones, are built up a **s.** house, ... *4152*
1Pe 2:5 priesthood, to offer up **s.** sacrifices, ... *4152*

SPIRITUALLY
Ro 8:6 but to be **s.** minded is life and *3588,4151*
1Co 2:14 because they are **s.** discerned........... *4153*
Re 11:8 which **s.** is called Sodom and Egypt, ... *4153*

SPIT See also SPAT; SPITTED; SPITTING.
Le 15:8 he that hath the issue **s.** upon him...... 7556
Nu 12:14 her father had but **s.** in her face,........ 3417
De 25:9 and **s.** in his face, and shall answer...... 3417
Job 30:10 me, and spare not to **s.** in my face. 7536
Mt 26:67 Then did they **s.** in his face, and........ *1716*
Mt 27:30 And they **s.** upon him, and took the.... *1716*
Mk 7:33 and he **s.**, and touched his tongue; *4429*
Mk 8:23 when he had **s.** on his eyes, and put... *4429*
Mk 10:34 **and shall s. upon him, and shall** ... *1716*
Mk 14:65 And some began to **s.** on him, and to.. *1716*
Mk 15:19 did **s.** upon him, and bowing their....... *1716*

SPITE See also DESPITE; SPITEFULLY.
Ps 10:14 thou beholdest mischief and **s.**, to....... 3708

SPITEFULLY
Mt 22:6 **servants, and entreated them s.**,.... *5195*
Lu 18:32 **shall be mocked, and s. entreated**,. *5195*

SPITTED See also SPAT.
Lu 18:32 **spitefully entreated, and s. on**:...... *1716*

SPITTING
Isa 50:6 hid not my face from shame and **s.**..... 7536

SPITTLE
1Sa 21:13 let his **s.** fall down upon his beard. 7388
Job 7:19 alone till I swallow down my **s.**?......... 7536
Joh 9:6 ground, and made clay of the **s.**, ... *4427*

SPOIL See also SPOILED; SPOILEST; SPOILETH; SPOILING; SPOILS.
Ge 49:27 and at night he shall divide the **s.**....... 7998
Ex 3:22 and ye shall **s.** the Egyptians............. 5337
Ex 15:9 will overtake, I will divide the **s.**; 7998
Nu 31:9 and took the **s.** of all their cattle,.......... 962
Nu 31:11 And they took all the **s.**, and all the.... 7998
Nu 31:12 and the **s.**, unto Moses, and Eleazer... 7998
Nu 31:53 (For the men of war had taken **s.**, ... 962
De 2:35 the **s.** of the cities which we took....... 7998
De 3:7 the cattle, and the **s.** of the cities,....... 7998
De 13:16 thou shalt gather all the **s.** of it into.... 7998
De 13:16 and all the **s.** thereof every whit, ... 7998
De 20:14 all the **s.** thereof, shalt thou take........ 7998
De 20:14 shalt eat the **s.** of thine enemies, ... 7998

Jos 8:2 only the **s.** thereof, and the cattle....... 7998
Jos 8:27 **s.** of that city Israel took for a prey.... 7998
Jos 11:14 the **s.** of these cities, and the cattle,... 7998
Jos 22:8 divide the **s.** of your enemies with...... 7998
Jg 5:30 the necks of them that take the **s.**? 7998
Jg 14:19 men of them, and took their **s.**, ... 2488
1Sa 14:30 had eaten freely to day of the **s.** of..... 7998
1Sa 14:32 And the people flew upon the **s.**,......... 7998
1Sa 14:36 and **s.** them until the morning light,...... 962
1Sa 15:19 but didst fly upon the **s.**, and didst 7998
1Sa 15:21 But the people took of the **s.**, sheep... 7998
1Sa 30:16 because of all the great **s.** that they.... 7998
1Sa 30:19 neither **s.**, nor any thing that they...... 7998
1Sa 30:20 cattle, and said, This is David's **s.**. 7998
1Sa 30:22 will not give them ought of the **s.**....... 7998
1Sa 30:26 of the **s.** unto the elders of Judah,...... 7998
1Sa 30:26 a present for you of the **s.** of the....... 7998
2Sa 3:22 and brought in a great **s.** with them:... 7998
2Sa 8:12 and of the **s.** of Hadadezer, son of...... 7998
2Sa 12:30 he brought forth the **s.** of the city...... 7998
2Sa 23:10 returned after him only to **s.**. 6584
2Ki 3:23 now therefore, Moab, to the **s.**........... 7998
2Ki 21:14 prey and a **s.** to all their enemies;...... 4933
1Ch 20:2 he brought also exceeding much **s.** 7998
2Ch 14:13 they carried away very much **s.**. 7998
2Ch 14:14 was exceeding much **s.** in them........... 961
2Ch 15:11 of the **s.** which they had brought,........ 7998
2Ch 20:25 came to take away the **s.** of them, ... 7998
2Ch 20:25 three days in gathering of the **s.**, ... 7998
2Ch 24:23 sent all the **s.** of them unto the king... 7998
2Ch 25:13 thousand of them, and took much **s.**. 961
2Ch 28:8 took also away much **s.** from them, ... 7998
2Ch 28:8 and brought the **s.** to Samaria........... 7998
2Ch 28:14 the **s.** before the princes and all the..... 961
2Ch 28:15 with the **s.** clothed all that were......... 7998
Ezr 9:7 to a **s.**, and to confusion of face, as...... 961
Es 3:13 to take the **s.** of them for a prey........ 7998
Es 8:11 to take the **s.** of them for a prey,....... 7998
Es 9:10 on the **s.** laid they not their hand......... 961
Job 29:17 and plucked the **s.** out of his teeth...... 2964
Ps 44:10 which hate us **s.** for themselves. 8154
Ps 68:12 that tarried at home divided the **s.**...... 7998
Ps 89:41 All that pass by the way **s.** him:......... 8155
Ps 109:11 and let the strangers **s.** his labour. 962
Ps 119:162 word, as one that findeth great **s.**....... 7998
Pr 1:13 we shall fill our houses with **s.**........... 7998
Pr 16:19 than to divide the **s.** with the proud.... 7998
Pr 22:23 and **s.** the soul of those that spoiled.... 6906
Pr 24:15 righteous; **s.** not his resting place;...... 7703
Pr 31:11 so that he shall have no need of **s.**. 7998
Ca 2:15 the little foxes, that **s.** the vines: 2254
Isa 3:14 the **s.** of the poor is in your houses.... 1500
Isa 8:4 the **s.** of Samaria shall be taken 7998
Isa 9:3 men rejoice when they divide the **s.**..... 7998
Isa 10:6 to take the **s.**, and to take the prey,... 7998
Isa 11:14 they shall **s.** them of the east............. 962
Isa 17:14 is the portion of them that **s.** us,........ 8154
Isa 33:1 when thou shalt cease to **s.**, thou....... 7703
Isa 33:4 your **s.** shall be gathered like the 7998
Isa 33:23 is the prey of a great **s.** divided; 7998
Isa 42:22 for a **s.**, and none saith, Restore. 4933
Isa 42:24 Who gave Jacob for a **s.**, and............ 4882
Isa 53:12 divide the **s.** with the strong; 7998
Jer 5:6 wolf of the evenings shall **s.** them,...... 7703
Jer 6:7 violence and **s.** is heard in her; 7701
Jer 15:13 thy treasures will I give to the **s.**........ 957
Jer 17:3 and all thy treasures to the **s.**, and....... 957
Jer 20:5 which shall **s.** them, and take them, ... 962
Jer 20:8 cried out, I cried violence and **s.**; 7701
Jer 30:16 and they that **s.** thee shall be a.......... 7701
Jer 30:16 shall be a **s.**, and all that prey............ 4933
Jer 47:4 cometh to **s.** all the Philistines, ... 7703
Jer 47:4 for the Lord will **s.** the Philistines,...... 7703
Jer 49:28 to Kedar, and **s.** the men of the east. . 7703
Jer 49:32 the multitude of their cattle a **s.**.......... 7998
Jer 50:10 And Chaldea shall be a **s.**: all that....... 7998
Jer 50:10 all that **s.** her shall be satisfied,......... 7998
Eze 7:21 to the wicked of the earth for a **s.**;..... 7998
Eze 14:15 they **s.** it, so that it be desolate, ... 7921
Eze 25:7 will deliver thee for a **s.** to the........... 957
Eze 26:5 it shall become a **s.** to the nations........ 957
Eze 26:12 they shall make a **s.** of thy riches, ... 7997
Eze 29:19 and take her **s.**, and take her prey; 7997
Eze 32:12 they shall **s.** the pomp of Egypt, ... 7703
Eze 38:12 to take a **s.**, and to take a prey; 7998
Eze 38:13 thee, Art thou come to take a **s.**? 7998
Eze 38:13 cattle and goods, to take a great **s.**? 7998
Eze 39:10 and they shall **s.** those that spoiled..... 7997
Eze 45:9 remove violence and **s.**, and............. 7701
Da 11:24 among them the prey, and **s.**, and...... 7998
Da 11:33 by captivity, and by **s.**, many days. 961
Ho 10:2 altars, he shall **s.** their images. 7703
Ho 13:15 he shall **s.** the treasure of all............ 8154
Na 2:9 the **s.** of silver, take the **s.** of gold:...... 962
Hab 2:8 of the people shall **s.** thee;................ 7997
Hab 2:17 and the **s.** of beasts, which made 7701
Zep 2:9 residue of my people shall **s.** them,...... 962
Zec 2:9 shall be a **s.** to their servants: 7998
Zec 14:1 thy **s.** shall be divided in the midst 7998
Mt 12:29 **man's house, and s. his goods,** *1283*
Mt 12:29 **man? and then he will s. his** *1283*
Mk 3:27 **man's house, and s. his goods,** *1283*
Mk 3:27 **and then he will s. his house.** *1283*
Col 2:8 Beware lest any man **s.** you............. *4812*

SPOILED
Ge 34:27 came upon the slain, and **s.** the city, ... 962
Ge 34:29 **s.** even all that was in the house. 962
Ex 12:36 And they **s.** the Egyptians................. 5337
De 28:29 be only oppressed and **s.** evermore,.... 1497
Jg 2:14 the hands of spoilers that **s.** them,...... 8155
Jg 2:16 of the hands of those that **s.** them........ 8154
1Sa 14:48 of the hands of them that **s.** them. 8154
1Sa 17:53 Philistines, and they **s.** their tents. 8155
2Ki 7:16 out, and **s.** the tents of the Syrians. 962
2Ch 14:14 and they **s.** all the cities; for there....... 962
Job 12:17 He leadeth counsellers away **s.**, ... 7758
Job 12:19 He leadeth princes away **s.**, and......... 7758
Ps 76:5 The stouthearted are **s.**, they have..... 7997
Pr 22:23 the soul of those that **s.** them........... 6906
Isa 13:16 their houses shall be **s.**, and their....... 8155
Isa 18:2 whose land the rivers have **s.**! 958
Isa 18:7 whose land the rivers have **s.**, to the.... 958
Isa 24:3 be utterly emptied, and utterly **s.**.......... 962
Isa 33:1 that spoilest, and thou wast not **s.**;..... 7703
Isa 33:1 cease to spoil, thou shalt be **s.**; 7703
Isa 42:22 But this is a people robbed and **s.**; 8154
Jer 2:14 he a homeborn slave? why is he **s.**? 957
Jer 4:13 Woe unto us! for we are **s.**................ 7703
Jer 4:20 is cried; for the whole land is **s.**.......... 7703
Jer 4:20 suddenly are my tents **s.**, and my....... 7703
Jer 4:30 when thou art **s.**, what wilt thou do?... 7703
Jer 9:19 heard out of Zion, How are we **s.**!....... 7703
Jer 10:20 My tabernacle is **s.**, and all my.......... 7703
Jer 21:12 deliver him that is **s.** out of the.......... 1497
Jer 22:3 deliver the **s.** out of the hand of the.... 1497
Jer 25:36 for the Lord hath **s.** their pasture. 7703
Jer 48:1 Woe unto Nebo! for it is **s.**............... 7703
Jer 48:15 Moab is **s.**, and gone up out of her...... 7703
Jer 48:20 tell ye it in Arnon, that Moab is **s.**, ... 7703
Jer 49:3 Howl, O Heshbon, for Ai is **s.**: cry,.... 7703
Jer 49:10 his seed is **s.**, and his brethren, and ... 7703
Jer 51:55 Because the Lord hath **s.** Babylon, ... 7703
Eze 18:7 hath **s.** none by violence, hath 1497
Eze 18:12 hath **s.** by violence, hath not 1497
Eze 18:16 neither hath **s.** by violence, but................
Eze 18:18 **s.** his brother by violence, and did...... 1497
Eze 23:46 give them to be removed and **s.**. 957
Eze 39:10 they shall spoil those that **s.** them, ... 7997
Ho 10:14 and all thy fortresses shall be **s.**......... 7703
Ho 10:14 as Shalman **s.** Beth-arbel in the.......... 7701
Am 3:11 thee, and thy palaces shall be **s.**. 962
Am 5:9 strengtheneth the **s.** against the......... 7701
Am 5:9 that the **s.** shall come against the 7701
Mic 2:4 and say, We be utterly **s.**: he hath 7703
Hab 2:8 thou hast **s.** many nations, all the 7997
Zec 2:8 me unto the nations which **s.** you; 7997
Zec 11:2 fallen; because the mighty are **s.**: 7703
Zec 11:3 for their glory is **s.**: a voice of the...... 7703
Zec 11:3 lions; for the pride of Jordan is **s.**....... 7703
Col 2:15 having **s.** principalities...powers, ... *554*

SPOILER See also SPOILERS.
Isa 16:4 to them from the face of the **s.**:........ 7703
Isa 16:4 the **s.** ceaseth, the oppressors are........ 7701
Isa 21:2 treacherously, and the **s.** spoileth. 7703
Jer 6:26 the **s.** shall suddenly come upon us..... 7703
Jer 15:8 of the young men a **s.** at noonday:...... 7703
Jer 48:8 the **s.** shall come upon every city, ... 7703
Jer 48:18 **s.** of Moab shall come upon thee, ... 7703
Jer 48:32 **s.** is fallen upon thy summer fruits...... 7703
Jer 51:56 Because the **s.** is come upon her,....... 7703

SPOILERS
Jg 2:14 the hands of **s.** that spoiled them,....... 8154
1Sa 13:17 the **s.** came out of the camp of the..... 7843
1Sa 14:15 and the **s.**, they also trembled, and..... 7843
2Ki 17:20 them into the hand of **s.**, until........... 8154
Jer 12:12 **s.** are come upon all high places......... 7703
Jer 51:48 the **s.** shall come unto her from the.... 7703
Jer 51:53 yet from me shall **s.** come unto her, ... 7703

SPOILEST
Isa 33:1 Woe to thee that **s.**, and thou wast..... 7703

SPOILETH
Ps 35:10 the needy from him that **s.** him? 1497
Isa 21:2 treacherously, and the spoiler **s.**.......... 7703
Ho 7:1 the troop of robbers **s.** without. 6584
Na 3:16 the cankerworm **s.**, and fleeth away.... 6584

SPOILING
Ps 35:12 evil for good to the **s.** of my soul. 7908
Isa 22:4 because of the **s.** of the daughter 7701
Jer 48:3 **s.** and great destruction.................... 7701
Hab 1:3 for **s.** and violence are before me: 7701
Heb 10:34 took joyfully the **s.** of your goods,........ *724*

SPOILS
Jos 7:21 among the **s.** a goodly Babylonish....... 7998
1Ch 26:27 Out of the **s.** won in battles did 7998
Isa 25:11 together with the **s.** of their hands. 698
Lu 11:22 **he trusted, and divideth his s.**........ *4661*
Heb 7:4 Abraham gave the tenth of the **s.**.......... *205*

SPOKE See SPAKE; SPOKEN; SPOKES; SPOKESMAN.

SPOKEN
Ge 12:4 as the Lord had **s.** unto him;............. 1696
Ge 18:19 that which he had **s.** of him............... 1696
Ge 19:21 this city, for the which thou hast **s.**. ... 1696
Ge 21:1 Lord did unto Sarah as he had **s.**........ 1696
Ge 21:2 time of which God had **s.** to him. 1696
Ge 24:51 son's wife, as the Lord hath **s.**. 1696
Ge 28:15 done that which I have **s.** to thee of. .. 1696
Ge 41:28 thing...I have **s.** unto Pharaoh:........... 1696
Ge 44:2 to the word that Joseph had **s.**........... 1696
Ex 4:10 nor since thou hast **s.** unto thy 1696
Ex 4:30 which the Lord had **s.** unto Moses,..... 1696
Ex 9:12 as the Lord had **s.** unto Moses, ... 1696
Ex 9:35 go; as the Lord had **s.** by Moses. 1696
Ex 10:29 Thou hast **s.** well, I will see thy......... 1696
Ex 19:8 All that the Lord hath **s.** we will do. ... 1696
Ex 32:13 all this land that I have **s.** of will I........ 559
Ex 32:34 place of which I have **s.** unto thee: 1696
Ex 33:17 do this thing also that thou hast **s.**:..... 1696
Ex 34:32 all that the Lord had **s.** with him in..... 1696
Le 10:11 which the Lord hath **s.** unto them....... 1696
Nu 1:48 the Lord had **s.** unto Moses, saying,... 1696
Nu 10:29 the Lord hath **s.** good concerning....... 1696
Nu 12:2 the Lord indeed **s.** only by Moses?..... 1696
Nu 12:2 hath he not **s.** also by us? And the 1696
Nu 14:17 be great, according as thou hast **s.**, ... 1696
Nu 14:28 as ye have **s.** in mine ears, so will I ... 1696
Nu 15:22 which the Lord hath **s.** unto Moses,.... 1696
Nu 21:7 for we have **s.** against the Lord, ... 1696
Nu 23:2 And Balak did as Balaam had **s.**; 1696
Nu 23:17 unto him, What hath the Lord **s.**?....... 1696
Nu 23:19 or hath he **s.**, and shall he not make... 1696
De 1:14 thing which thou hast **s.** is good for.... 1696
De 5:28 which they have **s.** unto thee:............ 1696
De 5:28 have well said all that they have **s.**. 1696
De 6:19 before thee, as the Lord hath **s.**. 1696
De 13:5 he hath **s.** to turn you away from 1696
De 18:17 Lord said unto me, They have well **s.** ....
De 18:17 that which they have **s.**................... 1696
De 18:21 word which the Lord hath not **s.**?........ 1696
De 18:22 thing which the Lord hath not **s.**, ... 1696
De 18:22 prophet hath **s.** it presumptuously:...... 1696
De 26:19 the Lord thy God, as he hath **s.**.......... 1696
Jos 6:8 when Joshua had **s.** unto the people,..... 559
Jos 21:45 the Lord had **s.** unto the house of 1696
Ru 2:13 for thou hast **s.** friendly unto thine...... 1696
1Sa 1:16 and grief have I **s.** hitherto................ 1696
1Sa 3:12 things which I have **s.** concerning....... 1696
1Sa 20:23 matter which thou and I have **s.** of, ... 1696
1Sa 25:30 the good that he hath **s.** concerning.... 1696
2Sa 2:27 unless thou hadst **s.**, surely then in..... 1696
2Sa 3:18 the Lord hath **s.** of David, saying,........ 559
2Sa 6:22 maidservants which thou hast **s.** of,...... 559
2Sa 7:19 hast **s.** also of thy servant's house...... 1696
2Sa 7:25 word that thou hast **s.** concerning....... 1696
2Sa 7:29 for thou, O Lord God, hast **s.** it:........ 1696

2Sa 14:19 ought that my lord the king hath s.: 1696
2Sa 17:6 Ahithophel hath s. after this 1696
1Ki 2:23 if Adonijah have not s. this word 1696
1Ki 12:9 this people, which have s. to me, 1696
1Ki 13:3 is the sign which the Lord hath s.; 1696
1Ki 13:11 words which he had s. unto the king, 1696
1Ki 14:11 the air eat: for the Lord hath s. it. 1696
1Ki 18:24 answered and said, It is well s. 1697
1Ki 21:4 the Jezreelite had s. to him: for 1696
1Ki 22:23 Lord hath s. evil concerning thee. 1696
1Ki 22:28 peace, the Lord hath not s. by me. 1696
2Ki 1:17 of the Lord which Elijah had s. 1696
2Ki 4:13 wouldest thou be s. for to the king, 1696
2Ki 7:18 the man of God had s. to the king, 1696
2Ki 19:21 the Lord hath s. concerning him; 1696
2Ki 20:9 will do the thing that he hath s.: 1696
2Ki 20:19 word of the Lord which thou hast s. 1696
1Ch 17:17 hast also s. of thy servant's house 1696
1Ch 17:23 thou hast s. concerning thy servant. 1696
2Ch 2:14 the wine, which my lord hath s. of, 559
2Ch 6:10 his word that he hath s.: 1696
2Ch 6:17 thou hast s. unto thy servant David. 1696
2Ch 10:9 people, which have s. to me, saying, 1696
2Ch 18:22 the Lord hath s. evil against thee. 1696
2Ch 18:27 then hath not the Lord s. by me. 1696
2Ch 36:22 word...s. by the mouth of Jeremiah
Ezr 8:22 we had s. unto the king, saying, 559
Ne 2:18 king's words that he had s. unto me. 559
Es 6:10 nothing fail of all...thou hast s. 1696
Es 7:9 who had s. good for the king, 1696
Job 21:3 and after that I have s., mock on. 1696
Job 32:4 Elihu had waited till Job had s., 1697
Job 33:2 my tongue hath s. in my mouth. 1696
Job 33:8 Surely thou hast s. in mine hearing, 559
Job 34:35 Job hath s. without knowledge, 1696
Job 40:5 Once have I s.; but I will not 1696
Job 42:7 Lord had s. these words unto Job, 1696
Job 42:7 for ye have not s. of me the thing 1696
Job 42:8 that ye have not s. of me the thing. 1696
Ps 50:1 God, even the Lord, hath s., and 1696
Ps 60:6 God hath s. in his holiness; I will 1696
Ps 62:11 God hath s. once; twice have I 1696
Ps 66:14 and my mouth hath s., when I was 1696
Ps 87:3 Glorious things are s. of thee, O 1696
Ps 108:7 God hath s. in his holiness; I will 1696
Ps 109:2 s. against me with a lying tongue. 1696
Ps 116:10 believed, therefore have I s.: I was 1696
Pr 15:23 a word s. in due season, how good
Pr 25:11 word fitly s. is like apples of gold 1696
Ec 7:21 no heed unto all words that are s.; 1696
Ca 8:8 the day when she shall be s. for? 1696
Isa 1:2 ear, O earth: for the Lord hath s., 1696
Isa 1:20 for the mouth of the Lord hath s. it. 1696
Isa 16:13 the word that the Lord hath s. 1696
Isa 16:14 But now the Lord hath s., saying, 1696
Isa 21:17 the Lord God of Israel hath s. it. 1696
Isa 22:25 be cut off: for the Lord hath s. it. 1696
Isa 23:4 O Zidon; for the sea hath s., even 559
Isa 24:3 for the Lord hath s. this word. 1696
Isa 25:8 the earth: for the Lord hath s. it. 1696
Isa 31:4 For thus hath the Lord s. unto me, 559
Isa 37:22 the word which the Lord hath s. 1696
Isa 38:7 will do this thing that he hath s.; 1696
Isa 38:15 hath both s. unto me, and himself 559
Isa 39:8 is the word...which thou hast s. 1696
Isa 40:5 for the mouth of the Lord hath s. it. 1696
Isa 45:19 I have not s. in secret, in a dark 1696
Isa 46:11 I have s. it, I will also bring it to 1696
Isa 48:15 I, even I, have s.; yea, I have 1696
Isa 48:16 I have not s. in secret from the 1696
Isa 58:14 for the mouth of the Lord hath s. it. 1696
Isa 59:3 your lips have s. lies, your tongue 1696
Jer 3:5 thou hast s. and done evil things as 1696
Jer 4:28 because I have s. it, I have purposed. 1696
Jer 9:12 the mouth of the Lord hath s. 1696
Jer 13:15 be not proud: for the Lord hath s. 1696
Jer 23:21 I have not s. to them, yet they 1696
Jer 23:35, 37 and, What hath the Lord s.? 1696
Jer 25:3 and I have s. unto you, rising early 1696
Jer 26:16 he hath s. to us in the name of the 1696
Jer 27:13 the Lord hath s. against the nation 1696
Jer 29:23 have s. lying words in my name, 1696
Jer 30:2 Write...all the words that I have s. 1696
Jer 32:24 what thou hast s. is come to pass; 1696
Jer 33:24 not what this people have s., saying, 1696
Jer 35:14 I have s. unto you, rising early 1696
Jer 35:17 because I have s. unto them, but 1696
Jer 36:2 write...all the words that I have s. 1696
Jer 36:4 which he had s. unto him, upon a 1696
Jer 38:1 words that Jeremiah had s. unto 1696
Jer 44:16 the word that thou hast s. unto us. 1696
Jer 44:25 your wives have both s. with your 1696
Jer 48:8 be destroyed, as the Lord hath s. 559
Jer 51:62 thou hast s. against this place, to 1696
Eze 5:13 I the Lord have s. it in my zeal, 1696
Eze 5:15 rebukes. I the Lord have s. it. 1696
Eze 5:17 upon thee. I the Lord have s. it. 1696
Eze 12:28 word which I have s. shall be done, 1696
Eze 13:7 have ye not s. a lying divination, 1696
Eze 13:7 Lord saith it; albeit I have not s.? 559
Eze 13:8 Because ye have s. vanity, and 1696
Eze 14:9 deceived when he hath s. a thing, 1696
Eze 17:21 know that I the Lord have s. it. 1696
Eze 17:24 I the Lord have s. and have done it. 1696
Eze 21:32 for I the Lord have s. it. 1696
Eze 22:14 I the Lord have s. it, and will do it. 1696
Eze 22:28 God, when the Lord hath not s. 1696
Eze 23:34 I have s. it, saith the Lord God. 1696
Eze 24:14 I the Lord have s. it: it shall come 1696
Eze 26:5 for I have s. it, saith the Lord God: 1696
Eze 26:14 for I the Lord have s. it, saith the 1696
Eze 28:10 for I have s. it, saith the Lord God. 1696
Eze 30:12 of strangers: I the Lord have s. it. 1696
Eze 34:24 among them; I the Lord have s. it. 1696
Eze 35:12 thy blasphemies which thou hast s. 559
Eze 36:5 in the fire of my jealousy have I s. 1696
Eze 36:6 I have s. in my jealousy and in my 1696
Eze 36:36 I the Lord have s. it, and I will do it. 1696
Eze 37:14 ye know that I the Lord have s. it, 1696
Eze 38:17 he of whom I have s. in old time 1696
Eze 38:19 and in the fire of my wrath have I s., 1696
Eze 39:5 for I have s. it, saith the Lord God. 1696
Eze 39:8 this is the day whereof I have s. 1696
Da 4:31 Nebuchadnezzar, to thee it is s.; 560
Da 10:11 when he had s. this word unto me, 1696
Da 10:15 when he had s. such words unto 1696
Da 10:19 And when he had s. unto me, I was 1696
Ho 7:13 yet they have s. lies against me. 1696
Ho 10:4 They have s. words, swearing 1696
Ho 12:10 I have also s. by the prophets, and 1696
Joe 3:8 far off: for the Lord hath s. it. 1696
Am 3:1 word that the Lord hath s. against 1696
Am 3:8 the Lord hath s., who can but 1696
Am 5:14 shall be with you, as ye have s. 559
Ob 12 shouldest thou have s. proudly in 6310
Ob 18 of Esau; for the Lord hath s. it. 1696
Mic 4:4 mouth of the Lord of hosts hath s. 1696
Mic 6:12 the inhabitants thereof have s. lies, 1696
Zec 10:2 For the idols have s. vanity, and the 1696
Mal 3:13 What have we s. so much against 1696
Mt 1:22 which was s. of the Lord by the *4483*
Mt 2:15 which was s. of the Lord by the *4483*
Mt 2:17 which was s. by Jeremy the prophet, *4483*
Mt 2:23 which was s. by the prophets, *4483*
Mt 3:3 that was s. of by the prophet Esaias, *4483*
Mt 4:14 which was s. by Esaias the prophet, *4483*
Mt 8:17 which was s. by Esaias the prophet, *4483*
Mt 12:17 which was s. by Esaias the prophet, *4483*
Mt 13:35 which was s. by the prophet, *4483*
Mt 21:4 which was s. by the prophet, *4483*
Mt 22:31 which was s. unto you by God, *4483*
Mt 24:15 s. of by Daniel the prophet, stand *4483*
Mt 26:65 saying, He hath s. blasphemy; *987*
Mt 27:9 was s. by Jeremy the prophet, *4483*
Mt 27:35 which was s. by the prophet, *4483*
Mk 1:42 And as soon as he had s., *2036*
Mk 5:36 Jesus heard the word that was s., *2980*
Mk 12:12 had s. the parable against them: *2036*
Mk 13:14 s. of by Daniel the prophet, *4483*
Mk 14:9 be s. of for a memorial of her. *2980*
Mk 16:19 after the Lord had s. unto them, *2980*
Lu 2:33 those things which were s. of him. *2980*
Lu 2:34 for a sign which shall be s. against; *483*
Lu 12:3 whatsoever ye have s. in darkness *2036*
Lu 12:3 ye have s. in the ear in closets *2980*
Lu 18:34 they the things which were s. *3004*
Lu 19:28 And when he had thus s., he went *2036*
Lu 20:19 had s. this parable against them. *2036*
Lu 24:25 all that the prophets have s.: *2980*
Lu 24:40 when he had thus s., he shewed *2036*
Joh 4:50 word that Jesus had s. unto him, *2036*
Joh 9:6 When he had thus s., he spat on the *2036*
Joh 11:13 had s. of taking of rest in sleep. *3004*
Joh 11:43 And when he thus had s., he cried *2036*
Joh 12:48 the word that I have s., the same *2980*
Joh 12:49 For I have not s. of myself; but *2980*
Joh 14:25 These things have I s. unto you, *2980*
Joh 15:3 the word which I have s. unto you. *2980*
Joh 15:11 These things have I s. unto you, *2980*
Joh 15:22 I had not come and s. unto them, *2980*
Joh 16:1 These things have I s. unto you, *2980*
Joh 16:25 have I s. unto you in proverbs: *2980*
Joh 16:33 These things I have s. unto you, *2980*
Joh 18:1 When Jesus had s. these words, *2036*
Joh 18:22 when he had thus s., one of the *2036*
Joh 18:23 If I have s. evil, bear witness of *2980*
Joh 20:18 he had s. these things unto her *2036*
Joh 21:19 And when he had s. this, he saith *2036*
Ac 1:9 when he had s. these things, while *2036*
Ac 2:16 which was s. by the prophet Joel; *2046*
Ac 3:21 God hath s. by the mouth of all *2980*
Ac 3:24 as many as have s., have likewise *2980*
Ac 8:24 none of these things...ye have s. *2046*
Ac 9:27 way, and that he had s. to him, *2980*
Ac 13:40 you, which is s. of in the prophets; *2046*
Ac 13:45 things which were s. by Paul, *3004*
Ac 13:46 should first have been s. to you. *2980*
Ac 16:14 the things which were s. of Paul. *2980*
Ac 19:36 these things cannot be s. against, *369*
Ac 19:41 when he had thus s., he dismissed *2036*
Ac 20:36 when he had thus s., he kneeled *2036*
Ac 23:9 a spirit or an angel hath s. to him, *2980*
Ac 26:30 And when he had thus s., the king *2036*
Ac 27:11 things which were s. by Paul. *3004*
Ac 27:35 he had thus s., he took bread, *2036*
Ac 28:22 that every where it is s. against. *483*
Ac 28:24 believed the things which were s., *3004*
Ac 28:25 after that Paul had s. one word, *2036*
Ro 1:8 that your faith is s. of throughout *2605*
Ro 4:18 according to that which was s., So *2046*
Ro 14:16 Let not then your good be evil s. of: *987*
Ro 15:21 To whom he was not s. of, they *312*
1Co 10:30 why am I evil s. of for that for *987*
1Co 14:9 how shall it be known what is s.? *2980*
2Co 4:13 believed, and therefore have I s.; *2980*
Heb 1:2 last days s. unto us by his Son, *2980*
Heb 2:2 word s. by angels was stedfast, *2980*
Heb 2:3 the first began to be s. by the Lord, *2980*
Heb 3:5 things which were to be s. after; *2980*
Heb 4:8 afterward have s. of another day. *2980*
Heb 7:13 he of whom these things are s. *3004*
Heb 8:1 things...we have s. this is the sum. *3004*
Heb 9:19 when Moses had s. every precept *2980*
Heb 12:19 should not be s. to them any more: *4369*
Heb 13:7 who have s. unto you the word of *2980*
Jas 5:10 who have s. in the name of the *2980*
1Pe 4:14 on their part he is evil s. of, but on *987*
2Pe 2:2 the way of truth shall be evil s. of. *987*
2Pe 3:2 s. before by the holy prophets, *4280*
Jude 15 which ungodly sinners have s. *2980*
Jude 17 were s. before of the apostles *4280*

SPOKES

1Ki 7:33 their felloes, and their s., were all 2840

SPOKESMAN

Ex 4:16 he shall be thy s. unto the people: 1696

SPONGE See SPUNGE.

SPOON See also SPOONS.

Nu 7:14 One s. of ten shekels of gold, full 3709
Nu 7:20 One s. of gold of ten shekels, full of 3709
Nu 7:26, 32,38,44,50,56,62,68,74,80 One golden s. of ten shekels, full of 3709

SPOONS

Ex 25:29 the dishes thereof, and s. thereof, 3709
Ex 37:16 the table, his dishes, and his s., 3709
Nu 4:7 thereon the dishes, and the s., and 3709
Nu 7:84 silver bowls, twelve s. of gold: 3709
Nu 7:86 The golden s. were twelve, full of 3709
Nu 7:86 the gold of the s. was an hundred 3709
1Ki 7:50 and the s., and the censers of pure 3709
2Ki 25:14 the snuffers and the s., and all the 3709
2Ch 4:22 and the s., and the censers, of pure 3709
2Ch 24:14 s. and vessels of gold and silver. 3709
Jer 52:18 the bowls, and the s., and all the 3709
Jer 52:19 the candlesticks, and the s., and 3709

SPORT See also SPORTING.

Jg 16:25 Samson, that he may make us s. 7832
Jg 16:25 house; and he made them s.: 6711
Jg 16:27 that beheld while Samson made s. 7832

Pr 10:23 It is as s. to a fool to do mischief:...... 7814
Pr 26:19 neighbour, and saith, Am...I in s.?...... 7832
Isa 57:4 Against whom do ye s. yourselves? 6026

SPORTING
Ge 26:8 behold, Isaac was s. with Rebekah...... 6711
2Pe 2:13 s. themselves with their own............ *1792*

SPOT See also SPOTS; SPOTTED.
Le 13:2 flesh a rising, a scab, or bright s., ... 934
Le 13:4 If the bright s. be white in the skin...... 934
Le 13:19 be a white rising, or a bright s.,........ 934
Le 13:23 But if the bright s. stay in his place,..... 934
Le 13:24 that burneth have a white bright s.,...... 934
Le 13:25 the hair in the bright s. be turned........ 934
Le 13:26 be no white hair in the bright s., ... 934
Le 13:28 And if the bright s. stay in his place, ... 934
Le 13:39 it is a freckled s. that groweth in......... 933
Le 14:56 and for a scab, and for a bright s.:........ 934
Nu 19:2 bring thee a red heifer without s.,....... 8549
Nu 28:3 lambs of the first year without s.......... 8549
Nu 28:9 lambs of the first year without s.,......... 8549
Nu 28:11 lambs of the first year without s.;....... 8549
Nu 29:17, 26 of the first year without s.:........... 8549
De 32:5 their s. is not...of his children:........... 3971
De 32:5 is not the s. of his children: they.............
Job 11:15 thou lift up thy face without s.;.......... 3971
Ca 4:7 fair, my love; there is no s. in thee. ... 3971
Eph 5:27 not having s., or wrinkle, or any......... *4696*
1Ti 6:14 keep this commandment without s.,....... *784*
Heb 9:14 offered himself without s. to God,......... *299*
1Pe 1:19 without blemish and without s.: *784*
2Pe 3:14 found of him in peace, without s., ... *784*

SPOTS
Le 13:38 bright s., even white bright s.;............ 934
Le 13:39 if the bright s. in the skin of their........ 934
Jer 13:23 his skin, or the leopard his s.?........... 2272
2Pe 2:13 S. they are and blemishes,................. *4696*
Jude 12 These are s. in your feasts of............. *4694*

SPOTTED
Ge 30:32 all the speckled and s. cattle, and....... 2921
Ge 30:32 s. and speckled among the goats: 2921
Ge 30:33 is not speckled and s. among the........ 2921
Ge 30:35 goats that were ringstraked and s.,...... 2921
Ge 30:35 goats that were speckled and s.......... 2921
Ge 30:39 ringstraked, speckled, and s............. 2921
Jude 23 even the garment s. by the flesh........ *4695*

SPOUSE See also ESPOUSED; SPOUSES.
Ca 4:8 with me from Lebanon, my s.,........... 3618
Ca 4:9 my heart, my sister, my s.; thou 3618
Ca 4:10 fair is thy love, my sister, my s.!........ 3618
Ca 4:11 Thy lips, O my s., drop as the 3618
Ca 4:12 garden inclosed is my sister, my s.;..... 3618
Ca 5:1 into my garden, my sister, my s.:....... 3618

SPOUSES
Ho 4:13 and your s. shall commit adultery. 3618
Ho 4:14 your s. when they commit adultery;..... 3618

SPOUTS See WATERSPOUTS.

SPRANG See also SPRUNG.
Mk 4:5 **and immediately it s. up, because..** *1816*
Mk 4:8 **yield fruit that s. up and increased,** *305*
Lu 8:7 **and the thorns s. up with it, and...** *4855*
Lu 8:8 **fell on good ground, and s. up,** *5453*
Ac 16:29 he called for a light, and s. in, and...... *1530*
Heb 7:14 that our Lord s. out of Juda; of *393*
Heb 11:12 Therefore s. there even of one, and ... *1080*

SPREAD See also OVERSPREAD; SPREADEST; SPREADETH; SPREADING.
Ge 10:18 of the Canaanites s. abroad. 6327
Ge 28:14 thou shalt s. abroad to the west,........ 6555
Ge 33:19 a field, where he had s. his tent,........ 5186
Ge 35:21 and s. his tent beyond the tower of..... 5186
Ex 9:29 I will s. abroad my hands unto the...... 6566
Ex 9:33 and s. abroad his hands unto the........ 6566
Ex 37:9 the cherubims s. out their wings on.... 6566
Ex 40:19 And he s. abroad the tent over the..... 6566
Le 13:5 and the plague s. not in the skin; 6581
Le 13:6 and the plague s. not in the skin, ... 6581
Le 13:7 if the scab s. much abroad in the........ 6581
Le 13:22 if it s. much abroad in the skin, ... 6581
Le 13:23 spot stay in his place, and s. not,....... 6581
Le 13:27 if it be s. much abroad in the skin, ... 6581
Le 13:28 his place, and s. not in the skin, ... 6581
Le 13:32 if the scall s. not, and there be in it.... 6581
Le 13:34 if the scall be not s. in the skin,......... 6581
Le 13:35 But if the scall s. much in the skin 6581
Le 13:36 behold, if the scall be s. in the skin, ... 6581
Le 13:51 if the plague be s. in the garment,...... 6581
Le 13:53 the plague be not s. in the garment, ... 6581
Le 13:55 colour, and the plague be not s.;....... 6581
Le 14:39 if the plague be s. in the walls of 6581
Le 14:44 if the plague be s. in the house, it...... 6581
Le 14:48 the plague hath not s. in the house,.... 6581
Nu 4:6 shall s. over it a cloth wholly of......... 6566
Nu 4:7 they shall s. a cloth of blue, and......... 6566
Nu 4:8 shall s. upon them a cloth of scarlet, ... 6566
Nu 4:11 altar they shall s. a cloth of blue, ... 6566
Nu 4:13 altar, and s. a purple cloth thereon: 6566
Nu 4:14 they shall s. upon it a covering of........ 6566
Nu 11:32 and they s. them all abroad for 7849
Nu 24:6 As the valleys are they s. forth, as...... 5186
De 22:17 shall s. the cloth before the elders...... 6566
Jg 8:25 And they s. a garment, and did cast.... 6566
Jg 15:9 Judah, and s. themselves in Lehi. 5203
Ru 3:9 s. therefore thy skirt over thine......... 6566
1Sa 30:16 were s. abroad upon all the earth, ... 5203
2Sa 5:18, 22 and s. themselves in the valley....... 5203
2Sa 16:22 So they s. Absalom a tent upon 5186
2Sa 17:19 s. a covering over the well's mouth, ... 6566
2Sa 17:19 and s. ground corn thereon; and......... 7849
2Sa 21:10 and s. it for her upon the rock,.......... 5186
2Sa 22:43 the street, and did s. them abroad...... 7554
1Ki 6:32 and s. gold upon the cherubims,......... 7286
1Ki 8:7 the cherubims s. forth their two......... 6566
1Ki 8:22 s. forth his hands toward heaven:....... 6566
1Ki 8:38 and s. forth his hands toward this....... 6566
1Ki 8:54 with his hands s. up to heaven........... 6566
2Ki 8:15 and s. it on his face, so...he died: 6566
2Ki 19:14 the Lord, and s. it before the Lord..... 6566
1Ch 14:9 Philistines came...s. themselves 6584
1Ch 14:13 Philistines yet again s. themselves 6584
1Ch 28:18 cherubims, that s. out their wings, ... 6566
2Ch 3:13 wings of...cherubims s. themselves..... 6566
2Ch 5:8 the cherubims s. forth their wings 6566
2Ch 6:12 of Israel, and s. forth his hands:........ 6566
2Ch 6:13 s. forth his hands toward heaven,....... 6566
2Ch 6:29 s. forth his hands in this house: 6566
2Ch 26:8 and his name s. abroad even to the 3212
2Ch 26:15 And his name s. far abroad; for he 3318
Ezr 9:5 s. out my hands unto the Lord my 6566
Job 29:19 My root was s. out by the waters, ... 6605
Job 37:18 thou with him s. out the sky, ... 7554
Ps 105:39 He s. a cloud for a covering; and 6566
Ps 140:5 they have s. a net by the wayside; 6566
Pr 1:17 Surely in vain the net is s. in the 2219
Isa 1:15 And when ye s. forth your hands, ... 6566
Isa 14:11 the worm is s. under thee, and the...... 3331
Isa 19:8 they that s. nets upon the waters....... 6566
Isa 25:7 the vail that is s. over all nations........ 5259
Isa 25:11 And he shall s. forth his hands in 6566
Isa 33:23 mast, they could not s. the sail:.......... 6566
Isa 37:14 the Lord, and s. it before the Lord...... 6566
Isa 42:5 he that s. forth the earth, and that..... 7554
Isa 58:5 to s. sackcloth and ashes under.......... 3331
Isa 65:2 I have s. out my hands all the day...... 6566
Jer 8:2 they shall s. them before the sun, ... 7849
Jer 10:9 Silver s. into plates is brought 7554
Jer 43:10 he shall s. his royal pavilion over........ 5186
Jer 48:40 and shall s. his wings over Moab......... 6566
Jer 49:22 and s. his wings over Bozrah: and...... 6566
La 1:10 The adversary hath s. out his hand..... 6566
La 1:13 he hath s. a net for my feet, he hath .. 6566
Eze 2:10 and he s. it before me; and it was....... 6566
Eze 12:13 My net also will I s. upon him, and..... 6566
Eze 16:8 I s. my skirt over thee, and covered... 6566
Eze 17:20 And I will s. my net upon him, and..... 6566
Eze 19:8 and s. their net over him:................ 6566
Eze 26:14 shalt be a place to s. nets upon; 4894
Eze 32:3 I will therefore s. out my net over 6566
Eze 47:10 shall be a place to s. forth nets;......... 4894
Ho 5:1 Mizpah, and a net s. upon Tabor........ 6566
Ho 7:12 go, I will s. my net upon them; 6566
Ho 14:6 His branches shall s., and his 3212
Joe 2:2 morning s. upon the mountains: 6566
Hab 1:8 horsemen shall s. themselves, ... 6335
Zec 1:17 prosperity shall yet be s. abroad; 6327
Zec 2:6 s. you abroad as the four winds 6566
Mal 2:3 seed, and s. dung upon your faces,...... 2219
Mt 9:31 s. abroad his fame in all that............ *1310*
Mt 21:8 s. their garments in the way; *4766*
Mk 1:28 immediately his fame s. abroad *1831*
Mk 6:14 (for his name was s. abroad:) and....... *5318*
Mk 11:8 many s. their garments in the way:..... *4766*
Lu 19:36 they s. their clothes in the way.......... *5291*
Ac 4:17 it s. no further among the people, ... *1268*
1Th 1:8 faith to God-ward is s. abroad;.......... *1831*

SPREADEST
Eze 27:7 which thou s. forth to be thy sail;....... 4666

SPREADETH
Le 13:8 the scab s. in the skin, then the......... 6581
De 32:11 As an eagle...s. abroad her wings,...... 6566
Job 9:8 Which alone s. out the heavens,......... 5186
Job 26:9 throne, and s. his cloud upon it.......... 6576
Job 36:30 Behold, he s. his light upon it,........... 6566
Job 41:30 he s. sharp pointed things upon.......... 7502
Pr 29:5 his neighbour s. a net for his feet........ 6566
Isa 25:11 that swimmeth s. forth his hands........ 6566
Isa 40:19 the goldsmith s. it over with gold, ... 7554
Isa 40:22 s. them out as a tent to dwell in: 4969
Isa 44:24 s. abroad the earth by myself;............ 7554
Jer 4:31 that s. her hands, saying, Woe is 6566
Jer 17:8 that s. out her roots by the river, ... 7971
La 1:17 Zion s. forth her hands, and there 6566

SPREADING See also OVERSPREADING; SPREADINGS.
Le 13:57 thing of skin; it is a s. plague: 6524
Ps 37:35 s. himself like a green bay tree.......... 6168
Eze 17:6 became a s. vine of low stature, ... 5628
Eze 26:5 be a place for the s. of nets in the 4894

SPREADINGS
Job 36:29 understand the s. of the clouds, ... 4666

SPRIGS
Isa 18:5 cut off the s. with pruning hooks,....... 2150
Eze 17:6 forth branches, and shot forth s......... 6288

SPRING See also DAYSPRING; OFFSPRING; SPRANG; SPRINGETH; SPRINGING; SPRINGS; SPRUNG.
Nu 21:17 sang this song, S. up, O well; 5927
De 8:7 and depths that s. out of valleys......... 3318
Jg 19:25 when the day began to s., they let 5927
1Sa 9:26 to pass about the s. of the day, ... 5927
2Ki 2:21 forth unto the s. of the waters,.......... 4161
Job 5:6 neither doth trouble s. out of the 6779
Job 38:27 bud of the tender herb to s. forth? 6779
Ps 85:11 Truth shall s. out of the earth; and..... 6779
Ps 92:7 When the wicked s. as the grass,....... 6524
Pr 25:26 fountain, and a corrupt s.................. 4726
Ca 4:12 a s. shut up, a fountain sealed. 1530
Isa 42:9 before they s. forth I tell you of......... 6779
Isa 43:19 now it shall s. forth; shall ye not........ 6779
Isa 44:4 they shall s. up as among the grass, ... 6779
Isa 45:8 let righteousness s. up together;......... 6779
Isa 58:8 thine health shall s. forth speedily:...... 6779
Isa 58:11 like a s. of water, whose waters 4161
Isa 61:11 that are sown in it to s. forth; 6779
Isa 61:11 and praise to s. forth before all the...... 6779
Eze 17:9 wither in all the leaves of her s.,........ 6780
Ho 13:15 and his s. shall become dry, and 4726
Joe 2:22 pastures of the wilderness do s.,......... 1876
Mk 4:27 **and the seed should s. and grow up,** *985*

SPRINGETH
1Ki 4:33 the hyssop that s. out of the wall: 3318
2Ki 19:29 year that which s. of the same;.......... 7823
Isa 37:30 year that which s. of the same:.......... 7823
Ho 10:4 thus judgment s. up as hemlock 6524

SPRINGING
Ge 26:19 and found there a well of s. water. 2416
2Sa 23:4 as the tender grass s. out of the earth ......
Ps 65:10 thou blessest the s. thereof............... 6780
Joh 4:14 **of water s. up into everlasting life..** *242*
Heb 12:15 lest any root of bitterness s. up *5453*

SPRINGS
De 4:49 the plain, under the s. of Pisgah. 794
Jos 10:40 and of the s., and all their kings; 794
Jos 12:8 and in the s., and in the wilderness,..... 794
Jos 15:19 land; give me also s. of water............ 1543
Jos 15:19 her the upper s., and the nether s........ 1543
Jg 1:15 land; give me also s. of water............ 1543
Jg 1:15 her the upper s. and the nether s......... 1543
Job 38:16 entered into the s. of the sea? 5033
Ps 87:7 be there: all my s. are in thee. 4599
Ps 104:10 He sendeth the s. into the valleys, ... 4599
Isa 35:7 and the thirsty land s. of water: 4002
Isa 41:18 and the dry land s. of water. 4161
Isa 49:10 s. of water shall he guide them. 4002

Jer 51:36 up her sea, and make her s. dry....... 4726

SPRINKLE See also SPRINKLED; SPRINKLETH; SPRINKLING.
Ex 9:8 let Moses s. it toward the heaven...... 2236
Ex 29:16 and s. it round about the altar. 2236
Ex 29:20 s. the blood upon the altar round........ 2236
Ex 29:21 s. it upon Aaron, and upon his........... 5137
Le 1:5 s. the blood round about upon the...... 2236
Le 1:11 s. his blood round about upon the....... 2236
Le 3:2 shall s. the blood upon the altar......... 2236
Le 3:8 s. the blood thereof round about........ 2236
Le 3:13 s. the blood thereof upon the altar...... 2236
Le 4:6 s. of the blood seven times before...... 5137
Le 4:17 s. it seven times before the Lord,...... 5137
Le 5:9 s. of the blood of the sin offering...... 5137
Le 7:2 he s. round about upon the altar. 2236
Le 14:7 s. upon him that is to be cleansed...... 5137
Le 14:16 shall s. of the oil with his finger........ 5137
Le 14:27 shall s. with his right finger some....... 5137
Le 14:51 water, and s. the house seven times:.. 5137
Le 16:14 and s. it with his finger upon the........ 5137
Le 16:14 he s. of the blood with his finger........ 5137
Le 16:15 and s. it upon the mercy seat, and..... 5137
Le 16:19 he shall s. of the blood upon it with.... 5137
Le 17:6 priest shall s. the blood upon the........ 2236
Nu 8:7 S. water of purifying upon them,........ 5137
Nu 18:17 shalt s. their blood upon the altar,...... 2236
Nu 19:4 s. of her blood directly before the...... 5137
Nu 19:18 s. it upon the tent, and upon all the.... 5137
Nu 19:19 the clean person shall s. upon the........ 5137
2Ki 16:15 and s. upon it all the blood of the........ 2236
Isa 52:15 So shall he s. many nations; the......... 5137
Eze 36:25 will I s. clean water upon you, and..... 2236
Eze 43:18 thereon, and to s. blood thereon. 2236

SPRINKLED
Ex 9:10 Moses s. it up toward heaven;........... 2236
Ex 24:6 half of the blood he s. on the altar...... 2236
Ex 24:8 the blood, and s. it on the people,...... 2236
Le 6:27 when there is s. of the blood............ 5137
Le 6:27 whereon it was s. in the holy place.... 5137
Le 8:11 he s....upon the altar seven times,..... 5137
Le 8:19, 24 and Moses s. the blood upon............ 2236
Le 8:30 s. it upon Aaron, and upon his............ 5137
Le 9:12 he s. round about upon the altar. 2236
Le 9:18 which he s. upon the altar round........ 2236
Nu 19:13 water of separation was not s. upon.... 2236
Nu 19:20 water...hath not been s. upon him;..... 2236
2Ki 9:33 of her blood was s. on the wall,......... 5137
2Ki 16:13 s. the blood of his peace offerings,..... 2236
2Ch 29:22 the blood, and s. it on the altar:......... 2236
2Ch 29:22 they s. the blood upon the altar: 2236
2Ch 29:22 they s. the blood upon the altar. 2236
2Ch 30:16 the priests s. the blood, which they.... 2236
2Ch 35:11 the priests s. the blood from their....... 2236
Job 2:12 s. dust upon their heads toward......... 2236
Isa 63:3 blood...be s. upon my garments,......... 5137
Heb 9:19 and s. both the book, and all the........ *4473*
Heb 9:21 s. with blood both the tabernacle,....... *4473*
Heb 10:22 hearts s. from an evil conscience........ *4473*

SPRINKLETH
Le 7:14 be the priest's that s. the blood......... 2236
Nu 19:21 he that s. the water of separation....... 5137

SPRINKLING
Heb 9:13 ashes of an heifer s. the unclean,....... *4472*
Heb 11:28 the passover, and the s. of blood,....... *4378*
Heb 12:24 to the blood of s., that speaketh........ *4473*
1Pe 1:2 and s. of the blood of Jesus Christ:..... *4473*

SPROUT
Job 14:7 be cut down, that it will s. again,....... 2498

SPRUNG See also SPRANG.
Ge 41:6 the east wind s. up after them........... 6779
Ge 41:23 the east wind, s. up after them:......... 6779
Le 13:42 a leprosy s. up in his bald head,......... 6524
Mt 4:16 and shadow of death light is s. up. *393*
Mt 13:5 **and forthwith they s. up, because..** *1816*
Mt 13:7 **the thorns s. up, and choked them:.** *305*
Mt 13:26 **But when the blade was s. up, and ..** *985*
Lu 8:6 **soon as it was s. up, it withered....** *5453*

SPUE See also SPEWING; SPUED.
Le 18:28 That the land s. not you out also,........ 6958
Le 20:22 to dwell therein, s. you not out.......... 6958
Jer 25:27 be drunken, and s., and fall, and........ 7006
Re 3:16 **I will s. thee out of my mouth.....** *1692*

SPUED
Le 18:28 as it s. out the nations that were....... 6958

SPUN
Ex 35:25 brought that which they had s.,........... 4299
Ex 35:26 them up in wisdom s. goats' hair. 2901

SPUNGE
Mt 27:48 a s., and filled it with vinegar, ... *4699*
Mk 15:36 ran and filled a s. full of vinegar. *4699*
Joh 19:29 and they filled a s. with vinegar, ... *4699*

SPY See also ESPY; SPIED; SPIES.
Nu 13:16 Moses sent to s. out the land............ 8446
Nu 13:17 Moses sent them to s. out the land.... 8446
Nu 21:32 And Moses sent to s. out Jaazer,........ 7270
Jos 2:1 of Shittim two men to s. secretly,...... 7270
Jos 6:25 Joshua sent to s. out Jericho. 7270
Jg 18:2 to s. out the land, and to search it;.... 7270
Jg 18:14 went to s. out the country of Laish,.... 7270
Jg 18:17 men that went to s. out the land........ 7270
2Sa 10:3 to search the city, and to s. it out,...... 7270
2Ki 6:13 Go and s. where he is, that I may...... 7200
1Ch 19:3 overthrow, and to s. out the land?...... 7200
Ga 2:4 came in privily to s. out our liberty..... *2684*

SQUARE See also FOURSQUARE; SQUARED; SQUARES; STONE-SQUARERS.
1Ki 7:5 all the doors and posts were s.,.......... 7251
Eze 43:16 s. in the four squares thereof. 7251
Eze 45:2 hundred in breadth, s. round about;.... 7251

SQUARED
Eze 41:21 The posts of the temple were s.,....... 7251

SQUARES
Eze 43:16 square in the four s. thereof............. 7253
Eze 43:17 and fourteen broad in the four s......... 7253

ST. See S.; SAINT.

STABILITY
Isa 33:6 shall be the s. of thy times,................ 530

STABLE See also UNSTABLE.
1Ch 16:30 the world also shall be s., that it....... 3559
Eze 25:5 will make Rabbah a s. for camels,....... 5116

STABLISH See also ESTABLISH; STABLISHED; STABLISHETH.
2Sa 7:13 I will s. the throne of his kingdom...... 3559
1Ch 17:12 and I will s. his throne for ever. 3559
1Ch 18:3 to s. his dominion by the river........... 5324
2Ch 7:18 Then will I s. the throne of thy........... 6965
Es 9:21 To s. this among them, that they....... 6965
Ps 119:38 S. thy word unto thy servant, who...... 6965
Ro 16:25 to s. you according to my gospel,........ *4741*
1Th 3:13 To the end he may s. your hearts...... *4741*
2Th 2:17 and s. you in every good word and..... *4741*
2Th 3:3 who shall s. you, and keep you......... *4741*
Jas 5:8 Be ye also patient; s. your hearts:...... *4741*
1Pe 5:10 make you perfect, s., strengthen,........ *4741*

STABLISHED See also ESTABLISHED.
2Ch 17:5 the Lord s. the kingdom in his........... 3559
Ps 93:1 the world also is s., that it cannot...... 3559
Ps 148:6 He hath also s. them for ever and...... 5975
Col 2:7 and s. in the faith, as ye have been...... *950*

STABLISHETH See also ESTABLISHETH.
Hab 2:12 blood, and s. a city by iniquity!.......... 3559
2Co 1:21 he which s. us with you in Christ,....... *950*

STACHYS (sta'-kis)
Ro 16:9 in Christ, and S. my beloved. *4720*

STACKS
Ex 22:6 in thorns, so that the s. of corn,........ 1430

STACTE (stac'-te)
Ex 30:34 Take unto thee sweet spices, s.,........ 5198

STAFF See also STAVES.
Ge 32:10 for with my s. I passed over this....... 4731
Ge 38:18 and thy s. that is in thine hand.......... 4294
Ge 38:25 the signet, and bracelets, and s........... 4294
Ex 12:11 feet, and your s. in your hand: 4731
Ex 21:19 and walk abroad upon his s., then....... 4938
Le 26:26 have broken the s. of your bread,...... 4294
Nu 13:23 bare it between two upon a s.; 4132
Nu 22:27 and he smote the ass with a s.,......... 4731
Jg 6:21 put forth the end of the s. that was.... 4938
1Sa 17:7 And the s. of his spear was like a...... 2671
1Sa 17:40 And he took his s. in his hand, and....... 4731
2Sa 3:29 is a leper, or that leaneth on a s.,...... 6418
2Sa 21:19 the s. of whose spear was like a......... 6086
2Sa 23:7 with iron and the s. of a spear;.......... 6086
2Sa 23:21 but he went down to him with a s.,.... 7626
2Ki 4:29 and take my s. in thine hand, and....... 4938
2Ki 4:29 lay my s. upon the face of the child.... 4938
2Ki 4:31 and laid the s. upon the face of the..... 4938
2Ki 18:21 thou trustest upon the s. of this......... 4938
1Ch 11:23 he went down to him with a s., ... 7626
1Ch 20:5 spear s. was like a weaver's beam...... 6086
Ps 23:4 rod and thy s. they comfort me. 4938
Ps 105:16 he brake the whole s. of bread. 4294
Isa 3:1 from Judah the stay and the s.,.......... 4938
Isa 9:4 the s. of his shoulder, the rod of........ 4294
Isa 10:5 and the s. in their hand is mine.......... 4294
Isa 10:15 or as if the s. should lift up itself,....... 4294
Isa 10:24 and shall lift up his s. against thee,..... 4294
Isa 14:5 hath broken the s. of the wicked,........ 4294
Isa 28:27 the fitches are beaten out with a s.,..... 4294
Isa 30:32 where the grounded s. shall pass,........ 4294
Isa 36:6 Lo, thou trustest in the s. of this....... 4938
Jer 48:17 How is the strong s. broken, and........ 4294
Eze 4:16 I will break the s. of bread in............ 4294
Eze 5:16 and will break your s. of bread: 4294
Eze 14:13 and will break the s. of the bread....... 4294
Eze 29:6 they have been a s. of reed to the 4938
Ho 4:12 and their s. declareth unto them:........ 4731
Zec 8:4 every man with his s. in his hand........ 4938
Zec 11:10 And I took my s., even Beauty,......... 4731
Zec 11:14 Then I cut asunder mine other s.,....... 4731
Mk 6:8 for their journey, save a s. only;........ *4464*
Heb 11:21 leaning upon the top of his s.............. *4464*

STAGGER See also STAGGERED; STAGGERETH.
Job 12:25 them to s. like a drunken man. 8582
Ps 107:27 fro, and s. like a drunken man, ... 5128
Isa 29:9 they s., but not with strong drink........ 5128

STAGGERED
Ro 4:20 He s. not at the promise of God *1252*

STAGGERETH
Isa 19:14 as a drunken man s. in his vomit........ 8582

STAID See STAYED.

STAIN
Job 3:5 and the shadow of death s. it;.......... 1350
Isa 23:9 to s. the pride of all glory, and to....... 2490
Isa 63:3 and I will s. all my raiment............ 1351

STAIRS
1Ki 6:8 with winding s. into the middle 3883
2Ki 9:13 it under him on the top of the s.,........ 4609
Ne 3:15 the s. that go down from the city....... 4609
Ne 9:4 up upon the s., of the Levites, ... 4608
Ne 12:37 up by the s. of the city of David,....... 4609
Ca 2:14 rock, in the secret places of the s.,..... 4095
Eze 40:6 east, and went up the s. thereof,....... 4609
Eze 43:17 his s. shall look toward the east......... 4609
Ac 21:35 And when he came upon the s., so...... *304*
Ac 21:40 Paul stood on the s., and beckoned..... *304*

STAKES
Isa 33:20 not one of the s. thereof shall ever..... 3489
Isa 54:2 thy cords, and strengthen thy s.; 3489

STALK See also STALKS.
Ge 41:5 ears of corn came up upon one s.,...... 7070
Ge 41:22 seven ears came up in one s., full...... 7070
Ho 8:7 reap the whirlwind: it hath no s.: 7054

STALKS
Jos 2:6 and hid them with the s. of flax, ... 6086

STALL See also STALLED; STALLS.
Am 6:4 calves out of the midst of the s.;........ 4770
Mal 4:2 and grow up as calves of the s.. 4770
Lu 13:15 **loose his ox or his ass from the s.,** *5336*

STALLED
Pr 15:17 than a s. ox and hatred therewith. 75

STALLS
1Ki 4:26 had forty thousand s. of horses 723
2Ch 9:25 had four thousand s. for horses 723
2Ch 32:28 and s. for all manner of beasts, and....... 723
Hab 3:17 there shall be no herd in the s.:.......... 7517

STAMMERERS
Isa 32:4 s. shall be ready to speak plainly. 5926

STAMMERING
Isa 28:11 with s. lips and another tongue 3934
Isa 33:19 of a s. tongue, that thou canst not...... 3932

STAMP See also STAMPED; STAMPING.
2Sa 22:43 I did **s.** them as the mire of the......... 1854
Eze 6:11 thine hand, and **s.** with thy foot, ... 7554

STAMPED
De 9:21 and burnt it with fire, and **s.** it,.......... 3807
2Ki 23:6 **s.** it small to powder, and cast the...... 1854
2Ki 23:15 **s.** it small to powder, and burned....... 1854
2Ch 15:16 Asa cut down her idol, and **s.** it,....... 1854
Eze 25:6 and **s.** with the feet, and rejoiced....... 7554
Da 7:7 **s.** the residue with the feet of it: 7512
Da 7:19 and **s.** the residue with his feet;......... 7512
Da 8:7 to the ground, and **s.** upon him: 7429
Da 8:10 to the ground, and **s.** upon them. 7429

STAMPING
Jer 47:3 noise of the **s.** of the hoofs of his....... 8161

STANCHED
Lu 8:44 immediately her issue of blood **s.**........ *2476*

STAND See also STANDEST; STANDETH; STANDING; STOOD; WITHSTAND.
Ge 19:9 And they said, **S.** back. And they....... 5066
Ge 24:13 I **s.** here by the well of water; and..... 5324
Ge 24:43 Behold, I **s.** by the well of water;....... 5324
Ex 7:15 thou shalt **s.** by the river's brink........ 5324
Ex 8:20 morning, and **s.** before Pharaoh;......... 3320
Ex 9:11 the magicians could not **s.** before......... 5975
Ex 9:13 morning, and **s.** before Pharaoh,......... 3320
Ex 14:13 Fear ye not, **s.** still, and see the........ 3320
Ex 17:6 I will **s.** before thee there upon the 5975
Ex 17:9 I will **s.** on the top of the hill with...... 5324
Ex 18:14 and all the people **s.** by thee from...... 5324
Ex 33:10 cloudy pillar **s.** at the tabernacle......... 5975
Ex 33:21 me, and thou shalt **s.** upon a rock: 5324
Le 18:23 shall any woman **s.** before a beast...... 5975
Le 19:16 shalt thou **s.** against the blood of......... 5975
Le 26:37 power to **s.** before your enemies........ 8617
Le 27:14 shall estimate it, so shall it **s.**. 6965
Le 27:17 to thy estimation it shall **s.**................ 6965
Nu 1:5 of the men that shall **s.** with you:....... 5975
Nu 9:8 **S.** still, and I will hear what the......... 5975
Nu 11:16 that they may **s.** there with thee......... 3320
Nu 16:9 and to **s.** before the congregation....... 5975
Nu 23:3 **S.** by thy burnt offering, and I.......... 3320
Nu 23:15 **S.** here by thy burnt offering, while.... 3320
Nu 27:21 shall **s.** before Eleazar the priest,....... 5975
Nu 30:4 then all her vows shall **s.**, and.......... 6965
Nu 30:4 she hath bound her soul shall **s.**. 6965
Nu 30:5 she hath bound her soul, shall **s.**: 6965
Nu 30:7 then her vows shall **s.**, and her.......... 6965
Nu 30:7 she bound her soul, shall **s.**............... 6965
Nu 30:9 have bound their souls, shall **s.**.......... 6965
Nu 30:11 then all her vows shall **s.**, and every... 6965
Nu 30:11 wherewith...bound her soul shall **s.**...... 6965
Nu 30:12 the bond of her soul, shall not **s.**:........ 6965
Nu 35:12 until he **s.** before the congregation...... 5975
De 5:31 But as for thee, **s.** thou here by me, .. 5975
De 7:24 no man be able to **s.** before thee,....... 3320
De 9:2 can **s.** before the children of Anak! 3320
De 10:8 to **s.** before the Lord to minister.......... 5975
De 11:25 no man be able to **s.** before you:........ 3320
De 18:5 to **s.** to minister in the name of......... 5975
De 18:7 do, which **s.** there before the Lord. 5975
De 19:17 shall **s.** before the Lord, before the 5975
De 24:11 Thou shalt **s.** abroad, and the man....... 5975
De 25:8 if he **s.** to it, and say, I like not to..... 5975
De 27:12 These shall **s.** upon mount Gerizim..... 5975
De 27:13 shall **s.** upon mount Ebal to curse;....... 5975
De 29:10 Ye **s.** this day all of you before the...... 5324
Jos 1:5 not any man be able to **s.** before........ 3320
Jos 3:8 Jordan, ye shall **s.** still in Jordan......... 5975
Jos 3:13 and they shall **s.** upon an heap........... 5975
Jos 7:12 could not **s.** before their enemies, ... 6965
Jos 7:13 canst not **s.** before thine enemies,....... 6965
Jos 10:8 not a man of them **s.** before thee. 5975
Jos 10:12 Sun, **s.** thou still upon Gibeon;........... 1826
Jos 20:4 shall **s.** at the entering of the gate...... 5975
Jos 20:6 until he **s.** before the congregation...... 5975
Jos 23:9 man hath been able to **s.** before you... 5975
Jg 2:14 could not...**s.** before their enemies...... 5975
Jg 4:20 **S.** in the door of the tent, and it........ 5975
1Sa 6:20 Who is able to **s.** before this holy....... 5975
1Sa 9:27 but **s.** thou still a while, that I may....... 5975
1Sa 12:7 Now therefore **s.** still, that I may........ 3320
1Sa 12:16 Now...**s.** and see this great thing, ... 3320
1Sa 14:9 then we will **s.** still in our place, ... 5975
1Sa 16:22 Let David, I pray thee, **s.** before me; ..5975
1Sa 19:3 And I will go out and **s.** beside my 5975
2Sa 1:9 **S.**, I pray thee, upon me, and slay..... 5975
2Sa 18:30 unto him, Turn aside, and **s.** here. 3320
1Ki 1:2 and let her **s.** before the king, and...... 5975
1Ki 8:11 the priests could not **s.** to minister..... 5975
1Ki 10:8 thy servants, which **s.** continually 5975
1Ki 17:1 of Israel liveth, before whom I **s.**, ... 5975
1Ki 18:15 of hosts liveth, before whom I **s.**,........ 5975
1Ki 19:11 **s.** upon the mount before the Lord. 5975
2Ki 3:14 Lord...liveth, before whom I **s.**,......... 5975
2Ki 5:11 will surely come out to me, and **s.**,...... 5975
2Ki 5:16 the Lord liveth, before whom I **s.**, I ... 5975
2Ki 6:31 if the head of Elisha...**s.** on him......... 5975
2Ki 10:4 before him: how then shall we **s.**? 5975
1Ch 21:16 angel of the Lord **s.** between the 5975
1Ch 23:30 to **s.** every morning to thank and 5975
2Ch 5:14 the priests could not **s.** to minister...... 5975
2Ch 9:7 which **s.** continually before thee, ... 5975
2Ch 20:9 we **s.** before this house, and in thy..... 5975
2Ch 20:17 **s.** ye still, and see the salvation of...... 5975
2Ch 29:11 Lord hath chosen you to **s.** before...... 5975
2Ch 34:32 Jerusalem and Benjamin to **s.** to it...... 5975
2Ch 35:5 **s.** in the holy place according to the.... 5975
Ezr 9:15 we cannot **s.** before thee because of... 5975
Ezr 10:13 and we are not able to **s.** without, ... 5975
Ezr 10:14 our rulers of all the congregation **s.**, ... 5975
Ne 7:3 while they **s.** by, let them shut the..... 5975
Ne 9:5 **S.** up and bless the Lord your God..... 6965
Es 3:4 Mordecai's matters would **s.**:............. 5975
Es 8:11 and to **s.** for their life, to destroy, ... 5975
Job 8:15 upon his house, but it shall not **s.**:...... 5975
Job 19:25 he shall **s.** at the latter day upon........ 6965
Job 30:20 I **s.** up, and thou regardest me 5975
Job 33:5 thy words in order before me, **s.** up. .. 3320
Job 37:14 Hearken unto this, O Job: **s.** still,....... 5975
Job 38:14 the seal; and they **s.** as a garment....... 3320
Job 41:10 who then is able to **s.** before me? 3320
Ps 1:5 the ungodly shall not **s.** in the........... 6965
Ps 4:4 **S.** in awe, and sin not: commune.............
Ps 5:5 foolish shall not **s.** in thy sight: 3320
Ps 20:8 but we are risen, and **s.** upright.......... 5749
Ps 24:3 or who shall **s.** in his holy place?........ 6965
Ps 30:7 made my mountain to **s.** strong:.......... 5975
Ps 33:8 inhabitants of the world **s.** in awe....... 1481
Ps 35:2 buckler, and **s.** up for mine help......... 6965
Ps 38:11 My lovers and my friends **s.** aloof....... 5975
Ps 38:11 my sore; and my kinsmen **s.** afar off. .. 5975
Ps 45:9 thy right hand did **s.** the queen in....... 5324
Ps 73:7 Their eyes **s.** out with fatness: 3318
Ps 76:7 and who may **s.** in thy sight when....... 5975
Ps 78:13 made the waters to **s.** as an heap....... 5324
Ps 89:28 my covenant shall **s.** fast with him........ 539
Ps 89:43 not made him to **s.** in the battle.......... 6965
Ps 94:16 who will **s.** up for me against the 3320
Ps 109:6 and let Satan **s.** at his right hand......... 5975
Ps 109:31 he shall **s.** at the right hand of the...... 5975
Ps 111:8 They **s.** fast for ever and ever, and 5564
Ps 122:2 Our feet shall **s.** within thy gates,....... 5975
Ps 130:3 iniquities, O Lord, who shall **s.**? 5975
Ps 134:1 which by night **s.** in the house of the .. 5975
Ps 135:2 Ye that **s.** in the house of the Lord,.... 5975
Ps 147:17 morsels: who can **s.** before his cold?... 5975
Pr 12:7 the house of the righteous shall **s.**. 5975
Pr 19:21 counsel of the Lord, that shall **s.**........ 6965
Pr 22:29 business? he shall **s.** before kings: 3320
Pr 22:29 he shall not **s.** before mean men. 3320
Pr 25:6 **s.** not in the place of great men: 5975
Pr 27:4 but who is able to **s.** before envy?...... 5975
Ec 4:15 second child that shall **s.** up in his 5975
Ec 8:3 of his sight: **s.** not in an evil thing; 5975
Isa 7:7 It shall not **s.**, neither shall it............. 6965
Isa 8:10 speak the word, and it shall not **s.**....... 6965
Isa 11:10 **s.** for an ensign of the people; 5975
Isa 14:24 as I have purposed, so shall it **s.**........ 6965
Isa 21:8 I **s.**...upon the watchtower................. 5975
Isa 27:9 groves and images shall not **s.** up. 6965
Isa 28:18 agreement with hell shall not **s.**;......... 6965
Isa 32:8 and by liberal thing shall he **s.**. 6965
Isa 40:8 word of our God shall **s.** for ever. 6965
Isa 44:11 gathered together, let them **s.** up;....... 5975
Isa 46:10 My counsel shall **s.**, and I will do 6965
Isa 47:12 **S.** now with thine enchantments,........ 5975
Isa 47:13 the monthly prognosticators, **s.** up,..... 5975
Isa 48:13 call unto them, they **s.** up together..... 5975
Isa 50:8 let us **s.** together: who is mine.......... 5975
Isa 51:17 awake, **s.** up, O Jerusalem, which....... 6965
Isa 61:5 strangers shall **s.** and feed your 5975
Isa 65:5 Which say, **S.** by thyself, come not..... 7126
Jer 6:16 **S.** ye in the ways, and see, and......... 5975
Jer 7:2 **S.** in the gate of the Lord's house, ... 5975
Jer 7:10 come and **s.** before me in this house, .. 5975
Jer 14:6 wild asses did **s.** in the high places, ... 5975
Jer 15:19 again, and thou shalt **s.** before me: 5975
Jer 17:19 Go and **s.** in the gate of the children... 5975
Jer 26:2 **S.** in the court of the Lord's house, ... 5975
Jer 35:19 want a man to **s.** before me for ever... 5975
Jer 44:28 shall know whose words shall **s.**,........ 6965
Jer 44:29 words shall surely **s.** against you........ 6965
Jer 46:4 and **s.** forth with your helmets; 3320
Jer 46:14 **S.** fast, and prepare thee; for the....... 3320
Jer 46:21 they did not **s.**, because the day of..... 5975
Jer 48:19 inhabitant of Aroer, **s.** by the way,a..... 5975
Jer 49:19 who is that shepherd that will **s.** 5975
Jer 50:44 who is that shepherd that will **s.** 5975
Jer 51:50 the sword, go away, **s.** not still:......... 5975
Eze 2:1 Son of man, **s.** upon thy feet, and I 5975
Eze 13:5 to **s.** in the battle in the day of the..... 5975
Eze 17:14 keeping of his covenant it might **s.**...... 5975
Eze 22:30 **s.** in the gap before me for the land,.... 5975
Eze 27:29 ships, they shall **s.** upon the land;....... 5975
Eze 29:7 madest all their loins to be at a **s.**. 5976
Eze 31:14 their trees **s.** up in their height, ... 5975
Eze 33:26 Ye **s.** upon your sword, ye work........ 5975
Eze 44:11 shall **s.** before them to minister unto...... 5975
Eze 44:15 and they shall **s.** before me to offer 5975
Eze 44:24 they shall **s.** in judgment; and........... 5975
Eze 46:2 and shall **s.** by the post of the gate,.... 5975
Eze 47:10 that the fishers shall **s.** upon it from..... 5975
Da 1:4 in them to **s.** in the king's palace,....... 5975
Da 1:5 they might **s.** before the king. 5975
Da 2:44 kingdoms, and it shall **s.** for ever. 6966
Da 7:4 and made **s.** upon the feet as a man,... 6966
Da 8:4 that no beasts might **s.** before him,...... 5975
Da 8:7 there was no power in the ram to **s.**.... 5975
Da 8:22 four kingdoms shall **s.** up out of the.... 5975
Da 8:23 dark sentences, shall **s.** up............... 5975
Da 8:25 shall also **s.** up against the Prince....... 5975
Da 10:11 I speak unto thee, and **s.** upright:........ 5975
Da 11:2 there shall **s.** up yet three kings in..... 5975
Da 11:3 And a mighty king shall **s.** up, that 5975
Da 11:4 when he shall **s.** up, his kingdom........ 5975
Da 11:6 neither shall he **s.**, nor his arm: 5975
Da 11:7 branch of her roots shall one **s.** up 5975
Da 11:14 many **s.** up against the king of the...... 5975
Da 11:16 will, and none shall **s.** before him: 5975
Da 11:16 and he shall **s.** in the glorious land,..... 5975
Da 11:17 she shall not **s.** on his side, neither..... 5975
Da 11:20 **s.** up in his estate a raiser of taxes..... 5975
Da 11:21 his estate shall **s.** up a vile person,..... 5975
Da 11:25 mighty army; but he shall not **s.**.......... 5975
Da 11:31 And arms shall **s.** on his part, and 5975
Da 12:1 And at that time shall Michael **s.** up,... 5975
Da 12:13 **s.** in thy lot at the end of the days. ... 5975
Am 2:15 shall he **s.** that handleth the bow;....... 5975
Mic 5:4 he shall **s.** and feed in the strength..... 5975
Na 1:6 Who can **s.** before his indignation?...... 5975
Na 2:8 **S.**, **s.**, shall they cry: but none shall ... 5975
Hab 2:1 I will **s.** upon my watch, and set me ... 5975
Zec 3:7 to walk among these that **s.** by.......... 5975
Zec 4:14 **s.** by the Lord of the whole earth....... 5975
Zec 14:4 his feet shall **s.** in that day upon......... 5975
Zec 14:12 away while they **s.** upon their feet,..... 5975
Mal 3:2 who shall **s.** when he appeareth? 5975
Mt 12:25 **divided against itself shall not s.**... *2476*
Mt 12:26 **how shall then his kingdom s.?**..... *2476*
Mt 12:47 mother and thy brethren **s.** without,..... *2476*
Mt 20:6 **Why s. ye here all the day idle?**.... *2476*
Mt 24:15 **the prophet, s. in the holy place,**... *2476*
Mk 3:3 had the withered hand, **S. forth.** *1453*
Mk 3:24 **itself, that kingdom cannot s.**. *2476*
Mk 3:25 **against itself, that house cannot s.**. *2476*
Mk 3:26 **and be divided, he cannot s., but**... *2476*
Mk 9:1 **there be some of them that s. here,** *2476*
Mk 11:25 **And when ye s. praying, forgive,**... *4739*
Lu 1:19 that **s.** in the presence of God; *3936*
Lu 6:8 **Rise up, and s. forth in the midst.**.. *2476*
Lu 8:20 mother and thy brethren **s.** without,... *2476*
Lu 11:18 **himself, how shall his kingdom s.?**. *2476*
Lu 13:25 **and ye begin to s. without, and to.** *2476*
Lu 21:36 **and to s. before the Son of man.**... *2476*
Joh 11:42 **of the people which s. by I said it,** .*4026*
Ac 1:11 why **s.** ye gazing up into heaven? *2476*
Ac 4:10 this man **s.** here before you whole...... *3936*
Ac 5:20 Go, **s.** and speak in the temple to *2476*

Ac 8:38 commanded the chariot to **s.** still: *2476*
Ac 10:26 **S.** up; I myself also am a man *450*
Ac 14:10 loud voice, **S.** upright on thy feet *450*
Ac 25:10 I **s.** at Caesar's judgment seat, ... *2476*
Ac 26:6 I **s.** and am judged for the hope of *2476*
Ac 26:16 **But rise, and s. upon thy feet: for.** *2476*
Ro 5:2 faith into this grace wherein we **s.**, ... *2476*
Ro 9:11 God according to election might **s.**, ... *3306*
Ro 14:4 up: for God is able to make him **s.** *2476*
Ro 14:10 we shall all **s.** before the judgment *3936*
1Co 2:5 should not **s.** in the wisdom of men, ... *1510*
1Co 15:1 I have received, and wherein ye **s.**; *2476*
1Co 15:30 why **s.** we in jeopardy every hour? ....
1Co 16:13 **s.** fast in the faith, quit you like *4739*
2Co 1:24 of your joy; for by faith ye **s.** *2476*
Ga 4:20 my voice; for I **s.** in doubt of you. *639*
Ga 5:1 **S.** fast therefore in the liberty *4739*
Eph 6:11 may be able to **s.** against the wiles *2476*
Eph 6:13 evil day, and having done all, to **s.** *2476*
Eph 6:14 **S.** therefore, having your loins girt *2476*
Php 1:27 that ye **s.** fast in one spirit, with *4739*
Php 4:1 so **s.** fast in the Lord, my dearly *4739*
Col 4:12 ye may **s.** perfect and complete in *2476*
1Th 3:8 we live, if ye **s.** fast in the Lord. *4739*
2Th 2:15 **s.** fast, and hold the traditions *4739*
Jas 2:3 **S.** thou there, or sit here under *2476*
1Pe 5:12 the true grace of God wherein ye **s.** .. *2476*
Re 3:20 **I s. at the door, and knock:** *2476*
Re 6:17 come; and who shall be able to **s.**? *2476*
Re 10:5 angel which I saw **s.** upon the sea *2476*
Re 15:2 **s.** on the sea of glass, having the *2476*
Re 18:15 shall **s.** afar off for the fear of her *2476*
Re 20:12 I saw the dead,...**s.** before God; *2476*

STANDARD See also STANDARDBEARER; STANDARDS.
Nu 1:52 and every man by his own **s.**, ... 1714
Nu 2:2 of Israel shall pitch by his own **s.**, ... 1714
Nu 2:3 they of the **s.** of the camp of Judah 1714
Nu 2:10 be the **s.** of the camp of Reuben 1714
Nu 2:18 be the **s.** of the camp of Ephraim 1714
Nu 2:25 The **s.** of the camp of Dan shall be 1714
Nu 10:14 went the **s.** of the camp...of Judah 1714
Nu 10:18 And the **s.** of the camp of Reuben 1714
Nu 10:22 the **s.** of the camp...of Ephraim 1714
Nu 10:25 And the **s.** of the camp...of Dan 1714
Isa 49:22 and set up my **s.** to the people: 5251
Isa 59:19 Spirit of the Lord shall lift up a **s.** 5127
Isa 62:10 stones; lift up a **s.** for the people. 5251
Jer 4:6 Set up the **s.** toward Zion: retire, ... 5251
Jer 4:21 How long shall I see the **s.**, and 5251
Jer 50:2 and publish, and set up a **s.**; 5251
Jer 51:12 Set...**s.** upon the walls of Babylon, ... 5251
Jer 51:27 Set ye up a **s.** in the land, blow the 5251

STANDARDBEARER
Isa 10:18 shall be as when a **s.** fainteth 5264

STANDARDS
Nu 2:17 every man in his place by their **s.** 1714
Nu 2:31 shall go hindmost with their **s.** 1714
Nu 2:34 so they pitched by their **s.**, and so 1714

STANDEST See also UNDERSTANDEST.
Ge 24:31 wherefore **s.** thou without? for I 5975
Ex 3:5 the place whereon thou **s.** is holy 5975
Jos 5:15 the place whereon thou **s.** is holy. 5975
Ps 10:1 Why **s.** thou afar off, O Lord? why 5975
Ac 7:33 for the place where thou **s.** is holy *2476*
Ro 11:20 broken off, and thou **s.** by faith. *2476*

STANDETH See also UNDERSTANDETH.
Nu 14:14 and that thy cloud **s.** over them, ... 5975
De 1:38 son of Nun, which **s.** before thee, ... 5975
De 17:12 that **s.** to minister there before the 5975
De 29:15 him that **s.** here with us this day 5975
Jg 16:26 pillars whereupon the house **s.**, ... 3559
Es 6:5 Behold, Haman **s.** in the court. 5975
Es 7:9 gallows...**s.** in the house of Haman. 5975
Ps 1:1 nor **s.** in the way of sinners, nor 5975
Ps 26:12 My foot **s.** in an even place: in the 5975
Ps 33:11 The counsel of the Lord **s.** for ever, ... 5975
Ps 82:1 God **s.** in the congregation of the 5324
Ps 119:161 but my heart **s.** in awe of thy word ....
Pr 8:2 She **s.** in the top of high places, by 5324
Ca 2:9 he **s.** behind our wall, he looketh 5975
Isa 3:13 The Lord **s.** up to plead, ... 5324
Isa 3:13 and **s.** to judge the people 5975
Isa 46:7 and set him in his place, and he **s.**; 5975
Isa 59:14 backward, and justice **s.** afar off: 5975
Da 12:1 prince which **s.** for the children of 5975
Zec 11:16 broken, nor feed that that **s.** still: 5324
Joh 1:26 but there **s.** one among you, whom *2476*
Joh 3:29 which **s.** and heareth him, ... *2476*
Ro 14:4 to his own master he **s.** or falleth *4739*
1Co 7:37 he that **s.** stedfast in his heart, ... *2476*
1Co 8:13 I will eat no flesh while the world **s.**, ...
1Co 10:12 let him that thinketh he **s.** take *2476*
2Ti 2:19 the foundation of God **s.** sure, ... *2476*
Heb 10:11 every priest **s.** daily ministering *2476*
Jas 5:9 behold, the judge **s.** before the door. .. *2476*
Re 10:8 the angel which **s.** upon the sea and *2476*

STANDING See also UNDERSTANDING.
Ex 22:6 stacks of corn, or the **s.** corn, ... 7054
Ex 26:15 tabernacle of shittim wood **s.** up 5975
Ex 36:20 tabernacle of shittim wood, **s.** up 5975
Le 26:1 neither rear you up a **s.** image, ... 4676
Nu 22:23, 31 angel of the Lord **s.** in the way, ... 5324
De 23:25 When thou comest into the **s.** corn 7054
De 23:25 sickle unto thy neighbour's **s.** corn 7054
Jg 15:5 into the **s.** corn of the Philistines, ... 7054
Jg 15:5 the shocks, and also the **s.** corn, ... 7054
1Sa 19:20 Samuel **s.** as appointed over them, ... 5975
1Sa 22:6 his servants were **s.** about him;) 5324
1Ki 13:25 and the lion **s.** by the carcase: 5975
1Ki 13:28 ass and the lion **s.** by the carcase: 5975
1Ki 22:19 and all the host of heaven **s.** by him 5975
2Ch 9:18 place, and two lions **s.** by the stays: ... 5975
2Ch 18:18 the host of heaven **s.** on his right 5975
Es 5:2 Esther the queen **s.** in the court, ... 5975
Ps 69:2 deep mire, where there is no **s.**: 4613
Ps 107:35 the wilderness into a **s.** water, ... 98
Ps 114:8 turned the rock into a **s.** water, ... 98
Da 8:6 I had seen **s.** before the river, ... 5975
Am 9:1 I saw the Lord **s.** upon the altar: 5324
Mic 1:11 he shall receive of you his **s.** 5979
Mic 5:13 thy **s.** images out of the midst of 4676
Zec 3:1 the high priest **s.** before the angel 5975
Zec 3:1 Satan **s.** at his right hand to resist 5975
Zec 6:5 from **s.** before the Lord of all the 3320
Mt 6:5 **to pray s. in the synagogues** *2476*
Mt 16:28 **There be some s. here, which shall.** *2476*
Mt 20:3 **others s. idle in the marketplace** .. *2476*
Mt 20:6 **went out, and found others s. idle,** *2476*
Mk 3:31 and, **s.** without, sent unto him, ... *2476*
Mk 13:14 **desolation,...s. where it ought not,** *2476*
Lu 1:11 **s.** on the right side of the altar of *2476*
Lu 5:2 And saw two ships **s.** by the lake: *2476*
Lu 9:27 **there be some s. here, which shall** *2476*
Lu 18:13 **publican, s. afar off, would not** *2476*
Joh 8:9 and the woman **s.** in the midst *2476*
Joh 19:26 disciple **s.** by, whom he loved, ... *3936*
Joh 20:14 herself back, and saw Jesus **s.**, ... *2476*
Ac 2:14 Peter, **s.** up with the eleven, lifted *2476*
Ac 4:14 the man which was healed **s.** with *2476*
Ac 5:23 keepers **s.** without before the doors: ... *2476*
Ac 5:25 put in prison are **s.** in the temple, ... *2476*
Ac 7:55 Jesus **s.** on the right hand of God *2476*
Ac 7:56 Son of man **s.** on the right hand of *2476*
Ac 22:20 I also was **s.** by, and consenting *2186*
Ac 24:21 voice, that I cried **s.** among them, ... *2476*
Heb 9:8 the first tabernacle was yet **s.** ... *2192,4714*
2Pe 3:5 earth **s.** out of the water and in *4921*
Re 7:1 four angels **s.** on the four corners *2476*
Re 11:4 two candlesticks **s.** before the God *2476*
Re 18:10 **S.** afar off for...fear of her torment, ... *2476*
Re 19:17 And I saw an angel **s.** in the sun; *2476*

STANK
Ex 7:21 and the river **s.**, and the Egyptians 887
Ex 8:14 upon heaps: and the land **s.** 887
Ex 16:20 morning, and it bred worms, and **s.**: 887
2Sa 10:6 saw that they **s.** before David, the 887

STAR See also STARGAZERS; STARS.
Nu 24:17 shall come a **S.** out of Jacob, and 3556
Am 5:26 your images, the **s.** of your god, ... 3556
Mt 2:2 for we have seen his **s.** in the east, ... *792*
Mt 2:7 what time the **s.** appeared. *792*
Mt 2:9 the **s.**, which they saw in the east, ... *792*
Mt 2:10 When they saw the **s.**, they rejoiced *792*
Ac 7:43 and the **s.** of your god Remphan, ... *798*
1Co 15:41 for one **s.** differeth from another *792*
1Co 15:41 differeth from another **s.** in glory. *792*
2Pe 1:19 the day **s.** arise in your hearts: *5459*
Re 2:28 **And I will give him the morning s.** . *792*
Re 8:10 there fell a great **s.** from heaven, ... *792*
Re 8:11 name of the **s.** is called Wormwood: *792*
Re 9:1 I saw a **s.** fall from heaven unto the *792*
Re 22:16 **and the bright and morning s.** *792*

STARE
Ps 22:17 bones: they look and **s.** upon me 7200

STARGAZERS
Isa 47:13 now the astrologers, the **s.**, ... 2374,3556

STARS
Ge 1:16 the night: he made the **s.** also. 3556
Ge 15:5 now toward heaven, and tell the **s.**, ... 3556
Ge 22:17 thy seed as the **s.** of the heaven, ... 3556
Ge 26:4 seed to multiply as the **s.** of heaven, ... 3556
Ge 37:9 eleven **s.** made obeisance to me 3556
Ex 32:13 your seed as the **s.** of heaven, and 3556
De 1:10 as the **s.** of heaven for multitude 3556
De 4:19 the sun, and the moon, and the **s.** 3556
De 10:22 made thee as the **s.** of heaven for 3556
De 28:62 ye were as the **s.** of heaven for 3556
Jg 5:20 the **s.** in their courses fought 3556
1Ch 27:23 Israel like to the **s.** of the heavens. 3556
Ne 4:21 the morning till the **s.** appeared 3556
Ne 9:23 thou as the **s.** of heaven, and 3556
Job 3:9 Let the **s.** of the twilight...be dark; 3556
Job 9:7 it riseth not; and sealeth up the **s.** 3556
Job 22:12 and behold the height of the **s.**, how ... 3556
Job 25:5 yea, the **s.** are not pure in his sight, ... 3556
Job 38:7 When the morning **s.** sang together, ... 3556
Ps 8:3 the moon and the **s.**, which thou 3556
Ps 136:9 The moon and **s.** to rule by night: 3556
Ps 147:4 He telleth the number of the **s.**; 3556
Ps 148:3 moon: praise him, all ye **s.** of light 3556
Ec 12:2 moon, or the **s.**, be not darkened 3556
Isa 13:10 For the **s.** of heaven and the 3556
Isa 14:13 will exalt my throne above the **s.** 3556
Jer 31:35 and of the **s.** for a light by night, ... 3556
Eze 32:7 and make the **s.** thereof dark; 3556
Da 8:10 host and of the **s.** to the ground, ... 3556
Da 12:3 as the **s.** for ever and ever. 3556
Joe 2:10 the **s.** shall withdraw their shining: 3556
Joe 3:15 the **s.** shall withdraw their shining 3556
Am 5:8 Seek him that maketh the seven **s.** 3598
Ob 4 thou set thy nest among the **s.**, ... 3556
Na 3:16 merchants above the **s.** of heaven: 3556
Mt 24:29 **and the s. shall fall from heaven,** ... *792*
Mk 13:25 **And the s. of heaven shall fall,** *792*
Lu 21:25 **and in the moon, and in the s.;** *798*
Ac 27:20 sun nor **s.** in many days appeared, ... *798*
1Co 15:41 moon, and another glory of the **s.**: *792*
Heb 11:12 as the **s.** of the sky in multitude, ... *798*
Jude 13 wandering **s.**, to whom is reserved *792*
Re 1:16 he had in his right hand seven **s.**: *792*
Re 1:20 **The mystery of the seven s. which** .. *792*
Re 1:20 **seven s. are the angels of the seven** *792*
Re 2:1 **he that holdeth the seven s. in his** .. *792*
Re 3:1 **Spirits of God, and the seven s.;** *792*
Re 6:13 the **s.** of heaven fell unto the earth, ... *792*
Re 8:12 moon, and the third part of the **s.**; *792*
Re 12:1 upon her head a crown of twelve **s.**: *792*
Re 12:4 the third part of the **s.** of heaven, ... *792*

STATE See also ESTATE.
Ge 43:7 The man asked us straitly of our **s.**, ...
2Ch 24:13 they set the house of God in his **s.**, ... 4971
Es 1:7 according to the **s.** of the king. 3027
Es 2:18 according to the **s.** of the king. 3027
Ps 39:5 at his best **s.** is altogether vanity 5324
Pr 27:23 to know the **s.** of thy flocks, and 6440
Pr 28:2 the **s.** thereof shall be prolonged. 3651
Isa 22:19 and from thy **s.** shall he pull thee 4612
Mt 12:45 **the last s. of that man is worse than...**
Lu 11:26 **the last s. of that man is worse than...**
Php 2:19 comfort, when I know your **s.** ... *3588,4012*
Php 2:20 will naturally care for your **s.** *3588,4012*
Php 4:11 in whatsoever **s.** I am, therewith to ....
Col 4:7 my **s.** shall Tychicus declare *3588,2596*

STATELY
Eze 23:41 satest upon a **s.** bed, and a table 3520

STATION
Isa 22:19 And I will drive thee from thy **s.**, ... 4673

STATURE
Nu 13:32 we saw in it are men of a great **s.** 4060
1Sa 16:7 or on the height of his **s.**; because 6967
2Sa 21:20 where was a man of great **s.**, that 4055
1Ch 11:23 an Egyptian, a man of great **s.**, ... 4060

1Ch 20:6 Gath, where was a man of great **s.**,.... 4060
Ca 7:7 This thy **s.** is like to a palm tree,....... 6967
Isa 10:33 high ones of **s.** shall be hewn down,.... 6967
Isa 45:14 and of the Sabeans, men of **s.**,.......... 4060
Eze 13:18 the head of every **s.** to hunt souls!..... 6967
Eze 17:6 became a spreading vine of low **s.**,..... 6967
Eze 19:11 her **s.** was exalted among the thick..... 6967
Eze 31:3 shadowing shroud,...of an high **s.**;...... 6967
Mt 6:27 **can add one cubit unto his s.?**....... *2244*
Lu 2:52 Jesus increased in wisdom and **s.**,....... *2244*
Lu 12:25 **can add to his s. one cubit?**.......... *2244*
Lu 19:3 press, because he was little of **s.**....... *2244*
Eph 4:13 unto the measure of the **s.** of the....... *2244*

STATUTE See also STATUTES.
Ex 15:25 there he made for them a **s.** and........ 2706
Ex 27:21 it shall be a **s.** for ever unto their....... 2708
Ex 28:43 it shall be a **s.** for ever unto him......... 2708
Ex 29:9 shall be theirs for a perpetual **s.**:........ 2708
Ex 29:28 and his sons' by a **s.** for ever from..... 2706
Ex 30:21 and it shall be a **s.** for ever to them,... 2706
Le 3:17 It shall be a perpetual **s.** for your....... 2708
Le 6:18 It shall be a **s.** for ever in your.......... 2706
Le 6:22 it is a **s.** for ever unto the Lord; it..... 2706
Le 7:34 and unto his sons by a **s.** for ever...... 2706
Le 7:36 by a **s.** for ever throughout their........ 2708
Le 10:9 be a **s.** for ever throughout your........ 2708
Le 10:15 sons' with thee, by a **s.** for ever;........ 2706
Le 16:29 this shall be a **s.** for ever unto you:.... 2708
Le 16:31 afflict your souls, by a **s.** for ever....... 2708
Le 16:34 shall be an everlasting **s.** unto you,..... 2708
Le 17:7 This shall be a **s.** for ever unto.......... 2708
Le 23:14 be a **s.** for ever throughout your......... 2708
Le 23:21 it shall be a **s.** for ever in all your...... 2708
Le 23:31 be a **s.** for ever throughout your......... 2708
Le 23:41 It shall be a **s.** for ever in your.......... 2708
Le 24:3 it shall be a **s.** for ever in your.......... 2708
Le 24:9 made by fire by a perpetual **s.**........... 2706
Nu 18:11, 19 with thee, by a **s.** for ever:........... 2706
Nu 18:23 be a **s.** for ever throughout your......... 2708
Nu 19:10 among them, for a **s.** for ever.......... 2708
Nu 19:21 it shall be a perpetual **s.** unto them,.... 2708
Nu 27:11 children of Israel a **s.** of judgment,...... 2708
Nu 35:29 things shall be for a **s.** of judgment..... 2708
Jos 24:25 set them a **s.** and an ordinance in........ 2706
1Sa 30:25 he made it a **s.** and an ordinance........ 2706
Ps 81:4 For this was a **s.** for Israel, and a...... 2706
Da 6:7 together to establish a royal **s.**,.......... 7010
Da 6:15 no decree nor **s.** which the king......... 7010

STATUTES
Ge 26:5 my commandments, my **s.**, and my..... 2708
Ex 15:26 commandments, and keep...his **s.**,...... 2706
Ex 18:16 do make them know the **s.** of God,..... 2706
Le 10:11 all the **s.** which the Lord hath........... 2706
Le 18:5 Ye shall therefore keep my **s.**, and..... 2708
Le 18:26 Ye shall therefore keep my **s.** and...... 2708
Le 19:19 Ye shall keep my **s.**. Thou shalt......... 2708
Le 19:37 Therefore shall ye observe all my **s.**... 2708
Le 20:8 ye shall keep my **s.**, and do them:...... 2708
Le 20:22 Ye shall therefore keep all my **s.**,........ 2708
Le 25:18 Wherefore ye shall do my **s.**, and....... 2708
Le 26:3 If ye walk in my **s.**, and keep my........ 2708
Le 26:15 And if ye shall despise my **s.**, or if....... 2708
Le 26:43 because their soul abhorred my **s.**...... 2708
Le 26:46 These are the **s.** and judgments and.... 2708
Nu 30:16 These are the **s.**, which the Lord........ 2706
De 4:1 unto the **s.** and unto the judgments,..... 2706
De 4:5 I have taught you **s.** and judgments,..... 2706
De 4:6 which shall hear all these **s.**, and........ 2706
De 4:8 that hath **s.** and judgments so............ 2706
De 4:14 me at that time to teach you **s.** and.... 2706
De 4:40 Thou shalt keep therefore his **s.**,......... 2706
De 4:45 are the testimonies, and the **s.**, and.... 2706
De 5:1 the **s.** and judgments which I speak.... 2706
De 5:31 all the commandments, and the **s.**,....... 2706
De 6:1 are the commandments, the **s.**, and.... 2706
De 6:2 all his **s.** and his commandments,........ 2708
De 6:17 his **s.**, which he hath commanded....... 2706
De 6:20 mean the testimonies, and the **s.**,........ 2706
De 6:24 commanded us to do all these **s.**,........ 2706
De 7:11 keep the commandments, and the **s.**,.. 2706
De 8:11 his **s.**, which I command thee this...... 2708
De 10:13 his **s.**, which I command thee this....... 2708
De 11:1 and keep his charge, and his **s.**,......... 2708
De 11:32 ye shall observe to do all the **s.**.......... 2706
De 12:1 These are the **s.** and judgments,......... 2706
De 16:12 thou shalt observe and do these **s.**..... 2706
De 17:19 the words of this law and these **s.**,...... 2706
De 26:16 hath commanded thee to do these **s.**.... 2706
De 26:17 to keep his **s.**, and...commandments,.. 2706
De 27:10 do his commandments and his **s.**,........ 2706
De 28:15 his **s.** which I command thee this........ 2708
De 28:45 keep his commandments and his **s.**...... 2708
De 30:10, 16 his commandments and his **s.**......... 2708
2Sa 22:23 as for his **s.**, I did not depart from..... 2708
1Ki 2:3 to walk in his ways, to keep his **s.**,..... 2708
1Ki 3:3 walking in the **s.** of David his............ 2708
1Ki 3:14 keep my **s.** and...commandments,......... 2706
1Ki 6:12 if thou wilt walk in my **s.**, and........... 2708
1Ki 8:58 his commandments, and his **s.**,............ 2706
1Ki 8:61 to walk in his **s.**, and to keep his........ 2706
1Ki 9:4 wilt keep my **s.** and my judgments:..... 2706
1Ki 9:6 keep my commandments and...**s.**......... 2708
1Ki 11:11 not kept my covenant and my **s.**,........ 2708
1Ki 11:33 to keep my **s.** and my judgments,........ 2708
1Ki 11:34 kept my commandments and my **s.**..... 2708
1Ki 11:38 keep my **s.** and my commandments,...... 2708
2Ki 17:8 And walked in the **s.** of the heathen,... 2708
2Ki 17:13 keep my commandments and my **s.**,.... 2708
2Ki 17:15 And they rejected his **s.**, and his........ 2706
2Ki 17:19 walked in the **s.** of Israel which.......... 2708
2Ki 17:34 neither do they after their **s.**, or......... 2708
2Ki 17:37 And the **s.**, and the ordinances,.......... 2706
2Ki 23:3 his testimonies and his **s.** with all....... 2708
1Ch 22:13 heed to fulfil the **s.** and judgments...... 2706
1Ch 29:19 thy testimonies, and thy **s.**, and to...... 2706
2Ch 7:17 observe my **s.** and my judgments;....... 2706
2Ch 7:19 if ye turn away, and forsake my **s.**...... 2708
2Ch 19:10 **s.** and judgments, ye shall even......... 2706
2Ch 33:8 to the whole law and the **s.** and.......... 2706
2Ch 34:31 his testimonies, and his **s.**, with all..... 2706
Ezr 7:10 to teach in Israel **s.** and judgments...... 2706
Ezr 7:11 of the Lord, and of his **s.** to Israel...... 2706
Ne 1:7 kept the commandments, nor the **s.**,... 2706
Ne 9:13 laws, good **s.** and commandments:...... 2706
Ne 9:14 **s.**, and laws, by the hand of Moses..... 2706
Ne 10:29 Lord, and his judgments and his **s.**;.... 2706
Ps 18:22 I did not put away his **s.** from me....... 2708
Ps 19:8 the **s.** of the Lord are right,............... 6490
Ps 50:16 hast thou to do to declare my **s.**,........ 2706
Ps 89:31 If they break my **s.**, and keep not...... 2708
Ps 105:45 That they might observe his **s.**,......... 2706
Ps 119:5 ways were directed to keep thy **s.**!..... 2706
Ps 119:8 I will keep thy **s.**: O forsake me not... 2706
Ps 119:12 art thou, O Lord: teach me thy **s.**...... 2706
Ps 119:16 I will delight myself in thy **s.**: I.......... 2708
Ps 119:23 thy servant did meditate in thy **s.**........ 2706
Ps 119:26 thou heardest me: teach me thy **s.**..... 2706
Ps 119:33 me, O Lord, the way of thy **s.**; and..... 2706
Ps 119:48 loved; and I will meditate in thy **s.**...... 2706
Ps 119:54 Thy **s.** have been my songs in the........ 2706
Ps 119:64 full of thy mercy: teach me thy **s.**...... 2706
Ps 119:68 and doest good; teach me thy **s.**........ 2706
Ps 119:71 afflicted; that I might learn thy **s.**...... 2706
Ps 119:80 Let my heart be sound in thy **s.**;......... 2706
Ps 119:83 smoke; yet do I not forget thy **s.**........ 2706
Ps 119:112 mine heart to perform thy **s.** alway,..... 2706
Ps 119:117 and I will have respect unto thy **s.**...... 2706
Ps 119:118 down all them that err from thy **s.**...... 2706
Ps 119:124 unto thy mercy, and teach me thy **s.**.... 2706
Ps 119:135 thy servant; and teach me thy **s.**........ 2706
Ps 119:145 hear me, O Lord: I will keep thy **s.**.... 2706
Ps 119:155 wicked: for they seek not thy **s.**......... 2706
Ps 119:171 when thou hast taught me thy **s.**......... 2706
Ps 147:19 his **s.** and...judgments unto Israel........ 2706
Jer 44:10 nor in my **s.**, that I set before you...... 2708
Jer 44:23 nor in his **s.**, nor in his testimonies;.... 2708
Eze 5:6 my **s.** more than the countries that..... 2708
Eze 5:6 refused my judgments and my **s.**,........ 2708
Eze 5:7 have not walked in my **s.**, neither....... 2708
Eze 11:12 for ye have not walked in my **s.**,......... 2706
Eze 11:20 That they may walk in my **s.**, and....... 2708
Eze 18:9 Hath walked in my **s.**, and hath.......... 2708
Eze 18:17 judgments, hath walked in my **s.**;........ 2708
Eze 18:19 hath kept all my **s.**, and hath done...... 2708
Eze 18:21 keep all my **s.**, and do that which is.... 2708
Eze 20:11 And I gave them my **s.**, and shewed... 2708
Eze 20:13 they walked not in my **s.**, and they..... 2708
Eze 20:16 walked...not in my **s.**, but polluted....... 2708
Eze 20:18 Walk...not in the **s.** of your fathers,..... 2706
Eze 20:19 Lord your God; walk in my **s.**,........... 2708
Eze 20:21 they walked not in my **s.**, neither....... 2708
Eze 20:24 but had despised my **s.**, and had........ 2708
Eze 20:25 gave them...**s.** that were not good,..... 2706
Eze 33:15 walk in the **s.** of live, without............ 2708
Eze 36:27 cause you to walk in my **s.**, and ye..... 2706
Eze 37:24 and observe my **s.**, and do them......... 2708
Eze 44:24 they shall keep my laws and my **s.**..... 2708
Mic 6:16 For the **s.** of Omri are kept, and all.... 2708
Zec 1:6 But my words and my **s.**, which I...... 2706
Mal 4:4 Israel, with the **s.** and judgments......... 2706

STAUNCHED See STANCHED.

STAVES See also HANDSTAVES.
Ex 25:13 thou shalt make **s.** of shittim wood,...... 905
Ex 25:14 thou shalt put the **s.** into the rings....... 905
Ex 25:15 The **s.** shall be in the rings of the........ 905
Ex 25:27 shall the rings be for places of the **s.**..... 905
Ex 25:28 shalt make the **s.** of shittim wood,........ 905
Ex 27:6 and thou shalt make **s.** for the altar,..... 905
Ex 27:6 **s.** of shittim wood, and overlay them.... 905
Ex 27:7 the **s.** shall be put into the rings,.......... 905
Ex 27:7 the **s.** shall be upon the two sides of.... 905
Ex 30:4 for places for the **s.** to bear it withal.... 905
Ex 30:5 shalt make the **s.** of shittim wood,........ 905
Ex 35:12 the ark, and the **s.** thereof, with the..... 905
Ex 35:13 The table, and his **s.**, and all his.......... 905
Ex 35:15 And the incense altar, and his **s.**,.......... 905
Ex 35:16 grate, his **s.**, and all his vessels the...... 905
Ex 37:4 And he made **s.** of shittim wood, and.... 905
Ex 37:5 he put the **s.** into the rings by the........ 905
Ex 37:14 places for the **s.** to bear the table........ 905
Ex 37:15 And he made the **s.** of shittim wood,.... 905
Ex 37:27 to be places for the **s.** to bear it.......... 905
Ex 37:28 And he made the **s.** of shittim wood,.... 905
Ex 38:5 grate of brass, to be places for the **s.**... 905
Ex 38:6 And he made the **s.** of shittim wood,.... 905
Ex 38:7 he put the **s.** into the rings on the........ 905
Ex 39:35 of the testimony, and the **s.** thereof,.... 905
Ex 39:39 grate...his **s.**, and all his vessels,......... 905
Ex 40:20 the ark, and set the **s.** on the ark,........ 905
Nu 4:6 blue, and shall put in the **s.** thereof...... 905
Nu 4:8 and shall put in the **s.** thereof............. 905
Nu 4:11 and shall put to the **s.** thereof:............ 905
Nu 4:14 badgers' skins, and put to the **s.** of it... 905
Nu 21:18 of the lawgiver, with their **s.**............. 4938
1Sa 17:43 that thou comest to me with **s.**?.......... 4731
1Ki 8:7 covered the ark and the **s.** thereof....... 905
1Ki 8:8 they drew out the **s.**, that the ends...... 905
1Ki 8:8 **s.** were seen out in the holy place....... 905
1Ch 15:15 upon their shoulders with the **s.**......... 4133
2Ch 5:8 covered the ark and the **s.** thereof....... 905
2Ch 5:9 And they drew out the **s.** of the ark,.... 905
2Ch 5:9 ends of the **s.** were seen from the ark.. 905
Hab 3:14 didst strike through with his **s.**.......... 4294
Zec 11:7 I took unto me two **s.**; the one I........ 4731
Mt 10:10 **coats, neither shoes, nor yet s.**....... *4464*
Mt 26:47 great multitude with swords and **s.**,..... *3586*
Mt 26:55 **against a thief with swords and s.**...*3586*
Mk 14:43 great multitude with swords and **s.**,..... *3586*
Mk 14:48 **swords and with s. to take me?**..... *3586*
Lu 9:3 **your journey, neither s., nor scrip,**.*4464*
Lu 22:52 **against a thief, with swords and s.?***3586*

STAY See also STAYED; STAYETH; STAYS.
Ge 19:17 neither **s.** thou in all the plain;........... 5975
Ex 9:28 let you go, and ye shall **s.** no longer... 5975
Le 13:5 the plague in his sight be at a **s.**,....... 5975
Le 13:23, 28 if the bright spot **s.** in his place,.... 5975
Le 13:37 if the scall be in his sight at a **s.**,....... 5975
Jos 10:19 And **s.** ye not, but pursue after your... 5975
Ru 1:13 would ye **s.** for them from having......... 5702
1Sa 15:16 **S.**, and I will tell thee what the......... 7503
1Sa 20:38 the lad, Make speed, haste, **s.** not....... 5975
2Sa 22:19 calamity: but the Lord was my **s.**....... 4937
2Sa 24:16 It is enough: **s.** now thine hand.......... 7503
1Ch 21:15 It is enough, **s.** now thine hand.......... 7503
Job 37:4 will not **s.** them when his voice.......... 6117
Job 38:37 who can **s.** the bottles of heaven,........ 7901
Ps 18:18 calamity: but the Lord was my **s.**........ 4937
Pr 28:17 flee to the pit; let no man **s.** him........ 8551
Ca 2:5 **S.** me with flagons, comfort me........... 5564
Isa 3:1 from Judah the **s.** and the staff,.......... 4937
Isa 3:1 the staff, the whole **s.** of bread,.......... 8172
Isa 3:1 bread, and the whole **s.** of water,........ 4937
Isa 10:20 no more...**s.** upon him that smote....... 4937
Isa 10:20 shall **s.** upon the Lord, the Holy.......... 8172
Isa 19:13 are the **s.** of the tribes thereof........... 6438
Isa 29:9 **S.** yourselves, and wonder; cry........... 4102
Isa 30:12 and perverseness, and **s.** thereon:...... 8172
Isa 31:1 **s.** on horses, and trust in chariots,..... 8172

Isa 48:2 and **s.**...upon the God of Israel; 5564
Isa 50:10 of the Lord, and **s.** upon his God. 8172
Jer 4:6 toward Zion: retire, **s.** not: 5975
Jer 20:9 with forbearing, and I could not **s.**.
Da 4:35 none can **s.** his hand, or say unto 4223
Ho 13:13 he should not **s.** long in the place 5975

STAYED
Ge 8:10 And he **s.** yet other seven days; 2342
Ge 8:12 And he **s.** yet other seven days; 3176
Ge 32:4 with Laban, and **s.** there until now: 309
Ex 10:24 your flocks and your herds be **s.**: 3322
Ex 17:12 Aaron and Hur **s.** up his hands, 8551
Nu 16:48, 50 and the plague was **s.**. 6113
Nu 25:8 plague was **s.** from the children of 6113
De 10:10 I **s.** in the mount, according to the 5975
Jos 10:13 the sun stood still, and the moon **s.**, 5975
1Sa 20:19 And when thou hast **s.** three days,
1Sa 24:7 David **s.** his servants with these 8156
1Sa 30:9 those that were left behind **s.**. 5975
2Sa 17:17 and Ahimaaz **s.** by En-rogel; for 5975
2Sa 24:21 plague may be **s.** from the people. 6113
2Sa 24:25 and the plague was **s.** from Israel. 6113
1Ki 22:35 the king was **s.** up in his chariot 5975
2Ki 4:6 not a vessel more. And the oil **s.**. 5975
2Ki 13:18 And he smote thrice, and **s.**. 5975
2Ki 15:20 back, and **s.** not there in the land. 5975
1Ch 21:22 plague may be **s.** from the people. 6113
2Ch 18:34 king...**s.** himself up in his chariot 5975
Job 38:11 here shall thy proud waves be **s.**? 7896
Ps 106:30 and so the plague was **s.**. 6113
Isa 26:3 peace, whose mind is **s.** on thee: 5564
La 4:6 moment, and no hands **s.** on her. 2342
Eze 31:15 and the great waters were **s.**: 3607
Hag 1:10 the heaven over you is **s.** from dew, 3607
Hag 1:10 and the earth is **s.** from her fruit. 3607
Lu 4:42 **s.** him, that he should not depart *2722*
Ac 19:22 he himself **s.** in Asia for a season. *1907*

STAYETH
Isa 27:8 he **s.** his rough wind in the day of 1898

STAYS
1Ki 10:19 there were **s.** on either side on 3027
1Ki 10:19 and two lions stood beside the **s.**. 3027
2Ch 9:18 **s.** on each side of the sitting place, 3027
2Ch 9:18 and two lions standing by the **s.**. 3027

STEAD See also BESTEAD; INSTEAD; STEADS; STEDFAST.
Ge 22:13 burnt offering in the **s.** of his son. 8478
Ge 30:2 Am I in God's **s.**, who hath withheld 8478
Ge 36:33 died, and Jobab...reigned in his **s.** 8478
Ge 36:34 and Husham...reigned in his **s.**. 8478
Ge 36:35 died, and Hadad...reigned in his **s.** 8478
Ge 36:36 and Samlah...reigned in his **s.**. 8478
Ge 36:37 died, and Saul...reigned in his **s.**. 8478
Ge 36:38 Baal-hanan...reigned in his **s.**. 8478
Ge 36:39 died, and Hadar reigned in his **s.**. 8478
Ex 29:30 And that son that is priest in his **s.** 8478
Le 6:22 his sons that is anointed in his **s.** 8478
Le 16:32 the priest's office in his father's **s.**, 8478
Nu 32:14 ye are risen up in your fathers' **s.**, 8478
De 2:12 before them, and dwelt in their **s.**; 8478
De 2:22 and dwelt in their **s.** even unto this 8478
De 2:23 them, and dwelt in their **s.**. 8478
De 10:6 in the priest's office in his **s.**. 8478
Jos 5:7 whom he raised up in their **s.**, 8478
2Sa 10:1 Hanun his son reigned in his **s.**. 8478
2Sa 16:8 Saul, in whose **s.** thou hast reigned; 8478
1Ki 1:30 shall sit upon my throne in my **s.**, 8478
1Ki 1:35 for he shall be king in my **s.**: 8478
1Ki 11:43 Rehoboam his son reigned in his **s.** 8478
1Ki 14:20 Nadab his son reigned in his **s.**. 8478
1Ki 14:27 Rehoboam made in their **s.** brasen 8478
1Ki 14:31 Adijam his son reigned in his **s.** 8478
1Ki 15:8 and Asa his son reigned in his **s.** 8478
1Ki 15:24 Jehoshaphat...reigned in his **s.**. 8478
1Ki 15:28 Baasha...reigned in his **s.**. 8478
1Ki 16:6 and Elah his son reigned in his **s.**. 8478
1Ki 16:10 And Zimri...and reigned in his **s.**. 8478
1Ki 16:28 and Ahab his son reigned in his **s.**. 8478
1Ki 22:40 Ahaziah his son reigned in his **s.**. 8478
1Ki 22:50 Jehoram his son reigned in his **s.** 8478
2Ki 1:17 And Jehoram reigned in his **s.** in 8478
2Ki 3:27 that should have reigned in his **s.**. 8478
2Ki 8:15 died: and Hazael reigned in his **s.**. 8478
2Ki 8:24 Ahaziah his son reigned in his **s.**. 8478
2Ki 10:35 Jehoahaz his son reigned in his **s.**. 8478
2Ki 12:21 Amaziah his son reigned in his **s.** 8478
2Ki 13:9 and Joash his son reigned in his **s.**. 8478
2Ki 13:24 Ben-hadad his son reigned in his **s.**. 8478
2Ki 14:16 Jeroboam his son reigned in his **s.**. 8478
2Ki 14:29 Zachariah his son reigned in his **s.**. 8478
2Ki 15:7 Jotham his son reigned in his **s.**, 8478
2Ki 15:10 And Shallum...reigned in his **s.** 8478
2Ki 15:14 Menahem...reigned in his **s.**. 8478
2Ki 15:22 Pekahiah his son reigned in his **s.**. 8478
2Ki 15:30 And Hoshea...reigned in his **s.**. 8478
2Ki 15:38 and Ahaz his son reigned in his **s.**. 8478
2Ki 16:20 Hezekiah his son reigned in his **s.** 8478
2Ki 19:37 Esarhaddon...reigned in his **s.** 8478
2Ki 20:21 Manasseh his son reigned in his **s.** 8478
2Ki 21:18 and Amon his son reigned in his **s.**. 8478
2Ki 21:24 made Josiah his son king in his **s.**. 8478
2Ki 21:26 Josiah his son reigned in his **s.**. 8478
2Ki 23:30 made him king in his father's **s.** 8478
2Ki 24:6 Jehoiachin his son reigned in his **s.** 8478
2Ki 24:17 his father's brother king in his **s.**. 8478
1Ch 1:44 dead, Jobab...reigned in his **s.** 8478
1Ch 1:45 dead, Husham...reigned in his **s.**. 8478
1Ch 1:46 dead, Hadad...reigned in his **s.** 8478
1Ch 1:47 dead, Samlah...reigned in his **s.** 8478
1Ch 1:48 dead, Shaul...reigned in his **s.**. 8478
1Ch 1:49 Baal-hanan...reigned in his **s.**. 8478
1Ch 1:50 was dead, Hadad reigned in his **s.**. 8478
1Ch 19:1 died, and his son reigned in his **s.**. 8478
1Ch 29:28 Solomon his son reigned in his **s.**. 8478
2Ch 1:8 and hast made me to reign in his **s.**. 8478
2Ch 9:31 Rehoboam his son reigned in his **s.** 8478
2Ch 12:16 and Abijah his son reigned in his **s.**. 8478
2Ch 14:1 and Asa his son reigned in his **s.**. 8478
2Ch 17:1 Jehoshaphat...reigned in his **s.**. 8478
2Ch 21:1 Jehoram his son reigned in his **s.**. 8478
2Ch 22:1 made Ahaziah...king in his **s.**: 8478
2Ch 24:27 Amaziah his son reigned in his **s.**. 8478
2Ch 26:23 Jotham his son reigned in his **s.**. 8478
2Ch 27:9 And Ahaz his son reigned in his **s.**. 8478
2Ch 28:27 Hezekiah his son reigned in his **s.** 8478
2Ch 32:33 Manasseh his son reigned in his **s.** 8478
2Ch 33:20 and Amon his son reigned in his **s.**. 8478
2Ch 33:25 made Josiah his son king in his **s.**. 8478
2Ch 36:1 Jehoahaz...king in his father's **s.**. 8478
2Ch 36:8 Jehoiachin his son reigned in his **s.**. 8478
Job 16:4 if your soul were in my soul's **s.**, I 8478
Job 33:6 according to thy wish in God's **s.**:
Job 34:24 number, and set others in their **s.**. 8478
Pr 11:8 and the wicked cometh in his **s.**. 8478
Ec 4:15 child that shall stand up in his **s.**. 8478
Isa 37:38 Esar-haddon...reigned in his **s.** 8478
Jer 29:26 thee priest in the **s.** of Jehoiada 8478
2Co 5:20 we pray you in Christ's **s.**, be ye *5228*
Phm 13 in they **s.** he might have ministered *5228*

STEADFAST See STEDFAST.

STEADS
1Ch 5:22 dwelt in their **s.** until the captivity. 8478

STEADY
Ex 17:12 his hands were **s.** until the going 530

STEAL See also STEALETH; STEALING; STOLE; STOLEN.
Ge 31:27 secretly, and **s.** away from me; 1589
Ge 44:8 should we **s.** out of thy lord's house; 1589
Ex 20:15 Thou shalt not **s.**. 1589
Ex 22:1 If a man shall **s.** an ox, or a sheep, 1589
Le 19:11 Ye shall not **s.**, neither deal falsely, 1589
De 5:19 Neither shalt thou **s.**. 1589
2Sa 19:3 as people being ashamed **s.** away 1589
Pr 6:30 if he **s.** to satisfy his soul when he 1589
Pr 30:9 or lest I be poor, and **s.**, and take 1589
Jer 7:9 Will ye **s.**, murder, and commit 1589
Jer 23:30 that **s.** my words every one from his 1589
Mt 6:19 **thieves break through and s.** *2813*
Mt 6:20 **do not break through nor s.** *2813*
Mt 19:18 **Thou shalt not s., Thou shalt not** *2813*
Mt 27:64 come by night, and **s.** him away, *2813*
Mk 10:19 **Do not kill, Do not s., Do not bear** *2813*
Lu 18:20 **Do not kill, Do not s., Do not bear** *2813*
Joh 10:10 **The thief cometh not, but for to s.,** *2813*
Ro 2:21 a man should not **s.**, dost thou **s.**? *2813*
Ro 13:9 shalt not kill, Thou shalt not **s.**, *2813*
Eph 4:28 Let him that stole **s.** no more: but *2813*

STEALERS See MENSTEALERS.

STEALETH
Ex 21:16 he that **s.** a man, and selleth him, 1589
Job 27:20 tempest **s.** him away in the night 1589
Zec 5:3 for every one that **s.** shall be cut off 1589

STEALING
De 24:7 If a man be found **s.** any of his 1589
Ho 4:2 and lying, and killing, and **s.**, and 1589

STEALTH
2Sa 19:3 them by **s.** that day into the city, 1589

STEDFAST
Job 11:15 yea, thou shalt be **s.**, and shalt not 3332
Ps 78:8 whose spirit was not **s.** with God 589
Ps 78:37 neither were they **s.** in his covenant. 589
Da 6:26 is the living God, and **s.** for ever, 7011
1Co 7:37 he that standeth **s.** in his heart, *1476*
1Co 15:58 my beloved brethren, be ye **s.**, *1476*
1Co 15:2 And our hope of you is **s.**, knowing, *949*
Heb 2:2 if the word spoken by angels were **s.**, *949*
Heb 3:14 of our confidence **s.** unto the end; *949*
Heb 6:19 anchor of the soul, both sure and **s.**, *949*
1Pe 5:9 Whom resist **s.** in the faith, *4731*

STEDFASTLY
Ru 1:18 she was **s.** minded to go with her, 553
2Ki 8:11 he settled his countenance **s.**, 7760
Lu 9:51 **s.** set his face to go to Jerusalem, *4741*
Ac 1:10 they looked **s.** toward heaven as *816*
Ac 2:42 they continued **s.** in the apostles' *4342*
Ac 6:15 looking **s.** on him, saw his face as *816*
Ac 7:55 looked up **s.** into heaven, and saw *816*
Ac 14:9 Paul speak: who **s.** beholding him, *816*
2Co 3:7 could not **s.** behold the face of *816*
2Co 3:13 could not **s.** look to the end of that *816*

STEDFASTNESS
Col 2:5 and the **s.** of your faith in Christ. *4733*
2Pe 3:17 the wicked, fall from your own **s.** *4740*

STEEL
2Sa 22:35 bow of **s.** is broken by mine arms. 5154
Job 20:24 and the bow of **s.** shall strike him 5154
Ps 18:34 bow of **s.** is broken by mine arms. 5154
Jer 15:12 the northern iron and the **s.**? 5178

STEEP
Eze 38:20 **s.** places shall fall, and every wall 4095
Mic 1:4 that are poured down a **s.** place. 4174
Mt 8:32 ran violently down a **s.** place into *2911*
Mk 5:13 herd ran violently down a **s.** place *2911*
Lu 8:33 herd ran violently down a **s.** place *2911*

STEM
Isa 11:1 forth a rod out of the **s.** of Jesse, 1508

STEP See also STEPPED; STEPPETH; STEPS.
1Sa 20:3 is but a **s.** between me and death. 6587
Job 31:7 If my **s.** hath turned out of the way, 838

STEPHANAS (stef'-a-nas)
1Co 1:16 baptized also the household of **S.**: *4734*
1Co 16:15 brethren, (ye know the house of **S.**, *4734*
1Co 16:17 I am glad of the coming of **S.** and *4734*
1Co *subscr.* was written from Philippi by **S.**, *4734*

STEPHEN (ste'-ven)
Ac 6:5 they chose **S.**, a man full of faith *4736*
Ac 6:8 and **S.**, full o faith and power, did *4736*
Ac 6:9 and of Asia, disputing with **S.**. *4736*
Ac 7:59 they stoned **S.**, calling upon God, *4736*
Ac 8:2 devout men carried **S.** to his burial, *4736*
Ac 11:19 the persecution that arose about **S.** *4736*
Ac 22:20 blood of thy martyr **S.** was shed, *4736*

STEPPED
Joh 5:4 the troubling of the water **s.** in *1684*

STEPPETH
Joh 5:7 coming, another **s.** down before *2597*

STEPS See also FOOTSTEPS.
Ex 20:26 thou go up by **s.** unto mine altar, 4609
2Sa 22:37 hast enlarged my **s.** under me; 6806
1Ki 10:19 The throne had six **s.**, and the top 4609
1Ki 10:20 and on the other upon the six **s.**: 4609
2Ch 9:18 And there were six **s.** to the throne, 4609
2Ch 9:19 and on the other upon the six **s.**. 4609
Job 14:16 For now thou numberest my **s.**: 6806
Job 18:7 **s.** of his strength shall be straitened, 6806
Job 23:11 My foot hath held his **s.**, his way 838
Job 29:6 When I washed my **s.** with butter, 1978
Job 31:4 see my ways, and count all my **s.**? 6806
Job 31:37 unto him the number of my **s.**; 6806
Ps 17:11 have now compassed us in our **s.**: 838
Ps 18:36 hast enlarged my **s.** under me, 6806

Ps 37:23 The **s.** of a good man are ordered...... 4703
Ps 37:31 his heart; none of his **s.** shall slide. 838
Ps 44:18 have our **s.** declined from thy way; 838
Ps 56:6 they mark my **s.**, when they wait....... 6119
Ps 57:6 have prepared a net for my **s.**; 6471
Ps 73:2 gone; my **s.** had well nigh slipped. 838
Ps 85:13 shall set us in the way of his **s.**.......... 6471
Ps 119:133 Order my **s.** in thy word: and let 6471
Pr 4:12 thy **s.** shall not be straitened; 6806
Pr 5:5 to death; her **s.** take hold on hell. 6806
Pr 16:9 way: but the Lord directeth his **s.**. 6806
Isa 26:6 the poor, and the **s.** of the needy. 6471
Jer 10:23 man that walketh to direct his **s.**. 6806
La 4:18 They hunt our **s.**, that we cannot 6806
Eze 40:22 they went up unto it by seven **s.**;........ 4609
Eze 40:26 there were seven **s.** to go up to it,..... 4609
Eze 40:31, 34,37 going up to it had eight **s.**. 4609
Eze 40:49 he brought me by the **s.** whereby....... 4609
Da 11:43 the Ethiopians shall be at his **s.**.......... 4703
Ro 4:12 walk in the **s.** of that faith of our....... *2487*
2Co 12:18 spirit? walked we not in the same **s.**?... *2487*
1Pe 2:21 that ye should follow his **s.**:............... *2487*

STERN

Ac 27:29 cast four anchors out of the **s.**, ... *4403*

STEWARD See also STEWARDS.

Ge 15:2 the **s.** of my house is this.......... 1121,4943
Ge 43:19 to the **s.** of Joseph's house,..... 376,834,5921
Ge 44:1 commanded the **s.** of his house..... 834,5921
Ge 44:4 far off, Joseph said unto his **s.**,...... 834,5921
1Ki 16:9 Arza **s.** of his house in Tirzah. 834,5921
Mt 20:8 **of the vineyard saith unto his s.**,... *2012*
Lu 8:3 the wife of Chuza Herod's **s.**, and....... *2012*
Lu 12:42 **then is that faithful and wise s.**,... *3623*
Lu 16:1 **a certain rich man, which had a s.**;*3623*
Lu 16:2 **for thou mayest be no longer s.**..... *3621*
Lu 16:3 **Then the s. said within himself**,.... *3622*
Lu 16:8 **the lord commended the unjust s.**,. *3622*
Tit 1:7 must be blameless, as the **s.** of God; .. *3622*

STEWARDS

1Ch 28:1 the **s.** over all the substance and........ 8269
1Co 4:1 and **s.** of the mysteries of God. *3623*
1Co 4:2 Moreover it is required in **s.**, that a.... *3623*
1Pe 4:10 **s.** of the manifold grace of God. *3623*

STEWARDSHIP

Lu 16:2 **give an account of thy s.; for thou** *3622*
Lu 16:3 **lord taketh away from me the s.**: .. *3622*
Lu 16:4 **when I am put out of the s., they**.. *3622*

STICK See also CANDLESTICK; STICKETH; STICKS; STUCK.

Ki 6:6 And he cut down a **s.**, and cast it....... 6086
Job 33:21 bones that were not seen **s.** out......... 8205
Job 41:17 they **s.** together, that they cannot 3920
Ps 38:2 For thine arrows **s.** fast in me, and..... 5181
La 4:8 is withered, it is become like a **s.**....... 6086
Eze 29:4 the fish of thy rivers to **s.** unto thy..... 1692
Eze 29:4 the fish of thy rivers shall **s.** unto....... 1692
Eze 37:16 thou son of man, take thee one **s.**, ... 6086
Eze 37:16 then take another **s.**, and write upon... 6086
Eze 37:16 For Joseph, the **s.** of Ephraim, and..... 6086
Eze 37:17 them one to another into one **s.**; 6086
Eze 37:19 Behold, I will take the **s.** of Joseph, ... 6086
Eze 37:19 with him, even with the **s.** of Judah, ... 6086
Eze 37:19 and make them one **s.**, and they 6086

STICKETH

Pr 18:24 is a friend that **s.** closer than a 1695

STICKS

Nu 15:32 they found a man that gathered **s.** 6086
Nu 15:33 they that found him gathering **s.**.......... 6086
1Ki 17:10 woman was there gathering of **s.**.......... 6086
1Ki 17:12 behold, I am gathering two **s.**, that..... 6086
Eze 37:20 the **s.** whereon thou writest shall 6086
Ac 28:3 Paul had gathered a bundle of **s.**, ... *5434*

STIFF See also STIFFHEARTED; STIFFNECKED.

De 31:27 thy rebellion and thy **s.** neck: 7186
Ps 75:5 on high: speak not with a **s.** neck. 6277
Jer 17:23 but made their neck **s.**, that they 7185

STIFFENED

2Ch 36:13 but he **s.** his neck, and hardened........ 7185

STIFFHEARTED

Eze 2:4 are impudent children and **s.**........ 2389,3820

STIFFNECKED

Ex 32:9 and, behold, it is a **s.** people: 7186,6203
Ex 33:3 thee; for thou art a **s.** people: 7186,6203
Ex 33:5 Ye are a **s.** people: I will come ... 7186,6203
Ex 34:9 among us; for it is a **s.** people; ... 7186,6203
De 9:6 for thou art a **s.** people. 7186,6203
De 9:13 and, behold, it is a **s.** people: 7186,6203
De 10:16 your heart, and be no more **s.**..... 7185,6203
2Ch 30:8 be ye not **s.**, as your fathers...... 7185,6203
Ac 7:51 Ye **s.** and uncircumcised in heart........ *4644*

STILL See also STILLED; STILLEST; STILLETH.

Ge 12:9 going on **s.** toward the south. 5265
Ge 41:21 but they were **s.** ill favoured, as at the......
Ex 9:2 and wilt hold them **s.**, ... 5750
Ex 14:13 not stand **s.**, and see the salvation of........
Ex 15:16 arm they shall be as **s.** as a stone; 1826
Ex 23:11 thou shalt let it rest and lie **s.**;.................
Le 13:57 And if it appear **s.** in the garment,...... 5750
Nu 9:8 them, Stand **s.**, and I will hear what ....
Nu 14:38 that went to search the land, lived **s.**. ......
Jos 3:8 Jordan, ye shall stand **s.** in Jordan.............
Jos 10:12 Sun, stand thou **s.** upon Gibeon; 1826
Jos 10:13 And the sun stood **s.**, and the moon ... 1826
Jos 10:13 So the sun stood **s.** in the midst of..........
Jos 11:13 cities that stood **s.** in their strength, ...
Jos 24:10 Balaam; therefore he blessed you **s.**..........
Jg 18:9 it is very good: and are ye **s.**?........... 2814
Ru 3:18 Then said she, Sit **s.**, my daughter, ...
1Sa 9:27 but stand thou **s.** a while, that I may.........
1Sa 12:7 Now therefore stand **s.**, that I may............
1Sa 12:25 But if ye shall **s.** do wickedly, ye shall.......
1Sa 14:9 then we will stand **s.** in our place, ...
1Sa 26:25 great things, and also shalt **s.** prevail.........
2Sa 2:23 Asahel fell down and died stood **s.**..............
2Sa 2:28 and all the people stood **s.**, and.................
2Sa 11:1 But David tarried **s.** at Jerusalem. ....
2Sa 14:32 but his hand is stretched out **s.**........... 5750
2Sa 16:5 came forth, and cursed **s.** as he came. ......
2Sa 18:30 And he turned aside, and stood **s.**. ....
2Sa 20:12 saw that all the people stood **s.**,................
2Sa 20:12 every one that came by him stood **s.**. ....
1Ki 19:12 and after the fire a **s.** small voice, ... 1827
1Ki 22:3 Gilead is ours, and we be **s.**, and ....
2Ki 2:11 And it came to pass, as they **s.** went on,...
2Ki 7:4 and if we sit **s.** here, we die also. ....
2Ki 12:3 the people **s.** sacrificed and burnt 5750
2Ki 15:4 burnt incense **s.** on the high places. 5750
2Ki 15:35 and burned incense **s.** in the high 5750
2Ch 20:17 stand ye **s.**, and see the salvation of.........
2Ch 22:9 no power to keep **s.** the kingdom. ....
2Ch 33:17 did sacrifice **s.** in the high places, ... 5750
Ne 12:39 they stood **s.** in the prison gate................
Job 2:3 **s.** he holdeth fast his integrity, ... 5750
Job 2:9 Dost thou **s.** retain thine integrity? 5750
Job 3:13 For now should I have lain **s.** and............
Job 4:16 It stood **s.**, but I could not discern...........
Job 20:13 but keep it **s.** within his mouth:................
Job 32:16 they spake not, but stood **s.**, and 5975
Job 37:14 stand **s.**, and consider the wondrous ... 5975
Ps 4:4 heart upon your bed, and be **s.**. 1826
Ps 8:2 thou mightest **s.** the enemy and 7673
Ps 23:2 leadeth me beside the **s.** waters.......... 4496
Ps 46:10 Be **s.**, and know that I am God: I 7503
Ps 49:9 That he should **s.** live for ever, and 5750
Ps 68:21 one as goeth on **s.** in his trespasses..........
Ps 76:8 the earth feared, and was **s.**,............... 8252
Ps 78:32 For all this they sinned **s.**, and 5750
Ps 83:1 thy peace, and be not **s.**, O God. 8252
Ps 84:4 they will be **s.** praising thee. 5750
Ps 92:14 They shall **s.** bring forth fruit in old 5750
Ps 107:29 so that the waves thereof are **s.**. 2814
Ps 139:18 when I awake, I am **s.** with thee.......... 5750
Ec 12:9 he **s.** taught the people knowledge;...... 5750
Isa 5:25 but his hand is stretched out **s.**........... 5750
Isa 9:12 but his hand is stretched out **s.**........... 5750
Isa 9:17, 21 but his hand is stretched out **s.**....... 5750
Isa 10:4 but his hand is stretched out **s.**.......... 5750
Isa 23:2 Be **s.**, ye inhabitants of the isle;.......... 1826
Isa 30:7 this, Their strength is to sit **s.**........... 7673
Isa 42:14 I have been **s.**, and refrained............ 2790
Jer 8:14 Why do we sit **s.**? assemble.....................
Jer 23:17 They say **s.** unto them that despise me, ...
Jer 27:11 I let remain **s.** in their own land, ...
Jer 31:20 I do earnestly remember him **s.** 5750
Jer 42:10 If ye will **s.** abide in this land, then..........
Jer 47:6 into thy scabbard, rest, and be **s.**........ 1826
Jer 51:50 the sword, go away, stand not **s.**; 5975
La 3:20 soul hath them **s.** in remembrance, ...
Eze 33:30 thy people **s.** are talking against thee ....
Eze 41:7 a winding about **s.** upward to the side ....
Eze 41:7 about the house went **s.** upward...............
Eze 41:7 breadth of the house was **s.** upward,.........
Hab 3:11 the sun and moon stood **s.** in....................
Zec 1:11 all the earth sitteth **s.**, and is at ....
Zec 11:16 nor feed that that standeth **s.**: ....
Mt 20:32 Jesus stood **s.**, and called them.......... *2476*
Mk 4:39 said unto the sea, **Peace, be s.**,.......... *5392*
Mk 10:49 Jesus stood **s.**, and commanded.......... *2476*
Lu 7:14 and they that bare him stood **s.**. *2476*
Joh 7:9 unto them, he abode **s.** in Galilee. ....
Joh 11:6 abode two days **s.** in the same place ....
Joh 11:20 him: but Mary sat **s.** in the house.............
Ac 8:38 commanded the chariot to stand **s.**........ *2476*
Ac 15:34 it pleased Silas to abide there **s.**...............
Ac 17:14 Silas and Timotheus abode there **s.**............
Ro 11:23 also, if they abide not **s.** in unbelief,..........
1Ti 1:3 thee to abide **s.** at Ephesus, when...... *4357*
Re 22:11 is unjust, let him be unjust **s.** *2089*
Re 22:11 which is filthy, let him be filthy **s.**......... *2089*
Re 22:11 righteous, let him be righteous **s.**. *2089*
Re 22:11 he that is holy, let him be holy **s.**........ *2089*

STILLED

Nu 13:30 Caleb **s.** the people before Moses,...... 2013
Ne 8:11 So the Levites **s.** all the people,......... 2814

STILLEST

Ps 89:9 waves thereof arise, thou **s.** them. 7623

STILLETH

Ps 65:7 Which **s.** the noise of the seas, ... 7623

STING See also STINGETH; STINGS.

1Co 15:55 O death, where is thy **s.**? O grave, ... *2759*
1Co 15:56 The **s.** of death is sin; and the........... *2759*

STINGETH

Pr 23:32 a serpent, and **s.** like an adder........... 6567

STINGS

Re 9:10 and there were **s.** in their tails:.......... *2759*

STINK See STANK; STINKETH.

Ge 34:30 have troubled me to make me to **s.**...... 887
Ex 7:18 shall die, and the river shall **s.**;............ 887
Ex 16:24 it did not **s.**, neither was there any 887
Ps 38:5 My wounds **s.** and are corrupt 887
Isa 3:24 of sweet smell there shall be **s.**; 4716
Isa 34:3 their **s.** shall come up out of their 889
Joe 2:20 his **s.** shall come up, and his ill............ 889
Am 4:10 made the **s.** of your camps to come...... 889

STINKETH

Isa 50:2 their fish **s.**, because there is no.......... 887
Joh 11:39 him, Lord, by this time he **s.**;............ *3605*

STINKING

Ec 10:1 to send forth a **s.** savour: so............... 887

STIR See also BESTIR; STIRRED; STIRRETH; STIRS.

Nu 24:9 a great lion: who shall **s.** him up? 6965
Job 17:8 the innocent shall **s.** up himself 5782
Job 41:10 is so fierce that dare **s.** him up: 5782
Ps 35:23 **S.** up thyself, and awake to my.......... 5782
Ps 78:38 and did not **s.** up all his wrath........... 5782
Ps 80:2 and Manasseh **s.** up thy strength,....... 5782
Pr 15:1 but grievous words **s.** up anger........... 5927
Ca 2:7 ye **s.** not up, nor awake my love,....... 5782
Ca 3:5 ye **s.** not up, nor awake my love,....... 5782
Ca 8:4 ye **s.** not up, nor awake my love,....... 5782
Isa 10:26 Lord of hosts shall **s.** up a scourge..... 5782
Isa 13:17 I will **s.** up the Medes against them, ... 5782
Isa 42:13 he shall **s.** up jealousy like a man 5782
Da 11:2 shall **s.** up all against the realm of....... 5782
Da 11:25 And he shall **s.** up his power and........ 5782
Ac 12:18 no small **s.** among the soldiers, ... *5017*
Ac 19:23 there arose no small **s.** about that *5017*
2Ti 1:6 that thou **s.** up the gift of God,............ *329*
2Pe 1:13 to **s.** you up by putting you in............ *1326*
2Pe 3:1 I **s.** up your pure minds by way of...... *1326*

STIRRED

Ex 35:21 every one whose heart **s.** him up, ... 5375
Ex 35:26 women whose heart **s.** them up in....... 5375
Ex 36:2 one whose heart **s.** him up to come 5375
1Sa 22:8 son hath **s.** up my servant against 6965
1Sa 26:19 Lord have **s.** thee up against me, ... 5496
1Ki 11:14 the Lord **s.** up an adversary unto 6965
1Ki 11:23 God **s.** him up another adversary,....... 6965
1Ki 21:25 whom Jezebel his wife **s.** up............. 5496

1Ch 5:26 the God of Israel **s.** up the spirit........ 5782
2Ch 21:16 the Lord **s.** up against Jehoram the..... 5782
2Ch 36:22 Lord **s.** up the spirit of Cyrus king..... 5782
Ezr 1:1 Lord **s.** up the spirit of Cyrus king..... 5782
Ps 39:2 good; and my sorrow was **s.**, ... 5916
Da 11:10 But his sons shall be **s.** up, and......... 1624
Da 11:10 then shall he return, and be **s.** up,...... 1624
Da 11:25 king of the south shall be **s.** up to...... 1624
Hag 1:14 And the Lord **s.** up the spirit of......... 5782
Ac 6:12 And they **s.** up the people, and the..... *4787*
Ac 13:50 the Jews **s.** up the devout and........... *3951*
Ac 14:2 Jews **s.** up the Gentiles, and............. *1892*
Ac 17:13 thither also, and **s.** up the people. *4531*
Ac 17:16 his spirit was **s.** in him, when............ *3947*
Ac 21:27 **s.** up all the people, and laid............. *4797*

STIRRETH
De 32:11 As an eagle **s.** up her nest,.............. 5782
Pr 10:12 Hatred **s.** up strifes: but love 5782
Pr 15:18 a wrathful man **s.** up strife: but.......... 1624
Pr 28:25 is of a proud heart **s.** up strife;.......... 1624
Pr 29:22 An angry man **s.** up strife, and a......... 1624
Isa 14:9 it **s.** up the dead for thee even all 5782
Isa 64:7 that **s.** up himself to take hold of......... 5782
Lu 23:5 He **s.** up the people, teaching............. *383*

STIRS
Isa 22:2 Thou that art full of **s.**, a.................. 8663

STOCK See also GAZINGSTOCK; STOCKS.
Le 25:47 to the **s.** of the stranger's family: 6133
Job 14:8 the **s.** thereof die in the ground; 1503
Isa 40:24 their **s.** shall not take root in the......... 1503
Isa 44:19 shall I fall down to the **s.** of a tree?...... 944
Jer 2:27 Saying to **s.**, Thou art my father; 6086
Jer 10:8 the **s.** is a doctrine of vanities............ 6086
Ac 13:26 children of the **s.** of Abraham, and...... *1085*
Php 3:5 the eighth day, of the **s.** of Israel, ... *1085*

STOCKS
Job 13:27 puttest my feet also in the **s.**, and...... 5465
Job 33:11 He putteth my feet in the **s.**, he 5465
Pr 7:22 a fool to the correction of the **s.**; 5914
Jer 3:9 adultery with stones and with **s.**.......... 6086
Jer 20:2 put him in the **s.** that were in the....... 4115
Jer 20:3 forth Jeremiah out of the **s.**............... 4115
Jer 29:26 put him in prison, and in the **s.**.......... 6729
Ho 4:12 My people ask counsel at their **s.**,...... 6086
Ac 16:24 and made their feet fast in the **s.**. *3586*

STOICKS (sto'-ics)
Ac 17:18 and of the **S.**, encountered him,......... *4770*

STOLE See also STOLEN.
Ge 31:20 Jacob **s.** away unawares to Laban....... 1589
2Sa 15:6 Absalom **s.** the hearts of the men....... 1589
2Ki 11:2 **s.** him from among the king's sons...... 1589
2Ch 22:11 **s.** him from among the king's sons...... 1589
Mt 28:13 and **s.** him away while we slept.......... *2813*
Eph 4:28 Let him that **s.** steal no more; but...... *2813*

STOLEN
Ge 30:33 that shall be counted **s.** with me......... 1589
Ge 31:19 Rachel had **s.** the images that were 1589
Ge 31:26 thou hast **s.** away unawares to me,..... 1589
Ge 31:30 wherefore hast thou **s.** my gods?........ 1589
Ge 31:32 knew not that Rachel had **s.** them. 1589
Ge 31:39 whether **s.** by day, or **s.** by night....... 1589
Ge 40:15 I was **s.** away out of the land of the.... 1589
Ex 22:7 and it be **s.** out of the man's house;.... 1589
Ex 22:12 if it be **s.** from him, he shall make...... 1589
Jos 7:11 have also **s.**, and dissembled also, ... 1589
2Sa 19:41 the men of Judah **s.** thee away,.......... 1589
2Sa 21:12 had **s.** them from the street of........... 1589
Pr 9:17 **S.** waters are sweet, and bread......... 1589
Ob 5 not have **s.** till they have enough? 1589

STOMACHER
Isa 3:24 of a **s.** a girding of sackcloth;............ 6614

STOMACH'S
1Ti 5:23 a little wine for they **s.** sake and........ *4751*

STONE See also BRIMSTONE; HEADSTONE; MILLSTONE; STONED; STONE'S; STONES; STONESQUARERS; STONEST; STONING; STUMBLINGSTONE.
Ge 2:12 there is bdellium and the onyx **s.**........... 68
Ge 11:3 And they had brick for **s.**, and slime 68
Ge 28:18 the **s.** that he had put for his pillows,..... 68
Ge 28:22 this **s.**, which I have set for a pillar, ... 68
Ge 29:2 a great **s.** was upon the well's mouth. 68
Ge 29:3 rolled the **s.** from the well's mouth. 68
Ge 29:3 put the **s.** again upon the well's............ 68
Ge 29:8 roll the **s.** from the well's mouth; 68
Ge 29:10 rolled the **s.** from the well's mouth, ... 68
Ge 31:45 And Jacob took a **s.**, and set it up for..... 68
Ge 35:14 talked with him, even a pillar of **s.**........ 68
Ge 49:24 is the shepherd, the **s.** of Israel:).......... 68
Ex 4:25 Zipporah took a sharp **s.**, and cut 6697
Ex 7:19 vessels of wood, and in vessels of **s.**...... 68
Ex 8:26 their eyes, and will they not **s.** us?..... 5619
Ex 15:5 they sank into the bottom as a **s.**. 68
Ex 15:16 arm they shall be as still as a **s.**; 68
Ex 17:4 they be almost ready to **s.** me........... 5619
Ex 17:12 they took a **s.**, and put it under him,...... 68
Ex 20:25 if thou wilt make me an altar of **s.**, ... 68
Ex 20:25 thou shalt not build it of hewn **s.**: ....
Ex 21:18 and one smite another with a **s.**, ... 68
Ex 24:10 it were a paved work of a sapphire **s.**, ...
Ex 24:12 and I will give thee tables of **s.**, and 68
Ex 28:10 Six of their names on one **s.**, and the..... 68
Ex 28:10 six names of the rest on the other **s.**, ... 68
Ex 28:11 With the work of an engraver in **s.**, ... 68
Ex 31:18 two tables of testimony, tables of **s.**,...... 68
Ex 34:1 Hew thee two tables of **s.** like unto 68
Ex 34:4 he hewed two tables of **s.** like unto 68
Ex 34:4 took in his hand the two tables of **s.**. 68
Le 20:2 of the land shall **s.** him with stones. 7275
Le 20:27 they shall **s.** them with stones: 7275
Le 24:14 and let all the congregation **s.** him. 7275
Le 24:16 congregation shall certainly **s.** him:...... 7275
Le 24:23 the camp, and **s.** him with stones. 7275
Le 26:1 neither shall ye set up any image of **s.** ... 68
Nu 14:10 all the congregation bade **s.** them 7275
Nu 15:35 congregation...**s.** him with stones 7275
Nu 35:17 if he smite him with throwing a **s.**, ... 68
Nu 35:23 Or with any **s.**, where with a man........... 68
De 4:13 he wrote them upon two tables of **s.**...... 68
De 4:28 work of men's hands, wood and **s.**,......... 68
De 5:22 he wrote them in two tables of **s.**,......... 68
De 9:9 the mount to receive the tables of **s.**,..... 68
De 9:10 delivered unto me two tables of **s.**.......... 68
De 9:11 Lord gave me the two tables of **s.**,......... 68
De 10:1 Hew thee two tables of **s.** like unto 68
De 10:3 and hewed two tables of **s.** like unto 68
De 13:10 thou shalt **s.** him with stones, that...... 5619
De 17:5 and shalt **s.** them with stones, till....... 5619
De 21:21 all the men of his city shall **s.** him...... 7275
De 22:21 the men of her city shall **s.** her with... 5619
De 22:24 ye shall **s.** them with stones that......... 5619
De 28:36 thou serve other gods, wood and **s.**....... 68
De 28:64 have known, even wood and **s.**............. 68
De 29:17 and their idols, wood and **s.**, silver 68
Jos 4:5 take ye up every man of you a **s.**........... 68
Jos 15:6 border went up to the **s.** of Bohan......... 68
Jos 18:17 descended to the **s.** of Bohan the son..... 68
Jos 24:26 took a great **s.**, and set it up there........ 68
Jos 24:27 this **s.** shall be a witness unto us;.......... 68
Jg 9:5 and ten persons, upon one **s.**:.............. 68
Jg 9:18 and ten persons, upon one **s.**, and.......... 68
1Sa 6:14 there, where there was a great **s.**: 68
1Sa 6:15 were, and put them on the great **s.**: 68
1Sa 6:18 even unto the great **s.** of Abel, whereon....
1Sa 6:18 which **s.** remaineth unto this day in..........
1Sa 7:12 Then Samuel took a **s.**, and set it.......... 68
1Sa 14:33 roll a great **s.** unto me this day............ 68
1Sa 17:49 and took thence a **s.**, and slang it,......... 68
1Sa 17:49 that the **s.** sunk into his forehead; 68
1Sa 17:50 Philistine with a sling and with a **s.**, ... 68
1Sa 20:19 and shalt remain by the **s.** Ezel............ 68
1Sa 25:37 within him, and he became as a **s.**......... 68
2Sa 17:13 be not one small **s.** found there.......... 6872
2Sa 20:8 at the great **s.** which is in Gibeon,......... 68
1Ki 1:9 and fat cattle by the **s.** of Zoheleth, ... 68
1Ki 6:7 built of **s.** made ready before it was........ 68
1Ki 6:18 all was cedar; there was no **s.** seen. 68
1Ki 6:36 court with three rows of hewed **s.**,..... 1496
1Ki 8:9 in the ark save the two tables of **s.**, ... 68
1Ki 21:10 carry him out, and **s.** him, that he...... 5619
2Ki 3:25 piece of land cast every man his **s.**, ... 68
2Ki 12:12 And to masons, and hewers of **s.**, ... 68
2Ki 12:12 buy timber and hewed **s.** to repair......... 68
2Ki 19:18 work of men's hands, wood and **s.**:.......... 68
2Ki 22:6 to buy timber and hewn **s.** to repair....... 68
1Ch 22:14 timber also and **s.** have I prepared;........ 68
1Ch 22:15 hewers and workers of **s.** and.............. 68
2Ch 2:14 brass, in iron, in **s.**, and in timber, ... 68
2Ch 34:11 to buy hewn **s.**, and timber for 68
Ne 4:3 shall even break down their **s.** wall. 68
Ne 9:11 as a **s.** into the mighty waters. 68
Job 28:2 and brass is molten out of the **s.**........... 68
Job 38:6 or who laid the corner **s.** thereof;.......... 68
Job 38:30 The waters are hid as with a **s.**, and...... 68
Job 41:24 His heart is as firm as a **s.**; yea, as 68
Ps 91:12 lest thou dash thy foot against a **s.**........ 68
Ps 118:22 The **s.** which the builders refused.......... 68
Ps 118:22 is become the head **s.** of the corner.........
Pr 17:8 A gift is as a precious **s.** in the eyes...... 68
Pr 24:31 the **s.** wall thereof was broken down. 68
Pr 26:8 As he that bindeth a **s.** in a sling,.......... 68
Pr 26:27 and he that rolleth a **s.**, it will return 68
Pr 27:3 A **s.** is heavy, and the sand weighty;...... 68
Isa 8:14 but for a **s.** of stumbling and for a 68
Isa 28:16 Zion for a foundation a **s.**, a tried **s.**,...... 68
Isa 28:16 a precious corner **s.**, a sure ....
Isa 37:19 work of men's hands, wood and **s.**:......... 68
Jer 2:27 and to a **s.**, Thou hast brought me 68
Jer 51:26 not take of thee a **s.** for a corner, ... 68
Jer 51:26 nor a **s.** for foundations; but thou 68
Jer 51:63 that thou shalt bind a **s.** to it, and.......... 68
La 3:9 inclosed my ways with hewn **s.**,......... 1496
La 3:53 the dungeon, and cast a **s.** upon me....... 68
Eze 1:26 as the appearance of a sapphire **s.**: 68
Eze 10:1 over them as it were a sapphire **s.**, ... 68
Eze 10:9 was as the colour of a beryl **s.**............ 68
Eze 16:40 and they shall **s.** thee with stones,....... 7275
Eze 20:32 the countries, to serve wood and **s.**........ 68
Eze 23:47 company shall **s.** them with stones,..... 7275
Eze 28:13 every precious **s.** was thy covering,....... 68
Eze 40:42 four tables were hewn **s.** for the........... 68
Da 2:34 that a **s.** was cut out without hands, ... 69
Da 2:35 the **s.** that smote the image became......... 69
Da 2:45 the **s.** was cut out of the mountain 69
Da 5:4 of brass, of iron, of wood, and of **s.**....... 69
Da 5:23 of brass, iron, wood, and **s.**, which........ 69
Da 6:17 And a **s.** was brought, and laid upon 69
Am 5:11 ye have built houses of hewn **s.**, ... 1496
Hab 2:11 For the **s.** shall cry out of the wall. 68
Hab 2:19 to the dumb **s.**, Arise, it shall teach! 68
Hag 2:15 a **s.** was laid upon a **s.** in the temple...... 68
Zec 3:9 behold the **s.** that I have laid before........ 68
Zec 3:9 upon one **s.** shall be seven eyes:........... 68
Zec 7:12 their hearts as an adamant **s.**............ 8068
Zec 12:3 make Jerusalem a burdensome **s.**........... 68
Mt 4:6 thou dash thy foot against a **s.**........... *3037*
Mt 7:9 **ask bread, will he give him a s.?** ... *3037*
Mt 21:42 **The s. which the builders rejected,** .*3037*
Mt 21:44 **fall on this s. shall be broken:** *3037*
Mt 24:2 **be left here one s. upon another,**... *3037*
Mt 27:60 rolled a great **s.** to the door of the *3037*
Mt 27:66 sealing the **s.**, and setting a watch. *3037*
Mt 28:2 came and rolled back the **s.** from......... *3037*
Mk 12:10 **The s. which the builders rejected**. *3037*
Mk 13:2 **not be left one s. upon another.** *3037*
Mk 15:46 and rolled a **s.** unto the door of the *3037*
Mk 16:3 roll us away the **s.** from the door *3037*
Mk 16:4 they saw that the **s.** was rolled........... *3037*
Lu 4:3 command this **s.** that it be made *3037*
Lu 4:11 thou dash thy foot against a **s.**........... *3037*
Lu 11:11 **is a father, will he give him a s.?**.. *3037*
Lu 19:44 **leave in thee one s. upon another;**. *3037*
Lu 20:6 all the people will **s.** us: for they......... *2642*
Lu 20:17 **The s. which the builders rejected,** .*3037*
Lu 20:18 **shall fall upon that s. be broken;**.. *3037*
Lu 21:6 **not be left one s. upon another,** *3037*
Lu 23:53 in a sepulchre that was hewn in **s.**,..... *2991*
Lu 24:2 they found the **s.** rolled away from *3037*
Joh 1:42 which is by interpretation, A **s.**........... *4074*
Joh 2:6 were set there six waterpots of **s.**,...... *3035*
Joh 8:7 **you, let him first cast a s. at her.** ..*3037*
Joh 10:31 Jews took...stones agains to **s.** him..... *3034*
Joh 10:32 **which of those works do ye s. me?** .*3034*
Joh 10:33 For a good work we **s.** thee not;.......... *3034*
Joh 11:8 the Jews of late sought to **s.** thee;....... *3034*
Joh 11:38 It was a cave, and a **s.** lay upon it...... *3037*
Joh 11:39 Jesus said, **Take ye away the s.** *3037*
Joh 11:41 they took away the **s.** from the........... *3037*
Joh 20:1 seeth the **s.** taken away from the *3037*
Ac 4:11 This is the **s.** which was set at.......... *3037*
Ac 14:5 them despitefully, and to **s.** them, ... *3036*
Ac 17:29 is like unto gold, or silver, or **s.**,......... *3037*
2Co 3:3 not in tables of **s.**, but in fleshy *3035*
Eph 2:20 himself being the chief corner **s.**;............
1Pe 2:4 whom coming, as unto a living **s.**,....... *3037*
1Pe 2:6 I lay in Sion a chief corner **s.**, elect, ... *3037*
1Pe 2:7 **s.** which the builders disallowed, ... *3037*

1Pe 2:8 And a s. of stumbling, and a rock of... 3037
Re 2:17 **and will give him a white s.,** 5586
Re 2:17 **and in the s. a new name written,** . 5586
Re 4:3 like a jasper and a sardine s.: 3037
Re 9:20 gold, and silver, and brass, and s.,........ 3035
Re 16:21 every s. about the weight of a talent:........
Re 18:21 mighty angel took up a s. like a 3037
Re 21:11 was like unto a s. most precious, ... 3037
Re 21:11 like a jasper s., clear as crystal;......... 3037

STONED

Ex 19:13 but he shall surely be s., or shot........ 5619
Ex 21:28 then the ox shall be surely s., and...... 5619
Ex 21:29 the ox shall be s., and his owner......... 5619
Ex 21:32 of silver, and the ox shall be s............ 5619
Nu 15:36 s. him with stones, and he died; 7275
Jos 7:25 And all Israel s. him with stones, ... 5619
Jos 7:25 after they had s. them with stones. 7275
1Ki 12:18 and all Israel s. him with stones,........ 7275
1Ki 21:13 s. him with stones, that he died........ 5619
1Ki 21:14 saying, Naboth is s., and is dead........ 5619
1Ki 21:15 Jezebel heard that Naboth was s., ... 5619
2Ch 10:18 children of Israel s. him with............ 7275
2Ch 24:21 and s. him with stones at the 7275
Mt 21:35 **and killed another, and s. another** ..3036
Joh 8:5 commanded; us, that such...be s........ 3036
Ac 5:26 lest they should have been s.. 3034
Ac 7:58 him out of the city, and s. him:........... 3036
Ac 7:59 they s. Stephen, calling upon God,...... 3036
Ac 14:19 having s. Paul, drew him out of 3034
2Co 11:25 once was I s., thrice I suffered........... 3034
Heb 11:37 They were s., they were sawn.......... 3034
Heb 12:20 it shall be s., or thrust through.......... 3036

STONE'S

Lu 22:41 from them about a s. cast,................ 3037

STONES See also CHALKSTONES; HAILSTONES; MILLSTONES; SLINGSTONES.

Ge 28:11 and he took of the s. of that place,........ 68
Ge 31:46 said unto his brethren, Gather s.;.......... 68
Ge 31:46 and they took s., and made an heap:...... 68
Ex 25:7 Onyx s., and s. to be set in the ephod, .. 68
Ex 28:9 And thou shalt take two onyx s., and..... 68
Ex 28:11 shalt thou engrave the two s. with......... 68
Ex 28:12 put the two s. upon the shoulders of....... 68
Ex 28:12 for s. of memorial unto the children....... 68
Ex 28:17 And thou shalt set in it settings of s., ... 68
Ex 28:17 even four rows of s.: the first row 68
Ex 28:21 the s. shall be with the names of the 68
Ex 31:5 And in cutting of s., to set them, and..... 68
Ex 35:9 onyx s., and s. to be set for the ephod, ..68
Ex 35:27 And the rulers brought onyx s., and....... 68
Ex 35:27 and s. to be set, for the ephod, and........ 68
Ex 35:33 And in the cutting of s., to set them, ... 68
Ex 39:6 wrought onyx s. inclosed in ouches......... 68
Ex 39:7 be s. for a memorial to the children....... 68
Ex 39:10 And they set in it four rows of s.: the.... 68
Ex 39:14 the s. were according to the names 68
Le 14:40 take away the s. in which the plague....... 68
Le 14:42 And they shall take other s., and put 68
Le 14:42 and put them in the place of those s.; 68
Le 14:43 after that he hath taken away the s.,....... 68
Le 14:45 break down the house, the s. of it,........ 68
Le 20:2 of the land shall stone him with s.......... 68
Le 20:27 death: they shall stone them with s.:...... 68
Le 21:20 or scabbed, or hath his s. broken;........ 810
Le 24:23 of the camp, and stone him with s.......... 68
Nu 14:10 bade stone them with s......................... 68
Nu 15:35 congregation shall stone him with s.......... 68
Nu 15:36 and stoned him with s., and he died;...... 68
De 8:9 a land whose s. are iron, and out of....... 68
De 13:10 thou shalt stone him with s., that he...... 68
De 17:5 shalt stone them with s., till they die. 68
De 21:21 of his city shall stone him with s., ... 68
De 22:21 shall stone her with s. that she die: 68
De 22:24 ye shall stone them with s. that they 68
De 23:1 He that is wounded in the s., or hath........
De 27:2 that thou shalt set thee up great s.,......... 68
De 27:4 that ye shall set up these s., which I 68
De 27:5 unto the Lord thy God, an altar of s.: 68
De 27:6 altar of the Lord thy God of whole s.: 68
De 27:8 write upon the s. all the words of.......... 68
Jos 4:3 the priests' feet stood firm, twelve s.,...... 68
Jos 4:6 saying, What mean ye by these s.?......... 68
Jos 4:7 these s. shall be for a memorial unto...... 68
Jos 4:8 took up twelve s. out of the midst of 68
Jos 4:9 Joshua set up twelve s. in the midst 68
Jos 4:20 those twelve s., which they took out...... 68
Jos 4:21 come, saying, What mean these s.? 68
Jos 7:25 And all Israel stoned him with s., ... 68
Jos 7:25 after they had stoned them with s. 68
Jos 7:26 raised over him a great heap of s.......... 68
Jos 8:29 and raise thereon a great heap of s.,...... 68
Jos 8:31 an altar of whole s., over which no......... 68
Jos 8:32 he wrote there upon the s. a copy of..... 68
Jos 10:11 Lord cast down great s. from heaven..... 68
Jos 10:18 Roll great s. upon the mouth of the 68
Jos 10:27 and laid great s. in the cave's mouth, ... 68
Jg 20:16 could sling s. at an hair breadth,............ 68
1Sa 17:40 chose him five smooth s. out of the 68
2Sa 12:30 a talent of gold with the precious s.. 68
2Sa 16:6 And he cast s. at David, and at all.......... 68
2Sa 16:13 and threw s. at him, and cast dust......... 68
2Sa 18:17 and laid a very great heap of s. upon 68
1Ki 5:17 and they brought great s., costly s., ... 68
1Ki 5:17 hewed s., to lay the foundation of.......... 68
1Ki 5:18 prepared timber and s. to build the......... 68
1Ki 7:9 All these were of costly s., according..... 68
1Ki 7:9 to the measures of hewed s., ... 1496
1Ki 7:10 was of costly s., even great s.............. 68
1Ki 7:10 s. of ten cubits, and s. of eight cubits. ... 68
1Ki 7:11 And above were costly s., after the....... 68
1Ki 7:11 after the measures of hewed s.,......... 1496
1Ki 7:12 was with three rows of hewed s., ... 1496
1Ki 10:2 and very much gold, and precious s.. 68
1Ki 10:10 very great store, and precious s............ 68
1Ki 10:11 of almug trees, and precious s.............. 68
1Ki 10:27 made silver to be in Jerusalem as s.,...... 68
1Ki 12:18 all Israel stoned him with s., that he...... 68
1Ki 15:22 and they took away the s. of Ramah, ... 68
1Ki 18:31 Elijah took twelve s., according to.......... 68
1Ki 18:32 with the s. he built an altar in the.......... 68
1Ki 18:38 the wood, and the s., and the dust, ... 68
1Ki 21:13 and stoned him with s., that he died. 68
2Ki 3:19 mar every good piece of land with s........ 68
2Ki 3:25 Kir-haraseth left they the s. thereof;...... 68
2Ki 16:17 and put it upon a pavement of s............ 68
1Ch 12:2 right hand and the left in hurling s.......... 68
1Ch 20:2 and there were precious s. in it; and...... 68
1Ch 22:2 he set masons to hew wrought s. to......... 68
1Ch 29:2 wood for things of wood; onyx s., ... 68
1Ch 29:2 and s. to be set, glistering................. 68
1Ch 29:2 glistering s., and of divers colours, ... 68
1Ch 29:2 manner of precious s., and marble s........ 68
1Ch 29:8 with whom precious s. were found........... 68
2Ch 1:15 gold at Jerusalem as plenteous as s.,...... 68
2Ch 3:6 garnished the house with precious s........ 68
2Ch 9:1 gold in abundance, and precious s........... 68
2Ch 9:9 great abundance, and precious s.............. 68
2Ch 9:10 brought algum trees and precious s.......... 68
2Ch 9:27 king made silver in Jerusalem as s., ... 68
2Ch 10:18 children of Israel stoned him with s.,....... 68
2Ch 16:6 they carried away the s. of Ramah,......... 68
2Ch 24:21 stoned him with s. at...commandment..... 68
2Ch 26:14 and bows, and slings to cast s. 68
2Ch 26:15 to shoot arrows and great s. withal......... 68
2Ch 32:27 and for gold, and for precious s.,........... 68
Ezr 5:8 which is builded with great s., and.......... 69
Ezr 6:4 With three rows of great s., and a.......... 69
Ne 4:2 they revive the s. out of the heaps......... 68
Job 5:23 be in league with the s. of the field:......... 68
Job 6:12 Is my strength the strength of s.? or 68
Job 8:17 the heap, and seeth the place of s.......... 68
Job 14:19 waters wear the s.: thou washest.......... 68
Job 22:24 the gold of Ophir as the s. of the....... 6697
Job 28:3 the s. of darkness, and the shadow of.... 68
Job 28:6 s. of it are the place of sapphires: 68
Job 40:17 the sinews of his s. are wrapped........ 6344
Job 41:30 Sharp s. are under him: he 2789
Ps 18:12 clouds passed, hail s. and coals of fire. ......
Ps 18:13 gave his voice; hail s. and coals of fire.......
Ps 102:14 thy servants take pleasure in her s., ... 68
Ps 137:9 thy little ones against the s.. 5553
Ps 144:12 our daughters may be as corner s., ... 2106
Ec 3:5 A time to cast away s., and a time to 68
Ec 3:5 a time to gather s. together; a time....... 68
Ec 10:9 Whoso removeth s. shall be hurt............ 68
Isa 5:2 it, and gathered out the s. thereof, ... 5619
Isa 9:10 but we will build with hewn s.: 1496
Isa 14:19 that go down to the s. of the pit; 68
Isa 27:9 when he maketh all the s. of the altar.... 68
Isa 34:11 of confusion, and the s. of emptiness........ 68
Isa 54:11 I will lay thy s. with fair colours, and 68
Isa 54:12 and all thy borders of pleasant s............ 68
Isa 57:6 Among the smooth s. of the stream is.......
Isa 60:17 and for wood brass, and for s. iron:....... 68
Isa 62:10 up the highway; gather out the s.;......... 68
Jer 3:9 committed adultery with s. and with....... 68
Jer 43:9 Take great s. in thine hand, and hide 68
Jer 43:10 set his throne upon these s. that I......... 68
La 3:16 broken my teeth with gravel s., ... 2687
La 4:1 s. of the sanctuary are poured out in...... 68
Eze 16:40 and they shall stone thee with s., ... 68
Eze 23:47 company shall stone them with s., ... 68
Eze 26:12 they shall lay thy s. and thy timber........ 68
Eze 27:22 and with all precious s., and gold........... 68
Eze 28:14 down in the midst of the s. of fire. 68
Eze 28:16 from the midst of the s. of fire. 68
Da 11:38 and with precious s., and pleasant 68
Mic 1:6 I will pour down the s. thereof into......... 68
Zec 5:4 the timber thereof and the s. thereof. 68
Zec 9:15 devour, and subdue with sling s.; 68
Zec 9:16 for they shall be as the s. of a crown, ... 68
Mt 3:9 able of these s. to raise up children 3037
Mt 4:3 that these s. be made bread............... 3037
Mk 5:5 crying, and cutting himself with s.. 3037
Mk 12:4 **and at him they cast s., and** 3036
Mk 13:1 see what manner of s. and what......... 3037
Lu 3:8 able of these s. to raise up children 3037
Lu 19:40 **the s. would immediately cry out** .. 3037
Lu 21:5 adorned with goodly s. and gifts,....... 3037
Joh 8:59 Then took they up s. to cast at him:.... 3037
Joh 10:31 the Jews took up s. again to stone...... 3037
1Co 3:12 gold, silver, precious s., wood, hay,.... 3037
2Co 3:7 death, written and engraven in s., ... 3037
1Pe 2:5 Ye also, as lively s., are built up a...... 3037
Re 17:4 decked with gold and precious s.......... 3037
Re 18:12 gold, and silver, and precious s.,......... 3037
Re 18:16 decked with gold, and precious s.,......... 3037
Re 21:19 with all manner of precious s............ 3037

STONESQUARERS

1Ki 5:18 builders did hew them, and the s........ 1382

STONEST

Mt 23:37 **s. them which are sent unto thee,** . 3036
Lu 13:34 **s. them that are sent unto thee;** 3036

STONING

1Sa 30:6 for the people spake of s. him, ... 5619

STONY

Ps 141:6 are overthrown in s. places............... 5553
Eze 11:19 take the s. heart out of their flesh, ... 68
Eze 36:26 away the s. heart out of your flesh, ... 68
Mt 13:5 **Some fell upon s. places, where** ... 4075
Mt 13:20 **received the seed into s. places,** 4075
Mk 4:5 **And some fell on s. ground, where** .4075
Mk 4:16 **which are sown on s. ground;** 4075

STOOD See also STOODEST; UNDERSTOOD; WITHSTOOD.

Ge 18:2 and, lo, three men s. by him: 5324
Ge 18:8 and he s. by them under the tree,...... 5975
Ge 18:22 Abraham s. yet before the Lord.......... 5975
Ge 19:27 place where he s. before the Lord:..... 5975
Ge 23:3 Abraham s. up...before his dead,........ 6965
Ge 23:7 And Abraham s. up, and bowed 6965
Ge 24:30 he s. by the camels at the well. 5975
Ge 28:13 And, behold, the Lord s. above it,...... 5324
Ge 37:7 my sheaf arose, and also s. upright;.... 5324
Ge 37:7 your sheaves s. round about, and.............
Ge 41:1 and, behold, he s. by the river. 5975
Ge 41:3 s. by the other kine upon the brink..... 5975
Ge 41:17 I s. upon the bank of the river:.......... 5975
Ge 41:46 years old when he s. before Pharaoh... 5975
Ge 43:15 to Egypt, and s. before Joseph. 5975
Ge 45:1 before all them that s. by him;........... 5324
Ge 45:1 And there s. no man with him, ... 5975
Ex 2:4 his sister s. afar off, to wit what......... 3320
Ex 2:17 but Moses s. up and helped them,...... 6965
Ex 5:20 met Moses...who s. in the way,.......... 5324
Ex 9:10 furnace, and s. before Pharaoh;.......... 5975
Ex 14:19 their face, and s. behind them: 5975
Ex 15:8 the floods s. upright as an heap, ... 5324
Ex 18:13 and the people s. by Moses from 5975
Ex 19:17 and they s. at the nether part of......... 3320
Ex 20:18 it, they removed, and s. afar off.......... 5975
Ex 20:21 And the people s. afar off, and........... 5975
Ex 32:26 Moses s. in the gate of the camp, ... 5975
Ex 33:8 and s. every man at his tent door,....... 5324
Ex 33:9 s. at the door of the tabernacle,.......... 5975
Ex 34:5 the cloud, and s. with him there,......... 3320
Le 9:5 drew near and s. before the Lord....... 5975

Book	Ref	Text	No.
Nu	11:32	And the people **s.** up all that day,	6965
Nu	12:5	**s.** in the door of the tabernacle,	5975
Nu	16:18	and **s.** in the door of the tabernacle	5975
Nu	16:27	and **s.** in the door of their tents,	5324
Nu	16:48	**s.** between the dead and the living;	5975
Nu	22:22	angel of the Lord **s.** in the way	3320
Nu	22:24	angel of the Lord **s.** in a path of	5975
Nu	22:26	further, and **s.** in a narrow place,	5975
Nu	23:6	lo, he **s.** by his burnt sacrifice, he,	5324
Nu	23:17	behold, he **s.** by his burnt offering,	5324
Nu	27:2	And they **s.** before Moses, and	5975
De	4:11	near and **s.** under the mountain;	5975
De	5:5	(I **s.** between the Lord and you at	5975
De	31:15	pillar of the cloud **s.** over the door	5975
Jos	3:16	waters which came…from above **s.**	5975
Jos	3:17	priests…**s.** firm on dry ground	5975
Jos	4:3	where the priests' feet **s.** firm,	4673
Jos	4:9	bare the ark of the covenant **s.**:	4673
Jos	4:10	which bare the ark **s.** in the midst	5975
Jos	5:13	these **s.** a man over against him with	5975
Jos	8:33	**s.** on this side the ark and on that	5975
Jos	10:13	And the sun **s.** still, and the moon	1826
Jos	10:13	So the sun **s.** still in the midst of	5975
Jos	11:13	cities that **s.** still in their strength,	5975
Jos	20:9	until he **s.** before the congregation	5975
Jos	21:44	**s.** not a man of all their enemies	5975
Jg	3:19	all that **s.** by him went out from	5975
Jg	6:31	Joash said unto all that **s.** against	5975
Jg	7:21	And they **s.** every man in his place	5975
Jg	9:7	he went and **s.** in the top of mount	5975
Jg	9:35, 44	**s.** in the entering of the gate of	5975
Jg	16:29	pillars upon which the house **s.**,	3559
Jg	18:16	Dan, **s.** by the entering of the gate	5324
Jg	18:17	priest **s.** in the entering of the gate	5324
Jg	20:28	Aaron, **s.** before it in those days,)	5975
1Sa	1:26	I am the woman that **s.** by thee	5324
1Sa	3:10	the Lord came, and **s.**, and called	3320
1Sa	4:20	women that **s.** by her said unto her,	5324
1Sa	6:14	**s.** there, where there was a great	5975
1Sa	10:23	and when he **s.** among the people,	3320
1Sa	16:21	came to Saul, and **s.** before him:	5975
1Sa	17:3	the Philistines **s.** on a mountain	5975
1Sa	17:3	Israel **s.** on a mountain on the other	5975
1Sa	17:8	he **s.** and cried unto the armies of	5975
1Sa	17:26	David spake to the men that **s.** by	5975
1Sa	17:51	David…**s.** upon the Philistine, and	5975
1Sa	22:7	his servants that **s.** about him,	5324
1Sa	22:17	unto the footmen that **s.** about him,	5324
1Sa	26:13	and **s.** on the top of an hill afar off;	5975
2Sa	1:10	So I **s.** upon him, and slew him,	5975
2Sa	2:23	where Asahel fell down…**s.** still.	5975
2Sa	2:25	troop, and **s.** on the top of an hill.	5975
2Sa	2:28	trumpet, and all the people **s.** still,	5975
2Sa	13:31	**s.** by with their clothes rent.	5324
2Sa	15:2	and **s.** beside the way of the gate:	
2Sa	18:4	And the king **s.** by the gate side,	5975
2Sa	18:30	And he turned aside, and **s.** still.	5975
2Sa	20:11	And one of Joab's men **s.** by him,	5975
2Sa	20:12	man saw that all the people **s.** still,	5975
2Sa	20:12	every one that came by him **s.** still.	5975
2Sa	20:15	the city, and it **s.** in the trench:	5975
2Sa	23:12	he **s.** in the midst of the ground,	3320
1Ki	1:28	presence, and **s.** before the king.	5975
1Ki	3:15	**s.** before the ark of the covenant of	5975
1Ki	3:16	unto the king, and **s.** before him.	5975
1Ki	7:25	It **s.** upon twelve oxen, three looking	5975
1Ki	8:14	all the congregation of Israel **s.**;)	5975
1Ki	8:22	Solomon **s.** before the altar of the	5975
1Ki	8:55	And he **s.**, and blessed all the	5975
1Ki	10:19	and two lions **s.** beside the stays.	5975
1Ki	10:20	twelve lions **s.** there on the one side	5975
1Ki	12:6	that **s.** before Solomon his father	5975
1Ki	12:8	with him, and which **s.** before him:	5975
1Ki	13:1	Jeroboam **s.** by the altar to burn	5975
1Ki	13:24	cast in the way, and the ass **s.** by it,	5975
1Ki	13:24	the lion also **s.** by the carcase.	5975
1Ki	19:13	and **s.** in the entering in of the cave	5975
1Ki	22:21	a spirit, and **s.** before the Lord,	5975
2Ki	2:7	went, and **s.** to view afar off:	5975
2Ki	2:7	afar off: and they two **s.** by Jordan.	5975
2Ki	2:13	back, and **s.** by the bank of Jordan;	5975
2Ki	3:21	and upward, and **s.** in the border.	5975
2Ki	4:12	had called her, she **s.** before him.	5975
2Ki	4:15	had called her, she **s.** in the door.	5975
2Ki	5:9	**s.** at the door of the house of Elisha.	5975
2Ki	5:15	and came, and **s.** before him:	5975
2Ki	5:25	went in, and **s.** before his master.	5975
2Ki	8:9	and came and **s.** before him, and	5975
2Ki	9:17	there **s.** a watchman on the tower	5975
2Ki	10:4	Behold, two kings **s.** not before him:	5975
2Ki	10:9	went out, and **s.**, and said to all the	5975
2Ki	11:11	And the guard **s.**, every man with	5975
2Ki	11:14	behold, the king **s.** by a pillar, as	5975
2Ki	13:21	he revived, and **s.** up on his feet.	6965
2Ki	18:17	and **s.** by the conduit of the upper	5975
2Ki	18:28	then Rab-shakeh **s.** and cried with	5975
2Ki	23:3	the king **s.** by a pillar, and made a	5975
2Ki	23:3	all the people **s.** to the covenant.	5975
1Ch	6:39	Asaph, who **s.** on his right hand,	5975
1Ch	6:44	the sons of Merari **s.** on the left hand:	
1Ch	21:1	And Satan **s.** up against Israel,	5975
1Ch	21:15	angel…**s.** by the threshingfloor	5975
1Ch	28:2	David the king **s.** up upon his feet,	6965
2Ch	3:13	and they **s.** on their feet, and their	5975
2Ch	4:4	It **s.** upon twelve oxen, three looking	5975
2Ch	5:12	harps, **s.** at the east end of the altar,	5975
2Ch	6:3	all the congregation of Israel **s.**.	5975
2Ch	6:12	he **s.** before the altar of the Lord	5975
2Ch	6:13	upon it he **s.**, and kneeled down	5975
2Ch	7:6	before them, and all Israel **s.**.	5975
2Ch	9:19	twelve lions **s.** there on the one side	5975
2Ch	10:6	old men that had **s.** before Solomon	5975
2Ch	10:8	young men…that **s.** before him.	
2Ch	13:4	And Abijah **s.** up upon mount	6965
2Ch	18:20	a spirit, and **s.** before the Lord,	5975
2Ch	20:5	Jehoshaphat **s.** in the congregation	5975
2Ch	20:13	And all Judah **s.** before the Lord,	5975
2Ch	20:19	**s.** up to praise the Lord God of	6965
2Ch	20:20	Jehoshaphat **s.** and said, Hear me,	5975
2Ch	20:23	Moab **s.** up against the inhabitants	5975
2Ch	23:13	king **s.** at his pillar at the entering	5975
2Ch	24:20	priest, which **s.** above the people,	5975
2Ch	28:12	**s.** up against them that came from	6965
2Ch	29:26	Levites **s.** with the instruments of	5975
2Ch	30:16	they **s.** in their place after their	5975
2Ch	34:31	the king **s.** in his place, and made	5975
2Ch	35:10	and the priests **s.** in their place,	5975
Ezr	2:63	till there **s.** up a priest with Urim	5975
Ezr	3:2	**s.** up Jeshua the son of Jozadak,	6965
Ezr	3:9	Then **s.** Jeshua with his sons and	5975
Ezr	10:10	Ezra the priest **s.** up, and said unto	6965
Ne	7:65	till there **s.** up a priest with Urim	5975
Ne	8:4	Ezra the scribe **s.** upon a pulpit of	5975
Ne	8:4	and beside him **s.** Mattithiah, and	5975
Ne	8:5	he opened it, all the people **s.** up:	5975
Ne	8:7	law: and the people **s.** in their place.	
Ne	9:2	and **s.** and confessed their sins,	5975
Ne	9:3	they **s.** up in their place, and read	6965
Ne	9:4	Then **s.** up upon the stairs, of the	6965
Ne	12:39	and they **s.** still in the prison gate.	5975
Ne	12:40	So **s.** the two companies of them	5975
Es	5:1	**s.** in the inner court of the king's	5975
Es	5:9	the king's gate, that he **s.** not up,	6965
Es	7:7	Haman **s.** up to make request for	5975
Es	8:4	Esther arose, and **s.** before the king,	5975
Es	9:16	together, and **s.** for their lives,	5975
Job	4:15	face; the hair of my flesh **s.** up:	5568
Job	4:16	It **s.** still, but I could not discern	5975
Job	29:8	and the aged arose, and **s.** up.	5975
Job	30:28	the sun: I **s.** up, and I cried in the	6965
Job	32:16	(for they spake not, but **s.** still,	5975
Ps	33:9	done; he commanded, and it **s.** fast.	5975
Ps	104:6	the waters **s.** above the mountains.	5975
Ps	106:23	not Moses his chosen **s.** before him	5975
Ps	106:30	Then **s.** up Phinehas, and executed	5975
Isa	6:2	Above it **s.** the seraphims: each one	5975
Isa	36:2	he **s.** by the conduit of the upper	5975
Isa	36:13	Then Rabshakeh **s.**, and cried with	5975
Jer	15:1	Moses and Samuel **s.** before me, yet	5975
Jer	18:20	I **s.** before thee to speak good for	5975
Jer	19:14	and he **s.** in the court of the Lord's	5975
Jer	23:18	hath **s.** in the counsel of the Lord,	5975
Jer	23:22	But if they had **s.** in my counsel,	5975
Jer	28:5	all the people that **s.** in the house of	5975
Jer	36:21	princes which **s.** beside the king.	5975
Jer	44:15	all the women that **s.** by, a great	5975
Jer	46:15	they **s.** not, because the Lord did	5975
Jer	48:45	They that fled **s.** under the shadow	5975
La	2:4	he **s.** with his right hand as an	5324
Eze	1:21	and when those **s.**, these **s.**; and	5975
Eze	1:24	when they **s.**, they let down their	5975
Eze	1:25	when they **s.**, and had let down	5975
Eze	3:23	the glory of the Lord **s.** there, as	5975
Eze	8:11	there **s.** before them seventy men	5975
Eze	8:11	in the midst of them **s.** Jaazaniah	5975
Eze	9:2	in, and **s.** beside the brasen altar.	5975
Eze	10:3	the cherubims **s.** on the right side	5975
Eze	10:4	and **s.** over the threshold of the house;	
Eze	10:6	went in, and **s.** beside the wheels.	5975
Eze	10:17	When they stood, these **s.**; and	5975
Eze	10:18	house, and **s.** over the cherubims.	5975
Eze	10:19	every one **s.** at the door of the east	5975
Eze	11:23	**s.** upon the mountain which is on	5975
Eze	21:21	king of Babylon **s.** at the parting	5975
Eze	37:10	lived, and **s.** up upon their feet,	5975
Eze	40:3	reed; and he **s.** in the gate.	5975
Eze	43:6	the house; and the man **s.** by me.	5975
Eze	47:1	of the house **s.** toward the east,	
Da	1:19	therefore **s.** they before the king.	5975
Da	2:2	they came and **s.** before the king.	5975
Da	2:31	was excellent, **s.** before thee;	6966
Da	3:3	and they **s.** before the image that	6966
Da	7:10	times ten thousand **s.** before him:	6966
Da	7:16	near unto one of them that **s.** by,	6966
Da	8:3	there **s.** before the river a ram	5975
Da	8:15	**s.** before me as the appearance of	5975
Da	8:17	So he came near where I **s.**: and	5977
Da	8:22	whereas four **s.** up for it, four	5975
Da	10:11	this word unto me, I **s.** trembling.	5975
Da	10:16	said unto him that **s.** before me,	5975
Da	11:1	**s.** to confirm and to strengthen	5975
Da	12:5	behold, there **s.** other two, the one	5975
Ho	10:9	there they **s.**: the battle in Gibeah	5975
Am	7:7	the Lord **s.** upon a wall made by a	5324
Ob	14	thou have **s.** in the crossway, to	5975
Hab	3:6	He **s.**, and measured the earth; he	5975
Hab	3:11	The sun and moon **s.** still in their	5975
Zec	1:8	he **s.** among the myrtle trees that	5975
Zec	1:10	man that **s.** among the myrtle trees	5975
Zec	1:11	angel…**s.** among the myrtle trees,	5975
Zec	3:3	garments, and **s.** before the angel.	5975
Zec	3:4	unto those that **s.** before him,	5975
Zec	3:5	And the angel of the Lord **s.** by	5975
Mt	2:9	**s.** over where the young child was	*2476*
Mt	12:46	mother and his brethren **s.** without,	*2476*
Mt	13:2	the whole multitude **s.** on the shore.	*2476*
Mt	20:32	And Jesus **s.** still, and called them,	*2476*
Mt	26:73	while came unto him they that **s.** by,	*2476*
Mt	27:11	And Jesus **s.** before the governor:	*2476*
Mt	27:47	Some of them that **s.** there, when	*2476*
Mk	10:49	Jesus **s.** still, and commanded him	*2476*
Mk	11:5	certain of them that **s.** there said	*2476*
Mk	14:47	of them that **s.** by drew a sword,	*3936*
Mk	14:60	the high priest **s.** up in the midst,	*450*
Mk	14:69	began to say to them that **s.** by,	*3936*
Mk	14:70	they that **s.** by said again to Peter,	*3936*
Mk	15:35	And some of them that **s.** by, when	*3936*
Mk	15:39	centurion, which **s.** over against	*3936*
Lu	4:16	sabbath day, and **s.** up for to read.	*450*
Lu	4:39	And he **s.** over her, and rebuked	*2186*
Lu	5:1	he **s.** by the lake of Gennesaret,	*2476*
Lu	6:8	**midst.** And he arose and **s.** forth.	*2476*
Lu	6:17	down with them, and **s.** in the plain,	*2476*
Lu	7:14	and they that bare him **s.** still.	*2476*
Lu	7:38	**s.** at his feet behind him weeping,	*2476*
Lu	9:32	and the two men that **s.** with him.	*4921*
Lu	10:25	behold, a certain lawyer **s.** up, and	*450*
Lu	17:12	that were lepers, which **s.** afar off:	*2476*
Lu	18:11	**Pharisee s. and prayed thus with**	*2476*
Lu	18:40	And Jesus **s.**, and commanded him	*2476*
Lu	19:8	and Zacchaeus **s.**, and said unto the	*2476*
Lu	19:24	**And he said unto them that s. by,**	*3936*
Lu	23:10	scribes **s.** and vehemently accused	*2476*
Lu	23:35	And the people **s.** beholding. And	*2476*
Lu	23:49	**s.** afar off, beholding these things.	*2476*
Lu	24:4	two men **s.** by them in shining	*2186*
Lu	24:36	Jesus…**s.** in the midst of them,	*2476*
Joh	1:35	Again the next day after John **s.**,	*2476*
Joh	6:22	people which **s.** on the other side of	*2476*
Joh	7:37	Jesus **s.** and cried, saying, **If any**	*2476*
Joh	11:56	themselves, as they **s.** in the temple,	*2476*
Joh	12:29	The people therefore, that **s.** by,	*2476*
Joh	18:5	which betrayed him, **s.** with them.	*2476*
Joh	18:16	But Peter **s.** at the door without.	*2476*
Joh	18:18	the servants and officers **s.** there,	*2476*
Joh	18:18	Peter **s.** with them, and warmed	*2476*
Joh	18:22	officers which **s.** by struck Jesus	*3936*
Joh	18:25	Peter **s.** and warmed himself.	*2476*

Joh 19:25 **s.** by the cross of Jesus his mother,..... *2476*
Joh 20:11 Mary **s.** without at the sepulchre........ *2476*
Joh 20:19 came Jesus and **s.** in the midst, and.... *2476*
Joh 20:26 **s.** in the midst, and said, **Peace be**.... *2476*
Joh 21:4 now come, Jesus **s.** on the shore: *2476*
Ac 1:10 men **s.** by them in white apparel; *2936*
Ac 1:15 days Peter **s.** up in the midst of the *450*
Ac 3:8 And he leaping up **s.**, and walked *2476*
Ac 4:26 The kings of the earth **s.** up, and....... *3936*
Ac 5:34 then **s.** there up one in the council, ... *450*
Ac 9:7 journeyed with him **s.** speechless,....... *2476*
Ac 9:39 all the widows **s.** by him weeping, ... *3936*
Ac 10:17 house, and **s.** before the gate, ... *2186*
Ac 10:30 **s.** before me in bright clothing, ... *2476*
Ac 11:13 which **s.** and said unto him, Send *2476*
Ac 11:28 And there **s.** up one of them named *450*
Ac 12:14 told how Peter **s.** before the gate....... *2476*
Ac 13:16 Then Paul **s.** up, and beckoning........... *450*
Ac 14:20 the disciples **s.** round about him, ... *2944*
Ac 16:9 There **s.** a man of Macedonia, and *2476*
Ac 17:22 Paul **s.** in the midst of Mars' hill 2476
Ac 21:40 Paul **s.** on the stairs, and beckoned...... 2476
Ac 22:13 Came unto me, and **s.**, and said........ *2186*
Ac 22:25 said unto the centurion that **s.** by, ... *2476*
Ac 23:2 them that **s.** by him to smite him *3936*
Ac 23:4 And they that **s.** by said, Revilest....... *3936*
Ac 23:11 night following the Lord **s.** by him, ... *2186*
Ac 24:20 in me, while I **s.** before the council,.... *2476*
Ac 25:7 Jews...from Jerusalem **s.** round.......... *4026*
Ac 25:18 whom when the accusers **s.** up, they .. *2476*
Ac 27:21 Paul **s.** forth in the midst of them,...... *2476*
Ac 27:23 For there **s.** by me this night the....... *3936*
2Ti 4:16 first answer no man **s.** with me,.......... *4836*
2Ti 4:17 Lord **s.** with me, and strengthened..... *3936*
Heb 9:10 Which **s.** only in meats and drinks,............
Re 5:6 **s.** a Lamb as it had been slain, ... *2476*
Re 7:9 **s.** before the throne, and before the ... *2476*
Re 7:11 angels **s.** round about the throne, ... *2476*
Re 8:2 seven angels which **s.** before God;....... *2476*
Re 8:3 angel came and **s.** at the altar,........... *2476*
Re 11:1 and the angel **s.**, saying, Rise, and *2476*
Re 11:11 them, and they **s.** upon their feet; *2476*
Re 12:4 and the dragon **s.** before the woman ... *2476*
Re 13:1 And I **s.** upon the sand of the sea, ... *2476*
Re 14:1 lo, a Lamb **s.** on the mount Sion, ... *2476*
Re 18:17 as many as trade by sea, **s.** afar off, ... *2476*

STOODEST
Nu 22:34 I knew not that thou **s.** in the way 5324
De 4:10 day that thou **s.** before the Lord 5975
Ob 11 day that thou **s.** on the other side, ... 5975

STOOL See also FOOTSTOOL; STOOLS.
2Ki 4:10 there a bed and a table, and a **s.**,........ 3678

STOOLS
Ex 1:16 women, and see them upon the **s.**;........ 70

STOOP See also STOOPED; STOOPETH; STOOPING.
Job 9:13 proud helpers do **s.** under him. 7817
Pr 12:25 in the heart of man maketh it **s.**:......... 7812
Isa 46:2 They **s.**, they bow down together;...... 7164
Mk 1:7 I am not worthy to **s.** down and......... *2955*

STOOPED
Ge 49:9 he **s.** down, he couched as a lion,....... 3766
1Sa 24:8 David **s.** with his face to the earth,..... 6915
1Sa 28:14 he **s.** with his face to the ground,....... 6915
2Ch 36:17 old man, or him that **s.** for age: 3486
Joh 8:6 But Jesus **s.** down, and with his.......... *2955*
Joh 8:8 again he **s.** down, and wrote on the *2955*
Joh 20:11 she **s.** down, and looked into the........ *3879*

STOOPETH
Isa 46:1 Bel boweth down, Nebo **s.**, their.......... 7164

STOOPING
Lu 24:12 and **s.** down, he beheld the linen........ *3879*
Joh 20:5 And he **s.** down, and looking in, saw... *3879*

STOP See also STOPPED; STOPPETH.
1Ki 18:44 down, that the rain **s.** thee not. 6113
2Ki 3:19 **s.** all wells of water, and mar every.... 5640
2Ch 32:3 to **s.** the water of the fountains.......... 5640
Ps 35:3 and **s.** the way against them that........ 5462
Ps 107:42 and all iniquity shall **s.** her mouth. 7092
Eze 39:11 and it shall **s.** the noses of the.......... 2629
2Co 11:10 no man shall **s.** me of this boasting..... *5420*

STOPPED See also UNSTOPPED.
Ge 8:2 the windows of heaven were **s.**,......... 5534
Ge 26:15 the Philistines had **s.** them, and 5640
Ge 26:18 for the Philistines had **s.** them after 5640
Le 15:3 or his flesh be **s.** from his issue, it 2856
2Ki 3:25 and they **s.** all the wells of water, ... 5640
2Ch 32:4 who **s.** all the fountains, and the......... 5640
2Ch 32:30 **s.** the upper watercourse of Gihon,..... 5640
Ne 4:7 that the breaches began to be **s.**, ... 5640
Ps 63:11 of them that speak lies shall be **s.**. 5534
Jer 51:32 that the passages are **s.**, and the......... 8610
Zec 7:11 **s.** their ears, that they should not 3513
Ac 7:57 **s.** their ears, and ran upon him.......... *4912*
Ro 3:19 that every mouth may be **s.**, and all.... *5420*
Tit 1:11 Whose mouths must be **s.**, who *1993*
Heb 11:33 promises, **s.** the mouths of lions,........ *5420*

STOPPETH
Job 5:16 hope, and iniquity **s.** her mouth.......... 7092
Ps 58:4 like the deaf adder that **s.** her ear;....... 331
Pr 21:13 Whoso **s.** his ears at the cry of the 331
Isa 33:15 that **s.** his ears from hearing of blood,... 331

STORE See also RESTORE; STOREHOUSE.
Ge 26:14 of herds, and great **s.** of servants:............
Ge 41:36 that food shall be for **s.** to the land..... 6487
Le 25:22 fruits come in ye shall eat of the old **s.**......
Le 26:10 And ye shall eat old **s.**, and bring....... 3462
De 28:5,17 shall be thy basket and thy **s.**. 4863
De 32:34 Is not this laid up in **s.** with me and..........
1Ki 9:19 the cities of **s.** that Solomon had, ... 4543
1Ki 10:10 and of spices very great **s.**, and ....
2Ki 20:17 which thy fathers have laid up in **s.** 686
1Ch 29:16 all this **s.** that we have prepared 1995
2Ch 8:4 all the **s.** cities, which he built in.......... 4543
2Ch 8:6 all the **s.** cities that Solomon had, ... 4543
2Ch 11:11 **s.** of victual, and of oil and wine. 214
2Ch 16:4 and all the **s.** cities of Naphtali. 4543
2Ch 17:12 in Judah castles, and cities of **s.**. 4543
2Ch 31:10 that which is left is this great **s.**.......... 1995
Ne 5:18 in ten days **s.** of all sorts of wine: 7235
Ps 144:13 be full, affording all manner of **s.**: ....
Isa 39:6 which thy fathers have laid up in **s.** 686
Am 3:10 who **s.** up violence and robbery in........ 686
Na 2:9 for there is none end of the **s.** and 8498
1Co 16:2 every one of you lay by him in **s.**, ... *2343*
1Ti 6:19 Laying up in **s.** for themselves a.......... *597*
2Pe 3:7 by the same word are kept in **s.**, ... *2343*

STORE-CITIES See STORE and CITIES.

STOREHOUSE See also STOREHOUSES.
Mal 3:10 Bring ye all the tithes into the **s.**, ... 214
Lu 12:24 **which neither have s. nor barn;**..... *5009*

STOREHOUSES
Ge 41:56 And Joseph opened all the **s.**, and........ 834
De 28:8 the blessing upon thee in thy **s.**,.......... 618
1Ch 27:25 and over the **s.** in the fields, in the 214
2Ch 32:28 **S.** also for the increase of corn, ... 4543
Ps 33:7 heap: he layeth up the depth in **s.**. 214
Jer 50:26 the utmost border, open her **s.**: 3965

STORIES
Ge 6:16 second, and third **s.** shalt thou make it. .....
Eze 41:16 galleries round about on their three **s.**,.......
Eze 42:3 was gallery against gallery in three **s.**. ....
Eze 42:6 For they were in three **s.**, but had not ......
Am 9:6 that buildeth his **s.** in the heaven,......... 4609

STORK
Le 11:19 the **s.**, the heron after her kind,......... 2624
De 14:18 And the **s.**, and the heron after her 2624
Ps 104:17 as for the **s.**, the fir trees are her 2624
Jer 8:7 the **s.** in the heaven knoweth her 2624
Zec 5:9 had wings like the wings of a **s.**: 2624

STORM
Job 21:18 chaff that the **s.** carrieth away. 5492
Job 27:21 as a **s.** hurleth him out of his place. ....
Ps 55:8 my escape from the windy **s.** and 5584
Ps 83:15 and make them afraid with they **s.**...... 5492
Ps 107:29 He maketh the **s.** a calm, so that 5591
Isa 4:6 for a covert from **s.**, and from rain, ... 2230
Isa 25:4 a refuge from the **s.**, a shadow from... 2230
Isa 25:4 blast...is as a **s.** against the wall......... 2230
Isa 28:2 tempest of hail and a destroying **s.**, ... 8178
Isa 29:6 great noise, with **s.** and tempest, ... 5492
Eze 38:9 shalt ascend and come like a **s.**, ... 7722
Na 1:3 in the whirlwind and in the **s.**, ... 8183
Mk 4:37 there arose a great **s.** of wind, and..... *2978*
Lu 8:23 there came down a **s.** of wind on *2978*

STORMY
Ps 107:25 raiseth the **s.** wind, which lifteth 5591
Ps 148:8 vapours: **s.** wind fulfilling his word: 5591
Eze 13:11 fall; and a **s.** wind shall rend it. 5591
Eze 13:13 even rend it with a **s.** wind in my....... 5591

STORY See also STORIES.
2Ch 13:22 in the **s.** of the prophet of Iddo.......... 4097
2Ch 24:27 in the **s.** of the book of the kings. 4097

STOUT See also STOUTHEARTED.
Job 4:11 the **s.** lion's whelps are scattered.............
Isa 10:12 punish the fruit of the **s.** heart of 1433
Da 7:20 look was more **s.** than his fellows. 7229
Mal 3:13 words have been **s.** against me, ... 2388

STOUTHEARTED
Ps 76:5 The **s.** are spoiled, they have 47,3820
Isa 46:12 Hearken unto me, ye **s.**, that 47,3820

STOUTNESS
Isa 9:9 say in the pride and **s.** of heart, ... 1433

STRAIGHT See also STRAIGHTWAY; STRAIT.
Jos 6:5 ascend up every man **s.** before him..........
Jos 6:20 the city, every man **s.** before him,............
1Sa 6:12 the kine took the **s.** way to the.......... 3474
2Ch 32:30 brought it **s.** down to the west side 3474
Ps 5:8 make thy way **s.** before my face. 3474
Pr 4:25 let thine eyelids look **s.** before thee. ... 3474
Ec 1:15 is crooked cannot be made **s.**. 8626
Ec 7:13 for who can make that **s.**, which he 8626
Isa 40:3 make **s.** in the desert a highway......... 3474
Isa 40:4 the crooked shall be made **s.**, and 4334
Isa 42:16 before them, and crooked things **s.**..... 4334
Isa 45:2 and make the crooked places **s.**: 3474
Jer 31:9 by the river of waters in a **s.** way. 3474
Eze 1:7 their feet were **s.** feet; and the sole.... 3474
Eze 1:9 they went every one **s.** forward. 5676
Eze 1:12 they went every one **s.** forward: 5676
Eze 1:23 the firmament were their wings **s.**,..... 3474
Eze 10:22 they went every one **s.** forward. 5676
Mt 3:3 of the Lord, make his paths **s.**. *2117*
Mk 1:3 way of the Lord, make his paths **s.**..... *2117*
Lu 3:4 way of the Lord, make his paths **s.**..... *2117*
Lu 3:5 and the crooked shall be made **s.**, ... *2117*
Lu 13:13 and immediately she was made **s.**, ... *461*
Joh 1:23 Make **s.** the way of the Lord, as........ *2116*
Ac 9:11 **into the street which is called S.**,.. *2117*
Ac 16:11 with a **s.** course to Samothracia, ... *2113*
Ac 21:1 came with a **s.** course unto Coos,........ *2113*
Heb 12:13 And make **s.** paths for your feet,........ *3717*

STRAIGHTLY See STRAITLY.

STRAIGHTWAY
1Sa 9:13 into the city, ye shall **s.** find him, ... 3651
1Sa 28:20 Saul fell **s.** all along on the earth, ... 4116
Pr 7:22 He goeth after her **s.**, as an ox.......... 6597
Da 10:17 **s.** there remained no strength in 6258
Mt 3:16 went up **s.** out of the water: and,....... *2117*
Mt 4:20 they **s.** left their nets, and followed.... *2112*
Mt 14:22 **s.** Jesus constrained his disciples *2112*
Mt 14:27 But **s.** Jesus spake unto them,........... *2112*
Mt 21:2 **s. ye shall find an ass tied, and a**.. *2112*
Mt 21:3 **of them; and s. he will send them.** .*2112*
Mt 25:15 **ability; and s. took his journey.** *2112*
Mt 27:48 And **s.** one of them ran, and took a *2112*
Mk 1:10 And **s.** coming up out of the water, ... *2112*
Mk 1:18 And **s.** they forsook their nets, and..... *2112*
Mk 1:20 And **s.** he called them: and they......... *2112*
Mk 1:21 **s.** on the sabbath day he entered *2112*
Mk 2:2 **s.** many were gathered together,.......... *2112*
Mk 3:6 **s.** took counsel with the Herodians *2112*
Mk 5:29 **s.** the fountain of her blood was *2112*
Mk 5:42 **s.** the damsel arose, and walked;.......... *2112*
Mk 6:25 And she came in **s.** with haste unto *2112*
Mk 6:45 And **s.** he constrained his disciples...... *2112*
Mk 6:54 out of the ship, **s.** they knew him,...... *2112*
Mk 7:35 And **s.** his oars were opened, and *2112*
Mk 8:10 **s.** he entered into a ship with his *2112*
Mk 9:15 **s.** all the people, when they beheld..... *2112*
Mk 9:20 he saw him, **s.** the spirit tare him;...... *2112*
Mk 9:24 **s.** the father of the child cried out, ... *2112*
Mk 11:3 **and s. he will send him hither**....... *2112*
Mk 14:45 he was come, he goeth **s.** to him, ... *2112*
Mk 15:1 **s.** in the morning the chief priests *2112*
Lu 5:39 **drunk old wine s. desireth new:**..... *2112*
Lu 8:55 came again, and she arose **s.**:........... *3916*

Lu 12:54 **s. ye say, There cometh a shower;** *2112*
Lu 14:5 **not s. pull him out on the sabbath** *2112*
Joh 13:32 **himself and shall s. glorify him** *2117*
Ac 5:10 Then fell she down s. at his feet, *3916*
Ac 9:20 And s. he preached Christ in the *2112*
Ac 16:33 was baptized, he and all his, s. *3916*
Ac 22:29 Then s. they departed from him *2112*
Ac 23:30 man, I sent s. to thee, and gave *1824*
Jas 1:24 s. forgetteth what manner of man *2112*

STRAIN See also RESTRAIN.
Mt 23:24 **blind guides, which s. at a gnat,** *1368*

STRAIT See also STRAIGHT; STRAITEST; STRAITS.
1Sa 13:6 Israel saw that they were in a s., 6887
2Sa 24:14 said unto Gad, I am in a great s. 6887
2Ki 6:1 dwell with thee is too s. for us. 6862
1Ch 21:13 said unto Gad, I am in a great s. 6887
Job 36:16 remove thee out of the s. into a 6862
Isa 49:20 ears, The place is too s. for me: 6862
Mt 7:13 **Enter ye in at the s. gate: for wide** *4728*
Mt 7:14 **s. is the gate, and narrow is the** *4728*
Lu 13:24 **Strive to enter in at the s. gate:** *4728*
Php 1:23 For I am in a s. betwixt two, *4912*

STRAITEN See also STRAITENED; STRAITENETH.
Jer 19:9 that seek their lives, shall s. them. 6693

STRAITENED
Job 18:7 steps of his strength shall be s., 3334
Job 37:10 the breadth of the waters is s. 4164
Pr 4:12 goest, thy steps shall not be s.; 3334
Eze 42:6 the building was s. more than 680
Mic 2:7 Jacob, is the spirit of the Lord s.? 7114
Lu 12:50 **am I s. till it be accomplished!** *4912*
2Co 6:12 Ye are not s. in us, but ye are *4729*
2Co 6:12 but ye are s. in your own bowels. *4729*

STRAITENETH
Job 12:23 the nations, and s. them again. 5148

STRAITEST
Ac 26:5 that after the most s. sect of our *196*

STRAITLY
Ge 43:7 The man asked us s. of our state,
Ex 13:19 had s. sworn the children of Israel,
Jos 6:1 Jericho was s. shut up because
1Sa 14:28 Thy father s. charged the people
Mt 9:30 Jesus s. charged them, saying, See
Mk 1:43 he s. charged him, and forthwith sent
Mk 3:12 And he s. charged them that they *4183*
Mk 5:43 he charged them s. that no man *4183*
Lu 9:21 he s. charged them, and commanded
Ac 4:17 let us s. threaten them, that they *547*
Ac 5:28 Did not we s. command you that ye

STRAITNESS
De 28:53, 55 in the siege, and in the s., 4689
De 28:57 things secretly in the siege and s., 4689
Job 36:16 broad place, where there is no s.; 4164
Jer 19:9 of his friend in the siege and s., 4689

STRAITS
Job 20:22 of his sufficiency he shall be in s. 3334
La 1:3 over took her between the s. 4712

STRAKE See also STRAKES; STRUCK.
Ac 27:17 s. sail, and so were driven *5465*

STRAKES
Ge 30:37 and pilled white s. in them, and 6479
Le 14:37 walls of the house with hollow s., 8258

STRANGE See also ESTRANGED; STRANGER.
Ge 35:2 Put away the s. gods..among you, 5236
Ge 35:4 gave unto Jacob all the s. gods 5236
Ge 42:7 but made himself s. unto them, 5234
Ex 2:22 I have been a stranger in a s. land. 5237
Ex 18:3 I have been an alien in a s. land: 5237
Ex 21:8 to sell her unto a s. nation he shall 5237
Ex 30:9 Ye shall offer no s. incense 2114
Le 10:1 and offered s. fire before the Lord, 2114
Nu 3:4 they offered s. fire before the Lord, 2114
Nu 26:61 they offered s. fire before the Lord. 2114
De 32:12 and there was no s. god with him. 5236
De 32:16 him to jealousy with s. gods, 2114
Jos 24:20 the Lord, and serve s. gods, then 5236
Jos 24:23 the s. gods which are among you, 5236
Jg 10:16 put away the s. gods from among 5236
Jg 11:2 thou art the son of a s. woman. 312
1Sa 7:3 then put away the s. gods and 5236
1Ki 11:1 Solomon loved many s. women, 5237
1Ki 11:8 likewise did he for all his s. wives, 5237
2Ki 19:24 have digged and drunk s. waters, 2114
2Ch 14:3 away the altars of the s. gods, 5236
2Ch 33:15 he took away the s. gods, and the 5236
Ezr 10:2 have taken s. wives of the people 5237
Ezr 10:10 and have taken s. wives, to increase 5237
Ezr 10:11 of the land, and from the s. wives. 5237
Ezr 10:14 all them which have taken s. wives 5237
Ezr 10:17 all the men that had taken s. wives 5237
Ezr 10:18 found that had taken s. wives: 5237
Ezr 10:44 All these had taken s. wives: and 5237
Ne 13:27 transgress…in marrying s. wives? 5237
Job 19:3 that ye make yourselves s. to me. 1970
Job 19:17 My breath is s. to my wife, 2114
Job 31:3 a s. punishment to the workers 5235
Ps 44:20 stretched out…hands to a s. god; 2114
Ps 81:9 There shall no s. god be in thee; 2114
Ps 81:9 shalt thou worship any s. god. 5236
Ps 114:1 Jacob from a people of s. language; 3937
Ps 137:4 sing the Lord's song in a s. land? 5236
Ps 144:11 me from the hand of s. children, 5236
Ps 144:7 from the hand of s. children; 5236
Pr 2:16 deliver thee from the s. woman, 2114
Pr 5:3 the lips of a s. woman drop as an 2114
Pr 5:20 son, be ravished with a s. woman, 2114
Pr 6:24 of the tongue of a s. woman. 5237
Pr 7:5 keep thee from the s. woman, 2114
Pr 20:16 a pledge of him for a s. woman. 5237
Pr 21:8 way of man is froward and s. 2114
Pr 22:14 mouth of s. women is a deep pit: 2114
Pr 23:27 and a s. woman is a narrow pit. 5237
Pr 23:33 thine eyes shall behold s. women, 2114
Pr 27:13 a pledge of him for a s. woman. 5237
Isa 17:10 and shalt set it with s. slips: 2114
Isa 28:21 he may do his work, his s. work; 2114
Isa 28:21 bring to pass his act, his s. act. 5237
Isa 43:12 there was no s. god among you: 2114
Jer 2:21 the degenerate plant of a s. vine 5237
Jer 5:19 and served s. gods in your land, 5236
Jer 8:19 images, and with s. vanities? 5236
Eze 3:5 not sent to a people of a s. speech 6012
Eze 3:6 Not to many people of a s. speech 6012
Da 11:39 most strong holds with a s. god, 5236
Ho 5:7 they have begotten s. children: 2114
Ho 8:12 they were counted as a s. thing. 2114
Zep 1:8 as are clothed with s. apparel 5237
Mal 2:11 married the daughter of a s. god. 5236
Lu 5:26 We have seen s. things to day. *3861*
Ac 7:6 seed should sojourn in a s. land; *245*
Ac 17:18 to be a setter forth of s. gods: *3581*
Ac 17:20 certain s. things to our ears: *3579*
Ac 26:11 I persecuted them…unto s. cities. *1854*
Heb 11:9 land of promise, as in a s. country, *245*
Heb 13:9 about with divers and s. doctrines. *3581*
1Pe 4:4 think it s.…ye run not with them *3579*
1Pe 4:12 think it not s. concerning the fiery *3579*
1Pe 4:12 some s. thing happened unto you: *3581*
Jude 7 and going after s. flesh, are set *2087*

STRANGELY
De 32:27 should behave themselves s., 5234

STRANGER See also STRANGER'S, STRANGERS.
Ge 15:13 be a s. in a land that is not theirs, 1616
Ge 17:8 the land wherein thou art a s., 4033
Ge 17:12 bought with money of any s., 1121,5235
Ge 17:27 bought with money of the s., 1121,5235
Ge 23:4 I am a s. and a sojourner with you: 1616
Ge 28:4 the land wherein thou art a s., 4033
Ge 37:1 land wherein his father was a s., 4033
Ex 2:22 I have been a s. in a strange land. 1616
Ex 12:19 whether he be a s., or born in the 1616
Ex 12:43 There shall no s. eat thereof: 1121,5235
Ex 12:48 when a s. shall sojourn with thee, 1616
Ex 12:49 the s. that sojourneth among you. 1616
Ex 20:10 nor thy s. that is within thy gates: 1616
Ex 22:21 Thou shalt neither vex a s., nor 1616
Ex 23:9 Also thou shalt not oppress a s. 1616
Ex 23:9 for ye know the heart of a s., seeing 1616
Ex 23:12 son of thy handmaid and the s., 1616
Ex 29:33 but a s. shall not eat there of, 2114
Ex 30:33 putteth any of it upon a s., 2114
Le 16:29 a s. that sojourneth among you: 1616
Le 17:12 any s. that sojourneth among you 1616
Le 17:15 be one of your own country, or a s., 1616
Le 18:26 any s. that sojourneth among you: 1616
Le 19:10 shalt leave them for the poor and s. 1616
Le 19:33 if a s. sojourn with thee in your land, 1616
Le 19:34 But the s. that dwelleth with you 1616
Le 22:10 There shall no s. eat of the holy 2114
Le 22:12 daughter…married unto a s., 376,2114
Le 22:13 but there shall no s. eat thereof. 2114
Le 23:22 them unto the poor, and the s. 1616
Le 24:16 as well the s., as he that is born in 1616
Le 24:22 as well for the s., as for one of your 1616
Le 25:6 thy s. that sojourneth with thee, 8453
Le 25:35 though he be a s., or a sojourner; 1616
Le 25:47 sojourner or s. wax rich by thee, 8453
Le 25:47 and sell himself unto the s. or 1616
Nu 1:51 s. that cometh nigh shall be put 2114
Nu 3:10, 38 s. that cometh nigh shall be put 2114
Nu 9:14 if a s. shall sojourn among you, 1616
Nu 9:14 for the s.., and for him that was born 1616
Nu 15:14 And if a s. sojourn with you, or 1616
Nu 15:15 for the s. that sojourneth with you, 1616
Nu 15:15 so shall the s. be before the Lord. 1616
Nu 15:16 for the s. that sojourneth with you. 1616
Nu 15:26 the s. that sojourneth among them; 1616
Nu 15:29 the s. that sojourneth among them. 1616
Nu 15:30 he be born in the land, or a s., 1616
Nu 16:40 no s., which is not of the seed 376,2114
Nu 18:4 a s. shall not come nigh unto you 376,2114
Nu 18:7 the s. that cometh nigh shall be 376,2114
Nu 19:10 s. that sojourneth among them, 1616
Nu 35:15 children of Israel, and for the s., 1616
De 1:16 brother, and the s. that is with him. 1616
De 5:14 nor thy s. that is within thy gates; 1616
De 10:18 and loveth the s., in giving him food 1616
De 10:19 Love ye therefore the s.: for ye 1616
De 14:21 shalt give it unto the s. that is in thy 1616
De 14:29 and the s., and the fatherless, and 1616
De 16:11, 14 the s., and the fatherless, and 1616
De 17:15 mayest not set a s. over thee, 376,5237
De 23:7 because thou wast a s. in his land. 1616
De 23:20 Unto a s. thou mayest lend upon 5237
De 24:17 not pervert the judgment of the s., 1616
De 24:19, 20,21 it shall be for the s., for the 1616
De 25:5 not marry without unto a s.: 376,2114
De 26:11 and the s. that is among you. 1616
De 26:12 s., the fatherless, and the widow, 1616
De 26:13 unto the s., to the fatherless, and to 1616
De 27:19 perverteth the judgment of the s., 1616
De 28:43 The s. that is within thee shall get 1616
De 29:11 and thy s. that is in thy camp, 1616
De 29:22 the s. that shall come from a far 5237
De 31:12 and thy s. that is within thy gates, 1616
Jos 8:33 as well the s., as he that was born 1616
Jos 20:9 for the s. that sojourneth among 1616
Jg 19:12 aside hither into the city of a s., 5237
Ru 2:10 knowledge of me, seeing I am a s.? 5237
2Sa 1:13 answered, I am the son of a s., 376,1616
2Sa 15:19 thou art a s., and also an exile 5237
1Ki 3:18 was no s. with us in the house, 2114
1Ki 8:41 Moreover concerning a s., that is 5237
1Ki 8:43 all that the s. calleth to thee for: 5237
2Ch 6:32 Moreover concerning the s., which 5237
2Ch 6:33 to all that the s. calleth to thee for; 5237
Job 15:19 and no s. passed among them. 2114
Job 19:15 and my maids, count me for a s. 2114
Job 31:32 The s. did not lodge in the street: 1616
Ps 39:12 I am a s. with thee, and a sojourner 1616
Ps 69:8 I am…a s. unto my brethren, 2114
Ps 94:6 They slay the widow and the s., 1616
Ps 119:19 I am a s. in the earth: hide not thy 1616
Pr 2:16 from the s. which flattereth with 5237
Pr 5:10 thy labours be in the house of a s., 5237
Pr 5:20 and embrace the bosom of a s.? 5237
Pr 6:1 hast stricken thy hand with a s., 2114
Pr 7:5 from the s. which flattereth with 5237
Pr 11:15 that is surety for a s. shall smart 2114
Pr 14:10 a s. doth not intermeddle with his 2114
Pr 20:16 his garment that surety for a s. 2114
Pr 27:2 a s., and not thine own lips. 5237
Pr 27:13 his garment that is surety for a s. 2114
Ec 6:2 eat thereof, but a s. eateth it: 376,5237
Isa 56:3 Neither let the son of the s., that 5236
Isa 56:6 Also the sons of the s., that join 5236
Isa 62:8 the sons of the s. shall not drink 5236
Jer 7:6 If ye oppress not the s., the 1616
Jer 14:8 thou be as a s. in the land, and 1616
Jer 22:3 no wrong, do no violence to the s., 1616
Eze 14:7 the s. that sojourneth in Israel, 1616

Eze 22:7 dealt by oppression with the s.. 1616
Eze 22:29 have oppressed the s. wrongfully 1616
Eze 44:9 s., uncircumcised in heart, 1121,5236
Eze 44:9 of any s. that is among the 1121,5236
Eze 47:23 in what tribe the s. sojourneth, 1616
Ob 12 in the day that he became a s.; 5235
Zec 7:10 widow, nor the fatherless, the s., 1616
Mal 3:5 turn aside the s. from his right, 1616
Mt 25:35 **I was a s., and ye took me in:** *3581*
Mt 25:38 **When saw we thee a s., and took** *3581*
Mt 25:43 **I was a s., and ye took me not in:** *3581*
Mt 25:44 **or a s., or naked, or sick, or in** *3581*
Lu 17:18 **to give glory to God, save this s.** *241*
Lu 24:18 Art thou only a s. in Jerusalem, *3939*
Joh 10:5 **And a s. will they not follow, but** *245*
Ac 7:29 was a s. in the land of Madian, *3941*

STRANGER'S
Le 22:25 Neither from a s. hand shall 1121,5236
Le 25:47 or to the stock of the s. family: 1616

STRANGERS See also STRANGERS'.
Ge 31:15 Are we not counted of him s.? for 5237
Ge 36:7 and the land wherein they were s. 4033
Ex 6:4 pilgrimage, wherein they were s. 1481
Ex 22:21 for ye were s. in the land of Egypt. 1616
Ex 23:9 ye were s. in the land of Egypt. 1616
Le 17:8, 10,13 s. which sojourn among you, 1616
Le 19:34 for ye were s. in the land of Egypt: 1616
Le 20:2 of the s. that sojourn in Israel, that 1616
Le 22:18 house of Israel, or of the s. in Israel, 1616
Le 25:23 ye are s. and sojourners with me. 1616
Le 25:45 the s. that do sojourn among you, 8453
De 10:19 ye were s. in the land of Egypt. 1616
De 24:14 thy s. that are in thy land within 1616
De 31:16 after the gods of the s. of the land, 5236
Jos 8:35 s. that were conversant among 1616
2Sa 22:45 S. shall submit themselves 1121,5236
2Sa 22:46 S. shall fade away, and they 1121,5236
1Ch 16:19 but few, even a few, and s. in it. 1481
1Ch 22:2 to gather together the s. that 1616
1Ch 29:15 For we are s. before thee, and 1616
2Ch 2:17 Solomon numbered all the s. 582,1616
2Ch 15:9 the s. with them out of Ephraim 1481
2Ch 30:25 the s. that came out of the land of 1616
Ne 9:2 Israel separated...from all s., 1121,5236
Ne 13:30 Thus cleansed I them from all s., 1121,5236
Ps 18:44 s. shall submit themselves, 1121,5236
Ps 18:45 The s. shall fade away, and be 1121,5236
Ps 54:3 For s. are risen up against me, 2114
Ps 105:12 yea, very few, and s. in it. 1481
Ps 109:11 and let the s. spoil his labour. 2114
Ps 146:9 The Lord preserveth the s.; he 1616
Pr 5:10 Lest s. be filled with thy wealth; 2114
Isa 1:7 land, s. devour it in your presence, 2114
Isa 1:7 it is desolate, as overthrown by s. 2114
Isa 2:6 themselves in the children of s. 5237
Isa 5:17 places of the fat ones shall s. eat. 1481
Isa 14:1 the s. shall be joined with them, 1616
Isa 25:2 a palace of s. to be no city; it 2114
Isa 25:5 shalt bring down the noise of s., as 2114
Isa 29:5 multitude of thy s....be like...dust, 2114
Isa 60:10 sons of s. shall build up thy walls, 5236
Isa 61:5 s. shall stand and feed your flocks, 2114
Jer 2:25 for I have loved s., and after them 2114
Jer 3:13 hast scattered thy ways to the s. 2114
Jer 5:19 so shall ye serve s. in a land that 2114
Jer 30:8 s. shall no more serve themselves 2114
Jer 35:7 days in the land where ye be s.. 1481
Jer 51:51 s. are come into the sanctuaries 2114
La 5:2 Our inheritance is turned to s., our 2114
Eze 7:21 into the hands of the s. for a prey, 2114
Eze 11:9 and deliver you into the hands of s., 2114
Eze 16:32 taketh s. instead of her husband! 2114
Eze 28:7 therefore I will bring s. upon thee, 2114
Eze 28:10 uncircumcised by the hand of s.. 2114
Eze 30:12 that is therein, by the hand of s.. 2114
Eze 31:12 And s., the terrible of the nations, 2114
Eze 44:7 brought into my sanctuary s., 1121,5236
Eze 47:22 to the s. that sojourn among you, 1616
Ho 7:9 S. have devoured his strength, 2114
Ho 8:7 it yield, the s. shall swallow it up. 2114
Joe 3:17 shall no s. pass through her any 2114
Ob 11 s. carried away captive his forces, 2114
Mt 17:25 **of their own children, or of s.?** *245*
Mt 17:26 Peter saith unto him, Of s.. Jesus *245*
Mt 27:7 the potter's field, to bury s. in *3581*
Joh 10:5 **for they know not the voice of s.** *245*
Ac 2:10 s. of Rome, Jews and proselytes, *1927*
Ac 13:17 dwelt as s. in...land of Egypt, *1722,3940*
Ac 17:21 s. which were there spent their *3581*
Eph 2:12 s. from the covenants of promise, *3581*
Eph 2:19 ye are no more s. and foreigners, *3581*
1Ti 5:10 up children, if she have lodged s., *3580*
Heb 11:13 confessed that they were s. and *3581*
Heb 13:2 Be not forgetful to entertain s.. *5381*
1Pe 1:1 to the s. scattered throughout *3927*
1Pe 2:11 I beseech you as s. and pilgrims, *3941*
3Jo 5 doest to the brethren, and to s.; *3581*

STRANGERS'
Pr 5:17 thine own, and not s. with thee. 2114

STRANGLED
Na 2:12 whelps, and s. for his lionesses, 2614
Ac 15:20 fornication, and from things s., *4156*
Ac 15:29 and from blood, and from things s., *4156*
Ac 21:25 and from s., and from fornication. *4156*

STRANGLING
Job 7:15 So that my soul chooseth s., and 4267

STRAW See also STRAWED.
Ge 24:25 We have both s. and provender 8401
Ge 24:32 s. and provender for the camels, 8401
Ex 5:7 give the people s. to make brick, 8401
Ex 5:7 go and gather s. for themselves. 8401
Ex 5:10 Pharaoh, I will not give you s.. 8401
Ex 5:11 get you s. where ye can find it: yet 8401
Ex 5:12 to gather stubble instead of s.. 8401
Ex 5:13 daily tasks, as when there was s.. 8401
Ex 5:16 is no s. given unto thy servants, 8401
Ex 5:18 for there shall no s. be given you, 8401
Jg 19:19 Yet there is both s. and provender 8401
1Ki 4:28 Barley also and s. for the horses 8401
Job 41:27 He esteemeth iron as s., and brass 8401
Isa 11:7 and the lion shall eat s. like the ox. 8401
Isa 25:10 even as s. is trodden down for the 4963
Isa 65:25 lion shall eat s. like the bullock: 8401

STRAWED See also STROWED.
Ex 32:20 powder, and s. it upon the water, 2219
Mt 21:8 the trees, and s. them in the way. *4766*
Mt 25:24 **gathering where thou hast not s.** *1287*
Mt 25:26 **and gather where I have not s.** *1287*
Mk 11:8 the trees, and s. them in the way. *4766*

STRAY See ASTRAY.

STREAKED See STRAKED.

STREAKS See STRAKES.

STREAM See also STREAMS.
Nu 21:15 at the s. of the brooks that goeth 793
Job 6:15 as the s. of brooks they pass away; 650
Ps 124:4 us, the s. had gone over our soul: 5158
Isa 27:12 of the river unto the s. of Egypt, 5158
Isa 30:28 his breath, as an overflowing s., 5158
Isa 30:33 like a s. of brimstone, doth kindle 5158
Isa 57:6 Among the smooth stones of the s. 5158
Isa 66:12 of the Gentiles like a flowing s. 5158
Da 7:10 A fiery s. issued and came forth 5103
Am 5:24 and righteousness as a mighty s.. 5158
Lu 6:48 **the s. beat vehemently upon that** *4215*
Lu 6:49 **against which the s. did beat** *4215*

STREAMS
Ex 7:19 the waters of Egypt, upon their s., 5104
Ex 8:5 thine hand with thy rod over the s., 5104
Ps 46:4 the s. whereof shall make glad the 6388
Ps 78:16 He brought s. also out of the rock, 5140
Ps 78:20 gushed out, and the s. overflowed; 5158
Ps 126:4 O Lord, as the s. in the south. 650
Ca 4:15 waters, and s. from Lebanon. 5140
Isa 11:15 and shall smite it in the seven s., 5158
Isa 30:25 rivers and s. of waters in the day 2988
Isa 33:21 us a place of broad rivers and s.; 2975
Isa 34:9 the s. thereof shall be burned into 5158
Isa 35:6 break out, and s. in the desert. 5158

STREET See also STREETS.
Ge 19:2 we will abide in the s. all night. 7339
De 13:16 of it into the midst of the s. thereof, 7339
Jos 2:19 the doors of thy house into the s., 2351
Jg 19:15 he sat him down in a s. of the city: 7339
Jg 19:17 wayfaring man in the s. of the city: 7339
Jg 19:20 upon me; only lodge not in the s.. 7339
2Sa 21:12 them from the s. of Beth-shan, 7339
2Sa 22:43 stamp them as the mire of the s., 2351
2Ch 29:4 them together into the east s., 7339
2Ch 32:6 him in the s. of the gate of the city, 7339
Ezr 10:9 sat in the s. of the house of God, 7339
Ne 8:1 s. that was before the water gate; 7339
Ne 8:3 s. that was before the water gate 7339
Ne 8:16 and in the s. of the water gate, and 7339
Ne 8:16 in the s. of the gate of Ephraim. 7339
Es 4:6 to Mordecai unto the s. of the city, 7339
Es 6:9,11 horseback through the s. of the 7339
Job 18:17 shall have no name in the s. 2351,6440
Job 29:7 when I prepared my seat in the s.! 7339
Job 31:32 stranger did not lodge in the s.. 2351
Pr 7:8 through the s. near her corner; 7784
Isa 42:2 his voice to be heard in the s.. 2351
Isa 51:23 as the s., to them that went over. 2351
Isa 59:14 truth is fallen in the s., and equity 7339
Jer 37:21 piece of bread out of the bakers' s., 2351
La 2:19 for hunger in the top of every s.. 2351
La 4:1 poured out in the top of every s.. 2351
Eze 16:24 thee an high place in every s.. 7339
Eze 16:31 makest thine high place in every s.; 7339
Da 9:25 the s. shall be built again, and the 7339
Ac 9:11 **the s. which is called Straight,** *4505*
Ac 12:10 out, and passed on through one s.; *4505*
Re 11:8 dead bodies shall lie in the s. of *4113*
Re 21:21 the s. of the city was pure gold, as it *4113*
Re 22:2 In the midst of the s. of it, and on *4113*

STREETS
2Sa 1:20 publish it not in the s. of Askelon; 2351
1Ki 20:34 shalt make s. for thee in Damascus, 2351
Ps 18:42 cast them out as the dirt in the s.. 2351
Ps 55:11 and guile depart not from her s. 7339
Ps 144:13 and ten thousands in our s.. 2351
Ps 144:14 there be no complaining in our s.. 7339
Pr 1:20 she uttereth her voice in the s. 7339
Pr 5:16 abroad, and rivers of waters in the s. 7339
Pr 7:12 Now is she without, now in the s., 7339
Pr 22:13 without, I shall be slain in the s.. 7339
Pr 26:13 a lion in the way; a lion is in the s. 7339
Ec 12:4 the doors shall be shut in the s., 7784
Ec 12:5 and the mourners go about the s. 7784
Ca 3:2 now, and go about the city in the s. 7784
Isa 5:25 were torn in the midst of the s.. 2351
Isa 10:6 them down like the mire of the s.. 2351
Isa 15:3 In their s. they shall gird themselves 2351
Isa 15:3 in their s., every one shall howl, 7339
Isa 24:11 is a crying for wine in the s.; all 2351
Isa 51:20 they lie at the head of all the s., as 2351
Jer 5:1 and fro through the s. of Jerusalem, 2351
Jer 7:17 of Judah and in the s. of Jerusalem? 2351
Jer 7:34 from the s. of Jerusalem, the voice 2351
Jer 9:21 and the young men from the s.. 7339
Jer 11:6 Judah, and in the s. of Jerusalem, 2351
Jer 11:13 the number of the s. of Jerusalem 2351
Jer 14:16 be cast out in the s. of Jerusalem 2351
Jer 33:10 Judah, and in the s. of Jerusalem, 2351
Jer 44:6 of Judah and in the s. of Jerusalem; 2351
Jer 44:9 Judah, and in the s. of Jerusalem? 2351
Jer 44:17 Judah, and in the s. of Jerusalem: 2351
Jer 44:21 Judah, and in the s. of Jerusalem, 2351
Jer 48:38 of Moab, and in the s. thereof: 7339
Jer 49:26 her young men shall fall in her s., 7339
Jer 50:30 shall her young men fall in the s., 7339
Jer 51:4 that are thrust through in her s. 2351
La 2:11 and the sucklings swoon in the s. 7339
La 2:12 swooned as the wounded in the s., 7339
La 2:21 the old lie on the ground in the s. 2351
La 4:5 delicately are desolate in the s. 2351
La 4:8 they are not known in the s. 2351
La 4:14 wandered as blind men in the s., 2351
La 4:18 steps, that we cannot go in our s. 7339
Eze 7:19 shall cast their silver in the s., 2351
Eze 11:6 filled the s. thereof with the slain. 2351
Eze 26:11 shall he tread down all thy s.: 2351
Eze 28:23 pestilence, and blood into her s.; 2351
Am 5:16 Wailing shall be in all the s.; 7339
Mic 7:10 trodden down as the mire of the s. 2351
Na 2:4 The chariots shall rage in the s., 2351
Na 3:10 dashed in pieces at...top of...the s. 2351
Zep 3:6 I made their s. waste, that none 2351
Zec 8:4 and old women dwell in the s. of 7339
Zec 8:5 s. of the city shall be full of boys 7339
Zec 8:5 and girls playing in the s. thereof. 7339
Zec 9:3 and fine gold as the mire of the s. 2351
Zec 10:5 in the mire of the s. in the battle: 2351

Mt 6:2 **in the synagogues and in the s.,** *4505*
Mt 6:5 **and in the corners of the s.,** *4113*
Mt 12:19 any man hears his voice in the s., ... *4113*
Mk 6:56 they laid the sick in the s., and............ *58*
Lu 10:10 **go your ways out into the s. of** *4113*
Lu 13:26 **and thou hast taught in our s..** *4113*
Lu 14:21 **out quickly into the s. and lanes** ... *4113*
Ac 5:15 brought forth the sick into the s., ... *4113*

STRENGTH
Ge 4:12 shall not...yield unto thee her s.;........ 3581
Ge 49:3 might, and the beginning of my s., ... 202
Ge 49:24 But his bow abode in s., and the 386
Ex 13:3 by s. of hand the Lord brought you 2392
Ex 13:14 By s. of hand the Lord brought us...... 2392
Ex 13:16 by s. of hand the Lord brought us 2392
Ex 14:27 sea returned to his s. when the........... 386
Ex 15:2 The Lord is my s. and song, and 5797
Ex 15:13 thou hast guided them in thy s........... 5797
Le 26:20 And your s. shall be spent in vain:...... 3581
Nu 23:22 hath as it were the s. of an unicorn. ... 8443
Nu 24:8 hath as it were the s. of an unicorn: ... 8443
De 21:17 for he is the beginning of his s.; 202
De 33:25 and as thy days, so shall thy s. be....... 1679
Jos 11:13 cities that stood still in their s., ... 8510
Jos 14:11 s. was then, even so is my s. now, ... 3581
Jg 5:21 soul, thou hast trodden down s.. 5797
Jg 8:21 for as the man is, so is his s.. 1369
Jg 16:5 and see wherein his great s. lieth, ... 3581
Jg 16:6 Tell me,...wherein thy great s. lieth,... 3581
Jg 16:9 the fire. So his s. was not known. 3581
Jg 16:15 told me wherein thy great s. lieth....... 3581
Jg 16:17 shaven, then my s. will go from me, ... 3581
Jg 16:19 him, and his s. went from him. 3581
1Sa 2:4 that stumbled are girded with s.......... 2428
1Sa 2:9 for by s. shall no man prevail............. 3581
1Sa 2:10 and he shall give s. unto his king,....... 5797
1Sa 15:29 the S. of Israel will not lie nor 5331
1Sa 28:20 and there was no s. in him; for he...... 3581
1Sa 28:22 and eat, that thou mayest have s.,...... 3581
2Sa 22:33 God is my s. and power: and he 4581
2Sa 22:40 hast girded me with s. to battle: 2428
1Ki 19:8 and went in the s. of that meat........... 3581
2Ki 9:24 Jehu drew a bow with his full s.,......... 3027
2Ki 18:20 I have counsel and s. for the war. 1369
2Ki 19:3 and there is not s. to bring forth. 3581
1Ch 16:11 Seek the Lord and his s., seek his 5797
1Ch 16:27 s. an gladness are in his place. 5797
1Ch 16:28 give unto the Lord glory and s.......... 5797
1Ch 26:8 able men for s. for the service,.......... 3581
1Ch 29:12 make great, and to give s. unto all. 2388
2Ch 6:41 place, thou, and the ark of thy s. 5797
2Ch 13:20 Neither did Jeroboam recover s.......... 3581
Ne 4:10 The s. of the bearers of burdens.......... 3581
Ne 8:10 for the joy of the Lord is your s.. 4581
Job 6:11 What is my s., that I should hope? 3581
Job 6:12 Is my s. the s. of stones? or is my...... 3581
Job 9:4 is wise in heart, and mighty in s. 3581
Job 9:19 If I speak of s., lo, he is strong: 3581
Job 12:13 With him is wisdom and s., he........... 1369
Job 12:16 With him is s. and wisdom: the.......... 5797
Job 12:21 weakeneth the s. of the mighty.......... 4206
Job 18:7 steps of his s. shall be straitened,........ 202
Job 18:12 His s. shall be hungerbitten, and.......... 202
Job 18:13 It shall devour the s. of his skin: 905
Job 18:13 firstborn of death shall devour his s...... 905
Job 21:23 One dieth in his full s., being............ 6106
Job 23:6 power? No; but he would not put s. in. .....
Job 26:2 savest...the arm that hath no s.?........ 5797
Job 30:2 the s. of their hands profit me,........... 3581
Job 36:5 he is mighty in s. and wisdom. 3581
Job 36:19 no, not gold, nor all the forces of s..... 3581
Job 37:6 and to the great rain of his s.. 5797
Job 39:11 trust him, because his s. is great?....... 3581
Job 39:19 Hast thou given the horse s.?........... 1369
Job 39:21 the valley, and rejoiceth in his s.......... 3581
Job 40:16 his s. is in his loins, and his force....... 3581
Job 41:22 In his neck remaineth s., and 5797
Ps 8:2 sucklings hast thou ordained s........... 5797
Ps 18:1 I will love thee, O Lord, my s............ 2391
Ps 18:2 my God, my s., in whom I will.......... 6697
Ps 18:32 It is God that girded me with s.,......... 2428
Ps 18:39 For thou hast girded me with s.......... 2428
Ps 19:14 O Lord, my s., and my redeemer.......... 6697
Ps 20:6 with...saving s. of his right hand. 1369
Ps 21:1 king shall joy in thy s., O Lord; 5797
Ps 21:13 Be...exalted, Lord, in thine own s...... 5797
Ps 22:15 My s. is dried up like a potsherd;....... 3581
Ps 22:19 O my s., haste thee to help me........... 360
Ps 27:1 Lord is the s. of my life; of whom...... 4581
Ps 28:7 The Lord is my s. and my shield;........ 5797
Ps 28:8 The Lord is their s., and he is the 5797
Ps 28:8 is the saving s. of his anointed........... 4581
Ps 29:1 give unto the Lord glory and s........... 5797
Ps 29:11 Lord will give s. unto his people; 5797
Ps 31:4 privily for me: for thou art my s.. 4581
Ps 31:10 my s. faileth because of mine 3581
Ps 33:16 man is not delivered by much s........... 3581
Ps 33:17 he deliver any by his great s.. 2428
Ps 37:39 is their s. in the time of trouble. 4581
Ps 38:10 heart panteth, my s. faileth me: 3581
Ps 39:13 O spare me, that I may recover s., ... 1082
Ps 43:2 For thou art the God of my s.: 4581
Ps 46:1 God is our refuge and s., a very 5797
Ps 52:7 the man that made not God his s.; 4581
Ps 54:1 thy name, and judge me by thy s.. 1369
Ps 59:9 Because of his s. will I wait upon........ 5797
Ps 59:17 Unto thee, O my s., will I sing: for 5797
Ps 60:7 Ephraim...is the s. of mine head; 4581
Ps 62:7 the rock of my s., and my refuge,....... 5797
Ps 65:6 by...s. setteth fast the mountains; 3581
Ps 68:28 Thy God hath commanded thy s.......... 5797
Ps 68:34 Ascribe ye s. unto God: his.............. 5797
Ps 68:34 Israel, and his s. is in the clouds. 5797
Ps 68:35 that giveth s....unto his people............ 5797
Ps 71:9 forsake me not when my s. faileth. 3581
Ps 71:16 I will go in the s. of the Lord God:..... 1369
Ps 71:18 I have shewed thy s. unto this............ 2220
Ps 73:4 in their death: but their s. is firm........ 193
Ps 73:26 but God is the s. of my heart, and 6697
Ps 74:13 Thou didst divide the sea by thy s...... 5797
Ps 77:14 declared thy s. among the people. 5797
Ps 78:4 the praises of the Lord, and his s.,..... 5807
Ps 78:51 chief of their s. in the tabernacles 202
Ps 78:61 And delivered his s. into captivity, ... 5797
Ps 80:2 and Manasseh stir up my s., ... 1369
Ps 81:1 Sing aloud unto God our s.: make....... 5797
Ps 84:5 is the man whose s. is in thee;.......... 5797
Ps 84:7 They go from s. to s., every one of ... 2428
Ps 86:16 give thy s. unto thy servant, and......... 5797
Ps 88:4 pit: I am as a man that hath no s.: 353
Ps 89:17 For thou art the glory of their s.:....... 5797
Ps 90:10 by reason of s. they be fourscore....... 1369
Ps 90:10 yet is their s. labour and sorrow; 7296
Ps 93:1 the Lord is clothed with s.,............... 5797
Ps 95:4 the s. of the hills is his also. 8443
Ps 96:6 s. and beauty are in his sanctuary....... 5797
Ps 96:7 give unto the Lord glory and s........... 5797
Ps 99:4 The king's s. also loveth judgment;..... 5797
Ps 102:23 He weakened my s. in the way; he..... 3581
Ps 103:20 ye his angels, that excel in s., that..... 3581
Ps 105:4 Seek the Lord, and his s.: seek his 5797
Ps 105:36 their land, the chief of all their s.......... 202
Ps 108:8 Ephraim...is the s. of mine head; 4581
Ps 110:2 send the rod of thy s. out of Zion:....... 5797
Ps 118:14 The Lord is my s. and song, and is 5797
Ps 132:8 thy rest; thou, and the ark of thy s.. .. 5797
Ps 138:3 strengthenedst...with s. in my soul. 5797
Ps 140:7 the Lord, the s. of my salvation, ... 5797
Ps 144:1 Blessed be the Lord my s., which....... 6697
Ps 147:10 delighteth not in...s. of the horse: 1369
Pr 8:14 I am understanding; I have s.............. 1369
Pr 10:29 The way of the Lord is s. to the........ 4581
Pr 14:4 increase is by the s. of the ox. 3581
Pr 20:29 glory of young men is their s............. 3581
Pr 21:22 and casteth down the s. of the........... 5797
Pr 24:5 a man of knowledge increaseth s.. 3581
Pr 24:10 day of adversity, thy s. is small. 3581
Pr 31:3 Give not thy s. unto women, nor 2428
Pr 31:17 She girdeth her loins with s., and........ 5797
Pr 31:25 S. and honour are her clothing;.......... 5797
Ec 9:16 said I, Wisdom is better than s........... 1369
Ec 10:10 edge, then must he put to more s. 2428
Ec 10:17 princes eat in due season, for s., ... 1369
Isa 5:22 men of s. to mingle strong drink: 2428
Isa 10:13 By the s. of my hand I have done 3581
Isa 12:2 Jehovah is my s. and my song; 5797
Isa 17:10 been mindful of the rock of thy s.,....... 4581
Isa 23:4 hath spoken, even the s. of the sea, ... 4581
Isa 23:10 of Tarshish: there is no more s........... 4206
Isa 23:14 Tarshish: for your s. is laid waste. 4581
Isa 25:4 For thou hast been a s. to the poor, ... 4581
Isa 25:4 a s. to the needy in his distress, ... 4581
Isa 26:4 Lord Jehovah is everlasting s.:.......... 6697
Isa 27:5 Or let him take hold of my s., ... 4581
Isa 28:6 for s. to them that turn the battle 1369
Isa 30:2 themselves in the s. of Pharaoh, ... 4581
Isa 30:3 the s. of Pharaoh be your shame,........ 4581
Isa 30:7 I cried...Their s. is to sit still. 7293
Isa 30:15 and in confidence shall be your s. 1369
Isa 33:6 of thy times, and s. of salvation: 2633
Isa 36:5 I have counsel and s. for war: 1369
Isa 37:3 and there is not s. to bring forth. 3581
Isa 40:9 tidings, lift up thy voice with s.;......... 3581
Isa 40:29 have no might be increaseth s.. 6109
Isa 40:31 the Lord shall renew their s.; 3581
Isa 41:1 and let the people renew their s.......... 3581
Isa 42:25 of his anger, and the s. of battle: 5807
Isa 44:12 worketh it with the s. of his arms: 3581
Isa 44:12 yea, he is hungry, and his s. faileth: ... 3581
Isa 45:24 Lord have I righteousness and s......... 5797
Isa 49:4 I have spent my s. for nought, and...... 3581
Isa 49:5 Lord, and my God shall be my s.. 5797
Isa 51:9 awake, put on s., O arm of the Lord; ..5797
Isa 52:1 awake; put on thy s., O Zion;............ 5797
Isa 62:8 hand, and by the arm of his s., ... 5797
Isa 63:1 travelling in...greatness of his s.? 3581
Isa 63:6 bring down their s. to the earth. 5332
Isa 63:15 where is thy zeal and thy s., the........ 1369
Jer 16:19 O Lord, my s., and my fortress, ... 5797
Jer 20:5 I will deliver all the s. of this city, ... 2633
Jer 51:53 should fortify the height of her s., ... 5797
La 1:6 they are gone without s. before 3581
La 1:14 he hath made my s. to fall, the.......... 3581
La 3:18 My s. and my hope is perished............ 5331
Eze 24:21 excellency of your s., the desire 5797
Eze 24:25 when I take from them their s., ... 4581
Eze 30:15 my fury upon Sin, the s. of Egypt; 4581
Eze 30:18 pomp of her s. shall cease in her:....... 5797
Eze 33:28 and the pomp of her s. shall cease;...... 5797
Da 2:37 thee a kingdom, power, and s.,........... 8632
Da 2:41 shall be in it of the s. of the iron,....... 5326
Da 10:8 and there remained no s. in me: 3581
Da 10:8 corruption, and I retained no s.......... 3581
Da 10:16 upon me, and I have retained no s...... 3581
Da 10:17 there remained no s. in me, neither.... 3581
Da 11:2 by his s. through his riches he........... 2394
Da 11:15 neither shall there be any s. to 3581
Da 11:17 to enter with the s. of his whole 8633
Da 11:31 shall pollute the sanctuary of s.,......... 4581
Ho 7:9 Strangers have devoured his s.,.......... 3581
Ho 12:3 by his s. he had power with God: 202
Joe 2:22 tree and the vine do yield their s.. 2428
Joe 3:16 the s. of the children of Israel. 4581
Am 3:11 shall bring down thy s. from thee, ... 5797
Am 6:13 taken to us horns by our own s.? 2392
Mic 5:4 and feed in the s. of the Lord,........... 5797
Na 3:9 Ethiopia and Egypt were her s.,.......... 6109
Na 3:11 seek s. because of the enemy............ 4581
Hab 3:19 The Lord God is my s., and he will 2428
Hag 2:22 destroy the s. of the kingdoms of....... 2392
Zec 12:5 shall be my s. in the Lord of hosts....... 556
Mk 12:30 **all thy mind, and with all thy s.** .. *2479*
Mk 12:33 all the soul, and with all the s.,.......... *2479*
Lu 1:51 He hath shewed s. with his arm;........ *2904*
Lu 10:27 all thy soul, and with all thy s.,........... *2479*
Ac 3:7 feet and ancle bones received s.......... *4732*
Ac 9:22 But Saul increased the more in s.,...... *1743*
Ro 5:6 For when we were yet without s.,........ *772*
1Co 15:56 is sin; and the s. of sin is the law....... *1411*
2Co 1:8 pressed out of measure, above s.,....... *1411*
2Co 12:9 **s. is made perfect in weakness** *1411*
Heb 9:17 of no s. at all while the testator.......... *2480*
Heb 11:11 Sara...received s. to conceive seed,.... *1411*
Re 1:16 was as the sun shineth in his s.. .... *1411*
Re 3:8 **thou hast a little s., and hast** *1411*
Re 5:12 and riches, and wisdom, and s., ... *2479*
Re 12:10 Now is come salvation, and s., and..... *1411*
Re 17:13 their power and s. unto the beast....... *1849*

STRENGTHEN See also STRENGTHENED; STRENGTHENETH; STRENGTHENING.
De 3:28 and encourage him, and s. him: 553
Jg 16:28 s. me, I pray thee, only this once, ... 2388
1Ki 20:22 Go, s. thyself, and mark, and see......... 2388
Ezr 6:22 to s. their hands in the work of the 2388
Ne 6:9 therefore, O God, s. my hands. 2388
Job 16:5 I would s. you with my mouth, and 553
Ps 20:2 sanctuary, and s. thee out of Zion; 5582
Ps 27:14 and he shall s. thine heart: 553

Ps 31:24 courage, and he shall s. your heart,...... 553
Ps 41:3 Lord will s. him upon the bed of........ 5582
Ps 68:28 s., O God, that which thou hast......... 5810
Ps 89:21 mine arm also shall s. him. 553
Ps 119:28 s....me according unto thy word......... 6965
Isa 22:21 robe, and s. him with thy girdle, ... 2388
Isa 30:2 to s....in the strength of Pharaoh, ... 5810
Isa 33:23 they could not well s. their mast, ... 2388
Isa 35:3 S. ye the weak hands, and confirm..... 2388
Isa 41:10 I will s. thee; yea, I will help thee; 553
Isa 54:2 thy cords, and s. thy stakes;............. 2388
Jer 23:14 they s. also the hands of evildoers,...... 2388
Eze 7:13 s. himself in the iniquity of his life. 2388
Eze 16:49 s. the hand of the poor and needy. 2388
Eze 30:24 s. the arms of the king of Babylon,..... 2388
Eze 30:25 s. the arms of the king of Babylon,..... 2388
Eze 34:16 and will s. that which was sick:.......... 2388
Da 11:1 I, stood to confirm and to s. him........ 4581
Am 2:14 and the strong shall not s. his force,..... 553
Zec 10:6 And I will s. the house of Judah, ... 1396
Zec 10:12 And I will s. them in the Lord; 1396
Lu 22:32 **art converted, s. thy brethren**........ *4741*
1Pe 5:10 perfect, stablish, s., settle you........... *4599*
Re 3:2 **and s. the things which remain,** *4741*

STRENGTHENED See also STRENGTHENEDST.

Ge 48:2 Israel s. himself, and sat upon 2388
Jg 3:12 Lord s. Eglon the king of Moab 2388
Jg 7:11 shall thine hands be s. to go down...... 2388
1Sa 23:16 the wood, and s. his hands in God...... 2388
2Sa 2:7 Therefore now let your hands be s., ... 2388
1Ch 11:10 s. themselves...in his kingdom, ... 2388
2Ch 1:1 Solomon...was s. in his kingdom,........ 2388
2Ch 11:17 So they s. the kingdom of Judah,........ 2388
2Ch 12:1 the kingdom, and had s. himself, ... 2394
2Ch 12:13 So king Rehoboam s. himself in.......... 2388
2Ch 13:7 s. themselves against Rehoboam.......... 553
2Ch 17:1 and s. himself against Israel. 2388
2Ch 21:4 s. himself, and slew all his brethren.... 2388
2Ch 23:1 seventh year Jehoiada s. himself,........ 2388
2Ch 24:13 house of God in his state, and s. it. 553
2Ch 25:11 Amaziah s. himself, and led forth........ 2388
2Ch 26:8 for he s. himself exceedingly. 2388
2Ch 28:20 and distressed him, but s. him not...... 2388
2Ch 32:5 Also he s. himself, and built up all...... 2388
Ezr 1:6 s. their hands with vessels of silver, ... 2388
Ezr 7:28 I was s. as the hand of the Lord my... 2388
Ne 2:18 s. their hands for this good work........ 2388
Job 4:3 and thou hast s. the weak hands. 2388
Job 4:4 and thou hast s. the feeble knees.......... 553
Ps 52:7 and s. himself in his wickedness. 5810
Ps 147:13 he hath s. the bars of thy gates; 2388
Pr 8:28 he s. the fountains of the deep: 5810
Eze 13:22 and s. the hands of the wicked, ... 2388
Eze 34:4 The diseased have ye not s., neither... 2388
Da 10:18 appearance of a man, and he s. me,.... 2388
Da 10:19 he had spoken unto me, I was s.. 2388
Da 10:19 my lord speak; for thou hast s. me..... 2388
Da 11:6 and he that s. her in these times........ 2388
Da 11:12 but he shall not be s. by it............... 5810
Ho 7:15 I have bound and s. their arms, ... 2388
Ac 9:19 he had received meat, he was s.......... *1765*
Eph 3:16 to be s. with might by his Spirit......... *2901*
Col 1:11 S. with all might, according to his....... *1412*
2Ti 4:17 Lord stood with me, and s. me;......... *1743*

STRENGTHENEDST

Ps 138:3 s. me with strength in my soul. 7292

STRENGTHENETH

Job 15:25 s. himself against the Almighty........... 1396
Ps 104:15 and bread which s. man's heart.......... 5582
Pr 31:17 with strength, and s. her arms. 553
Ec 7:19 Wisdom s. the wise more than ten 5810
Isa 44:14 the oak, which he s. for himself........... 553
Am 5:9 s. the spoiled against the strong,........ 1082
Php 4:13 things through Christ which s. me. *1743*

STRENGTHENING

Lu 22:43 an angel...from heaven, s. him........... *1765*
Ac 18:23 in order, s. all the disciples.............. *1991*

STRESS See DISTRESS.

STRETCH See also STRETCHED; STRETCHEST; STRETCHETH; STRETCHING.

Ex 3:20 s. out my hand, and smite Egypt........ 7971
Ex 7:5 I s. forth mine hand upon Egypt,........ 5186
Ex 7:19 s. out thine hand upon the waters 5186
Ex 8:5 S. forth thine hand with thy rod......... 5186
Ex 8:16 S. out thy rod, and smite the dust...... 5186
Ex 9:15 For now I will s. out my hand, that.... 7971
Ex 9:22 S....thine hand toward heaven, ... 5186
Ex 10:12 S. out thine hand over...Egypt.......... 5186
Ex 10:21 S. out thine hand toward heaven, ... 5186
Ex 14:16 and s. out thine hand over the sea,..... 5186
Ex 14:26 S. out thine hand over the sea, that.... 5186
Ex 25:20 cherubims...s. forth their wings.......... 6566
Jos 8:18 S. out the spear that is in thy........... 5186
1Sa 24:6 to s. forth mine hand against him, ... 7971
1Sa 26:9 s. forth his hand against the Lord's..... 7971
1Sa 26:11, 23 s....mine hand against the Lord's.... 7971
2Sa 1:14 not afraid to s. forth thine hand.......... 7971
2Ki 21:13 I will s. over Jerusalem the line 5186
Job 11:13 s. out thine hands toward him;........... 6566
Job 30:24 not s. out his hand to the grave, ... 7971
Job 39:26 s. her wings toward the south?.......... 6566
Ps 68:31 Ethiopia shall soon s. out her 7323
Ps 138:7 s....thine hand against the wrath 7971
Ps 143:6 I s. forth my hands unto thee: 6566
Isa 28:20 than that a man can s. himself 8311
Isa 31:3 the Lord shall s. out his hand, ... 5186
Isa 34:11 s. out upon it the line of confusion,..... 5186
Isa 54:2 and let them s. forth the curtains 5186
Jer 6:12 s....my hand upon the inhabitants 5186
Jer 10:20 none to s. forth my tent any more,...... 5186
Jer 15:6 will I s. out my hand against thee,...... 5186
Jer 51:25 I will s. out mine hand upon thee, ... 5186
Eze 6:14 So will I s. out my hand upon them, ... 5186
Eze 14:9 and I will s. out my hand upon him, ... 5186
Eze 14:13 then will I s. out mine hand upon it, ... 5186
Eze 25:7 I will s. out mine hand upon thee, ... 5186
Eze 25:13 also s. out mine hand upon Edom, ... 5186
Eze 25:16 s....mine hand upon the Philistines,..... 5186
Eze 30:25 s. it out upon the land of Egypt. 5186
Eze 35:3 I will s. out mine hand against thee,..... 5186
Da 11:42 He shall s. forth his hand also........... 7971
Am 6:4 s. themselves upon their couches, ... 5628
Zep 1:4 also s. out mine hand upon Judah, ... 5186
Zep 2:13 s. out his hand against the north, ... 5186
Mt 12:13 he to the man, **S. forth thine hand.** . *1614*
Mk 3:5 unto the man, **S. forth thine hand.** .. *1614*
Lu 6:10 unto the man, **S. forth thy hand.**..... *1614*
Joh 21:18 **old, thou shalt s. forth thy hands,**. *1614*
2Co 10:14 we s. not ourselves beyond our *5239*

STRETCHED See also OUTSTRETCHED; STRETCHEDST.

Ge 22:10 And Abraham s. forth his hand,.......... 7971
Ge 48:14 And Israel s. out his right hand,......... 7971
Ex 6:6 will redeem you with a s. out arm, ... 5186
Ex 8:6 Aaron s....his hand over the waters 5186
Ex 8:17 Aaron s. out his hand with his rod,..... 5186
Ex 9:23 Moses s....his rod toward heaven:...... 5186
Ex 10:13 Moses s. forth his rod over...Egypt,... 5186
Ex 10:22 Moses s....his hand toward heaven;.... 5186
Ex 14:21 Moses s. out his hand over the sea; ... 5186
Ex 14:27 Moses s. forth his hand over the sea, ..5186
De 4:34 a mighty hand and by a s. out arm, ... 5186
De 5:15 a mighty hand and by a s. out arm: 5186
De 7:19 mighty hand, and the s. out arm, ... 5186
De 9:29 mighty power and by thy s. out arm. .. 5186
De 11:2 mighty hand, and his s. out arm,........ 5186
Jos 8:18 Joshua s. out the spear that he had...... 5186
Jos 8:19 as soon as he had s. out his hand:...... 5186
Jos 8:26 back, wherewith he s. out the spear, .. 5186
2Sa 24:16 when the angel s. out his hand 7971
1Ki 6:27 s....the wings of the cherubims, ... 6566
1Ki 8:42 hand, and of thy s. out arm;)............. 5186
1Ki 17:21 he s. himself upon the child three....... 4058
2Ki 4:34 and he s. himself upon the child; 1457
2Ki 4:35 went up, and s. himself upon him: 1457
2Ki 17:36 with great power and a s. out arm,..... 5186
1Ch 21:16 sword...s. out over Jerusalem............ 5186
2Ch 6:32 mighty hand, and thy s. out arm; 5186
Job 38:5 or who hath s. the line upon it? 5186
Ps 44:20 s....our hands to a strange god; 6566
Ps 88:9 I have s. out my hands unto thee....... 7849
Ps 136:6 To him that s. out the earth above 7554
Ps 136:12 strong hand, and...a s. out arm: 5186
Pr 1:24 I have s. out my hand, and no man..... 5186
Isa 3:16 and walk with s. forth necks and 5186
Isa 5:25 s. forth his hand against them,........... 5186
Isa 5:25 away, but his hand is s. out still.......... 5186
Isa 9:12, 17,21 but his hand is s. out still. 5186
Isa 10:4 away, but his hand is s. out still.......... 5186
Isa 14:26 hand...s. out upon all the nations........ 5186
Isa 14:27 his hand is s. out, and who shall 5186
Isa 16:8 her branches are s. out, they are 5203
Isa 23:11 He s. out his hand over the sea, he.... 5186
Isa 42:5 the heavens, and s. them out; 5186
Isa 45:12 my hands, have s. out the heavens,.... 5186
Isa 51:13 that hath s. forth the heavens, and..... 5186
Jer 6:4 shadows of the evening are s. out. 5186
Jer 10:12 s. out the heavens by his discretion. ... 5186
Jer 32:17 by thy great power and s. out arm, ... 5186
Jer 32:21 strong hand, and with a s. out arm, ... 5186
Jer 51:15 and hath s. out the heaven by his....... 5186
La 2:8 he hath s. out a line, he hath not 5186
Eze 1:11 and their wings were s. upward; 6504
Eze 1:22 s. forth over their heads above. 5186
Eze 10:7 And one cherub s. forth his hand........ 7971
Eze 16:27 I have s. out my hand over thee, ... 5186
Eze 20:33 and with a s. out arm, and with fury... 5186
Eze 20:34 mighty hand, and with a s. out arm,.... 5186
Ho 7:5 he s. out his hand with scorners. 4900
Am 6:7 and the banquet of them that s. 5628
Zec 1:16 shall be s. forth upon Jerusalem. 5186
Mt 12:13 he s. it forth; and it was restored....... *1614*
Mt 12:49 And he s. forth his hand toward his *1614*
Mt 14:31 Jesus s. forth his hand, and caught *1614*
Mt 26:51 s. out his hand, and drew his sword,... *1614*
Mk 3:5 And he s. it out: and his hand was *1614*
Lu 22:53 **ye s. forth no hands against me:** ... *1614*
Ac 12:1 Herod the king s. forth his hands *1911*
Ac 26:1 Then Paul s. forth the hand, and........ *1614*
Ro 10:21 I have s. forth my hands unto a *1600*

STRETCHEDST

Ex 15:12 Thou s. out thy right hand, the.......... 5186

STRETCHEST

Ps 104:2 s. out the heavens like a curtain:........ 5186

STRETCHETH

Job 15:25 he s. out his hand against God,.......... 5186
Job 26:7 He s. out the north over the empty.... 5186
Pr 31:20 She s. out her hand to the poor;........ 6566
Isa 40:22 s. out the heavens as a curtain, ... 5186
Isa 44:13 The carpenter s. out his rule; he........ 5186
Isa 44:24 that s. forth the heavens alone;.......... 5186
Zec 12:1 Lord, which s. forth the heavens,........ 5186

STRETCHING

Isa 8:8 the s. out of his wings shall fill the 4298
Ac 4:30 By s. forth thine hand to heal; and *1614*

STREWED See STRAWED.

STRICKEN See also STRUCK.

Ge 18:11 Sarah were old and well s. in age; 935
Ge 24:1 Abraham was old, and well s. in age:.... 935
Jos 13:1 Now Joshua was old and s. in years; 935
Jos 13:1 Thou art old and s. in years, and......... 935
Jos 23:1 that Joshua waxed old and s. in age..... 935
Jos 23:2 unto them, I am old and s. in age: 935
Jg 5:26 and s. through his temples................ 2498
1Ki 1:1 king David was old and s. in years; 935
Pr 6:1 hast s. thy hand with a stranger,........ 8628
Pr 23:35 They have s. me, shalt thou say, ... 5221
Isa 1:5 Why should ye be s. any more? 5221
Isa 16:7 shall ye mourn; surely they are s.. 5218
Isa 53:4 yet we did esteem him s., smitten...... 5060
Isa 53:8 transgression of my people...he s....... 5061
Jer 5:3 thou hast s. them, but they have......... 5221
La 4:9 s. through for want of the fruits of 1856
Lu 1:7 both were now well s. in years. *4260*
Lu 1:18 man, and my wife well s. in years. *4260*

STRIFE See also STRIFES.

Ge 13:7 was a s. between the herdmen of....... 7379
Ge 13:8 said unto Lot, Let there be no s., ... 4808
Nu 27:14 of Zin, in the s. of the congregation, ... 4808
De 1:12 and your burden, and your s.? 7379
Jg 12:2 I and my people were at great s. 7379
2Sa 19:9 the people were at s. throughout........ 1777
Ps 31:20 a pavilion from the s. of tongues. 7379
Ps 55:9 have seen violence and s. in the city... 7379
Ps 80:6 us a s. unto our neighbours:.............. 4066
Ps 106:32 angered him...at the waters of s., ... 4808
Pr 15:18 A wrathful man stirreth up s. 4066
Pr 15:18 that is slow to anger appeaseth s.. 7379
Pr 16:28 A froward man soweth s.: and a 4066
Pr 17:1 an house full of sacrifices with s.. 7379
Pr 17:14 The beginning of s. is as when one..... 4066
Pr 17:19 loveth transgression that loveth s. 4683
Pr 20:3 honour for a man to cease from s....... 7379

Pr 22:10 yea, s. and reproach shall cease. 1779
Pr 26:17 meddleth with s. belonging not. 7379
Pr 26:20 is no talebearer, the s. ceaseth. 4066
Pr 26:21 is a contentious man to kindle s.. 7379
Pr 28:25 is of a proud heart stirreth up s. 4066
Pr 29:22 An angry man stirreth up s., and a 4066
Pr 30:33 forcing of wrath bringeth forth s. 7379
Isa 58:4 Behold, ye fast for s. and debate, 7379
Jer 15:10 a man of s. and a man of contention. 7379
Eze 47:19 even to the waters of s. in Kadesh, 4808
Eze 48:28 unto the waters of s. in Kadesh, 4808
Hab 1:3 and there are that raise up s. and. 7379
Lu 22:24 there was also a s. among them, *5379*
Ro 13:13 wantonness, not in s. and envying. *2054*
1Co 3:3 you envying and s., and divisions, *2054*
Ga 5:20 emulations, wrath, s., seditions, *2052*
Php 1:15 preach Christ even of envy and s.; *2054*
Php 2:3 Let nothing be done through s. or *2052*
1Ti 6:4 whereof cometh envy, s., railings, *2054*
Heb 6:16 oath...is to them an end of all s. *485*
Jas 3:14 envying and s. in your hearts, *2052*
Jas 3:16 For where envying and s. is, there *2052*

STRIFES
Pr 10:12 Hatred stirreth up s.: but love 4090
2Co 12:20 envyings, wrath, s., backbitings, *2052*
1Ti 6:4 about questions and s. of words, *3055*
2Ti 2:23 knowing that they do gender s. *3163*

STRIKE See also STRAKE; STRICKEN; STRIKETH; STRUCK.
Ex 12:7 and s. it on the two side posts. 5414
Ex 12:22 s. the lintel and the two side posts 5060
De 21:4 and shall s. off the heifer's neck
2Ki 5:11 and s. his hand over the place, 5130
Job 17:3 is he that will s. hands with me? 8628
Job 20:24 bow of steel shall s. him through. 2498
Ps 110:5 The Lord...shall s. through kings. 4272
Pr 7:23 Till a dart s. through his liver; as 6398
Pr 17:26 good, nor to s. princes for equity. 5221
Pr 22:26 Be not...one of them that s. hands, 8628
Hab 3:14 didst s. through with his staves. 5344
Mk 14:65 did s. him with the palms of their *906*

STRIKER
1Ti 3:3 Not given to wine, no s., not greedy *4131*
Tit 1:7 not given to wine, no s., not given to *4131*

STRIKETH
Job 34:26 He s. them as wicked men in the 5606
Pr 17:18 void of understanding s. hands, 8628
Re 9:5 a scorpion, when he s. a man. *3817*

STRING See also STRINGED; STRINGS.
Ps 11:2 ready their arrow upon the s., 3499
Mk 7:35 the s. of his tongue was loosed, *1199*

STRINGED
Ps 150:4 praise him with s. instruments 4482
Isa 38:20 my songs to the s. instrument 5058
Hab 3:19 chief singer on my s. instruments. 5058

STRINGS
Ps 21:12 arrows upon thy s. against the 4340
Ps 33:2 and an instrument of ten s..
Ps 92:3 Upon an instrument of ten s., and
Ps 144:9 and an instrument of ten s. will I.

STRIP See also STRIPPED.
Nu 20:26 s. Aaron of his garments, and put. 6584
1Sa 31:8 the Philistines came to s. the slain, 6584
1Ch 10:8 the Philistines came to s. the slain, 6584
Isa 32:11 s. you, and make you bare, and 6584
Eze 16:39 shall s. thee also of thy clothes, 6584
Eze 23:26 shall also s. thee out of thy clothes, 6584
Ho 2:3 Lest I s. her naked, and set her as 6584

STRIPE See also STRIPES.
Ex 21:25 wound for wound, s. for s. 2250

STRIPES
De 25:3 Forty s. he may give him, and 5221
De 25:3 him above these with many s., 4347
2Sa 7:14 with the s. of the children of men: 5061
Ps 89:32 rod, and their iniquity with s.. 5061
Pr 17:10 than an hundred s. into a fool. 5221
Pr 19:29 and s. for the back of fools. 4112
Pr 20:30 so do s. the inward parts of the 4347
Isa 53:5 and with his s. we are healed. 2250
Lu 12:47 will, shall be beaten with many s.
Lu 12:48 commit things worthy of s., shall *4127*
Lu 12:48 shall be beaten with few s.. For *4127*

Ac 16:23 they had laid many s. upon them, *4127*
Ac 16:33 of the night, and washed their s.; *4127*
2Co 6:5 In s., in imprisonments, in tumults, *4127*
2Co 11:23 in s. above measure, in prisons *4127*
2Co 11:24 times received I forty s. save one.
1Pe 2:24 by whose s. ye were healed. *3468*

STRIPLING
1Sa 17:56 Enquire...whose son this s. is. 5958

STRIPPED See also STRIPT.
Ex 33:6 children of Israel s. themselves 5337
Nu 20:28 Moses s. Aaron of his garments, 6584
1Sa 18:4 Jonathan s. himself of the robe 6584
1Sa 19:24 And he s. off his clothes also, and 6584
1Sa 31:9 off his head, and s. off his armour, 6584
1Ch 10:9 when they had s. him, they took 6584
2Ch 20:25 which they s. off for themselves, 5337
Job 19:9 He hath s. me of my glory, and 6584
Job 22:6 and s. the naked of their clothing. 6584
Mic 1:8 and howl, I will go s. and naked: 7758
Mt 27:28 And they s. him, and put on him a *1562*
Lu 10:30 which s. him of his raiment, and *1562*

STRIPT See also STRIPPED.
Ge 37:23 they s. Joseph out of his coat, his 6584

STRIVE See also STRIVED; STRIVETH; STRIVING.
Ge 6:3 My spirit shall not...s. with man, 1777
Ge 26:20 did s. with Isaac's herdmen, 7378
Ex 21:18 if men s. together, and one smite 7378
Ex 21:22 If men s., and hurt a woman with 5327
De 25:11 men s. together one with another, 5327
De 33:8 whom thou didst s. at the waters 7378
Jg 11:25 did he ever s. against Israel, or did 7378
Job 33:13 Why dost thou s. against him? for 7378
Ps 35:1 Lord, with them that s. with me: 3401
Pr 3:30 S. not with a man without cause, 7378
Pr 25:8 Go not forth hastily to s., lest thou. 7378
Isa 41:11 they that s. with thee shall perish. 7379
Isa 45:9 the potsherd s. with the potsherds
Ho 4:4 no man s., nor reprove another: 7378
Ho 4:4 are as they that s. with the priest. 7378
Mt 12:19 He shall not s., nor cry; neither *2051*
Lu 13:24 S. to enter in at the strait gate: *75*
Ro 15:30 ye s. together with me in your *4865*
2Ti 2:5 if a man also s. for masteries, yet *118*
2Ti 2:5 not crowned, except he s. lawfully. *118*
2Ti 2:14 s. not about words to no profit, *3054*
2Ti 2:24 servant of the Lord must not s.; *3164*

STRIVED See also STRIVEN; STROVE.
Ro 15:20 so have I s. to preach the gospel, *5389*

STRIVEN See also STRIVED.
Jer 50:24 thou hast s. against the Lord. 1624

STRIVETH
Isa 45:9 unto him that s. with his Maker! 7378
1Co 9:25 every man that s. for the mastery *75*

STRIVING See also STRIVINGS.
Php 1:27 one mind s. together for the faith *4866*
Col 1:29 s. according to his working, which *75*
Heb 12:4 resisted unto blood, s. against sin. *464*

STRIVINGS
2Sa 22:44 delivered me from the s. of my 7379
Ps 18:43 delivered me from the s. of the 7379
Tit 3:9 contentions, and s. about the law; *3163*

STROKE See also STROKES.
De 17:8 between s. and s., being matters 5061
De 19:5 his hand fetcheth a s. with the axe
De 21:5 controversy and every s. be tried: 5061
Es 9:5 enemies with the s. of the sword, 4347
Job 23:2 s. is heavier than my groaning. 3027
Job 36:18 he take thee away with his s.: 5607
Ps 39:10 Remove thy s. away from me: I 5061
Isa 14:6 the people...with a continual s., 4347
Isa 30:26 and healeth the s. of their wound. 4273
Eze 24:16 the desire of thine eyes with a s.: 4046

STROKES
Pr 18:6 and his mouth calleth for s.. 4112

STRONG See also STRONGER; STRONGEST.
Ge 49:14 Issachar is a s. ass couching 1634
Ge 49:24 were made s. by the hands of the 6339
Ex 6:1 a s. hand shall he let them go, 2389
Ex 6:1 a s. hand shall he drive them out 2389
Ex 10:19 Lord turned a mighty s. west wind, 2389

Ex 13:9 for with a s. hand hath the Lord 2389
Ex 14:21 sea to go back by a s. east wind 5794
Le 10:9 Do not drink wine nor s. drink, thou,
Nu 6:3 himself from wine and s. drink, and
Nu 6:3 or vinegar of s. drink, neither shall he
Nu 13:18 whether they be s. or weak, few 2389
Nu 13:19 whether in tents, or in s. holds; 4013
Nu 13:28 people be s. that dwell in the land, 5794
Nu 20:20 much people, and with a s. hand. 2389
Nu 21:24 the children of Ammon was s.. 5794
Nu 24:21 S. is thy dwellingplace, and thou 386
Nu 28:7 thou cause the s. wine to be poured
De 2:36 was not one city too s. for us: 7682
De 11:8 that ye may be s., and go in and 2388
De 14:26 for sheep, or for wine, or for s. drink,
De 29:6 have ye drunk wine or s. drink:
De 31:6 Be s. and of a good courage, fear 2388
De 31:7, 23 Be s. and of a good courage, for 2388
Jos 1:6 Be s. and of a good courage: for 2388
Jos 1:7 be thou s. and very courageous, 2388
Jos 1:9 Be s. and of a good courage; be 2388
Jos 1:18 only be s. and of a good courage. 2388
Jos 10:25 be s. and of good courage: for 2388
Jos 14:11 As yet I am as s. this day as I was 2389
Jos 17:13 children of Israel were waxen s., 2388
Jos 17:18 chariots, and though they be s.. 2389
Jos 19:29 to Ramah, and to the s. city Tyre; 4013
Jos 23:9 before you great nations and s.: 6099
Jg 1:28 came to pass, when Israel was s., 2388
Jg 6:2 mountains,...caves, and s. holds. 4679
Jg 9:51 was a s. tower within the city, 5797
Jg 13:4 and drink not wine nor s. drink, and
Jg 13:7 and now drink no wine nor s. drink,
Jg 13:14 neither let her drink wine or s. drink,
Jg 14:14 out of the s. came forth sweetness. 5794
Jg 18:26 Micah saw that they were too s. 2389
1Sa 1:15 have drunk neither wine nor s. drink,
1Sa 4:9 Be s., and quit yourselves like 2388
1Sa 14:52 when Saul saw any s. man, or any 1368
1Sa 23:14 abode in the wilderness in s. holds, 4679
1Sa 23:19 not David hide..with us in s. holds 4679
1Sa 23:29 and dwelt in s. holds at En-gedi. 4679
2Sa 3:6 Abner made himself s. for the 2388
2Sa 5:7 David took the s. hold of Zion: 4686
2Sa 10:11 If the Syrians be too s. for me, 2388
2Sa 10:11 if the children of Ammon be too s. 2388
2Sa 11:25 thy battle more s. against the city, 2388
2Sa 15:12 And the conspiracy was s.; for the 533
2Sa 16:21 the hands of all...with thee be s. 2388
2Sa 22:18 delivered me from my s. enemy, 5794
2Sa 22:18 me: for they were too s. for me. 553
2Sa 24:7 And came to the s. hold of Tyre, 4013
1Ki 2:2 be thou s. therefore, and shew 2388
1Ki 8:42 great name, and of thy s. hand, 2389
1Ki 19:11 and s. wind rent the mountains, 2389
2Ki 2:16 be with thy servants fifty s. men; 2428
2Ki 8:12 their s. holds wilt thou set on fire, 4013
2Ki 24:16 all that were s. and apt for war, 1368
1Ch 19:12 If the Syrians be too s. for me, 2388
1Ch 19:12 children of Ammon be too s. for 2388
1Ch 22:13 be s., and of good courage; dread 2388
1Ch 26:7 whose brethren were s. men, 2428
1Ch 26:9 had sons and brethren, s. men, 2428
1Ch 28:10 the sanctuary: be s., and do it. 2388
1Ch 28:20 his son, be s. and of good courage, 2388
2Ch 11:11 be fortified the s. holds, and put 4694
2Ch 11:12 and made them exceeding s., 2388
2Ch 11:17 Rehoboam the son of Solomon s., 559
2Ch 15:7 Be ye s. therefore, and let not your 2388
2Ch 16:9 shew himself s. in...behalf of them. 2388
2Ch 25:8 wilt go, do it, be s. for the battle: 2388
2Ch 26:15 marvellously helped, till he was s.. 2388
2Ch 26:16 But when he was s., his heart was 2394
2Ch 32:7 Be s. and courageous, be not 2388
Ezr 9:12 that ye may be s., and eat the good 2388
Ne 1:10 great power, and by thy s. hand. 2389
Ne 9:25 they took s. cities, and a fat land, 1219
Job 8:2 of thy mouth be like a s. wind? 3524
Job 9:19 If I speak of strength, lo, he is s.: 533
Job 30:21 with thy s. hand thou opposest 6108
Job 33:19 multitude of his bones with s. pain: 386
Job 37:18 spread out the sky, which is s., 2389
Job 39:28 crag of the rock, and the s. place. 4686
Job 40:18 His bones are as s. pieces of brass; 650
Ps 10:10 the poor may fall by his s. ones. 6099
Ps 18:17 delivered me from my s. enemy, 5794

Ps 18:17 me: for they were too s. for me ... 553
Ps 19:5 and rejoiceth as a s. man to run a ... 1368
Ps 22:12 s. bulls of Bashan have beset me ... 47
Ps 24:8 The Lord s. and mighty, the Lord ... 5808
Ps 30:7 made my mountain to stand s. ... 5797
Ps 31:2 be thou my s. rock, for an house ... 4581
Ps 31:21 marvellous kindness in a s. city ... 4692
Ps 35:10 the poor from him that is too s. ... 2389
Ps 38:19 are lively, and they are s.: and ... 6105
Ps 60:9 Who will bring me into the s. city? ... 4692
Ps 61:3 and a s. tower from the enemy ... 5797
Ps 71:3 Be thou my s. habitation, ... 6697
Ps 71:7 many; but thou art my s. refuge ... 5797
Ps 80:15 that thou madest s. for thyself ... 553
Ps 80:17 whom thou madest s. for thyself ... 553
Ps 89:8 who is a s. Lord like unto thee? ... 2626
Ps 89:10 thine enemies with thy s. arm ... 5797
Ps 89:13 s. is thy hand, and high is thy ... 5810
Ps 89:40 hast brought his s. holds to ruin ... 4013
Ps 108:10 Who will bring me into the s. city? ... 4013
Ps 136:12 With a s. hand, and with a ... 2389
Ps 144:14 That our oxen may be s. to labour; ...
Pr 7:26 many s. men have been slain by ... 6099
Pr 10:15 rich man's wealth is his s. city: ... 5797
Pr 11:16 honour: and s. men retain riches ... 6184
Pr 14:26 fear of the Lord is s. confidence: ... 5797
Pr 18:10 The name of the Lord is a s. tower: ... 5797
Pr 18:11 The rich man's wealth is his s. city, ... 5797
Pr 18:19 is harder to be won than a s. city: ... 5797
Pr 20:1 Wine is a mocker, s. drink is raging: ...
Pr 21:14 a reward in the bosom s. wrath ... 5794
Pr 24:5 A wise man is s.; yea, a man of ... 5797
Pr 30:25 The ants are a people not s., yet ... 5794
Pr 31:4 to drink wine; nor for princes s. drink: ...
Pr 31:6 Give s. drink unto him that is ready to ...
Ec 9:11 nor the battle to the s., neither yet ... 1368
Ec 12:3 the s. men shall bow themselves, ... 2428
Ca 8:6 for love is s. as death; jealousy is ... 5794
Isa 1:31 And the s. shall be as tow, and the ... 2634
Isa 5:11 that they may follow s. drink; that ...
Isa 5:22 men of strength to mingle s. drink: ...
Isa 8:7 waters of the river, s. and many, ... 6099
Isa 8:11 spake thus to me with a s. hand, ... 2393
Isa 17:9 shall his s. cities be as a forsaken ... 4581
Isa 23:11 city, to destroy the s. holds thereof ... 4581
Isa 24:9 s. drink shall be bitter to them that ...
Isa 25:3 shall the s. people glorify thee, ... 5794
Isa 26:1 We have a s. city; salvation will ... 5797
Isa 27:1 great and s. sword shall punish ... 2389
Isa 28:2 the Lord hath a mighty and s. one, ... 533
Isa 28:7 through s. drink are out of the way; ...
Isa 28:7 prophet have erred through s. drink, ...
Isa 28:7 are out of the way through s. drink; ...
Isa 28:22 lest your bands be made s.: for I ... 2388
Isa 29:9 they stagger, but not with s. drink ...
Isa 31:1 in horsemen,...they are very s.; ... 6105
Isa 31:9 and shall pass over to his s. hold ... 5553
Isa 35:4 of a fearful heart, be s., fear not: ... 2388
Isa 40:10 Lord God will come with s. hand, ... 2389
Isa 40:26 might, for that he is s. in power: ... 533
Isa 41:21 bring forth your s. reasons, saith ... 6110
Isa 53:12 shall divide the spoil with the s.; ... 6099
Isa 56:12 we will fill ourselves with s. drink; ...
Isa 60:22 and a small one a s. nation: ... 6099
Jer 8:16 sound of the neighing of his s. ones; ... 47
Jer 21:5 outstretched hand and...a s. arm, ... 2389
Jer 32:21 with wonders, and with a s. hand, ... 2389
Jer 47:3 of the hoofs of his s. horses, at the ... 47
Jer 48:14 mighty and s. men for the war? ... 2428
Jer 48:17 How is the s. staff broken, and the ... 5797
Jer 48:18 and he shall destroy thy s. holds ... 4013
Jer 48:41 the s. holds are surprised, and the ... 4679
Jer 49:19 against the habitation of the s. ... 386
Jer 50:34 Their Redeemer is s.; the Lord of ... 2389
Jer 50:44 Jordan unto the habitation of the s. ... 386
Jer 51:12 make the watch s., set up the ... 2388
La 2:2 s. holds of the daughter of Judah; ... 4013
La 2:5 he hath destroyed his s. holds, and ... 4013
Eze 3:8 thy face s. against their faces, ... 2389
Eze 3:8 forehead s. against their foreheads ... 2389
Eze 3:14 hand of the Lord was s. upon me ... 2388
Eze 7:24 make the pomp of the s. to cease; ... 5794
Eze 19:11 she had s. rods for the sceptres of ... 5797
Eze 19:12 s. rods were broken and withered; ... 5797
Eze 19:14 she hath no s. rod to be a sceptre ... 5797
Eze 22:14 endure, or can thine hands be s., ... 2388
Eze 26:11 s. garrisons shall go down to the ... 5797
Eze 26:17 city, which wast s. in the sea, ... 2389
Eze 30:21 to make it s. to hold the sword ... 2388
Eze 30:22 the s., and that which was broken; ... 2389
Eze 32:21 s. among the mighty shall speak ... 410
Eze 34:16 I will destroy the fat and the s.; ... 2389
Da 2:40 fourth kingdom shall be s. as iron: ... 8624
Da 2:42 the kingdom shall be partly s., and ... 8624
Da 4:11 The tree grew, and was s., and the ... 8631
Da 4:20 The tree...which grew, and was s., ... 8631
Da 4:22 king, that art grown and become s. ... 8631
Da 7:7 and terrible, and s. exceedingly; ... 8624
Da 8:8 when he was s., the great horn ... 6105
Da 10:19 be unto thee, be s., yea, be s. ... 2388
Da 11:5 the king of the south shall be s., ... 2388
Da 11:5 and he shall be s. above him, and ... 2388
Da 11:23 become s. with a small people ... 6105
Da 11:24 his devices against the s. holds, ... 4013
Da 11:32 that do know their God shall be s., ... 2388
Da 11:39 shall he do in the most s. holds ... 4581
Joe 1:6 is come up upon my land, s., ... 6099
Joe 2:2 a great people and a s., there hath ... 6099
Joe 2:5 as a s. people set in battle array ... 6099
Joe 2:11 for he is s. that executeth his word: ... 6099
Joe 3:10 spears: let the weak say, I am s. ... 1368
Am 2:9 spears, and he was s. as the oaks; ... 2634
Am 2:14 s. shall not strengthen his force, ... 2389
Am 5:9 the spoiled against the s., ... 5794
Mic 2:11 unto thee of wine and of s. drink; ... 7941
Mic 4:3 and rebuke s. nations afar off; ... 6099
Mic 4:7 her that was cast far off a s. nation: ... 6099
Mic 4:8 s. hold of the daughter of Zion, ... 6076
Mic 5:11 and throw down all thy s. holds: ... 4013
Mic 6:2 and ye s. foundations of the earth: ... 386
Na 1:7 a s. hold in the day of trouble; ... 4581
Na 2:1 make thy loins s., fortify thy power ... 2388
Na 3:12 s. holds shall be like fig trees with ... 4013
Na 3:14 for the siege, fortify thy s. holds: ... 4013
Na 3:14 the morter, make s. the brickkiln ... 2388
Hab 1:10 they shall deride every s. hold; ... 4013
Hag 2:4 Yet now be s., O Zerubbabel, saith ... 2388
Hag 2:4 be s., O Joshua, son of Josedech, ... 2388
Hag 2:4 and be s., all ye people of the land, ... 2388
Zec 8:9 Let your hands be s., ye that hear ... 2388
Zec 8:13 fear not, but let your hands be s. ... 2388
Zec 8:22 s. nations shall come to seek the ... 6099
Zec 9:3 Tyrus did build herself a s. hold, ... 4692
Zec 9:12 Turn you to the s. hold, ye ... 1225
Mt 12:29 **one enter into a s. man's house,** ... *2478*
Mt 12:29 **except he first bind the s. man?** ... *2478*
Mk 3:2 **can enter into a s. man's house,** ... *2478*
Mk 3:2 **he will first bind the s. man;** ... *2478*
Lu 1:15 drink neither wine nor s. drink; ... *4608*
Lu 1:80 child grew, and waxed s. in spirit, ... *2901*
Lu 2:40 child grew, and waxed s. in spirit, ... *2901*
Lu 11:21 **s. man armed keepeth his palace,** ... *2478*
Ac 3:16 his name hath made this man s., ... *4732*
Ro 4:20 was s. in faith, giving glory to God; ... *1743*
Ro 15:1 We...that are s. ought to bear the ... *1415*
1Co 4:10 we are weak, but ye are s.; ... *2478*
1Co 16:13 the faith, quit you like men, be s. ... *2901*
2Co 10:4 to the pulling down of s. holds;) ... *3794*
2Co 12:10 for when I am weak, then am I s. ... *1415*
2Co 13:9 when we are weak, and ye are s. ... *1415*
Eph 6:10 my brethren, be s. in the Lord, ... *1743*
2Th 2:11 God shall send them s. delusion, ... *1753*
2Ti 2:1 my son, be s. in the grace that is ... *1743*
Heb 5:7 with s. crying and tears unto him ... *2478*
Heb 5:12 need of milk, and not of s. meat ... *4731*
Heb 5:14 But s. meat belongeth to them that ... *4731*
Heb 6:18 we might have a s. consolation, ... *2478*
Heb 11:34 out of weakness were made s., ... *1743*
1Jo 2:14 young men, because ye are s., and ... *2478*
Re 5:2 I saw a s. angel proclaiming with ... *2478*
Re 18:2 he cried mightily with a s. voice, ... *3173*
Re 18:8 s. is the Lord God who judgeth ... *2478*

STRONG-DRINK See STRONG and DRINK.

STRONGER

Ge 25:23 shall be s. than the other people; ... 553
Ge 30:41 the s. cattle did conceive, ... 7194
Ge 30:42 were Laban's, and the s. Jacob's ... 7194
Nu 13:31 people; for they are s. than we ... 2389
Jg 14:18 honey? and what is s. than a lion? ... 5794
2Sa 1:23 eagles, they were s. than lions ... 1396
2Sa 3:1 but David waxed s....and the ... 2390
2Sa 3:1 but David waxed...s., and the ...
2Sa 13:14 but, being s. than she, forced her, ... 2388
1Ki 20:23 therefore they were s. than we; ... 2388
1Ki 20:23, 25 surely we shall be s. than they ... 2388
Job 17:9 that hath clean hands shall be s. ... 555
Job 17:9 that hath clean hands shall be...s., ...
Ps 105:24 made them s. than their enemies ... 6105
Ps 142:6 prosecutors; for they are s. than I ... 553
Jer 20:7 thou art s. than I, and hast ... 2388
Jer 31:11 hand of him that was s. than he ... 2388
Lu 11:22 **when a s. than he shall come** ... *2478*
1Co 1:25 the weakness of God is s. than men ... *2478*
1Co 10:22 to jealousy? are we s. than he? ... *2478*

STRONGEST

Pr 30:30 A lion is s. among beasts, ... 1368

STRONG-HOLD See STRONG and HOLD.

STRONGLY

Ezr 6:3 the foundations thereof be s. laid; ...

STROVE See also STRIVED.

Ge 26:20 Esek; because they s. with him ... 6229
Ge 26:21 another well, and s. for that also: ... 7378
Ge 26:22 another well;...for that they s. not: ... 7378
Ex 2:13 men of the Hebrews s. together: ... 5327
Le 24:10 of Israel s. together in the camp; ... 5327
Nu 20:13 children of Israel s. with the Lord, ... 7378
Nu 26:9 who s. against Moses and against ... 5327
Nu 26:9 when they s. against the Lord: ... 5327
2Sa 14:6 they two s. together in the field, ... 5327
Ps 60:*title* when he s. with Aram-naharaim ... 5327
Da 7:2 four winds of the heaven s. upon ... 1519
Joh 6:52 Jews...s. among themselves, ... *3164*
Ac 7:26 he shewed himself...as they s., ... *3164*
Ac 23:9 the Pharisees part arose, and s., ... *1264*

STROWED See also STRAWED.

2Ch 34:4 s. it upon the graves of them that ... 2236

STRUCK See also STRAKE; STRICKEN.

1Sa 2:14 And he s. it into the pan, or kettle, ... 5221
2Sa 12:15 the Lord s. the child that Uriah's ... 5062
2Sa 20:10 the ground, and s. him not again; ... 8138
2Ch 13:20 and the Lord s. him, and he died ... 5062
Mt 26:51 s. a servant of the high priest's, ... *3960*
Lu 22:64 him, they s. him on the face, ... *5180*
Joh 18:22 s. Jesus with the palm of his ... *1325,4475*

STRUGGLED

Ge 25:22 children s. together within her; ... 7533

STUBBLE

Ex 5:12 to gather s. instead of straw ... 7179
Ex 15:7 wrath, which consumed them as s. ... 7179
Job 13:25 and wilt thou pursue the dry s.? ... 7179
Job 21:18 They are as s. before the wind ... 8401
Job 41:28 slingstones are turned...into s. ... 7179
Job 41:29 Darts are counted as s.: he ... 7179
Ps 83:13 wheel; as the s. before the wind ... 7179
Isa 5:24 as the fire devoureth the s., and ... 7179
Isa 33:11 chaff, ye shall bring forth s. ... 7179
Isa 40:24 shall take them away as s. ... 7179
Isa 41:2 sword, and as driven s. to his bow ... 7179
Isa 47:14 Behold, they shall be as s.; the fire ... 7179
Jer 13:24 scatter them as the s. that passeth ... 7179
Joe 2:5 flame of fire that devoureth the s., ... 7179
Ob 18 flame, and the house of Esau for s., ... 7179
Na 1:10 they shall be devoured as s. ... 7179
Mal 4:1 all that do wickedly, shall be s. ... 7179
1Co 3:12 precious stones, wood, hay, s.; ... *2562*

STUBBORN

De 21:18 man have a s. and rebellious son, ... 5637
De 21:20 This our son is s. and rebellious, ... 5637
Jg 2:19 doings, nor from their s. way ... 7186
Ps 78:8 a s. and rebellious generation; ... 5637
Pr 7:11 (She is loud and s.; her feet abide ... 5637

STUBBORNNESS

De 9:27 look not unto the s. of this people, ... 7190
1Sa 15:23 and s. is an iniquity and idolatry ... 6484

STRUCK

1Sa 26:7 his spear s. in the ground at his ... 4600
Ps 119:31 I have s. unto thy testimonies: ... 1692
Ac 27:41 the forepart s. fast, and remained ... *2043*

STUDS

Ca 1:11 borders of gold with s. of silver ... 5351

STUDIETH

Pr 15:28 of the righteous s. to answer: ... 1897
Pr 24:2 For their heart s. destruction, and ... 1897

STUDY See also STUDIETH.
Ec 12:12 much s. is a weariness of the flesh..... 3854
1Th 4:11 that ye s. to be quiet, and to do........ *5389*
2Ti 2:15 S. to shew thyself approved unto....... *4704*

STUFF
Ge 31:37 thou hast searched all my s.,............ 3627
Ge 31:37 thou found of all thy household s.?...... 3627
Ge 45:20 Also regard not your s.; for the......... 3627
Ex 22:7 his neighbour money or s. to keep,...... 3627
Ex 36:7 s. they had was sufficient for all......... 4399
Jos 7:11 put it even among their own s............ 3627
1Sa 10:22 he hath hid himself among the s........ 3627
1Sa 25:13 and two hundred abode by the s......... 3627
1Sa 30:24 his part be that tarrieth by the s........ 3627
Ne 13:8 forth all the household s. of Tobiah..... 3627
Eze 12:3 prepare thee s. for removing,............ 3627
Eze 12:4 shalt thou bring forth thy s. by day..... 3627
Eze 12:4 in their sight, as s. for removing:....... 3627
Eze 12:7 I brought forth my s. by day,............. 3627
Eze 12:7 as s. for captivity, and in the even...... 3627
Lu 17:31 **housetop, and his s. in the house,** . *4632*

STUMBLE See also STUMBLED; STUMBLETH; STUMBLING.
Pr 3:23 safely, and thy foot shall not s.......... 5062
Pr 4:12 thou runnest, thou shalt not s............ 3782
Pr 4:19 they know not at whay they s............ 3782
Isa 5:27 shall be weary nor s. among them;..... 3782
Isa 8:15 And many among them shall s.,......... 3782
Isa 28:7 err in vision, they s. in judgment........ 6328
Isa 59:10 we s. at noon day as in the night;...... 3782
Isa 63:13 wilderness, that they should not s.?.... 3782
Jer 13:16 feet s. upon the dark mountains,........ 5062
Jer 18:15 caused them to s. in their ways......... 3782
Jer 20:11 therefore my persecutors shall s.,...... 3782
Jer 31:9 way, wherein they shall not s........... 3782
Jer 46:6 shall s., and fall toward the north....... 3782
Jer 50:32 the most proud shall s. and fall,......... 3782
Da 11:19 shall s. and fall, and not be found....... 3782
Na 2:5 they shall s. in their walk; they.......... 3782
Na 3:3 corpses; they s. upon their corpses:... 3782
Mal 2:8 have caused many to s. at the law;...... 3782
1Pe 2:8 even to them which s. at the word,..... *4350*

STUMBLED
1Sa 2:4 that s. are girded with strength.......... 3782
1Ch 13:9 to hold the ark; for the oxen s........... 8058
Ps 27:2 eat up my flesh, they s. and fell.......... 3782
Jer 46:12 man hath s. against the mighty,......... 3782
Ro 9:32 they s. at that stumblingstone;............ *4350*
Ro 11:11 Have they s. that they should fall?...... *4417*

STUMBLETH
Pr 24:17 thine heart be glad when he s........... 3782
Joh 11:9 **man walk in the day, he s. not,** *4350*
Joh 11:10 **if a man walk in the night, he s.,** .. *4350*
Ro 14:21 any thing whereby thy brother s.,....... *4350*

STUMBLING See also STUMBLINGBLOCK; STUMBLINGSTONE.
Isa 8:14 for a stone of s. and for a rock of...... 5063
Isa 57:14 take up the s. block out of the way.... 4383
1Pe 2:8 And a stone of s., and a rock of......... *4348*
1Jo 2:10 there is none occasion of s. in him...... *4625*

STUMBLINGBLOCK See also STUMBLINGBLOCKS.
Le 19:14 deaf, nor put a s. before the blind,..... 4383
Isa 57:14 [*in some editions*] s. out of the way..... 4383
Eze 3:20 iniquity, and I lay a s. before him,...... 4383
Eze 7:19 because it is the s. of their iniquity..... 4383
Eze 14:3 put the s. of their iniquity before......... 4383
Eze 14:4, 7 and putteth the s. of his iniquity....... 4383
Ro 11:9 made a snare, and a trap, and a s.,.... *4625*
Ro 14:13 no man put a s. or an occasion to....... *4348*
1Co 1:23 unto the Jews a s., and unto the........ *4625*
1Co 8:9 become a s. to them that are weak..... *4348*
Re 2:14 **to cast a s. before the children of** .. *4625*

STUMBLINGBLOCKS
Jer 6:21 I will lay s. before this people,........... 4383
Zep 1:3 sea, and the s. with the wicked;......... 4384

STUMBLINGSTONE
Ro 9:32 For they stumbled at that s.;...... *3037,4348*
Ro 9:33 I lay in Zion a s. and rock of...... *3037,4348*

STUMP
1Sa 5:4 only the s. of Dagon was left to him.........
Da 4:15 leave the s. of his roots in the........... 6136
Da 4:23 yet leave the s. of the roots thereof... 6136
Da 4:26 to leave the s. of the tree roots;........ 6136

SUAH (su'-ah)
1Ch 7:36 S., and Harnepher, and Shual,........... 5477

SUBDUE See also SUBDUED; SUBDUETH.
Ge 1:28 and replenish the earth, and s. it:....... 3533
1Ch 17:10 Moreover I will s....thine enemies...... 3665
Ps 47:3 He shall s. the people under us,......... 1696
Isa 45:1 holden, to s. nations before him;........ 7286
Da 7:24 first, and he shall s. three kings.......... 8214
Mic 7:19 he will s. our inquities; and thou....... 3533
Zec 9:15 devour, and s. with sling stones;........ 3533
Php 3:21 to s. all things unto himself............... *5293*

SUBDUED See also SUBDUEDST.
Nu 32:22 the land be s. before the Lord:........... 3533
Nu 32:29 and the land shall be s. before you;.... 3533
De 20:20 war with thee, until it be s................ 3381
Jos 18:1 And the land was s. before them........ 3533
Jg 3:30 So Moab was s. that day under the..... 3665
Jg 4:23 So God s. on that day Jabin the......... 3665
Jg 8:28 was Midian s. before the children....... 3665
Jg 11:33 the children of Ammon were s........... 3665
1Sa 7:13 So the Philistines were s., and they.... 3665
2Sa 8:1 smote the Philistines, and s. them:..... 3665
2Sa 8:11 of all nations which he s.;.................. 3533
2Sa 22:40 against me hast thou s. under me....... 3766
1Ch 18:1 smote the Philistines, and s. them,..... 3665
1Ch 20:4 of the giant: and they were s............ 3665
1Ch 22:18 and the land is s. before the Lord,..... 3533
Ps 18:39 thou hast s. under me those that......... 3766
Ps 81:14 should soon have s. their enemies,..... 3665
1Co 15:28 all things shall be s. unto him,........... *5293*
Heb 11:33 Who through faith s. kingdoms,.......... *2610*

SUBDUEDST
Ne 9:24 and thou s. before them the.............. 3665

SUBDUETH
Ps 18:47 me, and s. the people under me......... 1696
Ps 144:2 trust; who s. my people under me....... 7286
Da 2:40 in pieces and s. all things: and as....... 2827

SUBJECT See also SUBJECTED.
Lu 2:51 Nazareth, and was s. unto them:......... *5293*
Lu 10:17 devils are s. unto us through thy........ *5293*
Lu 10:20 **that the spirits are s. unto you;** *5293*
Ro 8:7 for it is not s. to the law of God,........ *5293*
Ro 8:20 the creature was made s. to vanity,.... *5293*
Ro 13:1 every soul be s. unto the higher........ *5293*
Ro 13:5 Wherefore ye must needs be s., not... *5293*
1Co 14:32 the prophets are s. to the prophets.... *5293*
1Co 15:28 the Son also himself be s. unto him..... *5293*
Eph 5:24 as the church is s. unto Christ,.......... *5293*
Col 2:20 the world, are ye s. to ordinances,..... *1379*
Tit 3:1 in mine to be s. to principalities......... *5293*
Heb 2:15 all their lifetime s. to bondage............ *1777*
Jas 5:17 Elias...a man s. to like passions......... *3663*
1Pe 2:18 Servants, be s. to your masters.......... *5293*
1Pe 3:22 powers being made s. unto him.......... *5293*
1Pe 5:5 all of you be s. one to another, and.... *5293*

SUBJECTED
Ro 8:20 who hath s. the same in hope,.......... 5293

SUBJECTION
Ps 106:42 brought into s. under their hand......... 3665
Jer 34:11 brought them into s. for servants........ 3533
Jer 34:16 to return, and brought them into s.,..... 3533
1Co 9:27 my body, and bring it into s............... *1396*
2Co 9:13 your professed s. unto the gospel....... *5292*
Ga 2:5 To whom we gave place by s., no,...... *5292*
1Ti 2:11 woman learn in silence with all s......... *5292*
1Ti 3:4 his children in s. with all gravity;....... *5292*
Heb 2:5 not put in s. the world to come,......... *5293*
Heb 2:8 Thou hast put all things in s. under..... *5293*
Heb 2:8 in that he put all in s. under him,........ *5293*
Heb 12:9 rather be in s. unto the Father of....... *5293*
1Pe 3:1 be in s. to our own husbands;............ *5293*
1Pe 3:5 in s. unto their own husbands:........... *5293*

SUBMIT See also SUBMITTED; SUBMITTING.
Ge 16:9 and s. thyself under her hands........... 6031
2Sa 22:45 Strangers shall s. themselves unto...... 3584
Ps 18:44 strangers shall s. themselves unto...... 3584
Ps 66:3 shall thine enemies s. themselves....... 3584
Ps 68:30 s. himself with pieces of silver:......... 7511
1Co 16:16 That ye s. yourselves unto such,......... *5293*
Eph 5:22 Wives, s. yourselves unto your own.... *5293*
Col 3:18 Wives, s. yourselves unto your own.... *5293*
Heb 13:17 rule over you, and s. yourselves:....... *5226*
Jas 4:7 S. yourselves therefore to God.......... *5293*
1Pe 2:13 S. yourselves to every ordinance........ *5293*
1Pe 5:5 s. yourselves unto the elder............... *5293*

SUBMITTED
1Ch 29:24 s. themselves unto Solomon....... 5414,3027
Ps 81:15 should have s. themselves unto.......... 3584
Ro 10:3 have not s. themselves unto the......... *5293*

SUBMITTING
Eph 5:21 S. yourselves one to another in......... *5293*

SUBORNED
Ac 6:11 Then they s. men, which said,........... *5260*

SUBSCRIBE See also SUBSCRIBED.
Isa 44:5 s. with his hand unto the Lord,.......... 3789
Jer 32:44 and s. evidences, and seal them,......... 3789

SUBSCRIBED
Jer 32:10 I s. the evidence, and sealed it,.......... 3789
Jer 32:12 witnesses that s. the book of the....... 3789

SUBSTANCE
Ge 7:4 living s. that I have made will I.......... 3351
Ge 7:23 And every living s. was destroyed...... 3351
Ge 12:5 all their s. that they had gathered,...... 7399
Ge 13:6 for their s. was great, so that they..... 7399
Ge 15:14 shall they come out with great s......... 7399
Ge 34:23 shall not their cattle and their s......... 7075
Ge 36:6 all his s., which he had got in the....... 7075
De 11:6 s. that was in their possession,.......... 3351
De 33:11 Bless, Lord, his s., and accept the..... 3428
Jos 14:4 for their cattle and for their s............ 7075
1Ch 27:31 rulers of the s. which was king........... 7399
1Ch 28:1 the stewards over all the s. and......... 7399
2Ch 21:17 away all the s. that was found in......... 7399
2Ch 31:3 portion of his s. for the burnt........... 7399
2Ch 32:29 God had given him s. very much......... 7399
2Ch 35:7 these were of the king's s................ 7399
Ezr 8:21 for our little ones, and for all our s..... 7399
Ezr 10:8 elders, all his s. should be forfeited,.... 7399
Job 1:3 His s. also was seven thousand.......... 4735
Job 1:10 and his s. is increased in the land....... 4735
Job 5:5 the robber swalloweth up their s......... 2428
Job 6:22 Give a reward for me of your s.?....... 3581
Job 15:29 rich, neither shall his s. continue,...... 2428
Job 20:18 according to his s. shall the.............. 2428
Job 22:20 Whereas our s. is not cut down,......... 7009
Job 30:22 upon it, and dissolvest my s.............. 7738
Ps 17:14 leave the rest of their s. to their babes. ....
Ps 105:21 his house, and ruler of all his s.......... 7075
Ps 139:15 My s. was not hid from thee,............. 6108
Ps 139:16 Thine eyes did see my s., yet........... 1564
Pr 1:13 We shall find all precious s., we......... 1952
Pr 3:9 Honour the Lord with thy s., and........ 1952
Pr 6:31 he shall give all the s. of his house..... 1952
Pr 8:21 those that love me to inherit s.;.......... 3426
Pr 10:3 casteth away the s. of the wicked....... 1942
Pr 12:27 the s. of a diligent man is precious..... 1952
Pr 28:8 and unjust gain increaseth his s.,........ 1952
Pr 29:3 with harlots spendeth his s............... 1952
Ca 8:7 give all the s. of his house for love,..... 1952
Isa 6:13 as an oak, whose s. is in them,......... 4678
Isa 6:13 the holy seed shall be the s. thereof... 4678
Jer 15:13 Thy s. and thy treasures will I........... 2428
Jer 17:3 I will give thy s. and all thy............. 2428
Ho 12:8 rich, I have found me out s............... 202
Ob 13 laid hands on their s. in the day of...... 2428
Mic 4:13 their s. unto the Lord of the whole..... 2428
Lu 8:3 ministered unto him of their s........... *5224*
Lu 15:13 **wasted his s. with riotous living** *3776*
Heb 10:34 a better and an enduring s............. *5223*
Heb 11:1 faith is the s. of things hoped for,....... *5287*

SUBTIL
Ge 3:1 the serpent was more s. than any...... 6175
2Sa 13:3 and Jonadab was a very s. man......... 2450
Pr 7:10 attire of an harlot, and s. of heart....... 5341

SUBTILLY
1Sa 23:22 told me that he dealeth very s.......... 6191
Ps 105:25 to deal s. with his servants............. 5230
Ac 7:19 The same dealt s. with our kindred,.... *2686*

SUBTILTY
Ge 27:35 The brother came with s., and........... 4820
2Ki 10:19 But Jehu did it in s., to the intent...... 6122
Pr 1:4 To give s. to the simple, to the......... 6195
Mt 26:4 that they might take Jesus by s.,........ *1388*

Ac 13:10 O full of all **s.** and all mischief, *1388*
2Co 11:3 beguiled Eve through his **s.**, *3834*

SUBTLE See SUBTIL.

SUBURBS
Le 25:34 field of the **s.** of their cities may 4054
Nu 35:2 unto the Levites **s.** for the cities 4054
Nu 35:3 and the **s.** of them shall be for their 4054
Nu 35:4 the **s.** of the cities, which ye shall 4054
Nu 35:5 shall be to them the **s.** of the cities. 4054
Nu 35:7 them shall ye give with their **s.** 4054
Jos 14:4 their **s.** for their cattle and for their 4054
Jos 21:2 with the **s.** thereof for our cattle. 4054
Jos 21:3 the Lord, these cities and their **s.** 4054
Jos 21:8 Levites these cities with their **s.**, 4054
Jos 21:11 with the **s.** thereof round about it. 4054
Jos 21:13 the priest Hebron with her **s.**, 4054
Jos 21:13 the slayer; and Libnah with her **s.**, 4054
Jos 21:14 And Jattir with her **s.**, 4054
Jos 21:14 and Eshtemoa with her **s.**, 4054
Jos 21:15 And Holon with her **s.**, 4054
Jos 21:15 and Debir with her **s.**, 4054
Jos 21:16 And Ain with her **s.**, 4054
Jos 21:16 and Juttah with her **s.**, 4054
Jos 21:16 and Beth-shemesh with her **s.**; 4054
Jos 21:17 of Benjamin, Gibeon with her **s.**, 4054
Jos 21:17 Geba with her **s.**, 4054
Jos 21:18 Anathoth with her **s.**, 4054
Jos 21:18 and Almon with her **s.**; four cities. 4054
Jos 21:19 were thirteen cities with their **s.** 4054
Jos 21:21 gave them Shechem with her **s.** in 4054
Jos 21:21 the slayer; and Gezer with her **s.**, 4054
Jos 21:22 And Kibzaim with her **s.**, 4054
Jos 21:22 and Beth-horon with her **s.**; 4054
Jos 21:23 tribe of Dan, Eltekeh with her **s.**, 4054
Jos 21:23 Gibbethon with her **s.**, 4054
Jos 21:24 Aijalon with her **s.**, 4054
Jos 21:24 Gath-rimmon with her **s.**; 4054
Jos 21:25 of Manesseh, Tanach with her **s.**, 4054
Jos 21:25 and Gath-rimmon with her **s.**; 4054
Jos 21:26 All the cities were ten with their **s.** 4054
Jos 21:27 gave Golan in Bashan with her **s.**, 4054
Jos 21:27 and Beesh-terah with her **s.**; 4054
Jos 21:28 of Issachar, Kishon with her **s.**, 4054
Jos 21:28 Dabareh with her **s.**, 4054
Jos 21:29 Jarmuth with her **s.**, 4054
Jos 21:29 En-gannim with her **s.**; four cities. 4054
Jos 21:30 tribe of Asher, Mishal with her **s.**, 4054
Jos 21:30 Abdon with her **s.**, 4054
Jos 21:31 Helkath with her **s.**, 4054
Jos 21:31 and Rehob with her **s.**; four cities. 4054
Jos 21:32 Kedesh in Galilee with her **s.**, 4054
Jos 21:32 and Hammoth-dor with her **s.**, 4054
Jos 21:32 and Kartan with her **s.**; 4054
Jos 21:33 were thirteen cities with their **s.** 4054
jos 21:34 of Zebulun, Jokneam with her **s.**, 4054
Jos 21:34 and Kartah with her **s.**, 4054
Jos 21:35 Dimnah with her **s.**, 4054
Jos 21:35 Nahalal with her **s.**; four cities. 4054
Jos 21:36 tribe of Reuben, Bezer with her **s.** 4054
Jos 21:36 and Jahazah with her **s.**, 4054
Jos 21:37 Kedemoth with her **s.**, 4054
Jos 21:37 and Mephaath with her **s.**; 4054
Jos 21:38 Ramoth in Gilead with her **s.**, 4054
Jos 21:38 slayer; and Mahanaim with her **s.**, 4054
Jos 21:39 Heshbon with her **s.**, 4054
Jos 21:39 Jazer with her **s.**; four cities in all. 4054
Jos 21:41 forty and eight cities with their **s.** 4054
Jos 21:42 cities were every one with their **s.** 4054
2Ki 23:11 chamberlain, which was in the **s.**, 6503
1Ch 5:16 towns, and in all the **s.** of Sharon, 4054
1Ch 6:55 and the **s.** thereof round about it. 4054
1Ch 6:57 Hebron,...and Libnah with her **s.**, 4054
1Ch 6:57 Jattir, and Eshtemoa, with their **s.**, 4054
1Ch 6:58 And Hilen with her **s.**, 4054
1Ch 6:58 Debir with her **s.**, 4054
1Ch 6:59 And Ashan with her **s.**, 4054
1Ch 6:59 and Beth-shemesh with her **s.** 4054
1Ch 6:60 of Benjamin; Geba with her **s.**, 4054
1Ch 6:60 and Alemeth with her **s.**, 4054
1Ch 6:60 and Anathoth with her **s.** 4054
1Ch 6:64 Levites these cities with their **s.** 4054
1Ch 6:67 Shechem...with her **s.**; 4054
1Ch 6:67 they gave also Gezer with her **s.**, 4054
1Ch 6:68 And Jokmeam with her **s.**, 4054
1Ch 6:68 and Beth-horon with her **s.**, 4054
1Ch 6:69 And Aijalon with her **s.**, 4054
1Ch 6:69 and Gath-rimmon with her **s.** 4054
1Ch 6:70 of Manasseh; Aner with her **s.**, 4054
1Ch 6:70 and Bileam with her **s.**, 4054
1Ch 6:71 Golan in Bashan with her **s.**, 4054
1Ch 6:71 and Ashtaroth with her **s.**: 4054
1Ch 6:72 of Issachar; Kedesh with her **s.**, 4054
1Ch 6:72 Daberath with her **s.**, 4054
1Ch 6:73 And Ramoth with her **s.**, 4054
1Ch 6:73 and Anem with her **s.**: 4054
1Ch 6:74 tribe of Asher; Mashal with her **s.**, 4054
1Ch 6:74 and Abdon with her **s.**, 4054
1Ch 6:75 And Hukok with her **s.**, 4054
1Ch 6:75 and Rehob with her **s.** 4054
1Ch 6:76 Kedesh in Galilee with her **s.**, 4054
1Ch 6:76 and Hammon with her **s.**, 4054
1Ch 6:76 and Kirjathaim with her **s.** 4054
1Ch 6:77 of Zebulun, Rimmon with her **s.**, 4054
1Ch 6:77 Tabor with her **s.**: 4054
1Ch 6:78 Bezer in the wilderness with her **s.**, 4054
1Ch 6:78 and Jahzah with her **s.**, 4054
1Ch 6:79 Kedemoth also with her **s.**, 4054
1Ch 6:79 and Mephaath with her **s.** 4054
1Ch 6:80 Ramoth in Gilead with her **s.**, 4054
1Ch 6:80 and Mahanaim with her **s.**, 4054
1Ch 6:81 And Heshbon with her **s.**, 4054
1Ch 6:81 and Jazer with her **s.** 4054
1Ch 13:2 which are in their cities and **s.**, 4054
2Ch 11:14 left their **s.** and their possession, 4054
2Ch 31:19 in the fields of the **s.** of their cities, 4054
Eze 27:28 The **s.** shall shake at the sound of 4054
Eze 45:2 round about for the **s.** thereof, 4054
Eze 48:15 for the city, for dwelling, and for **s.** 4054
Eze 48:17 the **s.** of the city shall be toward 4054

SUBVERT See also SUBVERTED; SUBVERTING.
La 3:36 to **s.** a man in his cause, the Lord 5791
Tit 1:11 who **s.** whole houses, teaching *396*

SUBVERTED
Tit 3:11 Knowing that he that is such is **s.**, *1612*

SUBVERTING
Ac 15:24 you with words, **s.** your souls, *384*
2Ti 2:14 profit, but to the **s.** of the hearers. *2692*

SUCCEED See also SUCCEEDED; SUCCEEDEST.
De 25:6 shall **s.** in the name of his brother 6965

SUCCEEDED
De 2:12 but the children of Esau **s.** them, 3423
De 2:21, 22 they **s.** them, and dwelt in their 3423

SUCCEEDEST
De 12:29 and thou **s.** them, and dwellest in 3423
De 19:1 and thou **s.** them, and dwellest in 3423

SUCCESS
Jos 1:8 and then thou shalt have good **s.** 7919

SUCCOR See SUCCOUR.

SUCCOTH (suc'-coth) See also SUCCOTH-BENOTH.
Ge 33:17 Jacob journeyed to **S.**, and built 5523
Ge 33:17 the name of the place is called **S.** 5523
Ex 12:37 journeyed from Rameses to **S.**, 5523
Ex 13:20 they took their journey from **S.**, 5523
Nu 33:5 from Rameses, and pitched in **S.** 5523
Nu 33:6 they departed from **S.**, and pitched 5523
Jos 13:27 Beth-nimrah, and **S.**, and Zaphon, 5523
Jg 8:5 men of **S.**, Give, I pray you, loaves 5523
Jg 8:6 And the princes of **S.** said, Are the 5523
Jg 8:8 as the men of **S.** had answered him. 5523
Jg 8:14 a young man of the men of **S.**, 5523
Jg 8:14 he described...the princes of **S.**, 5523
Jg 8:15 And he came unto the men of **S.**, 5523
Jg 8:16 with them he taught the men of **S.** 5523
1Ki 7:46 ground between **S.** and Zarthan. 5523
2Ch 4:17 ground between **S.** and Zeredathah. 5523
Ps 60:6 and mete out the valley of **S.** 5523
Ps 108:7 and mete out the valley of **S.** 5523

SUCCOTH-BENOTH (suc''-coth-be'-noth)
2Ki 17:30 And the men of Babylon made **S.**, 5524

SUCCOUR See also SUCCOURED.
2Sa 8:5 Syrians of Damascus came to **s.** 5826
2Sa 18:3 that thou **s.** us out of the city. 5826
Heb 2:18 is able to **s.** them that are tempted. *997*

SUCCOURED
2Sa 21:17 Abishai the son of Zeruiah **s.** him, 5826
2Co 6:2 the day of salvation have I **s.** thee: *997*

SUCCOURER
Ro 16:2 for she hath been a **s.** of many, *4368*

SUCH
Ge 4:20 was the father of **s.** as dwell in tents,
Ge 4:20 and of **s.** as have cattle.
Ge 4:21 the father of all **s.** as handle the harp
Ge 27:4 make me savoury meat, **s.** as I love,
Ge 27:9 meat for thy father, **s.** as he loveth:
Ge 27:14 savoury meat, **s.** as his father loved.
Ge 27:46 the daughters of Heth, **s.** as these
Ge 30:32 the goats: and of **s.** shall be my hire.
Ge 41:19 **s.** as I never saw in all the land of 2007
Ge 41:38 Can we find **s.** a one as this is, a
Ge 44:15 wot ye not that **s.** a man as I can
Ex 9:18 hail, **s.** as hath not been in Egypt 834
Ex 9:24 hail,. . .s. as there was none like it in 834
Ex 10:14 there were no **s.** locusts as they, 3651
Ex 10:14 neither after them shall be **s.**
Ex 11:6 cry. . .s. as there was none like it, 834
Ex 12:36 they lent unto them **s.** things as they
Ex 18:21 **s.** as fear God, men of truth, hating
Ex 18:21 and place **s.** over them, to be rulers of
Ex 34:10 **s.** as have not been done in all the
Le 10:19 and **s.** things have befallen me: 428
Le 11:34 that on which **s.** water cometh shall
Le 11:34 be drunk in every **s.** vessel shall be
Le 14:22 young pigeons, **s.** as he is able to get;
Le 14:30 young pigeons, **s.** as he can get;
Le 14:31 Even **s.** as he is able to get, the one
Le 20:6 that turneth after **s.** as have familiar
Le 22:6 touched any **s.** shall be unclean until
Le 27:9 man giveth of **s.** unto the Lord shall
Nu 8:16 instead of **s.** as open every womb,
De 4:32 hath been any **s.** thing as this great
De 5:29 O that there were **s.** an heart in 2888
De 13:11 shall do no more any **s.** wickedness
De 13:14 **s.** abomination is wrought among 2063
De 16:9 from **s.** time as thou beginnest to put
De 17:4 that **s.** abomination is wrought in 2063
De 19:20 commit no more any **s.** evil among
De 25:16 For all that do **s.** things, and all 428
Jg 3:2 **s.** as before knew nothing thereof;
Jg 13:23 have told us **s.** things as these.
Jg 18:23 that thou comest with **s.** a company?
Jg 19:30 was no **s.** deed done nor seen from 2063
Ru 4:1 Ho, **s.** a one! turn aside, sit down 6423
1Sa 2:23 unto them, Why do ye **s.** things? 428
1Sa 4:7 not been **s.** a thing heretofore. 2063
1Sa 21:2 servants to **s.** [6423] and **s.** a place. 492
1Sa 25:17 for he is **s.** a son of Belial, that a man
2Sa 9:8 look upon **s.** a dead dog as I am?
2Sa 12:8 given unto thee **s.** and **s.** things. 2007
2Sa 13:12 no **s.** thing ought to be done in 3651
2Sa 13:18 for with **s.** robes were the king's 3651
2Sa 14:13 then hast thou thought **s.** a thing 2063
2Sa 16:2 that **s.** as be faint in the wilderness
2Sa 19:36 recompense..with **s.** a reward? 2063
1Ki 10:10 no more **s.** abundance of spices 1931
1Ki 10:12 there came no **s.** almug trees, nor 3651
2Ki 6:8 In **s.**...a place shall be my camp. 6423
2Ki 6:8 and **s.** a place shall be my camp. 492
2Ki 6:9 Beware...thou pass not **s.** a place; 2088
2Ki 7:19 in heaven, might **s.** a thing be? 2088
2Ki 19:29 year **s.** things as grow of themselves,
2Ki 21:12 I am bringing **s.** evil upon Jerusalem
2Ki 23:22 there was not holden **s.** a passover. 2088
2Ki 25:15 bowls, and **s.** things as were of gold,
1Ch 12:33, 36 **s.** as went forth to battle, expert in
1Ch 29:25 bestowed upon him **s.** royal majesty
2Ch 1:12 **s.** as none of the kings have had 834
2Ch 4:6 **s.** things as they offered for the burnt
2Ch 9:9 **s.** spice as the queen of Sheba gave 1932
2Ch 9:11 there were none **s.** seen before in 1992
2Ch 11:16 **s.** as set their hearts to seek the Lord
2Ch 23:13 and **s.** as taught to sing praise.
2Ch 24:12 Jehoiada gave it to **s.** as did the work
2Ch 24:12 and also **s.** as wrought iron and brass
2Ch 30:5 long time in **s.** sort as it was written.
2Ch 35:18 keep **s.** a passover as Josiah kept,
Ezr 4:10, 11 side the river, and at **s.** a time. 3706
Ezr 4:17 the river, Peace, and at **s.** a time. 3706
Ezr 6:21 all **s.** as had separated themselves
Ezr 7:12 perfect peace, and at **s.** a time. 3706
Ezr 7:25 all **s.** as know the laws of thy God;
Ezr 7:27 put **s.** a thing as this in the king's
Ezr 8:31 and of **s.** as lay in wait by the way.

Ezr 9:13 hast given us s. deliverance as this;
Ezr 10:3 the wives, and s. as are born of them,
Ne 6:8 are no s. things done as thou sayest, 428
Ne 6:11 I said, Should s. a man as I flee? 3644
Es 2:9 with s. things as belonged to her, and
Es 4:11 s. to whom the king shall hold out 834
Es 4:14 the kingdom for s. a time as this?
Es 9:2 lay hand on s. as sought their hurt:
Es 9:27 upon all s. as joined themselves unto
Job 12:3 knoweth not s. things as these? 3644
Job 14:3 open thine eyes upon s. an one, 2088
Job 15:13 lettest s. words go out of thy mouth?
Job 16:2 I have heard many s. things: 428
Job 18:21 s. are the dwellings of the wicked, 428
Job 23:14 and many s. things are with him. 2007
Ps 25:10 and truth unto s. as keep his covenant
Ps 27:12 me, and s. as breathe out cruelty,
Ps 34:18 saveth s. as be of a contrite spirit.
Ps 37:14 slay s. as be of upright conversation.
Ps 37:22 s. as be blessed of him shall inherit
Ps 40:4 proud, nor s. as turn aside to lies.
Ps 40:16 let s. as love thy salvation say
Ps 50:21 I was altogether s. an one as thyself:
Ps 55:20 against s. as be at peace with him:
Ps 68:21 scalp of s. an one as goeth on still
Ps 70:4 let s. as love thy salvation say
Ps 73:1 even to s. as are of a clean heart.
Ps 103:18 To s. as keep his covenant, and to
Ps 107:10 S. as sit in darkness and in the
Ps 125:5 for s. as turn aside unto their crooked
Ps 139:6 S. knowledge is too wonderful for me;
Ps 144:15 is that people, that is in s. a case: 3602
Pr 11:20 s. as are upright in their way are his
Pr 28:4 s. as keep the law contend with them.
Pr 30:20 S. is the way of an adulterous 3651
Pr 31:8 all s. as are appointed to destruction.
Ec 4:1 the tears of s. as were oppressed,
Isa 9:1 dimness shall not be s. as was in her
Isa 10:20 s. as are escaped of the house of
Isa 20:6 Behold, s. is our expectation, 3541
Isa 37:30 eat this year s. as growth of itself;
Isa 58:5 Is it s. a fast that I have chosen? 2088
Isa 66:8 Who hath heard s. a thing? 2063
Isa 66:8 who hath seen s. things? 428
Jer 2:10 and see if there be s. a thing 2063
Jer 5:9, 29 avenged on s. a nation as this? 834
Jer 9:9 soul be avenged on s. a nation as 834
Jer 15:2 Lord; S. as are for death, to death;
Jer 15:2 and s. as for the sword, to the sword;
Jer 15:2 and s. as are for the famine, to the
Jer 15:2 and s. as are for the captivity, to the
Jer 18:13 heathen, who hath heard s. things: 428
Jer 21:7 and s. as are left in this city from the
Jer 38:4 in speaking s. words unto them: 428
Jer 43:11 deliver s. as are for death to death;
Jer 43:11 and s. as are for captivity to captivity;
Jer 43:11 s. as are for the sword to the sword.
Jer 44:14 shall return but s. as shall escape.
Eze 17:15 he escape that doeth s. things? 428
Eze 18:14 considereth, and doeth not s. like, 2007
Da 1:4 s. as had ability in them to stand in
Da 2:10 asked s. things at any magician, 1836
Da 10:15 he had spoken s. words unto me, 428
Da 11:32 And s. as do wickedly against the
Da 12:1 trouble, s. as never was since there 834
Am 5:16 and s. as are skilful of lamentation to
Mic 5:15 heathen, s. as they have not heard.
Zep 1:8 and all s. as are clothed with strange
Mt 9:8 had given s. power unto men. *5108*
Mt 18:5 **shall receive one s. little child in** *5108*
Mt 19:14 **for of s. is the kingdom of heaven.** *5108*
Mt 24:21 **s. as was not since the beginning** *3634*
Mt 24:44 **s. an hour as ye think not the Son**
Mt 26:18 **Go into the city to s. a man, and** *1170*
Mk 4:18 **thorns; s. as hear the word.** *3778*
Mk 4:20 **s. as hear the word, and receive** *3748*
Mk 4:33 with many s. parables spake he *5108*
Mk 6:2 even s. mighty works are wrought *5108*
Mk 7:8 **many other s. like things ye do.** *5108*
Mk 7:13 **and many s. like things do ye.** *5108*
Mk 9:37 **receive one of s. children in my** *5108*
Mk 10:14 **for of s. is the kingdom of God.** *5108*
Mk 13:7 **for s. things must needs be; but**
Mk 13:19 **s. as was not from the beginning** *3634*
Lu 9:9 is this, of whom I hear s. things? *3634*
Lu 10:7 **and drinking s. things as they give:**
Lu 10:8 **eat s. things as are set before you:**
Lu 11:41 **give alms of s. things as ye have;**
Lu 13:2 **because they suffered s. things?** *5108*
Lu 18:16 **for of s. is the kingdom of God.** *5108*
Joh 4:23 **Father seeketh s. to worship him.** *5108*
Joh 7:32 the people murmured s. things *5023*
Joh 8:5 us, that s. should be stoned: *5108*
Joh 9:16 man that is a sinner do s. miracles? *5108*
Ac 2:47 church daily s. as should be saved.
Ac 3:6 I none; but s. as I have give I thee:
Ac 15:24 whom we gave no s. commandment:
Ac 16:24 Who, having received s. a charge, *5108*
Ac 18:15 I will be no judge of s. matters. *5130*
Ac 21:25 that they observe no s. thing, *5108*
Ac 22:22 with s. a fellow from the earth: *5108*
Ac 25:18 accusation of s. things as I supposed:
Ac 25:20 I doubted of s. manner of questions,
Ac 26:29 and altogether s. as I am, except *5108*
Ac 28:10 they laded us with s. things as were
Ro 1:32 s. things are worthy of death, *5108*
Ro 2:2 them which commit s. things. *5108*
Ro 2:3 judgest them which do s. things, *5108*
Ro 16:18 they that are s. serve not our Lord *5108*
1Co 5:1 s. fornication as is not so much as *5108*
1Co 5:5 To deliver s. an one unto Satan for *5108*
1Co 5:11 with s. an one no not to eat. *5108*
1Co 6:11 And s. were some of you: but ye *5023*
1Co 7:15 is not under bondage in s. cases: *5108*
1Co 7:28 s. shall have trouble in the flesh: *5108*
1Co 10:13 taken you but s. as is common to man:
1Co 11:16 we have no s. custom, neither the *5108*
1Co 15:48 s. are they also that are earthy: *5108*
1Co 15:48 s. are they also that are heavenly. *5108*
1Co 16:16 that ye submit yourselves unto s., *5108*
1Co 16:18 acknowledge ye them that are s.. *5108*
2Co 2:6 Sufficient to s. a man is this *5108*
2Co 2:7 s. a one should be swallowed up *5108*
2Co 3:4 s. trust have we through Christ *5108*
2Co 3:12 Seeing then that we have s. hope, *5108*
2Co 10:11 Let s. an one think this, that, *3634*
2Co 10:11 s. as we are in word by letters *5108*
2Co 10:11 s. will we be also in deed when we *5108*
2Co 11:13 For s. are false apostles, deceitful *5108*
2Co 12:2 s. an one caught up to the third *5108*
2Co 12:3 And I knew s. a man, (whether in *5108*
2Co 12:5 Of s. an one will I glory: yet of *5108*
2Co 12:20 I shall not find you s. as I would, *3634*
2Co 12:20 found unto you s. as ye would not: *3634*
Ga 5:21 revellings, and s. like: *5125*
Ga 5:21 which do s. things shall not inherit *5108*
Ga 5:23 against s. there is no law. *5108*
Ga 6:1 restore s. an one in the spirit of *5108*
Eph 5:27 spot, or wrinkle, or any s. thing; *5108*
Php 2:29 gladness; and hold s. in reputation: *5108*
1Th 4:6 the Lord is the avenger of all s., *5130*
2Th 3:12 them that are s. we command and *5108*
1Ti 6:5 godliness: from s. withdraw thyself. *5108*
2Ti 3:5 power thereof: from s. turn away. *5128*
Tit 3:11 that he that is s. is subverted, and *5108*
Phm 9 being s. an one as Paul the aged, *5108*
Heb 5:12 are become s. as have need of milk,
Heb 7:26 s. an high priest became us, who *5108*
Heb 8:1 We have s. an high priest, who is *5108*
Heb 11:14 For they that say s. things declare *5108*
Heb 12:3 him that endured s. contradiction *5108*
Heb 13:5 content with s. things as ye have; *3588*
Heb 13:16 s. sacrifices God is well pleased. *5108*
Jas 4:13 to morrow we will go into s. a city, *3592*
Jas 4:16 boastings: all s. rejoicing is evil. *5108*
2Pe 1:17 there came s. a voice to him from *5107*
2Pe 3:14 seeing that ye look for s. things, *5023*
3Jo 8 We therefore ought to receive s., *5108*
Re 5:13 and s. as are in the sea, and all that
Re 16:18 s. as was not since men were upon *3634*
Re 20:6 on s. the second death hath no *5130*

SUCHATHITES (soo'-kath-ites)
1Ch 2:55 the Shimeathites, and S. 7756

SUCK See also SUCKED; SUCKING.
Ge 21:7 should have given children s.? 3243
De 32:13 him to s. honey out of the rock, 3243
De 33:19 s. of the abundance of the seas, 3243
1Sa 1:23 gave her son s. until she weaned 3243
1Ki 3:21 in the morning to give my child s., 3243
Job 3:12 why the breasts that I should s.? 3243
Job 20:16 He shall s. the poison of asps: 3243
Job 39:30 Her young ones also s. up blood: 5966
Isa 60:16 also s. the milk of the Gentiles, 3243
Isa 60:16 and shalt s. the breast of kings: 3243
Isa 66:11 That ye may s., and be satisfied 3243
Isa 66:12 then shall ye s., ye shall be borne 3243
La 4:3 they give s. to their young ones: 3243
Eze 23:34 shalt even drink it and s. it out, 4680
Joe 2:16 and those that s. the breasts: 3243
Mk 24:19 **and to them that give s. in those** *2337*
Mk 13:17 **them that give s. in those days!** *2337*
Lu 21:23 **them that give s., in those days!** *2337*
Lu 23:29 **and the paps which never gave s.** *2337*

SUCKED
Ca 8:1 that s. the breasts of my mother! 3243
Lu 11:27 and the paps which thou hast s.. *2337*

SUCKING
Nu 11:12 nursing father beareth the s. child, 3243
1Sa 7:9 Samuel took a s. lamb, and offered 2461
Isa 11:8 the s. child shall play on the hole 3243
Isa 49:15 Can a woman forget her s. child, 5764
La 4:4 The tongue of the s. child cleaveth 3243

SUCKLING See also SUCKLINGS.
De 32:25 the s. also with the man of gray 3243
1Sa 15:3 infant and s., ox and sheep, camel 3243
Jer 44:7 you man and woman, child and s., 3243

SUCKLINGS
1Sa 22:19 men and women, children and s., 3243
Ps 8:2 Out of the mouth of babes and s. 3243
La 2:11 and the s. swoon in the streets 3243
Mt 21:16 **Out of the mouth of babes and s.** *2337*

SUDDEN
Job 22:10 thee, and s. fear troubleth thee; 6597
Pr 3:25 Be not afraid of s. fear, neither of 6597
1Th 5:3 then s. destruction cometh upon *160*

SUDDENLY
Nu 6:9 if any man die very s. by him, 6597
Nu 12:4 And the Lord spake s. unto Moses, 6597
Nu 35:22 if he thrust him s. without enmity, 6621
De 7:4 against you, and destroy thee s. 4118
Jos 10:9 therefore came unto them s., and 6597
Jos 11:7 them by the waters of Merom s.; 6597
2Sa 15:14 lest he overtake us s., and bring 4116
2Ch 29:36 people: for the thing was done s. 6597
Job 5:3 root: but s. I cursed his habitation. 6597
Job 9:23 If the scourge slay s., he will laugh 6597
Ps 6:10 them return and be ashamed s. 7281
Ps 64:4 s. do they shoot at him, and fear 6597
Ps 64:7 arrow; s. shall they be wounded. 6597
Pr 6:15 shall his calamity come s.; 6597
Pr 6:15 s. shall he be broken without 6621
Pr 24:22 For their calamity shall rise s.; 6597
Pr 29:1 shall s. be destroyed, and that 6621
Ec 9:12 time, when it falleth s. upon them. 6597
Isa 29:5 yea, it shall be at an instant s. 6597
Isa 30:13 breaking cometh s. at an instant. 6597
Isa 47:11 desolation shall come upon thee s., 6597
Isa 48:3 them; I did them s., and they came 6597
Jer 4:20 s. are my tents spoiled, and my 6597
Jer 6:26 the spoiler shall s. come upon us. 6597
Jer 15:8 I have caused him to fall upon it s., 6597
Jer 18:22 shalt bring a troop s. upon them: 6597
Jer 49:19 s. make him run away from her: 7280
Jer 50:44 make them s. run away from her: 7280
Jer 51:8 Babylon is s. fallen and destroyed: 6597
Hab 2:7 Shall they not rise up s. that shall 6621
Mal 3:1 seek, shall s. come to his temple, 6597
Mk 9:8 s., when they had looked round *1819*
Mk 13:36 **coming s. he find you sleeping.** *1810*
Lu 2:13 And s. there was with the angel a *1810*
Lu 9:39 taketh him, and he s. crieth out; *1810*
Ac 2:2 s. there came a sound from heaven *869*
Ac 9:3 s. there shined round about him a *1810*
Ac 16:26 s. there was a great earthquake, *869*
Ac 22:6 s. there shone from heaven a great *1810*
Ac 28:6 swollen, or fallen down dead s. *869*
1Ti 5:22 Lay hands s. on no man, neither *5030*

SUE
Mt 5:40 **any man will s. thee at the law,** *2919*

SUFFER See also SUFFERED; SUFFEREST; SUFFERETH; SUFFERING.
Ex 12:23 will not s. the destroyer to come 5414
Ex 22:18 Thou shalt not s. a witch to live.
Le 2:13 shalt thou s. the salt...to be lacking

Le 19:17 neighbour,...not s. sin upon him. 5375
Le 22:16 Or s. them to bear the iniquity of 5375
Nu 21:23 Sihon would not s. Israel to pass 5414
Jos 10:19 s. them not to enter into their cities: 5414
Jg 1:34 would not s. them to come down to 5414
Jg 15:1 father would not s. him to go in. 5414
Jg 16:26 S. me that I may feel the pillars 3240
2Sa 14:11 not s. the revengers of blood to
1Ki 15:17 that he might not s. any to go out 5414
Es 3:8 not for the king's profit to s. them 3240
Job 9:18 will not s. me to take my breath, 5414
Job 21:3 S. me that I may speak; and after 5375
Job 24:11 tread their winepresses, and s. thirst.
Job 36:2 S. me a little, and I will shew thee 3803
Ps 9:13 consider my trouble which I s. of them
Ps 16:10 wilt thou s. thine Holy One to see 5414
Ps 34:10 young lions do lack, and s. hunger:
Ps 55:22 he shall never s. the righteous to 5414
Ps 88:15 I s. thy terrors I am distracted. 5375
Ps 89:33 from him, nor s. my faithfulness to fail.
Ps 101:5 and a proud heart will not I s. 3201
Ps 121:3 will not s. thy foot to be moved: 5414
Pr 10:3 will not s. the...righteous to famish:
Pr 19:15 sleep; and an idle soul shall s. hunger
Pr 19:19 great wrath shall s. punishment: 5375
Ec 5:6 S. not thy mouth to cause thy flesh 5414
Ec 5:12 the rich will not s. him to sleep. 3240
Eze 44:20 heads, nor s. their locks to grow long;
Mt 3:15 said unto him, **S. it to be so now:** *863*
Mt 8:21 s. me first to go and bury my *2010*
Mt 8:31 s. us to go away into the herd of *2010*
Mt 16:21 s. many things of the elders and *3958*
Mt 17:12 **also the Son of man s. of them.** *3958*
Mt 17:17 **with you? how long shall I s. you?** *430*
Mt 19:14 **S. little children, and forbid them** *863*
Mt 23:13 **neither s. ye them that are** *863*
Mk 7:12 **ye s. him no more to do ought for** *863*
Mk 8:31 Son of man must s. many things, *3958*
Mk 9:12 **man, that he must s. many things,** *3958*
Mk 9:19 **with you? how long shall I s. you?** *430*
Mk 10:14 **S. the little children to come unto** *863*
Mk 11:16 would not s. that any man should *863*
Lu 8:32 would s. them to enter into them. *2010*
Lu 9:22 **Son of man must s. many things,** *3958*
Lu 9:41 **shall I be with you, and s. you?** *430*
Lu 9:59 Lord, s. me first to go and bury my *2010*
Lu 17:25 **But first must he s. many things,** *3958*
Lu 18:16 **S. little children to come unto me,** *863*
Lu 22:15 **this passover with you before I s.** *3958*
Lu 22:51 answered and said, **S. ye thus far.** *1439*
Lu 24:46 **and thus it behoved Christ to s.,** *3958*
Ac 2:27 wilt thou s. thine Holy One to see *1325*
Ac 3:18 prophets, that Christ should s., *3958*
Ac 5:41 counted worthy to s. shame for his *818*
Ac 7:24 seeing one of them s. wrong, he
Ac 9:16 **him how great things he must s.** *3958*
Ac 13:35 shalt not s. thine Holy One to see *1325*
Ac 21:39 s. me to speak unto the people. *2010*
Ac 26:23 That Christ should s., and that he *3805*
Ro 8:17 If so be that we s. with him, that *4841*
1Co 3:15 shall be burned, he shall s. loss: *2210*
1Co 4:12 bless; being persecuted, we s. it: *430*
1Co 6:7 rather s. yourselves to be defrauded?
1Co 9:12 but s. all things, lest we should *4722*
1Co 10:13 will not s. you to be tempted above *1439*
1Co 12:26 whether one member s., all the *3958*
1Co 12:26 all the members s. with it; or one *4841*
2Co 1:6 same sufferings which we also s. *3958*
2Co 11:19 For ye s. fools gladly, seeing ye *430*
2Co 11:20 For ye s., if a man bring you into *430*
Ga 5:11 why do I yet s. persecution? then *1377*
Ga 6:12 should s. persecution for the cross *1377*
Php 1:29 on him, but also to s. for his sake; *3958*
Php 4:12 both to abound and to s. need. *5302*
1Th 3:4 before that we should s. tribulation;
2Th 1:5 kingdom of God, for which ye also s.
1Ti 2:12 I s. not a woman to teach, nor to *2010*
1Ti 4:10 we both labour and s. reproach,
2Ti 1:12 which cause I also s. these things: *3958*
2Ti 2:9 Wherein I s. trouble, as an evil doer, *2553*
2Ti 2:12 If we s., we shall also reign with *5278*
2Ti 3:12 Christ Jesus shall s. persecution. *1377*
Heb 11:25 Choosing rather to s. affliction *4778*
Heb 13:3 and them which s. adversity, as *2558*
Heb 13:22 s. the word of exhortation: for *430*
1Pe 2:20 when ye do well, and s. for it, ye *3958*
1Pe 3:14 if ye s. for righteousness' sake, *3958*
1Pe 3:17 that ye s. for well doing, than for *3958*
1Pe 4:15 let none of you s. as a murderer, or *3958*
1Pe 4:16 if any man s. as a Christian, let him
1Pe 4:19 let them that s. according to the *3958*
Re 2:10 **those things which thou shalt s.** *3958*
Re 11:9 not s. their dead bodies to be put in *863*

SUFFERED
Ge 20:6 s. I thee not to touch her. 5414
Ge 31:7 but God s. him not to hurt me. 5414
Ge 31:28 not s. me to kiss my sons and my 5203
De 8:3 and s. thee to hunger, and fed thee
De 18:14 thy God hath not s. thee so to do. 5414
Jg 3:28 Moab, and s. not a man to pass over. 5414
1Sa 24:7 and s. them not to rise against Saul. 5414
2Sa 21:10 and s. neither the birds of the air 5414
1Ch 16:21 He s. no man to do them wrong: 3240
Job 31:30 Neither have I s. my mouth to sin 5414
Ps 105:14 He s. no man to do them wrong: 3240
Jer 15:15 that for thy sake I have s. rebuke. 5375
Mt 3:15 **all righteousness.** Then he s. him *863*
Mt 19:8 **s. you to put away your wives:** *2010*
Mt 24:43 **have s. his house to be broken up** *1439*
Mt 27:19 for I have s. many things this day *3958*
Mk 1:34 and s. not the devils to speak, *863*
Mk 5:19 Howbeit Jesus s. him not, but saith *863*
Mk 5:26 s. many things of many physicians, *3958*
Mk 5:37 And he s. no man to follow him, *863*
Mk 10:4 s. to write a bill of divorcement, *2010*
Lu 4:41 rebuking...s. them not to speak: *1439*
Lu 8:32 enter into them. And he s. them. *2010*
Lu 8:51 he s. no man to go in, save Peter, *863*
Lu 12:39 **s. his house to be broken through** *863*
Lu 13:2 **because they s. such things?** *3958*
Lu 24:26 **not Christ to have s. these things,** *3958*
Ac 13:18 s. he their manners in the *5159*
Ac 14:16 s. all nations to walk in their own *1439*
Ac 16:7 but the Spirit s. them not. *1439*
Ac 17:3 that Christ must needs have s., *3958*
Ac 19:30 people, the disciples s. him not. *1439*
Ac 28:16 Paul was s. to dwell by himself *2010*
2Co 7:12 nor for his cause that s. wrong, but
2Co 11:25 was I stoned, thrice I s. shipwreck,
Ga 3:4 Have ye s. so many things in vain? *3958*
Php 3:8 I have s. the loss of all things, *2210*
1Th 2:2 even after that we had s. before, *4310*
1Th 2:14 s. like things of your...countrymen, *3958*
Heb 2:18 he himself hath s. being tempted, *3958*
Heb 5:8 he obedience by the things...he s.; *3958*
Heb 7:23 were not s. to continue by reason *2967*
Heb 9:26 For then must he often have s. *3958*
Heb 13:12 his own blood, s. without the gate. *3958*
1Pe 2:21 because Christ also s. for us, *3958*
1Pe 2:23 when he s., he threatened not; but *3958*
1Pe 3:18 Christ also hath once s. for sins, *3958*
1Pe 4:1 as Christ hath s. for us in the flesh *3958*
1Pe 4:1 for he that hath s. in the flesh hath *3958*
1Pe 5:10 after that ye have s. a while, make *3958*

SUFFEREST
Re 2:20 **thou s. that woman Jezebel,** *1439*

SUFFERETH
Ps 66:9 and s. not our feet to be moved. 5414
Ps 107:38 and s. not their cattle to decrease.
Mt 11:12 **kingdom of heaven s. violence,** *971*
Ac 28:4 sea, yet vengeance s. not to live. *1439*
1Co 13:4 Charity s. long, and is kind; *3114*

SUFFERING See also LONGSUFFERING; SUFFERINGS.
Ac 27:7 the wind not s. us, we sailed under *4330*
Heb 2:9 than the angels for the s. of death, *3804*
Jas 5:10 for an example of s. affliction, *2552*
1Pe 2:19 God endure grief, s. wrongfully. *3958*
Jude 7 s. the vengeance of eternal fire. *5254*

SUFFERINGS
Ro 8:18 I reckon that the s. of this present *3804*
2Co 1:5 as the s. of Christ abound in us, *3804*
2Co 1:6 enduring of the same s. which we *3804*
2Co 1:7 that as ye are partakers of the s., *3804*
Php 3:10 and the fellowship of his s., *3804*
Col 1:24 Who now rejoice in my s. for you, *3804*
Heb 2:10 their salvation perfect through s. *3804*
1Pe 1:11 testified beforehand the s. of Christ, *3804*
1Pe 4:13 as ye are partakers of Christ's s.; *3804*
1Pe 5:1 and a witness of the s. of Christ, *3804*

SUFFICE See also SUFFICED; SUFFICETH.
Nu 11:22 herds be slain for them, to s. them? 4672
Nu 11:22 gathered...for them, to s. them? 4672
De 3:26 Lord said unto me, Let it s. thee; 7227
1Ki 20:10 dust of Samaria...s. for handfuls 5606
Eze 44:6 it s. you of all your abominations, 7227
Eze 45:9 Let it s. you, O princes of Israel: 7227
1Pe 4:3 the time past of our life may s. us *713*

SUFFICED
Jg 21:14 and yet so they s. them not. 4672
Ru 2:14 corn, and she did eat, and was s., 7646
Ru 2:18 she had reserved after she was s., 7648

SUFFICETH
Joh 14:8 shew us the Father, and it s. us. *714*

SUFFICIENCY
Job 20:22 In the fullness of his s. he shall be 5607
2Co 3:5 of ourselves; but our s. is of God; *2426*
2Co 9:8 always having all s. in all things, *841*

SUFFICIENT
Ex 36:7 stuff they had was s. for all the 1767
De 15:8 surely lend him s. for his need, 1767
De 33:7 let his hands be s. for him; and 7227
Pr 25:16 eat so much as is s. for thee, lest 1767
Isa 40:16 And Lebanon is not s. to burn, nor 1767
Isa 40:16 the beasts thereof s. for a burnt 1767
Mt 6:34 **S. unto the day is the evil thereof** *713*
Lu 14:28 **cost, whether he have s. to finish it?**
Joh 6:7 pennyworth of bread is not s. for *714*
2Co 2:6 S. to such...is this punishment, *2425*
2Co 2:16 And who is s. for these things? *2425*
2Co 3:5 Not that we are s. of ourselves to *2425*
2Co 12:9 unto me, **My grace is s. for thee** *714*

SUFFICIENTLY
2Ch 30:3 had not sanctified themselves s., 4078
Isa 23:18 eat s., and for durable clothing. 7654

SUIT See also SUITS.
Jg 17:10 a s. of apparel, and thy victuals. 6187
2Sa 15:4 that every man which hath any s. 7379
Job 11:19 many shall make s. unto thee. 2470

SUITS
Isa 3:22 The changeable s. of apparel, and the 2470

SUKKIIMS (suk'-ke-ims)
2Ch 12:3 the Lubims, the S., and the 5525

SUM
Ex 21:30 be laid on him a s. of mney, 3724
Ex 30:12 takest the s. of the children of 7218
Ex 38:21 This is the s. of the tabernacle, 6485
Nu 1:2 Take ye the s. of the congregation 7218
Nu 1:49 Levi, neither take the s. of them 7218
Nu 4:2 Take the s. of the sons of Kohath 7218
Nu 4:22 Take...the s. of the sons of Gershon, 7218
Nu 26:2 Take the s. of all the congregation 7218
Nu 26:4 Take the s. of the people, from twenty
Nu 31:26 Take the s. of the prey that was 7218
Nu 31:49 have taken the s. of the men of war 7218
2Sa 24:9 the s. of the number of the people 4557
2Ki 22:4 that he may s. the silver which is 8552
1Ch 21:5 the s. of the number of the people 4557
Es 4:7 the s. of the money that Haman 6575
Ps 139:17 God! how great is the s. of them! 7218
Eze 28:12 Thou sealest up the s., full of 8508
Da 7:1 and told the s. of the matters. 7217
Ac 7:16 Abraham bought for a s. of money *5092*
Ac 22:28 a great s. obtained I this freedom. *2774*
Heb 8:1 we have spoken this is the s.: *2774*

SUMMER
Ge 8:22 cold and heat, and s. and winter, 7019
Jg 3:20 and he was sitting in a s. parlour, 4747
Jg 3:24 covereth his feet in his s. chamber. 4747
2Sa 16:1 and an hundred of s. fruits, and a 7019
2Sa 16:2 s. fruit for the young man to eat; 7019
Ps 32:4 is turned into the drought of s. 7019
Ps 74:17 thou hast made s. and winter. 7019
Pr 6:8 Provideth her meat in the s., and 7019
Pr 10:5 that gathereth in s. is a wise son: 7019
Pr 26:1 As snow in s., and as rain in 7019
Pr 30:25 they prepare their meat in the s.; 7019
Isa 16:9 for the shouting for thy s. fruits 7019
Isa 18:6 and the fowls shall s. upon them, 6972
Isa 28:4 as the hasty fruit before the s.; 7019
Jer 8:20 The harvest is past, the s. is ended, 7019
Jer 40:10 gather ye wine, and s. fruits, and 7019
Jer 40:12 gathered wine and s. fruits very 7019
Jer 48:32 spoiler is fallen upon thy s. fruits 7019

Da 2:35 the chaff of the **s.** threshingfloors; 7007
Am 3:15 winter house with the **s.** house; 7019
Am 8:1 me: and behold a basket of **s.** fruit. 7019
Am 8:2 And I said, A basket of **s.** fruit. 7019
Mic 7: they have gathered the **s.** fruits, 7019
Zec 14:8 sea: in **s.** and in winter shall it be 7019
Mt 24:32 **leaves, ye know that s. is nigh:** *2330*
Mr 13:28 **leaves, ye know that s. is near:** *2330*
Lu 21:30 **that s. is now nigh at hand.** *2330*

SUMPTUOUSLY See also PRESUMPTUOUSLY.
Lu 16:19 **fine linen, and fared s. every day:** *2988*

SUN See also SUNRISING.
Ge 15:12 And when the **s.** was going down, 8121
Ge 15:17 when the **s.** went down, and it was 8121
Ge 19:23 The **s.** was risen upon the earth 8121
Ge 28:11 all night, because the **s.** was set; 8121
Ge 32:31 as he passed over Penuel the **s.** rose 8121
Ge 37:9 the **s.** and the moon and the eleven 8121
Ex 16:21 when the **s.** waxed hot, it melted. 8121
Ex 17:12 until the going down of the **s.** 8121
Ex 22:3 If the **s.** be risen upon him, there 8121
Ex 22:26 unto him by that the **s.** goeth down: 8121
Le 22:7 And when the **s.** is down, he shall be 8121
Nu 2:3 toward the rising of the **s.** shall they
Nu 25:4 up before the Lord against the **s.**, 8121
De 4:19 and when thou seest the **s.**, and the 8121
De 11:30 the way where the **s.** goeth down, 8121
De 16:6 at the going down of the **s.**, at the 8121
De 17:3 either the **s.**, or moon, or any of the 8121
De 23:11 when the **s.** is down, he shall come 8121
De 24:13 again when the **s.** goeth down, 8121
De 24:15 neither shall the **s.** go down upon it; 8121
De 33:14 fruits brought forth by the **s.**, 8121
Jos 1:4 sea toward the going down of the **s.**, 8121
Jos 8:29 and as soon as the **s.** was down, 8121
Jos 10:12 **S.**, stand thou still upon Gibeon; 8121
Jos 10:13 And the **s.** stood still, and the moon 8121
Jos 10:13 **s.** stood still in the midst of heaven, 8121
Jos 10:27 the time of the going down of the **s.**, 8121
Jos 12:1 Jordan toward the rising of the **s.**, 8121
Jg 5:31 as the **s.** when he goeth forth in his 8121
Jg 8:13 from battle before the **s.** was up, 2775
Jg 9:33 as soon as the **s.** is up, thou shalt 8121
Jg 14:18 day before the **s.** went down, 2775
Jg 19:14 and the **s.** went down upon them 8121
1Sa 11:9 by that time the **s.** be hot, ye shall 8121
2Sa 2:24 the **s.** went down when they were 8121
2Sa 3:35 or ought else, till the **s.** be down. 8121
2Sa 12:11 with thy wives in the sight of this **s.** 8121
2Sa 12:12 before all Israel, and before the **s.** 8121
2Sa 23:4 of the morning, when the **s.** riseth, 8121
1Ki 22:36 host about the going down of the **s.**, 8121
2Ki 3:22 and the **s.** shone upon the water, 8121
2Ki 23:5 burned incense unto Baal, to the **s.**, 8121
2Ki 23:11 kings of Judah had given to the **s.**, 8121
2Ki 23:11 and burned the chariots of the **s.** 8121
2Ch 18:34 time of the **s.** going down he died. 8121
Ne 7:3 he opened until the **s.** be hot; 8121
Job 8:16 He is green before the **s.**, and his 8121
Job 9:7 Which commandeth the **s.**, and it 2775
Job 30:28 I went mourning without the **s.** 2535
Job 31:26 If I beheld the **s.** when it shined, 216
Ps 19:4 hath he set a tabernacle for the **s.**, 8121
Ps 50:1 the earth from the rising of the **s.** 8121
Ps 58:8 that they may not see the **s.** 8121
Ps 72:5 as long as the **s.** and moon endure, 8121
Ps 72:17 be continued as long as the **s.**: 8121
Ps 74:16 hast prepared the light and the **s.** 8121
Ps 84:11 For the Lord God is a **s.** and shield: 8121
Ps 89:36 and his throne as the **s.** before me. 8121
Ps 104:19 the **s.** knoweth his going down 8121
Ps 104:22 The **s.** ariseth, they gather 8121
Ps 113:3 From the rising of the **s.** unto the 8121
Ps 121:6 The **s.** shall not smite thee by day, 8121
Ps 136:8 The **s.** to rule by day: for his mercy 8121
Ps 148:3 Praise ye him, **s.** and moon: praise 8121
Ec 1:3 labour...he taketh under the **s.**? 8121
Ec 1:5 the **s.** also ariseth, and the **s.** goeth 8121
Ec 1:9 there is no new thing under the **s.** 8121
Ec 1:14 works that are done under the **s.**; 8121
Ec 2:11 and there was no profit under the **s.** 8121
Ec 2:17 work that is wrought under the **s.**: 8121
Ec 2:18 labour...I had taken under the **s.** 8121
Ec 2:19 shewed myself wise under the **s.** 8121
Ec 2:20 labour which I took under the **s.** 8121
Ec 2:22 he hath laboured under the **s.**? 8121
Ec 3:16 under the **s.** the place of judgment, 8121
Ec 4:1 the oppressions...done under the **s.** 8121
Ec 4:3 evil work that is done under the **s.** 8121
Ec 4:7 and I saw vanity under the **s.** 8121
Ec 4:15 the living which walk under the **s.**, 8121
Ec 5:13 sore evil...I have seen under the **s.**, 8121
Ec 5:18 labour that he taketh under the **s.** 8121
Ec 6:1 evil which I have seen under the **s.**, 8121
Ec 6:5 Moreover he hath not seen the **s.**, 8121
Ec 6:12 shall be after him under the **s.**? 8121
Ec 7:11 is profit to them that see the **s.** 8121
Ec 8:9 work that is done under the **s.**: 8121
Ec 8:15 hath no better thing under the **s.**, 8121
Ec 8:15 which God giveth him under the **s.** 8121
Ec 8:17 the work that is done under the **s.**: 8121
Ec 9:3 things that are done under the **s.**, 8121
Ec 9:6 any thing that is done under the **s.** 8121
Ec 9:9 he hath given thee under the **s.**, 8121
Ec 9:9 labour...thou takest under the **s.** 8121
Ec 9:11 I returned, and saw under the **s.**, 8121
Ec 9:13 wisdom have I seen...under the **s.**, 8121
Ec 10:5 evil which I have seen under the **s.**, 8121
Ec 11:7 it is for the eyes to behold the **s.**: 8121
Ec 12:2 While the **s.**, or the light, or the 8121
Ca 1:6 because the **s.** hath looked upon me: 8121
Ca 6:10 fair as the moon, clear as the **s.**, 2535
Isa 13:10 **s.** shall be darkened in his going 8121
Isa 24:34 confounded, and the **s.** ashamed, 2535
Isa 30:26 moon shall be as the light of the **s.**, 2535
Isa 30:26 light of the **s.** shall be sevenfold, 8121
Isa 38:8 is gone down in the **s.** dial of Ahaz, 8121
Isa 38:8 So the **s.** returned ten degrees, by 8121
Isa 41:25 from the rising of the **s.** shall he 8121
Isa 45:6 may know from the rising of the **s.**, 8121
Isa 49:10 shall the heat nor **s.** smite them: 8121
Isa 59:19 his glory from the rising of the **s.** 8121
Isa 60:19 The **s.** shall be no more thy light by 8121
Isa 60:20 Thy **s.** shall no more go down; 8121
Jer 8:2 they shall spread them before the **s.**, 8121
Jer 15:9 her **s.** is gone down while it was yet 8121
Jer 31:35 giveth the **s.** for a light by day, 8121
Eze 8:16 they worshipped the **s.** toward the 8121
Eze 32:7 I will cover the **s.** with a cloud, and 8121
Da 6:14 laboured till...going down of the **s.** 8122
Joe 2:10 the **s.** and the moon shall be dark, 8121
Joe 2:31 **s.** shall be turned into darkness, 8121
Joe 3:15 **s.** and the moon shall be darkened, 8121
Am 8:9 cause the **s.** to go down at noon, 8121
Jon 4:8 came to pass, when the **s.** did rise, 8121
Jon 4:8 the **s.** beat upon the head of Jonah, 8121
Mic 3:6 and the **s.** shall go down over the 8121
Na 3:17 when the **s.** ariseth they flee away, 8121
Hab 3:11 The **s.** and moon stood still in their 8121
Mal 1:11 from the rising of the **s.** even unto 8121
Mal 4:2 the **S.** of righteousness arise with 8121
Mt 5:45 **he maketh his s. to rise on the** *2246*
Mt 13:6 **And when the s. was up, they were** *2246*
Mt 13:43 **the righteous shine forth as the s.** *2246*
Mt 17:2 his face did shine as the **s.**, and his *2246*
Mt 24:29 **days shall the s. be darkened,** *2246*
Mk 1:3 when the **s.** did set, they brought *2246*
Mk 4:6 **But when the s. was up, it was** *2246*
Mk 13:24 **the s. shall be darkened, and the** *2246*
Mk 16:2 the sepulchre at the rising of the **s.** *2246*
Lu 4:40 Now when the **s.** was setting, all they *2246*
Lu 21:25 **And there shall be signs in the s.,** *2246*
Lu 23:45 And the **s.** was darkened, and the *2246*
Ac 2:20 **s.** shall be turned into darkness, *2246*
Ac 13:11 blind, not seeing the **s.** for a season *2246*
Ac 26:13 above the brightness of the **s.**, *2246*
Ac 27:20 when neither **s.** nor stars in many *2246*
1Co 15:41 There is one glory of the **s.**, and *2246*
Eph 4:26 not the **s.** go down upon your wrath: *2246*
Jas 1:11 For the **s.** is no sooner risen with a *2246*
Re 1:16 as the **s.** shineth in his strength. *2246*
Re 6:12 the **s.** became black as sackcloth of *2246*
Re 7:16 neither shall the **s.** light on them, *2246*
Re 8:12 the third part of the **s.** was smitten, *2246*
Re 9:2 the **s.** and the air were darkened by *2246*
Re 10:1 and his face was as it were the **s.**, *2246*
Re 12:1 a woman clothed with the **s.**, and *2246*
Re 16:8 poured out his vial upon the **s.**; *2246*
Re 19:17 I saw an angel standing in the **s.**; *2246*
Re 21:23 And the city had no need of the **s.**, *2246*
Re 22:5 no candle, neither light of the **s.**; *2246*

SUNDER See also ASUNDER; SUNDERED.
Ps 46:9 bow, and cutteth the spear in **s.**;
Ps 107:14 death, and break their bands in **s.**
Ps 107:16 of brass, and cut the bars of iron in **s.**
Isa 27:9 as chalkstones that are beaten in **s.**,
Isa 45:2 and cut in **s.** the bars of iron:
Na 1:13 thee, and will burst thy bonds in **s.**
Lu 12:46 **is not aware, and will cut him in s.,**

SUNDERED
Job 41:17 together, that they cannot be **s.** 6504

SUNDRY
Heb 1:1 at **s.** times and in divers manners *4181*

SUNG See also SANG.
Isa 26:1 In that day shall this song be **s.** in 7891
Mt 26:30 when they had **s.** an hymn, they *5214*
Mk 14:26 when they had **s.** an hymn, they *5214*
Re 5:9 they **s.** a new song, saying, Thou *103*
Re 14:3 **s.** as it were a new song before the *103*

SUNK See also SANK.
1Sa 17:49 the stone **s.** into his forehead; 2883
2Ki 9:24 and he **s.** down in his chariot 3766
Ps 9:15 heathen are **s.** down in the pit 2883
Jer 38:6 mire: so Jeremiah **s.** in the mire 2883
Jer 38:22 thy feet are **s.** in the mire, and they 2883
La 2:9 Her gates are **s.** into the ground; 2883
Ac 20:9 preaching, he **s.** down with sleep, *2702*

SUNRISING
Nu 21:11 is before Moab, toward the **s.** 4217,8121
Nu 34:15 Jericho eastward, toward the **s.** 4217
De 4:41,47 side Jordan toward the **s.**; 4217,8121
Jos 1:15 this side Jordan toward the **s.** 4217,8121
Jos 13:5 and all Lebanon, toward the **s.**, 4217,8121
Jos 19:12 Sarid eastward toward the **s.** 4217,8121
Jos 19:27 And turneth toward the **s.** to 4217,8121
Jos 19:34 upon Jordan toward the **s.** 4217,8121
Jg 20:43 against Gibeah toward the **s.** 4217,8121

SUP See also SUPPED.
Hab 1:9 faces shall **s.** up as the east wind, 4041
Lu 17:8 **Make ready wherewith I may s.,** *1172*
Re 3:20 **in to him, and will s. with him,** *1172*

SUPERFLUITY
Jas 1:21 filthiness and **s.** of naughtiness, *4050*

SUPERFLUOUS
Le 21:18 hath a flat nose, or any thing **s.**, 8311
Le 22:23 any thing **s.** or lacking in his parts, 8311
2Co 9:1 it is **s.** for me to write to you: *4053*

SUPERSCRIPTION
Mt 22:20 them, **Whose is this image and s.?** *1923*
Mk 12:16 them, **Whose is this image and s.?** *1923*
Mk 15:26 the **s.** of his accusation was written *1923*
Lu 20:24 **Whose image and s. hath it?** They *1923*
Lu 23:38 And a **s.** also was written over him *1923*

SUPERSTITION
Ac 25:19 against him of their own **s.**, and *1175*

SUPERSTITIOUS
Ac 17:22 that in all things ye are too **s.** *1174*

SUPPED
1Co 11:25 he took the cup, when he had **s.**, *1172*

SUPPER
Mk 6:21 birthday made a **s.** to his lords, *1173*
Lu 14:12 **thou makest a dinner or a s.,** *1173*
Lu 14:16 **A certain man made a great s.,** *1173*
Lu 14:17 **sent his servant at s. time to say** *1173*
Lu 14:24 **were bidden shall taste of my s.** *1173*
Lu 22:20 Likewise also the cup after **s.**, *1172*
Joh 12:2 There they made him a **s.**; and *1173*
Joh 13:2 **s.** being ended, the devil having *1173*
Joh 13:4 He riseth from **s.**, and laid aside *1173*
Joh 21:20 also leaned on his breast at **s.**, and *1173*
1Co 11:20 this is not to eat the Lord's **s.** *1173*
1Co 11:21 one taketh before other his own **s.** *1173*
Re 19:9 unto the marriage **s.** of the Lamb. *1173*
Re 19:17 unto the **s.** of the great God; *1173*

SUPPLANT See also SUPPLANTED.
Jer 9:4 for every brother will utterly **s.**, 6117

SUPPLANTED
Ge 27:36 for he hath **s.** me these two times: 6117

SUPPLE
Eze 16:4 thou washed in water to **s.** thee; 4935

SUPPLIANTS
Zep 3:10 the rivers of Ethiopia my **s.**, 6282

SUPPLICATION See also SUPPLICATIONS.
1Sa 13:12 I have not made **s.** unto the Lord: 2470
1Ki 8:28 prayer of thy servant, and to his **s.**, 8467
1Ki 8:30 And hearken thou to the **s.** of thy 8467
1Ki 8:33 make **s.** unto thee in this house: 2603
1Ki 8:38 prayer and **s.** soever be made by 8467
1Ki 8:45 in heaven their prayer and their **s.**, 8467
1Ki 8:45 and make **s.** unto thee in the land 2603
1Ki 8:49 their prayer and their **s.** in heaven 8467
1Ki 8:52 be open unto the **s.** of thy servant, 8467
1Ki 8:52 and unto the **s.** of thy people Israel, 8467
1Ki 8:54 all this prayer and **s.** unto the Lord, 8467
1Ki 8:59 I have made **s.** before the Lord, 2603
1Ki 9:3 have heard thy prayer and thy **s.**, 8467
2Ch 6:19 prayer of thy servant, and to his **s.**, 8467
2Ch 6:24 make **s.** before thee in this house; 2603
2Ch 6:29 what **s.** soever shall be made of 8467
2Ch 6:35 heavens their prayer and their **s.**, 8467
2Ch 33:13 and heard his **s.**, and brought him 8467
Es 4:8 the king, to make **s.** unto him, 2603
Job 8:5 and make thy **s.** to the Almighty; 2603
Job 9:15 but I would make **s.** to my judge 2603
Ps 6:9 The Lord hath heard my **s.**; the 8467
Ps 30:8 and unto the Lord I made **s.** 2603
Ps 55:1 and hide not thyself from my **s.** 8467
Ps 119:170 Let my **s.** come before thee: 8467
Ps 142:1 unto the Lord did I make my **s.** 2603
Isa 45:14 they shall make **s.** unto thee, 6419
Jer 36:7 present their **s.** before the Lord, 8467
Jer 37:20 let my **s.**, I pray thee, be accepted 8467
Jer 38:26 I presented my **s.** before the king, 8467
Jer 42:2 our **s.** be accepted before thee, and 8467
Jer 42:9 me to present your **s.** before him; 8467
Da 6:11 and making **s.** before his God. 2604
Da 9:20 presenting my **s.** before the Lord 8467
Ho 12:4 he wept, and made **s.** unto him: 2603
Ac 1:14 with one accord in prayer and **s.**, *1162*
Eph 6:18 with all prayer and **s.** in the Spirit, *1162*
Eph 6:18 perseverance and **s.** for all saints; *1162*
Php 4:6 by prayer and **s.** with thanksgiving *1162*

SUPPLICATIONS
2Ch 6:21 unto the **s.** of thy servant, and 8469
2Ch 6:39 their prayer and their **s.**, and 8467
Job 41:3 Will he make many **s.** unto thee? 8469
Ps 28:2 Hear the voice of my **s.**, when I cry 8469
Ps 28:6 he hath heard the voice of my **s.** 8469
Ps 31:22 heardest the voice of my **s.** when I 8469
Ps 86:6 and attend to the voice of my **s.** 8469
Ps 116:1 he hath heard my voice and my **s.** 8469
Ps 130:2 be attentive to the voice of my **s.** 8469
Ps 140:6 hear the voice of my **s.**, O Lord. 8469
Ps 143:1 prayer, O Lord, give ear to my **s.** 8469
Jer 3:21 weeping and **s.** of the children of 8469
Jer 31:9 and with **s.** will I lead them: 8469
Da 9:3 Lord God, to seek by prayer and **s.**, 8469
Da 9:17 prayer of thy servant, and his **s.**, 8469
Da 9:18 for we do not present our **s.** before 8469
Da 9:23 At the beginning of thy **s.** the 8469
Zec 12:10 the spirit of grace and of **s.**: and 8469
1Ti 2:1 that, first of all, **s.**, prayers, *1162*
1Ti 5:5 continueth in **s.** and prayers night *1162*
Heb 5:7 he had offered up prayers and **s.** *2428*

SUPPLIED
1Co 16:17 lacking on your part they have **s.** *378*
2Co 11:9 which came from Macedonia **s.** *4322*

SUPPLIETH
2Co 9:12 not only **s.** the want of the saints, *4322*
Eph 4:16 by that which every joint **s.**, *2024*

SUPPLY See also SUPPLIED; SUPPLIETH.
2Co 8:14 abundance...be a **s.** for their want,
2Co 8:14 also may be a **s.** for your want:
Php 1:19 the **s.** of the Spirit of Jesus Christ, *2024*
Php 2:30 to **s.** your lack of service toward *378*
Php 4:19 But my God shall **s.** all your need *4137*

SUPPORT
Ac 20:35 labouring ye ought to **s.** the weak, *482*
1Th 5:14 **s.** the weak, be patient toward all *472*

SUPPOSE See also SUPPOSED; SUPPOSING.
2Sa 13:32 not my Lord **s.** that they have slain 559
Lu 7:43 I **s.** that he, to whom he forgave *5274*
Lu 12:51 **S. ye that I am come to give** *1380*
Lu 13:2 **S. ye that these Galileans were** *1380*
Joh 21:25 I **s.** that even the world itelf *3633*
Ac 2:15 these are not drunken, as ye **s.**, *5274*
1Co 7:26 I **s.** therefore that this is good for *3543*
2Co 11:5 I **s.** I was not a whit behind the *3049*
Heb 10:29 much sorer punishment, **s.** ye, *1380*
1Pe 5:12 a faithful brother...as I **s.** *3049*

SUPPOSED
Mt 20:10 **s. that they should have received** *3543*
Mk 6:49 sea, they **s.** it had been a spirit, *1380*
Lu 3:23 being (as was **s.**) the son of Joseph, *3543*
Lu 24:37 and **s.** that they had seen a spirit. *1380*
Ac 7:25 For he **s.** his brethren would have *3543*
Ac 21:29 whom they **s.**...Paul had brought *3543*
Ac 25:18 accusation of such things as I **s.** *5282*
Php 2:25 I **s.** it necessary to send to you *2233*

SUPPOSING
Lu 2:44 they, **s.** him...in the company, *3543*
Joh 20:15 She, **s.** him to be the gardener, *1380*
Ac 14:19 out of the city, **s.** he had been dead *3543*
Ac 16:27 **s.** that the prisoners had been fled *3543*
Ac 27:13 **s.** that they had obtained their *1380*
Php 1:16 **s.** to add affliction to my bonds: *3633*
1Ti 6:5 truth, **s.** that gain is godliness: *3543*

SUPREME
1Pe 2:13 whether it be to the king, as **s.**; *5242*

SUR (sur)
2Ki 11:6 part shall be at the gate of **S.**; 5495

SURE See also ASSURE.
Ge 23:17 borders round about, were made **s.** 6965
Ge 23:20 were made **s.** unto Abraham for a 6965
Ex 3:19 I am **s.**...the king of Egypt will not 3045
Nu 32:23 and be **s.** your sin will find you out. 3045
De 12:23 be **s.** that thou eat not the blood: 2388
1Sa 2:35 and I will build him a **s.** house; 539
1Sa 20:7 be **s.**...evil is determined by him. 3045
1Sa 25:28 certainly make my lord a **s.** house; 539
2Sa 1:10 I was **s.** that he could not live 3045
2Sa 23:5 ordered in all things, and **s.** 8104
1Ki 11:38 and build thee a **s.** house, as I built 539
Ne 9:38 we make a **s.** covenant, and write 548
Job 24:22 riseth up, and no man is **s.** of life. 539
Ps 19:7 the testimony of the Lord is **s.**, 539
Ps 93:5 Thy testimonies are very **s.** 539
Ps 111:7 all his commandments are **s.** 539
Pr 6:3 thyself, and make **s.** thy friend. 7292
Pr 11:15 and he that hateth suretiship is **s.** 982
Pr 11:18 righteousness shall be a **s.** reward. 571
Isa 22:23 fasten him as a nail in a **s.** place; 539
Isa 22:25 nail that is fastened in the **s.** place 539
Isa 28:16 corner stone, a **s.** foundation: 3245
Isa 32:18 and in **s.** dwellings, and in quiet 4009
Isa 33:16 given him; his waters shall be **s.** 539
Isa 55:3 you, even the **s.** mercies of David. 539
Da 2:45 and the interpretation thereof **s.** 546
Da 4:26 thy kingdom shall be **s.** unto thee, 7011
Mt 27:64 sepulchre be made **s.** until the third *805*
Mt 27:65 your way, make it as **s.** as ye can. *805*
Mt 27:66 went, and made the sepulchre **s.**, *805*
Lu 10:11 **be ye s. of this, that the kingdom** *1097*
Joh 6:69 are **s.** that thou art that Christ, *1097*
Joh 16:30 Now are we **s.** that thou knowest *1492*
Ac 13:34 give you the **s.** mercies of David. *4103*
Ro 2:2 we are **s.** that the judgment of God *1492*
Ro 4:16 might be **s.** to all the seed; *949*
Ro 15:29 And I am **s.** that, when I come *1492*
2Ti 2:19 the foundation of God standeth **s.**, *4731*
Heb 6:19 of the soul, both **s.** and stedfast, *804*
2Pe 1:10 make your calling and election **s.** *949*
2Pe 1:19 also a more **s.** word of prophecy; *949*

SURELY
Ge 2:17 thou eatest thereof thou shalt **s.** die.
Ge 3:4 unto the woman, Ye shall not **s.** die:
Ge 9:5 **s.** your blood...will I require; 389
Ge 18:18 Abraham shall **s.** become a great and
Ge 20:7 know thou that thou shalt **s.** die, 3588
Ge 20:11 **S.** the fear of God is not in this 7535
Ge 26:11 or his wife shall **s.** be put to death.
Ge 28:16 said, **S.** the Lord is in this place; 403
Ge 28:22 me I will **s.** give the tenth unto thee.
Ge 29:14 **S.** thou art my bone and my flesh. 389
Ge 29:32 **S.** the Lord hath looked upon my 3588
Ge 30:16 **s.** I have hired thee with my son's
Ge 31:42 **s.** thou hadst sent me away now 3588
Ge 32:12 I will **s.** do thee good, and make thy
Ge 42:16 by the life of Pharaoh **s.** ye are spies.
Ge 43:10 **s.**...we had returned this second 3588
Ge 44:28 **S.** he is torn in pieces; and I saw 389
Ge 46:4 and I will also **s.** bring thee up again:
Ge 50:24 God will **s.** visit you, and bring you
Ge 50:25 God will **s.** visit you, and ye shall
Ex 2:14 and said, **S.** this thing is known. 403
Ex 3:7 I have **s.** seen the affliction of my
Ex 3:16 I have **s.** visited you, and seen that
Ex 4:25 **S.** a bloody husband art thou to 3588
Ex 11:1 he shall **s.** thrust you out hence
Ex 13:19 of Israel, saying, God will **s.** visit you;
Ex 18:18 Thou wilt **s.** wear away, both thou,
Ex 19:12 the mount shall be **s.** put to death:
Ex 19:13 touch it, but he shall **s.** be stoned, 3588
Ex 21:12 so that he die, shall be **s.** put to death.
Ex 21:15 or his mother, shall be **s.** put to death.
Ex 21:16 in his hand, he shall **s.** be put to death.
Ex 21:17 or his mother, shall **s.** be put to death.
Ex 21:20 his hand; he shall be **s.** punished.
Ex 21:22 he shall be **s.** punished, according as
Ex 21:28 then the ox shall be **s.** stoned, and his
Ex 21:36 he shall **s.** pay ox for ox; and the dead
Ex 22:6 the fire shall **s.** make restitution.
Ex 22:14 not with it, he shall **s.** make it good.
Ex 22:16 he shall **s.** endow her to be his wife.
Ex 22:19 with a beast shall **s.** be put to death.
Ex 22:23 at all unto me, I will **s.** hear their cry;
Ex 23:4 shalt **s.** bring it back to him again.
Ex 23:5 help him, thou shalt **s.** help with him.
Ex 23:33 it will **s.** be a snare unto thee. 3588
Ex 31:14 that defileth it shall **s.** be put to death:
Ex 31:15 day, he shall **s.** be put to death.
Ex 40:15 anointing shall **s.** be an everlasting
Le 20:2 Molech; he shall be put to death:
Le 20:9 or his mother shall be **s.** put to death:
Le 20:10 the adulteress shall be **s.** put to death.
Le 20:11 both of them shall **s.** be put to death;
Le 20:12 both of them shall **s.** be put to death:
Le 20:13 they shall **s.** be put to death; their
Le 20:15 a beast, he shall **s.** e put to death:
Le 20:16 beast: they shall **s.** be put to death;
Le 20:27 a wizard, shall **s.** be put to death:
Le 24:16 the Lord, he shall **s.** be put to death,
Le 24:17 any man shall **s.** be put to death.
Le 27:29 redeemed; but shall **s.** be put to death.
Nu 13:27 and **s.** it floweth with milk and honey;
Nu 14:23 **S.** they shall not see the land 518
Nu 14:35 I will **s.** do it unto all this evil 518
Nu 15:35 The man shall be **s.** put to death:
Nu 18:15 firstborn of man shalt thou **s.** redeem,
Nu 22:33 **s.** now also I had slain thee, and 3588
Nu 23:23 **S.** there is no enchantment against
Nu 26:65 They shall **s.** die in the wilderness.
Nu 27:7 thou shalt **s.** give them a possession of
Nu 32:11 **S.** none of the men that came up 518
Nu 35:16, 17,18 shall **s.** be put to death.
Nu 35:21 smote him shall **s.** be put to death;
Nu 35:31 death: but he shall be **s.** put to death.
De 1:35 **S.** there shall not one of these men 518
De 4:6 **S.** this great nation is a wise and
De 8:19 this day that ye shall **s.** perish. 3588
De 13:9 But thou shalt **s.** kill him; thine 3588
De 13:15 **s.** smite the inhabitants of that city
De 15:8 shalt **s.** lend him sufficient for his need,
De 15:10 Thou shalt **s.** give him, and thine
De 16:15 therefore thou shalt **s.** rejoice. 389
De 22:4 **s.** help him to lift them up again.
De 23:21 thy God will **s.** require it of thee;
De 30:18 that ye shall **s.** perish, and that 3588
De 31:18 And I will **s.** hide my face in that day
Jos 14:9 **S.** the land whereon thy feet have 518
Jg 3:24 said, **S.** he covereth his feet in his 389
Jg 4:9 And she said, I will **s.** go with thee:
Jg 6:16 **S.** I will be with thee, and thou 3588
Jg 11:31 of Ammon, shall **s.** be the Lord's,
Jg 13:22 We shall **s.** die, because we have seen
Jg 15:13 hand: but **s.** we will not kill thee.
Jg 20:39 **S.** they are smitten down before 389
Jg 21:5 saying, He shall **s.** be put to death.
Ru 1:10 **S.** we will return with thee unto 3588
1Sa 9:6 all that he saith cometh **s.** to pass:
1Sa 14:39 Jonathan my son, he shall **s.** die. 3588
1Sa 14:44 for thou shalt **s.** die, Jonathan.

1Sa 15:32 S. the bitterness of death is past. 403
1Sa 16:6 S. the Lord's anointed is before........... 389
1Sa 17:25 s. to defy Israel is he come up: 3588
1Sa 20:26 he is not clean; s. he is not clean. 3588
1Sa 20:31 him unto me, for he shall s. die. ....
1Sa 22:16 Thou shalt s. die, Ahimelech, thou,...........
1Sa 22:22 there, that he would s. tell Saul: ....
1Sa 24:20 well that thou shalt s. be king,..................
1Sa 25:21 S. in vain have I kept all that this 389
1Sa 25:34 s. there had not been left unto..... 3588,518
1Sa 28:2 S. thou shalt know what thy............. 3651
1Sa 29:6 S., as the Lord liveth, thou hast been.......
1Sa 30:8 for thou shalt s. overtake them, ...
2Sa 2:27 s. then in the meaning the people....... 3588
2Sa 9:7 s. shew the kindness for Jonathan....... 3588
2Sa 11:23 S. the men prevailed against us, ... 3588
2Sa 12:5 hath done this thing shall s. die: ....
2Sa 12:14 that is born unto thee shall s. die. ....
2Sa 15:21 s. in what place my lord the king 3588
2Sa 18:2 I will s. go forth with you myself also........
2Sa 20:18 They shall s. ask counsel at Abel:.............
2Sa 24:24 will s. buy it of thee at a price: 3588,518
1Ki 2:37 for certain that thou shalt s. die: ....
1Ki 2:42 any whither, that thou shalt s. die? ....
1Ki 8:13 I have s. built thee an house to.......... 403
1Ki 11:2 for s. they will turn away your heart 403
1Ki 11:11 I will s. rend the kingdom from thee, ...
1Ki 13:32 of Samaria, shall s. come to pass........ 3588
1Ki 18:15 I will s. shew myself unto him to 3588
1Ki 20:23, 25 s. we shall be stronger than 518
1Ki 22:32 they said, S. it is the king of Israel. 389
2Ki 1:4,6, 16 art gone up, but shalt s. die.......... 3588
2Ki 3:14 s., were it not that I regard the......... 3588
2Ki 3:23 the kings are s. slain, and they have ....
2Ki 5:11 He will s. come out to me, and stand,.......
2Ki 8:10 shewed me that he shall s. die.................
2Ki 8:14 me that thou shouldest s. recover. ....
2Ki 9:26 S. I have seen yesterday the blood of ....
2Ki 18:30 The Lord will s. deliver us, and this ....
2Ki 23:22 S. there was not holden such a.......... 3588
2Ki 24:3 S. at the commandment of the 389
Es 6:13 him, but shalt s. fall before him......... 3588
Job 8:6 s. now he would awake for thee,......... 3588
Job 13:3 S. I would speak to the Almighty,........ 199
Job 13:10 He will s. reprove you, if ye do ....
Job 14:18 And s. the mountain falling cometh....... 199
Job 18:21 S. such are the dwellings of the 389
Job 20:20 S. he shall not feel quietness in 3588
Job 28:1 S. there is a vein for the silver, and ... 3588
Job 31:36 S. I would take it upon my......... 518,3808
Job 33:8 S....hast spoken in mine hearing,......... 389
Job 34:12 Yea, s. God will not do wickedly,.......... 551
Job 34:31 S. it is meet to be said unto God,....... 3588
Job 35:13 S. God will not hear vanity, neither...... 389
Job 37:20 s. he shall be swallowed up............... 3588
Job 40:20 S. the mountains bring him forth........ 3588
Ps 23:6 S. goodness and mercy shall............... 389
Ps 32:6 s. in the floods of great waters 7535
Ps 39:6 S. every man walketh in a vain........... 389
Ps 39:6 s. they are disquieted in vain: he 389
Ps 39:11 like a moth: s. every man is vanity. 389
Ps 62:9 S. men of low degree are vanity,......... 389
Ps 73:18 S. thou didst set them in slippery 389
Ps 76:10 S. the wrath of man shall praise.......... 3588
Ps 77:11 s. I will remember thy wonders of old.......
Ps 85:9 S. his salvation is nigh them that 389
Ps 91:3 S. he shall deliver thee from the 3588
Ps 112:6 S. he shall not be moved for ever: 3588
Ps 131:2 S. I have behaved and quieted 518,3808
Ps 132:3 S. I will not come into...tabernacle....... 518
Ps 139:11 S. the darkness shall cover me:........... 389
Ps 139:19 S. thou wilt slay the wicked, O God: 518
Ps 140:13 S. the righteous shall give thanks......... 389
Pr 1:17 S. in vain the net is spread in the 3588
Pr 3:34 S. he scorneth the scorners: but 518
Pr 10:9 that walketh uprightly walketh s.......... 983
Pr 22:16 to the rich, shall s. come to want. 389
Pr 23:18 For s. there is an end; and thine...........
Pr 30:2 S. I am...brutish than any man, ... 3588
Pr 30:33 S. the churning of milk bringeth.......... 3588
Ec 4:16 S. this also is vanity and vexation....... 3588
Ec 7:7 S. oppression maketh a wise man....... 3588
Ec 8:12 s. I know it shall be well with them.... 3588
Ec 10:11 S. the serpent will bite without 518
Isa 7:9 s. ye shall not be established............ 3588
Isa 14:24 S. as I have thought, so shall....... 518,3808
Isa 16:7 ye mourn; s. they are stricken. 389
Isa 19:11 S. the princes of Zoan are fools, ... 389
Isa 22:14 S. this iniquity shall not be purged 518
Isa 22:17 mighty captivity, and will s. cover thee. .....
Isa 22:18 He will s. violently turn and toss thee ....
Isa 29:16 S. your turning of things upside........... 518
Isa 36:15 saying, The Lord will s. deliver us:..........
Isa 40:7 upon it: s. the people is grass. 403
Isa 45:14 S. God is in thee; and there is none...... 389
Isa 45:24 S., shall one say, in the Lord have I 389
Isa 49:4 s. my judgment is with the Lord,......... 403
Isa 49:18 shalt s. clothe thee with them all........ 3588
Isa 53:4 S. he hath borne our griefs, and.......... 403
Isa 54:15 they shall s. gather together, but not ....
Isa 60:9 S. the isles shall wait for me, and 3588
Isa 62:8 S. I will no more give thy corn to....... 518
Isa 63:8 For he said, S. they are my people, ... 389
Jer 2:35 s. his anger shall turn from me........... 389
Jer 3:20 S. as a wife treacherously 403
Jer 4:10 s. thou hast greatly deceived this........ 403
Jer 5:2 Lord liveth; s. they swear falsely......... 403
Jer 5:4 S. these are poor; they are foolish:...... 389
Jer 8:13 I will s. consume them, saith the.............
Jer 16:19 S. our fathers have inherited lies, ... 389
Jer 22:6 s. I...make thee a wilderness,...... 518,3808
Jer 22:22 s. then shalt thou be ashamed, and..... 3588
Jer 24:8 s. thus saith the Lord, So will I give... 3588
Jer 26:8 took him, saying, Thou shalt s. die. ....
Jer 26:15 ye shall s. bring innocent blood 3588
Jer 31:18 I have s. heard Ephraim bemoaning ....
Jer 31:19 S. after...I was turned, I repented;..... 3588
Jer 31:20 I will s. have mercy upon him, saith..........
Jer 32:4 shall s. be delivered into the hand of.........
Jer 34:3 not escape...but shalt s. be taken, ... 3588
Jer 36:16 will s. tell the king of all these words........
Jer 37:9 The Chaldeans shall s. depart from us: ......
Jer 38:3 This city shall s. be given into the...........
Jer 38:15 thee, wilt thou not s. put me to death?......
Jer 39:18 For I will s. deliver thee, and thou ....
Jer 44:25 We will s. perform our vows that we ....
Jer 44:25 ye will s. accomplish your vows, and.........
Jer 44:25 your vows, and s. perform your vows. ......
Jer 44:29 my words shall s. stand against................
Jer 46:18 S. as Tabor is among...mountains,....... 3588
Jer 49:12 but thou shalt s. drink of it. 3588
Jer 49:20 S. the least of the flock shall 518,3808
Jer 49:20 s. he...make their habitations....... 518,3808
Jer 50:45 S. the least of the flock shall 518,3808
Jer 50:45 s. he shall make their habitation.... 518,3808
Jer 51:14 S. I will fill thee with men, as...... 3588,518
Jer 51:56 God of recompences shall s. requite..........
La 3:3 S. against me is he turned; he 389
Eze 3:6 S., had I sent thee to them, ... 518,3808
Eze 3:18 say unto the wicked, Thou shalt s. die; .....
Eze 3:21 and he doth not sin, he shall s. live,..........
Eze 5:11 S., because thou hast defiled 518,3808
Eze 17:16 s. in the place where the king...... 518,3808
Eze 17:19 s. mine oath that he hath 518,3808
Eze 18:9 he is just, he shall s. live, saith the...........
Eze 18:13 he shall s. die; his blood shall be upon.......
Eze 18:17 iniquity of his father, he shall s. live..........
Eze 18:19 and hath done them, he shall s. live. ....
Eze 18:21, 28 he shall s. live, he shall not die............
Eze 20:33 s. with a mighty hand, and.......... 518,3808
Eze 31:11 heathen: he shall s. deal with him:............
Eze 33:8 O wicked man, thou shalt s. die; ....
Eze 33:13 to the righteous, that he shall s. live;........
Eze 33:14 unto the wicked, Thou shalt s. die;...........
Eze 33:15 he shall s. live, he shall not die................
Eze 33:16 is lawful and right; he shall s. live............
Eze 33:27 s. they that are in the wastes 518,3808
Eze 34:8 s. because my flock became a...... 518,3808
Eze 36:5 S. in the fire of my jealousy 518,3808
Eze 36:7 S. the heathen that are about....... 518,3808
Eze 38:19 S. in that day there shall be a...... 518,3808
Ho 5:9 made known that which shall s. be. 539
Ho 12:11 s. they are vanity: they sacrifice.......... 389
Am 3:7 S. the Lord God will do nothing, ... 3588
Am 5:5 for Gilgal shall s. go into captivity,...........
Am 7:11 Israel shall s. be led away captive out ....
Am 7:17 Israel shall s. go into captivity forth ....
Am 8:7 S. I will never forget any of their.............
Mic 2:12 I will s. assemble, O Jacob, all of thee;......
Mic 2:12 I will s. gather the remnant of Israel: ....
Hab 2:3 it will s. come, it will not tarry. ....
Zep 2:9 S. Moab shall be as Sodom, and 3588
Zep 3:7 I said, S. thou wilt fear me, thou......... 389
Mt 26:73 S. thou also art one of them:.............. *230*
Mk 14:70 to Peter, S. thou art one of them:......... *230*
Lu 1:1 things which are most s. believed....... *4135*
Lu 4:23 will s. say unto me this proverb, ... *3843*
Joh 17:8 known s. that I came out from....... *230*
Heb 6:14 S. blessing I will bless thee, and........ *2229*
Re 22:20 things saith, S. I come quickly........ *3483*

SURETIES

Pr 22:26 or of them that are s. for debts. 6148

SURETISHIP

Pr 11:15 it: and he that hateth s. is sure.......... 8628

SURETY See also SURETIES.

Ge 15:13 Know of a s. that thy seed shall be 3045
Ge 18:13 Shall I of a s. bear a child, which......... 552
Ge 26:9 said, Behold, of a s. she is thy wife: 389
Ge 43:9 I will be s. for him; of my hand.......... 6148
Ge 44:32 servant became s. for the lad unto...... 6148
Job 17:3 down now, put me in a s. with thee;.... 6148
Ps 119:122 Be s. for thy servant for good: let....... 6148
Pr 6:1 My son, if thou be s. for thy friend, ... 6148
Pr 11:15 He that is s. for a stranger shall 6148
Pr 17:18 becometh s. in the presence of his 6161
Pr 20:16 garment that is s. for a stranger: 6148
Pr 27:13 garment that is s. for a stranger, ... 6148
Ac 12:11 Now I know of a s., that the Lord *230*
Heb 7:22 made a s. of a better testament. *1450*

SURFEITING

Lu 21:34 hearts be overcharged with s.,........ *2897*

SURMISINGS

1Ti 6:4 cometh envy, strife, railings, evil s., ... *5283*

SURNAME See also SURNAMED.

Isa 44:5 s. himself by the name of Israel. 3655
Mt 10:3 whose s. was Thaddaeus; *1941*
Ac 10:5 for one Simon, whose s. is Peter: *1941*
Ac 10:32 hither Simon, whose s. is Peter; *1941*
Ac 11:13 call for Simon, whose s. is Peter;........ *1941*
Ac 12:12 of John, whose s. was Mark............. *1941*
Ac 15:37 them John, whose s. was Mark.......... *2564*

SURNAMED

Isa 45:4 I have s. thee, though thou hast 3655
Mk 3:16 And Simon he s. Peter;............. *2007,3686*
Mk 3:17 he s. them Boanerges, which *2007,3686*
Lu 22:3 Satan into Judah s. Iscariot,.............. *1941*
Ac 1:23 Barsabas, who was s. Justus, and....... *1941*
Ac 4:36 by the apostles was s. Barnabas,........ *1941*
Ac 10:18 whether Simon, which was s. Peter, ... *1941*
Ac 15:22 Judas s. Barsabas, and Silas, chief...... *1941*

SURPRISED

Isa 33:14 fearfulness hath s. the hypocrites......... 270
Jer 48:41 taken, and the strong holds are s., ... 8610
Jer 51:41 is the praise of the whole earth s.! 8610

SUSAH See HAZAR-SUSAH.

SUSANCHITES (su'-san-kites)

Ezr 4:9 the S., the Dehavites, and the........... 7801

SUSANNA (su-zan'-nah)

Lu 8:3 wife of...Herod's steward, and S., ... *4677*

SUSI (su'-si)

Nu 13:11 of Manasseh, Gaddi the son of S........ 5485

SUSIM See HAZAR-SUSIM.

SUSTAIN See also SUSTAINED.

1Ki 17:9 a widow woman there to s. thee. 3557
Ne 9:21 Yea, forty years didst thou s. them..... 3557
Ps 55:22 upon the Lord, and he shall s. thee: ... 3557
Pr 18:14 spirit of a man will s. his infirmity;...... 3557

SUSTAINED

Ge 27:37 with corn and wine have I s. him: 5564
Ps 3:4 I awaked; for the Lord s. me. 5564
Isa 59:16 and his righteousness, it s. him.......... 5564

SUSTENANCE

Jg 6:4 left no s. for Israel, neither sheep, ... 4241
2Sa 19:32 and he had provided the king of s....... 3557
Ac 7:11 and our fathers found no s.. .... *5527*

SWADDLED

La 2:22 those...I have s. and brought up 2946
Eze 16:4 wast not salted at all, nor s. at all. 2853

SWADDLING See also SWADDLINGBAND.

Lu 2:7 and wrapped him in s. clothes,........... *4683*
Lu 2:12 find the babe wrapped in s. clothes,.... *4683*

SWADDLINGBAND
Job 38:9 and thick darkness a s. for it, 2854

SWADDLING-CLOTHES See SWADDLING and CLOTHES.

SWALLOW See also SWALLOWED; SWALLOWETH.
Nu 16:30 open her mouth, and s. them up, 1104
Nu 16:34 said, Lest the earth s. us up also. 1104
2Sa 20:19 why wilt thou s. up the inheritance 1104
2Sa 20:20 me, that I should s. up or destroy. 1104
Job 7:19 me alone till I s. down my spittle? 1104
Job 20:18 he restore, and shall not s. it down: 1104
Ps 21:9 Lord shall s. them up in his wrath, 1104
Ps 56:1 O God: for man would s. me up; 7602
Ps 56:2 Mine enemies would daily s. me up: 7602
Ps 57:3 reproach of him that would s. me 7602
Ps 69:15 neither let the deep s. me up, and 1104
Ps 84:3 house, and the s. a net for herself, 1866
Pr 1:12 us s. them up alive as the grave; 1104
Pr 26:2 by wandering, as the s. by flying, 1866
Ec 10:12 the lips of a fool will s. up himself. 1104
Isa 25:8 He will s. up death in victory; and 1104
Isa 38:14 Like a crane or a s., so did I 5693
Jer 8:7 s. observe the time of their coming; 5693
Ho 8:7 yield, the strangers shall s. it up. 1104
Am 8:4 this, O ye that s. up the needy, 7602
Ob 16 drink, and they shall s. down, 3886
Jon 1:17 a great fish to s. up Jonah. 1104
Mt 23:24 **strain at a gnat, and s. a camel.** *2666*

SWALLOWED
Ex 7:12 but Aaron's rod s. up their rods. 1104
Ex 15:12 thy right hand, the earth s. them. 1104
Nu 16:32 and s. them up, and their houses, 1104
Nu 26:10 and s. them up together with Korah, 1104
De 11:6 s. them up, and their households, 1104
2Sa 17:16 lest the king be s. up, and all the 1104
Job 6:3 sea: therefore my words are s. up. 3886
Job 20:15 He hath s. down riches, and he 1104
Job 37:20 man speak, surely he shall be s. up. 1104
Ps 35:25 them not say, We have s. him up. 1104
Ps 106:17 The earth opened and s. up Dathan, 1104
Ps 124:3 Then they had s. us up quick, when 1104
Isa 28:7 they are s. up of wine, they are out 1104
Isa 49:19 that s. thee up shall be far away. 1104
Jer 51:34 he hath s. me up like a dragon, he 1104
Jer 51:44 mouth that which he hath s. up: 1105
La 2:2 Lord hath s. up all the habitations 1104
La 2:5 as an enemy: he hath s. up Israel, 1104
La 2:5 he hath s. up all her palaces: he 1104
La 2:16 We have s. her up: certainly this is 1104
Eze 36:3 and s. you up on every side, that 7602
Ho 8:8 Israel is s. up: now shall they be 1104
1Co 15:54 written, Death is s. up in victory. *2666*
2Co 2:7 be s. up with overmuch sorrow. *2666*
2Co 5:4 that mortality might be s. up of life. *2666*
Re 12:16 s. up the flood which the dragon *2666*

SWALLOWETH
Job 5:5 the robber s. up their substance. 7602
Job 39:24 He s. the ground with fierceness 1572

SWAN
Le 11:18 And the s., and the pelican, and 8580
De 14:16 owl, and the great owl, and the s., 8580

SWARE See also SWAREST.
Ge 21:31 because there they s. both of them. 7650
Ge 24:7 me, and that s. unto me, saying, 7650
Ge 24:9 s. to him concerning that matter. 7650
Ge 25:33 me this day; and he s. unto him: 7650
Ge 26:3 oath which I s. unto Abraham thy 7650
Ge 26:31 the morning, and s. one to another: 7650
Ge 31:53 Jacob s. by the fear of his father 7650
Ge 47:31 unto me. And he s. unto him. 7650
Ge 50:24 the land which he s. to Abraham, 7650
Ex 13:5 he s. unto thy fathers to give thee, 7650
Ex 13:11 he s. unto thee and to thy fathers, 7650
Ex 33:1 the land which I s. unto Abraham, 7650
Nu 14:16 the land which he s. unto them, 7650
Nu 14:23 land which I s. unto their fathers, 7650
Nu 14:30 I s. to make you dwell therein, 5375
Nu 32:10 kindled the same time, and he s., 7650
Nu 32:11 the land which I s. unto Abraham, 7650
De 1:8 land which the Lord s. unto your 7650
De 1:34 your words, and was wroth, and s., 7650
De 1:35 land, which I s. to give unto your 7650
De 2:14 the host, as the Lord s. unto them. 7650
De 4:21 s. that I should not go over Jordan, 7650
De 4:31 covenant...which he s. unto them. 7650
De 6:10 land which he s. unto thy fathers, 7650
De 6:18 which the Lord s. unto thy fathers, 7650
De 6:23 land which he s. unto our fathers. 7650
De 7:12 which he s. unto thy fathers: 7650
De 7:13 land which he s. unto thy fathers 7650
De 8:1 the Lord s. unto your fathers. 7650
De 8:18 his covenant which he s. unto thy 7650
De 9:5 which the Lord s. unto thy fathers, 7650
De 10:11 which I s. unto their fathers to give 7650
De 11:9, 21 the Lord s. unto your fathers 7650
De 26:3 which the Lord s. unto your fathers 7650
De 28:11 which the Lord s. unto thy fathers 7650
De 30:20 which the Lord s. unto thy fathers, 7650
De 31:20 land which I s. unto their fathers, 7650
De 31:21 them into the land which I s. 7650
De 31:23 into the land which I s. unto them: 7650
De 34:4 the land which I s. unto Abraham, 7650
Jos 1:6 which I s. unto their fathers to give 7650
Jos 5:6 the Lord s. that he would not shew 7650
Jos 5:6 land, which the Lord s. unto their 7650
Jos 6:22 all that she hath, as ye s. unto her. 7650
Jos 9:15 princes of the congregation s. unto 7650
Jos 9:20 of the oath which we s. unto them. 7650
Jos 14:9 And Moses s. on that day, saying, 7650
Jos 21:43 he s. to give unto their fathers; 7650
Jos 21:44 to all that he s. unto their fathers: 7650
Jg 2:1 land which I s. unto your fathers; 7650
1Sa 19:6 and Saul s., As the Lord liveth, he 7650
1Sa 20:3 And David s. moreover, and said, 7650
1Sa 24:22 And David s. unto Saul. And Saul 7650
1Sa 28:10 Saul s. to her by the Lord, saying, 7650
2Sa 3:35 while it was yet day, David s., 7650
2Sa 19:23 not die. And the king s. unto him. 7650
2Sa 21:17 Then the men of David s. unto him, 7650
1Ki 1:29 the king s., and said, As the Lord 7650
1Ki 1:30 Even as I s. unto thee by the Lord 7650
1Ki 2:8 and I s. to him by the Lord, saying, 7650
1Ki 2:23 Then King Solomon s. by the Lord, 7650
2Ki 25:24 Gedaliah s. to them, and to their 7650
2ch 15:14 s. unto the Lord with a loud voice, 7650
Ezr 10:5 according to this word. And they s. 7650
Ps 95:11 Unto whom I s. in my wrath that 7650
Ps 132:2 he s. unto the Lord, and vowed 7650
Jer 38:16 So Zedekiah the king s. secretly 7650
Jer 40:9 son of Shaphan s. unto them and to 7650
Eze 16:8 I s. unto thee, and entered into a 7650
Da 12:7 and s. by him that liveth for ever 7650
Mk 6:23 he s. unto her, Whatsoever thou *3660*
Lu 1:73 The oath which he s. to our father *3660*
Heb 3:11 So I s. in my wrath, They shall not *3660*
Heb 3:18 to whom s. he that they should not *3660*
Heb 6:13 by no greater, he s. by himself, *3660*
Heb 7:21 The Lord s. and will not repent, *3660*
Re 10:6 s. by him that liveth for ever and *3660*

SWAREST
Ex 32:13 to whom thou s. by thine own self, 7650
Nu 11:12 the land which thou s. unto their 7650
De 26:15 as thou s. unto our fathers, a land 7650
1Ki 1:17 thou s. by the Lord thy God unto 7650
Ps 89:49 thou s. unto David in thy truth? 7650

SWARM See also SWARMS.
Ex 8:24 there came a grievous s. of flies 6157
Ex 8:24 by reason of the s. of flies. 6157
Jg 14:8 was a s. of bees and honey in the 5712

SWARMS
Ex 8:21 I will send s. of flies upon thee, 6157
Ex 8:21 Egyptians shall be full of s. of flies, 6157
Ex 8:22 that no s. of flies shall be there; 6157
Ex 8:29 that the s. of flies may depart from 6157
Ex 8:31 and he removed the s. of flies from 6157

SWEAR See also FORSWEAR; SWARE; SWEARETH; SWEARING; SWORN.
Ge 21:23 therefore s. unto me here by God 7650
Ge 21:24 And Abraham said, I will s. 7650
Ge 24:3 I will make thee s. by the Lord, the 7650
Ge 24:37 And my master made me s., saying, 7650
Ge 25:33 And Jacob said, S. to me this day; 7650
Ge 47:31 And he said, S. unto me. And he 7650
Ge 50:5 My father made me s., saying, Lo, I 7650
Ge 50:6 according as he made thee s. 7650
Ex 6:8 I did s. to give it to Abraham, 5375
Le 5:4 Or if a soul s., pronouncing with 7650
Le 19:12 ye shall not s. by my name falsely, 7650
Nu 30:2 or s. an oath to bind his soul with 7650
De 6:13 him, and shalt s. by his name. 7650
De 10:20 thou cleave, and s. by his name. 7650
Jos 2:12 unto me by the Lord, since I 7650
Jos 2:17 oath which thou hast made us s. 7650
Jos 2:20 oath which thou hast made us to s. 7650
Jos 23:7 nor cause to s. by them, neither 7650
Jg 15:12 said unto them, S. unto me, that 7650
1Sa 20:17 Jonathan caused David to s. again, 7650
1Sa 24:21 S. now...unto me by the Lord, 7650
1Sa 30:15 S. unto me by God, that thou wilt 7650
2Sa 19:7 for I s. by the Lord, if thou go not 7650
1Ki 1:13 O king, s. unto thine handmaid, 7650
1Ki 1:51 Let king Solomon s. unto me to 7650
1Ki 2:42 I not make thee to s. by the Lord, 7650
1Ki 8:31 laid upon him to cause him to s., 422
2Ch 6:22 be laid upon him to make him s., 422
2Ch 36:13 who had made him s. by God: 7650
Ezr 10:5 to s. that they should do according 7650
Ne 13:25 and made them s. by God, saying, 7650
Isa 3:7 In that day shall he s., saying, I 5375
Isa 19:18 and s. to the Lord of hosts; one 7650
Isa 45:23 shall bow, every tongue shall s. 7650
Isa 48:1 which s. by the name of the Lord, 7650
Isa 65:16 earth shall s. by the God of truth; 7650
Jer 4:2 And thou shalt s., The Lord liveth, 7650
Jer 5:2 Lord liveth; surely they s. falsely. 7650
Jer 7:9 commit adultery, and s. falsely, 7650
Jer 12:16 to s. by my name, The Lord liveth; 7650
Jer 12:16 taught my people to s. by Baal; 7650
Jer 22:5 I s. by myself, saith the Lord, that 7650
Jer 32:22 thou didst s. to their fathers to give 7650
Ho 4:15 Beth-aven, nor s., The Lord liveth. 7650
Am 8:14 they that s. by the sin of Samaria, 7650
Zep 1:5 worship and that s. by the Lord, 7650
Zep 1:5 and that s. by Malcham; 7650
Mt 5:34 **S. not at all; neither by heaven;** *3660*
Mt 5:36 **Neither shalt thou s. by thy head,** *3660*
Mt 23:16 **Whosoever shall s. by the temple,** *3660*
Mt 23:16 **shall s. by the gold of the temple,** *3660*
Mt 23:18 **Whosoever shall s. by the altar, it** *3660*
Mt 23:20 **therefore shall s. by the altar,** *3660*
Mt 23:21 **And whoso shall s. by the temple,** *3660*
Mt 23:22 **And he that shall s. by heaven,** *3660*
Mt 26:74 Then began he to curse and to s., *3660*
Mk 14:71 But he began to curse and to s., *3660*
Heb 6:13 because he could s. by no greater, *3660*
Heb 6:16 For men verily s. by the greater: *3660*
Jas 5:12 all things, my brethren, s. not, *3660*

SWEARERS
Mal 3:5 and against false s., and against 7650

SWEARETH
Le 6:3 lieth concerning it, and s. falsely; 7650
Ps 15:4 He that s. to his own hurt, and 7650
Ps 63:11 one that s. by him shall glory: 7650
Ec 9:2 he that s., as he that feareth an 7650
Isa 65:16 he that s. in the earth shall swear 7650
Zec 5:3 every one that s. shall be cut off as 7650
Zec 5:4 of him that s. falsely by my name: 7650
Mt 23:18 **whosoever s. by the gift that is** *3660*
Mt 23:20 **s. by it, and by all things thereon.** *3660*
Mt 23:21 **s. by it, and by him that dwelleth** *3660*
Mt 23:22 **heaven, s. by the throne of God,** *3660*

SWEARING
Le 5:1 soul sin, and hear the voice of s., 423
Jer 23:10 because of s. the land mourneth; 423
Ho 4:2 By s., and lying, and killing, and 422
Ho 10:4 s. falsely in making a covenant: 422

SWEAT
Ge 3:19 In the s. of thy face shalt thou eat 2188
Eze 44:18 with any thing that causeth s. 3154
Lu 22:44 his s. was as it were great drops of *2402*

SWEEP See also SWEEPING; SWEPT.
Isa 14:23 and I will s. it with the besom of 2894
Isa 28:17 hail shall s. away the refuge of lies, 3261
Lu 15:8 **light a candle, and s. the house,** *4563*

SWEEPING
Pr 28:3 is like a s. rain that leaveth no 5502

SWEET See also SWEETER; SWEETSMELLING.
Ge 8:21 And the Lord smelled a s. savour; 5207
Ex 15:25 waters, the waters were made s.: 4985
Ex 25:6 anointing oil, and for s. incense, 5561
Ex 29:18 it is a s. savour, an offering made 5207

Ex 29:25 for a **s.** savour before the Lord:......... 5207
Ex 29:41 for a **s.** savour, an offering made........ 5207
Ex 30:7 burn thereon **s.** incense every 5561
Ex 30:23 and of **s.** cinnamon half so much,........ 1314
Ex 30:23 of **s.** calamus two hundred and fifty..... 1314
Ex 30:34 Take unto thee **s.** spices, stacte,........ 5561
Ex 30:34 **s.** spices with pure frankincense: 5561
Ex 31:11 and **s.** incense for the holy place: 5561
Ex 35:8 anointing oil,...for the **s.** incense, ... 5561
Ex 35:15 anointing oil, and the **s.** incense, ... 5561
Ex 35:28 anointing oil, and for the **s.** incense..... 5561
Ex 37:29 and the pure incense of **s.** spices,....... 5561
Ex 39:38 anointing oil, and the **s.** incense, ... 5561
Ex 40:27 And he burnt **s.** incense thereon; as.... 5561
Le 1:9, 13, 17 of a **s.** savour unto the Lord. ... 5207
Le 2:2 by fire, of a **s.** savour unto the Lord:.. 5207
Le 2:9 by fire, of a **s.** savour unto the Lord... 5207
Le 2:12 burnt on the altar for a **s.** savour. 5207
Le 3:5 by fire, of a **s.** savour unto the Lord... 5207
Le 3:16 made by fire for a **s.** savour:.......... 5207
Le 4:7 the horns of the altar of **s.** incense..... 5561
Le 4:31 for a **s.** savour unto the Lord; 5207
Le 6:15 it upon the altar for a **s.** savour, ... 5207
Le 6:21 offer for a **s.** savour unto the Lord. 5207
Le 8:21 a burnt sacrifice for a **s.** savour......... 5207
Le 8:28 were consecrations for a **s.** savour:..... 5207
Le 16:12 his hands full of **s.** incense beaten....... 5561
Le 17:6 fat for a **s.** savour unto the Lord. 5207
Le 23:13 fire unto the Lord for a **s.** savour:...... 5207
Le 23:18 by fire, of **s.** savour unto the Lord. 5207
Le 26:31 smell the savour of your **s.** odours....... 5207
Nu 4:16 for the light, and the **s.** incense, ... 5561
Nu 15:3 to make a **s.** savour unto the Lord, ... 5207
Nu 15:7 wine, for a **s.** savour unto the Lord. 5207
Nu 15:10, 13 fire, of a **s.** savour unto the Lord... 5207
Nu 15:14 by fire, of a **s.** savour unto the Lord;.. 5207
Nu 15:24 for a **s.** savour unto the Lord, ... 5207
Nu 18:17 fire, for a **s.** savour unto the Lord. 5207
Nu 28:2 by fire, for a **s.** savour unto me, ... 5207
Nu 28:6 in mount Sinai for a **s.** savour, ... 5207
Nu 28:8 by fire, of a **s.** savour unto the Lord... 5207
Nu 28:13 for a burnt offering of a **s.** savour,...... 5207
Nu 28:24 fire, of a **s.** savour unto the Lord: 5207
Nu 28:27 for a **s.** savour unto the Lord; 5207
Nu 29:2 for a **s.** savour unto the Lord; 5207
Nu 29:6 for a **s.** savour, a sacrifice made by 5207
Nu 29:8 unto the Lord for a **s.** savour; 5207
Nu 29:13 fire, of a **s.** savour unto the Lord; 5207
Nu 29:36 fire, of a **s.** savour unto the Lord: 5207
2Sa 23:1 and the **s.** psalmist of Israel, said, ... 5273
2Ch 2:4 and to burn before him **s.** incense,...... 5561
2Ch 13:11 burnt sacrifices and **s.** incense: 5561
2Ch 16:14 in the bed...filled with **s.** odours......... 1314
Ezr 6:10 **s.** savours unto the God of heaven, ... 5208
Ne 8:10 way, eat the fat, and drink the **s.**, ... 4477
Es 2:12 and six months with **s.** odours, ... 1314
Job 20:12 wickedness be **s.** in his mouth, ... 4985
Job 21:33 The clods of the valley shall be **s.** 4985
Job 38:31 bind the **s.** influences of Pleiades,....... 4575
Ps 55:14 We took **s.** counsel together, and....... 4985
Ps 104:34 My mediation of him shall be **s.** 6148
Ps 119:103 How **s.** are thy words unto my.......... 4452
Ps 141:6 hear my words; for they are **s.**........... 5276
Pr 3:24 lie down, and thy sleep shall be **s.**...... 6148
Pr 9:17 Stolen waters are **s.**, and bread 4985
Pr 13:19 desire accomplished is **s.** to the 6148
Pr 16:24 as an honeycomb, **s.** to the soul,........ 4966
Pr 20:17 Bread of deceit is **s.** to a man; but..... 6149
Pr 23:8 vomit up, and lose thy **s.** words.......... 5273
Pr 24:13 the honeycomb, which is **s.** to thy...... 4966
Pr 27:7 hungry soul every bitter thing is **s.**..... 4966
Ec 5:12 The sleep of a labouring man is **s.**, ... 4966
Ec 11:7 Truly the light is **s.**, and a pleasant..... 4966
Ca 2:3 and his fruit was **s.** to my taste. 4966
Ca 2:14 **s.** is thy voice, and thy countenance.... 6149
Ca 5:5 fingers with **s.** smelling myrrh,........... 5674
Ca 5:13 as a bed of spices, as **s.** flowers: 4840
Ca 5:13 lilies, dropping **s.** smelling myrrh......... 5674
Ca 5:16 His mouth is most **s.**: yea, he is 4477
Isa 3:24 instead of **s.** smell...shall be stink; 1314
Isa 5:20 put bitter for **s.**, and **s.** for bitter! 4966
Isa 23:16 make **s.** melody, sing many songs,...... 3190
Isa 43:24 hast brought me no **s.** cane with money,....
Isa 49:26 their own blood, as with **s.** wine: 6071
Jer 6:20 the **s.** cane from a far country?.......... 2896
Jer 6:20 nor your sacrifices **s.** unto me. 6148
Jer 31:26 and my sleep was **s.** unto me. 6148
Eze 6:13 offer **s.** savour to all their idols. 5207
Eze 16:19 set it before them for a **s.** savour:...... 5207
Eze 20:28 there also they made their **s.** savour,... 5207
Eze 20:41 will accept you with your **s.** savour,.... 5207
Da 2:46 an oblation and **s.** odours unto him...... 5208
Am 9:13 the mountains shall drop **s.** wine, ... 6071
Mic 6:15 and **s.** wine, but shalt not drink.......... 8492
Mk 16:1 and Salome, had bought **s.** spices, ...
2Co 2:15 are unto God a **s.** savour of Christ, ... *2175*
Php 4:18 an odour of a **s.** smell, a sacrifice *2175*
Jas 3:11 same place **s.** water and bitter?.......... *1099*
Re 10:9 it shall be in thy mouth **s.** as honey. ... *1099*
Re 10:10 and it was in my mouth **s.** as honey:... *1099*

SWEETER

Jg 14:18 What is **s.** than honey? and what........ 4966
Ps 19:10 **s.**...than honey and the honeycomb..... 4966
Ps 119:103 yea, **s.** than honey to my mouth!.............

SWEETLY

Job 24:20 the worm shall feed **s.** on him; he 4988
Ca 7:9 that goeth down **s.**, causing the 4339

SWEETNESS

Jg 9:11 Should I forsake my **s.**, and my 4987
Jg 14:14 and out of the strong came forth **s.**..... 4966
Pr 16:21 **s.** of the lips increaseth learning......... 4986
Pr 27:9 so doth the **s.** of a man's friend by 4986
Eze 3:3 was in my mouth as honey for **s.** 4966

SWEETSMELLING See also SWEET and SMELLING.

Eph 5:2 a sacrifice to God for a **s.** savour. *2175*

SWELL See also SWELLED; SWELLING; SWOLLEN.

Nu 5:21 thigh to rot, and thy belly to **s.**;......... 6639
Nu 5:22 to make thy belly to **s.**, and thy......... 6638
Nu 5:27 and her belly shall **s.**, and her thigh 6638
De 8:4 neither did thy foot **s.**, these forty...... 1216

SWELLED See also SWOLLEN.

Ne 9:21 waxed not old, and their feet **s.** not. ... 1216

SWELLING See also SWELLINGS.

Ps 46:3 the mountains shake with the **s.**......... 1346
Isa 30:13 **s.** out in a high wall, whose............... 1158
Jer 12:5 wilt thou do in the **s.** of Jordan? 1347
Jer 49:19 up like a lion from the **s.** of Jordan 1347
Jer 50:44 up like a lion from the **s.** of Jordan 1347
2Pe 2:18 speak great **s.** words of vanity,.......... *5246*
Jude 16 mouth speaketh great **s.** words, ... *5246*

SWELLINGS

2Co 12:20 backbitings, whisperings, **s.**,.............. *5450*

SWEPT

Jg 5:21 The river of Kishon **s.** them away, ... 1640
Jer 46:15 Why are thy valiant men **s.** away? 5502
Mt 12:44 **findeth it empty, s., and garnished,** *4563*
Lu 11:25 **he findeth it s. and garnished.** *4563*

SWERVED

1Ti 1:6 From which some having **s.** have *795*

SWIFT See also SWIFTER.

De 28:49 of the earth, as **s.** as the eagle flieth;........
1Ch 12:8 were as **s.** as the roes upon the......... 4116
Job 9:26 are passed away as the **s.** ships: 16
Job 24:18 He is **s.** as the waters; their 7031
Pr 6:18 feet...be **s.** in running to mischief,...... 4116
Ex 9:11 that the race is not to the **s.**, nor....... 7031
Isa 18:2 Go, ye **s.** messengers, to a nation...... 7031
Isa 19:1 the Lord rideth upon a **s.** cloud,......... 7031
Isa 30:16 flee: and, We will ride upon the **s.**;..... 7031
Isa 30:16 shall they that pursue you be **s.**......... 7043
Isa 66:20 upon mules, and upon **s.** beasts, ... 3753
Jer 2:23 thou art a **s.** dromedary traversing...... 7031
Jer 46:6 Let not the **s.** flee away, nor the 7031
Am 2:14 the flight shall perish from the **s.**,....... 7031
Am 2:15 and he that is **s.** of foot shall not........ 7031
Mic 1:13 bind the chariot to the **s.** beast: 7409
Mal 3:5 I will be a **s.** witness against the 4116
Ro 3:15 Their feet are **s.** to shed blood: *3691*
Jas 1:19 let every man be **s.** to hear, slow......... *5036*
2Pe 2:1 upon themselves **s.** destruction. *5031*

SWIFTER

2Sa 1:23 they were **s.** than eagles, they.......... 7043
Job 7:6 My days are **s.** than a weaver's 7043
Job 9:25 Now my days are **s.** than a post: 7043
Jer 4:13 his horses are **s.** than eagles. 7043
La 4:19 persecutors are **s.** than the eagles 7031
Hab 1:8 horses...are **s.** than the leopards, ... 7043

SWIFTLY

Ps 147:15 earth: his word runneth very **s.**. 4120
Isa 5:26 they shall come with speed **s.**............ 7031
Da 9:21 begin caused to fly **s.**, touched me...... 3288
Joe 3:4 **s.** and speedily will I return your........ 7031

SWIM

2Ki 6:6 it in thither; and the iron did **s.**.......... 6687
Ps 6:6 all the night make I my bed to **s.**; 7811
Isa 25:11 spreadeth forth his hands ot **s.**:.......... 7811
Eze 47:5 waters were risen, waters to **s.** in,..... 7813
Ac 27:42 lest any of them should **s.** out, ... *1579*
Ac 27:43 they which could **s.** should cast.......... *2860*

SWIMMEST

Eze 22:6 thy blood the land wherein thou **s.**,..... 6824

SWIMMETH

Isa 25:11 that **s.** spreadeth forth his hands 7811

SWINE See also SWINE'S.

Le 11:7 the **s.**, though he divide the hoof,....... 2386
De 14:8 the **s.**, because it divideth the hoof, ... 2386
Mt 7:6 **neither cast ye...pearls before s.**,.... *5519*
Mt 8:30 them an herd of my **s.** feeding........... *5519*
Mt 8:31 us to go away into the heard of **s.**....... *5519*
Mt 8:32 out, they went into the herd of **s.** *5519*
Mt 8:32 whole herd of **s.** ran violently down *5519*
Mk 5:11 a great heard of **s.** feeding. *5519*
Mk 5:12 Send us into the **s.**, that we may *5519*
Mk 5:13 went out, and entered into the **s.**........ *5519*
Mk 5:14 they that fed the **s.** fled, and told....... *5519*
Mk 5:16 the devil, and also concerning the **s.**.. *5519*
Lu 8:32 an herd of many **s.** feeding on the *5519*
Lu 8:33 of the man, and entered into the **s.**..... *5519*
Lu 15:15 **sent him into his fields to feed s.**... *5519*
Lu 15:16 **with the husks that the s. did eat:**... *5519*

SWINE'S

Pr 11:22 As a jewel of gold in a **s.** snout, so..... 2386
Isa 65:4 which eat **s.** flesh, and broth of.......... 2386
Isa 66:3 oblation, as if he offered **s.** blood;...... 2386
Isa 66:17 tree in the midst, eating **s.** flesh, ... 2386

SWOLLEN See also SWELLED.

Ac 28:6 looked when he should have **s.**, ... *4092*

SWOON See also SWOONED.

La 2:11 the sucklings **s.** in the streets of........ 5848

SWOONED

La 2:12 when they **s.** as the wounded in......... 5848

SWORD See also SWORDS.

Ge 3:24 a flaming **s.** which turned every 2719
Ge 27:40 And by thy **s.** shalt thou live, and........ 2719
Ge 31:26 as captives taken with the **s.**? 2719
Ge 34:25 brethren, took each man his **s.**, ... 2719
Ge 34:26 his son with the edge of the **s.**, ... 2719
Ge 48:22 hand of the Amorite with my **s.**. 2719
Ex 5:3 us with pestilence, or with the **s.**......... 2719
Ex 5:21 to put a **s.** in their hand to slay us...... 2719
Ex 15:9 I will draw my **s.**, my hand shall 2719
Ex 17:13 his people with the edge of the **s.**. 2719
Ex 18:4 delivered me from the **s.** of Pharaoh: .. 2719
Ex 22:24 hit, and I will kill you with the **s.**;...... 2719
Ex 32:27 Put every man his **s.** by his side, ... 2719
Le 26:6 shall the **s.** go through your land. 2719
Le 26:7 they shall fall before you by the **s.**,...... 2719
Le 26:8 enemies..fall before you by the **s.**,....... 2719
Le 26:25 And I will bring a **s.** upon you, that 2719
Le 26:33 and will draw out a **s.** after you: 2719
Le 26:36 they shall flee, as fleeing from a **s.**; 2719
Le 26:37 as it were before a **s.**, when none 2719
Nu 14:3 us unto this land, to fall by the **s.**,....... 2719
Nu 14:43 you, and ye shall fall by the **s.**........... 2719
Nu 19:16 is slain with a **s.** in the open fields,..... 2719
Nu 20:18 I come out against thee with the **s.**..... 2719
Nu 21:24 smote him with the edge of the **s.**, ... 2719
Nu 22:23 way, and his **s.** drawn in his hand:...... 2719
Nu 22:29 would there were a **s.** in mine hand,.... 2719
Nu 22:31 way, and his **s.** drawn in his hand:...... 2719
Nu 31:8 son of Beor they slew with the **s.**. 2719
De 13:15 of that city with the ege of the **s.**,........ 2719
De 13:15 cattle thereof, with...edge of the **s.**........ 2719
De 20:13 male thereof with the edge of the **s.**.... 2719
De 28:22 and with the **s.**, and with blasting, ... 2719
De 32:25 The **s.** without, and terror within, ... 2719
De 32:41 If I whet my glittering **s.**, and mine 2719
De 32:42 blood, and my **s.** shall devour flesh; 2719
De 33:29 and who is the **s.** of thy excellency! 2719

Jos 5:13 him with his **s.** drawn in his hand: 2719
Jos 6:21 and ass, with the edge of the **s.**......... 2719
Jos 8:24 were all fallen on the edge of the **s.**,.... 2719
Jos 8:24 and smote it with the edge of the **s.**.. 2719
Jos 10:11 children of Israel slew with the **s.**....... 2719
Jos 10:28, 30,32,35,37,39 the edge of the **s.**,...... 2719
Jos 11:10 smote the king thereof with the **s.**...... 2719
Jos 11:11 souls...therein with..edge of the **s.**, ... 2719
Jos 11:12 smote them with the edge of the **s.**, ... 2719
Jos 11:14 they smote with the edge of the **s.**,.... 2719
Jos 13:22 children of Israel slay with the **s.**........ 2719
Jos 19:47 and smote it with the edge of the **s.**, .. 2719
Jos 24:12 not with thy **s.**, nor with thy bow....... 2719
Jg 1:8 smitten it with the edge of the **s.**,...... 2719
Jg 1:25 smote the city with...edge of the **s.**; ... 2719
Jg 4:15 the edge of the **s.** before Barak; 2719
Jg 4:16 Sisera fell upon the edge of the **s.**; 2719
Jg 7:14 nothing else save the **s.** of Gideon...... 2719
Jg 7:18 The **s.** of the Lord, and of Gideon. ....
Jg 7:20 The **s.** of the Lord, and of Gideon. 2719
Jg 7:22 every man's against his fellow,........... 2719
Jg 8:10 twenty thousand men that drew **s.**....... 2719
Jg 8:20 But the youth drew not his **s.**: for...... 2719
Jg 9:54 thy **s.**, and slay men, that men 2719
Jg 18:27 smote them with the edge of the **s.**, ... 2719
Jg 20:2 thousand footmen that drew **s.**.......... 2719
Jg 20:15 and six thousand men that drew **s.**, ... 2719
Jg 20:17 hundred thousand men that drew **s.** 2719
Jg 20:25 thousand men; all these drew the **s.**..... 2719
Jg 20:35 hundred men: all these drew the **s.**...... 2719
Jg 20:37 all the city with the edge of the **s.**...... 2719
Jg 20:46 five thousand men that drew the **s.**;.... 2719
Jg 20:48 smote them with the edge of the **s.**, ... 2719
Jg 21:10 Jabesh-gilead with the edge of the **s.**,.. 2719
1Sa 13:22 was neither **s.** nor spear found in 2719
1Sa 14:20 every man's **s.** was against his........... 2719
1Sa 15:8 the people with the ege of the **s.**. 2719
1Sa 15:33 thy **s.** hath made women childless,...... 2719
1Sa 17:39 girded his **s.** upon his armour, ... 2719
1Sa 17:45 Thou comest to me with a **s.**, and...... 2719
1Sa 17:47 that the Lord saveth not with **s.** and... 2719
1Sa 17:50 was no **s.** in the hand of David. 2719
1Sa 17:51 upon the Philistine, and took his **s.**, ... 2719
1Sa 18:4 and his garments, even to his **s.**, ... 2719
1Sa 21:8 here under thine hand spear or **s.**........ 2719
1Sa 21:8 have neither brought my **s.** nor my..... 2719
1Sa 21:9 The **s.** of Goliath the Philistine,.......... 2719
1Sa 22:10 and gave him the **s.** of Goliath the...... 2719
1Sa 22:13 thou hast given him bread, and a **s.**, ... 2719
1Sa 22:19 smote he with the edge of the **s.**, ... 2719
1Sa 22:19 and sheep, with the edge of the **s.**. 2719
1Sa 25:13 men, Gird ye on every man his **s.**. 2719
1Sa 25:13 they girded on every man his **s.**;.......... 2719
1Sa 25:13 and David also girded on his **s.** 2719
1Sa 31:4 Draw thy **s.**, and thrust me through.... 2719
1Sa 31:4 Saul took a **s.**, and fell upon it. 2719
1Sa 31:5 dead, he fell likewise upon his **s.**,....... 2719
2Sa 1:12 because they were fallen by the **s.**....... 2719
2Sa 1:22 the **s.** of Saul returned not empty....... 2719
2Sa 2:16 thrust his **s.** in his fellow's side; 2719
2Sa 2:26 said, Shall the **s.** devour for ever? 2719
2Sa 3:29 or hat falleth on the **s.**, or that 2719
2Sa 11:25 for the **s.** devoureth one as well as..... 2719
2Sa 12:9 killed Uriah the Hittite with the **s.**, ... 2719
2Sa 12:9 hast slain him with the **s.** of the......... 2719
2Sa 12:10 the **s.** shall never depart from thine 2719
2Sa 15:14 the city with the edge of the **s.**.......... 2719
2Sa 18:8 more people that day than the **s.**......... 2719
2Sa 20:8 upon it a gridle with a **s.** fastened....... 2719
2Sa 20:10 Amasa took no heed to the **s.** that...... 2719
2Sa 21:16 he being girded with a new **s.**,.................
2Sa 23:10 and his hand clave unto the **s.**............ 2719
2Sa 24:9 valiant men that drew the **s.**;............. 2719
1Ki 1:51 will not slay his servant with the **s.**...... 2719
1Ki 2:8 not put thee to death with the **s.**......... 2719
1Ki 2:32 than he, and slew them with the **s.**,.... 2719
1Ki 3:24 And the king said, Bring me a **s.**....... 2719
1Ki 3:24 they brought a **s.** before the king. 2719
1Ki 19:1 slain all the prophets with the **s.**. 2719
1Ki 19:10, 14 slain thy prophets with the **s.**; 2719
1Ki 19:17 him that escapeth the **s.** of Hazael...... 2719
1Ki 19:17 that escapeth from the **s.** of Jehu 2719
2Ki 6:22 thou hast taken captive with thy **s.** 2719
2Ki 8:12 men wilt thou slay with the **s.**, and..... 2719
2Ki 10:25 smote them with the edge of the **s.**; ... 2719
2Ki 11:15 that followeth her kill with the **s.**........ 2719
2Ki 11:20 slew Athaliah with the **s.** beside the.... 2719
2Ki 19:7 to fall by the **s.** in his own land.......... 2719
2Ki 19:37 his sons smote him with the **s.**. 2719
1Ch 5:18 men able to bear buckler and **s.**, ... 2719
1Ch 10:4 Draw thy **s.**, and thrust me through.... 2719
1Ch 10:4 So Saul took a **s.**, and fell upon it....... 2719
1Ch 10:5 he fell likewise on the **s.**, and died...... 2719
1Ch 21:5 hundred thousand men...drew **s.** 2719
1Ch 21:5 and then thousand men that drew **s.**. .. 2719
1Ch 21:12 the **s.** of thine enemies overtaketh...... 2719
1Ch 21:12 else three days the **s.** of the Lord, ... 2719
1Ch 21:16 having a drawn **s.** in his hand............ 2719
1Ch 21:27 put up his **s.** again into the sheath...... 2719
1Ch 21:30 afraid because of the **s.** of the angel.... 2719
2Ch 20:9 evil cometh upon us, as the **s.**,.......... 2719
2Ch 21:4 slew all his brethren with the **s.**, ... 2719
2Ch 23:14 her, let him be slain with the **s.**. 2719
2Ch 23:21 they had slain Athaliah with the **s.**. 2719
2Ch 29:9 our fathers have fallen by the **s.**,........ 2719
2Ch 32:21 bowels slew him there with the **s.**. 2719
2Ch 36:17 slew their young men with the **s.** in.... 2719
2Ch 36:20 them that had escaped from the **s.**....... 2719
Ezr 9:7 to the **s.**, to captivity, and to a spoil, .. 2719
Ne 4:18 every one had his **s.** girded by his...... 2719
Es 9:5 enemies with the stroke of the **s.**,....... 2719
Job 1:15, 17 servants with the edge of the **s.**; ... 2719
Job 5:15 But he saveth the poor from the **s.**,.... 2719
Job 5:20 and in war from the power of the **s.**. .. 2719
Job 15:22 and he is waited for of the **s.**............ 2719
Job 19:29 Be ye afraid of the **s.**: for wrath 2719
Job 19:29 bringeth the punishment of the **s.**, ... 2719
Job 20:25 the glittering **s.** cometh out o his........ 1300
Job 27:14 be multiplied, it is for the **s.**:............. 2719
Job 33:18 his life from perishing by the **s.**.......... 7973
Job 36:12 not, they shall perish by the **s.**, ... 7973
Job 39:22 neither turneth...back from the **s.** 2719
Job 40:19 he that made him can make his **s.** 2719
Job 41:26 **s.** of him that layeth at him cannot...... 2719
Ps 7:12 If he turn not, he will whet his **s.**;...... 2719
Ps 17:13 from the wicked, which is thy **s.**: 2719
Ps 22:20 Deliver my soul from the **s.**; my 2719
Ps 37:14 The wicked have drawn out the **s.**,..... 2719
Ps 37:15 **s.** shall enter into their own heart,...... 2719
Ps 42:10 A with a **s.** in my bones, mine........... 7524
Ps 44:3 land in possession by their own **s.**, ... 2719
Ps 44:6 bow, neither shall my **s.** save me. 2719
Ps 45:3 Gird thy **s.** upon thy thigh, O most...... 2719
Ps 57:4 arrows, and their tongue a sharp **s.**. ... 2719
Ps 63:10 They shall fall by the **s.**: they shall 2719
Ps 64:3 Who whet their tongue like a **s.**, ... 2719
Ps 76:3 bow, the shield, and the **s.**, and the.... 2719
Ps 78:62 his people over also unto the **s.**; 2719
Ps 78:64 Their priests fell by the **s.**; and.......... 2719
Ps 89:43 hast also turned the edge of his **s.**,..... 2719
Ps 144:10 his servant from the hurtful **s.**. 2719
Ps 149:6 and a twoedged **s.** in their hand; 2719
Pr 5:4 wormwood, sharp as a twoedged **s.**. ... 2719
Pr 12:18 speaketh like the piercings of a **s.**....... 2719
Pr 25:18 his neighbour is a maul, and a **s.**, ... 2719
Ca 3:8 every man...his **s.** upon his thigh........ 2719
Isa 1:20 ye shall be devoured with the **s.** 2719
Isa 2:4 shall not lift up **s.** against nation, ... 2719
Isa 3:25 Thy men shall fall by the **s.**, and 2719
Isa 13:15 joined unto them shall fall by the **s.**..... 2719
Isa 14:19 are slain, thrust through with a **s.**,...... 2719
Isa 21:15 from the drawn **s.**, and from the 2719
Isa 22:2 slain men are not slain with the **s.**, ... 2719
Isa 27:1 great and strong **s.** shall punish.......... 2719
Isa 31:8 shall the Assyrian fall with the **s.**,....... 2719
Isa 31:8 and the **s.**, not of a mean man, shall... 2719
Isa 31:8 but he shall flee from the **s.**, and........ 2719
Isa 34:5 my **s.** shall be bathed in heaven: 2719
Isa 34:6 **s.** of the Lord is filled with blood,........ 2719
Isa 37:7 him to fall by the **s.** in his own land. ... 2719
Isa 37:38 his sons smote him with the **s.**; 2719
Isa 41:2 he gave them as the dust to his **s.**, ... 2719
Isa 49:2 made my mouth like a sharp **s.**; 2719
Isa 51:19 and the famine, and the **s.**: by 2719
Isa 65:12 will I number you to the **s.**, and......... 2719
Isa 66:16 by his **s.** will the Lord plead with....... 2719
Jer 2:30 your own **s.** hath devoured your......... 2719
Jer 4:10 the **s.** reacheth unto the soul............ 2719
Jer 5:12 neither shall we see **s.** nor famine: 2719
Jer 5:17 wherein thou trustedst, with the **s.**. 2719
Jer 6:25 for the **s.** of the enemy and fear is 2719
Jer 9:16 and I will send a **s.** after them, till I.... 2719
Jer 11:22 the young men shall die by the **s.**;...... 2719
Jer 12:12 for the **s.** of the Lord shall devour...... 2719
Jer 14:12 but I will consume them by the **s.**, ... 2719
Jer 14:13 Ye shall not see the **s.**, neither shall... 2719
Jer 14:15 **S.** and famine shall not be in this....... 2719
Jer 14:15 By **s.** and famine shall those............. 2719
Jer 14:16 because of the famine and the **s.**; 2719
Jer 14:18 then behold the slain with the **s.**! 2719
Jer 15:2 such as are for the **s.**, to the **s.**; 2719
Jer 15:3 the **s.** to slay, and the dogs to tear,.... 2719
Jer 15:9 will I deliver to the **s.** before their...... 2719
Jer 16:4 they shall be consumed by the **s.**, ... 2719
Jer 18:21 their blood by the force of the **s.**;....... 2719
Jer 18:21 their young men be slain be the **s.**....... 2719
Jer 19:7 I will cause them to fall by the **s.**....... 2719
Jer 20:4 shall fall by the **s.** of their enemies, ... 2719
Jer 20:4 and shall slay them with the **s.**........... 2719
Jer 21:7 from the **s.**, and from the famine,....... 2719
Jer 21:7 smite them with the edge of the **s.**;.... 2719
Jer 21:9 in this city shall die by the **s.**, and...... 2719
Jer 24:10 And I will send the **s.**, the famine,...... 2719
Jer 25:16 the **s.** that I will send among them. 2719
Jer 25:27 the **s.** which I will send among you. 2719
Jer 25:29 for I will call for a **s.** upon all the 2719
Jer 25:31 give them that are wicked to the **s.**, ... 2719
Jer 26:23 who slew him with the **s.**, and cast..... 2719
Jer 27:8 punish, saith the Lord, with the **s.**,..... 2719
Jer 27:13 die, thou and thy people, by the **s.**, ... 2719
Jer 29:17 I will send upon them the **s.**, the 2719
Jer 29:18 I will persecute them with the **s.**,....... 2719
Jer 31:2 The people which were left of the **s.**... 2719
Jer 32:24 because of the **s.**, and of the famine,... 2719
Jer 32:36 of the king of Babylon by the **s.**,........ 2719
Jer 33:4 down by the mounts, and by the **s.**;.... 2719
Jer 34:4 thee, Thou shalt not die by the **s.**; 2719
Jer 34:17 to the **s.**, to the pestilence, and......... 2719
Jer 38:2 in this city shall die by the **s.**, by 2719
Jer 39:18 and thou shalt not fall by the **s.**,......... 2719
Jer 41:2 the son of Shaphan with the **s.**,.......... 2719
Jer 42:16 that the **s.**, which ye feared, shall....... 2719
Jer 42:17 they shall die by the **s.**, by the.......... 2719
Jer 42:22 that ye shall die by the **s.**, by the....... 2719
Jer 43:11 and such as are for the **s.** to the **s.**. ... 2719
Jer 44:12, 12 by the **s.** and by the famine: 2719
Jer 44:13 have punished Jerusalem, by the **s.**,.... 2719
Jer 44:18 and have been consumed by the **s.** 2719
Jer 44:27 shall be consumed by the **s.** and......... 2719
Jer 44:28 a small number that escape the **s.** 2719
Jer 46:10 and the **s.** shall devour, and it shall..... 2719
Jer 46:14 for the **s.** shall devour round about 2719
Jer 46:16 our nativity, from the oppressing **s.**. ... 2719
Jer 47:6 O thou **s.** of the Lord, how long will... 2719
Jer 48:2 Madmen; the **s.** shall pursue thee....... 2719
Jer 48:10 that keepeth back his **s.** from blood. ... 2719
Jer 49:37 and I will send the **s.** after them, ... 2719
Jer 50:16 for fear of the oppressing **s.** they 2719
Jer 50:35 A **s.** is upon the Chaldeans, saith 2719
Jer 50:36 A **s.** is upon the liars; and they......... 2719
Jer 50:36 a **s.** is upon her mighty men; and....... 2719
Jer 50:37 A **s.** is upon their horses, and upon 2719
Jer 50:37 a **s.** is upon her treasures; and they.... 2719
Jer 51:10 that have escaped the **s.**, go away,..... 2719
La 1:20 abroad the **s.** bereaveth, at home 2719
La 2:21 my young men are fallen by the **s.**;...... 2719
La 4:9 that be slain with the **s.** are better 2719
La 5:9 because of the **s.** of the wilderness..... 2719
Eze 5:2 and I will draw out a **s.** after them. 2719
Eze 5:12 and a third part shall fall by the **s.**..... 2719
Eze 5:12 and I will draw out a **s.** after them. 2719
Eze 5:17 and I will bring the **s.** upon thee. 2719
Eze 6:3 I, even I, will bring a **s.** upon you, ... 2719
Eze 6:8 escape the **s.** among the nations,........ 2719
Eze 6:11 shall fall by the **s.**, by the famine,....... 2719
Eze 6:12 he that is near shall fall by the **s.**; 2719
Eze 7:15 The **s.** is without, and the pestilence... 2719
Eze 7:15 is in the field shall die with the **s.**;...... 2719
Eze 11:8 Ye have feared the **s.**; and I will 2719
Eze 11:8 bring a **s.** upon you, saith the Lord..... 2719
Eze 11:10 Ye shall fall by the **s.**; I will judge 2719
Eze 12:14 I will draw out the **s.** after them. 2719
Eze 12:16 leave a few men of them from the **s.**, ..2719
Eze 14:17 Or if I bring a **s.** upon that land, ... 2719
Eze 14:17 and say, **S.**, go through the land; 2719
Eze 14:21 Jerusalem, the **s.**, and the famine, ... 2719
Eze 17:21 all his bands shall fall by the **s.**, ... 2719
Eze 21:3 draw forth my **s.** out of his sheath,..... 2719

Eze 21:4 my **s.** go forth out of his sheath... 2719
Eze 21:5 drawn forth my **s.** out of his sheath: ... 2719
Eze 21:9 Say, A **s.**, a **s.** is sharpened, and ... 2719
Eze 21:11 **s.** is sharpened, and it is furbished,... 2719
Eze 21:12 terrors by reason of the **s.** shall be... 2719
Eze 21:13 what if the **s.** contemn even the rod? ...
Eze 21:14 and let the **s.** be doubled the third... 2719
Eze 21:14 time, the **s.** of the slain: it is the... 2719
Eze 21:14 **s.** of the great men that are slain, ... 2719
Eze 21:15 I have set the point of the **s.** against... 2719
Eze 21:19 **s.** of the king of Babylon may come: ... 2719
Eze 21:20 the **s.** may come to Rabbath of the... 2719
Eze 21:28 say thou, The **s.**, the **s.** is drawn: ... 2719
Eze 23:10 daughters, and slew her with the **s.**... 2719
Eze 23:25 and thy remnant shall fall by the **s.**:... 2719
Eze 24:21 whom ye have left shall fall by the **s.**. 2719
Eze 25:13 they of Dedan shall fall by the **s.**... 2719
Eze 26:6 in the field shall be slain by the **s.**; ... 2719
Eze 26:8 shall slay with the **s.** thy daughters... 2719
Eze 26:11 he shall slay thy people by the **s.**, ... 2719
Eze 28:23 judged in the midst of her by the **s.**... 2719
Eze 29:8 I will bring a **s.** upon thee, and cut... 2719
Eze 30:4 And the **s.** shall come upon Egypt, ... 2719
Eze 30:5 shall fall with them by the **s.**... 2719
Eze 30:6 Syene shall they fall in it by the **s.**,... 2719
Eze 30:17 and of Pi-beseth shall fall by the **s.** ... 2719
Eze 30:21 it, to make it strong to hold the **s.**. ... 2719
Eze 30:22 cause the **s.** to fall out of his hand... 2719
Eze 30:24 Babylon, and put my **s.** in his hand: ... 2719
Eze 30:25 put my **s.** into the hand of the king... 2719
Eze 31:17 unto them that be slain with the **s.**; ... 2719
Eze 31:18 with them that be slain by the **s.**... 2719
Eze 32:10 I shall brandish my **s.** before them; ... 2719
Eze 32:11 **s.** of the king of Babylon shall come... 2719
Eze 32:20 of them that are slain by the **s.**... 2719
Eze 32:20 she is delivered to the **s.**: draw her... 2719
Eze 32:21 lie uncircumcised, slain by the **s.**... 2719
Eze 32:22 all of them slain, fallen by the **s.**... 2719
Eze 32:23, 24 all of them slain, fallen by the **s.**, ... 2719
Eze 32:25 them uncircumcised, slain by the **s.**... 2719
Eze 32:26 them uncircumcised, slain by the **s.**,... 2719
Eze 32:28 with them that are slain with the **s.**. ... 2719
Eze 32:29 by them that were slain by the **s.**... 2719
Eze 32:30 with them that be slain by the **s.**,... 2719
Eze 32:31 and all his army slain by the **s.**, ... 2719
Eze 32:32 with them that are slain with the **s.**, ... 2719
Eze 33:2 when I bring the **s.** upon a land, if... 2719
Eze 33:3 he seeth the **s.** come upon the land, ... 2719
Eze 33:4 if the **s.** come, and take him away, ... 2719
Eze 33:6 if the watchman see the **s.** come, ... 2719
Eze 33:6 if the **s.** come, and take any person... 2719
Eze 33:26 Ye stand upon your **s.**, ye work... 2719
Eze 33:27 are in the wastes shall fall by the **s.**,... 2719
Eze 35:5 blood...of Israel by the force of the **s.**. 2719
Eze 35:8 they fall that are slain with the **s.**... 2719
Eze 38:8 that is brought back from the **s.**, ... 2719
Eze 38:21 And I will call for a **s.** against him ... 2719
Eze 38:21 every man's **s.** shall be against his... 2719
Eze 39:23 enemies: so fell they all by the **s.**... 2719
Da 11:33 yet they shall fall by the **s.**, and by... 2719
Ho 1:7 not save them by bow, nor by **s.**, ... 2719
Ho 2:18 and I will break the bow and the **s.**... 2719
Ho 7:16 their princes shall fall by the **s.**... 2719
Ho 11:6 And the **s.** shall abide on his cities,... 2719
Ho 13:16 they shall fall by the **s.**: their... 2719
Joe 2:8 and when they fall upon the **s.**, ... 7973
Am 1:11 did pursue his brother with the **s.**,... 2719
Am 4:10 young men have I slain with the **s.**, ... 2719
Am 7:9 the house of Jeroboam with the **s.**... 2719
Am 7:11 saith, Jeroboam shall die by the **s.**, ... 2719
Am 7:17 thy daughters shall fall by the **s.**,... 2719
Am 9:1 slay the last of them with the **s.**... 2719
Am 9:4 thence will I command the **s.**, and ... 2719
Am 9:10 sinners of my people...die by the **s.**,... 2719
Mic 4:3 shall not lift up a **s.** against nation,... 2719
Mic 5:6 waste...land of Assyria with the **s.**,... 2719
Mic 6:14 deliverest will I give up to the **s.**... 2719
Na 2:13 the **s.** shall devour thy young lions:... 2719
Na 3:3 horseman lifteth up...the bright **s.**... 2719
Na 3:15 the **s.** shall cut thee off, it shall eat... 2719
Zep 2:12 also, ye shall be slain by my **s.**... 2719
Hag 2:22 every one by the **s.** of his brother... 2719
Zec 9:13 made thee as the **s.** of a mighty man. ..2719
Zec 11:17 the **s.** shall be upon his arm, and... 2719
Zec 13:7 Awake, O **s.**, against my shepherd, ... 2719
Mt 10;34 **I came not to send peace, but a s.**...*3162*
Mt 26:51 drew his **s.**, and struck a servant... *3162*
Mt 26:52 **Put up again thy s. into his**... *3162*
Mt 26:52 **for all they that take the s.** ... *3162*
Mt 26:52 **shall perish with the s.**... *3162*
Mk 14:47 one of them that stood by drew a **s.**, .. *3162*
Lu 2:35 a **s.**...pierce through thy own soul ... *4501*
Lu 21:24 **shall fall by the edge of the s.**,... *3162*
Lu 22:36 **he that hath no s., let him sell**... *3162*
Lu 22:49 Lord, shall we smite with the **s.**? ... *3162*
Joh 18:10 Simon Peter having a **s.** drew it,... *3162*
Joh 18:11 Peter, **Put up thy s. into the**... *3162*
Ac 12:2 And he killed James...with the **s.**... *3162*
Ac 16:27 doors open, he drew out his **s.**, and... *3162*
Ro 8:35 or nakedness, or peril, or **s.**? ... *3162*
Ro 13:4 for he beareth not the **s.** in vain:... *3162*
Eph 6:17 **s.** of the Spirit, which is the word... *3162*
Heb 4:12 and sharper than any twoedged **s.**, ... *3162*
Heb 11:34 escaped the edge of the **s.**, out of... *3162*
Heb 11:37 tempted, were slain with the **s.**... *3162*
Re 1:16 mouth went a sharp twoedged **s.**:... *4501*
Re 2:12 **hath the sharp s. with two edges**;.. *4501*
Re 2:16 **them with the s. of my mouth**... *4501*
Re 6:4 was given unto him a great **s.**... *3162*
Re 6:8 to kill with **s.**, and with hunger, ... *4501*
Re 13:10 he that killeth with the **s.**... *3162*
Re 13:10 must be killed with the **s.**... *3162*
Re 13:14 beast, which had the wound by a **s.**, ... *3162*
Re 19:15 out of his mouth goeth a sharp **s.**, ... *4501*
Re 19:21 the remnant were slain with the **s.** ... *4501*
Re 19:21 which **s.** proceeded out of his mouth: ...

SWORDS
1Sa 13:19 Lest the Hebrews make them **s.**... 2719
2Ki 3:26 seven hundred men that drew **s.**, ... 2719
Ne 4:13 after their families with their **s.**,... 2719
Ps 55:21 than oil, yet were they drawn **s.**. ... 6609
Ps 59:7 their mouths: **s.** are in their lips:... 2719
Pr 30;14 a generation, whose teeth are as **s.**, ... 2719
Ca 3:8 all hold **s.**, being expert in war: ... 2719
Isa 2:4 shall beat their **s.** into plowshares,... 2719
Isa 21:15 For they fled from the **s.**, from the... 2719
Eze 16:40 thrust thee through with their **s.**. ... 2719
Eze 23:47 and dispatch them with their **s.**; ... 2719
Eze 28:7 draw their **s.** against the beauty of... 2719
Eze 30:11 shall draw their **s.** against Egypt, ... 2719
Eze 32:12 By the **s.** of the mighty will I cause... 2719
Eze 32:27 have laid their **s.** under their heads,... 2719
Eze 38:4 and shields, all of them handling **s.**... 2719
Joe 3:10 Beat your plowshares into **s.**, and... 2719
Mic 4:3 shall beat their **s.** into plowshares,... 2719
Mt 26:47 with him a great multitude with **s.** ... *3162*
Mt 26:55 **out as against a thief with s.**... *3162*
Mk 14:43 with him a great multitude with **s.** ... *3162*
Mk 14:48 **out, as against a thief, with s.** ... *3162*
Lu 22:38 said, Lord, behold, here are two **s.**... *3162*
Lu 22:52 **out, as against a thief, with s.** ... *3162*

SWORE See SWARE.

SWORN
Ge 22:16 By myself have I **s.** saith the Lord, ... 7650
Ex 13:19 straitly **s.** the children of Israel, ... 7650
Ex 17:16 Lord hath **s.** that the... 3027,5920,3676
Le 6:5 about which he hath **s.** falsely; ... 7650
De 7:8 keep the oath which he hath **s.** ... 7650
De 13:17 thee, as he hath **s.** unto thy fathers; ... 7650
De 19:8 as he hath **s.** unto thy fathers,... 7650
De 28:9 himself, as he hath **s.** unto thee, ... 7650
De 29:13 and as he hath **s.** unto thy fathers, ... 7650
De 31:7 Lord hath **s.** unto their fathers to... 7650
Jos 9:18 the princes...had **s.** unto them by... 7650
Jos 9:19 We have **s.** unto them by the Lord... 7650
Jg 2:15 and as the Lord had **s.** unto them:... 7650
Jg 21:1 the men of Israel had **s.** in Mizpeh, ... 7650
Jg 21:7 seeing we have **s.** by the Lord that ... 7650
Jg 21:18 for the children of Israel have **s.** ... 7650
1Sa 3:14 I have **s.** unto the house of Eli, ... 7650
1Sa 20:42 we have **s.** both of us in the name of.. 7650
2Sa 3:9 as the Lord hath **s.** to David, even... 7650
2Sa 21:2 children of Israel had **s.** unto them:... 7650
2Ch 15:15 for they had **s.** with all their heart, ... 7650
Ne 6:18 many in Judah **s.** unto him, ... 1167,7621
Ne 9:15 which thou hadst **s.** to give them... 5375
Ps 24:4 unto vanity, nor **s.** deceitfully... 7650
Ps 89:3 I have **s.** unto David my servant, ... 7650
Ps 89:35 Once have I **s.** by my holiness that... 7650
Ps 102:8 mad against me are **s.** against me... 7650
Ps 110:4 Lord hath **s.**, and will not repent, ... 7650
Ps 119:106 I have **s.**, and I will perform it, ... 7650
Ps 132:11 Lord hath **s.** in truth unto David;... 7650
Isa 14:24 The Lord of hosts hath **s.**, saying,... 7650
Isa 45:23 I have **s.** by myself, the word is ... 7650
Isa 54:9 I have **s.** that the waters of Noah... 7650
Isa 54:9 so have I **s.** that I would not be... 7650
Isa 62:8 Lord hath **s.** by his right hand, and... 7650
Jer 5:7 and **s.** by them that are no gods: ... 7650
Jer 11:5 the oath which I have **s.** unto your ... 7650
Jer 44:26 I have **s.** by my great name, saith ... 7650
Jer 49:13 I have **s.** by myself, saith the Lord, ... 7650
Jer 51:14 Lord of hosts hath **s.** by himself,... 7650
Eze 21:23 sight, to them that have **s.** oaths:... 7650
Am 4:2 Lord god hath **s.** by his holiness,... 7650
Am 6:8 The Lord God hath **s.** by himself,... 7650
Am 8:7 hath **s.** by the excellency of Jacob,... 7650
Mic 7:20 which thou has **s.** unto our fathers... 7650
Ac 2:30 God had **s.** with an oath to him,... *3660*
Ac 7:17 which God had **s.** to Abraham, the... *3660*
Heb 4:3 As I have **s.** in my wrath, if they ... *3660*

SYCAMINE
Lu 17:6 **ye might say unto the s. tree, Be**.. *4807*

SYCAMORE See SYCOMORE.

SYCHAR (si'-kar) See also SHECHEM.
Joh 4:5 city of Samaria, which is called **S.**,... *4965*

SYCHEM (si'-kem) See also SHECHEM.
Ac 7:16 And were carried over into **S.**, ... *4966*
Ac 7:16 sons of Emmor the father of **S.** ... *4966*

SYCOMORE See also SYCOMORES.
1Ki 10:27 as the **s.** trees that are in the vale, ... 3256
1Ch 27:28 **s.** trees that were in the low plains... 3256
2Ch 1:15 cedar trees made he as the **s.** trees... 3256
2Ch 9:27 cedar trees made he as the **s.** trees... 3256
Ps 78:47 hail, and their **s.** trees with frost... 3256
Am 7:14 herdman, and a gatherer of **s.** fruit: ... 3256
Lu 19:4 climbed up into a **s.** tree to see ... *4809*

SYCOMORES
Isa 9:10 the **s.** are cut down, but we will ... 8256

SYCOMORE-TREES See SYCOMORE and TREES.

SYENE (si-e'-ne)
Eze 29:10 from the tower of **S.** even unto ... 5482
Eze 30:6 from the tower of **S.** shall they fall ... 5482

SYNAGOGUE See also SYNAGOGUE'S; SYNAGOGUES.
Mt 12:9 thence, he went into their **s.**... *4864*
Mt 13:54 country, he taught them in their **s.**, ... *4864*
Mk 1:21 sabbath day he entered into the **s.**,... *4864*
Mk 1:23 in their **s.** a man with an unclean... *4864*
Mk 1:29 when they were come out of the **s.**, ... *4864*
Mk 3:1 And he entered again into the **s.**; ... *4864*
Mk 5:22 cometh one of the rulers of the **s.**,... *752*
Mk 5:36 unto the ruler of the **s.**, **Be not**... *752*
Mk 5:38 to the house of the ruler of the **s.**,... *752*
Mk 6:2 come, he began to teach in the **s.** ... *4864*
Lu 4:16 he went into the **s.** on the sabbath ... *4864*
Lu 4:20 eyes of all them that were in the **s.** ... *4864*
Lu 4:28 And all they in the **s.**, when they ... *4864*
Lu 4:33 in the **s.** there was a man, which ... *4864*
Lu 4:38 he arose out of the **s.**, and entered... *4864*
Lu 6:6 he entered into the **s.** and taught: ... *4864*
Lu 7:5 nation, and he hath built us a **s.**. ... *4864*
Lu 8:41 and he was a ruler of the **s.**: and ... *4864*
Lu 13:14 the ruler of the **s.** answered with... *752*
Joh 6:59 These things said he in the **s.**, as... *4864*
Joh 9:22 he should be put out of the **s.**... *656*
Joh 12:42 lest they should be put out of the **s.**... *656*
Joh 18:20 I ever taught in he **s.**, and in the ... *4864*
Ac 6:9 then there arose certain of the **s.**, ... *4864*
Ac 6:9 is called the **s.** of the Libertines,... *4864*
Ac 13:14 and went into the **s.** on the sabbath... *4864*
Ac 13:15 the rulers of the **s.** sent unto them, ... 752
Ac 13:42 the Jews were gone out of the **s.**, ... *4864*
Ac 14:1 both together into the **s.** of the... *4864*
Ac 17:1 where was a **s.** of the Jews:... *4864*
Ac 17:10 thither went into the **s.** of the Jews. ... *4864*
Ac 17:17 disputed he in the **s.** with the Jews,... *4864*
Ac 18:4 reasoned in the **s.** every sabbath,... *4864*
Ac 18:7 whose house joined hard to the **s.**... *4864*
Ac 18:8 Crispus, the chief ruler of the **s.**,... *752*
Ac 18:17 Sosthenes, the chief ruler of the **s.**, ... *752*
Ac 18:19 but he himself entered into the **s.**,... *4864*
Ac 18:26 he began to speak boldly in the **s.** ... *4864*
Ac 19:8 And he went into the **s.**, and spake ... *4864*
Ac 22:19 and beat in every **s.** them that... *4864*

Ac 26:11 I punished them oft in every s., ... *4864*
Re 2:9 **are not, but are the s. of Satan** ... *4864*
Re 3:9 **make them of the s. of Satan,** ... *4864*

SYNAGOGUE'S
Mk 5:35 came from the ruler of the s. house ... *752*
Lu 8:49 one from the ruler of the s. house, ... *752*

SYNAGOGUES
Ps 74:8 have burned up all the s. of God ... 4150
Mt 4:23 teaching in their s., and preaching ... *4864*
Mt 6:2 **as the hypocrites do in the s. and** .. *4864*
Mt 6:5 **love to pray standing in the s** ... *4864*
Mt 9:35 teaching in their s., and preaching ... *4864*
Mt 10:17 **they will scourge you in their s.;** ... *4864*
Mt 23:6 **and the chief seats in the s.,** ... *4864*
Mt 23:34 **them shall ye scourge in your s.,** ... *4864*
Mk 1:39 he preached in their s. throughout ... *4864*
Mk 12:39 **And the chief seats in the s., and** .. *4864*
Mk 13:9 **and in the s. ye shall be beaten:** ... *4864*
Lu 4:15 And he taught in their s., being ... *4864*
Lu 4:44 he preached in the s. of Galilee ... *4864*
Lu 11:43 **the uppermost seats in the s.,** ... *4864*
Lu 12:11 **when they bring you unto the s.,** ... *4864*
Lu 13:10 he was teaching in one of the s. ... *4864*
Lu 20:46 **and the highest seats in the s.,** ... *4864*
Lu 21:12 **delivering you up to the s., and** ... *4864*
Joh 16:2 **They shall put you out of the s** ... *656*
Ac 9:2 him letters to Damascus to the s., ... *4864*
Ac 9:20 he preached Christ in the s., that ... *4864*
Ac 13:5 preached the word of God in the s. ... *4864*
Ac 15:21 being read in the s. every sabbath ... *4864*
Ac 24:12 neither in the s., nor in the city: ... *4864*

SYNTYCHE (sin'-ti-ke)
Php 4:2 I beseech Euodias, and beseech S., ... *4941*

SYRACUSE (sir'-a-cuse)
Ac 28:12 landing at S., we tarried there ... *4946*

SYRIA (sir'-e-ah) See also ARAM; SYRIA-DAMASCUS; SYRIA-MAACHAH; SYRIAN.
Jg 10:6 and the gods of S., and the gods of ... 758
2Sa 8:6 put garrisons in S. of Damascus: ... 758
2Sa 8:12 Of S., and of Moab, and of the ... 758
2Sa 15:8 vow while I abode at Geshur in S., ... 758
1Ki 10:29 Hittites, and for the kings of S., ... 758
1Ki 11:25 Israel, and reigned over S. ... 758
1Ki 15:18 the son of Heion, king of S., that ... 758
1Ki 19:15 anoint Hazael to be king over S. ... 758
1Ki 20:1 Ben-hadad the king of S. gathered ... 758
1Ki 20:20 the king of S. escaped on an horse ... 758
1Ki 20:22 king of S. will come up against thee. ... 758
1Ki 20:23 servants of the king of S. said unto ... 758
1Ki 22:1 without war between S. and Israel. ... 758
1Ki 22:3 not out of the hand of the king of S.? ... 758
1Ki 22:31 king of S. commanded his thirty ... 758
2Ki 5:1 captain of the host of the king of S., ... 758
2Ki 5:1 Lord had given deliverance unto S. ... 758
2Ki 5:5 the king of S. said, Go to, go, and I ... 758
2Ki 6:8 king of S. warred against Israel, ... 758
2Ki 6:11 the heart of the king of S. was sore ... 758
2Ki 6:23 the bands of S. came no more into ... 758
2Ki 6:24 Ben-hadad king of S. gathered all ... 758
2Ki 7:5 uttermost part of the camp of S., ... 758
2Ki 8:7 Ben-hadad the king of S. was sick; ... 758
2Ki 8:9 Ben-hadad king of S. hath sent me ... 758
2Ki 8:13 that thou shalt be king over S. ... 758
2Ki 8:28 the war against Hazael king of S. ... 758
2Ki 8:29 he fought against Hazael king of S. ... 758
2Ki 9:14 Israel, because of Hazael king of S. ... 758
2Ki 9:15 he fought with Hazael king of S..) ... 758
2Ki 12:17 Then Hazael king of S. went up, and ... 758
2Ki 12:18 and sent it to Hazael king of S. ... 758
2Ki 13:3 into the hand of Hazael king of S., ... 758
2Ki 13:4 the king of S. oppressed them. ... 758
2Ki 13:7 the king of S. had destroyed them, ... 758
2Ki 13:17 the arrow of deliverance from S. ... 758
2Ki 13:19 then hadst thou smitten S. till thou ... 758
2Ki 13:19 now thou shalt smite S. but thrice. ... 758
2Ki 13:22 Hazael king of S. oppressed Israel ... 758
2Ki 13:24 So Hazael king of S. died; and ... 758
2Ki 15:37 against Judah Rezin the king of S., ... 758
2Ki 16:5 Then Rezin king of S. and Pekah ... 758
2Ki 16:6 Rezin king of S. recovered Elath ... 758
2Ki 16:6 recovered Elath to S., and drave the ... 758
2Ki 16:7 me out of the hand of the king of S., ... 758
2Ch 1:17 for the kings of S., by their means ... 758
2Ch 16:2 and sent to Ben-hadad king of S., ... 758
2Ch 16:7 thou hast relied on the king of S., ... 758
2Ch 16:7 king of S. escaped out of thine hand. ... 758
2Ch 18:10 With these thou shalt push S. until ... 758
2Ch 18:30 the king of S. had commanded the ... 758
2Ch 20:2 from beyond the sea on this side S.; ... 758
2Ch 22:5 to war against Hazael king of S. at ... 758
2Ch 22:6 he fought with Hazal king of S.. ... 758
2Ch 24:23 the host of S. came up against him: ... 758
2Ch 28:5 him into the hand of the king of S.; ... 758
2Ch 28:23 gods of the kings of S. help them, ... 758
Isa 7:1 Rezin the king of S., and Pekah the ... 758
Isa 7:2 S. is confederate with Ephraim. ... 758
Isa 7:4 for the fierce anger of Rezin with S., ... 758
Isa 7:5 Because S., Ephraim, and the son ... 758
Isa 7:8 For the head of S. is Damascus, and ... 758
Isa 17:3 Damascus, and the remnant of S. ... 758
Eze 16:57 thy reproach of the daughters of S., ... 758
Eze 27:16 S. was thy merchant by reason of ... 758
Ho 12:12 Joacb fled into the country of S., ... 758
Am 1:5 people of S. shall go into captivity ... 758
Mt 4:24 his fame went throughout all S. ... *4947*
Lu 2:2 when Cyrenius was governor of S..) ... *4947*
Ac 15:23 of the Gentiles in Antioch and S. ... *4947*
Ac 15:41 he went through S. and Cilicia, ... *4947*
Ac 18:18 brethren, and sailed thence into S., ... *4947*
Ac 20:3 as he was about to sail into S., he ... *4947*
Ac 21:3 sailed into S., and landed at Tyre: ... *4947*
Gal 1:21 I came into the regions of S. and ... *4947*

SYRIACK (sir'-e-ak) See also SYRIAN.
Da 2:4 the Chaldeans to the king in S., ... 762

SYRIA-DAMASCUS (sir''-e-ah-da-mas'-cus) See also SYRIA and DAMASCUS.
1Ch 18:6 David put garrisons in S.; ... 758,1834

SYRIA-MAACHAH (sir''-e-ah-ma'-a-kah)
1Ch 19:6 and out of S., and out of Zobah. ... 758

SYRIAN (sir'-e-un) See also ARAMITES; SYRIANS; SYROPHENICIAN.
Ge 25:20 of Bethuel the S. of Padan-aram, ... 761
Ge 25:20 the sister to Laban the S.. ... 761
Ge 28:5 unto Laban, son of Bethuel the S., ... 761
Ge 31:20 away unawares to Laban the S., ... 761
Ge 31:24 And God came to Laban the S. in a ... 761
De 26:5 a S. ready to perish was my father, ... 761
2Ki 5:20 master hath spared Naaman this S., ... 761
2Ki 18:26 to thy servants in the S. language; ... 762
Ezr 4:7 letter was written in the S. tongue, ... 762
Ezr 4:7 and interpreted in the S. tongue. ... 762
Isa 36:11 thy servant in the S. language; ... 762
Lu 4:27 **cleansed, saving Naaman the S.** ... *4948*

SYRIANS (sir'-e-uns)
2Sa 8:5 S. of Damascus came to succour ... 758
2Sa 8:5 David slew of the S. two and twenty ... 758
2Sa 8:6 the S. became servants to David, ... 758
2Sa 8:13 from smiting of the S. in the valley ... 758
2Sa 10:6 and hired the S. of Beth-rehob, ... 758
2Sa 10:6 and the S. of Zoba, twenty thousand ... 758
2Sa 10:8 the S. of Zoba, and or Rehob, and ... 758
2Sa 10:9 put them in array against the S. ... 758
2Sa 10:11 If the S. be too strong for me, then ... 758
2Sa 10:13 him, unto the battle against the S. ... 758
2Sa 10:14 of Ammon saw that the S. were fled, ... 758
2Sa 10:15 the S. saw that they were smitten ... 758
2Sa 10:16 the S. that were beyond the river: ... 758
2Sa 10:17 S. set themselves in array against ... 758
2Sa 10:18 And the S. fled before Israel; and ... 758
2Sa 10:18 of seven hundred chariots of the S., ... 758
2Sa 10:19 the S. feared to help the children of ... 758
1Ki 20:20 S. fled; and Israel pursued them: ... 758
1Ki 20:21 slew the S. with a great slaughter ... 758
1Ki 20:26 that Ben-hadad numbered the S., ... 758
1Ki 20:27 kids; but the s. filled the country, ... 758
1Ki 20:28 Because the S. have said, The Lord ... 758
1Ki 20:29 the children of Israel slew of the S. ... 758
1Ki 22:11 With these shalt thou push the S., ... 758
1Ki 22:35 up in his chariot against the S., ... 758
2Ki 5:2 the S. had gone out by companies, ... 758
2Ki 6:9 for thither the S. are come down. ... 758
2Ki 7:4 let us fall unto the host of the S. ... 758
2Ki 7:5 to go unto the camp of the S. ... 758
2Ki 7:6 made...host of the S. to hear a noise. ... 758
2Ki 7:10 We came to the camp of the S., and, ... 758
2Ki 7:12 you what the S. have done to us. ... 758
2Ki 7:14 the king sent after the host of the S., ... 758
2Ki 7:15 which the S. had cast away in their ... 758
2Ki 7:16 out, and spoiled the tents of the S.. ... 758
2Ki 8:28 and the S. wounded Joram. ... 761
2Ki 8:29 wounds which the S. had given him. ... 761
2Ki 9:15 wounds which the S. had given him, ... 761
2Ki 13:5 out from under the hand of the S. ... 758
2Ki 13:17 for thou shalt smite the S. in Aphek, ... 758
2Ki 16:6 and the S. came to Elath, and dwelt ... 758
2Ki 24:2 bands of the S., and bands of the ... 758
1Ch 18:5 the S. of Damascus came to help ... 758
1Ch 18:5 David slew of the S. two and twenty ... 758
1Ch 18:6 and the S. became David's servants, ... 758
1Ch 19:10 and put them in array against the S. ... 758
1Ch 19:12 If the S. be too strong for me, then ... 758
1Ch 19:14 nigh before the S. unto the battle; ... 758
1Ch 19:15 Ammon saw that the S. were fled, ... 758
1Ch 19:16 the S. saw that they were put to the ... 758
1Ch 19:16 the S. that were beyond the river: ... 758
1Ch 19:17 the battle in array against the S., ... 758
1Ch 19:18 But the S. fled before Israel; and ... 758
1Ch 19:18 David slew of the S. seven thousand ... 758
1Ch 19:19 the S. help the children of Ammon ... 758
2Ch 18:34 in his chariot against the S. until ... 758
2Ch 22:5 and the S. smote Joram. ... 761
2Ch 24:24 army of the S. came with a small ... 758
Isa 9:12 The S. before, and the philistines ... 758
Jer 35:11 and for fear of the army of the S.: ... 758
Am 9:7 from Caphtor, and the S. from Kir? ... 758

SYROPHENICIAN (sy''-ro-fe-ne'-she-un)
Mk 7:26 The woman was a Greek, a S. by ... *4949*

T.

TAANACH (ta'-a-nak) See also TANACH.
Jos 12:21 The king of T., one; the king of ... 8590
Jos 17:11 the inhabitants of T. and her towns, ... 8590
Jg 1:27 nor T. and her towns, nor the ... 8590
Jg 5:19 fought the kings of Canaan in T. ... 8590
1Ki 4:12 to him pertained T. and Megiddo, ... 8590
1Ch 7:29 T. and her towns, Megiddo and her ... 8590

TAANATH-SHILOH (ta''-a-nath-shi'-lo)
Jos 16:6 went about eastward unto T., ... 8387

TABBAOTH (tab'-ba-oth)
Ezr 2:43 of Hasupha, the children of T.. ... 2884
Ne 7:46 of Hashupha, the children of T., ... 2884

TABBATH (tab'-bath)
Jg 7:22 border of Abel-meholah, unto T.. ... 2888

TABEAL (tab'-e-al) See also TABEEL.
Isa 7:6 the midst of it, even the son of T. ... 2870

TABEEL (tab'-e-el) See also TABEAL.
Ezr 4:7 wrote Bishlam, Mithredath, T., ... 2870

TABER See TABERING.

TABERAH (tab'-e-rah)
Nu 11:3 called the name of the place T. ... 8404
De 9:22 And at T., and at Massah, and at ... 8404

TABERING
Na 2:7 of doves, t. upon their breasts, ... 8608

TABERNACLE See also TABERNACLES.
Ex 25:9 thee, after the pattern of the t., ... 4908
Ex 26:1 shalt make the t. with ten curtains ... 4908
Ex 26:6 the taches: and it shall be one t. ... 4908
Ex 26:7 hair to be a covering upon the t. ... 4908
Ex 26:9 curtain in the forefront of the t. ... 168
Ex 26:12 hang over the backside of the t. ... 4908
Ex 26:13 it shall hang over the sides of the t., .. 4908

Ex	26:15	boards for the **t.** of shittim wood	4908
Ex	26:17	make for all the boards of the **t.**	4908
Ex	26:18	shalt make the boards for the **t.**,	4908
Ex	26:20	second side of the **t.** on the north	4908
Ex	26:22	And for the sides of the **t.** westward...	4908
Ex	26:23	thou make for the corners of the **t.**	4908
Ex	26:26	the boards of the one side of the **t.**,	4908
Ex	26:27	boards of the other side of the **t.**,	4908
Ex	26:27	for the boards of the side of the **t.**,	4908
Ex	26:30	shalt rear up the **t.** according to the	4908
Ex	26:35	the side of the **t.** toward the south:	4908
Ex	27:9	thou shalt make the court of the **t.**	4908
Ex	27:19	vessels of the **t.** in all the service	4908
Ex	27:21	In the **t.** of...congregation without	168
Ex	28:43	come in unto...**t.** of...congregation,	168
Ex	29:4	door of the **t.** of the congregation,	168
Ex	29:10	before the **t.** of the congregation:	168
Ex	29:11	door of the **t.** of the congregation.	168
Ex	29:30	into the **t.** of the congregation	168
Ex	29:32	door of the **t.** of the congregation.	168
Ex	29:42	door of the **t.** of the congregation	168
Ex	29:43	the **t.** shall be sanctified by my glory	
Ex	29:44	sanctify the **t.** of the congregation,	168
Ex	30:16	service of the **t.** of the congregation;	168
Ex	30:18	between the **t.** of the congregation	168
Ex	30:20	go into the **t.** of the congregation,	168
Ex	30:26	anoint the **t.** of the congregation	168
Ex	30:36	testimony in...**t.** of...congregation,	168
Ex	31:7	**t.** of the congregation, and the ark	168
Ex	31:7	and all the furniture of the **t.**,	168
Ex	33:7	And Moses took the **t.**, and pitched it	168
Ex	33:7	called it...**T.** of the congregation.	168
Ex	33:7	out unto the **t.** of the congregation,	168
Ex	33:8	when Moses went out unto the **t.**,	168
Ex	33:8	Moses, until he was gone into the **t.**	168
Ex	33:8	pass, as Moses entered into the **t.**,	168
Ex	33:9	pillar...stood at the door of the **t.**,	168
Ex	33:10	cloudy pillar stand at the **t.** door:	168
Ex	33:11	Joshua...departed not out of the **t.**	168
Ex	35:11	The **t.**, his tent, and his covering,	4908
Ex	35:15	the door at the entering in of the **t.**,	4908
Ex	35:18	The pins of the **t.**, and the pins of	4908
Ex	35:21	work of the **t.** of the congregation,	168
Ex	36:8	that wrought the work of the **t.**	4908
Ex	36:13	with the taches: so it became one **t.**	4908
Ex	36:14	goats' hair for the tent over the **t.**	4908
Ex	36:20	boards for the **t.** of shittim wood,	4908
Ex	36:22	he make for all the boards of the **t.**	4908
Ex	36:23	And he made boards for the **t.**;	4908
Ex	36:25	And for the other side of the **t.**,	4908
Ex	36:27	And for the sides of the **t.** westward...	4908
Ex	36:28	made he for the corners of the **t.**	4908
Ex	36:31	the boards of the one side of the **t.**,	4908
Ex	36:32	boards of the other side of the **t.**,	4908
Ex	36:32	and five bars for the boards of the **t.**	4908
Ex	36:37	made an hanging for the **t.** door.	168
Ex	38:8	door of the **t.** of the congregation.	168
Ex	38:20	And all the pins of the **t.**, and of	4908
Ex	38:21	This is the sum of the **t.**, even of	4908
Ex	38:21	even of the **t.** of testimony, as it was	4908
Ex	38:30	door of the **t.** of the congregation,	168
Ex	38:31	and all the pins of the **t.**, and all	4908
Ex	39:32	**t.** of the tent of the congregation	4908
Ex	39:33	And they brought the **t.** unto Moses,	4908
Ex	39:38	and the hanging for the **t.** door,	168
Ex	39:40	the vessels of the service of the **t.**,	4908
Ex	40:2	**t.** of the tent of the congregation.	4908
Ex	40:5	put the hanging of the door to the **t.**	4908
Ex	40:6	**t.** of the tent of the congregation.	4908
Ex	40:9	anoint the **t.**, and all that is therein,	4908
Ex	40:12	door of the **t.** of the congregation,	168
Ex	40:17	month, that the **t.** was reared up,	4908
Ex	40:18	And Moses reared up the **t.**, and	4908
Ex	40:19	spread abroad the tent over the **t.**,	4908
Ex	40:21	And he brought the ark into the **t.**,	4908
Ex	40:22	upon the side of the **t.** northward,	4908
Ex	40:24	on the side of the **t.** southward.	4908
Ex	40:28	up the hanging at the door of the **t.**	4908
Ex	40:29	**t.** of the tent of the congregation,	4908
Ex	40:33	round about the **t.** and the altar,	4908
Ex	40:34,	35 the glory of the Lord filled the **t.**	4908
Ex	40:36	cloud was taken up from over the **t.**,	4908
Ex	40:38	cloud of the Lord was upon the **t.**	4908
Le	1:1	out of the **t.** of the congregation,	168
Le	1:3	door of the **t.** of the congregation	168
Le	1:5	door of the **t.** of the congregation.	168
Le	3:2	door of the **t.** of the congregation:	168
Le	3:13	before the **t.** of the congregation:	168
Le	4:4	door of the **t.** of the congregation	168
Le	4:5	bring it to the **t.** of...congregation:	168
Le	4:7	is in the **t.** of the congregation;	168
Le	4:7	door of the **t.** of the congregation.	168
Le	4:14	before the **t.** of the congregation.	168
Le	4:16	blood to the **t.** of the congregation:	168
Le	4:18	that is in the **t.** of the congregation,	168
Le	4:18	door of the **t.** of the congregation.	168
Le	6:16	court of the **t.** of the congregation	168
Le	6:26	court of the **t.** of the congregation.	168
Le	6:30	into the **t.** of the congregation	168
Le	8:3,4	door of the **t.** of the congregation.	168
Le	8:10	anointed the **t.** and all...therein,	4908
Le	8:31	door of the **t.** of the congregation:	168
Le	8:33	not go out of the door of the **t.**	168
Le	8:35	door of the **t.** of the congregation	168
Le	9:5	before the **t.** of the congregation:	168
Le	9:23	went into the **t.** of the congregation,	168
Le	10:7	door of the **t.** of the congregation,	168
Le	10:9	go into the **t.** of the congregation,	168
Le	12:6	door of the **t.** of the congregation,	168
Le	14:11	door of the **t.** of the congregation:	168
Le	14:23	door of the **t.** of the congregation,	168
Le	15:14	door of the **t.** of the congregation,	168
Le	15:29	door of the **t.** of the congregation.	168
Le	15:31	defile my **t.** that is among them.	4908
Le	16:7	door of the **t.** of the congregation.	168
Le	16:16	he do for the **t.** of the congregation,	168
Le	16:17	no man in the **t.** of the congregation	168
Le	16:20	place, and the **t.** of...congregation,	168
Le	16:23	come into the **t.** of...congregation,	168
Le	16:33	atonement for...**t.** of...congregation,	168
Le	17:4	door of the **t.** of the congregation,	168
Le	17:4	the Lord before the **t.** of the Lord;	4908
Le	17:5,	6,9 door of the **t.** of...congregation,	168
Le	19:21	door of the **t.** of the congregation,	168
Le	24:3	in the **t.** of the congregation,	168
Le	26:11	And I will set my **t.** among you:	4908
Nu	1:1	Sinai, in the **t.** of the congregation,	168
Nu	1:50	Levites over the **t.** of testimony,	4908
Nu	1:50	shall bear the **t.**, and all the vessels	4908
Nu	1:50	shall encamp round about the **t.**	4908
Nu	1:51	And when the **t.** setteth forward,	4908
Nu	1:51	and when the **t.** is to be pitched, the	4908
Nu	1:53	round about the **t.** of testimony,	4908
Nu	1:53	the charge of the **t.** of testimony.	4908
Nu	2:2	about the **t.** of the congregation	168
Nu	2:17	the **t.** of the congregation shall set	168
Nu	3:7	before the **t.** of the congregation,	168
Nu	3:7	to do the service of the **t.**	4908
Nu	3:8	of the **t.** of the congregation,	168
Nu	3:8	Israel, to do the service of the **t.**	4908
Nu	3:23	shall pitch behind the **t.** westward.	4908
Nu	3:25	in the **t.** of the congregation	168
Nu	3:25	shall be the **t.**, and the tent,	4908
Nu	3:25	door of the **t.** of the congregation,	168
Nu	3:26	of the court, which is by the **t.**	4908
Nu	3:29	on the side of the **t.** southward.	4908
Nu	3:35	on the side of the **t.** northward.	4908
Nu	3:36	shall be the boards of the **t.**, and	4908
Nu	3:38	before the **t.** toward the east, even	4908
Nu	3:38	before the **t.** of the congregation	168
Nu	4:3	work in the **t.** of the congregation	168
Nu	4:4	Kohath in the **t.** of...congregation,	168
Nu	4:15	Kohath in the **t.** of...congregation.	168
Nu	4:16	and the oversight of all the **t.**, and	4908
Nu	4:23	work in the **t.** of the congregation	168
Nu	4:25	shall bear the curtains of the **t.**	4908
Nu	4:25	and the **t.** of the congregation, his	168
Nu	4:25	door of the **t.** of the congregation,	168
Nu	4:26	which is by the **t.** and by the altar	4908
Nu	4:28	Gershon in the **t.** of...congregation:	168
Nu	4:30	work of the **t.** of the congregation	168
Nu	4:31	service in the **t.** of...congregation;	168
Nu	4:31	the boards of the **t.**, and the bars	4908
Nu	4:33	service, in the **t.** of...congregation,	168
Nu	4:35	work in the **t.** of the congregation:	168
Nu	4:37	service in the **t.** of the congregation,	168
Nu	4:39	work in the **t.** of the congregation,	168
Nu	4:41	service in the **t.** of the congregation,	168
Nu	4:43	work in the **t.** of the congregation,	168
Nu	4:47	burden in the **t.** of the congregation,	168
Nu	5:17	dust that is in the floor of the **t.**	4908
Nu	6:10,	13 door of the **t.** of...congregation:	168
Nu	6:18	door of the **t.** of the congregation,	168
Nu	7:1	that Moses had fully set up the **t.**,	4908
Nu	7:3	they brought them before the **t.**	4908
Nu	7:5	service of the **t.** of...congregation;	168
Nu	7:89	gone into the **t.** of the congregation	168
Nu	8:9	before the **t.** of the congregation:	168
Nu	8:15	service of the **t.** of the congregation:	168
Nu	8:19	Israel in the **t.** of the congregation,	168
Nu	8:22	service in the **t.** of the congregation	168
Nu	8:24	service of the **t.** of the congregation:	168
Nu	8:26	brethren in the **t.** of...congregation,	168
Nu	9:15	And on the day that the **t.** was	4908
Nu	9:15	reared up the cloud covered the **t.**,	4908
Nu	9:15	at even there was upon the **t.** as it	4908
Nu	9:17	the cloud was taken up from the **t.**,	168
Nu	9:18	as the cloud abode upon the **t.**	4908
Nu	9:19	the cloud tarried long upon the **t.**	4908
Nu	9:20	cloud was a few days upon the **t.**;	4908
Nu	9:22	that the cloud tarried upon the **t.**,	4908
Nu	10:3	door of the **t.** of the congregation.	168
Nu	10:11	was taken up from off the **t.** of the	4908
Nu	10:17	And the **t.** was taken down; and the	4908
Nu	10:17	Merari set forward, bearing the **t.**	4908
Nu	10:21	the other did set up the **t.** against	4908
Nu	11:16	them unto the **t.** of...congregation,	168
Nu	11:24	and set them round about the **t.**	168
Nu	11:26	but went not out into the **t.**: and	168
Nu	12:4	three unto the **t.** of...congregation.	168
Nu	12:5	and stood in the door of the **t.**, and	168
Nu	12:10	the cloud departed from off the **t.**;	168
Nu	14:10	appeared in the **t.** of...congregation	168
Nu	16:9	do the service of the **t.** of the Lord,	4908
Nu	16:18	door of the **t.** of the congregation	168
Nu	16:19	door of the **t.** of the congregation:	168
Nu	16:24	you up from about the **t.** of Korah,	4908
Nu	16:27	they gat up from the **t.** of Korah,	4908
Nu	16:42	toward the **t.** of the congregation:	168
Nu	16:43	before the **t.** of the congregation.	168
Nu	16:50	door of the **t.** of the congregation:	168
Nu	17:4	them up in the **t.** of...congregation	168
Nu	17:7	before the Lord in the **t.** of witness.	168
Nu	17:8	Moses went into the **t.** of witness;	168
Nu	17:13	near unto the **t.** of the Lord shall	4908
Nu	18:2	minister before the **t.** of witness.	168
Nu	18:3	charge, and the charge of all the **t.**	168
Nu	18:4	charge of the **t.** of the congregation,	168
Nu	18:4	for all the service of the **t.**: and a	168
Nu	18:6	service of the **t.** of the congregation.	168
Nu	18:21	service of the **t.** of the congregation.	168
Nu	18:22	come nigh the **t.** of...congregation,	168
Nu	18:23	service of the **t.** of the congregation,	168
Nu	18:31	service in the **t.** of the congregation.	168
Nu	19:4	before the **t.** of the congregation	168
Nu	19:13	himself, defileth the **t.** of the Lord;	4908
Nu	20:6	door of the **t.** of the congregation,	168
Nu	25:6	door of the **t.** of the congregation.	168
Nu	27:2	door of the **t.** of the congregation,	168
Nu	31:30	the charge of the **t.** of the Lord.	4908
Nu	31:47	the charge of the **t.** of the Lord;	4908
Nu	31:54	it into the **t.** of the congregation,	168
De	31:14	yourselves in...**t.** of...congregation,	168
De	31:14	in the **t.** of the congregation.	168
De	31:15	Lord appeared in the **t.** in a pillar of	168
De	31:15	cloud stood over the door of the **t.**	168
Jos	18:1	set up the **t.** of the congregation	168
Jos	19:51	door of the **t.** of the congregation.	168
Jos	22:19	wherein the Lord's **t.** dwelleth,	4908
Jos	22:29	Lord our God that is before his **t.**	4908
1Sa	2:22	door of the **t.** of the congregation.	168
2Sa	6:17	**t.** that David had pitched for it:	168
2Sa	7:6	have walked in a tent and in a **t.**	4908
1Ki	1:39	took an horn of oil out of the **t.**,	168
1Ki	2:28	Joab fled unto the **t.** of the Lord,	168
1Ki	2:29	was fled unto the **t.** of the Lord;	168
1Ki	2:30	Benaiah came to the **t.** of the Lord,	168
1Ki	8:4	and the **t.** of the congregation, and	168
1Ki	8:4	the holy vessels that were in the **t.**,	168
1Ch	6:32	place of the **t.** of the congregation	168
1Ch	6:48	of the **t.** of the house of God	4908
1Ch	9:19	keepers of the gate of the **t.**	168
1Ch	9:21	door of the **t.** of the congregation.	168
1Ch	9:23	the house of the **t.**, by wards	168
1Ch	16:39	priests, before the **t.** of the Lord	4908
1Ch	17:5	to tent, and from one **t.** to another.	4908
1Ch	21:29	For the **t.** of the Lord, which Moses...	4908
1Ch	23:26	they shall no more carry the **t.**, nor	4908

1Ch 23:32 charge of the **t.** of...congregation, ... 168
2Ch 1:3 there was the **t.** of the congregation..... 168
2Ch 1:5 he put before the **t.** of the Lord:........ 4908
2Ch 1:6 was at the **t.** of the congregation, ... 168
2Ch 1:13 before the **t.** of the congregation, ... 168
2Ch 5:5 and the **t.** of the congregation, ... 168
2Ch 5:5 the holy vessels that were in the **t.**,..... 168
2Ch 24:6 of Israel, for the **t.** of witness?........... 168
Job 5:24 know that thy **t.** shall be in peace; 168
Job 18:6 The light shall be dark in his **t.**, and..... 168
Job 18:14 confidence...be rooted out of his **t.**,....... 168
Job 18:15 It shall dwell in his **t.**, because it is...... 168
Job 19:12 me, and encamp round about my **t.**. 168
Job 20:26 go ill with him that is left in his **t.**........ 168
Job 29:4 the secret of God was upon my **t.**; 168
Job 31:31 If the men of my **t.** said not, Oh......... 168
Job 36:29 the clouds, or the noise of his **t.**?......... 5521
Ps 15:1 Lord, who shall abide in thy **t.**?.......... 168
Ps 19:4 In them hath he set a **t.** for the sun, ... 168
Ps 27:5 In the secret of his **t.** shall he hide 168
Ps 27:6 will I offer in his **t.** sacrifices of joy; 168
Ps 61:4 I will abide in thy **t.** for ever: I will...... 168
Ps 76:2 In Salem also is his **t.**, and his........... 5520
Ps 78:60 So that he forsook the **t.** of Shiloh,..... 4908
Ps 78:67 he refused the **t.** of Joseph, and 168
Ps 132:3 not come into the **t.** of my house,........ 168
Pr 14:11 the **t.** of the upright shall flourish......... 168
Isa 4:6 a **t.** for a shadow in the daytime 5521
Isa 16:5 upon it in truth in the **t.** of David,........ 168
Isa 33:20 a **t.** that shall not be taken down; 168
Jer 10:20 My **t.** is spoiled, and all my cords........ 168
La 2:4 in the **t.** of the daughter of Zion: 168
La 2:6 he hath violently taken away his **t.**,..... 7900
Eze 37:27 My **t.** also shall be with them:........... 4908
Eze 41:1 which was the breadth of the **t.**............. 168
Am 5:26 the **t.** of your Moloch and Chiun 5522
Am 9:11 day will I raise up the **t.** of David....... 5521
Ac 7:43 ye took up the **t.** of Moloch, and......... *4633*
Ac 7:44 Our fathers had the **t.** of witness in.... *4633*
Ac 7:46 to find a **t.** for the God of Jacob......... *4638*
Ac 15:16 will build again the **t.** of David, ... *4633*
2Co 5:1 our earthly house of this **t.** were........ *4636*
2Co 5:4 For we that are in this **t.** do graon, ... *4636*
Heb 8:2 and of the true **t.**, which the Lord...... *4633*
Heb 8:5 when he was about to make the **t.**. *4633*
Heb 9:2 For there was a **t.** made: the first,..... *4633*
Heb 9:3 **t.** which is called the Holiest of all;..... *4633*
Heb 9:6 priests went always into the first **t.**, ... *4633*
Heb 9:8 as the fist **t.** was yet standing: *4633*
Heb 9:11 by a greater and more perfect **t.**,....... *4633*
Heb 9:21 he sprinkled with blood both the **t.**, ... *4633*
Heb 13:10 no right to eat which serve the **t.**........ *4633*
2Pe 1:13 as long as I am in this **t.**, to stir *4638*
2Pe 1:14 shortly I must put off this my **t.**,.......... *4638*
Re 13:6 to blaspheme his name, and his **t.**, ... *4633*
Re 15:5 temple of the **t.** of the testimony........ *4633*
Re 21:3 the **t.** of God is with men, and he *4633*

TABERNACLES
Le 23:34 be the feast of **t.** for seven days........ 5521
Nu 24:5 tents, O Jacob, and thy **t.**, O Israel! ... 4908
De 16:13 observe the feast of **t.** seven days,..... 5521
De 16:16 feast of weeks, and in the feast of **t.**..... 5521
De 31:10 the year of release, in the feast of **t.**, ..5521
2Ch 8:13 feast of weeks, and in the feast of **t.**... 5521
Ezr 3:4 They kept also the feast of **t.**, as it is ..5521
Job 11:14 let not wickedness dwell in thy **t.**. 168
Job 12:6 The **t.** of robbers prosper, and they..... 168
Job 15:34 fire shall consume the **t.** of bribery....... 168
Job 22:23 put away iniquity far from thy **t.** 168
Ps 43:3 me unto thy holy hill, and to thy **t.**..... 4908
Ps 46:4 place of the **t.** of the most High......... 4908
Ps 78:51 of their strength in the **t.** of Ham: 168
Ps 83:6 **t.** of Edom, and the Ishamelites;.......... 168
Ps 84:1 How amiable are thy **t.**, O Lord of..... 4908
Ps 118:15 is in the **t.** of the righteous:................ 168
Ps 132:7 We will go into his **t.**: we will............ 4908
Da 11:45 he shall plant the **t.** of his palace 168
Ho 9:6 them: thorns shall be in their **t.**........... 168
Ho 12:9 will yet make thee to dwell in **t.**, ... 168
Zec 14:16 of hosts, and to keep the feast of **t.**..... 5521
Zec 14:18, 19 not up to keep the feast of **t.**........ 5521
Mal 2:12 the scholar, out of the **t.** of Jacob, ... 168
Mt 17:4 let us make here three **t.**; one for....... *4633*
Mk 9:5 let us make three **t.**; one for thee, ... *4633*
Lu 9:33 let us make three **t.**; one for thee, ... *4633*

Joh 7:2 the Jews' feast of **t.** was at hand........ *4634*
Heb 11:9 dwelling in **t.** with Isaac...Jacob,......... *4633*

TABITHA (tab'-ith-ah)
Ac 9:36 a certain disciple named **T.**,............... *5000*
Ac 9:40 him to the body said, **T.**, arise. *5000*

TABLE See also TABLES.
Ex 25:23 also make a **t.** of shittim wood:.......... 7979
Ex 25:27 places of the staves to bear the **t.**...... 7979
Ex 25:28 that the **t.** may be borne with them. ... 7979
Ex 25:30 thou shalt set upon the **t.** shewbread .. 7979
Ex 26:35 thou shalt set the **t.** without the vail, .. 7979
Ex 26:35 the candlestick over against the **t.** 7979
Ex 26:35 shalt put the **t.** on the north side. 7979
Ex 30:27 And the **t.** and all his vessels, and...... 7979
Ex 31:8 And the **t.** and his furniture, and the... 7979
Ex 35:13 The **t.**, and his staves, and all his........ 7979
Ex 37:10 And he made the **t.** of shittim wood:... 7979
Ex 37:14 places for the staves to ear the **t.**. 7979
Ex 37:15 them with gold, to bear the **t.**. 7979
Ex 37:16 the vessels which were upon the **t.**, ... 7979
Ex 39:36 The **t.**, and all the vessels thereof,..... 7979
Ex 40:4 And thou shalt bring in the **t.**, and...... 7979
Ex 40:22 And he put the **t.** in the tent of the.... 7979
Ex 40:24 over against the **t.**, on the side of...... 7979
Le 24:6 upon the pure **t.** before the Lord. 7979
Nu 3:31 charge shall be the ark, and the **t.**,..... 7979
Nu 4:7 upon the **t.** of shewbread they shall.... 7979
Jg 1:7 gathered their meat under my **t.** 7979
1Sa 20:29 he cometh not unto the king's **t.**. 7979
1Sa 20:34 Jonathan arose from the **t.** in fierce..... 7979
2Sa 9:7 and thou shalt eat bread at my **t.** 7979
2Sa 9:10 son shall eat bread alway at my **t.**. 7979
2Sa 9:11 he shall eat at my **t.**, as one of the..... 7979
2Sa 9:13 did eat continually at the king's **t.**; 7979
2Sa 19:28 them that did eat at thine own **t.**......... 7979
1Ki 2:7 them be of those that eat at thy **t.** 7979
1Ki 4:27 that came unto king Solomon's **t.**......... 7979
1Ki 7:48 the altar of gold, and the **t.** of gold, ... 7979
1Ki 10:5 the meat of his **t.**, and the sitting....... 7979
1Ki 13:20 it came to pass, as they sat at the **t.**, . 7979
1Ki 18:19 hundred, which eat at Jezebel's **t.**........ 7979
2Ki 4:10 us set for him there a bed, and a **t.**,... 7979
1Ch 28:16 tables of shewbread, for every **t.**; 7979
2Ch 9:4 the meat of his **t.**, and the sitting....... 7979
2Ch 13:11 set they in order upon the pure **t.**; 7979
2Ch 29:18 and the shewbread **t.**, with all the 7979
Ne 5:17 there were at my **t.** an hundred and ... 7979
Job 36:16 that which should be set on thy **t.** 7979
Ps 23:5 Thou preparest a **t.** before me in the .. 7979
Ps 69:22 Let their **t.** become a snare before...... 7979
Ps 78:19 God furnish a **t.** in the wilderness? 7979
Ps 128:3 like olive plants round about thy **t.**...... 7979
Pr 3:3 them upon the **t.** of thine heart:......... 3871
Pr 7:3 write them upon the **t.** of thine heart. . 3871
Pr 9:2 she hath also furnished her **t.**........... 7979
Ca 1:12 While the king sitteth at his **t.**, my...... 4524
Isa 21:5 Prepare the **t.**, watch in the............. 7979
Isa 30:8 Now go, write it before them in a **t.**, .. 3871
Isa 65:11 that prepare a **t.** or that troop, ... 7979
Jer 17:1 graven upon the **t.** of their heart, ... 3871
Eze 23:41 bed, and a **t.** prepared before it, ... 7979
Eze 39:20 Thus ye shall be filled at my **t.** with.... 7979
Eze 41:2 This is the **t.** that is before the Lord. ..7979
Eze 44:16 and they shall come near to my **t.**, ... 7979
Da 11:27 and they shall speak lies at one **t.**; 7979
Mal 1:7 The **t.** of the Lord is contemptible....... 7979
Mal 1:12 say, The **t.** of the Lord is polluted;..... 7979
Mt 15:27 which fall from their masters' **t.**, ... *5132*
Mk 7:28 yet the dogs under the **t.** eat of the.... *5132*
Lu 1:63 And he asked for a writing **t.**, and...... *4093*
Lu 16:21 fell from the rich man's **t.** *5132*
Lu 22:21 me is with me on the **t.** *5132*
Lu 22:30 may eat and drink at my **t.** in....... *5132*
Joh 12:2 of them that sat at the **t.** with him...........
Joh 13:28 Now no man at the **t.** knew for what.... *345*
Ro 11:9 saith, Let their **t.** be made a snare, ... *5132*
1Co 10:21 cannot be partakers of the Lord's **t.**,... *5132*
1Co 10:21 and of the **t.** of devils. *5132*
Heb 9:2 and the **t.**, and the shewbread; *5132*

TABLES
Ex 24:12 and I will give thee **t.** of stone,.......... 3871
Ex 31:18 two **t.** of testimony, **t.** of stone, ... 3871
Ex 32:15 two **t.** of the testimony were in his..... 3871
Ex 32:15 **t.** were written on both their sides;...... 3871
Ex 32:16 And the **t.** were the work of God,...... 3871
Ex 32:16 writing of God, graven upon the **t.**. 3871
Ex 32:19 and he cast the **t.** out of his hands, ... 3871
Ex 34:1 two **t.** of stone like unto the first: 3871
Ex 34:1 I will write upon these **t.** the words.... 3871
Ex 34:1 in the first **t.**, which thou brakest....... 3871
Ex 34:4 two **t.** of stone like unto the first; 3871
Ex 34:4 took in his hand the two **t.** of stone.... 3871
Ex 34:28 wrote upon the **t.** the words of the..... 3871
Ex 34:29 two **t.** of testimony in Moses' hand,.... 3871
De 4:13 he wrote them upon to **t.** of stone...... 3871
De 5:22 he wrote them in two **t.** of stone, ... 3871
De 9:9 the mount to receive the **t.** of stone, .. 3871
De 9:9 **t.** of the covenant which the Lord...... 3871
De 9:10 Delivered unto me two **t.** of stone...... 3871
De 9:11 Lord gave me the two **t.** of stone, ... 3871
De 9:11 stone, even the **t.** of the covenant...... 3871
De 9:15 two **t.** of the covenant were in my 3871
De 9:17 I took the two **t.**, and cast them out... 3871
De 10:1 two **t.** of stone like unto the first, ... 3871
De 10:2 I will write on the **t.** the words that.... 3871
De 10:2 in the first **t.** which thou brakest, ... 3871
De 10:3 two **t.** of stone like unto the first, ... 3871
De 10:3 having the two **t.** in mine hand. 3871
De 10:4 he wrote on the **t.**, according to the ... 3871
De 10:5 and put the **t.** in the ark which I had... 3871
1Ki 8:9 in the ark save the two **t.** of stone, ... 3871
1Ch 28:16 gave gold for the **t.** of shew bread,..... 7979
1Ch 28:16 likewise silver for the **t.** of silver:....... 7979
2Ch 4:8 He made also ten **t.**, and placed......... 7979
2Ch 4:19 **t.** whereon the shewbread was set; 7979
2Ch 5:10 nothing in the ark save the two **t.** 3871
Isa 28:8 For all **t.** are full of vomit and............ 7979
Eze 40:39 in the porch of the gate were two **t.**... 7979
Eze 40:39 this side, and two **t.** on that side,....... 7979
Eze 40:40 entry of the north gate, were two **t.**; .. 7979
Eze 40:40 the porch of the gate, were two **t.**. 7979
Eze 40:41 Four **t.** were on this side, and four..... 7979
Eze 40:41 and four **t.** on that side, by the side.... 7979
Eze 40:41 eight **t.**, whereupon they slew their 7979
Eze 40:42 four **t.** were of hewn stone for the 7979
Eze 40:43 and upon the **t.** was the flesh of the ... 7979
Hab 2:2 vision, and make it plain upon **t.**,........ 3871
Mt 21:12 the **t.** of the moneychangers, and......... *5132*
Mk 7:4 and pots, brasen vessels, and of **t.**. *2825*
Mk 11:15 the **t.** of the moneychangers,............. *5132*
Joh 2:15 money, and overthrew the **t.**;............. *5132*
Ac 6:2 leave the word of God, and serve **t.**. .. *5132*
2Co 3:3 living God; not in **t.** of stone. *4109*
2Co 3:3 but in fleshy **t.** of the heart............... *4109*
Heb 9:4 budded, and the **t.** of the covenant; *4109*

TABLETS
Ex 35:22 and earrings, and rings, and **t.**, all...... 3558
Nu 31:50 bracelets, rings, earrings, and **t.**, ... 3558
Isa 3:20 headbands, and the **t.**, and......... 1004,5315

TABOR (ta'-bor) See also AZNOTH-TABOR; CHISLOTH-TABOR.
Jos 19:22 And the coast reacheth to **T.**, and...... 8396
Jg 4:6 Go and draw toward mount **T.**, and.... 8396
Jg 4:12 Barak...was gone up to mount **T.**....... 8396
Jg 4:14 Barak went down from mount **T.**,........ 8396
Jg 8:18 men were they whom ye slew at **T.**? .. 8396
1Sa 10:3 thou shalt come to the plain of **T.**,....... 8396
1Ch 6:77 her suburbs, **T.** with her suburbs: 8396
Ps 89:12 **T.** and Hermon shall rejoice in thy...... 8396
Jer 46:18 as **T.** is among the mountains, and 8396
Ho 5:1 Mizpah, and a net spread upon **T.**. 8396

TABRET See also TABRETS.
Ge 31:27 with songs, with **t.**, and with harp?..... 8596
1Sa 10:5 and a **t.**, and a pipe, and a harp, ... 8596
Job 17:6 and aforetime I was a **t.**.................... 8611
Isa 5:12 the **t.**, and pipe, and wine, are in....... 8596

TABRETS
1Sa 18:6 to meet king Saul, with **t.**, with......... 8596
Isa 24:8 The mirth of **t.** ceaseth, the noise of... 8596
Isa 30:32 him, it shall be with **t.** and harps:....... 8596
Jer 31:4 shalt again be adorned with thy **t.**,....... 8596
Eze 28:13 the workmanship of thy **t.** and of........ 8596

TABRIMON (tab'-rim-on)
1Ki 15:18 them to Ben-hadad,...son of **T.**, ... 2886

TACHES (tatch'-ez)
Ex 26:6 thou shalt make fifty **t.** of gold,.......... 7165
Ex 26:6 the curtains together with the **t.** 7165
Ex 26:11 thou shalt make fifty **t.** of brass, ... 7165
Ex 26:11 and put the **t.** into the loops, and....... 7165
Ex 26:33 shalt hang up the vail under the **t.**,..... 7165

Ex 35:11 his covering, his **t.**, and his boards, ... 7165
Ex 36:13 And he made fifty **t.** of gold, and........ 7165
Ex 36:13 one unto another with the **t.**: so 7165
Ex 36:18 made fifty **t.** of brass to couple the...... 7165
Ex 39:33 all his furniture, his **t.**, his boards,...... 7165

TACHMONITE (tak'-mun-ite) See also HACHMONITE.
2Sa 23:8 The **T.** that sat in the seat, chief 8461

TACKLING See also TACKLINGS.
Ac 27:19 our own hand the **t.** of the ship. *4631*

TACKLINGS
Isa 33:23 Thy **t.** are loosed; they could not....... 2256

TADMOR (tad'-mor)
1Ki 9:18 Baalath, and **T.** in the wilderness, ... 8412
2Ch 8:4 he built **T.** in the wilderness, and........ 8412

TAHAN (ta'-han) See also TAHANITES.
Nu 26:35 **T.**, the family of the Tahanites........... 8465
1Ch 7:25 and Telah his son, and **T.** his son,....... 8465

TAHANITES (ta'-han-ites)
Nu 26:35 of Tahan, the family of the **T.**............ 8470

TAHAPANES (ta-hap'-a-neze) See also TAHPANHES; TAHPENES.
Jer 2:16 the children of Noph and **T.** have 8471

TAHATH (ta'-hath)
Nu 33:26 Makheloth, and encamped at **T.**. 8480
Nu 33:27 they departed from **T.**, and pitched..... 8480
1Ch 6:24 **T.** his son, Uriel his son, Uzziah........ 8480
1Ch 6:37 The son of **T.**, the son of Assir, ... 8480
1Ch 7:20 Bered his son, and **T.** his son,.......... 8480
1Ch 7:20 Eladah his son, and **T.** his son,.......... 8480

TAHPANHES (tah'-pan-heze) See also TAHPANES; TAHPENES; TEHAPHNEHES.
Jer 43:7 Lord: thus came they even to **T.**. 8471
Jer 43:8 of the Lord unto Jeremiah in **T.**, ... 8471
Jer 43:9 the entry of Pharaoh's house in **T.**,..... 8471
Jer 44:1 which dwell at Migdol, and at **T.**........ 8471
Jer 46:14 and publish in Noph and in **T.**............ 8471

TAHPENES (ta'-pe-neze) See also TAHPANHES.
1Ki 11:19 wife, the sister of **T.** the queen. 8472
1Ki 11:20 sister of **T.** bare him Genubath.......... 8472
1Ki 11:20 **T.** weaned in Pharaoh's house: 8472

TAHREA (tah'-re-ah) See also TAREA.
1Ch 9:41 and Melech, and **T.**, and Ahaz. 8475

TAHTIM-HODSHI (tah''-tim-hod'-shi)
2Sa 24:6 to Gilead, and to the land of **T.**;......... 8483

TAIL See also TAILS.
Ex 4:4 thine hand, and take it by the **t.**.......... 2180
De 28:13 thee the head, and not the **t.**;............ 2180
De 28:44 the head, and thou shalt be the **t.**. 2180
Jg 15:4 turned **t.** to **t.**, and put a firebrand 2180
Job 40:17 He moveth his **t.** like a cedar: the...... 2180
Isa 9:14 cut off from Israel head and **t.**, ... 2180
Isa 9:15 that teacheth lies, he is the **t.**. 2180
Isa 19:15 which the head or **t.**, branch or 2180
Re 12:4 his **t.** drew the third part of the......... *3769*

TAILS
Jg 15:4 in the midst between two **t.**. 2180
Isa 7:4 two **t.** of these smoking firebrands,..... 2180
Re 9:10 they had **t.** like unto scorpions,.......... *3769*
Re 9:10 and there were stings in their **t.** *3769*
Re 9:19 is in their mouth, and in their **t.**......... *3769*
Re 9:19 their **t.** were like unto serpents, ... *3769*

TAKE See also OVERTAKE; TAKEN; TAKEST; TAKETH; TAKING; TOOK; UNDERTAKE.
Ge 3:22 **t.** also of the tree of life, and eat, ... 3947
Ge 6:21 **t.** thou unto thee of all food that is..... 3947
Ge 7:2 clean beast thou shalt **t.** to thee by..... 3947
Ge 12:19 behold thy wife, **t.** her, and go thy..... 3947
Ge 13:9 if thou wilt **t.** the left hand, then I will.......
Ge 14:21 persons, and **t.** the goods to thyself.... 3947
Ge 14:23 I will not **t.** from a thread even to a ... 3947
Ge 14:28 I will not **t.** anything that is thine, ... 3947
Ge 14:24 Mamre; let them **t.** their portion. 3947
Ge 15:9 **T.** me an heifer of three years old,..... 3947
Ge 19:15 **t.** thy wife, and thy two daughters,..... 3947
Ge 19:19 lest some evil **t.** me, and I die:.......... 1692
Ge 21:30 lambs shalt thou **t.** of my hand,......... 3947
Ge 22:2 **T.** not thy son, thine only son.......... 3947
Ge 23:13 **t.** it of me, and I will bury my dead.... 3947
Ge 24:3 shalt not **t.** a wife unto my son of 3947
Ge 24:4 and **t.** a wife unto my son Isaac. 3947
Ge 24:7 and thou shalt **t.** a wife unto my son... 3947
Ge 24:37 shalt not **t.** a wife to my son of the 3947
Ge 24:38 kindred, and **t.** a wife unto my son. 3947
Ge 24:40 thou shalt **t.** a wife for my son of....... 3947
Ge 24:48 to **t.** my master's brother's daughter... 3947
Ge 24:51 Rebekah is before thee, **t.** her, and.... 3947
Ge 27:3 **t.**, I pray thee, thy weapons, thy 5375
Ge 27:3 the field, and **t.** me some venison;....... 6679
Ge 27:46 if Jacob **t.** a wife of the daughters....... 3947
Ge 28:1 shalt not **t.** a wife of the daughters..... 3947
Ge 28:2 **t.** thee a wife from thence of the 3947
Ge 28:6 to **t.** him a wife from thence; and....... 3947
Ge 28:6 shalt not **t.** a wife of the daughters..... 3947
Ge 30:15 **t.** away my son's mandrakes also?...... 3947
Ge 31:24 **T.** heed that thou speak not to 3947
Ge 31:29 **T.** thou heed that thou speak not 3947
Ge 31:31 **t.** by force thy daughters from........... 1497
Ge 31:32 is thine with me, and to it to thee. 3947
Ge 31:50 if thou shalt **t.** other wives beside 3947
Ge 33:11 **T.**, I pray thee, my blessing that is 3947
Ge 33:12 Let us **t.** our journey, and let us go..........
Ge 34:9 and **t.** our daughters unto you. 3947
Ge 34:16 we will **t.** your daughters to us,......... 3947
Ge 34:17 then will we **t.** our daughter, and 3947
Ge 34:21 let us **t.** their daughters to us for....... 3947
Ge 38:23 Let her **t.** it to her, lest we be.......... 3947
Ge 41:34 **t.** up he fifth part of the land of ....
Ge 42:33 and **t.** food for the famine of your....... 3947
Ge 42:36 not, and ye will **t.** Benjamin away:...... 3947
Ge 43:11 **t.** of the best fruits in the land in 3947
Ge 43:12 **t.** double money in your hand; and...... 3947
Ge 43:13 **T.** also your brother, and arise, go..... 3947
Ge 43:18 **t.** us for bondmen, and our asses. 3947
Ge 44:29 And if ye **t.** this also from me, and..... 3947
Ge 45:18 **t.** your father and your households, ... 3947
Ge 45:19 **t.** your wagons out of the land of....... 3947
Ex 2:9 **T.** this child away, and nurse it.......... 3212
Ex 4:4 thine hand, and **t.** it by the tail. 270
Ex 4:9 shalt **t.** of the water of the river, ... 3947
Ex 4:17 shalt **t.** this rod in thine hand,............ 3947
Ex 6:7 I will **t.** you to me for a people, and ... 3947
Ex 7:9 **T.** thy rod, and cast it before 3947
Ex 7:15 serpent shalt thou **t.** in thine hand...... 3947
Ex 7:19 **T.** thy rod, and stretch out thine........ 3947
Ex 8:8 that he may **t.** away the frogs from 5493
Ex 9:8 **T.** to you handfuls of ashes of the 3947
Ex 10:17 **t.** away from me this death only......... 5493
Ex 10:26 we **t.** to serve the Lord our God; 3947
Ex 10:28 **t.** heed to thyself, see my face no...... 3947
Ex 12:3 **t.** to them every man a lamb,............ 3947
Ex 12:4 **t.** it according to the number of the.... 3947
Ex 12:5 ye shall **t.** it out from the sheep,........ 3947
Ex 12:7 And they shall **t.** of the blood, and...... 3947
Ex 12:21 **t.** you a lamb according to your 3947
Ex 12:22 And ye shall **t.** a bunch of hyssop,...... 3947
Ex 12:32 Also **t.** your flocks and your herds,..... 3947
Ex 15:14 shall **t.** hold on the inhabitants of 270
Ex 15:15 trembling shall **t.** hold upon them;......... 270
Ex 16:16 **t.** ye every man or them which.......... 3947
Ex 16:33 **T.** a pot, and put an omer full of........ 3947
Ex 17:5 **t.** with thee of the elders of Israel;..... 3947
Ex 17:5 the river, **t.** in thine hand, and go. 3947
Ex 19:12 **T.** heed to yourselves, that ye go............
Ex 20:7 shalt not **t.** the name of the Lord....... 5375
Ex 21:10 If he **t.** him another wife; her............ 3947
Ex 21:14 thou shalt **t.** him from mine altar,....... 3947
Ex 22:26 at all **t.** thy neighbour's raiment 2254
Ex 23:8 And thou shalt **t.** no gift: for the 3947
Ex 23:25 **t.** sickness away from the midst......... 5493
Ex 25:2 his heart ye shall **t.** my offering. 3947
Ex 25:3 offering which ye shall **t.** of them: 3947
Ex 26:5 loops may **t.** hold one of another......... 6901
Ex 28:1 And **t.** thou unto thee Aaron thy 7126
Ex 28:5 And they shall **t.** gold, and blue, ... 3947
Ex 28:9 And thou shalt **t.** two onyx stones, ... 3947
Ex 29:1 **T.** one young bullock, and two........... 3947
Ex 29:5 And thou shalt **t.** the garments, ... 3947
Ex 29:7 Then shalt thou **t.** the anointing oil, ... 3947
Ex 29:12 shalt **t.** of the blood of the bullock, ... 3947
Ex 29:13 thou shalt **t.** all the fat that covereth... 3947
Ex 29:15 Thou shalt also **t.** one ram; and 3947
Ex 29:16 ram, and thou shalt **t.** his blood, ... 3947
Ex 29:19 And thou shalt **t.** the other ram; 3947
Ex 29:20 kill the ram, and to of his blood, ... 3947
Ex 29:21 **t.** of the blood that is upon the altar, .. 3947
Ex 29:22 **t.** of the ram the fat and the rump,..... 3947
Ex 29:26 thou shalt **t.** the breast of the ram...... 3947
Ex 29:31 shalt **t.** the ram of the consecration, ... 3947
Ex 30:16 thou shalt **t.** the atonement money 3947
Ex 30:23 **T.** thou also unto thee principal.......... 3947
Ex 30:34 **T.** unto thee sweet spices, stacte,...... 3947
Ex 33:23 And I will **t.** away mine hand,............ 5493
Ex 34:9 sin, and **t.** us for thine inheritance. ....
Ex 34:12 **T.** heed to thyself, lest thou make...........
Ex 34:16 **t.** of their daughters unto thy sons, ... 3947
Ex 35:5 **T.** ye from among you an offering 3947
Ex 40:9 And thou shalt **t.** the anointing oil,...... 3947
Le 2:2 **t.** thereout his handful of the flour...... 7061
Le 2:9 shall **t.** from the meat offering 7311
Le 3:4 and the fat...it shall he **t.** away. 5493
Le 3:9 shall he **t.** off hard by the backbone; 5493
Le 3:10, 15 and the fat...it shall he **t.** away...... 5493
Le 4:5 shall **t.** of the bullock's blood, ... 3947
Le 4:8 he shall **t.** off from it all the fat of...... 3318
Le 4:9 and the fat...it shall he **t.** away, ... 5493
Le 4:19 he shall **t.** all his fat from him,........... 7311
Le 4:25 **t.** of the blood of the sin offering........ 3947
Le 4:30 And the priest shall **t.** of the blood..... 3947
Le 4:31 he shall **t.** away all the fat thereof, ... 5493
Le 4:34 **t.** of the blood of the sin offering........ 3947
Le 4:35 he shall **t.** away all the fat thereof, ... 5493
Le 5:12 the priest shall **t.** his handful of it,...... 7061
Le 6:10 **t.** up the ashes which the fire hath 7311
Le 6:15 And he shall **t.** of it his handful,.......... 7311
Le 7:4 and the fat...it shall he **t.** away: 5493
Le 8:2 **T.** Aaron and his sons with him, ... 3947
Le 9:2 **T.**...a young calf for a sin offering, ... 3947
Le 9:3 **T.** ye a kid of the goats for a sin........ 3947
Le 10:12 **T.** the meat offering that remaineth.... 3947
Le 14:4 to **t.** for him that is to be cleansed..... 3947
Le 14:6 As for the living bird, he shall **t.** it, ... 3947
Le 14:10 **t.** two he lambs without blemish,........ 3947
Le 14:12 And the priest shall **t.** one he lamb,.... 3947
Le 14:14 the priest shall **t.** some of the blood..... 3947
Le 14:15 priest shall **t.** some of the log of oil, ... 3947
Le 14:21 **t.** one lamb for a trespass offering...... 3947
Le 14:24 **t.** the lamb of the trespass offering,.... 3947
Le 14:25 the priest shall **t.** some of the blood.... 3947
Le 14:40 **t.**...the stones in which the plague...... 2502
Le 14:42 And they shall **t.** other stones, and..... 3947
Le 14:42 he shall **t.** other mortar, and shall....... 3947
Le 14:49 And he shall **t.** to cleanse the house ... 3947
Le 14:51 he shall **t.** the cedar wood, and the..... 3947
Le 15:14 he shall **t.** to him two turtledoves,...... 3947
Le 15:29 she shall **t.** unto her two turtles,....... 3947
Le 16:5 And he shall **t.** of the congregation 3947
Le 16:7 And he shall **t.** the two goats, and...... 3947
Le 16:12 **t.** a censer full of burning coals of 3947
Le 16:14, 18 **t.** of the blood of the bullock, ... 3947
Le 18:17 shalt thou **t.** her son's daughter, ... 3947
Le 18:18 shalt thou **t.** a wife to her sister, ... 3947
Le 20:14 if a man **t.** a wife and her mother,...... 3947
Le 20:17 And if a man shall **t.** his sister, his 3947
Le 20:21 if a man shall **t.** his brother's wife, ... 3947
Le 21:7 shall not **t.** a wife that is a whore,...... 3947
Le 21:7 shall they **t.** a woman put away from... 3947
Le 21:13 he shall **t.** a wife in her virginity. 3947
Le 21:14 or an harlot, these shall he not **t.**......... 3947
Le 21:14 he shall **t.** a virgin of his own people... 3947
Le 22:5 a man of whom he may **t.** uncleanness, ...
Le 23:40 **t.** you on the first day the boughs 3947
Le 24:5 thou shalt **t.** fine flour, and bake 3947
Le 25:36 **T.** thou no usury of him, or 3947
Le 25:46 **t.** them as an inheritance for your.............
Nu 1:2 **T.** ye the sum of...congregation......... 5375
Nu 1:49 Levi, neither **t.** the sum of them........ 5375
Nu 1:51 the Levites shall **t.** it down: 3381
Nu 3:40 and **t.** the number of their names. 5375
Nu 3:41 thou shalt **t.** the Levite from me 3947
Nu 3:45 **T.** the Levites instead of all the 3947
Nu 3:47 shalt even **t.** five shekels apiece......... 3947
Nu 3:47 of the sanctuary shalt thou **t.** them: 3947
Nu 4:2 **T.** the sum of the sons of Kohath....... 5375
Nu 4:5 they shall **t.** down the covering vail,.... 3381
Nu 4:9 And they shall **t.** a cloth of blue, ... 3947
Nu 4:12 **t.** all the instruments of ministry, ... 3947
Nu 4:13 shall **t.** away the ashes from the altar,.......
Nu 4:22 **T.**...sum of the sons of Gershon, ... 5375
Nu 5:17 And the priest shall **t.** holy water 3947
Nu 5:17 and of the dust...the priest shall **t.**, ... 3947
Nu 5:25 priest shall **t.** the jealousy offering...... 3947
Nu 5:26 shall **t.** an handful of the offering, ... 7061
Nu 6:18 shall **t.** the hair of the head of his....... 3947

Nu 6:19 priest shall **t.** the sodden shoulder 3947
Nu 7:5 **T.** it of them, that they may be to 3947
Nu 8:6 **T.** the Levites from among the 3947
Nu 8:8 Then let them **t.** a young bullock 3947
Nu 8:8 shalt thou **t.** for a sin offering 3947
Nu 10:6 the south side shall **t.** their journey:
Nu 11:17 **t.** of the spirit which is upon thee, 680
Nu 16:3 Ye **t.** too much upon you, seeing all
Nu 16:6 **T.** you censers, Korah, and all his 3947
Nu 16:7 ye **t.** too much upon you, ye sons of
Nu 16:17 And **t.** every man his censer, and 3947
Nu 16:37 that he **t.** up the censers out of the 7311
Nu 16:46 **T.** a censer, and put fire therein 3947
Nu 17:2 and **t.** of every one of them a rod 3947
Nu 17:10 quite **t.** away their murmurings 3615
Nu 18:26 **t.** of the children of Israel the tithes 3947
Nu 19:4 Eleazar...shall **t.** of her blood 3947
Nu 19:6 And the priest shall **t.** cedar wood, 3947
Nu 19:17 **t.** of the ashes of the burnt heifer 3947
Nu 19:18 And a clean person shall **t.** hyssop, 3947
Nu 20:8 **T.** the rod, and gather thou the 3947
Nu 20:25 **T.** Aaron and Eleazar his son, and 3947
Nu 21:7 he **t.** away the serpents from us. 5493
Nu 23:12 Must I not **t.** heed to speak that
Nu 25:4 **T.** all the heads of the people, and 3947
Nu 26:2 **T.** the sum of all the congregation 5375
Nu 26:4 **T.** the sum of the people, from twenty
Nu 27:18 **T.** thee Joshua the son of Nun, 3947
Nu 31:26 **T.** the sum of the prey that was 5375
Nu 31:29 **T.** it of their half, and give it unto 3947
Nu 31:30 thou shalt **t.** one portion of fifty, of 3947
Nu 34:18 ye shall **t.** one prince of every tribe, 3947
Nu 35:31 **t.** no satisfaction for the life of a 3947
Nu 35:32 **t.** no satisfaction for him that is fled 3947
De 1:7 Turn you, and **t.** your journey, and go
De 1:13 **T.** you wise men, and 3051
De 1:40 **t.** your journey into the wilderness
De 2:4 **t.** ye good heed unto yourselves
De 2:24 Rise ye up, **t.** your journey, and pass
De 4:9 Only **t.** heed to thyself, and keep
De 4:15 **T.** ye...good heed unto yourselves;
De 4:23 **T.** heed unto yourselves, lest ye
De 4:34 assayed to go and **t.** him a nation 3947
De 5:11 shalt not **t.** the name of the Lord 5375
De 7:3 his daughter...**t.** unto thy son. 3947
De 7:15 **t.** away from thee all sickness, 5493
De 7:25 silver or gold...nor **t.** it unto thee, 3947
De 10:11 Arise, **t.** thy journey before the people,
De 11:16 **T.** heed to yourselves, that your
De 12:13 **T.** heed to thyself that thou offer
De 12:19 **T.** heed to thyself that thou forsake
De 12:26 and thy vows, thou shalt **t.**, and go 5375
De 12:30 **T.** heed to thyself that thou be
De 15:17 Then thou shalt **t.** an aul, and 3947
De 16:19 respect persons, neither **t.** a gift: 3947
De 20:7 the battle, and another man **t.** her. 3947
De 20:14 thereof, shalt thou **t.** unto thyself; 962
De 20:19 in making war against it to **t.** it, 8610
De 21:3 elders of that city...**t.** an heifer, 3947
De 22:6 shalt not **t.** the dam with the young: 3947
De 22:7 dam go, and **t.** the young to thee; 3947
De 22:13 If any man **t.** a wife, and go in unto 3947
De 22:15 **t.** and bring forth the tokens of the 3947
De 22:18 elders of that city shall **t.** that man 3947
De 22:30 man shall not **t.** his father's wife, 3947
De 24:4 may not **t.** her again to be his wife, 3947
De 24:6 shall **t.** the nether or the upper 2254
De 24:8 **T.** heed in the plague of leprosy,
De 24:17 **t.** a widow's raiment to pledge: 2254
De 25:5 unto her, and **t.** her to him to wife, 3947
De 25:7 man like not to **t.** his brother's wife, 3947
De 25:8 to it, and say, I like not to **t.** her; 3947
De 26:2 shalt **t.** of the first of all the fruit of 3947
De 26:4 **t.** the basket out of thine hand, 3947
De 27:9 **T.** heed, and hearken, O Israel; 5535
De 31:26 **T.** this book of the law, and put 3947
De 32:41 mine hand **t.** hold on judgment; 270
Jos 3:6 **T.** up the ark of the covenant, and 5375
Jos 3:12 **t.** you twelve men out of the tribes 3947
Jos 4:2 **T.** you twelve men...of the people, 3947
Jos 4:3 **T.** you hence out of the midst of 5375
Jos 4:5 **t.** ye up every man of you a stone 7311
Jos 6:6 **T.** up the ark of the covenant, and 5375
Jos 6:18 when ye **t.** of the accursed thing, 3947
Jos 7:13 **t.** away the accursed thing from 5493
Jos 7:14 the family which the Lord shall **t.** 3920
Jos 7:14 household which the Lord shall **t.** 3920
Jos 8:1 **t.** all the people of war with thee, 3947
Jos 8:2 shall ye **t.** for a prey unto yourselves:
Jos 8:29 **t.** his carcase down from a tree, 3381
Jos 9:11 **T.** victuals...for the journey, 3947
Jos 10:42 their land...Joshua **t.** at one time, 3920
Jos 11:12 all the kings of them, did Joshua **t.**, 3920
Jos 20:4 shall **t.** him into the city unto them, 622
Jos 22:5 **t.**...heed to do the commandment
Jos 22:19 and **t.** possession among us: but 270
Jos 23:11 **T.** good heed therefore unto your
Jg 4:6 **t.** with thee ten thousand men of 3947
Jg 5:30 the necks of them that **t.** the spoil?
Jg 6:20 **T.** the flesh and the unleavened 3947
Jg 6:25 **T.** thy father's young bullock, even 3947
Jg 6:26 **t.** the second bullock, and offer a 3947
Jg 7:24 **t.** before them the waters unto 3920
Jg 14:3 to **t.** a wife of the uncircumcised 3947
Jg 14:8 after a time he returned to **t.** her, 3947
Jg 14:15 ye called us to **t.** that we have? 3423
Jg 15:2 sister fairer than she? **t.** her, 1961
Jg 19:30 consider of it, **t.** advice, and speak
Jg 20:10 we will **t.** ten men of an hundred 3947
Ru 2:10 thou shouldest **t.** knowledge of me,
Ru 2:19 be he that did **t.** knowledge of thee.
1Sa 2:16 and then **t.** as much as thy soul 3947
1Sa 2:16 now: and if not, I will **t.** it by force. 3947
1Sa 6:7 **t.** two milch kine, on which there 3947
1Sa 6:8 **t.** the ark of the Lord, and lay it 3947
1Sa 8:11 He will **t.** your sons, and appoint 3947
1Sa 8:13 And he will **t.** your daughters to be 3947
1Sa 8:14 And he will **t.** your fields, and your 3947
1Sa 8:15 And he will **t.** the tenth of your seed,
1Sa 8:16 And he will **t.** your menservants, 3947
1Sa 8:17 He will **t.** the tenth of your sheep:
1Sa 9:3 **T.** now one of the servants with 3947
1Sa 9:5 for the asses, and **t.** thought for us.
1Sa 16:2 **T.** an heifer with thee, and say, I 3947
1Sa 17:17 **T.** now for thy brethren an ephah 3947
1Sa 17:18 brethren fare, and **t.** their pledge. 3947
1Sa 17:46 thee, and **t.** thine head from thee; 5493
1Sa 19:2 **t.** heed to thyself until...morning,
1Sa 19:14 Saul sent messengers to **t.** David, 3947
1Sa 19:20 Saul sent messengers to **t.** David: 3947
1Sa 20:21 are on this side of thee, **t.** them; 3947
1Sa 21:9 if thou wilt **t.** that, **t.** it: for there 3947
1Sa 23:23 **t.** knowledge of all the lurking places
1Sa 23:26 his men round about to **t.** them. 8610
1Sa 24:11 yet thou huntest my soul to **t.** it. 3947
1Sa 25:11 Shall I then **t.** my bread, and my 3947
1Sa 25:39 Abigail, to **t.** her to him to wife. 3947
1Sa 25:40 unto thee, to **t.** thee to him to wife. 3947
1Sa 26:11 **t.** thou now the spear that is at his 3947
2Sa 2:21 young men, and **t.** thee his armour. 3947
2Sa 4:11 and **t.** you away from the earth? 1197
2Sa 5:6 **t.** away the blind and the lame, 5493
2Sa 12:4 he spared to **t.** of his own flock 3947
2Sa 12:11 I will **t.** thy wives before thine eyes, 3947
2Sa 12:28 encamp against the city, and **t.** it: 3920
2Sa 12:28 lest I **t.** the city, and it be called 3920
2Sa 13:33 the king **t.** the thing to his heart, 7760
2Sa 15:20 return thou, and **t.** back thy brethren:
2Sa 16:9 me go over,...and **t.** off his head. 5493
2Sa 19:19 the king should **t.** it to his heart. 7760
2Sa 19:30 Yea, let him **t.** all, forasmuch as 3947
2Sa 20:6 **t.** thou thy lord's servants, and 3947
2Sa 24:10 **t.** away the iniquity of thy servant; 5674
2Sa 24:22 **t.** and offer up what seemeth good 3947
1Ki 1:33 **T.** with you the servants of your 3947
1Ki 2:4 thy children **t.** heed to their way,
1Ki 2:31 mayest **t.** away the innocent blood, 5493
1Ki 8:25 thy children **t.** heed to their way,
1Ki 11:31 to Jeroboam, **T.** thee ten pieces: 3947
1Ki 11:34 will not **t.** the whole kingdom out 3947
1Ki 11:35 I will **t.** the kingdom out of his 3947
1Ki 11:37 I will **t.** thee, and thou shalt reign 3947
1Ki 14:3 And **t.** with thee ten loaves, and 3947
1Ki 14:10 **t.** away the remnant of the house 1197
1Ki 16:3 **t.** away the posterity of Baasha, 1197
1Ki 18:40 them, **T.** the prophets of Baal; 8610
1Ki 19:4 now, O Lord, **t.** away my life; for 3947
1Ki 19:10, 14 they seek my life, to **t.** it away. 3947
1Ki 20:6 put it in their hand, and **t.** it away. 3947
1Ki 20:18 come out for peace, **t.** them alive; 8610
1Ki 20:18 be come out or war, **t.** them alive. 8610
1Ki 20:24 **T.** the kings away, every man out 5493
1Ki 21:15 **t.** possession of the vineyard of 3423
1Ki 21:16 the Jezreelite, to **t.** possession of it. 3423
1Ki 21:21 and will **t.** away thy posterity, 1197
1Ki 22:3 **t.** it not out of the hand of the king 3947
1Ki 22:26 **T.** Micaiah, and carry him back 3947
2Ki 2:1 when the Lord would **t.** up Elijah 5927
2Ki 2:3, 5 Lord will **t.** away thy master 3947
2Ki 4:1 creditor is come to **t.** unto him my 3947
2Ki 4:29 loins, and **t.** my staff in thine hand, 3947
2Ki 4:36 unto him, he said, **T.** up thy son. 5375
2Ki 5:15 thee, **t.** a blessing of thy servant. 3947
2Ki 5:16 And he urged him to **t.** it; but he 3947
2Ki 5:20 after him, and **t.** somewhat of him. 3947
2Ki 5:23 said, Be content, **t.** two talents. 3947
2Ki 6:2 and **t.** thence every man a beam, 3947
2Ki 6:7 Therefore said he, **T.** it up to thee. 7311
2Ki 6:32 hath sent to **t.** away mine head? 5493
2Ki 7:13 Let some **t.**,...five of the horses 3947
2Ki 8:8 **T.** a present in thine hand, and go, 3947
2Ki 9:1 and **t.** this box of oil in thine hand, 3947
2Ki 9:3 **t.** the box of oil, and pour it on his 3947
2Ki 9:17 **T.** an horseman, and send to meet 3947
2Ki 9:25 **T.** up, and cast him in the portion 5375
2Ki 9:26 **t.** and cast him into the plat of 5375
2Ki 10:6 **t.** ye the heads of the men your 3947
2Ki 10:14 And he said, **T.** them alive. 8610
2Ki 12:5 Let the priests **t.** it to them, 3947
2Ki 13:15 said unto him, **T.** bow and arrows. 3947
2Ki 13:18 And he said, **T.** the arrows. And he 3947
2Ki 18:32 Until I come and **t.** you...to a land 3947
2Ki 19:30 Judah, shall yet again **t.** root downward,
2Ki 20:7 And Isaiah said, **T.** a lump of figs. 3947
2Ki 20:18 of thy sons...shall they **t.** away; 3947
1Ch 7:21 came down to **t.** away their cattle. 3947
1Ch 17:13 not **t.** my mercy away from him, 5493
1Ch 21:23 said unto David, **T.** it to thee, and 3947
1Ch 21:24 I will not **t.** that which is thine for 5375
1Ch 28:10 **T.** heed now; for the Lord hath 7200
2Ch 6:16 **t.** heed to their way to walk in my
2Ch 18:25 **T.** ye Micaiah, and carry him back 3947
2Ch 19:6 to the judges, **T.** heed what ye do: 7200
2Ch 19:7 be upon you; **t.** heed and do it:
2Ch 20:25 his people came to **t.** away the spoil 962
2Ch 32:18 them; that they might **t.** the city. 3920
2Ch 33:8 they will **t.** heed to do all that I
Ezr 4:22 **T.** heed now that ye fail not to do 2095
Ezr 5:14 Cyrus the king **t.** out of the temple 5312
Ezr 5:15 **T.** these vessels, go, carry them 5376
Ezr 9:12 **t.** their daughters unto your sons, 5375
Ne 5:2 therefore we **t.** up corn for them, 3947
Ne 6:7 and let us **t.** counsel together.
Ne 10:30 nor **t.** their daughters for our sons: 3947
Ne 10:38 Levites, when the Levites **t.** tithes:
Ne 13:25 **t.** their daughters unto your sons, 5375
Es 4:4 to **t.** away his sackcloth from him: 5493
Es 6:10 and **t.** the apparel and the horse, 3947
Es 8:11 and to **t.** the spoil of them for a prey,
Es 3:13 and to **t.** the spoil of them for a prey.
Job 7:21 and **t.** away mine iniquity? 5674
Job 9:18 He will not suffer me to **t.** my breath,
Job 9:34 Let him **t.** his rod away from me, 5493
Job 10:20 alone, that I may **t.** comfort a little,
Job 11:18 and thou shalt **t.** thy rest in safety. 7901
Job 13:14 do I **t.** my flesh in my teeth, and 5375
Job 18:9 The gin shall **t.** him by the heel, 270
Job 21:12 they **t.** the timbrel and harp, and 5375
Job 23:10 But he knoweth the way that I **t.** 5978
Job 24:2 they violently **t.** away flocks, and 1497
Job 24:3 they **t.** the widow's ox for a pledge. 2254
Job 24:9 breast, and **t.** a pledge of the poor. 2254
Job 24:10 they **t.** away the sheaf from the 5375
Job 27:20 Terrors **t.** hold on him as waters, 5381
Job 30:17 season: and my sinews **t.** no rest. 7901
Job 31:36 I would **t.** it upon my shoulder, 5375
Job 32:22 my maker would soon **t.** me away. 5375
Job 36:17 judgment and justice **t.** hold on 8551
Job 36:18 he **t.** thee away with his stroke: 5496
Job 36:21 **T.** heed, regard not iniquity: for
Job 38:13 it might **t.** hold of the ends of the 270
Job 38:20 thou shouldest **t.** it to the bound 3947
Job 41:4 thou **t.** him for a servant for ever? 3947
Job 42:8 **t.** unto you now seven bullocks and 3947
Ps 2:2 and the rulers **t.** counsel together,
Ps 7:5 persecute my soul, and **t.** it; 5381
Ps 13:2 long shall I **t.** counsel in my soul, 7896
Ps 16:4 nor **t.** up their names into my lips. 5375
Ps 27:10 me, then the Lord will **t.** me up. 622
Ps 31:13 they devised to **t.** away my life. 3947

Ps 35:2 **T.** hold of shield and buckler, and....... 2388
Ps 39:1 I will **t.** heed to my ways, that I.............
Ps 50:9 will **t.** no bullock out of thy house, ... 3947
Ps 50:16 or thou shouldest **t.** my covenant 5375
Ps 51:11 and **t.** not thy holy spirit from me. 3947
Ps 52:5 he shall **t.** thee away, and pluck......... 2846
Ps 58:9 **t.** them away as with a whirlwind, ... 8175
Ps 69:20 I looked for some to **t.** pity, but there.......
Ps 69:24 wrathful anger **t.** hold of them. 5381
Ps 71:10 that lay wait for my soul **t.** counsel..........
Ps 71:11 persecute and **t.** him; for there is....... 8610
Ps 80:9 and didst cause it to **t.** deep root, ...
Ps 81:2 **T.** a psalm, and bring hither the......... 5375
Ps 83:12 **t.**...the houses of God in possession. ....
Ps 89:33 will I not utterly **t.** from him, ... 6331
Ps 102:14 thy servants **t.** pleasure in her stones, ...
Ps 102:24 **t.** me not away in the midst of my 5927
Ps 109:8 few; and let another **t.** his office. 3947
Ps 116:13 I will **t.** the cup of salvation, and........ 5375
Ps 119:43 **t.** not the word of truth utterly out...... 5337
Ps 139:9 If I **t.** the wings of the morning, ... 5375
Ps 139:20 thine enemies **t.** thy name in vain....... 5375
Pr 2:19 **t.** they hold of the paths of life. 5381
Pr 4:13 **T.** fast hold of instruction; let her....... 2388
Pr 5:5 to death; her steps **t.** hold on hell. 8551
Pr 5:22 own iniquities shall **t.** the wicked....... 3920
Pr 6:25 let her **t.** thee with her eyelids. 3947
Pr 6:27 Can a man **t.** fire in his bosom, and.... 2846
Pr 7:18 let us **t.** our fill of love until the..............
Pr 20:16 **T.** his garment that is surety for........ 3947
Pr 20:16 **t.** a pledge of him for a strange 2254
Pr 22:27 why should he **t.** away thy bed.......... 3947
Pr 25:4 **T.** away the dross from the silver, ... 1898
Pr 25:5 **T.** away the wicked from before......... 1898
Pr 27:13 **T.** his garment that is surety for........ 3947
Pr 27:13 **t.** a pledge of him for a strange 2254
Pr 30:9 and **t.** the name of my God in vain. 8610
Ec 5:15 and shall **t.** nothing of his labour,........ 5375
Ec 5:19 **t.** his portion, and to rejoice in his...... 5375
Ec 7:18 that thou shouldest **t.** hold of this; 270
Ec 7:21 **t.** no heed unto all words that are 5414
Ca 2:15 **T.** us the foxes, the little foxes, ... 270
Ca 7:8 I will **t.** hold of the boughs thereof:...... 270
Isa 1:25 thy dross, and **t.** away all thy tin:........ 5493
Isa 3:1 **t.** away from Jerusalem and from........ 5493
Isa 3:6 a man shall **t.** hold of his brother........ 8610
Isa 3:18 Lord will **t.** away the bravery of......... 5493
Isa 4:1 seven women shall **t.** hold of one 2388
Isa 4:1 thy name, to **t.** away our reproach....... 622
Isa 5:5 I will **t.** away the hedge thereof, ... 5493
Isa 5:23 and **t.** away the righteousness of the... 5493
Isa 7:4 unto him, **T.** heed, and be quiet;..............
Isa 8:1 **T.** thee a great roll, and write in........ 3947
Isa 8:10 **T.** counsel together, and it shall...............
Isa 10:2 to **t.** away the right from the poor........ 1497
Isa 10:6 give him a charge, to **t.** the spoil, ... 7997
Isa 10:6 to **t.** the prey, and to tread them......... 962
Isa 13:8 and sorrows shall **t.** hold of them;........ 270
Isa 14:2 And the people shall **t.** them, and....... 3947
Isa 14:2 they shall **t.** them captives, whose...........
Isa 14:4 shalt **t.** up this proverb against 5375
Isa 16:3 **T.** counsel, execute judgment;............. 935
Isa 18:4 I will **t.** my rest, and I will consider..........
Isa 18:5 **t.** away and cut down the branches..... 5493
Isa 23:16 **T.** an harp, go about the city,............ 3947
Isa 25:8 the rebuke of his people...**t.** away 5493
Isa 27:5 Or let him **t.** hold of my strength, ... 2388
Isa 27:6 them that come of Jacob to **t.** root: 2388
Isa 27:9 is all the fruit to **t.** away his sin;........ 5493
Isa 28:19 that it goeth forth it shall **t.** you:........ 3947
Isa 30:1 that **t.** counsel, but not of me;........... 6213
Isa 30:14 a sherd to **t.** fire from the hearth, ... 2846
Isa 30:14 or to **t.** water withal out of the pit...... 2834
Isa 33:23 spoil divided; the lame **t.** the prey........ 962
Isa 36:17 Until I come and **t.** you away to a....... 3947
Isa 37:31 of Judah shall...**t.** root downward,.............
Isa 38:21 Let them **t.** a lump of figs, and lay..... 5375
Isa 39:7 shalt beget, shall they **t.** away;.......... 3947
Isa 40:24 their stock shall not **t.** root in the....... 3947
Isa 40:24 the whirlwind shall **t.** them away........ 5375
Isa 44:14 for he will **t.** thereof, and warm......... 3947
Isa 45:21 yea, let them **t.** counsel together: ....
Isa 47:2 **T.** the millstones, and grind meal: 3947
Isa 47:3 I will **t.** vengeance, and I will not....... 3947
Isa 56:4 me, and **t.** hold of my covenant; 2388
Isa 57:13 all away; vanity shall **t.** them: 3947
Isa 57:14 **t.** up the stumbling block out of......... 7311
Isa 58:2 they **t.** delight in approaching to God.........
Isa 58:9 **t.** away from the midst of thee the..... 5493
Isa 64:7 up himself to **t.** hold of thee: for........ 2388
Isa 66:21 I will also **t.** of them for priests......... 3947
Jer 2:22 with nitre, and **t.** thee much sope,............
Jer 3:14 and I will **t.** you one of a city, ... 3947
Jer 4:4 and **t.** away the foreskins of your....... 5493
Jer 5:10 **t.** away her battlements; for they....... 5493
Jer 7:29 and **t.** up a lamentation on high.......... 5375
Jer 9:4 **T.** ye heed every one of his....................
Jer 9:10 mountains will I **t.** up a weeping.......... 5375
Jer 9:18 and **t.** up a wailing for us, that our 5375
Jer 13:4 **T.** the girdle that thou hast got,......... 3947
Jer 13:6 **t.** the girdle from thence, which......... 3947
Jer 13:21 shall not sorrows **t.** thee, as a............ 270
Jer 15:15 O Lord,...**t.** me not away in thy.......... 3947
Jer 15:19 if thou **t.** forth the precious from........ 3318
Jer 16:2 Thou shalt not **t.** thee a wife,............ 3947
Jer 17:21 **T.** heed to yourselves, and bear..............
Jer 18:22 they have digged a pit to **t.** me,......... 3920
Jer 19:1 and **t.** of the ancients of the people,..........
Jer 20:5 shall spoil them, and **t.** them, ... 3947
Jer 20:10 and we shall **t.** our revenge on him..... 3947
Jer 25:9 and **t.** all the families of the north,...... 3947
Jer 25:10 will **t.** from them the voice of mirth,........ 6
Jer 25:15 **T.** the wine cup of this fury at my....... 3947
Jer 25:28 if they refuse to **t.** the cup at thine..... 3947
Jer 29:6 **T.** ye wives, and beget sons and........ 3947
Jer 29:6 and **t.** wives for your sons, and give... 3947
Jer 32:3 king of Babylon, and he shall **t.** it;...... 3920
Jer 32:14 **T.** these evidences, this evidence....... 3947
Jer 32:24 are come unto the city to **t.** it; 3920
Jer 32:25 field for money, and **t.** witnesses;....... 5749
Jer 32:28 king of Babylon, and he shall **t.** it:...... 3920
Jer 32:44 **t.** witnesses in...land of Benjamin, ... 5749
Jer 33:26 not **t.** any of his seed to be rulers...... 3947
Jer 34:22 shall fight against it, and **t.** it,......... 3920
Jer 36:2 **T.** thee a roll of a book, and write...... 3947
Jer 36:14 **T.** in thine hand the roll wherein........ 3947
Jer 36:26 to **t.** Baruch the scribe and.............. 3947
Jer 36:28 **T.** thee again another roll, and........... 3947
Jer 37:8 fight against this city, and **t.** it,.......... 3920
Jer 38:3 Babylon's army, which shall **t.** it......... 3920
Jer 38:10 **T.** from hence thirty men with........... 3947
Jer 38:10 **t.** up Jeremiah the prophet out of........ 3947
Jer 39:12 **T.** him, and look well to him, and....... 3947
Jer 43:9 **T.** great stones in thine hand, and...... 3947
Jer 43:10 will send and **t.** Nebuchadrezzar......... 3947
Jer 44:12 I will **t.** the remnant of Judah,........... 3947
Jer 46:11 Go up into Gilead, and **t.** balm,.......... 3947
Jer 49:29 and their flocks shall they **t.** away: 3947
Jer 49:29 they shall **t.** to themselves their......... 5375
Jer 50:15 **t.** vengeance upon her; as she hath ....
Jer 51:8 **t.** balm for her pain, if so be she........ 3947
Jer 51:26 not **t.** of thee a stone for a corner,..... 3947
Jer 51:36 cause, and **t.** vengeance for thee:............
La 2:13 thing shall I **t.** to witness for thee? ....
Eze 4:1 **t.** thee a tile, and lay it before........... 3947
Eze 4:3 **t.** thou unto thee an iron pan, and...... 3947
Eze 4:9 **T.** thou also unto thee wheat, and....... 3947
Eze 5:1 son of man, **t.** thee a sharp knife, ... 3947
Eze 5:1 **t.** thee a barber's rasor, and cause..... 3947
Eze 5:1 then **t.** thee balances to weigh, and.... 3947
Eze 5:2 and thou shalt **t.** a third part, and....... 3947
Eze 5:3 shalt...**t.** thereof a few in number,........ 3947
Eze 5:4 Then **t.** of them again, and cast 3947
Eze 10:6 **T.** fire from between the wheels, ... 3947
Eze 11:18 **t.** away all the detestable things......... 5493
Eze 11:19 **t.** the stony heart out of their flesh,.... 5493
Eze 14:5 That I may **t.** the house of Israel 8610
Eze 15:3 will men **t.** a pin of it to hang any 3947
Eze 16:16 And of thy garments thou didst **t.**,........ 3947
Eze 16:39 and shall **t.** thy fair jewels, and.......... 3947
Eze 17:22 I will also **t.** of the highest branch...... 3947
Eze 19:1 **t.** thou up a lamentation for the 5375
Eze 21:26 the diadem, and **t.** off the crown: 7311
Eze 22:16 thou shalt **t.** thine inheritance ....
Eze 23:25 **t.** away thy nose and thine ears; 5493
Eze 23:25 **t.** thy sons and thy daughters;............ 3947
Eze 23:26 and **t.** away thy fair jewels............... 3947
Eze 23:29 and shall **t.** away all thy labour,.......... 3947
Eze 24:5 **T.** the choice of the flock, and........... 3947
Eze 24:8 fury to come up to **t.** vengeance: ....
Eze 24:16 I **t.** away from thee the desire of....... 3947
Eze 24:25 when I **t.** from them their strength,.... 3947
Eze 26:17 shall **t.** up a lamentation for thee, ... 5375
Eze 27:2 **t.** up a lamentation for Tyrus;............ 5375
Eze 27:32 shall **t.** up a lamentation for thee, ... 5375
Eze 28:12 **t.** up a lamentation upon the king 5375
Eze 29:19 and he shall **t.** her multitude,............ 5375
Eze 29:19 **t.** [7997] her spoil, and **t.** her prey; 962
Eze 30:4 they shall **t.** away her multitude, ... 3947
Eze 32:2 **t.** up a lamentation for Pharaoh.......... 5375
Eze 33:2 people...**t.** a man of their coasts,........ 3947
Eze 33:4 the sword come, and **t.** him away,....... 3947
Eze 33:6 **t.** any person from among them, ... 3947
Eze 36:24 **t.** you from among the heathen, ... 3947
Eze 36:26 I will **t.** away the stony heart out 5493
Eze 37:16 **t.** thee one stick, and write upon 3947
Eze 37:16 then **t.** another stick, and write.......... 3947
Eze 37:19 I will **t.** the stick of Joseph, which...... 3947
Eze 37:21 I will **t.** the children of Israel from...... 3947
Eze 38:12 To **t.** [7997] a spoil, and to **t.** a prey;... 962
Eze 38:13 thee, Art thou come to **t.** a spoil? 7997
Eze 38:13 gathered thy company to **t.** a prey?...... 962
Eze 38:13 gold, to **t.** away cattle and goods,....... 3947
Eze 38:13 and goods, to **t.** a great spoil? 3947
Eze 39:10 shall **t.** no wood out of the field, ... 5375
Eze 43:20 thou shalt **t.** of the blood thereof,........ 3947
Eze 43:21 shalt **t.** the bullock also of the sin....... 3947
Eze 44:22 they **t.** for their wives a widow,......... 3947
Eze 44:22 **t.** maidens of the seed of the house.... 3947
Eze 45:9 **t.** away your exactions from my......... 7311
Eze 45:18 thou shalt **t.** a young bullock............. 3947
Eze 45:19 **t.** of the blood of the sin offering,....... 3947
Eze 46:18 prince shall not **t.** of the people's 3947
Da 6:23 should **t.** Daniel up out of the den. 5267
Da 7:18 most High shall **t.** the kingdom, ... 6902
Da 7:26 they shall **t.** away his dominion, ... 5709
Da 11:15 and **t.** the most fenced cities: 3920
Da 11:18 unto the isles, and shall **t.** many:........ 3920
Da 11:31 shall **t.** away the daily sacrifice,........ 5493
Ho 1:2 to Hosea, Go, **t.** unto thee a wife of... 3947
Ho 1:6 but I will utterly **t.** them away........... 5375
Ho 2:9 and **t.** away my corn in the time 3947
Ho 2:17 will **t.** away the names of Baalim......... 5493
Ho 4:10 have left off to **t.** heed to the Lord..........
Ho 4:11 and new wine **t.** away the heart......... 3947
Ho 5:14 I will **t.** away, and none shall............ 5375
Ho 11:4 as they that **t.** off the yoke of their 7311
Ho 14:2 **T.** with you words, and turn to the..... 3947
Ho 14:2 **T.** away all iniquity, and receive......... 5375
Am 3:5 one **t.** up a snare from the earth,....... 5927
Am 4:2 he will **t.** you away with hooks, ... 5375
Am 5:1 this word which I **t.** up against you,.... 5375
Am 5:11 ye **t.** from him burdens of wheat:....... 3947
Am 5:12 they afflict the just, they **t.** a bribe, ... 3947
Am 5:23 **T.** thou away from me the noise of..... 5493
Am 6:10 And a man's uncle shall **t.** him up, ... 5375
Am 9:2 thence shall mine hand **t.** them; 3947
Am 9:3 I will search and **t.** them out thence;... 3947
Jon 1:12 **T.** me up, and cast me forth into 5375
Jon 4:3 O Lord, **t.**, I beseech thee, my life..... 3947
Mic 2:2 fields, and **t.** them by violence;.......... 5375
Mic 2:2 and houses, and **t.** them away: so...... 5375
Mic 2:4 one **t.** up a parable against you, ... 5375
Mic 2:6 them that they shall not **t.** shame....... 5253
Mic 6:14 and thou shalt **t.** hold, but shalt not.... 5253
Na 1:2 will **t.** vengeance on his adversaries, ...
Na 2:9 **T.** ye the spoil of silver, ... 962
Na 2:9 **t.** the spoil of gold: for there is none.... 962
Hab 1:10 for they shall heap dust, and **t.** it. 3920
Hab 1:15 They **t.** up all of them with the.......... 5927
Hab 2:6 not all these **t.** up a parable against 5375
Zep 3:11 I will **t.** away out of the midst of......... 5493
Hag 1:8 I will **t.** pleasure in it, and I will be...........
Hag 2:23 will I **t.** thee, O Zerubbabel, my......... 3947
Zec 1:6 they not **t.** hold of your fathers? 5381
Zec 3:4 **T.** away the filthy garments from 5493
Zec 6:10 **T.** of them of the captivity, even........ 3947
Zec 6:11 Then **t.** silver and gold, and make 3947
Zec 8:23 that ten men shall **t.** hold out of all..... 2388
Zec 8:23 **t.** hold of the skirt of him that is a 2388
Zec 9:7 I will **t.** away his blood out of his 5493
Zec 11:15 **T.** unto thee yet the instruments........ 3947
Zec 14:21 sacrifice shall come and **t.** of them,..... 3947
Mal 2:3 and one shall **t.** you away with it........ 5375
Mal 2:15 Therefore **t.** heed to your spirit, ...
Mal 2:16 therefore **t.** heed to your spirit, ...
Mt 1:20 fear not to **t.** unto thee Mary thy....... *3880*
Mt 2:13, 20 **t.** the young child and his mother,.. *3880*
Mt 5:40 **at the law, and t. away thy coat,..** *2983*
Mt 6:1 **T. heed that ye do not your alms** ....
Mt 6:25 **T. no thought for your life, what** ....

Mt 6:28 And why t. ye thought for raiment?
Mt 6:31 t. no thought, saying, What shall
Mt 6:34 T. therefore no thought for the
Mt 6:34 shall t. thought for the things of
Mt 9:6 t. up thy bed, and go unto thine 142
Mt 10:19 t. no thought how or what ye shall
Mt 11:12 and the violent t. it by force 726
Mt 11:29 T. my yoke upon you, and learn of 142
Mt 15:26 not meet to t. the children's bread, 2983
Mt 16:5 side, they had forgotten to t. bread. 2983
Mt 16:6 T. heed, and beware of the leaven
Mt 16:24 and t. up his cross, and follow me. 142
Mt 17:25 do the kings of the earth t. custom 2983
Mt 17:27 t. up the fish that first cometh up; 142
Mt 17:27 that t., and give unto them for me 2983
Mt 18:10 T. heed that ye despise not one of
Mt 18:16 then t. with thee one or two more, 3880
Mt 18:23 would t. account of his servants 4868
Mt 20:14 T. that thine is, and go thy way; I 142
Mt 22:13 hand and foot, and t. him away, 142
Mt 24:4 T. heed that no man deceive you
Mt 24:17 to t. any thing out of his house: 142
Mt 24:18 field return back to t. his clothes 142
Mt 25:28 T. therefore the talent from him, 142
Mt 26:4 they might t. Jesus by subtilty, 2902
Mt 26:26 and said, T., eat; this is my body 2983
Mt 26:45 Sleep on now, and t. your rest:
Mt 26:52 they that t. the sword shall perish. 2983
Mt 26:55 swords and staves for to t. me? 4815
Mk 2:9 or to say, Arise, and t. up thy bed, 142
Mk 2:11 unto thee, Arise, and t. up thy bed, 142
Mk 4:24 unto them, T. heed, what ye hear:
Mk 6:8 should t. nothing for their journey, 142
Mk 7:27 not meet to t. the children's bread, 2983
Mk 8:14 disciples had forgotten to t. bread, 2983
Mk 8:15 T. heed, beware of the leaven of
Mk 8:34 deny himself, and t. up his cross, 142
Mk 10:21 come, t. up the cross, and follow 142
Mk 12:19 that his brother should t. his wife, 2983
Mk 13:5 T. heed lest any man deceive you:
Mk 13:9 t. heed to yourselves: for they shall
Mk 13:11 t. no thought beforehand what ye shall
Mk 13:15 to t. any thing out of his house: 142
Mk 13:16 back again for to t. up his garment. 142
Mk 13:23 t. ye heed: behold, I have foretold
Mk 13:33 T. ye heed, watch and pray: for ye
Mk 14:1 how they might t. him be craft, 2902
Mk 14:22 and said, T., eat: this is my body 2983
Mk 14:36 to thee; t. away this cup from me: 3911
Mk 14:41 Sleep on now, and t. your rest: it is
Mk 14:44 t. him, and lead him away safely. 2902
Mk 14:48 swords and with staves to t. me? 4815
Mk 15:24 them, what every man should t. 142
Mk 15:36 Elias will come to t. him down 2507
Mk 16:18 They shall t. up serpents; and if 142
Lu 1:25 to t. away my reproach among men. 851
Lu 5:24 t. up thy couch, and go into thine 142
Lu 6:4 and did t. and eat the shewbread, 2983
Lu 6:29 thy cloke forbid not to t. thy coat.
Lu 8:18 T. heed therefore how ye hear: for
Lu 9:3 them, T. nothing for your journey, 142
Lu 9:23 himself, and t. up his cross daily, 142
Lu 10:35 and said unto him, T. care of him;
Lu 11:35 T. heed therefore that the light 4648
Lu 12:11 t. ye no thought how or what thing
Lu 12:15 T. heed, and beware of covetousness:
Lu 12:19 t. thine ease, eat, drink, and be.
Lu 12:22 T. no thought for your life, what
Lu 12:26 why t. ye thought for the rest?
Lu 14:9 with shame to t. the lowest room. 2722
Lu 16:6 T. thy bill, and sit down quickly, 1209
Lu 16:7 T. thy bill, and write fourscore. 1209
Lu 17:3 T. heed to yourselves: If thy
Lu 17:31 him not come down to t. it away: 142
Lu 19:24 T. from him the pound, and give it 142
Lu 20:20 that they might t. hold of his words, 1949
Lu 20:26 they could not t. hold of his words 1949
Lu 20:28 that his brother should t. his wife, 2983
Lu 21:8 T. heed that ye be not deceived:
Lu 21:34 t. heed to yourselves, lest at any
Lu 22:17 said, T. this, and divide it among 2983
Lu 22:36 he that hath a purse, let him t. it, 142
Joh 2:16 sold doves, T. these things hence; 142
Joh 5:8 him, Rise, t. up thy bed, and walk 142
Joh 5:11 unto me, T. up thy bed, and walk. 142
Joh 5:12 unto thee, T. up thy bed, and walk? 142
Joh 6:7 every one of them may t. a little 2983
Joh 6:15 would come and t. him by force, 726
Joh 7:30 Then they sought to t. him: but no 4084
Joh 7:32 chief priests sent officers to t. him. 4084
Joh 10:17 my life, that I might t. it again, 2983
Joh 10:18 and I have power to t. it again. 2983
Joh 10:39 they sought again to t. him; but he 4084
Joh 11:39 Jesus said, T. ye away the stone 142
Joh 11:48 t. away both our place and nation. 142
Joh 11:57 shew it, that they might t. him. 4084
Joh 16:15 he shall t. of mine, and shall 2983
Joh 17:15 shouldest t. them out of the world, 142
Joh 18:31 said Pilate unto them, T. ye him, 2983
Joh 19:6 them, T. ye him, and crucify him: 2983
Joh 19:38 he might t. away the body of Jesus: 142
Joh 20:15 hast laid him, and I will t. him away. 142
Ac 1:20 and his bishoprick let another t. 2983
Ac 1:25 he may t. part of this ministry and 2983
Ac 5:35 t. heed to yourselves what ye
Ac 12:3 he proceeded further to t. Peter 4815
Ac 15:14 to t. out of them a people for his 2983
Ac 15:37 determined to t. with them John, 4838
Ac 15:38 not good to t. him with them, who 4838
Ac 20:13 Assos, there intending to t. in Paul: 353
Ac 20:26 I t. you to record this day, that
Ac 20:28 T. heed therefore unto yourselves, and
Ac 21:24 Them t., and purify thyself with 3880
Ac 22:26 T. heed what thou doest: for this
Ac 23:10 t. him by force from among them. 726
Ac 24:8 t. knowledge of all these things,
Ac 27:33 Paul besought them all to t. meat, 3335
Ac 27:34 I pray you to t. some meat: for 4355
Ro 11:21 t. heed lest he also spare not thee.
Ro 11:27 when I shall t. away their sins. 851
Ro 15:24 I t. my journey into Spain, I will
1Co 3:10 let every man t. heed how he buildeth
1Co 6:7 Why do ye not rather t. wrong? Why
1Co 6:15 then t. the members of Christ, and 142
1Co 8:9 But t. heed lest by any means this
1Co 9:9 corn. Doth God t. care for oxen?
1Co 10:12 he standeth t. heed lest he fall.
1Co 11:24 T., eat: this is my body, which is 2983
2Co 8:4 t. upon us the fellowship of the
2Co 11:20 if a man t. of you, if a man exalt 2983
2Co 12:10 I t. pleasure in infirmities, in
Ga 5:15 t. heed that ye be not consumed one
Eph 6:13 t. unto you the whole armour of 353
Eph 6:17 t. the helmet of salvation, and the 1209
Col 4:17 T. heed to the ministry which thou
1Ti 3:5 shall he t. care of the church of God?)
1Ti 4:16 T. heed unto thyself, and unto the
2Ti 4:11 T. Mark, and bring him with thee: 353
Heb 3:12 T. heed, brethren, lest there be in
Heb 7:5 t. tithes of the people according to the
Heb 10:4 and of goats should t. away sins. 851
Heb 10:11 which can never t. away sins: 4014
Jas 5:10 T., my brethren, the prophets, who 2983
1Pe 2:20 your faults, ye shall t. it patiently?
1Pe 2:20 ye t. it patiently, this is acceptable
2Pe 1:19 whereunto ye do well that ye t. heed, as
1Jo 3:5 manifested to t. away our sins; 142
Re 3:11 hast, that no man t. thy crown. 2983
Re 5:9 Thou art worthy to t. the book, and 2983
Re 6:4 thereon to t. peace from the earth, 2983
Re 10:8 Go and t. the little book which is 2983
Re 10:9 said unto me, T. it, and eat it up; 2983
Re 22:17 let him t. the water of life freely. 2902
Re 22:19 if any man shall t. away from the 851
Re 22:19 God shall t. away his part out of the 851

TAKEN See also OVERTAKEN; UNTAKEN.

Ge 2:22 rib,...the Lord God had t. from man, 3947
Ge 2:23 because she was t. out of Man. 3947
Ge 3:19 ground; for out of it wast thou t. 3947
Ge 3:23 the ground from whence he was t. 3947
Ge 4:15 vengeance shall be t. on him sevenfold.
Ge 12:15 the woman was t. into Pharaoh's 3947
Ge 12:19 I might have t. her to me to wife: 3947
Ge 14:14 that his brother was t. captive,
Ge 18:27, 31 I have t. upon me to speak unto 2974
Ge 20:3 for the woman which thou hast t.; 3947
Ge 21:25 servants had violently t. away. 1497
Ge 27:33 where is he that hath t. venison, 6679
Ge 27:35 and hath t. away thy blessing. 3947
Ge 27:36 now he hath t. away my blessing. 3947
Ge 30:15 that thou hast t. my husband? 3947
Ge 30:23 God hath t. away my reproach: 622
Ge 31:1 Jacob hath t. way all that was 3947
Ge 31:9 God hath t. away the cattle of your 5337
Ge 31:16 which God hath t. from our father, 5337
Ge 31:26 as captives t. with the sword?
Ge 31:34 Rachel had t. the images, and put 3947
Ex 14:11 hast thou t. us away to die in the 3947
Ex 25:15 ark: they shall not be t. from it. 5493
Ex 40:36 the cloud was t. up from over the 5927
Ex 40:37 if the cloud were not t. up, then 5927
Ex 40:37 not till the day that it was t. up. 5927
Le 4:10 As it was t. off from the bullock 7311
Le 4:31 fat is t. away from off the sacrifice 7311
Le 4:35 as the fat of the lamb is t. away from 7311
Le 6:2 or in a thing t. away by violence, 1497
Le 7:34 and the heave shoulder have I t. 3947
Le 14:43 that he hath t. away the stones, 2502
Le 24:8 being t. from the children of Israel by
Nu 3:12 I have t. the Levites from among 3947
Nu 5:13 neither she be t. with the matter; 8610
Nu 8:16 of Israel, have I t. them unto me. 3947
Nu 8:18 And I have t. the Levites for all the 3947
Nu 9:17 when the cloud was t. up from the 5927
Nu 9:21 the cloud was t. up in the morning, 5927
Nu 9:21 by night that the cloud was t. up, 5927
Nu 9:22 when it was t. up, they journeyed. 5927
Nu 10:11 the cloud was t. up from off the 5927
Nu 10:17 the tabernacle was t. down; and 3381
Nu 16:15 I have not t. one ass from them, 5375
Nu 18:6 I have t. your brethren the Levites 3947
Nu 21:26 and t. all his land out of his hand, 3947
Nu 31:26 the sum of the prey that was t., 7628
Nu 31:49 servants have t. the sum of...men 5375
Nu 31:53 (For the men of war had t. spoil, every
Nu 36:3 be t. from the inheritance of our 1639
Nu 36:3 t. from the lot of our inheritance. 1639
Nu 36:4 shall their inheritance be t. away 1639
De 4:20 the Lord hath t. you, and brought 3947
De 20:7 a wife, and hath not t. her? 3947
De 21:10 and thou hast t. them captive,
De 24:1 When a man hath t. a wife, and 3947
De 24:5 When a man hath t. a new wife, he 3947
De 24:5 cheer up his wife which he hath t. 3947
De 26:14 neither have I t. away ought 1197
De 28:31 thine ass shall be violently t. away. 1497
Jos 7:11 have even t. of the accursed thing, 3947
Jos 7:15 that is t. with the accursed thing 3920
Jos 7:16 and the tribe of Judah was t. 3920
Jos 7:17 man by man; and Zabdi was t. 3920
Jos 7:18 Zerah, of the tribe of Judah, was t. 3920
Jos 8:8 shall be, when ye have t. the city 8610
Jos 8:21 that the ambush had t. the city, 3920
Jos 10:1 had heard how Joshua had t. Ai, 3920
Jg 1:8 against Jerusalem, and had t. it, 3920
Jg 11:36 Lord hath t. vengeance for thee 6213
Jg 14:9 had t. the honey out of the carcase 7287
Jg 15:6 because he had t. his wife, and 3947
Jg 17:2 shekels of silver...t. from thee, 3947
Jg 18:24 Ye have t. away my gods which I 3947
1Sa 4:11 the ark of God was t.; and the two 3947
1Sa 4:17 are dead, and the ark of God is t. 3947
1Sa 4:19 tidings that the ark of God was t., 3947
1Sa 4:21 because the ark of God was t., and 3947
1Sa 4:22 from Israel: for the ark of God is t. 3947
1Sa 7:14 cities which the Philistines had t. 3947
1Sa 10:20 near, the tribe of Benjamin was t. 3920
1Sa 10:21 the family of Matri was t., and Saul 3920
1Sa 10:21 and Saul the son of Kish was t. 3920
1Sa 12:3 his anointed: whose ox have I t.? 3947
1Sa 12:3 or whose ass have I t.? or whom 3947
1Sa 12:4 neither hast thou t. ought of any 3947
1Sa 14:41 And Saul and Jonathan were t. 3920
1Sa 14:42 my son. And Jonathan was t. 3920
1Sa 21:6 that was t. from before the Lord, 5493
1Sa 21:6 in the day when it was t. away. 3947
1Sa 30:2 And had t. the women captives,
1Sa 30:3 their daughters, were t. captives.
1Sa 30:5 David's two wives were t. captives,
1Sa 30:16 all the great spoil that they had t. 3947
1Sa 30:19 any thing that they had t. to them: 3947
2Sa 12:9 and hast t. his wife to be thy wife, 3947
2Sa 12:10 hast t. the wife of Uriah the Hittite 3947
2Sa 12:27 and have t. the city of waters 3920
2Sa 16:8 behold, thou art t. in thy mischief,
2Sa 18:9 t. up between the heaven and the 5414
2Sa 18:18 had t. and reared up...a pillar, 3947
2Sa 23:6 they cannot be t. with hands: 3947
1Ki 7:8 daughter, whom he had t. to wife, 3947

1Ki 9:9 and have **t.** hold upon other gods, 2388
1Ki 9:16 Egypt had gone up, and **t.** Gezer, 3920
1Ki 16:18 when Zimri saw that the city was **t.**, 3920
1Ki 21:19 thou killed, and also **t.** possession?
1Ki 22:43 the high places were not **t.** away; 5493
2Ki 2:9 before I be **t.** away from thee. 3947
2Ki 2:10 thou see me when I am **t.** from thee, 3947
2Ki 2:16 Spirit of the Lord hath **t.** him up, 5375
2Ki 4:20 when he had **t.** him, and brought 5375
2Ki 6:22 thou hast **t.** captive with thy sword
2Ki 12:3 But...high places were not **t.** away: 5493
2Ki 13:25 the cities, which he had **t.** out of 3947
2Ki 14:4 the high places were not **t.** away: 5493
2Ki 18:10 king of Israel, Samaria was **t.**. 3920
2Ki 18:22 altars Hezekiah hath **t.** away, 5493
2Ki 24:7 king of Babylon had **t.** from the 3947
1Ch 24:6 one principal household being **t.** 270
1Ch 24:6 for Eleazer, and one **t.** for Ithamar 270
2Ch 15:8 cities which he had **t.** from mount 3920
2Ch 15:17 the high places were not **t.** away 5493
2Ch 17:2 which Asa his father had **t.**. 3920
2Ch 19:3 hast **t.** away the groves out of the 1197
2Ch 20:33 the high places were not **t.** away: 5493
2Ch 28:11 have **t.** captive of your brethren:
2Ch 28:18 had **t.** Beth-shemesh, and Ajalon, 3920
2Ch 30:2 For the king had **t.** counsel, and
2Ch 32:12 Hezekiah **t.** away his high places 5493
Ezr 9:2 **t.** of their daughters...themselves, 5375
Ezr 10:2 **t.** strange wives of the people of 3427
Ezr 10:10 and have **t.** strange wives, 3427
Ezr 10:14 them which have **t.** strange wives 3427
Ezr 10:17 the men that had **t.** strange wives 3427
Ezr 10:18 found that had **t.** strange wives: 3427
Ezr 10:44 All these had **t.** strange wives: 5375
Ne 5:15 had **t.** of them bread and wine, 3947
Ne 6:18 son Johanan had **t.** the daughter of 3947
Es 2:15 who had **t.** her for his daughter, 3947
Es 2:16 Esther was **t.** unto king Ahasuerus 3947
Es 8:2 ring, which he had **t.** from Haman, 5674
Job 1:21 gave, and the Lord hath **t.** away; 3947
Job 16:12 he hath also **t.** me by my neck, and 247
Job 19:9 and **t.** the crown from my head 5493
Job 20:19 hath violently **t.** away an house 1497
Job 22:6 hast **t.** a pledge from thy brother 2254
Job 24:24 are **t.** out of the way as all other, 7092
Job 27:2 who hath **t.** away my judgment; 5493
Job 28:2 Iron is **t.** out of the earth, and 3947
Job 30:16 of affliction have **t.** hold upon me. 270
Job 34:5 God hath **t.** away my judgment. 5493
Job 34:20 and the mighty shall be **t.** away 5493
Ps 9:15 which they hid is their own foot **t.** 3920
Ps 10:2 let them be **t.** in the devices that 8610
Ps 40:12 iniquities have **t.** hold upon me, 5381
Ps 59:12 let them even be **t.** in their pride: 3920
Ps 83:3 They have **t.** crafty counsel against
Ps 85:3 Thou hast **t.** away all thy wrath: 5375
Ps 119:53 Horror hath **t.** hold upon me 270
Ps 119:111 testimonies have I **t.** as an heritage
Ps 119:143 and anguish have **t.** hold on me: 4672
Pr 3:26 shall keep thy foot from being **t.**. 3921
Pr 4:16 and their sleep is **t.** away, unless 1497
Pr 6:2 **t.** with the words of thy mouth. 3920
Pr 7:20 hath **t.** a bag of money with him, 3947
Pr 11:6 transgressors shall be **t.** in their 3920
Ec 2:18 labour which I had **t.** under the 6001
Ec 3:14 put to it, nor any thing **t.** from it: 1639
Ec 7:26 but the sinner shall be **t.** by her 3920
Ec 9:12 the fishes that are **t.** in an evil net, 270
Isa 6:6 he had **t.** with the tongs from off 3947
Isa 6:7 thine iniquity is **t.** away, and thy 5493
Isa 7:5 have **t.** evil counsel against thee,
Isa 8:4 spoil of Samaria shall be **t.** away 5375
Isa 8:15 broken, and be snared, and be **t.** 3920
Isa 10:27 that his burden shall be **t.** away 5493
Isa 10:29 have **t.** up their lodging at Geba; 3885
Isa 16:10 And gladness is **t.** away, and joy out 622
Isa 17:1 Damascus is **t.** away from being a 5493
Isa 21:3 pangs have **t.** hold upon me, as the 270
Isa 23:8 hath **t.** this counsel against Tyre,
Isa 24:18 of the pit shall be **t.** in the snare: 3920
Isa 28:13 and be broken, and snared, and **t.** 3920
Isa 33:20 tabernacle...shall not be **t.** down; 6813
Isa 36:7 altars Hezekiah hath **t.** away, 5493
Isa 41:9 have **t.** from the ends of the earth, 2388
Isa 49:24 the prey be **t.** from the mighty, or 3947
Isa 49:25 captives of the mighty shall be **t.** 3947
Isa 51:22 have **t.** out of thine hand the cup of 3947
Isa 52:5 my people is **t.** away for nought? 3947
Isa 53:8 He was **t.** from prison and from 3947
Isa 57:1 and merciful men are **t.** away, none 622
Isa 57:1 righteous is **t.** away from the evil to 622
Isa 64:6 like the wind, have **t.** us away. 5375
Jer 6:11 husbands with the wife shall be **t.**, 3920
Jer 6:24 anguish hath **t.** hold of us, and 2388
Jer 8:9 ashamed,...are dismayed and **t.**.
Jer 8:21 astonishment hath **t.** hold on me. 2388
Jer 12:2 planted them, yea, they have **t.** root:
Jer 16:5 **t.** away my peace from this people, 622
Jer 29:22 And of them shall be **t.** up a curse 3947
Jer 34:3 shalt surely be **t.**, and delivered 8610
Jer 38:23 shalt be **t.** by...the king of Babylon: 8610
Jer 38:28 until the day...Jerusalem was **t.** 3920
Jer 38:28 was there when Jerusalem was **t.**. 3920
Jer 39:5 and when they had **t.** him, they 3947
Jer 40:1 when he had **t.** him being bound in 3947
Jer 40:10 dwell in your cities that ye have **t.** 8610
Jer 48:1 Kiriathaim is confounded and **t.** 3920
Jer 48:7 thy treasures, thou shalt also be **t.** 3920
Jer 48:33 joy..is **t.** from the plentiful field, 622
Jer 48:41 Kerioth is **t.**, and the strong holds 3920
Jer 48:44 out of the pit shall be **t.** in the snare: 3920
Jer 48:46 for thy sons are **t.** captives, and thy 3947
Jer 49:20 Lord, that he hath **t.** against Edom; 3289
Jer 49:24 anguish and sorrows have **t.** her, 270
Jer 49:30 king of Babylon hath **t.** counsel
Jer 50:2 Babylon is **t.**, Bel is confounded, 3920
Jer 50:9 from thence she shall be **t.**: their 3920
Jer 50:24 thou art also **t.** O Babylon, and thou 3920
Jer 50:45 that he hath **t.** against Babylon: 3289
Jer 51:31 king of Babylon that his city is **t.** 3920
Jer 51:41 How is Sheshach **t.**! and how is the 3920
Jer 51:56 Babylon, and her mighty men are **t.**, 3920
La 2:6 hath violently **t.** away his tabernacle,
La 4:20 of the Lord, was **t.** in their pits, 3920
Eze 12:13 and he shall be **t.** in my snare: 8610
Eze 15:3 wood be **t.** thereof to do any work? 3947
Eze 16:17 Thou hast also **t.** thy fair jewels of 3947
Eze 16:20 **t.** thy sons and thy daughters, 3947
Eze 16:37 with whom thou hast **t.** pleasure,
Eze 17:12 and hath **t.** the king thereof, and 3947
Eze 17:13 And hath **t.** of the king's seed, and 3947
Eze 17:13 him, and hath **t.** an oath of him: 935
Eze 17:13 hath also **t.** the mighty of the land: 3947
Eze 17:20 and he shall be **t.** in my snare, and 8610
Eze 18:8 neither hath **t.** any increase, that 3947
Eze 18:13 upon usury, and hath **t.** increase: 3947
Eze 18:17 hath **t.** off his hand from the poor, 7725
Eze 19:4 he was **t.** in their it, and they 8610
Eze 19:8 net over him: he was **t.** in their pit 8610
Eze 21:23 the inquity, that they may be **t.** 8610
Eze 21:24 ye shall be **t.** with the hand 8610
Eze 22:12 have they **t.** gifts to shed blood; 3947
Eze 22:12 thou hast **t.** usury and increase, 3947
Eze 22:25 have **t.** the treasure and precious 3947
Eze 25:15 **t.** vengeance with a despiteful heart,
Eze 27:5 they have **t.** cedars from Lebann 3947
Eze 33:6 he is **t.** away in his inquity; but 3947
Eze 36:3 ye are **t.** up in the lips of talkers, 5927
Da 5:2 had **t.** out of the temple which 5312
Da 5:3 the golden vessels that were **t.** out 5312
Da 6:23 So Daniel was **t.** up out of the den, 5267
Da 7:12 they had their dominion **t.** away: 5709
Da 8:11 the daily sacrifice was **t.** away. 7311
Da 11:12 he hath **t.** away the multitude, 5375
Da 12:11 the daily sacrifice shall be **t.** away, 5493
Ho 4:3 the fishes...also shall be **t.** away. 622
Joe 3:5 ye have **t.** my silver and my gold, 3947
Am 3:4 of his den, if he have **t.** nothing? 3920
Am 3:5 earth, and have **t.** nothing at all? 3947
Am 3:12 children of Israel be **t.** out that 5337
Am 4:10 and have **t.** away your horses; 7628
Am 6:13 Have we not **t.** to us horns by our 3947
Mic 2:9 have ye **t.** away my glory for ever. 3947
Mic 4:9 pangs have **t.** thee as a woman in 2388
Zep 3:15 Lord hath **t.** away thy judgments, 5493
Zec 14:2 the city shall be **t.**, and the houses 3947
Mt 4:24 that were **t.** with divers diseases *4912*
Mt 9:15 **bridegroom shall be t. from them,** *522*
Mt 13:12 **from him shall be t. away even** *142*
Mt 16:7 It is because we have **t.** no bread. *2983*
Mt 21:43 **kingdom of God shall be t. from** *142*
Mt 24:40, 41 **one shall be t., and the other** *3880*
Mt 25:29 **be t. away even that which he** *142*
Mt 27:59 And when Joseph had **t.** the body, *2983*
Mt 28:12 with the elders, and had **t.** counsel, *2983*
Mk 2:20 **bridegroom shall be t. away from** *522*
Mk 4:25 **shall be t. even that which he** *142*
Mk 6:41 when he had **t.** the five loaves and *2983*
Mk 9:36 when he had **t.** him in his arms, he *1723*
Lu 1:1 as many have **t.** in hand to set *2021*
Lu 4:38 mother was **t.** with a great fever; *4912*
Lu 5:5 all the night, and have **t.** nothing: *2983*
Lu 5:9 of the fishes which they had **t.**: *4815*
Lu 5:18 bed a man which was **t.** with a palsy:
Lu 5:35 **bridegroom shall be t. away from** *522*
Lu 5:36 **the piece that was t. out of the new**
Lu 8:18 **from him shall be t. even that** *142*
Lu 8:37 for they were **t.** with great fear: *4912*
Lu 9:17 there was **t.** up of fragments that *142*
Lu 10:42 **shall not be t. away from her.** *851*
Lu 11:52 **have t. away the key of knowledge:** *142*
Lu 17:34, 35 **one shall be t., and the other** *3880*
Lu 17:36 **one shall be t., and the other left.** *3880*
Lu 19:8 **t.** any thing...by false accusation,
Lu 19:26 **he hath shall be t. away from him** *142*
Joh 7:44 some of them would have **t.** him; *4084*
Joh 8:3 unto him a woman **t.** in adultery; *2638*
Joh 8:4 this woman was **t.** in adultery, in *2638*
Joh 13:12 had **t.** his garments, and was set *2983*
Joh 19:31 and that they might be **t.** away *142*
Joh 20:1 and seeth the stone **t.** away from the *142*
Joh 20:2 They have **t.** away the Lord out of *142*
Joh 20:13 they have **t.** away my Lord, and I *142*
Ac 1:2 Until the day in which he was **t.** up, *353*
Ac 1:9 while they beheld, he was **t.** up; *1869*
Ac 1:11 Jesus, which is **t.** up from you into *353*
Ac 1:22 same day that he was **t.** up from us, *353*
Ac 2:23 ye have **t.**, and by wicked hands *2983*
Ac 8:7 and many **t.** with palsies, and that
Ac 8:33 his judgment was **t.** away: *142*
Ac 8:33 for his life is **t.** from the earth *142*
Ac 17:9 when they had **t.** security of Jason, *2983*
Ac 20:9 the third loft, and was **t.** up dead *142*
Ac 21:6 And when we had **t.** our leave one of *782*
Ac 23:27 This man was **t.** of the Jews, and *4815*
Ac 27:17 Which when they had **t.** up, they *142*
Ac 27:20 should be saved was then **t.** away. *4014*
Ac 27:33 fasting, having **t.** nothing. *4355*
Ac 27:40 when they had **t.** up the anchors, *4014*
Ro 9:6 the word of God hath **t.** none effect
1Co 5:2 done this deed might be **t.** away *1808*
1Co 10:13 There hath no temptation **t.** you *2983*
2Co 3:16 the Lord, the vail shall be **t.** away. *4014*
1Th 2:17 being **t.** from you for a short time *642*
2Th 2:7 let, until he be **t.** out of the way. *1096*
1Ti 5:9 not a widow be **t.** into the number *2639*
2Ti 2:26 who are **t.** captive by him at his will. *2221*
Heb 5:1 every high priest **t.** from among *2983*
2Pe 2:12 beasts, made to be **t.** and destroyed, *259*
Re 5:8 when he had **t.** the book, the four *2983*
Re 11:17 thou hast **t.** to thee thy great power, *2983*
Re 19:20 the beast was **t.**, and with him the *4084*

TAKER See also PARTAKER.

Isa 24:2 as with the **t.** of usury, so with the

TAKEST See also PARTAKEST.

Ex 4:9 the water which thou **t.** out of the 3947
Ex 30:12 thou **t.** the sum of the children 5375
Jg 4:9 the journey that thou **t.** shall not be 1980
1Ch 22:13 if thou **t.** heed to fulfil the statutes 8104
Ps 104:29 thou **t.** away their breath, they die, 622
Ec 9:9 labour...thou **t.** under the sun. 6001
Isa 58:3 our soul, and thou **t.** no knowledge?
Lu 19:21 **t. up that thou layedst not down,** *142*

TAKETH See also OVERTAKETH.

Ex 20:7 guiltless that **t.** his name in vain. 5375
De 5:11 guiltless that **t.** his name in vain. 5375
De 10:17 not persons, nor **t.** reward: 3947
De 24:6 for he **t.** a man's life to pledge 2254
De 25:11 hand, and **t.** him by the secrets: 2388
De 27:25 that **t.** reward to slay an innocent 3947
De 32:11 **t.** them, beareth them on her wings: 3947
Jos 7:14 tribe which the Lord **t.** shall come 3920
Jos 15:16 smiteth Kirjath-sepher, and **t.** it, 3920
Jg 1:12 smiteth Kirath-sepher, and **t.** it, 3920
1Sa 17:26 **t.** away the reproach from Israel? 5493
1Ki 14:10 as a man **t.** away dung, till it be 1197
Job 5:5 and **t.** it even out of the thorns, 3947

Job 5:13 He **t.** the wise in their...craftiness: 3920
Job 9:12 he **t.** away, who can hinder him? 2862
Job 12:20 **t.** away the understanding of the 3947
Job 12:24 He **t.** away the heart of the chief 5493
Job 21:6 and trembling **t.** hold on my flesh 270
Job 27:8 gained, when God **t.** away his soul? 7953
Job 40:24 He **t.** it with his eyes: his nose 3947
Ps 15:3 nor **t.** up a reproach against his 5375
Ps 15:5 nor **t.** reward against the innocent 3947
Ps 118:7 Lord **t.** my part with them that help
Ps 137:9 that **t.** and dasheth thy little ones 270
Ps 144:3 is man, that thou **t.** knowledge of him!
Ps 147:10 **t.** not pleasure in the legs of a man
Ps 147:11 Lord **t.** pleasure in them that fear
Ps 149:4 the Lord **t.** pleasure in his people:
Pr 1:19 which **t.** away the life of the owners 3947
Pr 16:32 his spirit than he that **t.** a city 3920
Pr 17:23 man **t.** a gift out of the bosom 3947
Pr 25:20 As he that **t.** away a garment in 5710
Pr 26:17 like one that **t.** a dog by the ears 2388
Pr 30:28 The spider **t.** hold with her hands, 8610
Ec 1:3 labour which he **t.** under the sun? 5998
Ec 2:23 yea, his heart **t.** not rest in the night
Ec 5:18 his labour that he **t.** under the sun 5998
Isa 13:14 and as a sheep that no man **t.** up: 6908
Isa 40:15 he **t.** up the isles as a very little 5190
Isa 44:14 and **t.** the cypress and the oak, 3947
Isa 51:18 there any that **t.** her by the hand 2388
Isa 56:6 polluting it,...**t.** hold of my covenant;... 2388
Eze 16:32 which **t.** strangers instead of her 3947
Eze 33:4 of the trumpet, and **t.** not warning;
Eze 33:5 that **t.** warning shall deliver his soul
Am 3:12 **t.** out of the mouth of the lion 5337
Mt 4:5 devil **t.** him up into the holy city, *3880*
Mt 4:8 devil **t.** him up into an exceeding *3880*
Mt 9:16 **in to fill it up t. from the garment,** *142*
Mt 10:38 **And he that t. not his cross, and** *2983*
Mt 12:45 **t. with himself seven other spirits** *3880*
Mt 17:1 after six days Jesus **t.** Peter, James, *3880*
Mk 2:21 **filled it up t. away from the old,** *142*
Mk 4:15 **t. away the word that was sown** *142*
Mk 5:40 he **t.** the father and the mother of *3880*
Mk 9:2 six days Jesus **t.** with him Peter, *3880*
Mk 9:18 wheresoever he **t.** him, he teareth *2638*
Mk 14:33 he **t.** with him Peter and James and *3880*
Lu 6:29 **him that t. away the cloke forbid** *142*
Lu 6:30 **of him that t. away thy goods ask** *142*
Lu 8:12 **t. away the word out of their** *142*
Lu 9:39 lo, a spirit **t.** him, and he suddenly *2983*
Lu 11:22 he **t.** from him all his armour *142*
Lu 11:26 and **t.** to him seven other spirits *3880*
Lu 16:3 **t.** away from me the stewardship: *851*
Joh 1:29 which **t.** away the sin of the world *142*
Joh 10:18 **No man t. it from me, but I lay it** *142*
Joh 15:2 **that beareth not fruit he t. away:** *142*
Joh 16:22 **and your joy no man t. from you** *142*
Joh 21:13 and **t.** bread, and giveth them, *2983*
Ro 3:5 unrighteous who **t.** vengeance? *2018*
1Co 3:19 **t.** the wise in their own craftiness *1405*
1Co 11:21 **t.** before other his own supper: *4301*
Heb 5:4 no man **t.** this honour unto himself, *2983*
Heb 10:9 He **t.** away the first, that he may *337*

TAKING
2Ch 19:7 respect of persons, nor **t.** of gifts 4727
Job 5:3 I have seen the foolish **t.** root: but
Ps 119:9 by **t.** heed thereto according to thy
Jer 50:46 At the noise of the **t.** of Babylon the 8610
Eze 25:12 the house of Judah by **t.** vengeance,
Ho 11:3 also to go, **t.** them by their arms; 3947
Mt 6:27 **Which of you by t. thought can**
Mk 13:34 **of man is as a man t. a far journey,**
Lu 4:5 **t.** him up into an high mountain, *321*
Lu 12:25 **And which of you with t. thought**
Lu 19:22 **man, t. up that I laid not down,** *142*
Joh 11:13 he had spoken of **t.** of rest in sleep
Ro 7:8 But sin, **t.** occasion by the *2983*
Ro 7:11 For sin, **t.** occasion by the *2983*
2Co 2:13 **t.** my leave of them, I went from
2Co 11:8 other churches, **t.** wages of them, *2983*
Eph 6:16 Above all, **t.** the shield of faith, *353*
2Th 1:8 **t.** vengeance on them that know *1325*
1Pe 5:2 flock...**t.** the oversight thereof, not by
3Jo 7 forth, **t.** nothing of the Gentiles. *2983*

TALE See also TALEBEARER; TALES.
Ex 5:8 And the **t.** of the bricks, which 4971
Ex 5:18 yet shall ye deliver the **t.** of bricks 8506
1Sa 18:27 they gave them in full **t.** to the king,
1Ch 9:28 bring them in and out by **t.** 4557
Ps 90:9 spend our years as a **t.** that is told 1899

TALEBEARER
Le 19:16 down as a **t.** among thy people: 7400
Pr 11:13 A **t.** revealeth secrets: but he 1980,7400
Pr 18:8 The words of a **t.** are as wounds, 5372
Pr 20:19 about as a **t.** revealeth secrets: 7400
Pr 26:20 there is no **t.**, the strife ceaseth 5372
Pr 26:22 The words of a **t.** are as wounds, 5372

TALENT See also TALENTS.
Ex 25:39 Of a **t.** of pure gold shall he make 3603
Ex 37:24 Of a **t.** of pure gold made he it, and 3603
Ex 38:27 hundred talents, a **t.** for a socket 3603
2Sa 12:30 a **t.** of gold with the precious stones: 3603
1Ki 20:39 or else thou shalt pay a **t.** of silver 3603
2Ki 5:22 give them, I pray thee, a **t.** of silver, 3603
2Ki 23:33 talents of silver, and a **t.** of gold 3603
1Ch 20:2 and found it to weigh a **t.** of gold, 3603
2Ch 36:3 talents of silver and a **t.** of gold 3603
Zec 5:7 there was lifted up a **t.** of lead: 3603
Mt 25:24 **he which had received the one t.** *5007*
Mt 25:25 **went and hid thy t. in the earth:** *5007*
Mt 25:28 **Take therefore the t. from him,** *5007*
Re 16:21 stone about the weight of a **t.** *5006*

TALENTS
Ex 38:24 offering, was twenty and nine **t.**, 3603
Ex 38:25 the silver...was an hundred **t.**, 3603
Ex 38:27 of the hundred **t.** of silver were cast 3603
Ex 38:27 hundred sockets of the hundred **t.**, 3603
Ex 38:29 brass of the offering was seventy **t.**, 3603
1Ki 9:14 sent to the king sixscore **t.** of gold 3603
1Ki 9:28 gold, four hundred and twenty **t.**, 3603
1Ki 10:10 an hundred and twenty **t.** of gold, 3603
1Ki 10:14 threescore and six **t.** of gold 3603
1Ki 16:24 of Shemer for two **t.** of silver, 3603
2Ki 5:5 and took with him ten **t.** of silver, 3603
2Ki 5:23 said, Be content, take two **t.** 3603
2Ki 5:23 bound two **t.** of silver in two bags, 3603
2Ki 15:19 gave Pul a thousand **t.** of silver, 3603
2Ki 18:14 unto Hezekiah..three hundred **t.** 3603
2Ki 18:14 of silver and thirty **t.** of gold 3603
2Ki 23:33 tribute of an hundred **t.** of silver, 3603
1Ch 19:6 Ammon sent a thousand **t.** of silver 3603
1Ch 22:14 an hundred thousand **t.** of gold, 3603
1Ch 22:14 a thousand thousand **t.** of silver; 3603
1Ch 29:4 Even three thousand **t.** of gold, of 3603
1Ch 29:4 seven thousand **t.** of refined silver, 3603
1Ch 29:7 of gold five thousand **t.** and ten 3603
1Ch 29:7 and of silver ten thousand **t.**, 3603
1Ch 29:7 and of brass eighteen thousand **t.**, 3603
1Ch 29:7 one hundred thousand **t.** of iron 3603
2Ch 3:8 gold, amounting to six hundred **t.** 3603
2Ch 8:18 four hundred and twenty **t.** of gold, 3603
2Ch 9:9 an hundred and twenty **t.** of gold, 3603
2Ch 9:13 and threescore and six **t.** of gold: 3603
2Ch 25:6 Israel for an hundred **t.** of silver 3603
2Ch 25:9 the hundred **t.** which I have given 3603
2Ch 27:5 same year an hundred **t.** of silver, 3603
2Ch 36:3 the land is an hundred **t.** of silver 3603
Ezr 7:22 Unto an hundred **t.** of silver, and 3604
Ezr 8:26 six hundred and fifty **t.** of silver, 3603
Ezr 8:26 and silver vessels an hundred **t.**, 3603
Ezr 8:26 and of gold an hundred **t.**; 3603
Es 3:9 I will pay ten thousand **t.** of silver 3603
Mt 18:24 **which owed him ten thousand t.** *5007*
Mt 25:15 **unto one he gave five t., and to** *5007*
Mt 25:16 **that had received the five t. went** *5007*
Mt 25:16 **same, and made them other five t.** *5007*
Mt 25:20 **And so he that had received five t.** *5007*
Mt 25:20 **came and brought other five t.,** *5007*
Mt 25:20 **thou deliveredst unto me five t.** *5007*
Mt 25:20 **gained beside them five t. more** *5007*
Mt 25:22 **He also that had received two t.** *5007*
Mt 25:22 **thou deliveredst unto me two t.** *5007*
Mt 25:22 **gained two other t. beside them.** *5007*
Mt 25:28 **give it unto him which hath ten t.** *5007*

TALES
Eze 22:9 men that carry **t.** to shed blood: 7400
Lu 24:11 words seemed to them as idle **t.**, *3026*

TALITHA (tal'-ith-ah)
Mk 5:41 hand, and said unto her, **T.** cumi; *5008*

TALK See also TALKED; TALKEST; TALKETH; TALKING.
Nu 11:17 come down and **t.** with thee there: 1696
De 5:24 this day that God doth **t.** with man 1696
De 6:7 **t.** of them when thou sittest in thine 1696
1Sa 2:3 **T.** no more so exceeding proudly; 1696
2Ki 18:26 and **t.** not...in the Jews' language 1696
1Ch 16:9 **t.** ye of all his wondrous works 7878
Job 11:2 should a man full of **t.** be justified? 8193
Job 13:7 God? and **t.** deceitfuly for him? 1696
Job 15:3 he reason with unprofitable **t.**? 1697
Ps 69:26 they **t.** to the grief of those whom 5608
Ps 71:24 also shall **t.** of thy righteousness 1897
Ps 77:12 all thy work, and **t.** of thy doings 7878
Ps 105:2 **t.** ye of all his wondrous works 7878
Ps 119:27 so shall I **t.** of thy wondrous works: 7878
Ps 145:11 thy kingdom, and **t.** of thy power; 1696
Pr 6:22 thou awakest, it shall **t.** with thee 7878
Pr 14:23 but the **t.** of the lips tendeth only 1697
Pr 24:2 and their lips **t.** of mischief 1696
Ec 10:13 the end of his **t.** is mischievous 6310
Jer 12:1 **t.** with thee of thy judgments: 1696
Eze 3:22 plain, and I will there **t.** with thee 1696
Da 10:17 the servant...**t.** with this my lord? 1696
Mt 22:15 they might entangle him in his **t.** *3056*
Joh 14:30 **Hereafter I will not t. much with** *2980*

TALKED
Ge 4:8 And Cain **t.** with Abel his brother: 559
Ge 17:3 on his face: and God **t.** with him, 1696
Ge 35:13 in the place where he **t.** with him 1696
Ge 35:14 in the place where he **t.** with him, 1696
Ge 45:15 after that his brethren **t.** with him 1696
Ex 20:22 that I have **t.** with you from heaven 1696
Ex 33:9 and the Lord **t.** with Moses 1696
Ex 34:29 his face shone while he **t.** with him 1696
Ex 34:31 unto him: and Moses **t.** with them 1696
De 5:4 The Lord **t.** with you face to face 1696
Jg 14:7 went down, and **t.** with the woman; 1696
1Sa 14:19 pass, while Saul **t.** unto the priest, 1696
1Sa 17:23 And as he **t.** with them, behold, 1696
1Ki 1:22 lo, while she yet **t.** with the king, 1696
2Ki 2:11 to pass, as they still went on, and **t.**, 1696
2Ki 6:33 And while he yet **t.** with them, 1696
2Ki 8:4 the king **t.** with Gehazi the servant 1696
2Ch 25:16 as he **t.** with him, that the king said 1696
Jer 38:25 princes hear...I have **t.** with thee, 1696
Da 9:22 informed me, and **t.** with me, and 1696
Zec 1:9 And the angel that **t.** with me said 1696
Zec 1:13 answered the angel that **t.** with me 1696
Zec 1:19 said unto the angel that **t.** with me, 1696
Zec 2:3 angel that **t.** with me went forth, 1696
Zec 4:1 angel that **t.** with me came again, 1696
Zec 4:4 spake to the angel that **t.** with me, 1696
Zec 4:5 the angel that **t.** with me answered 1696
Zec 5:5 angel that **t.** with me went forth, 1696
Zec 5:10 said I to the angel that **t.** with me, 1696
Zec 6:4 said unto the angel that **t.** with me, 1696
Mt 12:46 While he yet **t.** to the people, *2980*
Mk 6:50 And immediately **t.** with them, *2980*
Lu 9:30 there **t.** with him two men, which *4814*
Lu 24:14 they **t.** together of all these things *3656*
Lu 24:32 while he **t.** with us by the way, *2980*
Joh 4:27 marvelled...he **t.** with the woman: *2980*
Ac 10:27 as he **t.** with him, he went in, and *4926*
Ac 20:11 and **t.** a long while, even till break *3656*
Ac 26:31 aside, they **t.** between themselves, *2980*
Re 17:1 **t.** with me, saying unto me, Come *2980*
Re 21:9 **t.** with me, saying, Come hither, *2980*
Re 21:15 that **t.** with me had a golden reed *2980*

TALKERS
Eze 36:3 ye are taken up in the lips of **t.**, 3956
Tit 1:10 unruly and vain **t.** and deceivers, *3151*

TALKEST
Jg 6:17 me a sign that thou **t.** with me 1696
1Ki 1:14 while thou...**t.** there with the king, 1696
Joh 4:27 thou? or, Why **t.** thou with her? *2980*

TALKETH
Ps 37:30 and his tongue **t.** of judgment 1696
Joh 9:37 **him, and it is he that t. with thee.** *2980*

TALKING
Ge 17:22 And he left off **t.** with him, and 1696
1Ki 18:27 either he is **t.**, or he is pursuing, 7879
Es 6:14 while they were yet **t.** with him, 1696
Job 29:9 The princes refrained **t.**, and laid 4405
Eze 33:30 people still are **t.** against thee 1696
Mt 17:3 them Moses and Elias **t.** with him *4814*
Mk 9:4 Moses: and they were **t.** with Jesus *4814*

Eph 5:4 nor foolish **t.**, nor jesting, ... *3473*
Re 4:1 it were of a trumpet **t.** with me; *2980*

TALL See also TALLER.
De 2:10 a people great, and many, and **t.**, ... 7311
De 2:21 A people great, and many, and **t.**; 7311
De 9:2 A people great and **t.**, the children 7311
2Ki 19:23 will cut down the **t.** cedar trees 6967
Isa 37:24 I will cut down the **t.** cedars thereof, .. 6967

TALLER
De 1:28 people is greater and **t.** than we; 7311

TALMAI (tal'-mahee)
Nu 13:22 where Ahiman, Sheshai, and **T.**, ... 8526
Jos 15:14 Sheshai, and Ahiman, and **T.**, ... 8526
Jg 1:10 slew Sheshai, and Ahiman, and **T.** 8526
2Sa 3:3 the daughter of **T.** king of Geshur; 8526
2Sa 13:37 But Absalom fled, and went to **T.**, ... 8526
1Ch 3:2 the daughter of **T.** king of Geshur: 8526

TALMON (tal'-mon)
1Ch 9:17 Shallum, and Akkub, and **T.**, ... 2929
Ezr 2:42 children of Ater, the children of **T.**, ... 2929
Ne 7:45 children of Ater, the children of **T.**, ... 2929
Ne 11:19 the porters, Akkub, **T.**, and their 2929
Ne 12:25 Meshullam, **T.**, Akkub, were porters .. 2929

TAMAH (ta'-mah) See also THAMAH.
Ne 7:55 of Sisera, the children of **T.**, ... 8547

TAMAR (ta'-mar) See also BAAL-TAMAR; HAZAZON-TAMAR; THAMAR.
Ge 38:6 his firstborn, whose name was **T.** 8559
Ge 38:11 Judah to **T.** his daughter in law. 8559
Ge 38:11 **T.** went and dwelt in her father's 8559
Ge 38:13 And it was told **T.**, saying, Behold...... 8559
Ge 38:24 **T.** thy daughter in law hath played...... 8559
Ru 4:12 Pharez, whom **T.** bare unto Judah, ... 8559
2Sa 13:1 a fair sister, whose name was **T.**; 8559
2Sa 13:2 that he fell sick for his sister **T.**; 8559
2Sa 13:4 I love **T.**, my brother Absalom's 8559
2Sa 13:5 let my sister **T.** come, and give me 8559
2Sa 13:6 let **T.** my sister come, and make me... 8559
2Sa 13:7 David sent home to **T.**, saying, Go..... 8559
2Sa 13:8 So **T.** went to her brother Amnon's 8559
2Sa 13:10 And Amnon said unto **T.**, Bring the 8559
2Sa 13:10 **T.** took the cakes which she had........ 8559
2Sa 13:19 **T.** put ashes on her head, and rent...... 8559
2Sa 13:20 So **T.** remained desolate in her 8559
2Sa 13:22 because he had forced his sister **T.**....... 8559
2Sa 13:32 the day that he forced his sister **T.**...... 8559
2Sa 14:27 one daughter, whose name was **T.** 8559
1Ch 2:4 **T.** his daughter in law bare him 8559
1Ch 3:9 the concubines, and **T.** their sister...... 8559
Eze 47:19 from **T.** even to the waters of strife 8559
Eze 48:28 from **T.** unto the waters of strife in 8559

TAME See also TAMED.
Mk 5:4 neither could any man **t.** him. *1150*
Jas 3:8 But the tongue can no man **t.**; it is..... *1150*

TAMED
Jas 3:7 and of things in the sea, is **t.**, ... *1150*
Jas 3:7 and hath been **t.** of mankind: *1150*

TAMMUZ (tam'-muz)
Eze 8:14 there sat women weeping for **T.**. 8542

TANACH (ta'-nak) See also TAANACH.
Jos 21:25 Manasseh, **T.** with her suburbs, ... 8590

TANGLE See ENTANGLE.

TANHUMETH (tan'-hu-meth)
2Ki 25:23 the son of **T.**, the Netophthite, ... 8576
Jer 40:8 Kareah, and Seraiah the son of **T.**, ... 8576

TANNER
Ac 9:43 days in Joppa with one Simon a **t.** *1033*
Ac 10:6 He lodgeth with one Simon a **t.**, ... *1033*
Ac 10:32 in the house of one Simon a **t.** by the . *1033*

TAPESTRY
Pr 7:16 decked my bed with coverings of **t.**, ...
Pr 31:22 She maketh herself coverings of **t.**; ....

TAPHATH (ta'-fath)
1Ki 4:11 **T.**...daughter of Solomon to wife: 2955

TAPPUAH (tap'-pu-ah) See also BETH-TAPPUAH; EN-TAPPUAH.
Jos 12:17 The king of **T.**, one; the king of......... 8599
Jos 15:34 and En-gannim, **T.**, and Enam, ... 8599
Jos 16:8 from **T.** westward unto the river........ 8599
Jos 17:8 Now Manessah had the land of **T.** 8599
Jos 17:8 but **T.** on the border of Manasseh 8599
1Ch 2:43 the sons of Hebron; Korah, and **T.**, ... 8599

TARAH (ta'-rah)
Nu 33:27 from Tahath, and pitched at **T.** 8646
Nu 33:28 they removed from **T.**, and pitched...... 8646

TARALAH (tar'-a-lah)
Jos 18:27 And Rekem, and Irpeel, and **T.**, ... 8634

TARE See also TARES.
2Sa 13:31 king arose, and **t.** his garments, ... 7167
2Ki 2:24 **t.** forty and two children of them......... 1234
Mk 9:20 him, straightway the spirit **t.** him; *4682*
Lu 9:42 devil threw him down, and **t.** him. *4952*

TAREA (ta'-re-ah) See also TAHREA.
1Ch 8:35 and Melech, and **T.**, and Ahaz. 8390

TARES
Mt 13:25 **and sowed t. among the wheat,** *2215*
Mt 13:26 **fruit, then appeared the t. also** *2215*
Mt 13:27 **field? from whence then hath it t.?** . *2215*
Mt 13:29 **Nay; lest while ye gather up the t.,** *2215*
Mt 13:30 **Gather ye together first the t.,** *2215*
Mt 13:36 us the parable of the **t.** of the field. *2215*
Mt 13:38 **t. are the children of the wicked** .. *2215*
Mt 13:40 **t. are gathered and burned in the** .. *2215*

TARGET See also TARGETS.
1Sa 17:6 **t.** of brass between his shoulders. 3591
1Ki 10:16 shekels of gold went to one **t.** 6793
2Ch 9:15 of beaten gold went to one **t.** 6793

TARGETS
1Ki 10:16 two hundred **t.** of beaten gold:........... 6793
2Ch 9:15 two hundred **t.** of beaten gold:........... 6793
2Ch 14:8 had an army of men that bare **t.** and... 6793

TARPELITES (tar'-pel-ites)
Ezr 4:9 the Apharsathchites, the **T.**, the......... 2967

TARRIED
Ge 24:54 were with him, and **t.** all night; 3885
Ge 28:11 certain place, and **t.** there all night, ... 3885
Ge 31:54 bread, and **t.** all night in the mount..... 3885
Nu 9:19 cloud **t.** long upon the tabernacle 748
Nu 9:22 the cloud **t.** upon the tabernacle, ... 748
Jg 3:25 they **t.** till they were ashamed: 2342
Jg 3:26 And Ehud escaped while they **t.**, ... 4102
Jg 19:8 And they **t.** until afternoon, and 4102
Ru 2:7 that she **t.** a little in the house. 3427
1Sa 13:8 he **t.** seven days, according to the...... 3176
1Sa 14:2 Saul **t.** in the uttermost part of 3427
2Sa 11:1 But David **t.** still at Jerusalem........... 3427
2Sa 15:17 and **t.** in a place that was far off. 5975
2Sa 15:29 to Jerusalem: and they **t.** there. 3427
2Sa 20:5 but he **t.** longer than the set time 3186
2Ki 2:18 again to him, (for he **t.** at Jericho,) 3427
1Ch 20:1 Rabbah. But David **t.** at Jerusalem..... 3427
Ps 68:12 and she that **t.** at home divided the 5116
Mt 25:5 **While the bridegroom t., they all** .. *5549*
Lu 1:21 that he **t.** so long in the temple. *5549*
Lu 2:43 child Jesus **t.** behind in Jerusalem; *5278*
Joh 3:22 and there he **t.** with them, and *1304*
Ac 9:43 he **t.** many days in Joppa with one...... *3306*
Ac 15:33 after they had **t.** there a space, ... *4160*
Ac 18:18 Paul after this **t.** there yet a good *4357*
Ac 20:5 These going before **t.**...at Troas, ... *3306*
Ac 20:15 at Samos, and **t.** at Trogyllium; *3306*
Ac 21:4 disciples, we **t.** there seven days: *1961*
Ac 21:10 And as we **t.** there many days, ... *1961*
Ac 25:6 he had **t.** among them more than *1304*
Ac 27:33 the fourteenth day that ye have **t.** *4328*
Ac 28:12 at Syracuse, we **t.** there three days.... *1961*

TARRIEST
Ac 22:16 And now why **t.** thou? arise, and be ... *3195*

TARRIETH
1Sa 30:24 his part be that **t.** by the stuff; 3427
Mic 5:7 upon the grass, that **t.** not for man, ... 6960

TARRY See also TARRIED; TARRIEST; TARRIETH; TARRYING.
Ge 19:2 **t.** all night, and wash your feet, ... 3885
Ge 27:44 And **t.** with him a few days, until 3427
Ge 30:27 I have found favour in thine eyes, **t.** ....
Ge 45:9 Egypt: come down unto me, **t.** not: 5975
Ex 12:39 out of Egypt, and could not **t.**, ... 4102
Ex 24:14 **T.** ye here for us, until we come 3427
Le 14:8 **t.** abroad out of his tent seven days.... 3427
Nu 22:19 **t.** ye also here this night, that I may... 3427
Jg 5:28 why **t.** the wheels of his chariots? 309
Jg 6:18 I will **t.** until thou come again. 3427
Jg 19:6 and **t.** all night, and let thine 3885
Jg 19:9 evening, I pray you **t.** all night: 3885
Jg 19:10 But the man would not **t.** that night, ... 3885
Ru 1:13 **t.** for them till they were grown? 7663
Ru 3:13 **T.** this nght, and it shall be in the 3885
1Sa 1:23 **t.** until thou have weaned him; 3427
1Sa 10:8 seven days shalt thou **t.**, till I come 3176
1Sa 14:9 **T.** until we come to you; then we 1826
2Sa 10:5 **T.** at Jericho until your beards be 3427
2Sa 11:12 **T.** here to day also, and to morrow 3427
2Sa 15:28 **t.** in the plain of the wilderness, ... 4102
2Sa 18:14 Joab, I may not **t.** thus with thee. 3176
2Sa 19:7 there will not **t.** one with thee this 3885
2Ki 2:2 unto Elisha, **T.** here, I pray thee; 3427
2Ki 2:4 him, Elisha, **t.** here, I pray thee; 3427
2Ki 2:6 unto him, **T.**, I pray thee, here; 3427
2Ki 7:9 if we **t.** till the morning light, some..... 2442
2Ki 9:3 open the door, and flee, and **t.** not. 2442
2Ki 14:10 glory of this, and **t.** at home: for 3427
1Ch 19:5 **T.** at Jericho until your beards be 3427
Ps 101:7 he that telleth lies shall not **t.** in 3559
Pr 23:30 They that **t.** long at the wine; they 309
Isa 46:13 off, and my salvation shall not **t.**. 309
Jer 14:8 that turneth aside to **t.** for a night? 3885
Hab 2:3 not lie: though it **t.**, wait for it; 4102
Hab 2:3 it will surely come, it will not **t.**. 309
Mt 26:38 **t. ye here, and watch with me** *3306*
Mk 14:34 **unto death: t. ye here, and watch** .. *3306*
Lu 24:29 And he went in to **t.** with them. *3306*
Lu 24:49 **but t. ye in the city of Jerusalem,** .. *2523*
Joh 4:40 him that he would **t.** with them: *3306*
Joh 21:22 **If I will that he t. till I come,** *3306*
Ac 10:48 prayed they him to **t.** certain days...... *1961*
Ac 18:20 they desired him to **t.** longer time *3306*
Ac 28:14 desired to **t.** with them seven days: *1961*
1Co 11:33 together to eat, **t.** one for another...... *1551*
1Co 16:7 I trust to **t.** a while with you, if the.... *1961*
1Co 16:8 will **t.** at Ephesus until Pentecost. *1961*
1Ti 3:15 But if I **t.** long, that thou mayest *1019*
Heb 10:37 come will come, and will not **t.**. *5549*
Joh 21:23 If I will that he **t.** till...........................

TARRYING
Ps 40:17 deliverer; make no **t.**, O my God. 309
Ps 70:5 my deliverer; O Lord, make no **t.** 309

TARSHISH (tar'-shish) See also THARSHISH.
Ge 10:4 sons of Javan; Elishah, and **T.**, ... 8659
1Ch 1:7 the sons of Javan; Elishah and **T.** 8659
2Ch 9:21 For the king's ships went to **T.** 8659
2Ch 9:21 came the ships of **T.** bringing gold, ... 8659
2Ch 20:36 him to make ships to go to **T.** 8659
2Ch 20:37 they were not able to go to **T.** 8659
Es 1:14 Admatha, **T.**, Meres, Marsena, ... 8659
Ps 48:7 Thou breakest the ships of **T.** 8659
Ps 72:10 The kings of **T.** and of the isles 8659
Isa 2:16 And upon all the ships of **T.**, and 8659
Isa 23:1 Howl, ye ships of **T.**: for it is laid 8659
Isa 23:6 Pass ye over to **T.**; howl, ye............. 8659
Isa 23:10 land as a river, O daughter of **T.** 8659
Isa 23:14 Howl, ye ships of **T.**: for your 8659
Isa 60:9 for me, and the ships of **T.** first, ... 8659
Isa 66:19 them unto the nations, to **T.**, Pul, ... 8659
Jer 10:9 into plates is brought from **T.**, ... 8659
Eze 27:12 **T.** was thy merchant by reason of....... 8659
Eze 27:25 The ships of **T.** did sing of thee 8659
Eze 38:13 Dedan, and the merchants of **T.**, ... 8659
Jon 1:3 But Jonah rose up to flee unto **T.** 8659
Jon 1:3 and he found a ship going to **T.** 8659
Jon 1:3 unto it, to go with them unto **T.** 8659
Jon 4:2 Therefore I fled before unto **T.** 8659

TARSUS (tar'-sus)
Ac 9:11 **Judas for one called Saul, of T** *5018*
Ac 9:30 Caesarea, and sent him forth to **T.** *5019*
Ac 11:25 Then departed Barnabas to **T.**, ... *5019*
Ac 21:39 I am a man which am a Jew of **T.**, ... *5018*
Ac 22:3 man which am a Jew, born in **T.**, ... *5019*

TARTAK (tar'-tak)
2Ki 17:31 the Avites made Nibhaz and **T.**, ... 8662

TARTAN (tar'-tan)
2Ki 18:17 And the king of Assyria sent **T.** 8661
Isa 20:1 year that **T.** came unto Ashdod, ... 8661

TASCHITH See AL-TASCHITH.

TASK See also TASKMASTERS; TASKS.
Ex 5:14 fulfilled your **t.** in making brick 2706
Ex 5:19 from your bricks of your daily **t.** 1697

TASKMASTERS
Ex 1:11 they did set over them **t.** 8269,4522
Ex 3:7 their cry by reason of their **t.**; 5065
Ex 5:6 And Pharaoh commanded...the **t.** 5065
Ex 5:10 And the **t.** of the people went out, 5065
Ex 5:13 And the **t.** hasted them, saying, 5065
Ex 5:14 Pharaoh's **t.** had set over them, 5065

TASKS
Ex 5:13 Fulfill your works, your daily **t.**, 1697

TASTE See also TASTED; TASTETH.
Ex 16:31 **t.** of it was like wafers made with 2940
Nu 11:8 the **t.** of it was as the **t.** of fresh oil. 2940
1Sa 14:43 I did but **t.** a little honey with the 2938
2Sa 3:35 to me, and more also, if I **t.** bread, 2938
2Sa 19:35 **t.** what I eat or what I drink? 2938
Job 6:6 there any **t.** in the white of an egg? 2940
Job 6:30 my **t.** discern perverse things? 2441
Job 12:11 and the mouth **t.** his meat? 2938
Ps 34:8 O **t.** and see that the Lord is good: 2938
Ps 119:103 sweet are thy words unto my **t.**! 2441
Pr 24:13 honeycomb, which is sweet to thy **t.** 2441
Ca 2:3 and his fruit was sweet to my **t.** 2441
Jer 48:11 therefore his **t.** remained in him, 2940
Jon 3:7 beast, herd nor flock, **t.** any thing: 2938
Mt 16:28 **here, which shall not t. of death,** *1089*
Mk 9:1 **here, which shall not t. of death,** *1089*
Lu 9:27 **here, which shall not t. of death,** *1089*
Lu 14:24 **were bidden shall t. of my supper** *1089*
Joh 8:52 saying, he shall never **t.** of death. *1089*
Col 2:21 (Touch not; **t.** not; handle not; *1089*
Heb 2:9 should **t.** death for every man. *1089*

TASTED
1Sa 14:24 So none of the people **t.** any food. 2938
1Sa 14:29 because I **t.** a little of this honey. 2938
Da 5:2 Belshazzar, whiles he **t.** the wine, 2942
Mt 27:34 had **t.** thereof, he would not drink. *1089*
Joh 2:9 **t.** of the water that was made wine, *1089*
Heb 6:4 and have **t.** of the heavenly gift, and *1089*
Heb 6:5 And have **t.** the good word of God, *1089*
1Pe 2:3 ye have **t.** that the Lord is gracious. *1089*

TASTETH
Job 34:3 words, as the mouth **t.** meat. 2938

TATNAI (tat'-nahee)
Ezr 5:3,6 **T.**, governor on this side the 8674
Ezr 6:6 **T.**, governor behond the river, 8674
Ezr 6:13 **T.**, governor on this side the river, 8674

TATTLERS
1Ti 5:13 idle, but **t.** also and busybodies, *5397*

TAU (tawu)
Ps 119:169 *title* [ת] **T.**

TAUGHT
De 4:5 Behold, I have **t.** you statutes and 3925
De 31:22 day, and **t.** it the children of Israel. 3925
Jg 8:16 them he **t.** the men of Succoth. 3045
2Ki 17:28 **t.** them how they should fear the 3384
2Ch 6:27 thou hast **t.** them the good way, 3384
2Ch 17:9 they **t.** in Judah, and had the book 3925
2Ch 17:9 cities of Judah, and **t.** the people. 3925
2Ch 23:13 and such as **t.** to sing praise. 3045
2Ch 30:22 **t.** the good knowledge of the Lord: 7919
2Ch 35:3 unto the Levites that **t.** all Israel, 4000
Ne 8:9 and the Levites that **t.** the people, 995
Ps 71:17 thou hast **t.** me from my youth: 3925
Ps 119:102 judgments: for thou hast **t.** me. 3384
Ps 119:171 when thou hast **t.** me thy statutes. 3925
Pr 4:4 He **t.** me also, and said unto me, 3384
Pr 4:11 I have **t.** thee in the way of wisdom; 3384
Pr 31:1 prophecy that his mother **t.** him. 3256
Ec 12:9 he still **t.** the people knowledge; 3925
Isa 29:13 fear toward me is **t.** by the precept 3925
Isa 40:13 being his counsellor hath **t.** him? 3045
Isa 40:14 **t.** him in the path of judgment, 3925
Isa 40:14 and **t.** him knowledge, and shewed 3925
Isa 54:13 children shall be **t.** of the Lord; 3928
Jer 2:33 hast thou also **t.** the wicked ones 3925
Jer 9:5 have **t.** their tongue to speak lies, 3925
Jer 9:14 Baalim, which their fathers **t.** them: 3925
Jer 12:16 they **t.** my people to swear by Baal; 3925
Jer 13:21 thou hast **t.** them to be captains, 3925
Jer 28:16 hast **t.** rebellion against the Lord. 1696
Jer 29:32 hath **t.** rebellion against the Lord. 1696
Jer 32:33 though I **t.** them, rising up early 3925
Eze 23:48 be **t.** not to do after your lewdness. 3256
Ho 10:11 Ephraim is as an heifer that is **t.**, 3925
Ho 11:3 I **t.** Ephraim also to go, taking 8637
Zec 13:5 **t.** me to keep cattle from my youth.
Mt 5:2 he opened his mouth, and **t.** them, *1321*
Mt 7:29 he **t.** them as one having *2258,1321*
Mt 13:54 he **t.** them in their synagogue, *1321*
Mt 28:15 the money, and did as they were **t.** *1321*
Mk 1:21 entered into the synagogue, and **t.** *1321*
Mk 1:22 for he **t.** them as one that had *2258,1321*
Mk 2:13 resorted unto him, and he **t.** *2258,1321*
Mk 4:2 **t.** them many things by parables, *2258,1321*
Mk 6:30 had done, and what they had **t.** *2258,1321*
Mk 9:31 For he **t.** his disciples, and said *2258,1321*
Mk 10:1 he was wont, he **t.** them again. *2258,1321*
Mk 11:17 **t.**, saying unto them, **Is it not** *2258,1321*
Mk 12:35 said, while he **t.** in the temple, *2258,1321*
Lu 4:15 he **t.** in their synagogues, being *2258,1321*
Lu 4:31 **t.** them on the sabbath days. *2258,1321*
Lu 5:3 and **t.** the people out of the ship. *1321*
Lu 6:6 entered into the synagogue and **t.**: *1321*
Lu 11:1 pray, as John also **t.** his disciples. *1321*
Lu 13:26 **and thou hast t. in our streets.** *1321*
Lu 19:47 And he **t.** daily in the temple. *2258,1321*
Lu 20:1 as he **t.** the people in the temple. *1321*
Joh 6:45 **And they shall be all t. of God** *1318*
Joh 6:59 synagogue, as he **t.** in Capernaum. *1321*
Joh 7:14 went up into the temple, and **t.** *1321*
Joh 7:28 cried Jesus in the temple as he **t.**, *1321*
Joh 8:2 and he sat down, and **t.** them. *1321*
Joh 8:20 treasury, as he **t.** in the temple: *1321*
Joh 8:28 **as my Father hath t. me, I speak** *1321*
Joh 18:20 **I ever t. in the synagogue, and in** *1321*
Ac 4:2 grieved that they **t.** the people, *1321*
Ac 5:21 temple early in the morning, and **t.** *1321*
Ac 11:26 the church, and **t.** much people. *1321*
Ac 14:21 to that city, and had **t.** many, *3100*
Ac 15:1 down from Judaea **t.** the brethren, *1321*
Ac 18:25 **t.** diligently the things of the Lord, *1321*
Ac 20:20 you, and have **t.** you publickly, *1321*
Ac 22:3 **t.** according to the perfect manner *3811*
Ga 1:12 it of man, neither was I **t.** it. *1321*
Ga 6:6 Let him that is **t.** in the word *2727*
Eph 4:21 heard him, and...been **t.** by him, *1321*
Col 2:7 in the faith, as ye have been **t.**, *1321*
1Th 4:9 are **t.** of God to love one anther. *2312*
2Th 2:15 traditions which ye have been **t.**, *1321*
Tit 1:9 faithful word as he hath been **t.**, *1322*
1Joh 2:27 no lie, and even as it hath **t.** you, *1321*
Re 2:14 **t. Balac to cast a stumblingblock** *1321*

TAUNT See also TAUNTING.
Jer 24:9 and a proverb, a **t.** and a curse, 8148
Eze 5:15 So it shall be a reproach and a **t.**, 1422

TAUNTING
Hab 2:6 and a **t.** proverb against him, and 4426

TAVERNS
Ac 28:15 far as Appii forum,...The three **t.**; *4999*

TAXATION
2Ki 23:35 of every one according to his **t.**, to 6187

TAXED
2Ki 23:35 he **t.** the land to give the money 6186
Lu 2:1 that all the world should be **t.** *582*
Lu 2:3 all went to be **t.**, every one into his *582*
Lu 2:5 be **t.** with Mary his espoused wife, *582*

TAXES
Da 11:20 a raiser of **t.** in the glory of the 5065

TAXING
Lu 2:2 And this **t.** was first made when *583*
Ac 5:37 Judas of Galilee in the days of the **t.**, *583*

TEACH See also TAUGHT; TEACHER; TEACHEST; TEACHETH; TEACHING.
Ex 4:12 and **t.** thee what thou shalt say. 3384
Ex 4:15 and will **t.** you what ye shall do. 3384
Ex 18:20 thou shalt **t.** them ordinances and 2094
Ex 24:12 written; that thou mayest **t.** them. 3384
Ex 35:34 hath put in his heart that he may **t.**, 3384
Le 10:11 may **t.** the children of Israel all the 3384
Le 14:57 **t.** when it is unclean, and when it is 3384
De 4:1 the judgments, which I **t.** you, for 3925
De 4:9 but **t.** them thy sons, and thy sons' 3045
De 4:10 and that they may **t.** their children. 3925
De 4:14 me at that time to **t.** you statutes 3925
De 5:31 judgments, which thou shalt **t.** them, 3925
De 6:1 your God commanded to **t.** you, 3925
De 6:7 shalt **t.** them diligently unto thy 8150
De 11:19 And ye shall **t.** them your children, 3925
De 17:11 of the law which they shall **t.** thee, 3384
De 20:18 they **t.** you not to do after all their 3925
De 24:8 the priests the Levites shall **t.** you: 3384
De 31:19 you, and **t.** it the children of Israel: 3925
De 33:10 They shall **t.** Jacob thy judgments, 3384
Jg 3:2 Israel might know, to **t.** them war, 3925
Jg 13:8 and **t.** us what we shall do unto the 3384
1Sa 12:23 I will **t.** you the good and the right 3384
2Sa 1:18 bade them **t.** the children of Judah 3925
1Ki 8:36 that thou **t.** them the good way 3384
2Ki 17:27 **t.** them the manner of the God of 3384
2Ch 17:7 to **t.** in the cities of Judah. 3925
Ezr 7:10 and to **t.** in Israel statutes and 3925
Ezr 7:25 and **t.** ye them that know them not. 3046
Job 6:24 **T.** me, and I will hold my tongue: 3384
Job 8:10 Shall not they **t.** thee, and tell thee, 3384
Job 12:7 the beasts, and they shall **t.** thee; 3384
Job 12:8 to the earth, and it shall **t.** thee: 3384
Job 21:22 Shall any **t.** God knowledge? seeing 3925
Job 27:11 I will **t.** you by the hand of God: 3384
Job 32:7 multitude of years...**t.** wisdom. 3045
Job 33:33 peace, and I shall **t.** thee wisdom. 502
Job 34:32 That which I see not **t.** thou me: 3384
Job 37:19 **T.** us what we shall say unto him; 3045
Ps 25:4 thy ways, O Lord; **t.** me thy paths. 3925
Ps 25:5 Lead me in thy truth, and **t.** me: 3925
Ps 25:8 will he **t.** sinners in the way. 3384
Ps 25:9 and the meek will he **t.** his way. 3925
Ps 25:12 him shall he **t.** in the way that he 3384
Ps 27:11 **T.** me thy way, O Lord, and lead 3384
Ps 32:8 I will instruct thee and **t.** thee in the 3384
Ps 34:11 I will **t.** you the fear of the Lord. 3925
Ps 45:4 thy right hand shall **t.** thee terrible 3384
Ps 51:13 will I **t.** transgressors thy ways; 3925
Ps 60:*title* Michtam of David, to **t.**; when 3925
Ps 86:11 **T.** me thy way, O Lord; I will 3384
Ps 90:12 **t.** us to number our days, that we 3045
Ps 105:22 pleasure; and **t.** his senators wisdom.
Ps 119:12 thou, O Lord: **t.** me thy statutes. 3925
Ps 119:26 heardest me: **t.** me thy statutes. 3925
Ps 119:33 **T.** me, O Lord, the way of thy 3384
Ps 119:64 of thy mercy: **t.** me thy statutes. 3925
Ps 119:66 **T.** me...judgment and knowledge; 3925
Ps 119:68 and doest good; **t.** me thy statutes. 3925
Ps 119:108 O Lord, and **t.** me thy judgments. 3925
Ps 119:124 thy mercy, and **t.** me thy statutes. 3925
Ps 119:135 thy servant; and **t.** me thy statutes. 3925
Ps 132:12 my testimony that I shall **t.** them, 3925
Ps 143:10 **T.** me to do thy will; for thou art 3925
Pr 9:9 **t.** a just man, and he will increase 3045
Isa 2:3 he will **t.** us of his ways, and we 3384
Isa 28:9 Whom shall he **t.** knowledge? and 3384
Isa 28:26 him to discretion, and doth **t.** him. 3384
Jer 9:20 and **t.** your daughters wailing, and 3925
Jer 31:34 **t.** no more every man his neighbour, 3925
Eze 44:23 shall **t.** my people the difference 3384
Da 1:4 whom they might **t.** the learning 3925
Mic 3:11 and the priests thereof **t.** for hire, 3384
Mic 4:2 and he will **t.** us of his ways, and we 3384
Hab 2:19 Arise, it shall **t.**! Behold, it is laid 3384
Mt 5:19 **and shall t. men so, he shall be** *1321*
Mt 5:19 **whosoever shall do and t. them,** *1321*
Mt 11:1 to **t.** and to preach in their cities. *1321*
Mt 28:19 **Go ye therefore, and t. all nations,** *3100*
Mk 4:1 began again to **t.** by the sea side: *1321*
Mk 6:2 he began to **t.** in the synagogue: *1321*
Mk 6:34 he began to **t.** them many things. *1321*
Mk 8:31 he began to **t.** them, that the Son of *1321*
Lu 11:1 said unto him, Lord, **t.** us to pray, *1321*
Lu 12:12 **Holy Ghost shall t. you in the** *1321*
Joh 7:35 the Gentiles, and **t.** the Gentiles? *1321*
Joh 9:34 born in sins, and dost thou **t.** us? *1321*
Joh 14:26 **he shall t. you all things, and** *1321*
Ac 1:1 that Jesus began both to do and **t.**, *1321*
Ac 4:18 at all nor **t.** in the name of Jesus. *1321*
Ac 5:28 that ye should not **t.** in this name? *1321*
Ac 5:42 ceased not to **t.** and preach Jesus. *1321*

Ac 16:21 t. customs, which are not lawful......... *2605*
1Co 4:17 I t. every where in every church. *1321*
1Co 11:14 Doth not even nature itself t. you, ... *1321*
1Co 14:19 by my voice I might t. others also,...... *2727*
1Ti 1:3 some that they t. no other doctrine, ... *2085*
1Ti 2:12 But I suffer not a woman to t., nor *1321*
1Ti 3:2 given to hospitality, apt to t.; *1317*
1Ti 4:11 These things command and t............. *1321*
1Ti 6:2 benefit. These things t. and exhort...... *1321*
1Ti 6:3 If any man t. otherwise, and *2085*
2Ti 2:2 who shall be able to t. others also...... *1321*
2Ti 2:24 but be gentle unto all men, apt to t., .. *1317*
Tit 2:4 t. the young women to be sober, ... *4994*
Heb 5:12 ye have need that one t. you again..... *1321*
Heb 8:11 not t. every man his neighbour, ... *1321*
1Jo 2:27 ye need not that any man t. you: *1321*
Re 2:20 **to t. and to seduce my servants to** . *1321*

TEACHER See also TEACHERS.
1Ch 25:8 as the great, the t. as the scholar........ 995
Hab 2:18 the molten image, and a t. of lies,...... 3384
Joh 3:2 that thou art a t. come from God: *1320*
Ro 2:20 a t. of babes, which hast the form...... *1320*
1Ti 2:7 a t. of the Gentiles in faith and.......... *1320*
2Ti 1:11 an apostle, and a t. of the Gentiles. *1320*

TEACHERS
Ps 119:99 understanding than all my t.............. 3925
Pr 5:13 have not obeyed the voice of my t., ... 3384
Isa 30:20 not thy t. be removed into a corner.... 3384
Isa 30:20 but thine eyes shall see thy t.. 3384
Isa 43:27 t. have transgressed against me.......... 3887
Ac 13:1 at Antioch certain prophets and t.;...... *1320*
1Co 12:28 secondarily prophets, thirdly t.,.......... *1320*
1Co 12:29 are all prophets? are all t.? are all *1320*
Eph 4:11 and some, pastors and t.; *1320*
1Ti 1:7 Desiring to be t. of the law;............. *3547*
2Ti 4:3 shall they heap to themselves t.,.......... *1320*
Tit 2:3 to much wine, t. of good things; *2567*
Heb 5:12 when for the time ye ought to be t.,.... *1320*
2Pe 2:1 there shall be false t. among you,........ *5572*

TEACHEST
Ps 94:12 O Lord, and t. him out of thy law; 3925
Mt 22:16 true, and t. the way of God in truth, .. *1321*
Mk 12:14 men, but t. the way of God in truth:... *1321*
Lu 20:21 know that thou sayest and t. rightly,... *1321*
Lu 20:21 of any, but t. the way of God truly:.... *1321*
Ac 21:21 that thou t. all the Jews which are...... *1321*
Ro 2:21 Thou therefore which t. another,........ *1321*
Ro 2:21 t. thou not thyself? thou that............ *1321*

TEACHETH
2Sa 22:35 He t. my hands to war; so that a....... 3925
Job 35:11 Who t. us more than the beasts of....... 502
Job 36:22 by his power: who t. like him? 3384
Ps 18:34 He t. my hands to war, so that a....... 3925
Ps 94:10 he that t. man knowledge, shall not 3925
Ps 144:1 which t. my hands to war, and my 3925
Pr 6:13 his feet, he t. with his fingers; 3384
Pr 16:23 The heart of the wise t. his mouth, ... 7919
Isa 9:15 prophet that t. lies, he is the tail........ 3384
Isa 48:17 thy God which t. thee to profit, ... 3925
Ac 21:28 man, that t. all men every where *1321*
Ro 12:7 or he that t., on teaching;................ *1321*
1Co 2:13 the words which man's wisdom t.,....... *1318*
1Co 2:13 but which the Holy Ghost t............... *1318*
Ga 6:6 unto him that t. in all good things....... *2727*
1Jo 2:27 as the same anointing t. you of all...... *1321*

TEACHING
2Ch 15:3 without a t. priest, and without.......... 3384
Jer 32:33 them, rising up early and t. them, ... 3925
Mt 4:23 all Galilee, t. in their synagogues,....... *1321*
Mt 9:35 and villages, t. in their synagogues, ... *1321*
Mt 15:9 **t. for doctrines the commandments** *1321*
Mt 21:23 people came unto him as he was t.,..... *1321*
Mt 26:55 **sat daily with you t. in the temple,** *1321*
Mt 28:20 **T. them to observe all things** *1321*
Mk 6:6 he went round about the villages, t..... *1321*
Mk 7:7 **t. for doctrines the commandments** *1321*
Mk 14:49 **daily with you in the temple t.,** *1321*
Lu 5:17 pass on a certain day, as he was t.,.... *1321*
Lu 13:10 he was t. in one of the synagogues..... *1321*
Lu 13:22 through the cities and villages, t.,....... *1321*
Lu 21:37 day time he was t. in the temple;....... *1321*
Lu 23:5 the people, t. throughout all Jewry, ... *1321*
Ac 5:25 in the temple, and t. the people. *1321*
Ac 15:35 t. and preaching the word of the *1321*
Ac 18:11 t. the word of God among them. *1321*
Ac 28:31 t. those things which concern the....... *1321*
Ro 12:7 or he that teacheth, on t.; *1319*
Col 1:28 and t. every man in all wisdom; *1321*
Col 3:16 t. and admonishing one another.......... *1321*
Tit 1:11 t. things which they ought not, for *1321*
Tit 2:12 T. us that, denying ungodliness.......... *3811*

TEAR See also TARE; TEARETH; TEARS; TORN.
Jg 8:7 I will t. your flesh with the thorns...... 1758
Ps 7:2 Lest he t. my soul like a lion,............ 2963
Ps 35:15 they did t. me, and ceased not: 7167
Ps 50:22 lest I t. you in pieces, and there be.... 2963
Jer 15:3 sword to slay, and the dogs to t., ... 5498
Jer 16:7 shall men t. themselves for them 6536
Eze 13:20 and I will t. them from your arms, ... 7167
Eze 13:21 Your kerchiefs also will I t., and 7167
Ho 5:14 I, even I, will t. and go away; I will.... 2963
Ho 13:8 lion: the wild beast shall t. them. 1234
Am 1:11 and his anger did t. perpetually, ... 2963
Na 2:12 The lion did t. in pieces enough for 2963
Zec 11:16 the fat, and t. their claws in pieces..... 6561

TEARETH
De 33:20 t. the arm with the crown of the........ 2963
Job 16:9 He t. me in his wrath, who hateth...... 2963
Job 18:4 He t. himself in his anger: shall 2963
Mic 5:8 both treadeth down, and t. in pieces, .. 2963
Mk 9:18 he taketh him, he t. him: and he........ *4486*
Lu 9:39 and it t. him that he foameth again, ... *4682*

TEARS
2Ki 20:5 thy prayer, I have seen thy t.. 1832
Es 8:3 besought him with t. to put away....... 1058
Job 16:20 but mine eye poureth out t. unto God.......
Ps 6:6 to swim; I water my couch with t.. 1832
Ps 39:12 my cry; hold not thy peace at my t.. .. 1832
Ps 42:3 My t. have been my meat day and 1832
Ps 56:8 put thou my t. into thy bottle: are...... 1832
Ps 80:5 feedest them with the bread of t.; 1832
Ps 80:5 them t. to drink in great measure......... 1832
Ps 116:8 mine eyes from t., and my feet from .. 1832
Ps 126:5 They that sow in t. shall reap in joy. .. 1832
Ec 4:1 the t. of such as were oppressed, ... 1832
Isa 16:9 I will water thee with my t., O.......... 1832
Isa 25:8 Lord God will wipe away t. from off ... 1832
Isa 38:5 heard thy prayer, I have seen thy t.... 1832
Jer 9:1 and mine eyes a fountain of t., that 1832
Jer 9:18 that our eyes may run down with t.,... 1832
Jer 13:17 weep sore, and run down with t., ... 1832
Jer 14:17 Let mine eyes run down with t.......... 1832
Jer 31:16 weeping, and thine eyes from t.......... 1832
La 1:2 night, and her t. are on her cheeks: ... 1832
La 2:11 Mine eyes do fail with t., my 1832
La 2:18 let t. run down like a river day and 1832
Eze 24:16 weep, neither shall thy t. run down. ... 1832
Mal 2:13 covering...altar of the Lord with t., ... 1832
Mk 9:24 and said with t., Lord, I believe;........ *1144*
Lu 7:38 and began to wash his feet with t.,..... *1144*
Lu 7:44 **she hath washed my feet with t.,** .. *1144*
Ac 20:19 humility of mind, and with many t.,..... *1144*
Ac 20:31 every one night and day with t.. .... *1144*
2Co 2:4 I wrote unto you with many t.; not..... *1144*
2Ti 1:4 to see thee, being mindful of thy t.,..... *1144*
Heb 5:7 with strong crying and t. unto him...... *1144*
Heb 12:17 he sought it carefully with t.. .... *1144*
Re 7:17 and God shall wipe away all t. from *1144*
Re 21:4 and God shall wipe away all t. from *1144*

TEATS
Isa 32:12 They shall lament for the t., for......... 7699
Eze 23:3 bruised the t. of their virginity........... 1717
Eze 23:21 in bruising thy t. by the Egyptians...... 1717

TEBAH (te'-bah)
Ge 22:24 was Reumah, she bare also T.,.......... 2875

TEBALIAH (teb-a-li'-ah)
1Ch 26:11 Hilkiah the second, T. the third, ... 2882

TEBETH (te'-beth)
Es 2:16 month, which is the month T.,........... 2887

TEDIOUS
Ac 24:4 that I be not further t. unto thee, ... *1465*

TEETH
Ge 49:12 wine, and his t. white with milk. 8127
Nu 11:33 the flesh was yet between their t.,...... 8127
De 32:24 also send the t. of beasts upon them,.. 8127
1Sa 2:13 a fleshhook of three t. in his hand; 8127
Job 4:10 lions, and the t. of the young lions, ... 8127
Job 13:14 do I take my flesh in my t., and put ... 8127
Job 16:9 he gnasheth upon me with his t.; 8127
Job 19:20 I am escaped with the skin of my t..... 8127
Job 29:17 and plucked the spoil out of his t........ 8127
Job 41:14 his t. are terrible round about............ 8127
Ps 3:7 hast broken the t. of the ungodly. 8127
Ps 35:16 they gnashed upon me with their t.. ... 8127
Ps 37:12 and gnasheth upon him with his t.. 8127
Ps 57:4 whose t. are spears and arrows, ... 8127
Ps 58:6 Break their t., O God, in their 8127
Ps 58:6 break out the great t. of the young..... 4973
Ps 112:10 he shall gnash with his t., and 8127
Ps 124:6 not given us as a prey to their t.. 8127
Pr 10:26 As vinegar to the t., and as smoke..... 8127
Pr 30:14 generation, whose t. are as swords, ... 8127
Pr 30:14 their jaw t. as knives, to devour 4973
Ca 4:2 Thy t. are like a flock of sheep.......... 8127
Ca 6:6 Thy t. are as a flock of sheep which... 8127
Isa 41:15 threshing instrument having t.. 6374
Jer 31:29 the children's t. are set on edge. 8127
Jer 31:30 grape, his t. shall be set on edge. 8127
La 2:16 thee: they hiss and gnash the t.......... 8127
La 3:16 broken my t. with gravel stones,........ 8127
Eze 18:2 the children's t. are set on edge? 8127
Da 7:5 mouth of it between the t. of it: 8128
Da 7:7 it had great iron t.: it devoured 8128
Da 7:19 whose t. were of iron, and his nails.... 8128
Joe 1:6 whose t. are the t. of a lion, and 8127
Joe 1:6 hath the cheek t. of a great lion......... 4973
Am 4:6 have given you cleanness of t........... 8127
Mic 3:5 people err, that bite with their t., ... 8127
Zec 9:7 abominations from between his t.. 8127
Mt 8:12 **be weeping and gnashing of t.** *3599*
Mt 13:42, 50 **be wailing and gnashing of t** *3599*
Mt 22:13 **be weeping and gnashing of t** *3599*
Mt 24:51 **be weeping and gnashing of t** *3599*
Mt 25:30 **be weeping and gnashing of t** *3599*
Mt 27:44 with him, cast the same in his t.. .... *3679*
Mk 9:18 foameth, and gnasheth with his t., ... *3599*
Lu 13:28 **be weeping and gnashing of t.,** *3599*
Ac 7:54 they gnashed on him with their t........ *3599*
Re 9:8 and their t. were as...of lions. *3599*
Re 9:8 were as the t. of lions..........................

TEHAPHNEHES (te-haf'-ne-heze) See also TAHAPANES.
Eze 30:18 At T....the day shall be darkened, ... 8471

TEHINNAH (te-hin'-nah)
1Ch 4:12 and T. the father of Ir-nahash............ 8468

TEIL (teel)
Isa 6:13 as a t. tree, and as an oak, whose....... 424

TEKEL (te'-kel)
Da 5:25 Mene, Mene, T., Upharsin. 8625
Da 5:27 T.; Thou art weighed in the.............. 8625

TEKOA (te-ko'-ah) See also TEKOAH; TEKOITE.
1Ch 2:24 bare him Ashur the father of T.. 8620
1Ch 4:5 Ashur the father of T. had two.......... 8620
2Ch 11:6 even Beth-lehem, and Etam, and T..... 8620
2Ch 20:20 went forth into the wilderness of T.:... 8620
Jer 6:1 and blow the trumpet of T., and 8620
Am 1:1 who was among the herdmen of T.,..... 8620

TEKOAH (te-ko'-ah) See also TEKOA.
2Sa 14:2 And Joab sent to T., and fetched........ 8620
2Sa 14:4 woman of T. spake to the king, ... 8621
2Sa 14:9 woman of T. said unto the king,......... 8621

TEKOITE (te-ko'-ite) See also TEKOITES.
2Sa 23:26 Ira the son of Ikkesh the T.,............. 8621
1Ch 11:28 Ira the son of Ikkesh the T.,............. 8621
1Ch 27:9 was Ira the son of Ikkesh the T......... 8621

TEKOITES (te-ko'-ites)
Ne 3:5 next unto them the T. repaired;......... 8621
Ne 3:27 the T. repaired another piece, ... 8621

TEL See TEL-ABIB; TEL-HARESHA; TEL-MELAH.

TEL-ABIB (tel-a'-bib)
Eze 3:15 to them of the captivity at T., ... 8512

TELAH (te'-lah)
1Ch 7:25 and T. his son, and Tahan his son, ... 8520

TELAIM (tel'-a-im) See also TELEM.
1Sa 15:4 and numbered them in T., ... 2923

TELASSAR (te-las'-sar) See also THELASSAR.
Isa 37:12 children of Eden which were in T.?..... 8515

TELEM (te'-lem) See also TELAIM.
Jos 15:24 Ziph, and T., and Bealoth, 2928
Ezr 10:24 porters; Shallum, and T., and Uri. 2928

TEL-HARESHA (tel-ha-re'-shah) See also TEL-HARSA.
Ne 7:61 Tel-melah, T., Cherub, Addon, 8521

TEL-HARSA (tel-har'-sah) See also TEL-HARESHA.
Ezr 2:59 Tel-melah, T., Cherub, Addan, 8521

TELL See also FORETELL; TELLEST; TELLETH; TELLING; TOLD.
Ge 12:18 not t. me that she was thy wife? 5046
Ge 15:5 toward heaven, and t. the stars, 5608
Ge 21:26 neither didst thou t. me, neither 5046
Ge 22:2 mountains which I will t. thee of. 559
Ge 24:23 daughter art thou? t. me, I pray 5046
Ge 24:49 and truly with my master, t. me: 5046
Ge 24:49 and if not, t. me; that I may turn 5046
Ge 26:2 in the land which I shall t. thee of: 559
Ge 29:15 t. me, what shall thy wages be? 5046
Ge 31:27 and didst not t. me, that I might 5046
Ge 32:5 I have sent to t. my lord, that I may 5046
Ge 32:29 said, T. me, I pray thee, thy name. 5046
Ge 37:16 t. me, I pray thee, where they feed 5046
Ge 40:8 to God? t. me them, I pray you. 5608
Ge 43:6 to t. the man whether ye had yet 5046
Ge 43:22 we cannot t. who put our money 3045
Ge 45:13 shall t. my father of all my glory 5046
Ge 49:1 t. you that which shall befall you 5046
Ex 9:1 Go in unto Pharaoh, and t. him, 1696
Ex 10:2 mayest t. in the ears of thy sons, 5608
Ex 14:12 this the word that we did t. thee 1696
Ex 19:3 and t. the children of Israel; 5046
Le 14:35 house shall come and t. the priest, 5046
Nu 14:14 t. it to the inhabitants of this land: 559
Nu 21:1 heard t. that Israel came by the way
Nu 23:3 he sheweth me I will t. thee. 5046
De 17:11 judgment which they shall t. thee, 559
De 32:7 thy elders, and they will t. thee. 559
Jos 7:19 t. me now what thou hast done; 5046
Jg 14:16 my mother, and shall I t. it thee? 5046
Jg 16:6 T. me, I pray thee, wherein thy 5046
Jg 16:10 t. me, I pray thee, wherewith thou 5046
Jg 16:13 t. me wherewith thou mightest be 5046
Jg 20:3 T. us, how was this wickedness? 1696
Ru 3:4 he will t. thee what thou shalt do. 5046
Ru 4:4 it, then t. me, that I may know: 5046
1Sa 6:2 t. us wherewith we shall send it 3045
1Sa 9:8 the man of God, to t. us our way. 5046
1Sa 9:18 T. me,…where the seer's house is. 5046
1Sa 9:19 will t. thee all that is in thine heart. 5046
1Sa 10:15 T. me, I pray thee, what Samuel 5046
1Sa 14:43 T. me what thou hast done. 5046
1Sa 15:16 will t. thee what the Lord hath said 5046
1Sa 17:55 thy soul liveth, O king, I cannot t. 3045
1Sa 19:3 and what I see, that I will t. thee. 5046
1Sa 20:9 thee, then would not I t. to thee? 5046
1Sa 20:10 to Jonathan, Who shall t. me? or 5046
1Sa 22:22 there, that he would surely t. Saul: 5046
1Sa 23:11 Israel, I beseech thee, t. thy servant. 5046
1Sa 27:11 Lest they should t. on us, saying, 5046
2Sa 1:4 went the matter? I pray thee, t. me. 5046
2Sa 1:20 T. it not in Gath, publish it not in 5046
2Sa 7:5 Go and t. my servant David, Thus 559
2Sa 12:18 feared to t. him that the child was 5046
2Sa 12:18 if we t. him that the child is dead? 559
2Sa 12:22 Who can t. whether God will be 3045
2Sa 13:4 day to day? wilt thou not t. me? 5046
2Sa 15:35 shalt t. it to Zadok and Abiathar the 5046
2Sa 17:16 send quickly, and t. David, saying, 5046
2Sa 18:21 Go t. the king what thou hast seen 5046
1Ki 1:20 t. them who shall sit on the throne 5046
1Ki 14:3 he shall t. thee what shall become 5046
1Ki 14:7 t. Jeroboam, Thus saith the Lord 559
1Ki 18:8, 11 t. thy lord, Behold, Elijah is here. 559
1Ki 18:12 and so when I come and t. Ahab, 5046
1Ki 18:14 t. thy lord, Behold, Elijah is here: 559
1Ki 20:9 T. my lord the king, All that thou 559
1Ki 20:11 T. him, Let not him that girdeth 1696
1Ki 22:16 t. me nothing but that which is true 1696
1Ki 22:18 Did I not t. thee that he would 559
2Ki 4:2 t. me, what hast thou in the house? 5046
2Ki 7:9 may go and t. the king's household. 5046
2Ki 8:4 T. me, I pray thee, all the great 5608
2Ki 9:12 they said, It is false; t. us now. 5046
2Ki 9:15 of the city to go to t. it in Jezreel. 5046
2Ki 20:5 and t. Hezekiah the captain of my 559
2Ki 22:15 T. the man that sent you to me. 559
1Ch 17:4 Go and t. David my servant, Thus 559
1Ch 17:10 I t. thee that the Lord will build 5046
1Ch 21:10 Go and t. David, saying, Thus 1696
2Ch 18:17 Did I not t. thee that he would not 559
2Ch 34:23 T. ye the man that sent you to me. 559
Job 1:15, 16, 17, 19 escaped alone to t. thee. 5046
Job 8:10 not they teach thee, and t. thee, 559
Job 12:7 of the air, and they shall t. thee: 5046
Job 34:34 Let men of understanding t. me, 559
Ps 22:17 I may t. all my bones: they look 5608
Ps 26:7 and t. of all thy wondrous works. 5608
Ps 48:12 about her: t. the towers thereof. 5608
Ps 48:13 that ye may t. it to the generation 5608
Ps 50:12 I were hungry, I would not t. thee: 559
Pr 30:4 is his son's name, if thou canst t.? 3045
Ec 6:12 for who can t. a man what shall be 5046
Ec 8:7 for who can t. him when it shall be? 5046
Ec 10:14 a man cannot t. what shall be; and 5046
Ec 10:14 shall be after him, who can t. him? 5046
Ec 10:20 hath wings shall t. the matter. 5046
Ca 1:7 T. me, O thou whom my soul loveth, 5046
Ca 5:8 ye t. him, that I am sick of love. 5046
Isa 5:5 I will t. you what I will do to my 3045
Isa 6:9 and t. this people, Hear ye indeed, 559
Isa 19:12 let them t. thee now, and let them 5046
Isa 42:9 they spring forth I t. you of them. 8085
Isa 45:21 T. ye, and bring them near; yea, 5046
Isa 48:20 t. this, utter it even to the end of 8085
Jer 15:2 shalt t. them, Thus saith the Lord; 559
Jer 19:2 the words that I shall t. thee, 1696
Jer 23:27 they t. every man to his neighbour, 5608
Jer 23:28 hath a dream, let him t. a dream; 5608
Jer 23:32 do t. them, and cause my people 5608
Jer 28:13 Go and t. Hananiah, saying, Thus 559
Jer 34:2 Zedekiah king of Judah, and t. him, 559
Jer 35:13 Go and t. the men of Judah and the 559
Jer 36:16 We will surely t. the king of all 5046
Jer 36:17 T. us now, How didst thou write all 5046
Jer 48:20 t. ye it in Arnon,…Moab is spoiled, 5046
Eze 3:11 and speak unto them, and t. them, 559
Eze 12:23 T. them therefore, Thus saith the 559
Eze 17:12 t. them, Behold, the king of Babylon 559
Eze 24:19 t. us what these things are to us, 5046
Da 2:4 t. thy servants the dream, and we 560
Da 2:7 the king t. his servants the dream, 560
Da 2:9 t. me the dream, and I shall know 560
Da 2:36 and we will t. the interpretation 560
Da 4:9 t. me the visions of my dream that I 560
Joe 1:3 T. ye your children of it, and let 5608
Joe 1:3 and let your children t. their children,
Jon 1:8 T. us,…for whose cause this 5046
Jon 3:9 Who can t. if God will turn and 3045
Mt 8:4 saith unto him, **See thou t. no man;** 2036
Mt 10:27 **What I t. you in darkness, that** 3004
Mt 16:20 should t. no man that he was Jesus 2036
Mt 17:9 **T. the vision to no man, until the** 2036
Mt 18:15 **t. him his fault between thee and** 1650
Mt 18:17 **hear them, t. it unto the church:** 2036
Mt 21:5 T. ye the daughter of Sion, Behold, 2036
Mt 21:24 **you one thing, which if ye t. me,** 2036
Mt 21:24 **will t. you by what authority I do** 2046
Mt 21:27 Jesus, and said, We cannot t. 1492
Mt 21:27 **Neither t. I you by what authority** 3004
Mt 22:4 **T. them which are bidden, Behold,** 2036
Mt 22:17 T. us therefore, What thinkest thou? 2036
Mt 24:3 T. us, when shall these things be? 2036
Mt 26:63 t. us whether thou be the Christ, 2036
Mt 28:7 t. his disciples that he is risen from 2036
Mt 28:9 And as they went to t. his disciples, 518
Mt 28:10 **go t. my brethren that they go into** 518
Mk 1:30 fever, and anon they t. him of her. 3004
Mk 5:19 **t. them how great things the Lord** 312
Mk 7:36 them that they should t. no man: 2036
Mk 8:26 **town, nor t. it to any in the town.** 2036
Mk 8:30 that they should t. no man of him. 3004
Mk 9:9 t. no man what things they had 1334
Mk 10:32 and began to t. them what things 3004
Mk 11:29 **will t. you by what authority I do** 2046
Mk 11:33 and said unto Jesus, We cannot t. 1492
Mk 11:33 them, **Neither do I t. you by what** 3004
Mk 13:4 T. us, when shall these things be? 2036
Mk 16:7 t. his disciples and Peter that he 2036
Lu 4:25 **I t. you of a truth, many widows** 3004
Lu 5:14 And he charged him to **t. no man:** 2036
Lu 7:22 **t. John what things ye have seen** 518
Lu 7:42 **T. me…which of them will love** 2036
Lu 8:56 should t. no man what was done. 2036
Lu 9:21 them to t. no man that thing; 2036
Lu 9:27 **I t. you of a truth, there be some** 3004
Lu 10:24 **For I t. you, that many prophets** 3004
Lu 12:51 **I t. you, Nay; but rather division:** 3004
Lu 12:59 **I t. thee, thou shalt not depart** 3004
Lu 13:3, 5 **I t. you, Nay: but, except ye** 3004
Lu 13:27 **I t. you, I know you not whence** 3004
Lu 13:32 **Go ye, and t. that fox, Behold, I** 2036
Lu 17:34 **I t. you, in that night there shall** 3004
Lu 18:8 **I t. you that he will avenge them** 3004
Lu 18:14 **I t. you, this man went down to** 3004
Lu 19:40 **I t. you that, if these should hold** 3004
Lu 20:2 T. us, by what authority doest 2036
Lu 20:7 they could not t. whence it was 1492
Lu 20:8 **Neither t. I you by what authority** 3004
Lu 22:34 **I t. thee, Peter, the cock shall not** 3004
Lu 22:67 Art thou the Christ? t. us. And he 2036
Lu 22:67 them, **If I t. you, ye will not** 2036
Joh 3:8 **but canst not t. whence it cometh,** 1492
Joh 3:12 **if I t. you of heavenly things?** 2036
Joh 4:25 he is come, he will t. us all things. 312
Joh 8:14 **but ye cannot t. whence I come,** 1492
Joh 8:45 **And because I t. you the truth,** 3004
Joh 10:24 If thou be the Christ, t. us plainly. 2036
Joh 12:22 again Andrew and Philip t. Jesus. 3004
Joh 13:19 **Now I t. you before it come, that,** 3004
Joh 16:7 **Nevertheless I t. you the truth;** 3004
Joh 16:18 while? we cannot t. what he saith. 1492
Joh 18:34 **or did others t. it thee of me?** 2036
Joh 20:15 t. me where thou hast laid him, and 2036
Ac 5:8 T. me whether ye sold the land for 2036
Ac 10:6 t. thee what thou oughtest to do. 2980
Ac 11:14 Who shall t. thee words, whereby 2980
Ac 15:27 t. you the same things by mouth 518
Ac 17:21 either to t., or to hear some new 3004
Ac 22:27 him, T. me, art thou a Roman? 3004
Ac 23:17 he hath a certain thing to t. him. 518
Ac 23:19 him, What is that thou hast to t. me? 518
Ac 23:22 t. no man that thou hast shewed 1583
2Co 12:2 (whether in the body, I cannot t.; 1492
2Co 12:2 whether out of the body, I cannot t. 1492
2Co 12:3 or out of the body, I cannot t.: 1492
Ga 4:16 enemy, because I t. you the truth? 226
Ga 4:21 T. me, ye that desire to be under 3004
Ga 5:21 of the which I t. you before, as I 4302
Php 3:18 and now t. you even weeping, that 3004
Heb 11:32 time would fail me to t. of Gedeon, 1334
Re 17:7 t. thee the mystery of the woman, 2046

TELLEST
Ps 56:8 Thou t. my wanderings: put thou 5608

TELLETH
2Sa 7:11 Also the Lord t. thee that he will 5046
2Ki 6:12 t. the king of Israel the words that 5046
Ps 41:6 when he goeth abroad, he t. it. 1696
Ps 101:7 he that t. lies shall not tarry in my 1696
Ps 147:4 He t. the number of the stars; he 4487
Jer 33:13 the hands of him that t. them, 4487
Joh 12:22 Philip cometh and t. Andrew: and 3004

TELLING
Jg 7:15 Gideon heard the t. of the dream, 4557
2Sa 11:19 an end of t. the matters of the war 1696
2Ki 8:5 as he was t. the king how he had 5608

TEL-MELAH (tel-me'-lah)
Ezr 2:59 were they which went up from T., 8528
Ne 7:61 they which went up also from T., 8528

TEMA (te'-mah)
Ge 25:15 Hadar, and T., Jetur, Naphish, 8485
1Ch 1:30 and Dumah, Massa, Hadad, and T., 8485
Job 6:19 The troops of T. looked, the 8485
Isa 21:14 inhabitants…of T. brought water 8485
Jer 25:23 Dedan, and T., and Buz, and all 8485

TEMAN (te'-man) See also TEMANITE.
Ge 36:11 And the sons of Eliphaz were T., 8487
Ge 36:15 duke T., duke Omar, duke Zepho, 8487
Ge 36:42 Duke Kenaz, duke T., duke Mibzar, 8487
1Ch 1:36 The sons of Eliphaz; T., and Omar, 8487
1Ch 1:53 Duke Kenaz, duke T., duke Mibzar, 8487
Jer 49:7 Is wisdom no more in T.? is counsel 8487
Jer 49:20 against the inhabitants of T. 8487
Eze 25:13 I will make it desolate from T.; 8487
Am 1:12 But I will send a fire upon T., which 8487
Ob 9 And thy mighty men, O T., shall be 8487
Hab 3:3 God came from T., and the Holy 8487

TEMANI (te'-ma-ni) See also TEMANITE.
Ge 36:34 Husham of the land of **T.** reigned....... 8489

TEMANITE (te'-man-ite) See also TEMANI; TEMANITES.
Job 2:11 Eliphaz the **T.**, and Bildad the........... 8489
Job 4:1 Eliphaz the **T.** answered and said,...... 8489
Job 15:1 Then answered Eliphaz the **T.**, and..... 8489
Job 22:1 Eliphaz the **T.** answered and said,...... 8489
Job 42:7 the Lord said to Eliphaz the **T.**, My.... 8489
Job 42:9 So Eliphaz the **T.** and Bildad the........ 8489

TEMANITES (te'-man-ites)
1Ch 1:45 Husham of the land of the **T.**............ 8489

TEMENI (tem'-e-ni)
1Ch 4:6 Hopher, and **T.**, and Haahashtari........ 8488

TEMPER See also TEMPERED.
Eze 46:14 hin of oil, to **t.** with the fine flour;...... 7450

TEMPERANCE
Ac 24:25 as he reasoned of righteousness, **t.**,..... *1466*
Ga 5:23 Meekness, **t.**: against such there is.... *1466*
2Pe 1:6 And to knowledge **t.**; and to............. *1466*
2Pe 1:6 and to **t.** patience; and to patience...... *1466*

TEMPERATE
1Co 9:25 for the mastery is **t.** in all things........ 1467
Tit 1:8 of good men, sober, just, holy, **t.**;...... *1468*
Tit 2:2 the aged men be sober, grave, **t.**,...... *4998*

TEMPERED See also UNTEMPERED.
Ex 29:2 and cakes unleavened **t.** with oil,........ 1101
Ex 30:35 **t.** together, pure and holy:................ 4414
1Co 12:24 but God hath **t.** the body together,..... *4786*

TEMPEST
Job 9:17 For he breaketh me with a **t.**, and..... 8183
Job 27:20 **t.** stealeth him away in the night......... 5492
Ps 11:6 and brimstone, and an horrible **t.**......... 7307
Ps 55:8 from the windy storm and **t.**............. 5591
Ps 83:15 So persecute them with thy **t.**, and..... 5591
Isa 28:2 strong one, which as a **t.** of hail......... 2230
Isa 29:6 and great noise, with storm and **t.**,...... 5591
Isa 30:30 scattering, and **t.**, and hailstones........ 2230
Isa 32:2 the wind, and a covert from the **t.**;...... 2230
Isa 54:11 O thou afflicted, tossed with **t.**, and.... 5590
Am 1:14 a **t.** in the day of the whirlwind:......... 5591
Jon 1:4 there was a mighty **t.** in the sea,....... 5591
Jon 1:12 my sake this great **t.** is upon you....... 5591
Mt 8:24 there arose a great **t.** in the sea,....... *4578*
Ac 27:18 being exceedingly tossed with a **t.**,..... *5492*
Ac 27:20 and no small **t.** lay on us, all hope...... *5494*
Heb 12:18 blackness, and darkness, and **t.**,......... *2366*
2Pe 2:17 clouds that are carried with a **t.**;........ *2978*

TEMPESTUOUS
Ps 50:3 it shall be very **t.** round about him...... 8175
Jon 1:11 for the sea wrought, and was **t.**.......... 5490
Jon 1:13 wrought, and was **t.** against them...... 5490
Ac 27:14 there arose against it a **t.** wind,......... *5189*

TEMPLE See also TEMPLES.
1Sa 1:9 seat by a post of the **t.** of the Lord.... 1964
1Sa 3:3 lamp...went out in the **t.** of the Lord,.. 1964
2Sa 22:7 he did hear my voice out of his **t.**,...... 1964
1Ki 6:3 the porch before the **t.** of the house,.. 1964
1Ki 6:5 both of the **t.** and of the oracle:......... 1964
1Ki 6:17 the **t.** before it, was forty cubits......... 1964
1Ki 6:33 for the door of the **t.** posts of olive.... 1964
1Ki 7:21 up the pillars in the porch of the **t.**..... 1964
1Ki 7:50 doors of the house, to wit, of the **t.**.... 1964
2Ki 11:10 that were in the **t.** of the Lord.......... 1004
2Ki 11:11 king, from the right corner of the **t.**..... 1004
2Ki 11:11 to the left corner of the **t.**, along by... 1004
2Ki 11:11 along by the altar and the **t.**.............. 1004
2Ki 11:13 she came to the people into the **t.**....... 1004
2Ki 18:16 gold from the doors of the **t.** of the.... 1964
2Ki 23:4 bring forth out of the **t.** of the Lord.... 1964
2Ki 24:13 had made in the **t.** of the Lord,......... 1964
1Ch 6:10 office in the **t.** that Solomon built....... 1004
1Ch 10:10 fastened his head in...**t.** of Dagon....... 1004
2Ch 3:17 reared up the pillars before the **t.**,...... 1964
2Ch 4:7 set them in the **t.**, five on the right..... 1964
2Ch 4:8 and placed them in the **t.**, five on the.. 1964
2Ch 4:22 doors of the house of the **t.**, were of.. 1964
2Ch 23:10 hand, from the right side of the **t.**....... 1004
2Ch 23:10 to the left side of the **t.**, along by...... 1004
2Ch 23:10 along by the altar and the **t.**, by the.... 1004
2Ch 26:16 went into the **t.** of the Lord to burn... 1964
2Ch 27:2 entered not into the **t.** of the Lord..... 1964
2Ch 29:16 that they found in the **t.** of the Lord... 1964
2Ch 35:20 when Josiah had prepared the **t.**,........ 1004
2Ch 36:7 and put them in his **t.** at Babylon....... 1964
Ezr 3:6 the foundation of the **t.** of the Lord.... 1964
Ezr 3:10 the foundation of the **t.** of the Lord,... 1964
Ezr 4:1 builded the **t.** unto the Lord God......... 1964
Ezr 5:14 out of the **t.** that was in Jerusalem,.... 1965
Ezr 5:14 brought them into the **t.** of Babylon,... 1965
Ezr 5:14 king take out of the **t.** of Babylon,...... 1965
Ezr 5:15 them into the **t.** that is in Jerusalem,... 1965
Ezr 6:5 out of the **t.** which is at Jerusalem,...... 1965
Ezr 6:5 unto the **t.** which is at Jerusalem,....... 1965
Ne 6:10 in the house of God, within the **t.**,..... 1964
Ne 6:10 and let us shut the doors of the **t.**:..... 1964
Ne 6:11 go into the **t.** to save his life?............ 1964
Ps 5:7 will I worship toward thy holy **t.**......... 1964
Ps 11:4 The Lord is in his holy **t.**, the Lord's.. 1964
Ps 18:6 he heard my voice out of his **t.**, and... 1964
Ps 27:4 of the Lord, and to enquire in his **t.**.... 1964
Ps 29:9 in his **t.** doth every one speak of his... 1964
Ps 48:9 O God, in the midst of thy **t.**........... 1964
Ps 65:4 of thy house, even of thy holy **t.**........ 1964
Ps 68:29 Because of thy **t.** at Jerusalem shall.... 1964
Ps 79:1 thy holy **t.** have they defiled; they...... 1964
Ps 138:2 I will worship toward thy holy **t.**,....... 1964
Isa 6:1 lifted up, and his train filled the **t.**..... 1964
Isa 44:28 and to the **t.**, Thy foundation shall...... 1964
Isa 66:6 a voice from the **t.**, a voice of the...... 1964
Jer 7:4 words, saying, The **t.** of the Lord,...... 1964
Jer 7:4 **t.** of the Lord, The **t.** of the Lord,..... 1964
Jer 24:1 were set before the **t.** of the Lord,.... 1964
Jer 50:28 our God, the vengeance of his **t.**......... 1964
Jer 51:11 the Lord, the vengeance of his **t.**,....... 1964
Eze 8:16 at the door of the **t.** of the Lord,....... 1964
Eze 8:16 backs toward the **t.** of the Lord,......... 1964
Eze 41:1 Afterward he brought me to the **t.**,...... 1964
Eze 41:4 breadth, twenty cubits, before the **t.**:... 1964
Eze 41:15 with the inner **t.**, and the porches of... 1964
Eze 41:20 trees made, and on the wall of the **t.**.. 1964
Eze 41:21 The posts of the **t.** were squared,...... 1964
Eze 41:23 **t.** and the sanctuary had two doors...... 1964
Eze 41:25 made on them, on the doors of the **t.**,. 1964
Eze 42:8 the **t.** were an hundred cubits............ 1964
Da 5:2 of the **t.** which was in Jerusalem;....... 1965
Da 5:3 out of the **t.** of the house of God....... 1965
Am 8:3 songs of the **t.** shall be howlings........ 1964
Jon 2:4 I will look again toward thy holy **t.**..... 1964
Jon 2:7 came in unto thee, into thine holy **t.**... 1964
Mic 1:2 you, the Lord from his holy **t.**............ 1964
Hab 2:20 But the Lord is in his holy **t.**: let all... 1964
Hag 2:15 upon a stone in the **t.** of the Lord:..... 1964
Hag 2:18 foundation of the Lord's **t.** was laid,.... 1964
Zec 6:12 he shall build the **t.** of the Lord:........ 1964
Zec 6:13 he shall build the **t.** of the Lord;........ 1964
Zec 6:14 for a memorial in the **t.** of the Lord.... 1964
Zec 6:15 come and build in the **t.** of the Lord,.. 1964
Zec 8:9 was laid, that the **t.** might be built...... 1964
Mal 3:1 seek, shall suddenly come to his **t.**,..... 1964
Mt 4:5 setteth him on a pinnacle of the **t.**,...... *241*
Mt 12:5 **priests in the t. profane...sabbath,**.. *241*
Mt 12:6 **place is one greater than the t.**....... *241*
Mt 21:12 And Jesus went into the **t.** of God,...... *241*
Mt 21:12 them that sold and bought in the **t.**,..... *241*
Mt 21:14 and the lame came to him in the **t.**;..... *241*
Mt 21:15 and the children crying in the **t.**,......... *241*
Mt 21:23 And when he was come into the **t.**,....... *241*
Mt 23:16 **Whosoever shall swear by the t.**,... *3485*
Mt 23:16 **shall swear by the gold of the t.**,... *3485*
Mt 23:17 **or the t. that sanctifieth the gold?**. *3485*
Mt 23:21 **And whoso shall swear by the t.**,.... *3485*
Mt 23:35 **slew between the t. and the altar**.. *3485*
Mt 24:1 out, and departed from the **t.**............ *2411*
Mt 24:1 to shew him the buildings of the **t.**..... *2411*
Mt 26:55 **daily with you teaching in the t.**,.. *2411*
Mt 26:61 I am able to destroy the **t.** of God,..... *3485*
Mt 27:5 down the pieces of silver in the **t.**...... *3485*
Mt 27:40 Thou that destroyest the **t.**, and......... *3485*
Mt 27:51 the veil of the **t.** was rent in twain..... *3485*
Mk 11:11 into Jerusalem, and into the **t.**:.......... *2411*
Mk 11:15 Jesus went into the **t.**, and began to... *2411*
Mk 11:15 them that sold and bought in the **t.**,.... *2411*
Mk 11:16 carry any vessel through the **t.**.......... *2411*
Mk 11:27 as he was walking in the **t.**, there....... *2411*
Mk 12:35 and said, while he taught in the **t.**,..... *2411*
Mk 13:1 as he went out of the **t.**, one of his.... *2411*
Mk 13:3 mount of Olives over against the **t.**,.... *2411*
Mk 14:49 **daily with you in the t. teaching,**.. *2411*
Mk 14:58 destroy this **t.**...made with hands,...... *3485*
Mk 15:29 Ah, thou that destroyest the **t.**,......... *3485*
Mk 15:38 the veil of the **t.** was rent in twain..... *3485*
Lu 1:9 when he went into the **t.** of the Lord... *3485*
Lu 1:21 that he tarried so long in the **t.**.......... *3485*
Lu 1:22 that he had seen a vision in the **t.**...... *3485*
Lu 2:27 he came by the Spirit into the **t.**......... *2411*
Lu 2:37 which departed not from the **t.**, but.... *2411*
Lu 2:46 three days they found him in the **t.**,..... *2411*
Lu 4:9 and set him on a pinnacle of the **t.**,.... *2411*
Lu 11:51 **between the altar and the t.**......... *3624*
Lu 18:10 **men went up into the t. to pray;**... *2411*
Lu 19:45 And he went into the **t.**, and began..... *2411*
Lu 19:47 And he taught daily in the **t.**. But....... *2411*
Lu 20:1 as he taught the people in the **t.**,....... *2411*
Lu 21:5 And as some spake of the **t.**, how...... *2411*
Lu 21:37 day time he was teaching in the **t.**;..... *2411*
Lu 21:38 in the morning to him in the **t.**,......... *2411*
Lu 22:52 chief priests, and captains of the **t.**,.... *2411*
Lu 22:53 **I was daily with you in the t.**,...... *2411*
Lu 23:45 veil of the **t.** was rent in the midst..... *3485*
Lu 24:53 And were continually in the **t.**,.......... *2411*
Joh 2:14 found in the **t.** those that sold oxen.... *2411*
Joh 2:15 he drove them all out of the **t.**,......... *2411*
Joh 2:19 **Destroy this t., and in three days**.. *3485*
Joh 2:20 six years was this **t.** in building,......... *3485*
Joh 2:21 But he spake of the **t.** of his body...... *3485*
Joh 5:14 Jesus findeth him in the **t.**, and.......... *2411*
Joh 7:14 the feast Jesus went up into the **t.**,.... *2411*
Joh 7:28 cried Jesus in the **t.** as he taught,...... *2411*
Joh 8:2 morning he came again into the **t.**,..... *2411*
Joh 8:20 the treasury, as he taught in the **t.**..... *2411*
Joh 8:59 hid himself, and went out of the **t.**,..... *2411*
Joh 10:23 Jesus walked in the **t.** in Solomon's..... *2411*
Joh 11:56 themselves, as they stood in the **t.**,..... *2411*
Joh 18:20 **in the synagogue, and in the t.**,.... *2411*
Ac 2:46 daily with one accord in the **t.**,......... *2411*
Ac 3:1 John went up together into the **t.**....... *2411*
Ac 3:2 gate of the **t.**...is called Beautiful,....... *2411*
Ac 3:2 alms of them that entered...the **t.**;...... *2411*
Ac 3:3 and John about to go into the **t.**........ *2411*
Ac 3:8 and entered with them into the **t.**,....... *2411*
Ac 3:10 alms at the Beautiful gate of the **t.**..... *2411*
Ac 4:1 priests, and the captain of the **t.**,........ *2411*
Ac 5:20 and speak in the **t.** to the people........ *2411*
Ac 5:21 into the **t.** early in the morning,.......... *2411*
Ac 5:24 the captain of the **t.** and the chief........ *2411*
Ac 5:25 put in prison are standing in the **t.**,...... *2411*
Ac 5:42 daily in the **t.**, and in every house,...... *2411*
Ac 19:27 the **t.** of the great goddess Diana........ *2411*
Ac 21:26 with them entered into the **t.**,............ *2411*
Ac 21:27 Asia, when they saw him in the **t.**,...... *2411*
Ac 21:28 brought Greeks also into the **t.**,.......... *2411*
Ac 21:29 that Paul had brought into the **t.**.)....... *2411*
Ac 21:30 Paul, and drew him out of the **t.**:........ *2411*
Ac 22:17 while I prayed in the **t.**, I was in a...... *2411*
Ac 24:6 hath gone about to profane the **t.**........ *2411*
Ac 24:12 And they neither found me in the **t.**..... *2411*
Ac 24:18 Asia found me purified in the **t.**,.......... *2411*
Ac 25:8 neither against the **t.**, nor yet............ *2411*
Ac 26:21 the Jews caught me in the **t.**,............. *2411*
1Co 3:16 ye not that ye are the **t.** of God,........ *3485*
1Co 3:17 If any man defile the **t.** of God,.......... *3485*
1Co 3:17 destroy; for the **t.** of God is holy,....... *3485*
1Co 3:17 of God is holy, which **t.** ye are...............
1Co 6:19 body is the **t.** of the Holy Ghost......... *3485*
1Co 8:10 knowledge sit at meat in the idol's **t.**,.........
1Co 9:13 things live of the things of the **t.**?....... *2411*
2Co 6:16 hath the **t.** of God with idols?............ *3485*
2Co 6:16 for ye are the **t.** of the living God;...... *3485*
Eph 2:21 groweth unto an holy **t.** in the Lord:... *3485*
2Th 2:4 he as God sitteth in the **t.** of God,...... *3485*
Re 3:12 **make a pillar in the t. of my God**,. *3485*
Re 7:15 serve him day and night in his **t.**........ *3485*
Re 11:1 Rise, and measure the **t.** of God,........ *3485*
Re 11:2 the court which is without the **t.**........ *3485*
Re 11:19 the **t.** of God was opened in heaven,... *3485*
Re 11:19 was seen in his **t.** the ark of his......... *3485*
Re 14:15 another angel came out of the **t.**,....... *3485*
Re 14:17 another angel came out of the **t.**......... *3485*
Re 15:5 **t.** of the tabernacle of the testimony... *3485*
Re 15:6 the seven angels came out of the **t.**,... *3485*
Re 15:8 And the **t.** was filled with smoke........ *3485*
Re 15:8 no man was able to enter into the **t.**,.. *3485*
Re 16:1 I heard a great voice out of the **t.**....... *3485*
Re 16:17 great voice out of the **t.** of heaven,..... *3485*
Re 21:22 I saw no **t.** therein: for the Lord......... *3485*
Re 21:22 and the Lamb are the **t.** of it.............. *3485*

TEMPLES
Jg 4:21 and smote the nail into his t., and 7541
Jg 4:22 lay dead, and the nail was in his t. 7541
Jg 5:26 pierced and stricken through his t. 7541
Ca 4:3 t. are like a piece of a pomegranate 7541
Ca 6:7 a piece of a pomegranate are thy t. 7541
Ho 8:14 his Maker, and buildeth t.; 1964
Joe 3:5 have carried into your t. my goodly 1964
Ac 7:48 dwelleth not in t. made with 3485
Ac 17:24 dwelleth not in t. made with hands; 3485

TEMPORAL
2Co 4:18 the things which are seen are t.; 4340

TEMPT See also TEMPTED; TEMPTETH; TEMPTING.
Ge 22:1 things, that God did t. Abraham, 5254
Ex 17:2 me? wherefore do ye t. the Lord? 5254
De 6:16 Ye shall not t. the Lord your God, 5254
Isa 7:12 not ask, neither will I t. the Lord. 5254
Mal 3:15 that t. God are even delivered. 974
Mt 4:7 shall not t. the Lord thy God. 1598
Mt 22:18 said, Why t. ye me, ye hypocrites? 3985
Mk 12:15 said unto them, Why t. ye me? 3985
Lu 4:12 shalt not t. the Lord thy God. 1598
Lu 20:23 and said unto them, Why t. ye me? 3985
Ac 5:9 to t. the Spirit of the Lord? 3985
Ac 15:10 Now therefore why t. ye God, to 3985
1Co 7:5 t. you not for your incontinency. 3985
1Co 10:9 Neither let us t. Christ, as some of 1598

TEMPTATION See also TEMPTATIONS.
Ps 95:8 in the day of t. in the wilderness: 4531
Mt 6:13 lead us not into t., but deliver 3986
Mt 26:41 and pray, that ye enter not into t. 3986
Mk 14:38 ye and pray, lest ye enter into t. 3986
Lu 4:13 when the devil had ended all the t., 3986
Lu 8:13 believe, and in time of t. fall away. 3986
Lu 11:4 lead us not into t.; but deliver 3986
Lu 22:40 Pray that ye enter not into t. 3986
Lu 22:46 rise and pray, lest ye enter into t. 3986
1Co 10:13 There hath no t. taken you but such 3986
1Co 10:13 with the t....make a way to escape, 3986
Ga 4:14 And my t. which was in my flesh ye 3986
1Ti 6:9 will be rich fall into t. and a snare, 3986
Heb 3:8 in the day of t. in the wilderness: 3986
Jas 1:12 is the man that endureth t. 3986
Re 3:10 will keep thee from the hour of t., 3986

TEMPTATIONS
De 4:34 by t., by signs, and by wonders, 4531
De 7:19 The great t. which thine eyes saw, 4531
De 29:3 The great t. which thine eyes have 4531
Lu 22:28 have continued with me in my t. 3986
Ac 20:19 and t., which befell me by the lying 3986
Jas 1:2 all joy when ye fall into divers t.; 3986
1Pe 1:6 in heaviness through manifold t.: 3986
2Pe 2:9 how to deliver the godly out of t., 3986

TEMPTED
Ex 17:7 because they t. the Lord, saying, 5254
Nu 14:22 and have t. me now these ten times, 5254
De 6:16 your God, as ye t. him in Massah. 5254
Ps 78:18 they t. God in their heart by asking 5254
Ps 78:41 they turned back and t. God, and 5254
Ps 78:56 they t. and provoked the most high 5254
Ps 95:9 When your fathers t. me, proved me, 5254
Ps 106:14 wilderness, and t. God in the desert. 5254
Mt 4:1 wilderness to be t. of the devil. 3985
Mk 1:13 wilderness forty days, t. of Satan; 3985
Lu 4:2 Being forty days t. of the devil. 3985
Lu 10:25 lawyer stood up, and t. him, 1598
1Co 10:9 as some of them also t., and were 3985
1Co 10:13 not suffer you to be t. above that ye 3985
Ga 6:1 thyself, lest thou also be t. 3985
1Th 3:5 means the tempter have t. you, 3985
Heb 2:18 he himself hath suffered being t., 3985
Heb 2:18 is able to succour them that are t. 3985
Heb 3:9 When your fathers t. me, proved 3985
Heb 4:15 was in all points t. like as we are, 3985
Heb 11:37 they were sawn asunder, were t., 3985
Jas 1:13 say when he is t., I am t. of God: 3985
Jas 1:13 for God cannot be t. with evil, 551
Jas 1:14 every man is t., when he is drawn 3985

TEMPTER
Mt 4:3 And when the t. came to him, he 3985
1Th 3:5 means the t. have tempted you, 3985

TEMPTETH
Jas 1:13 with evil, neither t. he any man: 3985

TEMPTING
Mt 16:1 and t. desired him that he would 3985
Mt 19:3 came unto him, t. him, and saying 3985
Mt 22:35 asked him a question, t. him, 3985
Mk 8:11 of him a sign from heaven, t. him. 3985
Mk 10:2 a man to put away his wife? t. him. 3985
Lu 11:16 others, t. him, sought of him a sign 3985
Joh 8:6 This they said, t. him, that they 3985

TEN See also EIGHTEEN; FOURTEEN; NINETEEN; SEVENTEEN; SIXTEEN; TEN'S; TENS.
Ge 5:14 were nine hundred and t. years: 6235
Ge 16:3 after Abram had dwelt t. years in 6235
Ge 18:32 Peradventure t. shall be found 6235
Ge 24:10 the servant took t. camels of the 6235
Ge 24:22 hands of t. shekels weight of gold; 6235
Ge 24:55 with us a few days, at the least t.; 6218
Ge 31:7 and changed my wages t. times; 6235
Ge 31:41 hast changed my wages t. times. 6235
Ge 32:15 their colts, forty kine, and t. bulls, 6235
Ge 32:15 twenty she asses, and t. foals. 6235
Ge 42:3 Joseph's t. brethren went down to 6235
Ge 45:23 t. asses laden with the good things 6235
Ge 45:23 t. she asses laden with corn and 6235
Ge 46:27 into Egypt, were threescore and t.
Ge 50:3 mourned for him threescore and t. days.
Ge 50:22 Joseph lived an hundred and t. 6235
Ge 50:26 being an hundred and t. years old: 6235
Ex 15:27 and threescore and t. palm trees:
Ex 26:1 with t. curtains of fine twined linen, 6235
Ex 26:16 T. cubits shall be the length of a 6235
Ex 27:12 their pillars t., and their sockets t. 6235
Ex 34:28 the covenant, the t. commandments, 6235
Ex 36:8 t. curtains of fine twined linen, 6235
Ex 36:21 The length of a board was t. cubits, 6235
Ex 38:12 their pillars t., and their sockets t.; 6235
Le 26:8 you shall put t. thousand to flight: 7233
Le 26:26 t. women shall bake your bread 6235
Le 27:5, 7 and for the female t. shekels. 6235
Nu 7:14 One spoon of t. shekels of gold, 6235
Nu 7:20 One spoon of gold of t. shekels, 6235
Nu 7:26, 32,38,44,50,56,62,68,74,80 One golden spoon of t. shekels, full of 6235
Nu 7:86 weighing t. shekels apiece, after the 6235
Nu 11:19 neither t. days, nor twenty days; 6235
Nu 11:32 gathered least gathered t. homers: 6235
Nu 14:22 have tempted me now these t. times 6235
Nu 29:23 And on the fourth day t. bullocks, 6235
Nu 33:9 and threescore and t. palm trees;
De 4:13 perform, even t. commandments; 6235
De 10:4 the t. commandments, which the 6235
De 10:22 Egypt with threescore and t. persons; 6235
De 32:30 and two put t. thousand to flight, 7233
De 33:2 he came with t. thousands of saints: 7233
De 33:17 are the t. thousands of Ephraim, 7233
Jos 15:57 t. cities with their villages 6235
Jos 17:5 there fell t. portions to Manasseh, 6235
Jos 21:5 the half tribe of Manasseh, t. cities. 6235
Jos 21:26 the cities were t. with their suburbs 6235
Jos 22:14 with him t. princes, of each chief 6235
Jos 24:29 being an hundred and t. years old. 6235
Jg 1:4 of them in Bezek t. thousand men. 6235
Jg 1:7 Threescore and t. kings, having their
Jg 2:8 being an hundred and t. years old. 6235
Jg 3:29 that time about t. thousand men, 6235
Jg 4:6 and take with thee t. thousand men 6235
Jg 4:10 he went up with t. thousand men 6235
Jg 4:14 and t. thousand men after him. 6235
Jg 6:27 Gideon took t. men of his servants, 6235
Jg 7:3 and there remained t. thousand. 6235
Jg 8:30 Gideon had threescore and t. sons
Jg 9:2 which are threescore and t. persons,
Jg 9:4 him threescore and t. pieces of silver
Jg 9:5 being threescore and t. persons,
Jg 9:18 his sons, threescore and t. persons,
Jg 9:24 done to the threescore and t. sons of
Jg 12:11 and he judged Israel t. years. 6235
Jg 12:14 rode on threescore and t. ass colts:
Jg 17:10 I will give thee t. shekels of silver 6235
Jg 20:10 we will take t. men of an hundred 6235
Jg 20:10 and a thousand out of t. thousand, 7233
Jg 20:34 came against Gibeah t. thousand 6235
Ru 1:4 they dwelled there about t. years. 6235
Ru 4:2 he took t. men of the elders of the 6235
1Sa 1:8 am not I better to thee than t. sons? 6235
1Sa 6:19 thousand and threescore and t. men:
1Sa 15:4 and t. thousand men of Judah. 6235
1Sa 17:17 these t. loaves, and run to the camp 6235
1Sa 17:18 these t. cheeses unto the captain of 6235
1Sa 18:7 and David his t. thousands. 7233
1Sa 18:8 ascribed unto David t. thousands, 7233
1Sa 21:11 and David his t. thousands? 7233
1Sa 25:5 And David sent out t. young men, 6235
1Sa 25:38 it came to pass about t. days after, 6235
1Sa 29:5 and David his t. thousands? 7233
2Sa 15:16 And the king left t. women, which 6235
2Sa 18:3 thou art worth t. thousand of us: 6235
2Sa 18:11 have given thee t. shekels of silver, 6235
2Sa 18:15 And t. young men that bare Joab's 6235
2Sa 19:43 We have t. parts in the king, and 6235
2Sa 20:3 and the king took the t. women his 6235
1Ki 4:23 T. fat oxen, and twenty oxen out of 6235
1Ki 5:14 t. thousand a month by courses: 6235
1Ki 5:15 and t. thousand that bare burdens,
1Ki 6:3 t. cubits was the breadth thereof. 6235
1Ki 6:23 cherubims...each t. cubits high. 6235
1Ki 6:24 part of the other were t. cubits. 6235
1Ki 6:25 And the other cherub was t. cubits: 6235
1Ki 6:26 of the one cherub was t. cubits, 6235
1Ki 7:10 great stones, stones of t. cubits, 6235
1Ki 7:23 t. cubits from the one brim to the 6235
1Ki 7:24 t. in a cubit, compassing the sea 6235
1Ki 7:27 And he made t. bases of brass; four 6235
1Ki 7:37 this manner he made the t. bases: 6235
1Ki 7:38 Then made he t. layers of brass: 6235
1Ki 7:38 upon every one of the t. bases one 6235
1Ki 7:43 t. bases, and t. layers on the bases; 6235
1Ki 11:31 to Jeroboam, Take thee t. pieces: 6235
1Ki 11:31 and will give t. tribes to thee: 6235
1Ki 11:35 will give it unto thee, even t. tribes. 6235
1Ki 14:3 And take with thee t. loaves and 6235
2Ki 5:5 took with him t. talents of silver, 6235
2Ki 5:5 of gold, and t. changes of raiment. 6235
2Ki 13:7 but fifty horsemen, and t. chariots, 6235
2Ki 13:7 and t. thousand footmen; 6235
2Ki 14:7 in the valley of salt t. thousand, 6235
2Ki 15:17 and reigned t. years in Samaria. 6235
2Ki 20:9 the shadow go forward t. degrees, 6235
2Ki 20:9 degrees, or go back t. degrees? 6235
2Ki 20:10 the shadow to go down t. degrees: 6235
2Ki 20:10 shadow return backward t. degrees. 6235
2Ki 20:11 the shadow t. degrees backward, 6235
2Ki 24:14 valour, even t. thousand captives, 6235
2Ki 25:25 and t. men with him, and smote 6235
1Ch 6:61 tribe of Manasseh, by lot, t. cities. 6235
1Ch 21:5 t. thousand men that drew sword:
1Ch 29:7 talents and t. thousand drams, 7239
1Ch 29:7 and of silver t. thousand talents, 6235
2Ch 2:2 t. thousand men to bear burdens,
2Ch 2:18 t. thousand of them to be bearers of
2Ch 4:1 and t. cubits the height thereof. 6235
2Ch 4:2 a molten sea of t. cubits from brim 6235
2Ch 4:3 t. in a cubit, compassing the sea 6235
2Ch 4:6 He made also t. lavers, and put five 6235
2Ch 4:7 And he made t. candlesticks of gold 6235
2Ch 4:8 He made also t. tables, and placed 6235
2Ch 14:1 his days the land was quiet t. years. 6235
2Ch 25:11 of the children of Seir t. thousand. 6235
2Ch 25:12 And other t. thousand left alive did 6235
2Ch 27:5 and t. thousand measures of wheat, 6235
2Ch 27:5 of wheat, and t. thousand of barley. 6235
2Ch 29:32 was threescore and t. bullocks, an
2Ch 30:24 bullocks and t. thousand sheep: 6235
2Ch 36:9 reigned three months and t. days in 6235
2Ch 36:21 to fulfil threescore and t. years.
Ezr 1:10 a second sort four hundred and t., 6235
Ezr 8:12 with him an hundred and t. males. 6235
Ezr 8:24 and t. of their brethren with them, 6235
Ne 4:12 they said unto us t. times, From all 6235
Ne 5:18 once in t. days store of all sorts of 6235
Ne 11:1 bring one of t. to dwell in Jerusalem 6235
Es 3:9 will pay t. thousand talents of silver 6235
Es 9:10 The t. sons of Haman the son of 6235
Es 9:12 palace, and the t. sons of Haman; 6235
Es 9:13 let Haman's t. sons be hanged upon 6235
Es 9:14 and they hanged Haman's t. sons. 6235
Job 19:3 t. times have ye reproached me: ye 6235
Ps 3:6 be afraid of t. thousands of people, 7233
Ps 33:2 and an instrument of t. strings. 6218
Ps 90:10 our years are threescore years and t.;
Ps 91:7 and t. thousand at thy right hand; 7233
Ps 92:3 Upon an instrument of t. strings, 6218
Ps 144:9 instrument of t. strings will I sing 6218

Ps 144:13 and t. thousands in our streets: 7231
Ec 7:19 the wise more than t. mighty men...... 6235
Ca 5:10 the chiefest among t. thousand. 7233
Isa 5:10 t. acres of vineyard shall yield one...... 6235
Isa 38:8 dial of Ahaz, t. degreees backward. 6235
Isa 38:8 So the sun returned t. degrees, by..... 6235
Jer 41:1 even t. men with him, came unto....... 6235
Jer 41:2 and the t. men that were with him, ... 6235
Jer 41:8 But t. men were found among them.... 6235
Jer 42:7 And it came to pass after t. days, ... 6235
Eze 40:11 of the entry of the gate, t. cubits;...... 6235
Eze 41:2 breadth of the door was t. cubits; 6235
Eze 42:4 chambers was a walk of t. cubits........ 6235
Eze 45:1 the breadth shall be t. thousand. 6235
Eze 45:3 and the breadth of t. thousand:......... 6235
Eze 45:5 and the t. thousand of breadth,.......... 6235
Eze 45:14 cor, which is an homer of t. baths;..... 6235
Eze 45:14 for t. baths are an homer: 6235
Eze 48:9 and of t. thousand in breadth............ 6235
Eze 48:10 the west t. thousand in breadth, ... 6235
Eze 48:10 the east t. thousand in breadth, ... 6235
Eze 48:13 length, and t. thousand in breadth: 6235
Eze 48:13 and the breadth t. thousand. 6235
Eze 48:18 shall be t. thousand eastward, ... 6235
Eze 48:18 and t. thousand westward:................ 6235
Da 1:12 Prove thy servants,...t. days;............ 6235
Da 1:14 matter, and proved them t. days........ 6235
Da 1:15 end of t. days their countenances....... 6235
Da 1:20 he found them t. times better than..... 6235
Da 7:7 before it; and it had t. horns. 6236
Da 7:10 t. thousand times t. thousand............ 7240
Da 7:20 the t. horns that were in his head, ... 6236
Da 7:24 And the t. horns out of this kingdom... 6236
Da 7:24 are t. kings that shall arise:.............. 6236
Da 11:12 cast down many t. thousands:............ 7239
Am 5:3 forth by an hundred shall leave t., ... 6235
Am 6:9 there remain t. men in one house,...... 6235
Mic 6:7 with t. thousands of rivers of oil? 7233
Hag 2:16 twenty measures, there were...t........ 6235
Zec 1:12 these threescore and t. years?...............
Zec 5:2 and the breadth thereof t. cubits. 6235
Zec 8:23 t. men shall take hold out of all.......... 6235
Mt 18:24 **owed him t. thousand talents**........ *3463*
Mt 20:24 the t. heard it, they were moved....... *1176*
Mt 25:1 **heaven be likened unto t. virgins**... *1176*
Mt 25:28 **it unto him which hath t. talents**...*1176*
Mk 10:41 when the t. heard it, they began to *1176*
Lu 14:31 **able with t. thousand to meet him**. *1176*
Lu 15:8 **woman having t. pieces of silver**,... *1176*
Lu 17:12 met him t. men that were lepers,....... *1176*
Lu 17:17 said, **Were there not t. cleansed?**.... *1176*
Lu 19:13 **And he called his t. servants, and**.. *1176*
Lu 19:13 **and delivered them t. pounds, and**..*1176*
Lu 19:16 **thy pound hath gained t. pounds**...... *1176*
Lu 19:17 **have thou authority over t. cities**. . *1176*
Lu 19:24 **give it to him that hath t. pounds**. .*1176*
Lu 19:25 **him, Lord, he hath t. pounds**.)...... *1176*
Ac 23:23 and horsemen threescore and t., ...
Ac 25:6 among them more than t. days, ... *1176*
1Co 4:15 ye have t. thousand instructers in....... *3463*
1Co 14:19 t. thousand words in an unknown *3463*
Jude 14 with t. thousands of his saints, ... *3461*
Re 2:10 **ye shall have tribulation t. days**:... *1176*
Re 5:11 was t. thousand times t. thousand, ... *3461*
Re 12:3 having seven heads and t. horns, ... *1176*
Re 13:1 having seven heads and t. horns, ... *1176*
Re 13:1 and upon his horns t. crowns, and...... *1176*
Re 17:3 having seven heads and t. horns. *1176*
Re 17:7 hath the seven heads and t. horns....... *1176*
Re 17:12 t. horns...thou sawest are t. kings, ... *1176*
Re 17:16 the t. horns which thou sawest.......... *1176*

TEND See also ATTEND; CONTEND; EXTEND; INTEND; TENDETH.
Pr 21:5 the diligent t. only to plenteousness;.........

TENDER See also TENDERHEARTED.
Ge 18:7 and fetcht a calf t. and good, and 7390
Ge 29:17 Leah was t. eyed; but Rachel was...... 7390
Ge 33:13 knoweth that the children are t., ... 7390
De 28:54 that the man that is t. among you, ... 7390
De 28:56 The t. and delicate woman among 7390
De 32:2 as the small rain upon the t. herb, and......
2Sa 23:4 t. grass springing out of the earth ....
2Ki 22:19 Because thine heart was t., and......... 7401
1Ch 22:5 Solomon my son is young and t., ... 7390
1Ch 29:1 Solomon...is yet young and t., ... 7390
2Ch 34:27 Because thine heart was t., and......... 7401
Job 14:7 t. branch thereof will not cease.......... 3127
Job 38:27 the bud of the t. herb to spring forth?.......
Ps 25:6 Remember, O Lord, thy t. mercies ....
Ps 40:11 Withhold not thou thy t. mercies from.......
Ps 51:1 unto the multitude of thy t. mercies..........
Ps 69:16 to the multitude of thy t. mercies.............
Ps 77:9 he in anger shut up his t. mercies?...........
Ps 79:8 let thy t. mercies speedily prevent us: ......
Ps 103:4 with lovingkindness and t. mercies;...........
Ps 119:77 Let thy t. mercies come unto me, that......
Ps 119:156 Great are thy t. mercies, O Lord: ....
Ps 145:9 his t. mercies are over all his works. ....
Pr 4:3 t. and only beloved in the sight of 7390
Pr 12:10 the t. mercies of the wicked are cruel. ......
Pr 27:25 and the t. grass sheweth itself, and ....
Ca 2:13 with the t. grape give a good smell...........
Ca 2:15 vines: for our vines have t. grapes. ....
Ca 7:12 whether the t. grape appear,....................
Isa 47:1 thou shalt no more be called t. and..... 7390
Isa 53:2 grow up before him as a t. plant, ... 3126
Ezr 17:22 the top of his young twigs a t. one,.... 7390
Da 1:9 Daniel into favor and t. love ....
Da 4:15, 23 brass, in the t. grass of the field;.........
Mt 24:32 **When his branch is yet t., and**....... *527*
Mk 13:28 **When her branch is yet t., and**....... *527*
Lu 1:78 Through the t. mercy of our God;...... *4698*
Jas 5:11 is very pitiful, and of t. mercy. *3629*

TENDER-EYED See TENDER and EYED.

TENDERHEARTED
2Ch 13:7 Rehoboam was young and t.,...... 7390,3824
Eph 4:32 t., forgiving one another, even as....... *2155*

TENDERNESS
De 28:56 ground for delicateness and t.,........... 7391

TENDETH
Pr 10:16 The labour of the righteous t. to life: ....
Pr 11:19 As righteousness t. to life: so he that ....
Pr 11:24 more than is meet, but it t. to poverty......
Pr 14:23 the talk of the lips t. only to penury..........
Pr 19:23 The fear of the Lord t. to life: and he ....

TENONS
Ex 26:17 Two t. shall there be in one board, ... 3027
Ex 26:19 under one board for his two t.,.......... 3027
Ex 26:19 under another board for his two t....... 3027
Ex 36:22 One board had two t., equally 3027
Ex 36:24 under one board for his two t.,.......... 3027
Ex 36:24 under another board for his two t.,..... 3027

TENOR
Ge 43:7 according to the t. of these words:..... 6310
Ex 34:27 for after the t. of these words I have.. 6310

TEN'S
Ge 18:32 I will not destroy it for t. sake. 6235

TENS
Ex 18:21 rulers of fifties, and rulers of t........... 6235
Ex 18:25 rulers of fifties, and rulers of t........... 6235
De 1:15 over fifties, and captains over t.,........ 6235

TENT See also TENTMAKERS; TENTS.
Ge 9:21 and he was uncovered within his t.. 168
Ge 12:8 pitched his t., having Beth-el on the..... 168
Ge 13:3 place where his t. had been at the 168
Ge 13:12 and pitched his t. toward Sodom.......... 167
Ge 13:18 Then Abram removed his t., and......... 167
Ge 18:1 he sat in the t. door in the heat of....... 168
Ge 18:2 he ran to meet them from the t. door,.. 168
Ge 18:6 Abraham hastened into the t. unto 168
Ge 18:9 wife? And he said, Behold, in the t........ 168
Ge 18:10 And Sarah heard it in the t. door, ... 168
Ge 24:67 her into his mother Sarah's t., ... 168
Ge 26:17 pitched his t. in the valley of Gerar, ...
Ge 26:25 the Lord, and pitched his t. there: 168
Ge 31:25 Now Jacob had pitched his t. in the...... 168
Ge 31:33 into Jacob's t., and into Leah's t., ... 168
Ge 31:33 Then went he out of Leah's t.,............ 168
Ge 31:33 and entered into Rachel's t.. 168
Ge 31:34 And Laban searched all the t., but 168
Ge 33:18 and pitched his t. before the city.............
Ge 33:19 a field, where he had spread his t., ... 168
Ge 35:21 and spread his t. beyond the tower of... 168
Ex 18:7 welfare; and they came into the t.. 168
Ex 26:11 couple the t. together, that it may be... 168
Ex 26:12 remaineth of the curtains of the t.,....... 168
Ex 26:13 in the length of the curtains of the t.,... 168
Ex 26:14 a covering for the t. of rams' skins 168
Ex 26:36 an hanging for the door of the t.,......... 168
Ex 33:8 and stood every man at his t. door, ... 168
Ex 33:10 worshipped, every man in his t. door.... 168
Ex 35:11 The tabernacle, his t., and his............ 168
Ex 36:14 made curtains of goats' hair for the t.... 168
Ex 36:18 brass to couple the t. together, ... 168
Ex 36:19 a covering for the t. of rams' skins 168
Ex 39:32 the t. of the congregation finished:....... 168
Ex 39:33 the tabernacle unto Moses, the t., and.. 168
Ex 39:40 for the t. of the congregation, ... 168
Ex 40:2, 6 of the t. of the congregation............ 168
Ex 40:7 between the t. of the congregation....... 168
Ex 40:19 abroad the t. over the tabernacle, ... 168
Ex 40:19 and put the covering of the t. above..... 168
Ex 40:22 table in the t. of the congregation, ... 168
Ex 40:24 candlestick in...t. of...congregation, ... 168
Ex 40:26 altar in the t. of the congregation......... 168
Ex 40:29 of the t. of the congregation, ... 168
Ex 40:30 between the t. of the congregation....... 168
Ex 40:32 went into the t. of the congregation, ... 168
Ex 40:34 covered the t. of the congregation, ... 168
Ex 40:35 enter into the t. of the congregation,.... 168
Le 14:8 tarry abroad out of his t. seven days. ... 168
Nu 3:25 shall be the tabernacle, and the t.,........ 168
Nu 9:15 namely, the t. of the testimony: 168
Nu 11:10 every man in the door of his t. 168
Nu 19:14 is the law, when a man dieth in a t.. 168
Nu 19:14 into the t., and all that is in the t., ... 168
Nu 19:18 the water, and sprinkle it upon the t., .. 168
Nu 25:8 after the man of Israel into the t.,...... 6898
Jos 7:21 in the earth in the midst of my t.. 168
Jos 7:22 they ran unto the t.; and, behold, ... 168
Jos 7:22 it was hid in his t., and the silver 168
Jos 7:23 took them out of the midst of the t.,.... 168
Jos 7:24 and his t., and all that he had:............ 168
Jg 4:11 his t. unto the plain of Zaanaim, ... 168
Jg 4:17 Sisera fled away on his feet to the t..... 168
Jg 4:18 he had turned in unto her into the t., ... 168
Jg 4:20 Stand in the door of the t., and it 168
Jg 4:21 Heber's wife took a nail of the t., ... 168
Jg 4:22 And when he came into her t., behold,......
Jg 5:24 shall she be above women in the t.. 168
Jg 7:8 rest of Israel every man unto his t.,..... 168
Jg 7:13 host of Midian, and came unto a t.,...... 168
Jg 7:13 overturned it, that the t. lay along. 168
Jg 20:8 We will not any of us go to his t., ... 168
1Sa 4:10 and they fled every man into his t.:...... 168
1Sa 13:2 people he sent every man to his t........ 168
1Sa 17:54 but he put his armour in his t.. 168
2Sa 7:6 walked in a t. and in a tabernacle........ 168
2Sa 16:22 So they spread Absalom a t. upon........ 168
2Sa 18:17 all Israel fled every one to his t.......... 168
2Sa 19:8 Israel had fled every man to his t.. 168
2Sa 20:22 from the city, every man to his t.......... 168
2Ki 7:8 they went into one t., and did eat........ 168
2Ki 7:8 again, and entered into another t.. 168
1Ch 15:1 ark of God, and pitched for it a t.. 168
1Ch 16:1 and set it in the midst of the t. that..... 168
1Ch 17:5 but have gone from t. to t., and.......... 168
2Ch 1:4 had pitched a t. for it at Jerusalem. 168
2Ch 25:22 and they fled every man to his t.......... 168
Ps 78:60 the t. which he placed among men; 168
Isa 13:20 shall the Arabian pitch t. there; 167
Isa 38:12 from me as a shepherd's t.................. 168
Isa 40:22 them out as a t. to dwell in: 168
Isa 54:2 Enlarge the place of thy t., and let....... 168
Jer 10:20 none to stretch forth my t. any more, .. 168
Jer 37:10 they rise up every man in his t., ... 168

TENT-DOOR See TENT and DOOR.

TENTH
Ge 8:5 continually until the t. month: 6224
Ge 8:5 in the t. month, on the first day of..... 6224
Ge 28:22 I will surely give the t. unto thee......... 6237
Ex 12:3 In the t. day of this month they........ 6218
Ex 16:36 an omer is the t. part of an ephah...... 6224
Ex 29:40 with the one lamb a t. deal of flour..... 6241
Le 5:11 t. part of an ephah of fine flour.......... 6224
Le 6:20 the t. part of an ephah of fine flour...... 6224
Le 14:10 three t. deals of fine flour for a.......... 6241
Le 14:21 one t. deal of fine flour mingled 6241
Le 16:29 month, on the t. day of the month,...... 6218
Le 23:13 two t. deals of fine flour mingled........ 6241
Le 23:17 two wave loaves of two t. deals:......... 6241
Le 23:27 Also on the t. day of this seventh 6218
Le 24:5 two t. deals shall be in one cake. 6241
Le 25:9 the t. day of the seventh month,........ 6218

Le 27:32 the **t.** shall be holy unto the Lord....... 6224
Nu 5:15 the **t.** part of an ephah of barley........ 6224
Nu 7:66 On the **t.** day Ahiezer the son of........ 6224
Nu 15:4 meat offering of a **t.** deal of flour........ 6241
Nu 15:6 meat offering two **t.** deals of flour...... 6241
Nu 15:9 offering of three **t.** deals of flour...... 6241
Nu 18:21 children of Levi...the **t.** in Israel........ 4643
Nu 18:26 Lord, even a **t.** part of the tithe......... 4643
Nu 28:5 a **t.** part of an ephah of flour for a...... 6224
Nu 28:9 two **t.** deals of flour for a meat......... 6241
Nu 28:12 three **t.** deals of flour for a meat....... 6241
Nu 28:12 and two **t.** deals of flour for a meat...... 6241
Nu 28:13 a several **t.** deal of flour mingled........ 6241
Nu 28:20 three **t.** deals shall ye offer for a........ 6241
Nu 28:20 and two **t.** deals for a ram;............... 6241
Nu 28:21 A several **t.** deal shalt thou offer......... 6241
Nu 28:28 oil, three **t.** deals unto one bullock,...... 6241
Nu 28:28 bullock, two **t.** deals unto one ram,...... 6241
Nu 28:29 A several **t.** deal unto one lamb,........ 6241
Nu 29:3 oil, three **t.** deals for a bullock,.......... 6241
Nu 29:3 bullock, and two **t.** deals for a ram,.... 6241
Nu 29:4 And one **t.** deal for one lamb,............ 6241
Nu 29:7 on the **t.** day of this seventh month.... 6218
Nu 29:9 oil, three **t.** deals to a bullock,........... 6241
Nu 29:9 and two **t.** deals to one ram,............. 6241
Nu 29:10 A several **t.** deal for one lamb,.......... 6241
Nu 29:14 three **t.** deals unto every bullock of...... 6241
Nu 29:14 two **t.** deals to each ram of the two.... 6241
Nu 29:15 a several **t.** deal to each lamb of........ 6241
De 23:2 even to his **t.** generation shall he....... 6224
De 23:3 even to their **t.** generation shall......... 6224
Jos 4:19 on the **t.** day of the first month,......... 6218
1Sa 8:15 he will take the **t.** of your seed,......... 6237
1Sa 8:17 He will take the **t.** of your sheep:....... 6237
2Ki 25:1 year of his reign, in the **t.** month,...... 6218
2Ki 25:1 in the **t.** day of the month, that......... 6218
1Ch 12:13 Jeremiah the **t.**, Machbanai the.......... 6224
1Ch 24:11 to Jeshuah, the **t.** to Shecaniah,......... 6224
1Ch 25:17 **t.** to Shimei, he, his sons, and his....... 6224
1Ch 27:13 The **t.** captain for the **t.** month was.... 6224
Ezr 10:16 down in the first day of the **t.** month.. 6224
Es 2:16 into his house royal in the **t.** month,... 6224
Isa 6:13 But yet in it shall be a **t.**, and it......... 6224
Jer 32:1 **t.** year of Zedekiah king of Judah,....... 6224
Jer 39:1 **t.** month, came Nebuchadrezzar.......... 6224
Jer 52:4 year of his reign, in the **t.** month,...... 6224
Jer 52:4 in the **t.** day of the month, that......... 6218
Jer 52:12 month, in the **t.** day of the month,..... 6218
Eze 20:1 month, the **t.** day of the month, that... 6218
Eze 24:1 in the ninth year, in the **t.** month,...... 6224
Eze 24:1 in the **t.** day of the month, the.......... 6218
Eze 29:1 In the **t.** year, in the **t.** month,......... 6224
Eze 33:21 in the **t.** month, in the fifth day of...... 6224
Eze 40:1 year, in the **t.** day of the month,......... 6218
Eze 45:11 contain the **t.** part of an homer,......... 4643
Eze 45:11 the ephah the **t.** part of an homer:...... 6224
Eze 45:14 the **t.** part of a bath out of the cor,..... 4643
Zec 8:19 and the fast of the **t.**, shall be to........ 6224
Joh 1:39 day: for it was about the **t.** hour......... *1882*
Heb 7:2 also Abraham gave a **t.** part of all;...... *1181*
Heb 7:4 Abraham gave the **t.** of the spoils....... *1181*
Re 11:13 and the **t.** part of the city fell, and...... *1182*
Re 21:20 a topaz; the **t.**, a chrysoprasus;........ *1182*

TENTH-DEAL See TENTH and DEAL.

TEN-THOUSAND See TEN and THOUSAND.

TENTMAKERS
Ac 18:3 by their occupation they were **t.**........ *4635*

TENTS
Ge 4:20 the father of such as dwell in **t.**,.......... 168
Ge 9:27 and he shall dwell in the **t.** of Shem;.... 168
Ge 13:5 Abram, had flocks, and herds, and **t.**.... 168
Ge 25:27 was a plain man, dwelling in **t.**........... 168
Ge 31:33 and into the two maidservants' **t.**;........ 168
Ex 16:16 man for them which are in his **t.**.......... 168
Nu 1:52 children of Israel shall pitch their **t.**,..........
Nu 9:17 the children of Israel pitched their **t.**.........
Nu 9:18 tabernacle they rested in their **t.**..........
Nu 9:20 of the Lord they abode in their **t.**,............
Nu 9:22 children of Israel abode in their **t.**,...........
Nu 9:23 of the Lord they rested in the **t.**,.............
Nu 13:19 whether in **t.**, or in strong holds;........ 4264
Nu 16:26 from the **t.** of these wicked men,........ 168
Nu 16:27 out, and stood in the door of their **t.**,... 168
Nu 24:2 saw Israel abiding in his **t.** according.........
Nu 24:5 How goodly are thy **t.**, O Jacob,.......... 168
De 1:27 And ye murmured in your **t.**, and......... 168
De 1:33 you out a place to pitch your **t.** in,...........
De 5:30 to them, Get you into your **t.** again...... 168
De 11:6 their households, and their **t.**, and........ 168
De 16:7 in the morning, and go unto thy **t.**....... 168
De 33:18 going out; and, Issachar, in thy **t.**....... 168
Jos 3:14 the people removed from their **t.**,........ 168
Jos 22:4 return ye, and get you unto your **t.**,...... 168
Jos 22:6 away: and they went unto their **t.**........ 168
Jos 22:7 sent them away also unto their **t.**,........ 168
Jos 22:8 with much riches unto your **t.**, and........ 168
Jg 6:5 came up with their cattle and their **t.**,... 168
Jg 8:11 by the way of them that dwelt in **t.**...... 168
1Sa 17:53 Philistines, and...spoiled their **t.**......... 4264
2Sa 11:11 Israel, and Judah, abide in **t.**;............ 5521
2Sa 20:1 every man to his **t.**, O Israel.............. 168
1Ki 8:66 went unto their **t.** joyful and glad......... 168
1Ki 12:16 to your **t.**, O Israel: now see to thine... 168
1Ki 12:16 So Israel departed unto their **t.**............ 168
2Ki 7:7 left their **t.**, and their horses, and........ 168
2Ki 7:10 asses tied, and the **t.** as they were....... 168
2Ki 7:16 and spoiled the **t.** of the Syrians......... 4264
2Ki 8:21 and the people fled into their **t.**.......... 168
2Ki 13:5 children of Israel dwelt in their **t.**,........ 168
2Ki 14:12 and they fled every man to their **t.**....... 168
1Ch 4:41 smote their **t.**, and the habitations........ 168
1Ch 5:10 they dwelt in their **t.** throughout all...... 168
2Ch 7:10 he sent the people away into their **t.**,... 168
2Ch 10:16 every man to your **t.**, O Israel:............ 168
2Ch 10:16 So all Israel went to their **t.**............... 168
2Ch 14:15 They smote also the **t.** of cattle, and..... 168
2Ch 31:2 in the gates of the **t.** of the Lord......... 4264
Ezr 8:15 there abode we in **t.** three days:........ 2583
Ps 69:25 and let none dwell in their **t.**............... 168
Ps 78:55 tribes of Israel to dwell in their **t.**......... 168
Ps 84:10 than to dwell in the **t.** of wickedness.... 168
Ps 106:25 But murmured in their **t.**, and............ 168
Ps 120:5 that I dwell in the **t.** of Kedar!............ 168
Ca 1:5 as the **t.** of Kedar, as the curtains of.... 168
Ca 1:8 thy kids beside the shepherds' **t.**......... 4908
Jer 4:20 suddenly are my **t.** spoiled, and my........ 168
Jer 6:3 they shall pitch their **t.** against her....... 168
Jer 30:18 again the captivity of Jacob's **t.**,.......... 168
Jer 35:7 but all your days ye shall dwell in **t.**;.... 168
Jer 35:10 But we have dwelt in **t.**, and have....... 168
Jer 49:29 Their **t.** and their flocks shall they....... 168
Hab 3:7 I saw the **t.** of Cushan in affliction:...... 168
Zec 12:7 also shall save the **t.** of Judah first,...... 168
Zec 14:15 the beasts that shall be in these **t.**,...... 4264

TERAH (te'-rah) See also THARA.
Ge 11:24 and twenty years, and begat **T.**......... 8646
Ge 11:25 and Nahor lived after he begat **T.**........ 8646
Ge 11:26 **T.** lived seventy years, and begat........ 8646
Ge 11:27 these are the generations of **T.**:........... 8646
Ge 11:27 **T.** begat Abram, Nahor, and Haran;...... 8646
Ge 11:28 Haran died before his father **T.** in........ 8646
Ge 11:31 **T.** took Abram his son, and Lot.......... 8646
Ge 11:32 days of **T.** were two hundred and........ 8646
Ge 11:32 five years: and **T.** died in Haran.......... 8646
Jos 24:2 even **T.**, the father of Abraham,.......... 8646
1Ch 1:26 Serug, Nahor, **T.**,.......................... 8646

TERAPHIM (ter'-af-im)
Jg 17:5 and made an ephod, and **t.**, and........... 8655
Jg 18:14 is in these houses an ephod, and **t.**,..... 8655
Jg 18:17 image, and the ephod, and the **t.**,......... 8655
Jg 18:18 carved image, the ephod, and the **t.**,..... 8655
Jg 18:20 and he took the ephod, and the **t.**,...... 8655
Ho 3:4 without an ephod, and without **t.**:........ 8655

TERESH (te'-resh)
Es 2:21 chamberlains, Bigthan and **T.**,............. 8657
Es 6:2 had told of Bigthana and **T.**,............... 8657

TERMED
Isa 62:4 Thou shalt no more be **t.** Forsaken;...... 559
Isa 62:4 thy land any more be **t.** Desolate:........ 559

TERRACES
2Ch 9:11 king made of the algum trees **t.**.......... 4546

TERRESTRIAL
1Co 15:40 also celestial bodies, and bodies **t.**...... *1919*
1Co 15:40 and the glory of the **t.** is another........ *1919*

TERRIBLE
Ex 34:10 for it is a **t.** thing that I will do.......... 3372
De 1:19 all that great and **t.** wilderness,.......... 3372
De 7:21 is among you, a mighty God and **t.**...... 3372
De 8:15 through...great and **t.** wilderness,........ 3372
De 10:17 a great God, a mighty, and a **t.**,......... 3372
De 10:21 for thee these great and **t.** things,....... 3372
Jg 13:6 of an angel of God, very **t.**.................. 3372
2Sa 7:23 to do for you great things and **t.**,........ 3372
Ne 1:5 of heaven, the great and **t.** God,.......... 3372
Ne 4:14 the Lord, which is great and **t.**,............ 3372
Ne 9:32 great, the mighty, and the **t.** God,....... 3372
Job 37:22 the north: with God is **t.** majesty.......... 3372
Job 39:20 the glory of his nostrils is **t.**............... 367
Job 41:14 face? his teeth are **t.** round about......... 367
Ps 45:4 hand shall teach thee **t.** things............ 3372
Ps 47:2 For the Lord most high is **t.**; he is....... 3372
Ps 65:5 By **t.** things in righteousness wilt........ 3372
Ps 66:3 God, How **t.** art thou in thy works!...... 3372
Ps 66:5 he is **t.** in his doing toward the.......... 3372
Ps 68:35 O God, thou art **t.** out of thy holy....... 3372
Ps 76:12 he is **t.** to the kings of the earth......... 3372
Ps 99:3 them praise thy great and **t.** name;...... 3372
Ps 106:22 Ham, and **t.** things by the Red sea...... 3372
Ps 145:6 speak of the might of thy **t.** acts:........ 3372
Ca 6:4 **t.** as an army with banners.................. 366
Ca 6:10 and **t.** as an army with banners?........... 366
Isa 13:11 lay low the haughtiness of the **t.**........ 6184
Isa 18:2 to a people **t.** from their beginning....... 3372
Isa 18:7 to a people **t.** from their beginning........ 3372
Isa 21:1 from the desert, from a **t.** land........... 3372
Isa 25:3 the city of the **t.** nations shall fear........ 6184
Isa 25:4 the blast of the **t.** ones is as a storm.. 6184
Isa 25:5 the branch of the **t.** ones shall be........ 6184
Isa 29:5 multitude of the **t.** ones shall be as...... 6184
Isa 29:20 For the **t.** one is brought to nought,.... 6184
Isa 49:25 the prey of the **t.** shall be delivered:.... 6184
Isa 64:3 When thou didst **t.** things which we.... 3372
Jer 15:21 thee out of the hand of the **t.**............ 6184
Jer 20:11 Lord is with me as a mighty **t.** one:...... 6184
La 5:10 an oven because of the **t.** famine......... 2152
Eze 1:22 was as the colour of the **t.** crystal,...... 3372
Eze 28:7 upon thee, the **t.** of the nations:........ 6184
Eze 30:11 with him, the **t.** of the nations,........... 6184
Eze 31:12 the **t.** of the nations, have cut him...... 6184
Eze 32:12 the **t.** of the nations, all of them:........ 6184
Da 2:31 thee; and the form thereof was **t.**......... 1763
Da 7:7 a fourth beast, dreadful and **t.**,............ 574
Joe 2:11 day of the Lord is great and very **t.**;.... 3372
Joe 2:31 the great and the **t.** day of the Lord... 3372
Hab 1:7 They are **t.** and dreadful: their............ 366
Zep 2:11 The Lord will be **t.** unto them:........... 3372
Heb 12:21 so **t.** was the sight, that Moses.......... *5398*

TERRIBLENESS
De 26:8 and with great **t.**, and with signs,........ 4172
1Ch 17:21 thee a name of greatness and **t.**,........ 3372
Jer 49:16 Thy **t.** hath deceived thee, and the..... 8606

TERRIBLY
Isa 2:19, 21 he ariseth to shake **t.** the earth..... 6206
Na 2:3 and the fir trees shall be **t.** shaken..........

TERRIFIED
De 20:3 neither be ye **t.** because of them;........ 6206
Lu 21:9 **of wars and commotions, be not t.** *4422*
Lu 24:37 But they were **t.** and affrighted,.......... *4422*
Php 1:28 in nothing **t.** by your adversaries:........ *4426*

TERRIFIEST
Job 7:14 dreams, and **t.** me through visions:...... 1204

TERRIFY See also TERRIFIED; TERRIFIEST.
Job 3:5 let the blackness of the day **t.** it.......... 1204
Job 9:34 from me, and let not his fear **t.** me:..... 1204
Job 31:34 the contempt of families **t.** me,........... 2865
2Co 10:9 seem as if I would **t.** you by letters.... *1629*

TERROR See also TERRORS.
Ge 35:5 the **t.** of God was upon the cities........ 2847
Le 26:16 I will even appoint over you **t.**,............ 928
De 32:25 The sword without, and **t.** within,......... 367
De 34:12 the great **t.** which Moses shewed........ 4172
Jos 2:9 and that your **t.** is fallen upon us,........ 367
Job 31:23 destruction from God was a **t.** to......... 6343
Job 33:7 my **t.** shall not make thee afraid,.......... 367
Ps 91:5 not be afraid for the **t.** by night;......... 6343
Isa 10:33 hosts, shall lop the bough with **t.**......... 4637
Isa 19:17 of Judah shall be a **t.** unto Egypt,........ 2283
Isa 33:18 Thine heart shall meditate **t.**................ 367
Isa 54:14 and from **t.**; for it shall not come........ 4288
Jer 17:17 Be not a **t.** unto me: thou art my........ 4288

Jer 20:4 I will make thee a t. to thyself, ... 4032
Jer 32:21 strong hand,...and with great t.; 4172
Eze 26:17 which cause their t. to be on all.......... 2851
Eze 26:21 I will make thee a t., and thou............ 1091
Eze 27:36 thou shalt be a t., and never shalt...... 1091
Eze 28:19 thou shalt be a t., and never shalt...... 1091
Eze 32:23 which caused t. in the land of the........ 2851
Eze 32:24 which caused their t. in the land of..... 2851
Eze 32:25 their t. was caused in the land of........ 2851
Eze 32:26 they caused their t. in the land of......... 2851
Eze 32:27 the t. of the mighty in the land of 2851
Eze 32:30 with their t. they are ashamed of 2851
Eze 32:32 I have caused my t. in the land of....... 2851
Ro 13:3 rulers are not a t. to good works, ... *5401*
2Co 5:11 Knowing...the t. of the Lord, we *5401*
1Pe 3:14 be not afraid of their t., neither be *5401*

TERRORS
De 4:34 stretched out arm, and by great t.,...... 4172
Job 6:4 t. of God do set themselves in 1161
Job 18:11 T. shall make him afraid on every........ 1091
Job 18:14 shall bring him to the king of t............ 1091
Job 20:25 out of his gall: t. are upon him............ 367
Job 24:17 in the t. of the shadow of death......... 1091
Job 27:20 T. take hold on him as waters, a......... 1091
Job 30:15 T. are turned upon me: they............. 1091
Ps 55:4 the t. of death are fallen upon me......... 367
Ps 73:19 they are utterly consumed with t......... 1091
Ps 88:15 while I suffer thy t. I am distracted...... 367
Ps 88:16 over me; thy t. have cut me off.......... 1161
Jer 15:8 it suddenly, and t. upon the city.......... 928
La 2:22 a solemn day my t. round about,......... 4032
Eze 21:12 t. by reason of the sword shall be 4048

TERTIUS (tur'-she-us)
Ro 16:22 I T., who wrote this epistle, ... *5060*

TERTULLUS (tur-tul'-lus)
Ac 24:1 with a certain orator named T., ... *5061*
Ac 24:2 T. began to accuse him, saying,......... *5061*

TESTAMENT
Mt 26:28 **For this is my blood of the new t.,** .*1242*
Mk 14:24 **This is my blood of the new t.,** *1242*
Lu 22:20 **This cup is the new t. in my blood,** *1242*
1Co 11:25 **This cup is the new t. in my blood:** *1242*
2Co 3:6 us able ministers of the new t.; *1242*
2Co 3:14 away in the reading of the old t.; *1242*
Heb 7:22 Jesus made a surety of a better t........ *1242*
Heb 9:15 he is the mediator of the new t., ... *1242*
Heb 9:15 that were under the first t.,............... *1242*
Heb 9:16 For where a t. is, there must also of.. *1242*
Heb 9:17 For a t. is of force after men are *1242*
Heb 9:18 Whereupon neither the first t. was ....
Heb 9:20 This is the blood of the t. which *1242*
Re 11:19 seen in his temple the ark of his t....... *1242*

TESTATOR
Heb 9:16 necessity be the death of the t.. .... *1303*
Heb 9:17 strength at all while the t. liveth. *1303*

TESTIFIED See also TESTIFIEDST.
Ex 21:29 and it hath been t. to his owner,........ 5749
De 19:18 hath t. falsely against his brother;....... 6030
Ru 1:21 seeing the Lord hath t. against me, ... 6030
2Sa 1:16 for thy mouth hath t. against thee, ... 6030
2Ki 17:13 Yet the Lord t. against Israel, and...... 5749
2Ki 17:15 his testimonies which he t. against...... 5749
2Ch 24:19 Lord; and they t. against them: 5749
Ne 9:26 slew thy prophets which t. against...... 5749
Ne 13:15 and I t. against them in the day 5749
Ne 13:21 Then I t. against them, and said 5749
Joh 4:39 the saying of the woman, which t.,..... *3140*
Joh 4:44 For Jesus himself t., that a prophet *3140*
Joh 13:21 he was troubled in spirit, and t., ... *3140*
Ac 8:25 they had t. and preached the word *1263*
Ac 18:5 t. to the Jews that Jesus was *1263*
Ac 23:11 **thou hast t. of me in Jerusalem.** ... *1263*
Ac 28:23 and t. the kingdom of God, ... *1263*
1Co 15:15 we have t. of God that he raised.......... *3140*
1Th 4:6 also have forewarned you and t.,......... *1263*
1Ti 2:6 ransom for all, to be t. in due time..... *3142*
Heb 2:6 But one in a certain place t.,.............. *1263*
1Pe 1:11 it t. beforehand the sufferings of *4303*
1Jo 5:9 God which he hath t. of his Son......... *3140*
3Jo 3 and t. of the truth that is in thee, ... *3140*

TESTIFIEDST
Ne 9:29 And t. against them, that thou........... 5749
Ne 9:30 t. against them by thy spirit in thy 5749

TESTIFIETH
Ho 7:10 the pride of Israel t. to his face: 6030
Joh 3:32 hath seen and heard, that he t.;......... *3140*
Joh 21:24 disciple which t. of these things, ... *3140*
Heb 7:17 For he t., Thou art a priest for ever... *3140*
Re 22:20 He which t. these things saith, ... *3140*

TESTIFY See also TESTIFIED; TESTIFIETH; TESTIFYING.
Nu 35:30 one witness shall not t. against 6030
De 8:19 I t. against you this day that ye 5749
De 19:16 to t. against him that which is............ 6030
De 31:21 this song shall t. against them as a..... 6030
De 32:46 words which I t. among you this 5749
Ne 9:34 thou didst t. against them. 5749
Job 15:6 yea, thine own lips t. against thee. 6030
Ps 50:7 Israel, and I will t. against thee: 5749
Ps 81:8 my people, and I will t. unto thee: 5749
Isa 59:12 thee, and our sins t. against us:......... 6030
Jer 14:7 though our iniquities t. against us, ... 6030
Ho 5:5 pride of Israel doth t. to his face: 6030
Am 3:13 and t. in the house of Jacob, saith 5749
Mic 6:3 I wearied thee? t. against me. 6030
Lu 16:28 **that he may t. unto them, lest** *1263*
Joh 2:25 not that any should t. of man;............ *3140*
Joh 3:11 **know, and t. that we have seen;**.... *3140*
Joh 5:39 **and they are they which t. of me.** ..*3140*
Joh 7:7 **me it hateth, because I t. of it,** *3140*
Joh 15:26 **the Father, he shall t. of me**.......... *3140*
Ac 2:40 other words did he t. and exhort,........ *1263*
Ac 10:42 to t. that it is he which was.............. *1263*
Ac 20:24 to t. the gospel of the grace of God.... *1263*
Ac 26:5 if they would t., that after the *3140*
Ga 5:3 For I t. again to every man that is *3143*
Eph 4:17 t. in the Lord, that ye henceforth....... *3143*
1Jo 4:14 and do t. that the Father sent the...... *3140*
Re 22:16 **sent mine angel to t. unto you** *3140*
Re 22:18 I t. unto every man that heareth........ *4828*

TESTIFYING
Ac 20:21 T. both to the Jews, and also to *1263*
Heb 11:4 was righteous, God t. of his gifts: *3140*
1Pe 5:12 and t. that this is the true grace *1957*

TESTIMONIES
De 4:45 These are the t., and the statutes, ... 5713
De 6:17 his t., and his statutes, which he........ 5713
De 6:20 What mean the t., and the statutes,.... 5713
1Ki 2:3 his judgments, and his t., as it is 5715
2Ki 17:15 his t. which he testified against.......... 5715
2Ki 23:3 keep his commandments and his t. 5715
1Ch 29:19 keep thy commandments, thy t.,........ 5715
2Ch 34:31 keep his commandments, and his t., ... 5715
Ne 9:34 thy commandments and thy t.,............ 5715
Ps 25:10 as keep his covenant and his t.......... 5713
Ps 78:56 high God, and kept not his t.............. 5713
Ps 93:5 Thy t. are very sure: holiness 5713
Ps 99:7 they kept his t., and the ordinance 5713
Ps 119:2 Blessed are they that keep his t., ... 5713
Ps 119:14 have rejoiced in the way of thy t.,....... 5715
Ps 119:22 contempt; for I have kept thy t.......... 5713
Ps 119:24 Thy t. also are my delight and my...... 5713
Ps 119:31 I have stuck unto thy t.: O Lord,........ 5715
Ps 119:36 Incline my heart unto thy t., and......... 5715
Ps 119:46 I will speak of thy t. also before 5713
Ps 119:59 and turned my feet unto thy t.. 5713
Ps 119:79 and those that have known thy t.. 5713
Ps 119:95 me: but I will consider thy t.............. 5713
Ps 119:99 for thy t. are my meditation. 5715
Ps 119:111 Thy t. have I taken as an heritage...... 5715
Ps 119:119 dross: therefore I love thy t............... 5713
Ps 119:125 that I may know thy t.. 5713
Ps 119:129 Thy t. are wonderful: therefore 5715
Ps 119:138 Thy t. that thou hast commanded........ 5713
Ps 119:144 The righteousness of thy t. is............ 5715
Ps 119:146 save me, and I shall keep thy t.......... 5713
Ps 119:152 Concerning thy t., I have known of...... 5713
Ps 119:157 yet do I not decline from thy t............ 5715
Ps 119:167 My soul hath kept thy t.; and I........... 5713
Ps 119:168 I have kept thy precepts and thy t.. 5713
Jer 44:23 nor in his statutes, nor in his t.; 5715

TESTIMONY See also TESTIMONIES.
Ex 16:34 so Aaron laid it up before the T., ... 5715
Ex 25:16 thou shalt put into the ark the t........... 5715
Ex 25:21 in the ark thou shalt put the t.............. 5715
Ex 25:22 which are upon the ark of the t., ... 5715
Ex 26:33 within the vail the ark of the t.. 5715
Ex 26:34 mercy seat upon the ark of the t.......... 5715
Ex 27:21 the vail, which is before the t.,........... 5715
Ex 30:6 the vail that is by the ark of the t., ... 5715
Ex 30:6 the mercy seat that is over the t., ... 5715
Ex 30:26 therewith, and the ark of the t.,......... 5715
Ex 30:36 of it before the t. in the tabernacle...... 5715
Ex 31:7 the ark of the t., and the mercy seat .. 5715
Ex 31:18 two tables of t., tables of stone, ... 5715
Ex 32:15 the two tables of the t. were in his 5715
Ex 34:29 the two tables of t. in Moses' hand,..... 5715
Ex 38:21 even of the tabernacle of t., as it 5715
Ex 39:35 The ark of the t., and the staves 5715
Ex 40:3 shalt put therein the ark of the t.,....... 5715
Ex 40:5 the incense before the ark of the t., ... 5715
Ex 40:20 he took and put the t. into the ark, ... 5715
Ex 40:21 and covered the ark of the t.;............. 5715
Le 16:13 the mercy seat that is upon the t., ... 5715
Le 24:3 Without the vail of the t., in the 5715
Nu 1:50 Levites over the tabernacle of t.,......... 5715
Nu 1:53 round about the tabernacle of t., ... 5715
Nu 1:53 the charge of the tabernacle of t.. 5715
Nu 4:5 vail, and cover the ark of t. with it: 5715
Nu 7:89 seat that was upon the ark of t.,......... 5715
Nu 9:15 namely, the tent of the t.. 5715
Nu 10:11 up from off the tabernacle of the t...... 5715
Nu 17:4 of the congregation before the t.,........ 5715
Nu 17:10 Bring Aaron's rod again before...t.,..... 5715
Jos 4:16 priests that bear the ark of the t.,....... 5715
Ru 4:7 and this was a t. in Israel. 8584
2Ki 11:12 upon him, and gave him the t.. 5715
2Ch 23:11 him the crown, and gave him the t., ... 5715
Ps 19:7 the t. of the Lord is sure, making 5715
Ps 78:5 he established a t. in Jacob,and.......... 5715
Ps 81:5 he ordained in Joseph for a t.,............ 5715
Ps 119:88 so shall I keep the t. of thy mouth. 5715
Ps 122:4 unto the t. of Israel, to give thanks 5715
Ps 132:12 and my t. that I shall teach them, ... 5713
Isa 8:16 Bind up the t., seal the law among 8584
Isa 8:20 To the law and to the t.: if they 8584
Mt 8:4 **commanded, for a t. unto them.**...... *3142*
Mt 10:18 **a t. against them and the Gentiles.** *3142*
Mk 1:44 **commanded, for a t. unto them.**..... *3142*
Mk 6:11 **your feet for a t. against them.**...... *3142*
Mk 13:9 **for my sake, for a t. against them.**.*3142*
Lu 5:14 **commanded, for a t. unto them.**...... *3142*
Lu 9:5 **your feet for a t. against them.**...... *3142*
Lu 21:13 **And it shall turn to you for a t.**... *3142*
Joh 3:32 and no man receiveth his t.............. *3141*
Joh 3:33 He that hath received his t. hath........ *3141*
Joh 5:34 **But I receive not t. from man:**....... *3141*
Joh 8:17 **that the t. of two men is true.** *3141*
Joh 21:24 and we know that his t. is true........... *3141*
Ac 13:22 to whom also he gave t., and said, ... *3140*
Ac 14:3 which gave t. unto the word of his *3140*
Ac 22:18 **not receive thy t. concerning me.** .. *3141*
1Co 1:6 Even as the t. of Christ was.............. *3142*
1Co 2:1 declaring unto you the t. of God. *3142*
2Co 1:12 is this, the t. of our conscience,......... *3142*
2Th 1:10 our t. among you was believed)......... *3142*
2Ti 1:8 ashamed of the t. of our Lord, ... *3142*
Heb 3:5 a t. of those things which were to be.. *3142*
Heb 11:5 had this t., that he pleased God.......... *3140*
Re 1:2 God, and of the t. of Jesus Christ, ... *3141*
Re 1:9 God, and for the t. of Jesus Christ. *3141*
Re 6:9 God, and for the t. which they held: *3141*
Re 11:7 they shall have finished their t., ... *3141*
Re 12:11 Lamb, and by the word of their t.; *3141*
Re 12:17 God, and have the t. of Jesus Christ.. *3141*
Re 15:5 the tabernacle of the t. in heaven....... *3142*
Re 19:10 brethren that have the t. of Jesus:...... *3141*
Re 19:10 t. of Jesus is the spirit of prophecy..... *3141*

TETH (tayth)
Ps 119:65 *title* [ט] T...

TETRARCH
Mt 14:1 Herod the t. heard of the fame of *5076*
Lu 3:1 and Herod being t. of Galilee, and...... *5075*
Lu 3:1 his brother Philip t. of Ituraea and...... *5075*
Lu 3:1 and Lysanias the t. of Abilene, ... *5075*
Lu 3:19 Herod the t., being reproved by *5076*
Lu 9:7 Herod the t. heard of all that was *5076*
Ac 13:1 been brought up with Herod the t.. .... *5076*

THADDAEUS (thad-de'-us) See also JUDE; LEBBAEUS.
Mt 10:3 Lebbaeus, whose surname was T.; *2280*
Mk 3:18 the son of Alphaeus, and T., and........ *2280*

THAHASH (tha'-hash)
Ge 22:24 Gaham, and T., and Maachah. 8477

THAMAH (tha'-mah) See also TAMAH.
Ezr 2:53 of Sisera, the children of **T.** 8547

THAMAR (tha'-mar) See also TAMAR.
Mt 1:3 begat Phares and Zara of **T.**............. *2283*

THAN
Ge 3:1 more subtle **t.** any beast of the field ....
Ge 4:13 My punishment is greater **t.** I can bear......
Ge 19:9 we deal worse with thee, **t.** with them. .....
Ge 25:23 shall be stronger **t.** the other people; ....
Ge 26:16 us; for thou art much mightier **t.** we. ....
Ge 29:19 **t.** that I should give her to another..........
Ge 29:30 and he loved also Rachel more **t.** Leah, ...
Ge 34:19 more honourable **t.** all the house of..........
Ge 36:7 riches were more **t.** that they might ....
Ge 37:3 loved Joseph more **t.** all his children,........
Ge 37:4 their father loved him more **t.** all his.........
Ge 38:26 She hath been more righteous **t.** I; ....
Ge 39:9 none greater in this house **t.** I; 4480
Ge 41:40 in the throne will I be greater **t.** thou........
Ge 48:19 younger brother shall be greater **t.** he, ...
Ex 1:9 of Israel are more and mightier **t.** we: ......
Ex 14:12 **t.** that we should die in the wilderness. .....
Ex 18:11 that the Lord is greater **t.** all gods:..........
Ex 30:15 poor shall not give less **t.** half a shekel, ...
Ex 36:5 much more **t.** enough for the service ....
Le 13:3 sight be deeper **t.** the skin of his flesh, ...
Le 13:4 and in sight be not deeper **t.** the skin,.......
Le 13:20 it be in sight lower **t.** the skin, ...
Le 13:21 if it be not lower **t.** the skin, but be ... 4480
Le 13:25 it be in sight deeper **t.** the skin; 4480
Le 13:26 and it be no lower **t.** the other skin, ... 4480
Le 13:30 be in sight deeper **t.** the skin; and...... 4480
Le 13:31 it be not in sight deeper **t.** the skin; ... 4480
Le 13:32 be not in sight deeper **t.** the skin; 4480
Le 13:34 nor be in sight deeper **t.** the skin; 4480
Le 14:37 which in sight are lower **t.** the wall; 4480
Le 27:8 But if he be poorer **t.** thy estimation, ...
Nu 3:46 which are more **t.** the Levites; 5921
Nu 13:31 for they are stronger **t.** we. ....
Nu 14:12 a greater nation and mightier **t.** they. ....
Nu 22:15 more, and more honourable **t.** they...........
Nu 24:7 and his king shall be higher **t.** Agag. ....
De 1:28 The people is greater and taller **t.** we; ......
De 4:38 thee greater and mightier **t.** thou art,........
De 7:1 nations greater and mightier **t.** thou; ....
De 7:7 ye were more in number **t.** any people; .....
De 7:17 heart, These nations are more **t.** I; ....
De 9:1 nations greater and mightier **t.** thyself, ...
De 9:14 a nation mightier and greater **t.** they. ....
De 11:23 nations and mightier **t.** yourselves. ....
De 20:1 and a people more **t.** thou, be not ....
Jos 10:2 and because it was greater **t.** Ai, ... 4480
Jos 10:11 **t.** they whom the children of Israel...........
Jg 2:19 themselves more **t.** their fathers, ...
Jg 8:2 better **t.** the vintage of Abiezer? ....
Jg 11:25 art thou any thing better **t.** Balak the........
Jg 14:18 went down, What is sweeter **t.** honey?......
Jg 14:18 and what is stronger **t.** a lion? And he.......
Jg 15:2 is not her younger sister fairer **t.** she? ......
Jg 15:3 be more blameless **t.** the Philistines, ...
Jg 16:30 more **t.** they which he slew in his life..........
Ru 3:10 the latter end **t.** at the beginning, ... 4480
Ru 3:12 howbeit there is a kinsman nearer **t.** I.......
Ru 4:15 which is better to thee **t.** seven sons, ...
1Sa 1:8 am not I better to thee **t.** ten sons?..........
1Sa 9:2 of Israel a goodlier person **t.** he: ....
1Sa 9:2 he was higher **t.** any of the people...........
1Sa 10:23 he was higher **t.** any of the people............
1Sa 15:22 Behold, to obey is better **t.** sacrifice, ...
1Sa 15:22 and to hearken **t.** the fat of rams.............
1Sa 15:28 of thine, that is better **t.** thou.................
1Sa 18:30 wisely **t.** all the servants of Saul;.............
1Sa 24:17 to David, Thou art more righteous **t.** I: .....
1Sa 27:1 me **t.** that I should speedily escape..... 3588
2Sa 1:23 divided: they were swifter **t.** eagles, ...
2Sa 1:23 eagles, they were stronger **t.** lions. ....
2Sa 6:22 And I will yet be more vile **t.** thus, and.....
2Sa 13:14 but, being stronger **t.** she, forced her, ...
2Sa 13:15 he hated her was greater **t.** the love.........
2Sa 13:16 greater **t.** the other that thou didst...........
2Sa 17:14 is better **t.** the counsel of Ahithophel. ....
2Sa 18:8 more people that day **t.** the sword....... 834
2Sa 19:7 worse unto thee **t.** all the evil that...........
2Sa 19:43 have also more right in David **t.** ye:.........
2Sa 19:43 fiercer **t.** the words of the men of Israel....
2Sa 20:5 he tarried longer **t.** the set time......... 4480
2Sa 20:6 do us more harm **t.** did Absalom: 4480
2Sa 23:23 was more honourable **t.** the thirty, ... 4480
1Ki 1:37 greater **t.** the throne of my lord king ....
1Ki 1:47 name of Solomon better **t.** thy name, ...
1Ki 1:47 make his throne greater **t.** thy throne. ......
1Ki 2:32 men more righteous and better **t.** he,.........
1Ki 4:31 For he was wiser **t.** all men, ...
1Ki 4:31 **t.** Ethan the Ezrahite, and Heman, and......
1Ki 12:10 shall be thicker **t.** my father's loins. ....
1Ki 16:25 did worse **t.** all that..............................
1Ki 16:33 to anger **t.** all the kings of Israel that........
1Ki 19:4 life; for I am not better **t.** my fathers........
1Ki 20:23 therefore they were stronger **t.** we; ....
1Ki 20:23, 25 we shall be stronger **t.** they. ....
1Ki 21:2 give thee for it a better vineyard **t.** it;.......
2Ki 5:12 better **t.** all the waters of Israel?.............
2Ki 6:16 us are more **t.** they that be with them. .....
2Ki 9:35 no more of her **t.** the skull, ... 3588,518
2Ki 21:9 to do more evil **t.** did the nations 4480
1Ch 4:9 was more honourable **t.** his brethren: ....
1Ch 11:21 he was more honourable **t.** the two; ....
1Ch 24:4 Eleazar **t.** of the sons of Ithamar; 4480
2Ch 10:10 shall be thicker **t.** my father's loins. ....
2Ch 21:13 house, which were better **t.** thyself: ....
2Ch 20:25 more **t.** they could carry away: and...... 369
2Ch 25:9 is able to give thee much more **t.** this. ......
2Ch 29:34 to sanctify themselves **t.** the priests..........
2Ch 30:18 passover otherwise **t.** it was written. ....
2Ch 32:7 for there be more with us **t.** with him: ......
2Ch 33:9 and to do worse **t.** the heathen, ... 4480
Ezr 9:13 punished us less **t.** our iniquities..............
Es 1:19 unto another that is better **t.** she. ....
Es 2:17 favour in his sight more **t.** all the ....
Es 4:13 the king's house, more **t.** all the Jews. ......
Es 6:6 delight to do honour more **t.** to myself? .....
Job 3:21 dig for it more **t.** for hid treasures;...........
Job 4:17 Shall mortal man be more just **t.** God? ......
Job 4:17 shall a man be more pure **t.** his maker? .....
Job 6:3 be heavier **t.** the sand of the sea:............
Job 7:6 My days are swifter **t.** a weaver's............
Job 7:15 strangling, and death rather **t.** my life........
Job 9:25 Now my days are swifter **t.** a post: 4480
Job 11:6 God exacteth of thee less **t.** thine............
Job 11:8 deeper **t.** hell; what canst thou know? ....
Job 11:9 thereof is longer **t.** the earth, ... 4480
Job 11:9 the earth, and broader **t.** the sea. 4480
Job 11:17 age shall be clearer **t.** the noonday; ....
Job 15:10 aged men, much elder **t.** thy father...........
Job 23:2 stroke is heavier **t.** my groaning......... 5921
Job 23:12 his mouth more **t.** my necessary food........
Job 30:1 are younger **t.** I have me in derision, ...
Job 30:8 men; they were viler **t.** the earth....... 4480
Job 32:2 he justified himself rather **t.** God......... 4480
Job 32:4 spoken, because they were elder **t.** he. .....
Job 33:12 thee, that God is greater **t.** man. ....
Job 33:25 His flesh shall be fresher **t.** a child's: ....
Job 34:19 regardeth the rich more **t.**...poor?...... 6440
Job 34:23 will not lay upon man more **t.** right;..........
Job 35:2 My righteousness is more **t.** God's?..........
Job 35:5 the clouds which are higher **t.** thou...........
Job 35:11 Who teacheth us more **t.** the beasts of......
Job 35:11 and maketh us wiser **t.** the fowls of..........
Job 36:21 hast thou chosen rather **t.** affliction. ....
Job 42:12 latter end of Job more **t.** his beginning:.......
Ps 4:7 more **t.** in the time that their corn and......
Ps 8:5 made him a little lower **t.** the angels, ...
Ps 19:10 are they **t.** gold, yea, **t.** much fine gold: ....
Ps 19:10 sweeter also **t.** honey and...honeycomb. ......
Ps 37:16 is better **t.** the riches of many wicked. ......
Ps 40:5 they are more **t.** can be numbered. ....
Ps 40:12 are more **t.** the hairs of mine head: ....
Ps 45:2 Thou art fairer **t.** the children of men:.......
Ps 51:7 wash me, and I shall be whiter **t.** snow. ....
Ps 52:3 Thou lovest evil more **t.** good; and...........
Ps 52:3 lying rather **t.** to speak righteousness........
Ps 55:21 of his mouth were smoother **t.** butter........
Ps 55:21 his words were softer **t.** oil, yet were.......
Ps 61:2 lead me to the rock that is higher **t.** I. ......
Ps 62:9 they are altogether lighter **t.** vanity...........
Ps 63:3 thy lovingkindness is better **t.** life, 1232,1233
Ps 69:4 are more **t.** the hairs of mine head: ....
Ps 69:31 please the Lord better **t.** an ox or............
Ps 73:7 they have more **t.** heart could wish...........
Ps 76:4 excellent **t.** the mountains of prey. ....
Ps 84:10 in thy courts is better **t.** a thousand..........
Ps 84:10 **t.** to dwell in the tents of wickedness........
Ps 87:2 Zion more **t.** all the dwellings of Jacob, ...
Ps 89:27 higher **t.** the kings of the earth. ....
Ps 93:4 mightier **t.** the noise of many waters,........
Ps 93:4 yea, **t.** the mighty waves of the sea...........
Ps 105:24 made them stronger **t.** their enemies ....
Ps 118:8 trust . . . Lord **t.** to put confidence in man..
Ps 118:9 Lord **t.** to put confidence in princes. ....
Ps 119:72 unto me **t.** thousands of gold and.............
Ps 119:98 hast made me wiser **t.** mine enemies: ....
Ps 119:99 understanding **t.** all my teachers:.............
Ps 119:100 I understand more **t.** the ancients,...........
Ps 119:103 yea, sweeter **t.** honey to my mouth! ....
Ps 130:6 Lord more **t.** they that watch for the ....
Ps 130:6 I say, more **t.** they that watch for the.......
Ps 139:18 they are more in number **t.** the sand:.........
Ps 142:6 persecutors; for they are stronger **t.** I.......
Pr 3:14 it is better **t.** the merchandise of silver......
Pr 3:14 silver, and the gain thereof **t.** fine gold. .....
Pr 3:15 She is more precious **t.** rubies: and all.......
Pr 5:3 and her mouth is smoother **t.** oil: ....
Pr 8:10 and knowledge rather **t.** choice gold...........
Pr 8:11 For wisdom is better **t.** rubies; and all.......
Pr 8:19 is better **t.** gold, yea, **t.** fine gold; ....
Pr 11:24 is that withholdeth more **t.** is meet, ...
Pr 12:9 is better **t.** he that honoureth himself, ...
Pr 12:26 is more excellent **t.** his neighbour:............
Pr 15:16 **t.** great treasure and trouble therewith. .....
Pr 15:17 is, **t.** a stalled ox and hatred therewith. .....
Pr 16:8 **t.** great revenues without right. ....
Pr 16:16 much better is it to get wisdom **t.** gold!.....
Pr 16:16 rather to be chosen **t.** silver! ....
Pr 16:19 **t.** to divide the spoil with the proud.... 1229
Pr 16:32 slow to anger is better **t.** the mighty;.. 1229
Pr 16:32 his spirit **t.** he that taketh a city..............
Pr 17:1 **t.** an house full of sacrifices with ....
Pr 17:10 wise man **t.** an hundred stripes into a........
Pr 17:12 meet a man, rather **t.** a fool in his folly. ....
Pr 18:19 is harder to be won **t.** a strong city: ....
Pr 18:24 friend that sticketh closer **t.** a brother. ......
Pr 19:1 **t.** he that is perverse in his lips, and is .....
Pr 19:22 and a poor man is better **t.** a liar.............
Pr 21:3 acceptable to the Lord **t.** sacrifice. ....
Pr 21:9 **t.** with a brawling woman in a wide...........
Pr 21:19 **t.** with a contentious and an angry............
Pr 22:1 is rather to be chosen **t.** great riches, ...
Pr 22:1 loving favour rather **t.** silver and gold. ....
Pr 25:7 **t.** that thou shouldest be put lower in........
Pr 25:24 **t.** with a brawling woman and in a ....
Pr 26:12 there is more hope of a fool **t.** of him. ......
Pr 26:16 is wiser in his own conceit **t.** seven men....
Pr 27:3 a fool's wrath is heavier **t.** them both. ....
Pr 27:5 Open rebuke is better **t.** secret love. ....
Pr 27:10 that is near **t.** a brother far off................
Pr 28:6 **t.** he that is perverse in his ways, ...
Pr 28:23 favour **t.** he that flattereth with the..........
Pr 29:20 there is more hope of a fool **t.** of him, ...
Pr 30:2 Surely I am more brutish **t.** any man, ...
Ec 1:16 wisdom **t.** all they that have been....... 5921
Ec 2:9 increased more **t.** all that were before.......
Ec 2:16 wise more **t.** of the fool for ever;....... 5973
Ec 2:24 a man, **t.** that he should eat and drink, ...
Ec 2:25 else can hasten hereunto, more **t.** I?.........
Ec 3:22 **t.** that a man should rejoice in his own......
Ec 4:2 **t.** the living which are yet alive.......... 4480
Ec 4:3 Yea, better is he **t.** both they, which ....
Ec 4:6 **t.** both the hands full with travail............
Ec 4:9 Two are better **t.** one; because they.........
Ec 4:13 wise child **t.** an old and foolish king,.........
Ec 5:1 to hear, **t.** to give the sacrifice of fools:.....
Ec 5:5 **t.** that thou shouldest vow and not pay......
Ec 5:8 for he that is higher **t.** the highest...... 5921
Ec 5:8 and there be higher **t.** they.............. 5921
Ec 6:3 that an untimely birth is better **t.** he. ....
Ec 6:5 this hath more rest **t.** the other. ....
Ec 6:8 hath the wise more **t.** the fool?.......... 4480
Ec 6:9 sight of the eyes **t.** the wandering ....
Ec 6:10 with him that is mightier **t.** he. ....
Ec 7:1 A good name is better **t.** precious ....
Ec 7:1 day of death **t.** the day of one's birth. ....
Ec 7:2 **t.** to go to the house of feasting:.............
Ec 7:3 Sorrow is better **t.** laughter: for by..........
Ec 7:5 **t.** for a man to hear the song of fools........
Ec 7:8 is the end of a thing **t.** the beginning.........
Ec 7:8 in spirit is better **t.** the proud in spirit.......
Ec 7:10 the former days were better **t.** these?.......

Ec 7:19 the wise more **t.** mighty men which.........
Ec 7:26 I find more bitter **t.** death the woman, ...
Ec 8:15 thing under the sun, **t.** to eat,...... 3588,518
Ec 9:4 living dog is better **t.** a dead lion......... 4480
Ec 9:16 said I, Wisdom is better **t.** strength: ....
Ec 9:17 more **t.** the cry of him that ruleth............
Ec 9:18 Wisdom is better **t.** weapons of war:.........
Ca 1:2 mouth: for thy love is better **t.** wine.........
Ca 1:4 will remember thy love more **t.** wine: ....
Ca 4:10 how much better is thy love **t.** wine! ....
Ca 4:10 smell of thine ointments **t.** all spices! ....
Ca 5:9,9 thy beloved more **t.** another beloved, ...
Isa 13:12 a man more precious **t.** fine gold;.............
Isa 13:12 a man **t.** the golden wedge of Ophir.........
Isa 28:20 is shorter **t.** that a man can stretch..........
Isa 28:20 narrower **t.** that he can wrap himself..........
Isa 33:19 deeper speech **t.** thou canst perceive; ....
Isa 40:17 to him less **t.** nothing, and vanity. ....
Isa 52:14 visage was so marred more **t.** any man. ....
Isa 52:14 and his form more **t.** the sons of men: ......
Isa 54:1 **t.** the children of the married wife, ...
Isa 55:9 as the heavens are higher **t.** the earth,......
Isa 55:9 so are my ways higher **t.** your ways, ...
Isa 55:9 and my thoughts **t.** your thoughts............
Isa 56:5 better **t.** of sons and of daughters:.............
Isa 57:8 has discovered thyself to another **t.** me. ....
Isa 65:5 near to me; for I am holier **t.** thou. ....
Jer 3:11 herself more **t.** treacherous Judah..............
Jer 4:13 his horses are swifter **t.** eagles. ....
Jer 7:26 neck: they did worse **t.** their fathers..........
Jer 8:3 death shall be chosen rather **t.** life by........
Jer 16:12 ye have done worse **t.** your fathers; ....
Jer 20:7 thou art stronger **t.** I, and hast ....
Jer 31:11 hand of him that was stronger **t.** he. ....
Jer 46:23 they are more **t.** the grasshoppers, and.....
La 4:6 greater **t.** the punishment of the sin of ......
La 4:7 Her Nazarites were purer **t.** snow, they ....
La 4:7 they were whiter **t.** milk, they were ....
La 4:7 were more ruddy in body **t.** rubies, ...
La 4:8 Their visage is blacker **t.** a coal; they........
La 4:9 **t.** they that be slain with hunger: ....
La 4:19 are swifter **t.** the eagles of the heaven: .....
Eze 3:9 As an adamant harder **t.** flint have I..........
Eze 5:6 wickedness more **t.** the nations,............ 4480
Eze 5:6 statutes more **t.** the countries that 4480
Eze 5:7 multiplied more **t.** the nations that 4480
Eze 6:14 more desolate **t.** the wilderness ....
Eze 8:15 see greater abominations **t.** these. ....
Eze 15:2 What is the vine tree more **t.** any tree, ...
Eze 15:2 or **t.** a branch which is among the ....
Eze 16:47 wast corrupted more **t.** they in all thy ....
Eze 16:51 thine abominations more **t.** they, ...
Eze 16:52 committed more abominable **t.** they: ....
Eze 16:52 they are more righteous **t.** thou: yea,........
Eze 23:11 corrupt in her inordinate love **t.** she,.........
Eze 23:11 more **t.** her sister in her whoredoms.........
Eze 28:3 thou art wiser **t.** Daniel; there is no..........
Eze 36:11 do better unto you **t.** at your beginnings: ...
Eze 42:5 for the galleries were higher **t.** these, ...
Eze 42:5 **t.** the lower, and..................................
Eze 42:5 **t.** the middlemost of the building. ....
Eze 42:6 straitened more **t.** the lowest and the........
Da 1:10 faces worse liking **t.** the children........ 4480
Da 1:15 fatter in flesh **t.** all the children............ 4480
Da 1:20 better **t.** all the magicians and............ 5921
Da 2:30 that I have more **t.** any living, ... 4481
Da 3:19 seven times more **t.** it was wont........ 1768
Da 7:20 was more stout **t.** his fellows. 4481
Da 8:3 one was higher **t.** the other, and.......... 4480
Da 11:2 fourth shall be far richer **t.** they all: ....
Da 11:8 more years **t.** the king of the north. ....
Da 11:13 multitude greater **t.** the former, ... 4480
Ho 2:7 then was it better with me **t.** now. ....
Ho 6:6 of God more **t.** burnt offerings..................
Am 6:2 be they better **t.** these kingdoms? 4480
Am 6:2 or their border greater **t.** your border?......
Jon 4:3 for it is better for me to die **t.** to live. ......
Jon 4:8 said, It is better for me to die **t.** to live.....
Jon 4:11 are more **t.** sixscore thousand persons ......
Mic 7:4 upright is sharper **t.** a thorn hedge ....
Na 3:8 Art thou better **t.** populous No, that ....
Hab 1:8 horses also are swifter **t.** the leopards,......
Hab 1:8 are more fierce **t.** the evening wolves: ......
Hab 1:13 art of purer eyes **t.** to behold evil, and......
Hab 1:13 the man that is more righteous **t.** he? ....
Hag 2:9 shall be greater **t.** of the former,..............
Mt 3:11 that cometh after me is mightier **t.** I,........
Mt 5:37 is more **t.** these cometh of evil...........
Mt 5:47 only, what do ye more **t.** others?.........
Mt 6:25 Is not the life more **t.** meat, and the...
Mt 6:25 meat, and the body **t.** raiment?...........
Mt 6:26 them. Are ye not much better **t.** they?..
Mt 10:15 day of judgment, **t.** for that city.... *2228*
Mt 10:31 are of more value **t.** many sparrows.....
Mt 10:37 loveth father or mother more **t.** me *5228*
Mt 10:37 loveth son or daughter more **t.** me . *5228*
Mt 11:9 unto you, and more **t.** a prophet.........
Mt 11:11 hath not risen a greater **t.** John the.....
Mt 11:11 the kingdom of heaven is greater **t.** he..
Mt 11:22 at the day of judgment, **t.** for you.. *2228*
Mt 11:24 in the day of judgment, **t.** for thee. *2228*
Mt 12:6 place is one greater **t.** the temple........
Mt 12:12 much then is a man better **t.** a sheep?.
Mt 12:41 behold, a greater **t.** Jonas is here. ......
Mt 12:42 behold, a greater **t.** Solomon is here....
Mt 12:45 other spirits more wicked **t.** himself,...
Mt 12:45 state of that man is worse **t.** the first..
Mt 18:8 **t.** having two hands or two feet..... *2228*
Mt 18:9 **t.** having two eyes to be cast into.. *2228*
Mt 18:13 **t.** of the ninety and nine which...... *2228*
Mt 19:24 **t.** for a rich man to enter into the.. *2228*
Mt 21:36 sent other servants more **t.** the first:...
Mt 23:15 more the child of hell **t.** yourselves......
Mt 26:53 more **t.** twelve legions of angels?... *2228*
Mt 27:64 last error shall be worse **t.** the first:.........
Mk 1:7 cometh one mightier **t.** I after me,.............
Mk 4:31 is less **t.** all the seeds that be in the....
Mk 4:32 and becometh greater **t.** all herbs,.......
Mk 6:11 day of judgment, **t.** for that city.... *2228*
Mk 8:14 ship with them more **t.** one loaf. *1508*
Mk 9:43 **t.** having two hands to go into...... *2228*
Mk 9:45 **t.** having two feet to be cast into.... *2228*
Mk 9:47 **t.** having two eyes to be cast into.. *2228*
Mk 10:25 **t.** for a rich man to enter into the.. *2228*
Mk 12:31 other commandment greater **t.** these. ..
Mk 12:33 is more **t.** all whole burnt offerings ....
Mk 12:43 **t.** all they which have cast into the.....
Mk 14:5 for more **t.** three hundred pence, ... *1883*
Lu 3:13 no more **t.** that which is appointed...... *3844*
Lu 3:16 one mightier **t.** I cometh, the latchet........
Lu 7:26 you, and much more **t.** a prophet..........
Lu 7:28 a greater prophet **t.** John the Baptist...
Lu 7:28 the kingdom of God is greater **t.** he.....
Lu 10:12 day for Sodom, **t.** for that city...... *2228*
Lu 10:14 Sidon at the judgment, **t.** for you.. *2228*
Lu 11:22 a stronger **t.** he shall come upon him,..
Lu 11:26 other spirits more wicked **t.** himself;...
Lu 11:26 of that man is worse **t.** the first.........
Lu 11:31 behold, a greater **t.** Solomon is here....
Lu 11:32 behold, a greater **t.** Jonas is here. ......
Lu 12:7 are of more value **t.** many sparrows.....
Lu 12:23 The life is more **t.** meat,.....................
Lu 12:23 and the body is more **t.** raiment..........
Lu 12:24 more are ye better **t.** the fowls?...........
Lu 14:8 a more honourable man **t.** thou be ....
Lu 15:7 more **t.** over ninety and nine just.. *2228*
Lu 16:8 wiser **t.** the children of light......... *5228*
Lu 16:17 **t.** one tittle of the law to fail........ *2228*
Lu 17:2 **t.** that he should offend one of...... *2228*
Lu 18:14 house justified rather **t.** the other: . *2228*
Lu 18:25 **t.** for a rich man to enter into the.. *2228*
Lu 21:3 widow hath cast in more **t.** they all:....
Joh 1:50 thou shalt see greater things **t.** these..
Joh 3:19 loved darkness rather **t.** light,....... *2228*
Joh 4:1 and baptized more disciples **t.** John, ... *2228*
Joh 4:12 Art thou greater **t.** our father Jacob, ...
Joh 5:20 shew him greater works **t.** these, that..
Joh 5:36 I have greater witness **t.** that of John:.
Joh 7:31 he do more miracles **t.** these which ....
Joh 8:53 thou greater **t.** our father Abraham, ...
Joh 10:29 which gave them me, is greater **t.** all;.
Joh 12:43 of men more **t.** the praise of God....... *2260*
Joh 13:16 The servant is not greater **t.** his lord:..
Joh 13:16 is sent greater **t.** he that sent him.......
Joh 14:12 and greater works **t.** these shall he do;.
Joh 14:28 Father: for my Father is greater **t.** I..
Joh 15:13 Greater love hath no man **t.** this, that.
Joh 15:20 The servant is not greater **t.** his lord. ..
Joh 21:15 Jonas, lovest thou me more **t.** these?...
Ac 4:19 unto you more **t.** unto God, judge *2228*
Ac 5:29 ought to obey God rather **t.** men. *2228*
Ac 15:28 you no greater burden **t.** these *4133*
Ac 17:11 These were more noble **t.** those in..........
Ac 20:35 is more blessed to give **t.** to receive. ...
Ac 23:13 more **t.** forty which had made this...........
Ac 23:21 for him of them more **t.** forty men,..........
Ac 25:6 among them more **t.** ten days,........... *2228*
Ac 26:22 saying none other things **t.** those..............
Ac 27:11 **t.** those things which were spoken...... *2228*
Ro 1:25 the creature more **t.** the Creator,....... *3844*
Ro 3:9 are we better **t.** they? No, in no wise: ......
Ro 8:37 more **t.** conquerors through him.......... *5245*
Ro 12:3 more highly **t.** he ought to think;..............
Ro 13:11 nearer **t.** when we believed.............. *2228*
1Co 1:25 foolishness of God is wiser **t.** men;..........
1Co 1:25 weakness of God is stronger **t.** men. ....
1Co 3:11 can no man lay **t.** that is laid, ... *3844*
1Co 7:9 for it is better to marry **t.** to burn...... *2228*
1Co 9:15 **t.** that any man should make my *2228*
1Co 10:22 to jealousy? are we stronger **t.** he?..........
1Co 14:5 **t.** he that speaketh with tongues, ... *2228*
1Co 14:18 speak with tongues more **t.** ye all:...........
1Co 14:19 **t.** ten thousand words in an............... *2228*
1Co 15:10 laboured more abundantly **t.** they all:.........
2Co 1:13 **t.** what ye read or acknowledge; *2228*
Ga 1:8 **t.** that which we have preached *3844*
Ga 1:9 you **t.** that ye have received, ... *3844*
Ga 4:27 more children **t.** she which hath a........ *2228*
Eph 3:8 who am less **t.** the least of all saints, ...
Php 2:3 esteem other better **t.** themselves............
1Ti 1:4 rather **t.** godly edifying which is.......... *2228*
1Ti 5:8 the faith, and is worse **t.** an infidel...........
2Ti 3:4 pleasures more **t.** lovers of God;........ *2228*
Phm 21 thou wilt also do more **t.** I say. *5228*
Heb 1:4 Being made so much better **t.** angels, ...
Heb 1:4 a more excellent name **t.** they. *3844*
Heb 2:7 him a little lower **t.** the angels;............ *3844*
Heb 2:9 was made a little lower **t.** the angels... *3844*
Heb 3:3 worthy of more glory **t.** Moses, ... *3844*
Heb 3:3 house hath more honour **t.** the house........
Heb 4:12 sharper **t.** any twoedged sword,.......... *5228*
Heb 7:26 and made higher **t.** the heavens; ....
Heb 9:23 with better sacrifices **t.** these. *3844*
Heb 11:4 a more excellent sacrifice **t.** Cain,....... *3844*
Heb 11:25 **t.** to enjoy the pleasures of sin *2228*
Heb 11:26 greater riches **t.** the treasures in.............
Heb 12:24 better things **t.** that of Abel. *3844*
1Pe 1:7 more precious **t.** of gold that perisheth, ...
1Pe 3:17 for well doing, **t.** for evil doing. *2228*
2Pe 2:20 worse with them **t.** the beginning. ....
2Pe 2:21 **t.**, after they have known it, to............ *2228*
1Jo 3:20 God is greater **t.** our heart, and..............
1Jo 4:4 in you, **t.** he that is in the world *2228*
3Jo 4 no greater joy **t.** to hear that my..............
Re 2:19 and the last to be more **t.** the first. .....

THANK See also THANKED; THANKFUL; THANKING; THANKS; THANKWORTHY.

1Ch 16:4 to **t.** and praise the Lord God of........ 3034
1Ch 16:7 first this psalm to **t.** the Lord............ 3034
1Ch 23:30 morning to **t.** and praise the Lord,...... 3034
1Ch 29:13 our God, we **t.** thee, and praise thy.... 3034
2Ch 29:31 **t.** offerings into the house of the......... 8426
2Ch 29:31 brought...sacrifices and **t.** offerings; 8426
2Ch 33:16 peace offerings and **t.** offerings, ... 8426
Da 2:23 I **t.** thee, and praise thee, O thou 3029
Mt 11:25 and said, I **t.** thee, O Father, Lord. *1843*
Lu 6:32 which love you, what **t.** have ye?... *5485*
Lu 6:33 do good to you, what **t.** have ye?... *5485*
Lu 6:34 hope to receive, what **t.** have ye?... *5485*
Lu 10:21 and said, I **t.** thee, O Father, Lord. *1843*
Lu 17:9 he **t.** that servant because...... *2192,5485*
Lu 18:11 God, I **t.** thee, that I am not as..... *2168*
Joh 11:41 I **t.** thee that thou hast heard me.. *2168*
Ro 1:8 I **t.** my God through Jesus Christ....... *2168*
Ro 7:25 I **t.** God through Jesus Christ our....... *2168*
1Co 1:4 I **t.** my God always on your behalf,..... *2168*
1Co 1:14 I **t.** God that I baptized none of you,... *2168*
1Co 14:18 I **t.** my God, I speak with tongues...... *2168*
Php 1:3 **t.** my God upon every remembrance... *2168*
1Th 2:13 this cause also **t.** we God without....... *2168*
2Th 1:3 We are bound to **t.** God always for...... *2168*
1Ti 1:12 And I **t.** Christ Jesus our Lord,... *2192,5485*
2Ti 1:3 I **t.** God, whom I serve from my. *2192,5485*
Phm 4 I **t.** my God, making mention of......... *2168*

THANKED

2Sa 14:22 bowed himself, and **t.** the king:.......... 1288
Ac 28:15 saw, he **t.** God, and took courage. *2168*
Ro 6:17 But, God be **t.**, that ye were the....... *5485*

THANKFUL See also UNTHANKFUL.
Ps 100:4 be **t.** unto him, and bless his name. 3034
Ro 1:21 him not as God, neither were **t.**; *2168*
Col 3:15 called in one body; and be ye **t.** *2170*

THANKFULNESS
Ac 24:3 most noble Felix, with all **t.**. *2169*

THANKING
2Ch 5:13 heard in praising and **t.** the Lord; 3034

THANK-OFFERINGS See THANK and OFFERINGS.

THANKS See also THANKSGIVING.
2Sa 22:50 Therefore I will give **t.** unto thee, 3034
1Ch 16:8 Give **t.** unto the Lord, call upon his 3034
1Ch 16:34 O give **t.** unto the Lord; for he is 3034
1Ch 16:35 we may give **t.** to thy holy name, 3034
1Ch 16:41 by name, to give **t.** to the Lord, 3034
1Ch 25:3 to give **t.** and to praise the Lord. 3034
2Ch 31:2 to minister, and to give **t.**, and to 3034
Ezr 3:11 and giving **t.** unto the Lord; 3034
Ne 12:24 to praise and to give **t.**, according 3034
Ne 12:31 companies of them that gave **t.**, 8426
Ne 12:38 other company of them that gave **t.** 8426
Ne 12:40 companies of them that gave **t.** 8426
Ps 6:5 in the grave who shall give thee **t.**? 3034
Ps 18:49 will I give **t.** unto thee, O Lord, 3034
Ps 30:4 give **t.** at the remembrance of his 3034
Ps 30:12 I will give **t.** unto thee for ever. 3034
Ps 35:18 thee **t.** in the great congregation: 3034
Ps 75:1 Unto thee, O God, do we give **t.**, 3034
Ps 75:1 unto thee do we give **t.**: for that 3034
Ps 79:13 we thy people...give thee **t.** for ever: 3034
Ps 92:1 good thing to give **t.** unto the Lord, 3034
Ps 97:12 give **t.** at the remembrance of his 3034
Ps 105:1 O give **t.** unto the Lord; call upon 3034
Ps 106:1 O give **t.** unto the Lord; for he is 3034
Ps 106:47 to give **t.** unto thy holy name, and 3034
Ps 107:1 O give **t.** unto the Lord, for he is 3034
Ps 118:1, 29 O give **t.** unto the Lord: for he is 3034
Ps 119:62 At midnight I will rise to give **t.** 3034
Ps 122:4 give **t.** unto the name of the Lord. 3034
Ps 136:1 O give **t.** unto the Lord; for he is 3034
Ps 136:2 O give **t.** unto the God of gods: for 3034
Ps 136:3 O give **t.** to the Lord of lords: for 3034
Ps 136:26 O give **t.** unto the God of heaven: 3034
Ps 140:13 the righteous shall give **t.** unto thy 3034
Da 6:10 prayed, and gave **t.** before his God, 3029
Mt 15:36 and gave **t.**, and brake them, *2168*
Mt 26:27 And he took the cup, and gave **t.**, *2168*
Mk 8:6 took the seven loaves, and gave **t.**, *2168*
Mk 14:23 when he had given **t.**, he gave it to *2168*
Lu 2:38 gave **t.** likewise unto the Lord, *437*
Lu 17:16 his face at his feet, giving him **t.**: *2168*
Lu 22:17 And he took the cup, and gave **t.**, *2168*
Lu 22:19 And he took bread, and gave **t.**, *2168*
Joh 6:11 when he had given **t.**, he distributed *2168*
Joh 6:23 after that the Lord had given **t.**:) *2168*
Ac 27:35 gave **t.** to God in presence of them *2168*
Ro 14:6 to the Lord, for he giveth God **t.**; *2168*
Ro 14:6 he eateth not, and giveth God **t.**. *2168*
Ro 16:4 unto whom not only I give **t.**, but *2168*
1Co 10:30 of for that for which I give **t.**? *2168*
1Co 11:24 when he had given **t.**, he brake it, *2168*
1Co 14:16 say Amen at thy giving of **t.**, *2169*
1Co 14:17 thou verily givest **t.** well, but the *2168*
1Co 15:57 But **t.** be to God, which giveth us *5485*
2Co 1:11 **t.** may be given by many on our *2168*
2Co 2:14 Now **t.** be unto God, which always *5485*
2Co 8:16 But **t.** be to God, which put the *5485*
2Co 9:15 **T.** be unto God for his unspeakable *5485*
Eph 1:16 Cease not to give **t.** for you, *2168*
Eph 5:4 convenient: but rather giving of **t.**. *2169*
Eph 5:20 Giving **t.** always for all things *2168*
Col 1:3 We give **t.** to God and the Father *2168*
Col 1:12 Giving **t.** unto the Father, which *2168*
Col 3:17 giving **t.** to God and the Father by *2168*
1Th 1:2 We give **t.** to God always for you. *2168*
1Th 3:9 for what **t.** can we render to God *2169*
1Th 5:18 In every thing give **t.**: for this is *2168*
2Th 2:13 are bound to give **t.** alway to God *2168*
1Ti 2:1 intercessions, and giving of **t.**, *2169*
Heb 13:15 of our lips giving **t.** to his name. *3670*
Re 4:9 **t.** to him that sat on the throne, *2169*
Re 11:17 We give thee **t.**, O Lord God *2168*

THANKSGIVING See also THANKSGIVINGS.
Le 7:12 If he offer it for a **t.**, then he shall 8426
Le 7:12 with the sacrifice of **t.** unleavened 8426
Le 7:13 bread with the sacrifice of **t.** of his 8426
Le 7:15 his peace offerings for **t.** shall be 8426
Le 22:29 offer a sacrifice of **t.** unto the Lord, 8426
Ne 11:17 principal to begin the **t.** in prayer: 3034
Ne 12:8 Mattaniah, which was over the **t.**, 1960
Ne 12:46 songs of praise and **t.** unto God. 3034
Ps 26:7 may publish with the voice of **t.**, 8426
Ps 50:14 Offer unto God **t.**; and pay thy vows 8426
Ps 69:30 song, and will magnify him with **t.** 8426
Ps 95:2 us come before his presence with **t.**, 8426
Ps 100:4 Enter into his gates with **t.**, and 8426
Ps 107:22 them sacrifice the sacrifices of **t.**, 8426
Ps 116:17 I will offer to thee the sacrifice of **t.**, 8426
Ps 147:7 Sing unto the Lord with **t.**; sing 8426
Isa 51:3 gladness shall be found therein, **t.**, 8426
Jer 30:19 out of them shall proceed **t.** and the 8426
Am 4:5 offer a sacrifice of **t.** with leaven, 8426
Jon 2:9 unto thee with the voice of **t.**; 8426
2Co 4:15 through the **t.** of many redound to *2169*
2Co 9:11 which causeth through us **t.** to God. *2169*
Php 4:6 by prayer and supplication with **t.** *2169*
Col 2:7 taught, abounding therein with **t.**. *2169*
Col 4:2 and watch in the same with **t.**; *2169*
1Ti 4:3 to be received with **t.** of them which *2169*
1Ti 4:4 be refused, if it be received with **t.** *2169*
Re 7:12 and wisdom, and **t.**, and honour, *2169*

THANKSGIVINGS
Ne 12:27 both with **t.**, and with singing, 8426
2Co 9:12 also by many **t.** unto God; *2169*

THANKWORTHY
1Pe 2:19 this is **t.**, if a man for conscience *5485*

THARA (tha'-rah) See also TERAH.
Lu 3:34 which was the son of **T.**, which *2291*

THARSHISH (thar'-shish) See also TARSHISH.
1Ki 10:22 the king had at sea a navy of **T.** 8659
1Ki 10:22 in three years came the navy of **T.**, 8659
1Ki 22:48 Jehoshaphat made ships of **T.** to 8659
1Ch 7:10 Zethan, and **T.**, and Ahishahar. 8659

THAT See in the APPENDIX.

THE See in the APPENDIX; also NEVERTHELESS.

THEATRE
Ac 19:29 rushed with one accord into the **t.**. *2302*
Ac 19:31 not adventure himself into the **t.**. *2302*

THEBEZ (the'-bez)
Jg 9:50 Then went Abimelech to **T.**, and 8405
Jg 9:50 encamped against **T.**, and took it. 8405
2Sa 11:21 from the wall, that he died in **T.**? 8405

THEE See in the APPENDIX; also THEE-WARD.

THEE-WARD
1Sa 19:4 his works have been to **t.** very good:

THEFT See also THEFTS.
Ex 22:3 then he shall be sold for his **t.**. 1591
Ex 22:4 If the **t.** be certainly found in his 1591

THEFTS
Mt 15:19 **fornications, t., false witness,** *2829*
Mk 7:22 **T., covetousness, wickedness,** *2829*
Re 9:21 of their fornication, nor of their **t.** *2809*

THEIR See in the APPENDIX; also THEIRS.

THEIRS
Ge 15:13 a stranger in a land that is not **t.**, 1992
Ge 34:23 and every beast of **t.** be ours?
Ge 43:34 was five times so much as any of **t.**
Ex 29:9 the priest's office shall be **t.** for a 1992
Le 18:10 for **t.** is thine own nakedness 2007
Nu 16:26 and touch nothing of **t.**, lest ye be 1992
Nu 18:9 from the fire: every oblation of **t.**,
Nu 18:9 every meat offering of **t.**, and every
Nu 18:9 and every sin offering of **t.**, and
Nu 18:9 every trespass offering of **t.**, which
Jos 21:10 Levi, had: for **t.** was the first lot. 1992
1Ch 6:54 the Kohathites: for **t.** was the lot. 1992
2Ch 18:12 I pray thee, be like one of **t.**, and 1992
Jer 44:28 whose words shall stand, mine, or **t.** 1992
Eze 7:11 of their multitude, nor of any of **t.**. 1992
Eze 44:29 dedicated thing in Israel shall be **t.**. 1992
Hab 1:6 the dwellingplaces that are not **t.**.
Mt 5:3,10 **for t. is the kingdom of heaven.** *846*
1Co 1:2 Christ our Lord, both **t.** and ours:
2Ti 3:9 manifest unto...men, as **t.** also *3588,1565*

THELASAR (the-la'-sar) See also TELASSAR.
2Ki 19:12 of Eden which were in **T.**? 8515

THEM See in the APPENDIX; also THEMSELVES.

THEMSELVES
Ge 3:7 together, and made **t.** aprons. 1992
Ge 3:8 hid **t.** from the presence of the Lord
Ge 13:11 they separated **t.** the one from the
Ge 19:11 that they wearied **t.** to find the door.
Ge 21:28 set seven ewe lambs of the flock by **t.**
Ge 21:29 ewe lambs which thou hast set by **t.**?
Ge 30:40 and he put his own flocks by **t.**, 905
Ge 32:16 of his servants, every drove by **t.**; 905
Ge 33:6 their children, and they bowed **t.**
Ge 33:7 children came near, and bowed **t.**.
Ge 33:7 near and Rachel, and they bowed **t.**.
Ge 34:30 they shall gather **t.** together against
Ge 42:6 and bowed down **t.** before him with
Ge 43:26 and bowed **t.** to him to the earth.
Ge 43:32 him by himself, and for them by **t.**, 905
Ge 43:32 which did eat with him, by **t.**: 905
Ex 5:7 let them go and gather straw for **t.** 1992
Ex 11:8 and bow down **t.** unto me, saying,
Ex 12:39 they prepared for **t.** any victual. 1992
Ex 18:26 every small matter they judged **t.**. 1992
Ex 19:22 sanctify **t.**, lest the Lord break forth
Ex 26:9 thou shalt couple five curtains by **t.**, 905
Ex 26:9 and six curtains by **t.**, and shalt 905
Ex 32:1 the people gathered **t.** together unto
Ex 32:7 the land of Egypt, have corrupted **t.**
Ex 32:26 sons of Levi gathered **t.** together unto
Ex 33:6 of Israel stripped **t.** of their ornaments
Ex 36:16 and he coupled five curtains by **t.**. 905
Ex 36:16 and six curtains by **t.**. 905
Le 15:18 they shall both bathe **t.** in water, and
Le 22:2 that they separate **t.** from the holy
Nu 6:2 shall separate **t.** to vow a vow of a
Nu 6:2 Nazarite, to separate **t.** unto the Lord:
Nu 8:7 clothes, and so make **t.** clean. 1992
Nu 10:3 shall assemble **t.** to thee at the door
Nu 10:4 of Israel, shall gather **t.** unto thee.
Nu 11:32 them all abroad for **t.** round about 1992
Nu 16:3 gathered **t.** together against Moses
Nu 20:2 gathered **t.** together against Moses
Nu 27:3 gathered **t.** together against the Lord
De 7:20 that are left, and hide **t.** from thee,
De 9:12 forth out of Egypt have corrupted **t.**;
De 31:14 and presented **t.** in the tabernacle of
De 31:20 they shall have eaten and filled **t.**,
De 32:5 They have corrupted **t.**, their spot is
De 32:27 adversaries...behave **t.** strangely,
De 32:31 even our enemies **t.** being judges.
Jos 8:27 city Israel took for a prey unto **t.**, 1992
Jos 9:2 That they gathered **t.** together, to
Jos 10:5 king of Eglon, gathered **t.** together,
Jos 10:13 had avenged **t.** upon their enemies.
Jos 10:16 fled, and hid **t.** in a cave at Makkedah.
Jos 11:14 of Israel took for a prey unto **t.**; 1992
Jos 22:12 children of Israel gathered **t.** together
Jos 24:1 and they presented **t.** before God.
Jg 2:12 about them, and bowed **t.** unto them,
Jg 2:17 other gods, and bowed **t.** unto them:
Jg 2:19 corrupted **t.** more than their fathers,
Jg 5:2 when the people willingly offered **t.**
Jg 5:9 offered **t.** willingly among the people.
Jg 7:2 lest Israel vaunt **t.** against me, saying,
Jg 7:23 gathered **t.** together out of Naphtali,
Jg 7:24 men of Ephraim gathered **t.** together,
Jg 10:17 of Israel assembled **t.** together,
Jg 12:1 men of Ephraim gathered **t.** together,
Jg 15:9 in Judah, and spread **t.** in Lehi.
Jg 20:2 presented **t.** in the assembly of the
Jg 20:14 of Benjamin gathered **t.** together out
Jg 20:20 men of Israel put **t.** in array to fight
Jg 20:22 the men of Israel encouraged **t.**,
Jg 20:22 where they put **t.** in array the first
Jg 20:30 and put **t.** in array against Gibeah,
Jg 20:33 and put **t.** in array at Baal-tamar:
Jg 20:37 and the liers in wait drew **t.** along,
1Sa 2:5 were full have hired out **t.** for bread;

1Sa 3:13 because his sons made **t.** vile, and...... 1992
1Sa 4:2 the Philistines put **t.** in array against.........
1Sa 8:4 elders of Israel gathered **t.** together,..........
1Sa 13:5 Philistines gathered **t.** together to..........
1Sa 13:6 then the people did hide **t.** in caves, ...
1Sa 13:11 Philistines gathered **t.** together at............
1Sa 14:11 discovered **t.** unto the garrison of the........
1Sa 14:11 out of the holes where they had hid **t.**.......
1Sa 14:20 that were with him assembled **t.**, ...
1Sa 14:22 which had hid **t.** in mount Ephraim, ...
1Sa 21:4 have kept **t.** at least from women............
1Sa 22:2 discontented, gathered **t.** unto him;..........
1Sa 28:4 the Philistines gathered **t.** together, ...
2Sa 2:25 of Benjamin gathered **t.** together.............
2Sa 5:18, 22 and spread **t.** in the valley of...............
2Sa 10:8 and Maacah, were by **t.** in the field...... 905
2Sa 10:15 Israel, they gathered **t.** together. ....
2Sa 10:17 the Syrians set **t.** in array against............
2Sa 16:14 came weary, and refreshed **t.** there. ....
2Sa 22:45 Strangers shall submit **t.** unto me:............
1Ki 8:2 all the men of Israel assembled **t.**............
1Ki 8:47 they shall bethink **t.** in the land...............
1Ki 18:23 let them choose one bullock for **t.**, ... 1992
1Ki 18:28 and cut **t.** after their manner with............
1Ki 20:12 they set **t.** in array against the city..........
2Ki 2:15 bowed **t.** to the ground before him. ....
2Ki 7:12 out of the camp to hide **t.** in the field, ...
2Ki 8:20 of Judah, and made a king over **t.**....... 1992
2Ki 17:17 sold **t.** to do evil in the sight of the ....
2Ki 17:32 and made unto **t.** of the lowest of...............
2Ki 19:29 eat this year such things as grow of **t.**, ...
1Ch 11:1 Then all Israel gathered **t.** to David ....
1Ch 11:10 who strengthened **t.** with him in his............
1Ch 11:14 they set **t.** in the midst of that parcel, ...
1Ch 12:8 Gadites there separated **t.** unto David ....
1Ch 13:2 that they may gather **t.** unto us: ....
1Ch 14:9 spread **t.** in the valley of Rephaim. ....
1Ch 14:13 spread **t.** abroad in the valley. ....
1Ch 15:14 sanctified **t.** to bring up the ark of the.......
1Ch 19:6 that they had made **t.** odious to David, ...
1Ch 19:7 gathered **t.** together from their cities, ...
1Ch 19:9 were come were by **t.** in the field....... 905
1Ch 19:11 they set **t.** in array against the children .....
1Ch 21:20 and his four sons with him hid **t.**..............
1Ch 29:24 submitted **t.** unto Solomon the king..........
2Ch 3:13 spread **t.** forth twenty cubits: ....
2Ch 5:3 all the men of Israel assembled **t.**............
2Ch 6:37 Yet if they bethink **t.** in the land ....
2Ch 7:3 bowed **t.** with their faces to the..............
2Ch 7:14 shall humble **t.**, and pray, and seek..........
2Ch 12:6 Israel and the king humbled **t.**, ...
2Ch 12:7 the Lord saw that they humbled **t.**, ...
2Ch 12:7 They have humbled **t.**; therefore.............
2Ch 13:7 strengthened **t.** against Rehoboam ....
2Ch 14:13 that they could not recover **t.**;.......... 1992
2Ch 15:10 gathered **t.** together at Jerusalem ....
2Ch 20:4 And Judah gathered **t.** together, to ....
2Ch 20:25 jewels, which they stripped off for **t.**, ...
2Ch 20:26 assembled **t.** in the valley of Berachah:......
2Ch 21:8 of Judah, and made **t.** a king............. 1992
2Ch 29:15 their brethren, and sanctified **t.**, ...
2Ch 29:29 that were present with him bowed **t.**, ...
2Ch 29:34 the other priests had sanctified **t.**...........
2Ch 29:34 more upright in heart to sanctify **t.** ....
2Ch 30:3 had not sanctified **t.** sufficiently, ...
2Ch 30:3 had the people gathered **t.** together..........
2Ch 30:11 Manasseh and of Zebulun humbled **t.**,........
2Ch 30:15 were ashamed, and sanctified **t.**, ...
2Ch 30:18 and Zebulun, had not cleansed **t.**, ...
2Ch 30:24 great number of priests sanctified **t.**..........
2Ch 31:18 for in their set office they sanctified **t.**........
2Ch 32:8 rested **t.** upon the words of Hezekiah........
2Ch 35:14 afterward they made ready for **t.**,........ 1992
2Ch 35:14 the Levites prepared for **t.**, and........ 1992
Ezr 3:1 people gathered **t.** together as one ....
Ezr 6:20 brethren the priests, and for **t.**.......... 1992
Ezr 6:21 such as had separated **t.** unto them ....
Ezr 9:1 have not separated **t.** from the people.......
Ezr 9:2 taken of their daughters for **t.**, ... 1992
Ezr 9:2 mingled **t.** with the people of those...........
Ezr 10:7 that they should gather **t.** together ....
Ezr 10:9 gathered **t.** together unto Jerusalem...........
Ne 4:2 feeble Jews? will they fortify **t.**?........ 1992
Ne 8:1 people gathered **t.** together as one ....
Ne 8:16 and made **t.** booths, every one 1992
Ne 9:2 Israel separated **t.** from all strangers,........
Ne 9:25 and delighted **t.** in thy great goodness. ......

Ne 10:28 that had separated **t.** from the people........
Ne 11:2 that willingly offered **t.** to dwell at...........
Ne 12:28 of the singers gathered **t.** together, ...
Ne 12:30 the priests and the Levites purified **t.**,.......
Ne 13:22 Levites, that they should cleanse **t.**, ...
Es 8:11 in every city to gather **t.** together, ...
Es 8:13 that day to avenge **t.** on their enemies. .....
Es 9:2 Jews gathered **t.** together in their............
Es 9:15 gathered **t.** together on the fourteenth......
Es 9:16 king's provinces gathered **t.** together,........
Es 9:27 upon all such as joined **t.** unto them,.........
Es 9:31 had decreed for **t.** and for their.......... 5315
Job 1:6 came to present **t.** before the Lord,..........
Job 2:1 came to present **t.** before the Lord,.........
Job 3:14 which built desolate places for **t.**; ....
Job 6:4 terrors of God do set **t.** in array ....
Job 16:10 have gathered **t.** together against me. ....
Job 24:4 the poor of the earth hide **t.** together........
Job 24:16 had marked for **t.** in the daytime: ....
Job 29:8 the young men saw me, and hid **t.**:............
Job 30:14 the desolation they rolled **t.** upon me. ....
Job 34:22 the workers of iniquity may hide **t.**. ....
Job 39:3 They bow **t.**, they bring forth their...........
Job 41:23 they are firm in **t.**; they cannot be............
Job 41:25 by reason of breakings they purify **t.**........
Ps 2:2 The kings of the earth set **t.**, and the ......
Ps 3:6 have set **t.** against me round about. ....
Ps 9:20 nations may know **t.** to be but men. ....
Ps 18:44 strangers shall submit **t.** unto me. ....
Ps 35:15 rejoiced, and gathered **t.** together:............
Ps 35:15 gathered **t.** together against me. ....
Ps 35:26 dishonour that magnify **t.** against me. ....
Ps 37:11 delight **t.** in the abundance of peace..........
Ps 38:16 slippeth, they magnify **t.** against me.........
Ps 44:10 and they which hate us spoil for **t.**............
Ps 49:6 boast **t.** in the multitude of their..............
Ps 56:6 They gathered **t.** together, they hide ....
Ps 56:6 they hide **t.**, they mark my steps, ...
Ps 57:6 the midst whereof they are fallen **t.**. ....
Ps 59:4 They run and prepared **t.** without my........
Ps 64:5 They encourage **t.** in an evil matter: ....
Ps 64:8 their own tongue to fall upon **t.**:..............
Ps 66:3 thine enemies submit **t.** unto thee. ....
Ps 66:7 nations: let not the rebellious exalt **t.**. ....
Ps 80:6 and our enemies laugh among **t.**...............
Ps 81:15 should have submitted **t.** unto him: ....
Ps 94:4 all the workers of iniquity boast **t.**? ....
Ps 94:21 They gather **t.** together against the ....
Ps 97:7 graven images, that boast **t.** of idols: ....
Ps 104:22 sun ariseth, they gather **t.** together, ...
Ps 106:28 they joined **t.** also unto Baal-peor, ...
Ps 109:29 cover **t.** with their own confusion, ...
Ps 140:8 his wicked device; lest they exalt **t.**..........
Pr 23:5 for riches certainly make **t.** wings;............
Pr 28:28 when the wicked rise, men hide **t.**:...........
Ec 3:18 might see that they **t.** are beasts. 1992
Ec 11:3 of rain, they empty **t.** upon the earth: ....
Ec 12:3 and the strong men shall bow **t.**, and ....
Isa 2:6 please **t.** in the children of strangers. ....
Isa 3:9 they have rewarded evil unto **t.**. 1992
Isa 8:21 they shall be hungry, they shall fret **t.**,......
Isa 10:31 inhabitants of Gebim gather **t.** to flee. ....
Isa 15:3 they shall gird **t.** with sackcloth:...............
Isa 22:7 and the horsemen shall set **t.** in array ....
Isa 30:2 strengthen **t.** in the strength of................
Isa 46:2 but **t.** are gone into captivity. 5315
Isa 47:14 deliver **t.** from the power of the........ 5315
Isa 48:2 For they call **t.** of the holy city, and..........
Isa 48:2 and stay **t.** upon the God of Israel; ....
Isa 49:18 all these gather **t.** together, and...............
Isa 56:6 that join **t.** to the Lord, to serve him, ...
Isa 59:6 shall they cover **t.** with their works: ....
Isa 60:4 all they gather **t.** together, they come ....
Isa 60:14 bow **t.** down at the soles of thy feet; ....
Isa 66:17 They that sanctify **t.**, and purify ....
Isa 66:17 and purify **t.** in the gardens behind.............
Jer 2:24 that seek her will not weary **t.**;...............
Jer 4:2 and the nations shall bless **t.** in him, ...
Jer 5:7 assembled **t.** by troops in the harlot's........
Jer 5:22 and though the waves thereof toss **t.**, ...
Jer 7:19 do they not provoke **t.** to the ....
Jer 9:5 and weary **t.** to commit iniquity.................
Jer 11:17 done against **t.** to provoke me 1992
Jer 12:13 they have put **t.** to pain, but shall not ....
Jer 16:6 shall men lament for them, nor cut **t.**,.......
Jer 16:6 nor make **t.** bald for them:........................

Jer 16:7 Neither shall men tear **t.** for them in.........
Jer 25:14 great kings shall serve **t.** of them also: ......
Jer 27:7 and great kings shall serve **t.** of him. ....
Jer 30:8 shall no more serve **t.** of him: ....
Jer 30:21 And their nobles shall be of **t.**, and...........
Jer 34:10 none should serve **t.** of them any ....
Jer 41:5 their clothes rent, and having cut **t.**, ...
Jer 49:29 they shall take to **t.** their curtains,...... 1992
Jer 50:9 shall set **t.** in array against her; ....
La 2:10 they have girded **t.** with sackcloth: ....
La 4:14 they have polluted **t.** with blood, so..........
Eze 6:9 and they shall lothe **t.** for the evils 6440
Eze 7:18 They shall also gird **t.** with sackcloth.........
Eze 10:17 lifted up, these lifted up **t.** also: ....
Eze 10:22 of Chebar, their appearances and **t.**. ....
Eze 14:18 but they only shall be delivered **t.**...........
Eze 26:16 they shall clothe **t.** with trembling;............
Eze 27:30 they shall wallow **t.** in the ashes:..............
Eze 27:31 shall make **t.** utterly bald for thee,............
Eze 31:14 by the waters exalt **t.** for their height, ...
Eze 34:2 shepherds of Israel that do feed **t.**!..........
Eze 34:8 the shepherds fed **t.**, and fed not my ....
Eze 34:10 the shepherds feed **t.** any more;.......... 853
Eze 34:27 hand of those that served **t.** of them. ....
Eze 37:23 defile **t.** any more with their idols,...........
Eze 43:26 it; and they shall consecrate **t.**.......... 3027
Eze 44:18 gird **t.** with any thing that causeth ....
Eze 44:25 come at no dead person to defile **t.**: ....
Eze 44:25 had no husband, they may defile **t.**. ....
Eze 45:5 ministers of the house, have for **t.**...... 1992
Da 2:43 shall mingle **t.** with the seed of men: ....
Da 10:7 upon them, so that they fled to hide **t.**. .....
Da 11:6 end of years they shall join **t.** together; .....
Da 11:14 shall exalt **t.** to establish the vision; ....
Ho 1:11 together, and appoint **t.** one head, ... 1992
Ho 4:14 for **t.** are separated with whores, ... 1992
Ho 7:14 they assemble **t.** for corn and wine, ...
Ho 9:9 they have deeply corrupted **t.**, as in..........
Ho 9:10 and separated **t.** unto that shame; ....
Ho 10:10 they shall bind **t.** in their furrows. ....
Am 2:8 And they lay **t.** down upon clothes............
Am 6:4 and stretch **t.** upon their couches, and.........
Am 6:5 invent to **t.** instruments of............... 1992
Am 6:6 anoint **t.** with the chief ointments: ....
Am 6:7 that stretched **t.** shall be removed. ....
Am 9:3 they hide **t.** in the top of Carmel,............
Mic 3:4 have behaved **t.** ill in their doings. ....
Hab 1:7 and their dignity shall proceed of **t.**...........
Hab 1:8 and their horsemen shall spread **t.**, ...
Hab 2:13 people shall weary **t.** for very vanity?........
Zep 2:8 and magnified **t.** against their border. ....
Zep 2:10 magnified **t.** against the people of ....
Zec 4:12 pipes empty the golden oil out of **t.**? ....
Zec 11:5 slay them, and hold **t.** not guilty: and........
Zec 12:3 burden **t.** with it shall be cut in pieces,......
Zec 12:7 do not magnify **t.** against Judah. ....
Mt 9:3 of the scribes said within **t.**,............ *1438*
Mt 14:2 works do shew forth **t.** in him. ....
Mt 14:15 the villages, and buy **t.** victuals.......... *1438*
Mt 16:7 they reasoned among **t.**, saying,......... *1438*
Mt 19:12 **made t. eunuchs for the kingdom**.. *1438*
Mt 21:25 And they reasoned with **t.**, saying, ... *1438*
Mt 21:38 **they said among t., This is the**...... *1438*
Mt 23:4 **but they t. will not move them with** ....
Mk 1:27 they questioned among **t.**, saying,......... *848*
Mk 2:8 that they so reasoned within **t.**, ... *1438*
Mk 4:17 **have no root in t., and so endure** .. *1438*
Mk 6:14 mighty works do shew forth **t.** in him........
Mk 6:30 apostles gathered **t.** together unto ....
Mk 6:36 into the villages, and buy **t.** bread:...... *1438*
Mk 6:51 they were sore amazed in **t.** beyond ... *1438*
Mk 8:16 they reasoned among **t.**, saying, ... *240*
Mk 9:2 into an high mountain apart by **t.**:......... *3441*
Mk 9:8 any more, save Jesus only with **t.**. *1438*
Mk 9:10 they kept that saying with **t.**, ... *1438*
Mk 9:34 way they had disputed among **t.**, ... *240*
Mk 10:26 saying among **t.**, Who then can be....... *1438*
Mk 11:31 they reasoned with **t.**, saying, If we.... *1438*
Mk 12:7 **those husbandmen said among t.**,.. *1438*
Mk 14:4 some that had indignation within **t.**,..... *1438*
Mk 15:31 priests mocking said among **t.**............ *240*
Mk 16:3 they said among **t.**, Who shall roll *1438*
Lu 4:36 all amazed,and spake among **t.**, ... *240*
Lu 7:30 the counsel of God against **t.**,............ *1438*
Lu 7:49 with him began to say within **t.**,.......... *1438*
Lu 18:9 unto certain which trusted in **t.**........... *1438*

Lu 20:5 they reasoned with **t.**, saying, If we.... *1438*
Lu 20:14 **they reasoned among t., saying,**.... *1438*
Lu 20:20 which should feign **t.** just men, ... *1438*
Lu 22:23 they began to enquire among **t.**, ... *1438*
Lu 23:12 they were at enmity between **t.**. *1438*
Lu 24:12 beheld the linen clothes laid by **t.**, ... *3441*
Joh 6:52 Jews therefore strove among **t.**, ... *240*
Joh 7:35 Then said the Jews among **t.**, ... *1438*
Joh 11:55 before the passover, to purify **t.**. *1438*
Joh 11:56 spake among **t.**, as they stood in........ *240*
Joh 12:19 Pharisees therefore said among **t.**,...... *1438*
Joh 16:17 said some of his disciples among **t.**,...... *240*
Joh 17:13 **might have my joy fulfilled in t.**.... *848*
Joh 18:18 it was cold: and they warmed **t.**..............
Joh 18:28 they **t.** went not into the judgment....... *846*
Joh 19:24 They said therefore among **t.**, Let *240*
Ac 4:15 the council, they conferred among **t.**,.... *240*
Ac 5:36 of men, about four hundred, joined **t.**. ....
Ac 11:26 they assembled **t.** with the church, ...
Ac 15:32 and Silas, being prophets also **t.**, ... *846*
Ac 16:37 let them come **t.** and fetch us out. *846*
Ac 18:6 when they opposed **t.**, and blasphemed,.....
Ac 21:25 keep **t.** from things offered to idols,..........
Ac 23:12 and bound **t.** under a curse, ... *1438*
Ac 23:21 which have bound **t.** with an oath, ... *1438*
Ac 24:15 which they **t.** also allow, that there *846*
Ac 26:31 gone aside, they talked between **t.**,...... *240*
Ac 27:40 they committed **t.** unto the sea, and ....
Ac 27:43 swim should cast **t.** first into the sea,........
Ac 28:4 they said among **t.**, No doubt this....... *846*
Ac 28:25 And when they agreed not among **t.**,..... *846*
Ac 28:29 had great reasoning among **t.**. *1438*
Ro 1:22 Professing **t.** to be wise, they became.......
Ro 1:24 their own bodies between **t.**.............. *1438*
Ro 1:27 receiving in **t.** that recompence of *1438*
Ro 2:14 not the law, are a law unto **t.**.......... *1438*
Ro 10:3 submitted **t.** unto the righteousness of.......
Ro 13:2 resist shall receive to **t.** damnation. *1438*
1Co 6:9 nor abusers of **t.** with mankind,................
1Co 16:15 have addicted **t.** to the ministry *1438*
2Co 5:15 should not henceforth live unto **t.**, ... *1438*
2Co 8:3 their power they were willing of **t.**;...... *830*
2Co 10:12 with some that commend **t.**,.............. *1438*
2Co 10:12 but they measuring **t.** by **t.**,.............. *1438*
2Co 10:12 and comparing **t.** among **t.**,.............. *1438*
2Co 11:13 transforming **t.** into the apostles of ....
Ga 6:13 neither they **t.** who are circumcised...... *846*
Eph 4:19 given **t.** over unto lasciviousness, ... *1438*
Php 2:3 let each esteem other better than **t.**. .. *1438*
1Th 1:9 For they **t.** shew of us what manner *846*
1Ti 1:10 for them that defile **t.** with mankind, ...
1Ti 2:9 that women adorn **t.** in modest *1438*
1Ti 3:13 well purchase to **t.** a good degree, ... *1438*
1Ti 6:10 pierced **t.** through with many........... *1438*
1Ti 6:19 Laying up...for **t.** a good foundation *1438*
2Ti 2:25 instructing those that oppose **t.**;...............
2Ti 2:26 recover **t.** out of the snare of the devil,.....
2Ti 4:3 lusts shall they heap to **t.** teachers, ... *1438*
Tit 1:12 One of **t.**, even a prophet of their........ *846*
Heb 6:6 they crucify to **t.** the Son of God *1438*
Heb 9:23 the heavenly things **t.** with better *846*
1Pe 1:12 that not unto **t.**, but unto us they....... *1438*
1Pe 3:5 adorned **t.**, being in subjection unto *1438*
2Pe 2:1 and bring upon **t.** swift destruction...... *1438*
2Pe 2:13 sporting **t.** with their own deceivings.........
2Pe 2:19 **t.** are the servants of corruption: *846*
Jude 7 manner, giving **t.** over to fornication, ...
Jude 10 in those things they corrupt **t.**. ....
Jude 12 with you, feeding **t.** without fear: *1438*
Jude 19 These be they who separate **t.**, ... *1438*
Re 6:15 hid **t.** in the dens and in the rocks...... *1438*
Re 8:6 trumpets prepared **t.** to sound. *1438*

THEN

Ge 3:5 thereof, **t.** your eyes shall be opened, ...
Ge 4:26 **t.** began men to call upon the name...... 227
Ge 8:9 **T.** he put forth his hand, and took her,......
Ge 12:6 the Canaanite was **t.** in the land. 227
Ge 13:7 the Perizzite dwelled **t.** in the land. 227
Ge 13:9 the left hand, **t.** I will go to the right; ....
Ge 13:9 the right hand, **t.** I will go to the left. ....
Ge 13:11 **T.** Lot chose him all the plain of..............
Ge 13:16 **t.** shall thy seed also be numbered. ....
Ge 13:18 **T.** Abram removed his tent, and ....
Ge 17:17 **T.** Abraham fell upon his face, and...........
Ge 18:15 **T.** Sarah denied, saying, I laughed............
Ge 18:26 **t.** I will spare all the place for their..........
Ge 19:15 arose, **t.** the angels hastened Lot, ...
Ge 19:24 **T.** the Lord rained upon Sodom and.........
Ge 20:9 **T.** Abimelech called Abraham, and............
Ge 21:32 **t.** Abimelech rose up, and Phichol the.......
Ge 22:4 **T.** on the third day Abraham lifted up........
Ge 24:8 **t.** thou shalt be clear from this my...........
Ge 24:41 **T.** shalt thou be clear from this my...... 227
Ge 24:50 **T.** Laban and Bethuel answered and.........
Ge 25:1 **T.** again Abraham took a wife, and............
Ge 25:8 **T.** Abraham gave up the ghost, and ....
Ge 25:34 **T.** Jacob gave Esau bread and..................
Ge 26:12 **T.** Isaac sowed in that land, and...............
Ge 26:26 **T.** Abimelech went to him from Gerar, ...
Ge 27:41 hand; **t.** will I slay my brother Jacob. ....
Ge 27:45 **t.** I will send, and fetch thee from ....
Ge 28:9 **T.** went Esau unto Ishmael, and took........
Ge 28:21 in peace; **t.** shall the Lord be my God: ......
Ge 29:1 **T.** Jacob went on his journey, and ....
Ge 29:8 well's mouth; **t.** we water the sheep. ....
Ge 29:25 wherefore **t.** hast thou beguiled me? ....
Ge 30:14 **T.** Rachel said to Leah, Give me, I..........
Ge 31:8 wages; **t.** all the cattle bare speckled: ....
Ge 31:8 **t.** bare all the cattle ringstraked. ....
Ge 31:16 now **t.**, whatsoever God hath said unto......
Ge 31:17 **T.** Jacob rose up, and set his sons and......
Ge 31:25 **T.** Laban overtook Jacob. Now Jacob.........
Ge 31:33 **T.** went he out of Leah's tent, and ....
Ge 31:54 **T.** Jacob offered sacrifice upon the............
Ge 32:7 **T.** Jacob was greatly afraid and ....
Ge 32:8 **t.** the other company which is left ....
Ge 32:18 **T.** thou shalt say, They be thy servant......
Ge 33:6 **T.** the handmaidens came near, they.........
Ge 33:10 **t.** receive my present at my hand:............
Ge 34:16 **T.** will we give our daughters unto you,.....
Ge 34:17 **t.** will we take our daughter, and we.........
Ge 35:2 **T.** Jacob said unto his household, and........
Ge 37:28 **T.** there passed by Midianites..................
Ge 38:11 **T.** said Judah to Tamar his daughter ....
Ge 38:21 **T.** he asked the men of that place, ...
Ge 39:9 how **t.** can I do this great wickedness, ...
Ge 41:9 **T.** spake the chief butler unto Pharaoh, ...
Ge 41:14 **T.** Pharaoh sent and called Joseph, ...
Ge 42:25 **T.** Joseph commanded to fill their ....
Ge 42:34 **t.** shall I know that ye are no spies,..........
Ge 42:38 **t.** shall ye bring down my gray hairs ....
Ge 43:9 thee, **t.** let me bear the blame for ever: ....
Ge 44:8 **t.** should we steal out of thy lord's ....
Ge 44:11 **T.** they speedily took down every man ......
Ge 44:13 **T.** they rent their clothes, and laded ....
Ge 44:18 **T.** Judah came near unto him, and ....
Ge 44:26 brother be with us, **t.** will we go down:.....
Ge 44:32 **t.** I shall bear the blame to my father.........
Ge 45:1 **T.** Joseph could not refrain himself............
Ge 47:1 **T.** Joseph came and told Pharaoh, and.......
Ge 47:6 **t.** make them rulers over my cattle. ....
Ge 47:23 **T.** Joseph said unto the people, Behold,......
Ge 49:4 father's bed; **t.** defiledst thou it: 227
Ex 1:16 stools; if it be a son, **t.** ye shall kill him:....
Ex 1:16 but if it be a daughter, **t.** she shall live......
Ex 2:7 **T.** said his sister to Pharaoh's..................
Ex 4:25 **T.** Zipporah took a sharp stone, and..........
Ex 4:26 **t.** she said, A bloody husband thou....... 227
Ex 4:31 **t.** they bowed their heads and ....
Ex 5:15 **T.** the officers of the children of Israel ......
Ex 6:1 **T.** the Lord said unto Moses, Now...........
Ex 6:12 how **t.** shall Pharaoh hear me, who am......
Ex 7:9 **t.** thou shalt say unto Aaron, Take thy......
Ex 7:11 **T.** Pharaoh also called the wise men ....
Ex 8:8 **T.** Pharaoh called for Moses and ....
Ex 8:19 **T.** the magicians said unto Pharaoh, ...
Ex 9:1 **T.** the Lord said unto Moses, Go in..........
Ex 10:16 **T.** Pharaoh called for Moses and ....
Ex 12:21 **T.** Moses called for all the elders of..........
Ex 12:44 him, **t.** shall he eat thereof. 227
Ex 12:48 **t.** let him come near and keep it;......... 227
Ex 13:13 redeem it, **t.** thou shalt break his neck: .....
Ex 15:1 **T.** sang Moses and the children of 227
Ex 15:15 **T.** the dukes of Edom shall be 227
Ex 16:4 **T.** said the Lord unto Moses, Behold, ...
Ex 16:6 **t.** ye shall know that the Lord hath...........
Ex 16:7 **t.** ye shall see the glory of the Lord; ....
Ex 17:8 **T.** came Amalek, and fought with ....
Ex 18:2 **T.** Jethro, Moses' father in law, ...
Ex 18:23 **t.** thou shalt be able to endure, and all ......
Ex 19:5 **t.** ye shall be a peculiar treasure unto ....
Ex 21:3 **t.** his wife shall go out with him. ....
Ex 21:6 **T.** his master shall bring him unto ....
Ex 21:8 **t.** shall he let her be redeemed:................
Ex 21:11 **t.** shall she go out free without money. .....
Ex 21:13 **t.** I will appoint thee a place whither ....
Ex 21:19 **t.** shall he that smote him be quit:...........
Ex 21:23 follow, **t.** thou shalt give life for life, ...
Ex 21:28 **t.** the ox shall be surely stoned, and.........
Ex 21:30 **t.** he shall give for the ransom of his.........
Ex 21:35 **t.** they shall sell the live ox, and divide......
Ex 22:3 **t.** he shall be sold for his theft..................
Ex 22:8 **t.** the master of the house shall be ....
Ex 22:11 **T.** shall an oath of the Lord be ....
Ex 22:13 pieces, **t.** let him bring it for witness, ...
Ex 23:22 **t.** I will be an enemy unto thine ....
Ex 24:9 **T.** went up Moses, and Aaron, Nadab, ...
Ex 29:7 **T.** shalt thou take the anointing oil,...........
Ex 29:20 **T.** shalt thou kill the ram, and take of.......
Ex 29:34 **t.** thou shalt burn the remainder with........
Ex 30:12 **t.** shall they give every man a ransom.......
Ex 32:24 **t.** I cast it into the fire, and there came.....
Ex 32:26 **T.** Moses stood in the gate of the ....
Ex 34:20 him not, **t.** shalt thou break his neck.........
Ex 36:1 **T.** wrought Bezaleel and Aholiab, and........
Ex 40:34 **T.** a cloud covered the tent of the............
Ex 40:37 **t.** they journeyed not till the day that........
Le 1:14 **t.** he shall bring his offering of.................
Le 3:7 **t.** shall he offer it before the Lord. ....
Le 3:12 **t.** he shall offer it before the Lord. ....
Le 4:3 **t.** let him bring for his sin, which he ....
Le 4:14 **t.** the congregation shall offer a young.......
Le 4:28 **t.** he shall bring his offering, a kid of.........
Le 5:1 utter it, **t.** he shall bear his iniquity............
Le 5:3 knoweth of it, **t.** he shall be guilty. ....
Le 5:4 **t.** he shall be guilty in one of these...........
Le 5:7 **t.** he shall bring for his trespass, which .....
Le 5:11 **t.** he that sinned shall bring for his ....
Le 5:12 **T.** shall he bring it to the priest, and.........
Le 5:15 **t.** he shall bring for his trespass unto........
Le 6:4 **T.** it shall be, because he hath sinned,.......
Le 7:12 **t.** he shall offer with the sacrifice of..........
Le 10:3 **T.** Moses said unto Aaron, This is it.........
Le 12:2 **t.** she shall be unclean seven days;...........
Le 12:4 shall **t.** continue in the blood of her..........
Le 12:5 **t.** she shall be unclean two weeks, ...
Le 12:8 **t.** she shall bring two turtles, or two.........
Le 13:2 **t.** he shall be brought unto Aaron the........
Le 13:4 **t.** the priest shall shut him up that............
Le 13:5 **t.** the priest shall shut him up seven ....
Le 13:8 **t.** the priest shall pronounce him ....
Le 13:9 **t.** he shall be brought unto the priest; ....
Le 13:13 **T.** the priest shall consider: and, ...
Le 13:17 **t.** the priest shall pronounce him ....
Le 13:21 **t.** the priest shall shut him up seven ....
Le 13:22 **t.** the priest shall pronounce him ....
Le 13:25 **T.** the priest shall look upon it: and, ...
Le 13:26 **t.** the priest shall shut him up seven.........
Le 13:27 **t.** the priest shall pronounce him ....
Le 13:30 **T.** the priest shall see the plague: ....
Le 13:30 **t.** the priest shall pronounce him ....
Le 13:31 **t.** the priest shall shut up him that............
Le 13:34 **t.** the priest shall pronounce him ....
Le 13:36 **T.** the priest shall look on him: and, ...
Le 13:39 **T.** the priest shall look: and, behold, ...
Le 13:43 **T.** the priest shall look upon it: and, ...
Le 13:54 **T.** the priest shall command that they ....
Le 13:56 **t.** he shall rend it out of the garment, ...
Le 13:58 **t.** it shall be washed the second time, ...
Le 14:4 **T.** shall the priest command to take.........
Le 14:21 **t.** he shall take one lamb for a trespass .....
Le 14:36 **T.** the priest shall command that they ....
Le 14:38 **T.** the priest shall go out of the house......
Le 14:40 **T.** the priest shall command that they ....
Le 14:44 **T.** the priest shall come and look, and,......
Le 14:48 **t.** the priest shall pronounce the house......
Le 15:8 **t.** he shall wash his clothes, and bathe.......
Le 15:13 **t.** he shall number to himself seven ....
Le 15:16 **t.** he shall wash all his flesh in water,........
Le 15:28 **t.** she shall number to herself seven ....
Le 16:15 **T.** shall he kill the goat of the sin............
Le 17:15 until the even: **t.** shall he be clean..........
Le 17:16 his flesh; **t.** he shall bear his iniquity. ....
Le 19:23 **t.** ye shall count the fruit thereof as.........
Le 20:5 **T.** I will set my face against that man, ...
Le 22:14 **t.** he shall put the fifth part thereof..........
Le 22:27 **t.** it shall be seven days under the dam: ....
Le 23:10 **t.** ye shall bring a sheaf of the ....

Le 23:19 **T.** ye shall sacrifice one kid of the
Le 25:2 **t.** shall the land keep a sabbath unto
Le 25:9 **T.** shalt thou cause the trumpet of the
Le 25:21 **T.** I will command my blessing upon
Le 25:25 **t.** shall he redeem that which his
Le 25:27 **T.** let him count the years of the sale
Le 25:28 **t.** that which is sold shall remain in
Le 25:29 **t.** he may redeem it within a whole
Le 25:30 **t.** the house that is in the walled city
Le 25:33 **t.** the house that was sold, and the city
Le 25:35 with thee; **t.** thou shalt relieve him:
Le 25:41 **t.** shall he depart from thee, both he
Le 25:52 **t.** he shall count with him, and
Le 25:54 **t.** he shall go out in the year of jubilee,
Le 26:4 **T.** I will give you rain in due season,
Le 26:18 **t.** I will punish you seven times more
Le 26:24 **T.** will I also walk contrary unto you,
Le 26:28 **T.** I will walk contrary unto you also
Le 26:34 **T.** shall the land enjoy...sabbaths, 227
Le 26:34 **t.** shall the land rest, and enjoy her 227
Le 26:41 if **t.** their uncircumcised hearts be 227
Le 26:41 they **t.** accept of the punishment of 227
Le 26:42 **T.** will I remember my covenant with
Le 27:4 **t.** thy estimation shall be thirty
Le 27:5, 6 **t.** thy estimation shall be of the
Le 27:7 **t.** thy estimation shall be fifteen
Le 27:8 **t.** he shall present himself before the
Le 27:10 **t.** it and the exchange thereof shall be
Le 27:11 **t.** he shall present the beast before the
Le 27:13 **t.** he shall add a fifth part thereof unto
Le 27:14 **t.** the priest shall estimate it, whether
Le 27:15 **t.** he shall add the fifth part of the
Le 27:16 **t.** thy estimation shall be according to
Le 27:18 **t.** the priest shall reckon unto him the
Le 27:19 **t.** he shall add the fifth part of the
Le 27:23 **T.** the priest shall reckon unto him the
Le 27:27 **t.** he shall redeem it according to
Le 27:27 **t.** it shall be sold according to thy
Le 27:33 **t.** both it and the change thereof shall
Nu 2:7 **T.** the tribe of Zebulun: and Eliab the
Nu 2:14 **T.** the tribe of Gad: and the captain of
Nu 2:17 **T.** the tabernacle of the congregation
Nu 2:22 **T.** the tribe of Benjamin: and the
Nu 2:29 **T.** the tribe of Naphtali: and the
Nu 5:7 **T.** they shall confess their sin which
Nu 5:15 **T.** shall the man bring his wife unto
Nu 5:21 **T.** the priest shall charge the woman
Nu 5:25 **T.** the priest shall take the jealousy
Nu 5:27 **t.** it shall come to pass, that, if she be
Nu 5:28 **t.** she shall be free, and shall conceive
Nu 5:31 **T.** shall the man be guiltless from
Nu 6:9 **t.** he shall shave his head in the day of
Nu 7:89 **t.** he heard the voice of one speaking
Nu 8:8 **T.** let him take a young bullock with
Nu 9:17 **t.** after that the children of Israel
Nu 9:19 **t.** the children of Israel kept the
Nu 9:21 in the morning, **t.** they journeyed:
Nu 10:4 **t.** the princes, which are heads of
Nu 10:5 **t.** the camps that lie on the east parts
Nu 10:6 **t.** the camps that lie on the south side
Nu 10:9 **t.** ye shall blow an alarm with the
Nu 11:10 **T.** Moses heard the people weep
Nu 12:8 wherefore **t.** were ye not afraid to speak
Nu 14:5 **T.** Moses and Aaron fell on their faces
Nu 14:8 in us, **t.** he will bring us into this land,
Nu 14:13 **T.** the Egyptians shall hear it, (for
Nu 14:15 **t.** the nations which have heard the
Nu 14:45 **T.** the Amalekites came down, and the
Nu 15:4 **T.** shall he that offereth his offering
Nu 15:9 **T.** shall he bring with a bullock a
Nu 15:19 **T.** it shall be, that, when ye eat of the
Nu 15:24 **T.** it shall be, if ought be committed
Nu 15:27 **t.** he shall bring a she goat of the first
Nu 16:3 wherefore **t.** lift ye up yourselves
Nu 16:29 all men; **t.** the Lord hath not sent me.
Nu 16:30 **t.** ye shall understand that these men
Nu 18:26 **t.** ye shall offer up an heave offering of
Nu 18:30 **t.** it shall be counted unto the Levites
Nu 19:7 **T.** the priest shall wash his clothes,
Nu 19:12 **t.** the seventh day he shall not be
Nu 20:1 **T.** came the children of Israel, even
Nu 20:19 drink of thy water, **t.** I will pay for it:
Nu 21:1 **t.** he fought against Israel, and took
Nu 21:2 **t.** I will utterly destroy their cities.
Nu 21:17 **T.** Israel sang this song, Spring up, 227
Nu 22:31 **T.** the Lord opened the eyes of
Nu 27:1 **T.** came the daughters of Zelophehad,
Nu 27:8 **t.** ye shall cause his inheritance to
Nu 27:9, 10,11 **t.** ye shall give...inheritance unto
Nu 30:4 **t.** all her vows shall stand, and every
Nu 30:7 **t.** her vows shall stand, and her bonds
Nu 30:8 **t.** he shall make her vow which she
Nu 30:11 **t.** all her vows shall stand, and every
Nu 30:12 **t.** whatsoever proceedeth out of her
Nu 30:14 **t.** he establisheth all her vows, or all
Nu 30:15 them; **t.** he shall bear her iniquity
Nu 32:22 **t.** afterward ye shall return, and be
Nu 32:29 **t.** ye shall give them the land of Gilead
Nu 33:52 **T.** ye shall drive out all the inhabitants
Nu 33:55 **t.** it shall come to pass, that those
Nu 34:3 **T.** your south quarter shall be from
Nu 35:11 **T.** ye shall appoint you cities to be
Nu 35:24 **T.** the congregation shall judge
Nu 36:3 **t.** shall their inheritance be taken from
Nu 36:4 **t.** shall their inheritance be put unto
De 1:29 **T.** I said unto you, Dread not, neither
De 1:41 **T.** ye answered and said unto me, We
De 2:1 **T.** we turned, and took our journey
De 2:32 **T.** Sihon came out against us, he and
De 3:1 **T.** we turned, and went up the way to
De 3:20 **t.** shall ye return every man unto his
De 4:41 **T.** Moses severed three cities on 227
De 5:25 Lord our God any more, **t.** we shall die.
De 6:12 **T.** beware lest thou forget the Lord,
De 6:21 **T.** thou shalt say unto thy son, We
De 8:10 **t.** thou shalt bless the Lord thy God
De 8:14 **T.** thine heart be lifted up, and thou
De 9:9 **t.** I abode in the mount forty days and
De 9:23 **t.** ye rebelled against...commandment
De 11:17 **t.** the Lord's wrath be kindled against
De 11:23 **T.** will the Lord drive out all these
De 12:11 **T.** there shall be a place which the
De 12:21 **t.** thou shalt kill of thy herd and of thy
De 13:14 **T.** shalt thou enquire, and make
De 14:25 **T.** shalt thou turn it into money, and
De 15:12 **t.** in the seventh year thou shalt let
De 15:17 **T.** thou shalt take an aul, and thrust
De 17:5 **T.** shalt thou bring forth that man or
De 17:8 **t.** shalt thou arise, and get thee up
De 18:7 **T.** he shall minister in the name of the
De 19:9 **t.** shalt thou add three cities more for
De 19:12 **T.** the elders of his city shall send and
De 19:17 **T.** both the men, between whom the
De 19:19 **T.** shall ye do unto him, as he had
De 20:10 against it, **t.** proclaim peace unto it.
De 20:11 **t.** it shall be, that all the people that is
De 20:12 against thee, **t.** thou shalt besiege it:
De 21:2 **T.** thy elders and thy judges shall
De 21:12 **T.** thou shalt bring her home to thine
De 21:14 **t.** thou shalt let her go whither she
De 21:16 **T.** it shall be, when he maketh his
De 21:19 **T.** shall his father and his mother lay
De 22:2 **t.** thou shalt bring it unto thine own
De 22:8 **t.** thou shalt make a battlement for
De 22:15 **T.** shall the father of the damsel, and
De 22:21 **T.** they shall bring out the damsel to
De 22:22 **t.** they shall both of them die, both the
De 22:24 **T.** ye shall bring them both out unto
De 22:25 **t.** the man only that lay with her shall
De 22:29 **T.** the man that lay with her shall
De 23:9 **t.** keep thee from every wicked thing.
De 23:10 **t.** shall he go abroad out of the camp,
De 23:24 vineyard, **t.** thou mayest eat grapes
De 23:25 **t.** thou mayest pluck the ears with
De 24:1 **t.** let him write her a bill of
De 24:7 or selleth him; **t.** that thief shall die;
De 25:1 **t.** they shall justify the righteous, and
De 25:3 **t.** thy brother should seem vile unto
De 25:7 **t.** let his brother's wife go up to the
De 25:8 **T.** the elders of his city shall call him,
De 25:9 **T.** shall his brother's wife come unto
De 25:12 **T.** thou shalt cut off her hand, thine
De 26:13 **T.** thou shalt say before the Lord thy
De 28:59 **T.** the Lord will make thy plagues
De 29:20 but **t.** the anger of the Lord and his 227
De 29:25 **T.** men shall say, Because they have
De 30:3 That **t.** the Lord thy God will turn thy
De 31:17 **T.** my anger shall be kindled against
De 31:20 **t.** will they turn unto other gods, and
De 32:15 **t.** he forsook God which made him,
De 33:28 Israel **t.** shall dwell in safety alone:
Jos 1:8 for **t.** thou shalt make thy way 227
Jos 1:8 and **t.** thou shalt have good success. 227
Jos 1:10 **T.** Joshua commanded the officers of
Jos 1:15 **t.** ye shall return unto the land of your
Jos 2:15 **T.** she let them down by a cord
Jos 2:20 **t.** we will be quit of thine oath which
Jos 3:3 **t.** ye shall remove from your place,
Jos 4:4 **T.** Joshua called the twelve men,
Jos 4:7 **T.** ye shall answer them, That the
Jos 4:22 **T.** ye shall let your children know,
Jos 6:10 day I bid you shout; **t.** shall ye shout.
Jos 7:21 **t.** I coveted them, and took them; and,
Jos 8:7 **T.** ye shall rise up from the ambush,
Jos 8:21 **t.** they turned again, and slew the men
Jos 8:30 **T.** Joshua built an altar unto the 227
Jos 10:12 **T.** spake Joshua to the Lord in the 227
Jos 10:22 **T.** said Joshua, Open the mouth of the
Jos 10:29 **T.** Joshua passed from Makkedah,
Jos 10:33 **T.** Horam king of Gezer came up 227
Jos 14:6 **T.** the children of Judah came unto
Jos 14:11 as my strength was **t.**, even so is 227
Jos 14:12 **t.** I shall be able to drive them out,
Jos 15:1 This **t.** was the lot of the tribe of the
Jos 17:15 **t.** get thee up to the wood country, and
Jos 19:12 **t.** goeth out to Daberath, and goeth up
Jos 19:29 **t.** the coast turneth to Ramah, and to
Jos 19:34 And **t.** the coast turneth westward to
Jos 20:5 **t.** they shall not deliver the slayer up
Jos 20:6 **t.** shall the slayer return, and come 227
Jos 21:1 **T.** came near the heads of the fathers
Jos 22:1 **T.** Joshua called the Reubenites, 227
Jos 22:7 unto their tents, **t.** he blessed them,
Jos 22:19 **t.** pass ye over unto the land of the
Jos 22:21 **T.** the children of Reuben and the
Jos 23:16 **t.** shall the anger of the Lord be
Jos 24:9 **T.** Balak the son of Zippor, king of
Jos 24:20 **t.** he will turn and do you hurt, and
Jg 2:18 judges, **t.** the Lord was with the judge,
Jg 3:23 **T.** Ehud went forth through the porch,
Jg 4:8 If thou wilt go with me, **t.** I will go:
Jg 4:8 wilt not go with me, **t.** I will not go.
Jg 4:21 **T.** Jael Heber's wife took a nail of the
Jg 5:1 **T.** sang Deborah and Barak the son
Jg 5:8 new gods; **t.** was war in the gates: 227
Jg 5:11 **t.** shall the people of the Lord go down
Jg 5:13 **T.** he made him that remaineth 227
Jg 5:19 **t.** fought the kings of Canaan in 227
Jg 5:22 **T.** were the horsehoofs broken by 227
Jg 6:13 with us, why **t.** is all this befallen us?
Jg 6:17 **t.** shew me a sign that thou talkest
Jg 6:21 **T.** the angel of the Lord put forth the
Jg 6:21 **T.** the angel of the Lord departed out
Jg 6:24 **T.** Gideon built an altar there unto
Jg 6:27 **T.** Gideon took ten men of his
Jg 6:30 **T.** the men of the city said unto Joash,
Jg 6:33 **T.** all the Midianites and the
Jg 6:37 **t.** shall I know that thou wilt save
Jg 7:1 **T.** Jerubbaal, who is Gideon, and all
Jg 7:11 **T.** went he down with Phurah his
Jg 7:18 **t.** blow ye the trumpets also on every
Jg 7:24 **T.** all the men of Ephraim gathered
Jg 8:3 **T.** their anger was abated toward 227
Jg 8:7 **t.** I will tear your flesh with the thorns
Jg 8:18 **T.** said he unto Zebah and Zalmunna,
Jg 8:21 **T.** Zebah and Zalmunna said, Rise
Jg 8:22 **T.** the men of Israel said unto
Jg 9:12 **T.** said the trees unto the vine, Come
Jg 9:14 **T.** said all the trees unto the bramble,
Jg 9:15 you, **t.** come and put your trust in my
Jg 9:19 If ye **t.** have dealt truly and sincerely
Jg 9:19 **t.** rejoice ye in Abimelech, and let
Jg 9:23 **T.** God sent an evil spirit between
Jg 9:29 hand! **T.** would I remove Abimelech.
Jg 9:33 **t.** mayest thou do to them as thou
Jg 9:38 **T.** said Zebul unto him, Where is now
Jg 9:50 **T.** went Abimelech to Thebez, and
Jg 9:54 **T.** he called hastily unto the young
Jg 10:17 **T.** the children of Ammon were
Jg 11:3 **T.** Jephthah fled from his brethren,
Jg 11:11 **T.** Jephthah went with the elders of
Jg 11:17 **T.** Israel sent messengers unto the
Jg 11:18 **T.** they went along through the
Jg 11:29 **T.** the Spirit of the Lord came upon
Jg 11:31 **T.** it shall be, that whatsoever
Jg 12:3 **t.** are ye come up unto me this day,
Jg 12:4 **T.** Jephthah gathered together all the
Jg 12:6 **T.** said they unto him, Say now
Jg 12:6 **T.** they took him, and slew him at the

Jg 12:7 **T.** died Jephthah the Gileadite, and
Jg 12:10 **T.** died Ibzan, and was buried at
Jg 13:6 **T.** the woman came and told her
Jg 13:8 **T.** Manoah intreated the Lord, and
Jg 13:21 **T.** Manoah knew that he was an 227
Jg 14:3 **T.** his father and his mother said
Jg 14:5 **T.** went Samson down, and his
Jg 14:12 **t.** I will give you thirty sheets and
Jg 14:13 **t.** shall ye give me thirty sheets and
Jg 15:6 **T.** the Philistines said, Who hath
Jg 15:9 **T.** the Philistines went up, and
Jg 15:11 **T.** three thousand men of Judah went
Jg 16:1 **T.** went Samson to Gaza, and saw
Jg 16:7 **t.** shall I be weak, and be as another
Jg 16:8 **T.** the lords of the Philistines brought
Jg 16:11 **t.** shall I be weak, and be as another
Jg 16:17 **t.** my strength will go from me,
Jg 16:18 **T.** the lords of the Philistines came up
Jg 16:23 **T.** the lords of the Philistines
Jg 16:31 **T.** his brethren and all the house of
Jg 17:13 **T.** said Micah, Now know I that the
Jg 18:7 **T.** the five men departed, and came
Jg 18:14 **T.** answered the five men that went
Jg 18:18 **T.** said the priest unto them, What do
Jg 19:26 **T.** came the woman in the dawning of
Jg 19:28 **T.** the man took her up upon an ass,
Jg 20:1 **T.** all the children of Israel went out,
Jg 20:3 **T.** said the children of Israel, Tell us,
Jg 20:26 **T.** all the children of Israel, and all
Jg 21:16 **T.** the elders of the congregation said,
Jg 21:19 **T.** they said, Behold, there is a feast
Jg 21:21 **t.** come ye out of the vineyards,
Ru 1:6 **T.** she arose with her daughters in
Ru 1:9 **T.** she kissed them; and they lifted
Ru 1:18 her, **t.** she left speaking unto her.
Ru 1:21 why **t.** call ye me Naomi, seeing the
Ru 2:5 **T.** said Boaz unto his servant that
Ru 2:8 **T.** said Boaz unto Ruth, Hearest thou
Ru 2:10 **T.** she fell on her face, and bowed
Ru 2:13 **T.** she said, Let me find favour in thy
Ru 3:1 **T.** Naomi her mother in law said unto
Ru 3:13 **t.** will I do the part of a kinsman to
Ru 3:18 **T.** said she, Sit still, my daughter,
Ru 4:1 **T.** went Boaz up to the gate, and sat
Ru 4:4 redeem it, **t.** tell me, that I may know:
Ru 4:5 **T.** said Boaz, What day thou buyest
1Sa 1:8 **T.** said Elkanah her husband to her,
1Sa 1:11 **t.** I will give him unto the Lord all the
1Sa 1:17 **T.** Eli answered and said, Go in peace:
1Sa 1:22 be weaned, and **t.** I will bring him,
1Sa 2:16 **t.** take as much as thy soul desireth;
1Sa 2:16 **t.** he would answer him, Nay: but
1Sa 3:10 **T.** Samuel answered, Speak; for thy
1Sa 3:16 **T.** Eli called Samuel, and said,
1Sa 6:3 **t.** ye shall be healed, and it shall be 227
1Sa 6:4 **T.** said they, What shall be the
1Sa 6:6 **t.** do ye harden your hearts, as the
1Sa 6:9 **t.** he hath done us this great evil:
1Sa 6:9 **t.** we shall know that it is not his
1Sa 7:3 **t.** put away the strange gods and
1Sa 7:4 **T.** the children of Israel did put away
1Sa 7:12 **T.** Samuel took a stone, and set it
1Sa 8:4 **T.** all the elders of Israel gathered
1Sa 9:4 **t.** they passed through the land of
1Sa 9:7 **T.** said Saul to his servant, But,
1Sa 9:10 **T.** said Saul to his servant, Well said;
1Sa 9:18 **T.** Saul drew near to Samuel in the
1Sa 9:21 wherefore **t.** speakest thou so to me?
1Sa 10:1 **T.** Samuel took a vial of oil, and
1Sa 10:2 **t.** thou shalt find two men by Rachel's
1Sa 10:3 **T.** shalt thou go on forward from
1Sa 10:11 **t.** the people said one to another,
1Sa 10:25 **T.** Samuel told the people the manner
1Sa 11:1 **T.** Nahash the Ammonite came up,
1Sa 11:3 **t.**, if there be no man to save us, we
1Sa 11:4 **T.** came the messengers to Gibeah of
1Sa 11:14 **T.** said Samuel to the people, Come,
1Sa 12:8 **t.** the Lord sent Moses and Aaron,
1Sa 12:14 **t.** shall both ye and also the king that
1Sa 12:15 **t.** shall the hand of the Lord be
1Sa 12:21 **t.** should ye go after vain things,
1Sa 13:6 **t.** the people did hide themselves in
1Sa 14:8 **T.** said Jonathan, Behold, we will
1Sa 14:10 Come up unto us; **t.** we will go up:
1Sa 14:17 **T.** said Saul unto the people that were
1Sa 14:28 **T.** answered one of the people, and
1Sa 14:29 **T.** said Jonathan, My father hath
1Sa 14:33 **T.** they told Saul, saying, Behold, the
1Sa 14:36 **T.** said the priest, Let us draw near
1Sa 14:40 **T.** said he unto all Israel, Be ye on
1Sa 14:43 **T.** Saul said to Jonathan, Tell me
1Sa 14:46 **T.** Saul went up from following the
1Sa 15:10 **T.** came the word of the Lord unto
1Sa 15:14 What meaneth **t.** this bleating of the
1Sa 15:16 **T.** Samuel said unto Saul, Stay, and
1Sa 15:19 Wherefore **t.** didst thou not obey the
1Sa 15:30 **T.** he said, I have sinned: yet honour
1Sa 15:32 **T.** said Samuel, Bring ye hither to
1Sa 15:34 **T.** Samuel went to Ramah; and Saul
1Sa 16:8 **T.** Jesse called Abinadab, and made
1Sa 16:9 **T.** Jesse made Shammah to pass by
1Sa 16:13 **T.** Samuel took the horn of oil, and
1Sa 16:18 **T.** answered one of the servants, and
1Sa 17:9 kill me, **t.** will we be your servants:
1Sa 17:9 **t.** shall ye be our servants, and serve
1Sa 17:45 **T.** said David to the Philistine, Thou
1Sa 18:3 **T.** Jonathan and David made a
1Sa 18:30 **T.** the princes of the Philistines went
1Sa 19:5 wherefore **t.** wilt thou sin against
1Sa 19:22 **T.** went he also to Ramah, and came
1Sa 20:4 **T.** said Jonathan unto David,
1Sa 20:6 **t.** say, David earnestly asked leave of
1Sa 20:7 **t.** be sure that evil is determined by
1Sa 20:9 upon thee, **t.** would not I tell it thee?
1Sa 20:10 **T.** said David to Jonathan, Who
1Sa 20:12 I **t.** send not unto thee, and shew it 227
1Sa 20:13 **t.** I will shew it thee, and send thee
1Sa 20:18 **T.** Jonathan said to David, To
1Sa 20:19 **t.** thou shalt go down quickly, and
1Sa 20:21 **t.** come thou: for there is peace to
1Sa 20:30 **T.** Saul's anger was kindled against
1Sa 21:1 **T.** came David to Nob to Ahimelech
1Sa 21:14 **T.** said Achish unto his servants, Lo,
1Sa 21:14 wherefore **t.** have ye brought him to
1Sa 22:5 **T.** David departed, and came into the
1Sa 22:7 **T.** Saul said unto his servants that
1Sa 22:9 **T.** answered Doeg the Edomite,
1Sa 22:11 **T.** the king sent to call Ahimelech the
1Sa 22:14 **T.** Ahimelech answered the king, and
1Sa 22:15 I **t.** begin to enquire of God for 3117
1Sa 23:1 **T.** they told David, saying, Behold,
1Sa 23:3 how much more **t.** if we come to 3588
1Sa 23:4 **T.** David enquired of the Lord yet
1Sa 23:10 **T.** said David, O Lord God of Israel,
1Sa 23:12 **T.** said David, Will the men of Keilah
1Sa 23:13 **T.** David and his men, which were
1Sa 23:19 **T.** came up the Ziphites to Saul to
1Sa 24:2 **T.** Saul took three thousannd chosen
1Sa 24:4 **T.** David arose, and cut off the skirt
1Sa 25:11 Shall I **t.** take my bread, and my
1Sa 25:18 **T.** Abigail made haste, and took two
1Sa 25:31 my lord, **t.** remember thine handmaid,
1Sa 26:2 **T.** Saul arose, and went down to the
1Sa 26:6 **T.** answered David and said to
1Sa 26:8 **T.** said Abishai to David, God hath
1Sa 26:13 **T.** David went over to the other side,
1Sa 26:14 **T.** Abner answered and said, Who art
1Sa 26:15 wherefore **t.** hast thou not kept thy
1Sa 26:21 **T.** said Saul, I have sinned: return,
1Sa 26:25 **T.** Saul said to David, Blessed be
1Sa 27:6 **T.** Achish gave him Ziklag that day:
1Sa 28:7 **T.** said Saul unto his servants, Seek
1Sa 28:9 wherefore **t.** layest thou a snare for
1Sa 28:11 **T.** said the woman, Whom shall I
1Sa 28:16 **T.** said Samuel, Wherefore
1Sa 28:16 Wherefore **t.** dost thou ask of me,
1Sa 28:20 **T.** Saul fell straightway all along on
1Sa 28:25 **T.** they rose up, and went away that
1Sa 29:3 **T.** said the princes of the Philistines,
1Sa 29:6 **T.** Achish called David, and said unto
1Sa 30:4 **T.** David and the people that were
1Sa 30:22 **T.** answered all the wicked men and
1Sa 30:23 **T.** said David, Ye shall not do so, my
1Sa 31:4 **T.** said Saul unto his armourbearer,
2Sa 1:11 **T.** David took hold on his clothes,
2Sa 2:15 **T.** there arose and went over by
2Sa 2:20 **T.** Abner looked behind him, and
2Sa 2:22 how **t.** should I hold up my face to
2Sa 2:26 **T.** Abner called to Joab, and said,
2Sa 2:27 surely **t.** in the morning the people
2Sa 3:8 **T.** was Abner very wroth for the
2Sa 3:16 **T.** said Abner unto him, Go, return,
2Sa 3:18 Now **t.** do it: for the Lord hath
2Sa 3:24 **T.** Joab came to the king, and said,
2Sa 5:1 **T.** came all the tribes of Israel to
2Sa 5:24 that **t.** thou shalt bestir thyself: 227
2Sa 5:24 **t.** shall the Lord go out before thee, 227
2Sa 6:20 **T.** David returned to bless his
2Sa 7:18 **T.** went king David in, and sat before
2Sa 8:6 **T.** David put garrisons in Syria of
2Sa 8:10 **T.** Toi sent Joram his son unto king
2Sa 9:5 **T.** king David sent, and fetched him
2Sa 9:9 **T.** the king called to Ziba, Saul's
2Sa 9:11 **T.** said Ziba unto the king, According
2Sa 10:2 **T.** said David, I will shew kindness
2Sa 10:5 your beards be grown, and **t.** return,
2Sa 10:11 strong for me, **t.** thou shalt help me:
2Sa 10:11 for thee, **t.** I will come and help thee.
2Sa 10:14 **t.** fled they also before Abishai, and
2Sa 11:10 why **t.** didst thou not go down unto
2Sa 11:11 shall I **t.** go into mine house, to eat
2Sa 11:18 **T.** Joab sent and told David all the
2Sa 11:21 **t.** say thou, Thy servant Uriah the
2Sa 11:25 **T.** David said unto the messenger,
2Sa 12:18 how will he **t.** vex himself, if we tell
2Sa 12:20 **T.** David arose from the earth, and
2Sa 12:20 **t.** he came to his own house; and
2Sa 12:21 **T.** said his servants unto him, What
2Sa 13:7 **T.** David sent home to Tamar, saying,
2Sa 13:15 **T.** Amnon hated her exceedingly: so
2Sa 13:17 **T.** he called his servant that
2Sa 13:18 **T.** his servant brought her out, and
2Sa 13:26 **T.** said Absalom, If not, I pray thee,
2Sa 13:28 Smite Amnon; **t.** kill him, fear not:
2Sa 13:29 **T.** all the king's sons arose, and
2Sa 13:31 **T.** the king arose, and tare his
2Sa 14:11 **T.** said she, I pray thee, let the king
2Sa 14:12 **T.** the woman said, Let thine
2Sa 14:13 Wherefore **t.** hast thou thought
2Sa 14:17 **T.** thine handmaid said, The word of
2Sa 14:18 **T.** the king answered and said unto
2Sa 14:31 **T.** Joab arose, and came to Absalom
2Sa 15:2 **t.** Absalom called unto him, and said,
2Sa 15:8 to Jerusalem, **t.** I will serve the Lord.
2Sa 15:10 **t.** ye shall say, Absalom reigneth in
2Sa 15:19 **T.** said the king to Ittai the Gittite,
2Sa 15:33 **t.** thou shalt be a burden unto me:
2Sa 15:34 **t.** mayest thou for me defeat the
2Sa 16:4 **T.** said the king to Ziba, Behold,
2Sa 16:9 **T.** said Abishai the son of Zeruiah,
2Sa 16:10 Who shall **t.** say, Wherefore hast thou
2Sa 16:20 **T.** said Absalom to Ahithophel, Give
2Sa 16:21 **t.** shall the hands of all that are with
2Sa 17:5 **T.** said Absalom, Call now Hushai the
2Sa 17:13 **t.** shall all Israel bring ropes to that
2Sa 17:15 **T.** said Hushai unto Zadok and to
2Sa 17:22 **T.** David arose, and all the people that
2Sa 17:24 **T.** David came to Mahanaim. And
2Sa 18:14 **T.** said Joab, I may not tarry thus
2Sa 18:19 **T.** said Ahimaaz the son of Zadok,
2Sa 18:21 **T.** said Joab to Cushi, Go tell the
2Sa 18:22 **T.** said Ahimaaz the son of Zadok
2Sa 18:23 **T.** Ahimaaz ran by the way of the
2Sa 19:6 this day, **t.** it had pleased thee well. 227
2Sa 19:8 **T.** the king arose, and sat in the gate.
2Sa 19:12 wherefore **t.** are ye the last to bring
2Sa 19:35 wherefore **t.** should thy servant be
2Sa 19:40 **T.** the king went on to Gilgal, and
2Sa 19:42 wherefore **t.** be ye angry for this
2Sa 19:43 why **t.** did ye despise us, that our
2Sa 20:4 **T.** said the king to Amasa, Assemble
2Sa 20:16 **T.** cried a wise woman out of the
2Sa 20:17 **T.** he said unto him, Hear the words
2Sa 20:18 **T.** she spake, saying, They were wont
2Sa 20:22 **T.** the woman went unto all the
2Sa 21:1 **T.** there was a famine in the days of
2Sa 21:17 **T.** the men of David sware unto 227
2Sa 21:18 **t.** Sibbechai the Hushathite slew 227
2Sa 22:8 **T.** the earth shook and trembled; the
2Sa 22:43 **T.** did I beat them as small as the
2Sa 23:14 And David was **t.** in an hold, and 227
2Sa 23:14 the Philistines was **t.** in Beth-lehem.
2Sa 24:6 **T.** they came to Gilead, and to the
1Ki 1:5 **T.** Adonijah the son of Haggith
1Ki 1:13 throne? why **t.** doth Adonijah reign?
1Ki 1:28 **T.** king David answered and said,
1Ki 1:31 **T.** Bath-sheba bowed with her face to
1Ki 1:35 **T.** ye shall come up after him, that he
1Ki 2:12 **T.** sat Solomon upon the throne of

1Ki 2:20 **T.** she said, I desire one small petition
1Ki 2:23 **T.** king Solomon sware by the Lord,
1Ki 2:28 **T.** tidings came to Joab: for Joab had
1Ki 2:29 **T.** Solomon sent Benaiah the son of
1Ki 2:43 Why **t.** hast thou not kept the oath of
1Ki 3:14 did walk, **t.** I will lengthen thy days.
1Ki 3:16 **T.** came there two women, that 227
1Ki 3:23 **T.** said the king, The one saith, This
1Ki 3:26 **T.** spake the woman whose the living
1Ki 3:27 **T.** the king answered and said, Give
1Ki 6:10 **t.** he built chambers against all the
1Ki 6:12 **t.** will I perform my word with thee,
1Ki 7:7 **T.** he made a porch for the throne
1Ki 7:38 **T.** made he ten layers of brass: one
1Ki 8:1 **T.** Solomon assembled the elders 227
1Ki 8:12 **T.** spake Solomon, The Lord said 227
1Ki 8:32 **T.** hear thou in heaven, and do, and
1Ki 8:34, 36 **T.** hear thou in heaven, and
1Ki 8:39 **T.** hear thou in heaven thy
1Ki 8:45 **T.** hear thou in heaven their prayer
1Ki 8:49 **T.** hear thou their prayer and their
1Ki 9:5 **T.** I will establish the throne of thy
1Ki 9:7 **T.** will I cut off Israel out of the land
1Ki 9:11 that **t.** king Solomon gave Hiram 227
1Ki 9:24 built for her: **t.** did he build Millo 227
1Ki 11:7 **T.** did Solomon build an high place
1Ki 11:22 **T.** Pharaoh said unto them, But what
1Ki 12:5 for three days, **t.** come again to me.
1Ki 12:7 **t.** they will be thy servants for ever.
1Ki 12:18 **T.** king Rehoboam sent Adoram, who
1Ki 12:25 **T.** Jeroboam built Shechem in mount
1Ki 12:27 **t.** shall the heart of this people turn
1Ki 13:15 **T.** he said unto him, Come home with
1Ki 13:31 **t.** bury me in the sepulchre wherein
1Ki 15:18 **T.** Asa took all the silver and the gold
1Ki 15:22 **T.** king Asa made a proclamation
1Ki 16:1 **T.** the word of the Lord came to Jehu
1Ki 16:21 **T.** were the people of Israel 227
1Ki 18:21 follow him: but if Baal, **t.** follow him.
1Ki 18:22 **T.** said Elijah unto the people, I, even
1Ki 18:38 **T.** the fire of the Lord fell, and
1Ki 19:2 **T.** Jezebel sent a messenger unto
1Ki 19:5 behold, **t.** an angel touched him, and
1Ki 19:20 my mother, and **t.** I will follow thee.
1Ki 19:21 **T.** he arose, and went after Elijah,
1Ki 20:7 **T.** the king of Israel called all the
1Ki 20:14 **T.** he said, Who shall order the
1Ki 20:15 **T.** he numbered the young men of the
1Ki 20:33 **T.** he said, Go ye, bring him.
1Ki 20:33 **T.** Ben-hadad came forth to him; and
1Ki 20:34 **T.** said Ahab, I will send thee away
1Ki 20:36 **T.** said he unto him, Because thou
1Ki 20:37 **T.** he found another man, and said,
1Ki 20:39 **t.** shall thy life be for his life, or else
1Ki 21:10 **t.** carry him out, and stone him, that
1Ki 21:13 **T.** they carried him forth out of the
1Ki 21:14 **T.** they sent to Jezebel, saying,
1Ki 22:6 **T.** the king of Israel gathered the
1Ki 22:9 **T.** the king of Israel called an officer,
1Ki 22:47 There was **t.** no king in Edom: a
1Ki 22:49 **T.** said Ahaziah the son of Ahab 227
2Ki 1:1 **T.** Moab rebelled against Israel after
2Ki 1:9 **T.** the king sent unto him a captain of
2Ki 1:10 **t.** let fire come down from heaven,
2Ki 3:27 **T.** he took his eldest son that should
2Ki 4:3 **T.** he said, Go, borrow thee vessels
2Ki 4:7 **T.** she came and told the man of God.
2Ki 4:14 he said, What **t.** is to be done for her?
2Ki 4:20 sat on her knees till noon, and **t.** died.
2Ki 4:24 **T.** she saddled an ass, and said to her
2Ki 4:28 **T.** she said, Did I desire a son of my
2Ki 4:29 **T.** he said to Gehazi, Gird up thy
2Ki 4:35 **T.** he returned, and walked in the
2Ki 4:37 **T.** she went in, and fell at his feet,
2Ki 4:41 But he said, **T.** bring meal. And he
2Ki 5:13 how much rather **t.**, when he saith to
2Ki 5:14 **T.** went he down, and dipped himself
2Ki 5:17 Shall there not **t.**, I pray thee, be
2Ki 6:8 **T.** the king of Syria warred against
2Ki 6:31 **T.** he said, God do so and more also to
2Ki 7:1 **T.** Elisha said, Hear ye the word of
2Ki 7:2 **T.** a lord on whose hand the king
2Ki 7:4 **t.** the famine is in the city, and we
2Ki 7:9 **T.** they said one to anther, We do
2Ki 8:1 **T.** spake Elisha unto the woman,
2Ki 8:16 Jehoshaphat being **t.** king of Judah,
2Ki 8:22 **T.** Libnah revolted at the same 227
2Ki 9:3 **T.** take the box of oil, and pour it on
2Ki 9:3 **T.** open the door, and flee, and tarry
2Ki 9:11 **T.** Jehu came forth to the servants of
2Ki 9:13 **T.** they hasted, and took every man
2Ki 9:15 **t.** let none go forth nor escape out of
2Ki 9:19 **T.** he sent out a second on horseback,
2Ki 9:25 **T.** said Jehu to Bidkar his captain,
2Ki 10:4 before him: how **t.** shall we stand?
2Ki 10:6 **T.** he wrote a letter the second time
2Ki 12:7 **T.** king Jehoash called for Jehoiada
2Ki 12:17 **T.** Hazael king of Syria went up, 227
2Ki 13:17 **T.** Elisha said, Shoot, And he shot.
2Ki 13:19 **t.** hadst thou smitten Syria till thou 227
2Ki 14:8 **T.** Amaziah sent messengers to 227
2Ki 15:16 **T.** Menahem smote Tiphsah, and 227
2Ki 16:5 **T.** Rezen king of Syria, and Pekah 227
2Ki 17:5 **T.** the king of Assyria came up
2Ki 17:27 **T.** the king of Assyria commanded,
2Ki 17:28 **T.** one of the priests whom they had
2Ki 18:24 How **t.** wilt thou turn away the face of
2Ki 18:26 **T.** said Eliakim the son of Hilkiah,
2Ki 18:28 **T.** Rab-shakeh stood and cried with a
2Ki 18:31 **t.** eat ye every man of his own vine,
2Ki 18:37 **T.** came Eliakim the son of Hilkiah,
2Ki 19:20 **T.** Isaiah the son of Amoz sent to
2Ki 20:2 **T.** he turned his face to the wall, and
2Ki 20:14 **T.** came Isaiah the prophet unto king
2Ki 20:19 **T.** said Hezekiah unto Isaiah, Good is
2Ki 23:17 **T.** he said, What title is that that I see?
2Ki 24:1 **t.** he turned and rebelled against him.
1Ch 1:29 **t.** Kedar, and Adbeel, and Mibsam,
1Ch 2:24 **t.** Abiah Hezron's wife bare him
1Ch 6:32 **t.** they waited on their office according
1Ch 9:36 And his firstborn son Abdon, **t.** Zur,
1Ch 10:4 **T.** said Saul to his armourbearer,
1Ch 10:7 **t.** they forsook their cities, and fled:
1Ch 11:1 **T.** all Israel gathered themselves to
1Ch 11:16 And David was **t.** in the hold, and 227
1Ch 11:16 garrison was **t.** at Beth-lehem. 227
1Ch 12:3 The chief was Ahiezer, **t.** Joash, the
1Ch 12:18 **T.** the spirit came upon Amasai, who
1Ch 12:18 **T.** David received them, and made
1Ch 14:11 **T.** David said, God hath broken in
1Ch 14:15 that **t.** thou shalt go out to battle: 227
1Ch 15:2 **T.** David said, None ought to carry 227
1Ch 16:7 **T.** on that day David delivered first 227
1Ch 16:33 **T.** shall the trees of the wood sing 227
1Ch 17:2 **T.** Nathan said unto David, Do all
1Ch 18:6 **T.** David put garrisons in
1Ch 19:5 **T.** there went certain, and told David
1Ch 19:5 your beards be grown, and **t.** return.
1Ch 19:12 strong for me, **t.** thou shalt help me:
1Ch 19:12 strong for thee, **t.** I will help thee.
1Ch 19:15 city. **T.** Joab came to Jerusalem.
1Ch 21:3 why **t.** doth my lord require this
1Ch 21:16 **T.** David and the elders of Israel, who
1Ch 21:18 **T.** the angel of the Lord commanded
1Ch 21:22 **T.** David said to Ornan, Grant me the
1Ch 21:28 the Jebusite, **t.** he sacrificed there.
1Ch 22:1 **T.** David said, This is the house of
1Ch 22:6 **T.** he called for Solomon his son, and
1Ch 22:13 **T.** shalt thou prosper, if thou 227
1Ch 26:14 **T.** for Zechariah his son, a wise
1Ch 28:2 **T.** David the king stood up upon his
1Ch 28:11 **T.** David gave to Solomon his son the
1Ch 29:5 And who **t.** is willing to consecrate his
1Ch 29:6 **T.** the chief of the fathers and princes
1Ch 29:9 **T.** the people rejoiced, for that they
1Ch 29:23 **T.** Solomon sat on the throne of the
2Ch 1:2 **T.** Solomon spake unto all Israel, to
2Ch 1:13 **T.** Solomon came from his journey to
2Ch 2:6 who am I **t.**, that I should build him a
2Ch 2:11 **T.** Huram the king of Tyre answered
2Ch 3:1 **T.** Solomon began to build the house
2Ch 5:2 **T.** Solomon assembled the elders 227
2Ch 5:11 and did not **t.** wait by course:
2Ch 5:13 **t.** the house was filled with a cloud,
2Ch 6:1 **T.** said Solomon, the Lord hath 227
2Ch 6:17 Now **t.**, O Lord God of Israel, let thy
2Ch 6:23 **T.** hear thou from heaven, and do,
2Ch 6:25 **T.** hear thou from the heavens, and
2Ch 6:27 **T.** hear thou from heaven, and forgive
2Ch 6:29 **T.** what prayer or what supplication
2Ch 6:30 **T.** hear thou from heaven thy
2Ch 6:33 **T.** hear thou from the heavens, even
2Ch 6:35 **T.** hear thou from the heavens their
2Ch 6:39 **T.** hear thou from the heavens, even
2Ch 7:4 **T.** the king and all the people offered
2Ch 7:14 **t.** will I hear from heaven, and will
2Ch 7:18 **T.** will I stablish the throne of thy
2Ch 7:20 **T.** will I pluck them up by the roots
2Ch 8:12 **T.** Solomon offered burnt offerings 227
2Ch 8:17 **T.** went Solomon to Ezion-geber, 227
2Ch 10:18 **T.** king Rehoboam sent Hadoram that
2Ch 12:5 **T.** came Shemaiah the prophet to
2Ch 13:15 **T.** the men of Judah gave a shout:
2Ch 14:10 **T.** Asa went out against him, and
2Ch 16:2 **T.** Asa brought out silver and gold
2Ch 16:6 **T.** Asa the king took all Judah; and
2Ch 16:10 **T.** Asa was wroth with the seer, and
2Ch 18:16 **T.** he said, I did see all Israel
2Ch 18:20 **T.** there came out a spirit, and stood
2Ch 18:23 **T.** Zedekiah the son of Chenaanah
2Ch 18:25 **T.** the king of Israel said, Take ye
2Ch 18:27 **t.** hath not the Lord spoken by me.
2Ch 20:2 **T.** there came some that told
2Ch 20:9 affliction, **t.** thou wilt hear and help.
2Ch 20:14 **T.** upon Jahaziel the son of
2Ch 20:27 **T.** they returned, every man of Judah
2Ch 20:37 **T.** Eliezer the son of Dodavah of
2Ch 21:9 **T.** Jehoram went forth with his
2Ch 23:11 **T.** they brought out the king's son,
2Ch 23:13 **T.** Athaliah rent her clothes, and said,
2Ch 23:14 **T.** Jehoiada the priest brought out
2Ch 23:17 **T.** all the people went to the house of
2Ch 24:17 **T.** the king hearkened unto them.
2Ch 25:10 **T.** Amaziah separated them, to wit,
2Ch 25:16 **T.** the prophet forbare, and said, I
2Ch 25:17 **T.** Amaziah king of Judah took
2Ch 26:1 **T.** all the people of Judah took
2Ch 26:19 **T.** Uzziah was wroth, and had a
2Ch 28:12 **T.** certain of the heads of the children
2Ch 28:15 brethren: **t.** they returned to Samaria.
2Ch 29:12 **T.** the Levites arose, Mahath the son
2Ch 29:18 **T.** they went in to Hezekiah the king,
2Ch 29:20 **T.** Hezekiah the king rose early, and
2Ch 29:31 **T.** Hezekiah answered and said, Now
2Ch 30:15 **T.** they killed the passover on the
2Ch 30:27 **T.** the priests the Levites arose and
2Ch 31:1 **T.** all the children of Israel returned,
2Ch 31:9 **T.** Hezekiah questioned with the
2Ch 31:11 **T.** Hezekiah commanded to prepare
2Ch 32:18 **T.** they cried with a loud voice in the
2Ch 33:13 **T.** Manasseh knew that the Lord he
2Ch 34:18 **T.** Shaphan the scribe told the king,
2Ch 34:29 **T.** the king sent and gathered
2Ch 36:1 **T.** the people of the land took
Ezr 1:5 **T.** rose up the chief of the fathers of
Ezr 3:2 **T.** stood up Jeshua the son of
Ezr 3:9 **T.** stood Jeshua with his sons and his
Ezr 4:2 **T.** they came to Zerubbabel, and to
Ezr 4:4 **T.** the people of the land weakened
Ezr 4:9 **T.** wrote Rehum the chancellor, 116
Ezr 4:13 **t.** will they not pay toll, tribute, and
Ezr 4:17 **T.** sent the king an answer unto
Ezr 4:24 **T.** ceased the work of the house of 116
Ezr 5:1 **T.** the prophets, Haggai the prophet,
Ezr 5:2 **T.** rose up Zerubbabel the son of 116
Ezr 5:4 **T.** said we unto them after this 116
Ezr 5:5 **t.** they returned answer by letter 116
Ezr 5:9 **T.** asked we those elders, and said 116
Ezr 5:16 **T.** came the same Sheshbazzar, and 116
Ezr 6:1 **T.** Darius the king made a decree, 116
Ezr 6:13 **T.** Tatnai, governor on this side the 116
Ezr 8:16 **T.** sent I for Eliezer, for Ariel, for
Ezr 8:21 **T.** I proclaimed a fast there, at the
Ezr 8:24 **T.** I separated twelve of the chief of
Ezr 8:31 **T.** we departed from the river of
Ezr 9:4 **T.** were assembled unto me every one
Ezr 10:5 **T.** arose Ezra, and made the chief
Ezr 10:6 **T.** Ezra rose up from before the
Ezr 10:9 **T.** all the men of Judah and
Ezr 10:12 **T.** all the congregation answered and
Ne 2:2 of heart. **T.** I was very sore afraid
Ne 2:4 **T.** the king said unto me, For what
Ne 2:9 **T.** I came to the governors beyond the
Ne 2:14 **T.** I went on to the gate of the
Ne 2:15 **T.** went I up in the night by the
Ne 2:17 **T.** said I unto them, Ye see the
Ne 2:18 **T.** I told them of the hand of my God
Ne 2:20 **T.** answered I them, and said unto
Ne 3:1 **T.** Eliashib the high priest rose up
Ne 4:7 to be stopped, **t.** they were very wroth,
Ne 5:7 **T.** I consulted with myself, and I

Ne 5:8 **T.** held they their peace, and found
Ne 5:12 **T.** said they, We will restore them, and
Ne 5:12 **T.** I called the priests, and took an
Ne 6:5 **T.** sent Sanballat his servant unto me
Ne 6:8 **T.** I sent unto him, saying, There are
Ne 8:10 **T.** he said unto them, Go your way,
Ne 9:4 **T.** stood up upon the stairs, of the
Ne 9:5 **T.** the Levites, Jeshua, and Kadmiel,
Ne 12:31 **T.** I brought up the princes of Judah
Ne 13:9 **T.** I commanded, and they cleansed
Ne 13:11 **T.** contended I with the rulers, and
Ne 13:12 **T.** brought all Judah the tithe of the
Ne 13:17 **T.** I contended with the nobles of
Ne 13:21 **T.** I testified against them, and said
Ne 13:27 Shall we **t.** hearken unto you to do all
Es 1:13 **T.** the king said to the wise men,
Es 2:2 **T.** said the king's servants that
Es 2:13 **T.** thus came every maiden unto the
Es 2:18 **T.** the king made a great feast unto
Es 2:19 **t.** Mordecai sat in the king's gate.
Es 3:3 **T.** the king's servants, which were in
Es 3:5 reverence, **t.** was Haman full of wrath.
Es 3:12 **T.** were the king's scribes called on
Es 4:4 **T.** was the queen exceedingly grieved;
Es 4:5 **T.** called Esther for Hatach, one of the
Es 4:13 **T.** Mordecai commanded to answer
Es 4:14 **t.** shall there enlargement and
Es 4:15 **T.** Esther bade them return Mordecai
Es 5:3 **T.** said the king unto her, What wilt
Es 5:5 **T.** the king said, Cause Haman to
Es 5:7 **T.** answered Esther, and said, My
Es 5:9 **T.** went Haman forth that day joyful
Es 5:14 **T.** said Zeresh his wife and all his
Es 5:14 **t.** go thou in merrily with the king
Es 6:3 **T.** said the king's servants that
Es 6:10 **T.** the king said to Haman, Make
Es 6:11 **T.** took Haman the apparel and the
Es 6:13 **T.** said his wise men and Zeresh his
Es 7:3 **T.** Esther the queen answered and
Es 7:5 **T.** the king Ahasuerus answered and
Es 7:6 **T.** Haman was afraid before the king
Es 7:8 **T.** the king returned out of the palace
Es 7:8 **T.** said the king, Will he force the
Es 7:9 **T.** the king said, Hang him thereon.
Es 7:10 **T.** was the king's wrath pacified.
Es 8:4 **T.** the king held out the golden
Es 8:7 **T.** the king Ahasuerus said unto
Es 8:9 **T.** were the king's scribes called at
Es 9:13 **T.** said Esther, If it please the king,
Es 9:29 **T.** Esther the queen, the daughter of
Job 1:7,9 **T.** Satan answered the Lord, and
Job 1:20 **T.** Job arose, and rent his mantle, and
Job 2:9 **T.** said his wife unto him, Dost thou
Job 3:13 have slept: **t.** had I been at rest. 227
Job 4:1 **T.** Eliphaz the Temanite answered
Job 4:15 **T.** a spirit passed before my face; the
Job 6:10 **T.** should I yet have comfort; yea, I
Job 7:14 **T.** thou scarest me with dreams, and
Job 8:1 **T.** answered Bildad the Shuhite, and
Job 8:18 **t.** it shall deny him, saying, I have not
Job 9:1 **T.** Job answered and said,
Job 9:29 If I be wicked, why **t.** labour I in vain?
Job 9:35 **T.** would I speak, and not fear him;
Job 10:14 If I sin, **t.** thou markest me, and thou
Job 10:18 Wherefore **t.** hast thou brought me
Job 10:20 cease **t.**, and let me alone, that I may
Job 11:1 **T.** answered Zophar the Naamathite,
Job 11:10 or gather together, **t.** who can hinder
Job 11:11 also; will he not **t.** consider it?
Job 11:15 For **t.** shalt thou lift up thy face 227
Job 13:20 **t.** will I not hide myself from thee 227
Job 13:22 **T.** call thou, and I will answer: or let
Job 15:1 **T.** answered Eliphaz the Temanite,
Job 16:1 **T.** Job answered and said,
Job 16:22 **t.** I shall go the way whence I shall
Job 18:1 **T.** answered Bildad the Shuhite, and
Job 19:1 **T.** Job answered and said,
Job 20:1 **T.** answered Zophar the Naamathite,
Job 21:34 How **t.** comfort ye me in vain, seeing
Job 22:1 **T.** Eliphaz the Temanite answered
Job 22:24 **T.** shalt thou lay up gold as dust, and
Job 22:26 For **t.** shalt thou have thy delight 227
Job 22:29 **t.** thou shalt say, There is lifting up;
Job 23:1 **T.** Job answered and said,
Job 25:1 **T.** answered Bildad the Shuhite, and
Job 25:4 How **t.** can man be justified with God?
Job 27:12 it; why **t.** are ye thus altogether vain?

Job 28:20 Whence **t.** cometh wisdom? and where
Job 28:27 **T.** did he see it, and declare it; he 227
Job 29:11 the ear heard me, **t.** it blessed me;
Job 29:18 **T.** I said, I shall die in my nest, and I
Job 30:26 looked for good, **t.** evil came unto me:
Job 31:1 why **t.** should I think upon a maid?
Job 31:8 **T.** let me sow, and let another eat;
Job 31:10 **T.** let my wife grind unto another, and
Job 31:14 What **t.** shall I do when God riseth up?
Job 31:22 **T.** let mine arm fall from my shoulder
Job 32:2 **T.** was kindled the wrath of Elihu the
Job 32:5 three men, **t.** his wrath was kindled.
Job 33:16 **T.** he openeth the ears of men, and 227
Job 33:24 **T.** he is gracious unto him, and saith,
Job 34:29 quietness, who **t.** can make trouble?
Job 34:29 hideth his face, who **t.** can behold him?
Job 36:9 **T.** he sheweth them their work, and
Job 36:18 **t.** a great ransom cannot deliver thee.
Job 37:8 **T.** the beasts go into dens, and
Job 38:1 **T.** the Lord answered Job out of the
Job 38:21 thou it, because thou wast **t.** born? 227
Job 40:3 **T.** Job answered the Lord, and said,
Job 40:6 **T.** answered the Lord unto Job out of
Job 40:14 **T.** will I also confess unto thee that
Job 41:10 up: who **t.** is able to stand before me?
Job 42:1 **T.** Job answered the Lord, and said,
Job 42:11 **T.** came there unto him all his
Ps 2:5 **T.** shall he speak unto them in his 227
Ps 18:7 **T.** the earth shook and trembled; the
Ps 18:15 **T.** the channels of water were seen,
Ps 18:42 **T.** did I beat them small as the dust
Ps 19:13 **t.** shall I be upright, and I shall be 227
Ps 27:10 forsake me, **t.** the Lord will take me
Ps 39:3 burned: **t.** spake I with my tongue,
Ps 40:7 **T.** said I, Lo, I come: in the volume 227
Ps 43:4 **T.** will I go unto the altar of God,
Ps 50:18 a thief, **t.** thou consentedst with him,
Ps 51:13 **T.** will I teach transgressors thy ways;
Ps 51:19 **T.** shalt thou be pleased with the 227
Ps 51:19 **t.** shall they offer bullocks upon 227
Ps 55:6 for **t.** would I fly away, and be at rest,
Ps 55:7 Lo, **t.** would I wander far off, and
Ps 55:12 me, **t.** I could have borne it:
Ps 55:12 **t.** I would have hid myself from him:
Ps 56:9 **t.** shall mine enemies turn back: 227
Ps 67:6 **T.** shall the earth yield her increase;
Ps 69:4 **t.** I restored that which I took not 227
Ps 73:17 of God; **t.** understood I their end.
Ps 78:34 he slew them, **t.** they sought him: and
Ps 78:65 **T.** the Lord awaked as one out of
Ps 80:12 Why hast thou **t.** broken down her
Ps 89:19 **T.** thou spakest in vision to thy 227
Ps 89:32 **T.** will I visit their transgression with
Ps 96:12 **t.** shall all the trees of the wood 227
Ps 106:12 **T.** believed they his words; they sang
Ps 106:30 **T.** stood up Phinehas, and executed
Ps 107:6, 13 **T.** they cried unto the Lord in
Ps 107:19, 28 **T.** they cry unto the Lord in
Ps 107:30 **T.** are they glad because they be quiet;
Ps 116:4 **T.** called I upon the name of the Lord;
Ps 119:6 **T.** shall I not be ashamed, when I 227
Ps 119:92 I should **t.** have perished in mine 227
Ps 124:3 **T.** they had swallowed us up quick, 233
Ps 124:4 **T.** the waters had overwhelmed us, 233
Ps 124:5 **T.** the proud waters had gone over 233
Ps 126:2 **T.** was our mouth filled with 227
Ps 126:2 **t.** said they among the heathen, 227
Ps 142:3 within me, **t.** thou knewest my path
Pr 1:28 **T.** shall they call upon me, but I 227
Pr 2:5 **T.** shalt thou understand the fear 227
Pr 2:9 **T.** shalt thou understand 227
Pr 3:23 **T.** shalt thou walk in thy way safely, 227
Pr 8:30 **T.** I was by him, as one brought up
Pr 11:2 When pride cometh, **t.** cometh shame:
Pr 15:11 how much more **t.** the hearts of the
Pr 18:3 cometh, **t.** cometh also contempt,
Pr 20:14 he is gone his way, **t.** he boasteth. 227
Pr 20:24 how can a man **t.** understand his own
Pr 24:14 found it, **t.** there shall be a reward,
Pr 24:32 **T.** I saw, and considered it well: I
Ec 2:11 **T.** I looked on all the works that my
Ec 2:13 **T.** I saw that wisdom excelleth folly,
Ec 2:15 **T.** said I in my heart, As it happeneth
Ec 2:15 to me; and why was I **t.** more wise? 227
Ec 2:15 **T.** I said in my heart, that this also is
Ec 4:7 **T.** I returned, and I saw vanity under
Ec 4:11 if two lie together, **t.** they have heat:

Ec 8:15 **T.** I commended mirth, because a man
Ec 8:17 **T.** I beheld all the work of God, that a
Ec 9:16 **T.** said I, Wisdom is better than
Ec 10:10 edge, **t.** must he put to more strength:
Ec 12:7 **T.** shall the dust return to the earth
Ca 8:10 **t.** was I in his eyes as one that found 227
Isa 5:17 **T.** shall the lambs feed after their
Isa 6:5 **T.** said I, Woe is me! for I am undone;
Isa 6:6 **T.** flew one of the seraphims unto me,
Isa 6:8 us? **T.** said I, Here am I; send me.
Isa 6:11 **T.** said I, Lord, how long? And he
Isa 7:3 **T.** said the Lord unto Isaiah, Go forth
Isa 8:3 **T.** said the Lord to me, Call his name
Isa 14:25 **t.** shall his yoke depart from off them,
Isa 14:32 shall one **t.** answer the messengers of
Isa 24:23 **T.** the moon shall be confounded and
Isa 28:18 **t.** ye shall be trodden down by it
Isa 30:23 **T.** shall he give the rain of thy seed,
Isa 31:8 **T.** shall the Assyrian fall with the
Isa 32:16 **T.** judgment shall dwell in the
Isa 33:23 **t.** is the prey of a great spoil 227
Isa 35:5 **T.** the eyes of the blind shall be 227
Isa 35:6 **T.** shall the lame man leap as an 227
Isa 36:3 **T.** came forth unto him Eliakim,
Isa 36:9 How **t.** wilt thou turn away the face of
Isa 36:11 **T.** said Eliakim and Shebna and Joah
Isa 36:13 **T.** Rabshakeh stood, and cried with a
Isa 36:22 **T.** came Eliakim, the son of Hilkiah,
Isa 37:21 **T.** Isaiah the son of Amoz sent unto
Isa 37:36 **T.** the angel of the Lord went forth,
Isa 38:2 **T.** Hezekiah turned his face toward
Isa 38:4 **T.** came the word of the Lord to
Isa 39:3 **T.** came Isaiah the prophet unto king
Isa 39:4 **T.** said he, What have they seen in
Isa 39:5 **T.** said Isaiah to Hezekiah, Hear the
Isa 39:8 **T.** said Hezekiah to Isaiah, Good is
Isa 40:18 To whom **t.** will ye liken God? or what
Isa 40:25 To whom **t.** will ye liken me, or shall I
Isa 41:1 them come near; **t.** let them speak: 227
Isa 44:15 **T.** shall it be for a man to burn: for he
Isa 48:18 **t.** had thy peace been as a river, and
Isa 49:4 **T.** I said, I have laboured in vain, I
Isa 49:21 **T.** shalt thou say in thine heart, Who
Isa 58:8 **T.** shall thy light break forth as 227
Isa 58:9 **T.** shalt thou call, and the Lord 227
Isa 58:10 **t.** shall thy light rise in obscurity, and
Isa 58:14 **T.** shalt thou delight thyself in the 227
Isa 60:5 **T.** thou shalt see, and flow together, 227
Isa 63:11 **T.** he remembered the days of old,
Isa 66:12 **t.** shall ye suck, ye shall be borne
Jer 1:4 **T.** the word of the Lord came unto
Jer 1:6 **T.** said I, Ah, Lord God! behold, I
Jer 1:9 **T.** the Lord put forth his hand, and
Jer 1:12 **T.** said the Lord unto me, Thou hast
Jer 1:14 **T.** the Lord said unto me, Out of the
Jer 2:21 how **t.** art thou turned into the
Jer 4:1 of my sight, **t.** shalt thou not remove.
Jer 4:10 **T.** said I, Ah, Lord God! surely thou
Jer 5:7 to the full, they **t.** committed adultery,
Jer 5:19 **t.** shalt thou answer them, Like as ye
Jer 7:7 **T.** will I cause you to dwell in this
Jer 7:34 **T.** will I cause to cease from the cities
Jer 8:5 Why **t.** is this people of Jerusalem
Jer 8:22 why **t.** is not the health of the 3588
Jer 11:5 **T.** answered I, and said, So be it, O
Jer 11:6 **T.** the Lord said unto me, Proclaim all
Jer 11:12 **T.** shall the cities of Judah and
Jer 11:15 thou doest evil, **t.** thou rejoicest. 227
Jer 11:18 **t.** thou shewedst me their doings 227
Jer 12:5 **t.** how canst thou contend with horses?
Jer 12:5 **t.** how wilt thou do in the swelling of
Jer 12:16 **t.** shall they be built in the midst of my
Jer 13:7 **T.** I went to Euphrates, and digged,
Jer 13:8 **T.** the word of the Lord came unto
Jer 13:13 **T.** shalt thou say unto them, Thus
Jer 13:23 **t.** may ye also do good, that are
Jer 14:11 **T.** said the Lord unto me, Pray not
Jer 14:13 **T.** said I, Ah, Lord God! behold, the
Jer 14:14 **T.** the Lord said unto me, The
Jer 14:18 **t.** behold the slain with the sword!
Jer 14:18 **t.** behold them that are sick with
Jer 15:1 **T.** said the Lord unto me, Though
Jer 15:2 **t.** thou shalt tell them, Thus saith the
Jer 15:19 thou return, **t.** will I bring thee again,
Jer 16:11 **T.** shalt thou say unto them, Because
Jer 17:25 **T.** shall there enter into the gates of
Jer 17:27 **t.** will I kindle a fire in the gates

Jer 18:3 T. I went down to the potter's house,
Jer 18:5 T. the word of the Lord came to me,
Jer 18:10 t. I will repent of the good, wherewith
Jer 18:18 T. said they, Come, and let us devise
Jer 19:10 T. shalt thou break the bottle in the
Jer 19:14 T. came Jeremiah from Tophet,
Jer 20:2 T. Pashur smote Jeremiah the
Jer 20:3 T. said Jeremiah unto him, The Lord
Jer 20:9 T. I said, I will not mention of him,
Jer 21:3 T. said Jeremiah unto them, Thus
Jer 22:4 t. shall there enter in by the gates of
Jer 22:9 T. they shall answer, Because they
Jer 22:15 justice, and t. it was well with him? 227
Jer 22:16 and needy; t. it was well with him: 227
Jer 22:22 surely t. shalt thou be ashamed and 227
Jer 23:22 t. they should have turned them from
Jer 23:33 thou shalt t. say unto them, What
Jer 24:3 T. said the Lord unto me, What seest
Jer 25:17 T. took I the cup at the Lord's hand,
Jer 25:28 t. shalt thou say unto them, Thus
Jer 26:6 T. will I make this house like Shiloh,
Jer 26:10 t. they came up from the king's house
Jer 26:11 T. spake the priests and the prophets
Jer 26:12 T. spake Jeremiah unto all the
Jer 26:16 T. said the princes and all the people
Jer 26:17 T. rose up certain of the elders of the
Jer 27:7 t. many nations and great kings shall
Jer 27:22 t. will I bring them up, and restore
Jer 28:5 T. the prophet Jeremiah said unto the
Jer 28:9 t. shall the prophet be known, that the
Jer 28:10 T. Hananiah the prophet took the
Jer 28:12 T. the word of the Lord came unto
Jer 28:15 T. said the prophet Jeremiah unto
Jer 29:12 T. shall ye call upon me, and ye shall
Jer 29:30 T. came the word of the Lord unto
Jer 31:13 T. shall the virgin rejoice in the
Jer 31:36 t. the seed of Israel also shall cease
Jer 32:2 For t. the king of Babylon's army 227
Jer 32:8 T. I knew that this was the word of
Jer 32:26 T. came the word of the Lord unto
Jer 33:21 T. may also my covenant be broken
Jer 33:26 T. will I cast away the seed of 1571
Jer 34:6 T. Jeremiah the prophet spake all
Jer 34:10 more, t. they obeyed, and let them go.
Jer 35:3 T. I took Jaazaniah the son of
Jer 35:12 T. came the word of the Lord unto
Jer 36:4 T. Jeremiah called Baruch the son of
Jer 36:10 T. read Baruch in the book the words
Jer 36:12 T. he went down into the king's house,
Jer 36:13 T. Michaiah declared unto them all
Jer 36:18 T. Baruch answered them, He
Jer 36:19 T. said the princes unto Baruch, Go,
Jer 36:27 T. the word of the Lord came to
Jer 36:32 T. took Jeremiah another roll, and
Jer 37:5 T. Pharaoh's army was come forth out
Jer 37:6 T. came the word of the Lord unto the
Jer 37:12 T. Jeremiah went forth out of
Jer 37:14 T. said Jeremiah, It is false; I fall not
Jer 37:17 T. Zedekiah the king sent, and took
Jer 37:21 T. Zedekiah the king commanded
Jer 38:1 T. Shephatiah the son of Mattan, and
Jer 38:5 T. Zedekiah the king said, Behold, he
Jer 38:6 T. took they Jeremiah, and cast him
Jer 38:7 king t. sitting in the gate of Benjamin;
Jer 38:10 T. the king commanded Ebed-melech
Jer 38:14 T. Zedekiah the king sent, and took
Jer 38:15 T. Jeremiah said unto Zedekiah, If I
Jer 38:17 T. said Jeremiah unto Zedekiah, Thus
Jer 38:17 t. thy soul shall live, and this city shall
Jer 38:18 t. shall this city be given into the hand
Jer 38:24 T. said Zedekiah unto Jeremiah, Let
Jer 38:26 T. thou shalt say unto them, I
Jer 38:27 T. came all the princes unto Jeremiah
Jer 39:4 t. they fled, and went forth out of the
Jer 39:6 T. the king of Babylon slew the sons
Jer 39:9 T. Nebuzar-adan the captain of the
Jer 40:6 T. went Jeremiah unto Gedaliah the
Jer 40:8 T. they came to Gedaliah to Mizpah,
Jer 40:15 T. Johanan the son of Kareah spake
Jer 41:2 T. arose Ishmael the son of Nethaniah,
Jer 41:10 T. Ishmael carried away captive all
Jer 41:12 T. they took all the men, and went to
Jer 41:13 that were with him, t. they were glad.
Jer 41:16 T. took Johanan the son of Kareah,
Jer 42:1 T. all the captains of the forces, and
Jer 42:4 T. Jeremiah the prophet said unto

Jer 42:5 T. they said to Jeremiah, The Lord
Jer 42:8 T. called he Johanan the son of
Jer 42:10 abide in this land, t. will I build you,
Jer 42:16 T. it shall come to pass, that the
Jer 43:2 T. spake Azariah the son of Hoshaiah,
Jer 43:8 T. came the word of the Lord unto
Jer 44:15 T. all the men which knew that their
Jer 44:17 t. had we plenty of victuals, and were
Jer 44:20 T. Jeremiah said unto all the people,
Jer 47:2 t. the men shall cry, and all the
Jer 49:1 why t. doth their king inherit Gad,
Jer 49:2 t. shall Israel be heir unto them that
Jer 51:48 T. the heaven and the earth, and all
Jer 51:62 T. shalt thou say, O Lord, thou hast
Jer 52:7 T. the city was broken up, and all
Jer 52:9 T. they took the king, and carried
Jer 52:11 T. he put out the eyes of Zedekiah;
Jer 52:15 T. Nebuzar-adan the captain of the
La 3:54 mine head; t. I said, I am cut off
Eze 3:3 T. did I eat it; and it was in my
Eze 3:12 T. the spirit took me up, and I heard
Eze 3:15 T. I came to them of the captivity at
Eze 3:23 T. I arose, and went forth into the
Eze 3:24 T. the spirit entered into me, and set
Eze 4:14 T. said I, Ah Lord God! behold, my
Eze 4:15 T. he said unto me, Lo, I have given
Eze 5:1 t. take thee balances to weigh, and
Eze 5:4 T. take of them again, and cast them
Eze 6:13 T. shall ye know that I am the Lord,
Eze 7:26 t. shall they seek a vision of the
Eze 8:2 T. I beheld, and lo a likeness as the
Eze 8:5, 8,12 T. said he unto me, Son of man,
Eze 8:14 T. he brought me to the door of the
Eze 8:15 T. said he unto me, Hast thou seen
Eze 8:17 T. he said unto me, Hast thou seen
Eze 9:6 T. they began at the ancient men
Eze 9:9 T. said he unto me, The iniquity of
Eze 10:1 T. I looked, and, behold, in the
Eze 10:4 T. the glory of the Lord went up from
Eze 10:6 t. he went in, and stood beside the
Eze 10:18 T. the glory of the Lord departed from
Eze 11:2 T. said he unto me, Son of man, these
Eze 11:13 T. fell I down upon my face, and cried
Eze 11:22 T. did the cherubims lift up their
Eze 11:25 T. I spake unto them of the captivity
Eze 12:4 T. shalt thou bring forth thy stuff by
Eze 14:1 T. came certain of the elders of Israel
Eze 14:13 t. will I stretch out mine hand upon it,
Eze 16:9 T. washed I thee with water; yea, I
Eze 16:53 t. will I bring again the captivity of
Eze 16:55 t. thou and thy daughters shall return
Eze 16:61 T. thou shalt remember thy ways, and
Eze 18:13 shall he t. live? he shall not live: he
Eze 19:5 t. she took another of her whelps, and
Eze 19:8 T. the nations set against him on
Eze 20:2 T. came the word of the Lord unto
Eze 20:7 T. said I unto them, Cast ye away
Eze 20:8 t. I said, I will pour out my fury upon
Eze 20:13, 21 t. I said, I would pour out my fury
Eze 20:28 t. they saw every high hill, and all the
Eze 20:29 T. I said unto them, What is the high
Eze 20:49 T. said I, Ah Lord God! they say of
Eze 21:4 Seeing t. that I will cut off from thee
Eze 21:10 glitter: should we t. make mirth? 176
Eze 22:3 T. say thou, Thus saith the Lord
Eze 23:13 T. I saw that she was defiled, that
Eze 23:18 t. my mind was alienated from her,
Eze 23:39 t. they came the same day into my
Eze 23:43 T. said I unto her that was old in
Eze 24:11 T. set it empty upon the coals thereof,
Eze 24:20 T. I answered them, The word of the
Eze 26:16 T. all the princes of the sea shall come
Eze 28:25 t. shall they dwell in their land that I
Eze 32:4 T. will I leave thee upon the land,
Eze 32:14 T. will I make their waters deep, 227
Eze 32:15 t. shall they know that I am the Lord
Eze 33:4 T. whosoever heareth the sound of the
Eze 33:10 away in them, how should we t. live?
Eze 33:23 T. the word of the Lord came unto me,
Eze 33:29 T. shall they know that I am the Lord,
Eze 33:33 t. shall they know that a prophet hath
Eze 36:25 T. will I sprinkle clean water upon
Eze 36:31 T. shall ye remember your own evil
Eze 36:36 T. the heathen that are left round
Eze 37:9 T. said he unto me, Prophesy unto the
Eze 37:11 T. he said unto me, Son of man, these

Eze 37:14 t. shall ye know that I the Lord have
Eze 37:16 t. take another stick, and write upon
Eze 39:15 t. shall he set up a sign by it, till the
Eze 39:28 T. shall they know that I am the Lord
Eze 40:6 T. came he unto the gate which looketh
Eze 40:9 T. measured he the porch of the gate,
Eze 40:13 He measured t. the gate from the roof
Eze 40:17 T. brought me into the outward
Eze 40:19 T. he measured the breadth from the
Eze 41:3 T. went he inward, and measured the
Eze 42:1 T. he brought me forth into the utter
Eze 42:13 T. said he unto me, The north
Eze 42:14 t. shall they not go out of the holy
Eze 44:1 T. he brought me back the way of the
Eze 44:2 T. said the Lord unto me; This gate
Eze 44:4 T. brought he me the way of the
Eze 46:2 t. he shall go forth; but the gate shall
Eze 46:12 one shall t. open him the gate that
Eze 46:12 t. he shall go forth; and after his
Eze 46:17 t. it shall be his to the year of liberty;
Eze 46:20 T. said he unto me, This is the place
Eze 46:21 T. he brought me forth into the utter
Eze 46:24 T. said he unto me, These are the
Eze 47:2 T. brought he me out of the way of
Eze 47:6 T. he brought me, and caused me to
Eze 47:8 T. said he unto me, These waters
Da 1:10 t. shall ye make me endanger my
Da 1:11 T. said Daniel to Melzar, whom the
Da 1:13 T. let our countenances be looked
Da 1:18 t. the prince of the eunuchs brought
Da 2:2 T. the king commanded to call the
Da 2:4 T. spake the Chaldeans to the king in
Da 2:14 T. Daniel answered with counsel 116
Da 2:15 T. Arioch made the thing known to 116
Da 2:16 T. Daniel went in, and desired of the
Da 2:17 T. Daniel went to his house, and 116
Da 2:19 T. was the secret revealed unto 116
Da 2:19 T. Daniel blessed the God of heaven. 116
Da 2:25 T. Arioch brought in Daniel before 116
Da 2:35 T. was the iron, the clay, the brass, 116
Da 2:46 T. the king Nebuchadnezzar fell 116
Da 2:48 T. the king made Daniel a great 116
Da 2:49 T. Daniel requested of the king, and
Da 3:2 T. Nebuchadnezzar the king sent to
Da 3:3 T. the princes, the governors, and 116
Da 3:4 T. an herald cried aloud, To you it is
Da 3:13 T. Nebuchadnezzar in his rage and 116
Da 3:13 T. they brought these men before 116
Da 3:19 T. was Nebuchadnezzar full of fury, 116
Da 3:21 T. these men were bound in their 116
Da 3:24 T. Nebuchadnezzar the king was 116
Da 3:26 T. Nebuchadnezzar came near to 116
Da 3:26 T. Shadrach, Meshach, and 116
Da 3:28 T. Nebuchadnezzar spake, and said,
Da 3:30 T. the king promoted Shadrach, 116
Da 4:7 T. came in the magicians, the 116
Da 4:19 T. Daniel, whose name was 116
Da 5:3 T. they brought the golden vessels 116
Da 5:6 T. the king's countenance was 116
Da 5:8 T. came in all the king's wise men: 116
Da 5:9 T. was king Belshazzar greatly 116
Da 5:13 T. was Daniel brought in before the 116
Da 5:17 T. Daniel answered and said before 116
Da 5:24 T. was the part of the hand sent 116
Da 5:29 T. commanded Belshazzar, and they 116
Da 6:3 T. this Daniel was preferred above 116
Da 6:4 T. the presidents and princes 116
Da 6:5 T. said these men, We shall not find 116
Da 6:6 T. these presidents and princes 116
Da 6:11 T. these men assembled, and found 116
Da 6:12 T. they came near, and spake before 116
Da 6:13 T. answered they and said before 116
Da 6:14 T. the king, when he heard these 116
Da 6:15 T. these men assembled unto the 116
Da 6:16 T. the king commanded, and they 116
Da 6:18 T. the king went to his palace, and 116
Da 6:19 T. the king arose very early in the 116
Da 6:21 T. said Daniel unto the king, O king, 116
Da 6:23 T. was the king exceeding glad for 116
Da 6:25 T. king Darius wrote unto all people, 116
Da 7:1 t. he wrote the dream, and told the 116
Da 7:11 I beheld t. because of the voice of 116
Da 7:19 T. I would know the truth of the 116
Da 8:3 T. I lifted up mine eyes, and saw,
Da 8:13 T. I heard one saint speaking, and
Da 8:14 t. shall the sanctuary be cleansed.

Da	8:15	t., behold, there stood before me as	
Da	10:5	T. I lifted up mine eyes, and looked,	
Da	10:9	t. was I in a deep sleep on my face,	
Da	10:12	T. said he unto me, Fear not, Daniel:	
Da	10:16	t. I opened my mouth, and spake, and	
Da	10:18	T. there came again and touched me	
Da	10:20	T. said he, Knowest thou wherefore I	
Da	11:10	t. shall he return, and be stirred up,	
Da	11:19	T. he shall turn his face toward the	
Da	11:20	T. shall stand up in his estate a	
Da	11:28	T. shall he return into his land with	
Da	12:5	T. I Daniel looked, and, behold, there	
Da	12:8	t. said I, O my Lord, what shall be the	
Ho	1:9	T. said God, Call his name Lo-ammi:	
Ho	1:11	T. shall the children of Judah and the	
Ho	2:7	t. shall she say, I will go and return to	
Ho	2:7	t. was it better with me than now	227
Ho	3:1	T. said the Lord unto me, Go yet,	
Ho	5:13	t. went Ephraim to the Assyrian,	
Ho	6:3	T. shall he know, if we follow on	
Ho	7:1	t. the iniquity of Ephraim was	
Ho	10:3	Lord; what t. should a king do to us?	
Ho	11:1	Israel was a child, t. I loved him, and	
Ho	11:10	t. the children shall tremble from the	
Joe	2:18	T. will the Lord be jealous for his	
Joe	2:23	Be glad t., ye children of Zion, and	
Joe	3:17	t. shall Jerusalem be holy, and there	
Am	6:2	t. go down to Gath of the Philistines:	
Am	6:10	T. shall he say, Hold thy tongue: for	
Am	7:2	t. I said, O Lord God, forgive, I	
Am	7:5	T. said I, O Lord God, cease, I	
Am	7:8	T. said the Lord, Behold, I will set a	
Am	7:10	T. Amaziah the priest of Beth-el sent	
Am	7:14	T. answered Amos, and said to	
Am	8:2	T. said the Lord unto me, The end is	
Jon	1:5	T. the mariners were afraid, and cried	
Jon	1:8	T. said they unto him, Tell us, we	
Jon	1:10	T. were the men exceedingly afraid,	
Jon	1:11	T. said they unto him, What shall we	
Jon	1:16	T. the men feared the Lord	
Jon	2:1	T. Jonah prayed unto the Lord his	
Jon	2:4	T. I said, I am cast out of thy sight;	
Jon	4:4	T. said the Lord, Doest thou well to	
Jon	4:10	T. said the Lord, thou hast had pity	
Mic	3:4	T. shall they cry unto the Lord,	227
Mic	3:7	T. shall the seers be ashamed, and	
Mic	5:3	t. the remnant of his brethren shall	
Mic	5:5	t. shall we raise against him seven	
Mic	7:10	T. she that is mine enemy shall see it,	
Hab	1:11	T. shall his mind change, and he	227
Zep	3:9	t. will I turn to the people a pure	227
Zep	3:11	t. I will take away out of the midst	227
Hag	1:3	T. came the word of the Lord by	
Hag	1:12	T. Zerubbabel the son of Shealtiel,	
Hag	1:13	T. spake Haggai the Lord's	
Hag	2:13	T. said Haggai, If one that is	
Hag	2:14	T. answered Haggai, and said, So is	
Zec	1:9	T. said I, O my Lord, what are these?	
Zec	1:12	T. the angel of the Lord answered	
Zec	1:18	T. lifted I up mine eyes, and saw, and	
Zec	1:21	T. said I, What come these to do?	
Zec	2:2	T. said I, Whither goest thou? And	
Zec	3:7	t. thou shalt also judge my house,	
Zec	4:5	T. the angel that talked with me	
Zec	4:6	T. he answered and spake unto me,	
Zec	4:11	T. answered I, and said unto him,	
Zec	4:14	T. said he, These are the two	
Zec	5:1	T. I turned, and lifted up mine eyes,	
Zec	5:3	T. said he unto me, This is the curse	
Zec	5:5	T. the angel that talked with me went	
Zec	5:9	T. lifted I up mine eyes, and looked,	
Zec	5:10	T. said I to the angel that talked with	
Zec	6:4	T. I answered and said unto the	
Zec	6:8	T. cried he upon me, and spake unto	
Zec	6:11	T. take silver and gold, and make	
Zec	7:4	T. came the word of the Lord of hosts	
Zec	11:9	T. said I, I will not feed you: that that	
Zec	11:14	T. I cut asunder mine other staff, even	
Zec	13:3	t. his father and his mother that begat	
Zec	13:6	T. he shall answer, Those with which	
Zec	14:3	T. shall the Lord go forth, and fight	
Mal	1:6	if t. I be a father, where is mine	
Mal	3:4	T. shall the offering of Judah and	
Mal	3:16	T. they that feared the Lord spake	
Mal	3:18	T. shall ye return, and discern	
Mt	1:19	T. Joseph her husband,...a just	1161
Mt	1:24	T. Joseph being raised from sleep	1161
Mt	2:7	T. Herod, when he had privily	5119
Mt	2:16	T. Herod, when he saw that he was	5119
Mt	2:17	T. was fulfilled that which was	5119
Mt	3:5	T. went out to him Jerusalem, and	5119
Mt	3:13	T. cometh Jesus from Galilee to	5119
Mt	3:15	righteousness. T. he suffered him	5119
Mt	4:1	T. was Jesus led up of the spirit	5119
Mt	4:5	T. the devil taketh him up into the	5119
Mt	4:10	T. saith Jesus unto him, Get thee	5119
Mt	4:11	T. the devil leaveth him, and,	5119
Mt	5:24	and t. come and offer thy gift	5119
Mt	7:5	t. shalt thou see clearly to cast	5119
Mt	7:11	If ye t., being evil, know how to	3767
Mt	7:23	t. will I profess unto them, I	5119
Mt	8:26	T. he arose, and rebuked the winds	5119
Mt	9:6	(t. saith he to the sick of the palsy,)	5119
Mt	9:14	T. came to him the disciples of	5119
Mt	9:15	from them, and t. shall they fast	5119
Mt	9:29	T. touched he their eyes, saying,	5119
Mt	9:37	T. saith he unto his disciples, The	5119
Mt	11:20	T. began he to upbraid the cities	5119
Mt	12:12	How much t. is a man better	3767
Mt	12:13	T. saith he to the man, Stretch	5119
Mt	12:14	T. the Pharisees went out,...held	1161
Mt	12:22	T. was brought unto him one	5119
Mt	12:26	how shall t. his kingdom stand?	3767
Mt	12:28	t. the kingdom of God is come	686
Mt	12:29	and t. he will spoil his house	5119
Mt	12:38	T. certain of the scribes and of the	5119
Mt	12:44	T. he saith, I will return into	5119
Mt	12:45	T. goeth he, and taketh with	5119
Mt	12:47	T. one said unto him, Behold, thy	5119
Mt	13:19	t. cometh the wicked one, and	
Mt	13:26	fruit, t. appeared the tares also	5119
Mt	13:27	from whence t. hath it tares?	3767
Mt	13:28	Wilt thou t. that we go and	3767
Mt	13:36	T. Jesus sent the multitude away,	5119
Mt	13:43	T. shall the righteous shine forth	5119
Mt	13:52	T. said he unto them, Therefore	1161
Mt	13:56	Whence t. hath this man all these	3767
Mt	14:33	T. they that were in the ship came	1161
Mt	15:1	T. came to Jesus scribes and	5119
Mt	15:12	T. came his disciples, and said unto	5119
Mt	15:15	T. answered Peter and said unto	1161
Mt	15:21	T. Jesus went thence, and	2532
Mt	15:25	T. came she and worshipped him,	1161
Mt	15:28	T. Jesus answered and said unto	5119
Mt	15:32	T. Jesus called his disciples unto	1161
Mt	16:6	T. Jesus said unto them, Take	1161
Mt	16:12	T. understood they how that he	5119
Mt	16:20	T. charged he his disciples that	5119
Mt	16:22	T. Peter took him, and began to	2532
Mt	16:24	T. said Jesus unto his disciples,	5119
Mt	16:27	and t. he shall reward every	5119
Mt	17:4	T. answered Peter, and said unto	1161
Mt	17:10	Why t. say the scribes that Elias	3767
Mt	17:13	T. the disciples understood that	5119
Mt	17:17	T. Jesus answered and said, O	1161
Mt	17:19	T. came the disciples to Jesus	5119
Mt	17:26	unto him, T. are the children free	686
Mt	18:16	t. take with thee one or two more,	
Mt	18:21	T. came Peter to him, and said,	5119
Mt	18:27	T. the lord of that servant was	1161
Mt	18:32	T. his lord, after that he had	5119
Mt	19:7	did Moses t. command to give a	3767
Mt	19:13	T. were...brought unto him little	5119
Mt	19:23	T. said Jesus unto his disciples,	1161
Mt	19:25	saying, Who t. can be saved?	686
Mt	19:27	T. answered Peter and said unto	5119
Mt	20:20	T. came to him the mother of	5119
Mt	21:1	Olives, t. sent Jesus two disciples,	5119
Mt	21:25	us, Why did ye not t. believe him?	3767
Mt	22:8	T. saith he to his servants, The	5119
Mt	22:13	T. said the king to the servants,	5119
Mt	22:15	T. went the Pharisees, and took	5119
Mt	22:21	T. saith he unto them, Render	5119
Mt	22:35	T. one of them, which was a	2532
Mt	22:43	How t. doth David in spirit call	3767
Mt	22:45	If David t. call him Lord, how is	3767
Mt	23:1	T. spake Jesus to the multitude,	5119
Mt	23:32	Fill ye up t. the measure of your	2532
Mt	24:9	T. shall they deliver you up to be	5119
Mt	24:10	t. shall many be offended, and	5119
Mt	24:14	nations; and t. shall the end	5119
Mt	24:16	T. let them which be in Judaea	5119
Mt	24:21	t. shall be great tribulation, such	5119
Mt	24:23	T. if any man shall say unto you,	5119
Mt	24:30	t. shall appear the sign of the	5119
Mt	24:30	t. shall all the tribes of the earth	5119
Mt	24:40	T. shall two be in the field; the	5119
Mt	24:45	t. is a faithful and wise servant,	686
Mt	25:1	T. shall the kingdom of heaven	5119
Mt	25:7	T. all those virgins arose, and	5119
Mt	25:16	T. he that had received the five	1161
Mt	25:24	T. he which had received the one	1161
Mt	25:27	t. at my coming I should have	
Mt	25:31	t. shall he sit upon the throne of	5119
Mt	25:34	T. shall the King say unto them	5119
Mt	25:37	T. shall the righteous answer,	5119
Mt	25:41	T. shall he say also unto them on	5119
Mt	25:44	T. shall they also answer him,	5119
Mt	25:45	T. shall he answer them, saying,	5119
Mt	26:3	T. assembled together the chief	5119
Mt	26:14	T. one of the twelve, called Judas	5119
Mt	26:25	T. Judas, which betrayed him,	1161
Mt	26:31	T. saith Jesus unto them, All ye	5119
Mt	26:36	T. cometh Jesus with them unto a	5119
Mt	26:38	T. saith he unto them, My soul is	5119
Mt	26:45	T. cometh he to his disciples, and	5119
Mt	26:50	T. came they, and laid hands on	5119
Mt	26:52	T. said Jesus unto him, Put up	5119
Mt	26:54	But how t. shall the scripture be	3767
Mt	26:56	T. all the disciples forsook him,	5119
Mt	26:65	T. the high priest rent his clothes,	5119
Mt	26:67	T. did they spit in his face, and	5119
Mt	26:74	T. began he to curse and to swear,	5119
Mt	27:3	T. Judas, which had betrayed him,	5119
Mt	27:9	T. was fulfilled that which was	5119
Mt	27:13	T. said Pilate unto him, Hearest	5119
Mt	27:16	And they had t. a notable prisoner,	5119
Mt	27:22	What shall I do t. with Jesus	3767
Mt	27:25	T. answered all the people, and	2532
Mt	27:26	T. released he Barabbas unto	5119
Mt	27:27	T. the soldiers of the governor took	5119
Mt	27:38	T. were there two thieves crucified	5119
Mt	27:58	T. Pilate commanded the body to	5119
Mt	28:10	T. said Jesus unto them, Be not	5119
Mt	28:16	T. the eleven disciples went away	1161
Mk	2:20	and t. shall they fast in those	5119
Mk	3:27	man; and t. he will spoil his	5119
Mk	3:31	There came t. his brethren and his	3767
Mk	4:13	and how t. will ye know all	
Mk	4:28	first the blade, t. the ear, after	1534
Mk	7:1	T. came together unto him the	2532
Mk	7:5	T. the Pharisees and scribes	1899
Mk	10:8	so t. they are no more twain, but	
Mk	10:21	T. Jesus beholding him loved	1161
Mk	10:26	themselves, Who t. can be saved?	
Mk	10:28	T. Peter began to say unto him,	2532
Mk	11:31	say, Why t. did ye not believe him?	3767
Mk	12:18	T. come unto him the Sadducees,	2532
Mk	12:37	him Lord; and whence is he t. his	
Mk	13:14	t. let them that be in Judaea flee	5119
Mk	13:21	t. if any man shall say to you,	5119
Mk	13:26	t. shall they see the Son of man	5119
Mk	13:27	And t. shall he send his angels,	5119
Mk	14:63	T. the high priest rent his clothes,	1161
Mk	15:12	What will ye t. that I shall do unto	3767
Mk	15:14	T. Pilate said unto them, Why,	1161
Mk	16:19	So t. after the Lord had spoken	3767
Lu	1:34	T. said Mary unto the angel, How	1161
Lu	2:28	T. took he him up in his arms,	2532
Lu	3:7	T. said he to the multitude that	3767
Lu	3:10	him, saying, What shall we do t.?	3767
Lu	3:12	T. came also publicans to be	1161
Lu	5:35	and t. shall they fast in those	5119
Lu	5:36	t. both the new maketh a rent,	
Lu	6:9	T. said Jesus unto them, I will	3767
Lu	6:42	t. shalt thou see clearly to pull out	5119
Lu	7:6	T. Jesus went with them. And	1161
Lu	7:22	T. Jesus answering said unto	2532
Lu	7:31	Whereunto t. shall I liken the men	3767
Lu	8:12	t. cometh the devil, and taketh	1534
Lu	8:19	T. came to him his mother and	1161
Lu	8:24	T. he arose, and rebuked the wind	1161
Lu	8:33	T. went the devils out of the man,	1161
Lu	8:35	T. they went out to see what was	1161
Lu	8:37	T. the...multitude of the country	2532
Lu	9:1	T. he called his twelve disciples	1161
Lu	9:12	t. came the twelve, and said unto	1161
Lu	9:16	T. he took the five loaves and the	1161
Lu	9:46	T. there arose a reasoning among	1161
Lu	10:37	T. said Jesus unto him, Go, and	3767
Lu	11:13	If ye t., being evil, know how to	3767

Lu 11:26 T. goeth he, and taketh to him 5119
Lu 11:45 T. answered one of the lawyers, ... 1161
Lu 12:20 t. whose shall those things be, ... 1161
Lu 12:26 If ye t. be not able to do that 3767
Lu 12:28 If t. God so clothe the grass, ... 1161
Lu 12:41 T. Peter said unto him, Lord,........... 1161
Lu 12:42 Who t. is that faithful and wise...... 686
Lu 13:7 T. said he unto the dresser of his.. 1161
Lu 13:9 t. after that thou shall cut it down......
Lu 13:15 The Lord t. answered him, and 3767
Lu 13:18 T. said he, Unto what is the.......... 1161
Lu 13:23 T. said one unto him, Lord, are......... 1161
Lu 13:26 T. shall ye begin to say, We have.. 5119
Lu 14:10 t. shalt thou have worship in the... 5119
Lu 14:12 T. said he also to him that bade......... 1161
Lu 14:16 T. said he unto him, A certain 1161
Lu 14:21 T. the master of the house being... 5119
Lu 15:1 T. drew near...all the publicans.......... 1161
Lu 16:3 T. the steward said within himself, 1161
Lu 16:7 T. said he to another, And how...... 1899
Lu 16:27 T. he said, I pray thee, therefore,.. 1161
Lu 17:1 T. said he unto the disciples, It is 1161
Lu 18:26 heard it said, Who t. can be saved? 2532
Lu 18:28 T. Peter said, Lo, we have left all,..... 1161
Lu 18:31 T. he took unto him the twelve, ... 1161
Lu 19:15 t. he commanded these servants 1532
Lu 19:16 T. came the first, saying, Lord,..... 1161
Lu 19:23 Wherefore t. gavest not thou my ... 2532
Lu 20:5 say, Why t. believe ye him not?......... 3767
Lu 20:9 T. began he to speak to the people 1161
Lu 20:13 T. said the lord of the vineyard, ... 1161
Lu 20:17 What is this t. that is written, ... 3767
Lu 20:27 T. came to him certain of the........... 1161
Lu 20:39 T. certain of the scribes answering..... 1161
Lu 20:44 calleth...Lord, how is he t. his...... 2532
Lu 20:45 T. in the audience of all the 1161
Lu 21:10 T. said he unto them, Nation shall... 5119
Lu 21:20 t. know that the desolation........... 5119
Lu 21:21 T. let them which are in Judaea.... 5119
Lu 21:27 t. shall they see the Son of man.... 5119
Lu 21:28 t. look up, and lift up your heads;.......
Lu 22:3 T. entered Satan into Judas............... 1161
Lu 22:7 T. came the day of unleavened 1161
Lu 22:36 T. said he unto them, But now, ... 3767
Lu 22:52 T. Jesus said unto...chief priests, ... 1161
Lu 22:54 T. took they him, and led him, ... 1161
Lu 22:70 T. said they all, Art thou 1161
Lu 22:70 all, Art thou t. the Son of God? 3767
Lu 23:4 T. said Pilate to the chief priests........ 1161
Lu 23:9 T. he questioned...him in many.......... 1161
Lu 23:30 T. shall they begin to say to the 5119
Lu 23:34 T. said Jesus, Father, forgive.......... 1161
Lu 24:12 T. arose Peter, and ran unto the........ 1161
Lu 24:25 T. he said unto them, O fools, and... 1161
Lu 24:45 T. opened he their understanding, ... 5119
Joh 1:21 him, What t.? Art thou Elias? 3767
Joh 1:22 T. said they unto him, Who art......... 3767
Joh 1:25 Why baptizest thou t., if thou be......... 3767
Joh 1:38 T. Jesus turned, and saw them 1161
Joh 2:10 well drunk, t. that which is worse: 5119
Joh 2:18 T. answered the Jews and said 3767
Joh 2:20 T. said the Jews, Forty and six.......... 3767
Joh 3:25 T. there arose a question between 3767
Joh 4:5 T. cometh he to a city of Samaria, ... 3767
Joh 4:9 T. saith the woman of Samaria........... 3767
Joh 4:11 from whence t. hast thou that 3767
Joh 4:28 The woman t. left her waterpot, ... 3767
Joh 4:30 T. they went out of the city, and 3767
Joh 4:35 four months, and t. cometh harvest?....
Joh 4:45 T. when he was come into Galilee, ... 3767
Joh 4:48 T. said Jesus unto him, Except ye..... 3767
Joh 4:52 T. enquired he of them the hour 3767
Joh 5:4 whosoever t. first after...troubling....... 3767
Joh 5:12 T. asked they him, What man is 3767
Joh 5:19 T. answered Jesus and said unto 3767
Joh 6:5 When Jesus t. lifted up his eyes,......... 3767
Joh 6:14 T. those men, when they had seen...... 3767
Joh 6:21 T. they willingly received him into....... 3767
Joh 6:28 T. said they unto him, What shall....... 3767
Joh 6:30 What sign shewest thou t., that we 3767
Joh 6:32 T. Jesus said unto them, Verily, ... 3767
Joh 6:34 T. said they unto him, Lord, ... 3767
Joh 6:41 The Jews t. murmured at him, ... 3767
Joh 6:42 how is it t. that he saith, I came........ 3767
Joh 6:53 T. Jesus said unto them, Verily, ... 3767
Joh 6:67 T. said Jesus unto the twelve, Will.... 3767
Joh 6:68 T. Simon Peter answered him, ... 3767
Joh 7:6 T. Jesus said unto them, My time..... 3767
Joh 7:10 t. went he also up unto the feast, ... 5119
Joh 7:11 T. the Jews sought him at the 3767
Joh 7:25 T. said some of them of Jerusalem, ... 3767
Joh 7:28 T. cried Jesus in the temple as he...... 3767
Joh 7:30 T. they sought to take him: but no...... 3767
Joh 7:33 T. said Jesus unto them, Yet a 3767
Joh 7:33 and t. I go unto him that sent 3767
Joh 7:35 T. said the Jews among..................... 3767
Joh 7:45 T. came the officers to the chief........ 3767
Joh 7:47 T. answered them the Pharisees, ... 3767
Joh 8:12 T. spake Jesus again unto them, ... 3767
Joh 8:19 T. said they unto him, Where is.......... 3767
Joh 8:21 T. said Jesus again unto them, I 3767
Joh 8:22 T. said the Jews, Will he kill 3767
Joh 8:25 T. said they unto him, Who art.......... 3767
Joh 8:28 T. said Jesus unto them, When ye..... 5119
Joh 8:28 t. shall ye know that I am he, ... 3767
Joh 8:31 T. said Jesus to those Jews which 3767
Joh 8:31 t. are ye my disciples indeed; ....
Joh 8:41 T. said they to him, We be not.......... 3767
Joh 8:48 T. answered the Jews, and said 3767
Joh 8:52 T. said the Jews unto him, Now......... 3767
Joh 8:57 T. said the Jews unto him, Thou........ 3767
Joh 8:59 T. took they up stones to cast at 3767
Joh 9:12 T. said they unto him, Where is he? ... 3767
Joh 9:15 T. again the Pharisees also asked....... 3767
Joh 9:19 born blind? how t. doth he now see?... 3767
Joh 9:24 T. again called they the man that 3767
Joh 9:26 T. said they to him again, What 1161
Joh 9:28 T. they reviled him, and said,............ 3767
Joh 10:7 T. said Jesus unto them again,............ 3767
Joh 10:24 T. came the Jews round about him, ... 3767
Joh 10:31 T. the Jews took up stones again 3767
Joh 11:7 T. after that saith he to his............. 1899
Joh 11:12 T. said his disciples, Lord, if he 3767
Joh 11:14 T. said Jesus unto them plainly, ... 3767
Joh 11:16 T. said Thomas, which is called 3767
Joh 11:17 T. when Jesus came, he found that..... 3767
Joh 11:20 T. Martha, as soon as she heard........ 3767
Joh 11:21 T. said Martha unto Jesus, Lord, ... 3767
Joh 11:31 The Jews t. which were with her in.... 3767
Joh 11:32 T. when Mary was come where.......... 3767
Joh 11:36 T. said the Jews, Behold how he........ 3767
Joh 11:41 T. they took away the stone from 3767
Joh 11:45 T. many of the Jews which came....... 3767
Joh 11:47 T. gathered the chief priests and....... 3767
Joh 11:53 T. from that day forth they took 3767
Joh 11:56 T. sought they for Jesus, and 3767
Joh 12:1 T. Jesus six days before the............. 3767
Joh 12:3 T. took Mary a pound of ointment 3767
Joh 12:4 T. saith one of his disciples, Judas 3767
Joh 12:7 T. said Jesus, Let her alone:........... 3767
Joh 12:16 t. remembered they that these 5119
Joh 12:28 T. came there a voice from............... 3767
Joh 12:35 T. Jesus said unto them, Yet a 3767
Joh 13:6 T. cometh he to Simon Peter: and...... 3767
Joh 13:14 If I t., your Lord and Master,....... 3767
Joh 13:22 T. the disciples looked one on 3767
Joh 13:25 He t. lying on Jesus' breast saith........ 1161
Joh 13:27 T. said Jesus unto him, That thou....... 3767
Joh 13:30 He t. having received the sop went 3767
Joh 14:9 and how sayest thou t., Shew us ....
Joh 16:17 T. said some of his disciples............. 3767
Joh 18:3 Judas t., having received a band of 3767
Joh 18:6 As soon t. as he had said unto them, .. 3767
Joh 18:7 T. asked he them again, Whom 3767
Joh 18:10 T. Simon Peter having a sword.......... 3767
Joh 18:11 T. said Jesus unto Peter, Put up....... 3767
Joh 18:12 T. the band and the captain and 3767
Joh 18:16 T. went out that other disciple,......... 3767
Joh 18:17 T. saith the damsel that kept the 3767
Joh 18:19 The high priest t. asked Jesus of......... 3767
Joh 18:27 Peter t. denied again: and................. 3767
Joh 18:28 T. led they Jesus from Caiaphas......... 3767
Joh 18:29 Pilate t. went out unto them, and......... 3767
Joh 18:31 T. said Pilate unto them, Take ye 3767
Joh 18:33 T. Pilate entered into the judgment..... 3767
Joh 18:36 world, t. would my servants fight, ...
Joh 18:37 said unto him, Art thou a king t.?......... 3766
Joh 18:40 T. cried they all again, saying, ... 3767
Joh 19:1 T. Pilate therefore took Jesus,............ 5119
Joh 19:5 T. came Jesus forth, wearing the 3767
Joh 19:10 T. saith Pilate unto him, Speakest 3767
Joh 19:16 T. delivered he him therefore............ 5119
Joh 19:20 This title t. read many of the Jews: 3767
Joh 19:21 T. said the chief priests of the........... 3767
Joh 19:23 T. the soldiers, when they had 3767
Joh 19:27 T. saith he to the disciple, ... 1534
Joh 19:32 T. came the soldiers, and brake 3767
Joh 19:40 T. took they the body of Jesus, ... 3767
Joh 20:2 T. she runneth, and cometh to 3767
Joh 20:6 T. cometh Simon Peter following.......... 3767
Joh 20:8 T. went in also that other disciple, ... 5119
Joh 20:10 T. the disciples went away again 3767
Joh 20:19 T. the same day at evening, being...... 3767
Joh 20:20 T. were the disciples glad, when.......... 3767
Joh 20:21 T. said Jesus to them again, Peace 3767
Joh 20:26 t. came Jesus, the doors being shut, ...
Joh 20:27 T. said he to Thomas, Reach 1534
Joh 21:5 T. Jesus saith unto them, ... 3767
Joh 21:9 soon t. as they were come to land, ... 3767
Joh 21:13 Jesus t. cometh, and taketh bread, ... 3767
Joh 21:20 T. Peter, turning about, seeth the...... 1161
Joh 21:23 T. went this saying abroad among 3767
Ac 1:12 T. returned they unto Jerusalem 5119
Ac 2:38 T. Peter said unto them, Repent,........ 1161
Ac 2:41 T. they that gladly received his.......... 3767
Ac 3:6 T. Peter said, Silver and gold have...... 1161
Ac 4:8 T. Peter, filled with the Holy 5119
Ac 5:9 T. Peter said unto her, How is it 1161
Ac 5:10 T. fell she down straightway at his 1161
Ac 5:17 T. the high priest rose up, and all 1161
Ac 5:25 T. came one and told them, saying, ... 1161
Ac 5:26 T. went the captain with the 5119
Ac 5:29 T. Peter and the other apostles 1161
Ac 5:34 T. stood there up one in...council,....... 1161
Ac 6:2 T. the twelve called the multitude 1161
Ac 6:9 T. there arose certain of the 1161
Ac 6:11 T. they suborned men, which said, ... 5119
Ac 7:1 T. said the high priest, Are these....... 1161
Ac 7:4 T. came he out of the land of the....... 5119
Ac 7:14 T. sent Joseph, and called his............ 1161
Ac 7:29 T. fled Moses at this saying, and 1161
Ac 7:32 T. Moses trembled, and durst not 1161
Ac 7:33 T. said the Lord to him, Put off thy.... 1161
Ac 7:42 T. God turned, and gave them up 1161
Ac 7:57 T. they cried out with a loud voice, ... 1161
Ac 8:5 T. Philip went down to the city of...... 1161
Ac 8:13 T. Simon himself believed also: 1161
Ac 8:17 T. laid they their hands on them, ... 5119
Ac 8:24 T. answered Simon, and said,............ 1161
Ac 8:29 T. the Spirit said unto Philip, Go....... 1161
Ac 8:35 T. Philip opened his mouth, and......... 1161
Ac 9:13 T. Ananias answered, Lord, I have...... 1161
Ac 9:19 T. was Saul certain days with the........ 1161
Ac 9:25 T. the disciples took him by night,....... 1161
Ac 9:31 T. had the churches rest 3767
Ac 9:39 T. Peter arose and went with............ 1161
Ac 10:21 T. Peter went down to the men........... 1161
Ac 10:23 T. called he them in, and lodged 3767
Ac 10:34 T. Peter opened his mouth, and......... 1161
Ac 10:46 magnify God. T. answered Peter, ... 5119
Ac 10:48 T. prayed they him to tarry 5119
Ac 11:16 T. remembered I the word of the........ 1161
Ac 11:17 Forasmuch t. as God gave them 3767
Ac 11:18 T. hath God also to the Gentiles.......... 686
Ac 11:22 T. tidings of these things came 1161
Ac 11:25 T. departed Barnabas to Tarsus, ... 1161
Ac 11:29 T. the disciples, every man............... 1161
Ac 12:3 (T. were the days of unleavened 1161
Ac 12:15 even so. T. said they, It is his........... 1161
Ac 13:9 T. Saul, (who also is called Paul,)....... 1161
Ac 13:12 T. the deputy, when he saw what 5119
Ac 13:16 T. Paul stood up, and beckoning 1161
Ac 13:46 T. Paul and Barnabas waxed bold, ... 1161
Ac 14:13 T. the priest of Jupiter, which was 1161
Ac 15:12 T. all the multitude kept silence, ... 1161
Ac 15:22 T. pleased it the apostles and............ 5119
Ac 16:1 T. came he to Derbe and Lystra: 1161
Ac 16:29 T. he called for a light, and.............. 1161
Ac 17:14 t. immediately the brethren sent 5119
Ac 17:18 T. certain philosophers of the 1161
Ac 17:22 T. Paul stood in the midst of Mars' 1161
Ac 17:29 Forasmuch t. as we are in the........... 3767
Ac 18:9 T. spake the Lord to Paul in the 1161
Ac 18:17 T. all the Greeks took Sosthenes, ... 1161
Ac 18:18 and t. took his leave of the brethren, ...
Ac 19:3 Unto what t. were ye baptized? 3767
Ac 19:4 T. said Paul, John verily baptized 1161
Ac 19:13 T. certain of the vagabond Jews, ... 1161

Ac 19:36 Seeing **t.** that these things cannot... *3767*
Ac 21:13 **T.** Paul answered, What mean ye... *1161*
Ac 21:26 **T.** Paul took the men, and the... *5119*
Ac 21:33 **T.** the chief captain came near, ... *5119*
Ac 22:22 and **t.** lifted up their voices, and said,...
Ac 22:27 **T.** the chief captain came, and... *1161*
Ac 22:29 **T.** straightway they departed from... *3767*
Ac 23:3 **T.** said Paul unto him, God shall ... *5119*
Ac 23:5 **T.** said Paul, I wist not, brethren, ... *5037*
Ac 23:17 **T.** Paul called one of...centurions ... *1161*
Ac 23:19 **T.** the chief captain took him by... *1161*
Ac 23:22 captain **t.** let the young man depart,...
Ac 23:27 **t.** came I with an army, and rescued...
Ac 23:31 **T.** the soldiers, as it was... *3767*
Ac 24:10 **T.** Paul, after that...governor had... *1161*
Ac 25:2 **T.** the high priest and the chief of... *1161*
Ac 25:10 **T.** said Paul, I stand at Caesar's ... *1161*
Ac 25:12 **T.** Festus, when he had conferred... *5119*
Ac 25:22 **T.** Agrippa said...Festus, I would... *1161*
Ac 26:1 **T.** Agrippa said unto Paul, Thou... *1161*
Ac 26:1 **T.** Paul stretched forth the hand, ... *5119*
Ac 26:20 of Judaea, and **t.** to the Gentiles,...
Ac 26:28 **T.** Agrippa said unto Paul, ... *1161*
Ac 26:32 **T.** said Agrippa unto Festus, This ... *1161*
Ac 27:20 be saved was **t.** taken away. ... *3063*
Ac 27:29 **T.** fearing lest we should have... *5037*
Ac 27:32 **T.** the soldiers cut off the ropes of... *5119*
Ac 27:36 **T.** were they all of good cheer, and... *1161*
Ac 28:1 **t.** they knew that the island was ... *5119*
Ro 3:1 What advantage **t.** hath the Jew?... *3767*
Ro 3:6 for **t.** how shall God judge the world?...
Ro 3:9 What **t.**? are we better than they?... *3767*
Ro 3:27 Where is boasting **t.**? It is ... *3767*
Ro 3:31 Do we **t.** make void the law through... *3767*
Ro 4:1 What shall we say **t.** that Abraham... *3767*
Ro 4:9 Cometh this blessedness **t.** upon... *3767*
Ro 4:10 How was it **t.** reckoned? when he ... *3767*
Ro 5:9 Much more **t.**, being now justified ... *3767*
Ro 6:1 What shall we say **t.**? Shall we ... *3767*
Ro 6:15 What **t.**? shall we sin, because we... *3767*
Ro 6:18 Being **t.** made free from sin, ye... *1161*
Ro 6:21 fruit had ye **t.** in those things... *5119,3767*
Ro 7:3 So **t.** if, while her husband liveth, ... *686*
Ro 7:7 What shall we say **t.**? Is the law ... *3767*
Ro 7:13 **t.** that which is good made death... *3767*
Ro 7:16 If **t.** I do that which I would not, I... *1161*
Ro 7:17 **t.** it is no more I that do it, but sin ... *1161*
Ro 7:21 I find **t.** a law, that, when I would ... *686*
Ro 7:25 **t.** with the mind I myself serve the... *686*
Ro 8:8 So **t.** they that are in...flesh cannot ... *1161*
Ro 8:17 if children, **t.** heirs; heirs of God,... *2535*
Ro 8:25 **t.** do we with patience wait for it. ...
Ro 8:31 What shall we **t.** say to these... *3767*
Ro 9:14 What shall we say **t.**? Is there... *3767*
Ro 9:16 So **t.** it is not of him that willeth,... *686*
Ro 9:19 Thou wilt say **t.** unto me, Why... *3767*
Ro 9:30 What shall we say **t.**? That the... *3767*
Ro 10:14 **t.** shall they call on him in whom... *3767*
Ro 10:17 So **t.** faith cometh by hearing, and ... *686*
Ro 11:1 I say **t.**, Hath God cast away his... *3767*
Ro 11:5 Even so **t.** at this present time also... *3767*
Ro 11:6 if by grace, **t.** is it no more of works: ...
Ro 11:6 it be of works, **t.** is it no more grace: ...
Ro 11:7 What **t.**? Israel hath not obtained... *3767*
Ro 11:11 I say **t.**, Have they stumbled that... *3767*
Ro 11:19 Thou wilt say **t.**, The branches... *3767*
Ro 12:6 Having **t.** gifts differing according ... *1161*
Ro 13:3 thou **t.** not be afraid of the power?... *1161*
Ro 14:12 So **t.** every one of us shall give an... *686*
Ro 14:16 Let not **t.** your good be evil spoken... *3767*
Ro 15:1 We **t.** that are strong ought to bear... *1161*
1Co 3:5 Who **t.** is Paul, and who is... *3767*
1Co 3:7 So **t.** neither is he that planteth any...
1Co 4:5 **t.** shall every man have praise of... *5119*
1Co 5:10 **t.** must ye needs go out of the world ... *686*
1Co 6:4 If **t.** ye have judgments of things... *3767*
1Co 6:15 I **t.** take the members of Christ, ... *3767*
1Co 7:38 **t.** he that giveth her in marriage ... *2532*
1Co 9:18 What is my reward **t.**? Verily ... *3767*
1Co 10:19 What say I **t.**? that the idol is... *3767*
1Co 12:28 **t.** gifts of healings, helps, ... *1534*
1Co 13:10 **t.** that which is in part shall be ... *5119*
1Co 13:12 a glass, darkly; but **t.** face to face: ... *5119*
1Co 13:12 **t.** shall I know even as also I am ... *5119*
1Co 14:15 What is it **t.**? I will pray with the ... *3767*
1Co 14:26 How is it **t.**, brethren? when ye... *3767*
1Co 15:5 seen of Cephas, **t.** of the twelve; ... *1534*
1Co 15:7 seen of James; **t.** of all the apostles. ... *1534*
1Co 15:13 of the dead, **t.** is Christ not risen:... *3761*
1Co 15:14 not risen, **t.** is our preaching vain, ... *686*
1Co 15:16 rise not, **t.** is not Christ raised: ... *3761*
1Co 15:18 **T.** they also which are fallen... *686*
1Co 15:24 **T.** cometh the end, when he shall ... *1534*
1Co 15:28 **t.** shall the Son also himself be ... *5119*
1Co 15:29 why are they **t.** baptized for the dead? ...
1Co 15:54 **t.** shall be brought to pass the... *5119*
2Co 2:2 who is he **t.** that maketh me glad, ... *2532*
2Co 3:12 Seeing **t.** that we have such hope,... *3767*
2Co 4:12 So **t.** death worketh in us, but life... *3303*
2Co 5:14 if one died for all, **t.** were all dead: ... *686*
2Co 5:20 Now **t.** we are ambassadors for Christ, ...
2Co 6:1 We **t.**, as workers together with... *3767*
2Co 12:10 am weak, **t.** am I strong. ... *5119,1161,2532*
Ga 1:18 **T.** after three years I went up to... *1899*
Ga 2:1 **T.** fourteen years after I went up... *1899*
Ga 2:21 the law, **t.** Christ is dead in vain... *686*
Ga 3:9 So **t.** they which be of faith are...
Ga 3:19 Wherefore **t.** serveth the law? It... *3767*
Ga 3:21 law **t.** against the promises of God? ... *3767*
Ga 3:29 Christ's, **t.** are ye Abraham's seed, ... *686*
Ga 4:7 **t.** an heir of God through Christ... *2532*
Ga 4:8 Howbeit **t.**, when ye knew not ... *5119*
Ga 4:15 Where is **t.** the blessedness ye... *3767*
Ga 4:29 But as **t.** he that was born after... *5119*
Ga 4:31 So **t.**, brethren, we are not ... *686*
Ga 5:11 **t.** is the offense of the cross ceased. ... *686*
Ga 5:16 This I say **t.**, Walk in the Spirit, ... *1161*
Ga 6:4 **t.** shall he have rejoicing in ... *5119*
Eph 5:15 See **t.** that ye walk circumspectly, ... *3767*
Php 1:18 What **t.**? notwithstanding, every... *1063*
Col 3:1 If ye **t.** be risen with Christ, seek... *3767*
Col 3:4 **t.** shall ye also appear with him in ... *5119*
1Th 4:1 **t.** we beseech you, brethren, ... *3767*
1Th 4:17 **T.** we which are alive and remain... *1899*
1Th 5:3 **t.** sudden destruction cometh upon... *5119*
2Th 2:8 **t.** shall that Wicked be revealed, ... *5119*
1Ti 2:13 For Adam was first formed, **t.** Eve... *1534*
1Ti 3:2 A bishop **t.** must be blameless,... *3767*
1Ti 3:10 **t.** let them use the office of a... *1534*
Heb 2:14 Forasmuch **t.** as the children are... *3767*
Heb 4:8 **t.** would he not afterward have ...
Heb 4:14 Seeing **t.** that we have a great... *3767*
Heb 7:27 own sins, and **t.** for the people's: ... *1899*
Heb 8:7 **t.** should no place have been sought...
Heb 9:1 **T.** verily the first covenant had... *3767*
Heb 9:9 a figure for the time **t.** present, ... *3588*
Heb 9:26 For **t.** must he often have suffered ...
Heb 10:2 For **t.** would they not have ceased to...
Heb 10:7 **T.** said I, Lo, I come (in the ... *5119*
Heb 10:9 **T.** said he, Lo, I come to do thy... *5119*
Heb 12:8 **t.** are ye bastards, and not sons. ... *686*
Heb 12:26 Whose voice **t.** shook the earth: ... *5119*
Jas 1:15 **T.** when lust hath conceived, it... *1534*
Jas 2:4 Are ye not **t.** partial in yourselves, ... *2532*
Jas 2:24 Ye see **t.** how that by works a ... *5106*
Jas 3:17 above is first pure, **t.** peaceable, ... *1899*
Jas 4:14 a little time, and **t.** vanisheth away. ... *1899*
1Pe 4:1 Forasmuch **t.** as Christ hath... *3767*
2Pe 3:6 Whereby the world that **t.** was, ... *5119*
2Pe 3:11 Seeing **t.** that all these things ... *3767*
1Jo 1:5 This **t.** is the message which we... *2532*
1Jo 3:21 **t.** have we confidence toward God...
Re 3:16 **So t. because thou art lukewarm,** ...
Re 22:9 **T.** saith he unto me, See thou do... *2532*

THENCE See also THENCEFORTH.

Ge 2:10 from **t.** it was parted, and became... 8033
Ge 11:8 Lord scattered them abroad from **t.** ... 8033
Ge 11:9 **t.** did the Lord scatter them from... 8033
Ge 12:8 removed from **t.** unto a mountain ... 8033
Ge 18:16 And the men rose up from **t.**, and... 8033
Ge 18:22 the men turned their faces from **t.**,... 8033
Ge 20:1 And Abraham journeyed from **t.**... 8033
Ge 24:7 take a wife unto my son from **t.**... 8033
Ge 26:17 And Isaac departed **t.**, and pitched... 8033
Ge 26:22 he removed from **t.**, and digged... 8033
Ge 26:23 he went up from **t.** to Beer-sheba. ... 8033
Ge 27:9 fetch me from **t.** two good kids of... 8033
Ge 27:45 I will send, and fetch thee from **t.**. ... 8033
Ge 28:2 take thee a wife from **t.** of the... 8033
Ge 28:6 to take him a wife from **t.**;... 8033
Ge 30:32 removing from **t.** all the speckled ... 8033
Ge 42:2 thither, and buy for us from **t.**;... 8033
Ge 42:26 asses with the corn, and departed **t.**... 8033
Ge 49:24 (from **t.** is the shepherd, the stone... 8033
Nu 13:23 cut down from **t.** a branch with one ... 8033
Nu 13:24 children of Israel cut down from **t.**... 8033
Nu 21:16 And from **t.** they went to Beer: that... 8033
Nu 21:12, 13 From **t.** they removed, and... 8033
Nu 22:41 **t.** he might see the utmost part of... 8033
Nu 23:13 all: and curse me them from **t.**. ... 8033
Nu 23:27 mayest curse me them from **t.**. ... 8033
De 4:29 But if from **t.** thou shalt seek the... 8033
De 5:15 thy God brought thee out **t.** through... 8033
De 6:23 he brought us out from **t.**, that he... 8033
De 10:7 From **t.** they journeyed unto ... 8033
De 19:12 his city shall send and fetch him **t.**,... 8033
De 22:8 thine house, if any man fall from **t.**. ...
De 24:18 Lord thy God redeemed thee **t.** ... 8033
De 30:4 from **t.** will the Lord thy God... 8033
De 30:4 thee, and from **t.** will he fetch thee: ... 8033
Jos 6:22 and bring out **t.** the woman, and all ... 8033
Jos 15:4 From **t.** it passed toward Azmon, ...
Jos 15:14 And Caleb drove **t.** the three sons... 8033
Jos 15:15 he went up **t.** to the inhabitants ... 8033
Jos 18:13 went over from **t.** toward Luz, ... 8033
Jos 18:14 border was drawn **t.**, and compassed ...
Jos 19:13 And from **t.** passeth on along on ... 8033
Jos 19:34 and goeth out from **t.** to Hukkok,... 8033
Jg 1:11 And from **t.** he went against the ... 8033
Jg 1:20 expelled **t.** the three sons of Anak... 8033
Jg 8:8 he went up **t.** to Penuel, and spake ... 8033
Jg 18:11 there went from **t.** of the family of... 8033
Jg 18:13 passed **t.** unto mount Ephraim, ... 8033
Jg 19:18 from **t.** am I: and I went to... 8033
Jg 21:24 children of Israel departed **t.** at... 8033
Jg 21:24 went out from **t.** every man to his... 8033
1Sa 4:4 might bring from **t.** the ark of the ... 8033
1Sa 10:3 shalt thou go on forward from **t.**, ... 8033
1Sa 10:23 And they ran and fetched him **t.**... 8033
1Sa 17:49 took **t.** a stone, and slang it, and... 8033
1Sa 22:1 David therefore departed **t.**, and ... 8033
1Sa 22:3 David went **t.** to Mizpeh of Moab:... 8033
1Sa 23:29 And David went up from **t.**, an ... 8033
2Sa 6:2 bring up from **t.** the ark of God, ... 8033
2Sa 14:2 fetched **t.** a wise woman, and said... 8033
2Sa 16:5 **t.** came out a man of the family of... 8033
2Sa 21:13 he brought up from **t.** the bones of... 8033
1Ki 1:45 they are come up from **t.** rejoicing,... 8033
1Ki 2:36 and go not forth **t.** any whither. ... 8033
1Ki 9:28 to Ophir, and fetched from **t.** gold, ... 8033
1Ki 12:25 and went out from **t.**, and built... 8033
1Ki 19:19 So he departed **t.**, and found Elisha ... 8033
2Ki 2:21 shall not be from **t.** any more death... 8033
2Ki 2:23 he went up from **t.** unto Beth-el: ... 8033
2Ki 2:25 he went from **t.** to mount Carmel,... 8033
2Ki 2:25 and from **t.** he returned to Samaria... 8033
2Ki 6:2 and take **t.** every man a beam, ... 8033
2Ki 7:8 and carried **t.** silver, and gold,... 8033
2Ki 7:8 carried **t.** also, and went and hid it. ... 8033
2Ki 10:15 when he was departed **t.**, he lighted ... 8033
2Ki 17:27 priests whom ye brought from **t.**;... 8033
2Ki 17:33 whom they carried away from **t.**. ... 8033
2Ki 23:12 brake them down from **t.**, and cast... 8033
2Ki 24:13 he carried out **t.** all the treasures... 8033
1Ch 13:6 to bring up **t.** the ark of God the ... 8033
2Ch 8:18 and took **t.** four hundred and fifty... 8033
2Ch 26:20 they thrust him out from **t.**; yea, ... 8033
Ezr 6:6 beyond the river, be ye far from **t.**... 8536
Ne 1:9 yet will I gather them from **t.**, and ... 8033
Job 39:29 From **t.** she seeketh the prey, and... 8033
Isa 52:11 depart ye, go ye out from **t.**, ... 8033
Isa 65:20 be no more **t.** an infant of days,... 8033
Jer 5:6 one that goeth out **t.** shall be torn... 2007
Jer 13:6 and take the girdle from **t.**,... 8033
Jer 22:24 hand, yet would I pluck thee **t.**; ... 8033
Jer 36:29 cause to cease from **t.** man and beast? ...
Jer 37:12 separate himself **t.** in the midst of ... 8033
Jer 38:11 took **t.** old cast clouts and old rotten... 8033
Jer 43:12 he shall go forth from **t.** in peace. ... 8033
Jer 49:16 I will bring thee down from **t.**, saith... 8033
Jer 49:38 will destroy them from **t.** the king and..8033
Jer 50:9 her; from **t.** she shall be taken: ... 8033
Eze 11:18 all the abominations thereof from **t.**...
Ho 2:15 give her her vineyards from **t.**, ... 8033
Am 6:2 from **t.** go ye to Hamath the great: ... 8033
Am 9:2 hell, **t.** shall mine hand take them;... 8033
Am 9:2 to heaven, **t.** will I bring them down: .. 8033
Am 9:3 I will search and take them out **t.**;... 8033
Am 9:3 **t.** will I command the serpent, and... 8033
Am 9:4 **t.** will I command the sword, and it ... 8033

Ob 4 t. will I bring thee down, saith the 8033
Mt 4:21 going on from t., he saw other two 1564
Mt 5:26 by no means come out t., till 1564
Mt 9:9 as Jesus passed forth from t., he saw ..1564
Mt 9:27 when Jesus departed t., two blind 1564
Mt 10:11 and there abide till ye go t..................
Mt 11:1 he departed t. to teach and to preach.. 1564
Mt 12:9 when he was departed t., he went 1564
Mt 12:15 knew it,...withdrew himself from t...... 1564
Mt 13:53 these parables, he departed t.. 1564
Mt 14:13 he departed t. by ship into a desert.... 1564
Mt 15:21 Jesus went t., and departed into the ... 1564
Mt 15:29 Jesus departed from t., and came........ 1564
Mt 19:15 his hands on them, and departed t...... 1564
Mk 1:19 when he had gone a little farther t.,.... 1564
Mk 6:1 he went out from t., and came into 1564
Mk 6:11 when ye depart t., shake off the.... 1564
Mk 7:24 from t. he arose, and went into the 1564
Mk 9:30 they departed t., and passed............ 1564
Mk 10:1 And he rose from t., and cometh 1564
Lu 9:4 into, there abide, and t. depart....... 1564
Lu 12:59 thou shalt not depart t., till thou .. 1564
Lu 16:26 to us, that would come from t....... 1564
Joh 4:43 Now after two days he departed t.,.... 1564
Joh 11:54 went t. unto a country near to the 1564
Ac 7:4 from t., when his father was dead, ... 1564
Ac 13:4 and from t. they sailed to Cyprus....... 1564
Ac 14:26 And t. sailed to Antioch, from 1564
Ac 16:12 from t. to Philippi, which is the chief... 1564
Ac 18:7 he departed t., and entered into a 1564
Ac 18:18 sailed t. into Syria, and with him.............
Ac 20:15 And we sailed t., and came the.......... 1564
Ac 21:1 Rhodes, and from t. unto Patara: 1564
Ac 27:4 when we had launched from t., we..... 1564
Ac 27:12 more part advised to depart t. also,.... 1564
Ac 27:13 loosing t., they sailed close by Crete. ....
Ac 28:13 And from t. we fetched a compass, ... 3606
Ac 28:15 And from t., when the brethren......... 1564
2Co 2:13 them, I went from t. into Macedonia.........

THENCEFORTH

Le 22:27 and t. it shall be accepted for an........ 1973
2Ch 32:23 the sight of all nations from t....... 310,3651
Mt 5:13 it is t. good for nothing, but to be..2089
Joh 19:12 t. Pilate sought to release.......... 1537,5127

THEOPHILUS (the-of'-il-us)

Lu 1:3 thee in order, most excellent T.,........ 2321
Ac 1:1 treatise have I made, O T., of all....... 2321

THERE See also THEREABOUT; THEREAT; THEREBY; THEREFORE; THEREFROM; THEREIN; THEREOF; THEREON; THEREOUT; THEREUNTO; THEREUPON; THEREWITH.

Ge 1:3 Let t. be light: and t. was light...............
Ge 1:6 Let t. be a firmament in the midst............
Ge 1:14 said, Let t. be lights in the firmament ....
Ge 1:30 upon the earth, wherein t. is life, ...
Ge 2:5 t. was not a man to till the ground. ....
Ge 2:6 But t. went up a mist from the earth, ...
Ge 2:8 t. he put the man whom he had......... 8033
Ge 2:11 land of Havilah, where t. is gold:..............
Ge 2:12 t. is bdellium and the onyx stone........ 8033
Ge 2:20 Adam t. was not found an help meet.........
Ge 4:26 to Seth, to him also t. was born a son; .....
Ge 6:4 T. were giants in the earth in those..........
Ge 7:9 T. went in two and two unto Noah ....
Ge 9:11 shall t. any more be a flood to destroy ......
Ge 11:2 land of Shinar; and they dwelt t.. 8033
Ge 11:7 and t. confound their language, ... 8033
Ge 11:9 Lord did t. confound the language....... 8033
Ge 11:31 they came unto Haran, and dwelt t..... 8033
Ge 12:7 t. builded he an altar unto the Lord, ... 8033
Ge 12:8 t. he builded an altar unto the Lord, ... 8033
Ge 12:10 And t. was a famine in the land: and.........
Ge 12:10 down into Egypt to sojourn t.;.......... 8033
Ge 13:4 which he had made t. at the first: 8033
Ge 13:7 t. was a strife between the herdmen.........
Ge 13:8 said unto Lot, Let t. be no strife,............
Ge 13:18 built t. an altar unto the Lord. 8033
Ge 14:8 And t. went out the king of Sodom, ...
Ge 14:10 and Gomorrah fled, and fell t.;.......... 8033
Ge 14:13 And t. came one that had escaped, and .....
Ge 18:24 t. be fifty righteous within the city:..........
Ge 18:28 t. shall lack five of the fifty righteous: ....
Ge 18:28 If I find t. forty and five, I will.......... 8033
Ge 18:29 t. shall be forty found t.........................
Ge 18:30 t. shall thirty be found t.. 8033
Ge 18:30 I will not do it, if I find thirty t.. 8033
Ge 18:31 t. shall be twenty found t.. 8033
Ge 18:32 Peradventure ten shall be found t...... 8033
Ge 19:1 t. came two angels to Sodom at even;........
Ge 19:31 is old, and t. is not a man in the earth ......
Ge 21:31 t. they sware both of them. 8033
Ge 21:33 called t. on the name of the Lord,...... 8033
Ge 22:2 and offer him t. for a burnt offering 8033
Ge 22:9 Abraham built an altar t., and laid........ 8033
Ge 23:13 it of me, and I will bury my dead t..... 8033
Ge 24:23 is t. room in thy father's house for us ....
Ge 24:33 t. was set meat before him to eat: but ......
Ge 25:10 t. was Abraham buried, and Sarah...... 8033
Ge 25:24 behold, t. were twins in her womb. ....
Ge 26:1 And t. was a famine in the land,..............
Ge 26:8 when he had been t. a long time,......... 8033
Ge 26:17 in the valley of Gerar, and dwelt t...... 8033
Ge 26:19 found t. a well of springing water. 8033
Ge 26:25 he builded an altar t., and called......... 8033
Ge 26:25 the Lord, and pitched his tent t.: 8033
Ge 26:25 and t. Isaac's servants digged a well... 8033
Ge 26:28 said, Let t. be now an oath betwixt us. .....
Ge 28:11 place, and tarried t. all night, ... 8033
Ge 29:2 t. were three flocks of sheep lying 8033
Ge 31:14 Is t. yet any portion or inheritance for.......
Ge 31:46 and they did eat t. upon the heap....... 8033
Ge 32:4 with Laban, and stayed t. until now: ....
Ge 32:13 And he lodged t. that same night; 8033
Ge 32:24 and t. wrestled a man with him until; ....
Ge 32:29 my name? And he blessed him t. 8033
Ge 33:20 And he erected t. an altar, and......... 8033
Ge 35:1 Arise, go up to Beth-el, and dwell t.:.. 8033
Ge 35:1 and make t. an altar unto God, ... 8033
Ge 35:3 I will make t. an altar unto God, ... 8033
Ge 35:7 he built t. an altar, and called the....... 8033
Ge 35:7 because t. God appeared unto him,..... 8033
Ge 35:16 t. was but a little way to come to............
Ge 36:31 before t. reigned any king over the...........
Ge 37:24 pit was empty, t. was no water in it. ....
Ge 37:28 t. passed by Midianites merchantmen; ....
Ge 38:2 And Judah saw t. a daughter of a 8033
Ge 38:21 said, T. was no harlot in this place. ....
Ge 38:22 that t. was no harlot in this place. ....
Ge 39:9 T. is none greater in this house than I; .....
Ge 39:11 and t. was none of the men of the...........
Ge 39:11 of the men of the house t. within. 8033
Ge 39:20 and he was t. in the prison. 8033
Ge 39:22 whatsoever they did t., he was the..... 8033
Ge 40:8 a dream, and t. is no interpreter of it........
Ge 40:17 t. was of all manner of bakemeats ....
Ge 41:2 t. came up out of the river seven well.......
Ge 41:8 t. was none that could interpret them........
Ge 41:12 And t. was...with us a young man, ...
Ge 41:12 was t. with us a young man, an......... 8033
Ge 41:15 and t. is none that can interpret it:...........
Ge 41:18 t. came up out of the river seven kine, ...
Ge 41:24 t. was none that could declare it to me......
Ge 41:29 t. come seven years of great plenty..........
Ge 41:30 t. shall arise after them seven years of......
Ge 41:39 t. is none so discreet and wise as thou......
Ge 41:54 in all the land of Egypt t. was bread.. ....
Ge 42:1 Jacob saw that t. was corn in Egypt,.........
Ge 42:2 I have heard that t. is corn in Egypt: ....
Ge 42:16 proved, whether t. be any truth in you:.....
Ge 43:25 heart that they should eat bread t. 8033
Ge 43:30 into his chamber, and wept t............. 8033
Ge 44:14 to Joseph's house; for he was yet t.: .. 8033
Ge 45:1 And t. stood no man with him, while.........
Ge 45:6 and yet t. are five years, in the ....
Ge 45:6 which t. shall neither be earing nor............
Ge 45:11 And t. will I nourish thee; for yet....... 8033
Ge 45:11 for yet t. are five years of famine,.............
Ge 46:3 will t. make of thee a great nation: 8033
Ge 47:13 t. was no bread in all the land; for the ......
Ge 47:18 t. is not ought left in the sight of my ....
Ge 48:7 yet t. was but a little way to come............
Ge 48:7 and I buried her t. in the way of......... 8033
Ge 49:31 T. they buried Abraham and Sarah...... 8033
Ge 49:31 t. they buried Isaac and Rebekah 8033
Ge 49:31 his wife; and t. I buried Leah. 8033
Ge 50:5 of Canaan, t. shalt thou bury me. 8033
Ge 50:9 t. went up with him both chariots and ....
Ge 50:10 t. they mourned with a great and....... 8033
Ex 1:8 t. arose up a new king over Egypt, ...
Ex 1:10 when t. falleth out any war, they join........
Ex 2:1 t. went a man of the house of Levi,..........
Ex 2:12 and when he saw that t. was no man, ...
Ex 5:9 t. more work be laid upon the men,..........
Ex 5:13 daily tasks, as when t. was straw. ....
Ex 5:16 T. is no straw given unto thy ....
Ex 5:18 for t. shall no straw be given you,............
Ex 7:19 that t. may be blood throughout all ....
Ex 7:21 t. was blood throughout all the land ....
Ex 8:10 t. is none like unto the Lord our God........
Ex 8:15 when Pharaoh saw that t. was respite, ...
Ex 8:18 so t. were lice upon man, and upon ....
Ex 8:22 that no swarms of flies shall be t.;...... 8033
Ex 8:24 t. came a grievous swarm of flies into ....
Ex 8:31 from his people; t. remained not one.........
Ex 9:3 t. shall be a very grievous murrain. ....
Ex 9:4 t. shall nothing die of all that is the..........
Ex 9:7 t. was not one of the cattle of the ....
Ex 9:14 that t. is none like me in all the earth. ......
Ex 9:22 that t. may be hail in all the land of ....
Ex 9:24 So t. was hail, and fire mingled with ....
Ex 9:24 such as t. was none like it in all the..........
Ex 9:26 children of Israel were, was t. no hail. ......
Ex 9:28 t. be no more mighty thunderings and ....
Ex 9:29 neither shall t. be any more hail;..............
Ex 10:14 t. were no such locusts as they, ...
Ex 10:15 t. remained not any green thing in............
Ex 10:19 t. remained not one locust in all the..........
Ex 10:21 that t. may be darkness over the land.......
Ex 10:22 t. was a thick darkness in all the land.......
Ex 10:26 t. shall not an hoof be left behind; for ....
Ex 11:6 t. shall be a great cry throughout all ....
Ex 11:6 such as t. was none like it, nor shall.........
Ex 12:16 day t. shall be an holy convocation,...........
Ex 12:16 day t. shall be an holy convocation,...........
Ex 12:19 Seven days shall t. be no leaven found ......
Ex 12:30 and t. was a great cry in Egypt; ....
Ex 12:30 cry in Egypt; for t. was not a house ....
Ex 12:30 house where t. was not one dead. ....
Ex 12:43 T. shall no stranger eat thereof:...............
Ex 13:3 t. shall no leavened bread be eaten. ....
Ex 13:7 t. shall no leavened bread be seen with .....
Ex 13:7 neither shall t. be leaven seen with............
Ex 14:11 Because t. were no graves in Egypt, ...
Ex 14:28 t. remained not so much as one of.............
Ex 15:25 t. he made for them a statute and...... 8033
Ex 15:25 ordinance, and t. he proved them. 8033
Ex 15:27 They encamped t. by the waters........ 8033
Ex 16:14 wilderness t. lay a small round thing, ...
Ex 16:24 neither was t. any worm therein. ....
Ex 16:26 is the sabbath, in it t. shall be none. ....
Ex 16:27 that t. went out some of the people on......
Ex 17:1 t. was no water for the people to drink. ....
Ex 17:3 the people thirsted t. for water;......... 8033
Ex 17:6 I will stand before thee t. upon the..... 8033
Ex 17:6 t. shall come water out of it, that the........
Ex 19:2 t. Israel camped before the mount...... 8033
Ex 19:13 T. shall not an hand touch it, but he ....
Ex 19:16 that t. were thunders and lightnings, ...
Ex 21:30 If t. be laid on him a sum of money, ...
Ex 22:2 die, t. shall no blood be shed for him. ....
Ex 22:3 t. shall be blood shed for him; ....
Ex 23:26 T. shall nothing cast their young, nor ....
Ex 24:10 and t. was under his feet as it were a........
Ex 24:12 to me into the mount, and be t......... 8033
Ex 25:22 and t. I will meet with thee,....................
Ex 25:35 t. shall be a knop under two branches ....
Ex 26:17 Two tenons shall t. be in one board,.........
Ex 26:20 side t. shall be twenty boards:................
Ex 27:9 t. shall be hangings for the court of ....
Ex 27:11 t. shall be hangings of an hundred............
Ex 28:32 t. shall be an hole in the top of it, ...
Ex 29:42 meet you, to speak t. unto thee......... 8033
Ex 29:43 t. I will meet with the children of 8033
Ex 30:12 that t. be no plague among them, ...
Ex 30:34 of each shall t. be a like weight:...............
Ex 32:17 T. is a noise of war in the camp...............
Ex 32:24 into the fire, and t. came out this calf. ......
Ex 32:28 t. fell of the people that day about............
Ex 33:20 for t. shall no man see me, and live...........
Ex 33:21 Lord said, Behold, t. is a place by me, ...
Ex 34:2 present thyself t. to me in the top...... 8033
Ex 34:5 in the cloud, and stood with him t., ... 8033
Ex 34:28 he was t. with the Lord forty days 8033
Ex 35:2 day t. shall be to you an holy day,............
Ex 36:30 And t. were eight boards; and their ....

Ex 39:23 **t.** was an hole in the midst of the robe,.....
Ex 40:30 put water **t.**, to wash withal............. 8033
Le 6:27 when **t.** is sprinkled of the blood.............
Le 7:7 **t.** is one law for them: the priest that.......
Le 8:31 **t.** eat it with the bread that is in........ 8033
Le 9:24 **t.** came a fire out from before the Lord,....
Le 10:2 **t.** went out fire from the Lord, and..........
Le 11:36 pit, wherein **t.** is plenty of water,............
Le 13:10 **t.** be quick raw flesh in the rising;............
Le 13:19 place of the boil **t.** be a white rising,.........
Le 13:21 behold, **t.** be no white hairs therein, ...
Le 13:24 Or if **t.** be any flesh, in the......................
Le 13:24 in the skin whereof **t.** is a hot burning,......
Le 13:26 **t.** be no white hair in the bright spot, ...
Le 13:30 skin; and **t.** be in it a yellow thin hair;.......
Le 13:31 skin, and that **t.** is no black hair in it;........
Le 13:32 not, and **t.** be in it no yellow hair, ...
Le 13:37 **t.** is black hair grown up therein;.............
Le 13:42 if **t.** be in the bald head, or bald.................
Le 14:35 **t.** is as it were a plague in the house: ....
Le 16:17 **t.** shall be no man in the tabernacle ....
Le 16:23 place, and shall leave them **t.**. 8033
Le 17:3 what man soever **t.** be of the house of.......
Le 17:8, 10 man **t.** be of the house of Israel,.........
Le 17:13 man **t.** be of the children of Israel, ...
Le 20:14 that **t.** be no wickedness among you. ....
Le 21:1 **T.** shall none be defiled for the dead.........
Le 22:10 **T.** shall no stranger eat of the holy...........
Le 22:13 but **t.** shall no stranger eat thereof. ....
Le 22:21 **t.** shall be no blemish therein....................
Le 23:27 seventh month **t.** shall be a day of..............
Le 25:51 If **t.** be yet many years behind,.................
Le 25:52 **t.** remain but few years unto the year.......
Nu 1:4 you **t.** shall be a man of every tribe;.........
Nu 1:53 **t.** be no wrath upon the congregation........
Nu 5:13 and **t.** be no witness against her,.............
Nu 6:5 **t.** shall no rasor come upon his...............
Nu 8:19 **t.** be no plague among the children of........
Nu 9:6 **t.** were certain men, who were defiled......
Nu 9:15 at even **t.** was upon the tabernacle as.......
Nu 9:17 **t.** the children of Israel pitched.......... 8033
Nu 11:6 **t.** is nothing at all, beside this manna, ...
Nu 11:16 that they may stand **t.** with thee. 8033
Nu 11:17 come down and talk with thee **t.**. 8033
Nu 11:26 But **t.** remained two of the men in the......
Nu 11:27 **t.** ran a young man, and told Moses,........
Nu 11:31 **t.** went forth a wind from the Lord,..........
Nu 11:34 because **t.** they buried the people....... 8033
Nu 12:6 If **t.** be a prophet among you, I the ....
Nu 13:20 whether **t.** be wood therein, or not..........
Nu 13:28 we saw the children of Anak **t.**. 8033
Nu 13:33 **t.** we saw the giants, the sons of...... 8033
Nu 14:35 be consumed, and **t.** they shall die...... 8033
Nu 14:43 the Canaanites are **t.** before you, ... 8033
Nu 16:35 And **t.** came out a fire from the Lord,.......
Nu 16:46 for **t.** is wrath gone out from the Lord; .....
Nu 18:5 that **t.** be no wrath any more upon.........
Nu 19:18 and upon the persons that were **t.**,..... 8033
Nu 20:1 Miriam died **t.**, and was buried **t.**....... 8033
Nu 20:2 **t.** was no water for the congregation:........
Nu 20:4 we and our cattle should die **t.**? 8033
Nu 20:5 neither is **t.** any water to drink. ....
Nu 20:26 unto his people, and shall die **t.**. 8033
Nu 20:28 and Aaron died **t.** in the top of the..... 8033
Nu 21:5 the wilderness? for **t.** is no bread,............
Nu 21:5 neither is **t.** any water; ....
Nu 21:28 For **t.** is a fire gone out of Heshbon,..........
Nu 21:32 out the Amorites that were **t.**,.......... 8033
Nu 21:35 until **t.** was none left him alive:...............
Nu 22:5 **t.** is a people come out from Egypt: ....
Nu 22:11 **t.** is a people come out of Egypt,...........
Nu 22:29 I would **t.** were a sword in mine hand, ...
Nu 23:23 **t.** is no enchantment against Jacob,..........
Nu 23:23 is **t.** any divination against Israel:............
Nu 24:17 **t.** shall come a Star out of Jacob, and a....
Nu 26:62 **t.** was no inheritance given them.............
Nu 26:64 among these **t.** was not a man of them.......
Nu 26:65 And **t.** was not left a man of them,..........
Nu 31:5 **t.** were delivered out of the thousands......
Nu 31:16 **t.** was a plague among the.....................
Nu 31:49 and **t.** lacketh not one man of us. ....
Nu 32:26 shall be **t.** in the cities of Gilead:....... 8033
Nu 33:9 ten palm trees; and they pitched **t.**..... 8033
Nu 33:38 and died **t.**, in the fortieth year.......... 8033
Nu 35:6 **t.** shall be six cities for refuge, ...
De 1:2 (**T.** are eleven days' journey from............
De 1:28 seen the sons of the Anakims **t.**........ 8033
De 1:35 **t.** shall not one of these men of this.........
De 1:46 unto the days that ye abode **t.**................
De 2:36 **t.** was not one city too strong for us:.........
De 3:4 **t.** was not a city which we took not.........
De 3:24 what God is **t.** in heaven or in earth, ...
De 4:7 For what nation is **t.** so great, who...........
De 4:8 what nation is **t.** so great, that hath..........
De 4:28 **t.** ye shall serve gods, the work of..... 8033
De 4:32 whether **t.** hath been any such thing ....
De 4:35 he is God; **t.** is none else beside him. ....
De 4:39 the earth beneath: **t.** is none else.............
De 5:26 For who is **t.** of all flesh, that hath...........
De 5:29 O that **t.** were such a heart in them,.........
De 7:14 **t.** shall not be male nor female barren........
De 7:24 **t.** shall no man be able to stand before......
De 8:15 and drought, where **t.** was no water; ....
De 10:5 **t.** they be, as the Lord commanded.... 8033
De 10:6 **t.** Aaron died, and **t.** he was buried;... 8033
De 11:17 that **t.** be no rain, and that the land.........
De 11:25 **T.** shall no man be able to stand before.....
De 12:5 all your tribes to put his name **t.**,....... 8033
De 12:7 **t.** ye shall eat before the Lord your.... 8033
De 12:11 **t.** shall be a place which the Lord............
De 12:11 to cause his name to dwell **t.**;........... 8033
De 12:14 **t.** thou shalt offer thy burnt.............. 8033
De 12:14 **t.** thou shalt do all that I................ 8033
De 12:21 God hath chosen to put his name **t.**.... 8033
De 13:1 If **t.** arise among you a prophet, or a........
De 13:12 thy God hath given thee to dwell **t.**, ... 8033
De 13:17 **t.** shall cleave nought of the cursed..........
De 14:23 shall choose to place his name **t.**,....... 8033
De 14:24 God shall choose to set his name **t.**, ... 8033
De 14:26 shalt eat **t.** before the Lord thy God, .. 8033
De 15:4 when **t.** shall be no poor among you; ....
De 15:7 If **t.** be among you a poor man of one.......
De 15:9 **t.** be not a thought in thy wicked ....
De 15:21 And if **t.** be any blemish therein, as if ....
De 16:2 shall choose to place his name **t.**........ 8033
De 16:4 **t.** shall be no leavened bread seen............
De 16:4 neither shall **t.** any thing of the flesh, ...
De 16:6 **t.** thou shalt sacrifice the passover...... 8033
De 16:11 hath chosen to place his name **t.**. 8033
De 17:2 If **t.** be found among you, within ....
De 17:8 If **t.** arise a matter too hard for thee in .....
De 17:12 to minister **t.** before the Lord thy 8033
De 18:7 do, which stand **t.** before the Lord. 8033
De 18:10 **T.** shall not be found among you any.........
De 20:5 man is **t.** that hath built a new house,........
De 20:7 man is **t.** that hath betrothed a wife,.........
De 20:8 What man is **t.** that is fearful and ....
De 21:4 the heifer's neck **t.** in the valley:........ 8033
De 22:26 **t.** is in the damsel no sin worthy of..........
De 22:27 cried, and **t.** was none to save her. ....
De 23:10 **t.** be among you any man, that is not.........
De 23:17 **T.** shall be no whore of the daughters.......
De 25:1 If **t.** be a controversy between men, ...
De 26:2 shall choose to place his name **t.**. 8033
De 26:5 Egypt, and sojourned **t.** with a few...... 8033
De 26:5 **t.** a nation, great, mighty, and.......... 8033
De 27:5 **t.** shalt thou build an altar unto the..... 8033
De 27:7 peace offerings, and shalt eat **t.**, ... 8033
De 28:32 and **t.** shall be no might in thine hand.......
De 28:36 **t.** shalt thou serve other gods, ... 8033
De 28:64 and **t.** thou shalt serve other gods, ... 8033
De 28:65 shall give thee **t.** a trembling heart, ... 8033
De 28:68 **t.** ye shall be sold unto your enemies.. 8033
De 29:18 Lest **t.** should be among you man, or........
De 29:18 lest **t.** should be among you a root that.....
De 31:26 it may be **t.** for a witness against....... 8033
De 32:12 and **t.** was no strange god with him. ....
De 32:28 is **t.** any understanding in them. ....
De 32:36 is gone, and **t.** is none shut up, or left. .....
De 32:39 I, am he, and **t.** is no god with me: ....
De 32:39 neither is **t.** any that can deliver out ....
De 33:19 **t.** they shall offer sacrifices of........... 8033
De 33:21 **t.**, in a portion of the lawgiver, was.... 8033
De 33:26 **T.** is none like unto the God of.............
De 34:5 the servant of the Lord died **t.** in....... 8033
De 34:10 **t.** arose not a prophet since in Israel.........
Jos 1:5 **T.** shall not any man be able to stand........
Jos 2:1 house, named Rahab, and lodged **t.**...... 8033
Jos 2:2 **t.** came men in hither to night of the........
Jos 2:4 **T.** came men unto me, but I wist not........
Jos 2:11 neither did **t.** remain...more courage ....
Jos 2:16 and hide yourselves **t.** three days, ... 8033
Jos 2:22 mountain, and abode **t.** three days, ... 8033
Jos 3:1 lodged **t.** before they passed over. 8033
Jos 3:4 Yet **t.** shall be a space between you..........
Jos 4:8 lodged, and laid them down **t.**............. 8033
Jos 4:9 stood: and they are **t.** unto this day.... 8033
Jos 5:1 neither was **t.** spirit in them any more,......
Jos 5:13 **t.** stood a man over against him with ....
Jos 7:4 So **t.** went up thither of the people...........
Jos 7:13 **T.** is an accursed thing in the midst..........
Jos 8:11 **t.** was a valley between them and Ai.........
Jos 8:14 wist not that **t.** were liers in ambush.........
Jos 8:17 **t.** was not a man left in Ai or Beth-el,.......
Jos 8:32 And he wrote **t.** upon the stones........ 8033
Jos 8:35 **T.** was not a word of all that Moses ....
Jos 9:23 and **t.** shall none of you be freed.............
Jos 10:8 **t.** shall not a man of them stand before .....
Jos 10:14 And **t.** was no day like that before it..........
Jos 11:11 **t.** was not any left to breathe: and he ....
Jos 11:19 **T.** was not a city that made peace............
Jos 11:22 **T.** was none of the Anakims left in...........
Jos 11:22 in Gath, and in Ashod, **t.** remained. ....
Jos 13:1 **t.** remaineth yet very much land to be.......
Jos 14:12 day how the Anakims were **t.**,.......... 8033
Jos 17:1 **T.** was also a lot for the tribe of..............
Jos 17:2 **T.** was also a lot for the rest of the..........
Jos 17:5 And **t.** fell ten portions to Manasseh, ...
Jos 17:15 cut down for thyself **t.** in the land 8033
Jos 18:1 tabernacle of the congregation **t.**. 8033
Jos 18:2 **t.** remained among the children of ....
Jos 18:10 **t.** Joshua divided the land unto the...... 8033
Jos 21:44 **t.** stood not a man of all their enemies ......
Jos 21:45 **T.** failed not ought of any good thing.........
Jos 22:10 tribe of Manasseh built **t.** an altar....... 8033
Jos 22:17 **t.** was a plague in the congregation of.......
Jos 24:26 and set it up **t.** under an oak,........... 8033
Jg 1:7 him to Jerusalem, and **t.** he died. 8033
Jg 2:5 they sacrificed **t.** unto the Lord.......... 8033
Jg 2:10 **t.** arose another generation after them,......
Jg 3:29 of valour; and **t.** escaped not a man. ....
Jg 4:16 the sword; and **t.** was not a man left. ....
Jg 4:17 **t.** was peace between Jabin the king.........
Jg 4:20 of thee, and say, Is **t.** any man here?.........
Jg 5:8 was **t.** a shield or spear seen among.........
Jg 5:11 **t.** shall they rehearse the righteous...........
Jg 5:14 Out of Ephraim was **t.** a root of them ....
Jg 5:15 **t.** were great thoughts of heart................
Jg 5:16 **t.** were great searchings of heart. ....
Jg 5:27 he bowed, **t.** he fell down dead.......... 8033
Jg 6:11 **t.** came an angel of the Lord, and sat........
Jg 6:21 **t.** rose up fire out of the rock, and...........
Jg 6:24 then Gideon built an altar **t.** unto........ 8033
Jg 6:39 and upon all the ground let **t.** be dew........
Jg 6:40 only, and **t.** was dew on all the ground......
Jg 7:3 **t.** returned of the people twenty and.........
Jg 7:3 and **t.** remained ten thousand...................
Jg 7:4 and I will try them for thee **t.**:........... 8033
Jg 7:13 **t.** was a man that told a dream unto ....
Jg 8:10 **t.** fell an hundred and twenty..................
Jg 9:21 and went to Beer, and dwelt **t.**,......... 8033
Jg 9:36 **t.** come people down from the top..............
Jg 9:37 **t.** come people down by the middle ....
Jg 9:51 **t.** was a strong tower within the city, ...
Jg 10:1 **t.** arose to defend Israel Tola the son ....
Jg 11:3 **t.** were gathered vain men to Jephthah, ...
Jg 12:6 **t.** fell at that time of the Ephraimites, ...
Jg 13:2 **t.** was a certain man of Zorah, of the.........
Jg 14:3 **t.** never a woman among the daughters.....
Jg 14:8 **t.** was a swarm of bees and honey in........
Jg 14:10 and Samson made **t.** a feast; 8033
Jg 15:19 the jaw, and **t.** came water thereout; ....
Jg 16:1 to Gaza, and saw **t.** an harlot, ... 8033
Jg 16:9 **t.** were men lying in wait, abiding............
Jg 16:12 **t.** were liers in wait abiding in the............
Jg 16:17 **T.** hath not come a rasor upon mine ....
Jg 16:27 lords of the Philistines were **t.**;.......... 8033
Jg 16:27 **t.** were upon the roof about three ....
Jg 17:1 and **t.** was a man of mount Ephraim,..........
Jg 17:6 In those days **t.** was no king in Israel,........
Jg 17:7 And **t.** was a young man out of................
Jg 17:7 was a Levite, and he sojourned **t.**. 8033
Jg 18:1 In those days **t.** was no king in Israel:.......
Jg 18:2 house of Micah, they lodged **t.**. 8033
Jg 18:7 **t.** was no magistrate in the land, that........
Jg 18:10 where **t.** is no want of any thing ....
Jg 18:11 **t.** went from thence of the family ....
Jg 18:14 that **t.** is in these houses an ephod, ...

Jg 18:28 **t.** was no deliverer, because it was far......
Jg 19:1 days, when **t.** was no king in Israel, ...
Jg 19:1 **t.** was a certain Levite sojourning on..........
Jg 19:2 and was **t.** four whole months........... 8033
Jg 19:4 did eat and drink, and lodged **t.**. 8033
Jg 19:7 him: therefore he lodged **t.** again........ 8033
Jg 19:10 **t.** were with him two asses saddled, ...
Jg 19:15 for **t.** was no man that took them into.......
Jg 19:16 **t.** came an old man from his work ....
Jg 19:18 **t.** is no man that receiveth me to.............
Jg 19:19 **t.** is both straw and provender for our.......
Jg 19:19 and **t.** is bread and wine also for me, ...
Jg 19:19 servants: **t.** is no want of any thing. ....
Jg 19:30 **T.** was no such deed done, nor seen.........
Jg 20:16 **t.** were seven hundred chosen men ....
Jg 20:26 wept, and sat **t.** before the Lord, ... 8033
Jg 20:27 ark of the covenant of God was **t.**...... 8033
Jg 20:34 **t.** came against Gibeah ten thousand ....
Jg 20:38 Now **t.** was an appointed sign between......
Jg 20:44 **t.** fell of Benjamin eighteen thousand.........
Jg 21:1 **T.** shall not any...give his daughter...........
Jg 21:2 and abode **t.** till even before God, ... 8033
Jg 21:3 **t.** should be to day one tribe lacking ....
Jg 21:4 rose early, and built **t.** an altar, ... 8033
Jg 21:5 Who is **t.** among all the tribes of Israel......
Jg 21:6 **T.** is one tribe cut off from Israel this ....
Jg 21:8 What one is **t.** of the tribes of Israel.........
Jg 21:8 **t.** came none to the camp from................
Jg 21:9 **t.** were none of the inhabitants of.............
Jg 21:9 inhabitants of Jabesh-gilead **t.**............. 8033
Jg 21:17 **T.** must be an inheritance for them...........
Jg 21:19 **t.** is a feast of the Lord in Shiloh.............
Jg 21:25 In those days **t.** was no king in Israel:.......
Ru 1:1 that **t.** was a famine in the land...............
Ru 1:2 country of Moab, and continued **t.**. 8033
Ru 1:4 they dwelled **t.** about ten years.......... 8033
Ru 1:11 are **t.** yet any more sons in my womb, ...
Ru 1:17 will I die, and **t.** will I be buried:........ 8033
Ru 3:12 **t.** is a kinsman nearer than I. ....
Ru 4:1 to the gate, and sat him down **t.**......... 8033
Ru 4:4 for **t.** is none to redeem it beside thee; .....
Ru 4:17 saying, **T.** is a son born to Naomi;............
1Sa 1:1 Now **t.** was a certain man of ....
1Sa 1:3 the priests of the Lord, were **t.**............. 8033
1Sa 1:11 **t.** shall no rasor come upon his head. ....
1Sa 1:22 the Lord, and **t.** abide for ever. 8033
1Sa 1:28 And he worshipped the Lord **t.**.......... 8033
1Sa 2:2 **T.** is none holy as the Lord:......................
1Sa 2:2 for **t.** is none beside thee: ....
1Sa 2:2 neither is **t.** any rock like our God............
1Sa 2:27 And **t.** came a man of God unto Eli,..........
1Sa 2:31, 32 **t.** shall not be an old man in thine ....
1Sa 3:1 in those days; **t.** was no open vision. ....
1Sa 4:4 were **t.** with the ark of the covenant... 8033
1Sa 4:7 for **t.** hath not been such a thing..............
1Sa 4:10 and **t.** was a very great slaughter;............
1Sa 4:10 for **t.** fell of Israel thirty thousand...........
1Sa 4:12 **t.** ran a man of Benjamin out of the ....
1Sa 4:16 And he said, What is **t.** done, my son? ....
1Sa 4:17 and **t.** hath been also a great slaughter ......
1Sa 5:11 **t.** was a deadly destruction throughout ......
1Sa 5:11 the hand of God was very heavy **t.**...........
1Sa 6:7 kine, on which **t.** hath come no yoke,........
1Sa 6:14 the cart came...and stood **t.**, ... 8033
1Sa 6:14 where **t.** was a great stone: ....
1Sa 7:6 and said **t.**, We have sinned against 8033
1Sa 7:14 **t.** was peace between Israel and the.........
1Sa 7:17 to Ramah; for **t.** was his house;......... 8033
1Sa 7:17 and **t.** he judged Israel; and............... 8033
1Sa 7:17 **t.** he built an altar unto the Lord........ 8033
1Sa 9:1 Now **t.** was a man of Benjamin, whose......
1Sa 9:2 **t.** was not among the children of Israel......
1Sa 9:4 land of Shalim, and **t.** they were not: ....
1Sa 9:6 now, **t.** is in this city a man of God, ...
1Sa 9:7 **t.** is not a present to bring to the man ......
1Sa 9:12 **t.** is a sacrifice of the people to day ....
1Sa 10:3 and **t.** shall meet thee three men..............
1Sa 10:24 **t.** is none like him among all the ....
1Sa 10:26 and **t.** went with him a band of men,.........
1Sa 11:3 and then if **t.** be no man to save us, ...
1Sa 11:13 **T.** shall not a man be put to death............
1Sa 11:14 Gilgal, and renew the kingdom **t.**....... 8033
1Sa 11:15 **t.** they made Saul king before the....... 8033
1Sa 11:15 **t.** they sacrificed sacrifices of peace 8033
1Sa 11:15 **t.** Saul and all the men of Israel 8033
1Sa 13:19 **t.** was no smith found throughout all ....
1Sa 13:22 that **t.** was neither sword nor spear..........
1Sa 13:22 with Jonathan his son was **t.** found............
1Sa 14:4 **t.** was a sharp rock on the one side,..........
1Sa 14:6 for **t.** is no restraint to the Lord to...........
1Sa 14:15 And **t.** was trembling in the host, in..........
1Sa 14:17 and his armourbearer were not **t.**..............
1Sa 14:20 and **t.** was a very great discomfiture. ....
1Sa 14:25 and **t.** was honey upon the ground...........
1Sa 14:30 for had **t.** not been now a much...............
1Sa 14:34 him that night, and slew them **t.**....... 8033
1Sa 14:39 But **t.** was not a man among all the ....
1Sa 14:45 **t.** shall not one hair of his head fall to ....
1Sa 14:52 **t.** was sore war against the Philistines.......
1Sa 16:11 said, **T.** remaineth yet the youngest,.........
1Sa 17:3 and **t.** was a valley between them...........
1Sa 17:4 And **t.** went out a champion out of the ......
1Sa 17:23 behold, **t.** came up the champion, ...
1Sa 17:29 have I now done? Is **t.** not a cause?..........
1Sa 17:34 father's sheep, and **t.** came a lion, ...
1Sa 17:46 may know that **t.** is a God in Israel.........
1Sa 17:50 **t.** was no sword in the hand of David........
1Sa 18:10 and **t.** was a javelin in Saul's hand............
1Sa 19:8 **t.** was war again: and David went out, ...
1Sa 19:16 in, behold, **t.** was an image in the bed,.......
1Sa 20:3 **t.** is but a step between me and death. .....
1Sa 20:6 his city: for **t.** is a yearly sacrifice ....
1Sa 20:6 sacrifice **t.** for all the family............... 8033
1Sa 20:8 if **t.** be in me iniquity, slay me myself; ......
1Sa 20:12 behold, if **t.** be good toward David,...........
1Sa 20:21 come thou: for **t.** is peace to thee, ...
1Sa 20:29 he hath commanded me to be **t.**...............
1Sa 21:3 in mine hand, or what **t.** is present.............
1Sa 21:4 **T.** is no common bread under mine............
1Sa 21:4 mine hand, but **t.** is hallowed bread; ....
1Sa 21:6 hallowed bread: for **t.** was no bread ....
1Sa 21:6 was no bread **t.** but the shewbread,.... 8033
1Sa 21:7 of the servants of Saul was **t.** that day, ...
1Sa 21:8 is **t.** not here under thine hand spear ....
1Sa 21:9 it: for **t.** is no other save that here.............
1Sa 21:9 And David said, **T.** is none like that;..........
1Sa 22:2 **t.** were with him about four hundred..........
1Sa 22:8 **t.** is none that sheweth me that my ....
1Sa 22:8 and **t.** is none of you that is sorry ....
1Sa 22:22 when Doeg the Edomite was **t.**,............ 8033
1Sa 23:22 haunt is, and who hath seen him **t.**..... 8033
1Sa 23:27 But **t.** came a messenger unto Saul, ...
1Sa 24:11 and see that **t.** is neither evil nor ....
1Sa 25:2 And **t.** was a man in Maon, whose.............
1Sa 25:7 neither was **t.** ought missing unto.............
1Sa 25:10 **t.** be many servants now a days that.........
1Sa 25:13 **t.** went up after David about four ....
1Sa 25:34 surely **t.** had not been left unto Nabal ....
1Sa 26:15 **t.** came one of the people in to destroy.....
1Sa 27:1 **t.** is nothing better for me than that I ....
1Sa 27:5 the country, that I may dwell **t.**. 8033
1Sa 28:7 **t.** is a woman that hath a familiar ....
1Sa 28:10 **t.** shall no punishment happen to thee ....
1Sa 28:20 and **t.** was no strength in him; for he.........
1Sa 30:17 and **t.** escaped not a man of them, save.....
1Sa 30:19 And **t.** was nothing lacking to them,..........
1Sa 31:12 came to Jabesh, and burnt them **t.**...... 8033
2Sa 1:21 mountains of Gilboa, let **t.** be no dew, ...
2Sa 1:21 neither let **t.** be rain, upon you, nor...........
2Sa 1:21 **t.** the shield of the mighty is vilely 8033
2Sa 2:4 **t.** they anointed David king over the... 8033
2Sa 2:15 **t.** arose and went over by number............
2Sa 2:17 And **t.** was a very sore battle that day; ....
2Sa 2:18 And **t.** were three sons of Zeruiah............
2Sa 2:18 were three sons of Zeruiah **t.**;........... 8033
2Sa 2:23 and he fell down **t.**, and died in the 8033
2Sa 2:30 **t.** lacked of David's servants nineteen........
2Sa 3:1 **t.** was long war between the house of.......
2Sa 3:6 while **t.** was war between the house of.......
2Sa 3:27 smote him **t.** under the fifth rib,.......... 8033
2Sa 3:29 let **t.** not fail from the house of Joab ....
2Sa 3:38 Know ye not that **t.** is a prince and a........
2Sa 4:3 were sojourners **t.** until this day.)....... 8033
2Sa 5:13 **t.** were yet sons and daughters born to .....
2Sa 5:20 David smote them **t.**, and said, The..... 8033
2Sa 5:21 **t.** they left their images, and David..... 8033
2Sa 6:7 and God smote him **t.** for his error;.... 8033
2Sa 6:7 and **t.** he died by the ark of God........ 8033
2Sa 7:22 O Lord God: for **t.** is none like thee, ...
2Sa 7:22 neither is **t.** any God beside thee, ...
2Sa 9:1 Is **t.** yet any that is left of the house of.....
2Sa 9:2 **t.** was of the house of Saul a servant ....
2Sa 9:3 Is **t.** not yet any of the house of Saul, ...
2Sa 10:18 captain of their host, who died **t.**......... 8033
2Sa 11:8 **t.** followed him a mess of meat from.........
2Sa 11:17 **t.** fell some of the people of the...............
2Sa 12:1 **T.** were two men in one city; the one.......
2Sa 12:4 **t.** came a traveller unto the rich man, ...
2Sa 13:16 And she said unto him, **T.** is no cause:......
2Sa 13:30 sons, and **t.** is not one of them left...........
2Sa 13:34 **t.** came much people by the way of the.....
2Sa 13:38 to Geshur, and was **t.** three years...... 8033
2Sa 14:6 **t.** was none to part them, but the one.......
2Sa 14:11 **t.** shall not one hair of thy son fall to ....
2Sa 14:25 **t.** was none to be so much praised as ....
2Sa 14:25 crown of his head **t.** was no blemish ....
2Sa 14:27 unto Absalom **t.** were born three sons,......
2Sa 14:30 he hath barley **t.**; go and set it on...... 8033
2Sa 14:32 good for me to have been **t.** still:....... 8033
2Sa 14:32 if **t.** be any iniquity in me, let him kill........
2Sa 15:3 **t.** is no man deputed of the king to...........
2Sa 15:13 **t.** came a messenger to David, saying, ...
2Sa 15:21 even **t.** also will thy servant be.......... 8033
2Sa 15:28 until **t.** come word from you to certify.......
2Sa 15:29 to Jerusalem: and they tarried **t.**. 8033
2Sa 15:35 hast thou not **t.** with thee Zadok........ 8033
2Sa 15:36 have **t.** with them their two sons, ... 8033
2Sa 16:14 weary, and refreshed themselves **t.**.... 8033
2Sa 17:9 **T.** is a slaughter among the people ....
2Sa 17:12 **t.** shall not be left so much as one...........
2Sa 17:13 until **t.** be not one small stone found ....
2Sa 17:13 be not one small stone found **t.**......... 8033
2Sa 17:22 by the morning light **t.** lacked not one ....
2Sa 18:7 and **t.** was...a great slaughter that day ......
2Sa 18:7 was **t.** a great slaughter that day........ 8033
2Sa 18:8 the battle was **t.** scattered over the.... 8033
2Sa 18:11 and why didst thou not smite him **t.**.... 8033
2Sa 18:13 for **t.** is no matter hid from the king, ...
2Sa 18:25 he be alone, **t.** is tidings in his mouth........
2Sa 19:7 **t.** will not tarry one with thee this............
2Sa 19:17 **t.** were a thousand men of Benjamin ....
2Sa 19:18 And **t.** went over a ferry boat to carry ......
2Sa 19:22 shall **t.** any man be put to death this.........
2Sa 20:1 **t.** happened to be...a man of Belial, ...
2Sa 20:1 happened to be **t.** a man of Belial,....... 8033
2Sa 20:7 and **t.** went out after him Joab's men, ...
2Sa 21:1 **t.** was a famine in the days of David ....
2Sa 21:18 **t.** was again a battle with the ....
2Sa 21:19 **t.** was again a battle in Gob with the.........
2Sa 21:20 And **t.** was yet a battle in Gath, where.....
2Sa 22:9 **T.** went up a smoke out of his nostrils, ...
2Sa 22:42 They looked, but **t.** was none to save; ......
2Sa 23:9 defied the Philistines that were **t.**........ 8033
2Sa 24:9 and **t.** were in Israel eight hundred...........
2Sa 24:13 or that **t.** be three days' pestilence in.......
2Sa 24:15 **t.** died of the people from Dan even to......
2Sa 24:25 David built **t.** an altar unto the........... 8033
1Ki 1:2 Let **t.** be sought for my lord the king a .....
1Ki 1:14 thou yet talkest **t.** with the king,......... 8033
1Ki 1:34 anoint him **t.** king over Israel: 8033
1Ki 1:52 **t.** shall not an hair of him fall to the..........
1Ki 2:4 **t.** shall not fail thee (said he) a man on......
1Ki 2:33 shall **t.** be peace for ever from the ....
1Ki 2:36 house in Jerusalem, and dwell **t.**,......... 8033
1Ki 3:2 **t.** was no house built unto the name ....
1Ki 3:4 king went to Gibeon to sacrifice **t.**;..... 8033
1Ki 3:12 that **t.** was none like thee before thee, ...
1Ki 3:13 **t.** shall not be any among the kings...........
1Ki 3:16 Then came **t.** two women, that were ....
1Ki 3:18 **t.** was no stranger with us in the ....
1Ki 4:34 And **t.** came of all people to hear the ....
1Ki 5:4 that **t.** is neither adversary nor evil...........
1Ki 5:6 for thou knowest that **t.** is not among ....
1Ki 5:9 cause them to be discharged **t.**, ... 8033
1Ki 5:12 **t.** was peace between Hiram and...............
1Ki 6:7 **t.** was neither hammer nor axe nor...........
1Ki 6:18 all was cedar; **t.** was no stone seen. ....
1Ki 6:19 to set **t.** the ark of the covenant of..... 8033
1Ki 7:4 And **t.** were windows in three rows, ...
1Ki 7:24 brim of it round about **t.** were knops.........
1Ki 7:29 upon the ledges **t.** was a base above:........
1Ki 7:34 **t.** were four undersetters to the four ....
1Ki 7:35 top of the base was **t.** a round compass.....
1Ki 8:8 and **t.** they are unto this day. 8033
1Ki 8:9 **T.** was nothing in the ark save the ....
1Ki 8:9 which Moses put **t.** at Horeb,............ 8033
1Ki 8:21 I have set **t.** a place for the ark, ... 8033
1Ki 8:23 **t.** is no God like thee, in heaven above, ...
1Ki 8:25 **T.** shall not fail thee a man in my............
1Ki 8:29 hast said, My name shall be **t.**:.......... 8033

1Ki	8:35	heaven is shut up, and **t.** is no rain.	
1Ki	8:37	If **t.** be in the land famine,	
1Ki	8:37	If **t.** be pestilence, blasting, mildew,	
1Ki	8:37	locust, or if **t.** be caterpillar;	
1Ki	8:37	plague, whatsoever sickness **t.** be;	
1Ki	8:46	(for **t.** is no man that sinneth not.)	
1Ki	8:56	**t.** hath not failed one word of all his	
1Ki	8:60	Lord is God, and that **t.** is none else.	
1Ki	8:64	for **t.** he offered burnt offerings,	8033
1Ki	9:3	built, to put my name **t.** for ever;	8033
1Ki	9:3	mine heart shall be **t.** perpetually.	8033
1Ki	9:5	**T.** shall not fail thee a man upon the	
1Ki	10:3	**t.** was not any thing hid from the king.	
1Ki	10:5	the Lord; **t.** was no more spirit in her,	
1Ki	10:10	**t.** came no more such abundance of	
1Ki	10:12	**t.** came no such almug trees, nor were	
1Ki	10:19	**t.** were stays on either side on the	
1Ki	10:20	And twelve lions stood **t.** on the	8033
1Ki	10:20	**t.** was not the like made in any	
1Ki	11:16	six months did Joab remain **t.**	8033
1Ki	11:36	have chosen me to put my name **t.**	8033
1Ki	12:20	**t.** was none that followed the house of	
1Ki	13:1	**t.** came a man of God out of Judah by	
1Ki	13:11	**t.** dwelt an old prophet in Beth-el;	
1Ki	13:17	eat no bread nor drink water **t.**,	8033
1Ki	14:2	**t.** is Ahijah the prophet, which told	8033
1Ki	14:13	in him **t.** is found some good thing	
1Ki	14:21	tribes of Israel, to put his name **t.**	8033
1Ki	14:24	**t.** were also Sodomites in the land:	
1Ki	14:30	**t.** was war between Rehoboam and	
1Ki	15:6	**t.** was war between Rehoboam and	
1Ki	15:7	**t.** was war between Abijam and	
1Ki	15:16	**t.** was war between Asa and Baasha	
1Ki	15:19	**T.** is a league between me and thee,	
1Ki	15:32	**t.** was war between Asa and Baasha	
1Ki	17:1	**t.** shall not be dew nor rain these	
1Ki	17:4	the ravens to feed thee **t.**	8033
1Ki	17:7	because **t.** had been no rain in the land.	
1Ki	17:9	belongeth to Zidon, and dwell **t.**:	8033
1Ki	17:9	a widow woman **t.** to sustain thee.	8033
1Ki	17:10	the widow woman was **t.** gathering	8033
1Ki	17:17	sore, that **t.** was no breath left in him.	
1Ki	18:2	And **t.** was a sore famine in Samaria.	
1Ki	18:10	**t.** is no nation or kingdom, whither my	
1Ki	18:10	when they said, He is not **t.**; he took	
1Ki	18:26	But **t.** was no voice, nor any that	
1Ki	18:29	that **t.** was neither voice, nor any to	
1Ki	18:40	brook Kishon, and slew them **t.**	8033
1Ki	18:41	for **t.** is a sound of abundance of rain,	
1Ki	18:43	and looked, and said, **T.** is nothing.	
1Ki	18:44	**t.** ariseth a little cloud out of the sea,	
1Ki	18:45	and wind, and **t.** was a great rain.	
1Ki	19:3	to Judah, and left his servant **t.**	8033
1Ki	19:6	**t.** was a cake baken on the coals,	
1Ki	19:9	thither unto a cave, and lodged **t.**;	8033
1Ki	19:13	behold, **t.** came a voice unto him, and	
1Ki	20:1	**t.** were thirty and two kings with him,	
1Ki	20:13	**t.** came a prophet unto Ahab king of	
1Ki	20:17	**T.** are men come out of Samaria.	
1Ki	20:28	**t.** came a man of God, and spake unto	
1Ki	20:30	**t.** a wall fell upon twenty and seven	
1Ki	20:40	as thy servant was busy here and **t.**,	2008
1Ki	21:13	**t.** came in two men, children of	
1Ki	21:25	**t.** was none like unto Ahab, which did	
1Ki	22:7	Is **t.** not here a prophet of the Lord	
1Ki	22:8	**T.** is yet one man, Micaiah the son of	
1Ki	22:21	**t.** came forth a spirit, and stood before	
1Ki	22:36	**t.** went a proclamation throughout	
1Ki	22:47	**T.** was then no king in Edom: a	
2Ki	1:3	it not because **t.** is not a God in Israel,	
2Ki	1:6	**T.** came a man up to meet us, and said	
2Ki	1:6	it not because **t.** is not a God in Israel,	
2Ki	1:10	**t.** came down fire from heaven, and	
2Ki	1:14	Behold, **t.** came fire down from heaven,	
2Ki	1:16	**t.** is no God in Israel to enquire of	
2Ki	2:11	**t.** appeared a chariot of fire, and	
2Ki	2:16	**t.** be with thy servants fifty strong	
2Ki	2:21	the waters, and cast the salt in **t.**,	8033
2Ki	2:21	**t.** shall not be from thence any more	
2Ki	2:23	**t.** came forth little children out of the	
2Ki	2:24	**t.** came forth two she bears out of the	
2Ki	3:9	**t.** was no water for the host, and for	
2Ki	3:11	Is **t.** not here a prophet of the Lord,	
2Ki	3:20	**t.** came water by the way of Edom, and	
2Ki	3:27	**t.** was great indignation against Israel:	
2Ki	4:1	**t.** cried a certain woman of the wives	
2Ki	4:6	said unto her, **T.** is not a vessel more.	
2Ki	4:10	and let us set for him **t.** a bed, and	8033
2Ki	4:11	unto the chamber, and lay **t.**	8033
2Ki	4:31	but **t.** was neither voice, nor hearing.	
2Ki	4:38	**t.** was a dearth in the land; and the	
2Ki	4:40	thou man of God, **t.** is death in the pot.	
2Ki	4:41	eat. And **t.** was no harm in the pot	
2Ki	4:42	**t.** came a man from Baal-shalisha, and	
2Ki	5:8	know that **t.** is a prophet in Israel.	
2Ki	5:15	now I know that **t.** is no God in all the	
2Ki	5:17	Shall **t.** not then, I pray thee, be given	
2Ki	5:18	house of Rimmon to worship **t.**,	8033
2Ki	5:22	**t.** be come to me from mount Ephraim	
2Ki	6:2	let us make us a place **t.**, where	8033
2Ki	6:10	and saved himself **t.**, not once nor	8033
2Ki	6:25	**t.** was a great famine in Samaria:	
2Ki	6:26	**t.** cried a woman unto him, saying,	
2Ki	7:3	And **t.** were four leprous men at the	
2Ki	7:4	enter into the city,...we shall die **t.**	8033
2Ki	7:5	camp of Syria, behold, **t.** was no man	
2Ki	7:5	of Syria, behold,...was no man **t.**	8033
2Ki	7:10	Syrians, and, behold, **t.** was no man	
2Ki	7:10	was no man **t.**; neither voice of	8033
2Ki	9:2	out **t.** Jehu the son of Jehoshaphat	8033
2Ki	9:10	and **t.** shall be none to bury her.	
2Ki	9:16	went to Jezreel; for Joram lay **t.**	8033
2Ki	9:17	**t.** stood a watchman on the tower in	
2Ki	9:18	**t.** went one on horseback to meet him,	
2Ki	9:23	and said to Ahaziah, **T.** is treachery,	
2Ki	9:27	he fled to Megiddo, and died **t.**	8033
2Ki	9:32	**t.** looked out to him two or three	
2Ki	10:2	**t.** are with you chariots and horses,	
2Ki	10:8	**t.** came a messenger, and told him,	
2Ki	10:10	now that **t.** shall fall unto the earth	
2Ki	10:21	**t.** was not a man left that came not.	
2Ki	10:23	and look that **t.** be here with you none	
2Ki	11:16	king's house: and **t.** was she slain.	8033
2Ki	12:10	they saw that **t.** was much money they	
2Ki	12:13	Howbeit **t.** were not made for the house	
2Ki	13:6	**t.** remained the grove also in Samaria.	
2Ki	14:9	**t.** passed by a wild beast that was in	
2Ki	14:19	him to Lachish, and slew him **t.**	8033
2Ki	14:26	**t.** was not any shut up, nor any left,	
2Ki	15:20	and stayed not **t.** in the land.	8033
2Ki	16:6	to Elath, and dwelt **t.** to this day.	8033
2Ki	17:11	**t.** they burnt incense in all the high	8033
2Ki	17:18	**t.** was none left but the tribe of Judah	
2Ki	17:25	the beginning of their dwelling **t.**,	8033
2Ki	17:27	and let them go and dwell **t.**, and	8033
2Ki	18:18	**t.** came out to them Eliakim the son	
2Ki	19:3	and **t.** is not strength to bring forth.	
2Ki	19:32	this city, nor shoot an arrow **t.**,	8033
2Ki	20:13	**t.** was nothing in his house, nor in all	
2Ki	20:15	**t.** is nothing among my treasures that	
2Ki	22:7	**t.** was no reckoning made with them	
2Ki	23:16	spied the sepulchres that were **t.**	8033
2Ki	23:20	upon the high places that were **t.**	8033
2Ki	23:22	**t.** was not holden such a passover	
2Ki	23:25	like unto him was **t.** no king before	
2Ki	23:25	neither after him arose **t.** any like him.	
2Ki	23:27	which I said, My name shall be **t.**	8033
2Ki	23:34	and he came to Egypt, and died **t.**	8033
2Ki	25:3	**t.** was no bread for the people of the	
2Ki	25:23	**t.** came to Gedaliah to Mizpah,	
1Ch	3:4	**t.** he reigned seven years and six	8033
1Ch	4:23	**t.** they dwelt with the king for his	8033
1Ch	4:40	for they of Ham had dwelt **t.** of old.	8033
1Ch	4:41	the habitations that were found **t.**,	8033
1Ch	4:41	in their rooms: because **t.** was pasture	
1Ch	4:41	was pasture **t.** for their flocks.	8033
1Ch	4:43	escaped, and dwelt **t.** unto this day.	8033
1Ch	5:22	For **t.** fell down many slain, because	
1Ch	11:13	**t.** the Philistines were gathered	8033
1Ch	12:8	of the Gadites **t.** separated themselves	
1Ch	12:16	**t.** came of the children of Benjamin	
1Ch	12:17	seeing **t.** is no wrong in mine hands,	
1Ch	12:19	**t.** fell some of Manasseh to David,	
1Ch	12:20	to Ziklag, **t.** fell to him of Manasseh,	
1Ch	12:22	day by day **t.** came to David to help	
1Ch	12:39	**t.** they were with David three	8033
1Ch	12:40	abundantly: for **t.** was joy in Israel.	
1Ch	13:10	ark: and **t.** he died before God	8033
1Ch	14:11	and David smote them **t.**	8033
1Ch	14:12	when they had left their gods **t.**,	8033
1Ch	16:37	So he left **t.** before the ark of the	8033
1Ch	17:20	O Lord, **t.** is none like thee, neither is	
1Ch	17:20	neither is **t.** any God beside thee,	
1Ch	19:5	Then **t.** went certain, and told David	
1Ch	20:2	gold, and **t.** were precious stones in it;	
1Ch	20:4	that **t.** arose war at Gezer with the	
1Ch	20:5	**t.** was war again with the Philistines;	
1Ch	20:6	And yet again **t.** was war at Gath,	
1Ch	21:14	and **t.** fell of Israel seventy thousand	
1Ch	21:26	David built **t.** an altar unto the	8033
1Ch	21:28	the Jebusite, then he sacrificed **t.**	8033
1Ch	22:15	Moreover **t.** are workmen with thee in	
1Ch	22:16	brass, and the iron, **t.** is no number.	
1Ch	24:4	**t.** were more chief men found of the	
1Ch	24:4	**t.** were sixteen chief men of the house	
1Ch	26:31	**t.** were found among them mighty	
1Ch	27:24	**t.** fell wrath for it against Israel;	
1Ch	28:21	**t.** shall be with thee for all mannner of	
1Ch	29:15	as a shadow, and **t.** is none abiding.	
2Ch	1:3	for **t.** was the tabernacle of the	8033
2Ch	1:12	neither shall **t.** any after thee have the	
2Ch	5:9	And **t.** it is unto this day.	8033
2Ch	5:10	**T.** was nothing in the ark save the	
2Ch	6:5,6	that my name might be **t.**;	8033
2Ch	6:14	**t.** is no God like thee in the heaven,	
2Ch	6:16	**T.** shall not fail thee a man in my	
2Ch	6:20	thou wouldest put thy name **t.**;	8033
2Ch	6:26	heaven is shut up, and **t.** is no rain,	
2Ch	6:28	If **t.** be dearth in the land,	
2Ch	6:28	if **t.** be pestilence, if **t.** be blasting,	
2Ch	6:28	sore or whatsoever sickness **t.** be:	
2Ch	6:36	(for **t.** is no man which sinneth not,)	
2Ch	7:7	**t.** he offered burnt offerings, and	8033
2Ch	7:13	If I shut up heaven that **t.** be no rain,	
2Ch	7:16	that my name may be **t.** for ever:	8033
2Ch	7:16	mine heart shall be **t.** perpetually.	8033
2Ch	7:18	**T.** shall not fail thee a man to be ruler	
2Ch	8:2	the children of Israel to dwell **t.**	8033
2Ch	9:2	and **t.** was nothing hid from Solomon	
2Ch	9:4	Lord; **t.** was no more spirit in her.	
2Ch	9:9	neither was **t.** any such spice as the	
2Ch	9:11	**t.** were none such seen before in the	
2Ch	9:18	and **t.** were six steps to the throne,	
2Ch	9:19	twelve lions stood **t.** on the one	8033
2Ch	9:19	**T.** was not the like made in any	
2Ch	12:13	tribes of Israel, to put his name **t.**	8033
2Ch	12:15	**t.** were wars between Rehoboam and	
2Ch	13:2	And **t.** was war between Abijah and	
2Ch	13:7	**t.** are gathered unto him vain men,	
2Ch	13:8	**t.** are with you golden calves, which	
2Ch	13:17	**t.** fell down slain of Israel five hundred	
2Ch	14:9	**t.** came out against them Zerah the	
2Ch	14:14	**t.** was exceeding much spoil in them.	
2Ch	15:5	**t.** was no peace to him that went out	
2Ch	15:19	**t.** was no more war unto the five and	
2Ch	16:3	**T.** is a league between me and thee,	
2Ch	16:3	as **t.** was between my father and thy	
2Ch	18:6	Is **t.** not here a prophet of the Lord	
2Ch	18:7	**T.** is yet one man, by whom we may	
2Ch	18:20	then **t.** came out a spirit, and stood	
2Ch	19:3	**t.** are good things found in thee,	
2Ch	19:7	for **t.** is no iniquity with the Lord our	
2Ch	20:2	**t.** came some that told Jehoshaphat,	
2Ch	20:2	**T.** cometh a great multitude against	
2Ch	20:6	and in thine hand is **t.** not power and	
2Ch	20:26	**t.** they blessed the Lord: therefore	8033
2Ch	21:12	**t.** came a writing to him from Elijah	
2Ch	21:17	so that **t.** was never a son left him,	
2Ch	23:15	king's house, they slew her **t.**	8033
2Ch	24:11	they saw that **t.** was much money,	
2Ch	25:7	**t.** came a man of God to him, saying,	
2Ch	25:18	**t.** passed by a wild beast that was in	
2Ch	25:27	after him, and slew him **t.**	8033
2Ch	28:9	But a prophet of the Lord was **t.**,	8033
2Ch	28:10	but are **t.** not with you, even with you,	
2Ch	28:13	and **t.** is fierce wrath against Israel.	
2Ch	28:18	billages thereof: and they dwelt **t.**	8033
2Ch	30:13	And **t.** assembled at Jerusalem much	
2Ch	30:17	**t.** were many in the congregation that	
2Ch	30:26	So **t.** was great joy in Jerusalem: for	
2Ch	30:26	Israel **t.** was not the like in Jerusalem.	
2Ch	32:4	So **t.** was gathered much people	
2Ch	32:7	for **t.** be more with us than with him:	
2Ch	32:14	Who was **t.** among all the gods of	
2Ch	32:21	bowels slew him **t.** with the sword	8033
2Ch	32:25	therefore **t.** was wrath upon him, and	
2Ch	34:13	and of the Levites **t.** were scribes, and	
2Ch	35:18	And **t.** was no passover like to that	
2Ch	36:16	his people, till **t.** was no remedy.	
2Ch	36:23	Who is **t.** among you of all his people?	
Ezr	1:3	Who is **t.** among you of all his people?	

Ezr 2:63 till **t.** stood up a priest with Urim and
Ezr 2:65 of whom **t.** were seven thousand three
Ezr 2:65 and **t.** were among them two hundred
Ezr 4:20 **T.** have been mighty kings also over
Ezr 5:17 let **t.** be search made in the king's
Ezr 5:17 house, which is **t.** at Babylon, 8536
Ezr 6:2 And **t.** was found at Achmetha, in the
Ezr 6:12 hath caused his name to dwell **t.** 8536
Ezr 7:7 **t.** went up some of the children of
Ezr 7:23 should **t.** be wrath against the realm
Ezr 8:15 **t.** abode we in tents three days: 8033
Ezr 8:15 found **t.** none of the sons of Levi. 8033
Ezr 8:21 then I proclaimed a fast **t.**, at the 8033
Ezr 8:25 all Israel **t.** present, had offered:
Ezr 8:32 and abode **t.** three days. 8033
Ezr 9:14 **t.** should be no remnant nor escaping?
Ezr 10:1 **t.** assembled unto him out of Israel a
Ezr 10:2 **t.** is hope in Israel concerning this
Ezr 10:18 among the sons of the priests **t.** were
Ne 1:3 are left of the captivity **t.** in the 8033
Ne 1:9 though **t.** were of you cast out unto
Ne 1:9 I have chosen to set my name **t.** 8033
Ne 2:10 **t.** was come a man to seek the welfare
Ne 2:11 Jerusalem, and was **t.** three days. 8033
Ne 2:12 neither was **t.** any beast with me,
Ne 2:14 **t.** was no place for the beast that was
Ne 4:10 **t.** is much rubbish; so that we are not
Ne 5:1 **t.** was a great cry of the people and
Ne 5:2 **t.** were that said, We, our sons, and
Ne 5:3 Some also **t.** were that said, We have
Ne 5:4 **T.** were also that said, We have
Ne 5:17 **t.** were at my table an hundred and
Ne 6:1 that **t.** was no breach left therein;
Ne 6:7 **T.** is a king in Judah: and now shall
Ne 6:8 **T.** are no such things done as thou
Ne 6:11 and who is **t.**, that, being as I am,
Ne 6:18 **t.** were many in Judah sworn unto
Ne 7:65 till **t.** stood up a priest with Urim and
Ne 7:67 of whom **t.** were seven thousand three
Ne 8:17 so. And **t.** was very great gladness.
Ne 12:46 of old **t.** were chief of the singers,
Ne 13:16 **T.** dwelt men of Tyre also therein,
Ne 13:19 **t.** should no burden be brought in on
Ne 13:26 many nations was **t.** no king like him,
Es 1:18 thus shall **t.** arise too much contempt
Es 1:19 **t.** go a royal commandment from him,
Es 2:2 Let **t.** be fair young virgins sought for
Es 2:5 in...the palace **t.** was a certain Jew,
Es 3:8 **T.** is a certain people scattered
Es 3:12 **t.** was written according to all that
Es 4:3 **t.** was great mourning among the
Es 4:11 **t.** is one law of his to put him to death,
Es 4:14 **t.** enlargement and deliverance arise
Es 6:3 unto him, **T.** is nothing done for him.
Es 7:7 he saw that **t.** was evil determined
Job 1:1 **T.** was a man in the land of Uz,
Job 1:2 **t.** were born unto him seven sons and
Job 1:6 **t.** was a day when the sons of God
Job 1:8 that **t.** is none like him in the earth,
Job 1:13 **t.** was a day when his sons and his
Job 1:14 And **t.** came a messenger unto Job,
Job 1:16, 17,18 speaking, **t.** came also another,
Job 1:19 **t.** came a great wind from the
Job 2:1 Again **t.** was a day when the sons of
Job 2:3 that **t.** is none like him in the earth,
Job 3:3 was said, **T.** is a man child conceived.
Job 3:17 **T.** the wicked cease from 8033
Job 3:17 and **t.** the weary be at rest. 8033
Job 3:18 **T.** the prisoners rest together; they
Job 3:19 The small and great are **t.**; and 8033
Job 4:16 **t.** was silence, and I heard a voice,
Job 5:1 if **t.** be any that will answer thee;
Job 5:4 gate, neither is **t.** any to deliver them.
Job 5:19 in seven **t.** shall no evil touch thee.
Job 6:6 is **t.** any taste in the white of an egg?
Job 6:30 Is **t.** iniquity in my tongue? cannot
Job 7:1 Is **t.** not an appointed time to man
Job 9:33 Neither is **t.** any daysman betwixt us,
Job 10:7 **t.** is none that can deliver out of thine
Job 11:18 thou shalt be secure, because **t.** is hope; ...
Job 12:14 up a man, and **t.** can be no opening.
Job 12:24 in a wilderness where **t.** is no way.
Job 14:7 For **t.** is hope of a tree, if it be cut
Job 15:11 is **t.** any secret thing with thee?
Job 17:2 Are **t.** not mockers with me? and doth
Job 19:7 I cry aloud, but **t.** is no judgment.
Job 19:29 that ye may know **t.** is a judgment.
Job 20:21 **T.** shall none of his meat be left;
Job 21:33 him, as **t.** are innumerable before him.
Job 21:34 your answers **t.** remaineth falsehood?
Job 22:29 then thou shalt say, **T.** is lifting up;
Job 23:7 **T.** the righteous might dispute 8033
Job 23:8 Behold, I go forward, but he is not **t.**;
Job 25:3 Is **t.** any number of his armies? and
Job 28:1 Surely **t.** is a vein for the silver, and a
Job 28:7 **T.** is a path which no fowl knoweth,
Job 30:26 I waited for light, **t.** came darkness.
Job 31:2 what portion of God is **t.** from above?
Job 32:5 Elihu saw that **t.** was no answer in
Job 32:8 But **t.** is a spirit in man: and the
Job 32:12 **t.** was none of you that convinced Job.
Job 33:9 innocent; neither is **t.** iniquity in me.
Job 33:23 If **t.** be a messenger with him, an
Job 34:22 **T.** is no darkness, nor shadow of
Job 35:12 **T.** they cry, but none giveth 8033
Job 36:16 broad place, where **t.** is no straitness;
Job 36:18 Because **t.** is wrath, beware lest he
Job 38:26 the wilderness, wherein **t.** is no man;
Job 39:30 and where the slain are, **t.** is she. 8033
Job 41:33 Upon earth **t.** is not his like, who is
Job 42:11 Then came **t.** unto him all his
Ps 3:2 Many **t.** be which say of my soul,
Ps 3:2 **T.** is no help for him in God. Selah.
Ps 4:6 **T.** be many that say, Who will shew
Ps 5:9 **t.** is no faithfulness in their mouth;
Ps 6:5 For in death **t.** is no remembrance of
Ps 7:2 it in pieces, while **t.** is none to deliver.
Ps 7:3 if **t.** be iniquity in my hands;
Ps 14:1 hath said in his heart, **T.** is no God.
Ps 14:1 works, **t.** is none that doeth good.
Ps 14:2 if **t.** were any that did understand,
Ps 14:3 **t.** is none that doeth good, no, not one.
Ps 14:5 **T.** were they in great fear: for 8033
Ps 16:11 hand **t.** are pleasures for evermore.
Ps 18:8 **T.** went up a smoke out of his nostrils,
Ps 18:41 cried, but **t.** was none to save them:
Ps 19:3 **T.** is no speech nor language, where
Ps 19:6 **t.** is nothing hid from the heat thereof.
Ps 19:11 in keeping of them **t.** is great reward.
Ps 22:11 trouble is near; for **t.** is none to help.
Ps 30:9 What profit is **t.** in my blood, when I
Ps 32:2 and in whose spirit **t.** is no guile.
Ps 33:16 **T.** is no king saved by the multitude
Ps 34:9 for **t.** is no want to them that fear him.
Ps 36:1 **t.** is no fear of God before his eyes
Ps 36:12 **T.** are the workers of iniquity 8033
Ps 38:3 **T.** is no soundness in my flesh
Ps 38:3 neither is **t.** any rest in my bones
Ps 38:7 and **t.** is no soundness in my flesh.
Ps 45:12 the daughter of Tyre shall be **t.**
Ps 46:4 **T.** is a river, the streams whereof
Ps 48:6 Fear took hold upon them **t.**, and 8033
Ps 50:22 in pieces, and **t.** be none to deliver.
Ps 53:1 hath said in his heart, **T.** is no God.
Ps 53:1 iniquity: **t.** is none that doeth good.
Ps 53:2 if **t.** were any that did understand,
Ps 53:3 **t.** is none that doeth good, no, not one.
Ps 53:5 **T.** were they in great fear, where 8033
Ps 55:18 against me: for **t.** were many with me.
Ps 58:11 Verily **t.** is a reward for the righteous:
Ps 66:6 on foot: **t.** did we rejoice in him. 8033
Ps 68:27 **T.** is little Benjamin with their 8033
Ps 69:2 in deep mire, where **t.** is no standing:
Ps 69:20 some to take pity, but **t.** was none;
Ps 69:35 that they may dwell **t.**, and have it in
Ps 71:11 him; for **t.** is none to deliver him.
Ps 72:16 **T.** shall be an handful of corn in the
Ps 73:4 For **t.** are no bands in their death:
Ps 73:11 and is **t.** knowledge in the most High?
Ps 73:25 **t.** is none upon earth that I desire
Ps 74:9 our signs: **t.** is no more any prophet:
Ps 74:9 neither is **t.** among us any that
Ps 75:8 in the hand of the Lord **t.** is a cup,
Ps 76:3 **T.** brake he the arrows of the bow, 8033
Ps 79:3 and **t.** was none to bury them.
Ps 81:9 **T.** shall no strange god be in thee;
Ps 86:8 Among the gods **t.** is none like unto
Ps 86:8 are **t.** any works like unto thy works.
Ps 87:4 Ethiopia; this man was born **t.** 8033
Ps 87:6 people, that this man was born **t.** 8033
Ps 87:7 the players on instruments shall be **t.**
Ps 91:10 **T.** shall no evil befall thee, neither
Ps 92:15 and **t.** is no unrighteousness in him.
Ps 104:26 **T.** go the ships: 8033
Ps 104:26 **t.** is that leviathan, whom thou
Ps 105:31 spake, and **t.** came divers sorts of flies,
Ps 105:37 **t.** was not one feeble person among
Ps 106:11 enemies: **t.** was not one of them left.
Ps 107:12 fell down, and **t.** was none to help.
Ps 107:36 **t.** he maketh the hungry to dwell, 8033
Ps 107:40 in the wilderness, where **t.** is no way.
Ps 109:12 Let **t.** be none to extend mercy unto
Ps 109:12 let **t.** be any to favour his fatherless
Ps 112:4 **t.** ariseth light in the darkness:
Ps 122:5 For **t.** are set thrones of judgment, 8033
Ps 130:4 But **t.** is forgiveness with thee, that
Ps 130:7 for with the Lord **t.** is mercy, and with
Ps 132:17 **T.** will I make the horn of David 8033
Ps 133:3 for **t.** the Lord commanded the 8033
Ps 135:17 neither is **t.** any breath in their
Ps 137:1 river of Babylon, **t.** we sat down, 8033
Ps 137:3 For **t.** they that carried us away 8033
Ps 139:4 For **t.** is not a word in my tongue, but,
Ps 139:8 ascend up into heaven, thou art **t.** 8033
Ps 139:8 my bed in hell, behold, thou art **t.**
Ps 139:10 Even **t.** shall thy hand lead me, 8033
Ps 139:16 when as yet **t.** was none of them.
Ps 139:24 see if **t.** be any wicked way in me, and
Ps 142:4 **t.** was no man that would know me:
Ps 144:14 that **t.** be no breaking in, nor going
Ps 144:14 **t.** be no complaining in our streets.
Ps 146:3 the son of man, in whom **t.** is no help.
Pr 7:10 **t.** met him a woman with the attire of
Pr 8:8 **t.** is nothing froward or perverse in
Pr 8:24 **t.** were no depths, I was brought forth;
Pr 8:24 **t.** were no fountains abounding with
Pr 8:27 prepared the heavens, I was **t.**: 8033
Pr 9:18 he knoweth not that the dead are **t.**; 8033
Pr 10:19 In the multitude of words **t.** wanteth
Pr 11:10 when the wicked perish, **t.** is shouting
Pr 11:14 multitude of counsellers, **t.** is safety.
Pr 11:24 **T.** is that scattereth, and yet
Pr 11:24 **t.** is that withholdeth more than is
Pr 12:18 **T.** is that speaketh like the piercings
Pr 12:21 **T.** shall no evil happen to the just:
Pr 12:28 in the pathway thereof **t.** is no death.
Pr 13:7 **T.** is that maketh himself rich, yet
Pr 13:7 **t.** is that maketh himself poor, yet
Pr 13:23 **t.** is that is destroyed for want of
Pr 14:9 but among the righteous **t.** is favour.
Pr 14:12 **T.** is a way which seemeth right unto
Pr 14:23 In all labour **t.** is profit: but the talk
Pr 16:25 **T.** is a way that seemeth right unto a
Pr 16:27 and in his lips **t.** is as a burning fire.
Pr 17:16 is **t.** a price in the hand of a fool to
Pr 18:24 **t.** is a friend that sticketh closer than a
Pr 19:18 Chasten thy son while **t.** is hope, and
Pr 19:21 **T.** are many devices in a man's heart;
Pr 20:15 **T.** is gold, and a multitude of rubies:
Pr 21:20 **T.** is treasure to be desired and oil in
Pr 21:30 **T.** is no wisdom nor understanding
Pr 22:13 The slothful man saith, **T.** is a lion.
Pr 23:18 For surely **t.** is an end; and thine
Pr 24:6 in multitude of counsellers **t.** is safety.
Pr 24:14 found it, then **t.** shall be a reward,
Pr 24:20 **t.** shall be no reward to the evil man;
Pr 25:4 and **t.** shall come forth a vessel for the
Pr 26:12 **t.** is more hope of a fool than of him.
Pr 26:13 man saith, **T.** is a lion in the way;
Pr 26:20 no wood is, **t.** the fire goeth out: so
Pr 26:20 **t.** is no talebearer, the strife ceaseth.
Pr 26:25 **t.** are seven abominations in his heart.
Pr 28:12 men do rejoice, **t.** is great glory:
Pr 29:6 of an evil man **t.** is a snare:
Pr 29:9 he rage or laugh, **t.** is no rest.
Pr 29:18 Where **t.** is no vision, the people
Pr 29:20 **t.** is more hope of a fool than of him.
Pr 30:11 **T.** is a generation that curseth their
Pr 30:12 **T.** is a generation that are pure in
Pr 30:13 **T.** is a generation, O how lofty are
Pr 30:14 **T.** is a generation, whose teeth are as
Pr 30:15 **T.** are three things that are never
Pr 30:18 **T.** be three things which are too
Pr 30:24 **T.** be four things which are little upon
Pr 30:29 **T.** be three things which go well, yea,
Pr 30:31 king, against whom **t.** is no rising up.
Ec 1:9 **t.** is no new thing under the sun.
Ec 1:10 Is **t.** any thing whereof it may be said,

Ec 1:11 **T.** is no remembrance of former
Ec 1:11 neither shall **t.** be any remembrance
Ec 2:11 and **t.** was no profit under the sun
Ec 2:16 **t.** is no remembrance of the wise
Ec 2:21 **t.** is a man whose labour is in wisdom,
Ec 2:24 **T.** is nothing better for a man, than
Ec 3:1 To every thing **t.** is a season, and a
Ec 3:12 I know that **t.** is no good in them, but
Ec 3:16 judgment, that wickedness was **t.**; 8033
Ec 3:16 righteousness, that iniquity was **t.**. 8033
Ec 3:17 **t.** is a time...for every purpose and
Ec 3:17 is a time **t.** for every purpose and 8033
Ec 3:22 I perceive that **t.** is nothing better,
Ec 4:1 side of their oppressors **t.** was power;
Ec 4:8 **T.** is one alone, and...is not a second;
Ec 4:8 is one alone, and **t.** is not a second;
Ec 4:8 is **t.** no end of all his labour; neither
Ec 4:16 **T.** is no end of all the people, even of
Ec 5:7 words **t.** are also divers vanities:
Ec 5:8 regardeth; and **t.** be higher than they.
Ec 5:11 what good is **t.** to the owners thereof,
Ec 5:13 **T.** is a sore evil which I have seen
Ec 5:14 a son, and **t.** is nothing in his hand.
Ec 6:1 **T.** is an evil which I have seen under
Ec 6:11 **t.** be many things that increase vanity,
Ec 7:11 by it **t.** is profit to them that see the
Ec 7:15 **t.** is a just man that perisheth in his
Ec 7:15 **t.** is a wicked man that prolongeth his
Ec 7:20 For **t.** is not a just man upon earth,
Ec 8:4 the word of a king is, **t.** is power:
Ec 8:6 to every purpose **t.** is time and
Ec 8:8 **T.** is no man that hath power over the
Ec 8:8 and **t.** is no discharge in that war;
Ec 8:9 **t.** is a time wherein one man ruleth
Ec 8:14 **T.** is a vanity which is done upon the
Ec 8:14 that **t.** be just men, unto whom it
Ec 8:14 again, **t.** be wicked men, to whom it
Ec 8:16 **t.** is that neither day nor night seeth
Ec 9:2 **t.** is one event to the righteous, and
Ec 9:3 the sun, that **t.** is one event unto all:
Ec 9:4 is joined to all the living **t.** is hope:
Ec 9:10 for **t.** is no work, nor device, nor
Ec 9:14 **T.** was a little city, and few men
Ec 9:14 and **t.** came a great king against it,
Ec 9:15 **t.** was found in it a poor wise man,
Ec 10:5 **T.** is an evil which I have seen under
Ec 11:3 the tree falleth, **t.** it shall be 8033
Ec 12:12 of making many books **t.** is no end;
Ca 4:4 whereon **t.** hang a thousand bucklers,
Ca 4:7 all fair, my love; **t.** is no spot in thee.
Ca 6:6 **t.** is not one barren among them.
Ca 6:8 **T.** are threescore queens, and
Ca 7:12 bud forth: **t.** will I give thee my loves.
Ca 8:5 **t.** thy mother brought thee forth:
Ca 8:5 **t.** she brought thee forth that bare
Isa 1:6 unto the head **t.** is no soundness in it;
Isa 2:7 is **t.** any end of their treasures;
Isa 2:7 neither is **t.** any end of their chariots:
Isa 3:24 instead of sweet smell **t.** shall be stink;
Isa 4:6 **t.** shall be a tabernacle for a shadow
Isa 5:6 but **t.** shall come up briers and thorns:
Isa 5:8 lay field to field, till **t.** be no place,
Isa 6:12 **t.** be a great forsaking in the midst
Isa 7:23 where **t.** were a thousand vines at a
Isa 7:25 **t.** shall not come thither the fear of
Isa 8:20 it is because **t.** is no light in them.
Isa 9:7 and peace **t.** shall be no end,
Isa 10:14 **t.** was none that moved the wing, or
Isa 11:1 **t.** shall come forth a rod out of the
Isa 11:10 in that day **t.** shall be a root of Jesse,
Isa 11:16 **t.** shall be an highway for the remnant
Isa 13:20 shall the Arabian pitch tent **t.**; 8033
Isa 13:20 the shepherds make their fold **t.**. 8033
Isa 13:21 beasts of the desert shall lie **t.**; 8033
Isa 13:21 creatures; and owls shall dwell **t.**, 8033
Isa 13:21 and satyrs shall dance **t.** 8033
Isa 14:31 **t.** shall come from the north a smoke,
Isa 15:6 the grass faileth, **t.** is no green thing.
Isa 16:10 in the vineyard **t.** shall be no singing,
Isa 16:10 neither shall **t.** be shouting: the
Isa 17:9 Israel: and **t.** shall be desolation.
Isa 19:15 shall **t.** be any work for Egypt, which
Isa 19:19 In that day shall **t.** be an altar to the
Isa 19:23 In that day shall **t.** be a highway out
Isa 22:18 a large country: **t.** shalt thou die, 8033
Isa 22:18 **t.** the chariots of thy glory shall be 8033
Isa 23:1 laid waste, so that **t.** is no house,
Isa 23:10 of Tarshish: **t.** is no more strength.
Isa 23:12 **t.** also shalt thou have no rest. 8033
Isa 24:11 **T.** is a crying for wine in the streets;
Isa 24:13 **t.** shall be as the shaking of an olive
Isa 27:10 wilderness: **t.** shall the calf feed, 8033
Isa 27:10 **t.** shall he lie down, and consume 8033
Isa 28:8 filthiness, so that **t.** is no place clean.
Isa 28:10 line; here a little, and **t.** a little: 8033
Isa 28:13 line; here a little, and **t.** a little; 8033
Isa 29:2 and **t.** shall be heaviness and sorrow:
Isa 30:14 so that **t.** shall not be found in the
Isa 30:25 **t.** shall be upon every high mountain,
Isa 30:28 **t.** shall be a bridle in the jaws of the
Isa 33:21 But **t.** the glorious Lord will be 8033
Isa 34:12 the kingdom, but none shall be **t.**, 8033
Isa 34:14 the screech owl also shall rest **t.**, 8033
Isa 34:15 **T.** shall the great owl make her 8033
Isa 34:15 **t.** shall the vultures also be 8033
Isa 35:8 And an highway shall be **t.**, and a 8033
Isa 35:9 No lion shall be **t.**, nor any 8033
Isa 35:9 up thereon, it shall not be found **t.**; 8033
Isa 35:9 but the redeemed shall walk **t.**:
Isa 37:3 and **t.** is not strength to bring forth.
Isa 37:33 this city, nor shoot an arrow **t.**, 8033
Isa 39:2 **t.** was nothing in his house, nor in all
Isa 39:4 **t.** is nothing among my treasures that
Isa 39:8 **t.** shall be peace and truth in my days.
Isa 40:28 **t.** is no searching of his understanding.
Isa 41:17 and needy seek water, and **t.** is none,
Isa 41:26 yea, **t.** is none that sheweth,
Isa 41:26 yea, **t.** is none that declareth,
Isa 41:26 **t.** is none that heareth your words.
Isa 41:28 For I beheld, and **t.** was no man; even
Isa 41:28 among them, and **t.** was no counseller,
Isa 43:10 before me **t.** was no God formed,
Isa 43:10 formed, neither shall **t.** be after me.
Isa 43:11 Lord; and beside me **t.** is no saviour.
Isa 43:12 **t.** was no strange god among you:
Isa 43:13 **t.** is none that can deliver out of my
Isa 44:6 the last; and beside me **t.** is no God.
Isa 44:8 my witnesses. Is **t.** a God beside me?
Isa 44:8 Yea, **t.** is no God; I know not any.
Isa 44:19 neither is **t.** knowledge nor
Isa 44:20 say, Is **t.** not a lie in my right hand?
Isa 45:5 I am the Lord, and **t.** is none else,
Isa 45:5 **t.** is no God beside me: I girded thee,
Isa 45:6 the west, that **t.** is none beside me.
Isa 45:6 I am the Lord, and **t.** is none else.
Isa 45:14 thee; and **t.** is none else, **t.** is no God.
Isa 45:18 I am the Lord; and **t.** is none else.
Isa 45:21 and **t.** is no god else beside me; a just
Isa 45:21 and a Saviour; **t.** is none beside me.
Isa 45:22 for I am God, and **t.** is none else.
Isa 46:9 old: for I am God, and **t.** is none else;
Isa 46:9 I am God, and **t.** is none like me,
Isa 47:1 **t.** is no throne, O daughter of the
Isa 47:14 **t.** shall not be a coal to warm at, nor
Isa 48:16 from the time that it was, **t.** am I: 8033
Isa 48:22 **T.** is no peace, saith the Lord, unto
Isa 50:2 when I came, was **t.** no man?
Isa 50:2 when I called, was **t.** none to answer?
Isa 50:2 **t.** is no water, and dieth for thirst.
Isa 51:18 **T.** is none to guide her among all the
Isa 51:18 neither is **t.** any that taketh her by the
Isa 52:1 for henceforth **t.** shall no more come
Isa 52:4 aforetime into Egypt to sojourn **t.**; 8033
Isa 53:2 **t.** is no beauty that we should desire
Isa 57:10 yet saidst thou not, **T.** is no hope:
Isa 57:21 **T.** is no peace, saith my God, to the
Isa 59:8 and **t.** is no judgment in their goings:
Isa 59:11 we look for judgment, but **t.** is none;
Isa 59:15 him that **t.** was no judgment.
Isa 59:16 and he saw that **t.** was no man, and
Isa 59:16 wondered that **t.** was no intercessor:
Isa 63:3 and of the people **t.** was none with me:
Isa 63:5 And I looked, and **t.** was none to help;
Isa 63:5 and I wondered that **t.** was none to
Isa 64:7 **t.** is none that calleth upon thy name,
Isa 65:9 it, and my servants shall dwell **t.** 8033
Isa 65:20 **T.** shall be no more thence an infant
Jer 2:10 diligently, and see if **t.** be such a thing.
Jer 2:25 **T.** is no hope: no; for I have loved
Jer 3:3 and **t.** hath been no latter rain;
Jer 3:6 tree, and **t.** hath played the harlot. 8033
Jer 4:25 I beheld, and, lo, **t.** was no man, and
Jer 5:1 if **t.** be any that executeth judgment,
Jer 6:14 Peace, peace; when **t.** is no peace.
Jer 6:20 purpose cometh **t.** to me incense from
Jer 7:2 house, and proclaim **t.** this word, 8033
Jer 7:32 bury in Tophet, till **t.** be no place.
Jer 8:11 Peace, peace; where **t.** is no peace.
Jer 8:13 **t.** shall be no grapes on the vine, nor
Jer 8:14 cities, and let us be silent **t.** 8033
Jer 8:22 Is **t.** no balm in Gilead; is **t.** no
Jer 8:22 is...no physician **t.**? why then is 8033
Jer 10:6 as **t.** is none like unto thee, O Lord;
Jer 10:7 kingdoms, **t.** is none like unto thee.
Jer 10:13 **t.** is a multitude of waters in the
Jer 10:14 falsehood, and **t.** is no breath in them.
Jer 10:20 **t.** is none to stretch forth my tent any
Jer 11:23 **t.** shall be no remnant of them: for I
Jer 13:4 and hide it **t.** in a hole of the rock. 8033
Jer 13:6 which I commanded thee to hide **t.**. 8033
Jer 14:4 for **t.** was no rain in the earth, the
Jer 14:5 and forsook it, because **t.** was no grass.
Jer 14:6 eyes did fail, because **t.** was no grass.
Jer 14:19 smitten us, and **t.** is no healing for us?
Jer 14:19 looked for peace, and **t.** is no good;
Jer 14:22 Are **t.** any among the vanities of the
Jer 16:13 **t.** shall ye serve other gods day 8033
Jer 16:19 and things wherein **t.** is no profit.
Jer 17:25 **t.** enter into the gates of this city kings
Jer 18:2 **t.** I will cause thee to hear my 8033
Jer 18:12 And they said, **T.** is no hope: but we
Jer 19:2 proclaim **t.** the words that I shall 8033
Jer 19:11 in Tophet, till **t.** be no place to bury.
Jer 20:6 to Babylon, and **t.** thou shalt die, 8033
Jer 20:6 and shalt be buried **t.**, thou, and all 8033
Jer 22:1 of Judah, and speak **t.** this word, 8033
Jer 22:4 then shall **t.** enter in by the gates of
Jer 22:26 were not born; and **t.** shall ye die. 8033
Jer 26:20 And **t.** was also a man that prophesied
Jer 27:22 **t.** shall they be until the day that 8033
Jer 29:6 that ye may be increased **t.**, and 8033
Jer 30:13 **T.** is none to plead thy cause, that
Jer 31:6 For **t.** shall be a day, that the
Jer 31:17 **t.** is hope in thine end, saith the Lord,
Jer 31:24 **t.** shall dwell in Judah itself, and in
Jer 32:5 **t.** shall he be until I visit him, 8033
Jer 32:17 and **t.** is nothing too hard for thee:
Jer 32:27 flesh: is **t.** any thing too hard for me?
Jer 33:10 Again **t.** shall be heard in this place,
Jer 33:20 that **t.** should not be day and night in
Jer 36:12 the princes sat **t.**, even Elishama 8033
Jer 36:22 **t.** was a fire on the hearth burning
Jer 36:32 **t.** were added besides unto them many
Jer 37:10 **t.** remained, but wounded men among
Jer 37:13 a captain of the ward was **t.**, 8033
Jer 37:16 had remained **t.** many days; 8033
Jer 37:17 said, Is **t.** any word from the Lord?
Jer 37:17 and Jeremiah said, **T.** is: for, said he,
Jer 37:20 Jonathan the scribe, lest I die **t.**. 8033
Jer 38:6 in the dungeon **t.** was no water, but
Jer 38:9 for **t.** is no more bread in the city.
Jer 38:26 to Jonathan's house, to die **t.** 8033
Jer 38:28 he was **t.** when Jerusalem was taken.
Jer 41:1 **t.** they did eat bread together in 8033
Jer 41:3 the Chaldeans that were found **t.**, 8033
Jer 41:5 that **t.** came certain from Shechem,
Jer 42:14 of bread; and **t.** will we dwell: 8033
Jer 42:15 into Egypt, and go to sojourn **t.**; 8033
Jer 42:16 shall overtake you **t.** in the land of 8033
Jer 42:16 follow close after you **t.** in Egypt; 8033
Jer 42:16 in Egypt; and **t.** ye shall die. 8033
Jer 42:17 faces to go into Egypt to sojourn **t.**; 8033
Jer 43:2 Go not into Egypt to sojourn **t.** 8033
Jer 44:12, 14 the land of Egypt to sojourn **t.**, 8033
Jer 44:14 have a desire to return to dwell **t.** 8033
Jer 44:27 the famine, until **t.** be an end of them.
Jer 44:28 the land of Egypt to sojourn **t.**, 8033
Jer 46:17 They did cry **t.**, Pharaoh king of 8033
Jer 47:7 sea shore? **t.** hath he appointed it 8033
Jer 48:2 **T.** shall be no more praise of Moab:
Jer 48:38 **T.** shall be lamentation generally
Jer 49:18 the Lord, no man shall abide **t.**, 8033
Jer 49:23 **t.** is sorrow on the sea; it cannot be
Jer 49:33 for ever: **t.** shall no man abide
Jer 49:33 shall no man abide **t.**, nor any 8033
Jer 49:36 and **t.** shall be no nation whither the
Jer 50:3 out of the north **t.** cometh up a nation
Jer 50:20 be sought for, and **t.** shall be none;
Jer 50:39 beasts of the islands shall dwell **t.**,

Jer 50:40 so shall no man abide t., neither........ 8033
Jer 51:16 voice, t. is a multitude of waters in the.....
Jer 51:17 falsehood, and t. is no breath in them. ......
Jer 52:6 so that t. was no bread for the people.......
Jer 52:23 t. were ninety and six pomegranates.........
Jer 52:34 t. was a continual diet given him of..........
La 1:12 see if t. be any sorrow like unto my.........
La 1:17 hands, and t. is none to comfort her: ....
La 1:20 bereaveth, at home t. is as death.............
La 1:21 that I sigh: t. is none to comfort me: ....
La 3:29 in the dust; if so be t. may be hope..........
La 4:15 they shall no more sojourn t...................
La 5:8 t. is none that doth deliver us out of.........
Eze 1:3 hand of the Lord was t. upon him. 8033
Eze 1:25 And t. was a voice from the firmament.......
Eze 2:5 t. hath been a prophet among them. ....
Eze 2:10 t. was written therein lamentations, ...
Eze 3:15 sat, and remained t. astonished.......... 8033
Eze 3:22 hand of the Lord was t. upon me; 8033
Eze 3:22 plain, and I will t. talk with thee. 8033
Eze 3:23 the glory of the Lord stood t., as....... 8033
Eze 4:14 neither came t. abominable flesh into.........
Eze 7:11 neither shall t. be wailing for them. ....
Eze 7:25 shall seek peace, and t. shall be none.........
Eze 8:1 hand of the Lord...fell t. upon me. 8033
Eze 8:4 glory of the God of Israel was t., ... 8033
Eze 8:11 And t. stood before them seventy men......
Eze 8:14 t. sat women weeping for Tammuz..... 8033
Eze 10:1 t. appeared over them as it were a...........
Eze 10:8 t. appeared in the cherubims the form.........
Eze 12:13 not see it, though he shall die t.. 8033
Eze 12:24 t. shall be no more any vain vision nor......
Eze 12:28 T. shall none of my words be prolonged ....
Eze 13:10 saying, Peace; and t. was no peace; ....
Eze 13:11 t. shall be an overflowing shower; and.......
Eze 13:13 and t. shall be an overflowing shower........
Eze 13:16 and t. is no peace, saith the Lord God. .....
Eze 13:20 wherewith ye t. hunt the souls to....... 8033
Eze 17:7 T. was also another great eagle with.........
Eze 17:20 plead with him t. for his trespass....... 8033
Eze 20:28 and they offered t. their sacrifices, ... 8033
Eze 20:28 t. they presented the provocation........ 8033
Eze 20:28 t....they made their sweet savour,...... 8033
Eze 20:28 poured out t. their drink offerings....... 8033
Eze 20:35 t. will I plead with you face to face..... 8033
Eze 20:40 t. shall all the house of Israel, all of.... 8033
Eze 20:40 serve me: t. will I accept them,......... 8033
Eze 20:40 and t. will I require your offerings, ... 8033
Eze 20:43 t. shall ye remember your ways, ... 8033
Eze 22:20 and I will leave you t., and melt you. ....
Eze 22:25 T. is a conspiracy of her prophets in.........
Eze 23:2 t. were two women, the daughters of ....
Eze 23:3 t. were their breasts pressed, and...... 8033
Eze 23:3 t. they bruised the teats of their........ 8033
Eze 28:3 t. is no secret that they can hide from ......
Eze 28:24 t. shall be no more a pricking brier...........
Eze 29:14 they shall be t. a base kingdom.......... 8033
Eze 30:13 t. shall be no more a prince of the land .....
Eze 30:18 shall break t. the yokes of Egypt: 8033
Eze 32:22 Asshur is t. and all her company: 8033
Eze 32:24 T. is Elam and all her multitude.......... 8033
Eze 32:26 T. is Meshech, Tubal, and all her....... 8033
Eze 32:26 T. is Edom, her kings, and all her....... 8033
Eze 32:30 T. be the princes of the north, all 8033
Eze 34:5 scattered, because t. is no shepherd: ....
Eze 34:8 because t. was no shepherd, neither.........
Eze 34:14 t. shall they lie in a good fold, and...... 8033
Eze 34:26 season; t. shall be showers of blessing. .....
Eze 35:10 whereas the Lord was t.: 8033
Eze 37:2 t. were very many in the open valley;.......
Eze 37:7 t. was a noise, and behold a shaking, ...
Eze 37:8 but t. was no breath in them. ....
Eze 38:19 in that day t. shall be a great shaking........
Eze 39:11 give unto Gog a place t. of graves...... 8033
Eze 39:11 t. shall they bury Gog and all his........ 8033
Eze 39:28 have left none of them any more t...... 8033
Eze 40:3 t. was a man, whose appearance..............
Eze 40:16 t. were narrow windows to the little.........
Eze 40:17 court, and, lo, t. were chambers,............
Eze 40:25 t. were windows in it and in the arches.....
Eze 40:26 And t. were seven steps to go up to it,......
Eze 40:27 t. was a gate in the inner court toward......
Eze 40:29 t. were windows in it and in the arches.....
Eze 40:33 t. were windows therein and in the...........
Eze 40:49 t. were pillars by the posts, one on this ....
Eze 41:7 t. was an enlarging, and a winding............
Eze 41:25 t. were made on them, on the doors of.....

Eze 41:25 t. were thick planks upon the face of ....
Eze 41:26 t. were narrow windows and palm...........
Eze 42:13 t. shall they lay the most holy.......... 8033
Eze 42:14 t. they shall lay their garments.......... 8033
Eze 45:2 this t. shall be for the sanctuary five.........
Eze 46:19 t. was a place on the two sides 8033
Eze 46:21 corner of the court t. was a court. ....
Eze 46:22 of the court t. were courts joined............
Eze 46:23 t. was a row of building round about.........
Eze 47:2 t. ran out waters on the right side...........
Eze 47:9 t. shall be a very great multitude of..........
Eze 47:23 t. shall ye give him his inheritance,..... 8033
Eze 48:35 that day shall be, the Lord is t.. 8033
Da 2:9 the dream, t. is but one decree for you:....
Da 2:10 T. is not a man upon the earth that.........
Da 2:10 t. is no king, lord, nor ruler, that............
Da 2:11 t. is none other than can shew it before ....
Da 2:28 t. is a God in heaven that revealeth..........
Da 2:41 t. shall be in it of the strength of the........
Da 3:12 T. are certain Jews whom thou hast..........
Da 3:29 t. is no other God that can deliver.............
Da 4:31 mouth, t. fell a voice from heaven, ...
Da 5:11 T. is a man in thy kingdom, in whom........
Da 6:4 neither was t. any error or fault found.......
Da 7:8 t. came up among them another little........
Da 7:8 before whom t. were three of the ....
Da 7:14 And t. was given him dominion, and..........
Da 8:3 stood before the river a ram which...........
Da 8:4 neither was t. any that could deliver.........
Da 8:7 t. was no power in the ram to stand...........
Da 8:7 t. was none that could deliver the ram ......
Da 8:15 t. stood before me as the appearance........
Da 10:8 and t. remained no strength in me:............
Da 10:13 I remained t. with the kings of 8033
Da 10:17 t. remained no strength in me, ...
Da 10:17 in me, neither is t. breath left in me. ....
Da 10:18 t. came again and touched me one............
Da 10:21 t. is none that holdeth with me in these.....
Da 11:2 t. shall stand up yet three kings in............
Da 11:14 in those times t. shall many stand up ....
Da 11:15 neither shall t. be any strength to.............
Da 12:1 t. shall be a time of trouble, such as.........
Da 12:1 such as never was since t. was a nation ....
Da 12:5 t. stood other two, the one on this side.......
Da 12:11 t. shall be a thousand two hundred and......
Ho 1:10 people, t. it shall be said unto them, ...
Ho 2:15 she shall sing t., as in the days of...... 8033
Ho 4:1 because t. is no truth, nor mercy,............
Ho 4:9 And t. shall be, like people, like priest: .....
Ho 6:7 t. have they dealt treacherously......... 8033
Ho 6:10 t. is the whoredom of Ephraim, ... 8033
Ho 7:7 t. is none among them that calleth............
Ho 7:9 gray hairs are here and t. upon him, ...
Ho 9:12 them, that t. shall not be a man left:.........
Ho 9:15 in Gilgal: for t. I hated them: 8033
Ho 10:9 the days of Gibeah: t. they stood: 8033
Ho 12:4 in Beth-el, and t. he spake with us;.... 8033
Ho 12:11 Is t. iniquity in Gilead? surely they ....
Ho 13:4 but me: for t. is no saviour beside me.......
Ho 13:8 t. will I devour them like a lion:......... 8033
Joe 2:2 t. hath not been ever the like, neither.......
Joe 3:2 plead with them t. for my people 8033
Joe 3:12 t. will I sit to judge all the heathen...... 8033
Joe 3:17 t. shall no strangers pass through her ....
Am 3:6 shall t. be evil in a city, and the Lord........
Am 3:11 An adversary t. shall be even round..........
Am 4:7 when t. were yet three months to the.......
Am 5:2 her land; t. is none to raise her up............
Am 5:6 and t. be none to quench it in Beth-el. ......
Am 6:9 if t. remain ten men in one house,............
Am 6:10 of the house, Is t. yet any with thee? ....
Am 6:12 rock? will one plow t. with oxen? ....
Am 7:12 and t. eat bread, and prophesy t.:...... 8033
Am 8:3 t. shall be many dead bodies in every.........
Ob 7 thee: t. is none understanding in him. ....
Ob 17 deliverance, and t. shall be holiness; ....
Ob 18 and t. shall not be any remaining of...........
Jon 1:4 t. was a mighty tempest in the sea..........
Jon 4:5 and t. made him a booth, and sat....... 8033
Mic 3:7 their lips; for t. is no answer of God.........
Mic 4:9 is t. no king in thee? is thy counseller.......
Mic 4:10 to Babylon; t. shalt thou be delivered;.......
Mic 4:10 t. the Lord shall redeem thee from.... 8033
Mic 6:10 Are t. yet the treasures of wickedness.......
Mic 7:1 of the vintage: t. is no cluster to eat:........
Mic 7:2 and t. is none upright among men:............
Na 1:11 T. is one come out of thee, that ....

Na 2:9 for t. is none end of the store and glory....
Na 3:3 t. is a multitude of slain, and a great.........
Na 3:3 and t. is none end of their corpses; ....
Na 3:15 T shall the fire devour thee; the 8033
Na 3:19 T. is no healing of thy bruise; thy.............
Hab 1:3 and t. are that raise up strife and.............
Hab 2:19 t. is no breath at all in the midst of it........
Hab 3:4 and t. was the hiding of his power...... 8033
Hab 3:17 and t. shall be no herd in the stalls:..........
Zep 1:10 t. shall be the noise of a cry from the.......
Zep 1:14 mighty man shall cry t. bitterly. 8033
Zep 2:5 thee, that t. shall be no inhabitant. ....
Zep 2:15 heart, I am, and t. is none beside me: ......
Zep 3:6 are destroyed, so that t. is no man,..........
Zep 3:6 is no man, that t. is none inhabitant. ....
Hag 1:6 ye clothe you, but t. is none warm; ....
Hag 2:14 that which they offer t. is unclean. 8033
Hag 2:16 of twenty measures, t. were but ten:........
Hag 2:16 out of the press, t. were but twenty..........
Zec 1:8 and behind him were t. red horses, ...
Zec 5:7 behold, t. was lifted up a talent of lead:.....
Zec 5:9 and, behold, t. came out two women, ...
Zec 5:11 and set t. upon her own base............ 8033
Zec 6:1 behold, t. came four chariots out from.......
Zec 8:4 T. shall yet old men and old women..........
Zec 8:10 these days t. was no hire for man, ...
Zec 8:10 neither was t. any peace to him that.........
Zec 8:20 to pass, that t. shall come people, ...
Zec 10:2 troubled, because t. was no shepherd........
Zec 11:3 T. is a voice of the howling of the ....
Zec 12:11 that day shall t. be a great mourning.........
Zec 13:1 that day t. shall be a fountain opened........
Zec 14:4 and t. shall be a very great valley;............
Zec 14:9 that day shall t. be one Lord, and his........
Zec 14:11 t. shall be no more utter destruction;........
Zec 14:18 t. shall be the plague, wherewith the ....
Zec 14:20 that day sahll t. be upon the bells of.........
Zec 14:21 in that day t. shall be no more the...........
Mal 1:10 is t. even among you that would shut........
Mal 3:10 that t. may be meat in mine house, ...
Mal 3:10 t. shall not be room enough to receive ......
Mt 2:1 t. came wise men from the east to...........
Mt 2:13 be thou t. until I bring thee word:...... 1563
Mt 2:15 And was t. until the death of Herod:... 1563
Mt 2:18 In Rama was t. a voice heard, ...
Mt 4:25 t. followed him great multitudes of............
Mt 5:23 t. rememberest that thy brother.... 1563
Mt 5:24 Leave t. thy gift before the altar,.. 1563
Mt 6:21 is, t. will your heart be also.......... 1563
Mt 7:9 Or what man is t. of you, whom if......
Mt 7:13 and many t. be which go in thereat:...
Mt 7:14 unto life, and few t. be that find it......
Mt 8:2 t. came a leper and worshipped him,.........
Mt 8:5 t. came unto him a centurion, ...
Mt 8:12 t. shall be weeping and gnashing... 1563
Mt 8:24 t. arose a great tempest in the sea,..........
Mt 8:26 and the sea; and t. was a great calm.........
Mt 8:28 t. met him two possessed with devils,.......
Mt 8:30 and t. was a good way off from them..........
Mt 9:18 t. came a certain ruler, and worshipped.....
Mt 10:11 and t. abide till ye go thence. 1563
Mt 10:26 t. is nothing covered, that shall not.....
Mt 11:11 t. hath not risen a greater than John...
Mt 12:10 t. was a man which had his hand............
Mt 12:11 What man shall t. be among you,.........
Mt 12:39 t. shall no sign be given to it, but ....
Mt 12:45 and they enter in and dwell t......... 1563
Mt 13:42, 50 t. shall be wailing and gnashing 1563
Mt 13:58 he did not many mighty works t.......... 1563
Mt 14:23 evening was come, he was t. alone..... 1563
Mt 15:29 up into a mountain, and sat down t..... 1563
Mt 16:4 and t. shall no sign be given unto it, ...
Mt 16:28 T. be some standing here, which ....
Mt 17:3 t. appeared unto them Moses and ....
Mt 17:14 t. came to him a certain man, kneeling......
Mt 18:20 t. am I in the midst of them. 1563
Mt 19:2 him; and he healed them t.. 1563
Mt 19:12 For t. are some eunuchs, which ....
Mt 19:12 t. are some eunuchs, which were.........
Mt 19:12 t. be eunuchs, which have made..........
Mt 19:13 were t. brought unto him...children,..........
Mt 19:17 t. is none good but one, that is, God: ..
Mt 21:17 into Bethany; and he lodged t........... 1563
Mt 21:33 T. was a certain householder, which....
Mt 22:11 saw t. a man which had not on a .. 1563
Mt 22:13 t. shall be weeping and gnashing... 1563
Mt 22:23 which say that t. is no resurrection,..........

Mt	22:25	Now **t.** were with us seven brethren:
Mt	24:2	**T.** shall not be left here one stone
Mt	24:7	**t.** shall be famines, and pestilences,
Mt	24:22	shortened, **t.** should no flesh be
Mt	24:23	unto you, Lo, here is Christ, or **t.**.. *5602*
Mt	24:24	**t.** shall arise false Christs, and false
Mt	24:28	is, **t.** will the eagles be gathered *1563*
Mt	24:51	**t.** shall be weeping and gnashing *1563*
Mt	25:6	at midnight **t.** was a cry made,
Mt	25:9	least **t.** be not enough for us and
Mt	25:25	earth: lo, **t.** thou hast that is thine
Mt	25:30	**t.** shall be weeping and gnashing *1563*
Mt	26:5	least **t.** be an uproar among the people
Mt	26:7	**T.** came unto him a woman having
Mt	26:13	**t.** shall also this, that this woman
Mt	26:71	and said unto them that were **t.**, *1563*
Mt	27:36	sitting down they watched him **t.**; *1563*
Mt	27:38	were **t.** two thieves crucified with him,
Mt	27:45	from the sixth hour **t.** was darkness
Mt	27:47	Some of them that stood **t.**, when *1563*
Mt	27:55	many women were **t.** beholding *1563*
Mt	27:57	**t.** came a rich man of Arimathaea,
Mt	27:61	**t.** was Mary Magdalene, and the *1563*
Mt	28:2	behold, **t.** was a great earthquake: for
Mt	28:7	**t.** shall ye see him: lo, I have told *1563*
Mt	28:10	Galilee, and **t.** shall they see me *1563*
Mk	1:5	**t.** went out unto him all the land of
Mk	1:7	**T.** cometh one mightier than I after
Mk	1:11	**t.** came a voice from heaven, saying,
Mk	1:13	**t.** in the wilderness forty days, *1563*
Mk	1:23	**t.** was in their synagogue a man with
Mk	1:35	into a solitary place, and **t.** prayed *1563*
Mk	1:38	towns, that I may preach **t.** also: *1563*
Mk	1:40	**t.** came a leper to him, beseeching
Mk	2:2	that **t.** was no room to receive them,
Mk	2:6	**t.** were certain of the scribes sitting
Mk	2:6	scribes sitting **t.**, and reasoning *1563*
Mk	2:15	for **t.** were many, and they followed
Mk	3:1	and **t.** was a man...which had a
Mk	3:1	a man **t.** which had a withered *1563*
Mk	3:31	**T.** came then his brethren and his
Mk	4:1	**t.** was gathered unto him a great
Mk	4:3	Behold, **t.** went out a sower to sow:
Mk	4:22	For **t.** is nothing hid, which shall not
Mk	4:36	**t.** were also with him other little
Mk	4:37	**t.** arose a great storm of wind, and the
Mk	4:39	wind ceased, and **t.** was a great calm.
Mk	5:2	**t.** met him out of the tombs a man
Mk	5:11	**t.** was...nigh unto the mountains
Mk	5:11	was **t.** nigh unto the mountains *1563*
Mk	5:22	**t.** cometh one of the rulers of the
Mk	5:35	**t.** came from the ruler of the
Mk	6:5	he could **t.** do no mighty work, *1563*
Mk	6:10	**t.** abide till ye depart...that place *1563*
Mk	6:31	for **t.** were many coming and going,
Mk	7:4	And many other things **t.** be, which
Mk	7:15	**T.** is nothing from without a man,
Mk	8:12	**T.** shall no sign be given unto this
Mk	9:1	That **t.** be some of them that stand
Mk	9:4	**t.** appeared unto them Elias with
Mk	9:7	**t.** was a cloud that overshadowed
Mk	9:39	for **t.** is no man which shall do a
Mk	10:17	**t.** came one running, and kneeled to
Mk	10:18	**t.** is none good but one, that is, God
Mk	10:29	**T.** is no man that hath left house,
Mk	11:5	certain of them that stood **t.** *1563*
Mk	11:27	**t.** come to him the chief priests,
Mk	12:18	which say **t.** is no resurrection; and
Mk	12:20	**t.** were seven brethren: and the first
Mk	12:31	**T.** is none other commandment
Mk	12:32	hast said the truth: for **t.** is one God;
Mk	12:32	one God; and **t.** is none other but he:
Mk	12:42	And **t.** came a certain poor widow,
Mk	13:2	**t.** shall not be left one stone upon
Mk	13:8	and **t.** shall be earthquakes in divers
Mk	13:8	and **t.** shall be famines and troubles:
Mk	13:21	here is Christ; or, lo, he is **t.**; *1563*
Mk	14:2	day, lest **t.** be an uproar of the people.
Mk	14:3	**t.** came a woman having an alabaster
Mk	14:4	And **t.** were some that had indignation
Mk	14:13	**t.** shall meet you a man bearing a
Mk	14:15	prepared: **t.** make ready for us *1563*
Mk	14:51	**t.** followed him a certain young man,
Mk	14:57	**t.** arose certain, and bare false witness
Mk	14:66	**t.** cometh one of the maids of the high
Mk	15:7	And **t.** was one named Barabbas,
Mk	15:33	**t.** was darkness over the whole land
Mk	15:40	**T.** were also women looking on afar
Mk	16:7	**t.** shall ye see him, as he said unto *1563*
Lu	1:5	**T.** was in the days of Herod, the king
Lu	1:11	**t.** appeared unto him an angel of the
Lu	1:33	and of his kingdom **t.** shall be no end.
Lu	1:45	**t.** shall be a performance of those
Lu	1:61	**T.** is none of thy kindred that is
Lu	2:1	that **t.** went out a decree from Caesar
Lu	2:6	while they were **t.**, the days were *1563*
Lu	2:7	**t.** was no room for them in the inn.
Lu	2:8	**t.** were in the same country shepherds
Lu	2:13	And suddenly **t.** was with the angel a
Lu	2:25	**t.** was a man in Jerusalem, whose
Lu	2:36	And **t.** was one Anna, a prophetess, the
Lu	4:14	**t.** went out a fame of him through all
Lu	4:17	**t.** was delivered unto him the book
Lu	4:33	And in the synagogue **t.** was a man,
Lu	5:15	much the more went **t.** a fame abroad
Lu	5:17	that **t.** were Pharisees and doctors of
Lu	5:29	**t.** was a great company of publicans
Lu	6:6	**t.** was a man whose right hand *1563*
Lu	6:19	for **t.** went virtue out of him, and
Lu	7:12	behold, **t.** was a dead man carried out,
Lu	7:16	And **t.** came a fear on all: and they
Lu	7:28	**t.** is not a greater prophet than
Lu	7:41	**T.** was a certain creditor which had
Lu	8:23	**t.** came down a storm of wind on the
Lu	8:24	and they ceased, and **t.** was a calm.
Lu	8:27	**t.** met him out of the city a certain
Lu	8:32	And **t.** was...an herd of many swine
Lu	8:32	**t.** an herd of many swine feeding *1563*
Lu	8:41	behold, **t.** came a man named Jairus,
Lu	8:49	**t.** cometh one from the ruler of the
Lu	9:4	house ye enter into, **t.** abide, and *1563*
Lu	9:17	**t.** was taken up of fragments that
Lu	9:27	of a truth, **t.** be some standing here,
Lu	9:30	behold, **t.** talked with him two men,
Lu	9:34	While he thus spake, **t.** came a cloud,
Lu	9:35	And **t.** came a voice out of the cloud,
Lu	9:46	**t.** arose a reasoning among them,
Lu	10:6	And if the son of peace be **t.**, your *1563*
Lu	10:31	by chance **t.** came down a certain
Lu	11:26	they enter in, and dwell **t.**: and *1563*
Lu	11:29	and **t.** shall no sign be given it, but
Lu	12:1	when **t.** were gathered together an
Lu	12:2	For **t.** is nothing covered, that shall
Lu	12:18	**t.** will I bestow all my fruits and *1563*
Lu	12:34	treasure is, **t.** will your heart be 1563
Lu	12:52	**t.** shall be five in one house divided,
Lu	12:54	**T.** cometh a shower; and so it is.
Lu	12:55	**T.** will be heat; and it cometh to pass
Lu	13:1	**T.** were present at that season some
Lu	13:11	**t.** was a woman which had a spirit of
Lu	13:14	**T.** are six days in which men ought
Lu	13:23	him, Lord, are **t.** few that be saved?
Lu	13:28	**T.** shall be weeping and gnashing *1563*
Lu	13:30	**t.** are last which shall be first,
Lu	13:30	and **t.** are first which shall be last
Lu	13:31	The same day **t.** came certain of the
Lu	14:2	**t.** was a certain man before him
Lu	14:22	hast commanded, and yet **t.** is room
Lu	14:25	**t.** went great multitudes with him:
Lu	15:10	**t.** is joy in the presence of the angels
Lu	15:13	and **t.** wasted his substance with *1563*
Lu	15:14	**t.** arose a mighty famine in that land;
Lu	16:1	**T.** was a certain rich man, which had
Lu	16:19	**T.** was a certain rich man, which was
Lu	16:20	**t.** was a...beggar named Lazarus,
Lu	16:26	between us and you **t.** is a great gulf
Lu	17:12	**t.** met him ten men that were lepers,
Lu	17:17	Were **t.** not ten cleansed? but where
Lu	17:18	**T.** are not found that returned to give
Lu	17:21	shall they say, Lo here! or, lo **t.**! *1563*
Lu	17:23	say to you, See here; or, see **t.** *1563*
Lu	17:34	night **t.** shall be two men in one bed;
Lu	18:2	**T.** was in a city a judge, which feared
Lu	18:3	And **t.** was a widow in that city; and
Lu	18:29	**T.** is no man that hath left house, or
Lu	19:2	behold, **t.** was a man named Zacchaeus,
Lu	20:27	which deny that **t.** is any resurrection:
Lu	20:29	**T.** were therefore seven brethren: and
Lu	21:6	**t.** shall not be left one stone upon
Lu	21:7	what sign will **t.** be when these things
Lu	21:11	great signs shall **t.** be from heaven
Lu	21:18	**t.** shall not an hair of your head
Lu	21:23	**t.** shall be great distress in the land,
Lu	21:25	**t.** shall be signs in the sun, and in the
Lu	22:10	into the city, **t.** shall a man meet you,
Lu	22:12	room furnished: **t.** make ready. *1563*
Lu	22:24	**t.** was also a strife among them,
Lu	22:43	**t.** appeared an angel unto him from
Lu	23:27	**t.** followed him a great company of
Lu	23:32	**t.** were also two other, malefactors,
Lu	23:33	Calvary, **t.** they crucified him, *1563*
Lu	23:44	**t.** was a darkness over all the earth
Lu	23:50	behold, **t.** was a man named Joseph,
Lu	24:18	things which are come to pass **t.** *1722,846*
Joh	1:6	**T.** was a man sent from God, whose
Joh	1:26	**t.** standeth one among you, whom ye
Joh	1:46	Can **t.** any good thing come out of
Joh	2:1	the third day **t.** was a marriage in Cana
Joh	2:1	and the mother of Jesus was **t.** *1563*
Joh	2:6	**t.** were set...six waterpots of stone,
Joh	2:6	set **t.** six waterpots of stone, *1563*
Joh	2:12	they continued **t.** not many days. *1563*
Joh	3:1	**T.** was a man of the Pharisees, named
Joh	3:22	and **t.** he tarried with them, and *1563*
Joh	3:23	to Salim, because **t.** was much water
Joh	3:23	because...was much water **t.** *1563*
Joh	3:25	Then **t.** arose a question between some
Joh	4:6	Now Jacob's well was **t.** Jesus *1563*
Joh	4:7	**T.** cometh a woman of Samaria to
Joh	4:35	**T.** are yet four months, and then
Joh	4:40	them: and he abode **t.** two days. *1563*
Joh	4:46	And **t.** was a certain nobleman, whose
Joh	5:1	After this **t.** was a feast of the Jews;
Joh	5:2	Now **t.** is at Jerusalem by the sheep
Joh	5:5	And a certain man was **t.**, which *1563*
Joh	5:32	**T.** is another that beareth witness of
Joh	5:45	**t.** is one that accuseth you, even
Joh	6:3	and **t.** he sat with his disciples. *1563*
Joh	6:9	**T.** is a lad here, which hath five
Joh	6:10	Now **t.** was much grass in the place.
Joh	6:22	saw that **t.** was none other boat
Joh	6:22	saw that...was none other boat **t.**, *1563*
Joh	6:23	**t.** came other boats from Tiberias
Joh	6:24	therefore saw that Jesus was not **t.**, *1563*
Joh	6:64	**t.** are some of you that believe not.
Joh	7:4	**t.** is no man that doeth any thing in
Joh	7:12	**t.** was much murmuring among the
Joh	7:43	So **t.** was a division among the people
Joh	8:44	the truth, because **t.** is no truth in
Joh	8:50	**t.** is one that seeketh and judgeth.
Joh	9:16	And **t.** was a division among them.
Joh	10:16	**t.** shall be one fold, and one shepherd
Joh	10:19	**T.** was a division therefore again
Joh	10:40	at first baptized; and **t.** he abode. *1563*
Joh	10:42	And many believed on him **t.** *1563*
Joh	11:9	Are **t.** not twelve hours in the day?
Joh	11:10	stumbleth, because **t.** is no light in
Joh	11:15	for your sakes that I was not **t.**, *1563*
Joh	11:31	She goeth unto the grave to weep **t.** *1563*
Joh	11:54	and **t.** continued with his disciples *1563*
Joh	12:2	**T.** they made him a supper; and *1563*
Joh	12:9	Jews therefore knew that he was **t.** *1563*
Joh	12:20	**t.** were certain Greeks among them
Joh	12:26	I am, **t.** shall also my servant be: *1563*
Joh	12:28	Then came **t.** a voice from heaven,
Joh	13:23	**t.** was leaning on Jesus' bosom one of
Joh	14:3	that where I am, **t.** ye may be also
Joh	18:18	And the servants and officers stood **t.**,
Joh	19:25	Now **t.** stood by the cross of Jesus his
Joh	19:29	Now **t.** was set a vessel full of vinegar:
Joh	19:34	and forthwith came **t.** out blood and
Joh	19:39	**t.** came also Nicodemus, which at the
Joh	19:41	where he was crucified **t.** was a garden;
Joh	19:42	**T.** laid they Jesus therefore *1563*
Joh	21:2	**T.** were together Simon Peter, and
Joh	21:9	they saw a fire of coals **t.**, and fish
Joh	21:11	and for all **t.** were so many, yet was
Joh	21:25	**t.** are also many other things which
Ac	2:2	And suddenly **t.** came a sound from
Ac	2:3	And **t.** appeared unto them cloven
Ac	2:5	**t.** were dwelling at Jerusalem Jews,
Ac	2:41	**t.** were added unto them about three
Ac	4:12	Neither is **t.** salvation in any other:
Ac	4:12	**t.** is none other name under heaven
Ac	4:34	Neither was **t.** any among them that
Ac	5:16	**T.** came also a multitude out of the
Ac	5:34	Then stood **t.** up one in the council,
Ac	6:1	**t.** arose a murmuring of the Grecians

Ac 6:9 **t.** arose certain of the synagogue,
Ac 7:11 **t.** came a dearth over all the land of
Ac 7:12 Jacob heard that **t.** was corn in Egypt,
Ac 7:30 **t.** appeared to him in the wilderness
Ac 8:1 at that time **t.** was a great persecution
Ac 8:8 And **t.** was great joy in that city
Ac 8:9 But **t.** was a certain man, called Simon,
Ac 9:3 suddenly **t.** shined round about him a
Ac 9:10 **t.** was a certain disciple at Damascus,
Ac 9:18 **t.** fell from his eyes as it had been
Ac 9:33 **t.** he found a certain man named *1563*
Ac 9:36 now **t.** was at Joppa a certain disciple
Ac 9:38 had heard that Peter was **t.**, *1722,846*
Ac 10:1 **T.** was a certain man in Caesarea
Ac 10:13 **t.** came a voice to him, Rise, Peter;
Ac 10:18 surnamed Peter, were lodged **t.** *1759*
Ac 11:11 immediately **t.** were three men already
Ac 11:28 And **t.** stood up one of them named
Ac 11:28 spirit that **t.** should be great dearth
Ac 12:18 **t.** was no small stir among the soldiers,
Ac 12:19 from Judaea to Caesarea, and **t.** abode.
Ac 13:1 Now **t.** were in the church that was at
Ac 13:11 immediately **t.** fell on him a mist and a
Ac 13:25 **t.** cometh one after me, whose shoes
Ac 14:5 And when **t.** was an assault made both
Ac 14:7 And **t.** they preached the gospel. *1563*
Ac 14:8 And **t.** sat a certain man at Lystra,
Ac 14:19 **t.** came thither certain Jews from
Ac 14:28 **t.** they abode long time with the *1563*
Ac 15:5 **t.** rose up certain of the sect of the
Ac 15:7 And when **t.** had been much disputing,
Ac 15:33 And after they had tarried **t.** a space,
Ac 15:34 it pleased Silas to abide **t.** still. *847*
Ac 16:1 a certain disciple was **t.**, named *1563*
Ac 16:9 **T.** stood a man of Macedonia, and
Ac 16:15 come into my house, and abide **t.**
Ac 16:26 suddenly **t.** was a great earthquake, so
Ac 17:7 that **t.** is another king, one Jesus
Ac 17:14 Silas and Timotheus abode **t.** still. *1563*
Ac 17:21 and strangers which were **t.** *1927*
Ac 18:11 And he continued **t.** a year and six
Ac 18:18 Paul after this tarried **t.** yet a good
Ac 18:19 came to Ephesus, and left them **t.**: *847*
Ac 18:23 after he had spent some time **t.**, he
Ac 19:2 heard whether **t.** be any Holy Ghost.
Ac 19:14 **t.** were seven sons of one Sceva, a
Ac 19:21 After I have been **t.**, I must also *1563*
Ac 19:23 same time **t.** arose no small stir about
Ac 19:35 what man is **t.** that knoweth not how
Ac 19:38 the law is open, and **t.** are deputies:
Ac 19:40 this day's uproar, **t.** being no cause
Ac 20:3 **t.** abode three months. And when the
Ac 20:4 And **t.** accompanied him into Asia
Ac 20:8 And **t.** were many lights in the upper
Ac 20:9 **t.** sat in a window a certain young
Ac 20:13 Assos, **t.** intending to take in Paul: *1564*
Ac 20:22 things that shall befall me **t.** *1722,846*
Ac 21:3 for **t.** the ship was to unlade her *1566*
Ac 21:4 disciples, we tarried **t.** seven days: *847*
Ac 21:10 And as we tarried **t.** many days,
Ac 21:10 **t.** came down from Judaea a certain
Ac 21:16 **T.** went with us also certain of the
Ac 21:20 thousands of Jews **t.** are which believe;
Ac 21:40 when **t.** was made a great silence, he
Ac 22:5 were **t.** bound unto Jerusalem. *1566*
Ac 22:6 **t.** shone from heaven a great light
Ac 22:10 **t. it shall be told thee of all things** *1563*
Ac 22:12 report of all the Jews which dwelt **t.**,
Ac 23:7 he had so said, **t.** arose a dissension
Ac 23:8 say that **t.** is no resurrection,
Ac 23:9 **t.** arose a great cry: and the scribes
Ac 23:10 when **t.** arose a great dissension, the
Ac 23:21 for **t.** lie in wait for him of them more
Ac 24:11 that **t.** are yet but twelve days since
Ac 24:15 **t.** shall be a resurrection of the dead,
Ac 25:5 man, if **t.** be any wickedness in him.
Ac 25:9 **t.** be judged of these things before *1563*
Ac 25:11 it **t.** be none of these things whereof
Ac 25:14 when they had been **t.** many days, *1563*
Ac 25:14 **T.** is a certain man left in bonds by
Ac 25:20 and **t.** be judged of these matters. *1563*
Ac 27:6 And **t.** the centurion found a ship *1563*
Ac 27:12 attain to Phenice, and **t.** to winter;
Ac 27:14 after **t.** arose against it a tempestuous
Ac 27:22 **t.** shall be no loss of any man's life
Ac 27:23 For **t.** stood by me this night the angel
Ac 27:34 for **t.** shall not an hair fall from the
Ac 28:3 the fire, **t.** came a viper out of the heat,
Ac 28:12 at Syracuse, we tarried **t.** three days.
Ac 28:18 **t.** was no cause of death in me.
Ac 28:23 **t.** came many to him into his lodging;
Ro 2:11 **t.** is no respect of persons with God.
Ro 3:1 or what profit is **t.** of curcumcision?
Ro 3:10 **T.** is none righteous, no, not one:
Ro 3:11 **T.** is none that understandeth,
Ro 3:11 **t.** is none that seeketh after God.
Ro 3:12 **t.** is none that doeth good, no, not one.
Ro 3:18 **T.** is no fear of God before their eyes.
Ro 3:20 **t.** shall no flesh be justified in his
Ro 3:22 that believe: for **t.** is no difference:
Ro 4:15 where no law is, **t.** is no transgression.
Ro 5:13 sin is not imputed when **t.** is no law.
Ro 8:1 **T.** is therefore now no condemnation
Ro 9:14 Is **t.** unrighteousness with God? God
Ro 9:26 **t.** shall they be called the children *1563*
Ro 10:12 **t.** is no difference between the Jew
Ro 11:5 present time also **t.** is a remnant
Ro 11:26 **T.** shall come out of Sion the
Ro 13:1 For **t.** is no power but of God: the
Ro 13:9 if **t.** be any other commandment, it is
Ro 14:14 that **t.** is nothing unclean of itself:
Ro 15:12 saith, **T.** shall be a root of Jesse,
1Co 1:10 and that **t.** be no divisions among you:
1Co 1:11 that **t.** are contentions among you.
1Co 3:3 for whereas **t.** is among you envying,
1Co 5:1 reported...that **t.** is fornication
1Co 6:5 that **t.** is not a wise man among you?
1Co 6:7 **t.** is utterly a fault among you,
1Co 7:34 **T.** is difference also between a wife
1Co 8:4 and that **t.** is none other God but one.
1Co 8:5 For though **t.** be that are called gods,
1Co 8:5 (as **t.** be gods many, and lords many,)
1Co 8:6 But to us **t.** is but one God, the Father,
1Co 8:7 **t.** is not in every man that knowledge:
1Co 10:13 **T.** hath no temptation taken you but
1Co 11:18 I hear that **t.** be divisions among you;
1Co 11:19 **t.** must be also heresies among you,
1Co 12:4 **t.** are diversities of gifts, but the same
1Co 12:5 **t.** are differences of administrations,
1Co 12:6 **t.** are diversities of operations, but it
1Co 12:25 **t.** should be no schism in the body;
1Co 13:8 but whether **t.** be prophecies, they
1Co 13:8 whether **t.** be tongues, they shall
1Co 13:8 whether **t.** be knowledge, it shall
1Co 14:10 **T.** are, it may be, so many kinds of
1Co 14:23 **t.** come in those that are unlearned, or
1Co 14:24 **t.** come in one that believeth not, or
1Co 14:28 But if **t.** be no interpreter, let him
1Co 15:12 among you that **t.** is no resurrection
1Co 15:13 if **t.** be no resurrection of the dead,
1Co 15:39 but **t.** is one kind of flesh of men,
1Co 15:40 **T.** are also celestial bodies, and
1Co 15:41 **T.** is one glory of the sun, and
1Co 15:44 **T.** is a natural body,
1Co 15:44 and **t.** is a spiritual body.
1Co 16:2 that **t.** be no gatherings when I come.
1Co 16:9 unto me, and **t.** are many adversaries.
2Co 1:17 that with me **t.** should be yea yea, and
2Co 3:17 Spirit of the Lord is, **t.** is liberty. *1563*
2Co 8:11 that as **t.** was a readiness to will,
2Co 8:11 so **t.** may be a performance also out of
2Co 8:12 For if **t.** be first a willing mind, it is
2Co 8:14 for your want: that **t.** may be equality:
2Co 12:7 **t.** was given to me a thorn in the flesh,
2Co 12:20 lest **t.** be debates, envyings, wraths,
Ga 1:7 but **t.** be some that trouble you, and
Ga 3:21 for if **t.** had been a law given which
Ga 3:28 **T.** is neither Jew nor Greek,
Ga 3:28 **t.** is neither bond nor free,
Ga 3:28 **t.** is neither male nor female: for ye
Ga 5:23 temperance: against such **t.** is no law.
Eph 4:4 **T.** is one body, and one Spirit, even as
Eph 6:9 neither is **t.** respect of persons with
Php 2:1 If **t.** be therefore any consolation in
Php 4:8 if **t.** be any virtue...if **t.** be any praise,
Col 3:11 Where **t.** is neither Greek nor Jew,
Col 3:25 done: and **t.** is no respect of persons.
2Th 2:3 except **t.** come a falling away first,
2Th 3:11 **t.** are some which walk among you
1Ti 1:10 if **t.** be any other thing that is contrary
1Ti 2:5 For **t.** is one God, and one mediator
2Ti 2:20 **t.** are not only vessels of gold and of
2Ti 4:8 **t.** is laid up for me a crown of
Tit 1:10 **t.** are many unruly and vain talkers
Tit 3:12 for I have determined **t.** to winter. *1563*
Phm 23 **T.** salute thee Epaphras, my
Heb 3:12 lest **t.** be in any of you an evil heart of
Heb 4:9 **T.** remaineth therefore a rest to the
Heb 4:13 Neither is **t.** any creature that is not
Heb 7:8 **t.** he receiveth them, of whom it is *1563*
Heb 7:11 what further need was **t.** that another
Heb 7:12 **t.** is made of necessity a change also
Heb 7:15 of Melchisedec **t.** ariseth another
Heb 7:18 For **t.** is verily a disannulling of the
Heb 8:4 **t.** are priests that offer gifts according
Heb 9:2 For **t.** was a tabernacle made; the
Heb 9:16 **t.** must also of necessity be the death
Heb 10:3 in those sacrifices **t.** is a remembrance
Heb 10:18 these is, **t.** is no more offering for sin.
Heb 10:26 **t.** remaineth no more sacrifice for sins,
Heb 11:12 sprang **t.** even of one, and he as good
Heb 12:16 Lest **t.** be any fornicator, or profane
Jas 2:2 **t.** come unto your assembly a man
Jas 2:2 **t.** come in also a poor man in vile
Jas 2:3 and say to the poor, Stand thou **t.**, *1563*
Jas 2:19 Thou believest that **t.** is one God;
Jas 3:16 **t.** is confusion and every evil work. *1563*
Jas 4:12 **T.** is one lawgiver, who is able to save
Jas 4:13 such a city, and continue **t.** a year, *1563*
2Pe 1:17 **t.** came such a voice to him from the
2Pe 2:1 **t.** were false prophets also among the
2Pe 2:1 **t.** shall be false teachers among you,
2Pe 3:3 **t.** shall come in the last days scoffers,
1Jo 2:10 **t.** is none occasion of stumbling in
1Jo 2:18 even now are **t.** many antichrists;
1Jo 4:18 **T.** is no fear in love; but perfect love
1Jo 5:7 **t.** are three that bear record in heaven,
1Jo 5:8 **t.** are three that bear witness in earth,
1Jo 5:16 **T.** is a sin unto death: I do not say
1Jo 5:17 is sin: and **t.** is a sin not unto death.
2Jo 10 **t.** come any unto you, and bring not
Jude 4 **t.** are certain men crept in unawares,
Jude 18 **t.** should be mockers in the last time,
Re 2:14 **thou hast t. them that hold the** *1563*
Re 4:3 **t.** was a rainbow round about the
Re 4:5 **t.** were seven lamps of fire burning
Re 4:6 before the throne **t.** was a sea of glass
Re 6:4 **t.** went out another horse that was
Re 6:4 **t.** was given unto him a great sword.
Re 6:12 and, lo, **t.** was a great earthquake;
Re 7:4 **t.** were sealed an hundred and forty
Re 8:1 **t.** was silence in heaven about the
Re 8:3 **t.** was given unto him much incense,
Re 8:5 and **t.** were voices, and thunderings,
Re 8:7 **t.** followed hail and fire mingled with
Re 8:10 and **t.** fell a great star from heaven,
Re 9:2 and **t.** arose a smoke out of the pit,
Re 9:3 **t.** came out of the smoke locusts upon
Re 9:10 and **t.** were stings in their tails:
Re 9:12 **t.** come two woes more hereafter.
Re 10:6 that **t.** should be time no longer:
Re 11:1 **t.** was given me a reed like unto a rod:
Re 11:13 same hour was **t.** a great earthquake,
Re 11:15 **t.** were great voices in heaven, saying,
Re 11:19 **t.** was seen in his temple the ark of
Re 11:19 and **t.** were lightnings, and voices,
Re 12:1 **t.** appeared a great wonder in heaven;
Re 12:3 **t.** appeared another wonder in heaven;
Re 12:6 should feed her **t.** a thousand two *1563*
Re 12:7 **t.** was war in heaven: Michael and his
Re 13:5 And **t.** was given unto him a mouth
Re 14:8 And **t.** followed another angel, saying,
Re 16:2 **t.** fell a noisome and grievous sore
Re 16:17 **t.** came a great voice out of the temple
Re 16:18 And **t.** were voices, and thunders,
Re 16:18 **t.** was a great earthquake, such as
Re 16:21 **t.** fell upon men a great hail out of
Re 17:1 **t.** came one of the seven angels which
Re 17:10 **t.** are seven kings: five are fallen,
Re 20:11 and **t.** was found no place for them,
Re 21:1 passed away; and **t.** was no more sea.
Re 21:4 **t.** shall be no more death, neither
Re 21:4 neither shall **t.** be any more pain:
Re 21:9 **t.** came unto me one of the seven
Re 21:25 at all by day: for **t.** shall be no night
Re 21:25 shall be no night **t.** *1563*
Re 21:27 **t.** shall in no wise enter into it any
Re 22:2 of the river, was **t.** the tree of life,
Re 22:3 And **t.** shall be no more curse: but the
Re 22:5 **t.** shall be no night...and they need
Re 22:5 shall be no night **t.**; and they *1563*

THEREABOUT
Lu 24:4 they were much perplexed **t.**, *4012,5127*

THEREAT
Ex 30:19 wash their hands and their feet **t.**
Ex 40:31 washed their hands and their feet **t.**
Mt 7:13 **many there be which go in t.** *1223,846*

THEREBY
Ge 24:14 **t.** shall I know that thou hast shewed
Le 11:43 them, that ye should be defiled **t.**
Job 22:21 peace; **t.** good shall come unto thee.
Pr 20:1 whosoever is deceived **t.** is not wise.
Ec 10:9 cleaveth wood shall be endangered **t.**
Isa 33:21 oars, neither shall gallant ship pass **t.**
Jer 18:16 that passeth **t.** shall be astonished, 5921
Jer 19:8 that passeth **t.** shall be astonished 5921
Jer 51:43 doth any son of man pass **t.** 2004
Eze 12:5 wall in their sight, and carry out **t.**
Eze 12:12 dig through the wall to carry out **t.**
Eze 33:12 he shall not fall **t.** in the day that he
Eze 33:18 iniquity, he shall even die **t.**
Eze 33:19 is lawful and right, he shall live **t.**
Zec 9:2 And Hamath also shall border **t.**;
Joh 11:4 **of God might be glorified t.** *1223,846*
Eph 2:16 having slain the enmity **t.** *1722,846*
Heb 12:11 them which are exercised **t.** *1223,846*
Heb 12:15 you, and **t.** many be defiled; *1223,5026*
Heb 13:2 **t.** some have entertained angels *1223,5026*
1Pe 2:2 the word, that ye may grow **t.** *1722,846*

THEREFORE
Ge 2:24 **T.** shall a man leave…father 5921,3651
Ge 3:23 **T.** the Lord God sent him forth from
Ge 4:15 **T.** whosoever slayeth Cain, 3651
Ge 11:9 **T.** is the name of it called 5921,3651
Ge 12:12 **T.** it shall come to pass, when the
Ge 12:19 **t.** behold thy wife, take her, and go
Ge 17:9 Thou shalt keep my covenant **t.**, thou
Ge 18:5 for **t.** are ye come to your 5921,3651
Ge 18:12 **T.** Sarah laughed within herself,
Ge 19:8 **t.** came they under the 5921,3651
Ge 19:22 **T.** the name of the city was 5921,3651
Ge 20:6 **t.** suffered I thee not to touch 5921,3651
Ge 20:7 **t.** restore the man his wife; for he
Ge 20:8 **T.** Abimelech rose early in the
Ge 21:23 Now **t.** sware unto me here by God
Ge 23:15 me and thee? bury **t.** thy dead
Ge 24:65 **t.** she took a vail, and covered herself
Ge 25:30 **t.** was his name called Edom 5921,3651
Ge 26:33 **t.** the name of the city is 5921,3651
Ge 27:3 **t.** take, I pray thee, thy weapons,
Ge 27:8 Now **t.**, my son, obey my voice
Ge 27:28 **T.** God give thee of the dew of heaven.
Ge 27:43 Now **t.**, my son, obey my voice; and
Ge 29:15 shouldest thou **t.** serve me for nought?
Ge 29:32 now **t.** my husband will love me 3588
Ge 29:33 he hath **t.** given me this son also: 1571
Ge 29:34 **t.** was his name called Levi 5921,3651
Ge 29:35 **t.** she called his name Judah; 5921,3651
Ge 30:6 **t.** called she his name Dan 5921,3651
Ge 30:15 **T.** he shall lie with thee to night 3651
Ge 31:44 **t.** come thou, let us make a covenant,
Ge 31:48 **T.** was the name of it called 5921,3651
Ge 32:32 **T.** the children of Israel eat 5921,3651
Ge 33:10 for **t.** I have seen thy face, as 5921,3651
Ge 33:17 **t.** the name of the place is 5921,3651
Ge 34:21 **t.** let them dwell in the land, and
Ge 37:20 Come now **t.**, and let us slay him,
Ge 38:29 thee: **t.** his name was called Pharez.
Ge 41:33 **t.** let Pharaoh look out a man discreet
Ge 42:21 **t.** is this distress come upon 5921,3651
Ge 42:22 **t.**, behold,…his blood is required 1571
Ge 44:30 Now **t.** when I come to thy servant my
Ge 44:33 **t.**, I pray thee, let thy servant abide
Ge 45:5 Now **t.** be not grieved, nor angry with
Ge 47:4 **t.**, we pray thee, let thy servants dwell
Ge 50:5 **t.** let me go up, I pray thee, and bury
Ge 50:21 now **t.** fear ye not: I will nourish you,
Ex 1:11 **T.** they did set over them taskmasters
Ex 1:20 **T.** God dealt well with the midwives:
Ex 3:9 Now **t.**, behold, the cry of the children
Ex 3:10 Come now **t.**, and I will send thee
Ex 4:12 Now **t.** go, and I will be with thy
Ex 5:8 **t.** they cry, saying, Let us go 5921,3651
Ex 5:17 **t.** ye say, Let us go and do 5921,3651
Ex 5:18 Go **t.** now, and work; for there shall
Ex 9:19 Send **t.** now, and gather thy cattle,
Ex 10:17 Now **t.** forgive, I pray thee, my sin
Ex 12:17 **t.** shall ye observe this day in your
Ex 13:10 Thou shalt **t.** keep this ordinance in
Ex 13:15 **t.** I sacrifice to the Lord all 5921,3651
Ex 15:23 **t.** the name of it was called 3651
Ex 16:29 **t.** he giveth you on the sixth 3651
Ex 19:5 Now **t.**, if ye will obey my voice
Ex 31:14 Ye shall keep the sabbath **t.**; for it is
Ex 32:10 **t.** let me alone, that my wrath may
Ex 32:34 **T.** now go, lead the people unto the
Ex 33:5 **t.** now put off thy ornaments from
Ex 33:13 Now **t.**, I pray thee, if I have found
Le 8:35 **T.** shall ye abide at the door of the
Le 9:8 Aaron **t.** went unto the altar, and
Le 11:44 ye shall **t.** sanctify yourselves, and ye
Le 11:45 God: ye shall **t.** be holy, for I am holy.
Le 13:52 He shall **t.** burn that garment,
Le 16:4 **t.** shall he wash his flesh in water,
Le 17:12 **T.** I said unto the children of 5921,3651
Le 17:14 **t.** I said unto the children of Israel,
Le 18:5 Ye shall **t.** keep my statutes, and my
Le 18:25 **t.** I do visit the iniquity thereof upon
Le 18:26 Ye shall **t.** keep my statutes and my
Le 18:30 **T.** shall ye keep mine ordinance, that
Le 19:8 **T.** every one that eateth it shall bear
Le 19:37 **T.** shall ye observe all my statutes,
Le 20:7 Sanctify yourselves **t.**, and be ye holy:
Le 20:22 Ye shall **t.** keep all my statutes, and
Le 20:23 these things, and **t.** I abhorred them,
Le 20:25 Ye shall **t.** put difference between
Le 21:6 they do offer: **t.** they shall be holy
Le 21:8 Thou shalt sanctify him **t.**; for he
Le 22:9 They shall **t.** keep mine ordinance,
Le 22:9 for it, and die **t.**, if they profane it:
Le 22:31 **T.** shall ye keep my commandments
Le 25:17 Ye shall not **t.** oppress one another;
Nu 3:12 Israel: **t.** the Levites shall be mine;
Nu 11:18 **t.** the Lord will give you flesh, and ye
Nu 14:16 **t.** he hath slain them in the
Nu 14:43 Lord, **t.** the Lord will not be with you.
Nu 16:38 before the Lord, **t.** they are hallowed:
Nu 18:7 **T.** thou and thy sons with thee shall
Nu 18:24 **t.** I have said unto them. 5921,3651
Nu 18:30 **T.** thou shalt say unto them, When ye
Nu 20:12 **t.** ye shall not bring this 3651
Nu 21:7 **T.** the people came to Moses, and
Nu 22:5 He sent messengers **t.** unto Balaam
Nu 22:6 Come now **t.**, I pray thee, curse me
Nu 22:17 come **t.**, I pray thee, curse me this
Nu 22:19 now **t.**, I pray you, tarry ye also here
Nu 22:34 now **t.**, if I displease thee, I will get
Nu 24:11 **T.** now flee thou to thy place: I
Nu 24:14 come **t.**, and I will advertise thee
Nu 27:4 Give unto us **t.** a possession among
Nu 31:17 **t.** kill every male among the little
Nu 31:50 **t.** brought an oblation for the Lord,
Nu 35:34 Defile not **t.** the land which ye shall
De 2:4 take ye good heed unto yourselves **t.**:
De 4:1 Now **t.** hearken, O Israel, unto the
De 4:6 Keep **t.** and do them; for this is your
De 4:15 Take ye **t.** good heed unto yourselves:
De 4:37 **t.** he chose their seed after them, and
De 4:39 Know **t.** this day, and consider it in
De 4:40 Thou shalt keep **t.** his statutes, and
De 5:15 **t.** the Lord…commanded 5921,3651
De 5:25 **t.** why should we die? for this great
De 5:32 Ye shall observe to do **t.** as the Lord
De 6:3 Hear **t.**, O Israel, and observe to do it:
De 7:9 Know **t.** that the Lord thy God, he is
De 7:11 shalt **t.** keep the commandments,
De 8:6 **T.** thou shalt keep the
De 9:3 Understand **t.** this day, that the Lord
De 9:6 Understand **t.**, that the Lord thy God
De 9:26 I prayed **t.** unto the Lord, and said,
De 10:16 Circumcise **t.** the foreskin of your
De 10:19 Love ye **t.** the stranger: for ye were
De 11:1 **T.** thou shalt love the Lord thy God,
De 11:8 **T.** shall ye keep all the
De 11:18 **T.** shall ye lay up these my words in
De 14:7 hoof; **t.** they are unclean unto you.
De 15:11 **t.** I command thee, saying, 5921,3651
De 15:15 **t.** I command thee this thing to 5921,3651
De 16:2 Thou shalt **t.** sacrifice the passover
De 16:15 hands, **t.** thou shalt surely rejoice
De 18:2 **T.** shall they have no inheritance
De 23:14 before thee; **t.** shall thy camp be holy:
De 24:18, 22 **t.** I command thee to do 5921,3651
De 25:19 **T.** it shall be, when the Lord thy God
De 26:16 thou shalt **t.** keep and do them with
De 27:4 **T.** it shall be when ye be gone over
De 27:10 shalt **t.** obey the voice of the Lord
De 28:48 **T.** shalt thou serve thine enemies
De 29:9 Keep **t.** the words of this covenant,
De 30:19 **t.** choose life, that both thou and thy
De 31:19 Now **t.** write ye this song for you, and
De 31:22 Moses **t.** wrote this song the same
Jos 1:2 now **t.** arise, go over this Jordan,
Jos 2:12 Now **t.**, I pray you, swear unto me by
Jos 3:12 Now **t.** take you twelve men out of the
Jos 4:17 Joshua **t.** commanded the priests,
Jos 7:12 **T.** the children of Israel could not
Jos 7:14 In the morning **t.** ye shall be brought
Jos 8:6 the first: **t.** we will flee before them.
Jos 8:9 Joshua **t.** sent them forth: and they
Jos 9:6 now **t.** make ye a league with us.
Jos 9:11 **t.** now make ye a league with us.
Jos 9:19 Israel: now **t.** we may not touch them
Jos 9:23 now **t.** ye are cursed, and there shall
Jos 9:24 **t.** we were sore afraid of our lives
Jos 10:5 **T.** the five kings of the Amorites, the
Jos 10:9 Joshua **t.** came unto them suddenly,
Jos 13:7 **t.** divide this land for an inheritance
Jos 14:4 **t.** they gave no part unto the Levites
Jos 14:12 Now **t.** give me this mountain, whereof
Jos 14:14 Hebron **t.** became the inheritance of
Jos 17:1 of war, **t.** he had Gilead and Bashan.
Jos 17:4 **T.** according to the commandment of
Jos 18:6 shall **t.** describe the land into seven
Jos 19:9 **t.** the children of Simeon had their
Jos 19:47 **t.** the children of Dan went up to
Jos 22:4 **t.** now return ye, and get you unto
Jos 22:26 **T.** we said, Let us now prepare to
Jos 22:28 **T.** said we, that it shall be, when they
Jos 23:6 Be ye **t.** very courageous to keep and
Jos 23:11 Take good heed **t.** unto your selves,
Jos 23:15 **T.** it shall come to pass, that as all
Jos 24:10 **t.** he blessed you still: so I delivered
Jos 24:14 Now **t.** fear the Lord, and serve him in
Jos 24:18 **t.** will we also serve the Lord; for he
Jos 24:23 **t.** put away, said he, the strange gods
Jos 24:27 it shall be **t.** a witness unto you, lest
Jg 2:23 **T.** the Lord left those nations,
Jg 3:8 **T.** the anger of the Lord was hot
Jg 3:25 **t.** they took a key, and opened them:
Jg 6:32 **T.** on that day he called him
Jg 7:3 **t.** go to, proclaim in the ears of the
Jg 8:7 **T.** when the Lord hath delivered
Jg 9:16 Now **t.**, if ye have done truly and
Jg 9:32 Now **t.** up by night, thou and the
Jg 11:8 **T.** we turn again to thee now,
Jg 11:13 **t.** restore those lands again peaceably.
Jg 11:26 why **t.** did ye not recover them within
Jg 13:4 **t.** beware, I pray thee, and drink not
Jg 14:2 now **t.** get her for me to wife
Jg 15:2 her; **t.** I gave her to thy companion:
Jg 16:12 Delilah **t.** took new ropes, and bound
Jg 17:3 now **t.** I will restore it unto thee.
Jg 18:14 now **t.** consider what ye have to do.
Jg 19:7 urged him: **t.** he lodged there again.
Jg 20:13 Now **t.** deliver us the men, the
Jg 20:42 **T.** they turned their backs before the
Jg 21:20 **T.** they commanded the children of
Ru 3:3 Wash thyself **t.**, and anoint thee, and
Ru 3:9 spread **t.** thy skirt over thine
Ru 4:8 **T.** the kinsman said unto Boaz, Buy
1Sa 1:7 her; **t.** she wept, and did not eat
1Sa 1:13 **t.** Eli thought she had been drunken.
1Sa 1:28 **T.** also I have lent him to the Lord; as
1Sa 3:9 **T.** Eli said unto Samuel, Go, lie down:
1Sa 3:14 **t.** I have sworn unto the house of Eli,
1Sa 5:5 **T.** neither the priests of 5921,3651
1Sa 5:8 They sent **t.** and gathered all the
1Sa 5:10 **T.** they sent the ark of God to Ekron.
1Sa 6:7 Now **t.** make a new cart, and take two
1Sa 8:9 Now **t.** hearken unto their voice:
1Sa 9:13 Now **t.** get you up; for about this time
1Sa 10:12 **T.** it became a proverb, Is 5921,3651
1Sa 10:19 **t.** present yourselves before the Lord
1Sa 10:22 **T.** they enquired of the Lord further,
1Sa 11:10 **T.** the men of Jabesh said, To
1Sa 12:7 Now **t.** stand still, that I may reason
1Sa 12:13 now **t.** behold the king whom ye have
1Sa 12:16 Now **t.** stand and see this great 1571
1Sa 13:12 **T.** said I, The Philistines will come

1Sa 13:12 I forced myself **t.**, and offered a burnt
1Sa 14:41 **T.** Saul said unto the Lord God of
1Sa 15:1 now **t.** hearken thou unto the voice of
1Sa 15:25 Now **t.**, I pray thee, pardon my sin,
1Sa 17:51 **T.** David ran, and stood upon the
1Sa 18:13 **T.** Saul removed him from him, and
1Sa 18:22 thee: now **t.** be the king's son in law.
1Sa 19:2 now **t.**, I pray thee, take heed to
1Sa 20:8 **T.** thou shalt deal kindly with thy
1Sa 20:29 **T.** he cometh not unto the 5921,3651
1Sa 21:3 Now **t.** what is under thine hand? give
1Sa 22:1 David **t.** departed thence, and escaped
1Sa 23:2 **T.** David enquired of the Lord,
1Sa 23:20 Now **t.**, O king, come down according
1Sa 23:23 See **t.**, and take knowledge of all the
1Sa 23:28 **t.** they called that place 5921,3651
1Sa 24:15 The Lord **t.** be judge, and judge
1Sa 24:21 Swear now **t.** unto me by the Lord,
1Sa 25:17 **t.** know and consider what thou wilt
1Sa 25:26 Now **t.**, my lord, as the Lord liveth,
1Sa 26:4 David **t.** sent out spies, and
1Sa 26:8 now **t.** let me smite him, I pray thee,
1Sa 26:19 Now **t.**, I pray thee, let my lord the
1Sa 26:20 now **t.**, let not my blood fall to the
1Sa 27:12 him; **t.** he shall be my servant for ever.
1Sa 28:2 **T.** will I make thee keeper of mine
1Sa 28:15 **t.** I have called thee, that thou mayest
1Sa 28:18 **t.** hath the Lord done this 5921,3651
1Sa 28:22 Now **t.**, I pray thee, hearken thou also
1Sa 31:4 **T.** Saul took a sword, and fell upon it
2Sa 2:7 **T.** now let your hands be
2Sa 4:11 shall I not **t.** now require his blood
2Sa 5:20 **T.** he called the name of that 5921,3651
2Sa 6:21 Israel: **t.** will I play before the Lord.
2Sa 6:23 **T.** Michal the daughter of Saul had
2Sa 7:8 Now **t.** so shalt thou say unto my
2Sa 7:27 **t.** hath thy servant found in his heart
2Sa 7:29 **T.** now let it please thee to bless the
2Sa 9:10 Thou **t.**, and thy sons, and thy
2Sa 12:10 Now **t.** the sword shall never depart
2Sa 12:16 David **t.** besought God for the child;
2Sa 12:19 **t.** David said unto his servants, Is the
2Sa 12:28 Now **t.** gather the rest of the people
2Sa 13:13 Now **t.**, I pray thee, speak unto the
2Sa 13:33 **t.** let not my lord the king take the
2Sa 14:15 **t.** that I am come to speak of this
2Sa 14:7 **t.** the Lord thy God will be with thee.
2Sa 14:21 **t.**, bring the young man Absalom
2Sa 14:26 was heavy on him, **t.** he polled it:)
2Sa 14:29 **T.** Absalom sent for Joab, to have
2Sa 14:30 **T.** he said unto his servants, See,
2Sa 14:32 now **t.** let me see the king's face; and
2Sa 15:29 Zadok **t.** and Abiathar carried the ark
2Sa 15:35 **t.** it shall be, that what thing soever
2Sa 17:11 **T.** I counsel that all Israel be
2Sa 17:16 Now **t.** send quickly, and tell David,
2Sa 18:3 **t.** now it is better that thou succour us
2Sa 19:7 Now **t.** arise, go forth, and speak
2Sa 19:10 **t.** why speak ye not a word of bringing
2Sa 19:20 **t.**, behold, I am come the first this day
2Sa 19:23 **T.** the king said unto Shimei, Thou
2Sa 19:27 God: do **t.** what is good in thine eyes.
2Sa 19:28 what right **t.** have I yet to cry any
2Sa 22:25 **T.** the Lord hath recompensed me
2Sa 22:50 **T.** I will give thanks unto 5921,3651
2Sa 23:17 of their lives? **t.** he would not drink it.
2Sa 23:19 of three? **t.** he was their captain:
1Ki 1:12 now **t.** come, let me, I pray thee, give
1Ki 2:2 be thou strong **t.**, and show thyself a
1Ki 2:6 do **t.** according to thy wisdom, and let
1Ki 2:9 Now **t.** hold him not guiltless: for
1Ki 2:19 Bath-sheba **t.** went unto king
1Ki 2:24 Now **t.**, as the Lord liveth, which hath
1Ki 2:33 Their blood shall **t.** return upon the
1Ki 2:44 **t.** the Lord shall return thy wickedness
1Ki 3:9 Give **t.** thy servant an understanding
1Ki 5:6 Now **t.** command thou that they hew
1Ki 8:25 **T.** now, Lord God of Israel, keep
1Ki 8:61 your heart **t.** be perfect with the Lord
1Ki 9:9 **t.** hath the Lord brought upon 5921,3651
1Ki 10:9 **t.** made he thee king, to do judgment
1Ki 11:40 Solomon sought **t.** to kill Jeroboam.
1Ki 12:4 now **t.** make thou the grievous service
1Ki 12:18 **t.** king Rehoboam made speed to get
1Ki 12:24 They hearkened **t.** to the word of the
1Ki 13:26 **t.** the Lord hath delivered him unto
1Ki 14:10 **T.**, behold, I will bring evil upon the
1Ki 14:12 Arise thou **t.**, get thee to thine own
1Ki 18:19 Now **t.** send, and gather to me all
1Ki 18:23 Let them **t.** give us two bullocks; and
1Ki 20:23 **t.** they were stronger than we; 5921,3651
1Ki 20:28 **t.** will I deliver all this great multitude
1Ki 20:42 **t.** thy life shall go for his life, and thy
1Ki 22:19 Hear thou **t.** the word of the Lord: 3651
1Ki 22:23 Now **t.**, behold, the Lord hath put a
2Ki 1:4 Now **t.** thus saith the Lord, Thou 3651
2Ki 1:6 **t.** thou shalt not come down from 3651
2Ki 1:14 **t.** let my life now be precious in thy
2Ki 1:16 **t.** thou shalt not come down off that
2Ki 2:17 They sent **t.** fifty men; and they
2Ki 3:23 another: now **t.**, Moab, to the spoil.
2Ki 4:33 He went in **t.**, and shut the door upon
2Ki 5:15 now **t.**, I pray thee, take a blessing of
2Ki 5:27 leprosy **t.** of Naaman shall cleave unto
2Ki 6:7 **T.** said he, Take it up to thee. And he
2Ki 6:11 **T.** the heart of the king of Syria was
2Ki 6:14 **T.** sent he thither horses, and
2Ki 7:4 Now **t.** come, and let us fall unto the
2Ki 7:9 now **t.** come, that we may go and tell
2Ki 7:12 **t.** are they gone out of the camp to
2Ki 7:14 They took **t.** two chariot horses; and
2Ki 9:26 now **t.** take and cast him into the plat
2Ki 10:19 Now **t.** call unto me all the prophets of
2Ki 12:7 now **t.** receive no more money of your
2Ki 14:11 **T.** Jehoash king of Israel went up;
2Ki 15:16 they opened not to him, **t.** he smote it:
2Ki 17:4 **t.** the king of Assyria shut him up, and
2Ki 17:18 **T.** the Lord was very angry with
2Ki 17:25 **t.** the Lord sent lions among them,
2Ki 17:26 **t.** he hath sent lions among them, and
2Ki 18:23 Now **t.**, I pray thee, give pledges to my
2Ki 19:18 stone: **t.** they have destroyed them.
2Ki 19:19 Now **t.**, O Lord our God, I beseech thee,
2Ki 19:26 **T.** their inhabitants were of small
2Ki 19:28 **t.** I will put my hook in thy nose, and
2Ki 19:32 **T.** thus saith the Lord concerning 3651
2Ki 21:12 **T.** thus saith the Lord God of 3651
2Ki 22:17 **t.** my wrath shall be kindled against
2Ki 22:20 Behold **t.**, I will gather thee unto 3651
1Ch 10:14 **t.** he slew him, and turned the
1Ch 11:3 **T.** came all the elders of Israel to the
1Ch 11:7 **t.** they called it the city of 5921,3651
1Ch 11:19 brought it. **T.** he would not drink it.
1Ch 14:11 **t.** they called the name of 5921,3651
1Ch 14:14 **T.** David inquired again of God; and
1Ch 14:16 David **t.** did as God commanded him:
1Ch 17:7 **t.** thus shalt thou say unto my servant
1Ch 17:23 **T.** now, Lord, let the thing that thou
1Ch 17:25 **t.** thy servant hath found in 5921,3651
1Ch 17:27 Now **t.** let it please thee to bless the
1Ch 21:7 with this thing; **t.** he smote Israel
1Ch 21:12 **t.** advise thyself what word I shall
1Ch 22:5 I will **t.** now make preparation for it
1Ch 22:16 Arise **t.**, and be doing, and the Lord be
1Ch 22:19 arise **t.**, and build ye the sanctuary
1Ch 23:11 **t.** they were in one reckoning,
1Ch 24:2 **t.** Eleazar and Ithamar executed the
1Ch 28:8 Now **t.**, in the sight of all Israel the
1Ch 29:13 Now **t.**, our God, we thank thee, and
2Ch 2:7 Send me now **t.** a man cunning to
2Ch 2:15 Now **t.** the wheat, and the barley, the
2Ch 6:10 The Lord **t.** hath performed his word
2Ch 6:16 Now **t.**, O Lord God of Israel, keep
2Ch 6:19 Have respect **t.** to the prayer of thy
2Ch 6:21 Hearken **t.** unto the supplications of
2Ch 6:41 Now **t.** arise, O Lord God, into thy
2Ch 7:22 **t.** hath he brought all this 5921,3651
2Ch 9:8 **t.** made he thee king over them, to do
2Ch 10:4 now **t.** ease thou somewhat the
2Ch 12:5 **t.** have I also left you in the hand of
2Ch 12:7 **t.** I will not destroy them, but I will
2Ch 14:7 **T.** he saith unto Judah, Let us build
2Ch 15:7 Be ye strong **t.**, and let not your hands
2Ch 16:7 **t.** is the host of the king of 5921,3651
2Ch 16:9 **t.**...henceforth thou shalt have wars.
2Ch 17:5 **T.** the Lord stablished the kingdom in
2Ch 18:5 **T.** the king of Israel gathered
2Ch 18:12 let thy word **t.**, I pray thee, be like one
2Ch 18:16 them return **t.** every man to his house
2Ch 18:18 **T.** hear the word of the Lord; 3651
2Ch 18:22 now **t.**, behold, the Lord hath put a
2Ch 18:31 **T.** they compassed about him to fight:
2Ch 18:33 **t.** he said to his chariot man, Turn
2Ch 19:2 **t.** is wrath come upon thee from 2063
2Ch 20:26 **t.** the name of the same place 5921,3651
2Ch 28:11 Now hear me **t.**, and deliver the
2Ch 28:23 **t.** will I sacrifice to them, that they
2Ch 30:7 who **t.** gave them up to desolation, as
2Ch 30:17 **t.** the Levites had the charge of the
2Ch 32:15 Now **t.** let not Hezekiah deceive you,
2Ch 32:25 **t.** there was wrath upon him, and
2Ch 34:25 **t.** my wrath shall be poured out upon
2Ch 35:14 **t.** the Levites prepared for themselves,
2Ch 35:24 His servants **t.** took him out of that
2Ch 36:17 **T.** he brought upon them the king of
Ezr 2:62 **t.** were they, as polluted, put from the
Ezr 4:14 **t.** have we sent and certified 5921,1836
Ezr 5:17 Now **t.**, if it seem good to the king, let
Ezr 6:6 Now **t.**, Tatnai, governor beyond the
Ezr 9:12 **t.** give not your daughters unto their
Ezr 10:3 **t.** let us make a covenant with our God
Ezr 10:11 Now **t.** make confession unto the Lord
Ne 2:20 **t.** we his servants will arise and build:
Ne 4:13 **T.** set I in the lower places behind the
Ne 4:20 In what place **t.** ye hear the sound of
Ne 5:2 **t.** we take up corn for them, that we
Ne 6:7 Come now **t.**, and let us take counsel
Ne 6:9 Now **t.**, O God, strengthen my hands.
Ne 6:13 **T.** was he hired, that I should be
Ne 7:64 **t.** were they, as polluted, put from the
Ne 9:27 **T.** thou deliveredst them into the
Ne 9:28 **t.** leftest thou them in the hand of
Ne 9:30 **t.** gavest thou them into the hand of
Ne 9:32 Now **t.**, our God, the great, the mighty,
Ne 13:8 **t.** I cast forth all the household stuff
Ne 13:28 Horonite: **t.** I chased him from me.
Es 1:12 **t.** was the king very wroth, and his
Es 2:23 **t.** they were both hanged on a tree:
Es 3:8 **t.** it is not for the king's profit to suffer
Es 9:19 **T.** the Jews of the villages, 5921,3651
Es 9:26 **T.** for all the words of this 5921,3651
Job 5:17 **t.** despise not thou the chastening of
Job 6:3 **t.** my words are swallowed up 5921,3651
Job 6:28 Now **t.** be content, look upon me; for
Job 7:11 **T.** I will not refrain my mouth; I 1571
Job 9:22 This is one thing, **t.** I said it, 5921,3651
Job 10:15 confusion; **t.** see thou mine affliction;
Job 11:6 Know **t.** that God exacteth of thee less
Job 17:4 **t.** shalt thou not exalt them 5921,3651
Job 20:2 **T.** do my thoughts cause me to 3651
Job 20:21 **t.** shall no man look for his 5921,3651
Job 21:14 **T.** they say unto God, Depart from
Job 22:10 **T.** snares are round about 5921,3651
Job 23:15 **T.** am I troubled at his 5921,3651
Job 32:10 **T.** I said, Hearken to me; I also 3651
Job 34:10 **T.** hearken unto me, ye men of 3651
Job 34:25 **T.** he knoweth their works, and he 3651
Job 34:33 and not I: **t.** speak what thou knowest.
Job 35:14 is before him; **t.** trust thou in him.
Job 35:16 **T.** doth Job open his mouth in vain;
Job 37:24 Men do **t.** fear him: he respecteth 3651
Job 42:3 **t.** have I uttered that I understood 3651
Job 42:8 **T.** take unto you now seven bullocks
Ps 1:5 **T.** the ungodly shall not 5921,3651
Ps 2:10 Be wise now **t.**, O ye kings: be
Ps 7:7 for their sakes **t.** return thou on high.
Ps 16:9 **T.** my heart is glad, and my glory 3651
Ps 18:24 **T.** hath the Lord recompensed me
Ps 18:49 **T.** will I give thanks unto 5921,3651
Ps 21:12 **T.** shalt thou make them turn their
Ps 25:8 **t.** will he teach sinners in the 5921,3651
Ps 26:1 also in the Lord; **t.** I shall not slide.
Ps 27:6 **t.** will I offer in his tabernacle
Ps 28:7 **t.** my heart greatly rejoiceth; and
Ps 31:3 **t.** for thy name's sake lead me, and
Ps 36:7 **t.** the children of men put their trust
Ps 40:12 of mine head: **t.** my heart faileth me.
Ps 42:6 **t.** will I remember thee from 5921,3651
Ps 45:2 **t.** God hath blessed thee 5921,3651
Ps 45:7 **t.** God, thy God, hath anointed 5921,3651
Ps 45:17 **t.** shall the people praise thee 5921,3651
Ps 46:2 **T.** will not we fear, though the 5921,3651
Ps 55:19 have no changes, **t.** they fear not God.
Ps 59:5 Thou **t.**, O Lord God of hosts, the God
Ps 63:7 **t.** in the shadow of thy wings will I
Ps 73:6 **T.** pride compasseth them about as a
Ps 73:10 **T.** his people return hither: and 3651
Ps 78:21 **T.** the Lord heard this, and was 3651

Ps 78:33 **T.** their days did he consume in
Ps 91:14 his love upon me, **t.** will I deliver him:
Ps 106:23 **T.** he said that he would destroy them,
Ps 106:26 **T.** he lifted up his hand against them,
Ps 106:40 **T.** was the wrath of the Lord kindled
Ps 107:12 **T.** he brought down their heart with
Ps 110:7 **t.** shall he lift up the head 5921,3651
Ps 116:2 **t.** will I call upon him as long as I live.
Ps 116:10 I believed, **t.** have I spoken: I was 3588
Ps 118:7 **t.** shall I see my desire upon them that
Ps 119:104 **t.** I hate every false way. 5921,3651
Ps 119:119 dross: **t.** I love thy testimonies. 3651
Ps 119:127 **T.** I love thy commandments 5921,3651
Ps 119:128 **T.** I esteem all thy precepts 5921,3651
Ps 119:129 **t.** doth my soul keep them 5921,3651
Ps 119:140 is very pure: **t.** thy servant loveth it.
Ps 139:19 depart from me **t.**, ye bloody men.
Ps 143:4 **T.** is my spirit overwhelmed within
Pr 1:31 **T.** shall they eat of the fruit of their
Pr 4:7 is the principal thing; **t.** get wisdom:
Pr 5:7 Hear me now **t.**, O ye children, and
Pr 6:15 **T.** shall his calamity come 5921,3651
Pr 6:34 **t.** he will not spare in the day of
Pr 7:15 **T.** came I forth to meet thee, 5921,3651
Pr 7:24 Hearken unto me now **t.**, O ye
Pr 8:32 Now **t.** hearken unto me, O ye
Pr 17:11 **t.** a cruel messenger shall be sent
Pr 17:14 **t.** leave off contention, before it be
Pr 20:4 **t.** shall he beg in harvest and have
Pr 20:19 **t.** meddle not with him that flattereth
Ec 2:1 thee with mirth, **t.** enjoy pleasure:
Ec 2:17 **T.** I hated life; because the work that
Ec 2:20 **T.** I went about to cause my heart to
Ec 5:2 earth: **t.** let thy words be few. 5921,3651
Ec 8:6 **t.** the misery of man is great upon
Ec 8:11 **t.** the heart of the sons of men 5921,3651
Ec 11:10 **T.** remove sorrow from thy heart, and
Ca 1:3 **t.** do the virgins love thee. 5921,3651
Isa 1:24 **T.** saith the Lord, the Lord of hosts, 3651
Isa 2:6 **T.** thou hast forsaken thy people the
Isa 2:9 humbleth himself: **t.** forgive them not.
Isa 3:17 **T.** the Lord will smite with a scab the
Isa 5:13 **T.** my people are gone into 3651
Isa 5:14 **T.** hell hath enlarged herself, and 3651
Isa 5:24 **T.** as the fire devoureth the stubble, 3651
Isa 5:25 **T.** is the anger of the Lord 5921,3651
Isa 7:14 **T.** the Lord himself shall give you 3651
Isa 8:7 Now **t.**, behold, the Lord bringeth 3651
Isa 9:11 **T.** the Lord shall set up the
Isa 9:14 **T.** the Lord will cut off from Israel
Isa 9:17 **T.** the Lord shall have no joy 5921,3651
Isa 10:16 **T.** shall the Lord, the Lord of 5921,3651
Isa 10:24 **T.** thus saith the Lord God of 5921,3651
Isa 12:3 **T.** with joy shall ye draw water out of
Isa 13:7 **T.** shall all hands be faint, 5921,3651
Isa 13:13 **T.** I will shake the heavens, 5921,3651
Isa 15:4 **t.** the armed soldiers of Moab 5921,3651
Isa 15:7 **T.** the abundance they have 5921,3651
Isa 16:7 **T.** shall Moab howl for Moab, every 3651
Isa 16:9 **T.** I will bewail with the 5921,3651
Isa 17:10 **t.** shalt thou plant pleasant 5921,3651
Isa 21:3 **T.** are my loins filled with 5921,3651
Isa 22:4 **T.** said I, Look away from me; 5921,3651
Isa 24:6 **T.** hath the curse devoured the 5921,3651
Isa 24:6 **t.** the inhabitants of the earth 5921,3651
Isa 25:3 **T.** shall the strong people 5921,3651
Isa 26:14 **t.** hast thou visited and destroyed 3651
Isa 27:9 **t.** shall the iniquity of Jacob be 3651
Isa 27:11 **t.** he that made them will not 5921,3651
Isa 28:16 **T.** thus saith the Lord God, Behold, 3651
Isa 28:22 Now **t.** be ye not mockers, lest your
Isa 29:14 **T.**, behold, I will proceed to do a 3651
Isa 29:22 **T.** thus saith the Lord, who 3651
Isa 30:3 **T.** shall the strength of Pharaoh be
Isa 30:7 **t.** have I cried concerning this, 3651
Isa 30:13 **T.** this iniquity shall be to you as a 3651
Isa 30:16 upon horses; **t.** shall ye flee: 5921,3651
Isa 30:16 **t.** shall they that pursue you be 5921,3651
Isa 30:18 **t.** will the Lord wait, that he may 3651
Isa 30:18 unto you, and **t.** will he be exalted, 3651
Isa 36:8 Now **t.** give pledges, I pray thee, to
Isa 37:19 stone: **t.** they have destroyed them.
Isa 37:20 Now **t.**, O Lord our God, save us from
Isa 37:27 **T.** their inhabitants were of small
Isa 37:29 **t.** will I put my hook in thy nose, and
Isa 37:33 **T.** thus saith the Lord concerning 3651
Isa 38:20 **t.** we will sing my songs to the stringed

Isa 42:25 **T.** he hath poured upon him the fury
Isa 43:4 **t.** will I give men for thee, and people
Isa 43:12 **t.** ye are my witnesses, saith the Lord,
Isa 43:28 **T.** I have profaned the princes of the
Isa 47:8 **T.** hear now this, thou that art given
Isa 47:11 **T.** shall evil come upon thee; thou
Isa 50:7 **t.** shall I not be confounded: 5921,3651
Isa 50:7 **t.** have I set my face like a 5921,3651
Isa 51:11 **T.** the redeemed of the Lord shall
Isa 51:21 **T.** hear now this, thou afflicted. 3651
Isa 52:5 Now **t.**, what have I here, saith the
Isa 52:6 **T.** my people shall know my 3651
Isa 52:6 **t.** they shall know in that day that I 3651
Isa 53:12 **T.** will I divide him a portion with 3651
Isa 57:10 **t.** thou wast not grieved. 5921,3651
Isa 59:9 **T.** is judgment far from us, 5921,3651
Isa 59:16 **t.** his arm brought salvation unto
Isa 60:11 **T.** thy gates shall be open continually;
Isa 61:7 **t.** in their land they shall possess 3651
Isa 63:5 **t.** mine own arm brought salvation
Isa 63:10 **t.** he was turned to be their enemy,
Isa 65:7 **t.** will I measure their former work
Isa 65:12 **T.** will I number you to the sword,
Isa 65:13 **T.** thus saith the Lord God, 3651
Jer 1:17 Thou **t.** gird up thy loins, and arise,
Jer 2:19 know **t.** and see that it is an evil thing
Jer 2:33 **t.** hast thou also taught the wicked 3651
Jer 3:3 **T.** the showers have been withholden,
Jer 5:4 **T.** I said, Surely these are poor; they
Jer 5:27 **t.** they are become great, and 5921,3651
Jer 6:11 **T.** I am full of the fury of the Lord; I
Jer 6:15 **t.** they shall fall among them that 3651
Jer 6:18 **T.** hear, ye nations, and know, O 3651
Jer 6:21 **T.** thus saith the Lord, Behold, I 3651
Jer 7:14 **T.** will I do unto this house, which is
Jer 7:16 **T.** pray not thou for this people,
Jer 7:20 **T.** thus saith the Lord God; 3651
Jer 7:27 **T.** thou shalt speak all these words
Jer 7:32 **T.**, behold, the days come, saith 3651
Jer 8:10 **T.** will I give their wives unto 3651
Jer 8:12 **t.** shall they fall among them that 3651
Jer 9:7, 15 **T.** thus saith the Lord of hosts, 3651
Jer 10:21 **t.** they shall not prosper, and 5921,3651
Jer 11:8 **t.** I will bring upon them all the words
Jer 11:11 **T.** thus saith the Lord, Behold, I 3651
Jer 11:14 **T.** pray not thou for this people,
Jer 11:21 **T.** thus saith the Lord of the men 3651
Jer 11:22 **T.** thus saith the Lord of hosts, 3651
Jer 12:8 against me: **t.** have I hated it, 5921,3651
Jer 13:12 **T.** thou shalt speak unto them this
Jer 13:24 **T.** will I scatter them as the stubble
Jer 13:26 **T.** will I discover thy skirts upon thy
Jer 14:10 **t.** the Lord doth not accept them;
Jer 14:15 **T.** thus saith the Lord concerning 3651
Jer 14:17 **T.** thou shalt say this word unto
Jer 14:22 **t.** we will wait upon thee: for thou
Jer 15:6 **t.** will I stretch out my hand against
Jer 15:19 **T.** thus saith the Lord, If thou 3651
Jer 16:13 **T.** will I cast you out of this land into
Jer 16:14 **T.**, behold, the days come, saith 3651
Jer 16:21 **T.**, behold, I will this once cause 3651
Jer 18:11 Now **t.** go to, speak to the men of
Jer 18:13 **T.** thus saith the Lord; Ask ye 3651
Jer 18:21 **T.** deliver up their children to the 3651
Jer 19:6 **T.**, behold, the days come, saith 3651
Jer 20:11 **t.** my persecutors shall 5921,3651
Jer 22:18 **T.** thus saith the Lord concerning 3651
Jer 23:2 **T.** thus saith the Lord God of 3651
Jer 23:7 **T.**, behold, the days come, saith 3651
Jer 23:15 **T.** thus saith the Lord of hosts 3651
Jer 23:30 **T.**, behold, I am against the 3651
Jer 23:32 **t.** they shall not profit this people at
Jer 23:38 **T.** thus saith the Lord; Because
Jer 23:39 **T.**, behold, I, even I, will utterly 3651
Jer 25:8 **T.** thus saith the Lord of hosts; 3651
Jer 25:27 **T.** thou shalt say unto them, Thus
Jer 25:30 **T.** prophesy thou against them all
Jer 26:13 **T.** now amend your ways and your
Jer 27:9 **T.** hearken not ye to your prophet,
Jer 27:14 **T.** hearken not unto the words of the
Jer 28:16 **T.** thus saith the Lord; Behold, I 3651
Jer 29:20 Hear ye **t.** the word of the Lord, all ye
Jer 29:27 Now **t.** why hast thou not reproved
Jer 29:28 **t.** he sent unto us in Babylon, 5921,3651
Jer 29:32 **T.** thus saith the Lord; Behold, I 3651
Jer 30:10 **T.** fear thou not, O my servant Jacob,
Jer 30:16 **T.** all they that devour thee shall 3651

Jer 31:3 **t.** with lovingkindness have I 5921,3651
Jer 31:12 **T.** they shall come and sing in the
Jer 31:20 **t.** my bowels are troubled for 5921,3651
Jer 32:23 **t.** thou hast caused all this evil to
Jer 32:28 **T.** thus saith the Lord; 5921,3651
Jer 32:36 And now **t.** thus saith the Lord, the 3651
Jer 34:12 **T.** the word of the Lord came to
Jer 34:17 **T.** thus saith the Lord; Ye have 3651
Jer 35:17 **T.** thus saith the Lord God of hosts, 3651
Jer 35:19 **T.** thus saith the Lord of hosts, 3651
Jer 36:6 **T.** go thou, and read in the roll, which
Jer 36:14 **T.** all the princes sent Jehudi the son
Jer 36:30 **T.** thus saith the Lord of 3651
Jer 37:20 **T.** hear now, I pray thee, O my lord
Jer 38:4 **T.** the princes said unto the king, We
Jer 40:3 voice, **t.** this thing is come upon you
Jer 42:15 now **t.** hear the word of the Lord, 3651
Jer 42:22 **t.** know certainly that ye shall die
Jer 44:7 **T.** now thus saith the Lord, the God
Jer 44:11 **T.** thus saith the Lord of hosts, 3651
Jer 44:22 **t.** is your land a desolation, and an
Jer 44:23 **t.** this evil is happened unto 5921,3652
Jer 44:26 **T.** hear ye the word of the Lord, 3651
Jer 48:11 **t.** his taste remained in him, 5921,3651
Jer 48:12 **T.**, behold, the days come, saith. 5921,3651
Jer 48:31 **T.** will I howl for Moab, and 5921,3651
Jer 48:36 **T.** mine heart shall sound for 5921,3651
Jer 49:2 **T.**, behold, the days come, saith. 5921,3651
Jer 49:20 **T.** hear the counsel of the Lord, 5921,3651
Jer 49:26 **T.** her young men shall fall in her. 5921,3651
Jer 50:18 **T.** thus saith the Lord of hosts, 5921,3651
Jer 50:30 **T.** shall her young men fall in the. 5921,3651
Jer 50:39 **T.** the wild beasts of the desert 5921,3651
Jer 50:45 **T.** ye the counsel of the Lord, 5921,3651
Jer 51:7 wine; **t.** the nations are mad. 5921,3651
Jer 51:36 **T.** thus saith the Lord; Behold, I 3651
Jer 51:47 **T.**, behold, the days come, that I 3651
La 1:8 sinned; **t.** she is removed; 5921,3651
La 1:9 end; **t.** she came down wonderfully:
La 2:8 **t.** he made the rampart and the wall
La 3:21 to my mind, **t.** have I hope. 5921,3651
La 3:24 my soul; **t.** will I hope in him. 5921,3651
Eze 3:17 **t.** hear the word at my mouth, and
Eze 4:7 **T.** thou shalt set thy face toward the
Eze 5:7,8 **T.** thus saith the Lord God; 3651
Eze 5:10 **T.** the fathers shall eat the sons in 3651
Eze 5:11 **t.** will I also diminish thee; neither
Eze 7:20 **t.** have I set it far from them. 5921,3651
Eze 8:18 **T.** will I also deal in fury: mine eye
Eze 11:4 **T.** prophesy against them, 3651
Eze 11:7 **T.** thus saith the Lord God; Your 3651
Eze 11:16, 17 **T.** say, Thus saith the Lord God; 3651
Eze 12:3 **T.**, thou son of man, prepare thee
Eze 12:23 Tell them **t.**, Thus saith the Lord 3651
Eze 12:28 **T.** say unto them, Thus saith the 3651
Eze 13:8 **T.** thus saith the Lord God; 3651
Eze 13:8 **t.**, behold, I am against you, saith 3651
Eze 13:13 **T.** thus saith the Lord God; I will 3651
Eze 13:23 **T.** ye shall see no more vanity, 3651
Eze 14:4 **T.** speak unto them, and say unto 3651
Eze 14:6 **T.** say unto the house of Israel, 3651
Eze 15:6 **T.** thus saith the Lord God; As the 3651
Eze 16:27 **t.** I have stretched out my hand
Eze 16:34 given unto thee, **t.** thou art contrary.
Eze 16:37 **t.** I will gather all thy lovers, with 3651
Eze 16:43 **t.** I also will recompense thy way upon
Eze 16:50 **t.** I took them away as I saw good.
Eze 17:19 **T.** thus saith the Lord God; As I 3651
Eze 18:30 **T.** I will judge you, O house of 3651
Eze 20:27 **T.**, son of man, speak unto the 3651
Eze 21:4 **t.** shall my sword go forth out of his
Eze 21:6 Sigh **t.**, thou son of man, with the
Eze 21:12 my people: smite **t.** upon thy thigh.
Eze 21:14 Thou **t.**, son of man, prophesy, and
Eze 21:24 **T.** thus saith the Lord God; 3651
Eze 22:4 **t.** have I made thee a reproach 5921,3651
Eze 22:13 **t.** I have smitten mine hand at thy
Eze 22:19 **T.** thus saith the Lord God; 3651
Eze 22:19 **t.** I will gather you into the midst 3651
Eze 22:31 **T.** have I poured out mine indignation
Eze 23:22 **T.**, O Aholibah, thus saith the 3651
Eze 23:31 **t.** will I give her cup into thine hand.
Eze 23:35 **T.** thus saith the Lord God; 3651
Eze 23:35 **t.** bear thou also thy lewdness and thy
Eze 24:9 **T.** thus saith the Lord God; Woe 3651
Eze 25:4 **t.** I will deliver thee to the men of 3651
Eze 25:7 **t.** I will stretch out mine hand 3651

Eze 25:9 T., behold, I will open the side of 3651
Eze 25:13, 16 T. thus saith the Lord God; I 3651
Eze 26:3 T. thus saith the Lord God; 3651
Eze 28:6 T. thus saith the Lord God; 3651
Eze 28:7 t. I will bring strangers upon thee, 3651
Eze 28:16 t. I will cast thee as profane out of the
Eze 28:18 t. will I bring forth a fire from the
Eze 29:8 T. thus saith the Lord God; 3651
Eze 29:10 t. I am against thee, and against 3651
Eze 29:19 T. thus saith the Lord God; 3651
Eze 30:22 T. thus saith the Lord God; 3651
Eze 31:5 T. his height was exalted above 5921,3651
Eze 31:10 T. thus saith the Lord God; 3651
Eze 31:11 I have t. delivered him into the hand
Eze 32:3 I will t. spread out my net over thee
Eze 33:7 t. thou shalt hear the word at my
Eze 33:10 T., O thou son of man, speak unto the
Eze 33:12 T., thou son of man, say unto the
Eze 34:7 T., ye shepherds, hear the word of 3651
Eze 34:9 T., O ye shepherds, hear the word 3651
Eze 34:20 T. thus saith the Lord God unto 3651
Eze 34:22 T. will I save my flock, and they shall
Eze 35:6, 11 T., as I live, saith the Lord God, 3651
Eze 36:3 T. prophesy and say, Thus saith 3651
Eze 36:4 T., ye mountains of Israel, hear 3651
Eze 36:5 T. thus saith the Lord God; Surely 3651
Eze 36:6 Prophesy t. concerning the land of 3651
Eze 36:7 T. thus saith the Lord God; I have 3651
Eze 36:14 T. thou shalt devour men no more, 3651
Eze 36:22 T. say unto the house of Israel, 3651
Eze 37:12 T. prophesy and say unto them, 3651
Eze 38:14 T., son of man, prophesy and say 3651
Eze 39:1 T., thou son of man, prophesy
Eze 39:23 t. hid I my face from them, and gave
Eze 39:25 T. thus saith the Lord God; Now 3651
Eze 41:7 t. the breadth of the house 5921,3651
Eze 42:6 t. the building was straitened 5921,3651
Eze 44:2 hath entered in by it, t. it shall be shut.
Eze 44:12 t. have I lifted up mine hand 5921,3651
Da 1:8 t. he requested of the prince of the
Da 1:19 Azariah: t. stood they before the king.
Da 2:6 t. shew me the dream, and the 2006
Da 2:9 t. tell me the dream, and I shall 2006
Da 2:10 t. there is no king, lord, 3606,6903,1768
Da 2:24 T. Daniel went in unto 3606,6903,1768
Da 3:7 T. at that time, when all 3606,6903,1836
Da 3:19 t. he spake, and commanded that they
Da 3:22 T. because the king's 3606,6903,1836
Da 3:29 T. I make a decree, That every
Da 4:6 T. made I a decree to bring in all the
Da 8:8 T. the he goat waxed very great: and
Da 9:11 t. the curse is poured upon us, and the
Da 9:14 T. hath the Lord watched upon the
Da 9:17 Now t., O our God, hear the prayer of
Da 9:23 t. understand the matter, and consider
Da 9:25 Know t. and understand, that from the
Da 10:8 T. I was left alone, and saw this great
Da 11:30 t. he shall be grieved, and return, and
Da 11:44 t. he shall go forth with great fury to
Ho 2:2 let her t. put away her whoredoms out
Ho 2:6 T., behold, I will hedge up thy 3651
Ho 2:9 T. will I return, and take away my 3651
Ho 2:14 T., behold, I will allure her, and 3651
Ho 4:3 T. shall the land mourn, and 5921,3651
Ho 4:5 T. shalt thou fall in the day, and the
Ho 4:7 t. will I change their glory into shame.
Ho 4:13 t. your daughters...commit 5921,3651
Ho 4:14 t. the people that doth not understand
Ho 5:5 t. shall Israel and Ephraim fall in
Ho 5:10 t. I will pour out my wrath upon them
Ho 5:12 T. will I be unto Ephraim as a moth,
Ho 6:5 T. have I hewed them by the 5921,3651
Ho 8:6 workman made it; t. it is not God:
Ho 9:9 t. he will remember their iniquity, he
Ho 10:14 T. shall a tumult arise among thy
Ho 12:6 T. turn thou to thy God: keep mercy
Ho 12:14 t. shall he leave his blood upon him,
Ho 13:3 T. they shall be as the morning 3651
Ho 13:6 t. have they forgotten me 5921,3651
Ho 13:7 T. I will be unto them as a lion: as a
Joe 2:12 T. also now, saith the Lord, turn 1571
Am 2:14 T. the flight shall perish from the
Am 3:2 t. I will punish you for all 5921,3651
Am 3:11 T. thus saith the Lord God; An 3651
Am 4:12 T. thus will I do unto thee, O 3651
Am 5:11 Forasmuch t. as your treading is 3651
Am 5:13 T. the prudent shall keep silence 3651
Am 5:16 T. the Lord, the God of hosts, the 3651
Am 5:27 T. will I cause you to go into captivity
Am 6:7 T. now shall they go captive with 3651
Am 6:8 t. will I deliver up the city with all
Am 7:16 Now t. hear thou the word of the Lord:
Am 7:17 T. thus saith the Lord; Thy wife 3651
Jon 4:2 T. I fled...unto Tarshish: 5921,3651
Jon 4:3 T. now, O Lord, take, I beseech thee,
Mic 1:6 T. I will make Samaria as an heap of
Mic 1:8 T. I will wail and howl, I will go
Mic 1:14 T. shalt thou give presents to 3651
Mic 2:3 T. thus saith the Lord; Behold, 3651
Mic 2:5 T. thou shalt have none that shall 3651
Mic 3:6 T. night shall be unto you, that ye 3651
Mic 3:12 T. shall Zion for your sake be 3651
Mic 5:3 T. will he give them up, until the 3651
Mic 6:13 T. also will I make thee sick in
Mic 6:16 t. ye shall bear the reproach of my
Mic 7:7 T. I will look unto the Lord; I will
Hab 1:4 T. the law is slacked, and 5921,3651
Hab 1:4 righteous; t. wrong judgment 5921,3651
Hab 1:15 t. they rejoice and are glad. 5921,3651
Hab 1:16 T. they sacrifice unto their net, 5921,3651
Hab 1:17 Shall they t. empty their net, and 3651
Zep 1:13 T. their goods shall become a booty,
Zep 2:9 T. as I live, saith the Lord of 3651
Zep 3:8 T. wait ye upon me, saith the Lord, 3651
Hag 1:5 Now t. thus saith the Lord of hosts;
Hag 1:10 T. the heaven over you is 5921,3651
Zec 1:3 T. say thou unto them, Thus saith the
Zec 1:16 T. thus saith the Lord; I am 3651
Zec 7:12 t. came a great wrath from the Lord
Zec 7:13 T. it is come to pass, that as he cried,
Zec 8:19 feasts; t. love the truth and peace.
Zec 10:2 t. they went their way as a 5921,3651
Mal 2:9 T. have I also made you contemptible
Mal 2:15 T. take heed to your spirit, and let
Mal 2:16 t. take heed to your spirit, that ye deal
Mal 3:6 t. ye sons of Jacob are not consumed.
Mt 3:8 Bring forth t. fruits meet for 3767
Mt 3:10 t. every tree which bringeth not 3767
Mt 5:19 Whosoever t. shall break one of 3767
Mt 5:23 T. if thou bring thy gift to the 3767
Mt 5:48 ye t. perfect, even as your Father 3767
Mt 6:2 T. when thou doest thine alms, do 3767
Mt 6:8 Be not ye t. like unto them: for 3767
Mt 6:9 After this manner t. pray ye: Our 3767
Mt 6:22 if t. thine eye be single, thy whole 3767
Mt 6:23 If t. the light that is in thee be 3767
Mt 6:25 T. I say unto you, Take no 1223,5124
Mt 6:31 T. take no thought, saying, What 3767
Mt 6:34 Take t. no thought for the morrow 3767
Mt 7:12 T. all things whatsoever ye would 3767
Mt 7:24 T. whosoever heareth these sayings 3767
Mt 9:38 Pray ye t. the Lord of the harvest, 3767
Mt 10:16 be ye t. wise as serpents, and 3767
Mt 10:26 Fear them not t.: for there is 3767
Mt 10:31 Fear ye not t., ye are of more 3767
Mt 10:32 Whosoever t. shall confess me 3767
Mt 12:27 t. they shall be your judges 1223,5124
Mt 13:13 T. I to them in parables: 1223,5124
Mt 13:18 Hear ye t. the parable of the 3767
Mt 13:40 As t. the tares are gathered and 3767
Mt 13:52 T. every scribe which is 1223,5124
Mt 14:2 t. mighty works do shew forth 1223,5124
Mt 18:4 Whosoever t. shall humble himself 3767
Mt 18:23 T. is the kingdom of heaven 1223,5124
Mt 18:26 The servant t. fell down, and 3767
Mt 19:6 What t. God hath joined together, 3767
Mt 19:27 thee; what shall we have t.? 686
Mt 21:40 When the lord t. of the vineyard 3767
Mt 21:43 T. say? I unto you, The 1223,5124
Mt 22:9 Go ye t. into the highways, and as 3767
Mt 22:17 Tell us t., What thinkest thou? Is it 3767
Mt 22:21 Render t. unto Caesar the things 3767
Mt 22:28 T. in the resurrection whose wife 3767
Mt 23:3 t. whatsoever they bid you observe, 3767
Mt 23:14 t. ye shall receive the greater 1223,5124
Mt 23:20 Whoso t. shall swear by the altar, 3767
Mt 24:15 ye t. shall see the abomination 3767
Mt 24:42 Watch t.: for ye know not what 3767
Mt 24:44 T. be ye also ready: for in 1223,5124
Mt 25:13 Watch t., for ye know neither the 3767
Mt 25:27 Thou oughtest t. to have put my 3767
Mt 25:28 Take t. the talent from him, and 3767
Mt 27:17 T. when they were gathered 3767
Mt 27:64 Command t. that the sepulchre be 3767
Mt 28:19 Go ye t., and teach all nations, 3767
Mk 1:38 there also: for t. came I forth 1519,5124
Mk 2:28 T. the Son of man is Lord also of 5620
Mk 6:14 t. mighty works do shew forth 1223,5124
Mk 6:19 T. Herodias had a quarrel against
Mk 8:38 Whosoever t. shall be ashamed of 1063
Mk 10:9 What t. God hath joined together, 3767
Mk 11:24 T. I say unto you, What 1223,5124
Mk 12:6 Having yet t. one son, his 3767
Mk 12:9 What shall t. the lord of the 3767
Mk 12:23 In the resurrection t., when they 3767
Mk 12:24 Do ye not t. err, because ye 1223,5124
Mk 12:27 the living: ye t. do greatly err 3767
Mk 12:37 David t. himself calleth him Lord; 3767
Mk 13:35 Watch ye t.: for ye know not when 3767
Lu 1:35 t. also that holy thing which shall 1352
Lu 3:8 Bring forth t. fruits worthy of 3767
Lu 3:9 every tree t. which bringeth not 3767
Lu 4:7 If thou t. wilt worship me, all shall 3767
Lu 4:43 cities also: for t. am I sent 1519,5124
Lu 6:36 Be ye t. merciful, as your Father 3767
Lu 7:42 Tell me t., which of them will love 3767
Lu 8:18 Take heed t. how ye hear: for 3767
Lu 10:2 T. said he unto them, The harvest 3767
Lu 10:2 pray ye t. the Lord of the harvest,
Lu 10:40 alone? bid her t. that she help me. 3767
Lu 11:19 t. shall they be your judges 1223,5124
Lu 11:34 t. when thine eye is single, thy 3767
Lu 11:35 Take heed t. that the light which 3767
Lu 11:36 If thy whole body t. be full of 3767
Lu 11:49 T. also said the wisdom of God, I
Lu 12:3 T. whatsoever ye have spoken 473,5607
Lu 12:7 Fear not t.: ye are of more value 3767
Lu 12:22 T. I say unto you, Take no 1223,5124
Lu 12:40 Be ye t. ready also: for the Son of 3767
Lu 13:14 in them t. come and be healed, and 3767
Lu 14:20 a wife, and t. I cannot come 122,5124
Lu 15:28 t. came his father out, and 3767
Lu 16:11 If t. ye have not been faithful in 3767
Lu 16:27 I pray thee t., father, that thou 3767
Lu 19:12 He said t., a certain nobleman 3767
Lu 20:15 What t. shall the lord of the 3767
Lu 20:25 Render t. unto Caesar the things 5106
Lu 20:29 There were t. seven brethren: and 3767
Lu 20:33 T. in the resurrection whose wife 3767
Lu 20:44 David t. calleth him Lord, how is he
Lu 21:8 near: go ye not t. after them 3767
Lu 21:14 Settle it t. in your hearts, not to 3767
Lu 21:36 Watch ye t., and pray always, 3767
Lu 23:16 I will t. chastise him, and release 3767
Lu 23:20 Pilate t., willing to release Jesus, 3767
Lu 23:22 I will t. chastise him, and let him 3767
Joh 1:31 t. am I come baptizing with 1223,5124
Joh 2:22 When t. he was risen from the 3767
Joh 3:29 voice: this my joy t. is fulfilled. 3767
Joh 4:1 When t. the Lord knew how the 3767
Joh 4:6 Jesus t., being wearied with his 3767
Joh 4:33 T. said the disciples one to 3767
Joh 5:10 Jews t. said unto him that was 3767
Joh 5:16 And t. did the Jews persecute 1223,5124
Joh 5:18 T. the Jews sought the more to 1223,5124
Joh 6:13 T. they gathered them together, 3767
Joh 6:15 When Jesus t. perceived that they 3767
Joh 6:24 When the people t. saw that Jesus 3767
Joh 6:30 They said t. unto him, What sign 3767
Joh 6:43 Jesus t. answered and said unto 3767
Joh 6:45 Every man t. that hath heard, and 3767
Joh 6:52 Jews t. strove among themselves, 3767
Joh 6:60 Many t. of his disciples, when they 3767
Joh 6:65 T. said I unto you, that no 1223,5124
Joh 7:3 His brethren t. said unto him. 3767
Joh 7:22 Moses t. gave unto you 1223,5124
Joh 7:40 Many of the people t., when they 3767
Joh 8:13 The Pharisees t. said unto him, 3767
Joh 8:24 I said t. unto you, that ye shall 3767
Joh 8:36 If the Son t. shall make you free, 3767
Joh 8:47 ye t. hear them not, because 1223,5124
Joh 9:7 He went his way t., and washed, 3767
Joh 9:8 The neighbours t., and they which 3767
Joh 9:10 T. said they unto him, how were 3767
Joh 9:16 T. said some of the Pharisees, This 3767
Joh 9:23 T. said his parents, He is of 1223,5124
Joh 9:41 We see; t. your sin remaineth 3767
Joh 10:17 T. doth my Father love me, 1223,5124

Joh 10:19 was a division t. again among the 3767
Joh 10:39 T. they sought again to take him: 3767
Joh 11:3 T. his sisters sent unto him, ... 3767
Joh 11:6 he had heard t. that he was sick, ... 3767
Joh 11:33 When Jesus t. saw her weeping, ... 3767
Joh 11:38 Jesus t. again groaning in himself 3767
Joh 11:54 Jesus t. walked no more openly 3767
Joh 12:9 the Jews t. knew that he was there: ... 3767
Joh 12:17 people t. that was with him when 3767
Joh 12:19 The Pharisees t. said among 3767
Joh 12:21 The same came t. to Philip, which 3767
Joh 12:29 The people t., that stood by, and 3767
Joh 12:39 T. they could not believe, ... 1223,5124
Joh 12:50 I speak t., even as the Father, ... 3767
Joh 13:11 t. said he, Ye are not all clean 1223,5124
Joh 13:24 Simon Peter t. beckoned to him, ... 3767
Joh 13:31 T., when he was gone out, Jesus 3767
Joh 15:19 world, t. the world hateth 1223,5124
Joh 16:15 t. said I, that he shall take of .1223,5124
Joh 16:18 They said t., What is this that he 3767
Joh 16:22 And ye now t. have sorrow: but I .. 3767
Joh 18:4 Jesus t., knowing all things that 3767
Joh 18:8 if t. ye seek me, let these go their ..3767
Joh 18:25 They said t. unto him, Art not thou 3767
Joh 18:31 The Jews t. said unto him, It is not 3767
Joh 18:37 Pilate t. said unto him, Art thou a 3767
Joh 18:39 will ye t. that I release unto you 3767
Joh 19:1 Then Pilate t. took Jesus, and 3767
Joh 19:4 Pilate t. went forth again, and 3767
Joh 19:6 the chief priests t. and officers saw 3767
Joh 19:8 when Pilate t. heard that saying, ... 3767
Joh 19:11 t. he that delivered me unto ... 1223,5124
Joh 19:13 When Pilate t. heard that saying, ... 3767
Joh 19:16 Then delivered he him t. unto them 3767
Joh 19:24 They said t. among themselves, Let ... 3767
Joh 19:24 These things t. the soldiers did 3767
Joh 19:26 When Jesus t. saw his mother, and 3767
Joh 19:30 When Jesus t. had received the 3767
Joh 19:31 The Jews t., because it was the 3767
Joh 19:38 He came t., and took the body of 3767
Joh 19:42 There laid they Jesus t. because of 3767
Joh 20:3 Peter t. went forth, and that other 3767
Joh 20:25 other disciples t. said unto him, ... 3767
Joh 21:6 They cast t., and now they were not .. 3767
Joh 21:7 T. that disciple whom Jesus loved 3767
Ac 1:6 When they t. were come together, ... 3767
Ac 2:26 T. did my heart rejoice, and 1223,5124
Ac 2:30 T. being a prophet, and knowing 3767
Ac 2:33 T. being by the right hand of God 3767
Ac 2:36 T. let all the house of Israel know 3767
Ac 3:19 Repent ye t., and be converted, ... 3767
Ac 8:4 T. they that were scattered abroad 3767
Ac 8:22 Repent t. of this thy wickedness, ... 3767
Ac 10:20 Arise t., and get thee down, and go 235
Ac 10:29 T. came I unto you without 1352
Ac 10:29 I ask t. for what intent ye have 3767
Ac 10:32 Send t. to Joppa, and call hither 3767
Ac 10:33 Immediately t. I sent to thee; and 3767
Ac 10:33 t. are we all here present before 3767
Ac 12:5 Peter t. was kept in prison: but 3767
Ac 13:38 Be it known unto you t., men and 3767
Ac 13:40 Beware t., lest that come upon you 3767
Ac 14:3 Long time t. abode they speaking 3767
Ac 15:2 When t. Paul and Barnabas had no 3767
Ac 15:10 Now t. why tempt ye God, to put a 3767
Ac 15:27 We have sent t. Judas and Silas, ... 3767
Ac 16:11 T. loosing from Troas, we came 3767
Ac 16:36 go: now t. depart, and go in peace 3767
Ac 17:12 T. many of them believed; also of 3767
Ac 17:17 T. disputed he in the synagogue 3767
Ac 17:20 know t. what these things mean 3767
Ac 17:23 Whom t. ye ignorantly worship, ... 3767
Ac 19:32 Some t. cried one thing, and some 3767
Ac 20:11 When he t. was come up again, ... 3767
Ac 20:28 Take heed t. unto yourselves, and to ....
Ac 20:31 T. watch, and remember, that by 1352
Ac 21:22 What is it t.? the multitude must 3767
Ac 21:23 Do t. this that we say to thee: We 3767
Ac 23:15 Now t. ye with the council signify 3767
Ac 25:5 Let them t., said he, which among 3767
Ac 25:17 T., when they were come hither, ... 3767
Ac 26:22 Having t. obtained help of God, I 3767
Ac 28:20 for this cause t. have I called for 3767
Ac 28:28 Be it known t. unto you, that the 3767
Ro 2:1 T. thou art inexcusable, O man, ... 1352
Ro 2:21 Thou t. which teachest another, ... 3767
Ro 2:26 T. if the uncircumcision keep the 3767
Ro 3:20 T. by the deeds of the law there 1360
Ro 3:27 T. we conclude that a man is 3767
Ro 4:16 T. it is of faith, that it might 1233,5124
Ro 4:22 t. it was imputed to him for 1352
Ro 5:1 T. being justified by faith, we 3767
Ro 5:18 T. as by the offence of one 686,3767
Ro 6:4 T. we are buried with him by 3767
Ro 6:12 Let not sin t. reign in your mortal 3767
Ro 8:1 There is t. now no condemnation 686
Ro 8:12 T., brethren, we are debtors, ... 686,3767
Ro 9:18 T. hath he mercy on whom he 686,3767
Ro 11:22 Behold t. the goodness...of God: 3767
Ro 12:1 I beseech you t., brethren, by the 3767
Ro 12:20 T. if thine enemy hunger, feed 3767
Ro 13:2 Whosoever t. resisteth the power, ... 5620
Ro 13:7 Render t. to all their dues: 3767
Ro 13:10 t. love is the fulfilling of the law 3767
Ro 13:12 us t. cast off the works of darkness, .. 3767
Ro 14:8 whether we live t., or die, we are 3767
Ro 14:13 Let us not t. judge one another any 3767
Ro 14:19 Let us t. follow after the things 686,3767
Ro 15:17 t. whereof I may glory through 3767
Ro 15:28 When t. I have performed this, ... 3767
Ro 16:19 I am glad t. on your behalf: but yet 3767
1Co 3:21 T. let no man glory in men. For 5620
1Co 4:5 T. judge nothing before the time, ... 5620
1Co 5:7 Purge out t. the old leaven, that 3767
1Co 5:8 T. let us keep the feast, not with 5628
1Co 5:13 T. put away from among yourselves, ...
1Co 6:7 Now t. there is utterly a fault 3767
1Co 6:20 t. glorify God in your body, and in 1211
1Co 7:8 I say t. to the unmarried and 1160
1Co 7:26 I suppose t. that this is good for 3767
1Co 8:4 As concerning t. the eating of those 3767
1Co 9:26 I t. so run, not as uncertainly; so 5106
1Co 10:31 Whether t. ye eat, or drink, or 3767
1Co 11:20 ye come together t. into one place. 3767
1Co 12:15, 16 is it t. not of the body? .. 3756,3844,5124
1Co 14:11 T. if I know not the meaning of 3767
1Co 14:23 If t. the whole church be come 3767
1Co 15:11 T. whether it were I or they, so we ... 3767
1Co 15:58 T., my beloved brethren, be ye 5620
1Co 16:11 Let no man t. despise him: but 3767
1Co 16:18 t. acknowledge ye them that are 3767
2Co 1:17 When I t. was thus minded, did I 3767
2Co 4:1 T. seeing we have this 1223,5124
2Co 4:13 I believed, and t. have I spoken; 1352
2Co 4:13 we also believe, and t. speak; 1352
2Co 5:6 T. we are always confident, ... 3767
2Co 5:11 Knowing t. the terror of the Lord, ... 3767
2Co 5:17 T. if any man be in Christ, he is a 5620
2Co 7:1 Having t. these promises, dearly 3767
2Co 7:13 T. we were comforted in your 1223,5124
2Co 7:16 I rejoice t. that I have confidence in ....
2Co 8:7 T., as ye abound in every thing, ... 235
2Co 8:11 now t. perform the doing of it; 2532
2Co 9:5 T. I thought it necessary to exhort 3767
2Co 11:15 T. it is no great thing if his 3767
2Co 12:9 gladly t. will I rather glory in my 3767
2Co 12:10 T. I take pleasure in infirmities, ... 1352
2Co 13:10 T. I write these things being 1223,5124
Ga 2:17 is t. Christ the minister of sin? 686
Ga 3:5 He t. that ministereth to you the 3767
Ga 3:7 Know ye t. that they which are of 686
Ga 4:16 Am I t. become your enemy, ... 5620
Ga 5:1 Stand fast t. in the liberty 3767
Ga 6:10 As we have t. opportunity, let 685,3767
Eph 2:19 Now t. ye are no more strangers 686
Eph 4:1 I t., the prisoner of the Lord, ... 3767
Eph 4:17 This I say t., and testify in the 3767
Eph 5:1 Be ye t. followers of God, as dear 3767
Eph 5:7 Be not ye t. partakers with them. 3767
Eph 5:24 T. as the church is subject unto 235
Eph 6:14 Stand t., having your loins girt 3767
Php 2:1 If there be t. any consolation in 3767
Php 2:23 Him t. I hope to send presently, ... 3767
Php 2:28 I sent him t. the more carefully, ... 3767
Php 2:29 Receive him t. in the Lord with all 3767
Php 3:15 Let us t., as many as be perfect, be ... 3767
Php 4:1 T., my brethren dearly beloved 5620
Col 2:6 As ye have t. received Christ 3767
Col 2:16 Let no man t. judge you in meat, ... 3767
Col 3:5 Mortify t. your members which are 3767
Col 3:12 Put on t., as the elect of God, holy 3767
1Th 3:7 T., brethren, we were 1223,5124
1Th 4:8 He t. that despiseth, despiseth not 5105
1Th 5:6 T. let us not sleep, as do 686,3767
2Th 2:15 T., brethren, stand fast, and 686,3767
1Ti 2:1 I exhort t., that, first of all, ... 3767
1Ti 2:8 I will t. that men pray every where, ... 3767
1Ti 4:10 t. we both labour and suffer 1519,5124
1Ti 5:14 t. that the younger women marry, ... 3767
2Ti 1:8 Be not thou t. ashamed of the 3767
2Ti 2:1 Thou t., my son, be strong in the 3767
2Ti 2:3 Thou t. endure hardness, as a good 3767
2Ti 2:10 T. I endure all things for the elect's ....
2Ti 2:21 If a man t. purge himself from 3767
2Ti 4:1 I charge thee t. before God, and 3767
Phm 12 thou t. receive him, that is, mine own ....
Phm 15 he t. departed for a season, ... 1223,5124
Phm 17 If thou count me t. a partner, ... 3767
Heb 1:9 t. God, even thy God, hath 1223,5124
Heb 2:1 T. we ought to give the more 1223,5124
Heb 4:1 Let us t. fear, lest, a promise 3767
Heb 4:6 Seeing t. it remaineth that some 3767
Heb 4:9 remaineth t. a rest unto the people 686
Heb 4:11 labour t. to enter into that rest, ... 3767
Heb 4:16 Let us t. come boldly unto the 3767
Heb 6:1 T. leaving the principles of the ....
Heb 7:11 If t. perfection were by the 3767
Heb 9:23 It was t. necessary that the 3767
Heb 10:19 Having t., brethren, boldness to 3767
Heb 10:35 Cast not away t. your confidence, ... 3767
Heb 11:12 T. sprang there even of one, and 1352
Heb 13:13 Let us go forth t. unto him without 5106
Heb 13:15 By him t. let us offer the sacrifice 3767
Jas 4:4 whosoever t. will be a friend of the 3767
Jas 4:7 Submit yourselves t. to God 3767
Jas 4:17 T. to him that knoweth to do good, ... 3767
Jas 5:7 Be patient t., brethren, unto the 3767
1Pe 2:7 Unto you t. which believe he is 3767
1Pe 4:7 be ye t. sober, and watch unto 3767
1Pe 5:6 Humble yourselves t. under the 3767
2Pe 3:17 Ye t., beloved, seeing ye know 3767
1Jo 2:24 Let that t. abide in you, which ye 3767
1Jo 3:1 t. the world knoweth us not, ... 1223,5124
1Jo 4:5 t. speak they of the world, and ... 1223,5124
3Jo 8 We t. ought to receive such, that 3767
Jude 5 I will t. put you in remembrance, ...
Re 2:5 Remember t. from whence thou 3767
Re 3:3 Remember t. how thou hast 3767
Re 3:3 If t. thou shalt not watch, I will ... 3767
Re 3:19 chasten: be zealous t., and repent. .3767
Re 7:15 T. are they before the throne 1223,5124
Re 12:12 T. rejoice, ye heavens, and ye 1223,5124
Re 18:8 T. shall her plagues come in one 5124

THEREFROM

Jos 23:6 ye turn not aside t. to the right hand ....
2Ki 3:3 made Israel to sin; he departed not t. ......
2Ki 13:2 made Israel to sin; he departed not t.. ......

THEREIN See also THEREINTO.

Ge 9:7 in the earth, and multiply t. ....
Ge 18:24 for the fifty righteous that are t.? 7130
Ge 23:11 and the cave that is t., I give it thee; ....
Ge 23:17 field, and the cave was t., and all the ....
Ge 23:20 And the field, and the cave that is t., ...
Ge 34:10 be before you; dwell and trade ye t., ...
Ge 34:10 and get you possessions t. ....
Ge 34:21 dwell in the land, and trade t.; ....
Ge 47:27 they had possessions t., and grew, and .....
Ge 49:32 of the cave that is t. was from the ....
Ex 2:3 and with pitch, and put the child t.; ....
Ex 5:9 the men, that they may labour t.; ....
Ex 16:24 stink, neither was there any worm t.. ....
Ex 16:33 and put an omer full of manna t.; 8033
Ex 21:33 cover it, and an ox or an ass fall t.; 8033
Ex 29:29 his sons' after him, to be anointed t., ...
Ex 30:18 altar, and thou shalt put water t. 8033
Ex 31:14 for whosoever doeth any work t., that ......
Ex 35:2 doeth work t. shall be put to death ....
Ex 40:3 put t. the ark of the testimony, ... 8033
Ex 40:7 the altar, and shall put water t. 8033
Ex 40:9 the tabernacle, and all that is t., ...
Le 6:3 these that a man doeth, sinning t. 2077
Le 6:7 that he hath done in trespassing t. ....
Le 8:10 the tabernacle and all that was t., ...
Le 10:1 them his censer, and put fire t., ... 2004
Le 13:21 and, behold, there be no white hairs t., ...
Le 13:37 that there is black hair grown up t.; ....
Le 18:4 and keep mine ordinances, to walk t. ....
Le 18:30 and that ye defile not yourselves t. ....
Le 20:22 land, whither I bring you to dwell t., ...
Le 22:21 accepted; there shall be no blemish t. ....

Le 23:3 convocation; ye shall do no work **t.**
Le 23:7, 8 ye shall do no servile work **t.**
Le 23:21 you: ye shall do no servile work **t.**
Le 23:25 Ye shall do no servile work **t.**: but ye
Le 23:35, 36 ye shall do no servile work **t.**
Le 25:19 eat your fill, and dwell **t.** in safety. 5921
Le 26:32 your enemies which dwell **t.** shall be
Nu 4:16 all the tabernacle, and of all that **t.** is,
Nu 13:18 and the people that dwelleth **t.**, 5921
Nu 13:20 fat or lean, whether there be wood **t.**,
Nu 14:30 which I sware to make you dwell **t.**,
Nu 16:7 And put fire **t.**, and put incense in 2004
Nu 16:46 and put fire **t.** from off the altar, 5921
Nu 28:18 shall do no manner of servile work **t.**
Nu 29:7 your souls: ye shall not do any work **t.**
Nu 29:35 ye shall do no servile work **t.**
Nu 32:40 the son of Manasseh; and he dwelt **t.**
Nu 33:53 inhabitants of the land, and dwell **t.**
Nu 35:33 be cleansed of the blood that is shed **t.**,
De 2:10 The Emims dwelt **t.** in times past, a
De 2:20 of giants: giants dwelt **t.** in old time;
De 7:25 it unto thee, lest thou be snared **t.**
De 8:12 hast built goodly houses, and dwelt **t.**;
De 10:14 God, the earth also, with all that **t.** is.
De 11:31 and ye shall possess it, and dwell **t.**
De 13:15 destroying it utterly, and all that is **t.**,
De 15:21 And if there be any blemish **t.**, as if it
De 16:8 thy God: thou shalt do no work **t.**
De 17:14 and shalt possess it, and shalt dwell **t.**,
De 17:19 he shall read **t.** all the days of his life:
De 20:11 the people that is found **t.** shall be
De 26:1 and possessest it, and dwellest **t.**;
De 28:30 an house, and thou shalt not dwell **t.**
De 29:23 nor beareth, nor any grass groweth **t.**,
Jos 1:8 thou shalt meditate **t.** day and night,
Jos 1:8 do according to all that is written **t.**
Jos 6:17 even it, and all that are **t.**, to the Lord:
Jos 6:24 the city with fire, and all that was **t.**
Jos 10:28 them, and all the souls that were **t.**;
Jos 10:30 sword, and all the souls that were **t.**;
Jos 10:32 sword, and all the souls that were **t.**,
Jos 10:35 souls that were **t.** he utterly destroyed
Jos 10:37 thereof, and all the souls that were **t.**;
Jos 10:37 utterly, and all the souls that were **t.**
Jos 10:39 destroyed all the souls that were **t.**;
Jos 11:11 they smote all the souls that were **t.**
Jos 19:47 and dwelt **t.**, and called Leshem, Dan,
Jos 19:50 and he built the city, and dwelt **t.**
Jos 21:43 and they possessed it, and dwelt **t.**
Jg 2:22 keep the way of the Lord to walk **t.**,
Jg 8:25 did cast **t.** every man the earrings 8033
Jg 9:45 and slew the people that was **t.**, and
Jg 16:30 and upon all the people that were **t.**
Jg 18:7 and saw the people that were **t.**, 7130
Jg 18:28 And they built a city, and dwelt **t.**
1Sa 30:2 the women captives, that were **t.**
2Sa 12:31 brought forth the people that were **t.**,
1Ki 8:16 house, that my name might be **t.**; 8033
1Ki 11:24 they went to Damascus, and dwelt **t.**,
1Ki 12:25 in mount Ephraim, and dwelt **t.**;
2Ki 2:20 me a new cruse, and put salt **t.** 8033
2Ki 12:9 put **t.** all the money that was brought 8033
2Ki 13:6 who made Israel sin, but walked **t.**
2Ki 13:11 who made Israel sin: but he walked **t.**
2Ki 15:16 smote Tiphsah, and all that were **t.**,
2Ki 15:16 the women **t.** that were with child he
1Ch 16:32 let the fields rejoice, and all that is **t.**
1Ch 21:22 I may build an altar **t.** unto the Lord:
2Ch 2:3 cedars to build him an house to dwell **t.**,
2Ch 5:10 the two tables which Moses put **t.** at
2Ch 20:8 And they dwelt **t.**, and have built thee
2Ch 20:8 built thee a sanctuary **t.** for thy name,
Ezr 4:19 and sedition have been made **t.**
Ezr 6:2 and **t.** was a record thus written: 1459
Ne 6:1 and that there was no breach left **t.**;
Ne 7:4 but the people were few **t.**, and the
Ne 7:5 up at the first, and found written **t.**,
Ne 8:3 And he read **t.** before the street that
Ne 9:6 earth, and all things that are **t.**, 5921
Ne 9:6 the seas, and all that is **t.**, and thou
Ne 13:1 and **t.** was found written, that the
Ne 13:16 There dwelt men of Tyre also **t.**, which
Job 3:7 be solitary, let no joyful voice come **t.**
Job 20:18 be, and he shall not rejoice **t.**
Ps 24:1 the world, and they that dwell **t.**
Ps 37:29 the land, and dwell **t.** for ever. 5921
Ps 68:10 Thy congregation hath dwelt **t.**: thou,
Ps 69:34 seas, and every thing that moveth **t.**
Ps 69:36 they that love his name shall dwell **t.**
Ps 96:12 Let the field be joyful, and all that is **t.**
Ps 98:7 the world, and they that dwell **t.**
Ps 104:26 whom thou hast made to play **t.**
Ps 107:34 the wickedness of them that dwell **t.**
Ps 111:2 out of all them that have pleasure **t.**
Ps 119:35 thy commandments; for **t.** do I delight.
Ps 146:6 and earth, the sea, and all that **t.** is:
Pr 15:4 but perverseness **t.** is a breach in the
Pr 22:14 abhorred of the Lord shall fall **t.** 8033
Pr 26:27 Whoso diggeth a pit shall fall **t.**: and
Ec 2:21 yet to a man that hath not laboured **t.**
Isa 5:2 of it, and also made a winepress **t.**: 8432
Isa 7:6 it, and let us make a breach **t.** for us,
Isa 24:6 and they that dwell **t.** are desolate:
Isa 33:24 the people that dwell **t.** shall be
Isa 34:1 the earth hear, and all that is **t.**; 4393
Isa 34:17 to generation shall they dwell **t.**
Isa 35:8 men, though fools, shall not err **t.**
Isa 42:5 upon it, and spirit to them that walk **t.**
Isa 42:10 down to the sea, and all that is **t.**; 4393
Isa 44:23 mountains, O forest, and every tree **t.**
Isa 51:3 joy and gladness shall be found **t.**,
Isa 51:6 and they that dwell **t.** shall die in like
Isa 59:8 whosoever goeth **t.** shall not know
Jer 4:29 forsaken, and not a man dwell **t.** 2004
Jer 6:16 where is the good way, and walk **t.**,
Jer 6:16 But they said, We will not walk **t.**
Jer 8:16 in it; the city, and those that dwell **t.**
Jer 9:13 obeyed my voice, neither walked **t.**;
Jer 12:4 the wickedness of them that dwell **t.**?
Jer 17:24 the sabbath day, to do no work **t.**;
Jer 23:12 they shall be driven on, and fall **t.**:
Jer 27:11 Lord; and they shall till it, and dwell **t.**
Jer 36:2 write **t.** all the words that I have 413
Jer 36:29 Why hast thou written **t.**, saying, 5921
Jer 36:32 who wrote **t.** from the mouth of 5921
Jer 44:2 a desolation, and no man dwelleth **t.**,
Jer 47:2 overflow the land, and all that is **t.**; 4393
Jer 47:2 the city, and them that dwell **t.**
Jer 48:9 desolate, without any to dwell **t.** 2004
Jer 50:3 land desolate, and none shall dwell **t.**
Jer 50:39 dwell there, and the owls shall dwell **t.**
Jer 50:40 neither shall any son of man dwell **t.**
Jer 51:48 all that is **t.**, shall sing for Babylon:
Eze 2:9 me; and, lo, a roll of a book was **t.**;
Eze 2:10 there was written **t.** lamentations, 413
Eze 7:20 and of their detestable things **t.**
Eze 12:19 may be desolate from all that is **t.**, 4393
Eze 12:19 the violence of all them that dwell **t.**
Eze 14:22 **t.** shall be left a remnant that shall be
Eze 20:47 south to the north shall be burned **t.**
Eze 24:5 let them seethe the bones of it **t.** 8432
Eze 24:6 to the pot whose scum is **t.**, and whose
Eze 28:26 And they shall dwell safely **t.**, and 5921
Eze 30:12 the land waste, and all that is **t.**, 4393
Eze 32:15 I shall smite all them that dwell **t.**,
Eze 37:25 and they shall dwell **t.**, even they,
Eze 40:33 and there were windows **t.** and in the
Eze 42:14 When the priests enter **t.**, then shall
Eze 44:14 and for all that shall be done **t.**
Da 5:2 and his concubines, might drink **t.**
Ho 4:3 one that dwelleth **t.** shall languish,
Ho 14:9 but the transgressors shall fall **t.**
Am 6:8 up the city with all that is **t.** 4393
Am 8:8 and every one mourn that dwelleth **t.**?
Am 9:5 melt, and all that dwell **t.** shall mourn:
Mic 1:2 hearken, O earth, and all that **t.** is: 4393
Mic 7:13 desolate because of them that dwell **t.**,
Na 1:5 yea, the world, and all that dwell **t.**
Hab 2:8, 17 of the city, and of all that dwell **t.**
Hab 2:18 the maker of his work trusteth **t.**, 5921
Zec 2:4 the multitude of men and cattle **t.** 8432
Zec 6:6 black horses which are **t.** go forth into
Zec 13:8 two parts **t.** shall be cut off and die;
Zec 13:8 and die; but the third shall be left **t.**
Zec 14:21 come and take of them, and seethe **t.**
Mt 23:21 **by it, and by him that dwelleth t.**
Mk 10:15 **child, he shall not enter t.** *1519,846*
Mk 13:15 **down into the house, neither enter t.,**
Lu 10:9 **And heal the sick that are t.,** *1722,846*
Lu 18:17 **child shall in no wise enter t.** *1519,846*
Lu 19:45 to cast out them that sold **t.**, *1722,846*
Joh 12:6 the bag, and bare what was put **t.**
Ac 1:20 and let no man dwell **t.** *1722,846*
Ac 14:15 sea, and all things that are **t.** *1722,846*
Ac 17:24 made the world and all things **t.**, *1722,846*
Ac 27:6 sailing into Italy; and he put us **t.**
Ro 1:17 **t.** is the righteousness of God *1722,846*
Ro 6:2 dead to sin, live any longer **t.**? *1722,846*
Co 17:24 he is called, **t.** abide with God *1722,5129*
Eph 6:20 that **t.** I may speak boldly, as I *1722,846*
Php 1:18 and I **t.** do rejoice, yea, and will. *1722,5129*
Col 2:7 abounding **t.**...thanksgiving. *1722,846*
Heb 4:6 that some must enter **t.**, *1519,846*
Heb 10:8 not, neither hadst pleasure **t.**;
Heb 13:9 that have been occupied **t.** *1722,3639*
Jas 1:25 law of liberty, and continueth **t.**,
2Pe 2:20 they are again entangled **t.**, and *5125*
2Pe 3:10 the works that are **t.** shall be *1722,846*
Re 1:3 things which are written **t.** *1722,846*
Re 10:6 and the things that **t.** are, *1722,846*
Re 10:6 and the things which are **t.** *1722,846*
Re 11:1 altar, and them that worship **t.** *1722,846*
Re 13:12 earth and them which dwell **t.** *1722,846*
Re 21:22 And I saw no temple **t.**: for the *1722,846*

THEREINTO

Lu 21:21 **are in the countries enter t.** *1519,846*

THEREOF

Ge 2:17 thou eatest **t.** thou shalt surely die.
Ge 2:19 living creature, that was the name **t.**
Ge 2:21 ribs, and closed up the flesh instead **t.**;
Ge 3:5 doth know that in the day ye eat **t.**,
Ge 3:6 she took of the fruit **t.**, and did eat,
Ge 4:4 firstlings of his flock and of the fat **t.**
Ge 6:16 of the ark shalt thou set in the side **t.**
Ge 9:4 with the life **t.**, which is the blood **t.**,
Ge 40:10 the clusters **t.** brought forth ripe
Ge 40:18 and said, This is the interpretation **t.**
Ge 41:8 of Egypt, and all the wise men **t.**
Ge 45:16 the fame **t.** was heard in Pharaoh's
Ge 47:21 of Egypt even to the other end **t.**
Ex 3:20 which I will do in the midst **t.**
Ex 5:8 ye shall not diminish ought **t.**
Ex 9:18 been in Egypt since the foundation **t.**
Ex 10:26 **t.** must we take to serve the Lord our
Ex 12:9 his legs, and with the purtenance **t.**
Ex 12:43 there shall no stranger eat **t.**
Ex 12:44 circumcised him, then shall he eat **t.**
Ex 12:45 and an hired servant shall not eat **t.**
Ex 12:46 neither shall ye break a bone **t.**
Ex 12:48 no uncircumcised person shall eat **t.**
Ex 16:31 of Israel called the name **t.** Manna:
Ex 19:18 the smoke **t.** ascended as the smoke of
Ex 22:11 and the owner of it shall accept **t.**, and
Ex 22:12 make restitution unto the owner **t.**
Ex 22:14 or die, the owner **t.** being not with it,
Ex 22:15 if the owner **t.** be with it, he shall not
Ex 23:10 land, and shalt gather in the fruits **t.**
Ex 25:9 the pattern of all the instruments **t.**,
Ex 25:10 and a half shall be the length **t.**,
Ex 25:10 and a cubit and a half the breadth **t.**,
Ex 25:10 and a cubit and a half the height **t.**
Ex 25:12 it, and put them in the four corners **t.**
Ex 25:17 and a half shall be the length **t.**,
Ex 25:17 and a cubit and a half the breadth **t.**
Ex 25:19 the cherubims on the two ends **t.**
Ex 25:23 two cubits shall be the length **t.**,
Ex 25:23 and a cubit the breadth **t.**,
Ex 25:23 and a cubit and a half the height **t.**
Ex 25:25 make a golden crown to the border **t.**
Ex 25:26 corners that are on the four feet **t.**
Ex 25:29 shalt make the dishes **t.**, and spoons **t.**,
Ex 25:29 and covers **t.**, and bowls **t.**, to cover
Ex 25:37 thou shalt make the seven lamps **t.**
Ex 25:37 and they shall light the lamps **t.**, that
Ex 25:38 the tongs **t.**, and the snuffdishes **t.**
Ex 26:30 to the fashion **t.** which was shewed
Ex 27:1 and the height **t.** shall be three cubits.
Ex 27:2 horns of it upon the four corners **t.**
Ex 27:3 vessels **t.** thou shalt make of brass.
Ex 27:4 four brasen rings in...four corners **t.**
Ex 27:10 the twenty pillars **t.** and their twenty
Ex 27:19 of the tabernacle in all the service **t.**,
Ex 27:19 and all the pins **t.**, and all the pins of
Ex 28:7 It shall have the two shoulderpieces **t.**
Ex 28:7 joined at the two edges **t.**; and so it
Ex 28:8 of the same, according to the work **t.**;
Ex 28:16 doubled; a span shall be the length **t.**,
Ex 28:16 and a span shall be the breadth **t.**

Ex 28:26 of the breastplate in the border **t.**,
Ex 28:27 underneath, toward the forepart **t.**,
Ex 28:27 over against the other coupling **t.**,
Ex 28:28 bind the breastplate by the rings **t.**
Ex 28:32 hole in the top of it, in the midst **t.**:
Ex 28:33 of scarlet, round about the hem **t.**;
Ex 29:33 but a stranger shall not eat **t.**, because
Ex 29:41 according to the drink offering **t.**, for a
Ex 30:2 A cubit shall be the length **t.**,
Ex 30:2 a cubit the breadth **t.**: foursquare
Ex 30:2 and two cubits shall be the height **t.**
Ex 30:2 the horns **t.** shall be of the same.
Ex 30:3 overlay it with pure gold, the top **t.**,
Ex 30:3 and the sides **t.** round about, and the
Ex 30:3 and the horns **t.**; and thou shalt make
Ex 30:4 the crown of it, by the two corners **t.**,
Ex 30:37 according to the composition **t.**
Ex 35:12 The ark, and the staves **t.**, with the
Ex 36:29 coupled together at the head **t.**, to one
Ex 37:6 two cubits and a half was the length **t.**,
Ex 37:6 one cubit and a half the breadth **t.**.
Ex 37:8 he the cherubims on the two ends **t.**
Ex 37:10 wood: two cubits was the length **t.**,
Ex 37:10 and a cubit the breadth **t.**, and a cubit
Ex 37:10 and a cubit and a half the height **t.**
Ex 37:12 made a crown of gold for the border **t.**
Ex 37:13 four corners that were in…four feet **t.**.
Ex 37:18 six branches going out of the sides **t.**;
Ex 37:18 the candlestick out of the one side **t.**,
Ex 37:18 candlestick out of the other side **t.**
Ex 37:24 gold made he it, and all the vessels **t.**.
Ex 37:25 height of it; horns **t.** were of the same.
Ex 37:26 top of it, and the sides **t.** round about,
Ex 37:27 rings of gold for it under the crown **t.**
Ex 37:27 corners of it, upon the two sides **t.**,
Ex 38:1 wood: five cubits was the length **t.**,
Ex 38:1 and five cubits the breadth **t.**; it was
Ex 38:1 and three cubits the height **t.**.
Ex 38:2 he made the horns **t.** on the four
Ex 38:2 the horns **t.** were of the same: and he
Ex 38:3 all the vessels **t.** made he of brass.
Ex 38:4 of network under the compass **t.**
Ex 39:5 of the same, according to the work **t.**;
Ex 39:9 double: a span was the length **t.**,
Ex 39:9 a span the breadth **t.**, being doubled.
Ex 39:20 it, over against the other coupling **t.**,
Ex 39:35 ark of the testimony, and the staves **t.**,
Ex 39:36 The table, and all the vessels **t.**, and
Ex 39:37 pure candlestick, with the lamps **t.**,
Ex 39:37 be set in order, and all the vessels **t.**,
Ex 40:4 the candlestick, and light the lamps **t.**
Ex 40:9 shalt hallow it, and all the vessels **t.**
Ex 40:18 his sockets, and set up the boards **t.**,
Ex 40:18 and put in the bars **t.**, and reared up
Le 1:15 the blood **t.** shall be wrung out at the
Le 1:17 he shall cleave it with the wings **t.**,
Le 2:2 of the flour **t.**, and of the oil **t.**,
Le 2:2 with all the frankincense **t.**; and the
Le 2:9 from the meat offering a memorial **t.**,
Le 2:16 beaten corn **t.**, and part of the oil **t.**,
Le 2:16 with all the frankincense **t.**: it is an
Le 3:8 Aaron's sons shall sprinkle the blood **t.**
Le 3:9 the fat **t.**, and the whole rump, it shall
Le 3:13 Aaron shall sprinkle the blood **t.** upon
Le 3:14 And he shall offer **t.** his offering, even
Le 4:30 the priest shall take of the blood **t.**
Le 4:30 and shall pour out all the blood **t.** at
Le 4:31 he shall take away all the fat **t.**, as the
Le 4:34 and shall pour out all the blood **t.** at
Le 4:35 he shall take away all the fat **t.**, as the
Le 5:12 his handful of it, even a memorial **t.**,
Le 6:15 of the meat offering, and of the oil **t.**,
Le 6:16 remainder **t.** shall Aaron and his sons
Le 6:20 it in the morning, and half **t.** at night.
Le 6:27 shall touch the flesh **t.** shall be holy:
Le 6:27 when there is sprinkled of the blood **t.**
Le 6:29 males among the priests shall eat **t.**
Le 7:2 the blood **t.** shall he sprinkle round
Le 7:3 And he shall offer of it all the fat **t.**,
Le 7:6 male among the priests shall eat **t.**
Le 7:19 the flesh, all that be clean shall eat **t.**
Le 8:11 he sprinkled **t.** upon the altar seven
Le 9:13 him, with the pieces **t.**, and the head:
Le 9:17 took a handful **t.**, and burnt it upon
Le 11:39 he that toucheth the carcase **t.** shall
Le 13:4 and the hair **t.** be not turned white;
Le 13:18 which, even in the skin **t.**, was a boil,
Le 13:20 skin, and the hair **t.** be turned white:
Le 14:45 and the timber **t.**, and all the morter
Le 17:13 he shall even pour out the blood **t.**,
Le 17:14 the blood of it is for the life **t.**
Le 17:14 for the life of all flesh is the blood **t.**
Le 18:25 I do visit the iniquity **t.** upon it,
Le 19:23 count the fruit **t.** as uncircumcised:
Le 19:24 all the fruit **t.** shall be holy to praise
Le 19:25 fifth year shall ye eat of the fruit **t.**,
Le 19:25 it may yield unto you the increase **t.**
Le 22:13 but there shall no stranger eat **t.**.
Le 22:14 he shall put the fifth part **t.** unto it,
Le 22:24 neither shall ye make any offering **t.**
Le 23:10 and shall reap the harvest **t.**, then ye
Le 23:13 And the meat offering **t.** shall be two
Le 23:13 drink offering **t.** shall be of wine,
Le 24:5 fine flour, and bake twelve cakes **t.**
Le 25:3 vineyard, and gather in the fruit **t.**;
Le 25:7 land, shall all the increase **t.** be meat.
Le 25:10 all the land unto all the inhabitants **t.**
Le 25:12 eat the increase **t.** out of the field.
Le 25:16 years thou shalt increase the price **t.**,
Le 25:27 let him count the years of the sale **t.**,
Le 27:10 it and the exchange **t.** shall be holy.
Le 27:13 add a fifth part **t.** unto thy estimation.
Le 27:16 shall be according to the seed **t.**
Le 27:21 the possession **t.** shall be the priest's.
Le 27:31 he shall add thereto the fifth part **t.**.
Le 27:33 it and the change **t.** shall be holy;
Nu 1:50 testimony, and over all the vessels **t.**,
Nu 1:50 the tabernacle, and all the vessels **t.**;
Nu 2:6,8, 11 and those that were numbered **t.**,
Nu 3:25 the covering **t.**, and the hanging for
Nu 3:26 the cords of it for all the service **t.**
Nu 3:31 the hanging, and all the service **t.**
Nu 3:36 and the bars **t.**, and the pillars **t.**,
Nu 3:36 the sockets **t.**, and all the vessels **t.**,
Nu 4:6 of blue, and shall put in the staves **t.**.
Nu 4:8 and shall put in the staves **t.**
Nu 4:9 snuffdishes, and all the oil vessels **t.**,
Nu 4:10 they shall put it and all the vessels **t.**
Nu 4:11 skins, and shall put to the staves **t.**
Nu 4:14 shall put upon it all the vessels **t.**,
Nu 4:16 in the sanctuary, and in the vessels **t.**.
Nu 4:31 of the tabernacle, and the bars **t.**,
Nu 4:31 and the pillars **t.**, and sockets **t.**,
Nu 5:7 his trespass with the principal **t.**,
Nu 5:7 add unto it the fifth part **t.**, and give
Nu 5:26 of the offering, even the memorial **t.**,
Nu 7:1 sanctified it, and all…instruments **t.**,
Nu 7:1 both the altar and all the vessels **t.**,
Nu 7:13 the weight **t.** was an hundred
Nu 8:3 he lighted the lamps **t.** over against
Nu 8:4 unto the shaft **t.**, unto the flowers **t.**,
Nu 8:25 shall cease waiting upon the service **t.**,
Nu 9:3 and according to all the ceremonies **t.**,
Nu 9:14 and according to the manner **t.**, so
Nu 11:7 the colour **t.** as the colour of bdellium.
Nu 13:32 land that eateth up the inhabitants **t.**;
Nu 18:28 shall give **t.** the Lord's heave offering
Nu 18:29 offering of the Lord, of all the best **t.**,
Nu 18:29 even the hallowed part **t.** out of it.
Nu 18:30 ye have heaved the best **t.** from it,
Nu 21:25 in Heshbon, and in all the villages **t.**.
Nu 21:32 Jaazer, and they took the villages **t.**,
Nu 26:56 shall the possession **t.** be divided.
Nu 28:7 drink offering **t.** shall be the fourth
Nu 28:8 and as the drink offering **t.**, thou shalt
Nu 28:9 with oil, and the drink offering **t.**
Nu 29:19 and the meat offering **t.**, and their
Nu 32:33 with the cities **t.** in the coasts, even
Nu 32:41 went and took the small towns **t.**,
Nu 32:42 and took Kenath, and the villages **t.**,
Nu 34:2 the land of Canaan with the coasts **t.**:)
Nu 34:4 and the going forth **t.** shall be from
Nu 34:12 shall be your land with the coasts **t.**
De 3:11 nine cubits was the length **t.**, and
De 3:12 half mount Gilead, and the cities **t.**,
De 3:17 plain also, and Jordan, and the coast **t.**,
De 9:21 and I cast the dust **t.** into the brook
De 12:15 the unclean and the clean may eat **t.**,
De 13:15 all that is therein, and the cattle **t.**,
De 13:16 of it into the midst of the street **t.**,
De 13:16 city, and all the spoil **t.** every whit,
De 15:23 Only thou shalt not eat the blood **t.**;
De 20:13 smite every male **t.** with the edge of
De 20:14 is in the city, even all the spoil **t.**,
De 20:19 thou shalt not destroy the trees **t.** by
De 26:14 I have not eaten **t.** in my mourning,
De 26:14 neither have I taken away ought **t.** for
De 26:14 use, nor given ought **t.** for the dead:
De 28:30 and shalt not gather the grapes **t.**.
De 28:31 thine eyes, and thou shalt not eat **t.**
De 29:23 that the whole land **t.** is brimstone,
De 33:16 things of the earth and fulness **t.**,
Jos 6:2 thine hand Jericho, and the king **t.**,
Jos 6:26 he shall lay the foundation **t.** in his
Jos 7:14 come according to the families **t.**;
Jos 8:2 only the spoil **t.**, and the cattle **t.**,
Jos 9:1 and Hivite, and the Jebusite, heard **t.**;
Jos 10:2 Ai, and all the men **t.** were mighty.
Jos 10:28 and the king **t.** he utterly destroyed,
Jos 10:30 the king **t.**, into the hand of Israel;
Jos 10:30 but did unto the king **t.** as he did unto
Jos 10:37 and the king **t.**, and all the cities **t.**,
Jos 10:39 and the king **t.**, and all the cities **t.**;
Jos 10:39 so he did to Debir, and to the king **t.**;
Jos 11:10 and smote the king **t.** with the sword:
Jos 13:23 Reuben was Jordan, and the border **t.**.
Jos 13:23 families, the cities and the villages **t.**
Jos 15:7 and the goings out **t.** were at En-rogel:
Jos 15:12 was to the great sea, and the coast **t.**.
Jos 15:47 and the great sea, and the border **t.**.
Jos 16:3 and the goings out **t.** are at the sea.
Jos 16:8 and the goings out **t.** were at the sea.
Jos 18:12, 14 and the goings out **t.** were at
Jos 18:20 by the coasts **t.** round about,
Jos 19:14 outgoings **t.** are in the valley of
Jos 19:29 the outgoings **t.** are at the sea from
Jos 19:33 and the outgoings **t.** were at Jordan:
Jos 21:2 in, with the suburbs **t.** for our cattle.
Jos 21:11 with the suburbs **t.** round about it.
Jos 21:12 fields of the city, and the villages **t.**,
Jos 22:7 unto the other half **t.** gave Joshua
Jos 23:14 you, and not one thing hath failed **t.**
Jg 1:18 Judah took Gaza with the coast **t.**,
Jg 1:18 and Askelon with the coast **t.**,
Jg 1:18 and Ekron with the coast **t.**
Jg 1:26 a city, and called the name **t.** Luz:
Jg 1:26 which is the name **t.** unto this day.
Jg 3:2 least such as before knew nothing **t.**;
Jg 5:23 curse ye bitterly the inhabitants **t.**;
Jg 7:15 the dream, and the interpretation **t.**,
Jg 8:14 princes of Succoth, and the elders **t.**,
Jg 8:27 and Gideon made an ephod **t.**, and
Jg 14:9 he took **t.** in his hands, and went on
Jg 15:19 he called the name **t.** En-hakkore,
Jg 17:4 who made **t.** a graven image and a
1Sa 5:6 even Ashdod and the coasts **t.**.
1Sa 6:8 offering, in a coffer by the side **t.**;
1Sa 7:14 the coasts **t.** did Israel deliver out of
1Sa 17:51 sword, and drew it out of the sheath **t.**,
1Sa 20:20 I will shoot three arrows on the side **t.**,
1Sa 28:24 it, and did bake unleavened bread **t.**
2Sa 20:8 upon his loins in the sheath **t.**;
2Sa 23:16 nevertheless he would not drink **t.**,
1Ki 2:32 my father David not knowing **t.**, to
1Ki 3:27 in no wise slay it: she is the mother **t.**
1Ki 6:2 the length **t.** was threescore cubits,
1Ki 6:2 and the breadth **t.** twenty cubits,
1Ki 6:2 and the height **t.** thirty cubits.
1Ki 6:3 twenty cubits was the length **t.**,
1Ki 6:3 and ten cubits was the breadth **t.**
1Ki 6:20 and twenty cubits in the height **t.**: and
1Ki 6:38 finished throughout all the parts **t.**,
1Ki 7:2 the length **t.** was an hundred cubits,
1Ki 7:2 and the breadth **t.** fifty cubits,
1Ki 7:2 and the height **t.** thirty cubits,
1Ki 7:6 pillars; the length **t.** was fifty cubits,
1Ki 7:6 and the breadth **t.** thirty cubits: and
1Ki 7:21 pillar, and called the name **t.** Jachin:
1Ki 7:21 pillar, and called the name **t.** Boaz.
1Ki 7:26 brim **t.** was wrought like the brim of a
1Ki 7:27 base, and four cubits the breadth **t.**,
1Ki 7:30 the four corners **t.** had undersetters:
1Ki 7:31 the mouth **t.** was round after the work
1Ki 7:35 on the top of the base the ledges **t.**
1Ki 7:35 and the borders **t.** were of the same.
1Ki 7:36 For on the plates of the ledges **t.**, and
1Ki 7:36 and on the borders **t.**, he graved
1Ki 8:7 covered the ark and the staves **t.**

1Ki 13:26 him back from the way heard **t.**,
1Ki 15:21 when Baasha heard **t.**, that he left off
1Ki 15:22 stones of Ramah, and the timber **t.**,
1Ki 16:34 he laid the foundation **t.** in Abiram his
1Ki 16:34 and set up the gates **t.** in his youngest
1Ki 17:13 but made me **t.** a little cake first, 8033
2Ki 2:12 chariot of Israel, and the horsemen **t.**
2Ki 3:25 in Kir-haraseth left they the stones **t.**;
2Ki 4:39 gathered **t.** wild gourds his lap full,
2Ki 4:40 in the pot. And they could not eat **t.**
2Ki 4:42 and full ears of corn in the husk **t.**
2Ki 4:43 They shall eat, and shall leave **t.**
2Ki 4:44 them, and they did eat, and left **t.**,
2Ki 7:2, 19 thine eyes, but shalt not eat **t.**
2Ki 13:14 chariot of Israel, and the horsemen **t.**
2Ki 15:16 therein, and the coasts **t.** from Tirzah:
2Ki 16:10 according to all the workmanship **t.**
2Ki 17:24 Samaria, and dwelt in the cities **t.**
2Ki 18:8 unto Gaza, and the borders **t.**, from
2Ki 19:23 will cut down the tall cedar trees **t.**,
2Ki 19:23 and the choice fir trees **t.**: and I will
2Ki 19:29 plant vineyards, and eat the fruits **t.**
2Ki 22:16 place, and upon the inhabitants **t.**,
2Ki 22:19 place, and against the inhabitants **t.**,
2Ki 23:6 and cast the powder **t.** upon the graves
1Ch 2:23 the towns **t.**, even threescore cities.
1Ch 6:55 and the suburbs **t.** round about it.
1Ch 6:56 and the villages **t.**, they gave to Caleb
1Ch 7:28 Beth-el and the towns **t.**, and eastward
1Ch 7:28 westward Gezer, with the towns **t.**;
1Ch 7:28 Shechem also and the towns **t.**,
1Ch 7:28 unto Gaza and the towns **t.**
1Ch 8:12 built Ono, and Lod, with the towns **t.**
1Ch 9:27 opening **t.** every morning pertained to
1Ch 16:32 Let the sea roar, and the fulness **t.**
1Ch 21:27 up his sword again into the sheath **t.**
1Ch 23:26 nor any vessels of it for the service **t.**
1Ch 28:11 the houses **t.**, and of the treasuries **t.**,
1Ch 28:11 and of the upper chambers **t.**,
1Ch 28:11 and of the inner parlours **t.**, and of the
1Ch 28:15 candlestick, and for the lamps **t.**
1Ch 28:15 candlestick, and also for the lamps **t.**,
2Ch 3:7 the beams, the posts, and the walls **t.**,
2Ch 3:7 and the doors **t.**, with gold;
2Ch 3:8 and the breadth **t.** twenty cubits:
2Ch 4:1 of brass, twenty cubits the length **t.**,
2Ch 4:1 and twenty cubits the breadth **t.**,
2Ch 4:1 and ten cubits the height **t.**
2Ch 4:2 compass, and five cubits the height **t.**
2Ch 4:22 inner doors **t.** for the most holy place,
2Ch 5:8 covered the ark and the staves **t.**
2Ch 13:11 candlestick of gold with the lamps **t.**,
2Ch 13:19 from him, Beth-el with the towns **t.**,
2Ch 13:19 and Jeshanah with the towns **t.**,
2Ch 13:19 and Ephraim with the towns **t.**
2Ch 16:6 stones of Ramah, and the timber **t.**,
2Ch 28:18 and Shocho with the villages **t.**,
2Ch 28:18 and Timnah with the villages **t.**,
2Ch 28:18 Gimzo also and the villages **t.**: they
2Ch 29:18 burnt offering, with all the vessels **t.**,
2Ch 29:18 table, with all the vessels **t.**
2Ch 32:1 things, and the establishment **t.**,
2Ch 34:24 place, and upon the inhabitants **t.**,
2Ch 34:27 place, and against the inhabitants **t.**,
2Ch 36:19 and burnt all the palaces **t.** with fire,
2Ch 36:19 and destroyed all the goodly vessels **t.**
Ezr 4:12 and have set up the walls **t.**, and
Ezr 4:16 builded again, and the walls **t.** set up,
Ezr 6:3 let the foundations **t.** be strongly laid;
Ezr 6:3 the height **t.** threescore cubits,
Ezr 6:3 and the breadth **t.** threescore cubits;
Ezr 9:9 to repair the desolations **t.**, and to
Ezr 10:14 elders of every city, and the judges **t.**
Ne 1:3 and the gates **t.** are burned with fire.
Ne 2:3 the gates **t.** are consumed with fire?
Ne 2:13 the gates **t.** were consumed with fire.
Ne 2:17 and the gates **t.** are burned with fire:
Ne 3:3 the beams **t.**, and set up the doors **t.**,
Ne 3:3 the locks **t.**, and the bars **t.**
Ne 3:6 the beams **t.**, and set up the doors **t.**,
Ne 3:6 and the locks **t.**, and the bars **t.**
Ne 3:13 they built it, and set up the doors **t.**,
Ne 3:13 the locks **t.**, and the bars **t.**, and a
Ne 3:14 he built it, and set up the doors **t.**,
Ne 3:14 the locks **t.**, and the bars **t.**
Ne 3:15 and covered it, and set up the doors **t.**,
Ne 3:15 the locks **t.**, and the bars **t.**, and the

Ne 4:6 was joined together unto the half **t.**:
Ne 6:16 that when all our enemies heard **t.**,
Ne 9:36 to eat the fruit **t.** and the good **t.**,
Ne 11:25 at Kirjath-arba, and the villages **t.**,
Ne 11:25 and at Dibon, and in the villages **t.**,
Ne 11:25 at Jekabzeel, and in the villages **t.**,
Ne 11:27 at Beer-sheba, and in the villages **t.**,
Ne 11:28 and at Mekonah, and in the villages **t.**,
Ne 11:30 at Lachish, and the fields **t.**,
Ne 11:30 at Azekah, and in the villages **t.**
Ne 13:14 house of my God, and for the offices **t.**
Es 1:22 province according to the writing **t.**,
Es 2:22 Esther certified the king **t.** in
Es 3:12 province according to the writing **t.**,
Es 8:9 on the three and twentieth day **t.**;
Es 8:9 province according to the writing **t.**,
Es 9:18 together on the thirteenth day **t.**,
Es 9:18 and on the fourteenth **t.**; and on
Job 3:9 the stars of the twilight **t.** be dark;
Job 4:12 to me, and mine ear received a little **t.**
Job 4:16 but I could not discern the form **t.**
Job 9:6 her place, and the pillars **t.** trembled.
Job 9:24 he covereth the faces of the judges **t.**;
Job 11:9 The measure **t.** is longer than the
Job 14:7 the tender branch **t.** will not cease.
Job 14:8 the root **t.** wax old in the earth,
Job 14:8 and the stock **t.** die in the ground;
Job 15:29 he prolong the perfection **t.** upon
Job 24:2 take away the flocks, and feed **t.**
Job 24:13 the light; they know not the ways **t.**,
Job 24:13 nor abide in the paths **t.**
Job 26:5 the waters, and the inhabitants **t.**
Job 28:13 Man knoweth not the price **t.**; neither
Job 28:15 shall silver be weighed for the price **t.**
Job 28:22 heard the fame **t.** with our ears.
Job 28:23 God understandeth the way **t.**,
Job 28:23 and he knoweth the place **t.**
Job 31:17 and the fatherless hath not eaten **t.**;
Job 31:38 that the furrows likewise **t.** complain;
Job 31:39 If I have eaten the fruits **t.** without
Job 31:39 the owners **t.** to lose their life:
Job 36:27 down rain according to the vapour **t.**
Job 36:33 The noise **t.** sheweth concerning it,
Job 38:5 Who hath laid the measures **t.**, if
Job 38:6 are the foundations **t.** fastened?
Job 38:6 or who laid the corner stone **t.**;
Job 38:9 I made the cloud the garment **t.**,
Job 38:19 as for darkness, where is the place **t.**,
Job 38:20 thou shouldest take it to the bound **t.**,
Job 38:20 know the paths to the house **t.**?
Job 38:33 thou set the dominion **t.** in the earth?
Ps 19:6 there is nothing hid from the heat **t.**
Ps 24:1 earth is the Lord's and the fulness **t.**;
Ps 34:2 the humble shall hear **t.**, and be glad.
Ps 46:3 Though the waters **t.** roar and be
Ps 46:3 mountains shake with the swelling **t.**
Ps 48:12 go round about her: tell the towers **t.**
Ps 50:1 of the sun unto the going down **t.**
Ps 50:12 the world is mine, and the fulness **t.**
Ps 55:10 they go about it upon the walls **t.**
Ps 55:11 Wickedness is in the midst **t.**: deceit
Ps 60:2 heal the breaches **t.**; for it shaketh.
Ps 65:10 waterest the ridges **t.** abundantly:
Ps 65:10 thou settlest the furrows **t.**: thou
Ps 65:10 thou blessest the springing **t.**
Ps 71:15 days; for I know not the numbers **t.**
Ps 72:16 the fruit **t.** shall shake like Lebanon:
Ps 74:6 they break down the carved work **t.** at
Ps 75:3 all the inhabitants **t.** are dissolved:
Ps 75:8 but the dregs **t.**, all the wicked of the
Ps 80:10 the boughs **t.** were like the goodly
Ps 89:9 when the waves **t.** arise, thou stillest
Ps 89:11 for the world and the fulness **t.**, thou
Ps 96:11 let the sea roar, and the fulness **t.**
Ps 97:1 let the multitude of isles be glad **t.**
Ps 98:7 Let the sea roar, and the fulness **t.**;
Ps 102:14 in her stones, and favour the dust **t.**
Ps 103:16 and the place **t.** shall know it no more.
Ps 107:25 wind, which lifteth up the waves **t.**
Ps 107:29 a calm, so that the waves **t.** are still.
Ps 137:2 harps upon the willows in the midst **t.**
Ps 137:7 it, rase it, even to the foundation **t.**
Pr 1:19 taketh away the life of the owners **t.**
Pr 3:14 silver, and the gain **t.** than fine gold.
Pr 12:28 in the pathway **t.** there is no death.
Pr 14:12 but the end **t.** are the ways of death.
Pr 16:25 but the end **t.** are the ways of death.

Pr 16:33 the whole disposing **t.** is of the Lord.
Pr 18:21 they that love it shall eat the fruit **t.**
Pr 20:21 but the end **t.** shall not be blessed.
Pr 21:22 down the strength of the confidence **t.**
Pr 24:31 and nettles had covered the face **t.**,
Pr 24:31 the stone wall **t.** was broken down.
Pr 25:8 know not what to do in the end **t.**,
Pr 27:18 the fig tree shall eat the fruit **t.**
Pr 28:2 of a land many are the princes **t.**
Pr 28:2 knowledge the state **t.** shall be
Ec 5:11 what good is there to the owners **t.**,
Ec 5:13 riches kept for the owners **t.** to their
Ec 5:19 and hath given him power to eat **t.**,
Ec 6:2 God giveth him not power to eat **t.**,
Ec 7:8 end of a thing than the beginning **t.**
Ca 1:12 spikenard sendeth forth the smell **t.**
Ca 3:10 He made the pillars **t.** of silver,
Ca 3:10 the bottom **t.** of gold, the covering of
Ca 3:10 midst **t.** being paved with love, for the
Ca 4:16 that the spices **t.** may flow out.
Ca 7:8 tree, I will take hold of the boughs **t.**
Ca 8:6 the coals **t.** are coals of fire, which
Ca 8:11 every one for the fruit **t.** was to bring
Ca 8:12 and those that keep the fruit **t.** two
Isa 3:14 of his people, and the princes **t.**
Isa 4:4 blood of Jerusalem from the midst **t.**
Isa 5:2 it, and gathered out the stones **t.**,
Isa 5:5 I will take away the hedge **t.**, and
Isa 5:5 and break down the wall **t.**, and it
Isa 5:30 light is darkened in the heavens **t.**
Isa 6:13 holy seed shall be the substance **t.**
Isa 13:9 shall destroy the sinners **t.** out of it.
Isa 13:10 of heaven and the constellations **t.**
Isa 14:17 wilderness, and destroyed the cities **t.**;
Isa 15:8 of Moab: the howling **t.** unto Eglaim,
Isa 15:8 and the howling **t.** unto Beer-elim.
Isa 16:8 broken down the principal plants **t.**,
Isa 17:6 in the outmost fruitful branches **t.**,
Isa 19:3 of Egypt shall fail in the midst **t.**;
Isa 19:3 and I will destroy the counsel **t.**: and
Isa 19:10 shall be broken in the purposes **t.**,
Isa 19:13 they that are the stay of the tribes **t.**
Isa 19:14 a perverse spirit in the midst **t.**
Isa 19:14 caused Egypt to err in every work **t.**,
Isa 19:17 one that maketh mention **t.** shall
Isa 19:19 a pillar at the border **t.** to the Lord.
Isa 21:2 all the sighing **t.** have I made to cease.
Isa 22:11 have not looked unto the maker **t.**,
Isa 23:11 city to destroy the strong holds **t.**
Isa 23:13 wilderness: they set up the towers **t.**,
Isa 23:13 they raised up the palaces **t.**; and he
Isa 24:1 scattereth abroad the inhabitants **t.**
Isa 24:5 is defiled under the inhabitants **t.**;
Isa 24:20 transgression **t.** shall be heavy upon
Isa 27:10 down, and consume the branches **t.**
Isa 27:11 When the boughs **t.** are withered,
Isa 28:25 When he hath made plain the face **t.**,
Isa 30:27 his anger, and the burden **t.** is heavy:
Isa 30:33 the pile **t.** is fire and much wood;
Isa 31:4 for mount Zion, and for the hill **t.**
Isa 33:20 not one of the stakes **t.** shall ever be
Isa 33:20 shall any of the cords **t.** be broken.
Isa 34:9 streams **t.** shall be turned into pitch,
Isa 34:9 and the dust **t.** into brimstone, and
Isa 34:9 land **t.** shall become burning pitch.
Isa 34:10 the smoke **t.** shall go up for ever:
Isa 34:12 call the nobles **t.** to the kingdom,
Isa 34:13 and brambles in the fortresses **t.**
Isa 37:24 and I will cut down the tall cedars **t.**,
Isa 37:24 and the choice fir trees **t.**: and I will
Isa 37:30 plant vineyards, and eat the fruit **t.**
Isa 40:6 and all the godliness **t.** is as the flower
Isa 40:16 beasts **t.** sufficient for a burnt offering.
Isa 40:22 inhabitants **t.** are as grasshoppers;
Isa 41:9 called thee from the chief men **t.**, and
Isa 42:10 the isles, and the inhabitants **t.**
Isa 42:11 wilderness and the cities **t.** lift up
Isa 44:15 for he will take **t.**, and warm himself;
Isa 44:16 He burneth part **t.** in the fire; with
Isa 44:16 with part **t.** he eateth flesh; he
Isa 44:17 And the residue **t.** he maketh a god,
Isa 44:19 I have baked bread upon the coals **t.**
Isa 44:19 I make the residue **t.** an abomination?
Isa 44:26 I will raise up the decayed places **t.**
Isa 48:19 of thy bowels like the gravel **t.**;
Isa 62:1 the righteousness **t.** go forth as
Isa 62:1 and the salvation **t.** as a lamp that

Jer	1:13	and the face t. is toward the north.
Jer	1:15	against all the walls t. round about,
Jer	1:18	the princes t., against the priests t.,
Jer	2:7	to eat the fruit t. and the goodness t.;
Jer	4:26	and all the cities t. were broken down
Jer	5:1	know, and seek in the broad places t.
Jer	5:22	though the waves t. toss themselves,
Jer	5:31	and what will ye do in the end t.?
Jer	6:24	We have heard the fame t.: our hands
Jer	11:19	us destroy the tree with the fruit t.,
Jer	14:2	mourneth, and the gates t. languish;
Jer	14:8	the saviour t. in time of trouble, why
Jer	17:27	then will I kindle a fire in the gates t.,
Jer	19:8	and hiss because of all the plagues t.
Jer	19:12	the Lord, and to the inhabitants t.,
Jer	20:5	of this city, and all the labours t.,
Jer	20:5	and all the precious things t., and all
Jer	21:14	I will kindle a fire in the forest t., and
Jer	23:14	and the inhabitants t. as Gomorrah.
Jer	25:9	and against the inhabitants t., and
Jer	25:18	and the kings t., and the princes t., to
Jer	26:15	this city, and upon the inhabitants t.
Jer	29:7	in the peace t. shall ye have peace.
Jer	30:18	shall remain after the manner t.
Jer	31:23	the land of Judah and in the cities t.
Jer	31:24	itself, and in all the cities t. together,
Jer	31:35	the sea when the waves t. roar;
Jer	33:2	Thus saith the Lord the maker t.,
Jer	33:12	and in all the cities t., shall be a
Jer	34:1	Jerusalem, against all the cities t.,
Jer	34:18	twain, and passed between the parts t.,
Jer	46:8	destroy the city and the inhabitants t.
Jer	46:22	voice t. shall go like a serpent; for
Jer	48:9	the cities t. shall be desolate, without
Jer	48:38	of Moab, and in the streets t.:
Jer	49:13	the cities t. shall be perpetual wastes.
Jer	49:17	and shall hiss at all the plagues t.
Jer	49:18	Gomorrah and the neighbour cities t.,
Jer	49:21	the noise t. was heard in the Red sea.
Jer	49:32	bring their calamity from all sides t.,
Jer	50:29	it round about; let none t. escape:
Jer	50:40	Gomorrah and the neighbour cities t.,
Jer	51:28	the captains t., and all the rulers t.,
Jer	51:42	with the multitude of the waves t.
Jer	52:21	and the thickness t. was four fingers:
La	2:2	polluted the kingdom and the princes t.
La	4:11	it hath devoured the foundations t.
Eze	1:4	and out of the midst t. as the colour of
Eze	1:5	out of the midst t. came the likeness
Eze	4:9	in one vessel, and make thee bread t.,
Eze	4:9	and ninety days shalt thou eat t.
Eze	5:3	shalt also take t. a few in number,
Eze	5:4	for t. shall a fire come forth into all the
Eze	7:12	for wrath is upon all the multitude t.
Eze	7:13	is touching the whole multitude t.,
Eze	7:14	my wrath is upon all the multitude t.
Eze	9:4	that be done in the midst t.
Eze	10:7	and took t., and put it into the hands
Eze	11:6	have filled the streets t. with the slain.
Eze	11:9	I will bring you out of the midst t., and
Eze	11:11	shall ye be the flesh in the midst t.;
Eze	11:18	take away all the detestable things t.
Eze	11:18	all the abominations t. from thence.
Eze	13:14	the foundation t. shall be discovered,
Eze	13:14	ye shall be consumed in the midst t.
Eze	14:13	and will break the staff of the bread t.,
Eze	15:3	Shall wood be taken t. to do any work?
Eze	17:6	him, and the roots t. were under him:
Eze	17:9	shall he not pull up the roots t.
Eze	17:9	and cut off the fruit t., that it wither?
Eze	17:9	people to pluck it up by the roots t.
Eze	17:12	taken the king t., and the princes t.,
Eze	17:23	in the shadow of the branches t. shall
Eze	19:7	land was desolate, and the fulness t.,
Eze	20:29	the name t. is called Bamah unto this
Eze	22:21	and ye shall be melted in the midst t.
Eze	22:22	so shall ye be melted in the midst t.;
Eze	22:25	of her prophets in the midst t.,
Eze	22:25	made her many widows in the midst t.
Eze	22:27	Her princes in the midst t. are like
Eze	23:34	and thou shalt break the sherds t., and
Eze	24:4	Gather the pieces t. into it, even every
Eze	24:11	Then set it empty upon the coals t.,
Eze	27:9	wise men t. were in thee thy calkers:
Eze	31:15	and I restrained the floods t., and the
Eze	32:7	heaven, and made the stars t. dark;
Eze	32:12	all the multitude t. shall be destroyed.
Eze	32:13	I will destroy also all the beasts t.
Eze	38:13	Tarshish, with all the young lions t.,
Eze	40:6	the east, and went up the stairs t.,
Eze	40:9	and the posts t., two cubits; and the
Eze	40:20	the length t., and the breadth t.
Eze	40:21	little chambers t. were three on this
Eze	40:21	the posts t. and the arches t. were after
Eze	40:21	the length t. was fifty cubits, and the
Eze	40:22	and the arches t. were before them.
Eze	40:24	measured the posts t. and the arches t.
Eze	40:25	in it and in the arches t. round about,
Eze	40:26	it, and the arches t. were before them:
Eze	40:26	on that side, upon the posts t.
Eze	40:29	the little chambers t., and the posts t.,
Eze	40:29	and the arches t., according to these
Eze	40:29	in it and in the arches t. round about:
Eze	40:31	arches t. were toward the utter court;
Eze	40:31	and palm trees were upon the posts t.:
Eze	40:33	the little chambers t., and the posts t.,
Eze	40:33	and the arches t., were according to
Eze	40:33	and in the arches t. round about:
Eze	40:34	the arches t. were toward the outward
Eze	40:34	and the palm trees were upon the posts t.,
Eze	40:36	The little chambers t., the posts t.,
Eze	40:36	and the arches t., and the windows
Eze	40:37	posts t. were toward the utter court;
Eze	40:37	and palm trees were upon the posts t.,
Eze	40:38	the entries t. were by the posts of the
Eze	41:2	and he measured the length t., forty
Eze	41:4	he measured the length t., twenty
Eze	41:12	about, and the length t. ninety cubits.
Eze	41:13	and the building, with the walls t.,
Eze	41:15	and the galleries t. on the one side and
Eze	41:22	high, and the length t. two cubits;
Eze	41:22	and the corners t., and the length t.,
Eze	41:22	and the walls t., were of wood:
Eze	42:7	chambers, the length t. was fifty cubits.
Eze	43:11	form of the house, and the fashion t.,
Eze	43:11	and the goings out t.,
Eze	43:11	and the comings in t.,
Eze	43:11	and all the forms t.,
Eze	43:11	and all the ordinances t.,
Eze	43:11	and all the forms t.,
Eze	43:11	and all the laws t.: and write it in
Eze	43:11	that they may keep the whole form t.,
Eze	43:11	and all the ordinances t., and do them.
Eze	43:12	the whole limit t. round about shall
Eze	43:13	the breadth a cubit, and the border t.
Eze	43:13	by the edge t. round about shall be a
Eze	43:16	broad, square in the four squares t.
Eze	43:17	fourteen broad in the four squares t.;
Eze	43:17	the bottom t. shall be a cubit about;
Eze	43:20	And thou shalt take of the blood t., and
Eze	44:5	house of the Lord, and all the laws t.;
Eze	44:14	of the house, for all the service t.,
Eze	45:1	This shall be holy in all the borders t.
Eze	45:2	cubits round about for the suburbs t.
Eze	45:11	measure t. shall be after the homer.
Eze	46:8	and he shall go forth by the way t.
Eze	46:16	the inheritance t. shall be his sons';
Eze	47:11	But the miry places t., and
Eze	47:11	the marishes t. shall not be healed;
Eze	47:12	And by the river upon the bank t.,
Eze	47:12	neither shall the fruit t. be consumed:
Eze	47:12	and the fruit t. shall be for meat,
Eze	47:12	and the leaf t. for medicine.
Eze	48:10	sanctuary...shall be in the midst t.
Eze	48:15	and the city shall be in the midst t.
Eze	48:16	And these shall be the measures t.:
Eze	48:18	and the increase t. shall be for food
Eze	48:21	sanctuary...shall be in the midst t.
Da	1:5	at the end t. they might stand before
Da	2:5	the dream, with the interpretation t.,
Da	2:6	the dream, and the interpretation t.,
Da	2:6	the dream, and the interpretation t.
Da	2:9	ye can shew me the interpretation t.
Da	2:26	I have seen, and the interpretation t.?
Da	2:31	thee; and the form t. was terrible.
Da	2:36	and we will tell the interpretation t.
Da	2:45	certain, and the interpretation t. sure.
Da	3:1	cubits, and the breadth t. six cubits:
Da	4:7	known unto me the interpretation t.
Da	4:9	I have seen, and the interpretation t.
Da	4:10	the earth, and the height t. was great.
Da	4:11	and the height t. reached unto heaven.
Da	4:11	the sight t. to the end of all the earth;
Da	4:12	The leaves t. were fair, and the
Da	4:12	and the fruit t. much, and in it was
Da	4:12	of the heaven dwelt in the boughs t.,
Da	4:18	declare the interpretation t.,
Da	4:19	or the interpretation t., trouble thee.
Da	4:19	the interpretation t. to thine enemies.
Da	4:20	and the sight t. to all the earth;
Da	4:21	and the fruit t. much, and in it was
Da	4:23	yet leave the stump of the roots t. in
Da	5:7	and shew me the interpretation t.,
Da	5:8	known to the king the interpretation t.
Da	5:15	known unto me the interpretation t.:
Da	5:16	known to me the interpretation t.,
Da	7:4	I beheld till the wings t. were plucked,
Da	9:26	and the end t. shall be with a flood,
Ho	2:9	and take away my corn in the time t.,
Ho	2:9	and my wine in the season t.,
Ho	4:13	elms, because the shadow t. is good:
Ho	8:14	and it shall devour the palaces t.
Ho	9:4	all that eat t. shall be polluted:
Ho	10:5	for the people t. shall mourn over it,
Ho	10:5	and the priests t. that rejoiced on it,
Ho	10:5	for the glory t., because it is departed
Ho	14:7	the scent t. shall be as the wine of
Joe	1:7	away; the branches t. are made white.
Am	1:3,6	not turn away the punishment t.;
Am	1:7	which shall devour the palaces t.
Am	1:9	will not turn away the punishment t.;
Am	1:10	which shall devour the palaces t.
Am	1:11,	13 not turn away the punishment t.;
Am	1:14	and it shall devour the palaces t., with
Am	2:1	will not turn away the punishment t.;
Am	2:3	will cut off the judge from the midst t.,
Am	2:3	will slay all the princes t. with him,
Am	2:4,	6 not turn away the punishment t.;
Am	3:9	the great tumults in the midst t.,
Am	3:9	and the oppressed in the midst t.
Am	8:10	son, and the end t. as a bitter day.
Am	9:11	is fallen, and close up the breaches t.;
Am	9:14	plant vineyards, and drink the wine t.;
Jon	1:3	so he paid the fare t., and went down
Mic	1:6	pour down the stones t. into the valley,
Mic	1:6	and I will discover the foundations t.
Mic	1:7	the graven images t. shall be beaten
Mic	1:7	and all the hires t. shall be burned
Mic	1:7	and all the idols t. will I lay desolate:
Mic	3:11	The heads t. judge for reward,
Mic	3:11	and the priests t. teach for hire,
Mic	3:11	and the prophets t. divine for money:
Mic	5:6	the land of Nimrod in the entrances t.
Mic	6:12	For the rich men t. are full of violence,
Mic	6:12	the inhabitants t. have spoken lies,
Mic	6:16	and the inhabitants t. an hissing:
Na	1:8	will make an utter end of the place t.,
Na	2:5	they shall make haste to the wall t.,
Hab	2:18	that the maker t. hath graven it;
Zep	1:13	vineyards, but not drink the wine t.
Zep	3:5	The just Lord is in the midst t.; he
Zec	2:2	to see what is the breadth t.,
Zec	2:2	and what is the length t.
Zec	3:9	I will engrave the graving t., saith
Zec	4:2	lamps, which are upon the top t.
Zec	4:3	and the other upon the left side t.
Zec	4:7	forth the headstone t. with shoutings,
Zec	4:11	candlestick and upon the left side t.?
Zec	5:2	roll; the length t. is twenty cubits,
Zec	5:2	and the breadth t. ten cubits.
Zec	5:4	it with the timber t. and the stones t.
Zec	5:8	weight of lead upon the mouth t.
Zec	7:7	and the cities t. round about her, when
Zec	8:5	boys and girls playing in the streets t.
Zec	9:1	and Damascus shall be the rest t.
Zec	14:4	of Olives shall cleave in the midst t.
Mal	1:12	and the fruit t., even his meat, is
Mt	2:16	in Bethlehem, and in all the coasts t., ... 846
Mt	6:34	**unto the day is the evil t. ... 846**
Mt	12:36	**they shall give account t. in ... 4012,846**
Mt	13:32	**come and lodge in the branches t. ... 846**
Mt	13:44	**for joy t. goeth and selleth all that. 846**
Mt	14:13	and when the people had heard t., they
Mt	21:43	**a nation bringing forth the fruits t. 846**
Mt	22:7	**But when the king heard t., he was**
Mt	27:34	and when he had tasted t., he would
Mk	6:16	But when Herod heard t., he said, It is
Lu	19:33	owners t. said unto them, Why loose

Lu 21:20 **know that the desolation t. is nigh** *846*
Lu 22:16 **I will not any more eat t.,** *1538,846*
Joh 3:8 **thou hearest the sound t., but** *846*
Joh 4:12 the well, and drank **t.** himself, *1538,846*
Joh 6:50 **a man may eat t., and not die** *1538,846*
Joh 7:7 **of it, that the works t. are evil** *3012,846*
Ac 15:16 I will build again the ruins **t.**, and I *846*
Ro 6:12 that ye should obey it in the lusts **t.** *846*
Ro 13:14 for the flesh, to fulfil the lusts **t.**
1Co 9:7 and eateth not of the fruit **t.**? *846*
1Co 9:23 that I might be partaker **t.** with you. *846*
1Co 10:26 earth is the Lord's, and the fulness **t.** *846*
1Co 10:28 earth is the Lord's, and the fulness **t.** 846
2Ti 3:5 godliness, but denying the power **t.** *846*
Heb 7:18 weakness and unprofitableness **t.** *846*
Jas 1:11 the grass, and the flower **t.** falleth, *846*
1Pe 1:24 and the flower **t.** falleth away: *846*
1Pe 5:2 is among you, taking the oversight **t.**,
1Jo 2:17 world passeth away, and the lust **t.** *846*
Re 5:2 the book, and to loose the seals **t.**? *846*
Re 5:5 book, and to loose the seven seals **t.** *846*
Re 5:9 the book, and to open the seals **t.** *846*
Re 16:12 water **t.** was dried up, that the way *846*
Re 16:21 for the plague **t.** was exceeding great. *846*
Re 21:15 city, and the gates **t.**, and the wall **t.** *846*
Re 21:17 he measured the wall **t.**, an hundred *846*
Re 21:23 lighten it, and the Lamb is the light **t.** *846*

THEREON See also THEREUPON.
Ge 35:14 and he poured a drink offering **t.**, 5921
Ge 35:14 and he poured oil **t.** 5921
Ex 17:12 and put it under him, and he sat **t.**; 5921
Ex 20:24 shalt sacrifice **t.** thy burnt offerings, 5921
Ex 20:26 thy nakedness be not discovered **t.** 5921
Ex 30:7 Aaron shall burn **t.** sweet incense 5921
Ex 30:9 Ye shall offer no strange incense **t.**, 5921
Ex 30:9 shall ye pour drink offering **t.** 5921
Ex 40:27 And he burnt sweet incense **t.**; as 5921
Ex 40:35 because the cloud abode **t.**, and the 5921
Le 2:1 oil upon it, and put frankincense **t.** 5921
Le 2:6 part it in pieces, and pour oil **t.** 5921
Le 2:15 put oil upon it, lay frankincense **t.** 5921
Le 5:11 shall he put any frankincense **t.** 5921
Le 6:12 he shall burn **t.** the fat of the peace 5921
Le 10:1 put fire therein, and put incense **t.**, 5921
Le 11:38 and any part of their carcase fall **t.**, 5921
Nu 4:6 put **t.** the covering of badgers' skins, 5921
Nu 4:7 put **t.** the dishes, and the spoons, 5921
Nu 4:7 and the continual bread shall be **t.**: 5921
Nu 4:13 altar, and spread a purple cloth **t.**: 5921
Nu 5:15 oil upon it, nor put frankincense **t.**; 5921
Nu 9:22 upon the tabernacle, remaining **t.**, 5921
Nu 16:18 put fire in them, and laid incense **t.**, 5921
De 27:6 thou shalt offer burnt offerings **t.** 5921
Jos 8:29 and raise **t.** a great heap of stones, 5921
Jos 8:31 they offered **t.** burnt offerings unto 5921
Jos 22:23 or if to offer **t.** burnt offering or 5921
Jos 22:23 or if to offer peace offerings **t.**, let 5921
2Sa 17:10 mouth, and spread ground corn **t.**; 5921
2Sa 19:26 saddle me an ass, that I may ride **t.**, 5921
1Ki 6:35 carved **t.** cherubims and palm trees
1Ki 13:13 him the ass: and he rode **t.**, 5921
2Ki 16:12 to the altar, and offered **t.** 5921
1Ch 12:17 the God of our fathers look **t.**, and
1Ch 15:15 their shoulders with the staves **t.**, 5921
2Ch 3:5 and set **t.** palm trees and chains 5921
2Ch 3:14 linen, and wrought cherubims **t.** 5921
2Ch 33:16 and sacrificed **t.** peace offerings and 5921
Ezr 3:2 to offer burnt offerings **t.**, as it is 5921
Ezr 3:3 they offered burnt offerings **t.** unto 5921
Ezr 6:11 being set up, let him be hanged **t.**; 5921
Es 5:14 that Mordecai may be hanged **t.** 5921
Es 7:9 Then the king said, Hang him **t.** 5921
Isa 30:12 and perverseness, and stay **t.** 5921
Isa 35:9 nor any ravenous beast shall go up **t.**
Eze 15:3 a pin of it to hang any vessel **t.**? 5921
Eze 40:39 to slay **t.** the burnt offering and the 5921
Eze 43:18 make it, to offer burnt offerings **t.**, 5921
Eze 43:18 and to sprinkle blood **t.** 5921
Zec 4:2 and his seven lamps **t.**, and seven 5921
Mt 21:7 clothes, and they set him **t.** *1883,846*
Mt 21:19 found nothing **t.**, but leaves *1722,846*
Mt 23:20 **by it, and by all things t.** *1883,846*
Mt 23:22 **God, and by him that sitteth t.** *1883,846*
Mk 11:13 he might find any thing **t.** *1722,846*
Mk 14:72 And when he thought **t.**, he wept *1911*
Lu 13:6 **he came and sought fruit t.,** *1722,846*
Lu 19:35 upon the colt, and they set Jesus **t.** *1913*
Joh 12:14 had found a young ass, sat **t.**; *1909,846*
Joh 21:9 coals there, and fish laid **t.**, and *1945*
1Co 3:10 foundation, and another buildeth **t.** *2026*
Re 5:3 to open the book, neither to look **t.** *846*
Re 5:4 to read the book, neither to look **t.** *846*
Re 6:4 was given to him that sat **t.** *1909,846*
Re 21:12 and names written **t.**, which are the *1924*

THEREOUT
Le 2:2 he shall take **t.** his handful of the 8033
Jg 15:19 in the jaw, and there came water **t.**;

THERETO
Ex 25:24 make **t.** a crown of gold round about
Ex 29:41 shalt do **t.** according to the meat
Ex 30:38 shall make like unto that, to smell **t.**,
Le 5:16 and shall add the fifth part **t.**, 5921
Le 6:5 and shall add the fifth part more **t.**, 5921
Le 18:23 stand before a beast to lie down **t.**
Le 20:16 unto any beast, and lie down **t.**,
Le 27:27 and shall add a fifth part of it **t.** 5921
Le 27:31 shall add **t.** the fifth part thereof. 5921
Nu 3:36 vessels thereof, and all that serveth **t.**,
Nu 19:17 running water shall be put **t.** in a 5921
De 12:32 thou shalt not add **t.**, nor diminish 5921
Jg 11:17 king of Edom would not hearken **t.**
1Ch 22:14 prepared; and thou mayest add **t.** 5921
2Ch 10:14 your yoke heavy, but I will add **t.** 5921
2Ch 21:11 fornication, and compelled Judah **t.**
Ps 119:9 taking heed **t.** according to thy word.
Isa 44:15 a graven image, and falleth down **t.**
Mk 14:70 a Galilaean, and thy speech agreeth **t.**
Ga 3:15 no man disannulleth, or addeth **t.** *1928*

THEREUNTO
Ex 32:8 worshipped it, and have sacrificed **t.**,
Ex 36:36 he made **t.** four pillars of shittim
Ex 37:11 made **t.** a crown of gold round about
Ex 37:12 he made **t.** a border of an handbreadth
De 1:7 and unto all the places nigh **t.**, in the
Eph 6:18 and watching **t.** with all *1519,846,5124*
1Th 3:3 that we are appointed **t.** *1519,5124*
Heb 10:1 make the comers **t.** perfect. *4334*
1Pe 3:9 knowing that ye are **t.** called, *1519,5124*

THEREUPON
Ex 31:7 and the mercy seat that is **t.**,
Eze 16:16 colours, and playedst the harlot **t.**
Zep 2:7 the house of Judah; they shall feed **t.**
1Co 3:10 man take heed how he buildeth **t.** *2026*
1Co 3:14 work abide which he hath built **t.**, *2026*

THEREWITH
Ex 22:6 corn, or the field, be consumed **t.**;
Ex 30:26 the tabernacle of the congregation **t.**,
Ex 38:30 **t.** he made the sockets to the door
Le 7:7 that maketh atonement **t.** shall have it
Le 8:7 of the ephod, and bound it unto him **t.**
Le 15:32 goeth from him, and is defiled **t.**;
Le 18:23 lie with any beast to defile thyself **t.**
Le 22:8 he shall not eat to defile himself **t.**
De 16:3 shalt thou eat unleavened bread **t.** 5921
De 23:13 thou shalt dig **t.**, and shalt turn back
Jg 15:15 took it, and slew a thousand men **t.**
Jg 16:12 took new ropes, and bound him **t.**,
1Sa 12:3 any bribe to blind mine eyes **t.**? and
1Sa 17:51 and slew him, and cut off his head **t.**
1Sa 31:4 thy sword, and thrust me through **t.**;
2Sa 20:10 so he smote him **t.** in the fifth rib, and
2Ki 5:6 I have **t.** sent Naaman my servant to
2Ki 12:14 and repaired **t.** the house of the Lord
1Ch 10:4 thy sword, and thrust me through **t.**;
1Ch 23:5 which I made, said David, to praise **t.**
2Ch 16:6 and he built **t.** Geba and Mizpah.
Pr 15:16 than great treasure and trouble **t.**
Pr 15:17 love is, than a stalled ox and hatred **t.**
Pr 17:1 is a dry morsel, and quietness **t.**,
Pr 25:16 thee, lest thou be filled **t.**, and vomit it.
Ec 1:13 to the sons of man to be exercised **t.**
Ec 2:6 pools of water, to water **t.** the wood
Ec 10:9 removeth stones shall be hurt **t.**;
Isa 10:15 itself against him that heweth **t.**?
Eze 4:15 thou shalt prepare thy bread **t.** 5921
Joe 2:19 and oil, and ye shall be satisfied **t.** 854
Php 4:11 whatsoever state I am, **t.** to be content.
1Ti 6:8 and raiment let us be **t.** content *5125*
Jas 3:9 **T.** bless we God, even the *1722,846*
Jas 3:9 **t.** curse we men, which are *1722,846*
3Jo 10 not content **t.**, neither doth *1909,5125*

THESE
Ge 2:4 **T.** are the generations of the 428
Ge 6:9 **T.** are the generations of Noah: 428
Ge 9:19 **T.** are three sons of Noah: and of 428
Ge 10:1 **t.** are the generations of the sons 428
Ge 10:5 By **t.** were the isles of the Gentiles 428
Ge 10:20 **T.** are the sons of Ham, after their 428
Ge 10:29 all **t.** were the sons of Joktan. 428
Ge 10:31 **T.** are the sons of Shem, after their 428
Ge 10:32 **T.** are the families of the sons of 428
Ge 10:32 by **t.** were the nations divided in 428
Ge 11:10 **T.** are the generations of Shem: 428
Ge 11:27 **t.** are the generations of Terah: 428
Ge 14:2 That **t.** made war with Bera king
Ge 14:3 All **t.** were joined together in the 428
Ge 14:13 **t.** were confederate with Abram. 1992
Ge 15:1 After **t.** things the word of the 428
Ge 15:10 he took unto him all **t.**, and divided 428
Ge 19:8 only unto **t.** men do nothing; for 428
Ge 20:8 and told all **t.** things in their ears. 428
Ge 21:29 What mean **t.** seven ewe lambs
Ge 21:30 **t.** seven ewe lambs shalt thou take
Ge 22:1 after **t.** things, that God did tempt 428
Ge 22:20 pass after **t.** things, that it was told 428
Ge 22:23 **t.** eight Milcah did bear to Nahor, 428
Ge 23:1 **t.** were the years of the life of Sarah.
Ge 24:28 told. . .her mother's house **t.** things.
Ge 25:4 All **t.** were the children of Keturah. 428
Ge 25:7 And **t.** are the days of the years of 428
Ge 25:12 Now **t.** are the generations of 428
Ge 25:13 And **t.** are the names of the sons of 428
Ge 25:16 **T.** are the sons of Ishmael, and 428
Ge 25:16 **t.** are their names, by their towns, 428
Ge 25:17 And **t.** are the years of the life of 428
Ge 25:19 And **t.** are the generations of Isaac, 428
Ge 26:3 thy seed, I will give all **t.** countries, 411
Ge 26:4 give unto thy seed all **t.** countries; 411
Ge 27:36 hath supplanted me **t.** two times: 2088
Ge 27:42 **t.** words of Esau her elder son
Ge 27:46 as **t.** which are of the daughters 428
Ge 29:13 And he told Laban all **t.** things. 428
Ge 31:43 **T.** daughters are my daughters,
Ge 31:43 and **t.** children are my children,
Ge 31:43 and **t.** cattle are my cattle, and all that
Ge 31:43 I do this day unto **t.** my daughters. 428
Ge 32:17 thou? and whose are **t.** before thee? 428
Ge 33:8 **T.** are to find grace in the sight of my
Ge 34:21 **T.** men are peaceable with us; 428
Ge 35:26 **t.** are the sons of Jacob, which were 428
Ge 36:1 Now **t.** are the generations of Esau, 428
Ge 36:5 **t.** are the sons of Esau, which were 428
Ge 36:9 And **t.** are the generations of Esau 428
Ge 36:10 **T.** are the names of Esau's sons; 428
Ge 36:12 **t.** were the sons of Adah Esau's 428
Ge 36:13 **t.** are the sons of Reuel; Nahath, 428
Ge 36:13 **t.** were the sons of Bashemath 428
Ge 36:14 **t.** were the sons of Aholibamah, the 428
Ge 36:15 **T.** were the dukes of the sons of 428
Ge 36:16 **t.** are the dukes that came of 428
Ge 36:16 of Edom; **t.** were the sons of Adah. 428
Ge 36:17 **t.** are the sons of Reuel Esau's son; 428
Ge 36:17 **t.** are the dukes that came of Reuel 428
Ge 36:17 **t.** are the sons of Bashemath Esau's 428
Ge 36:18 **t.** are the sons of Aholibamah. 428
Ge 36:18 **t.** were the dukes that came of 428
Ge 36:19 **T.** are the sons of Esau, who is 428
Ge 36:19 Edom, and **t.** are their dukes. 428
Ge 36:20 **T.** are the sons of Seir the Horite, 428
Ge 36:21 **t.** are the dukes of the Horites, the 428
Ge 36:23 And the children of Shobal were **t.**; 428
Ge 36:24 **t.** are the children of Zibeon; both 428
Ge 36:25 And the children of Anah were **t.**; 428
Ge 36:26 And **t.** are the children of Dishon; 428
Ge 36:27 The children of Ezer are **t.**; Bilhan, 428
Ge 36:28 The children of Dishan are **t.**; Uz, 428
Ge 36:29 **T.** are the dukes that came of the 428
Ge 36:30 **T.** are the dukes that came of Hori, 428
Ge 36:31 **t.** are the kings that reigned in the 428
Ge 36:40 **t.** are the names of the dukes that 428
Ge 36:43 **t.** be the dukes of Edom, according 428
Ge 37:2 **T.** are the generations of Jacob. 428
Ge 38:25 man, whose **t.** are, am I with child: 428
Ge 38:25 whose are **t.**, the signet, and 428
Ge 39:7 it came to pass after **t.** things, that 428

Ge 39:17 unto him according to **t.** words, 428
Ge 40:1 And it came to pass after **t.** things, 428
Ge 42:36 away: all **t.** things are against me.
Ge 43:7 according to the tenor of **t.** words: 428
Ge 43:16 Bring **t.** men home, and slay, and
Ge 43:16 for **t.** men shall dine with me at noon.
Ge 44:6 he spake unto them **t.** same words. 411
Ge 44:7 Wherefore saith my lord **t.** words? 428
Ge 45:6 **t.** two years hath the famine been 2088
Ge 46:8 **t.** are the names of the children of 428
Ge 46:15 **T.** be the sons of Leah, which she 428
Ge 46:18 **T.** are the sons of Zilpah, whom 428
Ge 46:18 **t.** she bare unto Jacob, even 428
Ge 46:22 **T.** are the sons of Rachel, which 428
Ge 46:25 **T.** are the sons of Bilhah, which 428
Ge 46:25 and she bare **t.** unto Jacob: all the 428
Ge 48:1 And it came to pass after **t.** things, 428
Ge 48:8 Joseph's sons, and said, Who are **t.**? 428
Ge 49:28 All **t.** are the twelve tribes of Israel: 428
Ex 1:1 **t.** are the names of the children of 428
Ex 4:9 will not believe also **t.** two signs, 428
Ex 6:14 **T.** be the heads of their father's 428
Ex 6:14 Carmi: **t.** be the families of Reuben. 428
Ex 6:15 **t.** are the families of Simeon. 428
Ex 6:16 **t.** are the names of the sons of Levi 428
Ex 6:19 **t.** are the families of Levi according 428
Ex 6:24 **t.** are the families of the Korhites. 428
Ex 6:25 **t.** are the heads...of the Levites 428
Ex 6:26 **T.** are that Aaron and Moses, to 1931
Ex 6:27 **t.** are that Moses and Aaron. 1931
Ex 6:27 **T.** are they which spake to 1992
Ex 10:1 might shew **t.** my signs before him: 428
Ex 11:8 all **t.** thy servants shall come down 428
Ex 11:10 Moses and Aaron did all **t.** wonders 428
Ex 14:20 them, but it gave light by night to **t.**:
Ex 15:26 will put none of **t.** diseases upon thee,
Ex 19:6 **T.** are the words which thou shalt 428
Ex 19:7 laid before their faces all **t.** words 428
Ex 20:1 And God spake all **t.** words, saying, 428
Ex 21:1 Now **t.** are the judgments which 428
Ex 21:11 if he do not **t.** three unto her, then 428
Ex 24:8 with you concerning all **t.** words. 428
Ex 25:39 shall he make it, with all **t.** vessels. 428
Ex 28:4 **t.** are the garments which they shall 428
Ex 30:34 **t.** sweet spices with...frankincense:
Ex 32:4,8 **T.** be thy gods, O Israel, which 428
Ex 33:4 the people heard **t.** evil tidings, they
Ex 34:1 I will write upon **t.** tables the words
Ex 34:27 unto Moses, Write thou **t.** words: 428
Ex 34:27 for after the tenor of **t.** words I have 428
Ex 35:1 **T.** are the words which the Lord 428
Le 2:8 is made of **t.** things unto the Lord: 428
Le 5:4 then he shall be guilty in one of **t.** 428
Le 5:5 shall be guilty in one of **t.** things, 428
Le 5:13 sin that he hath sinned in one of **t.**, 428
Le 5:17 commit any of **t.** things which are
Le 6:3 any of all **t.** that a man doeth, sinning
Le 11:2 **T.** are the beasts which ye shall 2063
Le 11:4 **t.** shall ye not eat of them that 2088
Le 11:9 **T.** shall ye eat of all that are in 2088
Le 11:13 **t.** are they which ye shall have in 428
Le 11:21 Yet **t.** may ye eat of every 2088
Le 11:22 Even **t.** of them ye may eat; the 428
Le 11:24 And for **t.** ye shall be unclean: 428
Le 11:29 **T.** also shall be unclean unto you 2088
Le 11:31 **T.** are unclean to you among all 2088
Le 16:4 **t.** are holy garments; therefore 1992
Le 18:24 ye yourselves in any of **t.** things: 428
Le 18:24 for in all **t.** the nations are defiled 428
Le 18:26 not commit any of **t.** abominations; 428
Le 18:27 all **t.** abominations have the men 411
Le 18:29 commit any of **t.** abominations, 428
Le 18:30 any one of **t.** abominable customs,
Le 20:23 for they committed all **t.** things, 428
Le 21:14 or an harlot, **t.** shall he not take: 428
Le 22:22 ye shall not offer **t.** unto the Lord, 428
Le 22:25 the bread of your God of any of **t.**; 428
Le 23:2 convocations, even **t.** are my feasts. 428
Le 23:4, 37 **T.** are the feasts of the Lord, 428
Le 25:54 he be not redeemed in **t.** years, then 428
Le 26:14 will not do all **t.** commandments; 428
Le 26:23 not be reformed by me by **t.** things, 428
Le 26:46 **T.** are the statutes and judgments 428
Le 27:34 **T.** are the commandments, which 428
Nu 1:5 **t.** are the names of the men that 428
Nu 1:16 **T.** were the renowned of the 428
Nu 1:17 And Moses and Aaron took **t.** men 428
Nu 1:44 **T.** are those that were numbered, 428
Nu 2:9 their armies. **T.** shall first set forth.
Nu 2:32 **T.** are those which were numbered 428
Nu 3:1 **T.** also are the generations of 428
Nu 3:2 **t.** are the names of the sons of 428
Nu 3:3 **T.** are the names of the sons of 428
Nu 3:17 **t.** were the sons of Levi by their 428
Nu 3:18 **t.** are the names of the sons of 428
Nu 3:20 **T.** are the families of the Levites 428
Nu 3:21 **t.** are the families of...Gershonites. 428
Nu 3:27 **t.** are the families of...Kohathites. 428
Nu 3:33 **t.** are the families of Merari. 428
Nu 3:35 **t.** shall pitch on the side of the
Nu 4:15 **T.** things are the burden of the 428
Nu 4:37 **T.** were they that were numbered 428
Nu 4:41 **T.** are they that were numbered of 428
Nu 4:45 **T.** be those that were numbered of 428
Nu 5:23 priest shall write **t.** curses in a book, 428
Nu 13:4 **t.** were their names: of the tribe of 428
Nu 13:16 **T.** are the names of the men which 428
Nu 14:22 tempted me now **t.** ten times, and 2088
Nu 14:39 Moses told **t.** sayings unto all the 428
Nu 15:13 shall do **t.** things after this manner, 428
Nu 15:22 not observed all **t.** commandments, 428
Nu 16:14 thou put out the eyes of **t.** men? 1992
Nu 16:26 from the tents of **t.** wicked men, 428
Nu 16:28 hath sent me to do all **t.** works; 428
Nu 16:29 If **t.** men die the common death of 428
Nu 16:30 that **t.** men have provoked the Lord.
Nu 16:31 an end of speaking all **t.** words, 428
Nu 16:38 censers of **t.** sinners against their 428
Nu 21:25 And Israel took all **t.** cities: and 428
Nu 22:9 said, What men are **t.** with thee? 428
Nu 22:28 hast smitten me **t.** three times? 2088
Nu 22:32 smitten thine ass **t.** three times? 2088
Nu 22:33 and turned from me **t.** three times: 2088
Nu 24:10 blessed them **t.** three times. 2088
Nu 26:7, 14, 18, **T.** are the families of the 428
Nu 26:22 **T.** are the families of Judah 428
Nu 26:25 **T.** are the families of Issachar 428
Nu 26:27 **T.** are the families of the 428
Nu 26:30 **T.** are the sons of Gilead: of Jeezer, 428
Nu 26:34 **T.** are the families of Manasseh, 428
Nu 26:35 **T.** are the sons of Ephraim after 428
Nu 26:36 And **t.** are the sons of Shuthelah: 428
Nu 26:37 **T.** are the families of the sons of 428
Nu 26:37 **T.** are the sons of Joseph after their 428
Nu 26:41 **T.** are the sons of Benjamin after 428
Nu 26:42 **T.** are the sons of Dan after their 428
Nu 26:42 **T.** are the families of Dan after 428
Nu 26:47 **T.** are the families of the sons of 428
Nu 26:50 **T.** are the families of Naphtali 428
Nu 26:51 **T.** were the numbered of the 428
Nu 26:53 Unto **t.** the land shall be divided for 428
Nu 26:57 **t.** are they that were numbered of 428
Nu 26:58 **T.** are the families of the Levites: 428
Nu 26:63 **T.** are they that were numbered by 428
Nu 26:64 But among **t.** there was not a man 428
Nu 27:1 **t.** are the names of his daughters' 428
Nu 28:23 offer **t.** beside the burnt offering 428
Nu 29:39 **T.** things ye shall do unto the Lord 428
Nu 30:16 **T.** are the statutes, which the Lord 428
Nu 31:16 **t.** caused the children of Israel, 2007
Nu 33:1 **T.** are the journeys of the children 428
Nu 33:2 **t.** are their journeys according to 428
Nu 34:17 **T.** are the names of the men which 428
Nu 34:19 And the names of the men are **t.**: Of 428
Nu 34:29 **T.** are they whom the Lord 428
Nu 35:13 **t.** cities which ye shall give six cities
Nu 35:15 **T.** six cities shall be a refuge, both 428
Nu 35:24 blood according to **t.** judgments: 428
Nu 35:29 So **t.** things shall be for a statute of 428
Nu 36:13 **T.** are the commandments and the 428
De 1:1 **T.** be the words which Moses spake 428
De 1:35 shall not one of **t.** men of this evil 428
De 2:7 **t.** forty years the Lord thy God 2088
De 3:5 **t.** cities were fenced with high 428
De 3:21 God hath done unto **t.** two kings: 428
De 4:6 which shall hear all **t.** statutes, and 428
De 4:30 all **t.** things are come upon thee, 428
De 4:42 fleeing unto one of **t.** cities he might 411
De 4:45 **T.** are the testimonies, and the 428
De 5:22 **T.** words the Lord spake unto all 428
De 6:1 Now **t.** are the commandments, 2063
De 6:6 And **t.** words, which I command thee 428
De 6:24 commanded us to do all **t.** statutes, 428
De 6:25 to do all **t.** commandments before 2063
De 7:12 if ye hearken to **t.** judgments, and 428
De 7:17 heart, **T.** nations are more than I; 428
De 8:2 thy God led thee **t.** forty years in 2088
De 8:4 did thy foot swell, **t.** forty years. 2088
De 9:4,5 for the wickedness of **t.** nations 428
De 10:21 for thee **t.** great and terrible things, 428
De 11:18 ye lay up **t.** my words in your heart 438
De 11:22 keep all **t.** commandments which 2063
De 11:23 the Lord drive out all **t.** nations 428
De 12:1 **T.** are the statutes and judgments, 428
De 12:28 hear all **t.** words which I command 428
De 12:30 How did **t.** nations serve their gods? 428
De 14:4 **T.** are the beasts which ye shall 2063
De 14:7 **t.** ye shall not eat of them that 2088
De 14:9 **T.** ye shall eat of all that are in 2088
De 14:12 **t.** are they of which ye shall not eat: 2088
De 15:5 to do all **t.** commandments which 2063
De 16:12 shalt observe and do **t.** statutes 428
De 17:19 the words of this law and **t.** statutes, 428
De 18:12 that do **t.** things are an abomination 428
De 18:12 because of **t.** abominations the 428
De 18:14 For **t.** nations, which thou shalt 428
De 19:9 keep all **t.** commandments to do 2063
De 19:9 cities more for thee, beside **t.** three:
De 19:11 die, and fleeth into one of **t.** cities: 411
De 20:15 not of the cities of **t.** nations 428,2007
De 20:16 But of the cities of **t.** people, which 428
De 22:17 **t.** are the tokens of my daughter's 428
De 23:18 even both **t.** are abomination unto the
De 25:3 beat him above **t.** with many stripes,
De 26:16 commanded thee to do **t.** statutes 428
De 27:4 that ye shall set up **t.** stones, which I 428
De 27:12 **T.** shall stand upon mount Gerizim 428
De 27:13 **t.** shall stand upon mount Ebal to 428
De 28:2 all **t.** blessings shall come on thee, 428
De 28:15, 45 all **t.** curses shall come upon thee, 428
De 28:65 among **t.** nations shalt thou find no 1992
De 29:1 **T.** are the words of the covenant, 428
De 29:18 and serve the gods of **t.** nations; 1992
De 30:1 all **t.** things are come upon thee, 428
De 30:7 all **t.** curses upon thine enemies, 428
De 31:1 and spake **t.** words unto all Israel. 428
De 31:3 destroy **t.** nations from before thee, 428
De 31:17 Are not **t.** evils come upon us, 428
De 31:28 I may speak **t.** words in their ears, 428
De 32:45 an end of speaking all **t.** words 428
Jos 2:11 And as soon as we heard **t.** things, our
Jos 4:6 saying, What mean ye by **t.** stones? 428
Jos 4:7 **t.** stones shall be for a memorial 428
Jos 4:21 come, saying, What mean **t.** stones? 428
Jos 9:13 **t.** bottles of wine, which we filled, 428
Jos 9:13 **t.** our garments and our shoes are 428
Jos 10:16 But **t.** five kings fled, and hid 428
Jos 10:24 your feet upon the necks of **t.** kings. 428
Jos 10:42 **t.** kings and their land did Joshua 428
Jos 11:5 when all **t.** kings were met together, 428
Jos 11:14 And all the spoil of **t.** cities, and the 428
Jos 12:1 Now **t.** are the kings of the land, 428
Jos 12:7 **t.** are the kings of the country which 428
Jos 13:12 **t.** did Moses smite, and cast them out.
Jos 13:32 **T.** are the countries which Moses 428
Jos 14:1 And **t.** are the countries which the 428
Jos 14:10 as he said, **t.** forty and five years, 2088
Jos 17:2 **t.** were the male children of 428
Jos 17:3 **t.** are the names of his daughters, 428
Jos 17:9 **t.** cities of Ephraim are among the 428
Jos 19:8 the villages...round about **t.** cities 428
Jos 19:16, 31,48 **t.** cities with their villages. 428
Jos 19:51 **T.** are the inheritances, which 428
Jos 20:9 **T.** were the cities appointed for all 428
Jos 21:3 the Lord, **t.** cities and their suburbs. 428
Jos 21:8 unto the Levites **t.** cities with their 428
Jos 21:9 **t.** cities which are here mentioned 428
Jos 21:42 **T.** cities were every one with their 428
Jos 21:42 about them: thus were all **t.** cities 428
Jos 22:3 not left your brethren **t.** many days 428
Jos 23:3 done unto all **t.** nations because of 428
Jos 23:4 you by lot **t.** nations that remain, 428
Jos 23:7 That ye come not among **t.** nations, 428
Jos 23:7 **t.** that remain among you; neither 428
Jos 23:12 unto the remnant of **t.** nations, 428
Jos 23:12 even **t.** that remain among you, and 428
Jos 23:13 no more drive out any of **t.** nations 428
Jos 24:26 Joshua wrote **t.** words in the book 428
Jos 24:29 And it came to pass after **t.** things, 428

Jg 2:4 the angel of the Lord spake **t.** words.... 428
Jg 3:1 Now **t.** are the nations which the......... 428
Jg 9:3 all the men of Shechem all **t.** words: 428
Jg 13:23 he have shewed us all **t.** things, ... 428
Jg 13:23 have told us such things as **t.**........... 2063
Jg 16:15 hast mocked me **t.** three times, ... 2088
Jg 18:14 that there is in **t.** houses an ephod,...... 428
Jg 18:18 And **t.** went into Micah's house, and..... 428
Jg 19:13 draw near to one of **t.** places to lodge.......
Jg 20:17 sword: all **t.** were men of war. 2088
Jg 20:25 men; all **t.** drew the sword................ 428
Jg 20:35 hundred men: all **t.** drew the sword. 428
Jg 20:44 men; all **t.** were men of valour. 428
Jg 20:46 sword; all **t.** were men of valour.......... 428
Ru 3:17 **T.** six measures of barley gave he 428
Ru 4:18 **t.** are the generations of Pharez: 428
1Sa 4:8 out of the hand of **t.** mighty Gods?....... 428
1Sa 4:8 **t.** are the Gods that smote the........... 428
1Sa 6:17 **t.** are the golden emerods which.......... 428
1Sa 10:7 when **t.** signs are come unto thee,....... 428
1Sa 14:6 the garrison of **t.** uncircumcised:.......... 428
1Sa 14:8 Behold, we will pass over unto **t.** men, ...
1Sa 14:49 names of his two daughters were **t.**; ....
1Sa 16:10 Jesse, The Lord hath not chosen **t.**...... 428
1Sa 17:17 **t.** ten loaves, and run to the camp...... 2088
1Sa 17:18 And carry **t.** ten cheeses unto the........ 428
1Sa 17:39 said unto Saul, I cannot go with **t.** 428
1Sa 18:26 his servants told David **t.** words, ... 428
1Sa 21:5 been kept from us about **t.** three days,......
1Sa 21:12 David laid up **t.** words in his heart, ... 428
1Sa 23:2 Shall I go and smite **t.** Philistines?........ 428
1Sa 24:7 stayed his servants with **t.** words, and ......
1Sa 24:16 made an end of speaking **t.** words........ 428
1Sa 25:37 his wife had told him **t.** things, that...... 428
1Sa 29:3 What do **t.** Hebrews here? 428
1Sa 29:3 been with me **t.** days, or **t.** years, ... 2088
1Sa 29:4 not be with the heads of **t.** men? 1992
1Sa 31:4 **t.** uncircumcised come and thrust......... 428
2Sa 3:5 **T.** were born to David in Hebron......... 428
2Sa 3:39 **t.** men the sons of Zeruiah be too........ 428
2Sa 5:14 **t.** be the names of those that were...... 428
2Sa 7:17 According to all **t.** words, and............ 428
2Sa 7:21 hast thou done all **t.** great things,....... 2063
2Sa 13:21 king David heard of all **t.** things, ... 428
2Sa 14:19 he put all **t.** words in the mouth of....... 428
2Sa 16:2 unto Ziba, What meanest thou by **t.**? 428
2Sa 21:22 **T.** four were born to the giant in......... 428
2Sa 23:1 Now **t.** be the last words of David. 428
2Sa 23:8 **T.** be the names of the mighty men 428
2Sa 23:17 **T.** things did **t.** three mighty men. 428
2Sa 23:22 **T.** things did Benaiah the son of.......... 428
2Sa 24:17 but **t.** sheep, what have they done?...... 428
2Sa 24:23 All **t.** things did Araunah, as a king, ...
1Ki 4:2 **t.** were the princes which he had;........ 428
1Ki 4:8 And **t.** are their names: The son of...... 428
1Ki 7:9 All **t.** were of costly stones, according.. 428
1Ki 7:45 all **t.** vessels, which Hiram made 428
1Ki 8:59 And let **t.** my words, wherewith I........ 428
1Ki 9:13 What cities are **t.** which thou hast........ 428
1Ki 9:23 **T.** were the chief of the officers that.... 428
1Ki 10:8 happy are **t.** thy servants, which.......... 428
1Ki 10:10 abundance of spices as **t.** which 1931
1Ki 11:2 Solomon clave unto **t.** in love. 1992
1Ki 17:1 shall not be dew nor rain **t.** years, ... 428
1Ki 17:17 And it came to pass after **t.** things,...... 428
1Ki 18:36 have done all **t.** things at thy word......... 428
1Ki 20:19 So **t.** young men of the princes of........ 428
1Ki 21:1 And it came to pass after **t.** things,...... 428
1Ki 22:11 With **t.** shalt thou push the Syrians, ... 428
1Ki 22:17 the Lord said, **T.** have no master: 428
1Ki 22:23 the mouth of all **t.** thy prophets,.......... 428
2Ki 1:7 to meet you, and told you **t.** words?..... 428
2Ki 1:13 and the life of **t.** fifty thy servants,....... 428
2Ki 2:21 the Lord, I have healed **t.** waters: 428
2Ki 3:10, 13 called **t.** three kings together, ... 428
2Ki 6:20 Lord, open the eyes of **t.** men, that..... 428
2Ki 7:8 and when **t.** lepers came to the........... 428
2Ki 10:9 and slew him: but who slew all **t.**? 428
2Ki 17:41 So **t.** nations feared the Lord, and 428
2Ki 18:27 and to thee, to speak **t.** words?........... 428
2Ki 20:14 said unto him, What said **t.** men?.......... 428
2Ki 21:11 of Judah hath done **t.** abominations, ... 428
2Ki 23:16 proclaimed, who proclaimed **t.** words, ... 428
2Ki 23:17 and proclaimed **t.** things that thou........ 428
2Ki 25:16 the brass of all **t.** vessels was without .. 428
2Ki 25:17 like unto **t.** had the second pillar......... 428
2Ki 25:20 captain of the guard took **t.**, and ....
1Ch 1:23 All **t.** were the sons of Joktan. 428
1Ch 1:29 **T.** are their generations: The............. 428
1Ch 1:31 **T.** are the sons of Ishmael. 428,1992
1Ch 1:33 All **t.** are the sons of Keturah. 428
1Ch 1:43 **t.** are the kings that reigned in the....... 428
1Ch 1:54 Iram. **T.** are the dukes of Edom. 428
1Ch 2:1 **T.** are the sons of Israel; Reuben, ... 428
1Ch 2:18 her sons are **t.**; Jesher, and Shobab, ... 428
1Ch 2:23 **t.** belonged to the sons of Machir 428
1Ch 2:33 Zaza. **T.** were the sons of Jerahmeel. ... 428
1Ch 2:50 **T.** were the sons of Caleb the son of ... 428
1Ch 2:55 **T.** are the Kenites that came of......... 1992
1Ch 3:1 Now **t.** were the sons of David, ... 428
1Ch 3:4 **T.** six were born unto him in Hebron; ....
1Ch 3:5 And **t.** were born unto him in.............. 428
1Ch 3:9 **T.** were all the sons of David, beside........
1Ch 4:2 **T.** are the families of the 428
1Ch 4:3 And **t.** were of the father of Etam; 428
1Ch 4:4 **T.** are the sons of Hur, the................ 428
1Ch 4:6 **T.** were the sons of Naarah................ 428
1Ch 4:12 Ir-nahash. **T.** are the men of Rechah. ... 428
1Ch 4:18 And **t.** are the sons of Bithiah the........ 428
1Ch 4:22 And **t.** are ancient things. ....
1Ch 4:23 **T.** were the potters, and those.......... 1992
1Ch 4:31 **T.** were their cities unto the reign 428
1Ch 4:33 **T.** were their habitations, and............ 2063
1Ch 4:38 **T.** mentioned by their names were....... 428
1Ch 4:41 **t.** written by name came in the days 428
1Ch 5:14 **T.** are the children of Abihail the 428
1Ch 5:17 **t.** were reckoned by genealogies in the......
1Ch 5:24 **t.** were the heads of the house of........ 428
1Ch 6:17 And **t.** be the names of the sons of...... 428
1Ch 6:19 **t.** are the families of the Levites.......... 428
1Ch 6:31 **t.** are they whom David set over the ....
1Ch 6:33 **t.** are they that waited with their......... 428
1Ch 6:50 **t.** are the sons of Aaron; Eleazar his.... 428
1Ch 6:54 Now **t.** are their dwelling places 428
1Ch 6:64 to the Levites **t.** cities with their.............
1Ch 6:65 **t.** cities, which are called by their............
1Ch 7:8 All **t.** are the sons of Becher. 428
1Ch 7:11 All **t.** the sons of Jediael, by the.......... 428
1Ch 7:17 **T.** were the sons of Gilead, the son..... 428
1Ch 7:29 In **t.** dwelt the children of Joseph......... 428
1Ch 7:33 **T.** are the children of Japhlet. 428
1Ch 7:40 All **t.** were the children of Asher, ... 428
1Ch 8:6 And **t.** are the sons of Ehud: 428
1Ch 8:6 **t.** are the heads of the fathers 428,1992
1Ch 8:10 **T.** were his sons, heads of the........... 428
1Ch 8:28 **T.** were heads of the fathers, by 428
1Ch 8:28 chief men. **T.** dwelt in Jerusalem. 428
1Ch 8:32 **t.** also dwelt with their brethren......... 1992
1Ch 8:38 sons, whose names are **t.**, Azrikam,..... 428
1Ch 8:38 Hanan. All **t.** were the sons of Azel. 428
1Ch 8:40 fifty. All **t.** are the sons of Benjamin..... 428
1Ch 9:9 **t.** men were chief of the fathers in....... 428
1Ch 9:22 **t.** which were chosen to be porters in.......
1Ch 9:22 **T.** were reckoned by their................ 1992
1Ch 9:26 **t.** Levites, the four chief porters, ... 1992
1Ch 9:33 And **t.** are the singers, chief of the 428
1Ch 9:34 **T.** chief fathers of the Levites were 428
1Ch 9:34 generations; **t.** dwelt at Jerusalem........ 428
1Ch 9:44 had six sons, whose names are **t.**, ... 428
1Ch 9:44 Hanan: **t.** were the sons of Azel. 428
1Ch 10:4 lest **t.** uncircumcised come and........... 428
1Ch 11:10 **T.** also are the chief of the mighty 428
1Ch 11:19 shall I drink the blood of **t.** men that 428
1Ch 11:19 **T.** things did...three mightiest. 428
1Ch 11:19 things did **t.** three mightiest. ....
1Ch 11:24 **T.** things did Benaiah the son of.......... 428
1Ch 12:1 **t.** are they that came to David to 428
1Ch 12:14 **T.** were of the sons of Gad, captains.... 428
1Ch 12:15 **T.** are they that went over.......... 428,1992
1Ch 12:23 **t.** are the numbers of the bands 428
1Ch 12:38 **t.** men of war, that could keep rank, ... 428
1Ch 14:4 Now **t.** are the names of his children.... 428
1Ch 17:15 According to all **t.** words, and............ 428
1Ch 17:19 in making known all **t.** great things. ....
1Ch 18:11 that he brought from all **t.** nations; ....
1Ch 20:8 **T.** were born unto the giant in............ 411
1Ch 21:17 but as for **t.** sheep, what have they...... 428
1Ch 23:9 **T.** were the chief of the fathers of....... 428
1Ch 23:10 **T.** four were the sons of Shimei. 428
1Ch 23:24 **T.** were the sons of Levi after the 428
1Ch 24:1 **t.** are the divisions of the sons of............
1Ch 24:19 **T.** were the orderings of them in......... 428
1Ch 24:20 the rest of the sons of Levi were **t.**..........
1Ch 24:30 **T.** were the sons of the Levites 428
1Ch 24:31 **T.** likewise cast lots over against........ 1992
1Ch 25:5 All **t.** were the sons of Heman the....... 428
1Ch 25:6 All **t.** were under the hands of their 428
1Ch 26:8 All **t.** of the sons of Obed-edom: 428
1Ch 26:12 Among **t.** were the divisons of the 428
1Ch 26:19 **T.** are the divisions of the porters........ 428
1Ch 27:22 **T.** were the princes of the tribes of 428
1Ch 27:31 **t.** were the rulers of the substance 428
1Ch 29:17 I have willingly offered all **t.** things:...... 428
1Ch 29:19 and to do all **t.** things, and to build ....
2Ch 3:3 **t.** are the things wherein Solomon........ 428
2Ch 3:13 The wings of **t.** cherubims spread........ 428
2Ch 4:18 Solomon made all **t.** vessels in great..... 428
2Ch 5:5 **t.** did the priests and Levites bring...........
2Ch 8:10 **t.** were the chief of king Solomon's 428
2Ch 9:7 men, and happy are **t.** thy servants,..... 428
2Ch 14:7 Let us build **t.** cities, and make 428
2Ch 14:8 all **t.** were mighty men of valour.......... 428
2Ch 15:8 when Asa heard **t.** words, and the 428
2Ch 17:14 And **t.** are the numbers of them 428
2Ch 17:19 **T.** waited on the king, beside those...... 428
2Ch 18:10 With **t.** thou shalt push Syria until........ 428
2Ch 18:16 the Lord said, **T.** have no master; 428
2Ch 18:22 in the mouth of **t.** thy prophets, ... 428
2Ch 21:2 all **t.** were the sons of Jehoshaphat....... 428
2Ch 24:26 **t.** are they that conspired against......... 428
2Ch 29:32 **t.** were for a burnt offering to the........ 428
2Ch 32:1 After **t.** things, and the...................... 428
2Ch 35:7 **t.** were of the king's substance............ 428
2Ch 36:18 princes; all **t.** he brought to Babylon. ....
Ezr 1:11 **t.** did Sheshbazzar bring up with them.......
Ezr 2:1 **t.** are the children of the province........ 428
Ezr 2:59 **t.** were they which went up from.......... 428
Ezr 2:62 **T.** sought their register among............ 428
Ezr 4:21 to cause **t.** men to cease,.................. 479
Ezr 5:9 house, and to make up **t.** walls?......... 1836
Ezr 5:11 that was builded **t.** many years ago,..... 1836
Ezr 5:15 Take **t.** vessels, go, carry them into..... 412
Ezr 6:8 ye shall do to the elders of **t.** Jews 479
Ezr 6:8 expences be given unto **t.** men,........... 479
Ezr 7:1 Now after **t.** things, in the reign of 428
Ezr 8:1 **T.** are now the chief of their fathers,.... 428
Ezr 8:13 whose names are **t.**, Eliphelet, Jeiel, ... 428
Ezr 9:1 Now when **t.** were done, the princes.... 428
Ezr 9:14 with the people of **t.** abominations? 428
Ezr 10:44 All **t.** had taken strange wives: and...... 428
Ne 1:4 came to pass, when I heard **t.** words,... 428
Ne 1:10 Now **t.** are thy servants and thy 1992
Ne 4:2 and said, What do **t.** feeble Jews?............
Ne 5:6 when I heard their cry and **t.** words..... 428
Ne 6:6 be their king, according to **t.** words...... 428
Ne 6:7 to the king according to **t.** words......... 428
Ne 6:14 according to **t.** their works, ... 428
Ne 6:16 heathen...about us saw **t.** things,..............
Ne 7:6 **T.** are the children of the province, ... 428
Ne 7:61 **t.** were they which went up also from... 428
Ne 7:64 **T.** sought their register among............ 428
Ne 10:8 Shemaiah: **t.** were the priests. 428
Ne 11:3 **t.** are the chief of the province that...... 428
Ne 11:7 **t.** are the sons of Benjamin; Sallu 428
Ne 12:1 **t.** are the priests and the Levites 428
Ne 12:7 **T.** were the chief of the priests and 428
Ne 12:26 **T.** were in the days of Joiakim the....... 428
Ne 13:26 king of Israel sin by **t.** things?............. 428
Es 1:5 And when **t.** days were expired, the..... 428
Es 2:1 After **t.** things, when the wrath of 428
Es 3:1 After **t.** things did king Ahasuerus........ 428
Es 4:11 in unto the king **t.** thirty days............ 2088
Es 9:20 And Mordecai wrote **t.** things, and....... 428
Es 9:26 Wherefore they called **t.** days Purim..... 428
Es 9:27 that they would keep **t.** two days......... 428
Es 9:28 that **t.** days should be remembered...... 428
Es 9:28 and that **t.** days of Purim should not..... 428
Es 9:31 To confirm **t.** days of Purim in their..... 428
Es 9:32 confirmed **t.** matters of Purim; 428
Job 8:2 How long wilt thou speak **t.** things?...... 428
Job 10:13 And **t.** things hast thou hid in thine 428
Job 12:3 who knoweth not such things as **t.**?...... 428
Job 12:9 knoweth not in all **t.** that the hand 428
Job 19:3 **T.** ten times have ye reproached........ 2088
Job 26:14 Lo, **t.** are parts of his ways: but.......... 428
Job 32:1 **t.** three men ceased to answer Job,....... 428
Job 32:5 answer in the mouth of **t.** three men.........
Job 33:29 **t.** things worketh God oftentimes......... 428

Job 42:7 Lord had spoken t. words unto Job, ... 428
Ps 15:5 He that doeth t. things shall never ... 428
Ps 42:4 When I remember t. things, I pour ... 428
Ps 50:21 T. things hast thou done, and I ... 428
Ps 57:1 refuge, until t. calamities be overpast. ...
Ps 73:12 t. are the ungodly, who prosper in ... 428
Ps 104:27 T. wait all upon thee; that thou ...
Ps 107:24 T. see the works of the Lord, and ... 1992
Ps 107:43 is wise, and will observe t. things, ... 428
Pr 6:16 T. six things doth the Lord hate: ... 2007
Pr 24:23 T. things also belong to the wise. ... 428
Pr 25:1 T. are also proverbs of Solomon, ... 428
Ec 7:10 the former days were better than t.? ... 428
Ec 11:9 that for all t. things God will bring ... 428
Ec 12:12 by t., my son, be admonished: of ... 1992
Isa 7:4 two tails of t. smoking firebrands, ... 428
Isa 34:16 no one of t. shall fail, none shall ... 2007
Isa 36:12 and to thee to speak t. words? ... 428
Isa 36:20 they among all the gods of t. lands, ... 428
Isa 38:16 O Lord, by t. things men live, ... 5921
Isa 38:16 in all t. things is the life of my spirit: ...
Isa 39:3 said unto him, What said t. men? ... 428
Isa 40:26 behold who hath created t. things, ... 428
Isa 42:16 T. things will I do unto them, and ... 428
Isa 44:21 Remember t., O Jacob and Israel; ... 428
Isa 45:7 evil: I the Lord do all t. things. ... 428
Isa 47:7 didst not lay t. things to thy heart, ... 428
Isa 47:9 But t. two things shall come to thee. ... 428
Isa 47:13 save thee from t. things that shall ...
Isa 48:14 them hath declared t. things? ... 428
Isa 49:12 Behold, t. shall come from far: and, ... 428
Isa 49:12 t. from the north and from the west; ... 428
Isa 49:12 west; and t. from the land of Sinim. ... 428
Isa 49:18 all t. gather themselves together, and ...
Isa 49:21 Who hath begotten me t., seeing I ... 428
Isa 49:21 fro? and who hath brought up t.? ... 2004
Isa 49:21 left alone; t., where had they been? ... 428
Isa 51:19 T. two things are come unto thee; ... 2007
Isa 57:6 Should I receive comfort in t.? ... 428
Isa 60:8 Who are t. that fly as a cloud, and as ... 428
Isa 64:12 thou refrain thyself for t. things, ... 428
Isa 65:5 T. are a smoke in my nose, a fire ... 428
Jer 2:34 it by secret search, but upon all t. ... 428
Jer 3:7 said after she had done all t. things, ... 428
Jer 3:12 Go and proclaim t. words toward ... 428
Jer 4:18 have procured t. things unto thee; ... 428
Jer 5:4 I said, Surely t. are poor; they are ... 1992
Jer 5:5 t. have altogether broken the yoke, ... 1992
Jer 5:9 Shall I not visit for t. things? saith ... 428
Jer 5:19 Lord our God all t. things unto us? ... 428
Jer 5:25 have turned away t. things, ... 428
Jer 5:29 Shall I not visit for t. things? saith ... 428
Jer 7:2 that enter in at t. gates to worship ... 428
Jer 7:4 the temple of the Lord, are t. ... 1992
Jer 7:10 delivered to do all t. abominations? ... 428
Jer 7:13 because ye have done all t. works, ... 428
Jer 7:27 shall speak all t. words unto them: ... 428
Jer 9:9 Shall I not visit them for t. things? ... 428
Jer 9:24 for in t. things I delight, saith the ... 428
Jer 9:26 for all t. nations are uncircumcised, ...
Jer 10:11 earth, and from under t. heavens. ... 429
Jer 11:6 Proclaim all t. words in the cities of ... 428
Jer 13:22 Wherefore come t. things upon me? ... 428
Jer 14:22 for thou hast made all t. things. ... 428
Jer 16:10 shalt shew this people all t. words, ... 428
Jer 17:20 Jerusalem, that enter in by t. gates: ... 428
Jer 20:1 that Jeremiah prophesied t. things. ... 428
Jer 22:2 thy people that enter in by t. gates: ... 428
Jer 22:5 if ye will not hear t. words, I swear ... 428
Jer 23:21 I have not sent t. prophets, yet they ...
Jer 24:5 Like t. good figs, so will I ... 428
Jer 25:9 against all t. nations round about, ... 428
Jer 25:11 t. nations shall serve the king of ... 428
Jer 25:30 thou against them all t. words, ... 428
Jer 26:7 heard Jeremiah speaking t. words in ... 428
Jer 26:10 the princes of Judah heard t. things, ... 428
Jer 26:15 to speak all t. words in your ears. ... 428
Jer 27:6 now have I given all t. lands into the ... 428
Jer 27:12 of Judah according to all t. words, ... 428
Jer 28:14 iron upon the neck of all t. nations, ... 428
Jer 29:1 Now t. are the words of the letter ... 428
Jer 30:4 t. are the words that the Lord spake ... 428
Jer 30:15 I have done t. things unto thee. ... 428
Jer 31:21 of Israel, turn again to t. thy cities ... 428
Jer 32:14 Take t. evidences, this evidence of ... 428
Jer 34:6 spake all t. words unto Zedekiah ... 428
Jer 34:7 t. defenced cities remained of the ... 2007
Jer 36:16 surely tell the king of all t. words. ... 428
Jer 36:17 thou write all t. words at his mouth? ... 428
Jer 36:18 He pronounced all t. words unto me ... 428
Jer 36:24 his servants that heard all t. words. ... 428
Jer 38:9 t. men have done evil in all that they ... 428
Jer 38:12 Put now t. old cast clouts and rotten ...
Jer 38:16 hand of t. men that seek thy life. ... 428
Jer 38:24 Let no man know of t. words, and ... 428
Jer 38:27 told them according to all t. words ... 428
Jer 43:1 sent him to them, even all t. words, ... 428
Jer 43:10 set his throne upon t. stones that I ... 428
Jer 45:1 when he had written t. words in ... 428
Jer 51:60 all t. words that are written against ... 428
Jer 51:61 shalt see, and shalt read all t. words; ... 428
Jer 52:20 the brass of all t. vessels was without .. 428
Jer 52:22 the pomegranates were like unto t. ... 428
La 1:16 For t. things I weep; mine eye, mine ... 428
La 4:9 for t. pine away, stricken through ... 1992
La 5:17 for t. things our eyes are dim. ... 428
Eze 1:21 When those went, t. went; and when ...
Eze 1:21 when those stood, t. stood; and when ...
Eze 8:15 see greater abominations than t. ... 428
Eze 10:17 When they stood, t. stood; and when ...
Eze 10:17 were lifted up, t. lifted up themselves ...
Eze 11:2 t. are the men that devise mischief, ... 428
Eze 14:3 t. men have set up their idols in ... 428
Eze 14:14 Though t. three men, Noah, Daniel, ... 428
Eze 14:16, 18 Though t. three men were in it, ... 428
Eze 16:5 to do any of t. unto thee, to have ... 428
Eze 16:20 t. hast thou sacrificed unto them to be ...
Eze 16:30 seeing thou doest all t. things, the ... 428
Eze 16:43 but hast fretted me in all t. things; ... 428
Eze 17:12 Know ye not what t. things mean? ... 428
Eze 17:18 and hath done all t. things, he shall ... 428
Eze 18:10 doeth the like to any one of t. things, ... 428
Eze 18:13 he hath done all t. abominations; he ... 428
Eze 23:10 T. discovered her nakedness: ... 1992
Eze 23:30 I will do t. things unto thee, ... 428
Eze 24:19 not tell us what t. things are to us, ... 428
Eze 27:21 goats: in t. were they thy merchants. ...
Eze 27:24 T. were thy merchants in all sorts ... 1992
Eze 30:17 t. cities shall go into captivity. ... 2007
Eze 35:10 T. two nations and t. two countries ...
Eze 36:20 T. are the people of the Lord, and ... 428
Eze 37:3 me, Son of man, can t. bones live? ... 428
Eze 37:4 Prophesy upon t. bones, and say ... 428
Eze 37:5 saith the Lord God unto t. bones; ... 428
Eze 37:9 breathe upon t. slain, that they may ... 428
Eze 37:11 man, t. bones are the whole house of ... 428
Eze 37:18 shew us what thou meanest by t.? ... 428
Eze 40:24 thereof according to t. measures. ... 428
Eze 40:28 south gate according to t. measures; ... 428
Eze 40:29 thereof, according to t. measures: ... 428
Eze 40:32 the gate according to t. measures. ... 428
Eze 40:33 were according to t. measures: ... 428
Eze 40:35 it according to t. measures; ... 428
Eze 40:46 t. are the sons of Zadok among the ... 1992
Eze 42:5 the galleries were higher than t., ... 2007
Eze 42:9 under t. chambers was the entry ... 428
Eze 43:13 t. are the measures of the altar after ... 428
Eze 43:18 T. are the ordinances of the altar in ... 428
Eze 43:27 when t. days are expired, it shall ...
Eze 46:22 t. four corners were of one measure. ...
Eze 46:24 T. are the places of them that boil, ... 428
Eze 47:8 T. waters issue out toward the east ... 428
Eze 47:9 because t. waters shall come thither: ... 428
Eze 48:1 Now t. are the names of the tribes. ... 428
Eze 48:1 for t. are his sides east and west; a ...
Eze 48:16 t. shall be the measures thereof; ... 428
Eze 48:29 and t. are their portions, saith the ... 428
Eze 48:30 t. are the goings out of the city on ... 428
Da 1:6 among t. were of the children of ... 1992
Da 1:17 As for t. four children, God gave ... 428
Da 2:28 of thy head upon thy bed, are t.; ... 1836
Da 2:40 as iron that breaketh all t., shall it ... 459
Da 2:44 in the days of t. kings shall the ... 581
Da 2:44 and consume all t. kingdoms, ... 459
Da 3:12 t. men, O king, have not regarded ... 479
Da 3:13 they brought t. men before the king. ... 479
Da 3:21 t. men were bound in their coats, ... 479
Da 3:23 t. three men, Shadrach, Meshach, ... 479
Da 3:27 saw t. men, upon whose bodies the ... 479
Da 6:2 And over t. three presidents; of ... 4481
Da 6:5 Then said t. men, We shall not find ... 479
Da 6:6 Then t. presidents and princes ... 459
Da 6:11 Then t. men assembled, and found ... 479
Da 6:14 when he heard t. words, was sore ...
Da 6:15 t. men assembled unto the king, ... 479
Da 7:17 T. great beasts, which are four, are ... 459
Da 10:21 that holdeth with me in t. things, ... 428
Da 11:6 he that strengthened her in t. times. ...
Da 11:27 both t. kings' hearts shall be to do. ...
Da 11:41 t. shall escape out of his hand, even ... 428
Da 12:6 shall it be to the end of t. wonders? ...
Da 12:7 all t. things shall be finished. ... 428
Da 12:8 what shall be the end of t. things? ... 428
Ho 2:12 T. are my rewards that my lovers ... 1992
Ho 14:9 and he shall understand t. things? ... 428
Am 6:2 be they better than t. kingdoms? or ... 428
Mic 2:7 Lord straitened? are t. his doings? ... 428
Hab 2:6 Shall not all t. take up a parable ... 428
Hag 2:13 by a dead body touch any of t., ... 428
Zec 1:9 Then said I, O my lord, what are t.? ... 428
Zec 1:9 unto me, I will shew thee what t. be ... 428
Zec 1:10 T. are they whom the Lord hath ... 428
Zec 1:12 had indignation t. threescore and ... 2088
Zec 1:19 that talked with me, What be t.? ... 428
Zec 1:19 T. are the horns which have ... 428
Zec 1:21 Then said I, What come t. to do? ... 428
Zec 1:21 saying, T. are the horns which have ... 428
Zec 1:21 but t. are come to fray them, to cast ... 428
Zec 3:7 to walk among t. that stand by. ... 428
Zec 4:4 me, saying, What are t., my lord? ... 428
Zec 4:5 me, Knowest thou not what t. be? ... 428
Zec 4:11 What are t. two olive trees upon the ... 428
Zec 4:12 What be t. two olive branches which ...
Zec 4:13 said, Knowest thou not what t. be? ... 428
Zec 4:14 T. are the two anointed ones, that ... 428
Zec 5:10 me, Whither do t. bear the ephah? ... 1992
Zec 6:4 with me, What are t., my lord? ... 428
Zec 6:5 T. are the four spirits of the ... 428
Zec 6:8 t. that go toward the north country ...
Zec 7:3 as I have done t. so many years? ... 2088
Zec 8:6 remnant of this people in t. days, ... 1992
Zec 8:9 ye that hear in t. days t. words by ... 428
Zec 8:10 before t. days there was no hire ... 1992
Zec 8:12 this people to possess all t. things. ... 428
Zec 8:15 have I thought in t. days to do well. ... 428
Zec 8:16 T. are the things that ye shall do; ... 428
Zec 8:17 for all t. are things that I hate, ... 428
Zec 13:6 What are t. wounds in thine hands? ... 428
Zec 14:15 the beasts that shall be in t. tents, ... 1992
Mt 1:20 But while he thought on t. things, ... *5023*
Mt 2:3 Herod the king had heard t. things, ...
Mt 3:9 God is able of t. stones to raise up ... *5130*
Mt 4:3 command that t. stones be made ... *3778*
Mt 4:9 him, All t. things will I give thee, ... *5023*
Mt 5:19 **one of t. least commandments,** ... *5130*
Mt 5:37 **whatsoever is more than t. cometh** *5130*
Mt 6:29 **was not arrayed like one of t** ... *5130*
Mt 6:32 **all t. things do the Gentiles seek:)** *5023*
Mt 6:32 **that ye have need of all t. things** .. *5130*
Mt 6:33 **t. things shall be added unto you** . *5023*
Mt 7:24 **whosoever heareth t. sayings of** ... *5128*
Mt 7:26 **every one that heareth t. sayings** .. *5128*
Mt 7:28 when Jesus had ended t. sayings, ... *5128*
Mt 9:18 While he spake t. things unto them, ... *5023*
Mt 10:2 names of the twelve apostles are t.; ... *5023*
Mt 10:5 T. twelve Jesus sent forth, and ... *5128*
Mt 10:42 **unto one of t. little ones a cup of** . *5130*
Mt 11:25 **hast hid t. things from the wise** ... *5023*
Mt 13:34 All t. things spake Jesus unto the ... *5023*
Mt 13:51 **Have ye understood all t. things?** .. *5023*
Mt 13:53 when Jesus...finished t. parables, ... *5025*
Mt 13:54 this wisdom, and t. mighty works? ... *3588*
Mt 13:56 then hath this man all t. things? ... *5023*
Mt 15:20 **T. are the things which defile a** ... *5023*
Mt 18:6 **shall offend one of t. little ones** ... *5130*
Mt 18:10 **ye despise not one of t. little ones:** *5130*
Mt 18:14 **one of t. little ones should perish** .. *5130*
Mt 19:1 when Jesus had finished t. sayings, ... *5128*
Mt 19:20 All t. things have I kept from my ... *5023*
Mt 20:12 **T. last have wrought but one** ... *3778*
Mt 20:21 Grant that t. my two sons may sit, ... *3778*
Mt 21:16 unto him, Hearest thou what t. say? ... *3778*
Mt 21:23 authority doest thou t. things? ... *5023*
Mt 21:24, 27 **by what authority I do t** ... *5023*
Mt 22:22 had heard t. words, they marvelled, ...
Mt 22:40 **On t. two commandments hang** ...
Mt 23:23 **t. ought ye to have done, and not** . *5023*
Mt 23:36 **All t. things shall come upon this** . *5023*
Mt 24:2 unto them, **See ye not all t. things?** *5023*
Mt 24:3 Tell us, when shall t. things be? ... *5023*
Mt 24:6 **for all t. things must come to pass,** ...

Mt 24:8 All t. are the beginning of sorrows. 5023
Mt 24:33 ye, when ye shall see all t. things, 5023
Mt 24:34 pass, till all t. things be fulfilled 5023
Mt 25:40 one of the least of t. my brethren, 5130
Mt 25:45 did it not to one of the least of t., 5130
Mt 25:46 t. shall go away into everlasting 3778
Mt 26:1 Jesus had finished all t. sayings, 5128
Mt 26:62 what is it which t. witness against 3778
Mk 2:8 reason ye t. things in your hearts? 5023
Mk 4:11 all t. things are done in parables: 3588
Mk 4:15 And t. are they by the way side, 3778
Mk 4:16 t. are they likewise which are 3778
Mk 4:18 t. are they which are sown among 3778
Mk 4:20 t. are they which are sown on 3778
Mk 6:2 whence hath this man t. things? 5023
Mk 7:23 t. evil things come from within, 5023
Mk 8:4 can a man satisfy t. men with 5128
Mk 9:42 offend one of t. little ones that 3588
Mk 10:20 t. have I observed from my youth. 5023
Mk 11:28 what authority doest thou t. things? 5023
Mk 11:28 thee this authority to do t. things? 5023
Mk 11:29, 33 what authority I do t. things 5023
Mk 12:31 commandment greater than t. 5130
Mk 12:40 t. shall receive greater damnation. 3778
Mk 13:2 Seest thou t. great buildings? 5025
Mk 13:4 Tell us, when shall t. things be? 5023
Mk 13:4 when all t. things shall be fulfilled? 5023
Mk 13:8 t. are the beginnings of sorrows 5023
Mk 13:29 ye shall see t. things come to pass, 5023
Mk 13:30 not pass, till all t. things be done 5023
Mk 14:60 what is it which t. witness against 3778
Mk 16:17 t. signs shall follow them that 5023
Lu 1:19 and to shew thee t. glad tidings. 5023
Lu 1:20 that t. things shall be performed. 5023
Lu 1:65 all t. sayings were noised abroad 5023
Lu 2:19 But Mary kept all t. things, and 5023
Lu 2:51 his mother kept all t. sayings in 5023
Lu 3:8 God is able of t. stones to raise up 5130
Lu 4:28 when they heard t. things, were 5023
Lu 5:27 And after t. things he went forth, 5023
Lu 7:9 When Jesus heard t. things, he 5023
Lu 7:18 John shewed him of all t. things. 5130
Lu 8:8 And when he had said t. things, he 5023
Lu 8:13 and t. have no root, which for a 3778
Lu 8:21 are t. which hear the word of God, 3778
Lu 9:28 an eight days after t. sayings, 5128
Lu 9:44 Let t. sayings sink down into your 5128
Lu 10:1 After t. things the Lord appointed 5023
Lu 10:21 hast hid t. things from the wise 5023
Lu 10:36 Which now of t. three, thinkest 5130
Lu 11:27 as he spake t. things, a certain 5023
Lu 11:42 t. ought ye to have done, and not 5023
Lu 11:53 as he said t. things unto them, the 5023
Lu 12:27 was not arrayed like one of t. 5130
Lu 12:30 all t. things do the nations of the 5023
Lu 12:30 that ye have need of t. things 5130
Lu 12:31 t. things shall be added unto you 5023
Lu 13:2 Suppose ye that t. Galilaeans were 3778
Lu 13:7 t. three years I come seeking fruit ......
Lu 13:16 hath bound, lo, t. eighteen years........
Lu 13:17 when he had said t. things, all his 5023
Lu 14:6 not answer him again to t. things. 5023
Lu 14:15 sat at meat with him heard t. things, 5023
Lu 14:21 came, and shewed his lord t. 5023
Lu 15:26 and asked what t. things meant 5023
Lu 15:29 Lo, t. many years do I serve thee, 5118
Lu 16:14 Pharisees...heard all t. things: 5023
Lu 17:2 should offend one of t. little ones 5130
Lu 18:21 All t. have I kept from my youth 5023
Lu 18:22 Now when Jesus heard t. things, 5023
Lu 18:34 they understood none of t. things: 5130
Lu 19:11 And as they heard t. things, he 5023
Lu 19:15 he commanded t. servants to be 5128
Lu 19:40 that, if t. should hold their peace, 3778
Lu 20:2 authority doest thou t. things? 5023
Lu 20:8 by what authority I do t. things 5023
Lu 20:16 come and destroy t. husbandmen, 5128
Lu 21:4 all t. have of their abundance cast 3778
Lu 21:6 As for t. things which ye behold, 5023
Lu 21:7 Master, but when shall t. things be? 5023
Lu 21:7 when t. things shall come to pass? 5023
Lu 21:9 t. things must first come to pass; 5023
Lu 21:12 But before all t., they shall lay 5130
Lu 21:22 For t. be the days of vengeance, 3778
Lu 21:28 when t. things begin to come to 5130
Lu 21:31 when ye see t. things come to pass, 5023
Lu 21:36 worthy to escape all t. things 5023
Lu 23:31 if they do t. things in a green tree, 5023
Lu 23:49 stood afar off, beholding t. things. 5023
Lu 24:9 told all t. things unto the eleven, 5023
Lu 24:10 told t. things unto the apostles. 5023
Lu 24:14 they talked together of all t. things 5130
Lu 24:17 of communications are t. that ye 3778
Lu 24:18 are come to pass there in t. days? 5025
Lu 24:21 day since t. things were done. 5023
Lu 24:26 Christ to have suffered t. things, 5023
Lu 24:44 T. are the words which I spake 3778
Lu 24:48 And ye are witnesses of t. things 5130
Joh 1:28 T. things were done in Bethabara 5023
Joh 1:50 shalt see greater things than t. 5130
Joh 2:16 sold doves, Take t. things hence; 5023
Joh 2:18 seeing that thou doest t. things? 5023
Joh 3:2 for no man can do t. miracles that 5023
Joh 3:9 unto him, How can t. things be? 5023
Joh 3:10 Israel, and knowest not t. things? 5023
Joh 3:22 After t. things came Jesus and his 5023
Joh 5:3 In t. lay a great multitude of 5025
Joh 5:16 had done t. things on the sabbath 5023
Joh 5:19 t. also doeth the Son likewise 5023
Joh 5:20 shew him greater works than t., 5130
Joh 5:34 t. things I say, that ye might be 5023
Joh 6:1 After t. things Jesus went over the 5023
Joh 6:5 we buy bread, that t. may eat? 3778
Joh 6:59 T. things said he in the synagogue, 5023
Joh 7:1 t. things Jesus walked in Galilee: 5023
Joh 7:4 If thou do t. things, shew thyself to 5023
Joh 7:9 When he had said t. words unto 5023
Joh 7:31 will he do more miracles than t. 5130
Joh 8:20 T. words spake Jesus in the 5023
Joh 8:28 hath taught me, I speak t. things 5023
Joh 8:30 As he spake t. words, many 5023
Joh 9:22 T. words spake his parents, 5023
Joh 9:40 were with him heard t. words, 5023
Joh 10:19 among the Jews for t. sayings. 5128
Joh 10:21 T. are not the words of him that 5023
Joh 11:11 T. things said he: and after that he 5023
Joh 12:16 T. things understood not his 5023
Joh 12:16 that t. things were written of him, 5023
Joh 12:16 they had done t. things unto him. 5023
Joh 12:36 T. things spake Jesus, and 5023
Joh 12:41 T. things said Esaias, when he saw 5023
Joh 13:17 If ye know t. things, happy are ye 5023
Joh 14:12 greater works than t. shall he do; 5130
Joh 14:25 T. things have I spoken unto you, 5023
Joh 15:11 T. things have I spoken unto you, 5023
Joh 15:17 T. things I command you, that ye 5023
Joh 15:21 all t. things will they do unto you 5023
Joh 16:1 T. things have I spoken unto you, 5023
Joh 16:3 And t. things will they do unto 5023
Joh 16:4 t. things have I told you, that 5023
Joh 16:4 t. things I said not unto you at 5023
Joh 16:6 I have said t. things unto you, 5023
Joh 16:25 T. things have I spoken unto you 5023
Joh 16:33 T. things I have spoken unto you, 5023
Joh 17:1 T. words spake Jesus, and lifted up 5023
Joh 17:11 t. are in the world, and I come 3778
Joh 17:13 and t. things I speak in the world, 5023
Joh 17:20 Neither pray I for t. alone, but 5130
Joh 17:25 t. have known that thou hast sent 3778
Joh 18:1 When Jesus had spoken t. words, 5023
Joh 18:8 ye seek me, let t. go their way: 5128
Joh 19:24 T. things therefore the soldiers 5023
Joh 19:36 For t. things were done, that the 5023
Joh 20:18 he had spoken t. things unto her. 5023
Joh 20:31 But t. are written, that ye might 5023
Joh 21:1 After t. things Jesus shewed 5023
Joh 21:15 lovest thou me more than t.? 5130
Joh 21:24 which testifieth of t. things, 5130
Joh 21:24 and wrote t. things: and we know 5023
Ac 1:9 And when he had spoken t. things, 5023
Ac 1:14 T. all continued with one accord 3778
Ac 1:21 t. men which have companied 5130
Ac 1:24 whether of t. two thou hast chosen, 5130
Ac 2:7 not all t. which speak Galilaeans? 3778
Ac 2:13 said, T. men are full of new wine. ....
Ac 2:15 For t. are not drunken, as ye 3778
Ac 2:22 Ye men of Israel, hear t. words; 5128
Ac 3:24 have likewise foretold of t. days. 5025
Ac 4:16 What shall we do to t. men? for 5125
Ac 5:5 And Ananias hearing t. words fell 5128
Ac 5:5 on all them that heard t. things. 5023
Ac 5:11 upon as many as heard t. things, 5023
Ac 5:24 the chief priests heard t. things, 5128
Ac 5:32 we are his witnesses of t. things; 5130
Ac 5:35 intend to do as touching t. men. 5125
Ac 5:36 before t. days rose up Theudas, 5130
Ac 5:38 Refrain from t. men, and let them 5130
Ac 7:1 the high priest, Are t. things so? 5023
Ac 7:50 not my hand made all t. things? 5023
Ac 7:54 they heard t. things, they were cut 5023
Ac 8:24 that none of t. things which ye have ....
Ac 10:8 when he had declared all t. things............
Ac 10:44 While Peter yet spake t. words, 5023
Ac 10:47 that t. should not be baptized, 5128
Ac 11:12 t. six brethren accompanied me, 3778
Ac 11:18 When they heard t. things, they 5023
Ac 11:22 Then tidings of t. things came unto 846
Ac 11:27 in t. days came prophets from 5125
Ac 12:17 Go shew t. things unto James, and 5023
Ac 13:42 Gentiles besought that t. words 5023
Ac 14:15 saying, Sirs, why do ye t. things? 5130
Ac 14:15 turn from t. vanities unto the 5023
Ac 14:18 t. sayings scarce restrained they 5023
Ac 15:17 the Lord, who doeth all t. things. 5023
Ac 15:28 burden than t. necessary things; 5130
Ac 16:17 T. men are the servants of the most 3778
Ac 16:20 T. men, being Jews, do exceedingly 3778
Ac 16:38 serjeants told t. words unto the 5023
Ac 17:6 T....have turned the world upside 3778
Ac 17:7 t. all do contrary to the decrees of 3778
Ac 17:8 the city, when they heard t. things. 5023
Ac 17:11 T. were more noble than those in 3778
Ac 17:20 know...what t. things mean. 5023
Ac 18:1 After t. things Paul departed from 5023
Ac 19:21 After t. things were ended, Paul 5023
Ac 19:28 And when they heard t. sayings, they ....
Ac 19:36 that t. things cannot be spoken 5130
Ac 19:37 For ye have brought hither t. men, 5128
Ac 20:5 T. going before tarried for us at 3778
Ac 20:24 But none of t. things move me, ...
Ac 20:34 t. hands have ministered unto my 3778
Ac 21:12 And when we heard t. things, both 5023
Ac 21:38 before t. days madest an uproar, 5130
Ac 23:22 thou hast shewed t. things to me. 5023
Ac 24:8 take knowledge of all t. things, 5130
Ac 24:9 saying that t. things were so. 5023
Ac 24:20 Or else let t. same here say, if they 3778
Ac 24:22 And when Felix heard t. things, 5023
Ac 25:9 judged of t. things before me? 5130
Ac 25:11 if there be none of t. things ....
Ac 25:11 whereof t. accuse me, no man may 3778
Ac 25:20 and there be judged of t. matters. 5130
Ac 26:16 of t. things which thou hast seen, ...
Ac 26:21 For t. causes the Jews caught me 5130
Ac 26:26 For the king knoweth of t. things, 5130
Ac 26:26 that none of t. things are hidden 5130
Ac 26:29 such as I am, except t. bonds. 5130
Ac 27:31 Except t. abide in the ship, ye 3778
Ac 28:29 And when he had said t. words, 5023
Ro 2:14 t., having not the law, are a law 3778
Ro 8:31 What shall we then say to t. things? 5023
Ro 8:37 in all t. things we are more than 5125
Ro 9:8 t. are not the children of God: 5023
Ro 11:24 how much more shall t., which be 3778
Ro 11:31 so have t. also now not believed, 3778
Ro 14:18 he that in t. things serveth Christ 5125
Ro 15:23 having no more place in t. parts, 5125
Ro 15:23 having a great desire t. many years ....
1Co 4:6 And t. things, brethren, I have in 5023
1Co 4:14 I write not t. things to shame you, 5023
1Co 9:8 Say I t. things as a man? or saith 5023
1Co 9:15 But I have used none of t. things: 5130
1Co 9:15 neither have I written t. things, 5023
1Co 10:6 Now t. things were our examples, 5023
1Co 10:11 Now all t. things happened unto 5023
1Co 12:2 carried away unto t. dumb idols, 3588
1Co 12:11 But all t. worketh that one and the 5023
1Co 12:23 upon t. we bestow more abundant 5125
1Co 13:13 faith, hope, charity, t. three; 5023
1Co 13:13 but the greater of t. is charity. 5130
2Co 2:16 And who is sufficient for t. things? 5023
2Co 7:1 Having therefore t. promises, 5025
2Co 13:10 I write t. things being absent, 5023
Ga 2:6 But of t. who seemed to be somewhat, ...
Ga 4:24 for t. are the two covenants, one 3778
Ga 5:17 t. are contrary the one to the 5023
Ga 5:19 of the flesh are manifest, which are t.; ......
Eph 5:6 of t. things cometh the wrath of 5023

Php 4:8 be any praise, think on t. things......... 5023
Col 3:8 put off all t.; anger, wrath, malice, ...
Col 3:14 above all t. things put on charity, ... 5125
Col 4:11 T. only are my fellowworkers unto 3778
1Th 3:3 should be moved by t. afflictions: 5025
1Th 4:18 comfort one another with t. words...... 5125
2Th 2:5 yet with you, I told you t. things? 5023
1Ti 3:10 And let t. also first be proved; 3778
1Ti 3:14 T. things write I unto thee,.............. 5023
1Ti 4:6 in remembrance of t. things, ... 5023
1Ti 4:11 T. things command and teach............ 5023
1Ti 4:15 Meditate upon t. things; give............ 5023
1Ti 5:7 And t. things give in charge, that....... 5023
1Ti 5:21 that thou observe t. things without..... 5023
1Ti 6:2 T. things teach and exhort............... 5023
1Ti 6:11 thou, O man of God, flee t. things;..... 5023
2Ti 1:12 which cause I also suffer t. things: 5023
2Ti 2:14 Of t. things put them in 5023
2Ti 2:21 therefore purge himself from t.,......... 5130
2Ti 3:8 so do t. also resist the truth: 3778
Tit 2:15 T. things speak, and exhort, and........ 5023
Tit 3:8 t. things I will that thou affirm.......... 5130
Tit 3:8 T. things are good and profitable........ 5023
Heb 1:2 in t. last days spoken unto us by........ 5130
Heb 7:13 he of whom t. things are spoken........ 5023
Heb 9:6 t. things were thus ordained,............ 5130
Heb 9:23 should be purified with t.;................ 5125
Heb 9:23 with better sacrifices than t............. 5025
Heb 10:18 Now where remission of t. is, there ... 5130
Heb 11:13 T. all died in faith, not having........... 3778
Heb 11:39 And t. all, having obtained a good....... 3778
Jas 3:10 t. things ought not so to be. 5023
1Pe 1:20 manifest in t. last times for you, ... 3588
2Pe 1:4 that by t. ye might be partakers of..... 5130
2Pe 1:8 For if t. things be in you, and........... 5023
2Pe 1:9 he that lacketh t. things is blind, ... 5023
2Pe 1:10 for if ye do t. things, ye shall never.... 5023
2Pe 1:12 in remembrance of t. things, ... 5130
2Pe 1:15 t. things always in remembrance. 5130
2Pe 2:12 But t., as natural brute beasts, ... 3778
2Pe 2:17 T. are wells with out water, clouds...... 3778
2Pe 3:11 all t. things shall be dissolved, ... 5130
2Pe 3:16 speaking in them of t. things; 5130
2Pe 3:17 seeing ye know t. things before, ...
1Jo 1:4 And t. things write we unto you, ... 5023
1Jo 2:1 t. things write I unto you, that ye....... 5023
1Jo 2:26 T. things have I written unto you....... 5023
1Jo 5:7 Holy Ghost: and t. three are one. 3778
1Jo 5:8 blood: and t. three agree in one......... 3778
1Jo 5:13 T. things have I written unto you....... 5023
Jude 8 Likewise also t. filthy dreamers 3778
Jude 10 But t. speak evil of those things 3778
Jude 12 T. are spots in your feasts of............ 3778
Jude 14 prophesied of t., saying, Behold, ... 5125
Jude 16 T. are murmurers, complainers, ... 3778
Jude 19 T. be they who separate 3778
Re 2:1 **T. things saith he that holdeth** 3592
Re 2:8 **T. things saith the first and the** 3592
Re 2:12 **T. things saith he which hath the**.. 3592
Re 2:18 **T. things saith the Son of God,** 3592
Re 3:1 **T. things saith he that hath the** 3592
Re 3:7 **T. things saith he that is holy, he** . 3592
Re 3:14 **T. things saith the Amen, the** 3592
Re 7:1 after t. things I saw four angels......... 5023
Re 7:13 What are t. which are arrayed in........ 3778
Re 7:14 T. are they which came out of........... 3778
Re 9:18 By t. three was the third part of......... 5130
Re 9:20 were not killed by t. plagues yet........ 5025
Re 11:4 T. are the two olive trees, and the..... 3778
Re 11:6 T. have power to shut heaven, that.... 3778
Re 11:10 t. two prophets tormented them 3778
Re 14:4 T. are they which were not defiled..... 3778
Re 14:4 T. are they which follow the Lamb..... 3778
Re 14:4 T. were redeemed from among.......... 3778
Re 16:9 which hath power over t. plagues:...... 5025
Re 17:13 T. have one mind, and shall give........ 3778
Re 17:14 T. shall make war with the Lamb,....... 3778
Re 17:16 t. shall hate the whore, and shall........ 3778
Re 18:1 after t. things I saw another angel...... 5023
Re 18:15 The merchants of t. things, which...... 5130
Re 19:1 after t. things I heard a great............ 5023
Re 19:9 T. are the true sayings of God. 3778
Re 19:20 T. both were cast alive into a lake...... 3588
Re 21:5 for t. words are true and faithful. 3778
Re 22:6 T. sayings are faithful and true: 3778
Re 22:8 I John saw t. things, and heard.......... 5023
Re 22:8 angel which shewed me t. things........ 5023
Re 22:16 **angel to testify upon you t. things** 5023
Re 22:18 any man shall add unto t. things,........ 5023
Re 22:20 He which testifieth t. things saith,...... 5023

THESSALONIANS (thes-sa-lo'-ne-uns)
Ac 20:4 and of the T., Aristarchus and........... 2331
1Th*general* *title* Paul The Apostle To The T. 2331
1Th 1:1 unto the church of the T. which........ 2331
1Th*subscr.* The first epistle unto the T. was........ 2331
2Th*general* *title* Paul The Apostle To The T. 2331
2Th 1:1 unto the church of the T. in God........ 2331
2Th*subscr.* The second epistle to the T. was....... 2331

THESSALONICA (thes-sa-lo-ni'-cah) See also THESSALONIANS.
Ac 17:1 they came to T., where was a........... 2332
Ac 17:11 were more noble than those in T., ... 2332
Ac 17:13 the Jews of T. had knowledge 2332
Ac 27:2 Aristarchus, a Mecedonian of T.,......... 2331
Php 4:16 For even in T. ye sent once and........ 2332
2Ti 4:10 world, and is departed into T.; 2332

THEUDAS (thew'-das)
Ac 5:36 For before these days rose up T.,....... 2333

THEY See in the APPENDIX; also THEIR; THEM.

THICK See also THICKER.
Ex 10:22 there was a t. darkness in all the......... 653
Ex 19:9 Lo, I come unto thee in a t. cloud,...... 5645
Ex 19:16 and a t. cloud upon the mount,.......... 3515
Ex 20:21 Moses drew near unto the t. darkness ......
Le 23:40 and the boughs of t. trees, and.......... 5687
De 4:11 darkness, clouds, and t. darkness. ....
De 5:22 the cloud, and of the t. darkness, ...
De 32:15 art waxen fat, thou art grown t.,......... 5666
2Sa 18:9 under the t. boughs of a great oak,...........
2Sa 22:12 waters, and t. clouds of the skies. ....
1Ki 7:6 and the t. beam were before them. ....
1Ki 7:26 And it was an hand breadth t., ... 5672
1Ki 8:12 he would dwell in the t. darkness. ....
2Ki 8:15 he took a t. cloth, and dipped it in...........
2Ch 6:1 he would dwell in the t. darkness. ....
Ne 8:15 and branches of t. trees, to make....... 5687
Job 15:26 upon the t. bosses of his bucklers: 5672
Job 22:14 T. clouds are a covering to him,...............
Job 26:8 up the waters in his t. clouds; ....
Job 37:11 by watering he wearieth the t. cloud: ....
Job 38:9 t. darkness a swaddlingband for it,...........
Ps 18:11 dark waters and t. clouds of the...............
Ps 18:12 before him his t. clouds passed, ...
Ps 74:5 lifted up axes upon the t. trees. 5441
Isa 44:22 blotted out, as a t. cloud, thy.................
Eze 6:13 green tree, and under every t. oak,.... 5687
Eze 8:11 and a t. cloud of incense went up........ 6282
Eze 19:11 was exalted among the t. branches, ... 5688
Eze 20:28 high hill, and all the t. trees, ... 5687
Eze 31:3 his top was among the t. boughs.......... 5688
Eze 31:10 up his top among the t. boughs,......... 5688
Eze 31:14 up their top among the t. boughs, ... 5688
Eze 41:12 of the building was five cubits t.......... 7341
Eze 41:25 t. planks upon the face of the........... 5645
Eze 41:26 of the house, and t. planks......................
Joe 2:2 day of clouds and of t. darkness, ...
Hab 2:6 that ladeth himself with t. clay! ....
Zep 1:15 a day of clouds and t. darkness, ...
Lu 11:29 the people were gathered t. together, ...

THICKER
1Ki 12:10 finger shall be t. than my father's....... 5666
2Ch 10:10 finger shall be t. than my father's....... 5666

THICKET See also THICKETS.
Ge 22:13 a ram caught in a t. by his horns: 5442
Jer 4:7 The lion is come up from his t.,......... 5441

THICKETS
1Sa 13:6 hide themselves in caves, and in t., ... 2337
Isa 9:18 shall kindle in the t. of the forests, ... 5442
Isa 10:34 shall cut down the t. of the forest 5442
Jer 4:29 they shall go into the t., and climb 5645

THICKNESS
2Ch 4:5 the t. of it was an handbreadth, ... 5672
Jer 52:21 and the t. thereof was four fingers: 5672
Eze 41:9 The t. of the wall, which was for 7341
Eze 42:10 chambers were in the t. of the wall 7341

THIEF See also THIEVES.
Ex 22:2 If a t. be found breaking up, and........ 1590
Ex 22:7 if a t. be found, let him pay double..... 1590
Ex 22:8 If the t. be not found, then the.......... 1590
De 24:7 selleth him; then that t. shall die;....... 1590
Job 24:14 needy, and in the night is as a t......... 1590
Job 30:5 (they cried after them as after a t.;)... 1590
Ps 50:18 When thou sawest a t., then thou 1590
Pr 6:30 Men do not despise a t., if he steal.... 1590
Pr 29:24 Whoso is partner with a t. hateth....... 1590
Jer 2:26 As the t. is ashamed when he is........ 1590
Ho 7:1 the t. cometh in, and the troop of...... 1590
Joe 2:9 enter in at the windows like a t.. 1590
Zec 5:4 shall enter into the house of the t., ... 1590
Mt 24:43 **in what watch the t. would come,** . 2812
Mt 26:55 **Are ye come out as against a t.**..... 3027
Mk 14:48 **Are ye come out, as against a t.,**... 3027
Lu 12:33 **where no t. approacheth, neither**... 2812
Lu 12:39 **what hour the t. would come,** 2812
Lu 22:52 **Be ye come out, as against a t.,**.... 3027
Joh 10:1 **way, the same is a t. and a robber.** 2812
Joh 10:10 **The t. cometh not, but for to steal,** 2812
Joh 12:6 but because he was a t., and had the.. 2812
1Th 5:2 Lord so cometh as a t. in the night. ... 2812
1Th 5:4 day should overtake you as a t. 2812
1Pe 4:15 you suffer as a murderer, or as a t.,... 2812
2Pe 3:10 Lord will come as a t. in the night;..... 2812
Re 3:3 **watch, I will come on thee as a t.,** 2812
Re 16:15 **Behold, I come as a t.. Blessed is**.. 2812

THIEVES
Isa 1:23 rebellious, and companions of t. 1590
Jer 48:27 unto thee? was he found among t.?..... 1590
Jer 49:9 if t. by night, they will destroy till...... 1590
Ob 5 If t. came to thee, if robbers by 1590
Mt 6:19 **where t. break through and steal:** . 2812
Mt 6:20 **where t. do not break through nor** 2812
Mt 21:13 **but ye have made it a den of t..** 3027
Mt 27:38 there two t. crucified with him;.......... 3027
Mt 27:44 The t. also, which were crucified 3027
Mk 11:17 **but ye have made it a den of t..** 3027
Mk 15:27 And with him they crucify two t.;........ 3027
Lu 10:30 **to Jericho, and fell among t.,** 3027
Lu 10:36 **unto him that fell among the t.?** ... 3027
Lu 19:46 **but ye have made it a den of t.** 3027
Joh 10:8 **that ever came before me are t.** 2812
1Co 6:10 Nor t., nor covetous, nor drunkards, .. 2812

THIGH See also THIGHS.
Ge 24:2 pray thee, thy hand under my t. 3409
Ge 24:9 his hand under the t. of Abraham....... 3409
Ge 32:25 he touched the hollow of his t.; 3409
Ge 32:25 hollow of Jacob's t. was out of joint, ... 3409
Ge 32:31 him, and he halted upon his t. 3409
Ge 32:32 which is upon the hollow of the t., ... 3409
Ge 32:32 touched the hollow of Jacob's t. in....... 3409
Ge 47:29 I pray thee, thy hand under my t., ... 3409
Nu 5:21 the Lord doth make thy t. to rot,........ 3409
Nu 5:22 thy belly to swell, and thy t. to rot:.... 3409
Nu 5:27 shall swell, and her t. shall rot:.......... 3409
Jg 3:16 under his raiment upon his right t....... 3409
Jg 3:21 took the dagger from his right t.,....... 3409
Jg 15:8 And he smote them hip and t. with..... 3409
Ps 45:3 Gird thy sword upon thy t., O most ... 3409
Ca 3:8 man hath his sword upon his t........... 3409
Isa 47:2 bare the leg, uncover the t., ... 7785
Jer 31:19 instructed, I smote upon my t. 3409
Eze 21:12 smite therefore upon thy t................. 3409
Eze 24:4 good piece, the t., and the shoulder;... 3409
Re 19:16 and on his t. a name written, ... 3382

THIGHS
Ex 28:42 the loins even unto the t. they 3409
Ca 7:1 the joints of thy t. are like jewels,...... 3409
Da 2:32 silver, his belly and his t. of brass, ... 3410

THIMNATHAH (thim'-nath-ah) See also TIMNAH.
Jos 19:43 And Elon, and T., and Ekron, ... 8553

THIN
Ge 41:6 seven t. ears and blasted with the...... 1851
Ge 41:7 And the seven t. ears devoured the.... 1851
Ge 41:23 behold, seven ears, withered, t.,........ 1851
Ge 41:24 the t. ears devoured the seven good... 1851
Ge 41:27 the seven t. and ill favoured kine 7534
Ex 39:3 they did beat the gold into t. plates, ...
Le 13:30 and there be in it a yellow t. hair;...... 1851
1Ki 7:29 certain additions made of t. work. 4174
Isa 17:4 the glory of Jacob shall be made t., ... 1809

THINE See also THY.
Ge 13:14 Lift up now t. eyes, and look from the......

Ge 14:20 delivered **t.** enemies into thy hand.
Ge 14:23 that I will not take any thing that is **t.**,
Ge 15:4 him, saying, This shall not be **t.** heir;
Ge 15:4 out of **t.** own bowels shall be **t.** heir.
Ge 20:7 surely die, thou, and all that are **t.**
Ge 21:18 up the lad, and hold him in **t.** hand;
Ge 22:2 Take now thy son, **t.** only son Isaac,
Ge 22:12 Lay not **t.** hand upon the lad, neither
Ge 22:12 withheld thy son, **t.** only son from me.
Ge 22:16 hast not withheld thy son, **t.** only son:
Ge 30:27 if I have found favour in **t.** eyes, tarry:
Ge 31:12 he said, Lift up now **t.** eyes, and see,
Ge 31:32 discern thou what is **t.** with me,
Ge 38:18 and thy staff that is in **t.** hand.
Ge 40:13 days shall Pharaoh lift up **t.** head,
Ge 44:18 not **t.** anger burn against thy servant:
Ge 46:4 shall put his hand upon **t.** eyes.
Ge 47:19 Wherefore shall we die before **t.** eyes,
Ge 48:6 thou begettest after them, shall be **t.**,
Ge 49:8 shall be in the neck of **t.** enemies;
Ex 4:2 What is that in **t.** hand?
Ex 4:4 Put forth **t.** hand, and take it by the
Ex 4:6 him, Put now **t.** hand into thy bosom.
Ex 4:7 Put **t.** hand into thy bosom again.
Ex 4:17 And thou shalt take this rod in **t.** hand,
Ex 4:21 Pharaoh, which I have put in **t.** hand:
Ex 5:16 but the fault is in **t.** own people.
Ex 7:15 to a serpent shalt thou take in **t.** hand.
Ex 7:19 stretch out **t.** hand upon the waters of
Ex 8:3 shall go up and come into **t.** house,
Ex 8:3 and upon thy people, and into **t.** ovens,
Ex 8:5 Stretch forth **t.** hand with thy rod over
Ex 9:14 send all my plagues upon **t.** heart,
Ex 9:22 Stretch forth **t.** hand toward heaven,
Ex 10:12 Stretch out **t.** hand over the land of
Ex 10:21 Stretch out **t.** hand toward heaven,
Ex 13:9 be for a sign unto thee upon **t.** hand,
Ex 13:9 and for a memorial between **t.** eyes,
Ex 13:16 it shall be for a token upon **t.** hand,
Ex 13:16 and for frontlets between **t.** eyes:
Ex 14:16 and stretch out **t.** hand over the sea,
Ex 14:26 Stretch out **t.** hand over the sea, that
Ex 15:7 in the greatness of **t.** excellency thou
Ex 15:16 by the greatness of **t.** arm they shall
Ex 15:17 them in the mountain of **t.** inheritance,
Ex 17:5 thou smotest the river, take in **t.** hand,
Ex 20:24 offerings, thy sheep, and **t.** oxen:
Ex 22:30 Likewise shalt thou do with **t.** oxen,
Ex 23:1 put not **t.** hand with the wicked to be
Ex 23:4 meet **t.** enemy's ox or his ass going
Ex 23:12 that **t.** ox and **t.** ass may rest, and the
Ex 23:22 I will be an enemy unto **t.** enemies,
Ex 23:22 and an adversary unto **t.** adversaries.
Ex 23:27 I will make all **t.** enemies turn their
Ex 32:13 to whom thou swarest by **t.** own self,
Ex 34:9 our sin, and take us for **t.** inheritance.
Le 2:13 all **t.** offerings thou shalt offer salt.
Le 10:15 it shall be **t.**, and thy sons' with thee,
Le 18:10 for theirs is **t.** own nakedness.
Le 18:14 approach to his wife: she is **t.** aunt.
Le 19:17 shalt not hate thy brother in **t.** heart:
Le 27:23 he shall give **t.** estimation in that day,
Le 27:27 redeem it according to **t.** estimation,
Nu 5:20 have lain with thee beside **t.** husband:
Nu 10:35 Lord, and let **t.** enemies be scattered;
Nu 18:9 shall be **t.** of the most holy things,
Nu 18:11 And this is **t.**; the heave offering of
Nu 18:13 shall bring unto the Lord, shall be **t.**;
Nu 18:13 every one that is clean in **t.** house
Nu 18:14 thing devoted in Israel shall be **t.**
Nu 18:15 it be of men or beasts, shall be **t.**:
Nu 18:16 redeem, according to **t.** estimation,
Nu 18:18 And the flesh of them shall be **t.**,
Nu 18:18 breast and as the right shoulder are **t.**,
Nu 18:20 I am thy part and **t.** inheritance
Nu 22:30 Am not I **t.** ass, upon which thou hast
Nu 22:30 ridden ever since I was **t.** unto this
Nu 22:32 thou smitten **t.** ass these three times?
Nu 27:18 is the spirit, and lay **t.** hand upon him;
Nu 27:20 shalt put some of **t.** honour upon him,
De 2:24 I have given into **t.** hand Sihon the
De 3:21 **T.** eyes have seen all that the Lord
De 3:27 Pisgah, and lift up **t.** eyes westward,
De 3:27 eastward, and behold it with **t.** eyes:
De 4:9 the things which **t.** eyes have seen,
De 4:19 lest thou lift up **t.** eyes unto heaven,
De 4:39 consider it in **t.** heart, that the Lord
De 5:14 nor **t.** ox, nor **t.** ass,nor any of thy
De 6:5 the Lord thy God with all **t.** heart,
De 6:6 thee this day, shall be in **t.** heart:
De 6:7 of them when thou sittest in **t.** house,
De 6:8 bind them for a sign upon **t.** hand,
De 6:8 shall be as frontlets between **t.** eyes.
De 6:19 To cast out all **t.** enemies from before
De 7:13 and thy wine, and **t.** oil, the increase
De 7:16 **t.** eye shall have no pity upon them:
De 7:17 say in **t.** heart, These nations are
De 7:19 great temptations which **t.** eyes saw,
De 7:24 shall deliver their kings into **t.** hand,
De 7:26 bring an abomination into **t.** house,
De 8:2 thee, to know what was in **t.** heart,
De 8:5 Thou shalt also consider in **t.** heart,
De 8:14 Then **t.** heart be lifted up, and thou
De 8:17 And thou say in **t.** heart, My power
De 9:4 Speak not thou in **t.** heart, after that
De 9:5 or for the uprightness of **t.** heart, dost
De 9:26 destroy not the people and **t.** inheritance,
De 9:29 are thy people and **t.** inheritance,
De 10:21 things, which **t.** eyes have seen.
De 11:14 in thy corn, and thy wine, and **t.** oil.
De 11:19 when thou sittest in **t.** house, and
De 11:20 them upon the door posts of **t.** house,
De 12:17 offerings, or heave offering of **t.** hand;
De 12:18 in all that thou puttest **t.** hands unto.
De 13:6 thy friend, which is as **t.** own soul,
De 13:8 neither shall **t.** eye pity him, neither
De 13:9 **t.** hand shall be first upon him to
De 13:17 nought of the cursed thing to **t.** hand:
De 14:23 of thy corn, of thy wine, and of **t.** oil,
De 14:25 and bind up the money in **t.** hand,
De 14:26 shalt rejoice, thou, and **t.** household,
De 14:28 bring forth all the tithe of **t.** increase
De 14:29 bless thee in all the work of **t.** hand
De 15:3 but that which is **t.** with thy brother
De 15:3 with thy brother **t.** hand shall release,
De 15:7 thee, thou shalt not harden **t.** heart,
De 15:7 nor shut **t.** hand from thy poor brother:
De 15:8 thou shalt open **t.** hand wide unto
De 15:9 **t.** eye be evil against thy poor brother,
De 15:10 **t.** heart shall not be grieved when thou
De 15:10 in all that thou puttest **t.** hand unto.
De 15:11 open **t.** hand wide unto thy brother,
De 15:16 because he loveth thee and **t.** house,
De 16:10 tribute of a freewill offering of **t.** hand,
De 16:15 God shall bless thee in all **t.** increase,
De 16:15 and in all the works of **t.** hands,
De 18:4 of thy wine, and of **t.** oil, and the first
De 18:21 say in **t.** heart, How shall we know the
De 19:13 **T.** eye shall not pity him, but thou
De 19:14 of old time have set in **t.** inheritance,
De 19:21 **t.** eye shall not pity; but life shall go
De 20:1 goest out to battle against **t.** enemies,
De 20:13 thy God hath delivered it into **t.** hands,
De 20:14 thou shalt eat the spoil of **t.** enemies,
De 21:10 goest forth to war against **t.** enemies,
De 21:10 God hath delivered them into **t.** hands
De 21:12 thou shalt bring her home to **t.** house.
De 21:13 shall remain in **t.** house, and bewail
De 22:2 thou shalt bring it unto **t.** own house,
De 22:8 thou bring not blood upon **t.** house,
De 23:9 host goeth forth against **t.** enemies,
De 23:14 and to give up **t.** enemies before thee;
De 23:20 thee in all that thou settest **t.** hand to
De 23:24 eat grapes thy fill at **t.** own pleasure;
De 23:25 mayest pluck the ears with **t.** hand;
De 24:19 cuttest down **t.** harvest in thy field,
De 24:19 bless thee in all the work of **t.** hands.
De 24:20 When thou beatest **t.** olive tree, thou
De 25:12 off her hand, **t.** eye shall not pity her.
De 25:14 have in **t.** house divers measures,
De 25:19 given thee rest from all **t.** enemies
De 26:4 shall take the basket out of **t.** hand,
De 26:11 given unto thee, and unto **t.** house,
De 26:12 all the tithes of **t.** increase the third
De 26:16 keep and do them with all **t.** heart,
De 28:7 The Lord shall cause **t.** enemies that
De 28:8 in all that thou settest **t.** hand unto;
De 28:12 and to bless all the work of **t.** hand:
De 28:20 in all that thou settest **t.** hand unto
De 28:25 thee to be smitten before **t.** enemies:
De 28:31 **T.** ox shall be slain before **t.** eyes, and
De 28:31 **t.** ass shall be violently taken away
De 28:31 sheep shall be given unto **t.** enemies,
De 28:32 **t.** eyes shall look, and fail with
De 28:32 there shall be no might in **t.** hand.
De 28:34 shalt be mad for the sight of **t.** eyes
De 28:40 oil; for **t.** olive shall cast his fruit.
De 28:48 shalt thou serve **t.** enemies which
De 28:53 thou shalt eat the fruit of **t.** own body.
De 28:53 **t.** enemies shall distress thee:
De 28:55 **t.** enemies shall distress thee in all
De 28:57 **t.** enemy shall distress thee in thy
De 28:67 fear of **t.** heart wherewith thou shalt
De 28:67 for the sight of **t.** eyes which thou
De 29:3 temptations which **t.** eyes have seen,
De 30:2 with all **t.** heart, and with all thy soul;
De 30:4 If any of **t.** be driven out unto the
De 30:6 thy God will circumcise **t.** heart,
De 30:6 the Lord thy God with all **t.** heart,
De 30:7 put all these curses upon **t.** enemies,
De 30:9 plenteous in every work of **t.** hand,
De 30:10 the Lord thy God with all **t.** heart,
De 30:17 But if **t.** heart turn away, so that thou
De 33:10 whole burnt sacrifice upon **t.** altar.
De 33:29 **t.** enemies shall be found liars unto
De 34:4 caused thee to see it with **t.** eyes,
Jos 2:3 thee, which are entered into **t.** house:
Jos 2:17 We will be blameless of this **t.** oath
Jos 2:20 then we will be quit of **t.** oath which
Jos 6:2 I have given into **t.** hand Jericho,
Jos 7:13 canst not stand before **t.** enemies,
Jos 8:18 Ai; for I will give it into **t.** hand.
Jos 9:25 And now, behold, we are in **t.** hand:
Jos 10:8 I have delivered them into **t.** hand;
Jos 14:9 have trodden shall be **t.** inheritance,
Jos 17:18 But the mountain shall be **t.**; for it is
Jos 17:18 and the outgoings of it shall be **t.**:
Jg 4:7 and I will deliver him into **t.** hand.
Jg 4:9 thou takest shall not be for **t.** honour;
Jg 4:14 hath delivered Sisera into **t.** hand:
Jg 5:31 So let all **t.** enemies perish, O Lord:
Jg 6:39 Let not **t.** anger be hot against me,
Jg 7:7 deliver the Midianites into **t.** hand:
Jg 7:9 for I have delivered it into **t.** hand.
Jg 7:11 shall **t.** hands be strengthened
Jg 8:6 Zebah and Zalmunna now in **t.** hand,
Jg 8:6 we should give bread unto **t.** army?
Jg 8:15 Zebah and Zalmunna now in **t.** hand,
Jg 9:29 to Abimelech, Increase **t.** army, and
Jg 11:36 vengeance for thee of **t.** enemies,
Jg 12:1 burn **t.** house upon thee with fire.
Jg 16:15 thee, when **t.** heart is not with me?
Jg 18:19 lay **t.** hand upon thy mouth, and go
Jg 19:5 Comfort **t.** heart with a morsel of
Jg 19:6 all night, and let **t.** heart be merry
Jg 19:8 said, Comfort **t.** heart, I pray thee.
Jg 19:9 here, that **t.** heart may be merry;
Jg 19:22 forth the man that came into **t.** house,
Jg 20:28 I will deliver them into **t.** hand.
Ru 2:9 Let **t.** eyes be on the field that they do
Ru 2:10 Why have I found grace in **t.** eyes,
Ru 2:11 in law since the death of **t.** husband:
Ru 2:13 spoken friendly unto **t.** handmaid,
Ru 2:13 not like unto one of **t.** handmaidens.
Ru 3:9 answered, I am Ruth **t.** handmaid:
Ru 3:9 therefore thy skirt over **t.** handmaid;
Ru 4:11 that is come into **t.** house like Rachel
Ru 4:15 thy life, and a nourisher of **t.** old age:
1Sa 1:11 look on the affliction of **t.** handmaid,
1Sa 1:11 me, and not forget **t.** handmaid,
1Sa 1:11 wilt give unto **t.** handmaid a man
1Sa 1:16 Count not **t.** handmaid for a daughter
1Sa 1:18 Let **t.** handmaid find grace in thy
1Sa 2:31 days come, that I will cut off **t.** arm,
1Sa 2:31 shall not be an old man in **t.** house.
1Sa 2:32 not be an old man in **t.** house for ever.
1Sa 2:33 the man of **t.**, whom I shall not cut
1Sa 2:33 consume **t.** eyes, and to grieve **t.** heart:
1Sa 2:33 all the increase of **t.** house shall die
1Sa 2:36 every one that is left in **t.** house shall
1Sa 9:19 and will tell thee all that is in **t.** heart
1Sa 9:20 for **t.** asses that were lost three days
1Sa 14:7 unto him, Do all that is in **t.** heart:
1Sa 14:19 unto the priest, Withdraw **t.** hand.
1Sa 15:17 When thou wast little in **t.** own sight,
1Sa 15:28 and hath given it to a neighbour of **t.**,
1Sa 16:1 fill **t.** horn with oil, and go, I will send
1Sa 17:28 pride, and the naughtiness of **t.** heart;

1Sa 17:46 thee, and take **t.**, head from thee;
1Sa 20:3 that I have found grace in **t.** eyes;
1Sa 20:29 if I have found favour in **t.** eyes, let
1Sa 20:30 the son of Jesse to **t.** own confusion,
1Sa 21:3 Now therefore what is under **t.** hand?
1Sa 21:8 is there not here under **t.** hand spear
1Sa 22:14 bidding, and is honourable in **t.** house?
1Sa 23:4 deliver the Philistines into **t.** hand.
1Sa 24:4 I will deliver **t.** enemy into **t.** hand,
1Sa 24:10 this day **t.** eyes have seen how that the
1Sa 24:15 cause, and deliver me out of **t.** hand.
1Sa 24:18 Lord had delivered me into **t.** hand,
1Sa 24:20 Israel shall be established in **t.** hand.
1Sa 25:6 both to thee, and peace be to **t.** house,
1Sa 25:8 the young men find favour in **t.** eyes:
1Sa 25:8 whatsoever cometh to **t.** hand unto
1Sa 25:24 and let **t.** handmaid, I pray thee,
1Sa 25:24 speak in **t.** audience, and hear the
1Sa 25:24 and hear the words of **t.** handmaid.
1Sa 25:25 I **t.** handmaid saw not the young men
1Sa 25:26 avenging thyself with **t.** own hand,
1Sa 25:26 now let **t.** enemies, and they that
1Sa 25:27 now this blessing which **t.** handmaid
1Sa 25:28 forgive the trespass of **t.** handmaid:
1Sa 25:29 and the souls of **t.** enemies, them shall
1Sa 25:31 my lord, then remember **t.** handmaid.
1Sa 25:35 unto her, Go up in peace to **t.** house;
1Sa 25:41 let **t.** handmaid be a servant to wash
1Sa 26:8 hath delivered **t.** enemy into **t.** hand
1Sa 26:21 my soul was precious in **t.** eyes this
1Sa 27:5 If I have now found grace in **t.** eyes,
1Sa 28:16 from thee, and is become **t.** enemy?
1Sa 28:17 hath rent the kingdom out of **t.** hand,
1Sa 28:21 **t.** handmaid hath obeyed thy voice,
1Sa 28:22 also unto the voice of **t.** handmaid,
2Sa 1:14 not afraid to stretch forth **t.** hand to
2Sa 1:25 thou wast slain in **t.** high places.
2Sa 3:21 reign over all that **t.** heart desireth.
2Sa 4:8 Ish-bosheth the son of Saul **t.** enemy,
2Sa 5:19 deliver the Philistines into **t.** hand.
2Sa 7:3 the king, Go, do all that is in **t.** heart;
2Sa 7:9 have cut off all **t.** enemies out of thy
2Sa 7:11 thee to rest from all **t.** enemies.
2Sa 7:16 **t.** house and thy kingdom shall be
2Sa 7:21 according to **t.** own heart, hast thou
2Sa 11:10 didst thou not go down unto **t.** house?
2Sa 12:10 shall never depart from **t.** house;
2Sa 12:11 evil against thee out of **t.** own house,
2Sa 12:11 I will take thy wives before **t.** eyes,
2Sa 13:10 chamber, that I may eat of **t.** hand.
2Sa 14:7 family is risen against **t.** handmaid,
2Sa 14:8 Go to **t.** house, and I will give charge
2Sa 14:12 Let **t.** handmaid, I pray thee, speak
2Sa 14:17 Then **t.** handmaid said, The word of
2Sa 14:19 words in the mouth of **t.** handmaid:
2Sa 16:4 **t.** are all that pertained unto
2Sa 17:11 thou go to battle in **t.** own person.
2Sa 19:6 In that thou lovest **t.** enemies, and
2Sa 19:27 do therefore what is good in **t.** eyes.
2Sa 19:28 them that did eat at **t.** own table.
2Sa 20:17 him, Hear the words of **t.** handmaid.
2Sa 22:28 **t.** eyes are upon the haughty, that
2Sa 24:13 flee three months before **t.** enemies,
2Sa 24:16 people, It is enough: stay now **t.** hand.
2Sa 24:17 let **t.** hand, I pray thee, be against me,
1Ki 1:12 that thou mayest save **t.** own life, and
1Ki 1:13 O king, swear unto **t.** handmaid,
1Ki 1:17 by the Lord thy God unto **t.** handmaid,
1Ki 1:53 said unto him, Go to **t.** house.
1Ki 2:26 thee to Anathoth, unto **t.** own fields;
1Ki 2:37 thy blood shall be upon **t.** own head.
1Ki 2:44 wickedness which **t.** heart is privy to,
1Ki 2:44 thy wickedness upon **t.** own head;
1Ki 3:11 nor hast asked the life of **t.** enemies;
1Ki 3:20 beside me, while **t.** handmaid slept,
1Ki 3:26 it be neither mine nor **t.**, but divide it.
1Ki 8:18 it was in **t.** heart to build an house
1Ki 8:18 thou didst well that it was in **t.** heart.
1Ki 8:24 and hast fulfilled it with **t.** hand,
1Ki 8:29 That **t.** eyes may be open toward this
1Ki 8:31 the oath come before **t.** altar in this
1Ki 8:51 they be thy people, and **t.** inheritance,
1Ki 8:52 That **t.** eyes may be open unto the
1Ki 8:53 of the earth, to be **t.** inheritance,
1Ki 11:22 thou seekest to go to **t.** own country?
1Ki 12:16 now see to **t.** own house, David
1Ki 13:8 If thou wilt give me half **t.** house, I
1Ki 13:18 Bring him back with thee into **t.** house,
1Ki 14:12 therefore, get thee to **t.** own house:
1Ki 17:11 thee, a morsel of bread in **t.** hand.
1Ki 19:10, 14 thrown down **t.** altars, and slain thy
1Ki 20:4 thy saying, I am **t.**, and all that I have.
1Ki 20:6 they shall search **t.** house, and the
1Ki 20:6 that whatsoever is pleasant in **t.** eyes,
1Ki 20:13 I will deliver it into **t.** hand this day;
1Ki 20:28 all this great multitude into **t.** hand,
1Ki 21:7 eat bread, and let **t.** heart be merry:
1Ki 21:19 shall dogs lick thy blood, even **t.**. 859
1Ki 21:22 And will make **t.** house like the house
1Ki 22:34 Turn **t.** hand, and carry me out of the
2Ki 4:2 **T.** handmaid hath not any thing in
2Ki 4:16 of God, do not lie unto **t.** handmaid.
2Ki 4:29 and take my staff in **t.** hand, and go
2Ki 7:2, 19 thou shalt see it with **t.** eyes, but
2Ki 8:1 Arise, and go thou and **t.** household,
2Ki 8:8 Take a present in **t.** hand, and go,
2Ki 9:1 and take this box of oil in **t.** hand,
2Ki 10:5 do thou that which is good in **t.** eyes.
2Ki 10:15 If it be, give me **t.** hand.
2Ki 10:15 Is **t.** heart right, as my heart is with
2Ki 13:16 of Israel, Put **t.** hand upon the bow.
2Ki 14:10 and **t.** heart hath lifted thee up:
2Ki 19:16 Lord, bow down **t.** ear, and hear:
2Ki 19:16 open, Lord, **t.** eyes, and see: and hear
2Ki 19:22 voice, and lifted up **t.** eyes on high?
2Ki 20:1 Set **t.** house in order; for thou shalt
2Ki 20:15 said, What have they seen in **t.** house?
2Ki 20:17 days come, that all that is in **t.** house,
2Ki 22:19 Because **t.** heart was tender, and thou
2Ki 22:20 **t.** eyes shall not see all the evil which
1Ch 4:10 and that **t.** hand might be with me,
1Ch 12:18 **T.** are we, David, and on thy side,
1Ch 12:18 unto thee, and peace be to **t.** helpers;
1Ch 14:10 for I will deliver them into **t.** hand.
1Ch 17:2 unto David, Do all that is in **t.** heart;
1Ch 17:8 cut off all **t.** enemies from before thee,
1Ch 17:10 Moreover I will subdue all **t.** enemies.
1Ch 17:17 was a small thing in **t.** eyes, O God;
1Ch 17:19 according to **t.** own heart, hast thou
1Ch 17:22 Israel didst thou make **t.** own people
1Ch 21:12 sword of **t.** enemies overtaketh thee;
1Ch 21:15 It is enough, stay now **t.** hand.
1Ch 21:17 let **t.** hand, I pray thee, O Lord my
1Ch 21:24 not take that which is **t.** for the Lord,
1Ch 29:11 **T.**, O Lord, is the greatness, and the
1Ch 29:11 is in the heaven and in the earth is **t.**;
1Ch 29:11 **t.** is the kingdom, O Lord, and thou
1Ch 29:12 and in **t.** hand is power and might;
1Ch 29:12 and in **t.** hand it is to make great, and
1Ch 29:14 and of **t.** own have we given thee
1Ch 29:16 build thee an house for **t.** holy name
1Ch 29:16 cometh of **t.** hand, and is all **t.** own.
2Ch 1:11 Because this was in **t.** heart, and thou
2Ch 1:11 or honour, nor the life of **t.** enemies,
2Ch 6:8 as it was in **t.** heart to build an house
2Ch 6:8 didst well in that it was in **t.** heart:
2Ch 6:15 and hast fulfilled it with **t.** hand, as it
2Ch 6:20 That **t.** eyes may be open upon this
2Ch 6:22 the oath come before **t.** altar in this
2Ch 6:40 Now, my God, let,...**t.** eyes be open,
2Ch 6:40 let **t.** ears be attent unto the prayer
2Ch 6:42 turn not away the face of **t.** anointed:
2Ch 9:5 I heard in mine own land of **t.** acts,
2Ch 10:16 and now, David, see to **t.** own house.
2Ch 16:7 king of Syria escaped out of **t.** hand.
2Ch 16:8 Lord, he delivered them into **t.** hand.
2Ch 18:33 Turn **t.** hand, that thou mayest carry
2Ch 19:3 hast prepared **t.** heart to seek God.
2Ch 20:6 in **t.** hand is there not power and
2Ch 25:15 their own people out of **t.** hand?
2Ch 25:19 and **t.** heart lifteth thee up to boast:
2Ch 25:19 why shouldest thou meddle to **t.** hurt,
2Ch 26:18 neither shall it be for **t.** honour from
2Ch 34:27 Because **t.** heart was tender, and thou
2Ch 34:28 neither shall **t.** eyes see all the evil
Ezr 7:14 law of thy God which is in **t.** hand;
Ezr 7:25 wisdom of thy God, that is in **t.** hand,
Ne 1:6 Let **t.** ear now be attentive, and
Ne 1:6 and **t.** eyes open, that thou mayest
Ne 1:11 let now **t.** ear be attentive to the prayer
Ne 6:8 thou feignest them out of **t.** own heart.
Job 1:11 But put forth **t.** hand now, and touch
Job 1:12 upon himself put not forth **t.** hand
Job 2:5 But put forth **t.** hand now, and touch
Job 2:6 he is in **t.** hand; but save his life.
Job 2:9 Dost thou still retain **t.** integrity?
Job 5:25 **t.** offspring as the grass of the earth.
Job 7:8 **t.** eyes are upon me, and I am not.
Job 7:17 thou shouldest set **t.** heart upon him?
Job 10:3 shouldest despise the work of **t.** hands,
Job 10:7 none that can deliver out of **t.** hand.
Job 10:8 **T.** hands have made me and
Job 10:13 these things hast thou hid in **t.** heart:
Job 10:17 increasest **t.** indignation upon me;
Job 11:4 is pure, and I am clean in **t.** eyes.
Job 11:6 of thee less than **t.** iniquity deserveth.
Job 11:13 If thou prepare **t.** heart, and stretch
Job 11:13 and stretch out **t.** hands toward him;
Job 11:14 If iniquity be in **t.** hand, put it far
Job 11:17 And **t.** age shall be clearer than the
Job 13:21 Withdraw **t.** hand far from me: and
Job 13:24 thy face, and holdest me for **t.** enemy?
Job 14:3 thou open **t.** eyes upon such an one,
Job 14:15 have a desire to the work of **t.** hands.
Job 15:5 For thy mouth uttereth **t.** iniquity,
Job 15:6 **T.** own mouth condemneth thee, and
Job 15:6 yea, **t.** own lips testify against thee.
Job 15:12 Why doth **t.** heart carry thee away?
Job 22:5 great? and **t.** iniquities infinite?
Job 22:22 and lay up his words in **t.** heart.
Job 22:30 delivered by the pureness of **t.** hands.
Job 35:7 him? or what receiveth he of **t.** hand?
Job 40:14 that **t.** own right hand can save thee.
Job 41:8 Lay **t.** hand upon him, remember the
Ps 2:8 thee the heathen for **t.** inheritance,
Ps 6:1 O Lord, rebuke me not in **t.** anger,
Ps 7:6 Arise, O Lord, in **t.** anger, lift up
Ps 8:2 strength because of **t.** enemies
Ps 10:12 O God, lift up **t.** hand: forget not the
Ps 10:17 heart, thou wilt cause **t.** ear to hear:
Ps 16:10 wilt thou suffer **t.** Holy One to see
Ps 17:2 let **t.** eyes behold the things that are
Ps 17:6 incline **t.** ear unto me, and hear my
Ps 20:4 Grant thee according to **t.** own heart,
Ps 21:8 **T.** hand shall find out all **t.** enemies:
Ps 21:9 as a fiery oven in the time of **t.** anger:
Ps 21:12 make ready **t.** arrows upon thy strings
Ps 21:13 thou exalted, Lord, in **t.** own strength:
Ps 26:6 so will I compass **t.** altar, O Lord:
Ps 26:8 the place where **t.** honour dwelleth.
Ps 27:14 and he shall strengthen **t.** heart:
Ps 28:9 thy people, and bless **t.** inheritance:
Ps 31:2 Bow down **t.** ear to me; deliver me
Ps 31:5 Into **t.** hand I commit my spirit: thou
Ps 31:22 haste, I am cut off from before **t.** eyes:
Ps 37:4 he shall give thee the desire of **t.** heart,
Ps 38:2 For **t.** arrows stick fast in me, and thy
Ps 38:3 in my flesh because of **t.** anger;
Ps 39:10 I am consumed by the blow of **t.** hand.
Ps 44:3 **t.** arm,...the light of thy countenance,
Ps 45:5 **T.** arrows are sharp in the heart of the
Ps 45:10 and consider, and incline **t.** ear;
Ps 45:10 forget also **t.** own people, and thy
Ps 50:20 thou slanderest **t.** own mother's son.
Ps 50:21 and set them in order before **t.** eyes.
Ps 51:19 shall they offer bullocks upon **t.** altar.
Ps 56:7 in **t.** anger cast down the people, O
Ps 66:3 shall **t.** enemies submit themselves
Ps 68:9 thou didst confirm **t.** inheritance,
Ps 68:23 be dipped in the blood of **t.** enemies,
Ps 69:9 the zeal of **t.** house hath eaten me up;
Ps 69:24 Pour out **t.** indignation upon them,
Ps 71:2 incline **t.** ear unto me, and save me.
Ps 71:16 of thy righteousness, even of **t.** only.
Ps 74:1 why doth **t.** anger smoke against the
Ps 74:2 rod of **t.** inheritance, which thou hast
Ps 74:4 **T.** enemies roar in the midst of thy
Ps 74:16 The day is **t.**, the night also is **t.**: thou
Ps 74:22 Arise, O God, plead **t.** own cause:
Ps 74:23 Forget not the voice of **t.** enemies: the
Ps 77:15 hast with **t.** arm redeemed thy people,
Ps 77:17 a sound: **t.** arrows also went abroad.
Ps 79:1 heathen are come into **t.** inheritance;
Ps 83:2 For, lo, **t.** enemies make a tumult:
Ps 84:3 she may lay her young, even **t.** altars,
Ps 84:9 and look upon the face of **t.** anointed.
Ps 85:3 thyself from the fierceness of **t.** anger.
Ps 85:4 and cause **t.** anger toward us to cease.
Ps 85:5 wilt thou draw out **t.** anger to all
Ps 86:1 Bow down **t.** ear, O Lord, hear me: for
Ps 86:16 and save the son of **t.** handmaid.

Ps 88:2 before thee: incline **t.** ear unto my cry;
Ps 89:10 hast scattered **t.** enemies with thy
Ps 89:11 the heavens are **t.**, the earth also is **t.**:
Ps 89:38 thou hast been wroth with **t.** anointed
Ps 89:51 Wherewith **t.** enemies...reproached, O
Ps 89:51 reproached the footsteps of **t.** anointed
Ps 90:7 For we are consumed by **t.** anger, and
Ps 90:11 Who knoweth the power of **t.** anger?
Ps 91:8 Only with **t.** eyes shalt thou behold
Ps 92:9 For, lo, **t.** enemies, O Lord, for, lo,
Ps 92:9 **t.** enemies shall perish; all the
Ps 93:5 holiness becometh **t.** house, O Lord,
Ps 94:5 people, O Lord, and afflict **t.** heritage
Ps 102:2 am in trouble; incline **t.** ear unto me:
Ps 102:10 Because of **t.** indignation and thy
Ps 103:3 Who forgiveth all **t.** iniquities; who
Ps 104:28 thou openest **t.** hand, they are filled
Ps 106:5 that I may glory with **t.** inheritance
Ps 110:1 until I make **t.** enemies thy footstool
Ps 110:2 rule thou in the midst of **t.** enemies
Ps 116:16 servant, and the son of **t.** handmaid:
Ps 119:91 this day according to **t.** ordinances:
Ps 119:94 I am **t.**, save me; for I have sought
Ps 119:173 Let **t.** hand help me; for I have chosen
Ps 128:2 thou shalt eat the labour of **t.** hands:
Ps 128:3 a fruitful vine by the side of **t.** house:
Ps 130:2 let **t.** ears be attentive to the voice of
Ps 132:10 turn not away the face of **t.** anointed
Ps 138:7 thou shalt stretch forth **t.** hand against
Ps 138:8 forsake not the works of **t.** own hands.
Ps 139:5 and before, and laid **t.** hand upon me.
Ps 139:16 **T.** eyes did see my substance, yet
Ps 139:20 and **t.** enemies take thy name in vain.
Ps 144:6 shoot out **t.** arrows, and destroy them.
Ps 144:7 Send **t.** hand from above; rid me, and
Ps 145:16 Thou openest **t.** hand, and satisfiest
Pr 2:2 that thou incline **t.** ear unto wisdom,
Pr 2:2 and apply **t.** heart to understanding;
Pr 2:10 When wisdom entereth into **t.** heart,
Pr 3:1 let **t.** heart keep my commandments:
Pr 3:3 write them upon the table of **t.** heart:
Pr 3:5 Trust in the Lord with all **t.** heart;
Pr 3:5 lean not unto **t.** own understanding.
Pr 3:7 Be not wise in **t.** own eyes: fear the
Pr 3:9 with the firstfruits of all **t.** increase:
Pr 3:21 son, let not them depart from **t.** eyes:
Pr 3:27 it is in the power of **t.** hand to do it
Pr 4:4 unto me, Let **t.** heart retain my words:
Pr 4:9 give to **t.** head an ornament of grace:
Pr 4:20 words; incline **t.** ear unto my sayings.
Pr 4:21 Let them not depart from **t.** eyes;
Pr 4:21 keep them in the midst of **t.** heart
Pr 4:25 Let **t.** eyes look right on, and let
Pr 4:25 let **t.** eyelids look straight before thee.
Pr 5:1 and bow **t.** ear to my understanding:
Pr 5:9 Lest thou give **t.** honour unto others,
Pr 5:15 Drink waters out of **t.** own cistern, and
Pr 5:15 and running waters out of **t.** own well.
Pr 5:17 Let them be only **t.** own, and not
Pr 6:4 Give not sleep to **t.** eyes, nor slumber
Pr 6:4 eyes, nor slumber to **t.** eyelids.
Pr 6:21 Bind them continually upon **t.** heart,
Pr 6:25 Lust not after her beauty in **t.** heart;
Pr 7:2 live; and my law as the apple of **t.** eye.
Pr 7:3 write them upon the table of **t.** heart.
Pr 7:25 Let not **t.** heart decline to her ways, go
Pr 20:13 open **t.** eyes, and thou shalt be satisfied
Pr 22:17 Bow down **t.** ear, and hear the words
Pr 22:17 and apply **t.** heart unto my knowledge.
Pr 23:4 to be rich: cease from **t.** own wisdom.
Pr 23:5 thou set **t.** eyes upon that which is not?
Pr 23:12 Apply **t.** heart unto instruction, and
Pr 23:12 and **t.** ears to the words of knowledge.
Pr 23:15 if **t.** heart be wise, my heart shall
Pr 23:17 Let not **t.** heart envy sinners: but be
Pr 23:18 and **t.** expectation shall not be cut off
Pr 23:19 be wise, and guide **t.** heart in the way.
Pr 23:26 My son, give me **t.** heart, and let
Pr 23:26 heart, and let **t.** eyes observe my ways.
Pr 23:33 **T.** eyes shall behold strange women,
Pr 23:33 **t.** heart shall utter perverse things.
Pr 24:17 Rejoice not when **t.** enemy falleth, and
Pr 24:17 let not **t.** heart be glad when he
Pr 24:27 field; and afterwards build **t.** house.
Pr 25:7 of the prince whom **t.** eyes have seen.
Pr 25:10 shame, and **t.** infamy turn not away.
Pr 25:21 If **t.** enemy be hungry, give him bread
Pr 27:2 praise thee, and not **t.** own mouth;
Pr 27:2 a stranger, and not **t.** own lips.
Pr 27:10 **T.** own friend, and thy father's friend,
Pr 30:32 evil, lay **t.** hand upon thy mouth.
Ec 5:2 not **t.** heart be hasty to utter any thing
Ec 5:6 and destroy the work of **t.** hands?
Ec 7:18 also from this withdraw not **t.** hand:
Ec 7:22 oftentimes also **t.** own heart knoweth
Ec 11:6 in the evening withhold not **t.** hand:
Ec 11:9 and walk in the ways of **t.** heart, and
Ec 11:9 and in the sight of **t.** eyes: but know
Ca 4:9 ravished my heart with one of **t.** eyes,
Ca 4:10 smell of **t.** ointments than all spices!
Ca 6:5 Turn away **t.** eyes from me, for they
Ca 7:4 **t.** eyes like the fishpools in Heshbon,
Ca 7:5 **T.** head upon thee is like Carmel, and
Ca 7:5 and the hair of **t.** head like purple;
Ca 8:6 Set me as a seal upon **t.** heart, as a seal
Ca 8:6 as a seal upon **t.** arm; for love is
Isa 6:7 **t.** iniquity is taken away, and thy sin
Isa 12:1 **t.** anger is turned away, and thou
Isa 14:13 For thou hast said in **t.** heart, I will
Isa 26:11 fire of **t.** enemies shall devour them.
Isa 30:20 but **t.** eyes shall see thy teachers:
Isa 30:21 **t.** ears shall hear a word behind thee,
Isa 33:17 **T.** eyes shall see the king in...beauty:
Isa 33:18 **T.** heart shall meditate terror. Where
Isa 33:20 **t.** eyes shall see Jerusalem a quiet
Isa 37:17 Incline **t.** ear, O Lord, and hear; open
Isa 37:17 hear; open **t.** eyes, O Lord, and see:
Isa 37:23 thy voice, and lifted up **t.** eyes on high?
Isa 38:1 Set **t.** house in order: for thou shalt
Isa 39:4 he, What have they seen in **t.** house?
Isa 39:6 days come, that all that is in **t.** house,
Isa 42:6 will hold **t.** hand, and will keep thee,
Isa 43:24 hast wearied me with **t.** iniquities.
Isa 44:3 and my blessing upon **t.** offspring:
Isa 45:14 over unto thee, and they shall be **t.**:
Isa 47:6 and given them into **t.** hand:
Isa 47:8 that sayest in **t.** heart, I am, and none
Isa 47:9 great abundance of **t.** enchantments.
Isa 47:10 and thou hast said in **t.** heart, I am,
Isa 47:12 Stand now with **t.** enchantments, and
Isa 48:8 that time that **t.** ear was not opened:
Isa 49:18 Lift up **t.** eyes round about, and
Isa 49:20 the other, shall say again in **t.** ears,
Isa 49:21 Then shalt thou say in **t.** heart, Who
Isa 51:22 have taken out of **t.** hand the cup of
Isa 54:2 forth the curtains of **t.** habitations:
Isa 54:5 For thy Maker is **t.** husband; the Lord
Isa 57:10 thou hast found the life of **t.** hand;
Isa 58:7 thou hide not thyself from **t.** own flesh?
Isa 58:8 **t.** health shall spring forth speedily:
Isa 58:13 honour him, not doing **t.** own ways,
Isa 58:13 nor finding **t.** own pleasure, nor
Isa 58:13 pleasure, nor speaking **t.** own words:
Isa 60:4 Lift up **t.** eyes round about, and see:
Isa 60:5 **t.** heart shall fear, and be enlarged;
Isa 60:17 peace, and **t.** exactors righteousness.
Isa 60:20 the Lord shall be **t.** everlasting light,
Isa 62:8 thy corn to be meat for **t.** enemies;
Isa 63:2 Wherefore art thou red in **t.** apparel,
Isa 63:17 sake, the tribes of **t.** inheritance
Isa 63:19 We art **t.**: thou never barest rule
Isa 64:2 thy name known to **t.** adversaries,
Jer 2:2 of thy youth, the love of **t.** espousals,
Jer 2:19 **T.** own wickedness shall correct thee,
Jer 2:22 yet **t.** iniquity is marked before me,
Jer 2:37 from him, and **t.** hands upon **t.** head:
Jer 3:2 Lift up **t.** eyes unto the high places,
Jer 3:13 Only acknowledge **t.** iniquity, that
Jer 4:1 put away **t.** abominations out of my
Jer 4:14 wash **t.** heart from wickedness,
Jer 4:18 because it reacheth unto **t.** heart.
Jer 5:3 Lord, are not **t.** eyes upon the truth?
Jer 5:17 shall eat up **t.** harvest, and thy bread,
Jer 5:17 shall eat up thy flocks and **t.** herds:
Jer 6:9 turn back **t.** hand as a grapegatherer
Jer 7:29 Cut off **t.** hair, O Jerusalem, and cast
Jer 9:6 **T.** habitation is in the midst of
Jer 10:24 not in **t.** anger, lest thou bring me to
Jer 13:22 And if thou say in **t.** heart, Wherefore
Jer 13:22 For the greatness of **t.** iniquity are thy
Jer 13:27 I have seen **t.** adulteries, and thy
Jer 13:27 and **t.** abominations on the hills in
Jer 15:14 to pass with **t.** enemies into a land
Jer 17:4 discontinue from **t.** heritage that I
Jer 17:4 I will cause thee to serve **t.** enemies in
Jer 18:23 thus with them in the time of **t.** anger
Jer 20:4 enemies, and **t.** eyes shall behold it:
Jer 20:6 Pashur, and all that dwell in **t.** house
Jer 22:17 But **t.** eyes and **t.** heart are not but for
Jer 25:28 refuse to take the cup at **t.** hand to
Jer 28:7 now this word that I speak in **t.** ears,
Jer 30:14 one, for the multitude of **t.** iniquity;
Jer 30:15 Why criest thou for **t.** affliction? thy
Jer 30:15 for the multitude of **t.** iniquity:
Jer 30:16 all **t.** adversaries, every one of them,
Jer 31:16 from weeping, and **t.** eyes from tears:
Jer 31:17 And there is hope in **t.** end, saith the
Jer 31:21 set **t.** heart toward the highway, even
Jer 32:7 Hanameel the son of Shallum **t.** uncle
Jer 32:7 the right of redemption is **t.** to buy it
Jer 32:8 for the right of inheritance is **t.**, and
Jer 32:8 the redemption is **t.**; buy it for thyself
Jer 32:19 for **t.** eyes are open upon all the ways
Jer 34:3 **t.** eyes shall behold the eyes of the
Jer 36:14 Take in **t.** hand the roll wherein thou
Jer 38:12 rotten rags under **t.** armholes under
Jer 38:17 fire; and thou shalt live, and **t.** house:
Jer 40:4 the chains which were upon **t.** hand.
Jer 42:2 few of many, as **t.** eyes do behold us:)
Jer 43:9 Take great stones in **t.** hand, and
Jer 49:16 and the pride of **t.** heart, O thou that
Jer 51:13 abundant in treasures, **t.** end is come,
La 2:14 they have not discovered **t.** iniquity,
La 2:16 **t.** enemies have opened their mouth
La 2:17 caused **t.** enemy to rejoice over thee,
La 2:17 set up the horn of **t.** adversaries.
La 2:18 rest; let not the apple of **t.** eye cease.
La 2:19 pour out **t.** heart like water before
La 2:21 hast slain them in the day of **t.** anger;
La 3:56 hide not **t.** ear at my breathing, at my
La 4:22 The punishment of **t.** iniquity is
La 4:22 he will visit **t.** iniquity, O daughter of
Eze 3:10 speak unto thee receive in **t.** heart,
Eze 3:10 heart, and hear with **t.** ears.
Eze 3:18, 20 his blood will I require at **t.** hand.
Eze 3:24 me, Go, shut thyself within **t.** house.
Eze 4:7 and **t.** arm shall be uncovered,
Eze 5:1 and cause it to pass upon **t.** head and
Eze 5:9 like, because of all **t.** abominations.
Eze 5:11 and with all **t.** abominations, therefore
Eze 6:11 Smite with **t.** hand, and stamp with
Eze 7:3 upon thee all **t.** abominations.
Eze 7:4 **t.** abominations shall be in the midst
Eze 7:8 thee for all **t.** abominations.
Eze 7:9 thy ways and **t.** abominations that are
Eze 8:5 lift up **t.** eyes now the way toward the
Eze 10:2 fill **t.** hands with coals of fire between
Eze 16:6 saw thee polluted in **t.** own blood, I
Eze 16:7 are fashioned, and **t.** hair is grown,
Eze 16:12 thy forehead, and earrings in **t.** ears,
Eze 16:12 and a beautiful crown upon **t.** head.
Eze 16:15 But thou didst trust in **t.** own beauty,
Eze 16:22 **t.** abominations and thy whoredoms
Eze 16:27 and have diminished **t.** ordinary food,
Eze 16:30 How weak is **t.** heart, saith the Lord
Eze 16:31 buildest **t.** eminent place in the head
Eze 16:31 makest **t.** high place in every street;
Eze 16:39 shall throw down **t.** eminent place,
Eze 16:41 they shall burn **t.** houses with fire, and
Eze 16:43 will recompense thy way upon **t.** head,
Eze 16:43 lewdness above all **t.** abominations.
Eze 16:46 **t.** elder sister is Samaria, she and her
Eze 16:51 multiplied **t.** abominations more than
Eze 16:51 thy sisters in all **t.** abominations
Eze 16:52 bear **t.** own shame for thy sins that
Eze 16:54 That thou mayest bear **t.** own shame,
Eze 16:58 thy lewdness and **t.** abominations,
Eze 16:61 thy sisters, **t.** elder and thy younger:
Eze 21:14 prophesy, and smite **t.** hands together,
Eze 22:4 and hast defiled thyself in **t.** idols
Eze 22:14 Can **t.** heart endure, or can
Eze 22:14 can **t.** hands be strong, in the days
Eze 22:16 shalt take **t.** inheritance in thyself
Eze 23:25 shall take away thy nose and **t.** ears;
Eze 23:27 shalt not lift up **t.** eyes unto them,
Eze 23:31 will I give her cup into **t.** hand.
Eze 23:34 thereof, and pluck off **t.** own breasts:
Eze 24:16 the desire of **t.** eyes with a stroke:
Eze 24:17 bind the tire of **t.** head upon thee,
Eze 24:26 to cause thee to hear it with **t.** ears?
Eze 25:6 Because thou hast clapped **t.** hands,

Eze	27:6	of Bashan have they made t. oars;	
Eze	27:10	of Lud and of Phut were in t. army,	
Eze	27:11	The men of Arvad with t. army were	
Eze	27:15	isles were the merchandise of t. hand:	
Eze	28:2	Because t. heart is lifted up, and thou	
Eze	28:2	thou set t. heart as the heart of God:	
Eze	28:4	thy wisdom and with t. understanding	
Eze	28:5	t. heart is lifted up because of thy	
Eze	28:6	hast set t. heart as the heart of God;	
Eze	28:17	T. heart was lifted up because of thy	
Eze	28:18	by the multitude of t. iniquities, by	
Eze	33:8	but his blood will I require at t. hand.	
Eze	35:11	I will even do according to t. anger,	
Eze	35:11	according to t. envy which thou hast	
Eze	37:17	and they shall become one in t. hand.	
Eze	37:20	shall be in t. hand before their eyes.	
Eze	38:4	will bring thee forth, and all t. army,	
Eze	38:12	turn t. hand upon the desolate places	
Eze	39:3	t. arrows to fall out of thy right hand.	
Eze	40:4	me, Son of man, behold with t. eyes,	
Eze	40:4	eyes, and hear with t. ears,	
Eze	40:4	set t. heart upon all that I shall shew	
Eze	44:5	mark well, and behold with t. eyes,	
Eze	44:5	hear with t. ears all that I say unto	
Eze	44:30	cause the blessing to rest in t. house.	
Da	2:38	the heaven hath he given into t. hand,	
Da	3:17	and he will deliver us out of t. hand, O	
Da	4:19	interpretation thereof to t. enemies.	
Da	4:27	t. iniquities by shewing mercy to the	
Da	5:22	hast not humbled t. heart, though	
Da	9:16	t. anger and thy fury be turned away	
Da	9:18	O my God, incline t. ear, and hear;	
Da	9:18	open t. eyes, and behold our	
Da	9:19	defer not, for t. own sake, O my God:	
Da	10:12	thou didst set t. heart to understand,	
Ho	9:7	mad, for the multitude of t. iniquity.	
Ho	13:9	thyself; but in me is t. help.	
Ho	14:1	for thou hast fallen by t. iniquity.	
Joe	2:17	and give not t. heritage to reproach,	
Ob	3	The pride of t. heart hath deceived	
Ob	15	reward shall return upon t. own head.	
Jon	1:8	What is t. occupation? and whence	
Jon	2:7	came in unto thee, into t. holy temple.	
Mic	4:10	thee from the hand of t. enemies.	
Mic	4:13	of Zion: for I will make t. horn iron,	
Mic	5:9	T. hand shall be lifted up upon	
Mic	5:9	shall be lifted up upon t. adversaries,	
Mic	5:9	and all t. enemies shall be cut off.	
Mic	5:12	will cut off witchcrafts out of t. hand;	
Mic	5:13	more worship the work of t. hands.	
Mic	7:14	the flock of t. heritage, which dwell	
Na	3:13	be set wide open unto t. enemies:	
Hab	3:8	was t. anger against the rivers? was	
Hab	3:8	that thou didst ride upon t. horses	
Hab	3:11	at the light of t. arrows they went,	
Hab	3:13	even for salvation with t. anointed;	
Hab	3:15	walk through the sea with t. horses,	
Zep	3:15	judgments, he hath cast out t. enemy:	
Zep	3:16	and to Zion, Let not t. hands be slack.	
Zec	3:4	I have caused t. iniquity to pass from	
Zec	5:5	Lift up now t. eyes, and see what is	
Zec	13:6	What are these wounds in t. hands?	
Mt	5:25	**Agree with t. adversary quickly,**	*4675*
Mt	5:33	**perform unto the Lord t. oaths:**	*4675*
Mt	5:43	**thy neighbour, and hate t. enemy.**	*4675*
Mt	6:2	**Therefore when thou doest t. alms,**	
Mt	6:4	**That t. alms may be in secret:**	*4675*
Mt	6:13	**t. is the kingdom, and the power,**	*4675*
Mt	6:17	**when thou fastest, anoint t. head,**	*4675*
Mt	6:22	**if therefore t. eye be single, thy**	*4675*
Mt	6:23	**But if t. eye be evil, thy whole**	*4675*
Mt	7:3	**not the beam that is in t. own eye?**	*4674*
Mt	7:4	**me pull out the mote out of t. eye;**	*4675*
Mt	7:4	**behold, a beam is in t. own eye?**	*4675*
Mt	7:5	**cast out the beam out of t. own**	*4675*
Mt	9:6	**up thy bed, and go unto t. house.**	*4675*
Mt	12:13	to the man, **Stretch forth t. hand.**	*4675*
Mt	18:9	**if t. eye offend thee, pluck it out,**	*4675*
Mt	20:14	**Take that t. is, and go thy way: I**	*4674*
Mt	20:15	**Is t. eye evil, because I am good?**	*4675*
Mt	22:44	**I make t. enemies thy footstool?**	*4675*
Mt	25:25	**lo, there thou hast that is t.**	*4674*
Mk	2:11	**bed, and go thy way into t. house.**	*4675*
Mk	3:5	the man, **Stretch forth t. hand,**	*4675*
Mk	9:47	**if t. eye offend thee, pluck it out:**	*4675*
Mk	12:36	**I make t. enemies thy footstool.**	*4675*
Lu	4:7	wilt worship me, all shall be t.	*4675*
Lu	5:24	**up thy couch, and go into t. house.**	*4675*
Lu	5:33	Pharisees; but t. eat and drink?	*4674*
Lu	6:41	**not the beam that is in t. own eye?**	*2398*
Lu	6:42	**pull out the mote that is in t. eye.**	*4675*
Lu	6:42	**not the beam that is in t. own eye?**	*4675*
Lu	6:42	**out first the beam out of t. own**	*4675*
Lu	7:44	**I entered into t. house, thou gavest**	*4675*
Lu	8:39	**return to t. own house, and shew**	*4675*
Lu	11:34	**therefore when t. eye is single, thy**	*4675*
Lu	11:34	**but when t. eye is evil, thy body**	
Lu	12:19	**take t. ease, eat, drink, and be merry.**	
Lu	12:58	**When thou goest with t. adversary**	*4675*
Lu	13:12	**thou art loosed from t. infirmity**	*4675*
Lu	15:31	**with me, and all that I have is t.**	*4674*
Lu	19:22	**Out of t. own mouth will I judge**	*4675*
Lu	19:42	**but now they are hid from t. eyes.**	*4675*
Lu	19:43	**that t. enemies shall cast a trench**	*4675*
Lu	20:43	**I make t. enemies thy footstool**	*4675*
Lu	22:42	**not my will, but t., be done.**	*4674*
Joh	2:17	zeal of t. house hath eaten me up.	*4675*
Joh	8:10	**where are those t. accusers?**	*4675*
Joh	9:10	unto him, How were t. eyes opened?	*4675*
Joh	9:17	of him, that he hath opened t. eyes?	*4675*
Joh	9:26	he to thee? how opened he t. eyes?	*4675*
Joh	17:5	**glorify thou me with t. own self**	*4572*
Joh	17:6	**t. they were, and thou gavest them**	*4671*
Joh	17:9	**thou hast given me; for they are t.**	*4671*
Joh	17:10	**And all mine are t., and**	*4674*
Joh	17:10	**and t. are mine; and I am**	*3588,4674*
Joh	17:11	**keep through t. own name those**	*4675*
Joh	18:35	**T.** own nation and the chief	*4674*
Ac	2:27	wilt thou suffer t. Holy One to see	*4675*
Ac	4:30	By stretching forth t. hand to heal;	*4675*
Ac	5:3	Satan filled t. heart to lie to the	*4675*
Ac	5:4	it remained, was it not t. own?	*4671*
Ac	5:4	was it not in t. own power?	*3588,4674*
Ac	5:4	conceived this thing in t. heart?	*4675*
Ac	8:22	the thought of t. heart may be	*4671*
Ac	8:37	If thou believest with all t. heart,	*3588*
Ac	10:4	t. alms are come up for a memorial	*3588*
Ac	10:31	t. alms are had in remembrance	*4675*
Ac	13:35	shalt not suffer t. Holy One to see	*4675*
Ac	23:35	when t. accusers are also come.	*4675*
Ro	10:6	Say not in t. heart, Who shall	*4675*
Ro	10:9	shalt believe in t. heart that God	*4675*
Ro	11:3	and digged down t. altars;	*4675*
Ro	12:20	Therefore if t. enemy hunger, feed	*4675*
1Co	10:29	I say, not t. own, but of the other:	*1438*
1Ti	5:23	sake and t. ofter infirmities.	*4675*
Phm	19	unto me even t. own self besides.	*4572*
Heb	1:10	heavens are the works of t. hands:	*4675*
Heb	1:13	I make t. enemies thy footstool?	*4675*
Re	3:18	**and anoint t. eyes with eyesalve,**	*4675*

THING See also ANYTHING; NOTHING; SOMETHING; THINGS.

Ge	1:24	and creeping t., and beast of the earth	
Ge	1:25	every t. that creepeth upon the earth	
Ge	1:26	over every creeping t. that creepeth	
Ge	1:28	every living t. that moveth upon the	
Ge	1:30	every t. that creepeth upon the earth,	
Ge	1:31	God saw every t. that he had made.	
Ge	6:7	man, and beast, and the creeping t.,	
Ge	6:17	every t. that is in the earth shall die.	
Ge	6:19	And of every living t. of all flesh, two	
Ge	6:20	every creeping t. of the earth after his	
Ge	7:8	every t. that creepeth upon the earth,	
Ge	7:14,	21 every creeping t. that creepeth	
Ge	8:1	and every living t., and all the cattle	
Ge	8:17	Bring forth with thee every living t.	
Ge	8:17	every creeping t. that creepeth upon	
Ge	8:19	Every beast, every creeping t., and	
Ge	8:21	smite any more every t. living,	
Ge	9:3	Every moving t. that liveth shall be	
Ge	14:23	will not take any t. that is thine,	
Ge	18:14	Is any t. too hard for the Lord?	1697
Ge	18:17	hide from Abraham that t. which I do;	
Ge	19:21	thee concerning this t. also,	1697
Ge	19:22	cannot do any t. till thou be come	1697
Ge	20:10	thou, that thou hast done this t.?	1697
Ge	21:11	And the t. was very grievous in	1697
Ge	21:26	I wot not who hath done this t.	1697
Ge	22:12	neither do thou any t. unto him: for	
Ge	22:16	for because thou hast done this t.,	1697
Ge	24:50	The t. proceedeth from the Lord:	1697
Ge	30:31	Thou shalt not give me any t.	1697
Ge	30:31	if thou wilt do this t. for me, I will	1697
Ge	34:7	which t. ought not to be done.	3651
Ge	34:14	We cannot do this t., to give our	1697
Ge	34:19	man deferred not to do the t.,	1697
Ge	38:10	the t. which he did displeased the	
Ge	39:9	hath he kept back any t. from me	3972
Ge	39:23	looked not to any t. that was under	3972
Ge	41:28	This is the t. which I have spoken	1697
Ge	41:32	because the t. is established by God,	1697
Ge	41:37	t. was good in the eyes of Pharaoh,	1697
Ge	44:7	should do according to this t.	1697
Ex	1:18	Why have ye done this t., and have	1697
Ex	2:14	and said, Surely this t. is known.	1697
Ex	2:15	Now when Pharaoh heard this t.,	1697
Ex	9:5	the Lord shall do this t. in the land.	1697
Ex	9:6	the Lord did that t. on the morrow,	1697
Ex	10:15	remained not any green t. in the trees,	
Ex	12:24	observe this t. for an ordinance	1697
Ex	16:14	there lay a small round t., as small as	
Ex	16:16,	32 This is the t. which the Lord	1697
Ex	18:11	in the t. wherein they dealt proudly	1697
Ex	18:14	t. that thou doest to the people?	1697
Ex	18:17	The t. that thou doest is not good.	1697
Ex	18:18	for this t. is too heavy for thee;	1697
Ex	18:23	If thou shalt do this t., and God	1697
Ex	20:4	or any likeness of any t. that is in	
Ex	20:17	ass, nor any t. that is thy neighbour's.	
Ex	22:9	raiment, or for any manner of lost t.,	
Ex	22:15	if it be an hired t., it came for his	
Ex	29:1	this is the t. that thou shalt do	1697
Ex	33:17	this t. also that thou hast spoken:	1697
Ex	34:10	is a terrible t. that I will do with thee.	
Ex	35:4	the t. which the Lord commanded,	1697
Le	2:3,	10 it is a t. most holy of the offerings	
Le	4:13	the t. be hid from the eyes of the	1697
Le	5:2	Or if a soul touch any unclean t.,	1697
Le	5:5	confess that he hath sinned in that t.	
Le	5:16	harm that he hath done in the holy t.,	
Le	6:2	or in a t. taken away by violence, or	
Le	6:4	the t. which he hath deceitfully gotten,	
Le	6:4	to keep, or the lost t. which he found,	
Le	6:7	forgiven him for any t. of all that he	
Le	7:19	flesh that toucheth any unclean t.	
Le	7:21	soul that shall touch any unclean t.,	
Le	7:21	beast, or any abominable unclean t.,	
Le	8:5	the t. which the Lord commanded	1697
Le	9:6	the t. which the Lord commanded	1697
Le	11:10	living t. which is in the waters,	5315
Le	11:21	may ye eat of every flying creeping t.	
Le	11:35	every t. whereupon any part of their	
Le	11:41	every creeping t. that creepeth upon	
Le	11:43	abominable with any creeping t. that	
Le	11:44	creeping t. that creepeth upon the	
Le	12:4	she shall touch no hallowed t., nor	
Le	13:48	a skin, or in any t. made of skin;	4399
Le	13:49	or in the woof, or in any t. of skin;	3627
Le	13:52	linen, or any t. of skin, wherein the	3627
Le	13:53	or in the woof, or in any t. of skin:	3627
Le	13:54	wash the t. wherein the plague is,	
Le	13:57	or in the woof, or in any t. of skin;	3627
Le	13:58	woof, or whatsoever t. of skin it be,	3627
Le	13:59	warp, or woof, or any t. of skins,	3627
Le	15:4	and every t., whereon he sitteth,	3627
Le	15:6	he that sitteth on any t. whereon	3627
Le	15:10	toucheth any t. that was under him	
Le	15:20	And every t. that she lieth upon in	
Le	15:20	every t. also that she sitteth upon	
Le	15:22	toucheth any t. that she sat upon	3627
Le	15:23	or on any t. whereon she sitteth,	3627
Le	17:2	This is the t. which the Lord hath	1697
Le	19:8	hath profaned the hallowed t. of the	
Le	19:26	Ye shall not eat any t. with the blood:	
Le	20:17	it is a wicked t.; and they shall be cut	
Le	20:21	his brother's wife, it is an unclean t.	
Le	20:25	any manner of living t. that creepeth	
Le	21:18	hath a flat nose, or any t. superfluous,	
Le	22:4	whoso toucheth any t. that is unclean	
Le	22:5	whosoever toucheth any creeping t.	
Le	22:10	shall no stranger eat of the holy t.	
Le	22:10	servant, shall not eat of the holy t.	
Le	22:14	if a man eat of the holy t. unwittingly,	
Le	22:14	give it unto the priest with the holy t.	
Le	22:23	lamb that hath any t. superfluous or	
Le	23:37	offerings, every t. upon his day:	1697
Le	27:23	that day, as a holy t. unto the Lord.	
Le	27:28	no devoted t., that a man shall devote	
Le	27:28	every devoted t. is most holy unto the	

Nu 4:15 but they shall not touch any holy **t.**,
Nu 16:9 Seemeth it but a small **t.** unto you,
Nu 16:13 it a small **t.** that thou hast brought us
Nu 16:30 But if the Lord make a new **t.**, and the
Nu 17:13 cometh any **t.** near unto the tabernacle
Nu 18:7 office for every **t.** of the altar, 1697
Nu 18:14 **t.** devoted in Israel shall be thine.
Nu 18:15 **t.** that openeth the matrix in all flesh,
Nu 20:19 without doing any **t.** else, go 1697
Nu 22:38 now any power at all to say any **t.**? 3972
Nu 30:1 **t.**...the Lord hath commanded. 1697
Nu 31:23 Every **t.** that may abide the fire, 1697
Nu 32:20 If ye will do this **t.**, if ye will go 1697
Nu 35:22 him any **t.** without laying of wait, 3627
Nu 36:6 **t.** which the Lord doth command 1697
De 1:14 **t.** which thou hast spoken is good 1697
De 1:32 this **t.** ye did not believe the Lord 1697
De 4:18 The likeness of any **t.** that creepeth on
De 4:23, 25 image, or the likeness of any **t.**,
De 4:32 there hath been any such **t.** as this
De 4:32 been any such...as this great **t.** is, 1697
De 5:8 likeness of any **t.** that is in heaven
De 5:21 or any **t.** that is thy neighbour's.
De 7:26 house, lest thou be a cursed **t.** like it:
De 7:26 utterly abhor it; for it is a cursed **t.**.
De 8:9 thou shalt not lack any **t.** in it;
De 12:32 What **t.** soever I command you, 1697
De 13:14 if it be truth, and the **t.** certain, 1697
De 13:17 of the cursed **t.** to thine hand:
De 14:3 Thou shalt not eat any abominable **t.**.
De 14:19 every creeping **t.** that flieth is unclean
De 14:21 not eat of any **t.** that dieth of itself:
De 15:10 for this **t.** the Lord thy God shall 1697
De 15:15 I command thee this **t.** to day. 1697
De 16:4 shall there any **t.** of the flesh,
De 17:4 it be true, and the **t.** certain, 1697
De 17:5 have committed that wicked **t.**, 1697
De 18:22 if the **t.** follow not, nor come to pass, 1697
De 18:22 **t.** which the Lord hath not spoken, 1697
De 22:3 and with all lost **t.** of thy brother's,
De 22:20 But if this **t.** be true, and the tokens 1697
De 23:9 keep thee from every wicked **t.**. 1697
De 23:14 that he see no unclean **t.** in thee, 1697
De 23:19 usury of any **t.** that is lent upon 1697
De 24:10 dost lend thy brother any **t.**, 4859
De 24:18, 22 I command thee to do this **t.**. 1697
De 26:11 thou shalt rejoice in every good **t.**
De 31:13 children, which have not known any **t.**,
De 32:47 For it is not a vain **t.** for you; 1697
De 32:47 through this **t.** you shall prolong 1697
Jos 4:10 until every **t.** was finished that the 1697
Jos 6:18 keep yourselves from the accursed **t.**,
Jos 6:18 accursed, when ye take the accursed **t.**,
Jos 7:1 a trespass in the accursed **t.**
Jos 7:1 of Judah, took of the accursed **t.**
Jos 7:11 have even taken of the accursed **t.**,
Jos 7:13 is an accursed **t.** in the midst of thee,
Jos 7:13 away the cursed **t.** from among you.
Jos 7:15 he that is taken with the accursed **t.**
Jos 9:24 of you, and have done this **t.**. 1697
Jos 14:6 knowest the **t.** that the Lord said 1697
Jos 21:45 failed not ought of any good **t.** which 1697
Jos 22:20 commit a trespass in the accursed **t.**,
Jos 22:24 rather done it for fear of this **t.**, 1697
Jos 22:33 the **t.** pleased the children of Israel; 1697
Jos 23:14 not one **t.** hath failed of all the good 1697
Jos 23:14 and not one **t.** hath failed thereof. 1697
Jg 6:29 another, Who hath done this **t.**? 1697
Jg 6:29 the son of Joash hath done this **t.**. 1697
Jg 8:27 which **t.** became a snare unto Gideon,
Jg 11:25 are thou any **t.** better than Balak
Jg 11:37 father, Let this **t.** be done for me: 1697
Jg 13:4 drink, and eat not any unclean **t.**
Jg 13:7 drink, neither eat any unclean **t.**
Jg 13:14 not eat of any **t.** that cometh from the
Jg 13:14 strong drink, nor eat any unclean **t.**
Jg 18:7 put them to shame in any **t.**; 1697
Jg 18:10 where there is no want of any **t.** 1697
Jg 19:19 servants: there is no want of any **t.** 1697
Jg 19:24 unto this man do not so vile a **t.** 1697
Jg 20:9 the **t.** which we will do to Gibeah; 1697
Jg 21:11 And this is the **t.** that ye shall do, 1697
Ru 3:18 he have finished the **t.** this day. 1697
1Sa 3:11 Behold, I will do a **t.** in Israel, at 1697
1Sa 3:17 the **t.** that the Lord hath said unto 1697
1Sa 3:17 if thou hide any **t.** from me of all 1697
1Sa 4:7 hath not been such a **t.** heretofore.
1Sa 8:6 But the **t.** displeased Samuel, 1697
1Sa 12:16 stand and see this great **t.**, 1697
1Sa 14:12 up to us, and we will shew you a **t.** 1697
1Sa 15:9 every **t.** that was vile and refuse, 4399
1Sa 18:20 told Saul, and the **t.** pleased him. 1697
1Sa 18:23 a light **t.** to be the king's son in law,
1Sa 20:2 my father hide this **t.** from me? 1697
1Sa 20:26 Saul spake not any **t.** that day:
1Sa 20:39 But the lad knew not any **t.**: only
1Sa 21:2 man know any **t.** of the business 1697
1Sa 22:15 impute any **t.** unto his servant, 1697
1Sa 24:6 should do this **t.** unto my master, 1697
1Sa 25:15 hurt, neither missed we any **t.**, 1697
1Sa 26:16 **t.** is not good that thou hast done. 1697
1Sa 28:10 happen to thee for this **t.** 1697
1Sa 28:18 hath the Lord done this **t.** unto thee 1697
1Sa 30:19 any **t.** that they had taken to them:
2Sa 2:6 because ye have done this **t.** 1697
2Sa 3:13 but one **t.** I require of thee, that is, 1697
2Sa 7:19 yet a small **t.** in thy sight, O Lord
2Sa 11:11 soul liveth, I will not do this **t.** 1697
2Sa 11:25 Let not this **t.** displease thee, for 1697
2Sa 11:27 But the **t.** that David had done 1697
2Sa 12:5 the man that hath done this **t.** shall
2Sa 12:6 fourfold, because he did this **t.** 1697
2Sa 12:12 I will do this **t.** before all Israel, 1697
2Sa 12:21 What **t.** is this that thou hast done? 1697
2Sa 13:2 hard for him to do any **t.** to her.
2Sa 13:12 for no such **t.** ought to be done in 3651
2Sa 13:20 thy brother, regard not this **t.**. 1697
2Sa 13:33 the king take the **t.** to his heart, 1697
2Sa 14:13 thought such a **t.** against the people of
2Sa 14:13 speak this **t.** as one that is faulty, 1697
2Sa 14:15 speak of this **t.** unto my lord the 1697
2Sa 14:18 thee, the **t.** that I shall ask thee. 1697
2Sa 14:20 hath thy servant Joab done this **t.** 1697
2Sa 14:21 Behold now, I have done this **t.** 1697
2Sa 15:11 simplicity, and they knew not any **t.** 1697
2Sa 15:35 that what **t.** soever thou shalt hear 1697
2Sa 15:36 send unto me every **t.** that ye can 1697
2Sa 17:19 thereon; and the **t.** was not known. 1697
2Sa 24:3 my lord the king delight in this **t.**? 1697
1Ki 1:27 Is this **t.** done by my lord the king, 1697
1Ki 3:10 that Solomon had asked this **t.** 1697
1Ki 3:11 Because thou hast asked this **t.**, 1697
1Ki 10:3 was not any **t.** hid from the king, 1697
1Ki 11:10 commanded him concerning this **t.**, 1697
1Ki 12:24 to his house; for this **t.** is from me. 1697
1Ki 12:30 And this **t.** became a sin: for the 1697
1Ki 13:33 After this **t.** Jeroboam returned not 1697
1Ki 13:34 this **t.** became sin unto the house of 1697
1Ki 14:5 wife of Jeroboam cometh to ask a **t.** 1697
1Ki 14:13 there is found some good **t.** toward 1697
1Ki 15:5 turned not aside from any **t.** that he
1Ki 16:31 had been a light **t.** for him to walk in
1Ki 20:9 I will do: but this **t.** I may not do. 1697
1Ki 20:24 And do this **t.**, Take the kings away, 1697
1Ki 20:33 whether any **t.** would come from him,
2Ki 2:10 And he said, Thou hast asked a hard **t.**:
2Ki 3:18 but a light **t.** in the sight of the Lord:
2Ki 4:2 Thine handmaid hath not any **t.** in the
2Ki 5:13 had bid thee do some great **t.**, 1697
2Ki 5:18 this **t.** the Lord pardon thy servant, 1697
2Ki 5:18 Lord pardon thy servant in this **t.** 1697
2Ki 6:11 Syria was sore troubled for this **t.**; 1697
2Ki 7:2 windows in heaven, might this **t.** be? 1697
2Ki 7:19 in heaven, might such a **t.** be? 1697
2Ki 8:9 even of every good **t.** of Damascus,
2Ki 8:13 that he should do this great **t.**? 1697
2Ki 11:5 This is the **t.** that ye shall do; A 1697
2Ki 17:12 unto them, Ye shall not do this **t.** 1697
2Ki 20:9 will do the **t.** that he hath spoken:
2Ki 20:10 is a light **t.** for the shadow to go down
1Ch 2:7 who transgressed in the **t.** accursed.
1Ch 11:19 forbid it me, that I should do this **t.**:
1Ch 13:4 **t.** was right in the eyes of all the 1697
1Ch 17:17 yet this was a small **t.** in thine eyes,
1Ch 17:23 let the **t.** that thou hast spoken 1697
1Ch 21:3 why then doth my lord require this **t.**?
1Ch 21:7 God was displeased with this **t.**; 1697
1Ch 21:8 greatly, because I have done this **t.** 1697
1Ch 26:28 and whosoever had dedicated any **t.**,
2Ch 9:20 any **t.** accounted of in the days of
2Ch 11:4 house: for this **t.** is done of me. 1697
2Ch 16:10 in a rage with him because of this **t.**
2Ch 23:4 This is the **t.** that ye shall do; A 1697
2Ch 23:19 unclean in any **t.** should enter in. 1697
2Ch 29:36 people: for the **t.** was done suddenly 1697
2Ch 30:4 the **t.** pleased the king and all the 1697
Ezr 7:27 such a **t.** as this in the king's heart,
Ezr 9:3 when I heard this **t.**, I rent my 1697
Ezr 10:2 is hope in Israel concerning this **t.**
Ezr 10:13 that have transgressed in this **t.** 1697
Ne 2:19 What is this **t.** that ye do? will ye 1697
Ne 13:17 What evil **t.** is this that ye do, and 1697
Es 2:4 And the **t.** pleased the king; and he 1697
Es 2:22 the **t.** was known to Mordecai, who 1697
Es 5:14 And the **t.** pleased Haman; and he 1697
Es 6:13 friends every **t.** that had befallen him.
Es 8:5 the **t.** seem right before the king, 1697
Job 3:25 the **t.** which I greatly feared is come
Job 4:12 a **t.** was secretly brought to me, 1697
Job 6:8 God would grant me the **t.** that I long
Job 9:22 This is one **t.**, therefore I said it, He
Job 12:10 hand is the soul of every living **t.**,
Job 13:28 And he, as a rotten **t.**, consumeth, as a
Job 14:4 can bring a clean **t.** out of an unclean?
Job 15:11 is there any secret **t.** with thee? 1697
Job 22:28 Thou shalt also decree a **t.**, and it 562
Job 23:14 he performeth the **t.** that is appointed
Job 26:3 plentifully declared the **t.** as it is?
Job 28:10 and his eye seeth every precious **t.**.
Job 28:11 the **t.** that is hid bringeth he forth to
Job 33:32 (*In most editions*) If thou hast any **t.** to
Job 39:8 and he searcheth after every green **t.**.
Job 42:2 I know that thou canst do every **t.**,
Job 42:7 not spoken of me the **t.** that is right,
Job 42:8 not spoken of me the **t.** which is right,
Ps 2:1 and the people imagine a vain **t.**?
Ps 27:4 One **t.** have I desired of the Lord, that
Ps 33:17 An horse is a vain **t.** for safety:
Ps 34:10 the Lord shall not want any good **t.**.
Ps 38:20 because I follow the **t.** that good is.
Ps 69:34 seas, and every **t.** that moveth therein.
Ps 84:11 no good **t.** will he withhold from them
Ps 89:34 nor alter the **t.** that is gone out of my
Ps 92:1 It is a good **t.** to give thanks unto the
Ps 101:3 set no wicked **t.** before mine eyes: 1697
Ps 141:4 Incline not my heart to any evil **t.**, 1697
Ps 145:16 satisfiest the desire of every living **t.**.
Ps 150:6 **t.** that hath breath praise the Lord.
Pr 4:7 Wisdom is the principal **t.**; therefore
Pr 18:22 Whoso findeth a wife findeth a good **t.**,
Pr 22:18 For it is a pleasant **t.** if thou keep
Pr 25:2 is the glory of God to conceal a **t.** 1697
Pr 27:7 the hungry soul every bitter **t.** is sweet.
Ec 1:9 the **t.** that hath been, it is that which
Ec 1:9 and there is no new **t.** under the sun.
Ec 1:10 Is there any **t.** whereof it may be 1697
Ec 3:1 To every **t.** there is a season, and a
Ec 3:11 He hath made every **t.** beautiful in his
Ec 3:14 be put to it, nor any **t.** taken from it:
Ec 3:19 beasts; even one **t.** befalleth them:
Ec 5:2 thine heart be hasty to utter any **t.** 1697
Ec 6:5 not seen the sun, nor known any **t.**:
Ec 7:8 end of a **t.** than the beginning 1697
Ec 8:1 knoweth the interpretation of a **t.**? 1697
Ec 8:3 stand not in an evil **t.**; for he doeth 1697
Ec 8:5 commandment shall feel no evil **t.**: 1697
Ec 8:15 a man hath no better **t.** under the sun,
Ec 9:5 but the dead know not any **t.**,
Ec 9:6 any more a portion forever in any **t.**
Ec 11:7 A pleasant **t.** it is for the eyes to
Ec 12:14 with every secret **t.**, whether it be good,
Isa 7:13 Is it a small **t.** for you to weary men
Isa 15:6 the grass faileth, there is no green **t.**.
Isa 17:13 like a rolling **t.** before the whirlwind.
Isa 19:7 every **t.** sown by the brooks, shall
Isa 29:16 the **t.** framed say of him that framed it,
Isa 29:21 turn aside the just for a **t.** of nought.
Isa 38:7 will do this **t.** that he hath spoken; 1697
Isa 40:15 he taketh up the isles as a very little **t.**.
Isa 41:12 be as nothing, and as a **t.** of nought.
Isa 43:19 Behold, I will do a new **t.**: now it shall
Isa 49:6 a light **t.** that thou shouldest be my
Isa 52:11 out from thence, touch no unclean **t.**;
Isa 55:11 prosper in the **t.** whereto I sent it.
Isa 64:6 But we are all as an unclean **t.**, and
Isa 66:8 Who hath heard such a **t.**? who hath
Jer 2:10 diligently, and see if there be such a **t.**,
Jer 2:19 see that it is an evil **t.** and bitter,

Jer 5:30 horrible **t.** is committed in the land;
Jer 7:23 But this **t.** commanded I them, 1697
Jer 11:13 ye set up altars to that shameful **t.**,
Jer 14:14 a **t.** of nought, and the deceit of their
Jer 18:13 of Israel hath done a very horrible **t.**
Jer 22:4 if ye do this **t.** indeed, then shall 1697
Jer 23:14 prophets of Jerusalem an horrible **t.**
Jer 31:22 Lord hath created a new **t.** in the earth,
Jer 32:27 is there any **t.** too hard for me? 1697
Jer 33:14 I will perform that good **t.** which I 1697
Jer 38:5 he that can do any **t.** against you. 1697
Jer 38:14 unto Jeremiah, I will ask thee a **t.**; 1697
Jer 40:3 therefore this **t.** is come upon you 1697
Jer 40:16 Kareah, Thou shalt not do this **t.** 1697
Jer 42:3 walk, and the **t.** that we may do. 1697
Jer 42:4 that whatsoever **t.** the Lord shall 1697
Jer 42:21 nor any **t.** for the which he hath sent
Jer 44:4 not this abominable **t.** that I hate 1697
Jer 44:17 do whatsoever **t.** goeth forth out of 1697
La 2:13 What **t.** shall I take to witness for thee?
La 2:13 what **t.** shall I liken to thee, O
Eze 8:17 Is it a light **t.** to the house of Judah
Eze 14:9 deceived when he hath spoken a **t.**, 1697
Eze 16:47 but, as if that were a very little **t.**,
Eze 34:18 a small **t.** unto you to have eaten up
Eze 44:18 with any **t.** that causeth sweat.
Eze 44:29 every dedicated **t.** in Israel shall be
Eze 44:31 shall not eat of any **t.** that is dead of
Eze 47:9 every **t.** that liveth, which moveth, 5315
Eze 47:9 every **t.** shall live whither the river
Eze 48:12 shall be unto them a **t.** most holy
Da 2:5 Chaldeans, The **t.** is gone from me: 4406
Da 2:8 ye see the **t.** is gone from me. 4406
Da 2:11 is a rare **t.** that the king requireth, 4406
Da 2:15 Then Arioch made the **t.** known to 4406
Da 2:17 made the **t.** known to Hananiah, 4406
Da 3:29 which speak any **t.** amiss against the
Da 4:33 The same hour was the **t.** fulfilled 4406
Da 5:15 shew the interpretation of the **t.** 4406
Da 5:26 This is the interpretation of the **t.** 4406
Da 6:12 answered and said, The **t.** is true, 4406
Da 10:1 a **t.** was revealed unto Daniel, 1697
Da 10:1 and the **t.** was true, but the time 1697
Da 10:1 was long: and he understood the **t.**, 1697
Ro 6:10 seen an horrible **t.** in the house of
Ro 8:3 Israel hath cast off the **t.** that is good:
Ro 8:12 but they were counted as a strange **t.**
Am 6:13 Ye which rejoice in a **t.** of nought, 1697
Jon 3:7 beast, herd nor flock, taste any **t.**
Mal 1:14 sacrificeth unto the Lord a corrupt **t.**
Mt 8:33 and told every **t.**, and what was
Mt 18:19 **agree on earth as touching any t.** *4229*
Mt 19:16 Good Master, what good **t.** shall I do,
Mt 20:20 him, and desiring a certain **t.** of him
Mt 21:24 **I also will ask you one t., which if** *3056*
Mt 24:17 **to take any t. out of his house:**
Mk 1:27 themselves, saying, What **t.** is this?
Mk 4:22 **neither was any t. kept secret, but**
Mk 5:32 about to see her that had done this **t.**
Mk 7:18 **whatsoever t. from without entereth**
Mk 9:22 but if thou canst do any **t.**, have
Mk 10:21 and said unto him, **One t. thou lackest:**
Mk 11:13 haply he might find any **t.** thereon:
Mk 13:15 **to take any t. out of his house:**
Mk 16:8 neither said they any **t.** to any man;
Mk 16:18 **if they drink any deadly t., it shall**
Lu 1:35 also that holy **t.** which shall be born
Lu 2:15 see this **t.** which is come to pass, *4487*
Lu 6:9 unto them, **I will ask you one t.;**
Lu 8:17 **neither any t. hid, that shall not be**
Lu 9:21 them to tell no man that **t.**;
Lu 10:42 **But one t. is needful: and Mary**
Lu 12:11 **how or what t. ye shall answer.**
Lu 12:26 **not able to do that t. which is least,**
Lu 18:22 unto him, **Yet lackest thou one t.**
Lu 19:8 have taken any **t.** from any man by
Lu 20:3 them, **I will also ask you one t.** *3056*
Lu 22:23 of them it was that should do this **t.**
Lu 22:35 **and scrip, and shoes, lacked ye any t.?**
Joh 1:3 was not any **t.** made that was made
Joh 1:46 any good **t.** come out of Nazareth?
Joh 5:14 **more, lest a worse t. come unto thee.**
Joh 7:4 is no man that doeth any **t.** in secret,
Joh 9:25 one **t.** I know, that, whereas I was
Joh 9:30 Why herein is a marvellous **t.**, that ye
Joh 14:14 **If ye shall ask any t. in my name,**
Joh 18:34 **Sayest thou this t. of thyself, or did**

Ac 5:4 conceived this **t.** in thine heart? *4229*
Ac 10:14 never eaten any **t.** that is common
Ac 10:28 unlawful **t.** for a man that is a Jew to
Ac 12:12 And when he had considered the **t.**, he
Ac 17:21 either to tell, or to hear some new **t.**.)
Ac 17:25 as though he needed any **t.**, seeing
Ac 19:32 Some therefore cried one **t.**, and some
Ac 19:39 any **t.** concerning other matters,
Ac 21:25 concluded that they observe no such **t.**,
Ac 21:34 And some cried one **t.**, some another,
Ac 23:17 for he hath a certain **t.** to tell him.
Ac 25:8 Caesar, have I offended any **t.** at all.
Ac 25:11 committed any **t.** worthy of death,
Ac 25:26 no certain **t.** to write unto my lord.
Ac 26:8 be thought a **t.** incredible with you,
Ac 26:10 Which **t.** I also did in Jerusalem:
Ac 26:26 this **t.** was not done in a corner.
Ro 7:18 is, in my flesh,) dwelleth no good **t.**
Ro 8:33 Who shall lay any **t.** to the charge of
Ro 9:20 Shall the **t.** formed say to him that *4110*
Ro 13:6 attending continually upon this very **t.**
Ro 13:8 Owe no man any **t.**, but to love one
Ro 14:14 that esteemeth any **t.** to be unclean,
Ro 14:21 nor any **t.** whereby thy brother
Ro 14:22 condemneth not himself in that **t.**
1Co 1:5 in every **t.** ye are enriched by him,
1Co 1:10 that ye all speak the same **t.**, and that
1Co 2:2 not to know any **t.** among you,
1Co 3:7 neither is he that planteth any **t.**,
1Co 4:3 very small **t.** that I should be judged
1Co 8:2 man think that he knoweth any **t.**,
1Co 8:7 hour eat it as a **t.** offered unto an idol;
1Co 9:11 is it a great **t.** if we shall reap your
1Co 9:17 For if I do this **t.** willingly, I have a
1Co 10:19 say I then? that the idol is any **t.**,
1Co 10:19 offered in sacrifice to idols is any **t.**?
1Co 14:30 If any **t.** be revealed to another that
1Co 14:35 And if they will learn any **t.**, let
2Co 2:10 To whom ye forgive any **t.**, I forgive
2Co 2:10 for if I forgave any **t.**, to whom I
2Co 3:5 to think any **t.** as of ourselves;
2Co 5:5 wrought us for the selfsame **t.** is God,
2Co 6:3 Giving no offence in any **t.**, that
2Co 6:17 Lord, and touch not the unclean **t.**;
2Co 7:11 For behold this selfsame **t.**, that ye
2Co 7:14 For if I have boasted any **t.** to him of
2Co 8:7 Therefore, as ye abound in every **t.**, in
2Co 9:11 in every **t.** to all bountifulness,
2Co 10:5 every high **t.** that exalteth itself *5313*
2Co 11:15 it is no great **t.** if his ministers
2Co 12:8 For this **t.** I besought the Lord thrice,
Ga 4:18 affected always in a good **t.**
Ga 5:6 circumcision availeth any **t.**, nor
Ga 6:15 neither circumcision availeth any **t.**,
Eph 4:28 with his hands the **t.** which is good,
Eph 5:24 be to their own husbands in every **t.**
Eph 5:27 spot, or wrinkle, or any such **t.**;
Eph 6:8 whatsoever good **t.** any man doeth,
Php 1:6 Being confident of this very **t.**, that
Php 3:13 but this one **t.** I do, forgetting *1520*
Php 3:15 if in any **t.** ye be otherwise minded,
Php 3:16 the same rule, let us mind the same **t.**
Php 4:6 in every **t.** by prayer and supplication
1Th 1:8 that we need not to speak any **t.**
1Th 5:18 In every **t.** give thanks: for this is the
2Th 1:6 righteous **t.** with God to recompense
1Ti 1:10 and if there be any other **t.** that is
2Ti 1:14 good **t.** which was committed unto
Tit 2:8 having no evil **t.** to say of you.
Phm 6 by the acknowledging of every good **t.**
Heb 10:29 an unholy **t.**, and hath done despite
Heb 10:31 It is a fearful **t.** to fall into the hands
Heb 11:40 God having provided some better **t.**
Heb 13:9 it is a good **t.** that the heart be
Jas 1:7 he shall receive any **t.** of the Lord
1Pe 4:12 some strange **t.** happened unto you:
2Pe 3:8 be not ignorant of this one **t.**,
1Jo 2:8 which **t.** is true in him and in you:
1Jo 5:14 if we ask any **t.** according to his will,
Re 2:15 **of the Nicolaitanes, which t. I hate.**
Re 9:4 neither any green **t.**, neither any tree:
Re 21:27 enter into it any **t.** that defileth,

THINGS See also THINGS'.
Ge 7:23 and the creeping **t.**, and the fowl of the
Ge 9:3 the green herb have I given you all **t.**
Ge 15:1 After these **t.** the word of the Lord 1697
Ge 20:8 and told all these **t.** in their ears: 1697
Ge 22:1, 20 And it came to pass after these **t.**, 1697
Ge 24:1 the Lord had blessed Abraham in all **t.**
Ge 24:28 of her mother's house these **t.** 1697
Ge 24:53 brother and to her mother precious **t.** 1697
Ge 24:66 servant told Isaac all **t.** that he 1697
Ge 29:13 And he told Laban all these **t.** 1697
Ge 39:7 And it came to pass after these **t.**, 1697
Ge 40:1 And it came to pass after these **t.**, 1697
Ge 42:36 away: all these **t.** are against me.
Ge 45:23 ten asses laden with the good **t.** of
Ge 48:1 And it came to pass after these **t.**, 1697
Ex 10:2 what **t.** I have wrought in Egypt, and
Ex 12:36 unto them such **t.** as they required.
Ex 23:13 And in all **t.** that I have said unto you
Ex 25:22 of all **t.** which I will give thee in
Ex 28:38 may bear the iniquity of the holy **t.**
Ex 29:33 eat those **t.** wherewith the atonement
Ex 29:35 all **t.** which I have commanded thee:
Ex 40:4 order the **t.** that are to be set in order
Le 2:8 offering that is made of these **t.** unto
Le 4:2 **t.** which ought not to be done,
Le 4:13, 22 **t.** which should not be done,
Le 4:27 **t.** which ought not to be done,
Le 5:2 or the carcase of unclean creeping **t.**,
Le 5:5 he shall be guilty in one of these **t.**,
Le 5:15 ignorance, in the holy **t.** of the Lord;
Le 5:17 commit any of these **t.** which are
Le 8:36 Aaron and his sons did all the **t.** 1697
Le 10:19 Lord; and such **t.** have befallen me:
Le 11:23 But all other flying creeping **t.**, which
Le 11:29 unto you among the creeping **t.**
Le 11:42 hath more feet among all creeping **t.**
Le 14:11 that is to be made clean, and those **t.**,
Le 15:10 and he that beareth any of those **t.**
Le 15:27 whosoever toucheth those **t.** shall be
Le 18:24 not ye yourselves in any of these **t.**
Le 20:23 for they committed all these **t.**, and
Le 22:2 from the holy **t.** of the children of
Le 22:2 name in those **t.** which they hallow
Le 22:3 that goeth unto the holy **t.**, which the
Le 22:4 he shall not eat of the holy **t.**, until he
Le 22:6 and shall not eat of the holy **t.**, unless
Le 22:7 and shall afterward eat of the holy **t.**;
Le 22:12 not eat of an offering of the holy **t.**
Le 22:15 And they shall not profane the holy **t.**
Le 22:16 trespass, when they eat their holy **t.**
Le 26:23 will not be reformed by me by these **t.**
Nu 1:50 and over all **t.** that belong to it:
Nu 4:4 congregation, about the most holy **t.**
Nu 4:15 **t.** are the burden of the sons of Kohath
Nu 4:19 they approach unto the most holy **t.**
Nu 4:20 in to see when the holy **t.** are covered,
Nu 5:9 And every offering of all the holy **t.** of
Nu 5:10 every man's hallowed **t.** shall be his:
Nu 15:13 shall do these **t.** after this manner, in
Nu 18:8 hallowed **t.** of the children of Israel;
Nu 18:9 This shall be thine of the most holy **t.**,
Nu 18:19 All the heave offerings of the holy **t.**,
Nu 18:32 neither shall ye pollute the holy **t.** of
Nu 29:39 These **t.** ye shall do unto the Lord
Nu 31:20 of goats' hair, and all **t.** made of wood
Nu 35:29 So these **t.** shall be for a statute of
De 1:18 at that time all the **t.** which ye 1697
De 4:7 God is in all **t.** that we call upon him
De 4:9 the **t.** which thine eyes have seen, 1697
De 4:30 and all these **t.** are come upon thee 1697
De 6:11 and houses full of all good **t.**, which
De 10:21 for thee these great and terrible **t.**,
De 12:8 do after all the **t.** that we do here this
De 12:26 Only thy holy **t.** which thou hast, and
De 18:12 For all that do these **t.** are an
De 25:16 For all that do such **t.**, and all that do
De 26:13 I have brought away the hallowed **t.**
De 28:47 of heart, for the abundance of all **t.**;
De 28:48 in nakedness, and in want of all **t.**
De 28:57 for she shall eat them for want of all **t.**
De 29:29 secret **t.** belong unto the Lord our
De 29:29 **t.** which are revealed belong unto us
De 30:1 all these **t.** are come upon thee, 1697
De 32:35 the **t.** that shall come upon them make
De 33:13 for the precious **t.** of heaven, for the
De 33:14 the precious **t.** put forth by the moon,
De 33:15 chief **t.** of the ancient mountains,
De 33:15 for the precious **t.** of the lasting hills,
De 33:16 And for the precious **t.** of the earth
Jos 1:17 as we hearkened unto Moses in all **t.**

Jos 2:11 And as soon as we had heard these **t.**,
Jos 2:23 and told him all **t.** that befell them:
Jos 11:1 king of Hazor had heard those **t.**,
Jos 23:14 thing hath failed of all the good **t.** 1697
Jos 23:15 as all good **t.** are come upon you, 1697
Jos 23:15 the Lord bring upon you all evil **t.**, 1697
Jos 24:29 And it came to pass after these **t.**, 1697
Jg 13:23 would he have shewed us all these **t.**, 1697
Jg 13:23 time have told us such **t.** as these. 1697
Jg 18:27 took the **t.** which Micah had made, 1697
Ru 4:7 changing, for to confirm all **t.**; 1697
1Sa 2:23 unto them, Why do ye such **t.**? 1697
1Sa 3:12 against Eli all **t.** which I have spoken
1Sa 3:17 hide any thing from me of all the **t.**
1Sa 12:21 for then should ye go after vain **t.**,
1Sa 12:24 consider how great **t.** he hath done for
1Sa 15:21 the chief of the **t.** which should
1Sa 19:7 Jonathan shewed him all those **t.** 1697
1Sa 25:37 and his wife had told him these **t.**, 1697
1Sa 26:25 David: thou shalt both do great **t.**,
2Sa 7:21 hast thou done all these great **t.**, to
2Sa 7:23 and to do for you great **t.** and terrible,
2Sa 11:18 told David all the **t.** concerning 1697
2Sa 12:8 have given unto thee such and such **t.**.
2Sa 13:21 king David heard of all these **t.**, 1697
2Sa 14:20 to know all **t.** that are in the earth.
2Sa 23:5 covenant, ordered in all **t.** and sure:
2Sa 23:17 These **t.** did these three mighty men.
2Sa 23:22 These **t.** did Benaiah the son of
2Sa 24:12 saith the Lord, I offer thee three **t.**;
2Sa 24:23 all these **t.** did Araunah, as a king
1Ki 4:33 fowl, and of creeping **t.**, and of fishes.
1Ki 5:8 considered the **t.** which thou sentest
1Ki 7:51 the **t.** which David his father had
1Ki 15:15 brought in the **t.** which his father had
1Ki 15:15 the **t.** which himself had dedicated,
1Ki 17:17 And it came to pass after these **t.**, 1697
1Ki 18:36 I have done all these **t.** that thy 1697
1Ki 21:1 And it came to pass after these **t.**, 1697
1Ki 21:26 according to all **t.** as did the Amorites,
2Ki 8:4 the great **t.** that Elisha hath done.
2Ki 11:9 according to all **t.** that Jehoiada the
2Ki 12:4 All the money of the dedicated **t.** that
2Ki 12:18 all the hallowed **t.** that Jehoshaphat,
2Ki 12:18 and his own hallowed **t.**, and all the
2Ki 14:3 according to all **t.** as Joash his father
2Ki 17:9 did secretly those **t.** that were not 1697
2Ki 17:11 wrought wicked **t.** to provoke the 1697
2Ki 19:29 shall eat this year such **t.** as grow of
2Ki 20:13 them all the house of his precious **t.**,
2Ki 20:15 All the **t.** that are in mine house have
2Ki 23:17 proclaimed these **t.** that thou hast 1697
2Ki 25:15 and such **t.** as were of gold, in gold,
1Ch 4:22 And these are ancient **t.** 1697
1Ch 9:31 set office over the **t.** that were made in
1Ch 11:19 These **t.** did these three mightiest.
1Ch 11:24 These **t.** did Benaiah the son of
1Ch 17:19 in making known all these great **t.**.
1Ch 21:10 saith the Lord, I offer thee three **t.**
1Ch 23:13 he should sanctify the most holy **t.**, he
1Ch 23:28 and in the purifying of all holy **t.**, and
1Ch 26:20 over the treasures of the dedicated **t.**.
1Ch 26:26 all the treasures of the dedicated **t.**,
1Ch 28:12 of the treasuries of the dedicated **t.**
1Ch 28:14 gave of gold by weight for **t.** of gold,
1Ch 29:2 God the gold for **t.** to be made of gold,
1Ch 29:2 and the silver for **t.** of silver,
1Ch 29:2 and the brass for **t.** of brass,
1Ch 29:2 the iron for **t.** of iron,
1Ch 29:2 and wood for **t.** of wood;
1Ch 29:5 The gold for **t.** of gold,
1Ch 29:5 and the silver for **t.** of silver,
1Ch 29:14 for all **t.** come of thee, and of thine
1Ch 29:17 I have willingly offered all these **t.**
1Ch 29:19 and to do all these **t.**, and to build the
2Ch 3:3 **t.** wherein Solomon was instructed
2Ch 4:6 such **t.** as they offered for the burnt
2Ch 5:1 all the **t.** that David his father had
2Ch 12:12 and also in Judah **t.** went well. 1697
2Ch 15:18 of God the **t.** that his father had
2Ch 19:3 there are good **t.** found in thee, in 1697
2Ch 21:3 silver, and of gold, and of precious **t.**,
2Ch 23:8 according to all **t.** that Jehoiada the
2Ch 24:7 the dedicated **t.** of the house of the
2Ch 29:33 consecrated **t.** were six hundred oxen
2Ch 31:5 the tithe of all **t.** brought they in
2Ch 31:6 of holy **t.** which were consecrated

2Ch 31:12 tithes and the dedicated **t.** faithfully:
2Ch 31:14 of the Lord, and the most holy **t.**.
2Ch 32:1 After these **t.**, and the 1697
Ezr 1:6 with beasts, and with precious **t.**,
Ezr 2:63 should not eat of the most holy **t.**,
Ezr 7:1 Now after these **t.**, in the reign of 1697
Ezr 9:1 Now when these **t.** were done, the
Ne 6:8 are no such **t.** done as thou sayest, 1697
Ne 6:16 that were about us saw these **t.**,
Ne 7:65 should not eat of the most holy **t.**,
Ne 9:6 the earth, and all **t.** that are therein,
Ne 10:33 for the set feasts, and for the holy **t.**,
Ne 12:47 sanctified holy **t.** unto the Levites;
Ne 13:26 Solomon king of Israel sin by these **t.**?
Es 2:1 After these **t.**, when the wrath of 1697
Es 2:3 let their **t.** for purification be given 1697
Es 2:9 gave her her **t.** for purification, 1697
Es 2:9 with such **t.** as belonged to her, and 1697
Es 2:12 with other **t.** for the purifying of the 1697
Es 3:1 After these **t.** did king Ahasuerus 1697
Es 5:11 all the **t.** wherein the king had
Es 9:20 And Mordecai wrote these **t.**, 1697
Job 5:9 doeth great **t.** and unsearchable;
Job 5:9 marvellous **t.** without number:
Job 6:7 The **t.** that my soul refused to touch.
Job 6:30 cannot my taste discern perverse **t.**?
Job 8:2 How long wilt thou speak these **t.**?
Job 9:10 Which doeth great **t.** past finding out;
Job 10:13 these **t.** has thou hid in thine heart:
Job 12:3 yea, who knoweth not such **t.** as these?
Job 12:22 discovereth deep **t.** out of darkness,
Job 13:20 Only do not two **t.** unto me: then will I
Job 13:26 For thou writest bitter **t.** against me,
Job 14:19 thou washest away the **t.** which grow
Job 16:2 I have heard many such **t.**: miserable
Job 22:18 Yet he filled their houses with good **t.**
Job 23:14 me: and many such **t.** are with him.
Job 26:5 Dead **t.** are formed from under the
Job 33:29 these **t.** worketh God oftentimes with
Job 37:5 great **t.** doeth he, which we cannot
Job 41:30 sharp pointed **t.** upon the mire.
Job 41:34 He beholdeth all high **t.**: he is a king
Job 42:3 **t.** too wonderful for me, which I knew
Ps 8:6 thou hast put all **t.** under his feet:
Ps 12:3 the tongue that speaketh proud **t.**
Ps 15:5 He that doeth these **t.** shall never be
Ps 17:2 thine eyes behold the **t.** that are equal.
Ps 31:18 which speak grievous **t.** proudly and
Ps 35:11 laid to my charge **t.** that I knew not
Ps 38:12 seek my hurt speak mischievous **t.**,
Ps 42:4 When I remember these **t.**, I pour out
Ps 45:1 I speak of the **t.** which I have made
Ps 45:4 right hand shall teach thee terrible **t.**
Ps 50:21 These **t.** hast thou done, and I kept
Ps 57:2 God that performeth all **t.** for me.
Ps 60:3 Thou hast shewed thy people hard **t.**
Ps 65:5 By terrible **t.** in righteousness wilt
Ps 71:19 is very high, who hast done great **t.**
Ps 72:18 of Israel, who only doeth wondrous **t.**.
Ps 78:12 Marvellous **t.** did he in the sight of
Ps 86:10 thou art great, and doest wondrous **t.**
Ps 87:3 Glorious **t.** are spoken of thee, O city
Ps 94:4 long shall they utter and speak hard **t.**?
Ps 98:1 song; for he hath done marvellous **t.**
Ps 103:5 Who satisfieth thy mouth with good **t.**;
Ps 104:25 wherein are **t.** creeping innumerable,
Ps 106:21 which had done great **t.** in Egypt;
Ps 106:22 Ham, and terrible **t.** by the Red sea.
Ps 107:43 is wise, and will observe these **t.**,
Ps 113:6 to behold the **t.** that are in heaven,
Ps 119:18 may behold wondrous **t.** out of thy law.
Ps 119:128 thy precepts concerning all **t.** to be
Ps 126:2 The Lord hath done great **t.** for them.
Ps 126:3 The Lord hath done great **t.** for us;
Ps 131:1 great matters, or in **t.** too high for me.
Ps 148:10 all cattle; creeping **t.**, and flying fowl:
Pr 2:12 the man that speaketh froward **t.**;
Pr 3:15 and all the **t.** thou canst desire are not
Pr 6:16 These six **t.** doth the Lord hate: yea,
Pr 8:6 for I will speak of excellent **t.**; and
Pr 8:6 opening of my lips shall be right **t.**
Pr 8:11 all the **t.** that may be desired are not
Pr 15:28 of the wicked poureth out evil **t.**.
Pr 16:4 The Lord hath made all **t.** for himself:
Pr 16:30 shutteth his eyes to devise froward **t.**
Pr 22:20 Have not I written to thee excellent **t.**
Pr 23:16 rejoice, when thy lips speak right **t.**.

Pr 23:33 and thine heart shall utter perverse **t.**.
Pr 24:23 These **t.** also belong to the wise. It is
Pr 26:10 The great God that formed all **t.** both
Pr 28:5 that seek the Lord understand all **t.**.
Pr 28:10 the upright shall have good **t.** in
Pr 30:7 Two **t.** have I required of thee; deny
Pr 30:15 are three **t.** that are never satisfied,
Pr 30:15 yea, four **t.** say not, It is enough:
Pr 30:18 be three **t.** which are too wonderful
Pr 30:21 For three **t.** the earth is disquieted.
Pr 30:24 There be four **t.** which are little upon
Pr 30:29 There be three **t.** which go well, yea,
Ec 1:8 All **t.** are full of labour: man 1697
Ec 1:11 is no remembrance of former **t.**;
Ec 1:11 be any remembrance of **t.** that are
Ec 1:13 out by wisdom concerning all **t.** that
Ec 6:11 be many **t.** that increase vanity, 1697
Ec 7:15 All **t.** have I seen in the days of my
Ec 7:25 seek out wisdom, and the reason of **t.**,
Ec 9:2 All **t.** come alike to all: there is one
Ec 9:3 is an evil among all **t.** that are done
Ec 10:19 merry: but money answereth all **t.**
Ec 11:9 that for all these **t.** God will bring thee
Isa 12:5 Lord; for he hath done excellent **t.**
Isa 25:1 for thou hast done wonderful **t.**; thy
Isa 25:6 make unto all people a feast of fat **t.**,
Isa 25:6 of fat **t.** full of marrow, of wines on
Isa 29:16 Surely your turning of **t.** upside down
Isa 30:10 Prophesy not unto us right **t.**,
Isa 30:10 speak unto us smooth **t.**, prophesy
Isa 32:8 But the liberal deviseth liberal **t.**;
Isa 32:8 and by liberal **t.** shall he stand.
Isa 34:1 world, and all **t.** that come forth of it.
Isa 38:16 O Lord, by these **t.** men live,
Isa 38:16 in all these **t.** is the life of my spirit:
Isa 39:2 them the house of his precious **t.**,
Isa 40:26 and behold who hath created these **t.**,
Isa 41:22 let them shew the former **t.**, what they
Isa 41:22 of them; or declare us **t.** for to come.
Isa 41:23 Shew the **t.** that are to come hereafter,
Isa 42:9 Behold, the former **t.** are come to pass,
Isa 42:9 and new **t.** do I declare: before they
Isa 42:16 them, and crooked **t.** straight.
Isa 42:16 These **t.** will I do unto them, and 1697
Isa 42:20 Seeing many **t.**, but thou observest
Isa 43:9 declare this, and shew us former **t.**?
Isa 43:18 Remember ye not the former **t.**,
Isa 43:18 neither consider the **t.** of old.
Isa 44:7 and the **t.** that are coming, and shall
Isa 44:9 and their delectable **t.** shall not profit;
Isa 44:24 I am the Lord that maketh all **t.**;
Isa 45:7 create evil: I the Lord do all these **t.**.
Isa 45:11 Ask me of **t.** to come concerning my
Isa 45:19 I declare **t.** that are right.
Isa 46:9 Remember the former **t.** of old: for I
Isa 46:10 from ancient times the **t.** that are not
Isa 47:7 thou didst not lay these **t.** to thy heart,
Isa 47:9 these two **t.** shall come to thee in a
Isa 47:13 save thee from these **t.** that shall come
Isa 48:3 I have declared the former **t.** from the
Isa 48:6 I have shewed thee new **t.** from this
Isa 48:6 even hidden **t.**, and thou didst not
Isa 48:14 among them hath declared these **t.**?
Isa 51:19 These two **t.** are come unto thee; who
Isa 56:4 choose the **t.** that please me, and take
Isa 61:11 garden causeth the **t.** that are sown
Isa 64:3 terrible **t.** which we looked not for,
Isa 64:11 and all our pleasant **t.** are laid waste.
Isa 64:12 refrain thyself for these **t.**, O Lord?
Isa 65:4 of abominable **t.** is in their vessels;
Isa 66:2 For all those **t.** hath mine hand made,
Isa 66:2 and all those **t.** have been, saith the
Isa 66:8 such a thing? who hath seen such **t.**?
Jer 2:8 and walked after **t.** that do not profit
Jer 3:5 thou hast spoken and done evil **t.** as
Jer 3:7 said after she had done all these **t.**,
Jer 4:18 have procured these **t.** unto thee;
Jer 5:9 Shall I not visit for these **t.**? saith the
Jer 5:19 doeth the Lord our God all these **t.**
Jer 5:25 iniquities have turned away these **t.**,
Jer 5:25 your sins have withholden good **t.**
Jer 5:29 Shall I not visit for these **t.**? saith the
Jer 8:13 **t.** that I have given them shall pass
Jer 9:9 Shall I not visit them for these **t.**?
Jer 9:24 in these **t.** I delight, saith the Lord.
Jer 10:16 for he is the former of all **t.**; and Israel

Jer 13:22 Wherefore come these t. upon me?
Jer 14:22 thee: for thou hast made all these t.
Jer 16:18 of their detestable and abominable t.
Jer 16:19 and t. wherein there is no profit
Jer 17:9 The heart is deceitful above all t., and
Jer 18:13 the heathen, who hath heard such t.
Jer 20:1 that Jeremiah prophesied these t. 1697
Jer 20:5 and all the precious t. thereof, and all
Jer 21:14 it shall devour all t. round about it
Jer 26:10 princes of Judah heard these t., 1697
Jer 30:15 I have done these t. unto thee
Jer 31:5 and shall eat them as common t.
Jer 33:3 and shew thee great and mighty t.,
Jer 42:5 according to all t. for the which 1697
Jer 44:18 we have wanted all t., and have been
Jer 45:5 And seekest thou great t. for thyself?
Jer 51:19 them; for he is the former of all t.
La 1:7 all her pleasant t. that she had in the
La 1:10 out his hand upon all her pleasant t.
La 1:11 have given their pleasant t. for meat
La 1:16 For these t. I weep; mine eye, mine
La 2:14 prophets have seen vain and foolish t.
La 5:17 is faint; for these t. our eyes are dim
Eze 5:11 sanctuary with all thy detestable t.,
Eze 7:20 and of their detestable t. therein:
Eze 8:10 and behold every form of creeping t.,
Eze 11:5 for I know the t. that come into your
Eze 11:18 take away all the detestable t. thereof
Eze 11:21 after the heart of their detestable t.
Eze 11:25 all the t. that the Lord has shewed 1697
Eze 16:16 the like t. shall not come, neither shall
Eze 16:30 seeing thou doest all these t., the work
Eze 16:43 but hast fretted me I all these t.;
Eze 17:12 Know ye not what these t. mean?
Eze 17:15 shall he escape that doeth such t.? or
Eze 17:18 and hath done all these t., he shall not
Eze 18:10 doeth the like to any one of these t.,
Eze 20:40 your oblations, with all your holy t.
Eze 22:8 Thou hast despised mine holy t., and
Eze 22:25 taken the treasure and precious t.;
Eze 22:26 law, and have profaned mine holy t.
Eze 23:30 I will do these t. unto thee, because
Eze 24:19 thou not tell us what these t. are to us,
Eze 27:24 were thy merchants in all sorts of t.,
Eze 37:23 their idols, nor with their detestable t.,
Eze 38:10 time shall t. come into thy mind, 1697
Eze 38:20 and all creeping t. that creep upon the
Eze 42:13 the Lord shall eat the most holy t.
Eze 42:13 there shall they lay the most holy t.,
Eze 42:14 to those t. which are for the people
Eze 44:8 not kept the charge of mine holy t.
Eze 44:13 nor to come near to any of my holy t.,
Eze 44:30 the first of all the firstfruits of all t.,
Da 2:10 that asked such t. at any magician,
Da 2:22 He revealeth the deep and secret t.
Da 2:40 breaketh in pieces and subdueth all t.
Da 7:8 man, and a mouth speaking great t.
Da 7:16 know the interpretation of the t. 4406
Da 7:20 and a mouth that spake very great t.,
Da 10:21 none that holdeth with me in these t.,
Da 11:36 marvellous t. against the God of gods,
Da 11:38 with precious stones, and pleasant t.
Da 11:43 and over all the precious t. of Egypt:
Da 12:7 people, all these t. shall be finished.
Da 12:8 Lord, what shall be the end of these t.?
Ho 2:18 and with the creeping t. of the ground:
Ho 8:12 written to him the great t. of my law,
Ho 9:3 they shall eat unclean t. in Assyria.
Ho 14:9 and he shall understand t.
Joe 2:20 up, because he hath done great t.,
Joe 2:21 rejoice: for the Lord will do great t.
Joe 3:5 your temples my goodly pleasant t.
Ob 6 How are the t. of Esau searched out!
Ob 6 how are his hidden t. sought up!
Mic 7:15 will I shew unto him marvellous t.
Hab 1:14 as the creeping t., that have no ruler
Zep 1:2 utterly consume all t. from off the
Zec 4:10 who hath despised the day of small t.?
Zec 8:12 of this people to possess all these t.
Zec 8:16 These are the t. that ye shall do;
Zec 8:17 for all these are t. that I hate, saith
Mt 1:20 But while he thought on these t.,
Mt 2:3 Herod the king had heard these t.,
Mt 4:9 All these t. will I give thee, if thou
Mt 6:8 **knoweth what t. ye have need of**
Mt 6:32 **all these t. do the Gentiles seek:)**
Mt 6:32 **that ye have need of all these t**
Mt 6:33 **all these t. shall be added unto you**
Mt 6:34 **take thought for the t. of itself**
Mt 7:11 **is in heaven give good t. to them that**
Mt 7:12 **Therefore all t. whatsoever ye would**
Mt 9:18 While he spake these t. unto them,
Mt 11:4 **shew John again those t. which ye do**
Mt 11:25 **hast hid these t. from the wise and**
Mt 11:27 **All t. are delivered unto me of my**
Mt 12:34 **can ye, being evil, speak good t.?**
Mt 12:35 **of the heart bringeth forth good t**
Mt 12:35 **the evil treasure bringeth forth evil t**
Mt 13:3 he spake many t. unto them in
Mt 13:17 **desired to see those t. which ye see,**
Mt 13:17 **and to hear those t. which ye hear,**
Mt 13:34 All these t. spake Jesus unto the
Mt 13:35 I will utter t. which have been kept
Mt 13:41 **out of his kingdom all t. that offend,**
Mt 13:51 **Have ye understood all these t.?**
Mt 13:52 **out of his treasure t. new and old,**
Mt 13:56 then hath this man all these t.?
Mt 15:18 **those t. which proceed out of the**
Mt 15:20 **These are the t. which defile a man:**
Mt 16:21 and suffer many t. of the elders and
Mt 16:23 **savourest not the t. that be of God,**
Mt 17:11 **shall first come, and restore all t**
Mt 19:20 All these t. have I kept from my
Mt 19:26 **but with God all t. are possible**
Mt 21:15 saw the wonderful t. that he did,
Mt 21:22 **all t., whatsoever ye shall ask in**
Mt 21:23 authority doest thou these t.?
Mt 21:24, 27 **by what authority I do these t**
Mt 22:4 **all t. are ready: come unto the**
Mt 22:21 **Caesar the t. which are Caesar's;**
Mt 22:21 **unto God the t. that are God's**
Mt 23:20 **sweareth by it, and by all t. thereon**
Mt 23:36 **All these t. shall come upon this**
Mt 24:2 unto them, **See ye not all these t.?**
Mt 24:3 Tell us, when shall these t. be?
Mt 24:6 **for all these t. must come to pass,**
Mt 24:33 **ye, when ye shall see all these t.,**
Mt 24:34 **not pass, till all these t. be fulfilled**
Mt 25:21 **thou hast been faithful over a few t.,**
Mt 25:21 **I will make thee ruler over many t**
Mt 25:23 **thou hast been faithful over a few t.,**
Mt 25:23 **I will make thee ruler over many t**
Mt 27:13 many t. they witness against thee?
Mt 27:19 I have suffered many t. this day in
Mt 27:54 and those t. that were done,
Mt 28:11 priests all the t. that were done.
Mt 28:20 **to observe all t. whatsoever I have**
Mk 1:44 **those t. which Moses commanded,**
Mk 2:8 **Why reason ye these t. in your**
Mk 3:8 they had heard what great t. he did,
Mk 4:2 taught them many t. by parables,
Mk 4:11 **all these t. are done in parables:**
Mk 4:19 **lusts of other t. entering in, choke**
Mk 4:34 he expounded all t. to his disciples.
Mk 5:19 **tell them how great t. the Lord hath**
Mk 5:20 great t. Jesus had done for him:
Mk 5:26 And had suffered many t. of many
Mk 6:2 whence hath this man these t.?
Mk 6:20 he did many t., and heard him gladly.
Mk 6:30 unto Jesus, and told him all t.,
Mk 6:34 and he began to teach them many t.
Mk 7:4 many other t. there be, which they
Mk 7:8 **and many other such like t. ye do**
Mk 7:13 **and many such like t. do ye**
Mk 7:15 **but the t. which come out of him,**
Mk 7:23 **All these evil t. come from within,**
Mk 7:37 saying, He hath done all t. well: he
Mk 8:31 the Son of man must suffer many t.,
Mk 8:33 **savourest not the t. that be of God,**
Mk 8:33 **of God, but the t. that be of men**
Mk 9:9 tell no man what t. they had seen,
Mk 9:12 **cometh first, and restoreth all t.;**
Mk 9:12 **of man, that he must suffer many t.,**
Mk 9:23 **t. are possible to him that believeth**
Mk 10:27 **for with God all t. are possible**
Mk 10:32 tell them what t. should happen
Mk 11:11 had looked round about upon all t.
Mk 11:23 **those t. which he saith shall come**
Mk 11:24 **What t. soever ye desire, when ye**
Mk 11:28 what authority doest thou these t.?
Mk 11:28 thee this authority to do these t.?
Mk 11:29, 33 **by what authority I do these t**
Mk 12:17 **to Caesar the t. that are Caesar's**
Mk 12:17 **and to God the t. that are God's**
Mk 13:4 Tell us, when shall these t. be?
Mk 13:4 when all these t. shall be fulfilled?
Mk 13:7 **for such t. must needs be; but the**
Mk 13:23 **behold, I have foretold you all t**
Mk 13:29 **shall see these t. come to pass,**
Mk 13:30 **not pass, till all these t. be done**
Mk 14:36 **Father, all t. are possible unto thee;**
Mk 15:3 priests accused him of many t.
Mk 15:4 how many t. they witness against
Lu 1:1 in order a declaration of those t. *4229*
Lu 1:3 had perfect understanding of all t.
Lu 1:4 know the certainty of those t., *3056*
Lu 1:20 until the day that these t. shall be
Lu 1:45 of those t. which were told her
Lu 1:49 mighty hath done to me great t.
Lu 1:53 hath filled the hungry with good t.;
Lu 2:18 wondered at those t. which were told
Lu 2:19 But Mary kept all these t., and *4487*
Lu 2:20 praising God for all the t. that they
Lu 2:33 marvelled at those t. which were
Lu 2:39 had performed all t. according to the
Lu 3:18 other t. in his exhortation preached
Lu 4:28 when they heard these t., were filled
Lu 5:26 We have seen strange t. to day.
Lu 5:27 And after these t. he went forth,
Lu 6:46 **Lord, and do not the t. which I say?**
Lu 7:9 Jesus heard these t., he marvelled
Lu 7:18 John shewed him of all these t.
Lu 7:22 **tell John what t. ye have seen and**
Lu 8:8 when he had said these t., he cried,
Lu 8:39 **how great t. God hath done unto**
Lu 8:39 how great t. Jesus had done unto
Lu 9:9 who is this, of whom I hear such t.?
Lu 9:22 **Son of man must suffer many t.,**
Lu 9:36 any of those t. which they had seen
Lu 9:43 they wondered every one at all t.
Lu 10:1 After these t. the Lord appointed
Lu 10:7 **and drinking such t. as they give:**
Lu 10:8 **eat such t. as are set before you:**
Lu 10:21 **hid these t. from the wise and**
Lu 10:22 **All t. are delivered to me of my**
Lu 10:23 **eyes which see the t. that ye see:**
Lu 10:24 **desired to see those t. which ye see,**
Lu 10:24 **and to hear those t. which ye hear,**
Lu 10:41 **careful and troubled about many t**
Lu 11:27 as he spake these t., a certain
Lu 11:41 **give alms of such t. as ye have;**
Lu 11:41 **behold, all t. are clean unto you**
Lu 11:53 as he said these t. unto them,
Lu 11:53 to provoke him to speak of many t.
Lu 12:15 **of the t. which he possesseth**
Lu 12:20 **then whose shall those t. be, which**
Lu 12:30 **these t. do the nations of the world**
Lu 12:30 **that ye have need of these t**
Lu 12:31 **all these t. shall be added unto**
Lu 12:48 **and did commit t. worthy of stripes,**
Lu 13:2 **because they suffered such t.?**
Lu 13:17 And when he had said these t.,
Lu 13:17 glorious t. that were done by him.
Lu 14:6 not answer him again to these t.
Lu 14:15 sat at meat with him heard these t.,
Lu 14:17 **Come; for all t. are now ready**
Lu 14:21 **came, and shewed his lord these t**
Lu 15:26 **and asked what these t. meant**
Lu 16:14 were covetous, heard all these t.
Lu 16:25 **thy lifetime receivedst thy good t.,**
Lu 16:25 **and likewise Lazarus evil t.: but now**
Lu 17:9 **he did the t. that were commanded**
Lu 17:10 **he shall have done all those t. which**
Lu 17:25 **But first must he suffer many t.,**
Lu 18:22 Now when Jesus heard these t.,
Lu 18:27 **t. which are impossible with men are**
Lu 18:31 **t. that are written by the prophets**
Lu 18:34 they understood none of these t.
Lu 18:34 neither knew they the t. which were
Lu 19:11 as they heard these t., he added
Lu 19:42 **the t. which belong unto thy peace!**
Lu 20:2 authority doest thou these t.?
Lu 20:8 **by what authority I do these t**
Lu 20:25 **Caesar the t. which be Caesar's,**
Lu 20:25 **and unto God the t. which be God's**
Lu 21:6 **As for these t. which ye behold,**
Lu 21:7 Master, but when shall these t. be?
Lu 21:7 when these t. shall come to pass?
Lu 21:9 **for these t. must first come to pass;**
Lu 21:22 **t. which are written may be fulfilled**
Lu 21:26 **looking after those t. which are**

Lu 21:28 **when these t. begin to come to pass,**
Lu 21:31 **when ye see these t. come to pass,**
Lu 21:36 **these t. that shall come to pass,**
Lu 22:37 **the t. concerning me have an end**
Lu 22:65 many other **t.** blasphemously spake
Lu 23:8 because he had heard many **t.** of him;
Lu 23:14 touching those **t.** whereof ye accuse
Lu 23:31 **if they do these t. in a green tree,**
Lu 23:48 beholding the **t.** which were done,
Lu 23:49 stood afar off, beholding these **t.**.
Lu 24:9 and told all these **t.** unto the eleven,
Lu 24:10 which told these **t.** unto the apostles.
Lu 24:14 they talked together of all these **t.**
Lu 24:18 hast not known the **t.** which are come
Lu 24:19 And he said unto them, **What t.?** And
Lu 24:21 third day since these **t.** were done.
Lu 24:26 **not Christ to have suffered these t.,**
Lu 24:27 scriptures the **t.** concerning himself
Lu 24:35 they told what **t.** were done in the way,
Lu 24:44 **that all t. must be fulfilled, which**
Lu 24:48 **And ye are witnesses of these t.**.
Joh 1:3 All **t.** were made by him; and without
Joh 1:28 These **t.** were done in Bethabara
Joh 1:50 **thou shalt see greater t. than these.**
Joh 2:16 **Take these t. hence; make not**
Joh 2:18 us, seeing that thou doest these **t.**?
Joh 3:9 unto him, How can these **t.** be?
Joh 3:10 **Israel, and knowest not these t.?**
Joh 3:12 **If I have told you earthly t., and ye**
Joh 3:12 **ye believe if I tell you of heavenly t.?**
Joh 3:22 After these **t.** came Jesus and his
Joh 3:35 and hath given all **t.** into his hand.
Joh 4:25 when he is come, he will tell us all **t.**.
Joh 4:29 which told me all **t.** that ever I did:
Joh 4:45 seen all **t.** that he did at Jerusalem
Joh 5:16 done these **t.** on the sabbath day
Joh 5:19 **for what t. soever he doeth, these also**
Joh 5:20 **sheweth him all t. that himself doeth:**
Joh 5:34 **these t. I say, that ye might be saved.**
Joh 6:1 After these **t.** Jesus went over the
Joh 6:59 These **t.** said he in the synagogue,
Joh 7:1 After these **t.** Jesus walked in
Joh 7:4 If thou do these **t.**, shew thyself to
Joh 7:32 that the people murmured such **t.**
Joh 8:26 **I have many t. to say and to judge of**
Joh 8:26 **world those t. which I have heard of**
Joh 8:28 **hath taught me, I speak these t.**.
Joh 8:29 **I do always those t. that please him.**
Joh 10:6 they understood not what **t.** they were
Joh 10:41 but all **t.** that John spake of this man
Joh 11:11 These **t.** said he: and after that he *5023*
Joh 11:45 and had seen the **t.** which Jesus did,
Joh 11:46 and told them what **t.** Jesus had done
Joh 12:16 These **t.** understood not his disciples
Joh 12:16 they that these **t.** were written of him,
Joh 12:16 they had done these **t.** unto him
Joh 12:36 These **t.** spake Jesus, and departed,
Joh 12:41 These **t.** said Esaias, when he saw
Joh 13:3 Father had given all **t.** into his hands,
Joh 13:17 **If ye know these t., happy are ye**
Joh 13:29 Buy those **t.** that we have need of
Joh 14:25 **These t. have I spoken unto you,**
Joh 14:26 **he shall teach you all t., and bring all**
Joh 14:26 **and bring all t. to your remembrance,**
Joh 15:11 **These t. have I spoken unto you,**
Joh 15:15 **all t. that I have heard of my Father**
Joh 15:17 **These t. I command you, that ye**
Joh 15:21 **But all these t. will they do unto**
Joh 16:1 **These t. have I spoken unto you,**
Joh 16:3 **And these t. will they do unto you,**
Joh 16:4 **But these t. have I told you, that**
Joh 16:4 **these t. I said not unto you at the**
Joh 16:6 **I have said these t. unto you,**
Joh 16:12 **I have yet many t. to say unto you,**
Joh 16:13 **and he will shew you t. to come**
Joh 16:15 **All t. that the Father hath are mine:**
Joh 16:25 **These t. have I spoken unto you**
Joh 16:30 are we sure that thou knowest all **t.**,
Joh 16:33 **These t. have I spoken unto you,**
Joh 17:7 **that all t. whatsoever thou hast given**
Joh 17:13 **and these t. I speak in the world, that**
Joh 18:4 knowing all **t.** should come upon him,
Joh 19:24 these **t.** therefore the soldiers did.
Joh 19:28 that all **t.** were now accomplished.
Joh 19:36 For these **t.** were done, that the
Joh 20:18 he had spoken these **t.** unto her.
Joh 21:1 After these **t.** Jesus shewed himself
Joh 21:17 unto him, Lord, thou knowest all **t.**;
Joh 21:24 disciple which testifieth of these **t.**,
Joh 21:24 and wrote these **t.**: and we know
Joh 21:25 also many other **t.** which Jesus did,
Ac 1:3 **t.** pertaining to the kingdom of God:
Ac 1:9 And when he had spoken these **t.**,
Ac 2:44 together, and had all **t.** common;
Ac 3:18 But those **t.**, which God before had
Ac 3:21 the times of restitution of all **t.**, which
Ac 3:22 shall ye hear in all **t.** whatsoever he
Ac 4:20 speak the **t.** which we have seen and
Ac 4:25 rage, and the people imagine vain **t.**?
Ac 4:32 ought of the **t.** which he possessed
Ac 4:32 his own; but they had all **t.** common.
Ac 4:34 the prices of the **t.** that were sold,
Ac 5:5 on all them that heard these **t.**
Ac 5:11 and upon as many as heard these **t.**.
Ac 5:24 the chief priests heard these **t.**, *3056*
Ac 5:32 we are his witnesses of these **t.** *4487*
Ac 7:1 the high priest, Are these **t.** so?
Ac 7:50 Hath not my hand made all these **t.**?
Ac 7:54 When they heard these **t.**, they were
Ac 8:6 gave heed unto these **t.** which Philip
Ac 8:12 Philip preaching the **t.** concerning
Ac 8:24 none of these **t.** which ye have spoken
Ac 9:16 **shew him how great t. he must suffer.**
Ac 10:8 had declared all these **t.** unto them,
Ac 10:12 beasts, and creeping **t.**, and fowls
Ac 10:33 to hear all **t.** that are commanded thee
Ac 10:39 we are witnesses of all **t.** which he did
Ac 11:6 beasts, and creeping **t.**, and fowls
Ac 11:18 When they heard these **t.**,they held
Ac 11:22 Then tidings of these **t.** came unto
Ac 12:17 said, Go shew these **t.** unto James,
Ac 13:39 that believe are justified from all **t.**.
Ac 13:45 those **t.** which were spoken by Paul,
Ac 14:15 Sirs, why do ye these **t.**? We also
Ac 14:15 and the sea, and all **t.** that are therein:
Ac 15:4 and they declared all **t.** that God had
Ac 15:17 the Lord, who doeth all these **t.**
Ac 15:20 fornication, and from **t.** strangled,
Ac 15:27 also tell you the same **t.** by mouth
Ac 15:28 burden than these necessary **t.**;
Ac 15:29 and from blood, and from **t.** strangled,
Ac 16:14 unto the **t.** which were spoken of Paul.
Ac 17:8 the city, when they heard these **t.**
Ac 17:11 daily, whether these **t.** were so.
Ac 17:20 bringest certain strange **t.** to our ears:
Ac 17:20 know therefore what these **t.** mean.
Ac 17:22 that in all **t.** ye are too superstitious.
Ac 17:24 that made the world and all **t.** therein.
Ac 17:25 giveth to all life, and breath, and all **t.**
Ac 18:1 After these **t.** Paul departed from
Ac 18:17 And Gallio cared for none of those **t.**.
Ac 18:25 taught diligently the **t.** of the Lord,
Ac 19:8 the **t.** concerning the kingdom of God
Ac 19:21 After these **t.** were ended, Paul
Ac 19:36 these **t.** cannot be spoken against,
Ac 20:22 not knowing the **t.** that shall befall me
Ac 20:24 But none of these **t.** move me. *3056*
Ac 20:30 shall men arise, speaking perverse **t.**,
Ac 20:35 I have shewed you all **t.**, how that so
Ac 21:12 And when we heard these **t.**, both
Ac 21:19 particularly what **t.** God had wrought
Ac 21:24 and all may know that those **t.**,
Ac 21:25 themselves from **t.** offered to idols,
Ac 22:10 **told thee of all t. which are appointed**
Ac 23:22 thou hast shewed these **t.** to me.
Ac 24:8 take knowledge of all these **t.**,
Ac 24:9 saying that these **t.** were so.
Ac 24:13 they prove the **t.** whereof they now
Ac 24:14 all **t.** which are written in the law
Ac 24:22 when Felix heard these **t.**, having
Ac 25:9 be judged of these **t.** before me?
Ac 25:11 none of these **t.** whereof these accuse
Ac 25:18 accusation of such **t.** as I supposed:
Ac 26:2 touching all the **t.** whereof I am
Ac 26:9 many **t.** contrary to the name of Jesus
Ac 26:16 **both of these t. which thou hast seen,**
Ac 26:16 **of those t. in the which I will appear**
Ac 26:22 saying none other **t.** than those which
Ac 26:26 For the king knoweth of these **t.**,
Ac 26:26 that none of these **t.** are hidden
Ac 27:11 those **t.** which were spoken by Paul
Ac 28:10 us with such **t.** as were necessary.
Ac 28:24 And some believed the **t.** which were
Ac 28:31 teaching those **t.** which concern the
Ro 1:20 invisible **t.** of him from the creation
Ro 1:20 understood by the **t.** that are made,
Ro 1:23 fourfooted beasts, and creeping **t.**
Ro 1:28 do those **t.** which are not convenient;
Ro 1:30 inventors of evil **t.**, disobedient to
Ro 1:32 which commit such **t.** are worthy of
Ro 2:1 thou that judgest doest the same **t.**.
Ro 2:2 against them which commit such **t.**
Ro 2:3 that judgest them which do such **t.**.
Ro 2:14 nature the **t.** contained in the law,
Ro 2:18 approvest the **t.** that are more
Ro 3:19 that what **t.** soever the law saith
Ro 4:17 those **t.** which be not as though they
Ro 6:21 What fruit had ye then in those **t.**
Ro 6:21 for the end of those **t.** is death.
Ro 8:5 the flesh do mind the **t.** of the flesh;
Ro 8:5 after the Spirit the **t.** of the Spirit
Ro 8:28 we know that all **t.** work together for
Ro 8:31 What shall we then say to these **t.**?
Ro 8:32 not with him also freely give us all **t.**?
Ro 8:37 in all these **t.** we are more than
Ro 8:38 nor **t.** present, nor **t.** to come.
Ro 10:5 man which doeth those **t.** shall live
Ro 10:15 and bring glad tidings of good **t.**! *18*
Ro 11:36 through him, and to him, are all **t.**
Ro 12:16 Mind not high **t.**, but condescend to
Ro 12:17 Provide **t.** honest in the sight of all
Ro 14:2 one believeth that he may eat all **t.**
Ro 14:18 For he that in these **t.** serveth Christ
Ro 14:19 after the **t.** which make for peace,
Ro 14:19 **t.** wherewith one may edify another.
Ro 14:20 All **t.** indeed are pure; but it is evil
Ro 15:4 For whatsoever **t.** were written
Ro 15:17 in those **t.** which pertain to God.
Ro 15:18 not dare to speak of any of those **t.**
Ro 15:27 made partakers of their spiritual **t.**,
Ro 15:27 to minister unto them in carnal **t.**.
1Co 1:27 hath chosen the foolish **t.** of the world
1Co 1:27 hath chosen the weak **t.** of the world
1Co 1:27 to confound the **t.** which are mighty;
1Co 1:28 And base **t.** of the world, and
1Co 1:28 and **t.** which are despised, hath God
1Co 1:28 God chosen, yea, and **t.** which are not,
1Co 1:28 are not, to bring to nought **t.** that are:
1Co 2:9 **t.** which God hath prepared for them
1Co 2:10 searcheth all **t.**, yea, the deep **t.** of God.
1Co 2:11 For what man knoweth the **t.** of a man,
1Co 2:11 even so the **t.** of God knoweth no man,
1Co 2:12 know the **t.** that are freely given to us
1Co 2:13 Which **t.** also we speak, not in the
1Co 2:13 comparing spiritual **t.** with spiritual.
1Co 2:14 natural man receiveth not the **t.** of
1Co 2:15 But he that is spiritual judgeth all **t.**,
1Co 3:21 glory in men. For all **t.** are yours;
1Co 3:22 or death, or **t.** present, or **t.** to come;
1Co 4:5 to light the hidden **t.** of darkness,
1Co 4:6 these **t.**, brethren, I have in a figure
1Co 4:13 the offscouring of all **t.** unto this day.
1Co 4:14 I write not these **t.** to shame you,
1Co 6:3 much more **t.** that pertain to this life?
1Co 6:4 judgments of **t.** pertaining to this life,
1Co 6:12 All **t.** are lawful unto me, but all
1Co 6:12 unto me, but all **t.** are not expedient:
1Co 6:12 all **t.** are lawful for me, but I will not
1Co 7:1 concerning the **t.** whereof ye wrote
1Co 7:32 is unmarried careth for the **t.** that
1Co 7:33 married careth for the **t.** that are of
1Co 7:34 woman careth for the **t.** of the Lord,
1Co 7:34 married careth for the **t.** of the world,
1Co 8:1 Now as touching **t.** offered unto idols,
1Co 8:4 the eating of those **t.** that are offered
1Co 8:6 God, the Father, of whom are all **t.**,
1Co 8:6 Lord Jesus Christ, by whom are all **t.**,
1Co 8:10 eat those **t.** which are offered to idols;
1Co 9:8 Say I these **t.** as a man? or saith not
1Co 9:11 If we have sown unto you spiritual **t.**,
1Co 9:11 thing if we shall reap your carnal **t.**?
1Co 9:12 but suffer all **t.**, lest we should hinder
1Co 9:13 they which minister about holy **t.**
1Co 9:13 live of the **t.** of the temple? and they
1Co 9:15 But I have used none of these **t.**
1Co 9:15 neither have I written these **t.**,
1Co 9:22 I am made all **t.** to all men, that I
1Co 9:25 for the mastery is temperate in all **t.**
1Co 10:6 Now these **t.** were our examples,
1Co 10:6 intent we should not lust after evil **t.**,
1Co 10:11 all these **t.** happened unto them

1Co 10:20 that the **t.** which the Gentiles sacrifice,
1Co 10:23 All **t.** are lawful for me, but all
1Co 10:23 but all **t.** are not expedient:
1Co 10:23 all **t.** are lawful for me, but all
1Co 10:23 are lawful for me, but all **t.** edify not
1Co 10:33 Even as I please all men in all **t.**, not
1Co 11:2 that ye remember me in all **t.**,
1Co 11:12 also by the woman; but all **t.** of God.
1Co 13:7 Beareth all **t.**, believeth all **t.**,
1Co 13:7 hopeth all **t.**, endureth all **t.**.
1Co 13:11 became a man, I put away childish **t.**.
1Co 14:7 And even **t.** without life giving sound,
1Co 14:26 Let all **t.** be done unto edifying.
1Co 14:37 acknowledge that the **t.** that I write
1Co 14:40 all **t.** be done decently and in order.
1Co 15:27 For he hath put all **t.** under his feet.
1Co 15:27 he saith all **t.** are put under him,
1Co 15:27 which did put all **t.** under him.
1Co 15:28 when all **t.** shall be subdued unto him,
1Co 15:28 unto him that put all **t.** under him,
1Co 16:14 Let all your **t.** be done with charity.
2Co 1:13 For we write none other **t.** unto you,
2Co 1:17 or the **t.** that I purpose, do I purpose
2Co 2:9 you, whether ye be obedient in all **t.**
2Co 2:16 And who is sufficient for these **t.**?
2Co 4:2 have renounced the hidden **t.** of
2Co 4:15 For all **t.** are for your sakes, that the
2Co 4:18 we look not at the **t.** which are seen,
2Co 4:18 but at the **t.** which are not seen:
2Co 4:18 for the **t.** which are seen are temporal;
2Co 4:18 the **t.** which are not seen are eternal.
2Co 5:10 every one may receive the **t.** done in
2Co 5:17 new creature: old **t.** are passed away;
2Co 5:17 behold, all **t.** are become new.
2Co 5:18 all **t.** are of God, who hath reconciled
2Co 6:4 in all **t.** approving ourselves as the
2Co 6:10 nothing, and yet possessing all **t.**
2Co 7:11 In all **t.** ye have approved yourselves
2Co 7:14 but as we spake all **t.** to you in truth,
2Co 7:16 I have confidence in you in all **t.**
2Co 8:21 Providing for honest **t.**, not only in the
2Co 8:22 oftentimes proved diligent in many **t.**,
2Co 9:8 always having all sufficiency in all **t.**,
2Co 10:7 on **t.** after the outward appearance?
2Co 10:13 not boast of **t.** without our measure,
2Co 10:15 boasting of **t.** without our measure,
2Co 10:16 line of **t.** made ready to our hand.
2Co 11:6 made manifest among you in all **t.**
2Co 11:9 all **t.** I have kept myself from being
2Co 11:28 Beside those **t.** that are without, that
2Co 11:30 glory of the **t.** which concern mine
2Co 12:19 we do all **t.**, dearly beloved, for your
2Co 13:10 I write these **t.** being absent, lest
Ga 1:20 Now the **t.** which I write unto you,
Ga 2:18 For if I build again the **t.** which I
Ga 3:4 Have ye suffered so many **t.** in vain?
Ga 3:10 that continueth not in all **t.** which are
Ga 4:24 Which **t.** are an allegory: for these are
Ga 5:17 that ye cannot do the **t.** that ye would
Ga 5:21 which do such **t.** shall not inherit the
Ga 6:6 him that teacheth in all good **t.**
Eph 1:10 together in one all **t.** in Christ,
Eph 1:11 who worketh all **t.** after the counsel
Eph 1:22 And hath put all **t.** under his feet, and
Eph 1:22 be the head over all **t.** to the church,
Eph 3:9 who created all **t.** by Jesus Christ:
Eph 4:10 all heavens, that he might fill all **t.**.)
Eph 4:15 may grow up into him in all **t.**, which
Eph 5:6 because of these **t.** cometh the
Eph 5:12 those **t.** which are done of them in
Eph 5:13 But all **t.** that are reproved are made
Eph 5:20 Giving thanks always for all **t.** unto
Eph 6:9 ye masters, do the same **t.** unto them,
Eph 6:21 Lord, shall make known to you all **t.**
Php 1:10 ye may approve **t.** that are excellent;
Php 1:12 the **t.** which happened unto me have
Php 2:4 Look not every man on his own **t.**,
Php 2:4 but every man also on the **t.** of others.
Php 2:10 knee should bow, of **t.** in heaven,
Php 2:10 and **t.** in earth, and **t.** under the earth;
Php 2:14 Do all **t.** without murmurings and
Php 2:21 not the **t.** which are Jesus Christ's.
Php 3:1 To write the same **t.** to you, to me
Php 3:7 But what **t.** were gain to me, those I
Php 3:8 and I count all **t.** but loss for the
Php 3:8 whom I have suffered the loss of all **t.**,

Php 3:13 forgetting those **t.** which are behind,
Php 3:13 reaching forth unto those **t.** which
Php 3:19 is in their shame, who mind earthly **t.**.
Php 3:21 he is able even to subdue all **t.** unto
Php 4:8 brethren, whatsoever **t.** are true,
Php 4:8 whatsoever **t.** are honest,
Php 4:8 whatsoever **t.** are just,
Php 4:8 whatsoever **t.** are pure,
Php 4:8 whatsoever **t.** are lovely,
Php 4:8 whatsoever **t.** are of good report; if
Php 4:8 there be any praise, think on these **t.**.
Php 4:9 Those **t.**, which ye have both learned,
Php 4:12 in all **t.** I am instructed both to be
Php 4:13 I can do all **t.** through Christ which
Php 4:18 the **t.** which were sent from you, an
Col 1:16 For by him were all **t.** created, that are
Col 1:16 all **t.** were created by him, and for
Col 1:17 before all **t.**, and by him all **t.** consist.
Col 1:18 that in all **t.** he might have the
Col 1:20 him to reconcile all **t.** unto himself;
Col 1:20 they be **t.** in earth, or **t.** in heaven.
Col 2:17 Which are a shadow of **t.** to come;
Col 2:18 intruding into those **t.** which he hath
Col 2:23 **t.** have indeed a shew of wisdom
Col 3:1 Christ, seek those **t.** which are above,
Col 3:2 Set your affection on **t.** above,
Col 3:2 not on **t.** on the earth.
Col 3:4 And above all these **t.** put on charity,
Col 3:14 above all these **t.** put on charity,
Col 3:20 Children, obey your parents in all **t.**
Col 3:22 obey in all **t.** your masters according
Col 4:9 shall make known unto you all **t.**
1Th 2:14 have suffered like **t.** of your own
1Th 5:21 Prove all **t.**; hold fast that which is
2Th 2:5 yet with you, I told you these **t.**?
2Th 3:4 will do the **t.** which we command you.
1Ti 3:11 not slanderers sober, faithful in all **t.**
1Ti 3:14 These **t.** write I unto thee, hoping
1Ti 4:6 brethren in remembrance of these **t.**,
1Ti 4:8 but godliness is profitable unto all **t.**,
1Ti 4:11 These **t.** command and teach.
1Ti 4:15 Meditate upn these **t.**; give thyself
1Ti 5:7 And these **t.** give in charge, that
1Ti 5:13 speaking **t.** which they ought not.
1Ti 5:21 observe these **t.** without perferring
1Ti 6:2 benefit. These **t.** teach and exhort.
1Ti 6:11 thou, O man of God, flee these **t.**;
1Ti 6:13 sight of God, who quickeneth all **t.**,
1Ti 6:17 who giveth us richly all **t.** to enjoy;
2Ti 1:12 which cause I also suffer these **t.**
2Ti 1:18 how many **t.** he ministered unto me at
2Ti 2:2 **t.** that thou hast heard of me among
2Ti 2:7 Lord give thee understanding in all **t.**.
2Ti 2:10 I endure all **t.** for the elect's sake,
2Ti 2:14 these **t.** put them in remembrance,
2Ti 3:14 in the **t.** which thou hast learned
2Ti 4:5 But watch thou in all **t.**, endure
Tit 1:5 set in order the **t.** that are wanting,
Tit 1:11 teaching **t.** which they ought not, for
Tit 1:15 Unto the pure all **t.** are pure: but unto
Tit 2:1 **t.** which become sound doctrine:
Tit 2:3 too much wine, teachers of good **t.**;
Tit 2:7 In all **t.** shewing thyself a pattern of
Tit 2:9 and to please them well in all **t.**;
Tit 2:10 doctrine of God our Saviour in all **t.**.
Tit 2:15 These **t.** speak, and exhort, and
Tit 3:8 **t.** I will that thou affirm constantly,
Tit 3:8 **t.** are good and profitable unto
Heb 1:2 whom he hath appointed heir of all **t.**,
Heb 1:3 and upholding all **t.** by the word of his
Heb 2:1 earnestly to the **t.** which we have
Heb 2:8 put all **t.** in subjection under his feet.
Heb 2:8 we see not yet all **t.** put under him.
Heb 2:10 it became him, for whom are all **t.**,
Heb 2:10 and by whom are all **t.**, in bringing
Heb 2:17 in all **t.** it behoved him to be made like
Heb 2:17 high priest in **t.** pertaining to God,
Heb 3:4 man; but he that built all **t.** is God.
Heb 3:5 those **t.** which were to be spoken after;
Heb 4:13 **t.** are naked and opened unto the eyes
Heb 5:1 for men in **t.** pertaining to God,
Heb 5:8 learned he obedience by the **t.** which
Heb 5:11 Of whom we have many **t.** to say, and
Heb 6:9 we are persuaded better **t.** of you,
Heb 6:9 and **t.** that accompany salvation,
Heb 6:18 That by two immutable **t.**, in

Heb 7:13 he of whom these **t.** are spoken *4229*
Heb 8:1 **t.** which we have spoken this is the
Heb 8:5 example and shadow of heavenly **t.**,
Heb 8:5 make all **t.** according to the pattern
Heb 9:6 Now when these **t.** were thus
Heb 9:11 being come a high priest of good **t.**
Heb 9:22 all **t.** are by the law purged with blood
Heb 9:23 the patterns of **t.** in the heavens
Heb 9:23 the heavenly **t.** themselves with better
Heb 10:1 having a shadow of good **t.** to come,
Heb 10:1 and not the very image of the **t.**, *4229*
Heb 11:1 faith is the substance of **t.** hoped *4229*
Heb 11:1 for, the evidence of **t.** not seen.
Heb 11:3 so that **t.** which are seen were not
Heb 11:3 were not made of **t.** which do appear.
Heb 11:7 being warned of God of **t.** not seen as
Heb 11:14 they that say such **t.** declare plainly
Heb 11:20 Jacob and Esau concerning **t.** to come,
Heb 12:24 speaketh better **t.** than that of Abel.
Heb 12:27 removing of those **t.** that are shaken,
Heb 12:27 that are shaken, as of **t.** that are made,
Heb 12:27 those **t.** which cannot be shaken may
Heb 13:5 and be content with such **t.** as ye have:
Heb 13:18 in all **t.** willing to live honestly.
Jas 2:16 ye give them not those **t.** which are
Jas 3:2 For in many **t.** we offend all. If any
Jas 3:5 little member, and boasteth great **t.**.
Jas 3:7 and of serpents, and of **t.** in the sea, is
Jas 3:10 these **t.** ought not so to be.
Jas 5:12 But above all **t.**, my brethren, swear
1Pe 1:12 unto us they did minister the **t.**, *846*
1Pe 1:12 which **t.** the angels desire to look into.
1Pe 1:18 were not redeemed with corruptible **t.**,
1Pe 4:7 But the end of all **t.** is at hand: be ye
1Pe 4:8 And above all **t.** have fervent charity
1Pe 4:11 that God in all **t.** may be glorified
2Pe 1:3 given unto us all **t.** that pertain unto
2Pe 1:8 For if these **t.** be in you, and
2Pe 1:9 he that lacketh these **t.** is blind,
2Pe 1:10 for if ye do these **t.**, ye shall never
2Pe 1:12 always in remembrance of these **t.**,
2Pe 1:15 these **t.** always in remembrance.
2Pe 2:12 speak evil of the **t.** that they
2Pe 3:4 **t.** continue as they were from the
2Pe 3:11 that all these **t.** shall be dissolved,
2Pe 3:14 seeing that ye look for such **t.**,
2Pe 3:16 speaking in them of these **t.**;
2Pe 3:16 are some **t.** hard to be understood,
2Pe 3:17 seeing ye know these **t.** before,
1Jo 1:4 And these **t.** write we unto you,
1Jo 2:1 children, these **t.** write I unto you,
1Jo 2:15 neither the **t.** that are in the world.
1Jo 2:20 from the Holy One, and ye know all **t.**.
1Jo 2:26 These **t.** have I written unto you
1Jo 2:27 same anointing teacheth you of all **t.**,
1Jo 3:20 than our heart, and knoweth all **t.**
1Jo 3:22 and do those **t.** that are pleasing in his
1Jo 5:13 These **t.** have I written unto you
2Jo 8 not those **t.** which we have wrought,
2Jo 12 Having many **t.** to write unto you,
3Jo 2 above all **t.** that thou mayest prosper
3Jo 13 I had many **t.** to write, but I will not
Jude 10 speak evil of those **t.** which they know
Jude 10 in those **t.** they corrupt themselves.
Re 1:1 servants **t.** which must shortly come
Re 1:2 Christ, and of all **t.** that he saw.
Re 1:3 keep those **t.** which are written
Re 1:19 **Write the t. which thou hast seen, and**
Re 1:19 **thou hast seen, and the t. which are,**
Re 1:19 **and the t. which shall be hereafter;**
Re 2:1 **These t. saith he that holdeth the**
Re 2:8 **These t. saith the first and the last,**
Re 2:10 **Fear none of those t. which thou shalt**
Re 2:12 **These t. saith he which hath the sharp**
Re 2:14 **But I have a few t. against thee,**
Re 2:14 **to eat t. sacrificed unto idols, and to**
Re 2:18 **These t. saith the Son of God, who**
Re 2:20 **I have a few t. against thee,**
Re 2:20 **and to eat t. sacrificed unto idols**
Re 3:1 **These t. saith he that hath the seven**
Re 3:2 **and strengthen the t. which remain,**
Re 3:7 **These t. saith he that is holy, he that**
Re 3:14 **These t. saith the Amen, the faithful**
Re 4:1 shew these **t.** which must be hereafter.
Re 4:11 for thou hast created all **t.**, and for
Re 7:1 after these **t.** I saw four angels

Re 10:4 t. which the seven thunders uttered,
Re 10:6 heaven, and the t. that therein are,
Re 10:6 the earth, and the t. that therein are,
Re 10:6 the sea, and the t. which are therein,
Re 13:5 a mouth speaking great t. and
Re 18:1 And after these t. I saw another
Re 18:14 and all t. which were dainty and
Re 18:15 The merchants of these t., which
Re 19:1 after these t. I heard a great voice
Re 20:12 t. which were written in the books,
Re 21:4 for the former t. are passed away.
Re 21:5 said, Behold, I will make all t. new.
Re 21:7 that overcometh shall inherit all t.;
Re 22:6 the t. which must shortly be done.
Re 22:8 And I John saw these t., and
Re 22:8 angel which shewed me these t.
Re 22:16 **testify unto you these t. in the**
Re 22:18 If any man shall add unto these t.,
Re 22:19 the t. which are written in this book.
Re 22:20 He which testifieth these t. saith,

THINGS'
Col 3:6 For which t. sake the wrath of God

THINK See also BETHINK; THINKEST; THINKETH; THINKING; THOUGHT.
Ge 40:14 t. on me when it shall be well 2142
Nu 36:6 them marry to whom they t. best; 5869
2Sa 13:33 t. that all the king's sons are dead: 559
2Ch 13:8 And now ye t. to withstand the 559
Ne 5:19 T. upon me, my God, for good, 2142
Ne 6:6 that thou and the Jews t. to rebel: 2803
Ne 6:14 My God, t. thou upon Tobiah and 2142
Es 4:13 T. not with thyself that thou shalt 1819
Job 31:1 why then should I t. upon a maid? 995
Job 41:32 one would t. the deep to be hoary. 2803
Ec 8:17 though a wise man t. to know it, 559
Isa 10:7 so, neither doth his heart t. so; 2803
Jer 23:27 Which t. to cause my people to 2803
Jer 29:11 the thoughts that I t. toward you, 2803
Eze 38:10 and thou shalt t. an evil thought: 2803
Da 7:25 and t. to change times and laws: 5452
Jon 1:6 if so be that God will t. upon us, 6245
Zec 11:12 If ye t. good, give me my price; 5869
Mt 3:9 t. not to say within yourselves, *1380*
Mt 5:17 **T. not that I am come to destroy** *3543*
Mt 6:7 **they t. that they shall be heard for** *1380*
Mt 9:4 **Wherefore t. ye evil in your hearts** *1760*
Mt 10:34 **T. not that I am come to send** *3543*
Mt 18:12 **How t. ye? if a man have an** *1380*
Mt 21:28 **what t. ye? A certain man had** *1380*
Mt 22:42 Saying, **What t. ye of Christ? whose** *1380*
Mt 24:44 **such an hour as ye t. not the Son** *1380*
Mt 26:66 What t. ye? They answered and *1380*
Mk 14:64 heard the blasphemy: what t. ye? *5316*
Lu 12:40 **cometh at an hour when ye t. not** *1380*
Lu 13:4 **t. ye that they were sinners above** *1380*
Joh 5:39 **in them ye t. ye have eternal life:** *1380*
Joh 5:45 **Do not t. that I will accuse you to** *1380*
Joh 11:56 What t. ye, that he will not come to *1380*
Joh 16:2 **will t. that he doeth God service** *1380*
Ac 13:25 Whom t. ye that I am? I am not *5282*
Ac 17:29 not to t. that the Godhead is like *3543*
Ac 26:2 I t. myself happy, king Agrippa, *2233*
Ro 12:3 not to t. of himself more highly *5252*
Ro 12:3 more highly than he ought to t.; *5426*
Ro 12:3 but to t. soberly, according as God *5426*
1Co 4:6 not to t. of men above that which is *5426*
1Co 4:9 For I t. that God hath set forth us *1380*
1Co 7:36 if any man t. that he behaveth *3543*
1Co 7:40 I t. also that I have the Spirit of *1380*
1Co 8:2 if any man t. that he knoweth any *1380*
1Co 12:23 which we t. to be less honourable, *1380*
1Co 14:37 If any man t. himself to be a *1380*
2Co 3:5 to t. any thing as of ourselves; *3049*
2Co 10:2 I t. to be bold against some, which *3049*
2Co 10:2 which t. of us as if we walked *3049*
2Co 10:7 let him of himself t. this again, *3049*
2Co 10:11 Let such an one t. this, that, such *3049*
2Co 11:16 say again, Let no man t. me a fool; *1380*
2Co 12:6 man should t. of me above that *3049*
2Co 12:19 t. ye that we excuse ourselves unto *1380*
Ga 6:3 if a man t. himself to be something, *1380*
Eph 3:20 above all that we ask or t., *3539*
Php 1:7 is meet for me to t. this of you all, *5426*
Php 4:8 be any praise, t. on these things. *3049*
Jas 1:7 that man t. that he shall receive *3633*
Jas 4:5 Do ye t. that the scripture saith in *1380*
1Pe 4:4 t. it strange that ye run not with them
1Pe 4:12 t. it not strange concerning the fiery
2Pe 1:13 Yea, I t. it meet, as long as I am in *2233*

THINKEST
2Sa 10:3 T. thou that David doth honour 5869
1Ch 19:3 T. thou that David doth honour 5869
Job 35:2 T. thou this to be right, that thou 2803
Mt 17:25 him, saying, **What t. thou, Simon?** *1380*
Mt 22:17 Tell us therefore, What t. thou? *1380*
Mt 26:53 **T. thou that I cannot now pray to** *1380*
Lu 10:36 **Which now of these three, t. thou,** *1380*
Ac 28:22 desire to hear of thee what thou t. *5426*
Ro 2:3 And t. thou this, O man, that *3049*

THINKETH
2Sa 18:27 Me t. the running of the foremost 7200
Ps 40:17 needy; yet the Lord t. upon me: 2803
Pr 23:7 For as he t. in his heart, so is he: 8176
1Co 10:12 let him that t. he standeth take *1380*
1Co 13:5 is not easily provoked, t. no evil; *3049*
Php 3:4 If any other man t. that he hath *1380*

THINKING
2Sa 4:10 t....have brought good tidings, 1931,1961
2Sa 5:6 t., David cannot come in hither. 559

THIRD
Ge 1:13 and the morning were the t. day. 7992
Ge 2:14 name of the t. river is Hiddekel: 7992
Ge 6:16 and t. stories shalt thou make it 7992
Ge 22:4 t. day Abraham lifted up his eyes, 7992
Ge 31:22 told Laban on the t. day that Jacob 7992
Ge 32:19 he the second, and the t., and all 7992
Ge 34:25 came to pass on the t. day, when 7992
Ge 40:20 came to pass the t. day, which was 7992
Ge 42:18 Joseph said unto them the t. day, 7992
Ge 50:23 children of the t. generation: 8029
Ex 19:1 In the t. month, when the children 7992
Ex 19:11 And be ready against the t. day: 7992
Ex 19:11 t. day the Lord will come down in 7992
Ex 19:15 Be ready against the t. day: come 7969
Ex 19:16 it came to pass on the t. day in the 7992
Ex 20:5 unto the t. and fourth generation 8029
Ex 28:19 the t. row a ligure, an agate, and 7992
Ex 34:7 unto the t. and to the fourth 8029
Ex 39:12 the t. row, a ligure, an agate, and 7992
Le *general title* The T. Book Of Moses, Called
Le 7:17 flesh of the sacrifice on the t. day 7992
Le 7:18 be eaten at all on the t. day, 7992
Le 19:6 if ought remain until the t. day, it 7992
Le 19:7 if it be eaten at all on the t. day, it 7992
Nu 2:24 they shall go forward in the t. rank 7992
Nu 7:24 On the t. day Eliab the son of Helon, 7992
Nu 14:18 unto the t. and fourth generation 8029
Nu 15:6 mingled with the t. part of an hin 7992
Nu 15:7 offer the t. part of an hin of wine, 7992
Nu 19:12 purify himself with it on the t. day, 7992
Nu 19:12 if he purify not himself the t. day, 7992
Nu 19:19 upon the unclean on the t. day, 7992
Nu 28:14 and the t. part of an hin unto a ram, 7992
Nu 29:20 on the t. day eleven bullocks, two 7992
Nu 31:19 and your captives on the t. day, 7992
De 5:9 unto the t. and fourth generation 8029
De 23:8 of the Lord in their t. generation. 7992
De 26:12 tithes of thine increase the t. year, 7992
Jos 9:17 came unto their cities on the t. day. 7992
Jos 19:10 the t. lot came up for the children 7992
Jg 20:30 children of Benjamin on the t. day, 7992
1Sa 3:8 called Samuel again the t. time. 7992
1Sa 17:13 Abinadab, and the t. Shammah. 7992
1Sa 19:21 sent messengers agian the t. time, 7992
1Sa 20:5 myself in the field unto the t. day 7992
1Sa 20:12 to morrow any time, or the t. day, 7992
1Sa 30:1 were come to Ziklag on the t. day, 7992
2Sa 1:2 It came even to pass on the t. day, 7992
2Sa 3:3 the t., Absalom the son of Maacah 7992
2Sa 18:2 David sent forth a t. part of the 7992
2Sa 18:2 a t. part under the hand of Abishai 7992
2Sa 18:2 t. part under the hand of Ittai the 7992
1Ki *general title* Called,...T. Book Of The Kings
1Ki 3:18 the t. day after that I was delivered, 7992
1Ki 6:6 the t. was seven cubits broad: for 7992
1Ki 6:8 and out of the middle into the t. 7992
1Ki 12:12 came to Rehoboam the t. day, 7992
1Ki 12:12 saying, come to me again the t. day. 7992
1Ki 15:28 Even in the t. year of Asa king of 7969
1Ki 15:33 t. year of Asa king of Judah began 7969
1Ki 18:1 Lord came to Elijah in the t. year, 7992
1Ki 18:34 And he said, Do it the t. time. 8027
1Ki 18:34 And they did it the t. time. 8027
1Ki 22:2 it come to pass in the t. year, that 7992
2Ki 1:13 sent again a captain of the t. fifty 7992
2Ki 1:13 And the t. captain of fifty went up, 7992
2Ki 11:5 A t. part of you that enter in on the 7992
2Ki 11:6 a t. part shall be at the gate of Sur; 7992
2Ki 11:6 a t. part at the gate behind the 7992
2Ki 18:1 to pass in the t. year of Hoshea 7969
2Ki 19:29 in the t. year sow ye, and reap, and 7992
2Ki 20:5 t. day thou shalt go up unto the 7992
2Ki 20:8 the house of the Lord the t. day? 7992
1Ch 2:13 the second, and Shimma the t., 7992
1Ch 3:2 t., Absalom the son of Maachah the 7992
1Ch 3:15 t. Zedekiah, the fourth Shallum. 7992
1Ch 8:1 the second, and Aharah the t., 7992
1Ch 8:39 the second, and Eliphelet the t.. 7992
1Ch 12:9 Obadiah the second, Eliab the t., 7992
1Ch 23:19 Jahaziel the t., and Jekameam the 7992
1Ch 24:8 t. to Harim, the fourth to Seorim, 7992
1Ch 24:23 Jehaziel the t., Jekameam the 7992
1Ch 25:10 t. to Zaccur, he, his sons, and his 7992
1Ch 26:2 Zebadiah the t., Jathniel the fourth, 7992
1Ch 26:4 Joah the t., and Sacar the fourth, 7992
1Ch 26:11 Tebaliah the t., Zechariah 7992
1Ch 27:5 t. captain of the host for the 7992
1Ch 27:5 t. month was Benaiah the son of 7992
2Ch 10:12 came to Rehoboam on the t. day, 7992
2Ch 10:12 Come again to me on the t. day. 7992
2Ch 15:10 at Jerusalem in the t. month, in 7992
2Ch 17:7 in the t. year of his reign he sent 7969
2Ch 23:4 A t. part of you entering on the 7992
2Ch 23:5 t. part shall be at the king's house; 7992
2Ch 23:5 t. part at the gate of the foundation: 7992
2Ch 27:5 both the second year, and the t.. 7992
2Ch 31:7 t. month they began to lay the 7992
Ezr 6:15 house was finished on the t. day 8531
Ne 10:32 t. part of a shekel for the service 7992
Es 1:3 In the t. year of his reign, he made 7969
Es 5:1 Now it came to pass on the t. day, 7992
Es 8:9 called at that time in the t. month, 7992
Job 42:14 the name of the t., Keren-happuch. 7992
Isa 19:24 shall Israel be the t. with Egypt 7992
Isa 37:30 in the t. year sow ye, and reap, and 7992
Jer 38:14 t. entry that is in the house of the 7992
Eze 5:2 Thou shalt burn with fire a t. part 7992
Eze 5:2 thou shalt take a t. part, and smite 7992
Eze 5:2 a t. part thou shalt scatter in the 7992
Eze 5:12 A t. part of thee shall die with the 7992
Eze 5:12 a t. part shall fall by the sword 7992
Eze 5:12 I will scatter a t. part into all the 7992
Eze 10:14 and the t. the face of a lion, and the 7992
Eze 21:14 let the sword be doubled the t. time, 7992
Eze 31:1 the eleventh year, in the t. month, 7992
Eze 46:14 the t. part of an hin of oil, to temper 7992
Da 1:1 t. year of the reign of Jehoiakim 7969
Da 2:39 and another t. kingdom of brass, 8523
Da 5:7 shall be the t. ruler in the kingdom. 8523
Da 5:16, 29 be he t. ruler in the kingdom. 8531
Da 8:1 In the t. year of the reign of king 7969
Da 10:1 the t. year of Cyrus king of Persia 7969
Ho 6:2 t. day he will raise us up, and we 7992
Zec 6:3 And in the t. chariot white horses; 7992
Zec 13:8 die; but the t. shall be left therein. 7992
Zec 13:9 bring the t. part through the fire, 7992
Mt 16:21 and be raised again the t. day. *5154*
Mt 17:23 **and the t. day he shall be raised** *5154*
Mt 20:3 **And he went out about the t. hour,** *5154*
Mt 20:19 **and the t. day he shall rise again.** *5154*
Mt 22:26 also, and the t., unto the seventh. *5154*
Mt 26:44 and prayed the t. time, saying the *5154*
Mt 27:64 be made sure until the t. day, *5154*
Mk 9:31 **is killed, he shall rise the t. day.** *5154*
Mk 10:34 **and the t. day he shall rise again.** *5154*
Mk 12:21 he any seed: and the t. likewise. *5154*
Mk 14:41 he cometh the t. time, and saith *5154*
Mk 15:25 And it was the t. hour, and they *5154*
Lu 9:22 **be slain, and be raised the t. day.** *5154*
Lu 12:38 **watch, or come in the t. watch,** *5154*
Lu 13:32 **and the t. day I shall be perfected.** *5154*
Lu 18:33 **and the t. day he shall rise again.** *5154*
Lu 20:12 **And again he sent a t.: and they** *5154*
Lu 20:31 And the t. took her; and in like *5154*

Lu 23:22 And he said unto them the **t.** time,..... *5154*
Lu 24:7 crucified, and the **t.** day rise again..... *5154*
Lu 24:21 to day is the **t.** day since these.......... *5154*
Lu 24:46 **to rise from the dead the t. day:**.... *5154*
Joh 2:1 the **t.** day there was a marriage......... *5154*
Joh 21:14 **t.** time that Jesus shewed himself....... *5154*
Joh 21:17 He saith unto him the **t.** time, ... *5154*
Joh 21:17 he said unto him the **t.** time,............. *5154*
Ac 2:15 it is but the **t.** hour of the day........... *5154*
Ac 10:40 Him God raised up the **t.** day, and *5154*
Ac 20:9 and fell down from the **t.** loft,............ *5152*
Ac 23:23 at the **t.** hour of the night;................ *5154*
Ac 27:19 And the **t.** day we cast out with......... *5154*
1Co 15:4 he rose again the **t.** day according...... *5154*
2Co 12:2 an one caught up to the **t.** heaven...... *5154*
2Co 12:14 **t.** time I am ready to come to you; *5154*
2Co 13:1 is the **t.** time I am coming to you....... *5154*
3Jo *general title* The **T.** Epistle Of John.............. *5154*
Re 4:7 and the **t.** beast had a face as a man,.. *5154*
Re 6:5 when he had opened the **t.** seal, ... *5154*
Re 6:5 I heard the **t.** beast say, Come and *5154*
Re 8:7 the **t.** part of trees was burnt up,....... *5154*
Re 8:8 the **t.** part of the sea became blood; ... *5154*
Re 8:9 the **t.** part of the creatures which....... *5154*
Re 8:9 **t.** part of the ships were destroyed..... *5154*
Re 8:10 And the **t.** angel sounded, and there ... *5154*
Re 8:10 fell upon the **t.** part of the rivers,....... *5154*
Re 8:11 the **t.** part of the waters became........ *5154*
Re 8:12 the **t.** part of the sun was smitten, ... *5154*
Re 8:12 and the **t.** part of the moon, and the... *5154*
Re 8:12 moon, and the **t.** part of the stars; *5154*
Re 8:12 **t.** part of them was darkened, and....... *5154*
Re 8:12 the day shone not for a **t.** part of it, ... *5154*
Re 9:15 year, for to slay the **t.** part of men..... *5154*
Re 9:18 three was the **t.** part of men killed, ... *5154*
Re 11:14 behold, the **t.** woe cometh quickly...... *5154*
Re 12:4 tail drew the **t.** part of the stars of...... *5154*
Re 14:9 And the **t.** angel followed them, ... *5154*
Re 16:4 **t.** angel poured out his vial upon *5154*
Re 21:19 the **t.**, a chalcedony; the fourth, an..... *5154*

THIRDLY
1Co 12:28 secondarily prophets, **t.** teachers,....... *5154*

THIRST See also ATHIRST; THIRSTED; THIRSTETH.
Ex 17:3 our children and our cattle with **t.**?..... 6772
De 28:48 hunger, and in **t.**, and in nakedness, ... 6772
De 29:19 heart, to add drunkenness to **t.**.......... 6771
Jg 15:18 and now shall I die for **t.**, and fall....... 6772
2Ch 32:11 yourselves to die by famine and...**t.**, ... 6772
Ne 9:15 for them out of the rock for their **t.**, ... 6772
Ne 9:20 and gavest them water for their **t.**...... 6772
Job 24:11 their winepresses, and suffer **t.**.......... 6770
Ps 69:21 in my **t.** they gave me vinegar to....... 6772
Ps 104:11 the wild asses quench their **t.**........... 6772
Isa 5:13 their multitude dried up with **t.**......... 6772
Isa 41:17 and their tongue faileth for **t.**,............ 6772
Isa 49:10 They shall not hunger nor **t.**; 6770
Isa 50:2 there is no water, and dieth for **t.**...... 6772
Jer 2:25 unshod, and thy throat from **t.**............ 6773
Jer 48:18 down from thy glory, and sit in **t.**;...... 6772
La 4:4 to the roof of his mouth for **t.**............ 6772
Ho 2:3 like a dry land, and slay her with **t.**.... 6772
Am 8:11 famine of bread, nor a **t.** for water, ... 6772
Am 8:13 virgins and young men faint for **t.**....... 6772
Mt 5:6 **hunger and t. after righteousness:**. *1372*
Joh 4:13 **drinketh...this water shall t. again:** *1372*
Joh 4:14 **that I shall give him shall never t.;** *1372*
Joh 4:15 give me this water, that I **t.** not, ... *1372*
Joh 6:35 **that believeth on me shall never t.**. *1372*
Joh 7:37 **If any man t., let him come unto** .. *1372*
Joh 19:28 might be fulfilled, saith, **I t.**............. *1372*
Ro 12:20 feed him; if he **t.**, give him drink:....... *1372*
1Co 4:11 both hunger, and **t.**, and are naked, ... *1372*
2Co 11:27 watchings often, in hunger and **t.**, ... *1373*
Re 7:16 no more, neither **t.** any more; *1372*

THIRSTED
Ex 17:3 And the people **t.** there for water;...... 6770
Isa 48:21 And they **t.** not when he led them...... 6770

THIRSTETH
Ps 42:2 My soul **t.** for God, for the living....... 6770
Ps 63:1 my soul **t.** for thee, my flesh longeth .. 6770
Ps 143:6 my soul **t.** after thee, as a thirsty............
Isa 55:1 Ho, every one that **t.**, come ye to...... 6771

THIRSTY See also BLOODTHIRSTY.
Jg 4:19 a little water to drink; for I am **t.**....... 6770
2Sa 17:29 is hungry, and weary, and **t.**, ... 6771
Ps 63:1 longeth for thee in a dry and **t.** land,.........
Ps 107:5 Hungry and **t.**, their soul fainted 6771
Ps 143:6 soul thirsteth after thee, as a **t.** land.........
Pr 25:21 and if he be **t.**, give him water to......... 6771
Pr 25:25 As cold waters to a **t.** soul, so is good.....
Isa 21:14 brought water to him that was **t.**,....... 6771
Isa 29:8 or as when a **t.** man dreameth, and, ... 6771
Isa 32:6 will cause the drink of the **t.** to fail..... 6771
Isa 35:7 and the **t.** land springs of water: 6774
Isa 44:3 pour water upon him that is **t.**, ... 6771
Isa 65:13 shall drink, but ye shall be **t.**............. 6770
Eze 19:13 wilderness, in a dry and **t.** ground...... 6772
Mt 25:35 **I was t., and ye gave me drink:**..... *1372*
Mt 25:37 **thee? or t., and gave thee drink?** ... *1372*
Mt 25:42 **I was t., and ye gave me no drink:** .*1372*

THIRTEEN
Ge 17:25 his son was **t.** years old, ... 7969,6240
Nu 3:43 hundred and threescore and **t.**.......... 7969
Nu 3:46 hundred and threescore and **t.** of........ 7969
Nu 29:13 **t.** young bullocks, two rams, ... 7969,6240
Nu 29:14 every bullock of the **t.** bullocks, .. 7969,6240
Jos 19:6 **t.** cities and their villages:.......... 7969,6240
Jos 21:4 the tribe of Benjamin, **t.** cities. ... 7969,6240
Jos 21:6 Manasseh in Bashan, **t.** cities. 7969,6240
Jos 21:19 **t.** cities with their suburbs......... 7969,6240
Jos 21:33 **t.** cities with their suburbs......... 7969,6240
1Ki 7:1 building his own house **t.** years,.. 7969,6240
1Ch 6:60 their families were **t.** cities. 7969,6240
1Ch 6:62 Manasseh in Bashan, **t.** cities. ... 7969,6240
1Ch 26:11 and brethren of Hosah were **t.**.... 7969,6240
Eze 40:11 length of the gate, **t.** cubits........ 7969,6240

THIRTEENTH
Ge 14:4 in the **t.** year they rebelled. 7969,6240
1Ch 24:13 **t.** to Huppah, the fourteenth 7969,6240
1Ch 25:20 The **t.** to Shubael, he, his sons,.. 7969,6240
Es 3:12 scribes called on the **t.** day 7969,6240
Es 3:13 upon the **t.** day of the twelfth..... 7969,6240
Es 8:12 upon the **t.** day of the twelfth..... 7969,6240
Es 9:1 Adar, on the **t.** day of the same,. 7969,6240
Es 9:17 the **t.** day of the month Adar;..... 7969,6240
Es 9:18 together on the **t.** day hereof, ... 7969,6240
Jer 1:2 in the **t.** year of his reign. 7969,6240
Jer 25:3 the **t.** year of Josiah the son of... 7969,6240

THIRTIETH
2Ki 15:13 in the nine and **t.** year of Uzziah 7970
2Ki 15:17 In the nine and **t.** year of Azariah....... 7970
2Ki 25:27 seven and **t.** year of the captivity of.... 7970
2Ch 15:19 five and **t.** year of the reign of Asa..... 7970
2Ch 16:1 six and **t.** year of the reign of Asa...... 7970
Ne 5:14 two and **t.** year of Artaxerxes the 7970
Ne 13:6 the two and **t.** year of Artaxerxes 7970
Jer 52:31 seven and **t.** year of the captivity of.... 7970
Eze 1:1 Now it came to pass in the **t.** year, ... 7970

THIRTY See also THIRTYFOLD.
Ge 5:3 And Adam lived an hundred and **t.**....... 7970
Ge 5:5 were nine hundred and **t.** years: 7970
Ge 5:16 Jared eight hundred and **t.** years, ... 7970
Ge 6:15 cubits, and the height of it **t.** cubits. ... 7970
Ge 11:12 Arphaxad lived five and **t.** years,........ 7970
Ge 11:14 And Salah lived **t.** years, and begat..... 7970
Ge 11:16 And Eber lived four and **t.** years,........ 7970
Ge 11:17 Peleg four hundred and **t.** years,........ 7970
Ge 11:18 And Peleg lived **t.** years, and begat 7970
Ge 11:20 And Reu lived two and **t.** years, and... 7970
Ge 11:22 And Serug lived **t.** years, and begat.... 7970
Ge 18:30 there shall **t.** be found there............. 7970
Ge 18:30 I will not do it, if I find **t.** there. 7970
Ge 25:17 an hundred and **t.** and seven years: 7970
Ge 32:15 **T.** milch camels with their colts, ... 7970
Ge 41:46 And Joseph was **t.** years old when...... 7970
Ge 46:15 his daughters were **t.** and three. 7970
Ge 47:9 are an hundred and **t.** years: 7970
Ex 6:16 were an hundred **t.** and seven years. .. 7970
Ex 6:18 were an hundred **t.** and three years.... 7970
Ex 6:20 an hundred and **t.** and seven years. 7970
Ex 12:40 was four hundred and **t.** years. 7970
Ex 12:41 end of the four hundred and **t.** years,.. 7970
Ex 21:32 their masters **t.** shekels of silver,....... 7970
Ex 26:8 of one curtain shall be **t.** cubits,......... 7970
Ex 36:15 length of one curtain was **t.** cubits,..... 7970
Ex 38:24 and seven hundred and **t.** shekels,....... 7970
Le 12:4 of her purifying three and **t.** days; 7970
Le 27:4 thy estimation shall be **t.** shekels........ 7970
Nu 1:35 were **t.** and two thousand and two...... 7970
Nu 1:37 were **t.** and five thousand and four 7970
Nu 2:21 were **t.** and two thousand and two...... 7970
Nu 2:23 were **t.** and five thousand and four 7970
Nu 4:3, 23,30,35,39 **t.** years old and upward ... 7970
Nu 4:40 thousand and six hundred and **t.**......... 7970
Nu 4:43, 47 From **t.** years old and upward 7970
Nu 7:13, 19,25,31,37,43,49,55,61,67,73,79,85
an hundred and **t.** shekels,................. 7970
Nu 20:39 they mourned for Aaron **t.** days, ... 7970
Nu 26:7 thousand and seven hundred and **t.**..... 7970
Nu 26:37 them, **t.** and two thousand and five..... 7970
Nu 26:51 a thousand seven hundred and **t.**......... 7970
Nu 31:35 **t.** and two thousand persons in all, ... 7970
Nu 31:36 seven and **t.** thousand and five........... 7970
Nu 31:38 beeves were **t.** and six thousand; 7970
Nu 31:39 the asses were **t.** thousand and five.... 7970
Nu 31:40 the Lord's tribute was **t.** and two....... 7970
Nu 31:43 hundred thousand and **t.** thousand....... 7970
Nu 31:44 And **t.** and six thousand beeves, ... 7970
Nu 31:45 **t.** thousand asses and five hundred, ... 7970
De 2:14 brook Zered, was **t.** and eight years; .. 7970
De 34:8 Moses in the plains of Moab **t.** days: .. 7970
Jos 7:5 smote of them about **t.** and six men:... 7970
Jos 8:3 and Joshua chose out **t.** thousand 7970
Jos 12:24 one: all the kings **t.** and one............. 7970
Jg 10:4 had **t.** sons that rode on **t.** ass colts, .. 7970
Jg 10:4 and they had **t.** cities, which are 7970
Jg 12:9 he had **t.** sons, and **t.** daughters, ... 7970
Jg 12:9 took in **t.** daughters from abroad 7970
Jg 12:14 he had forty sons and **t.** nephews,....... 7970
Jg 14:11 they brought **t.** companions to be....... 7970
Jg 14:12 **t.** sheets and **t.** change of garments:... 7970
Jg 14:13 **t.** sheets and **t.** change of garments.... 7970
Jg 14:19 slew **t.** men of them, and took their.... 7970
Jg 20:31 in the field, about **t.** men of Israel. 7970
Jg 20:39 and kill of the men of Israel about **t.**... 7970
1Sa 4:10 fell of Israel **t.** thousand footmen. 7970
1Sa 9:22 which were about **t.** persons. 7970
1Sa 11:8 and the men of Judah **t.** thousand. 7970
1Sa 13:5 **t.** thousand chariots, and six............. 7970
2Sa 5:4 David was **t.** years old when he......... 7970
2Sa 5:5 he reigned **t.** and three years over 7970
2Sa 6:1 chosen men of Israel, **t.** thousand. 7970
2Sa 23:13 And three of the **t.** chief went down, .. 7970
2Sa 23:23 He was more honourable than the **t.**,.. 7970
2Sa 23:24 brother of Joab was one of the **t.**; 7970
2Sa 23:39 the Hittite: **t.** and seven in all........... 7970
1Ki 2:11 **t.** and three years reigned he in......... 7970
1Ki 4:22 day was **t.** measures of fine flour, ... 7970
1Ki 5:13 and the levy was **t.** thousand men. 7970
1Ki 6:2 and the height thereof **t.** cubits......... 7970
1Ki 7:2 and the height thereof **t.** cubits, ... 7970
1Ki 7:6 and the breadth thereof **t.** cubits: 7970
1Ki 7:23 and a line of **t.** cubits did compass it ... 7970
1Ki 16:23 the **t.** and first year of Asa king of 7970
1Ki 16:29 the **t.** and eighth year of Asa king 7970
1Ki 20:1 there were **t.** and two kings with 7970
1Ki 20:15 they were two hundred and **t.** two: 7970
1Ki 20:16 **t.** and two kings that helped him. 7970
1Ki 22:31 **t.** and to captains that had rule 7970
1Ki 22:42 Jehoshaphat was **t.** and five years....... 7970
2Ki 8:17 **T.** and two years old was he when...... 7970
2Ki 13:10 **t.** and seventh year of Joash king 7970
2Ki 15:8 **t.** and eighth year of Azariah king......... 7970
2Ki 18:14 of silver and **t.** talents of gold........... 7970
2Ki 22:1 and he reigned **t.** and one years in 7970
1Ch 3:4 he reigned **t.** and three years. 7970
1Ch 7:4 for war, six and **t.** thousand men:....... 7970
1Ch 7:7 and two thousand and **t.** and four. 7970
1Ch 11:15 Now three of the **t.** captain went 7970
1Ch 11:25 he was honourable among the **t.**,........ 7970
1Ch 11:42 of the Reubenites, and **t.** with him,..... 7970
1Ch 12:4 man among the **t.**, and over the **t.**; 7970
1Ch 12:34 and spear **t.** and seven thousand. 7970
1Ch 15:7 and his brethren and hundred and **t.**..... 7970
1Ch 19:7 hired **t.** and **t.**o thousand chariots, ... 7970
1Ch 23:3 the age of **t.** years and upward: 7970
1Ch 23:3 by man, was **t.** and eight thousand. 7970
1Ch 27:6 among the **t.**, and above the **t.** 7970
1Ch 29:27 **t.** and three years reigned he in......... 7970
2Ch 3:15 two pillars of **t.** and five cubits high, ... 7970
2Ch 4:2 a line of **t.** cubits did compass it......... 7970
2Ch 16:12 Asa in the **t.** and ninth year of his 7970
2Ch 20:31 he was **t.** and five years old when he.. 7970
2Ch 21:5 Jehoram was **t.** and two years old 7970

2Ch 21:20 **T.** and two years old was he when..... 7970
2Ch 24:15 an hundred and **t.** years old was he 7970
2Ch 34:1 in Jerusalem one and **t.** years. 7970
2Ch 35:7 to the number of **t.** thousand, and 7970
Ezr 1:9 **t.** chargers of gold, a thousand 7970
Ezr 1:10 **T.** basons of gold, silver basons of...... 7970
Ezr 2:35 thousand and six hundred and **t.**......... 7970
Ezr 2:42 in all an hundred **t.** and nine............. 7970
Ezr 2:65 three hundred **t.** and seven: 7970
Ezr 2:66 were seven hundred **t.** and six;.......... 7970
Ezr 2:67 camels, four hundred **t.** and five;........ 7970
Ne 7:38 three thousand nine hundred and **t.**..... 7970
Ne 7:45 of Shobai, and hundred **t.** and eight..... 7970
Ne 7:67 three hundred **t.** and seven: 7970
Ne 7:68 horses, seven hundred **t.** and six:....... 7970
Ne 7:69 camels, four hundred **t.** and five:........ 7970
Ne 7:70 hundred and **t.** priests' garments. 7970
Es 4:11 come in unto the king these **t.** days.... 7970
Jer 38:10 Take from hence **t.** men with thee, ... 7970
Jer 52:29 eight hundred **t.** and two persons: 7970
Eze 40:17 **t.** chambers were upon the 7970
Eze 41:6 one over another, and **t.** in order; 7970
Eze 46:22 of forty cubits long and **t.** broad: 7970
Da 6:7 of any God or man for **t.** days, ... 8533
Da 6:12 of any God or man within **t.** days, ... 8533
Da 12:12 hundred and five and **t.** days 7970
Zec 11:12 for my price **t.** pieces of silver.......... 7970
Zec 11:13 and I took the **t.** pieces of silver, ... 7970
Mt 13:23 **hundredfold, some sixty, some t.**... *5144*
Mt 26:15 with him for **t.** pieces of silver........... *5144*
Mt 27:3 brought again the **t.** pieces of silver.... *5144*
Mt 27:9 they took the **t.** pieces of silver, the.... *5144*
Mk 4:8 **forth, some t., and some sixty, and***5144*
Lu 3:23 began to be about **t.** years of age,...... *5144*
Joh 5:5 had an infirmity **t.** and eight years. *5144*
Joh 6:19 about five and twenty or **t.** furlongs, ... *5144*
Ga 3:17 four hundred and **t.** years after, ... *5144*

THIRTYFOLD
Mt 13:8 **some sixtyfold, some t.**................. *5144*
Mk 4:20 **forth fruit, some t., some sixty,**.... *5144*

THIRTY-THOUSAND See THIRTY and THOUSAND.

THIS See also THESE.
Ge 2:23 **T.** is now bone of my bones, and....... 2063
Ge 3:13 What is **t.** that thou hast done?.......... 2063
Ge 3:14 Because thou hast done **t.**, thou......... 2063
Ge 4:14 thou hast driven me out **t.** day from ....
Ge 5:1 **T.** is the book of the generations 2088
Ge 5:29 **T.** same shall comfort us 2088
Ge 6:15 **t.** is the fashion which thou shalt........ 2088
Ge 7:1 before me in **t.** generation. 2088
Ge 9:12 **T.** is the token of the covenant........... 2063
Ge 9:17 **T.** is the token of the covenant, ...
Ge 11:6 **t.** they begin to do: and now 2088
Ge 12:7 Unto thy seed will I give **t.** land:........ 2063
Ge 12:12 that they shall say, **T.** is his wife: 2063
Ge 12:18 What is **t.** that thou hast done 2063
Ge 15:2 house is **t.** Eliezer of Damascus?........ 1931
Ge 15:4 saying, **T.** shall not be thine heir; 2088
Ge 15:7 to give thee **t.** land to inherit it.......... 2063
Ge 15:18 Unto thy seed have I given **t.** land, ... 2063
Ge 17:10 **T.** is my covenant, which ye shall....... 2063
Ge 17:21 at **t.** set time in the next year. 2088
Ge 18:25 from thee to do after **t.** manner, ... 2088
Ge 18:32 and I will speak yet but **t.** once: 6471
Ge 19:5 men which came in to thee **t.** night? ....
Ge 19:9 **T.** one fellow came in to sojourn, ...
Ge 19:12 city, bring them out of **t.** place: ....
Ge 19:13 For we will destroy **t.** place, ... 2088
Ge 19:14 said, Up, get you out of **t.** place; 2088
Ge 19:14 for the Lord will destroy **t.** city.................
Ge 19:20 now, **t.** city is near to flee unto, ... 2063
Ge 19:21 accepted thee concerning **t.** thing 2088
Ge 19:21 that I will not overthrow **t.** city, ...
Ge 19:34 make him drink wine **t.** night also;...........
Ge 19:37 father of the Moabites unto **t.** day. ....
Ge 19:38 the children of Ammon unto **t.** day. ....
Ge 20:5 of my hands have I done **t.**. 2063
Ge 20:6 thou didst **t.** in the integrity of thy 2063
Ge 20:10 that thou hast done **t.** thing? 2088
Ge 20:11 the fear of God is not in **t.** place; 2088
Ge 20:13 **T.** is thy kindness which thou.............. 2088
Ge 21:10 Cast out **t.** bondwoman and her 2063
Ge 21:10 the son of **t.** bondwoman shall not 2063
Ge 21:26 I wot not who hath done **t.** thing:....... 2088
Ge 21:30 witness unto me, that I have digged **t.** well.
Ge 22:14 as it is said to **t.** day, ...
Ge 22:16 because thou hast done **t.** thing, ... 2088
Ge 23:19 after **t.**, Abraham buried Sarah.......... 3651
Ge 24:5 willing to follow me unto **t.** land: 2063
Ge 24:7 unto thy seed will I give **t.** land; 2063
Ge 24:8 then thou shalt be clear from **t.** my oath:...
Ge 24:12 send me good speed **t.** day, ...
Ge 24:41 shalt thou be clear from **t.** my oath,..........
Ge 24:42 And I came **t.** day unto the well..............
Ge 24:58 unto her, Wilt thou go with **t.** man?.... 2088
Ge 24:65 What man is **t.** that walketh in........... 1976
Ge 25:31 said, Sell me **t.** day thy birthright. ....
Ge 25:32 what profit shall **t.** birthright do 2088
Ge 25:33 And Jacob said, Swear to me **t.** day; ....
Ge 26:3 Sojourn in **t.** land, and I will be.......... 2063
Ge 26:10 What is **t.** thou hast done unto us? 2063
Ge 26:11 He that toucheth **t.** man or his 2088
Ge 26:33 the city is Beer-sheba unto **t.** day. 2088
Ge 28:15 will bring thee again into **t.** land; 2063
Ge 28:16 Surely the Lord is in **t.** place; and...... 2088
Ge 28:17 and said, How dreadful is **t.** place!...... 2088
Ge 28:17 **t.** is none other but the house of........ 2088
Ge 28:17 God, and **t.** is the gate of heaven. 2088
Ge 28:20 will keep me in **t.** way that I go,........ 2088
Ge 28:22 **t.** stone, which I have set for a 2063
Ge 29:25 What is **t.** thou hast done unto me?.... 2063
Ge 29:27 we will give thee **t.** also for the 2063
Ge 29:33 therefore given me **t.** son also: 2088
Ge 29:34 **t.** time will my husband be joined ....
Ge 30:31 if thou wilt do **t.** thing for me, I......... 2088
Ge 31:1 father's hath he gotten all **t.** glory............
Ge 31:13 arise, get thee out from **t.** land,......... 2063
Ge 31:38 **T.** twenty years have I been with....... 2088
Ge 31:43 what can I do **t.** day unto these my ....
Ge 31:48 **T.** heap is a witness between me 2088
Ge 31:48 witness between me and thee **t.** day.........
Ge 31:51 said to Jacob, Behold **t.** heap, ... 2088
Ge 31:51 behold **t.** pillar, which I have ....
Ge 31:52 **T.** heap be witness, and.................. 2088
Ge 31:52 **t.** pillar be witness, that I will not............
Ge 31:52 will not pass over **t.** heap to thee,...... 2088
Ge 31:52 **t.** heap (2088) and **t.** pillar unto 2063
Ge 32:2 them, he said, **T.** is God's host:......... 2088
Ge 32:10 my staff I passed over **t.** Jordan;........ 2088
Ge 32:19 On **t.** manner shall ye speak unto........ 2088
Ge 32:32 hollow of the thigh, unto **t.** day:......... 2088
Ge 33:8 What meanest thou by all **t.** drove...... 2088
Ge 34:4 saying, Get me **t.** damsel to wife. 2063
Ge 34:14 We cannot do **t.** thing, to give our...... 2088
Ge 34:15 in **t.** will we consent unto you: 2063
Ge 35:17 thou shalt have **t.** son also. 2088
Ge 35:20 pillar of Rachel's grave unto **t.** day...........
Ge 36:24 **t.** was that Anah that found the 1931
Ge 37:6 **t.** dream which I have dreamed:......... 2088
Ge 37:10 **t.** dream that thou hast dreamed?....... 2088
Ge 37:19 Behold, **t.** dreamer cometh. 1976
Ge 37:22 cast him into **t.** pit that is in the......... 2088
Ge 37:32 and said, **T.** have we found: 2063
Ge 38:21 There was no harlot in **t.** place. 2088
Ge 38:22 that there was no harlot in **t.** place..... 2088
Ge 38:23 behold, I sent **t.** kid, and thou 2088
Ge 38:28 thread, saying, **T.** came out first. 2088
Ge 38:29 **t.** breach be upon thee:.......................
Ge 39:9 is none greater in **t.** house than I; 2088
Ge 39:9 can I do **t.** great wickedness, and....... 2063
Ge 39:11 And it came to pass about **t.** time, ... 2088
Ge 39:19 **t.** manner did thy servant to me; 428
Ge 40:12 **T.** is the interpretation of it:.............. 2088
Ge 40:14 and bring me out of **t.** house: 2088
Ge 40:18 **T.** is the interpretation thereof:........... 2088
Ge 41:9 I do remember my faults **t.** day: ....
Ge 41:24 and I told **t.** unto the magicians;..............
Ge 41:34 Let Pharaoh do **t.**, and let him.................
Ge 41:28 **T.** is the thing which I have 1931
Ge 41:38 Can we find such a one as **t.** is,.......... 2088
Ge 41:39 as God hath shewed thee all **t.**, ... 2063
Ge 42:13 youngest is **t.** day with our father,............
Ge 42:18 **T.** do, and live; for I fear God: 2063
Ge 42:21 is **t.** distress come upon us. 2063
Ge 42:28 What is **t.** that God hath done 2063
Ge 42:32 youngest is **t.** day with our father............
Ge 43:10 we had returned **t.** second time. 2088
Ge 43:11 If it must be so now, do **t.**; 2063
Ge 43:29 Is **t.** your younger brother, of 2088
Ge 44:5 Is not **t.** it in which my lord 2088
Ge 44:7 should do according to **t.** thing;.......... 2088
Ge 44:15 What deed is **t.** that ye have done? 2088
Ge 44:29 And if ye take **t.** also from me,.......... 2088
Ge 45:17 Say unto thy brethren, **T.** do ye; 2063
Ge 45:19 Now thou art commanded, **t.** do ye; ... 2063
Ge 45:23 his father he sent after **t.** manner; 2063
Ge 47:23 I have bought you **t.** day and your...........
Ge 47:26 the land of Egypt unto **t.** day,............ 2088
Ge 48:4 will give **t.** land to thy seed after 2063
Ge 48:9 God hath given me in **t.** place........... 2088
Ge 48:15 fed me all my life long unto **t.** day,..... 2088
Ge 48:18 for **t.** is the firstborn; put thy........... 2088
Ge 49:28 **t.** is it that their father spake 2063
Ge 50:11 **T.** is a grievous mourning to the 2088
Ge 50:20 as it is **t.** day, to save much people 2088
Ge 50:24 bring you out of **t.** land unto the 2063
Ex 1:18 Why have ye done **t.** thing, and 2088
Ex 2:6 **T.** is one of the Hebrews' children...... 2088
Ex 2:9 Take **t.** child away, and nurse it......... 2088
Ex 2:12 he looked **t.** way and that way,.......... 3541
Ex 2:14 and said, Surely **t.** thing is known............
Ex 2:15 when Pharaoh heard **t.** thing, ... 2088
Ex 3:3 turn aside, and see **t.** great sight, ... 2088
Ex 3:12 and **t.** shall be a token unto thee,....... 2088
Ex 3:15 unto you: **t.** is my name for ever, ... 2088
Ex 3:15 and **t.** is my memorial unto all 2088
Ex 3:21 I will give **t.** people favour in the 2088
Ex 4:17 shalt take **t.** rod in thine hand,........... 2088
Ex 5:22 thou so evil entreated **t.** people? 2088
Ex 5:23 he hath done evil to **t.** people;............ 2088
Ex 7:17 In **t.** thou shalt know that I am.......... 2063
Ex 7:23 did he set his heart to **t.** also. 2063
Ex 8:19 Pharaoh, **T.** is the finger of God: 1931
Ex 8:23 to morrow shall **t.** sign be................ 2088
Ex 8:32 hardened his heart at **t.** time also, ... 2063
Ex 9:5 the Lord shall do **t.** thing in the 2088
Ex 9:14 For I will at **t.** time send all my......... 2063
Ex 9:16 for **t.** cause have I raised thee up,...... 2063
Ex 9:18 to morrow about **t.** time I will cause ....
Ex 9:27 unto them, I have sinned **t.** time: ....
Ex 10:6 were upon the earth unto **t.** day. 2088
Ex 10:7 How long shall **t.** man be a snare 2088
Ex 10:17 I pray thee, my sin only **t.** once,..............
Ex 10:17 take away from me **t.** death only........ 2088
Ex 12:2 **T.** month shall be unto you the 2088
Ex 12:3 In the tenth day of **t.** month they 2088
Ex 12:12 through the land of Egypt **t.** night, ... 2088
Ex 12:14 **t.** day shall be unto you for a 2088
Ex 12:17 in **t.** selfsame day have I brought 2088
Ex 12:17 therefore shall ye observe **t.** day..............
Ex 12:24 observe **t.** thing for an ordinance........ 2088
Ex 12:25 that ye shall keep **t.** service 2063
Ex 12:26 you, What mean ye by **t.** service? 2063
Ex 12:42 **t.** is that night of the Lord to be 2088
Ex 12:43 Aaron, **T.** is the ordinance of the 2063
Ex 13:3 Remember **t.** day, in which ye........... 2088
Ex 13:3 brought you out from **t.** place:............ 2088
Ex 13:4 **T.** day came ye out in the month ....
Ex 13:5 shalt keep **t.** service in **t.** month. 2088
Ex 13:8 **T.** is done because of that which..............
Ex 13:10 keep **t.** ordinance in his season.......... 2063
Ex 13:14 time to come, saying, What is **t.**?........ 2063
Ex 14:5 Why have we done **t.**, that we have ... 2063
Ex 14:12 Is not **t.** the word that we did tell...... 2088
Ex 15:1 the children of Israel **t.** song unto........ 2063
Ex 16:3 us forth into **t.** wilderness,................ 2088
Ex 16:3 to kill **t.** whole assembly with 2088
Ex 16:8 **T.** shall be, when the Lord shall give ....
Ex 16:15 **T.** is the bread which the Lord 1931
Ex 16:16 **T.** is the thing which the Lord............ 2088
Ex 16:23 **T.** is that which the Lord hath........... 1931
Ex 16:32 **T.** is the thing which the Lord............ 2088
Ex 17:3 Wherefore is **t.** that thou hast 2088
Ex 17:4 What shall I do unto **t.** people? 2088
Ex 17:14 Write **t.** for a memorial in a book, ... 2063
Ex 18:14 What is **t.** thing that thou doest 2088
Ex 18:18 and **t.** people that is with thee:.......... 2088
Ex 18:18 for **t.** thing is too heavy for thee; ....
Ex 18:23 If thou shalt do **t.** thing, and God........ 2088
Ex 18:23 all **t.** people shall also go to their 2088
Ex 21:31 according to **t.** judgment shall it be..... 2088
Ex 25:3 **t.** is the offering which ye shall.......... 2063
Ex 26:13 on **t.** side and on that side,............... 2088
Ex 28:17 carbuncle: **t.** shall be the first row. ....
Ex 29:1 **t.** is the thing that thou shalt do......... 2088
Ex 29:38 **t.** is that which thou shalt offer.......... 2088
Ex 29:42 **T.** shall be a continual burnt ....
Ex 30:13 **T.** they shall give, every one that....... 2088

Ex 30:31 **T.** shall be an holy anointing oil......... 2088
Ex 32:1 for as for **t.** Moses, the man that....... 2088
Ex 32:9 unto Moses, I have seen **t.** people, ... 2088
Ex 32:12 repent of **t.** evil against thy people. ....
Ex 32:13 all **t.** land that I have spoken of 2063
Ex 32:21 What did **t.** people unto thee, that...... 2088
Ex 32:23 for as for **t.** Moses, the man that....... 2088
Ex 32:24 the fire, and there came out **t.** calf. ....
Ex 32:29 bestow upon you a blessing **t.** day. ....
Ex 32:31 **t.** people have sinned a great sin........ 2088
Ex 33:12 sayest unto me, Bring up **t.** people:.... 2088
Ex 33:13 consider that **t.** nation is thy people. ....
Ex 33:17 I will do **t.** thing also that thou.......... 2088
Ex 34:11 that which I command thee **t.** day:...........
Ex 35:4 **T.** is the thing which the Lord.......... 2088
Ex 37:8 One cherub on the end of **t.** side, ... 2088
Ex 38:15 on **t.** hand and that hand, were.......... 2088
Ex 38:21 **T.** is the sum of the tabernacle, ... 428
Ex 39:10 and a carbuncle: **t.** was the first row..........
Le 4:20 a sin offering, so shall he do with **t.**:........
Le 6:9 **T.** is the law of the burnt offering: 2063
Le 6:14 **t.** is the law of the meat offering:....... 2063
Le 6:20 **T.** is the offering of Aaron and of....... 2088
Le 6:25 **T.** is the law of the sin offering:......... 2063
Le 7:1 **t.** is the law of the trespass 2063
Le 7:11 **t.** is the law of the sacrifice of peace... 2063
Le 7:35 **T.** is the portion of the anointing........ 2063
Le 7:37 **T.** is the law of the burnt offering, ... 2063
Le 8:5 **T.** is the thing which the Lord........... 2088
Le 8:34 As he hath done **t.** day, so the Lord... 2088
Le 9:6 **T.** is the thing which the Lord.......... 2088
Le 10:3 **T.** is it that the Lord spake,.............. 1031
Le 10:19 **t.** day have they offered their sin ....
Le 11:46 **T.** is the law of the beasts, and of...... 2063
Le 12:7 **T.** is the law for her that hath born 2063
Le 13:59 **T.** is the law of the plague of 2063
Le 14:2 **T.** shall be the law of the leper in 2063
Le 14:32 **T.** is the law of him in whom is the 2063
Le 14:54 **T.** is the law for all manner of........... 2063
Le 14:57 it is clean: **t.** is the law of leprosy. 2063
Le 15:3 **t.** shall be his uncleanness in his 2063
Le 15:32 **T.** is the law of him that hath an........ 2063
Le 16:29 **t.** shall be a statute for ever unto you: .....
Le 16:34 **t.** shall be an everlasting statute......... 2063
Le 17:2 **T.** is the thing which the Lord.......... 2063
Le 17:7 **T.** shall be a statute for ever unto...... 2063
Le 23:27 the tenth day of **t.** seventh month...... 2088
Le 23:34 fifteenth day of **t.** seventh month......... 2088
Le 24:10 **t.** son of the Israelitish woman and a.........
Le 25:13 In the year of **t.** jubile ye shall.......... 2063
Le 26:16 I also will do **t.** unto you; I will......... 2063
Le 26:18 if ye will not yet for all **t.** hearken 428
Le 26:27 if ye will not for all **t.** hearken 2063
Nu 4:4 **T.** shall be the service of the sons...... 2063
Nu 4:24, 28 **T.** is the service of the families 2063
Nu 4:31 And **t.** is the charge of their burden,... 2063
Nu 4:33 **T.** is the service of the families of....... 2063
Nu 5:19 free from **t.** bitter water that causeth........
Nu 5:22 **t.** water that causeth the curse shall ....
Nu 5:29 **T.** is the law of jealousies, when........ 2063
Nu 5:30 shall execute upon her all **t.** law......... 2063
Nu 5:31 **t.** woman shall bear her iniquity. 1931
Nu 6:13 And **t.** is the law of the Nazarite, ... 2063
Nu 6:20 **t.** is holy for the priest, with the........ 1931
Nu 6:21 **T.** is the law of the Nazarite who....... 2063
Nu 6:23 On **t.** wise ye shall bless the 3541
Nu 7:17 **t.** was the offering of Nahshon the........ 2088
Nu 7:23 **t.** was the offering of Nathaneel the.... 2088
Nu 7:29 **t.** was the offering of Eliab the son..... 2088
Nu 7:35 **t.** was the offering of Elizur the son.... 2088
Nu 7:41 **t.** was the offering of Shelumiel the 2088
Nu 7:47 **t.** was the offering of Eliasaph the....... 2088
Nu 7:53 **t.** was the offering of Elishama the 2088
Nu 7:59 **t.** was the offering of Gamaliel the...... 2088
Nu 7:65 **t.** was the offering of Abidan the........ 2088
Nu 7:71 **t.** was the offering of Ahiezer the....... 2088
Nu 7:77 **t.** was the offering of Pagiel the son ... 2088
Nu 7:83 **t.** was the offering of Ahira the son 2088
Nu 7:84, 88 **T.** was the dedication of the......... 2063
Nu 8:4 **t.** work of the candlestick was of........ 2088
Nu 8:24 **T.** is it that belongeth unto the 2063
Nu 9:3 In the fourteenth day of **t.** month,....... 2088
Nu 11:6 is nothing at all, beside **t.** manna, ... 2088
Nu 11:11 burden of all **t.** people upon me? 2088
Nu 11:12 Have I conceived all **t.** people? 2088
Nu 11:13 have flesh to give unto all **t.** people?... 2088
Nu 11:14 not able to bear all **t.** people alone,..... 2088
Nu 11:31 it were a day's journey on **t.** side,...... 3541
Nu 13:17 Get you up **t.** way southward, and...... 2088
Nu 13:27 and honey; and **t.** is the fruit of it. 2088
Nu 14:2 God we had died in **t.** wilderness!....... 2088
Nu 14:3 the Lord brought us unto **t.** land, ... 2063
Nu 14:8 then he will bring us into **t.** land, ... 2063
Nu 14:11 long will **t.** people provoke me? 2088
Nu 14:13 (for thou broughtest up **t.** people in 2088
Nu 14:14 tell it to the inhabitants of **t.** land: 2063
Nu 14:14 thou Lord art among **t.** people,........... 2088
Nu 14:15 shalt kill all **t.** people as one man, ... 2088
Nu 14:16 was not able to bring **t.** people into 2088
Nu 14:19 Pardon,...the iniquity of **t.** people 2088
Nu 14:19 and as thou hast forgiven **t.** people, ... 2088
Nu 14:27 I bear with **t.** evil congregation, ... 2063
Nu 14:29 carcases...fall in **t.** wilderness; 2088
Nu 14:32 they shall fall in **t.** wilderness. 2088
Nu 14:35 do it unto all **t.** evil congregation, ... 2063
Nu 14:35 in **t.** wilderness they shall be............... 2088
Nu 15:13 shall do these things after **t.** manner, ...
Nu 16:6 **T.** do; Take you censers, Korah, ... 2063
Nu 16:21 from among **t.** congregation,............... 2063
Nu 16:45 you up from among **t.** congregation,.... 2063
Nu 18:9 **T.** shall be thine of the most holy....... 2088
Nu 18:11 **t.** is thine; the heave offering of......... 2088
Nu 18:27 And **t.** your heave offering shall be...........
Nu 19:2 **T.** is the ordinance of the law............ 2063
Nu 19:14 **T.** is the law, when a man dieth in 2063
Nu 20:4 of the Lord into **t.** wilderness, ... 2088
Nu 20:5 to bring us in unto **t.** evil place?.......... 2088
Nu 20:10 we fetch you water out of **t.** rock? 2088
Nu 20:12 ye shall not bring **t.** congregation 2088
Nu 20:13 **T.** is the water of Meribah;................ 1992
Nu 21:2 deliver **t.** people into my hand, ... 2088
Nu 21:5 and our soul loatheth **t.** light bread. ....
Nu 21:17 Then Israel sang **t.** song, Spring 2088
Nu 22:1 plains of Moab on **t.** side Jordan...............
Nu 22:4 Now shall **t.** company lick up all that.........
Nu 22:6 I pray thee, curse me **t.** people; 2088
Nu 22:8 Lodge here **t.** night, and I will bring..........
Nu 22:17 I pray thee, curse me **t.** people. 2088
Nu 22:19 tarry ye also here **t.** night, that I may.......
Nu 22:24 a wall being on **t.** side, and a wall 2088
Nu 22:30 ever since I was thine unto **t.** day?..... 2088
Nu 23:23 according to **t.** time it shall be said of........
Nu 24:14 **t.** people shall do to thy people.......... 2088
Nu 24:23 Alas, who shall live when God doeth **t.**!.....
Nu 26:9 **T.** is that Dathan, and Abiram, ... 1931
Nu 27:12 Get thee up into **t.** mount Abarim, ... 2088
Nu 28:3 **T.** is the offering made by fire........... 2088
Nu 28:10 **T.** is the burnt offering of every...............
Nu 28:14 **t.** is the burnt offering of every 2063
Nu 28:17 the fifteenth day of **t.** month is the..... 2088
Nu 28:24 After **t.** manner ye shall offer daily,...... 428
Nu 29:7 day of **t.** seventh month an holy.......... 2088
Nu 30:1 **T.** is the thing which the Lord hath 2088
Nu 31:21 **T.** is the ordinance of the law............ 2063
Nu 32:5 **t.** land be given unto thy servants 2063
Nu 32:15 and ye shall destroy all **t.** people. 2088
Nu 32:19 is fallen to us on **t.** side Jordan ....
Nu 32:20 If ye will do **t.** thing, if ye will go....... 2088
Nu 32:22 **t.** land shall be your possession.......... 2063
Nu 32:32 inheritance on **t.** side Jordan may.............
Nu 34:2 (**t.** is the land that shall fall unto......... 2063
Nu 34:6 **t.** shall be your west border............... 2088
Nu 34:7 And **t.** shall be your north border:...... 2088
Nu 34:9 **t.** shall be your north border. 2088
Nu 34:12 **t.** shall be your land with the.............. 2063
Nu 34:13 **T.** is the land...ye shall inherit by....... 2063
Nu 34:15 inheritance on **t.** side Jordan near ....
Nu 35:5 **t.** shall be to them the suburbs of 2088
Nu 35:14 give three cities on **t.** side Jordan,............
Nu 36:6 **T.** is the thing which the Lord........... 2088
De 1:1 unto all Israel on **t.** side Jordan...............
De 1:5 On **t.** side Jordan, in the land of...............
De 1:5 began Moses to declare **t.** law, ... 2063
De 1:6 dwelt long enough in **t.** mount: 2088
De 1:10 ye are **t.** day as the stars of heaven..........
De 1:31 until ye came into **t.** place................... 2088
De 1:32 Yet in **t.** thing ye did not believe......... 2088
De 1:35 of these men of **t.** evil generation....... 2088
De 2:3 have compassed **t.** mountain long 2088
De 2:7 walking through **t.**...wilderness: 2088
De 2:18 through Ar, the coast of Moab, **t.** day:......
De 2:22 in their stead even unto **t.** day:.......... 2088
De 2:25 **T.** day will I begin to put the dread 2088
De 2:30 into thy hand, as appeareth **t.** day. 2088
De 3:8 land that was on **t.** side Jordan,................
De 3:12 **t.** land, which we possessed at 2063
De 3:14 Bashan-havoth-jair, unto **t.** day........... 2088
De 3:18 your God hath given you **t.** land......... 2063
De 3:26 no more unto me of **t.** matter.............. 2088
De 3:27 thou shalt not go over **t.** Jordan. 2088
De 3:28 he shall go over before **t.** people,....... 2088
De 4:4 God are alive every one of you **t.** day. ......
De 4:6 for **t.** is your wisdom and your 1931
De 4:6 Surely **t.** great nation is a wise 2088
De 4:8 so righteous as all **t.** law, which......... 2063
De 4:8 law, which I set before you **t.** day?...........
De 4:20 of inheritance, as ye are **t.** day. 2088
De 4:22 But I must die in **t.** land, I must 2088
De 4:26 earth to witness against you **t.** day, ...
De 4:32 any such thing as **t.** great thing.......... 2088
De 4:38 for an inheritance, as it is **t.** day. 2088
De 4:39 Know therefore **t.** day, and consider it ......
De 4:40 which I command thee **t.** day, that.............
De 4:41 three cities on **t.** side Jordan...................
De 4:44 **t.** is the law which Moses set............ 2063
De 4:46 On **t.** side Jordan, in the valley ....
De 4:47 which were on **t.** side Jordan...................
De 4:49 plain on **t.** side Jordan eastward, ...
De 5:1 which I speak in your ears **t.** day, ...
De 5:3 Lord made not **t.** covenant with......... 2063
De 5:3 who are all of us here alive **t.** day. ....
De 5:24 seen **t.** day that God doth talk........... 2088
De 5:25 for **t.** great fire will consume us: 2063
De 5:28 the voice of the words of **t.** people, ... 2088
De 6:6 words, which I command thee **t.** day,........
De 6:24 preserve us alive, as it is at **t.** day. 2088
De 7:11 which I command thee **t.** day,.................
De 8:1 which I command thee **t.** day shall ye.........
De 8:11 which I command thee **t.** day:.................
De 8:17 hand hath gotten me **t.** wealth. 2088
De 8:18 unto thy fathers, as it is **t.** day. 2088
De 8:19 I testify against you **t.** day that ye...........
De 9:1 Thou art to pass over Jordan **t.** day, ...
De 9:3 Understand therefore **t.** day, that the........
De 9:4 brought me in to possess **t.** land: 2088
De 9:6 God giveth thee not **t.** good land........ 2063
De 9:7 until ye came unto **t.** place, ye 2088
De 9:13 me, saying, I have seen **t.** people,...... 2088
De 9:27 unto the stubbornness of **t.** people,...... 2088
De 10:8 to bless in his name, unto **t.** day. 2088
De 10:13 I command thee **t.** day for thy good? ....
De 10:15 above all people, as it is **t.** day. 2088
De 11:2 And know ye **t.** day: for I speak not ....
De 11:4 hath destroyed them unto **t.** day; 2088
De 11:5 until ye came into **t.** place;................ 2088
De 11:8, 13 which I command you **t.** day, ...
De 11:26 I set before you **t.** day a blessing and ....
De 11:27 God, which I command you **t.** day: ....
De 11:28 the way which I command you **t.** day, ...
De 11:32 which I set before you **t.** day. ....
De 12:8 all the things that we do here **t.** day, ...
De 13:11 such wickedness as **t.** is among 2088
De 13:18 which I command thee **t.** day,..................
De 15:2 **t.** is the manner of the release: 2088
De 15:5 which I command thee **t.** day..................
De 15:10 **t.** thing the Lord thy God shall 2088
De 15:15 I command thee **t.** thing to day........... 2088
De 17:18 him a copy of **t.** law in a book 2063
De 17:19 to keep all the words of **t.** law and..... 2063
De 18:3 **t.** shall be the priest's due from.......... 2088
De 18:16 neither let me see **t.** great fire 2063
De 19:4 **t.** is the case of the slayer, which 2088
De 19:9 I command thee **t.** day, to love the...........
De 20:3 ye aproach **t.** day unto battle against.........
De 21:7 Our hands have not shed **t.** blood,....... 2088
De 21:20 **T.** our son is stubborn and................ 2088
De 22:14 I took **t.** woman, and when I came..... 2063
De 22:16 my daughter unto **t.** man to wife, ... 2088
De 22:20 But if **t.** thing be true, and the 2088
De 22:26 slayeth him, even so is **t.** matter:....... 2088
De 24:18, 22 I command thee to do **t.** thing. 2088
De 26:3 I profess **t.** day unto the Lord thy God,.....
De 26:9 he hath brought us into **t.** place, ... 2088
De 26:9 given us **t.** land, even a land that 2063
De 26:16 **T.** day the Lord thy God hath........... 2088
De 26:17 the Lord **t.** day to be thy God, ...
De 26:18 Lord hath avouched thee **t.** day to be........
De 27:1 which I command you **t.** day....................
De 27:3 upon them all the words of **t.** law,...... 2063
De 27:4 which I command you **t.** day, in ....
De 27:8 the stones all the words of **t.** law....... 2063

De 27:9 t. day thou art become the people...... 2088
De 27:10 which I command thee t. day..................
De 27:26 not all the words of t. law to do......... 2063
De 28:1, 13 which I command thee t. day, ...
De 28:14 words which I command thee t. day,.........
De 28:15 which I command thee t. day;..................
De 28:58 to do all the words of t. law that........ 2063
De 28:58 that are written in t. book, that......... 2088
De 28:58 fear t. glorious and fearful name,......... 2088
De 28:61 not written in the book of t. law, ... 2063
De 29:4 see, and ears to hear, unto t. day. 2088
De 29:7 when ye came unto t. place, Sihon..... 2088
De 29:9 therefore the words of t. covenant, ... 2063
De 29:10 stand t. day all of you before the Lord......
De 29:12 Lord thy God maketh with thee t. day: .....
De 29:14 do I make t. covenant and t. oath; 2063
De 29:15 him that standeth here with us t. day........
De 29:15 him that is not here with us t. day: ....
De 29:18 heart turneth...t. day from the Lord ....
De 29:19 he heareth the words of t. curse,....... 2063
De 29:29 curses that are written in t. book....... 2088
De 29:21 are written in t. book of the law: 2088
De 29:24 the Lord done thus unto t. land?........ 2063
De 29:24 the heat of t. great anger?................ 2088
De 29:27 Lord was kindled against t. land,........ 1931
De 29:27 curses that are written in t. book:...... 2088
De 29:28 into another land, as it is t. day. 2088
De 29:29 may do all the words of t. law. 2063
De 30:2 to all that I command thee t. day, ...
De 30:8 which I command thee t. day...................
De 30:10 are written in t. book of the law, ... 2088
De 30:11 For t. commandment which I............ 2063
De 30:11 which I command thee t. day, it is............
De 30:15 set before thee t. day life and good, ...
De 30:16 that I command thee t. day to love..........
De 30:18 I denounce unto you t. day, that ye.........
De 30:19 earth to record t. day against you,...........
De 31:2 hundred and twenty years old t. day;.........
De 31:2 Thou shalt not go over t. Jordan. 2088
De 31:7 thou must go with t. people unto 2088
De 31:9 Moses wrote t. law, and delivered...... 2063
De 31:11 read t. law before all Israel in their..... 2063
De 31:12 to do all the words of t. law:.......... 2063
De 31:16 t. people will rise up, and go a 2088
De 31:19 therefore write ye t. song for you, ... 2063
De 31:19 t. song may be a witness for me........ 2063
De 31:21 t. song shall testify against them 2063
De 31:22 Moses therefore wrote t. song the..... 2063
De 31:24 writing the words of t. law in a........ 2063
De 31:26 Take t. book of the law, and put........ 2088
De 31:27 while I am yet alive with you t. day,.........
De 31:30 of Israel the words of t. song,.......... 2063
De 32:27 and the Lord hath not done all t......... 2063
De 32:29 were wise, that they understood t., ... 2063
De 32:34 Is not t. laid up in store with me, ... 1931
De 32:44 words of t. song in the ears of the..... 2063
De 32:46 which I testify among you t. day, ... 2063
De 32:46 to do, all the words of t. law............ 2063
De 32:47 through t. thing ye shall prolong......... 2088
De 32:49 thee up into t. mountain Abarim,........ 2088
De 33:1 t. is the blessing, wherewith Moses.... 2063
De 33:7 t. is the blessing of Judah: and he 2063
De 34:4 T. is the land which I sware unto....... 2063
De 34:6 of his sepulchre unto t. day............. 2088
Jos 1:2 therefore arise, go over t. Jordan, ...
Jos 1:2 thou, and all t. people, unto the......... 2088
Jos 1:2 t. Lebanon even unto the great.......... 2088
Jos 1:6 unto t. people shalt thou divide for..... 2088
Jos 1:8 T. book of the law shall not depart..... 2088
Jos 1:11 days ye shall pass over t. Jordan,....... 2088
Jos 1:13 rest, and hath given you t. land. 2063
Jos 1:14 Moses gave you on t. side Jordan;...........
Jos 1:15 servant gave you on t. side Jordan.............
Jos 2:14 if ye utter not t. our business............ 2088
Jos 2:17 will be blameless of t. thine oath........ 2088
Jos 2:18 shalt bind t. line of scarlet thread....... 2088
Jos 2:20 And if thou utter t. our business, ... 2088
Jos 3:4 ye have not passed t. way heretofore........
Jos 3:7 T. day will I begin to magnify............ 2088
Jos 4:3 place, where ye shall lodge t. night...........
Jos 4:6 That t. may be a sign among you,...... 2063
Jos 4:9 and they are there unto t. day........... 2063
Jos 4:22 Israel came over t. Jordan on dry....... 2088
Jos 5:4 t. is the cause why Joshua did......... 2088
Jos 5:9 T. day have I rolled away the..................
Jos 5:9 place is called Gilgal unto t. day. 2088
Jos 6:25 dwelleth in Israel even unto t. day;..... 2088
Jos 6:26 that riseth up and buildeth t. city 2063
Jos 7:7 all brought t. people over Jordan, ... 2088
Jos 7:25 the Lord shall trouble thee t. day. 2088
Jos 7:26 a great heap of stones unto t. day...... 2088
Jos 7:26 The valley of Achor, unto t. day. 2088
Jos 8:20 had no power to flee t. way or that.... 2007
Jos 8:22 some on t. side, and some on that..... 2088
Jos 8:28 ever, even a desolation unto t. day..... 2088
Jos 8:29 stones, that remaineth unto t. day....... 2088
Jos 8:33 stood on t. side the ark and on that.... 2088
Jos 9:1 which were on t. side Jordan,..................
Jos 9:12 T. our bread we took hot for our....... 2088
Jos 9:20 T. we will do them; we will 2063
Jos 9:24 of you, and have done t. thing........... 2088
Jos 9:27 altar of the Lord, even unto t. day, ... 2088
Jos 10:13 Is not t. written in the book of.......... 1931
Jos 10:27 which remain until t. very day. 2088
Jos 11:6 for to morrow about t. time will I....... 2063
Jos 12:7 Israel smote on t. side Jordan on.............
Jos 13:2 T. is the land that yet remaineth:....... 2063
Jos 13:7 divide t. land for an inheritance.......... 2063
Jos 13:13 among the Israelites until t. day......... 2088
Jos 13:23 T. was the inheritance of the............ 2063
Jos 13:28 T. is the inheritance of the children ... 2063
Jos 13:29 t. was the possession of the half tribe ......
Jos 14:10 Lord spake t. word unto Moses,........ 2088
Jos 14:10 I am t. day fourscore and five years ....
Jos 14:11 I am as strong t. day as I was in the........
Jos 14:12 therefore give me t. mountain, ... 2088
Jos 14:14 Jephunneh the Kenezite...t. day,........ 2088
Jos 15:1 T. then was the lot of the tribe of the......
Jos 15:4 sea: t. shall be your south coast. 2088
Jos 15:12 T. is the coast of the children of........ 2088
Jos 15:20 T. is the inheritance of the tribe 2063
Jos 15:63 Judah at Jerusalem unto t. day.......... 2088
Jos 16:8 T. is the inheritance of the tribe 2063
Jos 16:10 the Ehraimites unto t. day, ... 2088
Jos 18:14 Judah: t. was the west quarter. 2063
Jos 18:19 of Jordan: t. was the south coast........ 2088
Jos 18:20 T. was the inheritance of the............ 2063
Jos 18:28 T. is the inheritance of the children 2063
Jos 19:8 T. is the inheritance of the tribe of..... 2063
Jos 19:16 T. is the inheritance of the children 2063
Jos 19:23, 31,39,48 T. is the inheritance of 2063
Jos 22:3 these many days unto t. day, ... 2088
Jos 22:7 their brethren on t. side Jordan...............
Jos 22:16 What trespass is t. that ye have 2088
Jos 22:16 turn away t. day from follwing the...........
Jos 22:16 ye might rebel t. day against the.............
Jos 22:17 we are not cleansed until t. day, ... 2088
Jos 22:18 turn away t. day from following the ....
Jos 22:22 the Lord, (save us not t. day,) 2088
Jos 22:24 rather done it for fear of t. thing,....... 2063
Jos 22:29 turn t. day from following the Lord, to......
Jos 22:31 T. day we perceive that the Lord is..........
Jos 22:31 not committed t. trespass against....... 2088
Jos 23:8 God, as ye have done unto t. day. 2088
Jos 23:9 to stand before you unto t. day.......... 2088
Jos 23:13 perish from off t. good land which 2063
Jos 23:14 t. day I am going the way of all the.........
Jos 23:15 destroyed you from off t. good land.... 2063
Jos 24:15 choose you t. day whom ye will serve;......
Jos 24:27 t. stone shall be a witness unto 2063
Jg 1:21 Benjamin in Jerusalem unto t. day. 2088
Jg 1:26 is the name thereof unto t. day.......... 2088
Jg 2:2 with the inhabitants of t. land; 2063
Jg 2:2 my voice: why have ye done t.? 2063
Jg 2:20 that t. people hath transgressed......... 2088
Jg 4:14 t. is the day in which the Lord hath.... 2088
Jg 6:13 us, why then is all t. befallen us?....... 2063
Jg 6:14 Go in t. thy might, and thou shalt 2088
Jg 6:20 cakes, and lay them upon t. rock, ... 1975
Jg 6:24 t. day it is yet in Ophrah of the 2088
Jg 6:26 thy God upon the to of t. rock, ... 2088
Jg 6:29 to another, Who hath done t. thing?.... 2088
Jg 6:29 the son of Joash hath done t. thing..... 2088
Jg 6:39 me, and I will speak but t. once:.............
Jg 6:39 thee, but t. once with the fleece; ....
Jg 7:4 T. shall go with thee, the same 2088
Jg 7:4 T. shall not go with thee, the same.... 2088
Jg 7:14 T. is nothing else save the sword....... 2063
Jg 8:9 in peace, I will break down t. tower. ....
Jg 9:18 up against my father's house t. day,..........
Jg 9:19 and with his house t. day,................... 2088
Jg 9:29 to God t. people were under my........ 2088
Jg 9:38 t. the people...thou hast despised? 2088
Jg 10:4 are called Havoth-jair unto t. day,........ 2088
Jg 10:15 us only, we pray thee, t. day. 2088
Jg 11:27 t. day between the children of Israel.........
Jg 11:37 Let t. thing be done for me: 2088
Jg 12:3 then are ye come up unto me t. day, .. 2088
Jg 13:23 as at t. time have told us such things........
Jg 15:6 Philistines said, Who hath done t.? 2063
Jg 15:7 Though ye have done t., yet will........ 2063
Jg 15:11 what is t. that thou hast done unto...... 2063
Jg 15:18 hast given t. great deliverance into..... 2063
Jg 15:29 which is in Lehi unto t. day.............. 2063
Jg 16:18 Come up t. once, for he hath ....
Jg 16:28 I pray thee, only t. once, O God,....... 2088
Jg 18:3 and what makest thou in t. place? 6311
Jg 18:12 place Mahaneh-dan unto t. day:.......... 2088
Jg 18:24 and what is t. that ye say unto me, ... 2088
Jg 19:11 let us turn in into t. city of the.......... 2063
Jg 19:23 seeing that t. man is come into.......... 2088
Jg 19:23 into mine house, do not t. folly.......... 2063
Jg 19:24 unto t. man do not so vile a thing. 2088
Jg 19:30 of the land of Egypt unto t. day:........ 2088
Jg 20:3 Tell us, how was t. wickedness?........ 2063
Jg 20:9 t. shall be the thing that we will do 2063
Jg 20:12 wickedness is t. that is done among.... 2063
Jg 20:16 Among all t. people there were.......... 2088
Jg 21:3 why is t. come to pass in Israel, ... 2063
Jg 21:6 one tribe cut off from Israel t. day............
Jg 21:11 And t. is the thing that ye shall do, ... 2063
Jg 21:22 ye did not give unto them at t. time, ...
Ru 1:19 them, and they said, Is t. Naomi? 2063
Ru 2:5 the reapers, Whose damsel is t.? 2063
Ru 3:13 Tarry t. night, and it shall be in the..........
Ru 3:18 he have finished the thing t. day. ....
Ru 4:7 t. was the manner in former time....... 2063
Ru 4:7 and t. was the testimony in Israel. 2063
Ru 4:9 ye are witnesses t. day, that I have..........
Ru 4:10 of his place: ye are witnesses t. day. ....
Ru 4:12 shall give thee of t. young woman. 2063
Ru 4:14 hath not left thee t. day without a ....
1Sa 1:3 t. man went up out of his city 1931
1Sa 1:27 For t. child I prayed; and the............ 2088
1Sa 2:20 give thee seed of t. woman for the..... 2063
1Sa 2:23 your evil dealings by all t. people......... 428
1Sa 2:34 And t. shall be a sign unto thee, ... 2088
1Sa 4:6 meaneth the noise of t. great shout 2063
1Sa 4:14 meaneth the noise of t. tumult? 2088
1Sa 5:5 of Dagon in Ashdod unto t. day. 2088
1Sa 6:9 then he hath done us t. great evil: 2063
1Sa 6:18 stone remaineth unto t. day in the...... 2088
1Sa 6:20 to stand before t. holy Lord God? 2088
1Sa 8:8 up out of Egypt even unto t. day, ... 2088
1Sa 8:11 T. will be the manner of the king 2088
1Sa 9:6 there is in t. city a man of God,.......... 2063
1Sa 9:13 up; for about t. time ye shall find him. ......
1Sa 9:16 To morrow about t. time I will send ....
1Sa 9:17 t. same shall reign over my people. 2088
1Sa 9:24 for unto t. time hath it been kept for ....
1Sa 10:11 What is t. that is come unto the 2088
1Sa 10:19 And ye have t. day rejected your God,......
1Sa 10:27 said, How shall t. man save us?......... 2088
1Sa 11:2 On t. condition will I make a............ 2063
1Sa 11:13 not a man be put to death t. day:........ 2088
1Sa 12:2 you from my childhood unto t. day. 2088
1Sa 12:5 and his anointed is witness t. day, ... 2088
1Sa 12:8 and made them dwell in t. place......... 2088
1Sa 12:16 stand and see t. great thing, ... 2088
1Sa 12:19 have added unto all our sins t. evil, ...
1Sa 12:20 ye have done all t. wickedness: 2063
1Sa 14:10 and t. shall be a sign unto us............ 2088
1Sa 14:28 the man that eateth any food t. day. ....
1Sa 14:29 because I tasted a little of t. honey..... 2088
1Sa 14:33 roll a great stone unto me t. day..............
1Sa 14:38 wherein t. sin hath been t. day.......... 2088
1Sa 14:45 hath wrought t. great salvation in....... 2088
1Sa 14:45 he hath wrought with God t. day........ 2088
1Sa 15:14 What meaneth then t. bleating of......... 2088
1Sa 15:16 the Lord hath said to me t. night. ....
1Sa 15:28 kingdom of Israel from thee t. day,..........
1Sa 16:8, 9 Neither hath the Lord chosen t...... 2088
1Sa 16:12 Arise, anoint him: for t. is he.......... 2088
1Sa 17:10 defy the armies of Israel t. day;......... 2088
1Sa 17:17 an ephah of t. parched corn,.............. 2088
1Sa 17:25 Have ye seen t. man that is come...... 2088
1Sa 17:26 the man that killeth t. Philistine, ... 1975
1Sa 17:26 who is t. uncircumcised Philistine, ... 2088

1Sa 17:27 answered him after **t.** manner, 2088
1Sa 17:32 will go and fight with **t.** Philistine. 2088
1Sa 17:33 not able to go against **t.** Philistine. 2088
1Sa 17:36 **t.** uncircumcised Philistine shall be 2088
1Sa 17:37 me out of the hand of **t.** Philistine. 2088
1Sa 17:46 **T.** day will the Lord deliver thee 2088
1Sa 17:46 the Philistines **t.** day unto the fowls 2088
1Sa 17:47 **t.** assembly shall know that the 2088
1Sa 17:55 host, Abner, whose son is **t.** youth? 2088
1Sa 18:21 Thou shalt **t.** day be my son in law in
1Sa 18:24 saying, On **t.** manner spake David 428
1Sa 20:2 should my father hide **t.** thing 2088
1Sa 20:3 Let not Jonathan know **t.**, lest he 2063
1Sa 20:21 the arrows are on **t.** side of thee, 2007
1Sa 21:5 it were sanctified **t.** day in the vessel.
1Sa 21:11 not **t.** David the king of the land? 2088
1Sa 21:15 have brought **t.** fellow to play the 2088
1Sa 21:15 shall **t.** fellow come into my house? 2088
1Sa 22:8, 13 me, to lie in wait, as at **t.** day? 2088
1Sa 22:15 thy servant knew nothing of all **t.**, 2063
1Sa 23:26 And Saul went on **t.** side of the 2088
1Sa 24:6 should do **t.** thing unto my master, 2088
1Sa 24:10 **t.** day thine eyes have seen 2088
1Sa 24:16 said, Is **t.** thy voice, my son David? 2088
1Sa 24:18 thou hast shewed **t.** day how that thou
1Sa 24:19 thou hast done unto me **t.** day. 2088
1Sa 25:21 have I kept all that **t.** fellow hath 2088
1Sa 25:24 my lord, upon me let **t.** iniquity be:
1Sa 25:25 regard **t.** man of Belial, even 2088
1Sa 25:27 **t.** blessing which thine handmaid 2063
1Sa 25:31 That **t.** shall be no grief unto thee, 2063
1Sa 25:32 which sent thee **t.** day to meet me: 2088
1Sa 25:33 hast kept me **t.** day from coming to 2088
1Sa 26:8 enemy into thine hand **t.** day:
1Sa 26:16 **T.** thing is not good that thou 2088
1Sa 26:17 said, Is **t.** thy voice, my son David? 2088
1Sa 26:19 driven me out **t.** day from abiding
1Sa 26:21 was precious in thine eyes **t.** day: 2088
1Sa 26:24 much set by **t.** day in mine eyes, 2088
1Sa 27:6 the kings of Judah unto **t.** day. 2088
1Sa 28:10 happen to thee for **t.** thing. 2088
1Sa 28:18 Lord done **t.** thing unto thee **t.** day. 2088
1Sa 29:3 Is not **t.** David, the servant of Saul 2088
1Sa 29:3 since he fell unto me unto **t.** day? 2088
1Sa 29:4 Make **t.** fellow return, that he may
1Sa 29:5 Is not **t.** David, of whom they sang 2088
1Sa 29:6 of thy coming unto me unto **t.** day: 2088
1Sa 29:8 I have been with thee unto **t.** day, 2088
1Sa 30:8 Shall I pursue after **t.** troop? shall I 2088
1Sa 30:15 thou bring me down to **t.** company? 2088
1Sa 30:15 will bring thee down to **t.** company. 2088
1Sa 30:20 cattle, and said, **T.** is David's spoil. 2088
1Sa 30:24 will hearken unto you in **t.** matter? 2088
1Sa 30:25 an ordinance for Israel unto **t.** day. 2088
2Sa 1:17 David lamented with **t.** 2063
2Sa 2:1 And it came to pass after **t.**, that 3651
2Sa 2:5 **t.** kindness unto your Lord, 2088
2Sa 2:6 I also will requite you **t.** kindness, 2088
2Sa 2:6 because ye have done **t.** thing. 2088
2Sa 3:8 shew kindness **t.** day unto the house
2Sa 3:8 with a fault concerning **t.** woman?
2Sa 3:38 great man fallen **t.** day in Israel? 2088
2Sa 3:39 I am **t.** day weak, though anointed
2Sa 4:3 were sojourners there until **t.** day.) 2088
2Sa 4:8 my lord the king **t.** day of Saul, 2088
2Sa 6:8 of the place Perez-uzzah to **t.** day. 2088
2Sa 7:6 even to **t.** day, but have walked in a 2088
2Sa 7:17 and according to all **t.** vision, so did 2088
2Sa 7:19 **t.** was yet a small thing in thy 2063
2Sa 7:19 And is **t.** the manner of man, O 2063
2Sa 7:27 found in his heart to pray **t.** prayer 2063
2Sa 7:28 promised **t.** goodness unto thy 2088
2Sa 8:1 And after **t.** it came to pass, that 3651
2Sa 10:1 And it came to pass after **t.**, that 3651
2Sa 11:3 Is not **t.** Bath-sheba, the daughter 2063
2Sa 11:11 soul liveth, I will not do **t.** thing. 2088
2Sa 11:25 Let not **t.** thing displease thee, for 2088
2Sa 12:5 hath done **t.** thing shall surely die: 2063
2Sa 12:6 because he did **t.** thing, and 2088
2Sa 12:11 thy wives in the sight of **t.** sun. 2063
2Sa 12:12 I will do **t.** thing before all Israel, 2088
2Sa 12:14 because by **t.** deed thou hast given 2088
2Sa 12:21 What thing is **t.** that thou hast 2088
2Sa 13:1 And it came to pass after **t.**, that 3651
2Sa 13:12 in Israel: do not thou **t.** folly. 2063
2Sa 13:16 **t.** evil in sending me away is 2063
2Sa 13:17 Put now **t.** woman out from me, 2063
2Sa 13:20 is thy brother; regard not **t.** thing. 2063
2Sa 13:32 **t.** hath been determined from the day
2Sa 14:3 and speak on **t.** manner unto him. 2088
2Sa 14:13 for the king doth speak **t.** thing as 2088
2Sa 14:15 come to speak of **t.** thing unto my 2088
2Sa 14:19 hand of Joab with thee in all **t.**? 2063
2Sa 14:20 To fetch about **t.** form of speech hath
2Sa 14:20 thy servant Joab done **t.** thing: 2088
2Sa 14:21 Behold now, I have done **t.** thing: 2088
2Sa 15:1 And it came to pass after **t.**, that 3651
2Sa 15:6 on **t.** manner did Absalom to all 2088
2Sa 15:20 should I **t.** day make thee go up and
2Sa 16:9 Why should **t.** dead dog curse my 2088
2Sa 16:11 more now may **t.** Benjamite do it?
2Sa 16:12 me good for his cursing **t.** day. 2088
2Sa 16:17 Is **t.** thy kindness to thy friend? 2088
2Sa 16:18 but whom the Lord, and **t.** people, 2088
2Sa 17:1 arise and pursue after David **t.** night: 2088
2Sa 17:6 hath spoken after **t.** manner: 2088
2Sa 17:7 hath given is not good at **t.** time. 2063
2Sa 17:16 Lodge not **t.** night in the plains of the
2Sa 18:18 it is called unto **t.** day, Absalom's 2088
2Sa 18:20 Thou shalt not bear tidings **t.** day, 2088
2Sa 18:20 **t.** day thou shalt bear no tidings, 2088
2Sa 18:31 Lord hath avenged thee **t.** day of all
2Sa 19:5 hast shamed **t.** day the faces of all thy
2Sa 19:5 which **t.** day have saved thy life,
2Sa 19:6 thou hast declared **t.** day, that thou
2Sa 19:6 **t.** day I perceive, that if Absalom had
2Sa 19:6 we had died **t.** day, then it had pleased
2Sa 19:7 will not tarry one with thee **t.** night:
2Sa 19:14 that they sent **t.** word unto the king,
2Sa 19:20 I am come the first **t.** day of all the
2Sa 19:21 not Shimei but put to death for **t.**, 2063
2Sa 19:22 ye should **t.** day be adversaries unto
2Sa 19:22 man be put to death **t.** day in Israel?
2Sa 19:22 that I am **t.** day king over Israel?
2Sa 19:35 I am **t.** day fourscore years old: and
2Sa 19:42 then be ye angry for **t.** matter? 2088
2Sa 21:18 it came to pass after **t.**, that there 3651
2Sa 22:1 unto the Lord the words of **t.** song. 2063
2Sa 23:5 for **t.** is all my salvation, and all my
2Sa 23:17 me, O Lord, that I should do **t.** 2063
2Sa 23:17 **t.** the blood of the men that went in
2Sa 24:3 lord the king delight in **t.** thing? 2088
1Ki 1:25 For he is gone down **t.** day, and hath
1Ki 1:27 **t.** thing done by my lord the king, 2088
1Ki 1:30 even so will I certainly do **t.** day. 2088
1Ki 1:41 Wherefore is **t.** noise of the city being
1Ki 1:45 **T.** is the noise that ye have heard. 1931
1Ki 1:48 given one to sit on my throne **t.** day,
1Ki 2:23 spoken **t.** word against his own 2088
1Ki 2:24 Adonijah shall be put to death **t.** day.
1Ki 2:26 not at **t.** time put thee to death: 2088
1Ki 3:6 hast kept for him **t.** great kindness, 2088
1Ki 3:6 to sit on his throne, as it is **t.** day. 2088
1Ki 3:9 to judge **t.** thy so great a people? 2088
1Ki 3:10 that Solomon had asked **t.** thing. 2088
1Ki 3:11 Because thou hast asked **t.** thing, 2088
1Ki 3:17 lord, I and **t.** woman dwell in one 2063
1Ki 3:18 that **t.** woman was delivered also: 2063
1Ki 3:19 **t.** woman's child died in the night; 2063
1Ki 3:22 **t.** said, No; but the dead is thy son, 2063
1Ki 3:23 one saith, **T.** is my son that liveth, 2063
1Ki 4:24 all the region on **t.** side the river,
1Ki 4:24 all the kings on **t.** side the river:
1Ki 5:7 Blessed be the Lord **t.** day, which hath
1Ki 5:7 a wise son over **t.** great people. 2088
1Ki 6:12 Concerning **t.** house which thou art 2088
1Ki 7:8 taken to wife, like unto **t.** porch. 2088
1Ki 7:28 of the bases was on **t.** manner: 2088
1Ki 7:37 After **t.** manner he made the ten 2063
1Ki 8:8 and there they are unto **t.** day. 2088
1Ki 8:24 it with thine hand, as it is **t.** day. 2088
1Ki 8:27 less **t.** house that I have builded? 2088
1Ki 8:29 eyes may be open toward **t.** house 2088
1Ki 8:29 servant shall make toward **t.** place. 2088
1Ki 8:30 they shall pray toward **t.** place: 2088
1Ki 8:31 come before thine altar in **t.** house: 2088
1Ki 8:33 supplication unto thee in **t.** house: 2088
1Ki 8:35 if they pray toward **t.** place, and 2088
1Ki 8:38 forth his hands toward **t.** house: 2088
1Ki 8:42 come and pray toward **t.** house; 2088
1Ki 8:43 that they may know that **t.** house, 2088
1Ki 8:54 an end of praying all **t.** prayer 2063
1Ki 8:61 his commandments, as **t.** day. 2088
1Ki 9:3 have hallowed **t.** house, which thou 2088
1Ki 9:7 **t.** house, which I have hallowed for
1Ki 9:8 And at **t.** house, which is high, 2088
1Ki 9:8 the Lord done thus unto **t.** land, 2063
1Ki 9:9 Lord brought upon them all **t.** evil. 2063
1Ki 9:13 the land of Cabul unto **t.** day. 2088
1Ki 9:15 **t.** is the reason of the levy which 2088
1Ki 9:21 tribute of bondservice unto **t.** day. 2088
1Ki 10:12 trees, nor were seen unto **t.** day. 2088
1Ki 11:10 had commanded him concerning **t.** 2088
1Ki 11:11 Forasmuch as **t.** is done of thee, 2063
1Ki 11:27 And **t.** was the cause that he lifted 2088
1Ki 11:39 will for **t.** afflict the seed of David, 2063
1Ki 12:6 that I may answer **t.** people? 2088
1Ki 12:7 be a servant unto **t.** people **t.** day, 2088
1Ki 12:9 ye that we may answer **t.** people, 2088
1Ki 12:10 shalt thou speak unto **t.** people 2088
1Ki 12:19 the house of David unto **t.** day. 2088
1Ki 12:24 his house; for **t.** thing is from me. 2088
1Ki 12:27 If **t.** people go up to do sacrifice in 2088
1Ki 12:27 the heart of **t.** people turn again 2088
1Ki 12:30 And **t.** thing became a sin: for the 2088
1Ki 13:3 **T.** is the sign which the Lord hath 2088
1Ki 13:8 bread nor drink water in **t.** place; 2088
1Ki 13:16 drink water with thee in **t.** place: 2088
1Ki 13:33 After **t.** thing Jeroboam returned 2088
1Ki 13:34 **t.** thing became sin unto the house 2088
1Ki 14:2 that I should be king over **t.** people. 2088
1Ki 14:15 root up Israel out of **t.** good land, 2063
1Ki 17:21 let **t.** child's soul come into him 2088
1Ki 17:24 by **t.** know that thou art a man of 2088
1Ki 18:36 be known **t.** day that thou art God 2088
1Ki 18:37 that **t.** people may know that thou 2088
1Ki 19:2 of them by to morrow about **t.** time.
1Ki 20:6 unto thee to morrow about **t.** time,
1Ki 20:7 see how **t.** man seeketh mischief: 2088
1Ki 20:9 will do: but **t.** thing I may not do. 2088
1Ki 20:12 when Ben-hadad heard **t.** message, 2088
1Ki 20:13 thou seen all **t.** great multitude? 2088
1Ki 20:13 deliver it into thine hand **t.** day; 2088
1Ki 20:24 And do **t.** thing, Take the kings 2088
1Ki 20:28 deliver all **t.** great multitude into 2088
1Ki 20:34 I will send thee away with **t.** covenant.
1Ki 20:39 unto me, and said, Keep **t.** man: 2088
1Ki 22:20 And one said on **t.** manner, and 3541
1Ki 22:27 Put **t.** fellow in the prison, and 2088
2Ki 1:2 whether I shall recover of **t.** disease. 2088
2Ki 2:19 the situation of **t.** city is pleasant, 2088
2Ki 2:22 the waters were healed unto **t.** day, 2088
2Ki 3:16 Lord, Make **t.** valley full of ditches. 2088
2Ki 3:18 **t.** is but a light thing in the sight 2063
2Ki 3:23 they said, **T.** is blood: the kings 2088
2Ki 4:9 that **t.** is an holy man of God, 1931
2Ki 4:12 his servant, Call **t.** Shunammite. 2063
2Ki 4:13 been careful for us with all **t.** care; 2063
2Ki 4:16 About **t.** season, according to the 2088
2Ki 4:36 and said, Call **t.** Shunammite. 2063
2Ki 4:43 I set **t.** before an hundred men? 2088
2Ki 5:6 when **t.** letter is come unto thee, 2088
2Ki 5:7 that **t.** man doth send unto me to 2088
2Ki 5:18 In **t.** thing the Lord pardon thy 2088
2Ki 5:18 Lord pardon thy servant in **t.** thing. 2088
2Ki 5:20 hath spared Naaman **t.** Syrian, 2088
2Ki 6:11 was sore troubled for **t.** thing; 2088
2Ki 6:18 Smite **t.** people, I pray thee, with 2088
2Ki 6:19 said unto them, **T.** is not the way, 2088
2Ki 6:19 neither is **t.** the city: follow me, 2090
2Ki 6:24 And it came to pass after **t.**, that 3651
2Ki 6:28 **T.** woman said unto me, Give thy 2063
2Ki 6:31 Shaphat shall stand on him **t.** day.
2Ki 6:33 said, Behold, **t.** evil is of the Lord; 2063
2Ki 7:1 To morrow about **t.** time shall a
2Ki 7:2 in heaven, might **t.** thing be? 2088
2Ki 7:9 **t.** day is a day of good tidings, and 1931
2Ki 7:18 to morrow about **t.** time in the gate of
2Ki 8:5 My lord, O king, **t.** is the woman, 2063
2Ki 8:5 and **t.** is her son, whom Elisha 2088
2Ki 8:8, 9 Shall I recover of **t.** disease? 2088
2Ki 8:13 that he should do **t.** great thing? 2088
2Ki 8:22 under the hand of Judah unto **t.** day 2088
2Ki 9:1 and take **t.** box of oil in thine hand, 2088
2Ki 9:11 came **t.** mad fellow to thee? 2088
2Ki 9:25 the Lord laid **t.** burden upon him; 2088
2Ki 9:26 and I will requite thee in **t.** plat, 2063
2Ki 9:27 Ahaziah the king of Judah saw **t.**,
2Ki 9:34 Go, see now **t.** cursed woman, and 2063
2Ki 9:36 **T.** is the word of the Lord, which 1931
2Ki 9:37 they shall not say, **T.** is Jezebel. 2063

2Ki 10:2 as soon as t. letter cometh to you,..... 2088
2Ki 10:6 to me to Jezreel by to morrow t. time. .....
2Ki 10:27 it a draught house unto t. day. 2088
2Ki 11:5 T. is the thing that ye shall do;.......... 2088
2Ki 14:7 the name of it Joktheel unto t. day. 2088
2Ki 14:10 up: glory of t., and tarry at home:...........
2Ki 15:12 T. was the word of the Lord............ 1931
2Ki 16:6 Elath, and dwelt there unto t. day...... 2088
2Ki 17:12 unto them, Ye shall not do t. thing. 2088
2Ki 17:23 own land to Assyria unto t. day. 2088
2Ki 17:34 t. day they do after the former......... 2088
2Ki 17:41 their fathers, so do they unto t. day. .. 2088
2Ki 18:19 What confidence is t. wherein thou..... 2088
2Ki 18:21 upon the staff of t. bruised reed,........ 2088
2Ki 18:22 before t. altar in Jerusalem?........... 2088
2Ki 18:25 Lord against t. place to destroy it? 2088
2Ki 18:25 Go up against t. land, and destroy...... 2063
2Ki 18:30 t. city shall not be delivered into........ 2063
2Ki 19:3 T. day is a day of trouble, and of....... 2088
2Ki 19:21 T. is the word that the Lord hath......... 2088
2Ki 19:29 And t. shall be a sign unto thee, Ye.... 2088
2Ki 19:29 shall eat t. year such things as grow of .....
2Ki 19:31 of the Lord of hosts shall do t.,......... 2063
2Ki 19:32 He shall not come into t. city, ... 2063
2Ki 19:33 and shall not come into t. city, ... 2063
2Ki 19:34 For I will defend t. city, to save it, ... 2063
2Ki 20:6 I will deliver thee and t. city out of 2063
2Ki 20:6 defend t. city for mine own sake, ...
2Ki 20:9 T. sign shalt thou have of the........... 2088
2Ki 20:17 have laid up in store unto t. day, ... 2088
2Ki 21:7 In t. house, and in Jerusalem,........... 2088
2Ki 21:15 forth out of Egypt, even unto t. day, .. 2088
2Ki 22:13 concerning the words of t. book......... 2088
2Ki 22:13 hearkened unto the words of t. book,.. 2088
2Ki 22:16 I will bring evil upon t. place, and 2088
2Ki 22:17 shall be kindled against t. place,......... 2088
2Ki 22:19 what I spake against t. place, ... 2088
2Ki 22:20 which I will bring upon t. place.......... 2088
2Ki 23:3 perform the words of t. covenant 2063
2Ki 23:3 that were written in t. book............. 2088
2Ki 23:21 written in the book of t. covenant. 2088
2Ki 23:23 wherein t. passover was holden to....... 2088
2Ki 23:27 and will cast off t. city Jerusalem........ 2063
2Ki 24:3 of the Lord came t. upon Judah,...............
1Ch 4:41 destroyed them utterly unto t. day, ... 2088
1Ch 4:43 and dwelt there unto t. day.............. 2088
1Ch 5:26 and to the river Gozan, unto t. day. ... 2088
1Ch 11:11 t. is the number of the mighty men...... 428
1Ch 11:19 it me, that I should do t. thing: 2063
1Ch 13:11 place is called Perez-uzza to t. day. 2088
1Ch 16:7 first t. psalm to thank the Lord...............
1Ch 17:5 I brought up Israel unto t. day;......... 2088
1Ch 17:15 according to all t. vision, so did 2088
1Ch 17:17 t. was a small thing in thine eyes, ... 2063
1Ch 17:19 hast thou done all t. greatness,.......... 2063
1Ch 17:26 hast promised t. goodness unto thy 2063
1Ch 18:1 Now after t. it came to pass, that 3651
1Ch 19:1 Now it came to pass after t., that 3651
1Ch 20:4 And it came to pass after t., that 3651
1Ch 21:3 then doth my lord require t. thing?..... 2063
1Ch 21:7 God was displeased with t. thing; 2088
1Ch 21:8 because I have done t. thing: 2088
1Ch 21:22 me the place of t. threshingfloor,.............
1Ch 22:1 T. is the house of the Lord God, ... 2088
1Ch 22:1 t. is the altar of the burnt offering...... 2088
1Ch 26:30 on t. side Jordan westward in all.............
1Ch 27:6 T. is that Benaiah, who was............. 1931
1Ch 28:7 any my judgments, as at t. day........... 2088
1Ch 28:8 that ye may possess t. good land, and.......
1Ch 28:19 All t., said David, the Lord made me........
1Ch 28:19 me, even all the works of t. pattern. ....
1Ch 29:5 consecrate his service t. day unto the ....
1Ch 29:14 to offer so willingly after t. sort?........ 2063
1Ch 29:16 all t. store that we have prepared 2088
1Ch 29:18 keep t. for ever in the imagination...... 2063
2Ch 1:10 out and come in before t. people:....... 2088
2Ch 1:10 for who can judge t. thy people, ... 2088
2Ch 1:11 Because t. was in thine heart, and...... 2063
2Ch 2:4 T. is an ordinance for ever to Israel.... 2063
2Ch 5:9 And there it is unto t. day............... 2088
2Ch 6:15 hast fulfilled it...as it is t. day.......... 2088
2Ch 6:18 how much less t. house which I.......... 2088
2Ch 6:20 eyes may be open upon t. house........ 2088
2Ch 6:20 thy servant prayeth toward t. place. ... 2088
2Ch 6:21 they shall make toward t. place:......... 2088
2Ch 6:22 come before thine altar in t. house; 2088
2Ch 6:24 supplication before thee in t. house;.... 2088
2Ch 6:26 yet if they pray toward t. place, and... 2088
2Ch 6:29 spread forth his hands in t. house:...... 2088
2Ch 6:32 if they come and pray in t. house;...... 2088
2Ch 6:33 know that t. house which I have 2088
2Ch 6:34 pray unto thee toward t. city............ 2063
2Ch 6:40 prayer that is made in t. place........... 2088
2Ch 7:12 chosen t. place to myself for an......... 2088
2Ch 7:15 prayer that is made in t. place........... 2088
2Ch 7:16 I chosen and sanctified t. house, ... 2088
2Ch 7:20 t. house, which I have sanctified 2088
2Ch 7:21 And t. house, which is high, shall....... 2088
2Ch 7:21 the Lord done thus unto t. land, ... 2063
2Ch 7:21 land, and unto t. house?.................. 2088
2Ch 7:22 he brought all t. evil upon them. 2063
2Ch 8:8 make to pay tribute until t. day.......... 2088
2Ch 10:6 me to return answer to t. people?...... 2088
2Ch 10:7 If thou be kind to t. people, and 2088
2Ch 10:9 we may return answer to t. people,.... 2088
2Ch 10:19 the house of David unto t. day. 2088
2Ch 11:4 house: for t. thing is done of me......... 2088
2Ch 14:11 name we go against t. multitude......... 2088
2Ch 16:10 rage with him because of t. thing. 2063
2Ch 18:19 one spake saying after t. manner,....... 3602
2Ch 18:26 Put t. fellow in the prison, and 2088
2Ch 19:10 t. do, and ye shall not trespass........... 3541
2Ch 20:1 It came to pass after t. also, that....... 3651
2Ch 20:2 from beyond the sea on t. side Syria;........
2Ch 20:7 out the inhabitants of t. land............. 2063
2Ch 20:9 we stand before t. house, and in......... 2088
2Ch 20:9 (for thy name is in t. house,) and....... 2088
2Ch 20:12 might against t. great company 2088
2Ch 20:15 by reason of t. great multitude; 2088
2Ch 20:17 shall not need to fight in t. battle: 2063
2Ch 20:26 valley of Berachah, unto t. day. 2088
2Ch 20:35 after t. did Jehoshaphat king of.......... 3651
2Ch 21:10 the hand of Judah unto t. day. 2088
2Ch 21:18 after all t. the Lord smote him in....... 2063
2Ch 23:4 T. is the thing that ye shall do;.......... 2088
2Ch 24:4 And it came to pass after t., that 3651
2Ch 24:18 Jerusalem for t. their trespass. 2063
2Ch 25:9 to give thee much more than t.. 2088
2Ch 25:16 because thou hast done t., and 2063
2Ch 28:22 the Lord: t. is that king Ahaz............ 1931
2Ch 29:9 our wives are in captivity for t........... 2088
2Ch 29:28 t. continued until the burnt offering..........
2Ch 30:9 shall come again unto t. land: 2063
2Ch 31:1 Now when all t. was finished, all......... 2063
2Ch 31:10 that which is left is t. great store....... 2088
2Ch 32:9 t. did Sennacherib king of Assyria....... 2088
2Ch 32:15 nor persuade you on t. manner,.......... 2063
2Ch 32:20 for t. cause Hezekiah the king, ... 2063
2Ch 32:30 T. same Hezekiah also stopped........... 1931
2Ch 33:7 In t. house, and in Jerusalem,............ 2088
2Ch 33:14 after t. he built a wall without........... 3651
2Ch 34:21 after all that is written in t. book. 2088
2Ch 34:24 I will bring evil upon t. place, and 2088
2Ch 34:25 shall be poured out upon t. place,....... 2088
2Ch 34:27 heardest his words against t. place. 2088
2Ch 34:28 evil that I will bring upon t. place, ... 2088
2Ch 34:31 which are written in t. book.............. 2088
2Ch 35:19 of Josiah was t. passover kept. 2088
2Ch 35:20 After all t., when Josiah had............ 2063
2Ch 35:21 I come not against thee t. day, but..........
2Ch 35:25 in their lamentations to t. day,...............
Ezr 1:9 t. is the number of them: thirty.......... 428
Ezr 3:12 foundation of t. house was laid........... 2088
Ezr 4:8 to Artaxerxes the king in t. sort: 3660
Ezr 4:10 rest that are on t. side the river, ...
Ezr 4:11 T. is the copy of the letter that 1836
Ezr 4:11 servants the men on t. side the ....
Ezr 4:13 if t. city be builded, and the walls....... 1791
Ezr 4:15 that t. city is a rebellious city, ... 1791
Ezr 4:15 which cause was t. city destroyed. 1791
Ezr 4:16 if t. city be builded again, and the 1791
Ezr 4:16 by t. means thou shalt have no........... 1836
Ezr 4:16 have no portion on t. side the river. ....
Ezr 4:19 that t. city of old time hath made 1791
Ezr 4:21 that t. city be not builded, until.......... 1791
Ezr 4:22 heed now that ye fail not to do t........ 1836
Ezr 5:3 governor on t. side the river, ...
Ezr 5:3 commanded you to build t. house, ... 1836
Ezr 5:3 and to make up t. wall! 1836
Ezr 5:4 we unto them after t. manner,........... 3660
Ezr 5:4 of the men that make t. building? 1836
Ezr 5:5 by letter concerning t. matter........... 1836
Ezr 5:6 governor on t. side the river, ...
Ezr 5:6 which were on t. side the river,..............
Ezr 5:8 and t. work goeth fast on, and........... 1791
Ezr 5:9 commanded you to build t. house, ... 1836
Ezr 5:12 Chaldean, who destroyed t. house, ... 1836
Ezr 5:13 a decree to build t. house of God....... 1836
Ezr 5:17 king to build t. house of God at 1791
Ezr 5:17 to us concerning t. matter. 1836
Ezr 6:7 work of t. house of God alone; 1791
Ezr 6:7 of the Jews build t. house of God....... 1791
Ezr 6:8 for the building of t. house of God:..... 1791
Ezr 6:11 that whosoever shall alter t. word, ... 1836
Ezr 6:11 his house be made a dunghill for t.. 1836
Ezr 6:12 to alter and to destroy t. house of...... 1791
Ezr 6:13 governor on t. side the river, ...
Ezr 6:15 t. house was finished on the third....... 1836
Ezr 6:16 dedication of t. house of God with...... 1836
Ezr 6:17 the dedication of t. house of God 1836
Ezr 7:6 T. Ezra went up from Babylon;.......... 1931
Ezr 7:11 t. is the copy of the letter that 2088
Ezr 7:17 speedily with t. money bullocks,......... 1836
Ezr 7:24 or ministers of t. house of God,.......... 1836
Ezr 7:27 a thing as t. in the king's heart, ... 2063
Ezr 8:1 t. is the genealogy of them that........... 428
Ezr 8:23 and besought our God for t................ 2063
Ezr 8:35 t. was a burnt offering unto the Lord. ....
Ezr 8:36 governors on t. side the river:.................
Ezr 9:2 hath been chief in t. trespass. 2088
Ezr 9:3 And when I heard t. thing, I rent....... 2088
Ezr 9:7 in a great trespass unto t. day;.......... 2088
Ezr 9:7 confusion of face, as it is t. day. 2088
Ezr 9:10 God, what shall we say after t.? 2063
Ezr 9:13 given us such deliverance as t.; 2063
Ezr 9:15 remain yet escaped, as it is t. day:..... 2063
Ezr 9:15 stand before thee because of t............ 2063
Ezr 10:2 hope in Israel concerning t. thing. 2063
Ezr 10:4 t. matter belongeth unto thee: we...........
Ezr 10:5 should do according to t. word.......... 2088
Ezr 10:9 God, trembling because of t. matter,.........
Ezr 10:13 neither is t. a work of one day or two:......
Ezr 10:13 that have transgressed in t. thing. 2088
Ezr 10:14 wrath of our God for t. matter be 2088
Ezr 10:15 were employed about t. matter: 2063
Ne 1:11 I pray thee, thy servant t. day,................
Ne 1:11 him mercy in the sight of t. man. 2088
Ne 2:2 t. is nothing else but sorrow of.......... 2088
Ne 2:18 their hands for t. good work....................
Ne 2:19 What is t. thing that ye do? will......... 2088
Ne 3:7 the governor on t. side the river.............
Ne 5:10 pray you, let us leave off t. usury. 2088
Ne 5:11 to them, even t. day, their lands,............
Ne 5:12 should do according to t. promise....... 2088
Ne 5:13 that performeth not t. promise,.......... 2088
Ne 5:13 people did according to t. promise. 2088
Ne 5:16 continued in the work of t. wall, ... 2063
Ne 5:18 for all t. required not I the bread 2088
Ne 5:18 bondage was heavy upon t. people....... 2088
Ne 5:19 all that I have done for t. people. 2088
Ne 6:4 unto me four times after t. sort; 2088
Ne 6:12 pronounced t. prophecy against me:..........
Ne 6:16 t. work was wrought of our God.......... 2063
Ne 7:7 men of the people of Israel was t.;...........
Ne 8:9 T. day is holy unto the Lord your............
Ne 8:10 for t. day is holy unto our Lord: ....
Ne 9:1 twenty and fourth day of t. month...... 2088
Ne 9:10 get thee a name, as it is t. day.......... 2088
Ne 9:18 T. is thy God that brought thee up...... 2088
Ne 9:32 of the kings of Assyria unto t. day...... 2088
Ne 9:36 Behold, we are servants t. day, and ....
Ne 9:38 because of all t. we make a sure........ 2063
Ne 13:4 And before t., Eliashib the priest, ... 2088
Ne 13:6 all t. time was not I at Jerusalem: 2088
Ne 13:14 me, O my god, concerning t., and...... 2088
Ne 13:17 What evil thing is t. that ye do, ... 2088
Ne 13:18 our God bring all t. evil upon us, ... 2088
Ne 13:18 upon us, and upon t. city? yet ye......... 2063
Ne 13:22 me, O my God, concerning t. also,...... 2063
Ne 13:27 unto you to do all t. great evil, ... 2063
Es 1:1 (t. is Ahasuerus which reigned,.......... 1931
Es 1:17 For t. deed of the queen shall come ....
Es 1:18 of Persia and Media say t. day 2088
Es 4:14 holdest thy peace at t. time, ... 2063
Es 4:14 the kingdom for such a time as t.? 2063
Es 4:15 them return Mordecai t. answer,..............
Es 5:4 Haman come t. day unto the banquet........
Es 5:13 Yet all t. availeth me nothing,........... 2088

Es 6:3 hath been done to Mordecia for **t.**?..... 2088
Es 6:9 let **t.** apparel and horse be delivered... 2088
Es 7:6 and enemy is **t.** wicked Haman.......... 2088
Es 9:4 **t.** man Mordecai waxed greater and.........
Es 9:13 also according unto **t.** day's decree, ...
Es 9:21 To stablish **t.** among them, that they ....
Es 9:26 had seen concerning **t.** matter, ... 3602
Es 9:26 Therefore for all the words of **t.** letter, ...
Es 9:29 confirm **t.** second letter of Purim........ 2063
Job 1:3 so that **t.** man was the greatest......... 1931
Job 1:22 In all **t.** Job sinned not, for............... 2063
Job 2:10 In all **t.** did not Job sin with his.......... 2063
Job 2:11 heard of all **t.** evil that was come 2063
Job 3:1 After **t.** opened Job his mouth, ... 3651
Job 4:6 Is not **t.** thy fear, thy confidence, thy........
Job 5:27 Lo **t.**, we have searched it, so it is;.... 2063
Job 8:19 **t.** is the joy of his way, and out of 1931
Job 9:22 **T.** is one thing, therefore I said it, ... 1931
Job 10:13 heart: I know that **t.** is with thee. 2063
Job 12:9 hand of the Lord hath wrought **t.**?...... 2063
Job 13:1 Lo, mine eye hath seen all **t.**, mine ear .....
Job 17:8 men shall be astonied at **t.**, and 2063
Job 18:21 **t.** is the place of him that knoweth 2088
Job 19:26 my skin worms destroy **t.** body, ... 2063
Job 20:2 answer, and for **t.** I make haste ....
Job 20:4 Knowest thou not **t.** of old, since 2063
Job 20:29 **T.** is the portion of a wicked man....... 2088
Job 21:2 and let **t.** be your consolations........... 2063
Job 27:13 **T.** is the portion of a wicked man........ 2088
Job 31:11 For **t.** is an heinous crime; yea, it...... 1931
Job 31:28 **T.** also were an iniquity to be........... 1931
Job 33:12 Behold, in **t.** thou art not just: I......... 2063
Job 34:16 thou hast understanding, hear **t.**:......... 2063
Job 35:2 Thinkest thou **t.** to be right, that 2063
Job 36:21 **t.** hast thou chosen rather than.......... 2088
Job 37:1 At **t.** also my heart trembleth, ... 2063
Job 37:14 Hearken unto **t.**, O Job: stand still,..... 2063
Job 38:2 Who is **t.** that darkeneth counsel........ 2088
Job 42:16 After **t.** lived Job an hundred and 2063
Ps 2:7 my Son; **t.** day have I begotten thee.........
Ps 7:3 O Lord my God, if I have done **t.**; 2063
Ps 11:6 **t.** shall be the portion of their cup. ....
Ps 12:7 preserve them from **t.** generation....... 2098
Ps 17:14 which have their portion in **t.** life,............
Ps 18:*title* the words of **t.** song in the day.......... 2063
Ps 23:31 shall be born, that he hath done **t.**............
Ps 24:6 **T.** is the generation of them that........ 2088
Ps 24:8 who is **t.** King of glory? The Lord....... 2088
Ps 24:10 Who is **t.** King of glory? The Lord 2088
Ps 27:3 me, in **t.** will I be confident.............. 2063
Ps 32:6 **t.** shall every one that is godly pray.... 2063
Ps 34:6 **T.** poor man cried, and the Lord........ 2088
Ps 35:22 **T.** thou hast seen, O Lord: keep not .. 2088
Ps 41:11 **t.** I know that thou favourest me,........ 2063
Ps 44:17 **t.** is come upon us; yet have we........ 2063
Ps 44:21 Shall not God search **t.** out? for he..... 2063
Ps 48:14 For **t.** God is our God for ever and 2088
Ps 49:1 Hear **t.**, all ye people; give ear, all.... 2063
Ps 49:13 **T.** their way is their folly: yet........... 2088
Ps 50:22 Now consider **t.**, ye that forget.......... 2063
Ps 51:4 I sinned, and done **t.** evil in thy sight:..2063
Ps 52:7 **t.** is the man that made not God his..........
Ps 56:9 back: **t.** I know; for God is for me. 2088
Ps 62:11 twice have I heard **t.**; that power....... 2098
Ps 68:16 **t.** is the hill which God desireth to...........
Ps 69:31 **T.** also shall please the Lord better ....
Ps 69:32 The humble shall see **t.**, and be glad:........
Ps 71:18 thy strength unto **t.** generation, ...
Ps 73:16 When I thought to know **t.**, it was...... 2063
Ps 74:2 **t.** mount Zion, wherein thou hast 2088
Ps 74:18 Remember **t.**, that the enemy 2063
Ps 77:10 And I said, **T.** is my infirmity: 1931
Ps 78:21 Therefore the Lord heard **t.**, and was ..1931
Ps 78:32 For all **t.** they sinned still, and........... 2063
Ps 78:54 even to **t.** mountain, which his........... 2088
Ps 78:59 When God heard **t.**, he was wroth, and.....
Ps 80:14 and behold, and visit **t.** vine; 2063
Ps 81:4 **t.** was a statute for Israel, and a........ 1931
Ps 81:5 **T.** he ordained in Joseph for a ....
Ps 87:4 Ethiopia; **t.** man was born there......... 2088
Ps 87:5 **T.** and that man was born in her: ....
Ps 87:6 that **t.** man was born there............. 2088
Ps 92:6 neither doth a fool understand **t.**. 2063
Ps 95:10 long was I grieved with **t.** generation, ...
Ps 102:18 **T.** shall be written for the................. 2088
Ps 104:25 so is **t.** great and wide sea, wherein ... 2088
Ps 109:20 Let **t.** be the reward of mine............ 2063
Ps 109:27 they may know that **t.** is thy hand;..... 2063
Ps 113:2 name of the Lord from **t.** time forth.........
Ps 115:18 will bless the Lord from **t.** time forth.........
Ps 118:20 **T.** gate of the Lord, into which.......... 2088
Ps 118:23 **T.** is the Lord's doing; it is.............. 2063
Ps 118:24 **T.** is the day which the Lord hath 2088
Ps 119:50 **T.** is my comfort in my affliction: 2063
Ps 119:56 **T.** I had, because I kept...precepts..... 2063
Ps 119:91 continue **t.** day according to thine............
Ps 121:8 and thy coming in from **t.** time forth, ...
Ps 132:14 **T.** is my rest for ever:..........................
Ps 149:9 **t.** honour have all his saints.............. 1931
Pr 6:3 Do **t.** now, my son, and deliver 2063
Pr 7:14 me; **t.** day have I payed my vows. ....
Pr 22:19 I have made known to thee **t.** day. ....
Ec 1:10 it may be said, See, **t.** is new? 2088
Ec 1:13 **t.** sore travail hath God given to 1931
Ec 1:17 I perceived that **t.** also is vexation...... 2088
Ec 2:1 and, behold, **t.** also is vanity. 1931
Ec 2:10 and **t.** was my portion of all my 2088
Ec 2:15 in my heart, that **t.** also is vanity. 2088
Ec 2:19 under the sun. **T.** is also vanity. 2088
Ec 2:21 **T.** also is vanity and a great evil. 2088
Ec 2:23 the night. **T.** is also vanity. 2088,1931
Ec 2:24 **T.** also I saw, that it was from the..... 2088
Ec 2:26 **T.** also is vanity and vexation of......... 2088
Ec 4:4 that for **t.** a man is envied of his........ 1931
Ec 4:4 **T.** is also vanity and vexation of......... 2088
Ec 4:8 **T.** is also vanity, yea, it is a sore....... 2088
Ec 4:16 **t.** also is vanity and vexation of.......... 2088
Ec 5:10 with increase: **t.** is also vanity. 2088
Ec 5:16 **t.** also is a sore evil, that in all 2090
Ec 5:19 in his labour; **t.** is the gift of God. 2090
Ec 6:2 it: **t.** is vanity, and it is an evil.......... 2088
Ec 6:5 **t.** hath more rest than the other. 2088
Ec 6:9 **t.** is also vanity and vexation of.......... 2088
Ec 6:12 what is good for man in **t.** life,..................
Ec 7:6 of the fool: **t.** also is vanity. 2088
Ec 7:10 not enquire wisely concerning **t.**? 2088
Ec 7:18 that thou shouldest take hold of **t.**; 2088
Ec 7:18 from **t.** withdraw not thine hand: 2088
Ec 7:23 all **t.** have I proved by wisdom: 2090
Ec 7:27 Behold, **t.** have I found, saith the 2088
Ec 7:29 **t.** only have I found, that God hath..... 2088
Ec 8:9 All **t.** have I seen, and applied my...... 2088
Ec 8:10 they had so done: **t.** is also vanity...... 2088
Ec 8:14 I said that **t.** also is vanity. 2088
Ec 9:1 For all **t.** I consider in my heart........ 2088
Ec 9:1 even to declare all **t.**, that the 2088
Ec 9:3 **T.** is an evil among all things that....... 2088
Ec 9:9 that is thy portion in **t.** life, and 2088
Ec 9:13 **T.** wisdom have I seen also under 2090
Ec 11:6 shall prosper, either **t.** or that, ... 2088
Ec 12:13 for **t.** is the whole duty of man. 2088
Ca 3:6 Who is **t.** that cometh out of the........ 2063
Ca 5:16 **T.** is my beloved, and **t.** is my 2088
Ca 7:7 **T.** thy statute is like to a palm.......... 2063
Ca 8:5 Who is **t.** that cometh up from the 2063
Isa 1:12 who hath required **t.** at your hand, ... 2063
Isa 3:6 and let **t.** ruin be under thy hand:....... 2063
Isa 5:25 For all **t.** his anger is not turned........ 2063
Isa 6:7 said, Lo, **t.** hath touched thy lips;......... 2088
Isa 6:9 And he said, Go, and tell **t.** people, ... 2088
Isa 6:10 Make the heart of **t.** people fat, and ... 2088
Isa 8:6 as **t.** people refuseth the waters of..... 2088
Isa 8:11 not walk in the way of **t.** people,........ 2088
Isa 8:12 them to whom **t.** people shall say,...... 2088
Isa 8:20 they speak not according to **t.** word,... 2088
Isa 9:5 but **t.** shall be with burning ....
Isa 9:7 the Lord of hosts will perform **t.**........ 2063
Isa 9:12 For all **t.** his anger is not turned........ 2063
Isa 9:16 the leaders of **t.** people cause them 2088
Isa 9:17, 21 all **t.** his anger is not turned......... 2063
Isa 10:4 For all **t.** his anger is not turned 2063
Isa 12:5 things: **t.** is known in all the earth...... 2063
Isa 14:4 take up **t.** proverb against the 2088
Isa 14:16 Is **t.** the man that made the earth 2088
Isa 14:26 **T.** is the purpose that is purposed........ 2063
Isa 14:26 **t.** is the hand that is stretched out 2063
Isa 14:28 king Ahaz died was **t.** burden. 2088
Isa 16:13 **T.** is the word that the Lord hath........ 2088
Isa 17:14 **T.** is the portion of them that spoil..... 2088
Isa 20:6 inhabitant of **t.** isle shall say in that.... 2088
Isa 22:14 **t.** iniquity shall not be purged from..... 2088
Isa 22:15 Go, get thee unto **t.** treasurer, even... 2088
Isa 23:7 Is **t.** your joyous city, whose............ 2063
Isa 23:8 hath taken **t.** counsel against Tyre,..... 2063
Isa 23:13 **t.** people was not, till the Assyrian..... 2088
Isa 24:3 for the Lord hath spoken **t.** word. 2088
Isa 25:6 And in **t.** mountain shall the Lord....... 2088
Isa 25:7 he will destroy in **t.** mountain the....... 2088
Isa 25:9 in that day, Lo, **t.** is our God; 2088
Isa 25:9 **t.** is the Lord; we have waited for...... 2088
Isa 25:10 in **t.** mountain shall the hand of the..... 2088
Isa 26:1 In that day shall **t.** song be sung 2088
Isa 27:9 By **t.** therefore shall the iniquity......... 2063
Isa 27:9 **t.** is all the fruit to take away his 2088
Isa 28:11 tongue will he speak to **t.** people........ 2088
Isa 28:12 **T.** is the rest wherewith ye may......... 2063
Isa 28:12 to rest; and **t.** is the refreshing:......... 2063
Isa 28:14 that rule **t.** people...in Jerusalem. 2088
Isa 28:29 **T.** also cometh forth from the Lord 2088
Isa 29:11, 12 saying, Read **t.**, I pray thee: 2088
Isa 29:13 Forasmuch as **t.** people draw near...... 2068
Isa 29:14 marvellous work among **t.** people, ... 2088
Isa 30:7 have I cried concerning **t.**, Their......... 2063
Isa 30:9 That **t.** is a rebellious people, lying..... 1931
Isa 30:12 Because ye despise **t.** word, and........ 2088
Isa 30:13 **t.** iniquity shall be to you as a........... 2088
Isa 30:21 **T.** is the way, walk ye in it, when...... 2088
Isa 36:4 What confidence is **t.** wherein thou..... 2088
Isa 36:6 in the staff of **t.** broken reed, ... 2088
Isa 36:7 Ye shall worship before **t.** altar?......... 2088
Isa 36:10 Lord against **t.** land to destroy it? 2063
Isa 36:10 unto me, Go up against **t.** land, and.... 2063
Isa 36:15 **t.** city shall not be delivered into........ 2063
Isa 37:3 **T.** day is a day of trouble, and of....... 2088
Isa 37:22 **T.** is the word which the Lord hath 2088
Isa 37:30 And **t.** shall be a sign unto thee, ... 2088
Isa 37:30 eat **t.** year such as growth of itself; ....
Isa 37:32 of the Lord of hosts shall do **t.**. 2063
Isa 37:33 He shall not come into **t.** city, nor....... 2063
Isa 37:34 and shall not come into **t.** city, saith ... 2063
Isa 37:35 For I will defend **t.** city to save it 2063
Isa 38:6 I will deliver thee and **t.** city out of 2063
Isa 38:6 of Assyria: and I will defend **t.** city..... 2063
Isa 38:7 **t.** shall be a sign unto thee from 2088
Isa 38:7 Lord will do **t.** thing that he hath 2088
Isa 38:19 he shall praise thee, as I do **t.** day: ....
Isa 39:6 have laid up in store until **t.** day,.......... 2088
Isa 41:20 the hand of the Lord hath done **t.**, ... 2063
Isa 42:22 **t.** is a people robbed and spoiled;....... 1931
Isa 42:23 Who among you will give ear to **t.**? 2063
Isa 43:9 who among them can declare **t.**, ... 2063
Isa 43:21 **T.** people have I formed for 2098
Isa 45:21 declared **t.** from ancient time? 2063
Isa 46:8 Remember **t.**, and shew yourselves 2063
Isa 47:8 Therefore hear now **t.**, thou that art... 2063
Isa 48:1 Hear ye **t.**, O house of Jacob, which... 2063
Isa 48:6 Thou hast heard, see all **t.**; and will..........
Isa 48:6 shewed thee new things from **t.** time, ...
Isa 48:16 Come ye near unto me, hear ye **t.**; 2063
Isa 48:20 tell **t.**, utter it even to the end of the.. 2063
Isa 50:11 **T.** shall ye have of mine hand; ye........ 2063
Isa 51:21 hear now **t.**, thou afflicted, and.......... 2063
Isa 54:9 **t.** is as the waters of Noah unto me: .. 2063
Isa 54:17 **T.** is the heritage of the servants of.... 2063
Isa 56:2 Blessed is the man that doeth **t.**, ... 2063
Isa 56:12 and to morrow shall be as **t.** day,....... 2088
Isa 58:4 ye shall not fast as ye do **t.** day, to ....
Isa 58:5 wilt thou call **t.** a fast, and an............ 2088
Isa 58:6 Is not **t.** the fast that I have chosen? .. 2088
Isa 59:21 me, **t.** is my covenant with them,....... 2063
Isa 63:1 Who is **t.** that cometh from Edom, ... 2088
Isa 63:1 **t.** that is glorious in his apparel,......... 2088
Isa 66:2 but to **t.** man will I look, even to 2088
Isa 66:14 And when ye see **t.**, your heart shall ....
Jer 1:10 **t.** day set thee over the nations......... 2088
Jer 1:18 have made thee **t.** day a defenced city,.......
Jer 2:12 Be astonished, O ye heavens, at **t.**,.... 2063
Jer 2:17 thou not procured **t.** unto thyself,....... 2063
Jer 3:4 thou not from **t.** time cry unto me,...........
Jer 3:10 yet for all **t.** her treacherous sister...... 2063
Jer 3:25 from our youth even unto **t.** day, ... 2088
Jer 4:8 For **t.** gird you with sackcloth,........... 2063
Jer 4:10 hast greatly deceived **t.** people and..... 2088
Jer 4:11 time shall it be said to **t.** people......... 2088
Jer 4:18 **t.** is thy wickedness, because it is 2063
Jer 4:28 For **t.** shall the earth mourn, and....... 2063
Jer 5:7 How shall I pardon thee for **t.**? thy..... 2063
Jer 5:9 be avenged on such a nation as **t.**? 2088
Jer 5:14 Because ye speak **t.** word, behold, I... 2088

Jer 5:14 **t.** people wood, and it shall devour 2088
Jer 5:20 Declare **t.** in the house of Jacob, ... 2063
Jer 5:21 Hear now **t.**, O foolish people, and 2063
Jer 5:23 But **t.** people hath a revolting and 2088
Jer 5:29 avenged on such a nation as **t.**? 2068
Jer 6:6 **t.** is the city to be visited; she is 1931
Jer 6:19 I will bring evil upon **t.** people, ... 2088
Jer 6:21 stumblingblocks before **t.** people, ... 2088
Jer 7:2 house, and proclaim there **t.** word, ... 2088
Jer 7:3 I will cause you to dwell in **t.** place..... 2088
Jer 7:6 shed not innocent blood in **t.** place,..... 2088
Jer 7:7 will I cause you to dwell in **t.** place,.... 2088
Jer 7:10 and stand before me in **t.** house, ... 2088
Jer 7:11 Is **t.** house, which is called by my 2088
Jer 7:14 Therefore will I do unto **t.** house, ...
Jer 7:16 pray not thou for **t.** people, neither..... 2088
Jer 7:20 shall be poured out upon **t.** place, ... 2088
Jer 7:23 But **t.** thing commanded I them, ... 2088
Jer 7:25 out of the land of Egypt unto **t.** day.... 2088
Jer 7:28 **T.** is a nation that obeyeth not the 2088
Jer 7:33 carcases of **t.** people shall be meat 2088
Jer 8:3 them that remain of **t.** evil family, ... 2063
Jer 8:5 then is **t.** people of Jerusalem 2088
Jer 9:9 be avenged on such a nation as **t.**? 2088
Jer 9:12 wise man, that may understand **t.**? 2063
Jer 9:15 even **t.** people, with wormwood, ... 2088
Jer 9:24 let him that glorieth glory in **t.**, ... 2063
Jer 10:18 inhabitants of the land at **t.** once, ... 2063
Jer 10:19 Truly **t.** is a grief, and I must bear 2088
Jer 11:2 Hear ye the words of **t.** covenant, ... 2088
Jer 11:3 not the words of **t.** covenant, ... 2088
Jer 11:5 with milk and honey, as it is **t.** day..... 2088
Jer 11:6 Hear ye the words of **t.** covenant, ... 2088
Jer 11:7 even unto **t.** day, rising early and 2088
Jer 11:8 them all the words of **t.** covenant, ... 2088
Jer 11:14 pray not thou for **t.** people, neither 2088
Jer 13:9 After **t.** manner will I mar the pride of ......
Jer 13:10 **T.** evil people, which refuse to 2088
Jer 13:10 shall even be as **t.** girdle, which is 2088
Jer 13:12 thou shalt speak unto them **t.** word; ... 2088
Jer 13:13 I will fill all the inhabitants of **t.** land, ...
Jer 13:25 **T.** is thy lot, the portion of thy 2088
Jer 14:10 Thus saith the Lord unto **t.** people, ... 2088
Jer 14:11 Pray not for **t.** people for their good. .. 2088
Jer 14:13 give you assured peace in **t.** place. 2088
Jer 14:15 and famine shall not be in **t.** land; 2063
Jer 14:17 thou shalt say **t.** word unto them; 2088
Jer 15:1 mind could not be toward **t.** people: 2088
Jer 15:20 unto **t.** people a fenced brasen wall: 2088
Jer 16:2 have sons or daughters in **t.** place. 2088
Jer 16:3 daughters that are born in **t.** place, ... 2088
Jer 16:3 fathers that begat them in **t.** land; 2088
Jer 16:5 away my peace from **t.** people, ... 2088
Jer 16:6 and the small shall die in **t.** land: 2063
Jer 16:9 cease out of **t.** place in your eyes, ... 2088
Jer 16:10 shew **t.** people all these words, ... 2088
Jer 16:10 Lord pronounced all **t.** great evil 2063
Jer 16:13 I cast you out of **t.** land into a land 2063
Jer 16:21 I will **t.** once cause them to know, ... 2063
Jer 17:24 burden through the gates of **t.** city 2063
Jer 17:25 enter into the gates of **t.** city kings..... 2063
Jer 17:25 and **t.** city shall remain for ever. 2088
Jer 18:6 cannot I do with you as **t.** potter? 2088
Jer 19:3 I will bring evil upon **t.** place, ... 2088
Jer 19:4 me, and have estranged **t.** place, ... 2088
Jer 19:4 **t.** place with the blood of innocents; 2088
Jer 19:6 **t.** place shall no more be called 2088
Jer 19:7 of Judah and Jerusalem in **t.** place; 2088
Jer 19:8 And I will make **t.** city desolate, ... 2063
Jer 19:11 Even so will I break **t.** people and 2088
Jer 19:11 **t.** city, as one breaketh a potter's 2063
Jer 19:12 Thus will I do unto **t.** place, saith 2088
Jer 19:12 and even make **t.** city as Tophet: 2063
Jer 19:15 I will bring upon **t.** city 2063
Jer 20:5 deliver all the strength of **t.** city, ... 2063
Jer 21:4 them into the midst of **t.** city 2063
Jer 21:6 will smite the inhabitants of **t.** city, ... 2063
Jer 21:7 such as are left in **t.** city from the 2063
Jer 21:8 And unto **t.** people thou shalt say, ... 2088
Jer 21:9 abideth in **t.** city shall die by the 2063
Jer 21:10 set my fact against **t.** city for evil, ... 2063
Jer 22:1 of Judah, and speak there **t.** word, ... 2088
Jer 22:3 shed innocent blood in **t.** place 2088
Jer 22:4 if ye do **t.** thing indeed, then shall 2088
Jer 22:4 enter in by the gates of **t.** house 2088
Jer 22:5 **t.** house shall become a desolation. 2088

Jer 22:8 many nations shall pass by **t.** city, ... 2063
Jer 22:8 Lord done thus unto **t.** great city? 2063
Jer 22:11 which went forth out of **t.** place; 2088
Jer 22:12 and shall see **t.** land no more 2063
Jer 22:16 was not **t.** to know me? saith the 1931
Jer 22:21 **T.** hath been thy manner from 2088
Jer 22:28 Is **t.** man Coniah a despised broken 2088
Jer 22:30 Write ye **t.** man childless, a man 2088
Jer 23:6 **t.** is his name whereby he shall be 2088
Jer 23:26 shall **t.** be in the heart of the prophets ......
Jer 23:32 shall not profit **t.** people at all, ... 2088
Jer 23:33 when **t.** people, or the prophet, or a.... 2088
Jer 23:38 Because ye say **t.** word, The burden .. 2088
Jer 24:5 whom I have sent out of **t.** place into.. 2088
Jer 24:6 I will bring them again to **t.** land: 2063
Jer 24:8 residue...that remain in **t.** land, ... 2063
Jer 25:3 even unto **t.** day, that is the three...... 2088
Jer 25:9 will bring them against **t.** land, ... 2063
Jer 25:11 **t.** whole land shall be a desolation, ... 2063
Jer 25:13 even all that is written in **t.** book, ... 2088
Jer 25:15 Take the wine cup of **t.** fury at my..... 2063
Jer 25:18 and a curse; as it is **t.** day; 2088
Jer 26:1 Judah came **t.** word from the Lord,..... 2088
Jer 26:6 will I make **t.** house like Shiloh, ... 2088
Jer 26:6 **t.** city a curse to all the nations 2063
Jer 26:9 **T.** house shall be like Shiloh, ... 2088
Jer 26:9 **t.** city shall be desolate without an...... 2063
Jer 26:11 **T.** man is worthy to die; for he 2088
Jer 26:11 he hath prophesied against **t.** city, ... 2063
Jer 26:12 me to prophesy against **t.** house 2088
Jer 26:12 and against **t.** city all the words 2063
Jer 26:15 upon yourselves, and upon **t.** city, ... 2063
Jer 26:16 **T.** man is not worthy to die: for 2088
Jer 26:20 against **t.** city and against **t.** land........ 2063
Jer 27:1 came **t.** word unto Jeremiah from 2088
Jer 27:16 to the priests and to all **t.** people, ... 2088
Jer 27:17 should **t.** city be laid waste? 2063
Jer 27:19 of the vessels that remain in **t.** city, ... 2063
Jer 27:22 up, and restore them to **t.** place. 2008
Jer 28:3 will I bring again into **t.** place all 2008
Jer 28:3 Babylon took away from **t.** place, ... 2008
Jer 28:4 And I will bring again to **t.** place 2008
Jer 28:6 captive, from Babylon into **t.** place...... 2008
Jer 28:7 hear thou now **t.** word that I speak 2008
Jer 28:15 makest **t.** people to trust in a lie. 2008
Jer 28:16 **t.** year thou shalt die, because thou ....
Jer 29:10 causing you to return to **t.** place. 2088
Jer 29:16 the people that dwelleth in **t.** city, ... 2063
Jer 29:28 saying, **T.** captivity is long: 1931
Jer 29:29 and Zephaniah the priest read **t.** letter.......
Jer 29:32 a man to dwell among **t.** people; 2088
Jer 30:17 **T.** is Zion, whom no man seeketh 1931
Jer 30:21 who is **t.**...engaged his heart...... 1931,2088
Jer 31:23 shall use **t.** speech in the land 1931,2088
Jer 31:26 Upon **t.** I awaked, and beheld; 2063
Jer 31:33 **t.** shall be the covenant that I will 2063
Jer 32:3 will give **t.** city into the hand of the 2063
Jer 32:8 that **t.** was the word of the Lord........ 1931
Jer 32:14 **t.** evidence of the purchase, both 2088
Jer 32:14 and **t.** evidence which is open; 2088
Jer 32:15 be possessed again in **t.** land. 2063
Jer 32:20 land of Egypt, even unto **t.** day, ... 2088
Jer 32:20 made thee a name, as at **t.** day; 2088
Jer 32:22 And hast given them **t.** land, ... 2063
Jer 32:23 all **t.** evil to come upon them: 2063
Jer 32:28 give **t.** city into the hand of the 2063
Jer 32:29 Chaldeans, that fight against **t.** city, ... 2063
Jer 32:29 shall come and set fire on **t.** city, ... 2063
Jer 32:31 For **t.** city hath been to me as a 2063
Jer 32:31 that they built it even unto **t.** day; 2088
Jer 32:35 they should do **t.** abomination, ... 2063
Jer 32:36 concerning **t.** city, whereof ye say; 2063
Jer 32:37 I will bring them again into **t.** place, ... 2088
Jer 32:41 will plant them in **t.** land assuredly...... 2063
Jer 32:42 as I have brought all **t.** great evil 2063
Jer 32:42 evil upon **t.** people, so will I bring 2088
Jer 32:43 fields shall be bought in **t.** land, ... 2063
Jer 33:4 concerning the houses of **t.** city, ... 2063
Jer 33:5 I have hid my face from **t.** city. 2063
Jer 33:10 there shall be heard in **t.** place, ... 2088
Jer 33:12 Again in **t.** place, which is desolate 2088
Jer 33:16 **t.** is the name wherewith she shall 2088
Jer 33:24 not what **t.** people have spoken, ... 2088
Jer 34:2 give **t.** city into the hand of the 2063
Jer 34:8 **T.** is the word that came unto ....
Jer 34:22 cause them to return to **t.** city; 2063

Jer 35:14 for unto **t.** day they drink none, ... 2088
Jer 35:16 **t.** people hath not hearkened unto 2088
Jer 36:1 **t.** word came unto Jeremiah from 2088
Jer 36:2 days of Josiah, even unto **t.** day. 2088
Jer 36:7 hath pronounced against **t.** people. 2088
Jer 36:29 Thou hast burned **t.** roll, saying, ... 2063
Jer 36:29 certainly come and destroy **t.** land, ... 2063
Jer 37:8 and fight against **t.** city, and take it, ... 2063
Jer 37:10 his tent, and burn **t.** city with fire. 2063
Jer 37:18 thy servants, or against **t.** people. 2088
Jer 37:19 against you, nor against **t.** land? 2063
Jer 38:2 He that remaineth in **t.** city shall 2063
Jer 38:3 **T.** city shall surely be given into 2063
Jer 38:4 thee, let **t.** man be put to death: 2088
Jer 38:4 men of war that remain in **t.** city, ... 2063
Jer 38:4 for **t.** man seeketh not the welfare 2088
Jer 38:4 welfare for **t.** people, but the hurt. 2088
Jer 38:16 Lord liveth, that made us **t.** soul, ... 2063
Jer 38:17 **t.** city shall not be burned with fire; 2063
Jer 38:18 **t.** city be given into the hand of the 2063
Jer 38:21 **t.** is the word that the Lord hath 2088
Jer 38:23 **t.** city to be burned with fire, ... 2063
Jer 39:16 bring my words upon **t.** city for evil, ... 2063
Jer 40:2 thy God hath pronounced **t.** evil 2063
Jer 40:2 evil upon **t.** place. 2088
Jer 40:3 **t.** thing is come upon you. 2088
Jer 40:4 I loose thee **t.** day from the chains ....
Jer 40:16 Thou shalt not do **t.** thing: for 2088
Jer 42:2 thy God, even for all **t.** remnant; 2063
Jer 42:10 If ye will still abide in **t.** land, then 2063
Jer 42:13 say, We will not dwell in **t.** land, ... 2063
Jer 42:18 and ye shall see **t.** place no more. 2088
Jer 42:19 that I have admonished you **t.** day. ....
Jer 42:21 now I have **t.** day declared it to you: ....
Jer 44:2 **t.** day they are a desolation, and 2088
Jer 44:4 do not **t.** abominable thing that 2088
Jer 44:6 wasted and desolate, as at **t.** day. 2088
Jer 44:7 Wherefore commit ye **t.** great evil ....
Jer 44:10 are not humbled even unto **t.** day, ... 2088
Jer 44:22 without an inhabitant, as at **t.** day...... 2088
Jer 44:23 therefore **t.** evil is happened unto 2063
Jer 44:23 happened unto you, as at **t.** day. 2088
Jer 44:29 And **t.** shall be a sign unto you, ... 2063
Jer 44:29 that I will punish you in **t.** place, ... 2088
Jer 45:4 I will pluck up, even **t.** whole land. 1931
Jer 46:7 Who is **t.** that cometh up as a 2088
Jer 46:10 **t.** is the day of the Lord God of 1931
Jer 50:17 and last **t.** Nebuchadrezzar king of 2088
Jer 50:25 **t.** is the work of the Lord god of 1931
Jer 51:6 for **t.** is the time of the Lord's 1931
Jer 51:59 And **t.** Seraiah was a quiet prince. ....
Jer 51:62 thou hast spoken against **t.** place, ... 2088
Jer 51:63 made an end of reading **t.** book, ... 2088
Jer 52:28 **T.** is the people...Nebuchadrezzar 2088
La 2:15 Is **t.** the city that men call The 2088
La 2:16 **t.** is the day that we looked for; 2088
La 2:20 to whom thou hast done **t.** 3541
La 3:21 **T.** I recall to my mind, therefore 2063
La 5:17 For **t.** our heart is faint; for these 2088
Eze 1:5 **t.** was their appearance; they had 2088
Eze 1:23 had two, which covered on **t.** side, ... 2007
Eze 1:28 **T.** was the appearance of the 1931
Eze 2:3 against me, even unto **t.** very day. 2088
Eze 3:1 eat **t.** roll, and go speak unto the 2063
Eze 3:3 fill thy bowels with **t.** roll that I 2063
Eze 4:3 **T.** shall be a sign to the house of 1931
Eze 5:5 **T.** is Jerusalem: I have set it in 2063
Eze 6:10 that I would do **t.** evil unto them. 2063
Eze 8:5 **t.** image of jealousy in the entry 2088
Eze 8:15, 17 Hast thou seen **t.**, O son of man? ....
Eze 10:15, 20 **T.** is the living creature that I 1931
Eze 11:2 and give wicked counsel in **t.** city: 2063
Eze 11:3 **t.** city is the caldron, and we be 1931
Eze 11:6 multiplied your slain in **t.** city, ... 2063
Eze 11:7 flesh, and **t.** city is the caldron: 1931
Eze 11:11 **T.** city shall not be your caldron, ... 1931
Eze 11:15 unto us is **t.** land given in 1931
Eze 12:10 **T.** burden concerneth the prince 2088
Eze 12:23 I will make **t.** proverb to cease, and ... 2088
Eze 16:20 **t.** of thy whoredoms a small matter. ....
Eze 16:43 shall not commit **t.** lewdness above all ....
Eze 16:44 shall use **t.** proverb against thee, ...
Eze 16:49 **t.** was the iniquity of thy sister 2088
Eze 17:7 **t.** vine did bend her roots toward 2063
Eze 18:2 use **t.** proverb concerning the land 2088
Eze 18:3 more to use **t.** proverb in Israel. 2088

Mk 1:27 saying, What thing is t.? what 3778
Mk 1:27 what new doctrine is t.? for with 5124
Mk 2:7 Why doth t. man thus speak 3778
Mk 2:12 We never saw it on t. fashion 3779
Mk 4:13 them, Know ye not t. parable? 5026
Mk 4:19 And the cares of t. world, and the 3588
Mk 4:41 What manner of man is t., that even 3778
Mk 5:32 to see her that had done t. thing 5124
Mk 5:39 Why make ye t. ado, and weep?
Mk 6:2 whence hath t. man these things? 5129
Mk 6:2 what wisdom is t. which is given 3588
Mk 6:3 Is not t. the carpenter, the son of 3778
Mk 6:35 T. is a desert place, and now the 3588
Mk 7:6 T. people honoureth me with their 3778
Mk 7:29 unto her, For t. saying go thy way; 5126
Mk 8:12 Why doth t. generation seek after 3778
Mk 8:12 sign be given unto t. generation 5026
Mk 8:38 t. adulterous and sinful generation; 5026
Mk 9:7 T. is my beloved Son: hear him 3778
Mk 9:21 is it ago since t. came unto him? 5124
Mk 9:29 T. kind can come forth by nothing, 5124
Mk 10:5 your heart he wrote you t. precept. 5026
Mk 10:7 t. cause shall a man leave his 5127
Mk 10:30 an hundredfold now in t. time, 5129
Mk 11:3 man say unto you, Why do ye t.? 5124
Mk 11:23 shall say unto t. mountain, Be 5129
Mk 11:28 who gave thee t. authority to do 5026
Mk 12:7 among themselves, T. is the heir; 3778
Mk 12:10 And have ye not read t. scripture; 5026
Mk 12:11 T. was the Lord's doing, and it is 3778
Mk 12:16 is t. image and superscription? 3778
Mk 12:30 t. is the first commandment 3778
Mk 12:30 the second is like, namely t., 3778
Mk 12:43 t. poor widow hath cast more in, 3778
Mk 13:19 which God created unto t. time, 3568
Mk 13:30 that t. generation shall not pass, 3778
Mk 14:4 Why was t. waste of the ointment 3778
Mk 14:9 t. gospel shall be preached 5124
Mk 14:9 t. also that she hath done shall be
Mk 14:22 and said, Take, eat: t. is my body 5124
Mk 14:24 T. is my blood of the new 5124
Mk 14:27 offended because of me t. night: 5026
Mk 14:30 I say unto thee, That t. day, 4594
Mk 14:30 even in t. night, before the cock 5026
Mk 14:36 thee; take away t. cup from me: 5124
Mk 14:58 destroy t. temple that is made 5126
Mk 14:69 that stood by, T. is one of them 3778
Mk 14:71 I know not t. man of whom ye 5126
Mk 15:39 Truly t. man was the Son of God 3778
Lu 1:18 angel, Whereby shall I know it? 5124
Lu 1:29 manner of salutation t. should be 3778
Lu 1:34 How shall t. be, seeing I know not 5124
Lu 1:36 t. is the sixth month with her, who 3778
Lu 1:43 And whence is t. to me, that the 5124
Lu 1:61 kindred that is called by t. name 5129
Lu 1:66 What manner of child shall t. be! 5124
Lu 2:2 (And t. taxing was first made when 3778
Lu 2:11 is born t. day in the city of David a 4594
Lu 2:12 t. shall be a sign unto you; ye shall 5124
Lu 2:15 t. thing which is come to pass, 5124
Lu 2:17 was told them concerning t. child 5127
Lu 2:34 t. child is set for the fall and rising 3778
Lu 3:20 Added yet t. above all, that he shut 5124
Lu 4:3 t. stone that it be made bread 5129
Lu 4:6 All t. power will I give thee, and 5026
Lu 4:21 T. day is...scripture fulfilled in 4594
Lu 4:21 is t. scripture fulfilled in your 3778
Lu 4:22 they said, Is not t. Joseph's son? 3778
Lu 4:23 will surely say unto me t. proverb, 5026
Lu 4:36 saying, What a word is t.! for 3778
Lu 5:6 And when they had t. done, they 5124
Lu 5:21 saying, Who is t. which speaketh 3778
Lu 6:3 Have ye not read so much as t., 5124
Lu 7:4 worthy for whom he should do t. 5124
Lu 7:8 my servant, Do t., and he doeth it 5124
Lu 7:17 t. rumour of him went forth 3778
Lu 7:27 T. is he, of whom it is written, 3778
Lu 7:31 I liken the men of t. generation? 5026
Lu 7:39 T. man, if he were a prophet, 3778
Lu 7:39 manner of woman t....that toucheth 3588
Lu 7:44 unto Simon, Seest thou t. woman? 5026
Lu 7:45 t. woman since the time I came in, 3778
Lu 7:46 t. woman hath anointed my feet 3778
Lu 7:49 Who is t. that forgiveth sins also? 3778
Lu 8:9 saying, What might t. parable be? 3778
Lu 8:11 Now the parable is t.: The seed is 3778
Lu 8:14 and riches and pleasures of t. life, 3588
Lu 8:25 another, What manner of man is t.! 3778
Lu 9:9 but who is t., of whom I hear such 3778
Lu 9:13 go and buy meat for all t. people 5126
Lu 9:35 T. is my beloved Son: hear him 3778
Lu 9:45 they understood not t. saying, 5127
Lu 9:48 shall receive t. child in my name 5124
Lu 9:54 his disciples James and John saw t.,
Lu 10:5 first say, Peace be to t. house 5129
Lu 10:11 notwithstanding be ye sure of t., 5124
Lu 10:20 Notwithstanding in t. rejoice not, 5129
Lu 10:28 right: t. do, and thou shalt live 5124
Lu 11:29 to say, T. is an evil generation: 3778
Lu 11:30 the Son of man be to t. generation. 5026
Lu 11:31 with the men of t. generation, 5026
Lu 11:32 the judgment with t. generation, 5026
Lu 11:50 may be required of t. generation; 5026
Lu 11:51 shall be required of t. generation 5026
Lu 12:18 And he said, T. will I do: I will 5124
Lu 12:20 t. night thy soul shall be required 5026
Lu 12:39 t. know, that if the goodman of 5124
Lu 12:41 speakest thou t. parable unto us, 5026
Lu 12:56 is it that ye do not discern t. time? 5126
Lu 13:6 He spake also t. parable; A certain 5026
Lu 13:7 I come seeking fruit on t. fig tree, 5026
Lu 13:8 Lord, let it alone t. year also, till I 5124
Lu 13:16 And ought not t. woman, being a 5026
Lu 13:16 be loosed from t. bond on the 5127
Lu 14:9 and say to thee, Give t. man place; 5129
Lu 14:30 T. man began to build, and was 3778
Lu 15:2 T. man receiveth sinners, and 3778
Lu 15:3 And he spake t. parable unto them, 5026
Lu 15:24 t. my son was dead, and is alive 3778
Lu 15:30 as soon as t. thy son was come, 3778
Lu 15:32 t. thy brother was dead, and is 3778
Lu 16:2 How is it that I hear t. of thee? 5124
Lu 16:8 children of t. world are in their 5127
Lu 16:24 for I am tormented in t. flame 5026
Lu 16:26 beside all t., between us and you 5125
Lu 16:28 also come into t. place of torment 5126
Lu 17:6 might say unto t. sycamine tree, 5026
Lu 17:18 give glory to God, save t. stranger. 3778
Lu 17:25 and be rejected of t. generation 5026
Lu 18:1 a parable unto them to t. end, 3588
Lu 18:5 because t. widow troubleth me, I 5026
Lu 18:9 he spake t. parable unto certain 5026
Lu 18:11 adulterers, or even as t. publican 3778
Lu 18:14 t. man went down to his house 3778
Lu 18:23 And when he heard t., he was very 5023
Lu 18:30 manifold more in t. present time, 5129
Lu 18:34 t. saying was hid from them, 5124
Lu 19:9 him, T. day is salvation come 4594
Lu 19:9 is salvation come to t. house, 5129
Lu 19:14 not have t. man to reign over us 5126
Lu 19:42 known,...at least in t. thy day, 5026
Lu 20:2 is he that gave thee t. authority? 5026
Lu 20:9 he to speak to the people t. parable; 5026
Lu 20:14 T. is the heir: come, let us kill 3778
Lu 20:17 What is t. then that is written, 5124
Lu 20:19 spoken t. parable against them 5026
Lu 20:34 The children of t. world marry, 5126
Lu 21:3 t. poor widow hath cast in more 3778
Lu 21:23 the land, and wrath upon t. people. 5129
Lu 21:32 T. generation shall not pass away, 3778
Lu 21:34 drunkenness, and cares of t. life,
Lu 22:15 to eat t. passover with you before 5124
Lu 22:17 Take t., and divide it among 5124
Lu 22:19 T. is my body which is given for 5124
Lu 22:19 you: t. do in remembrance of me 5124
Lu 22:20 T. cup is the new testament in my 5124
Lu 22:23 them it was that should do t. thing 5124
Lu 22:34 the cock shall not crow t. day, 4594
Lu 22:37 that t. is written must yet be 5124
Lu 22:42 be willing, remove t. cup from me: 5124
Lu 22:53 but t. is your hour, and the power 3778
Lu 22:56 said, T. man was also with him 3778
Lu 22:59 Of a truth t. fellow also was with 3778
Lu 23:2 We found t. fellow perverting the 5126
Lu 23:4 people, I find no fault in t. man 5129
Lu 23:5 beginning from Galilee to t. place 5602
Lu 23:14 Ye have brought t. man unto me, 5129
Lu 23:14 have found no fault in t. man 5126
Lu 23:18 Away with t. man, and release unto 5126
Lu 23:38 T. Is The King Of The Jews 3778
Lu 23:41 t. man hath done nothing amiss 3778
Lu 23:47 Certainly t. was a righteous man 3778
Lu 23:52 T. man went unto Pilate, and 3778
Lu 24:21 and beside all t., to day is the third 5125
Joh 1:15 T. was he of whom I spake, He 3778
Joh 1:19 t. is the record of John, when the 3778
Joh 1:30 T. is he of whom I said, After me 3778
Joh 1:34 bare record that t. is the Son of God 3778
Joh 2:11 T. beginning of miracles did Jesus 5026
Joh 2:12 After t. he went...to Capernaum, 5124
Joh 2:19 Destroy t. temple, and in three 5126
Joh 2:20 Forty and six years was t. temple 3778
Joh 2:22 that he had said t. unto them; 5124
Joh 3:19 And t. is the condemnation, that 3778
Joh 3:29 voice: t. my joy therefore is fulfilled 3778
Joh 4:13 drinketh of t. water shall thirst 5127
Joh 4:15 Sir, give me t. water, that I thirst 5124
Joh 4:20 fathers worshipped in t. mountain; 5124
Joh 4:21 shall neither in t. mountain, nor 5129
Joh 4:27 And upon t. came his disciples, and 5129
Joh 4:29 that ever I did: is not t. the Christ? 3778
Joh 4:42 know that t. is indeed the Christ, 3778
Joh 4:54 T. is again the second miracle 5124
Joh 5:1 After t. there was a feast of the 5023
Joh 5:28 Marvel not at t.: for the hour is 5124
Joh 6:6 And t. he said to prove him: for he 5124
Joh 6:14 T. is of a truth that prophet that 3778
Joh 6:29 T. is the work of God, that ye 5124
Joh 6:34 Lord, evermore give us t. bread 5126
Joh 6:39 t. is the Father's will which hath 5124
Joh 6:40 t. is the will of him that sent me, 5124
Joh 6:42 Is not t. Jesus, the son of Joseph, 3778
Joh 6:50 T. is the bread which cometh down 3778
Joh 6:51 if any man eat of t. bread, he shall 5127
Joh 6:52 How can t. man give us his flesh 3778
Joh 6:58 T. is that bread which came down 3778
Joh 6:58 he that eateth of t. bread shall live 5126
Joh 6:60 disciples, when they heard t., said,
Joh 6:60 T. is an hard saying; who can 3778
Joh 6:61 unto them, Doth t. offend you? 5124
Joh 7:8 Go ye up unto t. feast: I go not up. 5026
Joh 7:8 I go not up yet unto t. feast; for 5026
Joh 7:15 How knoweth t. man letters, 3778
Joh 7:25 Is not t. he, whom they seek to kill? 3778
Joh 7:26 indeed that t. is the very Christ? 3778
Joh 7:27 we know t. man whence he is: but 5126
Joh 7:31 these which t. man hath done? 3778
Joh 7:36 What manner of saying is t. that he 3778
Joh 7:39 (But t. spake he of the Spirit, which 5124
Joh 7:40 when they heard t. saying, 3588
Joh 7:40 said, Of a truth t. is the Prophet 3778
Joh 7:41 Others said, T. is the Christ. But 3778
Joh 7:46 Never man spake like t. man 3778
Joh 7:49 t. people who knoweth not the law 3778
Joh 8:4 t. woman was taken in adultery, 3778
Joh 8:6 T. they said, tempting him, that 5124
Joh 8:23 am from above: ye are of t. world; 5127
Joh 8:23 I am not of t. world 5127
Joh 8:40 heard of God: t. did not Abraham. 5124
Joh 9:2 who did sin, t. man, or his parents, 3778
Joh 9:3 Neither hath t. man sinned, nor 3778
Joh 9:8 Is not t. he that sat and begged? 3778
Joh 9:9 Some said, T. is he: others said, 3778
Joh 9:16 T. man is not of God, because he 3778
Joh 9:19 Is t. your son, who...was born blind? 3778
Joh 9:20 We know that t. is our son, and 3778
Joh 9:24 we know that t. man is a sinner 3778
Joh 9:29 as for t. fellow, we know not from 5126
Joh 9:33 If t. man were not of God, he 3778
Joh 9:39 judgment I am come into t. world 5126
Joh 10:6 T. parable spake Jesus unto them:
Joh 10:16 sheep I have,...are not of t. fold: 5026
Joh 10:18 T. commandment have I received 5026
Joh 10:41 John spake of t. man were true 5127
Joh 11:4 T. sickness is not unto death, but 3778
Joh 11:9 he seeth the light of t. world 5127
Joh 11:26 shall never die. Believest thou t.? 5124
Joh 11:37 Could not t. man, which opened 3778
Joh 11:37 even t. man should not have died? 3778
Joh 11:39 him, Lord, by t. time he stinketh: 2235
Joh 11:47 for t. man doeth many miracles 3778
Joh 11:51 And t. spake he not of himself: but 5124
Joh 12:5 t. ointment sold for three hundred 5124
Joh 12:6 T. he said, not that he cared for the 5124
Joh 12:7 day of my burying hath she kept t. 846
Joh 12:18 t. cause the people also met him, 5124
Joh 12:18 heard that he had done t. miracle 5124
Joh 12:25 he that hateth his life in t. world 5129

Joh 12:27 say? Father, save me from t. hour: 5026
Joh 12:27 for t. cause came I unto...hour. 5124
Joh 12:27 cause came I unto t. hour. 5026
Joh 12:30 T. voice came not because of me, 3778
Joh 12:31 Now is the judgment of t. world: 5127
Joh 12:31 the prince of t. world be cast out. 5127
Joh 12:33 T. he said, signifying what death 5124
Joh 12:34 lifted up? who is t. Son of man? 3778
Joh 13:1 out of t. world unto the Father, 5127
Joh 13:28 what intent he spake t. unto him. 5124
Joh 13:35 t. shall all men know that ye are 5129
Joh 14:30 for the prince of t. world cometh, 3127
Joh 15:12 T. is my commandment, That ye 3778
Joh 15:13 Greater love hath no man than t. 5026
Joh 15:25 But t. cometh to pass, that the word
Joh 16:11 the prince of t. world is judged, 5127
Joh 16:17 What is t. that he saith unto us, 5124
Joh 16:18 what is t. that he saith, A little 5124
Joh 16:30 by t. we believe that thou camest 5129
Joh 17:3 t. is life eternal, that they might 3778
Joh 18:17 also one of t. man's disciples? 5127
Joh 18:29 accusation bring ye against t. man? 5127
Joh 18:34 Sayest thou t. thing of thyself, or 5124
Joh 18:36 My kingdom is not of t. world: 5127
Joh 18:36 my kingdom were not of t. world, 5127
Joh 18:37 I am a king. To t. end was I born, 5124
Joh 18:37 for t. cause came I into the world, 5124
Joh 18:38 when he had said t., he went out 5124
Joh 18:40 saying, Not t. man, but Barabbas. 5126
Joh 19:12 If thou let t. man go, thou art not 5126
Joh 19:20 T. title then read many of the Jews: 5126
Joh 19:28 After t., Jesus knowing that all 5124
Joh 19:38 And after t. Joseph of Arimathaea, 5023
Joh 20:22 And when he had said t., he 5124
Joh 20:30 which are not written in t. book: 5129
Joh 21:1 and on t. wise shewed he himself. 3779
Joh 21:14 T. is now the third time that 5124
Joh 21:19 T. spake he, signifying by what 5124
Joh 21:19 when he had spoken t., he saith 5124
Joh 21:21 Lord, and what shall t. man do? 3778
Joh 21:23 Then went t. saying abroad 3778
Joh 21:24 T. is the disciple which testifieth 3778
Ac 1:6 wilt thou at t. time restore again 5129
Ac 1:11 t. same Jesus, which is taken up 3778
Ac 1:16 t. scripture must needs have been 5026
Ac 1:17 had obtained part of t. ministry. 5026
Ac 1:18 Now t. man purchased a field 3778
Ac 1:25 he may take part of t. ministry 5026
Ac 2:6 Now when t. was noised abroad, the 5026
Ac 2:12 one to another, What meaneth t.? 5124
Ac 2:14 t. known unto you, and hearken to 5124
Ac 2:16 t. is that which was spoken by the 5124
Ac 2:29 his sepulchre is with us unto t. day. 5026
Ac 2:31 seeing t. before spake of...resurrection
Ac 2:32 T. Jesus hath God raised up, 5126
Ac 2:33 he hath shed forth t., which ye 5124
Ac 2:37 they heard t., they were pricked in
Ac 2:40 Save yourselves from t. untoward 5026
Ac 3:12 men of Israel, why marvel ye at t.? 5129
Ac 3:12 we had made t. man to walk? 846
Ac 3:16 name hath made t. man strong, 5026
Ac 3:16 given him t. perfect soundness 5126
Ac 4:7 by what name, have ye done t.? 5124
Ac 4:9 If we t. day be examined of the 4594
Ac 4:10 by him doth t. man stand here 3778
Ac 4:11 T. is the stone which was set at 3778
Ac 4:17 speak...to no man in t. name. 5129
Ac 4:22 on whom t. miracle of healing was 5124
Ac 5:4 conceived t. thing in thine heart? 5124
Ac 5:20 to the people all the words of t. life. 5026
Ac 5:24 of them whereunto t. would grow. 5124
Ac 5:28 ye should not teach in t. name? 5129
Ac 5:28 to bring t. man's blood upon us. 5127
Ac 5:37 After t. man rose up Judas of 5126
Ac 5:38 for if t. (3778) counsel or t. work 5124
Ac 6:3 we may appoint over t. business. 5026
Ac 6:13 T. man ceaseth not to speak 5127
Ac 6:13 words against t. holy place, and 3778
Ac 6:14 t. Jesus of Nazareth shall destroy 5126
Ac 6:14 of Nazareth shall destroy t. place, 3778
Ac 7:4 he removed him into t. land, 5026
Ac 7:6 And God spake on t. wise, That 3779
Ac 7:7 forth, and serve me in t. place. 5129
Ac 7:29 Then fled Moses at t. saying, and 5129
Ac 7:35 T. Moses whom they refused, 5126
Ac 7:37 T. is that Moses, which said unto 3778
Ac 7:38 T. is he, that was in the church in 3778
Ac 7:40 for as for t. Moses, which brought 3778
Ac 7:60 Lord, lay not t. sin to their charge. 5026
Ac 7:60 And when he had said t., he fell 5124
Ac 8:10 T. man is the great power of God. 3778
Ac 8:19 Give me also t. power, that on 5026
Ac 8:21 neither part nor lot in t. matter: 5129
Ac 8:22 Repent...of t. thy wickedness, 5026
Ac 8:29 near, and join thyself to t. chariot. 5129
Ac 8:32 the scripture which he read was t., 3778
Ac 8:34 of whom speaketh the prophet t.? 5124
Ac 9:2 if he found any of t. way, whether 3588
Ac 9:13 I have heard by many of t. man, 5127
Ac 9:21 Is not t. he that destroyeth them 3778
Ac 9:21 called on t. name in Jerusalem, 5124
Ac 9:22 proving that t. is very Christ. 3778
Ac 9:36 t. woman was full of good works 3778
Ac 10:16 T. was done thrice: and the 5124
Ac 10:17 what t. vision which he had seen 3588
Ac 10:30 ago I was fasting until t. hour; 5026
Ac 11:10 And t. was done three times: and 5124
Ac 13:17 The God of t. people of Israel chose 5127
Ac 13:23 t. man's seed hath God according 5127
Ac 13:26 you is the word of t. salvation sent 5026
Ac 13:33 Son, t. day have I begotten thee. 4594
Ac 13:34 he said on t. wise, I will give you 3779
Ac 13:38 through t. man is preached unto you 5127
Ac 13:48 when the Gentiles heard t., they were
Ac 15:2 and elders about t. question. 5127
Ac 15:6 for to consider of t. matter. 5127
Ac 15:15 And to t. agree the words of the 5129
Ac 15:16 After t. I will return, and will 5023
Ac 15:23 they wrote letters by them after t. 3592
Ac 16:18 And t. did she many days. But 5124
Ac 16:36 the prison told t. saying to Paul, 5128
Ac 17:3 t. Jesus, whom I preach unto you, 3778
Ac 17:18 said, What will t. babbler say? 3778
Ac 17:19 May we know what t. new doctrine, 3778
Ac 17:23 I found an altar with t. inscription, 3739
Ac 17:30 times of t. ignorance God winked 3588
Ac 17:32 will hear thee again of t. matter. 5127
Ac 18:10 for I have much people in t. city. 5026
Ac 18:13 T. fellow persuadeth men to 3778
Ac 18:18 Paul after t. tarried there yet a good
Ac 18:21 t. feast that cometh in Jerusalem: 3588
Ac 18:25 T. man was instructed in the way 3778
Ac 19:5 When they heard t., they were baptized
Ac 19:10 t. continued by the space of two 5124
Ac 19:17 t. was known to all the Jews and 5124
Ac 19:25 by t. craft we have our wealth. 5026
Ac 19:26 t. Paul hath persuaded and turned 3778
Ac 19:27 not only t. our craft is in danger to 5124
Ac 19:40 in question for t. day's uproar, 4594
Ac 19:40 give an account of t. concourse. 5026
Ac 20:26 Wherefore I take you to record t. 4594
Ac 20:29 For I know t., that after my 5124
Ac 21:11 bind the man that owneth t. girdle, 3778
Ac 21:23 therefore t. that we say to thee: 5124
Ac 21:28 T. is the man, that teacheth all 3778
Ac 21:28 people, and the law, and t. place: 5126
Ac 21:28 and hath polluted t. holy place. 5127
Ac 22:3 in t. city at the feet of Gamaliel, 5026
Ac 22:3 toward God, as ye all are t. day. 4594
Ac 22:4 I persecuted t. way unto the death, 5026
Ac 22:22 gave him audience unto t. word, 5127
Ac 22:26 thou doest: for t. man is a Roman. 3778
Ac 22:28 a great sum obtained I t. freedom. 5026
Ac 23:1 conscience before God until t. day. 5026
Ac 23:9 saying, We find no evil in t. man: 5129
Ac 23:13 which had made t. conspiracy. 5026
Ac 23:17 Bring t. young man unto the chief 5126
Ac 23:18 to bring t. young man unto thee, 5126
Ac 23:25 he wrote a letter after t. manner: 5126
Ac 23:27 T. man was taken of the Jews, and 5126
Ac 24:2 unto t. nation by thy providence, 5129
Ac 24:5 found t. man a pestilent fellow, 5126
Ac 24:10 many years a judge unto t. nation, 5129
Ac 24:14 But t. I confess unto thee, that 5124
Ac 24:21 Except it be for t. one voice, that I 5026
Ac 24:21 called in question by you t. day. 4594
Ac 24:25 Go thy way for t. time; when I 3568
Ac 25:5 down with me, and accuse t. man, 846
Ac 25:24 ye see t. man, about whom all the 5126
Ac 26:2 I shall answer for myself t. day 4594
Ac 26:16 appeared unto thee for t. purpose, 5124
Ac 26:22 I continue unto t. day, witnessing 5026
Ac 26:26 t. thing was not done in a corner. 5124
Ac 26:29 but also all that hear me t. day, 4594
Ac 26:31 T. man doeth nothing worthy of 3778
Ac 26:32 T. man might have been set at 3778
Ac 27:10 I perceive that t. voyage will be 3588
Ac 27:21 to have gained t. harm and loss. 5026
Ac 27:23 stood by me t. night the angel of 5026
Ac 27:33 T. day is the fourteenth day that 4594
Ac 27:34 meat: for t. is for your health: 5124
Ac 28:4 No doubt t. man is a murderer, 3778
Ac 28:9 So when t. was done, others also, 5127
Ac 28:20 For t. cause therefore have I called 5026
Ac 28:20 of Israel I am bound with t. chain. 5026
Ac 28:22 for as concerning t. sect, we know 5026
Ac 28:26 Go unto t. people, and say, 5126
Ac 28:27 heart of t. people is waxed gross, 5127
Ro 1:26 For t. cause God gave them up 5124
Ro 2:3 And thinkest thou t., O man, that 5124
Ro 3:26 at t. time his righteousness: 3588,3568
Ro 4:9 Cometh t. blessedness then upon 3778
Ro 5:2 into t. grace wherein we stand, 5026
Ro 6:6 Knowing t., that our old man is 5124
Ro 7:24 me from the body of t. death? 5127
Ro 8:18 sufferings of t. present time are 3588
Ro 9:9 For t. is the word of promise, At 3778
Ro 9:9 At t. time will I come, and Sarah 5126
Ro 9:10 And not only t.; but when Rebecca
Ro 9:17 for t. same purpose...I raised thee 5124
Ro 10:6 is of faith speaketh on t. wise, 3779
Ro 11:5 t. present time...there is a remnant 3588
Ro 11:8 they should nor hear;) unto t. day. 4594
Ro 11:25 should be ignorant of t. mystery, 5124
Ro 11:27 For t. is my covenant unto them, 3778
Ro 12:2 And be not conformed to t. world: 5129
Ro 13:6 for t. cause pay ye tribute also: 5124
Ro 13:6 continually upon t. very thing. 5124
Ro 13:9 For t., Thou shalt not commit 3588
Ro 13:9 briefly comprehended in t. saying. 5129
Ro 14:9 For to t. end Christ both died, and 5124
Ro 14:13 but judge t. rather, that no man 5124
Ro 15:9 For t. cause I will confess to thee 5124
Ro 15:28 When therefore I have performed t., 5124
Ro 15:28 and have sealed to them t. fruit, 5126
Ro 16:22 I Tertius, who wrote t. epistle, 3588
1Co 1:12 Now t. I say, that every one of you 5124
1Co 1:20 where is the disputer of t. world? 5127
1Co 1:20 foolish the wisdom of t. world? 5127
1Co 2:6 yet not the wisdom of t. world, nor 5127
1Co 2:6 nor of the princes of t. world, that 5127
1Co 2:8 of the princes of t. world knew: 5127
1Co 3:12 man build upon t. foundation gold, 5126
1Co 3:18 seemeth to be wise in t. world, 5129
1Co 3:19 wisdom of t. world is foolishness 5127
1Co 4:11 t. present hour we both hunger, 3588
1Co 4:13 offscouring of all things unto t. day 737
1Co 4:17 For t. cause have I sent unto you 5124
1Co 5:2 he that hath done t. deed might be 5124
1Co 5:3 him that hath so done t. deed, 5124
1Co 5:10 with the fornicators of t. world, 5127
1Co 6:3 more things that pertain to t. life?
1Co 6:4 of things pertaining to t. life,
1Co 7:6 But I speak t. by permission, and 5124
1Co 7:7 one after t. manner, and another 3779
1Co 7:26 t. is good for the present distress, 5124
1Co 7:29 t. I say, brethren, the time is short: 5124
1Co 7:31 And they that use t. world, as not 5127
1Co 7:31 for the fashion of t. world passeth 5129
1Co 7:35 t. I speak for your own profit; not 5124
1Co 8:7 conscience of the idol unto t. hour 737
1Co 8:9 t. liberty of yours become a 3778
1Co 9:3 to them that do examine me is t., 3778
1Co 9:10 For our sakes, no doubt, t. is written:
1Co 9:12 If others be partakers of t. power 3588
1Co 9:12 we have not used t. power; 5026
1Co 9:17 if I do t. thing willingly, I have a 5124
1Co 9:23 t. I do for the gospel's sake, that I 5124
1Co 10:28 T. is offered in sacrifice unto idols, 5124
1Co 11:10 For t. cause ought the woman to 5124
1Co 11:17 in t. that I declare unto you I praise 5124
1Co 11:20 t. is not to eat the Lord's supper.
1Co 11:22 to you? shall I praise you in t.? 5129
1Co 11:24 t. is my body, which is broken for 5124
1Co 11:24 you: t. do in remembrance of me. 5124
1Co 11:25 T. cup is the new testament in my 5124
1Co 11:25 to do t., as oft as ye drink it, in 5124
1Co 11:26 For as often as ye eat t. bread, 5126
1Co 11:26 and drink t. cup, ye do shew the 5124
1Co 11:27 whosoever shall eat t. bread, and 5126
1Co 11:27 and drink t. cup of the Lord, 5126

1Co 11:30 **t.** cause many are weak and sickly...... *5124*
1Co 14:21 lips will I speak unto **t.** people;.......... *5129*
1Co 15:6 greater part remain unto **t.** present,..........
1Co 15:19 If in **t.** life only we have hope in......... *5126*
1Co 15:34 of God: I speak **t.** to your shame. ....
1Co 15:50 Now **t.** I say, brethren, that flesh....... *5124*
1Co 15:53 For **t.** corruptible must be put on....... *5124*
1Co 15:53 **t.** mortal must put on immortality....... *5124*
1Co 15:54 **t.** corruptible shall have put on *5124*
1Co 15:54 and **t.** mortal shall have put on *5124*
1Co 16:12 was not at all to come at **t.** time;....... *3568*
2Co 1:12 our rejoicing is **t.**, the testimony *3778*
2Co 1:15 in **t.** confidence I was minded to *5026*
2Co 2:1 But I determined **t.** with myself, ... *5124*
2Co 2:3 And I wrote **t.** same unto you, lest,.... *5124*
2Co 2:6 to such a man is **t.** punishment, ... *3778*
2Co 2:9 For to **t.** end also did I write, that *5124*
2Co 3:10 glorious had no glory in **t.** respect, ... *5129*
2Co 3:14 until **t.** day remaineth the same........... *4594*
2Co 3:15 But even unto **t.** day, when Moses..... *4594*
2Co 4:1 seeing we have **t.** ministry,................ *5026*
2Co 4:4 god of **t.** world hath blinded the *5127*
2Co 4:7 **t.** treasure in earthen vessels, ... *5126*
2Co 5:1 earthly house of **t.** tabernacle *3588*
2Co 5:2 in **t.** we groan, earnestly desiring......... *5129*
2Co 5:4 that are in **t.** tabernacle do groan, ... *3588*
2Co 7:3 I speak not **t.** to condemn you: for...........
2Co 7:11 behold **t.** selfsame thing, that ye *5124*
2Co 7:11 yourselves...be clear in **t.** matter. *3588*
2Co 8:5 **t.** they did, not as we hoped, but first.......
2Co 8:7 that ye abound in **t.** grace also........... *5124*
2Co 8:10 **t.** is expedient for you, who have....... *5124*
2Co 8:14 at **t.** time your abundance may.... *3588,3568*
2Co 8:19 to travel with us with **t.** grace, ... *5124*
2Co 8:20 Avoiding **t.**, that no man should *5124*
2Co 8:20 in **t.** abundance which is *5026*
2Co 9:3 you should be in vain in **t.** behalf;....... *5129*
2Co 9:4 in **t.** same confident boasting............. *3588*
2Co 9:6 But **t.** I say, He which soweth.............. *5124*
2Co 9:12 the administration of **t.** service........... *5026*
2Co 9:13 the experiment of **t.** ministration *5026*
2Co 10:7 let him of himself think **t.** again,......... *5124*
2Co 10:11 Let such an one think **t.**, that, such.... *5124*
2Co 11:10 man shall stop me of **t.** boasting in *3778*
2Co 11:17 in **t.** confidence of boasting................ *5026*
2Co 12:8 For **t.** thing I besought the Lord *5127*
2Co 12:13 to you? forgive me **t.** wrong............... *5026*
2Co 13:1 **T.** is the third time I am coming *5124*
2Co 13:9 **t.** also we wish, even your perfection.. *5124*
Ga 1:4 deliver us from **t.** present evil *3588*
Ga 3:2 **T.** only would I learn of you,............. *5124*
Ga 3:17 **t.** I say, that the covenant, that.......... *5124*
Ga 4:25 **t.** Agar is mount Sinai in Arabia, ... *3588*
Ga 5:8 **T.** persuasion cometh not of him.......... *3588*
Ga 5:14 is fulfilled in one word, even in **t.**;...... *3588*
Ga 5:16 **T.** I say then, Walk in the Spirit, and........
Ga 6:16 many as walk according to **t.** rule,....... *5129*
Eph 1:21 not only in **t.** world, but also in.......... *3588*
Eph 2:2 according to the course of **t.** world,...... *5127*
Eph 3:1 For **t.** cause, I Paul, the prisoner....... *5127*
Eph 3:8 is **t.** grace given, that I should........... *3778*
Eph 3:14 For **t.** cause I bow my knees unto...... *5127*
Eph 4:17 **T.** I say therefore, and testify in......... *5124*
Eph 5:5 **t.** ye know, that no whoremonger, ... *5124*
Eph 5:31 For **t.** cause shall a man leave his *5127*
Eph 5:32 **T.** is a great mystery: but I speak...... *5124*
Eph 6:1 parents in the Lord: for **t.** is right. *5124*
Eph 6:12 rulers of the darkness of **t.** world, ... *5127*
Php 1:6 Being confident of **t.** very thing,......... *5124*
Php 1:7 meet for me to think **t.** of you all,...... *5124*
Php 1:9 **t.** I pray, that your love may abound... *5124*
Php 1:19 that **t.** shall turn to my salvation *5124*
Php 1:22 flesh, **t.** is the fruit of my labour: *5124*
Php 1:25 having **t.** confidence, I know that.......... *5124*
Php 2:5 Let **t.** mind be in you, which was......... *5124*
Php 3:13 **t.** one thing I do, forgetting those............
Php 3:15 God shall reveal even **t.** unto you......... *5124*
Col 1:9 For **t.** cause we also, since the day *5124*
Col 1:27 the glory of **t.** mystery among the....... *5127*
Col 2:4 And **t.** I say, lest any man should....... *5124*
Col 3:20 **t.** is well pleasing unto the Lord.......... *5124*
Col 4:16 when **t.** epistle is read among you, ... *3588*
1Th 2:13 **t.** cause also thank we God without *5124*
1Th 3:5 For **t.** cause, when I could no............ *5124*
1Th 4:3 For **t.** is the will of God, even your.... *5124*
1Th 4:15 **t.** we say unto you by the word of *5124*
1Th 5:18 **t.** is the will of God in Christ Jesus..... *5124*
1Th 5:27 **t.** epistle be read unto all the holy...... *3588*
2Th 1:11 count you worthy of **t.** calling. *3588*
2Th 2:11 for **t.** cause God shall send them........ *5124*
2Th 3:10 **t.** we commanded you, that if any *5124*
2Th 3:14 man obey not our word by **t.** epistle, .. *3588*
1Ti 1:9 Knowing **t.**, that the law is not.......... *5124*
1Ti 1:15 **T.** is a faithful saying, and worthy....... *3588*
1Ti 1:16 for **t.** cause I obtained mercy, ... *5124*
1Ti 1:18 **T.** charge I commit unto thee, ... *5026*
1Ti 2:3 For **t.** is good and acceptable in.......... *5124*
1Ti 3:1 **T.** is a true saying, If a man desire..... *3588*
1Ti 4:9 **T.** is a faithful saying and worthy......... *3588*
1Ti 4:16 in doing **t.** thou shalt both save.......... *5124*
1Ti 6:7 we brought nothing into **t.** world, ... *3588*
1Ti 6:14 That thou keep **t.** commandment.......... *3588*
1Ti 6:17 them that are rich in **t.** world, ... *3588,3568*
2Ti 1:15 **T.** thou knowest, that all they *5124*
2Ti 2:4 himself with the affairs of **t.** life;..............
2Ti 2:19 standeth sure, having **t.** seal, ... *5026*
2Ti 3:1 **T.** know also, that in the last days...... *5124*
2Ti 3:6 **t.** sort are they which creep into......... *5130*
2Ti 4:10 me, having loved **t.** present world, ... *3588*
Tit 1:5 For **t.** cause left I thee in Crete,......... *5127*
Tit 1:13 **T.** witness is true. Wherefore............ *3778*
Tit 2:12 and godly, in **t.** present world;............ *3588*
Tit 3:8 **T.** is a faithful saying, and these......... *3588*
Heb 1:5 Son, **t.** day have I begotten thee? *4594*
Heb 3:3 For **t.** man was counted worthy of...... *3778*
Heb 4:4 place of the seventh day on **t.** wise, ... *3779*
Heb 4:5 And in **t.** place again, If they shall *5129*
Heb 5:4 man taketh **t.** honour unto himself, ... *3588*
Heb 6:3 And **t.** will he do, if God permit. *5124*
Heb 7:1 **t.** Melchisedec, king of Salem, ... *3778*
Heb 7:4 consider how great **t.** man was, ... *3778*
Heb 7:21 but **t.** with an oath by him that................
Heb 7:24 But **t.** man, because he continueth...... *3588*
Heb 7:27 **t.** he did once, when he offered up..... *5124*
Heb 8:1 which we have spoken **t.** is the sum: ....
Heb 8:3 **t.** man have somewhat...to offer. *5126*
Heb 8:10 **t.** is the covenant that I will make *3778*
Heb 9:8 The Holy Ghost **t.** signifying, that *5124*
Heb 9:11 that is to say, not of **t.** building;......... *5026*
Heb 9:15 for **t.** cause he is the mediator of *5124*
Heb 9:20 **T.** is the blood of the testament.......... *5124*
Heb 9:27 to die, but after **t.** the judgment:......... *5124*
Heb 10:12 **t.** man, after he had offered one *3778*
Heb 10:16 **T.** is the covenant that I will make *3778*
Heb 11:5 his translation he had **t.** testimony, ...
Heb 12:27 **t.** word, Yet once more, signifieth *3588*
Heb 13:19 I beseech you the rather to do **t.**, ... *5124*
Jas 1:3 Knowing **t.**, that the trying of your...........
Jas 1:25 **t.** man shall be blessed in his............. *3778*
Jas 1:26 heart, **t.** man's religion is vain. *5127*
Jas 1:27 before God and the Father is **t.**,.......... *3778*
Jas 2:5 the poor of **t.** world rich in faith,........ *5127*
Jas 3:15 **T.** wisdom descendeth not from.......... *3778*
Jas 4:15 we shall live, and do **t.**, or that.......... *5124*
1Pe 1:25 **t.** is the word which by the gospel *5124*
1Pe 2:19 For **t.** is thankworthy, if a man for *5124*
1Pe 2:20 patiently, **t.** is acceptable with God. *5124*
1Pe 3:5 For after **t.** manner in the old time..... *3779*
1Pe 4:6 **t.** cause was the gospel preached *5124*
1Pe 4:16 let him glorify God in **t.** behalf. *5129*
1Pe 5:12 that **t.** is the true grace of God.......... *5026*
2Pe 1:5 beside **t.**, giving all diligence,............. *5124*
2Pe 1:13 as long as I am in **t.** tabernacle, ... *5129*
2Pe 1:14 I must put off **t.** my tabernacle, ... *3588*
2Pe 1:17 **T.** is my beloved Son, in whom I *3778*
2Pe 1:18 **t.** voice which came from heaven *5026*
2Pe 1:20 Knowing **t.** first, that no prophecy...... *5124*
2Pe 3:1 **T.** second epistle, beloved, I now........ *5026*
2Pe 3:3 Knowing **t.** first, that there shall *5124*
2Pe 3:5 **t.** they willingly are ignorant of, ... *5124*
2Pe 3:8 be not ignorant of **t.** one thing, ... *5124*
1Jo 1:5 **T.** then is the message which we *3778*
1Jo 2:25 And **t.** is the promise that he hath...... *3778*
1Jo 3:3 every man that hath **t.** hope in him..... *5026*
1Jo 3:8 For **t.** purpose the Son of God was *5124*
1Jo 3:10 In **t.** the children of God are *5129*
1Jo 3:11 **t.** is the message that ye heard *2778*
1Jo 3:17 But whoso hath **t.** world's good, ... *3588*
1Jo 3:23 **t.** is his commandment, That we *3778*
1Jo 4:3 **t.** is that spirit of antichrist, ... *5124*
1Jo 4:9 In **t.** was manifested the love of.......... *5129*
1Jo 4:17 as he is, so are we in **t.** world........... *5129*
1Jo 4:21 **t.** commandment have we from.......... *5026*
1Jo 5:2 By **t.** we know that we love the *5129*
1Jo 5:3 **t.** is the love of God, that we keep..... *3778*
1Jo 5:4 **t.** is the victory that overcometh........ *3778*
1Jo 5:6 **T.** is he that came by water and *3778*
1Jo 5:9 **t.** is the witness of God which he....... *3778*
1Jo 5:11 **t.** is the record, that God hath.......... *3778*
1Jo 5:11 life, and **t.** life is in his Son. *3778*
1Jo 5:14 **t.** is the confidence that we have in *3778*
1Jo 5:20 **T.** is the true God, and eternal life. *3778*
2Jo 6 **t.** is love, that we walk after his *3778*
2Jo 6 **T.** is the commandment, That, as....... *3778*
2Jo 7 **T.** is a deceiver and an antichrist....... *3778*
2Jo 10 you, and bring not **t.** doctrine, ... *5026*
Jude 4 old ordained to **t.** condemnation, ... *5124*
Jude 5 though ye once knew **t.**, how *5124*
Re 1:3 that hear the words of **t.** prophecy, ... *3588*
Re 2:6 **t. thou hast, that thou hatest the** .. *5124*
Re 2:24 **as many as have not t. doctrine,** ... *5026*
Re 4:1 After **t.** I looked, and, behold, a......... *5023*
Re 7:9 After **t.** I beheld, and, lo, a great........ *5023*
Re 11:5 he must in **t.** manner be killed........... *3779*
Re 11:15 kingdoms of **t.** world are become *5026*
Re 18:18 What city is like unto **t.** great city! ....
Re 20:5 **T.** is the first resurrection. *3778*
Re 20:14 of fire. **T.** is the second death. *3778*
Re 22:7 sayings of the prophecy of **t.** book...... *5127*
Re 22:9 which keep the sayings of **t.** book: *5127*
Re 22:10 sayings of the prophecy of **t.** book:..... *5127*
Re 22:18 words of the prophecy of **t.** book, ... *5127*
Re 22:18 plagues that are written in **t.** book:..... *5129*
Re 22:19 words of the book of **t.** prophecy, ... *5129*
Re 22:19 which are written in **t.** book. *5026*

THISTLE See also THISTLES.
2Ki 14:9 The **t.** that was in Lebanon sent 2336
2Ki 14:9 Lebanon, and trode down the **t.**. 2336
2Ch 25:18 The **t.** that was in Lebanon sent 2336
2Ch 25:18 Lebanon, and trode down the **t.**. 2336
Ho 10:8 **t.** shall come up on their altars; 1863

THISTLES
Ge 3:18 and **t.** shall it bring forth to thee; 1863
Job 31:40 Let **t.** grow instead of wheat, ... 2336
Mt 7:16 **grapes of thorns, or figs of t.?**........ *5146*

THITHER See also THITHERWARD.
Ge 19:20 Oh, let me escape **t.**, (is it not a little..8033
Ge 19:22 Haste thee, escape **t.**; for I cannot..... 8033
Ge 19:22 do any thing till thou be come **t.** 8033
Ge 24:6 thou bring not my son **t.** again.......... 8033
Ge 24:8 only bring not my son **t.** again ....
Ge 29:3 **t.** were all the flocks gathered: 8033
Ge 39:1 which had brought him down **t.**. 8033
Ge 42:2 get you down **t.**, and buy for us......... 8033
Ex 10:26 serve the Lord, until we come **t.**. 8033
Ex 26:33 bring in **t.** within the vail the ark......... 8033
Nu 35:6 manslayer, that he may flee **t.**.......... 8033
Nu 35:11 that the slayer may flee **t.**, which....... 8033
Nu 35:15 any person unawares may flee **t.**. 8033
De 1:37 saying, Thou also shalt not go in **t.**..... 8033
De 1:38 before thee, he shall go in **t.**. 8033
De 1:39 they shall go in **t.**, and unto them....... 8033
De 4:42 that the slayer might flee **t.**, which..... 8033
De 12:5 ye seek, and **t.** thou shalt come: 8033
De 12:6 And **t.** ye shall bring your burnt 8033
De 12:11 **t.** shall ye bring all that I command...... 8033
De 19:3 parts, that every slayer may flee **t.**...... 8033
De 19:4 of the slayer, which shall flee **t.**, ... 8033
De 32:52 thou shalt not go **t.** unto the land 8033
De 34:4 but thou shalt not go over **t.**. 8033
Jos 7:3 not all the people to labour **t.**; 8033
Jos 7:4 So there went up **t.** of the people 8033
Jos 20:3 and unwittingly may flee **t.**................. 8033
Jos 20:9 person at unawares might flee **t.**, ... 8033
Jg 8:27 Israel went **t.** a whoring after it: 8033
Jg 9:51 and **t.** fled all the men and women,..... 8033
Jg 18:3 they turned in **t.**, and said unto.......... 8033
Jg 18:17 came in **t.**, and took the graven 8033
Jg 19:15 And they turned aside **t.**, to go in 8033
Jg 21:10 sent **t.** twelve thousand men of the..... 8033
1Sa 2:14 unto all the Israelites that came **t.**...... 8033
1Sa 5:8 the ark of the God of Israel about **t.**. ....
1Sa 9:6 new let us go **t.**; peradventure he 8033
1Sa 10:5 when thou art come **t.** to the city,........ 8033
1Sa 10:10 And when they came **t.** to the hill, ... 8033
1Sa 10:22 if the man should yet come **t.**.............. 1988
1Sa 19:23 he went **t.** to Naioth in Ramah:.......... 8033
1Sa 22:1 heard it, they went down **t.** to him. 8033
1Sa 30:7 brought **t.** the ephod to David.................

2Sa 2:2 So David went up t., and his two....... 8033
2Sa 4:6 came t. into the midst of the house, ...
1Ki 6:7 made ready before it was brought t. ....
1Ki 19:9 And he came t. unto a cave, and........ 8033
2Ki 2:8 they were divided hither and t., ... 2008
2Ki 2:14 waters, they parted hither and t......... 2008
2Ki 4:8 by, he turned in t. to eat bread. 8033
2Ki 4:10 to us, that he shall turn in t.. 8033
2Ki 4:11 And it fell on a day, that he came t., .. 8033
2Ki 6:6 cut down a stick, and cast it in t.; 8033
2Ki 6:9 for t. the Syrians are come down. 8033
2Ki 6:14 Therefore sent he t. horses, and........ 8033
2Ki 9:2 And when thou comest t., look out..... 8033
2Ki 17:27 Carry t. one of the priests whom ye... 8033
2Ch 1:6 Solomon went up t. to the brasen 8033
Ezr 10:6 when he came t., he did eat no bread, .8033
Ne 4:20 of the trumpet, resort ye t. unto us:... 8033
Ne 5:16 were gathered t. unto the work. 8033
Ne 13:9 t. brought I again the vessels of......... 8033
Job 1:21 womb, and naked shall I return t......... 8033
Job 6:20 they came t., and were ashamed........ 5704
Ec 1:7 rivers come, t. they return again........ 8033
Isa 7:24 and with bows shall men come t.; 8033
Isa 7:25 not come t. the fears of briers and..... 8033
Isa 32:20 that send forth t. the feet of the ox..........
Isa 55:10 from heaven, and returneth not t., ... 8033
Isa 57:7 t. wentest thou up to offer sacrifice.... 8033
Jer 22:11 He shall not return t. any more: 8033
Jer 22:27 to return, t. shall they not return....... 8033
Jer 31:8 a great company shall return t.. 2008
Jer 40:4 convenient for thee to go, t. go. 8033
Eze 1:20 they went, t. was their spirit to go:..... 8033
Eze 11:18 they shall come t., and they shall....... 8033
Eze 40:1 was upon me, and brought me t......... 8033
Eze 40:3 And he brought me t., and, behold, ... 8033
Eze 47:9 because these waters shall come t........ 8033
Joe 3:11 t. cause thy mighty ones to come....... 8033
Mt 2:22 Herod, he was afraid to go t. 1563
Mk 6:33 and ran afoot t. out of all cities, ... 1563
Lu 17:37 **t. will the eagles be gathered** 1563
Lu 21:2 poor widow casting in t. two mites. 1563
Joh 7:34 **and where I am, t. ye cannot come.** ....
Joh 7:36 and where I am, t. ye cannot come? ....
Joh 11:8 thee; and goest thou t. again? 1563
Joh 18:2 Jesus ofttimes resorted t. with his...... 1563
Joh 18:3 cometh t. with lanterns and torches..... 1563
Ac 8:30 Philip ran t. to him, and heard him 4370
Ac 14:19 came t. certain Jews from Antioch...... 1904
Ac 16:13 unto the women which resorted t.. ....
Ac 17:10 coming t. went into the synagogue 3854
Ac 17:13 they came t. also, and stirred up........ 1563
Ac 25:4 he himself would depart shortly t.. ....

THITHERWARD

Jg 18:15 And they turned t., and came to the... 8033
Jer 50:5 the way to Zion with their faces t.,..... 2008
Ro 15:24 to be brought on my way t. by you, ... 1563

THOMAS (tom'-us) See also DIDYMUS.

Mt 10:3 T., and Matthew the publican; 2381
Mk 3:18 T., and James the son of Alphaeus, ... 2381
Lu 6:15 T., James the son of Alphaeus, ... 2381
Joh 11:16 said T., which is called Didymus, ... 2381
Joh 14:5 T. saith unto him, Lord, we know...... 2381
Joh 20:24 But T., one of the twelve, called........ 2381
Joh 20:26 were within, and T. with them:.......... 2381
Joh 20:27 Then saith he to T., **Reach hither**.... 2381
Joh 20:28 T. answered and said unto him, ... 2381
Joh 20:29 T., **because thou hast seen me,**...... 2381
Joh 21:2 Peter, and T. called Didymus, ... 2381
Ac 1:13 T., Bartholomew, and Matthew,.......... 2381

THONGS

Ac 22:25 as they bound him with t., Paul 2438

THORN See also THORNS.

Job 41:2 or bore his jaw through with a t.? 2336
Pr 26:9 As a t. goeth up into the hand of a..... 2336
Isa 55:13 of the t. shall come up the fir tree, ... 5285
Eze 28:24 grieving t. of all that are round 6975
Ho 10:8 the t. and the thistle shall come up...... 6975
Mic 7:4 upright is sharper than a t. hedge:...... 4534
2Co 12:7 was given to me a t. in the flesh,....... 4647

THORN-HEDGE See THORN and HEDGE.

THORNS

Ge 3:18 T. also and thistles shall it bring......... 6975
Ex 22:6 If fire break out, and catch in t., so.... 6975
Nu 33:55 in your eyes, and t. in your sides,...... 6796
Jos 23:13 in your sides, and t. in your eyes,...... 6796
Jg 2:3 but they shall be as t. in your sides,.........
Jg 8:7 I will tear your flesh with the t.......... 6975
Jg 8:16 and t. of the wilderness and briers, ... 6975
2Sa 23:6 be all of them as t. thrust away, ... 6975
2Ch 33:11 took Manasseh among the t., ... 2336
Job 5:5 and taketh it even out of the t., ... 6791
Ps 58:9 Before your pots can feel the t., he 329
Ps 118:12 they are quenched as the fire of t. 6975
Pr 15:19 slothful man is as an hedge of t. 2312
Pr 22:5 T. and snares are in the way of......... 6791
Pr 24:31 all grown over with t., and nettles...... 7063
Ec 7:6 as the crackling of t. under a pot, ... 5518
Ca 2:2 As the lily among t., so is my love..... 2336
Isa 5:6 there shall come up briers and t......... 7898
Isa 7:19 upon all t., and upon all bushes.......... 5285
Isa 7:23 it shall even be for briers and t.......... 7898
Isa 7:24 the land shall become briers and t.. 7898
Isa 7:25 thither the fear of briers and t........... 7898
Isa 9:18 it shall devour the briers and t.,......... 7898
Isa 10:17 shall burn and devour his t. and his 7898
Isa 27:4 set the briers and t. against me in...... 7898
Isa 32:13 people shall come up t. and briers; 6975
Isa 33:12 t. cut up shall they be burned in the... 6975
Isa 34:13 t. shall come up in her palaces,......... 5518
Jer 4:3 ground, and sow not among t.. 6975
Jer 12:13 have sown wheat, but shall reap t. 6975
Eze 2:6 though briers and t. be with thee, ... 5544
Ho 2:6 I will hedge up thy way with t., ... 5518
Ho 9:6 t. shall be in their tabernacles........... 2336
Na 1:10 while they be folden together as t., ... 5518
Mt 7:16 **Do men gather grapes of t., or figs** . 173
Mt 13:7 **And some fell among t.;** 173
Mt 13:7 **the t. sprung up, and choked them:** .173
Mt 13:22 **also that received seed among the t.** 173
Mt 27:29 when they had platted a crown of t., ... 173
Mk 4:7 **And some fell among t.,** 173
Mk 4:7 **and the t. grew up, and choked it,** .. 173
Mk 4:18 **are they which are sown among t.;** ..173
Mk 15:17 platted a crown of t., and put it........... 174
Lu 6:44 **of t. men do not gather figs, nor of** .173
Lu 8:7 **And some fell among t.;** 173
Lu 8:7 **t. sprang up with it, and choked it**.. 173
Lu 8:14 **that which fell among t. are they,** .. 173
Joh 19:2 the soldiers platted a crown of t., ... 173
Joh 19:5 Jesus forth, wearing the crown of t., ... 174
Heb 6:8 that which beareth t. and briers is 173

THOROUGHLY See also THROUGHLY.

Ex 21:19 shall cause him to be t. healed........... 7495
2Ki 11:18 his images brake they in pieces t., ... 3190

THOSE

Ge 6:4 were giants in the earth in t. days;..... 1992
Ge 15:17 lamp that passed between t. pieces. 428
Ge 19:25 And he overthrew t. cities, and all....... 411
Ge 24:60 possess the gate of t. which hate them......
Ge 33:5 and said, Who are t. with thee?........... 428
Ge 41:35 gather all the food of t. good years 428
Ge 42:5 came to buy corn among t. that came: ......
Ge 50:3 the days of t. which are embalmed: ....
Ex 2:11 And it came to pass in t. days, ... 1992
Ex 4:21 thou do all t. wonders before Pharaoh, ...
Ex 29:33 they shall eat t. things wherewith the........
Ex 35:35 and of t. that devise cunning work............
Le 11:27 all four, t. are unclean unto you: 1992
Le 14:11 and t. things, before the Lord,................
Le 14:42 and put them in the place of t. stones; ......
Le 15:10 that beareth any of t. things shall............
Le 15:27 whosoever toucheth t. things shall be........
Le 22:2 t. things which they hallow unto me:..........
Nu 1:21 T. that were numbered of them, even.......
Nu 1:22 fathers, t. that were numbered of them, ...
Nu 1:23, 25,27,29,31,33,35,37,39,41,43
t. that were numbered of them, even of....
Nu 1:44 These are t. that were numbered,............
Nu 1:45 t. that were numbered of the children ....
Nu 2:4 t. that were numbered of them, were ....
Nu 2:5 t. that do pitch next unto him shall be.......
Nu 2:6, 8,11 t. that were numbered thereof, ...
Nu 2:12 And t. which pitch by him shall be the.........
Nu 2:13 t. that were numbered of them, were ....
Nu 2:15, 19,21,23,26 t. that were numbered of.......
Nu 2:27 t. that encamp by him shall be the............
Nu 2:28, 30 t. that were numbered of them,..............
Nu 2:32 all t. that were numbered of the..............
Nu 2:32 are t. which were numbered of the...........
Nu 3:22 T. that were numbered of them, ...
Nu 3:22 t. that were numbered of them were ....
Nu 3:34 And t. that were numbered of them,.........
Nu 3:38 But t. that encamp before the..................
Nu 3:43 t. that were numbered of them, were ....
Nu 3:46 for t. that are to be redeemed of the........
Nu 4:36 t. that were numbered of them by..............
Nu 4:38 t. that were numbered of the sons of........
Nu 4:40 Even t. that were numbered of them, ...
Nu 4:42 t. that were numbered of the families........
Nu 4:44 t. that were numbered of them after.........
Nu 4:45 These be t. that were numbered of.........
Nu 4:46 t. that were numbered of the Levites,.......
Nu 4:48 Even t. that were numbered of them, ...
Nu 9:7 And t. men said unto him, we are...... 1992
Nu 13:3 all t. men were heads of the children ....
Nu 14:22 t. men which have seen my glory, ... 582
Nu 14:37 t. men that did bring up the evil........... 582
Nu 18:16 And t. that are to be redeemed from a......
Nu 25:9 t. that died in the plague were twenty.......
Nu 26:18, 22,25,27 according to t. that were
numbered of them..................................
Nu 26:34 and t. that were numbered of them, ...
Nu 26:37, 43,47,54 according to t. that were
numbered of.......................................
Nu 26:62 t. that were numbered of them were ....
Nu 33:55 t. which ye let remain of them shall..........
De 7:22 will put out t. nations before thee 411
De 17:9 the judge that shall be in t. days, ... 1992
De 18:9 the abominations of t. nations. 1992
De 19:5 he shall flee unto one of t. cities,.......... 428
De 19:17 judges, which shall be in t. days;........ 1992
De 19:20 And t. which remain shall hear, and..........
De 26:3 the priest that shall be in t. days,....... 1992
De 29:3 the signs, and t. great miracles:......... 1992
De 29:29 but t. things which are revealed..............
De 32:21 with t. which are not a people; ....
Jos 3:16 t. that came down toward the sea of.........
Jos 4:20 t. twelve stones, which they took........ 428
Jos 10:22 and bring out t. five kings unto me 428
Jos 10:23 brought forth t. five kings unto him...... 428
Jos 10:24 brought out t. kings unto Joshua, ... 428
Jos 11:1 king of Hazor had heard t. things, ...
Jos 11:10 was the head of all t. kingdoms. 428
Jos 11:12 And all the cities of t. kings, and all..... 428
Jos 11:18 war a long time with all t. kings. 428
Jos 17:12 drive out the inhabitants of t. cities; 428
Jos 20:4 he that doth flee unto one of t. cities.... 428
Jos 20:6 high priest that shall be in t. days: 1992
Jos 21:16 nine cities out of t. two tribes............. 428
Jos 24:17 which did t. great signs in our sight, ... 428
Jg 2:16 of the hand of t. that spoiled them............
Jg 2:23 the Lord left t. nations, without........... 428
Jg 7:8 and retained t. three hundred men:...........
Jg 11:13 therefore restore t. lands again................
Jg 12:5 t. Ephraimites which were escaped...........
Jg 17:6 In t. days there was no king in.......... 1992
Jg 18:1 In t. days there was no king in.......... 1992
Jg 18:1 in t. days the tribe of the Danites 1992
Jg 19:1 it came to pass in t. days, when 1992
Jg 20:27 of God was there in t. days, ... 1992
Jg 20:28 of Aaron, stood before it in t. days,)... 1992
Jg 21:25 In t. days there was no king in.......... 1992
1Sa 3:1 the Lord was precious in t. days;........ 1992
1Sa 7:16 and judged Israel in all t. places.......... 428
1Sa 10:9 all t. signs came to pass that day.......... 428
1Sa 11:6 upon Saul when he heard t. tidings,....... 428
1Sa 17:11 Saul and all Israel heard t. words of..... 428
1Sa 17:28 whom hast thou left t. few sheep....... 2207
1Sa 18:23 Saul's servants spake t. words in......... 428
1Sa 19:7 Jonathan shewed him all t. things.......... 428
1Sa 25:9 according to all t. words in the............ 428
1Sa 25:12 came and told them all t. sayings.......... 428
1Sa 27:8 for t. nations were of old the............. 2007
1Sa 28:1 And it came to pass in t. days, that.... 1992
1Sa 28:3 had put away t. that had familiar 1992
1Sa 28:9 hath cut off t. that have familiar ....
1Sa 30:9 where t. that were left behind stayed.........
1Sa 30:20 they drave before t. other cattle, ... 1931
1Sa 30:22 of Belial, of t. that went with David, ...
2Sa 5:14 be the names of t. that were born unto.....
2Sa 16:23 which he counselled in t. days, ... 1992
1Ki 2:7 let them be of t. that eat at thy table:.......
1Ki 3:2 name of the Lord, until t. days. 1992
1Ki 4:27 t. officers provided victual for 428

1Ki	8:4	**t.** did the priests and the Levites	
1Ki	9:21	upon **t.** did Solomon levy a tribute of	
1Ki	21:27	when Ahab heard **t.** words, that he	428
2Ki	4:4	shalt pout out into all **t.** vessels,	428
2Ki	6:22	wouldest thou smite **t.** whom thou	
2Ki	10:32	In **t.** days the Lord began to cut	1992
2Ki	15:37	In **t.** days the Lord began to send	1992
2Ki	17:9	did secretly **t.** things that were not	
2Ki	18:4	unto **t.** days the children of Israel	1992
2Ki	20:1	In **t.** days was Hezekiah sick unto	1992
2Ki	24:15	**t.** carried he into captivity from	
1Ch	4:23	and **t.** that dwelt among plants and	
1Ch	16:42	and cymbals for **t.** that should make a	
2Ch	14:6	rest, and he had no war in **t.** years;	428
2Ch	15:5	**t.** times there was no peace to him	1992
2Ch	17:19	**t.** whom the king put in the fenced	
2Ch	20:29	on all the kingdoms of **t.** countries,	
2Ch	32:13	the gods of the nations of **t.** lands	
2Ch	32:14	among all the gods of **t.** nations	428
2Ch	32:24	In **t.** days Hezekiah was sick to	1992
Ezr	1:8	Even **t.** did Cyrus king of Persia bring	
Ezr	2:1	**t.** which had been carried away, whom	
Ezr	2:62	**t.** that were reckoned by genealogy	
Ezr	3:3	because of the people of **t.** countries:	
Ezr	5:9	Then asked we **t.** elders, and said	479
Ezr	5:14	**t.** did Cyrus the king take out of	1994
Ezr	7:19	**t.** deliver thou before the God of	
Ezr	8:35	children of **t.** that had been carried	
Ezr	9:2	themselves with the people of **t.** lands:	
Ezr	9:4	transgression of **t.** that had been	
Ezr	10:3	and of **t.** that trembled at the	
Ezr	10:8	congregation of **t.** that had been	
Ne	4:17	that bare burdens, with **t.** that laded,	
Ne	5:17	beside **t.** that came unto us from	
Ne	6:17	in **t.** days the nobles of Judah sent	1992
Ne	7:6	of **t.** that had been carried away, whom	
Ne	7:64	register among **t.** that were reckoned	
Ne	8:3	women, and **t.** that could understand;	
Ne	10:1	Now **t.** that sealed were, Nehemiah,	
Ne	13:15	In **t.** days saw I in Judah some	1992
Ne	13:23	In **t.** days also saw I Jews that had	1992
Es	1:2	That in **t.** days, when the king	1992
Es	2:21	In **t.** days, while Mordecai sat in	1992
Es	2:21	of **t.** which kept the door, were wroth,	
Es	3:9	the hands of **t.** that have the charge	
Es	9:5	they would unto **t.** that hated them	
Es	9:11	the number of **t.** that were slain in	
Job	5:11	To set up on high **t.** that be low; that	
Job	5:11	**t.** which mourn may be exalted to	
Job	21:22	seeing he judgeth **t.** that are high	
Job	24:13	are of **t.** that rebel against the light;	
Job	24:19	doth the grave **t.** which have sinned,	
Job	27:15	**T.** that remain of him shall be buried	
Ps	5:11	**t.** that put their trust in thee rejoice:	
Ps	13:4	**t.** that trouble me rejoice when I am	
Ps	17:7	thee from **t.** that rise up against them.	
Ps	18:30	is a buckler to all **t.** that trust in him	
Ps	18:39	subdued under me **t.** that rose up	
Ps	18:48	liftest me up above **t.** that rise up	
Ps	21:8	hand shall find out **t.** that hate thee.	
Ps	37:9	**t.** that wait upon the Lord, they shall	
Ps	40:16	Let all **t.** that seek thee rejoice and be	
Ps	50:5	**t.** that have made a covenant with me	
Ps	61:5	the heritage of **t.** that fear thy name.	
Ps	63:9	But **t.** that seek my soul, to destroy it,	
Ps	68:6	he bringeth out **t.** which are bound	
Ps	68:11	the company of **t.** that published it	
Ps	69:6	let not **t.** that seek thee be confounded	
Ps	69:26	they talk to the grief of **t.** whom thou	
Ps	70:4	Let all **t.** that seek rejoice and be	
Ps	74:23	the tumult of **t.** that rise up against	
Ps	79:11	preserve thou **t.** that are appointed to	
Ps	92:13	**T.** that be planted in the house of the	
Ps	102:20	to loose **t.** that are appointed to death;	
Ps	103:18	**t.** that remember his commandments	
Ps	106:46	of all **t.** that carried them captives.	
Ps	109:31	him from **t.** that condemn his soul.	
Ps	119:79	Let **t.** that fear thee turn unto me,	
Ps	119:79	**t.** that have known thy testimonies.	
Ps	119:132	usest to do unto **t.** that love thy name.	
Ps	123:4	the scorning of **t.** that are at ease,	
Ps	125:4	Do good, O Lord, unto **t.** that be good,	
Ps	139:21	I grieved with **t.** that rise up against	
Ps	140:9	As for the head of **t.** that compass me	
Ps	143:3	as **t.** that have been long dead	
Ps	145:14	raiseth up all **t.** that be bowed down	
Ps	147:11	fear him, in **t.** that hope in his mercy.	
Pr	1:12	whole, as **t.** that go down into the pit:	
Pr	4:22	they are life unto **t.** that find them,	
Pr	8:17	**t.** that seek me early shall find me	
Pr	8:21	may cause **t.** that love me to inherit	
Pr	22:23	spoil the soul of **t.** that spoiled them.	
Pr	24:11	death, and **t.** that are ready to be slain;	
Pr	26:28	A lying tongue hateth **t.** that are	
Pr	31:6	and wine unto **t.** that be of heavy	
Ec	1:11	are to come with **t.** that shall come	
Ec	5:14	**t.** riches perish by evil travail:	1931
Ec	7:28	a woman among all **t.** have I not	428
Ec	8:8	deliver **t.** that are given to it.	
Ec	12:3	**t.** that look out of the windows be	
Ca	7:9	the lips of **t.** that are asleep to speak.	
Ca	8:12	and **t.** that keep the fruit thereof two	
Isa	14:19	as the raiment of **t.** that are slain,	
Isa	27:7	him, as he smote **t.** that smote him?	
Isa	35:8	not pass over it; but it shall be for **t.**	
Isa	38:1	In **t.** days was Hezekiah sick unto	1992
Isa	40:11	gently lead **t.** that are with young	
Isa	56:8	beside **t.** that are gathered unto him.	
Isa	60:12	yea, **t.** nations shall be utterly wasted.	
Isa	64:5	**t.** that remember thee in thy ways:	
Isa	64:5	in **t.** is continuance, and we shall	1992
Isa	66:2	all **t.** things hath mine hand made,	428
Isa	66:2	all **t.** things have been, saith the	428
Isa	66:19	**t.** that escape of them unto the	1992
Jer	3:16	in **t.** days, saith the Lord, they	1992
Jer	3:18	In **t.** days the house of Judah	1992
Jer	4:12	full wind from **t.** places shall come	428
Jer	5:18	Nevertheless in **t.** days, saith the	1992
Jer	8:16	it; the city, and **t.** that dwell therein.	
Jer	14:15	and famine shall **t.** prophets be	1992
Jer	21:7	the hand of **t.** that seek their life:	
Jer	27:11	**t.** will I let remain still in their own	
Jer	31:29	In **t.** days they shall say no more,	1992
Jer	31:33	After **t.** days, saith the Lord, I will	1992
Jer	31:36	If **t.** ordinances depart from	428
Jer	33:15	In **t.** days, and at that time, will	1992
Jer	33:16	In **t.** days shall Judah be saved,	1992
Jer	38:22	**t.** women shall say, Thy friends	2007
Jer	39:9	and **t.** that fell away, that fell to him,	
Jer	46:26	the hand of **t.** that seek their lives,	
Jer	49:5	hosts, from all **t.** that be about thee;	
Jer	49:36	scatter them toward all **t.** winds;	428
Jer	50:4,	20 In **t.** days, and in that time,	1992
Jer	52:15	**t.** that fell away, that fell to the king	
La	2:22	**t.** that I have swaddled and brought	
La	3:62	The lips of **t.** that rose up against me,	
Eze	1:21	When **t.** went, these went; and when	
Eze	1:21	and when **t.** stood, these stood; and	
Eze	1:21	when **t.** were lifted up from the earth,	
Eze	18:11	that doeth not any of **t.** duties, but	428
Eze	22:5	**T.** that be near, and **t.** that be far	
Eze	28:26	upon all **t.** that despise them round	
Eze	33:24	that inhabit **t.** wastes of the land	428
Eze	34:27	hand of **t.** that served themselves of	
Eze	38:17	prophesied in **t.** days many years,	1992
Eze	39:10	shall spoil **t.** that spoiled them, and	
Eze	39:10	rob **t.** that robbed them, saith	
Eze	39:14	**t.** that remain on the face of the	
Eze	40:25	round about, like **t.** windows:	428
Eze	42:14	approach of **t.** things which are for	
Da	3:22	flame of the fire slew **t.** men that	479
Da	4:37	**t.** that walk in pride he is able to	1768
Da	6:24	**t.** men which had accused Daniel,	479
Da	10:2	In **t.** days I Daniel was mourning	1992
Da	11:4	up, even for others beside **t.**	428
Da	11:14	And in **t.** times there shall many	1992
Joe	2:16	children, and **t.** that suck the breasts:	
Joe	2:29	**t.** days will I pour out my spirit.	1992
Joe	3:1	For, behold, in **t.** days, and in that	1992
Ob	14	to cut off **t.** of his that did escape;	
Ob	14	have delivered up **t.** of his that did	
Zep	1:6	**t.** that have not sought the Lord,	
Zep	1:9	punish all **t.** that leap on the	
Hag	2:16	Since **t.** days were, when one came to	
Hag	2:22	chariots, and **t.** that ride in them;	
Zec	3:4	spake unto **t.** that stood before him,	
Zec	4:10	hand of Zerubbabel with **t.** seven;	428
Zec	7:5	even **t.** seventy years, did ye at	2088
Zec	8:23	In **t.** days it shall come to pass,	1992
Zec	11:16	which shall not visit **t.** that be cut off,	
Zec	13:6	**T.** with which I was wounded in the	
Zec	14:3	forth, and fight against **t.** nations,	1992
Mal	3:5	against **t.** that oppress the hireling	
Mt	3:1	In **t.** days came John the Baptist,	*1565*
Mt	4:24	**t.**...were possessed with devils,	*3588*
Mt	4:24	devils, and **t.** which were lunatick,	
Mt	4:24	lunatick, and **t.** that had the palsy;	
Mt	11:4	**shew John again t. things which ye**	
Mt	13:17	**desired to see t. things which ye see,**	
Mt	13:17	**and to hear t. things which ye hear,**	
Mt	15:18	**t. things which proceed out of the**	*3588*
Mt	15:30	with them **t.** that were lame, blind,	
Mt	16:23	**be of God, but t. that be of men**	*3588*
Mt	21:40	**will he do unto t. husbandmen?**	*1565*
Mt	21:41	miserably destroy **t.** wicked men,	*846*
Mt	22:7	**and destroyed t. murderers, and**	*1565*
Mt	22:10	**So t. servants went out into the**	*1565*
Mt	24:19	**to them that give suck in t. days!**	*1565*
Mt	24:22	**except t. days should be shortened,**	*1565*
Mt	24:22	**sake t. days shall be shortened**	*1565*
Mt	24:29	**after the tribulation of t. days**	*1565*
Mt	25:7	**Then all t. virgins arose, and**	*1565*
Mt	25:19	**the lord of t. servants cometh,**	*1565*
Mt	27:54	and **t.** things that were done, they	*3588*
Mk	1:9	And it came to pass in **t.** days, that	*1565*
Mk	1:44	**cleansing t. things which Moses**	
Mk	2:20	**then shall they fast in t. days.**	*1565*
Mk	6:55	about in beds **t.** that were sick,	*3588*
Mk	7:15	**t. are they that defile the man.**	*1565*
Mk	8:1	In **t.** days the multitude being very	*1565*
Mk	10:13	disciples rebuked **t.** that brought	*3588*
Mk	11:23	**shall believe that t. things which he**	
Mk	12:7	**But t. husbandmen said among**	*1565*
Mk	13:17	**to them that give suck in t. days!**	*1565*
Mk	13:19	**For in t. days shall be affliction,**	*1565*
Mk	13:20	**the Lord had shortened t. days,**	*3588*
Mk	13:24	**in t. days, after that tribulation,**	*3588*
Lu	1:1	a declaration of **t.** things which are	*3588*
Lu	1:4	know the certainty of **t.** things,	
Lu	1:24	after **t.** days his wife Elisabeth	*5025*
Lu	1:39	Mary arose in **t.** days, and went	*5025*
Lu	1:45	**t.** things which were told her from	*3588*
Lu	2:1	it came to pass in **t.** days, that	*1565*
Lu	2:18	wondered at **t.** things which were told	
Lu	2:33	marvelled at **t.** things which were	*3588*
Lu	4:2	And in **t.** days he did eat nothing:	*1565*
Lu	5:35	**and then shall they fast in t.**	*1565*
Lu	6:12	And it came to pass in **t.** days, that	*5025*
Lu	6:32	**sinners also love t. that love**	*3588*
Lu	7:28	**Among t. that are born of women**	
Lu	8:12	**T. by the way side are they that**	*3588*
Lu	9:36	close, and told no man in **t.** days	*1565*
Lu	9:36	any of **t.** things which they had seen	
Lu	10:24	**desired to see t. things which ye see,**	
Lu	10:24	**and to hear t. things which ye hear,**	
Lu	12:20	**then whose shall t. things be, which**	
Lu	12:37	**Blessed are t. servants, whom**	*1565*
Lu	12:38	**them so, blessed are t. servants.**	*1565*
Lu	13:4	**Or t. eighteen, upon whom the**	*1565*
Lu	14:7	a parable to **t.** which were bidden,	*3588*
Lu	14:24	**t. men which were bidden shall**	*1565*
Lu	17:10	**have done all t. things which**	*3588*
Lu	19:27	**t. mine enemies, which would**	*1565*
Lu	20:1	that on one of **t.** days, as he taught	*1565*
Lu	21:23	**to them that give suck, in t.**	*1565*
Lu	21:26	**looking after t. things which are**	*3588*
Lu	23:14	touching **t.** things whereof ye accuse	
Joh	2:14	in the temple **t.** that sold oxen	*3588*
Joh	6:14	Then **t.** men, when they had seen	*3588*
Joh	8:10	**where are t. thine accusers?**	*1565*
Joh	8:26	**t. things which I have heard of**	*5023*
Joh	8:29	**always t. things that please him.**	*3588*
Joh	8:31	said Jesus to **t.** Jews which believed	*3588*
Joh	10:32	**which of t. works do ye stone me?**	*846*
Joh	13:29	Buy **t.** things that we have need of	
Joh	17:11	**name t. whom thou hast given,**	*846*
Joh	17:12	**t. that thou gavest me I have,**	*846*
Ac	1:15	**t.** days Peter stood up in the	*5025*
Ac	2:18	pour out in **t.** days of my Spirit;	*1565*
Ac	3:18	But **t.** things, which God before had	
Ac	3:24	Samuel and **t.** that follow after,	*3588*
Ac	6:1	And in **t.** days, when the number	*5025*
Ac	7:41	made a calf in **t.** days, and offered	*1565*
Ac	8:6	unto **t.** things which Philip spake,	*3588*
Ac	9:37	to pass in **t.** days, that she was	*1565*
Ac	13:45	spake against **t.** things which were	*3588*
Ac	16:3	Jews which were in **t.** quarters:	*1565*
Ac	16:35	serjeants, saying, Let **t.** men go.	*1565*

Ac 17:11 noble than **t.** in Thessalonica, ... *3588*
Ac 17:11 daily, whether **t.** things were so......... *5023*
Ac 18:17 Gallio cared for none of **t.** things........ *5130*
Ac 20:2 when he had gone over **t.** parts, ... *1565*
Ac 21:5 when we had accomplished **t.** days, ... *3588*
Ac 21:15 **t.** days we took up our carriages,........ *5025*
Ac 21:24 all may know that **t.** things, whereof.........
Ac 26:16 **t.** things in the which I will appear.....
Ac 26:22 saying none other things than **t.** which.........
Ac 27:11 **t.** things which were spoken by *3588*
Ac 28:31 teaching **t.** things which concern......... *3588*
Ro 1:28 **t.** things which are not covenient;........ *3588*
Ro 4:17 calleth **t.** things which be not as......... *3588*
Ro 6:13 as **t.** that are alive from the dead,............
Ro 6:21 fruit had ye then in **t.** things which............
Ro 6:21 for the end of **t.** things is death. *1565*
Ro 10:5 man which doeth **t.** things shall live...... *846*
Ro 15:17 in **t.** things which pertain to God........ *3588*
Ro 15:18 **t.** things which Christ hath not.................
1Co 8:4 eating of **t.** things that are offered...... *3588*
1Co 8:10 eat **t.** things which are offered to....... *3588*
1Co 12:22 much more **t.** members of the body,... *3588*
1Co 12:23 **t.** members of the body, which we ....
1Co 14:23 there come in **t.** that are unlearned,..........
2Co 7:6 comforteth **t.** that are cast down,........ *3588*
2Co 11:28 Beside **t.** things that are without, ... *3588*
Eph 5:12 **t.** things which are done in secret. *3588*
Php 3:7 me, **t.** I counted loss for Christ. *5023*
Php 3:13 forgetting **t.** things...are behind,......... *3588*
Php 3:13 reaching forth unto **t.** things which......... *3588*
Php 4:3 help **t.** women which laboured with *846*
Php 4:9 **T.** things, which ye have both *5023*
Col 2:18 into **t.** things which he hath not seen, ...
Col 3:1 Christ, seek **t.** things which are *3588*
1Ti 4:10 all men, specially of **t.** that believe............
1Ti 5:8 specially for **t.** of his own house,......... *3588*
2Ti 2:25 instructing **t.**...oppose themselves; *3588*
2Ti 3:3 fierce, despisers of **t.** that are good, ...
Heb 3:5 testimony of **t.** things which were....... *3588*
Heb 5:14 **t.** who by reason of use have their..... *3588*
Heb 6:4 it is impossible for **t.** who were once .. *3588*
Heb 7:21 **t.** priests were made without an......... *3588*
Heb 7:27 needeth not daily, as **t.** high priests.... *3588*
Heb 8:10 the house of Israel after **t.** days,....... *1565*
Heb 10:1 can never with **t.** sacrifices.......... *3588,846*
Heb 10:3 in **t.** sacrifices...is a remembrance..*3588,846*
Heb 10:16 will make with them after **t.** days,...... *1565*
Heb 12:27 removing of **t.** things...are shaken,..... *3588*
Heb 12:27 **t.** things which cannot be shaken......... *3588*
Heb 13:11 For the bodies of **t.** beasts, whose..... *5130*
Jas 2:16 **t.** things which are needful to the....... *3588*
2Pe 2:6 ensample unto **t.** that after should...... *3588*
2Pe 2:18 **t.** that were clean escaped from......... *3588*
1Jo 3:22 **t.** things that are pleasing in his......... *3588*
2Jo 8 lose not **t.** things we have wrought,..........
Jude 10 **t.** things which they know not *3745*
Jude 10 **t.** things they corrupt themselves....... *5125*
Re 1:3 **t.** things...are written therein:........... *3588*
Re 2:10 Fear none of **t.** things which......... *3588*
Re 2:13 **t.** days wherein Antipas was my.... *3588*
Re 4:9 **t.** beasts give glory and honour.......... *3588*
Re 9:4 **t.** men which have not the seal of...... *3588*
Re 9:6 in **t.** days shall men seek death,......... *1565*
Re 10:4 **t.** things which the seven thunders ....
Re 13:14 means of **t.** miracles which he had...... *3588*
Re 20:12 **t.** things which were written in the..... *3588*

THOU See in the APPENDIX; also THEE; THY.

THOUGH See also ALTHOUGH.

Ge 31:30 **t.** thou wouldest needs be gone, ...
Ge 33:10 **t.** I had seen the face of God, and............
Ge 40:10 and it was as **t.** it budded, and her...........
Le 5:17 **t.** he wist it not, yet is he guilty, ...
Le 11:7 And the swine, **t.** he divide the hoof, ...
Le 25:35 **t.** he be a stranger, or a sojourner; ....
Nu 18:27 unto you, as **t.** it were the corn of the......
De 29:19 **t.** I walk in the imagination of........... 3588
Jos 17:18 **t.** they have iron chariots,................. 3588
Jos 17:18 chariots, and **t.** they be strong........... 3588
Jg 13:16 **T.** thou detain me, I will not eat.......... 518
Jg 15:3 **t.** I do them a displeasure................. 3588
Jg 15:7 **T.** ye have done this, yet will I be....... 518
Ru 2:13 **t.** I be not like unto one of thine.............
1Sa 14:39 **t.** it be in Jonathan my son,......... 3588,518
1Sa 20:20 side thereof, as **t.** I shot at a mark..........
1Sa 21:5 **t.** it were sanctified this day in 3588
2Sa 1:21 as **t.** he had not anointed with oil. ....
2Sa 3:39 am this day weak, **t.** anointed king; ....
2Sa 4:6 as **t.** they would have fetched wheat; ....
2Sa 18:12 **T.** I should receive a thousand........... 3863
1Ki 2:28 **t.** he turned not after Absalom................
1Ch 26:10 **t.** he was not the firstborn, yet his...........
2Ch 30:19 **t.** he be not cleansed according to the.......
Ne 1:9 **t.** there were of you cast unto 518
Ne 6:1 (**t.** at that time I had not set up......... 1571
Es 9:1 (**t.** it was turned to the contrary,...............
Job 8:7 **T.** thy beginning was small, yet thy ....
Job 9:15 **t.** I were righteous, yet would I 518
Job 9:21 **T.** I were perfect, yet would I not...........
Job 10:19 have been as **t.** I had not been; ....
Job 11:12 **t.** man be born like a wild ass's colt..........
Job 13:15 **T.** he slay me, yet will I trust in him: ....
Job 14:8 **T.** the root thereof wax old in the........ 518
Job 16:6 **T.** I speak, my grief is not 518
Job 16:6 and **t.** I forbear, what am I eased?............
Job 19:17 **t.** I entreated for the children's sake ....
Job 19:26 And **t.** after my skin worms destroy ....
Job 19:27 **t.** my reins be consumed within me. ....
Job 20:6 **T.** his excellency mount up to the.............
Job 20:12 **T.** wickedness be sweet in his 518
Job 20:12 mouth, **t.** he hide it under his tongue; ....
Job 20:13 **T.** he spare it, and forsake it not; but ....
Job 24:23 **T.** it be given him to be in safety, ...
Job 27:8 **t.** he hath gained, when God taketh.... 3588
Job 27:16 **T.** he heap up silver as the dust.......... 518
Job 30:24 grave, **t.** they cry in his destruction. 518
Job 39:16 young ones, as **t.** they were not hers:.......
Ps 23:4 **t.** I walk through the valley of........... 3588
Ps 27:3 **T.** an host should encamp against......... 518
Ps 27:3 **t.** war should rise against me, in.......... 518
Ps 35:14 **t.** he had been my friend or brother:.........
Ps 37:24 **T.** he fall, he shall not be utterly......... 3588
Ps 44:19 **T.** thou hast sore broken us in 3588
Ps 46:2 we fear, **t.** the earth be removed, ...
Ps 46:2 and **t.** the mountains be carried into..........
Ps 46:3 **T.** the waters thereof roar and be ....
Ps 46:3 **t.** the mountains shake with the ....
Ps 49:18 **T.** while he lived he blessed his 3588
Ps 68:13 **T.** ye have lien among the pots, ... 518
Ps 78:23 **T.** he had commanded the clouds.............
Ps 99:8 **t.** thou tookest vengeance of their ....
Ps 138:6 **T.** the Lord be high, yet hath he........ 3588
Ps 138:7 **T.** I walk in the midst of trouble,......... 518
Pr 6:35 content, **t.** thou givest many gifts....... 3588
Pr 11:21 **T.** hand join in hand, the wicked shall........
Pr 16:5 **t.** hand join in hand, he shall not be ....
Pr 27:22 **T.** thou shouldest bray a fool in a 518
Pr 28:6 is perverse in his ways, **t.** he be rich. ....
Pr 29:19 words: for **t.** he understand he will not......
Ec 6:6 **t.** he live a thousand years twice told, ...
Ec 8:12 **T.** a sinner do evil an hundred times, ...
Ec 8:17 because **t.** a man labour to seek it 834
Ec 8:17 **t.** a wise man think to know it, ... 518
Isa 1:18 **t.** your sins be as scarlet, they shall..... 518
Isa 1:18 **t.** they be red like crimson, they 518
Isa 10:22 **t.** thy people Israel be as the sand........ 518
Isa 12:1 **t.** thou wast angry with me, thine 3588
Isa 30:20 And **t.** the Lord give you the bread ....
Isa 35:8 men, **t.** fools, shall not err therein. ....
Isa 45:4 thee, **t.** thou hast not known me. ....
Isa 45:5 thee, **t.** thou hast not known me: ....
Isa 49:5 **T.** Israel be not gathered, yet shall I.........
Isa 63:16 **t.** Abraham be ignorant of us,............ 3588
Jer 2:22 For **t.** thou wash thee with nitre,......... 518
Jer 4:30 **T.** thou clothest thyself with............. 3588
Jer 4:30 **t.** thou deckest thee with ornaments... 3588
Jer 4:30 **t.** thou rentest thy face with............. 3588
Jer 5:2 **t.** they say, The Lord liveth; surely 518
Jer 5:22 **t.** the waves thereof toss themselves, ...
Jer 5:22 **t.** they roar, yet can they not pass over ....
Jer 11:11 **t.** they shall cry unto me, I will not ....
Jer 12:6 **t.** they speak fair words unto thee...... 3588
Jer 14:7 **t.** our iniquities testify against us, ... 518
Jer 15:1 **T.** Moses and Samuel stood before 518
Jer 22:24 **t.** Coniah the son of Jehoiakim...... 3588,518
Jer 30:11 **t.** I make a full end of all nations....... 3588
Jer 32:5 **t.** ye fight with the Chaldeans, ye....... 3588
Jer 32:33 **t.** I taught them, rising up early and ....
Jer 37:10 For **t.** ye had smitten the whole 518
Jer 46:23 the Lord, **t.** it cannot be searched;..... 3588
Jer 49:16 **t.** thou shouldest make thy nest.......... 3588
Jer 51:5 **t.** their land was filled with sin........... 3588
Jer 51:53 **T.** Babylon should mount up to 3588
Jer 51:53 **t.** she should fortify the height of....... 3588
La 3:32 But **t.** he cause grief, yet will he......... 518
Eze 2:6 **t.** briers and thorns be with thee,........ 3588
Eze 2:6 looks, **t.** they be a rebellious house. ... 3588
Eze 3:9 looks, **t.** they be a rebellious house. ....
Eze 8:18 **t.** they cry in mine ears with a loud ....
Eze 12:3 **t.** they be a rebellious house. 3518
Eze 12:13 shall he not see it, **t.** he shall die there. ....
Eze 14:14 **T.** these three men, Noah, Daniel, and......
Eze 14:16, 18 **T.** these three men were in it, as I......
Eze 14:20 **T.** Noah, Daniel, and Job, were in it, ...
Eze 26:21 **t.** thou be sought for, yet shalt thou ....
Eze 28:2 **t.** thou set thine heart as the heart of.......
Eze 32:25 **t.** their terror was caused in the 3588
Eze 32:26 **t.** they caused their terror in the......... 3588
Eze 32:27 **t.** they were the terror of the mighty.. 3588
Da 5:22 **t.** thou knewest all this; 3606,6903,1768
Da 9:9 **t.** we have rebelled against him;......... 3588
Ho 4:15 **T.** thou, Israel, play the harlot, ... 518
Ho 5:2 **t.** I have been a rebuker of them all..........
Ho 7:13 **t.** I have redeemed them, yet they............
Ho 7:15 **T.** I have bound and strengthened ....
Ho 8:10 Yea, **t.** they have hired among the...... 3588
Ho 9:12 **T.** they bring up their.................. 3588,518
Ho 9:16 yea, **t.** they bring forth, yet will I......... 3588
Ho 11:7 **t.** they called them to the most High,........
Ho 13:15 **T.** he be fruitful among his................. 3588
Am 5:22 **T.** ye offer me burnt offerings...... 3588,518
Am 9:2 **T.** they dig into hell, thence shall.. 3588,518
Am 9:2 **t.** they climb up to heaven, thence.3588,518
Am 9:3 **t.** they hide themselves in the top .3588,518
Am 9:3 **t.** they be hid from my sight in the 3588,518
Am 9:4 **t.** they go into captivity before..... 3588,518
Ob 4 **T.** thou exalt thyself as the eagle,. 3588,518
Ob 4 **t.** thou set thy nest among the..... 3588,518
Ob 16 they shall be as **t.** they had not been. ....
Mic 5:2 Beth-lehem Ephratah, **t.** thou be little ....
Na 1:12 **T.** they be quiet, and likewise............. 518
Na 1:12 **T.** I have afflicted thee, I will afflict ....
Hab 1:5 will not believe, **t.** it be told you. 3588
Hab 2:3 **t.** it tarry, wait for it; because it.......... 518
Zec 9:2 and Zidon, **t.** it be very wise............. 3588
Zec 10:6 be as **t.** I had not cast them off:.......... 834
Zec 12:3 **t.** all the people of the earth be ....
Mt 26:33 **T.** all men shall be offended *1499*
Mt 26:35 **T.** I should die with thee, yet will *2579*
Mt 26:60 **t.** many false witnesses came, yet found....
Lu 9:53 was as **t.** he would go to Jerusalem. ....
Lu 11:8 **T.** he will not rise and give him,... *1499*
Lu 16:31 **t.** one rose from the dead.......... *1437*
Lu 18:4 **T.** I fear not God, nor regard........ *1499*
Lu 18:7 him, **t.** he bear long with them?.... *2532*
Lu 24:28 as **t.** he would have gone further.............
Joh 4:2 (**T.** Jesus himself baptized not,............ *2544*
Joh 8:6 on the ground, as **t.** he heard them not. ....
Joh 8:14 **T.** I bear record of myself, yet...... *2579*
Joh 10:38 **t.** ye believe not me, believe the.... *2579*
Joh 11:25 **t.** he were dead, yet shall he......... *2579*
Joh 12:37 **t.** he had done so many miracles before.....
Ac 3:12 as **t.** by our own power or holiness we.....
Ac 13:28 **t.** they found no cause of death in him,......
Ac 13:41 **t.** a man declare it unto you............. *1437*
Ac 17:25 as **t.** he needed any thing, seeing he.........
Ac 17:27 **t.** he be not far from every one of...... *2544*
Ac 23:15 as **t.** ye would enquire something............
Ac 23:20 as **t.** they would enquire somewhat of ....
Ac 27:30 as **t.** they would have cast anchors out......
Ac 28:4 whom, **t.** he hath escaped the sea, ...
Ac 28:17 **t.** I have committed nothing against ....
Ro 4:11 believe, **t.** they be not circumcised; *1223*
Ro 4:17 things which be not as **t.** they were.........
Ro 7:3 **t.** she be married to another man. ....
Ro 9:6 Not as **t.** the word of God hath *3754*
Ro 9:27 **T.** the number of the children of *1437*
1Co 4:15 **t.** ye have ten thousand instructors...... *1437*
1Co 4:18 up, as **t.** I would not come to you. ....
1Co 5:3 judged already, as **t.** I were present, ...
1Co 7:29 that have wives be as **t.** they had none; ....
1Co 7:30 they that weep, as **t.** they wept not;.........
1Co 7:30 that rejoice, as **t.** they rejoiced not;.........
1Co 7:30 they that buy, as **t.** they possessed not; ....
1Co 8:5 **t.** there be that are called gods.......... *1512*
1Co 9:16 For **t.** I preach the gospel, I have *1437*
1Co 9:19 For **t.** I be free from all men, yet............
1Co 13:1 **T.** I speak with the tongues of........... *1437*
1Co 13:2 And **t.** I have the gift of prophecy, ... *1437*
1Co 13:2 **t.** I have all faith, so that I could....... *1437*
1Co 13:3 **t.** I bestow all my goods to feed *1437*

1Co 13:3 and t. I give my body to be burned, ... 1437
2Co 4:16 t. our outward man perish, yet the..... 1499
2Co 5:16 t. we have known Christ after the...... 1499
2Co 5:20 as t. God did beseech you by us:............
2Co 7:8 t. I made you sorry with a letter,....... 1499
2Co 7:8 I do not repent, t. I did repent:......... 1499
2Co 7:8 sorry, t. it were but for a season....... 1499
2Co 7:12 Wherefore, t. I wrote unto you, I...... 1499
2Co 8:9 that, t. he was rich, yet for your sakes.....
2Co 10:3 t. we walk in the flesh, we do not war......
2Co 10:8 t. I should boast somewhat more 1437
2Co 10:14 as t. we reached not unto you: ....
2Co 11:6 t. I be rude in speech, yet not in....... 1499
2Co 11:21 reproach, as t. we had been weak...... 3754
2Co 12:6 For t. I would desire to glory, I......... 1437
2Co 12:11 chiefest apostles, t. I be nothing........ 1499
2Co 12:15 t. the more abundantly I love you,...... 1499
2Co 13:4 For t. he was crucified through.......... 1487
2Co 13:7 is honest, t. we be as reprobates............
Ga 1:8 But t. we, or an angel from heaven,... 1437
Ga 3:15 T. it be but a man's covenant, yet...... 3676
Ga 4:1 from a servant, t. he be lord of all;........
Php 3:4 T. I might also have confidence in 2539
Php 3:12 Not as t. I had already attained,......... 3754
Col 2:5 t. I be absent in the flesh, yet am...... 1499
Col 2:20 as t. living in the world, are ye subject......
Phm 8 t. I might be much bold in Christ to.........
Heb 5:8 T. he were a Son, yet learned he....... 2539
Heb 6:9 salvation, t. we thus speak............... 1499
Heb 7:5 t. they come out of the loins of 2539
Heb 12:17 t. he sought it carefully with tears....... 2539
Jas 2:14 t. a man say he hath faith, and 1437
Jas 3:4 the ships, which t. they be so great,........
1Pe 1:6 ye greatly rejoice, t. now for a season, ...
1Pe 1:7 that perisheth, t. it be tried with fire, ...
1Pe 1:8 t. now ye see him, yet believing, ...
1Pe 4:12 t. some strange thing happened unto.........
2Pe 1:12 of these things, t. ye know them, ... 2539
2Jo 5 not as t. I wrote a new commandment ......
Jude 5 in remembrance, t. ye once knew this, ...

THOUGHT See also THOUGHTEST; THOUGHTS.

Ge 20:11 I t., Surely the fear of God is not........ 559
Ge 38:15 saw her, he t. her to be an harlot; 2803
Ge 48:11 I had not t. to see thy face:.............. 6419
Ge 50:20 as for you, ye t. evil against me; 2803
Ex 32:14 the evil which he t. to do unto his...... 1696
Nu 24:11 I t. to promote thee unto great 559
Nu 33:56 unto you, as I t. to do unto them........ 1819
De 15:9 be not a t. in thy wicked heart, ... 1697
De 19:19 as he had t. to have done unto his 2161
Jg 15:2 I verily t. that thou hadst utterly 559
Jg 20:5 by night, and t. to have slain me:........ 1819
Ru 4:4 I t. to advertise thee, saying, Buy 559
1Sa 1:13 Eli t. she had been drunken............. 2803
1Sa 9:5 for the asses, and take t. for us.......... 1672
1Sa 18:25 Saul t. to make David fall by the........ 2803
1Sa 20:26 for he t., Something hath befallen 559
2Sa 4:10 who t. that I would have given him a..........
2Sa 13:2 Amnon t. it hard for him to do............ 5869
2Sa 14:13 hast thou t. such a thing against......... 2803
2Sa 19:18 and to do what he t. good. 5869
2Sa 21:16 new sword, t. to have slain David........ 559
2Ki 5:11 I t., He will surely come out to me,..... 559
2Ch 11:22 for he t. to make him king......................
2Ch 32:1 and t. to win them for himself............. 559
Ne 6:2 But they t. to do me mischief............ 2803
Es 3:6 t. scorn to lay hands on Mordecai 5869
Es 6:6 Now Haman t. in his heart To............. 559
Job 12:5 despised in the t. of him that is at...... 6248
Job 42:2 no t. can be withholden from.............. 4209
Ps 48:9 We have t. of thy lovingkindness,........ 1819
Ps 49:11 Their inward t. is, that their houses..........
Ps 64:6 the inward t. of every one of them, ...
Ps 73:16 When I t. to know this, it was too 2803
Ps 119:59 I t. on my ways, and turned my 2803
Ps 139:2 thou understandest my t. afar off. 7454
Pr 24:9 The t. of foolishness is sin: and 2154
Pr 30:32 or if thou hast t. evil, lay thine 2161
Ec 10:20 not the king, no not in thy t.;............ 4093
Isa 14:24 Surely as I have t., so shall it come.... 1819
Jer 18:8 the evil that I t. to do unto them. 2803
Eze 38:10 and thou shalt think an evil t............ 4284
Da 4:2 I t. it good to shew the signs..... 8232,6925
Da 6:3 king t. to set him over the whole......... 6246
Am 4:13 declareth unto man what is his t., ... 7807
Zec 1:6 the Lord of hosts t. to do unto us,...... 2161
Zec 8:14 As I t. to punish you, when your 2161
Zec 8:15 again have I t. in these days to do 2161
Mal 3:16 Lord, and that t. upon his name......... 2803
Mt 1:20 But while he t. on these things,......... 1760
Mt 6:25 Take no t. for your life, what ye... 3309
Mt 6:27 you by taking t. can add one 3309
Mt 6:28 And why take ye t. for raiment?.... 3309
Mt 6:31 take no t., saying, What shall....... 3309
Mt 6:34 Take...no t. for the morrow: 3309
Mt 6:34 morrow shall take t. for the.......... 3309
Mt 10:19 take no t. how or what ye shall 3309
Mk 13:11 take no t. beforehand what ye........ 4305
Mk 14:72 And when he t. thereon, he wept....... 1911
Lu 7:7 neither t. I myself worthy to come ....
Lu 9:47 perceiving the t. of their heart,........... 1261
Lu 12:11 take ye no t. how or what thing...... 3309
Lu 12:17 And he t. within himself, saying,.. 1260
Lu 12:22 Take no t. for your life, what ye... 3309
Lu 12:25 you with taking t. can add to......... 3309
Lu 12:26 least, why take ye t. for the.......... 3309
Lu 19:11 they t. that the kingdom of God......... 1380
Joh 11:13 they t. that he had spoken of taking..... 1380
Joh 13:29 some of them t., because Judas had.... 1380
Ac 8:20 thou hast t. that the gift of God......... 3543
Ac 8:22 t. of thine heart may be forgiven........ 1963
Ac 10:19 While Peter t. on the vision, the........ 1760
Ac 12:9 the angel; but t. he saw a vision. 1380
Ac 15:38 Paul t. not good to take him with............
Ac 26:8 should it be t. a thing incredible......... 2919
Ac 26:9 I verily t. with myself, that I............. 1380
1Co 13:11 as a child, I t. as a child;................. 3049
2Co 9:5 I t. it necessary to exhort the 2233
2Co 10:5 every t. to the obedience of Christ;.... 3540
Php 2:6 t. it not robbery to be equal with......... 2233
1Th 3:1 we t. it good to be left at Athens....... 2106
Heb 10:29 shall he be t. worthy, who hath ....

THOUGHTEST

Ps 50:21 thou t. that I was altogether such....... 1819

THOUGHTS

Ge 6:5 the t. of his heart was only evil 4284
Jg 5:15 there were great t. of heart. 2711
1Ch 28:9 all the imaginations of the t. 4284
1Ch 29:18 of the t. of the heart of thy people, ... 4284
Job 4:13 t. from the visions of the night, ... 5587
Job 17:11 broken off, even the t. of my heart. ... 4180
Job 20:2 do my t. cause me to answer, ... 5587
Job 21:27 I know your t., and the devices 4284
Ps 10:4 after God: God is not in all his t.. 4209
Ps 33:11 t. of his heart to all generations. 4284
Ps 40:5 and thy t. which are to us-ward: 4284
Ps 56:5 all their t. are against me for evil. 4284
Ps 92:5 thy works! and thy t. are very deep. .. 4284
Ps 94:11 The Lord knoweth the t. of man, ... 4284
Ps 94:19 In the multitude of my t. within 8312
Ps 119:113 I hate vain t.: but thy law do I 5588
Ps 139:17 How precious...are thy t. unto me,....... 7454
Ps 139:23 heart: try me, and know my t. 8312
Ps 146:4 in that very day his t. perish. 6250
Pr 12:5 The t. of the righteous are right: 4284
Pr 15:26 t. of the wicked are an abomination 4284
Pr 16:3 and thy t. shall be established............ 4284
Pr 21:5 the t. of the diligent tend only to 4284
Isa 55:7 and the unrighteous man his t............ 4284
Isa 55:8 For my t. are not your t., neither...... 4284
Isa 55:9 your ways, and my t. than your t......... 4284
Isa 59:7 blood: their t. are t. of iniquity; 4284
Isa 65:2 was not good, after their own t.; 4284
Isa 66:18 for I know their works and their t...... 4284
Jer 4:14 How long shall thy vain t. lodge.......... 4284
Jer 6:19 people, even the fruit of their t.,......... 4284
Jer 23:20 have performed the t. of his heart:..... 4209
Jer 29:11 I know the t. that I think toward......... 4284
Jer 29:11 t. of peace, and not of evil, to........... 4284
Da 2:29 O king, thy t. came into thy mind 7476
Da 2:30 mightest know the t. of thy heart....... 7476
Da 4:5 t. upon my bed and the visions.......... 2031
Da 4:19 one hour, and his t. troubled him. 7476
Da 5:6 changed, and his t. troubled him, ... 7476
Da 5:10 let not thy t. trouble thee, nor 7476
Mic 4:12 they know not the t. of the Lord, ... 4284
Mt 9:4 And Jesus knowing their t. said,......... 1761
Mt 12:25 Jesus knew their t., and said unto 1761
Mt 15:19 out of the heart proceed evil t.,...... 1261
Mk 7:21 the heart of men, proceed evil t.,.. 1261
Lu 2:35 t. of many hearts may be revealed. ... 1261
Lu 5:22 But when Jesus perceived their t.,...... 1261
Lu 6:8 he knew their t., and said to the........ 1261
Lu 11:17 knowing their t., said unto them, ... 1270
Lu 24:38 and why do t. arise in your........... 1261
Ro 2:15 and their t. the mean while.............. 3053
1Co 3:20 Lord knoweth the t. of the wise, ... 1261
Heb 4:12 a discerner of the t. and intents of..... 1761
Jas 2:4 and are become judges of evil t.? 1261

THOUSAND See also THOUSANDS.

Ge 20:16 thy brother a t. pieces of silver:.......... 505
Ex 12:37 six hundred t. on foot that were.......... 505
Ex 32:28 people that day about three t. men. 505
Ex 38:25 a t. seven hundred and threescore 505
Ex 38:26 six hundred t. and three t. and five...... 505
Ex 38:28 t. seven hundred seventy and five......... 505
Ex 38:29 two t. and four hundred shekels. 505
Le 26:8 of you shall put ten t. to flight: 7233
Nu 1:21 forty and six t. and five hundred.......... 505
Nu 1:23 fifty and nine t. and three hundred. 505
Nu 1:25 and five t. six hundred and fifty........... 505
Nu 1:27 and fourteen t. and six hundred. 505
Nu 1:29 fifty and four t. and four hundred.......... 505
Nu 1:31 fifty and seven t. and four hundred....... 505
Nu 1:33 were forty t. and five hundred. 505
Nu 1:35 thirty and two t. and two hundred......... 505
Nu 1:37 thirty and five t. and four hundred. 505
Nu 1:39 and two t. and seven hundred............. 505
Nu 1:41 forty and one t. and five hundred.......... 505
Nu 1:43 fifty and three t. and four hundred. 505
Nu 1:46 numbered were six hundred t. and......... 505
Nu 1:46 three t. and five hundred and fifty........ 505
Nu 2:4 and fourteen t. and six hundred. 505
Nu 2:6 fifty and four t. and four hundred.......... 505
Nu 2:8 fifty and seven t. and four hundred......... 505
Nu 2:9 were an hundred t. and fourscore t....... 505
Nu 2:9 and six t. and four hundred,................ 505
Nu 2:11 forty and six t. and five hundred.......... 505
Nu 2:13 fifty and nine t. and three hundred. 505
Nu 2:15 five t. and six hundred and fifty. 505
Nu 2:16 were an hundred t. and fifty and one 505
Nu 2:16 one t. and four hundred and fifty, ... 505
Nu 2:19 were forty t. and five hundred. 505
Nu 2:21 thirty and two t. and two hundred.......... 505
Nu 2:23 thirty and five t. and four hundred. 505
Nu 2:24 were an hundred t. and eight t............ 505
Nu 2:26 and two t. and seven hundred............... 505
Nu 2:28 forty and one t. and five hundred.......... 505
Nu 2:30 fifty and three t. and four hundred. 505
Nu 2:31 camp of Dan were an hundred t. 505
Nu 2:31 fifty and seven t. and six hundred. 505
Nu 2:32 their hosts were six hundred t. 505
Nu 2:32 three t. and five hundred and fifty.......... 505
Nu 3:22 were seven t. and five hundred. 505
Nu 3:28 were eight t. and six hundred, ... 505
Nu 3:34 were six t. and two hundred................ 505
Nu 3:39 upward, were twenty and two t............. 505
Nu 3:43 two t. two hundred and threescore 505
Nu 3:50 t. three hundred and threescore 505
Nu 4:36 two t. seven hundred and fifty. 505
Nu 4:40 two t. and six hundred and thirty. 505
Nu 4:44 were three t. and two hundred............. 505
Nu 4:48 were eight t. and five hundred and........ 505
Nu 7:85 two t. and four hundred shekels, ... 505
Nu 11:21 I am, are six hundred t. footmen 505
Nu 16:49 were fourteen t. and seven hundred, ... 505
Nu 25:9 the plague were twenty and four t. 505
Nu 26:7 and three t. and seven hundred and 505
Nu 26:14 twenty and two t. and two hundred...... 505
Nu 26:18 of them, forty t. and five hundred......... 505
Nu 26:22 and sixteen t. and five hundred. 505
Nu 26:25 and four t. and three hundred. 505
Nu 26:27 threescore t. and five hundred. 505
Nu 26:34 fifty and two t. and seven hundred....... 505
Nu 26:37 thirty and two t. and five hundred......... 505
Nu 26:41 forty and five t. and six hundred........... 505
Nu 26:43 and four t. and four hundred 505
Nu 26:47 fifty and three t. and four hundred. 505
Nu 26:50 forty and five t. and four hundred. 505
Nu 26:51 children of Israel, six hundred t. 505
Nu 26:51 and a t. seven hundred and thirty. 505
Nu 26:62 of them were twenty and three t., ... 505
Nu 31:4 Of every tribe a t., throughout all......... 505
Nu 31:5 of Israel, a t. of every tribe,................ 505
Nu 31:5 every tribe, twelve t., armed for war. .. 505
Nu 31:6 them to the war, a t. of every tribe. 505
Nu 31:32 war had caught, was six hundred t....... 505

Nu 31:32 seventy **t.** and five **t.** sheep, 505
Nu 31:33 threescore and twelve **t.** beeves, 505
Nu 31:34 And threescore and one **t.** asses, 505
Nu 31:35 And thirty and two **t.** persons in all, 505
Nu 31:36 was in number three hundred **t.** 505
Nu 31:36 thirty **t.** and five hundred sheep: 505
Nu 31:38 the beeves were thirty and six **t.**; 505
Nu 31:39 were thirty **t.** and five hundred; 505
Nu 31:40 And the persons were sixteen **t.**; 505
Nu 31:43 congregation was three hundred **t.** 505
Nu 31:43 and thirty **t.** and seven **t.** and five 505
Nu 31:44 And thirty and six **t.** beeves, 505
Nu 31:45 And thirty **t.** asses and five hundred, 505
Nu 31:46 And sixteen **t.** persons;) 505
Nu 31:52 was sixteen **t.** seven hundred and 505
Nu 35:4 outward a **t.** cubits round about 505
Nu 35:5 city on the east side two **t.** cubits, 505
Nu 35:5 and on the south side two **t.** cubits, 505
Nu 35:5 and on the west side two **t.** cubits, 505
Nu 35:5 and on the north side two **t.** cubits; 505
De 1:11 make you a **t.** times so many more 505
De 7:9 commandments to a **t.** generations; 505
De 32:30 How should one chase a **t.**, and two 505
De 32:30 and two put ten **t.** to flight, except 505
Jos 3:4 it, about two **t.** cubits by measure: 505
Jos 4:13 About forty **t.** prepared for war 505
Jos 7:3 let about two or three **t.** men go up 505
Jos 7:4 of the people about three **t.** men: 505
Jos 8:3 chose out thirty **t.** mighty men of 505
Jos 8:12 And he took about five **t.** men, and 505
Jos 8:25 men and women, were twelve **t.**, 505
Jos 23:10 One man of you shall chase a **t.**: for 505
Jg 1:4 slew of them in Bezek ten **t.** men 505
Jg 3:29 slew...at that time about ten **t.** men, 505
Jg 4:6 with thee ten **t.** men of the children 505
Jg 4:10 went up with ten **t.** men at his feet: 505
Jg 4:14 Tabor, and ten **t.** men after him 505
Jg 5:8 spear seen among forty **t.** in Israel? 505
Jg 7:3 of the people twenty and two **t.**; 505
Jg 7:3 and there remained ten **t.** 505
Jg 8:10 with them, about fifteen **t.** men, 505
Jg 8:10 and twenty **t.** men that drew sword. 505
Jg 8:26 a **t.** and seven hundred shekels of 505
Jg 9:49 also, about a **t.** men and women. 505
Jg 12:6 the Ephraimites forty and two **t.** 505
Jg 15:11 Then three **t.** men of Judah went to 505
Jg 15:15 took it, and slew a **t.** men therewith 505
Jg 15:16 jaw of an ass have I slain a **t.** men 505
Jg 16:27 roof about three **t.** men and women. 505
Jg 20:2 hundred **t.** footmen that drew sword 505
Jg 20:10 of Israel, and an hundred of a **t.**, 505
Jg 20:10 a **t.**...to fetch victual for the people, 505
Jg 20:10 out of ten **t.**, to fetch victual for 7233
Jg 20:15 and six **t.** men that drew sword, 505
Jg 20:17 four hundred **t.** men that drew 505
Jg 20:21 that day twenty and two **t.** men. 505
Jg 20:25 of Israel again eighteen **t.** men; 505
Jg 20:34 against Gibeah ten **t.** chosen men 505
Jg 20:35 twenty and five **t.** and an hundred 505
Jg 20:44 fell of Benjamin eighteen **t.** men; 505
Jg 20:45 them in the highways five **t.** men; 505
Jg 20:45 unto Gidom, and slew two **t.** men of 505
Jg 20:46 twenty and five **t.** men that drew the 505
Jg 21:10 twelve **t.** men of the valiantest, 505
1Sa 4:2 army in the field about four **t.** men 505
1Sa 4:10 there fell of Israel thirty **t.** footmen. 505
1Sa 6:19 fifty **t.** and threescore and ten men: 505
1Sa 11:8 of Israel were three hundred **t.**, 505
1Sa 11:8 and the men of Judah thirty **t.** 505
1Sa 13:2 Saul chose him three **t.** men of 505
1Sa 13:2 two **t.** were with Saul in Michmash 505
1Sa 13:2 a **t.** were with Jonathan in Gibeah 505
1Sa 13:5 to fight with Israel, thirty **t.** chariots, 505
1Sa 13:5 six **t.** horsemen, and people as the 505
1Sa 15:4 in Telaim, two hundred **t.** footmen, 505
1Sa 15:4 footmen, and ten **t.** men of Judah 505
1Sa 17:5 the coat was five **t.** shekels of brass 505
1Sa 17:18 cheeses unto the captain of their **t.**, 505
1Sa 18:13 and made him his captain over a **t.**; 505
1Sa 24:2 Saul took three **t.** chosen men out of 505
1Sa 25:2 had three **t.** sheep, and a **t.** goats: 505
1Sa 26:2 three **t.** chosen men of Israel with 505
2Sa 6:1 the chosen men of Israel, thirty **t.** 505
2Sa 8:4 David took from him a **t.** chariots, 505
2Sa 8:4 horsemen, and twenty **t.** footmen: 505
2Sa 8:5 the Syrians two and twenty **t.** men. 505
2Sa 8:13 valley of salt, being eighteen **t.** men. 505
2Sa 10:6 Syrians of Zoba, twenty **t.** footmen, 505
2Sa 10:6 and of king Maacah a **t.** men, 505
2Sa 10:6 and of Ish-tob twelve **t.** men 505
2Sa 10:18 the Syrians, and forty **t.** horsemen, 505
2Sa 17:1 me now choose out twelve **t.** men, 505
2Sa 18:3 but now thou art worth ten **t.** of us: 505
2Sa 18:7 slaughter that day of twenty **t.** men 505
2Sa 18:12 I should receive a **t.** shekels of silver 505
2Sa 19:17 a **t.** men of Benjamin with him, 505
2Sa 24:9 Israel eight hundred **t.** valiant men 505
2Sa 24:9 of Judah were five hundred **t.** men. 505
2Sa 24:15 even to Beer-sheba seventy **t.** men 505
1Ki 3:4 **t.** burnt offerings did Solomon offer 505
1Ki 4:26 Solomon had forty **t.** stalls of horses 505
1Ki 4:26 chariots, and twelve **t.** horsemen. 505
1Ki 4:32 And he spake three **t.** proverbs: 505
1Ki 4:32 and his songs were a **t.** and five. 505
1Ki 5:11 gave Hiram twenty **t.** measures of 505
1Ki 5:13 and the levy was thirty **t.** men. 505
1Ki 5:14 Lebanon, ten **t.** a month by courses: 505
1Ki 5:15 and ten **t.** that bare burdens, 505
1Ki 5:15 and fourscore **t.** hewers in the 505
1Ki 5:16 three **t.** and three hundred, which 505
1Ki 7:26 of lilies: it contained three **t.** baths 505
1Ki 8:63 the Lord, two and twenty **t.** oxen, 505
1Ki 8:63 and an hundred and twenty **t.** sheep. 505
1Ki 10:26 had a **t.** and four hundred chariots, 505
1Ki 10:26 and twelve **t.** horsemen, whom he 505
1Ki 12:21 hundred and fourscore **t.** chosen 505
1Ki 19:18 Yet I have left me seven **t.** in Israel, 505
1Ki 20:15 the children of Israel, being seven **t.** 505
1Ki 20:29 the Syrians an hundred **t.** footmen 505
1Ki 20:30 upon twenty and seven **t.** of the men 505
2Ki 3:4 king of Israel an hundred **t.** lambs, 505
2Ki 3:4 an hundred **t.** rams, with the wool 505
2Ki 5:5 six **t.** pieces of gold, and ten changes 505
2Ki 13:7 ten chariots, and ten **t.** footmen; 505
2Ki 14:7 of Edom in the valley of salt ten **t.** 505
2Ki 15:19 gave Pul a **t.** talents of silver, 505
2Ki 18:23 and I will deliver thee two **t.** horses, 505
2Ki 19:35 an hundred fourscore and five **t.** 505
2Ki 24:14 men of valour, even ten **t.** captives, 505
2Ki 24:16 all the men of might, even seven **t.**, 505
2Ki 24:16 and craftsmen and smiths a **t.**, all 505
1Ch 5:18 four and forty **t.** seven hundred 505
1Ch 5:21 their cattle; of their camels fifty **t.**, 505
1Ch 5:21 of sheep two hundred and fifty **t.**, 505
1Ch 5:21 and of asses two **t.**, 505
1Ch 5:21 and of men an hundred **t.** 505
1Ch 7:2 two and twenty **t.** and six hundred. 505
1Ch 7:4 for war, six and thirty **t.** men: 505
1Ch 7:5 genealogies fourscore and seven **t.** 505
1Ch 7:7 twenty and two **t.** and thirty and 505
1Ch 7:9 was twenty **t.** and two hundred. 505
1Ch 7:11 were seventeen **t.** and two hundred 505
1Ch 7:40 battle was twenty and six **t.** men. 505
1Ch 9:13 a **t.** and seven hundred and 505
1Ch 12:14 hundred, and the greatest over a **t.** 505
1Ch 12:24 were six **t.** and eight hundred, 505
1Ch 12:25 the war, seven **t.** and one hundred 505
1Ch 12:26 children of Levi four **t.** and six 505
1Ch 12:27 were three **t.** and seven hundred; 505
1Ch 12:29 the kindred of Saul, three **t.** 505
1Ch 12:30 of Ephraim twenty **t.** and eight 505
1Ch 12:31 half tribe of Manasseh eighteen **t.**, 505
1Ch 12:33 war, fifty **t.**, which could keep rank: 505
1Ch 12:34 And of Naphtali a **t.** captains, and 505
1Ch 12:34 shield and spear thirty and seven **t.** 505
1Ch 12:35 in war twenty and eight **t.** and six 505
1Ch 12:36 to battle, expert in war, forty **t.** 505
1Ch 12:37 battle, an hundred and twenty **t.** 505
1Ch 16:15 he commanded to a **t.** generations; 505
1Ch 18:4 David took from him a **t.** chariots, 505
1Ch 18:4 and seven **t.** horsemen, 505
1Ch 18:4 and twenty **t.** footmen: David also 505
1Ch 18:5 the Syrians two and twenty **t.** men. 505
1Ch 18:12 in the valley of salt eighteen **t.** 505
1Ch 19:6 Ammon sent a **t.** talents of silver to 505
1Ch 19:7 they hired thirty and two **t.** chariots, 505
1Ch 19:18 slew of the Syrians seven **t.** men 505
1Ch 19:18 in chariots, and forty **t.** footmen, 505
1Ch 21:5 all they of Israel were a **t.** **t.** and 505
1Ch 21:5 an hundred **t.** men that drew sword: 505
1Ch 21:5 hundred threescore and ten **t.** men 505
1Ch 21:14 there fell of Israel seventy **t.** men 505
1Ch 22:14 Lord an hundred **t.** talents of gold, 505
1Ch 22:14 and a **t.** **t.** talents of silver; 505
1Ch 23:3 man by man, was thirty and eight **t.** 505
1Ch 23:4 four **t.** were to set forward the work 505
1Ch 23:4 and six **t.** were officers and judges: 505
1Ch 23:5 Moreover four **t.** were porters; 505
1Ch 23:5 and four **t.** praised the Lord with the 505
1Ch 26:30 of valour, a **t.** and seven hundred, 505
1Ch 26:32 were two **t.** and seven hundred chief 505
1Ch 27:1 course were twenty and four **t.** 505
1Ch 27:2 his course were twenty and four **t.** 505
1Ch 27:4 likewise were twenty and four **t.** 505
1Ch 27:5, 7,8,9,10,11,12,13,14,15 his course were twenty and four **t.** 505
1Ch 29:4 Even three **t.** talents of gold, of the 505
1Ch 29:4 and seven **t.** talents of refined silver, 505
1Ch 29:7 of God of gold five **t.** talents 505
1Ch 29:7 and ten **t.** drams, 7239
1Ch 29:7 and of silver ten **t.** talents, and of 505
1Ch 29:7 and of brass eighteen **t.** talents, 505
1Ch 29:7 and one hundred **t.** talents of iron. 7239,505
1Ch 7:21 even a **t.** bullocks, a **t.** rams, 7239,505
1Ch 7:21 **t.** lambs, with their drink offerings, 7239,505
2Ch 1:6 offered a **t.** burnt offerings upon it. 7239,505
2Ch 1:14 had a **t.** and four hundred chariots, 7239,505
2Ch 1:14 and twelve **t.** horsemen, which he 7239,505
2Ch 2:2 and ten **t.** men to bear burdens, 7239,505
2Ch 2:2 fourscore **t.** to hew in the 7239,505
2Ch 2:2 three **t.** and six hundred to 7239,505
2Ch 2:10 twenty **t.** measures of beaten 7239,505
2Ch 2:10 and twenty **t.** measures of barley, 7239,505
2Ch 2:10 barley, and twenty **t.** baths of 7239,505
2Ch 2:10 wine, and twenty **t.** baths of oil. 7239,505
2Ch 2:17 were found an hundred and fifty **t.** 7239,505
2Ch 2:17 and three **t.** and six hundred 7239,505
2Ch 2:18 and ten **t.** of them to be bearers of 7239,505
2Ch 2:18 and fourscore **t.** to be hewers in 7239,505
2Ch 2:18 three **t.** and six hundred overseers 7239,505
2Ch 4:5 it received and held three **t.** baths. 7239,505
2Ch 7:5 sacrifice of twenty and two **t.** 7239,505
2Ch 7:5 an hundred and twenty **t.** sheep: 7239,505
2Ch 9:25 Solomon had four **t.** stalls for 7239,505
2Ch 9:25 chariots, and twelve **t.** horsemen; 7239,505
2Ch 11:1 and fourscore **t.** chosen men, 7239,505
2Ch 12:3 chariots, and threescore **t.** 7239,505
2Ch 13:3 even four hundred **t.** chosen men: 7239,505
2Ch 13:3 with eight hundred **t.** chosen men, 7239,505
2Ch 13:17 Israel five hundred **t.** chosen men. 7239,505
2Ch 14:8 out of Judah three hundred **t.**; 7239,505
2Ch 14:8 two hundred and fourscore **t.**: 7239,505
2Ch 14:9 the Ethiopian with an host of a **t.** **t.**, 505
2Ch 15:11 hundred oxen and seven **t.** sheep 505
2Ch 17:11 seven **t.** and seven hundred rams, 505
2Ch 17:11 seven **t.** and seven hundred he goats 505
2Ch 17:14 men of valour three hundred **t.** 505
2Ch 17:15 him two hundred and fourscore **t.** 505
2Ch 17:16 hundred **t.** mighty men of valour 505
2Ch 17:17 with bow and shield two hundred **t.** 505
2Ch 17:18 fourscore **t.** ready prepared for the 505
2Ch 25:5 them three hundred **t.** choice men, 505
2Ch 25:6 hired also an hundred **t.** mighty men 505
2Ch 25:11 smote of the children of Seir ten **t.** 505
2Ch 25:12 ten **t.** left alive did the children of 505
2Ch 25:13 and smote three **t.** of them, and took 505
2Ch 26:12 valour were two **t.** and six hundred. 505
2Ch 26:13 was an army, three hundred **t.** and 505
2Ch 26:13 and seven **t.** and five hundred, that 505
2Ch 27:5 silver, and ten **t.** measures of wheat, 505
2Ch 27:5 and ten **t.** of barley. So much did 505
2Ch 28:6 an hundred and twenty **t.** in one day, 505
2Ch 28:8 of their brethren two hundred **t.**, 505
2Ch 29:33 six hundred oxen and three **t.** sheep 505
2Ch 30:24 a **t.** bullocks and seven **t.** sheep; 505
2Ch 30:24 a **t.** bullocks and ten **t.** sheep: 505
2Ch 35:7 present, to the number of thirty **t.**, 505
2Ch 35:7 and three **t.** bullocks: these were of 505
2Ch 35:8 two **t.** and six hundred small cattle, 505
2Ch 35:9 offerings five **t.** small cattle, 505
Ezr 1:9 of gold, a **t.** chargers of silver, 505
Ezr 1:10 and ten, and other vessels a **t.** 505
Ezr 1:11 silver were five **t.** and four hundred. 505
Ezr 2:3 two **t.** an hundred seventy and two. 505
Ezr 2:6 two **t.** eight hundred and twelve. 505
Ezr 2:7 a **t.** two hundred fifty and four. 505
Ezr 2:12 a **t.** two hundred twenty and two. 505
Ezr 2:14 of Bigvai, two **t.** fifty and six. 505

Ezr 2:31 a **t.** two hundred fifty and four. 505
Ezr 2:35 three **t.** and six hundred and thirty. 505
Ezr 2:37 children of Immer, a **t.** fifty and two. 505
Ezr 2:38 a **t.** two hundred forty and seven. 505
Ezr 2:39 of Harim, a **t.** and seventeen. 505
Ezr 2:64 forty and two **t.** three hundred and 505
Ezr 2:65 seven **t.** three hundred thirty and 505
Ezr 2:67 six **t.** seven hundred and twenty. 505
Ezr 2:69 threescore and one **t.** drams of gold, 505
Ezr 2:69 and five **t.** pound of silver, and one 505
Ezr 8:27 basons of gold, of a **t.** drams; 505
Ne 3:13 a **t.** cubits on the wall unto the dung 505
Ne 7:8 two **t.** an hundred seventy and two. 505
Ne 7:11 two **t.** and eight hundred and 505
Ne 7:12 a **t.** two hundred fifty and four. 505
Ne 7:17 two **t.** three hundred twenty and 505
Ne 7:19 Bigvai, two **t.** threescore and seven. 505
Ne 7:34 a **t.** two hundred fifty and four. 505
Ne 7:38 three **t.** nine hundred and thirty. 505
Ne 7:40 children of Immer, a **t.** fifty and two. 505
Ne 7:41 a **t.** two hundred forty and seven. 505
Ne 7:42 of Harim, a **t.** and seventeen. 505
Ne 7:66 two t. three hundred and threescore, 505
Ne 7:67 were seven **t.** three hundred and thirty. 505
Ne 7:69 **t.** seven hundred and twenty asses. 505
Ne 7:70 to the treasure a **t.** drams of gold, 505
Ne 7:71 the work twenty **t.** drams of gold, 7239
Ne 7:71 and two **t.** and two hundred pound 505
Ne 7:72 gave was twenty **t.** drams of gold, 505
Ne 7:72 and two **t.** pound of silver, and 7239
Es 3:9 I will pay ten **t.** talents of silver to 505
Es 9:16 slew of their foes seventy and five **t.**, 505
Job 1:3 substance also was seven **t.** sheep, 505
Job 1:3 three **t.** camels, and five hundred 505
Job 9:3 he cannot answer him one of a **t.** 505
Job 33:23 one among a **t.**, to shew unto man 505
Job 42:12 for he had fourteen **t.** sheep, and six 505
Job 42:12 sheep, and six **t.** camels, and a 505
Job 42:12 and a **t.** yoke of oxen, and a 505
Job 42:12 yoke of oxen, and a **t.** she asses. 505
Ps 50:10 mine, and the cattle upon a **t.** hills. 505
Ps 60:*title* Edom in the valley of salt twelve **t.** 505
Ps 68:17 The chariots of God are twenty **t.**, 7239
Ps 84:10 a day in thy courts is better than a **t.** 505
Ps 90:4 For a **t.** years in thy sight are but as 505
Ps 91:7 A **t.** shall fall at thy side, and ten 505
Ps 91:7 and ten **t.** at thy right hand; but it 7233
Ps 105:8 he commanded to a **t.** generations 505
Ec 6:6 though he live a **t.** years twice told, 505
Ec 7:28 one man among a **t.** have I found; 505
Ca 4:4 whereon there hang a **t.** bucklers, 505
Ca 5:10 ruddy, the chiefest among ten **t.** 7233
Ca 8:11 was to bring a **t.** pieces of silver. 505
Ca 8:12 thou, O Solomon, must have a **t.**, 505
Isa 7:23 were a **t.** vines at a **t.** silverlings, 505
Isa 30:17 One **t.** shall flee at the rebuke of one; 505
Isa 36:8 and I will give thee two **t.** horses, 505
Isa 37:36 a hundred and fourscore and five **t.** 505
Isa 60:22 A little one shall become a **t.**, and a 505
Jer 52:28 three **t.** Jews and three and twenty: 505
Jer 52:30 were four **t.** and six hundred 505
Eze 45:1 length of five and twenty **t.** reeds, 505
Eze 45:1 and the breadth shall be ten **t.** 505
Eze 45:3 the length of five and twenty **t.**, 505
Eze 45:3 the breadth of ten **t.**: and in it shall 505
Eze 45:5 And the five and twenty **t.** of length, 505
Eze 45:5 and the ten **t.** of breadth, shall also 505
Eze 45:6 possession of the city five **t.** broad, 505
Eze 45:6 and five and twenty **t.** long, over 505
Eze 47:3 eastward, he measured a **t.** cubits, 505
Eze 47:4, 4 Again he measured a **t.**, and 505
Eze 47:5 Afterward he measured a **t.**: and it 505
Eze 48:8 five and twenty **t.** reeds in breadth, 505
Eze 48:9 be of five and twenty **t.** in length, 505
Eze 48:9 in length, and of ten **t.** in breadth. 505
Eze 48:10 north five and twenty **t.** in length, 505
Eze 48:10 toward the west ten **t.** in breadth, 505
Eze 48:10 toward the east ten **t.** in breadth, 505
Eze 48:10 south five and twenty **t.** in length: 505
Eze 48:13 have five and twenty **t.** in length, 505
Eze 48:13 in length, and ten **t.** in breadth: 505
Eze 48:13 length shall be five and twenty **t.**, 505
Eze 48:13 and the breadth ten **t.** 505
Eze 48:15 five **t.**, that are left in the breadth 505
Eze 48:15 over against the five and twenty **t.**, 505
Eze 48:16 north side four **t.** and five hundred, 505
Eze 48:16 south side four **t.** and five hundred, 505
Eze 48:16 east side four **t.** and five hundred, 505
Eze 48:16 west side four **t.** and five hundred. 505
Eze 48:18 holy portion shall be ten **t.** eastward, 505
Eze 48:18 and ten **t.** westward: and it shall be 505
Eze 48:20 and twenty **t.** by five and twenty **t.** 505
Eze 48:21 the five and twenty **t.** of the oblation 505
Eze 48:21 over against the five and twenty **t.** 505
Eze 48:30 four **t.** and five hundred measures. 505
Eze 48:32 east side four **t.** and five hundred: 505
Eze 48:33 four **t.** and five hundred measures: 505
Eze 48:34 west side four **t.** and five hundred, 505
Eze 48:35 round about eighteen **t.** measures: 505
Da 5:1 a great feast to a **t.** of his lords, 506
Da 5:1 lords, and drank wine before the **t.** 506
Da 7:10 **t.** thousands ministered unto him, 506
Da 7:10 ten **t.** times ten **t.** stood before him: 7240
Da 8:14 Unto two **t.** and three hundred days; 505
Da 12:11 be a **t.** two hundred and ninety days. 505
Da 12:12 cometh to the **t.** three hundred and 505
Am 5:3 city that went out by a **t.** shall leave 505
Jon 4:11 sixscore **t.** persons that cannot 7239
Mt 14:21 had eaten were about five **t.** men, *4000*
Mt 15:38 they that did eat were four **t.** men, *5070*
Mt 16:9 **the five loaves of the five t.,** *4000*
Mt 16:10 **the seven loaves of the four t.,** *5070*
Mt 18:24 **which owed him ten t. talents** *3463*
Mk 5:13 (they were about two **t.**;) and were *1367*
Mk 6:44 the loaves were about five **t.** men. *4000*
Mk 8:9 that had eaten were about four **t.** *5070*
Mk 8:19 **brake the five loaves among five t.,** *4000*
Mk 8:20 **And when the seven among four t.,** *5070*
Lu 9:14 For they were about five **t.** men. *4000*
Lu 14:31 **be able with ten t. to meet him** *5505*
Lu 14:31 **against him with twenty t.?** *5505*
Joh 6:10 sat down, in number about five **t.** *4000*
Ac 2:41 unto them about three **t.** souls. *5153*
Ac 4:4 of the men was about five **t.** *5505*
Ac 19:19 and found it fifty **t.** pieces of silver, *3461*
Ac 21:38 four **t.** men that were murderers? *5070*
Ro 11:4 reserved to myself seven **t.** men, *2035*
1Co 4:15 ye have ten **t.** instructors in Christ, *3563*
1Co 10:8 fell in one day three and twenty **t.** *5505*
1Co 14:19 ten **t.** words in an unknown tongue. *3463*
2Pe 3:8 day is with the Lord as a **t.** years, *5507*
2Pe 3:8 years, and a **t.** years as one day. *5507*
Re 5:11 of them was ten **t.** times ten **t.**, *3461*
Re 7:4 forty and four **t.** of all the tribes *5505*
Re 7:5 tribe of Juda were sealed twelve **t.** *5505*
Re 7:5 of Reuben were sealed twelve **t.** *5505*
Re 7:5 tribe of Gad were sealed twelve **t.** *5505*
Re 7:6 tribe of Aser were sealed twelve **t.** *5505*
Re 7:6 of Nepthalim were sealed twelve **t.** *5505*
Re 7:6 of Manasses were sealed twelve **t.** *5505*
Re 7:7 of Simeon were sealed twelve **t.** *5505*
Re 7:7 tribe of Levi were sealed twelve **t.** *5505*
Re 7:7 of Issachar were sealed twelve **t.** *5505*
Re 7:8 of Zabulon were sealed twelve **t.** *5505*
Re 7:8 of Joseph were sealed twelve **t.** *5505*
Re 7:8 of Benjamin were sealed twelve **t.** *5505*
Re 9:16 horsemen were two hundred **t.** **t.** *3461*
Re 11:3 a **t.** two hundred and threescore *5507*
Re 11:13 were slain of men seven **t.** *5505*
Re 12:6 a **t.** two hundred and threescore *5507*
Re 14:1 him an hundred forty and four **t.**, *5505*
Re 14:3 the hundred and forty and four **t.**, *5505*
Re 14:20 of a **t.** and six hundred furlongs. *5507*
Re 20:2 Satan, and bound him a **t.** years, *5507*
Re 20:3 till the **t.** years should be fulfilled: *5507*
Re 20:4 and reigned with Christ a **t.** years. *5507*
Re 20:5 until the **t.** years were finished. *5507*
Re 20:6 and shall reign with him a **t.** years. *5507*
Re 20:7 when the **t.** years are expired, Satan *5507*
Re 21:16 with the reed, twelve **t.** furlongs. *5505*

THOUSANDS

Ge 24:60 be thou the mother of **t.** of millions, 505
Ex 18:21 to be rulers of **t.**, and rulers of 505
Ex 18:25 rulers of **t.**, rulers of hundreds, 505
Ex 20:6 shewing mercy unto **t.** of them that 505
Ex 34:7 Keeping mercy for **t.**, forgiving 505
Nu 1:16 their father, heads of **t.** in Israel. 505
Nu 10:4 which are heads of the **t.** of Israel, 505
Nu 10:36 O Lord, unto the many **t.** of Israel. 505
Nu 31:5 were delivered out of the **t.** of Israel, 505
Nu 31:14 the host, with the captains over **t.**, 505
Nu 31:48 which were over **t.** of the host, 505
Nu 31:48 the captains of **t.**, and captains of 505
Nu 31:52 of the captains of **t.**, and of the 505
Nu 31:54 took the gold of the captains of **t.** 505
De 1:15 heads over you, captains over **t.**, 505
De 5:10 shewing mercy unto **t.** of them that 505
De 33:2 and he came with ten **t.** of saints: 7233
De 33:17 and they are the ten **t.** of Ephraim, 7233
De 33:17 and they are the **t.** of Manasseh. 505
Jos 22:14 fathers among the ten **t.** of Israel. 505
Jos 22:21 unto the heads of the **t.** of Israel, 505
Jos 22:30 the **t.** of Israel which were with him, 505
2Sa 8:12 he will appoint him captains over **t.**, 505
2Sa 10:10 Lord by your tribes, and by your **t.** 505
2Sa 18:7 Saul hath slain his **t.**, 505
2Sa 18:7 and David his ten **t.** 505
2Sa 18:8 have ascribed unto David ten **t.**, 7233
2Sa 18:8 to me they have ascribed but **t.** 505
2Sa 21:11 Saul hath slain his **t.**, 505
2Sa 21:11 David his ten **t.**? 7233
2Sa 22:7 and make you all captains of **t.**, and 505
2Sa 23:23 out throughout all the **t.** of Judah. 505
2Sa 29:2 passed on by hundreds, and by **t.** 505
2Sa 29:5 Saul slew his **t.**, 505
2Sa 29:5 David his ten **t.**? 7233
2Sa 18:1 and set captains of **t.** and captains 505
2Sa 18:4 came out by hundreds and by **t.** 505
1Ch 12:20 captains of the **t.** that were of 505
1Ch 13:1 the captains of **t.** and hundreds, 505
1Ch 15:25 and the captains over **t.**, went to 505
1Ch 26:26 the captains over **t.** and hundreds, 505
1Ch 27:1 and captains of **t.** and hundreds, 505
1Ch 28:1 and the captains over the **t.**, and 505
1Ch 29:6 the captains of **t.** and of hundreds, 505
2Ch 1:2 to the captains of **t.** and of hundreds, 505
2Ch 17:14 of Judah, the captains of **t.**; Adnah 505
2Ch 25:5 and made them captains over **t.**, 505
Ps 3:6 not be afraid of ten **t.** of people, 7233
Ps 68:17 thousand, even **t.** of angels; 505
Ps 119:72 unto me than **t.** of gold and silver. 505
Ps 144:13 our sheep may bring forth **t.** 503
Ps 144:13 and ten **t.** in our streets: 7232
Jer 32:18 shewest lovingkindness unto **t.**, 505
Da 7:10 thousand **t.** ministered unto him, 506
Da 11:12 he shall cast down many ten **t.** 7239
Mic 5:2 thou be little among the **t.** of Judah, 505
Mic 6:7 the Lord be pleased with **t.** of rams, 505
Mic 6:7 or with ten **t.** of rivers of oil? shall 7233
Ac 21:20 **t.** of Jews there are which believe; *3461*
Jude 14 cometh with ten **t.** of his saints, *3461*
Re 5:11 times ten thousand, and **t.** of **t.**; *5505*

THOUSAND-THOUSAND See THOUSAND.

THREAD

Ge 14:23 take from a **t.** even to a shoelatchet, 2339
Ge 38:28 bound upon his hand a scarlet **t.**,
Ge 38:30 that had the scarlet **t.** upon his hand:
Jos 2:18 shalt bind this line of scarlet **t.** 2339
Jg 16:9 as a **t.** of tow is broken when it 6616
Jg 16:12 them from off his arms like a **t.** 2339
Ca 4:3 Thy lips are like a **t.** of scarlet, and 2339

THREATEN See also THREATENED; THREATENING.

Ac 4:17 let us straitly **t.** them, that they *546*

THREATENED

Ac 4:21 So when they had further **t.** them, *4324*
1Pe 2:23 again; when he suffered, he **t.** not; *546*

THREATENING See also THREATENINGS.

Eph 6:9 things unto them, forbearing **t.** *547*

THREATENINGS

Ac 4:29 And now, Lord, behold their **t.**: and *547*
Ac 9:1 And Saul, yet breathing out **t.** and *547*

THREE See also THIRTEEN; THREEFOLD; THREESCORE.

Ge 5:22 Methuselah **t.** hundred years, 7969
Ge 5:23 Enoch was **t.** hundred sixty and five 7969
Ge 6:10 Noah begat **t.** sons, Shem, Ham, 7969
Ge 6:15 the ark shall be **t.** hundred cubits, 7969
Ge 7:13 the **t.** wives of his sons with them, 7969
Ge 9:19 These are the **t.** sons of Noah: and 7969
Ge 9:28 after the flood **t.** hundred and fifty 7969
Ge 11:13 Salah four hundred and **t.** years, 7969
Ge 11:15 Eber four hundred and **t.** years, 7969
Ge 14:14 own house, **t.** hundred and eighteen, 7969
Ge 15:9 Take me an heifer of **t.** years old, 8027
Ge 15:9 and a she goat of **t.** years old, and a 8027
Ge 15:9 a ram of **t.** years old, and a 8027
Ge 18:2 and, lo, **t.** men stood by him: 7969

Ge 18:6 quickly **t.** measures of fine meal, ... 7969
Ge 29:2 there were **t.** flocks of sheep lying ... 7969
Ge 29:34 because I have born him **t.** sons: ... 7969
Ge 30:36 **t.** days' journey betwixt himself and ... 7969
Ge 38:24 came to pass about **t.** months after, ... 7969
Ge 40:10 And in the vine were **t.** branches: ... 7969
Ge 40:12 The **t.** branches are **t.** days: ... 7969
Ge 40:13 within **t.** days shall Pharaoh lift ... 7969
Ge 40:16 I had **t.** white baskets on my head: ... 7969
Ge 40:18 thereof: the **t.** baskets are **t.** days: ... 7969
Ge 40:19 within **t.** days shall Pharaoh lift ... 7969
Ge 42:17 them all together into ward **t.** days. ... 7969
Ge 45:22 gave **t.** hundred pieces of silver, ... 7969
Ge 46:15 his daughters were thirty and **t.** ... 7969
Ex 2:2 goodly child, she hid him **t.** months. ... 7969
Ex 3:18 **t.** days' journey into the wilderness, ... 7969
Ex 5:3 **t.** days' journey into the desert, and ... 7969
Ex 6:18 an hundred thirty and **t.** years. ... 7969
Ex 7:7 Aaron fourscore and **t.** years old, ... 7969
Ex 8:27 **t.** days' journey into the wilderness, ... 7969
Ex 10:22 in all the land of Egypt **t.** days: ... 7969
Ex 10:23 rose any from his place for **t.** days: ... 7969
Ex 15:22 they went **t.** days in the wilderness, ... 7969
Ex 21:11 And if he do not these **t.** unto her, ... 7969
Ex 23:14 **T.** times thou shalt keep a feast ... 7969
Ex 23:17 **T.** times in the year all thy males ... 7969
Ex 25:32, 32 **t.** branches of the candlestick ... 7969
Ex 25:33 **T.** bowls made like unto almonds, ... 7969
Ex 25:33 **t.** bowls made like almonds in the ... 7969
Ex 27:1 the height thereof shall be **t.** cubits. ... 7969
Ex 27:14, 15 pillars **t.**, and their sockets **t.** ... 7969
Ex 32:28 that day about **t.** thousand men. ... 7969
Ex 37:18, 18 **t.** branches of the candlestick ... 7969
Ex 37:19 **T.** bowls made after the fashion of ... 7969
Ex 37:19 and **t.** bowls made like almonds in ... 7969
Ex 38:1 and **t.** cubits the height thereof. ... 7969
Ex 38:14, 15 pillars **t.**, and their sockets **t.** ... 7969
Ex 38:26 **t.** thousand and five hundred and ... 7969
Le 12:4 of her purifying **t.** and thirty days; ... 7969
Le 14:10 **t.** tenth deals of fine flour for a ... 7969
Le 19:23 **t.** years shall it be as uncircumcised ... 7969
Le 25:21 it shall bring forth fruit for **t.** years. ... 7969
Le 27:6 estimation...be **t.** shekels of silver. ... 7969
Nu 1:23 and nine thousand and **t.** hundred. ... 7969
Nu 1:43 fifty and **t.** thousand and four. ... 7969
Nu 1:46 hundred thousand and **t.** thousand. ... 7969
Nu 2:13 and nine thousand and **t.** hundred. ... 7969
Nu 2:30 and **t.** thousand and four hundred. ... 7969
Nu 2:32 hundred thousand and **t.** thousand. ... 7969
Nu 3:50 **t.** hundred and threescore and five ... 7969
Nu 4:44 were **t.** thousand and two hundred. ... 7969
Nu 10:33 mount of the Lord **t.** days' journey: ... 7969
Nu 10:33 before them in the **t.** days' journey, ... 7969
Nu 12:4 Come out ye **t.** unto the tabernacle ... 7969
Nu 12:4 And they **t.** came out. ... 7969
Nu 15:9 offering of **t.** tenth deals of flour ... 7969
Nu 22:28 hast smitten me these **t.** times? ... 7969
Nu 22:32 smitten thine ass these **t.** times? ... 7969
Nu 22:33 and turned from me these **t.** times: ... 7969
Nu 24:10 blessed them these **t.** times. ... 7969
Nu 26:7 forty and **t.** thousand and seven ... 7969
Nu 26:25 and four thousand and **t.** hundred. ... 7969
Nu 26:47 were fifty and **t.** thousand and four ... 7969
Nu 26:62 twenty and **t.** thousand, all males ... 7969
Nu 28:12 **t.** tenth deals of flour for a meat ... 7969
Nu 28:20 **t.** tenth deals shall ye offer for a ... 7969
Nu 28:28 **t.** tenth deals unto one bullock, two ... 7969
Nu 29:3 **t.** tenth deals for a bullock, and ... 7969
Nu 29:9 **t.** tenth deals to a bullock, and two ... 7969
Nu 29:14 **t.** tenth deals unto every bullock of ... 7969
Nu 31:36 **t.** hundred thousand and seven ... 7969
Nu 31:43 **t.** hundred thousand and thirty ... 7969
Nu 33:8 **t.** days' journey in the wilderness ... 7969
Nu 33:39 hundred and twenty and **t.** years ... 7969
Nu 35:14 give **t.** cities on this side Jordan, ... 7969
Nu 35:14 **t.** cities shall ye give in the land of ... 7969
De 4:41 Moses severed **t.** cities on this side ... 7969
De 14:28 the end of **t.** years thou shalt bring ... 7969
De 16:16 **T.** times in a year shall all thy ... 7969
De 17:6 of two witnesses, or **t.** witnesses, ... 7969
De 19:2 separate **t.** cities for thee in the ... 7969
De 19:3 thee to inherit, into **t.** parts, ... 8027
De 19:7 shalt separate **t.** cities for thee. ... 7969
De 19:9 cities more for thee, beside these **t.** ...
De 19:9 thou add **t.** cities more for thee, ... 7969
De 19:15 or at the mouth of **t.** witnesses, ... 7969
Jos 1:11 within **t.** days ye shall pass over ... 7969
Jos 2:16 and hide yourselves there **t.** days, ... 7969
Jos 2:22 and abode there **t.** days, until the ... 7969
Jos 3:2 it came to pass after **t.** days, that ... 7969
Jos 7:3 about two or **t.** thousand men go up ... 7969
Jos 7:4 the people about **t.** thousand men: ... 7969
Jos 9:16 came to pass at the end of **t.** days ... 7969
Jos 15:14 drove thence the **t.** sons of Anak, ... 7969
Jos 17:11 and her towns, even **t.** countries. ... 7969
Jos 18:4 among you **t.** men for each tribe: ... 7969
Jos 21:32 Kartan with her suburbs; **t.** cities. ... 7969
Jg 1:20 thence the **t.** sons of Anak. ... 7969
Jg 7:6 their mouth, were **t.** hundred men: ... 7969
Jg 7:7 By the **t.** hundred men that lapped ... 7969
Jg 7:8 and retained those **t.** hundred men: ... 7969
Jg 7:16 **t.** hundred men into **t.** companies, ... 7969
Jg 7:20 the **t.** companies blew the trumpets, ... 7969
Jg 7:22 the **t.** hundred blew the trumpets, ... 7969
Jg 8:4 **t.** hundred men that were with him, ... 7969
Jg 9:22 had reigned **t.** years over Israel. ... 7969
Jg 9:43 and divided them into **t.** companies, ... 7969
Jg 10:2 judged Israel twenty and **t.** years, ... 7969
Jg 11:26 coasts of Arnon, **t.** hundred years? ... 7969
Jg 14:14 not in **t.** days expound the riddle. ... 7969
Jg 15:4 went and caught **t.** hundred foxes, ... 7969
Jg 15:11 **t.** thousand men of Judah went to ... 7969
Jg 16:15 hast mocked me these **t.** times, ... 7969
Jg 16:27 about **t.** thousand men and women, ... 7969
Jg 19:4 and he abode with him **t.** days: ... 7969
1Sa 1:24 him up with her, with **t.** bullocks, ... 7969
1Sa 2:13 a fleshhook of **t.** teeth in his hand: ... 7969
1Sa 2:21 bare **t.** sons and two daughters. ... 7969
1Sa 9:20 thine asses that were lost **t.** days ... 7969
1Sa 10:3 meet thee **t.** men going up to God ... 7969
1Sa 10:3 one carrying **t.** kids, and another ... 7969
1Sa 10:3 another carrying **t.** loaves of bread, ... 7969
1Sa 11:8 of Israel were **t.** hundred thousand, ... 7969
1Sa 11:11 put the people in **t.** companies; ... 7969
1Sa 13:2 Saul chose him **t.** thousand men of ... 7969
1Sa 13:17 of the Philistines in **t.** companies: ... 7969
1Sa 17:13 the **t.** eldest sons of Jesse went and ... 7969
1Sa 17:13 the names of his **t.** sons that went ... 7969
1Sa 17:14 and the **t.** eldest followed Saul. ... 7969
1Sa 20:19 when thou hast stayed **t.** days, ... 8027
1Sa 20:20 I will shoot **t.** arrows on the side ... 7969
1Sa 20:41 and bowed himself **t.** times: ... 7969
1Sa 21:5 kept from us about these **t.** days, ... 8032
1Sa 24:2 took **t.** thousand chosen men out ... 7969
1Sa 25:2 he had **t.** thousand sheep, and a ... 7969
1Sa 26:2 having **t.** thousand chosen men of ... 7969
1Sa 30:12 any water, **t.** days and **t.** nights. ... 7969
1Sa 30:13 because **t.** days agone I fell sick. ... 7969
1Sa 31:6 So Saul died, and his **t.** sons, and ... 7969
1Sa 31:8 Saul and his **t.** sons fallen in mount ... 7969
2Sa 2:18 there were **t.** sons of Zeruiah there, ... 7969
2Sa 2:31 so that **t.** hundred and threescore ... 7969
2Sa 5:5 he reigned thirty and **t.** years over ... 7969
2Sa 6:11 Obed-edom the Gittite **t.** months: ... 7969
2Sa 13:38 to Geshur, and was there **t.** years. ... 7969
2Sa 14:27 Absalom there were born **t.** sons, ... 7969
2Sa 18:14 And he took **t.** darts in his hand, ... 7969
2Sa 20:4 the men of Judah within **t.** days, ... 7969
2Sa 21:1 famine in the days of David **t.** years, ... 7969
2Sa 21:16 spear weighed **t.** hundred shekels ... 7969
2Sa 23:9 one of the **t.** mighty men with ... 7969
2Sa 23:13 **t.** of the thirty chief went down, ... 7991
2Sa 23:16 the **t.** mighty men brake through ... 7969
2Sa 23:17 things did these **t.** mighty men. ... 7969
2Sa 23:18 son of Zeruiah, was chief among **t.** ... 7992
2Sa 23:18 up his spear against **t.** hundred, ... 7969
2Sa 23:18 them, and had the name among **t.** ... 7969
2Sa 23:19 Was he not most honourable of **t.**? ... 7969
2Sa 23:19 he attained not unto the first **t.** ... 7969
2Sa 23:22 the name among **t.** mighty men. ... 7969
2Sa 23:23 but he attained not to the first **t.** ... 7969
2Sa 24:12 the Lord, I offer thee **t.** things; ... 7969
2Sa 24:13 wilt thou flee **t.** months before ... 7969
2Sa 24:13 that there be **t.** days' pestilence in ... 7969
1Ki 2:11 thirty and **t.** years reigned he in ... 7969
1Ki 2:39 came to pass at the end of **t.** years, ... 7969
1Ki 4:32 And he spake **t.** thousand proverbs: ... 7969
1Ki 5:16 **t.** thousand and **t.** hundred, which ... 7969
1Ki 6:36 court with **t.** rows of hewed stone, ... 7969
1Ki 7:4 And there were windows in **t.** rows, ... 7969
1Ki 7:4, 5 was against light in **t.** ranks. ... 7969
1Ki 7:12 was with **t.** rows of hewed stones, ... 7969
1Ki 7:25 oxen, **t.** looking toward the north, ... 7969
1Ki 7:25 and **t.** looking toward the west, ... 7969
1Ki 7:25 and **t.** looking toward the south, ... 7969
1Ki 7:25 and **t.** looking toward the east: ... 7969
1Ki 7:27 and **t.** cubits the height of it. ... 7969
1Ki 9:25 **t.** times in a year did Solomon offer ... 7969
1Ki 10:17 **t.** hundred shields of beaten gold; ... 7969
1Ki 10:17 **t.** pound of gold went to one shield: ... 7969
1Ki 10:22 once in **t.** years came the navy of ... 7969
1Ki 11:3 and **t.** hundred concubines: and ... 7969
1Ki 12:5 Depart yet for **t.** days, then come ... 7969
1Ki 15:2 **T.** years reigned he in Jerusalem. ... 7969
1Ki 17:21 himself upon the child **t.** times, ... 7969
1Ki 22:1 they continued **t.** years without war ... 7969
2Ki 2:17 they sought **t.** days, but found him ... 7969
2Ki 3:10, 13 called these **t.** kings together, ... 7969
2Ki 9:32 out to him two or **t.** eunuchs. ... 7969
2Ki 12:6 the **t.** and twentieth year of king ... 7969
2Ki 13:1 the **t.** and twentieth year of Joash ... 7969
2Ki 13:25 **T.** times did Joash beat him, and ... 7969
2Ki 17:5 to Samaria, and besieged it **t.** years. ... 7969
2Ki 18:10 at the end of **t.** years they took it: ... 7969
2Ki 18:14 **t.** hundred talents of silver and ... 7969
2Ki 23:31 Jehoahaz was twenty and **t.** years. ... 7969
2Ki 23:31 he reigned **t.** months in Jerusalem. ... 7969
2Ki 24:1 became his servant **t.** years: ... 7969
2Ki 24:8 he reigned in Jerusalem **t.** months. ... 7969
2Ki 25:17 the height of the chapiter **t.** cubits; ... 7969
2Ki 25:18 and the **t.** keepers of the door: ... 7969
1Ch 2:3 which **t.** were born unto him of the ... 7969
1Ch 2:16 Abishai, and Joab, and Asahel, **t.** ... 7969
1Ch 2:22 who had **t.** and twenty cities in the ... 7969
1Ch 3:4 he reigned thirty and **t.** years. ... 7969
1Ch 3:23 and Hezekiah, and Azrikam, **t.** ... 7969
1Ch 7:6 Bela, and Becher, and Jediael, **t.** ... 7969
1Ch 10:6 Saul died, and his **t.** sons, and all ... 7969
1Ch 11:11 **t.** hundred slain by him at one time. ... 7969
1Ch 11:12 who was one of the **t.** mighties. ... 7969
1Ch 11:15 **t.** of the thirty captains went down ... 7969
1Ch 11:18 the **t.** brake through the host of the ... 7969
1Ch 11:19 These things did these **t.** mightiest. ... 7969
1Ch 11:20 of Joab, he was chief of the **t.** ... 7969
1Ch 11:20 up his spear against **t.** hundred, ... 7969
1Ch 11:20 and had a name among the **t.** ... 7969
1Ch 11:21 Of the **t.**, he was more honourable ... 7969
1Ch 11:21 he attained not to the first **t.** ... 7969
1Ch 11:24 the name among the **t.** mighties. ... 7969
1Ch 11:25 but attained not to the first **t.** ... 7969
1Ch 12:27 **t.** thousand and seven hundred; ... 7969
1Ch 12:29 the kindred of Saul, **t.** thousand: ... 7969
1Ch 12:39 there they were with David **t.** days, ... 7969
1Ch 13:14 Obed-edom in his house **t.** months. ... 7969
1Ch 21:10 the Lord, I offer thee **t.** things: ... 7969
1Ch 21:12 Either **t.** years' famine; ... 7969
1Ch 21:12 or **t.** months to be destroyed before ... 7969
1Ch 21:12 else **t.** days the sword of the Lord, ... 7969
1Ch 23:8 Jehiel, and Zetham, and Joel, **t.** ... 7969
1Ch 23:9 and Haziel, and Haran, **t.** ... 7969
1Ch 23:23 Mahli, and Eder, and Jeremoth, **t.** ... 7969
1Ch 24:18 The **t.** and twentieth to Delaiah, ... 7969
1Ch 25:5 fourteen sons and **t.** daughters. ... 7969
1Ch 25:30 The **t.** and twentieth to Mahazioth, ... 7969
1Ch 29:4 Even **t.** thousand talents of gold, ... 7969
1Ch 29:27 thirty and **t.** years reigned he in ... 7969
2Ch 2:2 **t.** thousand and six hundred to ... 7969
2Ch 2:17 and **t.** thousand and six hundred ... 7969
2Ch 2:18 and **t.** thousand and six hundred ... 7969
2Ch 4:4 oxen, **t.** looking toward the north, ... 7969
2Ch 4:4 and **t.** looking toward the west, ... 7969
2Ch 4:4 and **t.** looking toward the south, ... 7969
2Ch 4:4 and **t.** looking toward the east: and ... 7969
2Ch 4:5 and held **t.** thousand baths. ... 7969
2Ch 6:13 **t.** cubits high, and had set it in the ... 7969
2Ch 7:10 **t.** and twentieth day of the seventh ... 7969
2Ch 8:13 solemn feasts, **t.** times in the year, ... 7969
2Ch 9:16 **t.** hundred shields made he of ... 7969
2Ch 9:16 **t.** hundred shekels of gold went to ... 7969
2Ch 9:21 every **t.** years once came the ships ... 7969
2Ch 10:5 Come again unto me after **t.** days. ... 7969
2Ch 11:17 the son of Solomon strong, **t.** years: ... 7969
2Ch 11:17 for **t.** years they walked in the way ... 7969
2Ch 13:2 He reigned **t.** years in Jerusalem. ... 7969
2Ch 14:8 out of Judah **t.** hundred thousand; ... 7969
2Ch 14:9 thousand, and **t.** hundred chariots; ... 7969
2Ch 17:14 men of valour **t.** hundred thousand. ... 7969
2Ch 20:25 they were **t.** days in gathering of ... 7969
2Ch 25:5 found them **t.** hundred thousand ... 7969
2Ch 25:13 and smote **t.** thousand of them, ... 7969

2Ch 26:13 **t.** hundred thousand and seven 7969
2Ch 29:33 oxen and **t.** thousand sheep 7969
2Ch 31:16 from **t.** years old and upward, 7969
2Ch 35:7 thousand, and **t.** thousand bullocks: 7969
2Ch 35:8 small cattle, and **t.** hundred oxen 7969
2Ch 36:2 was twenty and **t.** years old when 7969
2Ch 36:2 he reigned **t.** months in Jerusalem. 7969
2Ch 36:9 he reigned **t.** months and ten days 7969
Ezr 2:4 **t.** hundred seventy and two. 7969
Ezr 2:11 Bebai, six hundred and twenty and **t.** 7969
Ezr 2:17 of Bezai, **t.** hundred twenty and **t.** 7969
Ezr 2:19 two hundred twenty and **t.** 7969
Ezr 2:21 an hundred twenty and **t.** 7969
Ezr 2:25 seven hundred and forty and **t.** 7969
Ezr 2:28 and Ai, two hundred twenty and **t.** 7969
Ezr 2:32 of Harim, **t.** hundred and twenty. 7969
Ezr 2:34 Jericho, **t.** hundred forty and five 7969
Ezr 2:35 **t.** thousand and six hundred and 7969
Ezr 2:36 nine hundred seventy and **t.** 7969
Ezr 2:58 were **t.** hundred ninety and two. 7969
Ezr 2:64 forty and two thousand **t.** hundred 7969
Ezr 2:65 seven thousand **t.** hundred thirty 7969
Ezr 6:4 With **t.** rows of great stones, and a 8532
Ezr 8:5 and with him **t.** hundred males 7969
Ezr 8:15 there abode we in tents **t.** days: 7969
Ezr 8:32 Jerusalem, and abode there **t.** days. 7969
Ezr 10:8 would not come within **t.** days, 7969
Ezr 10:9 unto Jerusalem within **t.** days. 7969
Ne 2:11 Jerusalem, and was there **t.** days. 7969
Ne 7:9 **t.** hundred seventy and two. 7969
Ne 7:17 two thousand **t.** hundred twenty 7969
Ne 7:22 **t.** hundred twenty and eight. 7969
Ne 7:23 Bezai, **t.** hundred twenty and four. 7969
Ne 7:29 Beeroth, seven hundred forty and **t.** 7969
Ne 7:32 and Ai, an hundred twenty and **t.** 7969
Ne 7:35 of Harim, **t.** hundred and twenty. 7969
Ne 7:36 Jericho, **t.** hundred forty and five 7969
Ne 7:38 **t.** thousand nine hundred and 7969
Ne 7:39 nine hundred seventy and **t.** 7969
Ne 7:60 were **t.** hundred ninety and two. 7969
Ne 7:66 thousand **t.** hundred and threescore, 7969
Ne 7:67 **t.** hundred thirty and seven: 7969
Es 4:16 neither eat nor drink **t.** days, night 7969
Es 8:9 on the **t.** and twentieth day thereof; 7969
Es 9:15 slew **t.** hundred men at Shushan; 7969
Job 1:2 him seven sons and **t.** daughters. 7969
Job 1:3 and **t.** thousand camels, and five 7969
Job 1:4 their **t.** sisters to eat and to drink 7969
Job 1:17 The Chaldeans made out **t.** bands, 7969
Job 2:11 Job's **t.** friends heard of all this evil 7969
Job 32:1 these **t.** men ceased to answer Job, 7969
Job 32:3 against his **t.** friends was his wrath 7969
Job 32:5 answer in the mouth of these **t.** men, 7969
Job 42:13 also seven sons and **t.** daughters 7969
Pr 30:15 **t.** things that are never satisfied, 7969
Pr 30:18 **t.** things which are too wonderful 7969
Pr 30:21 For **t.** things the earth is disquieted, 7969
Pr 30:29 There be **t.** things which go well, 7969
Isa 15:5 Zoar, an heifer of **t.** years old: 7992
Isa 16:14 Within **t.** years, as the years of an 7969
Isa 17:6 two or **t.** berries in the top of the 7969
Isa 20:3 walked naked and barefoot **t.** years 7969
Jer 25:3 that is the **t.** and twentieth year, 7969
Jer 36:23 Jehudi had read **t.** or four leaves, 7969
Jer 48:34 as an heifer of **t.** years old: 7992
Jer 52:24 and the **t.** keepers of the door: 7969
Jer 52:28 **t.** thousand Jews and **t.** and twenty: 7969
Jer 52:30 In the **t.** and twentieth year of 7969
Eze 4:5 days, **t.** hundred and ninety days: 7969
Eze 4:9 **t.** hundred and ninety days shalt 7969
Eze 14:14 Though these **t.** men, Noah, Daniel, 7969
Eze 14:16, 18, Though these **t.** men were in it, 7969
Eze 40:10 **t.** on this side, and **t.** on that side; 7969
Eze 40:10 side; they **t.** were of one measure: 7969
Eze 40:21 **t.** of this side and **t.** on that side; 7969
Eze 40:48 the gate was **t.** cubits on this side, 7969
Eze 40:48 this side, and **t.** cubits on that side. 7969
Eze 41:6 the side chambers were **t.**, one 7969
Eze 41:16 round about on their **t.** stories, 7969
Eze 41:22 altar of wood was **t.** cubits high, 7969
Eze 42:3 gallery against gallery in **t.** stories. 7992
Eze 42:6 For they were in **t.** stories, but had 8027
Eze 48:31 **t.** gates northward; one gate of 7969
Eze 48:32 **t.** gates; and one gate of Joseph, 7969
Eze 48:33 hundred measures: and **t.** gates; 7969
Eze 48:34 five hundred, with their **t.** gates; 7969
Da 1:5 so nourishing them **t.** years, that at 7969
Da 3:23 these **t.** men, Shadrach, Meshach, 8532
Da 3:24 Did not we cast **t.** men bound into 8532
Da 6:2 And over these **t.** presidents; of 8532
Da 6:10 upon his knees **t.** times a day, 8532
Da 6:13 maketh his petition **t.** times a day 8532
Da 7:5 it had **t.** ribs in the mouth of it 8532
Da 7:8 whom there were **t.** of the first 8532
Da 7:20 came up, and before whom **t.** fell; 8532
Da 7:24 first, and he shall subdue **t.** kings. 8532
Da 8:14 thousand and **t.** hundred days; 7969
Da 10:2 Daniel was mourning **t.** full weeks. 7969
Da 10:3 till **t.** whole weeks were fulfilled 7969
Da 11:2 shall stand up yet **t.** kings in Persia; 7969
Da 12:12 thousand **t.** hundred and five and 7969
Am 1:3 For **t.** transgressions of Damascus, 7969
Am 1:6 For **t.** transgressions of Gaza, and 7969
Am 1:9 For **t.** transgressions of Tyrus, and 7969
Am 1:11 For **t.** transgressions of Edom, and 7969
Am 1:13 For **t.** transgressions of the children 7969
Am 2:1 For **t.** transgressions of Moab, and 7969
Am 2:4 For **t.** transgressions of Judah, and 7969
Am 2:6 For **t.** transgressions of Israel, and 7969
Am 4:4 and your tithes after **t.** years: 7969
Am 4:7 were yet **t.** months to the harvest: 7969
Am 4:8 So two or **t.** cities wandered unto 7969
Jon 1:17 belly of the fish **t.** days and nights. 7969
Jon 3:3 great city of **t.** days' journey. 7969
Zec 11:8 **T.** shepherds also I cut off in one 7969
Mt 12:40 **as Jonas was t. days and t. nights** *5140*
Mt 12:40 **t. days and t. nights in the heart** *5140*
Mt 13:33 **and hid in t. measures of meal,** *5140*
Mt 15:32 **continue with me now t. days,** *5140*
Mt 17:4 let us make here **t.** tabernacles; *5140*
Mt 18:16 **the mouth of two or t. witnesses** *5140*
Mt 18:20 **two or t. are gathered together in** *5140*
Mt 26:61 of God, and to build it in **t.** days. *5140*
Mt 27:40 and buildest it in **t.** days, save *5140*
Mt 27:63 alive, After **t.** days I will rise again. *5140*
Mk 8:2 **have now been with me t. days,** *5140*
Mk 8:31 killed, and after **t.** days rise again *5140*
Mk 9:5 and let us make **t.** tabernacles; one *5140*
Mk 14:5 for more than **t.** hundred pence, *5145*
Mk 14:58 within **t.** days I will build another *5140*
Mk 15:29 temple, and buildest it in **t.** days, *5140*
Lu 1:56 abode with her about **t.** months, *5140*
Lu 2:46 after **t.** days they found him in the *5140*
Lu 4:25 **shut up t. years and six months,** *5140*
Lu 9:33 and let us make **t.** tabernacles; one *5140*
Lu 10:36 **Which now of these t., thinkest** *5140*
Lu 11:5 **him, Friend, lend me t. loaves;** *5140*
Lu 12:52 **t. against two, and two against t.,** *5140*
Lu 13:7 **t. years, I come seeking fruit** *5140*
Lu 13:21 **and hid in t. measures of meal,** *5140*
Joh 2:6 containing two or **t.** firkins apiece. *5140*
Joh 2:19 **and in t. days I will raise it up** *5140*
Joh 2:20 and wilt thou rear it up in **t.** days? *5140*
Joh 12:5 ointment sold for **t.** hundred pence, *5145*
Joh 21:11 fishes, an hundred and fifty and **t.**: *5140*
Ac 2:41 them about **t.** thousand souls. *5153*
Ac 5:7 about the space of **t.** hours after, *5140*
Ac 7:20 up in his father's house **t.** months: *5140*
Ac 9:9 And he was **t.** days without sight, *5140*
Ac 10:19 unto him, Behold, **t.** men seek thee. *5140*
Ac 11:10 And this was done **t.** times: and all *5151*
Ac 11:11 **t.** men already come unto the house *5140*
Ac 17:2 **t.** sabbath days reasoned with them *5140*
Ac 19:8 boldly for the space of **t.** months, *5140*
Ac 20:3 And there abode **t.** months. And *5140*
Ac 20:31 the space of **t.** years I ceased not *5148*
Ac 25:1 after **t.** days he ascended from *5140*
Ac 28:7 and lodged us **t.** days courteously, *5140*
Ac 28:11 And after **t.** months we departed in *5140*
Ac 28:12 Syracuse, we tarried there **t.** days *5140*
Ac 28:15 as Appii forum, and The **t.** taverns: *5140*
Ac 28:17 after **t.** days Paul called the chief *5140*
1Co 10:8 in one day **t.** and twenty thousand. *5140*
1Co 13:13 faith, hope, charity, these **t.**; *5140*
1Co 14:27 let it be by two, or at the most by **t.**, *5140*
1Co 14:29 Let the prophets speak two or **t.**, *5140*
2Co 13:1 mouth of two or **t.** witnesses shall *5140*
Ga 1:18 Then after **t.** years I went up to *5140*
1Ti 5:19 but before two or **t.** witnesses. *5140*
Heb 10:28 mercy under two or **t.** witnesses: *5140*
Heb 11:23 was hid **t.** months of his parents, *5150*
Jas 5:17 space of **t.** years and six months. *5140*
1Jo 5:7 are **t.** that bear record in heaven *5140*
1Jo 5:7 Holy Ghost: and these **t.** are one. *5140*
1Jo 5:8 are **t.** that bear witness in earth, *5140*
1Jo 5:8 blood: and these **t.** agree in one. *5140*
Re 6:6 **t.** measures of barley for a penny; *5140*
Re 8:13 of the trumpet of the **t.** angels, *5140*
Re 9:18 By these **t.** was the third part of *5140*
Re 11:9 dead bodies **t.** days and an half, *5140*
Re 11:11 after **t.** days and an half the Spirit *5140*
Re 16:13 I saw **t.** unclean spirits like frogs *5140*
Re 16:19 great city was divided into **t.** parts, *5140*
Re 21:13 On the east **t.** gates; *5140*
Re 21:13 on the north **t.** gates; *5140*
Re 21:13 on the south **t.** gates; *5140*
Re 21:13 and on the west **t.** gates. *5140*

THREEFOLD

Ec 4:12 a **t.** cord is not quickly broken. 8027

THREE-HUNDRED See THREE and HUNDRED.

THREESCORE

Ge 25:7 an hundred **t.** and fifteen years. 7657
Ge 25:26 Isaac was **t.** years old when she 8346
Ge 46:26 all the souls were **t.** and six; 8346
Ge 46:27 came into Egypt, were **t.** and ten. 7657
Ge 50:3 mourned for him **t.** and ten days. 7657
Ex 15:27 water, and **t.** and ten palm trees: 7657
Ex 38:25 hundred and **t.** and fifteen shekels, 7657
Le 12:5 of her purifying **t.** and six days. 8346
Nu 1:27 were **t.** and fourteen thousand 7657
Nu 1:39 were **t.** and two thousand and 8346
Nu 2:4 were **t.** and fourteen thousand 7657
Nu 2:26 were **t.** and two thousand and 8346
Nu 3:43 two hundred and **t.** and thirteen. 7657
Nu 3:46 two hundred and **t.** and thirteen 7657
Nu 3:50 hundred and **t.** and five shekels, 8346
Nu 26:22 **t.** and sixteen thousand and five 7657
Nu 26:25 **t.** and four thousand and three 8346
Nu 26:27 them, **t.** thousand and five hundred. 8346
Nu 26:43 were **t.** and four thousand and 8346
Nu 31:33 **t.** and twelve thousand beeves, 7657
Nu 31:34 And **t.** and one thousand asses, 8346
Nu 31:37 six hundred and **t.** and fifteen. 7657
Nu 31:38 Lord's tribute was **t.** and twelve. 7657
Nu 31:39 the Lord's tribute was **t.** and one. 8346
Nu 33:9 water, and **t.** and ten palm trees; 7657
De 3:4 **t.** cities, all the region of Argob, ; 8346
De 10:22 Egypt with **t.** and ten persons; 7657
Jos 13:30 which are in Bashan, **t.** cities: 8346
Jg 1:7 **T.** and ten kings, having their 7657
Jg 8:14 thereof, even **t.** and seventeen men 7657
Jg 8:30 had **t.** and ten sons of his body 7657
Jg 9:2 which are **t.** and ten persons, reign 7657
Jg 9:4 they gave him **t.** and ten pieces 7657
Jg 9:5 Jerubbaal, being **t.** and ten persons, 7657
Jg 9:18 slain his sons, **t.** and ten persons, 7657
Jg 9:24 to the **t.** and ten sons of Jerubbaal 7657
Jg 12:14 that rode on **t.** and ten ass colts: 7657
1Sa 6:19 fifty thousand and **t.** and ten men: 7657
2Sa 2:31 three hundred and **t.** men died 8346
1Ki 4:13 **t.** great cities with walls and 8346
1Ki 4:22 fine flour, and **t.** measures of meal, 8346
1Ki 5:15 had **t.** and ten thousand that bare 7657
1Ki 6:2 the length thereof was **t.** cubits, 8346
1Ki 10:14 hundred and **t.** and six talents of gold, 8346
2Ki 25:19 and **t.** men of the people of the land 8346
1Ch 2:21 whom he married when he was **t.** 8346
1Ch 2:23 the towns thereof, even **t.** cities. 8346
1Ch 5:18 thousand seven hundred and **t.**, 8346
1Ch 9:13 and seven hundred and **t.**; 8346
1Ch 16:38 with their brethren, **t.** and eight; 8346
1Ch 21:5 **t.** and ten thousand men that drew 7657
1Ch 26:8 were **t.** and two of Obed-edom. 8346
2Ch 2:2 **t.** and ten thousand men to bear 7657
2Ch 2:18 **t.** and ten thousand of them to be 7657
2Ch 3:3 the first measure was **t.** cubits, 8346
2Ch 9:13 six hundred and **t.** and six talents 8346
2Ch 11:21 eighteen wives, and **t.** concubines; 8346
2Ch 11:21 and eight sons, and **t.** daughters.) 8346
2Ch 12:3 chariots, and **t.** thousand horsemen: 8346
2Ch 29:32 brought, was **t.** and ten bullocks, 7657
2Ch 36:21 sabbath, to fulfil **t.** and ten years. 7657
Ezr 2:9 of Zaccai, seven hundred and **t.** 8346
Ezr 2:64 two thousand three hundred and **t.**, 8346
Ezr 2:69 **t.** and one thousand drams of gold, 7239
Ezr 6:3 the height thereof **t.** cubits, and 8361
Ezr 6:3 and the breadth thereof **t.** cubits; 8361

Ezr 8:10 him an hundred and **t.** males. 8346
Ezr 8:13 Shemaiah, and with them **t.** males. 8346
Ne 7:14 of Zaccai, seven hundred and **t.**. 8346
Ne 7:18 six hundred **t.** and seven. 8346
Ne 7:19 Bigvai, two thousand **t.** and seven. 8346
Ne 7:66 two thousand three hundred and **t.**, 8346
Ne 7:72 and **t.** and seven priests' garments. 8346
Ne 11:6 four hundred **t.** and eight valiant 8346
Ps 90:10 of our years are **t.** years and ten; 7657
Ca 3:7 **t.** valiant men are about it, of the 7657
Ca 6:8 There are **t.** queens, and fourscore 7657
Isa 7:8 and within **t.** and five years shall 7657
Jer 52:25 and **t.** men of the people of the land, 7657
Eze 40:14 He made also posts of **t.** cubits, 7657
Da 3:1 gold, whose height was **t.** cubits, 8361
Da 5:31 being about **t.** and two years old. 8361
Da 9:25 weeks, and **t.** and two weeks: 8346
Da 9:26 And after **t.** and two weeks shall 8346
Zec 1:12 indignation these **t.** and ten years? 7657
Lu 24:13 from Jerusalem about **t.** furlongs. *1835*
Ac 7:14 his kindred, **t.** and fifteen souls. *1440*
Ac 23:23 and horsemen **t.** and ten, and *1440*
Ac 27:37 two hundred **t.** and sixteen souls. *1440*
1Ti 5:9 the number under **t.** years old, *1835*
Re 11:3 thousand two hundred and **t.** days, *1835*
Re 12:6 thousand two hundred and **t.** days. *1835*
Re 13:18 number is Six hundred **t.** and six. *5516*

THREESCORE-THOUSAND See THREESCORE and THOUSAND.

THREE-TRAVERNS See THREE and TAVERNS.

THREE-THOUSAND See THREE and THOUSAND.

THRESH See also THRESHED; THRESHETH; THRESHING.
Isa 41:15 thou shalt **t.** the mountains, and 1758
Jer 51:33 threshingfloor, it is time to **t.** her: 1869
Mic 4:13 Arise and **t.**, O daughter of Zion: 1758
Hab 3:12 thou didst **t.** the heathen in anger. 1758

THRESHED
Jg 6:11 Gideon **t.** wheat by the winepress, 2251
Isa 28:27 fitches are not **t.** with a threshing 1758
Am 1:3 they have **t.** Gilead with threshing 1758

THRESHETH
1Co 9:10 he that **t.** in hope should be partaker *248*

THRESHING See also THRESHINGFLOOR; THRESHINGPLACE.
Le 26:5 And your **t.** shall reach unto the 1786
2Sa 24:22 and **t.** instruments and other 4173
2Ki 13:7 had made them like the dust by **t.** 1758
1Ch 21:20 Now Ornan was **t.** wheat. 1758
1Ch 21:23 and the **t.** instruments for wood, 4173
Isa 21:10 O my **t.**, and the corn of my floor: 4098
Isa 28:27 not threshed with a **t.** instrument, 2742
Isa 28:28 because he will not ever be **t.** it, 1758
Isa 41:15 a new sharp **t.** instrument having 4173
Am 1:3 Gilead with **t.** instruments of iron: 2742

THRESHINGFLOOR See also THRESHINGFLOORS.
Ge 50:10 And they came to the **t.** of Atad, 1637
Nu 15:20 as ye do the heave offering of the **t.**, 1637
Nu 18:27 as though it were the corn of the **t.**, 1637
Nu 18:30 Levites as the increase of the **t.**, 1637
Ru 3:2 winnoweth barley to night in the **t.** 1637
2Sa 6:6 when they came to Nachon's **t.**, 1637
2Sa 24:18 unto the Lord in the **t.** of Araunah. 1637
2Sa 24:21 David said, To buy the **t.** of thee, 1637
2Sa 24:24 David bought the **t.** and the oxen 1637
1Ch 13:9 they came unto the **t.** of Chidon, 1637
1Ch 21:15 angel of the Lord stood by the **t.** 1637
1Ch 21:18 unto the Lord in the **t.** of Ornan 1637
1Ch 21:21 saw David, and went out of the **t.**, 1637
1Ch 21:22 Grant me the place of this **t.**, that 1637
1Ch 21:28 answered him in the **t.** of Ornan 1637
2Ch 3:1 had prepared in the **t.** of Ornan 1637
Jer 51:33 The daughter of Babylon is like a **t.**, 1637

THRESHINGFLOORS
1Sa 23:1 Keilah, and they rob the **t.** 1637
Da 2:35 like the chaff of the summer **t.**; 147

THRESHINGPLACE
2Sa 24:16 angel of the Lord was by the **t.** 1637

THRESHOLD See also THRESHOLDS.
Jg 19:27 and her hands were upon the **t.**. 5592
1Sa 5:4 his hands were cut off upon the **t.**; 4670
1Sa 5:5 tread on the **t.** of Dagon in Ashdod. 4670
1Ki 14:17 she came to the **t.** of the door, 5592
Eze 9:3 he was, to the **t.** of the house. 4670
Eze 10:4 and stood over the **t.** of the house; 4670
Eze 10:18 from off the **t.** of the house, 4670
Eze 40:6 and measured the **t.** of the gate, 5592
Eze 40:6 and the other **t.** of the gate, which 5592
Eze 40:7 the **t.** of the gate by the porch of 5592
Eze 43:8 setting of their **t.** by my thresholds, 5592
Eze 46:2 shall worship at the **t.** of the gate: 4670
Eze 47:1 waters issued out from under the **t.** 4670
Zep 1:9 punish all those that leap on the **t.**, 4670

THRESHOLDS
Ne 12:25 the ward at the **t.** of the gates. 624
Eze 43:8 setting of their threshold by my **t.**, 5592
Zep 2:14 desolation shall be in the **t.** 5592

THREW See also OVERTHREW; THREWEST.
2Sa 16:13 **t.** stones at him, and cast dust. 5619
2Ki 9:33 her down. So they **t.** her down: 8058
2Ch 31:1 **t.** down the high places and the 5422
Mk 12:42 widow, and she **t.** in two mites, *906*
Lu 9:42 devil **t.** him down, and tare him. *4952*
Ac 22:23 clothes, and **t.** dust into the air, *906*

THREWEST
Ne 9:11 persecutors thou **t.** into the deeps, 7993

THRICE
Ex 34:23 **T.** in the year shall all your 7969,6471
Ex 34:24 Lord thy God **t.** in the year. 7969,6471
2Ki 13:18 And he smote **t.**, and stayed. 7969,6471
2Ki 13:19 thou shalt smite Syria but **t.** 7969,6471
Mt 26:34 **crow, thou shalt deny me t.** *5151*
Mt 26:75 thou shalt deny me **t.**
Mk 14:30 **twice, thou shalt deny me t.**. *5151*
Mk 14:72 thou shalt deny me **t.**
Lu 22:34 **shalt t. deny that thou knowest** *5151*
Lu 22:61 cock crow, thou shalt deny me **t.**. *5151*
Joh 13:38 **crow, till thou hast denied me t.**. *5151*
Ac 10:16 This was done **t.**: and the vessel *5151*
2Co 11:25 **T.** was I beaten with rods, once *5151*
2Co 11:25 **t.** I suffered shipwreck, a night *5151*
2Co 12:8 this thing I besought the Lord **t.**, *5151*

THROAT
Ps 5:9 their **t.** is an open sepulchre; they 1627
Ps 69:3 weary of my crying: my **t.** is dried: 1627
Ps 115:7 neither speak they through their **t.**. 1627
Pr 23:2 And put a knife to thy **t.**, if thou 3930
Jer 2:25 unshod, and thy **t.** from thirst: 1627
Mt 18:28 **and took him by the t., saying,** *4155*
Ro 3:13 Their **t.** is an open sepulchre; *2995*

THRONE See also THRONES.
Ge 41:40 only in the **t.** will I be greater 3678
Ex 11:5 of Pharaoh that sitteth upon his **t.**, 3678
Ex 12:29 of Pharaoh that sat on his **t.** 3678
De 17:18 sitteth upon the **t.** of his kingdom, 3678
1Sa 2:8 make them inherit the **t.** of glory: 3678
2Sa 3:10 to set up the **t.** of David over Israel 3678
2Sa 7:13 will stablish the **t.** of his kingdom 3678
2Sa 7:16 thy **t.** shall be established for ever. 3678
2Sa 14:9 the king and his **t.** be guiltless. 3678
1Ki 1:13 me, and he shall sit upon my **t.**? 3678
1Ki 1:17 me, and he shall sit upon my **t.**. 3678
1Ki 1:20 who shall sit on the **t.** of my lord 3678
1Ki 1:24 me, and he shall sit upon my **t.**? 3678
1Ki 1:27 who should sit on the **t.** of my lord. 3678
1Ki 1:30 he shall sit upon my **t.** in my stead; 3678
1Ki 1:35 he may come and sit upon my **t.**; 3678
1Ki 1:37 Solomon, and make his **t.** greater 3678
1Ki 1:37 than the **t.** of my lord king David. 3678
1Ki 1:46 Solomon sitteth on the **t.** of the 3678
1Ki 1:47 and make his **t.** greater than thy **t.** 3678
1Ki 1:48 given one to sit on my **t.** this day, 3678
1Ki 2:4 (said he) a man on the **t.** of Israel. 3678
1Ki 2:12 sat Solomon upon the **t.** of David 3678
1Ki 2:19 and sat down on his **t.**, and caused 3678
1Ki 2:24 set me on the **t.** of David my father, 3678
1Ki 2:33 upon his **t.**, shall there be peace 3678
1Ki 2:45 the **t.** of David shall be established 3678
1Ki 3:6 hast given him a son to sit on his **t.**, 3678
1Ki 5:5 son, whom I will set upon thy **t.** in 3678
1Ki 7:7 he made a porch for the **t.** where he 3678
1Ki 8:20 my father, and sit on the **t.** of Israel, 3678
1Ki 8:25 in my sight to sit on the **t.** of Israel; 3678
1Ki 9:5 will establish the **t.** of thy kingdom 3678
1Ki 9:5 thee a man upon the **t.** of Israel. 3678
1Ki 10:9 thee, to set thee on the **t.** of Israel: 3678
1Ki 10:18 the king made a great **t.** of ivory 3678
1Ki 10:19 The **t.** had six steps, and the top of 3678
1Ki 10:19 the top of the **t.** was round behind: 3678
1Ki 16:11 reign, as soon as he sat on his **t.**, 3678
1Ki 22:10 king of Judah sat each on his **t.**, 3678
1Ki 22:19 I saw the Lord sitting on his **t.**, 3678
2Ki 10:3 sons, and set him on his father's **t.**, 3678
2Ki 10:30 shall sit on the **t.** of Israel. 3678
2Ki 11:19 And he sat on the **t.** of the kings. 3678
2Ki 13:13 and Jeroboam sat upon his **t.**: 3678
2Ki 15:12 sons shall sit on the **t.** of Israel 3678
2Ki 25:28 set his **t.** above the **t.** of the kings 3678
1Ch 17:12 and I will stablish his **t.** for ever. 3678
1Ch 17:14 and his **t.** shall be established for 3678
1Ch 22:10 establish the **t.** of his kingdom over 3678
1Ch 28:5 to sit upon the **t.** of the kingdom of 3678
1Ch 29:23 Solomon sat on the **t.** of the Lord 3678
2Ch 6:10 and am set on the **t.** of Israel, as 3678
2Ch 6:16 sight to sit upon the **t.** of Israel; 3678
2Ch 7:18 will I stablish the **t.** of thy kingdom, 3678
2Ch 9:8 in thee to set thee on his **t.**, 3678
2Ch 9:17 the king made a great **t.** of ivory, 3678
2Ch 9:18 And there were six steps to the **t.**, 3678
2Ch 9:18 gold, which were fastened to the **t.**, 3678
2Ch 18:9 Judah sat either of them on his **t.**, 3678
2Ch 18:18 I saw the Lord sitting upon his **t.**, 3678
2Ch 23:20 king upon the **t.** of the kingdom. 3678
Ne 3:7 unto the **t.** of the governor on this 3678
Es 1:2 king Ahasuerus sat on the **t.** of his 3678
Es 5:1 king sat upon his royal **t.** in the 3678
Job 26:9 He holdeth back the face of his **t.**, 3678
Job 36:7 with kings are they on the **t.**; yea, 3678
Ps 9:4 thou satest in the **t.** judging right. 3678
Ps 9:7 ever: he hath prepared his **t.** for 3678
Ps 11:4 temple, the Lord's **t.** is in heaven: 3678
Ps 45:6 Thy **t.**, O God, is for ever and ever: 3678
Ps 47:8 God sitteth upon the **t.** of his 3678
Ps 89:4 build up thy **t.** to all generations. 3678
Ps 89:14 are the habitation of thy **t.** 3678
Ps 89:29 and his **t.** as the days of heaven. 3678
Ps 89:36 and his **t.** as the sun before me. 3678
Ps 89:44 and cast his **t.** down to the ground. 3678
Ps 93:2 Thy **t.** is established of old: thou 3678
Ps 94:20 the **t.** of iniquity have fellowship 3678
Ps 97:2 are the habitation of his **t.** 3678
Ps 103:19 hath prepared his **t.** in the heavens; 3678
Ps 132:11 of thy body will I set upon thy **t.**. 3678
Ps 132:12 also sit upon thy **t.** for evermore. 3678
Pr 16:12 **t.** is established by righteousness. 3678
Pr 20:8 A king that sitteth in the **t.** of 3678
Pr 20:28 and his **t.** is upholden by mercy. 3678
Pr 25:5 his **t.** shall be established in 3678
Pr 29:14 his **t.** shall be established for ever. 3678
Isa 6:1 saw also the Lord sitting upon a **t.**, 3678
Isa 9:7 upon the **t.** of David, and upon his 3678
Isa 14:13 exalt my **t.** above the stars of God: 3678
Isa 16:5 in mercy shall the **t.** be established: 3678
Isa 22:23 a glorious **t.** to his father's house. 3678
Isa 47:1 there is no **t.**, O daughter of the 3678
Isa 66:1 The heaven is my **t.**, and the earth 3678
Jer 1:15 set every one his **t.** at the entering 3678
Jer 3:17 call Jerusalem the **t.** of the Lord; 3678
Jer 13:13 the kings that sit upon David's **t.**, 3678
Jer 14:21 do not disgrace the **t.** of thy glory: 3678
Jer 17:12 A glorious high **t.** from the 3678
Jer 17:25 princes sitting upon the **t.** of David, 3678
Jer 22:2 that sittest upon the **t.** of David, 3678
Jer 22:4 kings sitting upon the **t.** of David, 3678
Jer 22:30 sitting upon the **t.** of David, 3678
Jer 29:16 that sitteth upon the **t.** of David, 3678
Jer 33:17 upon the **t.** of the house of Israel; 3678
Jer 33:21 not have a son to reign upon his **t.**; 3678
Jer 36:30 none to sit upon the **t.** of David: 3678
Jer 43:10 will set his **t.** upon these stones. 3678
Jer 49:38 I will set my **t.** in Elam, and will 3678
Jer 52:32 set his **t.** above the **t.** of the kings 3678
La 5:19 **t.** from generation to generation. 3678
Eze 1:26 their heads was the likeness of a **t.**, 3678
Eze 1:26 upon the likeness of the **t.** was the 3678
Eze 10:1 appearance of the likeness of a **t.** 3678
Eze 43:7 the place of my **t.**, and the place of 3678
Da 5:20 he was deposed from his kingly **t.**, 3764
Da 7:9 his **t.** was like the fiery flame, and 3764
Jon 3:6 Nineveh, and he arose from his **t.**, 3678
Hag 2:22 I will overthrow the **t.** of kingdoms, 3678
Zec 6:13 and shall sit and rule upon his **t.**; 3678

Zec 6:13 he shall be a priest upon his **t.** 3678
Mt 5:34 **by heaven; for it is God's t.** *2362*
Mt 19:28 **man shall sit in the t. of his glory,** *2362*
Mt 23:22 **heaven, sweareth by the t. of God,** *2362*
Mt 25:31 **he sit upon the t. of his glory:** *2362*
Lu 1:32 unto him the **t.** of his father David: *2362*
Ac 2:30 raise up Christ to sit on his **t.**: *2362*
Ac 7:49 Heaven is my **t.**, and earth is my *2362*
Ac 12:21 in royal apparel, sat upon his **t.**, *968*
Heb 1:8 Thy **t.**, O God, is for ever and ever: *2362*
Heb 4:16 come boldly unto the **t.** of grace, *2362*
Heb 8:1 right hand of the **t.** of the Majesty *2362*
Heb 12:2 at the right hand of the **t.** of God. *2362*
Re 1:4 Spirits which are before his **t.**; *2362*
Re 3:21 **I grant to sit with me in my t.,** *2362*
Re 3:21 **set down with my Father in his t.** *2362*
Re 4:2 and, behold, a **t.** was set in heaven, *2362*
Re 4:2 and one sat on the **t.** *2362*
Re 4:3 was a rainbow round about the **t.**, *2362*
Re 4:4 about the **t.** were four and twenty *2362*
Re 4:5 out of the **t.** proceeded lightnings *2362*
Re 4:5 lamps of fire burning before the **t.**, *2362*
Re 4:6 before the **t.** there was a sea of *2362*
Re 4:6 and in the midst of the **t.**, *2362*
Re 4:6 and round about the **t.**, were four *2362*
Re 4:9 thanks to him that sat on the **t.**, *2362*
Re 4:10 down before him that sat on the **t.**, *2362*
Re 4:10 and cast their crowns before the **t.**, *2362*
Re 5:1 hand of him that sat on the **t.** a *2362*
Re 5:6 in the midst of the **t.** and of the *2362*
Re 5:7 hand of him that sat upon the **t.** *2362*
Re 5:11 of many angels round about the **t.** *2362*
Re 5:13 unto him that sitteth upon the **t.**, *2362*
Re 8:16 face of him that sitteth on the **t.**, *2362*
Re 7:9 stood before the **t.**, and before the *2362*
Re 7:10 our God which sitteth upon the **t.**, *2362*
Re 7:11 angels stood round about the **t.**, *2362*
Re 7:11 and fell before the **t.** on their faces, *2362*
Re 7:15 are they before the **t.** of God, *2362*
Re 7:15 he that sitteth on the **t.** shall dwell *2362*
Re 7:17 Lamb which is in the midst of the **t.** *2362*
Re 8:3 altar which was before the **t.** *2362*
Re 12:5 caught up unto God, and to his **t.** *2362*
Re 14:3 as it were a new song before the **t.**, *2362*
Re 14:5 without fault before the **t.** of God. *2362*
Re 16:17 from the **t.**, saying, It is done. *2362*
Re 19:4 worshipped God that sat on the **t.**, *2362*
Re 19:5 a voice came out of the **t.**, saying, *2362*
Re 20:11 I saw a great white **t.**, and him that *2362*
Re 21:5 he that sat upon the **t.** said, Behold, *2362*
Re 22:1 proceeding out of the **t.** of God and *2362*
Re 22:3 the **t.** of God and of the Lamb shall *2362*

THRONES
Ps 122:5 For there are set **t.** of judgment, 3678
Ps 122:5 the **t.** of the house of David. 3678
Isa 14:9 raised up from their **t.** all the kings 3678
Eze 26:16 sea shall come down from their **t.**, 3678
Da 7:9 I beheld till the **t.** were cast down, 3764
Mt 19:28 **ye also shall sit upon twelve t.,** *2362*
Lu 22:30 **sit on t. judging the twelve tribes** *2362*
Col 1:16 whether they be **t.**, or dominions, *2362*
Re 20:4 I saw **t.**, and they sat upon them, *2362*

THRONG See also THRONGED; THRONGING.
Mk 3:9 multitude, lest they should **t.** him. *2346*
Lu 8:45 the multitude **t.** thee and press *4912*

THRONGED
Mk 5:24 people followed him, and **t.** him. *4918*
Lu 8:42 But as he went the people **t.** him. *4846*

THRONGING
Mk 5:31 Thou seest the multitude **t.** thee, *4918*

THROUGH See also THROUGHOUT.
Ge 6:13 is filled with violence **t.** them; 6440
Ge 12:6 Abram passed **t.** the land unto the
Ge 13:17 walk **t.** the land in the length of it and
Ge 30:32 I will pass **t.** all thy flock to day,
Ge 41:36 that the land perish not **t.** the famine.
Ex 10:15 of the field, **t.** all the land of Egypt.
Ex 12:12 pass **t.** the land of Egypt this night,
Ex 12:23 will pass **t.** to smite the Egyptians;
Ex 13:17 God led them not **t.** the way of the
Ex 13:18 **t.** the way of the wilderness of the
Ex 14:16 ground **t.** the midst of the sea. 8432
Ex 14:24 of the Egyptians **t.** the pillar of fire
Ex 19:13 shall surely be stoned, or shot **t.**;
Ex 19:21 lest they break **t.** unto the Lord to
Ex 19:24 people break **t.** to come up unto the
Ex 21:6 shall bore his ear **t.** with an aul:
Ex 36:33 middle bar to shoot **t.** the boards 8432
Le 4:2 If a soul shall sin **t.** ignorance against
Le 4:13 congregation...Israel sin **t.** ignorance,
Le 4:22 and done somewhat **t.** ignorance
Le 4:27 the common people sin **t.** ignorance,
Le 5:15 a trespass, and sin **t.** ignorance,
Le 18:21 of thy seed pass **t.** the fire to Molech,
Le 26:6 neither shall the sword go **t.** your land.
Nu 13:32 **t.** which we have gone to search it,
Nu 14:7 land, which we passed **t.** to search it,
Nu 15:27 And if any soul sin **t.** ignorance,
Nu 15:29 law for him that sinneth **t.** ignorance,
Nu 20:17 us pass, I pray thee, **t.** thy country:
Nu 20:17 country: we will not pass **t.** the fields,
Nu 20:17 or **t.** the vineyards, neither will we
Nu 20:19 any thing else, go **t.** on my feet. 5674
Nu 20:20 And he said, Thou shalt not go **t.** 5674
Nu 20:21 to give Israel passage **t.** his border:
Nu 21:22 Let me pass **t.** thy land: we will not
Nu 21:23 not suffer Israel to pass **t.** his border:
Nu 24:8 and pierce them **t.** with his arrows.
Nu 25:8 the tent, and trust both of them **t.**,
Nu 25:8 Israel, and the woman **t.** her belly. 413
Nu 31:16 **t.** the counsel of Balaam, to commit
Nu 31:23 ye shall make it go **t.** the fire, and it
Nu 31:23 fire ye shall make go **t.** the water.
Nu 33:8 and passed **t.** the midst of the sea 8432
De 1:19 **t.** all that great and terrible wilderness,
De 2:4 are to pass **t.** the coast of your brethren
De 2:7 thy walking **t.** this great wilderness:
De 2:8 **t.** the way of the plain from Elath,
De 2:18 Thou art to pass over **t.** Ar, the coast
De 2:27 Let me pass **t.** thy land: I will go
De 2:28 drink: only I will pass **t.** on my feet;
De 5:15 thee out thence **t.** a mighty hand
De 8:15 **t.** that great and terrible wilderness,
De 9:26 thou hast redeemed **t.** thy greatness,
De 15:17 and trust it **t.** his ear unto the door,
De 18:10 son or his daughter to pass **t.** the fire,
De 29:16 **t.** the nations which ye passed by; ; ... 7130
De 31:29 him to anger **t.** the work of your hands.
De 32:47 **t.** this thing ye shall prolong your days
De 33:11 smite **t.** the loins of them that rise
Jos 1:11 Pass **t.** the host, and command the 7130
Jos 2:15 down by a cord **t.** the window: 1157
Jos 3:2 that the officers went **t.** the host; 7130
Jos 18:4 and they shall rise, and go **t.** the land,
Jos 18:8 Go and walk **t.** the land, and describe
Jos 18:9 the men went and passed **t.** the land,
Jos 18:12 went up **t.** the mountains westward;
Jos 24:17 all the people **t.** whom we passed: 7130
Jg 2:22 That **t.** them I may prove Israel,
Jg 3:23 Then Ehud went forth **t.** the porch,
Jg 5:6 and the travellers walked **t.** byways.
Jg 5:26 pierced and stricken **t.** his temples.
Jg 5:28 a window, and cried **t.** the lattice. 1157
Jg 9:54 And his young man thrust him **t.**,
Jg 11:16 **t.** the wilderness unto the Red sea,
Jg 11:17 Let me, I pray thee, pass **t.** thy land:
Jg 11:18 they went along **t.** the wilderness,
Jg 11:19 pray thee, **t.** thy land into my place.
Jg 11:20 trusted not Israel to pass **t.** his coast:
Jg 20:12 sent men **t.** all the tribe of Benjamin,
1Sa 9:4 And he passed **t.** mount Ephraim, and
1Sa 9:4 and passed **t.** the land of Shalisha,
1Sa 9:4 then they passed **t.** the land of Shalim,
1Sa 9:4 passed **t.** the land of the Benjamites,
1Sa 19:12 Michal let David down **t.** a window: 1157
1Sa 31:4 sword, and thrust me **t.** therewith;
1Sa 31:4 uncircumcised come and thrust me **t.**,
2Sa 2:29 men walked all that night **t.** the plain,
2Sa 2:29 over Jordan, and went **t.** all Bithron,
2Sa 4:7 and gat them away **t.** the plain all 1870
2Sa 6:16 daughter looked **t.** a window, 1157
2Sa 12:31 and made them pass **t.** the brickkiln:
2Sa 18:14 thrust them **t.** the heart of Absalom,
2Sa 20:14 And he went **t.** all the tribes of Israel
2Sa 22:13 **T.** the brightness before him were
2Sa 22:30 For by thee I have run **t.** a troop: by
2Sa 23:16 brake **t.** the host of the Philistines, 1234
2Sa 24:2 Go now **t.** all the tribes of Israel, 7751
2Sa 24:8 So when they had gone **t.** all the land,
2Ki 1:2 Ahaziah fell down **t.** a lattice in his 1157
2Ki 3:8 The way **t.** the wilderness of Edom.
2Ki 3:26 break **t.**...unto the king of Edom: 1234
2Ki 10:21 And Jehu sent **t.** all Israel: and all the
2Ki 16:3 and made his son to pass **t.** the fire,
2Ki 17:17 and their daughters to pass **t.** the fire,
2Ki 21:6 And he made his son pass **t.** the fire,
2Ki 23:10 daughter to pass **t.** the fire to Molech.
2Ki 24:20 **t.** the anger of the Lord it came to 5921
1Ch 10:4 sword, and thrust me **t.** therewith;
1Ch 11:18 brake **t.** the host of the Philistines, 1234
2Ch 19:4 he went out again **t.** the people from
2Ch 23:20 they came **t.** the high gate into 8432
2Ch 24:9 made a proclamation **t.** Judah and
2Ch 30:10 **t.** the country of Ephraim and
2Ch 31:18 their daughters, **t.** all the congregation:
2Ch 32:4 that ran **t.** the midst of the land, 8432
2Ch 33:6 caused his children to pass **t.** the fire
Ezr 6:14 they prospered **t.** the prophesying of
Ne 9:11 they went **t.** the midst of the sea 8432
Es 6:9 bring him on horseback **t.** the street
Es 6:11 brought him on horseback **t.** the street
Job 7:14 dreams, and terrifiest me **t.** visions:
Job 14:9 Yet **t.** the scent of water it will bud,
Job 20:24 the bow of steel shall strike him **t.**
Job 22:13 know? can he judge **t.** the dark cloud?
Job 24:16 In the dark they dig **t.** houses, 2864
Job 26:12 understanding he smiteth **t.** the proud.
Job 29:3 when by his light I walked **t.** darkness;
Job 29:7 I went out to the gate **t.** the city, 5921
Job 40:24 his eyes: his nose pierceth **t.** snares.
Job 41:2 nose? or bore his jaw **t.** with a thorn?
Ps 8:8 passeth **t.** the paths of the seas.
Ps 10:4 wicked, **t.** the pride of his countenance.
Ps 18:29 For by thee I have run **t.** a troop; and
Ps 19:4 Their line is gone out **t.** all the earth,
Ps 21:7 **t.** the mercy of the most High he shall
Ps 23:4 **t.** the valley of the shadow of death,
Ps 32:3 my bones waxed old **t.** my roaring all
Ps 44:5 **T.** thee will we push down our
Ps 44:5 **t.** thy name will we tread them under
Ps 60:12 **T.** God we shall do valiantly: for he it
Ps 66:3 **t.** the greatness of thy power shall
Ps 66:6 land: they went **t.** the flood on foot:
Ps 66:12 heads: we went **t.** fire and **t.** water:
Ps 68:7 thou didst march **t.** the wilderness;
Ps 73:9 their tongue walketh **t.** the earth.
Ps 78:13 the sea, and caused them to pass **t.**;
Ps 81:5 he went out **t.** the land of Egypt: 5921
Ps 84:6 passing **t.** the valley of Baca make it a
Ps 92:4 Lord, hast made me glad **t.** thy work:
Ps 106:9 **t.** the depths, as **t.** the wilderness.
Ps 107:39 and brought low **t.** oppression,
Ps 108:13 **T.** God we shall do valiantly: for he it
Ps 109:24 My knees are weak **t.** fasting: and
Ps 110:5 strike **t.** kings in the day of his wrath.
Ps 115:7 not: neither speak they **t.** their throat,
Ps 119:98 Thou **t.** thy commandments hast
Ps 119:104 **T.** thy precepts I get understanding:
Ps 136:14 Israel to pass **t.** the midst of it: 8432
Ps 136:16 which led his people **t.** the wilderness:
Pr 7:6 of my house I looked **t.** my casement,
Pr 7:8 Passing **t.** the street near her corner;
Pr 7:23 Till a dart strike **t.** his liver: as a bird
Pr 11:9 but **t.** knowledge shall the just be
Pr 18:1 **T.** desire a man, having separated
Pr 24:3 **T.** wisdom is an house builded; and
Ec 5:3 a dream cometh **t.** the multitude of
Ec 10:18 **t.** idleness of the hands the house
Ec 10:18 the hands the house droppeth **t.** 1811
Ca 2:9 shewing himself **t.** the lattice. 4480
Isa 8:8 And he shall pass **t.** Judah; he shall
Isa 8:21 And they shall pass **t.** it, hardly
Isa 9:19 **T.** the wrath of the Lord of hosts is
Isa 13:15 one that is found shall be thrust **t.**; 1856
Isa 14:19 are slain, thrust **t.** with a sword, 2944
Isa 16:8 they wandered **t.** the wilderness:
Isa 21:1 As whirlwinds in the south pass **t.**; so
Isa 23:10 Pass **t.** thy land as a river, O daughter
Isa 27:4 I would go **t.** them, I would burn
Isa 28:7 But they also have erred **t.** wine, and
Isa 28:7 **t.** strong drink are out of the way;
Isa 28:7 have erred **t.** strong drink,
Isa 28:7 are out of the way **t.** strong drink; 4480
Isa 28:15, 18 overflowing scourge shall pass **t.**,
Isa 30:31 For **t.** the voice of the Lord shall the
Isa 34:10 none shall pass **t.** it for ever and ever.

Isa 43:2 When thou passest **t.** the waters, I will
Isa 43:2 **t.** the rivers, they shall not overflow
Isa 43:2 when thou walkest **t.** the fire, thou 1119
Isa 48:21 not when he led them **t.** the deserts:
Isa 60:15 hated, so that no man went **t.** thee, 5674
Isa 62:10 Go **t.**, go **t.** the gates; prepare ye 5674
Isa 63:13 That led them **t.** the deep, as an horse
Jer 2:6 of Egypt, that led us **t.** the wilderness,
Jer 2:6 **t.** a land of deserts and of pits,
Jer 2:6 **t.** a land of drought, and of the shadow
Jer 2:6 **t.** a land that no man passed **t.**, and
Jer 3:9 **t.** the lightness of her whoredom,
Jer 5:1 Run ye to and fro **t.** the streets of
Jer 9:6 **t.** deceit they refuse to know me, saith
Jer 9:10 up, so that none can pass **t.** them;
Jer 9:12 a wilderness, that none passeth **t.**?
Jer 12:12 upon all high places **t.** the wilderness:
Jer 17:24 in no burden **t.** the gates of this city
Jer 32:35 their daughters to pass **t.** the fire unto
Jer 51:4 that are thrust **t.** in her streets 1856
Jer 51:52 **t.** all her land the wounded shall
Jer 52:3 **t.** the anger of the Lord it came to 5921
La 3:44 that our prayer should not pass **t.**
La 4:9 stricken **t.** for want of the fruits of the
La 4:21 the cup shall also pass **t.** unto thee:
Eze 5:17 and blood shall pass **t.** thee;
Eze 6:8 ye shall be scattered **t.** the countries.
Eze 9:4 Go **t.** the midst of the city, 5674
Eze 9:4 **t.** the midst of Jerusalem, and set a
Eze 9:5 Go ye after him **t.** the city, and smite:
Eze 12:5 Dig thou **t.** the wall in their sight, and
Eze 12:7 and in the even I digged **t.** the wall
Eze 12:12 they shall dig **t.** the wall to carry out
Eze 14:5 all estranged from me **t.** their idols.
Eze 14:15 noisome beasts to pass **t.** the land,
Eze 14:15 no man may pass **t.** because of the
Eze 14:17 land, and say, Sword, go **t.** the land;
Eze 16:14 for it was perfect **t.** my comeliness,
Eze 16:21 cause them to pass **t.** the fire for them?
Eze 16:36 discovered **t.** thy whoredoms with thy
Eze 16:40 and thrust thee **t.** with their swords.
Eze 20:23 and disperse them **t.** the countries;
Eze 20:26 **t.** the fire all that openeth the womb,
Eze 20:31 ye make your sons to pass **t.** the fire,
Eze 23:37 to pass for them **t.** the fire, to devour
Eze 29:11 No foot of man shall pass **t.** it, nor
Eze 29:11 foot of beast shall pass **t.** it, neither
Eze 29:12 will disperse them **t.** the countries.
Eze 30:23 will disperse them **t.** the countries.
Eze 33:28 be desolate, that none shall pass **t.**
Eze 34:6 My sheep wandered **t.** all the
Eze 36:19 they were dispersed **t.** the countries:
Eze 39:14 passing **t.** the land to bury with the
Eze 39:15 the passengers that pass **t.** the land,
Eze 41:19 made **t.** all the house round about. 413
Eze 46:19 he brought me **t.** the entry, which was
Eze 47:3 and he brought me **t.** the waters; 5674
Eze 47:4 and brought me **t.** the waters; 5674
Eze 47:4 a thousand, and brought me **t.**; 5674
Da 8:25 And **t.** his policy also he shall 5921
Da 9:7 **t.** all the countries whither thou hast
Da 11:2 strength **t.** his riches he shall stir up
Da 11:10 come, and overflow, and pass **t.**
Joe 3:17 no strangers pass **t.** her any more.
Am 2:10 led you forty years **t.** the wilderness,
Am 5:17 for I will pass **t.** thee, saith the 7130
Jon 3:7 proclaimed and published **t.** Nineveh
Mic 2:13 and have pass **t.** the gate, and are
Mic 5:8 if he go **t.**, both treadeth down, 5674
Na 1:12 be cut down, when he shall pass **t.**
Na 1:15 the wicked shall no more pass **t.** thee;
Na 3:4 that selleth nations **t.** her whoredoms,
Na 3:4 and familiar **t.** her witchcrafts.
Hab 1:6 shall march **t.** the breadth of the land,
Hab 3:12 didst march **t.** the land in indignation,
Hab 3:14 Thou didst strike **t.** with his staves
Hab 3:15 didst walk **t.** the sea with thine horses,
Hab 3:15 horses, **t.** the heap of great waters.
Zec 1:10 sent to walk to and fro **t.** the earth.
Zec 1:11 have walked to and fro **t.** the earth,
Zec 1:17 My cities **t.** prosperity shall yet be
Zec 4:10 run to and fro **t.** the whole earth.
Zec 4:12 **t.** the two golden pipes empty the 3027
Zec 5:6 is their resemblance **t.** all the earth.
Zec 6:7 might walk to and fro **t.** the earth:
Zec 6:7 hence, walk to and fro **t.** the earth.
Zec 6:7 So they walked to and fro **t.** the earth.
Zec 7:14 that no man passed **t.** nor returned:
Zec 9:8 no oppressor shall pass **t.** them any
Zec 9:15 drink, and made a noise as **t.** wine;
Zec 10:7 their heart shall rejoice as **t.** wine:
Zec 10:11 he shall pass **t.** the sea with affliction,
Zec 13:3 that begat him shall thrust him **t.**
Zec 13:9 I will bring the third part **t.** the fire,
Mt 6:19 **where thieves break t. and steal:** *1358*
Mt 6:20 **thieves do not break t. nor steal:** *1358*
Mt 9:34 devils **t.** the prince of the devils. *1722*
Mt 12:1 on the sabbath day **t.** the corn; *1223*
Mt 12:43 **he walketh t. dry places, seeking** *1223*
Mt 19:24 **camel to go t. the eye of a needle,** *1223*
Mk 2:23 **t.** the corn fields on the sabbath *1223*
Mk 6:55 ran **t.** that whole region round *4063*
Mk 7:13 **God of none effect t. your tradition,**
Mk 7:31 **t.** the midst of the coast of *303*
Mk 9:30 thence, and passed **t.** Galilee; *1223*
Mk 10:25 **camel to go t. the eye of a needle,** *1223*
Mk 11:16 carry any vessel **t.** the temple. *1223*
Lu 1:78 **T.** the tender mercy of our God; *1223*
Lu 2:35 sword shall pierce **t.** thy own soul *1330*
Lu 4:14 fame of him **t.** all the region *2596*
Lu 4:30 he passing **t.** the midst of them *1223*
Lu 5:19 let him down **t.** the tiling with his *1223*
Lu 6:1 that he went **t.** the corn fields; *1223*
Lu 9:6 and went **t.** the towns, preaching *2596*
Lu 10:17 are subject unto us **t.** thy name. *1722*
Lu 11:15 casteth out devils **t.** Beelzebub the *1722*
Lu 11:18 **I cast out devils t. Beelzebub.** *1722*
Lu 11:24 **he walketh t. dry places, seeking** *1223*
Lu 12:39 **suffered his house to be broken t.** *1358*
Lu 13:22 he went **t.** the cities and villages, *2596*
Lu 17:1 **woe unto him, t. whom they come!** *1223*
Lu 17:11 he passed **t.** the midst of Samaria *1223*
Lu 18:25 **for a camel to go t. a needle's eye,** *1223*
Lu 19:1 Jesus entered…passed **t.** Jericho. *1330*
Joh 1:7 that all men **t.** him might believe. *1223*
Joh 3:17 **the world t. him might be saved.** *1223*
Joh 4:4 And he must needs go **t.** Samaria. *1223*
Joh 8:59 **t.** the midst of them, and so passed *1223*
Joh 15:3 **ye are clean t. the word which** *1223*
Joh 17:11 **t. thine own name those whom** *1722*
Joh 17:17 **Sanctify them t. thy truth: thy** *1722*
Joh 17:29 **might be sanctified t. the truth.** *1722*
Joh 17:20 **shall believe on me t. their word;** *1223*
Joh 20:31 ye might have life **t.** his name. *1722*
Ac 1:2 after that he **t.** the Holy Ghost had *1223*
Ac 3:16 his name **t.** faith in his name *1909*
Ac 3:17 I wot that **t.** ignorance ye did it, *2596*
Ac 4:2 preached **t.** Jesus the resurrection *1722*
Ac 8:18 that **t.** laying on of the apostles' *1223*
Ac 8:40 passing **t.** he preached in all the *1223*
Ac 10:43 **t.** his name whosoever believeth *1223*
Ac 12:10 out, and passed on **t.** one street;
Ac 13:6 when they had gone **t.** the isle unto *1330*
Ac 13:38 that **t.** this man is preached unto *1223*
Ac 14:22 **t.** much tribulation enter into the *1223*
Ac 15:3 they passed **t.** Phenice and Samaria, *1330*
Ac 15:11 we believe that **t.** the grace of the *1223*
Ac 15:41 And he went **t.** Syria and Cilicia, *1350*
Ac 16:4 And as they went **t.** the cities, they *1279*
Ac 17:1 when they had passed **t.** Amphipolis *1653*
Ac 18:27 which had believed **t.** grace: *1223*
Ac 19:1 having passed **t.** the upper coasts *1330*
Ac 19:21 when he had passed **t.** Macedonia *1330*
Ac 20:3 purposed to return **t.** Macedonia. *1223*
Ac 21:4 who said to Paul **t.** the Spirit, that *1223*
Ro 1:8 I thank my god **t.** Jesus Christ for *1223*
Ro 1:24 uncleanness **t.** the lusts of their *1722*
Ro 2:23 **t.** breaking the law dishonourest *1223*
Ro 2:24 blasphemed among the Gentiles **t.** *1223*
Ro 3:7 abounded **t.** my lie unto his glory; *1722*
Ro 3:24 **t.** the redemption that is in Christ *1223*
Ro 3:25 a propitiation **t.** faith in his blood, *1223*
Ro 3:25 past, **t.** the forbearance of God; *1722*
Ro 3:30 faith, and uncircumcision **t.** faith. *1223*
Ro 3:31 then make void the law **t.** faith? *1223*
Ro 4:13 Abraham, or to his seed, **t.** the law, *1223*
Ro 4:13 but **t.** the righteousness of faith. *1223*
Ro 4:20 not at the promise of God **t.** unbelief;
Ro 5:1 peace with God **t.** our Lord Jesus *1223*
Ro 5:9 shall be saved from wrath **t.** him. *1223*
Ro 5:11 in God **t.** our Lord Jesus Christ, *1223*
Ro 5:15 if **t.** the offence of one many be dead,
Ro 5:21 grace reign **t.** righteousness *1223*
Ro 6:11 alive unto God **t.** Jesus Christ our *1722*
Ro 6:23 God is eternal life **t.** Jesus Christ *1722*
Ro 7:25 I thank God **t.** Jesus Christ our *1223*
Ro 8:3 do, in that it was weak **t.** the flesh, *1223*
Ro 8:13 if ye **t.** the Spirit do mortify the deeds
Ro 8:37 conquerors **t.** him that loved us. *1223*
Ro 11:11 rather **t.** their fall salvation is come
Ro 11:30 now obtained mercy **t.** their unbelief:
Ro 11:31 **t.** your mercy they also may obtain
Ro 11:36 and **t.** him, and to him, are all *1223*
Ro 12:3 For I say, **t.** the grace given unto me, *1223*
Ro 15:4 we **t.** patience and comfort of the *1223*
Ro 15:13 **t.** the power of the Holy Ghost *1722*
Ro 15:17 I may glory **t.** Jesus Christ in *1722*
Ro 15:19 **T.** mighty signs and wonders, by *1722*
Ro 16:27 be glory **t.** Jesus Christ for ever. *1223*
1Co 1:1 Jesus Christ **t.** the will of God, *1223*
1Co 4:15 I have begotten you **t.** the gospel. *1223*
1Co 8:11 **t.** thy knowledge shall the weak *1909*
1Co 10:1 cloud, and all passed **t.** the sea; *1223*
1Co 13:12 For now we see **t.** a glass, darkly; *1223*
1Co 15:57 the victory **t.** our Lord Jesus Christ. *1223*
1Co 16:5 you, when I shall pass **t.** Macedonia: *1330*
1Co 16:5 for I do pass **t.** Macedonia. *1330*
2Co 3:4 such trust have we **t.** Christ to *1223*
2Co 4:15 **t.** the thanksgiving of many *1223*
2Co 8:9 that ye **t.** his poverty might be rich.
2Co 9:11 causeth **t.** us thanksgiving to God. *1223*
2Co 10:4 but mighty **t.** God to the pulling down
2Co 11:3 beguiled Eve **t.** his subtilty, *1722*
2Co 11:33 **t.** a window in a basket was I let *1223*
2Co 12:7 **t.** the abundance of the revelations,
2Co 13:4 he was crucified **t.** weakness, *1537*
Ga 2:19 I **t.** the law am dead to the law, *1223*
Ga 3:8 would justify the heathen **t.** faith, *1537*
Ga 3:14 on the Gentiles **t.** Jesus Christ; *1722*
Ga 3:14 the promise of the Spirit **t.** faith. *1223*
Ga 4:7 son, then an heir of God **t.** Christ. *1223*
Ga 4:13 **t.** infirmity of the flesh I preached *1223*
Ga 5:5 For we **t.** the Spirit wait for the hope
Ga 5:10 confidence in you **t.** the Lord, *1722*
Eph 1:7 we have redemption **t.** his blood, *1223*
Eph 2:7 toward us **t.** Christ Jesus. *1722*
Eph 2:8 For by grace are ye saved **t.** faith; *1223*
Eph 2:18 **t.** him we both have access by one *1223*
Eph 2:22 an habitation of God **t.** the Spirit. *1722*
Eph 4:6 above all, and **t.** all, and in you all. *1223*
Eph 4:18 **t.** the ignorance that is in them, *1223*
Php 1:19 to my salvation **t.** your prayer, *1223*
Php 2:3 Let nothing be done **t.** strife or *2596*
Php 3:9 that which is **t.** the faith of Christ, *1223*
Php 4:7 hearts and minds **t.** Christ Jesus. *1722*
Php 4:13 I can do all things **t.** Christ which *1722*
Col 1:14 we have redemption **t.** his blood, *1223*
Col 1:20 peace **t.** the blood of his cross, *1223*
Col 1:22 In the body of his flesh **t.** death, to *1223*
Col 2:8 any man spoil you **t.** philosophy *1223*
Col 2:12 ye are risen with him **t.** the faith of *1223*
2Th 2:13 you to salvation **t.** sanctification. *1722*
2Th 2:16 consolation and good hope **t.** grace, *1722*
1Ti 6:10 pierced themselves **t.** with many *4044*
2Ti 1:10 immortality to light **t.** the gospel: *1223*
2Ti 3:15 salvation **t.** faith which is in Christ *1223*
Tit 1:3 manifested his word **t.** preaching, *1722*
Tit 3:6 on us abundantly **t.** Jesus Christ *1223*
Phm 22 that **t.** your prayers I shall be given *1223*
Heb 2:10 their salvation perfect **t.** sufferings. *1223*
Heb 2:14 that **t.** death he might destroy him *1223*
Heb 2:15 **t.** fear of death were all their lifetime
Heb 3:13 hardened **t.** the deceitfulness of sin.
Heb 6:12 who **t.** faith and patience inherit *1223*
Heb 9:14 who **t.** the eternal Spirit offered *1223*
Heb 10:10 **t.** the offering of the body of Jesus *1223*
Heb 10:20 **t.** the veil, that is to say, his flesh; *1223*
Heb 11:3 **T.** faith we understand that the
Heb 11:11 **T.** faith also Sara herself received
Heb 11:28 **T.** faith he kept the passover, and the
Heb 11:29 they passed **t.** the Red sea as by dry *1224*
Heb 11:33 Who **t.** faith subdued kingdoms, *1223*
Heb 11:39 obtained a good report **t.** faith. *1223*
Heb 12:20 be stoned, or thrust **t.** with a dart: *2700*
Heb 13:20 **t.** the blood of the everlasting *1722*
Heb 13:21 in his sight, **t.** Jesus Christ; *1223*
1Pe 1:2 **t.** sanctification of the spirit, unto *1722*
1Pe 1:5 of God **t.** faith unto salvation *1223*
1Pe 1:6 heaviness **t.** manifold temptations. *1722*
1Pe 1:22 in obeying the truth **t.** the Spirit *1223*
1Pe 4:11 may be glorified **t.** Jesus Christ, *1223*

2Pe 1:1 faith with us **t.** the righteousness *1722*
2Pe 1:2 unto you **t.** the knowledge of God, ... *1722*
2Pe 1:3 **t.** the knowledge of him that hath....... *1223*
2Pe 1:4 that is in the world **t.** lust................ *1722*
2Pe 2:3 **t.** covetousness shall they with.......... *1722*
2Pe 2:18 they allure **t.** the lusts of the flesh,..... *1722*
2Pe 2:18 **t.** much wantonness, those that................
2Pe 2:20 world **t.** the knowledge of the Lord *1722*
1Jo 4:9 world, that we might live **t.** him......... *1223*
Re 8:13 an angel flying **t.** the midst of............ *1722*
Re 18:3 rich **t.** the abundance of her............. *1537*
Re 22:14 may enter in **t.** the gates into the city.......

THROUGHLY See also THOROUGHLY.
Ge 11:3 us make brick, and burn them **t.**..............
Job 6:2 Oh that my grief were **t.** weighed,............
Ps 51:2 Wash me **t.** from mine iniquity,.......... 7235
Jer 6:9 they shall **t.** glean the remnant................
Jer 7:5 if ye **t.** amend your ways and your ....
Jer 7:5 if ye **t.** execute judgment between............
Jer 50:34 he shall **t.** plead their cause, that.............
Eze 16:9 I **t.** washed away thy blood from thee, ...
Mt 3:12 he will **t.** purge his floor, and gather... *1245*
Lu 3:17 he will **t.** purge his floor, and will....... *1245*
2Co 11:6 been **t.** made manifest among..... *1722,3956*
2Ti 3:17 **t.** furnished unto all good works......... *1822*

THROUGHOUT
Ge 41:29 great plenty **t.** all the land of Egypt: ....
Ge 41:46 and went **t.** all the land of Egypt. ....
Ge 45:8 and a ruler **t.** all the land of Egypt...........
Ex 5:12 abroad **t.** all the land of Egypt ....
Ex 7:19 may be blood **t.** all the land of Egypt, ...
Ex 7:21 was blood **t.** all the land of Egypt...........
Ex 8:16 become lice **t.** all the land of Egypt..........
Ex 8:17 became lice **t.** all the land of Egypt...........
Ex 9:9 upon beast, **t.** all the land of Egypt...........
Ex 9:16 name may be declared **t.** all the earth. ......
Ex 9:22 herb of the field, **t.** the land of Egypt.........
Ex 9:25 hail smote **t.** all the land of Egypt............
Ex 11:6 a great cry **t.** all the land of Egypt,...........
Ex 12:14 feast to the Lord **t.** your generations; ....
Ex 29:42 burnt offering **t.** your generations ....
Ex 30:8 before the Lord **t.** your generations. ....
Ex 30:10 upon it **t.** your generations:....................
Ex 30:21 and to his seed **t.** their generations...........
Ex 30:31 oil unto me **t.** your generations. ....
Ex 31:13 me and you **t.** your generations;...............
Ex 31:16 the sabbath **t.** their generations,..............
Ex 32:27 and out from gate to gate **t.** the camp, ...
Ex 34:3 let any man be seen **t.** all the mount;..........
Ex 35:3 kindle no fire **t.** your habitations.............
Ex 36:6 caused it to be proclaimed **t.** the camp, ...
Ex 37:19 **t.** the six branches going out of the ....
Ex 40:15 priesthood **t.** their generations. ....
Ex 40:38 house of Israel, **t.** all their journeys. ....
Le 3:17 your generations **t.** all your dwellings, ...
Le 7:36 a statute for ever **t.** their generations........
Le 10:9 a statute for ever **t.** your generations:.......
Le 17:7 ever unto them **t.** their generations. ....
Le 23:14 a statute for ever **t.** your generations.......
Le 23:21 all your dwellings **t.** your generations ....
Le 23:31 a statute for ever **t.** your generations........
Le 25:9 the trumpet sound **t.** all your land............
Le 25:10 proclaim liberty **t.** all the land unto...........
Le 25:30 him that bought it **t.** his generations:........
Nu 1:42 of Naphtali, **t.** their generations,...............
Nu 1:52 by his own standard, **t.** their hosts. ....
Nu 2:3 camp of Judah pitch **t.** their armies: ....
Nu 2:9 and four hundred, **t.** their armies.............
Nu 2:16 hundred and fifty, **t.** their armies.............
Nu 2:24 and an hundred, **t.** their armies................
Nu 2:32 numbered of the camps **t.** their hosts ....
Nu 3:39 **t.** their families, all the males from a.........
Nu 4:22 Gershon, **t.** the houses of their fathers, ...
Nu 4:38 the sons of Gershon, **t.** their families, ...
Nu 4:40 numbered of them, **t.** their families,..........
Nu 4:42 of the sons of Merari, **t.** their families, ...
Nu 10:8 ordinance for ever **t.** your generations. ......
Nu 10:25 of all the camps **t.** their hosts:................
Nu 11:10 the people weep **t.** their familes,...............
Nu 15:38 of their garments **t.** their generations. ....
Nu 18:23 a statute for ever **t.** your generations,.......
Nu 26:2 and upward, **t.** their father's house, ...
Nu 28:14 every month **t.** the months of the year. .....
Nu 28:21 for every lamb, **t.** the seven lambs: ....
Nu 28:24 ye shall offer daily, **t.** the seven days, ...
Nu 28:29 unto one lamb, **t.** the seven lambs;...........
Nu 29:4, 10 for one lamb, **t.** the seven lambs:.........
Nu 31:4 a thousand, **t.** all the tribes of Israel, ...
Nu 35:29 unto you **t.** your generations in all............
De 16:18 thy God giveth thee, **t.** thy tribes:.............
De 28:40 shalt have olive trees **t.** all thy coasts. ......
De 28:52 wherein thou trustedst, **t.** all thy land:.......
De 28:52 thee in all thy gates **t.** all thy land, ...
Jos 2:22 pursuers sought them **t.** all the way,..........
Jos 6:27 his fame was noised **t.** all the country. ......
Jos 16:1 up from Jericho **t.** mount Beth-el,.............
Jos 22:14 a prince **t.** all the tribes of Israel;............
Jos 24:3 and led him **t.** all the land of Canaan, ...
Jg 6:35 he sent messengers **t.** all Manasseh;.........
Jg 7:22 against his fellow, even **t.** the host: ....
Jg 7:24 sent messengers **t.** all mount Ephraim,......
Jg 20:6 and sent her **t.** all the country of the.........
Jg 20:10 an hundred **t.** all the tribes of Israel,.........
1Sa 5:11 a deadly destruction **t.** all the city;...........
1Sa 11:7 sent them **t.** all the coasts of Israel..........
1Sa 13:3 Saul blew the trumpet **t.** all the land, ...
1Sa 13:19 no smith found **t.** all the land of Israel: .....
1Sa 23:23 out **t.** all the thousands of Judah............
2Sa 8:14 **t.** all Edom put he garrisons, and all ....
2Sa 15:10 sent spies **t.** all the tribes of Israel, ...
2Sa 19:9 were at strife **t.** all the tribes of Israel, ...
1Ki 1:3 for a fair damsel **t.** all the coasts..............
1Ki 6:38 house finished **t.** all the parts thereof, ...
1Ki 15:22 made a proclamation **t.** all Judah;.............
1Ki 18:6 the land between them to pass **t.** it: ....
1Ki 22:36 there went a proclamation **t.** the host........
2Ki 17:5 of Assyria came up **t.** all the land, ...
1Ch 5:10 in their tents **t.** all the east land......... 5921
1Ch 6:54 their dwelling places **t.** their castles ....
1Ch 6:60 **t.** their families were thirteen cities. ....
1Ch 6:62 the sons of Gershom **t.** their families ....
1Ch 6:63 were given by lot, **t.** their families,............
1Ch 7:40 **t.** the genealogy of them that were............
1Ch 9:34 were chief **t.** their generations;................
1Ch 12:30 famous **t.** the house of their fathers. ....
1Ch 21:4 Joab departed, and went **t.** all Israel,.........
1Ch 21:12 destroying **t.** all the coasts of Israel. ....
1Ch 22:5 of fame and of glory **t.** all countries: ....
1Ch 26:6 that ruled **t.** the house of their father: ....
1Ch 27:1 by month **t.** all the months of the year, ...
2Ch 8:6 and **t.** all the land of his dominion. ....
2Ch 11:23 children **t.** all the countries of Judah.........
2Ch 16:9 run to and fro **t.** the whole earth,............
2Ch 17:9 went about **t.** all the cities of Judah,..........
2Ch 17:19 put in the fenced cities **t.** all Judah...........
2Ch 19:5 **t.** all the fenced cities of Judah,................
2Ch 20:3 and proclaimed a fast **t.** all Judah........ 5921
2Ch 25:5 fathers, **t.** all Judah and Benjamin: ....
2Ch 26:14 for them **t.** all the host shields, ...
2Ch 30:5 to make proclamation **t.** all Israel,............
2Ch 30:6 the king and his princes **t.** all Israel ....
2Ch 30:22 they did eat **t.** the feast seven days, ...
2Ch 31:20 And thus did Hezekiah **t.** all Judah, ...
2Ch 34:7 the idols **t.** all the land of Israel, ...
2Ch 36:22 a proclamation **t.** all his kingdom,.............
Ezr 1:1 a proclamation **t.** all his kingdom,..............
Ezr 10:7 And they made proclamation **t.** Judah ....
Es 1:20 shall be published **t.** all his empire, ...
Es 3:6 Jews that were **t.** the whole kingdom............
Es 9:2 cities **t.** all the provinces of the king.........
Es 9:4 his fame went out **t.** all the provinces;........
Es 9:28 and kept **t.** every generation ....
Ps 72:5 and moon endure, **t.** all generations ....
Ps 102:24 thy years are **t.** all generations. ....
Ps 135:13 memorial, O Lord, **t.** all generations. ....
Ps 145:13 dominion endureth **t.** all generations..........
Jer 17:3 high places for sin, **t.** all thy borders.........
Eze 38:21 against him **t.** all my mountains, ...
Mt 4:24 And his fame went **t.** all Syria: *1519*
Mk 1:28 fame spread abroad **t.** all the region.... *1519*
Mk 1:39 in their synagogues **t.** all Galilee,........ *1519*
Mk 14:9 **be preached t. the whole world,**..... *1519*
Lu 1:65 **t.** all the hill country of Judaea.......... *1722*
Lu 4:25 **great famine was t. all the land;** ... *1909*
Lu 7:17 of him went forth **t.** all Judaea, ... *1722*
Lu 7:17 and **t.** all the region round about. *1722*
Lu 8:1 he went **t.** every city and village. *2596*
Lu 8:39 and published **t.** the whole city how.... *2596*
Lu 23:5 the people, teaching **t.** all Jewry,........ *2596*
Joh 19:23 seam, woven from the top **t.**...... *1223,3650*
Ac 8:1 scattered abroad **t.** the regions of....... *2596*
Ac 9:31 had the churches rest **t.** all Judaea...... *2596*
Ac 9:32 as Peter passed **t.** all quarters, he...... *1223*
Ac 9:42 And it was known **t.** all Joppa;........... *2596*
Ac 10:37 which was published **t.** all Judaea,....... *2596*
Ac 11:28 be great dearth **t.** all the world:......... *1909*
Ac 13:49 was published **t.** all the region. *1223*
Ac 14:24 after they had passed **t.** Pisidia, ... *1330*
Ac 16:6 when they had gone **t.** Phrygia *1330*
Ac 19:26 but almost **t.** all Asia, this Paul ....
Ac 24:5 among all the Jews **t.** the world, ... *2596*
Ac 26:20 and **t.** all the coast of Judaea, ... *1519*
Ro 1:8 is spoken of **t.** the whole world........... *1722*
Ro 9:17 might be declared **t.** all the earth. *1722*
2Co 8:18 is in the gospel **t.** all the churches;..... *1223*
Eph 3:21 church by Christ Jesus **t.** all ages, ... *1519*
1Pe 1:1 to the strangers scattered **t.** Pontus,.........

THROW See also OVERTHROW; THREW; THROWING; THROWN.
Jg 2:2 ye shall **t.** down their altars:.............. 5422
Jg 6:25 **t.** down the altar of Baal that thy 2040
2Sa 20:15 battered the wall, to **t.** it down. 5307
2Ki 9:33 And he said, **T.** her down. So............ 8058
Jer 1:10 and to destroy, and to **t.** down, ... 2040
Jer 31:28 to **t.** down, and to destroy, and to...... 2040
Eze 16:39 shall **t.** down thine eminent place,...... 2040
Mic 5:11 and **t.** down all thy strong holds: 2040
Mal 1:4 They shall build, but I will **t.** down; 2040

THROWING
Nu 35:17 if he smite him with **t.** a stone,.......... 3027

THROWN See also OVERTHROWN.
Ex 15:1, 21 rider hath he **t.** into the sea........... 7411
Jg 6:32 because he hath **t.** down his altar. 5422
2Sa 20:21 his head shall be **t.** to thee over 7993
1Ki 19:10, 14 covenant, **t.** down thine altars, ... 2040
Jer 31:40 nor **t.** down any more for ever. 2040
Jer 33:4 which are **t.** down by the mounts, ... 5422
Jer 50:15 are fallen, her walls are **t.** down:......... 2040
La 2:2 he hath **t.** down in his wrath the........... 2040
La 2:17 hath **t.** down, and hath not pitied:........ 2040
Eze 29:5 leave thee **t.** into the wilderness, ...
Eze 38:20 the mountains shall be **t.** down, ... 2040
Na 1:6 and the rocks are **t.** down by him....... 5422
Mt 24:2 **another, that shall not be t. down**..*2647*
Mk 13:2 **another, that shall not be t. down**..*2647*
Lu 4:35 the devil had **t.** him in the midst, ... *4496*
Lu 21:6 **another, that shall not be t. down**..*2647*
Re 18:21 that great city Babylon be **t.** down, ... *906*

THRUST See also THRUSTETH.
Ex 11:1 he shall surely **t.** you out hence......... 1644
Ex 12:39 because they were **t.** out of Egypt, ... 1644
Nu 22:25 she **t.** herself unto the wall, and......... 3905
Nu 25:8 tent, and **t.** both of them through, ... 1856
Nu 35:20 But if he **t.** him of hatred, or hurl 1920
Nu 35:22 **t.** him suddenly without enmity, ... 1920
De 13:5 to **t.** thee out of the way which 5080
De 13:10 to **t.** thee away from the Lord thy...... 5080
De 15:17 **t.** it through his ear unto the door, ... 5414
De 33:27 he shall **t.** out the enemy from 1644
Jg 3:21 right thigh, and **t.** it into his belly: 8628
Jg 6:38 **t.** the fleece together, and wringed..... 2115
Jg 9:41 Zebul **t.** out Gaal and his brethren, ... 1644
Jg 9:54 his young man **t.** him through,........... 1856
Jg 11:2 they **t.** out Jephthah, and said............ 1644
1Sa 11:2 I may **t.** out all your right eyes,......... 5365
1Sa 31:4 and **t.** me through therewith;............... 1856
1Sa 31:4 come and **t.** me through, ... 1856
2Sa 2:16 and **t.** his sword in his fellow's side; ....
2Sa 18:14 and **t.** them through the heart of........... 8628
2Sa 23:6 be all of them as thorns **t.** away,......... 5074
1Ki 2:27 So Solomon **t.** out Abiathar from........ 1644
2Ki 4:27 Gehazi came near to **t.** her away........ 1920
1Ch 10:4 and **t.** me through therewith;............... 1856
2Ch 26:20 and they **t.** him out from thence; 926
Ps 118:13 Thou hast **t.** sore at me that I........... 1760
Isa 13:15 that is found shall be **t.** through; 1856
Isa 14:19 are slain, **t.** through with a sword,...... 2944
Jer 51:4 that are **t.** through in her streets. 1856
Eze 16:40 **t.** thee through with their swords....... 1333
Eze 34:21 ye have **t.** with side and with 1920
Eze 46:18 to **t.** them out of their possession;...... 3238
Joe 2:8 Neither shall one **t.** another; they....... 1766
Zec 13:3 begat him shall **t.** him through 1856
Lu 4:29 rose up and **t.** him out of the city,...... *1544*
Lu 5:3 would **t.** out a little from the land. *1877*
Lu 10:15 **heaven, shall be t. down to hell**..... *2601*

Lu 13:28 **of God, and you yourselves t. out..** *1544*
Joh 20:25 nails, and **t.** my hand into his side,....... *906*
Joh 20:27 **thy hand, and t. it into my side:**..... *906*
Ac 7:27 his neighbour wrong **t.** him away, ... *683*
Ac 7:39 not obey, but **t.** him from them, ... *683*
Ac 16:24 **t.** them into the inner prison, ... *906*
Ac 16:37 and now do they **t.** us out privily? *1544*
Ac 27:39 it were possible, to **t.** in the ship. *1856*
Heb 12:20 stoned, or **t.** through with a dart:....... *2700*
Re 14:15 **T.** in thy sickle, and reap: for............ *3992*
Re 14:16 cloud **t.** in his sickle on the earth;........ *906*
Re 14:18 **T.** in thy sharp sickle, and gather....... *3992*
Re 14:19 the angel **t.** in his sickle into the.......... *906*

TRUSTETH
Job 32:13 God **t.** him down, not man................ 5086

THUMB See also THUMBS.
Ex 29:20 and upon the **t.** of their right hand, ... 931
Le 8:23 and upon the **t.** of his right hand,.......... 931
Le 14:14, 17,25,28 the **t.** of his right hand, ... 931

THUMBS
Le 8:24 upon the **t.** of their right hands, ... 931
Jg 1:6 cut off his **t.** and his great toes. ... 931,3027
Jg 1:7 **t.** and their great toes cut off,...... 931,3027

THUMMIM (thum'-mim)
Ex 28:30 of judgment the Urim and the **T.**;....... 8550
Le 8:8 breastplate the Urim and the **T.**......... 8550
De 33:8 Let thy **T.** and thy Urim be with......... 8550
Ezr 2:63 a priest with Urim and with **T.**.. 8550
Ne 7:65 up a priest with Urim and **T.**............. 8550

THUNDER See also THUNDERBOLTS; THUNDERED; THUNDERETH; THUNDERINGS; THUNDERS.
Ex 9:23 the Lord sent **t.** and hail, and the....... 6963
Ex 9:29 and the **t.** shall cease, neither shall..... 6963
1Sa 2:10 of heaven shall he **t.** upon them: 7481
1Sa 7:10 the Lord thundered with a great **t.**..... 6963
1Sa 12:17 Lord, and he shall send **t.** and rain; 6963
1Sa 12:18 the Lord sent **t.** and rain that day: 6963
Job 26:14 but the **t.** of his power who can......... 7482
Job 28:26 a way for the lightning of the **t.** 6963
Job 38:25 or a way for the lightning of **t.**;.......... 6963
Job 39:19 hast thou clothed his neck with **t.**? 7483
Job 39:25 the **t.** of the captains, and the............ 7482
Job 40:9 thou **t.** with a voice like him? 7481
Ps 77:18 voice of thy **t.** was in the heaven: 7482
Ps 81:7 thee in the secret place of **t.**............ 7482
Ps 104:7 voice of thy **t.** they hasted away......... 7482
Isa 29:6 visited of the Lord of hosts with **t.**,..... 7482
Mk 3:17 Boanerges,...The sons of **t.** *1027*
Re 6:1 I heard, as it were the noise of **t.**, ... *1027*
Re 14:2 waters, and as a voice of a great **t.**..... *1027*

THUNDERBOLTS
Ps 78:48 the hail, and their flocks to hot **t.**....... 7565

THUNDERED
1Sa 7:10 the Lord **t.** with a great thunder 7481
2Sa 22:14 The Lord **t.** from heaven, and........... 7481
Ps 18:13 The Lord also **t.** in the heavens, ... 7481
Joh 12:29 and heard it, said that it **t.**......... *1027,1096*

THUNDERETH
Job 37:4 **t.** with the voice of his excellency: 7481
Job 37:5 God **t.** marvellously with his voice; 7481
Ps 29:3 the God of glory **t.**: the Lord is......... 7481

THUNDERINGS
Ex 9:28 be no more mighty **t.** and hail;.......... 6963
Ex 20:18 and all the people saw the **t.**, and....... 6963
Re 4:5 lightnings and **t.** and voices: *1027*
Re 8:5 and there were voices, and **t.**, and..... *1027*
Re 11:19 were lightnings, and voices, and **t.**,...... *1027*
Re 19:6 and as the voice of mighty **t.**,............ *1027*

THUNDERS
Ex 9:33 **t.** and hail ceased, and the rain.......... 6963
Ex 9:34 and the hail and the **t.** were ceased, ... 6963
Ex 19:16 that there were **t.** and lightnings, ... 6963
Re 10:3 cried, seven **t.** uttered their voices..... *1027*
Re 10:4 seven **t.** had uttered their voices,....... *1027*
Re 10:4 things which the seven **t.** uttered,...... *1027*
Re 16:18 were voices, and **t.**, and lightnings;..... *1027*

THUS
Ge 2:1 **T.** the heavens and the earth were..........
Ge 6:22 **T.** did Noah; according to all that ....
Ge 19:36 **T.** were both the daughters of Lot............
Ge 20:16 with all other: **t.** she was reproved. ....
Ge 24:30 **T.** spake the man unto me; that......... 3541
Ge 25:22 she said, If it be so, why am I **t.**?...... 2088
Ge 25:34 **t.** Esau despised his birthright. ....
Ge 31:8 If he said **t.**, The speckled shall.......... 3541
Ge 31:8 if he said **t.**, The ringstraked shall...... 3541
Ge 31:9 **T.** God hath taken away the cattle of........
Ge 31:32 **T.** they made a covenant at.....................
Ge 31:40 **T.** I was; in the day the drought..............
Ge 31:41 **T.** have I been twenty years in.......... 2088
Ge 32:4 **T.** shall ye speak unto my lord 3541
Ge 32:4 Thy servant Jacob saith **t.**, I have 3541
Ge 36:8 **T.** dwelt Esau in mount Seir: Esau ....
Ge 37:35 **T.** his father wept for him......................
Ge 42:25 the way: and **t.** did he unto them. 3651
Ge 45:9 **T.** saith thy son Joseph, God hath...... 3541
Ex 3:14 **T.** shalt thou say unto the............... 3541
Ex 3:15 **T.** shalt thou say unto the children...........
Ex 4:22 **T.** saith the Lord, Israel is my son, ... 3541
Ex 5:1 **T.** saith the Lord God of Israel,......... 3541
Ex 5:10 **T.** saith Pharaoh, I will not give 3541
Ex 5:15 dealest thou **t.** with thy servants?....... 3541
Ex 7:17 **T.** saith the Lord, In this thou........... 3541
Ex 8:1, 20 **T.** saith the Lord, Let my 3541
Ex 9:1, 13 **T.** saith the Lord God of the......... 3541
Ex 10:3 **T.** saith the Lord God of the............ 3541
Ex 11:4 **T.** saith the Lord, About midnight 3541
Ex 12:11 **t.** shall ye eat it; with your loins 3602
Ex 12:50 **T.** did all the children of Israel; as............
Ex 14:11 hast thou dealt **t.** with us, to carry..... 2063
Ex 14:30 **T.** the Lord saved Israel that day out..........
Ex 19:3 **T.** shalt thou say to the house of 3541
Ex 20:22 **T.** thou shalt say unto the................ 3541
Ex 26:17 **t.** shalt thou make for all the 3651
Ex 26:24 **t.** shall it be for them both; they......... 3651
Ex 29:35 **t.** shalt thou do unto Aaron, and to his......
Ex 32:27 **T.** saith the Lord God of Israel,......... 3541
Ex 36:22 **t.** did he make for all the boards 3651
Ex 36:29 **t.** he did to both of them in both the... 3651
Ex 39:32 **T.** was all the work of the tabernacle........
Ex 40:16 **T.** did Moses: according to all that...........
Le 15:31 **T.** shall ye separate the children of...........
Le 16:3 **T.** shall Aaron come into the holy....... 2063
Nu 4:19 **t.** do unto them, that they may live, ...
Nu 4:49 **t.** were they numbered of him, as the.......
Nu 8:7 **t.** shalt thou do unto them, to........... 3541
Nu 8:14 **T.** shalt thou separate the Levites............
Nu 8:26 **T.** shalt thou do unto the Levites....... 3602
Nu 10:28 **T.** were the journeyings of the........... 428
Nu 11:15 if thou deal **t.** with me, kill me, ... 3602
Nu 15:11 **T.** shall it be done for one bullock, ... 3602
Nu 18:26 **T.** speak unto the Levites, and say...........
Nu 18:28 **T.** ye also shall offer an heave........... 3651
Nu 20:14 **T.** saith thy brother Israel, Thou........ 3541
Nu 20:21 **T.** Edom refused to give Israel ....
Nu 21:31 **T.** Israel dwelt in the land of the............
Nu 22:16 **T.** saith Balak the son of Zippor, ... 3541
Nu 23:5 unto Balak, and **t.** thou shalt speak.... 3541
Nu 23:16 Go again into Balak, and say **t.**. 3541
Nu 32:8 **T.** did your fathers, when I sent 3541
De 7:5 **t.** shall ye deal with them; ye shall 3541
De 9:25 **T.** I fell down before the Lord forty..........
De 20:15 **T.** shalt thou do unto all the.............. 3651
De 29:24 the Lord done **t.** unto this land?......... 3662
De 32:6 Do ye **t.** requite the Lord, O............. 2063
Jos 2:4 said **t.**, There came men unto me, ... 3651
Jos 6:3 once. **T.** shalt thou do six days. 3541
Jos 7:10 liest thou **t.** upon thy face? 2088
Jos 7:13 for **t.** saith the Lord God of Israel, ... 3541
Jos 7:20 Israel, and **t.** and **t.** have I done: 2063
Jos 10:25 **t.** shall the Lord do to all your.......... 3602
Jos 16:5 according to their families was **t.**. ....
Jos 21:13 **T.** they gave to the children of Aaron........
Jos 21:42 them: **t.** were all these cities............ 3651
Jos 22:16 **T.** saith the whole congregation of...... 3541
Jos 24:2 **T.** saith the Lord God of Israel, ... 3541
Jg 6:8 **T.** saith the Lord God of Israel, I....... 3541
Jg 8:1 Why hast thou served us **t.**,........ 1697,2007
Jg 8:28 **T.** was Midian subdued before the............
Jg 9:56 **T.** God rendered the wickedness of..........
Jg 11:15 **T.** saith Jephthah, Israel took not 3541
Jg 11:33 **T.** the children of Ammon were ....
Jg 13:18 askest thou **t.** after my name, ... 2088
Jg 18:4 **T.**...dealeth Micah with me, ... 2090
Jg 18:4 and **t.** dealeth Micah with me, ... 2088
Jg 20:43 **T.** they inclosed the Benjamites ....
1Sa 2:27 **T.** saith the Lord, Did I plainly 3541
1Sa 9:9 **t.** he spake, Come, and let us go to ... 3541
1Sa 10:18 **T.** saith the Lord God of Israel, ... 3541
1Sa 11:9 **T.** shall ye say unto the men of......... 3541
1Sa 14:9 If they say **t.** unto us, Tarry until....... 3541
1Sa 14:10 But if they say **t.**, Come up unto us; .. 3541
1Sa 15:2 **T.** saith the Lord of hosts, I.............. 3541
1Sa 18:25 **T.** shall ye say to David, The king...... 3541
1Sa 20:7 If he say **t.**, It is well; thy servant 3541
1Sa 20:22 But if I say **t.** unto the young man, ... 3541
1Sa 25:6 **t.** shall ye say to him that liveth in 3541
1Sa 26:18 doth my lord **t.** pursue after his 2088
2Sa 6:22 I will yet be more vile than **t.**,.......... 2063
2Sa 7:5 **T.** saith the Lord, Shalt thou............ 3541
2Sa 7:8 **T.** saith the Lord of hosts, I took........ 3541
2Sa 11:25 T shalt thou say unto Joab, Let.......... 3541
2Sa 12:7 **T.** saith the Lord God of Israel, I....... 3541
2Sa 12:11 **T.** saith the Lord, Behold, I will......... 3541
2Sa 12:31 **t.** did he unto all the cities of the....... 3651
2Sa 15:26 But if he **t.** say, I have no delight 3541
2Sa 16:7 And **t.** said Shimei when he cursed,.... 3541
2Sa 17:15 **T.** and **t.** did Ahithophel counsel......... 2063
2Sa 17:15 and **t.** and **t.** have I counselled. 2063
2Sa 17:21 for **t.** hath Ahithophel counselled 3602
2Sa 18:14 Joab, I may not tarry **t.** with thee 3651
2Sa 18:33 **t.** he said, O my son Absalom, ... 3541
2Sa 24:12 **T.** saith the Lord, I offer thee 3541
1Ki 1:48 also **t.** said the king, Blessed be 3602
1Ki 2:30 **T.** saith the king, Come forth. 3541
1Ki 2:30 **T.** said Joab, and **t.** he answered........ 3541
1Ki 3:22 **T.** they spake before the king..................
1Ki 5:11 **t.** gave Solomon to Hiram year by...... 3541
1Ki 9:8 the Lord done **t.** unto this land, ... 3602
1Ki 11:31 for **t.** saith the Lord, the God of........ 3541
1Ki 12:10 **T.** shall thou speak unto this 3541
1Ki 12:10 **t.** shalt thou say unto them, My.......... 3541
1Ki 12:24 **T.** saith the Lord, Ye shall not go 3541
1Ki 13:2 O altar, altar, **t.** saith the Lord; 3541
1Ki 13:21 **T.** saith the Lord, Forasmuch as 3541
1Ki 14:5 **t.**...shalt thou say unto her: 2090
1Ki 14:5 and **t.** shalt thou say unto her:........... 2088
1Ki 14:7 **T.** saith the Lord God of Israel, ... 3541
1Ki 16:12 **T.** did Zimri destroy all the house............
1Ki 17:14 For **t.** saith the Lord God of Israel, ... 3541
1Ki 20:2 said unto him, **T.** saith Ben-hadad,...... 3541
1Ki 20:5 **T.** speaketh Ben-hadad, saying,.......... 3541
1Ki 20:13 **T.** saith the Lord, Hast thou seen...... 3541
1Ki 20:14 **T.** saith the Lord, Even by the.......... 3541
1Ki 20:28 **T.** saith the Lord, Because the 3541
1Ki 20:42 **T.** saith the Lord, Because thou.......... 3541
1Ki 21:19 **T.** saith the Lord, Hast thou killed,..... 3541
1Ki 21:19 **T.** saith the Lord, In the place........... 3541
1Ki 22:11 **T.** saith the Lord, With these shalt..... 3541
1Ki 22:27 **T.** saith the king, Put this fellow 3541
2Ki 1:4 Now therefore **t.** saith the Lord, ... 3541
2Ki 1:6 **T.** saith the Lord, Is it not because 3541
2Ki 1:11 **t.** hath the king said, Come down........ 3541
2Ki 1:16 **T.** saith the Lord, Forasmuch as 3541
2Ki 2:21 **T.** saith the Lord, I have healed......... 3541
2Ki 3:16 **T.** saith the Lord, Make this valley..... 3541
2Ki 3:17 **t.** saith the Lord, Ye shall not see...... 3541
2Ki 4:43 **t.** saith the Lord, They shall eat. 3541
2Ki 5:4 **T.** and **t.** said the maid that is of........ 2063
2Ki 7:1 **T.** saith the Lord, To morrow 3541
2Ki 9:3 **T.** saith the Lord, I have anointed....... 3541
2Ki 9:6 **T.** saith the Lord God of Israel, ... 3541
2Ki 9:12 he said, **T.** and **t.** spake he to me. 2063
2Ki 9:12 **T.** saith the Lord, I have anointed...... 3541
2Ki 9:18, 19 **T.** saith the king, Is it peace?......... 3541
2Ki 10:28 **T.** Jehu destroyed Baal out of............. 3541
2Ki 16:16 **T.** did Urijah the priest, according ....
2Ki 18:19 **T.** saith the great king, the king......... 3541
2Ki 18:29 **T.** saith the king, Let not 3541
2Ki 18:31 **t.** saith the king of Assyria, Make 3541
2Ki 19:3 **T.** saith Hezekiah, This day is a......... 3541
2Ki 19:6 **T.** shall ye say to your master,.......... 3541
2Ki 19:6 **T.** saith the Lord, Be not afraid of....... 3541
2Ki 19:10 **T.** shall ye speak to Hezekiah king 3541
2Ki 19:20 **T.** saith the Lord God of Israel, ... 3541
2Ki 19:32 **t.** saith the Lord concerning the......... 3541
2Ki 20:1 **T.** saith the Lord, Set thine house...... 3541
2Ki 20:5 **T.** saith the Lord, the God of David.... 3541
2Ki 21:12 **t.** saith the Lord God of Israel, ... 3541
2Ki 22:15 **T.** saith the Lord God of Israel, ... 3541
2Ki 22:16 **T.** saith the Lord, Behold, I will......... 3541
2Ki 22:18 of the Lord, **t.** shall ye say to him,..... 3541
2Ki 22:18 **T.** saith the Lord God of Israel, ... 3541
1Ch 15:28 **T.** all Israel brought up the ark of............
1Ch 17:4 **T.** saith the Lord, Thou shalt not........ 3541

1Ch 17:7 **t.** shalt thou say unto my servant....... 3541
1Ch 17:7 **T.** saith the Lord of hosts, I took....... 3541
1Ch 18:6, 13 **T.** the Lord preserved David..............
1Ch 21:10 **T.** saith the Lord, I offer thee.......... 3541
1Ch 21:11 **T.** saith the Lord, Choose thee.......... 3541
1Ch 24:4 Ithamar; and **t.** were they divided............
1Ch 24:5 **T.** were they divided by lot, one sort........
1Ch 29:26 **T.** David the son of Jesse reigned............
2Ch 4:18 **T.** Solomon made all these vessels ....
2Ch 5:1 **T.** all the work that Solomon made ....
2Ch 7:11 **T.** Solomon finished the house of the ....
2Ch 7:21 the Lord done **t.** unto this land, ... 3602
2Ch 10:10 **T.** shalt thou answer the people......... 3541
2Ch 10:10 **t.** shalt thou say unto them, My......... 3541
2Ch 11:4 **T.** saith the Lord, Ye shall not go 3541
2Ch 12:5 **T.** saith the Lord, Ye have forsaken.... 3541
2Ch 13:18 **T.** the children of Israel were brought.......
2Ch 18:10 **T.** saith the Lord, With these thou 3541
2Ch 18:26 **T.** saith the king, Put this fellow........ 3541
2Ch 19:9 **T.** shall ye do in the fear of the.......... 3541
2Ch 20:15 **T.** saith the Lord unto you, Be not..... 3541
2Ch 21:12 **T.** saith the Lord God of David thy..... 3541
2Ch 24:11 **T.** they did day by day, and.............. 3541
2Ch 24:20 **T.** saith God, Why transgress ye......... 3541
2Ch 24:22 **T.** Joash the king remembered not............
2Ch 31:20 **t.** did Hezekiah throughout all............ 2063
2Ch 32:10 **T.** saith Sennacherib king of.............. 3541
2Ch 32:22 **T.** the Lord saved Hezekiah and...............
2Ch 34:23 **T.** saith the Lord God of Israel, ... 3541
2Ch 34:24 **T.** saith the Lord, Behold, I will......... 3541
2Ch 34:26 **T.** saith the Lord God of Israel.......... 3541
2Ch 36:23 **T.** saith Cyrus king of Persia, All....... 3541
Ezr 1:2 **T.** saith Cyrus king of Persia, The...... 3541
Ezr 5:3 and said **t.** unto them, Who hath........ 3652
Ezr 5:7 unto him, wherein was written **t.**; 1836
Ezr 5:9 and said unto them **t.**, Who.............. 3660
Ezr 5:11 **t.** they returned us answer, saying, ... 3660
Ezr 6:2 therein was a record **t.** written: 3652
Ne 5:13 even **t.** be he shaken out, and.......... 3602
Ne 13:18 Did not your fathers **t.**, and did 3541
Ne 13:30 **T.** cleansed I them from all strangers, ...
Es 1:18 **T.** shall there arise too much..................
Es 2:13 **t.** came every maiden unto the 2088
Es 6:9 **T.** shall it be done to the man 3602
Es 6:11 **T.** shall it be done unto the man 3602
Es 9:5 **T.** the Jews smote all their enemies..........
Job 1:5 hearts. **T.** did Job continually............ 3602
Job 27:12 then are ye **t.** altogether vain?.......... 2088
Ps 38:14 **T.** I was as a man that heareth not,..........
Ps 63:4 **T.** will I bless thee while I live: 3651
Ps 73:15 If I say, I will speak **t.**; behold, ... 3644
Ps 73:21 **T.** my heart was grieved, and I 3588
Ps 106:20 **t.** they changed their glory into the..........
Ps 106:29 **T.** they provoked him to anger with..........
Ps 106:39 **T.** were they defiled with their own..........
Ps 128:4 **t.** shall the man be blessed that 3651
Isa 7:7 **T.** saith the Lord God, It shall.......... 3541
Isa 8:11 spake **t.** to me with a stong hand, ... 3541
Isa 10:24 **t.** saith the Lord God of hosts, ... 3541
Isa 21:6 **t.** hath the Lord said unto me, Go,..... 3541
Isa 21:16 For **t.** hath the Lord said unto me, ... 3541
Isa 22:15 **T.** saith the Lord God of hosts, Go, ... 3541
Isa 24:13 When **t.** it shall be in the midst of...... 3541
Isa 28:16 Therefore **t.** saith the Lord God,........ 3541
Isa 29:22 **t.** saith the Lord, who redeemed........ 3541
Isa 30:12 **t.** saith the Holy One of Israel, ... 3541
Isa 30:15 **t.** saith the Lord God, the Holy One... 3541
Isa 31:4 **t.** hath the Lord spoken unto me,....... 3541
Isa 36:4 **T.** saith the great king, the king of..... 3541
Isa 36:14 **T.** saith the king, Let no Hezekiah 3541
Isa 36:16 **t.** saith the king of Assyria, Make 3541
Isa 37:3 **T.** saith Hezekiah, This day is a......... 3541
Isa 37:6 **T.** shall ye say unto your master,....... 3541
Isa 37:6 **T.** saith the Lord, Be not afraid of..... 3541
Isa 37:10 **T.** shall ye speak to Hezekiah king 3541
Isa 37:21 **T.** saith the Lord God of Israel, ... 3541
Isa 37:33 **t.** saith the Lord concerning the......... 3541
Isa 38:1 **T.** saith the Lord, Set thine house...... 3541
Isa 38:5 **T.** saith the Lord, the God of David..... 3541
Isa 42:5 **T.** saith God the Lord, he that 3541
Isa 43:1 now **t.** saith the Lord that created...... 3541
Isa 43:14 **T.** saith the Lord, your redeemer,...... 3541
Isa 43:16 **T.** saith the Lord, which maketh a...... 3541
Isa 44:2 **T.** saith the Lord that made thee, ... 3541
Isa 44:6 **T.** saith the Lord the King of Israel, ... 3541
Isa 44:24 **T.** saith the Lord, thy redeemer, ... 3541
Isa 45:1 **T.** saith the Lord to his anointed, ... 3541
Isa 45:11 **T.** saith the Lord, the Holy One of..... 3541
Isa 45:14 **T.** saith the Lord, The labour of 3541
Isa 45:18 For **t.** saith the Lord that created....... 3541
Isa 47:15 **T.** shall they be unto thee with.......... 3651
Isa 48:17 **T.** saith the Lord, thy Redeemer,........ 3541
Isa 49:7 **T.** saith the Lord, the Redeemer of.... 3541
Isa 49:8 **T.** saith the Lord, In an acceptable 3541
Isa 49:22 **T.** saith the Lord God, Behold, I........ 3541
Isa 49:25 **t.** saith the Lord, Even the captives.... 3541
Isa 50:1 **T.** saith the Lord, Where is the bill 3541
Isa 51:22 **T.** saith thy Lord the Lord, and......... 3541
Isa 52:3 For **t.** saith the Lord, Ye have sold 3541
Isa 52:4 **t.** saith the Lord God, My people....... 3541
Isa 56:1 **T.** saith the Lord, Keep ye 3541
Isa 56:4 **t.** saith the Lord unto the eunuchs...... 3541
Isa 57:15 For **t.** saith the high and lofty One 3541
Isa 65:8 **T.** saith the Lord, As the new wine.... 3541
Isa 65:13 Therefore **t.** saith the Lord God,........ 3541
Isa 66:1 **T.** saith the Lord, The heaven is........ 3541
Isa 66:12 For **t.** saith the Lord, Behold, I will.... 3541
Jer 2:2 **T.** saith the Lord; I remember........... 3541
Jer 2:5 **T.** saith the Lord, What iniquity 3541
Jer 4:3 For **t.** saith the Lord to the men of.... 3541
Jer 4:27 For **t.** hath the Lord said, The 3541
Jer 5:13 them: **t.** shall it be done unto them..... 3541
Jer 5:14 **t.** saith the Lord God of hosts, ... 3541
Jer 6:6 For **t.** hath the Lord of hosts said, ... 3541
Jer 6:9 **T.** saith the Lord of hosts, They........ 3541
Jer 6:16 **T.** saith the Lord, Stand ye in the...... 3541
Jer 6:21 Therefore **t.** saith the Lord, Behold, ... 3541
Jer 6:22 **T.** saith the Lord, Behold, a people 3541
Jer 7:3 **T.** saith the Lord of hosts, the God.... 3541
Jer 7:20 Therefore **t.** saith the Lord God;........ 3541
Jer 7:21 **T.** saith the Lord of Hosts, the God ... 3541
Jer 8:4 say unto them, **T.** saith the Lord; 3541
Jer 9:7, 15 **t.** saith the Lord of hosts, ... 3541
Jer 9:17 **T.** saith the Lord of hosts, Consider ... 3541
Jer 9:22 **T.** saith the Lord, Even the 3541
Jer 9:23 **T.** saith the Lord, Let not the wise 3541
Jer 10:2 **T.** saith the Lord, Learn not the 3541
Jer 10:11 **T.** shall ye say unto them, The.......... 1836
Jer 10:18 For **t.** saith the Lord, Behold, I.......... 3541
Jer 11:3 **T.** saith the Lord God of Israel; 3541
Jer 11:11 Therefore **t.** saith the Lord, Behold, ... 3541
Jer 11:21 Therefore **t.** saith the Lord of the 3541
Jer 11:22 **t.** saith the Lord of hosts, Behold,...... 3541
Jer 12:14 **T.** saith the Lord against all mine....... 3541
Jer 13:1 **T.** saith the Lord unto me, Go and..... 3541
Jer 13:9 **T.** saith the Lord, After this............. 3541
Jer 13:12 **T.** saith the Lord God of Israel, ... 3541
Jer 13:13 **T.** saith the Lord, Behold, I will......... 3541
Jer 14:10 **T.** saith the Lord unto this people, ... 3541
Jer 14:10 **T.** have they loved to wander, ... 3651
Jer 14:15 **t.** saith the Lord concerning the.......... 3541
Jer 15:2 thou shalt tell them, **T.** saith the Lord;......
Jer 15:19 **t.** saith the Lord, If thou return, ... 3541
Jer 16:3 **t.** saith the Lord concerning the......... 3541
Jer 16:5 **t.** saith the Lord, Enter not into the... 3541
Jer 16:9 **t.** saith the Lord of hosts, the God...... 3541
Jer 17:5 **T.** saith the Lord; Cursed be the 3541
Jer 17:19 **T.** said the Lord unto me; Go and...... 3541
Jer 17:21 **T.** saith the Lord; Take heed to......... 3541
Jer 18:11 saying, **T.** saith the Lord; Behold,...... 3541
Jer 18:13 Therefore **t.** saith the Lord; Ask ye.... 3541
Jer 18:23 deal **t.** with them in the time of thine........
Jer 19:1 **T.** saith the Lord, Go and get a......... 3541
Jer 19:3 **T.** saith the Lord of hosts, the God.... 3541
Jer 19:11 them, **T.** saith the Lord of hosts; 3541
Jer 19:12 **T.** will I do unto this place, saith........ 3651
Jer 19:15 **T.** saith the Lord of hosts, the 3541
Jer 20:4 **t.** saith the Lord, Behold, I will 3541
Jer 21:3 them, **T.** shall ye say to Zedekiah:...... 3541
Jer 21:4 **T.** saith the Lord God of Israel; 3541
Jer 21:8 thou shalt say, **T.** saith the Lord;......... 3541
Jer 21:12 house of David, **t.** saith the Lord; 3541
Jer 22:1 **T.** saith the Lord; Go down to the 3541
Jer 22:3 **T.** saith the Lord; Execute ye 3541
Jer 22:6 **t.** saith the Lord unto the king's.......... 3541
Jer 22:8 Lord done **t.** unto this great city?....... 3602
Jer 22:11 For **t.** saith the Lord touching 3541
Jer 22:18 **t.** saith the Lord concerning............. 3541
Jer 22:30 **T.** saith the Lord, Write ye this......... 3541
Jer 23:2 **t.** saith the Lord God of Israel.......... 3541
Jer 23:15 Therefore **t.** saith the Lord of hosts.... 3541
Jer 23:16 **T.** saith the Lord of hosts, Hearken.... 3541
Jer 23:35 **T.** shall ye say every one to his......... 3541
Jer 23:37 **T.** shalt thou say to the prophet,........ 3541
Jer 23:38 therefore **t.** saith the Lord;.............. 3541
Jer 24:5 **T.** saith the Lord, the God of........... 3541
Jer 24:8 **t.** saith the Lord, So will I give.......... 3541
Jer 25:8 **t.** saith the Lord of hosts; Because..... 3541
Jer 25:15 **t.** saith the Lord God of Israel unto.... 3541
Jer 25:27 **T.** saith the Lord of hosts, the God.... 3541
Jer 25:28 **T.** saith the Lord of hosts; Ye shall 3541
Jer 25:32 **T.** saith the Lord of hosts, Behold,..... 3541
Jer 26:2 **T.** saith the Lord; Stand in the 3541
Jer 26:4 **T.** saith the Lord; If ye will not 3541
Jer 26:18 **T.** saith the Lord of hosts: Zion......... 3541
Jer 26:19 **T.** might we procure great evil ....
Jer 27:2 **T.** saith the Lord to me; Make.......... 3541
Jer 27:4 **T.** saith the Lord of hosts, the God.... 3541
Jer 27:4 **T.** shall ye say unto your masters; 3541
Jer 27:16 **T.** saith the Lord; Hearken not to 3541
Jer 27:19 For **t.** saith the Lord of hosts............ 3541
Jer 27:21 **t.** saith the Lord of hosts, the God..... 3541
Jer 28:2 **T.** speaketh the Lord of hosts, the..... 3541
Jer 28:11 **T.** saith the Lord; Even so will I........ 3602
Jer 28:13 **T.** saith the Lord; Thou hast............ 3541
Jer 28:14 **t.** saith the Lord of hosts, the God..... 3541
Jer 28:16 **t.** saith the Lord; Behold, I will 3541
Jer 29:4 **T.** saith the Lord of hosts, the God.... 3541
Jer 29:8 **t.** saith the Lord of hosts, the God..... 3541
Jer 29:10 For **t.** saith the Lord, That after 3541
Jer 29:16 that **t.** saith the Lord of the king........ 3541
Jer 29:17 **T.** saith the Lord of hosts; Behold,..... 3541
Jer 29:21 **T.** saith the Lord of hosts, the God.... 3541
Jer 29:24 **T.** shalt thou also speak to Shemaiah.........
Jer 29:25 **T.** speaketh the Lord of hosts, the 3541
Jer 29:31 **T.** saith the Lord concerning 3541
Jer 29:32 Therefore **t.** saith the Lord; Behold, ... 3541
Jer 30:2 **T.** speaketh the Lord God of Israel,.... 3541
Jer 30:5 **t.** saith the Lord; We have heard a..... 3541
Jer 30:12 **t.** saith the Lord, Thy bruise is.......... 3541
Jer 30:18 **T.** saith the Lord; Behold, I will......... 3541
Jer 31:2 **T.** saith the Lord, The people 3541
Jer 31:7 For **t.** saith the Lord; Sing with......... 3541
Jer 31:15 **T.** saith the Lord; A voice was 3541
Jer 31:16 **T.** saith the Lord; Refrain thy............ 3541
Jer 31:18 heard Ephraim bemoaning himself **t.**;.........
Jer 31:23 **T.** saith the Lord of hosts, the 3541
Jer 31:35 **T.** saith the Lord, which giveth the..... 3541
Jer 31:37 **T.** saith the Lord; If heaven above 3541
Jer 32:3 **T.** saith the Lord, Behold, I will......... 3541
Jer 32:14 **T.** saith the Lord of hosts, the God.... 3541
Jer 32:15 **t.** saith the Lord of hosts, the God..... 3541
Jer 32:28 **t.** saith the Lord; Behold, I will 3541
Jer 32:36 And now therefore **t.** saith the Lord, .. 3541
Jer 32:42 **t.** saith the Lord; Like as I have 3541
Jer 33:2 **T.** saith the Lord the maker.............. 3541
Jer 33:4 For **t.** saith the Lord, the God of....... 3541
Jer 33:10 **T.** saith the Lord; Again there........... 3541
Jer 33:12 **T.** saith the Lord of hosts; Again 3541
Jer 33:17 **t.** saith the Lord; David shall never; ... 3541
Jer 33:20 **T.** saith the Lord; If ye can break 3541
Jer 33:24 **t.** they have despised my people, that.......
Jer 33:25 **T.** saith the Lord; If my covenant....... 3541
Jer 34:2 **T.** saith the Lord, the God of Israel;... 3541
Jer 34:2 **T.** saith the Lord; Behold, I will......... 3541
Jer 34:4 **T.** saith the Lord of thee, Thou 3541
Jer 34:13 **T.** saith the Lord, the God of Israel;... 3541
Jer 34:17 **t.** saith the Lord; ye have not............ 3541
Jer 35:8 **T.** have we obeyed the voice of...............
Jer 35:13 **T.** saith the Lord of hosts, the 3541
Jer 35:17 **t.** saith the Lord God of hosts, the..... 3541
Jer 35:18 **T.** saith the Lord of hosts, the God.... 3541
Jer 35:19 Therefore **t.** saith the Lord of hosts,... 3541
Jer 36:29 **T.** saith the Lord; Thou hast............ 3541
Jer 36:30 **t.** saith the Lord of Jehoiakim king...... 3541
Jer 37:7 **T.** saith the Lord, the God of Israel;... 3541
Jer 37:7 **T.** shall ye say to the king of Judah, ... 3541
Jer 37:9 **T.** saith the Lord; Deceive not 3541
Jer 37:21 **T.** Jeremiah remained in the court of.........
Jer 38:2 **T.** saith the Lord, He that 3541
Jer 38:3 **T.** saith the Lord, This city shall........ 3541
Jer 38:4 **t.** he weakeneth the hands of..... 5921,3651
Jer 38:17 **T.** saith the Lord, the God of............ 3541
Jer 39:16 **T.** saith the Lord of hosts, the God.... 3541
Jer 42:9 **T.** saith the Lord, the God of Israel,... 3541
Jer 42:15 **T.** saith the Lord of hosts, the God.... 3541
Jer 42:18 For **t.** saith the Lord of hosts, the...... 3541
Jer 43:7 **t.** came they even to Tahpanhes. ....
Jer 43:10 **T.** saith the Lord of hosts, the 3541
Jer 44:2 **T.** saith the Lord of hosts, the God.... 3541
Jer 44:7 now **t.** saith the Lord, the God.......... 3541

Jer 44:11 **t.** saith the Lord of hosts, the God..... 3541
Jer 44:25 **T.** saith the Lord of hosts, the God.... 3541
Jer 44:30 **T.** saith the Lord; Behold, I will......... 3541
Jer 45:2 **T.** saith the Lord, the God of Israel,... 3541
Jer 45:4 **T.** shalt thou say unto him, The......... 3541
Jer 45:4 Lord saith **t.**; Behold, that which........ 3541
Jer 47:2 **T.** saith the Lord; Behold, waters...... 3541
Jer 48:1 Moab **t.** saith the Lord of hosts,........ 3541
Jer 48:40 **t.** saith the Lord; Behold, he shall...... 3541
Jer 48:47 **T.** far is the judgment of Moab.......... 2008
Jer 49:1 **t.** saith the Lord; Hath Israel no........ 3541
Jer 49:7 Edom, **t.** saith the Lord of hosts;....... 3541
Jer 49:12 For **t.** saith the Lord; Behold, they..... 3541
Jer 49:28 **t.** saith the Lord; Arise ye, go up to... 3541
Jer 49:35 **T.** saith the Lord of hosts; Behold,..... 3541
Jer 50:18 **t.** saith the Lord of hosts, the God..... 3541
Jer 50:33 **T.** saith the Lord of hosts; The......... 3541
Jer 51:1 **T.** saith the Lord; Behold, I will........ 3541
Jer 51:4 **T.** the slain shall fall in the land of...........
Jer 51:33 **t.** saith the Lord of hosts, the God..... 3541
Jer 51:36 **t.** saith the Lord; Behold, I will......... 3541
Jer 51:58 **T.** saith the Lord of hosts; The......... 3541
Jer 51:64 **T.** shall Babylon sink, and shall.......... 3602
Jer 51:64 **T.** far are the words of Jeremiah........ 2008
Jer 52:27 **T.** Judah was carried away captive...........
Eze 1:11 **T.** were their faces; and their wings.........
Eze 2:4 unto them, **T.** saith the Lord God...... 3541
Eze 3:11 **T.** saith the Lord God; whether......... 3541
Eze 3:27 **T.** saith the Lord God; He that.......... 3541
Eze 4:13 **t.** shall the children of Israel eat......... 3602
Eze 5:5 **T.** saith the Lord God; This is.......... 3541
Eze 5:7 **t.** saith the Lord God; Because ye...... 3541
Eze 5:8 **t.** saith the Lord God; Behold, I,........ 3541
Eze 5:13 **T.** shall mine anger be accomplished,........
Eze 6:3 **T.** saith the Lord God to the............. 3541
Eze 6:11 **T.** saith the Lord God; Smite with...... 3541
Eze 6:12 **t.** will I accomplish my fury upon..............
Eze 7:2 **t.** saith the Lord God unto the........... 3541
Eze 7:5 **T.** saith the Lord God; And evil, and.. 3541
Eze 11:5 unto me, Speak; **T.** saith the Lord;..... 3541
Eze 11:5 **T.** have ye said, O house of Israel:..... 3651
Eze 11:7 Therefore **t.** saith the Lord God;........ 3541
Eze 11:16 **T.** saith the Lord God; Although I...... 3541
Eze 11:17 **T.** saith the Lord God; I will even...... 3541
Eze 12:10 **T.** saith the Lord God; This............. 3541
Eze 12:19 **T.** saith the Lord God of the............ 3541
Eze 12:23 **T.** saith the Lord God; I will make..... 3541
Eze 12:28 **T.** saith the Lord God; There shall..... 3541
Eze 13:3 **T.** saith the Lord God; Woe unto....... 3541
Eze 13:8, 13 Therefore **t.** saith the Lord God;... 3541
Eze 13:15 **T.** will I accomplish my wrath upon...........
Eze 13:18 **T.** saith the Lord God; Woe to the..... 3541
Eze 13:20 Wherefore **t.** saith the Lord God;........ 3541
Eze 14:4 **T.** saith the Lord God; Every man..... 3541
Eze 14:6 **T.** saith the Lord God; Repent, and.... 3541
Eze 14:21 For **t.** saith the Lord God;................ 3541
Eze 15:6 Therefore **t.** saith the Lord God; As... 3541
Eze 16:3 say, **T.** saith the Lord God unto......... 3541
Eze 16:13 **T.** wast thou decked with gold and...........
Eze 16:19 and **t.** it was, saith the Lord God............
Eze 16:36 **T.** saith the Lord God; Because......... 3541
Eze 16:59 For **t.** saith the Lord God; I will........ 3541
Eze 17:3 **T.** saith the Lord God; A great.......... 3541
Eze 17:9 **T.** saith the Lord God; Shall it........... 3541
Eze 17:19 Therefore **t.** saith the Lord God; As... 3541
Eze 17:22 **T.** saith the Lord God; I will also....... 3541
Eze 20:3 **T.** saith the Lord God; Are ye........... 3541
Eze 20:5 **T.** saith the Lord God; In the day...... 3541
Eze 20:27 **T.** saith the Lord God; Yet in this...... 3541
Eze 20:30 **T.** saith the Lord God; Are ye........... 3541
Eze 20:39 **t.** saith the Lord God; Go ye, serve... 3541
Eze 20:47 **T.** saith the Lord God; Behold, I........ 3541
Eze 21:3 **T.** saith the Lord; Behold, I am.......... 3541
Eze 21:9 **T.** saith the Lord; Say, A sword, a..... 3541
Eze 21:24 **t.** saith the Lord God: Because ye...... 3541
Eze 21:26 **T.** saith the Lord God; Remove the.... 3541
Eze 21:28 **T.** saith the Lord God concerning....... 3541
Eze 22:3 **T.** saith the Lord God, The city.......... 3541
Eze 22:19 **t.** saith the Lord God; Because ye...... 3541
Eze 22:28 **T.** saith the Lord God, when the........ 3541
Eze 23:4 **T.** were their names; Samaria is..............
Eze 23:7 **T.** she committed her whoredoms............
Eze 23:21 **T.** thou calledst to remembrance the.........
Eze 23:22 **t.** saith the Lord; Behold, I.............. 3541
Eze 23:27 **T.** will I make thy lewdness to cease........
Eze 23:28 **t.** saith the Lord God; Behold, I........ 3541
Eze 23:32 **T.** saith the Lord God; Thou shalt...... 3541
Eze 23:35 Therefore **t.** saith the Lord God;........ 3541
Eze 23:39 **t.** have they one in the midst of......... 3541
Eze 23:46 **t.** saith the Lord God; I will bring...... 3541
Eze 23:48 **T.** will I cause lewdness to cease out........
Eze 24:3 **T.** saith the Lord God; Set on a......... 3541
Eze 24:6 Wherefore **t.** saith the Lord God;....... 3541
Eze 24:9 Therefore **t.** saith the Lord God;........ 3541
Eze 24:21 **T.** saith the Lord God; Behold, I........ 3541
Eze 24:24 **T.** Ezekiel is unto you a sign according......
Eze 25:3 **T.** saith the Lord God; Because......... 3541
Eze 25:6 For **t.** saith the Lord God; Because.... 3541
Eze 25:8, 12 **T.** saith the Lord God; Because..... 3541
Eze 25:13 **t.** saith the Lord God; I will also........ 3541
Eze 25:15 **T.** saith the Lord God; Because the.... 3541
Eze 25:16 **t.** saith the Lord God; Behold, I....... 3541
Eze 26:3 **t.** saith the Lord God; Behold, I am.... 3541
Eze 26:7 For **t.** saith the Lord God; Behold,..... 3541
Eze 26:15 **T.** saith the Lord God to Tyrus;........ 3541
Eze 26:19 **t.** saith the Lord God; When I shall.... 3541
Eze 27:3 **T.** saith the Lord God; O Tyrus,........ 3541
Eze 28:2 **T.** saith the Lord God; Because......... 3541
Eze 28:6 Therefore **t.** saith the Lord God;........ 3541
Eze 28:12 **T.** saith the Lord God; Thou............ 3541
Eze 28:22 **T.** saith the Lord God; Behold, I........ 3541
Eze 28:25 **T.** saith the Lord God; When I.......... 3541
Eze 29:3 **T.** saith the Lord God; Behold, I........ 3541
Eze 29:8 Therefore **t.** saith the Lord God;........ 3541
Eze 29:13 Yet **t.** saith the Lord God; At the....... 3541
Eze 29:19 Therefore **t.** saith the Lord God;........ 3541
Eze 30:2 **T.** saith the Lord God; Howl ye,........ 3541
Eze 30:6 **T.** saith the Lord; They also that....... 3541
Eze 30:10, 13 **T.** saith the Lord God; I will......... 3541
Eze 30:19 **T.** will I execute judgments in Egypt:........
Eze 30:22 Therefore **t.** saith the Lord God;........ 3541
Eze 31:7 **T.** was he fair in his greatness, in the.......
Eze 31:10 Therefore **t.** saith the Lord God;........ 3541
Eze 31:15 **T.** saith the Lord God; In the day............
Eze 31:18 To whom art thou **t.** like in glory....... 3602
Eze 32:3 **T.** saith the Lord God; I will............ 3541
Eze 32:11 For **t.** saith the Lord God; The.......... 3541
Eze 33:10 **T.** ye speak, saying If our.................. 3651
Eze 33:25 **T.** saith the Lord God; Ye eat........... 3541
Eze 33:27 Say thou **t.** unto them,.................... 3541
Eze 33:27 **T.** saith the Lord God; As I live,....... 3541
Eze 34:2 **T.** saith the Lord God unto the.......... 3541
Eze 34:10 **T.** saith the Lord God; Behold, I........ 3541
Eze 34:11, 17 **t.** saith the Lord God; Behold,....... 3541
Eze 34:20 **t.** saith the Lord God unto them;...... 3541
Eze 34:30 **T.** shall they know that I the Lord...........
Eze 35:3 **T.** saith the Lord God; Behold, O...... 3541
Eze 35:7 **T.** will I make mount Seir most...............
Eze 35:13 **T.** with your mouth ye have boasted.........
Eze 35:14 **T.** saith the Lord God; When the....... 3541
Eze 36:2, 3 **T.** saith the Lord God; Because...... 3541
Eze 36:4 **T.** saith the Lord God to the............ 3541
Eze 36:5 Therefore **t.** saith the Lord God;........ 3541
Eze 36:6 **T.** saith the Lord God; Behold, I........ 3541
Eze 36:7 **t.** saith the Lord God; I have lifted..... 3541
Eze 36:13 **T.** saith the Lord God; Because......... 3541
Eze 36:22 **T.** saith the Lord God; I do not......... 3541
Eze 36:33 **T.** saith the Lord God; In the day...... 3541
Eze 36:37 **T.** saith the Lord God; I will yet....... 3541
Eze 37:5 **T.** saith the Lord God unto these...... 3541
Eze 37:9 **T.** saith the Lord God; Come from..... 3541
Eze 37:12, 19,21 **T.** saith the Lord God;............ 3541
Eze 38:3 **T.** saith the Lord God; Behold, I........ 3541
Eze 38:10 **T.** saith the Lord God; It shall........... 3541
Eze 38:14 **T.** saith the Lord God; In that day..... 3541
Eze 38:17 **T.** saith the Lord God; Art thou he..... 3541
Eze 38:23 **T.** will I magnify myself, and sanctify........
Eze 39:1 **T.** saith the Lord God; Behold, I........ 3541
Eze 39:16 **T.** shall they cleanse the land..................
Eze 39:17 **t.** saith the Lord God; Speak unto....... 3541
Eze 39:20 **T.** ye shall be filled at my table with.........
Eze 39:25 **t.** saith the Lord God; Now will I....... 3541
Eze 43:18 **t.** saith the Lord God; These are....... 3541
Eze 43:20 **t.** shalt thou cleanse and purge it.............
Eze 44:6 **T.** saith the Lord God; O ye house..... 3541
Eze 44:9 **T.** saith the Lord God; No stranger,... 3541
Eze 45:9 **T.** saith the Lord God; Let it........... 3541
Eze 45:18 **T.** saith the Lord God; In the first..... 3541
Eze 46:1 **T.** saith the Lord God; The gate of.... 3541
Eze 46:15 **T.** shall they prepare the lamb, and..........
Eze 46:16 **T.** saith the Lord God; If the............. 3541
Eze 47:13 **T.** saith the Lord God; This shall....... 3541
Da 1:16 **T.** Melzar took away the portion of..........
Da 2:24 said **t.** unto him; Destroy not the....... 3652
Da 2:25 said **t.** unto him; I have found a......... 3652
Da 4:10 **T.** were the visions of mine head in..........
Da 4:14 He cried aloud, and said **t.**, Hew........ 3652
Da 6:6 and said **t.** unto him, King Darius,...... 3652
Da 7:5 they said **t.** unto it, Arise, devour...... 3652
Da 7:23 **T.** he said, The fourth beast shall....... 3652
Da 11:17 upright ones with him; **t.** shall he do:........
Da 11:39 **T.** shall he do in the most strong holds......
Ho 10:4 **t.** judgment springeth up as hemlock.........
Am 1:3, 6,11,13 **T.** saith the Lord; For........... 3541
Am 1:9 **T.** saith the Lord; For three transgressions.
Am 2:1, 4,6 **T.** saith the Lord; For three........ 3541
Am 2:11 Is it not even **t.**, O ye children of...... 2063
Am 3:11 Therefore **t.** saith the Lod God;........ 3541
Am 3:12 **T.** saith the Lord; As the shepherd..... 3541
Am 4:12 Therefore **t.** will I do unto thee, O..... 3541
Am 5:3 **t.** saith the Lord God; The city that.... 3541
Am 5:4 **t.** saith the Lord unto the house of..... 3541
Am 5:16 the Lord, saith **t.**; Wailing shall be...... 3541
Am 7:1, 4 **T.** hath the Lord God shewed........ 3541
Am 7:7 **T.** he shewed me: and, behold, the.... 3541
Am 7:11 For **t.** Amos saith, Jeroboam shall...... 3541
Am 7:17 **t.** saith the Lord; Thy wife shall......... 3541
Am 8:1 **T.** hath the Lord God shewed unto..... 3541
Ob 1 **T.** saith the Lord God concerning....... 3541
Mic 2:3 **t.** saith the Lord; Behold, against....... 3541
Mic 3:5 **T.** saith the Lord concerning the........ 3541
Mic 5:6 **t.** shall he deliver us from the.................
Na 1:12 **T.** saith the Lord; Though they.......... 3541
Na 1:12 yet **t.** shall they be cut down,............ 3651
Hag 1:2 **T.** speaketh the Lord of hosts,.......... 3541
Hag 1:5 therefore **t.** saith the Lord of hosts;.... 3541
Hag 1:7 **T.** saith the Lord of hosts; Consider... 3541
Hag 2:6 For **t.** saith the Lord of hosts; Yet..... 3541
Hag 2:11 **T.** saith the Lord of hosts; Ask now... 3541
Mal 1:4 **t.** saith the Lord of hosts, They shall.. 3541
Mal 1:13 **t.** ye brought an offering: should I...... 3541
Zec 1:3, 4 **T.** saith the Lord of hosts;............ 3541
Zec 1:14 **T.** saith the Lord of hosts; I am......... 3541
Zec 1:15 Therefore **t.** saith the Lord; I am....... 3541
Zec 1:17 **T.** saith the Lord of hosts; My........... 3541
Zec 2:8 For **t.** saith the Lord of hosts; After... 3541
Zec 3:7 **T.** saith the Lord of hosts; If thou..... 3541
Zec 6:12 **T.** speaketh the Lord of hosts,.......... 3541
Zec 7:9 **T.** speaketh the Lord of hosts,.......... 3541
Zec 7:14 **T.** the land was desolate after them,.........
Zec 8:2 **T.** saith the Lord of hosts; I was....... 3541
Zec 8:3 **T.** saith the Lord; I am returned........ 3541
Zec 8:4 **T.** saith the Lord of hosts; There....... 3541
Zec 8:6 **T.** saith the Lord of hosts; If it be...... 3541
Zec 8:7 **T.** saith the Lord of hosts; Behold,..... 3541
Zec 8:9 **T.** saith the Lord of hosts; Let.......... 3541
Zec 8:14 For **t.** saith the Lord of hosts; As I.... 3541
Zec 8:19 **T.** saith the Lord of hosts; The fast.... 3541
Zec 8:20 **T.** saith the Lord of hosts; It shall...... 3541
Zec 8:23 **T.** saith the Lord of hosts; In those.... 3541
Zec 11:4 **T.** saith the Lord my God; Feed........ 3541
Mt 2:5 for **t.** it is written by the prophet,...... *3779*
Mt 3:15 **for t. it becometh us to fulfil all** ... *3779*
Mt 15:6 **T. have ye...the commandment** *2532*
Mt 26:54 **be fulfilled, that t. it must be?** *3779*
Mk 2:7 this man **t.** speak blasphemies?.......... *3779*
Lu 1:25 **T.** hath the Lord dealt with me in...... *3779*
Lu 2:48 Son, why hast thou **t.** dealt with us?... *3779*
Lu 9:34 while he **t.** spake, there came a......... *5023*
Lu 11:45 **t.** saying thou reproachest us also...... *5023*
Lu 17:30 **Even t. shall it be in the** *2596,5023*
Lu 18:11 **and prayed t. with himself,** *5023*
Lu 19:28 when he had **t.** spoken, he went......... *5023*
Lu 19:31 **t. shall ye say unto him, Because** .. *3779*
Lu 22:51 answered and said, **Suffer ye t. far** ... *5127*
Lu 23:46 and having said **t.**, he gave up the...... *5028*
Lu 24:36 And as they **t.** spake, Jesus himself.... *5028*
Lu 24:40 when he had **t.** spoken, he shewed..... *5124*
Lu 24:46 said unto them, **T. it is written,** *3779*
Lu 24:46 **t. it behoved Christ to suffer,** *3779*
Joh 4:6 with his journey, sat **t.** on the well:.... *3779*
Joh 9:6 when he had **t.** spoken, he spat on..... *5023*
Joh 11:43 when he **t.** had spoken, cried........... *5023*
Joh 11:48 If we let him **t.** alone, all men will...... *3779*
Joh 13:21 When Jesus had **t.** said, he was......... *5023*
Joh 18:22 when he had **t.** spoken, one of the..... *5023*
Joh 20:14 when she had **t.** said, she turned....... *5023*
Ac 19:41 And when he had **t.** spoken, he......... *5023*

Ac 20:36 when he had **t.** spoken, he kneeled..... *5023*
Ac 21:11 **T.** saith the Holy Ghost, So shall....... *3592*
Ac 26:24 And as he **t.** spake for himself,.......... *5023*
Ac 26:30 when he had **t.** spoken, the king........ *5023*
Ac 27:35 when he had **t.** spoken, he took.......... *5023*
Ro 9:20 it, Why hast thou made me **t.**?.......... *3779*
1Co 14:25 **t.** are the secrets of his heart made.... *3779*
2Co 1:17 When I therefore was **t.** minded,........ *5124*
2Co 5:14 because we **t.** judge, that if one died... *5124*
Php 3:15 as many as be perfect, be **t.** minded:.. *5124*
Heb 6:9 salvation, though we **t.** speak.......... *3779*
Heb 9:6 when these things were **t.** ordained, ... *3779*
Re 9:17 **t.** I saw the horses in the vision, ... *3779*
Re 16:5 be, because thou hast judged **t.**. *5023*
Re 18:21 **T.** with violence shall that great.......... *3779*

THY See in the APPENDIX; also THINE; THYSELF.

THYATIRA (thi-a-ti'-rah)
Ac 16:14 a seller of purple, of the city of **T.**, ... *2363*
Re 1:11 **and unto T., and unto Sardis,** *2363*
Re 2:18 **angel of the church in T. write;** ... *2363*
Re 2:24 **you I say, and unto the rest in T.,** .*2363*

THYINE (thi'-ine)
Re 18:12 silk, and scarlet, and all **t.** wood,........ *2367*

THYSELF
Ge 13:9 separate **t.**, I pray thee, from me: if..........
Ge 14:21 the persons, and take the goods to **t.**.........
Ge 16:9 and submit **t.** under her hands. ....
Ge 33:9 brother; keep that thou hast unto **t.**..........
Ex 9:17 yet exaltest thou **t.** against my people, ...
Ex 10:3 thou refuse to humble **t.** before me ....
Ex 10:28 take heed to **t.**, see my face no more; ......
Ex 18:14 why sittest thou **t.** alone, and all the 859
Ex 18:18 thou art not able to perform it **t.** alone. .....
Ex 18:22 so shall it be easire for **t.**, and they..........
Ex 20:5 Thou shalt not bow down **t.** to them, ...
Ex 34:2 present **t.** there to me in the top of the.....
Ex 34:12 Take heed to **t.**, lest thou make a............
Le 9:7 and made an atonement for **t.**, and for.......
Le 18:20 neighbour's wife, to defile **t.** with her........
Le 18:23 with any beast to defile **t.** therewith:.........
Le 19:18 thou shalt love thy neighbour as **t.**:...........
Le 19:34 you, and thou shalt love him as **t.**;...........
Nu 11:17 thee, that thou bear it not **t.** alone.........
Nu 16:13 thou make **t.** altogether a prince over........
De 4:9 Only take heed to **t.**, and keep thy..........
De 5:9 shalt not bow down **t.** unto them, nor ....
De 9:1 nations greater and mightier than **t.**, ...
De 12:13 Take heed to **t.** that thou offer not thy......
De 12:19 take heed to **t.** that thou forsake not.........
De 12:30 Take heed to **t.** that thou be not..............
De 20:14 spoil thereof, shalt thou take unto **t.**; ....
De 22:1 go astray, and hide **t.** from them:............
De 22:3 do likewise: thou mayest not hide **t.** ....
De 22:4 by the way, and hide **t.** from them: ....
De 22:12 vesture, wherewith thou coverest **t.**. ....
De 23:13 when thou wilt ease **t.** abroad, thou..........
De 28:40 thou shalt not anoint **t.** with the oil;..........
Jos 17:15 had cut down for **t.** there in the land.........
Ru 3:3 Wash **t.** therefore, and anoint thee, ...
Ru 3:3 make not **t.** known unto the man,.............
Ru 4:6 redeem thou my right to **t.**; for I ....
1Sa 19:2 thee, take heed to **t.** until the morning. .....
1Sa 19:2 abide in a secret place, and hide **t.**: ....
1Sa 20:8 there be in me iniquity, slay me **t.**; 859
1Sa 20:19 to the place where thou didst hide **t.**..........
1Sa 25:26 from avenging **t.** with thine own hand,.......
2Sa 5:24 trees, that then thou shalt bestir **t.**...........
2Sa 7:24 hast confirmed to **t.** thy people Israel........
2Sa 13:5 down on thy bed, and make **t.** sick:..........
2Sa 14:2 I pray thee, feign **t.** to be a mourner, ...
2Sa 14:2 and anoint not **t.** with oil, but be as a.........
2Sa 18:13 and thou **t.** wouldest have set............. 859
2Sa 18:13 wouldest have set **t.** against me. ....
2Sa 22:26 merciful thou wilt shew **t.** merciful,...........
2Sa 22:26 upright man thou wilt shew **t.** upright........
2Sa 22:27 With the pure thou wilt shew **t.** pure; ....
2Sa 22:27 froward thou wilt shew **t.** unsavoury. ....
1Ki 2:2 strong therefore, and shew **t.** a man; ....
1Ki 2:3 and whithersoever thou turnest **t.**:............
1Ki 3:11 and hast not asked for **t.** long life;............
1Ki 3:11 niether hast asked riches for **t.**, nor..........
1Ki 3:11 **t.** understanding to discern judgment;........
1Ki 13:7 Come home with me, and refresh **t.**, ...
1Ki 14:2 and disguise **t.**, that thou be not known.....
1Ki 14:6 why feignest thou **t.** to be another? ....
1Ki 17:3 hide **t.** by the brook Cherith, that is ....
1Ki 18:1 year, saying, Go, shew **t.** unto Ahab;........
1Ki 20:22 Go strengthen **t.**, and mark, and see.........
1Ki 20:40 thy judgment be; **t.** hast decided it. ....
1Ki 21:20 sold **t.** to work evil in the sight of the.......
1Ki 22:25 go into an inner chamber to hide **t.**............
2Ki 22:19 thou hast humbled **t.** before the Lord. ....
1Ch 21:12 advise **t.** what word I shall bring..............
2Ch 1:11 asked wisdom and knowledge for **t.**, ...
2Ch 18:24 go into an inner chamber to hide **t.**...........
2Ch 20:37 thou hast joined **t.** with Ahaziah, ...
2Ch 21:13 house, which were better than **t.**: ....
2Ch 34:27 and thou didst humble **t.** before God, ...
2Ch 34:27 and humbledst **t.** before me, and..............
Es 4:13 Think not with **t.** that thou shalt 5315
Job 8:8 prepare **t.** to the search of their..............
Job 10:16 thou shewest **t.** marvellous upon me. ....
Job 15:8 dost thou restrain wisdom to **t.**?.......... 413
Job 22:21 Acquaint now **t.** with him, and be............
Job 30:21 hand thou opposest **t.** against me. ....
Job 40:10 Deck **t.** now with majesty and ....
Job 40:10 and array **t.** with glory and beauty. ....
Ps 7:6 lift up **t.** because o the rage of mine ....
Ps 10:1 why hidest thou **t.** in times of trouble? ......
Ps 18:25 merciful thou wilt shew **t.** merciful;...........
Ps 18:25 man thou wilt shew **t.** upright;..............
Ps 18:26 with the pure thou wilt shew **t.** pure;........
Ps 18:26 froward thou wilt shew **t.** froward. ....
Ps 35:23 Stir up **t.**, and awake to my judgment, ...
Ps 37:1 Fret not **t.** because of evildoers, ...
Ps 37:4 delight **t.** also in the Lord; and he ....
Ps 37:7 fret not **t.** because of him who................
Ps 37:8 fret not **t.** in any wise to do evil. ....
Ps 49:18 thee, when thou doest well to **t.** ....
Ps 50:21 I was altogether such an one as **t.**:...........
Ps 52:1 Why boastest thou **t.** in mischief, O..........
Ps 55:1 and hide not **t.** from my supplication. ....
Ps 60:1 displeased; O turn **t.** to us again. ....
Ps 80:15 branch that thou madest strong for **t.**........
Ps 80:17 man whom thou madest strong for **t.** ....
Ps 85:3 turned **t.** from the fierceness of thine.......
Ps 89:46 long, Lord? wilt thou hide **t.** forever?.......
Ps 94:1 whom vengeance belongeth, shew **t.** ....
Ps 94:2 Lift up **t.**, thou judge of the earth:..........
Ps 104:2 Who coverest **t.** with light as with a ....
Pr 6:3 Do this now my son, and deliver **t.**,..........
Pr 6:3 humble **t.**, and make sure thy friend. ....
Pr 6:5 Deliver **t.** as a roe from the hand of..........
Pr 9:12 thou be wise, thou shalt be wise for **t.**: .....
Pr 24:19 Fret not **t.** because of evil men,..............
Pr 24:27 and make it fit for **t.** in the field;.............
Pr 25:6 Put not forth **t.** in the presence of the.......
Pr 27:1 Boast not **t.** of to morrow; for thou...........
Pr 30:32 hast done foolishly in lifting up **t.**,............
Ec 7:16 over much; neither make **t.** over wise:.....
Ec 7:16 wise: why shouldest thou destroy **t.**? ....
Ec 7:22 thou **t.** likewise hast cursed others....... 859
Isa 26:20 hide **t.** as it were for a little moment, ...
Isa 33:3 at the lifting up of the **t.** the nations..........
Isa 45:15 Verily thou art a God that hidest **t.**,..........
Isa 52:2 Shake **t.** from the dust; arise, and sit........
Isa 52:2 loose **t.** from the bands of thy neck, ...
Isa 57:8 hast discovered **t.** to another than me, ...
Isa 57:9 off, and didst debase **t.** even unto hell. ......
Isa 58:7 thou hide not **t.** from thine own flesh? ....
Isa 58:14 Then shalt thou delight **t.** in the Lord;........
Isa 63:14 people, to make **t.** a glorious name. ....
Isa 64:12 Wilt thou refrain **t.** for these things,..........
Isa 65:5 say, Stand by **t.**, come not near to me; .....
Jer 2:17 Hast thou not procured this unto **t.**,..........
Jer 4:30 Though thou clothest **t.** with crimson, ...
Jer 4:30 in vain shalt thou make **t.** fair;...............
Jer 6:26 sackcloth, and wallow **t.** in ashes:............
Jer 17:4 And thou, even **t.**, shalt discontinue..........
Jer 20:4 I will make thee a terror to **t.**, and to.......
Jer 22:15 because thou closest **t.** in cedar?.............
Jer 32:8 the redemption is thine; but it for **t.** ....
Jer 45:5 And sekest thou great things for **t.**?.........
Jer 46:19 Egypt, furnish **t.** to go into captivity: ....
Jer 47:5 their valley: how long wilt thou cut **t.**? ......
Jer 47:6 put up **t.** into thy scabbard, rest, and........
La 2:18 give **t.** no rest; let not the apple of...........
La 3:44 Thou hast covered **t.** with a cloud, ...
La 4:21 be drunken, and shalt make **t.** naked.........
Eze 3:24 me, Go, shut **t.** within thine house. ....
Eze 16:17 thee, and madest to **t.** images of men, ...
Eze 22:4 defiled **t.** in thine idols which thou ....
Eze 22:16 thou shalt take thine inhertance in **t.** ....
Eze 23:40 for whom thou didst wash **t.**,..................
Eze 23:40 eyes, and deckedst **t.** with ornaments, ...
Eze 31:10 thou hast lifted up **t.** in height, and...........
Eze 38:7 and prepare for **t.**, thou, and all thy..........
Da 5:17 Let thy gifts be to **t.**, and give thy ....
Da 5:23 hast lifted up **t.** against the Lord of...........
Da 10:12 and to chasten **t.** before thy God, thy ....
Ho 13:9 O Israel, thou hast destroyed **t.**; but.........
Ob 4 Though thou exalt **t.** as the eagle, ...
Mic 1:10 house of Aphrah roll **t.** in the dust............
Mic 5:1 Now gather **t.** in troops, O daughter.........
Na 3:15 make **t.** many as the cankerworm,............
Na 3:15 make **t.** many as the locusts.................
Zec 2:7 Deliver **t.**, O Zion, that dwellest with........
Mt 4:6 be the Son of God, cast **t.** down: *4572*
Mt 5:33 **Thou shalt not forswear t., but shalt**...
Mt 8:4 **shew t. to the priest, and offer**...... *4572*
Mt 19:19 **Thou shalt love thy neighbour as t.**..*4572*
Mt 22:39 **Thou shalt love thy neighbour as t.**..*4572*
Mt 27:40 buildest it in three days, save **t.**......... *4572*
Mk 1:44 **shew t. to the priest, and offer for** .*4572*
Mk 12:31 **Thou shalt love thy neighbour as t.**..*4572*
Mk 15:30 Save **t.**, and come down from the....... *4572*
Lu 4:9 of God, cast **t.** down from hence:....... *4572*
Lu 4:23 **this proverb, Physician, heal t.** *4572*
Lu 5:14 **but go, and shew t. to the priest,** .. *4572*
Lu 6:42 **when thou t. beholdest not the**......... *846*
Lu 7:6 unto him, Lord, trouble not **t.**: for...........
Lu 10:27 thy mind; and thy neighbour as **t.** *4572*
Lu 17:8 **and gird t., and serve me, till I have** ...
Lu 23:37 be the king of the Jews, save **t.**.......... *4572*
Lu 23:39 If thou be Christ, save **t.** and us. *4572*
Joh 1:22 sent us. What sayest thou of **t.**? *4572*
Joh 7:4 these things, shew **t.** to the world...... *4572*
Joh 8:13 him, Thou bearest record of **t.**; *4572*
Joh 8:53 are dead: whom makest thou **t.**? *4572*
Joh 10:33 thou, being a man, makest **t.** God. *4572*
Joh 14:22 that thou wilt manifest **t.** unto us, ... *4572*
Joh 18:34 **Sayest thou this thing of t., or**...... *1438*
Joh 21:18 **thou wast young, thou girdedst t.,**.. *4572*
Ac 8:29 Go near, and join **t.** to this chariot...........
Ac 12:8 him, Gird **t.**, and bind on thy sandals. ....
Ac 16:28 Do **t.** no harm: for we are all here. *4572*
Ac 21:24 take, and purify **t.** with them,..................
Ac 21:24 that thou **t.** also walkest orderly, ... *846*
Ac 24:8 **t.** mayest take knowledge of all........... *846*
Ac 26:1 Thou art permitted to speak for **t.**........ *4572*
Ac 26:24 a loud voice, Paul, thou art beside **t.**;........
Ro 2:1 another, thou condemnest **t.**;.............. *4572*
Ro 2:5 treasurest up unto **t.** wrath against..... *4572*
Ro 2:19 thou **t.** art a guide of the blind,.......... *4572*
Ro 2:21 another, teachest thou not **t.**?............ *4572*
Ro 13:9 Thou shalt love thy neighbour as **t.**..... *1438*
Ro 14:22 thou faith? have it to **t.** before God..... *4572*
Ga 5:14 Thou shalt love thy neighbour as **t.**..... *1438*
Ga 6:1 considering **t.**, lest thou also be *4572*
1Ti 3:15 to behave **t.** in the house of God,.............
1Ti 4:7 exercise **t.** rather unto godliness. *4572*
1Ti 4:15 these things; give **t.** wholly to them;..........
1Ti 4:16 Take heed unto **t.**, and unto the *4572*
1Ti 4:16 doing this thou shalt both save **t.**, ... *4572*
1Ti 5:22 of other men's sins: keep **t.** pure. *4572*
1Ti 6:5 godliness: from such withdraw **t.**...............
2Ti 2:15 Study to show **t.** approved unto........... *4572*
Tit 2:7 showing **t.** a pattern of good works:.... *4572*
Jas 2:8 Thou shalt love thy neighbour as **t.**,.... *4572*

TIBERIAS (ti-be'-re-as)
Joh 6:1 of Galilee, which is the sea of **T.**........ *5085*
Joh 6:23 there came other boats from **T.**......... *5085*
Joh 21:1 to the disciples at the sea of **T.**; *5085*

TIBERIUS (ti-be'-re-us) See also CAESAR.
Lu 3:1 year of the reign of **T.** Caesar, ... *5086*

TIBHATH (tib'-hath)
1Ch 18:8 Likewise from **T.**, and from Chun,........ 2880

TIBNI (tib'-ni)
1Ki 16:21 the people followed **T.** the son of....... 8402
1Ki 16:22 people that followed **T.** the son of...... 8402
1Ki 16:22 so **T.** died, and Omri reigned. 8402

TIDAL (ti'-dal)
Ge 14:1 of Elam, and **T.** king of nations;......... 8413
Ge 14:9 Elam, and with **T.** king of nations,...... 8413

TIDE See EVENINGTIDE; EVENTIDE; NOONTIDE.

TIDINGS
Ge 29:13 when Laban heard the **t.** of Jacob....... 8088
Ex 33:4 when the people heard these evil **t.**,... 1697
1Sa 4:19 heard the **t.** that the ark of God......... 8052
1Sa 11:4 and told the **t.** in the ears of the........ 1697
1Sa 11:5 him the **t.** of the men of Jabesh. 1697
1Sa 11:6 upon Saul when he heard those **t.**, ... 1697
1Sa 27:11 nor woman alive, to bring **t.** to Gath, ...
2Sa 4:4 five years old when the **t.** came......... 8052
2Sa 4:10 thinking to have brought good **t.**, ... 1319
2Sa 4:10 have given him a reward for his **t.**...... 1309
2Sa 13:30 that **t.** came to David, saying, ... 8052
2Sa 18:19 me now run, and bear the king **t.**,....... 1319
2Sa 18:20 Thou shalt not bear **t.** this day, ... 1309
2Sa 18:20 but thou shalt bear **t.** another day: 1319
2Sa 18:20 but this day thou shalt bear no **t.**, ... 1319
2Sa 18:22 seeing that thou hast no **t.** ready? 1309
2Sa 18:25 be alone, there is **t.** in his mouth, ... 1309
2Sa 18:26 the king said, He also bringeth **t.** 1319
2Sa 18:27 man, and cometh with good **t.** 1309
2Sa 18:31 Cushi said, **T.**, my lord the king:........ 1319
1Ki 1:42 valiant man, and bringest good **t.**........ 1319
1Ki 2:28 Then **t.** came to Joab: for Joab 8052
1Ki 14:6 for I am sent to thee with heavy **t.**...........
2Ki 7:9 this day is a day of good **t.**, and we.... 1309
1Ch 10:9 to carry **t.** unto their idols, and to...... 1319
Ps 112:7 He shall not be afraid of evil **t.** 8052
Isa 40:9 O Zion, that bringest good **t.**, get....... 1319
Isa 40:9 O Jerusalem, that bringest good **t.**,...... 1319
Isa 41:27 one that bringeth good **t.**.................. 1319
Isa 52:7 feet of him that bringeth good **t.**, ... 1319
Isa 52:7 that bringeth good **t.** of good, that...... 1319
Isa 61:1 to preach good **t.** unto the meek; 1319
Jer 20:15 man who brought **t.** to my father, ... 1319
Jer 37:5 Jerusalem heard **t.** of them,............... 8088
Jer 49:23 Arpad: for they have heard evil **t.** 8052
Eze 21:7 that thou shalt answer, For the **t.**; 8052
Da 11:44 But **t.** out of the east and out of the... 8052
Na 1:15 feet of him that bringeth good **t.**, ... 1319
Lu 1:19 thee, and to shew thee these glad **t.**..... *2097*
Lu 2:10 I bring you good **t.** of great joy,......... *2097*
Lu 8:1 shewing the glad **t.** of the kingdom..... *2097*
Ac 11:22 **t.** of these things came unto the *3056*
Ac 13:32 And we declare unto you glad **t.**, ... *2097*
Ac 21:31 **t.** came unto the chief captain of......... *5334*
Ro 10:15 and bring glad **t.** of good things!......... *2097*
1Th 3:6 and brought us good **t.** of your faith.... *2097*

TIE See also TIED.
1Sa 6:7 no yoke, and **t.** the kine to the cart, ... 631
Pr 6:21 and **t.** them about thy neck. 6029

TIED
Ex 39:31 And they **t.** unto it a lace of blue, ... 5414
1Sa 6:10 milch kine, and **t.** them to the cart,...... 631
2Ki 7:10 but horses **t.**, and asses **t.**, and the 631
Mt 21:2 **straightway ye shall find an ass t.**,.*1210*
Mk 11:2 **ye shall find a colt t., whereon** *1210*
Mk 11:4 and found the colt **t.** by the door......... *1210*
Lu 19:30 **your entering ye shall find a colt t.**,.*1210*

TIGLATH-PILESER (tig''-lath-pi-le'-zur) See also TILGATH-PILNESER.
2Ki 15:29 Israel came **t.** king of Assyria, ... 8407
2Ki 16:7 So Ahaz sent messengers of **T.** 8407
2Ki 16:10 Ahaz went to Damascus to meet **T.**..... 8407

TIKVAH (tik'-vah) See also TIKVATH.
2Ki 22:14 wife of Shallum the son of **T.**,............ 8616
Ezr 10:15 and Jahaziah the son of **T.** were......... 8616

TIKVATH (tik'-vath) See also TIKVAH.
2Ch 34:22 the wife of Shallum the son of **T.**, ... 8616

TILE See also TILING.
Eze 4:1 son of man, take thee a **t.**, and lay it .. 3843

TILGATH-PILNESER (til''-gath-pil-ne'-zur) See also TIGLATH-PILESER.
1Ch 5:6 whom **T.** king of Assyria carried 8407
1Ch 5:26 and the spirit of **T.** king of Assyria, ... 8407
2Ch 28:20 **T.** king of Assyria came unto him,...... 8407

TILING
Lu 5:19 let him down through the **t.** wih......... *2766*

TILL See also TILLED; TILLER; TILLEST; TILLETH; UNTIL.
Ge 2:5 was not a man to **t.** the ground. 5647
Ge 3:19 **t.** thou return unto the ground;.......... 5704
Ge 3:23 to **t.** the ground from whence he........ 5647
Ge 19:22 I cannot do any thing **t.** thou be......... 5704
Ge 29:8 **t.** they roll the stone from the well's.........
Ge 38:11 house, **t.** Shelah my son be grown:...... 5704
Ge 38:17 give me a pledge, **t.** thou send it? 5704
Ex 15:16 **t.** thy people pass over, O Lord,........ 5704
Ex 15:16 **t.** the people pass over, which thou.... 5704
Ex 16:19 no man leave of it **t.** the morning. 5704
Ex 16:24 And they laid it up **t.** the morning, ... 5704
Ex 34:33 **t.** Moses had done speaking with them,.....
Ex 40:37 **t.** the day that it was taken up. 5704
Nu 12:15 **t.** Miriam was brought in again. 5704
De 17:5 stone them with stones, **t.** they die. ....
De 28:45 thee, **t.** thou be destroyed; 5704
Jos 5:6 **t.** all the people that were men of...... 5704
Jos 5:8 in the camp, **t.** they were whole. 5704
Jos 8:6 **t.** we have drawn them from the......... 5704
Jos 10:20 slaughter, **t.** they were consumed,...... 5704
Jg 3:25 they tarried **t.** they were ashamed:..... 5704
Jg 6:4 **t.** thou come unto Gaza, and left no.... 5704
Jg 11:33 even **t.** thou come to Minnith, ... 5704
Jg 16:3 Samson lay **t.** midnight, and arose 5704
Jg 19:26 where her lord was, **t.** it was light. 5704
Jg 21:2 and abode there **t.** even before God,... 5704
Ru 1:13 tarry for them **t.** they were grown?.... 5704
1Sa 10:8 shalt thou tarry, **t.** I come to thee,..... 5704
1Sa 16:11 will not sit down **t.** he come hither. 5704
1Sa 22:3 **t.** I know what God will do for me. 5704
2Sa 3:35 or ought else, **t.** the sun be down. 6440
2Sa 9:10 servants, shall **t.** the land for him. 5647
1Ki 14:10 taketh away dung, **t.** it be all gone. 5704
1Ki 18:28 **t.** the blood gushed out upon them. 5704
2Ki 2:17 they urged him **t.** he was ashamed, ... 5704
2Ki 4:20 he sat on her knees **t.** noon, and 5704
2Ki 7:9 if we tarry **t.** the morning light, ... 5704
2Ki 10:17 Samaria, **t.** he had destroyed him, ... 5704
2Ki 13:17 Aphek, **t.** thou have consumed........... 5704
2Ki 13:19 Syria **t.** thou hadst consumed it:......... 5704
2Ki 21:16 **t.** he had filled Jerusalem from one 5704
2Ch 26:15 helped, **t.** he was strong. 5704,3588
2Ch 29:34 help them, **t.** the work was ended, ... 5704
2Ch 36:16 his people, **t.** there was no remedy. ... 5704
Ezr 2:63 **t.** there stood up a priest with Urim ... 5704
Ezr 5:5 **t.** the matter came to Darius:........... 5705
Ezr 9:14 us **t.** thou hadst consumed us, ... 5704
Ne 2:7 me over **t.** I come into Judah;............ 5704
Ne 4:11 **t.** we come in the midst among.......... 5704
Ne 4:21 the morning **t.** the stars appeared...... 5704
Ne 7:65 **t.** there stood up a priest with Urim 5704
Ne 13:19 not be opened **t.** after the sabbath:..... 5704
Job 7:19 alone **t.** I swallow down my spittle? 5704
Job 8:21 **T.** he fill thy mouth with laughing, ... 5704
Job 14:6 **t.** he shall accomplish, as an............ 5704
Job 14:12 **t.** the heavens be no more, they......... 5704
Job 14:14 will I wait, **t.** my change comes. 5704
Job 27:5 **t.** I die I will not remove mine........... 5704
Job 32:4 Elihu had waited **t.** Job had spoken, ...
Ps 10:15 out his wickedness **t.** thou find none. ....
Ps 18:37 turn again **t.** they were consumed. 5704
Ps 68:30 **t.** every one submit himself with ....
Pr 7:23 **T.** a dart strike through his liver; 5704
Pr 29:11 a wise man keepeth it in **t.** afterwards.......
Ec 2:3 **t.** I might see what was that good...... 5704
Ca 2:7 nor awake my love, **t.** he please. 5704
Ca 3:5 nor awake my love, **t.** he please. 5704
Isa 5:8 field to field, **t.** there be no place, ... 5704
Isa 5:11 until night, **t.** wine inflame them! ....
Isa 22:14 not be purged from you **t.** ye die, ... 5704
Isa 23:13 **t.** the Assyrian founded it for them...........
Isa 30:17 **t.** ye be left as a beacon upon the top.......
Isa 38:13 I reckoned **t.** morning, that, as a........ 5704
Isa 42:4 **t.** he have set judgment in the........... 5704
Isa 62:7 give him no rest, **t.** he establish,......... 5704
Isa 62:7 **t.** he make Jerusalem a praise in......... 5704
Jer 7:32 bury in Tophet, **t.** there be no place. ....
Jer 9:16 them, **t.** I have consumed them. 5704
Jer 19:11 in Tophet, **t.** there be no place to bury .....
Jer 23:20 **t.** he have performed the thoughts...... 5704
Jer 24:10 **t.** they be consumed from off the 5704
Jer 27:11 they shall **t.** it, and dwell therein. 5647
Jer 49:9 they will destroy **t.** they have enough........
Jer 49:37 them, **t.** I have consumed them: 5704
Jer 52:3 **t.** he had cast them out from his......... 5704
Jer 52:11 in prison **t.** the day of his death. 5704
La 3:50 **T.** the Lord look down, and behold..... 5704
Eze 4:8 **t.** thou hast ended the days of thy...... 5704
Eze 4:14 even **t.** now have I not eaten of that... 5704
Eze 24:13 **t.** I have caused my fury to rest 5704
Eze 28:15 **t.** iniquity was found in thee. 5704
Eze 34:21 **t.** ye have scattered them abroad; 5704
Eze 39:15 **t.** the buriers have buried it in the...... 5704
Eze 39:19 And ye shall eat fat **t.** ye be full, and ....
Eze 39:19 and drink blood **t.** ye be drunken, of..........
Eze 47:20 **t.** a man come over against 5704
Da 2:9 before me, **t.** the time be changed:..... 5704
Da 2:34 sawest **t.** that a stone was cut out...... 5704
Da 4:23 field, **t.** seven times pass over him; 5704
Da 4:25 **t.** thou know that the most High 5704
Da 4:33 **t.** his hairs were grown like eagles'..... 5704
Da 5:21 **t.** he knew that the most high God..... 5704
Da 6:14 laboured **t.** the going down of the....... 5704
Da 7:4 **t.** the wings thereof were plucked, ... 5704
Da 7:9 **t.** the thrones were cast down,........... 5704
Da 7:11 beheld even **t.** the beast was slain, ... 5704
Da 10:3 **t.** three whole weeks were fulfilled. 5704
Da 11:36 **t.** the indignation be accomplished:...... 5704
Da 12:9 and sealed **t.** the time of the end. 5704
Da 12:13 But go thou thy way **t.** the end be: ....
Ho 5:15 **t.** they acknowledge their offence, ... 5704
Ho 10:12 **t.** he come and rain righteousness 5704
Ob 5 not have stolen **t.** they had enough? ....
Jon 4:5 **t.** he might see what would.............. 5704
Zep 3:3 gnaw not the bones **t.** the morrow. ....
Mt 1:25 not **t.** she had brought forth her......... *2193*
Mt 2:9 **t.** it came and stood over where the ... *2193*
Mt 5:18 **T. heaven and earth pass, one jot**.. *2193*
Mt 5:18 **pass from the law, t. all be fulfilled**..*2193*
Mt 5:26 **t. thou hast paid the uttermost** *2193*
Mt 10:11 **and there abide t. ye go thence**. *2193*
Mt 10:23 **Israel, t. the son of man be come**.. *2193*
Mt 12:20 **t.** he send forth judgment unto *2193*
Mt 13:33 **meal, t. the whole was leavened**..... *2193*
Mt 16:28 **t. they see the son of man coming**..*2193*
Mt 18:21 and I forgive him? **t.** seven times?...... *2193*
Mt 18:30 **prison, t. he should pay the debt**.. *2193*
Mt 18:34 **t. he should pay all that was due** .. *2193*
Mt 22:44 **t. I make thine enemies thy**........... *2193*
Mt 23:39 **t. ye shall say, Blessed is he that**.. *2193*
Mt 24:34 **pass, t. all these things be**........... *2193*
Mk 6:10 **abide t. ye depart from that place**. .*2193*
Mk 9:1 **t.** they have seen the kingdom of........ *2193*
Mk 9:9 **t.** the Son of man were risen *1508,3752*
Mk 12:36 **t. I make thine enemies thy**........... *2193*
Mk 13:30 **pass, t. all these things be done**. ... *3360*
Lu 1:80 **t.** the day of his shewing unto *2193*
Lu 9:27 **t. they see the kingdom of God**. *2193*
Lu 12:50 **straitened t. it be accomplished!**.... *2193*
Lu 12:59 **t. thou hast paid the very last mite**. .*2193*
Lu 13:8 **t. I shall dig about it, and dung**... *2193*
Lu 13:21 **meal, t. the whole was leavened**.... *2193*
Lu 15:8 **and seek diligently t. she find it?** .. *2193*
Lu 17:8 **me, t. I have eaten and drunken;** .. *2193*
Lu 19:13 **said unto them, Occupy t. I come**. .*2193*
Lu 20:43 **T. I make thine enemies thy**........... *2193*
Lu 21:32 **not pass away, t. all be fulfilled**.... *2193*
Joh 13:38 **crow, t. thou hast denied me thrice**. .*2193*
Joh 21:22 **If I will that he tarry t. I come**,.... *2193*
Ac 7:18 **T.** another king arose, which *891,3757*
Ac 8:40 the cities, **t.** he came to Caesarea. *2193*
Ac 20:11 even **t.** break of day, so he departed.... *891*
Ac 21:5 children, **t.** we were out of the city: ... *2193*
Ac 23:12 nor drink **t.** they had killed Paul. *2193*
Ac 23:21 nor drink **t.** they have killed him: *2193*
Ac 25:21 kept **t.** I might send him to Caesar. *2193*
Ac 28:23 prophets, from morning **t.** evening. *2193*
1Co 11:26 the Lord's death **t.** he come. *891,3757*
1Co 15:25 **t.** he hath put all enemies under... *891,3757*
Ga 3:19 **t.** the seed shall come to whom.... *891,3757*
Eph 4:13 **T.** we all come in the unity of the *3360*
Php 1:10 offence **t.** the day of Christ; *1519*
1Ti 4:13 **T.** I come, give attendance to............ *2193*
Heb 10:13 **t.** his enemies be made his footstool. .. *2193*
Re 2:25 **have already hold fast t. I come**. *891*
Re 7:3 **t.** we have sealed the servants of........ *891*
Re 15:8 **t.** the seven plagues of the seven *891*
Re 20:3 **t.** the thousand years shall be *891*

TILLAGE
1Ch 27:26 the work of the field for **t.** of the 5656
Ne 10:37 the tithes in all the cities of our **t.**...... 5656
Pr 13:23 Much food is in the **t.** of the poor: 5215

TILLED
Eze 36:9 you, and ye shall be **t.** and sown: 5647
Eze 36:34 And the desolate land shall be **t.**, 5647

TILLER
Ge 4:2 but Cain was a **t.** of the gound. 5647

TILLEST
Ge 4:12 When thou **t.** the ground, it shall 5647

TILLETH
Pr 12:11 He that **t.** his land shall be 5647
Pr 28:19 He that **t.** his land shall have plenty 5647

TILON (ti'-lon)
1Ch 4:20 and Rinnah, Ben-hanan, and **T.**, 8436

TIMAEUS (tim-me'-us) See also BARTIMAEUS.
Mk 10:46 blind Bartimaeus, the son of **T.** *5090*

TIMBER
Ex 31:5 and in carrying of **t.**, to work in all 6086
Le 14:45 the stones of it, and the **t.** thereof, 6086
1Ki 5:6 that can skill to hew **t.** like unto the 6086
1Ki 5:8 they desire concerning **t.** of cedar, 6086
1Ki 5:8 of cedar, and concerning **t.** of fir. 6086
1Ki 5:18 prepared **t.** and stones to build the 6086
1Ki 6:10 rested on the house with **t.** of cedar 6086
1Ki 15:22 stones of Ramah, and the **t.** thereof, 6086
2Ki 12:12 to buy **t.** and hewed stone to repair 6086
2Ki 22:6 to but **t.** and hewn stone to repair 6086
1Ch 14:1 and **t.** of cedars, with masons and 6086
1Ch 22:14 **t.** also and stone have I prepared; 6086
1Ch 22:15 and workers of stone and **t.**, and 6086
2Ch 2:8 can skill to cut **t.** in Lebanon; 6086
2Ch 2:9 to prepare me **t.** in abundance: 6086
2Ch 2:10 thy servants, the hewers that cut **t.**, 6086
2Ch 2:14 brass, in iron, in stone, and in **t.**, 6086
2Ch 16:6 stones of Ramah, and the **t.** thereof, 6086
2Ch 34:11 hewn stone, and **t.** for couplings, 6086
Ezr 5:8 stones, and **t.** is laid in the walls, 636
Ezr 6:4 of great stones, and a row of new **t.**: 636
Ezr 6:11 let **t.** be pulled down from his house, 636
Ne 2:8 he may give me **t.** to make beams 6086
Eze 26:12 thy stones and thy **t.** and thy dust 6086
Hab 2:11 beam out of the **t.** shall answer it 6086
Zec 5:4 the **t.** thereof and the stones thereof 6086

TIMBREL See also TIMBRELS.
Ex 15:20 of Aaron, took a **t.** in her hand; 8596
Job 21:12 They take the **t.** and harp, and 8596
Ps 81:2 a psalm, and bring hither the **t.** 8596
Ps 149:3 sing praises unto him with the **t.** 8596
Ps 150:4 Praise him with the **t.** and dance. 8596

TIMBRELS
Ex 15:20 women went out after her with **t.** 8596
Jg 11:34 came out to meet him with **t.** and 8596
2Sa 6:5 harps, and on psalteries, and on **t.** 8596
1Ch 13:8 and with psalteries, and with **t.**, 8596
Ps 68:25 were the damsels playing with **t.** 8608

TIME See also AFORETIME; BEFORETIME; DAYTIME; LIFETIME; MEALTIME; SOMETIME; TIMES; UNTIMELY.
Ge 4:3 And in process of **t.** it came to pass, 3117
Ge 17:21 shall bear unto thee at this set **t.**
Ge 18:10 thee according to the **t.** of life; 6256
Ge 18:14 At the **t.** appointed I will return
Ge 18:14 according to the **t.** of life, and 6256
Ge 21:2 at the set **t.** of which God had
Ge 21:22 it came to pass at that **t.**, that 6256
Ge 22:15 out of heaven the second **t.**, 6256
Ge 24:11 of water at the **t.** of the evening, 6256
Ge 24:11 the **t.** that women go out to draw 6256
Ge 26:8 when he had been there a long **t.**, 3117
Ge 29:7 neither is it **t.** that the cattle 6256
Ge 29:34 this **t.** will my husband be joined 6471
Ge 30:33 answer for me in **t.** to come, 3117
Ge 31:10 at the **t.** that the cattle conceived, 6256
Ge 38:1 came to pass at that **t.**, that Judah 6256
Ge 38:12 in process of **t.** the daughter of 3117
Ge 38:27 to pass in the **t.** of her travail, 6256
Ge 39:5 from the **t.** that he had made him
Ge 39:11 it came to pass about this **t.**, that 3117
Ge 41:5 he slept and dreamed the second **t.**:
Ge 43:10 we had returned this second **t.**. 6471
Ge 43:18 returned in our sacks at the first **t.** 8462
Ge 43:20 we came indeed down at the first **t.** 8462
Ge 47:29 the **t.** drew nigh that Israel must 3117
Ex 2:23 it came to pass in process of **t.**, 3117
Ex 8:32 hardened his heart at this **t.** also, 6471
Ex 9:5 And the Lord appointed a set **t.**,
Ex 9:14 will at this **t.** send all my plagues 6471
Ex 9:18 to morrow about this **t.** I will cause 6256
Ex 9:27 unto them, I have sinned this **t.**: 6471
Ex 13:14 thy son asketh thee in **t.** to come, 4279
Ex 21:19 he shall pay for the loss of his **t.**, 7674
Ex 21:29 push with his horn in **t.** past 8543,8032
Ex 21:36 hath used to push in **t.** past, 8543,8032
Ex 23:15 in the **t.** appointed of the month
Ex 34:18 thee, in the **t.** of the month Abib: 4150
Ex 34:21 in earing **t.** and in harvest thou shalt
Le 13:58 then it shall be washed the second **t.**,
Le 15:25 out of the **t.** of her separation, 6256
Le 15:25 run beyond the **t.** of her separation; 6256
Le 18:18 besides the other in her life **t.**.
Le 25:32 may the Levites redeem at any **t.**
Le 25:50 according to the **t.** of an hired servant
Le 26:5 vintage shall reach unto the sowing **t.**:
Nu 10:6 When ye blow an alarm the second **t.**,
Nu 13:20 **t.** was the **t.** of the firstripe grapes. 3117
Nu 14:14 them, by day **t.** in a pillar of a cloud,
Nu 20:15 we have dwelt in Egypt a long **t.** 3117
Nu 22:4 king of the Moabites at that **t.**. 6256
Nu 23:23 according to this **t.** it shall be said 6256
Nu 26:10 **t.** the fire devoured two hundred and
Nu 32:10 anger was kindled the same **t.**, 3117
Nu 35:26 if the slayer shall at any **t.** come
De 1:9 I spake unto you at that **t.**, saying, 6256
De 1:16 I charged your judges at that **t.**, 6256
De 1:18 I commanded you at that **t.** all the 6256
De 2:20 giants dwelt therein in old **t.**; and
De 2:34 And we took all his cities at that **t.**, 6256
De 3:4 And we took all his cities at that **t.**, 6256
De 3:8 we took at that **t.** out of the hand 6256
De 3:12 land, which we possessed at that **t.**, 6256
De 3:18 I commanded you at that **t.**, saying 6256
De 3:21 I commanded Joshua at that **t.**, 6256
De 3:23 And I besought the Lord at that **t.**. 6256
De 4:14 the Lord commanded me at that **t.** 6256
De 5:5 between the Lord and you at that **t.**, 6256
De 6:20 thy son asketh thee in **t.** to come, 4279
De 9:19 Lord hearkened unto me at that **t.** 6471
De 9:20 prayed for Aaron also the same **t.**. 6256
De 10:1 At that **t.** the Lord said unto me, 6256
De 10:8 At that **t.** the Lord separated the 6256
De 10:10 according to the first **t.**, forty days 3117
De 10:10 Lord hearkened unto me at that **t.** 6471
De 16:9 such **t.** as thou beginnest to put the
De 19:4 whom he hated not in **t.** past; 8543,8032
De 19:6 as he hated him not in **t.** past. 8543,8032
De 19:14 which they of old **t.** have set in thine
De 20:19 thou shalt besiege a city a long **t.** 3117
De 32:35 their foot shall slide in due **t.**: for 6256
Jos 2:5 about the **t.** of shutting of the gate,
Jos 3:15 all his banks all the **t.** of harvest, 3117
Jos 4:6, 21 ask their fathers in **t.** to come, 4279
Jos 5:2 At that **t.** the Lord said unto 6256
Jos 5:2 the children of Israel the second **t.**.
Jos 6:16 it came to pass at the seventh **t.**, 6471
Jos 6:26 Joshua adjured them at that **t.**, 6256
Jos 8:14 he and all his people, at a **t.** appointed,
Jos 10:27 at the **t.** of the boing down of the 6256
Jos 10:42 land did Joshua take at one **t.**, 6471
Jos 11:6 about this **t.** will I deliver then 6256
Jos 11:10 And Joshua at that **t.** turned back, 6256
Jos 11:18 Joshua made war a long **t.** with 3117
Jos 11:21 And at that **t.** came Joshua, and 6256
Jos 22:24 In **t.** to come your children might 4279
Jos 22:27 say to our children in **t.** to come, 4279
Jos 22:28 to our generations in **t.** to come, 4279
Jos 23:1 it came to pass a long **t.** after that 3117
Jos 24:2 the other side of the flood in old **t.**, 5769
Jg 3:29 slew of Moab at that **t.** about ten 6256
Jg 4:4 she judged Israel at that **t.** 6256
Jg 9:8 The trees went forth on a **t.** to anoint
Jg 10:14 you in the **t.** of your tribulation. 6256
Jg 11:4 it came to pass in process of **t.**, 3117
Jg 11:26 ye not recover them within that **t.**? 6256
Jg 12:6 fell at that **t.** of the Ephraimtes 6256
Jg 13:23 nor would as at this **t.** have told us 6256
Jg 14:4 for at that **t.** the Philistines had 6256
Jg 14:8 after a **t.** he returned to take her, 3117
Jg 15:1 in the **t.** of wheat harvest, that 3117
Jg 18:31 all the **t.** that the house of God was
Jg 20:15 Benjamin were numbered at that **t.**
Jg 21:14 Benjamin came again at that **t.**; 6256
Jg 21:22 ye did not give unto them at this **t.**, 6256
Jg 21:24 of Israel departed thence at that **t.** 6256
Ru 4:7 the manner in former **t.** in Israel 6440
1Sa 1:4 the **t.** was that Elkanah offered, 3117
1Sa 1:20 when the **t.** was come about after 3117
1Sa 3:2 And it came to pass at that **t.**, when 3117
1Sa 3:8 Lord called Samuel again the third **t.**
1Sa 4:20 And about the **t.** of her death the 6256
1Sa 7:2 that the **t.** was long; for it 3117
1Sa 9:13 for about this **t.** ye shall find him 3117
1Sa 9:16 To morrow about this **t.** I will 6256
1Sa 9:24 unto this **t.** hath it been kept for 4150
1Sa 11:9 To morrow, by that **t.** the sun be hot,
1Sa 13:8 according to the set **t.** that Samuel
1Sa 14:18 the ark of God was at that **t.** with 3117
1Sa 14:21 the Philistines before that **t.**, 8032
1Sa 18:19 came to pass at the **t.** when Merab 6256
1Sa 19:21 sent messengers again the third **t.**,
1Sa 20:12 my father about to morrow any **t.**, 6256
1Sa 20:35 at the **t.** appointed with David,
1Sa 26:8 I will not smite him the second **t.**
1Sa 27:7 the **t.** that David dwelt in the 4557,3117
2Sa 2:11 the **t.** that David was king in 4557,3117
2Sa 5:2 Also in **t.** past, when Saul was 865,8543
2Sa 7:6 since the **t.** that I brought up the 3117
2Sa 7:11 as since the **t.** that I commanded 3117
2Sa 11:1 at the **t.** when kings go forth to 6256
2Sa 14:2 woman that had a long **t.** mourned 3117
2Sa 14:29 when he sent again the second **t.**,
2Sa 17:7 hath given is not good at this **t.** 6471
2Sa 20:5 he tarried longer than the set **t.**
2Sa 20:18 They were wont to speak in old **t.**,
2Sa 23:8 hundred, whom he slew at one **t.** 6471
2Sa 23:13 came to David in the harvest **t.** unto
2Sa 23:20 in the midst of a pit in **t.** of snow: 3117
2Sa 24:15 morning even to the **t.** appointed: 6256
1Ki 1:6 had not displeased him at any **t.** in 3117
1Ki 2:26 will not at this **t.** put thee to death, 3117
1Ki 8:65 at that **t.** Solomon held a feast, 6256
1Ki 9:2 appeared to Solomon the second **t.**,
1Ki 11:29 at that **t.** when Jeroboam went 6256
1Ki 11:42 And the **t.** that Solomon reigned in 3117
1Ki 14:1 At that **t.** Abijah the son of 6256
1Ki 15:23 in the **t.** of his old age he was 6256
1Ki 18:29 until the **t.** of the offering of the
1Ki 18:34 And he said, Do it the second **t.**
1Ki 18:34 And they did it the second **t.**
1Ki 18:34 And he said, Do it the third **t.**
1Ki 18:34 And they did it the third **t.**
1Ki 18:36 **t.** of the offering of the evening
1Ki 18:44 And it came to pass at the seventh **t.**,
1Ki 19:2 them by to morrow about this **t.** 6256
1Ki 19:7 of the Lord came again the second **t.**,
1Ki 20:6 unto thee to morrow about this **t.**, 6256
2Ki 3:6 went out of Samaria the same **t.**, 3117
2Ki 4:16 according to the **t.** of life, thou 6256
2Ki 4:17 unto her, according to the **t.** of life. 6256
2Ki 5:26 Is it a **t.** to receive money, and to 6256
2Ki 7:1 To morrow about this **t.** shall a 6256
2Ki 7:18 to morrow about this **t.** in the gate 6256
2Ki 8:22 Libnah revolted at the same **t.** 6256
2Ki 10:6 Then he wrote a letter the second **t.**
2Ki 10:6 me to Jezreel by to morrow this **t.** 6256
2Ki 10:36 **t.** that Jehu reigned over Israel 3117
2Ki 16:6 At that **t.** Rezin king of Syria 6256
2Ki 18:16 At that **t.** did Hezekiah cut off the 6256
2Ki 20:12 that **t.** Berodach-baladan, the son 6256
2Ki 24:10 **t.** the servants of Nebuchadnezzar 6256
1Ch 9:20 was the ruler over them in **t.** past, 6440
1Ch 9:25 seven days from **t.** to **t.** with them 6256
1Ch 11:2 And moreover in **t.** past, even 8543
1Ch 11:11 hundred slain by him at one **t.** 6471
1Ch 12:22 at that **t.** day by day there came 6256
1Ch 17:10 since the **t.** that I commanded 3117
1Ch 20:1 the **t.** that kings go out to battle, 6256
1Ch 20:4 **t.** Sibbechai the Hushathite slew 227
1Ch 21:28 **t.** when David saw the the Lord 6256
1Ch 29:22 the son of David king the second **t.**,
1Ch 29:27 **t.** that he reigned over Israel was 3117
2Ch 7:8 at the same **t.** Solomon kept the 6256
2Ch 13:18 were brought under at the **t.**, 6256
2Ch 15:11 offered unto the Lord the same **t.**, 3117
2Ch 16:7 **t.** Hanani the seer came to Asa 6256
2Ch 16:10 some of the people the same **t.** 6256
2Ch 18:34 **t.** of the sun going down he died. 6256
2Ch 21:10 The same **t.** also did Libnah revolt 6256

2Ch 21:19 came to pass, that in process of **t.**, 3117
2Ch 24:11 at what **t.** the chest was brought 6256
2Ch 25:27 after the **t.** that Amaziah did turn 6256
2Ch 28:16 At that **t.** did king Ahaz send unto 6256
2Ch 28:22 And in the **t.** of his distress did he 6256
2Ch 30:3 they could not keep it at that **t.**, 6256
2Ch 30:5 they had not done it a long **t.** in
2Ch 30:26 since the **t.** of Solomon the son of 3117
2Ch 35:17 kept the pasover at that **t.**, 6256
Ezr 4:10, 11 side the river, and at such a **t.**.
Ezr 4:15 sedition with the same of old **t.** 3118
Ezr 4:17 the river, Peace, and at such a **t.**.
Ezr 4:19 it is found that this city of old **t.** 3118
Ezr 5:3 the same **t.** came to them Tatnai, 2166
Ezr 5:16 and since that **t.** even until now 116
Ezr 7:12 perfect peace, and at such at **t.**.
Ezr 8:34 the weight was written at that **t.** 6256
Ezr 10:13 many, and it is a **t.** of much rain 6256
Ne 2:6 to send me; and I set him a **t.** 2165
Ne 4:16 it came to pass from that **t.** forth, 3117
Ne 4:22 the same **t.** said I unto the people, 6256
Ne 5:14 from the **t.** that I was a appointed 3117
Ne 6:1 at that **t.** I had not set up the 6256
Ne 6:5 fifth **t.** with an open letter in his 6471
Ne 9:27 and in the **t.** of their trouble, when 6256
Ne 9:32 since the **t.** of the kings of Assyria 3117
Ne 12:44 And at that **t.** were some appointed 3117
Ne 13:6 in all this **t.** was not I at Jerusalem:
Ne 13:21 From that **t.** forth came they no 6256
Es 2:19 were gathered together the second **t.**,
Es 4:14 holdest thy peace at this **t.**, 6256
Es 4:14 to the kingdom for such a **t.** as this? 6256
Es 8:9 called at that **t.** in the third month, 6256
Es 9:27 according to their appointed **t.** 2165
Job 6:17 What **t.** they wax warm, they 6256
Job 7:1 appointed **t.** to man upon earth? 6635
Job 9:19 who shall set me a **t.** to plead?
Job 14:13 thou wouldest appoint me a set **t.**,
Job 14:14 days of my appointed **t.** will I wait, 6635
Job 15:32 shall be accomplished before his **t.**, 3117
Job 22:16 Which were cut down out of **t.**, 6256
Job 30:3 in former **t.** desolate and waste. 570
Job 38:23 reserved against the **t.** of trouble, 6256
Job 39:1 thou the **t.** when the wild goats 6256
Job 39:2 thou the **t.** when they bring forth? 6256
Job 39:18 What **t.** she lifteth up herself on 6256
Ps 4:7 in the **t.** that their corn and their 6256
Ps 21:9 a fiery oven in the **t.** of thine anger: 6256
Ps 27:5 **t.** of trouble he shall hide me in 3117
Ps 32:6 pray unto thee in a **t.** when thou 6256
Ps 37:19 shall not be ashamed in the evil **t.** 6256
Ps 37:39 is their strength in the **t.** of trouble. 6256
Ps 41:1 will deliver him in **t.** of trouble 3117
Ps 56:3 What **t.** I am afraid, I will trust in 3117
Ps 69:13 thee, O Lord, in an acceptable **t.** 6256
Ps 71:9 Cast me not off in the **t.** of old age: 6256
Ps 78:38 many a **t.** turned he his anger
Ps 81:3 **t.** appointed, on our solemn feast
Ps 81:15 their **t.** should have endured for 6256
Ps 89:47 Remember how short my **t.** is:
Ps 102:13 for the **t.** to favour her, yea, 6256
Ps 102:13 her, yea, the set **t.** is come.
Ps 105:19 Until the **t.** that his word came: 6256
Ps 113:2 from this **t.** forth and for evermore.
Ps 115:18 bless the Lord from this **t.** forth 6258
Ps 119:126 It is **t.** for thee, Lord, to work: 6256
Ps 121:8 and thy coming in from this **t.** forth,
Ps 129:1,2 Many a **t.** have they afflicted me 7227
Pr 25:13 cold of snow in the **t.** of harvest, 3117
Pr 25:19 an unfaithful man in **t.** of trouble 3117
Pr 31:25 and she shall rejoice in **t.** to come. 3117
Ec 1:10 it hath been already of old **t.**,
Ec 3:1 a **t.** to every purpose under the 6256
Ec 3:2 A **t.** to be born, and a **t.** to die; 6256
Ec 3:2 a **t.** to plant, and a **t.** to pluck up that. 6256
Ec 3:3 A **t.** to kill, and a **t.** to heal; 6256
Ec 3:3 a **t.** to break down, and a **t.** to build 6256
Ec 3:4 A **t.** to weep, and a **t.** to laugh; 6256
Ec 3:4 a **t.** to mourn, and a **t.** to dance 6256
Ec 3:5 A **t.** to cast away stones, and a 6256
Ec 3:5 and a **t.** to gather stones together; 6256
Ec 3:5 a **t.** to embrace, and a **t.** to refrain 6256
Ec 3:6 A **t.** to get, and a **t.** to lose; 6256
Ec 3:6 a **t.** to keep, and a **t.** to cast away; 6256
Ec 3:7 A **t.** to rend, and a **t.** to sew; 6256
Ec 3:7 a **t.** to keep silence, and a **t.** to speak; 6256
Ec 3:8 A **t.** to love, and a **t.** to hate; 6256
Ec 3:8 a **t.** of war, and a **t.** of peace. 6256
Ec 3:11 every thing beautiful in his **t.**: 6256
Ec 3:17 there is a **t.** there for every purpose 6256
Ec 7:17 shouldest thou die before thy **t.**? 6256
Ec 8:5 man's heart discerneth both **t.** and 6256
Ec 8:6 to every purpose there is **t.** and 6256
Ec 8:9 a **t.** wherein one man ruleth over 6256
Ec 9:11 **t.** and chance happeneth to them 6256
Ec 9:12 For man also knoweth not his **t.**: 6256
Ec 9:12 sons of men snared in an evil **t.**, 6256
Ca 2:12 **t.** of the singing of birds is come, 6256
Isa 11:11 shall set his hand again the second 6256
Isa 13:22 and her **t.** is near to come, and 6256
Isa 16:13 concerning Moab since that **t.** 227
Isa 18:7 In that **t.** shall the present be 6256
Isa 20:2 At the same **t.** spake the Lord by 6256
Isa 26:17 draweth near the **t.** of her delivery,
Isa 28:19 From the **t.** that it goeth forth it 1767
Isa 30:8 may be for the **t.** to come for ever 3117
Isa 33:2 salvation also in the **t.** of trouble. 6256
Isa 39:1 At that **t.** Merodach-baladan, the 6256
Isa 42:14 I have long **t.** holden my peace;
Isa 42:23 and hear for the **t.** to come? 268
Isa 44:8 have not I told thee from that **t.**, 227
Isa 45:21 hath declared this from ancient **t.**?
Isa 45:21 who hath told it from that **t.**? have 227
Isa 48:6 thee new things from this **t.**, 6258
Isa 48:8 from that **t.** that thine ear was not 227
Isa 48:16 from the **t.** that it was, there am I: 6256
Isa 49:8 an acceptable **t.** have I heard thee, 6256
Isa 60:22 I the Lord will hasten it in his **t.** 6256
Jer 1:13 Lord came unto me the second **t.**,
Jer 2:20 For of old **t.** I have broken thy yoke,
Jer 2:27 **t.** of their trouble they will say, 6256
Jer 2:28 save thee in the **t.** of thy trouble: 6256
Jer 3:4 thou not from this **t.** cry unto me. 6258
Jer 3:17 At that **t.** they shall call Jerusalem 6256
Jer 4:11 At that **t.** shall it be said to this 6256
Jer 6:15 at the **t.** that I visit them they shall 6256
Jer 8:1 At that **t.**, saith the Lord, they 6256
Jer 8:7 crane and...swallow observe the **t.** 6256
Jer 8:12 **t.** of their visitation they shall be 6256
Jer 8:15 and for a **t.** of health, and behold 6256
Jer 10:15 **t.** of their visitation they shall 6256
Jer 11:12 at all in the **t.** of their trouble. 6256
Jer 11:14 hear them in the **t.** that they cry 6256
Jer 13:3 Lord came unto me the second **t.**,
Jer 14:8 the saviour thereof in **t.** of trouble, 6256
Jer 14:19 and for the **t.** of healing, and behold 6256
Jer 15:11 **t.** of evil and in the **t.** of affliction. 6256
Jer 18:23 with them in the **t.** of thine anger. 6256
Jer 27:7 until the very **t.** of his land come: 6256
Jer 30:7 it is even the **t.** of Jacob's trouble; 6256
Jer 31:1 At the same **t.**, saith the Lord, will 6256
Jer 33:1 came unto Jeremiah the second **t.**,
Jer 33:15 at that **t.**, will I cause the Branch 6256
Jer 39:10 vineyards and fields at the same **t.** 3117
Jer 46:17 he hath passed the **t.** appointed.
Jer 46:21 them, and the **t.** of their visitation. 6256
Jer 49:8 him, the **t.** that I will visit him. 6256
Jer 49:19 and who will appoint me the **t.**? and
Jer 50:4 and in that **t.**, saith the Lord, 6256
Jer 50:16 the sickle in the **t.** of harvest: 6256
Jer 50:20 and in that **t.**, saith the Lord, the 6256
Jer 50:27 day is come, the **t.** of their visitation 6256
Jer 50:31 is come, the **t.** that I will visit thee. 6256
Jer 50:44 and who will appoint me the **t.**? and
Jer 51:6 is the **t.** of the Lord's vengeance; 6256
Jer 51:18 **t.** of their visitation they perish. 6256
Jer 51:33 threshingfloor, it is **t.** to thresh her: 6256
Jer 51:33 and the **t.** of her harvest is come. 6256
La 5:20 ever, and forsake us so long **t.**? 3117
Eze 4:10 from **t.** to **t.** shalt thou eat it 6256
Eze 4:11 hin: from **t.** to **t.** shalt thou drink. 6256
Eze 7:7 the **t.** is come, the day of trouble 6256
Eze 7:12 The **t.** is come, the day draweth 6256
Eze 16:8 behold, thy **t.** was the **t.** of love; 6256
Eze 16:57 as the **t.** of thy reproach of the 6256
Eze 21:14 the sword be doubled the third **t.**,
Eze 22:3 midst of it, that her **t.** may come, 6256
Eze 26:20 with the people of old **t.**, and
Eze 27:34 the **t.** when thou shalt be broken 6256
Eze 30:3 it shall be the **t.** of the heathen. 6256
Eze 35:5 sword in the **t.** of their calamity, 6256
Eze 35:5 it the **t.** that their iniquity had an 6256
Eze 38:10 same **t.** shall things come into thy 3117
Eze 38:17 of whom I have spoken in old **t.** 3117
Eze 38:18 come to pass at the same **t.** when 3117
Da 2:8 certainty that ye would gain the **t.**, 5732
Da 2:9 before me, till the **t.** be changed: 5732
Da 2:16 king that he would give him **t.**, 2166
Da 3:5 at what **t.** ye hear the sound of 5732
Da 3:7 at that **t.**, when all the people 2166
Da 3:8 at that **t.** certain Chaldeans came 2166
Da 3:15 at what **t.** ye hear the sound of 5732
Da 4:36 the same **t.** my reason returned 2166
Da 7:12 prolonged for a season and **t.** 5732
Da 7:22 **t.** came that the saints possessed 2166
Da 7:25 given into his hand until a **t.** and 5732
Da 7:25 and times and the dividing of **t.** 5732
Da 8:17 at the **t.** of the end shall be the 6256
Da 8:19 the **t.** appointed the end shall be.
Da 8:23 And in the latter **t.** of their kingdom,
Da 9:21 about the **t.** of the evening 6256
Da 10:1 true, but the **t.** appointed was long:
Da 11:24 the strong holds, even for a **t.** 6256
Da 11:27 end shall be at the **t.** appointed.
Da 11:29 At the **t.** appointed he shall return,
Da 11:35 white, even to the **t.** of the end: 6256
Da 11:35 because it is yet for a **t.** appointed.
Da 11:40 at the **t.** of the end shall the king 6256
Da 12:1 at that **t.** shall Michael stand up, 6256
Da 12:1 and there shall be a **t.** of trouble, 6256
Da 12:1 was a nation even to that same **t.** 6256
Da 12:1 that **t.** thy people to shall be delivered, 6256
Da 12:4 the book, even to the **t.** of the end: 6256
Da 12:7 be for a **t.**, times, and an half; 4150
Da 12:9 and sealed till the **t.** of the end. 6256
Da 12:11 the **t.** that the daily sacrifice shall 6256
Ho 2:9 away my corn in the **t.** thereof, 6256
Ho 9:10 in the fig tree at her first **t.** 7225
Ho 10:12 for it is **t.** to seek the Lord, till he 6256
Joe 3:1 in that **t.**, when I shall bring again 6256
Am 5:13 shall keep silence in that **t.**; 6256
Am 5:13 for it is and evil **t.** 6256
Jon 3:1 Lord came unto Jonah the second **t.**,
Mic 2:3 go haughtily: for this **t.** is evil. 6256
Mic 3:4 hide his face from them at that **t.**, 6256
Mic 5:3 the **t.** that she which travaileth 6256
Na 1:9 shall not rise up the second **t.** 6471
Hab 2:3 vision is yet for an appointed **t.**,
Zep 1:12 it shall come to pass at that **t.**, 6256
Zep 3:19 at that **t.** I will undo all that afflict 6256
Zep 3:20 At that **t.** will I bring you again, 6256
Zep 3:20 even in the **t.** that I gather you: for 6256
Hab 1:2 people say, The **t.** is not come, 6256
Hab 1:2 the **t.** that the Lord's house should 6256
Hab 1:4 Is it **t.** for you, O ye, to dwell in 6256
Zec 10:1 rain in the **t.** of the latter rain; 6256
Zec 14:7 that at evening **t.** it shall be light. 6256
Mal 3:11 your vine cast her fruit before the **t.**
Mt 1:11 about the **t.** they were carried *1909*
Mt 2:7 of them diligently what **t.** the star *5550*
Mt 2:16 according to the **t.** which he had *5550*
Mt 4:6 lest at any **t.** thou dash thy foot *3379*
Mt 4:17 that **t.** Jesus began to preach, *5119*
Mt 5:21 **that it was said by them of old t.,** *744*
Mt 5:25 **at any t. the adversary delivery** *3379*
Mt 5:27 **that it was said by them of old t.,** *744*
Mt 5:33 **it hath been said by them of old t.,** *744*
Mt 8:29 hither to torment us before the **t.**? *2540*
Mt 11:25 At that **t.** Jesus answered and said, *2540*
Mt 12:1 that **t.** Jesus went on the sabbath *2540*
Mt 13:15 **lest at any t. they should see** *3379*
Mt 13:30 **in the t. of harvest I will say to the** *2540*
Mt 14:1 At that **t.** Herod the tetrarch heard *2540*
Mt 14:15 place, and the **t.** is now past; *5610*
Mt 16:21 From that **t.** forth began Jesus to *5119*
Mt 18:1 At the same **t.** came the disciples *5610*
Mt 21:34 **when the t. of the fruit drew,** *2540*
Mt 24:21 **beginning of the world to this t.,** *2540*
Mt 25:19 **After a long t. the lord of those** *5550*
Mt 26:16 from that **t.** he sought opportunity *5119*
Mt 26:18 **Master saith, My t. is at hand;** *2540*
Mt 26:42 He went away again the second **t.**,
Mt 26:44 away again, and prayed the third **t.**,
Mk 1:15 **t. is fulfilled, and the kingdom** *2540*
Mk 4:12 **lest at any t. they...be converted,** *3379*
Mk 4:17 **and so endure but for a t.** *4340*
Mk 6:35 and now the **t.** is far passed: *5610*
Mk 10:30 **an hundred fold now in this t.,** *2540*
Mk 11:13 for the **t.** of figs was not yet. *2540*
Mk 13:19 **which God created unto this t.,** *3568*
Mk 13:33 **for ye know not when the t. is** *2540*

Mk 14:41 he cometh the third t., and saith unto
Mk 14:72 And the second t. the cock crew
Lu 1:10 were praying without at the t. of 5610
Lu 1:57 Now Elisabeth's full t. came that 5550
Lu 4:5 of the world in a moment of t. 5550
Lu 4:11 lest at any t. thou dash thy foot 3379
Lu 4:27 **were in Israel in the t. of Eliseus** 1909
Lu 7:45 **woman since the t. I came in hath**
Lu 8:13 **and in t. of temptation fall away** 2540
Lu 8:27 man, which had devils long t., and 5550
Lu 9:51 the t. was come that he should be 2250
Lu 12:1 In the mean t., when there were
Lu 12:56 **is it that ye do not discern this t.?** 2540
Lu 13:35 **until the t. come when ye shall say,**
Lu 14:17 **sent his servant at supper t. to say** 5610
Lu 15:29 **neither transgressed I at any t. thy**
Lu 16:16 **t. the kingdom of God is preached,** 5119
Lu 18:30 **manifold more in this present t.,** 2540
Lu 19:44 **knewest not the t. of thy visitation** 2540
Lu 20:9 **into a far country for a long t.** 5550
Lu 21:8 **Christ; and the t. draweth near:** 2540
Lu 21:34 **at any t.…hearts be overcharged** 3379
Lu 21:37 in the day t. he was teaching in 2250
Lu 23:7 also was at Jerusalem at that t. 2250
Lu 23:22 And he said unto them the third t.,
Joh 1:18 No man hath seen God at any t.; 4455
Joh 3:4 second t. into his mother's womb, 1208
Joh 5:6 had been now a long t. in that case, 5550
Joh 5:37 **neither heard his voice at any t.,** 4455
Joh 6:66 From that t. many of his disciples
Joh 7:6 unto them, **My t. is not yet come:** 2540
Joh 7:6 **come: but your t. is alway ready** 2540
Joh 7:8 **feast; for my t. is not yet full** 2540
Joh 11:39 him, Lord, by this t. he stinketh: 2235
Joh 14:9 **Have I been so long t. with you,** 5550
Joh 16:2 **the t. cometh, that whosoever** 5610
Joh 16:4 **when the t. shall come, ye may** 5610
Joh 16:25 **the t. cometh, when I shall no** 5610
Joh 21:14 now the third t. that Jesus shewed
Joh 21:16 saith to him again the second t.,
Joh 21:17 He saith unto him the third t., **Simon,**
Joh 21:17 said unto him the third t., Lovest thou
Ac 1:6 thou at this t. restore again the 5550
Ac 1:21 have companied with us all the t. 5550
Ac 7:13 And at the second t. Joseph was made
Ac 7:17 the t. of the promise drew nigh, 5550
Ac 7:20 In which t. Moses was born, and 2540
Ac 8:1 And at that t. there was a great 2250
Ac 8:11 of long t. he had bewitched them 5550
Ac 10:15 spake unto him again the second t.,
Ac 11:8 hath at any t. entered into my mouth.
Ac 12:1 Now about that t. Herod the king 2540
Ac 13:18 about the t. of forty years suffered 5550
Ac 14:3 Long t.…abode they speaking 5550
Ac 14:28 abode long t. wih the disciples. 5550
Ac 15:21 Moses of Old t. hath in every city 1074
Ac 17:21 spent their t. in nothing else, but 2119
Ac 18:20 him to tarry longer t. with them, 5550
Ac 18:23 after he had spent some t. there, he 5550
Ac 19:23 same t. there arose no small stir 2540
Ac 20:16 he would not spend the t. in Asia: 5551
Ac 24:25 answered, go thy way for this t.; 3568
Ac 27:9 when much t. was spent, and when 5550
Ro 3:26 I say, at this t. his righteousness: 2540
Ro 5:6 in due t. Christ died for…ungodly 2540
Ro 8:18 sufferings of this present t. are not 2540
Ro 9:9 At this t. will I come, and Sarah 2540
Ro 11:5 at this present t. also there is a 2540
Ro 13:11 And that, knowing the t., that now 2540
Ro 13:11 it is high t. to awake out of sleep: 5610
1Co 4:5 judge nothing before the t., until 2540
1Co 7:5 except it be with consent for a t., 2540
1Co 7:29 this I say, brethren, the t. is short: 2540
1Co 9:7 warfare any t. at his own charges? 4218
1Co 15:8 me also, as of one born out of due t.
1Co 16:12 was not all to come at this t.; 3598
1Co 16:12 when he shall have convenient t. 2119
2Co 6:2 I have heard thee in a t. accepted, 2540
2Co 6:2 now is the accepted t.; behold, now 2540
2Co 8:14 this t. your abundance may be a 2540
2Co 12:14 the third t. I am ready to come to you
2Co 13:1 This is the third t. I am coming to you
2Co 13:2 as if I were present, the second t.;
Ga 1:13 heard of my conversation in t. past 4218
Ga 4:2 until…t. appointed of the father. 4287
Ga 4:4 the fulness of the t. was come, 5550
Ga 5:21 as I have also told you in t. past,
Eph 2:2 in t. past ye walked according to 4218
Eph 2:11 that ye being in t. past Gentiles 4218
Eph 2:12 at that t. ye were without Christ, 2540
Eph 5:16 Redeeming the t., because the days 2540
Col 3:7 the which ye also walked some t., 4218
Col 4:5 that are without, redeeming the t. 2540
1Th 2:5 neither at any t. used we flattering 4218
1Th 2:17 from you for a short t. in presence, 2540
2Th 2:6 that he might be revealed in his t. 2540
1Ti 2:6 for all, to be testified in due t. 2540
1Ti 6:19 foundation against the t. to come, 3195
2Ti 4:3 the t. will come when they will not 2540
2Ti 4:6 the t. of my departure is at hand. 2540
2Ti *subscr.* brought before Nero the second t.
Phm 11 in t. past was to thee unprofitable, 4218
Heb 1:1 spake in t. past unto the fathers 3819
Heb 1:5, 13 of the angels said he at any t., 4218
Heb 2:1 at any t. we should let them slip. 4218
Heb 4:7 David, To day, after so long a t.; 5550
Heb 4:16 and find grace to help in t. of need. 2121
Heb 5:12 for the t. ye ought to be teachers, 5550
Heb 9:9 a figure for the t. then present, in 2540
Heb 9:10 on them until the t. of reformation. 2540
Heb 9:28 shall he appear the second t. without
Heb 11:32 t. would fail me to tell of Gibeon, 5550
Jas 4:14 that appeareth for a little t., and then
1Pe 1:5 ready to be revealed in the last t. 2540
1Pe 1:11 or what manner of t. the Spirit of 2540
1Pe 1:17 t. of your sojourning here in fear: 5550
1Pe 2:10 Which in t. past were not a people, 4218
1Pe 3:5 in the old t. the holy women also, 4218
1Pe 4:2 should live the rest of his t. in the 5550
1Pe 4:3 t. past of our life may suffice us to 5550
1Pe 4:17 the t. is come that judgment must 2540
1Pe 5:6 that he may exalt you in due t. 2540
2Pe 1:21 prophecy came not in old t. by th 4218
2Pe 2:3 whose judgment now of a long t. 1597
2Pe 2:13 count it pleasure to riot in the day t.
1Jo 2:18 Little children, it is the last t. 5610
1Jo 2:18 whereby we know…it is the last t. 5610
1Jo 4:12 No man hath seen God at any t. 4455
Jude 18 should be mockers in the last t., 5550
Re 1:3 therein: for the t. is at hand. 2540
Re 10:6 that there should be t. no longer: 5550
Re 11:18 is come, and the t. of the dead, 2540
Re 12:12 knoweth that he hath but a short t. 2540
Re 12:14 where she is nourished for a t., 2540
Re 12:14 and half a t., from the face of the 2540
Re 14:15 for the t. is come for thee to reap; 5610
Re 22:10 of this book: for the t. is at hand. 2540

TIMES See also BETIMES; OFTENTIMES; OFTTIMES SOMETIMES.

Ge 27:36 hath supplanted me these two t. 6471
Ge 31:7 me, and changed my wages ten t.; 4489
Ge 31:41 thou hast changed my wages ten t. 4489
Ge 33:3 himself to the ground seven t., 6471
Ge 43:34 five t. so much as any of theirs. 3027
Ex 23:14 Three t. thou shalt keep a feast unto
Ex 23:17 Three t. in the year all thy males 6471
Le 4:6 and sprinkle of the blood seven t. 6471
Le 4:17 sprinkle it seven t. before the Lord, 6471
Le 8:11 thereof upon the altar seven t., 6471
Le 14:7 cleansed from the leprosy seven t., 6471
Le 14:16 of the oil with his finger seven t. 6471
Le 14:27 oil that is in his left hand seven t. 6471
Le 14:51 and sprinkle the house seven t. 6471
Le 16:2 not at all t. into the holy place 6256
Le 16:14 the blood with his finger seven t. 6471
Le 16:19 upon it with his finger seven t., 6471
Le 19:26 ye use enchantment, nor observe t.
Le 25:8 unto thee, seven t. seven years; 6471
Le 26:18 punish you seven t. more for your
Le 26:21 bring seven t. more plagues upon
Le 26:24 punish you yet seven t. for your
Le 26:28 chastise you seven t. for your sins.
Nu 14:22 have tempted me now these ten t.,
Nu 19:4 of the congregation seven t.
Nu 22:28 thou hast smitten me these three t.?
Nu 22:32 these thou smitten thine ass three t.?
Nu 22:33 and turned from me these three t.
Nu 24:1 he went not, as at other t., to seek 6471
Nu 24:10 altogether blessed them these three t.
De 1:11 you a thousand t. so many more 6471
De 2:10 The Emims dwelt therein in t. past,
De 4:42 and hated him not in t. past; 8543
De 16:16 Three t. in a year shall all they 6471
De 18:10 divination, or an observer of t.,
De 18:14 hearkened unto observers of t., and
Jos 6:4 ye shall compass the city seven t., 6471
Jos 6:15 after the same manner seven t. 6471
Jos 6:15 they compassed the city seven t. 6471
Jg 13:25 began to move him at t. in the camp
Jg 16:15 hast mocked me these three t., 6471
Jg 16:20 I will go out as at other t. before, 6471
Jg 20:30 against Gibeah, as at other t. 6471
Jg 20:31 the people, and kill, as at other t., 6471
1Sa 3:10 and called as other t., Samuel, 6471
1Sa 18:10 with his hand, as at other t. 3117
1Sa 19:7 in his presence, as in t. past. 865,8543
1Sa 20:25 sat upon his seat, as at other t., 6471
1Sa 20:41 gound,…bowed himself three t. 6471
2Sa 3:17 ye sought for David in t. past 8543
1Ki 8:59 cause of his people Israel at all t., 3117
1Ki 9:25 three t. in a year did Solomon 6471
1Ki 17:21 himself upon the child three t., 6471
1Ki 18:43 And he said, go again seven t. 6471
1Ki 22:16 How many t. shall I adjure thee 6471
2Ki 4:35 and the child sneezed seven t., and 6471
2Ki 5:10 Go and wash in Jordan seven t., 6471
2Ki 5:14 dipped himself seven t. in Jordan, 6471
2Ki 13:19 shouldest have smitten five or six t.; 6471
2Ki 13:25 Three t. did Joash beat him, and 6471
2Ki 19:25 of ancient t. that I have formed it? 3117
2Ki 21:6 fire, and observed t., and used
1Ch 12:32 men that had understanding of the t.,
1Ch 21:3 his people an hundred t. so many 6471
1Ch 29:30 and the t. that went over him, and
2Ch 8:13 three t. in the year, even in the 6471
2Ch 15:5 in those t. there was no peace to him
2Ch 18:15 How many t. shall I adjure thee 6471
2Ch 33:6 also he observed t., and used
Ezr 10:14 in our cities come at appointed t., 6256
Ne 4:12 they said unto us ten t., From all 6471
Ne 6:4 they sent unto me four t. after 6471
Ne 9:28 many t. didst thou deliver them 6256
Ne 10:34 at t. appointed year by year, to 6256
Ne 13:31 the wood offering, at t. appointed, 6256
Es 1:13 to the wise men, which knew the t., 6256
Es 9:31 of Purim in their t. appointed, 2165
Job 19:3 ten t. have ye reproached me: 6471
Job 24:1 seeing t. are not hidden from the 6256
Ps 9:9 oppressed, a refuge in t. of trouble. 6256
Ps 10:1 hidest thou thyself in t. of trouble? 6256
Ps 12:6 in a furnance of earth, purified seven t.
Ps 31:15 My t. are in thy hand: deliver me 6256
Ps 34:1 I will bless the Lord at all t.: his 6256
Ps 44:1 in their days, in the t. of old. 3117
Ps 62:8 Trust in him at all t.; ye people, 6256
Ps 77:5 days of old, the years of ancient t.
Ps 106:3 that doeth righteousness at all t. 6256
Ps 106:43 Many t. did he deliver them; but 6471
Ps 119:20 hath unto thy judgments at all t. 6256
Ps 119:164 Seven t. a day do I praise thee because
Pr 5:19 her breasts satisfy thee at all t.; 6256
Pr 17:17 A friend loveth at all t., and a 6256
Pr 24:16 For a just man falleth seven t., and
Ec 8:12 a sinner do evil an hundred t.,
Isa 14:31 shall be alone in his appointed t. 4151
Isa 33:6 shall be the stability of thy t., 6256
Isa 37:26 ancient t., that I have formed it? 3117
Isa 46:10 from ancient t. the things that are not
Jer 8:7 heaven knoweth her appointed t.; 6256
Eze 12:27 he prophesieth of the t. that are far 6256
Da 1:20 he found them ten t. better than all
Da 2:21 changeth the t. and the seasons: 5732
Da 3:19 heat the furnace one seven t. more
Da 4:16 and let seven t. pass over him. 5732
Da 4:23 field, till seven t. pass over him; 5732
Da 4:25, 32 and seven t. shall pass over thee, 5732
Da 6:10 upon his knees three t. a day, 2166
Da 6:13 maketh his petition three t. a day. 2166
Da 7:10 ten thousand t. ten thousand stood
Da 7:25 and think to change t. and laws: 2166
Da 7:25 a time and t. and the dividing of 5732
Da 9:25 and the wall, even in troublous t. 6256
Da 11:6 he that strengthened her in these t. 6256
Da 11:14 in those t. there shall many stand 6256
Da 12:7 shall be for a time, t., and an half; 4150
Mt 16:3 **ye not discern…signs of the t.?** 2540
Mt 18:21 me, and I forgive him till seven t.? 2034
Mt 18:22 **say not unto thee, Until seven t.** 2034
Mt 18:22 **but, Until seventy t. seven.** 1441
Lu 17:4 **trespass against thee seven t. in a** 2034
Lu 17:4 **seven t. in a day turn again to thee,** 2034

Lu 21:24 **the t. of the Gentiles be fulfilled**... *2540*
Ac 1:7 **you to know the t. of the seasons,** ..*5550*
Ac 3:19 when the **t.** of refreshing shall.......... *2540*
Ac 3:21 until the **t.** of restitution of all.......... *5550*
Ac 11:10 And this was done three **t.**: and.......... *5151*
Ac 14:16 Who in **t.** past suffered all nations *1074*
Ac 17:26 determined...**t.** before appointed,........ *2540*
Ac 17:30 the **t.** of this ignorance God winked *5550*
Ro 11:30 in **t.** past have not believed God, ... *4218*
2Co 11:24 five **t.** received I forty stripes save..... *3999*
Ga 1:23 he which persecuted us in **t.** past....... *4218*
Ga 4:10 observe days, and months, and **t.**,....... *2540*
Eph 1:10 the dispensation of the fulness of **t.** *2540*
Eph 2:3 our conversation in **t.** past in the........ *4218*
1Th 5:1 of the **t.** and the seasons, brethren,.... *5550*
1Ti 4:1 latter **t.** some shall depart from.......... *5550*
1Ti 6:15 Which in his **t.** he shall shew, who *5550*
2Ti 3:1 the last days perilous **t.** shall come..... *5550*
Tit 1:3 hath in due **t.** manifested his word...... *5550*
Heb 1:1 who at sundry **t.** and in divers................
1Pe 1:20 manifest in these last **t.** for you, ... *5550*
Re 5:11 was ten thousand **t.** ten thousand, ...
Re 12:14 for a time, and **t.**, and half a time,...... *2540*

TIMNA (tim'-nah) See also TIMNATH.
Ge 36:12 **T.** was concubine to Eliphaz.............. 8555
Ge 36:22 Hemam; and Lotan's sister was **T.**. 8555
1Ch 1:36 Gatam, Henaz, and **T.**, and Amalekh... 8555
1Ch 1:39 Homam: and **T.** was Lotan's sister. 8555

TIMNAH (tim'-nah) See also TIMNA; TIMNATH; TIMNITE.
Ge 36:40 duke **T.**, duke Alvah, duke................ 8555
Jos 15:10 and passed on to **T.** 8553
Jos 15:57 Gibeah, and **T.**; ten cities with........... 8553
1Ch 1:51 the dukes of Edom were; duke **T.**,...... 8555
2Ch 28:18 and **T.** with the villages thereof,......... 8553

TIMNATH (tim'-nath) See also THIMNATHAH; TIMNAH; TIMNATH-HERES.
Ge 38:12 up unto his sheepshearers to **T.**,......... 8553
Ge 38:13 father in law goeth up to **T.** to........... 8553
Ge 38:14 place, which is by the way to **T.**; 8553
Jg 14:1 Samson went down to **T.**, and........... 8553
Jg 14:1, 2 a woman in **T.** of the daughters....... 8553
Jg 14:5 his father and his mother, to **T.**, ... 8553
Jg 14:5 and came to the vineyards of **T.**.......... 8553

TIMNATH-HERES (tim''-nath-he'-rez) See also TIMNATH-SERAH.
Jg 2:9 border of hs inheritance in **T.**, ... 8556

TIMNATH-SERAH (tim''-nath-se'-rabh) See also TIMNATH-HERES.
Jos 19:50 asked, even **T.** in mount Ephraim:...... 8556
Jos 24:30 border of his inheritance in **T.**, ... 8556

TIMNITE (tim'-nite)
Jg 15:6 Samson, the son in law of the **T.**, ... 8554

TIMON (ti'-mon)
Ac 6:5 **T.**, and Parmenas, and Nicolas a........ *5096*

TIMOTHEUS (tim-o'-the-us) See also TIMOTHY.
Ac 16:1 disciple was there, named **T.**,............ *5095*
Ac 17:14 but Silas and **T.** abode there still......... *5095*
Ac 17:15 a commandment unto Silas and **T.** *5095*
Ac 18:5 when Silas and **T.** were come from..... *5095*
Ac 19:22 ministered unto him, **T.** and............. *5095*
Ac 20:4 and Gaius of Derbe, and **T.**;............. *5095*
Ro 16:21 **T.** my workfellow, and Lucius,........... *5095*
1Co 4:17 this cause have I sent unto you **T.**, ... *5095*
1Co 16:10 if **T.** come, see that he may be with... *5095*
1Co *subscr.* Fortunatus, and Achaicus, and **T.**. *5095*
2Co 1:19 even by me and Silvanus and **T.**,........ *5095*
Php 1:1 Paul and **T.**, the servants of Jesus...... *5095*
Php 2:19 Jesus to send **T.** shortly unto you,...... *5095*
Col 1:1 the will of God, and **t.** our brother, ... *5095*
1Th 1:1 Silvanus, and **T.**, unto the church....... *5095*
1Th 3:2 sent **T.**, our brother, and minister...... *5095*
1Th 3:6 But now when **T.** came from you....... *5095*
2Th 1:1 Silvanus, and **T.**, unto the church....... *5095*
2Ti *subscr.* The second epistle unto **T.**, ... *5095*

TIMOTHY (tim'-o-thy) See also TIMOTHEUS.
2Co 1:1 **T.** our brother, unto the church......... *5095*
1Ti *general* *title* First Epistle Of Paul...To **T.** *5095*
1Ti 1:2 Unto **T.**, my own son in the faith: *5095*
1Ti 1:18 charge I commit unto thee, son **T.**, ... *5095*
1Ti 6:20 O **T.**, keep that which is committed.... *5095*
1Ti *subscr.* The first to **T.** was written from........ *5095*
2Ti *general* *title* Second Epistle Of Paul To **T.** *5095*
2Ti 1:2 To **T.**, my dearly beloved son: *5095*
Phm 1 and **T.** our brother, unto Philemon...... *5095*
Heb 13:23 our brother **T.** is set at liberty;.......... *5095*
Heb *subscr.* to the Hebrews from Italy by **T.**. *5095*

TIN
Nu 31:22 the brass, the iron, the **t.**, and the....... 913
Isa 1:25 away thy dross, take away all thy **t.**...... 913
Eze 22:18 all they are brass, and **t.**, and iron, ... 913
Eze 22:20 brass, and iron, and lead, and **t.**, ... 913
Eze 27:12 with silver, iron, **t.**, and lead, they....... 913

TINGLE
1Sa 3:11 every one that heareth it shall **t.**. 6750
2Ki 21:12 heareth of it, both his ears shall **t.**...... 6750
Jer 19:3 whosoever heareth, his ears shall **t.**.... 6750

TINKLING
Isa 3:16 and making a **t.** with their feet:.......... 5913
Isa 3:18 of their **t.** ornaments about their feet; ....
1Co 13:1 as sounding grass, or a **t.** cymbal......... *214*

TIP
Ex 29:20 the **t.** of the right ear of Aaron, ... 8571
Ex 29:20 the **t.** of the right ear of his sons, ... 8571
Le 8:23 it upon the **t.** of Aaron's right ear,...... 8571
Le 8:24 blood upon the **t.** of their right ear, ... 8571
Le 14:14 put it upon the **t.** of the right ear....... 8571
Le 14:17 put upon the **t.** of the right ear.......... 8571
Le 14:25 put it upon the **t.** of the right ear....... 8571
Le 14:28 upon the **t.** of the right ear of him...... 8571
Lu 16:24 **dip the t. of his finger in water,** *206*

TIPHSAH (tif'-sah)
1Ki 4:24 **T.** even to Azzah, over all the........... 8607
2Ki 15:16 Then Menahem smote **T.**, and all....... 8607

TIRAS (ti'-ras)
Ge 10:2 and Tubal, and Meshech, and **T.**. 8493
1Ch 1:15 and Tubal, and Meshech, and **T.**. 8493

TIRATHITES (ti'-rath-ites)
1Ch 2:55 the **T.**, the Shimeathites, and 8654

TIRE See also ATTIRE; RETIRE; TIRED; TIRES.
Eze 24:17 the **t.** of thine head upon thee, and..... 6287

TIRED See also RETIRED.
2Ki 9:30 painted her face, and **t.** her head,....... 3190

TIRES
Isa 3:18 and their round **t.** like the moon,........ 7720
Eze 24:23 your **t.** shall be upon your heads, ... 6287

TIRHAKAH (tur-ha'-kah)
2Ki 19:9 heard say of **T.** king of Ethiopia, ... 8640
Isa 37:9 say concerning **T.** king of Ethiopia, ... 8640

TIRHANAH (tur-ha'-nah)
1Ch 2:48 concubine, bare Sheber, and **T.**.......... 8647

TIRIA (tir'-e-ah)
1Ch 4:16 Jehaleleel; Ziph, and Ziphah, **T.**,......... 8493

TIRSHATHA (tur'-sha-thah)
Ezr 2:63 the **T.** said unto them, that they 8660
Ne 7:65 the **t.** said unto them, that they 8660
Ne 7:70 The **t.** gave to the treasure a............ 8660
Ne 8:9 And Nehemiah, which is the **T.**,.......... 8660
Ne 10:1 sealed were, Nehemiah, the **T.**, ... 8660

TIRZAH (tur'-zah)
Nu 26:33 Noah, Hoglah, Milcah, and **T.**........... 8656
Nu 27:1 and Hoglah, and Milcah, and **T.**.......... 8656
Nu 36:11 For Mahlah, **T.**, and Hoglah, and.......... 8656
Jos 12:24 The king of **T.**, one: all the kings....... 8656
Jos 17:3 and Noah, Hoglah, Milcah, and **T.**. 8656
1Ki 14:17 and departed, and came to **T.**............ 8656
1Ki 15:21 building of Ramah, and dwelt in **T.**....... 8656
1Ki 15:33 Ahijah to reign over all Israel in **T.**, ... 8656
1Ki 16:6 his fathers, and was buried in **T.**: 8656
1Ki 16:8 Baasha to reign over Israel in **T.**,......... 8656
1Ki 16:9 as he was in **T.**, drinking himself.......... 8656
1Ki 16:9 of Arza steward of his house in **T.**....... 8656
1Ki 16:15 did Zimri reign seven days in **T.**.......... 8656
1Ki 16:17 with him, and they besieged **T.**........... 8656
1Ki 16:23 years: six years reigned he in **T.**......... 8656
2Ki 15:14 the son of Gadi went up from **T.**,........ 8656
2Ki 15:16 and the coasts thereof from **T.**: 8656
Ca 6:4 art beautiful, O my love, as **T.**, ... 8656

TISHBITE (tish'-bite)
1Ki 17:1 And Elijah the **T.**, who was of........... 8664
1Ki 21:17, 28 the Lord came to Elijah the **T.**, ... 8664
2Ki 1:3 of the Lord said to Elijah the **T.**,........ 8664
2Ki 1:8 And he said, It is Elijah the **T.**. 8664
2Ki 9:36 spake by his servant Elijah the **T.**, ... 8664

TITHE See also TITHES; TITHING.
Le 27:30 all the **t.** of the land, whether of 4643
Le 27:32 concerning the **t.** of the herd, or of 4643
Nu 18:26 Lord, even a tenth part of the **t.**......... 4643
De 12:17 within thy gates the **t.** of thy corn, ... 4643
De 14:22 truly **t.** all the increase of thy seed,.... 6237
De 14:23 **t.** of thy corn, of thy wine, and of..... 4643
De 14:28 forth all the **t.** of thine increase.......... 4643
2Ch 31:5 the **t.** of things brought they in.......... 4643
2Ch 31:6 brought in the **t.** of oxen and sheep, ... 4643
2Ch 31:6 the **t.** of holy things which were......... 4643
Ne 10:38 the Levites shall bring up the **t.** of 4643
Ne 13:12 brought all Judah the **t.** of the corn..... 4643
Mt 23:23 **for ye pay t. of mint and anise** *586*
Lu 11:42 **ye t. mint and rue and all manner** .. *586*

TITHES
Ge 14:20 hand. And he gave him **t.** of all.......... 4643
Le 27:31 will at all redeem ought of his **t.**, ... 4643
Nu 18:24 But the **t.** of the children of Israel, ... 4643
Nu 18:26 the **t.** which I have given you from..... 4643
Nu 18:28 offering unto the Lord of all your **t.**, ... 4643
De 12:6 your **t.**, and heave offerings of your.... 4643
De 12:11 your **t.**, and the heave offering of....... 4643
De 26:12 the **t.** of thine increase the third 4643
2Ch 31:12 brought in the offerings and the **t.** 4643
Ne 10:37 the **t.** of our ground unto the............ 4643
Ne 10:37 have the **t.** in all the cities of our....... 6237
Ne 10:38 Levites, when the Levites take **t.**......... 6237
Ne 10:28 bring up the tithe of the **t.** unto.......... 4643
Ne 12:44 for the firstfruits, and for the **t.**, ... 4643
Ne 13:5 the vessels, and the **t.** of the corn,..... 4643
Am 4:4 and your **t.** after three years: 4643
Mal 3:8 robbed thee? In **t.** and offerings. 4643
Mal 3:10 ye all the **t.** into the storehouse, ... 4643
Lu 18:12 **I give t. of all that I possess**.......... *586*
Heb 7:5 to take **t.** of the people according to..... *586*
Heb 7:6 from them received **t.** of Abraham,..... *1183*
Heb 7:8 And here men that die receive **t.**; *1181*
Heb 7:9 receiveth **t.**, payed **t.** in Abraham....... *1183*

TITHING
De 26:12 made an end of **t.** all the tithes.......... 6237
De 26:12 third year, which is the year of **t.**,....... 4643

TITLE See also TITLES.
2Ki 23:17 said, What **t.** is that that I see? 6725
Joh 19:19 And Pilate wrote a **t.**, and put it *5102*
Joh 19:20 This **t.** then read many of the Jews: ... *5102*

TITLES
Job 32:21 let me give flattering **t.** unto man. ....
Job 32:22 For I know not to give flattering **t.**; ....

TITTLE
Mt 5:18 **one t. shall in no wise pass from**... *2762*
Lu 16:17 **pass, than one t. of the law to fail**. *2762*

TITUS (ti'-tus)
2Co 2:13 I found not **T.** my brother:............... *5103*
2Co 7:6 comforted us by the coming of **T.**;...... *5103*
2Co 7:13 the more joyed we for the joy of **T.**,.... *5103*
2Co 7:14 boasting, which I made before **T.**,....... *5103*
2Co 8:6 Insomuch that we desired **T.**, that....... *5103*
2Co 8:16 care into the heart of **T.** for you. *5103*
2Co 8:23 Whether any do enquire of **T.**, he *5103*
2Co 12:18 I desired **T.**, and with him I sent *5103*
2Co 12:18 brother. Did **T.** make a gain of you? ... *5103*
2Co *subscr.* of Macedonia, by **T.** and Lucas. *5103*
Ga 2:1 and took **T.** with me also................ *5103*
Ga 2:3 But neither **T.**, who was with me,....... *5103*
2Ti 4:10 to Galatia, **T.** unto Dalmatia. *5103*
Tit *general* *title* The Epistle Of Paul To **T.** *5103*
Tit 1:4 To **T.**, mine own son after the *5103*
Tit *subscr.* written to **T.**, ordained the first *5103*

TIZITE (ti'-zite)
1Ch 11:45 and Joha his brother, the **T.**,............. 8491

TO See in the APPENDIX; also ALLTO; HERETOFORE; HITHERTO; INTO; THERETO; TOGETHER; TOO; TOWARD; UNTO; WHERETO.

TOAH (to'-ah) See also NAHATH; TOHU.
1Ch 6:34 the son of Eliel, the son of **T.**, ... 8430

TOB (tob) See also ISH-TOB, TOB-ADONIJAH.
Jg 11:3 and dwelt in the land of **T.**................ 2897
Jg 11:5 Jephthah out of the land of **T.**............ 2897

TOB-ADONIJAH (tob''-ad-o-ni'-jah)
2Ch 17:8 and Tobijah, and T., Levites; 2899

TOBIAH (to-bi'-ah) See also TOBIJAH.
Ezr 2:60 of Delaiah, the children of T., 2900
Ne 2:10, 19 Horonite, and T. the servant, 2900
Ne 4:3 Now T. the Ammonite was by him, 2900
Ne 4:7 pass, that when Sanballat, and T., 2900
Ne 6:1 to pass, when Sanballat, and T., 2900
Ne 6:12 for T. and Sanballat and hired him. 2900
Ne 6:14 think thou upon T. and Sanballat 2900
Ne 6:17 Judah sent many letters unto T., 2900
Ne 6:17 the letters of T. came unto them. 2900
Ne 6:19 T. sent letters to put me in fear. 2900
Ne 7:62 the children of T., the children of 2900
Ne 13:4 of our God, was allied unto T. 2900
Ne 13:7 the evil that Eliashib did for T., 2900
Ne 13:8 forth all the household stuff of T. 2900

TOBIJAH (to-bi'-jah) See also TOBIAH.
2Ch 17:8 ad T., and Tob-adonijah, Levites; 2900
Zec 6:10 even of Heldai, of T., and of 2900
Zec 6:14 shall be to Helem, and to T., 2900

TOCHEN (to'-ken)
1Ch 4:32 and T., and Ashan, five cities: 8507

TO-DAY See DAY.

TOE See also TOES.
Ex 29:20 upon the great t. of their right foot, 931
Le 8:23 upon the great t. of his right foot. 931
Le 14:14 upon the great t. of his right foot: 931
Le 14:17 upon the great t. of his right foot, 931
Le 14:25 upon the great t. of his right foot: 931
Le 14:28 upon the great t. of his right foot, 931

TOES
Le 8:24 the great t. of their right feet: 931
Jg 1:6 off his thumbs and his great t.. 931, 7272
Jg 1:7 thumbs and...great t. cut off, 931, 7272
2Sa 21:20 finers, and on every foot six t., 676
1Ch 20:6 whose fingers and t. were four and 676
Da 2:41 whereas thou sawest the feet and t., 677
Da 2:42 And as the t. of the feet were part of 677

TOGARMAH (to-gar'-mah)
Ge 10:3 Ashkenaz, and Riphath, and T.. 8425
1Ch 1:6 Ashchenaz, and Riphath, and T.. 8425
Eze 27:14 the house of T. traded in thy fairs 8425
Eze 38:6 house of T. of the north quarters, 8425

TOGETHER See also ALTOGETHER.
Ge 1:9 heaven be gathered t. unto one place, 8425
Ge 1:10 gathering t. of the waters called he 8425
Ge 3:7 and they sewed fig leaves t., and 8425
Ge 13:6 them, that they might dwell t.: 3162
Ge 13:6 so that they could not dwell t.. 3162
Ge 14:3 were joined t. in the vale of Siddim,
Ge 22:6 and they went both of them t.. 3162
Ge 22:8 so they went both of them t.. 3162
Ge 22:19 rose up and went t. to Beer-sheba; 3162
Ge 25:22 children struggled t. within her;
Ge 29:7 the cattle should be gathered t.:
Ge 29:8 until all the flocks be gathered t.,
Ge 29:22 Laban gathered t. all the men of
Ge 34:30 gather themselves t. against me,
Ge 36:7 than that they might dwell t.; 3162
Ge 42:17 put them all t. into ward three days.
Ge 49:1 and said, Gather yourselves t.,
Ge 49:2 Gather yourselves t., and hear, ye
Ex 2:13 two men of the Hebrews strove t.:
Ex 3:16 and gather the elders of Israel t.
Ex 4:29 and gathered t. all the elders of the
Ex 8:14 they gathered them t. upon heaps:
Ex 15:8 the waters were gathered t.,
Ex 19:8 And all the people answered t., 3162
Ex 21:18 And if men strive t., and one smite
Ex 26:3 five curtains shall be coupled t.
Ex 26:6 and couple the curtains t. with the
Ex 26:11 and couple the tent t., that it may be
Ex 26:24 they shall be coupled t. beneath,
Ex 26:24 and they shall be coupled t. above 3162
Ex 28:7 and so it shall be joined t.
Ex 30:35 art of the apothecary, tempered t.,
Ex 32:1 gathered themselves t. unto Aaron,
Ex 32:26 gathered themselves t. unto him.
Ex 35:1 of the children of Israel t.,
Ex 36:18 taches of brass to couple the tent t.,
Ex 36:29 coupled t. at the head thereof, 3162
Ex 39:4 shoulderpieces for it, to couple it t.:
Ex 39:4 by the two edges was it coupled t..
Le 8:3 gather thou all the congregation t.
Le 8:4 and the assembly was gathered t.
Le 24:10 a man of Israel strove t. in the camp;
Le 26:25 ye are gathered t. within your cities,
Nu 1:18 assembled all the congregation t.
Nu 8:9 gather...the children of Israel t.:
Nu 10:7 congregation is to be gathered t.,
Nu 11:22 the fish of the sea be gathered t. for
Nu 14:35 that are gathered t. against me:
Nu 16:3 And they gathered themselves t.
Nu 16:11 all thy company are gathered t.
Nu 20:2 and they gathered themselves t.
Nu 20:8 and gather thou the assembly t.,
Nu 20:10 Aaron gathered the congregation t.
Nu 21:16 unto Moses, Gather the people t.,
Nu 21:23 but Sihon gathered all his people t.,
Nu 24:10 Balaam, and he smote his hands t.
Nu 26:10 and swallowed them up t. with Korah,
Nu 27:3 gathered themselves t. against
De 4:10 unto me, Gather me the people t.,
De 22:10 plough with an ox and an ass t.. 3162
De 22:11 sorts, as of woollen and linen t.. 3162
De 25:5 If brethren dwell t., and one of 3162
De 25:11 men strive t. one with another, 3162
De 31:12 Gather the people t., men, and
De 33:5 tribes of Israel were gathered t.. 3162
De 33:17 he shall push the people t. to the 3162
Jos 8:16 people that were in Ai were called t.
Jos 9:2 That they gathered themselves t., 3162
Jos 10:5 gathered themselves t., and went
Jos 10:6 mountains are gathered t. against us.
Jos 11:5 when all these kings were met t., 3162
Jos 11:5 came and pitched t. at the waters 3162
Jos 17:10 they met t. in Asher on the north,
Jos 18:1 of Israel assembled t. at Shiloh,
Jos 22:12 gathered themselves t. at Shiloh,
Jg 4:13 Sisera gathered t. all his chariots,
Jg 6:33 of the east were gathered t., 3162
Jg 6:38 and thrust the fleece t., and wringed
Jg 7:23 of Israel gathered themselves t.
Jg 7:24 of Ephraim gathered themselves t.,
Jg 9:6 the men of Shechem gathered t.,
Jg 9:47 of Shechem were gathered t.
Jg 10:17 children of Ammon were gathered t.,
Jg 10:17 of Israel assembled themselves t.,
Jg 11:20 but Sihon gathered all his people t.,
Jg 12:1 Ephraim gathered themselves t.,
Jg 12:4 Jephthah gathered t. all the men
Jg 16:23 Philistines gathered them t. for to
Jg 18:22 to Micah's house were gathered t.
Jg 19:6 did eat and drink both of them t. 3162
Jg 19:29 and divided her, t. with her bones,
Jg 20:1 was gathered t. as one man,
Jg 20:11 the city, knit t. as one man.
Jg 20:14 of Benjamin gathered themselves t.
1Sa 5:11 gathered t. all the lords of the
1Sa 7:6 And they gathered t. to Mizpeh,
1Sa 7:7 Israel were gathered t. to Mizpeh,
1Sa 8:4 of Israel gathered themselves t.,
1Sa 10:17 Samuel called the people t. unto
1Sa 11:11 that two of them were not left t.. 3162
1Sa 13:4 people were called t. after Saul to
1Sa 13:5 Philistines gathered...t. to fight
1Sa 13:11 Philistines gathered themselves t.
1Sa 15:4 And Saul gathered the people t.,
1Sa 17:1 Philistines gathered t. their armies
1Sa 17:1 and were gathered t. at Shochoh,
1Sa 17:2 men of Israel were gathered t., 3162
1Sa 17:10 give me a man, that we may fight t.. 3162
1Sa 23:8 Saul called all the people t. to war, 3162
1Sa 25:1 all the Israelites were gathered t.,
1Sa 28:1 Philistines gathered their armies t.
1Sa 28:4 Philistines gathered themselves t.,
1Sa 28:4 and Saul gathered all Israel t., and
1Sa 28:23 But his servants, t. with the woman,
1Sa 29:1 the Philistines gathered t. all their
1Sa 31:6 and all his men, that same day t.. 3162
2Sa 2:13 and met t. by the pool of Gibeon: 3162
2Sa 2:16 fellow's side; so they fell down t. 3162
2Sa 2:25 Benjamin gathered themselves t.
2Sa 2:30 he had gathered all the people t.,
2Sa 6:1 David gathered t. all the chosen men
2Sa 10:15 they gathered themselves t. 3162
2Sa 10:17 told David, he gathered all Israel t.,
2Sa 12:3 it grew up t. with him, and with 3162
2Sa 12:28 gather the rest of the people t.,
2Sa 12:29 David gathered all the people t.,
2Sa 14:6 and they two strove t. in the field,
2Sa 14:16 would destroy me and my son t. 3162
2Sa 20:14 they were gathered t., and went also
2Sa 21:9 they fell all seven t., and were put 3162
2Sa 23:9 were there gathered t. to battle,
2Sa 23:11 Philistines were gathered t. into a
1Ki 3:18 we were t.; there was no stranger 3162
1Ki 5:12 and they two made a league t.
1Ki 10:26 And Solomon gathered t. chariots
1Ki 11:1 t. with the daughter of Pharaoh,
1Ki 18:20 and gathered the prophets t. unto
1Ki 20:1 of Syria gathered all his host t.
1Ki 22:6 of Israel gathered the prophets t.,
2Ki 2:8 took his mantled, and wrapped it t.,
2Ki 3:10, 13 hath called these three kings t.,
2Ki 9:25 I and thou rode t. after Ahab his 6776
2Ki 10:18 Jehu gathered all the people t.,
1Ch 10:6 Saul...and all his house died t.. 3162
1Ch 11:13 Philistines were gathered t. to
1Ch 13:5 So David gathered all Israel t.,
1Ch 15:3 And David gathered all Israel t.
1Ch 16:35 and gather us t., and deliver us
1Ch 19:7 of Ammon gathered themselves t.
1Ch 22:2 David commanded to gather t. the
1Ch 23:2 he gathered t. all the princes of
2Ch 12:5 that were gathered t. to Jerusalem
2Ch 15:10 they gathered...t. at Jerusalem.
2Ch 18:5 of Israel gathered t. of prophets
2Ch 20:4 And Judah gathered themselves t.,
2Ch 24:5 he gathered t. the priests and the
2Ch 25:5 Amaziah gathered Judah t., and
2Ch 28:24 Ahaz gathered t. the vessels of the
2Ch 29:4 and gathered them t. into the east
2Ch 30:3 the people gathered themselves t.
2Ch 32:4 was gathered much people t.,
2Ch 32:6 gathered them t....in the street
2Ch 34:17 they have gathered t. the money
2Ch 34:29 sent and gathered t. all the elders
Ezr 2:64 whole congregation t. was forty 259
Ezr 3:1 gathered themselves t. as one man
Ezr 3:9 and his sons, the sons of Judah, t.. 259
Ezr 3:11 they sang t. by course in praising
Ezr 4:3 we ourselves t. will build unto the 3162
Ezr 6:20 and the Levites were purified t., 259
Ezr 7:28 gathered t. out of Israel chief men
Ezr 8:15 I gathered them t. to the river that
Ezr 10:7 should gather...t. unto Jerusalem;
Ezr 10:9 Benjamin gathered themselves t.
Ne 4:6 all the wall was joined t. unto the
Ne 4:8 conspired all of them t. to come 3162
Ne 6:2 Come, let us meet t. in some one of 3162
Ne 6:7 therefore, and let us take counsel t.. 3162
Ne 6:10 Let us meet t. in the house of God,
Ne 7:5 mine heart to gather t. the nobles,
Ne 7:66 whole congregation t. was forty 259
Ne 8:1 gathered themselves t. as one man
Ne 8:13 were gathered t. the chief of the
Ne 12:28 the singers gathered themselves t.,
Ne 13:11 And I gathered them t., and set
Es 2:3 gather t. all the fair young virgins
Es 2:8 many maidens were gathered t.
Es 2:19 virgins were gathered t. the second
Es 4:16 Go, gather t. all the Jews that are
Es 8:11 every city to gather themselves t.,
Es 9:2 The Jews gathered themselves t.
Es 9:15 in Shushan gathered themselves t.
Es 9:16 provinces gathered themselves t.
Es 9:18 that were at Shushan assembled t.
Job 2:11 they had made an appointment t. 3162
Job 3:18 There the prisoners rest t.; they 3162
Job 6:2 my calamity laid in the balances t.! 3162
Job 9:32 and we should come t. in judgment 3162
Job 10:8 have made me and fashioned me t. 3162
Job 11:10 cut off, and shut up, or gather t.,
Job 16:10 gathered themselves t. against me 3162
Job 17:16 pit, when our rest t. is in the dust. 3162
Job 19:12 His troops come t. and raise up 3162
Job 24:4 the poor of the earth hide . . . t. 3162
Job 30:7 the nettles they were gathered t.
Job 34:15 All flesh shall perish t., and man 3162
Job 38:7 When the morning stars sang t., 3162
Job 38:38 and the clods cleave fast t.?
Job 40:13 Hide them in the dust t.; and bind 3162

Job 40:17 sinews of his stones are wrapped t.
Job 41:15 pride, shut up t., as with a close seal
Job 41:17 they stick t., that they cannot be
Job 41:23 flakes of his flesh are joined t.
Ps 2:2 and the rulers take counsel t., 3162
Ps 14:3 aside, they are all t. become filthy: 3162
Ps 31:13 they took counsel t. against me, 3162
Ps 33:7 He gathereth the waters of the sea t.
Ps 34:3 me, and let us exalt his name t. 3162
Ps 35:15 and gathered themselves t.
Ps 35:15 the abjects gathered themselves t.
Ps 35:26 and brought to confusion t. 3162
Ps 37:38 transgressors shall be destroyed t. 3162
Ps 40:14 be ashamed and confounded t. 3162
Ps 41:7 All that hate me whisper t. against 3162
Ps 47:9 The princes . . . are gathered t., 3162
Ps 48:4 were assembled, they passed by t., 3162
Ps 49:2 Both low and high, rich and poor, t. 3162
Ps 50:5 Gather my saints t. unto me;
Ps 55:14 We took sweet counsel t. and 3162
Ps 56:6 They gather themselves t., they hide 3162
Ps 71:10 wait for my soul take counsel t., 3162
Ps 74:8 hearts, Let us destroy them t. 3162
Ps 83:5 have consulted t. with one consent: 3162
Ps 85:10 Mercy and truth are met t.
Ps 88:17 they compassed me about t. 3162
Ps 94:21 They gather themselves t. against
Ps 98:8 hands: let the hills be joyful t. 3162
Ps 102:22 When the people are gathered t., 3162
Ps 104:22 ariseth, they gather themselves t.,
Ps 122:3 as a city that is compact t. 3162
Ps 133:1 is for brethren to dwell t. in unity! 3162
Ps 140:2 are they gathered t. for war.
Ps 147:2 gathered t. the outcasts of Israel.
Pr 22:2 The rich and poor meet t.: the Lord is
Pr 29:13 poor and the deceitful man meet t.
Ec 3:5 and a time to gather stones t.;
Ec 4:5 fool foldeth his hands t., and eateth his
Ec 4:11 if two lie t., then they have heat:
Isa 1:18 Come now, and let us reason t., saith
Isa 1:28 and of the sinners shall be t., and 3162
Isa 1:31 spark, and they shall both burn t., 3162
Isa 8:10 Take counsel t., and it shall come to
Isa 9:11 him and join his enemies t.;
Isa 9:21 they t. shall be against Judah 3162
Isa 11:6 the young lion and the fatling t.; 3162
Isa 11:7 their young ones shall lie down t. 3162
Isa 11:12 gather t. the dispersed of Judah
Isa 11:14 shall spoil them of the east t. 3162
Isa 13:4 kingdoms of nations gathered t.
Isa 18:6 They shall be left t. unto the fowls 3162
Isa 22:3 All thy rulers are fled t., they are 3162
Isa 22:3 that are found in thee are bound t., 3162
Isa 22:9 gathered t. the waters of the lower
Isa 24:22 And they shall be gathered t., as
Isa 25:11 and he shall bring down their pride t.
Isa 26:19 t. with my dead body shall they arise.
Isa 27:4 them, I would burn them t. 3162
Isa 31:3 fall down, and they shall fail t. 3162
Isa 34:4 the heavens shall be rolled t. as
Isa 40:5 and all flesh shall see it t. 3162
Isa 41:1 let us come near t. to judgment. 3162
Isa 41:19 and the pine, and the box tree t. 3162
Isa 41:20 and consider, and understand t., 3162
Isa 41:23 may be dismayed, and behold it t. 3162
Isa 43:9 Let all the nations be gathered t., 3162
Isa 43:17 they shall lie down t., they shall not 3162
Isa 43:26 me in remembrance: let us plead t. 3162
Isa 44:11 let them all be gathered t., let
Isa 44:11 and they shall be ashamed t. 3162
Isa 45:8 let righteousness spring up t.; I 3162
Isa 45:16 go to confusion t. that are makers 3162
Isa 45:20 draw near t., ye that are escaped of 3162
Isa 45:21 near; yea, let them take counsel t. 3162
Isa 46:2 They stoop, they bow down t.; 3162
Isa 48:13 call unto them, they stand up t. 3162
Isa 49:18 all these gather themselves t., and
Isa 50:8 contend with me? let us stand t. 3162
Isa 52:8 with the voice t. shall they sing: 3162
Isa 52:9 Break forth into joy, sing t., ye
Isa 54:15 they shall surely gather t., but
Isa 54:15 whosoever shall gather t., against
Isa 60:4 all they gather themselves t., they
Isa 60:5 Then thou shalt see, and flow t.,
Isa 60:7 shall be gathered t. unto thee,
Isa 60:13 tree, the pine tree, and the box t., 3162
Isa 62:9 that have brought it t. shall drink
Isa 65:7 the inquities of your fathers t., 3162
Isa 65:25 the wolf and the lamb shall feed t., 259
Isa 66:17 the mouse, shall be consumed t., 3162
Jer 3:18 they shall come t. out of the land of 3162
Jer 4:5 cry, gather t., and say, Assemble
Jer 6:11 the assembly of young men t. 3162
Jer 6:12 with their fields and wives t. 3162
Jer 6:21 the sons t. shall fall upon them; 3162
Jer 13:14 even the fathers and the sons t., 3162
Jer 31:8 her that travaileth with child t. 3162
Jer 31:12 shall flow t. to the goodness of the 3162
Jer 31:13 dance, both young men and old t. 3162
Jer 31:24 and in all the cities thereof t., 3162
Jer 41:1 they did eat bread t. in Mizpah. 3162
Jer 46:12 mighty, and they are fallen both t. 3162
Jer 46:21 turned back, and are fled away t. 3162
Jer 48:7 with his priests and his princes t. 3162
Jer 49:3 and his priests and his princes t.
Jer 49:14 Gather ye t., and come against
Jer 50:4 they and the children of Judah t., 3162
Jer 50:29 Call t. the archers against
Jer 50:33 of Judah were oppressed t. 3162
Jer 51:27 call t. against her the kingdoms of
Jer 51:38 They shall roar t. like lions: they 3162
Jer 51:44 nations shall not flow t. any more
La 2:8 to lament; they languished t. 3162
Eze 21:14 prophesy, and smite thine hands t.,
Eze 21:17 I will also smite mine hands t., and I
Eze 29:5 thou shalt not be brought t., nor
Eze 37:7 bones came t., bone to his bone.
Da 2:35 and the gold, broken to pieces t., 2298
Da 3:2 king sent to gather t. the princes,
Da 3:3 gathered t. unto the dedication of
Da 3:27 counsellers, being gathered t.,
Da 6:6 presidents and princes assembled t.
Da 6:7 have consulted t. to establish
Da 11:6 they shall join themselves t.;
Ho 1:11 children of Israel be gathered t., 3162
Ho 11:8 me, my repentings are kindled t. 3162
Joe 3:11 gather yourselves t. round about:
Am 1:15 captivity, he and his princes t., 3162
Am 3:3 Can two walk t., except they be 3162
Mic 2:12 them t. as the sheep of Bozrah, 3162
Na 1:10 while they be folden t. as thorns,
Na 2:10 melteth, and the knees smite t.,
Zep 2:1 Gather yourselves t., yea,
Zep 2:1 yea, gather t., O nation not desired;
Zec 10:4 bow, out of him every oppressor t. 3162
Zec 12:3 people of the earth be gathered t.
Zec 14:14 round about shall be gathered t.,
Mt 1:18 before they came t., she was found *4905*
Mt 2:4 priests and scribes of the people t., *4863*
Mt 13:2 great multitudes were gathered t. *4863*
Mt 13:30 **Let both grow t. until the harvest:** *4886*
Mt 13:30 **Gather ye t. first the tares, and** *4816*
Mt 18:20 **three are gathered t. in my name,** *4863*
Mt 19:6 **What therefore God hath joined t.,** *4801*
Mt 22:10 **gathered t. all as many as they** *4863*
Mt 22:34 they were gathered t. *1909,3588,864*
Mt 22:41 the Pharisees were gathered t., *4863*
Mt 23:37 **I have gathered thy children t.,** *1996*
Mt 24:28 **will the eagles be gathered t.** *4863*
Mt 24:31 **gather t. his elect from the four** *1996*
Mt 26:3 Then assembled t. the chief priests, *4863*
Mt 27:17 when they were gathered t., *4863*
Mt 27:62 and Pharisees came t. unto Pilate, *4863*
Mk 1:33 city was gathered t. at the door. *1996*
Mk 2:2 many were gathered t., *4863*
Mk 2:15 and sinners sat also t. with Jesus *4873*
Mk 3:20 the multitude cometh t. again, *4905*
Mk 6:30 apostles gathered themselves t. *4863*
Mk 6:33 them, and came t. unto him. *4905*
Mk 7:1 came t. unto him the Pharisees, *4863*
Mk 9:25 that the people came running t., *1998*
Mk 10:9 **therefore God hath joined t.,** *4801*
Mk 12:28 having heard them reasoning t. *4802*
Mk 13:27 **gather t. his elect from the four** *1996*
Mk 14:56 him, but their witness agreed not t.
Mk 14:59 neither so did their witness agree t.
Mk 15:16 and they call t. the whole band. *4779*
Lu 5:15 great multitudes came t. to hear. *4905*
Lu 6:38 **pressed down, and shaken t.,**
Lu 8:4 much people were gathered t. *4896*
Lu 9:1 he called his twelve disciples t., *4779*
Lu 11:29 the people were gathered thick t., *1865*
Lu 12:1 were gathered t. an innumerable *1996*
Lu 13:11 was bowed t., and could in no wise *4794*
Lu 13:34 **I have gathered thy children t.,** *1996*
Lu 15:6 **he calleth t. his friends and** *4779*
Lu 15:9 **her friends and her neighbours t.,** *4779*
Lu 15:13 **the younger son gathered all t.,** *4863*
Lu 17:35 **women...be grinding t.;** *1909,3588,846*
Lu 17:37 **will the eagles be gathered t.** *4863*
Lu 22:55 were set down t., Peter sat down *4776*
Lu 22:66 priests and the scribes came t., *4863*
Lu 23:12 Herod were made friends t.: *3326,240*
Lu 23:13 he had called t. the chief priests *4779*
Lu 23:48 all the people that came t. to that *4836*
Lu 24:14 they talked t. of all these *4314,240*
Lu 24:15 they communed t. and reasoned,
Lu 24:33 and found the eleven gathered t., *4867*
Joh 4:36 **he that reapeth may rejoice t.** *3674*
Joh 6:13 Therefore they gathered them t., *4863*
Joh 11:52 gather t. in one the children of God *4863*
Joh 11:53 they took counsel t. for to put *4853*
Joh 20:4 So they ran both t.: and the *3674*
Joh 20:7 but wrapped t. in a place by itself. *1794*
Joh 21:2 There were t. Simon Peter, and *3674*
Ac 1:4 being assembled t. with them, *4811*
Ac 1:6 When they therefore were come t., *4905*
Ac 1:15 of names t. were about an *1909,3588,846*
Ac 2:6 abroad, the multitude came t., *4905*
Ac 2:44 all that believed were t., *1909,3588,846*
Ac 3:1 Peter and John went up t. *1909,3588,846*
Ac 3:11 all the people ran t. unto *4936,1909,846*
Ac 4:6 were gathered t. at Jerusalem. *4863*
Ac 4:26 rulers were gathered t. *1909,3588,846*
Ac 4:27 people of Israel, were gathered t., *4863*
Ac 4:31 where they were assembled t.; *4863*
Ac 5:9 it that ye have agreed t. to tempt *4856*
Ac 5:21 him, and called the council t., *4779*
Ac 10:24 called t. his kinsmen and near *4779*
Ac 10:27 and found many that were come t. *4905*
Ac 12:12 many were gathered t. praying. *4867*
Ac 13:44 came almost the whole city t. to *4863*
Ac 14:1 they went both t. into the *2596,3588,846*
Ac 14:27 and had gathered the church t., *4863*
Ac 15:6 And the apostles and elders came t. *4863*
Ac 15:30 they had gathered the multitude t., *4863*
Ac 16:22 multitude rose up t. against them: *4911*
Ac 19:19 arts brought their books t., *4851*
Ac 19:25 he called t. with the workmen *4867*
Ac 19:32 not wherefore they were come t. *4897*
Ac 20:7 disciples came t. to break bread, *4863*
Ac 20:8 where they were gathered t. *4863*
Ac 21:22 multitude must needs come t. *4905*
Ac 21:30 was moved, and the people ran t. *4890*
Ac 23:12 certain of the Jews banded t., *4966*
Ac 28:17 Paul called the chief of the Jews t. *4779*
Ac 28:17 and when they were come t., he *4905*
Ro 1:12 I may be comforted t. with you *4837*
Ro 3:12 they are t. become unprofitable; *260*
Ro 6:5 planted t. in the likeness of his *4854*
Ro 8:17 that we may be also glorified t. *4888*
Ro 8:22 groaneth and travaileth in pain t. *4944*
Ro 8:28 that all things work t. for good *4903*
Ro 15:30 strive t. with me in your prayers *4865*
1Co 1:10 that ye be perfectly joined t. in the *2675*
1Co 3:9 For we are labourers t. with God: *4904*
1Co 5:4 when ye are gathered t., and my *4863*
1Co 7:5 come t. again, that Satan *1909,3588,846*
1Co 11:17 that ye come t. not for the better, *4905*
1Co 11:18 when ye come t. in the church, I *4905*
1Co 11:20 When ye come t. therefore into one *4905*
1Co 11:33 when ye come t. to eat, tarry one *4905*
1Co 11:34 ye come not t. unto condemnation. *4905*
1Co 12:24 but God hath tempered the body t., *4786*
1Co 14:23 whole church be come t. into one *4905*
1Co 14:26 when ye came t., every one of you *4905*
2Co 1:11 Ye also helping t. by prayer for us, *4943*
2Co 6:1 We then, as workers t. with him, *4903*
2Co 6:14 Be ye not unequally yoked t. with *2086*
Eph 1:10 might gather t. in one all things *346*
Eph 2:5 hath quickened us t. with Christ, *4806*
Eph 2:6 And hath raised us up t., *4891*
Eph 2:6 made us sit t. in heavenly places *4776*
Eph 2:21 all the building fitly framed t. *4883*
Eph 2:22 In whom ye also are builded t. for *4925*
Eph 4:16 the whole body fitly joined t. and *4883*
Php 1:27 one mind striving t. for the faith *4866*
Php 3:17 Brethren, be followers t. of me, *4831*
Col 2:2 be comforted, being knit t. in love, *4822*
Col 2:13 hath he quickened t. with him, *4806*
Col 2:19 ministered, and knit t., *4822*

1Th 4:17 remain shall be caught up **t.** with... *260*
1Th 5:10 sheep, we should live **t.** with him. ... *260*
1Th 5:11 Wherefore comfort yourselves **t.**,... *240*
2Th 2:1 and by our gathering **t.** unto him,... *1997*
Heb 10:25 the assembling of ourselves **t.**, ... *1997*
Jas 5:3 Ye have heaped treasure **t.** for the...
1Pe 3:7 being heirs **t.** of the grace of life;... *4789*
1Pe 5:13 is at Babylon, elected **t.** with you,... *4899*
Re 6:14 as a scroll when it is rolled **t.**; ...
Re 16:16 he gathered them **t.** into a place ... *4863*
Re 19:17 Come and gather yourselves **t.** unto... *4863*
Re 19:19 armies, gathered **t.** to make war... *4863*
Re 20:8 Magog, to gather them **t.** to battle: ... *4863*

TOHU (to'-hu) See also NAHATH; TOAH.
1Sa 1:1 the son of Elihu, the son of **T.**, ... 8459

TOI (to'-i) See also TOU.
2Sa 8:9 When **T.** king of Hamath heard... 8583
2Sa 8:10 **T.** sent Joram his son unto king... 8583
2Sa 8:10 for Hadadezer had wars with **T.**... 8583

TOIL See also TOILED; TOILING.
Ge 5:29 our work and **t.** of our hands,... 6093
Ge 41:51 hath made me forget all my **t.**... 5999
Mt 6:28 **they t. not, neither do they spin:...** *2872*
Lu 12:27 **grow: they t. not, they spin not;...** *2872*

TOILED
Lu 5:5 Master, we have **t.** all the night,... *2872*

TOILING
Mk 6:48 And he saw them **t.** in rowing; for... *928*

TOKEN See also TOKENS.
Ge 9:12 This is the **t.** of the covenant which... 226
Ge 9:13 **t.** of a covenant between me and... 226
Ge 9:17 This is the **t.** of the covenant, which... 226
Ge 17:11 **t.** of the covenant betwixt me and... 226
Ex 3:12 this shall be a **t.** unto thee, that I... 226
Ex 12:13 the blood shall be to you for a **t.** ... 226
Ex 13:16 shall be for a **t.** upon thine hand,... 226
Nu 17:10 be kept for a **t.** against the rebels;... 226
Jos 2:12 father's house, and give me a true **t.**... 226
Ps 86:17 Shew me a **t.** for good; that they... 226
Mk 14:44 betrayed him had given them a **t.**,... *4958*
Php 1:28 to them an evident **t.** of perdition,... *1732*
2Th 1:5 a manifest **t.** of the righteous ... *1730*
2Th 3:17 which is the **t.** in every epistle: ... *4592*

TOKENS
De 22:15 forth the **t.** of the damsel's virginity...
De 22:17 are the **t.** of my daughter's virginity...
De 22:20 **t.** of virginity be not found for the...
Job 21:29 way? and do ye not know their **t.**, ... 226
Ps 65:8 uttermost parts are afraid at thy **t.**... 226
Ps 135:9 sent **t.** and wonders into the midst... 226
Isa 44:25 That frustrateth the **t.** of the liars,... 226

TOLA (to'-lah) See also TOLAITES.
Ge 46:13 sons of Issachar; **T.**, and Phuvah,... 8439
Nu 26:23 of **T.**, the family of the Tolaites: ... 8439
Jg 10:1 defend Israel **T.** the son of Puah,... 8439
1Ch 7:1 sons of Issachar were, **T.**, and ... 8439
1Ch 7:2 sons of **T.**; Uzzi, and Rephaiah, ... 8439
1Ch 7:2 their father's house, to wit, of **T.**... 8439

TOLAD (to'-lad) See also EL-TOLAD.
1Ch 4:29 Bilhah, and at Ezem, and at **T.**, ... 8434

TOLAITES (to'-lah-ites)
Nu 26:23 of Tola, the family of the **T.**... 8440

TOLD See also FORETOLD.
Ge 3:11 Who **t.** thee that thou wast naked? ... 5046
Ge 9:22 and **t.** his two brethren without... 5046
Ge 14:13 escaped, and **t.** Abram the Hebrew;... 5046
Ge 20:8 **t.** all these things in their ears:... 1696
Ge 22:3 the place of which God had **t.** him... 559
Ge 22:9 the place which God had **t.** him of;... 559
Ge 22:20 that it was **t.** Abraham, saying, ... 5046
Ge 24:28 **t.** them of her mother's house these... 5046
Ge 24:33 eat, until I have **t.** mine errand... 1696
Ge 24:66 servant **t.** Isaac all things that he ... 5608
Ge 26:32 her elder son were **t.** to Rebekah:... 5608
Ge 29:12 Jacob **t.** Rachel that he was her ... 5608
Ge 29:12 and she ran and **t.** her father... 5608
Ge 29:13 And he **t.** Laban all these things... 5608
Ge 31:20 in that he **t.** him not that he fled... 5046
Ge 31:22 **t.** Laban on the third day that... 5046
Ge 37:5 a dream, and he **t.** it his brethren: ... 5046
Ge 37:9 dream, and **t.** it his brethren, and... 5608
Ge 37:10 And he **t.** it to his father, and to... 5608
Ge 38:13 was **t.** Tamar, saying, Behold, thy... 5046
Ge 38:24 that it was **t.** Judah, saying, ... 5046
Ge 40:9 chief butler **t.** his dream to Joseph,... 5608
Ge 41:8 and Pharaoh **t.** them his dream;... 5608
Ge 41:12 we **t.** him, and he interpreted to us... 5608
Ge 41:24 and I **t.** this unto the magicians; ... 559
Ge 42:29 **t.** him all that befell unto them;... 5046
Ge 43:7 we **t.** him according to the tenor... 5046
Ge 44:24 we **t.** him the words of my lord... 5046
Ge 45:26 **t.** him, saying, Joseph is yet alive,... 5046
Ge 45:27 **t.** him all the words of Joseph,... 1696
Ge 47:1 Joseph came and **t.** Pharaoh, and... 5046
Ge 48:1 that one **t.** Joseph, Behold, thy ... 559
Ge 48:2 one **t.** Jacob, and said, Behold, ... 5046
Ex 4:28 Moses **t.** Aaron all the words of... 5046
Ex 5:1 Aaron went in, and **t.** Pharaoh, ... 559
Ex 14:5 it was **t.** the king of Egypt that the ... 5046
Ex 16:22 congregation came and **t.** Moses. ... 5046
Ex 18:8 Moses **t.** his father in law all that... 5608
Ex 19:9 Moses **t.** the words of the people... 5046
Ex 24:3 Moses came and **t.** the people all... 5608
Le 21:24 Moses **t.** it unto Aaron, and to his... 1696
Nu 11:24 **t.** the people the words of the Lord,... 1696
Nu 11:27 ran a young man, and **t.** Moses, ... 5046
Nu 13:27 **t.** him, and said, We came unto ... 5608
Nu 14:39 Moses **t.** these sayings unto all... 1696
Nu 23:26 said unto Balak, **T.** not I thee,... 1696
Nu 29:40 **t.** the children of Israel according... 559
De 17:4 And it be **t.** thee, and thou hast... 5046
Jos 2:2 And it was **t.** the king of Jericho,... 559
Jos 2:23 **t.** him all things that befell them:... 5608
Jos 9:24 it was certainly **t.** thy servants, ... 5046
Jos 10:17 it was **t.** Joshua, saying, The five... 5046
Jg 6:13 miracles which our fathers **t.** us... 5608
Jg 7:13 there was a man that **t.** a dream... 5608
Jg 9:7 And when they **t.** it to Jotham, ... 5046
Jg 9:25 by them: and it was **t.** Abimelech... 5046
Jg 9:42 the field; and they **t.** Abimelech... 5046
Jg 9:47 it was **t.** Abimelech, that all the men... 5046
Jg 13:6 woman came and **t.** her husband,... 559
Jg 13:6 was, neither **t.** he me his name: ... 5046
Jg 13:23 at this time have **t.** us such things... 8085
Jg 14:2 and **t.** his father and his mother, ... 5046
Jg 14:6 he **t.** not his father or his mother... 5046
Jg 14:9 he **t.** not them that he had taken... 5046
Jg 14:16 my people, and hast not **t.** it me... 5046
Jg 14:16 I have not **t.** it my father nor my ... 5046
Jg 14:17 on the seventh day, that he **t.** her,... 5046
Jg 14:17 she **t.** the riddle to the children of... 5046
Jg 16:2 it was **t.** the Gazites, saying, Samson...
Jg 16:10, 13 hast mocked me, and **t.** me lies: ... 1696
Jg 16:15 hast not **t.** me wherein thy great... 5046
Jg 16:17 That he **t.** her all his heart, and... 5046
Jg 16:18 saw that he had **t.** her all his heart,... 5046
Ru 3:16 she **t.** her all that the man had done... 5046
1Sa 3:13 **t.** him that I will judge his house... 5046
1Sa 3:18 Samuel **t.** him every whit, and hid... 5046
1Sa 4:13 man came into the city, and **t.** it, ... 5046
1Sa 4:14 man came in hastily, and **t.** Eli... 5046
1Sa 8:10 Samuel **t.** all the words of the Lord... 559
1Sa 9:15 Lord had **t.** Samuel in his ear a... 1540
1Sa 10:16 He **t.** us plainly that the asses... 5046
1Sa 10:16 Samuel spake, he **t.** him not... 5046
1Sa 10:25 Samuel **t.** the people the manner... 1696
1Sa 11:4 **t.** the tidings in the ears of the... 1696
1Sa 11:5 **t.** him the tidings of the men of... 5608
1Sa 14:1 side. But he **t.** not his father... 5046
1Sa 14:33 Then they **t.** Saul, saying, Behold,... 5046
1Sa 14:43 Jonathan **t.** him, and said, I did but... 5046
1Sa 15:12 it was **t.** Samuel, saying, Saul came... 5046
1Sa 18:20 they **t.** Saul, and the thing pleased... 5046
1Sa 18:24 the servants of Saul **t.** him, saying,... 5046
1Sa 18:26 his servants **t.** David these words, ... 5046
1Sa 19:2 and Jonathan **t.** David, saying, ... 5046
1Sa 19:11 Michal David's wife **t.** him, saying, ... 5046
1Sa 19:18 and **t.** him all that Saul had done to ... 5046
1Sa 19:19 **t.** Saul, saying, Behold, David is at... 5046
1Sa 19:21 when it was **t.** Saul, he sent other... 5046
1Sa 23:1 they **t.** David, saying, Behold, the... 5046
1Sa 23:7 it was **t.** Saul that David was come... 5046
1Sa 23:13 was **t.** Saul that David was escaped... 5046
1Sa 23:22 **t.** me that he dealeth very subtilly. ... 559
1Sa 23:25 they **t.** David: wherefore he came... 5046
1Sa 24:1 that it was **t.** him, saying, Behold,... 5046
1Sa 25:12 came and **t.** him all those sayings... 5046
1Sa 25:14 one of the young men **t.** Abigail, ... 5046
1Sa 25:19 But she **t.** not her husband Nabal... 5046
1Sa 25:36 she **t.** him nothing, less or more, ... 5046
1Sa 25:37 his wife had **t.** him these things, ... 5046
1Sa 27:4 **t.** Saul that David was fled to Gath:... 5046
2Sa 1:5 unto the young man that **t.** him,... 5046
2Sa 1:6 the young man that **t.** him said, As... 5046
2Sa 1:13 said unto the young man that **t.** him,... 5046
2Sa 2:4 And they **t.** David, saying, That the... 5046
2Sa 3:23 they **t.** Joab, saying, Abner the son... 5046
2Sa 4:10 When one **t.** me, saying, Behold, ... 5046
2Sa 6:12 And it was **t.** king David, saying, ... 5046
2Sa 10:5 When they **t.** it unto David, he sent... 5046
2Sa 10:17 was **t.** David, he gathered all Israel... 5046
2Sa 11:5 conceived, and sent and **t.** David,... 5046
2Sa 11:10 when they had **t.** David, saying,... 5046
2Sa 11:18 Then Joab sent and **t.** David all the... 5046
2Sa 14:33 Joab came to the king, and **t.** him:... 5046
2Sa 15:31 And one **t.** David, saying, Ahithophel... 5046
2Sa 17:17 and a wench went and **t.** them;... 5046
2Sa 17:17 and they went and **t.** king David. ... 5046
2Sa 17:18 a lad saw them, and **t.** Absalom; ... 5046
2Sa 17:21 went and **t.** king David, and said... 5046
2Sa 18:10 a certain man saw it, and **t.** Joab,... 5046
2Sa 18:11 Joab said unto the man that **t.** him,... 5046
2Sa 18:25 watchman cried, and **t.** the king... 5046
2Sa 19:1 And it was **t.** Joab, Behold, the king... 5046
2Sa 19:8 they **t.** unto all the people, saying, ... 5046
2Sa 21:11 it was **t.** David what Rizpah the... 5046
2Sa 24:13 So Gad came to David, and **t.** him,... 5046
1Ki 1:23 they **t.** the king, saying, Behold... 5046
1Ki 1:51 And it was **t.** Solomon, saying, ... 5046
1Ki 2:29 **t.** king Solomon that Joab was fled... 5046
1Ki 2:39 And they **t.** Shimei, saying, Behold,... 5046
1Ki 2:41 it was **t.** Solomon that Shimei had ... 5046
1Ki 8:5 that could not be **t.** nor numbered... 5608
1Ki 10:3 Solomon **t.** her all her questions:... 5046
1Ki 10:3 from the king, which he **t.** her not... 5046
1Ki 10:7 and, behold, the half was not **t.** me: ... 5046
1Ki 13:11 his sons came and **t.** him all the... 5608
1Ki 13:11 them they **t.** also to their father... 5608
1Ki 13:25 and **t.** it in the city where the old... 1696
1Ki 14:2 which **t.** me that I should be king... 1696
1Ki 18:13 Was it not **t.** my lord what I did... 5046
1Ki 18:16 went to meet Ahab, and **t.** him:... 5046
1Ki 19:1 Ahab **t.** Jezebel all that Elijah had... 5046
1Ki 20:17 Ben-hadad sent out, and they **t.** him, .. 5046
2Ki 1:7 meet you, and **t.** you these words?... 1696
2Ki 4:7 she came and **t.** the man of God... 5046
2Ki 4:27 hid it from me, and hath not **t.** me... 5046
2Ki 4:31 and **t.** him, saying, The child is not... 5046
2Ki 5:4 one went in, and **t.** his lord, saying,... 5046
2Ki 6:10 man of God **t.** him and warned him... 559
2Ki 6:13 was **t.** him, saying, Behold, he is... 5046
2Ki 7:10 they **t.** them, saying, We came to... 5046
2Ki 7:11 they **t.** it to the king's house within. ... 5046
2Ki 7:15 messengers returned,...**t.** the king. ... 5046
2Ki 8:6 king asked the woman, she **t.** him... 5608
2Ki 8:7 **t.** him, saying, The man of God is... 5046
2Ki 8:14 He **t.** me that thou shouldest surely... 559
2Ki 9:18 the watchman **t.**, saying, The... 5046
2Ki 9:20 watchman **t.**, saying, He came even... 5046
2Ki 9:36 they came again, and **t.** him... 5046
2Ki 10:8 there came a messenger, and **t.** him,... 5046
2Ki 12:10 **t.** the money that was found in... 4487
2Ki 12:11 they gave the money, being **t.**,... 8505
2Ki 18:37 **t.** him the words of Rab-shakeh... 5046
2Ki 23:17 the men of the city **t.** him, It is the... 559
1Ch 17:25 hast **t.** thy servant that thou wilt... 1540
1Ch 19:5 **t.** David how the men were served... 5046
1Ch 19:17 it was **t.** David; and he gathered... 5046
2Ch 2:2 Solomon **t.** out threescore and ten... 5608
2Ch 5:6 which could not be **t.** nor numbered... 5608
2Ch 9:2 Solomon **t.** her all her questions:... 5046
2Ch 9:2 from Solomon which he **t.** her not... 5046
2Ch 9:6 of thy wisdom was not **t.** me:... 5046
2Ch 20:2 came some that **t.** Jehoshaphat, ... 5046
2Ch 34:18 Then Shaphan the scribe **t.** the king... 5046
Ezr 8:17 I **t.** them what they should ... 7760,6310
Ne 2:12 neither **t.** I any man what my God... 5046
Ne 2:16 neither had I as yet **t.** it to the Jews,.. 5046
Ne 2:18 I **t.** them of the hand of my God... 5046
Es 2:22 who **t.** it unto Esther the queen;... 5046
Es 3:4 that they **t.** Haman, to see whether... 5046
Es 3:4 he had **t.** them that he was a Jew. ... 5046
Es 4:4 chamberlains came and **t.** it her. ... 5046
Es 4:7 And Mordecai **t.** him of all that had... 5046

Es 4:9 And Hatach came and t. Esther the.... 5046
Es 4:12 they t. to Mordecai Esther's words. ... 5046
Es 5:11 Haman t. them of the glory of his 5608
Es 6:2 that Mordecai had t. of Bigthana 5046
Es 6:13 Haman t. Zeresh his wife and all........ 5608
Es 8:1 Esther had t. what he was unto......... 5046
Job 15:18 wise men have t. from their fathers,... 5046
Job 37:20 Shall it be t. him that I speak? if a 5608
Ps 44:1 our fathers have t. us, what work 5608
Ps 52:*title* the Edomite came and t. Saul,........... 5046
Ps 78:3 known, and our fathers have t. us. 5608
Ps 90:9 we spend our years as a tale that is t.. .....
Ec 6:6 he live a thousand years twice t.,.............
Isa 7:2 And it was t. the house of David,....... 5046
Isa 36:22 t. him the words of Rabshakeh. 5046
Isa 40:21 not been t. you from the beginning?.... 5046
Isa 44:8 have not I t. thee from that time, ... 8085
Isa 45:21 who hath t. it from that time?............ 5046
Isa 52:15 that which had not been t. them 5608
Jer 36:20 and t. all the words in the ears of 5046
Jer 38:27 he t. them according to all these 5046
Da 4:7 and I t. the dream before them; 560
Da 4:8 before him I t. the dream, saying, ... 560
Da 7:1 and t. the sum of the matters. 560
Da 7:16 So he t. me, and made me know the.... 560
Da 8:26 the vision...which was t. is true: 560
Jon 1:10 the Lord, because he had t. them. 5046
Hab 1:5 not believe, though it be t. you.......... 5608
Zec 10:2 a lie, and have t. false dreams;.......... 1696
Mt 8:33 into the city, and t. every thing,.......... *518*
Mt 12:48 and said unto him that t. him,............ *2036*
Mt 14:12 buried it, and went and t. Jesus........... *518*
Mt 18:31 **t. unto their lord all that was done.** .*1285*
Mt 24:25 **Behold, I have t. you before.** *4280*
Mt 26:13 **done, be t. for a memorial of her.** ..*2980*
Mt 28:7 shall ye see him: lo, I have t. you. *2036*
Mk 5:14 t. it in the city, and in the country. *312*
Mk 5:16 they that saw it t. them how it.......... *1334*
Mk 5:33 him, and t. him all the truth. *2036*
Mk 6:30 t. him all things, both what they.......... *518*
Mk 9:12 he answered and t. them, **Elias** *2036*
Mk 16:10 t. them that had been with him, ... *518*
Mk 16:13 they went and t. it unto the residue: *518*
Lu 1:45 which were t. her from the Lord........ *2980*
Lu 2:17 was t. them concerning this child. *2980*
Lu 2:18 were t. them by the shepherds.......... *2980*
Lu 2:20 and seen, as it was t. unto them......... *2980*
Lu 8:20 it was t. him by certain which said, ... *518*
Lu 8:34 went and t. it in the city and in the...... *518*
Lu 8:36 which saw it t. them by what means *518*
Lu 9:10 t. him all that they had done. *1334*
Lu 9:36 and t. no man in those days any of *518*
Lu 13:1 some that t. him of the Galilaeans,....... *518*
Lu 18:37 they t. him, that Jesus of Nazareth *518*
Lu 24:9 t. all these things unto the eleven,....... *518*
Lu 24:10 t. these things unto the apostles. *3004*
Lu 24:35 t. what things were done in the *1834*
Joh 3:12 **If I have t. you earthly things,**....... *2036*
Joh 4:29 t. me all things that ever I did:.......... *2036*
Joh 4:39 He t. me all that ever I did.............. *2036*
Joh 4:51 and t. him, saying, Thy son liveth......... *518*
Joh 5:15 and t. the Jews that it was Jesus, ... *312*
Joh 8:40 **a man that hath t. you the truth,**.. *2980*
Joh 9:27 I have t. you already, and ye did........ *2036*
Joh 10:25 them, **I t. you, and ye believed**....... *2036*
Joh 11:46 and t. them what things Jesus had...... *2036*
Joh 14:2 **were not so, I would have t. you.** .. *2036*
Joh 14:29 **have t. you before it come to.** *2046*
Joh 16:4 **But these things have I t. you,**....... *2980*
Joh 16:4 **remember that I t. you of them**..... *2036*
Joh 18:8 **I have t. you that I am he:** *2036*
Joh 20:18 t. the disciples that she had seen......... *518*
Ac 5:22 the prison, they returned, and t. *518*
Ac 5:25 Then came one and t. them, saying,..... *518*
Ac 9:6 **be t. thee what thou must do.**........ *2980*
Ac 12:14 t. how Peter stood before the gate. *518*
Ac 16:36 keeper of the prison t. this saying......... *518*
Ac 16:38 serjeants t. these words unto the *312*
Ac 22:10 **it shall be t. thee of all things** *2980*
Ac 22:26 he went and t. the chief captain,.......... *518*
Ac 23:16 entered into the castle, and t. Paul. *518*
Ac 23:30 it was t. me how that the Jews.......... *3377*
Ac 27:25 it shall be even as it was t. me.......... *2980*
2Co 7:7 when he t. us your earnest desire, ... *312*
2Co 13:2 I t. you before, and foretell you, ... *4280*
Ga 5:21 as I have also t. you in time past, ... *4277*
Php 3:18 walk of whom I have t. you often,...... *3004*
1Th 3:4 we t. you before that we should *4302*
2Th 2:5 with you, I t. you these things? *3004*
Jude 18 that they t. you there should be......... *3004*

TOLERABLE

Mt 10:15 **It shall be more t. for the land of**... *414*
Mt 11:22 **It shall be more t. for Tyre and**...... *414*
Mt 11:24 **it shall be more t. for the land of**... *414*
Mk 6:11 **It shall be more t. for Sodom and**... *414*
Lu 10:12 **it shall be more t. in that day for**... *414*
Lu 10:14 **it shall be more t. for Tyre and** *414*

TOLL

Ezr 4:13 then will they not pay t., tribute, ... 4061
Ezr 4:20 t., tribute, and custom, was paid........ 4061
Ezr 7:24 it shall not be lawful to impose t., ... 4061

TOMB See also TOMBS.

Job 21:32 grave, and shall remain in the t.......... 1430
Mt 27:60 laid it in his own new t., which he...... *3419*
Mk 6:29 up his corpse, and laid it in a t.. .... *3419*

TOMBS

Mt 8:28 with devils, coming out of the t., ... *3419*
Mt 23:29 **ye build the t. of the prophets,**...... *5028*
Mk 5:2 there met him out of the t. a man...... *3419*
Mk 5:3 had his dwelling among the t.: and...... *3419*
Mk 5:5 and in the t., crying, and cutting........ *3418*
Lu 8:27 abode in any house, but in the t......... *3418*

TO-MORROW See MORROW.

TONGS

Ex 25:38 t. thereof, and the snuffdishes 4457
Nu 4:9 and his t., and his snuffdishes,........... 4457
1Ki 7:49 and the lamps, and the t. of gold,....... 4457
2Ch 4:21 the lamps, and the t., made he of 4457
Isa 6:6 which he had taken with the t. 4457
Isa 44:12 smith with the t. both worketh in....... 4621

TONGUE See also DOUBLETONGUED; TONGUES.

Ge 10:5 every one after his t., after their 3956
Ex 4:10 slow of speech, and of a slow t.......... 3956
Ex 11:7 Israel shall not a dog move his t., ... 3956
De 28:49 whose t. thou shalt not understand: 3956
Jos 10:21 none moved his t. against any of........ 3956
Jg 7:5 lappeth of the water with his t.,......... 3956
2Sa 23:2 by me, and his word was in my t.. 3956
Ezr 4:7 letter was written in the Syrian t., ... 762
Ezr 4:7 and interpreted in the Syrian t.. 762
Es 7:4 bondwomen, I had held my t.,........... 2790
Job 5:21 be hid from the scourge of the t. 3956
Job 6:24 Teach me, and I will hold my t.......... 2790
Job 6:30 Is there iniquity in my t.? cannot........ 3956
Job 13:19 if I hold my t., I shall give up the 2790
Job 15:5 thou choosest the t. of the crafty. 3956
Job 20:12 though he hide it under his t.;........... 3956
Job 20:16 asps: the viper's t. shall slay him. 3956
Job 27:4 wickedness, nor my t. utter deceit. 3956
Job 29:10 their t. cleaved to the roof of their..... 3956
Job 33:2 my t. hath spoken in my mouth. 3956
Job 41:1 or his t. with a cord which thou 3956
Ps 5:9 sepulchre; they flatter with their t.. 3956
Ps 10:7 under his t. is mischief and vanity. 3956
Ps 12:3 the t. that speaketh proud things:....... 3956
Ps 12:4 said, With our t. will we prevail: 3956
Ps 15:3 He that backbiteth not with his t., ... 3956
Ps 22:15 my t. cleaveth to my jaws; and thou... 3956
Ps 34:13 Keep thy t. from evil, and thy lips...... 3956
Ps 35:28 And my t. shall speak of thy 3956
Ps 37:30 and his t. talketh of judgment. 3956
Ps 39:1 my ways, that I sin not with my t. 3956
Ps 39:3 burned: then spake I with my t.,........ 3956
Ps 45:1 my t. is the pen of a ready writer. 3956
Ps 50:19 to evil, and thy t. frameth deceit........ 3956
Ps 51:14 my t. shall sing aloud of thy 3956
Ps 52:2 Thy t. deviseth mischiefs; like a......... 3956
Ps 52:4 words, O thou deceitful t.................. 3956
Ps 57:4 arrows, and their t. a sharp sword. 3956
Ps 64:3 Who whet their t. like a sword, and.... 3956
Ps 64:8 shall make their own t. to fall upon..... 3956
Ps 66:17 and he was extolled with my t.. 3956
Ps 68:23 and the t. of thy dogs in the same...... 3956
Ps 71:24 My t. also shall talk of thy............... 3956
Ps 73:9 their t. walketh through the earth....... 3956
Ps 109:2 spoken against me with a lying t.. 3956
Ps 119:172 My t. shall speak of thy word: for...... 3956
Ps 120:2 lying lips, and from a deceitful t.. 3956
Ps 120:3 be done unto thee, thou false t.?........ 3956
Ps 126:2 laughter, and our t. with singing:......... 3956
Ps 137:6 let my t. cleave to the roof of my 3956
Ps 139:4 For there is not a word in my t., ... 3956
Pr 6:17 A proud look, a lying t., and hands..... 3956
Pr 6:24 of the t. of a strange woman. 3956
Pr 10:20 t. of the just is as choice silver:......... 3956
Pr 10:31 but the froward t. shall be cut out. 3956
Pr 12:18 but the t. of the wise is health. 3956
Pr 12:19 but a lying t. is but for a moment......... 3956
Pr 15:2 The t. of the wise useth knowledge.... 3956
Pr 15:4 A wholesome t. is a tree of life: but ... 3956
Pr 16:1 answer of the t., is from the Lord...... 3956
Pr 17:4 a liar giveth ear to a naughty t.. 3956
Pr 17:20 a perverse t. falleth into mischief. 3956
Pr 18:21 and life are in the power of the t.: 3956
Pr 21:6 lying t. is a vanity tossed to and fro.... 3956
Pr 21:23 keepeth his mouth and his t. 3956
Pr 25:15 and a soft t. breaketh the bone.......... 3956
Pr 25:23 angry countenance a backbiting t.. 3956
Pr 26:28 A lying t. hateth those that are.......... 3956
Pr 28:23 than he that flattereth with the t.. 3956
Pr 31:26 and in her t. is the law of kindness..... 3956
Ca 4:11 honey and milk are under thy t.;........ 3956
Isa 3:8 their t. and their doings are against 3956
Isa 11:15 destroy the t. of the Egyptian sea;..... 3956
Isa 28:11 and another t. will he speak to this..... 3956
Isa 30:27 and his t. as a devouring fire:........... 3956
Isa 32:4 the t. of the stammerers shall be 3956
Isa 33:19 of a stammering t., that thou canst..... 3956
Isa 35:6 hart, and the t. of the dumb sing: 3956
Isa 41:17 none, and their t. faileth for thirst, ... 3956
Isa 45:23 knee shall bow, every t. shall swear. .. 3956
Isa 50:4 hath given me the t. of the learned..... 3956
Isa 54:17 every t. that shall rise against thee..... 3956
Isa 57:4 a wide mouth, and draw out the t.? 3956
Isa 59:3 your t. hath muttered perverseness..... 3956
Jer 9:5 have taught their t. to speak lies,....... 3956
Jer 9:8 Their t. is as an arrow shot out; it 3956
Jer 18:18 and let us smite him with the t., ... 3956
La 4:4 t. of the sucking child cleaveth to....... 3956
Eze 3:26 make thy t. cleave to the roof of thy .. 3956
Da 1:4 and the t. of the Chaldeans............... 3956
Ho 7:16 by the sword for the rage of their t.... 3956
Am 6:10 Then shall he say, Hold thy t. 2013
Mic 6:12 their t. is deceitful in their mouth. 3956
Hab 1:13 holdest thy t. when the wicked.......... 2790
Zep 3:13 shall a deceitful t. be found in............ 3956
Zec 14:12 their t. shall consume away in their 3956
Mk 7:33 and he spit, and touched his t.;.......... *1100*
Mk 7:35 and the string of his t. was loosed,...... *1100*
Lu 1:64 and his t. loosed, and he spake, and.... *1100*
Lu 16:24 **finger in water, and cool my t.** *1100*
Joh 5:2 called in the Hebrew t. Bethesda, ... *1447*
Ac 1:19 field is called in their proper t.,.......... *1258*
Ac 2:8 hear we every man in our own t.. .... *1258*
Ac 2:26 heart rejoice, and my t. was glad; *1100*
Ac 21:40 spake unto them in the Hebrew t., ... *1258*
Ac 22:2 he spake in the Hebrew t. to them,.... *1258*
Ac 26:14 and saying in the Hebrew t., **Saul,** *1258*
Ro 14:11 and every t. shall confess to God. *1100*
1Co 14:2 he that speaketh in an unknown t......... *1100*
1Co 14:4 He that speaketh in an unknown t. *1100*
1Co 14:9 except ye utter by the t. words.......... *1100*
1Co 14:13 him that speaketh in an unknown t. *1100*
1Co 14:14 For if I pray in an unknown t., my *1100*
1Co 14:19 thousand words in an unknown t.. .... *1100*
1Co 14:26 a psalm, hath a doctrine, hath a t., ... *1100*
1Co 14:27 If any man speak in an unknown t., ... *1100*
Php 2:11 every t. should confess that Jesus *1100*
Jas 1:26 be religious, and bridleth not his t., ... *1100*
Jas 3:5 Even so the t. is a little member, ... *1100*
Jas 3:6 the t. is a fire, a world of iniquity:...... *1100*
Jas 3:6 so is the t. among our members, ... *1100*
Jas 3:8 But the t. can no man tame; it is *1100*
1Pe 3:10 let him refrain his t. from evil,........... *1100*
1Jo 3:18 let us not love in word, neither in t.;.. *1100*
Re 5:9 out of every kindred, and t., and........ *1100*
Re 9:11 name in the Hebrew t. is Abaddon, ... *1447*
Re 9:11 the Greek t. hath his name Apollyon.........
Re 14:6 every nation, and kindred, and t.,....... *1100*
Re 16:16 in the Hebrew t. Armageddon. *1447*

TONGUES

Ge 10:20, 31 their families, after their t., ... 3956
Ps 31:20 in a pavilion from the strife of t.. 3956
Ps 55:9 Destroy, O Lord, and divide their t. ... 3956
Ps 78:36 they lied unto him with their t.. 3956

Ps 140:3 sharpened their **t.** like a serpent: 3956
Isa 66:18 that I will gather all nations and **t.**; 3956
Jer 9:3 they bend their **t.** like their bow for..... 3956
Jer 23:31 that use their **t.**, and say, He saith..... 3956
Mk 16:17 **they shall speak with new t.**;........ *1100*
Ac 2:3 there appeared unto them cloven **t.** *1100*
Ac 2:4 began to speak with other **t.**, as the ... *1100*
Ac 2:11 we do hear them speak in our **t.** the... *1100*
Ac 10:46 For they heard them speak with **t.**, ... *1100*
Ac 19:6 they spake with **t.**, and prophesied..... *1100*
Ro 3:13 with their **t.** they have used deceit; *1100*
1Co 12:10 spirits; to another divers kinds of **t.**;... *1100*
1Co 12:10 to another the interpretation of **t.**: *1100*
1Co 12:28 governments, diversities of **t.**........... *1100*
1Co 12:30 do all speak with **t.**? do all............... *1100*
1Co 13:1 Though I speak with the **t.** of men *1100*
1Co 13:8 fail; whether there be **t.**, they shall..... *1100*
1Co 14:5 I would that ye all spake with **t.**,........ *1100*
1Co 14:5 than he that speaketh with **t.**,............ *1100*
1Co 14:6 if I come unto you speaking with **t.**,..... *1100*
1Co 14:18 I speak with **t.** more than ye all: *1100*
1Co 14:21 With men of other **t.** and other lips..... *2084*
1Co 14:22 Wherefore **t.** are for a sign, not to *1100*
1Co 14:23 and all speak with **t.**, and there.......... *1100*
1Co 14:39 and forbid not to speak with **t.**........... *1100*
Re 7:9 kindreds, and people, and **t.**, stood..... *1100*
Re 10:11 many peoples, and nations, and **t.**,...... *1100*
Re 11:9 of the people and kindreds and **t.** *1100*
Re 13:7 all kindreds, and **t.**, and nations. *1100*
Re 16:10 and they gnawed their **t.** for pain, ... *1100*
Re 17:15 and multitudes, and nations, and **t.**. *1100*

TOO
Ge 18:14 Is any thing **t.** hard for the Lord? ....
Ex 12:4 the household be **t.** little for the lamb,.......
Ex 18:18 for this thing is **t.** heavy for thee;............
Ex 36:7 the work to make it, and **t.** much....... 3498
Nu 11:14 alone, because it is **t.** heavy for me. ....
Nu 16:3 Ye take **t.** much upon you, seeing ....
Nu 16:7 ye take **t.** much upon you, ye sons............
Nu 22:6 people; for they are **t.** mighty for me: ....
De 1:17 the cause that is **t.** hard for you, bring......
De 2:36 was not one city **t.** strong for us:............
De 12:21 his name there be **t.** far from thee, ... 7368
De 14:24 And if the way be **t.** long for thee, so.......
De 14:24 or if the place be **t.** far from thee,...........
De 17:8 arise a matter **t.** hard for thee in.............
Jos 17:15 mount Ephraim be **t.** narrow for thee. ....
Jos 19:9 of Judah was **t.** much for them:................
Jos 19:47 of Dan went out **t.** little for them: ....
Jos 22:17 Is the iniquity of Peor **t.** little for us, ...
Jg 7:2 people that are with thee are **t.** many for...
Jg 7:4 The people are yet **t.** many; bring them ....
Jg 18:26 saw that they were **t.** strong for him, ...
Ru 1:12 for I am **t.** old to have an husband...........
2Sa 3:39 sons of Zeruiah be **t.** hard for me: ....
2Sa 10:11 If the Syrians be **t.** strong for me,...........
2Sa 10:11 children of Ammon be **t.** strong for...........
2Sa 12:8 and if that had been **t.** little, I would........
2Sa 22:18 me: for they were **t.** strong for me...........
1Ki 1:36 Lord God of my lord the king say so **t.**. ....
1Ki 8:64 **t.** little to receive the burnt offerings, ...
1Ki 12:28 It is **t.** much for you to go up to ....
1Ki 19:7 because the journey is **t.** great for thee. ....
2Ki 3:26 saw that the battle was **t.** sore for him,.....
2Ki 6:1 we dwell with thee is **t.** strait for us. ....
1Ch 19:12 If the Syrians be **t.** strong for me,...........
1Ch 19:12 children of Ammon be **t.** strong for...........
2Ch 29:34 But the priests were **t.** few, so that they...
Es 1:18 shall there arise **t.** much contempt...... 1767
Job 42:3 things **t.** wonderful for me, which I ....
Ps 18:17 me: for they were **t.** strong for me. ....
Ps 35:10 from him that is **t.** strong for him,............
Ps 38:4 heavy burden they are **t.** heavy for me......
Ps 73:16 to know this, it was **t.** painful for me; ....
Ps 131:1 matters, or in things **t.** high for me. ....
Ps 139:6 Such knowledge is **t.** wonderful for me; .....
Pr 24:7 Wisdom is **t.** high for a fool: he................
Pr 30:18 three things which are **t.** wonderful...........
Isa 49:19 shall even now be **t.** narrow by reason......
Isa 49:20 ears, The place is **t.** strait for me:............
Jer 32:17 and there is nothing **t.** hard for thee: ....
Jer 32:27 flesh: is there any thing **t.** hard for me?.....
Ac 17:22 all things ye are **t.** superstitious. *1174*

TOOK See also OVERTOOK; TOOKEST; UNDERTOOK.
Ge 2:15 And the Lord God **t.** the man, and 3947
Ge 2:21 and he **t.** one of his ribs, and........... 3947
Ge 3:6 she **t.** of the fruit thereof, and did...... 3947
Ge 4:19 And Lamech **t.** unto him two wives: ... 3947
Ge 5:24 and he was not; for God **t.** him.......... 3947
Ge 6:2 they **t.** them wives of all which they ... 3947
Ge 8:9 he put forth his hand, and **t.** her, ... 3947
Ge 8:20 **t.** of every clean beast, and of every... 3947
Ge 9:23 Shem and Japheth **t.** a garment, ... 3947
Ge 11:29 Abram and Nahor **t.** them wives: 3947
Ge 11:31 Terah **t.** Abram his son, and Lot.......... 3947
Ge 12:5 Abram **t.** Sarai his wife, and Lot 3947
Ge 14:11 And they **t.** all the goods of Sodom..... 3947
Ge 14:12 they **t.** Lot, Abram's brother's son, ... 3947
Ge 15:10 And he **t.** unto him all these, and....... 3947
Ge 16:3 Abram's wife **t.** Hagar her maid 3947
Ge 17:23 And Abraham **t.** Ishmael his son,......... 3947
Ge 18:8 he **t.** butter, and milk, and the calf 3947
Ge 20:2 king of Gerar sent, and **t.** Sarah.......... 3947
Ge 20:14 And Abimelech **t.** sheep, and oxen,...... 3947
Ge 21:14 and **t.** bread, and a bottle of water, ... 3947
Ge 21:21 mother **t.** him a wife out of the land ... 3947
Ge 21:27 And Abraham **t.** sheep and oxen, ... 3947
Ge 22:3 **t.** two of his young men with him....... 3947
Ge 22:6 Abraham **t.** the wood of the burnt 3947
Ge 22:6 he **t.** the fire in his hand, and a.......... 3947
Ge 22:10 and **t.** the knife to slay his son. 3947
Ge 22:13 and Abraham went and **t.** the ram, ... 3947
Ge 24:7 which **t.** me from my father's house,... 3947
Ge 24:10 the servant **t.** ten camels of the......... 3947
Ge 24:22 that the man **t.** a golden earring of..... 3947
Ge 24:61 the servant **t.** Rebekah, and went....... 3947
Ge 24:65 therefore she **t.** a vail, and covered 3947
Ge 24:67 and **t.** Rebekah, and she became......... 3947
Ge 25:1 Then again Abraham **t.** a wife, and..... 3947
Ge 25:20 old when he **t.** Rebekah to wife. 3947
Ge 25:26 his hand **t.** hold on Esau's heel: ....
Ge 26:34 old when he **t.** to wife Judith the......... 3947
Ge 27:15 Rebekah **t.** goodly raiment of her 3947
Ge 27:36 he **t.** away my birthright; and, ... 3947
Ge 28:9 and **t.** unto the wives which he had 3947
Ge 28:11 and he **t.** of the stones of that place, .. 3947
Ge 28:18 **t.** the stone that he had put for his..... 3947
Ge 29:23 that he **t.** Leah his daughter, and 3947
Ge 30:9 she **t.** Zilpah her maid, and gave 3947
Ge 30:37 Jacob **t.** him rods of green poplar, ... 3947
Ge 31:23 And he **t.** his brethren with him, ... 3947
Ge 31:45 And Jacob **t.** a stone, and set it up..... 3947
Ge 31:46 they **t.** stones, and made an heap:...... 3947
Ge 32:13 **t.** of that which came to his hand 3947
Ge 32:22 that night, and **t.** his two wives, ... 3947
Ge 32:23 And he **t.** them, and sent them over... 3947
Ge 33:11 And he urged him, and he **t.** it. 3947
Ge 34:2 he **t.** her, and lay with her, and......... 3947
Ge 34:25 **t.** each man his sword, and came 3947
Ge 34:26 **t.** Dinah out of Shechem's house, ... 3947
Ge 34:28 They **t.** their sheep, and their oxen, ... 3947
Ge 34:29 and their wives **t.** they captive,................
Ge 36:2 Esau **t.** his wives of the daughters....... 3947
Ge 36:6 And Esau **t.** his wives, and his sons,... 3947
Ge 37:24 they **t.** him, and cast him into a pit:.... 3947
Ge 37:31 they **t.** Joseph's coat, and killed a....... 3947
Ge 38:2 and he **t.** her, and went in unto her.... 3947
Ge 38:6 Judah **t.** a wife for Er his firstborn,..... 3947
Ge 38:28 the midwife **t.** and bound upon his 3947
Ge 39:20 And Joseph's master **t.** him, and 3947
Ge 40:11 I **t.** the grapes, and pressed them 3947
Ge 41:42 Pharaoh **t.** off his ring from his.......... 5493
Ge 42:24 and **t.** from them Simeon, and 3947
Ge 42:30 and **t.** us for spies of the country. 5414
Ge 43:15 And the men **t.** that present, and....... 3947
Ge 43:15 they **t.** double money in their hand, ... 3947
Ge 43:34 he **t.** and sent messes unto them 5375
Ge 44:11 **t.** down every man his sack to the 3381
Ge 46:1 Israel **t.** his journey with all that................
Ge 46:6 And they **t.** their cattle, and their....... 3947
Ge 47:2 And he **t.** some of his brethren,......... 3947
Ge 48:1 and he **t.** with him his two sons,........ 3947
Ge 48:13 And Joseph **t.** them both, Ephraim...... 3947
Ge 48:22 I **t.** out of the hand of the Amorite..... 3947
Ge 50:25 Joseph **t.** an oath of the children..............
Ex 2:1 and **t.** to wife a daughter of Levi....... 3947
Ex 2:3 she **t.** for him an ark of bulrushes, ... 3947
Ex 2:9 the woman **t.** the child, and nursed.... 3947
Ex 4:6 when he **t.** it out, behold, his hand..... 3318
Ex 4:20 Moses **t.** his wife and his sons,.......... 3947
Ex 4:20 Moses **t.** the rod of God in his hand. .. 3947
Ex 4:25 Then Zipporah **t.** a sharp stone,......... 3947
Ex 6:20 Amram **t.** him Jochebed his father's 3947
Ex 6:23 Aaron **t.** him Elisheba, daughter of 3947
Ex 6:25 Eleazar...**t.** him one of the daughters .. 3947
Ex 9:10 And they **t.** ashes of the furnace, ... 3947
Ex 10:19 wind, which **t.** away the locusts, ... 5375
Ex 12:34 the people **t.** their dough before it...... 5375
Ex 13:19 Moses **t.** the bones of Joseph with 3947
Ex 13:20 they **t.** their journey from Succoth, ...
Ex 13:22 **t.** not away the pillar of the cloud....... 4185
Ex 14:6 and **t.** his people with him:............... 3947
Ex 14:7 he **t.** six hundred chosen chariots 3947
Ex 14:25 And **t.** off their chariot wheels, ... 5493
Ex 15:20 Miriam...**t.** a timbrel in her hand; 3947
Ex 16:1 And they **t.** their journey from Elim, ...
Ex 17:12 they **t.** a stone, and put it under 3947
Ex 18:2 Moses' father in law, **t.** Zipporah,....... 3947
Ex 18:12 **t.** a burnt offering and sacrifices for 3947
Ex 24:6 Moses **t.** half of the blood, and put..... 3947
Ex 24:7 And he **t.** the book of the covenant, ... 3947
Ex 24:8 Moses **t.** the blood, and sprinkled it.... 3947
Ex 32:20 he **t.** the calf which they had made, ... 3947
Ex 33:7 And Moses **t.** the tabernacle, and....... 3947
Ex 34:4 and **t.** in his hand the two tables of..... 3947
Ex 34:34 **t.** the vail off, until he came out......... 5493
Ex 40:20 he **t.** and put the testimony into......... 3947
Le 6:4 that which he **t.** violently away,................
Le 8:10 And Moses **t.** the anointing oil, ... 3947
Le 8:15 Moses **t.** the blood, and put it upon.... 3947
Le 8:16 And he **t.** all the fat that was upon 3947
Le 8:23 Moses **t.** of the blood of it, and put 3947
Le 8:25 he **t.** the fat, and the rump, and all..... 3947
Le 8:26 he **t.** one unleavened cake, and a 3947
Le 8:28 Moses **t.** them from off their hands, ... 3947
Le 8:29 Moses **t.** the breast, and waved it...... 3947
Le 8:30 And Moses **t.** of the anointing oil, ... 3947
Le 9:15 and **t.** the goat, which was the sin...... 3947
Le 9:17 offering, and **t.** an handful thereof,...........
Le 10:1 **t.** either of them his censer, and........ 3947
Nu 1:17 And Moses and Aaron **t.** these men.... 3947
Nu 3:49 Moses **t.** the redemption money of..... 3947
Nu 3:50 Of the firstborn...**t.** he the money; 3947
Nu 7:6 Moses **t.** the wagons and the oxen, ... 3947
Nu 10:12 children of Israel **t.** their journeys..............
Nu 10:13 they first **t.** their journey according...........
Nu 11:25 **t.** of the spirit that was upon him,........ 680
Nu 16:1 of Peleth, sons of Reuben, **t.** men:..... 3947
Nu 16:18 And they **t.** every man his censer, ... 3947
Nu 16:39 Eleazar...**t.** the brasen censers, ... 3947
Nu 16:47 And Aaron **t.** as Moses commanded, ... 3947
Nu 17:9 looked, and **t.** every man his rod........ 3947
Nu 20:9 Moses **t.** the rod from before the....... 3947
Nu 21:1 and **t.** some of them prisoners. 3947
Nu 21:25 And Israel **t.** all these cities: and........ 3947
Nu 21:32 and they **t.** the villages thereof, ... 3920
Nu 22:41 morning, that Balak **t.** Balaam,........... 3947
Nu 23:7 And he **t.** up his parable, and said, ... 5375
Nu 23:11 I **t.** thee to curse mine enemies, ... 3947
Nu 23:18 And he **t.** up his parable, and said, ... 5375
Nu 24:3, 15, 20 he **t.** up his parable, and said, .. 5375
Nu 24:21 and **t.** up his parable, and said, ... 5375
Nu 24:23 And he **t.** up his parable, and said, ... 5375
Nu 25:7 and **t.** a javelin in his hand: 3947
Nu 27:22 and he **t.** Joshua, and set him........... 3947
Nu 31:9 **t.** all the women of Midian captives,..........
Nu 31:9 and **t.** the spoil of all their cattle, ...
Nu 31:11 **t.** all the spoil, and all the prey, ... 3947
Nu 31:27 them that **t.** the war upon them......... 8610
Nu 31:47 Moses **t.** one portion of fifty, both...... 3947
Nu 31:51, 54 Moses and Eleazar...**t.** the gold..... 3947
Nu 32:39 Manasseh went to Gilead, and **t.** it, ... 3920
Nu 32:41 and **t.** the small towns thereof, ... 3920
Nu 32:42 And Nobah went and **t.** Kenath,......... 3920
Nu 33:12 they **t.** their journey out of the 5265
De 1:15 So I **t.** the chief of your tribes,.......... 3947
De 1:23 and I **t.** twelve men of you, one of...... 3947
De 1:25 And they **t.** of the fruit of the land 3947
De 2:1 **t.** our journey into the wilderness........ 5265
De 2:34 we **t.** all his cities at that time, ... 3920
De 2:35 cattle we **t.** for a prey unto ourselves, ...
De 2:35 the spoil of the cities which we **t.**........ 3920
De 3:4 we **t.** all his cities at that time, ... 3920
De 3:4 was not a city which we **t.** not.......... 3947
De 3:7 cities, we **t.** for a prey to ourselves.........
De 3:8 we **t.** at That time out of the hand 3947
De 3:14 son of Manasseh **t.** all the country...... 3947
De 9:17 I **t.** the two tables, and cast them 8610

De	9:21	I **t.** your sin, the calf which ye had	3947
De	10:6	children of Israel **t.** their journey	
De	22:14	I **t.** this woman, and when I came	3947
De	24:3	die, which **t.** her to be his wife;	3947
De	29:8	we **t.** their land, and gave it for an	3947
Jos	2:4	woman **t.** the two men, and hid	3947
Jos	3:6	they **t.** up the ark of the covenant,	5375
Jos	4:8	**t.** up twelve stones out of the midst	5375
Jos	4:20	stones, which they **t.** out of Jordan,	3947
Jos	6:12	priests **t.** up the ark of the Lord.	5375
Jos	6:20	before him, and they **t.** the city.	3920
Jos	7:1	of Judah, **t.** of the accursed thing:	3947
Jos	7:17	he **t.** the family of the Zarhites:	3920
Jos	7:21	then I coveted them, and **t.** them;	3947
Jos	7:23	**t.** them out of the midst of the tent,	3947
Jos	7:24	Joshua, and all Israel...**t.** Achan	3947
Jos	8:12	he **t.** about five thousand men,	3947
Jos	8:19	entered into the city, and **t.** it,	3920
Jos	8:23	And the king of Ai they **t.** alive,	8610
Jos	8:27	Israel **t.** for a prey unto themselves,	
Jos	9:4	**t.** old sacks upon their asses, and	3947
Jos	9:12	bread we **t.** hot for our provision	
Jos	9:14	men **t.** of their victuals, and asked	3947
Jos	10:27	they **t.** them down off the trees,	3381
Jos	10:28	Joshua **t.** Makkedah, and smote it	3920
Jos	10:32	**t.** it on the second day, and smote it	3920
Jos	10:35	they **t.** it on that day, and smote it	3920
Jos	10:37	they **t.** it, and smote it with the	3920
Jos	10:39	And he **t.** it, and the king thereof,	3920
Jos	11:10	time turned back, and **t.** Nazor,	3920
Jos	11:14	Israel **t.** for a prey unto themselves;	
Jos	11:16	So Joshua **t.** all that land, the	3947
Jos	11:17	all their kings he **t.**, and smote	3920
Jos	11:19	Gibeon: all other they **t.** in battle.	3947
Jos	11:23	So Joshua **t.** the whole land,	3947
Jos	15:17	Kenaz, the brother of Caleb, **t.** it:	3920
Jos	16:4	and Ephraim, **t.** their inheritance.	
Jos	19:47	to fight against Leshem, and **t.** it,	3920
Jos	24:3	I **t.** your father Abraham from	3947
Jos	24:26	**t.** a great stone, and set it up there	3947
Jg	1:13	Caleb's younger brother, **t.** it:	3920
Jg	1:18	Judah **t.** Gaza with the coast	3920
Jg	3:6	**t.** their daughters to be their wives,	3947
Jg	3:21	**t.** the dagger from his right thigh,	3947
Jg	3:25	therefore they **t.** a key, and opened	3947
Jg	3:28	**t.** the fords of Jordan toward Moab,	3920
Jg	4:21	Jael Heber's wife **t.** a nail of the	3947
Jg	4:21	**t.** an hammer in her hand, and	7760
Jg	5:19	Megiddo; they **t.** no gain of money.	3947
Jg	6:27	Gideon **t.** ten men of his servants,	3947
Jg	7:8	people **t.** victuals in their hand,	3947
Jg	7:24	**t.** the waters unto Beth-barah	3920
Jg	7:25	**t.** two princes of the Midianites,	3920
Jg	8:12	**t.** the two kings of Midian, Zebah	3920
Jg	8:16	And he **t.** the elders of the city,	3947
Jg	8:21	**t.** away the ornaments that were	3947
Jg	9:43	he **t.** the people, and divided them	3947
Jg	9:45	he **t.** the city, and slew the people	3920
Jg	9:48	Abimelech **t.** an axe in his hand,	3947
Jg	9:48	a bough from the trees, and **t.** it,	5375
Jg	9:50	encamped against Thebez, and **t.** it	3920
Jg	11:13	Israel **t.** away my land, when they	3947
Jg	11:15	Israel **t.** not away the land of Moab,	3947
Jg	12:5	the Gileadites **t.** the passages of	3920
Jg	12:6	Then they **t.** him, and slew him at	270
Jg	12:9	**t.** in thirty daughters from abroad	935
Jg	13:19	So Manoah **t.** a kid with a meat	3947
Jg	14:9	And he **t.** thereof in his hands, and	7287
Jg	14:19	men of them, and **t.** their spoil,	3947
Jg	15:4	**t.** firebrands, and turned tail to	3947
Jg	15:15	and put forth his hand, and **t.** it,	3947
Jg	16:3	**t.** the doors of the gate of the city,	270
Jg	16:12	Delilah therefore **t.** new ropes,	3947
Jg	16:21	the Philistines **t.** him, and put out	270
Jg	16:29	Samson **t.** hold of the two middle	
Jg	16:31	and **t.** him, and brought him up	5375
Jg	17:2	behold, the silver is with me: I **t.** it	3947
Jg	17:4	his mother **t.** two hundred shekels	3947
Jg	18:17	in thither, and **t.** the graven image,	3947
Jg	18:20	he **t.** the ephod, and the teraphim,	3947
Jg	18:27	**t.** the things which Micah had made,	3947
Jg	19:1	who **t.** to him a concubine out of	3947
Jg	19:15	no man that **t.** them into his house	622
Jg	19:25	the man **t.** his concubine, and	2388
Jg	19:28	the man **t.** her up upon an ass,	3947
Jg	19:29	he **t.** a knife, and laid hold on his	3947
Jg	20:6	And I **t.** my concubine, and cut her	270
Jg	21:23	**t.** them wives, according to their	5375
Ru	1:4	**t.** them wives of the women of Moab;	5375
Ru	2:18	she **t.** it up, and went into the city:	5375
Ru	4:2	he **t.** ten men of the elders of the	3947
Ru	4:13	So Boaz **t.** Ruth, and she was his	3947
Ru	4:16	Naomi **t.** the child, and laid it in	3947
1Sa	1:24	him, she **t.** him up with her,	5927
1Sa	2:14	brought up...priest **t.** for himself.	3947
1Sa	5:1	the Philistines **t.** the ark of God,	3947
1Sa	5:2	Philistines **t.** the ark of God, they	3947
1Sa	5:3	they **t.** Dagon, and set him in his	3947
1Sa	6:10	**t.** two milch kine, and tied them	3947
1Sa	6:12	the kine **t.** the straight way to the	
1Sa	6:15	the Levites **t.** down the ark of the	3381
1Sa	7:9	And Samuel **t.** a sucking lamb,	3947
1Sa	7:12	Then Samuel **t.** a stone, and set it	3947
1Sa	8:3	aside after lucre, and **t.** bribes,	3947
1Sa	9:22	Samuel **t.** Saul and his servant,	3947
1Sa	9:24	And the cook **t.** up the shoulder,	7311
1Sa	10:1	Then Samuel **t.** a vial of oil, and	3947
1Sa	11:7	And he **t.** a yoke of oxen, and hewed	3947
1Sa	14:32	**t.** sheep, and oxen, and calves, and	3947
1Sa	14:47	Saul **t.** the kingdom over Israel,	3920
1Sa	14:52	valiant man, he **t.** him unto him.	622
1Sa	15:8	**t.** Agag the king of the Amalekites	8610
1Sa	15:21	But the people **t.** of the spoil,	3947
1Sa	16:13	Then Samuel **t.** the horn of oil,	3947
1Sa	16:20	Jesse **t.** an ass laden with bread,	3947
1Sa	16:23	that David **t.** an harp, and played	3947
1Sa	17:20	and **t.**, and went, as Jesse had	5375
1Sa	17:34	bear, and **t.** a lamb out of the flock:	5375
1Sa	17:40	And he **t.** his staff in his hand,	3947
1Sa	17:49	and **t.** thence a stone, and slang it,	3947
1Sa	17:51	**t.** his sword, and drew it out of the	3947
1Sa	17:54	David **t.** the head of the Philistine,	3947
1Sa	17:57	Abner **t.** him, and brought him	3947
1Sa	18:2	Saul **t.** him that day, and would	3947
1Sa	19:13	Michal **t.** an image, and laid it in	3947
1Sa	24:2	Saul **t.** three thousand chosen men	3947
1Sa	25:18	haste, and **t.** two hundred loaves,	3947
1Sa	25:43	David also **t.** Ahinoam of Jezreel:	3947
1Sa	26:12	David **t.** the spear and the cruse of	3947
1Sa	27:9	**t.** away the sheep, and the oxen,	3947
1Sa	28:24	and **t.** flour, and kneaded it, and did	3947
1Sa	30:20	David **t.** all the flocks and the herds,	3947
1Sa	31:4	Therefore Saul **t.** a sword, and fell	3947
1Sa	31:12	**t.** the body of Saul and the bodies	3947
1Sa	31:13	they **t.** their bones, and buried them	3947
2Sa	1:10	I **t.** the crown that was upon his	3947
2Sa	1:11	Then David **t.** hold on his clothes,	
2Sa	2:8	**t.** Ish-bosheth the son of Saul,	3947
2Sa	2:32	they **t.** up Asahel, and buried him	5375
2Sa	3:15	and **t.** her from her husband, even	3947
2Sa	3:27	Joab **t.** him aside in the gate to speak	
2Sa	3:36	And all the people **t.** notice of it,	5384
2Sa	4:4	and his nurse **t.** him up, and fled:	5375
2Sa	4:7	beheaded him, and **t.** his head,	3947
2Sa	4:10	I **t.** hold of him, and slew him in	
2Sa	4:12	they **t.** the head of Ish-bosheth,	3947
2Sa	5:7	David **t.** the strong hold of Zion:	3920
2Sa	5:13	David **t.** him more concubines and	3947
2Sa	6:6	to the ark of God, and **t.** hold of it;	
2Sa	7:8	I **t.** thee from the sheepcote, from	3947
2Sa	7:15	as I **t.** it from Saul, whom I put	5493
2Sa	8:1	David **t.** Metheg-ammah out of	3947
2Sa	8:4	And David **t.** from him a thousand	3920
2Sa	8:7	David **t.** the shields of gold that	3947
2Sa	8:8	king David **t.** exceeding much brass.	3947
2Sa	10:4	Hanun **t.** David's servants,	3947
2Sa	11:4	David sent messengers, and **t.** her;	3947
2Sa	12:4	but **t.** the poor man's lamb, and	3947
2Sa	12:26	of Ammon, and **t.** the royal city.	3920
2Sa	12:29	and fought against it, and **t.** it	3920
2Sa	12:30	he **t.** their king's crown from off	3947
2Sa	13:8	And she **t.** flour, and kneaded it,	3947
2Sa	13:9	she **t.** a pan, and poured out before	3947
2Sa	13:10	Tamar **t.** the cakes which she had	3947
2Sa	13:11	he **t.** hold of her, and said unto	
2Sa	15:5	forth his hand, and **t.** him, and	2388
2Sa	17:19	woman **t.** and spread a covering	3947
2Sa	18:14	And he **t.** three darts in his hand.	3947
2Sa	18:17	And they **t.** Absalom, and cast him	3947
2Sa	20:3	the king **t.** the ten women his	3947
2Sa	20:9	Joab **t.** Amasa by the beard with	270
2Sa	20:10	Amasa **t.** no heed to the sword that	
2Sa	21:8	the king **t.** the two sons of Rizpah	3947
2Sa	21:10	the daughter of Aiah **t.** sackcloth,	3947
2Sa	21:12	David went and **t.** the bones of Saul	3947
2Sa	22:17	He sent from above, he **t.** me; he	3947
2Sa	23:16	and **t.** it, and brought it to David:	5375
1Ki	1:39	the priest **t.** an horn of oil out of	3947
1Ki	3:1	and **t.** Pharaoh's daughter, and	3947
1Ki	3:20	and **t.** my son from beside me,	3947
1Ki	4:15	he also **t.** Basmath the daughter of	3947
1Ki	8:3	and the priests **t.** up the ark.	5375
1Ki	11:18	and they **t.** men with them out of	3947
1Ki	12:28	Whereupon the king **t.** counsel,	
1Ki	13:29	the prophet **t.** up the carcase of	5375
1Ki	14:26	he **t.** away the treasures of the	3947
1Ki	14:26	king's house; he even **t.** away all:	3947
1Ki	14:26	he **t.** away all the shields of gold	3947
1Ki	15:12	he **t.** away the sodomites out of	5674
1Ki	15:18	Then Asa **t.** all the silver and the	3947
1Ki	15:22	they **t.** away the stones of Ramah,	5375
1Ki	16:31	he **t.** to wife Jezebel the daughter	3947
1Ki	17:19	And he **t.** him out of her bosom,	3947
1Ki	17:23	Elijah **t.** the child, and brought him	3947
1Ki	18:4	Obadiah **t.** an hundred prophets,	3947
1Ki	18:10	he **t.** an oath of the kingdom and	
1Ki	18:26	they **t.** the bullock which was	3947
1Ki	18:31	Elijah **t.** twelve stones, according	3947
1Ki	18:40	they **t.** them: and Elijah brought	8610
1Ki	19:21	**t.** a yoke of oxen, and slew them,	3947
1Ki	20:34	which my father **t.** from thy father,	3947
1Ki	20:41	**t.** the ashes away from his face;	
1Ki	22:46	father Asa, he **t.** out of the land	1197
2Ki	2:8	Elijah **t.** his mantle, and wrapped	3947
2Ki	2:12	and he **t.** hold of his own clothes, and	
2Ki	2:13	He **t.** up also the mantle of Elijah	7311
2Ki	2:14	he **t.** the mantle of Elijah that fell	3947
2Ki	3:26	he **t.** with him seven hundred men	3947
2Ki	3:27	**t.** his eldest son that should have	3947
2Ki	4:37	and **t.** up her son, and went out	5375
2Ki	5:5	**t.** with him ten talents of silver,	3947
2Ki	5:24	he **t.** them from their hand, and	3947
2Ki	6:7	And he put out his hand, and **t.** it.	3947
2Ki	6:8	**t.** counsel with his servants,	
2Ki	7:14	**t.** therefore two chariot horses;	3947
2Ki	8:9	him, and **t.** a present with him,	3947
2Ki	8:15	that he **t.** a thick cloth, and dipped	3947
2Ki	9:13	**t.** every man his garment, and put	3947
2Ki	10:7	they **t.** the king's sons, and slew	3947
2Ki	10:14	And they **t.** them alive, and slew	8610
2Ki	10:15	he **t.** him up to him into the chariot.	5927
2Ki	10:31	But Jehu **t.** no heed to walk in the law	
2Ki	11:2	**t.** Joash the son of Ahaziah, and	3947
2Ki	11:4	**t.** an oath of them in the house of	
2Ki	11:9	**t.** every man his men that were to	3947
2Ki	11:19	And he **t.** the rulers over hundreds,	3947
2Ki	12:9	But Jehoiada the priest **t.** a chest,	3947
2Ki	12:17	fought against Gath, and **t.** it:	3920
2Ki	12:18	Jehoash...**t.** all the hallowed	3947
2Ki	13:15	he **t.** unto him bow and arrows.	3947
2Ki	13:18	Take the arrows. And he **t.** them.	3947
2Ki	13:25	Jehoash...**t.** again out of the hand	3947
2Ki	14:7	**t.** Selah by war, and called the	8610
2Ki	14:13	king of Israel **t.** Amaziah king of	8610
2Ki	14:14	And he **t.** all the gold and silver,	3947
2Ki	14:21	all the people of Judah **t.** Azariah,	3947
2Ki	15:29	king of Assyria, and **t.** Ijon,	3947
2Ki	16:8	Ahaz **t.** the silver and gold that was	3947
2Ki	16:9	up against Damascus, and **t.** it,	8610
2Ki	16:17	**t.** down the sea from off the brasen	3381
2Ki	17:6	the king of Assyria **t.** Samaria,	3920
2Ki	18:10	at the end of three years they **t.** it:	3920
2Ki	18:13	cities of Judah, and **t.** them.	8610
2Ki	20:7	And they **t.** and laid it on the boil,	3947
2Ki	23:11	**t.** away the horses that the kings	7673
2Ki	23:16	**t.** the bones out of the sepulchres,	3947
2Ki	23:19	Josiah **t.** away, and did to them	5493
2Ki	23:30	the people of the land **t.** Jehoahaz	3947
2Ki	23:34	Jehoiakim, and **t.** Jehoahaz away:	3947
2Ki	24:12	the king of Babylon **t.** him in the	3947
2Ki	25:6	So they **t.** the king, and brought	8610
2Ki	25:14	they ministered, **t.** they away.	3947
2Ki	25:15	the captain of the guard **t.** away	3947
2Ki	25:18	the captain of the guard **t.** Seraiah	3947
2Ki	25:19	And out of the city he **t.** an officer	3947
2Ki	25:20	captain of the guard **t.** these,	3947
1Ch	2:19	Caleb **t.** unto him Ephrath, which	3947
1Ch	2:23	And he **t.** Geshur, and Aram, with	3947
1Ch	4:18	of Pharaoh, which Mered **t.**	3947
1Ch	5:21	they **t.** away their cattle; of their	
1Ch	7:15	And Machir **t.** to wife the sister of	3947

1Ch	10:4	So Saul **t.** a sword, and fell upon it	3947
1Ch	10:9	they **t.** his head, and his armour,	5375
1Ch	10:12	and **t.** away the body of Saul, and	5375
1Ch	11:5	David **t.** the castle of Zion, which	3920
1Ch	11:18	and **t.** it, and brought it to David:	5375
1Ch	14:3	David **t.** more wives at Jerusalem:	3947
1Ch	17:7	I **t.** thee from the sheepcote, even	3947
1Ch	17:13	him, as I **t.** it from him that was	5493
1Ch	18:1	**t.** Gath and her towns out of the	3947
1Ch	18:4	And David **t.** from him a thousand	3920
1Ch	18:7	And David **t.** the shields of gold	3947
1Ch	19:4	Hanun **t.** David's servants, and	3947
1Ch	20:2	David **t.** the crown of their king	3947
1Ch	23:22	brethren the sons of Kish **t.** them.	5375
1Ch	27:23	David **t.** not the number of them	5375
2Ch	5:4	and the Levites **t.** up the ark	5375
2Ch	8:18	**t.** thence four hundred and fifty	3947
2Ch	10:6	Rehoboam **t.** counsel with the old	
2Ch	10:8	**t.** counsel with the young men that	
2Ch	11:18	Rehoboam **t.** him Mahalath the	3947
2Ch	11:20	**t.** Maachah...daughter of Absalom;	3947
2Ch	11:21	(for he **t.** eighteen wives, and	5375
2Ch	12:4	And he **t.** the fenced cities which	3920
2Ch	12:9	**t.** away the treasures of the house	3947
2Ch	12:9	of the king's house; he **t.** all:	3947
2Ch	13:19	Jeroboam, and **t.** cities from him,	3920
2Ch	14:3	**t.** away the altars of the strange	5493
2Ch	14:5	he **t.** away out of all the cities of	5493
2Ch	15:8	he **t.** courage, and put away the	
2Ch	16:6	Then Asa the king **t.** all Judah;	3947
2Ch	17:6	**t.** away the high places and groves	
2Ch	22:11	king, **t.** Joash the son of Ahaziah,	3947
2Ch	23:1	**t.** the captains of hundreds, Azariah	3947
2Ch	23:8	**t.** every man his men that were to	3947
2Ch	23:20	he **t.** the captains of hundreds, and	3947
2Ch	24:3	Jehoiada **t.** for him two wives;	5375
2Ch	24:11	and emptied the chest, and **t.** it,	5375
2Ch	25:13	of them, and **t.** much spoil.	
2Ch	25:17	Amaziah king of Judah **t.** advice,	
2Ch	25:23	the king of Israel **t.** Amaziah king	8610
2Ch	25:24	he **t.** all the gold and the silver, and	
2Ch	26:1	all the people of Judah **t.** Uzziah,	3947
2Ch	28:8	**t.** also away much spoil from them,	
2Ch	28:15	**t.** the captives, and with the spoil	2388
2Ch	28:21	Ahaz **t.** away a portion out of the	
2Ch	29:16	And the Levites **t.** it, to carry it out	6901
2Ch	30:14	and **t.** away the altars that were in	
2Ch	30:14	the altars for incense **t.** they away,	
2Ch	30:23	whole assembly **t.** counsel to keep	
2Ch	32:3	He **t.** counsel with his princes and	
2Ch	33:11	**t.** Manasseh among the thorns,	3920
2Ch	33:15	And he **t.** away the strange gods,	
2Ch	34:33	Josiah **t.** away all the abominations	
2Ch	35:24	His servants therefore **t.** him out	5674
2Ch	36:1	the people of the land **t.** Jehoahaz	3947
2Ch	36:4	And Necho **t.** Jehoahaz his brother,	3947
Ezr	2:61	which **t.** a wife of the daughters	3947
Ezr	5:14	Nebuchadnezzar **t.** out of the	5312
Ezr	6:5	Nebuchadnezzar **t.** forth out of the	5312
Ezr	8:30	So **t.** the priests and the Levites	6901
Ne	2:1	and I **t.** up the wine, and gave it	5375
Ne	4:1	and **t.** great indignation, and mocked	
Ne	5:12	the priests, and **t.** an oath of them,	
Ne	7:63	**t.** one of the daughters of Barzillai	3947
Ne	9:25	And they **t.** strong cities, and a fat	3920
Es	2:7	dead, **t.** for his own daughter.	3947
Es	3:10	the king **t.** his ring from his hand,	5493
Es	6:11	Then **t.** Haman the apparel and	3947
Es	8:2	And the king **t.** off his ring, which	5493
Es	9:27	Jews ordained, and **t.** upon them,	6901
Job	1:15	fell upon them, and **t.** them away;	3947
Job	2:8	And he **t.** him a potsherd to scrape	3947
Ps	18:16	He sent from above, he **t.** me, he	3947
Ps	22:9	art he that **t.** me out of the womb:	1518
Ps	31:13	while they **t.** counsel together	
Ps	48:6	Fear **t.** hold upon them there, and	
Ps	55:14	We **t.** sweet counsel together, and	
Ps	56:*title*	the Philistines **t.** him in Gath	270
Ps	69:4	restored that which I **t.** not away.	1497
Ps	71:6	**t.** me out of my mother's bowels:	1491
Ps	78:70	and **t.** him from the sheepfolds:	3947
Pr	12:27	not that which he **t.** in hunting:	
Ec	2:20	to despair of all the labour which I **t.**	
Ca	5:7	walls **t.** away my veil from me.	5375
Isa	8:2	I **t.** unto me faithful witnesses to	
Isa	20:1	fought against Ashdod, and **t.** it:	3920
Isa	36:1	cities of Judah, and **t.** them.	8610
Isa	40:14	With whom **t.** he counsel, and who	
Jer	13:7	**t.** the girdle from the place where	3947
Jer	25:17	**t.** I the cup at the Lord's hand, and	3947
Jer	26:8	prophets and all the people **t.** him,	8610
Jer	27:20	Which Nebuchadnezzar...**t.** not,	3947
Jer	28:3	king of Babylon **t.** away from this	3947
Jer	28:10	Hananiah the prophet **t.** the yoke	3947
Jer	31:32	I **t.** them by the hand to bring	2388
Jer	32:10	and sealed it, and **t.** witnesses,	
Jer	32:11	I **t.** the evidence of the purchase,	3947
Jer	35:3	Then I **t.** Jaazaniah the son of	3947
Jer	36:14	Baruch...**t.** the roll in his hand,	3947
Jer	36:21	he **t.** it out of Elishama the scribe's	3947
Jer	36:32	Then **t.** Jeremiah another roll, and	3947
Jer	37:13	and he **t.** Jeremiah the prophet,	8610
Jer	37:14	so Irijah **t.** Jeremiah, and brought	8610
Jer	37:17	the king sent, and **t.** him out:	3947
Jer	38:6	Then **t.** they Jeremiah, and cast	3947
Jer	38:11	Ebed-melech **t.** the men with him,	3947
Jer	38:11	**t.** thence old cast clouts and old	3947
Jer	38:13	and **t.** him up out of the dungeon:	5927
Jer	38:14	**t.** Jeremiah the prophet unto him	3947
Jer	39:14	and **t.** Jeremiah out of the court	3947
Jer	40:2	captain of the guard **t.** Jeremiah,	3947
Jer	41:12	Then they **t.** all the men, and went	3947
Jer	41:16	Then **t.** Johanan the son of Kareah,	3947
Jer	43:5	**t.** all the remnant of Judah, that	3947
Jer	50:33	all that **t.** them captives held them	
Jer	50:43	anguish **t.** hold of him, and pangs	
Jer	52:9	Then they **t.** the king, and carried	8610
Jer	52:18	they ministered, **t.** they away.	3947
Jer	52:19	**t.** the captain of the guard away	3947
Jer	52:24	the captain of the guard **t.** Seraiah	3947
Jer	52:25	He **t.** also out of the city an eunuch,	3947
Jer	52:26	the captain of the guard **t.** them,	3947
La	5:13	They **t.** the young men to grind,	5375
Eze	3:12	Then the spirit **t.** me up, and I	5375
Eze	3:14	spirit lifted me up, and **t.** me away,	3947
Eze	8:3	and **t.** me by a lock of mine head;	3947
Eze	10:7	and **t.** thereof, and put it into the	5375
Eze	10:7	linen: who **t.** it, and went out.	3947
Eze	11:24	Afterwards the spirit **t.** me up,	5375
Eze	16:50	I **t.** them away as I saw good.	5493
Eze	17:3	**t.** the highest branch of the cedar:	3947
Eze	17:5	He **t.** also of the seed of the land,	3947
Eze	19:5	then she **t.** another of her whelps,	3947
Eze	23:10	they **t.** her sons and her daughters,	3947
Eze	23:13	was defiled, that they **t.** both one way,	
Eze	29:7	they **t.** hold of thee by thy hand,	8610
Eze	33:5	of the trumpet, and **t.** not warning;	
Eze	43:5	So the spirit **t.** me up, and brought	5375
Da	1:16	Melzar **t.** away the portion of their	5375
Da	3:22	those men that **t.** up Shadrach,	5267
Da	5:20	and they **t.** his glory from him:	5709
Da	5:31	And Darius...**t.** the kingdom,	6902
Ho	1:3	**t.** Gomer the daughter of Diblaim;	3947
Ho	12:3	**t.** his brother by the heel in the womb,	
Ho	13:11	and **t.** him away in my wrath.	3947
Am	7:15	And the Lord **t.** me as I followed the	3947
Jon	1:15	So they **t.** up Jonah, and cast him	5375
Zec	11:7	I **t.** unto me two staves; the one I	3947
Zec	11:10	I **t.** my staff, even Beauty, and cut	3947
Zec	11:13	And I **t.** the thirty pieces of silver,	3947
Mt	1:24	him, and **t.** unto him his wife:	*3880*
Mt	2:14	he **t.** the young child and his	*3880*
Mt	2:21	and **t.** the young child and his	*3880*
Mt	8:17	saying, Himself **t.** our infirmities,	*2983*
Mt	9:25	he went in, and **t.** her by the hand,	*2902*
Mt	13:31	**mustard seed, which a man t.,**	*2983*
Mt	13:33	**unto leaven, which a woman t.**	*2983*
Mt	14:12	disciples came, and **t.** up the body,	*142*
Mt	14:19	and **t.** the five loaves, and the two	*2983*
Mt	14:20	they **t.** up of the fragments that	*142*
Mt	15:36	he **t.** the seven loaves and the	*2983*
Mt	15:37	they **t.** up of the broken meat that	*142*
Mt	15:39	**t.** ship,...came into the coasts	*1684,1519*
Mt	16:9,	10 **and how many baskets ye t.**	*2983*
Mt	16:22	Then Peter **t.** him, and began to	*4355*
Mt	18:28	**and t. him by the throat, saying**	*2902*
Mt	20:17	**t.** the twelve disciples apart in the	*3880*
Mt	21:35	**the husbandmen t. his servants,**	*2983*
Mt	21:46	because they **t.** him for a prophet.	*2192*
Mt	22:6	**And the remnant t. his servants,**	*2902*
Mt	22:15	**t.** counsel how they might entangle	*2983*
Mt	24:39	**flood came, and t. them all away;**	*142*
Mt	25:1	**ten virgins, which t. their lamps,**	*2983*
Mt	25:3	**foolish t. their lamps, and t. no**	*2983*
Mt	25:4	**the wise t. oil in their vessels**	*2983*
Mt	25:15	**and straightway t. his journey.**	*589*
Mt	25:35	**I was a stranger, and ye t. me**	*4863*
Mt	25:38	**we thee a stranger, and t. thee**	*4863*
Mt	25:43	**a stranger, and ye t. me not in:**	*4863*
Mt	26:26	Jesus **t.** bread, and blessed it, and	*2983*
Mt	26:27	And he **t.** the cup, and gave thanks,	*2983*
Mt	26:37	And he **t.** with him Peter and the	*3880*
Mt	26:50	laid hands on Jesus, and **t.** him.	*2902*
Mt	27:1	and elders of the people **t.** counsel	*2983*
Mt	27:6	chief priests **t.** the silver pieces,	*2983*
Mt	27:7	they **t.** counsel, and bought with	*2983*
Mt	27:9	they **t.** the thirty pieces of silver,	*2983*
Mt	27:24	he **t.** water, and washed his hands	*2983*
Mt	27:27	**t.** Jesus into the common hall,	*3880*
Mt	27:30	**t.** the reed, and smote him on the	*2983*
Mt	27:31	they **t.** the robe off from him, and	*1562*
Mt	27:48	and **t.** a spunge, and filled it with	*2983*
Mt	28:15	So they **t.** the money, and did as	*2983*
Mk	1:31	he came and **t.** her by the hand,	*2902*
Mk	2:12	he arose, **t.** up the bed, and went	*142*
Mk	3:6	**t.** counsel with the Herodians	*4160*
Mk	4:36	**t.** him even as he was in the ship	*3880*
Mk	5:41	And he **t.** the damsel by the hand,	*2902*
Mk	6:29	they came and **t.** up his corpse, and	*142*
Mk	6:43	they **t.** up twelve baskets full of the	*142*
Mk	7:33	he **t.** him aside from the multitude,	*618*
Mk	8:6	he **t.** the seven loaves,and gave	*2983*
Mk	8:8	they **t.** up of the broken meat that	*142*
Mk	8:19,	20 **baskets full of fragments t. ye**	*142*
Mk	8:23	he **t.** the blind man by the hand,	*1949*
Mk	8:32	Peter **t.** him, and began to rebuke	*4355*
Mk	9:27	But Jesus **t.** him by the hand, and	*2902*
Mk	9:36	he **t.** a child, and set him in the	*2983*
Mk	10:16	he **t.** them up in his arms, put his	*1723*
Mk	10:32	he **t.** again the twelve, and began	*3880*
Mk	12:8	**they t. him, and killed him, and**	*2983*
Mk	12:20	the first **t.** a wife, and dying left no	*2983*
Mk	12:21	And the second **t.** her, and died,	*2983*
Mk	14:22	Jesus **t.** bread, and blessed, and	*2983*
Mk	14:23	he **t.** the cup, and when he had	*2983*
Mk	14:46	their hands on him, and **t.** him.	*2902*
Mk	14:49	**temple teaching, and ye t. me**	*2902*
Mk	15:20	they **t.** off the purple from him,	*1562*
Mk	15:46	**t.** him down, and wrapped him in	*2507*
Lu	2:28	Then **t.** he him up in his arms,	*1209*
Lu	5:25	and **t.** up that whereon he lay, and	*142*
Lu	8:54	**t.** her by the hand, and called,	*2902*
Lu	9:10	And he **t.** them, and went aside	*3880*
Lu	9:16	Then he **t.** the five loaves and the	*2983*
Lu	9:28	he **t.** Peter and John and James,	*3880*
Lu	9:47	**t.** a child, and set him by him,	*1949*
Lu	10:34	**him to an inn, and t. care of him**	*1959*
Lu	10:35	**he t. out two pence, and gave**	*1544*
Lu	13:19	**of mustard seed, which a man t.,**	*2983*
Lu	13:21	**is like leaven, which a woman t.**	*2983*
Lu	14:4	he **t.** him, and healed him, and let	*1949*
Lu	15:13	**t. his journey into a far country,**	*589*
Lu	18:31	Then he **t.** unto him the twelve,	*3830*
Lu	20:29	the first **t.** a wife, and died without	*2983*
Lu	20:30	And the second **t.** her to wife, and	*2983*
Lu	20:31	And the third **t.** her, and in like	*2983*
Lu	22:17	he **t.** the cup, and gave thanks,	*1209*
Lu	22:19	And he **t.** bread, and gave thanks,	*2983*
Lu	22:54	Then **t.** they him, and led him,	*4815*
Lu	23:53	And he **t.** it down, and wrapped it	*2507*
Lu	24:30	he **t.** bread, and blessed it, and	*2983*
Lu	24:43	he **t.** it, and did eat before them.	*2983*
Joh	5:9	was made whole, and **t.** up his bed,	*142*
Joh	6:11	And Jesus **t.** the loaves; and when	*2983*
Joh	6:24	they also **t.** shipping, and	*1684,1519*
Joh	8:59	**t.** they up stones to cast at him:	*142*
Joh	10:31	the Jews **t.** up stones again to stone	*941*
Joh	11:41	**t.** away the stone from the place	*142*
Joh	11:53	they **t.** counsel together for to put	*4823*
Joh	12:3	Then **t.** Mary a pound of ointment	*2983*
Joh	12:13	**T.** branches of palm trees, and	*2983*
Joh	13:4	and **t.** a towel, and girded himself	*2983*
Joh	18:12	and officers of the Jews **t.** Jesus,	*4815*
Joh	19:1	Pilate therefore **t.** Jesus, and	*2983*
Joh	19:16	they **t.** Jesus, and led him away.	*3880*
Joh	19:23	**t.** his garments, and made four	*2983*
Joh	19:27	disciple **t.** her unto his own home	*2983*
Joh	19:38	therefore, and **t.** the body of Jesus	*142*

Joh 19:40 Then **t.** they the body of Jesus, ... *2983*
Ac 1:16 was guide to them that **t.** Jesus. *4815*
Ac 3:7 And he **t.** him by the right hand, ... *4084*
Ac 4:13 they **t.** knowledge of them, that *1921*
Ac 5:33 heart, and **t.** counsel to slay them. *1011*
Ac 7:21 Pharaoh's daughter **t.** him up, and *337*
Ac 7:43 ye **t.** up the tabernacle of Moloch, ... *353*
Ac 9:23 the Jews **t.** counsel to kill him: *4823*
Ac 9:25 Then the disciples **t.** him by night, ... *2983*
Ac 9:27 But Barnabas **t.** him, and brought *1949*
Ac 10:26 Peter **t.** him up, sayng, Stand up; *1453*
Ac 12:25 and **t.** with them John, whose *4838*
Ac 13:29 they **t.** him down from the tree, ... *2507*
Ac 15:39 Barnabas **t.** Mark, and sailed unto *3880*
Ac 16:3 **t.** and circumcised him because of *2983*
Ac 16:33 he **t.** them the same hour of the *3880*
Ac 17:5 **t.** unto them certain lewd fellows *4355*
Ac 17:19 they **t.** him, and brought him unto *1949*
Ac 18:17 Then all the Greeks **t.** Sosthenes, ... *1949*
Ac 18:18 and then **t.** his leave of the brethren. ... *657*
Ac 18:26 **t.** him unto them, and expounded *4355*
Ac 19:13 **t.** upon them to call over them *2021*
Ac 20:14 we **t.** him in, and came to Mitylene *353*
Ac 21:6 we **t.** ship; and they returned *1910,1519*
Ac 21:11 **t.** Paul's girdle, and bound his own *142*
Ac 21:15 those days we **t.** up our carriages, ... *643*
Ac 21:26 Then Paul **t.** the men, and the *3880*
Ac 21:30 they **t.** Paul, and drew him out of *1949*
Ac 21:32 Who immediately **t.** soldiers and *3880*
Ac 21:33 captain came near, and **t.** him, ... *1949*
Ac 23:18 So he **t.** him, and brought him to *3880*
Ac 23:19 chief captain **t.** him by the hand, ... *1949*
Ac 23:31 as it was commanded them **t.** Paul, ... *353*
Ac 24:6 whom we **t.**, and would have *2902*
Ac 24:7 **t.** him away out of our hands, ... *520*
Ac 27:35 **t.** bread, and gave thanks to God *2983*
Ac 27:36 cheer, and they also **t.** some meat *4355*
Ac 28:15 he thanked God, and **t.** courage. *2983*
1Co 11:23 in which he was betrayed **t.** bread: *2983*
1Co 11:25 the same manner also he **t.** the cup, ...
Ga 2:1 and **t.** Titus with me also. *4838*
Php 2:7 **t.** upon him the form of a servant, ... *2983*
Col 2:14 and **t.** it out of the way, nailing *142*
Heb 2:14 himself likewise **t.** part of the *3348*
Heb 2:16 he **t.** not on him the nature of *1949*
Heb 2:16 he **t.** on him the seed of Abraham. *1949*
Heb 8:9 when I **t.** them by the hand to lead *1949*
Heb 9:19 he **t.** the blood of calves and of *2983*
Heb 10:34 **t.** joyfully the spoiling of your *4327*
Re 5:7 **t.** the book out of the right hand *4327*
Re 8:5 the angel **t.** the censer, and filled it *4327*
Re 10:10 I **t.** the little book out of the *4327*
Re 18:21 a mighty angel **t.** up a stone like a *142*

TOOKEST
Ps 99:8 though thou **t.** vengeance of their ....
Eze 16:18 And **t.** thy broidered garments, ... 3947

TOOL
Ex 20:25 if thou lift up thy **t.** upon it, thou 2719
Ex 32:4 and fashioned it with a graving **t.**, ...
De 27:5 shalt not lift up any iron **t.** upon them. ......
1Ki 6:7 any **t.** of iron heard in the house, ... 3627

TOOTH See also TEETH; TOOTH'S.
Ex 21:24 Eye for eye, **t.** for **t.**, hand for 8127
Ex 21:27 if he smite out his manservant's **t.**, ... 8127
Ex 21:27 or his maidservant's **t.**; he shall let 8127
Le 24:20 for breach, eye for eye, **t.** for **t.** 8127
De 19:21 **t.** for **t.**, hand for hand, foot for foot ... 8127
Pr 25:19 time of trouble is like a broken **t.** 8127
Mt 5:38 **eye for an eye, and a t. for a t.** *3599*

TOOTH'S
Ex 21:27 shall let him go free for his **t.** sake. 8127

TOP See also HOUSETOP; TOPS.
Ge 11:4 whose **t.** may reach unto heaven; 7218
Ge 28:12 and the **t.** of it reached to heaven: 7218
Ge 28:18 and poured oil upon the **t.** of it. 7218
Ex 17:9 I will stand on the **t.** of the hill 7218
Ex 17:10 Hur went up to the **t.** of the hill. 7218
Ex 19:20 mount Sinai, on the **t.** of the mount: ... 7218
Ex 19:20 Lord called Moses up to the **t.** of 7218
Ex 24:17 like...fire on the **t.** of the mount 7218
Ex 28:32 there shall be an hole in the **t.** of it, ... 7218
Ex 30:3 gold, the **t.** thereof, and the sides 1406
Ex 34:2 there to me n the **t.** of the mount. 7218
Ex 37:26 both the **t.** of it, and the sides 1406
Nu 14:40 up into the **t.** of the mountain. 7218
Nu 14:44 presumed to go up unto the hill **t.** 7218
Nu 20:28 died there in the **t.** of the mount: 7218
Nu 21:20 to the **t.** of Pisgah, which looketh 7218
Nu 23:9 from the **t.** of the rocks I see him, ... 7218
Nu 23:14 field of Zophim, to the **t.** of Pisgah, ... 7218
Nu 23:28 brought Balaam unto the **t.** of Peor, ... 7218
De 3:27 Get thee up into the **t.** of Pisgah. 7218
De 28:35 of thy foot unto the **t.** of thy head. 6936
De 33:16 and upon the **t.** of the head of him 6936
De 34:1 to the **t.** of Pisgah, that is over 7218
Jos 15:8 went up to the **t.** of the mountain 7218
Jos 15:9 was drawn from the **t.** of the hill 7218
Jg 6:26 an altar...upon the **t.** of this rock, ... 7218
Jg 9:7 stood in the **t.** of mount Gerizim, ... 7218
Jg 9:25 for him in the **t.** of the mountains, ... 7218
Jg 9:36 down from the **t.** of the mountains 7218
Jg 9:51 gat them up to the **t.** of the tower. 1406
Jg 15:8 dwelt in the **t.** of the rock Etam. 5585
Jg 15:11 went to the **t.** of the rock Etam, ... 5585
Jg 16:3 carried them up to the **t.** of an hill 7218
1Sa 9:25 with Saul upon the **t.** of the house. 1406
1Sa 9:26 called Saul to the **t.** of the house, ... 1406
1Sa 26:13 stood on the **t.** of an hill afar off; 7218
2Sa 2:25 troop, and stood on the **t.** of an hill. ... 7218
2Sa 15:32 was come to the **t.** of the mount, ... 7218
2Sa 16:1 was a little past the **t.** of the hill, ... 7218
2Sa 16:22 a tent upon the **t.** of the house; 1406
1Ki 7:17 were upon the **t.** of the pillars: 7218
1Ki 7:18 the chapiters that were upon the **t.**, ... 7218
1Ki 7:19 that were upon the **t.** of the pillars 7218
1Ki 7:22 the **t.** of the pillars was lily work: 7218
1Ki 7:35 in the **t.** of the base was there a 7218
1Ki 7:35 and on the **t.** of the base the ledges ... 7218
1Ki 7:41 were on the **t.** of the two pillars; 7218
1Ki 7:41 were upon the **t.** of the pillars; 7218
1Ki 10:19 and the **t.** of the throne was round 7218
1Ki 18:42 Elijah went up to the **t.** of Carmel; 7218
2Ki 1:9 behold, he sat on the **t.** of an hill. 7218
2Ki 9:13 under him on the **t.** of the stairs, ... 1634
2Ki 23:12 **t.** of the upper chamber of Ahaz, ... 1406
2Ch 3:15 that was on the **t.** of each of them 7218
2Ch 4:12 were on the **t.** of the two pillars, ... 7218
2Ch 4:12 which were on the **t.** of the pillars; 7218
2Ch 25:12 brought them unto the **t.** of the rock, .. 7218
2Ch 25:12 cast...down from the **t.** of the rock, ... 7218
Es 5:2 and touched the **t.** of the sceptre. 7218
Ps 72:16 upon the **t.** of the mountains; 7218
Ps 102:7 sparrow alone upon the house **t.** 1406
Pr 8:2 standeth in the **t.** of high places, ... 7218
Pr 23:34 he that lieth upon the **t.** of a mast. 7218
Ca 4:8 Lebanon: look from the **t.** of Amana, ... 7218
Ca 4:8 from the **t.** of Shenir and Hermon, ... 7218
Isa 2:2 established in the **t.** of...mountains, ... 7218
Isa 17:6 in the **t.** of the uppermost bough, ... 7218
Isa 30:17 a beacon upon the **t.** of a mountain, ... 7218
Isa 42:11 shout from the **t.** of the mountains. 7218
La 2:19 for hunger in the **t.** of every street. 7218
La 4:1 poured out in the **t.** of every street. ... 7218
Eze 17:4 cropped off the **t.** of his young twigs, .. 7218
Eze 17:22 off from the **t.** of his young twigs 7218
Eze 24:7 she set it upon the **t.** of a rock; 6706
Eze 24:8 set her blood upon the **t.** of a rock, ... 6706
Eze 26:4 and make her like the **t.** of a rock. 6706
Eze 26:14 will make thee like the **t.** of a rock: 6706
Eze 31:3 his **t.** was among the thick boughs. 6788
Eze 31:10 up his **t.** among the thick boughs, ... 6788
Eze 31:14 up their **t.** among the thick boughs, ... 6788
Eze 43:12 Upon the **t.** of the mountain the 7218
Am 1:2 and the **t.** of Carmel shall wither. 7218
Am 9:3 hide themselves in the **t.** of Carmel, ... 7218
Mic 4:1 in the **t.** of the mountains, ... 7218
Na 3:10 in pieces at the **t.** of all the streets: 7218
Zec 4:2 with a bowl upon the **t.** of it, and 7218
Zec 4:2 which are upon the **t.** thereof: 7218
Mt 27:51 in twain from the **t.** to the bottom; *509*
Mk 15:38 in twain from the **t.** to the bottom. *509*
Joh 19:23 seam, woven from the **t.** throughout *509*
Heb 11:21 leaning upon the **t.** of his staff. *206*

TOPAZ
Ex 28:17 first row shall be a sardius, a **t.**, ... 6357
Ex 39:10 first row was a sardius, a **t.**, and 6357
Job 28:19 **t.** of Ethiopia shall not equal it, ... 6357
Eze 28:13 sardius, **t.**, and the diamond, ... 6357
Re 21:20 the eighth, beryl; the ninth, a **t.**; *5116*

TOPHEL (to'-fel)
De 1:1 between Paran, and **T.**, and 8603

TOPHET (to'-fet) See also TOPHETH.
Isa 30:33 **T.** is ordained of old; yea, for the 8613
Jer 7:31 have built the high places of **T.**, ... 8612
Jer 7:32 that it shall no more be called **T.** 8612
Jer 7:32 for they shall bury in **T.**, till there 8612
Jer 19:6 place shall no more be called **T.**, ... 8612
Jer 19:11 and they shall bury them in **T.**, ... 8612
Jer 19:12 and even make this city as **T.**: 8612
Jer 19:13 shall be defiled as the place of **T.**, ... 8612
Jer 19:14 Then came Jeremiah from **T.**, ... 8612

TOPHETH (to'-feth) See also TOPHET.
2Ki 23:10 And he defiled **T.**, which is in the 8612

TOPS See also HOUSETOPS.
Ge 8:5 were the **t.** of the mountains seen. 7218
2Sa 5:24 going in the **t.** of the mulberry trees, .. 7218
1Ki 7:16 to set upon the **t.** of the pillars: 7218
2Ki 19:26 herb, as the grass on the house **t.**, ... 1406
1Ch 14:15 in the **t.** of the mulberry trees, ... 7218
Job 24:24 cut off as the **t.** of the ears of corn. ... 7218
Isa 2:21 into the **t.** of the ragged rocks. 5585
Isa 15:3 on the **t.** of their houses, and in 1406
Eze 6:13 in all the **t.** of the mountains, and 7218
Ho 4:13 upon the **t.** of the mountains, ... 7218
Joe 2:5 chariots on the **t.** of mountains shall 7218

TORCH See also TORCHES.
Zec 12:6 and like a **t.** of fire in a sheaf; 3940

TORCHES
Na 2:3 chariots shall be with flaming **t.** 6393
Na 2:4 they shall seem like **t.**, they shall 3940
Joh 18:3 with lanterns and **t.** and weapons. *2985*

TORE See TARE.

TORMENT See also TORMENTED; TORMENTS.
Mt 8:29 art thou come hither to **t.** us before *928*
Mk 5:7 thee by God, that thou **t.** me not *928*
Lu 8:28 high? I beseech thee, **t.** me not *928*
Lu 16:28 **they also come into this place of t.** .. *931*
1Jo 4:18 out fear, because fear hath **t.** *2851*
Re 9:5 their **t.** was as the **t.** of a scorpion, ... *929*
Re 14:11 the smoke of their **t.** ascendeth up *929*
Re 18:7 so much **t.** and sorrow give her: *929*
Re 18:10 Standing afar off for...fear of her **t.**, ... *929*
Re 18:15 stand afar off for the fear of her **t.**, ... *929*

TORMENTED
Mt 8:6 home sick of the palsy, grievously **t.** ... *928*
Lu 16:24 **tongue; for I am t. in this flame.** .. *3600*
Lu 16:25 **he is comforted, and thou art t.** ... *3600*
Heb 11:37 being destitute, afflicted, **t.**; *2558*
Re 9:5 that they should be **t.** five months: *928*
Re 11:10 these two prophets **t.** them that *928*
Re 14:10 he shall be **t.** with fire and brimstone *928*
Re 20:10 shall be **t.** day and night for ever *928*

TORMENTORS
Mt 18:34 **wroth, and delivered him to the t.** ... *930*

TORMENTS
Mt 4:24 taken with divers diseases and **t.**, ... *931*
Lu 16:23 **hell he lift up his eyes, being in t.,** .. *931*

TORN
Ge 31:39 That which was **t.** of beasts I 2966
Ge 44:28 Surely he is **t.** in pieces; and I 2963
Ex 22:13 If it be **t.** in pieces, then let him 2963
Ex 22:13 not make good that which was **t.** 2966
Ex 22:31 ye eat any flesh that is **t.** of beasts 2966
Le 7:24 fat of that which is **t.** with beasts, ... 2966
Le 17:15 or that which was **t.** with beasts, ... 2966
Le 22:8 dieth of itself, or is **t.** with beasts, ... 2966
1Ki 13:26 unto the lion, which hath **t.** him, ... 7665
1Ki 13:28 eaten the carcase, nor **t.** the ass. 7665
Isa 5:25 carcases were **t.** in the midst of 5478
Jer 5:6 out thence shall be **t.** in pieces: 2963
Eze 4:14 dieth of itself, or is **t.** in pieces; 2966
Eze 44:31 any thing that is dead of itself, or **t.**, ... 2966
Ho 6:1 for he hath **t.**, and he will heal us; 2963
Mal 1:13 and ye brought that which was **t.**, ... 1497
Mk 1:26 the unclean spirit had **t.** him, ... *4682*

TORTOISE
Le 11:29 mouse, and the **t.** after his kind, ... 6632

TORTURED
Heb 11:35 and others were **t.**, not accepting *5178*

TOSS See also TOSSED; TOSSINGS.
Isa 22:18 violently turn and **t.** thee like a......... 6802
Jer 5:22 the waves thereof **t.** themselves, ... 1607

TOSSED
Ps 109:23 I am **t.** up and down as the locust...... 5287
Pr 21:6 a vanity **t.** to and fro of them that...... 5086
Isa 54:11 O thou afflicted, **t.** with tempest, and........
Mt 14:24 the midst of the sea, **t.** with waves:..... *928*
Ac 27:18 exceedingly **t.** with a tempest,........... *5492*
Eph 4:14 **t.** to and fro, and carried about.......... *2831*
Jas 1:6 sea driven with the wind and **t.**.......... *4494*

TOSSINGS
Job 7:4 I am full of **t.** to and fro unto the....... 5076

TOTTERING
Ps 62:3 wall shall ye be, and as a **t.** fence. 1760

TOU (to'-u) See also TOI.
1Ch 18:9 **T.** king of Hamath heard how........... 8583
1Ch 18:10 (for Hadarezer had war with **T.**;)........ 8583

TOUCH See also TOUCHED; TOUCHETH; TOUCHING.
Ge 3:3 it, neither shall ye **t.** it, lest ye die..... 5060
Ge 20:6 suffered I thee not to **t.** her............. 5060
Ex 19:12 the mount, or **t.** the border of it: 5060
Ex 19:13 There shall not an hand **t.** it, but he ... 5060
Le 5:2 Or if a soul **t.** any unclean thing,........ 5060
Le 5:3 Or if he **t.** the uncleanness of man,..... 5060
Le 6:27 **t.** the flesh thereof shall be holy:......... 5060
Le 7:21 soul that shall **t.** any unclean thing...... 5060
Le 11:8 and their carcase ye shall not **t.**; 5060
Le 11:31 whosoever doth **t.** them, when they.... 5060
Le 12:4 she shall **t.** no hallowed thing, nor...... 5060
Nu 4:15 but they shall not **t.** any holy thing, ... 5060
Nu 16:26 **t.** nothing of theirs, lest ye be........... 5060
De 14:8 flesh, nor **t.** their dead carcase. 5060
Jos 9:19 now therefore we may not **t.** them. 5060
Ru 2:9 men that they shall not **t.** thee? 5060
2Sa 14:10 and he shall not **t.** thee any more........ 5060
2Sa 18:12 that none **t.** the young man Absalom.........
2Sa 23:7 man that shall **t.** them must be.......... 5060
1Ch 16:22 **T.** not mine anointed, and do my........ 5060
Job 1:11 and **t.** all that he hath, and he will...... 5060
Job 2:5 and **t.** his bone and his flesh, and he.... 5060
Job 5:19 in seven there shall no evil **t.** thee. 5060
Job 6:7 things that my soul refused to **t.** are.... 5060
Ps 105:15 **T.** not mine anointed, and do my........ 5060
Ps 144:5 **t.** the mountains, and they shall......... 5060
Isa 52:11 from thence, **t.** no unclean thing;........ 5060
Jer 12:14 that **t.** the inheritance which I have..... 5060
La 4:14 men could not **t.** their garments......... 5060
La 4:15 it is unclean; depart, depart **t.** not:....... 5060
Hag 2:12 and with his skirt do **t.** bread, or 5060
Hag 2:13 by a dead body **t.** any of these, ... 5060
Mt 9:21 If I may but **t.** his garment, I shall *680*
Mt 14:36 might only **t.** the hem of his garment:... *680*
Mk 3:10 they pressed upon him for to **t.** him, ... *680*
Mk 5:28 If I may **t.** but his clothes, I shall be *680*
Mk 6:56 **t.** if it were but the border of his......... *680*
Mk 8:22 him, and besought him to **t.** him.......... *680*
Mk 10:13 to him, that he should **t.** them:........... *680*
Lu 6:19 whole multitude sought to **t.** him: *680*
Lu 11:46 **t. not the burdens with one of**...... *4379*
Lu 18:15 also infants, that he would **t.** them: *680*
Joh 20:17 Jesus saith unto her, **T. me not;**......... *680*
1Co 7:1 is good for a man not to **t.** a woman. ... *680*
2Co 6:17 **t.** not the unclean thing: and I will *680*
Col 2:21 (**T.** not; taste not; handle not;............ *680*
Heb 11:28 destroyed the firstborn shall **t.**........... *2345*
Heb 12:20 And if so much as a beast **t.** the *2345*

TOUCHED
Ge 26:29 us no hurt, as we have not **t.** thee, ... 5060
Ge 32:25 him, he **t.** the hollow of his thigh; 5060
Ge 32:32 he **t.** the hollow of Jacob's thigh......... 5060
Le 22:6 The soul which hath **t.** any such......... 5060
Nu 19:18 and upon him that **t.** a bone, or one.... 5060
Nu 31:19 and whosoever hath **t.** any slain, ... 5060
Jg 6:21 **t.** the flesh and...unleavened cakes; 5060
1Sa 10:26 of men, whose hearts God had **t.**....... 5060
1Ki 6:27 the wing of the one **t.** the one wall,..... 5060
1Ki 6:27 the other cherub **t.** the other wall; 5060
1Ki 6:27 their wings **t.** one another in the........ 5060
1Ki 19:5 then an angel **t.** him, and said unto..... 5060
1Ki 19:7 and **t.** him, and said, Arise and eat; 5060
2Ki 13:21 let down, and **t.** the bones of Elisha,... 5060
Es 5:2 near, and **t.** the top of the sceptre. 5060
Job 19:21 for the hand of God hath **t.** me.......... 5060
Isa 6:7 and said, Lo, this hath **t.** thy lips; 5060
Jer 1:9 forth his hand, and **t.** my mouth......... 5060
Eze 3:13 creatures that **t.** one another,........... 5401
Da 8:5 earth, and **t.** not the ground:............. 5060
Da 8:18 but he **t.** me, and set me upright. 5060
Da 9:21 **t.** me about the time of the evening.... 5060
Da 10:10 an hand **t.** me, which set me upon...... 5060
Da 10:16 of the sons of men **t.** my lips: 5060
Da 10:18 **t.** me one like the appearance of a...... 5060
Mt 8:3 put forth his hand, and **t.** him,............ *680*
Mt 8:15 he **t.** her hand, and the fever left her: .. *680*
Mt 9:20 and **t.** the hem of his garment:........... *680*
Mt 9:29 Then **t.** he their eyes, saying,............ *680*
Mt 14:36 many as **t.** were made perfectly *680*
Mt 17:7 Jesus came and **t.** them, and said,........ *680*
Mt 20:34 on them, and **t.** their eyes:................ *680*
Mk 1:41 put forth his hand, and **t.** him, and....... *680*
Mk 5:27 the press behind, and **t.** his garment. ... *680*
Mk 5:30 press, and said, **Who t. my clothes?**.. *680*
Mk 5:31 thee, and sayest thou, Who **t.** me? *680*
Mk 6:56 as many as **t.** him were made whole..... *680*
Mk 7:33 ears, and he spit, and **t.** his tongue;..... *680*
Lu 5:13 he put forth his hand, and **t.** him. *680*
Lu 7:14 And he came and **t.** the bier: and *680*
Lu 8:44 and **t.** the border of his garment:......... *680*
Lu 8:45 And Jesus said, **Who t. me?** When...... *680*
Lu 8:45 thee, and sayest thou, Who **t.** me? *680*
Lu 8:46 Jesus said, **Somebody hath t. me:**..... *680*
Lu 8:47 people for what cause she had **t.** him,... *680*
Lu 22:51 And he **t.** his ear, and healed him. *680*
Ac 27:3 And the next day we **t.** at Sidon. *2609*
Heb 4:15 **t.** with...feeling of our infirmities; *4834*
Heb 12:18 unto the mount that might be **t.**,.......... *5584*

TOUCHETH
Ge 26:11 He that **t.** this man or his wife.......... 5060
Ex 19:12 whosoever **t.** the mount shall be 5060
Ex 29:37 whatsoever **t.** the altar shall be holy. .. 5060
Ex 30:29 whatsoever **t.** them shall be holy........ 5060
Le 6:18 every one that **t.** them shall be holy. .. 5060
Le 7:19 the flesh that **t.** any unclean thing....... 5060
Le 11:24 whosoever **t.** the carcase of them....... 5060
Le 11:26 one that **t.** them shall be unclean........ 5060
Le 11:27 whoso **t.** their carcase shall be........... 5060
Le 11:36 which **t.** their carcase shall be 5060
Le 11:39 he that **t.** the carcase thereof shall 5060
Le 15:5 whosoever **t.** his bed shall wash his.... 5060
Le 15:7 And he that **t.** the flesh of him that 5060
Le 15:10 whosoever **t.** any thing that was 5060
Le 15:11 whomsoever he **t.** that hath the.......... 5060
Le 15:12 that he **t.** which hath the issue, ... 5060
Le 15:19 whosoever **t.** her shall be unclean....... 5060
Le 15:21 whosoever **t.** her bed shall wash his ... 5060
Le 15:22 whosoever **t.** any thing that she......... 5060
Le 15:23 when he **t.** it, he shall be unclean........ 5060
Le 15:27 whosoever **t.** these thing shall be 5060
Le 22:4 whoso **t.** any thing that is unclean 5060
Le 22:5 Or whosoever **t.** any creeping thing, ... 5060
Nu 19:11 He that **t.** the dead body of any man... 5060
Nu 19:13 Whosoever **t.** the dead body of any 5060
Nu 19:16 And whosoever **t.** one that is slain...... 5060
Nu 19:21 he that **t.** the water of separation....... 5060
Nu 19:22 unclean person **t.** shall be unclean;...... 5060
Nu 19:22 the soul that **t.** it shall be unclean....... 5060
Jg 16:9 of tow is broken when it **t.** the fire..... 7306
Job 4:5 it **t.** thee, and thou art troubled. 5060
Ps 104:32 he **t.** the hills, and they smoke. 5060
Pr 6:29 **t.** her shall not be innocent. 5060
Eze 17:10 wither, when the east wind **t.** it? 5060
Ho 4:2 they break out, and blood **t.** blood....... 5060
Am 9:5 God of hosts is he that **t.** the land,..... 5060
Zec 2:8 he that **t.** you **t.** the apple of his eye. . 5060
Lu 7:39 manner of woman this is...**t.** him: *680*
1Jo 5:18 and that wicked one **t.** him not............ *680*

TOUCHING
Ge 27:42 Behold, thy brother Esau, as **t.** thee,........
Le 5:13 an atonement for him as **t.** his sin...... 5921
Nu 8:26 do unto the Levites **t.** their charge. ....
1Sa 20:23 And as **t.** the matter which thou and I.......
2Ki 22:18 As **t.** the words which thou hast heard; .....
Ezr 7:24 that **t.** any of the priests and Levites, ...
Job 37:23 **T.** the Almighty, we cannot find him ....
Ps 45:1 things which I have made **t.** the king:........
Isa 5:1 a song of my beloved **t.** his vineyard........
Jer 1:16 them **t.** all their wickedness, ... 5921
Jer 21:11 And **t.** the house of the king of Judah,.......
Jer 22:11 For thus saith the Lord **t.** Shallum....... 413
Eze 7:13 the vision is **t.** the whole multitude 413
Mt 18:19 **shall agree on earth as t. any**....... *4012*
Mt 22:31 **as t. the resurrection of the dead,**. *4012*
Mk 12:26 **And as t. the dead, that they**........ *4012*
Lu 23:14 no fault in this man **t.** those things............
Ac 5:35 ye intend to do as **t.** these men......... *1909*
Ac 21:25 As **t.** the Gentiles which believe......... *4012*
Ac 24:21 **T.** the resurrection of the dead I......... *4012*
Ac 26:2 **t.**...the things whereof I am accused... *4012*
Ro 11:28 but as **t.** the election, they are *2596*
1Co 8:1 as **t.** things offered unto idols, ... *4012*
1Co 16:12 As **t.** our brother Apollos, I greatly *4012*
2Co 9:1 as **t.** the ministering to the saints, ... *4012*
Php 3:5 Hebrews; as **t.** the law, a Pharisee;.... *2596*
Php 3:6 **t.** the righteousness which is in the *2596*
Col 4:10 Barnabas, (**t.** whom ye received......... *4012*
1Th 4:9 **t.** brotherly love ye need not that....... *4012*
2Th 3:4 have confidence in the Lord **t.** you, ... *1909*

TOW
Jg 16:9 as a thread of **t.** is broken when it 5296
Isa 1:31 the strong shall be as **t.**, and the 5296
Isa 43:17 extinct, they are quenched as **t.**......... 6594

TOWARD See also UNTOWARD.
Ge 2:14 which goeth **t.** the east of Assyria ....
Ge 12:9 journeyed, going on still **t.** the south.........
Ge 13:12 and pitched his tent **t.** Sodom........... 5704
Ge 15:5 Look now **t.** heaven, and tell the stars, ...
Ge 18:16 thence, and looked **t.** Sodom:..... 5921,6440
Ge 18:2 door, and bowed himself **t.** the ground, ...
Ge 18:22 faces from thence, and went **t.** Sodom:......
Ge 19:1 himself with his face **t.** the ground;...........
Ge 19:28 And he looked **t.** Sodom and...... 5921,6440
Ge 19:28 and **t.** all the land of the plain,.... 5921,6440
Ge 20:1 journeyed from thence **t.** the south...........
Ge 25:18 Egypt, as thou goest **t.** Assyria:..............
Ge 28:10 from Beer-sheba, and went **t.** Haran. ....
Ge 30:40 of the flocks **t.** the ringstraked. 413
Ge 31:2 behold, it was not **t.** him as before. ....
Ge 31:5 that it is not **t.** me as before; ....
Ge 31:21 and set his face **t.** the mount Gilead...........
Ge 48:13 in his right hand **t.** Israel's left hand,.........
Ge 48:13 in his left hand **t.** Israel's right hand..........
Ex 9:8 let Moses sprinkle it **t.** the heaven in........
Ex 9:10 and Moses sprinkled it up **t.** heaven;.........
Ex 9:22 Stretch forth thine hand **t.** heaven 5921
Ex 9:23 Stretched forth his rod **t.** heaven:....... 5921
Ex 10:21 Stretch out thine hand **t.** heaven, ... 5921
Ex 10:22 stretched forth his hand **t.** heaven; 5921
Ex 16:10 that they looked **t.** the wilderness, ... 413
Ex 25:20 **t.** the mercy seat shall the faces of...........
Ex 26:35 the side of the tabernacle **t.** the south: ......
Ex 28:27 **t.** the forepart thereof, over............. 4136
Ex 34:8 and bowed his head **t.** the earth, ...
Ex 36:25 which is **t.** the north corner, ...
Ex 39:20 underneath, **t.** the forepart of it, ... 4136
Le 9:22 lifted up his hand **t.** the people, ... 413
Le 13:41 the part of his head **t.** his face,................
Nu 2:3 on the east side **t.** the rising of the...........
Nu 3:38 before the tabernacle **t.** the east, ...
Nu 16:42 they looked **t.** the tabernacle of the...... 413
Nu 21:11 which is before Moab, **t.** the sunrising.......
Nu 21:20 which looketh **t.** Jeshimon......... 5921,6440
Nu 23:28 that looketh **t.** Jeshimon. 5921,6440
Nu 24:1 he set his face **t.** the wilderness......... 413
Nu 32:14 fierce anger of the Lord **t.** Israel. 413
Nu 34:15 Jericho eastward, **t.** the sunrising. ....
De 4:41, 47 this side Jordan **t.** the sunrising; ....
De 28:54 his eye shall be evil **t.** his brother, ...
De 28:54 and **t.** the wife of his bosom,..................
De 28:54 **t.** the remnant of his children which..........
De 28:56 be evil **t.** the husband of her bosom,.........
De 28:56 and **t.** her son, and **t.** her daughter, ...
De 28:57 **t.** her young one that cometh out.............
De 28:57 **t.** her children which she shall bear:..........
Jos 1:4 sea **t.** the going down of the sun, ...
Jos 1:15 on this side Jordan **t.** the sunrising. ....
Jos 3:16 came down **t.** the sea of the plain,...... 5921
Jos 8:18 the spear that is in thy hand **t.** Ai;....... 413
Jos 8:18 that he had in his hand **t.** the city. 413
Jos 12:1 side Jordan **t.** the rising of the sun,...........
Jos 13:5 and all Lebanon, **t.** the sunrising,.............
Jos 15:4 From thence it passed **t.** Azmon, and........
Jos 15:7 the border went up **t.** Debir from the........

Jos 15:7 so northward, looking **t.** Gilgal, 413
Jos 15:7 passed **t.** the waters of En-shemesh, 413
Jos 15:21 **t.** the coast of Edom southward 413
Jos 16:6 went out **t.** the sea to Michmethah
Jos 18:13 border went over from thence **t.** Luz,
Jos 18:17 and went forth **t.** Geliloth, 413
Jos 18:18 passed along **t.** the side over 413
Jos 19:11 And their border went up **t.** the sea,
Jos 19:12 from Sarid eastward **t.** the sunrising
Jos 19:18 And their border was **t.** Jezreel,
Jos 19:27 **t.** the sunrising to Beth-dagon,
Jos 19:27 **t.** the north side of Beth-emek,
Jos 19:34 Judah upon Jordan **t.** the sunrising.
Jg 3:28 and took the fords of Jordan **t.** Moab,
Jg 4:6 saying, Go and draw **t.** mount Tabor,
Jg 5:9 My heart is **t.** the governors of Israel,
Jg 5:11 acts **t.** the inhabitants of his villages
Jg 8:3 Then their anger was abated **t.** him,
Jg 13:20 went up **t.** heaven from off the altar,
Jg 19:9 now the day draweth **t.** evening,
Jg 19:18 **t.** the side of mount Ephraim; 5704
Jg 20:43 over against Gibeah **t.** the sunrising.
Jg 20:45 turned and fled **t.** the wilderness
1Sa 13:18 the valley of Zeboim **t.** the wilderness.
1Sa 17:30 he turned from him **t.** another, 413,4136
1Sa 17:48 David hasted, and ran **t.** the army
1Sa 20:12 if there be good **t.** David, and I 413
1Sa 20:41 arose out of a place **t.** the south, 681
2Sa 14:1 the king's heart was **t.** Absalom. 5921
2Sa 15:23 **t.** the way of the wilderness. 5921,6440
2Sa 24:5 of the river of Gad, and **t.** Jazer: 413
2Sa 24:20 his servants coming on **t.** him: 5921
1Ki 7:9 on the outside **t.** the great court. 5704
1Ki 7:25 oxen, three looking **t.** the north,
1Ki 7:25 north, and three looking **t.** the west,
1Ki 7:25 west, and three looking **t.** the south,
1Ki 7:25 south, and three looking **t.** the east:
1Ki 8:22 and spread forth his hands **t.** heaven:
1Ki 8:29 eyes may be opened **t.** this house 413
1Ki 8:29 **t.** the place of which thou hast said, 413
1Ki 8:29 thy servant shall make **t.** this place. 413
1Ki 8:30 when they shall pray **t.** this place: 413
1Ki 8:35 if they pray **t.** this place, and confess 413
1Ki 8:38 spread forth his hands **t.** this house: 413
1Ki 8:42 shall come and pray **t.** this house; 413
1Ki 8:44 Lord **t.** the city which thou hast 1870
1Ki 8:44 and **t.** the house that I have built
1Ki 8:48 and pray unto thee **t.** their land, 1870
1Ki 14:13 some good thing **t.** the Lord God 413
1Ki 18:43 Go up now, look **t.** the sea. 1870
2Ki 3:14 I would not look **t.** thee, nor see 413
2Ki 25:4 king went the way **t.** the plain. 1870
1Ch 9:24 **t.** the east, west, north, and south.
1Ch 12:15 both **t.** the east, and **t.** the west.
1Ch 26:17 a day, and **t.** Asuppim two and two.
2Ch 4:4 oxen, three looking **t.** the north,
2Ch 4:4 north, and three looking **t.** the west,
2Ch 4:4 west, and three looking **t.** the south.
2Ch 4:4 south, and three looking **t.** the east:
2Ch 6:13 and spread forth his hands **t.** heaven,
2Ch 6:20 thy servant prayeth **t.** this place. 413
2Ch 6:21 which they shall make **t.** this place: 413
2Ch 6:26 if they pray **t.** this place, and confess 413
2Ch 6:34 they pray unto thee **t.** this city 1870
2Ch 6:38 and pray **t.** their land, which thou 1870
2Ch 6:38 **t.** the city which thou hast chosen,
2Ch 6:38 and **t.** the house which I have built
2Ch 16:9 them whose heart is perfect **t.** him. 413
2Ch 20:24 Judah came **t.** the watch tower 5921
2Ch 24:16 done good in Israel, both **t.** God, 5973
2Ch 24:16 and **t.** his house.
2Ch 31:14 the Levite, the porter **t.** the east,
Ezr 3:11 mercy endureth for ever **t.** Israel. 5921
Ne 3:26 against the water gate **t.** the east,
Ne 12:31 hand upon the wall **t.** the dung gate:
Es 1:13 manner **t.** all that knew law and 6440
Es 8:4 held out the golden sceptre **t.** Esther.
Job 2:12 dust upon their heads **t.** heaven.
Job 11:13 stretch out thine hands **t.** him; 413
Job 39:26 and stretch her wings **t.** the south?
Ps 5:7 will I worship **t.** thy holy temple. 413
Ps 25:15 Mine eyes are ever **t.** the Lord; for 413
Ps 28:2 lift up my hands **t.** thy holy oracle. 413
Ps 66:5 his doing **t.** the children of men. 5921
Ps 85:4 cause thine anger **t.** us to cease. 5973
Ps 86:13 For great is thy mercy **t.** me: and 5921
Ps 98:3 and his truth **t.** the house of Israel:
Ps 103:11 is his mercy **t.** them that fear him. 5921
Ps 116:12 the Lord for all his benefits **t.** me? 5921
Ps 117:2 merciful kindness is great **t.** us: 5921
Ps 138:2 I will worship **t.** thy holy temple, 413
Pr 14:35 The king's favour is **t.** a wise servant:
Pr 23:5 they fly away as an eagle **t.** heaven.
Ec 1:6 The wind goeth **t.** the south, and 413
Ec 11:3 and if the tree fall **t.** the south, or
Ec 11:3 **t.** the north, in the place where the
Ca 7:4 Lebanon which looketh **t.** Damascus.
Ca 7:10 beloved's, and his desire is **t.** me. 5921
Isa 7:1 went up **t.** Jerusalem to war against
Isa 11:14 of the Philistines **t.** the west:
Isa 29:13 fear **t.** me is taught by the precept 854
Isa 38:2 turned his face **t.** the wall. 413
Isa 49:23 to thee with their face **t.** the earth,
Isa 63:7 great goodness **t.** the house of Israel,
Isa 63:15 bowels and of thy mercies **t.** me? 413
Isa 66:14 shall be known **t.** his servants, 854
Isa 66:14 and his indignation **t.** his enemies. 854
Jer 1:13 the face thereof is **t.** the north. 6440
Jer 3:12 proclaim these words **t.** the north,
Jer 4:6 Set up the standard **t.** Zion: retire,
Jer 4:11 **t.** the daughter of my people,
Jer 12:3 me, and tried mine heart **t.** thee: 854
Jer 15:1 mind could not be **t.** this people: 413
Jer 29:10 perform my good word **t.** you, 5921
Jer 29:11 the thoughts that I think **t.** you, 5921
Jer 31:21 set thine heart **t.** the highway, even
Jer 31:40 corner of the horse gate **t.** the east,
Jer 46:6 **t.** the north by the river Euphrates.
Jer 49:36 will scatter them **t.** all those winds;
La 2:19 lift up thy hands **t.** him for the 5921
Eze 1:23 straight, the one **t.** the other: 413
Eze 4:7 thy face **t.** the siege of Jerusalem, 413
Eze 6:2 thy face **t.** the mountains of Israel, 413
Eze 6:14 than the wilderness **t.** Diblath,
Eze 8:3 inner gate that looketh **t.** the north;
Eze 8:5 thine eyes now the way **t.** the north.
Eze 8:5 up mine eyes the way **t.** the north,
Eze 8:14 house which was **t.** the north; 5921
Eze 8:16 backs **t.** the temple of the Lord, 413
Eze 8:16 Lord, and their faces **t.** the east;
Eze 8:16 they worshipped the sun **t.** the east.
Eze 9:2 higher gate, which lieth **t.** the north,
Eze 12:14 scatter **t.** every wind all that are
Eze 16:42 So will I make my fury **t.** thee to rest,
Eze 16:63 when I am pacified **t.** thee for all that
Eze 17:6 whose branches turned **t.** him, 413
Eze 17:7 vine did bend her roots **t.** him, 5921
Eze 17:7 and shot forth her branches **t.** him, 5921
Eze 17:21 shall be scattered **t.** all winds:
Eze 20:46 of man, set thy face **t.** the south, 1870
Eze 20:46 and drop thy word **t.** the south, 413
Eze 21:2 man, set thy face **t.** Jerusalem, 413
Eze 21:2 drop thy word **t.** the holy places, 413
Eze 24:23 iniquities, and mourn one **t.** another. 413
Eze 33:25 and lift up your eyes **t.** your idols, 413
Eze 40:6 the gate which looketh **t.** the east, 1870
Eze 40:20 court that looked **t.** the north, 1870
Eze 40:22 of the gate that looketh **t.** the east; 1870
Eze 40:23 the gate **t.** the north, and **t.** the east: 1870
Eze 40:24 that he brought me **t.** the south, 1870
Eze 40:24 behold a gate **t.** the south: and he 1870
Eze 40:27 gate in the inner court **t.** the south: 1870
Eze 40:27 from gate to gate **t.** the south 1870
Eze 40:31 arches...were **t.** the utter court; 413
Eze 40:32 into the inner court **t.** the east: 1870
Eze 40:34 arches...were **t.** the outward court:
Eze 40:37 posts thereof were **t.** the utter court;
Eze 40:44 their prospect was **t.** the south: 1870
Eze 40:44 having the prospect **t.** the north. 1870
Eze 40:45 whose prospect is **t.** the south, 1870
Eze 40:46 whose prospect is **t.** the north is 1870
Eze 41:11 were **t.** the place that was left, 1870
Eze 41:11 one door **t.** the north, 1870
Eze 41:11 and another door **t.** the south: 1870
Eze 41:12 at the end **t.** the west was seventy 1870
Eze 41:14 and of the separate place **t.** the east,
Eze 41:19 face of a man was **t.** the palm tree 413
Eze 41:19 face of a young lion **t.** the palm tree 413
Eze 42:1 utter court, the way **t.** the north: 1870
Eze 42:1 before the building **t.** the north. 413
Eze 42:4 cubit; and their doors **t.** the north.
Eze 42:7 **t.** the utter court on the forepart 1870
Eze 42:10 the wall of the court **t.** the east, 1870
Eze 42:11 chambers which were **t.** the north, 1870
Eze 42:12 chambers that were **t.** the south 1870
Eze 42:12 directly before the wall **t.** the east, 1870
Eze 42:15 he brought me forth **t.** the gate 1870
Eze 42:15 whose prospect is **t.** the east, and 1870
Eze 43:1 the gate that looketh **t.** the east: 1870
Eze 43:4 gate whose prospect is **t.** the east. 1870
Eze 43:17 and his stairs shall look **t.** the east.
Eze 44:1 sanctuary which looketh **t.** the east;
Eze 46:1 inner court that looketh **t.** the east
Eze 46:12 him the gate that looketh **t.** the east,
Eze 46:19 priests, which looked **t.** the north:
Eze 47:1 of the house stood **t.** the east,
Eze 47:8 waters issue out **t.** the east country,
Eze 47:15 border of the land **t.** the north side,
Eze 48:10 **t.** the north five and twenty thousand
Eze 48:10 **t.** the west ten thousand in breadth,
Eze 48:10 **t.** the east ten thousand in breadth,
Eze 48:10 **t.** the south five and twenty thousand.
Eze 48:17 **t.** the north two hundred and fifty,
Eze 48:17 **t.** the south two hundred and fifty,
Eze 48:17 **t.** the east two hundred and fifty,
Eze 48:17 **t.** the west two hundred and fifty.
Eze 48:21 the oblation **t.** the east border, 5704
Eze 48:21 and twenty thousand **t.** the west 5921
Eze 48:28 and to the river **t.** the great sea. 5921
Da 4:2 the high God hath wrought **t.** me. 5974
Da 6:10 open in his chamber **t.** Jerusalem, 5049
Da 8:8 ones **t.** the four winds of heaven.
Da 8:9 exceeding great, **t.** the south, 413
Da 8:9 **t.** the east, and **t.** the pleasant land. 413
Da 8:18 deep sleep on my face **t.** the ground:
Da 10:9 my face, and my face **t.** the ground.
Da 10:15 unto me, I set my face **t.** the ground,
Da 11:4 be divided **t.** the four winds of heaven;
Da 11:19 his face **t.** the fort of his own land:
Da 11:29 shall return, and come **t.** the south;
Ho 3:1 the Lord **t.** the children of Israel, 854
Ho 5:1 for judgment is **t.** you, because ye
Joe 2:20 with his face **t.** the east sea, and 413
Joe 2:20 his hinder part **t.** the utmost sea, 413
Jon 2:4 will look again **t.** thy holy temple. 413
Zec 6:6 grisled go forth **t.** the south country. 413
Zec 6:8 these that go **t.** the north country 413
Zec 9:1 tribes of Israel, shall be **t.** the Lord.
Zec 14:4 thereof **t.** the east and **t.** the west,
Zec 14:4 mountain shall remove **t.** the north,
Zec 14:4 the north, and half of it **t.** the south.
Zec 14:8 half of them **t.** the former sea, 413
Zec 14:8 and half of them **t.** the hinder sea: 413
Mt 12:49 forth his hand **t.** his disciples, *1909*
Mt 14:14 moved with compassion **t.** them, *1909*
Mt 28:1 to dawn **t.** the first day of the week. *1519*
Mk 6:34 moved with compassion **t.** them, *1909*
Lu 2:14 on earth peace, good will **t.** men. *1722*
Lu 12:21 **himself, and is not rich t. God** *1519*
Lu 13:22 and journeying **t.** Jerusalem. *1519*
Lu 24:29 for it is **t.** evening, and the day is *4314*
Joh 6:17 went over the sea **t.** Capernaum. *1519*
Ac 1:10 looked stedfastly **t.** heaven as he *1519*
Ac 8:26 go **t.** the south unto the way that *2596*
Ac 20:21 to the Greeks, repentance **t.** God, *1519*
Ac 20:21 and faith **t.** our Lord Jesus Christ. *1519*
Ac 22:3 and was zealous **t.** God, as ye all are
Ac 24:15 And have hope **t.** God, which they *1519*
Ac 24:16 conscience void of offence **t.** God, *4314*
Ac 24:16 and **t.** men.
Ac 27:12 **t.** the south west and north west. *2596*
Ac 27:40 to the wind, and made **t.** shore. *1519*
Ac 28:14 days: and so we went **t.** Rome. *1519*
Ro 1:27 burned in their lust one **t.** another; *1519*
Ro 5:8 God commendeth his love **t.** us, *1519*
Ro 11:22 **t.** thee, goodness, if thou continue *1909*
Ro 12:16 of the same mind one **t.** another. *1519*
Ro 15:5 be likeminded one **t.** another *1722*
1Co 7:36 himself uncomely **t.** his virgin, *1909*
2Co 1:16 be brought on my way **t.** Judaea. *1519*
2Co 1:18 word **t.** you was not yea and nay. *4314*
2Co 2:8 would confirm your love **t.** him. *1519*
2Co 7:4 is my boldness of speech **t.** you, *4314*
2Co 7:7 your fervent mind **t.** me; *5228*
2Co 7:15 affection is more abundant **t.** you, *1519*
2Co 9:8 to make all grace abound **t.** you; *1519*
2Co 10:1 but being absent am bold **t.** you: *1519*
2Co 13:4 him by the power of God **t.** you. *1519*
Gal 2:8 was mighty in me **t.** the Gentiles:) *1519*
Eph 1:8 hath abounded **t.** us in all wisdom *1519*
Eph 2:7 in his kindness **t.** us through *1909*

Php 2:30 supply your lack of service **t.** me. *4314*
Php 3:14 I press **t.** the mark for the prize *2596*
Col 4:5 Walk in wisdom **t.** them that are *4314*
1Th 3:12 abound in love one **t.** another, *1519*
1Th 3:12 **t.** all men, even as we do **t.** you: *1519*
1Th 4:10 indeed ye do it **t.** all the brethren *1519*
1Th 4:12 ye may walk honestly **t.** them that *4314*
1Th 5:14 the weak, be patient **t.** all men. *4314*
2Th 1:3 of you all **t.** each other aboundeth *1519*
Tit 3:4 God our Saviour **t.** man appeared, *4814*
Phm 5 thou hast **t.** the Lord Jesus, *4314*
Phm 5 and **t.** all saints; *1519*
Heb 6:1 dead works, and of faith **t.** God, *1909*
Heb 6:10 which ye have shewed **t.** his name. *1519*
1Pe 2:19 for conscience **t.** God endure grief,
1Pe 3:21 of a good conscience **t.** God,) *1519*
1Jo 3:21 then have we confidence **t.** God. *4314*
1Jo 4:9 manifested the love of God **t.** us, *1722*

TOWEL
Joh 13:4 and took a **t.**, and girded himself. *3012*
Joh 13:5 wipe them with the **t.** wherewith *3012*

TOWER See also TOWERS; WATCHTOWER.
Ge 11:4 to, let us build us a city and a **t.**, 4026
Ge 11:5 down to see the city and the **t.**, 4026
Ge 35:21 his tent beyond the **t.** of Edar. 4026
Jg 8:9 peace, I will break down this **t.** 4026
Jg 8:17 he beat down the **t.** of Penuel, 4026
Jg 9:46 men of the **t.** of Shechem heard 4026
Jg 9:47 men of the **t.** of Shechem were 4026
Jg 9:49 men of the **t.** of Shechem died also, 4026
Jg 9:51 there was a strong **t.** within the city, 4026
Jg 9:51 gat them up to the top of the **t.** 4026
Jg 9:52 And Abimelech came unto the **t.**, 4026
Jg 9:52 went hard unto the door of the **t.** to 4026
2Sa 22:3 my high **t.**, and my refuge, my 4869
2Sa 22:51 He is the **t.** of salvation for his 1431
2Ki 5:24 when he came to the **t.**, he took 6076
2Ki 9:17 there stood a watchman on the **t.** 4026
2Ki 17:9 from the **t.** of the watchmen to the 4026
2Ki 18:8 from the **t.** of the watchmen to the 4026
2Ch 20:24 Judah came toward the watch **t.** in
Ne 3:1 even unto the **t.** of Meah they 4026
Ne 3:1 sanctified it, unto the **t.** of Hananeel. 4026
Ne 3:11 piece, and the **t.** of the furnaces. 4026
Ne 3:25 **t.** which lieth out from the king's 4026
Ne 3:26 the cast, and the **t.** that lieth out. 4026
Ne 3:27 against the great **t.** that lieth out, 4026
Ne 12:38 from beyond the **t.** of the furnaces 4026
Ne 12:39 fish gate, and the **t.** of Hananeel, 4026
Ne 12:39 and the **t.** of Meah, even unto the 4026
Ps 18:2 of my salvation, and my high **t.** 4869
Ps 61:3 and a strong **t.** from the enemy. 4026
Ps 144:2 my high **t.**, and my deliverer; 4869
Pr 18:10 name of the Lord is a strong **t.**: 4026
Ca 4:4 Thy neck is like the **t.** of David 4026
Ca 7:4 Thy neck is as a **t.** of ivory; thine 4026
Ca 7:4 thy nose is as the **t.** of Lebanon 4026
Isa 2:15 And upon every high **t.**, and upon 4026
Isa 5:2 and built a **t.** in the midst of it, 4026
Jer 6:27 I have set thee for a **t.** and a 969
Jer 31:38 from the **t.** of Hananeel unto the 4026
Eze 29:10 from the **t.** of Syene even unto the 4024
Eze 30:6 from the **t.** of Syene shall they fall 4024
Mic 4:8 And thou, O **t.** of the flock, the 4026
Hab 2:1 my watch, and set me upon the **t.**, 4692
Zec 14:10 and from the **t.** of Hananeel unto 4026
Mt 21:33 **a winepress in it, and built a t.,** *4444*
Mk 12:1 **for the winefat, and built a t.,** *4444*
Lu 13:4 **upon whom the t. in Siloam fell,** *4444*
Lu 14:28 **of you, intending to build a t.,** *4444*

TOWERS
2Ch 14:7 make about them walls, and **t.**, 4026
2Ch 26:9 Uzziah built **t.** in Jerusalem at the 4026
2Ch 26:10 Also he built **t.** in the desert, and 4026
2Ch 26:15 be on the **t.** and upon the bulwarks, 4026
2Ch 27:4 the forests he built castles and **t.** 4026
2Ch 32:5 broken, and raised it up to the **t.**, 4026
Ps 48:12 about her: tell the **t.** thereof. 4026
Ca 8:10 I am a wall, and my breasts like **t.** 4026
Isa 23:13 they set up the **t.** thereof, they 971
Isa 30:25 great slaughter, when the **t.** fall. 4026
Isa 32:14 the forts and **t.** shall be for dens 975
Isa 33:18 where is he that counted the **t.**? 4026
Eze 26:4 of Tyrus, and break down her **t.** 4026
Eze 26:9 his axes he shall break down thy **t.** 4026
Eze 27:11 the Gammadims were in thy **t.** 4026
Zep 1:16 cities, and against the high **t.** 6438
Zep 3:6 the nations: their **t.** are desolate; 6438

TO-WIT See WIT.

TOWN See also TOWNCLERK; TOWNS.
Jos 2:15 for her house was upon the **t.** wall 7023
1Sa 16:4 the elders of the **t.** trembled at his 7023
1Sa 23:7 entering into a **t.** that hath gates 5892
1Sa 27:5 a place in some **t.** in the country, 5892
Hab 2:12 him that buildeth a **t.** with blood, 5892
Mt 10:11 **city or t. ye shall enter,** *2968*
Mk 8:23 the hand, and led him out of the **t.**; *2968*
Mk 8:26 saying, **Neither go into the t., nor** *2968*
Mk 8:26 **nor tell it to any in the t.** *2968*
Lu 5:17 were come out of every **t.** of Galilee, *2968*
Joh 7:42 out of the **t.** of Bethlehem, where *2968*
Joh 11:1 the **t.** of Mary and her sister Martha. *2968*
Joh 11:30 Jesus was not yet come into the **t.**, *2968*

TOWNCLERK
Ac 19:35 And when the **t.** had appeased the *1122*

TOWNS
Ge 25:16 these are their names, by their **t.**, 2691
Nu 32:41 Jair...went and took the small **t.** 2333
De 3:5 beside unwalled **t.** a great many. 5892
Jos 13:30 **t.** of Jair, which are in Bashan, 2333
Jos 15:45 Ekron, with her **t.** and her villages: 1323
Jos 15:47 Ashdod with her **t.** and her villages, 1323
Jos 15:47 Gaza with her **t.** and her villages, 1323
Jos 17:11 in Asher Beth-shean and her **t.**, 1323
Jos 17:11 and Ibleam and her **t.**, 1323
Jos 17:11 the inhabitants of Dor and her **t.**, 1323
Jos 17:11 inhabitants of En-dor and her **t.**, 1323
Jos 17:11 inhabitants of Taanach and her **t.**, 1323
Jos 17:11 inhabitants of Megiddo and her **t.**, 1323
Jos 17:16 who are of Beth-shean and her **t.**, 1323
Jg 1:27 of Beth-shean and her **t.**, 1323
Jg 1:27 nor Taanach and her **t.**, 1323
Jg 1:27 the inhabitants of Dor and her **t.**, 1323
Jg 1:27 inhabitants of Ibleam and her **t.**, 1323
Jg 1:27 inhabitants of Megiddo and her **t.**: 1323
Jg 11:26 Israel dwelt in Heshbon and her **t.**, 1323
Jg 11:26 and in Aroer and her **t.**, and in all 1323
1Ki 4:13 to him pertained the **t.** of Jair the 2333
1Ch 2:23 and Aram, with the **t.** of Jair, 2333
1Ch 2:23 with Kenath, and the **t.** of Jair, 2333
1Ch 2:23 with Kenath, and the **t.** thereof, 1323
1Ch 5:16 in her **t.**, and in all the suburbs of 1323
1Ch 7:28 were, Beth-el and the **t.** thereof, 1323
1Ch 7:28 westward Gezer, with the **t.** thereof; 1323
1Ch 7:28 Shechem also and the **t.** thereof, 1323
1Ch 7:28 unto Gaza and the **t.** thereof: 1323
1Ch 7:29 Manasseh, Beth-shean and her **t.**,
1Ch 7:29 Taanach and her **t.**,
1Ch 7:29 Megiddo and her **t.**,
1Ch 7:29 Dor and her **t.**
1Ch 8:12 Ono, and Lod, with the **t.** thereof: 1323
1Ch 18:1 Gath and her **t.** out of the hand of 1323
2Ch 13:19 him, Beth-el with the **t.** thereof, 1323
2Ch 13:19 and Jeshanah with the **t.** thereof, 1323
2Ch 13:19 and Ephrain with the **t.** thereof. 1323
Es 9:19 that dwelt in the unwalled **t.** 5892
Jer 19:15 upon this city and upon all her **t.** 5892
Zec 2:4 inhabited as **t.** without walls for 6519
Mk 1:38 **Let us go into the next t., that I** *2969*
Mk 8:27 into the **t.** of Caesarea Philippi: *2968*
Lu 9:6 went through the **t.**, preaching the *2968*
Lu 9:12 they may go into the **t.** and country *2968*

TRACHONITIS (trak-o-ni'-tis)
Lu 3:1 of Ituraea and of the region of **T.**, *5139*

TRADE See also TRADED; TRADING.
Ge 34:10 dwell and **t.** ye therein, and get 5503
Ge 34:21 dwell in the land, and **t.** therein; 5503
Ge 46:32 for their **t.** hath been to feed cattle; 582
Ge 46:34 Thy servants' **t.** hath been about 582
Re 18:17 sailors, and as many as **t.** by sea, *2038*

TRADED
Eze 27:12 tin, and lead, they **t.** in thy fairs. 5414
Eze 27:13 they **t.** the persons of men and 5414
Eze 27:14 house of Togarmah **t.** in thy fairs 5414
Eze 27:17 **t.** in thy market wheat of Minnith, 5414
Mt 25:16 **talents went and t. with the same.** *2038*

TRADING
Lu 19:15 **much every man had gained by t.** *1281*

TRADITION See also TRADITIONS.
Mt 15:2 transgress the **t.** of the elders? *3862*
Mt 15:3 **commandment of God by your t.?** *3862*
Mt 15:6 **of God of none effect by your t.** *3862*
Mk 7:3 eat not, holding the **t.** of the elders. *3862*
Mk 7:5 according to the **t.** of the elders, *3862*
Mk 7:8 **ye hold the t. of men, as the** *3862*
Mk 7:9 **that ye may keep your own t.** *3862*
Mk 7:13 **God of none effect through your t.,** *3862*
Col 2:8 vain deceit, after the **t.** of men, *3862*
2Th 3:6 not after the **t.** which he received *3862*
1Pe 1:18 received by **t.** from your fathers;

TRADITIONS
Ga 1:14 zealous of the **t.** of my fathers. *3862*
2Th 2:15 hold the **t.**...ye have been taught, *3862*

TRAFFICK
Ge 42:34 brother, and ye shall **t.** in the land. 5503
1Ki 10:15 of the **t.** of the spice merchants, 4536
Eze 17:4 and carried it into a land of **t.**; 3667
Eze 28:5 by thy **t.** hast thou increased thy 7404
Eze 28:18 iniquities, by the iniquity of thy **t.**; 7404

TRAFFICKERS
Isa 23:8 **t.** are the honourable of the earth? 3669

TRAIN See also TRAINED.
1Ki 10:2 to Jerusalem with a very great **t.**, 2428
Pr 22:6 **T.** up a child in the way he should 2596
Isa 6:1 up, and his **t.** filled the temple. 7757

TRAINED
Ge 14:14 captive, he armed his **t.** servants, 2593

TRAITOR See also TRAITORS.
Lu 6:16 Iscariot, which was also the **t.** *4273*

TRAITORS
2Ti 3:4 **T.**, heady, highminded, lovers of *4273*

TRAMPLE
Ps 91:13 dragon shalt thou **t.** under feet. 7429
Isa 63:3 anger, and **t.** them in my fury; 7429
Mt 7:6 **they t. them under their feet,** *2662*

TRANCE
Nu 24:4,16 into a **t.**, but having his eyes open:
Ac 10:10 they made ready, he fell into a **t.**, *1611*
Ac 11:5 and in a **t.** I saw a vision, A certain *1611*
Ac 22:17 prayed in the temple, I was in a **t.**; *1611*

TRANQUILLITY
Da 4:27 it may be a lengthening of thy **t.** 7963

TRANSFERRED
1Co 4:6 I have in a figure **t.** to myself and *3345*

TRANSFIGURED
Mt 17:2 And was **t.** before them: and his *3339*
Mk 9:2 and he was **t.** before them. *3339*

TRANSFORMED
Ro 12:2 ye **t.** by the renewing of your mind, *3339*
2Co 11:14 Satan himself is **t.** into an angel *3345*
2Co 11:15 **t.** as...ministers of righteousness; *3345*

TRANSFORMING
2Co 11:13 **t.** themselves into the apostles of *3345*

TRANSGRESS See also TRANSGRESSED; TRANSGRESSEST; TRANGRESSETH; TRANSGRESSING.
Nu 14:41 do ye **t.** the commandment of the 5674
1Sa 2:24 ye make the Lord's people to **t.** 5674
2Ch 24:20 Why **t.** ye the commandments of 5674
Ne 1:8 If ye **t.**, I will scatter you abroad 4603
Ne 13:27 to **t.** against our God in marrying 4603
Ps 17:3 that my mouth shall not **t.** 5674
Ps 25:3 ashamed which **t.** without cause 898
Pr 28:21 a piece of bread that man will **t.** 6586
Jer 2:20 and thou saidst, I will not **t.**; 5647
Eze 20:38 and them that **t.** against me: 6586
Am 4:4 Come to Beth-el, and **t.**; at Gilgal 6586
Mt 15:2 thy disciples **t.** the tradition of the *3845*
Mt 15:3 **do ye also t. the commandment** *3845*
Ro 2:27 and circumcision dost **t.** the law? *3848*

TRANSGRESSED
De 26:13 I have not **t.** thy commandments, 5674
Jos 7:11 and they have also **t.** my covenant 5674
Jos 7:15 because he hath **t.** the covenant of 5674
Jos 23:16 When ye have **t.** the covenant of the 5674

Jg 2:20 this people hath **t.** my covenant 5674
1Sa 14:33 he said, Ye have **t.**: roll a great........... 898
1Sa 15:24 for I have **t.** the commandment of 5674
1Ki 8:50 wherein they have **t.** against thee,...... 6586
2Ki 18:12 their God, but **t.** his covenant,........... 5674
1Ch 2:7 Israel, who **t.** in...thing accursed........ 4603
1Ch 5:25 **t.** against the God of their fathers, ... 4603
2Ch 12:2 they had **t.** against the Lord,............. 4603
2Ch 26:16 for he **t.** against the Lord his God, ... 4603
2Ch 28:19 naked, and **t.** sore against the Lord. ... 4603
2Ch 36:14 people, **t.** very much after all the 4603
Ezr 10:10 Ye have **t.**, and have taken strange..... 4603
Ezr 10:13 many that have **t.** in this thing........... 6586
Isa 24:5 because they have **t.** the laws, ... 5674
Isa 43:27 thy teachers have **t.** against me. 6586
Isa 66:24 the men that have **t.** against me:........ 6586
Jer 2:8 the pastors also **t.** against me, and 6586
Jer 2:29 ye all have **t.** against me, saith the 6586
Jer 3:13 hast **t.** against the Lord thy God, ... 6586
Jer 33:8 whereby they have **t.** against me........ 6586
Jer 34:18 the men that have **t.** my covenant, ... 5674
La 3:42 We have **t.** and have rebelled: 6586
Eze 2:3 their fathers have **t.** against me, ... 6586
Eze 18:31 transgressions, whereby ye have **t.**...... 6586
Da 9:11 Yea, all Israel have **t.** thy law,............ 5674
Ho 6:7 they like men have **t.** the covenant: 5674
Ho 7:13 because they have **t.** against me: 6586
Ho 8:1 because they have **t.** my covenant, ... 5674
Zep 3:11 wherein thou hast **t.** against me: 6586
Lu 15:29 **neither t. I at any time thy**........... *3928*

TRANSGRESSEST
Es 3:3 Mordecai, Why **t.** thou the king's 5674

TRANSGRESSETH
Pr 16:10 his mouth **t.** not in judgment. 4603
Hab 2:5 Yea also, because he **t.** by wine, ... 898
1Jo 3:4 Whosoever committeth sin **t.**........ *458,4160*
2Jo 9 Whosoever **t.**, and abideth not in........ *3845*

TRANSGRESSING
De 17:2 Lord thy God, in **t.** his covenant, ... 5674
Isa 59:13 In **t.** and lying against the Lord,......... 6586

TRANSGRESSION See also TRANSGRESSIONS.
Ex 34:7 forgiving iniquity and **t.** and sin, ... 6588
Nu 14:18 forgiving iniquity and **t.**, and by no...... 6588
Jos 22:22 or if in **t.** against the Lord, (save 4604
1Sa 24:11 is neither evil nor **t.** in mine hand,...... 6588
1Ch 9:1 carried away to Babylon for their **t.** 4604
1Ch 10:13 So Saul died for his **t.** which he 4604
2Ch 29:19 in his reign did cast away in his **t.**, ... 4604
Ezr 9:4 the **t.** of those that had been............. 4604
Ezr 10:6 he mourned because of the **t.** of 4604
Job 7:21 why dost thou not pardon my **t.**,......... 6588
Job 8:4 he have cast them away for their **t.**; ... 6588
Job 13:23 make me to know my **t.** and my sin.... 6588
Job 14:17 My **t.** is sealed up in a bag, and......... 6588
Job 33:9 I am clean without **t.**, I am.............. 6588
Job 34:6 my wound is incurable without **t.**......... 6588
Ps 19:13 shall be innocent from the great **t.**....... 6588
Ps 32:1 Blessed is he whose **t.** is forgiven, ... 6588
Ps 36:1 The **t.** of the wicked saith within........ 6588
Ps 59:3 not for my **t.** nor for my sin, O Lord. ..6588
Ps 89:32 will I visit their **t.** with the rod, ... 6588
Ps 107:17 Fools because of their **t.**, and.......... 6588
Pr 12:13 The wicked is snared by the **t.** of......... 6588
Pr 17:9 He that covereth a **t.** seeketh love: 6588
Pr 17:19 He loveth **t.** that loveth strife: and 6588
Pr 19:11 and it is his glory to pass over a **t.**..... 6588
Pr 28:2 For the **t.** of a land many are the....... 6588
Pr 28:24 his mother, and saith, It is no **t.**; 6588
Pr 29:6 **t.** of an evil man there is a snare: 6588
Pr 29:16 are multiplied, **t.** increaseth:............. 6588
Pr 29:22 and a furious man aboundeth in **t.**........ 6588
Isa 24:20 **t.** thereof shall be heavy upon it;........ 6588
Isa 53:8 for the **t.** of my people was he 6588
Isa 57:4 are ye not children of **t.**, a seed of...... 6588
Isa 58:1 and shew my people their **t.**, and....... 6588
Isa 59:20 them that turn from **t.** in Jacob, ... 6588
Eze 33:12 not deliver him in the day of his **t.** 6588
Da 8:12 the daily sacrifice by reason of **t.**,........ 6588
Da 8:13 sacrifice, and the **t.** of desolation, ... 6588
Da 9:24 to finish the **t.**, and to make an end.... 6588
Am 4:4 at Gilgal multiply **t.**: and bring 6586
Mic 1:5 For the **t.** of Jacob is all this, and........ 6588
Mic 1:5 What is the **t.** of Jacob? is it not 6588
Mic 3:8 to declare unto Jacob his **t.**, and to...... 6588
Mic 6:7 shall I give my firstborn for my **t.**, ... 6588
Mic 7:18 passeth by the **t.** of the remnant of 6588
Ac 1:25 from which Judas by **t.** fell, that......... *3845*
Ro 4:15 for where no law is, there is no **t.**...... *3847*
Ro 5:14 after the similitude of Adam's **t.**, ... *3847*
1Ti 2:14 woman being deceived was in the **t.**..... *3847*
Heb 2:2 every **t.** and disobedience received *3847*
1Jo 3:4 the law: for sin is the **t.** of the law. *458*

TRANSGRESSIONS
Ex 23:21 not; for he will not pardon your **t.** 6588
Le 16:16 because of their **t.** in all their sins: 6588
Le 16:21 and all their **t.** in all their sins,........... 6588
Jos 24:19 not forgive your **t.** nor your sins. 6588
1Ki 8:50 all their **t.** wherein they have 6588
Job 31:33 If I covered my **t.** as Adam, by 6588
Job 35:6 if thy **t.** be multiplied, what doest....... 6588
Job 36:9 their **t.** that they have exceeded. 6588
Ps 5:10 out in the multitude of their **t.**; 6588
Ps 25:7 not the sins of my youth, nor my **t.**...... 6588
Ps 32:5 I will confess my **t.** unto the Lord; 6588
Ps 39:8 Deliver me from all my **t.**: make 6588
Ps 51:1 thy tender mercies blot out my **t.**........ 6588
Ps 51:3 For I acknowledge my **t.**: and my...... 6588
Ps 65:3 as for our **t.**, thou shalt purge them.... 6588
Ps 103:12 hath he removed our **t.** from us. 6588
Isa 43:25 blotteth out thy **t.** for mine own......... 6588
Isa 44:22 blotted out, as a thick cloud, thy **t.**,..... 6588
Isa 50:1 your **t.** is your mother put away. 6588
Isa 53:5 But he was wounded for our **t.**, he..... 6588
Isa 59:12 our **t.** are multiplied before thee,........ 6588
Isa 59:12 for our **t.** are with us; and as for 6588
Jer 5:6 because their **t.** are many, and their ... 6588
La 1:5 her for the multitude of her **t.** 6588
La 1:14 yoke of my **t.** is bound by his hand: 6588
La 1:22 hast done unto me for all my **t.** 6588
Eze 14:11 polluted any more with all their **t.**;....... 6588
Eze 18:22 All his **t.** that he hath committed,....... 6588
Eze 18:28 away from all his **t.** that he hath 6588
Eze 18:30 turn yourselves from all your **t.**; 6588
Eze 18:31 Cast away from you all your **t.**, ... 6588
Eze 21:24 in that your **t.** are discovered, so....... 6588
Eze 33:10 If our **t.** and our sins be upon us,....... 6588
Eze 37:23 things, nor with any of their **t.**.......... 6588
Eze 39:24 according to their **t.** have I done 6588
Am 1:3 For three **t.** of Damascus, and for...... 6588
Am 1:6 For three **t.** of Gaza, and for four, ... 6588
Am 1:9 For three **t.** of Tyrus, and for four, ... 6588
Am 1:11 For three **t.** of Edom, and for four, ... 6588
Am 1:13 For three **t.** of the children of........... 6588
Am 2:1 For three **t.** of Moab, and for four,..... 6588
Am 2:4 For three **t.** of Judah, and for four,..... 6588
Am 2:6 For three **t.** of Israel, and for four,..... 6588
Am 3:14 shall visit the **t.** of Israel upon him 6588
Am 5:12 your manifold **t.** and your mighty........ 6588
Mic 1:13 the **t.** of Israel were found in thee...... 6588
Ga 3:19 It was added because of **t.**, till the *3847*
Heb 9:15 the **t.** that were under the first.......... *3847*

TRANSGRESSOR See also TRANSGRESSORS.
Pr 21:18 and the **t.** for the upright. 898
Pr 22:12 overthroweth the words of the **t.**.......... 898
Isa 48:8 wast called a **t.** from the womb.......... 6586
Ga 2:18 I destroyed, I make myself a **t.** *3848*
Jas 2:11 kill, thou art become a **t.** of the law.... *3848*

TRANSGRESSORS
Ps 37:38 But the **t.** shall be destroyed............ 6586
Ps 51:13 Then will I teach **t.** thy ways; and...... 6586
Ps 59:5 be not merciful to any wicked **t.** 898
Ps 119:158 I beheld the **t.**, and was grieved; 898
Pr 2:22 and the **t.** shall be rooted out of it. 898
Pr 11:3 the perverseness of **t.** shall destroy...... 898
Pr 11:6 **t.** shall be taken in their own 898
Pr 13:2 the soul of the **t.** shall eat violence....... 898
Pr 13:15 favour: but the way of **t.** is hard.......... 898
Pr 23:28 and increaseth the **t.** among men. 898
Pr 26:10 the fool, and rewardeth **t.**................. 5674
Isa 1:28 the destruction of the **t.** and of the..... 6586
Isa 46:8 men; bring it again to mind, O ye **t.** ... 6586
Isa 53:12 and he was numbered with the **t.**; 6586
Isa 53:12 and made intercession for the **t.**......... 6586
Da 8:23 when the **t.** are come to the full, ... 6586
Ho 14:9 them: but the **t.** shall fall therein. 6586
Mk 15:28 And he was numbered with the **t.**......... *459*
Lu 22:37 **he was reckoned among the t.**:....... *459*
Jas 2:9 and are convinced of the law as **t.**...... *3848*

TRANSLATE See also TRANSLATED.
2Sa 3:10 To **t.** the kingdom from the house...... 5674

TRANSLATED
Col 1:13 hath **t.** us into the kingdom of his....... *3179*
Heb 11:5 By faith Enoch was **t.** that he............ *3346*
Heb 11:5 not found, because God had **t.** him: *3346*

TRANSLATION
Heb 11:5 for before his **t.** he had this *3331*

TRANSPARENT
Re 21:21 was pure gold, as it were **t.** glass. *1307*

TRAP See also TRAPS.
Job 18:10 and a **t.** for him in the way. 4434
Ps 69:22 for their welfare, let it become a **t.**..... 4170
Jer 5:26 they set a **t.**, they catch men. 4889
Ro 11:9 table he made a snare, and a **t.**, ... *2339*

TRAPS
Jos 23:13 shall be snares and **t.** unto you. 4170

TRAVAIL See also TRAVAILED; TRAVAILEST; TRAVAILETH; TRAVAILING; TRAVEL.
Ge 38:27 came to pass in the time of her **t.**, ... 3205
Ex 18:8 all the **t.** that had come upon them..... 8513
Nu 20:14 all the **t.** that hath befallen us: 8513
Ps 48:6 and pain, as of a woman in **t.**............ 3205
Ec 1:13 this sore **t.** hath God given to the 6045
Ec 2:23 days are sorrows, and his **t.** grief;...... 6045
Ec 2:26 to the sinner he giveth **t.**, to gather.... 6045
Ec 3:10 I have seen the **t.**, which God hath..... 6045
Ec 4:4 I considered all **t.**, and every right...... 5999
Ec 4:6 hands full with **t.** and vexation of........ 5999
Ec 4:8 is also vanity, yea, it is a sore **t.**........ 6045
Ec 5:14 But those riches perish by evil **t.** 6045
Isa 23:4 I **t.** not, nor bring forth children,........ 2342
Isa 53:11 He shall see of the **t.** of his soul, ... 5999
Isa 54:1 thou that didst not **t.** with child:......... 2342
Jer 4:31 heard a voice as of a woman in **t.**,....... 2470
Jer 6:24 us, and pain, as of a woman in **t.** 3205
Jer 13:21 sorrows take thee, as a woman in **t.**?.. 3205
Jer 22:23 thee, the pain as of a woman in **t.**! 3205
Jer 30:6 whether a man doth **t.** with child? 3205
Jer 30:6 on his loins, as a woman in **t.**,........... 3205
Jer 49:24 have taken her, as a woman in **t.** 3205
Jer 50:43 him, and pangs as of a woman in **t.** 3205
La 3:5 compassed me with gall and **t.**........... 8513
Mic 4:9 have taken thee as a woman in **t.**........ 3205
Mic 4:10 of Zion, like a woman in **t.**: 3205
Joh 16:21 **A woman...in t. hath sorrow**,........ *5088*
Ga 4:19 I **t.** in birth again until Christ be.......... *5605*
1Th 2:9 brethren, our labour and **t.**:................ *3449*
1Th 5:3 as **t.** upon a woman with child; *5604*
2Th 3:8 wrought with labour and **t.** night *3449*

TRAVAILED
Ge 35:16 Rachel **t.**, and she had hard labour,..... 3205
Ge 38:28 it came to pass, when she **t.**, that...... 3205
1Sa 4:19 dead, she bowed herself and **t.**; 3205
Isa 66:7 Before she **t.**, she brought forth; 2342
Isa 66:8 for as soon as Zion **t.**, she brought..... 2342

TRAVAILEST
Ga 4:27 forth and cry, thou that **t.** not: *5605*

TRAVAILETH
Job 15:20 wicked man **t.** with pain all his........... 2342
Ps 7:14 he **t.** with iniquity, and hath 2254
Isa 13:8 be in pain as a woman that **t.**........... 3205
Isa 21:3 as the pangs of a woman that **t.**......... 3205
Jer 31:8 and her that **t.** with child together: 3205
Mic 5:3 she which **t.** hath brought forth:......... 3205
Ro 8:22 and **t.** in pain together until now. *4944*

TRAVAILING
Isa 42:14 now will I cry like a **t.** woman; I........ 3205
Ho 13:13 The sorrows of a **t.** woman shall........ 3205
Re 12:2 being with child cried, **t.** in birth, ... *5605*

TRAVEL See also TRAVAIL; TRAVELLED; TRAVELLETH; TRAVELLING.
Nu 20:14 all the **t.** that hath befallen us: 8513
La 3:5 compassed me with gall and **t.**........... 8513
Ac 19:29 Macedonia, Paul's companions in **t.**, ... *4898*
2Co 8:19 chosen of the churches to **t.** with us ... *4898*

TRAVELLED
Ac 11:19 Stephen **t.** as far as Phenice, and....... *1330*

TRAVELLER See also TRAVELLERS.
2Sa 12:4 there came a **t.** unto the rich man, ... 1982
Job 31:32 but I opened my doors to the **t.** 734

TRAVELLERS
Jg 5:6 the **t.** walked through byways..... 1980,5410

TRAVELLETH
Pr 6:11 thy poverty come as one that **t.**,........ 1980
Pr 24:34 thy poverty come as one that **t.**;........ 1980

TRAVELLING
Isa 21:13 O ye **t.** companies of Dedanim. 736
Isa 63:1 **t.** in the greatness of his strength?..... 6808
Mt 25:14 **is as a man t. into a far country,**.... *589*

TRAVERSING
Jer 2:23 art a swift dromedary **t.** her ways; 8308

TREACHEROUS
Isa 21:2 **t.** dealer dealeth treacherously. 898
Isa 24:16 **t.** dealers have dealt treacherously;...... 898
Isa 24:16 the **t.** dealers have dealt very 898
Jer 3:7 And her **t.** sister Judah saw it. 901
Jer 3:8 yet her **t.** sister Judah feared not,........ 898
Jer 3:10 her **t.** sister Judah hath not................ 901
Jer 3:11 herself more than **t.** Judah................. 898
Jer 9:2 adulterers, an assembly of **t.** men......... 898
Zep 3:4 prophets are light and **t.** persons: 900

TREACHEROUSLY
Jg 9:23 Shechem dealt **t.** with Abimelech: 898
Isa 21:2 the treacherous dealer dealeth **t.**, ... 898
Isa 24:16 treacherous dealers have dealt **t.**; 898
Isa 24:16 dealers have dealt very **t.**.................. 898
Isa 33:1 wast not spoiled; and dealest **t.**, ... 898
Isa 33:1 and they dealt not **t.** with thee! 898
Isa 33:1 thou shalt make an end to deal **t.**,........ 898
Isa 33:1 they shall deal **t.** with thee................ 898
Isa 48:8 that thou wouldest deal very **t.**,............ 898
Jer 3:20 as a wife **t.** departeth from her............ 898
Jer 3:20 so have ye dealt **t.** with me................ 898
Jer 5:11 have dealt very **t.** against me,.............. 898
Jer 12:1 are all they happy that deal very **t.**? 898
Jer 12:6 even they have dealt **t.** with thee; 898
La 1:2 her friends have dealt **t.** with her,........ 898
Ho 5:7 have dealt **t.** against the Lord: 898
Ho 6:7 there have they dealt **t.** against me. 898
Hab 1:13 lookest thou upon them that deal **t.**, ... 898
Mal 2:10 we deal **t.** every man against his 898
Mal 2:11 Judah hath dealt **t.**, and an................. 898
Mal 2:14 against whom thou hast dealt **t.** 898
Mal 2:15 deal **t.** against the wife of his youth...... 898
Mal 2:16 to your spirit, that ye deal not **t.** 898

TREACHERY
2Ki 9:23 Ahaziah, There is **t.**, O Ahaziah. 4820

TREAD See also TREADER; TREADETH; TREADING; TRODDEN; TRODE.
De 11:24 the soles of your feet shall **t.** shall...... 1869
De 11:25 upon all the land...ye shall **t.** upon,...... 1869
De 33:29 thou shalt **t.** upon their high places. 1869
Jos 1:3 the sole of your feet shall **t.** upon,...... 1869
1Sa 5:5 **t.** on the threshold of Dagon in.......... 1869
Job 24:11 **t.** their winepresses, and suffer.......... 1869
Job 40:12 **t.** down the wicked in their place. 1915
Ps 7:5 let him **t.** down my life upon the 7429
Ps 44:5 will we **t.** them under that rise up........ 947
Ps 60:12 it is that shall **t.** down our enemies. 947
Ps 91:13 shalt **t.** upon the lion and adder:.......... 1869
Ps 108:13 it is that shall **t.** down our enemies. 947
Isa 1:12 this at your hand, to **t.** my courts? 7429
Isa 10:6 **t.** them down like the mire of..... 7760,4823
Isa 14:25 my mountains **t.** him under foot:.......... 947
Isa 16:10 treaders shall **t.** out no wine in.......... 1869
Isa 26:6 The foot shall **t.** it down, even the 7429
Isa 63:3 for I will **t.** them in mine anger,......... 1869
Isa 63:6 I will **t.** down the people in mine 947
Jer 25:30 shout, as they that **t.** the grapes,........ 1869
Jer 48:33 none shall **t.** with shouting; their........ 1869
Eze 26:11 shall he **t.** down all thy streets: 7429
Eze 34:18 ye must **t.** down with your feet the 7429
Da 7:23 shall **t.** it down, and break it in.......... 1759
Ho 10:11 and loveth to **t.** out the corn; 1758
Mic 1:3 **t.** upon the high places of the............ 1869
Mic 5:5 and when he shall **t.** in our palaces, ... 1869
Mic 6:15 thou shalt **t.** the olives, but thou........ 1869
Na 3:14 go into clay, and **t.** the morter,.......... 7429
Zec 10:5 which **t.** down their enemies in the 947
Mal 4:3 And ye shall **t.** down the wicked; 6072
Lu 10:19 **you power to t. on serpents and** *3961*
Re 11:2 holy city shall they **t.** under foot *3961*

TREADER See also TREADERS.
Am 9:13 the **t.** of grapes him that soweth........ 1869

TREADERS
Isa 16:10 the **t.** shall tread out no wine in......... 1869

TREADETH
De 25:4 the ox when he **t.** out the corn.......... 1758
Job 9:8 and **t.** upon the waves of the sea. 1869
Isa 41:25 morter, and as the potter **t.** clay. 7429
Isa 63:2 like him that **t.** in the winefat? 1869
Am 4:13 **t.** upon the high places of the earth. ... 1869
Mic 5:6 and when he **t.** within our borders...... 1869
Mic 5:8 **t.** down, and teareth in pieces, ... 7429
1Co 9:9 of the ox that **t.** out the corn............. *248*
1Ti 5:18 muzzle the ox that **t.** out the corn. *248*
Re 19:15 and he **t.** the winepress of the........... *3961*

TREADING
Ne 13:15 **t.** wine presses on the sabbath, ... 1869
Isa 7:25 and for the **t.** of lesser cattle............ 4823
Isa 22:5 is a day of trouble, and of **t.** down,..... 4001
Am 5:11 as your **t.** is upon the poor, ... 1318

TREASON
1Ki 16:20 and his **t.** that he wrought, ... 7195
2Ki 11:14 rent her clothes, and cried, **T.**, **T.**...... 7195
2Ch 23:13 rent their clothes, and said, **T.**, **T.**. 7195

TREASURE See also TREASURED; TREASURES; TREASUREST.
Ge 43:23 hath given you **t.** in your sacks: 4301
Ex 1:11 they built for Pharaoh **t.** cities, ... 4543
Ex 19:5 then ye shall be a peculiar **t.** unto me ....
De 28:12 shall open unto thee his good **t.**,.......... 214
1Ch 29:8 to the **t.** of the house of the Lord,....... 214
Ezr 2:69 their ability unto the **t.** of the work...... 214
Ezr 5:17 be search made in the king's **t.**.......... 1596
Ezr 7:20 it out of the king's **t.** house............. 1596
Ne 7:70 gave to the **t.** a thousand drams of....... 214
Ne 7:71 gave to the **t.** of the work twenty........ 214
Ne 10:38 to the chambers, into the **t.** house. 214
Ps 17:14 whose belly thou fillest with thy hid **t.**.......
Ps 135:4 himself, and Israel for his peculiar **t.** ....
Pr 15:6 house of the righteous is much **t.**........ 2633
Pr 15:16 Lord than great **t.** and trouble............ 214
Pr 21:20 There is **t.** to be desired and oil in....... 214
Ec 2:8 the peculiar **t.** of kings and of the............
Isa 33:6 the fear of the Lord is his **t.**............... 214
Eze 22:25 they have taken the **t.** and............... 2633
Da 1:2 vessels into the **t.** house of his god...... 214
Ho 13:15 spoil the **t.** of all pleasant vessels......... 214
Mt 6:21 **where your t. is, there will your**.... *2344*
Mt 12:35 **good t. of the heart bringeth**......... *2344*
Mt 12:35 **evil t. bringeth forth evil things.** ... *2344*
Mt 13:44 **heaven is like unto t. hid in a**....... *2344*
Mt 13:52 **out of his t. things new and old.** ... *2344*
Mt 19:21 **and thou shalt have t. in heaven:** .. *2344*
Mk 10:21 **and thou shalt have t. in heaven:** .. *2344*
Lu 6:45 **good t. of his heart bringeth**......... *2344*
Lu 6:45 **evil t. of his heart bringeth forth** .. *2344*
Lu 12:21 **he that layeth up t. for himself,**.... *2343*
Lu 12:33 **t. in the heavens that faileth not,**.. *2344*
Lu 12:34 **where your t. is, there will your**... *2344*
Lu 18:22 **and thou shalt have t. in heaven:** .. *2344*
Ac 8:27 who had the charge of all her **t.**,........ *1047*
2Co 4:7 we have this **t.** in earthen vessels, ... *2344*
Jas 5:3 heaped **t.** together for the last........... *2343*

TREASURE-CITIES See TREASURE and CITIES.

TREASURED
Isa 23:18 it shall not be **t.** nor laid up; for 686

TREASURE-HOUSE See TREASURE and HOUSE.

TREASURER See also TREASURERS.
Ezr 1:8 by the hand of Mithredath the **t.**, ... 1489
Isa 22:15 get thee unto this **t.**, even unto......... 5532

TREASURERS
Ezr 7:21 the **t.** which are beyond the river,...... 1490
Ne 13:13 And I made **t.** over the treasuries,....... 686
Da 3:2,3 judges, the **t.**, the counsellers, ... 1411

TREASURES
De 32:34 me, and sealed up among my **t.**? 214
De 33:19 the seas, and of **t.** hid in the sand. 8226
1Ki 7:51 he put among the **t.** of the house of..... 214
1Ki 14:26 he took away the **t.** of the house of 214
1Ki 14:26 Lord, and the **t.** of the king's house; 214
1Ki 15:18 in the **t.** of the house of the Lord, ... 214
1Ki 15:18 and the **t.** of the king's house, and....... 214
2Ki 12:18 in the **t.** of the house of the Lord, ... 214
2Ki 14:14 and in the **t.** in the king's house, ... 214
2Ki 16:8 and in the **t.** in the king's house, ... 214
2Ki 18:15 and in the **t.** of the king's house. 214
2Ki 20:13 and all that was found in his **t.**: 214
2Ki 20:15 among my **t.** that I have not shewed 214
2Ki 24:13 all the **t.** of the house of the Lord,....... 214
2Ki 24:13 and the **t.** of the king's house, and....... 214
1Ch 26:20 Ahijah was over the **t.** of the house...... 214
1Ch 26:20 over the **t.** of the dedicated things. 214
1Ch 26:22 were over the **t.** of the house of the 214
1Ch 26:24 the son of Moses, was ruler of the **t.** ... 214
1Ch 26:26 were over all the **t.** of the dedicated..... 214
1Ch 27:25 over the king's **t.** was Azmaveth the 214
2Ch 5:1 among the **t.** of the house of God. 214
2Ch 8:15 any matter, or concerning the **t.**.......... 214
2Ch 12:9 took away the **t.** of the house of the 214
2Ch 12:9 and the **t.** of the king's house; he 214
2Ch 16:2 gold out of the **t.** of the house of the.... 214
2Ch 25:24 and the **t.** of the king's house, the 214
2Ch 36:18 and the **t.** of the house of the Lord, ... 214
2Ch 36:18 and the **t.** of the king, and of his 214
Ezr 6:1 the **t.** were laid up in Babylon. 1596
Ne 12:44 over the chambers for the **t.**,............... 214
Job 3:21 and dig for it more than for hid **t.**;...... 4301
Job 38:22 entered into the **t.** of the snow? 214
Job 38:22 or hast thou seen the **t.** of the hail,...... 214
Pr 2:4 and searchest for her as for hid **t.**; 4301
Pr 8:21 substance, and I will fill their **t.**......... 214
Pr 10:2 **T.** of wickedness profit nothing: but 214
Pr 21:6 The getting of **t.** by a lying tongue....... 214
Isa 2:7 neither is there any end of their **t.**;...... 214
Isa 10:13 people, and have robbed their **t.**, ... 6259
Isa 30:6 their **t.** upon the bunches of camels,..... 214
Isa 39:2 and all that was found in his **t.**: 214
Isa 39:4 there is nothing among my **t.** that I...... 214
Isa 45:3 I will give thee the **t.** of darkness, ... 214
Jer 10:13 bringeth forth the wind out of his **t.** 214
Jer 15:13 Thy substance and thy **t.** will I give 214
Jer 17:3 substance and all thy **t.** to the spoil,..... 214
Jer 20:5 and all the **t.** of the kings of Judah 214
Jer 41:8 we have **t.** in the field, of wheat, ... 4301
Jer 48:7 trusted in thy works and in thy **t.**, ... 214
Jer 49:4 that trusted in her **t.**, saying, Who....... 214
Jer 50:37 a sword is upon her **t.**; and they 214
Jer 51:13 abundant in **t.**, thine end is come, ... 214
Jer 51:16 bringeth the wind out of his **t.** 214
Eze 28:4 gotten gold and silver into thy **t.**.......... 214
Da 11:43 have power over the **t.** of gold and..... 4362
Mic 6:10 Are there yet the **t.** of wickedness........ 214
Mt 2:11 and when they had opened their **t.**, ... *2344*
Mt 6:19 **not up for yourselves t. upon earth,**..*2344*
Mt 6:20 **up for yourselves t. in heaven,** *2344*
Co 2:3 whom are hid all the **t.** of wisdom *2344*
Heb 11:26 greater riches than the **t.** in Egypt: *2344*

TREASUREST
Ro 2:5 **t.** up unto thyself wrath against.......... *2343*

TREASURIES
1Ch 9:26 and **t.** of the house of God. 214
1Ch 28:11 thereof, and of the **t.** thereof,............ 1597
1Ch 28:12 about, of the **t.** of the house of God,.... 214
1Ch 28:12 of the **t.** of the dedicated things:.......... 214
2Ch 32:27 and he made himself **t.** for silver, ... 214
Ne 13:12 the new wine and the oil unto the **t.** 214
Ne 13:13 And I made treasurers over the **t.**, ... 214
Es 3:9 to bring it into the king's **t.**............... 1595
Es 4:7 had promised to pay to the king's **t.**.... 1595
Ps 135:7 he bringeth the wind out of his **t.** 214

TREASURY See also TREASURIES.
Jos 6:19 shall come into the **t.** of the Lord. 214
Jos 6:24 into the **t.** of the house of the Lord....... 214
Jer 38:11 the house of the king under the **t.**, ... 214
Mt 27:6 lawful for to put them into the **t.**,....... *2878*
Mk 12:41 And Jesus sat over against the **t.**, ... *1049*
Mk 12:41 the people cast money into the **t.**....... *1049*
Mk 12:43 **all they which have cast into the t.** ..*1049*
Lu 21:1 men casting their gifts into the **t.** *1049*
Joh 8:20 These words spake Jesus in the **t.**,...... *1049*

TREAT See ENTREAT; INTREAT.

TREATISE
Ac 1:1 The former **t.** have I made, O.......... *3056*

TREE See also TREES.
Ge 1:11 the fruit **t.** yielding fruit after his........ 6086

Ge 1:12 t. yielding fruit, whose seed was in..... 6086
Ge 1:29 face of all the earth, and every t.,...... 6086
Ge 1:29 is the fruit of a t. yielding seed;......... 6086
Ge 2:9 grow every t. that is pleasant to the... 6086
Ge 2:9 the t. of life also in the midst of the ... 6086
Ge 2:9 t. of knowledge of good and evil. 6086
Ge 2:16 every t. of the garden thou mayest..... 6086
Ge 2:17 of the t. of the knowledge of good...... 6086
Ge 3:1 Ye shall not eat of every t. of the 6086
Ge 3:3 of the fruit of the t. which is in the 6086
Ge 3:6 woman saw that the t. was good........ 6086
Ge 3:6 a t. to be desired to make one wise, .. 6086
Ge 3:11 Hast thou eaten of the t., whereof I ... 6086
Ge 3:12 she gave me of the t., and I did eat. .. 6086
Ge 3:17 and hast eaten of the t., of which I..... 6086
Ge 3:22 take also of the t. of life, and eat,...... 6086
Ge 3:24 way, to keep the way of the t. of life.. 6086
Ge 18:4 and rest yourselves under the t.: 6086
Ge 18:8 and he stood by them under the t., ... 6086
Ge 30:37 and of the hazel and chesnut t.; ....
Ge 40:19 thee, and shall hang thee on a t.;....... 6086
Ex 9:25 field, and brake every t. of the field...... 6086
Ex 10:5 shall eat every t. which groweth for.... 6086
Ex 15:25 the Lord shewed him a t., which........ 6086
Le 27:30 of the fruit of the t., is the Lord's:..... 6086
Nu 6:4 eat nothing...made of the vine t., ...
De 12:2 the hills, and under every green t.: 6086
De 19:5 with the axe to cut down the t., ... 6086
De 20:19 (for the t. of the field is man's life)..... 6086
De 21:22 death, and thou hang him on a t.:........ 6086
De 21:23 not remain all night upon the t.,......... 6086
De 22:6 be before thee in the way in any t.,...... 6086
De 24:20 When thou beatest thine olive t., thou.......
Jos 8:29 the king of Ai he hanged on a t.......... 6086
Jos 8:29 take his carcase down from the t., ... 6086
Jg 4:5 And she dwelt under the palm t. of..........
Jg 9:8 they said unto the olive t., Reign thou.......
Jg 9:9 But the olive t. said unto them, Should......
Jg 9:10 And the trees said to the fig t., ... 6086
Jg 9:11 But the fig t. said unto them,........... 6086
1Sa 14:2 Gibeah under a pomegranate t. ....
1Sa 22:6 Saul abode in Gibeah under a t. in 815
1Sa 31:13 buried them under a t. at Jabesh, ... 815
1Ki 4:25 under his vine and under his fig t., ...
1Ki 4:33 the cedar t. that is in Lebanon........... 6086
1Ki 6:23 he made two cherubims of olive t......... 6086
1Ki 6:31 the oracle he made doors of olive t.:..... 6086
1Ki 6:32 The two doors also were of olive t.; ... 6086
1Ki 6:33 door of the temple posts of olive t.,..... 6086
1Ki 6:34 And the two doors were of fir t.: 6086
1Ki 14:23 high hill, and under every green t....... 6086
1Ki 19:4 and sat down under a juniper t.:...............
1Ki 19:5 he lay and slept under a juniper t., ...
2Ki 3:19 and shall fell every good t., and........... 6086
2Ki 16:4 hills, and under every green t............ 6086
2Ki 17:10 hills, and under every green t............ 6086
2Ki 18:31 vine, and every one of his fig t., ...
2Ch 3:5 greater house he cieled with fir t., ... 6086
2Ch 28:4 hills, and under every green t.,........... 6086
Es 2:23 they were both hanged on a t.:............ 6086
Job 14:7 For there is hope of a t., if it be cut.... 6086
Job 19:10 hope hath he removed like a t.. 6086
Job 24:20 wickedness shall be broken as a t....... 6086
Ps 1:3 be like a t. planted by the rivers........ 6086
Ps 37:35 himself like a green bay t., ...
Ps 52:8 like a green olive t. in the house of God: ...
Ps 92:12 shall flourish like the palm t.:..................
Pr 3:18 She is a t. of life to them that lay 6086
Pr 11:30 fruit of the righteous is a t. of life; 6086
Pr 13:12 the desire cometh, it is a t. of life....... 6086
Pr 15:4 A wholesome tongue is a t. of life: 6086
Pr 27:18 Whoso keepeth the fig t. shall eat ....
Ec 11:3 and if the t. fall toward the south, ... 6086
Ec 11:3 the place where the t. falleth, there.... 6086
Ec 12:5 and the almond t. shall flourish,..............
Ca 2:3 As the apple t. among the trees of..... 6086
Ca 2:13 The fig t. putteth forth her green............
Ca 7:7 thy stature is like to a palm t., ...
Ca 7:8 I will go up to the palm t., I will............
Ca 8:5 raised thee up under the apple t.:.............
Isa 6:13 as a teil t., and as an oak, whose............
Isa 17:6 as the shaking of an olive t., two or..........
Isa 24:13 be as the shaking of an olive t., and..........
Isa 34:4 as a falling fig from the fig t.. ....
Isa 36:16 his vine, and every one of his fig t., ...
Isa 40:20 chooseth a t. that will not rot;........... 6086
Isa 41:19 wilderness the cedar, the shittah t.,..... 6086
Isa 41:19 and the myrtle, and the oil t.;.................
Isa 41:19 I will set in the desert the fir t., ...
Isa 41:19 the pine, and the box t. together:.............
Isa 44:19 I fall down to the stock of a t.?.......... 6086
Isa 44:23 O forest, and every t. therein: 6086
Isa 55:13 the thorn shall come up the fir t.,...............
Isa 55:13 brier shall come up the myrtle t...............
Isa 56:3 eunuch say, Behold, I am a dry t. 6086
Isa 57:5 with idols under every green t.,......... 6086
Isa 60:13 shall come unto thee, the fir t., ...
Isa 60:13 the pine t., and the box together,..............
Isa 65:22 as the days of a t. are the days of...... 6086
Isa 66:17 gardens behind one t. in the midst,...........
Jer 1:11 said, I see a rod of an almond t.. ....
Jer 2:20 and under every green t. thou.......... 6086
Jer 3:6 mountain and under every green t., ... 6086
Jer 3:13 the strangers under every green t.,.... 6086
Jer 8:13 not figs on the fig t., and the leaf.............
Jer 10:3 one cutteth a t. out of the forest,....... 6086
Jer 10:5 They are upright as the palm t., ...
Jer 11:16 A green olive t., fair, and of goodly.........
Jer 11:19 Let us destroy the t. with the fruit...... 6086
Jer 17:8 be as a t. planted by the waters, ... 6086
Eze 6:13 under every green t., and under 6086
Eze 15:2 What is the vine t. more than any t.,... 6086
Eze 15:6 As the vine t. among the trees of 6086
Eze 17:5 waters, and set it as a willow t...............
Eze 17:24 Lord have brought down the high t.,... 6086
Eze 17:24 have exalted the low t., have 6086
Eze 17:24 have dried up the green t., and have .. 6086
Eze 17:24 and have made the dry t. to flourish: .. 6086
Eze 20:47 green t. in thee, and every dry t.: 6086
Eze 21:10 the rod of my son, as every t.............. 6086
Eze 31:8 nor any t. in the garden of God was ... 6086
Eze 34:27 t. of the field shall yield her fruit,....... 6086
Eze 36:30 I will multiply the fruit of the t., ... 6086
Eze 41:18 a palm t. was between a cherub..............
Eze 41:19 toward the palm t. on the one side, ...
Eze 41:19 toward the palm t. on the other side:........
Da 4:10 a t. in the midst of the earth. 363
Da 4:11 The t. grew, and was strong, and........ 363
Da 4:14 Hew down the t., and cut off his......... 363
Da 4:20 The t. that thou sawest, which grew, ... 363
Da 4:23 Hew the t. down, and destroy it; yet ... 363
Da 4:26 leave the stump of the t. roots;........... 363
Ho 9:10 as the firstripe in the fig t. at her............
Ho 14:6 and his beauty shall be as the olive t.,.......
Ho 14:8 I am like a green fir t.. From me.............
Joe 1:7 vine waste, and barked my fig t.: ....
Joe 1:12 dried up, and the fig t. languisheth; ....
Joe 1:12 the pomegranate t., the palm t. ....
Joe 1:12 the apple t., even all the trees of.............
Joe 2:22 spring, for the t. beareth her fruit, ... 6086
Joe 2:22 the fig t. and the vine do yield.................
Mic 4:4 under his vine and under his fig t.; ....
Hab 3:17 the fig t. shall not blossom,......................
Hag 2:19 and the fig t., and the pomegranate, ...
Hag 2:19 the olive t., hath not brought forth: 6086
Zec 3:10 under the vine and under the fig t. ....
Zec 11:2 Howl, fir t.; for the cedar is fallen; ....
Mt 3:10 every t. which bringeth not forth........ *1186*
Mt 7:17 **good t. bringeth forth good fruit:** .. *1186*
Mt 7:17 **corrupt t. bringeth forth evil**......... *1186*
Mt 7:18 **good t. cannot bring forth evil** *1186*
Mt 7:18 **corrupt t. bring forth good fruit,** ... *1186*
Mt 7:19 **every t. that bringeth not forth**..... *1186*
Mt 12:33 **Either make the t. good,and his**.... *1186*
Mt 12:33 **or else make the t. corrupt, and**.... *1186*
Mt 12:33 **for the t. is known by his fruit.** *1186*
Mt 13:32 **among herbs, and becometh a t.,** *1186*
Mt 21:19 when he saw a fig t. in the way, he.... *4808*
Mt 21:19 presently the fig t. withered away. *4808*
Mt 21:20 How soon is the fig t. withered *4808*
Mt 21:21 **do this which is done to the fig t.,** .*4808*
Mt 24:32 **Now learn a parable of the fig t.;** .. *4808*
Mk 11:13 seeing a fig t. afar off having leaves, ... *4808*
Mk 11:20 the fig t. dried up from the roots. *4808*
Mk 11:21 fig t....thou cursedst is withered *4808*
Mk 13:28 **Now learn a parable of the fig t.;** .. *4808*
Lu 3:9 every t. therefore which bringeth....... *1186*
Lu 6:43 **good t. bringeth not forth corrupt** . *1186*
Lu 6:43 **corrupt t. bring forth good fruit**..... *1186*
Lu 6:44 **every t. is known by his own fruit.** .*1186*
Lu 13:6 **certain man had a fig t. planted** *4808*
Lu 13:7 **come seeking fruit on this fig t.,** ... *4808*
Lu 13:19 **it grew, and waxed a great t.;** *1186*
Lu 17:6 **ye might say unto this sycamine t.,**.....
Lu 19:4 climbed up into a sycomore t. to........ *4809*
Lu 21:29 **Behold the fig t., and all the trees;** *4808*
Lu 23:31 **they do these things in a green t.,** . *3586*
Joh 1:48 **when thou wast under the fig t., I.** *4808*
Joh 1:50 **thee, I saw thee under the fig t.,** ... *4808*
Ac 5:30 whom ye slew and hanged on a t.. .... *3586*
Ac 10:39 whom they slew and hanged on a t.: ... *3586*
Ac 13:29 they took him down from the t., ... *3586*
Ro 11:17 and thou, being a wild olive t.,............... *65*
Ro 11:17 of the root and fatness of the olive t.; ....
Ro 11:24 cut out of the olive t. which is wild........ *65*
Ro 11:24 to nature into a good olive t.:............ *2565*
Ro 11:24 be graffed into their own olive t.?............
Ga 3:13 is every one that hangeth on a t.: *3586*
Jas 3:12 Can the fig t., my brethren, bear *4808*
1Pe 2:24 our sins in his own body on the t.,...... *3586*
Re 2:7 **will I give to eat of the t. of life,** .. *3586*
Re 6:13 a fig t. casteth her untimely figs, ... *4808*
Re 7:1 nor on the sea, nor on any t.. .... *1186*
Re 9:4 any green thing, neither any t.; *1186*
Re 22:2 the river, was there the t. of life, ... *3586*
Re 22:2 leaves of the t. were for the healing ... *3586*
Re 22:14 may have right to the t. of life, and *3586*

TREES See also AXLETREES.

Ge 3:2 We may eat of the fruit of the t......... 6086
Ge 3:8 God amongst the t. of the garden....... 6086
Ge 23:17 all the t. that were in the field, that.... 6086
Ex 10:15 all the fruit of the t. which the hail..... 6086
Ex 10:15 not any green thing in the t., ... 6086
Ex 15:27 and threescore and ten palm t.: ....
Le 19:23 planted all manner of t. for food, ... 6086
Le 23:40 first day the boughs of goodly t., ... 6086
Le 23:40 branches of palm t.,...............................
Le 23:40 and the boughs of thick t., and 6086
Le 26:4 t. of the field shall yield their fruit. 6086
Le 26:20 neither shall the t. of the land yield 6086
Nu 24:6 t. of lign aloes which the Lord hath...........
Nu 24:6 as cedar t. beside the waters ....
Nu 33:9 and threescore and ten palm t.; ....
De 6:11 vineyards and olive t., which thou ....
De 8:8 and barley, and vines, and fig t., ...
De 16:21 plant thee a grove of any t. near........ 6086
De 20:19 thou shalt not destroy the t............... 6086
De 20:20 the t. which thou knowest that they.... 6086
De 20:20 they be not t. for meat, thou shalt 6086
De 28:40 shall have olive t. throughout all thy..........
De 28:42 All thy t. and fruit of thy land........... 6086
De 34:3 of Jericho, the city of palm t., unto...........
Jos 10:26 them, and hanged them on five t.:...... 6086
Jos 10:26 hanging upon the t. until...evening..... 6086
Jos 10:27 and they took them down off the t., ... 6086
Jg 1:16 went up out of the city of palm t.............
Jg 3:13 and possessed the city of palm t. ....
Jg 9:8 t. went forth on a time to anoint.......... 6086
Jg 9:9 and go to be promoted over the t.? 6086
Jg 9:10 And the t. said to the fig tree, Come .. 6086
Jg 9:11 and go to be promoted over the t.?.... 6086
Jg 9:12 Then said the t. unto the vine, ... 6086
Jg 9:13 and go to be promoted over the t.? 6086
Jg 9:14 said all the t. unto the bramble, ... 6086
Jg 9:15 And the bramble said unto the t.,....... 6086
Jg 9:48 and cut down a bough from the t., ... 6086
2Sa 5:11 and cedar t., and carpenters, and....... 6086
2Sa 5:23 over against the mulberry t....................
2Sa 5:24 in the tops of the mulberry t., ...
1Ki 4:33 he spake of t., from the cedar........... 6086
1Ki 5:6 hew me cedar t. out of Lebanon; ....
1Ki 5:10 Hiram gave Solomon cedar t. 6086
1Ki 5:10 fir t. according to all his desire. 6086
1Ki 6:29 figures of cherubims and palm t...............
1Ki 6:32 carvings of cherubims and palm t. ....
1Ki 6:32 cherubims, and upon the palm t. ....
1Ki 6:35 thereon cherubims and palm t. ....
1Ki 7:36 cherubims, lions, and palm t., ...
1Ki 9:11 furnished Solomon with cedar t. 6086
1Ki 9:11 and fir t., and with gold, according 6086
1Ki 10:11 Ophir great plenty of almug t., ... 6086
1Ki 10:12 king made of the almug t. pillars 6086
1Ki 10:12 there came no such almug t., nor....... 6086
1Ki 10:27 sycomore t. that are in the vale, ...
2Ki 3:25 water, and felled all the good t.: 6086
2Ki 19:23 cut down the tall cedar t. thereof, ...
2Ki 19:23 and the choice fir t. thereof: and.............
1Ch 14:14 them over against the mulberry t. ....
1Ch 14:15 in the tops of the mulberry t., ...

1Ch 16:33 Then shall the t. of the wood sing...... 6086
1Ch 22:4 Also cedar t. in abundance: for......... 6086
1Ch 27:28 the olive t. and the sycomore t..............
2Ch 1:15 as stones, and cedar t. made he as..........
2Ch 1:15 the sycomore t. that are in the vale.........
2Ch 2:8 also cedar t., (6086) fir t., and algum t., ...
2Ch 3:5 set thereon palm t. and chains.................
2Ch 9:10 algum t. and precious stones. 6086
2Ch 9:11 king made of the algum t. terraces..... 6086
2Ch 9:27 cedar t. made he as the sycomore...........
2Ch 9:27 made he as the sycomore t. that................
2Ch 28:15 to Jericho, the city of palm t.,................
Ezr 3:7 to bring cedar t. from Lebanon to...... 6086
Ne 8:15 and branches of thick t., to make....... 6086
Ne 9:25 and fruit t. in abundance:................. 6086
Ne 10:35 the firstfruits of all fruit of all t., ... 6086
Ne 10:37 and the fruit of all manner of t., of...... 6086
Job 40:21 He lieth under the shady t., in the............
Job 40:22 The shady t. cover him with their............
Ps 74:5 lifted up axes upon the thick t. 6086
Ps 78:47 and their sycomore t. with frost..............
Ps 96:12 shall all the t. of the wood rejoice...... 6086
Ps 104:16 The t. of the Lord are full of sap;...... 6086
Ps 104:17 the stork, the fir t. are her house. ....
Ps 105:33 their vines also and their fig t.;...............
Ps 105:33 and brake the t. of their coasts.......... 6086
Ps 148:9 hills; fruitful t., and all cedars: 6086
Ec 2:5 I planted t. in them of all kind of......... 6086
Ec 2:6 the wood that bringeth forth t. 6086
Ca 2:3 tree among the t. of the wood,.......... 6086
Ca 4:14 with all t. of frankincense;................. 6086
Isa 7:2 as the t. of the wood are moved........ 6086
Isa 10:19 the rest of the t. of his forest shall..... 6086
Isa 14:8 Yea, the fir t. rejoice at thee, and............
Isa 37:24 and the choice fir t. thereof:.....................
Isa 44:14 among the t. of the forest:................ 6086
Isa 55:12 all the t. of the field shall clap their.... 6086
Isa 61:3 might be called t. of righteousness;...... 352
Jer 5:17 eat up thy vines and thy fig t.....................
Jer 6:6 Hew ye down t., and cast a mount..... 6097
Jer 7:20 upon the t. of the field, and upon....... 6086
Jer 17:2 their groves by the green t. upon....... 6086
Eze 15:2 a branch which is among the t. of...... 6086
Eze 15:6 vine tree among the t. of the forest,... 6086
Eze 17:24 t. of the field shall know that I the.... 6086
Eze 20:28 every high hill, and all the thick t., ... 6086
Eze 27:5 thy ship boards of fir t. of Senir:...............
Eze 31:4 rivers unto all the t. of the field......... 6086
Eze 31:5 above all the t. of the field,.............. 6086
Eze 31:8 the fir t. were not like his boughs,..... 6086
Eze 31:8 and the chesnut t. were not like his.... 6086
Eze 31:9 so that all the t. of Eden, that........... 6086
Eze 31:14 that none of all the t. by the waters... 6086
Eze 31:14 neither their t. stand up in their......... 352
Eze 31:15 all the t. of the field fainted for.......... 6086
Eze 31:16 all the t. of Eden, the choice and....... 6086
Eze 31:18 in greatness among the t. of Eden?.... 6086
Eze 31:18 brought down with the t. of Eden....... 6086
Eze 40:16 and upon each post were palm t..............
Eze 40:22 their arches, and their palm t., ...
Eze 40:26 it had palm t., one on this side, and..........
Eze 40:31, 34,37 palm t. were upon the posts ....
Eze 41:18 made with cherubims and palm t., ...
Eze 41:20 were cherubims and palm t. made, ...
Eze 41:25 the temple, cherubims and palm t.,...........
Eze 41:26 windows and palm t. on the one...............
Eze 47:7 were very many t. on the one side..... 6086
Eze 47:12 shall grow all t. for meat, whose......... 6086
Ho 2:12 I will destroy her vines and her fig t.,.........
Joe 1:12 even all the t. of the field, are........... 6086
Joe 1:19 hath burned all the t. of the field......... 6086
Am 4:9 your vineyards and your fig t....................
Na 2:3 the fir t. shall be terribly shaken. ....
Na 3:12 strong holds shall be like fig t..................
Zec 1:8 he stood among the myrtle t. that ....
Zec 1:10 that stood among the myrtle t. ....
Zec 1:11 that stood among the myrtle t., ...
Zec 4:3 two olive t. by it, one upon the right ....
Zec 4:11 What are these two olive t. upon the ....
Mt 3:10 ax is laid unto the root of the t.......... *1186*
Mt 21:8 cut down branches from the t., and.... *1186*
Mk 8:24 and said, I see men as t., walking...... *1186*
Mk 11:8 cut down branches off the t., and....... *1186*
Lu 3:9 axe is laid unto the root of the t. *1186*
Lu 21:29 **Behold the fig tree, and all the t.;** ..*1186*
Joh 12:13 Took branches of palm t., and.................
Jude 12 t. whose fruit withereth, without........ *1186*
Re 7:3 earth, neither the sea, nor the t., ... *1186*
Re 8:7 the third part of t. was burnt up, ... *1186*
Re 11:4 These are the two olive t., and the two ....

TREMBLE See also TREMBLED; TREMBLETH; TREMBLING.
De 2:25 and shall t., and be in anguish............ 7264
De 20:3 faint, fear not, and do not t.,............. 2648
Ezr 10:3 those that t. at the commandment........ 2730
Job 9:6 place, and the pillars thereof t. 6426
Job 26:11 The pillars of heaven t. and are 7322
Ps 60:2 Thou hast made the earth to t.;......... 7493
Ps 99:1 Lord reigneth; let the people t........... 7264
Ps 114:7 T., thou earth, at the presence of...... 2342
Ec 12:3 the keepers of the house shall t.,....... 2111
Isa 5:25 the hills did t., and their carcases....... 7264
Isa 14:16 the man that made the earth to t.,...... 7264
Isa 32:11 T., ye women that are at ease; be..... 2729
Isa 64:2 nations may t. at thy presence!........... 7264
Isa 66:5 of the Lord, ye that t. at his word; 2730
Jer 5:22 will ye not t. at my presence,............ 2342
Jer 10:10 at his wrath the earth shall t., ... 7493
Jer 33:9 they shall fear and t. for all the.......... 7264
Jer 51:29 the land shall t. and sorrow: for......... 7493
Eze 26:16 shall t. at every moment, and be......... 2729
Eze 26:18 Now shall the isles t. in the day of..... 2729
Eze 32:10 they shall t. at every moment,........... 2729
Da 6:26 men t. and fear before the God of...... 2112
Ho 11:10 children shall t. from the west. 2729
Ho 11:11 shall t. as a bird out of Egypt, and..... 2729
Joe 2:1 all the inhabitants of the land t.......... 7264
Joe 2:10 before them; the heavens shall t. 7493
Am 8:8 Shall not the land t. for this, and........ 7264
Hab 3:7 curtains of the land of Midian did t. 7264
Jas 2:19 the devils also believe, and t............ *5425*

TREMBLED
Ge 27:33 And Isaac t. very exceedingly,........... 2729
Ex 19:16 the people that was in the camp t. 2729
Jg 5:4 earth t., and the heavens dropped,...... 7493
1Sa 4:13 his heart t. for the ark of God. 2730
1Sa 14:15 and the spoilers, they also t.,............ 2729
1Sa 16:4 elders of the town t. at his coming. 2729
1Sa 28:5 was afraid, and his heart greatly t. 2729
2Sa 22:8 Then the earth shook and t.; the 7493
Ezr 9:4 every one that t. at the words of........ 2730
Ps 18:7 Then the earth shook and t.; the 7493
Ps 77:18 the world: the earth t. and shook. 7264
Ps 97:4 the world: the earth saw, and t. 2342
Jer 4:24 the mountains, and, lo, they t.,.......... 7493
Jer 8:16 the whole land t. at the sound of......... 7493
Da 5:19 t. and feared before him:................... 2112
Hab 3:10 mountains saw thee, and they t. 2342
Hab 3:16 When I heard, my belly t.; my 7264
Hab 3:16 I t. in myself, that I might rest in 7264
Mk 16:8 for they t. and were amazed...... *2192,5156*
Ac 7:32 Then Moses t., and durst not..... *1790,1096*
Ac 24:25 Felix t., and answered, Go thy... *1719,1096*

TREMBLETH
Job 37:1 At this also my heart t., and is.......... 2729
Ps 104:32 He looketh on the earth, and it t......... 7460
Ps 119:120 My flesh t. for fear of thee; and 5568
Isa 66:2 contrite spirit, and t. at my word. 2730

TREMBLING
Ex 15:15 t. shall take hold upon them;............. 7460
De 28:65 shall give thee there a t. heart, ... 7268
1Sa 13:7 and all the people followed him t.. 2729
1Sa 14:15 And there was t. in the host, in.......... 2731
1Sa 14:15 quaked: so it was a very great t.. 2731
Ezr 10:9 t. because of this matter, and for 7460
Job 4:14 Fear came upon me, and t., which 7460
Job 21:6 and t. taketh hold on my flesh. 6427
Ps 2:11 Lord with fear, and rejoice with t.. 7460
Ps 55:5 Fearfulness and t. are come upon....... 7460
Isa 51:17 drunken the dregs of the cup of t.,..... 8653
Isa 51:22 out of thine hand the cup of t., ... 8653
Jer 30:5 We have heard a voice of t., of 2731
Eze 12:18 drink thy water with t. and with......... 7269
Eze 26:16 shall clothe themselves with t.; 2731
Da 10:11 this word unto me, I stood t.. 7460
Ho 13:1 When Ephraim spake t., he.............. 7578
Zec 12:2 I will make Jerusalem a cup of t......... 7478
Mk 5:33 But the woman fearing and t., ... *5141*
Lu 8:47 she came t., and falling down *5141*
Ac 9:6 he t. and astonished said, Lord,......... *5141*
Ac 16:29 and sprang in, and came t.,........ *1096,1790*
1Co 2:3 and in fear, and in much t................. *5156*
2Co 7:15 with fear and t. ye received him. *5156*
Eph 6:5 with fear and t., in singleness of........ *5156*
Php 2:12 your own salvation with fear and t...... *5156*

TRENCH
1Sa 17:20 he came to the t., as the host was..... 4570
1Sa 26:5 Saul lay in the t., and the people........ 4570
1Sa 26:7 Saul lay sleeping with the t., and........ 4570
2Sa 20:15 the city, and it stood in the t............. 2426
1Ki 18:32 and he made a t. about the altar, ... 8585
1Ki 18:35 and he filled the t. also with water. 8585
1Ki 18:38 up the water that was in the t............ 8585
Lu 19:43 **enemies shall cast a t. about thee**.. *5482*

TRESPASS See also TRESPASSED; TRESPASSES; TRESPASSING.
Ge 31:36 What is my t.? what is my sin, that.... 6588
Ge 50:17 the t. of thy brethren, and their.......... 6588
Ge 50:17 forgive the t. of thy servants of the.... 6588
Ex 22:9 For all manner of t., whether it be..... 6588
Le 5:6 he shall bring his t. offering unto......... 817
Le 5:7 then he shall bring for his t., which...... 817
Le 5:15 If a soul commit a t., and sin............. 4604
Le 5:15 shall bring for his t. unto the Lord 817
Le 5:15 of the sanctuary, for a t. offering: 817
Le 5:16 him with the ram of the t. offering, ... 817
Le 5:18 for a t. offering, unto the priest:.......... 817
Le 5:19 It is a t. offering: he hath certainly....... 817
Le 6:2 and commit a t. against the Lord,....... 4604
Le 6:5 in the day of his t. offering.................. 819
Le 6:6 bring his t. offering unto the Lord,....... 817
Le 6:6 for a t. offering, unto the priest:.......... 817
Le 6:17 sin offering, and as the t. offering. 817
Le 7:1 this is the law of the t. offering: 817
Le 7:2 shall they kill the t. offering:............... 817
Le 7:5 unto the Lord: it is a t. offering. 817
Le 7:7 sin offering is, so is the t. offering: 817
Le 7:37 and of the t. offering, and of the.......... 817
Le 14:12 lamb, and offer him for a t. offering...... 817
Le 14:13 is the priest's, so is the t. offering: 817
Le 14:14 some of the blood of the t. offering, ... 817
Le 14:17 upon the blood of the t. offering: 817
Le 14:21 take one lamb for a t. offering to be..... 817
Le 14:24 take the lamb of the t. offering,............ 817
Le 14:25 shall kill the lamb of the t. offering,...... 817
Le 14:25 some of the blood of the t. offering,..... 817
Le 14:28 place of the blood fo the t. offering...... 817
Le 19:21 bring his t. offering unto the Lord,....... 817
Le 19:21 even a ram for a t. offering. 817
Le 19:22 the ram of the t. offering before the..... 817
Le 22:16 them to bear the iniquity of t.,............. 819
Le 26:40 with their t. which they trespassed..... 4604
Nu 5:6 commit, to do a t. against the Lord, ... 4604
Nu 5:7 shall recompense his t. with the 817
Nu 5:8 kinsman to recompense the t. unto, ... 817
Nu 5:8 t. be recompensed unto the Lord,......... 817
Nu 5:12 and commit a t. against him, ... 4604
Nu 5:27 have done t. against her husband, ... 4604
Nu 6:12 of the first year for a t. offering: 817
Nu 18:9 every t. offering of theirs, which 817
Nu 31:16 to commit t. against the Lord in......... 4604
Jos 7:1 children of Israel committed a t. in..... 4604
Jos 22:16 What t. is this...ye have committed 4604
Jos 22:20 Achan the son of Zerah commit a t...... 4604
Jos 22:31 have not committed this t. against...... 4604
1Sa 6:3 any wise return him a t. offering: 817
1Sa 6:4 What shall be the t. offering which....... 817
1Sa 6:8 ye return him for a t. offering, ... 817
1Sa 6:17 for a t. offering unto the Lord;............ 817
1Sa 25:28 forgive the t. of thine handmaid: 6588
1Ki 8:31 any man t. against his neighbour, ... 2398
2Ki 12:16 t. money and sin money was not......... 817
1Ch 21:3 will he be a cause of t. to Israel?.......... 819
2Ch 19:10 warn them that they t. not against....... 816
2Ch 19:10 this do, and ye shall not t. 816
2Ch 24:18 and Jerusalem for this their t. 819
2Ch 28:13 add more to our sins and to our t.......... 819
2Ch 28:13 our t. is great, and there is fierce......... 819
2Ch 28:22 he t. yet more against the Lord:........ 4603
2Ch 33:19 all his sins, and his t., and the........... 4604
Ezr 9:2 rulers hath been chief in this t........... 4604
Ezr 9:6 t. is grown up unto the heavens. 819
Ezr 9:7 we been in a great t. unto this day; 819
Ezr 9:13 our evil deeds, and for our great t.,..... 819
Ezr 10:10 wives, to increase the t. of Israel. 819
Ezr 10:19 a ram of the flock for their t............. 819
Eze 15:8 because they have committed a t., ... 4604

Eze 17:20 will plead with him there for his t....... 4604
Eze 18:24 in his t. that he hath trespassed,........ 4604
Eze 20:27 have committed a t. against me, ... 4604
Eze 40:39 the sin offering and the t. offering........ 817
Eze 42:13 the sin offering, and the t. offering;...... 817
Eze 44:29 the sin offering, and the t. offering;...... 817
Eze 46:20 the priests shall boil the t. offering....... 817
Da 9:7 their t. that they have trespassed....... 4604
Mt 18:15 **if thy brother shall t. against thee,.** *264*
Lu 17:3 **If thy brother t. against thee, rebuke.***264*
Lu 17:4 **if he t. against thee seven times in..***264*

TRESPASSED
Le 5:19 certainly t. against the Lord............... 816
Le 26:40 trespass which they t. against me,...... 4604
Nu 5:7 unto him against whom he hath t......... 816
De 32:51 Because ye t. against me among........ 4603
2Ch 26:18 the sanctuary; for thou hast t.;.......... 4603
2Ch 29:6 For our fathers have t., and done....... 4603
2Ch 30:7 t. against the Lord God of their......... 4603
2Ch 33:23 but Amon t. more and more. 819
Ezr 10:2 We have t. against our God, and........ 4603
Eze 17:20 that he hath t. against me................ 4604
Eze 18:24 in his trespass that he hath t.,........... 4604
Eze 39:23 because they t. against me,............... 4603
Eze 39:26 whereby they have t. against me,........ 4603
Da 9:7 that they have t. against thee............ 4603
Ho 8:1 my covenant, and t. against my law. ....

TRESPASSES
Ezr 9:15 we are before thee in our t.: for 819
Ps 68:21 as one as goeth on still in his t........... 817
Eze 39:26 and all their t. whereby they have....... 4604
Mt 6:14 **For if ye forgive men their t.,.......** *3900*
Mt 6:15 **But if ye forgive not men their t.,.** *3900*
Mt 6:15 **will your Father forgive your t. ....** *3900*
Mt 18:35 **not every one his brother their t. ..** *3900*
Mk 11:25 **heaven may forgive you your t.....** *3900*
Mk 11:26 **which is in heaven forgive your t. ..***3900*
2Co 5:19 not imputing their t. unto them;......... *3900*
Eph 2:1 who were dead in t. and sin;............ *3900*
Col 2:13 him, having forgiven you all t.; *3900*

TRESPASSING
Le 6:7 all that he hath done in t. therein......... 819
Eze 14:13 land sinneth against me by t............. 4603

TRESPASS-MONEY See TRESPASS and MONEY.

TRESPASS-OFFERING See TRESPASS and OFFERING.

TRIAL
Job 9:23 laugh at the t. of the innocent. 4531
Eze 21:13 Because it is a t., and what if the........ 974
2Co 8:2 How that in a great t. of affliction....... *1382*
Heb 11:36 others had t. of cruel mockings.......... *3984*
1Pe 1:7 That the t. of your faith, being *1383*
1Pe 4:12 the fiery t. which is to try you,................

TRIBE See also TRIBES.
Ex 31:2 the son of Hur, of the t. of Judah:...... 4294
Ex 31:6 son of Ahisamach, of the t. of Dan: 4294
Ex 35:30 the son of Hur, of the t. of Judah;...... 4294
Ex 35:34 son of Ahisamach, of the t. of Dan. 4294
Ex 38:22 the son of Hur, of the t. of Judah,....... 4294
Ex 38:23 son of Ahisamach, of the t. of Dan, ... 4294
Le 24:11 daughter of Dibri, of the t. of Dan:)..... 4294
Nu 1:4 there shall be a man of every t.;........ 4294
Nu 1:5 of the t. of Reuben; Elizur the son of ......
Nu 1:21 of them, even of the t. of Reuben, ... 4294
Nu 1:23 of them, even of the t. of Simeon, ... 4294
Nu 1:25 of them, even of the t. of Gad,.......... 4294
Nu 1:27 of them, even of the t. of Judah,........ 4294
Nu 1:29 of them, even of the t. of Issachar, ... 4294
Nu 1:31 of them, even of the t. of Zebulun,..... 4294
Nu 1:33 of them, even of the t. of Ephraim, ... 4294
Nu 1:35 of them, even of the t. of Manasseh, .. 4294
Nu 1:37 of them, even of the t. of Benjamin, ... 4294
Nu 1:39 of them, even of the t. of Dan,.......... 4294
Nu 1:41 of them, even of the t. of Asher, ... 4294
Nu 1:43 of them, even of the t. of Naphtali, ... 4294
Nu 1:47 Levites after the t. of their fathers..... 4294
Nu 1:49 shalt not number the t. of Levi,......... 4294
Nu 2:5 unto him shall be the t. of Issachar:.... 4294
Nu 2:7 Then the t. of Zebulun: and Eliab....... 4294
Nu 2:12 by him shall be the t. of Simeon: 4294
Nu 2:14 Then the t. of Gad: and the captain.... 4294
Nu 2:20 by him shall be the t. of Manasseh: 4294
Nu 2:22 Then the t. of Benjamin: and the 4294
Nu 2:27 by him shall be the t. of Asher: 4294
Nu 2:29 Then the t. of Naphtali: and the......... 4294
Nu 3:6 Bring the t. of Levi near, and........... 4294
Nu 4:18 Cut ye not off the t. of the families 7626
Nu 7:12 of Amminadab, of the t. of Judah:....... 4294
Nu 10:15 of the t. of the children of Issachar...... 4294
Nu 10:16 of the t. of the children of Zebulun..... 4294
Nu 10:19 of the t. of the children of Simeon...... 4294
Nu 10:20 host of the t. of the children of Gad.... 4294
Nu 10:23 the t. of the children of Manasseh...... 4294
Nu 10:24 the t. of the children of Benjamin....... 4294
Nu 10:26 of the t. of the children of Asher........ 4294
Nu 10:27 of the t. of the children of Naphtali..... 4294
Nu 13:2 of every t. of their fathers shall ye..... 4294
Nu 13:4 of the t. of Reuben, Shammua the...... 4294
Nu 13:5 Of the t. of Simeon, Shaphat the........ 4294
Nu 13:6 Of the t. of Judah, Caleb the son of.... 4294
Nu 13:7 Of the t. of Issachar, Igal the son 4294
Nu 13:8 Of the t. of Ephraim, Oshea the son... 4294
Nu 13:9 Of the t. of Benjamin, Palti the son 4294
Nu 13:10 Of the t. of Zebulun, Gaddiel the........ 4294
Nu 13:11 Of the t. of Joseph, namely, of the 4294
Nu 13:11 of the t. of Manasseh, Gaddi the........ 4294
Nu 13:12 Of the t. of Dan, Ammiel the son of... 4294
Nu 13:13 Of the t. of Asher, Sethur the son of.. 4294
Nu 13:14 Of the t. of Naphtali, Nahbi the son.... 4294
Nu 13:15 Of the t. of Gad, Geuel the son of 4294
Nu 18:2 thy brethren also of the t. of Levi, ... 4294
Nu 18:2 t. of thy father, bring thou with 7626
Nu 31:4 Of every t. a thousand,....................... 4294
Nu 31:5 a thousand of every t., twelve........... 4294
Nu 31:6 to the war, a thousand of every t.,..... 4294
Nu 32:33 and unto half the t. of Manasseh 7626
Nu 34:13 the nine tribes, and to the half t. 4294
Nu 34:14 the t. of the children of Reuben 4294
Nu 34:14 and the t. of the children of Gad 4294
Nu 34:14 and half the t. of Manasseh have........ 4294
Nu 34:15 and the half t. have received their...... 4294
Nu 34:18 shall take one prince of every t.,........ 4294
Nu 34:19 Of the t. of Judah, Caleb the son of.... 4294
Nu 34:20 of the t. of the children of Simeon,..... 4294
Nu 34:21 Of the t. of Benjamin, Elidad the........ 4294
Nu 34:22 of the t. of the children of Dan, ... 4294
Nu 34:23 the t. of the children of Manasseh, ... 4294
Nu 34:24 the t. of the children of Ephraim,....... 4294
Nu 34:25 the t. of the children of Zebulun,........ 4294
Nu 34:26 the t. of the children of Issachar, ... 4294
Nu 34:27 of the t. of the children of Asher,....... 4294
Nu 34:28 the t. of the children of Naphtali, ... 4294
Nu 36:3 be put to the inheritance of the t. 4294
Nu 36:4 be put unto the inheritance of the t. ... 4294
Nu 36:4 inheritance of the t. of our fathers...... 4294
Nu 36:5 t. of the sons of Joseph hath said........ 4294
Nu 36:6 t. of their father shall they marry. 4294
Nu 36:7 of Israel remove from t. to t.............. 4294
Nu 36:7 inheritance of the t. of his fathers....... 4294
Nu 36:8 in any t. of the children of Israel,....... 4294
Nu 36:8 of the family of the t. of her father, ... 4294
Nu 36:9 remove from one t. to another t.; 4294
Nu 36:12 the t. of the family of their father....... 4294
De 1:23 twelve men of you, one of a t.: 7626
De 3:13 gave I unto the half t. of Manasseh; ... 7626
De 10:8 the Lord separated the t. of Levi, ... 7626
De 18:1 all the t. of Levi, shall have no part.... 7626
De 29:8 and to the half t. of Manasseh. 7626
De 29:18 man, or woman, or family, or t.,........ 7626
Jos 1:12 to half the t. of Manasseh, spake 7626
Jos 3:12 of Israel, out of every t. a man.......... 7626
Jos 4:2 of the people, out of every t. a man, .. 7626
Jos 4:4 of Israel, out of every t. a man:.......... 7626
Jos 4:12 half the t. of Manasseh, passed over... 7626
Jos 7:1 for Achan,...of the t. of Judah,........... 4294
Jos 7:14 that the t. which the Lord taketh 7626
Jos 7:16 and the t. of Judah was taken: 7626
Jos 7:18 and Achan,...of the t. of Judah,.......... 4294
Jos 12:6 and the half t. of Manasseh................ 7626
Jos 13:7 tribes, and the half t. of Manasseh, ... 7626
Jos 13:14 unto the t. of Levi he gave none........ 7626
Jos 13:15 the t. of the children of Reuben 4294
Jos 13:24 gave inheritance unto the t. of Gad,.... 4294
Jos 13:29 unto the half t. of Manasseh:............. 7626
Jos 13:29 half tribe of the children of Manasseh.. 4294
Jos 13:33 unto the t. of Levi Moses gave not 7626
Jos 14:2 the nine tribes, and for the half t.. 4294
Jos 14:3 an half t. on the other side Jordan: 4294
Jos 15:1, 20,21 the t. of the children of Judah.... 4294
Jos 16:8 of the t. of the children of Ephraim..... 4294
Jos 17:1 also a lot for the t. of Manasseh; 4294
Jos 18:4 among you three men for each t. 7626
Jos 18:7 and half the t. of Manasseh, have........ 7626
Jos 18:11, 21 t. of the children of Benjamin........ 4294
Jos 19:1 for the t. of the children of Simeon..... 4294
Jos 19:8 of the t. of the children of Simeon....... 4294
Jos 19:23 of the t. of the children of Issachar..... 4294
Jos 19:24 for the t. of the children of Asher 4294
Jos 19:31 of the t. of the children of Asher........ 4294
Jos 19:39 of the t. of the children of Naphtali..... 4294
Jos 19:40 out for the t. of the children of Dan.... 4294
Jos 19:48 of the t. of the children of Dan 4294
Jos 20:8 the plain out of the t. of Reuben, ... 4294
Jos 20:8 in Gilead out of the t. of Gad, ... 4294
Jos 20:8 Bashan out of the t. of Mansseh. 4294
Jos 21:4 had by lot out of the t. of Judah,........ 4294
Jos 21:4 and out of the t. of Simeon,................ 4294
Jos 21:4 and out of the t. of Benjamin,............. 4294
Jos 21:5 of the families of the t. of Ephraim, ... 4294
Jos 21:5 and out of the t. of Dan, ... 4294
Jos 21:5 out of the half t. of Manasseh, ten 4294
Jos 21:6 of the families of the t. of Issachar, ... 4294
Jos 21:6 and out of the t. of Asher,................. 4294
Jos 21:6 and out of the t. of Naphtali, ... 4294
Jos 21:6 the half t. of Manasseh in Bashan,...... 4294
Jos 21:7 families had out of the t. of Reuben, ... 4294
Jos 21:7 and out of the t. of Gad, ... 4294
Jos 21:7 and out of the t. of Zebulun, twelve.... 4294
Jos 21:9 of the t. of the children of Judah, ... 4294
Jos 21:9 of the t. of the children of Simeon,..... 4294
Jos 21:17 out of the t. of Benjamin, Gibeon 4294
Jos 21:20 their lot out of the t. of Ephraim,....... 4294
Jos 21:23 And out of the t. of Dan, Eltekeh........ 4294
Jos 21:25 of the half t. of Manasseh, Tanach...... 4294
Jos 21:27 the other half t. of Manasseh, they..... 4294
Jos 21:28 out of the t. of Issachar, Kishon 4294
Jos 21:30 and out of the t. of Asher, Mishal 4294
Jos 21:32 out of the t. of Naphtali, Kedesh......... 4294
Jos 21:34 out of the t. of Zebulun, Jokneam 4294
Jos 21:36 out of the t. of Reuben, Bezer with..........
Jos 21:38 And out of the t. of Gad, Ramoth....... 4294
Jos 22:1 and the half t. of Manasseh,.............. 4294
Jos 22:7 the one half of the t. of Manasseh...... 7626
Jos 22:9 the half t. of Manasseh returned, ... 7626
Jos 22:10 the half t. of Manasseh built there...... 7626
Jos 22:11 the half t. of Manasseh have built....... 7626
Jos 22:13, 15 and to the half t. of Manasseh,...... 7626
Jos 22:21 the half t. of Manasseh answered,....... 7626
Jg 18:1 the t. of the Danites sought them...... 7626
Jg 18:19 be a priest unto a t. and a family in.... 7626
Jg 18:30 sons were priests to the t. of Dan...... 7626
Jg 20:12 men through all the t. of Benjamin,..... 7626
Jg 21:3 be to day one t. lacking in Israel?...... 7626
Jg 21:6 There is one t. cut off from Israel...... 7626
Jg 21:17 a t. be not destroyed out of Israel...... 7626
Jg 21:24 every man to his t. and to his family,.. 7626
1Sa 9:21 the families of the t. of Benjamin? 7626
1Sa 10:20 near, the t. of Benjamin was taken. 7626
1Sa 10:21 caused the t. of Benjamin to come...... 7626
1Ki 7:14 widow's son of the t. of Naphtali,....... 4294
1Ki 11:13 but will give one t. to thy son 7626
1Ki 11:32 have one t. for my servant David's..... 7626
1Ki 11:36 And unto his son will I give one t.,..... 7626
1Ki 12:20 of David, but the t. of Judah only. 7626
1Ki 12:21 Judah, with the t. of Benjamin, ... 7626
2Ki 17:18 none left but the t. of Judah only......... 7626
1Ch 5:18 Gadites, and half the t. of Manasseh,.. 7626
1Ch 5:23 children of the half t. of Manasseh...... 7626
1Ch 5:26 Gadites, and the half t. of Manasseh,.. 7626
1Ch 6:60 And out of the t. of Benjamin;.......... 4294
1Ch 6:61 were left of the family of that t.,........ 4294
1Ch 6:61 were cities given out of the half t.,..... 4294
1Ch 6:61 out of the half t. of Manasseh, by lot, ...
1Ch 6:62 families out of the t. of Issachar,........ 4294
1Ch 6:62 and out of the t. of Asher,................. 4294
1Ch 6:62 and out of the t. of Naphtali, ... 4294
1Ch 6:62 out of the t. of Manasseh in Bashan,... 4294
1Ch 6:63 families, out of the t. of Reuben,......... 4294
1Ch 6:63 and out of the t. of Gad, ... 4294
1Ch 6:63 and out of the t. of Zebulun, twelve.... 4294
1Ch 6:65 of the t. of the children of Judah, ... 4294
1Ch 6:65 of the t. of the children of Simeon, ... 4294
1Ch 6:65 the t. of the children of Benjamin, ... 4294
1Ch 6:66 coasts out of the t. of Ephraim. 4294
1Ch 6:70 of the half t. of Manasseh; Aner 4294
1Ch 6:71 family of the half t. of Manasseh, ... 4294
1Ch 6:72 And out of the t. of Issachar; 4294
1Ch 6:74 And out of the t. of Asher; Mashal..... 4294

1Ch 6:76 And out of the t. of Naphtali; 4294
1Ch 6:77 were given out of the t. of Zebulun, ... 4294
1Ch 6:78 given them out of the t. of Reuben,.... 4294
1Ch 6:80 And out of the t. of Gad; Ramoth....... 4294
1Ch 12:31 of the half t. of Manasseh eighteen..... 4294
1Ch 12:37 and of the half t. of Manasseh, ... 7626
1Ch 23:14 sons were named of the t. of Levi...... 7626
1Ch 26:32 Gadites, and the half t. of Manasseh, .. 7626
1Ch 27:20 of the half t. of Manasseh, Joel the..... 7626
1Ch 27:21 Of the half t. of Manasseh in Gilead,.........
Ps 78:67 and chose not the t. of Ephraim:........ 7626
Ps 78:68 But chose the t. of Judah, the 7626
Eze 47:23 in what t. the stranger sojourneth, ... 7626
Lu 2:36 of Phanuel, of the t. of Aser: *5443*
Ac 13:21 Saul...a man of the t. of Benjamin, ... *5443*
Ro 11:1 of Abraham, of the t. of Benjamin. *5443*
Php 3:5 of Israel, of the t. of Benjamin,............ *5443*
Heb 7:13 spoken pertaineth to another t.,.......... *5443*
Heb 7:14 of which t. Moses spake nothing........ *5443*
Re 5:5 the Lion of the t. of Juda, the Root.... *5443*
Re 7:5 Of the t. of Juda were sealed twelve... *5443*
Re 7:5 Of the t. of Reuben were sealed........ *5443*
Re 7:5 Of the t. of Gad were sealed twelve... *5443*
Re 7:6 Of the t. of Aser were sealed twelve.. *5443*
Re 7:6 Of the t. of Nepthalim were sealed..... *5443*
Re 7:6 Of the t. of Manasses were sealed..... *5443*
Re 7:7 Of the t. of Simeon were sealed *5443*
Re 7:7 Of the t. of Levi were sealed twelve... *5443*
Re 7:7 Of the t. of Issachar were sealed....... *5443*
Re 7:8 Of the t. of Zabulon were sealed........ *5443*
Re 7:8 Of the t. of Joseph were sealed *5443*
Re 7:8 Of the t. of Benjamin were sealed...... *5443*

TRIBES
Ge 49:16 people, as one of the t. of Israel........ 7626
Ge 49:28 All these are the twelve t. of Israel: ... 7626
Ex 24:4 according to the twelve t. of Israel. 7626
Ex 28:21 they be according to the twelve t....... 7626
Ex 39:14 name, according to the twelve t......... 7626
Nu 1:16 princes of the t. of their fathers,........ 4294
Nu 7:2 who were the princes of the t., ... 4294
Nu 24:2 in his tents according to their t.;........ 7626
Nu 26:55 names of the t. of their fathers.......... 4294
Nu 30:1 spake unto the heads of the t............ 4294
Nu 30:31 4 throughout all the t. of Israel,......... 4294
Nu 32:28 and the chief fathers of the t. of 4294
Nu 33:54 according to the t. of your fathers...... 4294
Nu 34:13 commanded to give unto the nine t.,... 4294
Nu 34:15 two t. and the half tribe...received 4294
Nu 36:3 to any of the sons of the other t........ 7626
Nu 36:9 every one of the t. of the children....... 4294
De 1:13 and known among your t., ... 7626
De 1:15 So I took the chief of your t., wise..... 7626
De 1:15 tens, and officers among your t.......... 7626
De 5:23 even all the heads of your t., and....... 7626
De 12:5 God shall choose out of all your t....... 7626
De 12:14 Lord shall choose in one of thy t.,...... 7626
De 16:18 God giveth thee, throughout thy t.: 7626
De 18:5 hath chosen him out of all thy t., ... 7626
De 29:10 captains of your t., your elders, ... 7626
De 29:21 unto evil out of all the t. of Israel,...... 7626
De 31:28 unto me all the elders of your t., ... 7626
De 33:5 t. of Israel were gathered together..... 7626
Jos 3:12 twelve men out of the t. of Israel,....... 7626
Jos 4:5 according to the number of the t........ 7626
Jos 4:8 according unto the number of the t..... 7626
Jos 7:14 be brought according to your t.:.......... 7626
Jos 7:16 and brought Israel by their t.; 7626
Jos 11:23 to their divisions by their t................ 7626
Jos 12:7 Joshua gave unto the t. of Israel 7626
Jos 13:7 for an inheritance unto the nine t., ... 7626
Jos 14:1 heads of the fathers of the t. of......... 4294
Jos 14:2 for the nine t., and for the half.......... 4294
Jos 14:3 had given the inheritance of two t., ... 4294
Jos 14:4 the children of Joseph were two t.,...... 4294
Jos 18:2 And there remained...seven t., ... 7626
Jos 19:51 heads of the fathers of the t. of......... 4294
Jos 21:1 heads of the fathers of the t. of......... 4294
Jos 21:16 nine cities out of those two t............ 7626
Jos 22:14 throughout all the t. of Israel;........... 4294
Jos 23:4 to be an inheritance for your t., ... 7626
Jos 24:1 Joshua gathered all the t. of Israel...... 7626
Jg 18:1 not fallen unto them among the t........ 7626
Jg 20:2 people, even of all the t. of Israel, ... 7626
Jg 20:10 throughout all the t. of Israel,............ 7626
Jg 20:12 t. of Israel sent men through all......... 7626
Jg 21:5 is there among all the t. of Israel....... 7626
Jg 21:8 What one is there of the t. of Israel... 7626
Jg 21:15 made a breach in the t. of Israel. 7626
1Sa 2:28 choose him out of all the t. of Israel... 7626
1Sa 9:21 of the smallest of the t. of Israel? 7626
1Sa 10:19 before the Lord by your t.,.............. 7626
1Sa 10:20 all the t. of Israel to come near, ... 7626
1Sa 15:17 made the head of the t. of Israel,....... 7626
2Sa 5:1 came all the t. of Israel to David........ 7626
2Sa 7:7 I a word with any of the t. of Israel,... 7626
2Sa 15:2 servant is of one of the t. of Israel..... 7626
2Sa 15:10 spies throughout all the t. of Israel, ... 7626
2Sa 19:9 strife throughout all the t. of Israel, ... 7626
2Sa 20:14 he went through all the t. of Israel..... 7626
2Sa 24:2 Go now through all the t. of Israel, ... 7626
1Ki 8:1 Israel, and all the heads of the t., ... 4294
1Ki 8:16 no city out of all the t. of Israel......... 7626
1Ki 11:31 and will give ten t. to thee:............... 7626
1Ki 11:32 chosen out of all the t. of Israel:)....... 7626
1Ki 11:35 will give it unto thee, even ten t........ 7626
1Ki 14:21 did choose out of all the t. of Israel, ... 7626
1Ki 18:31 of the t. of the sons of Jacob,............ 7626
2Ki 21:7 I have chosen out of all t. of Israel, ... 7626
1Ch 27:16 Furthermore over the t. of Israel: 7626
1Ch 27:22 were the princes of the t. of Israel..... 7626
1Ch 28:1 princes of Israel,...princes of the t.,.... 7626
1Ch 29:6 and princes of the t. of Israel, ... 7626
2Ch 5:2 Israel, and all the heads of the t., ... 4294
2Ch 6:5 no city among all the t. of Israel 7626
2Ch 11:16 out of all the t. of Israel such as set... 7626
2Ch 12:13 chosen out of all the t. of Israel, ... 7626
2Ch 33:7 chosen before all the t. of Israel, ... 7626
Ezr 6:17 to the number of the t. of Israel. 7625
Ps 78:55 t. of Israel to dwell in their tents. 7626
Ps 105:37 one feeble person among their t......... 7626
Ps 122:4 the t. go up, the t. of the Lord, ... 7626
Isa 19:13 that are the stay of the t. thereof....... 7626
Isa 49:6 servant to raise up the t. of Jacob, ... 7626
Isa 63:17 sake, the t. of thine inheritance. 7626
Eze 37:19 and the t. of Israel his fellows, ... 7626
Eze 45:8 house of Israel according to their t.. ... 7626
Eze 47:13 according to the twelve t. of Israel: 7626
Eze 47:21 you according to the t. of Israel. 7626
Eze 47:22 with you among the t. of Israel.......... 7626
Eze 48:1 Now these are the names of the t.. 7626
Eze 48:19 serve it out of all the t. of Israel....... 7626
Eze 48:23 As for the rest of the t., from the....... 7626
Eze 48:29 divide by lot unto the t. of Israel........ 7626
Eze 48:31 after the names of the t. of Israel: 7626
Ho 5:9 among the t. of Israel have I made..... 7626
Hab 3:9 according to the oaths of the t.,......... 4294
Zec 9:1 of man, as of all the t. of Israel, ... 7626
Mt 19:28 judging the twelve t. of Israel....... *5443*
Mt 24:30 all the t. of the earth mourn, ... *5443*
Lu 22:30 judging the twelve t. of Israel....... *5443*
Ac 26:7 Unto which promise our twelve t., ... *1429*
Jas 1:1 the twelve t. which are scattered....... *5443*
Re 7:4 all the t. of the children of Israel....... *5443*
Re 21:12 are the names of the twelve t. of....... *5443*

TRIBULATION See also TRIBULATIONS.
De 4:30 When thou art in t., and all these....... 6862
Jg 10:14 deliver you in the time of your t.. 6869
1Sa 26:24 and let him deliver me out of all t.. 6869
Mt 13:21 for when t. or persecution ariseth . *2347*
Mt 24:21 For then shall be great t., such..... *2347*
Mt 24:29 after the t. of those days shall *2347*
Mk 13:24 that t., the sun...be darkened, ... *2347*
Joh 16:33 In the world ye shall have t.: but .. *2347*
Ac 14:22 through much t. enter into the.......... *2347*
Ro 2:9 T. and anguish upon every soul of...... *2347*
Ro 5:3 knowing that t. worketh patience;....... *2347*
Ro 8:35 shall t., or distress, or persecution, ... *2347*
Ro 12:12 Rejoicing in hope; patient in t.; *2347*
2Co 1:4 Who comforteth us in all our t., ... *2347*
2Co 7:4 I am exceeding joyful in all our t.. ...... *2347*
1Th 3:4 before that we should suffer t.;.......... *2346*
2Th 1:6 t. to them that trouble you; *2347*
Re 1:9 your brother, and companion in t.,....... *2347*
Re 2:9 thy works, and t., and poverty, ... *2347*
Re 2:10 and ye shall have t. ten days:........ *2347*
Re 2:22 adultery with her into great t., ... *2347*
Re 7:14 they which came out of great t., ... *2347*

TRIBULATIONS
1Sa 10:19 of all your adversities and your t.;...... 6869
Ro 5:3 only so, but we glory in t. also;......... *2347*
Eph 3:13 that ye faint not at my t. for you, ... *2347*
2Th 1:4 persecutions and t. that ye endure...... *2347*

TRIBUTARIES
De 20:11 found therein shall be t. unto thee,..... 4522
Jg 1:30 dwelt among them, and became t.. 4522
Jg 1:33 Beth-anath became t. unto them. 4522
Jg 1:35 prevailed, so that they became t.. 4522

TRIBUTARY See also TRIBUTARIES.
La 1:1 provinces, how is she become t.! 4522

TRIBUTE See also DISTRIBUTE.
Ge 49:15 and became a servant unto t.. 4522
Nu 31:28 levy a t. unto the Lord of the men..... 4371
Nu 31:37 the Lord's t. of the sheep was six....... 4371
Nu 31:38 the Lord's t. was threescore and........ 4371
Nu 31:39 which the Lord's t. was threescore..... 4371
Nu 31:40 the Lord's t. was thirty and two 4371
Nu 31:41 Moses gave the t., which was the...... 4371
De 16:10 a t. of a freewill offering of thine........ 4530
Jos 16:10 unto this day, and serve under t.. 4522
Jos 17:13 that they put the Canaanites to t.;...... 4522
Jg 1:28 that they put the Canaanites to t.,...... 4522
2Sa 20:24 And Adoram was over the t.: and 4522
1Ki 4:6 the son of Abda was over the t.. 4522
1Ki 9:21 Solomon levy a t. of bondservice......... 4522
1Ki 12:18 sent Adoram, who was over the t.; 4522
2Ki 23:33 put the land to a t. of an hundred....... 6066
2Ch 8:8 make to pay t. until this day............. 4522
2Ch 10:18 sent Hadoram that was over the t.; 4522
2Ch 17:11 brought...presents, and t. silver;........ 4853
Ezr 4:13 then will they not pay toll, t., and 1093
Ezr 4:20 t., and custom, was paid unto them. ... 1093
Ezr 6:8 even of the t. beyond the river,......... 4061
Ezr 7:24 lawful to impose toll, t., or custom, ... 1093
Ne 5:4 borrowed money for the king's t., ... 4060
Es 10:1 Ahasuerus laid a t. upon the land, ... 4522
Pr 12:24 but the slothful shall be under t.. 4522
Mt 17:24 they that receive t. money came........ *1323*
Mt 17:24 said, Doth not your master pay t.? *1323*
Mt 17:25 of the earth take custom or t.? *2778*
Mt 22:17 Is it lawful to give t. unto Caesar, ... *2778*
Mt 22:19 Shew me the t. money. And they..... *2778*
Mk 12:14 Is it lawful to give t. to Caesar, or..... *2778*
Lu 20:22 lawful for us to give t. unto Caesar,.... *5411*
Lu 23:2 and forbidding to give t. to Caesar,..... *5411*
Ro 13:6 For for this cause pay ye t. also: *5411*
Ro 13:7 t. to whom t. is due; custom to......... *5411*

TRICKLETH
La 3:49 Mine eye t. down, and ceaseth.......... 5064

TRIED
De 21:5 controversy and every stroke be t...........
2Sa 22:31 perfect; the word of the Lord is t. 6884
Job 23:10 when he hath t. me, I shall come 974
Job 34:36 is that Job may be t. unto the end, ... 974
Ps 12:6 as silver t. in a furnace of earth, ... 6884
Ps 17:3 thou hast t. me, and shalt find........... 6884
Ps 18:30 perfect: the word of the Lord is t. 6884
Ps 66:10 thou hast t. us, as silver is t............ 6884
Ps 105:19 came: the word of the Lord t. him. 6884
Isa 28:16 a stone, and a t. stone, a precious....... 976
Jer 12:3 me, and t. mine heart toward thee:...... 974
Da 12:10 purified, and made white, and t.;........ 6884
Zec 13:9 and will try them as gold is t............. 974
Heb 11:17 when he was t., offered up Isaac: *3985*
Jas 1:12 for when he is t., he shall receive...... *1384*
1Pe 1:7 though it be t. with fire, might be *1381*
Re 2:2 thou hast t. them which say they .. *3985*
Re 2:10 you into prison, that ye may be t.; .*3985*
Re 3:18 to buy of me gold t. in the fire, ... *4448*

TRIEST
1Ch 29:17 my God, that thou t. the heart, and..... 974
Jer 11:20 that t. the reins and the heart,............ 974
Jer 20:12 that t. the righteous, and seest the...... 974

TRIETH
Job 34:3 For the ear t. words, as the mouth...... 974
Ps 7:9 for the righteous God t. the hearts 974
Ps 11:5 The Lord t. the righteous: but the....... 974
Pr 17:3 for gold: but the Lord t. the hearts....... 974
1Th 2:4 but God, which t. our hearts. *1381*

TRIMMED
2Sa 19:24 dressed his feet, nor t. his beard, ... 6213
Mt 25:7 virgins arose, and t. their lamps.... *2885*

TRIMMEST
Jer 2:33 Why **t.** thou thy way to seek love?..... 3190

TRIUMPH See also TRIUMPHED; TRIUMPHING.
2Sa 1:20 daughters of the uncircumcised **t.**....... 5937
Ps 25:2 let not mine enemies **t.** over me.......... 5970
Ps 41:11 mine enemy doth not **t.** over me........ 7321
Ps 47:1 unto God with the voice of **t.**............ 7440
Ps 60:8 Philistia, **t.** thou because of me.......... 7321
Ps 92:4 I will **t.** in the works of thy hands...... 7442
Ps 94:3 how long shall the wicked **t.**?;........... 5937
Ps 106:47 holy name, and to **t.** in thy praise....... 7623
Ps 108:9 my shoes; over Philistia will I **t.**........ 7321
2Co 2:14 always causeth us to **t.** in Christ,........ *2358*

TRIUMPHED
Ex 15:1 the Lord, for he hath **t.** gloriously:..... 1342
Ex 15:21 the Lord, for he hath **t.** gloriously:..... 1342

TRIUMPHING
Job 20:5 That the **t.** of the wicked is short,...... 7445
Col 2:15 of them openly, **t.** over them in it...... *2358*

TROAS (tro'-as)
Ac 16:8 passing by Mysia came down to **T.**,..... *5174*
Ac 16:11 Therefore loosing from **T.**, we........... *5174*
Ac 20:5 going before tarried for us at **T.**......... *5174*
Ac 20:6 came unto them to **T.** in five days;..... *5174*
2Co 2:12 I came to **T.** to preach Christ's........... *5174*
2Ti 4:13 cloke that I left at **T.** with Carpus,...... *5174*

TROD See TRODDEN; TRODE.

TRODDEN
De 1:36 give the land that he hath **t.** upon,...... 1869
Jos 14:9 land whereon thy feet have **t.** shall...... 1869
Jg 5:21 soul, thou hast **t.** down strength......... 1869
Job 22:15 old way which wicked men have **t.**?.... 1869
Job 28:8 The lion's whelps have not **t.** it, nor.... 1869
Ps 119:118 hast **t.** down all them that err............ 5541
Isa 5:5 thereof, and it shall be **t.** down:......... 4823
Isa 14:19 the pit; as a carcase **t.** under feet........ 947
Isa 18:2 a nation meted out and **t.** down,......... 4001
Isa 18:7 nation meted out and **t.** under foot,.... 4001
Isa 25:10 Moab shall be **t.** down under him,....... 1758
Isa 25:10 straw is **t.** down for the dunghill......... 1758
Isa 28:3 of Ephraim, shall be **t.** under feet;...... 7429
Isa 28:18 then ye shall be **t.** down by it............ 4823
Isa 63:3 I have **t.** the winepress alone; and...... 1869
Isa 63:18 our adversaries have **t.** down thy......... 947
Jer 12:10 they have **t.** my portion underfoot,....... 947
La 1:15 hath **t.** under foot all my mighty......... 5541
La 1:15 the Lord hath **t.** the virgin, the.......... 1869
Eze 34:19 which ye have **t.** with your feet:........ 7429
Da 8:13 and the host to be **t.** under foot?....... 4823
Mic 7:10 shall she be **t.** down as the mire of..... 4823
Mt 5:13 **and to be t. under foot of men**....... *2662*
Lu 8:5 **it was t. down, and the fowls of**.... *2662*
Lu 21:24 **Jerusalem shall be t. down of the**.. *3961*
Heb 10:29 who hath **t.** under foot the Son of....... *2662*
Re 14:20 winepress was **t.** without the city,....... *3961*

TRODE
Jg 9:27 their vineyards, and **t.** the grapes,...... 1869
Jg 20:43 and **t.** them down with ease over........ 1869
2Ki 7:17 20 people **t.** upon him in the gate,....... 7429
2Ki 9:33 horses: and he **t.** her under foot......... 7429
2Ki 14:9 in Lebanon, and **t.** down the thistle...... 7429
2Ch 25:18 in Lebanon, and **t.** down the thistle...... 7429
Lu 12:1 that they **t.** one upon another,........... *2662*

TROGYLLIUM (tro-jil'-le-um)
Ac 20:15 at Samos, and tarried at **T.**;................. *5175*

TROOP See also TROOPS.
Ge 30:11 And Leah said, A **t.** cometh: and........ 1409
Ge 49:19 Gad, a **t.** shall overcome him: but....... 1416
1Sa 30:8 Shall I pursue after this **t.**? shall I....... 1416
2Sa 2:25 after Abner, and became one **t.**,............ 92
2Sa 3:22 and Joab came from pursuing a **t.**,........ 1416
2Sa 22:30 by thee I have run through a **t.**: by..... 1416
2Sa 23:11 were gathered together into a **t.**,........ 2416
2Sa 23:13 the **t.** of the Philistines pitched in........ 2416
Ps 18:29 by thee I have run through a **t.**;.......... 1416
Isa 65:11 that prepare a table for that **t.**,........... 1409
Jer 18:22 bring a **t.** suddenly upon them:........... 1416
Ho 7:1 the **t.** of robbers spoileth without......... 1416
Am 9:6 and hath founded his **t.** in the earth;...... 92

TROOPS
Job 6:19 The **t.** of Tema looked, the.................. 734
Job 19:12 His **t.** come together, and raise up..... 1416
Jer 5:7 assembled themselves by **t.** in the............
Ho 6:9 as **t.** of robbers wait for a man,.......... 1416
Mic 5:1 Now gather thyself in **t.**,................... 1413
Mic 5:1 O daughter of **t.**: he hath laid............ 1416
Hab 3:16 he will invade them with his **t.**...................

TROPHIMUS (trof'-im-us)
Ac 20:4 and of Asia, Tychicus and **T.**............. *5161*
Ac 21:29 before with him in the city **T.** an......... *5161*
2Ti 4:20 but **T.** have I left at Miletum sick....... *5161*

TROTH See BETROTH.

TROUBLE See also TROUBLED; TROUBLES; TROUBLEST; TROUBLETH; TROUBLING.
Jos 6:18 camp of Israel a curse, and **t.** it......... 5916
Jos 7:25 us? the Lord shall **t.** thee this day...... 5916
Jg 11:35 thou art one of them that **t.** me:......... 5916
2Ki 19:3 This day is a day of **t.**, and of............ 6869
1Ch 22:14 in my **t.** I have prepared for the.......... 6040
2Ch 15:4 they in their **t.** did turn unto the........ 6862
2Ch 29:8 and he hath delivered them to **t.**,........ 2189
2Ch 32:18 to affright them, and to **t.** them;........... 926
Ne 9:27 and in the time of their **t.**, when......... 6869
Ne 9:32 let not all the **t.** seem little before...... 8513
Job 3:26 neither was I quiet; yet **t.** came.......... 7267
Job 5:6 doth **t.** spring out of the ground;.......... 5999
Job 5:7 Yet man is born unto **t.**, as the........... 5999
Job 14:1 is of few days, and full of **t.**............... 7267
Job 15:24 **T.** and anguish shall make him............ 6862
Job 27:9 his cry when **t.** cometh upon him?......... 6869
Job 30:25 weep for him that was in **t.**?...... 7186,3117
Job 34:29 quietness, who then can make **t.**?........ 7561
Job 38:23 reserved against the time of **t.**,........... 6862
Ps 3:1 how are they increased that **t.** me!...... 6862
Ps 9:9 oppressed, a refuge in times of **t.**......... 6869
Ps 9:13 consider my **t.** which I suffer of.......... 6040
Ps 10:1 hidest thou thyself in times of **t.**?....... 6869
Ps 13:4 those that **t.** me rejoice when I am..... 6862
Ps 20:1 Lord hear thee in the day of **t.**;.......... 6869
Ps 22:11 Be not far from me; for **t.** is near;...... 6869
Ps 27:5 in the time of **t.** he shall hide me........ 7451
Ps 31:7 for thou hast considered my **t.**;............ 6040
Ps 31:9 upon me, O Lord, for I am in **t.**:......... 6887
Ps 32:7 thou shalt preserve me from **t.**;.......... 6862
Ps 37:39 is their strength in the time of **t.**........ 6869
Ps 41:1 Lord will deliver him in time of **t.**....... 7451
Ps 46:1 strength, a very present help in **t.**....... 6869
Ps 50:15 And call upon me in the day of **t.**:....... 6869
Ps 54:7 he hath delivered me out of all **t.**:....... 6869
Ps 59:16 and refuge in the day of my **t.**.............. 6862
Ps 60:11 Give us help from **t.**: for vain is.......... 6862
Ps 66:14 hath spoken, when I was in **t.**............. 6862
Ps 69:17 from thy servant; for I am in **t.**:......... 6887
Ps 73:5 They are not in **t.** as other men;.......... 5999
Ps 77:2 day of my **t.** I sought the Lord:........... 6869
Ps 78:33 in vanity, and their years in **t.**............ 928
Ps 78:49 wrath, and indignation, and **t.**,............ 6869
Ps 81:7 Thou calledst in **t.**, and I delivered...... 6869
Ps 86:7 day of my **t.** I will call upon thee:........ 6869
Ps 91:15 I will be with him in **t.**; I will deliver... 6869
Ps 102:2 me in the day when I am in **t.**;............ 6862
Ps 107:6, 13 cried unto the Lord in their **t.**,....... 6862
Ps 107:19 they cry unto the Lord in their **t.**,....... 6862
Ps 107:26 their soul is melted because of **t.**......... 7451
Ps 107:28 they cry unto the Lord in their **t.**,....... 6862
Ps 108:12 Give us help from **t.**: for vain is the.... 6862
Ps 116:3 upon me: I found **t.** and sorrow.......... 6869
Ps 119:143 **T.** and anguish have taken hold.......... 6862
Ps 138:7 Though I walk in the midst of **t.**,........ 6869
Ps 142:2 him; I shewed before him my **t.**.......... 6869
Ps 143:11 sake bring my soul out of **t.**.............. 6869
Pr 11:8 The righteous is delivered out of **t.**,...... 6869
Pr 12:13 but the just shall come out of **t.**........... 6869
Pr 15:6 in the revenues of the wicked is **t.**...... 5916
Pr 15:16 great treasure and **t.** therewith.......... 4103
Pr 25:19 in an unfaithful man in time of **t.**........ 6869
Isa 1:14 they are a **t.** unto me; I am weary....... 2960
Isa 8:22 behold **t.** and darkness, dimness.......... 6869
Isa 17:14 And behold at eveningtide **t.**;.............. 1091
Isa 22:5 For it is a day of **t.**, and of.................. 4103
Isa 26:16 Lord, in **t.** have they visited thee,....... 6862
Isa 30:6 Into the land of **t.** and anguish,........... 6869
Isa 33:2 our salvation also in the time of **t.**....... 6869
Isa 37:3 This day is a day of **t.**, and of............ 6869
Isa 46:7 answer, nor save him out of his **t.**....... 6869
Isa 65:23 in vain, nor bring forth for **t.**;............. 928
Jer 2:27 in the time of their **t.** they will say,..... 7451
Jer 2:28 can save thee in the time of thy **t.**:..... 7451
Jer 8:15 a time of health, and behold **t.**!.......... 1205
Jer 11:12 them at all in the time of their **t.**........ 7451
Jer 11:14 that they cry unto me for their **t.**........ 7451
Jer 14:8 the saviour thereof in time of **t.**,......... 6869
Jer 14:19 the time of healing, and behold **t.**!...... 1205
Jer 30:7 it is even the time of Jacob's **t.**;.......... 6869
Jer 51:2 for in the day of **t.** they shall be.......... 7451
La 1:21 mine enemies have heard of my **t.**;....... 7451
Eze 7:7 is come, the day of **t.** is near,.............. 4103
Eze 32:13 neither shall the foot of man **t.** them... 4103
Eze 32:13 nor the hoofs of beasts **t.** them.......... 1804
Da 4:19 the interpretation thereof, **t.** thee......... 927
Da 5:10 let not thy thoughts **t.** thee, nor let...... 927
Da 11:44 and out of the north shall **t.** him:......... 926
Da 12:1 and there shall be a time of **t.**,........... 6869
Na 1:7 good, a strong hold in the day of **t.**;... 6869
Hab 3:16 that I might rest in the day of **t.**:........ 6869
Zep 1:15 of wrath, a day of **t.** and distress,...... 6869
Mt 26:10 them, **Why t. ye the woman?**.. *2873,3930*
Mk 14:6 **Let her alone; why t. ye her?**.. *2873,3930*
Lu 7:6 unto him, Lord, **t.** not thyself:............ *4660*
Lu 8:49 is dead; **t.** not the Master.................. *4660*
Lu 11:7 **shall answer and say, T. me not:**... *2873*
Ac 15:19 sentence is, that we **t.** not them,........ *3926*
Ac 16:20 Jews, do exceedingly **t.** our city,......... *1613*
Ac 20:10 **T.** not yourselves; for his life is.......... *2350*
1Co 7:28 such shall have **t.** in the flesh:........... *2347*
2Co 1:4 comfort them which are in any **t.**,....... *2347*
2Co 1:8 our **t.** which came to us in Asia,......... *2347*
Ga 1:7 but there be some that **t.** you, and...... *5015*
Ga 5:12 were even cut off which **t.** you............. *387*
Ga 6:17 henceforth let no man **t.** me:....... *2873,3930*
2Th 1:6 tribulation to them that **t.** you;........... *2346*
2Ti 2:9 Wherein I suffer **t.**, as an evil doer,..... *2553*
Heb 12:15 of bitterness springing up **t.** you,........ *1776*

TROUBLED See also TROUBLEDST.
Ge 34:30 Ye have **t.** me to make me to stink.... 5916
Ge 41:8 the morning that his spirit was **t.**;...... 6470
Ge 45:3 for they were **t.** at his presence............ 926
Ex 14:24 and **t.** the host of the Egyptians,......... 2000
Jos 7:25 Joshua said, Why hast thou **t.** us?....... 5916
1Sa 14:29 My father hath **t.** the land: see,......... 5916
1Sa 16:14 evil spirit from the Lord **t.** him.......... 1204
1Sa 28:21 Saul, and saw that he was sore **t.**,......... 926
2Sa 4:1 feeble, and all the Israelites were **t.**...... 926
1Ki 18:18 he answered, I have not **t.** Israel;...... 5916
2Ki 6:11 king of Syria was sore **t.** for this........ 5590
Ezr 4:4 Judah, and **t.** them in building,........... 1089
Job 4:5 it toucheth thee, and thou art **t.**........... 926
Job 21:4 why should not my spirit be **t.**?.......... 7114
Job 23:15 Therefore am I **t.** at his presence:........ 926
Job 34:20 the people shall be **t.** at midnight,...... 1607
Ps 30:7 didst hide thy face, and I was **t.**.......... 926
Ps 38:6 I am **t.**; I am bowed down greatly;...... 5753
Ps 46:3 the waters thereof roar and be **t.**,...... 2560
Ps 48:5 they were **t.**, and hasted away............ 926
Ps 77:3 I remembered God, and was **t.**:........... 1993
Ps 77:4 I am so **t.** that I cannot speak............ 6470
Ps 77:16 afraid: the depths also were **t.**............ 7264
Ps 83:17 Let them be confounded and **t.** for....... 926
Ps 90:7 anger, and by thy wrath are we **t.**........ 926
Ps 104:29 Thou hidest thy face, they are **t.**:........ 926
Pr 25:26 the wicked is as a **t.** fountain,............ 7515
Isa 32:10 Many days and years shall ye be **t.**,..... 7264
Isa 32:11 are at ease; be **t.**, ye careless ones:.... 7264
Isa 57:20 But the wicked are like the **t.** sea,....... 1644
Jer 31:20 my bowels are **t.** for him; I will......... 1993
La 1:20 my bowels are **t.**; mine heart is.......... 2560
La 2:11 my bowels are **t.**, my liver is poured.. 2560
Eze 7:27 of the people of the land shall be **t.**:..... 926
Eze 26:18 isles that are in the sea shall be **t.**....... 926
Eze 27:35 afraid, they shall be **t.** in their.......... 7481
Da 2:1 wherewith his spirit was **t.**, and......... 6470
Da 2:3 my spirit was **t.** to know the dream.... 6470
Da 4:5 and the visions of my head **t.** me......... 927
Da 4:19 one hour, and his thoughts **t.** him......... 927
Da 5:6 his thoughts **t.** him, so that the........... 927
Da 5:9 Then was king Belshazzar greatly **t.**,.... 927
Da 7:15 and the visions of my head **t.** me......... 927
Da 7:28 Daniel, my cogitations much **t.** me,....... 927
Zec 10:2 they were **t.**, because there was no..... 6031
Mt 2:3 had heard these things, he was **t.**,....... *5015*

Mt 14:26 they were t., saying, It is a spirit;...... *5015*
Mt 24:6 see that ye be not t.: for all these ..*2360*
Mk 6:50 For they all saw him, and were t.:..... *5015*
Mk 13:7 and rumours of wars, be ye not t.: .*2360*
Lu 1:12 when Zacharias saw him, he was t.,.... *5015*
Lu 1:29 she was t. at his saying, and cast....... *1298*
Lu 10:41 careful and t. about many things: . *5182*
Lu 24:38 Why are ye t.? and why do *5015*
Joh 5:4 into the pool, and t. the water:.......... *5015*
Joh 5:7 have no man, when the water is t.,.... *5015*
Joh 11:33 groaned in the spirit,...was t.,.... *5015,1438*
Joh 12:27 Now is my soul t.; and what shall . *5015*
Joh 13:21 he was t. in spirit, and testified, ... *5015*
Joh 14:1 Let not your heart be t.: ye believe *5015*
Joh 14:27 Let not your heart be t., neither ... *5015*
Ac 15:24 out from us have t. you with words,... *5015*
Ac 17:8 they t. the people and the rulers of.... *5015*
2Co 4:8 We are t. on every side, yet not........ *2346*
2Co 7:5 rest, but we were t. on every side;.... *2346*
2Th 1:7 And to you who are t. rest with us, ... *2346*
2Th 2:2 or be t., neither by spirit, nor by....... *2360*
1Pe 3:14 afraid of their terror, neither be t.;..... *5015*

TROUBLEDST
Eze 32:2 and t. the waters with thy feet, ... 1804

TROUBLER
1Ch 2:7 Achar, the t. of Israel, who................ 5916

TROUBLES
De 31:17 evils and t. shall befall them;............. 6869
De 31:21 evils and t. are befallen them, ... 6869
Job 5:19 He shall deliver thee in six t.: yea,...... 6869
Ps 25:17 The t. of my heart are enlarged: O 6869
Ps 25:22 Israel, O God, out of all his t. 6869
Ps 34:6 him, and saved him out of all his t...... 6869
Ps 34:17 delivereth them out of all their t. 6869
Ps 71:20 hast shewed me great and sore t., ... 6869
Ps 88:3 For my soul is full of t.: and my 7451
Pr 21:23 tongue keepeth his soul from t. 6869
Isa 65:16 because the former t. are forgotten, ... 6869
Mk 13:8 and there shall be famines and t. .. *5016*

TROUBLEST
Mk 5:35 dead: why t. thou the Master any...... *4660*

TROUBLETH
1Sa 16:15 an evil spirit from God t. thee.......... 1204
1Ki 18:17 him, Art thou he that t. Israel?.......... 5916
Job 22:10 about thee, and sudden fear t. thee;..... 926
Job 23:16 heart soft, and the Almighty t. me: 926
Pr 11:17 he that is cruel t. his own flesh. 5916
Pr 11:29 that t. his own house shall inherit....... 5916
Pr 15:27 is greedy of gain t. his own house;...... 5916
Da 4:9 is in thee, and no secret t. thee, ... 598
Lu 18:5 yet because this widow t. me, .*3930,2873*
Ga 5:10 but he that t. you shall bear his......... *5015*

TROUBLING
Job 3:17 There the wicked cease from t.; 7267
Joh 5:4 the t. of the water stepped in was...... *5015*

TROUBLOUS
Da 9:25 and the wall, even in t. times............ 5916

TROUGH See also TROUGHS.
Ge 24:20 emptied her pitcher into the t.,.......... 8268

TROUGHS See also KNEADINGTROUGHS.
Ge 30:38 watering t. when the flocks came....... 8268
Ex 2:16 filled the t. to water their father's...... 7298

TROW
Lu 17:9 were commanded him? I t. not...... *1380*

TRUCEBREAKERS
2Ti 3:3 Without natural affection, t., false *786*

TRUE
Ge 42:11 we are t. men, thy servants are no 3651
Ge 42:19 If ye be t. men, let one of your......... 3651
Ge 42:31 We are t. men; we are no spies: 3651
Ge 42:33 shall I know that ye are t. men;......... 3651
Ge 42:34 are no spies, but that ye are t. men: .. 3651
De 17:4 it be t., and the thing certain, ... 571
De 22:20 But if this thing be t., and the tokens... 571
Jos 2:12 house, and give me a t. token:............ 571
Ru 3:12 it is t. that I am thy near kinsman: 551
2Sa 7:28 art that God, and thy words be t., ... 571
1Ki 10:6 It was a t. report that I heard in 571
1Ki 22:16 tell me nothing but that which is t......... 571
2Ch 9:5 It was a t. report which I heard in....... 571
2Ch 15:3 Israel hath been without the t. God,..... 571
Ne 9:13 them right judgments, and t. laws,....... 571
Ps 19:9 the judgments of the Lord are t. 571
Ps 119:160 Thy word is t. from the beginning:....... 571
Pr 14:25 A t. witness delivereth souls: but a....... 571
Jer 10:10 But the Lord is the t. God, he is the ... 571
Jer 42:5 Lord be a t. and faithful witness 571
Eze 18:8 hath executed t. judgment between...... 571
Da 3:14 Is it t., O Shadrach, Meshach, and..... 6656
Da 3:24 said unto the king, T., O king, ... 3330
Da 6:12 The thing is t., according to the......... 3330
Da 8:26 the morning which was told is t.:........ 571
Da 10:1 and the thing was t., but the time......... 571
Zec 7:9 Execute t. judgment, and shew 571
Mt 22:16 Master, we know that thou art t., ... *227*
Mk 12:14 Master, we know that thou art t.,......... *227*
Lu 16:11 commit to your trust the t. riches? ..*228*
Joh 1:9 That was the t. Light, which lighteth.... *228*
Joh 3:33 hath set to his seal that God is t. *227*
Joh 4:23 when the t. worshippers shall *228*
Joh 4:37 herein is that saying t., One sow, ... *228*
Joh 5:31 of myself, my witness is not t.......... *227*
Joh 5:32 which he witnesseth of me is t. *227*
Joh 6:32 my Father giveth you the t. bread .. *228*
Joh 7:18 glory that sent him, the same is t., ..*227*
Joh 7:28 but he that sent me is t., whom ye . *228*
Joh 8:13 of thyself; thy record is not t........... *227*
Joh 8:14 of myself, yet my record is t. *227*
Joh 8:16 yet if I judge, my judgment is t....... *227*
Joh 8:17 that the testimony of two men is t....*227*
Joh 8:26 he that sent me is t.; and I speak ... *227*
Joh 10:41 that John spake of this man were t........ *227*
Joh 15:1 I am the t. vine, and my Father is.. *228*
Joh 17:3 might know thee the only t. God. ... *228*
Joh 19:35 it bear record, and his record is t.: *228*
Joh 19:35 he knoweth that he saith t., that ye *227*
Joh 21:24 and we know that his testimony is t.... *227*
Ac 12:9 that it was t. which was done by the..... *227*
Ro 3:4 let God be t., but every man a liar; *227*
2Co 1:18 but as God is t., our word toward...... *4103*
2Co 6:8 report: as deceivers, and yet t.; *227*
Eph 4:24 righteousness and t. holiness. *3588,225*
Php 4:3 I intreat thee also, t. yokefellow, ... *1103*
Php 4:8 brethren, whatsoever things are t., ... *227*
1Th 1:9 idols to serve the living and t. God; *228*
1Ti 3:1 This is a t. saying, If a man desire *4103*
Tit 1:13 This witness is t.. Wherefore............. *227*
Heb 8:2 sanctuary, and of the t. tabernacle, ... *228*
Heb 9:24 which are the figures of the t.;............ *228*
Heb 10:22 Let us draw near with a t. heart in...... *228*
1Pe 5:12 that this is the t. grace of God........... *227*
2Pe 2:22 them according to the t. proverb, ... *227*
1Jo 2:8 which thing is t. in him and in you: *227*
1Jo 2:8 past, and the t. light now shineth.......... *228*
1Jo 5:20 that we may know him that is t.,......... *228*
1Jo 5:20 and we are in him that is t., even in *228*
1Jo 5:20 This is the t. God, and eternal life. *228*
3Jo 12 and ye know that our record is t.. .... *227*
Re 3:7 saith he that is holy, he that is t., .. *228*
Re 3:14 the faithful and t. witness, the *228*
Re 6:10 How long, O Lord, holy and t.,........... *228*
Re 15:3 just and t. are thy ways, thou King....... *228*
Re 16:7 t. and righteous are thy judgments....... *228*
Re 19:2 t. and righteous are his judgments: *228*
Re 19:9 me, These are the t. sayings of God. ... *228*
Re 19:11 him was called Faithful and T.,........... *228*
Re 21:5 for these words are t. and faithful........ *228*
Re 22:6 These sayings are faithful and t.: *228*

TRULY
Ge 4:24 t. Lamech seventy and sevenfold..............
Ge 24:49 deal kindly and t. with my master, ... 571
Ge 47:29 and deal kindly and t. with me;........... 571
Ge 48:19 but t. his younger brother shall be....... 199
Nu 14:21 But as t. as I live, all the earth........... 199
Nu 14:28 As t. as I live, saith the Lord, as ye.........
De 14:22 thou shalt t. tithe all the increase ....
Jos 2:14 will deal kindly and t. with thee. 571
Jos 2:24 T. the Lord hath delivered into........... 3588
Jg 9:16 if ye have done t. and sincerely, in 571
Jg 9:19 ye then have dealt t. and sincerely....... 571
1Sa 20:3 but t. as the Lord liveth, and as thy..... 199
Job 36:4 For t. my words shall not be false: 551
Ps 62:1 T. my soul waiteth upon God:............ 389
Ps 73:1 T. God is good to Israel, even to 389
Ps 116:16 O Lord, t. I am thy servant; I am 577
Pr 12:22 they that deal t. are his delight. 530
Ec 11:7 T. the light is sweet, and a pleasant ....
Jer 3:23 T. in vain is salvation hoped for........... 403
Jer 3:23 t. in the Lord...is the salvation of........ 403
Jer 10:19 but I said, T. this is a grief, and I........ 389
Jer 28:9 that the Lord hath t. sent him............. 571
Eze 18:9 hath kept my judgments, to deal t.;...... 571
Mic 3:8 t. I am full of power by the spirit......... 199
Mt 9:37 The harvest t. is plenteous, but *3303*
Mt 17:11 Elias t. shall first come, and......... *3303*
Mt 27:54 saying, T. this was the Son of God. *230*
Mk 14:38 spirit t. is ready, but the flesh *3303*
Mk 15:39 T. this man was the Son of God........... *230*
Lu 10:2 The harvest t. is great, but the...... *3303*
Lu 11:48 T. ye bear witness that ye allow *686*
Lu 20:21 teachest the way of God t........... *1909,225*
Lu 22:22 t. the Son of man goeth, as it *3303*
Joh 4:18 thy husband: in that saidst thou t....*227*
Joh 20:30 many other signs t. did Jesus *3303*
Ac 1:5 For John t. baptized with water;... *3303*
Ac 3:22 For Moses t. said unto the fathers, ... *3303*
Ac 5:23 The prison t. found we shut with *3303*
2Co 12:12 T. the signs of an apostle were........... *3303*
Heb 7:23 they t. were many priests, because *3303*
Heb 11:15 And t., if they had been mindful of..... *3303*
1Jo 1:3 t. our fellowship is with...Father. *1161*

TRUMP See also TRUMPET.
1Co 15:52 twinkling of an eye, at the last t.: *4536*
1Th 4:16 archangel, and with the t. of God: *4536*

TRUMPET See also TRUMP; TRUMPETS.
Ex 19:13 when the t. soundeth long, they......... 3104
Ex 19:16 the voice of the t. exceeding loud;...... 7782
Ex 19:19 the voice of the t. sounded long,........ 7782
Ex 20:18 lightnings, and the noise of the t.,...... 7782
Le 25:9 cause the t. of the jubile to sound 7782
Le 25:9 make the t. sound throughout all........ 7782
Nu 10:4 And if they blow but with one t., then.......
Jos 6:5 when ye hear the sound of the t., ... 7782
Jos 6:20 people heard the sound of the t.,....... 7782
Jg 3:27 that he blew a t. in the mountain 7782
Jg 6:34 upon Gideon, and he blew a t.;.......... 7782
Jg 7:16 he put a t. in every man's hand, ... 7782
Jg 7:18 When I blow with a t., I and all 7782
1Sa 13:3 Saul blew the t. throughout all the...... 7782
2Sa 2:28 So Joab blew a t., and all the people... 7782
2Sa 6:15 and with the sound of the t.............. 7782
2Sa 15:10 soon as ye hear the sound of the t.. ... 7782
2Sa 18:16 Joab blew the t., and the people 7782
2Sa 20:1 blew a t., and said, We have no part .. 7782
2Sa 20:22 he blew a t., and they retired from..... 7782
1Ki 1:34 blow ye with the t., and say, God...... 7782
1Ki 1:39 they blew the t.; and all the people 7782
1Ki 1:41 when Joab heard the sound of the t., .. 7782
Ne 4:18 he that sounded the t. was by me. 7782
Ne 4:20 place...ye hear the sound of the t.,..... 7782
Job 39:24 he that it is the sound of the t........... 7782
Ps 47:5 the Lord with the sound of a t........... 7782
Ps 81:3 Blow up the t. in the new moon, in.... 7782
Ps 150:3 Praise him with the sound of the t.:.... 7782
Isa 18:3 and when he bloweth a t., hear ye. 7782
Isa 27:13 that the great t. shall be blown,......... 7782
Isa 58:1 spare not, lift up thy voice like a t.,..... 7782
Jer 4:5 and say, Blow ye the t. in the land:..... 7782
Jer 4:19 heard, O my soul, the sound of the t., .7782
Jer 4:21 and hear the sound of the t.? 7782
Jer 6:1 and blow the t. in Tekoa, and set up .. 7782
Jer 6:17 Hearken to the sound of the t. 7782
Jer 42:14 war, nor hear the sound of the t., ... 7782
Jer 51:27 blow the t. among the nations, ... 7782
Eze 7:14 They have blown the t., even to......... 8628
Eze 33:3 blow the t., and warn the people;....... 7782
Eze 33:4 heareth the sound of the t., ... 7782
Eze 33:5 He heard the sound of the t., and 7782
Eze 33:6 if the watchman...blow not the t., ... 7782
Ho 5:8 in Gibeah, and the t. in Ramah: 2689
Ho 8:1 Set the t. to thy mouth. He shall 7782
Joe 2:1 Blow ye the t. in Zion, and sound 7782
Joe 2:15 Blow the t. in Zion, sanctify a fast,..... 7782
Am 2:2 and with the sound of the t. 7782
Am 3:6 Shall a t. be blown in the city, and 7782
Zep 1:16 a day of t. and alarm against the 7782
Zec 9:14 and the Lord God shall blow the t., ... 7782
Mt 6:2 alms, do not sound a t. before *4537*
Mt 24:31 angels with a great sound of a t., .. *4536*
1Co 14:8 if the t. give an uncertain sound,........ *4536*
1Co 15:52 for the t. shall sound, and the dead...........
Heb 12:19 And the sound of a t., and the voice... *4536*

Re 1:10 behind me a great voice, as of a **t.**, ... *4536*
Re 4:1 as it were of a **t.** talking with me; *4536*
Re 8:13 voices of the **t.** of the three angels, ... *4536*
Re 9:14 to the sixth angel which had the **t.**, ... *4536*

TRUMPETERS
2Ki 11:14 the princes and the **t.** by the king. 2689
2Ch 5:13 as the **t.** and singers were as one, ... 2689
2Ch 29:28 singers sang, and the **t.** sounded: 2690
Re 18:22 musicians, and of pipers, and **t.**, ... *4538*

TRUMPETS
Le 23:24 a sabbath a memorial of blowing of **t.**, ...
Nu 10:2 Make thee two **t.** of silver; of a 2689
Nu 10:8 the priests, shall blow with the **t.**; 2689
Nu 10:9 ye shall blow an alarm with the **t.**; 2689
Nu 10:10 blow with the **t.** over your burnt 2689
Nu 29:1 it is a day of blowing the **t.** unto you, ...
Nu 31:6 and the **t.** to blow in his hand. 2689
Jos 6:4 shall bear before the ark seven **t.** 7782
Jos 6:4 the priests shall blow with the **t.**, ... 7782
Jos 6:6 priests bear seven **t.** of rams' horns 7782
Jos 6:8 seven priests bearing the seven **t.** 7782
Jos 6:8 the Lord, and blew with the **t.** 7782
Jos 6:9 the priests that blew with the **t.**, ... 7782
Jos 6:9 going on, and blowing with the **t.** 7782
Jos 6:13 And seven priests bearing seven **t.** 7782
Jos 6:13 continually, and blew with the **t.** 7782
Jos 6:13 going on, and blowing with the **t.** 7782
Jos 6:16 when the priests blew with the **t.**, ... 7782
Jos 6:20 when the priests blew with the **t.** 7782
Jg 7:8 victuals in their hand, and their **t.** 7782
Jg 7:18 blow ye the **t.** also on every side of 7782
Jg 7:19 and they blew the **t.**, and brake the 7782
Jg 7:20 the three companies blew the **t.**, ... 7782
Jg 7:20 the **t.** in their right hands to blow 7782
Jg 7:22 And the three hundred blew the **t.**, ... 7782
2Ki 9:13 blew with **t.**, saying, Jehu is king. 7782
2Ki 11:14 of the land rejoiced, and blew with **t.** ....
2Ki 12:13 snuffers, basons, **t.**, any vessels of 2689
1Ch 13:8 and with cymbals, and with **t.** 2689
1Ch 15:24 did blow with the **t.** before the ark 2689
1Ch 15:28 sound of the cornet, and with **t.**, ... 2689
1Ch 16:6 priests with **t.** continually before 2689
1Ch 16:42 with **t.** and cymbals for those that 2689
2Ch 5:12 twenty priests sounding with **t.**:) 2689
2Ch 5:13 they lifted up their voice with the **t.** ....
2Ch 7:6 the priests sounded **t.** before them, ...
2Ch 13:12 his priests with sounding **t.** to cry 2689
2Ch 13:14 and the priests sounded with the **t.** 2689
2Ch 15:14 with shouting, and with **t.**, and with 2689
2Ch 20:28 harps and **t.** unto the house of the 2689
2Ch 23:13 the princes and the **t.** by the king: 2689
2Ch 23:13 land rejoiced, and sounded with **t.**, ... 2689
2Ch 29:26 of David, and the priests with the **t.** .. 2689
2Ch 29:27 the song...began also with the **t.**, ... 2689
Ezr 3:10 the priests in their apparel with **t.**, ... 2689
Ne 12:35 certain of the priests' sons with **t.**; 2689
Ne 12:41 Zechariah, and Hananiah, with **t.**; 2689
Job 39:25 He saith among the **t.**, Ha, ha; and 7782
Ps 98:6 With **t.** and sound of cornet make 2689
Re 8:2 and to them were given seven **t.** *4536*
Re 8:6 the seven **t.** prepared themselves to ... *4536*

TRUST See also TRUSTED; TRUSTEST; TRUSTETH; TRUSTING.
Jg 9:15 and put your **t.** in my shadow: 2620
Ru 2:12 whose wings thou art come to **t.** 2620
2Sa 22:3 God of my rock; in him will I **t.** 2620
2Sa 22:31 a buckler to all them that **t.** in him. 2620
2Ki 18:20 Now on whom dost thou **t.**, that 982
2Ki 18:21 of Egypt unto all that **t.** on him. 982
2Ki 18:22 me, We **t.** in the Lord our God: 982
2Ki 18:24 put thy **t.** on Egypt for chariots and 982
2Ki 18:30 Hezekiah make you **t.** in the Lord, ... 982
1Ch 5:20 because they put their **t.** in him. 982
2Ch 32:10 Whereon do ye **t.**, that ye abide in 982
Job 4:18 he put no **t.** in his servants; and his 539
Job 8:14 whose **t.** shall be a spider's web. 4009
Job 13:15 he slay me, yet will I **t.** in him: 3176
Job 15:15 he putteth no **t.** in his saints; yea, ... 539
Job 15:31 not him that is deceived **t.** in vanity: 539
Job 35:14 him; therefore **t.** thou in him. 2342
Job 39:11 Wilt thou **t.** him, because his 982
Ps 2:12 all they that put their **t.** in him. 2620
Ps 4:5 and put your **t.** in the Lord. 982
Ps 5:11 that put their **t.** in thee rejoice: 2620
Ps 7:1 my God, in thee do I put my **t.** 2620
Ps 9:10 thy name will put their **t.** in thee: 982
Ps 11:1 In the Lord put I my **t.**: how say 2620
Ps 16:1 O God: for in thee do I put my **t.** 2620
Ps 17:7 them which put their **t.** in thee 2620
Ps 18:2 God, my strength, in whom I will **t.**; ... 2620
Ps 18:30 buckler to all those that **t.** in him. 2620
Ps 20:7 Some **t.** in chariots, and some in ....
Ps 25:2 O my God, I **t.** in thee: let me 982
Ps 25:20 ashamed; for I put my **t.** in thee. 2620
Ps 31:1 In thee, O Lord, do I put my **t.**; let ... 2620
Ps 31:6 lying vanities: but I **t.** in the Lord. 982
Ps 31:19 wrought for them that **t.** in thee 2620
Ps 34:22 none of them that **t.** in him shall 2620
Ps 36:7 children of men put their **t.** under 2620
Ps 37:3 **T.** in the Lord, and do good; so 982
Ps 37:5 **t.** also in him; and he shall bring it 982
Ps 37:40 save them, because they **t.** in him. 2620
Ps 40:3 it, and fear, and shall **t.** in the Lord. 982
Ps 40:4 man that maketh the Lord his **t.**, ... 4009
Ps 44:6 For I will not **t.** in my bow, neither 982
Ps 49:6 They that **t.** in their wealth, and 982
Ps 52:8 I **t.** in the mercy of God for ever and ... 982
Ps 55:23 half their days; but I will **t.** in thee 982
Ps 56:3 time I am afraid, I will **t.** in thee 982
Ps 56:4 his word, in God I have put my **t.**; 982
Ps 56:11 In God have I put my **t.**: I will not 982
Ps 61:4 I will **t.** in the covert of thy wings. 2620
Ps 62:8 **T.** in him at all times; ye people, ... 982
Ps 62:10 **T.** not in oppression, and become 982
Ps 64:10 in the Lord, and shall **t.** in him; 2620
Ps 71:1 In thee, O Lord, do I put my **t.**: let ... 2620
Ps 71:5 thou art my **t.** from my youth. 4009
Ps 73:28 I have put my **t.** in the Lord God, ... 4268
Ps 91:2 fortress: my God; in him will I **t.** 982
Ps 91:4 and under his wings shalt thou **t.**: 2620
Ps 115:9 O Israel, **t.** thou in the Lord: he is 982
Ps 115:10 O house of Aaron, **t.** in the Lord: 982
Ps 115:11 Ye that fear the Lord, **t.** in the Lord: ... 982
Ps 118:8, 9 It is better to **t.** in the Lord than 2620
Ps 119:42 reproacheth me: for I **t.** in thy word. 982
Ps 125:1 They that **t.** in the Lord shall be as 982
Ps 141:8 in thee is my **t.**; leave not my soul 2620
Ps 143:8 in thee do I **t.**: cause me to know 982
Ps 144:2 my shield, and he in whom I **t.**; 2620
Ps 146:3 Put not your **t.** in princes, nor in 982
Pr 3:5 **T.** in the Lord with all thine heart; 982
Pr 22:19 That thy **t.** may be in the Lord, I 4009
Pr 28:25 he that putteth his **t.** in the Lord 982
Pr 29:25 whoso putteth his **t.** in the Lord shall ... 982
Pr 30:5 unto them that put their **t.** in him. 2620
Pr 31:11 her husband doth safely **t.** in her, ... 982
Isa 12:2 I will **t.**, and not be afraid: for 982
Isa 14:32 the poor of his people shall **t.** in it. 2620
Isa 26:4 **T.** ye in the Lord for ever: for in 982
Isa 30:2 and to **t.** in the shadow of Egypt! 2620
Isa 30:3 the **t.** in the shadow of Egypt your 2622
Isa 30:12 **t.** in oppression and perverseness, ... 982
Isa 31:1 and **t.** in chariots, because they are 982
Isa 36:5 now on whom dost thou **t.**, that thou 982
Isa 36:6 king of Egypt to all that **t.** in him. 982
Isa 36:7 to me, We **t.** in the Lord our God: 982
Isa 36:9 put thy **t.** on Egypt for chariots and 982
Isa 36:15 Hezekiah make you **t.** in the Lord, ... 982
Isa 42:17 ashamed, that **t.** in graven images, ... 982
Isa 50:10 let him **t.** in the name of the Lord, ... 982
Isa 51:5 me, and on mine arm shall they **t.** 3176
Isa 57:13 he that putteth his **t.** in me shall 2620
Isa 59:4 they **t.** in vanity, and speak lies; 982
Jer 7:4 **T.** ye not in lying words,...The temple.. 982
Jer 7:8 ye **t.** in lying words, that cannot 982
Jer 7:14 wherein ye **t.**, and unto the place 982
Jer 9:4 and **t.** ye not in any brother: 982
Jer 28:15 thou makest this people to **t.** in a lie. ... 982
Jer 29:31 and he caused you to **t.** in a lie: 982
Jer 39:18 thou hast put thy **t.** in me, saith the 982
Jer 46:25 Pharaoh, and all them that **t.** in him: 982
Jer 49:11 alive; and let thy widows **t.** in me. 982
Eze 16:15 thou didst **t.** in thine own beauty, ... 982
Eze 33:13 if he **t.** to his own righteousness, ... 982
Ho 10:13 because thou didst **t.** in thy way, ... 982
Am 6:1 and **t.** in the mountain of Samaria, ... 982
Mic 7:5 **T.** ye not in a friend, put ye not 539
Na 1:7 he knoweth them that **t.** in him. 2620
Zep 3:12 shall **t.** in the name of the Lord. 2620
Mt 12:21 in his name shall the Gentiles **t.** *1679*
Mk 10:24 **for them that t. in riches to enter** ..*3982*
Lu 16:11 **commit your t. the true riches?** *4100*
Joh 5:45 **you, even Moses, in whom ye t.** ... *1679*
Ro 15:12 in him shall the Gentiles **t.** *1679*
Ro 15:24 for I **t.** to see you in my journey, ... *1679*
1Co 16:7 but I **t.** to tarry a while with you, ... *1679*
2Co 1:9 that we should not **t.** in ourselves, ... *3982*
2Co 1:10 in whom we **t.** that he will yet *1679*
2Co 1:13 I **t.** ye shall acknowledge even to *1679*
2Co 3:4 such **t.** have we through Christ to *4006*
2Co 5:11 I **t.** also are made manifest in *1679*
2Co 10:7 if any man **t.** to himself that he *3982*
2Co 13:6 I **t.** that he shall know that we are *1679*
Php 2:19 But I **t.** in the Lord Jesus to send *1679*
Php 2:24 I **t.** in the Lord that I also myself *3982*
Php 3:4 whereof he might **t.** in the flesh, ... *3982*
1Th 2:4 to be put in **t.** with the gospel, ... *4100*
1Ti 1:11 which was committed to my **t.** *4100*
1Ti 4:10 because we **t.** in the living God, ... *1679*
1Ti 6:17 nor **t.** in uncertain riches, but in *1679*
1Ti 6:20 that which is committed to thy **t.**, ...
Phm 22 for I **t.** that through your prayers *1679*
Heb 2:13 again, I will put my **t.** in him. *3982*
Heb 13:18 we **t.** we have a good conscience, ... *3982*
2Jo 12 but I **t.** to come unto you, and *1679*
3Jo 14 But I **t.** I shall shortly see thee, ... *1679*

TRUSTED See also TRUSTEDST.
De 32:37 gods, their rock in whom they **t.**, ... 2620
Jg 11:20 Sihon **t.** not Israel to pass through 539
Jg 20:36 they **t.** unto the liers in wait which 982
2Ki 18:5 He **t.** in the Lord God of Israel; so 982
Ps 13:5 But I have **t.** in thy mercy; my 982
Ps 22:4 Our fathers **t.** in thee: they **t.**, and 982
Ps 22:5 they **t.** in thee, and were not 982
Ps 22:8 He **t.** on the Lord that he would 1556
Ps 26:1 I have **t.** also in the Lord; therefore 982
Ps 28:7 my heart **t.** in him, and I am helped: 982
Ps 31:14 But I **t.** in thee, O Lord: I said, ... 982
Ps 33:21 because we have **t.** in his holy name. ... 982
Ps 41:9 own familiar friend, in whom I **t.**, ... 982
Ps 52:7 but **t.** in the abundance of his riches, ... 982
Ps 78:22 in God, and **t.** not in his salvation: 982
Isa 47:10 For thou hast **t.** in thy wickedness: 982
Jer 13:25 forgotten me, and **t.** in falsehood. 982
Jer 48:7 because thou hast **t.** in thy works 982
Jer 49:4 that **t.** in her treasures, saying, ... 982
Da 3:28 his servants that **t.** in him, and 7365
Zep 3:2 she **t.** not in the Lord; she drew 982
Mt 27:43 He **t.** in God; let him deliver him *3982*
Lu 11:22 **him all his armour wherein he t.**,.. *3982*
Lu 18:9 unto certain which **t.** in themselves *3982*
Lu 24:21 we **t.** that it had been he which *1679*
Eph 1:12 of his glory, who first **t.** in Christ *4276*
Eph 1:13 in whom ye also **t.**, after that ye ....
1Pe 3:5 holy women also, who **t.** in God, ... *1679*

TRUSTEDST
De 28:52 walls come down, wherein thou **t.**, ... 982
Jer 5:17 thy fenced cities, wherein thou **t.**, ... 982
Jer 12:5 the land of peace, wherein thou **t.**, ... 982

TRUSTEST
2Ki 18:19 confidence is this wherein thou **t.**? 982
2Ki 18:21 thou **t.** upon the staff of this bruised 982
2Ki 19:10 God in whom thou **t.** deceive thee, ... 982
Isa 36:4 confidence is this wherein thou **t.**? 982
Isa 36:6 thou **t.** in the staff of this broken 982
Isa 37:10 Let not thy God, in whom thou **t.**, ... 982

TRUSTETH
Job 40:23 he **t.** that he can draw up Jordan 982
Ps 21:7 For the king **t.** in the Lord, and 982
Ps 32:10 but he that **t.** in the Lord, mercy 982
Ps 34:8 blessed is the man that **t.** in him. 2620
Ps 57:1 for my soul **t.** in thee: yea, in the 2620
Ps 84:12 blessed is the man that **t.** in thee. 982
Ps 86:2 save thy servant that **t.** in thee. 982
Ps 115:8 so is every one that **t.** in them. 982
Ps 135:18 so is every one that **t.** in them. 982
Pr 11:28 He that **t.** in his riches shall fall: 982
Pr 16:20 ynoso **t.** in the Lord, happy is he 982
Pr 28:26 He that **t.** in his own heart is a fool: 982
Isa 26:3 on thee: because he **t.** in thee 982
Jer 17:5 Cursed be the man that **t.** in man, ... 982
Jer 17:7 Blessed is the man that **t.** in...Lord, ... 982
Hab 2:18 the maker of his work **t.** therein, ... 982
1Ti 5:5 indeed, and desolate, **t.** in God, ... *1679*

TRUSTING
Ps 112:7 his heart is fixed, **t.** in the Lord. 982

TRUSTY
Job 12:20 removeth away the speech of the t., ... 539

TRUTH See also TRUTH'S.
Ge 24:27 my master of his mercy and his t.: ... 571
Ge 32:10 of all the t., which thou hast shewed ... 571
Ge 42:16 whether there be any t. in you: ... 571
Ex 18:21 such as fear God, men of t., hating ... 571
Ex 34:6 and abundant in goodness and t., ... 571
De 13:14 and, behold, if it be t., and the thing ... 571
De 32:4 a God of t. and without iniquity, ... 530
Jos 24:14 serve him in sincerity and in t.: ... 571
Jg 9:15 If in t. ye anoint me king over you, ... 571
1Sa 12:24 serve him in t. with all your heart: ... 571
1Sa 21:5 Of a t. women have been kept ... 3588,518
2Sa 2:6 shew kindness and t. unto you: ... 571
2Sa 15:20 mercy and t. be with thee. ... 571
1Ki 2:4 walk before me in t. with all their ... 571
1Ki 3:6 as he walked before thee in t., ... 571
1Ki 17:24 word of the Lord in thy mouth is t. ... 571
2Ki 19:17 Of a t., Lord, the kings of Assyria ... 551
2Ki 20:3 how I have walked before thee in t. ... 571
2Ki 20:19 good, if peace and t. be in my days? ... 571
2Ch 18:15 that thou say nothing but the t. ... 571
2Ch 31:20 and right and t. before the Lord ... 571
Es 9:30 with words of peace and t., ... 571
Job 9:2 I know it is so of a t.: but how ... 551
Ps 15:2 and speaketh the t. in his heart. ... 571
Ps 25:5 Lead me in thy t., and teach me: ... 571
Ps 25:10 paths of the Lord are mercy and t. ... 571
Ps 26:3 eyes: and I have walked in thy t. ... 571
Ps 30:9 praise thee? shall it declare thy t.? ... 571
Ps 31:5 hast redeemed me, O Lord God of t.. ... 571
Ps 33:4 and all his works are done in t.. ... 530
Ps 40:10 thy t. from the great congregation. ... 571
Ps 40:11 and thy t. continually preserve me. ... 571
Ps 43:3 O send out thy light and thy t.: let ... 571
Ps 45:4 because of t. and meekness and ... 571
Ps 51:6 thou desirest t. in the inward parts: ... 571
Ps 54:5 mine enemies: cut them off in thy t. ... 571
Ps 57:3 send forth his mercy and his t. ... 571
Ps 57:10 heavens, and thy t. unto the clouds. ... 571
Ps 60:4 be displayed because of the t.. ... 7189
Ps 61:7 O prepare mercy and t., which may ... 571
Ps 69:13 hear me, in the t. of thy salvation. ... 571
Ps 71:22 thee with the psaltery, even thy t., ... 571
Ps 85:10 Mercy and t. are met together; ... 571
Ps 85:11 T. shall spring out of the earth; ... 571
Ps 86:11 way, O Lord; I will walk in thy t.: ... 571
Ps 86:15 and plenteous in mercy and t.. ... 571
Ps 89:14 mercy and t. shall go before thy face. ... 571
Ps 89:49 thou swarest unto David in thy t.? ... 530
Ps 91:4 his t....be thy shield and buckler. ... 571
Ps 96:13 and the people with his t. ... 530
Ps 98:3 remembered his mercy and his t. ... 530
Ps 100:5 his t. endureth to all generations. ... 530
Ps 108:4 and thy t. reacheth unto the clouds. ... 571
Ps 111:8 and are done in t. and uprightness. ... 571
Ps 117:2 the t. of the Lord endureth for ever. ... 571
Ps 119:30 I have chosen the way of t.: thy ... 530
Ps 119:43 take not the word of t. utterly out ... 571
Ps 119:142 righteousness, and thy law is the t. ... 571
Ps 119:151 and all thy commandments are t. ... 571
Ps 132:11 Lord hath sworn in t. unto David; ... 571
Ps 138:2 thy lovingkindness and for thy t. ... 571
Ps 145:18 him, to all that call upon him in t.. ... 571
Ps 146:6 therein is: which keepeth t. for ever: ... 571
Pr 3:3 Let not mercy and t. forsake thee: ... 571
Pr 8:7 For my mouth shall speak t.; and ... 571
Pr 12:17 He that speaketh t. sheweth forth ... 530
Pr 12:19 the lip of t. shall be established ... 571
Pr 14:22 t. shall be to them that devise good. ... 571
Pr 16:6 By mercy and t. iniquity is purged: ... 571
Pr 20:28 Mercy and t. preserve the king: and ... 571
Pr 22:21 the certainty of the words of t.; ... 571
Pr 22:21 mightest answer the words of t. ... 571
Pr 23:23 Buy the t., and sell it not; also ... 571
Ec 12:10 was upright, even words of t.. ... 571
Isa 5:9 Of a t. many houses shall be ... 518,3808
Isa 10:20 Lord, the Holy One of Israel, in t.. ... 571
Isa 16:5 sit upon it in t. in the tabernacle ... 571
Isa 25:1 of old are faithfulness and t. ... 544
Isa 26:2 which keepeth the t. may enter in. ... 529
Isa 37:18 Of a t., Lord, the kings of Assyria ... 551
Isa 38:3 walked before thee in t. and with a ... 571
Isa 38:18 into the pit cannot hope for thy t. ... 571
Isa 38:19 children shall make known thy t. ... 571
Isa 39:8 shall be peace and t. in my days. ... 571
Isa 42:3 shall bring forth judgment unto t. ... 571
Isa 43:9 or let them hear, and say, It is t. ... 571
Isa 48:1 but not in t., nor in righteousness ... 571
Isa 59:4 for justice, nor any pleadeth for t.: ... 530
Isa 59:14 for t. is fallen in the street, and ... 571
Isa 59:15 t. faileth; and he that departeth ... 571
Isa 61:8 I will direct their work in t., and I ... 571
Isa 65:16 shall bless himself in the God of t.; ... 543
Isa 65:16 earth shall swear by the God of t.; ... 543
Jer 4:2 The Lord liveth, in t., in judgment, ... 571
Jer 5:1 judgment, that seeketh the t.; ... 530
Jer 5:3 Lord, are not thine eyes upon the t.? ... 530
Jer 7:28 t. is perished, and is cut off from ... 530
Jer 9:3 not valiant for the t. upon the earth; ... 530
Jer 9:5 and will not speak the t. ... 571
Jer 26:15 for of a t. the Lord hath sent me ... 571
Jer 33:6 them the abundance of peace and t.. ... 571
Da 2:47 Of a t. it is, that your God is a God ... 7187
Da 4:37 whose works are t., and his ways ... 7187
Da 7:16 and asked him the t. of all this. ... 3330
Da 7:19 know the t. of the fourth beast, ... 3321
Da 8:12 it cast down the t. to the ground; ... 571
Da 9:13 iniquities, and understand thy t.. ... 571
Da 10:21 which is noted in the scripture of t. ... 571
Da 11:2 And now will I shew thee the t. ... 571
Ho 4:1 because there is no t., nor mercy, ... 571
Mic 7:20 Thou wilt perform the t. to Jacob, ... 571
Zec 8:3 Jerusalem shall be called a city of t.; ... 571
Zec 8:8 God, in t. and in righteousness. ... 571
Zec 8:16 Speak ye every man the t. to his ... 571
Zec 8:16 execute the judgment of t. and ... 571
Zec 8:19 therefore love the t. and peace. ... 571
Mal 2:6 The law of t. was in his mouth, and ... 571
Mt 14:33 Of a t. thou art the Son of God. ... *230*
Mt 15:27 she said, T., Lord: yet the dogs ... *3483*
Mt 22:16 and teachest the way of God in t., ... *225*
Mk 5:33 before him, and told him all the t. ... *225*
Mk 12:14 but teachest the way of God in t. ... *225*
Mk 12:32 Well, Master, thou hast said the t. ... *225*
Lu 4:25 **I tell you of a t., many widows** ... *225*
Lu 9:27 **But I tell you of a t., there be** ... *230*
Lu 12:44 **a t. I say unto you, that he will** ... *230*
Lu 21:3 **Of a t. I say unto you, that this** ... *230*
Lu 22:59 Of a t. this fellow also was with ... *225*
Joh 1:14 of the Father,) full of grace and t. ... *225*
Joh 1:17 grace and t. came by Jesus Christ. ... *225*
Joh 3:21 **that doeth t. cometh to the light,** ... *225*
Joh 4:23 **the Father in spirit and t.** ... *225*
Joh 4:24 **worship him in spirit and in t.** ... *225*
Joh 5:33 **and he bare witness unto the t.** ... *225*
Joh 6:14 This is of a t. that prophet that ... *230*
Joh 7:40 said, Of a t. this is the Prophet. ... *230*
Joh 8:32 **And ye shall know the t., and the** ... *225*
Joh 8:32 **and the t. shall make you free.** ... *225*
Joh 8:40 **a man that hath told you the t.,** ... *225*
Joh 8:44 **beginning, and abode not in the t.,** ... *225*
Joh 8:44 **because there is no t. in him.** ... *225*
Joh 8:45 **because I tell you the t., ye believe** ... *225*
Joh 8:46 **And if I say the t., why do ye not** ... *225*
Joh 14:6 **I am the way, the t., and the life:** ... *225*
Joh 14:17 **Even the Spirit of t.; whom the** ... *225*
Joh 15:26 **the Father, even the Spirit of t.,** ... *225*
Joh 16:7 **Nevertheless I tell you the t.; It is** ... *225*
Joh 16:13 **when he, the Spirit of t., is come,** ... *225*
Joh 16:13 **he will guide you into all t.: for he** ... *225*
Joh 17:17 **Sanctify them through thy t.** ... *225*
Joh 17:17 **thy word is t.** ... *225*
Joh 17:19 **might be sanctified through the t.** ... *225*
Joh 18:37 **I should bear witness unto the t.** ... *225*
Joh 18:37 **Every one that is of the t. heareth** ... *225*
Joh 18:38 Pilate saith unto him, What is t.? ... *225*
Ac 4:27 of a t. against thy holy child Jesus, ... *225*
Ac 10:3 Of a t. I perceive that God is no ... *225*
Ac 26:25 forth the words of t. and soberness. ... *225*
Ro 1:18 who hold the t. in unrighteousness; ... *225*
Ro 1:25 Who changed the t. of God into a lie, ... *225*
Ro 2:2 judgment of God is according to t. ... *225*
Ro 2:8 contentious, and do not obey the t. ... *225*
Ro 2:20 knowledge and of the t. in the law. ... *225*
Ro 3:7 if the t. of God hath more abounded ... *225*
Ro 9:1 I say the t. in Christ, I lie not, my ... *225*
Ro 15:8 the circumcision for the t. of God, ... *225*
1Co 5:8 unleavened bread of sincerity and t.. ... *225*
1Co 13:6 in iniquity, but rejoiceth in the t.; ... *225*
1Co 14:25 report that God is in you of a t. ... *3689*
2Co 4:2 but by manifestation of the t. ... *225*
2Co 6:7 By the word of t., by the power of ... *225*
2Co 7:14 as we spake all things to you in t., ... *225*
2Co 7:14 I made before Titus, is found a t. ... *225*
2Co 11:10 As the t. of Christ is in me, no man ... *225*
2Co 12:6 not be a fool; for I will say the t. ... *225*
2Co 13:8 nothing against the t., but the t. ... *225*
Ga 2:5 the t. of the gospel might continue ... *225*
Ga 2:14 according to the t. of the gospel, ... *225*
Ga 3:1 you, that ye should not obey the t., ... *225*
Ga 4:16 enemy, because I tell you the t.? ... *226*
Ga 5:7 you that ye should not obey the t.? ... *225*
Eph 1:13 after that ye heard the word of t., ... *225*
Eph 4:15 speaking the t. in love, may grow ... *226*
Eph 4:21 taught by him, as the t. is in Jesus: ... *225*
Eph 4:25 speak every man t. with his ... *226*
Eph 5:9 goodness and righteousness and t.;) ... *226*
Eph 6:14 having your loins girt about with t., ... *226*
Php 1:18 whether in pretence, or in t., Christ ... *226*
Col 1:5 in the word of the t. of the gospel; ... *226*
Col 1:6 and knew the grace of God in t.: ... *226*
1Th 2:13 but as it is in t., the word of God, ... *230*
2Th 2:10 they received not the love of the t., ... *225*
2Th 2:12 be damned who believed not the t., ... *225*
2Th 2:13 of the Spirit and belief of the t. ... *225*
1Ti 2:4 come unto the knowledge of the t. ... *225*
1Ti 2:7 (I speak the t. in Christ, and lie not;) ... *225*
1Ti 3:15 God, the pillar and ground of the t. ... *225*
1Ti 4:3 them which believe and know the t. ... *225*
1Ti 6:5 corrupt minds,...destitute of the t. ... *225*
2Ti 2:15 rightly divide the word of t. ... *225*
2Ti 2:18 Who concerning the t. have erred, ... *225*
2Ti 2:25 to the acknowledging of the t.; ... *225*
2Ti 3:7 to come to the knowledge of the t. ... *225*
2Ti 3:8 Moses, so do these also resist the t. ... *225*
2Ti 4:4 turn away their ears from the t., ... *225*
Tit 1:1 of the t. which is after godliness; ... *225*
Tit 1:14 of men, that turn from the t. ... *225*
Heb 10:26 received the knowledge of the t., ... *225*
Jas 1:18 will begat he us with the word of t., ... *225*
Jas 3:14 glory not, and lie not against the t. ... *225*
Jas 5:19 if any of you do err from the t., and ... *225*
1Pe 1:22 purified your souls in obeying the t. ... *225*
2Pe 1:12 and be established in the present t. ... *225*
2Pe 2:2 the way of t. shall be evil spoken of. ... *225*
1Jo 1:6 darkness, we lie, and do not the t. ... *225*
1Jo 1:8 ourselves, and the t. is not in us. ... *225*
1Jo 2:4 is a liar, and the t. is not in him. ... *225*
1Jo 2:21 unto you because ye know not the t., ... *225*
1Jo 2:21 know it, and that no lie is of the t.. ... *225*
1Jo 2:27 of all things, and is t., and is no lie, ... *227*
1Jo 3:18 in tongue; but in deed and in t.. ... *225*
1Jo 3:19 we know that we are of the t., and ... *225*
1Jo 4:6 Hereby know we the spirit of t., and ... *225*
1Jo 5:6 witness, because the Spirit is t. ... *225*
2Jo 1 her children, whom I love in the t. ... *225*
2Jo 1 also all they that have known the t.; ... *225*
2Jo 3 Son of the Father, in t. and love. ... *225*
2Jo 4 I found of thy children walking in t., ... *225*
3Jo 1 Gaius, whom I love in the t.. ... *225*
3Jo 3 and testified of the t. that is in thee, ... *225*
3Jo 3 even as thou walkest in the t.. ... *225*
3Jo 4 to hear that my children walk in t.. ... *225*
3Jo 8 we might be fellowhelpers to the t.. ... *225*
3Jo 12 report of all men, and of the t. itself: ... *225*

TRUTH'S
Ps 115:1 for thy mercy, and for thy t. sake. ... 571
2Jo 2 For the t. sake, that dwelleth in us, ... *225*

TRY See also TRIED; TRIEST; TRIETH; TRYING.
Jg 7:4 and I will t. them for thee there: ... 6884
2Ch 32:31 God left him, to t. him, that he ... 5254
Job 7:18 morning, and t. him every moment? ... 974
Job 12:11 Doth not the ear t. words? and the ... 974
Ps 11:4 his eyelids t. the children of men. ... 974
Ps 26:2 me; t. my reins and my heart. ... 6884
Ps 139:23 t. me, and know my thoughts: ... 974
Jer 6:27 thou mayest know and t. their way. ... 974
Jer 9:7 I will melt them, and t. them; ... 974
Jer 17:10 Lord search the heart, I t. the reins, ... 974
La 3:40 Let us search and t. our ways, ... 2713
Da 11:35 fall, to t. them, and to purge, and ... 6684
Zec 13:9 and will t. them as gold is tried: ... 974
1Co 3:13 the fire shall t. every man's work. ... *1381*
1Pe 4:12 fiery trial which is to t. you, ... *4314,3986*
1Jo 4:1 t. the spirits whether they are of ... *1381*
Re 3:10 **t. them that dwell upon the earth.** 3985

TRYING
Jas 1:3 **t.** of your faith worketh patience. *1383*

TRYPHENA (tri-fe'-nah)
Ro 16:12 Salute **T.** and Tryphosa, who............ *5170*

TRYPHOSA (tri-fo'-sah)
Ro 16:12 Salute Tryphena and **T.**, who *5173*

TUBAL (tu'-bal) See also TUBAL-CAIN.
Ge 10:2 and **T.**, and Meshech, and Tiras......... 8422
1Ch 1:5 and **T.**, and Meshech, and Tiras......... 8422
Isa 66:19 to **T.**, and Javan, to isles afar off,....... 8422
Eze 27:13 **T.**, and Meshech, they were thy.......... 8422
Eze 32:26 There is Meshech, **T.**, and all her...... 8422
Eze 38:2 chief prince of Meshech and **T.**,......... 8422
Eze 38:3 chief prince of Meshech and **T.**........... 8422
Eze 39:1 chief prince of Meshech and **T.**........... 8422

TUBAL-CAIN (tu'-bal-cain)
Ge 4:22 And Zillah, she also bare **T.**, an......... 8423
Ge 4:22 and the sister of **T.** was Naamah......... 8423

TUMBLED
Jg 7:13 bread **t.** into the host of Midian, ... 2015

TUMULT See also TUMULTS.
1Sa 4:14 What meaneth the noise of this **t.**? 1995
2Sa 18:29 I saw a great **t.**, but I knew not......... 1995
2Ki 19:28 against me and thy **t.** is come up 7600
Ps 65:7 waves, and the **t.** of the people. 1995
Ps 74:23 the **t.** of those that rise up against...... 7588
Ps 83:2 For, lo, thine enemies make a **t.**......... 1993
Isa 33:3 the noise of the **t.** the people fled; 1995
Isa 37:29 thy **t.**, is come up into mine ears, ... 7600
Jer 11:16 with the noise of a great **t.** he hath 1999
Ho 10:14 shall a **t.** arise among thy people,....... 7588
Am 2:2 and Moab shall die with **t.**, with......... 7588
Zec 14:13 a great **t.** from the Lord shall be........ 4103
Mt 27:24 but that rather a **t.** was made, he....... *2351*
Mk 5:38 and seeth the **t.**, and them that *2351*
Ac 21:34 not know the certainty for the **t.**,....... *2351*
Ac 24:18 neither with multitude, nor with **t.**...... *2351*

TUMULTS
Am 3:9 the great **t.** in the midst thereof,........ 4103
2Co 6:5 in imprisonments, in **t.**, in labours,...... *181*
2Co 12:20 strifes,...whisperings, swellings, **t.** *181*

TUMULTUOUS
Isa 13:4 a **t.** noise of the kingdoms of............ 7588
Isa 22:2 that art full of stirs, a **t.** city, a.......... 1993
Jer 48:45 of the head of the **t.** ones.......... 1121,7588

TURN See also OVERTURN; RETURN; TURNED; TURNEST; TURNETH; TURNING.
Ge 19:2 my lords, **t.** in, I pray you, into 5493
Ge 24:49 that I may **t.** to the right hand, or...... 6437
Ge 27:44 until thy brother's fury **t.** away: 7725
Ge 27:45 Until my brother's anger **t.** away........ 7725
Ex 3:3 I will now **t.** aside, and see this.......... 5493
Ex 14:2 that they **t.** and encamp before 7725
Ex 23:27 thine enemies **t.** their backs unto thee.......
Ex 32:12 **T.** from thy fierce wrath, and............ 7725
Le 13:16 Or if the raw flesh **t.** again, and be..... 7725
Le 19:4 **T.** ye not unto idols, nor make to...... 6437
Nu 14:25 To morrow **t.** you, and get you 6437
Nu 20:17 will not **t.** to the right hand nor 5186
Nu 21:22 we will not **t.** into the fields, or into ... 5186
Nu 22:23 Balaam smote the ass, to **t.** her......... 5186
Nu 22:26 was no way to **t.** either to the right..... 5186
Nu 32:15 if ye **t.** away from after him, he......... 7725
Nu 34:4 your border shall **t.** from the south..... 5437
De 1:7 **T.** you, and take your journey, ... 6437
De 1:40 **t.** you, and take your journey into 6437
De 2:3 long enough: **t.** you northward........... 6437
De 2:27 I will neither **t.** unto the right nor 5493
De 4:30 if thou **t.** to the Lord thy God, ... 7725
De 5:32 ye shall not **t.** aside to the right......... 5493
De 7:4 will **t.** away thy son from following 5493
De 11:16 ye **t.** aside, and serve other gods,...... 5493
De 11:28 **t.** aside out of the way which I.......... 5493
De 13:5 spoken to **t.** you away from the 5627
De 13:17 Lord may **t.** from the fierceness of..... 7725
De 14:25 Then shalt thou **t.** it into money,....... 5414
De 16:7 and thou shalt **t.** in the morning, ... 6437
De 17:17 himself, that his heart **t.** not away: 5493
De 17:20 and that he **t.** not aside from the........ 5493
De 23:13 shalt **t.** back and cover that which...... 7725
De 23:14 in thee, and **t.** away from thee. 7725
De 30:3 Lord thy God will **t.** thy captivity, ... 7725
De 30:10 **t.** unto the Lord thy God with all 7725
De 30:17 But if thine heart **t.** away, as that 6437
De 31:20 then will they **t.** unto other gods, ... 6437
De 31:29 **t.** aside from the way I have 5493
Jos 1:7 **t.** not from it to the right hand or to... 5493
Jos 22:16, 18 **t.** away this day from following...... 7725
Jos 22:23 altar to **t.** from following the Lord, ... 7725
Jos 22:29 **t.** this day from following the Lord, ... 7725
Jos 23:6 that ye **t.** not aside therefrom to........ 5493
Jos 24:20 then he will **t.** and do you hurt, ... 7725
Jg 4:18 **T.** in, my lord, **t.** in to me; fear......... 5493
Jg 11:8 Therefore we **t.** again to thee now, ... 7725
Jg 19:11 **t.** into this city of the Jebusites,......... 5493
Jg 19:12 will not **t.** aside hither into the city...... 5493
Jg 20:8 will we any of us **t.** into his house, ... 5493
Ru 1:11 And Naomi said, **T.** again, my 7725
Ru 1:12 **T.** again, my daughter, go your.......... 7725
Ru 4:1 such a one! **t.** aside, sit down here...... 5493
1Sa 12:20 **t.** not aside from following the Lord,... 5493
1Sa 12:21 **t.** ye not aside: for then should ye...... 5493
1Sa 14:7 **t.** thee; behold, I am with thee.......... 5186
1Sa 15:25 pardon my sin,...**t.** again with me, ... 7725
1Sa 15:30 and **t.** again with me, that I may........ 7725
1Sa 22:17 **T.**, and slay the priests of the 5437
1Sa 22:18 **T.** thou, and fall upon the priests. 5437
2Sa 2:21 **T.** thee aside to thy right hand or 5186
2Sa 2:21 not **t.** aside from following of him. 5493
2Sa 2:22 **T.** thee aside from following me: 5493
2Sa 2:23 Howbeit he refused to **t.** aside:.......... 5493
2Sa 14:19 none can **t.** to the right hand or to the......
2Sa 14:24 Let him **t.** to his own house, and 5437
2Sa 15:31 **t.** the...of Ahithophel into foolishness. ....
2Sa 18:30 unto him, **T.** aside, and stand............ 5437
2Sa 19:37 servant, I pray thee, **t.** back again,..... 7725
1Ki 8:33 shall **t.** again to thee, and confess....... 7725
1Ki 8:35 thy name, and **t.** from their sin, ... 7725
1Ki 9:6 shall at all **t.** from following me, ... 7725
1Ki 11:2 they will **t.** away your heart after 5186
1Ki 12:27 heart of this people **t.** again unto........ 7725
1Ki 13:9 not **t.** again by the same way that 7725
1Ki 13:17 nor **t.** again to go by the way that....... 7725
1Ki 17:3 thee hence, and **t.** thee eastward, ... 6437
1Ki 22:34 **T.** thine hand, and carry me out......... 2015
2Ki 1:6 Go, **t.** again unto the king that........... 7725
2Ki 4:10 to us, that he shall **t.** in thither.......... 5493
2Ki 9:18, 19 with peace? **t.** thee behind me....... 5437
2Ki 17:13 **T.** ye from your evil ways, and.......... 7725
2Ki 18:24 then wilt thou **t.** away the face of......... 7725
2Ki 19:28 I will **t.** thee back by the way............ 7725
2Ki 20:5 **T.** again, and tell Hezekiah the 7725
1Ch 12:23 **t.** the kingdom of Saul to him. 5437
1Ch 14:14 up after them; **t.** away from them, ... 5437
2Ch 6:26 thy name, and **t.** from their sin, ... 7725
2Ch 6:37 **t.** and pray unto thee in the land of 7725
2Ch 6:42 **t.** not away...face of thine anointed: 7725
2Ch 7:14 face, and **t.** from thy wicked ways; 7725
2Ch 7:19 But if ye **t.** away, and forsake my 7725
2Ch 15:4 they in their trouble did **t.** unto the 7725
2Ch 18:33 **T.** thine hand, that thou mayest 2015
2Ch 25:27 that Amaziah did **t.** away from........... 5493
2Ch 29:10 that his fierce wrath may **t.** away....... 7725
2Ch 30:6 **t.** again unto the Lord God of............ 7725
2Ch 30:8 fierceness of his wrath may **t.** away.... 7725
2Ch 30:9 if ye **t.** again unto the Lord, your....... 7725
2Ch 30:9 not **t.** away his face from you, ... 5493
2Ch 35:22 Josiah would not **t.** his face from 5437
Ne 1:9 But if ye **t.** unto me, and keep my 7725
Ne 4:4 **t.** their reproach upon their own 7725
Ne 9:26 against them to **t.** them to thee, ... 7725
Es 2:12 when every maid's **t.** was come to 8447
Es 2:15 Now when the **t.** of Esther, the........... 8447
Job 5:1 to which of the saints wilt thou **t.**? 6437
Job 14:6 **T.** from him, that he may rest, till...... 8159
Job 23:13 in one mind, and who can **t.** him?....... 7725
Job 24:4 They **t.** the needy out of the way:....... 5186
Job 34:15 and man shall **t.** again unto dust......... 7725
Ps 4:2 long will ye **t.** my glory into shame? ....
Ps 7:12 If he **t.** not, he will whet his 7725
Ps 18:37 I **t.** again till they were consumed. 7725
Ps 21:12 shalt thou make them **t.** their back, ...
Ps 22:27 remember and **t.** unto the Lord: 7725
Ps 25:16 **T.** thee unto me, and have mercy 6437
Ps 40:4 proud, nor such as **t.** aside to lies. 7750
Ps 44:10 us to **t.** back from the enemy: 7725
Ps 56:9 thee, then shall mine eyes **t.** back: 7725
Ps 60:1 displeased; O **t.** thyself to us again. 7725
Ps 69:16 **t.** unto me according to the............. 6437
Ps 80:3 **T.** us again, O God, and cause thy 7725
Ps 80:7 **T.** us again, O God of hosts, and 7725
Ps 80:19 **T.** us again, O Lord God of hosts,...... 7725
Ps 85:4 **T.** us, O God of our salvation, and 7725
Ps 85:8 but let them not **t.** again to folly. 7725
Ps 86:16 O **t.** unto me, and have mercy........... 6437
Ps 101:3 hate...work of them that **t.** aside;....... 7750
Ps 104:9 that they **t.** not again to cover the....... 7725
Ps 106:23 to **t.** away his wrath, lest he should.... 7725
Ps 119:37 **T.** away mine eyes from................... 5674
Ps 119:39 **T.** away my reproach which I fear: 5674
Ps 119:79 those that fear thee **t.** unto me,......... 7725
Ps 125:5 As for such as **t.** aside unto their....... 5186
Ps 126:4 **T.** again our captivity, O Lord, as 7725
Ps 132:10 **t.** not away the face of thine 7725
Ps 132:11 he will not **t.** from it; Of the fruit....... 7725
Pr 1:23 **T.** you at my reproof: behold, I 7725
Pr 4:15 by it, **t.** from it, and pass away.......... 7847
Pr 4:27 **T.** not to the right hand nor to 5186
Pr 9:4,16 is simple, let him **t.** in hither: 5493
Pr 24:18 he **t.** away his wrath from him. 7725
Pr 25:10 and thine infamy **t.** not away, ... 7725
Pr 29:8 but wise men **t.** away wrath. 7725
Ec 3:20 the dust, and all **t.** to dust again. 7725
Ca 2:17 **t.**, my beloved, and be thou like a...... 5437
Ca 6:5 **T.** away thine eyes from me, for......... 5437
Isa 1:25 And I will **t.** my hand upon thee,........ 7725
Isa 10:2 **t.** aside the needy from judgment, ... 5186
Isa 13:14 every man **t.** to his own people, ... 6437
Isa 14:27 out, and who shall **t.** it back?............ 7725
Isa 19:6 they shall **t.** the rivers far away; 2186
Isa 22:18 surely violently **t.** and toss thee 6801
Isa 23:17 Tyre, and she shall **t.** to her hire, ... 7725
Isa 28:6 them that **t.** the battle to the gate. 7725
Isa 29:21 and **t.** aside the just for a thing of 5186
Isa 30:11 of the way, **t.** aside out of the path, ... 5186
Isa 30:21 ye in it, when ye **t.** to the right hand,.......
Isa 30:21 and when ye **t.** to the left.........................
Isa 31:6 **T.** ye unto him from whom the.......... 7725
Isa 36:9 wilt thou **t.** away the face of one........ 7725
Isa 37:29 **t.** thee back by the way by which....... 7725
Isa 58:13 **t.** away thy foot from the sabbath,...... 7725
Isa 59:20 **t.** from transgression in Jacob,.......... 7725
Jer 2:24 in her occasion who can **t.** her way? ... 7725
Jer 2:35 surely his anger shall **t.** from me........ 7725
Jer 3:7 these things, **T.** thou unto me. 7725
Jer 3:14 **T.**, O backsliding children, saith 7725
Jer 3:19 and shalt not **t.** away from me. 7725
Jer 4:28 repent, neither will I **t.** back from it.... 7725
Jer 6:9 **t.** back thine hand as a...................... 7725
Jer 8:4 shall he **t.** away, and not return?......... 7725
Jer 13:16 he **t.** it into the shadow of death, ... 7760
Jer 18:8 **t.** from their evil, I will repent of 7725
Jer 18:20 to **t.** away thy wrath from them. 7725
Jer 21:4 I will **t.** back the weapons of war 5437
Jer 25:5 **T.** ye again now every one from 7725
Jer 26:3 and **t.** every man from his evil way,.... 7725
Jer 29:14 and I will **t.** away your captivity, ... 7725
Jer 31:13 I will **t.** their mourning into joy, ... 2015
Jer 31:18 **t.** thou me, and I shall be turned;........ 7725
Jer 31:21 **t.** again, O virgin of Israel, **t.** 7725
Jer 32:40 that I will not **t.** away from them, ... 7725
Jer 44:5 ear to **t.** from their wickedness,........... 7725
Jer 49:8 Flee ye, **t.** back, dwell deep, O 6437
Jer 50:16 shall **t.** every one to his people,......... 6437
La 2:14 inquity, to **t.** away thy captivity;.......... 7725
La 3:35 To **t.** aside the right of a man........... 5186
La 3:40 ways, and **t.** again to the Lord........... 7725
La 5:21 **T.** thou us unto thee, O Lord, and 7725
Eze 3:19 he **t.** not from his wickedness, nor 7725
Eze 3:20 righteous man doth **t.** from his........... 7725
Eze 4:8 shalt not **t.** thee from one side to....... 2015
Eze 7:22 My face will I **t.** also from them,........ 5437
Eze 8:6 **t.** thee yet again, and thou shalt......... 7725
Eze 8:13 **T.** thee yet again, and thou shalt........ 7725
Eze 8:15 **t.** thee yet again, and thou shalt......... 7725
Eze 14:6 and **t.** yourselves from your idols; 7725
Eze 14:6 and **t.** away your face from all your 7725
Eze 18:21 the wicked will **t.** from all his sins 7725
Eze 18:30 and **t.** yourselves from all your 7725
Eze 18:32 wherefore **t.** yourselves, and live 7725
Eze 33:9 the wicked of his way to **t.** from it; 7725
Eze 33:9 if he do not **t.** from his way, he......... 7725
Eze 33:11 but that the wicked **t.** from his way.... 7725
Eze 33:11 **t.** ye, **t.** ye from your evil ways; for... 7725
Eze 33:14 if he **t.** from his sin, and do that 7725
Eze 33:19 the wicked **t.** from his wickedness,..... 7725
Eze 36:9 am for you, and I will **t.** unto you,...... 6437
Eze 38:4 I will **t.** thee back, and put hooks....... 7725
Eze 38:12 to **t.** thine hand upon the desolate 7725

Eze 39:2 I will **t.** thee back, and leave but........ 7725
Da 9:13 we might **t.** from our iniquities,.......... 7725
Da 11:18 shall he **t.** his face unto the isles, ... 7725
Da 11:18 he shall cause it to **t.** upon him............ 7725
Da 11:19 shall **t.** his face toward the fort of 7725
Da 12:3 they that **t.** many to righteousness, as........
Ho 5:4 their doings to **t.** unto their God: 7725
Ho 12:6 Therefore **t.** thou to thy God: keep 7725
Ho 14:2 you words, and **t.** to the Lord: 7725
Joe 2:12 **t.** ye even to me with all your heart, .. 7725
Joe 2:13 and **t.** unto the Lord your God: 7725
Am 1:3,6 will not **t.** away the punishment 7725
Am 1:8 I will **t.** mine hand against Ekron:....... 7725
Am 1:9, 11,13 not **t.** away the punishment....... 7725
Am 2:1,4, 6 not **t.** away the punishment 7725
Am 2:7 and **t.** aside the way of the meek: 5186
Am 5:7 Ye who **t.** judgment to wormwood, ... 2015
Am 5:12 they **t.** aside the poor in the gate 5186
Am 8:10 will **t.** your feasts into mourning,......... 2015
Jon 3:8 let them **t.** every one from his evil 7725
Jon 3:8 can tell if God will **t.** and repent,......... 7725
Jon 3:8 and **t.** away from his fierce anger, ... 7725
Mic 7:19 He will **t.** again, he will have............. 7725
Zep 2:7 them, and **t.** away their captivity. 7725
Zep 3:9 **t.** to the people a pure languege, ... 2015
Zep 3:20 when I **t.** back your captivity............. 7725
Zec 1:3 **T.** ye unto me, saith the Lord of......... 7725
Zec 1:3 I will **t.** unto you, saith the Lord of 7725
Zec 1:4 **T.** ye now from your evil ways, ... 7725
Zec 9:12 **T.** you to the strong hold, ye 7725
Zec 10:9 with their children, and **t.** again.......... 7725
Zec 13:7 **t.** mine hand upon the little ones. 7725
Mal 2:6 did **t.** many away from iniquity............ 7725
Mal 3:5 that **t.** aside the stranger from his 5186
Mal 4:6 **t.** the heart of the fathers to the........ 7725
Mt 5:39 **cheek, t. to him the other also.**...... *4762*
Mt 5:42 **borrow of thee t. not thou away.** *654*
Mt 7:6 **feet, and t. again and rend you,** *4762*
Mk 13:16 **is in the field not t. back again**..... *1994*
Lu 1:16 Israel shall he **t.** to the Lord their...... *1994*
Lu 1:17 to **t.** the hearts of the fathers to the... *1994*
Lu 10:6 **it: if not, it shall t. to you again.** ... *344*
Lu 17:4 **and seven times in a day t. again**.. *1994*
Lu 21:13 **it shall t. to you for a testimony.**.... *576*
Ac 13:8 **t.** away the deputy from the faith. *1294*
Ac 13:46 life, lo, we **t.** to the Gentiles............. *4762*
Ac 14:15 ye should **t.** from these vanities.......... *1994*
Ac 26:18 **to t. them from darkness to light,**..*1994*
Ac 26:20 they should repent and **t.** to God, ... *1994*
Ro 11:26 **t.** away ungodliness from Jacob:........... *654*
2Co 3:16 when it shall **t.** to the Lord,............... *1994*
Ga 4:9 how **t.** ye again to the weak and........ *1994*
Php 1:19 that this shall **t.** to my salvation........... *576*
2Ti 3:5 power thereof: from such **t.** away. *665*
2Ti 4:4 they shall **t.** away their ears from *654*
Tit 1:14 of men, that **t.** from the truth. *654*
Heb 12:25 we **t.** away from him that speaketh *654*
Jas 3:3 and we **t.** about their whole body. *3329*
2Pe 2:21 to **t.** from the holy commandment....... *1994*
Re 11:6 over waters to **t.** them to blood, ... *4762*

TURNED See OVERTURNED; RETURNED.

Ge 3:24 flaming sword which **t.** every way, ... 2015
Ge 18:22 men **t.** their faces from thence,.......... 6437
Ge 19:3 they **t.** in unto him, and entered 5493
Ge 38:1 and **t.** in to a certain Adullamite, ... 5186
Ge 38:16 And he **t.** unto her by the way, ... 5186
Ge 42:24 he **t.** himself about from them, ... 5437
Ex 3:4 Lord saw that he **t.** aside to see, ... 5493
Ex 4:7 it was **t.** again as his other flesh. 7725
Ex 7:15 the rod which was **t.** to a serpent 2015
Ex 7:17 river, and they shall be **t.** to blood. 2015
Ex 7:20 were in the river were **t.** to blood...... 2015
Ex 7:23 And Pharaoh **t.** and went into his 6437
Ex 10:6 he **t.** himself, and went out from......... 6437
Ex 10:19 Lord **t.** a mighty strong west wind, ... 2015
Ex 14:5 servants was **t.** against the people,..... 2015
Ex 32:8 They have **t.** aside quickly out of 5493
Ex 32:15 Moses **t.**, and went down from the...... 6437
Ex 33:11 And he **t.** again into the camp:........... 7725
Le 13:3 the hair in the plague is **t.** white, ... 2015
Le 13:4 the hair thereof be not **t.** white;.......... 2015
Le 13:10 skin, and it have **t.** the hair white,...... 2015
Le 13:13 hath the plague: it is all **t.** white: 2015
Le 13:17 if the plague be **t.** into white; 2015
Le 13:20 and the hair thereof be **t.** white; 2015
Le 13:25 hair in the bright spot be **t.** white,...... 2015
Nu 14:43 ye are **t.** away from the Lord,........... 7725
Nu 20:21 wherefore Israel **t.** away from him...... 5186
Nu 21:33 they **t.** and went up by the way of 6437
Nu 22:23 the ass **t.** aside out of the way, ... 5186
Nu 22:33 and the ass saw me, and **t.** from me... 5186
Nu 22:33 unless she had **t.** from me, surely 5186
Nu 25:4 anger of the Lord may be **t.** away 7725
Nu 25:11 hath **t.** my wrath away from the.......... 7725
Nu 33:7 and **t.** again unto Pi-hahiroth,............. 7725
De 1:24 **t.** and went up into the mountain,....... 6437
De 2:1 Then we **t.**, and took our journey......... 6437
De 2:8 we **t.** and passed by the way of the.... 6437
De 3:1 Then we **t.**, and went up the way 6437
De 9:12 are quickly **t.** aside out of the way...... 5493
De 9:15 **t.** and came down from the mount,..... 6437
De 9:16 **t.** aside quickly out of the way........... 5493
De 10:5 **t.** myself and came down from the...... 6437
De 23:5 the Lord thy God **t.** the curse into 2015
De 31:18 that they are **t.** unto other gods......... 6437
Jos 7:12 **t.** their backs before the enemies, ... 6437
Jos 7:26 the Lord **t.** from the fierceness of 7725
Jos 8:20 fled to the wilderness **t.** back 2015
Jos 8:21 they **t.** again, and slew the men of 7725
Jos 11:10 And Joshua at that time **t.** back,......... 7725
Jos 19:12 And **t.** from Sarid eastward toward..... 7725
Jg 2:17 they **t.** quickly out of the way............ 5493
Jg 3:19 himself **t.** again from the quarries 7725
Jg 4:18 And when he had **t.** in unto her.......... 5493
Jg 8:33 that the children of Israel **t.** again,...... 7725
Jg 14:8 he **t.** aside to see the carcase of......... 5493
Jg 15:4 tail to tail, and put a firebrand............ 6437
Jg 18:3 they **t.** in thither, and said unto 5493
Jg 18:15 they **t.** thitherward, and came to......... 5493
Jg 18:21 So they **t.** and departed, and put......... 6437
Jg 18:23 they **t.** their faces, and said unto......... 5437
Jg 18:26 **t.** and went back unto his house.......... 6437
Jg 19:15 they **t.** aside thither, to go in and....... 5493
Jg 20:41 when the men of Israel **t.** again, ... 2015
Jg 20:42 they **t.** their backs before the men 6437
Jg 20:45 **t.** and fled toward the wilderness 6437
Jg 20:47 six hundred men **t.** and fled to the...... 6437
Jg 20:48 the men of Israel **t.** again upon 7725
Ru 3:8 man was afraid, and **t.** himself: 3943
Ru 4:1 And he **t.** aside, and sat down. 5493
1Sa 6:12 **t.** not aside to the right hand or to..... 5493
1Sa 8:3 but **t.** aside after lucre, and took......... 5186
1Sa 10:6 and shalt be **t.** into another man......... 2015
1Sa 10:9 that when he had **t.** his back to go 6437
1Sa 13:17 one company **t.** unto the way that 6437
1Sa 13:18 And another company **t.** the way to 6437
1Sa 13:18 another company **t.** to the way of....... 6437
1Sa 14:21 they also **t.** to be with the Israelites ... 6437
1Sa 14:47 whithersoever he **t.** himself, he.......... 6437
1Sa 15:11 he is **t.** back from following me,........ 7725
1Sa 15:27 as Samuel **t.** about to go away, he....... 5437
1Sa 15:31 So Samuel **t.** again after Saul; and 7725
1Sa 17:30 he **t.** from him toward another,........... 5437
1Sa 22:18 Doeg the Edomite **t.**, and he fell......... 5437
1Sa 25:12 David's young men **t.** their way, ... 2015
2Sa 1:22 the bow of Jonathan **t.** not back, ... 7734
2Sa 2:19 going he **t.** not to the right hand 5186
2Sa 18:30 And he **t.** aside, and stood still. 5437
2Sa 19:2 victory that day was **t.** into mourning........
2Sa 22:38 and **t.** not again until I had.................. 7725
1Ki 2:15 howbeit the kingdom is **t.** about,.......... 5437
1Ki 2:28 for Joab had **t.** after Adonijah,............ 5186
1Ki 2:28 though he **t.** not after Absalom. 5186
1Ki 8:14 And the king **t.** his face about, and 5437
1Ki 10:13 **t.** and went to her own country, ... 6437
1Ki 11:3 and his wives **t.** away his heart........... 5186
1Ki 11:4 wives **t.** away his heart after other 5186
1Ki 11:9 heart was **t.** from the Lord God of 5186
1Ki 15:5 **t.** not aside from any thing that he 5493
1Ki 18:37 thou hast **t.** their heart back again...... 5437
1Ki 20:39 a man **t.** aside, and brought a man........ 5493
1Ki 21:4 upon his bed, and **t.** away his face,...... 5437
1Ki 22:32 they **t.** aside to fight against him: 5493
1Ki 22:33 they **t.** back from pursuing him. 7725
1Ki 22:43 he **t.** not aside from it, doing that........ 5493
2Ki 1:5 the messengers **t.** back unto him,........ 7725
2Ki 1:5 them, Why are ye now **t.** back? 7725
2Ki 2:24 he **t.** back, and looked on them,.......... 6437
2Ki 4:8 by, he **t.** in thither to eat bread. 5493
2Ki 4:11 he **t.** into the chamber, and lay.......... 5493
2Ki 5:12 So he **t.** and went away in a rage,....... 6437
2Ki 5:26 man **t.** again from his chariot............. 2015
2Ki 9:23 And Joram **t.** his hands, and fled, ... 2015
2Ki 15:20 So the king of Assyria **t.** back, and..... 7725
2Ki 16:18 **t.** he from the house of the Lord 5437
2Ki 20:2 Then he **t.** his face to the wall, and.... 5437
2Ki 22:2 **t.** not aside to the right hand or to..... 5493
2Ki 23:16 as Josiah **t.** himself, he spied the........ 6437
2Ki 23:25 that **t.** to the Lord with all his 7725
2Ki 23:26 Lord **t.** not from the fierceness of...... 7725
2Ki 23:34 **t.** his name to Jehoiakim, and took...... 5437
2Ki 24:1 he **t.** and rebelled against him............ 7725
1Ch 10:14 **t.** the kingdom unto David the son...... 5437
1Ch 21:20 Ornan **t.** back, and saw the angel; 7725
2Ch 6:3 the king **t.** his face, and blessed.......... 5437
2Ch 9:12 she **t.**, and went away to her own...... 2015
2Ch 12:12 the wrath of the Lord **t.** from him, ... 7725
2Ch 18:32 they **t.** back...from pursuing him. 7725
2Ch 20:10 they **t.** from them, and destroyed........ 5493
2Ch 29:6 have **t.** away their faces from the....... 5437
2Ch 29:6 of the Lord, and **t.** their backs........... 5414
2Ch 36:4 and **t.** his name to Jehoiakim. 5437
Ezr 6:22 **t.** the heart of the king of Assyria 5437
Ezr 10:14 God for this matter be **t.** from us....... 7725
Ne 2:15 and viewed the wall, and **t.** back, ... 7725
Ne 9:35 **t.** they from their wicked works.......... 7725
Ne 13:2 God **t.** the curse into a blessing. 2015
Es 9:1 (though it was **t.** to the contrary, ... 2015
Es 9:22 month which was **t.** unto them from.... 2015
Job 6:18 paths of their way are **t.** aside;........... 3943
Job 16:11 **t.** me over into the hands of the 3399
Job 19:19 whom I loved are **t.** against me. 2015
Job 20:14 Yet his meat in his bowels is **t.**, it is.... 2015
Job 28:5 and under it is **t.** up as it were fire..... 2015
Job 30:15 Terrors are **t.** upon me: they pursue .. 2015
Job 30:31 My harp also is **t.** to mourning, and.........
Job 31:7 If my step hath **t.** out of the way, ... 5186
Job 34:27 Because they **t.** back from him, ... 5493
Job 37:12 is **t.** round about by his counsels: 2015
Job 38:14 It is **t.** as clay to the seal; and they.... 2015
Job 41:22 sorrow is **t.** into joy before him. 1750
Job 41:28 are **t.** with him into stubble............... 2015
Job 42:10 the Lord **t.** the captivity of Job, ... 7725
Ps 9:3 When mine enemies are **t.** back, ... 7725
Ps 9:17 The wicked shall be **t.** into hell, ... 7725
Ps 30:11 hast **t.** for me my mourning into 2015
Ps 32:4 my moisture is **t.** into the drought...... 2015
Ps 35:4 let them be **t.** back and brought......... 5472
Ps 44:18 Our heart is not **t.** back, neither 5472
Ps 66:6 He **t.** the sea into dry land: they......... 2015
Ps 66:20 which hath not **t.** away my prayer, ... 5493
Ps 70:2 let them be **t.** backward, and put 5472
Ps 70:3 Let them be **t.** back for a reward 7725
Ps 78:9 bows, **t.** back in the day of battle. 2015
Ps 78:38 many a time **t.** he his anger away,...... 7725
Ps 78:41 Yea, they **t.** back and tempted God, ... 7725
Ps 78:44 And had **t.** their rivers into blood; 2015
Ps 78:57 But **t.** back, and dealt unfaithfully 5472
Ps 78:57 were **t.** aside like a deceitful bow. 2015
Ps 81:14 and **t.** my hand against their............... 7725
Ps 85:3 hast **t.** thyself from the fierceness 7725
Ps 89:43 hast also **t.** the edge of his sword, ... 7725
Ps 105:25 He **t.** their heart to hate his people, .. 2015
Ps 105:29 He **t.** their waters into blood, and 2015
Ps 114:8 **t.** the rock into a standing water, ... 2015
Ps 119:59 **t.** my feet unto thy testimonies........... 7725
Ps 126:1 the Lord **t.** again the captivity of........ 7725
Ps 129:5 and **t.** back that hate Zion................. 5472
Ec 2:12 **t.** myelf to behold wisdom, and........... 6437
Ca 6:1 whither is thy beloved **t.** aside? 6437
Isa 5:25 all this his anger is not **t.** away,......... 7725
Isa 9:1, 17,21 his anger is not **t.** away, but 7725
Isa 10:4 For all this his anger is not **t.** away. ... 7725
Isa 12:1 with me, thine anger is **t.** away, ... 7725
Isa 21:4 my pleasure hath he **t.** into fear.......... 7760
Isa 28:27 neither is a cart wheel **t.** about........... 5437
Isa 29:17 Lebanon...**t.** into a fruitful field, ... 7725
Isa 34:9 streams...shall be **t.** into pitch, ... 2015
Isa 38:2 Hezekiah **t.** his face toward the.......... 5437
Isa 42:17 They shall be **t.** back, they shall 5472
Isa 44:20 a deceived heart hath **t.** him aside, ... 5186
Isa 50:5 rebellious, neither **t.** away back.......... 5472
Isa 53:6 have **t.** every one to his own way; 6437
Isa 59:14 judgment is **t.** away backward,............ 5253
Isa 63:10 he was **t.** to be their enemy,.............. 2015
Jer 2:21 art thou **t.** into the degenerate plant ... 2015
Jer 2:27 they have **t.** their back unto me,......... 6437
Jer 3:10 sister Judah hath not **t.** unto me.......... 7725
Jer 4:8 anger of the Lord is not **t.** back.......... 7725
Jer 5:25 Your iniquities have **t.** away these 5186

Jer 6:12 houses shall be t. unto others,.......... 5437
Jer 8:6 every one t. to his course, as the...... 7725
Jer 11:10 They are t. back to the iniquities of.... 7725
Jer 23:22 have t. them from their evil way,...... 7725
Jer 30:6 and all faces are t. into paleness?...... 2015
Jer 31:18 turn thou me, and I shall be t.;.......... 7725
Jer 31:19 after that I was t., I repented;.......... 7725
Jer 32:33 they have t. unto me the back, and.... 6437
Jer 34:11 But afterward they t., and caused...... 7725
Jer 34:15 ye were now t., and had done right.... 7725
Jer 34:16 But ye t. and polluted my name,........ 7725
Jer 38:22 mire, and they are t. away back......... 5472
Jer 46:5 them dismayed and t. away back?....... 5472
Jer 46:21 they also are t. back, and are fled...... 6437
Jer 48:39 hath Moab t. the back with shame!...... 6437
Jer 50:6 t. them away on the mountains:......... 7725
La 1:13 net for my feet, he hath t. me back:... 7725
La 1:20 mine heart is t. within me; for I......... 2015
La 3:3 Surely against me is he t.;............... 7725
La 3:11 He hath t. aside my ways, and.......... 5493
La 5:2 Our inheritance is t. to strangers,...... 2015
La 5:15 our dance is t. into mourning............ 2015
La 5:21 thee, O Lord, and we shall be t.;....... 7725
Eze 1:9 they t. not when they went;.............. 5437
Eze 1:12, 17 and they t. not when they went..... 5437
Eze 10:11 they t. not as they went, but to the... 5437
Eze 10:11 followed it; they t. not as they went.. 5437
Eze 10:16 same wheels also t. not from beside... 5437
Eze 17:6 whose branches t. toward him,.......... 6437
Eze 26:2 she is t. unto me: I shall be............ 5437
Eze 42:19 He t. about to the west side, and....... 5437
Da 9:16 anger and thy fury be t. away............ 7725
Da 10:8 my comeliness was t. in me into........ 2015
Da 10:16 vision my sorrows are t. upon me,...... 2015
Ho 7:8 people; Ephraim is a cake not t.......... 2015
Ho 11:8 mine heart is t. within me, my.......... 2015
Ho 14:4 mine anger is t. away from him......... 7725
Joe 2:31 The sun shall be t. into darkness,...... 2015
Am 6:12 for ye have t. judgment into gall,....... 2015
Jon 3:10 that they t. from their evil way;......... 7725
Na 2:2 t. away the excellency of Jacob,......... 7725
Hab 2:16 Lord's right hand shall be t. unto....... 5437
Zep 1:6 that are t. back from the Lord;.......... 5472
Hag 2:17 yet ye t. not to me, saith the Lord...........
Zec 5:1 Then I t., and lifted up mine eyes,...... 7725
Zec 6:1 And I t., and lifted up mine eyes,........ 7725
Zec 14:10 All the land shall be t. as a plain........ 5437
Mt 2:22 t. aside into the parts of Galilee:......... *402*
Mt 9:22 But Jesus t. him about, and when...... *1994*
Mt 16:23 But he t., and said unto Peter, **Get**...... *4772*
Mk 5:30 t. him about in the press, and said,.... *1994*
Mk 8:33 when he had t. about and looked on.... *1994*
Lu 2:45 they t. back again to Jerusalem,......... *5290*
Lu 7:9 t. him about, and said unto the.......... *4762*
Lu 7:44 he t. to the woman, and said unto...... *4762*
Lu 9:55 But he t., and rebuked them, and...... *4762*
Lu 10:23 And he t. him unto his disciples,......... *4762*
Lu 14:25 him: and he t., and said unto them,.... *4762*
Lu 17:15 t. back, and with a loud voice............ *5290*
Lu 22:61 Lord t., and looked upon Peter.......... *4762*
Joh 1:38 Then Jesus t., and saw them............. *4762*
Joh 16:20 **your sorrow shall be t. into joy**..... *1096*
Joh 20:14 she t. herself back, and saw Jesus...... *4762*
Joh 20:16 She t. herself, and saith unto him,...... *4762*
Ac 2:20 The sun shall be t. into darkness,...... *4762*
Ac 7:39 hearts t. back again into Egypt,......... *4762*
Ac 7:42 Then God t., and gave them up to..... *4762*
Ac 9:35 Saron saw him, and t. to the Lord...... *1994*
Ac 11:21 believed, and t. unto the Lord........... *1994*
Ac 15:19 among the Gentiles are t. to God:...... *1994*
Ac 16:18 grieved, t. and said to the spirit,........ *1994*
Ac 17:6 that have t. the world upside down...... *387*
Ac 19:26 and t. away much people,.................. *3179*
1Th 1:9 and how ye t. to God from idols to..... *1994*
1Ti 1:6 have t. aside unto vain jangling;......... *1824*
1Ti 5:15 are already t. aside after Satan........... *1824*
2Ti 1:15 are in Asia be t. away from me;.......... *654*
2Ti 4:4 truth, and shall be t. unto fables.......... *654*
Heb 11:34 t. to flight the armies of the aliens...... *2827*
Heb 12:13 which is lame be t. out of the way;.... *1624*
Jas 3:4 t. about with a very small helm,......... *3329*
Jas 4:9 let...laughter be t. to mourning,......... *3344*
2Pe 2:22 dog is t. to his own vomit again;......... *1994*
Re 1:12 I t. to see the voice that spake with... *1994*
Re 1:12 And being t., I saw seven golden....... *1994*

TURNEST
1KI 2:3 and whithersoever thou t. thyself:...... 6437
Job 15:13 thou t. thy spirit against God,........... 7725
Ps 90:3 Thou t. man to destruction; and......... 7725

TURNETH See also OVERTURNETH; RETURNETH.
Le 20:6 the soul that t. after such as have...... 6437
De 29:18 whose heart t. away his day from....... 6437
Jos 7:8 Israel t. their backs before their......... 2015
Jos 19:27 And t. toward the sunrising to.......... 7725
Jos 19:29 And then the coast t. to Ramah,........ 7725
Jos 19:29 Tyre; and the coast t. to Hosah;........ 7725
Jos 19:34 And then the coast t. westward to..... 7725
Job 39:22 neither t. he back from the sword...... 7725
Ps 107:33 He t. rivers into a wilderness, and..... 7760
Ps 107:35 He t. the wilderness into a standing.... 7760
Ps 146:9 the way of the wicked he t. upside..... 5791
Pr 15:1 A soft answer t. away wrath: but....... 7725
Pr 17:8 whithersoever it t., it prospereth........ 6437
Pr 21:1 he t. it whithersoever he will............. 5186
Pr 26:14 As the door t. upon his hinges, so...... 5437
Pr 28:9 that t. away his ear from hearing....... 5493
Pr 30:30 beasts, and t. not away for any:......... 7725
Ec 1:6 south, and t. about unto the north;..... 5437
Ca 1:7 should I be as one that t. aside......... 5844
Isa 9:13 the people t. not unto him that.......... 7725
Isa 24:1 it waste, and t. it upside down,......... 5753
Isa 44:25 that t. wise men backward, and......... 7725
Jer 14:8 as a wayfaring man that t. aside......... 5186
Jer 49:24 feeble, and t. herself to flee, and....... 6437
La 1:8 yea, she sigheth, and t. backward...... 7725
La 3:3 t. his hand against me all the day....... 7725
Eze 18:24, 26 t. away from his righteousness,...........
Eze 18:27 man t. away from his wickedness............
Eze 18:28 t. away from all his transgressions...........
Eze 33:12 day that he t. from his wickedness;.... 7725
Eze 33:18 righteous t. from his righteousness,.... 7725
Am 5:8 and t. the shadow of death into.......... 2015

TURNING See also RETURNING.
2Ki 21:13 wiping it, and t. it upside down......... 2015
2Ch 26:9 gate, and at the t. of the wall,.......... 4740
2Ch 36:13 heart from t. unto the Lord God........ 7257
Ne 3:19 the armoury at the t. of the wall......... 4740
Ne 3:20 from the t. of the wall unto the door... 4740
Ne 3:24 of Azariah unto the t. of the wall,....... 4740
Ne 3:25 over against the t. of the wall,.......... 4740
Pr 1:32 the t. away of the simple shall slay..... 4878
Isa 29:16 your t. of things upside down............ 2017
Eze 41:24 two leaves apiece, two t. leaves;........ 4142
Mic 2:4 t. away he hath divided our fields....... 7725
Lu 23:28 But Jesus t. unto them said,............... *4762*
Joh 21:20 Peter, t. about, seeth the disciple....... *1994*
Ac 3:26 in t. away every one of you from......... *654*
Ac 9:40 t. him to the body said, Tabitha,......... *1994*
Jas 1:17 variableness, neither shadow of t....... *5157*
2Pe 2:6 t. the cities of Sodom...into ashes...... *5077*
Jude 4 t. the grace of our God into.............. *3346*

TURTLE See also TURTLEDOVE; TURTLES.
Ca 2:12 the voice of the t. is heard in our....... 8449
Jer 8:6 and the t. and the crane and the........ 8449

TURTLEDOVE See also TURTLEDOVES.
Ge 15:9 old, and a t., and a young pigeon....... 8449
Le 12:6 pigeon, or a t., for a sin offering,....... 8449
Ps 74:19 O deliver not the soul of thy t. unto... 8449

TURTLEDOVES
Le 1:14 he shall bring his offering of t.,.......... 8449
Le 5:7 two t., or two young pigeons, unto..... 8449
Le 5:11 But if he be not able to bring two t.,.. 8449
Le 14:22 And two t., or two young pigeons,..... 8449
Le 14:30 And he shall offer the one of the t.,.... 8449
Le 15:14 say he shall take to him two t.,......... 8449
Lu 2:24 A pair of t., or two young pigeons...... *5167*

TURTLES
Le 12:8 lamb, then she shall bring two t.,........ 8449
Le 15:29 day she shall take unto her two t.,...... 8449
Nu 6:10 eighth day he shall bring two t.,.......... 8449

TUTORS
Ga 4:2 But is under t. and governors............ *2012*

TWAIN See also TWO.
1Sa 18:21 my son in law in the one of the t....... 8147
2Ki 4:33 and shut the door upon them t.,........ 8147
Isa 6:2 wings; with t. he covered his face,..... 8147
Isa 6:2 and with t. he covered his feet,......... 8147
Isa 6:2 and with t. he did fly...................... 8147
Jer 34:18 when they cut the calf in t., and........ 8147
Eze 21:19 both t. shall come forth out of one..... 8147
Mt 5:41 **thee to go a mile, go with him t.**... *1417*
Mt 19:5 **and they t. shall be one flesh?**....... *1417*
Mt 19:6 **Wherefore they are no more t.,**..... *1417*
Mt 21:31 **Whether of them t. did the will of**.. *1417*
Mt 27:21 Whether of the t. will ye that I.......... *1417*
Mt 27:51 the veil of the temple was rent in t.... *1417*
Mk 10:8 **And they t. shall be one flesh: so**.. *1417*
Mk 10:8 **so then they are no more t., but**.... *1417*
Mk 15:38 the veil of the temple was rent in t.... *1417*
Eph 2:15 make in himself of t. one new man,.... *1417*

TWELFTH
Nu 7:78 On the t. day Ahira the son of.... 8147,6240
1Ki 19:19 before him, and he with the t..... 8147,6240
2Ki 8:25 In the t. year of Joram the son.... 8147,6240
2Ki 17:1 In the t. year of Ahaz king of..... 8147,6240
2Ki 25:27 in the t. month, on the seven..... 8147,6240
1Ch 24:12 to Eliashib, the t. to Jakim,........ 8147,6240
1Ch 25:19 The t. to Hashabiah, he, his........ 8147,6240
1Ch 27:15 The t. captain for the t. month... 8147,6240
2Ch 34:3 and in the t. year he began to.... 8147,6240
Ezr 8:31 the t. day of the first month,...... 8147,6240
Es 3:7 the t. year of king Ahasuerus,.... 8147,6240
Es 3:7 to the t. month, that is, the....... 8147,6240
Es 3:13 thirteenth day of the t. month,.... 8147,6240
Es 8:12 thirteenth day of the t. month,... 8147,6240
Es 9:1 Now in the t. month, that is,..... 8147,6240
Jer 52:31 in the t. month, in the five and... 8147,6240
Eze 29:1 in the t. day of the month, the... 8147,6240
Eze 32:1 it came to pass in the t. year,.... 8147,6240
Eze 32:1 t. month, in the first day of the.. 8147,6240
Eze 32:17 came to pass also in the t. year,..8147,6240
Eze 33:21 it came to pass in the t. year of.. 8147,6240
Re 21:20 a jacinth; the t., an amethyst............ *1428*

TWELVE
Ge 5:8 nine hundred and t. years:......... 8147,6240
Ge 14:4 T. years they served................ 8147,6240
Ge 17:20 t. princes shall he beget, and I... 8147,6240
Ge 25:16 t. princes according to their....... 8147,6240
Ge 35:22 Now the sons of Jacob were t..... 8147,6240
Ge 42:13 Thy servants are t. brethren,..... 8147,6240
Ge 42:32 We be t. brethren, sons of our.... 8147,6240
Ge 49:28 these are the t. tribes of Israel:.. 8147,6240
Ex 15:27 where were t. wells of water,.... 8147,6240
Ex 24:4 under the hill, and t. pillars,...... 8147,6240
Ex 24:4 according to the t. tribes of........ 8147,6240
Ex 28:21 of the children of Israel, t.,........ 8147,6240
Ex 28:21 be according to the t. tribes....... 8147,6240
Ex 39:14 of the children of Israel, t.,........ 8147,6240
Ex 39:14 according to the t. tribes.......... 8147,6240
Le 24:5 and bake t. cakes thereof:.......... 8147,6240
Nu 1:44 princes of Israel, being t. men:... 8147,6240
Nu 7:3 covered wagons, and t. oxen;..... 8147,6240
Nu 7:84 of Israel: t. chargers of silver,.... 8147,6240
Nu 7:84 t. silver bowls, t. spoons of gold:..8147,6240
Nu 7:86 The golden spoons were t., full.. 8147,6240
Nu 7:87 were t. bullocks, the rams t.,..... 8147,6240
Nu 7:87 the lambs of the first year t.,..... 8147,6240
Nu 7:87 of the goats for sin offering t...... 8147,6240
Nu 17:2 house of their fathers t. rods:..... 8147,6240
Nu 17:6 fathers' houses, even t. rods:...... 8147,6240
Nu 29:17 ye shall offer t. young bullocks,.. 8147,6240
Nu 31:5 t. thousand armed for war.......... 8147,6240
Nu 31:33 And threescore and t. thousand......... 8147
Nu 31:38 Lord's tribute was threescore and t... 8147
Nu 33:9 were t. fountains of water,........ 8147,6240
De 1:23 and I took t. men of you, one of. 8147,6240
Jos 3:12 take you t. men out of the.......... 8147,6240
Jos 4:2 Take you t. men out of the.......... 8147,6240
Jos 4:3 t. stones, and ye shall carry....... 8147,6240
Jos 4:4 Then Joshua called the t. men,... 8147,6240
Jos 4:8 t. stones out of the midst of...... 8147,6240
Jos 4:9 Joshua set up t. stones in the..... 8147,6240
Jos 4:20 And those t. stones, which they. 8147,6240
Jos 8:25 and women, were t. thousand,... 8147,6240
Jos 18:24 t. cities with their villages:........ 8147,6240
Jos 19:15 t. cities with their villages.......... 8147,6240
Jos 21:7 the tribe of Zebulun, t. cities...... 8147,6240
Jos 21:40 were by their lot t. cities........... 8147,6240
Jg 19:29 with her bones, into t. pieces,.... 8147,6240
Jg 21:10 sent thither t. thousand men of.... 8147,6240
2Sa 2:15 by number t. of Benjamin,......... 8147,6240
2Sa 2:15 and t. of the servants of David.. 8147,6240
2Sa 10:6 of Ish-tob t. thousand men......... 8147,6240
2Sa 17:1 me now choose out t. thousand.. 8147,6240
1Ki 4:7 had t. officers over all Israel,..... 8147,6240
1Ki 4:26 and t. thousand horsemen........... 8147,6240
1Ki 7:15 a line of t. cubits did compass.... 8147,6240

1Ki 7:25 It stood upon **t.** oxen, three....... 8147,6240
1Ki 7:44 sea, and **t.** oxen under the sea; .. 8147,6240
1Ki 10:20 **t.** lions stood there on the one ... 8147,6240
1Ki 10:26 **t.** thousand horsemen, whom...... 8147,6240
1Ki 11:30 on him, and rent it in **t.** pieces: .. 8147,6240
1Ki 16:23 to reign over Israel, **t.** years:..... 8147,6240
1Ki 18:31 And Elijah took **t.** stones,.......... 8147,6240
1Ki 19:19 plowing with **t.** yoke of oxen...... 8147,6240
2Ki 3:1 of Judah, and reigned **t.** years...... 8147,6240
2Ki 21:1 Manasseh was **t.** years old when..8147,6240
1Ch 6:63 the tribe of Zebulun, **t.** cities...... 8147,6240
1Ch 9:22 gates were two hundred and **t.**.. 8147,6240
1Ch 15:10 brethren an hundred and **t.**........ 8147,6240
1Ch 25:9 his brethren and sons were **t.**....... 8147,6240
1Ch 25:10, 11,12,13,14,15,16,17,18,19,20,
21,22,23,24,25,26,27,28,29,30
sons, and his brethren, **t.**............ 8147,624
1Ch 25:31 sons, and his brethren, were **t.** . 8147,6240
2Ch 1:14 and **t.** thousand horsemen,......... 8147,6240
2Ch 4:4 It stood upon **t.** oxen, three...... 8147,6240
2Ch 4:15 One sea, and **t.** oxen under it..... 8147,6240
2Ch 9:19 **t.** lions stood there on the one ... 8147,6240
2Ch 9:25 and **t.** thousand horsemen;......... 8147,6240
2Ch 12:3 With **t.** hundred chariots, and............. 505
2Ch 33:1 Manasseh was **t.** years old.......... 8147,6240
Ezr 2:6 thousand eight hundred and **t.**...... 8147,6240
Ezr 2:18 of Jorah, an hundred and **t.**........ 8147,6240
Ezr 6:17 **t.** he goats, according to the 8648,6236
Ezr 8:24 I separated **t.** of the chief.......... 8147,6240
Ezr 8:35 **t.** bullocks for all Israel, ninety ... 8147,6240
Ezr 8:35 **t.** he goats for a sin offering:...... 8147,6240
Ne 5:14 **t.** years, I and my brethren 8147,6240
Ne 7:24 of Hariph, an hundred and **t.**..... 8147,6240
Es 2:12 that she had been **t.** months,...... 8147,6240
Ps 60:*title* the valley of salt **t.** thousand....... 8147,6240
Jer 52:20 and **t.** brasen bulls that were...... 8147,6240
Jer 52:21 a fillet of **t.** cubits did compass ... 8147,6240
Eze 43:16 altar shall be **t.** cubits long,........ 8147,6240
Eze 43:16 **t.** broad, square in the four........ 8147,6240
Eze 47:13 to the **t.** tribes of Israel: 8147,6240
Da 4:29 end of **t.** months he walked in 8648,6236
Mt 9:20 with an issue of blood **t.** years,.......... *1427*
Mt 10:1 called unto him his **t.** disciples, ... *1427*
Mt 10:2 the names of the **t.** apostles are......... *1427*
Mt 10:5 These **t.** Jesus sent forth, and........... *1427*
Mt 11:1 of commanding his **t.** disciples,........... *1427*
Mt 14:20 that remained **t.** baskets full............. *1427*
Mt 19:28 **ye also shall sit upon t. thrones,** ... *1427*
Mt 19:28 **judging the t. tribes of Israel.**....... *1427*
Mt 20:17 took the **t.** disciples apart in the......... *1427*
Mt 26:14 Then one of the **t.**, called Judas *1427*
Mt 26:20 was come, he sat down with the **t.**..... *1427*
Mt 26:47 lo, Judas, one of the **t.**, came, and...... *1427*
Mt 26:53 **me more than t. legions of angels?** .*1427*
Mk 3:14 he ordained **t.**, that they should be..... *1427*
Mk 4:10 that were about him with the **t.** *1427*
Mk 5:25 had an issue of blood **t.** years,........... *1427*
Mk 5:42 for she was of the age of **t.** years. *1427*
Mk 6:7 And he called unto him the **t.**, and....... *1427*
Mk 6:43 they took up **t.** baskets full of the *1427*
Mk 8:19 **ye up?** They say unto him, **T.**........... *1427*
Mk 9:35 And he sat down, and called the **t.**, ... *1427*
Mk 10:32 he took again the **t.**, and began to...... *1427*
Mk 11:11 went out unto Bethany with the **t.**..... *1427*
Mk 14:10 Judas Iscariot, one of the **t.**, went...... *1427*
Mk 14:17 evening he cometh with the **t.**........... *1427*
Mk 14:20 **It is one of the t., that dippeth** *1427*
Mk 14:43 spake, cometh Judas, one of the **t.**, ... *1427*
Lu 2:42 when he was **t.** years old, they.......... *1427*
Lu 6:13 of them he chose **t.**, whom also he..... *1427*
Lu 8:1 of God: and the **t.** were with him, ... *1427*
Lu 8:42 daughter, about **t.** years of age, ... *1427*
Lu 8:43 having an issue of blood **t.** years, ... *1427*
Lu 9:1 he called his **t.** disciples together,...... *1427*
Lu 9:12 then came the **t.**, and said unto *1427*
Lu 9:17 that remained to them **t.** baskets........ *1427*
Lu 18:31 Then he took unto him the **t.**, and...... *1427*
Lu 22:3 being of the number of the **t.**........... *1427*
Lu 22:14 and the **t.** apostles with him............. *1427*
Lu 22:30 **judging the t. tribes of Israel.**...... *1427*
Lu 22:47 one of the **t.**, went before them,........ *1427*
Joh 6:13 filled **t.** baskets with the fragments..... *1427*
Joh 6:67 Then said Jesus unto the **t.**, **Will ye** .. *1427*
Joh 6:70 **Have not I chosen you t., and one** ..*1427*
Joh 6:71 betray him, being one of the **t.**.......... *1427*
Joh 11:9 **Are there not t. hours in the day?** ..*1427*
Joh 20:24 But Thomas, one of the **t.**, called....... *1427*
Ac 6:2 Then the **t.** called the multitude of...... *1427*
Ac 7:8 and Jacob begat the **t.** patriarchs. *1427*
Ac 19:7 And all the men were about **t.**......... *1177*
Ac 24:11 yet but **t.** days since I went up to......... *1177*
Ac 26:7 Unto which promise our **t.** tribes,....... *1429*
1Co 15:5 seen of Cephas, then of the **t.**: *1427*
Jas 1:1 to the **t.** tribes which are scattered..... *1427*
Re 7:5 of Juda were sealed **t.** thousand. *1427*
Re 7:5 of Reuben were sealed **t.** thousand. *1427*
Re 7:5 of Gad were sealed **t.** thousand.......... *1427*
Re 7:6 of Aser were sealed **t.** thousand......... *1427*
Re 7:6 Nepthalim were sealed **t.** thousand. *1427*
Re 7:6 Manasses were sealed **t.** thousand...... *1427*
Re 7:7 of Simeon were sealed **t.** thousand. *1427*
Re 7:7 of Levi were sealed **t.** thousand. *1427*
Re 7:7 Issachar were sealed **t.** thousand........ *1427*
Re 7:8 of Zabulon were sealed **t.** thousand..... *1427*
Re 7:8 of Joseph were sealed **t.** thousand. *1427*
Re 7:8 Benjamin were sealed **t.** thousand......... *1427*
Re 12:1 upon her head a crown of **t.** stars: *1427*
Re 21:12 great and high, and had **t.** gates,........ *1427*
Re 21:12 at the gates **t.** angels, and names....... *1427*
Re 21:12 of the **t.** tribes of the children of........ *1427*
Re 21:14 wall of the city had **t.** foundations, ... *1427*
Re 21:14 the names of the **t.** apostles of the *1427*
Re 21:16 with the reed, **t.** thousand furlongs. *1427*
Re 21:21 the **t.** gates were **t.** pearls; every *1427*
Re 22:2 life, which bare **t.** manner of fruits,..... *1427*

TWELVE-HUNDRED See TWELVE and HUNDRED.

TWELVE-THOUSAND See TWELVE and THOUSAND.

TWENTIETH

Ge 8:14 the seven and **t.** day of the month,..... 6242
Ex 12:18 the one and **t.** day of the month at..... 6242
Nu 10:11 on the **t.** day of the second month,..... 6242
1Ki 15:9 **t.** year of Jeroboam king of Israel....... 6242
2Ki 12:6 three and **t.** year of being Jehoash...... 6242
2Ki 13:1 In the three and **t.** year of Joash the... 6242
2Ki 15:30 **t.** year of Jotham the son of Uzziah. ... 6242
2Ki 25:27 the seven and **t.** day of the month,..... 6242
1Ch 24:16 to Pethahiah, the **t.** to Jehezekel, ... 6242
1Ch 24:17 The one and **t.** to Jachin, the two....... 6242
1Ch 24:17 to Jachin, the two and **t.** to Gamul,..... 6242
1Ch 24:18 The three and **t.** to Delaiah, the 6242
1Ch 24:18 the four and **t.** to Maaziah. 6242
1Ch 25:27 The **t.** to Eliathah, he, his sons, ... 6242
1Ch 25:28 The one and **t.** to Hothir, he, his 6242
1Ch 25:29 The two and **t.** to Giddalti, he, his 6242
1Ch 25:30 The three and **t.** to Mahazioth, he,..... 6242
1Ch 25:31 The four and **t.** to Romamti-ezer,....... 6242
2Ch 7:10 and **t.** day of the seventh month 6242
Ezr 10:9 on the **t.** day of the month;.............. 6242
Ne 1:1 the month Chisleu, in the **t.** year, ... 6242
Ne 2:1 in the **t.** year of Artaxerxes the.......... 6242
Ne 5:14 from the **t.** year even unto the two 6242
Es 8:9 on the three and **t.** day thereof;.......... 6242
Jer 25:3 day, that is the three and **t.** year, ... 6242
Jer 52:30 and **t.** year of Nebuchadrezzar........... 6242
Jer 52:31 in the five and **t.** day of the month, ... 6242
Eze 29:17 to pass in the seven and **t.** year,......... 6242
Eze 40:1 five and **t.** year of our captivity,......... 6242
Da 10:4 four and **t.** day of the first month, ... 6242
Hag 1:15 and **t.** day of the sixth month, ... 6242
Hag 2:1 in the one and **t.** day of the month, ... 6242
Hag 2:10, 18 and **t.** day of the ninth month,...... 6242
Hag 2:20 four and **t.** day of the ninth month,..... 6242
Zec 1:7 and **t.** day of the eleventh month,....... 6242

TWENTY See also TWENTY'S.

Ge 6:3 shall be an hundred and **t.** years. 6242
Ge 11:24 And Nahor lived nine and **t.** years, ... 6242
Ge 18:31 there shall be **t.** found there............ 6242
Ge 23:1 hundred and seven and **t.** years old: ... 6242
Ge 31:38 **t.** years have I been with thee; thy 6242
Ge 31:41 have I been **t.** years in thy house; I.... 6242
Ge 32:14 hundred she goats, and **t.** he goats,.... 6242
Ge 32:14 two hundred ewes, and **t.** rams, ... 6242
Ge 32:15 bulls, **t.** she asses, and ten foals. 6242
Ge 37:28 Ishmeelites for **t.** pieces of silver: 6242
Ex 26:2 curtain shall be eight and **t.** cubits, ... 6242
Ex 26:18 **t.** boards on the south side............... 6242
Ex 26:19 of silver under the **t.** boards;............ 6242
Ex 26:20 north side there shall be **t.** boards: 6242
Ex 27:10 And the **t.** pillars thereof and their...... 6242
Ex 27:10 their **t.** sockets shall be of brass; 6242
Ex 27:11 his **t.** pillars and their **t.** sockets of..... 6242
Ex 27:16 shall be an hanging of **t.** cubits,.......... 6242
Ex 30:13 (a shekel is **t.** gerahs:) an half........... 6242
Ex 30:14 from **t.** years old and above, shall....... 6242
Ex 36:9 one curtain was **t.** and eight cubits, ... 6242
Ex 36:23 **t.** boards for the south side............... 6242
Ex 36:24 he made under the **t.** boards; two 6242
Ex 36:25 north corner, he made **t.** boards, ... 6242
Ex 38:10 Their pillars were **t.**, ... 6242
Ex 38:10 and their brasen sockets **t.**;............... 6242
Ex 38:11 their pillars were **t.**, ... 6242
Ex 38:11 and their sockets of brass **t.**;............. 6242
Ex 38:18 **t.** cubits was the length, and the........ 6242
Ex 38:24 the offering, was **t.** and nine talents, ... 6242
Ex 38:26 from **t.** years old and upward, ... 6242
Le 27:3 male from **t.** years old even unto 6242
Le 27:5 years old even unto **t.** years old,........ 6242
Le 27:5 shall be of the male **t.** shekels, ... 6242
Le 27:25 **t.** gerahs shall be the shekel. 6242
Nu 1:3 From **t.** years old and upward, all....... 6242
Nu 1:18, 20,22,24,26,28,30,32,34,36,38,40,
42,45 from **t.** years old and upward, ...
Nu 3:39 upward, were **t.** and two thousand...... 6242
Nu 3:43 **t.** and two thousand two hundred 6242
Nu 3:47 them: (the shekel is **t.** gerahs:).......... 6242
Nu 7:86 was an hundred and **t.** shekels............ 6242
Nu 7:88 were **t.** and four bullocks, the........... 6242
Nu 8:24 **t.** and five years old and upward 6242
Nu 11:19 days, neither ten days, nor **t.** days; 6242
Nu 14:29 from **t.** years old and upward, ... 6242
Nu 18:16 the sanctuary, which is **t.** gerahs........ 6242
Nu 25:9 plague were **t.** and four thousand. 6242
Nu 26:2 from **t.** years old and upward, ... 6242
Nu 26:4 from **t.** years old and upward; 6242
Nu 26:14 **t.** and two thousand and two............. 6242
Nu 26:62 of them were **t.** and three thousand,... 6242
Nu 32:11 from **t.** years old and upward, ... 6242
Nu 33:39 an hundred and **t.** and three years...... 6242
De 31:2 I am an hundred and **t.** years old 6242
De 34:7 hundred and **t.** years old when he 6242
Jos 15:32 all the cities are **t.** and nine, with....... 6242
Jos 19:30 **t.** and two cities with their villages. 6242
Jg 4:3 **t.** years he mightily oppressed the...... 6242
Jg 7:3 of the people **t.** and two thousand; 6242
Jg 8:10 hundred and **t.** thousand men that 6242
Jg 10:2 he judged Israel **t.** and three years, ... 6242
Jg 10:3 and judged Israel **t.** and two years...... 6242
Jg 11:33 come to Minneth, even **t.** cities, ... 6242
Jg 15:20 the days of the Philistines **t.** years..... 6242
Jg 16:31 And he judged Israel **t.** years. 6242
Jg 20:15 **t.** and six thousand men that drew...... 6242
Jg 20:21 that day **t.** and two thousand men. 6242
Jg 20:35 **t.** and five thousand and an hundred.... 6242
Jg 20:46 **t.** and five thousand men that drew...... 6242
1Sa 7:2 time was long; for it was **t.** years:...... 6242
1Sa 14:14 was about **t.** men, within as it were.... 6242
2Sa 3:20 to David to Hebron, and **t.** men......... 6242
2Sa 8:4 and **t.** thousand footmen: 6242
2Sa 8:5 Syrians two and **t.** thousand men......... 6242
2Sa 9:10 had fifteen sons and **t.** servants. 6242
2Sa 10:6 of Zoba, **t.** thousand footmen,............ 6242
2Sa 18:7 slaughter that day of **t.** thousand........ 6242
2Sa 19:17 sons and his **t.** servants with him; 6242
2Sa 21:20 six toes, four and **t.** in number; 6242
2Sa 24:8 end of nine months and **t.** days. 6242
1Ki 4:23 and **t.** oxen out of the pastures,......... 6242
1Ki 5:11 gave Hiram **t.** thousand measures....... 6242
1Ki 5:11 and **t.** measures of pure oil: 6242
1Ki 6:2 and the breadth thereof **t.** cubits,....... 6242
1Ki 6:3 **t.** cubits was the length thereof, ... 6242
1Ki 6:16 he built **t.** cubits on the sides of......... 6242
1Ki 6:20 forepart was **t.** cubits in length, ... 6242
1Ki 6:20 and **t.** cubits in breadth, ... 6242
1Ki 6:20 **t.** cubits in the height thereof: and..... 6242
1Ki 8:63 Lord, two and **t.** thousand oxen, ... 6242
1Ki 8:63 an hundred and **t.** thousand sheep. 6242
1Ki 9:10 came to pass at the end of **t.** years, ... 6242
1Ki 9:11 king Solomon gave Hiram **t.** cities 6242
1Ki 9:28 gold, four hundred and **t.** talents, ... 6242
1Ki 10:10 an hundred and **t.** talents of gold,....... 6242
1Ki 14:20 reigned were two and **t.** years:.......... 6242
1Ki 15:33 Israel in Tirzah, **t.** and four years....... 6242
1Ki 16:8 the **t.** and sixth year of Asa king of 6242
1Ki 16:10, 15 **t.** and seventh year of Asa king..... 6242
1Ki 16:29 Israel in Samaria **t.** and two years. 6242
1Ki 20:30 there a wall fell upon **t.** and seven...... 6242
1Ki 22:42 and he reigned **t.** and five years in 6242
2Ki 4:42 of the firstfruits, **t.** loaves of barley, ... 6242
2Ki 8:26 Two and **t.** years old was Ahaziah...... 6242

2Ki 10:36 in Samaria was **t.** and eight years....... 6242
2Ki 14:2 He was **t.** and five years old when 6242
2Ki 14:2 **t.** and nine years in Jerusalem. 6242
2Ki 15:1 **t.** and seventh year of Jeroboam 6242
2Ki 15:27 in Samaria, and reigned **t.** years......... 6242
2Ki 15:33 Five and **t.** years old was he when..... 6242
2Ki 16:2 **T.** years old was Ahaz when he......... 6242
2Ki 18:2 **T.** and five years old was he when..... 6242
2Ki 18:2 he reigned **t.** and nine years in.......... 6242
2Ki 21:19 Amon was **t.** and two years old.......... 6242
2Ki 23:31 Jehoahaz was **t.** and three years......... 6242
2Ki 23:36 Jehoiakim was **t.** and five years.......... 6242
2Ki 24:18 Zedekiah was **t.** and one years old...... 6242
1Ch 2:22 and **t.** cities in the land of Gilead....... 6242
1Ch 7:2 and **t.** thousand and six hundred......... 6242
1Ch 7:7 **t.** and two thousand and thirty and 6242
1Ch 7:9 was **t.** thousand and two hundred....... 6242
1Ch 7:40 was **t.** and six thousand men............ 6242
1Ch 12:28 father's house **t.** and two captains....... 6242
1Ch 12:30 of Ephraim **t.** thousand and eight........ 6242
1Ch 12:35 war **t.** and eight thousand and six........ 6242
1Ch 12:37 battle, an hundred and **t.** thousand...... 6242
1Ch 15:5 his brethren an hundred and **t.**:.......... 6242
1Ch 15:6 his brethren two hundred and **t.**:......... 6242
1Ch 18:4 and **t.** thousand footmen:.................. 6242
1Ch 18:5 Syrians two and **t.** thousand men........ 6242
1Ch 20:6 fingers and toes were four and **t.**, ... 6242
1Ch 23:4 **t.** and four thousand were to set......... 6242
1Ch 23:24 from the age of **t.** years and upward.. 6242
1Ch 23:27 were numbered from **t.** years old 6242
1Ch 27:1, 2 course were **t.** and four thousand. 6242
1Ch 27:4 course...were **t.** and four thousand. 6242
1Ch 27:5, 7,8,9,10,11,12,13,14,15
course were **t.** and four thousand. 6242
1Ch 27:23 them from **t.** years old and under:...... 6242
2Ch 2:10 **t.** thousand measures of...wheat,........ 6242
2Ch 2:10 **t.** thousand measures of barley, ... 6242
2Ch 2:10 and **t.** thousand baths of wine,........... 6242
2Ch 2:10 and **t.** thousand baths of oil.............. 6242
2Ch 3:3 cubits, and the breadth **t.** cubits......... 6242
2Ch 3:4 the breadth of the house, **t.** cubits,..... 6242
2Ch 3:4 the height was an hundred and **t.**: 6242
2Ch 3:8 the breadth of the house, **t.** cubits,..... 6242
2Ch 3:8 and the breadth thereof **t.** cubits: 6242
2Ch 3:11 the cherubims were **t.** cubits long:....... 6242
2Ch 3:13 spread themselves forth **t.** cubits:........ 6242
2Ch 4:1 brass, **t.** cubits the length thereof,....... 6242
2Ch 4:1 **t.** cubits the breadth thereof, and....... 6242
2Ch 5:12 an hundred and **t.** priests sounding..... 6242
2Ch 7:5 of **t.** and two thousand oxen, and 6242
2Ch 7:5 an hundred and **t.** thousand sheep: 6242
2Ch 8:1 came to pass at the end of **t.** years, ... 6242
2Ch 9:9 an hundred and **t.** talents of gold, ... 6242
2Ch 11:21 and begat **t.** and eight sons, and 6242
2Ch 13:21 and begat **t.** and two sons, and.......... 6242
2Ch 20:31 and he reigned **t.** and five years in 6242
2Ch 25:1 Amaziah was **t.** and five years old 6242
2Ch 25:1 he reigned **t.** and nine years in.......... 6242
2Ch 25:5 them from **t.** years old and above,...... 6242
2Ch 27:1 Jotham was **t.** and five years old......... 6242
2Ch 27:8 He was five and **t.** years old when 6242
2Ch 28:1 Ahaz was **t.** years old when he.......... 6242
2Ch 28:6 an hundred and **t.** thousand in one...... 6242
2Ch 29:1 when he was five and **t.** years old, ... 6242
2Ch 29:1 nine and **t.** years in Jerusalem. 6242
2Ch 31:17 Levites...**t.** years old and upward, ... 6242
2Ch 33:21 Amon was two and **t.** years old 6242
2Ch 36:2 Jehoahaz was **t.** and three years......... 6242
2Ch 36:5 Jehoiakim was **t.** and five years.......... 6242
2Ch 36:11 Zedekiah was one and **t.** years old....... 6242
Ezr 1:9 of silver, nine and **t.** knives,.............. 6242
Ezr 2:11 of Bebai, six hundred **t.** and three........ 6242
Ezr 2:12 thousand two hundred **t.** and two. 6242
Ezr 2:17 Bezai, three hundred **t.** and three....... 6242
Ezr 2:19 Hashum, two hundred **t.** and three....... 6242
Ezr 2:21 Beth-lehem, an hundred **t.** and three... 6242
Ezr 2:23 Anathoth, an hundred **t.** and eight. 6242
Ezr 2:26 and Gaba, six hundred **t.** and one........ 6242
Ezr 2:27 Michmas, an hundred **t.** and two. 6242
Ezr 2:28 And Ai, two hundred **t.** and three........ 6242
Ezr 2:32 of Harim, three hundred and **t.**............ 6242
Ezr 2:33 and Ono, seven hundred **t.** and five. ... 6242
Ezr 2:41 of Asaph, an hundred **t.** and eight....... 6242
Ezr 2:67 six thousand seven hundred and **t.**....... 6242
Ezr 3:8 Levites,...**t.** years old and upward, ... 6242
Ezr 8:11 and with him **t.** and eight males. 6242
Ezr 8:19 his brethren and their sons, **t.**;.......... 6242
Ezr 8:20 two hundred and **t.** Nethinims:........... 6242
Ezr 8:27 **t.** basons of gold, of a thousand......... 6242
Ne 6:15 was finished in the **t.** and fifth day...... 6242
Ne 7:16 of Bebai, six hundred **t.** and eight....... 6242
Ne 7:17 two thousand three hundred **t.** and..... 6242
Ne 7:22 Hashum, three hundred **t.** and eight.... 6242
Ne 7:23 Bezai, three hundred **t.** and four. 6242
Ne 7:27 Anathoth, an hundred **t.** and eight. 6242
Ne 7:30 and Gaba, six hundred **t.** and one. 6242
Ne 7:31 an hundred and **t.** and two.................. 6242
Ne 7:32 and Ai, an hundred **t.** and three. 6242
Ne 7:35 of Harim, three hundred and **t.**.. 6242
Ne 7:37 and Ono, seven hundred **t.** and one. ... 6242
Ne 7:69 seven hundred and **t.** asses.............. 6242
Ne 7:71 work **t.** thousand drams of gold,......... 7239
Ne 7:72 was **t.** thousand drams of gold, ... 7239
Ne 9:1 **t.** and fourth day of the month........... 6242
Ne 11:8 Sallai, nine hundred **t.** and eight. 6242
Ne 11:12 were eight hundred **t.** and two:........... 6242
Ne 11:14 valour, an hundred **t.** and eight: 6242
Es 1:1 and seven and **t.** provinces:) 6242
Es 8:9 an hundred **t.** and seven provinces,..... 6242
Es 9:30 hundred **t.** and seven provinces of...... 6242
Ps 68:17 chariots of God are **t.** thousand,......... 7239
Jer 52:1 Zedekiah was one and **t.** years old...... 6242
Jer 52:28 thousand Jews and three and **t.**.......... 6242
Eze 4:10 shall be by weight, **t.** shekels a day: ... 6242
Eze 8:16 were about five and **t.** men, with 6242
Eze 11:1 door of the gate five and **t.** men; 6242
Eze 40:13 the breadth was five and **t.** cubits,...... 6242
Eze 40:21, 25 the breadth five and **t.** cubits. 6242
Eze 40:29 long, and five and **t.** cubits broad. 6242
Eze 40:30 about were five and **t.** cubits long....... 6242
Eze 40:33 long, and five and **t.** cubits broad. 6242
Eze 40:36 and the breadth five and **t.** cubits. 6242
Eze 40:49 length of the porch was **t.** cubits, ... 6242
Eze 41:2 cubits, and the breadth, **t.** cubits........ 6242
Eze 41:4 the length thereof, **t.** cubits; 6242
Eze 41:4 the breadth, **t.** cubits, before the 6242
Eze 41:10 of **t.** cubits round about the house...... 6242
Eze 42:3 the **t.** cubits which were for the......... 6242
Eze 45:1 length of five and **t.** thousand reeds, ... 6242
Eze 45:3 the length of five and **t.** thousand, ... 6242
Eze 45:5 the five and **t.** thousand of length, ... 6242
Eze 45:5 for a possession for **t.** chambers. 6242
Eze 45:6 and five and **t.** thousand long, over....... 6242
Eze 45:12 And the shekel shall be **t.** gerahs: 6242
Eze 45:12 **t.** shekels, five and **t.** shekels,............ 6242
Eze 48:8 of five and **t.** thousand reeds in.......... 6242
Eze 48:9 of five and **t.** thousand in length, ... 6242
Eze 48:10 the north five and **t.** thousand............ 6242
Eze 48:10 the south five and **t.** thousand 6242
Eze 48:13 have five and **t.** thousand in length, ... 6242
Eze 48:13 length shall be five and **t.** thousand,.... 6242
Eze 48:15 against the five and **t.** thousand,......... 6242
Eze 48:20 shall be five and **t.** thousand............. 6242
Eze 48:20 by five and **t.** thousand:.................... 6242
Eze 48:21, 21 against the five and **t.** thousand 6242
Da 6:1 an hundred and **t.** princes, ... 6243
Da 10:13 withstood me one and **t.** days:............ 6242
Hag 2:16 one came to an heap of **t.** measures, .. 6242
Hag 2:16 out of the press, there were but **t.**...... 6242
Zec 5:2 the length thereof is **t.** cubits, and...... 6242
Lu 14:31 **against him with t. thousand?**....... *1501*
Joh 6:19 about five and **t.** or thirty furlongs, ... *1501*
Ac 1:15 were about an hundred and **t.**,)........... *1501*
Ac 27:28 sounded, and found it **t.** fathoms: *1501*
1Co 10:8 in one day three and **t.** thousand......... *1501*
Re 4:4 the throne were four and **t.** seats:........ *1501*
Re 4:4 I saw four and **t.** elders sitting,........... *1501*
Re 4:10 The four and **t.** elders fall down.......... *1501*
Re 5:8 the four and **t.** elders fell down........... *1501*
Re 5:14 the four and **t.** elders fell down........... *1501*
Re 11:16 four and **t.** elders, which sat before *1501*
Re 19:4 the four and **t.** elders and the four....... *1501*

TWENTY'S

Ge 18:31 I will not destroy it for **t.** sake. 6242

TWENTY-THOUSAND See TWENTY and THOUSAND.

TWICE

Ge 41:32 was doubled unto Pharaoh **t.**; 6471
Ex 16:5 **t.** as much as they gather daily........... 4932
Ex 16:22 they gathered **t.** as much bread, ... 4932
Nu 20:11 with his rod he smote the rock **t.**........ 6471
1Sa 18:11 avoided out of his presence **t.**............ 6471
1Ki 11:9 which had appeared unto him **t.**, ... 6471
2Ki 6:10 saved himself...not once nor **t.**.. 8147
Ne 13:20 without Jerusalem once or **t.**.. 8147
Job 33:14 For God speaketh once, yea **t.**, yet.... 8147
Job 40:5 Once have I spoken;...yea, **t.**; but I.... 8147
Job 42:10 gave Job **t.** as much as he had.......... 4932
Ps 62:11 **t.** have I heard this; that power......... 8147
Ec 6:6 he live a thousand years **t.** told,......... 6471
Mk 14:30 **before the cock crow t., thou shalt.** *1364*
Mk 14:72 Before the cock crow **t.**, thou shalt *1364*
Lu 18:12 **I fast t. in the week, I give tithes.** *1364*
Jude 12 without fruit, **t.** dead, plucked up *1364*

TWIGS

Eze 17:4 cropped off the top of his young **t.**, ... 3242
Eze 17:22 off from the top of his young **t.** a 3127

TWILIGHT

1Sa 30:17 David smote them from the **t.** 5399
2Ki 7:5 they rose up in the **t.**, to go unto....... 5399
2Ki 7:7 they arose and fled in the **t.**, and 5399
Job 3:9 the stars of the **t.** thereof be dark;...... 5399
Job 24:15 of the adulterer waiteth for the **t.**,...... 5399
Pr 7:9 In the **t.**, in the evening, in the 5399
Eze 12:6 and carry it forth in the **t.**:............... 5939
Eze 12:7 I brought it forth in the **t.**, and I......... 5939
Eze 12:12 bear upon his shoulder in the **t.**, ... 5939

TWINED

Ex 26:1 with ten curtains of fine **t.** linen, ... 7806
Ex 26:31 and fine **t.** linen of cunning work: 7806
Ex 26:36 and scarlet, and fine **t.** linen,............. 7806
Ex 27:9 shall be hangings...of fine **t.** linen 7806
Ex 27:16 and scarlet, and fine **t.** linen,............. 7806
Ex 27:18 height five cubits of fine **t.** linen,........ 7806
Ex 28:6 of scarlet, and fine **t.** linen, with 7806
Ex 28:8 and scarlet, and fine **t.** linen. 7806
Ex 28:15 of scarlet, of fine **t.** linen, shalt thou ... 7806
Ex 36:8 made ten curtains of fine **t.** linen, ... 7806
Ex 36:35 and scarlet, and fine **t.** linen:............. 7806
Ex 36:37 and scarlet, and fine **t.** linen, of 7806
Ex 38:9 of the court were of fine **t.** linen, ... 7806
Ex 38:16 round about were of fine **t.** linen. 7806
Ex 38:18 and scarlet, and fine **t.** linen:............. 7806
Ex 39:2 and scarlet, and fine **t.** linen.............. 7806
Ex 39:5 and scarlet, and fine **t.** linen;............. 7806
Ex 39:8 and scarlet, and fine **t.** linen.............. 7806
Ex 39:24 purple, and scarlet, and **t.** linen.......... 7806
Ex 39:28 and linen breeches of fine **t.** linen,....... 7806
Ex 39:29 And a girdle of fine **t.** linen, and blue, . 7806

TWINKLING

1Co 15:52 In a moment, in the **t.** of an eye, ... *4493*

TWINS

Ge 25:24 behold, there were **t.** in her womb. 8380
Ge 38:27 that, behold, **t.** were in her womb...... 8380
Ca 4:2 whereof every one bear **t.**, and.......... 8382
Ca 4:5 like two young roes that are **t.**,......... 8380
Ca 6:6 whereof every one beareth **t.**, and....... 8382
Ca 7:3 like two young roes that are **t.**.. 8380

TWO See also TWAIN; TWOEDGED; TWOFOLD.

Ge 1:16 And God made **t.** great lights; 8147
Ge 4:19 Lamech took unto him **t.** wives:......... 8147
Ge 5:18 lived an hundred sixty and **t.** years, ... 8147
Ge 5:20 nine hundred sixty and **t.** years:......... 8147
Ge 5:26 seven hundred eighty and **t.** years,...... 8147
Ge 5:28 an hundred eighty and **t.** years, ... 8147
Ge 6:19 **t.** of every sort shalt thou bring.......... 8147
Ge 6:20 **t.** of every sort shall come unto.......... 8147
Ge 7:2 of beasts that are not clean by **t.**, ... 8147
Ge 7:9 There went in **t.** and **t.** unto Noah 8147
Ge 7:15 into the ark, **t.** and **t.** of all flesh, ... 8147
Ge 9:22 and told his **t.** brethren without.......... 8147
Ge 10:25 And unto Eber were born **t.** sons:...... 8147
Ge 11:10 begat Arphaxad **t.** years after the flood:.....
Ge 11:19 after he begat Reu **t.** hundred.................
Ge 11:20 And Reu lived **t.** and thirty years, ... 8147
Ge 11:21 Reu lived...**t.** hundred and seven years,......
Ge 11:23 Serug lived...**t.** hundred years..................
Ge 11:32 were **t.** hundred and five years: ....
Ge 19:1 And there came **t.** angels to Sodom.... 8147
Ge 19:8 I have **t.** daughters which have not..... 8147
Ge 19:15 take thy wife, and thy **t.** daughters,.... 8147
Ge 19:16 upon the hand of his **t.** daughters; 8147
Ge 19:30 and his **t.** daughters with him; 8147
Ge 19:30 in a cave, he and his **t.** daughters.......... 8147
Ge 22:3 took **t.** of his young men with him,..... 8147
Ge 24:22 and **t.** bracelets for her hands of ten... 8147
Ge 25:23 her, **T.** nations are in thy womb,......... 8147

Ge 25:23 and **t.** manner of people shall be 8147
Ge 27:9 fetch me from thence **t.** good kids...... 8147
Ge 27:36 hath supplanted me these **t.** times: 6471
Ge 29:16 Laban had **t.** daughters: the names 8147
Ge 31:33 into the **t.** maidservants' tents; 8147
Ge 31:41 fourteen years for thy **t.** daughters, ... 8147
Ge 32:7 herds, and the camels, into **t.** bands; .. 8147
Ge 32:10 and now I am become **t.** bands. 8147
Ge 32:14 **T.** hundred she goats, and twenty he........
Ge 32:14 **t.** hundred ewes, and twenty rams, ...
Ge 32:22 that night, and took his **t.** wives,........ 8147
Ge 32:22 and his **t.** womenservants, and.......... 8147
Ge 33:1 Rachel, and unto the **t.** handmaids. 8147
Ge 34:25 that **t.** of the sons of Jacob, Simeon.... 8147
Ge 40:2 was wroth against **t.** of his officers, ... 8147
Ge 41:1 to pass at the end of **t.** full years, that......
Ge 41:50 And unto Joseph were born **t.** sons..... 8147
Ge 42:37 Slay my **t.** sons, if I bring him not...... 8147
Ge 44:27 know that my wife bare me **t.** sons: ... 8147
Ge 45:6 these **t.** years hath the famine been in.......
Ge 46:27 born him in Egypt, were **t.** souls:....... 8147
Ge 48:1 and he took with him his **t.** sons, ... 8147
Ge 48:5 thy **t.** sons, Ephraim and Manasseh, ... 8147
Ge 49:14 couching down between **t.** burdens: ....
Ex 2:13 **t.** men of the Hebrews strove 8147
Ex 4:9 will not believe also these **t.** signs, ... 8147
Ex 12:7 and strike it on the **t.** side posts 8147
Ex 12:22 and the **t.** side posts with the blood.... 8147
Ex 12:23 the lintel, and on the **t.** side posts, ... 8147
Ex 16:22 much bread, **t.** omers for one man: ... 8147
Ex 16:29 on the sixth day the bread of **t.** days; ....
Ex 18:3 her **t.** sons; of which the name of....... 8147
Ex 18:6 thy wife, and her **t.** sons with her. 8147
Ex 21:21 if he continue a day or **t.**, he shall not.......
Ex 25:10 **t.** cubits and a half shall be the length ....
Ex 25:12 **t.** rings shall be in the one side of...... 8147
Ex 25:12 and **t.** rings in the other side of it. 8147
Ex 25:17 **t.** cubits and a half shall be the length ....
Ex 25:18 shalt make **t.** cherubims of gold, ... 8147
Ex 25:18 in the **t.** ends of the mercy seat.......... 8147
Ex 25:19 cherubims on the **t.** ends thereof.......... 8147
Ex 25:22 from between the **t.** cherubims 8147
Ex 25:23 **t.** cubits shall be the length thereof,..........
Ex 25:35, 35,35 a knop under **t.** branches of...... 8147
Ex 26:17 **T.** tenons shall there be in one 8147
Ex 26:19 boards; **t.** sockets under one board..... 8147
Ex 26:19 under one board for his **t.** tenons, ... 8147
Ex 26:19 and **t.** sockets under another board..... 8147
Ex 26:19 another board for his **t.** tenons. 8147
Ex 26:21 silver; **t.** sockets under one board, ... 8147
Ex 26:21 and **t.** sockets under another board..... 8147
Ex 26:23 **t.** boards shalt thou make for the 8147
Ex 26:23 of the tabernacle in the **t.** sides...............
Ex 26:24 they shall be for the **t.** corners. 8147
Ex 26:25 **t.** sockets under one board, ... 8147
Ex 26:25 and **t.** sockets under another board..... 8147
Ex 26:27 tabernacle, for the **t.** sides westward. ....
Ex 27:7 be upon the **t.** sides of the altar,.......... 8147
Ex 28:7 It shall have the **t.** shoulderpieces 8147
Ex 28:7 joined at the **t.** edges thereof; 8147
Ex 28:9 And thou shalt take **t.** onxy stones, ... 8147
Ex 28:11 engrave the **t.** stones with the.......... 8147
Ex 28:12 the **t.** stones upon the shoulders of..... 8147
Ex 28:12 upon his **t.** shoulders for a 8147
Ex 28:14 **t.** chains of pure gold at the ends; 8147
Ex 28:23 the breastplate **t.** rings of gold,.......... 8147
Ex 28:23 put the **t.** rings on the **t.** ends of the .. 8147
Ex 28:24 put the **t.** wreathen chains of gold 8147
Ex 28:24 the **t.** rings which are on the ends 8147
Ex 28:25 **t.** ends of the **t.** wreathen chains 8147
Ex 28:25 thou shalt fasten in the **t.** ouches, ... 8147
Ex 28:26 thou shalt make **t.** rings of gold, ... 8147
Ex 28:26 put them upon the **t.** ends of the 8147
Ex 28:27 **t.** other rings of gold thou shalt 8147
Ex 28:27 them on the **t.** sides of the ephod 8147
Ex 29:1 and **t.** rams without blemish, ... 8147
Ex 29:3 with the bullock and the **t.** rams......... 8147
Ex 29:13, 22 the **t.** kidneys, and the fat that 8147
Ex 29:38 **t.** lambs of the first year day by day ... 8147
Ex 30:2 **t.** cubits shall be the height thereof:..........
Ex 30:4 **t.** golden rings shalt thou make to 8147
Ex 30:4 of it, by the **t.** corners thereof,.......... 8147
Ex 30:4 upon the **t.** sides of it shalt thou 8147
Ex 30:23 even **t.** hundred and fifty shekels,............
Ex 30:23 calamus **t.** hundred and fifty shekels,.........
Ex 31:18 **t.** tables of testimony, tables of.......... 8147
Ex 32:15 the **t.** tables of the testimony were..... 8147

Ex 34:1 Hew thee **t.** tables of stone like......... 8147
Ex 34:4 he hewed **t.** tables of stone like 8147
Ex 34:4 in his hand the **t.** tables of stone......... 8147
Ex 34:29 with the **t.** tables of testimony in........ 8147
Ex 36:22 One board had **t.** tenons, equally........ 8147
Ex 36:24 boards; **t.** sockets under one board..... 8147
Ex 36:24 under one board for his **t.** tenons, ... 8147
Ex 36:24 **t.** sockets under another board for...... 8147
Ex 36:24 another board for his **t.** tenons. 8147
Ex 36:26 silver; **t.** sockets under one board, ... 8147
Ex 36:26 and **t.** sockets under another board..... 8147
Ex 36:28 **t.** boards made he for the corners of... 8147
Ex 36:28 of the tabernacle in the **t.** sides................
Ex 36:30 under every board **t.** sockets............ 8147
Ex 37:1 **t.** cubits and a half was the length of.........
Ex 37:3 even **t.** rings upon the one side of........ 8147
Ex 37:3 **t.** rings upon the other side of it. 8147
Ex 37:6 **t.** cubits and a half was the length............
Ex 37:7 And he made **t.** cherubims of gold, ... 8147
Ex 37:7 on the **t.** ends of the mercy seat;....... 8147
Ex 37:8 the cherubims on the **t.** ends.............. 8147
Ex 37:10 **t.** cubits was the length thereof,..............
Ex 37:21, 21,21 a knop under **t.** branches of...... 8147
Ex 37:25 and **t.** cubits was the height of it;............
Ex 37:27 And he made **t.** rings of gold for it 8147
Ex 37:27 crown thereof, by the **t.** corners of..... 8147
Ex 37:27 upon the **t.** sides thereof, to be 8147
Ex 38:29 **t.** thousand and four hundred shekels. ....
Ex 39:4 by the **t.** edges was it coupled........... 8147
Ex 39:16 **t.** ouches of gold, and **t.** gold rings; 8147
Ex 39:16 put the **t.** rings in the **t.** ends of the ... 8147
Ex 39:17 they put the **t.** wreathen chains of...... 8147
Ex 39:17 in the **t.** rings on the ends of the 8147
Ex 39:18 **t.** ends of the **t.** wreathen chains 8147
Ex 39:18 they fastened in the **t.** ouches, ... 8147
Ex 39:19 And they made **t.** rings of gold, ... 8147
Ex 39:19 on the **t.** ends of the breastplate, ... 8147
Ex 39:20 they made **t.** other golden rings, ... 8147
Ex 39:20 them on the **t.** sides of the ephod 8147
Le 3:4, 10,15 the **t.** kidneys, and the fat 8147
Le 4:9 the **t.** kidneys, and the fat that is....... 8147
Le 5:7, 11 **t.** turtledoves, or **t.** young pigeons, .8147
Le 7:4 the **t.** kidneys, and the fat that is 8147
Le 8:2 **t.** rams, and a basket of unleavened.... 8147
Le 8:16 and the **t.** kidneys, and their fat, ... 8147
Le 8:25 and the **t.** kidneys, and their fat, ... 8147
Le 12:5 she shall be unclean **t.** weeks, as in..........
Le 12:8 **t.** turtles, or **t.** young pigeons; 8147
Le 14:4 cleansed **t.** birds alive and clean, ... 8147
Le 14:10 he shall take **t.** he lambs without........ 8147
Le 14:22 **t.** turtledoves, or **t.** young pigeons, ... 8147
Le 14:49 take to cleanse the house **t.** birds,...... 8147
Le 15:14 **t.** turtledoves, or **t.** young pigeons, ... 8147
Le 15:29 her **t.** turtles, or **t.** young pigeons,..... 8147
Le 16:1 after the death of the **t.** sons of......... 8147
Le 16:5 **t.** kids of the goats for a sin............... 8147
Le 16:7 And he shall take the **t.** goats, and..... 8147
Le 16:8 shall cast lots upon the **t.** goats; 8147
Le 23:13 **t.** tenth deals of fine floor mingled...... 8147
Le 23:17 **t.** wave loaves of **t.** tenth deals: 8147
Le 23:18 one young bullock, and **t.** rams: 8147
Le 23:19 **t.** lambs of the first year for a 8147
Le 23:20 before the Lord, with the **t.** lambs:....... 8147
Le 24:5 **t.** tenth deals shall be in one cake. 8147
Le 24:6 And thou shalt set them in **t.** rows, ... 8147
Nu 1:35 were thirty and **t.** thousand.............. 8147
Nu 1:35 thousand and **t.** hundred. ....
Nu 1:39 **t.** thousand and seven hundred. 8147
Nu 2:21 were thirty and **t.** thousand.............. 8147
Nu 2:21 thousand and **t.** hundred. ....
Nu 2:26 **t.** thousand and seven hundred. 8147
Nu 3:34 were six thousand and **t.** hundred............
Nu 3:39 were twenty and **t.** thousand. 8147
Nu 3:43 were twenty and **t.** thousand............. 8147
Nu 3:43 **t.** hundred and threescore and.................
Nu 3:46 be redeemed of the **t.** hundred and...........
Nu 4:36 were **t.** thousand seven hundred and.........
Nu 4:40 were **t.** thousand and six hundred and ....
Nu 4:44 were three thousand and **t.** hundred..........
Nu 6:10 **t.** turtles, or **t.** young pigeons, ... 8147
Nu 7:3 a wagon for **t.** of the princes, and 8147
Nu 7:7 **T.** wagons and four oxen he gave......... 8147
Nu 7:17, 23,29,35,41,47,53,59,65,71,
77,83 offerings, **t.** oxen, five rams,..... 8147
Nu 7:85 silver vessels weighed **t.** thousand and ......
Nu 7:89 from between the **t.** cherubims: 8147

Nu 9:22 Or whether it were **t.** days, or a..............
Nu 10:2 Make thee **t.** trumpets of silver; of..... 8147
Nu 11:19 shall not eat one day, nor **t.** days, ...
Nu 11:26 there remained **t.** of the men in 8147
Nu 11:31 it were **t.** cubits high upon the face of.......
Nu 13:23 bare it between **t.** upon a staff;.......... 8147
Nu 15:6 offering **t.** tenth deals of flour, ... 8147
Nu 16:2 **t.** hundred and fifty princes of the............
Nu 16:17 **t.** hundred and fifty censers;...................
Nu 16:35 the **t.** hundred and fifty men that.............
Nu 22:22 and his **t.** servants were with him. 8147
Nu 26:10 devoured **t.** hundred and fifty men:...........
Nu 26:14 twenty and **t.** thousand and............... 8147
Nu 26:14 thousand and **t.** hundred. ....
Nu 26:34 **t.** thousand and seven hundred. 8147
Nu 26:37 and **t.** thousand and five hundred. 8147
Nu 28:3, 9 **t.** lambs of the first year without 8147
Nu 28:9 **t.** tenth deals of flour for a meat 8147
Nu 28:11 **t.** young bullocks, and one ram, ... 8147
Nu 28:12 **t.** tenth deals of flour for a meat 8147
Nu 28:19 **t.** young bullocks, and one ram, and.... 8147
Nu 28:20 and **t.** tenth deals for a ram; 8147
Nu 28:27 **t.** young bullocks, one ram, seven....... 8147
Nu 28:28 **t.** tenth deals unto one ram,............... 8147
Nu 29:3 and **t.** tenth deals for a ram, ... 8147
Nu 29:9 and **t.** tenth deals to one ram,............ 8147
Nu 29:13 **t.** rams, and fourteen lambs of the...... 8147
Nu 29:14 **t.** tenth deals to each ram of the....... 8147
Nu 29:14 deals to each ram of the **t.** rams, ... 8147
Nu 29:17 twelve young bullocks, **t.** rams, ... 8147
Nu 29:20 third day eleven bullocks, **t.** rams,...... 8147
Nu 29:23 fourth day ten bullocks, **t.** rams, ... 8147
Nu 29:26 the fifth day nine bullocks, **t.** rams,..... 8147
Nu 29:29 sixth day eight bullocks, **t.** rams,......... 8147
Nu 29:32 day seven bullocks, **t.** rams,............... 8147
Nu 31:27 And divide the prey into **t.** parts; 2673
Nu 31:35 and **t.** thousand persons in all, ... 8147
Nu 31:40 tribute was thirty and **t.** persons. 8147
Nu 34:15 The **t.** tribes and the half tribe have ... 8147
Nu 35:5 on the east side **t.** thousand cubits, ...
Nu 35:5 the south side **t.** thousand cubits,............
Nu 35:5 on the west side **t.** thousand cubits,..........
Nu 35:5 the north side **t.** thousand cubits; ....
Nu 35:6 ye shall add forty and **t.** cities. 8147
De 3:8 out of the hand of the **t.** kings........... 8147
De 3:21 God hath done unto these **t.** kings:..... 8147
De 4:13 wrote them upon **t.** tables of stone..... 8147
De 4:47 Bashan, **t.** kings of the Amorites, ... 8147
De 5:22 he wrote them in **t.** tables of stone,.... 8147
De 9:10 delivered unto me **t.** tables of stone.... 8147
De 9:11 Lord gave me the **t.** tables of stone,... 8147
De 9:15 and the **t.** tables of the covenant........ 8147
De 9:15 were in my **t.** hands. 8147
De 9:17 I took the **t.** tables, and cast them 8147
De 9:17 cast them out of my **t.** hands, and....... 8147
De 10:1 Hew the **t.** tables of stone like unto.... 8147
De 10:3 hewed **t.** tables of stone like unto....... 8147
De 10:3 having the **t.** tables in mine hand......... 8147
De 14:6 and cleaveth the cleft into **t.** claws,..... 8147
De 17:6 At the mouth of **t.** witnesses, or......... 8147
De 18:3 the shoulder, and the **t.** cheeks, and ....
De 19:15 at the mouth of **t.** witnesses, or at..... 8147
De 21:15 If a man have **t.** wives, one beloved, .. 8147
De 32:30 and **t.** put ten thousand to flight, ... 8147
Jos 2:1 sent out to Shittim **t.** men to spy 8147
Jos 2:4 And the woman took the **t.** men, ... 8147
Jos 2:10 unto the **t.** kings of the Amorites, ... 8147
Jos 2:23 So the **t.** men returned, and............. 8147
Jos 3:4 **t.** thousand cubits by measure: ....
Jos 6:22 the **t.** men that had spied out the 8147
Jos 7:3 let about **t.** or three thousand men go.......
Jos 7:21 and **t.** hundred shekels of silver, and.........
Jos 9:10 to the **t.** kings of the Amorites, ... 8147
Jos 14:3 given the inheritance of **t.** tribes 8147
Jos 14:4 children of Joseph were **t.** tribes, ... 8147
Jos 15:60 **t.** cities with their villages................. 8147
Jos 19:30 twenty and **t.** cities with their............ 8147
Jos 21:16 nine cities out of those **t.** tribes. 8147
Jos 21:25, 27 with her suburbs; **t.** cities. 8147
Jos 24:12 even the **t.** kings of the Amorites;....... 8147
Jg 3:16 him a dagger which had **t.** edges, ... 8147
Jg 5:30 prey; to every man a damsel or **t.**;...........
Jg 7:3 the people twenty and **t.** thousand;..... 8147
Jg 7:25 took **t.** princes of the Midianites,........ 8147
Jg 8:12 and took the **t.** kings of Midian, ... 8147
Jg 9:44 **t.** other companies ran upon all the..... 8147

Jg 10:3 judged Israel twenty and **t.** years. 8147
Jg 11:37 let me alone **t.** months, that I may 8147
Jg 11:38 and he sent her away for **t.** months: ... 8147
Jg 11:39 came to pass at the end of **t.** months, ..8147
Jg 12:6 Ephraimites forty and **t.** thousand. 8147
Jg 15:4 put a firebrand...between **t.** tails. 8147
Jg 15:13 they bound him with **t.** new cords, ... 8147
Jg 16:3 the gate of the city, and the **t.** posts, .. 8147
Jg 16:28 of the Philistines for my **t.** eyes, ... 8147
Jg 16:29 Samson took hold of the **t.** middle 8147
Jg 17:4 took **t.** hundred shekels of silver, ...
Jg 19:10 were with him **t.** asses saddled, ... 6771
Jg 20:21 day twenty and **t.** thousand men. 8147
Jg 20:45 and slew **t.** thousand men of them. ....
Ru 1:1 he, and his wife, and his **t.** sons. 8147
Ru 1:2 the name of his **t.** sons Mahlon and 8147
Ru 1:3 and she was left, and her **t.** sons. 8147
Ru 1:5 the woman was left of her **t.** sons 8147
Ru 1:7 her **t.** daughters in law with her; 8147
Ru 1:8 said unto her **t.** daughters in law, ... 8147
Ru 1:19 So they **t.** went until they came to 8147
Ru 4:11 **t.** did build the house of Israel: 8147
1Sa 1:2 he had **t.** wives; the name of the 8147
1Sa 1:3 And the **t.** sons of Eli, Hophni and 8147
1Sa 2:21 bare three sons and **t.** daughters. 8147
1Sa 2:34 that shall come upon thy **t.** sons, ... 8147
1Sa 4:4, 11 the **t.** sons of Eli, Hophni and 8147
1Sa 4:17 and thy **t.** sons also, Hophni and 8147
1Sa 6:7 take **t.** milch kine, on which there 8147
1Sa 6:10 took **t.** milch kine, and tied them. 8147
1Sa 10:2 thou shalt find **t.** men by Rachel's 8147
1Sa 10:4 and give thee **t.** loaves of bread; 8147
1Sa 11:11 **t.** of them were not left together. 8147
1Sa 13:1 when he had reigned **t.** years over 8147
1Sa 13:2 **t.** thousand were with Saul in ....
1Sa 14:49 names of his **t.** daughters were 8147
1Sa 15:4 **t.** hundred thousand footmen, and ....
1Sa 18:27 slew of the Philistines **t.** hundred men; ......
1Sa 23:18 they **t.** made a covenant before 8147
1Sa 25:13 and **t.** hundred abode by the stuff. ....
1Sa 25:18 haste, and took **t.** hundred loaves, ...
1Sa 25:18 **t.** bottles of wine, and five sheep 8147
1Sa 25:18 **t.** hundred cakes of figs, and laid them ......
1Sa 27:3 David with his **t.** wives, Ahinoam 8147
1Sa 28:8 and he went, and **t.** men with him, ... 8147
1Sa 30:5 And David's **t.** wives were taken. 8147
1Sa 30:10 **t.** hundred abode behind, which were ....
1Sa 30:12 of figs, and **t.** clusters of raisins: 8147
1Sa 30:18 and David rescued his **t.** wives. 8147
1Sa 30:21 David came to the **t.** hundred men, ...
2Sa 1:1 David...abode **t.** days in Ziklag; 8147
2Sa 2:2 up thither, and his **t.** wives also, ... 8147
2Sa 2:10 over Israel, and reigned **t.** years. 8147
2Sa 4:2 Saul's son had **t.** men that were 8147
2Sa 8:2 even with **t.** lines measured he to 8147
2Sa 8:5 the Syrians **t.** and twenty thousand 8147
2Sa 12:1 There were **t.** men in one city; the 8147
2Sa 13:23 it came to pass after **t.** full years, ...
2Sa 14:6 And thy handmaid had **t.** sons, ... 8147
2Sa 14:6 and they **t.** strove together in the 8147
2Sa 14:26 **t.** hundred shekels after the king's ....
2Sa 14:28 dwelt **t.** full years in Jerusalem, ...
2Sa 15:11 with Absalom went **t.** hundred men ....
2Sa 15:27 peace, and your **t.** sons with you, ... 8147
2Sa 15:36 have there with them their **t.** sons, ... 8147
2Sa 16:1 upon them **t.** hundred loaves of bread, ...
2Sa 18:24 David sat between the **t.** gates: 8147
2Sa 21:8 the king took the **t.** sons of Rizpah 8147
2Sa 23:20 he slew **t.** lionlike men of Moab: 8147
1Ki 2:5 what he did to the **t.** captains of 8147
1Ki 2:32 fell upon **t.** men more righteous 8147
1Ki 2:39 **t.** of the servants of Shimei ran 8147
1Ki 3:16 Then came there **t.** women, that 8147
1Ki 3:18 the house, save we **t.** in the house 8147
1Ki 3:25 said, Divide the living child in **t.**, ... 8147
1Ki 5:12 and they **t.** made a league together 8147
1Ki 5:14 Lebanon, and **t.** months at home: 8147
1Ki 6:23 the oracle he made **t.** cherubims 8147
1Ki 6:32 The **t.** doors also were of olive tree; .. 8147
1Ki 6:34 And the **t.** doors were of fir tree: 8147
1Ki 6:34 the **t.** leaves of the one door were 8147
1Ki 6:34 the **t.** leaves of the other door were ... 8147
1Ki 7:15 For he cast **t.** pillars of brass, of 8147
1Ki 7:16 made **t.** chapiters of molten brass, ... 8147
1Ki 7:18 **t.** rows round about upon the one 8147
1Ki 7:20 the chapiters upon the **t.** pillars 8147

1Ki 7:20 the pomegranates were **t.** hundred in ....
1Ki 7:24 the knops were cast in **t.** rows, ... 8147
1Ki 7:26 it contained **t.** thousand baths. ....
1Ki 7:41 The **t.** pillars, and the 8147
1Ki 7:41 the **t.** bowls of the chapiters that ....
1Ki 7:41 were on top of the **t.** pillars; 8147
1Ki 7:41 **t.** networks, to cover the **t.** bowls 8147
1Ki 7:42 pomegranates for the **t.** networks, ... 8147
1Ki 7:42 **t.** rows of pomegranates for one 8147
1Ki 7:42 cover the **t.** bowls of the chapiters 8147
1Ki 8:7 spread forth their **t.** wings over 8147
1Ki 8:9 the ark save the **t.** tables of stone, ... 8147
1Ki 8:63 **t.** and twenty thousand oxen, and 8147
1Ki 9:10 Solomon had built the **t.** houses, ... 8147
1Ki 10:16 king Solomon made **t.** hundred targets ....
1Ki 10:19 and **t.** lions stood beside the stays. 8147
1Ki 11:29 and they **t.** were alone in the field: 8147
1Ki 12:28 counsel, and made **t.** calves of gold, ... 8147
1Ki 14:20 reigned were **t.** and twenty years: 8147
1Ki 15:25 and reigned over Israel **t.** years. 8147
1Ki 16:8 to reign over Israel in Tirzah, **t.** years. .....
1Ki 16:21 of Israel divided into **t.** parts: 2677
1Ki 16:24 of Shemer for **t.** talents of silver, ...
1Ki 16:29 in Samaria twenty and **t.** years. 8147
1Ki 17:12 I am gathering **t.** sticks, that I 8147
1Ki 18:21 long halt ye between **t.** opinions? 8147
1Ki 18:23 them therefore give us **t.** bullocks; 8147
1Ki 18:32 would contain **t.** measures of seed. ....
1Ki 20:1 were thirty and **t.** kings of him, ... 8147
1Ki 20:15 and they were **t.** hundred ....
1Ki 20:15 hundred and thirty **t.**: 8147
1Ki 20:16 the thirty and **t.** kings that helped 8147
1Ki 20:27 them the **t.** little flocks of kids; 8147
1Ki 21:10 set **t.** men, sons of Belial, before 8147
1Ki 21:13 there came in **t.** men, children of 8147
1Ki 22:31 his thirty and **t.** captains that had 8147
1Ki 22:51 and reigned **t.** years over Israel. ....
2Ki 1:14 burnt up the **t.** captains of the 8147
2Ki 2:6 leave thee. And they **t.** went on. 8147
2Ki 2:7 off: and they **t.** stood by Jordan. 8147
2Ki 2:8 they **t.** went over on dry ground. 8147
2Ki 2:12 clothes, and rent them in **t.** pieces. 8147
2Ki 2:24 forth **t.** she bears out of the wood, ... 8147
2Ki 2:24 tare forty and **t.** children of them. 8147
2Ki 4:1 come to take unto him my **t.** sons 8147
2Ki 5:17 servant **t.** mules' burden of earth? ....
2Ki 5:22 mount Ephraim **t.** young men of 8147
2Ki 5:22 silver, and **t.** changes of garments. 8147
2Ki 5:23 said, Be content, take **t.** talents. ....
2Ki 5:23 bound **t.** talents of silver in **t.** bags, ... 8147
2Ki 5:23 with **t.** changes of garments, and 8147
2Ki 5:23 laid them upon **t.** of his servants; 8147
2Ki 7:1 **t.** measures of barley for a shekel, in ....
2Ki 7:14 took therefore **t.** chariot horses; 8147
2Ki 7:16 and **t.** measures of barley for a shekel, ...
2Ki 7:18 **T.** measures of barley for a shekel, ...
2Ki 8:17 Thirty and **t.** years old was he 8147
2Ki 8:26 **T.** and twenty years old was 8147
2Ki 9:32 out to him **t.** or three eunuchs 8147
2Ki 10:4 **t.** kings stood not before him: 8147
2Ki 10:8 Lay ye them in **t.** heaps at the 8147
2Ki 10:14 **t.** and forty men; neither left he 8147
2Ki 11:7 **t.** parts of all you that go forth on 8147
2Ki 15:2 **t.** and fifty years in Jerusalem. 8147
2Ki 15:23 Israel in Samaria, and reigned **t.** years. ......
2Ki 15:27 In the **t.** and fiftieth year of Azariah 8147
2Ki 17:16 them molten images, even **t.** calves, ... 8147
2Ki 18:23 deliver thee **t.** thousand horses, ...
2Ki 21:5 **t.** courts of the house of the Lord. 8147
2Ki 21:19 Amon was twenty and **t.** years old 8147
2Ki 21:19 he reigned **t.** years in Jerusalem. 8147
2Ki 23:12 made in the **t.** courts of the house 8147
2Ki 25:4 the way of the gate between **t.** walls, ...
2Ki 25:16 The **t.** pillars, one sea, and the 8147
1Ch 1:19 And unto Eber were born **t.** sons: 8147
1Ch 4:5 the father of Tekoa had **t.** wives, ... 8147
1Ch 5:21 of sheep **t.** hundred and fifty thousand, ...
1Ch 5:21 of asses **t.** thousand, and of men an ....
1Ch 7:2 **t.** and twenty thousand and six 8147
1Ch 7:7 twenty and **t.** thousand and thirty 8147
1Ch 7:9 was twenty thousand and **t.** hundred. ....
1Ch 7:11 thousand and **t.** hundred soldiers, ...
1Ch 9:22 the gates were **t.** hundred and twelve. ......
1Ch 11:21 was more honourable than the **t.**; 8147
1Ch 11:22 he slew **t.** lionlike men of Moab: 8147
1Ch 12:28 house twenty and **t.** captains. 8147

1Ch 12:32 the heads of them were **t.** hundred; ....
1Ch 15:6 his brethren **t.** hundred and twenty: ....
1Ch 15:8 the chief, and his brethren **t.** hundred: ......
1Ch 18:5 Syrians **t.** and twenty thousand 8147
1Ch 19:7 thirty and **t.** thousand chariots, ... 8147
1Ch 24:17 the **t.** and twentieth to Gamul, ... 8147
1Ch 25:7 was **t.** hundred fourscore and eight. ....
1Ch 25:29 The **t.** and twentieth to Giddalti, ... 8147
1Ch 26:8 were threescore...**t.** of Obed-edom. 8147
1Ch 26:17 day, and toward Assuppim **t.** and **t.** ... 8147
1Ch 26:18 the causeway, and **t.** at Parbar. 8147
1Ch 26:32 **t.** thousand and seven hundred chief ....
2Ch 3:10 made **t.** cherubims of image work, ... 8147
2Ch 3:15 he made before the house **t.** pillars 8147
2Ch 4:3 **T.** rows of oxen were cast, when it 8147
2Ch 4:12 the **t.** pillars, and the pommels, and 8147
2Ch 4:12 which were on the top of the **t.** pillars, ...
2Ch 4:12 **t.** wreaths to cover the **t.** pommels 8147
2Ch 4:13 pomegranates on the **t.** wreaths; 8147
2Ch 4:13 **t.** rows of pomegranates on each 8147
2Ch 4:13 to cover the **t.** pommels of the 8147
2Ch 5:10 nothing in the ark save the **t.** tables 8147
2Ch 7:5 of twenty and **t.** thousand oxen, ... 8147
2Ch 8:10 even **t.** hundred and fifty, that bare ....
2Ch 9:15 king Solomon made **t.** hundred targets ......
2Ch 9:18 and **t.** lions standing by the stays: 8147
2Ch 13:21 and begat twenty and **t.** sons, and 8147
2Ch 14:8 drew bows, **t.** hundred and fourscore ....
2Ch 17:15 with him **t.** hundred and fourscore ....
2Ch 17:16 **t.** hundred thousand mighty men of ....
2Ch 17:17 bow and shield **t.** hundred thousand. ....
2Ch 21:5 Jehoram was thirty and **t.** years 8147
2Ch 21:19 after the end of **t.** years, his bowels ... 8147
2Ch 21:20 Thirty and **t.** years old was he when ... 8147
2Ch 22:2 Forty and **t.** years old was Ahaziah 8147
2Ch 24:3 And Jehoiada took for him **t.** wives; 8147
2Ch 26:3 and he reigned fifty and **t.** years in 8147
2Ch 26:12 men of valour were **t.** thousand and six .....
2Ch 28:8 brethren **t.** hundred thousand, ...
2Ch 29:32 rams, and **t.** hundred lambs: ....
2Ch 33:5 **t.** courts of the house of the Lord, ... 8147
2Ch 33:21 Amon was **t.** and twenty years old ....
2Ch 33:21 and reigned **t.** years in Jerusalem. ....
2Ch 35:8 **t.** thousand and six hundred small ....
Ezr 2:3 of Parosh, **t.** thousand an hundred ....
Ezr 2:3 thousand an hundred seventy...**t.** 8147
Ezr 2:4 three hundred seventy and **t.**, ... 8147
Ezr 2:6 **t.** thousand eight hundred and twelve ....
Ezr 2:7 a thousand **t.** hundred fifty and four ....
Ezr 2:10 of Bani, six hundred forty and **t.** 8147
Ezr 2:12 a thousand **t.** hundred twenty ....
Ezr 2:12 hundred twenty and **t.** 8147
Ezr 2:14 Bigvai, **t.** thousand fifty and six. ....
Ezr 2:19 Hashum, **t.** hundred twenty and three. ......
Ezr 2:24 children of Azmaveth, forty and **t.** 8147
Ezr 2:27 Michmas, an hundred twenty and **t.** 8147
Ezr 2:28 and Ai, **t.** hundred twenty and three. ....
Ezr 2:29 The children of Nebo, fifty and **t.** 8147
Ezr 2:31 a thousand **t.** hundred fifty and four. ....
Ezr 2:37 of Immer, a thousand fifty and **t.** 8147
Ezr 2:38 thousand **t.** hundred forty and seven. ....
Ezr 2:58 were three hundred ninety and **t.** 8147
Ezr 2:60 of Nekoda, six hundred fifty and **t.** 8147
Ezr 2:64 and **t.** thousand three hundred and ....
Ezr 2:65 among them **t.** hundred singing men ....
Ezr 2:66 their mules, **t.** hundred forty and five; ....
Ezr 6:17 **t.** hundred rams, four hundred lambs; ....
Ezr 8:4 and with him **t.** hundred males. ....
Ezr 8:9 him **t.** hundred and eighteen males. ....
Ezr 8:20 **t.** hundred and twenty Nethinims: ....
Ezr 8:27 and **t.** vessels of fine copper, ... 8147
Ezr 10:13 is this a work of one day or **t.**: 8147
Ne 5:14 **t.** and thirtieth year of Artaxerxes 8147
Ne 6:15 the month Elul, in fifty and **t.** days. 8147
Ne 7:8 **t.** thousand an hundred seventy...**t.** ... 8147
Ne 7:9 three hundred seventy and **t.** 8147
Ne 7:10 of Arah, six hundred fifty and **t.** 8147
Ne 7:11 **t.** thousand and eight hundred and ....
Ne 7:12 a thousand **t.** hundred fifty and four. ....
Ne 7:17 of Azgad, **t.** thousand three 8147
Ne 7:17 three hundred twenty and **t.** 8147
Ne 7:19 **t.** thousand threescore and seven. ....
Ne 7:28 of Beth-azmaveth, forty and **t.** 8147
Ne 7:31 an hundred and twenty and **t.** 8147
Ne 7:33 men of the other Nebo, fifty and **t.** 8147
Ne 7:34 a thousand **t.** hundred fifty and four. ....

Ne 7:40 of Immer, a thousand fifty and t.. 8147
Ne 7:41 a thousand t. hundred forty and seven.
Ne 7:60 were three hundred ninety and t.. 8147
Ne 7:62 of Nekoda, six hundred forty and t.. 8147
Ne 7:66 together was forty and t. thousand
Ne 7:67 t. hundred forty and five singing men
Ne 7:68 their mules, t. hundred forty and five:
Ne 7:71 drams of gold, and t. thousand
Ne 7:71 and t. hundred pound of silver.
Ne 7:72 gold, and t. thousand pound of silver.
Ne 11:12 were eight hundred twenty and t.: 8147
Ne 11:13 the fathers, t. hundred forty and
Ne 11:13 the fathers,...hundred forty and t.: 8147
Ne 11:18 were t. hundred fourscore and four.
Ne 11:19 were an hundred seventy and t.. 8147
Ne 12:31 t. great companies of them that 8147
Ne 12:40 stood the t. companies of them that 8147
Ne 13:6 t. and thirtieth year of Artaxerxes 8147
Es 2:21 t. of the king's chamberlains, 8147
Es 6:2 t. of the king's chamberlains, the 8147
Es 9:27 keep these t. days according to 8147
Job 13:20 Only do not t. things unto me: then 8147
Job 42:7 thee and against thy t. friends: 8147
Pr 30:7 T. things have I required of thee; 8147
Pr 30:15 The horseleach hath t. daughters, 8147
Ec 4:9 T. are better than one; because 8147
Ec 4:11 Again, if t. lie together, then they 8147
Ec 4:12 against him, t. shall withstand him; 8147
Ca 4:5 Thy t. breasts are like t. young roes 8147
Ca 6:13 As it were the company of t. armies.
Ca 7:3 Thy t. breasts are like t. young 8147
Ca 8:12 that keep the fruit thereof t. hundred.
Isa 7:4 for the t. tails of these smoking 8147
Isa 7:21 nourish a young cow, and t. sheep; 8147
Isa 17:6 t. or three berries in the top of the 8147
Isa 22:11 also a ditch between the t. walls for
Isa 36:8 I will give thee t. thousand horses, if
Isa 45:1 to open before him the t. leaved gates;
Isa 47:9 these t. things shall come to thee 8147
Isa 51:19 These t. things are come unto thee; 8147
Jer 2:13 my people have committed t. evils; 8147
Jer 3:14 you one of a city, and t. of a family, 8147
Jer 24:1 t. baskets of figs were set before the 8147
Jer 28:3 Within t. full years will I bring again
Jer 28:11 within the space of t. full years.
Jer 33:24 t. families...the Lord hath chosen, 8147
Jer 39:4 by the gate betwixt the t. walls:
Jer 52:7 way of the gate between the t. walls,
Jer 52:20 The t. pillars, one sea, and twelve 8147
Jer 52:29 eight hundred thirty and t. persons: 8147
Eze 1:11 t. wings of every one were joined 8147
Eze 1:11 and t. covered their bodies. 8147
Eze 1:23, 23 every one had t., which covered 8147
Eze 21:19 son of man, appoint thee t. ways, 8147
Eze 21:21 the way, at the head of the t. ways, 8147
Eze 23:2 there were t. women, the daughters 8147
Eze 35:10 hast said, These t. nations and 8147
Eze 35:10 these t. countries shall be mine, 8147
Eze 37:22 they shall be no more t. nations, 8147
Eze 37:22 they be divided into t. kingdoms 8147
Eze 40:9 and the posts thereof, t. cubits; 8147
Eze 40:39 porch of the gate were t. tables on 8147
Eze 40:39 this side, and t. tables on that side,
Eze 40:40 of the north gate, were t. tables; 8147
Eze 40:40 porch of the gate, were t. tables. 8147
Eze 41:3 the post of the door, t. cubits; 8147
Eze 41:18 and every cherub had t. faces; 8147
Eze 41:22 and the length thereof t. cubits; 8147
Eze 41:23 and the sanctuary had t. doors. 8147
Eze 41:24 And the doors had t. leaves apiece, 8147
Eze 41:24 leaves apiece, t. turning leaves; 8147
Eze 41:24 t. leave for the one door,
Eze 41:24 and t. leaves for the other door. 8147
Eze 43:14 to the lower settle shall be t. cubits, 8147
Eze 45:15 out of the flock, out of t. hundred,
Eze 46:19 was a place on the t. sides westward.
Eze 47:13 Israel: Joseph shall have t. portions.
Eze 48:17 toward the north t. hundred and fifty,
Eze 48:17 toward the south t. hundred and fifty,
Eze 48:17 toward the east t. hundred and fifty,
Eze 48:17 toward the west t. hundred and fifty.
Da 5:31 about threescore and t. years old. 8648
Da 8:3 the river a ram which had t. horns:
Da 8:3 the t. horns were high; but one was
Da 8:6 came to the ram that had t. horns,
Da 8:7 the ram, and brake his t. horns: 8147
Da 8:14 t. thousand and three hundred days;
Da 8:20 ram...thou sawest having t. horns
Da 9:25 and threescore and t. weeks: 8147
Da 9:26 after threescore and t. weeks shall 8147
Da 12:5 there stood other t., the one on this 8147
Da 12:11 thousand t. hundred and ninety days.
Ho 6:2 After t. days will he revive us: in the
Ho 10:10 themselves in their t. furrows. 8147
Am 1:1 Israel, t. years before the earthquake.
Am 3:3 Can t. walk together, except they 8147
Am 3:12 out of the mouth of the lion t. legs, 8147
Am 4:8 So t. or three cities wandered unto 8147
Zec 4:3 t. olive trees by it, one upon the 8147
Zec 4:11 What are these t. olive trees upon 8147
Zec 4:12 What be these t. olive branches 8147
Zec 4:12 through the t. golden pipes empty 8147
Zec 4:14 These are the t. anointed ones, 8147
Zec 5:9 behold, there came out t. women, 8147
Zec 6:1 out from between t. mountains; 8147
Zec 11:7 And I took unto me t. staves; the 8147
Zec 13:8 t. parts therein shall be cut off and 8147
Mt 2:16 from t. years old and under, *1332*
Mt 4:18 saw t. brethren, Simon called *1417*
Mt 4:21 thence, he saw other t. brethren, *1417*
Mt 6:24 **No man can serve t. masters: for** *1417*
Mt 8:28 met him t. possessed with devils, *1417*
Mt 9:27 t. blind men followed him, crying, *1417*
Mt 10:10 **neither t. coats, neither shoes, nor** *1417*
Mt 10:29 **t. sparrows sold for a farthing?** *1417*
Mt 11:2 Christ, he sent t. of his disciples, *1417*
Mt 14:17 here but five loaves, and t. fishes. *1417*
Mt 14:19 the five loaves, and the t. fishes, *1417*
Mt 18:8 **having t. hands or t. feet to be** *1417*
Mt 18:9 **having t. eyes to be cast into hell.** *1417*
Mt 18:16 **take with thee one or t. more,** *1417*
Mt 18:16 **mouth of t. or three witnesses** *1417*
Mt 18:19 **if t. of you shall agree on earth as** *1417*
Mt 18:20 **For where t. or three are gathered** *1417*
Mt 20:21 Grant that...my t. sons may sit, *1417*
Mt 20:24 indignation against the t. brethren. *1417*
Mt 20:30 t. blind men sitting by the way side, *1417*
Mt 21:1 Olives, then sent Jesus t. disciples, *1417*
Mt 21:28 **A certain man had t. sons: and he** *1417*
Mt 22:40 **On these t. commandments hang** *1417*
Mt 24:40 **Then shall t. be in the field; the** *1417*
Mt 24:41 **T. women shall be grinding at the** *1417*
Mt 25:15 **he gave five talents, to another t.,** *1417*
Mt 25:17 **likewise, he that had received t.,** *1417*
Mt 25:17 **he also gained the other t.** *1417*
Mt 25:22 **that had received t. talents came** *1417*
Mt 25:22 **thou deliveredst unto me t. talents:** *1417*
Mt 25:22 **I have gained t. other talents** *1417*
Mt 26:2 **after that t. days is the feast of** *1417*
Mt 26:37 Peter and the t. sons of Zebedee, *1417*
Mt 26:60 At the last came t. false witnesses, *1417*
Mt 27:38 the t. thieves crucified with him, *1417*
Mk 5:13 (they were about t. thousand;) *1367*
Mk 6:7 to send them forth by t. and t.; *1417*
Mk 6:9 sandals; and not put on t. coats. *1417*
Mk 6:37 t. hundred pennyworth of bread, *1250*
Mk 6:38 knew, they say, Five, and t. fishes. *1417*
Mk 6:41 the five loaves and the t. fishes, *1417*
Mk 6:41 t. fishes divided he among them all. *1417*
Mk 9:43 **having t. hands to go into hell,** *1417*
Mk 9:45 **having t. feet to be cast into hell,** *1417*
Mk 9:47 **having t. eyes to be cast into hell** *1417*
Mk 11:1 he sendeth forth t. of his disciples, *1417*
Mk 11:4 in a place where t. ways met; *296*
Mk 12:42 widow, and she threw in t. mites, *1417*
Mk 14:1 After t. days was the feast of the *1417*
Mk 14:13 he sendeth forth t. of his disciples, *1417*
Mk 15:27 with him they crucify t. thieves; *1417*
Mk 16:12 in another form unto t. of them, *1417*
Lu 2:24 turtledoves, or t. young pigeons. *1417*
Lu 3:11 He that hath t. coats, let him impart *1417*
Lu 5:2 saw t. ships standing by the lake: *1417*
Lu 7:19 calling unto him t. of his disciples *1417*
Lu 7:41 **creditor which had t. debtors:** *1417*
Lu 9:3 **neither have t. coats apiece.** *1417*
Lu 9:13 more but five loaves and t. fishes; *1417*
Lu 9:16 took the five loaves and the t. fishes, *1417*
Lu 9:30 there talked with him t. men, *1417*
Lu 9:32 the t. men that stood with him. *1417*
Lu 10:1 seventy others, and sent them t.
Lu 10:1 and sent them...t. before his face *1417*
Lu 10:35 **he departed, he took out t. pence,** *1417*
Lu 12:6 **five sparrows sold for t. farthings,** *1417*
Lu 12:52 **three against t., and t. against** *1417*
Lu 15:11 he said, **A certain man had t. sons:** *1417*
Lu 16:13 **No servant can serve t. masters:** *1417*
Lu 17:34 **there shall be t. men in one bed;** *1417*
Lu 17:35 **T. women shall be grinding** *1417*
Lu 17:36 **T. men shall be in the field; the** *1417*
Lu 18:10 **T. men went up into the temple to** *1417*
Lu 19:29 Olives, he sent t. of his disciples, *1417*
Lu 21:2 widow casting in thither t. mites. *1417*
Lu 22:38 Lord, behold, here are t. swords. *1417*
Lu 23:32 there were also t. other, malefactors, *1417*
Lu 24:4 t. men stood by them in shining *1417*
Lu 24:13 t. of them went that same day to a *1417*
Joh 1:35 John stood, and t. of his disciples; *1417*
Joh 1:37 the t. disciples heard him speak, *1417*
Joh 1:40 One of the t. which heard John *1417*
Joh 2:6 containing t. or three firkins apiece. *1417*
Joh 4:40 them: and he abode there t. days. *1417*
Joh 4:43 after t. days he departed thence, *1417*
Joh 6:7 T. hundred pennyworth of bread *1250*
Joh 6:9 barley loaves, and t. small fishes: *1417*
Joh 8:17 **that the testimony of t. men is** *1417*
Joh 11:6 he abode t. days still in the same *1417*
Joh 19:18 crucified him, and t. other with him, *1417*
Joh 20:12 And seeth t. angels in white sitting, *1417*
Joh 21:2 and t. other of his disciples. *1417*
Joh 21:8 but as it were t. hundred cubits,) *1250*
Ac 1:10 t. men stood by them in white *1417*
Ac 1:23 they appointed t., Joseph called *1417*
Ac 1:24 of these t. thou hast chosen, *1417*
Ac 7:29 of Madian, where he begat t. sons. *1417*
Ac 9:38 they sent unto him t. men, desiring *1417*
Ac 10:7 called t. of his household servants, *1417*
Ac 12:6 was sleeping between t. soldiers, *1417*
Ac 12:6 bound with t. chains: and the *1417*
Ac 19:10 continued by the space of t. years; *1417*
Ac 19:22 he sent into Macedonia t. of them *1417*
Ac 19:34 the space of t. hours cried out, *1417*
Ac 21:33 him to be bound with t. chains; *1417*
Ac 23:23 he called unto him t. centurions, *1417*
Ac 23:23 Make ready t. hundred soldiers to *1250*
Ac 23:23 spearmen t. hundred, at the third *1250*
Ac 24:27 after t. years Porcius Festus came *1333*
Ac 27:37 t. hundred threescore and sixteen *1250*
Ac 27:41 into a place where t. seas met, *1337*
Ac 28:30 Paul dwelt t. whole years in his *1333*
1Co 6:16 for t., saith he, shall be one flesh. *1417*
1Co 14:27 let it be by t., or at the most by *1417*
1Co 14:29 Let the prophets speak t. or three, *1417*
2Co 13:1 the mouth of t. or three witnesses *1417*
Ga 4:22 Abraham had t. sons, the one by a *1417*
Ga 4:24 for these are the t. covenants; the *1417*
Eph 5:31 wife, and they t. shall be one flesh. *1417*
Php 1:23 For I am in a strait betwixt t., *1417*
1Ti 5:19 but before t. or three witnesses. *1417*
Heb 6:18 That by t. immutable things, in *1417*
Heb 10:28 mercy under t. or three witnesses: *1417*
Re 2:12 **the sharp sword with t. edges;** *1366*
Re 9:12 there come t. woes more hereafter. *1417*
Re 9:16 t. hundred thousand thousand: *1417*
Re 11:2 under foot forty and t. months. *1417*
Re 11:3 give power unto my t. witnesses, *1417*
Re 11:3 t. hundred and threescore days, *1250*
Re 11:4 These are the t. olive trees, and *1417*
Re 11:4 the t. candlesticks standing before *1417*
Re 11:10 these t. prophets tormented them *1417*
Re 12:6 thousand t. hundred and threescore *1417*
Re 12:14 given t. wings of a great eagle, *1417*
Re 13:5 to continue forty and t. months. *1417*
Re 13:11 and he had t. horns like a lamb, *1417*

TWOEDGED

Ps 149:6 and a t. sword in their hand; 6374
Pr 5:4 wormwood, sharp as a t. sword. 6310
Heb 4:12 and sharper than any t. sword, *1366*
Re 1:16 of his mouth went a sharp t. sword: *1366*

TWOFOLD

Mt 23:15 **make him t. more the child of hell.** *1366*

TWO-HUNDRED See TWO and HUNDRED.

TWO-LEAVED See TWO and LEAVED.

TWO-THOUSAND See TWO and THOUSAND.

TYCHICUS (tik'-ik-us)

Ac 20:4 and of Asia, T. and Trophimus. *5190*
Eph 6:21 T., a beloved brother and faithful *5190*
Eph *subscr.* Rome unto the Ephesians by T.. *5190*

Co 4:7 All my state shall **T.** declare unto....... *5190*
Co *subscr.* from Rome to the Colossians by **T.** *5190*
2Ti 4:12 And **T.** have I sent to Ephesus........... *5190*
Tit 3:12 send Artemas unto thee, or **T.**, ... *5190*

TYRANNUS (ti-ran'-nus)
Ac 19:9 daily in the school of one **T.**.............. *5181*

TYRE (tire) See also TYRUS.
Jos 19:29 Ramah, and to the strong city **T.**; 6865
2Sa 5:11 Hiram king of **T.** sent messengers...... 6865
2Sa 24:7 And came to the strong hold of **T.**,...... 6865
1Ki 5:1 Hiram king of **T.** sent his servants...... 6865
1Ki 7:13 sent and fetched Hiram out of **T.**. 6865
1Ki 7:14 and his father was a man of **T.**, ... 6876
1Ki 9:11 king of **T.** had furnished Solomon 6865
1Ki 9:12 Hiram came out from **T.** to see the 6865
1Ch 14:1 Hiram king of **T.** sent messengers...... 6865
1Ch 22:4 they of **T.** brought much cedar 6876
2Ch 2:3 sent to Huram the king of **T.**,............ 6865
2Ch 2:11 the king of **T.** answered in writing,..... 6865
2Ch 2:14 his father was a man of **T.**, skilful 6876
Ezr 3:7 to them of **T.**, to bring cedar trees...... 6876
Ne 13:16 There dwelt men of **T.** also therein, ... 6876
Ps 45:12 daughter of **T.** shall be there with 6865
Ps 83:7 with the inhabitants of **T.**;................ 6865
Ps 87:4 Philistia, and **T.**, with Ethiopia; 6865
Isa 23:1 The burden of **T.**. Howl, ye ships 6865
Isa 23:5 be sorely pained at the report of **T.**.... 6865
Isa 23:8 hath taken his counsel against **T.**,....... 6865
Isa 23:15 **T.** shall be forgotten seventy years,.... 6865
Isa 23:15 years shall **T.** sing as an harlot. 6865
Isa 23:17 years, that the Lord will visit **T.**, ... 6865
Joe 3:4 ye to do with me, O **T.**, and Zidon, ... 6865
Mt 11:21 **had been done in T. and Sidon,**..... *5184*
Mt 11:22 **be more tolerable for T. and Sidon** *5184*
Mt 15:21 into the coasts of **T.** and Sidon. *5184*
Mk 3:8 they about **T.** and Sidon, a great......... *5184*
Mk 7:24 into the borders of **T.** and Sidon, ... *5184*
Mk 7:31 departing from the coasts of **T.** and..... *5184*
Lu 6:17 from the sea coast of **T.** and............ *5184*
Lu 10:13 **works had been done in T. and** *5184*
Lu 10:14 **be more tolerable for T. and Sidon** *5184*
Ac 12:20 highly displeased with them of **T.** *5185*
Ac 21:3 sailed into Syria, and landed at **T.**:...... *5184*
Ac 21:7 we had finished our course from **T.**, ... *5184*

TYRUS (ti'-rus) See also TYRE.
Jer 25:22 And all the kings of **T.**, and all the 6865
Jer 27:3 to the king of **T.**, and to the king....... 6865
Jer 47:4 and to cut off from **T.** and Zidon 6865
Eze 26:2 **T.** hath said against Jerusalem, ... 6865
Eze 26:3 I am against thee, O, **T.**, and will....... 6865
Eze 26:4 they shall destroy the walls of **T.**, ... 6865
Eze 26:7 will bring upon **T.** Nebuchadrezzar...... 6865
Eze 26:15 Thus saith the Lord God to **T.**; 6865
Eze 27:2 man, take up a lamentation for **T.**;...... 6865
Eze 27:3 say unto **T.**, O thou art situate 6865
Eze 27:3 O **T.**, thou hast said, I am of perfect .. 6865
Eze 27:8 thy wise men, O **T.**, that were in....... 6865
Eze 27:32 saying, What city is like **T.**, like........ 6865
Eze 28:2 of man, say unto the prince of **T.**, ... 6865
Eze 28:12 a lamentation upon the king of **T.**, ... 6865
Eze 29:18 to serve a great service against **T.**: 6865
Eze 29:18 he no wages, nor his army, for **T.**,....... 6865
Ho 9:13 Ephraim, as I saw **T.**, is planted in..... 6865
Am 1:9 For three transgressions of **T.**, and 6865
Am 1:10 I will send a fire on the wall of **T.**, ... 6865
Zec 9:2 **T.**, and Zidon, though it be very 6865
Zec 9:3 **T.** did build herself a strong hold,....... 6865

TZADDI (tsaw-day')
Ps 119:137 *title* [צ] **T.**......................................

U.

UCAL (u'-cal)
Pr 30:1 Ithiel, even unto Ithiel and **U.**, ... 401

UEL (u'-el)
Ezr 10:34 of Bani; Maadai, Amram, and **U.**, ... 177

ULAI (u-lahee)
Da 8:2 vision, and I was by the river of **U.**. 195
Da 8:16 man's voice between the banks of **U.**,.... 195

ULAM (u'-lam)
1Ch 7:16 and his sons were **U.** and Rakem......... 198
1Ch 7:17 And the sons of **U.**; Bedan. These....... 198
1Ch 8:39 his brother were, **U.** his firstborn, ... 198
1Ch 8:40 the sons of **U.** were mighty men of...... 198

ULLA (ul'-lah)
1Ch 7:39 And the sons of **U.**; Arah, and............ 5925

UMMAH (um'-mah)
Jos 19:30 **U.** also, and Aphek, and Rehob:......... 5981

UNACCUSTOMED
Jer 31:18 as a bullock **u.** to the yoke: 3808,3925

UNADVISEDLY
Ps 106:33 so that he spake **u.** with his lips.......... 981

UNAWARES
Ge 31:20 Jacob stole away **u.** to Laban....... 3820,3824
Ge 31:26 thou hast stolen away **u.** to me,.. 3820,3824
Nu 35:11 which killeth any person at **u.**............ 7684
Nu 35:15 that killeth any person **u.** may flee...... 7684
De 4:42 should kill his neighbour **u.**, ... 1097,1847
Jos 20:3 slayer that killeth any person **u.**......... 7684
Jos 20:9 killeth any person at **u.** might flee 7684
Ps 35:8 destruction come upon him at **u.**; 3045
Lu 21:34 **and so that day come upon you u.**.. *160*
Ga 2:4 of false brethren **u.** brought in,.......... *3920*
Heb 13:2 some have entertained angels **u.**. *2990*
Jude 4 there are certain men crept in **u.**, ... *3921*

UNBELIEF
Mt 13:58 works there because of their **u.**.......... *570*
Mt 17:20 said unto them, **Because of your u.** ... *570*
Mk 6:6 he marvelled because of their **u.**......... *570*
Mk 9:24 Lord, I believe; help thou mine **u.**. *570*
Mk 16:14 upbraided them with their **u.** and........ *570*
Ro 3:3 shall their **u.** make the faith of God...... *570*
Ro 4:20 at the promise of God through **u.**; *570*
Ro 11:20 because of **u.** they were broken off,..... *570*
Ro 11:23 also, if they abide not still in **u.**, ... *570*
Ro 11:30 obtained mercy through their **u.** *543*
Ro 11:32 God hath concluded them all in **u.**, ... *543*
1Ti 1:13 because I did it ignorantly in **u.**. *570*
Heb 3:12 be in any of you an evil heart of **u.**, ... *570*
Heb 3:19 they could not enter in because of **u.**.... *570*
Heb 4:6 entered not in because of **u.**: *543*
Heb 4:11 fall after the same example of **u.**. *543*

UNBELIEVERS
Lu 12:46 **him his portion with the u.**.............. *571*
1Co 6:6 with brother, and that before the **u.**. *571*
1Co 14:23 in those that are unlearned, or **u.**, ... *571*
2Co 6:14 unequally yoked together with **u.** *571*

UNBELIEVING
Ac 14:2 the **u.** Jews stirred up the Gentiles, ... *544*
1Co 7:14 the **u.** husband is sanctified by the....... *571*
1Co 7:14 **u.** wife is sanctified by the husband:.... *571*
1Co 7:15 But if the **u.** depart, let him depart. *571*
Tit 1:15 are defiled and **u.** is nothing pure;........ *571*
Re 21:8 But the fearful, and **u.**, and the........... *571*

UNBLAMEABLE
Col 1:22 to present you holy and **u.** and........... *299*
1Th 3:13 stablish your hearts **u.** in holiness *299*

UNBLAMEABLY
1Th 2:10 justly and **u.** we behaved ourselves...... *274*

UNCERTAIN
1Co 14:8 For if the trumpet gave an **u.** sound, ... *82*
1Ti 6:17 nor rust in **u.** riches, but in the *83*

UNCERTAINLY
1Co 9:26 I therefore so run, not as **u.**; so fight *82*

UNCHANGEABLE
Heb 7:24 ever, hath an **u.** priesthood. *531*

UNCIRCUMCISED
Ge 17:14 And the **u.** man child whose flesh....... 6189
Ge 34:14 give our sister to one that is **u.**; 6190
Ex 6:12 hear me, who am of **u.** lips?............... 6189
Ex 6:30 I am of **u.** lips, and how shall............ 6189
Ex 12:48 for no **u.** person shall eat thereof......... 6189
Le 19:23 shall count the fruit thereof as **u.**: 6189
Le 19:23 three years shall it be as **u.** unto 6189
Le 26:41 if then their **u.** hearts be humbled, ... 6189
Jos 5:7 for they were **u.**, because................. 6189
Jg 14:3 to take a wife of the **u.** Philistines?..... 6189
Jg 15:18 and fall into the hand of the **u.**? 6189
1Sa 14:6 over unto the garrison of these **u.**........ 6189
1Sa 17:26 who is this **u.** Philistine, that he......... 6189
1Sa 17:36 this **u.** Philistine shall be as one of 6189
1Sa 31:4 lest these **u.** come and thrust me....... 6189
2Sa 1:20 the daughters of the **u.** triumph.......... 6189
1Ch 10:4 lest these **u.** come and abuse me. 6189
Isa 52:1 into thee the **u.** and the unclean......... 6189
Jer 6:10 ear is **u.**, and they cannot hearken: 6189
Jer 9:25 which are circumcised with the **u.**, ... 6190
Jer 9:26 for all these nations are **u.**, and 6189
Jer 9:26 house of Israel are **u.** in the heart....... 6189
Eze 28:10 Thou shalt die the deaths of the **u.**..... 6189
Eze 31:18 thou shalt lie in the midst of the **u.**..... 6189
Eze 32:19 down, and be thou laid with the **u.**. 6189
Eze 32:21 they lie **u.**, slain by the sword........... 6189
Eze 32:24 are gone down **u.** into the nether....... 6189
Eze 32:25 All of them **u.**, slain by the sword: 6189
Eze 32:26 all of them **u.**, slain by the sword,...... 6189
Eze 32:27 the mighty that are fallen of the **u.**, ... 6189
Eze 32:28 be broken in the midst of the **u.**, ... 6189
Eze 32:29 they shall lie with the **u.**, and with 6189
Eze 32:30 and they lie **u.** with them that be 6189
Eze 32:32 shall be laid in the midst of the **u.**....... 6189
Eze 44:7 **u.** in heart, and **u.** in flesh, to be....... 6189
Eze 44:9 stranger, **u.** in heart, nor **u.** in flesh, .. 6189
Ac 7:51 Ye stiffnecked and **u.** in heart and........ *564*
Ac 11:3 Thou wentest in to men **u.**,......... *203,2192*
Ro 4:11 which he had yet being **u.**..... *1722,3588,203*
Ro 4:12 which he had being yet **u.**.... *1722,3588,203*
1Co 7:18 let him not become **u.**...................... *1986*

UNCIRCUMCISION
Ro 2:25 law, thy circumcision is made **u.**.......... *203*
Ro 2:26 if the **u.** keep the righteousness *203*
Ro 2:26 shall not his **u.** be counted for............. *203*
Ro 2:27 And shall not **u.** which is by nature, ... *203*
Ro 3:30 by faith, and **u.** through faith............... *203*
Ro 4:9 or upon the **u.** also? for we say that..... *203*
Ro 4:10 he was in circumcision, or in **u.**? *203*
Ro 4:10 Not in circumcision, but in **u.**.............. *203*
1Co 7:18 Is any called in **u.**? let him not be........ *203*
1Co 7:19 is nothing, and **u.** is nothing,............... *203*
Ga 2:7 gospel of the **u.** was committed unto.... *203*
Ga 5:6 availeth any thing, nor **u.**; but faith *203*
Ga 6:15 availeth any thing, nor **u.**, but a *203*
Eph 2:11 who are called **U.** by that which *203*
Col 2:13 your sins and the **u.** of your flesh, ... *203*
Col 3:11 Greek nor Jew, circumcision nor **u.**, ... *203*

UNCLE See also UNCLE'S.
Le 10:4 the sons of Uzziel the **u.** of Aaron,..... 1730
Le 25:49 Either his **u.**, or his uncle's son, ... 1730
1Sa 10:14 Saul's **u.** said unto him and to his........ 1730
1Sa 10:15 Saul's **u.** said, Tell me, I pray thee,..... 1730
1Sa 10:16 Saul said unto his **u.**, He told us........ 1730
1Sa 14:50 Abner, the son of Ner, Saul's **u.**. 1730
1Ch 27:32 David's **u.** was a counsellor, ... 1730
Es 2:15 of Abihail the **u.** of Mordecai, ... 1730
Jer 32:7 Hanameel...thine **u.** shall come 1730
Am 6:10 And a man's **u.** shall take him up, ... 1730

UNCLEAN
Le 5:2 Or if a soul touch any **u.** thing,.......... 2931
Le 5:2 whether it be a carcass of an **u.** beast,. 2931
Le 5:2 a carcase of **u.** cattle, or the carcase .. 2931
Le 5:2 or the carcase of **u.** creeping things, ... 2931
Le 5:2 he also shall be **u.**, and guilty............ 2931
Le 7:19 flesh that toucheth any **u.** thing.......... 2931
Le 7:21 soul that shall touch any **u.** thing, ... 2932
Le 7:21 of man, or any **u.** beast,................... 2931
Le 7:21 or any abominable **u.** thing, and 2931
Le 10:10 unholy, and between **u.** and clean;...... 2931
Le 11:4,5, 6 not the hoof; he is **u.** unto you. 2931
Le 11:7 not the cud; he is **u.** to you. 2931

Le 11:8 ye not touch; they are **u.** to you. 2930
Le 11:24 And for these ye shall be **u.**:............ 2930
Le 11:24 of them shall be **u.** until the even. 2930
Le 11:25 his clothes, and be **u.** until the even. .. 2930
Le 11:26 cheweth the cud, are **u.** unto you:...... 2931
Le 11:26 that toucheth them shall be **u.**.......... 2930
Le 11:27 on all four, those are **u.** unto you:...... 2931
Le 11:27 carcase shall be **u.** until the even. 2930
Le 11:28 clothes, and be **u.** until the even: 2930
Le 11:28 the even: they are **u.** unto you:......... 2931
Le 11:29 shall be **u.** unto you among the.......... 2931
Le 11:31 are **u.** to you among all that creep:..... 2931
Le 11:31 be dead, shall be **u.** until the even...... 2930
Le 11:32 are dead, doth fall, it shall be **u.**; 2930
Le 11:32 and it shall be **u.** until the even; 2930
Le 11:33 whatsoever is in it shall be **u.**;........... 2930
Le 11:34 such water cometh shall be **u.**........... 2930
Le 11:34 in every such vessel shall be **u.**......... 2930
Le 11:35 their carcase falleth shall be **u.**; 2930
Le 11:35 are **u.**, and shall be **u.** unto you........ 2931
Le 11:36 toucheth their carcase shall be **u.**...... 2930
Le 11:38 thereon, it shall be **u.** unto you......... 2931
Le 11:39 thereof shall be **u.** until the even........ 2930
Le 11:40 clothes, and be **u.** until the even: 2930
Le 11:40 clothes, and be **u.** until the even. 2930
Le 11:43 ye make yourselves **u.** with them,....... 2930
Le 11:47 a difference between the **u.** and.......... 2931
Le 12:2 then she shall be **u.** seven days; 2930
Le 12:2 for her infirmity shall she be **u.**......... 2930
Le 12:5 then she shall be **u.** two weeks, ... 2930
Le 13:3 on him, and pronounce him **u.** 2930
Le 13:8 the priest shall pronounce him **u.** 2930
Le 13:11 the priest shall pronounce him **u.**, ... 2930
Le 13:11 shall not shut him up: for he is **u.**...... 2931
Le 13:14 appeareth in him, he shall be **u.**......... 2930
Le 13:15 flesh, and pronounce him to be **u.** 2930
Le 13:15 for the raw flesh is **u.**: it is a............ 2931
Le 13:20, 22,25,27,30 pronounce him **u.** 2930
Le 13:36 not seek for yellow hair; he is **u.** 2931
Le 13:44 He is a leprous man, he is **u.**: 2931
Le 13:44 shall pronounce him utterly **u.**; 2930
Le 13:45 upper lip, and shall cry, **U.**, **u.** 2931
Le 13:46 him he shall be defiled; he is **u.**......... 2931
Le 13:51 plague is a fretting leprosy; it is **u.**...... 2931
Le 13:55 the plague be not spread; it is **u.** 2931
Le 13:59 it clean, or to pronounce it **u.**............ 2930
Le 14:36 that is in the house be not made **u.**..... 2930
Le 14:40 shall cast them into an **u.** place.......... 2931
Le 14:41 without the city into an **u.** place:........ 2931
Le 14:44 leprosy in the house: it is **u.**............ 2931
Le 14:45 out of the city into an **u.** place........... 2931
Le 14:46 shut up shall be **u.** until the even. 2930
Le 14:57 To teach when it is **u.**, and when......... 2931
Le 15:2 flesh, because of his issue he is **u.**...... 2931
Le 15:4 he lieth that hath the issue, is **u.**: 2930
Le 15:4 whereon he sitteth, shall be **u.** 2930
Le 15:5, 6,7,8 and be **u.** until the even. 2930
Le 15:9 that hath the issue shall be **u.** 2930
Le 15:10 him shall be **u.** until the even: 2930
Le 15:10, 11,16,17,18 be **u.** until the even. 2930
Le 15:19 toucheth her shall be **u.** until the........ 2930
Le 15:20 upon in her separation shall be **u.**........ 2930
Le 15:20 also that she sitteth upon shall be **u.**.... 2930
Le 15:21, 22 and be **u.** until the even.............. 2930
Le 15:23 it, he shall be **u.** until the even................
Le 15:24 him, he shall be **u.** seven days; 2930
Le 15:24 bed whereon he lieth shall be **u.** 2930
Le 15:25 of her separation: she shall be **u.** 2931
Le 15:26 she sitteth upon shall be **u.**,............. 2931
Le 15:27 toucheth those things shall be **u.**,........ 2930
Le 15:27 in water, and be **u.** until the even. 2930
Le 15:33 him that lieth with her that is **u.** 2931
Le 17:15 in water, and be **u.** until the even: 2930
Le 20:21 brother's wife, it is an **u.** thing: 5079
Le 20:25 between clean beasts and **u.**, ... 2931
Le 20:25 and between **u.** fowls and clean: 2931
Le 20:25 I have separated from you as **u.** 2930
Le 22:4 toucheth any thing that is **u.** by 2931
Le 22:5 whereby he may be made **u.**, or a........ 2930
Le 22:6 hath touched any such shall be **u.**........ 2930
Le 27:11 if it be any **u.** beast, of which they..... 2931
Le 27:27 if it be of an **u.** beast, then he shall.... 2931
Nu 6:7 not make himself **u.** for his father,....... 2930
Nu 9:10 be **u.** by reason of a dead body, ... 2931
Nu 18:15 the firstling of **u.** beasts shalt 2931
Nu 19:7 priest shall be **u.** until the even. 2930
Nu 19:8 and shall be **u.** until the even. 2930
Nu 19:10 clothes, and be **u.** until the even:....... 2930
Nu 19:11 any man shall be **u.** seven days. 2930
Nu 19:13 upon him, he shall be **u.**;................. 2931
Nu 19:14 in the tent, shall be **u.** seven days...... 2930
Nu 19:15 no covering bound upon it, is **u.**......... 2931
Nu 19:16 or a grave, shall be **u.** seven days...... 2930
Nu 19:17 for an **u.** person they shall take of...... 2931
Nu 19:19 shall sprinkle upon the **u.** on the 2931
Nu 19:20 But the man that shall be **u.**, and....... 2930
Nu 19:20 sprinkled upon him; he is **u.**............. 2931
Nu 19:21 separation shall be **u.** until even. 2930
Nu 19:22 whatsoever the **u.** person toucheth...... 2931
Nu 19:22 person toucheth shall be **u.**;............. 2930
Nu 19:22 toucheth it shall be **u.** until even. 2930
De 12:15 **u.** and the clean may eat thereof,....... 2931
De 12:22 the **u.** and the clean shall eat of......... 2931
De 14:7 therefore they are **u.** unto you. 2931
De 14:8 not the cud, it is **u.** unto you: 2931
De 14:10 ye may not eat; it is **u.** unto you. 2931
De 14:19 creeping thing that flieth is **u.** unto..... 2931
De 15:22 **u.** and the clean person shall eat........ 2931
De 23:14 that he see no **u.** thing in thee, ... 6172
De 26:14 away ought thereof for any **u.** use, ... 2931
Jos 22:19 if the land of your possession be **u.**, ... 2931
Jg 13:4 drink, and eat not any **u.** thing: 2931
Jg 13:7 drink, neither eat any **u.** thing:........... 2932
Jg 13:14 strong drink, nor eat any **u.** thing:...... 2932
2Ch 23:19 none which was **u.** in any thing.......... 2931
Ezr 9:11 an **u.** land with the filthiness of.......... 5079
Job 14:4 bring a clean thing out of an **u.**?......... 2931
Job 36:14 and their life is among the **u.**............ 6945
Ec 9:2 and to the clean, and to the **u.**; 2931
Isa 6:5 because I am a man of **u.** lips, and..... 2931
Isa 6:5 in the midst of a people of **u.** lips:...... 2931
Isa 35:8 the **u.** shall not pass over it; but it 2931
Isa 52:1 thee the uncircumcised and the **u.**....... 2931
Isa 52:11 out from thence, touch no **u.** thing; 2931
Isa 64:6 But we are all as an **u.** thing, and...... 2931
La 4:15 unto them, Depart ye; it is **u.**; 2931
Eze 22:26 between the **u.** and the clean, ... 2931
Eze 44:23 between the **u.** and the clean. 2931
Ho 9:3 they shall eat **u.** things in Assyria....... 2931
Hag 2:13 If one that is **u.** by a dead body......... 2931
Hag 2:13 touch any of these, shall it be **u.**? 2930
Hag 2:13 answered and said, It shall be **u.**....... 2930
Hag 2:14 that which they offer there is **u.** 2931
Zec 13:2 **u.** spirit to pass out of the land.......... 2932
Mt 10:1 gave them power against **u.** spirits,...... *169*
Mt 12:43 **the u. spirit is gone out of a man,**.. *169*
Mk 1:23 synagogue a man with an **u.** spirit;....... *169*
Mk 1:26 And when the **u.** spirit had torn him,..... *169*
Mk 1:27 commandeth he even the **u.** spirits,...... *169*
Mk 3:11 **u.** spirits, when they saw him, fell....... *169*
Mk 3:30 they said, He hath an **u.** spirit,.......... *169*
Mk 5:2 of the tombs a man with an **u.** spirit,.... *169*
Mk 5:8 **out of the man, thou u. spirit**......... *169*
Mk 5:13 the **u.** spirits went out, and entered..... *169*
Mk 6:7 gave them power over **u.** spirits;.......... *169*
Mk 7:25 young daughter had an **u.** spirit, ... *169*
Lu 4:33 which had a spirit of an **u.** devil,......... *169*
Lu 4:36 power he commandeth the **u.** spirits,..... *169*
Lu 6:18 that were vexed with **u.** spirits: *169*
Lu 8:29 commanded the **u.** spirit to come.......... *169*
Lu 9:42 Jesus rebuked the **u.** spirit, and........... *169*
Lu 11:24 **the u. spirit is gone out of a man,**.. *169*
Ac 5:16 which were vexed with **u.** spirits: *169*
Ac 8:7 For **u.** spirits, crying with loud voice, ... *169*
Ac 10:14 any thing that is common or **u.** *169*
Ac 10:28 not call any man common or **u.** *169*
Ac 11:8 nothing common or **u.** hath at any......... *169*
Ro 14:14 that there is nothing **u.** of itself: *2839*
Ro 14:14 any thing to be **u.**, to him it is **u.** *2839*
1Co 7:14 else were your children **u.**; but *169*
2Co 6:17 Lord, and touch not the **u.** thing;......... *169*
Eph 5:5 nor **u.** person, nor covetous man,......... *169*
Heb 9:13 of an heifer sprinkling the **u.**, ... *2840*
Re 16:13 I saw three **u.** spirits like frogs........... *169*
Re 18:2 a cage of every **u.** and hateful bird....... *169*

UNCLEANNESS See also UNCLEANNESSES.

Le 5:3 Or if he touch the **u.** of man, ... 2932
Le 5:3 whatsoever **u.** it be that a man.......... 2932
Le 7:20 the Lord, having his **u.** upon him, ... 2932
Le 7:21 as the **u.** of man, or any unclean........ 2932
Le 14:19 that is to be cleansed from his **u.**;....... 2932
Le 15:3 And this shall be his **u.** in his issue:.... 2932
Le 15:3 stopped from his issue, it is his **u.**...... 2932
Le 15:25 all the days of the issue of her **u.**........ 2932
Le 15:26 unclean, as the **u.** of her separation. ... 2932
Le 15:30 the Lord for the issue of her **u.**......... 2932
Le 15:31 the children of Israel from their **u.**;...... 2932
Le 15:31 they die not in their **u.**, when they..... 2932
Le 16:16 of the **u.** of the children of Israel, ... 2932
Le 16:16 among them in the midst of their **u.**.... 2932
Le 16:19 from the **u.** of the children of Israel. ... 2932
Le 18:19 as she is put apart for her **u.**............ 2932
Le 22:3 having his **u.** upon him, that soul........ 2932
Le 22:5 or a man of whom he may take **u.**,....... 2930
Le 22:5 whatsoever **u.** he hath;.................... 2932
Nu 5:19 if thou hast not gone aside to **u.** 2932
Nu 19:13 be unclean; his **u.** is yet upon him...... 2932
De 23:10 reason of **u.** that chanceth him by 7137
De 24:1 he hath found some **u.** in her: 6172
2Sa 11:4 for she was purified from her **u.**: 2932
2Ch 29:16 out all the **u.** that they found............ 2932
Ezr 9:11 from end to another with their **u.**........ 2932
Eze 36:17 me as the **u.** of a removed woman. 2932
Eze 39:24 According to their **u.** and according..... 2932
Zec 13:1 of Jerusalem for sin and **u.**................. 5079
Mt 23:27 **of dead men's bones, and of all u.**... *167*
Ro 1:24 God also gave them up to **u.** through ... *167*
Ro 6:19 yielded your members servants to **u.**.... *167*
2Co 12:21 and have not repented of the **u.** and..... *167*
Ga 5:19 are these; Adultery, fornication, **u.**,...... *167*
Eph 4:19 to work all **u.** with greediness............ *167*
Eph 5:3 But fornication, and all **u.**, or.............. *167*
Col 3:5 upon the earth; fornication, **u.**,........... *167*
1Th 2:3 not of deceit, nor of **u.**, nor in guile: *167*
1Th 4:7 For God hath not called us unto **u.**, ... *167*
2Pe 2:10 after the flesh in the lust of **u.**,.......... *3394*

UNCLEANNESSES

Eze 36:29 will also save you from all your **u.**...... 2932

UNCLE'S

Le 20:20 if a man shall lie with his **u.** wife,....... 1733
Le 20:20 hath uncovered his **u.** nakedness:....... 1730
Le 25:49 Either his uncle, or his **u.** son, may.... 1733
Es 2:7 that is, Esther his **u.** daughter:.......... 1733
Jer 32:8 Hanameel mine **u.** son came to me...... 1733
Jer 32:9 the field of Hanameel my **u.** son, ... 1733
Jer 32:12 the sight of Hanameel mine **u.** son, ... 1733

UNCLOTHED

2Co 5:4 not for that we would be **u.**, but........ *1562*

UNCOMELY

1Co 7:36 behaveth himself **u.** toward a virgin,..... *807*
1Co 12:23 our **u.** parts have more abundant......... *809*

UNCONDEMNED

Ac 16:37 They have beaten us openly **u.**, ... *178*
Ac 22:25 a man that is a Roman, and **u.**?........... *178*

UNCORRUPTIBLE See also INCORRUPTIBLE.

Ro 1:23 changed the glory of the **u.** God.......... *862*

UNCORRUPTNESS

Tit 2:7 in doctrine shewing **u.**, gravity,............ *90*

UNCOVER See also UNCOVERED; UNCOVERETH.

Le 10:6 **U.** not your heads, neither rend......... 6544
Le 18:6 kin to him, to **u.** their nakedness: 1540
Le 18:7 of thy mother, shalt thou not **u.**:........ 1540
Le 18:7 thou shalt not **u.** her nakedness. 1540
Le 18:8 thy father's wife shalt thou not **u.**:...... 1540
Le 18:9, 10 nakedness thou shalt not **u.** 1540
Le 18:11 thou shalt not **u.** her nakedness. 1540
Le 18:12 not **u.** the nakedness of thy father's.... 1540
Le 18:13 **u.** the nakedness of thy mother's 1540
Le 18:14 not **u.** the nakedness of thy father's.... 1540
Le 18:15 **u.** the nakedness of thy daughter 1540
Le 18:15 thou shalt not **u.** her nakedness. 1540
Le 18:16 **u.** the nakedness of thy brother's....... 1540
Le 18:17 not **u.** the nakedness of a woman....... 1540
Le 18:17 daughter, to **u.** her nakedness;........... 1540
Le 18:18 to vex her, to **u.** her nakedness,........ 1540
Le 18:19 unto a woman to **u.** her nakedness,...... 1540
Le 20:18 her sickness, and shall **u.** her............ 1540
Le 20:19 **u.** the nakedness of thy mother's 1540
Le 21:10 shall not **u.** his head, nor rend his 6544
Nu 5:18 Lord, and **u.** the woman's head,......... 6544
Ru 3:4 and **u.** his feet, and lay thee down;...... 1540
Isa 47:2 and grind meal: **u.** thy locks,............ 1540
Isa 47:2 make bare the leg, **u.** the thigh, ... 1540
Zep 2:14 for he shall **u.** the cedar work. 6168

UNCOVERED

Ge 9:21 and he was **u.** within his tent. 1540
Le 20:11 wife hath **u.** his father's nakedness: 1540
Le 20:17 he hath **u.** his sister's nakedness;....... 1540
Le 20:18 and she hath **u.** the fountain of her..... 1540
Le 20:20 he hath **u.** his uncle's nakedness: 1540
Le 20:21 he hath **u.** his brother's nakedness; 1540
Ru 3:7 and **u.** his feet, and laid her down. 1540
2Sa 6:20 who **u.** himself to day in the eyes of... 1540
Isa 20:4 foot, even with their buttocks **u.**,....... 2834
Isa 22:6 horsemen, and Kir **u.** the shield......... 6168
Isa 47:3 Thy nakedness shall be **u.**, yea,......... 1540
Jer 49:10 bare, I have **u.** his secret places, ... 1540
Eze 4:7 thine arm shall be **u.**, and thou.......... 2834
Hab 2:16 also, and let thy foreskin be **u.**................
Mk 2:4 they **u.** the roof where he was:........... *648*
1Co 11:5 or prophesieth with her head **u.** *177*
1Co 11:13 that a woman pray unto God **u.**? *177*

UNCOVERETH

Le 20:19 sister; for he **u.** his near kin: 6168
De 27:20 because he **u.** his father's skirt: 1540
2Sa 6:20 fellows shamelessly **u.** himself! 1540

UNCTION

1Jo 2:20 ye have an **u.** from the Holy One,...... *5545*

UNDEFILED

Ps 119:1 Blessed are the **u.** in the way, ... 8549
Ca 5:2 sister, my love, my dove, my **u.**.......... 8535
Ca 6:9 My dove, my **u.** is but one; she is 8535
Heb 7:26 who is holy, harmless, **u.**, separate...... *283*
Heb 13:4 is honourable in all, and the bed **u.** *283*
Jas 1:27 Pure religion and **u.** before God *283*
1Pe 1:4 an inheritance incorruptible, and **u.**,...... *283*

UNDER See also UNDERGIRDING; UNDERNEATH; UNDERSETTERS; UNDERSTAND; UNDERTAKE.

Ge 1:7 which were **u.** the firmament............ 8478
Ge 1:9 waters **u.** the heaven be gathered 8478
Ge 6:17 the breath of life, from **u.** heaven;...... 8478
Ge 7:19 hills, that were **u.** the whole heaven, .. 8478
Ge 16:9 and submit thyself **u.** her hands. 8478
Ge 18:4 and rest yourselves **u.** the tree:......... 8478
Ge 18:8 and he stood by them **u.** the tree,........ 8478
Ge 19:8 came they **u.** the shadow of my roof.........
Ge 21:15 cast the child **u.** one of the shrubs. 8478
Ge 24:2 I pray thee, thy hand **u.** my thigh: 8478
Ge 24:9 servant put his hand **u.** the thigh of.... 8478
Ge 35:4 Jacob hid them **u.** the oak which 8478
Ge 35:8 buried beneath Beth-el **u.** an oak:....... 8478
Ge 39:23 to any thing that was **u.** his hand; ....
Ge 41:35 lay up corn **u.** the hand of Pharaoh, ... 8478
Ge 47:29 I pray thee, thy hand **u.** my thigh, ... 8478
Ge 49:25 blessings of the deep that lieth **u.**,...... 8478
Ex 6:6,7 out from **u.** the burdens of the 8478
Ex 17:12 they took a stone, and put it **u.** him, .. 8478
Ex 17:14 of Amalek from **u.** heaven.................. 8478
Ex 18:10 from **u.** the hand of the Egyptians. 8478
Ex 20:4 or that is in the water **u.** the earth:.... 8478
Ex 21:20 with a rod, and he die **u.** his hand;..... 8478
Ex 23:5 hateth thee lying **u.** his burden, ... 8478
Ex 24:4 and builded an altar **u.** the hill, ... 8478
Ex 24:10 and there was **u.** his feet as it were... 8478
Ex 25:35, 35,35 **u.** two branches of the same,.... 8478
Ex 26:19 of silver **u.** the twenty boards; 8478
Ex 26:19 two sockets **u.** one board for his........ 8478
Ex 26:19 two sockets **u.** another board for 8478
Ex 26:21 of silver; two sockets **u.** one board,..... 8478
Ex 26:21 and two sockets **u.** another board...... 8478
Ex 26:25 two sockets **u.** one board, and two..... 8478
Ex 26:25 and two sockets **u.** another board....... 8478
Ex 26:33 hang up the vail **u.** the taches, ... 8478
Ex 27:5 **u.** the compass of the altar beneath, ... 8478
Ex 30:4 thou make to it **u.** the crown of it, ... 8478
Ex 36:24 he made **u.** the twenty boards;.......... 8478
Ex 36:24 two sockets **u.** one board for his........ 8478
Ex 36:24 two sockets **u.** another board for 8478
Ex 36:26 two sockets **u.** one board, and two..... 8478
Ex 36:26 and two sockets **u.** another board...... 8478
Ex 36:30 silver, **u.** every board of two sockets.. 8478
Ex 37:21, 21,21 **u.** two branches of the same,.... 8478
Ex 37:27 of gold for it **u.** the crown thereof, ... 8478
Ex 38:4 grate of network **u.** the compass......... 8478
Le 15:10 any thing that was **u.** him shall be...... 8478
Le 22:27 it shall be seven days **u.** the dam;...... 8478
Le 27:32 of whatsoever passeth **u.** the rod, ... 8478
Nu 3:36 **u.** the custody and charge of the sons.......
Nu 4:28, 33 **u.** the hand of Ithamar the son of.........
Nu 6:18 in the fire which is **u.** the sacrifice...... 8478
Nu 7:8 **u.** the hand of Ithamar the son of............
Nu 16:31 clave asunder that was **u.** them: 8478
Nu 22:27 the Lord, she fell down **u.** Balaam:....... 8478
Nu 31:49 men of war which are **u.** our charge, ...
Nu 33:1 **u.** the hand of Moses and Aaron. ....
De 2:25 that are **u.** the whole heaven,............ 8478
De 3:17 sea, **u.** Ashdoth-pisgah eastward. 8478
De 4:11 near and stood **u.** the mountain;......... 8478
De 4:19 all nations **u.** the whole heaven. 8478
De 4:49 the plain, **u.** the springs of Pisgah. 8478
De 7:24 destroy their name from **u.** heaven:.... 8478
De 9:14 out their name from **u.** heaven: 8478
De 12:2 the hills, and **u.** every green tree:...... 8478
De 25:19 of Amalek from **u.** heaven;................ 8478
De 28:23 earth that is **u.** thee shall be iron. 8478
De 29:20 blot out his name from **u.** heaven. 8478
Jos 7:21 of my tent, and the silver **u.** it. 8478
Jos 7:22 hid in his tent, and the silver **u.** it...... 8478
Jos 11:3 to the Hivite **u.** Hermon in the land.... 8478
Jos 11:17 of Lebanon **u.** mount Hermon:........... 8478
Jos 12:3 from the south, **u.** Ashdoth-pisgah:..... 8478
Jos 13:5 from Baal-gad **u.** mount Hermon 8478
Jos 16:10 unto this day, and serve **u.** tribute. ....
Jos 24:26 and set it up there **u.** an oak,............ 8478
Jg 1:7 gathered their meat **u.** my table:........ 8478
Jg 3:16 he did gird it **u.** his raiment upon 8478
Jg 3:30 that day **u.** the hand of Israel. 8478
Jg 4:5 dwelt **u.** the palm tree of Deborah...... 8478
Jg 6:11 sat **u.** an oak which was in Ophrah, ... 8478
Jg 6:19 brought it out unto him **u.** the oak,...... 8478
Jg 9:29 to God this people were **u.** my hand!........
Ru 2:12 **u.** whose wings thou art come to 8478
1Sa 7:11 them, until they came **u.** Beth-car. 8478
1Sa 14:2 **u.** a pomegranate tree which is in 8478
1Sa 21:3 therefore what is **u.** thine hand?......... 8478
1Sa 21:4 is no common bread **u.** mine hand. 8478
1Sa 21:8 here **u.** thine hand spear or sword? ... 8478
1Sa 22:6 abode in Gibeah **u.** a tree in Ramah, ... 8478
1Sa 31:13 buried them **u.** a tree at Jabesh, ... 8478
2Sa 2:23 spear smote him **u.** the fifth rib,.......... 413
2Sa 3:27 and smote him there **u.** the fifth rib, ...
2Sa 4:6 they smote him **u.** the fifth rib: 413
2Sa 12:31 were therein, and put them **u.** saws, ...
2Sa 12:31 **u.** harrows of iron, and **u.** axes of iron,.....
2Sa 18:2 part of the people **u.** the hand of Joab, ...
2Sa 18:2 third part **u.** the hand of Abishai the ....
2Sa 18:2 third part **u.** the hand of Ittai the ....
2Sa 18:9 the mule went **u.** the thick boughs 8478
2Sa 18:9 the mule that was **u.** him went away... 8478
2Sa 22:10 and darkness was **u.** his feet............ 8478
2Sa 22:37 Thou hast enlarged my steps **u.** me;... 8478
2Sa 22:39 yea, they are fallen **u.** my feet. 8478
2Sa 22:40 me hast thou subdued **u.** me............ 8478
2Sa 22:48 bringeth down the people **u.** me,........ 8478
1Ki 4:25 man **u.** his vine and **u.** his fig tree, ... 8478
1Ki 5:3 put them **u.** the soles of his feet........ 8478
1Ki 7:24 **u.** the brim of it round about there..... 8478
1Ki 7:30 **u.** the laver were undersetters 8478
1Ki 7:32 **u.** the borders were four wheels;......... 8478
1Ki 7:44 sea, and twelve oxen **u.** the sea; 8478
1Ki 8:6 **u.** the wings of the cherubims. 413,478
1Ki 13:14 and found him sitting **u.** an oak:..... 413,478
1Ki 14:23 high hill, and **u.** every green tree... 413,478
1Ki 18:23, 23 lay it on wood, and put no fire **u.**:........
1Ki 18:25 of your gods, but put no fire **u.**. ....
1Ki 19:4 and sat down **u.** a juniper tree:.......... 8478
1Ki 19:5 he lay and slept **u.** a juniper tree, ... 8478
2Ki 8:20, 22 Edom revolted from **u.** the hand.... 8478
2Ki 9:13 it **u.** him on the top of the stairs,....... 8478
2Ki 9:33 the horses: and he trode her **u.** foot.........
2Ki 13:5 they went out from **u.** the hand of........ 8478
2Ki 14:27 the name of Israel from **u.** heaven:..... 8478
2Ki 16:4 the hills, and **u.** every green tree....... 8478
2Ki 16:17 off the brasen oxen that were **u.** it,.... 8478
2Ki 17:7 from **u.** the hand of Pharaoh king....... 8478
2Ki 17:10 high hill, and **u.** every green tree:...... 8478
1Ch 10:12 their bones **u.** the oak in Jabesh,......... 8478
1Ch 17:1 the ark...remaineth **u.** curtains........... 8478
1Ch 24:19 their manner, **u.** Aaron their father,..........
1Ch 25:2 the sons of Asaph **u.** the hands of...... 5921
1Ch 25:3 six, **u.** the hands of their father 5921
1Ch 25:6 were **u.** the hands of their father 5921
1Ch 26:28 it was **u.** the hand of Shelomith, ... 5921
1Ch 27:23 from twenty years old and **u.**: 4295
2Ch 4:3 **u.** it was the similitude of oxen,......... 8478
2Ch 4:15 One sea, and twelve oxen **u.** it.......... 8478
2Ch 5:7 even **u.** the wings of the cherubims:... 8478
2Ch 13:18 Israel were brought **u.** at that time,..........
2Ch 21:8 revolted from **u.** the dominion of........ 8478
2Ch 21:10 revolted from **u.** the hand of Judah 8478
2Ch 21:10 did Libnah revolt from **u.** his hand;..... 8478
2Ch 26:11 **u.** the hand of Hananiah, one of......... 5921
2Ch 26:13 And **u.** their hand was an army,.......... 5921
2Ch 28:4 the hills, and **u.** every green tree....... 8478
2Ch 28:10 to keep **u.** the children of Judah..............
2Ch 31:13 overseers **u.** the hand of Cononiah ....
Ne 2:14 the beast that was **u.** me to pass. 8478
Ne 8:17 made booths, and sat **u.** the booths:.........
Job 9:13 proud helpers do stoop **u.** him. 8478
Job 20:12 though he hide it **u.** his tongue; 8478
Job 26:5 are formed from **u.** the waters, ... 8478
Job 26:8 and the cloud is not rent **u.** them. 5921
Job 28:5 **u.** it is turned up as it were fire. 8478
Job 28:24 and seeth **u.** the whole heaven; 8478
Job 30:7 **u.** the nettles they were gathered 8478
Job 37:3 He directeth it **u.** the whole heaven,.... 8478
Job 40:21 He lieth **u.** the shady trees, in the 8478
Job 41:11 whatsoever is **u.** the whole heaven is.. 8478
Job 41:30 Sharp stones are **u.** him: he............... 8478
Ps 8:6 thou hast put all things **u.** his feet: 8478
Ps 10:7 **u.** his tongue is mischief and............ 8478
Ps 17:8 hide me **u.** the shadow of thy wings, ...
Ps 18:9 and darkness was **u.** his feet. 8478
Ps 18:36 Thou hast enlarged my steps **u.** me,... 8478
Ps 18:38 to rise: they are fallen **u.** my feet. 8478
Ps 18:39 subdued **u.** me those that rose up...... 8478
Ps 18:47 and subdueth the people **u.** me,......... 8478
Ps 36:7 their trust **u.** the shadow of thy wings.......
Ps 44:5 we tread them **u.** that rise up against........
Ps 45:5 whereby the people fall **u.** thee.......... 8478
Ps 47:3 He shall subdue the people **u.** us, ... 8478
Ps 47:3 and the nations **u.** our feet............... 8478
Ps 91:1 shall abide **u.** the shadow of the..............
Ps 91:4 and **u.** his wings shalt thou trust: 8478
Ps 91:13 dragon shalt thou trample **u.** feet. ....
Ps 106:42 into subjection **u.** their hand............. 8478
Ps 140:3 adders' poison is **u.** their lips............. 8478
Ps 144:2 who subdueth my people **u.** me. 8478
Pr 12:24 but the slothful shall be **u.** tribute............
Pr 22:27 take away thy bed from **u.** thee?........... 8478
Ec 1:3 labour which he taketh **u.** the sun? 8478
Ec 1:9 there is no new thing **u.** the sun. 8478
Ec 1:13 all things that are done **u.** heaven:...... 8478
Ec 1:14 the works that are done **u.** the sun; ... 8478
Ec 2:3 they should do **u.** the heaven all the ... 8478
Ec 2:11 and there was no profit **u.** the sun. 8478
Ec 2:17 work that is wrought **u.** the sun is 8478
Ec 2:18 which I had taken **u.** the sun:............ 8478
Ec 2:19 shewed myself wise **u.** the sun. 8478
Ec 2:20 the labour which I took **u.** the sun...... 8478
Ec 2:22 he hath laboured **u.** the sun?............ 8478
Ec 3:1 time to every purpose **u.** the heaven; . 3478
Ec 3:16 **u.** the sun the place of judgment, ... 8478
Ec 4:1 that are done **u.** the sun:................. 8478
Ec 4:3 evil work that is done **u.** the sun. 8478
Ec 4:7 and I saw vanity **u.** the sun.............. 8478
Ec 4:15 the living which walk **u.** the sun,......... 8478
Ec 5:13 evil which I have seen **u.** the sun,....... 8478
Ec 5:18 labour that he taketh **u.** the sun......... 8478
Ec 6:1 evil which I have seen **u.** the sun,....... 8478
Ec 6:12 what shall be after him **u.** the sun?..... 8478
Ec 7:6 the crackling of thorns **u.** the pot, ... 8478
Ec 8:9 every work that is done **u.** the sun:...... 8478
Ec 8:15 hath no better thing **u.** the sun, ... 8478
Ec 8:15 which God giveth him **u.** the sun........ 8478
Ec 8:17 the work that is done **u.** the sun:....... 8478
Ec 9:3 all things that are done **u.** the sun, ... 8478
Ec 9:6 any thing that is done **u.** the sun........ 8478
Ec 9:9 he hath given thee **u.** the sun, all....... 8478
Ec 9:9 labour...thou takest **u.** the sun........... 8478
Ec 9:11 and saw **u.** the sun, that the race is ... 8478
Ec 9:13 wisdom have I seen also **u.** the sun,... 8478
Ec 10:5 evil which I have seen **u.** the sun,....... 8478
Ca 2:3 I sat down **u.** his shadow with great ....
Ca 2:6 His left hand is **u.** my head, and 8478
Ca 4:11 honey and milk are **u.** thy tongue;....... 8478
Ca 8:3 His left hand should be **u.** my head,.... 8478
Ca 8:5 I raised thee up **u.** the apple tree:....... 8478
Isa 3:6 and let this ruin be **u.** thy hand:......... 8478
Isa 10:4 shall bow down **u.** the prisoners,........ 8478

Isa 10:4 they shall fall **u.** the slain. For all....... 8478
Isa 10:16 and **u.** his glory he shall kindle a........ 8478
Isa 14:11 the worm is spread **u.** thee, and........ 8478
Isa 14:19 pit; as a carcase trodden **u.** feet..............
Isa 14:25 my mountains tread him **u.** foot: ....
Isa 18:7 meted out and trodden **u.** foot, ...
Isa 24:5 also is defiled **u.** the inhabitants 8478
Isa 25:10 Moab shall be trodden down **u.** him, ... 8478
Isa 28:3 of Ephraim, shall be trodden **u.** feet:.........
Isa 28:15 **u.** falsehood have we hid ourselves:.........
Isa 34:15 and hatch, and gather **u.** her shadow:........
Isa 57:5 with idols **u.** every green tree, ... 8478
Isa 57:5 valleys **u.** the clifts of the rocks?........ 8478
Isa 58:5 spread sackcloth and ashes **u.** him?..........
Jer 2:20 high hill and **u.** every green tree 8478
Jer 3:6 and **u.** every green tree, and....... 413,8478
Jer 3:13 the strangers **u.** every green tree ..... ,8478
Jer 10:11 earth, and from **u.** these heavens. 8460
Jer 12:10 have trodden my portion **u.** foot,.............
Jer 27:8 will not put their neck **u.** the yoke..............
Jer 27:11 that bring their neck **u.** the yoke.............
Jer 27:12 your necks **u.** the yoke of the king...........
Jer 33:13 pass again **u.** the hands of him........... 5921
Jer 38:11 of the king **u.** the treasury, ... 413,8478
Jer 38:12 rags **u.** thine armholes **u.** the 413,8478
Jer 48:45 fled stood **u.** the shadow of Heshbon ....
Jer 52:20 bulls that were **u.** the bases,............. 8478
La 1:15 trodden **u.** foot all my mighty men...........
La 3:34 crush **u.** his feet all the prisoners....... 8478
La 3:66 them in anger from **u.** the heavens..... 8478
La 4:20 **U.** his shadow we shall live among...........
La 5:5 Our necks are **u.** persecution: we 5921
La 5:13 and the children fell **u.** the wood. ....
Eze 1:8 the hands of a man **u.** their wings 8478
Eze 1:23 **u.** the firmament were their wings...... 8478
Eze 6:13 mountains, and **u.** every green tree, ... 8478
Eze 6:13 **u.** every thick oak, the place where.... 8478
Eze 10:2 even **u.** the cherub, and fill 413,8478
Eze 10:8 of a man's hand **u.** their wings.......... 8478
Eze 10:20 creature that I saw **u.** the God of........ 8478
Eze 10:21 hands of a man was **u.** their wings. 8478
Eze 17:6 and the roots thereof were **u.** him;..... 8478
Eze 17:23 **u.** it shall dwell all fowl of every 8478
Eze 20:37 I will cause you to pass **u.** the rod, ... 8478
Eze 24:5 and burn also the bones **u.** it, and...... 8478
Eze 31:6 **u.** his branches did all the beasts 8478
Eze 31:6 and **u.** his shadow dwelt all great ....
Eze 31:17 that dwelt **u.** his shadow in the midst........
Eze 32:27 laid their swords **u.** their heads,........... 8478
Eze 42:9 **u.** these chambers was the entry 8478
Eze 46:23 with boiling places **u.** the rows 8478
Eze 47:1 issued out from **u.** the threshold 8478
Eze 47:1 the waters came down from **u.**............ 8478
Da 4:12 beasts of...field had shadow **u.** it,........ 8460
Da 4:14 let the beasts get away from **u.** it, ... 8478
Da 4:21 **u.** which the beasts of the field.......... 8460
Da 7:27 the kingdom **u.** the whole heaven,...... 8460
Da 8:13 and the host to be trodden **u.** foot? ....
Da 9:12 for **u.** the whole heaven hath not 8478
Ho 4:12 gone a whoring from **u.** their God. 8478
Ho 4:13 **u.** oaks and poplars and elms, ... 8478
Ho 14:7 They that dwell **u.** his shadow shall ....
Joe 1:17 The seed is rotten **u.** their clods,....... 8478
Am 2:13 I am pressed **u.** you, as a cart is 8478
Ob 7 bread have laid a wound **u.** thee: 8478
Jon 4:5 booth, and sat **u.** it in the shadow, ... 8478
Mic 1:4 mountains shall be molten **u.** him, ... 8478
Mic 4:4 man **u.** his vine and **u.** his fig tree; 8478
Zec 3:10 **u.** the vine and **u.** the fig tree.......... 8478
Mal 4:3 be ashes **u.** the soles of your feet...... 8478
Mt 2:16 from two years old and **u.**, ... *2736*
Mt 5:13 **and to be trodden u. foot of men**... *2662*
Mt 5:15 **a candle, and put it u. a bushel,**.... *5259*
Mt 7:6 **they trample them u. their feet,**.... *1722*
Mt 8:8 thou shouldest come **u.** my roof:........ *5259*
Mt 8:9 For I am a man **u.** authority,............ *5259*
Mt 8:9 having soldiers **u.** me: and I say *5259*
Mt 23:37 **her chickens u. her wings, and**..... *5259*
Mk 4:21 **to be put u. a bushel, or u. a bed?**. *5259*
Mk 4:32 **air may lodge u. the shadow of it**...*5259*
Mk 6:11 **shake off the dust u. your feet for**..*5270*
Mk 7:28 yet the dogs **u.** the table eat of the.... *5270*
Lu 7:6 thou shouldest enter **u.** my roof:........ *5259*
Lu 7:8 I also am a man set **u.** authority, ... *5259*
Lu 7:8 having **u.** me soldiers, and I say *5259*
Lu 8:16 **a vessel, or putteth it u. a bed;**..... *5270*
Lu 11:33 **neither u. a bushel, but on a**........ *5259*
Lu 13:34 **gather her brood u. her wings,**...... *5259*
Lu 17:24 **out of the one part u. heaven,**....... *5259*
Lu 17:24 **unto the other part u. heaven;**...... *5259*
Joh 1:48 **when thou wast u. the fig tree, I**.. *5259*
Joh 1:50 **thee, I saw thee u. the fig tree,**..... *5273*
Ac 2:5 out of every nation **u.** heaven............ *5259*
Ac 4:12 none other name **u.** heaven given....... *5259*
Ac 8:27 of a great authority **u.** Candace queen.......
Ac 23:12 and bound themselves **u.** a curse,........ *332*
Ac 23:14 bound ourselves **u.** a great curse,....... *332*
Ac 27:4 we sailed **u.** Cyprus, because the....... *5284*
Ac 27:7 we sailed **u.** Crete, over against *5284*
Ac 27:16 running **u.** a certain island which........ *5295*
Ac 27:30 **u.** colour as though they would have.........
Ro 3:9 Gentiles, that they are all **u.** sin;........ *5259*
Ro 3:13 the poison of asps is **u.** their lips: *5259*
Ro 3:19 saith to them who are **u.** the law: *1722*
Ro 6:14 ye are not **u.** the law, but **u.** grace. ... *5259*
Ro 6:15 we are not **u.** the law, but **u.** grace? .. *5259*
Ro 7:14 but I am carnal, sold **u.** sin. *5259*
Ro 16:20 bruise Satan **u.** your feet shortly........ *5259*
1Co 6:12 not be brought **u.** the power of any. ... *5259*
1Co 7:15 sister is not **u.** bondage in such cases: ......
1Co 9:20 that are **u.** the law, as **u.** the law, ... *5259*
1Co 9:20 gain them that are **u.** the law; *5259*
1Co 9:21 to God, but **u.** the law to Christ,) *1772*
1Co 9:27 I keep **u.** my body, and bring it *5299*
1Co 10:1 all our fathers were **u.** the cloud, ... *5259*
1Co 14:34 commanded to be **u.** obedience, ... *5293*
1Co 15:25, 27 hath put all enemies **u.** his feet....... *5259*
1Co 15:27 he saith all things are put **u.** him,....... *5259*
1Co 15:27 which did put all things **u.** him. *5293*
1Co 15:28 unto him that put all things **u.** him,..... *5293*
2Co 11:32 the governor **u.** Aretas the king..............
Ga 3:10 works of the law are **u.** the curse: *5259*
Ga 3:22 hath concluded all **u.** sin, that............ *5259*
Ga 3:23 faith came, we were kept **u.** the law,.. *5259*
Ga 3:25 we are no longer **u.** a schoolmaster.... *5259*
Ga 4:2 is **u.** tutors and governors until the..... *5259*
Ga 4:3 **u.** the elements of the world; *5259*
Ga 4:4 made of a woman, made **u.** the law, ... *5259*
Ga 4:5 redeem them that were **u.** the law, ... *5259*
Ga 4:21 ye that desire to be **u.** the law, do ye. *5259*
Ga 5:18 of the Spirit, ye are not **u.** the law. *5259*
Eph 1:22 And hath put all things **u.** his feet, ... *5259*
Php 2:10 in earth, and things **u.** the earth, ... *2709*
Col 1:23 every creature which is **u.** heaven;..... *5259*
1Ti 5:9 number **u.** threescore years old, ... *1640*
1Ti 6:1 servants as are **u.** the yoke count *5259*
Heb 2:8 all things in subjection **u.** his feet. *5270*
Heb 2:8 he put all in subjection **u.** him,.................
Heb 2:8 left nothing that is not put **u.** him. *506*
Heb 2:8 see not yet all things put **u.** him. *5293*
Heb 7:11 **u.** it the people received the law,)....... *1909*
Heb 9:15 the transgressions that were **u.** the *1909*
Heb 10:28 mercy **u.** two or three witnesses: *1909*
Heb 10:29 trodden **u.** foot the Son of God,......... *2662*
Jas 2:3 there, or sit here **u.** my footstool:...... *5259*
1Pe 5:6 **u.** the mighty hand of God,............... *5259*
Jude 6 in everlasting chains **u.** darkness *5259*
Re 5:3 nor in earth, neither **u.** the earth, ... *5270*
Re 5:13 and on the earth, and **u.** the earth,..... *5270*
Re 6:9 I saw **u.** the altar the souls of them.... *5270*
Re 11:2 shall they tread **u.** foot forty and two........
Re 12:1 the sun, and the moon **u.** her feet,..... *5270*

UNDERGIRDING

Ac 27:17 up, they used helps, **u.** the ship;........ *5269*

UNDERNEATH

Ex 28:27 on the two sides of the ephod **u.**. 4295
Ex 39:20 on the two sides of the ephod **u.**, ... 4295
De 33:27 **u.** are the everlasting arms:............. 8478

UNDERSETTERS

1Ki 7:30 the four corners thereof had **u.**.......... 3802
1Ki 7:30 under the laver were **u.** molten, ... 3802
1Ki 7:34 were four **u.** to the four corners 3802
1Ki 7:34 the **u.** were of the very base itself. 3802

UNDERSTAND See also UNDERSTANDEST; UNDERSTANDETH; UNDERSTANDING; UNDERSTOOD.

Ge 11:7 may not **u.** one another's speech....... 8085
Ge 41:15 canst **u.** a dream to interpret it:........ 8085
Nu 16:30 **u.** that these men have provoked 3045
De 9:3 **U.** therefore this day, that the Lord.... 3045
De 9:6 **U.** therefore, that the Lord thy.......... 3045
De 28:49 whose tongue thou shalt not **u.**;........ 8085
2Ki 18:26 the Syrian language; for we **u.** it:....... 8085
1Ch 28:19 Lord made me **u.** in writing by his 7919
Ne 8:3 women, and those that could **u.**;......... 995
Ne 8:7 caused the people to **u.** the law:.......... 995
Ne 8:8 and caused them to **u.** the reading. 995
Ne 8:13 even to **u.** the words of the law......... 7919
Job 6:24 me to **u.** wherein I have erred. 995
Job 23:5 and **u.** what he would way unto me...... 995
Job 26:14 thunder of his power who can **u.**? 995
Job 32:9 neither do the aged **u.** judgment. 995
Job 36:29 any **u.** the spreadings of the clouds, ... 995
Ps 14:2 see if there were any that did **u.**,....... 7919
Ps 19:12 Who can **u.** his errors? cleanse 995
Ps 53:2 see if there were any that did **u.**,....... 7919
Ps 82:5 They knew not, neither will they **u.**; 995
Ps 92:6 not; neither doth a fool **u.** this. 995
Ps 94:8 **U.**, ye brutish among the people:......... 995
Ps 107:43 **u.** the lovingkindness of the Lord......... 995
Ps 119:27 to **u.** the way of thy precepts: 995
Ps 119:100 I **u.** more than the ancients, because.... 995
Pr 1:6 To **u.** a proverb, and the 995
Pr 2:5 shalt thou **u.** the fear of the Lord, ... 995
Pr 2:9 Then shalt thou **u.** righteousness, ... 995
Pr 8:5 O ye simple, **u.** wisdom: and, ye 995
Pr 14:8 of the prudent is to **u.** his way:........... 995
Pr 19:25 and he will **u.** knowledge..................... 995
Pr 20:24 how can a man then **u.** his own way? ... 995
Pr 28:5 Evil men **u.** not judgment: but they...... 995
Pr 28:5 they that seek the Lord **u.** all things. ... 995
Pr 29:19 for though he **u.** he will not answer...... 995
Isa 6:9 people, Hear ye indeed, but **u.** not; 995
Isa 6:10 and **u.** with the heart, and convert,...... 995
Isa 28:9 whom shall he make to **u.** doctrine? 995
Isa 28:19 be a vexation only to **u.** the report. 995
Isa 32:4 also of the rash shall **u.** knowledge,....... 995
Isa 33:19 tongue, that thou canst not **u.**............... 998
Isa 36:11 the Syrian language; for we **u.** it:........ 8085
Isa 41:20 and consider, and **u.** together,........... 7919
Isa 43:10 believe me, and **u.** that I am he: 995
Isa 44:18 their hearts, that they cannot **u.** 7919
Isa 56:11 they are shepherds that cannot **u.**.......... 995
Jer 9:12 is the wise man, that may **u.** this? 995
Eze 3:6 whose words thou canst not **u.**.......... 8085
Da 8:16 make this man to **u.** the vision. 995
Da 8:17 he said unto me, **U.**, O son of man:..... 995
Da 9:13 our iniquities, and **u.** thy truth.......... 7919
Da 9:23 therefore **u.** the matter, and.............. 995
Da 9:25 Know therefore and **u.**, that from....... 7919
Da 10:11 **u.** the words that I speak unto thee, ... 995
Da 10:12 that thou didst set thine heart to **u.**, ... 995
Da 10:14 make thee **u.** what shall befall thy........ 995
Da 11:33 they that **u.** among the people........... 7919
Da 12:10 and none of the wicked shall **u.**; 995
Da 12:10 but the wise shall **u.**. 995
Ho 4:14 people that doth not **u.** shall fall. 995
Ho 14:9 is wise, and he shall **u.** these things?.... 995
Mic 4:12 Lord, neither **u.** they his counsel:........ 995
Mt 13:13 **they hear not, neither do they u.**... *4920*
Mt 13:14 **ye shall hear, and shall not u.;**..... *4920*
Mt 13:15 **and should u. with their heart,**....... *4920*
Mt 15:10 and said unto them, **Hear, and u.:**.... *4920*
Mt 15:17 **Do not ye yet u., that whatsoever**.. *3539*
Mt 16:9 **ye not yet u., neither remember**.... *3539*
Mt 16:11 **How is it that ye do not u. that I**.. *3539*
Mt 24:15 **place (whoso readeth, let him u.:)**. *3539*
Mk 4:12 **hearing they may hear, and not u.** .*4920*
Mk 7:14 **unto me every one of you, and u.:**. *4920*
Mk 8:17 **perceive ye not yet, neither u.?**..... *4920*
Mk 8:21 them, **How is it that ye do not u.?**..*4920*
Mk 13:14 **(let him that readeth u.,) then let**. *3539*
Mk 14:68 not, neither **u.** I what thou sayest. *1987*
Lu 8:10 **and hearing they might not u.** *4920*
Lu 24:45 that they might **u.** the scriptures,....... *4920*
Joh 8:43 **Why do ye not u. my speech?**........ *1097*
Joh 12:40 nor **u.** with their heart, and be *3539*
Ac 24:11 Because that thou mayest **u.**, that...... *1097*
Ac 28:26 ye shall hear, and shall not **u.**............ *4920*
Ac 28:27 **u.** with their heart, and should be *4920*
Ro 15:21 they that have not heard shall **u.**........ *4920*
1Co 12:3 Wherefore I give you to **u.**, that no.... *1107*
1Co 13:2 of prophecy, and **u.** all mysteries. *1492*
Eph 3:4 **u.** my knowledge in mystery of.......... *3539*
Php 1:12 I would ye should **u.**, brethren, ... *1097*
Heb 11:3 Through faith we **u.** that the *3539*
2Pe 2:12 speak evil of things that they **u.** not;...... *50*

UNDERSTANDEST

Job 15:9 what **u.** thou, which is not in us?......... 995

Ps 139:2 thou **u.** my thought afar off. 995
Jer 5:15 not, neither **u.** what they say. 8085
Ac 8:30 said, **U.** thou what thou readest? *1097*

UNDERSTANDETH

1Ch 28:9 and **u.** all the imaginations of the 995
Job 28:23 God **u.** the way thereof, and he 995
Ps 49:20 Man that is in honour, and **u.** not, 995
Pr 8:9 They are all plain to him that **u.**, 995
Pr 14:6 knowledge is easy unto him that **u.**. 995
Jer 9:24 that he **u.** and knoweth me, that I 7919
Mt 13:19 **word of the kingdom, and u. it** *4920*
Mt 13:23 **he that heareth the word, and u** *4920*
Ro 3:11 There is none that **u.**, there is none *4920*
1Co 14:2 for no man **u.** him; howbeit in the *191*
1Co 14:16 seeing he **u.** not what thou sayest? *1492*

UNDERSTANDING

Ex 31:3 of God, in wisdom, and in **u.**, 8394
Ex 35:31 spirit of God, in wisdom, in **u.**, 8394
Ex 36:1 whom the Lord put wisdom and **u.** 8394
De 1:13 Take you wise men, and **u.**, and 995
De 4:6 your **u.** in the sight of the nations, 998
De 4:6 nation is a wise and **u.** people. 995
De 32:28 neither is there any **u.** in them. 8394
1Sa 25:3 and she was a woman of good **u.**, 7922
1Ki 3:9 Give...thy servant an **u.** heart 8085
1Ki 3:11 asked for thyself **u.** to discern 995
1Ki 3:12 given thee a wise and an **u.** heart; 995
1Ki 4:29 God gave Solomon wisdom and **u.** 8394
1Ki 7:14 he was filled with wisdom, and **u.**, 8394
1Ch 12:32 were men that had **u.** of the times, 998
1Ch 22:12 the Lord give thee wisdom and **u.**, 998
2Ch 2:12 son, endued with prudence and **u.**, 998
2Ch 2:13 a cunning man, endued with **u.**, 998
2Ch 26:5 who had **u.** in the visions of God: 995
Ezr 8:16 and for Elnathan, men of **u.** 995
Ezr 8:18 us they brought us a man of **u.**, 7922
Ne 8:2 and all that could hear with **u.**, 995
Ne 10:28 having knowledge, and having **u.**; 995
Job 12:3 But I have **u.** as well as you; I am 3824
Job 12:12 wisdom; and in length of days **u.** 8394
Job 12:13 strength, he hath counsel and **u.** 8394
Job 12:20 taketh away the **u.** of the aged. 2940
Job 17:4 thou hast hid their heart from **u.**: 7922
Job 20:3 of my **u.** causeth me to answer. 998
Job 26:12 by his **u.** he smiteth through the 8394
Job 28:12, 20 and where is the place of **u.**? 998
Job 28:28 and to depart from evil is **u.** 998
Job 32:8 of the Almighty giveth them **u.** 995
Job 34:10 hearken unto me, ye men of **u.**: 3824
Job 34:16 If now thou hast **u.**, hear this: 998
Job 34:34 Let men of **u.** tell me, and let a 3824
Job 38:4 the earth? declare, if thou hast **u.** 998
Job 38:36 or who hath given **u.** to the heart? 998
Job 39:17 neither hath he imparted to her **u.** 998
Ps 32:9 or as the mule, which have no **u.**: 995
Ps 47:7 the earth: sing ye praises with **u.** 7919
Ps 49:3 of my heart shall be of **u.** 8394
Ps 111:10 a good **u.** have all they that do his 7922
Ps 119:34 Give me **u.**, and I shall keep thy 995
Ps 119:73 give me **u.**, that I may learn thy 995
Ps 119:99 more **u.** than all my teachers: 7919
Ps 119:104 Through thy precepts I get **u.**: 995
Ps 119:125 give me **u.**, that I may know thy 995
Ps 119:130 light; it giveth **u.** unto the simple. 995
Ps 119:144 give me **u.**, and I shall live. 995
Ps 119:169 give me **u.** according to thy word. 995
Ps 147:5 of great power: his **u.** is infinite. 8394
Pr 1:2 to perceive the words of **u.**; 998
Pr 1:5 a man of **u.** shall attain unto wise 995
Pr 2:2 and apply thine heart to **u.**; 8394
Pr 2:3 and liftest up thy voice for **u.**; 8394
Pr 2:6 mouth cometh knowledge and **u.** 8394
Pr 2:11 preserve thee, **u.** shall keep thee: 8394
Pr 3:4 good **u.** in the sight of God and 7922
Pr 3:5 and lean not unto thine own **u.** 998
Pr 3:13 and the man that getteth **u.** 8394
Pr 3:19 earth; by **u.** hath he established the 8394
Pr 4:1 of a father, and attend to know **u.** 998
Pr 4:5 Get wisdom, get **u.**: forget it not; 998
Pr 4:7 and with all thy getting get **u.** 998
Pr 5:1 and bow thine ear to my **u.**: 8394
Pr 6:32 adultery with a woman lacketh **u.**: 3820
Pr 7:4 sister; and call **u.** thy kinswoman: 998
Pr 7:7 youths, a young man void of **u.**, 3820
Pr 8:1 cry? and **u.** put forth her voice? 8394
Pr 8:5 and, ye fools, be ye of an **u.** heart. 995
Pr 8:14 wisdom: I am **u.**; I have strength. 998
Pr 9:4 as for him that wanteth **u.**, she 3820
Pr 9:6 live; and go in the way of **u.** 998
Pr 9:10 and the knowledge of the holy is **u.** 998
Pr 9:16 as for him that wanteth **u.**, she 3820
Pr 10:13 In the lips of him that hath **u.** 995
Pr 10:13 the back of him that is void of **u.** 3820
Pr 10:23 but a man of **u.** hath wisdom. 8394
Pr 11:12 but a man of **u.** holdeth his peace. 8394
Pr 12:11 vain persons is void of **u.** 3820
Pr 13:15 Good **u.** giveth favour: but the 7922
Pr 14:29 is slow to wrath is of great **u.**: 8394
Pr 14:33 in the heart of him that hath **u.**: 995
Pr 15:14 that hath **u.** seeketh knowledge: 995
Pr 15:21 a man of **u.** walketh uprightly. 8394
Pr 15:32 he that heareth reproof getteth **u.** 3820
Pr 16:16 **u.** rather to be chosen than silver! 998
Pr 16:22 **U.** is a wellspring of life unto 7922
Pr 17:18 A man void of **u.** striketh hands, 3820
Pr 17:24 is before him that hath **u.**; but the 995
Pr 17:27 and a man of **u.** is of an excellent 8394
Pr 17:28 his lips is esteemed a man of **u.** 995
Pr 18:2 A fool hath no delight in **u.**, but 8394
Pr 19:8 he that keepeth **u.** shall find good. 8394
Pr 19:25 and reprove one that hath **u.**, and 995
Pr 20:5 but a man of **u.** will draw it out. 8394
Pr 21:16 wandereth out of the way of **u.** 7919
Pr 21:30 no wisdom nor **u.** nor counsel 8394
Pr 23:23 wisdom, and instruction, and **u.** 998
Pr 24:3 and by **u.** it is established: 8394
Pr 24:30 vineyard of the man void of **u.**; 3820
Pr 28:2 by a man of **u.** and knowledge the 995
Pr 28:11 the poor that hath **u.** searcheth him 995
Pr 28:16 The prince that wanteth **u.** is also 8394
Pr 30:2 man, and have not the **u.** of a man. 998
Ec 9:11 nor yet riches to men of **u.**, nor yet 995
Isa 11:2 spirit of wisdom and **u.**, the spirit 998
Isa 11:3 shall make him of quick **u.** in the 7306
Isa 27:11 on fire: for it is a people of no **u.**: 998
Isa 29:14 **u.** of their prudent men shall be hid. 998
Isa 29:16 him that framed it, He had no **u.**? 995
Isa 29:24 erred in spirit shall come to **u.**, 998
Isa 40:14 and shewed to him the way of **u.**? 8394
Isa 40:28 there is no searching of his **u.** 8394
Isa 44:19 is there knowledge nor **u.** to say, I 8394
Jer 3:15 feed you with knowledge and **u.** 7919
Jer 4:22 children, and they have none **u.**: 995
Jer 5:21 O foolish people, and without **u.**; 3820
Jer 51:15 stretched out the heaven by his **u.** 8394
Eze 28:4 with thine **u.** thou hast gotten thee 8394
Da 1:4 in knowledge, and **u.** science, 995
Da 1:17 Daniel had **u.** in all visions and 995
Da 1:20 in all matters of wisdom and **u.**, 998
Da 2:21 knowledge to them that know **u.**: 999
Da 4:34 mine **u.** returned unto me, and I 4486
Da 5:11 father light and **u.** and wisdom, 7924
Da 5:12 and **u.**, interpreting of dreams, 7924
Da 5:14 **u.** and excellent wisdom is found in 7924
Da 8:23 **u.** dark sentences, shall stand up. 995
Da 9:22 come forth to give thee skill and **u.** 998
Da 10:1 the thing, and had **u.** of the vision. 998
Da 11:35 And some of them of **u.** shall fall, 7919
Ho 13:2 idols according to their own **u.**, 8394
Ob 7 under thee: there is none **u.** in him. 8394
Ob 8 and **u.** out of the mount of Esau? 8394
Mt 15:16 said, **Are ye also yet without u.?** *801*
Mk 7:18 them, **Are ye so without u. also?** *801*
Mk 12:33 all the heart, and with all the **u.**, *4907*
Lu 1:3 having had perfect **u.** of all things *3877*
Lu 2:47 him were astonished at his **u.** *4907*
Lu 24:45 Then opened he their **u.**, that they *3563*
Ro 1:31 Without **u.**, covenantbreakers, *801*
1Co 1:19 to nothing the **u.** of the prudent. *4907*
1Co 14:14 prayeth, but my **u.** is unfruitful. *3563*
1Co 14:15 and I will pray with the **u.** also: *3563*
1Co 14:15 and I will sing with the **u.** also. *3563*
1Co 14:19 rather speak five words with my **u.**, *3563*
1Co 14:20 Brethren, be not children in **u.** *5424*
1Co 14:20 be ye children, but in **u.** be men. *5424*
Eph 1:18 eyes of your **u.** being enlightened; *1271*
Eph 4:18 Having the **u.** darkened, being *1271*
Eph 5:17 **u.** what the will of the Lord is. *4920*
Php 4:7 peace of God, which passeth all **u.**, *3563*
Col 1:9 in all wisdom and spiritual **u.**; *4907*
Col 2:2 riches of the full assurance of **u.**, *4907*
1Ti 1:7 **u.** neither what they say, nor *4920*
2Ti 2:7 Lord give thee **u.** in all things. *4907*
1Jo 5:20 is come, and hath given us an **u.**, *1271*
Re 13:18 him that hath **u.** count the number *3563*

UNDERSTOOD

Ge 43:23 knew not that Joseph **u.** them; 8085
De 32:29 they were wise, that they **u.** this, 7919
1Sa 4:6 they **u.** that the ark of the Lord 3045
1Sa 26:4 **u.** that Saul was come in very deed. 3045
2Sa 3:37 all the people and all Israel **u.** that 3045
Ne 8:12 **u.** the words that were declared 995
Ne 13:7 **u.** of the evil that Eliashib did for 995
Job 13:1 this, mine ear hath heard and **u.** it. 995
Job 42:3 have I uttered that I **u.** not; 995
Ps 73:17 of God; then **u.** I their end. 995
Ps 81:5 I heard a language that I **u.** not. 3045
Ps 106:7 Our fathers **u.** not thy wonders in 7919
Isa 40:21 ye not **u.** from the foundations of 995
Isa 44:18 They have not known nor **u.**: for he 995
Da 8:27 at the vision, but none **u.** it. 995
Da 9:2 I Daniel **u.** by books the number of 995
Da 10:1 and he **u.** the thing, and had 995
Da 12:8 And I heard, but I **u.** not: then said 995
Mt 13:51 them, **Have ye u. all these things?** *4920*
Mt 16:12 Then **u.** they how that he bade *4920*
Mt 17:13 the disciples **u.** that he spake unto *4920*
Mt 26:10 When Jesus **u.** it, he said unto *1097*
Mk 9:32 But they **u.** not that saying, and *50*
Lu 2:50 **u.** not the saying which he spake *4920*
Lu 9:45 they **u.** not this saying, and it was *50*
Lu 18:34 And they **u.** none of these things: *4920*
Joh 8:27 **u.** not that he spake to them of *1097*
Joh 10:6 **u.** not what things they were which *1097*
Joh 12:16 These things **u.** not his disciples at *1097*
Ac 7:25 his brethren would have **u.** how *4920*
Ac 7:25 deliver them: but they **u.** not. *4920*
Ac 23:27 having **u.** that he was a Roman. *3129*
Ac 23:34 when he **u.** that he was of Cilicia; *4441*
Ro 1:20 **u.** by the things that are made, *3539*
1Co 13:11 I **u.** as a child, I thought as a child: *5426*
1Co 14:9 by the tongue words easy to be **u.**, *2154*
2Pe 3:16 are some things hard to be **u.**, *1425*

UNDERTAKE See also UNDERTOOK.

Isa 38:14 Lord, I am oppressed; **u.** for me. 6148

UNDERTOOK

Es 9:23 Jews **u.** to do as they had begun, 6901

UNDO See also UNDONE.

Isa 58:6 to **u.** the heavy burdens, and to let 5425
Zep 3:19 that time I will **u.** all that afflict 6213

UNDONE

Nu 21:29 thou art **u.**, O people of Chemosh: 6
Jos 11:15 he left nothing **u.** of all that the 5493
Isa 6:5 Woe is me! for I am **u.**; because 1820
Mt 23:23 **done, and not to leave the other u**
Lu 11:42 **done, and not to leave the other u**

UNDRESSED

Le 25:5 gather the grapes of thy vine **u.** 5139
Le 25:11 the grapes in it of thy vine **u.** 5139

UNEQUAL

Eze 18:25, 29 are not your ways **u.**? 3808,8505

UNEQUALLY

2Co 6:14 not **u.** yoked together with *2086*

UNFAITHFUL

Pr 25:19 Confidence in an **u.** man in time of 898

UNFAITHFULLY

Ps 78:57 and dealt **u.** like their fathers: 898

UNFEIGNED

2Co 6:6 by the Holy Ghost, by love **u.**, *505*
1Ti 1:5 of a good conscience, and of faith **u.** *505*
2Ti 1:5 the **u.** faith that is in thee, which *505*
1Pe 1:22 Spirit unto **u.** love of the brethren, *505*

UNFRUITFUL

Mt 13:22 **the word, and he becometh u** *175*
Mk 4:19 **choke the word, and it becometh u.** *175*
1Co 14:14 but my understanding is **u.** *175*
Eph 5:11 with the **u.** works of darkness, *175*
Tit 3:14 necessary uses, that they be not **u.** *175*
2Pe 1:8 nor **u.** in the knowledge of our Lord. *175*

UNGIRDED

Ge 24:32 he **u.** his camels, and gave straw 6605

UNGODLINESS
Ro 1:18 revealed from heaven against all **u.** *763*
Ro 11:26 and shall turn away **u.** from Jacob: *763*
2Ti 2:16 for they will increase unto more **u.** *763*
Tit 2:12 denying **u.** and worldly lusts, we *763*

UNGODLY
2Sa 22:5 floods of **u.** men made me afraid; 1100
2Ch 19:2 Shouldest thou help the **u.**, and 7563
Job 16:11 God hath delivered me to the **u.**, ... 5760
Job 34:18 wicked? and to princes, Ye are **u.**? 7563
Ps 1:1 walketh not in the counsel of the **u.**,.... 7563
Ps 1:4 The **u.** are not so: but are like the 7563
Ps 1:5 **u.** shall not stand in the judgment, ... 7563
Ps 1:6 but the way of the **u.** shall perish 7563
Ps 3:7 hast broken the teeth of the **u.** 7563
Ps 18:4 floods of **u.** men made me afraid. 1100
Ps 43:1 cause against an **u.** nation: 3808,2623
Ps 73:12 these are the **u.**, who prosper in 7563
Pr 16:27 An **u.** man diggeth up evil: and in 1100
Pr 19:28 An **u.** witness scorneth judgment: 1100
Ro 4:5 on him that justifieth the **u.**, his *765*
Ro 5:6 in due time Christ died for the **u.** *765*
1Ti 1:9 for the **u.** and for sinners, for *765*
1Pe 4:18 where shall the **u.** and the sinner *765*
2Pe 2:5 in the flood upon the world of the **u.**; ... *765*
2Pe 2:6 unto those that after should live **u.**; *764*
2Pe 3:7 judgment and perdition of **u.** men *765*
Jude 4 **u.** men, turning the grace of our God ... *765*
Jude 15 to convince all that are **u.** among *763*
Jude 15 all their **u.** deeds which they have *763*
Jude 15 which they have **u.** committed, ... *764*
Jude 15 speeches which **u.** sinners have *765*
Jude 18 walk after their own **u.** lusts *763*

UNHOLY
Le 10:10 difference between holy and **u.**, ... 2455
1Ti 1:9 for **u.** and profane, for murderers of..... *462*
2Ti 3:2 to parents, unthankful, **u.**, ... *462*
Heb 10:29 he was sanctified, an **u.** thing, ... *2839*

UNICORN See also UNICORNS.
Nu 23:22 as it were the strength of an **u.** 7214
Nu 24:8 as it were the strength of an **u.** 7214
Job 39:9 Will the **u.** be willing to serve thee, ... 7214
Job 39:10 Canst thou bind the **u.** with his 7214
Ps 29:6 Lebanon and Sirion like a young **u.** 7214
Ps 92:10 thou exalt like the horn of an **u.**: 7214

UNICORNS
De 33:17 his horns are like the horns of **u.** 7214
Ps 22:21 heard me from the horns of the **u.** 7214
Isa 34:7 the **u.** shall come down with them, ... 7214

UNITE See also UNITED.
Ps 86:11 **u.** my heart to fear thy name. 3161

UNITED
Ge 49:6 mine honour, be not thou **u.** 3161

UNITY
Ps 133:1 brethren to dwell together in **u.**! 3162
Eph 4:3 to keep the **u.** of the Spirit in the *1775*
Eph 4:13 we all come in the **u.** of the faith, ... *1775*

UNJUST
Ps 43:1 me from the deceitful and **u.** man. 5766
Pr 11:7 and the hope of **u.** men perisheth. 205
Pr 28:8 **u.** gain increaseth his substance, ... 8636
Pr 29:27 An **u.** man is an abomination to 5766
Zep 3:5 not; but the **u.** knoweth no shame. 5767
Mt 5:45 **rain on the just and on the u.** *94*
Lu 16:8 **the lord commended the u. steward,** .. *93*
Lu 16:10 **is u. in the least is u. also in much** .. *94*
Lu 18:6 said, **Hear what the u. judge saith.** ... *93*
Lu 18:11 **as other men are, extortioners, u.,** ... *94*
Ac 24:15 of the dead, both of the just and **u.** *94*
1Co 6:1 go to law before the **u.**, and not *94*
1Pe 3:18 suffered for sins, the just for the **u.**, ... *94*
2Pe 2:9 to reserve the **u.** unto the day of *94*
Re 22:11 He that is **u.**, let him be **u.** still: 91

UNJUSTLY
Ps 82:2 How long will ye judge **u.**, and 5766
Isa 26:10 of uprightness will he deal **u.** 5765

UNKNOWN
Ac 17:23 this inscription, To The **U.** God. *57*
1Co 14:2 he that speaketh in an **u.** tongue ....
1Co 14:4 in an **u.** tongue edifieth himself; ....
1Co 14:13 that speaketh in an **u.** tongue pray............
1Co 14:14 if I pray in an **u.** tongue, my spirit...........
1Co 14:19 ten thousand words in an **u.** tongue. ....
1Co 14:27 If any man speak in an **u.** tongue, let........
2Co 6:9 As **u.**, and yet well known; as dying, ... *50*
Gal 1:22 was **u.** by face unto the churches of *50*

UNLADE
Ac 21:3 the ship was to **u.** her burden. *670*

UNLAWFUL
Ac 10:28 an **u.** thing for a man that is a Jew....... *111*
2Pe 2:8 day to day with their **u.** deeds:) *459*

UNLEARNED
Ac 4:13 that they were **u.** and ignorant men, ... *62*
1Co 14:16 the **u.** say Amen at thy giving of *2399*
1Co 14:23 there come in those that are **u.**, ... *2399*
1Co 14:24 one that believeth not, or one **u.**, ... *2399*
2Ti 2:23 foolish and **u.** questions avoid, ... *521*
2Pe 3:16 that are **u.** and unstable wrest, ... *261*

UNLEAVENED
Ge 19:3 did bake **u.** bread, and they did 4682
Ex 12:8 night, roast with fire, and **u.** bread; 4682
Ex 12:15 Seven days shall ye eat **u.** bread; 4682
Ex 12:17 shall observe the feast of **u.** bread; 4682
Ex 12:18 ye shall eat **u.** bread, until the one 4682
Ex 12:20 habitations shall ye eat **u.** bread. 4682
Ex 12:39 they baked **u.** cakes of the dough 4682
Ex 13:6 Seven days thou shalt eat **u.** bread, ... 4682
Ex 13:7 **U.** bread shall be eaten seven 4682
Ex 23:15 shalt keep the feast of **u.** bread: 4682
Ex 23:15 thou shalt eat **u.** bread seven days, ... 4682
Ex 29:2 **u.** bread, and cakes **u.** tempered 4682
Ex 29:2 and wafers **u.** anointed with oil: 4682
Ex 29:23 out of the basket of the **u.** bread 4682
Ex 34:18 feast of **u.** bread shalt thou keep. 4682
Ex 34:18 Seven days thou shalt eat **u.** bread, ... 4682
Le 2:4 **u.** cakes of fine flour mingled with 4682
Le 2:4 oil, or **u.** wafers anointed with oil. 4682
Le 2:5 a pan, it shall be of fine flour **u.**, ... 4682
Le 6:16 with **u.** bread shall it be eaten in 4682
Le 7:12 **u.** cakes mingled with oil, ... 4682
Le 7:12 and **u.** wafers anointed with oil, ... 4682
Le 8:2 rams, and a basket of **u.** bread; 4682
Le 8:26 And out of the basket of **u.** bread. 4682
Le 8:26 he took one **u.** cake, and a cake of 4682
Le 23:6 the feast of **u.** bread unto the Lord: ... 4682
Le 23:6 seven days ye must eat **u.** bread. 4682
Nu 6:15 and a basket of **u.** bread, cakes of 4682
Nu 6:15 wafers of **u.** bread anointed with 4682
Nu 6:17 Lord, with the basket of **u.** bread: 4682
Nu 6:19 and one **u.** cake out of the basket, ... 4682
Nu 6:19 one **u.** wafer, and shall put them 4682
Nu 9:11 eat it with **u.** bread and bitter 4682
Nu 28:17 seven days shall **u.** bread be eaten. 4682
De 16:3 seven days shalt thou eat **u.** bread 4682
De 16:8 Six days thou shalt eat **u.** bread: 4682
De 16:16 in the feast of **u.** bread, and in the 4682
Jos 5:11 **u.** cakes, and parched corn in the 4682
Jg 6:19 and **u.** cakes of an ephah of flour: 4682
Jg 6:20 Take the flesh and the **u.** cakes, ... 4682
Jg 6:21 touched the flesh and the **u.** cakes; 4682
Jg 6:21 the flesh and the **u.** cakes 4682
1Sa 28:24 kneaded it, and did bake **u.** bread 4682
2Ki 23:9 did eat of the **u.** bread among their 4682
1Ch 23:29 for the **u.** cakes, and for that which 4682
2Ch 8:13 year, even in the feast of **u.** bread, ... 4682
2Ch 30:13 people to keep the feast of **u.** bread ... 4682
2Ch 30:21 the feast of **u.** bread seven days 4682
2Ch 35:17 the feast of **u.** bread seven days. 4682
Ezr 6:22 the feast of **u.** bread seven days 4682
Eze 45:21 seven days; **u.** bread shall be eaten. ... 4682
Mt 26:17 first day of the feast of **u.** bread *106*
Mk 14:1 of the passover, and of **u.** bread: *106*
Mk 14:12 the first day of **u.** bread, when they *106*
Lu 22:1 Now the feast of **u.** bread drew nigh, ... *106*
Lu 22:7 Then came the day of **u.** bread, ... *106*
Ac 12:3 (Then were the days of **u.** bread.) *106*
Ac 20:6 Philippi after the days of **u.** bread, ... *106*
1Co 5:7 ye may be a new lump, as ye are **u.** *106*
1Co 5:8 the **u.** bread of sincerity and truth. *106*

UNLESS
Le 22:6 **u.** he wash his flesh with 3588,518
Nu 22:33 **u.** she had turned from me, surely 194
2Sa 2:27 **u.** thou hadst spoken, surely 3588,3884
Ps 27:13 **u.** I had believed to see the 3884
Ps 94:17 **U.** the Lord had been my help, my 3884
Ps 119:92 **U.** thy law had been my delights, I..... 3884
Pr 4:16 **u.** they cause some to fall. 518,3808
1Co 15:2 **u.** ye have believed in vain. *1622,1508*

UNLOOSE See also LOOSE.
Mk 1:7 not worthy to stoop down and **u.** *3089*
Lu 3:16 whose shoes I am not worthy to **u.** *3089*
Joh 1:27 shoe's latchet I am not worthy to **u.** .. *3089*

UNMARRIED
1Co 7:8 say therefore to the **u.** and widows, ... *22*
1Co 7:11 and if she depart, let her remain **u.**, ... *22*
1Co 7:32 He that is **u.** careth for the things *22*
1Co 7:34 The **u.** woman careth for the things *22*

UNMERCIFUL
Ro 1:31 natural affection, implacable, **u.** *415*

UNMINDFUL
De 32:18 Rock that begat thee thou art **u.**, ... 7876

UNMOVEABLE
Ac 27:41 stuck fast, and remained **u.**, ... *761*
1Co 15:58 brethren, be ye stedfast, **u.**, ... *277*

UNNI (un'-ni)
1Ch 15:18 and Jehiel, and **U.**, Eliab, and 6042
1Ch 15:20 and Jehiel, and **U.**, and Eliab, and 6042
Ne 12:9 Also Bakbukiah and **U.**, their 6042

UNOCCUPIED
Jg 5:6 the highways were **u.**, and the 2308

UNPERFECT
Ps 139:16 did see my substance, yet being **u.**; ....

UNPREPARED
2Co 9:4 come with me, and find you **u.**, ... *532*

UNPROFITABLE
Job 15:3 Should he reason with **u.** talk? or 5532
Mt 25:30 **cast ye the u. servant into outer** *888*
Lu 17:10 **you, say, We are u. servants:** *888*
Ro 3:12 way, they are together become **u.**; *889*
Tit 3:9 the law; for they are **u.** and vain. *512*
Phm 11 Which in time past was to thee **u.**, ... *890*
Heb 13:17 with grief: for that is **u.** for you. *255*

UNPROFITABLENESS
Heb 7:18 for the weakness and **u.** thereof. *512*

UNPUNISHED
Pr 11:21 hand, the wicked shall not be **u.**: 5352
Pr 16:5 join in hand, he shall not be **u.** 5352
Pr 17:5 is glad at calamities shall not be **u.** 5352
Pr 19:5,9 A false witness shall not be **u.**, ... 5352
Jer 25:29 name, and should ye be utterly **u.**? 5352
Jer 25:29 Ye shall not be **u.**; for I will call for 5352
Jer 30:11 will not leave thee altogether **u.** 5352
Jer 46:28 yet will I not leave thee wholly **u.** 5352
Jer 49:12 thou he that shall altogether go **u.**? 5352
Jer 49:12 thou shalt not go **u.**, but thou shalt 5352

UNQUENCHABLE
Mt 3:12 will burn up the chaff with **u.** fire. *762*
Lu 3:17 the chaff he will burn with fire **u.** *762*

UNREASONABLE
Ac 25:27 seemeth to me **u.** to send a prisoner, ... *249*
2Th 3:2 delivered from **u.** and wicked men: *824*

UNREBUKEABLE
1Ti 6:14 commandment without spot, **u.**, ... *423*

UNREPROVEABLE
Col 1:22 unblameable and **u.** in his sight: *410*

UNRIGHTEOUS
Ex 23:1 the wicked to be an **u.** witness, ... 2555
Job 27:7 riseth up against me as the **u.** 5767
Ps 71:4 the hand of the **u.** and cruel man, ... 5765
Isa 10:1 unto them that decree **u.** decrees, ... 205
Isa 55:7 way, and the **u.** man his thoughts: 205
Lu 16:11 **not been faithful in the u. mammon** .. *94*
Ro 3:5 Is God **u.** who taketh vengeance? *94*
1Co 6:9 **u.** shall not inherit the kingdom of *94*
Heb 6:10 God is not **u.** to forget your work *94*

UNRIGHTEOUSNESS
Le 19:15 Ye shall do no **u.** in judgment: 5766
Le 19:35 Ye shall do no **u.** in judgment, in 5766
Ps 92:15 my rock, and there is no **u.** in him, ... 5766
Jer 22:13 that buildeth his house by **u.**, ... 3808,6664
Lu 16:9 **friends of the mammon of u.**; *93*
Joh 7:18 **same is true, and no u. is in him.** *93*

Ro 1:18 all ungodliness and **u.** of men, *93*
Ro 1:18 of men, who hold the truth in **u.**; *93*
Ro 1:29 Being filled with all **u.**, fornication, *93*
Ro 2:8 but obey **u.**, indignation and wrath, *93*
Ro 3:5 if our **u.** commend the righteousness *93*
Ro 6:13 as instruments of **u.** unto sin: *93*
Ro 9:14 we say then? Is there **u.** with God? *93*
2Co 6:14 hath righteousness with **u.**? *458*
2Th 2:10 deceivableness of **u.** in them that *93*
2Th 2:12 not the truth, but had pleasure in **u.** *93*
Heb 8:12 For I will be merciful to their **u.**, *93*
2Pe 2:13 And shall receive the reward of **u.**, *93*
2Pe 2:15 Bosor, who loved the wages of **u.**; *93*
1Jo 1:9 sins, and to cleanse us from all **u.** *93*
1Jo 5:17 All **u.** is sin: and there is a sin not *93*

UNRIGHTEOUSLY
De 25:16 all that do **u.**, are an abomination 5766

UNRIPE
Job 15:33 shake off his **u.** grape as the vine, 1154

UNRULY
1Th 5:14 brethren, warn them that are **u.**, *813*
Tit 1:6 children not accused of riot or **u.** *506*
Tit 1:10 there are many **u.** and vain talkers *506*
Jas 3:8 it is an **u.** evil, full of deadly poison *183*

UNSATIABLE
Eze 16:28 because thou wast **u.**; yea, 1115,7654

UNSAVOURY
2Sa 22:27 froward thou wilt shew thyself **u.** 6617
Job 6:6 Can that which is **u.** be eaten 8602

UNSEARCHABLE
Job 5:9 doeth great things and **u.**; 369,2714
Ps 145:3 praised; and his greatness is **u.** 369,2714
Pr 25:3 and the heart of kings is **u.** 369,2714
Ro 11:33 how **u.** are his judgments, and his *419*
Eph 3:8 Gentiles the **u.** riches of Christ; *421*

UNSEEMLY
Ro 1:27 with men working that which is **u.**, *808*
1Co 13:5 Doth not behave itself **u.**, seeketh not

UNSHOD
Jer 2:25 Withhold thy foot from being **u.**, *3182*

UNSKILFUL
Heb 5:13 every one that useth milk is **u.** in *552*

UNSPEAKABLE
2Co 9:15 Thanks be unto God for his **u.** gift. *411*
2Co 12:4 into paradise, and heard **u.** words, *731*
1Pe 1:8 with joy **u.** and full of glory: *412*

UNSPOTTED
Jas 1:27 to keep himself **u.** from the world *784*

UNSTABLE
Ge 49:4 **U.** as water, thou shalt not excel; 6349
Jas 1:8 A double minded man is **u.** in all *182*
2Pe 2:14 cease from sin; beguiling **u.** souls: *793*
2Pe 3:16 that are unlearned and **u.** wrest, *793*

UNSTOPPED
Isa 35:5 and the ears of the deaf shall be **u.** 6605

UNTAKEN
2Co 3:14 remaineth the same vail **u.** *3361,348*

UNTEMPERED
Eze 13:10 others daubed it with **u.** morter: 8602
Eze 13:11 them which daub it with **u.** morter, 8602
Eze 13:14 that ye have daubed with **u.** morter, 8602
Eze 13:15 that have daubed it with **u.** morter, 8602
Eze 22:28 have daubed them with **u.** morter, 8602

UNTHANKFUL
Lu 6:35 **is kind unto the u. and to the evil.** *884*
2Ti 3:2 disobedient to parents, **u.**, unholy, *884*

UNTIL See also TILL.
Ge 8:5 continually **u.** the tenth month: 5704
Ge 8:7 **u.** the waters were dried up from 5704
Ge 24:19 **u.** they have done drinking. 5704,515
Ge 24:33 **u.** I have told mine errand. 5704,515
Ge 26:13 and grew **u.** he became very great: 5704
Ge 27:44 **u.** thy brother's fury turn 5704,834
Ge 27:45 **U.** thy brother's anger turn 5704
Ge 28:15 **u.** I have done that which I 5703,834
Ge 29:8 **u.** all the flocks be gathered 5704
Ge 32:4 Laban, and stayed there **u.** now: 5704
Ge 32:24 with him **u.** the breaking of the day. 5704
Ge 33:3 **u.** he came near to his brother. 5704
Ge 33:14 **u.** I come unto my lord unto Seir. 5704
Ge 34:5 held his peace **u.** they were come. 5704
Ge 39:16 by her, **u.** his lord came home 5704
Ge 41:49 very much, **u.** he left numbering; 5704
Ge 46:34 cattle from our youth even **u.** now, 5704
Ge 49:10 his feet, **u.** Shiloh come; 5704,3588
Ex 9:18 foundation thereof even **u.** now 5704
Ex 10:26 serve the Lord, **u.** we come thither 5704
Ex 12:6 keep it up **u.** the fourteenth day of 5704
Ex 12:10 nothing of it remain **u.**...morning; 5704
Ex 12:10 which remaineth of it **u.**...morning 5704
Ex 12:15 the first day **u.** the seventh day, 5704
Ex 12:18 **u.** the one and twentieth day of the 5704
Ex 12:22 door of his house **u.** the morning. 5704
Ex 10:20 of them left of it **u.** the morning, 5704
Ex 10:23 for you to be kept **u.** the morning. 5704
Ex 10:35 **u.** they came to a land inhabited; 5704
Ex 10:35 **u.** they came unto the borders of 5704
Ex 17:12 **u.** the going down of the sun 5704
Ex 23:18 sacrifice remain **u.** the morning. 5704
Ex 23:30 **u.** thou be increased, and inherit 5704
Ex 24:14 for us, **u.** we come again unto you: 5704
Ex 33:8 **u.** he was gone into the tabernacle. 5704
Ex 34:34 he took the vail off, **u.** he came out 5704
Ex 34:35 **u.** he went in to speak with him. 5704
Le 7:15 not leave any of it **u.** the morning. 5704
Le 8:33 **u.** the days of your consecration be 5704
Le 11:24 them shall be unclean **u.** the even. 5704
Le 11:25 clothes, and be unclean **u.** the even. 5704
Le 11:27 shall be unclean **u.** the even. 5704
Le 11:28 clothes, and be unclean **u.** the even: 5704
Le 11:31 dead, shall be unclean **u.** the even. 5704
Le 11:32 and it shall be unclean **u.** the even; 5704
Le 11:39 shall be unclean **u.** the even. 5704
Le 11:40 clothes, and be unclean **u.** the even: 5704
Le 11:40 clothes, and be unclean **u.** the even. 5704
Le 12:4 **u.** the days of her purifying be 5704
Le 14:46 up shall be unclean **u.** the even. 5704
Le 15:5, 6,7 and be unclean **u.** the even. 5704
Le 15:8 and be unclean **u.** the even.
Le 15:10 him shall be unclean **u.** the even: 5704
Le 15:10, 16,17,18,19,21,22,23,27, be unclean **u.** 5704
Le 15:11 and be unclean **u.** the even.
Le 16:17 **u.** he come out, and have made an 5704
Le 17:15 water, and be unclean **u.** the even: 5704
Le 19:6 if ought remain **u.** the third day, it 5704
Le 19:13 with thee all night **u.** the morning. 5704
Le 22:4 of the holy things, **u.** he be clean. 5704
Le 22:6 any such shall be unclean **u.** even, 5704
Le 22:30 leave none of it **u.** the morrow: 5704
Le 23:14 **u.** the selfsame day that ye have 5704
Le 25:22 eat...of old fruit **u.** the ninth year; 5704
Le 25:22 **u.** her fruits come in ye shall 5704
Le 25:28 bought it **u.** the year of jubile: 5704
Nu 4:3 and upward even **u.** fifty years old, 5704
Nu 4:23 and upward **u.** fifty years old shalt 5704
Nu 6:5 **u.** the days be fulfilled, in the 5704
Nu 9:15 appearance of fire, **u.** the morning. 5704
Nu 11:20 **u.** it come out at your nostrils, and 5704
Nu 14:19 people, from Egypt even **u.** now. 5704
Nu 14:33 **u.** your carcases be wasted in the 5704
Nu 19:7 priest shall be unclean **u.** the even. 5704
Nu 19:8 and shall be unclean **u.** the even. 5704
Nu 19:10 clothes, and be unclean **u.** the even: 5704
Nu 19:21 separation shall be unclean **u.** even. 5704
Nu 19:22 toucheth it shall be unclean **u.** even. 5704
Nu 20:17 **u.** we have passed thy borders. 5704
Nu 21:22 way, **u.** we be past thy borders. 5704
Nu 21:35 **u.** there was none left him alive: 5704
Nu 23:24 not lie down **u.** he eat of the prey, 5704
Nu 24:22 **u.** Asshur shall carry thee away 5704
Nu 32:13 **u.** all the generation, that had 5704
Nu 32:17 **u.** we have brought them unto 5704
Nu 32:18 **u.** the children of Israel have 5704
Nu 32:21 **u.** he hath driven out his enemies 5704
Nu 35:12 **u.** he stand before the congregation 5704
Nu 35:28 **u.** the death of the high priest: 5704
Nu 35:32 land, **u.** the death of the priest. 5704
De 1:31 went, **u.** ye came into this place 5704
De 2:14 **u.** we were come over the brook 5704
De 2:14 **u.** all the generation of the men of 5704
De 2:15 the host, **u.** they were consumed. 5704
De 2:29 **u.** I shall pass over Jordan into the 5704
De 3:3 we smote him **u.** none was left 5704
De 3:20 **U.** the Lord have given rest unto 5704
De 3:20 you, and **u.** they also possess the land
De 7:20 **u.** they that are left, and hide 5704
De 7:23 destruction, **u.** they be destroyed. 5704
De 7:24 thee, **u.** thou have destroyed them. 5704
De 9:7 **u.** ye came unto this place, ye have 5704
De 9:21 even **u.** it was as small as dust: 5704
De 11:5 **u.** ye came into this place; 5704
De 16:4 remain all night **u.** the morning.
De 20:20 war with thee, **u.** it be subdued. 5704
De 22:2 thee **u.** thy brother seek after it, 5704
De 28:20 for to do, **u.** thou be destroyed, 5704
De 28:20 and **u.** thou perish quickly; 5704
De 28:21 **u.** he have consumed thee from off 5704
De 28:22 shall pursue thee **u.** thou perish. 5704
De 28:24 upon thee, **u.** thou be destroyed. 5704
De 28:48 neck, **u.** he have destroyed thee. 5704
De 28:51 of thy land, **u.** thou be destroyed: 5704
De 28:51 sheep, **u.** he have destroyed thee. 5704
De 28:52 **u.** thy high and fenced walls come 5704
De 28:61 upon thee, **u.** thou be destroyed. 5704
De 31:24 in a book, **u.** they were finished, 5704
De 31:30 of this song, **u.** they were ended. 5704
Jos 1:15 **U.** the Lord have given your 5704
Jos 2:16 days, **u.** the pursuers be returned: 5704
Jos 2:22 **u.** the pursuers were returned: 5704
Jos 3:17 **u.** all the people were passed clean 5704
Jos 4:10 **u.** every thing was finished that 5704
Jos 4:23 **u.** ye were passed over, as the Lord 5704
Jos 4:23 before us, **u.** we were gone over: 5704
Jos 5:1 of Israel, **u.** we were passed over, 5704
Jos 6:10 mouth, **u.** the day I bid you shout; 5704
Jos 7:6 the ark of the Lord **u.** the eventide, 5704
Jos 7:13 **u.** ye take away the accursed thing 5704
Jos 8:24 the sword, **u.** they were consumed, 5704
Jos 8:26 **u.** he had utterly destroyed all the 5704
Jos 8:29 he hanged on a tree **u.** eventide: 5704
Jos 10:13 **u.** the people had avenged 5704
Jos 10:26 upon the trees **u.** the evening, 5704
Jos 10:27 which remain **u.** this very day. 5704
Jos 10:33 **u.** he had left him none remaining. 5704
Jos 11:8 **u.** they left them none remaining 5704
Jos 11:14 **u.** they had destroyed them, 5704
Jos 13:13 among the Israelites **u.** this day. 5704
Jos 20:6 **u.** he stand before the congregation 5704
Jos 20:6 **u.** the death of the high priest that 5704
Jos 20:9 **u.** he stood before the congregation 5704
Jos 22:17 we are not cleansed **u.** this day, 5704
Jos 23:13 **u.** ye perish from off this good land 5704
Jos 23:15 **u.** he have destroyed you from off 5704
Jg 4:24 **u.** they had destroyed Jabin king 5704
Jg 5:7 in Israel, **u.** that I Deborah arose, 5704
Jg 6:18 **u.** I come unto thee, and bring 5704
Jg 13:15 **u.** we shall have made ready a kid 5704
Jg 18:30 **u.** the day of the captivity of the 5704
Jg 19:8 they tarried **u.** afternoon, and they 5704
Jg 19:25 her all the night **u.** the morning: 5704
Jg 20:23 and wept before the Lord **u.** even, 5704
Jg 20:26 fasted that day **u.** even, and offered 5704
Ru 1:19 went **u.** they came to Beth-lehem. 5704
Ru 2:7 even from the morning **u.** now, 5704
Ru 2:17 she gleaned in the field **u.** even, 5704
Ru 2:21 they have ended all my 5704,518
Ru 3:3 **u.** he shall have done eating and 5704
Ru 3:13 liveth: lie down **u.** the morning. 5704
Ru 3:14 she lay at his feet **u.** the morning: 5704
Ru 3:18 **u.** thou know how the matter 5704,834
Ru 3:18 **u.** he have finished the thing 3588,518
1Sa 1:22 not go up **u.** the child be weaned, 5704
1Sa 1:23 tarry **u.** thou have weaned him; 5704
1Sa 1:23 her son suck **u.** she weaned him. 5704
1Sa 3:15 And Samuel lay **u.** the morning, 5704
1Sa 7:11 **u.** they came under Beth-car. 5704
1Sa 9:13 the people will not eat **u.** he come, 5704
1Sa 11:11 Ammonites **u.** the heat of the day: 5704
1Sa 14:9 Tarry **u.** we come to you; then we 5704
1Sa 14:24 that eateth any food **u.** evening 5704
1Sa 14:36 spoil them **u.** the morning light, 5704
1Sa 15:7 Havilah **u.** thou comest to Shur,
1Sa 15:18 against them **u.** they be consumed 5704
1Sa 15:35 to see Saul **u.** the day of his death: 5704
1Sa 17:52 **u.** thou come to the valley, 5704
1Sa 19:2 heed to thyself **u.** the morning, 5704
1Sa 19:23 **u.** he came to Naioth in Ramah. 5704
1Sa 20:41 with another, **u.** David exceeded. 5704
1Sa 25:36 less or more, **u.** the morning light. 5704
1Sa 30:4 **u.** they had no more power to 5704,834

2Sa 1:12 and fasted **u.** even, for Saul, and........ 5704
2Sa 4:3 were sojourners there **u.** this day.)..... 5704
2Sa 5:25 from Geba **u.** thou come to Gazer...... 5704
2Sa 10:5 Jericho **u.** your beards be grown,...... 5704
2Sa 15:24 **u.** all the people had done passing...... 5704
2Sa 15:28 **u.** there come word from you to........ 5704
2Sa 17:13 **u.** there be not one small stone.... 5704,834
2Sa 19:7 befell thee from thy youth **u.** now. 5704
2Sa 19:24 king departed **u.** the day he came 5704
2Sa 21:10 **u.** water dropped upon them out of 5704
2Sa 22:38 not again **u.** I had consumed them...... 5704
2Sa 23:10 **u.** his hand was weary,............. 5704,3588
1Ki 3:1 **u.** he had made an end of building...... 5704
1Ki 3:2 name of the Lord, **u.** those days........ 5704
1Ki 5:3 **u.** the Lord put them under the......... 5704
1Ki 6:22 **u.** he had finished all the house:......... 5704
1Ki 10:7 **u.** I came, and mine eyes had seen 5704
1Ki 11:16 **u.** he had cut off every male in.......... 5704
1Ki 11:40 in Egypt **u.** the death of Solomon......... 5704
1Ki 15:29 breathed, **u.** he had destroyed him, ... 5704
1Ki 17:14 **u.** the day that the Lord sendeth 5704
1Ki 18:26 Baal from morning even **u.** noon, ... 5704
1Ki 18:29 **u.** the time of the offering of the........ 5704
1Ki 22:11 **u.** thou have consumed them............ 5704
1Ki 22:27 of affliction, **u.** I come in peace.......... 5704
2Ki 6:25 **u.** an ass's head was sold for............ 5704
2Ki 7:3 another, Why sit we here **u.** we die? .. 5704
2Ki 8:6 that she left the land, even **u.** now..... 5704
2Ki 8:11 stedfastly, **u.** he was ashamed: 5704
2Ki 10:8 in of the gate **u.** the morning.............. 5704
2Ki 10:11 **u.** he left him none remaining............ 5704
2Ki 17:20 **u.** he had cast them out of his........... 5704
2Ki 17:23 **U.** the Lord removed Israel out of...... 5704
2Ki 18:32 **U.** I come and take you away to a...... 5704
2Ki 24:20 **u.** he had cast them out from his 5704
1Ch 5:22 in their steads **u.** the captivity........... 5704
1Ch 6:32 **u.** Solomon had built the house of 5704
1Ch 12:22 **u.** it was a great host, like the host.... 5704
1Ch 19:5 at Jericho **u.** your beards be grown,.... 5704
1Ch 28:20 **u.** thou hast finished all the work 5704
2Ch 8:8 make to pay tribute **u.** this day.......... 5704
2Ch 8:16 of the Lord, and **u.** it was finished...... 5704
2Ch 9:6 **u.** I came, and mine eyes had seen 5704
2Ch 16:12 **u.** his disease was exceeding great: 5704
2Ch 18:10 push Syria **u.** they be consumed 5704
2Ch 18:26 of affliction, **u.** I return in peace......... 5704
2Ch 18:34 against the Syrians **u.** the even:......... 5704
2Ch 21:15 **u.** thy bowels fall out by reason of 5704
2Ch 24:10 the chest, **u.** they had made an end..... 5704
2Ch 29:28 **u.** the burnt offering was finished....... 5704
2Ch 29:34 **u.** the other priests had sanctified 5704
2Ch 31:1 **u.** they had utterly destroyed them..... 5704
2Ch 35:14 burnt offerings and the fat **u.** night; 5704
2Ch 36:16 **u.** the wrath of the Lord arose 5704
2Ch 36:20 **u.** the reign of the kingdom of........... 5704
2Ch 36:21 **u.** the land had enjoyed her............... 5704
Ezr 4:5 even **u.** the reign of Darius king of..... 5704
Ezr 4:21 **u.** another commandment shall be....... 5704
Ezr 5:16 **u.** now hath it been in building,.......... 5704
Ezr 8:29 **u.** ye weigh them before the chief...... 5704
Ezr 9:4 astonied **u.** the evening sacrifice......... 5704
Ezr 10:14 **u.** the fierce wrath of our God for...... 5704
Ne 7:3 be opened **u.** the sun be hot; 5704
Ne 8:3 gate from the morning **u.** midday, ... 5704
Ne 12:23 **u.** the days of Johanan the son of....... 5704
Job 14:13 me secret, **u.** thy wrath be past, ... 5704
Job 26:10 **u.** the day and night come to an 5704
Ps 36:2 **u.** his iniquity be found to be hateful.........
Ps 57:1 **u.** these calamities be overpast 5704
Ps 71:18 **u.** I have shewed thy strength unto 5704
Ps 73:17 **U.** I went into the sanctuary of God; .. 5704
Ps 94:13 **u.** the pit be digged for the wicked..... 5704
Ps 104:23 and to his labour **u.** the evening......... 5704
Ps 105:19 **U.** the time that his word came: 5704
Ps 110:1 **u.** I make thine enemies thy............. 5704
Ps 112:8 **u.** he see his desire upon his............ 5704
Ps 123:2 **u.** that he have mercy upon us 5704
Ps 132:5 **U.** I find out a place for the Lord,...... 5704
Pr 7:18 take our fill of love **u.** the morning: 5704
Ca 2:17 **U.** the day break, and the shadows..... 5704
Ca 3:11 **u.** I had brought him into my............ 5704
Ca 4:6 **U.** the day break, and the shadows..... 5704
Ca 8:4 nor awake my love, **u.** he please........ 5704
Isa 5:11 that continue **u.** night, till wine ....
Isa 6:11 **U.** the cities be wasted without 5704
Isa 26:20 **u.** the indignation be overpast............ 5704
Isa 32:15 **U.** the spirit be poured upon us 5704
Isa 36:17 **U.** I come and take you away to a...... 5704
Isa 39:6 have laid up in store **u.** this day,........ 5704
Isa 62:1 **u.** the righteousness...go forth as........ 5704
Jer 23:20 not return, **u.** he have executed,........ 5704
Jer 27:7 **u.** the very time of his land come:....... 5704
Jer 27:8 **u.** I have consumed them by his 5704
Jer 27:22 they be **u.** the day that I visit them, ... 5704
Jer 30:24 shall not return, **u.** he have done it, ... 5704
Jer 30:24 **u.** he hath performed the intents of.... 5704
Jer 32:5 and there shall he be **u.** I visit him, ... 5704
Jer 36:23 **u.** all the roll was consumed in the..... 5704
Jer 37:21 **u.** all the bread in the city were......... 5704
Jer 38:28 **u.** the day that Jerusalem was 5704
Jer 44:27 famine, **u.** there be an end of them 5704
Jer 52:34 a portion **u.** the day of his death, ... 5704
Eze 21:27 more, **u.** he come whose right it is;.... 5704
Eze 33:22 **u.** he came to me in the morning; 5704
Eze 46:2 shall not be shut **u.** the evening......... 5704
Da 4:32 **u.** thou know that the most High 5704
Da 7:22 **U.** the Ancient of days came, and....... 5704
Da 7:25 **u.** a time...times and the dividing....... 5704
Da 9:27 desolate,...**u.** the consummation,........ 5704
Ho 7:4 the dough, **u.** it be leavened............. 5704
Mic 5:3 **u.** the time...she which travaileth....... 5704
Mic 7:9 **u.** he plead my cause, and execute....... 5704
Zep 3:8 **u.** the day that I rise up to the prey: ....
Mt 1:17 **u.** the carrying away into Babylon *2193*
Mt 2:13 be thou there **u.** I bring thee word: *2193*
Mt 2:15 was there **u.** the death of Herod: *2193*
Mt 11:12 **days of John the Baptist u. now**.... *2193*
Mt 11:13 **and the law prophesied u. John**...... *2193*
Mt 11:23 **would have remained u. this day**... *3360*
Mt 13:30 **both grow together u. the harvest:** .*3360*
Mt 17:9 **u. the Son of man be risen again** .. *2193*
Mt 18:22 **say not unto thee, U. seven times:**. *2193*
Mt 18:22 **times: but, U. seventy times seven**..*2193*
Mt 24:38 **u. the day that Noe entered into**..... *891*
Mt 24:39 **And knew not u. the flood came,**... *2193*
Mt 26:29 **u. that day when I drink it new** *2193*
Mt 27:64 be made sure **u.** the third day, ... *2193*
Mt 28:15 among the Jews **u.** this day.............. *3360*
Mk 14:25 **u. that day that I drink it new**...... *2193*
Mk 15:33 the whole land **u.** the ninth hour *2193*
Lu 1:20 **u.** the day that these things shall be..... *891*
Lu 13:35 **u. the time...when ye shall say,**..... *2193*
Lu 15:4 **that which is lost, u. he find it?**...... *2193*
Lu 16:16 **and the prophets were u. John:**..... *2193*
Lu 17:27 **u. the day that Noe entered into**..... *891*
Lu 21:24 **u. the times of the Gentiles be**........ *891*
Lu 22:16 **u. it be fulfilled in the kingdom of**.*2193*
Lu 22:18 **u. the kingdom of God shall come**..*2193*
Lu 23:44 over all the earth **u.** the ninth hour..... *2193*
Lu 24:49 **u. ye be endued with power from** .. *2193*
Joh 2:10 hast kept the good wine **u.** now......... *2193*
Joh 9:18 **u.** they called the parents of him........ *2193*
Ac 1:2 **U.** the day in which he was taken........ *891*
Ac 2:35 **U.** I make thy foes thy footstool *2193*
Ac 3:21 **u.** the times of restitution of all........... *891*
Ac 10:30 ago I was fasting **u.** this hour; *3360*
Ac 13:20 fifty years, **u.** Samuel the prophet *2193*
Ac 20:7 continued his speech **u.** midnight........ *3360*
Ac 21:26 **u.**...an offering should be offered......... *2193*
Ac 23:1 conscience before God **u.** this day........ *891*
Ac 23:14 eat nothing **u.** we have slain Paul *2193*
Ro 5:13 (For **u.** the law sin was in the world: ... *891*
Ro 8:22 travaileth in pain together **u.** now *891*
Ro 11:25 **u.** the fulness of the Gentiles.............. *891*
1Co 4:5 **u.** the Lord come, who both will......... *2193*
1Co 16:8 will tarry at Ephesus **u.** Pentecost...... *2193*
2Co 3:14 **u.** this day remaineth the same vail...... *891*
Ga 4:2 **u.** the time appointed of the father....... *891*
Ga 4:19 again **u.** Christ be formed in you, ... *891*
Eph 1:14 **u.**...redemption of the purchased........ *1519*
Php 1:5 gospel from the first day **u.** now;......... *891*
Php 1:6 it **u.** the day of Jesus Christ: *891*
2Th 2:7 let, **u.** he be taken out of the way...... *2193*
1Ti 6:14 **u.** the appearing of our Lord............. *3360*
Heb 1:13 **u.** I make thine enemies thy.............. *2193*
Heb 9:10 them **u.** the time of reformation.......... *3360*
Jas 5:7 **u.** he receive the early and latter *2193*
2Pe 1:19 **u.** the day dawn, and the day star...... *2193*
1Jo 2:9 brother, is in darkness even **u.** now.... *2193*
Re 6:11 **u.** their fellowservants also and.......... *2193*
Re 17:17 **u.** the words of God...be fulfilled......... *891*
Re 20:5 **u.**...thousand years were finished....... *2193*

UNTIMELY
Job 3:16 a hidden **u.** birth I had not been;........ 5309
Ps 58:8 like the **u.** birth of a woman, that........ 5309
Ec 6:3 that an **u.** birth is better than he........ 5309
Re 6:13 as a fig tree casteth her **u.** figs,.......... *3653*

UNTO See in the APPENDIX; also HEREUNTO; THEREUNTO; WHEREUNTO.

UNTOWARD
Ac 2:40 from this **u.** generation..................... *4646*

UNWALLED
De 3:5 beside **u.** towns a great many............ 6521
Es 9:19 villages, that dwelt in the **u.** towns, ... 6519
Eze 38:11 will go up to the land of **u.** villages; ....

UNWASHEN
Mt 15:20 **to eat with u. hands defileth not a**.. *449*
Mk 7:2 defiled, that is...with **u.**, hands,............ *449*
Mk 7:5 elders, but eat bread with **u.** hands?..... *449*

UNWEIGHED
1Ki 7:47 And Solomon left all the vessels **u.**, ...

UNWISE
De 32:6 O foolish people and **u.**?............ 3808,2450
Ho 13:13 he is an **u.** son; for he should..... 3808,2450
Ro 1:14 both to the wise, and to the **u.** *453*
Eph 5:17 Wherefore be ye not **u.**, but............... *878*

UNWITTINGLY
Le 22:14 if a man eat of the holy thing **u.**,......... 7684
Jos 20:3 any person unawares and **u.**........ 1097,1847
Jos 20:5 he smote his neighbour **u.**, ... 1097,1847

UNWORTHILY
1Co 11:27 and drink this cup of the Lord, **u.**,....... *371*
1Co 11:29 For he that eateth and drinketh **u.**, ... *371*

UNWORTHY
Ac 13:46 **u.** of everlasting life,.................. *3756,514*
1Co 6:2 **u.** to judge the smallest matters?.......... *370*

UP See in the APPENDIX; also UPBRAID; UPHOLD; UPON; UPPER; UPRIGHT; UPRISING; UPROAR; UPSIDE; UPWARD.

UPBRAID See also UPBRAIDED; UPBRAIDETH.
Jg 8:15 with whom ye did **u.** me, saying, ... 2778
Mt 11:20 Then began he to **u.** the cities........... *3679*

UPBRAIDED
Mk 16:14 and **u.** them with their unbelief.......... *3679*

UPBRAIDETH
Jas 1:5 to all men liberally, and **u.** not;.......... *3679*

UPHARSIN (u-far'-sin) See also PERES.
Da 5:25 written, Mene, Mene, Tekel, **U.**........ 6537

UPHAZ (u'-faz)
Jer 10:9 Tarshish, and gold from **U.**, the 210
Da 10:5 were girded with fine gold of **U.**:.......... 210

UPHELD
Isa 63:5 unto me; and my fury, it **u.** me 5564

UPHOLD See also UPHELD; UPHOLDEN; UPHOLDEST; UPHOLDETH; UPHOLDING.
Ps 51:12 and **u.** me with thy free spirit............ 5564
Ps 54:4 Lord is with them that **u.** my soul...... 5564
Ps 119:116 **U.** me according unto thy word,......... 5564
Pr 29:23 but honour shall **u.** the humble in....... 8551
Isa 41:10 I will **u.** thee with the right hand of.... 8551
Isa 42:1 Behold my servant, whom I **u.**;........... 8551
Isa 63:5 I wondered...there was none to **u.**: 5564
Eze 30:6 They also that **u.** Egypt shall fall;....... 5564

UPHOLDEN
Job 4:4 Thy words have **u.** him that was........ 6965
Pr 20:28 and his throne is **u.** by mercy............ 5582

UPHOLDEST
Ps 41:12 me, thou **u.** me in mine integrity,....... 8551

UPHOLDETH
Ps 37:17 but the Lord **u.** the righteous............ 5564
Ps 37:24 for the Lord **u.** him with his hand....... 5564
Ps 63:8 after thee: thy right hand **u.** me......... 8551
Ps 145:14 Lord **u.** all that fall, and raiseth......... 5564

UPHOLDING
Heb 1:3 **u.** all things by the word of his.......... *5342*

UPON See in the APPENDIX; also THEREUPON; WHEREUPON.

UPPER See also UPPERMOST.
Ex 12:7 on the **u.** door post of the houses, ... 4947

Le 13:45 shall put a covering upon his **u.** lip, ... 8222
De 24:6 the nether or the **u.** millstone to 7393
Jos 15:19 And he gave her the **u.** springs, ... 5942
Jos 16:5 unto Beth-horon the **u.**; 5945
Jg 1:15 Caleb gave her the **u.** springs and 5942
2Ki 1:2 a lattice in his **u.** chamber that 5944
2Ki 18:17 stood by the conduit of the **u.** pool, ... 5945
2Ki 23:12 the top of the **u.** chamber of Ahaz, ... 5944
1Ch 7:24 Beth-horon the nether, and the **u.**, ... 5945
1Ch 28:11 and of the **u.** chambers thereof, ... 5944
2Ch 3:9 he overlaid the **u.** chambers with 5944
2Ch 8:5 Also he built Beth-horon the **u.**, ... 5945
2Ch 32:30 also stopped the **u.** watercourse of..... 5945
Isa 7:3 end of the conduit of the **u.** pool 5945
Isa 36:2 stood by the conduit of the **u.** pool..... 5945
Eze 42:5 Now the **u.** chambers were shorter: ... 5945
Zep 2:14 shall lodge in the **u.** lintels of it; 3730
Mk 14:15 **shew you a large u. room furnished** *508*
Lu 22:12 **shew you a large u. room furnished:** *508*
Ac 1:13 they went up into an **u.** room, ... *5253*
Ac 9:37 they laid her in an **u.** chamber *5253*
Ac 9:39 brought him into the **u.** chamber: *5253*
Ac 19:1 having passed through the **u.** coasts..... *510*
Ac 20:8 many lights in the **u.** chamber, ... *5250*

UPPERMOST
Ge 40:17 **u.** basket there was of all manner 5945
Isa 17:6 berries in the top of the **u.** bough, ...
Isa 17:9 a forsaken bough, and an **u.** branch, ...
Mt 23:6 **love the u. rooms at feasts, and** *4411*
Mk 12:39 **and the u. rooms at feasts:** *4411*
Lu 11:43 **love the u. seats in...synagogues,** ... *4410*

UPRIGHT
Ge 37:7 lo, my sheaf arose, and also stood **u.**; ....
Ex 15:8 the floods stood **u.** as an heap, ...
Le 26:13 of your yoke, and made you go **u.** 6968
1Sa 29:6 thou hast been **u.**, and thy going 3477
2Sa 22:24 was also **u.** before him, and have 8549
2Sa 22:26 merciful, and with the **u.** man 8549
2Sa 22:26 thou wilt shew thyself **u.** 8552
2Ch 29:34 the Levites were more **u.** in heart 3477
Job 1:1 and that man was perfect and **u.**, ... 3477
Job 1:8 a perfect and an **u.** man, one that 3477
Job 2:3 a perfect and an **u.** man, one that 3477
Job 8:6 If thou wert pure and **u.**; surely 3477
Job 12:4 just **u.** man is laughed to scorn 8549
Job 17:8 **U.** men shall be astonied at this, ... 3477
Ps 7:10 God, which saveth the **u.** in heart 3477
Ps 11:2 may privily shoot at the **u.** in heart..... 3477
Ps 11:7 his countenance doth behold the **u.** 3477
Ps 18:23 I was also **u.** before him, and I 8549
Ps 18:25 thyself merciful; with an **u.** man 8549
Ps 18:25 thou wilt shew thyself **u.**; 8549,8552
Ps 19:13 then shall I be **u.**, and I shall be 8552
Ps 20:8 fallen: but we are risen, and stand **u.** ....
Ps 25:8 Good and **u.** is the Lord: therefore..... 3477
Ps 32:11 for joy, all ye that are **u.** in heart....... 3477
Ps 33:1 for praise is comely for the **u.** 3477
Ps 36:10 thy righteousness to the **u.** in heart.... 3477
Ps 37:14 slay such as be of **u.** conversation 3477
Ps 37:18 Lord knoweth the days of the **u.**: 8549
Ps 37:37 perfect man, and behold the **u.**: 3477
Ps 49:14 **u.** shall have dominion over them 3477
Ps 64:10 and all the **u.** in heart shall glory 3477
Ps 92:15 To shew that the Lord is **u.**: he is 3477
Ps 94:15 all the **u.** in heart shall follow it 3477
Ps 97:11 and gladness for the **u.** in heart 3477
Ps 111:1 heart, in the assembly of the **u.**, ... 3477
Ps 112:2 generation of the **u.** shall be blessed... 3477
Ps 112:4 Unto the **u.** there ariseth light in........ 3477
Ps 119:137 O Lord, and **u.** are thy judgments 3477
Ps 125:4 to them that are **u.** in their hearts...... 3477
Ps 140:13 the **u.** shall dwell in thy presence 3477
Pr 2:21 For the **u.** shall dwell in the land, ... 3477
Pr 10:29 of the Lord is strength to the **u.**: 8537
Pr 11:3 The integrity of the **u.** shall guide 3477
Pr 11:6 righteousness of the **u.** shall deliver.... 3477
Pr 11:11 By the blessing of the **u.** the city is..... 3477
Pr 11:20 are **u.** in their way are his delight 8549
Pr 12:6 mouth of the **u.** shall deliver them....... 3477
Pr 13:6 keepeth him that is **u.** in the way: 8537
Pr 14:11 tabernacle of the **u.** shall flourish........ 3477
Pr 15:8 the prayer of the **u.** is his delight 3477
Pr 16:17 The highway of the **u.** is to depart 3477
Pr 21:18 and the transgressor for the **u.** 3477
Pr 21:29 as for the **u.**, he directeth his way 3477
Pr 28:10 the **u.** shall have good things in 8549
Pr 29:10 The bloodthirsty hate the **u.**: but 8535
Pr 29:27 is **u.** in the way is abomination to....... 3477
Ec 7:29 found, that God had made man **u.**; 3477
Ec 12:10 that which was written was **u.**, ... 3476
Ca 1:4 more than wine: the **u.** love thee 4339
Isa 26:7 thou, most **u.**, dost weigh the path 3477
Jer 10:5 They are **u.** as the palm tree, but 4749
Da 8:18 but he touched me, and set me **u.** 5977
Da 10:11 I speak unto thee, and stand **u.**: 5977
Da 11:17 kingdom, and **u.** ones with him; 3477
Mic 7:2 and there is none **u.** among men: 3477
Mic 7:4 **u.** is sharper than a thorn hedge: 3477
Hab 2:4 which is lifted up is not **u.** in him: 3474
Ac 14:10 a loud voice, Stand **u.** on thy feet *3717*

UPRIGHTLY
Ps 15:2 He that walketh **u.**, and worketh 8549
Ps 58:1 do ye judge **u.**, O ye sons of men?..... 4339
Ps 75:2 the congregation I will judge **u.** 4339
Ps 84:11 withhold from them that walk **u.** 8549
Pr 2:7 is a buckler to them that walk **u.** 8537
Pr 10:9 He that walketh **u.** walketh surely: 8537
Pr 15:21 man of understanding walketh **u.** 3474
Pr 28:18 Whoso walketh **u.** shall be saved: 8549
Isa 33:15 righteously, and speaketh **u.**; 4339
Am 5:10 they abhor him that speaketh **u.** 8549
Mic 2:7 do good to him that walketh **u.**? 3477
Ga 2:14 they walked not **u.** according to *3716*

UPRIGHTNESS
De 9:5 or for the **u.** of thine heart, dost 3476
1Ki 3:6 and in **u.** of heart with thee; 3483
1Ki 9:4 in integrity of heart, and in **u.**, ... 3476
1Ch 29:17 the heart, and hast pleasure in **u.** 3476
1Ch 29:17 **u.** of mine heart I have willingly 4339
Job 4:6 thy hope, and the **u.** of thy ways? 8537
Job 33:3 shall be of the **u.** of my heart: 3476
Job 33:23 thousand, to shew unto man his **u.** 3476
Ps 9:8 judgment to the people in **u.** 4339
Ps 25:21 Let integrity and **u.** preserve me; 3476
Ps 111:8 ever, and are done in truth and **u.** 3477
Ps 119:7 I will praise thee with **u.** of heart, ... 3476
Ps 143:10 good; lead me into the land of **u.** 4334
Pr 2:13 Who leave the paths of **u.**, to walk 3476
Pr 14:2 He that walketh in his **u.** feareth 3476
Pr 28:6 is the poor that walketh in his **u.**, ... 8537
Isa 26:7 The way of the just is **u.**: thou, ... 4339
Isa 26:10 land of **u.** will he deal unjustly, ... 5229
Isa 57:2 beds, each one walking in his **u.** 5228

UPRISING
Ps 139:2 my downsitting and mine **u.**, ... 6965

UPROAR
1Ki 1:41 noise of the city being in an **u.**? 1993
Mt 26:5 there be an **u.** among the people *2351*
Mk 14:2 lest there be an **u.** of the people *2351*
Ac 17:5 and set all the city on an **u.**, ... *2350*
Ac 19:40 called in question for this day's **u.**, ... *4714*
Ac 20:1 And after the **u.** was ceased, Paul *2351*
Ac 21:31 that all Jerusalem was in an **u.** *4797*
Ac 21:38 before these days madest an **u.**, ... *387*

UPSIDE
2Ki 21:13 wiping it, and turning it **u.** 5921,6440
Ps 146:9 way of the wicked he turneth **u.** down. .....
Isa 24:1 waste, and turneth it **u.** down, ... 5921,6440
Isa 29:16 your turning of things **u.** down shall ....
Ac 17:6 that have turned the world **u.** down *389*

UPWARD
Ge 7:20 Fifteen cubits **u.** did the waters 4605
Ex 38:26 from twenty years old and **u.**, ... 4605
Nu 1:3 From twenty years old and **u.**, all 4605
Nu 1:18, 20,22,24,26,28,30,32,34,36,38,40,
42,45 from twenty years old and **u.**, ... 4605
Nu 3:15 every male from a month old and **u.** ... 4605
Nu 3:22, 28,34,39,40,43 a month old and **u.**, ... 4605
Nu 4:3, 23,30,35,39,43,47 years old and **u.** 4605
Nu 8:24 twenty and five years old and **u.** 4605
Nu 14:29 from twenty years old and **u.**, ... 4605
Nu 26:2 from twenty years old and **u.**, ... 4605
Nu 26:4 from twenty years old and **u.**; 4605
Nu 26:62 all males from a month old and **u.** 4605
Nu 32:11 from twenty years old and **u.**, ... 4605
Jg 1:36 to Akrabbim, from the rock, and **u.** ... 4605
1Sa 9:2 from his shoulders and **u.** he was 4605
1Sa 10:23 people from his shoulders and **u.** 4605
2Ki 3:21 were able to put an armour, and **u.**, ... 4605
2Ki 19:30 root downward, and bear fruit **u.** 4605
1Ch 23:3 the age of thirty years and **u.** 4605
1Ch 23:24 the age of twenty years and **u.** 4605
2Ch 31:16 males, from three years old and **u.**, ... 4605
2Ch 31:17 from twenty years old and **u.**, ... 4605
Ezr 3:8 from twenty years old and **u.**, ... 4605
Job 5:7 unto trouble, as the sparks fly **u.** 1361
Ec 3:21 the spirit of man that goeth **u.**, ... 4605
Isa 8:21 king and their God, and look **u.** 4605
Isa 37:31 root downward, and bear fruit **u.** 4605
Isa 38:14 mine eyes fail with looking **u.** 4791
Eze 1:11 their wings were stretched **u.**; 4605
Eze 1:27 the appearance of his loins even **u.**, ... 4605
Eze 8:2 from his loins even **u.**, as the 4605
Eze 41:7 a winding about still **u.** to the side 4605
Eze 41:7 went still **u.** round about the 4605
Eze 41:7 breadth of the house was still **u.**, ... 4605
Eze 43:15 altar and **u.** shall be four horns 4605
Hag 2:15 you, consider from this day and **u.**, ... 4605
Hag 2:18 Consider now from this day and **u.**, ... 4605

UR (ur)
Ge 11:28 his nativity, in **U.** of the Chaldees 218
Ge 11:31 with them from **U.** of the Chaldees, ... 218
Ge 15:7 thee out of **U.** of the Chaldees, ... 218
1Ch 11:35 the Hararite, Eliphal the son of **U.**, ... 218
Ne 9:7 him forth out of **U.** of the Chaldees, ... 218

URBANE (ur'-bane)
Ro 16:9 Salute **U.**, our helper in Christ, ... *3779*

URGE See also URGED.
Lu 11:53 the Pharisees began to **u.** him *1758*

URGED
Ge 33:11 and he **u.** him, and he took it 6484
Jg 16:16 daily with her words, and **u.** him, ... 509
Jg 19:7 depart, his father in law **u.** him: 6484
2Ki 2:17 they **u.** him till he was ashamed, ... 6484
2Ki 5:16 And he **u.** him to take it; but he 6484
2Ki 5:23 he **u.** him, and bound two talents 6555

URGENT
Ex 12:33 the Egyptians were **u.** upon the 2388
Da 3:22 the king's commandment was **u.**, ... 2685

URI (u'-ri)
Ex 31:2 by name Bezaleel the son of **U.**, ... 221
Ex 35:30 by name Bezaleel the son of **U.**, ... 221
Ex 38:22 And Bezaleel the son of **U.**, the son..... 221
1Ki 4:19 Geber the son of **U.** was in the 221
1Ch 2:20 And Hur begat **U.**, and **U.** begat 221
2Ch 1:5 that Bezaleel the son of **U.**, the son 221
Ezr 10:24 Shallum, and Telem, and **U.** 221

URIAH (u-ri'-ah) See also URIAH'S; URIAS; URIJAH.
2Sa 11:3 Eliam, the wife of **U.** the Hittite? 223
2Sa 11:6 saying, Send me **U.** the Hittite 223
2Sa 11:6 And Joab sent **U.** to David. 223
2Sa 11:7 And when **U.** was come unto him, ... 223
2Sa 11:8 And David said to **U.**, Go down to 223
2Sa 11:8 And **U.** departed out of the king's 223
2Sa 11:9 **U.** slept at the door of the king's 223
2Sa 11:10 **U.** went not down unto his house, ... 223
2Sa 11:10 David said unto **U.**, Camest thou 223
2Sa 11:11 **U.** said unto David, The ark, and 223
2Sa 11:12 David said to **U.**, Tarry here to day 223
2Sa 11:12 So **U.** abode in Jerusalem that day, ... 223
2Sa 11:14 Joab, and sent it by the hand of **U.** 223
2Sa 11:15 Set ye **U.** in the forefront of the 223
2Sa 11:16 he assigned **U.** unto a place where 223
2Sa 11:17 David; and **U.** the Hittite died also 223
2Sa 11:21 Thy servant **U.** the Hittite is dead 223
2Sa 11:24 thy servant **U.** the Hittite is dead 223
2Sa 11:26 the wife of **U.** heard that **U.** her 223
2Sa 12:9 killed **U.** the Hittite with the sword, ... 223
2Sa 12:10 taken the wife of **U.** the Hittite to 223
2Sa 23:39 **U.** the Hittite: thirty and seven in 223
1Ki 15:5 in the matter of **U.** the Hittite 223
1Ch 11:41 **U.** the Hittite, Zabad the son of 223
Ezr 8:33 the hand of Meremoth the son of **U.** 223
Isa 8:2 witnesses to record, **U.** the priest, ... 223

URIAH'S (u-ri'-ahz)
2Sa 12:15 Lord struck the child that **U.** wife 223

URIAS (u-ri'-as) See also URIAH.
Mt 1:6 her that had been the wife of **U.**; *3774*

URIEL (u'-re-el)
1Ch 6:24 Tahath his son, **U.** his son, Uzziah 222

1Ch 15:5 the sons of Kohath; **U.** the chief......... 222
1Ch 15:11 and for the Levites for **U.**, Asaiah,....... 222
2Ch 13:2 the daughter of **U.** of Gibeah.......... 222

URIJAH (u-ri'-jah) See also URIAH.
2Ki 16:10 Ahaz sent to **U.** the priest the........... 223
2Ki 16:11 And **U.** the priest built an altar........... 223
2Ki 16:11 **U.** the priest made it against king........ 223
2Ki 16:15 Ahaz commanded **U.** the priest,........... 223
2Ki 16:16 Thus did **U.** the priest, according to..... 223
Ne 3:4 repaired Meremoth the son of **U.**, ... 223
Ne 3:21 repaired Meremoth the son of **U.** 223
Ne 8:4 and Anaiah, and **U.**, and Hilkiah,.......... 223
Jer 26:20 **U.** the son of Shemaiah of................. 223
Jer 26:21 when **U.** heard it, he was afraid, ... 223
Jer 26:23 they fetched forth **U.** out of Egypt,...... 223

URIM (u'-rim)
Ex 28:30 the breastplate of judgment the **U.**....... 224
Le 8:8 he put in the breastplate the **U.** 224
Nu 27:21 judgment of **U.** before the Lord:......... 224
De 33:8 thy Thummim and thy **U.** be with........ 224
1Sa 28:6 neither by dreams, nor by **U.**, nor....... 224
Ezr 2:63 till there stood up a priest with **U.**........ 224
Ne 7:65 till there stood up a priest with **U.**........ 224

US See in the APPENDIX; also US-WARD.

USE See also ABUSE; USED; USES; USEST; USETH; USING.
Le 7:24 may be used in any other **u.**: 4399
Le 19:26 neither shall ye **u.** enchantment, ... 5172
Nu 10:2 mayest **u.** them for the calling of the ....
Nu 15:39 after which ye **u.** to go a whoring:...........
De 26:14 ought thereof for any unclean **u.**,.............
2Sa 1:18 children of Judah the **u.** of the bow:..........
1Ch 12:2 **u.** both the right hand and the........... 3231
1Ch 28:15 to the **u.** of every candlestick............. 5656
Jer 23:31 that **u.** their tongues, and say, He...... 3947
Jer 31:23 shall **u.** this speech in the land of......... 559
Jer 46:11 in vain shalt thou **u.** many medicines;........
Eze 12:23 more **u.** it as a proverb in Israel; 4912
Eze 16:44 shall **u.** this proverb against thee,........ 4911
Eze 18:2 **u.** this proverb concerning the.......... 4911
Eze 18:3 more to **u.** this proverb in Israel.......... 4911
Eze 21:21 of the two ways, to **u.** divination:....... 7080
Mt 5:44 **them which despitefully u. you,** *1908*
Mt 6:7 **ye pray, u. not vain repetitions,** ....
Lu 6:28 **them which despitefully u. you,** *1908*
Ac 14:5 to **u.** them despitefully, and to........... *5195*
Ro 1:26 did change the natural **u.** into that....... *5540*
Ro 1:27 leaving...natural **u.** of the woman, ... *5540*
1Co 7:21 mayest be made free, **u.** it rather. *5530*
1Co 7:31 they that **u.** this world, as not........... *5530*
2Co 1:17 thus minded, did I **u.** lightness? *5530*
2Co 3:12 we **u.** great plainness of speech: *5530*
2Co 13:10 being present I...**u.** sharpness, ... *5530*
Ga 5:13 **u.** not liberty for an occasion to the.........
Eph 4:29 is good to the **u.** of edifying, ... *5532*
1Ti 1:8 is good, if a man **u.** it lawfully; *5530*
1Ti 3:10 then let them **u.** the office of a deacon, ...
1Ti 5:23 **u.** a little wine for thy stomach's.......... *5530*
2Ti 2:21 and meet for the master's **u.**,..................
Heb 5:14 those who by reason of **u.** have......... *1838*
1Pe 4:9 **U.** hospitality one to another............. *5382*

USED See also ABUSED; MISUSED.
Ex 21:36 the ox hath **u.** to push in time past,..........
Le 7:24 may be **u.** in any other use:.............. 6213
Jg 14:10 a beast, for so **u.** the young men to do. ....
Jg 14:20 whom he had **u.** as his friend. ....
2Ki 17:17 **u.** divination and enchantments. ....
2Ki 21:6 times, and **u.** enchantments,....................
2Ch 33:6 times, and **u.** enchantments,....................
2Ch 33:6 and **u.** witchcraft, and dealt with a...........
Jer 2:24 A wild ass **u.** to the wilderness,.......... 3928
Eze 22:29 people of the land have **u.** oppression,.......
Eze 35:11 envy which thou hast **u.** out of thy..... 6213
Ho 12:10 multiplied visions, and **u.** similitudes,.........
Mk 2:18 and of the Pharisees **u.** to fast:.......... *1510*
Ac 8:9 in the same city **u.** sorcery, ... *3096*
Ac 19:19 of them also which **u.** curious arts...... *4238*
Ac 27:17 they **u.** helps, undergirding the ship; *5530*
Ro 3:13 their tongues they have **u.** deceit; *1387*
1Co 9:12 we have not **u.** this power;.................. *5530*
1Co 9:15 But I have **u.** none of these things: *5530*
1Th 2:5 time **u.** we flattering words,....... *1096,1722*
1Ti 3:13 that have **u.** the office of a deacon...... *1247*
Heb 10:33 companions of them that were so **u.**...... *390*

USES
Tit 3:14 good works for necessary **u.**,............ *5532*

USEST
Ps 119:132 as thou **u.** to do unto those that 4941

USETH
De 18:10 or that **u.** divination, or an observer ....
Es 6:8 be brought which the king **u.** to wear,........
Pr 15:2 of the wise **u.** knowledge aright: ....
Pr 18:23 The poor **u.** intreaties; but the 1696
Jer 22:13 that **u.** his neighbour's service ....
Eze 16:44 every one that **u.** proverbs shall..............
Heb 5:13 For one that **u.** milk is unskillful.......... *3348*

USING See also ABUSING.
Col 2:22 Which all are to perish with the **u.**;)..... *671*
1Pe 2:16 not **u.** your liberty for a cloke of......... *2192*

USURER
Ex 22:25 thou shalt not be to him as an **u.**, ... 5383

USURP
1Ti 2:12 nor to **u.** authority over the man, ... *831*

USURY
Ex 22:25 shalt thou lay upon him **u.** 5392
Le 25:36 Take thou no **u.** of him, or increase:... 5392
Le 25:37 not give him thy money upon **u.**, ... 5392
De 23:19 not lend upon **u.** to thy brother; 5391
De 23:19 **u.** of money, **u.** of victuals,............... 5392
De 23:19 **u.** of any thing that is lent upon......... 5392
De 23:19 any thing that is lent upon **u.**............. 5391
De 23:20 a stranger thou mayest lend upon **u.**;.. 5391
De 23:20 thou shalt not lend upon **u.**: 5391
Ne 5:7 Ye exact **u.**, every one of his............ 5383
Ne 5:10 I pray you, let us leave off this **u.**......... 5383
Ps 15:5 putteth not out his money to **u.**, ... 5392
Pr 28:8 He that by **u.** and unjust gain 5392
Isa 24:2 as with the taker of **u.**, so with 5383
Isa 24:2 so with the giver of **u.** to him............ 5378
Jer 15:10 I have neither lent on **u.**, nor men 5383
Jer 15:10 nor men have lent to me on **u.**; 5383
Eze 18:8 thou hath not given forth upon **u.**, ... 5392
Eze 18:13 Hath given forth upon **u.**, and hath..... 5392
Eze 18:17 hath not received **u.** nor increase, ... 5392
Eze 22:12 thou hast taken **u.** and increase, ... 5392
Mt 25:27 **have received mine own with u.** *5110*
Lu 19:23 **have required mine own with u.?**... *5110*

US-WARD
Ps 40:5 and thy thoughts which are to **u.** 413
Eph 1:19 his power to **u.** who believed, ... *1519,2248*
2Pe 3:9 but is longsuffering to **u.**, not..... *1519,2248*

UTHAI (u'-thahee)
1Ch 9:4 **U.** the son of Ammihud, the son....... 5793
Ezr 8:14 **U.**, and Zabbud, and with them.......... 5793

UTMOST See also OUTMOST; UTTERMOST.
Ge 49:26 the **u.** bound of the everlasting hills: ....
Nu 22:36 Arnon, which is in the **u.** coast.......... 7097
Nu 22:41 might see the **u.** part of the people 7097
Nu 23:13 shalt see but the **u.** part of them, ... 7097
De 34:2 the land of Judah, unto the **u.** sea, ... 314
Jer 9:26 and all that are in the **u.** corners,....... 7112
Jer 25:23 and all that are in the **u.** corners,....... 7112
Jer 49:32 them that are in the **u.** corners;........ 7112
Jer 50:26 against her from the **u.** border,.......... 7093
Joe 2:20 his hinder part toward the **u.** sea,........ 314
Lu 11:31 **from the u. parts of the earth to**... *4009*

UTTER See also OUTER; UTTERED; UTTERETH; UTTERING; UTTERMOST.
Le 5:1 if he do not **u.** it, then he shall.......... 5046
Jos 2:14 yours, if ye **u.** not this our business ... 5046
Jos 2:20 And if thou **u.** this our business, ... 5046
Jg 5:12 Deborah: awake, awake, **u.** a song: 1696
1Ki 20:42 I appointed to **u.** destruction, ...
Job 8:10 and **u.** words out of their heart? 3318
Job 15:2 a wise man **u.** vain knowledge, ... 6030
Job 27:4 nor my tongue **u.** deceit.................. 1897
Job 33:3 lips shall **u.** knowledge clearly............ 4448
Ps 78:2 I will **u.** dark sayings of old:............. 5042
Ps 94:4 long shall they **u.** and speak hard 5042
Ps 106:2 Who can **u.** the mighty acts of the...... 4448
Ps 119:171 My lips shall **u.** praise, when............ 5042
Ps 145:7 shall abundantly **u.** the memory.......... 5042
Pr 14:5 but a false witness will **u.** lies........... 6315
Pr 23:33 heart shall **u.** perverse things........... 1696
Ec 1:8 are full of labour; man cannot **u.** it:..... 1696
Ec 5:2 hasty to **u.** any thing before God:....... 3318
Isa 32:6 and to **u.** error against the Lord, ... 1696
Isa 48:20 **u.** it even to the end of the earth;...... 3318
Jer 1:16 I will **u.** my judgments against 1696
Jer 25:30 **u.** his voice from his holy 5414
Eze 24:3 **u.** a parable unto the rebellious.......... 4911
Eze 40:31, 37 were toward the **u.** court; 2435
Eze 42:1 brought me forth into the **u.** court,...... 2435
Eze 42:3 pavement...was for the **u.** court,...... 2435
Eze 42:7 toward the **u.** court on the forepart 2435
Eze 42:8 chambers that were in the **u.** court..... 2435
Eze 42:9 goeth into them from the **u.** court...... 2435
Eze 42:14 of the holy place into the **u.** court, ... 2435
Eze 44:19 they go forth into the **u.** court,.......... 2435
Eze 44:19 even into the **u.** court of the people,... 2435
Eze 46:20 bear them not out into the **u.** court, ... 2435
Eze 46:21 brought me forth into the **u.** court,..... 2435
Eze 47:2 **u.** gate by the way that looketh......... 2531
Joe 2:11 Lord shall **u.** his voice before his 5414
Joe 3:16 and **u.** his voice from Jerusalem; 5414
Am 1:2 and **u.** his voice from Jerusalem; 5414
Na 1:8 he will make an **u.** end of the place 3617
Na 1:9 he will make an **u.** end: affliction......... 3617
Zec 14:11 shall be no more **u.** destruction;..............
Mt 13:35 **u.** things which have been kept......... *2044*
1Co 14:9 except ye **u.** by the tongue words...... *1325*
2Co 12:4 it is not lawful for a man to **u.**........... *2980*

UTTERANCE
Ac 2:4 tongues, as the Spirit gave them **u.**...... *669*
1Co 1:5 ye are enriched by him, in all **u.**, ... *3056*
2Co 8:7 in faith, and **u.**, and knowledge, ... *3056*
Eph 6:19 that **u.** may be given unto me, that *3056*
Col 4:3 would open unto us a door of **u.**, ... *3056*

UTTERED
Nu 30:6 vowed, or **u.** ought out of her lips,..... 4008
Nu 30:8 that which she **u.** with her lips, ... 4008
Jg 11:11 Jephthah **u.** all his words before......... 1696
2Sa 22:14 and the most High **u.** his voice........... 5414
Ne 6:19 me, and **u.** my words to him.............. 3318
Job 26:4 To whom hast thou **u.** words? and 5046
Job 42:3 have I **u.** that I understood not;......... 5046
Ps 46:6 he **u.** his voice, the earth melted 5414
Ps 66:14 Which my lips have **u.**, and my.......... 4475
Jer 48:34 Jahaz, have they **u.** their voice, ... 5414
Jer 51:55 waters, a noise of their voice is **u.** 5414
Hab 3:10 the deep **u.** his voice, and lifted up...... 5414
Ro 8:26 with groanings which cannot be **u.** *215*
Heb 5:11 things to say, and hard to be **u.**,......... *3004*
Re 10:3 seven thunders **u.** their voices.......... *2980*
Re 10:4 seven thunders had **u.** their voices, ... *2980*
Re 10:4 which the seven thunders **u.**, ... *2980*

UTTERETH
Job 15:5 For thy mouth **u.** thine iniquity,........... 502
Ps 19:2 Day unto day **u.** speech, and night 5042
Pr 1:20 she **u.** her voice in the streets: 5414
Pr 1:21 the city she **u.** her words, saying, ... 559
Pr 10:18 and he that **u.** a slander, is a fool....... 3318
Pr 29:11 A fool **u.** all his mind: but a wise 3318
Jer 10:13 When he **u.** his voice, there is a........ 5414
Jer 51:16 When he **u.** his voice, there is a........ 5414
Mic 7:3 he **u.** his mischievous desire: 1696

UTTERING
Isa 59:13 conceiving and **u.** from the heart........ 1897

UTTERLY
Ex 17:14 I will **u.** put out the remembrance of........
Ex 22:17 father **u.** refuse to give her unto him, ...
Ex 22:20 only, he shall be **u.** destroyed.................
Ex 23:24 but thou shalt **u.** overthrow them, ...
Le 13:44 priest...pronounce him **u.** unclean;..........
Le 26:44 I abhor them, to destroy them **u.**,...... 3615
Nu 15:31 that soul shall be **u.** cut off; ....
Nu 21:2 then I will **u.** destroy their cities. ....
Nu 21:3 they **u.** destroyed them and their..............
Nu 30:12 husband hath **u.** made them void..............
De 2:34 and **u.** destroyed the men, and the...........
De 3:6 And we **u.** destroyed them, as we............
De 3:6 **u.** destroying the men, women, ...
De 4:26 ye shall soon **u.** perish from off the ....
De 4:26 upon it, but shall **u.** be destroyed.............
De 7:2 smite them, and **u.** destroy them; ....
De 7:26 but thou shalt **u.** detest it, and thou.........
De 7:26 and thou shalt **u.** abhor it; for it is a ....
De 12:2 Ye shall **u.** destroy all the places, ...
De 13:15 destroying it **u.**, and all that is...................

De 20:17 But thou shalt **u.** destroy them;
De 31:29 death ye will **u.** corrupt yourselves,
Jos 2:10 and Og, whom ye **u.** destroyed.
Jos 6:21 they **u.** destroyed all that was in
Jos 8:26 until he had **u.** destroyed all the
Jos 10:1 taken Ai, and had **u.** destroyed it;
Jos 10:28 the king thereof he **u.** destroyed,
Jos 10:35 therein he **u.** destroyed that day,
Jos 10:37 destroyed it **u.**, and all the souls
Jos 10:39 and **u.** destroyed all the souls that
Jos 10:40 but **u.** destroyed all that breathed,
Jos 11:11 of the sword, **u.** destroying them:
Jos 11:12 he **u.** destroyed them, as Moses
Jos 11:20 that he might destroy them **u.**,
Jos 11:21 destroyed them **u.** with their cities.
Jos 17:13 tribute; but did not **u.** drive them out
Jg 1:17 Zephath, and **u.** destroyed it.
Jg 1:28 and did not **u.** drive them out.
Jg 15:2 thought that thou hadst **u.** hated her:
Jg 21:11 Ye shall **u.** destroy every male,
1Sa 15:3 and **u.** destroy all that they have,
1Sa 15:8 **u.** destroyed all the people with the
1Sa 15:9 good, and would not **u.** destroy them:
1Sa 15:9 and refuse, that they destroyed **u.**
1Sa 15:15 and the rest we have **u.** destroyed.
1Sa 15:18 Go and **u.** destroy the sinners the
1Sa 15:20 have **u.** destroyed the Amalekites.
1Sa 15:21 which should have been **u.** destroyed,
1Sa 27:12 his people Israel **u.** to abhor him;
2Sa 17:10 is as the heart of a lion, shall **u.** melt:
2Sa 23:7 they shall be **u.** burned with fire in the
1Ki 9:21 also were not able **u.** to destroy,
2Ki 19:11 to all lands, by destroying them **u.**:
1Ch 4:41 destroyed them **u.** unto this day,
2Ch 20:23 Seir, **u.** to slay and destroy them:
2Ch 31:1 until they had **u.** destroyed them
2Ch 32:14 nations that my fathers **u.** destroyed,
Ne 9:31 thou didst not **u.** consume them,
Ps 37:24 fall, he shall not be **u.** cast down:
Ps 73:19 they are **u.** consumed with terrors.
Ps 89:33 my lovingkindness will I not **u.** take
Ps 119:8 thy statutes: O forsake me not **u.**. 3966
Ps 119:43 word of truth **u.** out of my mouth; 3966
Ca 8:7 for love, it would **u.** be contemned.
Isa 2:18 And the idols he shall **u.** abolish. 3632
Isa 6:11 man, and the land be **u.** desolate,
Isa 11:15 shall **u.** destroy the tongue of the
Isa 24:3 shall be **u.** emptied, and **u.** spoiled:
Isa 24:19 The earth is **u.** broken down, the
Isa 34:2 he hath **u.** destroyed them, he
Isa 37:11 all lands by destroying them **u.**;
Isa 40:30 and the young men shall **u.** fall:
Isa 56:3 **u.** separated me from his people:
Isa 60:12 yea, those nations shall be **u.** wasted.
Jer 9:4 for every brother will **u.** supplant,
Jer 12:17 I will **u.** pluck up and destroy that
Jer 14:19 Hast thou **u.** rejected Judah? hath
Jer 23:39 behold, I, even I, will **u.** forget you,
Jer 25:9 about, and will **u.** destroy them,
Jer 25:29 and should ye be **u.** unpunished?
Jer 50:21 waste and **u.** destroy after them,
Jer 50:26 up as heaps, and destroy her **u.**:
Jer 51:3 men; destroy ye **u.** all her host.
Jer 51:58 walls of Babylon shall be **u.** broken,
La 5:22 But thou hast **u.** rejected us; thou
Eze 9:6 Slay **u.** old and young, both maids,
Eze 17:10 shall it not **u.** wither, when the east
Eze 27:31 make themselves **u.** bald for thee,
Eze 29:10 of Egypt **u.** wast and desolate,
Da 11:44 destroy, and **u.** to make away many.
Ho 1:6 Israel; but I will **u.** take them away.
Ho 10:15 shall the king of Israel **u.** be cut off.
Am 9:8 I will not **u.** destroy the house of
Mic 2:4 and say, We be **u.** spoiled: 7703
Na 1:15 through thee; he is **u.** cut off. 3605
Zep 1:2 will **u.** consume all thing from off
Zec 11:17 his right eye shall be **u.** darkened.
1Co 6:7 there is **u.** a fault among you, *3654*
2Pe 2:12 and shall **u.** perish in their own *2704*
Re 18:8 she shall be **u.** burned with fire: *2618*

UTTERMOST See also UTMOST.
Ex 26:4 in the **u.** edge of another curtain, 7020
Ex 36:11 in the **u.** side of another curtain, 7020
Ex 36:17 upon the **u.** edge of the curtain 7020
Nu 11:1 were in the **u.** parts of the camp. 7097
Nu 20:16 a city in the **u.** of thy border: 7097
De 11:24 unto the **u.** sea shall your coast be. 314
Jos 15:1 was the **u.** part of the south coast. 7097
Jos 15:5 of the sea at the **u.** part of Jordan: 7097
Jos 15:21 the **u.** cities of the tribe of the 7097
1Sa 14:2 tarried in the **u.** part of Gibeah 7097
1Ki 6:24 from the **u.** part of the one wing 7098
1Ki 6:24 wing unto the **u.** part of the other 7098
2Ki 7:5 the **u.** part of the camp of Syria, 7097
2Ki 7:8 came to the **u.** part of the camp, 7097
Ne 1:9 out unto the **u.** part of the heaven, 7097
Ps 2:8 and the **u.** parts of the earth for thy 657
Ps 65:8 that dwell in the **u.** parts are afraid 7098
Ps 139:9 dwell in the **u.** parts of the sea; 319
Isa 7:18 the **u.** part of the rivers of Egypt, 7097
Isa 24:16 From the **u.** part of the earth have 3671
Mt 5:26 **till thou hast paid the u. farthing.** *2078*
Mt 12:42 **from the u. parts of the earth** *4009*
Mk 13:27 **from the u. part of the earth** *206*
Mk 13:27 **to the u. part of heaven.** *206*
Ac 1:8 **unto the u. part of the earth.** *2078*
Ac 24:22 I will know the **u.** of your matter. *1231*
1Th 2:16 wrath is come upon them to the **u.** *5056*
Heb 7:25 able also to save them to the **u.** *3838*

UZ (uz)
Ge 10:23 children of Aram; **U.**, and Hul, 5780
Ge 36:28 children of Dishan are these; **U.**, 5780
1Ch 1:17 Aram, and **U.**, and Hul, and Gether, 5780
1Ch 1:42 The sons of Dishan; **U.**, and Aran. 5780
Job 1:1 There was a man in the land of **U.**, 5780
Jer 25:20 and all the kings of the land of **U.**, 5780
La 4:21 that dwellest in the land of **U.**; 5780

UZAI (u'-zahee)
Ne 3:25 Palal the son of **U.**, over against 186

UZAL (u'-zal)
Ge 10:27 Hadoram, and **U.**, and Diklah, 187
1Ch 1:21 Hadoram also, and **U.**, and Diklah, 187

UZZA (uz'-zah) See also UZZAH.
2Ki 21:18 own house, in the garden of **U.**: 5798
2Ki 21:26 his sepulchre in the garden of **U.**: 5798
1Ch 6:29 son, Shimei his son, **U.** his son, 5798
1Ch 8:7 he removed them, and begat **U.**, 5798
1Ch 13:7 and **U.** and Ahio drave the cart. 5798
1Ch 13:9 **U.** put forth his hand to hold the 5798
1Ch 13:10 the Lord was kindled against **U.**, 5798
1Ch 13:11 Lord had made a breach upon **U.**: 5798
Ezr 2:49 The children of **U.**, the children of 5798
Ne 7:51 the children of **U.**, the children of 5798

UZZAH (uz'-zah) See also PEREZ-UZZAH; UZZA.
2Sa 6:3 **U.** and Ahio, the sons of Abinadab, 5798
2Sa 6:6 **U.** put forth his hand to the ark of 5798
2Sa 6:7 the Lord was kindled against **U.**; 5798
2Sa 6:8 Lord had made a breach upon **U.**: 5798

UZZEN-SHERAH (uz''-zen-she'-rah)
1Ch 7:24 built Beth-horon...and **U.**.) 242

UZZI (uz'-zi)
1Ch 6:5 Bukki, and Bukki begat **U.**, 5813
1Ch 6:6 **U.** begat Zerahiah, and Zerahiah 5813
1Ch 6:51 Bukki his son, **U.** his son, Zerahiah 5813
1Ch 7:2 sons of Tola; **U.**, and Rephaiah, 5813
1Ch 7:3 And the sons of **U.**; Izrahiah: 5813
1Ch 7:7 sons of Bela; Ezbon, and **U.**, and 5813
1Ch 9:8 and Elah the son of **U.**, the son of 5813
Ezr 7:4 Zerahiah, the son of **U.**, the son of 5813
Ne 11:22 was **U.** the son of Bani, the son 5813
Ne 12:19 Joiarib, Mattenai; of Jedaiah, **U.**; 5813
Ne 12:42 Elezar, and **U.**, and Jehohanan, 5813

UZZIA (uz-zi'-ah)
1Ch 11:44 **U.** the Ashterathite, Shama and 5814

UZZIAH (uz-zi'-ah) See also OZIAS.
2Ki 15:13 the nine and thirtieth year of **U.** 5818
2Ki 15:30 year of Jotham the son of **U.** 5818
2Ki 15:32 Jotham the son of **U.**...to reign. 5818
2Ki 15:34 to all that his father **U.** had done 5818
1Ch 6:24 Uriel his son, **U.** his son, and 5818
1Ch 27:25 was Jehonathan the son of **U.** 5818
2Ch 26:1 all the people of Judah took **U.**, 5818
2Ch 26:3 Sixteen years old was **U.** when he 5818
2Ch 26:8 the Ammonites gave gifts to **U.** 5818
2Ch 26:9 **U.** built towers in Jerusalem at 5818
2Ch 26:11 **U.** had an host of fighting men, 5818
2Ch 26:14 **U.** prepared for them...shields, 5818
2Ch 26:18 And they withstood **U.** the king, 5818
2Ch 26:18 It appertaineth not unto thee, **U.**, 5818
2Ch 26:19 **U.** was wroth, and had a censer in 5818
2Ch 26:21 **U.** the king was a leper unto the 5818
2Ch 26:22 Now the rest of the acts of **U.**, first 5818
2Ch 26:23 So **U.** slept with his fathers, and 5818
2Ch 27:2 according to all his father **U.** did: 5818
Eze 10:21 and Shemaiah, and Jehiel, and **U.** 5818
Ne 11:4 of Judah; Athaiah the son of **U.**, 5818
Isa 1:1 in the days of **U.**, Jotham, Ahaz, 5818
Isa 6:1 In the year that king **U.** died I saw 5818
Isa 7:1 the son of Jotham, the son of **U.**, 5818
Ho 1:1 in the days of **U.**, Jotham, Ahaz, 5818
Am 1:1 in the days of **U.** king of Judah, 5818
Zec 14:5 the earthquake in the days of **U.** 5818

UZZIEL (uz-zi'-el) See also UZZIELITES.
Ex 6:18 and Izhar, and Hebron, and **U.** 5816
Ex 6:22 And the sons of **U.**; Mishael, and 5816
Le 10:4 the sons of **U.** the uncle of Aaron, 5816
Nu 3:19 and Izehar, Hebron, and **U.** 5816
Nu 3:30 shall be Elizaphan the son of **U.** 5816
1Ch 4:42 Rephaiah, and **U.**, the sons of Ishi 5816
1Ch 6:2 Amram, Izhar, and Hebron, and **U.** 5816
1Ch 6:18 and Izhar, and Hebron, and **U.** 5816
1Ch 7:7 Ezbon, and Uzzi, and **U.**, and 5816
1Ch 15:10 Of the sons of **U.**; Amminadab 5816
1Ch 23:12 Amram, Izhar, Hebron, and **U.**, 5816
1Ch 23:20 Of the sons of **U.**; Micah the first, 5816
1Ch 24:24 Of the sons of **U.**; Michah: 5816
1Ch 25:4 Bukkiah, Mattaniah, **U.**, Shebuel, 5816
2Ch 29:14 of Jeduthun; Shemaiah, and **U.** 5816
Ne 3:8 Next unto him repaired **U.** the son 5816

UZZIELITES (uz-zi'-el-ites)
Nu 3:27 and the family of the **U.** 5817
1Ch 26:23 the Hebronites, and the **U.** 5817

V.

VAGABOND See also VAGABONDS.
Ge 4:12 a **v.** shalt thou be in the earth. 5110
Ge 4:14 a fugitive and a **v.** in the earth; 5110
Ac 19:13 Then certain of the **v.** Jews, *4022*

VAGABONDS
Ps 109:10 Let his children be continually **v.**, 5128

VAIL See also VAILS; VEIL.
Ge 24:65 therefore she took a **v.**, and 6809
Ge 38:14 and covered her with a **v.**, and 6809
Ge 38:19 laid by her **v.** from her, and put on 6809
Ex 26:31 And thou shalt make a **v.** of blue, 6532
Ex 26:33 thou shalt hang up the **v.** under 6532
Ex 26:33 bring in thither within the **v.** the 6532
Ex 26:33 **v.** shall divide unto you between 6532
Ex 26:35 shalt set the table without the **v.**, 6532
Ex 27:21 of the congregation without the **v.**, 6532
Ex 30:6 the **v.** that is by the ark of the 6532
Ex 34:33 them, he put a **v.** on his face 4533
Ex 34:34 took the **v.** off, until he came out. 4533
Ex 34:35 Moses put the **v.** upon his face 4533
Ex 35:12 seat, and the **v.** of the covering, 6532
Ex 36:35 he made a **v.** of blue, and purple, 6532
Ex 38:27 sanctuary,...the sockets of the **v.**; 6532
Ex 39:34 skins, and the **v.** of the covering, 6532
Ex 40:3 and cover the ark with the **v.** 6532
Ex 40:21 and set up the **v.** of the covering, 6532
Ex 40:22 northward, without the **v.** 6532
Ex 40:26 of the congregation before the **v.**: 6532
Le 4:6 before the **v.** of the sanctuary 6532
Le 4:17 before the Lord, even before the **v.** 6532
Le 16:2 holy place within the **v.** before the 6532

Le 16:12 small, and bring it within the v.: 6532
Le 16:15 and bring his blood within the v., 6532
Le 21:23 Only he shall not go in unto the v., 6532
Le 24:3 Without the v. of the testimony, in 6532
Nu 4:5 shall take down the covering v., 6532
Nu 18:7 of the altar, and within the v., 6532
Ru 3:15 Bring the v. that thou hast upon 4304
2Ch 3:14 And he made the v. of blue, and 6532
Isa 25:7 v. that is spread over all nations. 4541
2Co 3:13 which put a v. over his face, that *2571*
2Co 3:14 the same v. untaken away in the *2571*
2Co 3:14 which v. is done away in Christ.
2Co 3:15 read, the v. is upon their heart. *2571*
2Co 3:16 Lord, the v. shall be taken away. *2571*

VAILS
Isa 3:23 linen, and the hoods, and the v. 7289

VAIN See also VAINGLORY.
Ex 5:9 let them not regard v. words. 8267
Ex 20:7 name of the Lord thy God in v.; 7723
Ex 20:7 guiltless that taketh his name in v. 7723
Le 26:16 ye shall sow your seed in v., for 7385
Le 26:20 your strength shall be spent in v.: 7385
De 5:11 name of the Lord thy God in v.: 7723
De 5:11 guiltless that taketh his name in v. 7723
De 32:47 For it is not a v. thing for you; 7386
Jg 9:4 Abimelech hired v. and light 7386
Jg 11:3 were gathered v. men to Jephthah, 7386
1Sa 12:21 then should ye go after v. things, 8414
1Sa 12:21 profit nor deliver; for they are v. 8414
1Sa 25:21 in v. have I kept all that this 8267
2Sa 6:20 one of the v. fellows shamelessly 7386
2Ki 17:15 became v., and went after the 1891
2Ki 18:20 sayest, (but they are but v. words,) 8193
2Ch 13:7 are gathered unto him v. men, 7386
Job 9:29 wicked, why then labour I in v.? 1892
Job 11:11 For he knoweth v. men: he seeth 7723
Job 11:12 For v. man would be wise, though 5014
Job 15:2 a wise man utter v. knowledge, and 7307
Job 16:3 Shall v. words have an end? or 7307
Job 21:34 How then comfort ye me in v., 1892
Job 27:12 then are ye thus altogether v.? 1891
Job 35:16 doth Job open his mouth in v.: 1892
Job 39:16 her labour is in v. without fear; 7385
Job 41:9 the hope of him is in v.: shall not 3576
Ps 2:1 and the people imagine a v. thing? 7385
Ps 26:4 I have not sat with v. persons, 7723
Ps 33:17 An horse is a v. thing for safety: 8267
Ps 39:6 every man walketh in a v. shew:
Ps 39:6 surely they are disquieted in v.: 1892
Ps 60:11 trouble: for v. is the help of man. 7723
Ps 62:10 and become not v. in robbery: 1891
Ps 73:13 I have cleansed my heart in v., 7385
Ps 89:47 hast thou made all men in v.? 7723
Ps 108:12 trouble: for v. is the help of man 7723
Ps 119:113 I hate v. thoughts: but thy law do I
Ps 127:1 they labour in v. that build it: 7723
Ps 127:1 the watchman waketh but in v. 7723
Ps 127:2 It is v. for you to rise up early, to 7723
Ps 139:20 thine enemies take thy name in v. 7723
Pr 1:17 Surely in v. the net is spread in 2600
Pr 12:11 he that followeth v. persons is 7386
Pr 28:19 he that followeth after v. persons 7386
Pr 30:9 and take the name of my God in v.
Pr 31:30 is deceitful, and beauty is v.: but 1892
Ec 6:12 all the days of his v. life which he 1892
Isa 1:13 Bring no more v. oblations; 7723
Isa 30:7 For the Egyptians shall help in v., 1892
Isa 36:5 thou, (but they are but v. words) 8193
Isa 45:18 he created it not in v., he formed 8414
Isa 45:19 Seek ye me in v.: I the Lord speak 8414
Isa 49:4 Then I said, I have laboured in v., 7385
Isa 49:4 strength for nought, and in v.: 1892
Isa 65:23 They shall not labour in v., nor 7385
Jer 2:5 after vanity, and are become v.? 1891
Jer 2:30 v. have I smitten your children; 7723
Jer 3:23 Truly in v. is salvation hoped for 8267
Jer 4:14 thy v. thoughts lodge within thee? 205
Jer 4:30 in v. shalt thou make thyself fair; 7723
Jer 6:29 the fire; the founder melteth in v.: 7723
Jer 8:8 us? Lo, certainly in v. made he it; 8267
Jer 8:8 it; the pen of the scribes is in v. 8267
Jer 10:3 customs of the people are in v.: 1892
Jer 23:16 unto you: they make you v.: 1891
Jer 46:11 in v. shalt thou use many 7723
Jer 50:9 man; none shall return in v. 7387
Jer 51:58 and the people shall labour in v., 7385
La 2:14 have seen v. and foolish things 7723
La 4:17 eyes as yet failed for our v. help: 1892
Eze 6:10 said in v. that I would do this evil 2600
Eze 12:24 shall be no more any v. vision 7723
Eze 13:7 Have ye not seen a v. vision, and 7723
Zec 10:2 false dreams; they comfort in v.: 1892
Mal 3:14 have said, It is v. to serve God: 7723
Mt 6:7 **when ye pray, use not v. repetitions,**
Mt 15:9 **But in v. they do worship me,** *3155*
Mk 7:7 **Howbeit in v. do they worship me,** *3155*
Ac 4:25 and the people imagine v. things? *2756*
Ro 1:21 became v. in their imaginations, *3154*
Ro 13:4 for he beareth not the sword in v.: *1500*
1Co 3:20 of the wise, that they are v. *3152*
1Co 15:2 you, unless ye have believed in v. *1500*
1Co 15:10 bestowed upon me was not in v.; *2756*
1Co 15:14 risen, then is our preaching v., *2756*
1Co 15:14 and your faith is also v. *2756*
1Co 15:17 be not raised, your faith is v.; *3152*
1Co 15:58 your labour is not in v. in the Lord. *2756*
2Co 6:1 receive not the grace of God in v. *2756*
2Co 9:3 boasting of you should be in v. *2761*
Ga 2:2 I should run, or had run, in v. *2756*
Ga 2:21 the law, then Christ is dead in v. *1432*
Ga 3:4 many things in v.? if it be yet in v. *1500*
Ga 4:11 bestowed upon you labour in v. *1500*
Ga 5:26 Let us not be desirous of v. glory, *2755*
Eph 5:6 man deceive you with v. words: *2756*
Php 2:16 not run in v., neither laboured in v. *2756*
Col 2:8 through philosophy and v. deceit. *2756*
1Th 2:1 in unto you, that it was not in v.: *2756*
1Th 3:5 you, and our labour be in v. *2756*
1Ti 1:6 have turned aside unto v. jangling; *3150*
1Ti 6:20 avoiding profane and v. babblings, *2757*
2Ti 2:16 shun profane and v. babblings: for *2757*
Tit 1:10 unruly and v. talkers and deceivers, *3151*
Tit 3:9 for they are unprofitable and v. *3152*
Jas 1:26 own heart, this man's religion is v. *3152*
Jas 2:20 O v. man, that faith without works *2756*
Jas 4:5 think that the scripture saith in v., *2761*
1Pe 1:18 your v. conversation received by *3152*

VAINGLORY See also VAIN and GLORY.
Php 2:3 be done through strife or v.; *2754*

VAINLY
Col 2:18 v. puffed up by his fleshly mind, *1500*

VAJEZATHA (va-jez'-a-thah)
Es 9:9 and Arisai, and Aridai, and V., 2055

VALE See also VALLEY.
Ge 14:3 together in the v. of Siddim, 6010
Ge 14:8 with them in the v. of Siddim; 6010
Ge 14:10 v. of Siddim was full of slimepits; 6010
Ge 37:14 sent him out of the v. of Hebron, 6010
De 1:7 in the hills, and in the v., and in 8219
Jos 10:40 of the south, and of the v., and of 8219
1Ki 10:27 sycomore trees that are in the v., 8219
2Ch 1:15 sycomore trees that are in the v. 8219
Jer 33:13 in the cities of the v., and in the 8219

VALIANT See also VALIANTEST.
1Sa 14:52 any strong man, or any v. man, 2428
1Sa 16:18 a mighty v. man, and a man of war, 2428
1Sa 18:17 only be thou v. for me, and 1121,2428
1Sa 26:15 said to Abner, Art not thou a v. man?
1Sa 31:12 All the v. men arose, and went all 2428
2Sa 2:7 strengthened, and be ye v.: 1121,2428
2Sa 11:16 where he knew that v. men were 2428
2Sa 13:28 be courageous, and be 1121,2428
2Sa 17:10 he also that is v., whose heart 1121,2428
2Sa 17:10 and they be with him are v. men. 2428
2Sa 23:20 of Jehoiada, the son of a v. man, 2428
2Sa 24:9 eight hundred thousand v. men 2428
1Ki 1:42 Come in; for thou art a v. man, 2428
1Ch 5:18 tribe of Manasseh, of v. men, 2428
1Ch 7:2 were v. men of might in their 1368
1Ch 7:5 of Issachar were v. men of might, 1368
1Ch 10:12 They arose, all the v. men, and 2428
1Ch 11:22 the son of a v. man of Kabzeel, 2428
1Ch 11:26 Also the v. of the armies were, 1368
1Ch 28:1 all the v. men, unto Jerusalem. 2428
2Ch 13:3 with an army of v. men of war, 1368
2Ch 26:17 of the Lord, that were v. men: 2428
2Ch 28:6 day, which were all v. men; 2428
Ne 11:6 threescore and eight v. men. 2428
Ca 3:7 threescore v. men are about it, of 1368
Ca 3:7 are about it, of the v. of Israel. 1368
Isa 10:13 the inhabitants like a v. man: 3524
Isa 33:7 their v. ones shall cry without: 691
Jer 9:3 they are not v. for the truth upon 1396
Jer 46:15 Why are thy v. men swept away? 47
Na 2:3 red, the v. men are in scarlet: 2428
Heb 11:34 waxed v. in fight, turned to flight *2478*

VALIANTEST
Jg 21:10 thousand men of the v., 1121,2428

VALIANTLY
Nu 24:18 enemies; and Israel shall do v. 2428
1Ch 19:13 and let us behave ourselves v. 2388
Ps 60:12 Through God we shall do v.: for 2428
Ps 108:13 Through God we shall do v.: for he 2428
Ps 118:15, 16 right hand of the Lord doeth v. 2428

VALLEY See also VALE; VALLEYS.
Ge 14:17 at the v. of Shaveh, which is the 6010
Ge 26:17 pitched his tent in the v. of Gerar, 5158
Ge 26:19 Isaac's servants digged in the v., 5158
Nu 14:25 the Canannites dwelt in the v.) 6010
Nu 21:12 and pitched in the v. of Zared. 5158
Nu 21:20 from Bamoth in the v., that is in 1516
Nu 32:9 they went up unto the v. of Eshcol, 5158
De 1:24 and came unto the v. of Eshcol, 5158
De 3:16 unto the river Arnon half the v., 5158
De 3:29 So we abode in the v. over against 1516
De 4:46 in the v. over against Beth-peor, in 1516
De 21:4 down the heifer unto a rough v., 5158
De 21:4 off the heifer's neck there in the v.: 5158
De 21:6 heifer that is beheaded in the v.: 5158
De 34:3 and the plain of the v. of Jericho, 1237
De 34:6 he buried him in a v. in the land of 1516
Jos 7:24 brought them unto the v. of Achor. 6010
Jos 7:26 place was called, The v. of Achor, 6010
Jos 8:11 was a v. between them and Ai. 1516
Jos 8:13 that night into the midst of the v. 6010
Jos 10:12 and thou, Moon, in the v. of Ajalon. 6010
Jos 11:2 the v., and in the borders of Dor 8219
Jos 11:8 unto the v. of Mizpeh eastward; 1237
Jos 11:16 all the land of Goshen, and the v., 8219
Jos 11:16 of Israel, and the v. of the same; 8219
Jos 11:17 Baal-gad in the v. of Lebanon 1237
Jos 12:7 from Baal-gad in the v. of Lebanon 1237
Jos 13:19 in the mount of the v., 6010
Jos 13:27 And in the v., Beth-aram, and 6010
Jos 15:7 toward Debir from the v. of Achor, 6010
Jos 15:8 up by the v. of the son of Hinnom 1516
Jos 15:8 before the v. of Hinnom westward, 1516
Jos 15:8 of the v. of the giants northward: 6010
Jos 15:33 in the v., Eshtaol, and Zoreah, 8219
Jos 17:16 the land of the v. have chariots of 6010
Jos 17:16 they who are of the v. of Jezreel. 6010
Jos 18:16 before the v. of the son of Hinnom, 1516
Jos 18:16 the v. of the giants on the north, 6010
Jos 18:16 descended to the v. of Hinnom, to 1516
Jos 18:21 Beth-hoglah, and the v. of Keziz, 6010
Jos 19:14 are in the v. of Jiphthah-el: 1516
Jos 19:27 to the v. of Jiphthah-el toward the 1516
Jg 1:9 and in the south, and in the v. 8219
Jg 1:19 drive out the inhabitants of the v., 6010
Jg 1:34 suffer them to come down to the v.: 6010
Jg 5:15 he was sent on foot into the v. 6010
Jg 6:33 and pitched in the v. of Jezreel. 6010
Jg 7:1 them, by the hill of Moreh, in the v. 6010
Jg 7:8 Midian was beneath him in the v. 6010
Jg 7:12 of the east lay along in the v. like 6010
Jg 16:4 loved a woman in the v. of Sorek, 5158
Jg 18:28 in the v. that lieth by Beth-rehob. 6010
1Sa 6:13 their wheat harvest in the v.: 6010
1Sa 13:18 that looketh to the v. of Zeboim 1516
1Sa 15:5 of Amalek, and laid wait in the v. 5158
1Sa 17:2 and pitched by the v. of Elah, 6010
1Sa 17:3 and there was a v. between them. 1516
1Sa 17:19 of Israel, were in the v. of Elah, 6010
1Sa 17:52 until thou come to the v., and to 1516
1Sa 21:9 thou slewest in the v. of Elah, 6010
1Sa 31:7 were on the other side of the v., 6010
2Sa 5:18, 22 themselves in the v. of Rephaim. 6010
2Sa 8:13 of the Syrians in the v. of salt, 1516
2Sa 23:13 pitched in the v. of Rephaim. 6010
2Ki 2:16 some mountain, or into some v. 1516
2Ki 3:16 Lord, Make this v. full of ditches. 5158
2Ki 3:17 yet that v. shall be filled with water, 5158
2Ki 14:7 He slew of Edom in the v. of salt 1516
2Ki 23:10 in the v. of the children of Hinnom, 1516

1Ch 4:14 the father of the **v.** of Charashim; 1516
1Ch 4:39 even unto the east side of the **v.**, 1516
1Ch 10:7 men of Israel that were in the **v.** 6010
1Ch 11:15 encamped in the **v.** of Rephaim. 6010
1Ch 14:9 themselves in the **v.** of Rephaim. 6010
1Ch 14:13 spread themselves abroad in the **v.** 6010
1Ch 18:12 of the Edomites in the **v.** of salt 1516
2Ch 14:10 in array in the **v.** of Zephathah 1516
2Ch 20:26 themselves in the **v.** of Berachah; 6010
2Ch 20:26 was called, The **v.** of Berachah, 6010
2Ch 25:11 went to the **v.** of salt, and smote of 1516
2Ch 26:9 at the **v.** gate, and at the turning of 1516
2Ch 28:3 in the **v.** of the son of Hinnom, 1516
2Ch 33:6 fire in the **v.** of the son of Hinnom: 1516
2Ch 33:14 west side of Gihon, in the **v.**, even 5158
2Ch 35:22 came to fight in the **v.** of Megiddo. 1237
Ne 2:13 out by night by the gate of the **v.**, 1516
Ne 2:15 and entered by the gate of the **v.**, 1516
Ne 3:13 The **v.** gate repaired Hanun, and 1516
Ne 11:30 Beer-sheba unto the **v.** of Hinnom. 1516
Ne 11:35 Lod, and Ono, the **v.** of craftsmen. 1516
Job 21:33 The clods of the **v.** shall be sweet 5158
Job 39:21 He paweth in the **v.**, and rejoiceth 6010
Ps 23:4 through the **v.** of the shadow of 1516
Ps 60:*title* smote of Edom in the **v.** of salt 1516
Ps 60:6 and mete out the **v.** of Succoth. 6010
Ps 84:6 Who passing through the **v.** of Baca 6010
Ps 108:7 and mete out the **v.** of Succoth. 6010
Pr 30:17 ravens of the **v.** shall pick it out, 5158
Ca 6:11 of nuts to see the fruits of the **v.**, 5158
Isa 17:5 ears in the **v.** of Rephaim. 6010
Isa 22:1 The burden of the **v.** of vision. 1516
Isa 22:5 God of hosts in the **v.** of vision, 1516
Isa 28:4 which is on the head of the fat **v.**, 1516
Isa 28:21 be wroth as in the **v.** of Gibeon, 6010
Isa 40:4 Every **v.** shall be exalted, and 1516
Isa 63:14 As a beast goeth down into the **v.**, 1237
Isa 65:10 **v.** of Achor a place for the herds to 6010
Jer 2:23 see thy way in the **v.**, know what 1516
Jer 7:31 is in the **v.** of the son of Hinnom, 1516
Jer 7:32 nor the **v.** of the son of Hinnom, 1516
Jer 7:32 but the **v.** of slaughter: for they 1516
Jer 19:2 unto the **v.** of the son of Hinnom, 1516
Jer 19:6 nor The **v.** of the son of Hinnom, 1516
Jer 19:6 but The **v.** of slaughter. 1516
Jer 21:13 O inhabitant of the **v.**, and rock of 6010
Jer 31:40 the whole **v.** of the dead bodies, and 6010
Jer 32:35 are in the **v.** of the son of Hinnom, 1516
Jer 32:44 in the cities of the **v.**, and in the 8219
Jer 47:5 off with the remnant of their **v.**: 6010
Jer 48:8 **v.** also shall perish, and the plain 6010
Jer 49:4 thy flowing **v.**, O backsliding 6010
Eze 37:1 midst of the **v.** which was full of 1237
Eze 37:2 were very many in the open **v.**; 1237
Eze 39:11 **v.** of the passengers on the east of 1516
Eze 39:11 shall call it The **v.** of Hamon-gog 1516
Eze 39:15 buried it in the **v.** of Hamon-gog. 1516
Ho 1:5 bow of Israel in the **v.** of Jezreel. 6010
Ho 2:15 the **v.** of Achor for a door of hope: 6010
Joe 3:2 down into the **v.** of Jehoshaphat, 6010
Joe 3:12 come up to the **v.** of Jehoshaphat: 6010
Joe 3:14 multitudes in the **v.** of decision: 6010
Joe 3:14 Lord is near in the **v.** of decision. 6010
Joe 3:18 and shall water the **v.** of Shittim. 5158
Mic 1:6 the stones thereof into the **v.**, 1516
Zec 12:11 in the **v.** of Megiddon. 1237
Zec 14:4 and there shall be a very great **v.**; 1516
Zec 14:5 shall flee to the **v.** of the mountains; 1516
Zec 14:5 the **v.** of the mountains shall reach 1516
Lu 3:5 Every **v.** shall be filled, and every *5327*

VALLEYS

Nu 24:6 As the **v.** are they spread forth, as 5158
De 8:7 and depths that spring out of **v.** 1237
De 11:11 possess it, is a land of hills and **v.**, 1237
Jos 9:1 Jordan, in the hills, and in the **v.**, 8219
Jos 12:8 In the mountains, and in the **v.**, 8219
1Ki 20:28 hills, but he is not God of the **v.**, 6010
1Ch 12:15 they put to flight all them of the **v.**, 6010
1Ch 27:29 over the herds that were in the **v.** 6010
Job 30:6 To dwell in the cliffs of the **v.**, in 5158
Job 39:10 or will he harrow the **v.** after thee? 6010
Ps 65:13 **v.** also are covered over with corn; 6010
Ps 104:8 they go down by the **v.** unto the 1237
Ps 104:10 He sendeth the springs into the **v.**, 5158
Ca 2:1 of Sharon, and the lily of the **v.** 6010
Isa 7:19 rest all of them in the desolate **v.**, 5158
Isa 22:7 choicest **v.** shall be full of chariots, 6010
Isa 28:1 head of the fat **v.** of them that are 1516
Isa 41:18 fountains in the midst of the **v.**: 1237
Isa 57:5 slaying the children in the **v.** 5158
Jer 49:4 Wherefore gloriest thou in the **v.** 6010
Eze 6:3 hills, to the rivers, and to the **v.**; 1516
Eze 7:16 the mountains like doves of the **v.**, 1516
Eze 31:12 in all the **v.** his branches are fallen, 1516
Eze 32:5 and fill the **v.** with thy height. 1516
Eze 35:8 in thy hills, and in thy **v.**, and in all 1516
Eze 36:4, 6 hills, to the rivers, and to the **v.**, 1516
Mic 1:4 the **v.** shall be cleft, as wax before 6010

VALOUR

Jos 1:14 all the mighty men of **v.**, and 2428
Jos 6:2 thereof, and the mighty men of **v.** 2428
Jos 8:3 thirty thousand mighty men of **v.**, 2428
Jos 10:7 him, and all the mighty men of **v.** 2428
Jg 3:29 men, all lusty, and all men of **v.**; 2428
Jg 6:12 with thee, thou mighty man of **v.** 2428
Jg 11:1 Jephthah...was a mighty man of **v.**, 2428
Jg 18:2 men from their coasts, men of **v.**, 2428
Jg 20:44 men; all these were men of **v.** 2428
Jg 20:46 the sword; all these were men of **v.** 2428
1Ki 11:28 Jeroboam was a mighty man of **v.**: 2428
2Ki 5:1 he was also a mighty man in **v.**, but 2428
2Ki 24:14 and all the mighty men of **v.**, 2428
1Ch 5:24 mighty men of **v.**, famous men, and 2428
1Ch 7:7 of their fathers, mighty men of **v.**; 2428
1Ch 7:9, 11 their fathers, mighty men of **v.** 2428
1Ch 7:40 choice and mighty men of **v.**, chief 2428
1Ch 8:40 of Ulam were mighty men of **v.**, 2428
1Ch 12:21 for they were all mighty men of **v.**, 2428
1Ch 12:25 mighty men of **v.** for the war, 2428
1Ch 12:28 Zadok, a young man mighty of **v.**, 2428
1Ch 12:30 eight hundred, mighty men of **v.**, 2428
1Ch 26:6 for they were mighty men of **v.** 2428
1Ch 26:30 and his brethren, man of **v.**, 2428
1Ch 26:31 among them mighty men of **v.** at 2428
1Ch 26:32 his brethren, men of **v.**, were two 2428
2Ch 13:3 men, being mighty men of **v.** 2428
2Ch 14:8 all these were mighty men of **v.** 2428
2Ch 17:13 the men of war, mighty men of **v.**, 2428
2Ch 17:14 with him mighty men of **v.** three 2428
2Ch 17:16 thousand mighty men of **v.** 2428
2Ch 17:17 Eliada a mighty man of **v.**, and 2428
2Ch 25:6 mighty men of **v.** out of Israel 2428
2Ch 26:12 fathers of the mighty men of **v.** 2428
2Ch 32:21 cut all all the mighty men of **v.**, 2428
Ne 11:14 their brethren, mighty men of **v.**, 2428

VALUE See also VALUED; VALUEST.

Le 27:8 priest, and the priest shall **v.** him; 6186
Le 27:8 that vowed shall the priest **v.** him. 6186
Le 27:12 And the priest shall **v.** it, whether 6186
Job 13:4 lies, ye are all physicians of no **v.** 457
Mt 10:31 **of more v. than many sparrows.** *1308*
Mt 27:9 of the children of Israel did **v.**; *5091*
Lu 12:7 **of more v. than many sparrows.** *1308*

VALUED

Le 27:16 barley seed shall be **v.** at fifty shekels
Job 28:16 be **v.** with the gold of Ophir, 5541
Job 28:19 neither shall it be **v.** with pure gold. 5541
Mt 27:9 the price of him that was **v.**, *5091*

VALUEST

Le 27:12 as thou **v.** it, who art the priest, so 6187

VANIAH (va-ni'-ah)

Ezr 10:36 **V.**, Meremoth, Eliashib, 2057

VANISH See also VANISHED; VANISHETH.

Job 6:17 time they wax warm, they **v.** 6789
Isa 51:6 heavens shall **v.** away like smoke, 4414
1Co 13:8 be knowledge, it shall **v.** away. *2673*
Heb 8:13 waxeth old is ready to **v.** away. *854*

VANISHED

Jer 49:7 the prudent? is their wisdom **v.**? 5628
Lu 24:31 and he **v.** out of their sight. *1096,855*

VANISHETH

Job 7:9 As the cloud is consumed and **v.** 3212
Jas 4:14 for a little time, and then **v.** away. *853*

VANITIES

De 32:21 me to anger with their **v.** 1892
1Ki 16:13, 26 of Israel to anger with their **v.** 1892
Ps 31:6 hated them that regard lying **v.** 1892
Ec 1:2 Vanity of **v.**, saith the Preacher, 1892
Ec 1:2 Preacher, vanity of **v.**; all is vanity. 1892
Ec 5:7 words there are also divers **v.** 1892
Ec 12:8 Vanity of **v.**, saith the preacher; all 1892
Jer 8:19 images, and with strange **v.**? 1892
Jer 10:8 the stock is a doctrine of **v.** 1892
Jer 14:22 any among the **v.** of the Gentiles 1892
Jon 2:8 that observe lying **v.** forsake their 1892
Ac 14:15 from these **v.** unto the living God, *3152*

VANITY See also VANITIES.

2Ki 17:15 they followed **v.**, and became vain, 1892
Job 7:3 I made to possess months of **v.**, 7723
Job 7:16 let me alone; for my days are **v.** 1892
Job 15:31 him that is deceived trust in **v.** 7723
Job 15:31 for **v.** shall be his recompence. 7723
Job 15:35 mischief, and bring forth **v.**, 205
Job 31:5 If I have walked with **v.**, or if my 7723
Job 35:13 Surely God will not hear **v.**, neither 7723
Ps 4:2 how long will ye love **v.**, and seek 7385
Ps 10:7 under his tongue is mischief and **v.** 205
Ps 12:2 They speak **v.** every one with his 7723
Ps 24:4 hath not lifted up his soul unto **v.**, 7723
Ps 39:5 at his best state is altogether **v.** 1892
Ps 39:11 a moth: surely every man is **v.** 1892
Ps 41:6 come to see me, he speaketh **v.** 7723
Ps 62:9 Surely men of low degree are **v.**, 1892
Ps 62:9 they are altogether lighter than **v.** 1892
Ps 78:33 their days did he consume in **v.**, 1892
Ps 94:11 thoughts of man, that they are **v.** 1892
Ps 119:37 mine eyes from beholding **v.**; 7723
Ps 144:4 Man is like to **v.**: his days are as 1892
Ps 144:8 Whose mouth speaketh **v.**, and 7723
Ps 144:11 children, whose mouth speaketh **v.**, 7723
Pr 13:11 Wealth gotten by **v.** shall be 1892
Pr 21:6 treasures by a lying tongue is a **v.** 1892
Pr 22:8 that soweth iniquity shall reap **v.** 205
Pr 30:8 Remove far from me **v.** and lies: 7723
Ec 1:2 **V.** of vanities, saith the Preacher, 1892
Ec 1:2 saith the Preacher, **v.** of vanities; 1892
Ec 1:2 saith the Preacher,...all is **v.** 1892
Ec 1:14 all is **v.** and vexation of spirit. 1892
Ec 2:1 and, behold, this also is **v.** 1892
Ec 2:11 all was **v.** and vexation of spirit, 1892
Ec 2:15 in my heart, that this also is **v.** 1892
Ec 2:17 for all is **v.** and vexation of spirit. 1892
Ec 2:19 under the sun. This is also **v.** 1892
Ec 2:21 This also is **v.** and a great evil. 1892
Ec 2:23 rest in the night. This is also **v.** 1892
Ec 2:26 also is **v.** and vexation of spirit. 1892
Ec 3:19 above a beast: for all is **v.** 1892
Ec 4:4 is also **v.** and vexation of spirit. 1892
Ec 4:7 and I saw **v.** under the sun. 1892
Ec 4:8 this is also **v.**, yea, it is a sore 1892
Ec 4:16 also is **v.** and vexation of spirit. 1892
Ec 5:10 with increase: this is also **v.** 1892
Ec 6:2 this is **v.**, and it is an evil disease. 1892
Ec 6:4 for he cometh in with **v.**, and 1892
Ec 6:9 is also **v.** and vexation of spirit. 1892
Ec 6:11 be many things that increase **v.**, 1892
Ec 7:6 laughter of the fool: this is also **v.** 1892
Ec 7:15 have I seen in the days of my **v.**: 1892
Ec 8:10 they had so done: this is also **v.** 1892
Ec 8:14 There is a **v.** which is done upon 1892
Ec 8:14 I said that this also is **v.** 1892
Ec 9:9 all the days of the life of thy **v.**, 1892
Ec 9:9 the sun, all the days of thy **v.** 1892
Ec 11:8 be many. All that cometh is **v.** 1892
Ec 11:10 for childhood and youth are **v.** 1892
Ec 12:8 **V.** of vanities, saith the preacher; 1892
Ec 12:8 saith the preacher; all is **v.** 1892
Isa 5:18 draw iniquity with cords of **v.**, 7723
Isa 30:28 sift the nations with the sieve of **v.** 7723
Isa 40:17 to him less than nothing, and **v.** 8414
Isa 40:23 the judges of the earth as **v.** 8414
Isa 41:29 they are all **v.**; their works are 205
Isa 44:9 a graven image are all of them **v.**, 8414
Isa 57:13 all away; **v.** shall take them: 1892
Isa 58:9 of the finger, and speaking **v.**; 205
Isa 59:4 they trust in **v.**, and speak lies; 8414
Jer 2:5 me, and have walked after **v.**, 1892
Jer 10:15 They are **v.**, and the work of errors: 1892
Jer 16:19 our fathers have inherited lies, **v.**, 1892
Jer 18:15 they have burned incense to **v.**, 7723
Jer 51:18 They are **v.**, the work of errors: 1892
Eze 13:6 They have seen **v.** and lying 7723
Eze 13:8 Because ye have spoken **v.**, and 7723
Eze 13:9 be upon the prophets that see **v.**, 7723

Eze 13:23 ye shall see no more v., nor divine..... 7723
Eze 21:29 Whiles they see v. unto thee,............ 7723
Eze 22:28 seeing v., and divining lies unto 7723
Ho 12:11 in Gilead? surely they are v.: 7723
Hab 2:13 weary themselves for very v.?.......... 7385
Zec 10:2 For the idols have spoken v., and........ 205
Ro 8:20 creature was made subject to v.,......... *3153*
Eph 4:17 walk, in the v. of their mind,............ *3153*
2Pe 2:18 speak great swelling words of v. *3153*

VANTAGE See ADVANTAGE.

VAPOUR See also VAPOURS.
Job 36:27 rain according to the v. thereof: 108
Job 36:33 the cattle also concerning the v.......... 5927
Ac 2:19 blood, and fire, and v. of smoke: *822*
Jas 4:14 a v., that appeareth for a little time,..... *822*

VAPOURS
Ps 135:7 He causeth the v. to ascend from....... 5387
Ps 148:8 Fire, and hail; snow, and v.;............. 7008
Jer 10:13 he causeth the v. to ascend from 5387
Jer 51:16 he causeth the v. to ascend from 5387

VARIABLENESS
Jas 1:17 with whom is no v., neither *3883*

VARIANCE
Mt 10:35 **a man at v. against his father,** *1369*
Ga 5:20 v., emulations, wrath, strife, ... *2054*

VASHNI (vash'-ni)
1Ch 6:28 sons of Samuel: the firstborn V., ... 2059

VASHTI (vash'-ti)
Es 1:9 V. the queen made a feast for the...... 2060
Es 1:11 bring V. the queen before the king..... 2060
Es 1:12 the queen V. refused to come at the .. 2060
Es 1:15 unto the queen V. according to law, ... 2060
Es 1:16 V. the queen hath not done wrong 2060
Es 1:17 commanded V. the queen to be 2060
Es 1:19 That V. come no more before king..... 2060
Es 2:1 he remembered V., and what she 2060
Es 2:4 the king be queen instead of V.. 2060
Es 2:17 and made her queen instead of V....... 2060

VAU (vawv)
Ps 119:41 *title* [ו] V...

VAUNT See also VAUNTETH.
Jg 7:2 lest Israel v. themselves against......... 6286

VAUNTETH
1Co 13:4 charity v. not itself, is not puffed....... *4068*

VEHEMENT
Ca 8:6 of fire, which hath a most v. flame. 3050
Jon 4:8 that God prepared a v. east wind; 2759
2Co 7:11 yea, what fear, yea, what v. desire,.... *1972*

VEHEMENTLY
Mk 14:31 But he spake the more v., If I.... *1722,4053*
Lu 6:48 **stream beat v. upon that house,** *4366*
Lu 6:49 **which the stream did beat v.,** *4366*
Lu 11:53 Pharisees began to urge him v.,......... *1171*
Lu 23:10 scribes stood and v. accused him......... *2159*

VEIL See also VAIL.
Ca 5:7 the keepers...took away my v. 7289
Mt 27:51 v. of the temple was rent in twain...... *2665*
Mk 15:38 v. of the temple was rent in twain...... *2665*
Lu 23:45 v. of the temple was rent in twain...... *2665*
Heb 6:19 entereth into that within the v.; *2665*
Heb 9:3 after the second v., the tabernacle...... *2665*
Heb 10:20 consecrated for us, through the v.,..... *2665*

VEIN
Job 28:1 Surely there is a v. for the silver, ... 4161

VENGE See AVENGE; REVENGE.

VENGEANCE
Ge 4:15 v. shall be taken on him sevenfold...... 5358
De 32:35 To me belongeth v., and 5359
De 32:41 I will render v. to mine enemies, ... 5359
De 32:43 will render v. to his adversaries, ... 5359
Jg 11:36 the Lord hath taken v. for thee of...... 5360
Ps 58:10 shall rejoice when he seeth the v.: 5359
Ps 94:1 Lord God, to whom v. belongeth;....... 5360
Ps 94:1 O God, to whom v. belongeth, shew.... 5360
Ps 99:8 thou tookest v. of their inventions. 5358
Ps 149:7 To execute v. upon the heathen,........ 5360
Pr 6:34 he will not spare in the day of v......... 5359
Isa 34:8 For it is the day of the Lord's v.,........ 5359
Isa 35:4 your God will come with v., even....... 5359
Isa 47:3 I will take v., and I will not meet....... 5359
Isa 59:17 he put on the garments of v. for........ 5359
Isa 61:2 Lord, and the day of v. of our God;.... 5359
Isa 63:4 For the day of v. is in mine heart,...... 5359
Jer 11:20 heart, let me see thy v. on them: 5360
Jer 20:12 heart, let me see thy v. on them: 5360
Jer 46:10 a day of v., that he may avenge him... 5360
Jer 50:15 for it is the v. of the Lord: 5360
Jer 50:15 take v. upon her; as she hath............ 5358
Jer 50:28 declare in Zion the v. of the Lord...... 5360
Jer 50:28 Lord our God, the v. of his temple..... 5360
Jer 51:6 for this is the time of the Lord's v.;.... 5360
Jer 51:11 v. of the Lord, the v. of his temple. ... 5360
Jer 51:36 thy cause, and take v. for thee; 5360
La 3:60 Thou hast seen all their v. and all...... 5360
Eze 24:8 cause fury to come up to take v.;......... 5359
Eze 25:12 the house of Judah by taking v.,......... 5359
Eze 25:14 I will lay my v. upon Edom by the...... 5360
Eze 25:14 they shall know my v., saith the 5360
Eze 25:15 taken v. with a despiteful heart,......... 5359
Eze 25:17 great v. upon them with furious 5360
Eze 25:17 when I shall lay my v. upon them...... 5360
Mic 5:15 execute v. in anger and fury upon 5359
Na 1:2 will take v. on his adversaries,.......... 5358
Lu 21:22 **For these be the days of v., that** ... *1557*
Ac 28:4 the sea, yet v. suffereth not to live. ... *1349*
Ro 3:5 Is God unrighteous who taketh v.? *3709*
Ro 12:19 V. is mine; I will repay, saith the....... *1557*
2Th 1:8 In flaming fire taking v. on them *1557*
Heb 10:30 V. belongeth unto me, I will............. *1557*
Jude 7 suffering the v. of eternal fire............ *1349*

VENISON
Ge 25:28 Esau, because he did eat of his v.: 6718
Ge 27:3 to the field, and take me some v.;...... 6720
Ge 27:5 went to the field to hunt for v., ... 6718
Ge 27:7 Bring me v., and made me savoury 6718
Ge 27:19 sit and eat of my v., that thy soul 6718
Ge 27:25 to me, and I will eat of my son's v., ... 6718
Ge 27:31 father arise, and eat of his son's v., ... 6718
Ge 27:33 where is he that hath taken v., and 6718

VENOM
De 32:33 dragons, and the cruel v. of asps........ 7219

VENOMOUS
Ac 28:4 saw the v. beast hang on his hand,...........

VENT See also INVENT; PREVENT.
Job 32:19 belly is as wine which hath no v.;....... 6605

VENTURE See also ADVENTURE.
1Ki 22:34 a certain man drew a bow at a v.,...... 8537
2Ch 18:33 a certain man drew a bow at a v.,...... 8537

VERIFIED
Ge 42:20 so shall your words be v., and ye 539
1Ki 8:26 let thy word, I pray thee, be v.,.......... 539
2Ch 6:17 God of Israel, let thy word be v., ... 539

VERILY
Ge 42:21 We are v. guilty concerning our 61
Ex 31:13 V. my sabbaths ye shall keep: for......... 389
Jg 15:2 I v. thought that thou hadst utterly 559
1Ki 1:43 V. our lord king David hath made......... 61
2Ki 4:14 V. she hath no child, and her 61
1Ch 21:24 I will v. buy it for the full price:......... 7069
Job 19:13 acquaintance are v. estranged............ 389
Ps 37:3 the land, and v. thou shalt be fed......... 530
Ps 39:5 v. every man at his best state is 389
Ps 58:11 V. there is a reward for the 389
Ps 58:11 v. he is a God that judgeth in the 389
Ps 66:19 But v. God hath heard me; he hath...... 403
Ps 73:13 V. I have cleansed my heart in............ 389
Isa 45:15 V. thou art a God that hidest.............. 403
Jer 15:11 V. it shall be well with thy.......... 518,3808
Jer 15:11 v. I will cause the enemy to entreat..... 518
Mt 5:18 **For v. I say unto you, Till heaven** .. *281*
Mt 5:26 **V. I say unto thee, Thou shalt by** ... *281*
Mt 6:2, 5,16 **V. I say unto you, They have**... *281*
Mt 8:10 **V. I say unto you, I have not found** .*281*
Mt 10:15 **V. I say unto you, It shall be more** . *281*
Mt 10:23 **for v. I say unto you, Ye shall not** .. *281*
Mt 10:42 **v. I say unto you, he shall in no** .. *281*
Mt 11:11 **V. I say unto you, Among them**...... *281*
Mt 13:17 **For v. I say unto you, That many** ... *281*
Mt 16:28 **V. I say unto you, There be some** ... *281*
Mt 17:20 **for v. I say unto you, If ye have** *281*
Mt 18:3 **V. I say unto you, Except ye be** *281*
Mt 18:13 **v. I say unto you, he rejoiceth** *281*
Mt 18:18 **V. I say unto you, Whatsoever ye** ... *281*
Mt 19:23 **V. I say unto you, That a rich man** .*281*
Mt 19:28 **V. I say unto you, That ye which** ... *281*
Mt 21:21 **V. I say unto you, If ye have faith,** .*281*
Mt 21:31 **V. I say unto you, That the** *281*
Mt 23:36 **V. I say unto you, All these things** . *281*
Mt 24:2 **v. I say unto you, There shall not** .. *281*
Mt 24:34 **V. I say unto you, This generation** ..*281*
Mt 24:47 **V. I say unto you, That he shall** *281*
Mt 25:12 **V. I say unto you, I know you not** .. *281*
Mt 25:40, 45 **V. I say unto you, Inasmuch as** .. *281*
Mt 26:13 **V. I say unto you, Wheresoever** *281*
Mt 26:21 **V. I say unto you, that one of you** .. *281*
Mt 26:34 **V. I say unto thee, That this night,** .*281*
Mk 3:28 **V. I say unto you, All sins shall be** . *281*
Mk 6:11 **V. I say unto you, It shall be more** . *281*
Mk 8:12 **v. I say unto you, There shall no** *281*
Mk 9:1 **V. I say unto you, That there be** *281*
Mk 9:12 **Elias v. cometh first, and restoreth** *3303*
Mk 9:41 **v. I say unto you, he shall not lose** .*281*
Mk 10:15 **V. I say unto you, Whosoever shall** *281*
Mk 10:29 **V. I say unto you, There is no man** .*281*
Mk 11:23 **v. I say unto you, That whosoever** .. *281*
Mk 12:43 **V. I say unto you, That this poor** ... *281*
Mk 13:30 **V. I say unto you, that this** *281*
Mk 14:9 **V. I say unto you, Wheresoever** *281*
Mk 14:18 **V. I say unto you, One of you** *281*
Mk 14:25 **V. I say unto you, I will drink no** ... *281*
Mk 14:30 **V. I say unto thee, That this day,** ... *281*
Lu 4:24 **V. I say unto you, No prophet is** *281*
Lu 11:51 **v. I say unto you, It shall be** *3483*
Lu 12:37 **v. I say unto you, that he shall** *281*
Lu 13:35 **and v. I say unto you, Ye shall not** . *281*
Lu 18:17 **V. I say unto you, Whosoever shall** .*281*
Lu 18:29 **V. I say unto you, There is no man** .*281*
Lu 21:32 **V. I say unto you, This generation** ..*281*
Lu 23:43 **V. I say unto thee, To day shalt** *281*
Joh 1:51 **V., v., I say unto you, Hereafter ye** . *281*
Joh 3:3,5 **V., v., I say unto thee, Except a** *281*
Joh 3:11 **V., v., I say unto thee, We speak**..... *281*
Joh 5:19 **V., v., I say unto you, The Son can** .*281*
Joh 5:24 **V.,v., I say unto you, He that** *281*
Joh 5:25 **V., v., I say unto you, The hour is** .. *281*
Joh 6:26 **V., v., I say unto you, Ye seek me,** . *281*
Joh 6:32 **V., v., I say unto you, Moses gave** .. *281*
Joh 6:47 **V., v., I say unto you, He that** *281*
Joh 6:53 **V., v., I say unto you, Except ye** *281*
Joh 8:34 **V., v., I say unto you, Whosoever** ... *281*
Joh 8:51 **V., v., I say unto you, If a man**...... *281*
Joh 8:58 **V., v., I say unto you, Before** *281*
Joh 10:1 **V., v., I say unto you, He that** *281*
Joh 10:7 **V., v., I say unto you, I am the** *281*
Joh 12:24 **V., v., I say unto you, Except a** *281*
Joh 13:16 **V., v., I say unto you, The servant** ..*281*
Joh 13:20 **V., v., I say unto you, He that** *281*
Joh 13:21 **V., v., I say unto you, that one of** .. *281*
Joh 13:38 **V., v., I say unto thee, The cock** *281*
Joh 14:12 **V., v., I say unto you, He that** *281*
Joh 16:20 **V., v., I say unto you, That ye** *281*
Joh 16:23 **V., v., I say unto you, Whatsoever**.. *281*
Joh 21:18 **V., v., I say unto thee, When thou**.. *281*
Ac 16:37 nay v.; but let them come................... *1063*
Ac 19:4 John v. baptized with the baptism........ *3303*
Ac 22:3 I am v. a man which am a Jew, born... *3303*
Ac 26:9 I v. thought with myself, that..... *3303,3767*
Ro 2:25 For circumcision v. profiteth, if........... *3303*
Ro 10:18 Yes v., their sound went into all *3304*
Ro 15:27 It hath pleased them v.; and their........ *1063*
1Co 5:3 For I v., as absent in body, but *3303*
1Co 9:18 V. that, when I preach the gospel, I.........
1Co 14:17 For thou v. givest thanks well, ... *3303*
Ga 3:21 v. righteousness should have been...... *3689*
1Th 3:4 For v., when we were with you, we... *2532*
Heb 2:16 v. he took not on him the nature of.... *1222*
Heb 3:5 Moses v. was faithful in all his........... *3303*
Heb 6:16 For men v. swear by the greater: *3303*
Heb 7:5 v. they that are of the sons of Levi, ... *3303*
Heb 7:18 For there is v. a disannulling of the *3303*
Heb 9:1 Then v. the first covenant had also..... *3303*
Heb 12:10 For they v. for a few days chastened... *3303*
1Pe 1:20 Who v. was foreordained before the.... *3303*
1Jo 2:5 him v. is the love of God perfected: *230*

VERITY
Ps 111:7 The works of his hands are v. and....... 571
1Ti 2:7 of the Gentiles in faith and v.............. *225*

VERMILION

Jer 22:14 with cedar, and painted with v. 8350
Eze 23:14 of the Chaldeans pourtrayed with v., 8350

VERY

Ge 1:31 made, and, behold, it was v. good. 3966
Ge 4:5 And Cain was v. wroth, and his 3966
Ge 12:14 the woman that she was v. fair. 3966
Ge 13:2 And Abram was v. rich in cattle, in. 3966
Ge 18:20 because their sin is v. grievous; 3966
Ge 21:11 thing was v. grievous in Abraham's 3966
Ge 24:16 the damsel was v. fair to look upon, 3966
Ge 26:13 and grew until he became v. great: 3966
Ge 27:21 whether thou be my v. son Esau or 2088
Ge 27:24 he said, Art thou my v. son Esau? 2088
Ge 27:33 Isaac trembled v. exceedingly, 1419
Ge 34:7 they were v. wroth, because he 3966
Ge 41:19 and v. ill favoured and leanfleshed, 3966
Ge 41:31 following; for it shall be v. grievous. 3966
Ge 41:49 v. much, until he left numbering; 3966
Ge 47:13 for the famine was v. sore, so that 3966
Ge 50:9 and it was a v. great company. 3966
Ge 50:10 a great and v. sore lamentation: 3966
Ex 1:20 multiplied, and waxed v. mighty. 3966
Ex 8:28 only ye shall not go v. far away:
Ex 9:3 shall be a v. grievous murrain. 3966
Ex 9:16 And in v. deed for this cause have I 199
Ex 9:18 cause it to rain a v. grievous hail, 3966
Ex 9:24 and fire...with the hail, v. grievous, 3966
Ex 10:14 v. grievous were they; before them 3966
Ex 11:3 Moses was v. great in the land of 3966
Ex 12:38 and herds, even v. much cattle. 3966
Ex 30:36 thou shalt beat some of it v. small, 1854
Nu 6:9 any man die v. suddenly by him, 6621
Nu 11:33 the people with a v. great plague. 3966
Nu 12:3 the man Moses was v. meek, above 3966
Nu 13:28 the cities are walled, and v. great: 3966
Nu 16:15 Moses was v. wroth, and said unto 3966
Nu 22:17 promote thee unto v. great honour, 3966
Nu 32:1 had a v. great multitude of cattle: 3966
De 9:20 the Lord was v. angry with Aaron 3966
De 9:21 stamped it, and ground it v. small, 3190
De 20:15 the cities which are v. far off from 3966
De 27:8 all the words of this law v. plainly. 3190
De 28:43 shall get up above thee v. high; 4605
De 28:43 and thou shalt come down v. low. 4295
De 28:54 tender among you, and v. delicate, 3966
De 30:14 But the word is v. nigh unto thee, 3966
De 32:20 they are a v. froward generation,
Jos 1:7 be thou strong and v. courageous, 3966
Jos 3:16 an heap v. far from the city Adam, 3966
Jos 8:4 go not v. far from the city, but be ye 3966
Jos 9:9 From a v. far country thy servants 3966
Jos 9:13 by reason of the v. long journey 3966
Jos 9:22 We are v. far from you; when ye 3966
Jos 10:20 them with a v. great slaughter, 3966
Jos 10:27 which remain until this v. day. 6106
Jos 11:4 with horses and chariots v. many. 3966
Jos 13:1 there remaineth yet v. much land 3966
Jos 22:8 your tents, and with v. much cattle, 3966
Jos 22:8 iron, and with v. much raiment: 3966
Jos 23:6 Be ye therefore v. courageous to 3966
Jg 3:17 Moab: and Eglon was a v. fat man. 3966
Jg 11:33 vineyards, with a v. great slaughter. 3966
Jg 11:35 thou hast brought me v. low, and
Jg 13:6 of an angel of God, v. terrible: 3966
Jg 18:9 the land, and, behold, it is v. good: 3966
Ru 1:20 hath dealt v. bitterly with me. 3966
1Sa 2:17 sin of the young men was v. great. 3966
1Sa 2:22 Now Eli was v. old, and heard all 3966
1Sa 4:10 and there was a v. great slaughter; 3966
1Sa 5:9 the city with a v. great destruction: 3966
1Sa 5:11 hand of God was v. heavy there 3966
1Sa 14:15 so it was a v. great trembling. 430
1Sa 14:20 there was a v. great discomfiture. 3966
1Sa 14:31 and the people were v. faint. 3966
1Sa 18:8 And Saul was v. wroth, and the 3966
1Sa 18:15 that he behaved himself v. wisely, 3966
1Sa 19:4 have been to thee-ward v. good: 3966
1Sa 20:7 but if he be v. wroth, then be sure
1Sa 23:22 is told me that he dealeth v. subtilly.
1Sa 25:2 and the man was v. great, and he 3966
1Sa 25:15 But the men were v. good unto us, 3966
1Sa 25:34 For in v. deed, as the Lord God of 199
1Sa 25:36 him, for he was v. drunken: 5704,3966
1Sa 26:4 that Saul was come in v. deed. 3559
2Sa 1:26 v. pleasant hast thou been unto 3966
2Sa 2:17 there was a v. sore battle that day; 3966
2Sa 3:8 Then was Abner v. wroth for the 3966
2Sa 11:2 the woman was v. beautiful to look 3966
2Sa 12:15 bare unto David, and it was v. sick.
2Sa 13:3 and Jonadab was a v. subtil man. 3966
2Sa 13:21 of all these things, he was v. wroth. 3966
2Sa 13:36 and all his servants wept v. sore. 3966
2Sa 18:17 a v. great heap of stones upon him: 3966
2Sa 19:32 Now Barzillai was a v. aged man, 3966
2Sa 19:32 for he was a v. great man. 3966
2Sa 24:10 for I have done v. foolishly. 3966
1Ki 1:4 And the damsel was v. fair, and 3966
1Ki 1:6 and he also was a v. goodly man; 3966
1Ki 1:15 and the king was v. old; and 3966
1Ki 7:34 undersetters were of the v. base
1Ki 10:2 to Jerusalem with a v. great train, 3966
1Ki 10:2 and v. much gold, and precious 3966
1Ki 10:10 and of spices v. great store, and 3966
1Ki 19:10, 14 I have been v. jealous for the Lord
1Ki 21:26 he did v. abominably in following 3966
2Ki 14:26 of Israel, that it was v. bitter: 3966
2Ki 17:18 the Lord was v. angry with Israel. 3966
2Ki 21:16 shed innocent blood v. much, 3966
1Ch 9:13 v. able men for the work of the
1Ch 18:8 brought David v. much brass, 3966
1Ch 21:8 servant; for I have done v. foolishly. 3966
1Ch 21:13 Lord; for v. great are his mercies: 3966
1Ch 23:17 sons of Rehabiah were v. many. 4605
2Ch 6:18 God in v. deed dwell with men on 552
2Ch 7:8 with him, a v. great congregation, 3966
2Ch 9:1 with a v. great company, and 3966
2Ch 14:13 they carried away v. much spoil. 3966
2Ch 16:8 host, with v. many chariots and 3966
2Ch 16:14 they made a v. great burning. 5704,3966
2Ch 20:35 king of Israel, who did v. wickedly:
2Ch 24:24 Lord delivered a v. great host 3966
2Ch 30:13 month, a v. great congregation. 3966
2Ch 32:29 had given him substance v. much. 3966
2Ch 33:14 and raised it up a v. great height, 3966
2Ch 36:14 transgressed v. much after all the
Ezr 10:1 a v. great congregation of men 3966
Ezr 10:1 children: for the people wept v. sore.
Ne 1:7 We have dealt v. corruptly against
Ne 2:2 heart. Then I was v. sore afraid, 3966
Ne 4:7 stopped, then they were v. wroth, 3966
Ne 5:6 I was v. angry when I heard their 3966
Ne 8:17 And there was v. great gladness. 3966
Es 1:12 therefore was the king v. wroth, 3966
Job 1:3 asses, and a v. great household; 3966
Job 2:13 saw that his grief was v. great. 3966
Job 15:10 the grayheaded and v. aged men, 3453
Job 32:6 said, I am young, and ye are v. old; 3453
Ps 5:9 their inward part is v. wickedness; 1942
Ps 35:8 into that v. destruction let him fall.
Ps 46:1 a v. present help in trouble. 3966
Ps 50:3 v. tempestuous round about him. 3966
Ps 71:19 righteousness...O God, is v. high, 5704
Ps 79:8 us: for we are brought v. low. 3966
Ps 89:2 shalt thou establish in the v. heavens.
Ps 92:5 and thy thoughts are v. deep. 3966
Ps 93:5 Thy testimonies are v. sure: 3966
Ps 104:1 O Lord my God, thou art v. great; 3966
Ps 105:12 but a few men in number; yea, v. few,
Ps 119:107 I am afflicted v. much: 5704,3966
Ps 119:138 are righteous and v. faithful. 3966
Ps 119:140 Thy word is v. pure: therefore 3966
Ps 142:6 my cry; for I am brought v. low: 3966
Ps 146:4 in that v. day his thoughts perish.
Ps 147:15 earth: his word runneth v. swiftly. 5704
Pr 17:9 a matter separateth v. friends.
Pr 27:15 continual dropping in a v. rainy 5464
Isa 1:9 left unto us a v. small remnant, 4592
Isa 5:1 hath a vineyard in a v. fruitful hill:
Isa 10:25 For yet a v. little while, and the 4213
Isa 16:6 the pride of Moab; he is v. proud: 3966
Isa 16:14 the remnant shall be v. small and 4213
Isa 24:16 dealers have dealt v. treacherously. 899
Isa 29:17 Is it not yet a v. little while, and 4213
Isa 30:19 he will be v. gracious unto thee at the
Isa 31:1 because they are v. strong; 3966
Isa 33:17 behold the land that is v. far off. 4801
Isa 40:15 up the isles as a v. little thing. 1851
Isa 47:6 hast thou v. heavily laid thy yoke. 3966
Isa 48:8 thou wouldest deal v. treacherously, 898
Isa 52:13 and extolled, and be v. high. 3966
Isa 64:9 Be not wroth v. sore, O Lord, 3966
Isa 64:12 thy peace, and afflict us v. sore? 3966
Jer 2:12 be ye v. desolate, saith the Lord. 3966
Jer 4:19 I am pained at my v. heart; my 7023
Jer 5:11 dealt v. treacherously against me,
Jer 12:1 happy that deal v. treacherously? 899
Jer 14:17 breach, with a v. grievous blow. 3966
Jer 18:13 Israel hath done a v. horrible thing. 3966
Jer 20:15 born unto thee; making him v. glad.
Jer 24:2 One basket had v. good figs, even 3966
Jer 24:2 other basket had v. naughty figs, 3966
Jer 24:3 I said, Figs; the good figs, v. good; 3966
Jer 24:3 and the evil, v. evil, that cannot be 3966
Jer 27:7 until the v. time of his land come:
Jer 40:12 wine and summer fruits v. much. 3966
Jer 46:20 Egypt is like a v. fair heifer, but 3304
La 5:22 thou art v. wroth against us. 5704,3966
Eze 2:3 against me, even unto this v. day. 6106
Eze 16:47 as if that were a v. little thing, 6985
Eze 27:25 made v. glorious in the midst of 3966
Eze 33:32 art unto them as a v. lovely song 5690
Eze 37:2 were v. many in the open valley; 3966
Eze 37:2 valley; and, lo, they were v. dry. 3966
Eze 40:2 set me upon a v. high mountain, 3966
Eze 47:7 were v. many trees on the one side. 3966
Eze 47:9 shall be a v. great multitude of fish, 3966
Da 2:12 the king was angry and v. furious, 7690
Da 6:19 the king arose v. early in the morning,
Da 7:20 mouth that spake v. great things, 7260
Da 8:8 the he goat waxed v. great: 5704,3960
Da 11:25 a v. great and mighty army; 5704,3960
Joe 2:11 army: for his camp is v. great: 3960
Joe 2:11 Lord is great and v. terrible; 3960
Am 5:20 v. dark, and no brightness in it? 651
Jon 4:1 exceedingly, and he was v. angry.
Hab 2:13 people shall labour in the v. fire, 1767
Hab 2:13 weary themselves for v. vanity? 1767
Zec 1:15 I am v. sore displeased with the
Zec 8:4 his staff in his hand for v. age. 7230
Zec 9:2 and Zidon, though it be v. wise. 3966
Zec 9:5 shall see it, and be v. sorrowful, 3966
Zec 14:4 and there shall be a v. great valley; 3966
Mt 10:30 **But the v. hairs of your head are** *2532*
Mt 15:28 made whole from that v. hour. *1565*
Mt 17:18 child was cured from that v. hour. *1565*
Mt 18:31 **was done, they were v. sorry,** *4970*
Mt 21:8 a v. great multitude spread their *4118*
Mt 24:24 **they shall deceive the v. elect** *2532*
Mt 26:7 box of v. precious ointment, *927*
Mt 26:37 began to be sorrowful and v. heavy. *85*
Mk 8:1 the multitude being v. great, and *3827*
Mk 14:3 ointment of spikenard v. precious; *4185*
Mk 14:33 be sore amazed, and to be v. heavy; *85*
Mk 16:2 v. early in the morning the first *3029*
Mk 16:4 rolled away: for it was v. great. *4970*
Lu 1:3 of all things from the v. first,
Lu 9:5 **shake off the v. dust from your** *2532*
Lu 9:5 **Even the v. dust of your city, which**
Lu 12:7 **But even the v. hairs of your head** *2532*
Lu 12:59 **till thou hast paid the v. last mite**
Lu 18:23 heard this, he was v. sorrowful: *4970*
Lu 18:23 sorrowful: for he was v. rich. *4970*
Lu 18:24 saw that he was v. sorrowful, *4036*
Lu 19:17 **hast been faithful in a v. little,** *1646*
Lu 19:48 were v. attentive to hear him. *1582*
Lu 24:1 v. early in the morning, they came
Joh 7:26 indeed that this is the v. Christ? *230*
Joh 8:4 was taken in adultery, in the v. act. *1888*
Joh 12:3 ointment of spikenard, v. costly, *4186*
Joh 14:11 **else believe me for the v. works' sake.**
Ac 9:22 proving that this is v. Christ. *846*
Ac 10:10 he became v. hungry, and would *4361*
Ac 24:2 that v. worthy deeds are done unto *2735*
Ac 25:10 no wrong, as thou v. well knowest. *2566*
Ro 10:20 Esaias is v. bold, and saith, I was *662*
Ro 13:6 continually upon this v. thing. *846*
1Co 4:3 it is a v. small thing that I should *1646*
2Co 9:2 your zeal hath provoked v. many. *4119*
2Co 11:5 behind the v. chiefest apostles. *5228*
2Co 12:11 I behind the v. chiefest apostles, *3029*
2Co 12:15 I will v. gladly spend and be spent *2236*
Php 1:6 Being confident of this v. thing, that *846*
1Th 5:13 to esteem them v. highly in love *5228*
1Th 5:23 the v. God of peace sanctify you. *846*
2Ti 1:17 he sought me out v. diligently, *4708*
2Ti 1:18 at Ephesus, thou knowest v. well. *957*
Heb 10:1 and not the v. image of the things, *846*

Jas 3:4 turned about with a **v.** small helm,...... *1646*
Jas 5:11 that the Lord is **v.** pitiful, and, of....... *4184*

VESSEL See also VESSELS.
Le 6:28 earthen **v.** wherein it is sodden......... 3627
Le 11:32 whether it be any **v.** of wood, or........ 3627
Le 11:32 whatsoever **v.** it be, wherein any 3627
Le 11:33 every earthen **v.**, whereinto any of..... 3627
Le 11:34 in every such **v.** shall be unclean....... 3627
Le 14:5 the birds be killed in an earthen **v.** 3627
Le 14:50 an earthen **v.** over running water: 3627
Le 15:12 And the **v.** of earth, that he toucheth.. 3627
Le 15:12 every **v.** of wood shall be rinsed in..... 3627
Nu 5:17 take holy water in an earthen **v.**;........ 3627
Nu 19:15 And every open **v.**, which hath no....... 3627
Nu 19:17 water shall be put thereto in a **v.**: 3627
De 23:24 but thou shalt not put any in thy **v.**...... 3627
1Sa 21:5 were sanctified this day in the **v.**........ 3627
1Ki 17:10 I pray thee, a little water in a **v.**,....... 3627
2Ki 4:6 unto her son, Bring me yet a **v.**......... 3627
2Ki 4:6 unto her, There is not a **v.** more. 3627
Ps 2:9 them in pieces like a potter's **v.**. 3627
Ps 31:12 out of mind: I am like a broken **v.**...... 3627
Pr 25:4 shall come forth a **v.** for the finer....... 3627
Isa 30:14 it as the breaking of the potters' **v.**...... 5035
Isa 66:20 bring an offering in a clean **v.** into 3627
Jer 18:4 And the **v.** that he made of clay was... 3627
Jer 18:4 so he made it again another **v.**, as....... 3627
Jer 19:11 as one breaketh a potter's **v.**, that...... 3627
Jer 22:28 is he a **v.** wherein is no pleasure? 3627
Jer 25:34 and ye shall fall like a pleasant **v.**. 3627
Jer 32:14 and put them in an earthen **v.**, that..... 3627
Jer 48:11 hath not been emptied from **v.** to **v.**, .. 3627
Jer 48:38 have broken Moab like a **v.** wherein.... 3627
Jer 51:34 he hath made me an empty **v.**, he...... 3627
Eze 4:9 and fitches, and put them in one **v.**,.... 3627
Eze 15:3 a pin of it to hang any **v.** thereon?...... 3627
Ho 8:8 as a **v.** wherein is no pleasure. 3627
Mk 11:16 carry any **v.** through the temple. *4632*
Lu 8:16 **a candle, covereth it with a v.**,....... *4632*
Joh 19:29 there was set a **v.** full of vinegar:....... *4632*
Ac 9:15 **he is a chosen v. unto me, to bear**..*4632*
Ac 10:11 a certain **v.** descending unto him, ... *4632*
Ac 10:16 the **v.** was received up again into *4632*
Ac 11:5 saw a vision, A certain **v.** descend,..... *4632*
Ro 9:21 lump to make one **v.** unto honour, ... *4632*
1Th 4:4 to possess his **v.** in sanctification........ *4632*
2Ti 2:21 he shall be a **v.** unto honour,............ *4632*
1Pe 3:7 unto the wife, as unto the weaker **v.**,.. *4632*

VESSELS
Ge 43:11 best fruits in the land in your **v.**,......... 3627
Ex 7:19 both in **v.** of wood, and in **v.** of stone. ......
Ex 25:39 shall he make it, with all these **v.**....... 3627
Ex 27:3 **v. thereof thou shalt make of brass**..... 3627
Ex 27:19 All the **v.** of the tabernacle in all 3627
Ex 30:27 And the table and all his **v.**, ... 3627
Ex 30:27 and the candlestick and his **v.**, ... 3627
Ex 30:28 And the altar...with all his **v.**,............ 3627
Ex 35:13 and his staves, and all his **v.**, and....... 3627
Ex 35:16 grate, his staves, and all his **v.**, ... 3627
Ex 37:16 he made the **v.** which were upon.......... 3627
Ex 37:24 pure gold made he it, and all the **v.** 3627
Ex 38:3 And he made all the **v.** of the altar, ... 3627
Ex 38:3 all the **v.** thereof made he of brass. 3627
Ex 38:30 for it, and all the **v.** of the altar,........ 3627
Ex 39:36 The table, and all the **v.** thereof,......... 3627
Ex 39:37 all the **v.** thereof, and the oil for 3627
Ex 39:39 brass, his staves, and all his **v.**, ... 3627
Ex 39:40 and all the **v.** of the service of the...... 3627
Ex 40:9 hallow it, and all the **v.** thereof: 3627
Ex 40:10 all his **v.**, and sanctify the altar: 3627
Le 8:11 anointed the altar and all his **v.**, ... 3627
Nu 1:50 over all the **v.** thereof, and over all..... 3627
Nu 1:50 tabernacle, and all the **v.** thereof; 3627
Nu 3:31 the **v.** of the sanctuary wherewith 3627
Nu 3:36 all the **v.** thereof, and all that 3627
Nu 4:9 all the oil **v.** thereof, wherewith 3627
Nu 4:10 put it and all the **v.** thereof within 3627
Nu 4:14 shall put upon it all the **v.** thereof,...... 3627
Nu 4:14 the basons, all the **v.** of the altar;........ 3627
Nu 4:15 and all the **v.** of the sanctuary, ... 3627
Nu 4:16 sanctuary, and in the **v.** thereof. 3627
Nu 7:1 the altar and all the **v.** thereof, ... 3627
Nu 7:85 the silver **v.** weighed two thousand...... 3627
Nu 18:3 come nigh the **v.** of the sanctuary...... 3627
Nu 19:18 and upon all the **v.**, and upon the 3627
Jos 6:19 and gold, and **v.** of brass and iron,...... 3627
Jos 6:24 and the **v.** of brass and of iron,.......... 3627
Ru 2:9 go unto the **v.**, and drink of that 3627
1Sa 9:7 for the bread is spent in our **v.**,......... 3627
1Sa 21:5 the **v.** of the young men are holy, ... 3627
2Sa 8:10 brought with him **v.** of silver, ... 3627
2Sa 8:10 and **v.** of gold, and **v.** of brass:.......... 3627
2Sa 17:28 beds, and basons, and earthen **v.**, ... 3627
1Ki 7:45 all these **v.**, which Hiram made.......... 3627
1Ki 7:47 Solomon left all the **v.** unweighed, ... 3627
1Ki 7:48 Solomon made all the **v.** that............ 3627
1Ki 7:51 silver, and the gold, and the **v.**, ... 3627
1Ki 8:4 holy **v.** that were in the tabernacle, ... 3627
1Ki 10:21 Solomon's drinking **v.** were of gold, ... 3627
1Ki 10:21 all the **v.** of the house of the forest 3627
1Ki 10:25 present, **v.** of silver, and **v.** of gold,.... 3627
1Ki 15:15 the Lord, silver, and gold, and **v.**....... 3627
2Ki 4:3 Go, borrow thee **v.** abroad of all 3627
2Ki 4:3 even empty **v.**; borrow not a few. 3627
2Ki 4:4 and shalt pour out into all those **v.**....... 3627
2Ki 4:5 who brought the **v.** to her; and she..........
2Ki 4:6 to pass, when the **v.** were full, ... 3627
2Ki 7:15 way was full of garments and **v.**,......... 3627
2Ki 12:13 any **v.** of gold, or **v.** of silver, of the... 3627
2Ki 14:14 all the **v.** that were found in the......... 3627
2Ki 23:4 all the **v.** that were made for Baal, ... 3627
2Ki 24:13 cut in pieces all the **v.** of gold........... 3627
2Ki 25:14 all the **v.** of brass wherewith they 3627
2Ki 25:16 all these **v.** was without weight. 3627
1Ch 9:28 the charge of the ministering **v.**, ... 3627
1Ch 9:29 were appointed to oversee the **v.**, ... 3627
1Ch 18:8 and the pillars, and the **v.** of brass...... 3627
1Ch 18:10 all manner of **v.** of gold and silver....... 3627
1Ch 22:19 the holy **v.** of God, into the house...... 3627
1Ch 23:26 any **v.** of it for the service thereof....... 3627
1Ch 28:13 for all the **v.** of service in the house ... 3627
2Ch 4:18 Solomon made all these **v.** in great..... 3627
2Ch 4:19 Solomon made all the **v.** that were...... 3627
2Ch 5:5 holy **v.** that were in the tabernacle, ... 3627
2Ch 9:20 the drinking **v.** of king Solomon.......... 3627
2Ch 9:20 all the **v.** of the house of the forest 3627
2Ch 9:24 **v.** of silver, and **v.** of gold, and.......... 3627
2Ch 15:18 dedicated, silver, and gold, and **v.**. 3627
2Ch 24:14 made **v.** for the house of the Lord,..... 3627
2Ch 24:14 even **v.** to minister, and to offer 3627
2Ch 24:14 spoons, and **v.** of gold and silver. 3627
2Ch 25:24 all the **v.** that were found in the......... 3627
2Ch 28:24 together the **v.** of the house of God,... 3627
2Ch 28:24 cut in pieces the **v.** of the house of..... 3627
2Ch 29:18 offering, with all the **v.** thereof, ... 3627
2Ch 29:18 table, with all the **v.** thereof. 3627
2Ch 29:19 Moreover all the **v.**, which king 3627
2Ch 36:7 Nebuchadnezzar also carried...**v.** of...... 3627
2Ch 36:10 goodly **v.** of the house of the Lord, ... 3627
2Ch 36:18 all the **v.** of the house of God,........... 3627
2Ch 36:19 destroyed all the goodly **v.** thereof....... 3627
Ezr 1:6 their hands with **v.** of silver, with....... 3627
Ezr 1:7 Cyrus...brought forth the **v.** of............. 3627
Ezr 1:10 and ten, and other **v.** a thousand. 3627
Ezr 1:11 All the **v.** of gold and of silver were.... 3627
Ezr 5:14 the **v.** also of gold and silver of the.... 3984
Ezr 5:15 Take these **v.**, go, carry them into..... 3984
Ezr 6:5 golden and silver **v.** of the house......... 3984
Ezr 7:19 The **v.** also that are given thee for 3984
Ezr 8:25 silver, and the gold, and the **v.**, ... 3627
Ezr 8:26 and silver **v.** an hundred talents, ... 3627
Ezr 8:27 two **v.** of fine copper, precious as....... 3627
Ezr 8:28 **v.** are holy also; and the silver........... 3627
Ezr 8:30 the silver, and the gold, and the **v.**,....... 3627
Ezr 8:33 and the **v.** weighed in the house......... 3627
Ne 10:39 where are the **v.** of the sanctuary,....... 3627
Ne 13:5 the frankincense, and the **v.**, and........ 3627
Ne 13:9 I again the **v.** of the house of God, ... 3627
Es 1:7 they gave them drink in **v.** of gold,...... 3627
Es 1:7 **v.** being diverse one from another,) 3627
Isa 18:2 **v.** of bulrushes upon the waters, ... 3627
Isa 22:24 the issue, all **v.** of small quantity, ... 3627
Isa 22:24 the **v.** of cups, even to all the **v.** of 3627
Isa 52:11 clean, that bear the **v.** of the Lord...... 3627
Isa 65:4 abominable things is in their **v.**;........... 3627
Jer 14:3 they returned with their **v.** empty;...... 3627
Jer 27:16 **v.** of the Lord's house shall now 3627
Jer 27:18 **v.** which are left in the house of.......... 3627
Jer 27:19 concerning the residue of the **v.**......... 3627
Jer 27:21 concerning the **v.** that remain in.......... 3627
Jer 28:3 bring again into this place all the **v.**...... 3627
Jer 28:6 to bring again the **v.** of the Lord's...... 3627
Jer 40:10 and put them in your **v.**, and dwell 3627
Jer 48:12 and shall empty his **v.**, and break 3627
Jer 49:29 and all their **v.**, and their camels; 3627
Jer 52:18 all the **v.** of brass wherewith they 3627
Jer 52:20 the brass of all these **v.** was without.... 3627
Eze 27:13 the persons of men and **v.** of brass..... 3627
Da 1:2 part of the **v.** of the house of God:..... 3627
Da 1:2 he brought the **v.** into the treasure..... 3627
Da 5:2 to bring the golden and silver **v.**.......... 3984
Da 5:3 Then they brought the golden **v.**......... 3984
Da 5:23 have brought the **v.** of his house........ 3984
Da 11:8 precious **v.** of silver and of gold; 3627
Ho 13:15 spoil the treasure of all pleasant **v.**.. 3627
Hag 2:16 to draw out fifty **v.** out of the press,.........
Mt 13:48 **gathered the good into v., but cast**... *30*
Mt 25:4 **wise took oil in their v. with their**.... *30*
Mk 7:4 cups, and pots, and brazen **v.**, and..........
Ro 9:22 **v.** of wrath fitted to destruction: *4632*
Ro 9:23 of his glory on the **v.** of mercy, ... *4632*
2Co 4:7 have this treasure in earthen **v.**, ... *4632*
2Ti 2:20 are not only **v.** of gold and of silver, ... *4632*
Heb 9:21 and all the **v.** of the ministry. *4632*
Re 2:27 **as the v. of a potter shall they be**.. *4632*
Re 18:12 wood, and all manner **v.** of ivory, ... *4632*
Re 18:12 manner **v.** of most precious wood,...... *4632*

VESTMENTS
2Ki 10:22 forth **v.** for all the worshippers 3830
2Ki 10:22 And he brought them forth **v.**. 4403

VESTRY
2Ki 10:22 unto him that was over the **v.**, ... 4458

VESTURE See also VESTURES.
De 22:12 upon the four quarters of thy **v.**, ... 3682
Ps 22:18 them, and cast lots upon my **v.**.......... 3830
Ps 102:26 as a **v.** shalt thou change them, ... 3830
Mt 27:35 and upon my **v.** did they cast lots....... *2441*
Joh 19:24 and for my **v.** they did cast lots. *2441*
Heb 1:12 as a **v.** shalt thou fold them up, ... *4018*
Re 19:13 clothed with a **v.** dipped in blood: *2440*
Re 19:16 on his **v.** and on his thigh a name....... *2440*

VESTURES
Ge 41:42 arrayed him in **v.** of fine linen,............ 899

VEX See also VEXED.
Ex 22:21 thou shalt neither **v.** a stranger, ... 3238
Le 18:18 take a wife to her sister, to **v.** her, ... 6887
Le 19:33 in your land, ye shall not **v.** him......... 3238
Nu 25:17 **V.** the Midianites, and smite 6887
Nu 25:18 For they **v.** you with their wiles,......... 6887
Nu 33:55 shall **v.** you in the land wherein.......... 6887
2Sa 12:18 how will he then **v.** himself, ... 6213,7451
2Ch 15:6 God did **v.** them with all adversity. 2000
Job 19:2 How long will ye **v.** my soul, and 3013
Ps 2:5 and **v.** them in his sore displeasure. 926
Isa 7:6 us go up against Judah, and **v.** it, ... 6973
Isa 11:13 and Judah shall not **v.** Ephraim........... 6887
Eze 32:9 I will also **v.** the hearts of many.......... 3707
Hab 2:7 and awake that shall **v.** thee,.............. 2111
Ac 12:1 hands to **v.** certain of the church. *2559*

VEXATION See also VEXATIONS.
De 28:20 shall send upon thee cursing, **v.**, ... 4103
Ec 1:14 all is vanity and **v.** of spirit............... 7469
Ec 1:17 that this also is **v.** of spirit............... 7475
Ec 2:11 all was vanity and **v.** of spirit,........... 7469
Ec 2:17 for all is vanity and **v.** of spirit. 7469
Ec 2:22 labour, and of the **v.** of his heart, ... 7475
Ec 2:26 also is vanity and **v.** of spirit.............. 7469
Ec 4:4 This is also vanity and **v.** of spirit....... 7469
Ec 4:6 full with travail and **v.** of spirit. 7469
Ec 4:16 this also is vanity and **v.** of spirit........ 7475
Ec 6:9 this is also vanity and **v.** of spirit........ 7469
Isa 9:1 shall not be such as was in her **v.**, ... 4164
Isa 28:19 shall be a **v.** only to understand 2113
Isa 65:14 and shall howl for **v.** of spirit. 7667

VEXATIONS
2Ch 15:5 but great **v.** were upon all the 4103

VEXED
Nu 20:15 Egyptians **v.** us, and our fathers:........ 7489
Jg 2:18 that oppressed them and **v.** them. 1766
Jg 10:8 they **v.** and oppressed the children 7492
Jg 16:16 so that his soul was **v.** unto death: 7114
1Sa 14:47 he turned himself, he **v.** them............ 7561
2Sa 13:2 Amnon was so **v.**, that he fell sick...... 3334

2Ki 4:27 for her soul is **v.** within her:............. 4843
Ne 9:27 of their enemies, who **v.** them:.......... 6887
Job 27:2 Almighty, who hath **v.** my soul; 4843
Ps 6:2 heal me; for my bones are **v.**............. 926
Ps 6:3 My soul is also sore **v.**: but thou......... 926
Ps 6:10 enemies be ashamed and sore **v.**: 926
Isa 63:10 rebelled, and **v.** his holy Spirit: 6087
Eze 22:5 which art infamous and much **v.**. 4103
Eze 22:7 in thee have they **v.** the fatherless...... 3238
Eze 22:29 and have **v.** the poor and needy: 3238
Mt 15:22 is grievously **v.** with a devil.............. *1139*
Mt 17:15 for he is lunatick, and sore **v.**:............ *3958*
Lu 6:18 that were **v.** with unclean spirits: *3791*
Ac 5:16 which were **v.** with unclean spirits:..... *3791*
2Pe 2:7 **v.** with the filthy conversation of........ *2669*
2Pe 2:8 **v.** his righteous soul from day to *928*

VIAL See also VIALS.
1Sa 10:1 Then Samuel took a **v.** of oil, and....... 6378
Re 16:2 poured out his **v.** upon the earth; *5357*
Re 16:3 poured out his **v.** upon the sea; *5357*
Re 16:4 poured out his **v.** upon the rivers *5357*
Re 16:8 poured out his **v.** upon the sun; *5357*
Re 16:10 poured out his **v.** upon the seat *5357*
Re 16:12 out his **v.** upon the great river........... *5357*
Re 16:17 poured out his **v.** into the air;............ *5357*

VIALS
Re 5:8 and golden **v.** full of odours, which...... *5357*
Re 15:7 seven golden **v.** full of the wrath of..... *5357*
Re 16:1 pour out the **v.** of the wrath of God.... *5357*
Re 17:1 angels which had the seven **v.**, ... *5357*
Re 21:9 the seven **v.** full of the seven last....... *5357*

VICTORY
2Sa 19:2 the **v.** that day was turned into.......... 8668
2Sa 23:10 the Lord wrought a great **v.** that........ 8668
2Sa 23:12 and the Lord wrought a great **v.**. 8668
1Ch 29:11 and the glory, and the **v.**, and the 5331
Ps 98:1 holy arm, hath gotten him the **v.**, ... 3467
Isa 25:8 He will swallow up death in **v.**;......... 5331
Mt 12:20 he send forth judgment unto **v.**.......... *3534*
1Co 15:54 Death is swallowed up in **v.**.............. *3534*
1Co 15:55 thy sting? O grave, where is thy **v.**? ... *3534*
1Co 15:57 **v.** through our Lord Jesus Christ......... *3534*
1Jo 5:4 the **v.** that overcometh the world, ... *3529*
Re 15:2 had gotten the **v.** over the beast, ... *3528*

VICTUAL See also VICTUALS.
Ex 12:39 prepared for themselves any **v.**.......... 6720
Jg 20:10 to fetch **v.** for the people, that they.... 6720
1Ki 4:27 those officers provided **v.** for king 3557
2Ch 11:11 captains in them, and store of **v.**, ... 3978
2Ch 11:23 he gave them **v.** in abundance............ 4202

VICTUALS
Ge 14:11 and Gomorrah, and all their **v.**,.......... 400
Le 25:37 nor lend him thy **v.** for increase........... 400
De 23:19 usury of money, usury of **v.**, usury 400
Jos 1:11 people, saying, Prepare you **v.**;.......... 6720
Jos 9:11 Take **v.** with you for the journey,....... 6720
Jos 9:14 And the men took up their **v.**, and....... 6718
Jg 7:8 the people took **v.** in their hand. 6720
Jg 17:10 and a suit of apparel, and thy **v.**.......... 4241
1Sa 22:10 and gave him **v.**, and gave him 6720
1Ki 4:7 provided **v.** for the king and his 3557
1Ki 11:18 appointed him **v.**, and gave him......... 3899
Ne 10:31 ware or any **v.** on the sabbath day........ 7668
Ne 13:15 in the day wherein they sold **v.**......... 6718
Jer 40:5 captain of the guard gave him **v.**.......... 737
Jer 44:17 for then had we plenty of **v.**, and 3899
Mt 14:15 villages, and buy themselves **v.**.......... *1033*
Lu 9:12 about, and lodge, and get **v.**:............ *1979*

VIEW See also VIEWED.
Jos 2:1 Go **v.** the land, even Jericho............. 7200
Jos 7:2 saying, Go up and **v.** the country. 7270
2Ki 2:7 went, and stood to **v.** afar off: 5048
2Ki 2:15 prophets...were to **v.** at Jericho 5048

VIEWED
Jos 7:2 And the men went up and **v.** Ai. 7270
Ezr 8:15 and I **v.** the people, and the priests, ... 995
Ne 2:13 and **v.** the walls of Jerusalem, ... 7663
Ne 2:15 night by the brook, and **v.** the wall, ... 7663

VIGILANT
1Ti 3:2 husband of one wife, **v.**, sober, of *3524*
1Pe 5:8 Be sober, be **v.**; because your........... *1127*

VILE See also REVILE; VILER; VILEST.
De 25:3 thy brother should seem **v.** unto 7034
Jg 19:24 this man do not so **v.** a thing............ 5039
1Sa 3:13 his sons made themselves **v.**, and....... 7043
1Sa 15:9 but every thing that was **v.** and 5240
2Sa 6:22 I will yet be more **v.** than thus, ... 7043
Job 18:3 and reputed **v.** in your sight?........... 2933
Job 40:4 I am **v.**; what shall I answer thee?...... 7043
Ps 15:4 eyes a **v.** person is contemned; 959
Isa 32:5 The **v.** person shall be no more 5036
Isa 32:6 the **v.** person will speak villany, ... 5036
Jer 15:19 forth the precious from the **v.**,........... 2151
Jer 29:17 will make them like **v.** figs, that 8182
La 1:11 and consider; for I am become **v.**. 2151
Da 11:21 estate shall stand up a **v.** person,......... 959
Na 1:14 make thy grave; for thou art **v.**........... 7043
Na 3:6 filth upon thee, and make thee **v.**, ... 5034
Ro 1:26 gave them up unto **v.** affections: *819*
Php 3:21 Who shall change our **v.** body, ... *5014*
Jas 2:2 in also a poor man in **v.** raiment: *4508*

VILELY
2Sa 1:21 of the mighty is **v.** cast away,............ 1602

VILER
Job 30:8 men: they were **v.** than the earth....... 5217

VILEST
Ps 12:8 when the **v.** men are exalted............. 2149

VILLAGE See also VILLAGES.
Mt 21:2 **Go into the v. over against you,** *2968*
Mk 11:2 **Go your way into the v. over** *2968*
Lu 8:1 went throughout every city and **v.**, ... *2968*
Lu 9:52 entered into a **v.** of the Samaritans, ... *2968*
Lu 9:56 **them.** And they went to another **v.**.... *2968*
Lu 10:38 that he entered into a certain **v.**......... *2968*
Lu 17:12 And as he entered into a certain **v.**,..... *2968*
Lu 19:30 **Go ye into the v. over against you;** .*2968*
Lu 24:13 same day to a **v.** called Emmaus, ... *2968*
Lu 24:28 And they drew nigh unto the **v.**, ... *2968*

VILLAGES
Ex 8:13 out of the **v.**, and out of the fields...... 2691
Le 25:31 houses of the **v.** which have no wall.... 2691
Nu 21:25 Heshbon, and in all the **v.** thereof....... 1323
Nu 21:32 they took the **v.** thereof, and drove 1323
Nu 32:42 took Kenath, and the **v.** thereof, ... 1323
Jos 13:23 the cities and the **v.** thereof. 2691
Jos 13:28 families, the cities, and their **v.**.......... 2691
Jos 15:32 are twenty and nine, with their **v.**. 2691
Jos 15:36 fourteen cities with their **v.**............... 2691
Jos 15:41 sixteen cities with their **v.**................ 2691
Jos 15:44 Mareshah; nine cities with their **v.**...... 2691
Jos 15:45 Ekron, with her towns and her **v.**:........ 2691
Jos 15:46 that lay near Ashdod, with their **v.**: 2691
Jos 15:47 Ashdod with her towns and her **v.**,...... 2691
Jos 15:47 Gaza with her towns and her **v.**, ... 2691
Jos 15:51 Giloh; eleven cities with their **v.**........ 2691
Jos 15:54 and Zior; nine cities with their **v.**......... 2691
Jos 15:57 Timnah; ten cities with their **v.**......... 2691
Jos 15:59 Eltekon: six cities with their **v.**. 2691
Jos 15:60 Rabbah; two cities with their **v.**........... 2691
Jos 15:62 En-gedi; six cities with their **v.**. 2691
Jos 16:9 all the cities with their **v.**.................. 2691
Jos 18:24 Gaba; twelve cities with their **v.**:......... 2691
Jos 18:28 fourteen cities with their **v.**............... 2691
Jos 19:6 thirteen cities and their **v.**:................ 2691
Jos 19:7 Ashan; four cities and their **v.**:........... 2691
Jos 19:8 all the **v.** that were round about......... 2691
Jos 19:15 twelve cities with their **v.**. 2691
Jos 19:16 families, these cities with their **v.**. 2691
Jos 19:22 Jordan: Sixteen cities with their **v.**........ 2691
Jos 19:23 families, the cities and their **v.**........... 2691
Jos 19:30 twenty and two cities with their **v.**. 2691
Jos 19:31 families, these cities with their **v.**. 2691
Jos 19:38 nineteen cities with their **v.**............... 2691
Jos 19:39 families, the cities and their **v.**........... 2691
Jos 19:48 families, these cities with their **v.**. 2691
Jos 21:12 fields of the city, and the **v.** thereof, ... 2691
Jg 5:7 The inhabitants of the **v.** ceased,........ 6520
Jg 5:11 the inhabitants of his **v.** in Israel: 6520
1Sa 6:18 of fenced cities, and of country **v.**,........ 3724
1Ch 4:32 And their **v.** were, Etam, and Ain, ... 2691
1Ch 4:33 all their **v.** that were round about 2691
1Ch 6:56 fields of the city, and the **v.** thereof, ... 2691
1Ch 9:16 dwelt in the **v.** of the Netophathites. ... 2691
1Ch 9:22 by their genealogy in their **v.**,............. 2691
1Ch 9:25 brethren, which were in their **v.**,......... 2691
1Ch 27:25 and the cities, and in the **v.**, and......... 3723
2Ch 28:18 and Shocho with the **v.** thereof, ... 1323
2Ch 28:18 and Timnah with the **v.** thereof, ... 1323
2Ch 28:18 Gimzo also and the **v.** thereof: and 1323
Ne 6:2 together in some one of the **v.** 3715
Ne 11:25 And for the **v.**, with their fields,......... 2691
Ne 11:25 Kirjath-arba, and in the **v.** thereof,........ 2691
Ne 11:25 at Dibon, and in the **v.** thereof,........... 1323
Ne 11:25 at Jekabzeel, and in the **v.** thereof, ... 1323
Ne 11:27 Beer-sheba, and in the **v.** thereof, ... 1323
Ne 11:28 at Mekonah, and in the **v.** thereof, ... 1323
Ne 11:30 and in their **v.**, at Lachish, ... 2691
Ne 11:30 at Azekah, and in the **v.** thereof.......... 1323
Ne 11:31 Aija, and Beth-el, and in their **v.**, ... 1323
Ne 12:28 and from the **v.** of Netophathi;............ 2691
Ne 12:29 for the singers had builded them **v.**...... 2691
Es 9:19 Therefore the Jews of the **v.**, that...... 6521
Ps 10:8 in the lurking places of the **v.**: 2691
Ca 7:11 the field; let us lodge in the **v.**........... 3723
Isa 42:11 the **v.** that Kedar doth inhabit:........... 2691
Eze 38:11 go up to the land of unwalled **v.**; 6519
Hab 3:14 with his staves the head of his **v.**: 6518
Mt 9:35 went about all the cities and **v.**, ... *2968*
Mt 14:15 that they may go into the **v.**, and *2968*
Mk 6:6 and he went round about the **v.**, ... *2968*
Mk 6:36 and into the **v.**, and buy themselves.... *2968*
Mk 6:56 he entered, into the **v.**, or cities, or ... *2968*
Lu 13:22 he went through the cities and **v.**, ... *2968*
Ac 8:25 preached the gospel in many **v.**........... *2968*

VILLANY
Isa 32:6 For the vile person will speak **v.**, ... 5039
Jer 29:23 they have committed **v.** in Israel, ... 5039

VINE See also VINEDRESSERS; VINES; VINEYARD.
Ge 40:9 dream, behold, a **v.** was before me;..... 1612
Ge 40:10 And in the **v.** were three branches: 1612
Ge 49:11 Binding his foal unto the **v.**, and......... 1612
Ge 49:11 his ass's colt unto the choice **v.**; 8321
Le 25:5 the grapes of thy **v.** undressed: 5139
Le 25:11 the grapes in it of thy **v.** undressed. ... 5139
Nu 6:4 eat nothing...made of the **v.** tree,......... 3196
De 32:32 For their **v.** is of the **v.** of Sodom, ... 1612
Jg 9:12 Then said the trees unto the **v.**, ... 1612
Jg 9:13 the **v.** said unto them, Should I.......... 1612
Jg 13:14 of any thing that cometh of the **v.**, ... 1612
1Ki 4:25 every man under his **v.** and under 1612
2Ki 4:39 to gather herbs, and found a wild **v.**,.... 1612
2Ki 18:31 eat ye every man of his own **v.**, and... 1612
2Ch 26:10 and **v.** dressers in the mountains, ... 3755
Job 15:33 off his unripe grape as the **v.**, and...... 1612
Ps 80:8 hast brought a **v.** out of Egypt:........... 1612
Ps 80:14 and behold, and visit this **v.**;............ 1612
Ps 128:3 Thy wife shall be as a fruitful **v.** by..... 1612
Ca 6:11 to see whether the **v.** flourished,........ 1612
Ca 7:8 breasts shall be as clusters of the **v.**,.. 1612
Ca 7:12 let us see if the **v.** flourish, whether ... 1612
Isa 5:2 and planted it with the choicest **v.**, ... 8321
Isa 16:8 languish, and the **v.** of Sibmah: 1612
Isa 16:9 weeping of Jazer the **v.** of Sibmah: 1612
Isa 24:7 wine mourneth, the **v.** languisheth, ... 1612
Isa 32:12 pleasant fields, for the fruitful **v.** 1612
Isa 34:4 as the leaf falleth off from the **v.**, ... 1612
Isa 36:16 and eat ye every one of his **v.**, and 1612
Jer 2:21 Yet I had planted thee a noble **v.**, ... 8321
Jer 2:21 degenerate plant of a strange **v.** 1612
Jer 6:9 glean the remnant of Israel as a **v.**: 1612
Jer 8:13 there shall be no grapes on the **v.**, ... 1612
Jer 48:32 O **v.** of Sibmah, I will weep for thee ... 1612
Eze 15:2 What is the **v.** tree more than any...... 1612
Eze 15:6 As the **v.** tree among the trees of...... 1612
Eze 17:6 a spreading **v.** of low stature,........... 1612
Eze 17:6 so it became a **v.**, and brought forth ... 1612
Eze 17:7 this **v.** did bend her roots toward 1612
Eze 17:8 fruit, that it might be a goodly **v.**. 1612
Eze 19:10 Thy mother is like a **v.** in thy blood, ... 1612
Ho 10:1 Israel is an empty **v.**, he bringeth........ 1612
Ho 14:7 as the corn, and grow as the **v.**: 1612
Joe 1:7 He hath laid my **v.** waste, and........... 1612
Joe 1:12 The **v.** is dried up, and the fig tree..... 1612
Joe 2:22 and the **v.** do yield their strength. 1612
Mic 4:4 sit every man under his **v.** and 1612
Na 2:2 out, and marred their **v.** branches....... 2156
Hag 2:19 as yet the **v.**, and the fig tree, and..... 1612
Zec 3:10 man his neighbour under the **v.**.......... 1612
Zec 8:12 the **v.** shall give her fruit, and the 1612
Mal 3:11 neither shall your **v.** cast her fruit 1612

Mt 26:29 **henceforth of this fruit of the v.,** *288*
Mk 14:25 **drink no more of the fruit of the v.,** *288*
Lu 22:18 **not drink of the fruit of the v.,** *288*
Joh 15:1 **I am the true v., and my Father is** . *288*
Joh 15:4 **of itself, except it abide in the v.;** ... *288*
Joh 15:5 **I am the v., ye are the branches:** *288*
Jas 3:12 bear olive berries? either a v., figs? *288*
Re 14:18 gather the clusters of the v. of........... *288*
Re 14:19 and gathered the v. of the earth, ... *288*

VINEDRESSERS See also VINE and DRESSERS.
2Ki 25:12 the land to be v. and husbandmen. 3755
Isa 61:5 shall be your plowmen and your v.. 3755
Jer 52:16 the land for v. and for husbandmen..... 3755
Joe 1:11 howl, O ye v., for the wheat and for... 3755

VINEGAR
Nu 6:3 no v. of wine, or v. of strong drink, ... 2558
Ru 2:14 bread, and dip thy morsel in the v.. 2558
Ps 69:21 my thirst they gave me v. to drink. 2558
Pr 10:26 As v. to the teeth, and as smoke to ... 2558
Pr 25:20 and as v. upon nitre, so is he that...... 2558
Mt 27:34 v. to drink mingled with gall: *3690*
Mt 27:48 took a spunge, and filled it with v.,..... *3690*
Mk 15:36 ran and filled a spunge full of v., ... *3690*
Lu 23:36 coming to him, and offering him v.,....... *3690*
Joh 19:29 there was set a vessel full of v.: *3690*
Joh 19:29 and they filled a spunge with v.,.......... *3690*
Joh 19:30 when Jesus...had received the v.,......... *3690*

VINES
Nu 20:5 place of seed, or of figs, or of v.,....... 1612
De 8:8 A land of wheat, and barley, and v., ... 1612
Ps 78:47 He destroyed their v. with hail, ... 1612
Ps 105:33 He smote their v. also and their fig 1612
Ca 2:13 the v. with the tender grape give a..... 1612
Ca 2:15 the little foxes, that spoil the v.: 3754
Ca 2:15 for our v. have tender grapes............ 3754
Isa 7:23 were a thousand v. at a thousand....... 1612
Jer 5:17 they shall eat up thy v. and thy fig 1612
Jer 31:5 yet plant v. upon the mountains 3754
Ho 2:12 destroy her v. and her fig trees, ... 1612
Hab 3:17 neither shall fruit be in the v.; 1612

VINEYARD See also VINEYARDS.
Ge 9:20 husbandman, and he planted a v.: 3754
Ex 22:5 shall cause a field or v. to be eaten, ... 3754
Ex 22:5 of the best of his own v., shall he 3754
Ex 23:11 manner thou shalt deal with thy v.,..... 3754
Le 19:10 And thou shalt not glean thy v., ... 3754
Le 19:10 thou gather every grape of thy v.;....... 3754
Le 25:3 six years thou shalt prune thy v.,....... 3754
Le 25:4 sow thy field, nor prune thy v.. 3754
De 20:6 man is he that hath planted a v., ... 3754
De 22:9 Thou shalt not sow thy v. with.......... 3754
De 22:9 and the fruit of thy v., be defiled......... 3754
De 23:24 thou comest into thy neighbour's v., ... 3754
De 24:21 thou gatherest the grapes of thy v.,...... 3754
De 28:30 thou shalt plant a v., and shalt not...... 3754
1Ki 21:1 that Naboth the Jezreelite had a v., ... 3754
1Ki 21:2 Give me thy v., that I may have it 3754
1Ki 21:2 give thee for it a better v. than it;....... 3754
1Ki 21:6 Give me thy v. for money; or else, ... 3754
1Ki 21:6 I will give thee another v. for it: 3754
1Ki 21:6 I will not give thee my v.. 3754
1Ki 21:7 I will give thee the v. of Naboth 3754
1Ki 21:15 take possession of the v. of Naboth 3754
1Ki 21:16 up to go down to the v. of Naboth 3754
1Ki 21:18 behold, he is in the v. of Naboth, ... 3754
Ps 80:15 the v. which thy right hand hath......... 3657
Pr 24:30 and by the v. of the man void of 3754
Pr 31:16 fruit of her hands she planteth a v.. 3754
Ca 1:6 but mine own v. have I not kept. 3754
Ca 8:11 Solomon had a v. at Baal-hamon;......... 3754
Ca 8:11 he let out the v. unto keepers; 3754
Ca 8:12 My v., which is mine, is before me: ... 3754
Isa 1:8 of Zion is left as a cottage in a v., ... 3754
Isa 3:14 ye have eaten up the v.; the spoil 3754
Isa 5:1 song of my beloved touching his v.. 3754
Isa 5:1 hath a v. in a very fruitful hill: 3754
Isa 5:3 I pray you, betwixt me and my v.. 3754
Isa 5:4 have been done more to my v., ... 3754
Isa 5:5 tell you what I will do to my v.:.......... 3754
Isa 5:7 v. of the Lord of hosts is the house.... 3754
Isa 5:10 ten acres of v. shall yield one bath, ... 3754
Isa 27:2 sing ye unto her, A v. of red wine. 3754
Jer 12:10 Many pastors have destroyed my v.,.... 3754
Jer 35:7 house, nor sow seed, nor plant v., ... 3754
Jer 35:9 neither have we v., nor field, nor....... 3754
Mic 1:6 the field, and as plantings of a v.: 3754
Mt 20:1 **to hire labourers into his v.** *290*
Mt 20:2 **a day, he sent them into his v..** *290*
Mt 20:4 **unto them; Go ye also into the v.,** .. *290*
Mt 20:7 **unto them, Go ye also into the v.;** .. *290*
Mt 20:8 **the lord of the v. saith unto his** *290*
Mt 21:28 **said, Son, go work to day in my v..** . *290*
Mt 21:33 **householder, which planted a v.,** *290*
Mt 21:39 **cast him out of the v., and slew** *290*
Mt 21:40 **the lord therefore of the v. cometh,** . *290*
Mt 21:41 and will let out his v. unto other.......... *290*
Mk 12:1 **A certain man planted a v., and set** . *290*
Mk 12:2 **husbandmen of the fruit of the v.** ... *290*
Mk 12:8 **him, and cast him out of the v..** *290*
Mk 12:9 **shall therefore the lord of the v. do?** *290*
Mk 12:9 **and will give the v. unto others.** *290*
Lu 13:6 **man had a fig tree planted in his v.;** *290*
Lu 13:7 **said he unto the dresser of his v.,** ... *289*
Lu 20:9 **A certain man planted a v., and let.** . *290*
Lu 20:10 **give him of the fruit of the v.:** *290*
Lu 20:13 **Then said the lord of the v., What..** *290*
Lu 20:15 **So they cast him out of the v., and..** *290*
Lu 20:15 **shall the lord of the v. do unto** *290*
Lu 20:16 **and shall give the v. to others.** *290*
1Co 9:7 who planteth a v., and eateth not of..... *290*

VINEYARDS
Nu 16:14 us inheritance of fields and v.: 3754
Nu 20:17 the fields, or through the v., ... 3754
Nu 21:22 turn into the fields, or into the v.; 3754
Nu 22:24 the Lord stood in a path of the v., ... 3754
De 6:11 v. and olive trees, which thou............ 3754
De 28:39 Thou shalt plant v., and dress 3754
Jos 24:13 v. and oliveyards which ye planted...... 3754
Jg 9:27 and gathered their v., and trode the.... 3754
Jg 11:33 cities, and unto the plain of the v., ... 3754
Jg 14:5 and came to the v. of Timnath: 3754
Jg 15:5 corn, with the v. and olives............... 3754
Jg 21:20 saying, Go and lie in wait in the v.; 3754
Jg 21:21 then come ye out of the v., and.......... 3754
1Sa 8:14 will take your fields, and your v., ... 3754
1Sa 8:15 tenth of your seed, and of your v., ... 3754
1Sa 22:7 give every one of you fields and v., ... 3754
2Ki 5:26 garments, and oliveyards, and v., ... 3754
2Ki 18:32 and wine, a land of bread and v., ... 3754
2Ki 19:29 year sow ye, and reap, and plant v.,... 3754
1Ch 27:27 the v. of Shimei the Ramathite:.......... 3754
1Ch 27:27 over the increase of the v. for the...... 3754
Ne 5:3 We have mortgaged our lands, v., ... 3754
Ne 5:4 and that upon our lands and v............ 3754
Ne 5:5 other men have our lands and v.. 3754
Ne 5:11 even this day, their lands, their v., ... 3754
Ne 9:25 wells digged, v., and oliveyards, ... 3754
Job 24:18 he beholdeth not the way of the v.. 3754
Ps 107:37 And sow the fields, and plant v., ... 3754
Ec 2:4 me houses; I planted me v.: 3754
Ca 1:6 they made me the keeper of the v.;...... 3754
Ca 1:14 of camphire in the v. of En-gedi. 3754
Ca 7:12 Let us get up early to the v.; let us ... 3754
Isa 16:10 in the v. there shall be no singing,...... 3754
Isa 36:17 and wine, a land of bread and v.. 3754
Isa 37:30 plant v., and eat the fruit thereof. 3754
Isa 65:21 they shall plant v., and eat the fruit 3754
Jer 32:15 and v. shall be possessd again in 3754
Jer 39:10 gave them v. and fields at the same.... 3754
Eze 28:26 shall build houses, and plant v.;......... 3754
Ho 2:15 I will give her her v. from thence,...... 3754
Am 4:9 when your gardens and your v. and 3754
Am 5:11 ye have planted pleasant v., but ye..... 3754
Am 5:17 And in all v. shall be wailing: for I...... 3754
Am 9:14 and they shall plant v., and drink......... 3754
Zep 1:13 they shall plant v., but not drink 3754

VINTAGE
Le 26:5 threshing shall reach unto the v., ... 1210
Le 26:5 the v. shall reach unto the sowing 1210
Jg 8:2 better than the v. of Abi-ezer?........... 1210
Job 24:6 they gather the v. of the wicked. 3754
Isa 16:10 I have made their v. shouting to cease. .....
Isa 24:13 grapes when the v. is done. 1210
Isa 32:10 for the v. shall fail, the gathering........ 1210
Jer 48:32 summer fruits and upon thy v.. 1210
Mic 7:1 as the grapegleanings of the v.: 1210
Zec 11:2 the forest of the v. is come down....... 1208

VIOL See also VIOLS.
Isa 5:12 And the harp, and the v., the........... 5035
Am 6:5 That chant to the sound of the v., ... 5035

VIOLATED
Eze 22:26 Her priests have v. my law, and 2554

VIOLENCE
Ge 6:11 and the earth was filled with v.. 2555
Ge 6:13 the earth is filled with v. through 2555
Le 6:2 or in a thing taken away by v., or 1498
2Sa 22:3 saviour; thou savest me from v.......... 2555
Ps 11:5 him that loveth v. his soul hateth. 2555
Ps 55:9 I have seen v. and strife in the city. ... 2555
Ps 58:2 ye weigh the v. of your hands in........ 2555
Ps 72:14 their soul from deceit and v.: 2555
Ps 73:6 v. covereth them as a garment. 2555
Pr 4:17 and drink the wine of v.. 2555
Pr 10:6, 11 but v. covereth the mouth of the ... 2555
Pr 13:2 of the transgressors shall eat v.. 2555
Pr 28:17 A man that doeth v. to the blood 6231
Isa 53:9 because he had done no v.,................ 2555
Isa 59:6 and the act of v. is in their hands. 2555
Isa 60:18 V. shall no more be heard in thy........ 2555
Jer 6:7 v. and spoil is heard in her; before 2555
Jer 20:8 I cried out, I cried v. and spoil; 2555
Jer 22:3 no wrong, do no v. to the stranger,..... 2554
Jer 22:17 for oppression, and for v., to do it...... 4835
Jer 51:35 The v. done to me and to my flesh..... 2555
Jer 51:46 come a rumour, and v. in the land,..... 2555
Eze 7:11 V. is risen up into a rod of.............. 2555
Eze 7:23 crimes, and the city is full of v.. 2555
Eze 8:17 they have filled the land with v., ... 2555
Eze 12:19 of the v. of all them that dwell........... 2555
Eze 18:7 hath spoiled none by v., hath............ 1500
Eze 18:12 hath spoiled by v., hath not............... 1500
Eze 18:16 neither hath spoiled by v., but........... 1500
Eze 18:18 spoiled his brother by v., and did 1499
Eze 28:16 filled the midst of thee with v.,.......... 2555
Eze 45:9 remove v. and spoil, and execute 2555
Joe 3:19 v. against the children of Judah, ... 2555
Am 3:10 who store up v. and robbery in.......... 2555
Am 6:3 cause the seat of v. to come near; 2555
Ob 10 thy v. against thy brother Jacob 2555
Jon 3:8 from the v. that is in their hands. 2555
Mic 2:2 covet fields, and take them by v.; 1497
Mic 6:12 rich men thereof are full of v.,.......... 2555
Hab 1:2 even cry out unto thee of v., and........ 2555
Hab 1:3 for spoiling and v. are before me:........ 2555
Hab 1:9 They shall come all for v.: their 2555
Hab 2:8 for the v. of the land, of the city,....... 2555
Hab 2:17 the v. of Lebanon shall cover thee,..... 2555
Hab 2:17 for the v. of the land, of the city,....... 2555
Zep 1:9 fill their masters' houses with v.......... 2555
Zep 3:4 they have done v. to the law. 2554
Mal 2:16 one covereth v. with his garment, ... 2555
Mt 11:12 **kingdom of heaven suffereth v.,** *971*
Lu 3:14 Do v. to no man, neither accuse *1286*
Ac 5:26 and brought them without v.: *970*
Ac 21:35 the soldiers for the v. of the people. *970*
Ac 24:7 with great v. took him away out of....... *970*
Ac 27:41 broken with the v. of the waves. *970*
Heb 11:34 Quenched the v. of fire, escaped......... *1411*
Re 18:21 v. shall that great city Babylon be *3731*

VIOLENT
2Sa 22:49 delivered me from the v. man. 2555
Ps 7:16 v. dealing shall come down upon 2555
Ps 18:48 hast delivered me from the v. man. 2555
Ps 86:14 the assemblies of v. men have........... 6184
Ps 140:1,4 preserve me from the v. man;............ 2555
Ps 140:11 evil shall hunt the v. man to............... 2555
Pr 16:29 A v. man enticeth his neighbor, and.... 2555
Ec 5:8 v. perverting of judgment and............ 1499
Mt 11:12 **and the v. take it by force.** *973*

VIOLENTLY
Ge 21:25 servants had v. taken away. 1497
Le 6:4 restore that which he took v. 1500
De 28:31 thine ass shall be v. taken away......... 1497
Job 20:19 he hath v. taken away an house 1497
Job 24:2 they v. take away flocks, and feed...... 1497
Isa 22:18 v. turn and toss thee like a ball...............
La 2:6 v. taken away his tabernacle,............ 2554
Mt 8:32 of swine ran v. down a steep place..........
Mk 5:13 the herd ran v. down a steep place...........
Lu 8:33 the herd ran v. down a steep place..........

VIOLS
Isa 14:11 the grave, and the noise of thy v.: 5035
Am 5:23 will not hear the melody of thy v......... 5035

VIPER See also VIPER'S; VIPERS.
Isa 30:6 the v. and fiery flying serpent, ... 660
Isa 59:5 is crushed breaketh out into a v.. ... 660
Ac 28:3 there came a v. out of the heat, ... *2191*

VIPER'S
Job 20:16 asps: the v. tongue shall slay him. ... 660

VIPERS
Mt 3:7 O generation of v., who hath... *2191*
Mt 12:34 **O generation of v., how can ye,** ... *2191*
Mt 23:33 **ye generation of v., how can ye** ... *2191*
Lu 3:7 O generation of v., who hath... *2191*

VIRGIN See also VIRGIN'S; VIRGINS.
Ge 24:16 was very fair to look upon, a v., ... 1330
Ge 24:43 v. cometh forth to draw water, ... 5959
Le 21:3 for his sister a v., that is nigh ... 1330
Le 21:14 he shall take a v. of his own people ... 1330
De 22:19 an evil name upon a v. of Israel: ... 1330
De 22:23 damsel that is a v. be betrothed... 1330
De 22:28 If a man find a damsel that is a v., ... 1330
De 32:25 both the young man and the v., the ... 1330
2Sa 13:2 for she was a v.; and Amnon... 1330
1Ki 1:2 for my lord the king a young v.: ... 1330
2Ki 19:21 The v. the daughter of Zion hath... 1330
Isa 7:14 Behold, a v. shall conceive, and ... 5959
Isa 23:12 O thou oppressed v., daughter of ... 1330
Isa 37:22 The v., the daughter of Zion, hath ... 1330
Isa 47:1 O v. daughter of Babylon, sit on ... 1330
Isa 62:5 For as a young man marrieth a v., ... 1330
Jer 14:17 v. daughter of my people is broken ... 1330
Jer 18:13 the v. of Israel hath done a very ... 1330
Jer 31:4 thou shalt be built, O v. of Israel: ... 1330
Jer 31:13 shall the v. rejoice in the dance, ... 1330
Jer 31:21 O v. of Israel, turn again to these ... 1330
Jer 46:11 balm, O v., the daughter of Egypt: ... 1330
La 1:15 the Lord hath trodden the v., the ... 1330
La 2:13 thee, O v. daughter of Zion? ... 1330
Joe 1:8 Lament like a v. girded with... 1330
Am 5:2 The v. of Israel is fallen; she shall ... 1330
Mt 1:23 Behold, a v. shall be with child, ... *3933*
Lu 1:27 To a v. espoused to a man whose ... *3933*
1Co 7:28 if a v. marry, she hath not sinned ... *3933*
1Co 7:34 also between a wife and a v.. ... *3933*
1Co 7:36 himself uncomely toward his v., ... *3933*
1Co 7:37 his heart that he will keep his v., ... *3933*
2Co 11:2 you as a chaste v. to Christ. ... *3933*

VIRGINITY
Le 21:13 he shall take a wife in her v.. ... 1331
De 22:15 forth the tokens of the damsel's v. ... 1331
De 22:17 are the tokens of my daughter's v.. ... 1331
De 22:20 tokens of v. be not found for the ... 1331
Jg 11:37 bewail my v., I and my fellows. ... 1331
Jg 11:38 and bewailed her v. upon the ... 1331
Eze 23:3 they bruised the teats of their v.. ... 1331
Eze 23:8 they bruised the breasts of her v., ... 1331
Lu 2:36 husband seven years from her v.; ... *3932*

VIRGIN'S
Lu 1:27 and the v. name was Mary... *3933*

VIRGINS
Ex 22:17 according to the dowry of v.. ... 1330
Jg 21:12 four hundred young v., that had ... 1330
2Sa 13:18 the king's daughters that were v. ... 1330
Es 2:2 Let there be fair young v. sought ... 1330
Es 2:3 together all the fair young v. unto ... 1330
Es 2:17 in his sight more than all the v.; ... 1330
Es 2:19 the v. were gathered together ... 1330
Ps 45:14 the v. her companions that follow ... 1330
Ca 1:3 therefore do the v. love thee... 5959
Ca 6:8 and v. without number. ... 5959
Isa 23:4 up young men, nor bring up v.. ... 1330
La 1:4 priests sigh, her v. are afflicted, ... 1330
La 1:18 my v. and my young men are ... 1330
La 2:10 the v. of Jerusalem hang down ... 1330
La 2:21 my v. and my young men are ... 1330
Am 8:13 the fair v. and young men faint for ... 1330
Mt 25:1 **of heaven be likened unto ten v.,** ... *3933*
Mt 25:7 **all those v. arose, and trimmed** ... *3933*
Mt 25:11 **Afterward came also the other v.,** .. *3933*
Ac 21:9 same man had four daughters, v., ... *3933*
1Co 7:25 Now concerning v. I have no ... *3933*
Re 14:4 with women; for they are v.. ... *3933*

VIRTUE
Mk 5:30 that v. had gone out of him, ... *1411*
Lu 6:19 for there went v. out of him, and ... *1411*
Lu 8:46 **that v. has gone out of me** ... *1411*
Php 4:8 there be any v., and if there be any ... *703*
2Pe 1:3 that hath called us to glory and v.: ... *703*
2Pe 1:5 diligence, add to your faith v.; ... *703*
2Pe 1:5 and to v. knowledge: ... *703*

VIRTUOUS
Ru 3:11 know that thou art a v. woman. ... 2428
Pr 12:4 A v. woman is a crown to her ... 2428
Pr 31:10 Who can find a v. woman? for her ... 2428

VIRTUOUSLY
Pr 31:29 Many daughters have done v., but ... 2428

VISAGE
Isa 52:14 his v. was so marred more than ... 4758
La 4:8 Their v. is blacker than a coal; ... 8389
Da 3:19 the form of his v. was changed ... 600

VISIBLE See also INVISIBLE.
Col 1:16 that are in earth, v. and invisible, ... *3707*

VISION See also DIVISION; VISIONS.
Ge 15:1 Lord came unto Abram in a v., ... 4236
Nu 12:6 myself known unto him in a v., ... 4758
Nu 24:4, 16 saw the v. of the Almighty, ... 4236
1Sa 3:1 those days; there was no open v. ... 2377
1Sa 3:15 Samuel feared to shew Eli the v. ... 4758
2Sa 7:17 according to all this v., so did ... 2384
1Ch 17:15 according to all this v., so did ... 2377
2Ch 32:32 they are written in the v. of Isaiah ... 2377
Job 20:8 chased away as a v. of the night. ... 2384
Job 33:15 in a v. of the night, when deep ... 2384
Ps 89:19 thou spakest in v. to thy holy one, ... 2377
Pr 29:18 Where there is no v., the people ... 2377
Isa 1:1 The v. of Isaiah the son of Amoz, ... 2377
Isa 21:2 grievous v. is declared unto me; ... 2380
Isa 22:1 The burden of the valley of v.. ... 2384
Isa 22:5 God of hosts in the valley of v., ... 2384
Isa 28:7 they err in v., they stumble in ... 7203
Isa 29:7 shall be as a dream of a night v.. ... 2377
Isa 29:11 the v. of all is become unto you as ... 2380
Jer 14:14 they prophesy unto you a false v. ... 2377
Jer 23:16 they speak a v. of their own heart, ... 2377
La 2:9 also find no v. from the Lord ... 2377
Eze 7:13 v. is touching the whole multitude ... 2377
Eze 7:26 shall they seek a v. of the prophet; ... 2377
Eze 8:4 to the v. that I saw in the plain ... 4758
Eze 11:24 brought me in a v. by the Spirit of ... 4758
Eze 11:24 the v. that I had seen went up from ... 4758
Eze 12:22 prolonged, and every v. faileth? ... 2377
Eze 12:23 at hand, and the effect of every v. ... 2377
Eze 12:24 be no more any vain v. nor flattering .. 2377
Eze 12:27 The v. that he seeth is for many ... 2377
Eze 13:7 Have ye not seen a vain v., and ... 4236
Eze 43:3 appearance of the v. which I saw, ... 4758
Eze 43:3 according to the v. that I saw when ... 4758
Eze 43:3 were like the v. that I saw by the ... 4758
Da 2:19 revealed unto Daniel in a night v.. ... 2376
Da 7:2 and said, I saw in my v. by night, ... 2376
Da 8:1 Belshazzar a v. appeared unto me, ... 2377
Da 8:2 I saw in a v.; and it came to pass, ... 2377
Da 8:2 I saw in a v., and I was by the river ... 2377
Da 8:13 shall be the v. concerning the ... 2377
Da 8:15 even I Daniel, had seen the v., and ... 2377
Da 8:16 this man to understand the v.. ... 4758
Da 8:17 the time of the end shall be the v. ... 4758
Da 8:26 v. of the evening and the morning ... 4758
Da 8:26 wherefore shut thou up the v.; for ... 2377
Da 8:27 I was astonished at the v., but ... 4758
Da 9:21 whom I had seen in the v. at the ... 2377
Da 9:23 the matter, and consider the v. ... 2377
Da 9:24 and to seal up the v. and prophecy, ... 2377
Da 10:1 and had understanding of the v.. ... 4758
Da 10:7 And I Daniel alone saw the v.: for ... 4759
Da 10:7 that were with me saw not the v.; ... 4759
Da 10:8 left alone, and saw this great v., ... 4759
Da 10:14 for yet the v. is for many days. ... 2377
Da 10:16 by the v. my sorrows are turned ... 4758
Da 11:14 themselves to establish the v.; ... 2377
Ob 1 The v. of Obadiah. Thus saith the ... 2377
Mic 3:6 you, that ye shall not have a v.; ... 2377
Na 1:1 The book of the v. of Nahum the ... 2377
Hab 2:2 Write the v., and make it plain ... 2377
Hab 2:3 the v. is yet for an appointed time, ... 2377
Zec 13:4 be ashamed every one of his v., ... 2384
Mt 17:9 **Tell the v. to no man, until the** ... *3705*
Lu 1:22 he had seen a v. in the temple: ... *3701*
Lu 24:23 they had also seen a v. of angels, ... *3701*
Ac 9:10 and to him said the Lord in a v., ... *3705*
Ac 9:12 **seen in a v. a man named Ananias** . *3705*
Ac 10:3 He saw in a v. evidently about the ... *3705*
Ac 10:17 what this v. which he had seen ... *3705*
Ac 10:19 While Peter thought on the v., the ... *3705*
Ac 11:5 and in a trance I saw a v., a certain ... *3705*
Ac 12:9 angel; but thought he saw a v. ... *3705*
Ac 16:9 a v. appeared to Paul in the night; ... *3705*
Ac 16:10 And after he had seen the v., ... *3705*
Ac 18:9 Lord to Paul in the night by a v., ... *3705*
Ac 26:19 disobedient unto the heavenly v.: ... *3705*
Re 9:17 I saw the horses in the v., and ... *3076*

VISIONS See also DIVISIONS.
Ge 46:2 unto Israel in the v. of the night, ... 4759
2Ch 9:29 v. of Iddo the seer against ... 2378
2Ch 26:5 understanding in the v. of God: ... 7200
Job 4:13 thoughts from the v. of the night, ... 2384
Job 7:14 and terrifest me through v.: ... 2384
Eze 1:1 were opened, and I saw v. of God ... 4759
Eze 8:3 brought me in the v. of God to ... 4759
Eze 13:16 which see v. of peace for her, and ... 2377
Eze 40:2 In the v. of God brought he me ... 4759
Eze 43:3 and the v. were like the vision ... 4759
Da 1:17 understanding in all v. and ... 2377
Da 2:28 v. of thy head upon thy bed, are ... 2376
Da 4:5 and the v. of my head trouble me ... 2376
Da 4:9 tell me the v. of my dream that I ... 2376
Da 4:10 Thus were the v. of mine head in ... 2376
Da 4:13 I saw in the v. of my head upon my ... 2376
Da 7:1 and v. of his head upon his bed: ... 2376
Da 7:7 After this I saw in the night v., ... 2376
Da 7:13 I saw in the night v., and, behold, ... 2376
Da 7:15 and the v. of my head troubled me. .. 2376
Ho 12:10 I have multiplied v., and used ... 2377
Joe 2:28 your young men shall see v.: ... 2384
Ac 2:17 and your young men shall see v., ... *3706*
2Co 12:1 I will come to v. and revelations ... *3701*

VISIT See also VISITED; VISITEST; VISITETH; VISITING.
Ge 50:24 God will surely v. you, and bring ... 6485
Ge 50:25 God will surely v. you, and ye shall ... 6485
Ex 13:19 God will surely v. you; and ye shall ... 6485
Ex 32:34 the day when I v. I will v. their sin ... 6485
Le 18:25 I do v. the iniquity thereof upon it, ... 6485
Job 5:24 and thou shalt v. thy habitation, ... 6485
Job 7:18 thou shouldest v. him evey ... 6485
Ps 59:5 Israel, awake to v. all the heathen: ... 6485
Ps 80:14 heaven, and behold, and v. this ... 6485
Ps 89:32 Then will I v. their transgression ... 6485
Ps 106:4 people: O v. me with thy salvation; ... 6485
Isa 23:17 that the Lord will v. Tyre, and she ... 6485
Jer 3:16 it; neither shall they v. it; ... 6485
Jer 5:9,29 Shall I not v. for these things? ... 6485
Jer 6:15 time that I v. them they shall be ... 6485
Jer 9:9 Shall I not v. them for these things? ... 6485
Jer 14:10 their iniquity, and v. their sins. ... 6485
Jer 15:15 and v. me, and revenge me of my ... 6485
Jer 23:2 v. upon you the evil of your doings, ... 6485
Jer 27:22 they be until the day that I v. them, ... 6485
Jer 29:10 at Babylon I will v. you, ... 6485
Jer 32:5 and there shall he be until I v. him, ... 6485
Jer 49:8 him, the time that I will v. him. ... 6485
Jer 50:31 is come, the time that I will v. thee. ... 6485
La 4:22 he will v. thine iniquity, O daughter ... 6485
Ho 2:13 will v. upon her the days of Baalim, ... 6485
Ho 8:13 their iniquity, and v. their sins: ... 6485
Ho 9:9 their iniquity, he will v. their sins. ... 6485
Am 3:14 shall v. the transgressions of Israel ... 6485
Am 3:14 I will also v. the altars of Beth-el: ... 6485
Zep 2:7 the Lord their God shall v. them, ... 6485
Zec 11:16 shall not v. those that be cut off, ... 6485
Ac 7:23 to v. his brethren the children of ... *1980*
Ac 15:14 God at the first did v. the Gentiles, ... *1980*
Ac 15:36 Let us go again and v. our brethren ... *1980*
Jas 1:27 To v. the fatherless and widows in ... *1980*

VISITATION
Nu 16:29 visited after the v. of all men; ... 6486
Job 10:12 thy v. hath preserved my spirit ... 6486
Isa 10:3 And what will ye do in the day of v., .. 6486
Jer 8:12 the time of their v. they shall be ... 6486
Jer 10:15 time of their v. they shall perish. ... 6486
Jer 11:23 Anathoth, even the year of their v., ... 6486
Jer 23:12 them, even the year of their v., ... 6486
Jer 46:21 upon them, and the time of their v.. ... 6486
Jer 48:44 upon Moab, the year of their v., ... 6486
Jer 50:27 day is come, the time of their v.. ... 6486

Jer 51:18 time of their v. they shall perish. 6486
Ho 9:7 The days of v. are come, the days 6486
Mic 7:4 of thy watchmen and thy v. cometh; ... 6486
Lu 19:44 **knewest not the time of thy v.** *1984*
1Pe 2:12 behold, glorify God in the day of v...... *1984*

VISITED
Ge 21:1 the Lord v. Sarah as he had said, ... 6485
Ex 3:16 I have surely v. you, and seen that..... 6485
Ex 4:31 Lord had ve the children of Israel, ... 6485
Nu 16:29 if they be v. after the visitation of 6485
Jg 15:1 that Samson v. his wife with a kid; 6485
Ru 1:6 the Lord had v. his people in giving 6485
1Sa 2:21 And the Lord v. Hannah, so that she .. 6485
Job 35:15 it is not so, he hath v. in his anger; 6485
Ps 17:3 thou hast v. me in the night; thou 6485
Pr 19:23 he shall not be v. with evil................ 6485
Isa 24:22 after many days shall they be v.......... 6485
Isa 26:14 hast thou v. and destroyed them, ... 6485
Isa 26:16 Lord, in trouble have they v. thee, ... 6485
Isa 29:6 Thou shalt be v. of the Lord of.......... 6485
Jer 6:6 Jerusalem: this is the city to be v.; 6485
Jer 23:2 them away, and have not v. them: 6485
Eze 38:8 After many days thou shalt be v......... 6485
Zec 10:3 the Lord of hosts hath v. his flock 6485
Mt 25:36 **I was sick, and ye v. me: I was in**.. *1980*
Mt 25:43 **and in prison, and ye v. me not**..... *1980*
Lu 1:68 hath v. and redeemed his people, ... *1980*
Lu 1:78 dayspring from on high hath v. us, ... *1980*
Lu 7:16 and, That God hath v. his people. *1980*

VISITEST
Ps 8:4 the son of man, that thou v. him? 6485
Ps 65:9 Thou v. the earth, and waterest it: 6485
Heb 2:6 the son of man, that thou v. him? *1980*

VISITETH
Job 31:14 when he v., what shall I answer......... 6485

VISITING
Ex 20:5 v. the iniquity of the fathers upon........ 6485
Ex 34:7 v. the iniquity of the fathers upon........ 6485
Nu 14:18 v. the iniquity of the fathers upon........ 6485
De 5:9 v. the iniquity of the fathers upon........ 6485

VOCATION See also CONVOCATION.
Eph 4:1 walk worthy of the v. wherewith......... *2821*

VOICE See also VOICES.
Ge 3:8 they heard the v. of the Lord God...... 6963
Ge 3:10 I heard thy v. in the garden, and........ 6963
Ge 3:17 hearkened unto the v. of thy wife, ... 6963
Ge 4:10 v. of thy brother's blood crieth unto.... 6963
Ge 4:23 wives, Adah and Zillah, hear my v.; 6963
Ge 16:2 hearkened to the v. of Sarai. 6963
Ge 21:12 unto thee, hearken unto her v.; 6963
Ge 21:16 over against him, and lift up her v., ... 6963
Ge 21:17 And God heard the v. of the lad; 6963
Ge 21:17 God hath heard the v. of the lad 6963
Ge 22:18 because thou hast obeyed my v.. 6963
Ge 26:5 that Abraham obeyed my v., and........ 6963
Ge 27:8 obey my v. according to that which..... 6963
Ge 27:13 only obey my v., and go fetch me 6963
Ge 27:22 The v. is Jacob's v., but the hands 6963
Ge 27:38 And Esau lifted up his v., and wept. ... 6963
Ge 27:43 Now therefore, my son, obey my v.; .. 6963
Ge 29:11 and lifted up his v., and wept. 6963
Ge 30:6 me, and hath also heard my v., ... 6963
Ge 39:14 with me, and I cried with a loud v. 6963
Ge 39:15 he heard that I lifted up my v. and 6963
Ge 39:18 as I lifted up my v. and cried, that 6963
Ex 3:18 they shall hearken to thy v.: and........ 6963
Ex 4:1 me, nor hearken unto my v. 6963
Ex 4:8 hearken to the v. of the first sign, ... 6963
Ex 4:8 will believe the v. of the latter sign..... 6963
Ex 4:9 signs, neither hearken unto thy v., ... 6963
Ex 5:2 should obey his v. to let Israel go? 6963
Ex 15:26 hearken to the v. of the Lord thy....... 6963
Ex 18:19 Hearken now unto my v., I will 6963
Ex 18:24 to the v. of his father in law, ... 6963
Ex 19:5 if ye will obey my v. indeed, and........ 6963
Ex 19:16 v. of the trumpet exceeding loud; 6963
Ex 19:19 the v. of the trumpet sounded long, ... 6963
Ex 19:19 and God answered him by a v.. 6963
Ex 23:21 Beware of him, and obey his v., ... 6963
Ex 23:22 if thou shalt indeed obey his v., ... 6963
Ex 24:3 all the people answered with one v., ... 6963
Ex 32:18 v. of them that shout for mastery, ... 6963
Ex 32:18 the v. of them that cry for being........ 6963
Le 5:1 hear the v. of swearing, and is a........ 6963
Nu 7:89 he heard the v. of one speaking......... 6963
Nu 14:1 the congregation lifted up their v., ... 6963
Nu 14:22 and have not hearkened to my v.; 6963
Nu 20:16 he heard our v., and sent an angel, ... 6963
Nu 21:3 Lord hearkened to the v. of Israel, ... 6963
De 1:34 Lord heard the v. of your words, ... 6963
De 1:45 Lord would not hearken to your v., ... 6963
De 4:12 ye heard the v. of the words, but....... 6963
De 4:12 no similitude; only ye heard a v. 6963
De 4:30 and shalt be obedient unto his v.; 6963
De 4:33 v. of God speaking out of the midst 6963
De 4:36 he made thee to hear his v., that 6963
De 5:22 the thick darkness, with a great v.; 6963
De 5:23 ye heard the v. out of the midst of..... 6963
De 5:24 we have heard his v. out of the 6963
De 5:25 if we hear the v. of the Lord our 6963
De 5:26 hath heard the v. of the living God 6963
De 5:28 Lord heard the v. of your words, ... 6963
De 5:28 I have heard the v. of the words of 6963
De 8:20 obedient unto the v. of the Lord 6963
De 9:23 him not, nor hearkened to his v. 6963
De 13:4 commandments, and obey his v., ... 6963
De 13:18 shalt hearken to the v. of the Lord..... 6963
De 15:5 hearken to the v. of the Lord thy....... 6963
De 18:16 not hear again the v. of the Lord 6963
De 21:18 will not obey the v. of his father, ... 6963
De 21:18 or the v. of his mother, and that, ... 6963
De 21:20 rebellious, he will not obey our v.; 6963
De 26:7 Lord heard our v., and looked on....... 6963
De 26:14 hearkened to the v. of the Lord my.... 6963
De 26:17 and to hearken unto his v.: 6963
De 27:10 obey the v. of the Lord thy God, ... 6963
De 27:14 all the men of Israel with a loud v., ... 6963
De 28:1 hearken. . .unto the v. of the Lord..... 6963
De 28:2 hearken unto the v. of the Lord thy.... 6963
De 28:15 not hearken unto the v. of the Lord.... 6963
De 28:45 not unto the v. of the Lord thy.......... 6963
De 28:62 not obey the v. of the Lord thy God. .. 6963
De 30:2 obey his v. according to all that I 6963
De 30:8 return and obey the v. of the Lord, ... 6963
De 30:10 hearken unto the v. of the Lord thy.... 6963
De 30:20 that thou mayest obey his v., and....... 6963
De 33:7 said, Hear, Lord, the v. of Judah........ 6963
Jos 5:6 they obeyed not the v. of the Lord:.... 6963
Jos 6:10 nor make any noise with your v., ... 6963
Jos 10:14 hearkened unto the v. of a man: 6963
Jos 22:2 have obeyed my v. in all that I 6963
Jos 24:24 we serve, and his v. will we obey, ... 6963
Jg 2:2 but ye have not obeyed my v.: why.... 6963
Jg 2:4 that the people lifted up their v., ... 6963
Jg 2:20 have not hearkened unto my v.; 6963
Jg 6:10 but ye have not obeyed my v. 6963
Jg 9:7 lifted up his v. and cried, and said 6963
Jg 13:9 God hearkened to the v. of Manoah; ... 6963
Jg 18:3 knew the v. of the young man the 663
Jg 18:25 Let not thy v. be heard among us, ... 6963
Jg 20:13 hearken to the v. of their brethren 6963
Ru 1:9 they lifted up their v. and wept.......... 6963
Ru 1:14 they lifted up their v. and wept......... 6963
1Sa 1:13 moved, but her v. was not heard: 6963
1Sa 2:25 not unto the v. of their father, ... 6963
1Sa 8:7 Hearken unto the v. of the people in... 6963
1Sa 8:9 therefore hearken unto their v.: 6963
1Sa 8:19 refused to obey the v. of Samuel; 6963
1Sa 8:22 Hearken unto their v., and make 6963
1Sa 12:1 have hearkened unto your v. in all...... 6963
1Sa 12:14 serve him, and obey his v., and not.... 6963
1Sa 12:15 ye will not obey the v. of the Lord, ... 6963
1Sa 15:1 the v. of the words of the Lord. 6963
1Sa 15:19 thou not obey the v. of the Lord, ... 6963
1Sa 15:20 I have obeyed the v. of the Lord, ... 6963
1Sa 15:22 as in obeying the v. of the Lord? 6963
1Sa 15:24 the people, and obeyed their v. 6963
1Sa 19:6 hearkened unto the v. of Jonathan: 6963
1Sa 24:16 said, Is this thy v., my son David? 6963
1Sa 24:16 And Saul lifted up his v., and wept. 6963
1Sa 25:35 I have hearkened to thy v., and 6963
1Sa 26:17 And Saul knew David's v., and said,.... 6963
1Sa 26:17 Is this thy v., my son David? And 6963
1Sa 26:17 David said, It is my v. my lord, ... 6963
1Sa 28:12 Samuel, she cried with a loud v.: 6963
1Sa 28:18 obeyedst not the v. of the Lord, ... 6963
1Sa 28:21 thine handmaid hath obeyed thy v. 6963
1Sa 28:22 unto the v. of thine handmaid, ... 6963
1Sa 28:23 and he hearkened unto their v. 6963
1Sa 30:4 him lifted up their v. and wept, ... 6963
2Sa 3:32 the king lifted up his v., and wept, ... 6963
2Sa 12:18 he would not hearken unto our v.: 6963
2Sa 13:14 he would not hearken unto her v.: 6963
2Sa 13:36 and lifted up their v. and wept: 6963
2Sa 15:23 all the country wept with a loud v., ... 6963
2Sa 19:4 the king cried with a loud v., O my 6963
2Sa 19:35 any more the v. of singing men 693
2Sa 22:7 he did hear my v. out of his temple, ... 6963
2Sa 22:14 and the most High uttered his v. 6963
1Ki 8:55 congregation of Israel with a loud v. 6963
1Ki 17:22 the Lord heard the v. of Elijah; and 6963
1Ki 18:26 But there was no v., nor any that 6963
1Ki 18:29 that there was neither v. nor any 6963
1Ki 19:12 and after the fire a still small v. 6963
1Ki 19:13 there came a v. unto him, and said, ... 6963
1Ki 20:25 he hearkened unto their v., and did 6963
1Ki 20:36 hast not obeyed the v. of the Lord, ... 6963
2Ki 4:31 there was neither v., nor hearing. 6963
2Ki 7:10 no man there, neither v. of man, ... 6963
2Ki 10:6 and if ye will hearken unto my v., ... 6963
2Ki 18:12 they obeyed not the v. of the Lord..... 6963
2Ki 18:28 a loud v. in the Jews languge, ... 6963
2Ki 19:22 whom hast thou exalted thy v., ... 6963
1Ch 15:16 by lifting up the v. with joy. 6963
2Ch 5:13 lifted up their v. with the trumpets 6963
2Ch 15:14 sware unto the Lord with a loud v., ... 6963
2Ch 20:19 of Israel with a loud v. on high. 6963
2Ch 30:27 and their v. was heard, and their........ 6963
2Ch 32:18 with a loud v. in the Jews' speech 6963
Ezr 3:12 their eyes, wept with a loud v.; 6963
Ezr 10:12 answered and said with a loud v. 6963
Ne 9:4 cried with a loud v. unto the Lord 6963
Job 2:12 they lifted up their v., and wept; 6963
Job 3:7 solitary, let no joyful v. come therein. ....
Job 3:18 hear not the v. of the oppressor. 6963
Job 4:10 the lion, and the v. of the fierce lion, .. 6963
Job 4:16 there was silence, and I heard a v., ... 6963
Job 9:16 that he had hearkened unto my v.. 6963
Job 30:31 organ into the v. of them that weep.... 6963
Job 33:8 I have heard the v. of thy words, ... 6963
Job 34:16 hearken to the v. of my words. 6963
Job 37:2 Hear attentively the noise of his v.. 6963
Job 37:4 After it a v. roareth: he thundereth 6963
Job 37:4 with the v. of his excellency; 6963
Job 37:4 not stay them when his v. is heard..... 6963
Job 37:5 marvellously with his v.; great 6963
Job 38:34 thou lift up thy v. to the clouds, ... 6963
Job 40:9 thou thunder with a v. like him? 6963
Ps 3:4 I cried unto the Lord wth my v., ... 6963
Ps 5:2 Hearken unto the v. of my cry, my 6963
Ps 5:3 My v. shalt thou hear in the............. 6963
Ps 6:8 hath heard the v. of my weeping. 6963
Ps 18:6 he heard my v. out of his temple, ... 6963
Ps 18:13 and the Highest gave his v.; 6963
Ps 19:3 where their v. is not heard. 6963
Ps 26:7 with the v. of thanksgiving, ... 6963
Ps 27:7 O Lord, when I cry with my v.: 6963
Ps 28:2 Hear the v. of my supplications, ... 6963
Ps 28:6 heard the v. of my supplications. 6963
Ps 29:3 v. of the Lord is upon the waters: 6963
Ps 29:4 The v. of the Lord is powerful; the 6963
Ps 29:4 the v. of the Lord is full of majesty. ... 6963
Ps 29:5 v. of the Lord breaketh the cedars; 6963
Ps 29:7 v. of the Lord divideth the flames....... 6963
Ps 29:8 The v. of the Lord shaketh the........... 6963
Ps 29:9 v. of the Lord maketh the hinds to 6963
Ps 31:22 heardest the v. of my supplications 6963
Ps 42:4 with the v. of joy and praise, with a.... 6963
Ps 44:16 For the v. of him that reproacheth...... 6963
Ps 46:6 he uttered his v., the earth melted. 6963
Ps 47:1 unto God with the v. of triumph. 6963
Ps 55:3 Because of the v. of the enemy, ... 6963
Ps 55:17 cry aloud: and he shall hear my v.. 6963
Ps 58:5 not hearken to the v. of charmers, ... 6963
Ps 64:1 Hear my v., O God, in my prayer: 6963
Ps 66:8 the v. of his praise to be heard: 6963
Ps 66:19 attended to the v. of my prayer. 6963
Ps 68:33 lo, he doth send out his v., ... 6963
Ps 68:33 and that a mighty v.. 6963
Ps 74:23 Forget not the v. of thine enemies: 6963
Ps 77:1 I cried unto God with my v., even...... 6963
Ps 77:1 unto God with my v.; and he gave...... 6963
Ps 77:18 The v. of thy thunder was in the........ 6963
Ps 81:11 people would not hearken to my v.; 6963
Ps 86:6 attend to the v. of my supplications. ... 6963
Ps 93:3 the floods have lifted up their v.; 6963
Ps 95:7 hand. To day if ye will hear his v., ... 6963

Ps	98:5	the harp, and the **v.** of a psalm.	6963
Ps	102:5	By reason of the **v.** of my groaning.	6963
Ps	103:20	hearkening unto the **v.** of his word.	6963
Ps	104:7	at the **v.** of thy thunder they hasted.	6963
Ps	106:25	not unto the **v.** of the Lord.	6963
Ps	116:1	Lord, because he hath heard my **v.**	6963
Ps	118:15	The **v.** of rejoicing and salvaton is	6963
Ps	119:149	Hear my **v.** according unto thy	6963
Ps	130:2	Lord, hear my **v.**: let thine ears	6963
Ps	130:2	thine ears be attentive to the **v.** of	6963
Ps	140:6	hear the **v.** of my supplications,	
Ps	141:1	give ear unto my **v.**, when I cry	6963
Ps	142:1	I cried unto the Lord with my **v.**;	6963
Ps	142:1	with my **v.** unto the Lord did I	6963
Pr	1:20	she uttereth her **v.** in the streets:	6963
Pr	2:3	liftest up thy **v.** for understanding;	6963
Pr	5:13	not obeyed the **v.** of my teachers,	6963
Pr	8:1	understanding put forth her **v.**?	6963
Pr	8:4	and my **v.** is to the sons of man.	6963
Pr	27:14	blesseth his friend with a loud **v.**,	6963
Ec	5:3	a fool's **v.** is known by multitude of	6963
Ec	5:6	should God be angry at thy **v.**,	6963
Ec	10:20	a bird of the air shall carry the **v.**,	6963
Ec	12:4	he shall rise up at the **v.** of the bird,	6963
Ca	2:8	The **v.** of my beloved! behold, he	6963
Ca	2:12	the **v.** of the turtle is heard in our	6963
Ca	2:14	me hear thy **v.**; for sweet is thy **v.**,	6963
Ca	5:2	**v.** of my beloved that knocketh,	6963
Ca	8:13	the companions hearken to thy **v.**:	6963
Isa	6:4	moved at the **v.** of him that cried,	6963
Isa	6:8	Also I heard the **v.** of the Lord,	6963
Isa	10:30	Lift up thy **v.**, O daughter of	6963
Isa	13:2	exalt the **v.** unto them, shake the	6963
Isa	15:4	their **v.** shall be heard even unto	6963
Isa	24:14	They shall lift up their **v.**, they shall	6963
Isa	28:23	Give ye ear, and hear my **v.**;	6963
Isa	29:4	thy **v.** shall be, as of one that hath a	6963
Isa	30:19	unto thee at the **v.** of thy cry;	6963
Isa	30:30	cause his glorious **v.** to be heard,	6963
Isa	30:31	through the **v.** of the Lord shall the	6963
Isa	31:4	he will not be afraid of their **v.**, nor	6963
Isa	32:9	hear my **v.**, ye careless daughers;	6963
Isa	36:13	cried with a loud **v.** in the Jews'	6963
Isa	37:23	whom hast thou exalted thy **v.**,	6963
Isa	40:3	The **v.** of him that crieth in the	6963
Isa	40:6	The **v.** said, Cry. And he said,	6963
Isa	40:9	tidings, lift up thy **v.** with strength;	6963
Isa	42:2	nor cause his **v.** to he heard in the	6963
Isa	42:11	and the cities thereof lift up their **v.**,	
Isa	48:20	with a **v.** of singing declare ye, tell	6963
Isa	50:10	that obeyeth the **v.** of his servant,	6963
Isa	51:3	thanksgiving, and the **v.** of melody.	6963
Isa	52:8	Thy watchmen shall lift up the **v.**;	6963
Isa	52:8	with the **v.** together shall they sing:	6963
Isa	58:1	not, lift up thy **v.** like a trumpet,	6963
Isa	58:4	make your **v.** to be heard on high.	6963
Isa	65:19	the **v.** of weeping shall be no more	6963
Isa	65:19	heard in her, nor the **v.** of crying.	6963
Isa	66:6	A **v.** of noise from the city,	6963
Isa	66:6	a **v.** from the temple,	6963
Isa	66:6	a **v.** of the Lord that rendereth	6963
Jer	3:13	and ye have not obeyed my **v.**, saith	6963
Jer	3:21	A **v.** was heard upon the high	6963
Jer	3:25	have not obeyed the **v.** of the Lord	6963
Jer	4:15	For a **v.** declareth from Dan, and	6963
Jer	4:16	give out their **v.** against the cities	6963
Jer	4:31	heard a **v.** as of a woman in travail,	6963
Jer	4:31	the **v.** of the daughter of Zion, that	6963
Jer	6:23	their **v.** roareth like the sea; and	6963
Jer	7:23	Obey my **v.**, and I will be your God,	6963
Jer	7:28	that obeyeth not the **v.** of the Lord	6963
Jer	7:34	the **v.** of mirth,...the **v.** of gladness,	6963
Jer	7:34	the **v.** of the bridegroom, and	6963
Jer	7:34	the **v.** of the bride: for the land	6963
Jer	8:19	the **v.** of the cry of the daughter of	6963
Jer	9:10	can men hear the **v.** of the cattle;	6963
Jer	9:13	and have not obeyed my **v.**, neither	6963
Jer	9:19	a **v.** of wailing is heard out of Zion,	6963
Jer	10:13	When he uttereth his **v.**, there is a	6963
Jer	11:4	iron furnace, saying, Obey my **v.**,	6963
Jer	11:7	and protesting, saying, Obey my **v.**	6963
Jer	16:9	the **v.** of mirth,...the **v.** of gladness.	6963
Jer	16:9	the **v.** of the bridegroom, and	6963
Jer	16:9	and the **v.** of the bride.	6963
Jer	18:10	that it obey not my **v.**, then I will	6963
Jer	18:19	hearken to he **v.** of them that	6963
Jer	22:20	and lift up thy **v.** in Bashan, and cry	6963
Jer	22:21	that thou obeyedst not my **v.**	6963
Jer	25:10	the **v.** of mirth,...the **v.** of gladness,	6963
Jer	25:10	the **v.** of the bridegroom, and	6963
Jer	25:10	and the **v.** of the bride, the sound	6963
Jer	25:30	high, and utter his **v.** from his holy	6963
Jer	25:36	A **v.** of the cry of the shepherds, and	6963
Jer	26:13	obey the **v.** of the Lord your God;	6963
Jer	30:5	We have heard a **v.** of trembling, of	6963
Jer	30:19	the **v.** of them that make merry:	6963
Jer	31:15	A **v.** was heard in Ramah	6963
Jer	31:16	Refrain thy **v.** from weeping, and	6963
Jer	32:23	but they obeyed not thy **v.**, neither	6963
Jer	33:11	The **v.** of joy, and the **v.** of gladness,	6963
Jer	33:11	the **v.** of the bridegroom, and	6963
Jer	33:11	and the **v.** of the bride, the	6963
Jer	33:11	**v.** of them that shall say, Praise the	6963
Jer	35:8	we obeyed the **v.** of Jonadab the	6963
Jer	38:20	I beseech thee, the **v.** of the Lord,	6963
Jer	40:3	Lord, and have not obeyed his **v.**,	6963
Jer	42:6	we will obey the **v.** of the Lord our	6963
Jer	42:6	when we obey the **v.** of the Lord our	6963
Jer	42:13	neither obey the **v.** of the Lord your	6963
Jer	42:21	have not obeyed the **v.** of the Lord	6963
Jer	43:4	obeyed not the **v.** of the Lord, to	6963
Jer	43:7	they obeyed not the **v.** of the Lord:	6963
Jer	44:23	have not obeyed the **v.** of the Lord,	6963
Jer	46:22	**v.** thereof shall go like a serpent;	6963
Jer	48:3	A **v.** of crying shall be from	6963
Jer	48:34	Jahaz, have they uttered their **v.**,	6963
Jer	50:28	**v.** of them that flee and escape out	6963
Jer	50:42	their **v.** shall roar like the sea, and	6963
Jer	51:16	When he uttereth his **v.**, there is a	6963
Jer	51:55	destroyed out of her the great **v.**;	6963
Jer	51:55	a noise of their **v.** is uttered:	6963
La	3:56	Thou hast heard my **v.**: hide not	6963
Eze	1:24	waters, the **v.** of the Almighty,	6963
Eze	1:24	the **v.** of speech, as the noise of	6963
Eze	1:25	a **v.** from the firmament that was	6963
Eze	1:28	and I heard a **v.** of one that spake.	6963
Eze	3:12	behind me a **v.** of a great rushing,	6963
Eze	8:18	they cry in mine ears with a loud **v.**,	6963
Eze	9:1	also in mine ears with a loud **v.**,	6963
Eze	10:5	as the **v.** of the Almighty God when	6963
Eze	11:13	cried with a loud **v.**, and said, Ah	6963
Eze	19:9	that his **v.** should no more be heard	6963
Eze	21:22	to lift up the **v.** with shouting, to	6963
Eze	23:42	a **v.** of a multitide being at ease	6963
Eze	27:30	cause their **v.** to be heard against	6963
Eze	33:32	song of one that hath a pleasant **v.**	6963
Eze	43:2	and his **v.** was like a noise of many	6963
Da	4:31	there fell a **v.** from heaven, saying,	7032
Da	6:20	he cried with a lamentable **v.** unto	7032
Da	7:11	the **v.** of the great words which the	7032
Da	8:16	I heard a man's **v.** between the	6963
Da	9:10	have we obeyed the **v.** of the Lord	6963
Da	9:11	that they might not obey thy **v.**;	6963
Da	9:14	he doeth: for we obeyed not his **v.**	6963
Da	10:6	and the **v.** of his words like the	6963
Da	10:6	like the **v.** of a multitude.	6963
Da	10:9	Yet heard I the **v.** of his words:	6963
Da	10:9	when I heard the **v.** of his words,	6963
Joe	2:11	shall utter his **v.** before his army:	6963
Joe	3:16	and utter his **v.** from Jerusalem;	6963
Am	1:2	and utter his **v.** from Jerusalem;	6963
Jon	2:2	cried I, and thou heardest my **v.**	6963
Jon	2:9	thee with the **v.** of thanksgiving;	6963
Mic	6:1	and let the hills hear thy **v.**	6963
Mic	6:9	The Lord's **v.** crieth unto the city,	6963
Na	2:7	lead her as with the **v.** of doves,	6963
Na	2:13	**v.** of thy messengers shall no more	6963
Hab	3:10	the deep uttered his **v.**, and lifted	6963
Hab	3:16	my lips quivered at the **v.**	6963
Zep	1:14	even the **v.** of the day of the Lord:	6963
Zep	2:14	their **v.** shall sing in the windows;	6963
Zep	3:2	She obeyed not the **v.**; she received	6963
Hag	1:12	obeyed the **v.** of the Lord their God,	6963
Zec	6:15	diligently obey the **v.** of the Lord	6963
Zec	11:3	**v.** of the howling of the shepherds;	6963
Zec	11:3	a **v.** of the roaring of young lions;	6963
Mt	2:18	In Rama was there a **v.** heard,	*5456*
Mt	3:3	**v.** of one crying in the wilderness,	*5456*
Mt	3:17	And lo a **v.** from heaven, saying,	*5456*
Mt	12:19	any man hear his **v.** in the streets.	*5456*
Mt	17:5	and behold a **v.** out of the cloud,	*5456*
Mt	27:46	Jesus cried with a loud **v.**, saying,	*5456*
Mt	27:50	he had cried again with a loud **v.**,	*5456*
Mk	1:3	**v.** of one crying in the wilderness,	*5456*
Mk	1:11	And there came a **v.** from heaven,	*5456*
Mk	1:26	cried with a loud **v.**, he came out of	*5456*
Mk	5:7	cried with a loud **v.**, and said, What	*5456*
Mk	9:7	a **v.** came out of the cloud, saying,	*5456*
Mk	15:34	hour Jesus cried with a loud **v.**,	*5456*
Mk	15:37	Jesus cried with a loud **v.**, and gave	*5456*
Lu	1:42	And she spake out with a loud **v.**,	*5456*
Lu	1:44	**v.** of thy salutation sounded in mine	*5456*
Lu	3:4	**v.** of one crying in the wilderness,	*5456*
Lu	3:22	a **v.** came from heaven, which said,	*5456*
Lu	4:33	devil, and cried out with a loud **v.**,	*5456*
Lu	8:28	with a loud **v.** said. What have I to	*5456*
Lu	9:35	there came a **v.** out of the cloud,	*5456*
Lu	9:36	when the **v.** was past, Jesus was	*5456*
Lu	11:27	certain woman...lifted up her **v.**,	*5456*
Lu	17:15	and with a loud **v.** glorified God,	*5456*
Lu	19:37	praise God with a loud **v.** for all the	*5456*
Lu	23:46	when Jesus had cried with a loud **v.**,	*5456*
Joh	1:23	**v.** of one crying in the wilderness,	*5456*
Joh	3:29	because of the bridegroom's **v.**:	*5456*
Joh	5:25	**shall hear the v. of the Son of God.**	*5456*
Joh	5:28	**are in the graves shall hear his v.,**	*5456*
Joh	5:37	**Ye have neither heard his V. at**	*5456*
Joh	10:3	**openeth; and the sheep hear his v.:**	*5456*
Joh	10:4	**follow him: for they know his v.**	*5456*
Joh	10:5	**they know not the v. of strangers.**	*5456*
Joh	10:16	**and they shall hear my v.; and**	*5456*
Joh	10:27	**My sheep hear my v., and I know**	*5456*
Joh	11:43	he cried with a loud **v.**, **Lazarus,**	*5456*
Joh	12:28	Then came there a **v.** from heaven,	*5456*
Joh	12:30	**This v. came not because of me,**	*5456*
Joh	18:37	**that is of the truth heareth my v.**	*5456*
Ac	2:14	lifted up his **v.**, and said unto them,	*5456*
Ac	4:24	they lifted up their **v.** to God with	*5456*
Ac	7:31	the **v.** of the Lord came unto him,	*5456*
Ac	7:57	Then they cried out with a loud **v.**,	*5456*
Ac	7:60	cried with a loud **v.**, Lord, lay not	*5456*
Ac	8:7	spirits, crying with loud **v.**, came	*5456*
Ac	9:4	and heard a **v.** saying unto him,	*5456*
Ac	9:7	hearing a **v.**, but seeing no man.	*5456*
Ac	10:13	there came a **v.** to him, Rise, Peter;	*5456*
Ac	10:15	the **v.** spake unto him again the	*5456*
Ac	11:7	And I heard a **v.** saying unto me,	*5456*
Ac	11:9	But the **v.** answered me again from	*5456*
Ac	12:14	And when she knew Peter's **v.**, she	*5456*
Ac	12:22	is the **v.** of a god, and not of a man.	*5456*
Ac	14:10	Said with a loud **v.**, Stand upright	*5456*
Ac	16:28	Paul cried with a loud **v.**, saying,	*5456*
Ac	19:34	one **v.** about the space of two hours	*5456*
Ac	22:7	heard a **v.** saying unto me, **Saul**	*5456*
Ac	22:9	heard not the **v.** of him that spake	*5456*
Ac	22:14	shouldest hear the **v.** of his mouth.	*5456*
Ac	24:21	Except it be for this one **v.**, that I	*5456*
Ac	26:10	death, I gave my **v.** against them.	*5586*
Ac	26:14	I heard a **v.** speaking unto me, and	*5456*
Ac	26:24	Festus said with a loud **v.**, Paul,	*5456*
1Co	14:11	if I know not the meaning of the **v.**,	*5456*
1Co	14:19	that by my **v.** I might teach others	
Ga	4:20	you now, and to change my **v.**;	*5456*
1Th	4:16	with the **v.** of the archangel, and	*5456*
Heb	3:7	saith, To day if ye will hear his **v.**,	*5456*
Heb	3:15	said, To day if ye will hear his **v.**,	*5456*
Heb	4:7	said, To day if ye will hear his **v.**,	*5456*
Heb	12:19	of a trumpet, and the **v.** of words;	*5456*
Heb	12:19	which **v.** they that heard intreated	
Heb	12:26	Whose **v.** then shook the earth:	*5456*
2Pe	1:17	came such a **v.** to him from the	*5456*
2Pe	1:18	this **v.** which came from heaven we	*5456*
2Pe	2:16	dumb ass speaking with man's **v.**	*5456*
Re	1:10	and heard behind me a great **v.**, as	*5456*
Re	1:12	I turned to see the **v.** that spake	*5456*
Re	1:15	his **v.** as the sound of many waters.	*5456*
Re	3:20	**if any man hear my v., and open**	*5456*
Re	4:1	the first **v.** which I heard was as it	*5456*
Re	5:2	angel proclaiming with a loud **v.**,	*5456*
Re	5:11	I heard the **v.** of many angels round	*5456*
Re	5:12	Saying with a loud **v.**, Worthy is the	*5456*
Re	6:6	I heard a **v.** in th midst of the four	*5456*
Re	6:7	I heard the **v.** of the fourth beast	*5456*
Re	6:10	And they cried with a loud **v.**,	*5456*
Re	7:2	he cried with a loud **v.** to the four	*5456*
Re	7:10	And cried with a loud **v.**, saying,	*5456*
Re	8:13	saying with a loud **v.**, Woe, woe,	*5456*
Re	9:13	I heard a **v.** from the four horns of	*5456*
Re	10:3	cried with a loud **v.**, as when a lion	*5456*
Re	10:4	I heard a **v.** from heaven saying	*5456*
Re	10:7	days of the **v.** of the seventh angel,	*5456*

Re 10:8 **v.** which I heard from heaven spake.... *5456*
Re 11:12 they heard a great **v.** from heaven...... *5456*
Re 12:10 I heard a loud **v.** saying in heaven, ... *5456*
Re 14:2 And I heard a **v.** from heaven, as....... *5456*
Re 14:2 as the **v.** of many waters, and.......... *5456*
Re 14:2 and as the **v.** of a great thunder:........ *5456*
Re 14:2 heard the **v.** of harpers harping.......... *5456*
Re 14:7 Saying with a loud **v.**, Fear God,........ *5456*
Re 14:9 them, saying with a loud **v.**,............. *5456*
Re 14:13 I heard a **v.** from heaven saying......... *5456*
Re 14:15 loud **v.** to him that sat on the cloud, ... *5456*
Re 16:1 a great **v.** out of the temple saying..... *5456*
Re 16:17 a great **v.** out of the temple of.......... *5456*
Re 18:2 he cried mightily with a strong **v.**,...... *5456*
Re 18:4 I heard another **v.** from heaven,.......... *5456*
Re 18:22 the **v.** of harpers, and musicians,......... *5456*
Re 18:23 the **v.** o the bridegroom and of the..... *5456*
Re 19:1 I heard a great **v.** of much people....... *5456*
Re 19:5 And a **v.** came out of the throne, ... *5456*
Re 19:6 it were the **v.** of a great multitude,..... *5456*
Re 19:6 and as the **v.** of many waters, ... *5456*
Re 19:6 as the **v.** of mighty thunderings,......... *5456*
Re 19:17 and he cried with a loud **v.**, saying..... *5456*
Re 21:3 a great **v.** out of heaven saying, ... *5456*

VOICES
Jg 21:2 lifted up their **v.**, and wept sore;........ 6963
1Sa 11:4 people lifted up their **v.**, and wept. 6963
Lu 17:13 And they lifted up their **v.**, and.......... *5456*
Lu 23:23 And they were instant with loud **v.**,.... *5456*
Lu 23:23 **v.** of them and of the chief priests...... *5456*
Ac 13:27 nor yet the **v.** of the prophets which... *5456*
Ac 14:11 they lifted up their **v.**, saying in the.... *5456*
Ac 22:22 and then lifted up their **v.**, and said,.... *5456*
1Co 14:10 so many kinds of **v.** in the world, ... *5456*
Re 4:5 lightnings and thunderings and **v.**........ *5456*
Re 8:5 and there were **v.**, and thunderings,..... *5456*
Re 8:13 of the other **v.** of the trumpet of........ *5456*
Re 10:3 seven thunders uttered their **v.**........... *5456*
Re 10:4 seven thunders had uttered their **v.**, ... *5456*
Re 11:15 and there were great **v.** in heaven,...... *5456*
Re 11:19 lightnings, and **v.**, and thunderings,..... *5456*
Re 16:18 there were **v.**, and thunders, and....... *5456*

VOID See also AVOID.
Ge 1:2 the earth was without form, and **v.**; 922
Nu 30:12 made them **v.** on the day he heard..... 6565
Nu 30:12 her husband hath made them **v.**; 6565
Nu 30:13 or her husband may make it **v.**. 6565
Nu 30:15 make them **v.** after that he hath......... 6565
De 32:28 For they are a nation **v.** of counsel,......... 6
1Ki 22:10 in a **v.** place in the entrance of the...... 1637
2Ch 18:9 sat in a **v.** place at the entering......... 1637
Ps 89:39 made **v.**...covenant of thy servant......... 5010
Ps 119:126 for they have made **v.** thy law. 6565
Pr 7:7 a young man **v.** of understanding, ... 2638
Pr 10:13 of him that is **v.** of understanding. 2638
Pr 11:12 He that is **v.** of wisdom despiseth........ 2638
Pr 12:11 vain persons is **v.** of understanding. 2638
Pr 17:18 a man **v.** of understanding striketh...... 2638
Pr 24:30 of the man **v.** of understanding;.......... 2638
Isa 55:11 it shall not return unto me **v.**, but...... 7387
Jer 4:23 and, lo, it was without form, and **v.**;..... 922
Jer 19:7 make **v.** the counsel of Judah and....... 1238
Na 2:10 She is empty, and **v.**, and waste: 4003
Ac 24:16 conscience **v.** of offence toward God,.... *677*
Ro 3:31 make **v.** the law through faith?........... *2673*
Ro 4:14 faith is made **v.**, and the promise *2758*
1Co 9:15 man should make my glorying **v.**......... *2758*

VOLUME
Ps 40:7 in the **v.** of the book it is written 4039
Heb 10:7 (in the **v.** of the book it is written *2777*

VOLUNTARILY
Eze 46:12 peace offerings **v.** unto the Lord, ... 5071

VOLUNTARY
Le 1:3 offer it of his own **v.** will at the.......... 7522
Le 7:16 offering be a vow, or a **v.** offering, ... 5071
Eze 46:12 shalt prepare a **v.** burnt offering......... 5071
Col 2:18 you of your reward in a **v.** humility..... *2309*

VOMIT See also VOMITED; VOMITETH.
Job 20:15 and he shall **v.** them up again: 6958
Pr 23:8 thou hast eaten shalt thou **v.** up,......... 6958
Pr 25:16 thou be filled therewith, and **v.** it. 6958
Pr 26:11 a dog returneth to his **v.**, so a fool..... 6892
Isa 19:14 drunken man staggereth in his **v.**........ 6892
Isa 28:8 For all tables are full of **v.** and.......... 6892
Jer 48:26 Moab also shall wallow in his **v.**, and... 6892
2Pe 2:22 dog is turned to his own **v.** again; *1829*

VOMITED
Jon 2:10 it **v.** out Jonah upon the dry land. 6958

VOMITETH
Le 18:25 land itself **v.** out her inhabitants. 6958

VOPHSI (vof'-si)
Nu 13:14 of Naphtali, Nahbi the son of **V.**......... 2058

VOUCH See AVOUCH.

VOW See also VOWED; VOWEST; VOWETH; VOWS.
Ge 28:20 Jacob vowed a **v.**, saying, If God........ 5088
Ge 31:13 where thou vowedst a **v.** unto me: 5088
Le 7:16 the sacrifice of his offering be a **v.**,..... 5088
Le 22:21 unto the Lord to accomplish his **v.**,..... 5088
Le 22:23 for a **v.** it shall not be accepted.......... 5088
Le 27:2 a man shall make a singular **v.**, the..... 5088
Nu 6:2 shall separate themselves to **v.** a........ 5087
Nu 6:2 **v.** of a Nazarite, to separate............. 5088
Nu 6:5 the days of the **v.** of his separation...... 5088
Nu 6:21 according to the **v.** which he vowed, ... 5088
Nu 15:3, 8 a sacrifice in performing a **v.**, or...... 5088
Nu 21:2 Israel vowed a **v.** unto the Lord,........ 5088
Nu 30:2 If a man **v.**...unto the Lord, ... 5087
Nu 30:2 **v.** unto the Lord, or swear 5088
Nu 30:3 a woman also **v.**...unto the Lord, ... 5087
Nu 30:3 **v.** unto the Lord, and bind............... 5088
Nu 30:4 her father hear her **v.**, and her bond... 5088
Nu 30:8 shall make her **v.** which she vowed,.... 5088
Nu 30:9 But every **v.** of a widow, and of her.... 5088
Nu 30:13 Every **v.**, and every binding oath to.... 5088
De 12:11 vows which ye **v.** unto the Lord:........ 5087
De 23:18 of the Lord thy God for any **v.**: 5088
De 23:21 thou shalt **v.**...unto the Lord 5087
De 23:21 **v.** unto the Lord thy God, ... 5088
De 23:22 But if thou shalt forbear to **v.**, it........ 5088
Jg 11:30 Jephtah vowed a **v.** unto the Lord, ... 5088
Jg 11:39 according to his **v.** which he had 5088
1Sa 1:11 And she vowed a **v.**, and said,........... 5088
1Sa 1:21 Lord the yearly sacrifice, and his **v.**,... 5088
2Sa 15:7 pray thee, let me go and pay my **v.**,... 5088
2Sa 15:8 servant vowed a **v.** while I abode....... 5088
Ps 65:1 unto thee shall the **v.** be performed. ... 5088
Ps 76:11 **V.**, and pay unto the Lord your......... 5087
Ec 5:4 When thou vowest a **v.** unto God, ... 5088
Ec 5:5 is it that thou shouldest not **v.**,.......... 5087
Ec 5:5 that thou shouldest **v.** and not pay...... 5087
Isa 19:21 yea, they shall **v.**...unto the Lord,....... 5087
Ac 18:18 head in Cenchrea: for he had a **v.**........ *2171*
Ac 21:23 four men which have a **v.** on them;..... *2171*

VOWED See also VOWEDST.
Ge 28:20 And Jacob **v.** a vow, saying, If God..... 5087
Le 27:8 according to his ability that **v.** shall..... 5087
Nu 6:21 law of the Nazarite who hath **v.**, and... 5087
Nu 6:21 according to the vow which he **v.**. 5087
Nu 21:2 And Israel **v.** a vow unto the Lord,..... 5087
Nu 30:6 at all an husband, when she **v.**,.......... 5088
Nu 30:8 shall make her vow which she **v.**,....... 5088
Nu 30:10 if she **v.** in her husband's house, ... 5087
De 23:23 as thou hast **v.** unto the Lord thy....... 5087
Jg 11:30 Jephtah **v.** a vow unto the Lord, ... 5087
Jg 11:39 to his vow which he had **v.**:.............. 5087
1Sa 1:11 And she **v.** a vow, and said, O Lord, .. 5087
2Sa 15:7 I have **v.** unto the Lord, in Hebron..... 5087
2Sa 15:8 thy servant **v.** a vow while I abode..... 5087
Ps 132:2 **v.** unto the mighty God of Jacob;....... 5087
Ec 5:4 pay that which thou hast **v.**. 5087
Jer 44:25 perform our vows that we have **v.**,..... 5087
Jon 2:9 I will pay that that I have **v.**............. 5087

VOWEDST
Ge 31:13 and where thou **v.** a vow unto me: 5087

VOWEST
De 12:17 nor any of thy vows which thou **v.**,..... 5087
Ec 5:4 When thou **v.** a vow unto God, defer .. 5087

VOWETH
Mal 1:14 and **v.**, and sacrificeth unto the......... 5087

VOWS
Le 22:18 offer his oblation for all his **v.**, ... 5088
Le 23:38 beside all your **v.**, and beside all 5088
Nu 29:39 beside your **v.**, and your freewill 5088
Nu 30:4 then all her **v.** shall stand, and.......... 5088
Nu 30:5 not any of her **v.**, or of her bonds 5088
Nu 30:7 then her **v.** shall stand, and her 5088
Nu 30:11 then all her **v.** shall stand, and.......... 5088
Nu 30:12 out of her lips concerning her **v.**,........ 5088
Nu 30:14 then he establisheth all her **v.**, or....... 5088
De 12:6 your **v.**, and your freewill offerings, ... 5088
De 12:11 all your choice **v.** which ye vow 5088
De 12:17 nor any of thy **v.** which thou 5088
De 12:26 and thy **v.**, thou shalt take, and go 5088
Job 22:27 thee, and thou shall pay they **v.**. 5088
Ps 22:25 I will pay my **v.** before them that....... 5088
Ps 50:14 and pay thy **v.** unto the most High: 5088
Ps 56:12 Thy **v.** are upon me, O God: I will..... 5088
Ps 61:5 For thou, O God, hast heard my **v.**: ... 5088
Ps 61:8 that I may daily perform my **v.**. 5088
Ps 66:13 offerings: I will pay thee my **v.**, ... 5088
Ps 116:14, 18 I will pay my **v.** unto the Lord....... 5088
Pr 7:14 me; this day have I payed my **v.**........ 5088
Pr 20:25 holy, and after **v.** to make enquiry....... 5088
Pr 31:2 womb? and what, the son of my **v.**?.... 5088
Jer 44:25 will surely perform our **v.** that we...... 5088
Jer 44:25 ye will surely accomplish your **v.**,....... 5088
Jer 44:25 and surely perform your **v.**................ 5088
Jon 1:16 sacrifice unto the Lord, and made **v.**.. 5088
Na 1:15 thy solemn feasts, perform thy **v.**:...... 5088

VOYAGE
Ac 27:10 I perceive that this **v.** will be with...... *4144*

VULTURE See also VULTURE'S; VULTURES.
Le 11:14 the **v.**, and the kite after his kind; 1676
De 14:13 the kite, and the **v.** after his kind, ... 1772

VULTURE'S
Job 28:7 which the **v.** eye hath not seen: 344

VULTURES
Isa 34:15 the **v.** also be gathered, every........... 1772

W.

WAFER See also WAFERS.
Ex 29:23 and one **w.** out of the basket of........ 7550
Le 8:26 a cake of oiled bread, and one **w.**,....... 7550
Nu 6:19 the basket, and one unleavened **w.**, ... 7550

WAFERS
Ex 16:31 of it was like **w.** made with honey. 6838
Ex 29:2 **w.** unleavened anointed with oil:......... 7550
Le 2:4 unleavened **w.** anointed with oil.......... 7550
Le 7:12 unleavened **w.** anointed with oil,......... 7550
Nu 6:15 **w.** of unleavened bread anointed 7550

WAG See also WAGGING.
Jer 18:16 be astonished, and **w.** his head. 5110
La 2:15 **w.** their head at the daughter of......... 5128
Zep 2:15 her shall hiss, and **w.** his hand........... 5128

WAGES
Ge 29:15 tell me, what shall thy **w.** be?........... 4909
Ge 30:28 Appoint me thy **w.**, and I will give...... 7939
Ge 31:7 and changed my **w.** ten times; 4909
Ge 31:8 The speckled shall be thy **w.**:............ 7939
Ge 31:41 hast changed my **w.** ten times. 4909
Ex 2:9 me, and I will give thee thy **w.**.......... 7939
Le 19:13 **w.** of him that is hired shall not 6468
Jer 22:13 neighbour's service without **w.**,........... 2600
Eze 29:18 yet had he no **w.**, nor his army, for.... 7939
Eze 29:19 and it shall be the **w.** for his army...... 7939
Hag 1:6 and he that earneth **w.** earneth.......... 7936
Hag 1:6 earneth **w.** to put it into a bag........... 7936
Mal 3:5 that oppress the hireling in his **w.**, ... 7939
Lu 3:14 and be content with your **w.**. *3800*
Joh 4:36 **And he that reapeth receiveth w.**,.. *3408*

Ro 6:23 For the **w.** of sin is death; but the *3800*
2Co 11:8 other churches, taking **w.** of them, ... *3800*
2Pe 2:15 loved the **w.** of unrighteousness; *3408*

WAGGING
Mt 27:39 by reviled him, **w.** their heads *2795*
Mk 15:29 by railed on him, **w.** their heads......... *2795*

WAGON See also WAGONS.
Nu 7:3 a **w.** for two of the princes, and for.... 5699

WAGONS
Ge 45:19 take you **w.** out of the land of 5699
Ge 45:21 Joseph gave them **w.** according to...... 5699
Ge 45:27 when he saw the **w.** which Joseph...... 5699
Ge 46:5 in the **w.** which Pharaoh had sent....... 5699
Nu 7:3 before the Lord, six covered **w.**,........ 5699
Nu 7:6 Moses took the **w.** and the oxen,........ 5699
Nu 7:7 Two **w.** and four oxen he gave unto ... 5699
Nu 7:8 four **w.** and eight oxen he gave.......... 5699
Eze 23:24 against thee with chariots, **w.**, ... 7393

WAIL See also BEWAILED; WAILED; WAILING.
Eze 32:18 **w.** for the multitude of Egypt, ... 5091
Mic 1:8 Therefore I will **w.** and howl, I.......... 5594
Re 1:7 kindreds of the earth shall **w.** *2875*

WAILED
Mk 5:38 and them that wept and **w.** greatly....... *214*

WAILING
Es 4:3 and fasting, and weeping, and **w.**;....... 4553
Jer 9:10 will I take up a weeping and **w.**, ... 5092
Jer 9:18 haste, and take up a **w.** for us,........... 5092
Jer 9:19 a voice of **w.** is heard out of Zion,...... 5092
Jer 9:20 and teach your daughters **w.**, ... 5092
Eze 7:11 neither shall there be **w.** for them. 5089
Eze 27:31 bitterness of heart and bitter **w.**......... 4553
Eze 27:32 in their **w.** they shall take up a.......... 5204
Am 5:16 **W.** shall be in all streets; and............ 4553
Am 5:16 as are skilful of lamentation to **w.**....... 4553
Am 5:17 And in all vineyards shall be **w.**:.......... 4553
Mic 1:8 I will make a **w.** like the dragons, ... 4553
Mt 13:42, 50 **be w. and gnashing of teeth**...... *2805*
Re 18:15 of her torment, weeping and **w.**,........ *3996*
Re 18:19 cried, weeping and **w.**, saying,........... *3996*

WAIT See also AWAIT; WAITED; WAITETH; WAITING.
Ex 21:13 if a man lie not in **w.**, but God.......... 6658
Nu 3:10 shall **w.** on their priest's office: 8104
Nu 8:24 in to **w.** upon the service of the......... 6633
Nu 35:20 or hurl at him by laying of **w.**,........... 6660
Nu 35:22 him any thing without laying of **w.**, ... 6660
De 19:11 and lie in **w.** for him, and rise up......... 693
Jos 8:4 ye shall lie in **w.** against the city,......... 693
Jos 8:13 liers in **w.** on the west of the city, ... 6119
Jg 9:25 set liers in **w.** for him in the top of...... 693
Jg 9:32 with thee, and lie in **w.** in the field:...... 693
Jg 9:34 and they laid **w.** against Shechem......... 693
Jg 9:35 were with him, from lying in **w.**......... 3993
Jg 9:43 laid **w.** in the field, and looked,............ 693
Jg 16:2 laid **w.** for him all night in the gate....... 693
Jg 16:9 Now there were men lying in **w.**, ... 693
Jg 16:12 there were liers in **w.** abiding in........... 693
Jg 20:29 Israel set liers in **w.** round about......... 693
Jg 20:33 liers in **w.** of Israel came forth............ 693
Jg 20:36 they trusted unto the liers in **w.**.......... 693
Jg 20:37 liers in **w.** hasted, and rushed upon...... 693
Jg 20:37 liers in **w.** drew themselves along, ... 693
Jg 20:38 men of Israel and the liers in **w.**,......... 693
Jg 21:20 go and lie in **w.** in the vineyards;......... 693
1Sa 15:2 how he laid **w.** for him in the way, ...
1Sa 15:5 Amalek, and laid **w.** in the valley. 693
1Sa 22:8 my servant against me, to lie in **w.**,...... 693
1Sa 22:13 should rise against me, to lie in **w.**,..... 693
2Ki 6:33 I **w.** for the Lord any longer?........... 3176
1Ch 23:28 was to **w.** on the sons of Aaron......... 3027
2Ch 5:11 and did not then **w.** by course: 8104
2Ch 13:10 the Levites **w.** upon their business: ....
Ezr 8:31 and of such as lay in **w.** by the way. 693
Job 14:14 of my appointed time will I **w.**.. 3176
Job 17:13 If I **w.**, the grave is mine house:........ 6960
Job 31:9 if I have laid **w.** at my neighbour's 693
Job 38:40 and abide in the covert to lie in **w.**? 695
Ps 10:9 He lieth in **w.** secretly as a lion in 693
Ps 10:9 he lieth in **w.** to catch the poor: he...... 693
Ps 25:3 none that **w.** on thee be ashamed:...... 6960
Ps 25:5 on thee do I **w.** all the day. 6960
Ps 25:21 preserve me; for I **w.** on thee. 6960
Ps 27:14 **w.** on the Lord: be of good.............. 6960
Ps 27:14 thine heart: **w.**, I say, on the Lord. 6960
Ps 37:7 Lord, and **w.** patiently for him: 2342
Ps 37:9 but those that **w.** upon the Lord, ... 6960
Ps 37:34 **w.** on the Lord, and keep his way,..... 6960
Ps 39:7 And now, Lord, what **w.** I for?.......... 6960
Ps 52:9 and I will **w.** on thy name; for it is..... 6960
Ps 56:6 steps, when they **w.** for my soul........ 6960
Ps 59:3 For, lo, they lie in **w.** for my soul:....... 693
Ps 59:9 his strength will I **w.** upon thee: 8104
Ps 62:5 My soul, **w.** thou only upon God;....... 1826
Ps 69:3 eyes fail while I **w.** for my God. 3176
Ps 69:6 Let not them that **w.** on thee, ... 6960
Ps 71:10 and they that lay **w.** for my soul 8104
Ps 104:27 These **w.** all upon thee; that thou....... 7663
Ps 123:2 so our eyes **w.** upon the Lord our............
Ps 130:5 I **w.** for the Lord, my soul doth **w.**, ... 6960
Ps 145:15 The eyes of all **w.** upon thee; and...... 7663
Pr 1:11 let us lay **w.** for blood, let us lurk......... 693
Pr 1:18 And they lay **w.** for their own blood; 693
Pr 7:12 and lieth in **w.** at every corner.).......... 693
Pr 12:6 the wicked are to lie in **w.** for blood:.... 693
Pr 20:22 **w.** on the Lord, and he shall save 6960
Pr 23:28 She also lieth in **w.** as for a prey,........ 693
Pr 24:15 Lay not **w.**, O wicked man, against...... 693
Isa 8:17 and I will **w.** upon the Lord, that 2442
Isa 30:18 therefore will the Lord **w.**, that he..... 2442
Isa 30:18 blessed are all they that **w.** for him. ... 2442
Isa 40:31 they that **w.** upon the Lord shall........ 6960
Isa 42:4 and the isles shall **w.** for his law. 3176
Isa 49:23 not be ashamed that **w.** for me. 6960
Isa 51:5 the isles shall **w.** upon me, and on...... 6960
Isa 59:9 **w.** for light, but behold obscurity;...... 6960
Isa 60:9 Surely the isles shall **w.** for me,......... 6960
Jer 5:26 they lay **w.**, as he that setteth.......... 7789
Jer 9:8 but in heart he layeth his **w.**............. 696
Jer 14:22 therefore we will **w.** upon thee: for 6960
La 3:10 was unto me as a bear lying in **w.**, ... 693
La 3:25 Lord is good unto them that **w.** 6960
La 3:26 quietly **w.** for the salvation of the....... 1748
La 4:19 laid **w.** for us in the wilderness. 693
Ho 6:9 as troops of robbers **w.** for a man, ... 2442
Ho 7:6 like an oven, whiles they lie in **w.**:....... 693
Ho 12:6 and **w.** on thy God continually. 6960
Mc 7:2 they all lie in **w.** for blood; they........... 693
Mc 7:7 **w.** for the God of my salvation: 3176
Hab 2:3 though it tarry, **w.** for it; because 2442
Zep 3:8 Therefore **w.** ye upon me, saith the.... 2442
Mk 3:9 a small ship should **w.** on him............ *4342*
Lu 11:54 Laying **w.** for him, and seeking to *1748*
Lu 12:36 **like...men that w. for their lord,** ... *4327*
Ac 1:4 **w. for the promise of the Father,** .. *4037*
Ac 20:3 the Jews laid **w.** for him, ... *1096,1917*
Ac 20:19 by the lying in **w.** of the Jews:........... *1917*
Ac 23:16 son heard of their lying in **w.**,.......... *1747*
Ac 23:21 for there lie in **w.** for him of them...... *1748*
Ac 23:30 the Jews laid **w.** for the man, ... *1917*
Ac 25:3 laying **w.** in the way to kill......... *4160,1747*
Ro 8:25 then do we with patience **w.** for it. *553*
Ro 12:7 let us **w.** on our ministering: ....
1Co 9:13 they which **w.** at the altar are............ *4332*
Gal 5:5 **w.** for the hope of righteousness by *553*
Eph 4:14 whereby they lie in **w.** to deceive;....... *3180*
1Th 1:10 And to **w.** for his Son from heaven, ... *362*

WAITED
Ge 49:18 I have **w.** for thy salvation, O Lord. ... 6960
1Ki 20:38 and **w.** for the king by the way,......... 5975
2Ki 5:2 and she **w.** on Naaman's wife. 1961,6440
1Ch 6:32 and then they **w.** on their office......... 5975
1Ch 6:33 they that **w.** with their children.......... 5975
1Ch 9:18 **w.** in the king's gate eastward: ....
2Ch 7:6 the priests **w.** on their offices: the...... 5975
2Ch 17:19 These **w.** on the king, beside those.... 8334
2Ch 35:15 and the porters **w.** at every gate;............
Ne 12:44 priests and for the Levites that **w.**. 5975
Job 6:19 the companies of Sheba **w.** for them. .. 6960
Job 15:22 and he is **w.** for of the sword. 6822
Job 29:21 Unto me men gave ear, and **w.**, ... 3176
Job 29:23 And they **w.** for me as for the rain; 3176
Job 30:26 when I **w.** for light, there came 3176
Job 32:4 Elihu had **w.** till Job had spoken, ... 2442
Job 32:11 Behold, I **w.** for your words; I 3176
Job 32:16 When I had **w.**, (for they spake not, ... 3176
Ps 40:1 I **w.** patiently for the Lord; and he...... 6960
Ps 106:13 they **w.** not for his counsel: 2442
Ps 119:95 wicked have **w.** for me to destroy...... 6960
Isa 25:9 we have **w.** for him, and he will.......... 6960
Isa 25:9 we have **w.** for him, we will be glad ... 6960
Isa 26:8 O Lord, have we **w.** for thee; 6960
Isa 33:2 we have **w.** for thee: be thou their..... 6960
Eze 19:5 when she saw that she had **w.**,.......... 3176
Mic 1:12 of Maroth **w.** carefully for good:......... 2342
Zec 11:11 poor of the flock that **w.** upon me 8104
Mk 15:43 also **w.** for the kingdom of God,......... *4327*
Lu 1:21 And the people **w.** for Zacharias,........ *4328*
Lu 23:51 himself **w.** for the kingdom of God...... *4327*
Ac 10:7 them that **w.** on him continually; *4342*
Ac 10:24 And Cornelius **w.** for them, and......... *4328*
Ac 17:16 while Paul **w.** for them at Athens, ... *1551*
1Pe 3:20 of God **w.** in the days of Noah,......... *1551*

WAITETH
Job 24:15 the adulterer **w.** for the twilight, ... 8104
Ps 33:20 Our soul **w.** for the Lord: he is 2442
Ps 62:1 Truly my soul **w.** upon God: from...... 1747
Ps 65:1 Praise **w.** for thee, O God, in Sion: 1747
Ps 130:6 My soul **w.** for the Lord more than ....
Pr 27:18 he that **w.** on his master shall be 8104
Isa 64:4 prepared for him that **w.** for him........ 2442
Da 12:12 Blessed is he that **w.**, and cometh to.. 2442
Mic 5:7 man, nor **w.** of the sons of men......... 3176
Ro 8:19 **w.** for the manifestation of the *553*
Jas 5:7 husbandman **w.** for the precious......... *1551*

WAITING
Nu 8:25 cease **w.** upon the service thereof, ... 6635
Pr 8:34 gates, **w.** at the posts of my doors....... 8104
Lu 2:25 **w.** for the consolation of Israel: *4327*
Lu 8:40 him: for they were all **w.** for him. *4328*
Joh 5:3 **w.** for the moving of the water.......... *1551*
Ro 8:23 **w.** for the adoption, to wit, the *553*
1Co 1:7 **w.** for the coming of our Lord Jesus..... *553*
2Th 3:5 and into the patient **w.** for Christ. ....

WAKE See also AWAKE; WAKED; WAKENED; WAKENETH; WAKETH; WAKING.
Jer 51:39, 57 a perpetual sleep, and not **w.**, ... 6974
Joe 3:9 **w.** up the mighty men, let all the....... 5782
1Th 5:10 whether we **w.** or sleep, we should.... *1127*

WAKED
Zec 4:1 with me came again, and **w.** me,........ 5782

WAKENED
Joe 3:12 Let the heathen be **w.**, and come....... 5782
Zec 4:1 a man that is **w.** out of his sleep,....... 5782

WAKENETH
Isa 50:4 he **w.** morning by morning, ... 5782
Isa 50:4 **w.** mine ear to hear as the learned..... 5782

WAKETH
Ps 127:1 the watchman **w.** but in vain. 8245
Ca 5:2 I sleep, but my heart **w.**: it is the...... 5782

WAKING
Ps 77:4 Thou holdest mine eyes **w.**: I am....... 8109

WALK See also WALKED; WALKEST; WALKETH; WALKING.
Ge 13:17 Arise, **w.** through the land in the 1980
Ge 17:1 **w.** before me, and be thou perfect. 1980
Ge 24:40 The Lord, before whom I **w.**, will 1980
Ge 48:15 fathers Abraham and Isaac did **w.**,...... 1980
Ex 16:4 whether they will **w.** in my law, or...... 3212
Ex 18:20 the way wherein they must **w.**, ... 3212
Ex 21:19 and **w.** abroad upon his staff,............ 1980
Le 18:3 shall ye **w.** in their ordinances. 3212
Le 18:4 mine ordinances, to **w.** therein:.......... 3212
Le 20:23 ye shall not **w.** in the manners of....... 3212
Le 26:3 If ye **w.** in my statutes, and keep....... 3212
Le 26:12 I will **w.** among you, and will be 1980
Le 26:21 ye **w.** contrary unto me, and will........ 3212
Le 26:23 but will **w.** contrary unto me; 1980
Le 26:24 will I also **w.** contrary unto you, ... 1980
Le 26:27 unto me, but **w.** contrary unto me;...... 1980
Le 26:28 Then I will **w.** contrary unto you........ 1980
De 5:33 Ye shall **w.** in all the ways which........ 3212
De 8:6 to **w.** in his ways, and to fear him. 3212
De 8:19 **w.** after other gods, and serve 1980
De 10:12 to **w.** in all his ways, and to love 3212
De 11:22 to **w.** in all his ways, and to cleave...... 3212
De 13:4 Ye shall **w.** after the Lord your God, .. 3212
De 13:5 thy God commanded thee to **w.** in....... 3212
De 19:9 thy God, and to **w.** ever in his ways;.. 3212
De 26:17 be thy God, and to **w.** in his ways,...... 3212
De 28:9 Lord thy God, and **w.** in his ways. 1980

De 29:19 I **w.** in the imagination of mine 3212
De 30:16 Lord thy God, to **w.** in his ways, 3212
Jos 18:8 Go and **w.** through the land, and 1980
Jos 22:5 God, and to **w.** in all his ways. 3212
Jg 2:22 the way of the Lord to **w.** therein, 3212
Jg 5:10 in judgment, and **w.** by the way. 1980
1Sa 2:30 should **w.** before me for ever: 1980
1Sa 2:35 he shall **w.** before mine anointed 1980
1Sa 8:5 and thy sons **w.** not in thy ways: 1980
1Ki 2:3 to **w.** in his ways, to keep his 3212
1Ki 2:4 to **w.** before me in truth with all 3212
1Ki 3:14 if thou wilt **w.** in my ways, to keep 3212
1Ki 3:14 as thy father David did **w.**, 1980
1Ki 6:12 if thou wilt **w.** in my statutes, 3212
1Ki 6:12 my commandments to **w.** in them; 3212
1Ki 8:23 thy servants that **w.** before thee 1980
1Ki 8:25 **w.** before me as thou hast walked 3212
1Ki 8:36 good way wherein they should **w.**, 3212
1Ki 8:58 unto him, to **w.** in all his ways, 3212
1Ki 8:61 Lord our god, to **w.** in his statutes, 3212
1Ki 9:4 if thou wilt **w.** before me, as David 3212
1Ki 11:38 wilt **w.** in my ways, and do that 1980
1Ki 16:31 a light thing for him to **w.** in the 3212
2Ki 10:31 no heed to **w.** in the law of the Lord 3212
2Ki 23:3 the Lord, to **w.** after the Lord, 3212
2Ch 6:14 that **w.** before thee with all their 1980
2Ch 6:16 heed to their way to **w.** in my law, 3212
2Ch 6:27 good way, wherein they should **w.**: 3212
2Ch 6:31 to **w.** in thy ways, so long as they 3212
2Ch 7:17 for thee, if thou wilt **w.** before me, 3212
2Ch 34:31 the Lord, and to **w.** after the Lord, 3212
Ne 5:9 ye not to **w.** in the fear of our God 3212
Ne 10:29 into an oath, to **w.** in God's law, 3212
Ps 12:8 The wicked **w.** on every side, 1980
Ps 23:4 though I **w.** through the valley 3212
Ps 26:11 for me, I will **w.** in mine integrity: 3212
Ps 48:12 **W.** about Zion, and go round 5437
Ps 56:13 I may **w.** before God in the light 1980
Ps 78:10 God, and refused to **w.** in his law; 3212
Ps 82:5 they **w.** on in darkness: 1980
Ps 84:11 from them that **w.** uprightly. 1980
Ps 86:11 O Lord; I will **w.** in thy truth: 1980
Ps 89:15 they shall **w.**, O Lord, in the light 1980
Ps 89:30 and **w.** not in my judgments; 3212
Ps 101:2 I will **w.** within my house with a 1980
Ps 115:7 feet have they, but they **w.** not: 1980
Ps 116:9 I will **w.** before the Lord in the 1980
Ps 119:1 who **w.** in the law of the Lord. 1980
Ps 119:3 no iniquity: they **w.** in his ways. 1980
Ps 119:45 I will **w.** at liberty: for I seek thy 1980
Ps 138:7 I **w.** in the midst of trouble, thou 1980
Ps 143:8 know the way wherein I shoud **w.**; 3212
Pr 1:15 **w.** not thou in the way with them; 3212
Pr 2:7 buckler to them that **w.** uprightly. 1980
Pr 2:13 to **w.** in the ways of darkness; 3212
Pr 2:20 thou mayest **w.** in the way of good 3212
Pr 3:23 shalt thou **w.** in thy way safely, 3212
Ec 4:15 the living which **w.** under the sun, 1980
Ec 6:8 knoweth to **w.** before the living? 1980
Ec 11:9 and **w.** in the ways of thine heart, 1980
Isa 2:3 ways, and we will **w.** in his paths: 3212
Isa 2:5 let us **w.** in the light of the Lord. 3212
Isa 3:16 **w.** with stretched forth necks and 3212
Isa 8:11 not **w.** in the way of this people, 3212
Isa 30:2 That **w.** to go down into Egypt, 1980
Isa 30:21 This is the way, ye **w.** in it, when 3212
Isa 35:9 but the redeemed shall **w.** there: 1980
Isa 40:31 and they shall **w.**, and not faint. 3212
Isa 42:5 and spirit to them that **w.** therein: 1980
Isa 42:24 for they would not **w.** in his ways, 1980
Isa 50:11 **w.** in the light of your fire, and in 3212
Isa 59:9 brightness, but we **w.** in darkness. 1980
Jer 3:17 neither shall they **w.** any more 3212
Jer 3:18 shall **w.** with the house of Israel, 3212
Jer 6:16 is the good way, and **w.** therein, 3212
Jer 6:16 they said, We will not **w.** therein. 3212
Jer 6:25 into the field, nor **w.** by the way; 3212
Jer 7:6 **w.** after other gods to your hurt: 3212
Jer 7:9 **w.** after other gods whom ye know 1980
Jer 7:23 **w.** ye in all the ways that I have 1980
Jer 9:4 neighbour will **w.** with slanders. 1980
Jer 13:10 which **w.** in the imagination of 1980
Jer 13:10 and **w.** after others gods, to serve 1980
Jer 16:12 **w.** every one after the imagination 1980
Jer 18:12 we will **w.** after our own devices, 1980
Jer 18:15 to **w.** in paths, in a way not cast 1980

Jer 23:14 commit adultery, and **w.** in lies: 1980
Jer 26:4 hearken to me, to **w.** in my law, 1980
Jer 31:9 cause them to **w.** by the rivers of 1980
Jer 42:3 us the way wherein we may **w.**, 1980
La 5:18 is desolate, the foxes **w.** upon it. 1980
Eze 11:20 That they may **w.** in my statutes, 3212
Eze 20:18 **W.** ye not in the statutes of your 3212
Eze 20:19 **w.** in my statutes, and keep my 3212
Eze 33:15 **w.** in the statutes of life, without 1980
Eze 36:12 I will cause men to **w.** upon you, 3212
Eze 36:27 cause you to **w.** in my statutes, 3212
Eze 37:24 they shall also **w.** in my judgments, 3212
Eze 42:4 chambers was a **w.** often cubits 4109
Da 4:37 those that **w.** in pride he is able to 1981
Da 9:10 to **w.** in his laws, which he set 3212
Ho 11:10 They shall **w.** after the Lord: he 3212
Ho 14:9 right, and the just shall **w.** in them: 3212
Joe 2:8 they shall **w.** every one in his path: 3212
Am 3:3 Can two **w.** together, except they 3212
Mic 4:2 ways, and we will **w.** in his paths: 3212
Mic 4:5 will **w.** every one in the name of his 3212
Mic 4:5 will **w.** in the name of the Lord our 3212
Mic 6:8 and to **w.** humbly with thy God? 3212
Mic 6:16 Ahab, and ye **w.** in their counsels; 3212
Na 2:5 they shall stumble in their **w.**: 1979
Hab 3:15 didst **w.** through the sea with 1869
Hab 3:19 me to **w.** upon mine high places. 1869
Zep 1:17 that they shall **w.** like blind men, 1980
Zec 1:10 to **w.** to and fro through the earth. 1980
Zec 3:7 If thou wilt **w.** in my ways, and if 3212
Zec 3:7 to **w.** among these that stand by. 4108
Zec 6:7 **w.** to and fro through the earth: 1980
Zec 6:7 **w.** to and fro through the earth. 1980
Zec 10:12 shall **w.** up and down in his name, 1980
Mt 9:5 **thee; or to say, Arise, and w.:** *4043*
Mt 11:5 **and the lame w., the lepers are** *4043*
Mt 15:31 the lame to **w.**, and the blind to see: *4043*
Mk 2:9 **and take up thy bed, and w.?** *4043*
Mk 7:5 Why **w.** not thy disciples according *4043*
Lu 5:23 **thee; or to say, Rise up and w.?** *4043*
Lu 7:22 **that the blind see, the lame w.,** *4043*
Lu 11:44 **the men that w. over them are not** *4043*
Lu 13:33 **I must w. to day, and to morrow,** *4198*
Lu 20:46 **which desire to w. in long robes,** *4043*
Lu 24:17 **ye have one to another, as ye w.,** *4043*
Joh 5:8 him, **Rise, take up thy bed, and w** *4043*
Joh 5:11 unto me, Take up thy bed, and **w.** *4043*
Joh 5:12 thee, Take up thy bed, and **w.**? *4043*
Joh 7:1 for he would not **w.** in Jewry, *4043*
Joh 8:12 **me shall not w. in darkness,** *4043*
Joh 11:9 **If any man w. in the day, he** *4043*
Joh 11:10 **But if a man w. in the night, he** *4043*
Joh 12:35 **W. while ye have the light, lest** *4043*
Ac 3:6 Christ of Nazareth rise up and **w.** *4043*
Ac 3:12 we had made this man to **w.**? *4043*
Ac 14:16 all nations to **w.** in their own ways. *4198*
Ac 21:21 neither to **w.** after the customs. *4043*
Ro 4:12 also **w.** in the steps of that faith *4748*
Ro 6:4 should **w.** in newness of life. *4043*
Ro 8:1 who **w.** not after the flesh, but *4043*
Ro 8:4 who **w.** not after the flesh, but *4043*
Ro 13:13 Let us **w.** honestly, as in the day; *4043*
1Co 3:3 are ye not carnal, and **w.** as men? *4043*
1Co 7:17 called every one, so let him **w.** *4043*
2Co 5:7 (For we **w.** by faith, not by sight:) *4043*
2Co 6:16 dwell in them, and **w.** in them; *1704*
2Co 10:3 For though we **w.** in the flesh, we *4043*
Ga 5:16 **W.** in the Spirit, and ye shall not *4043*
Ga 5:25 Spirit, let us also **w.** in the Spirit. *4748*
Ga 6:16 many as **w.** according to this rule, *4748*
Eph 2:10 that we should **w.** in them. *4043*
Eph 4:1 that ye **w.** worthy of the vocation *4043*
Eph 4:17 **w.** not as other Gentiles **w.**, *4043*
Eph 5:2 **w.** in love, as Christ also hath loved *4043*
Eph 5:8 in the Lord; **w.** as children of light: *4043*
Eph 5:15 See then that ye **w.** circumspectly, *4043*
Php 3:16 let us **w.** by the same rule, let us *4748*
Php 3:17 mark them which **w.** so as ye have *4043*
Php 3:18 (For many **w.**, of whom I have told *4043*
Col 1:10 That ye might **w.** worthy of the *4043*
Col 2:6 Jesus the Lord, so **w.** ye in him: *4043*
Col 4:5 **W.** in wisdom toward them that *4043*
1Th 2:12 That ye would **w.** worthy of God, *4043*
1Th 4:1 ye ought to **w.** and to please God, *4043*
1Th 4:12 **w.** honestly toward them that are *4043*
2Th 3:11 which **w.** among you disorderly, *4043*

2Pe 2:10 them that **w.** after the flesh in the *4198*
1Jo 1:6 with him, and **w.** in darkness, *4043*
1Jo 1:7 But if we **w.** in the light, as he is in *4043*
1Jo 2:6 in him ought himself also so to **w.**, *4043*
2Jo 6 we **w.** after this commandments. *4043*
2Jo 6 the beginning, ye should **w.** in it. *4043*
3Jo 4 hear that my children **w.** in truth. *4043*
Jude 18 **w.** after their own ungodly lusts. *4198*
Re 3:4 **they shall w. with me in white:** *4043*
Re 9:20 neither can see, nor hear, nor **w.**: *4043*
Re 16:15 lest he **w.** naked, and they see his *4043*
Re 21:24 are saved shall **w.** in the light of it: *4043*

WALKED See also WALKEDST.

Ge 5:22 Enoch **w.** with God after he begat 1980
Ge 5:24 Enoch **w.** with God: and he was 1980
Ge 6:9 generations, and Noah **w.** with God. 1980
Ex 2:5 her maidens **w.** along by the river's 1980
Ex 14:29 children of Israel **w.** upon dry land 1980
Le 26:40 they have **w.** contrary unto me; 1980
Le 26:41 I also have **w.** contrary unto them, 3212
Jos 5:6 **w.** forty years in the wilderness, 1980
Jg 2:17 the way which their fathers **w.** in, 1980
Jg 5:6 the travellers **w.** through byways. 3212
Jg 11:16 **w.** through the wilderness unto the 3212
1Sa 8:3 And his sons **w.** not in his ways, 1980
1Sa 12:2 I have **w.** before you from my 1980
2Sa 2:29 and his men **w.** all that night 1980
2Sa 7:6 **w.** in a tent and in a tabernacle. 1980
2Sa 7:7 I have **w.** with all the children of 1980
2Sa 11:2 and **w.** upon the roof of the king's 1980
1Ki 3:6 as he **w.** before thee in truth, and 1980
1Ki 8:25 me as thou hast **w.** before me. 1980
1Ki 9:4 as David thy father **w.**, in integrity 1980
1Ki 11:33 have not **w.** in my ways, to do that 1980
1Ki 15:3 and he **w.** in all the sins of his 3212
1Ki 15:26 and **w.** in the way of his father, and 3212
1Ki 15:34 and **w.** in the way of Jeroboam, and 3212
1Ki 16:2 hast **w.** in the way of Jeroboam, 3212
1Ki 16:26 he **w.** in all the way of Jeroboam 3212
1Ki 22:43 And he **w.** in all the ways of Asa his 3212
1Ki 22:52 and **w.** in the way of his father, and 3212
2Ki 4:35 and **w.** in the house to and fro; 3212
2Ki 8:18 he **w.** in the way of the kings of 3212
2Ki 8:27 he **w.** in the way of the house of 3212
2Ki 13:6 made Israel sin, but **w.** therein: 1980
2Ki 13:11 made Israel sin: but he **w.** therein. 1980
2Ki 16:3 But he **w.** in the way of the kings 3212
2Ki 17:8 **w.** in the statutes of the heathen, 3212
2Ki 17:19 **w.** in the statutes of Israel which 3212
2Ki 17:22 children of Israel **w.** in all the sins 3212
2Ki 20:3 **w.** before thee in truth and with a 1980
2Ki 21:21 And he **w.** in all the way that his 3212
2Ki 21:21 in all the way that his father **w.** in, 1980
2Ki 21:22 and **w.** not in the way of the Lord. 1980
2Ki 22:2 and **w.** in all the way of David his 3212
1Ch 17:6 I have **w.** with all Israel, 1980
1Ch 17:8 thee whithersoever thou hast **w.**,
2Ch 6:16 law as thou hast **w.** before me. 3212
2Ch 7:17 before me, as David thy father **w.**, 1980
2Ch 11:17 they **w.** in the way of David and 1980
2Ch 17:3 he **w.** in the first ways of his father 1980
2Ch 17:4 **w.** in his commandments, and not 1980
2Ch 20:32 And he **w.** in the way of Asa his 3212
2Ch 21:6 And he **w.** in the way of the kings 3212
2Ch 21:12 thou hast not **w.** in the ways of 1980
2Ch 21:13 hast **w.** in the way of the kings of 3212
2Ch 22:3 also **w.** in the ways of the house of 1980
2Ch 22:5 He **w.** also after their counsel, and 1980
2Ch 28:2 he **w.** in the ways of the kings of 3212
2Ch 34:2 **w.** in the ways of David his father, 3212
Es 2:11 Mordecai **w.** every day before the 1980
Job 29:3 his light I **w.** through darkness; 3212
Job 31:5 If I have **w.** wth vanity, or if my 1980
Job 31:7 and mine heart **w.** after mine eyes, 1980
Job 38:16 thou **w.** in the search of the depth? 1980
Ps 26:1 for I have **w.** in mine integrity: 1980
Ps 26:3 eyes: and I have **w.** in thy truth. 1980
Ps 55:14 and **w.** unto the house of God in 1980
Ps 81:12 they **w.** in their own counsels. 3212
Ps 81:13 and Israel had **w.** in my ways! 1980
Ps 142:3 In the way wherein I **w.** have they 1980
Isa 9:2 people that **w.** in darkness have 1980
Isa 20:3 my servant Isaiah hath **w.** naked 1980
Isa 38:3 how I have **w.** before thee in truth 1980
Jer 2:5 and have **w.** after vanity, and are 3212

Jer 2:8 w. after things that do not profit. 1980
Jer 7:24 but w. in the counsels and in the 3212
Jer 8:2 and after whom they have w., and 1980
Jer 9:13 obeyed my voice, neither w. therein; 1980
Jer 9:14 w. after the imagination of their 3212
Jer 11:8 w. every one in the imagination of 3212
Jer 16:11 have w. after others gods, and have 3212
Jer 32:23 thy voice, neither w. in thy law; 1980
Jer 44:10 have they feared, nor w. in my law, 1980
Jer 44:23 of the Lord, nor w. in his law, nor 1980
Eze 5:6 statutes, they have not w. in them. 1980
Eze 5:7 and have not w. in my statutes, 1980
Eze 11:12 for ye have not w. in my statutes, 1980
Eze 16:47 hast thou not w. after their ways, 1980
Eze 18:9 Hath w. in my statutes, and hath 1980
Eze 18:17 judgments, hath w. in my statutes; 1980
Eze 20:13 they w. not in my statutes, and 1980
Eze 20:16 and w. not in my statutes, but 1980
Eze 20:21 they w. not in my statutes, neither 1980
Eze 23:31 hast w. in the way of they sister; 1980
Eze 28:14 hast w. up and down in the midst 1980
Da 4:29 w. in the palace of the kingdom 1981
Ho 5:11 he...w. after the commandment. 1980
Am 2:4 the which their fathers have w.: 1980
Na 2:11 even the old lion, w., and the lion's 1980
Zec 1:11 We have w. to and fro through the 1980
Zec 6:7 w. to and fro through the earth. 1980
Mal 2:6 he w. with me in peace and equity 1980
Mal 3:14 w. mournfully before the Lord 1980
Mt 14:29 he w. on the water, to go to Jesus. *4043*
Mk 1:16 Now as he w. by the sa of Gailiee, *4043*
Mk 5:42 the damsel arose, and w., for she *4043*
Mk 16:12 form unto two of them, as they w., *4043*
Joh 1:36 looking upon Jesus as he w., he *4043*
Joh 5:9 whole, and took up his bed, and w. *4043*
Joh 6:66 back, and w. no more with him. *4043*
Joh 7:1 these things Jesus w. in Galilee: *4043*
Joh 10:23 Jesus w. in the temple in Solomon's *4043*
Joh 11:54 w. no more openly among the *4043*
Ac 3:8 he leaping up stood, and w., and *4043*
Ac 14:8 mother's womb, who never had w. *4043*
Ac 14:10 on thy feet. And he leaped and w. *4043*
2Co 10:2 as if we w. according to the flesh. *4043*
2Co 12:18 you? w. we not in the same spirit? *4043*
2Co 12:18 spirit? w. we not in the same steps? *4043*
Ga 2:14 they w. not uprightly according to *3716*
Eph 2:2 in time past ye w. according to the *4043*
Col 3:7 In the which ye also w. some time, *4043*
1Pe 4:3 we w. in lasciviousness, lusts, *4198*
1Jo 2:6 also so to walk, even as he w. *4043*

WALKEDST
Joh 21:18 **and w. whither thou wouldest:** *4043*

WALKEST
De 6:7 and when thou w. by the way, 3212
De 11:19 and when thou w. by the way, 3212
1Ki 2:42 out, and w. abroad any whither, 1980
Isa 43:2 when thou w. through the fire, 3212
Ac 21:24 w. orderly, and keepest the law. *4748*
Ro 14:15 meat, now w. thou not charitably. *4043*
3Jo 3 thee, even as thou w. in the truth. *4043*

WALKETH
Ge 24:65 man is this that w. in the field to 1980
De 23:14 Lord thy God w. in the midst of 1980
1Sa 12:2 behold, the king w. before you: 1980
Job 18:8 own feet, and he w. upon a snare. 1980
Job 22:14 and he w. in the circuit of heaven. 1980
Job 34:8 iniquity, and w. with wicked men. 3212
Ps 1:1 that w. not in the counsel of the 1980
Ps 15:2 He that w. uprightly, and worketh 1980
Ps 39:6 Surely every man w. in a vain shew: 1980
Ps 73:9 and their tongue w. through the 1980
Ps 91:6 the pestilence that w. in darkness; 1980
Ps 101:6 he that w. in perfect way, he shall 1980
Ps 104:3 who w. upon the wings of the wind: 1980
Ps 128:1 the Lord; that w. in his ways. 1980
Pr 6:12 man, w. with a froward mouth. 1980
Pr 10:9 that w. [1980] uprightly w. surely: 3212
Pr 13:20 He that w. with wise men shall be 1980
Pr 14:2 He that w. in his uprightness 1980
Pr 15:21 of understanding w. uprightly 1980
Pr 19:1 the poor that w. in his integrity, 1980
Pr 20:7 The just man w. in his integrity: 1980
Pr 28:6 poor that w. in his uprightness, 1980
Pr 28:18 Whoso w. uprightly shall be saved: 1980
Pr 28:26 but whoso w. wisely, he shall be 1980
Ec 2:14 but the fool w. in darkness: and I 1980
Ec 10:3 when he that is a fool w. by the way, 1980
Isa 33:15 He that w. righteously, and 1980
Isa 50:10 that w. in darkness, and hath no 1980
Isa 65:2 w. in a way that was not good, 1980
Jer 10:23 in man that w. to direct his steps. 1980
Jer 23:17 one that w. after the imagination 1980
Eze 11:21 whose heart w. after the heart of 1980
Mic 2:7 do good to him that w. uprightly? 1980
Mt 12:43 **he w. through dry places, seeking** *1330*
Lu 11:24 **he w. through dry places, seeking** *1330*
Joh 12:35 **he that w. in darkness knoweth** *4043*
2Th 3:6 every brother that w. disorderly, *4043*
1Pe 5:8 w. about, seeking whom he may *4043*
1Jo 2:11 w. in darkness, and knoweth not *4043*
Re 2:1 **who w. in the midst of the seven** *4043*

WALKING
Ge 3:8 of the Lord God w. in the garden 1980
De 2:7 he knoweth thy w. through this 3212
1Ki 3:3 w. in the statutes of David his 3212
1Ki 16:19 in w. in the way of Jeroboam, and 3212
Job 1:7 and from w. up and down in it. 1980
Job 2:2 and from w. up and down in it. 1980
Job 31:26 or the moon w. in brightness: 1980
Ec 10:7 and princes w. as servants upon the 1980
Isa 3:16 w. and mincing as they go, and 1980
Isa 20:2 he did so, w. naked and barefoot. 1980
Isa 57:2 each one w. in his uprightness. 1980
Jer 6:28 revolters, w. with slanders: 1980
Da 3:25 loose, w. in the midst of the fire, 1981
Mic 2:11 man w. in the spirit and falsehood 1980
Mt 4:18 Jesus, w. by the sea of Galilee, *4043*
Mt 14:25 went unto them, w. on the sea. *4043*
Mt 14:26 the disciples saw him w. on the sea, *4043*
Mk 6:48 cometh unto them w. upon the sea, *4043*
Mk 6:49 when they saw him w. upon the sea, *4043*
Mk 8:24 up, and said, I see men as trees, w. *4043*
Mk 11:27 and as he was w. in the temple, *4043*
Lu 1:6 w. in all the commandments and *4198*
Joh 6:19 they see Jesus w. on the sea, and *4043*
Ac 3:8 into the temple, w., and leaping, *4043*
Ac 3:9 saw him w. and praising God: *4043*
Ac 9:31 w. in the fear of the Lord, and in *4198*
2Co 4:2 not w. in craftiness, nor handling *4043*
2Pe 3:3 scoffers, w. after their own lusts. *4198*
2Jo 4 found of thy children w. in truth, *4043*
Jude 16 w. after heir own lusts; *4198*

WALL See also WALLED; WALLS.
Ge 49:6 selfwill they digged down a w. 7794
Ge 49:22 whose branches run over the w.: 7791
Ex 14:22, 29 waters were a w. unto them 2346
Le 14:37 in sight are lower than the w.: 7023
Le 25:31 which have no w. round about 2346
Nu 22:24 vineyards, a w. being on this side, 1447
Nu 22:24 this side, and a w. on that side. 1447
Nu 22:25 she thrust herself unto the w., 7023
Nu 22:25 Balaam's foot against the w.: 7023
Nu 35:4 shall reach from the w. of the city 7023
Jos 2:15 her house was upon the town w., 2346
Jos 2:15 and she dwelt upon the w. 2346
Jos 6:5 w. of the city shall fall down flat, 2346
Jos 6:20 shout, that the w. fell down flat, 2346
1Sa 18:11 I will smite David even to the w. 7023
1Sa 19:10 to smite David even to the w. with 7023
1Sa 19:10 he smote the javelin into the w.: 7023
1Sa 20:25 times, even upon a seat by the w.: 7023
1Sa 25:16 w. unto us both by night and day, 2346
1Sa 25:22, 34 that pisseth against the w. 7023
1Sa 31:10 his body to the w. of Beth-shan. 2346
1Sa 31:12 his sons from the w. of Beth-shan, 2346
2Sa 11:20 that they would shoot from the w.? 2346
2Sa 11:21 a millstone upon him from the w., 2346
2Sa 11:21 Thebez? why went ye nigh the w.? 2346
2Sa 11:24 shooters shot from off the w. upon 2346
2Sa 18:24 the roof over the gate unto the w., 2346
2Sa 20:15 were with Joab battered the w., 2346
2Sa 20:21 shall be thrown to thee over the w. 2346
2Sa 22:30 by my God have I leaped over a w. 7791
1Ki 3:1 the w. of Jerusalem round about. 2346
1Ki 4:33 that springeth out of the w.: 7023
1Ki 6:5 And against the w. of the house he 7023
1Ki 6:6 in the w. of the house he made
1Ki 6:27 of the one touched the one w., 7023
1Ki 6:27 other cherub touched the other w.; 7023
1Ki 6:31 side posts were a fifth part of the w.
1Ki 6:33 of olive tree, a fourth part of the w.
1Ki 9:15 Millo, and the w. of Jerusalem, 2346
1Ki 14:10 him that pisseth against the w., 7023
1Ki 16:11 not one that pisseth against a w., 7023
1Ki 20:30 w. fell upon twenty and seven 2346
1Ki 21:21 him that pisseth against the w., 7023
1Ki 21:23 eat Jezebel by the w. of Jezreel. 2426
2Ki 3:27 for a burnt offering upon the w. 2346
2Ki 4:10 chamber, I pray thee, on the w.; 7023
2Ki 6:26 Israel was passing by upon the w., 2346
2Ki 6:30 he passed by upon the w., and the 2346
2Ki 9:8 him that pisseth against the w., 7023
2Ki 9:33 her blood was sprinkled on the w., 7023
2Ki 14:13 brake down the w. of Jerusalem 2346
2Ki 18:26 of the people that are on the w. 2346
2Ki 18:27 me to the men which sit on the w., 2346
2Ki 20:2 Then he turned his face to the w., 7023
2Ch 3:11, 12 reaching to the w. of the house: 7023
2Ch 25:23 brake down the w. of Jerusalem 2346
2Ch 26:6 and brake down the w. of Gath, 2346
2Ch 26:6 w. of Jabneh, and the w. of Ashdod, 2346
2Ch 26:9 turning of the w., and fortified them.
2Ch 27:3 on the w. of Ophel he built much. 2346
2Ch 32:5 built up all the w. that was broken, 2346
2Ch 32:5 the towers, and another w. without, 2346
2Ch 32:18 of Jerusalem that were on the w., 2346
2Ch 33:14 built a w. without the city of David, 2346
2Ch 36:19 brake down the w. of Jerusalem, 2346
Ezr 5:3 this house, and to make up this w.? 846
Ezr 9:9 a w. in Judah and in Jerusalem. 1447
Ne 1:3 w. of Jerusalem also is broken 2346
Ne 2:8 and for the w. of the city, and for 2346
Ne 2:15 by the brook, and viewed the w., 2346
Ne 2:17 let us build up the w. of Jerusalem, 2346
Ne 3:8 Jerusalem unto the broad w. 2346
Ne 3:13 a thousand cubits on the w. unto 2346
Ne 3:15 w. of the pool of Siloah by the king's 2346
Ne 3:19 the armoury at the turning of the w.
Ne 3:20 turning of the w. unto the door of the
Ne 3:24 of Azariah unto the turning of the w.,
Ne 3:25 over against the turning of the w.,
Ne 3:27 out, even unto the w. of Ophel. 2346
Ne 4:1 heard that we builded the w., 2346
Ne 4:3 even break down their stone w. 2346
Ne 4:6 So built we the w.; and all the 2346
Ne 4:6 all the w. was joined together unto 2346
Ne 4:10 that we are not able to build the w. 2346
Ne 4:13 I in the lower places behind the w., 2346
Ne 4:15 we returned all of us to the w., 2346
Ne 4:17 They which builded on the w., and 2346
Ne 4:19 we are separated upon the w., one 2346
Ne 5:16 continued in the work of this w., 2346
Ne 6:1 heard that I had builded the w., 2346
Ne 6:6 which cause thou buildest the w., 2346
Ne 6:15 w. was finished in the twenty and 2346
Ne 7:1 when the w. was built, and I had 2346
Ne 12:27 dedication of the w. of Jerusalem. 2346
Ne 12:30 people, and the gates, and the w. 2346
Ne 12:31 the princes of Judah upon the w., 2346
Ne 12:31 right hand upon the w. toward the 2346
Ne 12:37 at the going up of the w., above the 2346
Ne 12:38 the half of the people upon the w., 2346
Ne 12:28 furnaces even unto the broad w.; 2346
Ne 13:21 them, Why lodge ye about the w.? 2346
Ps 18:29 by my God have I leaped over a w. 7791
Ps 62:3 as a bowing w. shall ye be, and as 7023
Pr 18:11 as an high w. in his own conceit. 2346
Pr 24:31 the stone w. thereof was broken. 1444
Ca 2:9 he standeth behind our w., he 3796
Ca 8:9 If she be a w., we will build upon 2346
Ca 8:10 I am a w., and my breasts like 2346
Isa 2:15 high tower, upon every fenced w., 2346
Isa 5:5 breakdown the w. thereof, and it 1447
Isa 22:10 ye broken down to fortify the w. 2346
Isa 25:4 ones is as a storm against the w. 7023
Isa 30:13 swelling out in a high w., whose 2346
Isa 36:11 of the people that are on the w. 2346
Isa 36:12 me to the men that sit upon the w., 2346
Isa 38:2 turned his face toward the w., 7023
Isa 59:10 We grope for the w. like the blind, 7023
Jer 15:20 this people a fenced brasen w.: 2346
Jer 49:27 kindle a fire in the w. of Damascus, 2346
Jer 51:44 yea, the w. of Babylon shall fall. 2346
La 2:8 to destroy the w. of the daughter 2346
La 2:8 the rampart and the w. to lament; 2346
La 2:18 O w. of the daughter of Zion, let 2346
Eze 4:3 set it for a w. of iron between thee 7023
Eze 8:7 I looked, behold a hole in the w. 7023

Eze 8:8 me, Son of man, dig now in the w...... 7023
Eze 8:8 when I had digged in the w.,............ 7023
Eze 8:10 pourtrayed upon the w. round 7023
Eze 12:5 Dig thou through the w. in their 7023
Eze 12:7 I digged through the w. with mine....... 7023
Eze 12:12 shall dig through the w. to carry 7023
Eze 13:10 one built up a w., and, lo, others 2434
Eze 13:12 when the w. was fallen, shall it not..... 7023
Eze 13:14 will I break down the w. that ye 7023
Eze 13:15 accomplish my wrath upon the w.,........ 7023
Eze 13:15 The w. is no more, neither they 7023
Eze 23:14 saw men pourtrayed upon the w., ... 7023
Eze 38:20 every w. shall fall to the ground......... 2346
Eze 40:5 a w. on the outside of the house.......... 2346
Eze 41:5 he measured the w. of the house, ... 7023
Eze 41:6 they entered into the w. which.......... 7023
Eze 41:6 not hold in the w. of the house.......... 7023
Eze 41:9 The thickness of the w., which was.... 7023
Eze 41:12 w. of the building was five cubits 7023
Eze 41:17 all the w. round about within and 7023
Eze 41:20 made, and on the w. of the temple..... 7023
Eze 42:7 And the w. that was without over 1447
Eze 42:10 thickness of the w. of the court 1444
Eze 42:12 the way directly before the w............ 1448
Eze 42:20 it had a w. round about, five 2346
Eze 43:8 and the w. between me and them, ... 7023
Da 5:5 upon the plaister of the w. of the....... 3797
Da 9:25 shall be built again, and the w., ... 2742
Ho 2:6 and make a w., that she shall not....... 1447
Joe 2:7 climb the w. like men of war;............ 2346
Joe 2:9 they shall run upon the w., they 2346
Am 1:7 will send a fire on the w. of Gaza,....... 2346
Am 1:10 will send a fire on the w. of Tyrus, ... 2346
Am 1:14 kindle a fire in the w. of Rabbah, ... 2346
Am 5:19 and leaned his hand on the w., ... 7023
Am 7:7 upon a w. made by a plumbline,.......... 2346
Na 2:5 make haste to the w. thereof, and........ 2346
Na 3:8 sea, and her w. was from the sea?...... 2346
Hab 2:11 the stone shall cry out of the w.,........ 7023
Zec 2:5 will be unto her a w. of fire round....... 2346
Ac 9:25 let down by the w. in a basket. *5038*
Ac 23:3 shall smite thee, thou whited w.: *5109*
2Co 11:33 a basket was I let down by the w., ... *5038*
Eph 2:14 broken down the middle w. of ....
Re 21:12 And had a w. great and high, and........ *5038*
Re 21:14 the w. of the city had twelve.............. *5038*
Re 21:15 gates thereof, and the w. thereof. *5038*
Re 21:17 And he measured the w. thereof, ... *5038*
Re 21:18 building of the w....was of jasper:....... *5038*
Re 21:19 foundations of the w. of the city......... *5038*

WALLED See also UNWALLED.
Le 25:29 sell a dwelling house in a w. city,........ 2346
Le 25:30 w. city shall be established for ever.... 2346
Nu 13:28 and the cities are w., and very 1219
De 1:28 are great and w. up to heaven;........... 1219

WALLOW See also WALLOWED; WALLOWING.
Jer 6:26 sackcloth, and w. thyself in ashes:....... 6428
Jer 25:34 w. yourselves in the ashes, ye 6428
Jer 48:26 Moab also shall w. in his vomit, ... 5606
Eze 27:30 shall w. themselves in the ashes: 6428

WALLOWED
2Sa 20:12 Amasa w. in blood in the midst of 1556
Mk 9:20 on the ground and w. foaming. *2947*

WALLOWING
2Pe 2:22 was washed to her w. in the mire. *2946*

WALLS
Le 14:37 plague be in the w. of the house......... 7023
Le 14:39 plague be spread in the w. of the 7023
De 3:5 cities were fenced with high w.,.......... 2346
De 28:52 thy high and fenced w. come down, ... 2346
1Ki 4:13 great cities with w. and brasen 2346
1Ki 6:5 against the w. of the house round 7023
1Ki 6:6 be fastened in the w. of the house. 7023
1Ki 6:15 he built the w. of the house within 7023
1Ki 6:15 the house, and the w. of the ceiling: ... 7023
1Ki 6:16 and the w. with boards of cedar: 7023
1Ki 6:29 he carved all the w. of the house 7023
2Ki 25:4 way of the gate between two w., ... 2346
2Ki 25:10 brake down the w. of Jerusalem......... 2346
1Ch 29:4 to overlay the w. of the houses 7023
2Ch 3:7 the w. thereof, and the doors............ 7023
2Ch 3:7 and graved cherubims on the w.. 7023
2Ch 8:5 fenced cities, with w., gates, and....... 2346
2Ch 14:7 make about them w., and towers, ... 2346
Ezr 4:12 and have set up the w. thereof, ... 7791
Ezr 4:13 be builded, and the w. set up again, ... 7791
Ezr 4:16 again, and the w. thereof set up. 7791
Ezr 5:8 and timber is laid in the w., and......... 3797
Ezr 5:9 house, and to make up these w.? 846
Ne 2:13 and viewed the w. of Jerusalem, ... 2346
Ne 4:7 the w. of Jerusalem were made up, ... 2346
Job 24:11 Which make oil within their w.,.......... 7791
Ps 51:18 build thou the w. of Jerusalem. 2346
Ps 55:10 go about it upon the w. thereof: 2346
Ps 122:7 Peace be within thy w., and............. 2426
Pr 25:28 is broken down, and without w.. 2346
Ca 5:7 keepers of the w. took away my veil .. 2346
Isa 22:5 breaking down the w., and of........... 7023
Isa 22:11 also a ditch between the two w. 2346
Isa 25:12 fortress of the high fort of thy w. 2346
Isa 26:1 salvation will God appoint for w. 2346
Isa 49:16 thy w. are continually before me. 2346
Isa 56:5 within my w. a place and a name 2346
Isa 60:10 of strangers shall build up thy w., ... 2346
Isa 60:18 thou shalt call thy w. Salvation,.......... 2346
Isa 62:6 I have set watchmen upon thy w.,........ 2346
Jer 1:15 all the w. thereof round about, ... 2346
Jer 1:18 brasen w. against the whole land,....... 2346
Jer 5:10 Go ye up upon her w., and destroy; ... 8284
Jer 21:4 which besiege you without the w.,....... 2346
Jer 39:4 by the gate betwixt the two w.:.......... 2346
Jer 39:8 brake down the w. of Jerusalem......... 2346
Jer 50:15 are fallen, her w. are thrown down:.... 2346
Jer 51:12 standard upon the w. of Babylon, ... 2346
Jer 51:58 broad w. of Babylon shall be utterly.... 2346
Jer 52:7 way of the gate between the two w.,... 2346
Jer 52:14 brake down all the w. of Jerusalem.... 2346
La 2:7 of the enemy the w. of her palaces;.... 2346
Eze 26:4 they shall destroy the w. of Tyrus,....... 2346
Eze 26:9 set engines of war against thy w.,....... 2346
Eze 26:10 thy w. shall shake at the noise of....... 2346
Eze 26:12 they shall break down thy w., and....... 2346
Eze 27:11 thine army were upon thy w. round...... 2346
Eze 27:11 hanged their shields upon thy w.......... 2346
Eze 33:30 are talking against thee by the w........ 7023
Eze 38:11 all of them dwelling without w., ... 2346
Eze 41:13 the building, with the w. thereof, ... 7023
Eze 41:22 and the w. thereof, were of wood: 7023
Eze 41:25 like as were made upon the w.;........... 7023
Mic 7:11 the day that thy w. are to be built,...... 1447
Zec 2:4 inhabited as towns without w....................
Heb 11:30 By faith the w. of Jericho fell............ *5038*

WANDER See also WANDERED; WANDEREST; WANDERETH; WANDERING.
Ge 20:13 me to w. from my father's house, ... 8582
Nu 14:33 children shall w. in the wilderness 7462
Nu 32:13 he made them w. in the wilderness 5128
De 27:18 he that maketh the blind to w. out 7686
Job 12:24 causeth them to w. in a wilderness..... 8582
Job 38:41 unto God, they w. for lack of meat...... 8582
Ps 55:7 then would I w. far off, and remain...... 5074
Ps 59:15 them w. up and down for meat, ... 5128
Ps 107:40 them to w. in the wilderness,............ 8582
Ps 119:10 not w. from thy commandments. 7686
Isa 47:15 shall w. every one to his quarter;........ 8582
Jer 14:10 Thus have they loved to w., they....... 5128
Jer 48:12 that shall cause him to w., and 6808
Am 8:12 And they shall w. from sea to sea, ... 5128

WANDERED
Ge 21:14 and w. in the wilderness of............... 8582
Jos 14:10 of Israel w. in the wilderness: 1980
Ps 107:4 They w. in the wilderness in a 8582
Isa 16:8 they w. through the wilderness:......... 8582
La 4:14 They have w. as blind men in the 5128
La 4:15 when they fled away and w., they 5128
Eze 34:6 My sheep w. through all the 7686
Am 4:8 or three cities w. unto one city,......... 5128
Heb 11:37 they w. about in sheepskins and......... *4022*
Heb 11:38 they w. in deserts, and in................. *4105*

WANDERERS
Jer 48:12 that I will send unto him w., that........ 6808
Ho 9:17 shall be w. among the nations........... 5074

WANDEREST
Jer 2:20 under every green tree thou w.,......... 6808

WANDERETH
Job 15:23 He w. abroad for bread, saying,......... 5074
Pr 21:16 The man that w. out of the way of..... 8582
Pr 27:8 As a bird that w. from her nest, so.... 5074
Pr 27:8 so is a man that w. from his place...... 5074
Isa 16:3 outcasts; bewray not him that w.. 5074
Jer 49:5 none shall gather up him that w.. 5074

WANDERING See also WANDERINGS.
Ge 37:15 behold, he was w. in the field:........... 8582
Pr 26:2 As the bird by w., as the swallow 5110
Ec 6:9 the eyes than the w. of the desire:...... 1981
Isa 16:2 as a w. bird cast out of the nest, ... 5074
1Ti 5:13 w. about from house to house; *4022*
Jude 13 w. stars, to whom is reserved the...... *4107*

WANDERINGS
Ps 56:8 Thou tellest my w.: put thou my......... 5112

WANT See also WANTED; WANTETH; WANTING; WANTS.
De 28:48 nakedness, and in w. of all thing: 2640
De 28:57 shall eat them for w. of all things 2640
Jg 18:10 a place where there is no w. of......... 4270
Jg 19:19 there is no w. of any thing............... 4270
Job 24:8 embrace...rock for w. of a shelter. 1097
Job 30:3 For w. and famine they were 2639
Job 31:19 seen any perish for w. of clothing,...... 1097
Ps 23:1 is my shepherd; I shall not w.. 2637
Ps 34:9 is no w. to them that fear him........... 4270
Ps 34:10 Lord shall not w. any good thing. 2637
Pr 6:11 and thy w. as an armed man. 4270
Pr 10:21 but fools die for w. of wisdom. 2638
Pr 13:23 is destroyed for w. of judgment. 3808
Pr 13:25 the belly of the wicked shall w........... 2637
Pr 14:28 but in the w. of people is the............. 657
Pr 21:5 every one that is hasty only to w.......... 4270
Pr 22:16 to the rich, shall surely come to w.. ... 4270
Pr 24:34 and thy w. as an armed man. 4270
Isa 34:16 shall fail, none shall w. her mate: 6485
Jer 33:17 never w. a man to sit upon the............ 3772
Jer 33:18 Levites w. a man before me to offer... 3772
Jer 35:19 not w. a man to stand before me for... 3772
La 4:9 for w. of the fruits of the field. ....
Eze 4:17 they may w. bread and water, and 2637
Am 4:6 and w. of bread in all your places: 2640
Mk 12:44 **she of her w. did cast in all that** ... *5304*
Lu 15:14 **land; and he began to be in w.** *5302*
2Co 8:14 may be a supply for their w., ... *5303*
2Co 8:14 also may be a supply for your w. *5303*
2Co 9:12 only supplieth the w. of the saints, ... *5303*
Php 4:11 Not that I speak in respect of w. *5304*

WANTED
Jer 44:18 we have w. all things, and have 2637
Joh 2:3 when they w. wine, the mother of...... *5302*
2Co 11:9 I was present with you, and w., I *5302*

WANTETH
De 19:8 for his need, in that which he w......... 2637
Pr 9:4 for him that w. understanding,........... 2638
Pr 9:16 as for him that w. understanding, ... 2638
Pr 10:19 of words there w. not sin: but........... 2308
Pr 28:16 The prince that w. understanding 2638
Ec 6:2 so that he w. nothing for his soul....... 2638
Ca 7:2 round goblet, which w. not liquor: 2637

WANTING
2Ki 10:19 and all his priests; let none be w......... 6485
2Ki 10:19 whosoever shall be w., he shall not 6485
Pr 19:7 with words, yet they are w. to him. ... 3808
Ec 1:15 which is w. cannot be numbered. 2642
Da 5:27 in the balances, and art found w......... 2627
Tit 1:5 set in order the things that are w.,...... *3007*
Tit 3:13 that nothing be w. unto them. *3007*
Jas 1:4 be perfect and entire, w. nothing. *3007*

WANTON
Isa 3:16 stretched forth necks and w. eyes,....... 8265
1Ti 5:11 begun to wax w. against Christ,......... *2691*
Jas 5:5 pleasure on the earth, and been w.;.... *4684*

WANTONNESS
Ro 13:13 not in chambering and w., not in *766*
2Pe 2:18 through much w., those that were *766*

WANTS
Jg 19:20 let all thy w. lie upon me; only 4270
Php 2:25 and he that ministered to my w. *5532*

WAR See also WARFARE; WARRED; WARRETH; WARRING; WARS.
Ge 14:2 these made w. with Bera king of........ 4421
Ex 1:10 when there falleth out any w.,............ 4421
Ex 13:17 the people repent when they see w.,.. 4421
Ex 15:3 The Lord is a man of w.: the Lord....... 4421
Ex 17:16 the Lord will have w. with Amalek 4421

Ex 32:17 There is a noise of w. in the camp. 4421
Nu 1:3 able to go forth to w. in Israel: 6635
Nu 1:20, 22,24,26,28,30,32,34,36,38,40,42 all that were able to go forth to w.; 6635
Nu 1:45 were able to go forth to w. in Israel; 6635
Nu 10:9 if ye go to w. in your land against 4421
Nu 26:2 that are able to go to w. in Israel. 6635
Nu 31:3 some of yourselves unto the w. 6635
Nu 31:4 of Israel, shall ye send to the w. 6635
Nu 31:5 twelve thousand armed for w.. 6635
Nu 31:6 And Moses sent them to the w., a 6635
Nu 31:6 of Eleazer the priest, to the w., 6635
Nu 31:21 men of w. which went to the battle, 4421
Nu 31:27 them that took the w. upon them, 4421
Nu 31:28 the men of w. which went out to 4421
Nu 31:32 which the men of w. had caught, 6635
Nu 31:36 of them that went out to w., 6635
Nu 31:49 men of w. which are under our 4421
Nu 31:53 the men of w. had taken spoil, 6635
Nu 32:6 Shall your brethren go to w., and 4421
Nu 32:20 go armed before the Lord to w., 4421
Nu 32:27 over, every man armed for w., 6635
De 1:41 on every man his weapons of w., 4421
De 2:14 generation of the men of w. were 4421
De 2:16 all the men of w. were consumed 4421
De 3:18 all that are meet for the w. 2428
De 4:34 signs, and by wonders, and by w., 4421
De 20:12 but will make w. against thee, then 4421
De 20:19 in making w. against it to take it, 3898
De 20:20 the city that maketh w. with thee, 4421
De 21:10 When thou goest forth to w. 4421
De 24:5 new wife, he shall not go out to w., 6635
Jos 4:13 forty thousand prepared for w. 6635
Jos 5:4 even all the men of w., died in the 4421
Jos 5:6 all the people that were men of w., 4421
Jos 6:3 compass the city, all ye men of w., 4421
Jos 8:1 take all the people of w. with thee, 4421
Jos 8:3 arose, and all the people of w., to 4421
Jos 8:11 even the people of w. that were 4421
Jos 10:5 Gibeon, and made w. against it. 3898
Jos 10:7 and all the people of w. with him, 4421
Jos 10:24 captains of the men of w. which 4421
Jos 11:7 and all the people of w. with him, 4421
Jos 11:18 Joshua made w. a long time with 4421
Jos 11:23 And the land rested from w.. 4421
Jos 14:11 even so is my strength now, for w., 4421
Jos 14:15 And the land had rest from w. 4421
Jos 17:1 he was a man of w., therefore he 4421
Jos 22:12 to go up to w. against them. 6635
Jg 3:2 might know, to teach them w., 4421
Jg 3:10 judged Israel, and went out to w. 4421
Jg 5:8 gods; then was w. in the gates: 3901
Jg 11:4, 5 the children of Ammon made w. 3898
Jg 11:27 doest me wrong to w. against me: 3898
Jg 18:11 appointed with weapons of w. 4421
Jg 18:16 appointed with their weapons of w., 4421
Jg 18:17 were appointed with weapons of w.. 4421
Jg 20:17 sword: all these were men of w. 4421
Jg 21:22 not to each man his wife in the w., 4421
1Sa 8:12 and to make his instruments of w. 4421
1Sa 14:52 was sore w. against the Philistines 4421
1Sa 16:18 and a man of w., and prudent in 4421
1Sa 17:33 and he a man of w. from his youth. 4421
1Sa 18:5 Saul set him over the men of w., 4421
1Sa 19:8 there was w. again: and David 4421
1Sa 23:8 called all the people together to w., 4421
1Sa 28:15 Philistines make w. against me, 3898
2Sa 1:27 and the weapons of w. perished! 4421
2Sa 3:1 long w. between the house of Saul 4421
2Sa 3:6 was w. between the house of Saul 4421
2Sa 11:7 did, and how the w. prospered. 4421
2Sa 11:18 all the things concerning the w. 4421
2Sa 11:19 end of telling the matters of the w. 4421
2Sa 17:8 thy father is a man of w., and will 4421
2Sa 21:15 Philistines had yet w. again with 4421
2Sa 22:35 He teacheth my hands to w.; so 4421
1Ki 2:5 and shed the blood of w. in peace, 4421
1Ki 2:5 put the blood of w. upon his girdle 4421
1Ki 9:22 but they were men of w., and his 4421
1Ki 14:30 there was w. between Rehoboam 4421
1Ki 15:6 there was w. between Rehoboam 4421
1Ki 15:7 there was w. between Abijam and 4421
1Ki 15:16, 32 there was w. between Asa and 4421
1Ki 20:18 or whether they be come out for w., 4421
1Ki 22:1 continued three years without w. 4421
2Ki 8:28 to the w. against Hazael king of 4421
2Ki 13:25 hand of Jehoahaz his father by w. 4421
2Ki 14:7 took Selah by w., and called the 4421
2Ki 16:5 Israel came up to Jerusalem to w. 4421
2Ki 18:20 counsel and strength for the w.. 4421
2Ki 24:16 that were strong and apt for w., 4421
2Ki 25:4 men of w. fled by night by the way 4421
2Ki 25:19 that was set over the men of w., 4421
1Ch 5:10 in the days of Saul they made w. 4421
1Ch 5:18 to shoot with bow, and skilful in w., 4421
1Ch 5:18 threescore, that went out ot the w. 6635
1Ch 5:19 they made w. with the Hagarites, 4421
1Ch 5:22 slain, because the w. was of God. 4421
1Ch 7:4 were bands of soldiers for w., six 4421
1Ch 7:11 fit to go out for w. and battle. 6635
1Ch 7:40 of them that were apt to the w. and 6635
1Ch 12:1 the mighty men, helpers of the w. 4421
1Ch 12:8 and men of w. fit for the battle, 6635
1Ch 12:23 that were ready armed to the w., 6635
1Ch 12:24 hundred, ready armed to the w. 6635
1Ch 12:25 mighty men of valour for the w., 6635
1Ch 12:33 forth to battle, expert in w., 4421
1Ch 12:33 with all instruments of w., fifty 4421
1Ch 12:35 of the Danites expert in w. twenty 4421
1Ch 12:36 battle, expert in w., forty thousand. 4421
1Ch 12:37 all manner of instruments of w. 6635
1Ch 12:38 All these men of w., that could 4421
1Ch 18:10 (for Hadarezer had w. with Tou;) 4421
1Ch 20:4 there arose w. at Gezer with the 4421
1Ch 20:5 And there was w. again with the 4421
1Ch 20:6 yet again there was w. at Gath, 4421
1Ch 28:3 thou hast been a man of w., and 4421
2Ch 6:34 If thy people go out to w. against 4421
2Ch 8:9 they were men of w., and chief of 4421
2Ch 13:2 w. between Abijah and Jeroboam. 4421
2Ch 13:3 with an army of valiant men of w., 4421
2Ch 14:6 and he had no w. in those years; 4421
2Ch 15:19 And there was no more w. unto the 4421
2Ch 17:10 made no w. against Jehoshaphat. 3898
2Ch 17:13 and the men of w., mighty men of 4421
2Ch 17:18 ready prepared for the w. 6635
2Ch 18:3 and we will be with thee in the w.. 4421
2Ch 22:5 son of Ahab king of Israel to w. 4421
2Ch 25:5 choice men, able to go forth to w., 6635
2Ch 26:11 men, that went out to w. by bands, 6635
2Ch 26:13 that made w. with mighty power, 4421
2Ch 28:12 them that came from the w., 6635
2Ch 32:6 And he set captains of w. over the 4421
2Ch 33:14 and put captains of w. in all the 2428
2Ch 35:21 the house wherewith I have w.: 4421
Job 5:20 in w. from the power of the sword. 4421
Job 10:17 changes and w. are against me. 6635
Job 38:23 against the day of battle and w.? 4421
Ps 18:34 He teacheth my hands to w., so 4421
Ps 27:3 though w. should rise against me, 4421
Ps 55:21 butter, but w. was in his heart: 7128
Ps 68:30 thou the people that delight in w. 7128
Ps 120:7 but when I speak, they are for w. 4421
Ps 140:2 are they gathered together for w.. 4421
Ps 144:1 teacheth my hands to w., 4421,7128
Pr 20:18 and with good advice make w. 4421
Pr 24:6 counsel thou shalt make thy w.: 4421
Ec 3:8 a time of w., and a time of peace. 4421
Ec 8:8 there is no discharge in that w.; 4421
Ec 9:18 is better than weapons of w.: but 7128
Ca 3:8 hold swords, being expert in w.: 4421
Isa 2:4 neither shall they learn w. any 4421
Isa 3:2 mighty man, and the man of w., 4421
Isa 3:25 sword, and thy mighty in the w.. 4421
Isa 7:1 toward Jerusalem to w. against it, 4421
Isa 21:15 and from the grievousness of w.. 4421
Isa 36:5 I have counsel and strength for w.: 4421
Isa 37:9 come forth to make w. with thee. 3898
Isa 41:12 they that w. against thee shall be 4421
Isa 42:13 stir up jealousy like a man of w.: 4421
Jer 4:19 of the trumpet, the alarm of w.. 4421
Jer 6:4 Prepare ye w. against her; arise, 4421
Jer 6:23 set in array as men for w. against 4421
Jer 21:2 king of Babylon maketh w. 3898
Jer 21:4 I will turn back the weapons of w. 4421
Jer 28:8 of w., and of evil, and of pestilence. 4421
Jer 38:4 the hands of the men of w. that 4421
Jer 39:4 saw them, and all the men of w., 4421
Jer 41:3 found there, and the men of w. 4421
Jer 41:16 even mighty men of w., and the 4421
Jer 42:14 Egypt, where we shall see no w., 4421
Jer 48:14 mighty and strong men for the w.? 4421
Jer 49:2 cause an alarm of w. to be heard in 4421
Jer 49:26 all the men of w. shall be cut off in 4421
Jer 50:30 all her men of w. shall be cut off in 4421
Jer 51:20 my battle axe and weapons of w.: 4421
Jer 51:32 and the men of w. are affrighted. 4421
Jer 52:7 all the men of w. fled, and went 4421
Jer 52:25 had the charge of the men of w.; 4421
Eze 17:17 company make for him in the w., 4421
Eze 26:9 engines of w. against thy walls, 6904
Eze 27:10 in thine army, thy men of w.: 4421
Eze 27:27 all thy men of w., that are in thee, 4421
Eze 32:27 to hell with their weapons of w.: 4421
Eze 39:20 mighty men, and with all men of w., 4421
Da 7:21 horn made w. with the saints, 7129
Da 9:26 unto the end of the w. desolations 4421
Joe 2:7 shall climb the wall like men of w.; 4421
Joe 3:9 Prepare w., wake up the mighty 4421
Joe 3:9 let all the men of w. draw near; 4421
Mic 2:8 by securely as men averse from w.. 4421
Mic 3:5 they even prepare w. against him. 4421
Mic 4:3 neither shall they learn w. any 4421
Lu 14:31 **to make w. against another king,** *4171*
Lu 23:11 Herod with his men of w. set him *4753*
2Co 10:3 flesh, we do not w. after the flesh: *4754*
1Ti 1:18 them mightest w. a good warfare; *4754*
Jas 4:1 lusts that w. in your members? *4754*
Jas 4:2 ye fight and w., yet ye have not, *4170*
1Pe 2:11 lusts, which w. against the soul; *4754*
Re 11:7 pit shall make w. against them, *4171*
Re 12:7 there was w. in heaven: Michael *4171*
Re 12:17 went to make w. with the remnant *4171*
Re 13:4 who is able to make w. with him? *4170*
Re 13:7 him to make w. with the saints, *4171*
Re 17:14 These...make w. with the Lamb, *4170*
Re 19:11 he doth judge and make w. *4170*
Re 19:19 to make w. against him that sat *4171*

WARD See also BACKWARD; DOWNWARD; EASTWARD; FORWARD; FROWARD; GOD-WARD; INWARD; NORTHWARD; ONWARD; OUTWARD; REREWARD; REWARD; SEATWARD; SOUTHWARD; THEEWARD; THITHERWARD; TOWARD; UPWARD; USWARD; WARDROBE; WARDS; WESTWARD; YOUWARD.

Ge 40:3 he put them in w. in the house of 4929
Ge 40:4 and they continued a season in w. 4929
Ge 40:7 with him in the w. of his lord's 4929
Ge 41:10 put me in w. in the captain of the 4929
Ge 42:17 he put them altogether into w. 4929
Le 24:12 they put him in w., that the mind 4929
Nu 15:34 they put him in w., because it was 4929
2Sa 20:3 put them in w., and fed them, 4931
1Ch 12:29 kept the w. of the house of Saul. 4931
1Ch 25:8 And they cast lots, w. against 4931
1Ch 25:8 against w., as well the small as the 4931
1Ch 26:16 of the going up, w. against w.. 4929
Ne 12:24 the man of God, w. over against w.. 4929
Ne 12:25 porters keeping the w. at the 4929
Ne 12:45 porters kept the w. of their God, 4931
Ne 12:45 and the w. of the purification, 4931
Isa 21:8 I am set in my w. whole nights: 4931
Jer 37:13 a captain of the w. was there, 6488
Eze 19:9 they put him in w. in chains, 5474
Ac 12:10 past the first and the second w. *5438*

WARDROBE

2Ki 22:14 son of Harhas, keeper of the w.; 899
2Ch 34:22 son of Hasrah, keeper of the w.; 899

WARDS See also INWARDS; REWARDS.

1Ch 9:23 house of the tabernacle, by w. 4931
1Ch 26:12 having w. one against another, 4931
Ne 13:30 appointed the w. of the priests and 4931

WARE See also AWARE; BEWARE; WARES.

Ne 10:31 the people of the land bring w. or 4728
Ne 13:16 brought fish, and all manner of w., 4377
Ne 13:20 sellers of all kind of w. lodged 4465
Lu 8:27 devils long time, and w. no clothes, *1737*
Ac 14:6 They were w. of it, and fled unto *4894*
2Ti 4:15 Of whom be thou w. also; for he *5442*

WARES See also UNAWARES.

Jer 10:17 Gather up thy w. out of the land, 3666
Eze 27:16, 18 of the w. of thy making: 4639
Eze 27:33 thy w. went forth out of the seas, 5801
Jon 1:5 forth the w. that were in the ship 3627

WARFARE

1Sa 28:1 their armies together for w., 6635
1Sa 40:2 her, that her w. is accomplished, 6635
1Co 9:7 who goeth a w. any time at his *4754*
2Co 10:4 weapons of our w. are not carnal, *4752*
1Ti 1:18 by them mightest war a good w.; *4752*

WARM See also LUKEWARM; WARMED; WARMETH; WARMING.
2Ki 4:34 the flesh of the child waxed **w.**......... 2552
Job 6:17 What time they wax **w.**, they........... 2215
Job 37:17 How thy garments are **w.**, when........ 2525
Ec 4:11 but how can one be **w.** alone? 3179
Isa 44:15 will take thereof, and **w.** himself; 2552
Isa 44:16 Aha, I am **w.**, I have seen the fire: 2552
Isa 47:14 there shall not be a coal to **w.** at, ... 2552
Hag 1:6 clothe you, but there is none **w.**; 2527

WARMED
Job 31:20 he were not **w.** with the fleece of 2552
Mk 14:54 and **w.** himself at the fire.................. 2328
Joh 18:18 was cold: and they **w.** themselves: 2328
Joh 18:18 stood with them, and **w.** himself. 2328
Joh 18:25 Simon Peter stood and **w.** himself. 2328
Jas 2:16 in peace, be ye **w.** and filled;............ 2328

WARMETH
Job 39:14 the earth, and **w.** them in dust, ... 2552
Isa 44:16 yea, he **w.** himself, and saith, Aha,..... 2552

WARMING
Mk 14:67 when she saw Peter **w.** himself, ... 2328

WARN See also WARNED; WARNING.
2Ch 19:10 **w.** them that they trespass not.......... 2094
Eze 3:18 nor speakest to **w.** the wicked............ 2094
Eze 3:19 Yet if thou **w.** the wicked, and he 2094
Eze 3:21 if thou **w.** the righteous man, that 2094
Eze 33:3 the trumpet, and **w.** the people;......... 2094
Eze 33:7 my mouth, and **w.** them from me....... 2094
Eze 33:8 dost not speak to **w.** the wicked 2094
Eze 33:9 if thou **w.** the wicked of his way to..... 2094
Ac 20:31 I ceased not to **w.** every one night..... 3560
1Co 4:14 but as my beloved sons I **w.** you. 3560
1Th 5:14 **w.** them that are unruly, comfort 3560

WARNED
2Ki 6:10 of God told him and **w.** him of, ... 2094
Ps 19:11 by them is thy servant **w.**: and in....... 2094
Eze 3:21 shall surely live, because he is **w.**; 2094
Eze 33:6 trumpet, and the people be not **w.**; 2094
Mt 2:12 being **w.** of God in a dream that 5537
Mt 2:22 being **w.** of God in a dream, he 5537
Mt 3:7 **w.** you to flee from the wrath to........ 5263
Lu 3:7 **w.** you to flee from the wrath to........ 5263
Ac 10:22 **w.** from God by an holy angel to......... 5537
Heb 11:7 being **w.** of God of things not seen..... 5537

WARNING
Jer 6:10 whom shall I speak, and give **w.**, ... 5749
Eze 3:17 mouth, and give them **w.** from me...... 2094
Eze 3:18 givest him not **w.**, nor speakest......... 2094
Eze 3:20 because thou hast not given him **w.**.... 2094
Eze 33:4 of the trumpet, and taketh not **w.**; 2094
Eze 33:5 of the trumpet, and took not **w.**;......... 2094
Eze 33:5 taketh **w.** shall deliver his soul........... 2094
Col 1:28 **w.** every man, and teaching every...... 3560

WARP
Le 13:48 Whether it be in the **w.**, or woof; 8359
Le 13:49, 51 either in the **w.**, or in the woof, ... 8359
Le 13:52 whether the **w.** or woof, in woolen..... 8359
Le 13:53 either in the **w.**, or in the woof, or..... 8359
Le 13:56 or out of the **w.**, or out of the woof: .. 8359
Le 13:57 either in the **w.**, or in the woof, or..... 8359
Le 13:58 the garment, either **w.**, or woof, or.... 8359
Le 13:59 either in the **w.**, or woof, or any........ 8359

WARRED
Nu 31:7 they **w.** against the Midianites, ... 6633
Nu 31:42 Moses divided from the men that **w.**,.. 6633
Jos 24:9 Moab, arose and **w.** against Israel, ... 3898
1Ki 14:19 the acts of Jeroboam, how he **w.**,....... 3898
1Ki 20:1 Samaria, and **w.** against it................ 3898
1Ki 22:45 that he shewed, and how he **w.**, ... 3898
2Ki 6:8 the king of Syria **w.** against Israel, ... 3898
2Ki 14:28 how he **w.**, and how he recovered...... 3898
2Ch 26:6 and **w.** against the Philistines,............ 3898

WARRETH
2Ti 2:4 No man that **w.** entangleth himself...... 4754

WARRING
2Ki 19:8 king of Assyria **w.** against Libnah: 3898
Isa 37:8 king of Assyria **w.** against Libnah: 3898
Ro 7:23 **w.** against the law of my mind,............ 497

WARRIOR See also WARRIORS.
Isa 9:5 battle of the **w.** is with confused 5431

WARRIORS
1Ki 12:21 chosen men, which were **w.**,....... 6213,4421
2Ch 11:1 chosen men, which were **w.**,....... 6213,4421

WARS
Nu 21:14 in the book of the **w.** of the Lord,...... 4421
Jg 3:1 had not known all the **w.** of Canaan; ... 4421
2Sa 8:10 for Hadadezer had **w.** with Toi. 4421
1Ki 5:3 the **w.** which were about him on........ 4421
1Ch 22:8 abundantly, and hast made great **w.**.... 4421
2Ch 12:15 there were **w.** between Rehoboam 4421
2Ch 16:9 henceforth thou shalt have **w.**............ 4421
2Ch 27:7 the acts of Jotham, and all his **w.**, ... 4421
Ps 46:9 maketh **w.** to cease unto the end of.... 4421
Mt 24:6 **hear of w. and rumours of w.** 4171
Mk 13:7 **hear of w. and rumours of w.**,...... 4171
Lu 21:9 **shall hear of w. and commotions,**.. 4171
Jas 4:1 whence come **w.** and fightings 4171

WAS See in the APPENDIX; also WAST; WERE.

WASH See also UNWASHEN; WASHED; WASHEST; WASHING; WASHPOT.
Ge 18:4 **w.** your feet, and rest yourselves....... 7364
Ge 19:2 tarry all night, and **w.** your feet, ... 7364
Ge 24:32 water to **w.** his feet, and the men's.... 7364
Ex 2:5 daughter of Pharaoh came...to **w.**........ 7364
Ex 19:10 and let them **w.** their clothes,............ 3526
Ex 29:4 and shalt **w.** them with water. 7364
Ex 29:17 and **w.** the inwards of him, and his..... 7364
Ex 30:18 his foot also of brass, to **w.** withal:..... 7364
Ex 30:19 and his sons shall **w.** their hands........ 7364
Ex 30:20 they shall **w.** with water, that they..... 7364
Ex 30:21 they shall **w.** their hands and their...... 7364
Ex 40:12 and **w.** them with water. 7364
Ex 40:30 and put water there, to **w.** withal. 7364
Le 1:9 and his legs shall he **w.** in water: 7364
Le 1:13 But he shall **w.** the inwards and......... 7364
Le 6:27 thou shalt **w.** that whereon it was 3526
Le 9:14 he did **w.** the inwards and the 7364
Le 11:25, 28 of them shall **w.** his clothes, ... 3526
Le 11:40, 40 carcase of it shall **w.** his clothes,.... 3526
Le 13:6, 34 and he shall **w.** his clothes, and..... 3526
Le 13:54 **w.** the thing wherein the plague is,..... 3526
Le 13:58 of skin it be, which thou shalt **w.**, ... 3526
Le 14:8 to be cleansed shall **w.** his clothes,..... 3526
Le 14:8 and **w.** himself in water, that he......... 7364
Le 14:9 and he shall **w.** his clothes, also......... 3526
Le 14:9 also he shall **w.** his flesh in water,...... 7364
Le 14:47 in the house shall **w.** his clothes;........ 3526
Le 14:47 in the house shall **w.** his clothes......... 3526
Le 15:5 toucheth...bed shall **w.** his clothes, ... 3526
Le 15:6, 7 hath the issue shall **w.** his clothes,... 3526
Le 15:8 he shall **w.** his clothes, and bathe....... 3526
Le 15:10 of those things shall **w.** his clothes, ... 3526
Le 15:11 he shall **w.** his clothes, and bathe....... 3526
Le 15:13 **w.** his clothes, and bathe his flesh...... 3526
Le 15:16 he shall **w.** all his flesh in water, ... 7364
Le 15:21 her bed shall **w.** his clothes,.............. 3526
Le 15:22 she sat upon shall **w.** his clothes, ... 3526
Le 15:27 and shall **w.** his clothes, and bathe...... 3526
Le 16:4 shall he **w.** his flesh in water, and 7364
Le 16:24 **w.** his flesh with water in the holy...... 7364
Le 16:26 the scapegoat shall **w.** his clothes,...... 3526
Le 16:28 burneth them shall **w.** his clothes, ... 3526
Le 17:15 he shall both **w.** his clothes, and 3526
Le 17:16 if he **w.** them not, nor bathe his 3526
Le 22:6 unless he **w.** his flesh with water. 7364
Nu 8:7 and let them **w.** their clothes,............. 3526
Nu 19:7 Then the priest shall **w.** his clothes, ... 3526
Nu 19:8 that burneth her shall **w.** his clothes ... 3526
Nu 19:10 of the heifer shall **w.** his clothes,........ 3526
Nu 19:19 purify himself, and **w.** his clothes, ... 3526
Nu 19:21 of separation shall **w.** his clothes; 3526
Nu 31:24 **w.** your clothes on the seventh day, ... 3526
De 21:6 **w.** their hands over the heifer 7364
De 23:11 on, he shall **w.** himself with water: 7364
Ru 3:3 **W.** thyself therefore, and anoint.......... 7364
1Sa 25:41 to **w.** the feet of the servants of my... 7364
2Sa 11:8 down to thy house, and **w.** thy feet. ... 7364
2Ki 5:10 Go and **w.** in Jordan seven times,....... 7364
2Ki 5:12 may I not **w.** in them, and be clean? ... 7364
2Ki 5:13 he saith to thee, **W.**, and be clean? 7364
2Ch 4:6 and five on the left, to **w.** in them:..... 7364
2Ch 4:6 the sea was for the priests to **w.** in. ... 7364
Job 9:30 If I **w.** myself with snow water, and ... 7364
Ps 26:6 I will **w.** mine hands in innocency: 7364
Ps 51:2 **W.** me throughly from mine............. 3526
Ps 51:7 **w.** me, and I shall be whiter than....... 3526
Ps 58:10 **w.** his feet in the blood of the 7364
Isa 1:16 **W.** you, make you clean; put away..... 7364
Jer 2:22 though thou **w.** thee with nitre, ... 3526
Jer 4:14 **w.** thine heart from wickedness, ... 3526
Eze 23:40 for whom thou didst **w.** thyself, ... 7364
Mt 6:17 **anoint thine head, and w. thy**....... 3538
Mt 15:2 **w.** not their hands when they eat....... 3538
Mk 7:3 except they **w.** their hands oft, eat..... 3538
Mk 7:4 except they **w.**, they eat not.............. 907
Lu 7:38 began to **w.** his feet with tears, ... 1026
Joh 9:7 him, **Go, w. in the pool of Siloam,**..3538
Joh 9:11 Go to the pool of Siloam, and **w.**......... 3538
Joh 13:5 and began to **w.** the disciples' feet,..... 3538
Joh 13:6 him, Lord, dost thou **w.** my feet?......... 3538
Joh 13:8 him, Thou shalt never **w.** my feet. 3538
Joh 13:8 **If I w. thee not, thou hast no part**.3538
Joh 13:10 **needeth not save to w. his feet,**..... 3538
Joh 13:14 **ought to w. one another's feet.**...... 3538
Ac 22:16 be baptized, and **w.** away thy sins,....... 628

WASHED See also UNWASHEN.
Ge 43:24 water, and they **w.** their feet; 7364
Ge 43:31 And he **w.** his face, and went out,....... 7364
Ge 49:11 he **w.** his garments in wine, and 3526
Ex 19:14 people; and they **w.** their clothes. 3526
Ex 40:31 Aaron and his sons **w.** their hands...... 7364
Ex 40:32 came near unto the altar, they **w.**; 7364
Le 8:6 his sons, and **w.** them with water....... 7364
Le 8:21 he **w.** the inwards and the legs in....... 7364
Le 13:55 the plague, after that it is **w.**:........... 3526
Le 13:58 it shall be **w.** the second time, and...... 3526
Le 15:17 shall be **w.** with water, and be........... 3526
Nu 8:21 purified, and they **w.** their clothes; 3526
Jg 19:21 they **w.** their feet, and did eat and 7364
2Sa 12:20 David arose from the earth, and **w.**, ... 7364
2Sa 19:24 his beard, nor **w.** his clothes, ... 3526
1Ki 22:38 one **w.** the chariot in the pool of........ 7857
1Ki 22:38 his blood; and they **w.** his armour; 7364
2Ch 4:6 burnt offering they **w.** in them;........... 1740
Job 29:6 When I **w.** my steps with butter, ... 7364
Ps 73:13 and **w.** my hands in innocency. 7364
Pr 30:12 yet is not **w.** from their filthiness. 7364
Ca 5:3 I have **w.** my feet; how shall I........... 7364
Ca 5:12 rivers of waters, **w.** with milk, and..... 7364
Isa 4:4 Lord shall have **w.** away the filth........ 7364
Eze 16:4 thou **w.** in water to supple thee; 7364
Eze 16:9 Then **w.** I thee with water; yea, ... 7364
Eze 16:9 I throughly **w.** away thy blood 7857
Eze 40:38 where they **w.** the burnt offering........ 1740
Mt 27:24 **w.** his hands before the multitude, ... 633
Lu 7:44 **she hath w. my feet with tears,**..... 1026
Lu 11:38 he had not first **w.** before dinner. 907
Joh 9:7 and **w.**, and came seeing. 3538
Joh 9:11 I went and **w.**, and I received sight. ... 3538
Joh 9:15 mine eyes, and I **w.**, and do see. 3538
Joh 13:10 **He that is w. needeth not save to**.. 3068
Joh 13:12 So after he had **w.** their feet, and 3538
Joh 13:14 **and Master, have w. your feet;**...... 3538
Ac 9:37 whom when they had **w.**, they laid 3068
Ac 16:33 of the night, and **w.** their stripes;....... 3068
1Co 6:11 but ye are **w.**, but ye are sanctified,..... 628
1Ti 5:10 if she have **w.** the saints' feet, if........ 3538
Heb 10:22 and our bodies **w.** with pure water. 3068
2Pe 2:22 sow that was **w.** to her wallowing 3068
Re 1:5 **w.** us from our sins in his own 3068
Re 7:14 and have **w.** their robes and made...... 4150

WASHEST
Job 14:19 thou **w.** away the things which........... 7857

WASHING See also WASHINGS.
Le 13:56 somewhat dark after the **w.** of it;....... 3526
2Sa 11:2 roof he saw a woman **w.** herself; 7364
Ne 4:23 that every one put them off for **w.**. 4325
Ca 4:2 which came up from the **w.**;............... 7367
Ca 6:6 of sheep which go up from the **w.**, ... 7367
Mk 7:4 received to hold, as the **w.** of cups, ... 909
Mk 7:8 **of men, as the w. of pots and cups:**. 909
Lu 5:2 of them, and were **w.** their nets.......... 637
Eph 5:26 cleanse it with the **w.** of water by...... 3067
Tit 3:5 by the **w.** of regeneration, and........... 3067

WASHINGS
Heb 9:10 in meats and drinks, and divers **w.**,...... 909

WASHPOT
Ps 60:8 Moab is my w.; over Edom....... 5518,7366
Ps 108:9 Moab is my w.; over Edom....... 5518,7366

WAST See also WERT.
Ge 3:11 Who told thee that thou w. naked?..........
Ge 3:19 ground; for out of it w. thou taken:..........
Ge 33:10 of God, and thou w. pleased with me.........
Ge 40:13 manner when thou w. his butler......... 1961
De 5:15 w. a servant in the land of Egypt,...... 1961
De 15:15 that thou w. a bondman in the land..... 1961
De 16:12 that thou w. a bondman in Egypt:...... 1961
De 23:7 thou w. a stranger in his land........... 1961
De 24:18 remember that thou w. a bondman..... 1961
De 24:22 thou w. a bondman in the land of....... 1961
De 25:18 thee, when thou w. faint and weary;.........
De 28:60 of Egypt, which thou w. afraid of;............
Ru 3:2 with whose maidens thou w.?............ 1961
1Sa 15:17 When thou w. little in thine own sight,......
1Sa 15:17 w. thou not made the head of the.............
2Sa 1:14 How w. thou not afraid to stretch..............
2Sa 1:25 thou w. slain in thine high places.............
2Sa 5:2 thou w. he that leddest out and........... 1961
1Ch 11:2 thou w. he that leddest out and...............
Job 15:7 or w. thou made before the hills?..............
Job 38:4 Where w. thou when I laid the.......... 1961
Job 38:21 thou it, because thou w. then born?............
Ps 99:8 thou w. a God that forgavest them..... 1961
Ps 114:5 Jordan, that thou w. driven back?..............
Isa 12:1 though thou w. angry with me, thine..........
Isa 14:3 wherein thou w. made to serve,................
Isa 33:1 spoilest, and thou w. not spoiled;.............
Isa 43:4 Since thou w. precious in my sight,..........
Isa 48:8 and w. called a transgressor from the........
Isa 54:6 of youth, when thou w. refused,..............
Isa 57:10 hand; therefore thou w. not grieved..........
Jer 2:36 as thou w. ashamed of Assyria..................
Jer 50:24 O Babylon, and thou w. not aware:..........
Eze 16:4 day thou w. born thy navel was not..........
Eze 16:4 neither w. thou washed in water to..........
Eze 16:5 thou w. cast out in the open field,............
Eze 16:5 person, in the day that thou w. born.........
Eze 16:6, 6 thee when thou w. in thy blood,............
Eze 16:7 whereas thou w. naked and bare..............
Eze 16:13 Thus w. thou decked with gold and..........
Eze 16:13 thou w. exceeding beautiful, and thou........
Eze 16:22 when thou w. naked and bare,........... 1961
Eze 16:22 and w. polluted in thy blood........... 1961
Eze 16:28 Assyrians, because thou w. unsatiable;.......
Eze 16:29 yet thou w. not satisfied herewith..............
Eze 16:47 thou w. corrupted more than they...........
Eze 21:30 in the place where thou w. created,..........
Eze 24:13 thou w. not purged, thou shalt not..........
Eze 26:17 that w. inhabited of seafaring men,..........
Eze 26:17 which w. strong in the sea, she and..........
Eze 27:25 thou w. replenished, and made very..........
Eze 28:3 thee in the day that thou w. created.........
Eze 28:14 thou w. upon the holy mountain......... 1961
Eze 28:15 Thou w. perfect in thy ways from the.......
Eze 28:15 from the day that thou w. created,...........
Ob 11 even thou w. as one of them...................
Mt 26:69 Thou also w. with Jesus of Galilee...... *2258*
Mk 14:67 thou also w. with Jesus of Nazareth.... *2258*
Joh 1:48 **thou w. under the fig tree**............ *5607*
Joh 9:34 Thou w. altogether born in sins, and.........
Joh 21:18 **thou w. young, thou girdedst**........ *2258*
Re 5:9 for thou w. slain, and hast redeemed........
Re 11:17 God Almighty, which art, and w.,........ *2258*
Re 16:5 Lord, which art, and w., and shalt...... *2258*

WASTE See also WASTED; WASTES; WASTETH; WASTING.
Le 26:31 And I will make your cities w.,.......... 2723
Le 26:33 be desolate, and your cities w.,.......... 2723
Nu 21:30 we have laid them w. even unto........ 8074
De 32:10 and in the w. howling wilderness;....... 8414
1Ki 17:14 The barrel of meal shall not w.,.......... 3615
2Ki 19:25 to lay w. fenced cities into ruinous..... 7582
1Ch 17:9 of wickedness w. them any more,....... 1086
Ne 2:3 of my fathers' sepulchres, lieth w.,...... 2720
Ne 2:17 how Jerusalem lieth w., and the......... 2720
Job 30:3 in former time desolate and w........... 4875
Job 38:27 satisfy the desolate and w. ground;...... 4875
Ps 79:7 and laid w. his dwelling place............ 8074
Ps 80:13 boar out of the wood doth w. it,......... 3765
Isa 5:6 I will lay it w.: it shall not be............ 1326
Isa 5:17 w. places of the fat ones shall............ 2723
Isa 15:1 in the night Ar of Moab is laid w.,....... 7703
Isa 15:1 the night Kir if Moab is laid w.,......... 7703
Isa 23:1 for it is laid w., so that there is no..... 7703
Isa 23:14 for your strength is laid w................ 7703
Isa 24:1 and maketh it w., and turneth it......... 1110
Isa 33:8 The highways lie w., the.................. 8074
Isa 34:10 to generation it shall lie w.;................ 2717
Isa 37:18 Assyria have laid w. all the nations,.... 2717
Isa 37:26 be to lay w. defenced cities into.......... 7582
Isa 42:15 I will make w. mountains and............ 2717
Isa 49:17 they that made thee w. shall go......... 2717
Isa 49:19 thy w. and thy desolate places,........... 2723
Isa 51:3 he will comfort all her w. places;........ 2723
Isa 52:9 ye w. places of Jerusalem:................. 2723
Isa 58:12 thee shall build the old w. places:....... 2723
Isa 61:4 they shall repair the w. cities, the...... 2721
Isa 64:11 our pleasant things are laid w............ 2723
Jer 2:15 yelled, and they made his land w.:....... 8047
Jer 4:7 and thy cities shall be laid w.,............ 5327
Jer 27:17 should this city be laid w.?............... 2723
Jer 46:19 Noph shall be w. and desolate........... 8047
Jer 49:13 a reproach, a w., and a curse;............ 2721
Jer 50:21 w. and utterly destroy after them,....... 2717
Eze 5:14 Moreover I will make thee w.,............ 2723
Eze 6:6 dwellingplaces...shall be laid w.,......... 2717
Eze 6:6 your altars may be laid w. and........... 2717
Eze 12:20 are inhabited shall be laid w.,............ 2717
Eze 19:7 palaces, and he laid w. their cities;...... 2717
Eze 26:2 be replenished, now she is laid w.:....... 2717
Eze 29:9 of Egypt shall be desolate and w.;...... 2723
Eze 29:10 of Egypt utterly w. and desolate,........ 2723
Eze 29:12 among the cities that are laid w.......... 2717
Eze 30:12 I will make the land w., and all.......... 8074
Eze 35:4 I will lay thy cities w., and thou.......... 2723
Eze 36:35 the w. and desolate and ruined.......... 2720
Eze 36:38 so shall the w. cities be filled with...... 2720
Eze 38:8 which have been always w.:................ 2723
Joe 1:7 He hath laid my vine w., and.............. 8047
Am 7:9 of Israel shall be laid w.;.................. 2717
Am 9:14 and they shall build the w. cities,........ 8074
Mic 5:6 shall w. the land of Assyria with......... 7489
Na 2:10 She is empty, and void, and w.:.......... 1110
Na 3:7 thee, and say, Nineveh is laid w.:...... 7703
Zep 3:6 I made their street w., that none....... 2717
Hag 1:4 houses, and this house lie w.?............ 2720
Hag 1:9 Because of mine house that is w.,...... 2720
Mal 1:3 mountains and his inheritance w......... 8077
Mt 26:8 To what purpose is this w.?................ *684*
Mk 14:4 Why was this w. of the ointment.......... *684*

WASTED
Nu 14:33 carcases be w. in the wilderness........ 8552
Nu 24:22 the Kenite shall be w., until.............. 1197
De 2:14 the men of war were w. out from....... 8552
1Ki 17:16 And the barrel of meal w. not,.......... 3615
1Ch 20:1 w. the country of the children of........ 7843
Ps 137:3 they that w. us required of us........... 8437
Isa 6:11 cities be w. without inhabitant,.......... 7582
Isa 19:5 the river shall be w. and dried up........ 2717
Isa 60:12 those nations shall be utterly w.......... 2717
Jer 44:6 and they are w. and desolate, as......... 2723
Eze 30:7 the midst of the cities that are w........ 2717
Joe 1:10 The field is w., the land mourneth;...... 7703
Joe 1:10 land mourneth; for the corn is w.:....... 7703
Lu 15:13 **there w. his substance with riotous** *1287*
Lu 16:1 **unto him that he had w. his goods.** *1287*
Ga 1:13 the church of God, and w. it:............ *4199*

WASTENESS
Zep 1:15 a day of w. and desolation, a day....... 7722

WASTER
Pr 18:9 brother to him that is a great w.......... 7843
Isa 54:16 I have created the w. to destroy......... 7843

WASTES
Isa 61:4 And they shall build the old w.,.......... 2723
Jer 49:13 cities thereof shall be perpetual w....... 2723
Eze 33:24 those w. of the land of Israel............ 2723
Eze 33:27 they that are in the w. shall fall by..... 2723
Eze 36:4 to the desolate w., and to the cities..... 2723
Eze 36:10 and the w. shall be builded:.............. 2723
Eze 36:33 cities, and the w. shall be builded....... 2723

WASTETH
Job 14:10 But man dieth, and w. away:............. 2522
Ps 91:6 destruction that w. at noonday.......... 7736
Pr 19:26 He that w. his father, and................ 7703

WASTING
Isa 59:7 w. and destruction are in their........... 7701
Isa 60:18 w. nor destruction within thy............ 7701

WATCH See also WATCHED; WATCHES; WATCHETH; WATCHFUL; WATCHING; WATCHMAN; WATCHTOWER.
Ge 31:49 the Lord w. between me and thee,..... 6822
Ex 14:24 in the morning w. the Lord looked....... 821
Jg 7:19 in the beginning of the middle w.;....... 821
Jg 7:19 they had but newly set the w........... 8104
1Sa 11:11 midst of the host in the morning w...... 821
1Sa 19:11 unto David's house, to w. him,.......... 8104
2Sa 13:34 the young man that kept the w.......... 6822
2Ki 11:5 keepers of the w. of the king's......... 4931
2Ki 11:6 shall ye keep the w. of the house,...... 4931
2Ki 11:7 they shall keep the w. of the house.... 4931
2Ch 20:24 Judah came toward the w. tower........ 4707
2Ch 23:6 shall keep the w. of the Lord............ 4931
Ezr 8:29 W. ye, and keep them, until ye........ 8245
Ne 4:9 set a w. against them day and.......... 4929
Ne 7:3 of Jerusalem, every one in his w.,...... 4929
Job 7:12 that thou settest a w. over me?......... 4929
Job 14:16 dost thou not w. over my sin?........... 8104
Ps 90:4 it is past, and as a w. in the night........ 821
Ps 102:7 I w., and am as a sparrow alone........ 8245
Ps 130:6 than they that w. for the morning:...... 8104
Ps 130:6 than they that w. for the morning....... 8104
Ps 141:3 Set a w., O Lord, before my mouth;.. 8108
Isa 21:5 the table, w. in the watchtower,........ 6822
Isa 29:20 all that w. for iniquity are cut off:....... 8245
Jer 5:6 a leopard shall w. over their cities:..... 8245
Jer 31:28 so will I w. over them, to build, and... 8245
Jer 44:27 I will w. over them for evil, and not... 8245
Jer 51:12 make the w. strong, set up the......... 4929
Na 2:1 w. the way, make thy loins strong,...... 6822
Hab 2:1 I will stand upon my w., and set......... 4931
Hab 2:1 will w. to see what he will say.......... 6822
Mt 14:25 fourth w. of the night Jesus went....... *5438*
Mt 24:42 **W. therefore: for ye know not**....... *1127*
Mt 24:43 **in what w. the thief would come,**.. *5438*
Mt 25:13 **W. therefore, for ye know neither**. *1127*
Mt 26:38 **tarry ye here, and w. with me**........ *1127*
Mt 26:40 **could ye not w. with me one hour?** *1127*
Mt 26:41 **W. and pray, that ye enter not**...... *1127*
Mt 27:65 Ye have a w.: go your way, make....... *2892*
Mt 27:66 sealing the stone, and setting a w...... *2892*
Mt 28:11 some of the w. came into the city,...... *2892*
Mk 6:48 about the fourth w. of the night......... *5438*
Mk 13:33 **Take ye heed, w. and pray: for ye**.... *69*
Mk 13:34 **and commanded the porter to w**... *1127*
Mk 13:35 **W. ye therefore: for ye know not**.. *1127*
Mk 13:37 **I say unto you I say unto all, W**... *1127*
Mk 14:34 **unto death: tarry ye here, and w**... *1127*
Mk 14:37 **couldest not thou w. one hour?**..... *1127*
Mk 14:38 **W. ye and pray, lest ye enter into**.. *1127*
Lu 2:8 keeping w. over their flock by........... *5438*
Lu 12:38 **if he shall come in the second w.,**.. *5438*
Lu 12:38 **or come in the third w., and find**.. *5438*
Lu 21:36 **W. ye therefore, and pray always,**.... *69*
Ac 20:31 Therefore w., and remember, that...... *1127*
1Co 16:13 W. ye, stand fast in the faith, quit....... *1127*
Col 4:2 w. in the same with thanksgiving;........ *1127*
1Th 5:6 others; but let us w. and be sober....... *1127*
2Ti 4:5 But w. thou in all things, endure......... *3525*
Heb 13:17 they w. for your souls, as they that....... *69*
1Pe 4:7 sober, and w. unto prayer................ *3525*
Re 3:3 **If therefore thou shalt not w., I**.... *1127*

WATCHED
Ps 59:*title* and they w. the house to kill him....... 8104
Jer 20:10 All my familiars w. for my halting,...... 8104
Jer 31:28 that like as I have w. over them,........ 8245
La 4:17 w. for a nation that could not save....... 6822
Da 9:14 hath the Lord w. upon the evil,.......... 8245
Mt 24:43 **he would have w., and would not**.. *1127*
Mt 27:36 sitting down they w. him there;.......... *5083*
Mk 3:2 they w. him, whether he would........... *3906*
Lu 6:7 the scribes and Pharisees w. him,....... *3906*
Lu 12:39 **he would have w., and not have**.... *1127*
Lu 14:1 the sabbath day, that they w. him....... *3906*
Lu 20:20 they w. him, and sent forth spies,....... *3906*
Ac 9:24 they w. the gates day and night to...... *3906*

WATCHER See also WATCHERS.
Da 4:13 a w. and an holy one came down....... 5894
Da 4:23 the king saw a w. and an holy one..... 5894

WATCHERS
Jer 4:16 that w. come from a far country, ... 5341
Da 4:17 matter is by the decree of the w., ... 5894

WATCHES
Ne 7:3 w. of the inhabitants of Jerusalem,....... 4931
Ne 12:9 were over against them in the w......... 4931
Ps 63:6 meditate on thee in the night w........... 821
Ps 119:148 Mine eyes prevent the night w.,........... 821
La 2:19 beginning of the w. pour out thine 821

WATCHETH
Ps 37:32 The wicked w. the righteous, and....... 6822
Eze 7:6 the end is come: it w. for thee;......... 6974
Re 16:15 Blessed is he that w., and keepeth..... *1127*

WATCHFUL
Re 3:2 **Be w., and strengthen the things**... *1127*

WATCHING See also WATCHINGS.
1Sa 4:13 sat upon a seat by the wayside w......... 6822
Pr 8:34 heareth me, w. daily at my gates,....... 8245
La 4:17 in our w. we have watched for a........ 6822
Mt 27:54 they that were with him, w. Jesus,...... *5083*
Lu 12:37 **lord when he cometh shall find w.** .*1127*
Eph 6:18 and w. thereunto with all..................... *69*

WATCHINGS
2Co 6:5 in tumults, in labours, in w., in............ *70*
2Co 11:27 painfulness, in w. often, in hunger......... *70*

WATCHMAN See also WATCHMAN'S; WATCHMEN.
2Sa 18:24 the w. went up to the roof over the ... 6822
2Sa 18:25 And the w. cried, and told the king. ... 6822
2Sa 18:26 the w. saw another man running: 6822
2Sa 18:26 and the w. called unto the porter, ... 6822
2Sa 18:27 And the w. said, Me thinketh the....... 6822
2Ki 9:17 there stood a w. on the tower in 6822
2Ki 9:18 the w. told, saying, The messenger.... 6822
2Ki 9:20 And the w. told, saying, He came 6822
Ps 127:1 city, the w. waketh but in vain. 8104
Isa 21:6 set a w., let him declare what he....... 6822
Isa 21:11, 11 W., what of the night?................. 8104
Isa 21:12 The w. said, The morning cometh,..... 8104
Eze 3:17 thee a w. unto the house of Israel:..... 6822
Eze 33:2 coasts, and set him for their w......... 6822
Eze 33:6 But if the w. see the sword come, ... 6822
Eze 33:7 thee a w. unto the house of Israel;..... 6822
Ho 9:8 w. of Ephraim was with my God:....... 6822

WATCHMAN'S
Eze 33:6 blood will I require at the w. hand...... 6822

WATCHMEN
1Sa 14:16 w. of Saul in Gibeah of Benjamin........ 6822
2Ki 17:9 from the tower of the w. to the......... 5341
2Ki 18:8 from the tower of the w. to the......... 5341
Ca 3:3 The w. that go about the city........... 8104
Ca 5:7 The w. that went about the city......... 8104
Isa 52:8 Thy w. shall lift up the voice;........... 6822
Isa 56:10 His w. are blind: they are all............ 6822
Isa 62:6 I have set w. upon thy walls, O.......... 8104
Jer 6:17 I set w. over you, saying, Hearken 6822
Jer 31:6 the w. upon the mount Ephraim......... 5341
Jer 51:12 the watch strong, set up the w.,........ 8104
Mic 7:4 the day of thy w. and thy visitation;.... 6822

WATCHTOWER See also WATCH and TOWER.
Isa 21:5 the table, watch in the w., eat,.......... 6844
Isa 21:8 I stand continually upon the w. in........ 4707

WATER See also WATERCOURSE; WATERED; WATEREST; WATERETH; WATERFLOOD; WATERING; WATERPOT; WATERS; WATERSPOUTS; WATERSPRINGS.
Ge 2:10 went out of Eden to w. the garden;.... 8248
Ge 16:7 found her by a fountain of w. in......... 4325
Ge 18:4 Let a little w., I pray you, be........... 4325
Ge 21:14 and took bread, and a bottle of w.,...... 4325
Ge 21:15 And the w. was spent in the bottle,.... 4325
Ge 21:19 her eyes, and she saw a well of w., ... 4325
Ge 21:19 went, and filled the bottle with w., ... 4325
Ge 21:25 Abimelech because of a well of w., ... 4325
Ge 24:11 by a well of w. at the time of the........ 4325
Ge 24:11 time that women go out to draw w..........
Ge 24:13 I stand here by the well of w.; 4325
Ge 24:13 of the city come out to draw w.......... 4325
Ge 24:17 thee, drink a little w. of thy pitcher. ... 4325
Ge 24:19 I will draw w. for thy camels also,...........
Ge 24:20 ran again unto the well to draw w., ...
Ge 24:32 and w. to wash his feet, and the........ 4325
Ge 24:43 I stand by the well of w.; and it......... 4325
Ge 24:43 virgin cometh forth to draw w., ...
Ge 24:43 a little w. of thy pitcher to drink; 4325
Ge 24:45 down unto the well, and drew w. ....
Ge 26:18 Isaac digged again the wells of w., ... 4325
Ge 26:19 found there a well of springing w.. 4325
Ge 26:20 herdmen, saying, The w. is ours:....... 4325
Ge 26:32 said unto him, We have found w.. 4325
Ge 29:7 w. ye the sheep, and go and feed 8248
Ge 29:8 mouth; then we w. the sheep............ 8248
Ge 37:24 was empty, there was no w. in it........ 4325
Ge 43:24 and gave them w., and they washed... 4325
Ge 49:4 Unstable as w., thou shalt not excel; .. 4325
Ex 2:10 Because I drew him out of the w.. 4325
Ex 2:16 and they came and drew w., and filled.......
Ex 2:16 troughs to w. their father's flock. 8248
Ex 2:19 and also drew w. enough for us, ...
Ex 4:9 shalt take of the w. of the river, ... 4325
Ex 4:9 the w. which thou takest out of the 4325
Ex 7:15 lo, he goeth out unto the w.; and........ 4325
Ex 7:18 lothe to drink of the w. of the river.... 4325
Ex 7:19 upon all their pools of w., that they.... 4325
Ex 7:21 not drink of the w. of the river;......... 4325
Ex 7:24 digged round about the river for w...... 4325
Ex 7:24 for they could not drink of the w. of... 4325
Ex 8:20 lo, he cometh forth to the w.; and....... 4325
Ex 12:9 nor sodden at all with w., but roast.... 4325
Ex 15:22 in the wilderness, and found no w.. 4325
Ex 15:27 where were twelve wells of w., ... 4325
Ex 17:1 was no w. for the people to drink. 4325
Ex 17:2 said, Give us w. that we may drink. ... 4325
Ex 17:3 the people thirsted there for w.; 4325
Ex 17:6 there shall come w. out of it, that...... 4325
Ex 20:4 that is in the w. under the earth: 4325
Ex 23:25 shall bless thy bread, and thy w.;........ 4325
Ex 29:4 and shalt wash them with w.. 4325
Ex 30:18 and thou shalt put w. therein.............. 4325
Ex 30:20 they shall wash with w., that they...... 4325
Ex 32:20 powder, and strawed it upon the w...... 4325
Ex 34:28 did neither eat bread, nor drink w.. 4325
Ex 40:7 the altar, and shalt put w. therein. 4325
Ex 40:12 and wash them with w.. 4325
Ex 40:30 and put w. there, to wash withal.......... 4325
Le 1:9 and his legs shall he wash in w........... 4325
Le 1:13 the inwards and the legs with w......... 4325
Le 6:28 be both scoured, and rinsed in w.. 4325
Le 8:6 his sons, and wash them with w.. 4325
Le 8:21 the inwards and the legs in w.;........... 4325
Le 11:32 is done, it must be put into w., and.... 4325
Le 11:34 on which such w. cometh shall be 4325
Le 11:36 wherein there is plenty of w., shall..... 4325
Le 11:38 But if any w. be put upon the seed, ... 4325
Le 14:5 an earthen vessel over running w....... 4325
Le 14:6 was killed over the running w.:.......... 4325
Le 14:8 and wash himself in w., that he 4325
Le 14:9 he shall wash his flesh in w., and....... 4325
Le 14:50 an earthen vessel over running w....... 4325
Le 14:51 in the running w., and sprinkle the 4325
Le 14:52 with the running w., and with the....... 4325
Le 15:5, 6,7,8,10 and bathe himself in w., ... 4325
Le 15:11 hath not rinsed his hands in w., ... 4325
Le 15:11 his clothes, and bathe himself in w., ... 4325
Le 15:12 vessel of wood shall be rinsed in w...... 4325
Le 15:13 and bathe his flesh in running w., ... 4325
Le 15:16 he shall wash all his flesh in w., ... 4325
Le 15:17 shall be washed with w., and be 4325
Le 15:18 shall both bathe themselves in w., ... 4325
Le 15:21, 22,27 and bathe himself in w., ... 4325
Le 16:4 shall he wash his flesh in w., and so... 4325
Le 16:24 shall wash his flesh with w. in the...... 4325
Le 16:26, 28 and bathe his flesh in w., ... 4325
Le 17:15 and bathe himself in w., and be 4325
Le 22:6 unless he wash his flesh with w.. 4325
Nu 5:17 And the priest shall take holy w. in 4325
Nu 5:17 shall take, and put it into the w. 4325
Nu 5:18 bitter w. that causeth the curse: 4325
Nu 5:19 be thou free from this bitter w. 4325
Nu 5:22 And this w. that causeth the curse..... 4325
Nu 5:23 blot them out with the bitter w.:.......... 4325
Nu 5:24 the woman to drink the bitter w. 4325
Nu 5:24 the w. that causeth the curse shall..... 4325
Nu 5:26 cause the woman to drink the w.. 4325
Nu 5:27 he hath made her to drink the w........ 4325
Nu 5:27 the w. that causeth the curse shall..... 4325
Nu 8:7 Sprinkle w. of purifying upon............ 4325
Nu 19:7 and he shall bathe his flesh in w.,........ 4325
Nu 19:8 her shall wash his clothes in w., ... 4325
Nu 19:8 bathe his flesh in w., and shall be....... 4325
Nu 19:9 of Israel for a w. of separation:.......... 4325
Nu 19:13 the w. of separation was not............ 4325
Nu 19:17 running w. shall be put thereto in....... 4325
Nu 19:18 take hyssop, and dip it in the w. 4325
Nu 19:19 clothes, and bathe himself in w., ... 4325
Nu 19:20 the w. of separation hath not been 4325
Nu 19:21 that sprinkleth the w. of separation..... 4325
Nu 19:21 that toucheth the w. of separation 4325
Nu 20:2 was no w. for the congregation:......... 4325
Nu 20:5 neither is there any w. to drink. 4325
Nu 20:8 it shall give forth his w., and thou 4325
Nu 20:8 forth to them w. out of the rock: 4325
Nu 20:10 we fetch you w. out of this rock?....... 4325
Nu 20:11 and the w. came out abundantly, ... 4325
Nu 20:13 This is the w. of Meribah; because...... 4325
Nu 20:17 will we drink of the w. of the wells: ... 4325
Nu 20:19 if I and my cattle drink of thy w., ... 4325
Nu 20:24 my word at the w. of Meribah........... 4325
Nu 21:5 is no bread, neither is there any w.; ... 4325
Nu 21:16 together, and I will give them w.. 4325
Nu 24:7 pour the w. out of his buckets, and 4325
Nu 27:14 sanctify me at the w. before their 4325
Nu 27:14 is the w. of Meribah in Kadesh in 4325
Nu 31:23 purified with the w. of separation: 4325
Nu 31:23 ye shall make go through the w.. 4325
Nu 33:9 Elim were twelve fountains of w., ... 4325
Nu 33:14 was no w. for the people to drink. 4325
De 2:6 also buy w. of them for money, ... 4325
De 2:28 and give me w. for money, that I....... 4325
De 8:7 good land, a land of brooks and w., ... 4325
De 8:15 drought, where there was no w.; 4325
De 8:15 forth w. out of the rock of flint; 4325
De 9:9 neither did eat bread nor drink w....... 4325
De 9:18 did neither eat bread, nor drink w., ... 4325
De 11:4 he made the w. of the Red sea to 4325
De 11:11 drinketh w. of the rain of heaven: 4325
De 12:16, 24 pour it upon the earth as w.. 4325
De 15:23 shalt pour it upon the ground as w.. 4325
De 23:4 met you not with bread and with w. ... 4325
De 23:11 on, he shall wash himself with w.: 4325
De 29:11 wood unto the drawer of thy w.:......... 4325
Jos 2:10 dried up the w. of the Red sea for 4325
Jos 3:8 to the brink of the w. of Jordan, ... 4325
Jos 3:15 were dipped in the brim of the w., ... 4325
Jos 7:5 people melted, and became as w.......... 4325
Jos 9:21 and drawers of w. unto all the........... 4325
Jos 9:23 and drawers of w. for the house of..... 4325
Jos 9:27 drawers of w. for the congregation, ... 4325
Jos 15:9 the fountain of the w. of Nephtoah, ... 4325
Jos 15:19 land; give me also springs of w.......... 4325
Jos 16:1 unto the w. of Jericho on the east, ... 4325
Jg 1:15 land; give me also springs of w.......... 4325
Jg 4:19 Give me,...a little w. to drink;............ 4325
Jg 5:4 the clouds also dropped w................. 4325
Jg 5:11 of archers in the places of drawing w., ...
Jg 5:25 He asked w., and she gave him 4325
Jg 6:38 out of the fleece, a bowl full of w........ 4325
Jg 7:4 bring them down unto the w., and...... 4325
Jg 7:5 down the people unto the w............. 4325
Jg 7:5 Every one that lappeth of the w.......... 4325
Jg 7:6 down upon their knees to drink w.. 4325
Jg 15:19 jaw, and there came w. thereout;........ 4325
1Sa 7:6 drew w., and poured it out before...... 4325
1Sa 9:11 maidens going out to draw w.,........... 4325
1Sa 25:11 I then take my bread, and my w., ... 4325
1Sa 26:11 and the cruse of w., and let us go........ 4325
1Sa 26:12 the cruse of w. from Saul's bolster; 4325
1Sa 26:16 cruse of w. that was at his bolster. 4325
1Sa 30:11 eat; and they made him drink w.;......... 4325
1Sa 30:12 eaten no bread, nor drunk any w., ... 4325
2Sa 14:14 and are as w. spilt on the ground, ... 4325
2Sa 17:20 They be gone over the brook of w.. ... 4325
2Sa 17:21 Arise, and pass quickly over the w.. ... 4325
2Sa 21:10 until w. dropped upon them out of...... 4325
2Sa 23:15 of the w. of the well of Beth-lehem, ... 4325
2Sa 23:16 and drew w. out of the well of........... 4325
1Ki 13:8 bread nor drink w. in this place: 4325
1Ki 13:9 Eat no bread, nor drink w., nor......... 4325
1Ki 13:16 will I eat bread nor drink w. with 4325
1Ki 13:17 eat no bread nor drink w. there, ... 4325
1Ki 13:18 he may eat bread and drink w.. 4325
1Ki 13:19 bread in his house, and drank w......... 4325
1Ki 13:22 hast eaten bread and drunk w. in 4325
1Ki 13:22 Eat no bread, and drink no w.; 4325
1Ki 14:15 Israel, as a reed is shaken in the w., .. 4325
1Ki 17:10 I pray thee, a little w. in a vessel, ... 4325
1Ki 18:4 and fed them with bread and w..)........ 4325
1Ki 18:5 unto all fountains of w., and unto 4325

1Ki 18:13 and fed them with bread and w.? 4325
1Ki 18:33 Fill four barrels with w., and pour...... 4325
1Ki 18:35 the w. ran round about the altar; 4325
1Ki 18:35 he filled the trench also with w.. 4325
1Ki 18:38 up the w. that was in the trench. 4325
1Ki 19:6 coals, and a cruse of w. at his head. ... 4325
1Ki 22:27 affliction and with w. of affliction. 4325
2Ki 2:19 the w. is naught, and the ground......... 4325
2Ki 3:9 there was no w. for the host, and...... 4325
2Ki 3:11 poured w. on the hands of Elijah. 4325
2Ki 3:17 that valley shall be filled with w., ... 4325
2Ki 3:19 good tree, and stop all wells of w.,...... 4325
2Ki 3:20 there came w. by the way of Edom, ... 4325
2Ki 3:20 and the country was filled with w.. 4325
2Ki 3:22 and the sun shone upon the w., ... 4325
2Ki 3:22 the Moabites saw the w. on the......... 4325
2Ki 3:25 they stopped all the wells of w., ... 4325
2Ki 6:5 beam the axe head fell into the w....... 4325
2Ki 6:22 set bread and w. before them, that..... 4325
2Ki 8:15 a thick cloth, and dipped it in w., ... 4325
2Ki 20:20 and brought w. into the city, are........ 4325
1Ch 11:17 of the w. of the well of Beth-lehem, ... 4325
1Ch 11:18 drew w. out of...well of Beth-lehem,... 4325
2Ch 18:26 affliction and with w. of affliction, ... 4325
2Ch 32:4 Assyria come, and find much w.? 4325
Ezr 10:6 he did eat no bread, nor drink w......... 4325
Ne 3:26 against the w. gate toward the east, ... 4325
Ne 8:1 street that was before the w. gate; 4325
Ne 8:3 street that was before the w. gate 4325
Ne 8:16 and in the street of the w. gate, ... 4325
Ne 9:15 forth w. for them out of the rock 4325
Ne 9:20 and gavest them w. for their thirst. 4325
Ne 12:37 even unto the w. gate eastward. 4325
Ne 13:2 of Israel with bread and with w.,........ 4325
Job 8:11 can the flag grow without w.?............ 4325
Job 9:30 I wash myself with snow w.,............. 1119
Job 14:9 through the scent of w. it will bud,..... 4325
Job 15:16 which drinketh iniquity like w.? 4325
Job 22:7 not given w. to the weary to drink, ... 4325
Job 34:7 who drinketh up scorning like w.? 4325
Job 36:27 he maketh small the drops of w. 4325
Ps 1:3 a tree planted by the rivers of w.,....... 4325
Ps 6:6 I w. my couch with my tears............. 4529
Ps 22:14 I am poured out like w., and all 4325
Ps 42:1 hart panteth after the w. brooks. 4325
Ps 63:1 and thirsty land, where no w. is;........ 4325
Ps 65:9 the river of God, which is full of w..... 4325
Ps 66:12 went through fire and through w.: 4325
Ps 72:6 as showers that w. the earth............ 2222
Ps 77:17 The clouds poured out w.: the........... 4325
Ps 79:3 Their blood have they shed like w. 4325
Ps 88:17 came round about me daily like w.;...... 4325
Ps 107:35 the wilderness into a standing w., ... 4325
Ps 109:18 let it come into his bowels like w.,...... 4325
Ps 114:8 turned the rock into a standing w.,...... 4325
Pr 8:24 no fountains abounding with w.. 4325
Pr 17:14 is as when one letteth out w. 4325
Pr 20:5 the heart of man is like deep w.; 4325
Pr 21:1 of the Lord, as the rivers of w.: 4325
Pr 25:21 he be thirsty, give him w. to drink: 4325
Pr 27:19 As in w. face answereth to face, so..... 4325
Pr 30:16 the earth that is not filled with w.; 4325
Ec 2:6 I made me pools of w.,.................... 4325
Ec 2:6 to w. therewith the wood that........... 8248
Isa 1:22 dross, thy wine mixed with w........... 4325
Isa 1:30 and as a garden that hath no w. 4325
Isa 3:1 bread, and the whole stay of w.,........ 4325
Isa 12:3 draw w. out of the wells of salvation... 4325
Isa 14:23 for the bittern, and pools of w.: 4325
Isa 16:9 I will w. thee with my tears, O 7301
Isa 21:14 brought w. to him that was thirsty, ... 4325
Isa 22:11 two walls for the w. of the old pool: .. 4325
Isa 27:3 I will w. it every moment: lest 8248
Isa 30:14 or to take w. withall out of the pit...... 4325
Isa 30:20 adversity, and the w. of affliction,....... 4325
Isa 32:2 as rivers of w. in a dry place, as........ 4325
Isa 35:7 and the thirsty land springs of w......... 4325
Isa 37:25 I have digged, and drunk w.; and....... 4325
Isa 41:17 When the poor and needy seek w., ... 4325
Isa 41:18 make the wilderness a pool of w., ... 4325
Isa 41:18 and the dry land springs of w.......... 4325
Isa 44:3 pour w. upon him that is thirsty,........ 4325
Isa 44:4 as willows by the w. courses............ 4325
Isa 44:12 he drinketh no w., and is faint. 4325
Isa 49:10 by the springs of w. shall he guide 4325
Isa 50:2 stinketh, because there is no w., ... 4325
Isa 58:11 like a spring of w., whose waters....... 4325
Isa 63:12 dividing the w. before them, to.......... 4325
Jer 2:13 broken cisterns, that can hold no w.. .. 4325
Jer 8:14 and given us w. of gall to drink,......... 4325
Jer 9:15 and give them w. of gall to drink........ 4325
Jer 13:1 thy loins, and put it not in w.. 4325
Jer 14:3 came to the pits, and found no w.; 4325
Jer 23:15 and make them drink the w. of gall:.... 4325
Jer 38:6 in the dungeon there was no w.,........ 4325
La 1:16 mine eye runneth down with w.,......... 4325
La 2:19 pour out thine heart like w. before 4325
La 3:48 eye runneth down with rivers of w. 4325
La 5:4 We have drunken our w. for money;.... 4325
Eze 4:11 shalt drink also w. by measure, ... 4325
Eze 4:16 and they shall drink w. by measure,...... 4325
Eze 4:17 That they may want bread and w., ... 4325
Eze 7:17 and all knees shall be weak as w........ 4325
Eze 12:18 drink thy w. with trembling and 4325
Eze 12:19 drink their w. with astonishment, ... 4325
Eze 16:4 neither wast thou washed in w. to 4325
Eze 16:9 Then washed I thee with w.; yea,...... 4325
Eze 17:7 he might w. it by the furrows of........ 8248
Eze 21:7 and all knees shall be weak as w........ 4325
Eze 24:3 set it on, and also pour w. into it: 4325
Eze 26:12 and thy dust in the midst of the w...... 4325
Eze 31:14 in their height, all that drink w.: 4325
Eze 31:16 of Lebanon, all that drink w., ... 4325
Eze 32:6 also w. with thy blood the land 8248
Eze 36:25 will I sprinkle clean w. upon you, ... 4325
Da 1:12 us pulse to eat, and w. to drink. 4325
Ho 2:5 that give me my bread and my w., ... 4325
Ho 5:10 my wrath upon them that like w.. 4325
Ho 10:7 is cut off as the foam upon the w.. 4325
Joe 3:18 and shall w. the valley of Shittim. 8248
Am 4:8 unto one city, to drink w.; 4325
Am 8:11 famine of bread, not a thirst for w.,.... 4325
Jon 3:7 let them not feed, nor drink w.: 4325
Na 2:8 Nineveh is of old like a pool of w.: 4325
Hab 3:10 overflowing of the w. passed by:......... 4325
Zec 9:11 out of the pit wherein is no w.. 4325
Mt 3:11 I indeed baptize you with w. unto...... *5204*
Mt 3:16 went up straightway out of the w.: *5204*
Mt 10:42 **these little ones a cup of cold w.** ....
Mt 14:28 bid me come unto thee on the w......... *5204*
Mt 14:29 he walked on the w., to go to Jesus. .. *5204*
Mt 17:15 into the fire, and oft into the w.......... *5204*
Mt 27:24 he took w., and washed his hands...... *5204*
Mk 1:8 I indeed have baptized you with w.: *5204*
Mk 1:10 coming up out of the w., he saw......... *5204*
Mk 9:41 **cup of w. to drink in my name,** *5204*
Mk 14:13 **you a man bearing a pitcher of w**... *5204*
Lu 3:16 all, I indeed baptize you with w.; *5204*
Lu 7:44 **thou gavest me no w. for my feet:** . *5204*
Lu 8:23 they were filled with w., and were in........
Lu 8:24 wind and the raging of the w.:........... *5204*
Lu 8:25 commandeth even the winds and w.,.... *5204*
Lu 16:24 **dip the tip of his finger in w.,** *5204*
Lu 22:10 **meet you, bearing a pitcher of w**... *5204*
Joh 1:26 them, saying, I baptize with w.: *5204*
Joh 1:31 am I come baptizing with w.. .... *5204*
Joh 1:33 he that sent me to baptize with w., ... *5204*
Joh 2:7 them, **Fill the waterpots with w**...... *5204*
Joh 2:9 tasted the w. that was made wine, ... *5204*
Joh 2:9 servants which drew the w. knew;) *5204*
Joh 3:5 **Except a man be born of w. and of** *5204*
Joh 3:23 because there was much w. there: *5204*
Joh 4:7 a woman of Samaria to draw w.......... *5204*
Joh 4:10 **he would have given thee living w.**. *5204*
Joh 4:11 then hast thou that living w.? *5204*
Joh 4:13 **Whosoever drinketh of this w**........ *5204*
Joh 4:14 **whosoever drinketh of the w. that** .. *5204*
Joh 4:14 **w. that I shall give him shall be**.... *5204*
Joh 4:14 **him a well of w. springing up** *5204*
Joh 4:15 Sir, give me this w., that I thirst *5204*
Joh 4:46 Galilee, where he made the w. wine... *5204*
Joh 5:3 waiting for the moving of the w.. .... *5204*
Joh 5:4 into the pool, and troubled the w. *5204*
Joh 5:4 first after the troubling of the w.......... *5204*
Joh 5:7 when the w. is troubled, to put me *5204*
Joh 7:38 **belly shall flow rivers of living w**.. *5204*
Joh 13:5 that he poureth w. into a bason, ... *5204*
Joh 19:34 came there out blood and w.............. *5204*
Ac 1:5 **For John truly baptized with w**..... *5204*
Ac 8:36 way, they came unto a certain w.:....... *5204*
Ac 8:36 See, here is w.; what doth hinder *5204*
Ac 8:38 they went down both into the w., ... *5204*
Ac 8:39 they were come up out of the w., ... *5204*
Ac 10:47 Can any man forbid w., that these...... *5204*
Ac 11:16 said, **John indeed baptized with w**...*5204*
Eph 5:26 the washing of w. by the word, ... *5204*
1Ti 5:23 Drink no longer w., but use a little..... *5202*
Heb 9:19 of calves and of goats, with w., and.... *5204*
Heb 10:22 our bodies washed with pure w.......... *5204*
Jas 3:11 at the same place sweet w. and bitter?......
Jas 3:12 both yield salt w. and fresh. *5204*
1Pe 3:20 is, eight souls were saved by w.. .... *5204*
2Pe 2:17 These are wells without w., clouds *504*
2Pe 3:5 standing out of the w. and in the w.... *5204*
2Pe 3:6 being overflowed with w., perished:.... *5204*
1Jo 5:6 is he that came by w. and blood, ... *5204*
1Jo 5:6 not by w. only, but by w. and blood. .. *5204*
1Jo 5:8 earth, the spirit, and the w., and *5204*
Jude 12 clouds they are without w., carried *504*
Re 12:15 out of his mouth w. as a flood *5204*
Re 16:12 and the w. thereof was dried up, ... *5204*
Re 21:6 the fountain of the w. of life freely. ... *5204*
Re 22:1 shewed me a pure river of w. of life,.. *5204*
Re 22:17 will, let him take the w. of life freely. . *5204*

WATER-BROOKS See WATER and BROOKS.

WATERCOURSE See also WATER and COURSES.
2Ch 32:20 the upper w. of Gihon, ... 4161,4325
Job 38:25 w. for the overflowing of waters, ... 8585

WATERED See also WATEREDST.
Ge 2:6 w. the whole face of the ground. 8248
Ge 13:10 that it was well w. every where,......... 4945
Ge 29:2 out of that well they w. the flocks:..... 8248
Ge 29:3 the well's mouth, and w. the sheep, ... 8248
Ge 29:10 w. the flock of Laban his mother's...... 8248
Ex 2:17 helped them, and w. their flock. 8248
Ex 2:19 enough for us, and w. the flock. 8248
Pr 11:25 watereth shall be w. also himself. 3384
Isa 58:11 and thou shalt be like a w. garden, ... 7302
Jer 31:12 their soul shall be as a w. garden;...... 7302
1Co 3:6 I have planted, Apollos w.; but *4222*

WATEREDST
De 11:10 w. it with thy foot, as a garden of...... 8248

WATEREST
Ps 65:9 Thou visitest the earth, and w. it:...... 7783
Ps 65:10 Thou w. the ridges thereof............... 7301

WATERETH
Ps 104:13 He w. the hills from his chambers: 8248
Pr 11:25 he that w. shall be watered also.......... 7301
Isa 55:10 w. the earth, and maketh it bring........ 7301
1Co 3:7 any thing, neither he that w.; *4222*
1Co 3:8 planteth and he that w. are one: *4222*

WATERFLOOD
Ps 69:15 Let not the w. overflow me, ... 7641,4325

WATERING
Ge 30:38 in the gutters in the w. troughs 4325
Job 37:11 by w. he wearieth the thick cloud:....... 7377
Lu 13:15 **stall, and lead him away to w.?** *4222*

WATERPOT See also WATERPOTS.
Joh 4:28 The woman then left her w., and....... *5201*

WATERPOTS
Joh 2:6 were set there six w. of stone, ... *5201*
Joh 2:7 unto them, **Fill the w. with water**... *5201*

WATERS
Ge 1:2 moved upon the face of the w.. 4325
Ge 1:6 firmament in the midst of the w.,........ 4325
Ge 1:6 and let it divide the w. from the w..... 4325
Ge 1:7 divided the w. which were under........ 4325
Ge 1:7 from the w. which were above the 4325
Ge 1:9 Let the w. under the heaven be......... 4325
Ge 1:10 together of the w. called he Seas: 4325
Ge 1:20 Let the w. bring forth abundantly 4325
Ge 1:21 the w. brought forth abundantly, ... 4325
Ge 1:22 multiply, and fill the w. in the seas, ... 4325
Ge 6:17 bring a flood of w. upon the earth, ... 4325
Ge 7:6 the flood of w. was upon the earth. 4325
Ge 7:7 ark, because of the w. of the flood. 4325
Ge 7:10 that the w. of the flood were upon 4325
Ge 7:17 the w. increased, and bare up the 4325
Ge 7:18 w. prevailed, and were increased 4325
Ge 7:18 ark went upon the face of the w.. 4325
Ge 7:19 w. prevailed exceedingly upon the 4325
Ge 7:20 cubits upward did the w. prevail;........ 4325
Ge 7:24 the w. prevailed upon the earth 4325

Ge	8:1	the earth, and the **w.** asswaged;	4325
Ge	8:3	the **w.** returned from off the earth	4325
Ge	8:3	and fifty days the **w.** were abated	4325
Ge	8:5	the **w.** decreased continually until	4325
Ge	8:7	until the **w.** were dried up from off	4325
Ge	8:8	to see if the **w.** were abated from	4325
Ge	8:9	the **w.** were on the face of the whole	4325
Ge	8:11	Noah knew that the **w.** were abated	4325
Ge	8:13	**w.** were dried up from off the earth	4325
Ge	9:11	off any more by the **w.** of a flood;	4325
Ge	9:15	the **w.** shall no more become a flood	4325
Ex	7:17	upon the **w.** which are in the river,	4325
Ex	7:19	thine hand upon the **w.** of Egypt,	4325
Ex	7:20	smote the **w.** that were in the river,	4325
Ex	7:20	all the **w.**…in the river were turned	4325
Ex	8:6	out his hand over the **w.** of Egypt;	4325
Ex	14:21	dry land, and the **w.** were divided.	4325
Ex	14:22	the **w.** were a wall unto them on	4325
Ex	14:26	**w.** may come…upon the Egyptians,	4325
Ex	14:28	the **w.** returned, and covered the	4325
Ex	14:29	the **w.** were a wall unto them on	4325
Ex	15:8	the **w.** were gathered together,	4325
Ex	15:10	they sank as lead in the mighty **w.**	4325
Ex	15:19	brought again the **w.** of the sea	4325
Ex	15:23	could not drink of the **w.** of Marah,	4325
Ex	15:25	which when he had cast into the **w.**,	4325
Ex	15:25	the **w.** were made sweet:	4325
Ex	15:27	and they encamped there by the **w.**	4325
Le	11:9	shall ye eat of all that are in the **w.**	4325
Le	11:9	hath fins and scales in the **w.**, in	4325
Le	11:10	of all that move in the **w.**, and of	4325
Le	11:10	any living thing which is in the **w.**,	4325
Le	11:12	hath no fins nor scales in the **w.**,	4325
Le	11:46	living creature…moveth in the **w.**,	4325
Nu	21:22	will not drink of the **w.** of the well:	4325
Nu	24:6	and as cedar trees beside the **w.**	4325
Nu	24:7	and his seed shall be in many **w.**,	4325
De	4:18	that is in the **w.** beneath the earth:	4325
De	5:8	that is in the **w.** beneath the earth:	4325
De	10:7	to Jotbath, a land of rivers of **w.**	4325
De	14:9	shall eat of all that are in the **w.**	4325
De	32:51	Israel at the **w.** of Meribah-Kadesh,	4325
De	33:8	didst strive at the **w.** of Meribah;	4325
Jos	3:13	shall rest in the **w.** of the Jordan,	4325
Jos	3:13	**w.** of the Jordan shall be cut off	4325
Jos	3:13	from the **w.** that come down from	4325
Jos	3:16	the **w.** which came down from above	4325
Jos	4:7	the **w.** of Jordan were cut off before	4325
Jos	4:7	the **w.** of Jordan were cut off:	4325
Jos	4:18	the **w.** of Jordan returned unto	4325
Jos	4:23	God dried up the **w.** of Jordan from	4325
Jos	5:1	Lord had dried up the **w.** of Jordan	4325
Jos	11:5	pitched together at the **w.** of Merom,	4325
Jos	11:7	against them by the **w.** of Merom	4325
Jos	15:7	toward the **w.** of En-shemesh,	4325
Jos	18:15	out to the well of **w.** of Nephtoah:	4325
Jg	5:19	in Taanach by the **w.** of Megiddo;	4325
Jg	7:24	them the **w.** unto Beth-barah	4325
Jg	7:24	took the **w.** unto Beth-barah and	4325
2Sa	5:20	before me, as the breach of **w.**	4325
2Sa	12:27	and have taken the city of **w.**	4325
2Sa	22:12	dark **w.**, and thick clouds of the	4325
2Sa	22:17	he drew me out of many **w.**;	4325
2Ki	2:8	smote the **w.**, and they were divided	4325
2Ki	2:14	and smote the **w.**, and said, Where	4325
2Ki	2:14	when he also had smitten the **w.**,	4325
2Ki	2:21	forth unto the spring of the **w.**,	4325
2Ki	2:21	the Lord, I have healed these **w.**;	4325
2Ki	2:22	the **w.** were healed unto this day,	4325
2Ki	5:12	better than all the **w.** of Israel?	4325
2Ki	18:31	ye every one the **w.** of his cistern:	4325
2Ki	19:24	have digged and drunk strange **w.**,	4325
1Ch	14:11	hand like the breaking forth of **w.**	4325
2Ch	32:3	men to stop the **w.** of the fountains	4325
Ne	9:11	as a stone into the mighty **w.**	4325
Job	3:24	are poured out like the **w.**	4325
Job	5:10	and sendeth **w.** upon the fields:	4325
Job	11:16	remember it as **w.** that pass away:	4325
Job	12:15	Behold, he withholdeth the **w.**,	4325
Job	14:11	As the **w.** fail from the sea, and the	4325
Job	14:19	The **w.** wear the stones: thou	4325
Job	22:11	and abundance of **w.** cover thee.	4325
Job	24:18	He is swift as the **w.**; their portion	4325
Job	24:19	and heat consume the snow **w.**: so	4325
Job	26:5	are formed from under the **w.**,	4325
Job	26:8	He bindeth up the **w.** in his thick	4325
Job	26:10	compassed the **w.** with bounds,	4325
Job	27:20	Terrors take hold on him as **w.**,	4325
Job	28:4	even the **w.** forgotten of the foot:	
Job	28:25	he weigheth the **w.** by measure.	4325
Job	29:19	My root was spread out by the **w.**,	4325
Job	30:14	upon me as a wide breaking in of **w.**:	
Job	37:10	breadth of the **w.** is straitened.	4325
Job	38:25	for the overflowing of **w.**,	
Job	38:30	The **w.** are hid as with a stone,	4325
Job	38:34	abundance of **w.** may cover thee?	4325
Ps	18:11	round about him were dark **w.** and	4325
Ps	18:15	Then the channels of **w.** were seen,	4325
Ps	18:16	me, he drew me out of many **w.**	4325
Ps	23:2	he leadeth me beside the still **w.**	4325
Ps	29:3	voice of the Lord is upon the **w.**:	4325
Ps	29:3	the Lord is upon many **w.**	4325
Ps	32:6	surely in the floods of great **w.** they	4325
Ps	33:7	He gathereth the **w.** of the sea	4325
Ps	46:3	Though the **w.** thereof roar and be	4325
Ps	58:7	Let them melt away as **w.** which	4325
Ps	69:1	the **w.** are come in unto my soul.	4325
Ps	69:2	I am come into deep **w.**, where	4325
Ps	69:14	hate me, and out of the deep **w.**	4325
Ps	73:10	and **w.** of a full cup are wrung out	4325
Ps	74:13	the heads of the dragons in the **w.**	4325
Ps	77:16	**w.** saw thee, O God, the **w.** saw thee;	4325
Ps	77:19	sea, and thy path in the great **w.**,	4325
Ps	78:13	he made the **w.** to stand as an heap.	4325
Ps	78:16	caused **w.** to run down like rivers.	4325
Ps	78:20	the rock, that the **w.** gushed out,	4325
Ps	81:7	I proved thee at the **w.** of Meribah.	4325
Ps	93:4	mightier than the noise of many **w.**,	4325
Ps	104:3	beams of his chambers in the **w.**:	4325
Ps	104:6	the **w.** stood above the mountains.	4325
Ps	105:29	He turned their **w.** into blood, and	4325
Ps	105:41	the rock, and the **w.** gushed out;	4325
Ps	106:11	And the **w.** covered their enemies:	4325
Ps	106:32	angered him also at the **w.** of strife,	4325
Ps	107:23	ships, that do business in great **w.**;	4325
Ps	114:8	the flint into a fountain of **w.**	4325
Ps	119:136	Rivers of **w.** run down mine eyes,	4325
Ps	124:4	Then the **w.** had overwhelmed us,	4325
Ps	124:5	proud **w.** had gone over our soul.	4325
Ps	136:6	stretched…the earth above the **w.**:	4325
Ps	144:7	and deliver me out of great **w.**,	4325
Ps	147:18	his wind to blow, and the **w.** flow.	4325
Ps	148:4	ye **w.** that be above the heavens.	4325
Pr	5:15	Drink **w.** out of thine own cistern,	4325
Pr	5:15	running **w.** out of thine own well.	
Pr	5:16	and rivers of **w.** in the streets.	4325
Pr	8:29	that the **w.** should not pass his	4325
Pr	9:17	Stolen **w.** are sweet, and bread	4325
Pr	18:4	of a man's mouth are as deep **w.**,	4325
Pr	25:25	As cold **w.** to a thirsty soul, so is	4325
Pr	30:4	hath bound the **w.** in a garment?	4325
Ec	11:1	Cast thy bread upon the **w.**: for	4325
Ca	4:15	a well of living **w.**, and streams	4325
Ca	5:12	eyes of doves by the rivers of **w.**,	4325
Ca	8:7	Many **w.** cannot quench love,	4325
Isa	8:6	the **w.** of Shiloah that go softly,	4325
Isa	8:7	up upon them the **w.** of the river,	4325
Isa	11:9	the Lord, as the **w.** cover the sea.	4325
Isa	15:6	the **w.** of Nimrim shall be desolate:	4325
Isa	15:9	**w.** of Dimon shall be full of blood:	4325
Isa	17:12	like the rushing of mighty **w.**!	4325
Isa	17:13	rush like the rushing of many **w.**:	4325
Isa	18:2	in vessels of bulrushes upon the **w.**,	4325
Isa	19:5	And the **w.** shall fail from the sea,	4325
Isa	19:8	they that spread nets upon the **w.**	4325
Isa	22:9	gathered…the **w.** of the lower pool.	4325
Isa	23:3	And by great **w.** the seed of Sihor,	4325
Isa	28:2	a flood of mighty **w.** overflowing,	4325
Isa	28:17	**w.** shall overflow the hiding place.	4325
Isa	30:25	high hill, rivers and streams of **w.**	4325
Isa	32:20	Blessed…ye that sow beside all **w.**,	4325
Isa	33:16	be given him; his **w.** shall be sure.	4325
Isa	35:6	the wilderness shall **w.** break out,	4325
Isa	36:16	every one the **w.** of his own cistern;	4325
Isa	40:12	measured the **w.** in the hollow of	4325
Isa	43:2	When thou passest through the **w.**,	4325
Isa	43:16	sea, and a path in the mighty **w.**;	4325
Isa	43:20	because I give **w.** in the wilderness,	4325
Isa	48:1	come forth out of the **w.** of Judah,	4325
Isa	48:21	caused the **w.** to flow out of the rock.	4325
Isa	48:21	rock also, and the **w.** gushed out.	4325
Isa	51:10	the sea, the **w.** of the great deep;	4325
Isa	54:9	this is as the **w.** of Noah unto me:	4325
Isa	54:9	the **w.** of Noah should no more go	4325
Isa	55:1	that thirsteth, come ye to the **w.**,	4325
Isa	57:20	whose **w.** cast up mire and dirt.	4325
Isa	58:11	spring of water, whose **w.** fail not.	4325
Isa	64:2	the fire causeth the **w.** to boil,	4325
Jer	2:13	forsaken…the fountain of living **w.**,	4325
Jer	2:18	of Egypt, to drink the **w.** of Sihor?	4325
Jer	2:18	to drink the **w.** of the river?	4325
Jer	6:7	As a fountain casteth out her **w.**,	4325
Jer	9:1	Oh that my head were **w.**, and mine	4325
Jer	9:18	and our eyelids gush out with **w.**	4325
Jer	10:13	is a multitude of **w.** in the heavens,	4325
Jer	14:3	have sent their little ones to the **w.**:	4325
Jer	15:18	me as a liar, and as **w.** that fail?	4325
Jer	17:8	shall be as a tree planted by the **w.**,	4325
Jer	17:13	the Lord, the fountain of living **w.**	4325
Jer	18:14	the cold flowing **w.** that come from	4325
Jer	31:9	them to walk by the rivers of **w.**	4325
Jer	41:12	by the great **w.** that are in Gibeon.	4325
Jer	46:7	whose **w.** are moved as the rivers?	4325
Jer	46:8	his **w.** are moved like the rivers;	4325
Jer	47:2	**w.** rise up out of the north, and	4325
Jer	48:34	for the **w.** also of Nimrim shall be	4325
Jer	50:38	A drought is upon her **w.**; and they	4325
Jer	51:13	O thou that dwellest upon many **w.**,	4325
Jer	51:16	is a multitude of **w.** in the heavens;	4325
Jer	51:55	her waves do roar like great **w.**,	4325
La	3:54	**W.** flowed over mine head; then I	4325
Eze	1:24	wings, like the noise of great **w.**,	4325
Eze	17:5	he placed it by great **w.**, and set it	4325
Eze	17:8	planted in a good soil by great **w.**,	4325
Eze	19:10	in thy blood, planted by the **w.**	4325
Eze	19:10	of branches by reason of many **w.**	4325
Eze	26:19	thee, and great **w.** shall cover thee;	4325
Eze	27:26	have brought thee into great **w.**:	4325
Eze	27:34	by the seas in the depths of the **w.**,	4325
Eze	31:4	The **w.** made him great, the deep	4325
Eze	31:5	because of the multitude of **w.**,	4325
Eze	31:7	for his root was by great **w.**	4325
Eze	31:14	none of all the trees by the **w.** exalt	4325
Eze	31:15	and the great **w.** were stayed:	4325
Eze	32:2	troubledst the **w.** with thy feet and	4325
Eze	32:13	thereof from beside the great **w.**;	4325
Eze	32:14	Then will I make their **w.** deep, and	4325
Eze	34:18	and to have drunk of the deep **w.**,	4325
Eze	43:2	voice was like a noise of many **w.**	4325
Eze	47:1	**w.** issued out from under the	4325
Eze	47:1	the **w.** came down from under from	4325
Eze	47:2	there ran out **w.** on the right side.	4325
Eze	47:3	and he brought me through the **w.**	4325
Eze	47:3	the **w.** were to the ancles.	4325
Eze	47:4	and brought me through the **w.**	4325
Eze	47:4	the **w.** were to the knees.	4325
Eze	47:4	through; the **w.** were to the loins.	4325
Eze	47:5	for the **w.** were risen, **w.** to swim in,	4325
Eze	47:8	These **w.** issue out toward the east	4325
Eze	47:8	the sea, the **w.** shall be healed.	4325
Eze	47:9	these **w.** shall come thither:	4325
Eze	47:12	their **w.** they issued out of the	4325
Eze	47:19	even to the **w.** of strife in Kadesh,	4325
Eze	48:28	unto the **w.** of strife in Kadesh,	4325
Da	12:6,	7 was upon the **w.** of the river,	4325
Joe	1:20	for the rivers of **w.** are dried up,	4325
Joe	3:18	rivers of Judah shall flow with **w.**,	4325
Am	5:8	that calleth for the **w.** of the sea,	4325
Am	5:24	But let judgment run down as **w.**,	4325
Am	9:6	he that calleth for the **w.** of the sea,	4325
Jon	2:5	The **w.** compassed me about, even	4325
Mic	1:4	as the **w.** that are poured down a	4325
Na	3:3	that had the **w.** round about it,	4325
Na	3:14	Draw thee **w.** for the siege, fortify	4325
Hab	2:14	of the Lord, as the **w.** cover the sea.	4325
Hab	3:15	through the heap of great **w.**	4325
Zec	14:8	**w.** shall go out from Jerusalem;	4325
Mt	8:32	the sea, and perished in the **w.**	*5204*
Mk	9:22	him into the fire, and into the **w.**,	*5204*
2Co	11:26	in perils of **w.**, in perils of robbers,	*4215*
Re	1:15	his voice as the sound of many **w.**	*5204*
Re	7:17	them unto living fountains of **w.**	*5204*
Re	8:10	and upon the fountains of **w.**;	*5204*
Re	8:11	and the third part of the **w.** became	*5204*
Re	8:11	and many men died of the **w.**,	*5204*
Re	11:6	have power over **w.** to turn them to	*5204*
Re	14:2	heaven, as the voice of many **w.**	*5204*
Re	14:7	the sea, and the fountains of **w.**	*5204*

Re 16:4 upon...rivers and fountains of w.; *5204*
Re 16:5 I heard the angel of the w. say, ... *5204*
Re 17:1 whore that sitteth upon many w. *5204*
Re 17:15 The w. which thou sawest, where *5204*
Re 19:6 and as the voice of many w., ... *5204*

WATERSPOUTS
Ps 42:7 unto deep at the noise of thy w. 6794

WATERSPRINGS
Ps 107:33 and the w. into dry ground; 4161,4325
Ps 107:35 and dry ground into w.. 4161,4325

WAVE See also WAVED; WAVES.
Ex 29:24 shalt w. them...before the Lord. 5130
Ex 29:24 for a w. offering before the Lord........ 8573
Ex 29:26 and w. it...before the Lord: 5130
Ex 29:26 for a w. offering before the Lord:....... 8573
Ex 29:27 the breast of the w. offering, ... 8573
Le 7:30 for a w. offering before the Lord........ 8573
Le 7:34 w. breast and the heave shoulder....... 8573
Le 8:27 for a w. offering before the Lord........ 8573
Le 8:29 it for a w. offering before the Lord:.... 8573
Le 9:21 for a w. offering before the Lord;....... 8573
Le 10:14 w. breast and heave shoulder shall 8573
Le 10:15 w. breast shall they bring with the 8573
Le 10:15 the fat, to w. it...before the Lord;...... 5130
Le 10:15 for a w. offering before the Lord;....... 8573
Le 14:12 annd w. them...before the Lord: 5130
Le 14:12 for a w. offering before the Lord:....... 8573
Le 14:24 shall w. them...before the Lord: 5130
Le 14:24 for a w. offering before the Lord:....... 8573
Le 23:11 w. the sheaf before the Lord,............ 5130
Le 23:11 after...sabbath the priest shall w. it. ... 5130
Le 23:12 when ye w. the sheaf an he lamb 5130
Le 23:15 the sheaf of the w. offering;.............. 8573
Le 23:17 two w. loaves of two tenth deals:....... 8573
Le 23:20 priest shall w. them with the bread..... 5130
Le 23:20 for a w. offering before the Lord,....... 8573
Nu 5:25 w. the offering before the Lord,......... 5130
Nu 6:20 And the priest shall w. them for a...... 5130
Nu 6:20 for a w. offering before the Lord:....... 8573
Nu 6:20 the w. breast and heave shoulder:....... 8573
Nu 18:11 the w. offerings of the children of...... 8573
Nu 18:18 w. breast and as the right shoulder..... 8573
Jas 1:6 is like a w. of the sea driven with *2830*

WAVED
Ex 29:27 of the heave offering, which is w.,...... 5130
Le 7:30 the breast may be w. for a wave 5130
Le 8:27 w. them for a wave offering before....... 5130
Le 8:29 w. it for a wave offering before the 5130
Le 9:21 Aaron w. for a wave offering before.... 5130
Le 14:21 for a trespass offering to be w.,......... 8573

WAVE-LOAF See WAVE and LOAF.

WAVE-OFFERING See WAVE and OFFERING.

WAVERETH
Jas 1:6 he that w. is like a wave of the sea.... *1252*

WAVERING
Heb 10:23 profession of our faith without w.;........ *186*
Jas 1:6 let him ask in faith, nothing w.. .... *1252*

WAVES
2Sa 22:5 the w. of death compassed me, ... 4867
Job 9:8 treadeth upon the w. of the sea......... 1116
Job 38:11 here shall thy proud w. be stayed? 1530
Ps 42:7 all thy w. and thy billows are gone 4867
Ps 65:7 of the seas, the noise of their w., ... 1530
Ps 88:7 hast afflicted me with all thy w.. 4867
Ps 89:9 when the w. thereof arise, thou 1530
Ps 93:3 voice; the floods lift up their w.. 1796
Ps 93:4 yea, than the mighty w. of the sea. 4867
Ps 107:25 which lifteth up the w. thereof........... 1530
Ps 107:29 so that the w. thereof are still. 1530
Isa 48:18 righteousness as the w. of the sea: 1530
Isa 51:15 divided the sea, whose w. roared:....... 1530
Jer 5:22 the w. thereof toss themselves, yet...... 1530
Jer 31:35 the sea when the w. thereof roar;........ 1530
Jer 51:42 with the multitude of the w.............. 1530
Jer 51:55 her w. do roar like great waters, ... 1530
Eze 26:3 the sea causeth his w. to come up. 1530
Jon 2:3 billows and thy w. passed over me. 1530
Zec 10:11 and shall smite the w. in the sea, ... 1530
Mt 8:24 the ship was covered with the w........ *2949*
Mt 14:24 midst of the sea, tossed with w. *2949*
Mk 4:37 the w. beat into the ship, so that it..... *2949*
Lu 21:25 **the sea and the w. roaring;**........... *4535*
Ac 27:41 broken with the violence of the w.. .... *2949*
Jude 13 Raging w. of the sea, foaming out *2949*

WAX See also WAXED; WAXEN; WAXETH; WAXING.
Ex 22:24 And my wrath shall w. hot, and I............
Ex 32:10 that my wrath may w. hot against ....
Ex 32:11 why doth thy wrath w. hot against...........
Ex 32:22 not the anger of my lord w. hot:..............
Le 25:47 if a sojourner or stranger w. rich.............
Le 25:47 that dwelleth by him w. poor,.................
1Sa 3:2 his eyes began to w. dim, that he ....
Job 6:17 What time they w. warm, they ....
Job 14:8 Though the root thereof w. old in.........
Ps 22:14 my heart is like w.; it is melted in...... 1749
Ps 68:2 as w. melteth before the fire, so let ... 1749
Ps 97:5 The hills melted like w. at the........... 1749
Ps 102:26 all of them shall w. old like a garment; ......
Isa 17:4 the fatness of his flesh shall w. lean.........
Isa 29:22 neither shall his face now w. pale............
Isa 50:9 they all shall w. old as a garment; ....
Isa 51:6 earth shall w. old like a garment, ...
Jer 6:24 our hands w. feeble: anguish hath.............
Mic 1:4 shall be cleft, as w. before the fire, ... 1749
Mt 24:12 **the love of many shall w. cold.** *5594*
Lu 12:33 **yourselves bags which w. not old,** ..*3822*
1Ti 5:11 to w. wanton against Christ, ... *2691*
2Ti 3:13 and seducers shall w. worse and........ *4298*
Heb 1:11 all shall w. old as doth a garment; *3822*

WAXED See also WAXEN.
Ge 18:12 After I am w. old shall I have...................
Ge 26:13 And the man w. great, and went.............
Ge 41:56 the famine w. sore in the land of............
Ex 1:7 multiplied and w. exceeding mighty;..........
Ex 1:20 people multiplied, and w. very mighty. ......
Ex 16:21 when the sun w. hot, it melted..............
Ex 19:19 long, and w. louder and louder,.................
Ex 32:19 Moses' anger w. hot, and he cast.............
Nu 11:23 Is the Lord's hand w. short? thou.............
De 8:4 Thy raiment w. not old upon thee, ...
De 32:15 But Jeshurun w. fat, and kicked: ....
Jos 23:1 Joshua w. old and stricken in age. ....
1Sa 2:5 hath many children is w. feeble..............
2Sa 3:1 David w. stronger and stronger, ... 1980
2Sa 3:1 the house of Saul w. weaker and........ 1980
2Sa 21:15 Philistines: and David w. faint.................
2Ki 4:34 and the flesh of the child w. warm............
1Ch 11:9 So David w. greater and greater: 1980
2Ch 13:21 Abijah w. mighty, and married ....
2Ch 17:12 And Jehoshaphat w. great................. 1980
2Ch 24:15 Jehoiada w. old, and was full of..............
Ne 9:21 their clothes w. not old, and their............
Es 9:4 Mordecai w. greater and greater........ 1980
Ps 32:3 bones w. old through my roaring.............
Jer 49:24 Damascus is w. feeble, and.....................
Jer 50:43 of them, and his hands w. feeble:.............
Da 8:8 Therefore the he goat w. very great: ....
Da 8:9 horn, which w. exceeding great,................
Da 8:10 And it w. great, even to the host of ....
Mt 13:15 **For this people's heart is w. gross,** .*3975*
Lu 1:80 child grew, and w. strong in spirit, ... *2901*
Lu 2:40 child grew, and w. strong in spirit, ... *2901*
Lu 13:19 **and it grew, and w. a great tree;** ... *1096*
Ac 13:46 Then Paul and Barnabas w. bold, ... *3955*
Ac 28:27 the heart of this people is w. gross, ... *3975*
Heb 11:34 made strong, w. valiant in fight,......... *1096*
Re 18:3 merchants of the earth are w. rich *4147*

WAXEN See also WAXED.
Ge 19:13 the cry of them is w. great before............
Le 25:25 If thy brother be w. poor, and.................
Le 25:35 And if thy brother be w. poor, and...........
Le 25:39 that dwelleth by thee be w. poor,............
De 29:5 clothes are not w. old upon you, ...
De 29:5 thy shoe is not w. old upon thy foot. ....
De 31:20 and filled themselves, and w. fat; ....
De 32:15 thou art w. fat, thou art grown.................
Jos 17:13 children of Israel were w. strong,..............
Jer 5:27 are become great, and w. rich..................
Jer 5:28 They are w. fat, they shine: yea, ...
Eze 16:7 thou hast increased and w. great, ...

WAXETH
Ps 6:7 it w. old because of all mine.....................
Heb 8:13 and w. old is ready to vanish............. *1095*

WAXING
Php 1:14 w. confident by my bonds, are........... *3982*

WAY See also ALWAY; AWAY; CAUSEWAY; HIGHWAY; PATHWAY; STRAIGHTWAY; WAYFARING; WAYMARKS; WAYS; WAYSIDE.
Ge 3:24 sword which turned every w.,.................
Ge 3:24 to keep the w. of the tree of life...............
Ge 6:12 for all flesh had corrupted his w...............
Ge 12:19 thy wife, take her, and go thy w..............
Ge 14:11 their victuals, and went their w.......... 3212
Ge 16:7 by the fountain in the w. to Shur. 1870
Ge 18:16 them to bring them on the w.. 7971
Ge 18:19 they shall keep the w. of the Lord, ... 1870
Ge 18:33 And the Lord went his w., as soon..... 3212
Ge 21:16 over against him a good w. off,................
Ge 24:27 I being in the w., the Lord led me 1870
Ge 24:40 with thee, and prosper thy w.; 1870
Ge 24:42 thou do prosper my w. which I go:..... 1870
Ge 24:48 had led me in the right w. to take...... 1870
Ge 24:56 the Lord hath prospered my w.; 1870
Ge 24:61 took Rebekah, and went his w........... 3212
Ge 24:62 Isaac came from the w. of the well...... 935
Ge 25:34 and rose up, and went his w.: 3212
Ge 28:20 will keep me in this w. that I go, ... 1870
Ge 32:1 And Jacob went on his w., and the 1870
Ge 33:16 that day on his w. unto Seir............... 1870
Ge 35:3 with me in the w. which I went. 1870
Ge 35:16 but a little w. to come to Ephrath. 776
Ge 35:19 was buried in the w. to Ephrath,........ 1870
Ge 38:14 which is by the w. to Timnath;........... 1870
Ge 38:16 And he turned unto her by the w.,........ 1870
Ge 38:21 that was openly by the w. side?......... 1870
Ge 42:25 to give them provision for the w.: 1870
Ge 42:38 if mischief befall him by the w. in........ 1870
Ge 45:21 gave them provision for the w.. 1870
Ge 45:23 and meat for his father by the w........ 1870
Ge 45:24 See that ye fall not out by the w........ 1870
Ge 48:7 in the land of Canaan in the w., ... 1870
Ge 48:7 a little w. to come unto Ephrath: 776
Ge 48:7 buried her...in the w. of Ephrath;........ 1870
Ge 49:17 Dan shall be a serpent by the w., an .. 1870
Ex 2:12 he looked this w. and that w.,........... 3541
Ex 4:24 came to pass by the w. in the inn, ... 1870
Ex 5:20 and Aaron, who stood in the w., ... 7125
Ex 13:17 w. of the land of the Philistines.......... 1870
Ex 13:18 w. of the wilderness of the Red sea:... 1870
Ex 13:21 of a cloud, to lead them the w.;......... 1870
Ex 18:8 had come upon them by the w.,......... 1870
Ex 18:20 the w. wherein they must walk,.......... 1870
Ex 18:27 he went his w. unto his own land. ....
Ex 23:20 to keep thee in the w., and to............ 1870
Ex 32:8 out of the w. which I commanded....... 1870
Ex 33:3 lest I consume thee in the w.. 1870
Ex 33:13 shew me now thy w., that I may 1870
Nu 13:17 Get you up this w. southward, and..........
Nu 14:25 wilderness by...w. of the Red sea. 1870
Nu 20:17 we will go by the king's high w.,........ 1870
Nu 20:19 unto him, We will go by the high w. ....
Nu 21:1 Israel came by the w. of the spies;...... 1870
Nu 21:4 Hor by the w. of the Red sea,........... 1870
Nu 21:4 much discouraged because of the w.. .. 1870
Nu 21:22 will go along by the king's high w.,..... 1870
Nu 21:33 and went up by the w. of Bashan:...... 1870
Nu 22:22 stood in the w. for an adversary 1870
Nu 22:23 angel of the Lord standing in the w., .. 1870
Nu 22:23 the ass turned aside out of the w.,...... 1870
Nu 22:23 the ass, to turn her into the w.. 1870
Nu 22:26 no w. to turn either to the right 1870
Nu 22:31 angel of the Lord standing in the w., .. 1870
Nu 22:32 because thy w. is perverse before,...... 1870
Nu 22:34 not that thou stoodest in the w.......... 1870
Nu 24:25 place: and Balak also went his w........ 1870
De 1:2 Horeb by the w. of mount Seir.......... 1870
De 1:19 w. of the mountain of the Amorites, ... 1870
De 1:22 again by the w. we must go up,......... 1870
De 1:31 in all the w. that ye went, until ye 1870
De 1:33 Who went in the w. before you, to..... 1870
De 1:33 shew you by what w. ye should go,.... 1870
De 1:40 wilderness by the w. of the Red sea... 1870
De 2:1 wilderness by the w. of the Red sea,.. 1870
De 2:8 the w. of the plain from Elath,.......... 1870
De 2:8 by the w. of the wilderness of Moab... 1870
De 2:27 I will go along by the high w., I........ 1870
De 3:1 and went up the w. to Bashan:.......... 1870
De 6:7 when thou walkest by the w., and...... 1870
De 8:2 w. which the Lord thy God led thee 1870
De 9:12 quickly turned aside out of the w. 1870
De 9:16 turned aside quickly out of the w. 1870
De 11:19 when thou walkest by the w., when.... 1870

De	11:28	but turn aside out of the **w.** which I	1870
De	11:30	the **w.** where the sun goeth down,	1870
De	13:5	to thrust thee out of the **w.** which	1870
De	14:24	And if the **w.** be long for thee, so	1870
De	17:16	henceforth return no more that **w.**	1870
De	19:3	Thou shalt prepare thee a **w.**, and	1870
De	19:6	because the **w.** is long, and slay	1870
De	22:4	ass or his ox fall down by the **w.**,	1870
De	22:6	chance to be before thee in the **w.**	1870
De	23:4	bread and with water in the **w.**,	1870
De	24:9	God did unto Miriam by the **w.**,	1870
De	25:17	Amalek did unto thee by the **w.**,	1870
De	25:18	How he met thee by the **w.**, and	1870
De	27:18	the blind to wander out of the **w.**	1870
De	28:7	shall come out against thee one **w.**,	1870
De	28:25	shalt go out one **w.** against them,	1870
De	28:68	the **w.** whereof I spake unto thee,	1870
De	31:29	and turn aside from the **w.** which I	1870
Jos	1:8	thou shalt make thy **w.** prosperous,	1870
Jos	2:7	the **w.** to Jordan unto the fords:	1870
Jos	2:16	and afterward may ye go your **w.**	1870
Jos	2:22	sought them throughout all the **w.**,	1870
Jos	3:4	know the **w.** by which ye must go:	1870
Jos	3:4	have not passed this **w.** heretofore.	1870
Jos	5:4	died in the wilderness by the **w.**,	1870
Jos	5:5	in the wilderness by the **w.** as they	1870
Jos	5:7	not circumcised them by the **w.**	1870
Jos	8:15	fled by the **w.** of the wilderness.	1870
Jos	8:20	no power to flee this **w.** or that **w.**	2008
Jos	10:10	**w.** that goeth up to Beth-horon,	1870
Jos	12:3	the east, the **w.** to Beth-jeshimoth;	1870
Jos	23:14	I am going the **w.** of all the earth:	1870
Jos	24:17	us in all the **w.** wherein we went,	1870
Jg	2:17	**w.** which their fathers walked in,	1870
Jg	2:19	doings, nor from their stubborn **w.**	1870
Jg	2:22	they will keep the **w.** of the Lord	1870
Jg	5:10	in judgment, and walk by the **w.**	1870
Jg	8:11	**w.** of them that dwelt in tents	1870
Jg	9:25	that came along that **w.** by them:	1870
Jg	18:5	**w.** which we go shall be prosperous	1870
Jg	18:6	the Lord is your **w.** wherein ye go.	1870
Jg	18:22	a good **w.** from the house of Micah,	
Jg	18:26	the children of Dan went their **w.**	1870
Jg	19:5	of bread, and afterward go your **w.**	
Jg	19:9	morrow get you early on your **w.**,	1870
Jg	19:14	they passed on and went their **w.**;	3212
Jg	19:27	house, and went out to go his **w.**	1870
Jg	20:42	unto the **w.** of the wilderness;	1870
Ru	1:7	on the **w.** to return unto...Judah.	1870
Ru	1:12	Turn again, my daughters, go your **w.**;	
1Sa	1:18	woman went her **w.**, and did eat,	1870
1Sa	6:9	goeth up by the **w.** of his own coast	1870
1Sa	6:12	the kine took the straight **w.**	1870
1Sa	6:12	to the **w.** of Beth-shemesh,	1870
1Sa	9:6	shew us our **w.** that we should go	1870
1Sa	9:8	to the man of God, to tell us our **w.**	1870
1Sa	12:23	teach you the good and the right **w.**	1870
1Sa	13:17	unto the **w.** that leadeth to Ophrah,	1870
1Sa	13:18	turned the **w.** to Beth-horon:	1870
1Sa	13:18	turned to the **w.** of the border that	1870
1Sa	15:2	how he laid wait for him in the **w.**,	1870
1Sa	15:20	gone the **w.** which the Lord sent	1870
1Sa	17:52	fell down by the **w.** to Shaaraim,	1870
1Sa	20:22	arrows are beyond thee; go thy **w.**:	3212
1Sa	24:3	came to the sheepcotes by the **w.**,	1870
1Sa	24:7	out of the cave, and went on his **w.**	1870
1Sa	25:12	David's young men turned their **w.**,	1870
1Sa	26:3	which is before Jeshimon, by the **w.**	1870
1Sa	26:25	So David went on his **w.**, and Saul	1870
1Sa	28:22	strength, when thou goest on thy **w.**	1870
1Sa	30:2	them away, and went on their **w.**	1870
2Sa	2:24	the **w.** of the wilderness of Gibeon.	1870
2Sa	13:30	to pass, while they were in the **w.**	1870
2Sa	13:34	much people by the **w.** of the hill	1870
2Sa	15:2	and stood beside the **w.** of the gate:	1870
2Sa	15:23	toward the **w.** of the wilderness.	1870
2Sa	16:13	David and his men went by the **w.**,	1870
2Sa	18:23	Ahimaaz ran by the **w.** of the plain,	1870
2Sa	19:36	servant will go a little **w.** over Jordan	
2Sa	22:31	As for God, his **w.** is perfect;	1870
2Sa	22:33	and he maketh my **w.** perfect.	1870
1Ki	1:49	rose up, and went every man his **w.**	1870
1Ki	2:2	I go the **w.** of all the earth: be thou	1870
1Ki	2:4	If thy children take heed to their **w.**,	1870
1Ki	8:25	thy children take heed to their **w.**,	1870
1Ki	8:32	to bring his **w.** upon his head;	1870

1Ki	8:36	good **w.** wherein they should walk,	1870
1Ki	11:29	the Shilonite found him in the **w.**;	1870
1Ki	13:9	by the same **w.** that thou camest.	1870
1Ki	13:10	went another **w.**, and returned not	1870
1Ki	13:10	by the **w.** that he came to Beth-el.	1870
1Ki	13:12	said unto them, What **w.** went he?	1870
1Ki	13:12	see what **w.** the man of God went,	1870
1Ki	13:17	to go by the **w.** that thou camest.	1870
1Ki	13:24	a lion met him by the **w.**, and slew	1870
1Ki	13:24	and his carcase was cast in the **w.**,	1870
1Ki	13:25	and saw the carcase cast in the **w.**,	1870
1Ki	13:26	that brought him back from the **w.**	1870
1Ki	13:28	and found his carcase cast in the **w.**,	1870
1Ki	13:33	returned not from his evil **w.**	1870
1Ki	15:26	and walked in the **w.** of his father,	1870
1Ki	15:34	and walked in the **w.** of Jeroboam,	1870
1Ki	16:2	hast walked in the **w.** of Jeroboam,	1870
1Ki	16:19	in walking in the **w.** of Jeroboam,	1870
1Ki	16:26	he walked in all the **w.** of Jeroboam	1870
1Ki	18:6	Ahab went one **w.** by himself,	1870
1Ki	18:6	and Obadiah went another **w.** by	1870
1Ki	18:7	And as Obadiah was in the **w.**,	1870
1Ki	19:15	return on thy **w.** to the wilderness	1870
1Ki	20:38	and waited for the king by the **w.**,	1870
1Ki	22:24	Which **w.** went the Spirit of	2088
1Ki	22:52	and walked in the **w.** of his father,	1870
1Ki	22:52	and in the **w.** of his mother,	1870
1Ki	22:52	and in the **w.** of Jeroboam the son	1870
2Ki	2:23	and as he was going up by the **w.**,	1870
2Ki	3:8	he said, Which **w.** shall we go up?	1870
2Ki	3:8	The **w.** through the wilderness of	1870
2Ki	3:20	there came water by the **w.** of Edom,	1870
2Ki	4:29	take my staff...and go thy **w.**:	
2Ki	5:19	So he departed from him a little **w.**	776
2Ki	6:19	This is not the **w.**, neither is this	1870
2Ki	7:15	all the **w.** was full of garments	1870
2Ki	8:18	in the **w.** of the kings of Israel,	1870
2Ki	8:27	in the **w.** of the house of Ahab,	1870
2Ki	9:27	fled by the **w.** of the garden house.	1870
2Ki	10:12	at the shearing house in the **w.**,	1870
2Ki	11:16	**w.** by the which the horses came	1870
2Ki	11:19	by the **w.** of the gate of the guard	1870
2Ki	16:3	in the **w.** of the kings of Israel,	1870
2Ki	19:28	by the **w.** by which thou camest.	1870
2Ki	19:33	By the **w.** that he came, by the same	1870
2Ki	21:21	walked in all the **w.** that his father	1870
2Ki	21:22	walked not in the **w.** of the Lord	1870
2Ki	22:2	and walked in all the **w.** of David	1870
2Ki	25:4	**w.** of the gate between two walls,	1870
2Ki	25:4	king went the **w.** toward the plain.	1870
2Ch	6:16	thy children take heed to their **w.**	1870
2Ch	6:23	recompensing his **w.** upon his own	1870
2Ch	6:27	thou hast taught them the good **w.**,	1870
2Ch	6:34	by the **w.** that thou shalt send them,	1870
2Ch	11:17	they walked in the **w.** of David and	1870
2Ch	18:23	Which **w.** went the Spirit of the	1870
2Ch	20:32	he walked in the **w.** of Asa his	1870
2Ch	21:6,	13 in the **w.** of the kings of Israel,	1870
Ezr	8:21	to seek of him a right **w.** for us,	1870
Ezr	8:22	us against the enemy in the **w.**	1870
Ezr	8:31	and of such as lay in wait by the **w.**	1870
Ne	8:10	Go your **w.**, eat the fat, and drink the	
Ne	8:12	all the people went their **w.** to eat, and	
Ne	9:12	to give them light in the **w.** wherein	1870
Ne	9:19	them by day, to lead them in the **w.**;	1870
Ne	9:19	and the **w.** wherein they should go.	1870
Es	4:17	So Mordecai went his **w.**, and did	
Job	3:23	given to a man whose **w.** is hid,	1870
Job	6:18	The paths of their **w.** are turned	1870
Job	8:19	Behold, this is the joy of his **w.**,	1870
Job	12:24	a wilderness where there is no **w.**	1870
Job	16:22	go the **w.** whence I shall not return.	734
Job	17:9	righteous...shall hold on his **w.**,	1870
Job	18:10	and a trap for him in the **w.**	5410
Job	19:8	He hath fenced up my **w.** that I	734
Job	19:12	and raise up their **w.** against me,	1870
Job	21:29	not asked them that go by the **w.**?	1870
Job	21:31	Who shall declare his **w.** to his face?	1870
Job	22:15	Hast thou marked the old **w.** which	734
Job	23:10	he knoweth the **w.** that I take:	1870
Job	23:11	his **w.** have I kept, and not	1870
Job	24:4	They turn the needy out of the **w.**	1870
Job	24:18	not the **w.** of the vineyards.	1870
Job	24:24	are taken out of the **w.** as all other,	1870
Job	28:23	God understandeth the **w.** thereof,	1870
Job	28:26	**w.** for the lightning of the thunder:	1870

Job	29:25	I chose out their **w.**, and sat chief,	1870
Job	31:7	my step hath turned out of the **w.**,	1870
Job	36:23	Who hath enjoined him his **w.**?	1870
Job	38:19	is the **w.** where light dwelleth?	1870
Job	38:24	By what **w.** is the light parted,	1870
Job	38:25	a **w.** for the lightning of thunder;	1870
Ps	1:1	nor standeth in the **w.** of sinners,	1870
Ps	1:6	knoweth the **w.** of the righteous:	1870
Ps	1:6	the **w.** of the ungodly shall perish.	1870
Ps	2:12	angry, and ye perish from the **w.**,	1870
Ps	5:8	make thy **w.** straight before my face	1870
Ps	18:30	As for God, his **w.** is perfect:	1870
Ps	18:32	strength, and maketh my **w.** perfect.	1870
Ps	25:8	will he teach sinners in the **w.**	1870
Ps	25:9	and the meek will he teach his **w.**	1870
Ps	25:12	teach in the **w.** that he shall choose.	1870
Ps	27:11	Teach me thy **w.**, O Lord, and lead	1870
Ps	32:8	thee in the **w.** which thou shalt go:	1870
Ps	35:3	and stop the **w.** against them that	
Ps	35:6	Let their **w.** be dark and slippery:	1870
Ps	36:4	himself in a **w.** that is not good;	1870
Ps	37:5	Commit thy **w.** unto the Lord:	1870
Ps	37:7	of him who prospereth in his **w.**,	1870
Ps	37:23	Lord: and he delighteth in his **w.**	1870
Ps	37:34	Wait on the Lord, and keep his **w.**,	1870
Ps	44:18	our steps declined from thy **w.**;	734
Ps	49:13	This their **w.** is their folly: yet	1870
Ps	67:2	thy **w.** may be known upon earth,	1870
Ps	77:13	Thy **w.**, O God, is in the sanctuary:	1870
Ps	77:19	Thy **w.** is in the sea, and thy path	1870
Ps	78:50	He made a **w.** to his anger;	5410
Ps	80:12	they which pass by the **w.** do pluck	1870
Ps	85:13	shall set us in the **w.** of his steps.	1870
Ps	86:11	Teach me thy **w.**, O Lord; I will	1870
Ps	89:41	All that pass by the **w.** spoil him:	1870
Ps	101:2	behave myself wisely in a perfect **w.**	1870
Ps	101:6	he that walketh in a perfect **w.**, he	1870
Ps	102:23	He weakened my strength in the **w.**;	1870
Ps	107:4	in the wilderness in a solitary **w.**;	1870
Ps	107:7	he led them forth by the right **w.**,	1870
Ps	107:40	the wilderness, where there is no **w.**	1870
Ps	110:7	shall drink of the brook in the **w.**:	1870
Ps	119:1	Blessed are the undefiled in the **w.**,	1870
Ps	119:9	shall a young man cleanse his **w.**?	734
Ps	119:14	rejoiced in...**w.** of thy testimonies	1870
Ps	119:27	to understand the **w.** of thy precepts:	1870
Ps	119:29	Remove from me the **w.** of lying:	1870
Ps	119:30	I have chosen the **w.** of truth: thy	1870
Ps	119:32	run the **w.** of thy commandments,	1870
Ps	119:33	Teach me,...the **w.** of thy statutes;	1870
Ps	119:37	and quicken thou me in thy **w.**	1870
Ps	119:101	my feet from every evil **w.**,	734
Ps	119:104	therefore I hate every false **w.**	734
Ps	119:128	be right; and I hate every false **w.**	734
Ps	139:24	if there be any wicked **w.** in me,	1870
Ps	139:24	and lead me in the **w.** everlasting.	1870
Ps	142:3	In the **w.** wherein I walked have	734
Ps	143:8	cause me to know the **w.** wherein	1870
Ps	146:9	**w.** of the wicked he turneth upside	1870
Pr	1:15	walk not thou in the **w.** with them;	1870
Pr	1:31	eat of the fruit of their own **w.**,	1870
Pr	2:8	and preserveth the **w.** of his saints.	1870
Pr	2:12	deliver thee from the **w.** of the evil	1870
Pr	2:20	mayest walk in the **w.** of good men,	1870
Pr	3:23	shalt thou walk in thy **w.** safely,	1870
Pr	4:11	taught thee in the **w.** of wisdom;	1870
Pr	4:14	go not in the **w.** of evil men.	1870
Pr	4:19	**w.** of the wicked is as darkness:	1870
Pr	5:8	Remove thy **w.** far from her, and	1870
Pr	6:23	of instruction are the **w.** of life:	1870
Pr	7:8	and he went the **w.** to her house,	1870
Pr	7:27	Her house is the **w.** to hell, going	1870
Pr	8:2	by the **w.** in the places of the paths.	1870
Pr	8:13	the evil **w.**, and the froward mouth,	1870
Pr	8:20	I lead in the **w.** of righteousness, in	734
Pr	8:22	me in the beginning of his **w.**,	1870
Pr	9:6	and go in the **w.** of understanding.	1870
Pr	10:17	He is in the **w.** of life that keepeth	734
Pr	10:29	The **w.** of the Lord is strength to	1870
Pr	11:5	of the perfect shall direct his **w.**	1870
Pr	11:20	upright in their **w.** are his delight.	1870
Pr	12:15	The **w.** of a fool is right in his own	1870
Pr	12:26	the **w.** of the wicked seduceth them.	1870
Pr	12:28	In the **w.** of righteousness is life;	734
Pr	13:6	him that is upright in the **w.**	1870
Pr	13:15	but the **w.** of transgressors is hard.	1870

Pr 14:8 the prudent is to understand his w. 1870
Pr 14:12 a w. which seemeth right unto a........ 1870
Pr 15:9 w. of the wicked is an abomination..... 1870
Pr 15:10 unto him that forsaketh the w............ 734
Pr 15:19 The w. of the slothful man is............ 1870
Pr 15:19 the w. of the righteous man is made 734
Pr 15:24 The w. of life is above to the wise,....... 734
Pr 16:9 A man's heart deviseth his w.: but..... 1870
Pr 16:17 keepeth his w. preserveth his soul. 1870
Pr 16:25 w. that seemeth right unto a man,....... 1870
Pr 16:29 him into the w. that is not good.......... 1870
Pr 16:31 be found in the w. of righteousness. ... 1870
Pr 19:3 foolishness of man perverteth his w.... 1870
Pr 20:14 but when he is gone his w., then he.........
Pr 20:24 man then understand his own w.?....... 1870
Pr 21:1 Every w. of a man is right in his.......... 1870
Pr 21:8 w. of man is froward and strange: 1870
Pr 21:16 man that wandereth out of the w. of... 1870
Pr 21:29 for the upright, he directeth his w..... 1870
Pr 22:5 snares are in the w. of the froward: ... 1870
Pr 22:6 Train up a child in the w. he should.... 1870
Pr 23:19 and guide thine heart in the w.......... 1870
Pr 26:13 man saith, There is a lion in the w.; ... 1870
Pr 28:10 righteous to go astray in an evil w.,.... 1870
Pr 29:27 and he that is upright in the w. is 1870
Pr 30:19 The w. of an eagle in the air; the....... 1870
Pr 30:19 w. of a serpent upon a rock; the........ 1870
Pr 30:19 w. of a ship in the midst of the sea; ... 1870
Pr 30:19 and the w. of a man with a maid........ 1870
Pr 30:20 Such is the w. of an adulterous.......... 1870
Ec 9:7 Go thy w., eat thy bread with joy, ...
Ec 10:3 he that is a fool walketh by the w., ... 1870
Ec 11:5 not what is the w. of the spirit, ... 1870
Ec 12:5 high, and fears shall be in the w., ... 1870
Ca 1:8 go thy w. forth by the footsteps..............
Isa 3:12 err, and destroy the w. of thy paths. .. 1870
Isa 8:11 not walk in the w. of this people, ... 1870
Isa 9:1 afflict her by the w. of the sea, ... 1870
Isa 15:5 w. of Horonaim they shall raise up 1870
Isa 26:7 The w. of the just is uprightness: 734
Isa 26:8 in the w. of thy judgments, O Lord,...... 734
Isa 28:7 strong drink are out of the w.; 8582
Isa 28:7 of the w. through strong drink;.......... 8582
Isa 30:11 Get you out of the w., turn 1870
Isa 30:21 This is the w., walk ye in it,............. 1870
Isa 35:8 an highway shall be there, and a w.,... 1870
Isa 35:8 shall be called The w. of holiness; 1870
Isa 37:29 the w. by which thou camest............ 1870
Isa 37:34 By the w. that he came, by the......... 1870
Isa 40:3 Prepare ye the w. of the Lord,.......... 1870
Isa 40:14 to him the w. of understanding?......... 1870
Isa 40:27 My w. is hid from the Lord, and my... 1870
Isa 41:3 w. that he had not gone with his 734
Isa 42:16 blind by a w. that they knew not;........ 1870
Isa 43:16 which maketh a w. in the sea, and..... 1870
Isa 43:19 even make a w. in the wilderness, ... 1870
Isa 48:15 he shall make his w. prosperous. 1870
Isa 48:17 by the w. that thou shouldest go........ 1870
Isa 49:11 I will make all my mountains a w., ... 1870
Isa 51:10 a w. for the ransomed to pass over?... 1870
Isa 53:6 turned every one to his own w.;........ 1870
Isa 55:7 Let the wicked forsake his w., and..... 1870
Isa 56:11 they all look to their own w., every.... 1870
Isa 57:10 wearied in the greatness of thy w.; 1870
Isa 57:14 ye up, cast ye up, prepare the w., ... 1870
Isa 57:14 block out of the w. of my people........ 1870
Isa 57:17 on frowardly in the w. of his heart. 1870
Isa 59:8 The w. of peace they knew not; and... 1870
Isa 62:10 prepare ye the w. of the people;......... 1870
Isa 65:2 walketh in a w. that was not good,...... 1870
Jer 2:17 God, when he led thee by the w.? 1870
Jer 2:18 hast thou to do in the w. of Egypt, ... 1870
Jer 2:18 hast thou to do in the w. of Assyria,... 1870
Jer 2:23 see thy w. in the valley, know what ... 1870
Jer 2:33 trimmest thou thy w. to seek love? ... 1870
Jer 2:36 about so much to change thy w.? 1870
Jer 3:21 for they have perverted their w., ... 1870
Jer 4:7 of the Gentiles is on his w.;............. 5265
Jer 4:18 Thy w. and thy doings have.............. 1870
Jer 5:4 they know not the w. of the Lord, ... 1870
Jer 5:5 they have known the w. of the Lord,.. 1870
Jer 6:16 the old paths, where is the good w.,... 1870
Jer 6:25 into the field, nor walk by the w.; 1870
Jer 6:27 thou mayest know and try their w....... 1870
Jer 10:2 Learn not the w. of the heathen, ... 1870
Jer 10:23 that the w. of man is not in himself: ... 1870
Jer 12:1 doth the w. of the wicked prosper? 1870
Jer 18:11 ye now every one from his evil w., ... 1870
Jer 18:15 walk in paths, in a w. not cast up;...... 1870
Jer 21:8 the w. of life, and the w. of death...... 1870
Jer 23:12 their w. shall be unto them as.......... 1870
Jer 23:22 have turned them from their evil w.,... 1870
Jer 25:5 now every one from his evil w., ... 1870
Jer 25:35 shepherds shall have no w. to flee,..... 4498
Jer 26:3 turn every man from his evil w.,......... 1870
Jer 28:11 the prophet Jeremiah went his w........ 1870
Jer 31:9 the rivers of waters in a straight w.,... 1870
Jer 31:21 even the w. which thou wentest: 1870
Jer 32:39 give them one heart, and one w.,....... 1870
Jer 35:15 ye now every man from his evil w.,.... 1870
Jer 36:3 return every man from his evil w.; 1870
Jer 36:7 return every one from his evil w.:...... 1870
Jer 39:4 by the w. of the king's garden, by...... 1870
Jer 39:4 and he went out the w. of the plain. ... 1870
Jer 42:3 God may shew us the w. wherein 1870
Jer 48:19 of Aroer, stand by the w., and espy; .. 1870
Jer 50:5 They shall ask the w. to Zion with 1870
Jer 52:7 w. of the gate between the...walls,..... 1870
Jer 52:7 they went by the w. of the plain. 1870
Eze 3:18 the wicked from his wicked w., ... 1870
Eze 3:19 nor from his wicked w., he shall die ... 1870
Eze 7:27 I will do unto them after their w., ... 1870
Eze 8:5 eyes now the w. toward the north....... 1870
Eze 8:5 mine eyes the w. toward the north,.... 1870
Eze 9:2 from the w. of the higher gate,.......... 1870
Eze 9:10 I will recompense their w. upon......... 1870
Eze 11:21 I will recompense their w. upon......... 1870
Eze 13:22 not return from his wicked w., ... 1870
Eze 14:22 shall see their w. and their doings:..... 1870
Eze 16:25 high place at every head of the w.,..... 1870
Eze 16:27 which are ashamed of thy lewd w....... 1870
Eze 16:31 place in the head of every w.,........... 1870
Eze 16:43 I also will recompense thy w. upon...... 1870
Eze 18:25 say, The w. of the Lord is not equal... 1870
Eze 18:25 Is not my w. equal? are not your....... 1870
Eze 18:29 The w. of the Lord is not equal. 1870
Eze 21:16 Go thee one w. or other, either on..........
Eze 21:19 it at the head of the w. to the city. 1870
Eze 21:20 Appoint a w., that the sword may 1870
Eze 21:21 stood at the parting of the w.,........... 1870
Eze 22:31 their own w. have I recompensed........ 1870
Eze 23:13 defiled, that they took both one w.,.... 1870
Eze 23:31 hast walked in the w. of thy sister; 1870
Eze 33:8 to warn the wicked from his w., ... 1870
Eze 33:9 warn the wicked of his w. to turn 1870
Eze 33:9 if he do not turn from his w., he........ 1870
Eze 33:11 that the wicked turn from his w......... 1870
Eze 33:17 The w. of the Lord is not equal: 1870
Eze 33:17 as for them, their w. is not equal....... 1870
Eze 33:20 The w. of the Lord is not equal. 1870
Eze 36:17 defiled it by their own w. and by........ 1870
Eze 36:17 their w. was before me as the........... 1870
Eze 36:19 according to their w. and according..... 1870
Eze 42:1 court, the w. toward the north: 1870
Eze 42:4 breadth inward, a w. of one cubit;...... 1870
Eze 42:11 And the w. before them was like the .. 1870
Eze 42:12 was a door in the head of the w., ... 1870
Eze 42:12 even the w. directly before the wall.... 1870
Eze 43:2 Israel came from the w. of the east: ... 1870
Eze 43:4 into the house by the w. of the gate... 1870
Eze 44:1 brought me back the w. of the gate.... 1870
Eze 44:3 enter by the w. of the porch of that ... 1870
Eze 44:3 shall go out by the w. of the same. 1870
Eze 44:4 he me the w. of the north gate.......... 1870
Eze 46:2 shall enter by the w. of the porch 1870
Eze 46:8 by the w. of the porch of that gate,..... 1870
Eze 46:8 he shall go forth by the w. thereof. 1870
Eze 46:9 in by the w. of the north gate 1870
Eze 46:9 out by the w. of the south gate; 1870
Eze 46:9 entereth by the w. of the south gate... 1870
Eze 46:9 forth by the w. of the north gate: 1870
Eze 46:9 not return by the w. of the gate 1870
Eze 47:2 out of the w. of the gate northward,... 1870
Eze 47:2 and led me about the w. without........ 1870
Eze 47:2 by the w. that looketh eastward;........ 1870
Eze 47:15 the w. of Hethlon, as men go to 1870
Eze 48:1 to the coast of the w. of Hethlon, ... 1870
Da 12:9 And he said, Go thy w., Daniel: for..........
Da 12:13 go thou thy w. till the end be: for thou .....
Ho 2:6 I will hedge up thy w. with thorns,..... 1870
Ho 6:9 of priests murder in the w. by........... 1870
Ho 10:13 because thou didst trust in thy w., ... 1870
Ho 13:7 as a leopard by the w. will I observe .. 1870
Am 2:7 and turn aside the w. of the meek:..... 1870
Jon 3:8 turn every one from his evil w., ... 1870
Jon 3:10 that they turned from their evil w.; 1870
Na 1:3 Lord hath his w. in the whirlwind....... 1870
Na 2:1 watch the w., make thy loins strong, .. 1870
Zec 10:2 they went their w. as a flock, they..........
Mal 2:8 But ye are departed out of the w.;..... 1870
Mal 3:1 he shall prepare the w. before me:..... 1870
Mt 2:12 into their own country another w.. 3598
Mt 3:3 Prepare ye the w. of the Lord,.......... 3598
Mt 4:15 by the w. of the sea, beyond Jordan, .. 3598
Mt 5:24 **gift before the altar, and go thy w.;....**
Mt 5:25 **whiles thou art in the w. with him;**3598
Mt 7:13 **broad is the w., that leadeth to.....** 3598
Mt 7:14 **narrow is the w., which leadeth....** 3598
Mt 8:4 **but go thy w., shew thyself to the.......**
Mt 8:13 said unto the centurion, **Go thy w.;..........**
Mt 8:28 no man might pass by that w.. 3598
Mt 8:30 a good w. off from them an herd........ 3112
Mt 10:5 **Go not into the w. of the Gentiles,**.3598
Mt 11:10 **shall prepare thy w. before thee.....** 3598
Mt 13:4 **some seeds fell by the w. side,......** 3598
Mt 13:19 **which received seed by the w. side.** 3598
Mt 13:25 **sowed tares...and went his w...............**
Mt 15:32 **fastings, lest they faint in the w..** 3598
Mt 20:4 **give you. And they went their w..........**
Mt 20:14 **Take that thine is, and go thy w..........**
Mt 20:17 twelve disciples apart in the w.,......... 3598
Mt 20:30 blind men sitting by the w. side, ... 3598
Mt 21:8 spread their garments in the w.; 3598
Mt 21:8 trees, and strawed them in the w....... 3598
Mt 21:19 when he saw a fig tree in the w., ... 3598
Mt 21:32 **came...in the w. of righteousness,**..3598
Mt 22:16 and teachest the w. of God in truth, ... 3598
Mt 22:22 and left him, and went their w...............
Mt 27:65 go your w., make it as sure as ye can. .....
Mk 1:2 shall prepare thy w. before thee. 3598
Mk 1:3 Prepare ye the w. of the Lord,.......... 3598
Mk 1:44 **but go thy w., shew thyself to the.......**
Mk 2:11 **bed, and go thy w. into thine house.....**
Mk 4:4 **he sowed, some fell by the w. side,**.3598
Mk 4:15 **And these are they by the w. side,**..3598
Mk 7:29 unto her, **For this saying go thy w.;.....**
Mk 8:3 **houses, they will faint by the w....** 3598
Mk 8:27 by the w. he asked his disciples,......... 3598
Mk 9:33 **it that ye disputed...by the w.?......** 3598
Mk 9:34 by the w. they had disputed among 3598
Mk 10:17 when he was gone forth into the w.,... 3598
Mk 10:21 **go thy w., sell whatsoever thou hast,...**
Mk 10:32 in the w. going up to Jerusalem; 3598
Mk 10:52 **Go thy w.; thy faith hath made thee....**
Mk 10:52 and followed Jesus in the w............... 3598
Mk 11:2 **Go your w. into the village over.........**
Mk 11:4 they went their w., and found the colt.......
Mk 11:8 spread their garments in the w......... 3598
Mk 11:8 trees, and strawed them in the w......... 3598
Mk 12:12 and they left him, and went their w.. ....
Mk 12:14 teachest the w. of God in truth:......... 3598
Mk 16:7 But go your w., tell his disciples and ....
Lu 1:79 guide our feet into the w. of peace..... 3598
Lu 3:4 Prepare ye the w. of the Lord,........... 3598
Lu 4:30 through the midst of them went his w.,.....
Lu 5:19 find by what w. they might bring him........
Lu 7:22 **your w., and tell John what things......**
Lu 7:27 **shall prepare thy w. before thee....** 3598
Lu 8:5 **he sowed, some fell by the w. side;**.3598
Lu 8:12 **by the w. side are they that hear;..** 3598
Lu 8:39 And he went his w., and published..... 3598
Lu 9:57 as they went in the w., a certain 3598
Lu 10:4 **and salute no man by the w..........** 3598
Lu 10:31 **down a certain priest that w.........** 3598
Lu 12:58 **thou art in the w., give diligence...** 3598
Lu 14:32 **the other is yet a great w. off.......** 4206
Lu 15:20 **when he was yet a great w. off,....** 3112
Lu 17:19 **Arise, go thy w.: thy faith hath..........**
Lu 18:35 blind man sat by the w. side 3598
Lu 19:4 to see him: for he was to pass that w.. .....
Lu 19:32 And they that were sent went their w.,.....
Lu 19:36 they spread their clothes in the w.. 3598
Lu 20:21 but teachest the w. of God truly: 3598
Lu 22:4 he went his w., and communed with.........
Lu 24:32 while he talked with us by the w.,....... 3598
Lu 24:35 what things were done in the w.,........ 3598
Joh 1:23 Make straight the w. of the Lord, ... 3598
Joh 4:28 and went her w. into the city, ...
Joh 4:50 unto him, **Go thy w.; thy son liveth......**
Joh 4:50 spoken unto him, and he went his w........
Joh 8:21 **I go my w., and ye shall seek me,.......**

Joh 9:7 He went his w. therefore, and washed,
Joh 10:1 **but climbeth up some other w.,**
Joh 11:28 when she had so said, she went her w.,
Joh 14:4 **I go ye know, and the w. ye know** *3598*
Joh 14:5 and how can we know the w.? *3598*
Joh 14:6 **I am the w., the truth, and the** *3598*
Joh 16:5 **I go my w. to him that sent me;**
Joh 18:8 **ye seek me, let these go their w.**
Ac 8:26 w. that goeth...from Jerusalem *3598*
Ac 8:36 as they went on their w., they came *3598*
Ac 8:39 and he went on his w. rejoicing. *3598*
Ac 9:2 that if he found any of this w., *3598*
Ac 9:15 **Go thy w.: for he is a chosen**
Ac 9:17 Ananias went his w., and entered into
Ac 9:17 that appeared unto thee in the w. *3598*
Ac 9:27 how he had seen the Lord in the w., *3598*
Ac 15:3 brought on their w. by the church, *4311*
Ac 16:17 shew unto us the w. of salvation. *3598*
Ac 18:25 instructed in the w. of the Lord; *3598*
Ac 18:26 him the w. of God more perfectly. *3598*
Ac 19:9 but spake evil of that w. before the *3598*
Ac 19:23 arose no small stir about that w. *3598*
Ac 21:5 we departed and went our w.; *4311*
Ac 21:5 and they all brought us on our w., *4311*
Ac 22:4 persecuted this w. unto the death, *3598*
Ac 24:14 after the w. which they call heresy, *3598*
Ac 24:22 more perfect knowledge of that w., *3598*
Ac 24:25 answered, Go thy w. for this time;
Ac 25:3 laying wait in the w. to kill him. *3598*
Ac 26:13 I saw in the w. a light from heaven, *3598*
Ro 3:2 Much every w.: chiefly, because *5158*
Ro 3:12 They are all gone out of the w., they
Ro 3:17 w. of peace have they not known: *3598*
Ro 14:13 an occasion to fall in his brother's w.
Ro 15:24 be brought on my w. thitherward *4311*
1Co 10:13 temptation...make a w. to escape, *1545*
1Co 12:31 I unto you a more excellent w. *3598*
1Co 16:7 I will not see you now by the w.; *3938*
2Co 1:16 brought on my w. toward Judaea. *4311*
Php 1:18 every w., whether in pretence, or *5158*
Col 2:14 took it out of the w., nailing it to *3319*
1Th 3:11 Christ, direct our w. unto you. *3598*
2Th 2:7 until he be taken out of the w. *3319*
Heb 5:2 on them that are out of the w.; *4105*
Heb 9:8 the w. into the holiest of all was *3598*
Heb 10:20 By a new and living w., which he *3598*
Heb 12:13 is lame be turned out of the w.; *1624*
Jas 1:24 beholdeth himself, and goeth his w., *1624*
Jas 2:25 had sent them out another w.? *3598*
Jas 5:20 the sinner from the error of his w. *3598*
2Pe 2:2 w. of truth shall be evil spoken of. *3598*
2Pe 2:15 Which have forsaken the right w., *3598*
2Pe 2:15 following the w. of Balaam the son *3598*
2Pe 2:21 known the w. of righteousness, *3598*
2Pe 3:1 minds by w. of remembrance: *1722*
Jude 11 they have gone in the w. of Cain, *3598*
Re 16:12 the w. of the kings of the east. *3598*

WAYFARING

Jg 19:17 he saw a w. man in the street of 732
2Sa 12:4 the w. man that was come unto him; 732
Isa 33:8 lie waste, the w. man ceaseth: 5674,734
Isa 35:8 the w. men, though fools, 1980,1870
Jer 9:2 a lodging place of w. men; 732
Jer 14:8 as a w. man that turneth aside to 732

WAYMARKS

Jer 31:21 Set thee up w., make thee high 6725

WAYS See also ALWAYS; HIGHWAYS.

Ge 19:2 rise up early, and go on your w. 1870
Le 20:4 people...do any w. hide their eyes
Le 26:22 your high w. shall be desolate. 1870
Nu 30:15 if he shall any w. make them void
De 5:33 walk in all the w. which the Lord 1870
De 8:6 to walk in his w., and to fear him. 1870
De 10:12 to walk in all his w., and to love 1870
De 11:22 to walk in all his w., and to cleave 1870
De 19:9 thy God, and to walk ever in his w.; 1870
De 26:17 to walk in his w., and to keep his 1870
De 28:7 way, and flee before thee seven w. 1870
De 28:9 Lord thy God, and walk in his w. 1870
De 28:25 and flee seven w. before them: 1870
De 28:29 thou shalt not prosper in thy w. 1870
De 30:16 to walk in his w., and to keep his 1870
De 32:4 for all his w. are judgment: 1870
Jos 22:5 to walk in all his w., and to keep 1870
1Sa 8:3 And his sons walked not in his w., 1870
1Sa 8:5 and thy sons walk not in thy w.: 1870
1Sa 18:14 behaved...wisely in all his w.; 1870
2Sa 22:22 For I have kept the w. of the Lord, 1870
1Ki 2:3 God, to walk in his w., to keep his 1870
1Ki 3:14 And if thou wilt walk in my w., to 1870
1Ki 8:39 to every man according to his w., 1870
1Ki 8:58 to walk in all his w., and to keep 1870
1Ki 11:33 and have not walked in my w., to do 1870
1Ki 11:38 and wilt walk in my w., and do that 1870
1Ki 22:43 he walked in all the w. of Asa his 1870
2Ki 17:13 Turn ye from your evil w., and 1870
2Ch 6:30 every man according unto all his w., 1870
2Ch 6:31 to walk in thy w., so long as they 1870
2Ch 7:14 and turn from their wicked w.; 1870
2Ch 13:22 acts of Abijah, and his w., and his 1870
2Ch 17:3 in the first w. of his father David, 1870
2Ch 17:6 was lifted up in the w. of the Lord: 1870
2Ch 21:12 walked in the w. of Jehoshaphat 1870
2Ch 21:12 nor in the w. of Asa king of Judah, 1870
2Ch 22:3 in the w. of the house of Ahab: 1870
2Ch 27:6 prepared his w. before the Lord 1870
2Ch 27:7 acts of Jotham,...and his w., 1870
2Ch 28:2 in the w. of the kings of Israel, 1870
2Ch 28:26 the rest of his acts and of all his w., 1870
2Ch 32:13 any w. able to deliver their lands
2Ch 34:2 and walked in the w. of David his 1870
Job 4:6 and the uprightness of thy w.? 1870
Job 13:15 maintain mine own w. before him. 1870
Job 21:14 desire not the knowledge of thy w. 1870
Job 22:3 that thou makest thy w. perfect? 1870
Job 22:28 the light shall shine upon thy w. 1870
Job 24:13 they know not the w. thereof, nor 1870
Job 24:23 yet his eyes are upon their w. 1870
Job 26:14 these are parts of his w.: but how 1870
Job 30:12 me the w. of their destruction. 734
Job 31:4 Doth not he see my w., and count 1870
Job 34:11 man to find according to his w. 734
Job 34:21 his eyes are upon the w. of man, 1870
Job 34:27 would not consider any of his w.: 1870
Job 40:19 He is the chief of the w. of God: 1870
Ps 10:5 His w. are always grievous; 1870
Ps 18:21 For I have kept the w. of the Lord, 1870
Ps 25:4 Shew me thy w., O Lord; teach me 1870
Ps 39:1 I said, I will take heed to my w., 1870
Ps 51:13 will I teach transgressors thy w.; 1870
Ps 81:13 and Israel had walked in my w.! 1870
Ps 84:5 in whose heart are the w. of them. 4546
Ps 91:11 thee, to keep thee in all thy w. 1870
Ps 95:10 and they have not known my w. 1870
Ps 103:7 He made known his w. unto Moses, 1870
Ps 119:3 do no iniquity: they walk in his w. 1870
Ps 119:5 O that my w. were directed to keep 1870
Ps 119:15 and have respect unto thy w. 734
Ps 119:26 I have declared my w., and thou 1870
Ps 119:59 I thought on my w., and turned my 1870
Ps 119:168 for all my w. are before thee. 1870
Ps 125:5 as turn aside unto their crooked w.,
Ps 128:1 the Lord; that walketh in his w. 1870
Ps 138:5 shall sing in the w. of the Lord: 1870
Ps 139:3 and art acquainted with all my w. 1870
Ps 145:17 The Lord is righteous in all his w., 1870
Pr 1:19 the w. of every one that is greedy of 734
Pr 2:13 to walk in the w. of darkness; 1870
Pr 2:15 Whose w. are crooked, and they 734
Pr 3:6 In all thy w. acknowledge him, 1870
Pr 3:17 Her w. are w. of pleasantness, and 1870
Pr 3:31 and choose none of his w. 1870
Pr 4:26 and let all thy w. be established. 1870
Pr 5:6 path of life, her w. are moveable, 4570
Pr 5:21 the w. of man are before the eyes 1870
Pr 6:6 consider her w., and be wise: 1870
Pr 7:25 not thine heart decline to her w., 1870
Pr 8:32 blessed are they that keep my w. 1870
Pr 9:15 passengers...go right on their w. 734
Pr 10:9 he that perverteth his w. shall be 1870
Pr 14:2 but he that is perverse in his w. 1870
Pr 14:12 the end thereof are the w. of death. 1870
Pr 14:14 shall be filled with his own w.: 1870
Pr 16:2 All the w. of a man are clean in his 1870
Pr 16:7 When a man's w. please the Lord, 1870
Pr 16:25 the end thereof are the w. of death. 1870
Pr 17:23 to pervert the w. of judgment. 734
Pr 19:16 he that despiseth his w. shall die. 1870
Pr 22:25 Lest thou learn his w., and get a 734
Pr 23:26 and let thine eyes observe my w. 1870
Pr 28:6 than he that is perverse in his w., 1870
Pr 28:18 that is perverse in his w. shall fall 1870
Pr 31:3 nor thy w. to that which destroyeth 1870
Pr 31:27 well to the w. of her household, 1979
Ec 11:9 and walk in the w. of thine heart, 1870
Ca 3:2 in the broad w. I will seek him 7339
Isa 2:3 and he will teach us of his w., and 1870
Isa 42:24 for they would not walk in his w., 1870
Isa 45:13 and I will direct all his w. 1870
Isa 49:9 They shall feed in the w., and their 1870
Isa 55:8 neither are your w. my w., saith 1870
Isa 55:9 so are my w. higher than your w., 1870
Isa 57:18 I have seen his w., and will heal 1870
Isa 58:2 daily, and delight to know my w., 1870
Isa 58:13 not doing thine own w., nor finding 1870
Isa 63:17 thou made us to err from thy w., 1870
Isa 64:5 that remember thee in thy w.: 1870
Isa 66:3 they have chosen their own w., and 1870
Jer 2:23 swift dromedary traversing her w.; 1870
Jer 2:33 also taught the wicked ones thy w. 1870
Jer 3:2 In the w. hast thou sat for them, as 1870
Jer 3:13 scattered thy w. to the strangers 1870
Jer 6:16 Stand ye in the w., and see, and ask 1870
Jer 7:3 Amend your w. and your doings, 1870
Jer 7:5 amend your w. and your doings; 1870
Jer 7:23 walk ye in all the w. that I have 1870
Jer 12:16 diligently learn the w. of my people, 1870
Jer 15:7 since they return not from their w. 1870
Jer 16:17 For mine eyes are upon all their w. 1870
Jer 17:10 give every man according to his w., 1870
Jer 18:11 and make your w. and your doings 1870
Jer 18:15 caused them to stumble in their w. 1870
Jer 23:12 as slippery w. in the darkness:
Jer 26:13 amend your w. and your doings, 1870
Jer 32:19 upon all the w. of the sons of men: 1870
Jer 32:19 give every one according to his w., 1870
La 1:4 The w. of Zion do mourn, because 1870
La 3:9 inclosed my w. with hewn stone, 1870
La 3:11 He hath turned aside my w., and 1870
La 3:40 Let us search and try our w., and 1870
Eze 7:3 will judge thee according to thy w., 1870
Eze 7:4 will recompense thy w. upon thee, 1870
Eze 7:8 will judge thee according to thy w., 1870
Eze 7:9 recompense thee according to thy w. 1870
Eze 14:23 ye see their w. and their doings: 1870
Eze 16:47 hast thou not walked after their w., 1870
Eze 16:47 more than they in all thy w. 1870
Eze 16:61 Then thou shalt remember thy w., 1870
Eze 18:23 that he should return from his w., 1870
Eze 18:25 equal? are not your w. unequal? 1870
Eze 18:29 of Israel, are not my w. equal? 1870
Eze 18:29 are not your w. unequal? 1870
Eze 18:30 every one according to his w., 1870
Eze 20:43 there shall ye remember your w., 1870
Eze 20:44 not according to your wicked w., 1870
Eze 21:19 son of man, appoint thee two w., 1870
Eze 21:21 at the head of the two w., to use 1870
Eze 24:14 according to thy w., and according 1870
Eze 28:15 Thou wast perfect in thy w. from 1870
Eze 33:11 turn ye, turn ye from your evil w.; 1870
Eze 33:20 will judge you every one after his w. 1870
Eze 36:31 ye remember your own evil w., 1870
Eze 36:32 and confounded for your own w., 1870
Da 4:37 are truth, and his w. judgment: 735
Da 5:23 whose are all thy w., hast thou not 735
Ho 4:9 I will punish them for their w., 1870
Ho 9:8 is a snare of a fowler in all his w., 1870
Ho 12:2 punish Jacob according to his w.; 1870
Ho 14:9 for the w. of the Lord are right, and 1870
Joe 2:7 shall march every one on his w., 1870
Mic 4:2 he will teach us of his w., and we 1870
Na 2:4 against another in the broad w.:
Hab 3:6 did bow: his w. are everlasting. 1979
Hag 1:5, 7 Lord of hosts; Consider your w. 1870
Zec 1:4 Turn ye now from your evil w., 1870
Zec 1:6 to do unto us, according to our w., 1870
Zec 3:7 If thou wilt walk in my w., and if 1870
Mal 2:9 as ye have not kept my w., but 1870
Mt 8:33 fled, and went their w. into the city,
Mt 22:5 **made light of it, and went their w**
Mk 11:4 in a place where two w. met; *296*
Lu 1:76 face of the Lord to prepare his w.; *3598*
Lu 3:5 the rough w. shall be made smooth: *3598*
Lu 10:3 **Go your w.: behold, I send you forth**
Lu 10:10 **go your w. out into the streets of**
Joh 11:46 them went their w. to the Pharisees,
Ac 2:28 made known to me the w. of life; *3598*

Ac 13:10 not cease to pervert the right w. of.... *3598*
Ac 14:16 all nations to walk in their own w....... *3598*
Ro 3:16 and misery are in their w.:............... *3598*
Ro 11:33 and his w. past finding out!.............. *3598*
1Co 4:17 of my w. which be in Christ,.............. *3598*
Heb 3:10 and they have not known my w......... *3598*
Jas 1:8 man is unstable in all his w.............. *3598*
Jas 1:11 the rich man fade away in his w.......... *4197*
2Pe 2:2 shall follow their pernicious w.;............ *684*
Re 15:3 just and true are thy w., thou King..... *3598*
Re 16:1 Go your w., and pour out the vials of.......

WAYSIDE See also WAY and SIDE.
1Sa 4:13 Eli sat upon a seat by the w. 3197,1870
Ps 140:5 have spread a net by the w.; 3027,4570

WE See in the APPENDIX; also OUR; US.

WEAK See also WEAKER.
Nu 13:18 whether they be strong or w.,........... 7504
Jg 16:7, 11 then shall I be w., and be as.......... 2470
Jg 16:17 I shall become w., and be like any...... 2470
2Sa 3:39 And I am this day w., though............ 7390
2Sa 17:2 while he is weary and w. handed,....... 7504
2Ch 15:7 and let not your hands be w.:............. 7503
Job 4:3 hast strengthened the w. hands. 7504
Ps 6:2 upon me, O Lord; for I am w.:........... 536
Ps 109:24 My knees are w. through fasting;....... 3782
Isa 14:10 Art thou also become w. as we?......... 2470
Isa 35:3 Strengthen ye the w. hands, and......... 7504
Eze 7:17 all knees shall be w. as water............ 3212
Eze 16:30 How w. is thine heart, saith the.......... 535
Eze 21:7 all knees shall be w. as water:........... 3212
Joe 3:10 let the w. say, I am strong.............. 2523
Mt 26:41 **is willing, but the flesh is w.**......... *772*
Mk 14:38 **truly is ready, but the flesh is w.**..... *772*
Ac 20:35 ye ought to support the w.,............... *770*
Ro 4:19 being not w. in faith, he considered...... *770*
Ro 8:3 in that it was w. through the flesh, ... *770*
Ro 14:1 Him that is w. in the faith receive......... *770*
Ro 14:2 another, who is w., eateth herbs. *770*
Ro 14:21 or is offended, or is made w............... *770*
Ro 15:1 to bear the infirmities of the w.,.......... *102*
1Co 1:27 chosen the w. things of the world........ *772*
1Co 4:10 we are w., but ye are strong;............ *772*
1Co 8:7 their conscience being w. is defiled. *772*
1Co 8:9 stumblingblock to them that are w.. ..... *770*
1Co 8:10 the conscience of him which is w......... *772*
1Co 8:11 shall the w. brother perish, ... *770*
1Co 8:12 and wound their w. conscience,........... *770*
1Co 9:22 To the w. became I as w.,................. *770*
1Co 9:22 that I might gain the w.: I am............. *770*
1Co 11:30 many are w. and sickly among you,...... *770*
2Co 10:10 but his bodily presence is w., and........ *770*
2Co 11:21 as though we had been w.................. *770*
2Co 11:29 Who is w., and I am not w.? who is *770*
2Co 12:10 for when I am w., then am I strong. *770*
2Co 13:3 which to you-ward is not w., but is....... *770*
2Co 13:4 For we also are w. in him, but we....... *770*
2Co 13:9 when we are w., and ye are strong:...... *770*
Ga 4:9 to the w. and beggarly elements,......... *772*
1Th 5:14 support the w., be patient toward........ *772*

WEAKEN See also WEAKENED; WEAKENETH.
Isa 14:12 which didst w. the nations! 2522

WEAKENED
Ezr 4:4 w. the hands of...people of Judah, ... 7503
Ne 6:9 hands shall be w. from the work, ... 7503
Ps 102:23 He w. my strength in the way; he...... 6031

WEAKENETH
Job 12:21 w. the strength of the mighty............ 7503
Jer 38:4 he w. the hands of the men of war..... 7503

WEAKER
2Sa 3:1 house of Saul waxed w. and w.. 1800
1Pe 3:7 the wife, as unto the w. vessel, ... *772*

WEAK-HANDED See WEAK and HANDED.

WEAKNESS
1Co 1:25 w. of God is stronger than men........... *772*
1Co 2:3 I was with you in w., and in fear,........ *769*
1Co 15:43 it is sown in w.; it is raised in power: .. *769*
2Co 12:9 **my strength is made perfect in w.**.... *769*
2Co 13:4 though he was crucified through w.,...... *769*
Heb 7:18 for the w. and unprofitableness............ *772*
Heb 11:34 out of w. were made strong, ... *769*

WEALTH See also COMMONWEALTH.
Ge 34:29 their w., and all their little ones, ... 2428
De 8:17 mine hand hath gotten me this w.. 2428
De 8:18 he that giveth thee power to get w., .. 2428
Ru 2:1 a mighty man of w., of the family....... 2428
1Sa 2:32 the w. which God shall give Israel: ....
2Ki 15:20 even of all the mighty men of w.,........ 2428
2Ch 1:11 not asked riches, w., or honour, ... 5233
2Ch 1:12 I will give thee riches, and w., and..... 5233
Ezr 9:12 nor seek their peace or their w. 2896
Es 10:3 seeking the w. of his people, and....... 2896
Job 21:13 They spend their days in w., and in.... 2896
Job 31:25 rejoiced because my w. was great, ... 2428
Ps 44:12 not increase thy w. by their price...........
Ps 49:6 They that trust in their w., and 2428
Ps 49:10 perish, and leave their w. to others. .. 2428
Ps 112:3 W. and riches...be in his house:......... 1952
Pr 5:10 strangers be filled with thy w.;.......... 3581
Pr 10:15 rich man's w. is his strong city: 1952
Pr 13:11 W. gotten by vanity shall be.............. 1952
Pr 13:22 the w. of the sinner is laid up for........ 2428
Pr 18:11 rich man's w. is his strong city, ... 1952
Pr 19:4 W. maketh many friends; but the......... 1952
Ec 5:19 God hath given riches and w., ... 5233
Ec 6:2 to whom God hath given riches, w., ... 5233
Zec 14:14 w. of all the heathen round about....... 2428
Ac 19:25 that by this craft we have our w.. ...... *2142*
1Co 10:24 his own, but every one another's w.........

WEALTHY
Ps 66:12 broughtest us out into a w. place. 7310
Jer 49:31 get you up unto the w. nation, ... 7961

WEANED
Ge 21:8 And the child grew and was w.:......... 1580
Ge 21:8 the same day that Isaac was w. 1580
1Sa 1:22 will not go up until the child be w., ... 1580
1Sa 1:23 tarry until thou have w. him;............. 1580
1Sa 1:23 gave her son suck until she w. him..... 1580
1Sa 1:24 And when she had w. him, she.......... 1580
1Ki 11:20 Tahpenes w. in Pharaoh's house: 1580
Ps 131:2 as a child that is w. of his mother: 1580
Ps 131:2 my soul is even as a w. child,............ 1580
Isa 11:8 w. child shall put his hand on the 1580
Isa 28:9 them that are w. from the milk,.......... 1580
Ho 1:8 Now when she had w. Lo-ruhamah, ... 1580

WEAPON See also WEAPONS.
Nu 35:18 smite him with an hand w. of............ 3627
De 23:13 shalt have a paddle upon thy w.; 240
2Ch 23:10 man having his w. in his hand,........... 7973
Ne 4:17 and with the other hand held a w. 7973
Job 20:24 He shall flee from the iron w., and..... 5402
Isa 54:17 No w. that is formed against thee 3627
Eze 9:1 with his destroying w. in his hand. 3627
Eze 9:2 man a slaughter w. in his hand; 3627

WEAPONS
Ge 27:3 therefore take, I pray thee, thy w.,.... 3627
De 1:41 girded on every man his w. of war,..... 3627
Jg 18:11 six hundred men appointed with w........ 3627
Jg 18:16 men appointed with their w. of war, ... 3627
Jg 18:17 that were appointed with w. of war. ... 3627
1Sa 21:8 my sword nor my w. with me, ... 3627
2Sa 1:27 fallen, and the w. of war perished! 3627
2Ki 11:8 every man with his w. in his hand: 3627
2Ki 11:11 every man with his w. in his hand,...... 3627
2Ch 23:7 every man with his w. in his hand; 3627
Ec 9:18 Wisdom is better that w. of war: 3627
Isa 13:5 and the w. of his indignation, to.......... 3627
Jer 21:4 I will turn back the w. of war that........ 3627
Jer 22:7 against thee, every one with his w.: ... 3627
Jer 50:25 forth the w. of his indignation: 3627
Jer 51:20 art my battle axe and w. of war:......... 3627
Eze 32:27 down to hell with their w. of war: 3627
Eze 39:9 shall set on fire and burn the w., ... 5402
Eze 39:10 for they shall burn the w. with fire: 5402
Joh 18:3 with lanterns and torches and w......... *3696*
2Co 10:4 w. of our warfare are not carnal,........ *3696*

WEAR See also WARE; WEARETH; WEARING.
Ex 18:18 Thou wilt surely w. away, both.......... 5034
De 22:5 woman shall not w. that which........... 1961
De 22:11 not w. a garment of divers sorts,......... 3847
1Sa 2:28 incense, to w. an ephod before me?.... 5375
1Sa 22:18 persons that did w. a linen ephod....... 5375
Es 6:8 brought which the king useth to w.,..... 3847
Job 14:19 The waters w. the stones: thou......... 7833
Isa 4:1 bread, and w. our own apparel: 3847
Da 7:25 w. out the saints of the most High, ... 1080
Zec 13:4 w. a rough garment to deceive: 3847
Mt 11:8 **they that w. soft clothing are in**.... *5409*
Lu 9:12 when the day began to w. away,......... *2827*

WEARETH
Jas 2:3 to him that w. the gay clothing, ... *5409*

WEARIED
Ge 19:11 w. themselves to find the door. 3811
Isa 43:23 offering, nor w. thee with incense. 3021
Isa 43:24 hast w. me with thine iniquities.......... 3021
Isa 47:13 Thou art w. in the multitude of.......... 3811
Isa 57:10 w. in the greatness of thy way: 3021
Jer 4:31 soul is w. because of murderers......... 5888
Jer 12:5 and they have w. thee, then how 3811
Jer 12:5 thou trustedst, they w. thee,....................
Eze 24:12 She hath w. herself with lies, and....... 3811
Mic 6:3 wherein have I w. thee? testify........... 3811
Mal 2:17 w. the Lord with your words. 3021
Mal 2:17 ye say, Wherein have we w. him?...... 3021
Joh 4:6 being w. with his journey, sat............ *2872*
Heb 12:3 ye be w. and faint in your minds. *2577*

WEARIETH
Job 37:11 by watering he w. the thick cloud:...... 2959
Ec 10:15 the foolish w. every one of them,........ 3021

WEARINESS
Ec 12:12 much study is a w. of the flesh.......... 3024
Mal 1:13 said also, Behold, what a w. is it! 4972
2Co 11:27 In w. and painfulness, in.................. *2873*

WEARING
1Sa 14:3 priest in Shiloh, w. an ephod. 5375
Joh 19:5 Jesus forth, w. the crown of thorns, ... *5409*
1Pe 3:3 plaiting the hair, and of w. of gold, ... *4025*

WEARISOME
Job 7:3 and w. nights are appointed to me...... 5999

WEARY See also WEARIED; WEARIETH; WEARISOME.
Ge 27:46 I am w. of my life because of the....... 6973
De 25:18 when thou wast faint and w.; 3023
Jg 4:21 for he was fast asleep and w. 5774
Jg 8:15 bread unto thy men that are w.? 3286
2Sa 16:14 that were with him, came w.,............ 5889
2Sa 17:2 upon him while he is w. and weak...... 3023
2Sa 17:29 The people is hungry, and w., ... 5889
2Sa 23:10 Philistines until his hand was w.,........ 3021
Job 3:17 and there the w. be at rest............... 3019
Job 10:1 My soul is w. of my life; I will........... 5354
Job 16:7 But now he hath made me w............. 3811
Job 22:7 not given water to the w. to drink,..... 5889
Ps 6:6 I am w. with my groaning; all the....... 3021
Ps 68:9 thine inheritance, when it was w........ 3811
Ps 69:3 I am w. of my crying: my throat........ 3021
Pr 3:11 neither be w. of his correction:........... 6973
Pr 25:17 lest he be w. of thee, and so hate...... 7646
Isa 1:14 unto me; I am w. to bear them. 3811
Isa 5:27 None shall be w. nor stumble............ 5889
Isa 7:13 a small thing for you to w. men, ... 3811
Isa 7:13 but will ye w. my God also?.............. 3811
Isa 16:12 that Moab is w. on the high place, ... 3811
Isa 28:12 ye may cause the w. to rest; 5889
Isa 32:2 shadow of a great rock in a w. land. ... 5889
Isa 40:28 earth, fainteth not, neither is w.? 3021
Isa 40:30 the youths shall faint and be w., ... 3021
Isa 40:31 they shall run, and not be w.; and 3021
Isa 43:22 thou hast been w. of me, O Israel....... 3021
Isa 46:1 they are a burden to the w. beast. 5889
Isa 50:4 word in season to him that is w. 3287
Jer 2:24 all they that seek her will not w.......... 3286
Jer 6:11 the Lord; I am w. with holding in:...... 3811
Jer 9:5 w. themselves to commit iniquity. 3811
Jer 15:6 thee, I am w. with repenting............. 3811
Jer 20:9 I was w. with forbearing, and I.......... 3811
Jer 31:25 For I have satiated the w. soul, ... 5889
Jer 51:58 in the fire, and they shall be w.. 3286
Jer 51:64 upon her: and they shall be w.. 3286
Hab 2:13 the people shall w. themselves for...... 3286
Lu 18:5 **her continual coming she w. me**.... *5299*
Ga 6:9 And let us not be w. in well doing:..... *1573*
2Th 3:13 brethren, be not w. in well doing. *1573*

WEASEL
Le 11:29 the w., and the mouse, and the 2467

WEATHER
Job 37:22 Fair w. cometh out of the north:........ 2091
Pr 25:20 taketh away a garment in cold w.,....... 3117
Mt 16:2 **evening, ye say, It will be fair w.**.. *2105*
Mt 16:3 **morning. It will be foul w. to day:** .*5494*

WEAVE See also WEAVEST; WOVE; WOVEN.
Isa 19:9 and they that w. networks, shall be...... 707
Isa 59:5 eggs, and w. the spider's web:.......... 707

WEAVER See also WEAVER'S.
Ex 35:35 and in fine linen, and of the w., ... 707
Isa 38:12 I have cut off like a w. my life: he....... 707

WEAVER'S
1Sa 17:7 of his spear was like a w. beam; 707
2Sa 21:19 of whose spear was like a w. beam...... 707
1Ch 11:23 hand was a spear like a w. beam; 707
1Ch 20:5 spear staff was like a w. beam........... 707
Job 7:6 days are swifter than a w. shuttle,............

WEAVEST
Jg 16:13 If thou w. the seven locks of my......... 707

WEB See also WEBS.
Jg 16:13 locks of my head with the w.. 4545
Jg 16:14 pin of the beam, and with the w. 4545
Job 8:14 whose trust shall be a spider's w. 1004
Isa 59:6 eggs, and weave the spider's w. 6980

WEBS
Isa 59:4 w. shall not become garments, ... 6980

WED See WEDDING; WEDLOCK.

WEDDING
Mt 22:3 **them that were bidden to the w.**.... 1062
Mt 22:8 **The w. is ready, but they which**.... 1062
Mt 22:10 **the w. was furnished with guests.**.. 1062
Mt 22:11 **which had not on a w. garment:**.... 1062
Mt 22:12 **in hither not having a w. garment?** 1062
Lu 12:36 **when he will return from the w.;**.. 1062
Lu 14:8 **art bidden of any man to a w.,**...... 1062

WEDGE
Jos 7:21 w. of gold of fifty shekels weight,....... 3956
Jos 7:24 the w. of gold, and his sons, and his.... 3956
Isa 13:12 a man than the golden w. of Ophir...........

WEDLOCK
Eze 16:38 as women that break w. and shed...... 5003

WEEDS
Jon 2:5 w. were wrapped about my head........ 5488

WEEK See also WEEKS.
Ge 29:27 Fulfil her w., and we will give thee..... 7620
Ge 29:28 Jacob did so, and fulfilled her w. 7620
Da 9:27 the covenant with many for one w........ 7620
Da 9:27 and in the midst of the w. he shall 7620
Mt 28:1 toward the first day of the w.,........... 4521
Mk 16:2 the morning the first day of the w.,.... 4521
Mk 16:9 risen early the first day of the w.,...... 4521
Lu 18:12 **I fast twice in the w., I give tithes** 4521
Lu 24:1 Now upon the first day of the w., ... 4521
Joh 20:1 the first day of the w. cometh Mary... 4521
Joh 20:19 being the first day of the w., when..... 4521
Ac 20:7 And upon the first day of the w., ... 4521
1Co 16:2 Upon the first day of the w. let every.. 4521

WEEKS
Ex 34:22 thou shalt observe the feast of w., ... 7620
Le 12:5 then she shall be unclean two w.,....... 7620
Nu 28:26 after your w. be out, ye shall have....... 7620
De 16:9 Seven w. shalt thou number unto....... 7620
De 16:9 begin to number the seven w. from.... 7620
De 16:10 keep the feast of w. unto the Lord...... 7620
De 16:16 in the feast of w., and in the feast...... 7620
2Ch 8:13 in the feast of w., and in the feast...... 7620
Jer 5:24 us the appointed w. of the harvest. 7620
Da 9:24 Seventy w. are determined upon........ 7620
Da 9:25 the Prince shall be seven w., ... 7620
Da 9:25 and threescore and two w.: the 7620
Da 9:26 threescore and two w. shall Messiah... 7620
Da 10:2 Daniel was mourning three full w. 7620
Da 10:3 till three whole w. were fulfilled. 7620

WEEP See also WEEPEST; WEEPETH; WEEPING; WEPT.
Ge 23:2 mourn for Sarah, and to w. for her..... 1058
Ge 43:30 and he sought where to w.; and he 1058
Nu 11:10 people w. throughout their families, ... 1058
Nu 11:13 for they w. unto me, saying, Give....... 1058
1Sa 11:5 What aileth the people that they w.?.... 1058
1Sa 30:4 until they had no more power to w..... 1058
2Sa 1:24 daughters of Israel, w. over Saul,........ 1058
2Sa 12:21 thou didst fast and w. for the child. 1058
2Ch 34:27 rend thy clothes, and w. before me; ... 1058
Ne 8:9 Lord your God; mourn not, nor w...... 1058
Job 27:15 death: and his widows shall not w.. 1058
Job 30:25 Did not I w. for him that was in......... 1058
Job 30:31 organ into the voice of them that w.. . 1058
Ec 3:4 A time to w., and a time to laugh; 1058
Isa 15:2 to Dibon, the high places, to w.: 1065
Isa 22:4 I will w. bitterly, labour not to........... 1065
Isa 30:19 thou shalt w. no more: he will be....... 1058
Isa 33:7 the ambassadors of peace shall w....... 1058
Jer 9:1 that I might w. day and night for........ 1058
Jer 13:17 my soul shall w. in secret places for... 1058
Jer 13:17 and mine eye shall w. sore, and......... 1830
Jer 22:10 W. ye not for the dead, neither 1058
Jer 22:10 w. sore for him that goeth away: 1058
Jer 48:32 will w. for thee with the weeping of.... 1058
La 1:16 For these things I w.; mine eye,........ 1058
Eze 24:16 neither shalt thou mourn nor w.,......... 1058
Eze 24:23 ye shall not mourn nor w.; but ye....... 1058
Eze 27:31 shall w. for thee with bitterness......... 1058
Joe 1:5 Awake, ye drunkards, and w.; and 1058
Joe 2:17 w. between the porch and the altar, ... 1058
Mic 1:10 ye it not at Gath, w. ye not at all: 1058
Zec 7:3 Should I w. in the fifth month,........... 1058
Mk 5:39 **Why make ye this ado, and w.?**..... 2799
Lu 6:21 **Blessed are ye that w. now: for ye** .2799
Lu 6:25 **now! for ye shall mourn and w.**. ... 2799
Lu 7:13 on her, and said unto her, **W. not,** 2799
Lu 8:52 he said, **W. not; she is not dead,** 2799
Lu 23:28 **Daughters of Jerusalem, w. not for** 2799
Lu 23:28 **but w. for yourselves, and for your** 2799
Joh 11:31 She goeth unto the grave to w. 2799
Joh 16:20 **you, That ye shall w. and lament,**..2799
Ac 21:13 What mean ye to w. and to break...... 2799
Ro 12:15 rejoice, and w. with them that w.. 2799
1Co 7:30 they that w., as though they wept...... 2799
Jas 4:9 Be afflicted, and mourn, and w.: 2799
Jas 5:1 w. and howl for your miseries that..... 2799
Re 5:5 W. not: behold, the Lion of the tribe .. 2799
Re 18:11 merchants of the earth shall w............ 2799

WEEPEST
1Sa 1:8 to her, Hannah, why w. thou? 1058
Joh 20:13 Woman, why w. thou? ....
Joh 20:15 unto her, **Woman, why w. thou?**..... 2799

WEEPETH
2Sa 19:1 w. and mourneth for Absalom........... 1058
2Ki 8:12 And Hazael said, Why w. my lord?..... 1058
Ps 126:6 He that goeth forth and w., bearing.... 1058
La 1:2 She w. sore in the night, and her....... 1058

WEEPING
Nu 25:6 were w. before the door of the.......... 1058
De 34:8 days of w. and mourning for Moses.... 1065
2Sa 3:16 husband went with her along w......... 1058
2Sa 15:30 they went up, w. as they went up....... 1058
Ezr 3:13 the noise of the w. of the people: 1065
Ezr 10:1 w. and casting himself down............. 1058
Es 4:3 and fasting, and w., and wailing; 1065
Job 16:16 My face is foul with w., and on my 1065
Ps 6:8 Lord hath heard the voice of my w...... 1065
Ps 30:5 w. may endure for a night, but joy 1065
Ps 102:9 and mingled my drink with w.,........... 1065
Isa 15:3 one shall howl, w. abundantly. 1065
Isa 15:5 Luhith with w. shall they go it up;....... 1065
Isa 16:9 I will bewail with the w. of Jazer........ 1065
Isa 22:12 did the Lord God of hosts call to w., .. 1065
Isa 65:19 voice of w. shall be no more heard..... 1065
Jer 3:21 w. and supplications of the................ 1065
Jer 9:10 will I take up a w. and wailing, ... 1065
Jer 31:9 They shall come with w., and with..... 1065
Jer 31:15 Ramah, lamentation, and bitter w.; 1065
Jer 31:15 Rahel w. for her children refused 1058
Jer 31:16 Refrain thy voice from w., and 1065
Jer 41:6 them, w. all along as he went:........... 1058
Jer 48:5 Luhith continual w. shall go up;......... 1065
Jer 48:32 weep for thee with the w. of Jazer:..... 1065
Jer 50:4 of Judah together, going and w.: 1058
Eze 8:14 there sat women w. for Tammuz. 1058
Joe 2:12 fasting, and with w., and with........... 1065
Mal 2:13 with tears, with w., and with crying.... 1065
Mt 2:18 lamentation, and w., and great........... 2805
Mt 2:18 Rachel w. for her children, and.......... 2799
Mt 8:12 **shall be w. and gnashing of teeth**.. 2805
Mt 22:13 **shall be w. and gnashing of teeth**.. 2805
Mt 24:51 **shall be w. and gnashing of teeth**.. 2805
Mt 25:30 **shall be w. and gnashing of teeth**.. 2805
Lu 7:38 stood at his feet behind him w.,......... 2799
Lu 13:28 **shall be w. and gnashing of teeth,** . 2805
Joh 11:33 When Jesus therefore saw her w.,....... 2799
Joh 11:33 Jews also w. which came with her,...... 2799
Joh 20:11 stood without at the sepulchre w.:...... 2799
Ac 9:39 and all the widows stood by him w.,... 2799
Php 3:18 often, and now tell you even w.,......... 2799
Re 18:15 fear of her torment, w. and wailing,.... 2799
Re 18:19 w. and wailing, saying, Alas, alas 2799

WEIGH See also WEIGHED; WEIGHETH; WEIGHING.
1Ch 20:2 and found it to w. a talent of gold, ... 4948
Ezr 8:29 ye w. them before the chief of the..... 8254
Ps 58:2 ye w. the violence of your hands........ 6424
Isa 26:7 dost w. the path of the just............... 6424
Isa 46:6 w. silver in the balance, and hire........ 8254
Eze 5:1 then take thee balances to w., and...... 4948

WEIGHED See also UNWEIGHED.
Ge 23:16 Abraham w. to Ephron the silver, ... 8254
Nu 7:85 all the silver vessels w. two thousand ....
1Sa 2:3 and by him actions are w.................. 8505
1Sa 17:7 spear's head w. six hundred shekels of......
2Sa 14:26 he w. the hair of his head at two 8254
2Sa 21:16 spear w. three hundred shekels ....
Ezr 8:25 And w. unto them the silver, and....... 8254
Ezr 8:26 I even w. unto their hand six 8254
Ezr 8:33 the vessels w. in the house of our...... 8254
Job 6:2 that my grief were throughly w.,........ 8254
Job 28:15 silver be w. for the price thereof. 8254
Job 31:6 Let me be w. in an even balance, ... 8254
Isa 40:12 and w. the mountains in scales, ... 8254
Jer 32:9 w. him the money, even seventeen 8254
Jer 32:10 w. him the money in the balances. 8254
Da 5:27 Thou art w. in the balances, and........ 8625
Zec 11:12 they w. for my price thirty pieces 8254

WEIGHETH
Job 28:25 he w. the waters by measure. 8505
Pr 16:2 eyes; but the Lord w. the spirits. 8505

WEIGHING
Nu 7:85 charges of silver w. an hundred and.........
Nu 7:86 full of incense, w. ten shekels apiece, ...

WEIGHT See also WEIGHTS.
Ge 24:22 golden earring of half a shekel w.,...... 4948
Ge 24:22 her hands of ten shekels w. of gold; ... 4948
Ge 43:21 of his sack, our money in full w.: 4948
Ex 30:34 of each shall there be a like w.: ....
Le 19:35 in meteyard, in w., or in measure. 4948
Le 26:26 deliver you your bread again by w.:..... 4948
Nu 7:13, 19,25 w. whereof was an hundred ....
Nu 7:31 charger of the w. of an hundred......... 4948
Nu 7:37 w. whereof was an hundred and......... 4948
Nu 7:43 charger of the w. of an hundred......... 4948
Nu 7:49 w. whereof was an hundred and......... 4948
Nu 7:55 charger of the w. of an hundred.......... 4948
Nu 7:61, 67,73,79 w. whereof was an 4948
De 25:15 shalt have a perfect and just w., a......... 68
Jos 7:21 wedge of gold of fifty shekels w.,....... 4948
Jg 8:26 w. of the golden earrings that he 4948
1Sa 17:5 w. of the coat was five thousand 4948
2Sa 12:30 the w. thereof was a talent of gold..... 4948
2Sa 14:26 hundred shekels after the king's w......... 68
2Sa 21:16 the w. of whose spear weighed........... 4948
2Sa 21:16 hundred shekels of brass in w., ... 4948
1Ki 7:47 neither was the w. of the brass 4948
1Ki 10:14 Now the w. of gold that came to........ 4948
2Ki 25:16 of all these vessels was without w...... 4948
1Ch 21:25 six hundred shekels of gold by w. 4948
1Ch 22:3 brass in abundance without w.; 4948
1Ch 22:14 and of brass and iron without w.; 4948
1Ch 28:14 of gold by w. for things of gold, for.... 4948
1Ch 28:14 for all instruments of silver by w.,....... 4948
1Ch 28:15 Even the w. for the candlesticks of....... 4948
1Ch 28:15 of gold, by w. for every candlestick, ... 4948
1Ch 28:15 for the candlesticks of silver by w., ... 4948
1Ch 28:16 by w. he gave gold for the tables of ... 4948
1Ch 28:17 he gave gold by w. for every bason;... 4948
1Ch 28:17 silver by w. for every bason of.......... 4948
1Ch 28:18 altar of incense refined gold by w.;..... 4948
2Ch 3:9 And the w. of the nails was fifty 4948
2Ch 4:18 for the w. of the brass could not be.... 4948
2Ch 9:13 Now the w. of gold that came to........ 4948
Ezr 8:30 and the Levites the w. of the silver, ... 4948
Ezr 8:34 By number and by w. of every one: ... 4948
Ezr 8:34 and all the w. was written at that....... 4948
Job 28:25 To make the w. for the winds; and..... 4948
Pr 11:1 Lord: but a just w. is his delight. 68

Pr 16:11 A just w. and balance are the........... 6425
Jer 52:20 all these vessels was without w.. 4948
Eze 4:10 thou shalt eat shall be by w.. 4946
Eze 4:16 and they shall eat bread by w.,.......... 4948
Zec 5:8 he cast the w. of lead upon the............ 68
Joh 19:39 aloes, about an hundred pound w.. ....
2Co 4:17 exceeding and eternal w. of glory: *922*
Heb 12:1 let us lay aside every w., and the *3591*
Re 16:21 every stone about the w. of a talent: .. *5006*

WEIGHTIER
Mt 23:23 **omitted the w. matters of the law,**.. *926*

WEIGHTS
Le 19:36 Just balances, just w., a just................ 68
De 25:13 shalt not have in thy bag divers w.,....... 68
Pr 16:11 all the w. of the bag are his work.......... 68
Pr 20:10 Divers w., and divers measures,............ 68
Pr 20:23 Divers w. are an abomination unto......... 68
Mic 6:11 and with the bag of deceitful w.?.......... 68

WEIGHTY See also WEIGHTIER.
Pr 27:3 A stone is heavy, and the sand w.;..... 5192
2Co 10:10 his letters, say they, are w. and.......... *926*

WELFARE
Ge 43:27 he asked them of their w., and.......... 7965
Ex 18:7 they asked each other of their w.;...... 7965
1Ch 18:10 to king David, to enquire of his w., ... 7965
Ne 2:10 the w. of the children of Israel. 2896
Job 30:15 my w. passeth away as a cloud.......... 3444
Ps 69:22 should have been for their w.,........... 7965
Jer 38:4 seeketh not the w. of this people,...... 7965

WELL See also FAREWELL; WELFARE; WELL-BELOVED; WELLFAVOURED; WELLPLEASING; WELL'S; WELLS; WELLSPRING.
Ge 4:7 If thou doest w., shalt thou not be 3190
Ge 4:7 if thou doest not w., sin lieth at the.... 3190
Ge 12:13 it may be w. with me for thy sake; 3190
Ge 12:16 And he entreated Abram w. for her.... 3190
Ge 13:10 of Jordan, that it was w. watered............
Ge 16:14 the w. was called Beer-lahai-roi;.......... 875
Ge 18:11 were old and w. stricken in age;.............
Ge 21:19 her eyes, and she saw a w. of water;...... 875
Ge 21:25 Abimelech because of a w. of water, ... 875
Ge 21:30 unto me, that I have digged this w....... 875
Ge 24:1 was old, and w. stricken in age:..............
Ge 24:11 by a w. of water at the time of the...... 875
Ge 24:13 I stand here by the w. of water;........ 5869
Ge 24:16 she went down to the w., and filled.... 5869
Ge 24:20 and ran again unto the w. to draw 875
Ge 24:29 ran out unto the man, unto the w......... 5869
Ge 24:30 he stood by the camels at the w.. 5869
Ge 24:42 And I came this day unto the w.,........ 5869
Ge 24:43 Behold, I stand by the w. of water;.... 5869
Ge 24:45 she went down unto the w., and......... 5869
Ge 24:62 from the way of the w. Lahai-roi; 875
Ge 25:11 Isaac dwelt by the w. Lahai-roi. 883
Ge 26:19 and found there a w. of springing......... 875
Ge 26:20 he called the name of the w. Esek;...... 875
Ge 26:21 they digged another w., and strove...... 875
Ge 26:22 digged another w.; and for that they..... 875
Ge 26:25 there Isaac's servants digged a w.. 875
Ge 26:32 told him concerning the w. which......... 875
Ge 29:2 looked, and behold a w. in the field, ... 875
Ge 29:2 for out of that w. they watered the...... 875
Ge 29:6 And he said unto them, Is he w.? 7965
Ge 29:6 And they said, He is w.: and,........... 7965
Ge 29:17 was beautiful and w. favoured........... 3303
Ge 32:9 and I will deal w. with thee:............. 3190
Ge 37:14 see whether it be w. with thy 7965
Ge 37:14 w. with the flocks; and bring me........ 7965
Ge 39:6 a goodly person, and w. favoured......... 3303
Ge 40:14 think on me when it shall be w.......... 3190
Ge 41:2 the river seven w. favoured kine........ 3303
Ge 41:4 the seven w. favoured and fat kine. 3303
Ge 41:18 kine, fatfleshed and w. favoured;........ 3303
Ge 43:27 Is your father w., the old man of 7965
Ge 45:16 and it pleased Pharaoh w., and his............
Ge 49:22 even a fruitful bough by a w.;........... 5869
Ex 1:20 God dealt w. with the midwives:........ 3190
Ex 2:15 Midian: and he sat down by a w.......... 875
Ex 4:14 brother? I know that he can speak w.. ......
Ex 10:29 Thou hast spoken w., I will see thy.... 3651
Le 24:16 as w. the stranger, as he that is born ....
Le 24:22 w. for the stranger, as for one of your.......
Nu 11:18 for it was w. with us in Egypt: 2895
Nu 13:30 it; for we are w. able to overcome it. ....
Nu 21:16 the w. whereof the Lord spake unto..... 875
Nu 21:17 Spring up, O w.; sing ye unto it: 875
Nu 21:18 The princes digged the w., the 875
Nu 21:22 not drink of the waters of the w.:........ 875
Nu 36:5 of the sons of Joseph hath said w....... 3651
De 1:17 shall hear the small as w. as the great; .....
De 1:23 And the saying pleased me w.: ....
De 3:20 unto your brethren, as w. as unto you, ...
De 4:40 that it may go w. with thee, and........ 3190
De 5:14 maidservant may rest as w. as thou..........
De 5:16 that it may go w. with thee, in the..... 3190
De 5:28 w. said all that they have spoken. 3190
De 5:29 that it might be w. with them, and 3190
De 5:33 and that it may be w. with you, ... 2895
De 6:3, 18 that it may be w. with thee, and.... 3190
De 7:18 shalt w. remember what the Lord thy.......
De 12:25, 28 that it may go w. with thee, ... 3190
De 15:16 house, because he is w. with thee;..... 2895
De 18:17 They have w. spoken that which........ 3190
De 19:13 Israel, that it may go w. with thee. 2895
De 20:8 his brethren's heart faint as w. as his........
De 22:7 that it may be w. with thee, and........ 3190
Jos 8:33 of the Lord, as w. the stranger,..............
Jos 18:15 to the w. of waters of Nephtoah: 4599
Jg 7:1 and pitched beside the w. of Harod:.... 5878
Jg 9:16 if ye have dealt w. with Jerubbaal....... 2895
Jg 14:3 for me; for she pleaseth me w..................
Jg 14:7 and she pleased Samson w.....................
Jg 20:48 sword, as w. the men of every city, ...
Ru 3:1 thee, that it may be w. with thee? 3190
Ru 3:13 thee the part of a kinsman, w.;.......... 2896
1Sa 9:10 said Saul to his servant, W. said; 2896
1Sa 16:16 with his hand, and thou shalt be w.. ... 2895
1Sa 16:17 me now that a man can play w., ... 3190
1Sa 16:23 so Saul was refreshed, and was w.,.... 2895
1Sa 18:26 it pleased David w. to be the ....
1Sa 19:22 came to a great w. that is in Sechu:..... 953
1Sa 20:7 If he say thus, It is w.; thy servant.... 2896
1Sa 24:18 that thou hast dealt w. with me: 2896
1Sa 24:19 enemy, will he let him go w. away?.... 2896
1Sa 24:20 I know w....thou shalt surely be king, ...
1Sa 25:31 shall have dealt w. with my lord,........ 3190
2Sa 3:13 he said, W.; I will make a league 2896
2Sa 3:26 him again from the w. of Sirah: 953
2Sa 6:19 Israel, as w. to the women as men,..........
2Sa 11:25 devoureth one as w. as another: 2090
2Sa 17:4 the saying pleased Absalom w.,................
2Sa 17:18 which had a w. in his court;................... 375
2Sa 17:21 that they came up out of the w., and.... 375
2Sa 18:28 and said unto the king, All is w......... 7965
2Sa 19:6 then it had pleased thee w.....................
2Sa 23:15 the water of the w. of Beth-lehem, ... 953
2Sa 23:16 water out of the w. of Beth-lehem, ... 953
1Ki 2:18 W.; I will speak for thee unto the 2896
1Ki 8:18 thou didst w. that it was in thine......... 3190
1Ki 18:24 answered and said, It is w. spoken. 2896
2Ki 4:23 And she said, It shall be w.. 7965
2Ki 4:26 and say unto her, Is it w. with thee? .. 7965
2Ki 4:26 is it w. with thy husband?................. 7965
2Ki 4:26 is it w. with the child? 7965
2Ki 4:26 And she answered, It is w................ 7965
2Ki 5:21 to meet him, and said, Is all w.? 7965
2Ki 5:22 And he said, All is w.. My master......... 7965
2Ki 7:9 said one to another, We do not w.: 3651
2Ki 9:11 and one said unto him, Is all w.?........ 7965
2Ki 10:30 thou hast done w. in executing 2895
2Ki 25:24 and it shall be w. with you............... 3190
1Ch 11:17 the water of the w. of Beth-lehem, ... 953
1Ch 11:18 water out of the w. of Beth-lehem, ... 953
1Ch 25:8 ward, as w. the small as the great,..........
1Ch 26:13 cast lots, as w. the small as the great, ...
2Ch 6:8 thou didst w. in that it was in............ 2895
2Ch 12:12 and also in Judah things went w.. 2896
2Ch 31:15 as w. to the great as to the small:............
Ne 2:13 even before the dragon w., and to....... 5869
Job 12:3 I have understanding as w. as you;........ 71
Job 33:31 Mark w., O Job, hearken unto me:..... 7181
Ps 48:13 Mark ye w. her bulwarks, ...
Ps 49:18 when thou doest w. to thyself. 3190
Ps 73:2 gone; my steps had w. nigh slipped...... 369
Ps 78:29 So they did eat, and were w. filled: 3966
Ps 84:6 the valley of Baca make it a w.;......... 4599
Ps 87:7 As w. the singers as the players on..........
Ps 119:65 Thou hast dealt w. with thy.............. 2896
Ps 128:2 be, and it shall be w. with thee. 2896
Ps 139:14 and that my soul knoweth right w.. ....
Pr 5:15 running waters out of thine own w.. 875
Pr 10:11 of a righteous man is a w. of life:....... 4726
Pr 11:10 When it goeth w. with the................ 2898
Pr 13:10 but with the w. advised is wisdom...........
Pr 14:15 the prudent man looketh w. to his 995
Pr 24:32 I saw, and considered it w.: I looked ....
Pr 27:23 flocks, and look w. to thy herds.............
Pr 30:29 There be three things which go w.,.... 3190
Pr 31:27 She looketh w. to the ways of her...... 6822
Ec 8:12 be w. with them that fear God, ... 2896
Ec 8:13 it shall not be w. with the wicked,...... 2896
Ca 4:15 of gardens, a w. of living waters,......... 875
Isa 1:17 Learn to do w.; seek judgment, ... 3190
Isa 3:10 that it shall be w. with him: 2896
Isa 3:24 instead of w. set hair baldness;.......... 4639
Isa 25:6 of wines on the lees w. refined................
Isa 33:23 not w. strengthen their mast,............. 3651
Isa 42:21 w. pleased for his righteousness'........ 2654
Jer 1:12 Lord unto me, Thou hast w. seen: 3190
Jer 7:23 you, that it may be w. unto you......... 3190
Jer 15:11 Verily it shall be w. with thy 2896
Jer 15:11 to entreat thee w. in the time of evil ....
Jer 22:15 and then it was w. with him?............. 2896
Jer 22:16 needy; then it was w. with him:......... 2896
Jer 38:20 so it shall be w. unto thee, and thy 3190
Jer 39:12 Take him, and look w. to him,.................
Jer 40:4 and I will look w. unto thee: ....
Jer 40:9 and it shall be w. with you................ 3190
Jer 42:6 that it may be w. with us, when we ... 2896
Jer 44:17 we plenty of victuals, and were w., ... 2896
Eze 24:5 under it, and make it boil w., ... 7571
Eze 24:10 consume the flesh, and spice it w.,...........
Eze 33:32 and can play w. on an instrument: ....
Eze 44:5 Son of man, mark w., and ....
Eze 44:5 mark w. the entering in of the................
Eze 47:14 shall inherit it, one as w. as another: ....
Da 1:4 was no blemish, but w. favoured,....... 2896
Da 3:15 the image which I have made; w.............
Jon 4:4 Lord, Doest thou w. to be angry? 3190
Jon 4:9 thou w. to be angry for the gourd?..... 3190
Jon 4:9 he said, I do w. to be angry, even 3190
Zec 8:15 I thought in these days to do w.. 3190
Mt 3:17 Son, in whom I am w. pleased.......... *2106*
Mt 12:12 **is lawful to do w. on the sabbath**.. *2573*
Mt 12:18 in whom my soul is w. pleased: *2106*
Mt 15:7 **w. did Esaias prophesy of you,**...... *2573*
Mt 17:5 Son, in whom I am w. pleased;.......... *2106*
Mt 25:21 **W. done, thou good and faithful**.... *2095*
Mt 25:23 **him, W. done, good and faithful**.... *2095*
Mk 1:11 Son, in whom I am w. pleased........... *2106*
Mk 7:6 **W. hath Esaias prophesied of**........ *2573*
Mk 7:9 **w. ye reject the commandment**........ *2573*
Mk 7:37 He hath done all things w................. *2573*
Mk 12:28 that he had answered them w.,........... *2573*
Mk 12:32 W., Master, thou hast said the.......... *2573*
Lu 1:7 were now w. stricken in years........... *4260*
Lu 1:18 and my wife w. stricken in years........ *4260*
Lu 3:22 Son; in thee I am w. pleased............. *2106*
Lu 6:26 **all men shall speak w. of you!** *2573*
Lu 13:9 **And if it bear fruit, w.: and**...............
Lu 19:17 **unto him, W., thou good servant:**.. *2095*
Lu 20:39 said, Master, thou hast w. said........... *2573*
Joh 2:10 and when men have w. drunk,........... *3184*
Joh 4:6 Now Jacob's w. was there. Jesus *4077*
Joh 4:6 his journey, sat thus on the w.: *4077*
Joh 4:11 to draw with, and the w. is deep: *5421*
Joh 4:12 father Jacob, which gave us the w.,..... *5421*
Joh 4:14 **a w. of water springing up into**..... *4077*
Joh 4:17 **Thou hast w. said, I have no**......... *2573*
Joh 8:48 Say we not w. that thou art a........... *2573*
Joh 11:12 Lord, if he sleep, he shall do w.. .... *4982*
Joh 13:13 **Master and Lord: and ye say w.;**... *2573*
Joh 18:23 **but if w., why smitest thou me?**.... *2573*
Ac 10:33 thou hast w. done that thou art *2573*
Ac 10:47 the Holy Ghost as w. as we? *2532*
Ac 15:29 ye shall do w.. Fare ye w.. .... *2095*
Ac 16:2 was w. reported of by the brethren.... *3140*
Ac 25:10 wrong, as thou very w. knowest. *2573*
Ac 28:25 W. spake the Holy Ghost by............ *2573*
Ro 2:7 by patient continuance in w. doing......... *18*
Ro 11:20 W.; because of unbelief they *2573*
1Co 7:37 he will keep his virgin, doeth w.. .... *2573*
1Co 7:38 giveth her in marriage doeth w.; *2573*
1Co 9:5 a wife, as w. as other apostles, ... *2532*
1Co 10:5 of them God was not w. pleased: *2106*
1Co 14:17 For thou verily givest thanks w., ... *2573*
2Co 6:9 As unknown, and yet w. known; *1921*
2Co 11:4 ye might w. bear with him.............. *2573*

Ga 4:17 zealously affect you, but not w.; *2573*
Ga 5:7 Ye did run w.; who did hinder you *2573*
Ga 6:9 let us not be weary in w. doing: *2570*
Eph 6:3 That it may be w. with thee, and....... *2095*
Php 4:14 Notwithstanding ye have w. done,....... *2573*
Col 3:20 this is w. pleasing unto the Lord........ *2101*
2Th 3:13 be not weary in w. doing.................. *2569*
1Ti 3:4 One that ruleth w. his own house,....... *2573*
1Ti 3:12 children and their own houses w.. ...... *2573*
1Ti 3:13 used the office of a deacon w. *2573*
1Ti 5:10 **W.** reported of for good works; if *3140*
1Ti 5:17 the elders that rule w. be counted....... *2573*
2Ti 1:18 meat Ephesus, thou knowest very w.... *957*
Tit 2:9 please them w. in all things;....... *1510,2101*
Heb 4:2 preached, as w. as unto them:........... *2509*
Heb 13:16 such sacrifices God is w. pleased. *2100*
Jas 2:8 thy neighbour as thyself, ye do w....... *2573*
Jas 2:19 there is one God; thou doest w. *2573*
1Pe 2:14 for the praise of them that do w. *17*
1Pe 2:15 that with w. doing ye may put to *15*
1Pe 2:20 when ye do w., and suffer for it, ye *15*
1Pe 3:6 ye are, as long a ye do w., and *15*
1Pe 3:17 ye suffer for w. doing, than for evil *15*
1Pe 4:19 of their souls to him in w. doing,........... *16*
2Pe 1:17 Son, in whom I am w. pleased........... *2106*
2Pe 1:19 ye do w. that ye take heed, as unto ... *2573*
3Jo 6 after a godly sort, thou shalt do w...... *2573*

WELLBELOVED

Ca 1:13 A bundle of myrrh is my w. unto 1730
Isa 5:1 Now will I sing to my w. a song of..... 3039
Isa 5:1 My w. hath a vineyard in a very........ 3039
Mk 12:6 **yet therefore one son, his w., he**...... *27*
Ro 16:5 Salute my w. Epaenetus, who is the...... *27*
3Jo 1 The elder unto the w. Gaius, whom....... *27*

WELL-DOING See WELL and DOING.

WELLFAVOURED See also WELL and FAVOURED.

Na 3:4 whoredoms of the w. harlot, ... 2896,2580

WELL-NIGH See WELL and NIGH.

WELLPLEASING See also WELL and PLEASING.

Php 4:18 a sacrifice acceptable, w. to God........ *2101*
Heb 13:21 you that which is w. in his sight,........ *2101*

WELL'S

Ge 29:2 great stone was upon the w. mouth. 875
Ge 29:3 rolled the stone from the w. mouth,..... 875
Ge 29:3 the stone again upon the w. mouth 875
Ge 29:8 roll the stone from the w. mouth: 875
Ge 29:10 rolled the stone from the w. mouth,..... 875
2Sa 17:19 a covering over the w. mouth, ... 875

WELLS

Ge 26:15 the w. which his father's servants........ 875
Ge 26:18 Isaac digged again the w. of water, ... 875
Ex 15:27 where were twelve w. of water, ... 5869
Nu 20:17 we drink of the water of the w.: 875
De 6:11 w. digged, which thou diggest not,........ 953
2Ki 3:19 and stop all w. of water, and mar....... 4599
2Ki 3:25 they stopped all the w. of water, ... 4599
2Ch 26:10 the desert, and digged many w.: 953
Ne 9:25 w. digged, vineyards, and.................. 953
Isa 12:3 water out of the w. of salvation. 4599
2Pe 2:17 These are w. without water, ... *4077*

WELLSPRING

Pr 16:22 Understanding is a w. of life unto....... 4726
Pr 18:4 and the w. of wisdom as a flowing...... 4726

WEN

Le 22:22 maimed, or having a w., or scurvy, ... 2990

WENCH

2Sa 17:17 and a w. went and told them;............ 8198

WENT See also OUTWENT; WENTEST.

Ge 2:6 there w. up a mist from the earth, ... 5927
Ge 2:10 a river w. out of Eden of water 3318
Ge 4:16 Cain w. out from the presence of....... 3318
Ge 7:7 And Noah w. in, and his sons, and....... 935
Ge 7:9 There w. in two and two unto Noah...... 935
Ge 7:15 they w. in unto Noah into the ark, ... 935
Ge 7:16 they that w. in, w. in male and 935
Ge 7:18 the ark w. upon the face of the 3212
Ge 8:7 a raven, which w. forth to and fro, ... 3318
Ge 8:18 Noah w. forth, and his sons, and........ 3318
Ge 8:19 their kinds, w. forth out of the ark. 3318
Ge 9:18 of Noah, that w. forth of the ark,....... 3318
Ge 9:23 and w. backward, and covered the...... 3212
Ge 10:11 Out of that land w. forth Asshur, ... 3318
Ge 11:31 they w. forth with him from Ur 3318
Ge 12:4 unto him; and Lot w. with him; 3212
Ge 12:5 they w. forth to go into the land of..... 3318
Ge 12:10 and Abram w. down into Egypt to....... 3381
Ge 13:1 Abram w. up out of Egypt, he, and 5927
Ge 13:3 he w. on his journeys from the 3212
Ge 13:5 which w. with Abram, had flocks,....... 1980
Ge 14:8 there w. out the king of Sodom, ... 3318
Ge 14:11 their victuals, and w. their way.......... 3212
Ge 14:17 king of Sodom w. out to meet him 3318
Ge 14:24 of the men which w. with me, ... 1980
Ge 15:17 when the sun w. down, and it was....... 935
Ge 16:4 and he w. in unto Hagar, and she 935
Ge 17:22 and God w. up from Abraham............ 5927
Ge 18:16 Abraham w. with them to bring 1980
Ge 18:22 thence, and w. toward Sodom: 3212
Ge 18:33 And the Lord w. his way, as soon as.. 3212
Ge 19:6 Lot w. out at the door unto them,...... 3318
Ge 19:14 Lot w. out, and spake unto his sons ... 3318
Ge 19:28 the smoke of the country w. up as..... 5927
Ge 19:30 Lot w. up out of Zoar, and dwelt 5927
Ge 19:33 and the firstborn w. in, and lay............ 935
Ge 21:16 And she w., and sat her down over.... 3212
Ge 21:19 and she w., and filled the bottle 3212
Ge 22:3 w. unto the place of which God had.... 3212
Ge 22:6 and they w. both of them together. 3212
Ge 22:8 so they w. both of them together. 3212
Ge 22:13 Abraham w. and took the ram, and..... 3212
Ge 22:19 and w. together to Beer-sheba. 3212
Ge 23:10 all that w. in at the gate of his city, ... 935
Ge 23:18 all that w. in at the gate of his city. 935
Ge 24:10 he arose, and w. to Mesopotamia,....... 3212
Ge 24:16 and she w. down to the well, and....... 3381
Ge 24:45 and she w. down unto the well, and.... 3381
Ge 24:61 took Rebekah, and w. his way. 3212
Ge 24:63 Isaac w....to meditate in the field....... 3318
Ge 25:22 And she w. to enquire of the Lord. 3212
Ge 25:34 drink, and rose up, and w. his way:.... 3212
Ge 26:1 Isaac w. unto Abimelech king of......... 3212
Ge 26:13 man waxed great, and w. forward, ... 3212
Ge 26:23 w. up from thence to Beer-sheba. 5927
Ge 26:26 Abimelech w. to him from Gerar,........ 1980
Ge 27:5 Esau w. to the field to hunt for 3212
Ge 27:14 And he w., and fetched, and brought .. 3212
Ge 27:22 Jacob w. near...Isaac his father;......... 5066
Ge 28:5 he w. to Padan-aram unto Laban, ... 3212
Ge 28:9 Then w. Esau unto Ishmael, and......... 3212
Ge 28:10 Jacob w. out from Beer-sheba, ... 3318
Ge 28:10 and w. toward Haran........................ 3212
Ge 29:1 Then Jacob w. on his journey, ... 5375,7272
Ge 29:10 that Jacob w. near, and rolled the....... 5066
Ge 29:23 her to him: and he w. in unto her........ 935
Ge 29:30 And he w. in also unto Rachel, and...... 935
Ge 30:4 to wife: and Jacob w. in unto her......... 935
Ge 30:14 to Reuben w. in the days of wheat..... 3212
Ge 30:16 and Leah w. out to meet him, ... 3318
Ge 31:19 And Laban w. to shear his sheep: 1980
Ge 31:33 And Laban w. into Jacob's tent, ... 935
Ge 31:33 Then w. he out of Leah's tent, and 3318
Ge 32:1 And Jacob w. on his way, and the 1980
Ge 32:21 So w. the present over before him: 5674
Ge 34:1 w. out to see the daughters of the 3318
Ge 34:6 w. out unto Jacob to commune 3318
Ge 34:24 that w. out of the gate of his city;...... 3318
Ge 34:24 that w. out of the gate of his city....... 3318
Ge 34:26 out of Shechem's house, and w. out.... 3318
Ge 35:3 with me in the way which I w.. 1980
Ge 35:13 God w. up from him in the place........ 5927
Ge 35:22 Reuben w. and lay with Bilhah........... 3212
Ge 36:6 w. into the country from the face....... 3212
Ge 37:12 brethren w. to feed their father's 3212
Ge 37:17 And Joseph w. after his brethren,....... 3212
Ge 38:1 Judah w. down from his brethren, ... 3381
Ge 38:2 he took her, and w. in unto her. 935
Ge 38:9 he w. in unto his brother's wife,.......... 935
Ge 38:11 Tamar w. and dwelt in her father's..... 3212
Ge 38:12 w. up unto his sheepshearers to 5927
Ge 38:19 she arose, and w. away, and laid........ 3212
Ge 39:11 Joseph w. unto the house to do his 935
Ge 41:45 Joseph w. out over all the land of....... 3318
Ge 41:46 Joseph w. out from the presence of.... 3318
Ge 41:46 and w. throughout all the land of........ 5674
Ge 42:3 ten brethren w. down to buy corn...... 3381
Ge 43:15 w. down to Egypt, and stood before... 3381
Ge 43:31 he washed his face, and w. out,......... 3318
Ge 44:28 And the one w. out from me, and 3318
Ge 45:25 And they w. up out of Egypt, and...... 5927
Ge 46:29 w. up to meet Israel his father, to...... 5927
Ge 47:10 and w. out from before Pharaoh. 3318
Ge 49:4 thou it: he w. up to my couch. 5927
Ge 50:7 Joseph w. up to bury his father:........... 5927
Ge 50:7 w. up all the servants of Pharaoh, ... 5927
Ge 50:9 there w. up with him both chariots 5927
Ge 50:14 w. up with him to bury his father, ... 5927
Ge 50:18 his brethren also w. and fell down...... 3212
Ex 2:1 w. a man of the house of Levi,........... 3212
Ex 2:8 w. and called the child's mother. 3212
Ex 2:11 he w. out unto his brethren, and........ 3318
Ex 2:13 And when he w. out the second day, .. 3318
Ex 4:18 Moses w. and returned to Jethro 3212
Ex 4:27 he w., and met him in the mount 3212
Ex 4:29 Moses and Aaron w. and gathered...... 3212
Ex 5:1 Moses and Aaron w. in, and told......... 935
Ex 5:10 taskmasters of the people w. out, ... 3318
Ex 7:10 and Aaron w. in unto Pharaoh, ... 935
Ex 7:23 turned and w. into his house,.............. 935
Ex 8:12 and Aaron w. out from Pharaoh: 3318
Ex 8:30 And Moses w. out from Pharaoh,....... 3318
Ex 9:33 w. out of the city from Pharaoh, ... 3318
Ex 10:6 himself, and w. out from Pharaoh. 3318
Ex 10:14 the locusts w. up over all the land...... 5927
Ex 10:18 And he w. out from Pharaoh, ... 3318
Ex 11:8 he w. out from Pharaoh in a great...... 3318
Ex 12:28 And the children of Israel w. away, ... 3212
Ex 12:38 multitude w. up also with them;......... 5927
Ex 12:41 w. out from the land of Egypt. 3318
Ex 13:18 w. up harnessed out of the land......... 5927
Ex 13:21 Lord w. before them by day in a........ 1980
Ex 14:8 Israel w. out with an high hand.......... 3318
Ex 14:19 God which w. before the camp of....... 1980
Ex 14:19 removed and w. behind them; 3212
Ex 14:19 cloud w. from before their face,......... 5265
Ex 14:22 children of Israel w. into the midst....... 935
Ex 14:23 w. in after them to the midst of 935
Ex 15:19 Pharaoh w. in with his chariots............ 935
Ex 15:19 Israel w. on dry land in the midst....... 1980
Ex 15:20 w. out after her with timbrels,........... 3318
Ex 15:22 w. out into the wilderness of Shur;..... 3318
Ex 15:22 w. three days in the wilderness, ... 3212
Ex 16:27 w. out some of the people on the....... 3318
Ex 17:10 Hur w. up to the top of the hill.......... 5927
Ex 18:7 Moses w. out to meet his father in..... 3318
Ex 18:27 he w. his way into his own land......... 3212
Ex 19:3 Moses w. up unto God, and the......... 5927
Ex 19:14 Moses w. down from the mount 3381
Ex 19:20 top of the mount; and Moses w. up.... 5927
Ex 19:25 So Moses w. down unto the people, ... 3381
Ex 24:9 They w. up Moses, and Aaron, ... 5927
Ex 24:13 Moses w. up into the mount of God. .. 5927
Ex 24:15 Moses w. up into the mount, and a 5927
Ex 24:18 w. into the midst of the cloud, ... 935
Ex 32:15 and w. down from the mount, ... 3381
Ex 33:7 w. out unto the tabernacle................ 3318
Ex 33:8 Moses w. out unto the tabernacle, ... 3318
Ex 34:4 and w. up unto mount Sinai,............. 5927
Ex 34:34 w. in before the Lord to speak............ 935
Ex 34:35 until he w. in to speak with him. 935
Ex 38:26 every one that w. to be numbered, ... 5674
Ex 40:32 When they w. into the tent of the........ 935
Ex 40:36 the children of Israel w. onward......... 5265
Le 9:8 Aaron therefore w. unto the altar,...... 7121
Le 9:23 and Aaron w. into the tabernacle 935
Le 10:2 there w. out fire from the Lord, ... 3318
Le 10:5 So they w. near, and carried them 7126
Le 16:23 on when he w. into the holy place, ... 935
Le 24:10 w. out among the children of............ 3318
Nu 8:22 after that w. the Levites in to do......... 935
Nu 10:14 place w. the standard of the camp...... 5265
Nu 10:33 the covenant of the Lord w. before 5265
Nu 10:34 day, when they w. out of the camp. ... 5265
Nu 11:8 the people w. about, and gathered...... 7751
Nu 11:24 Moses w. out, and told the people 3318
Nu 11:26 but w. not out unto the tabernacle:..... 3318
Nu 11:31 w. forth a wind from the Lord,........... 5265
Nu 13:21 So they w. up, and searched the........ 5927
Nu 13:26 And they w. and came to Moses,....... 3212
Nu 13:31 the men that w. up with him said, ... 5927
Nu 14:24 into the land whereinto he w.; 935
Nu 14:38 men that w. to search the land, ... 1980
Nu 16:25 Moses rose up and w. unto Dathan 3212
Nu 16:33 w. down alive into the pit, and the 3381

Nu	17:8	**w.** into the tabernacle of witness;	935
Nu	20:6	Moses and Aaron **w.** from the	935
Nu	20:15	our fathers **w.** down into Egypt,	3381
Nu	20:27	they **w.** up into mount Hor in the	5927
Nu	21:16	And from thence they **w.** to Beer:	
Nu	21:18	the wilderness they **w.** to Mattanah:	
Nu	21:23	and **w.** out against Israel into the	3318
Nu	21:33	and **w.** up by the way of Bashan:	5927
Nu	21:33	the king of Bashan **w.** out against	3318
Nu	22:14	rose up, and they **w.** unto Balak,	935
Nu	22:21	and **w.** with the princes of Moab.	3212
Nu	22:22	anger was kindled because he **w.**:	1980
Nu	22:23	of the way, and **w.** into the field:	3212
Nu	22:26	the angel of the Lord **w.** further,	5674
Nu	22:32	I **w.** out to withstand thee,	3318
Nu	22:35	**w.** with the princes of Balak.	3212
Nu	22:36	he **w.** out to meet him unto a city	3318
Nu	22:39	And Balaam **w.** with Balak, and	3212
Nu	23:3	thee. And he **w.** to an high place.	3212
Nu	24:1	he **w.** not, as at other times, to	1980
Nu	24:25	and **w.** and returned to his place:	3212
Nu	24:25	place: and Balak also **w.** his way.	1980
Nu	25:8	he **w.** after the man of Israel into	935
Nu	26:4	**w.** forth out of the land of Egypt	3318
Nu	31:13	**w.** forth to meet them without the	3318
Nu	31:21	men of war which **w.** to the battle,	935
Nu	31:27	upon them, who **w.** out to battle,	3318
Nu	31:28	men of war which **w.** out to battle:	3318
Nu	31:36	portion of them that **w.** out to war,	3318
Nu	32:9	**w.** up unto the valley of Eshcol,	5927
Nu	32:39	the son of Manasseh **w.** to Gilead,	3212
Nu	32:41	Jair...**w.** and took the small towns	1980
Nu	32:42	Nobah **w.** and took Kenath, and the	1980
Nu	33:1	**w.** forth out of the land of Egypt	3318
Nu	33:3	Israel **w.** out with an high hand	3318
Nu	33:8	**w.** three days' journey in the	3212
Nu	33:23	And they **w.** from Kehelathah, and	5265
Nu	33:29	And they **w.** from Mithcah, and	5265
Nu	33:33	And they **w.** from Hor-hagidgad,	5265
Nu	33:38	the priest **w.** up into mount Hor	5927
De	1:19	we **w.** through all that great and	3212
De	1:24	and **w.** up into the mountain,	5927
De	1:31	in all the way that ye **w.**, until ye	1980
De	1:33	Who **w.** in the way before you, to	1980
De	1:43	**w.** presumptuously up into the	5927
De	2:13	And we **w.** over the brook Zered.	5674
De	3:1	and **w.** up the way to Bashan:	5927
De	5:5	fire, and **w.** not up into the mount;)	5927
De	10:3	**w.** up into the mount, having the two	5927
De	10:22	Thy fathers **w.** down into Egypt	3381
De	26:5	he **w.** down into Egypt, and	3381
De	29:26	For they **w.** and served other gods,	3212
De	31:1	Moses **w.** and spake these words	3212
De	31:14	And Moses and Joshua **w.**, and	3212
De	33:2	from his right hand **w.** a fiery law	
De	34:1	**w.** up from the plains of Moab	5927
Jos	2:1	they **w.**, and came into an harlot's	3212
Jos	2:5	it was dark, that the men **w.** out:	3318
Jos	2:5	whither the men **w.** I wot not:	1980
Jos	2:22	And they **w.**, and came unto the	3212
Jos	3:2	the officers **w.** through the host;	5974
Jos	3:6	ark...and **w.** before the people.	3212
Jos	5:13	and Joshua **w.** unto him, and said	3212
Jos	6:1	none **w.** out, and none came in.	3318
Jos	6:9	armed men **w.** before the priests	1980
Jos	6:13	ark of the Lord **w.** on continually,	1980
Jos	6:13	and the armed men **w.** before them;	1980
Jos	6:20	that the people **w.** up into the city,	5927
Jos	6:23	young men that were spies **w.** in,	935
Jos	7:2	And the men **w.** up and viewed Ai	5927
Jos	7:4	So there **w.** up thither of the people	5927
Jos	8:9	and they **w.** to lie in ambush, and	3212
Jos	8:10	numbered the people, and **w.** up,	5927
Jos	8:11	of war that were with him, **w.** up,	5927
Jos	8:13	Joshua **w.** that night into the	3212
Jos	8:14	of the city **w.** out against Israel	3318
Jos	8:17	Beth-el, and **w.** not out after Israel:	3318
Jos	9:4	**w.** and made as if they had been	3212
Jos	9:6	they **w.** to Joshua unto the camp	3212
Jos	10:5	and **w.** up, they and all their hosts,	5927
Jos	10:9	and **w.** up from Gilgal all night.	5927
Jos	10:24	men of war which **w.** with him,	1980
Jos	10:36	And Joshua **w.** up from Eglon,	5927
Jos	11:4	they **w.** out, they and all their	3318
Jos	14:8	my brethren that **w.** up with me	5927
Jos	15:3	And it **w.** out to the south side to	3318
Jos	15:3	to Hezron, and **w.** up to Adar,	5927
Jos	15:4	**w.** out unto the river of Egypt;	3318
Jos	15:6	the border **w.** up to Beth-hogla,	5927
Jos	15:6	border **w.** up to the stone of Bohan	5927
Jos	15:7	the border **w.** up toward Debir	5927
Jos	15:8	border **w.** up by the valley of the	5927
Jos	15:8	**w.** up to the top of the mountain	5927
Jos	15:9	and **w.** out to the cities of mount	3318
Jos	15:10	and **w.** down to Beth-shemesh,	3381
Jos	15:11	**w.** out unto the side of Ekron	3318
Jos	15:11	Baalah, and **w.** out unto Jabneel;	3318
Jos	15:15	he **w.** up thence to the inhabitants	5927
Jos	16:6	the border **w.** out toward the sea	3318
Jos	16:6	border **w.** about eastward unto	5437
Jos	16:7	**w.** down from Janohah to Ataroth,	3381
Jos	16:7	to Jericho, and **w.** out at Jordan.	3318
Jos	16:8	The border **w.** out from Tappuah	3212
Jos	17:7	border **w.** along on the right hand	1980
Jos	18:8	and the men arose, and **w.** away:	3212
Jos	18:8	Joshua charged them that **w.**	1980
Jos	18:9	**w.** and passed through the land,	3212
Jos	18:12	border **w.** up to the side of Jericho	5927
Jos	18:12	and **w.** up through the mountains	5927
Jos	18:13	**w.** over from thence toward Luz,	5674
Jos	18:15	and the border **w.** out on the west,	3318
Jos	18:15	and **w.** out to the well of waters of	3318
Jos	18:17	north, and **w.** forth to En-shemesh,	3318
Jos	18:17	**w.** forth toward Geliloth, which is	3318
Jos	18:18	and **w.** down unto Arabah:	3381
Jos	19:11	their border **w.** up toward the sea,	5927
Jos	19:47	coast of the children of Dan **w.** out	3318
Jos	19:47	children of Dan **w.** up to fight	5927
Jos	22:6	away: and they **w.** unto their tents.	3212
Jos	24:4	his children **w.** down into Egypt.	3381
Jos	24:11	ye **w.** over Jordan, and came unto	5674
Jos	24:17	us in all the way wherein we **w.**,	1980
Jg	1:3	thy lot. So Simeon **w.** with him	3212
Jg	1:4	And Judah **w.** up; and the Lord	5927
Jg	1:9	children of Judah **w.** down to fight	3381
Jg	1:10	Judah **w.** against the Canaanites	3212
Jg	1:11	**w.** against...inhabitants of Debir:	3212
Jg	1:16	**w.** up out of the city of palm trees	5927
Jg	1:16	**w.** and dwelt among the people	3212
Jg	1:17	Judah **w.** with Simeon his brother,	3212
Jg	1:22	they also **w.** up against Beth-el:	5927
Jg	1:26	**w.** unto the land of the Hittites,	3212
Jg	2:6	**w.** every man unto his inheritance	3212
Jg	2:15	Whithersoever they **w.** out, the	3318
Jg	2:17	they **w.** a whoring after other gods,	
Jg	3:10	judged Israel, and **w.** out to war:	3318
Jg	3:13	Amalek, and **w.** and smote Israel,	3212
Jg	3:19	that stood by him **w.** out from him.	3318
Jg	3:22	the haft also **w.** in after the blade;	935
Jg	3:23	Ehud **w.** forth through the porch,	3318
Jg	3:27	**w.** down with him from the mount,	3381
Jg	3:28	they **w.** down after him, and took	3381
Jg	4:9	and **w.** with Barak to Kedesh.	3212
Jg	4:10	**w.** up with the ten thousand men	5927
Jg	4:10	and Deborah **w.** up with him.	5927
Jg	4:14	So Barak **w.** down from mount	3381
Jg	4:18	Jael **w.** out to meet Sisera, and said	3318
Jg	4:21	**w.** softly unto him, and smote the	935
Jg	6:19	Gideon **w.** in, and made ready a kid,	935
Jg	6:33	gathered together, and **w.** over,	5674
Jg	7:11	Then **w.** he down with Phurah,	3381
Jg	8:8	And he **w.** up thence to Penuel,	5927
Jg	8:11	And Gideon **w.** up by the way of	5927
Jg	8:27	Israel **w.** thither a whoring after it:	
Jg	8:29	**w.** and dwelt in his own house	3212
Jg	8:33	and **w.** a whoring after Baalim,	
Jg	9:1	son of Jerubbaal **w.** to Shechem	3212
Jg	9:5	he **w.** unto his father's house at	935
Jg	9:6	**w.**, and made Abimelech king,	3212
Jg	9:7	he **w.** and stood in the top of mount	3212
Jg	9:8	The trees **w.** forth on a time to	1980
Jg	9:21	ran away, and fled, and **w.** to Beer,	3212
Jg	9:26	brethren, and **w.** over to Shechem:	5674
Jg	9:27	And they **w.** out into the fields,	3318
Jg	9:27	and **w.** into the house of their god,	935
Jg	9:35	And Gaal the son of Ebed **w.** out,	3318
Jg	9:39	And Gaal **w.** out before the men	3318
Jg	9:42	the people **w.** out into the field;	3318
Jg	9:50	Then **w.** Abimelech to Thebez,	3212
Jg	9:52	**w.** hard unto the door of the tower	5066
Jg	11:3	Jephthah, and **w.** out with him.	3318
Jg	11:5	of Gilead **w.** to fetch Jephthah out	3212
Jg	11:11	Then Jephthah **w.** with the elders	3212
Jg	11:18	**w.** along through the wilderness,	3212
Jg	11:38	she **w.** with her companions, and	3212
Jg	11:40	the daughters of Israel **w.** yearly	3212
Jg	12:1	together, and **w.** northward,	5674
Jg	13:11	And Manoah...**w.** after his wife,	3212
Jg	13:20	the flame **w.** up toward heaven	5927
Jg	14:1	And Samson **w.** down to Timnath,	3381
Jg	14:5	Then **w.** Samson down, and his	3381
Jg	14:7	And he **w.** down, and talked with	3381
Jg	14:9	in his hands, and **w.** on eating,	3212
Jg	14:10	So his father **w.** down unto the	3381
Jg	14:18	day before the sun **w.** down,	935
Jg	14:19	and he **w.** down to Ashkelon,	3381
Jg	14:19	and he **w.** up to his father's house	5927
Jg	15:4	Samson **w.** and caught three	3212
Jg	15:8	he **w.** down and dwelt in the top of	3381
Jg	15:9	Then the Philistines **w.** up, and	5927
Jg	15:11	of Judah **w.** to the top of the rock	3381
Jg	16:1	Then **w.** Samson to Gaza, and	3212
Jg	16:1	an harlot, and **w.** in unto her.	935
Jg	16:3	posts, and **w.** away with them,	5265
Jg	16:14	**w.** away with the pin of the beam,	5265
Jg	16:19	him, and his strength **w.** from him.	5493
Jg	17:10	thy victuals. So the Levite **w.** in.	3212
Jg	18:11	**w.** from thence of the family of	5265
Jg	18:12	And they **w.** up, and pitched in	5927
Jg	18:14	men that **w.** to spy out the country	1980
Jg	18:17	And the five men that **w.** to spy	1980
Jg	18:17	to spy out the land **w.** up,	5927
Jg	18:18	And these **w.** into Micah's house,	935
Jg	18:20	and **w.** in the midst of the people.	935
Jg	18:26	the children of Dan **w.** their way:	3212
Jg	18:26	and **w.** back unto his house.	7725
Jg	19:2	**w.** away from him unto her	3212
Jg	19:3	husband arose, and **w.** after her,	3212
Jg	19:14	they passed on and **w.** their way;	3212
Jg	19:14	the sun **w.** down upon them when	935
Jg	19:15	when he **w.** in, he sat him down	935
Jg	19:18	I **w.** to Beth-lehem-judah, but I	3212
Jg	19:23	master of the house, **w.** out unto	3318
Jg	19:27	house, and **w.** out to go his way:	3318
Jg	20:1	all the children of Israel **w.** out,	3318
Jg	20:18	and **w.** up to the house of God,	5927
Jg	20:20	the men of Israel **w.** out to battle	3318
Jg	20:23	children of Israel **w.** up and wept	5927
Jg	20:25	Benjamin **w.** forth against them	3318
Jg	20:26	**w.** up, and came unto the house	5927
Jg	20:30	children of Israel **w.** up against	5927
Jg	20:31	the children of Benjamin **w.** out	3318
Jg	21:23	they **w.** and returned unto their	3212
Jg	21:24	**w.** out from thence every man to	3318
Ru	1:1	**w.** to sojourn in the country of	3212
Ru	1:7	Wherefore she **w.** forth out of the	3318
Ru	1:7	**w.** on the way to return unto the	3212
Ru	1:19	So they two **w.** until they came to	3212
Ru	1:21	I **w.** out full, and the Lord hath	1980
Ru	2:3	she **w.**, and came, and gleaned in	3212
Ru	2:18	took it up, and **w.** into the city:	935
Ru	3:6	And she **w.** down unto the floor,	3381
Ru	3:7	he **w.** to lie down at the end of the	935
Ru	3:15	it on her: and she **w.** into the city.	935
Ru	4:1	Then **w.** Boaz up to the gate, and	5927
Ru	4:13	and when he **w.** in unto her, the	935
1Sa	1:3	And this man **w.** up out of his city	5927
1Sa	1:7	**w.** up to the house of the Lord,	5927
1Sa	1:18	So the woman **w.** her way, and did	3212
1Sa	1:21	**w.** up to offer unto the Lord the	5927
1Sa	1:22	But Hannah **w.** not up; for she	5927
1Sa	2:11	Elkanah **w.** to Ramah to his house,	3212
1Sa	2:20	And they **w.** unto their own home.	1980
1Sa	3:3	ere the lamp of God **w.** out in the	3518
1Sa	3:5	again. And he **w.** and lay down.	3212
1Sa	3:6	And Samuel arose and **w.** to Eli,	3212
1Sa	3:8	he arose and **w.** to Eli, and said,	3212
1Sa	3:9	So Samuel **w.** and lay down in his	3212
1Sa	4:1	Now Israel **w.** out against the	3318
1Sa	5:12	cry of the city **w.** up to heaven.	5927
1Sa	6:12	**w.** along the highway, lowing as	1980
1Sa	6:12	the highway, lowing as they **w.**,	1980
1Sa	6:12	the Philistines **w.** after them unto	1980
1Sa	7:7	Philistines **w.** up against Israel.	5927
1Sa	7:11	men of Israel **w.** out of Mizpeh,	3318
1Sa	7:16	he **w.** from year to year in circuit	1980
1Sa	9:9	when a man **w.** to enquire of God,	3212
1Sa	9:10	**w.** unto the city where the man of	3212

1Sa 9:11 as they **w.** up the hill to the city, 5927
1Sa 9:14 And they **w.** up into the city: and 5927
1Sa 9:26 they **w.** out both of them, he and 3318
1Sa 10:14 and to his servant, Whither **w.** ye? 1980
1Sa 10:26 Saul also **w.** home to Gibeah; and 1980
1Sa 10:26 there **w.** with him a band of men, 3212
1Sa 11:15 And all the people **w.** to Gilgal; 3212
1Sa 13:7 And some of the Hebrews **w.** over 5674
1Sa 13:10 Saul **w.** out to meet him that he 3318
1Sa 13:20 all the Israelites **w.** down to the 3381
1Sa 13:23 Philistines **w.** out to the passage 3318
1Sa 14:16 **w.** on beating down one another. 3212
1Sa 14:19 the Philistines **w.** on and increased: 3212
1Sa 14:21 **w.** up with them into the camp 5927
1Sa 14:46 Then Saul **w.** up from following 5927
1Sa 14:46 Philistines **w.** to their own place 1980
1Sa 15:34 Then Samuel **w.** to Ramah; and 3212
1Sa 15:34 Saul **w.** up to his house to Gibeah 5927
1Sa 16:13 Samuel rose up, and **w.** to Ramah. 3212
1Sa 17:4 **w.** out a champion out of the camp 3318
1Sa 17:7 one bearing a shield **w.** before 1980
1Sa 17:12 man **w.** among men for an old man 935
1Sa 17:13 sons of Jesse **w.** and followed 3212
1Sa 17:13 three sons that **w.** to the battle 1980
1Sa 17:15 David **w.** and returned from Saul 1980
1Sa 17:20 **w.**, as Jesse had commanded him; 3212
1Sa 17:35 I **w.** out after him, and smote him, 3318
1Sa 17:41 that bare the shield **w.** before him.
1Sa 18:5 David **w.** out whithersoever Saul 3318
1Sa 18:13 he **w.** out and came in before the 3318
1Sa 18:16 he **w.** out and came in before them. 3318
1Sa 18:27 Wherefore David arose and **w.**, he 3212
1Sa 18:30 princes of the Philistines **w.** forth: 3318
1Sa 18:30 came to pass, after they **w.** forth, 3318
1Sa 19:8 David **w.** out, and fought with the 3318
1Sa 19:12 and he **w.**, and fled, and escaped. 3212
1Sa 19:18 he and Samuel **w.** and dwelt in 3212
1Sa 19:22 Then **w.** he also to Ramah, and 3212
1Sa 19:23 he **w.** thither to Naioth in Ramah: 3212
1Sa 19:23 and he **w.** on, and prophesied, 3212
1Sa 20:11 **w.** out both of them into the field. 3318
1Sa 20:35 Jonathan **w.** out into the field at 3318
1Sa 20:42 and Jonathan **w.** into the city. 935
1Sa 21:10 and **w.** to Achish to king of Gath. 935
1Sa 22:1 it, they **w.** down thither to him. 3381
1Sa 22:3 And David **w.** thence to Mizpeh of 3212
1Sa 23:5 David and his men **w.** to Keilah, 3212
1Sa 23:13 **w.** whithersoever they could go. 1980
1Sa 23:16 and **w.** to David into the wood, 3212
1Sa 23:18 And Jonathan **w.** to his house. 1980
1Sa 23:24 arose, and **w.** to Ziph before Saul: 3212
1Sa 23:25 Saul...and his men **w.** to seek him. 3212
1Sa 23:26 Saul **w.** on this side of the mountain, 3212
1Sa 23:28 and **w.** against the Philistines: 3212
1Sa 23:29 And David **w.** up from thence, 5927
1Sa 24:2 **w.** to seek David and his men 3212
1Sa 24:3 and Saul **w.** in to cover his feet: 935
1Sa 24:7 of the cave, and **w.** on his way. 3212
1Sa 24:8 afterward, and **w.** out of the cave, 3318
1Sa 24:22 And Saul **w.** home; but David 3212
1Sa 25:1 **w.** down to the wilderness of 3381
1Sa 25:12 turned their way, and **w.** again, 7725
1Sa 25:13 there **w.** up after David about 5927
1Sa 25:42 damsels of hers that **w.** after her; 1980
1Sa 25:42 she **w.** after the messengers of 3212
1Sa 26:2 **w.** down to the wilderness of Ziph, 3381
1Sa 26:13 David **w.** over to the other side, 5674
1Sa 26:25 So David **w.** on his way, and Saul 3212
1Sa 27:8 And David and his men **w.** up, and 5927
1Sa 28:8 and he **w.**, and two men with him, 3212
1Sa 28:25 rose up, and **w.** away that night. 3212
1Sa 29:11 the Philistines **w.** up to Jezreel. 5927
1Sa 30:2 them away, and **w.** on their way. 3212
1Sa 30:9 David **w.**, he and the six hundred 3212
1Sa 30:21 and they **w.** forth to meet David, 3318
1Sa 30:22 of those that **w.** with David, 1980
1Sa 30:22 Because they **w.** not with us, we 1980
1Sa 31:3 And the battle **w.** sore against Saul,
1Sa 31:12 men arose, and **w.** all night, and 3212
2Sa 1:4 said unto him, How **w.** the matter? 1961
2Sa 2:2 David **w.** up thither, and his two 5927
2Sa 2:12 **w.** out from Mahanaim to Gibeon. 3318
2Sa 2:13 servants of David, **w.** out, and met 3318
2Sa 2:15 and **w.** over by number twelve of 5674
2Sa 2:24 sun **w.** down when they were come 935
2Sa 2:29 **w.** through all Bithron, and they 3212
2Sa 2:32 And Joab and his men **w.** all night, 3212
2Sa 3:16 her husband **w.** with her along 3212
2Sa 3:19 Abner **w.** also to speak in the ears 3212
2Sa 3:21 Abner away; and he **w.** in peace. 3212
2Sa 4:5 **w.**, and came about the heat of the 3212
2Sa 5:6 king and his men **w.** to Jerusalem 3212
2Sa 5:10 David **w.** on, and grew great, and 3212
2Sa 5:17 of it, and **w.** down to the hold. 3381
2Sa 6:2 arose, and **w.** with all the people 3212
2Sa 6:4 God: and Ahio **w.** before the ark. 1980
2Sa 6:12 David **w.** and brought up the ark 3212
2Sa 7:18 Then **w.** king David in, and sat 935
2Sa 7:23 God **w.** to redeem for a people to 1980
2Sa 8:3 as he **w.** to recover his border at 3212
2Sa 8:6, 14 David whithersoever he **w.** 1980
2Sa 10:16 the host of Hadarezer **w.** before them.
2Sa 11:9 and **w.** not down to his house. 3381
2Sa 11:10 Uriah **w.** not down unto his house, 3381
2Sa 11:13 even he **w.** out to lie on his bed 3318
2Sa 11:13 but **w.** not down to his house. 3381
2Sa 11:17 And the men of the city **w.** out, 3318
2Sa 11:21 why **w.** ye nigh the wall? then say. 5066
2Sa 11:22 So the messenger **w.**, and came 3212
2Sa 12:16 David fasted, and **w.** in, and lay 935
2Sa 12:17 of his house arose, and **w.** to him,
2Sa 12:24 **w.** in unto her, and lay with her: 935
2Sa 12:29 **w.** to Rabbah, and fought against it, 3212
2Sa 13:8 So Tamar **w.** to her brother 3212
2Sa 13:9 they **w.** out every man from him. 3318
2Sa 13:19 on her head, and **w.** on crying. 3212
2Sa 13:37 Absalom fled, and **w.** to Talmai, 3212
2Sa 13:38 So Absalom fled, and **w.** to Geshur, 3212
2Sa 14:23 So Joab arose and **w.** to Geshur, 3212
2Sa 15:9 So he arose, and **w.** to Hebron. 3212
2Sa 15:11 with Absalom **w.** two hundred 1980
2Sa 15:11 and they **w.** in their simplicity, and 1980
2Sa 15:16, 17 And the king **w.** forth, and all 3318
2Sa 15:24 and Abiather **w.** up, until all the 5927
2Sa 15:30 David **w.** up by the ascent of mount 5927
2Sa 15:30 wept as he **w.** up, and had his head 5927
2Sa 15:30 head covered, and he **w.** barefoot: 1980
2Sa 15:30 man his head, and they **w.** up, 5927
2Sa 15:30 weeping as they **w.** up. 5927
2Sa 16:13 David and his men **w.** by the way, 3212
2Sa 16:13 Shimei **w.** along on the hill's side 1980
2Sa 16:13 and cursed as he **w.**, and threw 1980
2Sa 16:22 Absalom **w.** in unto his father's 935
2Sa 17:17 and a wench **w.** and told them; 980
2Sa 17:17 and they **w.** and told king David. 3212
2Sa 17:18 they **w.** both of them away quickly, 3212
2Sa 17:18 his court; whither they **w.** down. 3381
2Sa 17:21 well, and **w.** and told king David, 3212
2Sa 17:25 that **w.** in to Abigail the daughter 935
2Sa 18:6 people **w.** out into the field against 3318
2Sa 18:9 mule **w.** under the thick boughs 935
2Sa 18:9 mule that was under him **w.** away. 5674
2Sa 18:24 the watchman **w.** up to the roof 3212
2Sa 18:33 **w.** up to the chamber over the 5927
2Sa 18:33 as he **w.**, thus he said, O my son 3212
2Sa 19:17 **w.** over Jordan before the king. 6743
2Sa 19:18 there **w.** over a ferry boat to carry 5674
2Sa 19:19 the king **w.** out of Jerusalem, 3318
2Sa 19:31 and **w.** over Jordan with the king, 5674
2Sa 19:39 all the people **w.** over Jordan. 5674
2Sa 19:40 Then the king **w.** on to Gilgal, 5674
2Sa 19:40 and Chimham **w.** on with him: and 5674
2Sa 20:2 So every man of Israel **w.** up from 5927
2Sa 20:3 them, but **w.** not in unto them. 935
2Sa 20:5 So Amasa **w.** to assemble the men 3212
2Sa 20:7 there **w.** out after him Joab's men, 3318
2Sa 20:7 they **w.** out of Jerusalem, to pursue 3318
2Sa 20:8 in Gibeon, Amasa **w.** before them. 935
2Sa 20:8 and as he **w.** forth it fell out 3318
2Sa 20:13 all the people **w.** on after Joab, to 5674
2Sa 20:14 **w.** through all the tribes of Israel 5674
2Sa 20:14 together, and **w.** also after him. 935
2Sa 20:22 woman **w.** unto all the people in her 935
2Sa 21:12 David **w.** and took the bones of 3212
2Sa 21:15 David **w.** down, and his servants 3381
2Sa 22:9 There **w.** up a smoke out of his 5927
2Sa 23:13 three of the thirty chief **w.** down, 3381
2Sa 23:17 that **w.** in jeopardy of their lives? 1980
2Sa 23:20 he **w.** down also and slew a lion 3381
2Sa 23:21 but he **w.** down to him with a staff, 3381
2Sa 24:4 captains of the host **w.** out from 3318
2Sa 24:7 they **w.** out to the south of Judah, 3318
2Sa 24:19 **w.** up as the Lord commanded 5927
2Sa 24:20 and Araunah **w.** out, and bowed 3318
1Ki 1:15 Bath-sheba **w.** in unto the king 935
1Ki 1:38 and the Pelethites, **w.** down, and 3381
1Ki 1:49 up, and **w.** every man his way 3212
1Ki 1:50 **w.**, and caught hold of the horns of 3212
1Ki 2:8 the day when I **w.** to Mahanaim: 3212
1Ki 2:19 Bath-sheba therefore **w.** unto king 935
1Ki 2:34 the son of Jehoiada **w.** up, and 5927
1Ki 2:40 **w.** to Gath to Achish to seek his 3212
1Ki 2:40 and Shimei **w.**, and brought his 3212
1Ki 2:46 which **w.** out, and fell upon him, 3318
1Ki 3:4 the king **w.** to Gibeon to sacrifice 3212
1Ki 6:8 they **w.** up with winding stairs 5927
1Ki 8:66 **w.** unto their tents joyful and glad 3212
1Ki 10:5 **w.** up unto the house of the Lord; 5927
1Ki 10:13 turned and **w.** to her own country 3212
1Ki 10:16 shekels of gold **w.** to one target 5927
1Ki 10:17 three pound of gold **w.** to one 5927
1Ki 10:29 And a chariot...**w.** out of Egypt. 3318
1Ki 11:5 Solomon **w.** after Ashtoreth the 3212
1Ki 11:6 **w.** not full after the Lord, as did
1Ki 11:24 they **w.** to Damascus, and dwelt 3212
1Ki 11:29 Jeroboam **w.** out of Jerusalem, 3318
1Ki 12:1 And Rehoboam **w.** to Shechem: 3212
1Ki 12:25 and **w.** out from thence, and built 3318
1Ki 12:30 people **w.** to worship before the 3212
1Ki 13:10 So he **w.** another way, and returned 3212
1Ki 13:12 said unto them, What way **w.** he? 1980
1Ki 13:12 seen what way the man of God **w.**, 1980
1Ki 13:14 And **w.** after the man of God, 3212
1Ki 13:19 he **w.** back with him, and did eat 7725
1Ki 13:28 he **w.** and found his carcase cast 3212
1Ki 14:4 **w.** to Shiloh, and came to the 3212
1Ki 14:28 king **w.** into the house of the Lord, 935
1Ki 15:17 king of Israel **w.** up against Judah, 5927
1Ki 16:10 Zimri **w.** in and smote him, and 935
1Ki 16:17 And Omri **w.** up from Gibbethon, 5927
1Ki 16:18 he **w.** into the palace of the king's 935
1Ki 16:31 and **w.** and served Baal, and 3212
1Ki 17:5 So he **w.** and did according unto 3212
1Ki 17:5 **w.** and dwelt by the brook Cherith, 3212
1Ki 17:10 So he arose and **w.** to Zarephath 3212
1Ki 17:15 she **w.** and did according to the 3212
1Ki 18:2 Elijah **w.** to shew himself unto 3212
1Ki 18:6 Ahab **w.** one way by himself, and 1980
1Ki 18:6 and Obadiah **w.** another way by 1980
1Ki 18:16 So Obadiah **w.** to meet Ahab, and 3212
1Ki 18:16 and Ahab **w.** to meet Elijah. 3212
1Ki 18:42 Ahab **w.** up to eat and to drink. 5927
1Ki 18:42 Elijah **w.** up to the top of Carmel; 5927
1Ki 18:43 he **w.** up, and looked, and said, 5927
1Ki 18:45 And Ahab rode, and **w.** to Jezreel. 3212
1Ki 19:3 that, he arose, and **w.** for his life, 3212
1Ki 19:4 he himself **w.** a day's journey into 1980
1Ki 19:8 **w.** in the strength of that meat 3212
1Ki 19:13 his face in his mantle, and **w.** out, 3318
1Ki 19:21 **w.** after Elijah, and ministered 3212
1Ki 20:1 he **w.** up and besieged Samaria, 5927
1Ki 20:16 And they **w.** out at noon. But 3318
1Ki 20:17 of the provinces **w.** out first; 3318
1Ki 20:21 king of Israel **w.** out, and smote 3318
1Ki 20:26 **w.** up to Aphek, to fight against 5927
1Ki 20:27 all present, and **w.** against them: 3212
1Ki 20:39 Thy servant **w.** out into the midst 3318
1Ki 20:43 the king of Israel **w.** to his house 3212
1Ki 21:27 lay in sackcloth, and **w.** softly. 1980
1Ki 22:24 the son of Chenaanah **w.** near, 5674
1Ki 22:24 Which way **w.** the Spirit of the 5674
1Ki 22:29 of Judah **w.** up to Ramoth-gilead 5927
1Ki 22:30 himself, and **w.** into the battle. 935
1Ki 22:36 And there **w.** a proclamation 5674
1Ki 22:48 but they **w.** not; for the ships 1980
2Ki 1:9 And he **w.** up to him: and, behold, 5927
2Ki 1:13 the third captain of fifty **w.** up, 5927
2Ki 1:15 **w.** down with him unto the king. 3381
2Ki 2:1 Elijah **w.** with Elisha from Gilgal. 3212
2Ki 2:2 thee. So they **w.** down to Beth-el. 3381
2Ki 2:6 leave thee. And they two **w.** on. 3212
2Ki 2:7 of the sons of the prophets **w.**, 1980
2Ki 2:8 they two **w.** over on dry ground. 5674
2Ki 2:11 it came to pass, as they still **w.** on, 1980
2Ki 2:11 Elijah **w.** up by a whirlwind into 5927
2Ki 2:13 **w.** back, and stood by the bank of 7725
2Ki 2:14 and thither: and Elisha **w.** over. 5674
2Ki 2:21 he **w.** forth unto the spring of the 3318
2Ki 2:23 he **w.** up from thence unto Beth-el: 5927
2Ki 2:25 **w.** from thence to mount Carmel, 3212
2Ki 3:6 king Jehoram **w.** out of Samaria 3318

2Ki 3:7 he **w.** and sent to Jehoshaphat.......... 3212
2Ki 3:9 So the king of Israel **w.**, and the........ 3212
2Ki 3:12 the king of Edom **w.** down to him. 3381
2Ki 3:24 **w.** forward smiting the Moabites, ... 5221
2Ki 3:25 howbeit the slingers **w.** about it, ... 5437
2Ki 4:5 So she **w.** from him, and shut the 3212
2Ki 4:18 that he **w.** out to his father to the...... 3318
2Ki 4:21 And she **w.** up, and laid him on 5927
2Ki 4:21 the door upon him, and **w.** out. 3318
2Ki 4:25 **w.** and came unto the man of God....... 3212
2Ki 4:31 he **w.** again to meet him, and told 7725
2Ki 4:33 He **w.** in therefore, and shut the 935
2Ki 4:34 And he **w.** up, and lay upon the......... 5927
2Ki 4:35 **w.** up, and stretched himself upon 5927
2Ki 4:37 Then she **w.** in, and fell at his feet, ... 935
2Ki 4:37 and took up her son, and **w.** out. 3318
2Ki 4:39 **w.** out into the field to gather herbs, .. 3318
2Ki 5:4 And one **w.** in, and told his lord, ... 935
2Ki 5:11 Naaman was wroth, and **w.** away, ... 3212
2Ki 5:12 So he turned and **w.** away in a rage.... 3212
2Ki 5:14 Then **w.** he down, and dipped 3381
2Ki 5:25 But he **w.** in, and stood before his....... 935
2Ki 5:25 said, Thy servant **w.** no whither. 1980
2Ki 5:26 **W.** not mine heart with thee, when 1980
2Ki 5:27 **w.** out from his presence a leper........ 3318
2Ki 6:4 So he **w.** with them. And when 3212
2Ki 6:23 away, and they **w.** to their master...... 3212
2Ki 6:24 and **w.** up, and besieged Samaria........ 5927
2Ki 7:8 carried thence. . .and **w.** and hid it....... 935
2Ki 7:8 they **w.** into one tent, and did eat........ 935
2Ki 7:8 and raiment, and **w.** and hid it; 3212
2Ki 7:15 they **w.** after them unto Jordan: 3212
2Ki 7:16 the people **w.** out, and spoiled the...... 3318
2Ki 8:2 and she **w.** with her household, ... 3212
2Ki 8:3 she **w.** forth to cry unto the king 3318
2Ki 8:9 So Hazael **w.** to meet him, and......... 3212
2Ki 8:21 So Joram **w.** over to Zair, and all 5674
2Ki 8:28 he **w.** with Joram the son of Ahab 3212
2Ki 8:29 king Joram **w.** back to be healed 7725
2Ki 8:29 of Judah **w.** down to see Joram.......... 3381
2Ki 9:4 the prophet, **w.** to Ramoth-gilead. 3212
2Ki 9:6 he arose, and **w.** into the house: 935
2Ki 9:16 in a chariot, and **w.** to Jezreel; 3212
2Ki 9:18 So there **w.** one on horseback to 3212
2Ki 9:21 Ahaziah king of Judah **w.** out, ... 3318
2Ki 9:21 they **w.** out against Jehu, and met...... 3318
2Ki 9:24 and the arrow **w.** out at his heart, ... 3318
2Ki 9:35 And they **w.** to bury her: but they 3212
2Ki 10:9 he **w.** out, and stood, and said to....... 3318
2Ki 10:23 Jehu **w.**, and Jehonadab the son of....... 935
2Ki 10:24 when they **w.** in to offer sacrifices 935
2Ki 10:25 **w.** to the city of the house of Baal. 3212
2Ki 11:16 she **w.** by the way by the which the..... 935
2Ki 11:18 people of the land **w.** into the house..... 935
2Ki 12:17 Then Hazael king of Syria **w.** up, ... 5927
2Ki 12:18 and he **w.** away from Jerusalem. 5927
2Ki 13:5 they **w.** out from under the hand.......... 3318
2Ki 14:11 Jehoash king of Israel **w.** up; and 5927
2Ki 15:14 the son of Gadi **w.** up from Tirzah,...... 5927
2Ki 16:9 Assyria **w.** up against Damascus,........ 5927
2Ki 16:10 king Ahaz **w.** to Damascus to.............. 3212
2Ki 17:5 **w.** up to Samaria, and besieged it....... 5927
2Ki 17:15 **w.** after...heathen that were found...... 3212
2Ki 18:7 he prospered whithersoever he **w.**...... 3318
2Ki 18:17 they **w.** up and came to Jerusalem...... 5927
2Ki 19:1 and **w.** into the house of the Lord......... 935
2Ki 19:14 **w.** up into the house of the Lord, ... 5927
2Ki 19:35 that the angel of the Lord **w.** out, ... 3318
2Ki 19:36 and **w.** and returned, and dwelt at...... 3212
2Ki 22:14 **w.** unto Huldah the prophetess, ... 3212
2Ki 23:2 king **w.** up into the house of the 5927
2Ki 23:29 king of Egypt **w.** up against the 5927
2Ki 23:29 and king Josiah **w.** against him; 3212
2Ki 24:12 **w.** out to the king of Babylon, ... 3318
2Ki 25:4 king **w.** the way toward the plain. 3212
1Ch 2:21 Hezron **w.** in to the daughter of 935
1Ch 4:39 they **w.** to the entrance of Gedor,........ 3212
1Ch 4:42 hundred men, **w.** to mount Seir, ... 1980
1Ch 5:18 threescore, that **w.** out to the war. 3318
1Ch 5:25 **w.** a whoring after the gods of the...........
1Ch 6:15 And Jehozadak **w.** into captivity,......... 1980
1Ch 7:23 And when he **w.** in to his wife, she....... 935
1Ch 7:23 because it **w.** evil with his house........ 1961
1Ch 10:3 And the battle **w.** sore against Saul,..........
1Ch 11:4 and all Israel **w.** to Jerusalem. 3212
1Ch 11:6 Joab the son of Zeruiah **w.** first up, ... 5927
1Ch 11:15 captains **w.** down to the rock to......... 3381
1Ch 11:22 he **w.** down and slew a lion in a pit 3381
1Ch 11:23 he **w.** down to him with a staff, and.... 3381
1Ch 12:15 These are they that **w.** over Jordan.... 5674
1Ch 12:17 And David **w.** out to meet them,......... 3318
1Ch 12:20 As he **w.** to Ziklag, there fell to......... 3212
1Ch 12:33 Zebulun, such as **w.** forth to battle, ... 3318
1Ch 12:36 of Asher, such as **w.** forth to battle, ... 3318
1Ch 13:6 And David **w.** up, and all Israel, to..... 5927
1Ch 14:8 the Philistines **w.** up to seek David..... 5927
1Ch 14:8 of it, and **w.** out against them............ 3318
1Ch 14:17 the fame of David **w.** out into all........ 3318
1Ch 15:25 **w.** to bring up the ark of the............. 1980
1Ch 16:20 when they **w.** from nation to nation, ... 1980
1Ch 17:21 whom god **w.** to redeem to be his...... 1980
1Ch 18:3 as he **w.** to stablish his dominion......... 3212
1Ch 18:6, 13 David whithersoever he **w.**.. 1980
1Ch 19:5 then there **w.** certain, and told 3212
1Ch 19:16 host of Hadarezer **w.** before them. ....
1Ch 21:4 and **w.** throughout all Israel, and 1980
1Ch 21:19 David **w.** up at the saying of Gad, ... 5927
1Ch 21:21 and **w.** out of the threshingfloor, ... 3318
1Ch 27:1 in and **w.** out month by month........... 3318
1Ch 29:30 and the times that **w.** over him,......... 5674
2Ch 1:3 **w.** to the high place that was at......... 3212
2Ch 1:6 **w.** up thither to the brasen altar 5927
2Ch 8:3 Solomon **w.** to Hamath-zobah, ... 3212
2Ch 8:17 Then **w.** Solomon to Ezion-geber, ... 1980
2Ch 8:18 **w.** with the servants of Solomon.......... 935
2Ch 9:4 **w.** up into the house of the Lord; 5927
2Ch 9:12 and **w.** away to her own land,............ 3212
2Ch 9:15 shekels of...gold **w.** to one target....... 5927
2Ch 9:16 shekels of gold **w.** to one shield......... 5927
2Ch 9:21 the king's ships **w.** to Tarshish 1980
2Ch 10:1 And Rehoboam **w.** to Shechem: 3212
2Ch 10:16 So all Israel **w.** to their tents............ 3212
2Ch 12:12 and also in Judah things **w.** well, ... 1961
2Ch 14:10 Then Asa **w.** out against him, and...... 3318
2Ch 15:2 And he **w.** out to meet Asa, and....... 3318
2Ch 15:5 was no peace to him that **w.** out, ... 3318
2Ch 17:9 **w.** about throughout all the cities 5437
2Ch 18:2 certain years he **w.** down to Ahab...... 3381
2Ch 18:12 messenger that **w.** to call Micaiah...... 1980
2Ch 18:23 Which way **w.** the Spirit of the 5674
2Ch 18:28 of Judah **w.** up to Ramoth-gilead......... 5927
2Ch 18:29 himself; and they **w.** to the battle. 935
2Ch 19:2 the seer **w.** out to meet him, ... 3318
2Ch 19:4 **w.** out again through the people......... 3318
2Ch 20:20 and **w.** forth into the wilderness of..... 3318
2Ch 20:20 and as they **w.** forth, Jehoshaphat....... 3318
2Ch 20:21 as they **w.** out before the army, and... 3318
2Ch 21:9 Jehoram **w.** forth with his princes, ... 5674
2Ch 22:5 **w.** with Jehoram the son of Ahab 3212
2Ch 22:6 **w.** down to see Jehoram the son........ 3381
2Ch 22:7 he **w.** out with Jehoram against.......... 3318
2Ch 23:2 And they **w.** about in Judah, and 5437
2Ch 23:17 the people **w.** to the house of Baal,...... 935
2Ch 25:11 people, and **w.** to the valley of salt, ... 3212
2Ch 25:21 So Joash the king of Israel **w.** up; 5927
2Ch 26:6 he **w.** forth and warred against the..... 3318
2Ch 26:11 men, that **w.** out to war by bands, ... 3318
2Ch 26:16 **w.** into the temple of the Lord to 935
2Ch 26:17 Azariah the priest **w.** in after him, ... 935
2Ch 28:9 **w.** out before the host that came 3318
2Ch 29:16 the priests **w.** into the inner part of 935
2Ch 29:18 they **w.** in to Hezekiah the king,.......... 935
2Ch 29:20 **w.** up to the house of the Lord.......... 5927
2Ch 30:6 posts **w.** with the letters from the...... 3212
2Ch 31:1 **w.** out to the cities of Judah,............ 3318
2Ch 34:22 **w.** to Huldah the prophetess, the....... 3212
2Ch 34:30 **w.** up into the house of the Lord, ... 5927
2Ch 35:20 and Josiah **w.** out against him. 3318
Ezr 2:1 that **w.** up out of the captivity, ... 5927
Ezr 2:59 they which **w.** up from Tel-melah, ... 5927
Ezr 4:23 **w.** up in haste to Jerusalem unto 236
Ezr 5:8 we **w.** into the provinces of Judea, ... 236
Ezr 7:6 This Ezra **w.** up from Babylon; 5927
Ezr 7:7 there **w.** up some of the children of.... 5927
Ezr 8:1 that **w.** up with me from Babylon, ... 5927
Ezr 10:6 **w.** into the chamber of Johanan.......... 3212
Ne 2:13 I **w.** out by night by the gate of........... 3318
Ne 2:14 I **w.** on to the gate of the fountain,..... 5674
Ne 2:15 **w.** I up in the night by the brook, ... 5927
Ne 2:16 the rulers knew not whither I **w.**, ... 1980
Ne 7:6 that **w.** up out of the captivity, ... 5927
Ne 7:61 which **w.** up also from Tel-melah,....... 5927
Ne 8:12 all the people **w.** their way to eat, ... 3212
Ne 8:16 the people **w.** forth, and brought........ 3318
Ne 9:11 **w.** through the midst of the sea on..... 5674
Ne 9:24 so the children **w.** in and possessed 935
Ne 12:1 Levites that **w.** up with Zerubbabel..... 5927
Ne 12:31 one **w.** on the right hand upon the...... 1980
Ne 12:32 after them **w.** Hoshaiah, and half........ 3212
Ne 12:37 they **w.** up by the stairs of the city 5927
Ne 12:38 gave thanks **w.** over against them. 1980
Es 2:14 In the evening she **w.**, and on the 935
Es 3:15 The posts **w.** out, being hastened....... 3318
Es 4:1 **w.** out into the midst of the city, ... 3318
Es 4:6 Hatach **w.** forth to Mordecai unto...... 3318
Es 4:17 So Mordecai **w.** his way, and did........ 5674
Es 5:9 Then **w.** Haman forth that day........... 3318
Es 7:7 his wrath **w.** into the palace gardens: ....
Es 7:8 word **w.** out of the king's mouth, ... 3318
Es 8:14 upon mules and camels **w.** out, ... 3318
Es 8:15 Mordecai **w.** out from the presence 3318
Es 9:4 his fame **w.** out throughout all the 1980
Job 1:4 sons **w.** and feasted in their houses, ... 1980
Job 1:12 Satan **w.** forth from the presence 3318
Job 2:7 So **w.** Satan forth from the presence... 3318
Job 18:20 they that **w.** before were affrighted..... 6923
Job 29:7 When I **w.** out to the gate through..... 3318
Job 30:28 I **w.** mourning without the sun: I........ 1980
Job 31:34 and **w.** not out of the door? 3318
Job 42:9 Zophar the Naamathite **w.**,................ 3212
Ps 18:8 **w.** up a smoke out of his nostrils, ... 5927
Ps 42:4 I **w.** with them to the house of.......... 1718
Ps 66:6 they **w.** through the flood on foot: 5674
Ps 66:12 we **w.** through fire and through........... 935
Ps 68:25 The singers **w.** before, the 6923
Ps 73:17 Until I **w.** into the sanctuary of............ 935
Ps 77:17 thine arrows also **w.** abroad. 1980
Ps 81:5 when he **w.** out through the land......... 3318
Ps 105:13 **w.** from one nation to another, ... 1980
Ps 106:32 it **w.** ill with Moses for their sakes: ....
Ps 106:39 **w.** a whoring with their own....................
Ps 114:1 When Israel **w.** out of Egypt, the....... 3318
Ps 119:67 Before I was afflicted I **w.** astray: 7683
Ps 133:2 that **w.** down to the skirts of his......... 3381
Pr 7:8 and he **w.** the way to her house, ... 6805
Pr 24:30 I **w.** by the field of the slothful, ... 5674
Ec 2:20 I **w.** about to cause my heart to......... 5437
Ca 5:7 watchmen that **w.** about the city 5437
Ca 6:11 I **w.** down into the garden of nuts 3381
Isa 7:1 **w.** up toward Jerusalem to war.......... 5927
Isa 8:3 I **w.** unto the prophetess; and she 7126
Isa 37:1 and **w.** into the house of the Lord........ 935
Isa 37:14 Hezekiah **w.** up unto the house of 5927
Isa 37:36 the angel of the Lord **w.** forth, ... 3318
Isa 37:37 departed, and **w.** and returned,........... 3212
Isa 48:3 they **w.** forth out of my mouth, ... 3318
Isa 51:23 the street, to them that **w.** over. 5674
Isa 52:4 My people **w.** down aforetime into........ 3381
Isa 57:17 he **w.** on frowardly in the way of 3212
Isa 60:15 so that no man **w.** through thee, ... 5674
Jer 3:8 but **w.** and played the harlot also......... 3212
Jer 7:24 and **w.** backward, and not forward...... 1961
Jer 11:10 they **w.** after other gods to serve....... 1980
Jer 13:5 So I **w.**, and hid it by Euphrates, ... 3212
Jer 13:7 Then I **w.** to Euphrates, and............. 3212
Jer 18:3 I **w.** down to the potter's house,......... 3381
Jer 22:11 which **w.** forth out of this place;.......... 3318
Jer 26:21 afraid, and fled, and **w.** into Egypt; 935
Jer 28:4 of Judah, that **w.** into Babylon, ... 935
Jer 28:11 prophet Jeremiah **w.** his way............. 3212
Jer 31:2 when I **w.** to cause him to rest.......... 1980
Jer 36:12 he **w.** down into the king's house, ... 3381
Jer 36:20 they **w.** in to the king into the 935
Jer 37:4 in and **w.** out among the people: 3318
Jer 37:12 Jeremiah **w.** forth out of Jerusalem 3318
Jer 38:8 **w.** forth out of the king's house, ... 3318
Jer 38:11 **w.** into the house of the king under...... 935
Jer 39:4 **w.** forth out of the city by night,......... 3318
Jer 39:4 and he **w.** out the way of the plain. 3318
Jer 40:6 Then **w.** Jeremiah unto Gedaliah 935
Jer 41:6 Ishmael...**w.** forth from Mizpah.......... 3318
Jer 41:6 them, weeping all along as he **w.**: 1980
Jer 41:12 **w.** to fight with Ishmael the son......... 3212
Jer 41:14 and **w.** unto Johanan the son of.......... 3212
Jer 41:15 men, and **w.** to the Ammonites........... 3212
Jer 44:3 in that they **w.** to burn incense, ... 3212
Jer 51:59 when he **w.** with Zedekiah the............ 3212
Jer 52:7 **w.** forth out of the city by night by..... 3318

Jer 52:7 and they w. by the way of the plain.... 3212
Eze 1:9 they turned not when they w.;......... 3212
Eze 1:9 they w. every one straight forward..... 3212
Eze 1:12 they w. every one straight forward:.... 3212
Eze 1:12 the spirit was to go, they w.;........... 3212
Eze 1:12 and they turned not when they w...... 3212
Eze 1:13 it w. up and down among the........... 1980
Eze 1:13 out of the fire w. forth lightning........ 3318
Eze 1:17 When they w., they w. upon their...... 3212
Eze 1:17 and they turned not when they w...... 3212
Eze 1:19 living creatures w., the wheels w...... 3212
Eze 1:20 the spirit was to go, they w.,........... 3212
Eze 1:21 When those w., these w.; and when... 3212
Eze 1:24 when they w., I heard the noise......... 3212
Eze 3:14 I w. in bitterness, in the heat of my... 3212
Eze 3:23 and w. forth into the plain:............... 3318
Eze 8:10 So I w. in and saw; and behold........... 935
Eze 8:11 a thick cloud of incense w. up. 5927
Eze 9:2 they w. in, and stood beside the......... 935
Eze 9:7 they w. forth, and slew in the city...... 3318
Eze 10:2 the city. And he w. in in my sight. 935
Eze 10:3 of the house, when the man w. in;....... 935
Eze 10:4 glory of the Lord w. up from the 7311
Eze 10:6 then he w. in, and stood beside the 935
Eze 10:7 linen: who took it, and w. out. 3318
Eze 10:11 When they w., they w. upon their...... 3212
Eze 10:11 they turned not as they w., but to 3212
Eze 10:11 it; they turned not as they w.. 3212
Eze 10:16 the cherubims w., the wheels w. by... 3212
Eze 10:19 when they w. out, the wheels also..... 3318
Eze 10:22 w. every one straight forward. 3212
Eze 11:23 glory of the Lord w. up from the 5927
Eze 11:24 vision that I had seen w. up from........ 5927
Eze 16:14 thy renown w. forth among the.......... 3318
Eze 19:6 he w. up and down among the.......... 1980
Eze 20:16 for their heart w. after their idols....... 1980
Eze 23:44 Yet they w. in unto her, as they go..... 935
Eze 23:44 so w. they in unto Aholah and unto...... 935
Eze 24:12 scum w. not forth out of her:............ 3318
Eze 25:3 of Judah, when they w. into captivity; ....
Eze 27:33 thy wares w. forth out of the seas, ... 3318
Eze 31:15 day when he w. down to the grave..... 3381
Eze 31:17 They also w. down into hell with........ 3381
Eze 36:20 whither they w., they profaned my 935
Eze 36:21 among the heathen, whither they w...... 935
Eze 36:22 among the heathen, whither ye w.. 935
Eze 39:23 w. into captivity for their iniquity:.............
Eze 40:6 and w. up the stairs thereof, and 5927
Eze 40:22 they w. unto it be seven steps;......... 5927
Eze 40:49 the steps whereby they w. up to it:..... 5927
Eze 41:3 Then w. he inward, and measured....... 935
Eze 41:7 winding...of the house w. still upward ....
Eze 44:10 far from me, when Israel w. astray,.... 8582
Eze 44:10 which w. astray away from me after... 8582
Eze 44:15 children of Israel w. astray from me, .. 8582
Eze 47:3 line in his hand w. forth eastward,...... 3318
Eze 48:11 my charge, which w. not astray......... 8582
Eze 48:11 the children of Israel w. astray, ... 8582
Eze 48:11 as the Levites w. astray.................. 8582
Da 2:13 decree w. forth that the wise men...... 5312
Da 2:16 Then Daniel w. in, and desired of....... 5954
Da 2:17 Then Daniel w. to the house, and......... 236
Da 2:24 Daniel w. in unto Arioch, whom......... 5954
Da 2:24 he w. and said thus unto him;............. 236
Da 6:10 was signed, he w. into his house;........ 5954
Da 6:18 Then the king w. to his palace, ... 236
Da 6:18 him: and his sleep w. from him.......... 5075
Da 6:19 w. in haste unto the den of lions. 236
Ho 1:3 So he w. and took Gomer the 3212
Ho 2:13 she w. after her lovers, and forgat 3212
Ho 5:13 then w. Ephraim to the Assyrian,........ 3212
Ho 9:10 but they w. to Baal-peor, and 935
Ho 11:2 called them, so they w. from them:.... 1980
Am 5:3 city that w. out by a thousand.......... 3318
Am 5:3 that which w. forth by an hundred...... 3318
Am 5:19 or w. into the house, and leaned his..... 935
Jon 1:3 the Lord, and w. down to Joppa;........ 3381
Jon 1:3 fare thereof, and w. down into it,....... 3381
Jon 2:6 I w. down to the bottoms of the 3381
Jon 3:3 arose, and w. unto Nineveh, ... 3212
Jon 4:5 So Jonah w. out of the city, and......... 3318
Na 3:10 carried away, she w. into captivity:...... 1980
Hab 3:5 Before him w. the pestilence, and 3212
Hab 3:5 burning coals w. forth at his feet....... 3318
Hab 3:11 the light of thine arrows they w.,........ 1980
Zec 2:3 angel that talked with me w. forth,..... 3318
Zec 2:3 another angel w. out to meet him,....... 3318
Zec 5:5 angel that talked with me w. forth,..... 3318
Zec 6:7 And the bay w. forth, and sought to... 3318
Zec 8:10 peace to him that w. out or came in... 3318
Zec 10:2 they w. their way as a flock, they...... 5265
Mt 2:9 saw in the east, w. before them, ... 4254
Mt 3:5 Then w. out to him Jerusalem, ... 1607
Mt 3:16 w. up straightway out of the water: 305
Mt 4:23 And Jesus w. about all Galilee, ... 4013
Mt 4:24 his fame w. throughout all Syria; 565
Mt 5:1 he w. up into a mountain: 305
Mt 8:32 out, they w. into the herd of swine:..... 565
Mt 8:33 fled, and w. their ways into the city, ... 565
Mt 9:25 he w. in, and took her by the hand,.... 1525
Mt 9:26 fame...w. abroad into all that land...... 1831
Mt 9:32 As they w. out, behold, they............ 1831
Mt 9:35 Jesus w. about all the cities and......... 4013
Mt 11:7 What w. ye out into the............... 1831
Mt 11:8 what w. ye out for to see? A man.. 1831
Mt 11:9 But what w. ye out for to see? A... 1831
Mt 12:1 Jesus w. on the sabbath through........ 4198
Mt 12:9 thence, he w. into their synagogue: 2064
Mt 12:14 Then the Pharisees w. out, and......... 1831
Mt 13:1 same day w. Jesus out of the house,.... 1831
Mt 13:2 so that he w. into a ship, and sat;...... 1684
Mt 13:3 Behold, a sower w. forth to sow;... 1831
Mt 13:25 among the wheat, and w. his way... 565
Mt 13:36 away, and w. into the house: 2064
Mt 13:46 w. and sold all that he had, and 565
Mt 14:12 buried it, and w. and told Jesus. 2064
Mt 14:14 Jesus w. forth, and saw a great 1831
Mt 14:23 he w. up into a mountain apart to......... 305
Mt 14:25 of the night Jesus w. unto them, ... 565
Mt 15:21 Then Jesus w. thence, and................ 1831
Mt 15:29 and w. up into a mountain, and sat....... 305
Mt 18:13 and nine which w. not astray........ 4105
Mt 18:28 But the same servant w. out, and.. 1831
Mt 18:30 but w. and cast him into prison,..... 565
Mt 19:22 that saying, he w. away sorrowful:....... 565
Mt 20:1 which w. out early in the............ 1821
Mt 20:3 he w. out about the third hour,........ 1821
Mt 20:4 give you. And they w. their way..... 565
Mt 20:5 Again he w. out about the sixth 1831
Mt 20:6 the eleventh hour he w. out,......... 1831
Mt 21:6 And the disciples w., and did as......... 4198
Mt 21:9 the multitudes that w. before, ... 4254
Mt 21:12 Jesus w. into the temple of God,......... 1525
Mt 21:17 and w. out of the city into Bethany;.... 1831
Mt 21:29 but afterward he repented, and w... 565
Mt 21:30 and said, I go, sir: and w. not....... 565
Mt 21:33 and w. into a far country: 589
Mt 22:5 made light of it, and w. their 565
Mt 22:10 servants w. out into the............... 1831
Mt 22:15 Then w. the Pharisees, and took........ 4198
Mt 22:22 and left him, and w. their way........... 565
Mt 24:1 Jesus w. out, and departed from 1831
Mt 25:1 w. forth to meet the bridegroom.... 1831
Mt 25:10 And while they w. to buy, the 565
Mt 25:10 were ready w. in with him to the .. 1525
Mt 25:16 five talents w. and traded with the .4198
Mt 25:18 one w. and digged in the earth, ... 565
Mt 25:25 w. and hid thy talent in the earth:.. 565
Mt 26:14 Iscariot, w. unto the chief priests,...... 4198
Mt 26:30 w. out into the mount of Olives. 1831
Mt 26:39 he w. a little farther, and fell on 4281
Mt 26:42 He w. away again the second time, ... 565
Mt 26:44 And he left them, and w. away again,... 565
Mt 26:58 the high priest's palace, and w. in, ... 1525
Mt 26:75 And he w. out, and wept bitterly. 1831
Mt 27:5 and w. and hanged himself................ 565
Mt 27:53 w. into the holy city, and appeared..... 1525
Mt 27:58 He w. to Pilate, and begged the 4344
Mt 27:66 So they w., and made the sepulchre... 4198
Mt 28:9 as they w. to tell his disciples, ... 4198
Mt 28:16 disciples w. away into Galilee, ... 4198
Mk 1:5 w. out unto him all the land of........... 1607
Mk 1:20 hired servants, and w. after him.......... 565
Mk 1:21 And they w. into Capernaum; and 1531
Mk 1:35 he w. out, and departed into a.......... 1831
Mk 1:45 he w. out, and began to publish it 1831
Mk 2:12 bed, and w. forth before them all; 1831
Mk 2:13 he w. forth again by the sea side; 1831
Mk 2:23 he w. through the corn fields on 3899
Mk 2:23 as they w., to pluck the ears of.. 3598,4160
Mk 2:26 How he w. into the house of God.. 1525
Mk 3:6 And the Pharisees w. forth, and.......... 1831
Mk 3:19 him: and they w. into an house.......... 2064
Mk 3:21 it, they w. out to lay hold on him:...... 1831
Mk 4:3 Behold, there w. out a sower to 1831
Mk 5:13 And the unclean spirits w. out,.......... 1831
Mk 5:14 they w. out to see what it was that.... 1831
Mk 5:24 Jesus w. with him; and much............ 565
Mk 6:1 he w. out from thence, and came......... 1831
Mk 6:6 he w. round about the villages,.......... 4013
Mk 6:12 they w. out, and preached that.......... 1831
Mk 6:24 she w. forth, and said unto her.......... 1831
Mk 6:27 he w. and beheaded him in the........... 565
Mk 6:51 he w. up unto them into the ship;........ 305
Mk 7:24 w. into the borders of Tyre and 565
Mk 8:27 Jesus w. out, and his disciples, ... 1831
Mk 10:22 that saying, and w. away grieved:........ 565
Mk 10:32 and Jesus w. before them: and 4254
Mk 10:46 w. out of Jericho with his disciples....... 1607
Mk 11:4 they w. their way, and found the......... 565
Mk 11:9 they that w. before, and they that...... 4254
Mk 11:11 he w. out unto Bethany with the........ 1831
Mk 11:15 and Jesus w. into the temple, and 1525
Mk 11:19 was come, he w. out of the city. 1607
Mk 12:1 and w. into a far country.............. 589
Mk 12:12 and they left him, and w. their way...... 565
Mk 13:1 And as he w. out of the temple, ... 1607
Mk 14:10 twelve, w. unto the chief priests, ... 565
Mk 14:16 his disciples w. forth, and came 1831
Mk 14:26 w. out into the mount of Olives. 1831
Mk 14:35 he w. forward a little, and fell on 4281
Mk 14:39 again he w. away, and prayed, and........ 565
Mk 14:68 and he w. out into the porch; and 1831
Mk 15:43 and w. in boldly unto Pilate, and 1525
Mk 16:8 they w. out quickly, and fled from 1831
Mk 16:10 she w. and told them that had........... 4198
Mk 16:12 walked, and w. into the country.......... 4198
Mk 16:13 w. and told it unto the residue: 565
Mk 16:20 And they w. forth, and preached......... 1831
Lu 1:9 he w. into the temple of the Lord. 1525
Lu 1:39 w. into the hill country with haste, ... 4198
Lu 2:1 there w. out a decree from Caesar....... 1831
Lu 2:3 all w. to be taxed, every one into 4198
Lu 2:4 And Joseph also w. up from Galilee,..... 305
Lu 2:41 his parents w. to Jerusalem every 4198
Lu 2:42 they w. up to Jerusalem after the 305
Lu 2:44 the company, w. a day's journey; 2064
Lu 2:51 he w. down with them, and came......... 2597
Lu 4:14 there w. out a fame of him through.... 1831
Lu 4:16 he w. into the synagogue on the 1525
Lu 4:30 the midst of them w. his way,........... 4198
Lu 4:37 fame of him w. out into every place..... 1607
Lu 4:42 he departed and w. into a desert......... 4198
Lu 5:15 the more w. there a fame abroad....... 1330
Lu 5:19 they w. upon the housetop, and let...... 305
Lu 5:27 And after these things he w. forth,..... 1831
Lu 6:1 that he w. through the corn fields; 1279
Lu 6:4 he w. into the house of God,.......... 1525
Lu 6:12 he w. out into a mountain to pray, ... 1831
Lu 6:19 for there w. virtue out of him, and..... 1831
Lu 7:6 Then Jesus w. with them. And 4198
Lu 7:11 that he w. into a city called Nain,....... 4198
Lu 7:11 many of his disciples w. with him,...... 4848
Lu 7:17 rumour of him w. forth throughout 1831
Lu 7:24 What w. ye out into the................. 1831
Lu 7:25, 26 But what w. ye out for to see?.. 1831
Lu 7:36 he w. into the Pharisee's house, ... 1525
Lu 8:1 that he w. throughout every city......... 1353
Lu 8:2 out of whom w. seven devils,............ 1831
Lu 8:5 A sower w. out to sow his seed: 1831
Lu 8:22 w. into a ship with his disciples:......... 1684
Lu 8:27 And when he w. forth to land,........... 1831
Lu 8:33 Then w. the devils out of the man,..... 1831
Lu 8:34 w. and told it in the city and in the...... 565
Lu 8:35 they w. out to see what was done;...... 1831
Lu 8:37 and he w. up into the ship, and 1681
Lu 8:39 And he w. his way, and published........ 565
Lu 8:42 as he w. the people thronged him. 5217
Lu 9:6 and w. through the towns,................ 1330
Lu 9:10 w. aside privately into a desert 5298
Lu 9:28 and w. up into a mountain to pray......... 305
Lu 9:52 they w., and entered into a village....... 4198
Lu 9:56 And they w. to another village........... 4198
Lu 9:57 as they w. in the way, a certain man.. 4198
Lu 10:30 man w. down from Jerusalem to ... 2597
Lu 10:34 And w. to him, and bound up his .. 4334
Lu 10:38 as they w., that he entered into a...... 4198
Lu 11:37 he w. in, and sat down to meat. 1525
Lu 13:22 w. through the cities and villages, ... 1279
Lu 14:1 as he w. into the house of one of....... 2064
Lu 14:25 w. great multitudes with him: and 4848

Lu 15:15 w. and joined himself to a citizen.. 4198
Lu 16:30 if one w. unto them from the........ 4198
Lu 17:11 as he w. to Jerusalem, that he.......... 4198
Lu 17:14 as they w., they were cleansed. 5217
Lu 17:29 day that Lot w. out of Sodom it.... 1831
Lu 18:10 Two men w. up into the temple to .. 305
Lu 18:14 this man w. down to his house...... 2597
Lu 18:39 they which w. before rebuked him,..... 4254
Lu 19:12 nobleman w. into a far country..... 4198
Lu 19:28 he w. before, ascending up to 4198
Lu 19:32 they that were sent w. their way,........ 565
Lu 19:36 as he w., they spread their clothes..... 4198
Lu 19:45 he w. into the temple, and began...... 1525
Lu 20:9 w. into a far country for a long....... 589
Lu 21:37 at night he w. out, and abode in the ... 1831
Lu 22:4 he w. his way, and communed with...... 565
Lu 22:13 they w., and found as he had said........ 565
Lu 22:39 w., as he was wont, to the mount...... 4198
Lu 22:47 one of the twelve, w. before them, ... 4281
Lu 22:62 Peter w. out, and wept bitterly.......... 1831
Lu 23:52 This man w. unto Pilate, and............ 4344
Lu 24:13 two of them w. that same day to a..... 4198
Lu 24:15 drew near, and w. with them. 4848
Lu 24:24 were with us w. to the sepulchre, ... 565
Lu 24:28 unto the village, whither they w.:....... 4198
Lu 24:29 And he w. in to tarry with them. 1525
Joh 2:12 this he w. down to Capernaum, ... 2597
Joh 2:13 and Jesus w. up to Jerusalem,............ 305
Joh 4:28 w. her way into the city, and saith....... 565
Joh 4:30 Then they w. out of the city, and....... 1831
Joh 4:43 departed thence, and w. into Galilee..... 565
Joh 4:45 for they also w. unto the feast........... 2064
Joh 4:47 he w. unto him, and besought him 565
Joh 4:50 unto him, and he w. his way. 4198
Joh 5:1 and Jesus w. up to Jerusalem............. 305
Joh 5:4 For an angel w. down at a certain...... 2597
Joh 6:1 Jesus w. over the sea of Galilee, ... 565
Joh 6:3 And Jesus w. up into a mountain, ... 424
Joh 6:16 disciples w. down unto the sea, ... 2597
Joh 6:17 w. over...sea toward Capernaum........ 2064
Joh 6:21 was at the land whither they w.......... 5217
Joh 6:22 Jesus w. not with his disciples 4897
Joh 6:66 time many of his disciples w. back,....... 565
Joh 7:10 then w. he also up unto the feast, ... 305
Joh 7:14 feast Jesus w. up into the temple,........ 305
Joh 7:53 every man w. unto his own house...... 4198
Joh 8:1 Jesus w. unto the mount of Olives...... 4198
Joh 8:9 w. out one by one, beginning at......... 1831
Joh 8:59 himself, and w. out of the temple,...... 1831
Joh 9:7 He w. his way therefore, and............. 565
Joh 9:11 I w. and washed, and I received.......... 565
Joh 10:40 w. away again beyond Jordan into 565
Joh 11:20 was coming, w. and met him:............ 5221
Joh 11:28 she had so said, she w. her way, ... 565
Joh 11:31 she rose up hastily and w. out,.......... 1831
Joh 11:46 some of them w. their ways to the 565
Joh 11:54 w. thence unto a country near to 565
Joh 11:55 many w. out of the country up to 305
Joh 12:11 of him many of the Jews w. away,...... 5217
Joh 12:13 trees, and w. forth to meet him,......... 1831
Joh 13:3 come from God, and w. to God; 5217
Joh 13:30 having received the sop w...out: 1831
Joh 18:1 w. forth with his disciples over the..... 1831
Joh 18:4 w. forth, and said unto them, ... 1831
Joh 18:6 they w. backward, and fell to the......... 565
Joh 18:15 w. in with Jesus into the palace of...... 4897
Joh 18:16 Then w. out that other disciple, ... 1831
Joh 18:28 w. not into the judgment hall, ... 1525
Joh 18:29 Pilate then w. out unto them, and 1831
Joh 18:38 he w. out again unto the Jews, ... 1831
Joh 19:4 Pilate therefore w. forth again, and..... 1831
Joh 19:9 w. again into the judgment hall, ... 1525
Joh 19:17 w. forth into a place called............... 1831
Joh 20:3 Peter therefore w. forth, and that 1831
Joh 20:5 clothes lying; yet w. he not in. 1525
Joh 20:6 w. into the sepulchre, and seeth 1525
Joh 20:8 Then w. in also that other disciple,...... 1525
Joh 20:10 disciples w. away again unto their........ 565
Joh 21:3 They w. forth, and entered into a 1831
Joh 21:11 Simon Peter w. up, and drew the 305
Joh 21:23 Then w. this saying abroad among........ 1831
Ac 1:10 toward heaven as he w. up,.............. 4198
Ac 1:13 they w. up into an upper room,........... 305
Ac 1:21 Lord Jesus w. in and out........... 1525,1831
Ac 3:1 Now Peter and John w. up together..... 305
Ac 4:23 they w. to their own company, ... 2064
Ac 5:26 w. the captain with the officers, ... 565
Ac 7:15 So Jacob w. down into Egypt, and...... 2597
Ac 8:4 w. every where preaching the 1330
Ac 8:5 Then Philip w. down to the city of 2718
Ac 8:27 And he arose and w.: and, behold, ... 4198
Ac 8:36 And as they w. on their way, they 4198
Ac 8:38 they w. down both into the water, ... 2597
Ac 8:39 and he w. on his way rejoicing.......... 4198
Ac 9:1 the Lord, w. unto the high priest, ... 4334
Ac 9:17 Ananias w. his way, and entered 565
Ac 9:29 but they w. about to slay him............ 2021
Ac 9:39 Peter arose and w. with them............ 4905
Ac 10:9 as they w. on their journey, and 3596
Ac 10:9 Peter w. up upon the housetop to........ 305
Ac 10:21 Then Peter w. down to the men......... 2597
Ac 10:23 morrow Peter w. away with them, ... 1831
Ac 10:27 he w. in, and found many that........... 1525
Ac 10:38 who w. about doing good, and........... 1330
Ac 12:9 And he w. out, and followed him;....... 1831
Ac 12:10 they w. out, and passed on through..... 1831
Ac 12:17 and w. into another place............... 4198
Ac 12:19 And he w. down from Judea to 2718
Ac 13:11 he w. about seeking some to lead 4013
Ac 13:14 and w. into the synagogue on the....... 1525
Ac 14:1 w. both together into the synagogue... 1525
Ac 14:25 Perga, they w. down into Attalia:........ 2597
Ac 15:24 certain which w. out from us have...... 1831
Ac 15:38 and w. not with them to the work...... 4905
Ac 15:41 he w. through Syria and Cilicia, ... 1330
Ac 16:4 as they w. through the cities, they..... 1279
Ac 16:13 on the sabbath we w. out of the 1831
Ac 16:16 as we w. to prayer, a certain 4198
Ac 16:40 And they w. out of the prison, and..... 1831
Ac 17:2 his manner was, w. in unto them, ... 1525
Ac 17:10 w. into the synagogue of the Jews. 549
Ac 18:22 church, he w. down to Antioch. 2597
Ac 18:23 w. over all the country of Galatia 1330
Ac 19:8 And he w. into the synagogue, ... 1525
Ac 19:12 the evil spirits w. out of them. 1831
Ac 20:10 Paul w. down, and fell on him, and..... 2597
Ac 20:13 we w. before the ship, and sailed....... 4281
Ac 21:2 we w. aboard, and set forth............. 1910
Ac 21:5 we departed and w. our way; and 4198
Ac 21:15 carriages, and w. up to Jerusalem. 305
Ac 21:16 There w. with us also certain of 4905
Ac 21:18 Paul w. in with us unto James; 1524
Ac 21:31 And as they w. about to kill him, ... 2212
Ac 22:5 w. to Damascus, to bring them.......... 4198
Ac 22:26 he w. and told the chief captain, ... 4334
Ac 23:16 he w. and entered into the castle, ... 3854
Ac 23:19 and w. with him aside privately, ... 402
Ac 24:11 days since I w. up to Jerusalem........... 305
Ac 25:6 days, he w. down unto Caesarea;........ 2597
Ac 26:12 as I w. to Damascus with authority...... 4198
Ac 26:21 temple, and w. about to kill me. 3987
Ac 28:14 days: and so we w. toward Rome. 2064
Ro 10:18 their sound w. into all the earth, ... 1831
2Co 2:13 I w. from thence into Macedonia. 1831
2Co 8:17 of his own accord he w. unto you........ 1831
Ga 1:17 Neither w. I up to Jerusalem to........... 424
Ga 1:17 but I w. into Arabia, and returned........ 565
Ga 1:18 Then after three years I w. up to........ 424
Ga 2:1 I w. up again to Jerusalem with........... 305
Ga 2:2 And I w. up by revelation, and........... 305
1Ti 1:3 when I w. into Macedonia,................ 4198
1Ti 1:18 to the prophecies which w. before........ 4254
Heb 9:6 the priests w. always into the........... 1524
Heb 9:7 into the second w. the high priest ....
Heb 11:8 obeyed; and he w. out, ... 1831
Heb 11:8 not knowing whither he w................ 2064
1Pe 3:19 he w. and preached unto the............ 4198
1Jo 2:19 They w. out from us, but they were... 1831
1Jo 2:19 they w. out, that they might be made ....
3Jo 7 for his name's sake they w. forth, ... 1831
Re 1:16 his mouth w. a sharp twoedged 1607
Re 6:2 he w. forth conquering, and to........... 1831
Re 6:4 there w. out another horse that......... 1831
Re 10:9 I w. unto the angel, and said unto........ 565
Re 12:17 w. to make war with the remnant of 565
Re 16:2 the first w., and poured out his vial...... 565
Re 20:9 they w. upon the breadth of the 305

WENTEST

Ge 49:4 thou w. up to thy father's bed; 5927
Jg 5:4 Lord, when thou w. out of Seir; 3318
Jg 8:1 when thou w. to fight with the 1980
1Sa 10:2 asses which thou w. to seek are 1980
2Sa 7:9 with thee whithersoever thou w.,....... 1980
2Sa 16:17 why w. thou not with thy friend? 1980
2Sa 19:25 Wherefore w. not thou with me, ... 1980
Ps 68:7 thou w. forth before thy people, ... 3318
Isa 57:7 even thither w. thou up to offer......... 5927
Isa 57:9 thou w. to the king with ointment, ... 7788
Jer 2:2 thou w. after me in the wilderness, ... 3212
Jer 31:21 even the way which thou w.: 1980
Hab 3:13 Thou w. forth for the salvation of........ 3318
Ac 11:3 Thou w. in to men uncircumcised,...... 1525

WEPT

Ge 21:16 and lift up her voice, and w............ 1058
Ge 27:38 Esau lifted up his voice, and w.. 1058
Ge 29:11 and lifted up his voice, and w.. 1058
Ge 33:4 neck, and kissed him: and they w....... 1058
Ge 37:35 Thus his father w. for him. 1058
Ge 42:24 himself about from them, and w.; 1058
Ge 43:30 into his chamber, and w. there. 1058
Ge 45:2 And he w. aloud: 5414,853,6963,1065
Ge 45:14 brother Benjamin's neck, and w.; 1058
Ge 45:14 and Benjamin w. upon his neck......... 1058
Ge 45:15 his brethren, and w. upon them: 1058
Ge 46:29 and w. on his neck a good while. 1058
Ge 50:1 and w. upon him, and kissed him. 1058
Ge 50:17 Joseph w. when they spake unto........ 1058
Ex 2:6 child: and, behold, the babe w.. 1058
Nu 11:4 children of Israel also w. again,.......... 1058
Nu 11:18 ye have w. in the ears of the Lord, ... 1058
Nu 11:20 and have w. before him, saying,......... 1058
Nu 14:1 cried; and the people w. that night. 1058
De 1:45 returned and w. before the Lord;......... 1058
De 34:8 the children of Israel w. for Moses..... 1058
Jg 2:4 people lifted up their voice, and w...... 1058
Jg 14:16 And Samson's wife w. before him,...... 1058
Jg 14:17 she w. before him the seven days, ... 1058
Jg 20:23 and w. before the Lord until even, ... 1058
Jg 20:26 came unto the house of God, and w.,.. 1058
Jg 21:2 lifted up their voices, and w. sore; 1058
Ru 1:9 they lifted up their voice, and w......... 1058
Ru 1:14 lifted up their voice, and w. again:...... 1058
1Sa 1:7 therefore she w., and did not eat. 1058
1Sa 1:10 prayed unto the Lord, and w. sore. 1058
1Sa 11:4 people lifted up their voices, and w..... 1058
1Sa 20:41 w. one with another, until David 1058
1Sa 24:16 Saul lifted up his voice, and w.. 1058
1Sa 30:4 him lifted up their voice and w.,......... 1058
2Sa 1:12 they mourned, and w., and fasted 1058
2Sa 3:32 and w. at the grave of Abner; 1058
2Sa 3:32 of Abner; and all the people w........... 1058
2Sa 3:34 all the people w. again over him......... 1058
2Sa 12:22 child was yet alive, I fasted and w...... 1058
2Sa 13:36 and lifted up their voice and w.......... 1058
2Sa 13:36 and all his servants w. very sore......... 1058
2Sa 15:23 all the country w. with a loud voice, ... 1058
2Sa 15:30 mount Olivet, and w. as he went up, .. 1058
2Sa 18:33 the chamber over the gate, and w...... 1058
2Ki 8:11 ashamed: and the man of God w.. 1058
2Ki 13:14 and w. over his face, and said, O my.. 1058
2Ki 20:3 thy sight. And Hezekiah w. sore. 1058
2Ki 22:19 rent thy clothes, and w. before me;.... 1058
Ezr 3:12 their eyes, w. with a loud voice;......... 1058
Ezr 10:1 for the people w. very sore. 1058
Ne 1:4 words, that I sat down and w.,.......... 1058
Ne 8:9 For all the people w., when they 1058
Job 2:12 they lifted up their voice, and w.;........ 1058
Ps 69:10 When I w., and chastened my soul..... 1058
Ps 137:1 we w., when we remembered Zion..... 1058
Isa 38:3 thy sight. And Hezekiah w. sore. 1058
Ho 12:4 he w. and made supplication unto....... 1058
Mt 26:75 and he went out, and w. bitterly. 2799
Mk 5:38 them that w. and wailed greatly. 2799
Mk 14:72 when he thought thereon, he w.. 2799
Mk 16:10 with him as they mourned and w........ 2799
Lu 7:32 to you, and ye have not w.. 2799
Lu 8:52 all w., and bewailed her: but he......... 2799
Lu 19:41 he beheld the city, and w. over it, ... 2799
Lu 22:62 Peter went out, and w. bitterly.......... 2799
Joh 11:35 Jesus w.................................. 1145
Joh 20:11 and as she w., she stooped down,...... 2799
Ac 20:37 And they all w. sore, and fell on..1096,2805
1Co 7:30 that weep, as though they w. not;...... 2799
Re 5:4 And I w. much, because no man 2799

WERE See in the APPENDIX; also WERT.

WERT See also WAST.

Job 8:6 If thou w. pure and upright; surely...........

Ca 8:1 O that thou **w.** as my brother, that
Ro 11:17 olive tree, **w.** graffed in among them,
Ro 11:24 For if thou **w.** cut out of the olive tree
Ro 11:24 and **w.** graffed contrary to nature into
Re 3:15 **hot: I would thou w. cold or hot** *1498*

WEST See also WESTERN; WESTWARD.
Ge 12:8 having Beth-el on the **w.**, and Hai 3220
Ge 28:14 thou shalt spread abroad to the **w.** 3220
Ex 10:19 turned a mighty strong **w.** wind, 3220
Ex 27:12 the **w.** side shall be hangings of fifty 3220
Ex 38:12 the **w.** side were hangings of fifty 3220
Nu 2:18 On the **w.** side shall be the standard 3220
Nu 34:6 this shall be your **w.** border. 3220
Nu 35:5 on the **w.** side two thousand cubits, 3220
De 33:23 possess thou the **w.** and the south. 3220
Jos 8:9 Beth-el and Ai, on the **w.** side of Ai: 3220
Jos 8:12 and Ai, on the **w.** side of the city. 3220
Jos 8:13 liers in wait on the **w.** of the city, 3220
Jos 11:2 in the borders of Dor on the **w.**, 3220
Jos 11:3 on the east and on the **w.**, 3220
Jos 12:7 on this side Jordan on the **w.** 3220
Jos 15:12 the **w.** border was to the great sea, 3220
Jos 18:14 of Judah: this was the **w.** quarter. 3220
Jos 18:15 and the border went out on the **w.**, 3220
Jos 19:34 reacheth to Asher on the **w.** side, 3220
1Ki 7:25 and three looking toward the **w.**, 3220
1Ch 9:24 toward the east, **w.**, north, and 3220
1Ch 12:15 the east, and toward the **w.** 4628
2Ch 4:4 and three looking toward the **w.**, 3220
2Ch 32:30 to the **w.** side of the city of David. 4628
2Ch 33:14 on the **w.** side of Gihon, in the 4628
Ps 75:6 from the east, nor from the **w.**, 4628
Ps 103:12 As far as the east is from the **w.**, 4628
Ps 107:3 from the east, and from the **w.**, 4628
Isa 11:14 of the Philistines toward the **w.**; 3220
Isa 43:5 east, and gather thee from the **w.**; 4628
Isa 45:6 and from the **w.**, that there is none 4628
Isa 49:12 and from the **w.**; and these from 3220
Isa 59:19 the name of the Lord from the **w.**, 4628
Eze 41:12 end toward the **w.** was seventy 3220
Eze 42:19 He turned about to the **w.** side, 3220
Eze 45:7 city, from the **w.** side westward, 3220
Eze 45:7 from the **w.** border unto the east 3220
Eze 47:20 **w.** side also shall be the great sea 3220
Eze 47:20 Hamath. This is the **w.** side. 3220
Eze 48:1 for these are his sides east and **w.**; 3220
Eze 48:2 from the east side unto the **w.** side, 3220
Eze 48:3 the east side even unto the **w.** side, 3220
Eze 48:4, 5 the east side unto the **w.** side, 3220
Eze 48:6 the east side even unto the **w.** side, 3220
Eze 48:7, 8 the east side unto the **w.** side, 3220
Eze 48:8 from the east side unto the **w.** side: 3220
Eze 48:10 and toward the **w.** ten thousand in 3220
Eze 48:16 the **w.** side four thousand and five 3220
Eze 48:17 toward the **w.** two hundred and 3220
Eze 48:21 and twenty thousand toward the **w.** 3220
Eze 48:23, 24,25,26,27 east side unto the **w.** 3220
Eze 48:34 At the **w.** side four thousand and 3220
Da 8:5 an he goat came from the **w.** on 4628
Ho 11:10 children shall tremble from the **w.** 3220
Zec 8:7 and from the **w.** country; 3996,8121
Zec 14:4 toward the east and toward the **w.**, 3220
Mt 8:11 **shall come from the east and w.,** *1424*
Mt 24:27 **and shineth even unto the w.;** *1424*
Lu 12:54 **ye see a cloud rise out of the w.,** *1424*
Lu 13:29 **from the east, and from the w.,** *1424*
Ac 27:12 toward the south **w.** and north *3047*
Ac 27:12 toward the south...and north **w.** *5566*
Re 21:13 gates; and on the **w.** three gates *1424*

WESTERN
Nu 34:6 and as for the **w.** border, ye shall 3220

WESTWARD
Ge 13:14 southward, and eastward, and **w.** 3220
Ex 26:22 for the sides of the tabernacle **w.** 3220
Ex 26:27 the tabernacle, for the two sides **w.** 3220
Ex 36:27 for the sides of the tabernacle **w.** 3220
Ex 36:32 of the tabernacle for the sides **w.** 3220
Nu 3:23 pitch behind the tabernacle **w.** 3220
De 3:27 of Pisgah, and lift up thine eyes **w.**, 3220
Jos 5:1 were on the side of Jordan **w.**, and 3220
Jos 15:8 before the valley of Hinnom **w.**, 3220
Jos 15:10 from Baalah **w.** unto mount Seir, 3220
Jos 16:3 down **w.** to the coast of Japhleti, 3220
Jos 16:8 Tappuah **w.** unto the river Kanah; 3220
Jos 18:12 went up through the mountains **w.**; 3220
Jos 19:26 and reacheth to Carmel **w.**, and to 3220
Jos 19:34 coast turneth **w.** to Aznoth-tabor, 3220
Jos 22:7 brethren on this side Jordan **w.** 3220
Jos 23:4 even unto the great sea **w.** 3996,8121
1Ch 7:28 and **w.** Gezer, with the towns 4628
1Ch 26:16 and Hosah the lot came forth **w.**, 4628
1Ch 26:18 At Parbar **w.**, four at the causeway, 4628
1Ch 26:30 of Israel on this side Jordan **w.** 4628
Eze 45:7 of the city, from the west side **w.**, 3220
Eze 46:19 was a place on the two sides **w.** 3220
Eze 48:18 eastward, and ten thousand **w.** 3220
Eze 48:21 and **w.** over against the five and 3220
Da 8:4 I saw the ram pushing **w.**, and 3220

WEST-WIND See WEST and WIND.

WET
Job 24:8 They are **w.** with the showers of 7372
Da 4:15, 23 be **w.** with the dew of heaven, 6647
Da 4:25 **w.** thee with the dew of heaven, 6647
Da 4:33 and his body was **w.** with the dew 6647
Da 5:21 and his body was **w.** with the dew 6647

WHALE See also WHALE'S; WHALES.
Job 7:12 Am I a sea, or a **w.**, that thou 8577
Eze 32:2 and thou art as a **w.** in the seas: 8565

WHALE'S
Mt 12:40 **and three nights in the w. belly;** *2785*

WHALES
Ge 1:21 And God created great **w.**, and 8577

WHAT See also SOMEWHAT; WHATSOEVER.
Ge 2:19 to see **w.** he would call them: 4100
Ge 3:13 **W.** is this that thou hast done? 4100
Ge 4:10 And he said, **W.** hast thou done? 4100
Ge 9:24 **w.** his younger son had done 853,834
Ge 12:18 **W.** is this that thou hast done 4100
Ge 15:2 Lord God, **w.** wilt thou give me, 4100
Ge 20:9 him, **W.** hast thou done unto us? 4100
Ge 20:9 and **w.** have I offended thee, that 4100
Ge 20:10 **W.** sawest thou, that thou hast 4100
Ge 21:17 unto her, **W.** aileth thee, Hagar? 4100
Ge 21:29 **W.** mean these seven ewe lambs 4100
Ge 23:15 **w.** is that betwixt me and thee? 4100
Ge 24:65 **W.** man is this that walketh in 4310
Ge 25:32 **w.** profit shall this birthright do 4100
Ge 26:10 **W.** is this thou hast done unto us? 4100
Ge 27:37 and **w.** shall I do now unto thee, 4100
Ge 27:46 land, **w.** good shall my life do me? 4100
Ge 29:15 tell me, **w.** shall thy wages be? 4100
Ge 29:25 **W.** is this thou hast done unto me? 4100
Ge 30:31 And he said, **W.** shall I give thee? 4100
Ge 31:26 **W.** hast thou done, that thou hast 4100
Ge 31:32 discern thou **w.** is thine with me, 4100
Ge 31:36 **W.** is my trespass? **w.** is my sin, 4100
Ge 31:37 **w.** hast thou found of all thy...stuff? 4100
Ge 31:43 **w.** can I do this day unto these my 4100
Ge 32:27 he said unto him, **W.** is thy name? 4100
Ge 33:8 **W.** meanest thou by all this drove 4310
Ge 33:15 And he said, **W.** needeth it? let 4100
Ge 34:11 **w.** ye shall say unto me I will give 834
Ge 37:10 **W.** is this dream that thou hast 4100
Ge 37:15 him, saying, **W.** seekest thou? 4100
Ge 37:20 see **w.** will become of his dreams. 4100
Ge 37:26 **W.** profit is it if we slay our brother, 4100
Ge 38:16 And she said, **W.** wilt thou give me, 4100
Ge 38:18 said, **W.** pledge shall I give thee? 834
Ge 39:8 not **w.** is with me in the house, 4100
Ge 41:25 Pharaoh **w.** he is about to do. 853,834
Ge 41:28 **W.** God is about to do he sheweth 834
Ge 41:55 unto Joseph; **w.** he saith to you, do 834
Ge 42:28 **W.** is this that God hath done 4100
Ge 44:15 **W.** deed is this that ye have done? 4100
Ge 44:16 **W.** shall we say unto my lord? 4100
Ge 44:16 **w.** shall we speak? or how shall we 4100
Ge 46:33 shall say, **W.** is your occupation? 4100
Ge 47:3 brethren, **W.** is your occupation? 4100
Ex 2:4 afar off, to wit **w.** would be done to him.
Ex 3:13 shall say to me, **W.** is his name? 4100
Ex 3:13 **w.** shall I say unto them? 4100
Ex 4:2 unto him, **W.** is that in thine hand? 4100
Ex 4:12 and teach thee **w.** thou shalt say. 834
Ex 4:15 will teach you **w.** ye shall do. 853,834
Ex 6:1 see **w.** I will do to Pharaoh: 834
Ex 10:2 **w.** things I have wrought in 853,834
Ex 10:26 with **w.** we must serve the Lord, 4100
Ex 12:26 you, **W.** mean ye by this service? 4100
Ex 13:14 in time to come, saying, **W.** is this? 4100
Ex 15:24 Moses, saying, **W.** shall we drink? 4100
Ex 16:7 **w.** are we, that ye murmur against 4100
Ex 16:8 **w.** are we? your murmurings are 4100
Ex 16:15 manna: for thy wist not **w.** it was. 4100
Ex 17:4 **W.** shall I do unto this people? 4100
Ex 18:14 **W.** is this thing that thou doest to 4100
Ex 19:4 seen **w.** I did unto the Egyptians, 834
Ex 23:11 **w.** they leave the beasts of the field
Ex 32:1 we wot not **w.** is become of him. 4100
Ex 32:21 **W.** did this people unto thee, that 4100
Ex 32:23 we wot not **w.** is become of him. 4100
Ex 33:5 that I may know **w.** to do unto thee. 4100
Le 15:9 **w.** saddle soever he rideth upon 834
Le 17:3 **W.** man soever there be of...Israel, 376
Le 22:4 **W.** man soever of the seed of Aaron 376
Le 25:20 **W.** shall we eat the seventh year? 4100
Nu 9:8 hear **w.** the Lord will command 4100
Nu 10:32 that **w.** goodness the Lord shall do 834
Nu 13:18 And see the land, **w.** it is; and the 4100
Nu 13:19 **w.** the land is that they dwell in, 4100
Nu 13:19 **w.** cities they be that they dwell in, 4100
Nu 13:20 **w.** the land is, whether it be fat or 4100
Nu 15:34 declared **w.** should be done to him. 4100
Nu 16:11 and **w.** is Aaron, that ye murmur 4100
Nu 21:14 **W.** he did in the Red sea, and in 853
Nu 22:9 **W.** men are these with thee? 4310
Nu 22:19 may know **w.** the Lord will say 4100
Nu 22:28 **W.** have I done unto thee, that 4100
Nu 23:11 **W.** hast thou done unto me? 4100
Nu 23:17 him, **W.** hath the Lord spoken? 4100
Nu 23:23 of Israel, **W.** hath God wrought! 4100
Nu 24:13 **w.** the Lord saith, that will I speak? 834
Nu 24:14 **w.** this people shall do to thy people 834
Nu 26:10 **w.** time the fire devoured two hundred
Nu 31:50 **w.** every man hath gotten, of 834
De 1:22 again by **w.** way must we go up, 834
De 1:22 and into **w.** cities we shall come. 853
De 1:33 shew you by **w.** way ye should go, 834
De 3:24 for **w.** God is there in heaven or 4310
De 4:3 eyes have seen **w.** the Lord did 853,834
De 4:7 For **w.** nation is there so great, 4310
De 4:8 And **w.** nation is there so great, 4310
De 6:20 **W.** mean the testimonies, and 4100
De 7:18 remember **w.** the Lord thy God 853,834
De 8:2 to know **w.** was in thine heart, 853,834
De 10:12 **w.** doth the Lord thy God require 4100
De 11:4 **w.** he did unto the army of Egypt, 834
De 11:5 **w.** he did unto you in the wilderness, 834
De 11:6 **w.** he did unto Dathan and Abiram, 834
De 12:32 **W.** thing soever I command you, 853
De 20:5 **W.** man is there that hath built a 4310
De 20:6 **w.** man is he that hath planted a 4310
De 20:7 **w.** man is there that hath betrothed 4310
De 20:8 **W.** man is there that is fearful 4310
De 24:9 **w.** the Lord...did unto Miriam 853,834
De 25:17 **w.** Amalek did unto thee 853,834
De 29:24 **w.** meaneth the heat of this great 4100
De 32:20 I will see **w.** their end shall be: 4100
Jos 2:10 **w.** ye did unto the two kings of the 834
Jos 4:6 **W.** mean ye by these stones? 4100
Jos 4:21 saying, **W.** mean these stones? 4100
Jos 5:14 **W.** saith my lord unto his servant? 4100
Jos 7:8 O Lord, **w.** shall I say, when Israel 4100
Jos 7:9 **w.** wilt thou do unto thy great 4100
Jos 7:19 tell me now **w.** thou hast done; 4100
Jos 9:3 Gibeon heard **w.** Joshua had 853,834
Jos 15:18 said unto her, **w.** wouldest thou? 4100
Jos 22:16 **W.** trespass is this that ye have 4100
Jos 22:24 **W.** have ye to do with the Lord 4100
Jos 24:7 seen **w.** I have done in Egypt: 853,834
Jg 1:14 Caleb said unto her, **W.** wilt thou? 4100
Jg 7:11 And thou shalt hear **w.** they say; 4100
Jg 8:2 **W.** have I done now in comparison 4100
Jg 8:3 **w.** was I able to do in comparison 4100
Jg 8:18 **W.** manner of men were they 375
Jg 9:48 **W.** ye have seen me do, make 4100
Jg 10:18 **W.** man is he that will begin to 4310
Jg 11:12 **W.** hast thou to do with me, that 4100
Jg 13:8 teach us **w.** we shall do unto the 4100
Jg 13:17 **W.** is thy name, that when thy 4310
Jg 14:6 or his mother **w.** he had done. 853,834
Jg 14:18 down, **W.** is sweeter than honey? 4100
Jg 14:18 **w.** is stronger than a lion? And he 4100
Jg 15:11 **w.** is this that thou hast done unto 4100

Jg 16:5 **w.** means we may prevail against 4100
Jg 18:3 and **w.** makest thou in this place?....... 4100
Jg 18:3 and **w.** hast thou here? 4100
Jg 18:8 said unto them, **W.** say ye? 4100
Jg 18:14 therefore consider **w.** ye have to do. .. 4100
Jg 18:18 the priest unto them, **W.** do ye?........ 4100
Jg 18:23 **W.** aileth thee, that thou comest........ 4100
Jg 18:24 gone away: and **w.** have I more?........ 4100
Jg 18:24 **w.** is this that ye say unto me, ... 4100
Jg 18:24 ye say unto me, **W.** aileth thee? 4100
Jg 19:24 them **w.** seemeth good unto you: ....
Jg 20:12 **W.** wickedness is this that is done...... 4100
Jg 21:8 **W.** one is there of the tribes of......... 4310
Ru 2:18 in law saw **w.** she had gleaned:...... 853,834
Ru 3:4 he will tell thee **w.** thou shalt do.... 853,834
Ru 4:5 **W.** day thou buyest the field ....
1Sa 1:23 do **w.** seemeth thee good; tarry...............
1Sa 3:17 **W.** is the thing that the Lord 4100
1Sa 3:18 let him do **w.** seemeth him good. ....
1Sa 4:6, 14 **W.** meaneth the noise of this 4100
1Sa 4:16 he said, **W.** is there done, my son?.... 4100
1Sa 5:8 **W.** shall we do with the ark of the..... 4100
1Sa 6:2 **W.** shall we do to the ark of the........ 4100
1Sa 6:4 **W.** shall be the trespass offering........ 4100
1Sa 9:7 we go, **w.** shall we bring the man?..... 4100
1Sa 9:7 to the man of God: **w.** have we?........ 4100
1Sa 10:2 saying, **W.** shall I do for my son?....... 4100
1Sa 10:8 shew thee **w.** thou shalt do........... 853,834
1Sa 10:11 **W.** is this that is come unto the........ 4100
1Sa 10:15 thee, **w.** Samuel said unto you........... 4100
1Sa 11:5 **W.** aileth the people that they 4100
1Sa 13:11 Samuel said, **W.** hast thou done?........ 4100
1Sa 14:40 Saul, do **w.** seemeth good unto thee. ....
1Sa 14:43 Tell me **w.** thou hast done................ 4100
1Sa 15:14 **W.** meaneth then this bleating of........ 4100
1Sa 15:16 tell thee **w.** the Lord hath said 853,834
1Sa 16:3 will shew thee **w.** thou shalt do: 853,834
1Sa 17:26 **W.** shall be done to the man that...... 4100
1Sa 17:29 David said, **W.** have I now done?....... 4100
1Sa 18:8 **w.** can he have more but the kingdom? .....
1Sa 18:18 and **w.** is my life, or my father's........ 4310
1Sa 19:3 and **w.** I see, that I will tell thee........ 4100
1Sa 20:1 Jonathan, **W.** have I done?................ 4100
1Sa 20:1 **w.** is mine iniquity? 4100
1Sa 20:1 **w.** is my sin before thy father, that 4100
1Sa 20:10 or **w.** if thy father answer thee.......... 4100
1Sa 20:32 shall he be slain? **w.** hath he done?..... 4100
1Sa 21:2 and **w.** I have commanded thee: 834
1Sa 21:3 **w.** is under thine hand? give............. 4100
1Sa 21:3 in mine hand, or **w.** there is present.........
1Sa 22:3 till I know **w.** God will do for me. 4100
1Sa 25:17 and consider **w.** thou wilt do; 4100
1Sa 26:18 his servant? **w.** have I done? for......... 4100
1Sa 26:18 or **w.** evil is in mine hand?................ 4100
1Sa 28:2 know **w.** thy servant can do.......... 853,834
1Sa 28:9 thou knowest **w.** Saul hath done,.... 853,834
1Sa 28:13 Be not afraid: for **w.** sawest thou?....... 4100
1Sa 28:14 said unto her, **W.** form is he of?....... 4100
1Sa 28:15 make known unto me **w.** I shall do..... 4100
1Sa 29:3 **W.** do these Hebrews here? And 4100
1Sa 29:8 unto Achish, But **w.** have I done? 4100
1Sa 29:8 **w.** hast thou found in thy servant....... 4100
2Sa 3:24 king, and said, **W.** hast thou done?..... 4100
2Sa 7:18 and **w.** is in my house, that thou........ 4310
2Sa 7:20 **w.** can David say more unto thee?...... 4100
2Sa 7:23 **w.** one nation in the earth is like........ 4310
2Sa 9:8 **W.** is thy servant, that thou............. 4100
2Sa 12:21 **W.** thing is this that thou hast 4100
2Sa 14:5 said unto her, **W.** aileth thee? 4100
2Sa 15:2 and said, Of **w.** city art thou? 4310
2Sa 15:21 surely in **w.** place my Lord the king..... 834
2Sa 15:35 **w.** thing soever thou shalt hear.......... 3605
2Sa 16:2 Ziba, **W.** meanest thou by these?....... 4100
2Sa 16:10 **W.** have I to do with you, ye sons..... 4100
2Sa 16:20 counsel among you **w.** we shall do...... 4100
2Sa 17:5 let us hear likewise **w.** he saith.......... 4100
2Sa 18:4 **W.** seemeth you best I will do. 834
2Sa 18:21 Go tell the king **w.** thou hast seen. 834
2Sa 18:29 tumult, but I knew not **w.** it was........ 4100
2Sa 19:18 and to do **w.** he thought good..................
2Sa 19:22 **W.** have I to do with you, ye sons..... 4100
2Sa 19:27 do therefore **w.** is good in thine eyes.......
2Sa 19:28 **W.** right therefore have I yet to 4100
2Sa 19:35 can thy servant taste **w.** I eat 853,834
2Sa 19:35 I eat or **w.** I drink? can I hear....... 853,834
2Sa 19:37 **w.** shall seem good unto thee........ 853,834

2Sa 21:3 Gibeonites, **W.** shall I do for you?...... 4100
2Sa 21:4 **W.** ye shall say, that will I do for....... 4100
2Sa 21:11 was told David **w.** Rizpah the........ 853,834
2Sa 24:13 **w.** answer I shall return to him......... 4100
2Sa 24:17 these sheep, **w.** have they done? 4100
2Sa 24:22 offer up **w.** seemeth good unto him: ....
1Ki 1:16 the king said, **W.** wouldest thou? 4100
1Ki 2:5 **w.** Joab the son of Jeruiah did........ 853,834
1Ki 2:5 **w.** he did to the two captains of the...... 834
1Ki 2:9 knowest **w.** thou oughtest to do..... 853,834
1Ki 3:5 God said, Ask **w.** I shall give thee...... 4100
1Ki 8:38 **W.** prayer and supplication................ 3605
1Ki 9:13 **W.** cities are these which thou 4100
1Ki 11:22 But **w.** hast thou lacked with me,....... 4100
1Ki 12:9 **W.** counsel give ye that we may........ 4100
1Ki 12:16 **W.** portion have we in David? 4100
1Ki 13:12 unto them, **W.** way went he?....... 335,2088
1Ki 13:12 seen **w.** way the man of God went,...... 834
1Ki 14:3 thee **w.** shall become of the child. 4100
1Ki 14:14 of Jeroboam that day: but **w.**? 4100
1Ki 16:5 acts of Baasha, and **w.** he did, ... 834
1Ki 17:18 **W.** have I to do with thee, O thou..... 4100
1Ki 18:9 **W.** have I sinned, that thou 4100
1Ki 18:13 **w.** I did when Jezebel slew the...... 853,834
1Ki 19:9, 13 **W.** dost thou here, Elijah? 4100
1Ki 19:20 again: for **w.** have I done to thee?...... 4100
1Ki 20:22 mark, and see **w.** thou doest:........ 853,834
1Ki 22:14 **w.** the Lord saith unto me,..... 3588,853,834
2Ki 1:7 **W.** manner of man was he which 4100
2Ki 2:9 Elisha, Ask **w.** I shall do for thee,...... 4100
2Ki 3:13 Israel, **W.** have I to do with thee?...... 4100
2Ki 4:2 unto her, **W.** shall I do for thee?...... 4100
2Ki 4:2 tell me, **w.** hast thou in the house?..... 4100
2Ki 4:13 this care; **w.** is to be done for thee?... 4100
2Ki 4:14 said, **W.** then is to be done for her? ... 4100
2Ki 4:43 **W.**, should I set this before an 4100
2Ki 6:28 said unto her, **W.** aileth thee? 4100
2Ki 6:33 **w.** should I wait for the Lord any......... 4100
2Ki 7:12 shew you **w.** the Syrians have 853,834
2Ki 8:13 But **w.**, is thy servant a dog, that 4100
2Ki 8:14 to him, **W.** said Elisha to thee?.......... 4100
2Ki 9:18, 19 **W.** hast thou to do with peace?..... 4100
2Ki 9:22 **W.** peace, so long as the.................. 4100
2Ki 18:19 **W.** confidence is this wherein thou 4100
2Ki 19:11 heard **w.** the kings of Assyria........ 853,834
2Ki 20:8 **W.** shall be the sign that the Lord...... 4100
2Ki 20:14 **W.** said these men? and from............ 4100
2Ki 20:15 **W.** have they seen in thine house?..... 4100
2Ki 22:19 heardest **w.** I spake against this 834
2Ki 23:17 **W.** title is that that I see? 4100
1Ch 12:32 to know **w.** Israel ought to do; 4100
1Ch 17:16 Lord God, and **w.** is mine house, ... 4310
1Ch 17:18 **W.** can David speak more to thee 4100
1Ch 17:21 **w.** one nation in the earth is like........ 4310
1Ch 21:12 **w.** word I shall bring again to............ 4100
1Ch 21:17 as for these sheep, **w.** have they done?.....
1Ch 29:14 who am I, and **w.** is my people,......... 4310
2Ch 1:7 him, Ask **w.** I shall give thee............ 4100
2Ch 6:29 Then **w.** prayer or...supplication.......... 834
2Ch 6:29 **w.** supplication soever shall be.................
2Ch 10:6 **W.** counsel give ye me to return......... 349
2Ch 10:9 **W.** advice give ye that we may.......... 4100
2Ch 10:16 **W.** portion have we in David? 4100
2Ch 18:13 liveth, even **w.** my God saith, ... 853,834
2Ch 19:6 the judges, Take heed **w.** ye do:.......... 4100
2Ch 19:10 **w.** cause soever shall come to you..... 3602
2Ch 20:12 us; neither know we **w.** to do: 4100
2Ch 24:11 **w.** time the chest was brought unto..........
2Ch 25:9 **w.** shall we do for the hundred.......... 4100
2Ch 32:13 Know ye not **w.** I and my fathers....... 4100
2Ch 35:21 **W.** have I to do with thee, thou 4100
Ezr 5:4 **W.** are the names of the men that...... 4479
Ezr 6:8 **w.** ye shall do to the elders 3964,1768
Ezr 8:17 **w.** they should say unto Iddo, ... 1697
Ezr 9:10 God, **w.** shall we say after this?......... 4100
Ne 2:4 for **w.** dost thou make request? 4100
Ne 2:12 **w.** my God had put in my heart......... 4100
Ne 2:16 not whither I went, or **w.** I did;......... 4100
Ne 2:19 **W.** is this thing that ye do? will ye..... 4100
Ne 4:2 **W.** do these feeble Jews? will they..... 4100
Ne 4:20 In **w.** place therefore ye hear the 834
Ne 13:17 **W.** evil thing is this that ye do, ... 4100
Es 1:15 **W.** shall we do unto the queen 4100
Es 2:1 Vashti, and **w.** she had done, ... 853,834
Es 2:1 and **w.** was decreed against her. 853,834
Es 2:11 did, and **w.** should become of her....... 4100

Es 2:15 but **w.** Hegai...appointed. 853,834
Es 4:5 to Mordecai, to know **w.** it was, ... 4100
Es 5:3 her, **W.** wilt thou, queen Esther?....... 4100
Es 5:3 and **w.** is thy request? it shall be 4100
Es 5:6 **W.** is thy petition? and it shall be 4100
Es 5:6 and **w.** is thy request? even to 4100
Es 6:3 **W.** honour and dignity hath been......... 4100
Es 6:6 **W.** shall be done unto the man 4100
Es 7:2 **W.** is thy petition, queen Esther?....... 4100
Es 7:2 **w.** is thy request? and it shall be 4100
Es 8:1 Esther had told **w.** he was unto her.... 4100
Es 9:5 did **w.** they would unto those that 4100
Es 9:12 **w.** have they done in the rest of......... 4100
Es 9:12 now **w.** is thy petition? and it shall 4100
Es 9:12 **w.** is thy request further? and it 4100
Job 2:10 **W.**? shall we receive good at the 1571
Job 6:11 **W.** is my strength, that I should 4100
Job 6:11 **w.** is mine end, that I should............. 4100
Job 6:17 **W.** time they wax warm, they vanish: ....
Job 6:25 **w.** doth your arguing reprove?........... 4100
Job 7:17 **W.** is man, that thou shouldest 4100
Job 7:20 **w.** shall I do unto thee, O thou.......... 4100
Job 9:12 will say unto him, **W.** doest thou? 4100
Job 11:8 high as heaven; **w.** canst thou do?...... 4100
Job 11:8 than hell; **w.** canst thou know? 4100
Job 13:2 **W.** ye know, the same do I know also: .....
Job 13:13 speak, and let come on me **w.** will. 4100
Job 15:9 **W.** knowest thou, that we know 4100
Job 15:9 **w.** understandest thou, which is not..........
Job 15:12 and **w.** do thy eyes wink at,............... 4100
Job 15:14 **W.** is man, that he should be 4100
Job 16:3 or **w.** emboldeneth thee that thou....... 4100
Job 16:6 though I forbear, **w.** am I eased? 4100
Job 21:15 **W.** is the Almighty, that we.............. 4100
Job 21:15 **w.** profit should we have, if we pray... 4100
Job 21:21 **w.** pleasure hath he in his house 4100
Job 21:31 shall repay him **w.** he hath done? ....
Job 22:17 **w.** can the Almighty do for them? 4100
Job 23:5 understand **w.** he would say unto 4100
Job 23:13 and **w.** his soul desireth, even that he.......
Job 27:8 **w.** is the hope of the hypocrite,.......... 4100
Job 31:2 **w.** portion of God is there from.......... 4100
Job 31:2 **w.** inheritance of the Almighty from..........
Job 31:14 **W.** then shall I do when God............. 4100
Job 31:14 visiteth, **w.** shall I answer him?.......... 4100
Job 32:11 whilst ye searched out **w.** to say,.............
Job 34:4 know among ourselves **w.** is good. 4100
Job 34:7 **W.** man is like Job, who drinketh 4310
Job 34:33 therefore speak **w.** thou knowest. 4100
Job 35:3 **W.** advantage will it be unto thee?...... 4100
Job 35:3 and, **W.** profit shall I have, if I be 4100
Job 35:6 **W.** doest thou against him? or if 4100
Job 35:6 multiplied, **w.** doest thou unto him? 4100
Job 35:7 be righteous, **w.** givest thou him?....... 4100
Job 35:7 or **w.** receiveth he of thine hand?........ 4100
Job 37:19 Teach us **w.** we shall say unto him;..... 4100
Job 38:24 By **w.** way is the light parted,...... 335,2088
Job 39:18 **W.** time she lifted up herself on high, ...
Job 40:4 I am vile; **w.** shall I answer thee? 4100
Ps 8:4 **W.** is man, that thou art mindful 4100
Ps 11:3 destroyed, **w.** can the righteous do? ... 4100
Ps 25:12 **W.** man is he that feareth the........... 4310
Ps 30:9 **W.** profit is there in my blood, ... 4100
Ps 34:12 **W.** man is he that desireth life, ... 4310
Ps 39:4 the measure of my days, **w.** it is;........ 4310
Ps 39:7 Lord, **w.** wait I for? my hope is in........ 4100
Ps 44:1 us, **w.** work thou didst in their days, ...
Ps 46:8 **w.** desolations he hath made in the 834
Ps 50:16 **W.** hast thou to do to declare my....... 4100
Ps 56:3 **W.** time I am afraid, I will trust in............
Ps 56:4 I will not fear **w.** flesh can do............ 4100
Ps 56:11 not be afraid **w.** man can do unto........ 4100
Ps 66:16 and I will declare **w.** he hath done 834
Ps 85:8 hear **w.** God the Lord will speak: 4100
Ps 89:48 **W.** man is he that liveth, and............ 4310
Ps 114:5 **W.** ailed thee, O thou sea, that 4100
Ps 116:12 **W.** shall I render unto the Lord......... 4100
Ps 118:6 not fear: **w.** can man do unto me?....... 4100
Ps 120:3 **W.** shall be given unto thee?............ 4100
Ps 120:3 **w.** shall be done unto thee, thou........ 4100
Ps 144:3 Lord, **w.** is man, that thou takest........ 4100
Pr 4:19 they know not at **w.** they stumble. 4100
Pr 10:32 the righteous know **w.** is acceptable:.........
Pr 23:1 diligently **w.** is before thee:........... 853,834
Pr 25:8 thou know not **w.** to do in the end 4100
Pr 27:1 knowest not **w.** a day may bring 4100

Pr 30:4 w. is his name, and w. is his son's..... 4100
Pr 31:2 W., my son? and.......................... 4100
Pr 31:2 and w., the son of my womb? 4100
Pr 31:2 and w., the son of my vows? 4100
Ec 1:3 W. profit hath a man of all his 4100
Ec 2:2 mad: and of mirth, W. doeth it?......... 4100
Ec 2:3 I might see w. was that good for......... 335
Ec 2:12 w. can the man do that cometh.......... 4100
Ec 2:22 For w. hath man of all his labour,....... 4100
Ec 3:9 W. profit hath he that worketh in....... 4100
Ec 3:22 him to see w. shall be after him? 4100
Ec 5:11 and w. good is there to the owners.... 4100
Ec 5:16 and w. profit hath he that hath 4100
Ec 6:8 w. hath the wise more than the 4100
Ec 6:8 w. hath the poor, that knoweth to...... 4100
Ec 6:11 vanity, w. is man the better? 4100
Ec 6:12 who knoweth w. is good for man in.... 4100
Ec 6:12 can tell a man w. shall be after him 4100
Ec 7:10 W. is the cause that the former......... 4100
Ec 8:4 may say unto him, W. doest thou? 4100
Ec 10:14 a man cannot tell w. shall be;............ 4100
Ec 10:14 w. shall be after him, who can tell...... 4100
Ec 11:2 not w. evil shall be upon the earth. 4100
Ec 11:5 not w. is the way of the spirit, ... 4100
Ca 5:9 W. is thy beloved more than............. 4100
Ca 5:9 w. is thy beloved more than.............. 4100
Ca 6:13 W. will ye see in the Shulamite? 4100
Ca 8:8 w. shall we do for our sister in the..... 4100
Isa 1:11 To w. purpose is the multitude of...... 4100
Isa 3:15 W. mean ye that ye beat my people ... 4100
Isa 5:4 W. could have been done more to...... 4100
Isa 5:5 you w. I will do to my vineyard: 853,834
Isa 10:3 And w. will ye do in the day of.......... 4100
Isa 14:32 W. shall one then answer the 4100
Isa 19:12 w. the Lord of hosts hath purposed.... 4100
Isa 21:6 let him declare w. he seeth. 834
Isa 21:11 Seir, Watchman, w. of the night? 4100
Isa 21:11 night? Watchman, w. of the night?...... 4100
Isa 22:1 W. aileth thee now, that thou art 4100
Isa 22:16 W. hast thou here? and whom 4100
Isa 33:13 ye that are far off, w. I have done;...... 834
Isa 36:4 W. confidence is this wherein thou 4100
Isa 37:11 w. the kings of Assyria have done 834
Isa 38:15 W. shall I say? he hath both............. 4100
Isa 38:22 W. is the sign that I shall go up........ 4100
Isa 39:3 W. said these men? and from........... 4100
Isa 39:4 W. have they seen in thine house? 4100
Isa 40:6 W. shall I cry? All flesh is grass, ... 4100
Isa 40:18 w. likeness will ye compare unto......... 4100
Isa 41:22 and shew us w. shall happen: 853,834
Isa 41:22 the former things, w. they be,........... 4100
Isa 45:9 fashioneth it, W. makest thou? 4100
Isa 45:10 unto his father, W. begettest thou? 4100
Isa 45:10 W. hast thou brought forth?.............. 4100
Isa 52:5 w. have I here, saith the Lord,........... 4100
Isa 64:4 w. he hath prepared for him that..............
Jer 1:11 saying, Jeremiah, w. seest thou? 4100
Jer 1:13 second time, saying, W. seest thou?... 4100
Jer 2:5 W. iniquity have your fathers 4100
Jer 2:18, 18 w. hast thou to do in the way of.... 4100
Jer 2:23 valley, know w. thou hast done:......... 4100
Jer 4:30 thou art spoiled, w. wilt thou do? 4100
Jer 5:15 neither understandest w. they say...... 4100
Jer 5:31 w. will ye do in the end thereof?........ 4100
Jer 6:18 O congregation, w. is among.......... 853,834
Jer 6:20 To w. purpose cometh there to 4100
Jer 7:12 and see w. I did to it for the......... 853,834
Jer 7:17 thou not w. they do in the cities 4100
Jer 8:6 saying, W. have I done?................... 4100
Jer 8:9 Lord; and w. wisdom is in them? 4100
Jer 9:12 for w. the land perisheth and is 4100
Jer 11:15 W. hath my beloved to do in mine...... 4100
Jer 13:21 W. wilt thou say when he shall.......... 4100
Jer 16:10 w. is our iniquity: or w. is our sin...... 4100
Jer 18:7 At w. instant I shall speak concerning ....
Jer 18:9 And at w. instant I shall speak.................
Jer 23:25 heard w. the prophets said, ... 853,834
Jer 23:28 W. is the chaff to the wheat? saith..... 4100
Jer 23:33 W. is the burden of the Lord?........... 4100
Jer 23:33 then say unto them, W. burden?......... 4100
Jer 23:35 W. hath the Lord answered?............. 4100
Jer 23:35 and, W. hath the Lord spoken?.......... 4100
Jer 23:37 W. hath the Lord answered thee? 4100
Jer 23:37 and, W. hath the Lord spoken?.......... 4100
Jer 24:3 W. seest thou, Jeremiah? And I......... 4100
Jer 32:24 w. thou hast spoken is come to.......... 834
Jer 33:24 not w. this people have spoken,......... 4100
Jer 37:18 W. have I offended against thee,........ 4100
Jer 38:25 Declare unto us now w. thou hast...... 4100
Jer 38:25 also w. the king said unto thee: 4100
Jer 48:19 escapeth, and say, W. is done?.......... 4100
La 2:13 W. thing shall I take to witness for..... 4100
La 2:13 w. thing shall I liken to thee,............ 4100
La 2:13 w. shall I equal to thee, that I may..... 4100
La 5:1 O Lord, w. is come upon us: 4100
Eze 2:8 man, hear w. I say unto thee; 853,834
Eze 8:6 Son of man, seest thou w. they do?.... 4100
Eze 8:12 w. the ancients of the house of 834
Eze 12:9 said unto thee, W. doest thou? 4100
Eze 12:22 w. is that proverb that ye have......... 4100
Eze 15:2 W. is the vine tree more than any...... 4100
Eze 17:12 know ye not w. these things mean?.... 4100
Eze 18:2 W. mean ye, that ye use this........... 4100
Eze 19:2 W. is thy mother? A lioness: she 4100
Eze 20:29 W. is the high place whereunto ye 4100
Eze 21:13 w. if the sword condemn even the...... 4100
Eze 24:19 tell us w. these things are to us, ... 4100
Eze 27:32 W. city is like Tyrus, like the............ 4100
Eze 33:30 hear w. is the word that cometh 4100
Eze 37:18 shew w. thou meanest by these? 4100
Eze 47:23 in w. tribe the stranger sojourneth, ... 834
Da 2:22 he knoweth w. is in the darkness, ... 4101
Da 2:23 me now w. we desired of thee: 1768
Da 2:28 w. shall be in the latter days. 4101
Da 2:29 w. should come to pass hereafter:...... 4101
Da 2:29 known to thee w. shall come to pass. ..4101
Da 2:45 w. shall come to pass hereafter: 4101
Da 3:5, 15 w. time ye hear the sound of the... 1768
Da 4:35 or say unto him, W. doest thou?........ 4101
Da 8:19 know w. shall be in the last end..... 853,834
Da 10:14 w. shall befall thy people in the..... 853,834
Da 12:8 w. shall be the end of these............. 4100
Ho 6:4 Ephraim, w. shall I do unto thee?....... 4100
Ho 6:4 O Judah, w. shall I do unto thee? 4100
Ho 9:5 W. will ye do in the solemn day,........ 4100
Ho 9:14 them, O Lord: w. wilt thou give? 4100
Ho 10:3 w. then should a king do to us? 4100
Ho 14:8 W. have I to do any more with.......... 4100
Joe 3:4 w. have ye to do with me, O Tyre,.... 4100
Am 4:13 unto man w. is his thought, that 4100
Am 5:18 of the Lord! to w. end is it for you?... 4100
Am 7:8 said unto me, Amos, w. seest thou?... 4100
Am 8:2 he said, Amos, w. seest thou?.......... 4100
Jon 1:6 him, W. meanest thou, O sleeper? 4100
Jon 1:8 W. is thine occupation? and.............. 4100
Jon 1:8 comest thou? w. is thy country? 4100
Jon 1:8 and of w. people art thou? 335,2088
Jon 1:11 W. shall we do unto thee, that the..... 4100
Jon 4:5 see w. would become of the city........ 4100
Mic 1:5 W. is the transgression of Jacob? 4310
Mic 1:5 w. are the high places of Judah?........ 4310
Mic 6:1 Hear ye now w. the Lord saith; 834
Mic 6:3 people, w. have I done unto thee?...... 4100
Mic 6:5 w. Balak king of Moab consulted,....... 4100
Mic 6:5 w. Balaam...son of Beor answered 4100
Mic 6:8 shewed thee, O man, w. is good;........ 4100
Mic 6:8 w. doth the Lord require of thee,....... 4100
Na 1:9 W. do ye imagine against the 4100
Hab 2:1 and will watch to see w. he will say.... 4100
Hab 2:1 and w. I shall answer when I am........ 4100
Hab 2:18 W. profiteth the graven image that..... 4100
Zec 1:9 Then said I, O my lord, w. are.......... 4100
Zec 1:9 me, I will shew thee w. these be....... 4100
Zec 1:19 that talked with me, W. be these?...... 4100
Zec 1:21 Then said I, W. come these to do? 4100
Zec 2:2 to see w. is the breadth thereof,........ 4100
Zec 2:2 and w. is the length thereof. 4100
Zec 4:2 And said unto me, W. seest thou?...... 4100
Zec 4:4 me, saying, W. are these, my lord?... 4100
Zec 4:5 me, Knowest thou not w. these be?... 4100
Zec 4:11 W. are these two olive trees upon 4100
Zec 4:12 W. be these two olive branches......... 4100
Zec 4:13 Knowest thou not w. these be? And... 4100
Zec 5:2 W. seest thou? And I answered, ... 4100
Zec 5:5 and see w. is this that goeth forth...... 4100
Zec 5:6 And I said, W. is it? And he said, ... 4100
Zec 6:4 with me, W. are these, my lord? 4100
Zec 13:6 him, W. are these wounds in thine..... 4100
Mal 1:13 also, Behold, w. a weariness is it! ....
Mal 3:13 say, W. have we spoken so much...... 4100
Mal 3:14 w. profit is it that we have kept........ 4100
Mt 2:7 diligently w. time...star appeared........ 3588
Mt 5:46 which love you, w. reward have 5101
Mt 5:47 only, w. do ye more than others? .. 5101
Mt 6:3 know w. thy right hand doeth: 5101
Mt 6:8 Father knoweth w. things ye 3739
Mt 6:25 w. ye shall eat, or w. ye shall 5101
Mt 6:25 for your body, w. ye shall put on...5101
Mt 6:31 saying, W. shall we eat? or, ... 5101
Mt 6:31 or, W. shall we drink? or, ... 5101
Mt 7:2 with w. measure ye mete, it shall .. 3739
Mt 7:2 w. judgment ye judge, ye shall 3739
Mt 7:9 w. man is there of you, whom if ... 5101
Mt 8:27 saying, W. manner of man is this, ... 4217
Mt 8:29 W. have we to do with thee, Jesus,..... 5101
Mt 8:33 w. was befallen to the possessed 3588
Mt 9:13 go ye and learn w. that meaneth, .. 5101
Mt 10:19 thought how or w. ye shall 5101
Mt 10:19 that same hour w. ye shall speak...5101
Mt 10:27 W. I tell you in darkmes, that 3739
Mt 10:27 w. ye hear in the ear, that 3739
Mt 11:7 W. went ye out in the wilderness .. 5101
Mt 11:8 But w. went ye out for to see? A ... 5101
Mt 11:9 But w. went ye out for to see? A ... 5101
Mt 12:3 Have ye not read w. David did, ... 5101
Mt 12:7 if ye had known w. this 5101
Mt 12:11 W. man shall there be among 5101
Mt 16:26 For w. is a man profited, if he 5101
Mt 16:26 w. shall a man give in exchange 5101
Mt 17:25 W. thinkest thou, Simon? of 5101
Mt 18:31 his fellowservants saw w. was 3588
Mt 19:6 W. therefore God hath joined 3739
Mt 19:16 w. good thing shall I do, that I......... 5101
Mt 19:20 from my youth up: w. lack I yet?......... 5101
Mt 19:27 thee; w. shall we have therefore?....... 5101
Mt 20:15 me to do w. I will with mine 3739
Mt 20:21 he said unto her, W. wilt thou? 5101
Mt 20:22 and said, Ye know not w. ye ask..... 5101
Mt 20:32 W. will ye that I shall do unto 5101
Mt 21:16 Hearest thou w. these say? and......... 5101
Mt 21:23 By w. authority doest thou these 4169
Mt 21:24, 27 by w. authority I do these 4169
Mt 21:28 But w. think ye? A certain man 5101
Mt 21:40 cometh, w. will he do unto those.... 5101
Mt 22:17 us therefore, W. thinkest thou? 5101
Mt 22:42 W. think ye of Christ? whose son .. 5101
Mt 24:3 w. shall be the sign of thy coming, ... 5101
Mt 24:42 for ye know not w. hour your 4169
Mt 24:43 known in w. watch the thief 4169
Mt 26:8 To w. purpose is this waste? 5101
Mt 26:15 W. will ye give me, and I will............ 5101
Mt 26:40 W., could ye not watch with me 3779
Mt 26:62 w. is it which these witness............. 5101
Mt 26:65 w. further need have we of.............. 5101
Mt 26:66 W. think ye? They answered and....... 5101
Mt 26:70 saying, I know not w. thou sayest....... 5101
Mt 27:4 W. is that to us? see thou to that. 5101
Mt 27:22 W. shall I do then with Jesus 5101
Mt 27:23 said, Why, w. evil hath he done? 5101
Mk 1:24 w. have we to do with thee, thou 5101
Mk 1:27 amazed,...saying, W. thing is this? 5101
Mk 1:27 w. new doctrine is this? 5101
Mk 2:25 Have ye never read w. David did, .. 5101
Mk 3:8 had heard w. great things he did, ... 3745
Mk 4:24 Take heed w. ye hear: ....
Mk 4:24 with w. measure ye mete, it shall .. 3739
Mk 4:30 w. comparison shall we compare ... 4169
Mk 4:41 W. manner of man is this, that..... 5101,686
Mk 5:7 W. have I to do with thee, Jesus, ... 5101
Mk 5:9 he asked him, W. is thy name? 5101
Mk 5:14 out to see w. it was that was done..... 5101
Mr 5:33 knowing w. was done in her, came...... 3739
Mk 6:2 w. wisdom is this which is given 5101
Mk 6:10 In w. place soever ye enter into 3699
Mk 6:24 unto her mother, W. shall I ask?........ 5101
Mk 6:30 w. they had done, and w. they had 3745
Mk 8:36 For w. shall it profit a man, if 5101
Mk 8:37 Or w. shall a man give in 5101
Mk 9:6 For he wist not w. to say; for they 5101
Mk 9:9 tell no man w. things they had........... 3739
Mk 9:10 w. the rising from the dead should 5101
Mk 9:16 scribes, W. question ye with 5101
Mk 9:33 W. was it that ye disputed 5101
Mk 10:3 W. did Moses command you? 5101
Mk 10:9 W. therefore God hath joined 3739
Mk 10:17 w. shall I do that I may inherit 5101
Mk 10:32 w. things should happen unto him,....... 3588
Mk 10:36 W. would ye that I should do for .. 5101
Mk 10:38 unto them, Ye know not w. ye ask: ..5101
Mk 10:51 W. wilt thou that I should do 5101

Mk 11:5 them, W. do ye, loosing the colt? 5101
Mk 11:24 W. things soever ye desire, when 3745
Mk 11:28 By w. authority doest thou these 4169
Mk 11:29, 33 w. authority I do these things 4169
Mk 12:9 W. shall therefore the lord of the 5101
Mk 13:1 Master, see w. manner of stones 4217
Mk 13:1 stones and w. buildings are here! 4217
Mk 13:4 w. shall be the sign when all these 5101
Mk 13:11 beforehand w. ye shall speak, 5101
Mk 13:37 And w. I say unto you I say unto 3739
Mk 14:8 She hath done w. she could: she 3739
Mk 14:36 not w. I will, but w. thou wilt. 5101
Mk 14:40 neither wist they w. to answer him, 5101
Mk 14:60 w. is it which these witness thee 5101
Mk 14:63 W. need we any further witnesses? 5101
Mk 14:64 heard the blasphemy: w. think ye? 5101
Mk 14:68 understand I w. thou sayest. 5101
Mk 15:12 W. will ye then that I shall do unto 5101
Mk 15:14 them, Why w. evil hath he done? 5101
Mk 15:24 them, w. every man should take, 5101
Lu 1:29 mind w. manner of salutation this 4217
Lu 1:66 W. manner of child shall this 5101,686
Lu 3:10 him, saying, W. shall w. do then? 5101
Lu 3:12 unto him, Master, w. shall we do? 5101
Lu 3:14 of him, saying, And w. shall we do? 5101
Lu 4:34 w. have we to do with thee, thou 5101
Lu 4:36 saying, W. a word is this! for with 5101
Lu 5:19 by w. way they might bring him 4169
Lu 5:22 W. reason ye in your hearts? 5101
Lu 6:3 W. David did, when himself was 3739
Lu 6:11 another w. they might do to Jesus. 5101
Lu 6:32 which love you, w. thank have 4169
Lu 6:33 do good to you, w. thank have 4169
Lu 6:34 hope to receive, w. thank have 4169
Lu 7:22 tell John w. things ye have seen 3739
Lu 7:24 John, W. went ye out into the 5101
Lu 7:25, 26 But w. went ye out for to 5101
Lu 7:31 generation?...to w. are they like? 5101
Lu 7:39 and w. manner of woman this is 4217
Lu 8:9 saying, W. might this parable be? 5101
Lu 8:25 W. manner of man is this! 5101,686
Lu 8:28 W. have I to do with thee, Jesus. 5101
Lu 8:30 asked him, saying, W. is thy name? 5101
Lu 8:34 they that fed them saw w. was done, 3588
Lu 8:35 they went out to see w. was done; 3588
Lu 8:36 by w. means he that was possessed 4459
Lu 8:47 for w. cause she had touched him, 3739
Lu 8:56 they should tell no man w. was done. 3588
Lu 9:25 For w. is a man advantaged, if 5101
Lu 9:33 for Elias: not knowing w. he said. 3739
Lu 9:55 Ye know not w. manner of spirit 3634
Lu 10:25 w. shall I do to inherit eternal life? 5101
Lu 10:26 W. is written in the law? how 5101
Lu 12:11 how or w. thing ye shall answer, 5101
Lu 12:11 ye shall answer, or w. ye shall 5101
Lu 12:12 the same hour w. ye ought to say 3739
Lu 12:17 W. shall I do, because I have no 5101
Lu 12:22 for your life, w. ye shall eat; 5101
Lu 12:22 for the body, w. ye shall put on. 5101
Lu 12:29 And seek not ye w. ye shall eat, 5101
Lu 12:29 ye shall eat, or w. ye shall drink, 5101
Lu 12:39 w. hour the thief would come, 4169
Lu 12:49 w. will I, if it be already kindled? 5101
Lu 12:57 yourselves judge ye not w. is 3588
Lu 13:18 w. is the kingdom of God like? 5101
Lu 14:31 Or w. king, going to make war 5101
Lu 15:4 W. man of you, having an hundred 5101
Lu 15:8 Either w. woman having ten 5101
Lu 15:26 and asked w. these things meant 5101
Lu 16:3 W. shall I do? for my lord taketh 5101
Lu 16:4 I am resolved w. to do, that, 5101
Lu 18:6 Hear w. the unjust judge saith 5101
Lu 18:18 w. shall I do to inherit eternal life? 5101
Lu 18:36 passed by, he asked w. it meant. 5101
Lu 18:41 W. wilt thou that I shall do unto 5101
Lu 19:48 could not find w. they might do: 5101
Lu 20:2 by w. authority doest thou these 4169
Lu 20:8 by w. authority I do these 4169
Lu 20:13 W. shall I do? I will send my 5101
Lu 20:15 W. therefore shall the lord of the 5101
Lu 20:17 W. is this then that is written, 5101
Lu 21:7 w. sign will there be when these 5101
Lu 21:14 mediate before w. ye shall answer:
Lu 22:49 about him saw w. would follow, 3588
Lu 22:60 Man, I know not w. thou sayest. 3739
Lu 22:71 W. need we any further witness? 5101
Lu 23:22 Why, w. evil hath he done? I have 5101
Lu 23:31 tree, w. shall be done in the dry? 5101
Lu 23:34 for they know not w. they do. 5101
Lu 23:47 the centurion saw w. was done, 3588
Lu 24:17 W. manner of communications 5101
Lu 24:19 he said unto them, W. things? 4169
Lu 24:35 they told w. things were done in the 3588
Joh 1:21 him, W. then? Art thou Elias? 5101
Joh 1:22 sent us. W. sayest thou of thyself? 5101
Joh 1:38 and saith unto them, W. seek ye? 5101
Joh 2:4 Woman, w. have I to do with 5101
Joh 2:18 W. sign shewest thou unto us, 5101
Joh 2:25 man: for he knew w. was in man. 5101
Joh 3:32 w. he hath seen and heard, that he 3739
Joh 4:22 Ye worship ye know not w.: we 3739
Joh 4:22 we know w. we worship: for 3739
Joh 4:27 W. seekest thou? or, why talkest 5101
Joh 5:12 W. man is that which said unto 3739
Joh 5:19 but w. he seeth the Father do: 5100
Joh 5:19 for w. things soever he doeth, 5100
Joh 6:6 he himself knew w. he would do. 5101
Joh 6:9 but w. are they among so many? 5101
Joh 6:28 W. shall we do, that we might work 5101
Joh 6:30 W. sign shewest thou then, that 5101
Joh 6:30 believe thee? w. dost thou work? 5101
Joh 6:62 W. and if ye shall see the Son of
Joh 7:36 W. manner of saying is this that 5101
Joh 7:51 it hear him, and know w. he doeth? 5101
Joh 8:5 be stoned: but w. sayest thou? 5101
Joh 9:17 W. sayest thou of him, that he hath 5101
Joh 9:21 But by w. means he now seeth, we 4459
Joh 9:26 to him again, W. did he to thee? 5101
Joh 10:6 understood not w. things they were 5101
Joh 11:46 told them w. things Jesus had done. 3739
Joh 11:47 W. do we? for this man doeth 5101
Joh 11:56 W. think ye, that he will not come 5101
Joh 12:6 the bag, and bare w. was...therein. 3588
Joh 12:27 w. shall I say? Father, save me 5101
Joh 12:33 signifying w. death he should die. 4169
Joh 12:49 w. I should say, and w. I should 5101
Joh 13:7 W. I do thou knowest not now; 3739
Joh 13:12 Know ye w. I have done to you? 5101
Joh 13:28 knew for w. intent he spake this 5101
Joh 15:7 ye shall ask w. ye will, and it 3739
Joh 15:15 knoweth not w. his lord doeth: 5101
Joh 16:17 W. is this that he saith unto us, 5101
Joh 16:18 therefore, W. is this that he saith, 5101
Joh 16:18 we cannot tell w. he saith. 5101
Joh 18:21 me, w. I have said unto them: 5101
Joh 18:21 behold, they know w. I said. 5101
Joh 18:29 W. accusation bring ye against 5101
Joh 18:32 signifying w. death he should die. 4169
Joh 18:35 thee unto me: w. hast thou done? 5101
Joh 18:38 Pilate saith unto him, W. is truth? 5101
Joh 19:22 W. I have written I have written. 3739
Joh 21:19 by w. death he should glorify God. 4169
Joh 21:21 Lord, and w. shall this man do? 5101
Joh 21:22, 23 till I come, w. is that to thee? 5101
Ac 2:12 one to another, W. meaneth this? 5101
Ac 2:37 Men and brethren, w. shall we do? 5101
Ac 4:7 By w. power, or by w. name, 4169
Ac 4:9 by w. means he is made whole; 5101
Ac 4:16 W. shall we do to these men? for 5101
Ac 5:7 his wife, not knowing w. was done, 3588
Ac 5:35 w. ye intend to do as touching 5101
Ac 7:40 we wot not w. is become of him. 5101
Ac 7:49 w. house will ye build me? saith 4169
Ac 7:49 or, w. is the place of my rest? 5101
Ac 8:30 Understandest...w. thou readest? 3739
Ac 8:36 w. doth hinder me to be baptized? 5101
Ac 9:6 Lord, w. wilt thou have me to do? 5101
Ac 9:6 it shall be told thee w. thou 5101
Ac 10:4 was afraid, and said, W. is it, Lord? 5101
Ac 10:6 tell thee w. thou oughtest to do. 5101
Ac 10:15 W. God hath cleansed, that call not 3739
Ac 10:17 w. this vision which he had seen 5101
Ac 10:21 w. is the cause wherefore ye are 5101
Ac 10:29 for w. intent ye have sent for me? 5101
Ac 11:9 W. God hath cleansed, that call 3739
Ac 11:17 w. was I, that I could withstand 5101
Ac 12:18 soldiers, w....become of Peter. 5101,686
Ac 13:12 deputy, when he saw w. was done, 3588
Ac 14:11 the people saw w. Paul had done, 3739
Ac 15:12 declaring w. miracles and wonders 3745
Ac 16:30 Sirs, w. must I do to be saved? 5101
Ac 17:18 some said, W. will this babbler say? 5101
Ac 17:19 we know not w. this new doctrine, 5101
Ac 17:20 therefore w. these things mean. 5101
Ac 19:3 Unto w. then were ye baptized? 5101
Ac 19:35 w. man is there that knoweth not 5101
Ac 20:18 after w. manner I have been with 4459
Ac 21:13 W. mean ye to weep and to break 5101
Ac 21:19 w. things God had wrought among 3739
Ac 21:22 W. is it therefore? the multitude 5101
Ac 21:33 who he was, and w. he had done. 5101
Ac 22:10 And I said, W. shall I do, Lord? 5101
Ac 22:15 men of w. thou hast seen and heard. 3739
Ac 22:26 saying, Take heed w. thou doest: 5101
Ac 23:19 W. is that thou hast to tell me? 5101
Ac 23:30 thee w. they had against him. 3588
Ac 23:34 he asked of w. province he was. 4169
Ac 28:22 to hear of thee w. thou thinkest: 3739
Ro 3:1 W. advantage then hath the Jew? 5101
Ro 3:1 w. profit is there of circumcision? 5101
Ro 3:3 For w. if some did not believe? 5101
Ro 3:5 w. shall we say? Is God 5101
Ro 3:9 W. then? are we better than they? 5101
Ro 3:19 w. things soever the law saith, 3745
Ro 3:27 By w. law? of works? Nay: but 4169
Ro 4:1 W. shall we say then that 5101
Ro 4:3 w. saith the scripture? Abraham 5101
Ro 4:21 w. he had promised, he was able 3739
Ro 6:1 W. shall we say then? Shall we 5101
Ro 6:15 W. then? shall we sin, because we 5101
Ro 6:21 W. fruit had ye there in those 5101
Ro 7:7 W. shall we say then? Is the law 5101
Ro 7:15 not; for w. I would, that do I not; 3739
Ro 7:15 do I not; but w. I hate, that do I. 3739
Ro 8:3 w. the law could not do, in that it 3588
Ro 8:24 for w. a man seeth, why doth he yet
Ro 8:26 know not w. we should pray for 5101
Ro 8:27 knoweth w. is the mind of the Spirit, 5101
Ro 8:31 W. shall we then say to these 5101
Ro 9:14 W. shall we say then? Is there 5101
Ro 9:22 W. if God, willing to shew his wrath,
Ro 9:30 W. shall we say then? That the 5101
Ro 10:8 But w. saith it? The word is nigh 5101
Ro 11:2 w. the scripture saith of Elias? 5101
Ro 11:4 But w. saith the answer of God 5101
Ro 11:7 W. then? Israel hath not obtained 5101
Ro 11:15 w. shall the receiving of them be, 5101
Ro 12:2 that ye may prove w. is that good, 5101
1Co 2:11 w. man knoweth the things of a 5101
1Co 3:13 every man's work of w. sort it is. 3697
1Co 4:7 w. hast thou that thou didst not 5101
1Co 4:21 W. will ye? shall I come unto you 5101
1Co 5:12 For w. have I to do to judge them 5101
1Co 6:16 W.? know ye not that he which is 2228
1Co 6:19 W.? know ye not that your body is 2228
1Co 7:16 for w. knowest thou, O wife, 5101
1Co 7:36 him do w. he will, he sinneth not: 3739
1Co 9:18 W. is my reward then? Verily that 5101
1Co 10:15 as to wise men; judge ye w. I say. 3739
1Co 10:19 W. say I then? that the idol is any 5101
1Co 11:22 W.? have ye not houses to eat...in? 1063
1Co 11:22 W. shall I say to you? shall I 5101
1Co 14:6 w. shall I profit you, except I shall 5101
1Co 14:7 it be known w. is piped or harped? 3588
1Co 14:9 how shall it be known w. is spoken? 3588
1Co 14:15 W. is it then? I will pray with the 5101
1Co 14:16 understandeth not w. thou sayest? 5101
1Co 14:36 W.? came the word of God out 2228
1Co 15:2 keep in memory w. I preached 5101
1Co 15:10 by the grace of God I am w. I am: 3739
1Co 15:29 Else w. shall they do which are 5101
1Co 15:32 w. advantage it me, if the dead 5101
1Co 15:35 and with w. body do they come? 4169
2Co 1:13 that w. ye read or acknowledge; 3739
2Co 6:14 w. fellowship hath righteousness 5101
2Co 6:14 w. communion hath light with 5101
2Co 6:15 w. concord hath Christ with Belial? 5101
2Co 6:15 w. part hath he that believeth with 5101
2Co 6:16 w. agreement hath the temple of 5101
2Co 7:11 w. carefulness it wrought in you, 4214
2Co 7:11 in you, yea, w. clearing of yourselves,
2Co 7:11 of yourselves, yea, w. indignation,
2Co 7:11 yea, w. fear, yea, w. vehement desire,
2Co 7:11 desire, yea, w. zeal, yea, w. revenge!
2Co 11:12 But w. I do, that I will do, that I 3739
2Co 12:13 w. is it wherein ye were inferior 5101
Ga 4:30 Nevertheless w. saith the scripture? 5101
Eph 1:18 know w. is the hope of his calling, 5101
Eph 1:18 w. the riches of the glory of his 5101
Eph 1:19 w. is the exceeding greatness of 5101
Eph 3:9 w. is the fellowship of the mystery, 5101

Eph 3:18 with all saints w. is the breadth, ... 5101
Eph 4:9 w. is it but that he also descended 5101
Eph 5:10 Proving w. is acceptable unto the 5101
Eph 5:17 w. the will of the Lord is 5101
Php 1:18 W. then? notwithstanding, every 5101
Php 1:22 yet w. I shall choose I wot not. 5101
Php 3:7 But w. things were gain to me, ... 3748
Col 1:27 w. is the riches of the glory of 5101
Col 2:1 knew w. great conflict I have for 2245
1Th 1:5 know w. manner of men we were 3634
1Th 1:9 w. manner of entering in we had 3697
1Th 2:19 For w. is our hope, or joy, or 5101
1Th 3:9 for w. thanks can we render to 5101
1Th 4:2 know w. commandments we gave 5101
2Th 2:6 w. withholdeth that he might be 3588
1Ti 1:7 understanding neither w. they say, ... 3739
2Ti 2:7 Consider w. I say; and the Lord give .. 3739
2Ti 3:11 Lystra; w. persecutions I endured: 3634
Heb 2:6 W. is man, that thou art mindful 5101
Heb 7:11 w. further need was there that 5101
Heb 11:32 w. shall I more say? for the time 5101
Heb 12:7 for w. son is he whom the father 5101
Heb 13:6 not fear w. man shall do unto me. 5101
Jas 1:24 forgetteth w. manner of man he 3697
Jas 2:14 W. doth it profit, my brethren, ... 5101
Jas 2:16 to the body; w. doth it profit? 5101
Jas 4:14 not w. shall be on the morrow 3588
Jas 4:14 For w. is your life? It is even a 4169
1Pe 1:11 Searching w., or...manner of 1519,5101
1Pe 1:11 or w. manner of time the Spirit 4169
1Pe 2:20 For w. glory is it, if, when ye be 4169
1Pe 4:17 w. shall the end be of them that 5101
2Pe 3:11 w. manner of persons ought ye to 4217
1Jo 3:1 w. manner of love the Father hath 4217
1Jo 3:2 not yet appear w. we shall be: 5101
Jude 10 but w. they know naturally, as 3745
Re 1:11 **W. thou seest, write in a book** 3739
Re 2:7, 11,17,29 **hear w. the Spirit** 5101
Re 3:3 **shalt not know w. hour I will** 4169
Re 6:13, 22 **hear w. the Spirit saith** 5101
Re 7:13 W. are these which are arrayed in 5101
Re 18:18 W. city is like unto this great city! 5101

WHATSOEVER
Ge 2:19 w. Adam called every living 3605,834
Ge 8:19 and w. creepeth upon the earth, ... 3605
Ge 19:12 and w. thou hast in the city, ... 3605,834
Ge 31:16 w. God hath said unto thee, do. ... 3605,834
Ge 39:22 w. they did there, he was the 3605,834
Ex 13:2 firstborn, w. openeth the womb 3605
Ex 21:30 ransom...w. is laid upon him. 3605,834
Ex 29:37 w. toucheth the altar shall be holy. 3605
Ex 30:29 w. toucheth them shall be holy. 3605
Le 5:3 w. uncleanness it be that a man 3605
Le 5:4 w....a man shall pronounce 3605,834
Le 6:27 W. shall touch the flesh thereof 3605
Le 7:27 W. soul it be that eateth any 3605
Le 11:3 W. parteth the hoof, and is 3605
Le 11:9 w. hath fins and scales in the 3605
Le 11:12 W. hath no fins nor scales in the 3605
Le 11:27 w. goeth upon his paws, among the 3605
Le 11:32 upon w. any of them, when they 3605
Le 11:32 w. vessel it be, wherein any work is ... 3605
Le 11:33 w. is in it shall be unclean; 3605
Le 11:42 W. goeth upon the belly, ... 3605
Le 11:42 and w. goeth upon all fours, ... 3605
Le 11:42 or w. hath more feet among all 3605
Le 13:58 w. thing of skin it be, which thou 3605
Le 15:26 w. she sitteth upon shall be 3605,3627
Le 17:8 W. man there be of the house of 376,834
Le 17:10 w. man there be of the house of 376,834
Le 17:13 w. man there be of the children 376,834
Le 21:18 w. man he be that hath a blemish, ... 3605
Le 22:5 w. uncleanness he hath; 3605
Le 22:18 W. he be of the house of Israel, ... 376,834
Le 22:20 w. hath a blemish, that shall ye 3605
Le 23:29 w. soul it be that shall not be 3605
Le 23:30 w. soul it be that doeth any work in ... 3605
Le 27:32 even of w. passeth under the rod, ... 3605
Nu 5:10 w. any man giveth the priest, it 834
Nu 18:13 and w. is first ripe in the land, ... 3605,834
Nu 19:22 w. the unclean person toucheth 3605
Nu 22:17 I will do w. thou sayest unto 3605,834
Nu 23:3 w. he sheweth me I will tell 1697,4100
Nu 30:12 then w. proceeded out of her lips 3605
De 2:37 w. the Lord our God forbad us. 3605
De 12:8 man w. is right in his own eyes. 3605
De 12:15 w. thy soul lusteth after, according 3605
De 12:20 eat flesh, w. thy soul lusteth after. 3605
De 12:21 thy gates w. thy soul lusteth after. 3605
De 14:10 w. hath not fins and scales ye 3605,834
De 14:26 money for w. thy soul lusteth 3605,834
De 14:26 or for w. thy soul desireth: 3605,834
Jg 10:15 us w. seemeth good unto thee; 3605
Jg 11:31 w. cometh forth of the doors of my 834
1Sa 14:36 Do w. seemeth good unto thee. 3605
1Sa 20:4 W. thy soul desireth, I will even 4100
1Sa 25:8 w. cometh to thine hand unto 853,834
2Sa 3:36 as w. the king did pleased all 3605,834
2Sa 15:15 ready to do w. my lord the king ... 3605,834
2Sa 19:38 w. thou shalt require of me, ... 3605,834
1Ki 8:37 w. plague, w. sickness there be; 3605
1Ki 10:13 Sheba all her desire, w. she asked, ... 834
1Ki 20:6 that w. is pleasant in thine eyes, ... 3605
2Ch 6:28 w. sore or w. sickness there be: 3605
2Ch 9:12 Sheba all her desire, w. she asked, ... 3605
Ezr 7:18 w. shall seem good to thee, ... 1401,1768
Ezr 7:20 And w. more shall be needful for the ....
Ezr 7:21 w. Ezra the priest, the scribe 3605,3627
Ezr 7:23 W. is commanded by the God 3605,3627
Es 2:13 w. she desired was given 853,3605,834
Job 37:12 do w. he commandeth them 3605,834
Job 41:11 w. is under the whole heaven is mine. ......
Ps 1:3 and w. he doeth shall prosper. 3605,834
Ps 8:8 w. passeth through the paths of the ....
Ps 115:3 hath done w. he hath pleased 3605,834
Ps 135:6 W. the Lord pleased, that did 3605,834
Ec 2:10 w. my eyes desireth I kept not 3605,834
Ec 3:14 w. God doeth, it shall be for 3605,834
Ec 8:3 for he doeth w. pleaseth him. 3605,834
Ec 9:10 W. thy hand findeth to do, do it ... 3605,834
Jer 1:7 w. I commanded thee thou shalt ... 3605,834
Jer 42:4 that w. thing the Lord shall 3605
Jer 44:17 w. thing goeth forth out of our 853,3605
Mt 5:37 **w. is more than these cometh of** ... 3588
Mt 7:12 **w. ye would that men should** ... 3745,302
Mt 10:11 **into w. city or town ye** 3729,302
Mt 14:7 to give her w. she would ask. 3739,1437
Mt 15:5 **w. thou mightest be profited.** ..3739,1437
Mt 15:17 **w. entereth in at the mouth** 3956
Mt 16:19 **w. thou shalt bind on earth** ... 3739,1487
Mt 16:19 **w. thou shalt loose on earth** 1487
Mt 17:12 **have done unto him w. they** 3745
Mt 18:18 **W. ye shall bind on earth** 3745,1437
Mt 18:18 **w. ye shall loose on earth** 3745,1437
Mt 20:4 **and w. is right I will give** 3739,1437
Mt 20:7 **w. is right that shall ye** 3739,1437
Mt 21:22 **w. ye shall ask in prayer,** 3745,302
Mt 23:3 **w. they bid you observe,** 3745,302
Mt 28:20 **things w. I have commanded** 3745
Mk 6:22 Ask of me w. thou wilt, and I 3739,1437
Mk 6:23 W. thou shalt ask of me, I will ... 3739,1437
Mk 7:11 **by w. thou mightest be profited** 1437
Mk 7:18 **w. thing from without entereth** 3956
Mk 9:13 **have done unto him w. they** 3745
Mk 10:21 **sell w. thou hast, and give to the** .. 3745
Mk 10:35 do for us w. we shall desire 3739,1437
Mk 11:23 **pass; he shall have w. he saith.** 3739,302
Mk 13:11 **w. shall be given you in that** .. 3739,1437
Lu 4:23 w. we have heard done in 3745
Lu 9:4 **w. house ye enter into, there** ... 3739,302
Lu 10:5 **And into w. house ye enter,** 3739,302
Lu 10:8, **10 into w. city ye enter, and** 3739,302
Lu 10:35 w. thou spendest more, when ... 3748,302
Lu 12:3 **w. ye have spoken in darkness** 3745
Joh 2:5 W. he saith unto you, do it. 3748,302
Joh 5:4 made whole of w. disease he had. 1221
Joh 11:22 w. thou wilt ask of God, God 3748,302
Joh 12:50 **w. I speak therefore, even as the** ... 3739
Joh 14:13 **w. ye shall ask in my name,** 3748,302
Joh 14:26 **remembrance, w. I have said unto** ..3739
Joh 15:14 **friends, if ye do w. I command** 3745
Joh 15:16 **w. ye shall ask of the Father** 3748,302
Joh 16:13 **w. he shall hear, that shall he** ..3745,302
Joh 16:23 **W. ye shall ask the Father in** .. 3748,302
Joh 17:7 **w. thou hast given me are of thee.** .3745
Ac 3:22 in all things w. he shall say 3748,302
Ac 4:28 to do w. thy hand and thy counsel 3745
Ro 14:23 faith: for w. is not of faith is sin 3956
Ro 15:4 w. things were written aforetime 3745
Ro 16:2 ye assist her in w. business she ... 3739,302
1Co 10:25 W. is sold in the shambles, that 3956
1Co 10:27 w. is set before you, eat, asking 3956
1Co 10:31 w. ye do, do all to the glory of God. .. 5100
Ga 2:6 (w. they were, it maketh no 3697,4219
Ga 6:7 w. a man soweth, that shall he ... 3739,1437
Eph 5:13 w. doth make manifest is light. 3956
Eph 6:8 w. good thing any man 3739,1437,5100
Php 4:8 brethren, w. things are true, ... 3745
Php 4:8 w. things are honest, ... 3745
Php 4:8 w. things are just, ... 3745
Php 4:8 w. things are pure, ... 3745
Php 4:8 w. things are lovely, ... 3745
Php 4:8 w. things are of good report; 3745
Php 4:11 w. state I am, therewith to be 3588,3739
Col 3:17 w. ye do in word or deed, ... 3956,3754,5100
Col 3:23 w. ye do, do it heartily, as .. 3956,3754,1437
1Jo 3:22 w. we ask, we receive of him. ... 3739,1437
1Jo 5:4 w. is born of God overcometh the 3956
1Jo 5:15 w. we ask, we know that we 3739,302
3Jo 5 w. thou doest to the brethren, ... 3739,1437
Re 18:22 craftsman, of w. craft he be, shall 3956
Re 21:27 w. worketh abomination, or maketh ....

WHEAT See also WHEATEN.
Ge 30:14 went in the days of w. harvest, ... 2406
Ex 9:32 the w. and the rie were not smitten ... 2406
Ex 34:22 the first fruits of w. harvest, and the .. 2406
Nu 18:12 best of the wine, and of the w., ... 1715
De 8:8 A land of w., and barley, and 2406
De 32:14 with the fat of kidneys of w.; 2406
Jg 6:11 his son Gideon threshed w. by the 2406
Jg 15:1 after, in the time of w. harvest, ... 2406
Ru 2:23 barley harvest and of w. harvest; 2406
1Sa 6:13 were reaping their w. harvest in 2406
1Sa 12:17 Is it not w. harvest to day? I will 2406
2Sa 4:6 they would have fetched w.; 2406
2Sa 17:28 vessels, and w., and barley, and 2406
1Ki 5:11 twenty thousand measures of w. 2406
1Ch 21:20 Now Ornan was threshing w.. 2406
1Ch 21:23 and the w. for the meat offering; 2406
2Ch 2:10 thousand measures of beaten w., ... 2406
2Ch 2:15 the w., and the barley, the oil, and 2406
2Ch 27:5 and ten thousand measures of w., ... 2406
Ezr 6:9 w., salt, wine, and oil, according 2591
Ezr 7:22 and to an hundred measures of w., ... 2591
Job 31:40 Let thistles grow instead of w., ... 2406
Ps 81:16 them also with the finest of the w. 2406
Ps 147:14 filleth thee with the finest of the w. 2406
Pr 27:22 bray a fool in a mortar among w. 7383
Ca 7:2 an heap of w. set about with lilies. 2406
Isa 28:25 cast in the principal w. and the 2406
Jer 12:13 They have sown w., but shall reap 2406
Jer 23:28 what is the chaff to the w.? saith 1250
Jer 31:12 for w., and for wine, and for oil, ... 1715
Jer 41:8 in the field, of w., and of barley, ... 2406
Eze 4:9 Take thou also unto thee w., and 2406
Eze 27:17 traded in thy market w. of Minnith, ... 2406
Eze 45:13 part of an ephah of an homer of w., ... 2406
Joe 1:11 for the w. and for the barley; 2406
Joe 2:24 the floors shall be full of w., and 1250
Am 5:11 ye take from him burdens of w.: 1250
Am 8:5 sabbath, that we may set forth w., ... 1250
Am 8:6 yea, and sell the refuse of the w.? 1250
Mt 3:12 and gather his w. into the garner; 4621
Mt 13:25 **and sowed tares among the w.,** 4621
Mt 13:29 **ye root up also the w. with them.** .. 4621
Mt 13:30 **but gather the w. into my barn.** 4621
Lu 3:17 will gather the w. into his garner; 4621
Lu 16:7 **said, An hundred measures of w.** 4621
Lu 22:31 **you, that he may sift you as w.:** 4621
Joh 12:24 **a corn of w. fall into the ground** ... 4621
Ac 27:38 and cast out the w. into the sea 4621
1Co 15:37 it may chance of w., or of some 4621
Re 6:6 A measure of w. for a penny, and 4621
Re 18:13 and oil, and fine flour, and w., ... 4621

WHEATEN
Ex 29:2 of w. flour shalt thou make them 2406

WHEEL See also WHEELS.
1Ki 7:32 height of a w. was a cubit and half 212
1Ki 7:33 was like the work of a chariot w.: 212
Ps 83:13 God, make them like a w.; as the 1534
Pr 20:26 and bringeth the w. over them 212
Ec 12:6 or the w. broken at the cistern 1534
Isa 28:27 neither is a cart w. turned about 212
Isa 28:28 break it with the w. of his cart, ... 1536

Eze 1:15 behold one **w.** upon the earth by......... 212
Eze 1:16 it were a **w.** in the middle of a **w.**...... 212
Eze 10:9 cherubim, one **w.** by one cherub,......... 212
Eze 10:9 another **w.** by another cherub: 212
Eze 10:10 a **w.** had been in the midst of a **w.**..... 212
Eze 10:13 unto them in my hearing, O **w.**......... 1534

WHEELS
Ex 14:25 took off their chariot **w.**, that they....... 212
Jg 5:28 why tarry the **w.** of his chariots?........ 6471
1Ki 7:30 And every base had four brasen **w.**,..... 212
1Ki 7:32 under the borders were four **w.**; 212
1Ki 7:32 axletrees of the **w.** were joined to 212
1Ki 7:33 work of the **w.** was like the work of...... 212
Isa 5:28 and their **w.** like a whirlwind: 1534
Jer 18:3 he wrought a work on the **w.**. 70
Jer 47:3 and at the rumbling of his **w.**, the 1534
Eze 1:16 appearance of the **w.** and their 212
Eze 1:19 creatures went, the **w.** went by them:.. 212
Eze 1:19 the earth, the **w.** were lifted up. 212
Eze 1:20 the **w.** were lifted up over against........ 212
Eze 1:20 of the living creature was in the **w.**...... 212
Eze 1:21 **w.** were lifted up over against them: 212
Eze 1:21 of the living creature was in the **w.**...... 212
Eze 3:13 noise of the **w.** over against them, ... 212
Eze 10:2 Go in between the **w.**, even under 1534
Eze 10:6 Take fire from between the **w.**, ... 1534
Eze 10:6 went in, and stood beside the **w.**......... 212
Eze 10:9 the four **w.** by the cherubims,............. 212
Eze 10:9 appearance of the **w.** was as the........... 212
Eze 10:12 the **w.** were full of eyes round about,... 212
Eze 10:12 even the **w.** that they four had........... 212
Eze 10:13 As for the **w.**, it was cried unto 212
Eze 10:16 cherubims went, the **w.** went by 212
Eze 10:16 the same **w.** also turned not from.......... 212
Eze 10:19 out, the **w.** also were beside them,....... 212
Eze 11:22 wings, and the **w.** beside them; and...... 212
Eze 23:24 with chariots, wagons, and **w.**, ... 1534
Eze 26:10 of the horsemen, and of the **w.**,......... 1534
Da 7:9 flame, and his **w.** as burning fire. 1535
Na 3:2 the noise of the rattling of the **w.**, ... 212

WHELM See OVERWHELM.

WHELP See WHELPS.
Ge 49:9 Judah is a lion's **w.**: from the............ 1482
De 33:22 Dan is a lion's **w.**: he shall leap.......... 1482
Na 2:11 the lion's **w.**, and none made them 1482

WHELPS
2Sa 17:8 as a bear robbed of her **w.** in the field: .....
Job 4:11 the stout lion's **w.** are scattered......... 1121
Job 28:8 The lion's **w.** have not trodden it, ... 1121
Pr 17:12 Let a bear robbed of her **w.** meet a..........
Jer 51:38 lions: they shall yell as lions' **w.**.......... 1484
Eze 19:2 she nourished her **w.** among 1482
Eze 19:3 she brought one of her **w.**: it 1482
Eze 19:5 she took another of her **w.**, and......... 1482
Ho 13:8 as a bear that is bereaved of her **w.**, ...
Na 2:12 tear in pieces enough for his **w.**,......... 1484

WHEN See also WHENSOEVER.
Ge 2:4 of the earth **w.** they were created, ...
Ge 3:6 **w.** the woman saw that the tree was ....
Ge 4:8 **w.** they were in the field, that Cain ....
Ge 4:12 **W.** thou tillest the ground, it............. 3588
Ge 5:2 Adam, in the day **w.** they were created.....
Ge 6:1 **w.** men began to multiply on the......... 3588
Ge 6:4 **w.** the sons of God came in unto.......... 834
Ge 7:6 **w.** the flood of waters was upon the ....
Ge 9:14 **w.** I bring a cloud over the earth, that ......
Ge 12:4 years old **w.** he departed out of Haran. .....
Ge 12:11 **w.** he was come near to enter into 834
Ge 12:12 **w.** the Egyptians shall see thee, ... 3588
Ge 12:14 **w.** Abram was come into Egypt, the.........
Ge 14:14 **w.** Abram heard that his brother......... 3588
Ge 15:11 **w.** the fowls came down upon the ....
Ge 15:12 And **w.** the sun was going down, ... 1961
Ge 15:17 **w.** the sun went down, and it was...... 1961
Ge 16:4, 5 **w.** she was that she had conceived, ...
Ge 16:6 **w.** Sarai dealt hardly with her, she ....
Ge 16:16 **w.** Hagar bare Ishmael to Abram...............
Ge 17:1 **w.** Abram was ninety years old........... 1961
Ge 17:24, 25 **w.** he was circumcised in the flesh ....
Ge 18:2 **w.** he saw them, he ran to meet.............
Ge 19:15 And **w.** the morning arose, then......... 3644
Ge 19:17 **w.** they had brought them forth ....
Ge 19:23 the earth **w.** Lot entered into Zoar. ....
Ge 19:29 **w.** God destroyed the cities of the............
Ge 19:29 **w.** he overthrew the cities in the ....
Ge 19:33, 35 **w.** she lay down, nor **w.** she arose. .....
Ge 20:13 **w.** God caused me to wander from 834
Ge 21:5 **w.** his son Isaac was born unto him. ....
Ge 24:19 And **w.** she had done giving him drink, ...
Ge 24:30 **w.** he heard the words of Rebekah..............
Ge 24:30 **w.** he saw the earring and bracelets..........
Ge 24:36 a son to my master **w.** she was old...... 310
Ge 24:41 **w.** thou comest to thy kindred;...............
Ge 24:43 that **w.** the virgin cometh forth to draw.....
Ge 24:52 **w.** Abraham's servant heard their............
Ge 24:64 **w.** she saw Isaac, she lighted off the ....
Ge 25:20 years old **w.** he took Rebekah to wife, ...
Ge 25:24 **w.** her days to be delivered were............
Ge 25:26 threescore years old **w.** she bare them......
Ge 26:8 **w.** he had been there a long time,...... 3588
Ge 26:34 and Esau was forty years old **w.** ....
Ge 27:1 it came to pass that **w.** Issac was old,........
Ge 27:5 Rebekah heard **w.** Isaac spake to Esau......
Ge 27:34 **w.** Esau heard the words of his father,......
Ge 27:40 **w.** thou shalt have the dominion 834
Ge 28:6 **W.** Esau saw that Isaac had blessed ....
Ge 29:10 **w.** Jacob saw Rachel the daughter........ 834
Ge 29:13 **w.** Laban heard the tidings of Jacob ....
Ge 29:31 **w.** the Lord saw that Leah was hated, ...
Ge 30:1 **w.** Rachel saw that she bare Jacob no ....
Ge 30:9 **W.** Leah saw that she had left.................
Ge 30:25 **w.** Rachel had born Joseph, that 834
Ge 30:30 **w.** shall I provide for mine own 4970
Ge 30:33 **w.** it shall come for my hire before..... 3588
Ge 30:38 troughs **w.** the flocks came to drink,... 3588
Ge 30:38 conceive **w.** they came to drink...............
Ge 30:42 **w.** the cattle were feeble, he put them.......
Ge 31:49 **w.** we are absent one from another. ... 3588
Ge 32:2 **w.** Jacob saw them, he said, This 834
Ge 32:17 **W.** Esau my brother meeteth........... 3588
Ge 32:19 speak unto Esau, **w.** ye find him. ....
Ge 32:25 And **w.** he saw that he prevailed not.........
Ge 33:18 Canaan, **w.** he came from Padan-aram; ......
Ge 34:2 And **w.** Shechem the son of Hamor the .....
Ge 34:7 came out of the field **w.** they heard it: ......
Ge 34:25 **w.** they were sore, that two of the sons....
Ge 35:1 **w.** thou fleddest from the face of Esau......
Ge 35:7 **w.** he fled from the face of his................
Ge 35:9 **w.** he came out of Padan-aram, and..........
Ge 35:17 **w.** she was in hard labour, that the...........
Ge 35:22 **w.** Israel dwelt in that land, that ....
Ge 37:4 **w.** his brethren saw that their father.........
Ge 37:18 **w.** they saw him afar off, even before.......
Ge 37:23 **w.** Joseph was come unto his............. 834
Ge 38:5 he was at Chezib, **w.** she bare him............
Ge 38:9 **w.** he went in unto his brother's.......... 518
Ge 38:15 **W.** Judah saw her, he thought her to........
Ge 38:25 **w.** she was brought forth, she.................
Ge 38:28 **w.** she travailed, that the one put out ....
Ge 39:13 **w.** she saw that he had left his ....
Ge 39:15 **w.** he heard that I had lifted up my...........
Ge 39:19 **w.** his master heard the words of his ....
Ge 40:13 manner **w.** thou wast his butler. 834
Ge 40:14 on me **w.** it shall be well with thee, ... 834
Ge 40:16 **W.** the chief baker saw that the...............
Ge 41:21 And **w.** they had eaten them up, ...
Ge 41:46 years old **w.** he stood before Pharaoh ....
Ge 41:55 **w.** all the land of Egypt was famished, ...
Ge 42:1 **w.** Jacob saw that there was corn in ....
Ge 42:21 **w.** he besought us, and we would not ....
Ge 42:35 **w.** both they and their father saw the ....
Ge 43:2 **w.** they had eaten up the corn 834
Ge 43:16 **w.** Joseph saw Benjamin with them,.........
Ge 43:21 **w.** we came to the inn, that we......... 3588
Ge 43:26 **w.** Joseph came home, they brought ....
Ge 44:4 And **w.** they were gone out of the city,.....
Ge 44:4 **w.** thou dost overtake them, say unto.........
Ge 44:24 **w.** we came up unto thy servant.......... 3588
Ge 44:30 **w.** I came to thy servant my father, ...
Ge 44:31 **w.** he seeth that the lad is not with us, ...
Ge 45:27 **w.** he saw the wagons that Joseph had......
Ge 46:33 **w.** Pharaoh shall call you, and............ 3588
Ge 47:15 **w.** money failed in the land of Egypt, ...
Ge 47:18 **W.** the year was ended, they came ....
Ge 48:7 **w.** I came from Padan, Rachel died by ......
Ge 48:7 **w.** yet there was but a little way 5750
Ge 48:17 **w.** Joseph saw that his father laid his ....
Ge 49:33 **w.** Jacob had made an end of..................
Ge 50:4 **w.** the days of his mourning were past, ...
Ge 50:11 And **w.** the inhabitants of the land, ...
Ge 50:15 **w.** Joseph's brethren saw that their ....
Ge 50:17 Joseph wept **w.** they spake unto him.........
Ex 1:10 that, **w.** there falleth out any war,...... 3588
Ex 1:16 **W.** ye do the office of a midwife to the .....
Ex 2:2 and **w.** she saw him that he was a...........
Ex 2:3 And **w.** she could not longer hide him, ...
Ex 2:5 **w.** she saw the ark among the flags,.........
Ex 2:6 **w.** she had opened it, she saw the ....
Ex 2:11 **w.** Moses was grown, that he went out.....
Ex 2:12 and **w.** he saw that there was no man, ...
Ex 2:13 and **w.** he went out the second day, ...
Ex 2:15 Now **w.** Pharaoh heard this thing, ...
Ex 2:18 And **w.** they came to Reuel their father,....
Ex 3:4 **w.** the Lord saw that he turned aside........
Ex 3:12 **W.** thou hast brought forth the ....
Ex 3:13 **w.** I came unto the children of Israel,........
Ex 3:21 that, **w.** ye go, ye shall not go empty: ......
Ex 4:6 **w.** he took it out, behold, his hand was.....
Ex 4:14 **w.** he seeth thee, he will be glad in his .....
Ex 4:21 **W.** thou goest to return into Egypt, ...
Ex 4:31 **w.** they heard that the Lord had ....
Ex 5:13 daily tasks, as **w.** they were straw....... 834
Ex 6:28 day **w.** the Lord spake unto Moses in ....
Ex 7:5 **w.** I stretch forth mine hand upon ....
Ex 7:7 years old, **w.** they spake unto Pharaoh. .....
Ex 7:9 **W.** Pharaoh shall speak unto you,....... 3588
Ex 8:9 **w.** shall I intreat for thee, and for 4970
Ex 8:15 **w.** Pharaoh saw that there was respite,.....
Ex 9:34 **w.** Pharaoh saw that the rain and the........
Ex 10:13 and **w.** it was morning, the east wind........
Ex 11:1 **w.** he shall let you go, he shall surely ....
Ex 12:13 **w.** I see the blood, I will pass over ....
Ex 12:13 you, **w.** I smite the land of Egypt. ....
Ex 12:23 **w.** he seeth the blood upon the lintel, ...
Ex 12:25 **w.** ye be come to the land which 3588
Ex 12:26 **w.** your children shall say unto you,.... 3588
Ex 12:27 **w.** he smote the Egyptians, and...............
Ex 12:44 **w.** thou hast circumcised him, then..........
Ex 12:48 And **w.** a stranger shall sojourn.......... 3588
Ex 13:5 **w.** the Lord shall bring thee into........ 3588
Ex 13:8 unto me **w.** I came forth out of Egypt. ......
Ex 13:11 **w.** the Lord shall bring thee into.......... 3588
Ex 13:14 **w.** thy son asketh thee in time to....... 3588
Ex 13:15 **w.** Pharaoh would hardly let us go,...... 3588
Ex 13:17 pass, **w.** Pharaoh had let the people go, ...
Ex 13:17 the people repent **w.** they see war, ...
Ex 14:10 **w.** Pharaoh drew nigh, the children of.......
Ex 14:18 **w.** I have gotten me honour upon.............
Ex 14:27 his strength **w.** the morning appeared;.......
Ex 15:23 **w.** they came to Marah, they could not .....
Ex 15:25 **w.** he had cast into the waters, the ....
Ex 16:3 of Egypt, **w.** we sat by the flesh pots, ...
Ex 16:3 and **w.** we did eat bread to the full; ....
Ex 16:8 **w.** the Lord shall give you in the flesh ....
Ex 16:14 **w.** the dew that lay was gone up,............
Ex 16:15 And **w.** the children of Israel saw it, ...
Ex 16:18 And **w.** they did mete it with an omer,......
Ex 16:21 and **w.** the sun waxed hot, it melted. ....
Ex 16:32 **w.** I brought you forth from the land.........
Ex 17:11 pass, **w.** Moses held up his hand, ... 834
Ex 17:11 and **w.** he let down his hand, ... 834
Ex 18:1 **W.** Jethro, the priest of Midian,......... 3588
Ex 18:14 **w.** Moses' father in law saw all that he.......
Ex 18:16 **W.** they have a matter, they come..... 3588
Ex 19:1 **w.** the children of Israel were gone ....
Ex 19:9 people may hear **w.** I speak with thee, ...
Ex 19:13 **w.** the trumpet soundeth long, they..........
Ex 19:19 And **w.** the voice of the trumpet........ 1961
Ex 20:18 **w.** the people saw it, they removed,..........
Ex 22:27 **w.** he crieth unto me, that I will 3588
Ex 23:16 **w.** thou hast gathered in thy labours ....
Ex 28:29 **w.** he goeth in unto the holy place,...........
Ex 28:30 heart, **w.** he goeth in before the Lord: ......
Ex 28:35 **w.** he goeth in unto the holy place...........
Ex 28:35 and **w.** he cometh out, that he die not.......
Ex 28:43 **w.** they come in unto the tabernacle ....
Ex 28:43 or **w.** they come near unto the altar to......
Ex 29:30 **w.** he cometh into the tabernacle of 834
Ex 29:36 **w.** thou hast made an atonement for..........
Ex 30:7 **w.** he dresseth the lamps, he shall..........
Ex 30:8 **w.** Aaron lighteth the lamps at even,.........
Ex 30:12 **W.** thou takest the sum of the........... 3588
Ex 30:12 the Lord, **w.** thou numberest them; ....
Ex 30:12 them, **w.** thou numberest them. ....
Ex 30:15 **w.** they give an offering unto the Lord, ...
Ex 30:20 **W.** they go into the tabernacle of the........

Ex 30:20 or **w.** they come near to the altar to
Ex 31:18 **w.** he made an end of communing
Ex 32:1 **w.** the people saw that Moses delayed
Ex 32:5 **w.** Aaron saw it, he built an altar
Ex 32:17 **w.** Joshua heard the noise of the
Ex 32:25 **w.** Moses saw that the people were
Ex 32:34 nevertheless in the day **w.** I visit I
Ex 33:4 **w.** the people heard these evil tidings,
Ex 33:8 **w.** Moses went out unto the tabernacle,
Ex 34:24 **w.** thou shalt go up to appear before
Ex 34:29 **w.** Moses came down from mount
Ex 34:29 **w.** he came down from the mount,
Ex 34:30 **w.** Aaron and all the children of Israel
Ex 34:34 **w.** Moses went in before the Lord to
Ex 40:32 **W.** they went into the tent of the
Ex 40:32 **w.** they came near unto the altar, they
Ex 40:36 **w.** the cloud was taken up from over
Le 2:1 **w.** any will offer a meat offering unto
Le 2:8 and **w.** it is presented unto the priest,
Le 4:14 **W.** the sin, which they have sinned
Le 4:22 **W.** a ruler hath sinned, and done 834
Le 5:3,4 **w.** he knoweth of it, then he shall be
Le 5:5 **w.** he shall be guilty in one of 3588
Le 6:20 the Lord in the day **w.** he is anointed;
Le 6:21 **w.** it is baken, thou shalt bring it in:
Le 6:27 **w.** there is sprinkled of the blood 834
Le 7:35 **w.** he presented them to minister unto
Le 9:24 **w.** all the people saw, they shouted,
Le 10:9 **w.** ye go into the tabernacle of the
Le 10:20 **w.** Moses heard that, he was content
Le 11:31 doth touch them, **w.** they be dead,
Le 11:32 any of them, **w.** they are dead, doth
Le 12:6 **w.** the days of her purifying are
Le 13:2 **W.** a man shall have in the skin of 3588
Le 13:3 **w.** the hair in the plague is turned
Le 13:9 **W.** the plague of leprosy is in a 3588
Le 13:14 **w.** raw flesh appeareth in him, he 3117
Le 13:20 and if, **w.** the priest seeth it, behold,
Le 14:34 **W.** ye be come into the land of 3588
Le 14:57 To teach **w.** it is unclean, and 3117
Le 14:57 and **w.** it is clean: this is the law of 3117
Le 15:2 **W.** any man hath a running issue 3588
Le 15:13 **w.** he that hath an issue is cleansed 3588
Le 15:23 **w.** he toucheth it, he shall be unclean
Le 15:31 **w.** they defile my tabernacle that is
Le 16:1 **w.** they offered before the Lord, and
Le 16:17 **w.** he goeth in to make an atonement
Le 16:20 **w.** he hath made the end of reconciling
Le 16:23 put on **w.** he went into the holy place,
Le 18:28 spue not you out also, **w.** ye defile it,
Le 19:9 **w.** ye reap the harvest of your land,
Le 19:23 and **w.** ye shall come into the land, 3588
Le 20:4 **w.** he giveth of his seed unto Molech,
Le 22:7 **w.** the sun is down, he shall be clean,
Le 22:16 trespass, **w.** they eat their holy things:
Le 22:27 **W.** a bullock, or a sheep, or a goat, is
Le 22:29 And **w.** ye will offer a sacrifice of 3588
Le 23:10 **W.** ye be come into the land which 3588
Le 23:12 offer that day **w.** ye wave the sheaf
Le 23:22 **w.** ye reap the harvest of your land,
Le 23:39 **w.** ye have gathered in the fruit of the
Le 23:43 **w.** I brought them out of the land of
Le 24:16 **w.** he blasphemeth the name of the
Le 25:2 **W.** ye come into the land which I 3588
Le 26:17 ye shall flee **w.** none pursueth you.
Le 26:25 **w.** ye are gathered together within
Le 26:26 And **w.** I have broken the staff of your
Le 26:35 in your sabbaths, **w.** ye dwelt upon it
Le 26:36 and they shall fall **w.** none pursueth.
Le 26:37 before a sword, **w.** none pursueth:
Le 26:44 **w.** they be in the land of their enemies,
Le 27:2 **W.** a man shall make a singular 3588
Le 27:14 **w.** a man shall sanctify his house 3588
Le 27:21 the field, **w.** it goeth out in the jubile,
Nu 1:51 And **w.** the tabernacle setteth forward,
Nu 1:51 And **w.** the tabernacle is to be pitched,
Nu 3:4 **w.** they offered strange fire before the
Nu 4:5 **w.** the camp setteth forward, Aaron
Nu 4:15 **w.** Aaron and his sons have made an
Nu 4:19 **w.** they approach unto the most holy
Nu 4:20 to see **w.** the holy things are covered,
Nu 5:6 **W.** a man or a woman shall 3588
Nu 5:21 **w.** the Lord doth make thy thigh to
Nu 5:27 and **w.** he hath made her to drink the
Nu 5:29 **w.** a wife goeth aside to another 834
Nu 5:30 Or **w.** the spirit of jealousy cometh 834
Nu 6:2 **W.** either man or woman shall 3588
Nu 6:7 brother, or for his sister, **w.** they die:
Nu 6:13 **w.** the days of his separation are
Nu 7:84 altar, in the day **w.** it was anointed,
Nu 7:89 and **w.** Moses was gone into the
Nu 8:2 **W.** thou lightest the lamps, the seven
Nu 8:19 **w.** the children of Israel come nigh
Nu 9:17 **w.** the cloud was taken up from 6310
Nu 9:19 And **w.** the cloud tarried long upon the
Nu 9:20 **w.** the cloud was a few days upon 834
Nu 9:21 **w.** the cloud abode from even unto 834
Nu 9:22 but **w.** it was taken, they journeyed
Nu 10:3 But **w.** they shall blow with them,
Nu 10:5 **W.** ye blow an alarm, then the camps
Nu 10:6 **W.** ye blow an alarm the second time
Nu 10:7 **w.** the congregation is to be gathered
Nu 10:28 to their armies, **w.** they set forward.
Nu 10:34 by day, **w.** they went out of the camp.
Nu 10:35 came to pass, **w.** the ark set forward,
Nu 10:36 **w.** it rested, he said, Return, O Lord,
Nu 11:1 And **w.** the people complained, it
Nu 11:2 and **w.** Moses prayed unto the Lord,
Nu 11:9 And **w.** the dew fell upon the camp
Nu 11:25 that, **w.** the spirit rested upon them,
Nu 12:12 **w.** he cometh out of his mother's 834
Nu 15:2 **W.** ye be come into the land of 3588
Nu 15:8 **w.** thou preparest a bullock for a 3588
Nu 15:18 **W.** ye come into the land whither I
Nu 15:19 **w.** ye eat of the bread of the land, ye
Nu 15:28 **w.** he sinneth by ignorance before the
Nu 16:4 And **w.** Moses heard it, he fell upon his
Nu 16:42 **w.** the congregation was gathered
Nu 18:26 **W.** ye take of the children of 3588
Nu 18:30 **W.** ye have heaved the best thereof
Nu 18:32 **w.** ye have heaved from it the best of
Nu 19:14 the law, **w.** a man dieth in a tent: 3588
Nu 20:3 we had died **w.** our brethren died
Nu 20:16 **w.** we cried unto the Lord, he heard
Nu 20:29 And **w.** all the congregation saw that
Nu 21:1 And **w.** king Arad the Canaanite,
Nu 21:8 bitten, **w.** he looketh upon it, shall live.
Nu 21:9 **w.** he behold the serpent of brass, he
Nu 22:25, 27 And **w.** the ass saw the angel of
Nu 22:36 And **w.** Balak heard that Balaam was
Nu 23:17 **w.** he came to him, behold, he stood
Nu 24:1 And **w.** Balaam saw that it pleased
Nu 24:20 **w.** he looked upon Amalek, he took
Nu 24:23 Alas, who shall live **w.** God doeth this!
Nu 25:7 And **w.** Phinehas, the son of Eleazar,
Nu 26:9 **w.** they strove against the Lord:
Nu 26:10 with Korah, **w.** that company died,
Nu 26:61 **w.** they offered strange fire before the
Nu 26:64 **w.** they numbered the children of 834
Nu 27:13 **w.** thou hast seen it, thou also shalt
Nu 28:26 **w.** ye bring a new meat offering unto
Nu 30:6 had at all a husband, **w.** she vowed,
Nu 32:1 **w.** they saw the land of Jazer, and the
Nu 32:8 **w.** I sent them from Kadesh-barnea
Nu 32:9 For **w.** they went up unto the valley of
Nu 33:39 years old **w.** he died in mount Hor.
Nu 33:51 **W.** ye are passed over Jordan 3588
Nu 34:2 them, **W.** ye come into the land of 3588
Nu 35:10 **W.** ye be come over Jordan unto 3588
Nu 35:19 **w.** he meeteth him, he shall slay him.
Nu 35:21 slay the murderer, **w.** he meeteth him.
Nu 36:4 And **w.** the jubile of the children of 518
De 1:19 **w.** we departed from Horeb, we went
De 1:41 **w.** ye had girded on every man his
De 2:8 **w.** we passed by from our brethren
De 2:12 **w.** they had destroyed them from
De 2:16 **w.** all the men of war were 834
De 2:19 **w.** thou comest nigh over against the
De 2:22 **w.** he destroyed the Horims from 834
De 4:10 **w.** the Lord said unto me, Gather me
De 4:19 **w.** thou seest the sun, and the moon,
De 4:25 **W.** thou shalt beget children, and 3588
De 4:30 **W.** thou art in tribulation, and all
De 5:23 **w.** ye heard the voice out of the midst
De 5:28 of your words, **w.** ye spake unto me;
De 6:7 of them **w.** thou sitteth in thine house.
De 6:7 and **w.** thou walkest by the way,
De 6:7 and **w.** thou liest down,
De 6:7 and **w.** thou risest up
De 6:10 **w.** the Lord thy God shall have 3588
De 6:11 **w.** thou shalt have eaten and be full;
De 6:20 **w.** thy son asketh thee in time to 3588
De 7:1 **W.** the Lord thy God shall bring 3588
De 7:2 **w.** the Lord thy God shall deliver
De 8:10 **W.** thou hast eaten and art full, then
De 8:12 Lest **w.** thou hast eaten and art full,
De 8:13 **w.** thy herds and thy flocks multiply,
De 9:9 **W.** I was gone up into the mount to
De 9:23 Likewise **w.** the Lord sent you from
De 11:19 of them **w.** thou sittest in thine house,
De 11:19 and **w.** thou walkest by the way,
De 11:19 **w.** thou liest down, and **w.** thou risest
De 11:29 **w.** the Lord thy God hath brought 3588
De 12:10 But **w.** ye go over Jordan, and dwell
De 12:10 **w.** he giveth you rest from all your
De 12:20 **W.** the Lord thy God shall enlarge 3588
De 12:25 **w.** thou shalt do that which is right 3588
De 12:28 **w.** thou doest that which is good 3588
De 12:29 **W.** the Lord thy God shall cut off 3588
De 13:18 **W.** thou shalt hearken to the voice 3588
De 14:24 **w.** the Lord thy God hath blessed 3588
De 15:4 **w.** there shall be no poor among 3588
De 15:10 shall not be grieved **w.** thou givest
De 15:13 And **w.** thou sendest him out free 3588
De 15:18 **w.** thou sendest him away free from
De 16:3 **w.** thou camest forth out of the land
De 17:14 **W.** thou art come unto the land 3588
De 17:18 **w.** he sitteth upon the throne of his
De 18:9 **W.** thou art come into the land 3588
De 18:22 **W.** the prophet speaketh in the 834
De 19:1 **W.** the Lord thy God hath cut off 3588
De 19:5 As **w.** a man goeth into the wood 834
De 20:1 **W.** thou goest out to battle 3588
De 20:2 **w.** ye are come nigh unto the battle,
De 20:9 **w.** the officers have made an end of
De 20:10 **W.** thou comest nigh unto a city 3588
De 20:13 **w.** the Lord thy God hath delivered it
De 20:19 **W.** thou shalt besiege a city a 3588
De 21:9 **w.** thou shalt do that which is right 3588
De 21:10 **W.** thou goest forth to war against 3588
De 21:16 **w.** he maketh his sons to inherit 3117
De 21:18 **w.** they have chastened him will not
De 22:8 **W.** thou buildest a new house, 3588
De 22:14 **w.** I came to her, I found her not a
De 22:26 for as **w.** a man riseth against his
De 23:4 way, **w.** ye came forth out of Egypt;
De 23:9 **W.** the host goeth forth against 3588
De 23:11 **w.** evening cometh on, he shall wash
De 23:11 **w.** the sun is down, he shall come into
De 23:13 **w.** thou wilt ease thyself abroad, thou
De 23:21 **W.** thou shalt vow a vow unto the 3588
De 23:24 **W.** thou comest into thy 3588
De 23:25 **W.** thou comest into the standing 3588
De 24:1 **W.** a man hath taken a wife, and 3588
De 24:2 **w.** she is departed out of his house,
De 24:5 **W.** a man hath taken a new wife, 3588
De 24:10 **W.** thou dost lend thy brother any 3588
De 24:13 pledge again **w.** the sun goeth down,
De 24:19 **W.** thou cuttest down thine 3588
De 24:20 **W.** thou beatest thine olive tree, 3588
De 24:21 **W.** thou gatherest the grapes of 3588
De 25:4 the ox **w.** he treadeth out the corn.
De 25:11 **W.** men strive together one with 3588
De 25:17 **w.** ye were come forth out of Egypt;
De 25:18 thee, **w.** thou wast faint and weary;
De 25:19 **w.** the Lord thy God hath given thee
De 26:1 **w.** thou art come in unto the land 3588
De 26:7 **w.** we cried unto the Lord God of our
De 26:12 **W.** thou hast made an end of 3588
De 27:2 **w.** ye shall pass over Jordan unto 834
De 27:3 this law, **w.** thou art pased over,
De 27:4 it shall be **w.** ye be gone over Jordan,
De 27:12 people, **w.** ye are come over Jordan;
De 28:6 Blessed shalt thou be **w.** thou comest
De 28:6 blessed shalt thou be **w.** thou goest
De 28:19 Cursed shalt thou be **w.** thou comest
De 28:19 cursed shalt thou be **w.** thou goest out.
De 29:7 **w.** ye came unto this place, Sihon the
De 29:19 **w.** he heareth the words of this curse,
De 29:22 **w.** they see the plagues of that land,
De 29:25 **w.** he brought them forth out of the
De 30:1 **w.** all these things are come upon 3588
De 31:11 **W.** all Israel is come to appear before
De 31:20 **w.** I shall have brought them into 3588
De 31:21 **w.** many evils and troubles are 3588
De 31:24 **w.** Moses had made an end of writing
De 32:8 **W.** the most High divided to the
De 32:8 **w.** he separated the sons of Adam, he
De 32:19 And **w.** the Lord saw it, he abhorred
De 32:36 **w.** he seeth that their power is 3588
De 33:5 **w.** the heads of the people and the

De 34:7 and twenty years old **w.** he died:............
Jos 2:5 **w.** it was dark, that the men went out:.....
Jos 2:10 sea for you, **w.** ye came out of Egypt;......
Jos 2:14 **w.** the Lord hath given us the land,..........
Jos 2:18 **w.** we come into the land, thou shalt........
Jos 3:3 **W.** ye see the ark of the covenant of........
Jos 3:8 **W.** ye are come to the brink of the..........
Jos 3:14 **w.** the people removed from their...........
Jos 4:1 **w.** all the people were clean passed..... 834
Jos 4:6 **w.** your children ask their fathers....... 3588
Jos 4:7 **w.** it passed over Jordan, the waters of......
Jos 4:11 **w.** all the people were clean passed..... 834
Jos 4:18 **w.** the priests that bare the ark of the......
Jos 4:21 **W.** your children shall ask their.......... 834
Jos 5:1 **w.** all the kings of the Amorites,.............
Jos 5:8 **w.** they had done circumcising all......... 834
Jos 5:13 to pass, **w.** Joshua was by Jericho,..........
Jos 6:5 **w.** they make a long blast with the...........
Jos 6:5 **w.** ye hear the sound of the trumpet,.........
Jos 6:8 **w.** Joshua had spoken unto the people,......
Jos 6:16 **w.** the priests blew with the trumpets,......
Jos 6:18 **w.** ye take of the accursed thing, and........
Jos 6:20 shouted **w.** the priests blew with the........
Jos 6:20 **w.** the people heard the sound of the........
Jos 7:8 **w.** Israel turneth their backs............. 6310
Jos 7:21 **W.** I saw among the spoils a goodly...........
Jos 8:5 **w.** they come out against us, as at..... 3588
Jos 8:8 shall be, **w.** ye have taken the city,..........
Jos 8:13 **w.** they had set the people, even all.........
Jos 8:14 **w.** the king of Ai saw it, that they............
Jos 8:20 **w.** the men of Ai looked behind them,........
Jos 8:21 **w.** Joshua and all Israel saw that the.........
Jos 8:24 **w.** Israel had made an end of slaying..........
Jos 8:24 **w.** they were all fallen on the edge of.......
Jos 9:1 **w.** all the kings which were on this...........
Jos 9:3 **w.** the inhabitants of Gibeon heard...........
Jos 9:22 far from you; **w.** ye dwell among?............
Jos 10:1 **w.** Adoni-zedec king of Jerusalem.............
Jos 10:12 in the day **w.** the Lord delivered up..........
Jos 10:20 **w.** Joshua and the children of Israel..........
Jos 10:24 **w.** they brought out those kings unto........
Jos 11:1 **w.** Jabin king of Hazor had heard.............
Jos 11:5 **w.** all these kings were met together,.......
Jos 14:7 **w.** Moses the servant of the Lord sent......
Jos 17:13 **w.** the children of Israel were............ 3588
Jos 19:49 **W.** they had made an end of dividing........
Jos 20:4 **w.** he that doth flee unto one of those........
Jos 22:7 **w.** Joshua sent them away also.......... 3588
Jos 22:10 **w.** they came unto the borders of............
Jos 22:12 **w.** the children of Israel heard of it,..........
Jos 22:28 **w.** they should so say to us or to....... 3588
Jos 22:30 **w.** Phinehas the priest, and the princes.....
Jos 23:16 **W.** ye have transgressed the covenant......
Jos 24:7 And **w.** they cried unto the Lord,............
Jg 1:14 it came to pass, **w.** she came to him,........
Jg 1:25 **w.** he shewed them the entrance into........
Jg 1:28 **w.** Israel was strong, that they put the......
Jg 2:4 **w.** the angel of the Lord spake these.........
Jg 2:6 And **w.** Joshua had let the people go,........
Jg 2:18 **w.** the Lord raised them up judges,.... 3588
Jg 2:19 **w.** the judge was dead, that they............
Jg 2:21 nations which Joshua left **w.** he died:.........
Jg 3:9, 15 **w.** the children of Israel cried unto.........
Jg 3:18 **w.** he had made an end to offer the..... 834
Jg 3:24 **W.** he was gone out, his servants came;....
Jg 3:24 **w.** they saw that, behold, the doors of......
Jg 3:27 pass, **w.** he was come, that he blew a.......
Jg 4:1 sight of the Lord, **w.** Ehud was dead...........
Jg 4:18 **w.** he had turned in unto her into the........
Jg 4:20 **w.** any man doth come and enquire...... 518
Jg 4:22 And **w.** he came into her tent, behold,......
Jg 5:2 **w.** the people willingly offered.................
Jg 5:4 Lord, **w.** thou wentest out of Seir,............
Jg 5:4 **w.** thou marchedst out of the field of........
Jg 5:26 **w.** she had pierced and stricken...............
Jg 5:31 the sun **w.** he goeth forth in his might.......
Jg 6:3 And so it was, **w.** Israel had sown,...... 518
Jg 6:7 **w.** the children of Israel cried unto...... 3588
Jg 6:22 **w.** Gideon perceived that he was an.........
Jg 6:28 **w.** the men of the city arose early in........
Jg 6:29 **w.** they enquired and asked, they said,......
Jg 7:13 And **w.** Gideon was come, behold,............
Jg 7:15 **w.** Gideon heard the telling of the..........
Jg 7:17 **w.** I come to the outside of the camp,........
Jg 7:18 **W.** I blow with a trumpet, I and all..........
Jg 8:1 **w.** thou wentest to fight with the....... 3588
Jg 8:3 toward him, **w.** he had said that..............
Jg 8:7 **w.** the Lord hath delivered Zeba and.........
Jg 8:9 **W.** I come again in peace, I will break......
Jg 8:12 And **w.** Zeba and Zalmunna fled,...............
Jg 9:7 And **w.** they told it to Jotham, he went.....
Jg 9:22 **W.** Abimelech had reigned three years......
Jg 9:30 **w.** Zebul the ruler of the city heard..........
Jg 9:33 **W.** he and the people that is with him.......
Jg 9:36 And **w.** Gaal saw the people, he said to.....
Jg 9:46 And **w.** all the men of the tower of...........
Jg 9:55 And **w.** the men of Israel saw that...........
Jg 11:5 **w.** the children of Ammon made.......... 834
Jg 11:7 unto me now **w.** ye are in distress?..... 834
Jg 11:13 **w.** they came up out of Egypt, from.........
Jg 11:16 But **w.** Israel came up from Egypt, and.....
Jg 11:31 **w.** I return in peace from the children.......
Jg 11:35 to pass, **w.** he saw her, that he rent his....
Jg 12:2 **w.** I called you, ye delivered me not.........
Jg 12:3 And **w.** I saw that ye delivered me not,.....
Jg 12:5 **w.** those Ephraimites which were.............
Jg 13:17 **w.** thy sayings come to pass we........ 3588
Jg 13:20 **w.** the flame went up toward heaven.........
Jg 14:11 **w.** they saw him, that they brought..........
Jg 15:5 And **w.** he had set the brands on fire,.......
Jg 15:14 **w.** he came unto Lehi, the Philistines........
Jg 15:17 **w.** he had made an end of speaking,.........
Jg 15:19 **w.** he had drunk, his spirit came again.......
Jg 16:2 **w.** it is day, we shall kill him............ 5704
Jg 16:9 of tow is broken **w.** it toucheth the fire.....
Jg 16:15 thee, **w.** thine heart is not with me?.........
Jg 16:16 **w.** she pressed him daily with her...... 3588
Jg 16:18 **w.** Delilah saw that he had told her all.......
Jg 16:24 **w.** the people saw him, they praised..........
Jg 16:25 pass, **w.** their hearts were merry,...... 3588
Jg 17:3 **w.** he had restored the eleven hundred......
Jg 18:2 who **w.** they came to mount Ephraim,........
Jg 18:3 **W.** they were by the house of Micah,.......
Jg 18:10 **W.** ye go, ye shall come unto a people.......
Jg 18:22 **w.** they were a good way from the...........
Jg 18:26 **w.** Micah saw that they were too strong....
Jg 19:1 days, **w.** there was no king in Israel,........
Jg 19:3 **w.** the father of the damsel saw him,........
Jg 19:5 **w.** they arose early in the morning,..........
Jg 19:7 And **w.** the man rose up to depart, his.......
Jg 19:9 And **w.** the man rose up to depart,.........
Jg 19:11 **w.** they were by Jebus, the day was far....
Jg 19:14 upon them **w.** they were by Gibeah,........
Jg 19:15 **w.** he went in, he sat him down in a..........
Jg 19:17 **w.** he had lifted up his eyes, he saw a......
Jg 19:25 **w.** the day began to spring, they let.........
Jg 19:29 **w.** he was come into his house, he...........
Jg 20:10 **w.** they come to Gibeah of Benjamin..........
Jg 20:39 **w.** the men of Israel retired in the............
Jg 20:40 **w.** the flame began to arise up out of........
Jg 20:41 **w.** the men of Israel turned again,............
Jg 21:22 **w.** their fathers or their brethren....... 3588
Ru 1:1 pass in the days **w.** the judges ruled,........
Ru 1:18 **W.** she saw that she was stedfastly..........
Ru 1:19 **w.** they were come to Beth-lehem, that.....
Ru 2:9 **w.** thou art athirst, go unto the...............
Ru 2:15 **w.** she was risen up to glean, Boaz..........
Ru 3:4 be, **w.** he lieth down, that thou shalt.........
Ru 3:7 And **w.** Boaz had eaten and drunk,...........
Ru 3:15 And **w.** she held it, he measured six.........
Ru 3:16 And **w.** she came to her mother in law,.....
Ru 4:13 **w.** he went in unto her, the Lord gave......
1Sa 1:4 **w.** the time was that Elkanah offered,.......
1Sa 1:7 **w.** she went up to the house of......... 1767
1Sa 1:20 **w.** the time was come about after............
1Sa 1:24 **w.** she had weaned him, she took........ 834
1Sa 2:13 that, **w.** any man offered sacrifice,............
1Sa 2:19 **w.** she came up with her husband to.........
1Sa 2:27 **w.** they were in Egypt in Pharaoh's..........
1Sa 3:2 **w.** Eli was laid down in his place,............
1Sa 3:12 **w.** I begin, I will also make an end...........
1Sa 4:2 **w.** they joined battle, Israel was..............
1Sa 4:3 **w.** the people were come into the.............
1Sa 4:3 **w.** it cometh among us, it may save us.....
1Sa 4:5 **w.** the ark of the covenant of the............
1Sa 4:6 **w.** the Philistines heard the noise of.........
1Sa 4:13 **w.** he came, lo, Eli sat upon a seat by......
1Sa 4:13 **w.** the man came into the city, and..........
1Sa 4:14 **w.** Eli heard the noise of the crying, he.....
1Sa 4:18 **w.** he made mention of the ark of God,.....
1Sa 4:19 **w.** she heard the tidings that the ark........
1Sa 5:2 **W.** the Philistines took the ark of............
1Sa 5:3 **w.** they of Ashdod arose early on the........
1Sa 5:4 **w.** they arose early on the morrow..........
1Sa 5:7 **w.** the men of Ashdod saw that it was......
1Sa 6:6 **w.** he had wrought wonderfully............ 834
1Sa 6:16 **w.** the five lords of the Philistines had.......
1Sa 7:7 And **w.** the Philistines heard that the........
1Sa 7:7 **w.** the children of Israel heard it, they......
1Sa 8:1 **w.** Samuel was old, that he made........ 834
1Sa 8:6 **w.** they said, Give us a king to........... 834
1Sa 9:5 **w.** they were come to the land of Zuph,....
1Sa 9:9 **w.** a man went to enquire of God,...........
1Sa 9:14 and **w.** they were come into the city,........
1Sa 9:17 **w.** Samuel saw Saul, the Lord said..........
1Sa 9:25 **w.** they were come down from the...........
1Sa 10:2 **W.** thou art departed from me to day,.......
1Sa 10:5 **w.** thou art come thither to the city,.........
1Sa 10:7 **w.** these signs are come unto thee,.... 3588
1Sa 10:9 **w.** he had turned his back to go from........
1Sa 10:10 And **w.** they came thither to the hill,........
1Sa 10:11 **w.** all that knew him beforetime saw.........
1Sa 10:13 And **w.** he had made an end of................
1Sa 10:14 **w.** we saw that they were no where,.........
1Sa 10:20 **w.** Samuel had caused all the tribes..........
1Sa 10:21 **W.** he had caused the tribe of.................
1Sa 10:21 **w.** they sought him, he could not be.........
1Sa 10:23 **w.** he stood among the people, he was......
1Sa 11:6 upon Saul **w.** he heard those tidings,.........
1Sa 11:8 **w.** he numbered them in Bezek, the..........
1Sa 12:8 **W.** Jacob was come into Egypt,........... 834
1Sa 12:9 **w.** they forgat the Lord their God, he........
1Sa 12:12 **w.** ye saw that Nahash the king of the......
1Sa 12:12 **w.** the Lord your God was your king........
1Sa 13:1 and **w.** he had reigned two years over.......
1Sa 13:6 **W.** the men of Israel saw that they..........
1Sa 14:17 And **w.** they had numbered, behold,..........
1Sa 14:22 **w.** they heard that the Philistines fled,......
1Sa 14:26 And **w.** the people were come into the......
1Sa 14:27 not **w.** his father charged the people.........
1Sa 14:52 **w.** Saul saw any strong man, or any..........
1Sa 15:2 in the way, **w.** he came up from Egypt......
1Sa 15:6 Israel, **w.** they came up out of Egypt........
1Sa 15:12 **w.** Samuel rose early to meet Saul...........
1Sa 15:17 **W.** thou wast little in thine own.......... 518
1Sa 16:6 **w.** they were come, that he looked on......
1Sa 16:16 **w.** the evil spirit from God is upon...........
1Sa 16:23 **w.** the evil spirit from God was upon........
1Sa 17:11 **w.** Saul and all Israel heard those.............
1Sa 17:24 **w.** they saw the man, fled from him,........
1Sa 17:28 heard **w.** he spake unto the men;..............
1Sa 17:31 **w.** the words were heard which David.......
1Sa 17:35 **w.** he arose against me, I caught him........
1Sa 17:42 **w.** the Philistine looked about, and..........
1Sa 17:48 **w.** the Philistine arose, and came....... 3588
1Sa 17:51 **w.** the Philistines saw their champion........
1Sa 17:55 **w.** Saul saw David go forth against...........
1Sa 18:1 **w.** he had made an end of speaking..........
1Sa 18:6 **w.** David was returned from the...............
1Sa 18:15 Wherefore **w.** Saul saw that he behaved....
1Sa 18:19 **w.** Merab Saul's daughter should have.......
1Sa 18:26 **w.** his servants told David these words,....
1Sa 19:14 **w.** Saul sent messengers to take David,....
1Sa 19:16 And **w.** the messengers were come in,......
1Sa 19:20 and **w.** they saw the company of the.........
1Sa 19:21 **w.** it was told Saul, he sent other.............
1Sa 20:12 **w.** I have sounded my father about..... 3588
1Sa 20:15 **w.** the Lord hath cut off the enemies........
1Sa 20:19 And **w.** thou hast stayed three days,.........
1Sa 20:19 hide thyself **w.** the business was in...........
1Sa 20:24 **w.** the new moon was come, the king.......
1Sa 20:37 **w.** the lad was come to the place of the....
1Sa 21:6 in the day **w.** it was taken away.............
1Sa 22:1 **w.** his brethren and all his father's............
1Sa 22:6 **W.** Saul heard that David was.................
1Sa 22:17 because they knew **w.** he fled,.......... 3588
1Sa 22:22 **w.** Doeg the Edomite was there,....... 3588
1Sa 23:6 **w.** Abiathar the son of Ahimelech fled.......
1Sa 23:25 **w.** Saul heard that, he pursued after.........
1Sa 24:1 **w.** Saul was returned from following..... 834
1Sa 24:8 **w.** Saul looked behind him, David............
1Sa 24:16 **w.** David had made an end of speaking......
1Sa 24:18 as **w.** the Lord had delivered me...............
1Sa 25:9 And **w.** David's young men came, they.......
1Sa 25:15 with them, **w.** we were in the fields:........
1Sa 25:23 **w.** Abigail saw David, she hasted,............
1Sa 25:30 **w.** the Lord shall have done to my..... 3588
1Sa 25:31 **w.** the Lord shall have dealt well with.......

1Sa 25:37 **w.** the wine was gone out of Nabal,
1Sa 25:39 **w.** David heard that Nabal was dead,
1Sa 25:40 **w.** the servants of David were come
1Sa 26:20 as **w.** one doth hunt a partridge in 834
1Sa 28:5 **w.** Saul saw the host of the Philistines,
1Sa 28:6 And **w.** Saul enquired of the Lord,
1Sa 28:12 **w.** the woman saw Samuel, she cried
1Sa 28:22 strength, **w.** thou goest on thy way. 3588
1Sa 30:1 **w.** David and his men were come to
1Sa 30:12 **w.** he had eaten, his spirit came again
1Sa 30:16 **w.** he had brought him down, behold,
1Sa 30:21 **w.** David came near to the people, he
1Sa 30:26 **w.** David came to Ziklag, he sent of
1Sa 31:5 **w.** his armourbearer saw that Saul
1Sa 31:7 **w.** the men of Israel that were on the
1Sa 31:8 **w.** the Philistines came to strip the
1Sa 31:11 **w.** the inhabitants of Jabesh-gilead
2Sa 1:1 **w.** David was returned from the
2Sa 1:2 **w.** he came to David, that he fell to the
2Sa 1:7 **w.** he looked behind him, he saw me,
2Sa 2:10 old **w.** he began to reign over Israel,
2Sa 2:24 down **w.** they were come to the hill of
2Sa 2:30 **w.** he had gathered all the people
2Sa 3:13 **w.** thou comest to see my face
2Sa 3:23 **W.** Joab and all the host that was
2Sa 3:26 **w.** Joab was come out from David, he
2Sa 3:27 **w.** Abner was returned to Hebron,
2Sa 3:28 afterward **w.** David heard it, he said,
2Sa 3:35 **w.** all the people came to cause David
2Sa 4:1 **w.** Saul's son heard... Abner was dead
2Sa 4:4 **w.** the tidings came of Saul and
2Sa 4:7 For **w.** they came into the house, he
2Sa 4:10 **W.** one told me, saying, Behold, Saul
2Sa 4:11 **w.** wicked men have slain a 3588
2Sa 5:2 **w.** Saul was king over us, thou wast
2Sa 5:4 David was thirty years old **w.** he began
2Sa 5:17 **w.** the Philistines heard that they had
2Sa 5:23 **w.** David enquired of the Lord, he
2Sa 5:24 **w.** thou hearest the sound of a going
2Sa 6:6 And **w.** they came to Nachon's
2Sa 6:13 **w.** they that bare the ark of the 3588
2Sa 7:1 **w.** the king sat in his house, and 3588
2Sa 7:12 **w.** thy days be fulfilled, and thou 3588
2Sa 8:5 **w.** the Syrians of Damascus came to
2Sa 8:9 **W.** Toi king of Hamath heard that
2Sa 8:13 **w.** he returned from smiting of the
2Sa 9:2 **w.** they had called him unto David,
2Sa 9:6 Now **w.** Mephibosheth, the son of
2Sa 10:5 **W.** they told it unto David, he sent to
2Sa 10:6 **w.** the children of Ammon saw that
2Sa 10:7 **w.** David heard of it, he sent Joab, and
2Sa 10:9 **W.** Joab saw that the front of the
2Sa 10:14 **w.** the children of Ammon saw that
2Sa 10:15 **w.** the Syrians saw that they were
2Sa 10:17 **w.** it was told David, he gathered all
2Sa 10:19 **w.** all the kings that were servants to
2Sa 11:1 time **w.** the kings go forth to battle,
2Sa 11:7 **w.** Uriah was come unto him, David
2Sa 11:10 **w.** they had told David, saying, Uriah
2Sa 11:13 And **w.** David had called him, he did
2Sa 11:16 **w.** Joab observed the city, that he
2Sa 11:19 **W.** thou hast made an end of telling
2Sa 11:20 so nigh unto the city **w.** ye did fight?
2Sa 11:26 **w.** the wife of Uriah heard that Uriah
2Sa 11:27 **w.** the mourning was past, David sent
2Sa 12:19 **w.** David saw that his servants
2Sa 12:20 **w.** he required, they set bread before
2Sa 12:21 **w.** the child was dead, thou didst 834
2Sa 13:5 **w.** thy father cometh to see thee, say
2Sa 13:6 and **w.** the king was come to see him,
2Sa 13:11 **w.** she had brought them unto him to
2Sa 13:21 But **w.** king David heard of all these
2Sa 13:28 ye now **w.** Ammon's heart is merry
2Sa 13:28 and **w.** I say unto you, Smite Ammon;
2Sa 14:4 **w.** the woman of Tekoah spake to the
2Sa 14:26 **w.** he polled his head, (for it was at
2Sa 14:29 **w.** he sent again the second time, he
2Sa 14:33 **w.** he had called for Absalom, he came
2Sa 15:2 **w.** any man that had a controversy
2Sa 15:5 **w.** any man came nigh to him to do
2Sa 15:32 **w.** David was come to the top of the
2Sa 16:1 **w.** David was a little past the top of
2Sa 16:5 And **w.** king David came to Bahurim,
2Sa 16:7 thus said Shimei **w.** he cursed, Come
2Sa 16:16 **w.** Hushai the Archite, David's 834
2Sa 17:6 And **w.** Hushai was come to Absalom,

2Sa 17:9 **w.** some of them be overthrown at the
2Sa 17:20 **w.** Absalom's servants came to the
2Sa 17:20 **w.** they had sought and could not find
2Sa 17:23 **w.** Ahithophel saw that his counsel
2Sa 17:27 **w.** David was come to Mahanaim,
2Sa 18:5 **w.** the king gave all the captains
2Sa 18:29 **W.** Joab sent the king's servant, and
2Sa 19:3 steal away **w.** they flee in battle
2Sa 19:25 **w.** he was come to Jerusalem to 3588
2Sa 19:39 **w.** the king was come over, the king
2Sa 20:8 **W.** they were at the great stone
2Sa 20:12 **w.** the man saw that all the people
2Sa 20:12 **w.** he saw that every one that came
2Sa 20:13 **W.** he was removed out of the
2Sa 20:17 **w.** he was come near unto her, the
2Sa 21:12 **w.** the Philistines had slain Saul 3117
2Sa 21:21 **w.** he defied Israel, Jonathan the son
2Sa 22:5 **W.** the waves of death compassed 3588
2Sa 23:4 of the morning, **w.** the sun riseth,
2Sa 23:9 **w.** they defied the Philistines that
2Sa 24:8 So **w.** they had gone through all the
2Sa 24:11 **w.** David was up in the morning, the
2Sa 24:16 **w.** the angel stretched out his hand
2Sa 24:17 **w.** he saw the angel that smote the
1Ki 1:21 **w.** my lord the king shall sleep with
1Ki 1:23 **w.** he was come in before the king, he
1Ki 1:41 And **w.** Joab heard the sound of the
1Ki 2:7 to me **w.** I fled because of Absalom
1Ki 2:8 in the day **w.** I went to Mahanaim:
1Ki 3:21 **w.** I rose in the morning to give my
1Ki 3:21 but **w.** I had considered it in the
1Ki 5:7 **w.** Hiram heard...words of Solomon,
1Ki 6:7 **w.** it was in building, was built of
1Ki 7:24 were cast in two rows, **w.** it was cast
1Ki 8:9 **w.** the Lord made a covenant with 834
1Ki 8:9 **w.** they came out of the land of Egypt.
1Ki 8:10 **w.** the priests were come out of the
1Ki 8:21 **w.** he brought them out of the land of
1Ki 8:30 **w.** they shall pray toward this 834
1Ki 8:30 and **w.** thou hearest, forgive
1Ki 8:33 **W.** thy people Israel be smitten down
1Ki 8:35 **W.** heaven is shut up, and there is no
1Ki 8:35 there sin, **w.** thou afflictest them: 3588
1Ki 8:42 **w.** he shall come and pray toward this
1Ki 8:53 **w.** thou broughtest our fathers out of
1Ki 8:54 **w.** Solomon had made an end of
1Ki 9:1 **w.** Solomon had finished the building
1Ki 9:10 **w.** Solomon had built the two houses,
1Ki 10:1 **w.** the queen of Sheba heard of the
1Ki 10:2 and **w.** she was come to Solomon, she
1Ki 10:4 **w.** the queen of Sheba had seen all
1Ki 11:4 **w.** Solomon was old, that his 6256
1Ki 11:15 **w.** David was in Edom, and Joab the
1Ki 11:21 **w.** Hadad heard in Egypt that David
1Ki 11:24 a band, **w.** David slew them of Zobah:
1Ki 11:29 **w.** Jeroboam went out of Jerusalem,
1Ki 12:2 **w.** Jeroboam the son of Nebat, who
1Ki 12:16 So **w.** all Israel saw that the king
1Ki 12:20 **w.** all Israel heard that Jeroboam was
1Ki 12:21 **w.** Rehoboam was come to Jerusalem,
1Ki 13:4 **w.** king Jeroboam heard the saying of
1Ki 13:24 **w.** he was gone, a lion met him by the
1Ki 13:26 **w.** the prophet that brought him back
1Ki 13:31 **W.** I am dead, then bury me in the
1Ki 14:5 it shall be, **w.** she cometh in, that she
1Ki 14:6 **w.** Ahijah heard the sound of her feet,
1Ki 14:12 and **w.** thy feet enter into the city, the
1Ki 14:17 **w.** she came to the threshold of the
1Ki 14:21 one years old **w.** he began to reign,
1Ki 14:28 **w.** the king went into the house 1767
1Ki 15:21 it came to pass, **w.** Baasha heard
1Ki 15:29 **w.** he reigned, that he smote all the
1Ki 16:11 **w.** he began to reign, as soon as he sat
1Ki 16:18 **w.** Zimri saw that the city was taken,
1Ki 17:10 **w.** he came to the gate of the city,
1Ki 18:4 **w.** Jezebel cut off the prophets of
1Ki 18:10 and **w.** they said, He is not there;
1Ki 18:12 and so **w.** I come and tell Ahab
1Ki 18:13 **w.** Jezebel slew the prophets of the
1Ki 18:17 **w.** Ahab saw Elijah, that Ahab said
1Ki 18:29 **w.** midday was past, and they
1Ki 18:39 **w.** all the people saw it, they fell on
1Ki 19:3 **w.** he saw that, he arose, and went for
1Ki 19:13 **w.** Elijah heard it, that he wrapped
1Ki 19:15 **w.** thou comest, anoint Hazael to be
1Ki 20:12 **w.** Ben-hadad heard this message,

1Ki 21:15 **w.** Jezebel heard that Naboth was
1Ki 21:16 **w.** Ahab heard that Naboth was dead,
1Ki 21:27 to pass, **w.** Ahab heard those words,
1Ki 22:25 **w.** thou shalt go into an inner 834
1Ki 22:32, 33 **w.** the captains of the chariots
1Ki 22:42 five years old **w.** he began to reign;
2Ki 1:5 **w.** the messengers turned back unto
2Ki 2:1 **w.** the Lord would take up Elijah into
2Ki 2:9 came to pass, **w.** they were gone over,
2Ki 2:10 thou see me **w.** I am taken from thee,
2Ki 2:14 **w.** he also had smitten the waters,
2Ki 2:15 **w.** the sons of the prophets which
2Ki 2:17 **w.** they urged him till he was ashamed,
2Ki 2:18 **w.** they came again to him, (for he
2Ki 3:5 it came to pass, **w.** Ahab was dead,
2Ki 3:15 came to pass, **w.** the minstrel played,
2Ki 3:20 **w.** the meat offering was offered,
2Ki 3:21 **w.** all the Moabites heard that the
2Ki 3:24 **w.** they came to the camp of Israel,
2Ki 3:26 **w.** the king of Moab saw that the
2Ki 4:4 **w.** thou art come in, thou shalt shut
2Ki 4:6 came to pass, **w.** the vessels were full,
2Ki 4:10 and it shall be, **w.** he cometh to us,
2Ki 4:12 **w.** he had called her, she stood before
2Ki 4:15 **w.** he had called her, she stood in the
2Ki 4:18 **w.** the child was grown, it fell on a
2Ki 4:20 **w.** he had taken him, and brought
2Ki 4:25 **w.** the man of God saw her afar off,
2Ki 4:27 **w.** she came to the man of God to the
2Ki 4:32 **w.** Elisha was come into the house,
2Ki 4:36 **w.** she was come in unto him, he said,
2Ki 5:6 Now **w.** this letter is come unto thee,
2Ki 5:7 **w.** the king of Israel had read the
2Ki 5:8 **w.** Elisha the man of God had heard
2Ki 5:13 **w.** he saith to thee, Wash, and be 3588
2Ki 5:18 **w.** my master goeth into the house
2Ki 5:18 **w.** I bow down myself in the house of
2Ki 5:21 **w.** Naaman saw him running after
2Ki 5:24 **w.** he came to the tower, he took them
2Ki 5:26 **w.** the man turned again from his 3588
2Ki 6:4 **w.** they came to Jordan, they cut down
2Ki 6:15 **w.** the servant of the man of God was
2Ki 6:18 **w.** they came down to him, Elisha
2Ki 6:20 **w.** they were come into Samaria.
2Ki 6:21 **w.** he saw them, My father, shall I
2Ki 6:23 **w.** they had eaten and drunk, he sent
2Ki 6:30 **w.** the king heard the words of the
2Ki 6:32 **w.** the messenger cometh, shut the
2Ki 7:5 **w.** they were come to the uttermost
2Ki 7:8 **w.** these lepers came to the uttermost
2Ki 7:12 **W.** they come out of the city, we 3588
2Ki 7:17 who spake **w.** the king came down to
2Ki 8:6 **w.** the king asked the woman, she
2Ki 8:17 old was he **w.** he began to reign;
2Ki 8:26 old was Ahaziah **w.** he began to reign;
2Ki 8:29 **w.** he fought against Hazael king of
2Ki 9:2 **w.** thou comest thither, look out there
2Ki 9:5 **w.** he came, behold, the captains of
2Ki 9:15 **w.** he fought with Hazael king of
2Ki 9:22 **w.** Joram saw Jehu, that he said, Is it
2Ki 9:25 **w.** I and thou rode together after
2Ki 9:27 **w.** Ahaziah the king of Judah saw
2Ki 9:30 And **w.** Jehu was come to Jezreel,
2Ki 9:34 **w.** he was come in, he did eat and
2Ki 10:7 pass, **w.** the letter came to them, that
2Ki 10:15 **w.** he was departed thence, he lighted
2Ki 10:17 **w.** he came to Samaria, he slew all that
2Ki 10:24 And **w.** they went in to offer sacrifices
2Ki 11:1 **w.** Athaliah the mother of Ahaziah
2Ki 11:13 **w.** Athaliah heard the noise of the
2Ki 11:14 **w.** she looked, behold, the king stood
2Ki 11:21 was Jehoash **w.** he began to reign.
2Ki 12:10 **w.** they saw that there was much
2Ki 13:21 and **w.** the man was let down, and
2Ki 14:2 five years old **w.** he began to reign,
2Ki 15:2, 33 old **w.** he began to reign,
2Ki 16:2 old was Ahaz **w.** he began to reign,
2Ki 16:12 And **w.** the king was come from
2Ki 18:2 old was he **w.** he began to reign;
2Ki 18:17 **w.** they were come up, they came and
2Ki 18:18 **w.** they had called to the king, there
2Ki 18:32 **w.** he persuadeth you, saying, The 3588
2Ki 19:1 to pass, **w.** king Hezekiah heard it,
2Ki 19:9 **w.** he heard say of Tirhakah king of
2Ki 19:35 **w.** they arose early in the morning,
2Ki 21:1 years old **w.** he began to reign,

2Ki 21:19 two years old **w.** he began to reign,
2Ki 22:1 eight years old **w.** he began to reign,
2Ki 22:11 **w.** the king had heard the words of
2Ki 22:19 **w.** thou heardest what I spake against
2Ki 23:29 him at Megiddo, **w.** he had seen him.
2Ki 23:31 three years old **w.** he began to reign;
2Ki 23:36 five years old **w.** he began to reign;
2Ki 24:8 years old **w.** he began to reign, and
2Ki 24:18 one years old **w.** he began to reign,
2Ki 25:23 **w.** all the captains of the armies, they
1Ch 1:44 **w.** Bela was dead, Jobab the son of
1Ch 1:45 And **w.** Jobab was dead, Husham of
1Ch 1:46 **w.** Husham was dead, Hadad the son
1Ch 1:47 **w.** Hadad was dead, Samlah of
1Ch 1:48 **w.** Samlah was dead, Shaul of
1Ch 1:49 **w.** Shaul was dead, Baal-hanan the
1Ch 1:50 **w.** Baal-hanan was dead, Hadad
1Ch 2:19 **w.** Azubah was dead, Caleb took unto
1Ch 2:21 **w.** he was threescore years old;
1Ch 5:7 **w.** the genealogy of their generations
1Ch 6:15 **w.** the Lord carried away Judah and
1Ch 7:23 **w.** he went in to his wife, she conceived,
1Ch 10:5 **w.** his armourbearer saw that Saul
1Ch 10:7 **w.** all the men of Israel that were in
1Ch 10:8 **w.** the Philistines came to strip the
1Ch 10:9 **w.** they had stripped him, they took
1Ch 10:11 **w.** all Jabesh-gilead heard all that the
1Ch 11:2 time past, even **w.** Saul was king,
1Ch 12:15 **w.** it had overflown all his banks;
1Ch 12:19 **w.** he came with the Philistines
1Ch 13:9 **w.** they came unto the threshingfloor
1Ch 14:8 **w.** the Philistines heard that David
1Ch 14:12 And **w.** they had left their gods there,
1Ch 14:15 **w.** thou shalt hear a sound of going
1Ch 15:26 **w.** God helped the Levites that bare
1Ch 16:2 **w.** David had made an end of offering
1Ch 16:19 **W.** ye were but few, even a few, and
1Ch 16:20 **w.** they went from nation to nation,
1Ch 17:11 **w.** thy days be expired that thou 3588
1Ch 18:5 **w.** the Syrians of Damascus came
1Ch 18:9 **w.** Tou king of Hamath heard how
1Ch 19:6 **w.** the children of Ammon saw that
1Ch 19:8 **w.** David heard of it, he sent Joab,
1Ch 19:10 Now **w.** Joab saw that the battle was
1Ch 19:15 **w.** the children of Ammon saw that
1Ch 19:16 **w.** the Syrians saw that they were
1Ch 19:17 **w.** David had put the battle in array
1Ch 19:19 **w.** the servants of Hadarezer saw that
1Ch 20:7 **w.** he defied Israel, Jonathan the son
1Ch 21:28 that time **w.** David saw that the Lord
1Ch 23:1 **w.** David was old and full of days, he
2Ch 4:3 of oxen were cast, **w.** it was cast
2Ch 5:10 **w.** the Lord made a covenant with 834
2Ch 5:10 of Israel, **w.** they came out of Egypt
2Ch 5:11 **w.** the priests were come out of the
2Ch 5:13 **w.** they lifted up their voice with the
2Ch 6:21 heaven; and **w.** thou hearest, forgive.
2Ch 6:26 **W.** the heaven is shut up, and there
2Ch 6:26 sin, **w.** thou dost afflict them, 3588
2Ch 6:27 **w.** thou hast taught them the good 3588
2Ch 6:29 **w.** every one shall know his own 834
2Ch 7:1 **w.** Solomon had made an end of
2Ch 7:3 **w.** all the children of Israel saw how
2Ch 7:6 **w.** David praised by their ministry;
2Ch 9:1 **w.** the queen of Sheba heard of the
2Ch 9:1 **w.** she was come to Solomon, she
2Ch 9:3 **w.** the queen of Sheba had seen the
2Ch 10:2 **w.** Jeroboam the son of Nebat, who
2Ch 10:16 **w.** all Israel saw that the king would
2Ch 11:1 **w.** Rehoboam was come to Jerusalem,
2Ch 12:1 **w.** Reboboam had established the
2Ch 12:7 **w.** the Lord saw that they humbled
2Ch 12:11 **w.** the king entered into the house 1767
2Ch 12:12 **w.** he humbled himself, the wrath of
2Ch 12:13 forty years old **w.** he began to reign,
2Ch 13:7 **w.** Rehoboam was young and
2Ch 13:14 **w.** Judah looked back, behold, the
2Ch 15:4 **w.** they in their trouble did turn
2Ch 15:8 **w.** Asa heard these words, and the
2Ch 15:9 **w.** they saw that the Lord his God was
2Ch 16:5 **w.** Baasha heard it, that he left off
2Ch 18:14 **w.** he was come to the king, the king
2Ch 18:24 **w.** thou shalt go into an inner 834
2Ch 18:31, 32 **w.** the captains of the chariots
2Ch 19:8 **w.** they returned to Jerusalem.
2Ch 20:9 **w.** evil cometh upon us, as the sword,
2Ch 20:10 **w.** they came out of the land of Egypt,
2Ch 20:21 **w.** he had consulted with the people,
2Ch 20:22 **w.** they began to sing and to 6256
2Ch 20:23 **w.** they had made an end of the
2Ch 20:24 **w.** Judah came toward the watch
2Ch 20:25 **w.** Jehoshaphat and his people came
2Ch 20:29 **w.** they had heard that the Lord
2Ch 20:31 and five years **w.** he began to reign,
2Ch 21:4 **w.** Jehoram was risen up to the
2Ch 21:5 two years old **w.** he began to reign,
2Ch 21:20 old was he **w.** he began to reign,
2Ch 22:2 was Ahaziah **w.** he began to reign,
2Ch 22:6 **w.** he fought with Hazael king of
2Ch 22:7 **w.** he was come, he went out with
2Ch 22:8 **w.** Jehu was executing judgment
2Ch 22:9 **w.** they had slain him, they buried
2Ch 22:10 **w.** Athaliah the mother of Ahaziah
2Ch 23:7 **w.** he cometh in, and **w.** he goeth out
2Ch 23:12 **w.** Athaliah heard the noise of the
2Ch 23:15 **w.** she was come to the entering of the
2Ch 24:1 seven years old **w.** he began to reign,
2Ch 24:11 and **w.** they saw that there was much
2Ch 24:14 **w.** they had finished it, they brought
2Ch 24:15 and was full of days **w.** he died;
2Ch 24:15 thirty years old was he **w.** he died.
2Ch 24:22 **w.** he died, he said, The Lord look
2Ch 24:25 **w.** they were departed from him, (for
2Ch 25:1 five years old **w.** he began to reign,
2Ch 25:3 **w.** the kingdom was established to 834
2Ch 26:3 old was Uzziah **w.** he began to reign,
2Ch 26:16 **w.** he was strong, his heart was lifted
2Ch 27:1 five years old **w.** he began to reign,
2Ch 27:8 twenty years old **w.** he began to reign,
2Ch 28:1 twenty years old **w.** he began to reign,
2Ch 29:1 to reign **w.** he was five and twenty
2Ch 29:22 **w.** they had killed the rams, they
2Ch 29:27 **w.** the burnt offering began, the 6256
2Ch 29:29 **w.** they had made an end of offering,
2Ch 31:1 **w.** all this was finished, all Israel that
2Ch 31:8 **w.** Hezekiah and the princes came
2Ch 32:2 **w.** Hezekiah saw that Sennacherib
2Ch 32:21 **w.** he was come into the house of his
2Ch 33:1 twelve years old **w.** he began to reign,
2Ch 33:12 **w.** he was in affliction, he besought
2Ch 33:21 twenty years old **w.** he began to reign,
2Ch 34:1 eight years old **w.** he began to reign,
2Ch 34:7 **w.** he had broken down the altars and
2Ch 34:8 **w.** he had purged the land, and the
2Ch 34:9 **w.** they came to Hilkiah the high
2Ch 34:14 **w.** they brought out the money that
2Ch 34:19 **w.** the king had heard the word of the
2Ch 34:27 **w.** thou heardest his words against
2Ch 35:20 **w.** Josiah had prepared the temple, 834
2Ch 36:2 three years old **w.** he began to reign,
2Ch 36:5 five years old **w.** he began to reign,
2Ch 36:9 eight years old **w.** he began to reign,
2Ch 36:10 **w.** the year was expired, king
2Ch 36:11 twenty years old **w.** he began to reign,
Ezr 2:68 **w.** they came to the house of the Lord
Ezr 3:1 **w.** the seventh month was come, and
Ezr 3:10 **w.** the builders laid the foundation of
Ezr 3:11 **w.** they praised the Lord, because the
Ezr 3:12 **w.** the foundation of this house was
Ezr 4:1 **w.** the adversaries of Judah and
Ezr 4:23 Now **w.** the copy of king 4481,1768
Ezr 9:1 Now **w.** these things were done, the
Ezr 9:3 **w.** I heard this thing, I rent my
Ezr 10:1 **w.** Ezra had prayed, and **w.** he had
Ezr 10:6 **w.** he came thither, he did eat no
Ne 1:4 **w.** I heard these words, that I sat
Ne 2:3 **w.** the city, the place of my fathers' 834
Ne 2:6 be? and **w.** wilt thou return? 4970
Ne 2:10 **W.** Sanballat the Horonite, and
Ne 2:19 **w.** Sanballat the Horonite, and Tobiah
Ne 4:1 **w.** Sanballat heard that we builded 834
Ne 4:7 **w.** Sanballat, and Tobiah, and the 834
Ne 4:12 **w.** the Jews which dwelt by them 834
Ne 4:15 **w.** our enemies heard that it was 834
Ne 5:6 **w.** I heard their cry and these 834
Ne 6:1 **w.** Sanballat, and Tobiah, and 834
Ne 6:16 **w.** all our enemies heard thereof 834
Ne 7:1 **w.** the wall was built, and I had set 834
Ne 7:73 **w.** the seventh month came, the
Ne 8:5 **w.** he opened it, all the people stood
Ne 8:9 **w.** they heard the words of the law.
Ne 9:18 **w.** they had made them a molten 3588
Ne 9:27 **w.** they cried unto thee, thou heardest
Ne 9:28 **w.** they returned, and cried unto thee,
Ne 10:38 the Levites, **w.** the Levites take tithes:
Ne 13:3 **w.** they had heard the law, that they
Ne 13:19 **w.** the gates of Jerusalem began to 834
Es 1:2 **w.** the king Ahasuerus sat on the
Es 1:4 **W.** he shewed the riches of his
Es 1:5 **w.** these days were expired, the king
Es 1:10 **w.** the heart of the king was merry
Es 1:17 in their eyes, **w.** it shall be reported,
Es 1:20 **w.** the king's decree, which he shall
Es 2:1 **w.** the wrath of king Ahasuerus was
Es 2:7 **w.** her father and mother were dead,
Es 2:8 **w.** the king's commandment and his
Es 2:8 and **w.** many maidens were gathered
Es 2:12 **w.** every maid's turn was come to
Es 2:15 **w.** the turn of Esther, the daughter of
Es 2:19 **w.** the virgins were gathered together
Es 2:20 as **w.** she was brought up with him 834
Es 2:23 **w.** inquisition was made of the matter,
Es 3:4 **w.** they spake daily unto him, and he
Es 3:5 **w.** Haman saw that Mordecai bowed
Es 4:1 **W.** Mordecai perceived all that was
Es 5:2 **w.** the king saw Esther the queen
Es 5:9 **w.** Haman saw Mordecai in the king's
Es 5:10 **w.** he came home, he sent and called
Es 9:1 **w.** the king's commandment and 834
Es 9:25 **w.** Esther came before the king, he
Job 1:5 **w.** the days of their feasting were 3588
Job 1:6 was a day **w.** the sons of God came
Job 1:13 **w.** his sons and his daughters were
Job 2:1 was a day **w.** the sons of God came
Job 2:11 Now **w.** Job's three friends heard of
Job 2:12 **w.** they lifted up their eyes afar off,
Job 3:11 the ghost **w.** I came out of the belly?
Job 3:22 glad, **w.** they can find the grave? 3588
Job 4:13 night, **w.** deep sleep falleth upon men,
Job 5:21 afraid of destruction **w.** it cometh. 3588
Job 6:5 the wild ass bray **w.** he hath grass?
Job 6:17 **w.** it is hot, they are consumed out of
Job 7:4 **W.** I lie down, I say, 4970
Job 7:4 **W.** shall I arise, and the night 4970
Job 7:13 **W.** I say, My bed shall comfort 3588
Job 11:3 **w.** thou mockest, shall no man make
Job 16:22 **W.** a few years are come, then I 3588
Job 17:16 **w.** our rest together is in the dust. 518
Job 20:23 **W.** he is about to fill his belly, God
Job 21:6 Even **w.** I remember I am afraid, 518
Job 21:21 **w.** the number of his months is cut off
Job 22:29 **W.** men are cast down, then thou 3588
Job 23:10 **w.** he hath tried me, I shall come forth
Job 23:15 **w.** I consider, I am afraid of him.
Job 27:8 **w.** God taketh away his soul? 3588
Job 27:9 cry **w.** trouble cometh upon him? 3588
Job 28:26 **W.** he made a decree for the rain, and
Job 29:2 as in the days **w.** God preserved me;
Job 29:3 **W.** his candle shined upon my head,
Job 29:3 **w.** by his light I walked through
Job 29:4 **w.** the secret of God was upon my
Job 29:5 **W.** the Almighty was yet with 5750
Job 29:5 **w.** my children were about me;
Job 29:6 **W.** I washed my steps with butter,
Job 29:7 **W.** I went out to the gate through the
Job 29:7 **w.** I prepared my seat in the street!
Job 29:11 **W.** the ear heard me, then it 3588
Job 29:11 **w.** the eye saw me, it gave witness to
Job 30:26 **W.** I looked for good, then evil 3588
Job 30:26 **w.** I waited for light, there came
Job 31:13 **w.** they contended with me;
Job 31:14 shall I do **w.** God riseth up? and 3588
Job 31:14 **w.** he visiteth, what shall I answer 3588
Job 31:21 **w.** I saw my help in the gate: 3588
Job 31:26 If I beheld the sun **w.** it shined, or 3588
Job 31:29 lifted up myself **w.** evil found him: 3588
Job 32:5 **W.** Elihu saw there was no answer in
Job 32:16 **W.** I had waited, (for they spake not,
Job 33:15 night, **w.** deep sleep falleth upon men,
Job 34:29 **W.** he giveth quietness, who then can
Job 34:29 **w.** he hideth his face, who then can
Job 36:13 they cry not **w.** he bindeth them. 3588
Job 36:20 **w.** people are cut off in their place.
Job 37:4 stay them **w.** his voice is heard. 3588
Job 37:15 Dost thou know **w.** God disposed
Job 37:17 warm, **w.** he quieteth the earth by the
Job 38:4 wast thou **w.** I laid the foundations
Job 38:7 **W.** the morning stars sang together,

Job 38:8 the sea with doors, **w.** it break forth,
Job 38:9 **W.** I made the cloud the garment
Job 38:38 **W.** the dust groweth into hardness,
Job 38:40 **W.** they couch in their dens, and 3588
Job 38:41 **w.** his young ones cry unto God, 3588
Job 39:1 **w.** the wild goats of the rock bring
Job 39:1 thou mark **w.** the hinds do calve?
Job 39:2 thou the time **w.** they bring forth?
Job 41:25 **W.** he riseth up himself, the mighty
Job 42:10 of Job, **w.** he prayed for his friends:
Ps 2:12 **w.** his wrath is kindled but a little. 3588
Ps 3:*title* **w.** he fled from Absalom his son.
Ps 4:1 Hear me **w.** I call, O God of my
Ps 4:1 hast enlarged me **w.** I was in distress;
Ps 4:3 the Lord will hear **w.** I call unto him.
Ps 8:3 **W.** I consider thy heavens, the 3588
Ps 9:3 **W.** mine enemies are turned back
Ps 9:12 **W.** he maketh inquisition for 3588
Ps 10:9 poor, **w.** he draweth him into his net.
Ps 12:8 side, **w.** the vilest men are exalted.
Ps 13:4 trouble me rejoice **w.** I am moved. 3588
Ps 14:7 **w.** the Lord bringeth back the
Ps 17:15 satisfied, **w.** I awake, with thy likeness.
Ps 20:9 Lord: let the king hear us **w.** we call.
Ps 21:12 **w.** thou shalt make ready thine arrows
Ps 22:9 **w.** I was upon my mother's breasts.
Ps 22:24 but **w.** he cried unto me, he heard.
Ps 27:2 **W.** the wicked, even mine enemies
Ps 27:7 **w.** I cry with my voice: have mercy
Ps 27:8 **W.** thou saidst, Seek ye my face; my
Ps 27:10 **W.** my father and my mother 3588
Ps 28:2 my supplications, **w.** I cry unto thee,
Ps 28:2 **w.** I lift up my hands toward thy holy
Ps 30:9 in my blood, **w.** I go down to the pit?
Ps 31:22 my supplications **w.** I cried unto thee.
Ps 32:3 **W.** I kept silence, my bones 3588
Ps 32:6 in a time **w.** thou mayest be found:
Ps 34:*title* **w.** he changed his behaviour before
Ps 35:13 **w.** they were sick, my clothing was
Ps 37:33 nor condemn him **w.** he is judged.
Ps 37:34 **w.** the wicked are cut off, thou shalt
Ps 38:16 **w.** my foot slippeth, they magnify
Ps 39:11 **W.** thou with rebukes dost correct
Ps 41:5 me, **W.** shall he die, and his name 4970
Ps 41:6 **w.** he goeth abroad, he telleth it.
Ps 42:2 **w.** shall I come and appear before 4970
Ps 42:4 **W.** I remember these things, I pour
Ps 49:5 **w.** the iniquity of my heels shall
Ps 49:16 Be not thou afraid **w.** one is made 3588
Ps 49:16 rich, **w.** the glory of his house is 3588
Ps 49:17 **w.** he dieth he shall carry nothing 3588
Ps 49:18 thee, **w.** thou doest well to thyself, 3588
Ps 50:18 **W.** thou sawest a thief, then thou 518
Ps 51:*title* **w.** Nathan the prophet came unto
Ps 51:4 mightest be justified **w.** thou speakest,
Ps 51:4 speakest, and be clear **w.** thou judgest.
Ps 52:*title* **w.** Doeg the Edomite came and told
Ps 53:6 **W.** God bringeth back the captivity of
Ps 54:*title* **w.** the Ziphims came and said to
Ps 56:*title* **w.** the Philistines took him in Gath.
Ps 56:6 my steps, **w.** they wait for my soul. 834
Ps 56:9 **W.** I cry unto thee, then shall mine
Ps 57:*title* **w.** he fled from Saul in the cave.
Ps 58:7 **w.** he bendeth his bow to shoot his
Ps 58:10 rejoice **w.** he seeth the vengeance: 3588
Ps 59:*title* **w.** Saul sent, and they watched the
Ps 60:*title* **w.** he strove with Aram-naharaim
Ps 60:*title* **w.** Joab returned, and smote of Edom
Ps 61:2 thee, **w.** my heart is overwhelmed:
Ps 63:6 **W.** I remember thee upon my bed, 518
Ps 65:9 corn, **w.** thou hast so provided for it.
Ps 66:14 hath spoken, **w.** I was in trouble.
Ps 68:7 God, **w.** thou wentest forth before thy
Ps 68:7 **w.** thou didst march through the
Ps 68:9 thine inheritance, **w.** it was weary.
Ps 68:14 **W.** the Almighty scattered kings in
Ps 69:10 **W.** I wept, and chastened my soul
Ps 71:9 forsake me not **w.** my strength faileth.
Ps 71:18 also **w.** I am old and grayheaded, 5704
Ps 71:23 greatly rejoice **w.** I sing unto thee; 3588
Ps 72:12 shall deliver the needy **w.** he crieth;
Ps 73:3 **w.** I saw the prosperity of the wicked.
Ps 73:16 **w.** I thought to know this, it was too
Ps 73:20 a dream **w.** one awaketh; so, O Lord,
Ps 73:20 **w.** thou awakest, thou shalt despise
Ps 75:2 **W.** I shall receive the congregation 3588

Ps 76:7 in thy sight **w.** once thou art angry?
Ps 76:9 **W.** God arose to judgment, to save all
Ps 78:34 **W.** he slew them, then they sought 518
Ps 78:42 **w.** he delivered them from the 834
Ps 78:59 **W.** God heard this, he was wroth, and
Ps 81:5 **w.** he went out through the land of
Ps 87:6 count, **w.** he writeth up the people,
Ps 89:9 **w.** the waves thereof arise, thou stillest
Ps 90:4 are but as yesterday **w.** it is past, 3588
Ps 92:7 **W.** the wicked spring as the grass,
Ps 92:7 and **w.** all the workers of iniquity do
Ps 94:8 and ye fools, **w.** will ye be wise? 4970
Ps 94:18 **W.** I said, My foot slippeth; thy 518
Ps 95:9 **W.** your fathers tempted me, 834
Ps 101:2 O **w.** wilt thou come unto me? I 4970
Ps 102:*title* **w.** he is overwhelmed, and 3588
Ps 102:2 me in the day **w.** I am in trouble;
Ps 102:2 the day **w.** I call answer me speedily.
Ps 102:16 **W.** the Lord shall build up Zion, 3588
Ps 102:22 **W.** the people are gathered together,
Ps 105:12 **W.** they were but a few men in
Ps 105:13 **W.** they went from one nation to
Ps 105:38 Egypt was glad **w.** they departed: for
Ps 106:44 their affliction, **w.** he heard their cry:
Ps 109:7 **W.** he shall be judged, let him be
Ps 109:23 gone like the shadow **w.** it declineth:
Ps 109:25 **w.** they looked upon me they shaked
Ps 109:28 **w.** they arise, let them be ashamed;
Ps 114:1 **W.** Israel went out of Egypt, the
Ps 119:6 **w.** I have respect unto all thy
Ps 119:7 **w.** I shall have learned thy righteous
Ps 119:32 **w.** thou shalt enlarge my heart. 3588
Ps 119:74 fear thee will be glad **w.** they see me;
Ps 119:82 saying, **W.** wilt thou comfort me? 4970
Ps 119:84 **w.** wilt thou execute judgement on 4970
Ps 119:171 **w.** thou hast taught me thy 3588
Ps 120:7 but **w.** I speak, they are for war. 3588
Ps 122:1 I was glad **w.** they said unto me, Let
Ps 124:2 our side, **w.** men rose up against us:
Ps 124:3 **w.** their wrath was kindled against
Ps 126:1 **W.** the Lord turned again the
Ps 137:1 yea, we wept, **w.** we remembered Zion.
Ps 138:3 the day **w.** I cried thou answeredst me,
Ps 138:4 **w.** they hear the words of thy 3588
Ps 139:15 **w.** I was made in secret, and 834
Ps 139:16 **w.** as yet there was none of them.
Ps 139:18 **w.** I awake, I am still with thee.
Ps 141:1 ear unto my voice, **w.** I cry unto thee.
Ps 141:6 **W.** their judges are overthrown in
Ps 141:7 as **w.** one cutteth and cleaveth wood.
Ps 142:*title* A Prayer **w.** he was in the cave.
Ps 142:3 **W.** my spirit was overwhelmed
Pr 1:26 I will mock **w.** your fear cometh;
Pr 1:27 **W.** your fear cometh as desolation,
Pr 1:27 **w.** distress and anguish cometh upon
Pr 2:10 **W.** wisdom entereth into thine 3588
Pr 3:24 **W.** thou liest down, thou shalt not 518
Pr 3:25 of the wicked, **w.** it cometh. 3588
Pr 3:27 **w.** it is in the power of thine hand to
Pr 3:28 will give; **w.** thou hast it by thee.
Pr 4:8 honour, **w.** thou dost embrace her. 3588
Pr 4:12 **W.** thou goest, thy steps shall not be
Pr 4:12 **w.** thou runnest, thou shalt not 518
Pr 5:11 **w.** thy flesh and thy body are
Pr 6:3 **w.** thou art come into the hand of 3588
Pr 6:9 **w.** wilt thou arise out of thy sleep? 4970
Pr 6:22 **W.** thou goest, it shall lead thee;
Pr 6:22 **w.** thou sleepest, it shall keep thee;
Pr 6:22 **w.** thou awakest, it shall talk with
Pr 6:30 satisfy his soul **w.** he is hungry; 3588
Pr 8:24 **W.** there were no depths, I was
Pr 8:24 **w.** there were no fountains abounding
Pr 8:27 **W.** he prepared the heavens, I was
Pr 8:27 **w.** he set a compass upon the face of
Pr 8:28 **W.** he established the clouds above:
Pr 8:28 **w.** he strengthened the fountains of
Pr 8:29 **W.** he gave to the sea his decree that
Pr 8:29 **w.** he appointed the fountains of the
Pr 11:2 **W.** pride cometh, then cometh shame:
Pr 11:7 **W.** a wicked man dieth, his
Pr 11:10 **W.** it goeth well with the righteous,
Pr 11:10 **w.** the wicked perish, there is shouting.
Pr 13:12 **w.** the desire cometh, it is a tree of
Pr 14:7 **w.** thou perceivest not in him the lips
Pr 16:7 **W.** a man's ways please the Lord, he
Pr 17:14 strife is as **w.** one letteth out water:

Pr 17:28 **w.** he holdeth his peace, is counted
Pr 18:3 **W.** the wicked cometh, then cometh
Pr 20:14 but **w.** he is gone his way, then he
Pr 21:11 **W.** the scorner is punished, the
Pr 21:11 **w.** the wise is instructed, he receiveth
Pr 21:27 **w.** he bringeth it with a wicked 3588
Pr 22:6 and **w.** he is old, he will not depart 3588
Pr 23:1 **W.** thou sittest to eat with a ruler, 3588
Pr 23:16 rejoice, **w.** thy lips speak right things.
Pr 23:22 not thy mother **w.** she is old. 3588
Pr 23:31 not thou upon the wine **w.** it is red, 3588
Pr 23:31 **w.** it giveth his colour in the cup, 3588
Pr 23:31 in the cup, **w.** it moveth itself aright.
Pr 23:35 **w.** shall I awake? I will seek it 4970
Pr 24:14 **w.** thou hast found it, then there 518
Pr 24:17 Rejoice not **w.** thine enemy falleth,
Pr 24:17 thine heart be glad **w.** he stumbleth:
Pr 25:8 **w.** thy neighbour hath put thee to
Pr 26:25 **W.** he speaketh fair, believe him 3588
Pr 28:1 The wicked flee **w.** no man pursueth:
Pr 28:12 **W.** righteous men do rejoice, there is
Pr 28:12 **w.** the wicked rise, a man is hidden.
Pr 28:28 **W.** the wicked rise, men hide
Pr 28:28 **w.** they perish, the righteous increase.
Pr 29:2 **W.** the righteous are in authority, the
Pr 29:2 **w.** the wicked beareth rule, the people
Pr 29:16 **W.** the wicked are multiplied,
Pr 30:22 For a servant **w.** he reigneth; and 3588
Pr 30:22 and a fool **w.** he is filled with meat; 3588
Pr 30:23 odious woman **w.** she is married: 3588
Pr 31:23 **w.** he sitteth among the elders of the
Ec 4:10 woe to him that is alone **w.** he falleth:
Ec 5:1 Keep thy foot **w.** thou goest to the 834
Ec 5:4 **W.** thou vowest a vow unto God, 834
Ec 5:11 **W.** goods increase, they are increased
Ec 8:7 can tell him **w.** it shall be? 3588,834
Ec 8:16 **W.** I applied mine heart to know 834
Ec 9:12 time, **w.** it falleth suddenly upon them.
Ec 10:3 **w.** he that is a fool walketh by the
Ec 10:16 to thee, O land, **w.** thy king is a child,
Ec 10:17 land, **w.** thy king is the son of nobles,
Ec 12:1 **w.** thou shalt say, I have no 834
Ec 12:3 day **w.** the keepers of the house shall
Ec 12:4 **w.** the sound of the grinding is low,
Ec 12:5 **w.** they shall be afraid of that which is
Ca 5:6 my soul failed **w.** he spake: I sought
Ca 8:1 **w.** I should find thee without, I would
Ca 8:8 in the day **w.** she shall be spoken for?
Isa 1:12 **W.** ye come to appear before me, 3588
Isa 1:15 **w.** ye spread forth your hands, I will
Isa 1:15 **w.** ye make many prayers, I will 3588
Isa 2:19, 21 **w.** he ariseth to shake terribly the
Isa 3:6 **W.** a man shall take hold of his 3588
Isa 4:4 **W.** the Lord shall have washed 518
Isa 5:4 **w.** I looked that it should bring forth
Isa 6:13 in them, **w.** they cast their leaves: 834
Isa 8:19 **w.** they shall say unto you, Seek 3588
Isa 8:21 **w.** they shall be hungry, they shall 3588
Isa 9:1 **w.** at the first he lightly afflicted 6256
Isa 9:3 men rejoice **w.** they divide the spoil.
Isa 10:12 **w.** the Lord hath performed his 3588
Isa 10:18 be as **w.** a standardbearer fainteth.
Isa 13:19 be as **w.** God overthrew Sodom and
Isa 16:12 **w.** it is seen that Moab is weary on 3588
Isa 17:5 be as **w.** the harvestman gathereth the
Isa 18:3 **w.** he lifteth up an ensign on the
Isa 18:3 and **w.** he bloweth a trumpet, hear ye.
Isa 18:5 afore the harvest, **w.** the bud is perfect.
Isa 20:1 (**w.** Sargon the king of Assyria sent
Isa 24:13 **W.** thus it shall be in the midst of 3588
Isa 24:13 grapes **w.** the vintage is done. 518
Isa 24:23 **w.** the Lord of hosts shall reign in 3588
Isa 25:4 **w.** the blast of the terrible ones is 3588
Isa 26:9 **w.** thy judgments are in the earth. 834
Isa 26:11 **w.** thy hand is lifted up, they will not
Isa 26:16 **w.** thy chastening was upon them.
Isa 27:8 In measure, **w.** it shooteth forth, thou
Isa 27:9 **w.** he maketh all the stones of the
Isa 27:11 **W.** the boughs thereof are withered,
Isa 28:4 which **w.** he that looketh upon it seeth,
Isa 28:15, 18 **w.** the overflowing scourge 3588
Isa 28:25 **W.** he hath made plain the face 518
Isa 29:8 **w.** an hungry man dreameth, and, 834
Isa 29:8 as **w.** a thirsty man dreameth, and, 834
Isa 29:23 **w.** he seeth his children, the work 3588
Isa 30:19 **w.** he shall hear it, he will answer

Isa	30:21	in it, **w.** ye turn to the right hand,	3588
Isa	30:21	hand, and **w.** ye turn to the left.	3588
Isa	30:25	the great slaughter, **w.** the towers fall.	
Isa	30:29	the night **w.** a holy solemnity is kept;	
Isa	30:29	**w.** one goeth with a pipe to come into	
Isa	31:3	**W.** the Lord shall stretch out his	
Isa	31:4	**w.** a multitude of shepherds is	834
Isa	32:7	even **w.** the needy speaketh right.	
Isa	32:19	**W.** it shall hail, coming down on the	
Isa	33:1	**w.** thou shalt cease to spoil, thou shalt	
Isa	33:1	**w.** thou shalt make an end to deal	
Isa	37:1	**w.** king Hezekiah heard it, that he	
Isa	37:9	And **w.** he heard it, he sent messengers	
Isa	37:36	**w.** they arose early in the morning,	
Isa	38:9	**w.** he had been sick, and was	
Isa	41:17	**W.** the poor and needy seek water,	
Isa	41:28	no counseller, that, **w.** I ask of them,	
Isa	43:2	**W.** thou passest through the	3588
Isa	43:2	**w.** thou walkest through the fire,	3588
Isa	43:12	**w.** there was no strange god among	
Isa	48:7	the day **w.** thou heardest them not;	
Isa	48:13	**w.** I call unto them, they stand up	
Isa	48:21	thirsted not **w.** he led them through	
Isa	50:2	**w.** I came, was there no man?	
Isa	50:2	**w.** I called, was there none to answer?	
Isa	52:8	**w.** the Lord shall bring again Zion.	
Isa	53:2	and **w.** we shall see him, there is no	
Isa	53:10	**w.** thou shalt make his soul an	518
Isa	54:6	youth, **w.** thou wast refused, saith	3588
Isa	57:13	**W.** thou criest, let thy companies	
Isa	57:20	troubled sea, **w.** it cannot rest,	3588
Isa	58:7	**w.** thou seest the naked, that thou	3588
Isa	59:19	**W.** the enemy shall come in like a	3588
Isa	64:2	**w.** the melting fire burneth, the fire	
Isa	64:3	**W.** thou didst terrible things which	
Isa	65:12	because **w.** I called, ye did not answer;	
Isa	65:12	**w.** I spake, ye did not hear; but did	
Isa	66:4	because **w.** I called, none did answer;	
Isa	66:4	**w.** I spake, they did not hear: but	
Isa	66:14	**w.** ye see this, your heart shall rejoice,	
Jer	2:2	**w.** thou wentest after me in the	
Jer	2:7	**w.** ye entered, ye defiled my land, and	
Jer	2:17	God, **w.** he led thee by the way?	6256
Jer	2:20	**w.** upon every high hill and under	3588
Jer	2:26	thief is ashamed **w.** he is found,	3588
Jer	3:8	**w.** for all the causes whereby	3588
Jer	3:16	**w.** ye be multiplied and increased	3588
Jer	4:30	**w.** thou art spoiled, what wilt thou do?	
Jer	5:7	**w.** I had fed them to the full, they then	
Jer	5:19	**w.** ye shall say, Wherefore doeth	3588
Jer	6:14	Peace, peace; **w.** there is no peace.	
Jer	6:15	ashamed **w.** they had committed	3588
Jer	8:11	Peace, peace; **w.** there is no peace.	
Jer	8:12	ashamed **w.** they had committed	3588
Jer	8:18	**W.** I would comfort myself against	
Jer	10:13	**W.** he uttereth his voice, there is a	
Jer	11:15	**w.** thou doest evil, then thou	3588
Jer	12:1	thou, O Lord, **w.** I plead with thee:	3588
Jer	13:21	thou say **w.** he shall punish thee?	3588
Jer	13:27	be made clean? **w.** shall it once be?	
Jer	14:12	**W.** they fast, I will not hear their	3588
Jer	14:12	**w.** they offer burnt offering and an	3588
Jer	16:10	**w.** thou shalt show this people all	3588
Jer	17:6	and shall not see **w.** good cometh;	3588
Jer	17:8	and shall not see **w.** heat cometh,	3588
Jer	18:22	**w.** thou shalt bring a troop	3588
Jer	21:1	**w.** king Zedekiah sent unto him	
Jer	22:23	thou be **w.** pangs come upon thee,	
Jer	23:33	**w.** this people, or the prophet, or a	3588
Jer	25:12	**w.** seventy years are accomplished,	
Jer	26:8	**w.** Jeremiah had made an end of	
Jer	26:10	**W.** the princes of Judah heard these	
Jer	26:21	**w.** Jehoiakim the king, with all his	
Jer	26:21	**w.** Urijah heard it, he was afraid, and	
Jer	27:20	**w.** he carried away captive Jeconiah	
Jer	28:9	**w.** the word of the prophet shall come	
Jer	29:13	**w.** ye shall search for me with all	3588
Jer	31:2	Israel, **w.** I went to cause him to rest.	
Jer	31:23	**w.** I shall bring again their captivity;	
Jer	31:35	the sea **w.** the waves thereof roar;	
Jer	32:16	**w.** I had delivered the evidence of the	
Jer	34:1	**w.** Nebuchadnezzar king of Babylon,	
Jer	34:7	**W.** the king of Babylon's army fought	
Jer	34:10	**w.** all the princes, and all the people,	
Jer	34:14	**w.** he hath served thee six years, thou	
Jer	34:18	**w.** they cut the calf in twain, and	
Jer	35:11	**w.** Nebuchadrezzar king of Babylon	
Jer	36:11	**W.** Michaiah the son of Gemariah, the	
Jer	36:13	**w.** Baruch read the book in the ears of	
Jer	36:16	**w.** they had heard all the words, they	
Jer	36:23	**w.** Jehudi had read three or four	
Jer	37:5	**w.** the Chaldeans that besieged	
Jer	37:11	**w.** the army of the Chaldeans was	
Jer	37:13	**w.** he was in the gate of Benjamin, a	
Jer	37:16	**W.** Jeremiah was entered into	3588
Jer	38:7	**w.** Ebed-melech the Ethiopian, one of	
Jer	38:28	was there **w.** Jerusalem was taken.	834
Jer	39:4	**w.** Zedekiah the king of Judah saw	834
Jer	39:5	**w.** they had taken him, they brought	
Jer	40:1	**w.** he had taken him being bound in	
Jer	40:7	Now **w.** all the captains of the forces	
Jer	40:11	**w.** all the Jews that were in Moab,	
Jer	41:7	**w.** they came into the midst of the	
Jer	41:11	But **w.** Johanan the son of Kareah,	
Jer	41:13	that **w.** all the people which were with	
Jer	42:6	**w.** we obey the voice of the Lord	3588
Jer	42:18	you, **w.** ye shall enter into Egypt:	
Jer	42:20	**w.** ye sent me unto the Lord your	3588
Jer	43:1	**w.** Jeremiah had made an end of	
Jer	43:11	**w.** he cometh, he shall smite the land	
Jer	44:19	**w.** we burned incense to the	3588
Jer	45:1	**w.** he had written these words in a	
Jer	51:16	**W.** he uttereth his voice, there is a	
Jer	51:55	**w.** her waves do roar like great waters,	
Jer	51:59	**w.** he went with Zedekiah the king of	
Jer	51:61	**W.** thou comest to Babylon, and shalt	
Jer	51:63	**w.** thou hast made an end of reading	
Jer	52:1	twenty years old **w.** he began to reign,	
La	1:7	**w.** her people fell into the hand of the	
La	2:12	**w.** they swooned as the wounded in	
La	2:12	**w.** their soul was poured out into their	
La	3:8	**w.** I cry and shout, he shutteth	3588
La	3:37	pass, **w.** the Lord commanded it not?	
La	4:15	**w.** they fled away and wandered,	3588
Eze	1:9	another; they turned not **w.** they went;	
Eze	1:12	and they turned not **w.** they went.	
Eze	1:17	**W.** they went, they went upon their	
Eze	1:17	and they turned not **w.** they went.	
Eze	1:19	**w.** the living creatures went, the	
Eze	1:19	**w.** the living creatures were lifted up	
Eze	1:21	**W.** those went, these went; and	
Eze	1:21	**w.** those stood, these stood; and	
Eze	1:21	**w.** those were lifted up from the earth,	
Eze	1:24	**w.** they went, I heard the noise of	
Eze	1:24	**w.** they stood, they let down their	
Eze	1:25	**w.** they stood, and had let down their	
Eze	1:28	**w.** I saw it, I fell upon my face, and	
Eze	2:2	into me **w.** he spake unto me,	834
Eze	2:9	**w.** I looked, behold, an hand was sent	
Eze	3:18	**W.** I say unto the wicked, Thou shalt	
Eze	3:20	**W.** a righteous man doth turn from	
Eze	3:27	**w.** I speak with thee, I will open thy	
Eze	4:6	And **w.** thou hast accomplished them,	
Eze	5:2	**w.** the days of the siege are fulfilled:	
Eze	5:13	**w.** I have accomplished my fury in	
Eze	5:15	**w.** I shall execute judgments in thee in	
Eze	5:16	**W.** I shall send upon them the evil	
Eze	6:8	**w.** ye shall be scattered through the	
Eze	6:13	**w.** their slain men shall be among	
Eze	8:7	**w.** I looked, behold a hole in the wall.	
Eze	8:8	**w.** I had digged in the wall, behold a	
Eze	10:3	of the house, **w.** the man went in;	
Eze	10:5	the Almighty God **w.** he speaketh.	
Eze	10:6	that **w.** he had commanded the man	
Eze	10:9	**w.** I looked, behold the four wheels	
Eze	10:11	**W.** they went, they went upon their	
Eze	10:16	**w.** the cherubims went, the wheels	
Eze	10:16	**w.** the cherubims lifted up their wings	
Eze	10:17	**W.** they stood, these stood; and	
Eze	10:17	**w.** they were lifted up, these lifted up	
Eze	10:19	**w.** they went out, the wheels also were	
Eze	11:13	**w.** I prophesied, that Pelatiah the son	
Eze	12:15	**w.** I shall scatter them among the	
Eze	13:12	Lo, **w.** the wall is fallen, shall it not	
Eze	14:9	**w.** he hath spoken a thing,	3588
Eze	14:13	**w.** the land sinneth against me by	3588
Eze	14:21	**w.** I send my four sore judgments	3588
Eze	14:23	**w.** ye see their ways and their doings:	
Eze	15:5	**w.** it was whole, it was meet for no	
Eze	15:5	**w.** the fire hath devoured it, and	3588
Eze	15:7	**w.** I set my face against them.	
Eze	16:6	**w.** I passed by thee, and saw thee	
Eze	16:6	thee **w.** thou wast in thy blood, Live;	
Eze	16:6	thee **w.** thou wast in thy blood, Live.	
Eze	16:8	**w.** I passed by thee, and looked upon	
Eze	16:22	**w.** thou wast naked and bare, and	
Eze	16:53	**W.** I shall bring again their captivity,	
Eze	16:55	**W.** thy sisters, Sodom and her	
Eze	16:61	**w.** thou shalt receive thy sisters, thine	
Eze	16:63	**w.** I am pacified toward thee for all	
Eze	17:10	wither, **w.** the east wind toucheth it?	
Eze	17:18	**w.**, lo, he had given his hand, and	
Eze	18:19	**W.** the son hath done that which is	
Eze	18:24	**w.** the righteous turneth away from	
Eze	18:26	**W.** a righteous man turneth away	
Eze	18:27	**w.** the wicked man turneth away	
Eze	19:5	**w.** she saw that she had waited, and	
Eze	20:5	In the day **w.** I chose Israel, and	
Eze	20:5	**w.** I lifted up mine hand unto them,	
Eze	20:28	**w.** I had brought them into the land,	
Eze	20:31	For **w.** ye offer your gifts,	
Eze	20:31	**w.** ye make your sons to pass through	
Eze	20:41	**w.** I bring you out from the people,	
Eze	20:42	**w.** I shall bring you into the land of	
Eze	20:44	**w.** I have wrought with you for my	
Eze	21:7	**w.** they say unto thee, Wherefore	3588
Eze	21:25	**w.** iniquity shall have an end,	6256
Eze	21:29	**w.** their iniquity shall have an end.	6256
Eze	22:28	God, **w.** the Lord hath not spoken.	
Eze	23:5	played the harlot **w.** she was mine;	
Eze	23:11	And **w.** her sister Aholibah saw this,	
Eze	23:14	**w.** she saw men pourtrayed upon the	
Eze	23:39	**w.** they had slain their children to	
Eze	24:24	**w.** this cometh ye shall know that I	
Eze	24:25	**w.** I take from them their strength,	
Eze	25:3	**w.** it was profaned; and against	3588
Eze	25:3	land of Israel, **w.** it was desolate;	3588
Eze	25:3	Judah, **w.** they went into captivity;	3588
Eze	25:17	**w.** I shall lay my vengeance upon	
Eze	26:10	**w.** he shall enter into thy gates, as	
Eze	26:15	**w.** the wounded cry, **w.** the slaughter	
Eze	26:19	**W.** I shall make thee a desolate city,	
Eze	26:19	**w.** I shall bring up the deep upon	
Eze	26:20	**W.** I shall bring thee down with	
Eze	27:33	**W.** thy wares went forth out of the	
Eze	27:34	time **w.** thou shalt be broken by the	
Eze	28:22	**w.** I shall have executed judgments in	
Eze	28:25	**W.** I shall have gathered the house of	
Eze	28:26	**w.** I have executed judgments upon	
Eze	29:7	**W.** they took hold of thee by thy hand,	
Eze	29:7	and **w.** they leaned upon thee, thou	
Eze	29:16	**w.** they shall look after them:	
Eze	30:4	**w.** the slain shall fall in Egypt, and	
Eze	30:8	Lord, **w.** I have set a fire in Egypt,	
Eze	30:8	**w.** all her helpers shall be destroyed.	
Eze	30:18	**w.** I shall break there the yokes of	
Eze	30:25	**w.** I shall put my sword into the hand	
Eze	31:5	multitude of waters, **w.** he shot forth.	
Eze	31:15	the day **w.** he went down to the grave	
Eze	31:16	**w.** I cast him down to hell with them	
Eze	32:7	**w.** I shall put thee out, I will cover	
Eze	32:9	**w.** I shall bring thy destruction	
Eze	32:10	**w.** I shall brandish my sword before	
Eze	32:15	**W.** I shall make the land of Egypt	
Eze	32:15	**w.** I shall smite all them that dwell	
Eze	33:2	**W.** I bring the sword upon a	3588
Eze	33:3	**w.** he seeth the sword come unto the	
Eze	33:8	**W.** I say unto the wicked, O wicked	
Eze	33:13	**W.** I shall say to the righteous, that	
Eze	33:14	**w.** I say unto the wicked, Thou shalt	
Eze	33:18	**W.** the righteous turneth from his	
Eze	33:29	**w.** I have laid the land most desolate,	
Eze	33:33	**w.** this cometh to pass, (lo, it will	
Eze	34:5	of the field, **w.** they were scattered.	
Eze	34:27	**w.** I have broken the bands of their	
Eze	35:11	among them, **w.** I have judged thee.	834
Eze	35:14	**W.** the whole earth rejoiceth, I will	
Eze	36:17	**w.** the house of Israel dwelt in their	
Eze	36:20	And **w.** they entered unto the heathen,	
Eze	36:20	**w.** they said to them, These are the	
Eze	36:23	**w.** I shall be sanctified in you before	
Eze	37:8	**w.** I beheld, lo, the sinews and the	
Eze	37:13	**w.** I have opened your graves, O my	
Eze	37:18	**w.** the children of thy people shall	3588
Eze	37:28	**w.** my sanctuary shall be in the midst	
Eze	38:14	day **w.** my people of Israel dwelleth	
Eze	38:16	**w.** I shall be sanctified in thee, O Gog,	
Eze	38:18	**w.** Gog shall come against the	3117

Eze 39:15 w. any seeth a man's bone, then shall
Eze 39:26 w. they dwelt safely in their land, and
Eze 39:27 W. I have brought them again from
Eze 42:14 W. the priests enter therein, then
Eze 42:15 w. he had made an end of measuring
Eze 43:3 I saw w. I came to destroy the city:
Eze 43:18 in the day w. they shall make it,
Eze 43:23 W. thou hast made an end of
Eze 43:27 w. these days are expired, it shall be,
Eze 44:7 w. ye offer my bread, the fat and the
Eze 44:10 far from me, w. Israel went astray,
Eze 44:15 w. the children of Israel went astray
Eze 44:17 w. they enter in at the gates of the
Eze 44:19 w. they go forth into the utter court,
Eze 44:21 w. they enter into the inner court.
Eze 45:1 w. ye shall divide by lot the land for
Eze 46:8 w. the prince shall enter, he shall go
Eze 46:9 w. the people of the land shall come
Eze 46:10 in the midst of them, w. they go in,
Eze 46:10 and w. they go forth, shall go forth.
Eze 47:3 w. the man that had the line in his
Eze 47:7 w. I had returned, behold, at the bank
Eze 48:11 w. the children of Israel went astray,
Da 3:7 w. all the people heard the sound 1768
Da 5:20 w. his heart was lifted up, and his 1768
Da 6:10 w. Daniel knew that the writing was 1768
Da 6:14 king, w. he heard these words, 1768
Da 6:20 w. he came to the den, he cried with
Da 8:2 pass, w. I saw, that I was at Shushan
Da 8:8 w. he was strong, the great horn was
Da 8:15 w. I, even I Daniel, had seen the
Da 8:17 w. he came, I was afraid, and fell
Da 8:23 w. the transgressors are come to the
Da 10:9 And w. I heard the voice of his words,
Da 10:11 w. he had spoken this word unto me,
Da 10:15 w. he had spoken such words unto
Da 10:19 w. he had spoken unto me, I was
Da 10:20 w. I am gone forth, lo, the prince of
Da 11:4 w. he shall stand up, his kingdom
Da 11:12 w. he hath taken away the multitude,
Da 11:34 w. they shall fall, they shall be holpen
Da 12:7 w. he held up his right hand and his
Da 12:7 and w. he shall have accomplished to
Ho 1:8 w. she had weaned Lo-ruhamah, she
Ho 2:15 day w. she came up out of the land of
Ho 4:14 your daughters w. they commit 3588
Ho 4:14 spouses w. they commit adultery: 3588
Ho 5:13 W. Ephraim saw his sickness, and
Ho 6:11 w. I returned the captivity of my
Ho 7:1 W. I would have healed Israel, then
Ho 7:12 W. they shall go, I will spread my 834
Ho 7:14 w. they howled upon their beds: 3588
Ho 9:12 also to them w. I depart from them!
Ho 10:10 w. they shall bind themselves in their
Ho 11:1 W. Israel was a child, then I 3588
Ho 11:10 w. he shall roar, then the children 3588
Ho 13:1 W. Ephraim spake trembling, he
Ho 13:1 but w. he offended in Baal, he died.
Joe 2:8 w. they fall upon the sword, they
Joe 3:1 w. I shall bring again the captivity 834
Am 3:4 roar in the forest, w. he hath no prey?
Am 4:7 w. there were yet three months to the
Am 4:9 w. your gardens and your vineyards
Am 7:2 w. they had made an end of eating 518
Am 8:5 W. will the new moon be gone, 4970
Jon 2:7 W. my soul fainted within me I
Jon 4:2 w. I was yet in my country? 5704
Jon 4:7 w. the morning rose the next day,
Jon 4:8 it came to pass, w. the sun did arise,
Mic 2:1 w. the morning is light, they practise
Mic 5:5 w. the Assyrian shall come into 3588
Mic 5:5 w. he shall tread in our palaces, 3588
Mic 5:6 w. he cometh into our land, 3588
Mic 5:6 w. he treadeth within our borders. 3588
Mic 7:1 w. they have gathered the summer
Mic 7:8 enemy: w. I fall, I shall arise; 3588
Mic 7:8 w. I sit in darkness, the Lord shall be
Na 1:12 cut down, w. he shall pass through.
Na 3:17 w. the sun ariseth they flee away, and
Hab 1:13 w. the wicked devoureth the man that
Hab 2:1 I shall answer w. I am reproved. 5921
Hab 3:16 W. I heard, my belly trembled; my
Hab 3:16 w. he cometh up unto the people, he
Zep 3:20 w. I turn back your captivity before
Hag 1:9 w. ye brought it home, I did blow upon
Hag 2:5 with you w. ye came out of Egypt,
Hag 2:16 w. one came to an heap of twenty
Hag 2:16 w. one came to the pressfat for to
Zec 7:2 W. they had sent unto the house of
Zec 7:5 W. ye fasted and mourned in the 3588
Zec 7:6 w. ye did eat, and w. ye did drink, 3588
Zec 7:7 w. Jerusalem was inhabited and in
Zec 7:7 w. men inhabited the south and the
Zec 8:14 w. your fathers provoked me to wrath,
Zec 9:1 w. the eyes of man, as of all the 3588
Zec 9:13 W. I have bent Judah for me, filled 3588
Zec 12:2 w. they shall be in the siege both
Zec 13:3 that w. any shall yet prophesy. 3588
Zec 13:3 thrust him through w. he prophesieth.
Zec 13:4 of his vision, w. he hath prophesied;
Zec 14:3 w. he fought in the day of battle. 3117
Mal 2:17 w. ye say, Every one that doeth evil is
Mal 3:2 and who shall stand w. he appeareth?
Mal 3:17 that day w. I make up my jewels; 834
Mt 1:18 W. as his mother Mary was espoused
Mt 2:1 w. Jesus was born in Bethlehem of
Mt 2:3 W. Herod the king had heard these
Mt 2:4 And w. he had gathered all the chief
Mt 2:7 w. he had privily called the wise men,
Mt 2:8 w. ye have found him, bring me *1875*
Mt 2:9 W. they had heard the king, they
Mt 2:10 W. they saw the star, they rejoiced
Mt 2:11 w. they were come into the house, they
Mt 2:11 w. they had opened their treasures,
Mt 2:13 w. they were departed, behold, the
Mt 2:14 W. he arose, he took the young child
Mt 2:16 Herod, w. he saw that he was mocked
Mt 2:19 w. Herod was dead, behold, an angel
Mt 2:22 w. he heard that Archelaus did reign
Mt 3:7 w. he saw many of the Pharisees and
Mt 3:16 Jesus, w. he was baptized, went up
Mt 4:2 w. he had fasted forty days and forty
Mt 4:3 w. the tempter came to him, he said,
Mt 4:12 w. Jesus had heard that John was
Mt 5:1 w. he was set, his disciples came unto
Mt 5:11 **w. men shall revile you, and** *3752*
Mt 6:2 **w. thou doest thine alms, do not** *3752*
Mt 6:3 **w. thou doest alms, let not thy left**
Mt 6:5 **w. thou prayest, thou shalt not** *3752*
Mt 6:6 **thou, w. thou prayest, enter into** *3752*
Mt 6:6 **w. thou hast shut thy door, pray to**
Mt 6:7 **w. ye pray, use not vain repetitions,**
Mt 6:16 **w. ye fast, be not, as the** *3752*
Mt 6:17 **w. thou fastest, anoint thine head,**
Mt 7:28 w. Jesus had ended these sayings, *3753*
Mt 8:1 W. he was come down from the
Mt 8:5 w. Jesus was entered into Capernaum,
Mt 8:10 W. Jesus heard it, he marvelled, and
Mt 8:14 w. Jesus was come into Peter's house,
Mt 8:16 W. the even was come, they brought
Mt 8:18 Now w. Jesus saw great multitudes
Mt 8:23 w. he was entered into a ship, his
Mt 8:28 w. he was come to the other side into
Mt 8:32 w. they were come out, they went into
Mt 8:34 w. they saw him, they besought him
Mt 9:8 But w. the multitudes saw it, they
Mt 9:11 w. the Pharisees saw it, they said
Mt 9:12 w. Jesus heard that, he said unto
Mt 9:15 **w. the bridegroom shall be taken** *3752*
Mt 9:22 w. he saw her, he said, **Daughter, be**
Mt 9:23 w. Jesus came into the ruler's house,
Mt 9:25 w. the people were put forth, *3753*
Mt 9:27 w. Jesus departed thence, two blind
Mt 9:28 w. he was come into the house, the
Mt 9:31 But they, w. they were departed,
Mt 9:33 w. the devil was cast out, the dumb
Mt 9:36 w. he saw the multitudes, he was
Mt 10:1 w. he had called unto him his twelve
Mt 10:12 **w. ye come into an house, salute it.**
Mt 10:14 **w. ye depart out of that house or city,**
Mt 10:19 **w. they deliver you up, take no** *3752*
Mt 10:23 **w. they persecute you in this city,** *3752*
Mt 11:1 w. Jesus had made an end of *3753*
Mt 11:2 w. John had heard in the prison the
Mt 12:2 w. the Pharisees saw it, they said
Mt 12:3 **David did, w. he was an hungred,** *3753*
Mt 12:9 w. he was departed thence, he went *3753*
Mt 12:15 But w. Jesus knew it, he withdrew *3753*
Mt 12:24 w. the Pharisees heard it, they said,
Mt 12:43 **W. the unclean spirit is gone out** *3752*
Mt 12:44 **w. he is come, he findeth it empty,**
Mt 13:4 **w. he sowed, some seeds fell** *1722,3588*
Mt 13:6 **And w. the sun was up, they were**
Mt 13:19 **W. any one heareth the word of the**
Mt 13:21 **w. tribulation or persecution ariseth**
Mt 13:26 **But w. the blade was sprung up,** *3753*
Mt 13:32 **w. it is grown, it is the greatest** *3752*
Mt 13:44 **the which w. a man hath found, he**
Mt 13:46 **w. he hath found one pearl of great**
Mt 13:48 **w. it was full, they drew to shore,** *3753*
Mt 13:53 that w. Jesus had finished these *3753*
Mt 13:54 w. he was come into his own country,
Mt 14:5 w. he would have put him to death, he
Mt 14:6 w. Herod's birthday was kept, they
Mt 14:13 W. Jesus heard of it, he departed
Mt 14:13 w. the people had heard thereof, they
Mt 14:15 w. it was evening, his disciples came
Mt 14:23 w. he had sent the multitudes away,
Mt 14:23 w. the evening was come, he was
Mt 14:26 w. the disciples saw him walking on
Mt 14:29 w. Peter was come down out of the
Mt 14:30 w. he saw the wind boisterous, he was
Mt 14:32 w. they were come into the ship, the
Mt 14:34 w. they were gone over, they came
Mt 14:35 w. the men of that place had
Mt 15:2 their hands w. they eat bread. *3752*
Mt 15:31 w. they saw the dumb to speak,
Mt 16:2 **W. it is evening, ye say, it will be fair.**
Mt 16:5 w. his disciples were come to the
Mt 16:8 Which w. Jesus perceived, he said
Mt 16:13 W. Jesus came into the coasts of
Mt 17:6 w. the disciples heard it, they fell on
Mt 17:8 w. they had lifted up their eyes, they
Mt 17:14 w. they were come to the multitude,
Mt 17:24 w. they were come to Capernaum,
Mt 17:25 w. he was come into the house, *3753*
Mt 17:27 **w. thou hast opened his mouth, thou**
Mt 18:24 **w. he had begun to reckon, one was**
Mt 18:31 **w. his fellowservants saw what was**
Mt 19:1 that w. Jesus had finished these *3753*
Mt 19:22 w. the young man heard that saying,
Mt 19:25 W. his disciples heard it, they were
Mt 19:28 **w. the Son of man shall sit in the** *3752*
Mt 20:2 **w. he had agreed with the labourers**
Mt 20:8 **So w. even was come, the lord of the**
Mt 20:9 **w. they came that were hired about**
Mt 20:10 **But w. the first came, they supposed**
Mt 20:11 **And w. they had received it, they**
Mt 20:24 w. the ten heard it, they were moved
Mt 20:30 w. they heard that Jesus passed by,
Mt 21:1 And w. they drew nigh unto *3753*
Mt 21:10 w. he was come into Jerusalem, all
Mt 21:15 w. the chief priests and scribes saw
Mt 21:19 w. he saw a fig tree in the way, he
Mt 21:20 And w. the disciples saw it, they
Mt 21:23 And w. he was come into the temple,
Mt 21:32 **ye, w. ye had seen it, repented not**
Mt 21:34 **w. the time of the fruit drew near.** *3753*
Mt 21:38 **But w. the husbandmen saw the son,**
Mt 21:40 **W. the lord therefore of the** *3752*
Mt 21:45 w. the chief priests and Pharisees had
Mt 21:46 w. they sought to lay hands on him,
Mt 22:7 **w. the king heard thereof, he was**
Mt 22:11 **w. the king came in to see the guests,**
Mt 22:22 W. they had heard these words, they
Mt 22:25 the first, w. he had married a wife,
Mt 22:33 And w. the multitude heard this, they
Mt 22:34 w. the Pharisees had heard that he
Mt 23:15 **w. he is made, ye make him** *3752*
Mt 24:3 Tell us, w. shall these things be? *4218*
Mt 24:15 **W. ye therefore shall see the** *3752*
Mt 24:32 **W. his branch is yet tender, and** *3752*
Mt 24:33 **w. ye shall see all these things,** *3752*
Mt 24:46 **w. he cometh shall find so doing.**
Mt 24:50 **come in a day w. he looketh not for**
Mt 25:31 **W. the Son of man shall come in** *3752*
Mt 25:37 **w. saw we thee an hungred, and** *4218*
Mt 25:38 **W. saw we thee a stranger, and** *4218*
Mt 25:39 **Or w. saw we thee sick, or in** *4218*
Mt 25:44 **w. saw we thee an hungred, or** *4218*
Mt 26:1 w. Jesus had finished all these *3753*
Mt 26:6 w. Jesus was in Bethany, in the house
Mt 26:8 But w. his disciples saw it, they had
Mt 26:10 W. Jesus understood it, he said unto
Mt 26:20 Now w. the even was come, he sat
Mt 26:29 **until that day w. I drink it new** *3752*
Mt 26:30 And w. they had sung an hymn, they
Mt 26:71 w. he was gone out into the porch,

Book	Ref	Context	No.
Mt	27:1	**W.** the morning was come, all the	
Mt	27:2	**w.** they had bound him, they led him	
Mt	27:3	**w.** he saw that he was condemned,	
Mt	27:12	**w.** he was accused of the chief...	1722,3588
Mt	27:17	**w.** they were gathered together,	
Mt	27:19	**W.** he was set down on the judgment	
Mt	27:24	**W.** Pilate saw that he could prevail	
Mt	27:26	and **w.** he had scourged Jesus, he	
Mt	27:29	**w.** they had platted a crown of thorns,	
Mt	27:33	**w.** they were come unto a place called	
Mt	27:34	**w.** he had tasted thereof, he would not	
Mt	27:47	**w.** they heard that, said, This man	
Mt	27:50	**w.** he had cried again with a loud	
Mt	27:54	**w.** the centurion, and they that were	
Mt	27:57	**W.** the even was come, there came a	
Mt	27:59	**w.** Joseph had taken the body, he	
Mt	28:11	Now, **w.** they were going, behold,	
Mt	28:12	And **w.** they were assembled with the	
Mt	28:17	**w.** they saw him, they worshipped	
Mk	1:19	And **w.** he had gone a little farther	
Mk	1:26	**w.** the unclean spirit had torn him,	
Mk	1:29	**w.** they were come out of the	
Mk	1:32	**w.** the sun did set, they brought	3753
Mk	1:37	**w.** they had found him, they said unto	
Mk	2:4	**w.** they could not come nigh unto him	
Mk	2:4	**w.** they had broken it up, they let	
Mk	2:5	**W.** Jesus saw their faith, he said	
Mk	2:8	immediately **w.** Jesus perceived in his	
Mk	2:16	**w.** the scribes and Pharisees saw him	
Mk	2:17	**W.** Jesus heard it, he saith unto	
Mk	2:20	**w. the bridegroom shall be taken**	3752
Mk	2:25	**w. he had need, and was an**	3753
Mk	3:5	**w.** he had looked round about on	
Mk	3:8	**w.** they had heard what great things	
Mk	3:11	unclean spirits, **w.** they saw him,	3752
Mk	3:21	**w.** his friends heard of it, they went	
Mk	4:6	**w. the sun was up, it was scorched;**	
Mk	4:10	**w.** he was alone, they that were	3753
Mk	4:15	**but w. they have heard, Satan**	3752
Mk	4:16	**w. they have heard the word,**	3752
Mk	4:17	**w. affliction or persecution ariseth for**	
Mk	4:29	**w. the fruit is brought forth,**	
Mk	4:31	**w. it is sown in the earth, is less**	
Mk	4:32	**But w. it is sown, it groweth up,**	
Mk	4:34	**w.** they were alone, he expounded all	
Mk	4:35	the same day, **w.** the even was come,	
Mk	4:36	**w.** they had sent away the multitude,	
Mk	5:2	**w.** he was come out of the ship,	
Mk	5:6	**w.** he saw Jesus afar off, he ran and	
Mk	5:18	**w.** he was come unto the ship, he that	
Mk	5:21	**w.** Jesus was passed over again by	
Mk	5:22	and **w.** he saw him, he fell at his feet,	
Mk	5:27	**W.** she heard of Jesus, came in the	
Mk	5:39	**w.** he was come in, he saith unto	
Mk	5:40	**w.** he had put them all out, he taketh	
Mk	6:2	And **w.** the sabbath day was come, he	
Mk	6:11	**w. ye depart thence, shake off the**	
Mk	6:16	**w.** Herod heard thereof, he said, It is	
Mk	6:20	**w.** he heard him, he did many things,	
Mk	6:21	**w.** a convenient day was come, that	
Mk	6:22	**w.** the daughter of the said Herodias	
Mk	6:29	**w.** his disciples heard of it, they came	
Mk	6:34	And Jesus, **w.** he came out, saw much	
Mk	6:35	And **w.** the day was now far spent, his	
Mk	6:38	**w.** they knew, they say, Five, and two	
Mk	6:41	**w.** he had taken the five loaves and	
Mk	6:46	And **w.** he had sent them away, he	
Mk	6:47	**w.** even was come, the ship was in the	
Mk	6:49	**w.** they saw him walking upon the	
Mk	6:53	**w.** they had passed over, they came	
Mk	6:54	**w.** they were come out of the ship,	
Mk	7:2	**w.** they saw some of his disciples eat	
Mk	7:4	**w.** they come from the market, except	
Mk	7:14	**w.** he had called all the people unto	
Mk	7:17	**w.** he was entered into the house	3753
Mk	7:30	**w.** she was come to her house, she	
Mk	8:17	**w.** Jesus knew it, he saith unto	
Mk	8:19	**W. I brake the five loaves among**	5753
Mk	8:20	**w. the seven among four thousand,**	5753
Mk	8:23	**w.** he had spit on his eyes, and put his	
Mk	8:33	**w.** he had turned about and looked	
Mk	8:34	**w.** he had called the people unto him	
Mk	8:38	**w. he cometh in the glory of his...**	3752
Mk	9:8	**w.** they had looked round about, they	
Mk	9:14	**w.** he came to his disciples, he saw a	
Mk	9:15	all the people, **w.** they beheld him,	
Mk	9:20	**w.** he saw him, straightway the spirit	
Mk	9:25	**W.** Jesus saw the people came	
Mk	9:28	**w.** he was come into the house, his	
Mk	9:36	**w.** he had taken him in his arms, he	
Mk	10:14	But **w.** Jesus saw it, he was much	
Mk	10:17	**w.** he was gone forth into the way,	
Mk	10:41	**w.** the ten heard it, they began to be	
Mk	10:47	**w.** he heard that it was Jesus of	
Mk	11:1	**w.** they came nigh to Jerusalem,	3753
Mk	11:11	**w.** he had looked round about upon all	
Mk	11:12	**w.** they were come from Bethany,	
Mk	11:13	**w.** he came to it, he found nothing but	
Mk	11:19	**w.** even was come he went out of	3753
Mk	11:24	**things soever ye desire, w. ye pray,**	
Mk	11:25	**w. ye stand praying, forgive, if ye..**	3752
Mk	12:14	**w.** they were come, they say unto him,	
Mk	12:23	therefore, **w.** they shall rise,	3752
Mk	12:25	**w. they shall rise from the dead,...**	3752
Mk	12:34	And **w.** Jesus saw that he answered	
Mk	13:4	Tell us, **w.** shall these things be?	4218
Mk	13:4	sign **w.** all these things shall be	3752
Mk	13:7	**And w. ye shall hear of wars and..**	3752
Mk	13:11	**w. they shall lead you, and deliver**	3752
Mk	13:14	**w. ye shall see the abomination of**	3752
Mk	13:28	**W. her branch is yet tender, and...**	3752
Mk	13:29	**w. ye shall see these things come..**	3752
Mk	13:33	**for ye know not w. the time is...**	4218
Mk	13:35	**w. the master of the house cometh,**	4218
Mk	14:11	And **w.** they heard it, they were glad,	
Mk	14:12	**w.** they killed the passover, his	3753
Mk	14:23	**w.** he had given thanks, he gave it to	
Mk	14:26	And **w.** they had sung an hymn, they	
Mk	14:40	**w.** he returned, he found them asleep	
Mk	14:67	**w.** she saw Peter warming himself,	
Mk	14:72	And **w.** he thought thereon, he wept	
Mk	15:15	Jesus, **w.** he had scourged him, to be	
Mk	15:20	**w.** they had mocked him, they	3753
Mk	15:24	And **w.** he had crucified him, they	
Mk	15:33	**w.** the sixth hour was come, there was	
Mk	15:35	**w.** they heard it, said, Behold, he	
Mk	15:39	**w.** the centurion, which stood over	
Mk	15:41	**w.** he was in Galilee, followed him,	3753
Mk	15:42	now **w.** the even was come, because it	
Mk	15:45	**w.** he knew it of the centurion, he gave	
Mk	16:1	**w.** the sabbath was past, Mary	
Mk	16:4	And **w.** they looked, they saw that the	
Mk	16:9	**w.** Jesus was risen early in the first	
Mk	16:11	**w.** they had heard that he was alive,	
Lu	1:9	**w.** he went into the temple of the Lord.	
Lu	1:12	**w.** Zacharias saw him, he was	
Lu	1:22	**w.** he came out, he could not speak	
Lu	1:29	**w.** she saw him, she was troubled at	
Lu	1:41	**w.** Elisabeth heard the salutation	5613
Lu	2:2	**w.** Cyrenius was governor of Syria.	
Lu	2:17	**w.** they had seen it, they made known	
Lu	2:21	**w.** eight days were accomplished	3753
Lu	2:22	**w.** the days of her purification	3753
Lu	2:27	**w.** the parents brought in the	1722,3588
Lu	2:39	**w.** they had performed all things	5613
Lu	2:42	**w.** he was twelve years old, they	3753
Lu	2:43	**w.** they had fulfilled the days, as they	
Lu	2:45	**w.** they found him not, they turned	
Lu	2:48	**w.** they saw him, they were amazed:	
Lu	3:21	**w.** all the people were	1722,3588
Lu	4:2	and **w.** they were ended, he afterward	
Lu	4:13	**w.** the devil had ended all the	
Lu	4:17	**w.** he had opened the book, he found	
Lu	4:25	**w. the heaven was shut up three ..**	3753
Lu	4:25	**w. great famine was throughout....**	5613
Lu	4:28	synagogue, **w.** they heard these	
Lu	4:35	**w.** the devil had thrown him in the	
Lu	4:40	Now **w.** the sun was setting, all they	
Lu	4:42	And **w.** it was day, he departed and	
Lu	5:4	**w.** he had left speaking, he said	5613
Lu	5:6	**w.** they had this done, they inclosed a	
Lu	5:8	**W.** Simon Peter saw it, he fell down	
Lu	5:11	**w.** they had brought their ships to	
Lu	5:12	**w.** he was in a certain city,	1722,3588
Lu	5:19	**w.** they could not find by what way	
Lu	5:20	**w.** he saw their faith, he said unto	
Lu	5:22	**w.** Jesus perceived their thoughts,	
Lu	5:35	**w. the bridegroom shall be taken..**	3752
Lu	6:3	**did, w. himself was an hungred,...**	3698
Lu	6:13	**w.** it was day, he called unto him	3753
Lu	6:22	**are ye w. men shall hate you, and..**	3752
Lu	6:22	**w. they shall separate you from....**	3752
Lu	6:26	**w. all men shall speak well of you:**	3752
Lu	6:42	**w. thou thyself beholdest not the**	
Lu	6:48	**w. the flood arose, the stream beat**	
Lu	7:1	**w.** he had ended all his sayings in	1893
Lu	7:3	**w.** he heard of Jesus, he sent unto him	
Lu	7:4	**w.** they came to Jesus, they besought	
Lu	7:6	**w.** he was now not far from the house,	
Lu	7:9	**W.** Jesus heard these things, he	
Lu	7:12	**w.** he came nigh to the gate of the	5613
Lu	7:13	And **w.** the Lord saw her, he had	
Lu	7:20	**W.** the men were come unto him, they	
Lu	7:24	And **w.** the messengers of John were	
Lu	7:37	**w.** she knew that Jesus sat at meat in	
Lu	7:39	**w.** the Pharisee which had bidden	
Lu	7:42	**w. they had nothing to pay, he**	
Lu	8:4	And **w.** much people were gathered	
Lu	8:8	**w.** he had said these things, he cried,	
Lu	8:13	**w. they hear, receive the word**	3752
Lu	8:14	**w. they have heard, go forth, and are..**	
Lu	8:16	**No man, w. he hath lighted a candle,..**	
Lu	8:27	**w.** he went forth to land, there met	
Lu	8:28	**W.** he saw Jesus, he cried out, and	
Lu	8:34	**W.** they that fed them saw what was	
Lu	8:40	that, **w.** Jesus was returned,	1722,3588
Lu	8:45	**W.** all denied, Peter and they that	
Lu	8:47	**w.** the woman saw that she was not	
Lu	8:50	**w.** Jesus heard it, he answered him	
Lu	8:51	**w.** he came into the house, he suffered	
Lu	9:5	**w. ye go out of that city, shake off the**	
Lu	9:10	apostles, **w.** they were returned, told	
Lu	9:11	the people, **w.** they knew it, followed	
Lu	9:12	**w.** the day began to wear away, then	
Lu	9:26	**w. he shall come in his own glory,.**	3752
Lu	9:32	and **w.** they were awake, they saw his	
Lu	9:36	**w.** the voice was past, Jesus	1722,3588
Lu	9:37	**w.** they were come down from the hill,	
Lu	9:51	**w.** the time was come that he....	1722,3588
Lu	9:54	**w.** his disciples James and John saw	
Lu	10:31	**w. he saw him, he passed by on the**	
Lu	10:32	**a Levite, w. he was at the place, came**	
Lu	10:33	**w. he saw him, he had compassion on..**	
Lu	10:35	**on the morrow w. he departed, he**	
Lu	10:35	**w. I come again, I will repay..**	1722,3588
Lu	11:1	**w.** he ceased, one of his disciples	5613
Lu	11:2	**W. ye pray, say, Our Father which**	3752
Lu	11:14	**w.** the devil was gone out, the dumb	
Lu	11:21	**W. a strong man armed keepeth....**	3752
Lu	11:22	**w. a stronger than he shall come..**	1875
Lu	11:24	**W. the unclean spirit is gone out..**	3752
Lu	11:25	**w. he cometh, he findeth it swept and..**	
Lu	11:29	**w.** the people were gathered thick	
Lu	11:33	**No man, w. he hath lighted a candle,..**	
Lu	11:34	**w. thine eye is single, thy whole...**	1875
Lu	11:34	**w. thine eye is evil, thy body also..**	3752
Lu	11:36	**w. the bright shining of a candle...**	3752
Lu	11:38	**w.** the Pharisee saw it, he marvelled	
Lu	12:1	**w.** they were gathered together an	
Lu	12:11	**w. they bring you...the synagogues**	3752
Lu	12:36	**w. he will return from the**	4218
Lu	12:36	**that w. he cometh and knocketh,**	
Lu	12:37	**w. he cometh shall find watching:**	
Lu	12:40	**cometh at an hour w. ye think not**	
Lu	12:43	**his lord w. he cometh shall find**	
Lu	12:46	**come in a day w. he looketh not for**	
Lu	12:46	**at an hour w. he is not aware, and will**	
Lu	12:54	**W. ye see a cloud rise out of the...**	3752
Lu	12:55	**w. ye see the south wind blow, ye..**	3753
Lu	12:58	**W. thou goest with thine**	5613
Lu	13:12	**w.** Jesus saw her, he called her to him,	
Lu	13:17	**w.** he had said these things, all his	
Lu	13:25	**W. once the master of the house is**	
Lu	13:28	**w. ye shall see Abraham, and**	3752
Lu	13:35	**until the time come w. ye shall**	3753
Lu	14:7	**w.** he marked how they chose out the	
Lu	14:8	**W. thou art bidden of any man to.**	3752
Lu	14:10	**w. thou art bidden, go and sit**	3752
Lu	14:10	**w. he that bade thee cometh, he...**	3752
Lu	14:12	**W. thou makest a dinner or a**	3752
Lu	14:13	**But w. thou makest a feast, call...**	3752
Lu	14:15	**w.** one of them that sat at meat with	
Lu	15:5	**w. he hath found it, he layeth it on**	
Lu	15:6	**And w. he cometh home, he calleth**	
Lu	15:9	**w. she hath found it, she calleth her...**	
Lu	15:14	**w. he had spent all, there arose a**	
Lu	15:17	**w. he came to himself, he said, How...**	
Lu	15:20	**w. he was yet a great way off, his**	

Lu 16:4 **w. I am put out of the**... *3752*
Lu 16:9 **w. ye fail, they may receive you**... *3752*
Lu 17:7 **w. he is come from the field, Go and**...
Lu 17:10 **w. ye shall have done all those**... *3752*
Lu 17:14 w. he saw them, he said unto them, Go...
Lu 17:15 w. he saw that he was healed, turned...
Lu 17:20 w. he was demanded of the Pharisees,...
Lu 17:20 w. the kingdom of God should... *4218*
Lu 17:22 **w. ye shall desire to see one of**... *3753*
Lu 17:30 **the day w. the Son of man is revealed**..
Lu 18:8 **w. the Son of man cometh, shall he**...
Lu 18:15 w. his disciples saw it, they rebuked...
Lu 18:22 w. Jesus heard these things, he...
Lu 18:23 w. he heard this, he was very...
Lu 18:24 w. Jesus saw that he was very...
Lu 18:40 w. he was come near, he asked him,...
Lu 18:43 w. they saw it, gave praise unto God...
Lu 19:5 And w. Jesus came to the place, he... *5613*
Lu 19:7 w. they saw it, they all murmured,...
Lu 19:15 **w. he was returned, having**... *1722,3588*
Lu 19:28 w. he had thus spoken, he went before,...
Lu 19:29 w. he was come nigh to Bethphage... *5613*
Lu 19:37 w. he was come nigh, even now at the...
Lu 19:41 w. he was come near, he beheld... *5613*
Lu 20:13 **will reverence him w. they see him**...
Lu 20:14 **w. the husbandmen saw him, they**...
Lu 20:16 And w. they heard it, they said, God...
Lu 20:37 **w. he calleth the Lord the God of**... *5613*
Lu 21:7 w. shall these things be? and what... *4218*
Lu 21:7 w. these things shall come to pass... *3752*
Lu 21:9 **But w. ye shall hear of wars and**.. *3752*
Lu 21:20 **w. ye...see Jerusalem compassed**... *3752*
Lu 21:28 **w. these things begin to come to pass**,.
Lu 21:30 **W. they now shoot forth, ye see**... *3752*
Lu 21:31 **w. ye see these things come to**... *3752*
Lu 22:7 w....passover must be killed... *1722,3739*
Lu 22:10 **w. ye are entered into the city, there**...
Lu 22:14 w. the hour was come, he sat... *3753,3588*
Lu 22:32 **w. thou are converted, strengthen**.. *4218*
Lu 22:35 **W. I sent you without purse, and**.. *3753*
Lu 22:40 w. he was at the place, he said unto...
Lu 22:45 w. he rose up from prayer, and was...
Lu 22:49 W. they which were about him saw...
Lu 22:53 **W. I was daily with you in the temple**,.
Lu 22:55 w. they had kindled a fire in the midst...
Lu 22:64 And w. they had blindfolded him,...
Lu 28:6 W. Pilate heard of Galilee, he asked...
Lu 28:8 w. Herod saw Jesus, he was...glad:...
Lu 28:13 w. he had called together the chief...
Lu 28:33 w. they were come to the place,... *3753*
Lu 28:42 w. thou comest into thy kingdom... *3752*
Lu 28:46 w. Jesus had cried with a loud voice,...
Lu 28:47 w. the centurion saw what was done,...
Lu 24:6 unto you w. he was yet in Galilee,...
Lu 24:23 w. they found not his body, they came,...
Lu 24:40 w. he had thus spoken, he shewed...
Joh 1:19 w. the Jews sent priests and... *3753*
Joh 1:42 w. Jesus beheld him, he said, **Thou art**...
Joh 1:48 **w. thou was under the fig tree, I saw**..
Joh 2:3 w. they wanted wine, the mother of...
Joh 2:9 W. the ruler of the feast had... *5613*
Joh 2:10 w. men have well drunk, then that... *3752*
Joh 2:15 w. he had made a scourge of small...
Joh 2:22 W. therefore he was risen from... *3753*
Joh 2:23 w. he was in Jerusalem at the... *5613*
Joh 2:23 w. they saw the miracles which he did...
Joh 3:4 How can a man be born w. he is old?...
Joh 4:1 W. therefore the Lord knew how... *5613*
Joh 4:21 **w. ye shall neither in this**... *3753*
Joh 4:23 **w. the true worshippers shall**... *3753*
Joh 4:25 w. he is come, he will tell us all... *3752*
Joh 4:40 w. the Samaritans were come unto... *5613*
Joh 4:45 Then w. he was come into Galilee,... *3753*
Joh 4:47 W. he heard that Jesus was come out...
Joh 4:52 hour w. he began to amend... *1722,3739*
Joh 4:54 w. he was come out of Judaea into...
Joh 5:6 W. Jesus saw him lie, and knew that...
Joh 5:7 no man, w. the water is troubled,... *3752*
Joh 5:25 **w. the dead shall hear the voice**... *3753*
Joh 6:5 W. Jesus then lifted up his eyes, and...
Joh 6:11 w. he had given thanks, he distributed...
Joh 6:12 W. they were filled, he said unto... *5613*
Joh 6:14 w. they had seen the miracle that...
Joh 6:15 W. Jesus therefore perceived that they...
Joh 6:16 w. even was now come, his... *5613*
Joh 6:19 So w. they had rowed about five and...
Joh 6:22 w. the people which stood on the other...
Joh 6:24 W. the people therefore saw that... *3753*
Joh 6:25 w. they had found him on the... *4218*
Joh 6:25 him, Rabbi, w. camest thou hither?...
Joh 6:60 disciples, w. they had heard this, said,...
Joh 6:61 W. Jesus knew in himself that his...
Joh 7:9 W. he had said these words unto...
Joh 7:10 w. his brethren were gone up, then... *5613*
Joh 7:27 w. Christ cometh, no man knoweth... *3752*
Joh 7:31 W. Christ cometh, will he do more... *3752*
Joh 7:40 the people. . .w. they heard this saying...
Joh 8:3 w. they had set her in the midst,...
Joh 8:7 w. they continued asking him, he... *5613*
Joh 8:10 W. Jesus had lifted up himself, and...
Joh 8:28 **W. ye have lifted up the Son of**... *3752*
Joh 8:44 **W. he speaketh a lie, he speaketh**. *3752*
Joh 9:4 **night cometh, w. no man can**... *3753*
Joh 9:6 W. he had thus spoken, he spat on...
Joh 9:14 sabbath day w. Jesus made the... *3753*
Joh 9:35 w. he had found him, he said unto him,...
Joh 10:4 **w. he putteth forth his own sheep**. *3752*
Joh 11:4 W. Jesus heard that, he said, **This**...
Joh 11:6 W. he had heard therefore that he... *5613*
Joh 11:17 w. Jesus came, he found that he had...
Joh 11:28 w. she had so said, she went her way,...
Joh 11:31 w. they saw Mary, that she rose up...
Joh 11:32 w. Mary was come where Jesus... *5613*
Joh 11:33 W. Jesus therefore saw her... *5613*
Joh 11:43 And w. he thus had spoken, he cried...
Joh 12:12 w. they heard that Jesus was coming...
Joh 12:14 Jesus, w. he had found a young ass,...
Joh 12:16 but w. Jesus was glorified, then... *3753*
Joh 12:17 w. he called Lazarus out of his... *3753*
Joh 12:41 w. he saw his glory, and spake of... *3753*
Joh 13:1 w. Jesus knew that his hour was come...
Joh 13:19 **w. it is come to pass, ye may**... *3752*
Joh 13:21 W. Jesus had thus said, he was...
Joh 13:26 **I shall give a sop, w. I have dipped it**..
Joh 13:26 w. he had dipped the sop, he gave... *3753*
Joh 13:31 w. he was gone out, Jesus said,... *3753*
Joh 14:29 **w. it is come to pass, ye might**... *3752*
Joh 15:26 **w. the Comforter is come, whom I**. *3752*
Joh 16:4 **w. the time shall come, ye may**... *3752*
Joh 16:8 **w. he is come, he will reprove**...
Joh 16:13 **w. he, the Spirit of truth, is come**,. *3752*
Joh 16:21 **w. she is in travail hath sorrow**,... *3752*
Joh 16:25 **w. I shall no more speak unto**... *3753*
Joh 18:1 W. Jesus had spoken these words, he...
Joh 18:22 w. he had thus spoken, one of the...
Joh 18:38 w. he had said this, he went out again...
Joh 19:6 W. the chief priests therefore and... *3753*
Joh 19:8, 13 W. Pilate therefore heard that... *3753*
Joh 19:23 w. they had crucified Jesus, took... *3753*
Joh 19:26 W. Jesus therefore saw his mother,...
Joh 19:30 W. Jesus therefore had received... *3753*
Joh 19:33 But w. they came to Jesus, and... *5613*
Joh 20:1 Magdalene early, w. it was yet dark,...
Joh 20:14 w. she had thus said, she turned...
Joh 20:19 w. the doors were shut where the...
Joh 20:20 And w. he had so said, he shewed...
Joh 20:20 disciples glad, w. they saw the Lord...
Joh 20:22 w. he had said this, he breathed on...
Joh 20:24 was not with them w. Jesus came... *3753*
Joh 21:4 w. the morning was now come, Jesus...
Joh 21:7 w. Simon Peter heard that it was the...
Joh 21:15 w. they had dined, Jesus saith to... *3753*
Joh 21:18 **W. thou wast young, thou**... *3753*
Joh 21:18 **w. thou shalt be old, thou shalt**... *3752*
Joh 21:19 w. he had spoken this, he saith unto...
Ac 1:6 W. they therefore were come together...
Ac 1:9 w. he had spoken these things, while...
Ac 1:13 And w. they were come in, they... *3753*
Ac 2:1 w. the day of Pentecost was... *1722,3588*
Ac 2:6 Now w. this was noised abroad, the...
Ac 2:37 w. they heard this, they were pricked...
Ac 3:12 w. Peter saw it, he answered unto the...
Ac 3:13 w. he was determined to let him go...
Ac 3:19 w. the times of refreshing shall... *3704*
Ac 4:7 w. they had set them in the midst, they...
Ac 4:13 Now w. they saw the boldness of Peter...
Ac 4:15 But w. they had commanded to go...
Ac 4:21 w. they had further threatened them,...
Ac 4:24 w. they heard that, they lifted up their...
Ac 4:31 w. they had prayed, the place was...
Ac 5:7 w. his wife, not knowing what was...
Ac 5:21 w. they heard that, they entered into...
Ac 5:22 But w. the officers came, and found...
Ac 5:23 w. we had opened, we found no man...
Ac 5:24 w. the high priest and the captain... *5613*
Ac 5:27 w. they had brought them, they set...
Ac 5:33 W. they heard that, they were cut to...
Ac 5:40 w. they had called the apostles, and...
Ac 6:1 w. the number of the disciples was...
Ac 6:6 w. they had prayed, they laid their...
Ac 7:2 Abraham, w. he was in Mesopotamia,...
Ac 7:4 w. his father was dead, he removed... *3326*
Ac 7:5 after him, w. as yet he had no child...
Ac 7:12 w. Jacob heard that there was corn in...
Ac 7:17 w. the time of the promise drew... *2531*
Ac 7:21 w. he was cast out, Pharaoh's daughter...
Ac 7:23 w. he was full forty years old, it... *5613*
Ac 7:30 w. forty years were expired, there...
Ac 7:31 W. Moses saw it, he wondered at the...
Ac 7:54 W. they heard these things, they were...
Ac 7:60 And w. he had said this, he fell asleep...
Ac 8:12 w. they believed Philip preaching... *3753*
Ac 8:13 w. he was baptized, he continued with...
Ac 8:14 w. the apostles which were at...
Ac 8:15 Who, w. they were come down, prayed...
Ac 8:18 w. Simon saw that through laying on...
Ac 8:25 w. they had testified and preached the...
Ac 8:39 w. they were come up out of...water,. *3753*
Ac 9:8 w. his eyes were opened, he saw no...
Ac 9:19 w. he had received meat, he was...
Ac 9:26 w. Saul was come to Jerusalem, he...
Ac 9:30 w. the brethren knew, they brought...
Ac 9:37 whom w. they had washed, they laid...
Ac 9:39 W. he was come, they brought him...
Ac 9:40 eyes: and w. she saw Peter, she sat up...
Ac 9:41 w. he had called the saints and widows,...
Ac 10:4 w. he looked on him, he was afraid,...
Ac 10:7 w. the angel which spake unto... *5613*
Ac 10:8 w. he had declared all these things...
Ac 10:32 who, w. he cometh, shall speak unto...
Ac 11:2 w. Peter was come up to Jerusalem,... *3753*
Ac 11:6 which w. I had fastened mine eyes,...
Ac 11:18 W. they heard these things, they held...
Ac 11:20 w. they were come to Antioch, spake...
Ac 11:23 w. he came, and had seen the grace...
Ac 11:26 w. he had found him, he brought him...
Ac 12:4 w. he had apprehended him, and put...
Ac 12:6 w. Herod would have brought him... *3753*
Ac 12:10 W. they were past the first and the...
Ac 12:11 w. Peter was come to himself, he said,...
Ac 12:12 w. he had considered the thing, he...
Ac 12:14 w. she knew Peter's voice, she opened...
Ac 12:16 w. they had opened the door, and saw...
Ac 12:19 w. Herod had sought for him, and...
Ac 12:25 w. they had fulfilled their ministry,...
Ac 13:3 w. they had fasted and prayed, and...
Ac 13:5 w. they were at Salamis, they...
Ac 13:6 w. they had gone through the isle...
Ac 13:12 w. he saw what was done, believed,...
Ac 13:13 w. Paul and his company loosed from...
Ac 13:14 w. they departed from Perga, they...
Ac 13:17 w. they dwelt as strangers in... *1722,3588*
Ac 13:19 w. he had destroyed seven nations in...
Ac 13:22 w. he had removed him, he raised up...
Ac 13:24 W. John had first preached before his...
Ac 13:29 w. they had fulfilled all that was... *5613*
Ac 13:42 w. the Jews were gone out of the...
Ac 13:43 w. the congregation was broken up,...
Ac 13:45 w. the Jews saw the multitudes, they...
Ac 13:48 w. the Gentiles heard this, they were...
Ac 14:5 w. there was an assault made both... *5613*
Ac 14:11 w. the people saw what Paul had done,...
Ac 14:14 Which w. the apostles, Barnabas and...
Ac 14:21 And w. they had preached the gospel...
Ac 14:23 w. they had ordained them elders in...
Ac 14:25 w. they had preached the word in...
Ac 14:27 w. they had come, and had gathered...
Ac 15:2 W. therefore Paul and Barnabas had...
Ac 15:4 w. they were come to Jerusalem, they...
Ac 15:7 w. there had been much disputing,...
Ac 15:30 So w. they were dismissed, they came...
Ac 15:30 w. they had gathered the multitude...
Ac 15:31 Which w. they had read, they rejoiced...
Ac 16:6 w. they had gone throughout Phrygia...
Ac 16:15 w. she was baptized, and her... *5613*
Ac 16:19 w. her masters saw that the hope of...
Ac 16:23 w. they had laid many stripes upon...
Ac 16:34 w. he had brought them into his...

Ac 16:35 **w.** it was day, the magistrates sent the
Ac 16:38 **w.** they heard that they were Romans
Ac 16:40 **w.** they had seen the brethren, they
Ac 17:1 **w.** they had passed through
Ac 17:6 **w.** they found them not, they drew
Ac 17:8 the city, **w.** they heard these things
Ac 17:9 **w.** they had taken security of Jason,
Ac 17:13 But **w.** the Jews of Thessalonica *5613*
Ac 17:16 **w.** he saw the city wholly given to
Ac 17:32 **w.** they heard of the resurrection of
Ac 18:5 **w.** Silas and Timotheus were come *5613*
Ac 18:6 **w.** they opposed themselves, and
Ac 18:12 **w.** Gallio was the deputy of Achaia,
Ac 18:14 **w.** Paul was now about to open his
Ac 18:20 **W.** they desired him to tarry longer
Ac 18:22 **w.** he had landed at Caesarea, and
Ac 18:26 **w.** Aquila and Priscilla had heard,
Ac 18:27 **w.** he was disposed to pass into
Ac 18:27 **w.** he was come, helped them much
Ac 19:5 **W.** they heard this, they were baptized
Ac 19:6 **w.** Paul had laid his hands upon them,
Ac 19:9 But **w.** divers were hardened, and *5613*
Ac 19:21 **w.** he had passed through Macedonia
Ac 19:28 And **w.** they heard these sayings, they
Ac 19:30 **w.** Paul would have entered in unto
Ac 19:34 But **w.** they knew that he was a Jew,
Ac 19:35 **w.** the townclerk had appeased the
Ac 19:41 **w.** he had thus spoken, he dismissed
Ac 20:2 **w.** he had gone over those parts, and
Ac 20:3 **w.** the Jews laid wait for him, as he
Ac 20:7 **w.** the disciples came together to
Ac 20:11 **W.** he therefore was come again, and
Ac 20:14 And **w.** he met with us at Assos, *5613*
Ac 20:18 **w.** they were come to him, he said *5613*
Ac 20:36 **w.** he had thus spoken, he kneeled,
Ac 21:3 Now **w.** we had discovered Cyprus, we
Ac 21:5 **w.** we had accomplished those *3753*
Ac 21:6 **w.** we had taken our leave one of
Ac 21:7 **w.** we had finished our course from
Ac 21:11 **w.** he was come unto us, he took Paul's
Ac 21:12 **w.** we heard these things, both we, *5613*
Ac 21:14 **w.** he would not be persuaded, we
Ac 21:17 **w.** we were come to Jerusalem, the
Ac 21:19 **w.** he had saluted them, he declared
Ac 21:20 **w.** they heard it, they glorified the
Ac 21:27 And **w.** the seven days were almost *5613*
Ac 21:27 **w.** they saw him in the temple, stirred
Ac 21:32 **w.** they saw the chief captain and the
Ac 21:34 **w.** he could not know the certainty for
Ac 21:35 **w.** he came upon the stairs, so it *3753*
Ac 21:40 **w.** he had given him licence, Paul
Ac 21:40 **w.** there was made a great silence, he
Ac 22:2 **w.** they heard that he spake in the
Ac 22:11 **w.** I could not see for the glory of *5613*
Ac 22:17 **w.** I was come again to Jerusalem,
Ac 22:20 And **w.** the blood of thy martyr *3753*
Ac 22:26 **W.** the centurion heard that, he went
Ac 23:6 **w.** Paul perceived that the one part
Ac 23:7 **w.** he had so said, there arose a
Ac 23:10 **w.** there arose a great dissension, the
Ac 23:12 **w.** it was day, certain of the Jews
Ac 23:16 **w.** Paul's sister's son heard of their
Ac 23:28 **w.** I would have known the cause
Ac 23:30 **w.** it was told me how that the Jews
Ac 23:33 Who, **w.** they came to Caesarea, and
Ac 23:34 **w.** the governor had read the letter,
Ac 23:34 **w.** he understood that he was of
Ac 23:35 **w.** thine accusers are also come *3752*
Ac 24:2 **w.** he was called forth, Tertullus
Ac 24:22 **w.** Felix heard these things, having
Ac 24:22 **W.** Lysias the chief captain shall *3752*
Ac 24:24 **w.** Felix came with his wife Drusilla,
Ac 24:25 **w.** I have a convenient season, I will
Ac 25:1 **w.** Festus was come into the province,
Ac 25:6 **w.** he had tarried among them more
Ac 25:7 **w.** he was come, the Jews which came
Ac 25:12 **w.** he had conferred with the council,
Ac 25:14 **w.** they had been there many *5613*
Ac 25:15 About whom, **w.** I was at Jerusalem,
Ac 25:17 **w.** they were come hither, without
Ac 25:18 Against whom **w.** the accusers stood
Ac 25:21 **w.** Paul had appealed to be reserved
Ac 25:23 **w.** Agrippa was come, and Bernice,
Ac 25:25 **w.** I found that he had committed
Ac 26:10 **w.** they were put to death, I gave my
Ac 26:14 **w.** we were all fallen to the earth, I

Ac 26:30 **w.** he had thus spoken, the king rose
Ac 26:31 **w.** they were gone aside, they talked
Ac 27:1 **w.** it was determined that we *5613*
Ac 27:4 **w.** we had launched from thence, we
Ac 27:5 **w.** we had sailed over the sea of
Ac 27:7 **w.** we had sailed slowly many days,
Ac 27:9 Now **w.** much time was spent, and
Ac 27:9 **w.** sailing was now dangerous,
Ac 27:13 **w.** the south wind blew softly,
Ac 27:15 **w.** the ship was caught, and could not
Ac 27:17 **w.** they had taken up, they used helps,
Ac 27:20 **w.** neither sun nor stars in many days
Ac 27:27 **w.** the fourteenth night was come, *5613*
Ac 27:28 **w.** they had gone a little further, they
Ac 27:30 **w.** they had let down the boat into the
Ac 27:35 And **w.** he had thus spoken, he took
Ac 27:35 **w.** he had broken it, he began to eat.
Ac 27:38 **w.** they had eaten enough, they
Ac 27:39 **w.** it was day, they knew not the *3753*
Ac 27:40 **w.** they had taken up the anchors, they
Ac 28:1 **w.** they were escaped, then they knew
Ac 28:3 **w.** Paul had gathered a bundle of
Ac 28:4 And **w.** the barbarians saw the *5613*
Ac 28:6 they looked **w.** he should have swollen,
Ac 28:9 So **w.** this was done, others also,
Ac 28:10 **w.** we departed, they laded us with
Ac 28:15 **w.** the brethren heard of us, they came
Ac 28:15 **w.** Paul saw, he thanked God, and
Ac 28:16 And **w.** we came to Rome, the *3753*
Ac 28:17 **w.** they were come together, he said
Ac 28:18 Who, **w.** they had examined me,
Ac 28:19 **w.** the Jews spake against it, I was
Ac 28:23 **w.** they had appointed him a day,
Ac 28:25 And **w.** they agreed not among
Ac 28:29 **w.** he had said these words, the Jews
Ro 1:21 **w.** they knew God, they glorified him
Ro 2:14 For **w.** the Gentiles, which have *3752*
Ro 2:16 In the day **w.** God shall judge the *3753*
Ro 3:4 overcome **w.** thou art judged *1723,3588*
Ro 4:10 **w.** he was in circumcision, or in
Ro 4:19 **w.** he was about an hundred years
Ro 5:6 **w.** were yet without strength, in
Ro 5:10 if, **w.** were enemies, we were
Ro 5:13 sin is not imputed **w.** there is no law.
Ro 6:20 For **w.** ye were the servants of sin, *3753*
Ro 7:5 For **w.** we were in the flesh, the *3753*
Ro 7:9 but **w.** the commandment came, sin
Ro 7:21 **w.** I would do good, evil is present
Ro 9:10 **w.** Rebecca also had conceived by one,
Ro 11:27 **w.** I shall take away their sins. *3752*
Ro 13:11 nearer than **w.** we believed. *3753*
Ro 15:28 **W.** therefore I have performed this,
Ro 15:29 **w.** I come unto you, I shall come in the
1Co 2:1 And I, brethren, **w.** I came to you,
1Co 5:4 **w.** ye are gathered together, and my
1Co 8:12 **w.** ye so sin against the brethren, and
1Co 9:18 **w.** I preach the gospel, I may make
1Co 9:27 **w.** I have preached to others, I myself
1Co 11:18 **w.** ye come together in the church, I
1Co 11:20 **W.** ye come together therefore into
1Co 11:24 **w.** he had given thanks, he brake it,
1Co 11:25 he took the cup, **w.** he had supped, *3326*
1Co 11:32 But **w.** we are judged, we are
1Co 11:33 **w.** ye come together to eat, tarry one
1Co 11:34 rest will I set in order **w.** I come. *5613*
1Co 13:10 **w.** that which is perfect is come, *3752*
1Co 13:11 **W.** I was a child, I spake as a child, *3753*
1Co 13:11 **w.** I became a man, I put away *3753*
1Co 14:16 **w.** thou shalt bless with the spirit, *1437*
1Co 14:26 **w.** ye come together, every one of *3752*
1Co 15:24 **w.** he shall have delivered up the *3752*
1Co 15:24 **w.** he shall have put down all rule, *3752*
1Co 15:27 **w.** he saith all things are put under *3752*
1Co 15:28 **w.** all things shall be subdued unto *3752*
1Co 15:54 So **w.** this corruptible shall have *3752*
1Co 16:2 there be no gatherings **w.** I come *3752*
1Co 16:3 **w.** I come, whomsoever ye shall *3752*
1Co 16:5 **w.** I shall pass through Macedonia: *3752*
1Co 16:12 **w.** he shall have convenient time *3752*
2Co 1:17 **W.** I therefore was thus minded, I did
2Co 2:3 lest, **w.** I came, I should have sorrow
2Co 2:12 **w.** I came to Troas to preach Christ's
2Co 3:15 **w.** Moses is read, the vail is upon *2259*
2Co 3:16 **w.** it shall turn to the Lord, *2259*
2Co 7:5 **w.** we were come into Macedonia, our
2Co 7:7 **w.** he told us your earnest desire,

2Co 10:2 I may not be bold **w.** I am present
2Co 10:6 **w.** your obedience is fulfilled. *3752*
2Co 10:11 in word by letters **w.** we are absent,
2Co 10:11 we be also in deed **w.** we are present.
2Co 10:15 **w.** your faith is increased, that we
2Co 11:9 And **w.** I was present with you, and
2Co 12:10 **w.** I am weak, then am I strong. *3752*
2Co 12:20 **w.** I come, I shall not find you such as
2Co 12:21 **w.** I come again, my God will humble
2Co 13:9 For we are glad, **w.** we are weak, *3752*
Ga 1:15 But **w.** it pleased God, who *3753*
Ga 2:7 **w.** they saw that the gospel of the
Ga 2:9 And **w.** James, Cephas, and John, who
Ga 2:11 **w.** Peter was come to Antioch, I *3753*
Ga 2:12 **w.** they were come, he withdrew *3753*
Ga 2:14 But **w.** I saw that they walked not *3753*
Ga 4:3 so we, **w.** we were children, were in 3753
Ga 4:4 But **w.** the fulness of the time was *3753*
Ga 4:8 **w.** ye knew not God, ye did service
Ga 4:18 and not only **w.** I am present *1722,3588*
Ga 6:3 to be something, **w.** he is nothing,
Eph 1:20 **w.** he raised him from the dead, and
Eph 2:5 Even **w.** we were dead in sins, hath
Eph 3:4 **w.** ye read, ye may understand my
Eph 4:8 **W.** he ascended up on high, he led
Php 2:19 good comfort, **w.** I know your state
Php 2:28 **w.** ye see him again, ye may rejoice,
Php 4:15 **w.** I departed from Macedonia, no *3753*
Col 3:4 **W.** Christ, who is our life, shall *3752*
Col 3:7 some time, **w.** ye lived in them. *3753*
Col 4:16 **w.** this epistle is read among you, *3752*
1Th 2:6 **w.** we might have been burdensome,
1Th 2:13 **w.** ye received the word of God which
1Th 3:1 **w.** we could no longer forbear, we
1Th 3:4 **w.** we were with you, we told you *3753*
1Th 3:5 **w.** I could no longer forbear, I sent
1Th 3:6 **w.** Timotheus came from you unto us,
1Th 5:3 For **w.** they shall say, Peace and *3752*
2Th 1:7 **w.** the Lord Jesus shall be *1722,3739*
2Th 1:10 **W.** he shall come to be glorified *3752*
2Th 2:5 **w.** I was yet with you, I told ye these
2Th 3:10 even **w.** we were with you, this we *3753*
1Ti 1:3 **w.** I went into Macedonia, that thou
1Ti 5:11 for **w.** they have begun to wax *3752*
2Ti *subscr.* **w.** Paul was brought before Nero *3753*
2Ti 1:5 **W.** I call to remembrance the
2Ti 1:17 But **w.** he was in Rome, he sought me
2Ti 4:3 **w.** they will not endure sound *3753*
2Ti 4:13 **w.** thou comest, bring with thee, and
Tit 3:12 **W.** I shall send Artemas unto *3752*
Heb 1:3 **w.** he had by himself purged our sins,
Heb 1:6 **w.** he bringeth in the firstbegotten *3752*
Heb 3:9 **W.** your fathers tempted me, *3756*
Heb 3:16 some, **w.** they had heard, did provoke:
Heb 5:7 **w.** he had offered up prayers and
Heb 5:12 For **w.** for the time ye ought to be
Heb 6:13 **w.** God made promise to Abraham,
Heb 7:10 father, **w.** Melchisedec met him. *3753*
Heb 7:27 he did once, **w.** he offered up himself
Heb 8:5 of God **w.** he was about to make the
Heb 8:8 **w.** I will make a new covenant with
Heb 8:9 **w.** I took them by the hand to lead
Heb 9:6 **w.** these things were thus ordained,
Heb 9:19 **w.** Moses had spoken every precept to
Heb 10:5 **w.** he cometh into the world, he saith,
Heb 10:8 **w.** he said, Sacrifice and offering and
Heb 11:8 **w.** he was called to go out into a place
Heb 11:11 of a child **w.** she was passed age,
Heb 11:17 Abraham, **w.** he was tried, offered
Heb 11:21 **w.** he was a dying, blessed both the
Heb 11:22 By faith Joseph, **w.** he died, made
Heb 11:23 Moses, **w.** he was born, was hid three
Heb 11:24 Moses, **w.** he was come to years,
Heb 11:31 **w.** she had received the spies with
Heb 12:5 nor faint **w.** thou art rebuked of him:
Heb 12:17 **w.** he would have inherited the
Jas 1:2 **w.** ye fall into divers temptations; *3752*
Jas 1:12 **w.** he is tried, he shall receive the
Jas 1:13 Let no man say **w.** he is tempted,
Jas 1:14 **w.** he is drawn away of his own lust,
Jas 1:15 **w.** lust hath conceived, it bringeth
Jas 1:15 sin, **w.** it is finished, bringeth forth
Jas 2:21 **w.** he had offered Isaac his son upon
Jas 2:25 **w.** she had received the messengers,
1Pe 1:11 **w.** it testified beforehand the
1Pe 2:20 **w.** ye be buffeted for your faults, ye

1Pe	2:20	**w.** ye do well, and suffer for it, ye take	
1Pe	2:23	**w.** he was reviled, reviled not again;	
1Pe	2:23	**w.** he suffered, he threatened not; but	
1Pe	3:20	**w.** once the longsuffering of God	*3753*
1Pe	4:3	**w.** we walked in lasciviousness, lusts,	
1Pe	4:13	**w.** his glory shall be revealed,	*1722,3588*
1Pe	5:4	**w.** the chief Shepherd shall appear,	
2Pe	1:16	**w.** we made known unto you the power	
2Pe	1:17	**w.** there came such a voice to him	
2Pe	1:18	**w.** we were with him in the holy	
2Pe	2:18	**w.** they speak great swelling words of	
1Jo	2:28	**w.** he shall appear, we may have	*3752*
1Jo	3:2	**w.** he shall appear, we shall be like	*1437*
1Jo	5:2	**w.** we love God, and keep his	*3752*
3Jo	3	**w.** the brethren came and testified of	
Jude	3	**w.** I gave all diligence to write unto	
Jude	9	**w.** contending with the devil he	*3753*
Jude	12	**w.** they feast with you, feeding	
Re	1:17	**w.** I saw him, I fell at his feet as	*3753*
Re	4:9	**w.** those beasts give glory and	*3752*
Re	5:8	And **w.** he had taken the book, the	*3753*
Re	6:1	I saw **w.** the Lamb opened one of	*3753*
Re	6:3	**w.** he had opened the second seal, I	*3753*
Re	6:5	**w.** he had opened the third seal, I	*3753*
Re	6:7	**w.** he had opened the fourth seal, I	*3753*
Re	6:9	**w.** he had opened the fifth seal, I	*3753*
Re	6:12	**w.** he had opened the sixth seal,	*3753*
Re	6:13	**w.** she is shaken of a mighty wind	
Re	6:14	as a scroll **w.** it is rolled together;	
Re	8:1	**w.** he had opened the seventh seal,	*3753*
Re	9:5	scorpion, **w.** he striketh a man.	*3752*
Re	10:3	a loud voice, as **w.** a lion roareth:	
Re	10:3	**w.** he had cried, seven thunders	*3753*
Re	10:4	And **w.** the seven thunders had	*3753*
Re	10:7	**w.** he shall begin to sound, the	*3752*
Re	11:7	**w.** they shall have finished their	*3752*
Re	12:13	**w.** the dragon saw that he was	*3753*
Re	17:6	**w.** I saw her, I wondered with great	
Re	17:8	**w.** they behold the beast that was, and	
Re	17:10	**w.** he cometh, he must continue a	*3752*
Re	18:9	**w.** they shall see the smoke of their	*3752*
Re	18:18	**w.** they saw the smoke of her burning,	
Re	20:7	**w.** the thousand years are expired,	*3752*
Re	22:8	And **w.** I had heard and seen, I fell	*3753*

WHENCE

Ge	3:23	ground from **w.** he was taken.	834,8033
Ge	16:8	Sarai's maid, **w.** comest thou?	335,2088
Ge	24:5	the land from **w.** thou camest?	834,8033
Ge	29:4	unto them, My brethren, **w.** be ye?	370
Ge	42:7	he said unto them, **W.** come ye?	370
Nu	11:13	**W.** should I have flesh to give unto	370
Nu	23:13	**w.** thou mayest see them:	834,8033
De	9:28	land **w.** thou broughtest us out	834,8033
De	11:10	Egypt, from **w.** ye came out,	834,8033
Jos	2:4	me, but I wist not **w.** they were:	370
Jos	9:8	Who are ye? and from **w.** come ye?	370
Jos	20:6	unto the city from **w.** he fled.	834,8033
Jg	13:6	but I asked him not **w.** he was,	335,2088
Jg	17:9	said unto him, **W.** comest thou?	370
Jg	19:17	goest thou? and **w.** comest thou?	370
1Sa	25:11	whom I know not **w.** they be?	834,2088
1Sa	30:13	belongest thou?...**w.** art thou?	335,2088
2Sa	1:3	unto him, From **w.** comest thou?	335,2088
2Sa	1:13	man that told him, **W.** art thou?	335,2088
2Ki	5:25	him, **W.** comest thou, Gehazi?	370
2Ki	6:27	not help thee, **w.** shall I help thee?	370
2Ki	20:14	and from **w.** came they unto thee?	370
Ne	4:12	From all places **w.** ye shall return	834
Job	1:7	said unto Satan, **W.** comest thou?	370
Job	2:2	unto Satan, From **w.** comest	335,2088
Job	10:21	Before I go **w.** I shall not return,	
Job	16:22	go the way **w.** I shall not return	
Job	28:20	**W.** then cometh wisdom? and	370
Ps	121:1	the hills, from **w.** cometh my help	370
Ec	1:7	the place from **w.** the rivers come,	
Isa	30:6	**w.** come the young and the old lion,	1992
Isa	39:3	and from **w.** came they unto thee?	370
Isa	47:11	shalt not know from **w.** it riseth:	
Isa	51:1	look unto the rock **w.** ye are hewn,	
Isa	51:1	the hole of the pit **w.** ye are digged	
Jer	29:14	**w.** I caused you to be carried	834,8033
Jon	1:8	and **w.** comest thou? what is thy	370
Na	3:7	**w.** shall I seek comforters for thee?	370
Mt	12:44	**my house from w. I came out;**	*3606*
Mt	13:27	**thy field? from w. hath it tares?**	*4159*
Mt	13:54	**W.** hath this man this wisdom,	*4159*
Mt	13:56	**W.** then hath this man all these	*4159*
Mt	15:33	**W.** should we have so much bread	*4159*
Mt	21:25	**The baptism of John, w. was it?**	*4159*
Mk	6:2	**w.** hath this man these things?	*4159*
Mk	8:4	**w.** can a man satisfy these men	*4159*
Mk	12:37	**Lord; and w. is he then his son?**	*4159*
Lu	1:43	And **w.** is this to me, that the	*4159*
Lu	11:24	**unto my house w. I came out.**	*3606*
Lu	13:25	**you, I know you not w. ye are:**	*4159*
Lu	13:27	**tell you, I know you not w. ye are;**	*4159*
Lu	20:7	that they could not tell **w.** it was	*4159*
Joh	1:48	unto him, **W.** knowest thou me?	*4159*
Joh	2:9	wine, and knew not **w.** it was:	*4159*
Joh	3:8	**but canst not tell w. it cometh,**	*4159*
Joh	4:11	**w.** then hast thou that living water?	*4159*
Joh	6:5	**W. shall we buy bread, that these**	*4159*
Joh	7:27	Howbeit we know this man **w.** he is:	*4159*
Joh	7:27	cometh, no man knoweth **w.** he is.	*4159*
Joh	7:28	**know me, and ye know w. I am:**	*4159*
Joh	8:14	**for I know w. I came, and whither**	*4159*
Joh	8:14	**ye cannot tell w. I come, and**	*4159*
Joh	9:29	fellow, we know not from **w.** he is.	*4159*
Joh	9:30	that ye know not from **w.** he is,	*4159*
Joh	19:9	saith unto Jesus, **W.** art thou?	*4159*
Ac	14:26	to Antioch, from **w.** they had been	*3606*
Php	3:20	**w.** also we look for the Saviour,	*3739*
Heb	11:15	country from **w.** they came out,	*3739*
Heb	11:19	from **w.** also he received him in a	*3606*
Jas	4:1	**w.** come wars and fightings	*4159*
Re	2:5	**therefore from w. thou art fallen,**	*4159*
Re	7:13	in white robes? and **w.** came they?	*4159*

WHENSOEVER

Ge	30:41	**w.** the stronger cattle did conceive,	3605
Mk	14:7	**w. ye will ye may do them good:**	*3752*
Ro	15:24	**W.** I take my journey into	*5613,1437*

WHERE See also WHEREABOUT; WHEREAS; WHEREBY; WHEREFORE; WHEREIN; WHEREINSOEVER; WHEREINTO; WHEREOF; WHEREON; WHERESOVER; WHERETO; WHEREUNTO; WHEREUPON; WHEREWITH; WHEREWITHAL.

Ge	2:11	of Havilah, **w.** there is gold:	834,8033
Ge	3:9	and said unto him, **W.** art thou?	335
Ge	4:9	unto Cain, **W.** is Abel thy brother?	335
Ge	13:3	place **w.** his tent had been at the	834
Ge	13:10	that it was well watered every **w.**,	
Ge	13:14	look from the place **w.** thou art	834,8033
Ge	18:9	unto him, **W.** is Sarah thy wife?	346
Ge	19:5	**W.** are the men which came in to	346
Ge	19:27	place **w.** he stood before the Lord:	834
Ge	20:15	before thee: dwell **w.** it pleaseth thee.	
Ge	21:17	the voice of the lad **w.** he is.	834
Ge	22:7	**w.** is the lamb for a burnt offering?	346
Ge	27:33	**w.** is he that hath taken venison,	645
Ge	31:13	Bethel, **w.**...anointedst the pillar,	834
Ge	31:13	**w.** thou vowedst a vow unto me:	834
Ge	33:19	field, **w.** he had spread his tent,	834
Ge	35:13	in the place **w.** he talked with him.	834
Ge	35:14	in the place **w.** he talked with him,	
Ge	35:15	the place **w.** God spake with him,	834
Ge	35:27	**w.** Abraham and Isaac sojourned.	834
Ge	37:16	I pray thee, **w.** they feed their flocks.	375
Ge	38:21	**W.** is the harlot, that was openly	346
Ge	39:20	**w.** the king's prisoners were bound:	834
Ge	40:3	the place **w.** Joseph was bound	834
Ge	43:30	and he sought **w.** to weep; and he	
Ex	2:20	**w.** is he? why is it that ye have	346
Ex	5:11	ye, get you straw **w.** ye can find it:	834
Ex	9:26	Goshen, **w.** the children. . .were,	834,8033
Ex	12:13	a token upon the houses **w.** ye are:	834
Ex	12:30	a house **w.** there was not one dead	834
Ex	15:27	**w.** were twelve wells of water,	8033
Ex	18:5	**w.** he encamped at the mount	834,8033
Ex	20:21	the thick darkness **w.** God was.	834,8033
Ex	20:24	**w.** I record my name I will come	834
Ex	27:18	cubits, and the breadth fifty every **w.**,	
Ex	29:42	**w.** I will meet you, to speak	834,8033
Ex	30:6	**w.** I will meet with thee.	834,8033
Ex	30:36	**w.** I will meet with thee: it	834,8033
Le	4:12	place, **w.** the ashes are poured out;	413
Le	4:12	**w.** the ashes are poured out shall	5921
Le	4:24	in the place **w.** they kill the burnt	834
Le	4:33	**w.** they kill the burnt offering	834
Le	6:25	place **w.** the burn offering is killed.	834
Le	7:2	place **w.** they kill the burnt offering	834
Le	14:13	place **w.** he shall kill the sin offering	834
Nu	9:17	in the place **w.** the cloud abode,	834
Nu	13:22	**w.** Ahiman, Sheshai, and Talmai,	8033
Nu	17:4	**w.** I will meet with you.	834,8033
Nu	22:26	**w.** was no way to turn either to the	834
Nu	33:14	**w.** was no water for the people to	8033
Nu	33:54	place **w.** his lot falleth;	413,834,8033
De	1:31	**w.** thou hast seen how that the	834
De	8:15	drought, **w.** there was no water;	834
De	11:10	**w.** thou sowedst thy seed, and	834
De	11:30	by the way **w.** the sun goeth down, in	
De	18:6	of all Israel, **w.** he sojourned,	834,8033
De	23:16	one of thy gates, **w.** it liketh him best:	
De	32:37	**W.** are their gods, their rocks in	335
Jos	4:3	place **w.** the priests' feet stood firm,	
Jos	4:3	place, **w.** ye shall lodge this night.	834
Jos	4:8	unto the place **w.** they lodged,	413
Jos	4:9	in the place **w.** the feet of the priests	
Jg	5:27	**w.** he bowed, there he fell down	834
Jg	6:13	**w.** be all his miracles which our	346
Jg	9:38	**W.** is now thy mouth, wherewith	346
Jg	17:8	to sojourn **w.** he could find a place:	834
Jg	17:9	to sojourn **w.** I could find a place.	834
Jg	18:10	**w.** there is no want of any thing.	834
Jg	19:26	man's house **w.** her lord was,	834,8033
Jg	20:22	**w.** they put themselves in array	834,8033
Ru	1:7	out of the place **w.** she was,	834,8033
Ru	1:16	and **w.** thou lodgest, I will lodge:	834
Ru	1:17	**W.** thou diest, will I die, and there	834
Ru	2:19	her, **W.** hast thou gleaned to day?	645
Ru	2:19	**w.** wroughtest thou? blessed be he	375
Ru	3:4	mark the place **w.** he shall lie,	834,8033
1Sa	3:3	**w.** the ark of God was, and	834,8033
1Sa	6:14	there, **w.** there was a great stone:	8033
1Sa	9:10	city **w.** the man of God was.	834,8033
1Sa	9:18	thee, **w.** the seer's house is.	335,2088
1Sa	10:5	God, **w.** is the garrison of the	834,8033
1Sa	10:14	when we saw that they were no **w.**	370
1Sa	14:11	out of the holes **w.** they hid	834,8033
1Sa	19:3	my father in the field **w.** thou art,	834
1Sa	19:22	said, **W.** are Samuel and David?	375
1Sa	20:19	to the place **w.** thou didst hide	834,8033
1Sa	23:22	and see his place **w.** his haunt is,	834
1Sa	23:23	lurking places **w.** he hideth	834,8033
1Sa	24:3	by the way, **w.** was a cave; and Saul	8033
1Sa	26:5	the place **w.** Saul had pitched:	834,8033
1Sa	26:5	David beheld the place **w.** Saul	834,8033
1Sa	26:16	And now see **w.** the king's spear is,	335
1Sa	30:9	Besor, **w.** those that were left behind	
1Sa	30:31	places **w.** David himself and	834,8033
2Sa	2:23	to the place **w.** Asahel fell down	834,8033
2Sa	9:4	the king said unto him, **W.** is he?	375
2Sa	11:16	**w.** he knew that valiant men were	834
2Sa	15:32	the mount, **w.** he worshipped	834,8033
2Sa	16:3	said, And **w.** is thy master's son?	346
2Sa	17:12	place **w.** he shall be found,	834,8033
2Sa	17:20	said, **W.** is Ahimaaz and Jonathan?	346
2Sa	18:7	**W.** the people of Israel were slain	8033
2Sa	21:12	**w.** the Philistines had hanged	834,8033
2Sa	21:19	**w.** Elhanan the son of Jaare-oregim,	
2Sa	21:20	**w.** was a man of great stature, that	
2Sa	23:11	**w.** was a piece of ground full of	8033
1Ki	4:28	the place **w.** the officers were,	834,8033
1Ki	7:7	the throne **w.** he might judge,	834,8033
1Ki	7:8	his house **w.** he dwelt had	834,8033
1Ki	13:25	in the city **w.** the old prophet dwelt.	834
1Ki	17:19	him up into a loft **w.** he abode,	834,8033
1Ki	21:19	**w.** dogs licked the blood of Naboth	834
2Ki	2:14	said, **W.** is the Lord God of Elijah?	346
2Ki	4:8	Shunem, **w.** was a great woman;	8033
2Ki	6:1	**w.** we dwelt with thee is too	834,8033
2Ki	6:2	a place there, **w.** we may dwell.	8033
2Ki	6:6	the man of God said, **W.** fell it?	575
2Ki	6:13	Go and spy **w.** he is, that I may	351
2Ki	18:34	**W.** are the gods of Hamath, and	346
2Ki	18:34	**w.** are the gods of Sepharvaim,	346
2Ki	19:13	**W.** is the king of Hamath, and the	346
2Ki	23:7	**w.** the women wove hangings	834,8033
2Ki	23:8	**w.** the priests had burned	834,8033
1Ch	11:4	is Jebus; **w.** the Jebusites were,	8033
1Ch	11:13	**w.** was a parcel of ground full of	
1Ch	13:2	abroad unto our brethren every **w.**,	
1Ch	20:6	Gath, **w.** was a man of great stature,	
2Ch	3:1	**w.** the Lord appeared unto David	834
2Ch	25:4	of Moses, **w.** the Lord commanded,	834
2Ch	36:20	**w.** they were servants to him and his	
Ezr	1:4	in any place **w.** he sojourneth,	834,8033
Ezr	6:1	**w.** the treasures were laid up in	8536

Ezr 6:3 the place w. they offered sacrifices,.... 1768
Ne 10:39 w. are the vessels of the sanctuary, ... 8033
Ne 13:5 w. aforetime they laid the meat 8033
Es 1:6 W. were white, green, and blue..............
Es 7:5 Who is he, and w. is he, that durst...... 335
Job 4:7 or w. were the righteous cut off? 375
Job 9:24 thereof; if not, w., and who is he?....... 645
Job 10:22 order, and w. the light is as darkness. ......
Job 12:24 in a wilderness w. there is no way. ....
Job 14:10 giveth up the ghost, and w. is he? 346
Job 15:23 abroad for bread, saying, W. is it? 346
Job 17:15 w. is now my hope? as for my 346,645
Job 20:7 have seen him shall say, W. is he? 335
Job 21:28 say, W. is the house of the prince?...... 346
Job 21:28 w. are the dwelling places of the 346
Job 23:3 Oh that I knew w. I might find him!..........
Job 23:9 w. he doth work, but I cannot behold........
Job 28:1 and a place for gold w. they fine it. ....
Job 28:12 But w. shall wisdom be found?........... 370
Job 28:12 and w. is...understanding?........... 335,2088
Job 28:20 w. is the place of understanding? 335
Job 34:22 w. the workers of iniquity may 8033
Job 35:10 W. is God my maker, who giveth 335
Job 36:16 broad place, w. there is no straitness:.......
Job 38:4 W. wast thou when I laid the............. 375
Job 38:19 W. is the way w. light dwelleth? 335
Job 38:19 darkness, w. is the place thereof, ... 335
Job 38:26 it to rain on the earth, w. no man is;........
Job 39:30 and w. the slain are, there is she. 834
Job 40:20 w. all the beasts of the field play.......... 8033
Ps 19:3 language, w. their voice is not heard.........
Ps 26:8 the place w. thine honour dwelleth. ....
Ps 42:3 say unto me, W. is thy God?.............. 346
Ps 42:10 say daily unto me, W. is thy God? 346
Ps 53:5 there in great fear, w. no fear was: ....
Ps 63:1 a dry and thirsty land, w. no water is; ......
Ps 69:2 in deep mire, w. there is no standing: ....
Ps 69:2 deep waters, w. the floods overflow me. ...
Ps 79:10 W. is their God? let him be known 346
Ps 81:5 w. I heard a language that I ....
Ps 84:3 herself, w. she may lay her young, ... 834
Ps 89:49 w. are thy former lovingkindnesses, ... 346
Ps 104:17 W. the birds make their nests:..... 834,8033
Ps 107:40 the wilderness, w. there is no way. ....
Ps 115:2 heathen say, W. is now their God? 346
Pr 11:14 W. no counsel is, the people fall: but ....
Pr 14:4 W. no oxen are, the crib is clean: but.......
Pr 15:17 is a dinner of herbs w. love is, ... 8033
Pr 26:20 W. no wood is, the fire goeth out: 657
Pr 26:20 w. there is no talebearer, the strife ....
Pr 29:18 W. there is no vision the people ....
Ec 1:5 hasteth to his place w. he arose......... 8033
Ec 8:4 W. the word of a king is, there is........ 834
Ec 8:10 in the city w. they had so done: 834
Ec 11:3 place w. the tree falleth, there it shall.......
Ca 1:7 w. thou feedest, w. thou makest 349
Isa 7:23 w. there were a thousand vines at 834
Isa 10:3 and w. will ye leave your glory? 575
Isa 19:12 W. are they?...thy wise men?............ 335
Isa 19:12 w. are thy wise men? and let them 645
Isa 29:1 to Ariel, the city w. David dwelt! ....
Isa 30:32 w. the grounded staff shall pass; ....
Isa 33:18 W. is the scribe? w. is the receiver?.... 346
Isa 33:18 w. is he that counted the towers?........ 346
Isa 35:7 the habitation of dragons, w. each lay,.......
Isa 36:19 W. are the gods of Hamath and........... 346
Isa 36:19 w. are the gods of Sepharvaim?........... 346
Isa 37:13 W. is the king of Hamath, and the 346
Isa 49:21 left alone; these, w. had they been? 375
Isa 50:1 W. is the bill of your mother's 335
Isa 51:13 and w. is the fury of the oppressor? 346
Isa 57:8 lovedst their bed w. thou sawest it..... 3027
Isa 63:11 W. is he that brought them up out....... 346
Isa 63:11 w. is he that put his holy Spirit 346
Isa 63:15 w. is thy zeal and thy strength, the...... 346
Isa 64:11 house w. our fathers praised thee, ... 834
Isa 66:1 w. is the house that ye build unto........ 335
Isa 66:1 and w. is the place of my rest? 335
Jer 2:6 W. is the Lord that brought us up 346
Jer 2:6 through, and w. no man dwelt?.......... 8033
Jer 2:8 priests said not, W. is the Lord? 346
Jer 2:28 w. are thy gods that thou hast made 346
Jer 3:2 see w. thou hast not been lien with...... 375
Jer 6:16 paths, w. is the good way, and walk..... 335
Jer 7:12 w. I set my name at the first,...... 834,8033
Jer 13:7 from the place w. I hid it: 834,8033
Jer 13:20 w. is the flock that was given thee,....... 346
Jer 16:13 w. I will not shew you favour............. 834
Jer 17:15 W. is the word of the Lord? let it.......... 346
Jer 22:26 country, w. ye were not born; 834,8033
Jer 35:7 in the land w. ye be strangers. 834,8033
Jer 36:19 and let no man know w. ye be............ 375
Jer 37:19 W. are now your prophets which......... 346
Jer 38:9 die for hunger in the place w. he 8478
Jer 39:5 w. he gave judgment upon him. ....
Jer 42:14 of Egypt, w. we shall see no war, ... 834
Jer 52:9 w. he gave judgment upon him. ....
La 2:12 mothers, W. is corn and wine?............ 346
Eze 3:15 of Chebar, and I sat w. they sat, ... 8033
Eze 6:13 place w. they did offer sweet........ 834,8033
Eze 8:3 w. was the seat of the image of ... 834,8033
Eze 11:16 countries w. they shall come........ 834,8033
Eze 11:17 w. ye have been scattered, and I......... 834
Eze 13:12 W. is the daubing wherewith ye 346
Eze 17:10 wither in the furrows w. it grew. 5921
Eze 17:16 in the place w. the king dwelleth that........
Eze 20:38 out of the country w. they sojourn, ...
Eze 21:30 in the place w. thou wast created, ... 834
Eze 34:12 w. they have been scattered,....... 834,8033
Eze 40:38 w. they washed the burnt offering...... 8033
Eze 42:13 w. the priests that approach........ 834,8033
Eze 43:7 w. I will dwell in the midst of...... 834,8033
Eze 46:20 place w. the priests shall boil....... 834,8033
Eze 46:20 w. they shall bake the meat................ 834
Eze 46:24 w. the ministers of the house........ 834,833
Da 8:17 So he came near w. I stood: and when......
Ho 1:10 the place w. it was said unto them,...... 834
Ho 13:10 w. is any other that may save thee...... 645
Joe 2:17 among the people, W. is their God? 346
Am 3:5 upon the earth, w. no gin is for him? ....
Mic 7:10 unto me, W. is the Lord thy God?....... 346
Na 2:11 W. is the dwelling of the lions, and...... 346
Na 2:11 w. the lion, even the old lion, ... 834,8033
Na 3:17 place is not known w. they are. 335
Zep 3:19 land w. they have been put to shame. ....
Zec 1:5 Your fathers, w. are they? and........... 346
Mal 1:6 I be a father, w. is mine honour?......... 346
Mal 1:6 and if I be a master, w. is my fear? 346
Mal 2:17 or, W. is the God of judgment? 346
Mt 2:2 W. is he that is born King of the *4226*
Mt 2:4 of them w. Christ should be born........ *4226*
Mt 2:9 stood over w. the young child was. *3757*
Mt 6:19 **w. moth and rust doth corrupt,**....... *3699*
Mt 6:19 **w. thieves break through and steal:** *3699*
Mt 6:20 **w. neither moth nor rust doth**...... *3699*
Mt 6:20 **w. thieves do not break through**.... *3699*
Mt 6:21 **w. your treasure is, there will**...... *3699*
Mt 8:20 **man hath not w. to lay his head** .. *4226*
Mt 13:5 **w. they had not much earth:**......... *3699*
Mt 18:20 **For w. two or three are gathered**.. *3757*
Mt 25:24 **reaping w. thou hast not sown,**..... *3699*
Mt 25:24 **and gathering w. thou hast not**...... *3606*
Mt 25:26 **knewest that I reap w. I sowed**....... *3699*
Mt 25:26 **and gather w. I have not strawed:**.. *3606*
Mt 26:17 W. wilt thou that we prepare for........ *4226*
Mt 26:57 w. the scribes and the elders were..... *3699*
Mt 28:6 Come, see the place w. the Lord lay. .. *3699*
Mt 28:16 w. Jesus had appointed them............ *3757*
Mk 2:4 uncovered the roof w. he was: *3699*
Mk 4:5 **ground, w. it had not much earth;** .. *3699*
Mk 4:15 **the way side, w. the word is sown;** .. *3699*
Mk 5:40 and entereth in w. the damsel was *3699*
Mk 6:55 were sick, w. they heard he was. *3699*
Mk 9:44, 46 **W. their worm dieth not, and**.. *3699*
Mk 9:48 **W. their worm dieth not, and**....... *3699*
Mk 11:4 without in a place w. two ways met; *296*
Mk 13:14 **standing w. it ought not, (let him**. *3699*
Mk 14:12 W. wilt thou that we go and............. *4226*
Mk 14:14 **saith, W. is the guestchamber,**...... *4226*
Mk 14:14 **w. I shall eat the passover with**.... *3699*
Mk 15:47 of Joses beheld w. he was laid.......... *4226*
Mk 16:6 behold the place w. they laid him. *3699*
Mk 16:20 went forth, and preached every w., ... *3837*
Lu 4:16 w. he had been brought up: *3757*
Lu 4:17 found the place w. it was written, ... *3757*
Lu 8:25 said unto them, **W. is your faith?**.... *4226*
Lu 9:6 the gospel, and healing every w......... *3837*
Lu 9:58 **man hath not w. to lay his head** *4226*
Lu 10:33 **as he journeyed, came w. he was;**. *2596*
Lu 12:17 **no room w. to bestow my fruits?**... *4226*
Lu 12:33 **w. no thief approacheth, neither**... *3699*
Lu 12:34 **w. your treasure is, there will**...... *3699*
Lu 17:17 **ten cleansed? but w. are the nine?**. *4226*
Lu 17:37 and said unto him, W., Lord? *4226*
Lu 22:9 him, W. wilt thou that we prepare? *4226*
Lu 22:10 **into the house w. he entereth in**.... *3757*
Lu 22:11 **thee, W. is the guestchamber**........ *4226*
Lu 22:11 **w. I shall eat the passover with**.... *3699*
Joh 1:28 Jordan, w. John was baptizing,........... *3699*
Joh 1:38 Master,) w. dwellest thou? *4226*
Joh 1:39 They came and saw w. he dwelt, ... *4226*
Joh 3:8 **The wind bloweth w. it listeth,**...... *3699*
Joh 4:20 the place w. men ought to worship..... *3699*
Joh 4:46 Galilee, w. he made the water wine.... *3699*
Joh 6:23 the place w. they did eat bread,......... *3699*
Joh 6:62 **man ascend up w. he was before?**.. *3699*
Joh 7:11 at the feast, and said, W. is he? *4226*
Joh 7:34 **w. I am, thither ye cannot come** .. *3699*
Joh 7:36 w. I am, thither ye cannot come?....... *3699*
Joh 7:42 town of Bethlehem w. David was?...... *3699*
Joh 8:10 her, **Woman, w. are those thine**.... *4226*
Joh 8:19 said unto him, W. is thy Father?........ *4226*
Joh 9:12 him, W. is he? He said, I know not.... *4226*
Joh 10:40 the place w. John at first baptized; *3699*
Joh 11:6 days still in the same place w. he was.......
Joh 11:30 in that place w. Martha met him. *3699*
Joh 11:32 when Mary was come w. Jesus was,... *3699*
Joh 11:34 And said, **W. have ye laid him?**....... *4226*
Joh 11:41 the place w. the dead was laid,.......... *3757*
Joh 11:57 if any man knew w. he were, he......... *4226*
Joh 12:1 w. Lazarus was which had been......... *3699*
Joh 12:26 **and w. I am, there shall also my**... *3699*
Joh 14:3 **that w. I am, there ye may be**........ *3699*
Joh 17:24 **given me, be with me w. I am:**........ *3699*
Joh 18:1 w. was a garden, into the which he *3699*
Joh 19:18 W. they crucified him, and two.......... *3699*
Joh 19:20 place w. Jesus was crucified was........ *3699*
Joh 19:41 the place w. he was crucified there..... *3699*
Joh 20:2 we know not w. they have laid *4226*
Joh 20:12 feet, w. the body of Jesus had lain. *3699*
Joh 20:13 I know not w. they have laid him. *4226*
Joh 20:15 tell me w. thou hast laid him, and I *4226*
Joh 20:19 w. the disciples were assembled *3699*
Ac 1:13 w. abode both Peter, and James, ... *3757*
Ac 2:2 all the house w. they were sitting. *3757*
Ac 4:31 w. they were assembled............ *1722,3739*
Ac 7:29 of Madian, w. he begat two sons. *3757*
Ac 7:33 w. thou standest is holy *1722,3739*
Ac 8:4 went every w. preaching the word. *1330*
Ac 11:11 come unto the house w. I was,... *1722,3739*
Ac 12:12 w. many were together praying. *3757*
Ac 15:36 city w. we have preached.......... *1722,3739*
Ac 16:13 w. prayer was wont to be made;......... *3757*
Ac 17:1 w. was a synagogue of the Jews: *3699*
Ac 17:30 all men every w. to repent: *3837*
Ac 20:6 days; w. we abode seven days. *3757*
Ac 20:8 w. they were gathered together......... *3757*
Ac 21:28 men every w. against the people,........ *3837*
Ac 25:10 seat, w. I ought to be judged: *3757*
Ac 27:41 falling into a place w. two seas met, ... *1337*
Ac 28:14 W. we found brethren, and were *3757*
Ac 28:22 that every w. it is spoken against....... *3837*
Ro 3:27 W. is boasting then? It is *4226*
Ro 4:15 for w. no law is, there is no............. *3757*
Ro 5:20 But w. sin abounded, grace did.......... *3757*
Ro 9:26 place w. it was said unto them, ... *3757*
Ro 15:20 not w. Christ was named, lest I......... *3699*
1Co 1:20 W. is the wise? w. is the scribe? *4226*
1Co 1:20 w. is the disputer of this world?......... *4226*
1Co 4:17 I teach every w. in every church. *3837*
1Co 12:17 were an eye, w. were the hearing? *4226*
1Co 12:17 hearing, w. were the smelling? *4226*
1Co 12:19 one member, w. were the body?........ *4226*
1Co 15:55 O death, w. is thy sting? O grave, ... *4226*
1Co 15:55 sting? O grave, w. is thy victory? *4226*
2Co 3:17 and w. the Spirit of the Lord is, ... *3757*
Ga 4:15 W. is then the blessedness ye........... *5101*
Php 4:12 every w. and in all things I........ *1722,3956*
Col 3:1 w. Christ sitteth on the right............ *3757*
Col 3:11 W. there is neither Greek nor........... *3699*
1Ti 2:8 that men pray every w., ... *1722,5117*
Heb 9:16 w. a testament is, there must also *3699*
Heb 10:18 w. remission of these is, there is....... *3699*
Jas 3:16 w. envying and strife is, there is....... *3699*
1Pe 4:18 w. shall the ungodly and the............ *4226*
2Pe 3:4 W. is the promise of his coming? *4226*
Re 2:13 **thy works, and w. thou dwellest,**.. *4226*
Re 2:13 **dwellest, even w. Satan's seat is:**.. *3699*

Re 2:13 **among you, w. Satan dwelleth** *3699*
Re 11:8 **w.** also our Lord was crucified *3699*
Re 12:6 **w.** she hath a place prepared of *3699*
Re 12:14 **w.** she is nourished for a time, and *3699*
Re 17:15 **w.** the whore sitteth, are peoples, *3757*
Re 20:10 **w.** the beast and the false prophet *3699*

WHEREABOUT
1Sa 21:2 thing of the business **w.** I send thee, 834

WHEREAS
Ge 31:37 **W.** thou hast searched all my 3588
De 19:6 **w.** he was not worthy of death,
De 28:62 **w.** ye were as the stars of heaven 834
1Sa 24:17 good, **w.** I have rewarded thee evil.
2Sa 7:6 **W.** I have not dwelt in any house 3588
2Sa 15:20 **W.** thou camest but yesterday, should
1Ki 8:18 **W.** it was in thine heart to 3282,834
1Ki 12:11 **w.** my father did lade you with a
2Ki 13:19 **w.** now thou shalt smite Syria but 6258
2Ch 10:11 **w.** my father put a heavy yoke 6258
2Ch 28:13 **w.** we have offended against the 3588
Job 22:20 **W.** our substance is not cut down, 518
Ec 4:14 **w.** also he that is born in his 3588
Isa 37:21 **W.** thou hast prayed to me 834
Isa 60:15 **W.** thou hast been forsaken and 8478
Jer 4:10 **w.** the sword reacheth unto the soul.
Eze 13:7 **W.** ye say, The Lord saith it:
Eze 16:7 **W.** thou wast naked and bare.
Eze 16:34 **w.** none followeth thee to commit
Eze 35:10 possess it; **w.** the Lord was there:
Eze 36:34 **w.** it lay desolate in the sight 8478,834
Da 2:41 **w.** thou sawest the feet and toes, 1768
Da 2:43 **w.** thou sawest iron mixed with 1768
Da 4:23 **w.** the king saw a watcher and an 1768
Da 4:26 **w.** they commanded to leave the 1768
Da 8:22 **w.** four stood up for it, four
Mal 1:4 **W.** Edom saith, We are 3588
Joh 9:25 that, **w.** I was blind, now I see.
1Co 3:3 **w.** there is among you envying, *3699*
Jas 4:14 **W.** ye know not what shall be on *3748*
1Pe 2:12 **w.** they speak against you as *1722,3759*
1Pe 3:16 **w.** they speak evil of you, as of *1722,3759*
2Pe 2:11 **W.** angels, which are greater in *3699*

WHEREBY
Ge 15:8 **w.** shall I know that I shall inherit 4100
Ge 44:5 drinketh, and **w.** indeed he divineth?
Le 22:5 **w.** he may be made unclean, 834
Nu 5:8 **w.** an atonement shall be made for 834
Nu 17:5 **w.** they murmur against you. 834
De 7:19 **w.** the Lord thy God brought thee 834
De 28:20 doings, **w.** thou hast forsaken me. 834
1Sa 20:33 **w.** Jonathan knew that it was
Ps 45:5 **w.** the people fall under thee.
Ps 45:8 **w.** they have made thee glad 4482
Ps 68:9 **w.** thou didst confirm thine
Jer 3:8 **w.** backsliding Israel committed 834
Jer 17:19 **w.** the kings of Judah come in, 834
Jer 23:6 is his name **w.** he shall be called, 834
Jer 33:8 **w.** they have sinned against me; 834
Jer 33:8 iniquities, **w.** they have sinned, 834
Jer 33:8 **w.** they have transgressed against 834
Eze 18:31 **w.** ye have transgressed; and 834
Eze 20:25 judgments **w.** they should not live;
Eze 39:26 **w.** they have trespassed against 834
Eze 40:49 by the steps **w.** they went up to it: 834
Eze 46:9 the way of the gate **w.** he came in, 834
Eze 47:13 border, **w.** ye shall inherit the land 834
Zep 2:8 **w.** they have reproached my people, 834
Lu 1:18 **W.** shall I know this? for I *2596,5101*
Lu 1:78 **w.** the dayspring from on high *1722,3739*
Ac 4:12 men, **w.** we must be saved *1722,3739*
Ac 11:14 **w.** thou and all thy house shall *1722,3739*
Ac 19:40 **w.** we may give an account of *4012,3757*
Ro 8:15 **w.** we cry, Abba, Father. *1722,3739*
Ro 14:21 thing **w.** thy brother stumbleth, *1722,3739*
Eph 3:4 **W.**, when ye read, ye may *4314,3739*
Eph 4:14 **w.** they lie in wait to deceive; *4314*
Eph 4:30 **w.** ye are sealed unto the day *1722,3739*
Php 3:21 **w.** he is able even to subdue all *3588*
Heb 12:28 grace, **w.** we may serve God *1223,3739*
2Pe 1:4 **W.** are given unto us...great *1223,3739*
2Pe 3:6 **W.** the world that then was, *1223,3739*
1Jo 2:18 **w.** we know that it is the last time *3606*

WHEREFORE See also THEREFORE.
Ge 10:9 **w.** it is said, Even as Nimrod 5921,3651
Ge 16:14 **W.** the well was called 5921,3651
Ge 18:13 **W.** did Sarah laugh, saying, Shall 4100
Ge 21:10 **W.** she said unto Abraham, Cast out
Ge 21:31 **W.** he called that place 5921,3651
Ge 24:31 **w.** standest thou without? for I 4100
Ge 26:27 unto them, **W.** come ye to me, 4069
Ge 29:25 **w.** then hast thou beguiled 4100,2063
Ge 31:27 **W.** didst thou flee away secretly, 4100
Ge 31:30 yet, **w.** hast thou stolen my gods? 4100
Ge 32:29 **W.** is it that thou dost ask after my 4100
Ge 38:10 the Lord: **w.** he slew him also.
Ge 40:7 saying, **W.** look ye so sadly to day? 4069
Ge 43:6 **W.** dealt ye so ill with me, as to 4100
Ge 44:4 **W.** have ye rewarded evil for good? 4100
Ge 44:7 him, **W.** saith my lord these words? 4100
Ge 47:19 **W.** shall we die before thine eyes, 4100
Ge 47:22 **w.** they sold not their lands. 5921,3651
Ge 50:11 **w.** the name of it was called 5921,3651
Ex 2:13 wrong, **W.** smitest thou thy fellow? 4100
Ex 5:4 **W.** do ye, Moses and Aaron, let the 4100
Ex 5:14 **W.** have ye not fulfilled your task 4069
Ex 5:15 **W.** dealest thou thus with thy 4100
Ex 5:22 **w.** hast thou so evil entreated this 4100
Ex 6:6 **W.** say unto the children of Israel, 3651
Ex 14:11 **w.** hast thou dealt with us, 4100,2063
Ex 14:15 **W.** criest thou unto me? speak 4100
Ex 17:2 **W.** the people did chide with Moses,
Ex 17:2 with me? **w.** do ye tempt the Lord? 4100
Ex 17:3 **W.** is this that thou hast brought 4100
Ex 20:11 day: **w.** the Lord blessed the 5921,3651
Ex 31:16 **W.** the children of Israel shall keep
Ex 32:12 **W.** should the Egyptians speak, 4100
Le 10:17 **W.** have ye not eaten the sin 4069
Le 13:25 **w.** the priest shall pronounce him
Le 25:18 **W.** ye shall do my statutes, and keep
Nu 9:7 **w.** are we kept back, that we may 4100
Nu 11:11 **W.** hast thou afflicted thy servant? 4100
Nu 11:11 and **w.** have I not found favour in 4100
Nu 12:8 **w.** then were ye not afraid to speak 4069
Nu 14:3 **w.** hath the Lord brought us into 4100
Nu 14:41 **W.** now do ye transgress the 4100
Nu 16:3 **w.** then lift ye up yourselves 4069
Nu 20:5 **w.** have ye made us to come up out 4100
Nu 20:21 **w.** Israel turned away from him.
Nu 21:5 **W.** have ye brought us up out of 4100
Nu 21:14 **W.** it is said in the book of 5921,3651
Nu 21:27 **W.** they that speak in proverbs 5921,3651
Nu 22:32 **W.** hast thou smitten thine ass 4100
Nu 22:37 **w.** camest thou not unto me? am I 4100
Nu 25:12 **W.** say, Behold, I give unto him 3651
Nu 32:5 **W.**, said they, if we have found grace
Nu 32:7 And **w.** discourage ye the heart of 4100
De 7:12 **W.** it shall come to pass, if ye
De 10:9 **W.** Levi hath no part nor 5921,3651
De 19:7 **W.** I command thee, saying, 5921,3651
De 29:24 **W.** hath the Lord done thus 5921,4100
Jos 5:9 **W.** the name of the place is called
Jos 7:5 **w.** the hearts of the people melted,
Jos 7:7 **w.** hast thou at all brought this 4100
Jos 7:10 **w.** liest thou thus upon thy face? 4100
Jos 7:26 **W.** the name of that place 5921,3651
Jos 9:11 **W.** our elders and all the inhabitants
Jos 9:22 **W.** have ye beguiled us, saying, 4100
Jos 10:3 **W.** Adoni-zedec king of Jerusalem
Jg 2:3 **W.** I also said, I will not drive them
Jg 10:13 gods: **w.** I will deliver you no more. 3651
Jg 11:27 **W.** I have not sinned against thee,
Jg 12:1 **W.** passedst thou over to fight 4069
Jg 12:3 **w.** then are ye come up unto me 4100
Jg 15:19 **w.** he called the name thereof 5921,3651
Jg 18:12 **w.** they called that place 5921,3651
Ru 1:7 **W.** she went forth out of the place
1Sa 1:20 **W.** it came to pass, when the time
1Sa 2:17 **W.** the sin of the young men was
1Sa 2:29 **W.** kick ye at my sacrifice and at 4100
1Sa 2:30 **W.** the Lord God of Israel saith, 3651
1Sa 4:3 **W.** hath the Lord smitten us to 4100
1Sa 6:5 **W.** ye shall make images of your
1Sa 6:6 **W.** then do ye harden your hearts, 4100
1Sa 9:21 **w.** then speakest thou so to me? 4100
1Sa 14:27 **W.** he put forth the end of the rod
1Sa 15:19 **W.** then didst thou not obey the 4100
1Sa 16:19 **W.** Saul sent messengers unto Jesse,
1Sa 18:15 **W.** when Saul saw that he behaved
1Sa 18:21 **W.** Saul said to David, Thou shalt this
1Sa 18:27 **W.** David arose and went, he and his
1Sa 19:5 **w.** then wilt thou sin against 4100
1Sa 19:24 **W.** they say, Is Saul also 5921,3651
1Sa 20:27 **W.** cometh not the son of Jesse to 4069
1Sa 20:31 **W.** now send and fetch him unto me,
1Sa 20:32 **W.** shall he be slain? what hath 4100
1Sa 21:14 **w.** then have ye brought him to me? 4100
1Sa 23:25 **w.** he came down into a rock, and
1Sa 23:28 **W.** Saul returned from pursuing after
1Sa 24:9 **W.** hearest thou men's words, 4100
1Sa 24:19 **w.** the Lord reward thee good for that
1Sa 25:8 **W.** let the young men find favour in
1Sa 25:36 **w.** she told him nothing, less or more,
1Sa 26:15 **w.** then hast thou not kept thy 4100
1Sa 26:18 **W.** doth my lord thus pursue after 4100
1Sa 27:6 **w.** Ziklag pertaineth unto the 3651
1Sa 28:9 **w.** then layest thou a snare for my 4100
1Sa 28:16 **W.** then dost thou ask of me, 4100
1Sa 29:7 **W.** now return, and go in peace,
1Sa 29:10 **W.** now rise up early in the
2Sa 2:16 together: **w.** that place was called
2Sa 2:22 **w.** should I smite thee to the 4100
2Sa 2:23 **w.** Abner with the hinder end of the
2Sa 3:7 **W.** hast thou gone in unto my 4069
2Sa 5:8 **W.** they said, The blind and 5921,3651
2Sa 7:22 **W.** thou art great, O Lord 5921,3651
2Sa 10:4 **W.** Hanun took David's servants,
2Sa 11:20 **W.** approached ye so nigh unto 4069
2Sa 12:9 **W.** hast thou despised the 4069
2Sa 12:23 now he is dead, **w.** should I fast? 4100
2Sa 14:13 **W.** then hast thou thought such a 4100
2Sa 14:31 **W.** have thy servants set my field 4100
2Sa 14:32 say, **W.** am I come from Geshur? 4100
2Sa 15:19 **W.** goest thou also with us? return 4100
2Sa 16:10 they say, **W.** hast thou done so? 4069
2Sa 18:22 **W.** wilt thou run, my son, 4100,2088
2Sa 19:12 **w.** then are ye the last to bring 4100
2Sa 19:25 **W.** wentest not thou with me, 4100
2Sa 19:35 **w.** then should thy servant be yet 4100
2Sa 19:42 **W.** then be ye angry for this 4100
2Sa 21:3 **W.** David said unto the Gibeonites,
2Sa 24:21 **W.** is my lord the king come to 4069
1Ki 1:2 **W.** his servants said unto him, Let
1Ki 1:11 **W.** Nathan spake unto Bath-sheba
1Ki 1:41 **W.** is this noise of the city being 4069
1Ki 11:11 **W.** the Lord said unto Solomon,
1Ki 12:15 **W.** the king hearkened not unto the
1Ki 16:16 **w.** all Israel made Omri, the captain
1Ki 20:9 **W.** he said unto the messengers of
1Ki 22:34 **w.** he said unto the driver of his
2Ki 4:23 **W.** wilt thou go to him to day? 4069
2Ki 4:31 **W.** he went again to meet him, and
2Ki 5:7 **w.** consider, I pray you, and 3588,389
2Ki 5:8 **W.** hast thou rent thy clothes? 4100
2Ki 7:7 **W.** they arose and fled in the twilight,
2Ki 9:11 **w.** came this mad fellow to thee? 4069
2Ki 9:36 **W.** they came again, and told him
2Ki 17:26 **W.** they spake to the king of Assyria,
2Ki 19:4 **w.** lift up thy prayers for the remnant
1Ch 13:11 **w.** that place is called Perez-uzza to
1Ch 19:4 **W.** Hanun took David's servants, and
1Ch 21:4 **W.** Joab departed, and went
1Ch 29:10 **W.** David blessed the Lord before all
2Ch 5:3 **W.** all the men of Israel assembled
2Ch 19:7 **W.** now let the fear of the Lord be
2Ch 22:4 **W.** he did evil in the sight of the Lord
2Ch 25:10 **W.** their anger was greatly kindled
2Ch 25:15 **W.** the anger of the Lord was kindled
2Ch 28:5 **W.** the Lord his God delivered him
2Ch 29:8 **W.** the wrath of the Lord was upon
2Ch 29:34 **w.** their brethren the Levites did help
2Ch 33:11 **W.** the Lord brought upon them the
Ne 2:2 **W.** the king said unto me, Why is
Es 3:6 **w.** Haman sought to destroy all the
Es 9:26 **W.** they called these days 5921,3651
Job 3:20 **W.** is light given to him that is in 4100
Job 10:2 **w.** thou contendest with me. 5921,4100
Job 10:18 **W.** then hast thou brought me 4100
Job 13:14 **W.** do I take my flesh in my 5921,4100
Job 13:24 **W.** hidest thou thy face, and 4100
Job 18:3 **W.** we are counted as beasts, and 4069
Job 21:7 **W.** do the wicked live, become old, 4069
Job 32:6 **w.** I was afraid, and durst not 5921,3651
Job 33:1 **W.**, Job, I pray thee, hear my 199
Job 42:6 **W.** I abhor myself, and 5921,3651
Ps 10:13 **W.** doth the wicked contemn 5921,4100
Ps 44:24 **W.** hidest thou thy face, and 4100

Ps 49:5 W. should I fear in the days of evil,.... 4100
Ps 79:10 W. should the heathen say, Where..... 4100
Ps 89:47 W. hast thou made all men.......... 5921,4100
Ps 115:2 W. should the heathen say, Where..... 4100
Pr 17:16 W. is there a price in the.......... 4100,2088
Ec 3:22 W. I perceive that there is nothing..........
Ec 4:2 W. I praised the dead which are..............
Ec 5:6 w. should God be angry at thy.......... 4100
Isa 5:4 w., when I looked that it should.......... 4069
Isa 10:12 W. it shall come to pass, that when..........
Isa 16:11 W. my bowels shall sound......... 5921,3651
Isa 24:15 W. glorify ye the Lord in the..... 5921,3651
Isa 28:14 W. hear the word of the Lord, ye...... 3651
Isa 29:13 W. the Lord said, Forasmuch as..............
Isa 30:12 W. thus saith the Holy One of.......... 3651
Isa 37:4 w. lift up thy prayer for the remnant.........
Isa 50:2 W., when I came, was there no.......... 4069
Isa 55:2 W. do ye spend money for that......... 4100
Isa 58:3 W. have we fasted, say they, and...... 4100
Isa 58:3 w. have we afflicted our soul, and thou......
Isa 63:2 W. art thou red in thine apparel,........ 4069
Jer 2:9 W. I will yet plead with you,............ 3651
Jer 2:29 W. will ye plead with me? ye all......... 4100
Jer 2:31 w. say my people, We are lords;....... 4069
Jer 5:6 W. a lion out of the forest.......... 5921,3651
Jer 5:14 W. thus saith the Lord God of.......... 3651
Jer 5:19 W. doeth the Lord our God....... 8478,4100
Jer 12:1 W. doth the way of the wicked.......... 4069
Jer 12:1 w. are all they happy that deal very..........
Jer 13:22 W. come these things upon me?........ 4069
Jer 16:10 W. hath the Lord pronounced..... 5921,4100
Jer 20:18 W. came I forth out of the womb....... 4100
Jer 22:8 W. hath the Lord done thus....... 5921,4100
Jer 22:28 w. are they cast out, he and his......... 4069
Jer 23:12 W. their way shall be unto them........ 3651
Jer 27:17 w. should this city be laid waste,....... 4100
Jer 30:6 w. do I see every man with his......... 4069
Jer 32:3 W. dost thou prophesy, and say,......... 4069
Jer 37:15 W. the princes were wroth with..............
Jer 40:15 w. should he slay thee, that all the..... 4100
Jer 44:6 W. my fury and mine anger was.............
Jer 44:7 W. commit ye this great evil............ 4100
Jer 46:5 W. have I seen them dismayed.......... 4069
Jer 49:4 W. gloriest thou in the valleys,.......... 4100
Jer 51:52 W., behold, the days come, saith....... 3651
La 3:39 W. doth a living man complain, a........ 4100
La 5:20 W. dost thou forget us forever,......... 4100
Eze 5:11 W., as I live, saith the Lord God;...... 3651
Eze 7:24 W. I will bring the worst of the...............
Eze 13:20 W. thus saith the Lord God;............ 3651
Eze 16:35 W., O harlot, hear the word of the..... 3651
Eze 18:32 w. turn yourselves, and live ye...............
Eze 20:10 W. I caused them to go forth out of.........
Eze 20:25 W. I gave them also statutes that............
Eze 20:30 W. say unto the house of Israel,........ 3651
Eze 21:7 W. sighest thou? that thou......... 5981,4100
Eze 23:9 W. I have delivered her unto the....... 3651
Eze 24:6 W. thus saith the Lord God; Woe...... 3651
Eze 33:25 W. say unto them, Thus saith the...... 3651
Eze 36:18 W. I poured my fury upon them..............
Eze 43:8 w. I have consumed them in mine............
Da 3:8 W. at that time certain...... 3605,6903,1836
Da 4:27 W., O king, let my counsel be........... 3861
Da 6:9 W. king Darius signed....... 3605,6903,1836
Da 8:26 w. shut thou up the vision; for it.............
Da 10:20 Knowest thou w. I come unto thee?... 4100
Joe 2:17 w. should they say among the........... 4100
Jon 1:14 W. they cried unto the Lord, and............
Hab 1:13 w. lookest thou upon them that......... 4100
Mal 2:14 Yet ye say, W.? Because the..... 5921,4100
Mal 2:15 w. one? That he might seek a.......... 4100
Mt 6:30 W., if God so clothe the grass of... 1161
Mt 7:20 W. by their fruits ye shall....... 686,1065
Mt 9:4 W. think ye evil in your........ 2443,5101
Mt 12:12 W. it is lawful to do well on the... 5620
Mt 12:31 W. I say unto you, All.......... 1223,5124
Mt 14:31 faith, w. didst thou doubt?..... 1519,5101
Mt 18:8 W. if thy hand or thy foot offend.. 1161
Mt 19:6 W. they are no more twain, but.... 5620
Mt 23:31 W. ye be witnesses unto............ 5620
Mt 23:34 W., behold, I send unto you... 1223,5124
Mt 24:26 W. if they shall say unto you,....... 3767
Mt 26:50 Friend, w. art thou come?..... 1909,3739
Mt 27:8 W. that field was called, The field...... 1352
Lu 7:7 W. neither thought I myself............ 1352
Lu 7:47 W. I say unto thee, Her sins,...3739,5484
Lu 19:23 W. then gavest not thou my.......... 1302
Joh 9:27 hear: w. would ye hear it again?........ 5101
Ac 1:21 W. of these men which have............ 3767
Ac 6:3 W., brethren, look ye out among....... 3767
Ac 10:21 is the cause w. ye are come?..... 1223,3739
Ac 13:35 W. he saith also in another psalm,...... 1352
Ac 15:19 W. my sentence is, that we trouble.... 1352
Ac 19:32 w. they were come together...... 5101,1752
Ac 19:38 W. if Demetrius, and the.......... 3303,3767
Ac 20:26 W. I take you to record this day,....... 1352
Ac 22:24 w. they cried so against him...... 1223,3739
Ac 22:30 w. he was accused of the Jews.......... 5101
Ac 23:28 the cause w. they accused him,.. 1223,3739
Ac 24:26 w. he sent for him the oftener,.......... 1352
Ac 25:26 W. I have brought him forth before.... 1352
Ac 26:3 w. I beseech thee to hear me........... 1352
Ac 27:25 W., sirs, be of good cheer: for I.......... 1352
Ac 27:34 W. I pray you to take some meat:..... 1352
Ro 1:24 W. God also gave them up to............ 1352
Ro 5:12 W., as by...man sin entered....... 1223,5124
Ro 7:4 W., my brethren, ye also are............ 5620
Ro 7:12 W. the law is holy, and the.............. 5620
Ro 9:32 W.? Because they sought it not......... 1302
Ro 13:5 W. ye must needs be subject, not....... 1352
Ro 15:7 W. receive ye one another, as........... 1352
1Co 4:16 W. I beseech you, be ye followers..... 3767
1Co 8:13 W., if meat make my brother to........ 1355
1Co 10:12 W. let him that thinketh he.............. 5620
1Co 10:14 W., my dearly beloved, flee from....... 1355
1Co 11:27 W. whosoever shall eat this bread,..... 5620
1Co 11:33 W., my brethren, when ye come......... 5620
1Co 12:3 W. I give you to understand, that...... 1352
1Co 14:13 W. let him that speaketh in an........... 1355
1Co 14:22 W. tongues are for a sign, not to......... 5620
1Co 14:39 W., brethren, covet to prophesy,........ 5620
2Co 2:8 W. I beseech you that ye would........ 1352
2Co 5:9 W. we labour, that, whether............. 1352
2Co 5:16 W. henceforth know we no man........... 5620
2Co 6:17 W. come out from among them,........ 1352
2Co 7:12 W., though I wrote unto you, I did...... 686
2Co 8:24 W. shew ye to them, and before the.. 3767
2Co 11:11 W.? because I love you not? God........ 1302
Ga 3:19 W. then serveth the law? It was........ 5101
Ga 3:24 W. the law was our schoolmaster........ 5620
Ga 4:7 W. thou art no more a servant,......... 5620
Eph 1:15 W. I also, after I heard of......... 1223,5124
Eph 2:11 W. remember, that ye being in.......... 1352
Eph 3:13 W. I desire that ye faint not at my..... 1352
Eph 4:8 W. he saith, When he ascended......... 1352
Eph 4:25 W. putting away lying, speak............. 1352
Eph 5:14 W. he saith, Awake thou that............ 1352
Eph 5:17 W. be ye not unwise, but.......... 1223,5124
Eph 6:13 W. take unto you the whole....... 1223,5124
Php 2:9 W. God also hath highly exalted......... 1352
Php 2:12 W., my beloved, as ye have always.... 5620
Col 2:20 W. if ye be dead with Christ from...... 3767
1Th 2:18 W. we would have come unto you,..... 1352
1Th 3:1 W. when we could no longer............ 1352
1Th 4:18 W. comfort one another with............ 5620
1Th 5:11 W. comfort yourselves together,......... 1352
2Th 1:11 W. also we pray always for........ 1519,3739
2Ti 1:6 W. I put thee in remembrance..... 1223,3739
Tit 1:13 W. rebuke them sharply, that..... 1223,3739
Phm 8 W., though I might be much bold....... 1352
Heb 2:17 W. in all things it behoved him to....... 3606
Heb 3:1 W., holy brethren, partakers of......... 3606
Heb 3:7 W. (as the Holy Ghost saith, To........ 1352
Heb 3:10 W. I was grieved with that............ 1352
Heb 7:25 W. he is able also to save them......... 3606
Heb 8:3 w. it is of necessity that this man........ 3606
Heb 10:5 W. when he cometh into the............ 1352
Heb 11:16 w. God is not ashamed to be called.... 1352
Heb 12:1 W. seeing we also are compassed...... 5105
Heb 12:12 W. lift up the hands which hang......... 1352
Heb 12:28 W. we receiving a kingdom which....... 1352
Heb 13:12 W. Jesus also, that he might............ 1352
Jas 1:19 W., my beloved brethren, let........... 5620
Jas 1:21 W. lay apart all filthiness and............ 1352
Jas 4:6 W. he saith, God resisteth the............ 1352
1Pe 1:13 W. gird up the loins of your mind,....... 1352
1Pe 2:1 W. laying aside all malice, and........... 3767
1Pe 2:6 W. also it is contained in the............. 1352
1Pe 4:19 W. let them that suffer according....... 5620
2Pe 1:10 W. the rather, brethren, give............ 1352
2Pe 1:12 W. I will not be negligent to put........ 1352
2Pe 3:14 W., beloved, seeing that ye look......... 1352
1Jo 3:12 w. slew he him? Because his...... 5484,5101
3Jo 10 W., if I come, I will............... 1223,3739
Re 17:7 W. didst thou marvel: I will tell......... 1302

WHEREIN See also WHEREINSOEVER; WHEREINTO.

Ge 1:30 w. there is life, I have given every...... 834
Ge 6:17 w. is the breath of life, from under...... 834
Ge 7:15 of all flesh, w. is the breath of life......... 834
Ge 17:8 the land w. thou art a stranger, all..........
Ge 21:23 the land w. thou hast sojourned........... 834
Ge 28:4 the land w. thou art a stranger,...............
Ge 36:7 the land w. they were strangers,..............
Ge 37:1 in the land w. his father was a................
Ex 1:14 w. they made them serve, was with..... 834
Ex 6:4 pilgrimage, w. they were strangers...... 834
Ex 12:7 of the houses, w. they shall eat it........ 834
Ex 18:11 in the thing w. they dealt proudly........ 834
Ex 18:20 shew them the way w. they must walk,......
Ex 22:27 w. shall he sleep? and it shall........... 4100
Ex 33:16 w. shall it be known here that I......... 4100
Le 4:23 w. he hath sinned, come to his............ 834
Le 5:18 w. he erred and wist it not, and it....... 834
Le 6:28 vessel w. it is sodden shall be............ 834
Le 11:32 w. any work is done, it must be put..... 834
Le 11:36 w. there is plenty of water, shall be........
Le 13:46 days w. the plague shall be in him....... 834
Le 13:52 any thing of skin, w. the plague is:...... 834
Le 13:54 wash the thing w. the plague is,.......... 834
Le 13:57 burn that w. the plague is with fire...... 834
Le 18:3 land of Egypt w. ye dwelt shall ye...... 834
Nu 12:11 upon us, w. we have done foolishly,..... 834
Nu 12:11 foolishly, and w. we have sinned.......... 834
Nu 19:2 w. is no blemish, and upon which......... 834
Nu 31:10 burnt all their cities w. they dwelt,..........
Nu 33:55 vex you in the land w. ye dwell........... 834
Nu 35:33 shall not pollute the land w. ye are:..... 834
Nu 35:34 shall inhabit, w. I dwell:............. 834,8432
De 8:9 A land w. thou shalt eat bread........... 834
De 8:15 wilderness, w. were fiery serpents,..........
De 12:2 w. the nations which ye shall......... 834,8033
De 12:7 w. the Lord thy God hath blessed........ 834
De 17:1 or sheep, w. is blemish, or any........... 834
De 28:52 w. thou trustedst, throughout...... 834,2004
Jos 8:24 wilderness w. they chased them.......... 834
Jos 10:27 cave w. they had been hid,......... 834,8033
Jos 22:19 w. the Lord's tabernacle............. 834,8033
Jos 22:33 land w. the children of Reuben............ 834
Jos 24:17 us in all the way w. we went, and....... 834
Jg 16:5 see w. his great strength lieth,.......... 4100
Jg 16:6 w. thy great strength lieth, and......... 4100
Jg 16:15 told me w. thy great strength lieth..... 4100
Jg 18:6 the Lord is your way w. ye go............ 834
1Sa 6:15 w. the jewels of gold were, and put..... 834
1Sa 14:38 see w. this sin hath been this day...... 4100
2Sa 7:7 all the places w. I have walked........... 834
1Ki 2:26 afflicted in all w. my father was.......... 834
1Ki 8:21 ark, w. is the covenant of the...... 834,8033
1Ki 8:36 the good way w. they should walk,...... 834
1Ki 8:50 w. they have transgressed against....... 834
1Ki 13:31 sepulchre w. the man of God is........... 834
2Ki 12:2 w. Jehoiada the priest instructed......... 834
2Ki 14:6 w. the Lord commanded, saying,......... 834
2Ki 17:29 in their cities w. they dwelt......... 834,8033
2Ki 18:19 confidence is this w. thou trustest?...... 834
2Ki 23:23 w. this passover was holden to the..........
2Ch 3:3 w. Solomon was instructed for the...........
2Ch 6:11 w. is the covenant of the Lord,.... 834,8033
2Ch 6:27 good way, w. they should walk;.......... 834
2Ch 8:1 w. Solomon had built the house of....... 834
2Ch 33:19 the places w. he built high places,........ 834
Ezr 5:7 unto him, w. was written thus;.......... 1459
Ne 6:6 W. was written, It is reported.................
Ne 9:12 light in the way w. they should go........ 834
Ne 9:19 light, and the way w. they should go...... 834
Ne 13:15 them in the day w. they sold victuals........
Es 5:11 w. the king had promoted him,.............. 834
Es 8:11 W. the king granted the Jews.............. 834
Es 9:22 days w. the Jews rested from their...... 834
Job 3:3 Let the day perish w. I was born, and......
Job 6:16 of the ice, and w. the snow is hid:...........
Job 6:24 me to understand w. I have erred...... 4100
Job 38:26 on the wilderness, w. there is no man;......
Ps 74:2 this mount Zion, w. thou hast dwelt..........
Ps 90:15 to the days w. thou hast afflicted us,........
Ps 90:15 and the years w. we have seen evil.........
Ps 104:20 w. all the beasts of the forest do.............
Ps 104:25 wide sea, w. are things creeping........ 8033
Ps 142:3 In the way w. I walked have they...... 2098

Ps 143:8 to know the way w. I should walk;..... 2098
Ec 2:19 all my labour w. I have laboured,............
Ec 2:19 w. I have shewed myself wise under.........
Ec 2:22 w. he hath laboured under the sun?..........
Ec 3:9 worketh in that w. he laboureth?......... 834
Ec 8:9 is a time w. one man ruleth over......... 834
Isa 2:22 for w. is he to be accounted of?........ 4100
Isa 14:3 bondage w. thou wast made to........... 834
Isa 33:21 w. shall go no galley with oars,................
Isa 36:4 confidence is this w. thou trustest?...... 834
Isa 47:12 w. thou hast laboured from thy........... 834
Isa 65:12 did choose that w. I delighted not........ 834
Jer 5:17 fenced cities, w. thou trustedst,... 834,2004
Jer 7:14 called by my name, w. ye trust, and.... 834
Jer 12:5 the land of peace, w. thou trustedst,.........
Jer 16:19 vanity, and things w. there is no profit.........
Jer 20:14 Cursed be the day w. I was born:....... 834
Jer 20:14 not the day w. my mother bare me...... 834
Jer 22:28 idol? is he a vessel w. is no pleasure?.......
Jer 31:9 way, w. they shall not stumble:...............
Jer 36:14 roll w. thou hast read in the ears of...... 834
Jer 41:9 pit w. Ishmael had cast all the dead...... 834
Jer 42:3 shew us the way w. we may walk,...... 834
Jer 48:38 Moab like a vessel w. is no pleasure,........
Jer 51:43 a land w. no man dwelleth,................. 834
Eze 20:34 the countries w. ye are scattered,....... 834
Eze 20:41 countries w. ye have been scattered;.........
Eze 20:43 doings, w. ye have been defiled;......... 834
Eze 23:19 w. she had played the harlot in the...... 834
Eze 26:10 enter into a city w. is made a breach........
Eze 32:6 thy blood the land w. thou swimmest,........
Eze 37:23 w. they have sinned, and will............ 834
Eze 37:25 servant, w. your fathers have dwelt;.... 834
Eze 42:14 their garments w. they minister;.......... 834
Eze 44:19 their garments w. they ministered,....... 834
Ho 2:13 w. she burned incense to them, and..... 834
Ho 8:8 Gentiles as a vessel w. is no pleasure.......
Jon 4:11 w. are more than sixscore thousand..........
Mic 6:3 thee? and w. I have wearied thee?..... 4100
Zep 3:11 w. thou hast transgressed against......... 834
Zec 9:11 prisoners out of the pit w. is no water......
Mal 1:2 Yet ye say, W. hast thou loved us?.... 4100
Mal 1:6 W. have we despised thy name?........ 4100
Mal 1:7 W. have we polluted thee? In that...... 4100
Mal 2:17 ye say, W. have we wearied him?...... 4100
Mal 3:7 But ye said, W. shall we return?........ 4100
Mal 3:8 ye say, W. have we robbed thee?...... 4100
Mt 11:20 w. most of his mighty works...... *1722,3739*
Mt 25:13 **w. the Son of man cometh**..... *1722,3739*
Mk 2:4 w. the sick of the palsy lay........ *1909,3739*
Lu 1:4 w. thou hast been instructed......... *4012,3739*
Lu 1:25 in the days w. he looked on me,........ *3739*
Lu 11:22 **all his armour w. he trusted,**..*1909,3739*
Lu 23:53 w. never man before was laid........... *3757*
Joh 19:41 w. was never man yet laid........ *1722,3757*
Ac 2:8 own tongue, w. we were born?.. *1722,3757*
Ac 7:4 into this land, w. ye now dwell.. *1519,3757*
Ac 10:12 W....all manner of fourfooted...... *1722,3757*
Ro 2:1 for w. thou judgest another,........ *1722,3757*
Ro 5:2 into this grace w. we stand,....... *1722,3757*
Ro 7:6 being dead w. we were held;..... *1722,3757*
1Co 7:20 same calling w. he was called..... *1722,3757*
1Co 7:24 w. he is called, therein abide...... *1722,3757*
1Co 15:1 have received, and w. ye stand;. *1722,3757*
2Co 11:12 that w. they glory, they may be.. *1722,3757*
2Co 12:13 For what is it w. ye were inferior to... *3757*
Eph 1:6 w. he hath made us accepted..... *1722,3757*
Eph 1:8 W. he hath abounded toward us......... *3757*
Eph 2:2 W. in time past ye walked......... *1722,3757*
Eph 5:18 drunk with wine, w. is excess;... *1722,3757*
Php 4:10 w. ye were also careful, but....... *1909,3757*
Col 2:12 w. also ye are risen with him..... *1722,3757*
2Ti 2:9 W. I suffer trouble, as an evil.... *1722,3757*
Heb 6:17 W. God, willing more............... *1722,3757*
Heb 9:2 first, w. was the candlestick,........ *1722,3757*
Heb 9:4 w. was the golden pot that had... *1722,3757*
1Pe 1:6 W. ye greatly rejoice, though..... *1722,3757*
1Pe 3:20 w. few, that is, eight souls........ *1519,3757*
1Pe 4:4 W. they think it strange that...... *1722,3757*
1Pe 5:12 true grace of God w. ye stand.... *1519,3757*
2Pe 3:12 w. the heavens being on fire...... *1223,3757*
2Pe 3:13 w. dwelleth righteousness.......... *1722,3757*
Re 2:13 **w. Antipas was my...martyr,**.. *1722,3757*
Re 18:19 w. were made rich all that had... *1722,3757*

WHEREINSOEVER

2Co 11:21 w. any is bold, (I speak....... *1722,3739,302*

WHEREINTO

Le 11:33 w. any of them falleth,......... 834,413,8432
Nu 14:24 into the land w. he went;......... 824,8432
Joh 6:22 one w. his disciples...entered,.... *1519,3739*

WHEREOF

Ge 3:11 w. I commanded thee that thou.......... 834
Le 6:30 w. any of the blood is brought into....... 834
Le 13:24 skin w. there is a hot burning, and...........
Le 27:9 w. men bring an offering unto the........ 834
Nu 5:3 their camps, in the midst w. I dwell..... 834
Nu 7:19, 37,49,61,67,73,79 weight w. was an hundred and thirty shekels,.................
Nu 7:25 the weight w. was an hundred.................
Nu 21:16 well w. the Lord spake unto Moses,.... 834
De 13:2 to pass, w. he spake unto thee,......... 834
De 28:27 itch w. thou canst not be healed.......... 834
De 28:68 by the way w. I spake unto thee,........ 834
Jos 14:12 w. the Lord spake in that day;........... 834
Jos 20:2 w. I spake unto you by the hand of...... 834
Jos 22:9 w. they were possessed, according...... 834
1Sa 10:16 of the kingdom, w. Samuel spake,........ 834
1Sa 13:2 w. two thousand were with Saul in..........
2Sa 12:30 weight w. was a talent of gold with..........
2Ki 13:14 sick of this sickness w. he died........... 834
2Ki 17:12 w. the Lord had said unto them,......... 834
2Ch 3:8 w. was according to the breadth..............
2Ch 6:20 place w. thou hast said that thou......... 834
2Ch 24:14 w. were made vessels for the house of.....
2Ch 33:4 w. the Lord had said, In Jerusalem..... 834
Ne 12:31 w. one went on the right hand upon.........
Job 6:4 poison w. drinketh up my spirit:.......... 834
Ps 46:4 w. shall make glad the city of God,...........
Ps 57:6 midst w. they are fallen themselves..........
Ps 126:3 great things for us; w. we are glad.........
Ec 1:10 Is there any thing w. it may be said,.........
Ca 4:2 w. every one bear twins, and none is........
Ca 6:6 w. every one beareth twins, and there......
Jer 32:36 concerning this city, w. ye say, It......... 834
Jer 32:43 this land, w. ye say, It is desolate....... 834
Jer 42:16 and the famine, w. ye were afraid........ 834
Eze 32:15 be destitute of that w. it was full,.............
Eze 39:8 this is the day w. I have spoken.......... 834
Da 9:2 w. the word of the Lord came to............ 834
Ho 2:12 w. she hath said, These are my.......... 834
Lu 23:14 those things w. ye accuse him:................
Ac 2:32 raised up, w. we all are witnesses...... *3739*
Ac 3:15 raised from the dead; w. we are........ *3739*
Ac 17:19 new doctrine, w. thou speakest, is?..........
Ac 17:31 w. he hath given assurance unto all..........
Ac 21:24 w. they were informed concerning............
Ac 24:8 all these things, w. we accuse him..... *3739*
Ac 24:13 things w. they now accuse......... *4012,3739*
Ac 25:11 of these things w. these accuse me,... *3739*
Ac 26:2 things w. I am accused of the Jews:... *3739*
Ro 4:2 he hath w. to glory; but not before...........
Ro 6:21 w. ye are now ashamed?........... *1909,3739*
Ro 15:17 w. I may glory through Jesus Christ.........
1Co 7:1 things w. ye wrote unto me:...... *4012,3739*
2Co 9:5 your bounty, w. ye had notice before,.......
Eph 3:7 W. I was made a minister,................ *3739*
Php 3:4 he hath w. he might trust in the flesh,.......
Col 1:5 w. ye heard before in the word of...... *3739*
Col 1:23 w. I Paul am made a minister;........... *3739*
Col 1:25 W. I am made a minister,................ *3739*
1Ti 1:7 they say, nor w. they affirm....... *4012,5101*
1Ti 6:4 words, w. cometh envy, strife,... *1537,3739*
Heb 2:5 world to come, w. we speak...... *4012,3739*
Heb 10:15 W. the Holy Ghost also is a witness.........
Heb 12:8 chastisement, w. all are partakers,...... *3739*
Heb 13:10 w. they have no right to eat...... *1537,3739*
1Jo 4:3 w. ye have heard that it should.......... *3739*

WHEREON

Ge 28:13 land w. thou liest, to thee will...... 834,5921
Ex 3:5 place w. thou standest is holy...... 834,5921
Ex 8:21 also the ground w. they are......... 834,5921
Le 6:27 wash that w. it was sprinkled....... 834,5921
Le 15:4 every thing, w. he sitteth,.......... 834,5921
Le 15:6 sitteth on any thing w. he sat...... 834,5921
Le 15:17 w. is the seed of copulation,........ 834,5921
Le 15:23 or on any thing w. she sitteth,..... 834,5921
Le 15:24 all the bed w. he lieth shall be..... 834,5921
Le 15:26 bed w. she lieth all the days of.... 834,5921
De 11:24 w. the soles of your feet shall tread..... 834
Jos 5:15 place w. thou standest is holy...... 834,5921
Jos 14:9 land w. thy feet have trodden shall...... 834

1Sa 6:18 Abel, w. they set down the ark.... 834,5921
2Ch 4:19 tables w. the shewbread was set;....... 5921
2Ch 32:10 W. do ye trust, that ye abide..... 5921,4100
Es 7:8 upon the bed w. Esther was......... 834,5921
Job 24:23 him to be in safety, w. he resteth;..........
Ca 4:4 w. there hang a thousand bucklers,...... 5921
Isa 36:6 w. if a man lean, it will go........... 834,5921
Eze 37:20 sticks w. thou writest shall be...... 834,5921
Mk 11:2 **a colt tied, w. never man sat;**..*1909,3739*
Lu 4:29 the hill w. their city was built,.... *1909,3739*
Lu 5:25 and took up that w. he lay, and.. *1909,3739*
Lu 19:30 **a colt tied, w. never man sat:**.*1909,3739*
Joh 4:38 **reap w. ye bestowed no labour:**..... *3739*

WHERESOEVER

Le 13:12 to his foot, w. the priest looketh;....... 3605
2Ki 8:1 and sojourn w. thou canst sojourn:....... 834
2Ki 12:5 w. any breach shall be found........ 834,8033
1Ch 17:6 W. I...walked with all Israel,......... 3605,834
Jer 40:5 go w. it seemeth convenient........ 413,3605
Da 2:38 w. the children of men dwelt,..... 3606,1768
Mt 24:28 **w. the carcase is, there will**... *3699,1437*
Mt 26:13 **W. this gospel shall be**.......... *3699,1437*
Mk 9:18 w. he taketh him, he teareth....... *3699,302*
Mk 14:9 **W. this gospel shall be**........... *3699,302*
Mk 14:14 **w. he shall go in, say ye**....... *3699,1437*
Lu 17:37 **W. the body is, thither will the**..... *3699*

WHERETO See also WHEREUNTO.

Job 30:2 w. might the strength of their........... 4100
Isa 55:11 prosper in the thing w. I sent it.......... 834
Php 3:16 w. we have already attained,...... *1519,3739*

WHEREUNTO

Nu 36:3 the tribe w. they are received:...............
Nu 36:4 of the tribe w. they are recieved:........ 834
De 4:26 perish from off the land w. ye go......... 834
2Ch 8:11 w. the ark of the Lord hath come........ 834
Es 10:2 w. the king advanced him,.................. 834
Ps 71:3 w. I may continually resort:...................
Jer 22:27 the land w. they desire to return,........ 834
Eze 5:9 w. I will not do any more the like,....... 834
Eze 20:29 is the high place w. ye go?........... 834,8033
Mt 11:16 **w. shall I liken this generation?**....... *5101*
Mk 4:30 **W. shall we liken the kingdom of**. *5101*
Lu 7:31 **W. then shall I liken the men of**... *5101*
Lu 13:18 **like? and w. shall I resemble it?**.... *5101*
Lu 13:20 **W. shall I liken the kingdom of**.... *5101*
Ac 5:24 of them w. this would grow............ *5101*
Ac 13:2 for the work w. I have called them..... *3739*
Ac 27:8 nigh w. was the city of Lasea............ *3739*
Ga 4:9 w. ye desire again to be in............... *3739*
Col 1:29 W. I also labour, striving........... *1519,3739*
2Th 2:14 W. he called you by our gospel,.. *1519,3739*
1Ti 2:7 W. I am ordained a preacher,...... *1519,3739*
1Ti 4:6 doctrine, w. thou hast attained........... *3739*
1Ti 6:12 w. thou art also called, and........ *1519,3739*
2Ti 1:11 W. I am appointed a preacher,... *1519,3739*
1Pe 2:8 w. also they were appointed........ *1519,3739*
1Pe 3:21 like figure w. even baptism doth.......... *3739*
2Pe 1:19 w. ye do well that ye take heed, as.... *3739*

WHEREUPON

Le 11:35 w. any part of their carcase......... 834,5921
Jg 16:26 pillars w. the house standeth,...... 834,5921
1Ki 7:48 of gold, w. the shewbread was,.... 834,5921
1Ki 12:28 W. the king took counsel, and made.........
2Ch 12:6 W. the princes of Israel and the king........
Job 38:6 W. are the foundations.............. 5921,4100
Eze 9:3 from the cherub, w. he was,....... 834,5921
Eze 23:41 w. thou hast set thine incense and...... 5921
Eze 24:25 that w. they set their minds, their sons.....
Eze 40:41 tables, w. they slew their sacrifices...... 413
Eze 40:42 w. also they laid the instruments......... 413
Am 4:7 and the piece w. it rained not...... 834,5921
Mt 14:7 W. he promised with an oath to........ *3606*
Ac 24:18 W. certain Jews from Asia......... *1722,3739*
Ac 26:12 W. as I went to Damascus with.. *1722,3739*
Ac 26:19 W., O king Agrippa, I was not.......... *3606*
Heb 9:18 W. neither the first testament was..... *3606*

WHEREWITH See also WHEREWITHAL.

Ge 27:41 blessing w. his father blessed him:....... 834
Ex 3:9 the oppression w. the Egyptians.......... 834
Ex 4:17 thine hand, w. thou shalt do signs........ 834
Ex 16:32 may see the bread w. I have fed you.... 834
Ex 17:5 thy rod, w. thou smotest the river,...... 834
Ex 29:33 things w. the atonement was made,..... 834
Nu 3:31 of the sanctuary w. they minister,........ 834

Nu 3:48 w. the odd number of them is to be.........
Nu 4:9 thereof, w. they minister unto it:......... 834
Nu 4:12 w. they minister in the sanctuary,......... 834
Nu 4:14 w. they minister about it, even the...... 834
Nu 16:39 w. they that were burnt had offered;.... 834
Nu 25:18 w. they have beguiled you in the......... 834
Nu 30:4 her bond w. she hath bound her soul.... 834
Nu 30:4 bond w. she hath bound her soul......... 834
Nu 30:5 bonds w. she hath bound her soul,....... 834
Nu 30:6 of her lips, w. she bound her soul;....... 834
Nu 30:7 w. she bound her soul shall stand. 834
Nu 30:8 lips, w. she bound her soul, of none..... 834
Nu 30:9 w. they have bound their souls,........... 834
Nu 30:11 w. she bound her soul shall stand. 834
Nu 35:17 throwing a stone, w. he may die, ... 834
Nu 35:18 weapon of wood, w. he may die, ... 834
Nu 35:23 with any stone, w. a man may die, ... 834
De 9:19 w. the Lord was wroth against you...... 834
De 15:14 w. the Lord thy God hath blessed........ 834
De 22:12 of thy vesture, w. thou coverest 834
De 28:53 w. thine enemies shall distress thee: 834
De 28:55 w. thine enemies shall distress thee..... 834
De 28:57 w. thine enemy shall distress thee....... 834
De 28:67 of thine heart w. thou shalt fear, ... 834
De 33:1 w. Moses the man of God blessed......... 834
Jos 8:26 w. he stretched out the spear, until...... 834
Jg 6:15 my Lord, w. shall I save Israel?......... 4100
Jg 9:4 w. Abimelech hired vain and light............
Jg 9:9 w. by me they honour God and man,.... 834
Jg 9:38 is now thy mouth, w. thou saidst,......... 834
Jg 16:6 w. thou mightest be bound to........... 4100
Jg 16:10 thee, w. thou mightest be bound.......... 4100
Jg 16:13 tell me w. thou mightest be bound. 4100
1Sa 6:2 tell us w. we shall send it to his 4100
1Sa 8:8 w. they have forsaken me, and served......
1Sa 29:4 for w. should he reconcile himself....... 4100
2Sa 13:15 hatred w. he hated her was greater 834
2Sa 13:15 than the love w. he had loved her......... 834
2Sa 21:3 w. shall I make the atonement,.......... 4100
1Ki 8:59 w. I have made supplication before....... 834
1Ki 15:22 thereof, w. Baasha had builded;........... 834
1Ki 15:26 in his sin w. he made Israel to sin. 834
1Ki 15:30 w. he provoked the Lord God of........... 834
1Ki 15:34 in his sin w. he made Israel to sin. 834
1Ki 16:26 in his sin w. he made Israel to sin, ... 834
1Ki 21:22 w. thou hast provoked me to anger,..... 834
1Ki 22:22 And the Lord said unto him, W.? 4100
2Ki 13:12 w. he fought against Amaziah.............. 834
2Ki 21:16 his sin w. he made Judah to sin,.......... 834
2Ki 23:26 w. his anger was kindled against.......... 834
2Ki 25:14 vessels of brass w. they ministered,..... 834
1Ch 18:8 w. Solomon made the brasen sea, ... 834
2Ch 2:17 w. David his father had numbered........ 834
2Ch 16:6 thereof, w. Baasha was building;.......... 834
2Ch 18:20 And the Lord said unto him, W.? 4100
2Ch 35:21 but against the house w. I have war: ....
Ne 9:34 w. thou didst testify against them. 834
Job 15:3 with speeches w. he can do no good? ....
Ps 79:12 w. they have reproached thee, O......... 834
Ps 89:51 W. thine enemies have reproached,...... 834
Ps 89:51 w. they have reproached the.............. 834
Ps 93:1 strength, w. he hath girded himself:? ....
Ps 109:19 a girdle w. he is girded continually............
Ps 119:42 w. to answer him that reproacheth..... 1697
Ps 129:7 W. the mower filleth not his hand;............
Ca 3:11 crown w. his mother crowned him............
Isa 28:12 w. ye may cause the weary to rest; ....
Isa 37:6 w. the servants of the king of............ 834
Jer 18:10 w. I said I would benefit them............ 834
Jer 19:9 w. their enemies, and they that seek.... 834
Jer 21:4 w. ye fight against the king of............ 834
Jer 33:16 is the name w. she shall be called,....... 834
Jer 52:18 vessels of brass w. they ministered,..... 834
La 1:12 w. the Lord hath afflicted me in the..... 834
Eze 13:12 Where is the daubing w. ye have......... 834
Eze 13:20 w. ye there hunt the souls to make...... 834
Eze 16:19 and oil, and honey, w. I fed thee,............
Eze 29:20 labour w. he served against it, ... 834
Eze 32:16 lamentation w. they shall lament her: ....
Eze 36:18 their idols w. they had polluted it: ....
Eze 40:42 instruments w. they slew the burnt....... 834
Da 2:1 dreams, w. his spirit was troubled, ...
Mic 6:6 W. shall I come before the Lord, ... 4100
Zec 14:12 plague w. the Lord shall smite all 834
Zec 14:18 w. the Lord will smite the heathen....... 834
Mal 2:5 to him for the fear w. he feared me, ... 834
Mt 5:13 **w. shall it be salted?** *1722,5101*
Mk 3:28 **w. soever they shall blaspheme:**..... *3745*
Mk 9:50 **saltness, w. will ye season it?** .*1722,5101*
Lu 14:34 **w. shall it be seasoned?** *1722,5101*
Lu 17:8 **Make ready w. I may sup, and**...... *5101*
Joh 13:5 with the towel w. he was girded. *3739*
Joh 17:26 **the love w. thou hast loved me**...... *3739*
Ro 14:19 things w. one may edify another...............
2Co 1:4 w. we ourselves are comforted of...... *3739*
2Co 7:7 w. he was comforted in you, ... *3739*
2Co 10:2 w. I think to be bold against some,..... *3739*
Ga 5:1 liberty w. Christ hath made us free, ... *3739*
Eph 2:4 for his great love w. he loved us,........ *3739*
Eph 4:1 of the vocation w. ye are called, ... *3739*
Eph 6:16 w. ye shall be able to quench.... *1722,3739*
1Th 3:9 joy w. we joy for your sakes before.... 3739
Heb 10:29 w. he was sanctified, an unholy... *1722,3739*

WHEREWITHAL

Ps 119:9 w. shall a young man cleanse his........ 4100
Mt 6:31 **drink? or, W. shall we be clothed?** *5101*

WHET

De 32:41 If I w. my glittering sword, and......... 8150
Ps 7:12 he turn not, he will w. his sword; 3913
Ps 64:3 Who w. their tongue like a sword,...... 8150
Ec 10:10 blunt, and he do not w. the edge, ... 7043

WHETHER

Ge 18:21 see w. they have done altogether............
Ge 24:21 to wit w. the Lord had made his............
Ge 27:21 w. thou be my very son Esau or not. ....
Ge 31:39 w. stolen by day, or stolen by night..........
Ge 37:14 w. it be well with thy brethren, and..........
Ge 37:32 now w. it be thy son's coat or no..........
Ge 42:16 proved, w. there be any truth in you: ....
Ge 43:6 the man w. ye had yet a brother? 5750
Ex 4:18 Egypt, and see w. they be yet alive. .. 5750
Ex 12:19 w. he be a stranger, or born in the ....
Ex 16:4 w. they will walk in my law, or no............
Ex 19:13 w. it be beast or man, it shall not........ 518
Ex 21:31 W. he have gored a son, or have 176
Ex 22:4 hand alive, w. it be ox, or ass, ... 5704
Ex 22:8 to see w. he have put his hand 518,3808
Ex 22:9 w. it be for ox, for ass, for sheep, ...
Ex 34:19 cattle, w. ox or sheep, that is male. ....
Le 3:1 w. it be a male or female, he shall....... 518
Le 5:1 w. he hath seen or known of it; 176
Le 5:2 w. it be a carcase of an unclean........... 176
Le 7:26 blood, w. it be of fowl or of beast, ...
Le 11:32 w. it be any vessel of wood, or ....
Le 11:35 w. it be oven, or ranges for pots, they......
Le 13:47 w. it be a woolen garment, or a linen........
Le 13:48 W. it be in the warp, or woof, of......... 176
Le 13:48 w. in a skin, or any thing made of 176
Le 13:52 w. warp or woof, in woollen or in........ 176
Le 13:55 w. it be bare within or without. ....
Le 15:3 w. his flesh run with his issue, or his.......
Le 16:29 w. it be one of your own country, or ....
Le 17:15 w. it be one of your own country, or ....
Le 18:9 w. she be born at home, or born ....
Le 22:28 And w. it be cow or ewe, ye shall not ......
Le 27:12 shall value it, w. it be good or bad:...... 996
Le 27:14 estimate it, w. it be good or bad: 996
Le 27:26 w. it be ox, or sheep: it is the........... 518
Le 27:30 w. of the seed of the land, or of the.........
Le 27:33 not search w. it be good or bad, ... 996
Nu 9:21 w. it was by day or by night that......... 176
Nu 9:22 Or w. it were two days, or a month,.... 176
Nu 11:23 w. my word shall come to pass unto.........
Nu 13:18 w. they be strong or weak, few or...........
Nu 13:19 they dwell in, w. it be good or bad;..........
Nu 13:19 w. in tents, or in strong holds; ....
Nu 13:20 what the land is, w. it be fat or lean, ...
Nu 13:20 lean, w. there be wood therein, or not......
Nu 15:30 w. he be born in the land, or a.......... 4480
Nu 18:15 w. it be of men or beasts, shall be ....
De 4:32 w. there hath been any such thing as........
De 8:2 w. thou wouldest keep his ....
De 13:3 to know w. ye love the Lord with ....
De 18:3 a sacrifice, w. it be ox or sheep; 518
De 22:6 w. they be young ones, or eggs,..............
De 24:14 w. he be of thy brethren, or of thy..........
Jos 24:15 w. the gods which your fathers 518
Jg 2:22 w. they will keep the way of the Lord.......
Jg 3:4 know w. they would hearken unto the.......
Jg 9:2 W. is better for you, either that 4100
Jg 18:5 may know w. our way which we go..........
Ru 3:10 not young men, w. poor or rich........... 518
2Sa 12:22 Who can tell w. God will be gracious ....
2Sa 15:21 w. in death or life, even there also 518
1Ki 20:18 W. they be come out for peace, ... 518
1Ki 20:18 or w. they be come out for war, ... 518
1Ki 20:33 observe w. any thing would come.............
2Ki 1:2 w. I shall recover of this disease. 518
2Ch 14:11 w. with many, or with them that 996
2Ch 15:13 be put to death, w. small or great,..... 4480
2Ch 15:13 small or great, w. man or woman. ....
Ezr 2:59 their seed, w. they were of Israel:....... 518
Ezr 5:17 w. it be so, that a decree was made... 2006
Ezr 7:26 judgment...w. it be unto death, or...... 2006
Ne 7:61 their seed, w. they were of Israel........ 518
Es 3:4 w. Mordecai's matters would stand:..........
Es 4:11 w. man or woman, shall come unto...........
Es 4:14 w. thou art come to the kingdom......... 518
Job 34:29 w. it be done against a nation, or...........
Job 34:33 w. thou refuse, or w. thou choose; 3588
Job 37:13 w. for correction, or for his land,......... 518
Pr 20:11 w. his work be pure, and w. it be 518
Pr 29:9 man, w. he rage or laugh, there is no ....
Ec 2:19 w. he shall be a wise man or a fool? ....
Ec 5:12 is sweet, w. he eat little or much: 518
Ec 11:6 knowest not w. shall prosper, ... 335
Ec 11:6 or w. they both shall be alike good. 518
Ec 12:14 things, w. it be good, or w. it be evil... 518
Ca 6:11 and to see w. the vine flourished,............
Ca 7:12 flourish, w. the tender grape appear, ...
Jer 30:6 and see w. a man doth travail with....... 518
Jer 42:6 W. it be good, or w. it be evil, we....... 518
Eze 2:5 w. they...hear, or w. they will forbear,..518
Eze 2:7 w. they...hear, or w. they will forbear:..518
Eze 3:11 w. they...hear, or w. they will forbear...518
Eze 44:31 or torn, w. it be fowl or beast........... 4480
Mt 9:5 **w. is easier, to say, Thy sins be**.... *5101*
Mt 21:31 **W. of them twain did the will of**.. *5101*
Mt 23:17 **for w. is greater, the gold, or the**.. *5101*
Mt 23:19 **w. is greater, the gift, or the altar**.*5101*
Mt 26:63 thou tell us w. thou be the Christ, ... *1487*
Mt 27:21 W. of the twain will ye that I........... *5101*
Mt 27:49 w. Elias will come to save him. *1487*
Mk 2:9 **W. it is easier to say to the sick of**.*5101*
Mk 3:2 w. he would heal him on the *1487*
Mk 15:36 w. Elias will come to take him down.. *1487*
Mk 15:44 him w. he had been any while dead. ... *1487*
Lu 3:15 w. he were the Christ, or not; *3379*
Lu 5:23 **W. is easier, to say, Thy sins be**.... *5101*
Lu 6:7 w. he would heal on the sabbath........ *1487*
Lu 14:28 **w. he have sufficient to finish it?**.. *1487*
Lu 14:31 **w. he be able with ten thousand to**.*1487*
Lu 22:27 **w. is greater, he that sitteth at**...... *5101*
Lu 23:6 asked w. the man were a Galilaean..... *1487*
Joh 7:17 **of the doctrine, w. it be of God,**.... *4220*
Joh 7:17 **or w. I speak of myself**.....................
Joh 9:25 W. he be a sinner or no, I know........ *1487*
Ac 1:24 w. of these two thou hast........... *3739,1520*
Ac 4:19 W. it be right in the sight of God....... *1487*
Ac 5:8 w. ye sold the land for so much? *1487*
Ac 9:2 w. they were men or women *5037*
Ac 10:18 and asked w. Simon, which was......... *1487*
Ac 17:11 daily, w. those things were so......... *1487*
Ac 19:2 heard w. there be any Holy Ghost...... *1487*
Ac 25:20 him w. he would go to Jerusalem, ... *1487*
Ro 6:16 ye obey; w. of sin unto death,........... *2273*
Ro 12:6 w. prophecy, let us prophesy *1535*
Ro 14:8 w. we live, we live unto the *1437,5037*
Ro 14:8 w. we die, we die unto the........ *1437,5037*
Ro 14:8 w. we live therefore, or die, we . *1437,5037*
1Co 1:16 I know not w. I baptized any other..... *1487*
1Co 3:22 W. Paul, or Apollos, or Cephas, or...... *1535*
1Co 7:16 w. thou shalt save thy husband?......... *1487*
1Co 7:16 man, w. thou shalt save thy wife? *1487*
1Co 8:5 gods, w. in heaven or in earth,.......... *1535*
1Co 10:31 W. therefore ye eat, or drink, or....... *1535*
1Co 12:13 body, w. we be Jews or Gentiles, ... *1535*
1Co 12:13 w. we be bond or free; and have *1535*
1Co 12:26 And w. one member suffer, all the *1535*
1Co 13:8 w. there be prophecies, they shall...... *1535*
1Co 13:8 w. there be tongues, they shall.......... *1535*
1Co 13:8 w. there be knowledge, it shall.......... *1535*
1Co 14:7 w. pipe or harp, except they give a.... *1535*
1Co 15:11 Therefore w. it were I or they, so..... *1535*
2Co 1:6 And w. we be afflicted, it is for your .. *1535*
2Co 1:6 w. we be comforted, it is for your...... *1535*

2Co 2:9 **w.** ye be obedient in all things *1487*
2Co 5:9 **w.** present or absent, we may be *1535*
2Co 5:10 he hath done, **w.** it be good or bad *1535*
2Co 5:13 **w.** we be beside ourselves, it is to *1535*
2Co 5:13 **w.** we be sober, it is for your cause *1535*
2Co 8:23 **W.** any do enquire of Titus, he is *1535*
2Co 12:2 (**w.** in the body, I cannot tell; *1535*
2Co 12:2 or **w.** out of the body, I cannot tell: *1535*
2Co 12:3 (**w.** in the body, or out of the body, *1535*
2Co 13:5 yourselves, **w.** ye be in the faith; *1487*
Eph 6:8 the Lord, **w.** he be bond or free *1535*
Php 1:18 **w.** in pretence, or in truth, Christ *1535*
Php 1:20 body, **w.** it be by life, or by death *1535*
Php 1:27 **w.** I come and see you, or else be *1535*
Col 1:16 **w.** they be thrones, or dominions, *1535*
Col 1:20 **w.** they be things in earth, or things *1535*
1Th 5:10 **w.** we wake or sleep, we should live *1535*
2Th 2:15 taught, **w.** by word, or our epistle *1535*
1Pe 2:13 **w.** it be to the king, as supreme; *1535*
1Jo 4:1 try the spirits **w.** they are of God: *1487*

WHICH See also WHO.
Ge 1:7 the waters **w.** were under the 834
Ge 1:7 waters **w.** were above the firmament: 834
Ge 1:21 **w.** the waters brought forth 834
Ge 1:29 **w.** is upon the face of all the earth, 834
Ge 1:29 in the **w.** is the fruit of a tree 834
Ge 2:2 ended his work **w.** he had made; 834
Ge 2:2 from all his work **w.** he had made 834
Ge 2:3 from all his work **w.** God created 834
Ge 2:11 is it **w.** compasseth the whole land of
Ge 2:14 that is it **w.** goeth toward the east of
Ge 2:22 rib, **w.** the Lord God had taken 834
Ge 3:1 beast...**w.** the Lord God had made 834
Ge 3:3 tree **w.** is in the midst of the garden, 834
Ge 3:17 the tree, of **w.** I commanded thee, 834
Ge 3:24 flaming sword **w.** turned every way,
Ge 4:11 earth, **w.** hath opened her mouth 834
Ge 5:29 ground **w.** the Lord hath cursed 834
Ge 6:2 them wives of all **w.** they chose 834
Ge 6:4 became mighty men **w.** were of old, 834
Ge 6:15 fashion **w.** thou shalt make it of: 834
Ge 7:23 **w.** was upon the face of the ground, 834
Ge 8:6 window of the ark **w.** he had made: 834
Ge 8:7 forth a raven, **w.** went forth to and fro
Ge 8:12 **w.** returned not again unto him any
Ge 9:4 life thereof, **w.** is the blood thereof,
Ge 9:12 covenant **w.** I make between me 834
Ge 9:15 covenant, **w.** is between me and you 834
Ge 9:17 the covenant, **w.** I have established 834
Ge 11:5 **w.** the children of men builded 834
Ge 11:6 **w.** they have imagined to do 3605,834
Ge 13:4 altar, **w.** he had made there at the 834
Ge 13:5 Lot also, **w.** went with Abram,
Ge 13:15 For all the land **w.** thou seest, to 834
Ge 13:18 the plain of Mamre, **w.** is in Hebron,
Ge 14:2 and the king of Bela, **w.** is Zoar 1931
Ge 14:3 vale of Siddim, **w.** is the salt sea 1931
Ge 14:6 El-paran, **w.** is by the wilderness 1931
Ge 14:7 came to Enmishpat, **w.** is Kadesh,
Ge 14:15 **w.** is on the left hand of Damascus 834
Ge 14:17 of Shaveh, **w.** is the king's dale 1931
Ge 14:20 **w.** hath delivered thine enemies 834
Ge 14:24 that **w.** the young men have eaten, 834
Ge 14:24 of the men **w.** went with me, 834
Ge 16:15 son's name, **w.** Hagar bare, Ishmael 834
Ge 17:10 is my covenant, **w.** ye shall keep, 834
Ge 17:12 any stranger, **w.** is not of thy seed 834
Ge 17:21 **w.** Sarah shall bare unto thee at a 834
Ge 18:8 milk, and the calf **w.** he had dressed, 834
Ge 18:10 the tent door, **w.** was behind him 1931
Ge 18:13 a surety bear a child, **w.** am old? 589
Ge 18:17 from Abraham that thing **w.** I do; 834
Ge 18:19 that **w.** he hath spoken of him 834
Ge 18:21 to the cry of it, **w.** is come unto me;
Ge 18:27 Lord, **w.** am but dust and ashes: 595
Ge 19:5 **w.** came in to thee this night? 834
Ge 19:8 daughters **w.** have not known man; 834
Ge 19:14 sons in law, **w.** married his daughters,
Ge 19:15 and thy two daughters, **w.** are here;
Ge 19:19 **w.** thou hast shewed unto me in 834
Ge 19:21 city for the **w.** thou hast spoken 834
Ge 19:25 and that **w.** grew upon the ground
Ge 19:29 the cities in the **w.** Lot dwelt 834,2004
Ge 20:3 for the woman **w.** thou hast taken; 834
Ge 20:13 is thy kindness **w.** thou shalt show 834
Ge 21:2 set time of **w.** God had spoken to 834
Ge 21:9 **w.** she had born unto Abraham, 834
Ge 21:25 well...**w.** Abimelech's servants had 834
Ge 21:29 seven ewe lambs **w.** thou hast st 834
Ge 22:2 the mountains **w.** I will tell thee of 834
Ge 22:3 the place of **w.** God had told him
Ge 22:9 to the place **w.** God had told him of; 834
Ge 22:17 as the sand **w.** is upon the sea shore; 834
Ge 23:9 **w.** he hath, **w.** is inthe end of his 834
Ge 23:16 the silver, **w.** he had named in the 834
Ge 23:17 the field of Ephron, **w.** was in 834
Ge 23:17 Machpelah, **w.** was before Mamre, 834
Ge 23:17 field, and the cave **w.** was therein, 834
Ge 24:7 **w.** took me from my father's house, 834
Ge 24:7 **w.** took me from my father's house, 834
Ge 24:7 my kindred, and **w.** spake unto me, 834
Ge 24:24 the son of Milcah, **w.** she bare unto 834
Ge 24:42 thou do, prosper my way **w.** I go:
Ge 24:48 **w.** had led me in the right way to 834
Ge 24:60 possess the gate of those **w.** hate them
Ge 25:6 of the concubines, **w.** Abraham had,
Ge 25:7 years of Abraham's life **w.** he lived, 834
Ge 25:9 the Hittite, **w.** is before Mamre; 834
Ge 25:10 The field **w.** Abraham purchased
Ge 26:2 in the land **w.** I shall tell thee of: 834
Ge 26:3 oath **w.** I sware unto Abraham thy 834
Ge 26:15 the wells **w.** his father's servants 834
Ge 26:18 **w.** they had digged in the days of 834
Ge 26:18 by **w.** his father had called them 834
Ge 26:32 concerning the well **w.** they had 834
Ge 26:35 **W.** were a grief of mind unto Isaac
Ge 27:8 according to that **w.** I command 834
Ge 27:15 **w.** were with her in the house,
Ge 27:17 and the bread, **w.** she had prepared, 834
Ge 27:27 of a field **w.** the Lord hath blessed: 834
Ge 27:45 forget that **w.** thou hast done to him: 834
Ge 27:46 **w.** are of the daughters of the land, 834
Ge 28:4 land...**w.** God gave unto Abraham 834
Ge 28:9 and took unto the wives **w.** he had
Ge 28:15 done that **w.** I have spoken to thee 834
Ge 28:22 this stone, **w.** I have set for a pillar, 834
Ge 29:27 service **w.** thou shalt serve with me 834
Ge 30:26 knowest my service **w.** I have done 834
Ge 30:30 little **w.** thou hadst before I came, 834
Ge 30:37 white appear **w.** was in the rods 834
Ge 30:38 set the rods **w.** he had pilled before 834
Ge 31:1 of that **w.** was our father's hath he 834
Ge 31:10 the rams **w.** leaped upon the cattle
Ge 31:12 the rams **w.** leap upon the cattle are
Ge 31:16 riches **w.** God hath taken from our 834
Ge 31:18 and all his goods **w.** he had gotten, 834
Ge 31:18 **w.** he had gotten in Padan-aram, 834
Ge 31:39 **w.** was torn of beasts I brought not
Ge 31:43 their children **w.** they have born? 834
Ge 31:51 **w.** I have cast betwixt me and thee; 834
Ge 32:8 other company **w.** is left shall escape
Ge 32:9 the Lord **w.** saidst unto me, Return
Ge 32:10 **w.** thou hast shewed unto thy 834
Ge 32:12 the sand...**w.** cannot be numbered 834
Ge 32:13 took of that **w.** came to his hand a
Ge 32:32 Israel eat not of the sinew **w.** shrank,
Ge 32:32 **w.** is upon the hollow of the thigh, 834
Ge 33:5 the children **w.** God hath graciously 834
Ge 33:8 thou by all this drove **w.** I met? 834
Ge 33:18 Shechem, **w.** is in the land of Canaan, 834
Ge 34:1 of Leah, **w.** she bare unto Jacob, 834
Ge 34:7 **w.** things ought not to be done 3651
Ge 34:28 asses, and that **w.** was in the city, 834
Ge 34:28 the city, and that **w.** was in the field 834
Ge 35:3 was with me in the way **w.** I went 834
Ge 35:4 strange gods **w.** were in their hand, 834
Ge 35:4 their earrings **w.** were in their ears; 834
Ge 35:4 under the oak **w.** was by Shechem 834
Ge 35:6 Luz, **w.** is in the land of Canaan, 834
Ge 35:12 And the land **w.** I gave Abraham 834
Ge 35:19 way to Ephrath, **w.** is Bethlehem 1958
Ge 35:26 of Jacob, **w.** were born to him in 834
Ge 35:27 **w.** is Hebron, where Abraham and 834
Ge 36:5 **w.** were born unto him in the land 834
Ge 36:6 **w.** he had got in the land of Canaan; 834
Ge 37:6 you, this dream **w.** I have dreamed: 834
Ge 38:10 thing **w.** he did displeased the Lord: 834
Ge 38:14 place, **w.** is by the way to Timnath; 834
Ge 39:1 **w.** had brought him down thither 834
Ge 39:6 he had, save the bread **w.** he did eat, 834
Ge 39:17 **w.** thou hast brought unto us, 834
Ge 39:19 his wife, **w.** she spake unto him, 834
Ge 39:23 that **w.** he did, the Lord made it to 834
Ge 40:5 of Egypt, **w.** were bound in prison 834
Ge 40:20 day, **w.** was Pharaoh's birthday,
Ge 41:28 **w.** I have spoken unto Pharaoh: 834
Ge 41:36 **w.** shall be in the land of Egypt; 834
Ge 41:43 in the second chariot **w.** he had; 834
Ge 41:48 **w.** were in the land of Egypt, and 834
Ge 41:48 field, **w.** was round about every city, 834
Ge 41:50 sons...**w.** Asenath...bare unto him 834
Ge 42:9 the dreams **w.** he dreamed of them, 834
Ge 42:38 him by the way in the **w.** ye go, 834
Ge 43:2 corn **w.** they had brought out of 834
Ge 43:26 the present **w.** was in their hand 834
Ge 43:32 the Egyptians **w.** did eat with him,
Ge 44:5 not this it in **w.** my lord drinketh, 834
Ge 44:8 **w.** we found in our sacks' mouths, 834
Ge 45:6 in...**w.** there shall neither be earing 834
Ge 45:27 Joseph, **w.** he had said unto them: 834
Ge 45:27 wagons **w.** Joseph had sent to carry 834
Ge 46:5 wagons **w.** Pharaoh had sent to 834
Ge 46:6 **w.** they had gotten in the land of 834
Ge 46:8 children of Israel, **w.** came into Egypt,
Ge 46:15 of Leah, **w.** she bare unto Jacob 834
Ge 46:20 **w.** Asenath...bare unto him 834
Ge 46:22 of Rachel, **w.** were born to Jacob: 834
Ge 46:25 Bilhah, **w.** Laban gave unto Rachel 834
Ge 46:26 into Egypt, **w.** came out of his loins,
Ge 46:27 Joseph, **w.** were born him in Egypt, 834
Ge 46:27 **w.** came into Egypt, were threescore
Ge 46:31 **w.** were in the land of Canaan, are 834
Ge 47:14 for the corn **w.** they brought: 834
Ge 47:22 their portion **w.** Pharaoh gave them: 834
Ge 47:26 priests only, **w.** became not Pharaoh's
Ge 48:5 **w.** were born unto thee in the land of
Ge 48:6 issue, **w.** thou begettest after them, 834
Ge 48:15 the God **w.** fed me all my life long
Ge 48:16 The angel **w.** redeemed me from all
Ge 48:22 **w.** I took out of the hand of the 834
Ge 49:1 that **w.** shall befall you in the last 834
Ge 49:30 of Machpelah, **w.** is before Mamre, 834
Ge 49:30 **w.** Abraham bought with the field of 834
Ge 50:3 the days of those **w.** are embalmed:
Ge 50:5 my grave **w.** I have digged for me 834
Ge 50:10 threshingfloor of Atad, **w.** is beyond 834
Ge 50:11 Abel-mizraim, **w.** is beyond Jordan 834
Ge 50:13 **w.** Abraham bought with the field 834
Ge 50:15 us all the evil **w.** we did unto him 834
Ge 50:24 land **w.** he sware unto Abraham, 834
Ex 1:1 of Israel, **w.** came into Egypt;
Ex 1:8 over Egypt, **w.** knew not Joseph 834
Ex 1:15 of **w.** the name of one was Shiphrah, 834
Ex 3:7 of my people **w.** are in Egypt, and 834
Ex 3:16 and seen that **w.** is done to you in 834
Ex 3:20 my wonders **w.** I will do in the 834
Ex 4:9 water **w.** thou takest out of the river 834
Ex 4:18 unto my brethren **w.** are in Egypt, 834
Ex 4:19 the men are dead **w.** sought thy life
Ex 4:21 **w.** I have put in thine hand: 834
Ex 4:28 signs **w.** he had commanded him 834
Ex 4:30 the words **w.** the Lord had spoken 834
Ex 5:8 bricks, **w.** they did make heretofore, 834
Ex 5:14 **w.** Pharaoh's taskmasters had set 834
Ex 6:7 God, **w.** bringeth you out from under
Ex 6:8 concerning the **w.** I did swear to 834
Ex 6:27 are they **w.** spake to Pharaoh king of
Ex 7:15 the rod **w.** was turned to a serpent 834
Ex 7:17 the waters **w.** are in the river, 834
Ex 8:3 **w.** shall go up and come into thine
Ex 8:12 the frogs **w.** he had brought against 834
Ex 8:22 of Goshen, in **w.** my people dwell, 834
Ex 9:3 is upon the cattle **w.** is in the field, 834
Ex 9:19 beast **w.** shall be found in the field, 834
Ex 10:2 signs **w.** I have done among them; 834
Ex 10:5 eat the residue of that **w.** is escaped,
Ex 10:5 **w.** remaineth unto you from the hail,
Ex 10:5 every tree **w.** groweth for you out of
Ex 10:6 **w.** neither thy fathers, nor thy 834
Ex 10:15 fruit of the trees **w.** the hail left: 834
Ex 10:19 west wind, **w.** took away the locusts,
Ex 10:21 Egypt, even darkness **w.** may be felt
Ex 12:10 and that **w.** remaineth of it until the
Ex 12:16 save that **w.** every man must eat, 834
Ex 12:19 whosoever eateth that **w.** is leavened,
Ex 12:25 the land **w.** the Lord will give you, 834
Ex 12:39 dough **w.** they brought forth out of 834
Ex 13:3 day, in **w.** ye came out from Egypt, 834
Ex 13:5 **w.** he sware unto thy fathers to give 834
Ex 13:8 of that **w.** the Lord did unto me

Ex 13:12 cometh of a beast w. thou hast; 834
Ex 14:13 Lord, w. he will shew to you to day:.... 834
Ex 14:19 w. went before the camp of Israel, ...
Ex 14:31 work w. the Lord did put upon the 834
Ex 15:7 wrath w. consumed them as stubble. 834
Ex 15:13 the people w. thou hast redeemed:..... 2098
Ex 15:16 pass over, w. thou hast purchased...... 2098
Ex 15:17 w. thou hast made for thee to dwell ....
Ex 15:17 Lord, w. thy hands have established. ....
Ex 15:25 w. when he had cast into the waters, ...
Ex 15:26 wilt do that w. is right in his sight, ...
Ex 15:26 diseases, w. I have brought upon the ... 834
Ex 16:1 of Sin, w. is between Elim and Sinai, ... 834
Ex 16:5 shall prepare that w. they bring in; 834
Ex 16:8 w. ye murmur against him: 834
Ex 16:15 w. the Lord hath given you to eat. 834
Ex 16:16 thing w. the Lord hath commanded, ... 834
Ex 16:16 man for them w. are in his tents. 834
Ex 16:23 This is that w. the Lord hath said, ... 834
Ex 16:23 bake that w. ye will bake to day, ... 834
Ex 16:23 that w. remaineth over lay up for you ....
Ex 16:26 on the seventh day, w. is the sabbath, ...
Ex 16:32 the thing w. the Lord commandeth, ... 834
Ex 18:3 w. the name of the one was Gershom; ..834
Ex 18:9 w. the Lord had done to Israel, ... 834
Ex 19:6 These are the words w. thou shalt....... 834
Ex 19:7 words w. the Lord commanded 834
Ex 19:22 priests also, w. come near to the Lord, ...
Ex 20:2 w. have brought thee out of the 834
Ex 20:12 the land w. the Lord thy God giveth 834
Ex 21:1 w. thou shalt set before them. 834
Ex 22:9 w. another challengeth to be his, ... 834
Ex 22:13 shall not make good that w. was torn........
Ex 23:16 w. thou hast sown in the field: 834
Ex 23:16 w. is in the end of the year, ...
Ex 23:20 into the place w. I have prepared. 834
Ex 23:28 thee, w. shall drive out the Hivite, ...
Ex 24:3 the words w. the Lord hath said.......... 834
Ex 24:5 of Israel, w. offered burnt offerings, ...
Ex 24:8 w. the Lord hath made with you.......... 834
Ex 24:12 commandments w. I have written; 834
Ex 25:3 offering w. ye shall take of them; 834
Ex 25:16 the testimony w. I shall give thee. 834
Ex 25:22 w. are upon the ark of the testimony,... 834
Ex 25:22 of all things w. I will give thee in......... 834
Ex 25:40 w. was shewed thee in the mount......... 834
Ex 26:10 of the curtain w. coupleth the second........
Ex 26:13 that w. remaineth in the length of the ....
Ex 26:30 w. was shewed thee in the mount........ 834
Ex 27:21 the vail, w. is before the testimony, ... 834
Ex 28:4 the garments w. they shall make; 834
Ex 28:8 girdle of the ephod, w. is upon it, ... 834
Ex 28:24 w. are on the ends of the breastplate........
Ex 28:26 w. is in the side of the ephod inward.... 834
Ex 28:38 w. the children of Israel shall hallow..... 834
Ex 29:27 w. is waved, and w. is heaved up, of ... 834
Ex 29:27 even of that w. is for Aaron, ... 834
Ex 29:27 and of that w. is for his sons: 834
Ex 29:35 things w. I have commanded thee: 834
Ex 29:38 w. thou shalt offer upon the altar; 834
Ex 30:37 for the perfume w. thou shalt make, ... 834
Ex 32:1 make us gods, w. shall go before us; 834
Ex 32:2 w. are in the ears of your wives, ... 834
Ex 32:3 earrings w. were in their ears, ... 834
Ex 32:4 w. brought thee up out of the land....... 834
Ex 32:7 w. thou broughtest out of the land 834
Ex 32:8 of the way w. I commanded them: 834
Ex 32:8 w. have brought up out of the land 834
Ex 32:11 w. thou hast brought forth out of the.... 834
Ex 32:14 of the evil w. he thought to do............ 834
Ex 32:20 took the calf w. they had made, and..... 834
Ex 32:23 Make us gods, w. shall go before us: ... 834
Ex 32:32 out of thy book w. thou hast written. ... 834
Ex 32:34 place of w. I have spoken unto thee: 834
Ex 32:35 they made the calf, w. Aaron made. 834
Ex 33:1 people w. thou hast brought up out....... 834
Ex 33:1 the land w. I sware unto Abraham, ... 834
Ex 33:7 every one w. sought the Lord went out.....
Ex 33:7 w. was without the camp. 834
Ex 34:1 in the first tables, w. thou brakest. 834
Ex 34:10 people among w. thou art shall see 834
Ex 34:11 that w. I commanded thee this day: 834
Ex 34:34 Israel that w. he was commanded. 834
Ex 35:1 words w. the Lord hath commanded, ... 834
Ex 35:4 the thing w. the Lord commanded, ... 834
Ex 35:25 and brought that w. they had spun, ...

Ex 35:29 w. the Lord had commanded to be....... 834
Ex 36:3 w. the children of Israel had brought 834
Ex 36:4 man from his work w. they made; 834
Ex 36:5 w. the Lord commanded to make.......... 834
Ex 36:12 the curtain w. was in the coupling........ 834
Ex 36:17 of the curtain w. coupleth the second. ....
Ex 36:25 w. is toward the north corner, he made.....
Ex 37:16 the vessels w. were upon the table, ... 834
Ex 38:8 w. assembled at the door of the 834
Ex 39:19 w. was on the side of the ephod 834
Le 1:8,12 is on the fire w. is upon the altar: 834
Le 2:10 And that w. is left of the meat offering......
Le 2:11 w. ye shall bring unto the Lord, ... 834
Le 3:4 w. is by the flanks, and the caul......... 834
Le 3:5 w. is upon the wood that is on the......... 834
Le 3:10, 15 w. is by the flanks, and the caul...... 834
Le 4:2 things w. ought not to be done, ... 834
Le 4:3 for his sin, w. he hath sinned, ... 834
Le 4:7 w. is in the tabernacle of the 834
Le 4:7 w. is at the door of the tabernacle 834
Le 4:9 w. is by the flanks, and the caul 834
Le 4:13 things w. should not be done, ... 834
Le 4:14 sin, w. they have sinned against it, ... 834
Le 4:18 of the altar w. is before the Lord, ... 834
Le 4:18 w. is at the door of the tabernacle 834
Le 4:22 things w. should not be done, ... 834
Le 4:27 things w. ought not to be done, ... 834
Le 4:28 Or of his sin, w. he hath sinned, ... 834
Le 4:28 for his sin w. he hath sinned.............. 834
Le 5:6 Lord for his sin w. he hath sinned, ... 834
Le 5:7 his trespass, w. he hath committed, ... 834
Le 5:8 offer that w. is for the sin offering 834
Le 5:10 him for his sin w. he hath sinned, ... 834
Le 5:17 things w. are forbidden to be done....... 834
Le 6:2 that w. was delivered him to keep, ...
Le 6:3 Or have found that w. was lost, and ....
Le 6:4 restore that w. he took violently.......... 834
Le 6:4 thing w. he hath deceitfully gotten, ... 834
Le 6:4 that w. was delivered him to keep, ... 834
Le 6:4 or the lost thing w. he found, ... 834
Le 6:5 that about w. he hath sworn falsely; 834
Le 6:10 the ashes w. the fire hath consumed 834
Le 6:15 w. is upon the meat offering, and 834
Le 6:20 w. they shall offer unto the Lord in...... 834
Le 7:4 w. is by the flanks, and the caul that.... 834
Le 7:8 burnt offering w. he hath offered. 834
Le 7:11 w. he shall offer unto the Lord, ... 834
Le 7:21 offerings, w. pertain unto the Lord, ... 834
Le 7:24 the fat of that w. is torn with beasts, ...
Le 7:25 of w. men offer an offering made by..... 834
Le 7:36 W. the Lord commanded to be............ 834
Le 7:38 W. the Lord commanded Moses in....... 834
Le 8:5 is the thing w. the Lord commanded 834
Le 8:30 of the blood w. was upon the altar, ... 834
Le 8:32 And that w. remaineth of the flesh and......
Le 8:36 w. the Lord commanded by the........... 834
Le 9:5 brought that w. Moses commanded 834
Le 9:6 is the thing w. the Lord commanded 834
Le 9:8 the sin offering, w. was for himself. 834
Le 9:12 w. he sprinkled round about upon the........
Le 9:15 w. was the sin offering for the 834
Le 9:18 offerings, w. was for the people: 834
Le 9:18 w. he sprinkled upon the altar round.........
Le 9:19 and that w. covereth the inwards, ...
Le 9:24 w. when all the people saw, they ....
Le 10:1 Lord, w. he commanded them not. 834
Le 10:6 burning w. the Lord hath kindled. 834
Le 10:11 statutes w. the Lord hath spoken 834
Le 10:14 w. are given out of the sacrifices of..........
Le 10:16 sons of Aaron w. were left alive, ...
Le 11:2 These are the beasts w. ye shall eat 834
Le 11:10 any living thing w. is in the waters, ... 834
Le 11:13 they w. ye shall have in abomination ....
Le 11:21 w. have legs above their feet, to 834
Le 11:23 creeping things, w. have four feet, ... 834
Le 11:26 of every beast w. divideth the hoof, ... 834
Le 11:34 Of all meat w. may be eaten, ... 834
Le 11:34 that on w. such water cometh shall 834
Le 11:36 that w. toucheth their carcase shall be.......
Le 11:37 any sowing seed w. is to be sown, ... 834
Le 11:39 if any beast, of w. ye may eat, die; 834
Le 13:18 The flesh also, in w., even in the skin.......
Le 13:58 of skin it be, w. thou shalt wash, ... 834
Le 14:32 get that w. pertaineth to his cleansing. ......
Le 14:34 w. I give to you for a possession, ... 834
Le 14:37 w. in sight are lower than the wall; ....

Le 14:40 the stones in w. the plague is, ... 834
Le 15:12 that he toucheth w. hath the issue, ... 834
Le 16:2 the mercy seat, w. is upon the ark; 834
Le 16:6 of the sin offering, w. is for himself, ... 834
Le 16:9 the goat upon w. the Lord's lot fell, ... 834
Le 16:10 on w. the lot fell to be the scapegoat, .. 834
Le 16:11 of the sin offering, w. is for himself, ... 834
Le 16:11 of the sin offering, w. is for himself: 834
Le 16:23 w. he put on when he went into the...... 834
Le 17:2 thing w. the Lord hath commanded, ... 834
Le 17:5 w. they offer in the open field, ... 834
Le 17:8 the strangers w. sojourn among you..... 834
Le 17:13 w. hunteth and catcheth any beast 834
Le 17:15 soul that eateth that w. died of itself, ...
Le 17:15 that w. was torn with beasts, whether ......
Le 18:5 w. if a man do, he shall live in them: 834
Le 18:24 are defiled w. I cast out before you: ....
Le 18:27 the land done, w. were before you, ... 834
Le 18:30 w. were committed before you, ... 834
Le 19:22 Lord for his sin, w. he hath done: 834
Le 19:22 sin w. he hath done shall be forgiven ....
Le 19:36 w. brought you out of the land of 834
Le 20:8 I am the Lord w. sanctify you. ....
Le 20:23 the nation, w. I cast out before you. 834
Le 20:24 w. have separated you from other........ 834
Le 20:25 w. I have separated from you as 834
Le 21:3 virgin,...w. hath had no husband; 834
Le 21:8 I the Lord, w. sanctify you, am holy. ....
Le 22:2 things w. they hallow unto me: 834
Le 22:3 w. the children of Israel hallow unto..... 834
Le 22:6 The soul w. hath touched any such 834
Le 22:8 w. dieth of itself, or is torn with beasts, ...
Le 22:15 Israel, w. they offer unto the Lord; 834
Le 22:18 w. they will offer unto the Lord for a ... 834
Le 22:24 offer unto the Lord that w. is bruised, ...
Le 22:32 I am the Lord w. hallow you, ...
Le 23:2 w. ye shall proclaim to be holy 834
Le 23:4 w. ye shall proclaim in their seasons..... 834
Le 23:10 unto the land w. I give unto you, ... 834
Le 23:37 w. ye shall proclaim to be holy............ 834
Le 23:38 offerings, w. ye give unto the Lord. 834
Le 25:2 come into the land w. I give you, ... 834
Le 25:5 That w. groweth of its own accord ....
Le 25:11 neither reap that w. groweth of itself ....
Le 25:25 he redeem that w. his brother sold. ....
Le 25:28 then that w. is sold shall remain in ....
Le 25:31 w. have no wall round about them. 834
Le 25:38 w. brought you forth out of the land...... 834
Le 25:42 w. I brought forth out of the land of..... 834
Le 25:44 thy bondmaids, w. thou shalt have, ... 834
Le 25:45 with you, w. they begat in your land: ....
Le 26:13 w. brought you forth out of the 834
Le 26:22 w. shall rob you of your children, and ....
Le 26:32 enemies w. dwell therein shall be ....
Le 26:40 trespass w. they trespassed against...... 834
Le 26:46 and laws, w. the Lord made 834
Le 27:11 of w. they do not offer a sacrifice 834
Le 27:22 the Lord a field w. he hath brought, ...
Le 27:22 w. is not of the fields of his................ 834
Le 27:26 w. should be the Lord's firstling. 834
Le 27:29 devoted, w. shall be devoted of men, ... 834
Le 27:34 w. the Lord commanded Moses for...... 834
Nu 1:17 these men w. are expressed by their.... 834
Nu 1:44 w. Moses and Aaron numbered, and..... 834
Nu 2:12 those w. pitch by him shall be the...........
Nu 2:32 those w. were numbered of the ....
Nu 3:3 the priests w. were anointed, whom ....
Nu 3:26 the court, w. is by the tabernacle, ... 834
Nu 3:39 w. Moses and Aaron numbered at........ 834
Nu 3:46 Israel, w. are more than the Levites; ....
Nu 4:26 the court, w. is by the tabernacle 834
Nu 4:37 w. Moses and Aaron did number 834
Nu 5:7 confess their sin w. they have done: 834
Nu 5:9 Israel, w. they bring unto the priest, ... 834
Nu 5:18 hands, w. is the jealousy offering: 1958
Nu 6:5 in the w. he separateth himself 834
Nu 6:18 in the fire w. is under the sacrifice........ 834
Nu 6:21 according to the vow w. he vowed, ... 834
Nu 8:4 pattern w. the Lord had shewed Moses, ...
Nu 10:4 w. are heads of the thousands of.............
Nu 10:25 w. was the rereward of all the camps........
Nu 10:29 unto the place of w. the Lord said, ... 834
Nu 11:5 fish, w. we did eat in Egypt freely; 834
Nu 11:12 the land w. thou swarest unto their...... 834
Nu 11:17 take of the spirit w. is upon thee, ... 834
Nu 11:20 despised the Lord w. is among you, ... 834

Nu 12:3 men w. were upon the face of the 834
Nu 13:2 w. I give unto the children of Israel: 834
Nu 13:16 w. Moses sent to spy out the land. 834
Nu 13:24 w. the children of Israel cut down 834
Nu 13:32 of the land w. they had searched 834
Nu 13:32 through w. we have gone to search 834
Nu 13:33 of Anak, w. come of the giants:
Nu 14:6 w. were of them that searched the
Nu 14:7 w. we passed through to search it, 834
Nu 14:8 us; a land w. floweth with milk and 834
Nu 14:11 the signs w. I have shewed among 834
Nu 14:15 nations w. have heard the fame of 834
Nu 14:16 the land w. he sware unto them, 834
Nu 14:22 of those men w. have seen my glory,
Nu 14:22 w. I did in Egypt and in the 834
Nu 14:23 the land w. I sware unto their fathers,
Nu 14:27 congregation, w. murmur against 834
Nu 14:27 Israel, w. they murmur against me 834
Nu 14:29 w. have murmured against me, 834
Nu 14:30 w. I sware to make you dwell 834
Nu 14:31 ones, w. ye said should be a prey,
Nu 14:31 know the land w. ye have despised. 834
Nu 14:34 the days in w. ye search the land, 834
Nu 14:36 w. Moses sent to search the land, 834
Nu 14:38 w. were of the men that went to
Nu 14:40 place w. the Lord hath promised: 834
Nu 14:45 the Canaanites w. dwell in that hill,
Nu 15:2 habitations, w. I give unto you. 834
Nu 15:22 w. the Lord hath spoken unto 834
Nu 15:39 after w. ye use to go a whoring: 834
Nu 15:41 w. brought you out of the land of 834
Nu 16:11 For w. cause both thou and all thy
Nu 16:12 Eliab: w. said, We will not come up:
Nu 16:40 w. is not of the seed of Aaron, come 834
Nu 18:9 theirs, w. they shall render unto me, 834
Nu 18:12 w. they shall offer unto the Lord, 834
Nu 18:13 w. they shall bring unto the Lord. 834
Nu 18:15 flesh, w. they bring unto the Lord, 834
Nu 18:16 the sanctuary, w. is twelve gerahs. 1958
Nu 18:19 w. the children of Israel offer unto 834
Nu 18:21 for their service w. they serve, 834
Nu 18:24 w. they offer as an heave offering 834
Nu 18:26 the tithes w. I have given you from 834
Nu 18:28 w. ye receive of the children of 834
Nu 19:2 law w. the Lord hath commanded, 834
Nu 19:2 and upon w. never came yoke 834
Nu 19:15 w. hath no covering bound upon it, 834
Nu 20:12 unto the land w. I have given them. 834
Nu 20:24 unto the land w. I have given unto 834
Nu 21:1 the Canaanite, w. dwelt in the south,
Nu 21:11 the wilderness w. is before Moab, 834
Nu 21:13 w. is in the wilderness that cometh 834
Nu 21:20 Pisgah, w. looketh toward Jeshimon.
Nu 21:30 Nophah, w. reacheth unto Medeba. 834
Nu 21:34 the Amorites, w. dwelt at Heshbon. 834
Nu 22:5 Pethor, w. is by the river of the land 834
Nu 22:11 w. covereth the face of the earth:
Nu 22:20 the word w. I shall say unto thee, 834
Nu 22:30 upon w. thou hast ridden ever since 834
Nu 22:36 Moab, w. is in the border of Arnon, 834
Nu 22:36 Arnon, w. is in the utmost coast. 834
Nu 23:12 w. the Lord hath put in my mouth? 834
Nu 24:4 said, w. heard the words of God, 834
Nu 24:4 w. saw the vision of the Almighty,
Nu 24:6 lign aloes w. the Lord hath planted,
Nu 24:12 messengers w. thou sentest unto 834
Nu 24:16 w. heard the words of God, and knew
Nu 24:16 w. saw the vision of the Almighty,
Nu 25:18 w. was slain in the day of the plague
Nu 26:4 w. went forth out of the land of Egypt.
Nu 26:9 w. were famous in the congregation,
Nu 27:12 land w. I have given unto the 834
Nu 27:17 W. may go out before them, and 834
Nu 27:17 and w. may go in before them, and 834
Nu 27:17 and w. may lead them out, and 834
Nu 27:17 w. may bring them in; that the 834
Nu 27:17 not as sheep w. have no shepherd. 834
Nu 28:3 fire w. ye shall offer unto the Lord; 834
Nu 28:6 w. was ordained in mount Sinai for a
Nu 28:23 w. is for a continual burnt offering. 834
Nu 30:1 thing w. the Lord hath commanded. 834
Nu 30:8 shall make her vow w. she vowed, 834
Nu 30:8 and that w. she uttered with her lips,
Nu 30:14 or all her bonds, w. are upon her: 834
Nu 30:16 w. the Lord commanded Moses, 834
Nu 31:12 plains of Moab, w. are by Jordan 834
Nu 31:14 hundreds, w. came from the battle.
Nu 31:21 the men of war w. went to the battle,
Nu 31:21 w. the Lord commanded Moses; 834
Nu 31:28 the men of war w. went out to battle:
Nu 31:30 w. keep the charge of the tabernacle
Nu 31:32 prey w. the men of war had caught 834
Nu 31:36 w. was the portion of them that went
Nu 31:38, 39,40 of w. the Lord's tribute was
Nu 31:41 w. was the Lord's heave offering,
Nu 31:42 w. Moses divided from the men 834
Nu 31:47 w. kept the charge of the tabernacle
Nu 31:48 officers w. were over thousands 834
Nu 31:49 men of war w. are under our charge, 834
Nu 32:4 country w. the Lord smote before 834
Nu 32:7 land w. the Lord hath given them? 834
Nu 32:9 land w. the Lord hath given them. 834
Nu 32:11 the land w. I sware unto Abraham, 834
Nu 32:24 w. hath proceeded out of your mouth.
Nu 32:38 unto the cities w. they builded. 834
Nu 32:39 the Amorite w. was in it. 834
Nu 33:1 w. went forth out of the land of 834
Nu 33:4 firstborn, w. the Lord had smitten 834
Nu 33:6 w. is in the edge of the wilderness. 834
Nu 33:7 w. is before Baal-zephon: 834
Nu 33:36 wilderness of Zin, w. is Kadesh. 1958
Nu 33:40 Canaanite, w. dwelt in the south 1931
Nu 33:55 those w. ye let remain of them shall 834
Nu 34:13 This is the land w. ye shall inherit 834
Nu 34:13 w. the Lord commanded to give 834
Nu 34:17 w. shall divide the land unto you: 834
Nu 35:4 w. ye shall give unto the Levites, 834
Nu 35:6 w. ye shall appoint for the manslayer,
Nu 35:6 w. ye shall give unto the Levites 834
Nu 35:7 cities w. ye shall give to the Levites 834
Nu 35:8 the cities w. ye shall give shall be 834
Nu 35:8 to his inheritance w. he inheriteth. 834
Nu 35:11 w. killeth any person at unawares.
Nu 35:13 And of these cities w. ye shall give, 834
Nu 35:14 of Canaan, w. shall be cities of refuge.
Nu 35:25 w. was anointed with the holy oil. 834
Nu 35:31 a murderer, w. is guilty of death: 834
Nu 35:34 the land w. ye shall inhabit, 834
Nu 36:6 thing w. the Lord doth command 834
Nu 36:13 w. the Lord commanded by the 834
De 1:1 w. Moses spake unto all Israel 834
De 1:4 the Amorites, w. dwelt in Heshbon, 834
De 1:4 w. dwelt at Astaroth in Edrei: 834
De 1:8 the land w. the Lord sware unto 834
De 1:14 thing w. thou hast spoken is good 834
De 1:18 time all the things w. ye shall do. 834
De 1:19 wilderness, w. ye saw by the way 834
De 1:20 w. the Lord our God doth give unto 834
De 1:25 w. the Lord our God doth give us 834
De 1:30 Lord your God w. goeth before you,
De 1:35 land, w. I sware to give unto your 834
De 1:38 son of Nun, w. standeth before thee,
De 1:39 ones, w. ye said should be a prey, 834
De 1:39 w. in that day had no knowledge 834
De 1:44 Amorites, w. dwelt in that mountain,
De 2:4 the children of Esau, w. dwelt in Seir;
De 2:8 children of Esau, w. dwelt in Seir,
De 2:11 W. also were accounted giants, 1992
De 2:12 w. the Lord gave unto them. 834
De 2:14 the space in w. we came from 834
De 2:22 the children of Esau, w. dwelt in Seir,
De 2:23 And the Avims w. dwelt in Hazerim,
De 2:23 w. came forth out of Caphtor,
De 2:29 the children of Esau w. dwell in Seir,
De 2:29 Moabites w. dwell in Ar, did unto me;)
De 2:29 into the land w. the Lord our God 834
De 2:35 the spoil of the cities w. we took 834
De 2:36 Aroer, w. is by the brink of the river 834
De 3:2 the Amorites, w. dwelt at Heshbon. 834
De 3:4 not a city w. we took not from them, 834
De 3:9 (W. Hermon the Sidonians call
De 3:12 land, w. we possessed at that time,
De 3:12 w. is by the river Arnon, and half 834
De 3:13 w. was called the land of giants, 1931
De 3:16 w. is the border of the children of
De 3:19 your cities w. I have given you; 834
De 3:20 w. the Lord your God hath given 834
De 3:20 possession, w. I have given you. 834
De 3:28 inherit the land w. thou shalt see. 834
De 4:1 judgments, w. I teach you, for to do 834
De 4:1 possess the land w. the Lord God
De 4:2 unto the word w. I command you, 834
De 4:2 Lord your God w. I command you. 834
De 4:6 w. shall hear all these statutes, and 834
De 4:8 law, w. I set before you this day? 834
De 4:9 the things w. thine eyes have seen, 834
De 4:13 w. he commanded you to perform, 834
De 4:19 w. the Lord thy God hath divided 834
De 4:21 w. the Lord thy God giveth thee for 834
De 4:23 covenant...w. he made with you, 834
De 4:23 w. the Lord thy God hath forbidden 834
De 4:28 w. neither see, nor hear, nor eat, 834
De 4:31 fathers w. he sware unto them. 834
De 4:32 that are past, w. were before thee, 834
De 4:40 w. I command thee this day, 834
De 4:40 w. the Lord thy God giveth thee, 834
De 4:42 w. should kill his neighbour 834
De 4:44 law w. Moses set before the children 834
De 4:45 w. Moses spake unto the children of 834
De 4:47 w. were on this side Jordan toward 834
De 4:48 w. is by the bank of the river Arnon 834
De 4:48 unto mount Sion, w. is Hermon. 1931
De 5:1 w. I speak in your ears this day, 834
De 5:6 God, w. brought thee out of the land 834
De 5:16 land w. the Lord thy God giveth 834
De 5:28 w. they have spoken unto thee: 834
De 5:31 judgments, w. thou shalt teach them, 834
De 5:31 them in the land w. I give them 834
De 5:33 w. the Lord your God...commanded 834
De 5:33 in the land w. ye shall possess. 834
De 6:1 w. the Lord your God commanded 834
De 6:2 commandments, w. I command thee, 834
De 6:6 words, w. I command thee this day, 834
De 6:10 land w. he sware unto thy fathers, 834
De 6:10 goodly cities, w. thou buildest not, 834
De 6:11 good things, w. thou filledst not, 834
De 6:11 wells digged, w. thou diggedst not, 834
De 6:11 olive trees, w. thou plantedst not; 834
De 6:12 w. brought thee forth out of the 834
De 6:14 the people w. are round about you; 834
De 6:17 w. he hath commanded thee. 834
De 6:18 shalt do that w. is right and good 834
De 6:18 w. the Lord sware unto thy fathers, 834
De 6:20 w. the Lord our God...commanded 834
De 6:23 land w. he sware unto our fathers. 834
De 7:8 w. he had sworn unto your fathers, 834
De 7:9 w. keepeth covenant and mercy 834
De 7:11 w. I command thee this day, to do 834
De 7:12 land w. he sware unto thy fathers: 834
De 7:13 land w. he sware unto thy fathers 834
De 7:15 diseases of Egypt, w. thou knowest, 834
De 7:16 w. the Lord thy God shall deliver 834
De 7:19 temptations w. thine eyes saw, 834
De 8:1 commandments w. I command thee 834
De 8:1 land w. the Lord sware unto your 834
De 8:2 way w. the Lord thy God led thee 834
De 8:3 with manna, w. thou knewest not, 834
De 8:10 good land w. he hath given thee. 834
De 8:11 w. I command thee this day: 834
De 8:14 w. brought thee forth out of the land
De 8:16 manna, w. thy fathers knew not, 834
De 8:18 w. he sware unto thy fathers, as it 834
De 8:20 nations w. the Lord destroyeth 834
De 9:3 God, is he w. goeth over before thee;
De 9:5 w. the Lord sware unto thy fathers, 834
De 9:9 covenant w. the Lord made with 834
De 9:10 words w. the Lord spake with you 834
De 9:12 out of the way w. I commanded them;
De 9:12 w. thou hast brought forth out of 834
De 9:16 way w. the Lord had commanded 834
De 9:18 your sins w. ye sinned, in doing 834
De 9:21 your sin, the calf w. ye had made, 834
De 9:23 the land w. I have given you; 834
De 9:26 w. thou hast redeemed through thy 834
De 9:26 w. thou hast brought forth out of 834
De 9:28 into the land w. he promised them, 834
De 9:29 w. thou broughtest out by thy 834
De 10:2 in the first tables w. thou brakest, 834
De 10:4 w. the Lord spake unto you in the 834
De 10:5 the tables in the ark w. I had made; 834
De 10:11 w. I sware unto their fathers to 834
De 10:13 w. I command thee this day for 834
De 10:17 w. regardeth not persons, nor 834
De 10:21 terrible things, w. thine eyes have 834
De 11:2 known, and w. have not seen the 834
De 11:2 your children w. have not known, 834
De 11:3 acts, w. he did in the midst of Egypt 834
De 11:7 great acts of the Lord w. he did 834

De 11:8 commandments **w.** I command you....... 834
De 11:9 **w.** the Lord sware unto your fathers.... 834
De 11:12 A land **w.** the Lord thy God careth...... 834
De 11:13 commandments **w.** I command you....... 834
De 11:17 good land **w.** the Lord giveth you. 834
De 11:21 **w.** the Lord sware unto your fathers.... 834
De 11:22 commandments **w.** I command you,...... 834
De 11:27 **w.** I command you this day:............... 834
De 11:28 the way **w.** I command you this day,.... 834
De 11:28 other gods, **w.** ye have not known....... 834
De 11:30 **w.** dwell in the champaign over..............
De 11:31 **w.** the Lord your God giveth you, ... 834
De 11:32 judgments **w.** I set before you this....... 834
De 12:1 **w.** ye shall observe to do in the land,... 834
De 12:1 **w.** the Lord God of thy fathers hath..... 834
De 12:2 the nations **w.** ye shall possess 834
De 12:5 **w.** the Lord your God shall choose 834
De 12:9 **w.** the Lord your God giveth you. 834
De 12:10 **w.** the Lord your God giveth you 834
De 12:11 **w.** the Lord your God shall choose 834
De 12:11 vows **w.** ye vowed unto the Lord: 834
De 12:14 the place **w.** the Lord shall choose....... 834
De 12:15 Lord thy God **w.** he hath given thee:.... 834
De 12:17 nor any of thy vows **w.** thou vowest, ... 834
De 12:18 **w.** the Lord thy God shall choose, ... 834
De 12:21 **w.** the Lord thy God hath chosen 834
De 12:21 flock, **w.** the Lord hath given thee, ... 834
De 12:25 do that **w.** is right in the sight of the ....
De 12:26 Only thy holy things **w.** thou hast, ... 834
De 12:26 the place **w.** the Lord shall choose:...... 834
De 12:28 all these words **w.** I command thee,..... 834
De 12:28 doest that **w.** is good and right in............
De 12:31 abomination...**w.** he hateth, ... 834
De 13:2 other gods, **w.** thou hast not known,.... 834
De 13:5 **w.** brought you out of the land of............
De 13:5 of the way **w.** the Lord thy God......... 834
De 13:6 friend, **w.** is as thine own soul, ... 834
De 13:6 other gods, **w.** thou hast not known,.... 834
De 13:7 the people **w.** are round about you,...... 834
De 13:10 **w.** brought thee out of the land of...........
De 13:12 **w.** the Lord thy God hath given 834
De 13:13 other gods, **w.** ye have not known,...... 834
De 13:18 commandments **w.** I command thee...... 834
De 13:18 do that **w.** is right in the eyes of the.........
De 14:4 are the beasts **w.** ye shall eat: 834
De 14:12 these are they of **w.** ye shall not eat: ... 834
De 14:23 in the place **w.** he shall choose to........ 834
De 14:24 **w.** the Lord thy God shall choose 834
De 14:25 **w.** the Lord thy God shall choose: 834
De 14:29 the widow, **w.** are within thy gates, ... 834
De 14:29 work of thine hand **w.** thou doest. 834
De 15:3 that **w.** is thine with thy brother.......... 834
De 15:4 land **w.** the Lord thy God giveth.......... 834
De 15:5 **w.** I command thee this day,............... 834
De 15:7 land **w.** the Lord thy God giveth.......... 834
De 15:8 for his need, in that **w.** he wanteth. 834
De 15:20 the place **w.** the Lord shall choose,...... 834
De 16:2 the place **w.** the Lord shall choose....... 834
De 16:4 **w.** thou sacrificedst the first day at 834
De 16:5 **w.** the Lord thy God giveth thee: 834
De 16:6 **w.** the Lord thy God shall choose 834
De 16:7 place **w.** the Lord thy God shall 834
De 16:10 **w.** thou shalt give unto the Lord 834
De 16:11 **w.** the Lord thy God hath chosen 834
De 16:15 the place **w.** the Lord shall choose: 834
De 16:16 God in the place **w.** he shall choose; 834
De 16:17 Lord thy God **w.** he hath given thee..... 834
De 16:18 **w.** the Lord thy God giveth thee, ... 834
De 16:20 That **w.** is altogether just shalt thou..........
De 16:20 land **w.** the Lord thy God giveth.......... 834
De 16:21 thy God, **w.** thou shalt make thee........ 834
De 16:22 image; **w.** the Lord thy God hateth. 834
De 17:2 **w.** the Lord thy God giveth thee, ... 834
De 17:3 heaven, **w.** I have not commanded; 834
De 17:5 **w.** have committed that wicked 834
De 17:8 **w.** the Lord thy God shall choose. 834
De 17:10 sentence, **w.** they of that place 834
De 17:10 place **w.** the Lord shall choose 834
De 17:11 of the law **w.** they shall teach thee,...... 834
De 17:11 judgment **w.** they shall tell thee, ... 834
De 17:11 sentence **w.** they shall shew thee, ... 834
De 17:14 land **w.** the Lord thy God giveth thee,.. 834
De 17:15 over thee, **w.** is not thy brother. 834
De 17:18 out of that **w.** is before the priests ....
De 18:6 the place **w.** the Lord shall choose; 834
De 18:7 do, **w.** stand there before the Lord...........

De 18:8 that **w.** cometh of the sale of his.............
De 18:9 land **w.** the Lord thy God giveth.......... 834
De 18:14 these nations, **w.** thou shalt possess,.... 834
De 18:17 spoken that **w.** they have spoken......... 834
De 18:19 my words **w.** he shall speak in my....... 834
De 18:20 **w.** shall presume to speak a word in 834
De 18:20 **w.** I have not commanded him to ....
De 18:21 word **w.** the Lord hath not spoken?...... 834
De 18:22 thing **w.** the Lord hath not spoken, ... 834
De 19:2,3 **w.** the Lord thy God giveth thee to 834
De 19:4 the slayer, **w.** shall flee thither,........... 834
De 19:8 land **w.** he promised to give unto......... 834
De 19:9 them, **w.** I command thee this day,...... 834
De 19:10 land, **w.** the Lord thy God giveth thee.. 834
De 19:14 **w.** they of old time have set in thine.... 834
De 19:14 **w.** thou shalt inherit in the land.......... 834
De 19:16 testify against him that **w.** is wrong; ....
De 19:17 judges, **w.** shall be in those days; 834
De 19:20 And those **w.** remain shall hear,...............
De 20:1 **w.** brought thee up out of the land....... 834
De 20:14 **w.** the Lord thy God hath given 834
De 20:15 all the cities **w.** are very far off from.........
De 20:15 **w.** are not of the cities of these 834
De 20:16 **w.** the Lord thy God doth give thee..... 834
De 20:18 **w.** they have done unto their gods;...... 834
De 20:20 Only the trees **w.** thou knowest that.... 834
De 21:1 land **w.** the Lord thy God giveth......... 834
De 21:2 cities **w.** are round about him that........ 834
De 21:3 the city **w.** is next unto the slain man, ...
De 21:3 **w.** had not been wrought with,............ 834
De 21:3 and **w.** hath not drawn in the yoke;..... 834
De 21:4 valley, **w.** is neither eared nor sown,..... 834
De 21:9 do that **w.** is right in the sight of the ....
De 21:16 his sons to inherit that **w.** he hath, ... 834
De 21:16 the hated, **w.** is indeed the firstborn: ....
De 21:18 **w.** will not obey the voice of his father,.....
De 21:23 **w.** the Lord thy God giveth thee 834
De 22:3 of thy brother's, **w.** he hath lost,......... 834
De 22:5 wear that **w.** pertaineth unto a man, ...
De 22:9 fruit of thy seed **w.** thou hast sown,..... 834
De 22:28 is a virgin, **w.** is not betrothed,........... 834
De 23:13 and cover that **w.** cometh from thee: ....
De 23:15 the servant **w.** is escaped from his........ 834
De 23:16 in that place **w.** he shall choose........... 834
De 23:23 That **w.** is gone out of thy lips thou 834
De 23:23 **w.** thou hast promised with thy...............
De 24:3 die, **w.** took her to be his wife;........... 834
De 24:4 former husband, **w.** sent her away, ... 834
De 24:4 **w.** the Lord thy God giveth thee for 834
De 24:5 cheer up his wife **w.** he hath taken. 834
De 25:6 the firstborn **w.** she beareth shall.............
De 25:6 in the name of his brother **w.** is dead,.......
De 25:15, 19 land **w.** the Lord thy God giveth 834
De 26:1 the land **w.** the Lord giveth thee for..... 834
De 26:2 **w.** thou shalt bring of thy land............ 834
De 26:2 place **w.** the Lord God shall choose...... 834
De 26:3 **w.** the Lord sware unto our father....... 834
De 26:10 **w.** thou, O Lord, hast given me. 834
De 26:11 good thing **w.** the Lord hath given 834
De 26:12 third year, **w.** is the year of tithing,..........
De 26:13 **w.** thou hast commanded me: 834
De 26:15 and the land **w.** thou hast given us,...... 834
De 26:19 above all nations **w.** he hath made,....... 834
De 27:1 commandments **w.** I command you....... 834
De 27:2, 3 **w.** the Lord thy God giveth thee, ... 834
De 27:4 stones, **w.** I command you this day, ... 834
De 27:10 statutes, **w.** I command thee this day. .. 834
De 28:1 commandments **w.** I command you........ 834
De 28:8 land **w.** the Lord thy God giveth.......... 834
De 28:11 **w.** the Lord sware unto thy fathers...... 834
De 28:13 thy God, **w.** I command thee this day,.. 834
De 28:14 words **w.** I command thee this day,...... 834
De 28:15 statutes **w.** I command thee this day; ... 834
De 28:33 nation **w.** thou knowest not eat up; 834
De 28:34 sight of thine eyes **w.** thou shalt see. ... 834
De 28:36 thy king **w.** thou shalt set over thee,.... 834
De 28:36 nation **w.** neither thou nor thy fathers ....
De 28:45 his statutes **w.** he commanded thee...... 834
De 28:48 **w.** the Lord shall send against thee,..... 834
De 28:50 **w.** shall not regard the person of......... 834
De 28:51 **w.** also shall not leave thee either........ 834
De 28:52, 53 **w.** the Lord thy God hath given...... 834
De 28:54 of his children **w.** he shall leave:.......... 834
De 28:56 **w.** would not adventure to set the 834
De 28:57 her children **w.** she shall hear: 834
De 28:60 of Egypt, **w.** thou wast afraid of;......... 834

De 28:61 **w.** is not written in the book of this..... 834
De 28:64 **w.** neither thou nor thy fathers 834
De 28:67 sight of thine eyes **w.** thou shalt see. ... 834
De 29:1 **w.** he made with them in Horeb..............
De 29:1 **w.** the Lord commanded Moses to.......... 834
De 29:3 **w.** thine eyes have seen, the signs, ... 834
De 29:12 **w.** the Lord thy God maketh with........ 834
De 29:16 through...nations **w.** ye passed by;....... 834
De 29:17 and gold, **w.** were among them:) 834
De 29:22 **w.** the Lord hath laid upon it; 834
De 29:23 **w.** the Lord overthrew in his anger,..... 834
De 29:25 **w.** he made with them when he 834
De 29:29 those things **w.** are revealed belong..........
De 30:1 the curse, **w.** I have set before thee, ... 834
De 30:5 the land **w.** thy fathers possessed,....... 834
De 30:7 that hate thee, **w.** persecuted thee........ 834
De 30:8 commandments **w.** I commanded.......... 834
De 30:10 statutes **w.** are written in this book ....
De 30:11 commandment **w.** I command thee 834
De 30:20 **w.** the Lord sware unto thy fathers,..... 834
De 31:5 **w.** I have commanded you................. 834
De 31:7 land **w.** the Lord hath sworn unto........ 834
De 31:9 **w.** bare the ark of the covenant of...........
De 31:11 God in the place **w.** he shall choose, ... 834
De 31:13 children **w.** have not known any 834
De 31:16 covenant **w.** I have made with them..........
De 31:18 evils **w.** they shall have wrought,.......... 834
De 31:20 land **w.** I sware unto their fathers,........ 834
De 31:21 their imagination **w.** they go about, ... 834
De 31:21 them into the land **w.** I sware. 834
De 31:23 into the land **w.** I sware unto them: 834
De 31:25 **w.** bare the ark of the covenant of....... 834
De 31:29 from the way **w.** I have commanded..... 834
De 32:15 then he forsook God **w.** made him,...........
De 32:21 jealously with that **w.** is not God;............
De 32:21 with those **w.** are not a people; ....
De 32:38 **W.** did eat the fat of their.................. 834
De 32:46 all the words **w.** I testify among you 834
De 32:46 **w.** ye shall command your children....... 834
De 32:49 Nebo, **w.** is in the land of Moab, ... 834
De 32:49 Canaan, **w.** I give unto the children...... 834
De 32:52 land **w.** I give the children of Israel..... 834
De 34:4 the land **w.** I sware unto Abraham, ... 834
De 34:11 the wonders, **w.** the Lord sent him...... 834
De 34:12 the great terror **w.** Moses shewed....... 834
Jos 1:2 unto the land **w.** I do give to them,...... 834
Jos 1:6 **w.** I sware unto their fathers to give.... 834
Jos 1:7 **w.** Moses my servant commanded 834
Jos 1:11 **w.** the Lord your God giveth you to..... 834
Jos 1:13 word **w.** Moses the servant of the 834
Jos 1:14 in the land **w.** Moses gave you on this.. 834
Jos 1:15 **w.** the Lord your God giveth them:...... 834
Jos 1:15 **w.** Moses the Lord's servant gave 834
Jos 2:3 **w.** are entered into thine house:.......... 834
Jos 2:6 **w.** she had laid in order upon the............
Jos 2:7 they **w.** pursued after them were......... 834
Jos 2:17 oath **w.** thou hast made us swear. 834
Jos 2:18 window **w.** thou didst let us down by:... 834
Jos 2:20 oath **w.** thou hast made us to swear..... 834
Jos 3:4 know the way by **w.** ye must go: 834
Jos 3:16 the waters **w.** came down from above.......
Jos 4:9 priests **w.** bare the ark of the covenant .....
Jos 4:10 priests **w.** bare the ark stood in the..........
Jos 4:20 stones **w.** they took out of Jordan,....... 834
Jos 4:23 sea, **w.** he dried up from before us,..... 834
Jos 5:1 **w.** were on the side of Jordan............. 834
Jos 5:1 the Canaanites, **w.** were by the sea, ... 834
Jos 5:6 men of war, **w.** came out of Egypt, ...
Jos 5:6 land, **w.** the Lord sware unto their....... 834
Jos 6:25 **w.** Joshua sent to spy out Jericho. 834
Jos 7:2 Jericho to Ai, **w.** is beside Beth-aven,... 834
Jos 7:11 my covenant **w.** I commanded them: 834
Jos 7:14 household **w.** the Lord shall take 834
Jos 7:14 tribe **w.** the Lord taketh shall come...... 834
Jos 7:14 the family **w.** the Lord shall take 834
Jos 8:27 Lord...**w.** he commanded Joshua. 834
Jos 8:31 over **w.** no man hath lifted up any.........
Jos 8:32 **w.** he wrote in the presence of the...... 834
Jos 8:33 **w.** bare the ark of the covenant of the ......
Jos 8:35 **w.** Joshua read not before all the 834
Jos 9:1 kings **w.** were on this side Jordan, ... 834
Jos 9:10 king of Bashan, **w.** was at Ashtaroth. ... 834
Jos 9:13 And these bottles of wine **w.** we filled, . 834
Jos 9:20 of the oath **w.** we sware unto them...... 834
Jos 9:27 in the place **w.** he should choose. 834
Jos 10:11 more **w.** died with hailstones than........ 834

Book	Ref	Context	No.
Jos	10:20	the rest **w.** remained of them entered	
Jos	10:24	of the men of war **w.** went with him,	
Jos	10:27	mouth, **w.** remain until this very day.	
Jos	10:32	of Israel, **w.** took it on the second day,	
Jos	12:1	**w.** the children of Israel smote,	834
Jos	12:2	**w.** is upon the bank of the river	834
Jos	12:2	**w.** is the border of the children of	
Jos	12:4	**w.** was of the remnant of the giants,	
Jos	12:7	**w.** Joshua and the children of	834
Jos	12:7	**w.** Joshua gave unto the tribes of	
Jos	12:9	the king of Ai, **w.** is beside Beth-el,	834
Jos	13:3	From Sihor, **w.** is before Egypt,	834
Jos	13:3	**w.** is counted to the Canaanite:	
Jos	13:8	inheritance, **w.** Moses gave them,	834
Jos	13:10	Amorites, **w.** reigned in Heshbon,	834
Jos	13:12	**w.** reigned in Ashtaroth and in	834
Jos	13:21	Amorites, **w.** reigned in Heshbon,	834
Jos	13:21	and Reba, **w.** were dukes of Sihon,	
Jos	13:30	towns of Jair, **w.** are in Bashan,	834
Jos	13:32	countries **w.** Moses did distribute	834
Jos	14:1	**w.** the children of Israel inherited	834
Jos	14:1	**w.** Eleazar the priest, and Joshua	
Jos	14:15	**w.** Arba was a great man among the	
Jos	15:7	**w.** is on the south side of the river:	834
Jos	15:8	**w.** is at the end of the valley of the	834
Jos	15:9	to Baalah, **w.** is Kirjath-jearim:	1958
Jos	15:10	of mount Jearim, **w.** is Chesalon,	834
Jos	15:13	father of Anak, **w.** city is Hebron.	1958
Jos	15:25	Kerioth, and Hezron, **w.** is Hazor,	1958
Jos	15:49	and Kirjath-sannah, **w.** is Debir,	1958
Jos	15:54	and Kirjath-arba, **w.** is Hebron,	1958
Jos	15:60	Kirjath-baal, **w.** is Kirjath-jearim,	1958
Jos	17:5	**w.** were on the other side of Jordan;	834
Jos	18:2	tribes, **w.** had not yet received their	834
Jos	18:3	**w.** the Lord God of your fathers	834
Jos	18:7	**w.** Moses the servant of the Lord	834
Jos	18:13	to the side of Luz, **w.** is Beth-el,	1958
Jos	18:14	Kirjath-baal, **w.** is Kirjath-jearim,	1958
Jos	18:16	and **w.** is in the valley of the giants	834
Jos	18:17	**w.** is over against the going up of	834
Jos	18:28	and Jebusi, **w.** is Jerusalem,	1958
Jos	19:50	they gave him the city **w.** he asked,	834
Jos	19:51	**w.** Eleazar the priest, and Joshua	834
Jos	20:7	and Kirjath-arba, **w.** is Hebron,	1958
Jos	21:4	the priest, **w.** were of the Levites,	
Jos	21:9	these cities **w.** are mentioned by	834
Jos	21:10	**W.** the children of Aaron, being of	
Jos	21:11	father of Anak, **w.** city is Hebron,	1958
Jos	21:20	Levites **w.** remained of the children	
Jos	21:40	**w.** were remaining of the families of	
Jos	21:43	land **w.** he sware to give unto their	834
Jos	21:45	good thing **w.** the Lord had spoken	834
Jos	22:4,5	**w.** Moses the servant of the Lord	834
Jos	22:9	Shiloh, **w.** is in the land of Canaan,	834
Jos	22:17	from **w.** we are not cleansed until	834
Jos	22:28	of the Lord, **w.** our fathers made,	834
Jos	22:30	of Israel **w.** were with him, heard	834
Jos	23:13	**w.** the Lord your God hath given	834
Jos	23:14	things **w.** the Lord your God spake	834
Jos	23:15	**w.** the Lord your God promised you;	834
Jos	23:15	**w.** the Lord your God hath given	834
Jos	23:16	your God, **w.** he commanded you,	834
Jos	23:16	good land **w.** he hath given unto you	834
Jos	24:5	according to that **w.** I did among	834
Jos	24:8	**w.** dwelt on the other side Jordan;	
Jos	24:12	**w.** drave them out from before you,	
Jos	24:13	you a land for **w.** ye did not labour,	834
Jos	24:13	cities **w.** ye built not, and ye dwell in	834
Jos	24:13	olive yards **w.** ye planted not do ye	834
Jos	24:14,	15 the gods **w.** your fathers served	834
Jos	24:17	**w.** did those great signs in our sight,	834
Jos	24:18	the Amorites **w.** dwelt in the land:	
Jos	24:23	strange gods **w.** are among you,	834
Jos	24:27	words of the Lord **w.** he spake unto	834
Jos	24:30	**w.** is in mount Ephraim, on the north	834
Jos	24:31	**w.** had known all the works of the	834
Jos	24:32	**w.** the children of Israel brought up	834
Jos	24:32	parcel of ground **w.** Jacob bought	834
Jos	24:33	his son, **w.** was given him in mount	834
Jg	1:16	Judah, **w.** lieth in the south of Arad;	834
Jg	1:26	**w.** is the name thereof unto this	1931
Jg	2:1	land **w.** I sware unto your fathers;	834
Jg	2:10	after them, **w.** knew not the Lord,	834
Jg	2:10	nor yet the works **w.** he had done	834
Jg	2:12	**w.** brought them out of the land of	
Jg	2:16	**w.** delivered them out of the hand of	

Book	Ref	Context	No.
Jg	2:17	the way **w.** their fathers walked in,	834
Jg	2:20	my covenant **w.** I commanded their	834
Jg	2:21	nations **w.** Joshua left when he died:	834
Jg	3:1	are the nations **w.** the Lord left,	834
Jg	3:4	**w.** he commanded their fathers by	834
Jg	3:16	made him a dagger **w.** had two edges,	
Jg	3:20	**w.** he had made for himself alone:	834
Jg	3:31	**w.** slew of the Philistines six hundred	
Jg	4:2	was Sisera, **w.** dwelt in Harosheth	
Jg	4:11	**w.** was of the children of Hobab the	
Jg	4:11	plain of Zaanaim, **w.** is by Kedesh	834
Jg	4:14	in **w.** the Lord hath delivered Sisera	834
Jg	6:2	the dens **w.** are in the mountains,	834
Jg	6:8	children of Israel, **w.** said unto them,	
Jg	6:11	sat under an oak **w.** was in Ophrah,	834
Jg	6:13	miracles **w.** our fathers told us of,	834
Jg	6:26	the grove **w.** thou shalt cut down.	834
Jg	8:27	**w.** thing became a snare unto Gideon,	
Jg	8:35	goodness **w.** he had shewed unto	835
Jg	9:2	**w.** are threescore and ten persons,	
Jg	9:4	and light persons, **w.** followed him.	
Jg	9:13	my wine, **w.** cheereth God and man,	
Jg	9:24	their brother, **w.** slew them;	834
Jg	9:24	**w.** aided him in the killing of his	834
Jg	9:56	Abimelech **w.** he did unto his father,	834
Jg	10:4	**w.** are called Havoth-jair unto this	
Jg	10:4	day, **w.** are in the land of Gilead.	834
Jg	10:8	land of the Amorites, **w.** is in Gilead.	834
Jg	10:14	unto the gods **w.** ye have chosen;	834
Jg	11:24	possess that **w.** Chemosh thy god	834
Jg	11:28	words of Jephthah **w.** he sent him.	834
Jg	11:36	**w.** hath proceeded out of thy mouth;	834
Jg	11:39	to his vow **w.** he had vowed:	834
Jg	12:5	those Ephraimites **w.** were escaped	
Jg	13:8	the man of God **w.** thou didst send	834
Jg	14:19	unto them **w.** expounded the riddle.	
Jg	15:19	**w.** is in Lehi unto this day.	834
Jg	16:8	green withs **w.** had not been dried,	834
Jg	16:24	of our country, **w.** slew many of us.	834
Jg	16:29	pillars upon **w.** the house stood,	834
Jg	16:29	and on **w.** it was borne up, of the one	
Jg	16:30	So the dead **w.** he slew at his death	834
Jg	16:30	than they **w.** he slew in his life.	834
Jg	17:2	from thee; about **w.** thou cursedst,	
Jg	17:6	man did that **w.** was right in his own	
Jg	18:5	way **w.** we go shall be prosperous.	834
Jg	18:16	**w.** were of the children of Dan, stood	834
Jg	18:24	have taken away my gods **w.** I made,	834
Jg	18:27	took the things **w.** Micah had made,	834
Jg	18:27	and the priest **w.** he had, and came	834
Jg	18:31	Micah's graven image, **w.** he made,	834
Jg	19:10	against Jebus, **w.** is Jerusalem;	1958
Jg	19:14	Gibeah, **w.** belongeth to Benjamin.	834
Jg	19:16	even, **w.** was also of mount Ephraim;	
Jg	19:19	young man **w.** is with thy servants:	
Jg	20:9	the thing **w.** we will do to Gibeah;	834
Jg	20:13	children of Belial, **w.** are in Gibeah,	834
Jg	20:15	**w.** were numbered seven hundred	
Jg	20:18	**W.** of us shall go up first to the	4310
Jg	20:31	of **w.** one goeth up to the house of	834
Jg	20:36	wait **w.** they had set beside Gibeah.	834
Jg	20:42	them **w.** came out of the cities they	834
Jg	20:46	all **w.** fell that day of Benjamin were	
Jg	21:12	Shiloh, **w.** is in the land of Canaan.	834
Jg	21:14	them wives **w.** they had saved alive	834
Jg	21:19	**w.** is on the north side of Beth-el	834
Jg	21:25	did that **w.** was right in his own eyes.	
Ru	1:22	her, **w.** returned out of the country of	
Ru	2:9	that **w.** the young men have drawn.	834
Ru	2:11	**w.** thou knewest not heretofore.	834
Ru	4:3	**w.** was our brother Elimelech's:	834
Ru	4:11	**w.** two did build the house of Israel:	834
Ru	4:12	the seed **w.** the Lord shall give thee	834
Ru	4:14	Lord, **w.** hath not left thee this day	834
Ru	4:15	daughter in law **w.** loveth thee,	834
Ru	4:15	**w.** is better to thee than seven	834,1931
1Sa	1:27	me my petition **w.** I asked of him:	834
1Sa	2:20	for the loan **w.** is lent to the Lord.	834
1Sa	2:29	offering, **w.** I have commanded in	834
1Sa	2:32	wealth **w.** God shall give Israel:	834
1Sa	2:35	to that **w.** is in mine heart and in my	834
1Sa	3:11	at **w.** both the ears of every one that	834
1Sa	3:12	Eli all things **w.** I have spoken	834
1Sa	3:13	for the iniquity **w.** he knoweth;	834
1Sa	4:4	**w.** dwelleth between the cherubims:	
1Sa	6:4	offering **w.** we shall return to him?	834

Book	Ref	Context	No.
1Sa	6:7	kine, on **w.** there hath come no yoke,	834
1Sa	6:8	**w.** ye return him for a trespass	834
1Sa	6:17	golden emerods **w.** the Philistines	834
1Sa	6:18	**w.** stone remaineth unto this day in	
1Sa	7:14	cities **w.** the Philistines had taken	834
1Sa	8:8	to all the works **w.** they have done	834
1Sa	8:18	king **w.** ye shall have chosen you;	834
1Sa	9:22	bidden, **w.** were about thirty persons.	
1Sa	9:23	Bring the portion **w.** I gave thee,	834
1Sa	9:23	of **w.** I said unto thee, Set it by thee.	834
1Sa	9:24	shoulder, and that **w.** was upon it,	
1Sa	9:24	Behold that **w.** is left! set it before	
1Sa	10:2	asses **w.** thou wentest to seek are	834
1Sa	10:4	**w.** thou shalt receive of their hands.	
1Sa	11:11	that they **w.** remained were scattered,	
1Sa	12:7	**w.** he did to you and to your fathers.	834
1Sa	12:8	**w.** brought forth your fathers out of	
1Sa	12:16	**w.** the Lord will do before your	834
1Sa	12:17	**w.** ye have done in the sight of the	834
1Sa	12:21	things, **w.** cannot profit nor deliver;	834
1Sa	13:5	as the sand **w.** is on the sea shore in	834
1Sa	13:13	thy God, **w.** he commanded thee:	834
1Sa	13:14	that **w.** the Lord commanded thee.	834
1Sa	14:2	pomegranate tree **w.** is in Migron:	834
1Sa	14:4	**w.** Jonathan sought to go over unto	834
1Sa	14:14	**w.** Jonathan and his armourbearer	834
1Sa	14:14	land, **w.** a yoke of oxen might plow.	
1Sa	14:21	**w.** went up with them into the	834
1Sa	14:22	men of Israel **w.** had hid themselves	
1Sa	14:30	of their enemies **w.** they found?	834
1Sa	14:39	as the Lord liveth, **w.** saveth Israel,	
1Sa	15:2	I remember that **w.** Amalek did to	834
1Sa	15:14	the lowing of the oxen **w.** I hear?	834
1Sa	15:20	gone the way **w.** the Lord sent me,	834
1Sa	15:21	**w.** should have been utterly destroyed,	
1Sa	16:4	Samuel did that **w.** the Lord spake,	834
1Sa	16:16	thy servants, **w.** are before thee,	
1Sa	16:19	thy son, **w.** is with the sheep.	834
1Sa	17:1	at Shochoh, **w.** belongeth to Judah,	834
1Sa	17:31	words were heard **w.** David spake,	834
1Sa	17:40	them in a shepherd's bag **w.** he had,	834
1Sa	20:23	matter **w.** thou and I have spoken	834
1Sa	20:27	**w.** was the second day of the month,	
1Sa	20:36	out now the arrows **w.** I shoot.	834
1Sa	20:37	of the arrow **w.** Jonathan had shot,	834
1Sa	22:9	**w.** was set over the servants of	1931
1Sa	22:14	as David, **w.** is the king's son in law,	
1Sa	23:13	his men, **w.** were about six hundred,	
1Sa	23:19	**w.** is on the south of Jeshimon?	834
1Sa	24:4	the day of **w.** the Lord said unto thee,	834
1Sa	25:7	now thy shepherds **w.** were with us,	834
1Sa	25:27	this blessing **w.** thine handmaid	834
1Sa	25:32	**w.** sent thee this day to meet me:	834
1Sa	25:33	be thou, **w.** hast kept me this day	834
1Sa	25:34	**w.** hath kept me back from hurting	834
1Sa	25:35	hand that **w.** she had brought him,	834
1Sa	25:44	the son of Laish, **w.** was of Gallim.	834
1Sa	26:1	Hachilah, **w.** is before Jeshimon?	834
1Sa	26:3	Hachilah, **w.** is before Jeshimon,	834
1Sa	28:21	words **w.** thou spakest unto me.	834
1Sa	29:1	by a fountain **w.** is in Jezreel.	834
1Sa	29:3	**w.** hath been with me these days,	834
1Sa	29:4	to his place **w.** thou hast appointed	834
1Sa	30:10	**w.** were so faint that they could not	834
1Sa	30:14	the coast **w.** belongeth to Judah,	834
1Sa	30:17	men, **w.** rode upon camels, and fled.	834
1Sa	30:20	**w.** they drave before those other	
1Sa	30:21	**w.** were so faint that they could	834
1Sa	30:23	that **w.** the Lord hath given us,	834
1Sa	30:27	To them **w.** were in Beth-el, and to	834
1Sa	30:27	to them **w.** were in south Ramoth,	834
1Sa	30:27	and to them **w.** were in Jattir,	834
1Sa	30:28	And to them **w.** were in Aroer,	834
1Sa	30:28	and to them **w.** were in Siphmoth,	834
1Sa	30:28	and to them **w.** were in Eshtemoa,	834
1Sa	30:29	to them **w.** were in Rachal, and to	834
1Sa	30:29,	29 them **w.** were in the cities of the	834
1Sa	30:30	to them **w.** were in Hormah, and to	834
1Sa	30:30	and to them **w.** were in Chor-ashan,	834
1Sa	30:30	and to them **w.** were in Athach,	834
1Sa	30:31	to them **w.** were in Hebron, and to	834
1Sa	31:11	**w.** the Philistines had done to Saul;	
2Sa	2:15	**w.** pertained to Ish-bosheth the son	
2Sa	2:16	Helkath-hazzurim, **w.** is in Gibeon.	834
2Sa	2:32	of his father, **w.** is in Beth-lehem.	834
2Sa	3:8	**w.** against Judah do shew kindness	834

2Sa 3:14 wife Michal, **w.** I espoused to me........ 834
2Sa 3:26 **w.** brought him again from the well..........
2Sa 4:8 thine enemy, **w.** sought thy life;.......... 834
2Sa 5:6 **w.** spake unto David, saying, Except.........
2Sa 6:4 of Abinadab **w.** was at Gibeah, ... 834
2Sa 6:21 Lord, **w.** chose me before thy father, ... 834
2Sa 6:22 maidservants **w.** thou hast spoken........ 834
2Sa 7:12 **w.** shall proceed out of thy bowels,...... 834
2Sa 7:23 **w.** thou redeemest to thee from.......... 834
2Sa 8:11 **W.** also king David did dedicate unto.........
2Sa 8:11 of all nations **w.** he subdued;............... 834
2Sa 9:3 hath yet a son, **w.** is lame on his feet. ......
2Sa 10:12 Lord do that **w.** seemeth him good...........
2Sa 12:3 **w.** he had bought and nourished.......... 834
2Sa 13:10 took the cakes **w.** she had made,......... 834
2Sa 13:23 Baal-hazor, **w.** is beside Ephraim:........ 834
2Sa 14:7 they shall quench my coal **w.** is left,..... 834
2Sa 14:13 speak this thing as one **w.** is faulty,..........
2Sa 14:14 **w.** cannot be gathered up again;.......... 834
2Sa 15:4 every man **w.** hath any suit or cause.... 834
2Sa 15:7 **w.** I have vowed unto the Lord, in........ 834
2Sa 15:16 left ten women, **w.** were concubines,.... 834
2Sa 15:18 six hundred men **w.** came after........... 834
2Sa 16:11 my son **w.** came forth of my bowels,.... 834
2Sa 16:21 **w.** he had left to keep the house;........ 834
2Sa 16:23 **w.** he counselled in those days,........... 834
2Sa 17:10 they **w.** be with him are valiant........... 834
2Sa 17:18 Bahurim, **w.** had a well in his court; ....
2Sa 17:25 **w.** Amasa was a man's son, whose..........
2Sa 18:18 a pillar, **w.** is in the king's dale:........... 834
2Sa 18:28 **w.** hath delivered up the men that 834
2Sa 19:5 **w.** this day have saved thy life,................
2Sa 19:16 a Benjamite, **w.** was of Bahurim, ... 834
2Sa 19:19 remember that **w.** thy servant did........ 834
2Sa 19:38 that **w.** shall seem good unto thee:...........
2Sa 20:5 set time **w.** he had appointed him. 834
2Sa 20:8 the great stone **w.** is in Gibeon, ... 834
2Sa 21:12 **w.** had stolen them from the street...... 834
2Sa 21:16 **w.** was of the sons of the giant, ... 834
2Sa 21:18 **w.** was of the sons of the giant. 834
2Sa 22:44 a people **w.** I knew not shall serve me. .....
2Sa 23:15 of Beth-lehem, **w.** is by the gate! 834
2Sa 24:2 of the host, **w.** was with him, ... 834
2Sa 24:24 God of that **w.** doth cost me nothing.........
1Ki 1:8 mighty men **w.** belonged to David,....... 834
1Ki 1:9 of Zoheleth, **w.** is by En-rogel,............ 834
1Ki 1:48 **w.** hath given one to sit on my........... 834
1Ki 2:4 word **w.** he spake concerning me,........ 834
1Ki 2:8 **w.** cursed me with a grievous............ 1931
1Ki 2:24 liveth, **w.** hath established me,............ 834
1Ki 2:27 **w.** he spake concerning the house of.... 834
1Ki 2:31 the innocent blood, **w.** Joab shed, ... 834
1Ki 2:44 wickedness **w.** thine heart is privy to,... 834
1Ki 2:46 **w.** went out, and fell upon him, that ....
1Ki 3:8 thy people **w.** thou hast chosen, ... 834
1Ki 3:13 thee that **w.** thou hast not asked, ... 834
1Ki 3:21 it was not my son, **w.** I did bear. 834
1Ki 3:28 judgment **w.** the king had judged; 834
1Ki 4:2 These were the princes **w.** he had;...... 834
1Ki 4:7 **w.** provided victuals for the king and.........
1Ki 4:11 **w.** had Taphath the daughter of...............
1Ki 4:12 **w.** is by Zartanah beneath Jezreel,............
1Ki 4:13 son of Manasseh, **w.** are in Gilead; 834
1Ki 4:13 region of Argob, **w.** is in Bashan, ... 834
1Ki 4:19 the only officer **w.** was in the land. 834
1Ki 4:20 sand **w.** is by the sea in multitude,....... 834
1Ki 4:34 earth, **w.** had heard of his wisdom. 834
1Ki 5:3 for the wars **w.** were about him........... 834
1Ki 5:7 **w.** hath given unto David a wise son.... 834
1Ki 5:8 things **w.** thou sentest to me for: 834
1Ki 5:16 Solomon's officers **w.** were over the..... 834
1Ki 5:16 **w.** ruled over the people that wrought.. 834
1Ki 6:1 month Zif, **w.** is the second month, ... 1931
1Ki 6:2 house **w.** king Solomon built for........... 834
1Ki 6:12 this house **w.** thou art building, ... 834
1Ki 6:12 **w.** I spake unto David thy father: 834
1Ki 6:20 covered the altar **w.** was of cedar.............
1Ki 6:38 Bul, **w.** is the eighth month,.............. 1931
1Ki 7:8 the porch, **w.** was of the like work...........
1Ki 7:17 chapiters **w.** were upon the top of 834
1Ki 7:20 the belly **w.** was by the network: 834
1Ki 7:41 chapiters **w.** were upon the tops of...... 834
1Ki 7:45 **w.** Hiram made to king Solomon.......... 834
1Ki 7:51 the things **w.** David his father had...........
1Ki 8:1 out of the city of David, **w.** is Zion..... 1958
1Ki 8:2 **w.** is the seventh month.................. 1931

1Ki 8:9 **w.** Moses put there at Horeb, ... 834
1Ki 8:15 **w.** spake with his mouth unto 834
1Ki 8:21 Lord, **w.** he made with our fathers,...... 834
1Ki 8:26 **w.** thou spakest unto thy servant......... 834
1Ki 8:28 **w.** thy servant prayeth before thee 834
1Ki 8:29 the place of **w.** thou hast said, ... 834
1Ki 8:29 prayer **w.** thy servant shall make......... 834
1Ki 8:34 **w.** thou gavest unto their fathers.......... 834
1Ki 8:36 **w.** thou hast given unto thy people 834
1Ki 8:38 **w.** shall know every man the plague..... 834
1Ki 8:40 land **w.** thou gavest unto our fathers. ... 834
1Ki 8:43 house **w.** I have builded, is called by 834
1Ki 8:44 toward the city **w.** thou hast chosen, ... 834
1Ki 8:48 enemies, **w.** led them away captive, ... 834
1Ki 8:48 **w.** thou gavest unto their fathers, ... 834
1Ki 8:48 the city **w.** thou hast chosen, and 834
1Ki 8:48 house **w.** I have built for thy name:...... 834
1Ki 8:51 **w.** thou broughtest forth out of........... 834
1Ki 8:56 **w.** he promised by the hand of Moses .. 834
1Ki 8:58 **w.** he commanded our fathers. 834
1Ki 8:63 **w.** he offered unto the Lord, two and... 834
1Ki 9:1 desire **w.** he was pleased to do, ... 834
1Ki 9:3 this house **w.** thou hast built, ... 834
1Ki 9:6 statutes **w.** I have set before you, ... 834
1Ki 9:7 of the land **w.** I have given them; 834
1Ki 9:7 **w.** I have hallowed for my name,......... 834
1Ki 9:8 And at this house, **w.** is high,..................
1Ki 9:12 cities **w.** Solomon had given him;......... 834
1Ki 9:13 are these **w.** thou hast given me,........ 834
1Ki 9:15 the levy **w.** king Solomon raised;......... 834
1Ki 9:19 **w.** Solomon desired to build in 834
1Ki 9:20 **w.** were not of the children of Israel, ... 834
1Ki 9:23 **w.** bare rule over the people that............
1Ki 9:24 unto her house **w.** Solomon had........... 834
1Ki 9:25 the altar **w.** he built unto the Lord, ... 834
1Ki 9:26 Ezion-geber, **w.** is beside Eloth, ... 834
1Ki 10:3 from the king, **w.** he told her not. 834
1Ki 10:5 by **w.** he went up into the house of...... 834
1Ki 10:7 exceedeth the fame **w.** I heard............ 834
1Ki 10:8 **w.** stand continually before thee, ...
1Ki 10:9 **w.** delighted in thee, to set thee on 834
1Ki 10:10 **w.** the queen of Sheba gave to king 834
1Ki 10:13 **w.** Solomon gave her of his royal......... 834
1Ki 10:24 wisdom, **w.** God had put in his heart. ... 834
1Ki 11:2 nations concerning **w.** the Lord said 834
1Ki 11:8 **w.** burnt incense and sacrificed unto..........
1Ki 11:9 **w.** had appeared unto him twice,..............
1Ki 11:10 not that **w.** the Lord commanded. 834
1Ki 11:11 **w.** I have commanded thee,................ 834
1Ki 11:13 Jerusalem's sake **w.** I have chosen. 834
1Ki 11:18 **w.** gave him an house, and appointed........
1Ki 11:23 **w.** fled from his lord Hadadezer........... 834
1Ki 11:32 the city **w.** I have chosen out of all...... 834
1Ki 11:33 to do that **w.** is right in mine eyes,..........
1Ki 11:37 city **w.** I have chosen me to put my...... 834
1Ki 12:4 his heavy yoke **w.** he put upon us,....... 834
1Ki 12:8 the old men, **w.** they had given him, ... 834
1Ki 12:8 with him, and **w.** stood before him:...... 834
1Ki 12:9 yoke **w.** thy father did put upon us 834
1Ki 12:15 **w.** the Lord spake by Ahijah the.......... 834
1Ki 12:17 Israel **w.** dwelt in the cities of Judah, ...
1Ki 12:21 chosen men, **w.** were warriors,.................
1Ki 12:28 **w.** brought thee up out of the land....... 834
1Ki 12:31 **w.** were not of the sons of Levi. 834
1Ki 12:32 the high places **w.** he had made.......... 834
1Ki 12:33 upon the altar **w.** he had made in.......... 834
1Ki 12:33 month **w.** he had devised of his own..... 834
1Ki 13:3 the sign **w.** the Lord hath spoken; 834
1Ki 13:4 **w.** had cried against the altar in........... 834
1Ki 13:4 hand, **w.** he put forth against him, ... 834
1Ki 13:5 sign **w.** the man of God had given......... 834
1Ki 13:11 the words **w.** he had spoken unto 834
1Ki 13:12 God went, **w.** came from Judah. 834
1Ki 13:21 **w.** the Lord thy God commanded........... 834
1Ki 13:22 **w.** the Lord did say to thee, Eat no 834
1Ki 13:26 the lion, **w.** hath torn him, and slain..........
1Ki 13:26 of the Lord, **w.** he spake unto him....... 834
1Ki 13:32 For the saying **w.** he cried by the........ 834
1Ki 13:32 high places **w.** are in the cities of 834
1Ki 14:2 **w.** told me that I should be king 1931
1Ki 14:8 that only **w.** was right in mine eyes;........
1Ki 14:15 land, **w.** he gave to their fathers,.......... 834
1Ki 14:18 **w.** he spake by the hand of his............ 834
1Ki 14:20 the days **w.** Jeroboam reigned were 834
1Ki 14:21 the city **w.** the Lord did choose out 834
1Ki 14:22 their sins **w.** they had committed,........ 834

1Ki 14:24 nations **w.** the Lord cast out before...... 834
1Ki 14:26 shields of gold **w.** Solomon had made.... 834
1Ki 14:27 **w.** kept the door of the king's house.........
1Ki 15:3 father, **w.** he had done before him: 834
1Ki 15:5 **w.** was right in the eyes of the Lord,........
1Ki 15:11 Asa did that **w.** was right in the eyes........
1Ki 15:15 the things **w.** his father had dedicated, ...
1Ki 15:15 the things **w.** himself had dedicated,..........
1Ki 15:20 hosts **w.** he had against the cities 834
1Ki 15:23 did, and the cities **w.** he had built, ... 834
1Ki 15:27 **w.** belonged to the Philistines; 834
1Ki 15:29 **w.** he spake by his servant Ahijah........ 834
1Ki 15:30 sins of Jeroboam **w.** he sinned,............ 834
1Ki 15:30 and **w.** he made Israel sin,................. 834
1Ki 16:12 **w.** he spake against Baasha by............ 834
1Ki 16:13 of Elah his son, by **w.** they sinned, ... 834
1Ki 16:13 and by **w.** they made Israel to sin,....... 834
1Ki 16:15 **w.** belonged to the Philistines. 834
1Ki 16:19 his sins **w.** he sinned in doing evil......... 834
1Ki 16:19 his sin, **w.** he did, to make Israel 834
1Ki 16:24 the name of the city **w.** he built, ... 834
1Ki 16:27 rest of the acts of Omri **w.** he did, ... 834
1Ki 16:32 Baal, **w.** he had built in Samaria. 834
1Ki 16:34 **w.** he spake by Joshua the son of 834
1Ki 17:9 to Zarephath, **w.** belongeth to Zidon, ... 834
1Ki 17:16 of the Lord, **w.** he spake by Elijah....... 834
1Ki 18:3 **w.** was the governor of his house. 834
1Ki 18:19 four hundred, **w.** eat at Jezebel's table.......
1Ki 18:26 took the bullock **w.** was given them,.........
1Ki 18:26 leaped upon the altar **w.** was made. 834
1Ki 19:3 Beer-sheba, **w.** belongeth to Judah,....... 834
1Ki 19:18 knees **w.** have not bowed unto Baal, ... 834
1Ki 19:18 every mouth **w.** hath not kissed 834
1Ki 20:19 and the army **w.** followed them. 834
1Ki 20:34 **w.** my father took from thy father,....... 834
1Ki 21:1 had a vineyard, **w.** was in Jezreel, ... 834
1Ki 21:4 **w.** Naboth the Jezreelite had spoken..... 834
1Ki 21:11 letters **w.** she had sent unto them. 834
1Ki 21:15 **w.** he refused to give thee for............. 834
1Ki 21:18 king of Israel, **w.** is in Samaria:........... 834
1Ki 21:25 Ahab, **w.** did sell himself to work......... 834
1Ki 22:13 of them, and speak that **w.** is good..........
1Ki 22:16 but that **w.** is true in the name of the ....
1Ki 22:24 **W.** way went the spirit of the...... 335,2088
1Ki 22:38 the word of the Lord **w.** he spake. 834
1Ki 22:39 and the ivory house **w.** he made,.......... 834
1Ki 22:43 **w.** was right in the eyes of the Lord..........
1Ki 22:46 **w.** remained in the days of his father........
2Ki 1:4,6 that bed on **w.** thou art gone up, ... 834
2Ki 1:7 was he **w.** came up to meet you,......... 834
2Ki 1:16 off that bed on **w.** thou art gone up,..... 834
2Ki 1:17 of the Lord **w.** Elijah had spoken. 834
2Ki 1:18 of the acts of Ahaziah **w.** he did, ... 834
2Ki 2:15 of the prophets **w.** were to view at...... 834
2Ki 2:22 the saying of Elijah **w.** he spake. 834
2Ki 3:3 son of Nebat, **w.** made Israel to sin; 834
2Ki 3:8 he said, **W.** way shall we go........ 335,2088
2Ki 3:11 **w.** poured water on the hands of......... 834
2Ki 4:4 and thou shalt set aside that **w.** is full. .....
2Ki 4:9 of God **w.** passeth by us continually. ....
2Ki 5:20 at his hands that **w.** he brought: 834
2Ki 6:10 place **w.** the man of God told him 834
2Ki 6:11 **w.** of us is for the king of Israel? 4310
2Ki 7:13 that remain, **w.** are left in the city, ... 834
2Ki 7:15 **w.** the Syrians had cast away in 834
2Ki 8:21 Edomites **w.** compassed him about, ...
2Ki 8:29 **w.** the Syrians had given him............... 834
2Ki 9:5 And Jehu said, Unto **w.** of all us? 4310
2Ki 9:15 **w.** the Syrians had given him, ... 834
2Ki 9:19 second on horseback, **w.** came to them, ...
2Ki 9:27 going up to Gur, **w.** is by Ibleam......... 834
2Ki 9:36 **w.** he spake by his servant Elijah......... 834
2Ki 10:5 do thou that **w.** is good in thine eyes. ....
2Ki 10:6 men of the city, **w.** brought them up.........
2Ki 10:10 **w.** the Lord spake concerning the........ 834
2Ki 10:10 that **w.** he spake by his servant........... 834
2Ki 10:17 of the Lord, **w.** he spake to Elijah. 834
2Ki 10:30 executing that **w.** is right in mine eyes, ...
2Ki 10:31 of Jeroboam, **w.** made Israel to sin....... 834
2Ki 10:33 Aroer, **w.** is by the river Arnon, ... 834
2Ki 11:2 among the king's sons **w.** were slain;.........
2Ki 11:16 by the way by the **w.** the horses came......
2Ki 12:2 **w.** was right in the sight of the Lord........
2Ki 12:20 house of Millo, **w.** goeth down to Silla.......
2Ki 13:2 **w.** was evil in the sight of the Lord,.........
2Ki 13:2 son of Nebat, **w.** made Israel to sin;.........

2Ki 13:11 w. was evil in the sight of the Lord;
2Ki 13:25 w. he had taken out of the hand of 834
2Ki 14:3 w. is right in the sight of the Lord,
2K 14:5 w. had slain the king his father.
2Ki 14:6 unto that w. is written in the book
2Ki 14:11 Beth-shemesh, w. belongeth to 834
2Ki 14:15 of the acts of Jehoash w. he did, 834
2Ki 14:21 Azariah, w. was sixteen years old, 1931
2Ki 14:24 w. was evil in the sight of the Lord:
2Ki 14:25 w. he spake by the hand of his 834
2Ki 14:25 prophet, w. was of Gath-hepher. 834
2Ki 14:28 and Hamath, w. belonged to Judah,
2Ki 15:3 w. was right in the sight of the Lord,
2Ki 15:9 w. was evil in the sight of the Lord:
2Ki 15:12 the Lord w. he spake unto Jehu, 834
2Ki 15:15 and his conspiracy w. he made, 834
2Ki 15:18, 24,28 that w. was evil in the sight of
2Ki 15:34 w. was right in the sight of the Lord:
2Ki 16:2 w. was right in the sight of the Lord
2Ki 16:7 king of Israel, w. rise up against me.
2Ki 16:14 altar, w. was before the Lord, 834
2Ki 16:19 rest of the acts of Ahaz w. he did, 834
2Ki 17:2 w. was evil in the sight of the Lord,
2Ki 17:7 w. had brought them up out of the
2Ki 17:8 kings of Israel, w. they had made. 834
2Ki 17:13 law w. I commanded your fathers, 834
2Ki 17:13 and w. I sent to you by my servants 834
2Ki 17:15 w. he testified against them; and 834
2Ki 17:19 statutes of Israel w. they made. 834
2Ki 17:22 all the sins of Jeroboam w. he did; 834
2Ki 17:25 among them, w. slew some of them. 834
2Ki 17:26 The nations w. thou hast removed, 834
2Ki 17:29 high places w. the Samaritans had 834
2Ki 17:32 w. sacrificed for them in the 1961
2Ki 17:34 w. the Lord commanded the 834
2Ki 17:37 commandment, w. he wrote for you, 834
2Ki 18:3 w. was right in the sight of the Lord,
2Ki 18:6 w. the Lord commanded Moses 834
2Ki 18:9 w. was the seventh year of Hoshea 1958
2Ki 18:14 w. thou puttest on me will I bear. 834
2Ki 18:16 w. Hezekiah king of Judah had 834
2Ki 18:17 w. is in the highway of the fuller's 834
2Ki 18:18 Hilkiah, w. was over the household, 834
2Ki 18:21 Egypt, on w. if a man lean, it will go 834
2Ki 18:27 sent me to the men w. sit on the wall,
2Ki 18:37 Hilkiah, w. was over...household, 834
2Ki 19:2 Eliakim, w. was over the household, 834
2Ki 19:4 words w. the Lord thy God hath 834
2Ki 19:6 of the words w. thou hast heard, 834
2Ki 19:6 with w. the servants of the king of 834
2Ki 19:12 them w. my fathers have destroyed; 834
2Ki 19:12 of Eden w. were in Thelasar? 834
2Ki 19:15 w. dwellest between the cherubims,
2Ki 19:16 w. hath sent him to reproach the 834
2Ki 19:20 That w. thou hast prayed to me 834
2Ki 19:28 by the way by w. thou camest. 834
2Ki 19:29 year that w. springeth of the same;
2Ki 20:3 done that w. is good in thy sight.
2Ki 20:11 by w. it had gone down in the dial of 834
2Ki 20:17 that w. thy fathers have laid up in 834
2Ki 20:18 w. thou shalt beget, shall they take 834
2Ki 20:19 of the Lord w. thou hast spoken 834
2Ki 21:2 w. was evil in the sight of the Lord, 834
2Ki 21:3 high places w. Hezekiah his father 834
2Ki 21:4 of the Lord, of w. the Lord said, 834
2Ki 21:7 house, of w. the Lord said to David, 834
2Ki 21:7 w. I have chosen out of all tribes 834
2Ki 21:8 of the land w. I gave their fathers; 834
2Ki 21:11 Amorites did, w. were before him, 834
2Ki 21:15 done that w. was evil in my sight,
2Ki 21:16 w. was evil in the sight of the Lord.
2Ki 21:20 w. was evil in the sight of the Lord,
2Ki 21:25 of the acts of Amon w. he did, 834
2Ki 22:2 w. was right in the sight of the Lord,
2Ki 22:4 sum the silver w. is brought into the
2Ki 22:4 w. the keepers of the door have 834
2Ki 22:5 work w. is in the house of the Lord, 834
2Ki 22:13 all that w. is written concerning us.
2Ki 22:16 book w. the king of Judah hath 834
2Ki 22:18 w. sent you to enquire of the Lord,
2Ki 22:18 the words w. thou hast heard; 834
2Ki 22:20 evil w. I will bring upon this place 834
2Ki 23:2 covenant w. was found in the house of
2Ki 23:8 w. were on a man's left hand at the 834
2Ki 23:10 w. is in the valley of the children of 834
2Ki 23:11 w. was in the suburbs, and burned 834
2Ki 23:12 w. the kings of Judah had made, 834
2Ki 23:12 the altars w. Manasseh had made 834
2Ki 23:13 w. were on the right hand of the 834
2Ki 23:13 w. Solomon the king of Israel had 834
2Ki 23:15 high place w. Jeroboam the son of 834
2Ki 23:16 Lord w. the man of God proclaimed, 834
2Ki 23:17 man of God, w. came from Judah, 834
2Ki 23:19 w. the kings of Israel had made to 834
2Ki 23:24 w. were written in the book that
2Ki 23:27 city Jerusalem w. I have chosen, 834
2Ki 23:27 the house of w. I said, My name shall 834
2Ki 23:32, 37 did that w. was evil in the sight of
2Ki 24:2 w. he spake by his servants the 834
2Ki 24:4 blood; w. the Lord would not pardon.
2Ki 24:9 w. was evil in the sight of the Lord,
2Ki 24:13 w. Solomon king of Israel had made 834
2Ki 24:19 w. was evil in the sight of the Lord,
2Ki 25:4 walls, w. is by the king's garden: 834
2Ki 25:8 w. is the nineteenth year of king 1958
2Ki 25:16 w. Solomon had made for the house 834
2Ki 25:19 w. were found in the city, and the 834
2Ki 25:19 w. mustered the people of the land,
1Ch 1:46 w. smote Midian in the field of Moab,
1Ch 2:3 w. three were born unto him of the
1Ch 2:19 unto him Ephrath, w. bare him Hur.
1Ch 2:42 w. was the father of Ziph; 1931
1Ch 2:55 of the scribes w. dwelt at Jabez;
1Ch 3:1 w. were born unto him in Hebron; 834
1Ch 4:10 granted him that w. he requested. 834
1Ch 4:11 w. was the father of Eshton. 1931
1Ch 4:18 daughter of Pharaoh, w. Mered 834
1Ch 6:61 w. were left of the family of that tribe,
1Ch 6:65 w. are called by their names. 834
1Ch 9:22 these w. were chosen to be porters in
1Ch 9:25 brethren, w. were in the villages,
1Ch 10:13 w. he committed against the Lord, 834
1Ch 10:13 word of the Lord, w. he kept not, 834
1Ch 11:4 went to Jerusalem, w. is Jebus; 1958
1Ch 11:5 of Zion, w. is the city of David. 1958
1Ch 12:31 w. were expressed by name, 834
1Ch 12:32 w. were men that had understanding
1Ch 12:33 fifty thousand, w. could keep rank:
1Ch 13:2 and Levites w. are in their cities
1Ch 13:6 Kirjath-jearim, w. belonged to 834
1Ch 14:4 of his children w. had in Jerusalem; 834
1Ch 15:3 place, w. he had prepared for it. 834
1Ch 16:15 the word w. he commanded to a 834
1Ch 16:16 of the covenant w. he made with 834
1Ch 16:40 Lord, w. he commanded Israel; 834
1Ch 17:11 after thee, w. shall be of thy sons; 834
1Ch 19:13 Lord do that w. is good in his sight.
1Ch 19:18 seven thousand men w. fought in
1Ch 20:4 at w. time Sibbechai the 227
1Ch 21:19 w. he spake in the name of the 834
1Ch 21:23 king do that w. is good in his eyes:
1Ch 21:24 take that w. is thine for the Lord, 834
1Ch 21:29 w. Moses made in the wilderness, 834
1Ch 22:13 w. the Lord charged Moses with 834
1Ch 23:4 Of w. twenty and four thousand 428
1Ch 23:5 with the instruments w. I made, 834
1Ch 23:29 and for that w. is baked in the pan,
1Ch 23:29 in the pan, and for that w. is fried,
1Ch 25:2 w. prophesied according to the order
1Ch 26:22 w. were over the treasures of the
1Ch 26:26 W. Shelomith and his brethren 1931
1Ch 26:26 w. David the king, and the chief 834
1Ch 27:1 w. came in and went out month by
1Ch 27:31 substance w. was king David's. 834
1Ch 29:3 w. I have given to the house of my
1Ch 29:17 joy thy people, w. are present here, to
1Ch 29:19 for the w. I have made provision. 834
2Ch 1:3 w. Moses the servant of the Lord 834
2Ch 1:4 to the place w. David had prepared
2Ch 1:6 w. was at the tabernacle of the
2Ch 1:14 w. he placed in the chariot cities,
2Ch 2:5 And the house w. I build is great: 834
2Ch 2:9 house w. I am about to build shall 834
2Ch 2:11 in writing, w. he sent to Solomon,
2Ch 2:14 device w. shall be put to him, 834
2Ch 2:15 wine, w. my lord hath spoken of, 834
2Ch 3:5 w. he overlaid with fine gold, and
2Ch 4:3 of oxen, w. did compass it round
2Ch 4:12 chapiters w. were on the top of the two
2Ch 4:12 w. were on the top of the pillars; 834
2Ch 4:13 chapiters w. were upon the pillars 834
2Ch 5:2 of the city of David, w. is Zion. 1958
2Ch 5:3 feast w. was in the seventh month. 1931
2Ch 5:6 and oxen, w. could not be told nor 834
2Ch 5:10 two tables w. Moses put therein 834
2Ch 5:12 Also the Levites w. were the singers,
2Ch 6:4 his hands fulfilled that w. he spake 834
2Ch 6:9 thy son w. shall come forth out of thy
2Ch 6:14 w. keepest covenant, and shewest
2Ch 6:15 Thou w. hast kept with thy servant
2Ch 6:15, 16 father that w. thou hast promised 834
2Ch 6:17 w. thou hast spoken unto thy 834
2Ch 6:18 less this house w. I have built! 834
2Ch 6:19 w. thy servant prayeth before thee: 834
2Ch 6:20 the prayer w. thy servant prayeth 834
2Ch 6:21 w. they shall make toward this 834
2Ch 6:25 w. thou gavest to them and to their 834
2Ch 6:27 w. thou hast given unto thy people 834
2Ch 6:31 w. thou gavest unto our fathers 834
2Ch 6:32 w. is not of thy people Israel, 834
2Ch 6:33 house w. I have built is called by thy 834
2Ch 6:34 this city w. thou hast chosen, 834
2Ch 6:34 house w. I have built for thy name; 834
2Ch 6:36 (for there is no man w. sinneth not,) 834
2Ch 6:38 w. thou gavest unto their fathers, 834
2Ch 6:38 toward the city w. thou hast chosen, 834
2Ch 6:38 house w. I have built for thy name: 834
2Ch 6:39 thy people w. have sinned against 834
2Ch 7:6 w. David the king had made to 834
2Ch 7:7 brasen altar w. Solomon had made 834
2Ch 7:14 people, w. are called by my name, 834
2Ch 7:19 w. I have set before you, and shall go 834
2Ch 7:20 of my land w. I have given them; 834
2Ch 7:20 w. I have sanctified for my name, 834
2Ch 7:21 And this house, w. is high, shall be 834
2Ch 7:22 w. brought them forth out of the 834
2Ch 8:2 w. Huram had restored to Solomon, 834
2Ch 8:4 store cities, w. he built in Hamath. 834
2Ch 8:7 the Jebusites, w. were not of Israel, 834
2Ch 8:12 w. he had built before the porch, 834
2Ch 9:2 from Solomon w. he told her not. 834
2Ch 9:4 his ascent by w. he went up into the 834
2Ch 9:5 a true report w. I heard in mine 834
2Ch 9:7 w. stand continually before thee,
2Ch 9:8 w. delighted in thee to set thee on 834
2Ch 9:10 w. brought gold from Ophir, 834
2Ch 9:12 that w. she had brought unto the 834
2Ch 9:14 w. chapmen and merchants brought.
2Ch 9:18 gold, w. were fastened to the throne,
2Ch 10:8 counsel w. the old men gave him, 834
2Ch 10:9 w. have spoken to me, saying, Ease 834
2Ch 10:15 w. he spake by the hand of Ahijah 834
2Ch 11:1 men, w. were warriors, to fight
2Ch 11:10 w. are in Judah and in Benjamin, 834
2Ch 11:15 and for the calves w. he had made 834
2Ch 11:19 W. bare him children; Jeush, and
2Ch 11:20 w. bare him Abijah, and Attai, and
2Ch 12:4 cities w. pertained to Judah, 834
2Ch 12:9 the shields of gold w. Solomon had 834
2Ch 12:10 Instead of w. king Rehoboam made
2Ch 12:13 the city w. the Lord had chosen out 834
2Ch 13:4 w. is in mount Ephraim, and said, 834
2Ch 13:8 w. Jeroboam made you for gods. 834
2Ch 13:10 the priests, w. minister unto the Lord,
2Ch 14:2 w. was good, and right in the eyes of
2Ch 15:8 cities w. he had taken from mount 834
2Ch 15:11 time, of the spoil w. they had brought,
2Ch 16:14 w. he had made for himself in the 834
2Ch 16:14 in the bed w. was filled with sweet 834
2Ch 17:2 w. Asa his father had taken. 834
2Ch 18:23 W. way went the Spirit of the 335,2088
2Ch 20:2 in Hazazon-tamar; w. is En-gedi. 1958
2Ch 20:11 w. thou hast given us to inherit. 834
2Ch 20:22 Seir, w. were come against Judah;
2Ch 20:25 w. they stripped off for themselves,
2Ch 20:32 w. was right in the sight of the Lord.
2Ch 21:6 w. was evil in the eyes of the Lord.
2Ch 21:9 the Edomites w. compassed him in,
2Ch 21:13 house, w. were better than thyself:
2Ch 22:6 of the wounds w. were given him 834
2Ch 23:9 w. were in the house of God. 834
2Ch 23:19 that none w. was unclean in any thing
2Ch 24:2 w. was right in the sight of the Lord.
2Ch 24:20 the priest, w. stood above the people,
2Ch 24:22 kindness w. Jehoiada his father 834
2Ch 25:2 w. was right in the sight of the Lord,
2Ch 25:9 talents w. I have given to the army 834
2Ch 25:13 of the army w. Amaziah sent back, 834

Book	Ref	Context	No.
2Ch	25:15	w. said unto me, Why hast thou	
2Ch	25:15	w. could not deliver their own	834
2Ch	25:21	Beth-shemesh, w. belongeth...Judah	834
2Ch	26:4	w. was right in the sight of the Lord,	
2Ch	26:23	burial w. belonged to the kings;	834
2Ch	27:2	w. was right in the sight of the Lord,	
2Ch	28:1	w. was right in the sight of the Lord,	
2Ch	28:6	in one day, w. were all valiant men;	
2Ch	28:11	w. ye have taken captive of your	834
2Ch	28:15	the men w. were expressed by name	834
2Ch	28:23	the gods of Damascus, w. smote him:	
2Ch	29:2	w. was right in the sight of the Lord,	
2Ch	29:6	w. was evil in the eyes of the Lord	
2Ch	29:19	w. king Ahaz in his reign did cast	834
2Ch	29:32	w. the congregation brought,	834
2Ch	30:7	w. trespassed against the Lord God	834
2Ch	30:8	w. he hath sanctified for ever:	834
2Ch	30:16	w. they received of the hands of the	
2Ch	31:6	holy things w. were consecrated unto	
2Ch	31:10	and that w. is left is this great store	
2Ch	31:12	over w. Cononiah the Levite was ruler,	
2Ch	31:19	w. were in the fields of the suburbs of	
2Ch	31:20	that w. was good and right and truth	
2Ch	32:3	fountains w. were without the city:	834
2Ch	32:19	w. were the work of the hands of man.	
2Ch	32:21	w. cut off all the mighty men of valour,	
2Ch	33:2	w. was evil in the sight of the Lord,	
2Ch	33:3	w. Hezekiah his father had broken	834
2Ch	33:7	idol w. he had made, in the house of	834
2Ch	33:7	of w. God had said to David and to	834
2Ch	33:7	w. I have chosen before all the tribes	834
2Ch	33:8	land w. I have appointed for your	834
2Ch	33:11	w. took Manasseh among the thorns,	
2Ch	33:22	w. was evil in the sight of the Lord,	
2Ch	33:22	w. Manasseh his father had made,	834
2Ch	34:2	w. was right in the sight of the Lord,	
2Ch	34:9	w. the Levites that kept the door	834
2Ch	34:11	houses w. the kings of Judah had	834
2Ch	34:24	w. they have read before the king of	834
2Ch	34:26	the words w. thou hast heard;	834
2Ch	34:31	covenant w. are written in this book.	
2Ch	35:3	all Israel, w. were holy unto the Lord,	
2Ch	35:3	the house w. Solomon the son of	834
2Ch	35:26	w. was written in the law of the Lord,	
2Ch	36:5	w. was evil in the sight of the Lord	
2Ch	36:8	and his abominations w. he did,	834
2Ch	36:8	w. was found in him, behold, they are	
2Ch	36:9	w. was evil in the sight of the Lord.	
2Ch	36:12	w. was evil in the sight of the Lord	
2Ch	36:14	w. he had hallowed in Jerusalem.	834
2Ch	36:23	house in Jerusalem, w. is in Judah.	834
Ezr	1:2	house at Jerusalem, w. is in Judah.	834
Ezr	1:3	go up to Jerusalem, w. is in Judah,	834
Ezr	1:3	is the God,) w. is in Jerusalem.	834
Ezr	1:5	of the Lord w. is in Jerusalem.	834
Ezr	1:7	w. Nebuchadnezzar had brought	834
Ezr	2:1	of those w. had been carried away,	
Ezr	2:2	W. came with Zerubbabel:	834
Ezr	2:59	were they w. went up from Tel-melah,	
Ezr	2:61	w. took a wife of the daughters of	834
Ezr	2:68	of the Lord w. is at Jerusalem,	834
Ezr	4:2	of Assur, w. brought us up hither.	
Ezr	4:12	that the Jews w. came up from	1768
Ezr	4:15	time: for w. cause was this city	1836
Ezr	4:18	The letter w. ye sent unto us hath	1768
Ezr	4:20	w. have ruled over all countries	
Ezr	4:24	house of God w. is at Jerusalem.	1768
Ezr	5:2	the house of God w. is at Jerusalem	1768
Ezr	5:6	w. were on this side the river,	1768
Ezr	5:8	w. is builded with great stones,	1931
Ezr	5:11	w. a great king of Israel builded and	
Ezr	5:14	w. Nebuchadnezzar took out of	1768
Ezr	5:16	house of God w. is at Jerusalem:	1768
Ezr	5:17	house, w. is there at Babylon,	1768
Ezr	6:5	w. Nebuchadnezzar took forth out	1768
Ezr	6:5	the temple w. is at Jerusalem,	
Ezr	6:5	unto the temple w. is at Jerusalem,	1768
Ezr	6:6	w. are beyond the river, be ye far	1768
Ezr	6:9	And that w. they have need of both	
Ezr	6:9	the priests w. are at Jerusalem,	1768
Ezr	6:12	house of God w. is at Jerusalem.	1768
Ezr	6:13	that w. Darius the king had sent,	1768
Ezr	6:15	w. was in the sixth year of the	1768
Ezr	6:18	service of God, w. is at Jerusalem;	1768
Ezr	6:21	w. were come again out of captivity,	
Ezr	7:6	w. the Lord God of Israel had	834
Ezr	7:8	w. was in the seventh year of the	1958
Ezr	7:13	w. are minded of their...freewill	1768
Ezr	7:14	law of thy God w. is in thine hand;	1768
Ezr	7:15	w. the king and his counsellers	1768
Ezr	7:16	of their God w. is in Jerusalem:	1768
Ezr	7:17	of your God w. is in Jerusalem.	1768
Ezr	7:20	w. thou shalt have occasion to	1768
Ezr	7:21	treasurers w. are beyond the river,	1768
Ezr	7:25	w. may judge all the people that	1768
Ezr	7:27	w. hath put such a thing as this in	834
Ezr	7:27	of the Lord w. is in Jerusalem:	834
Ezr	8:25	w. the king, and his counsellers, and	
Ezr	8:35	w. were come out of captivity, offered	
Ezr	9:11	W. thou hast commanded by thy	834
Ezr	9:11	land unto w. ye go to possess it, is	834
Ezr	9:11	w. have filled it from one end to	834
Ezr	10:14	all them w. have taken strange wives	
Ne	1:2	w. were left of the captivity,	834
Ne	1:6	w. I pray before thee now, day and	834
Ne	1:6	w. we have sinned against thee:	834
Ne	1:7	w. thou commandedst thy servant	834
Ne	2:8	place w. appertained to the house,	834
Ne	2:13	Jerusalem, w. were broken down,	834
Ne	2:18	of my God w. was good upon me;	834
Ne	3:25	tower w. lieth out from the king's	
Ne	4:2	of the rubbish w. are burned?	1992
Ne	4:3	Even that w. they build, if a fox	834
Ne	4:12	when the Jews w. dwelt by them came,	
Ne	4:14	the Lord, w. is great and terrible,	
Ne	4:17	They w. builded on the wall, and they	
Ne	4:23	men of the guard w. followed me,	834
Ne	5:8	Jews, w. were sold unto the heathen;	
Ne	5:18	Now that w. was prepared for me	834
Ne	6:6	w. cause thou buildest the wall,	3651
Ne	7:5	of them w. came up at the first,	
Ne	7:61	they w. went up also from Tel-melah,	
Ne	7:63	w. took one of the daughters of	834
Ne	7:72	w. the rest of the people gave was	834
Ne	8:1	w. the Lord had commanded to	834
Ne	8:4	w. they had made for the purpose;	834
Ne	8:9	Nehemiah, w. is the Tirshatha,	1931
Ne	8:14	law w. the Lord had commanded	834
Ne	9:5	w. is exalted above all blessing and	
Ne	9:15	w. thou hadst sworn to give them	834
Ne	9:23	w. thou hadst promised to their	834
Ne	9:26	slew thy prophets w. testified	834
Ne	9:29	(w. if a man do, he shall live in	834
Ne	9:35	fat land w. thou gavest before them,	834
Ne	10:29	w. was given by Moses the servant	834
Ne	12:8	w. was over the thanksgiving, he	
Ne	12:37	gate, w. was over against them,	
Ne	13:5	w. was commanded to be given to the	
Ne	13:15	w. they brought into Jerusalem on the	
Ne	13:16	of Tyre also therein, w. brought fish,	
Es	1:1	(this is Ahasuerus w. reigned, from	
Es	1:2	w. was in Shushan the palace,	834
Es	1:9	house w. belonged to king Ahasuerus.	
Es	1:13	to the wise men, w. knew the times,	
Es	1:14	and Media, w. saw the king's face,	
Es	1:14	and w. sat the first in the kingdom,)	
Es	1:18	w. have heard of the deed of the	834
Es	1:20	the king's decree w. he shall make,	834
Es	2:4	the maiden w. pleaseth the king be	834
Es	2:6	w. had been carried away with	834
Es	2:9	maidens w. were meet to be given her,	
Es	2:14	chamberlain, w. kept the concubines:	
Es	2:16	tenth month, w. is the month Tebeth,	
Es	2:21	of those w. kept the door, were wroth,	
Es	3:3	servants, w. were in the king's	834
Es	3:13	month, w. is the month Adar,	1931
Es	4:6	city, w. was before the king's gate.	834
Es	4:16	king, w. is not according to the law:	834
Es	6:8	brought w. the king useth to wear,	834
Es	6:8	crown royal w. is set upon his head:	834
Es	7:9	w. Haman had made for Mordecai,	834
Es	8:2	ring, w. he had taken from Haman,	834
Es	8:5	w. he wrote to destroy the Jews	834
Es	8:5	w. are in all the king's provinces:	834
Es	8:8	writing w. is written in the king's	834
Es	8:9	w. are from India unto Ethiopia,	834
Es	8:11	the Jews w. were in every city	834
Es	8:12	month, w. is the month Adar.	1931
Es	9:13	to the Jews w. are in Shushan	834
Es	9:22	w. was turned unto them from	834
Es	9:25	w. he devised against the Jews,	834
Es	9:26	w. they had seen concerning this	4100
Es	9:26	matter, and w. had come unto them,	4100
Job	3:3	night in w. it was said, There is a man	
Job	3:14	w. built desolate places...themselves;	
Job	3:16	been; as infants w. never saw light	
Job	3:21	W. long for death, but it cometh not;	
Job	3:22	W. rejoice exceedingly, and are glad,	
Job	3:25	thing w. I greatly feared is come upon	
Job	3:25	that w. I was afraid is come unto	834
Job	4:14	w. made all my bones to shake.	
Job	4:19	dust, w. are crushed before the moth?	
Job	4:21	their excellency w. is in them go away?	
Job	5:1	to w. of the saints wilt thou turn?	4310
Job	5:9	W. doeth great things and	
Job	5:11	those w. mourn may be exalted to	
Job	6:6	Can that w. is unsavoury be eaten	
Job	6:16	W. are blackish by reason of the ice,	
Job	6:26	one that is desperate, w. are as wind?	
Job	9:5	W. removeth the mountains, and	
Job	9:5	w. overturneth them in his anger	834
Job	9:6	W. shaketh the earth out of her place,	
Job	9:7	W. commandeth the sun, and it riseth	
Job	9:8	W. alone spreadeth out the heavens,	
Job	9:9	W. maketh Arcturus, Orion, and	
Job	9:10	W. doeth greater things past finding	
Job	11:6	and they are double to that w. is!	
Job	14:19	things w. grow out of the dust of the	
Job	15:9	understandest thou, w. is not in	1931
Job	15:14	and he w. is born of a woman, that he	
Job	15:16	man, w. drinketh iniquity like water?	
Job	15:17	and that w. I have seen I will declare;	
Job	15:18	W. wise men have told from their	834
Job	15:28	and in houses w. no man inhabiteth,	
Job	15:28	w. are ready to become heaps.	834
Job	16:8	wrinkles, w. is a witness against me:	
Job	20:7	they w. have seen him shall say,	
Job	20:9	eye also w. saw him shall see him no	
Job	20:11	w. shall lie down with him in the dust.	
Job	20:18	That w. he laboured for shall be	
Job	20:19	away an house w. he builded not;	
Job	20:20	he shall not save of that w. he desired.	
Job	21:27	devices w. ye wrongfully imagine	
Job	22:15	way w. wicked men have trodden?	834
Job	22:16	W. were cut down out of time,	834
Job	22:17	W. said unto God, Depart from us:	
Job	23:5	the words w. he would answer me,	
Job	24:11	W. make oil within their walls, and	
Job	24:16	w. they have marked for themselves in	
Job	24:19	doth the grave those w. have sinned	
Job	25:6	and the son of man, w. is a worm?	
Job	27:11	w. is with the Almighty will I not	834
Job	27:13	w. they shall receive of the Almighty,	
Job	28:7	There is a path w. no fowl knoweth,	
Job	28:7	w. the vulture's eye hath not seen:	
Job	29:16	cause w. I knew not I searched out	
Job	32:19	my belly is as wine w. hath no vent;	
Job	33:27	that w. was right, and it profited me	
Job	34:8	W. goeth in company with...workers	
Job	34:32	That w. I see not teach thou me:	
Job	35:5	the clouds w. are higher than thou.	
Job	36:16	and that w. should be set on thy table	
Job	36:24	magnify his work, w. men behold	834
Job	36:28	W. the clouds do drop and distil	834
Job	37:5	doeth he, w. we cannot comprehend.	
Job	37:16	of him w. is perfect in knowledge?	
Job	37:18	w. is strong, and as a molten looking	
Job	37:21	the bright light w. is in the clouds:	1931
Job	38:23	W. I have reserved against the	834
Job	38:24	W. scattereth the east wind upon the	
Job	39:14	W. leaveth her eggs in the earth,	3588
Job	40:15	behemoth, w. I made with thee;	834
Job	41:1	with a cord w. thou lettest down?	
Job	42:3	too wonderful for me, w. I knew not.	
Job	42:8	spoken of me the thing w. is right,	
Ps	1:4	the chaff w. the wind driveth away	834
Ps	3:2	Many there be w. say of my soul,	
Ps	7:*title*	David, w. he sang unto the Lord,	834
Ps	7:10	w. saveth the upright in heart.	
Ps	7:15	fallen into the ditch w. he made.	
Ps	8:3	the stars, w. thou hast ordained;	834
Ps	9:11	to the Lord, w. dwelleth in Zion:	
Ps	9:13	trouble w. I suffer of them that hate	
Ps	9:15	net w. they hid is their own foot	2098
Ps	9:16	by the judgment w. he executeth:	
Ps	17:7	them w. put their trust in thee from	
Ps	17:13	soul from the wicked, w. is thy sword:	
Ps	17:14	From men w. are thy hand, O Lord,	

Book	Ref	Context	No.
Ps	17:14	**w.** have their portion in this life,	
Ps	18:17	enemy, and from them **w.** hated me:	
Ps	19:5	**W.** is as a bridegroom coming out of	
Ps	21:11	device, **w.** they are not able to perform	
Ps	25:3	ashamed **w.** transgress without	
Ps	28:3	**w.** speak peace to their neighbours,	
Ps	31:18	**w.** speak grievous things proudly	
Ps	31:19	**w.** thou hast laid up for them that	834
Ps	31:19	**w.** thou hast wrought for them that	
Ps	32:8	thee in the way **w.** thou shalt go:	2098
Ps	32:9	the mule, **w.** have no understanding:	
Ps	35:7	**w.** without cause they have digged	
Ps	35:10	**w.** deliverest the poor from him that	
Ps	35:27	**w.** hath pleasure in the prosperity of	
Ps	40:5	wonderful works **w.** thou hast done,	
Ps	40:5	and thy thoughts **w.** are to us-ward:	
Ps	41:9	I trusted, **w.** did eat of my bread,	
Ps	44:10	they **w.** hate us spoil for themselves	
Ps	45:1	**w.** I have made touching the king:	
Ps	51:8	that the bones **w.** thou hast broken	
Ps	58:5	**W.** will not hearken to the voice of	834
Ps	58:7	away as waters **w.** run continually:	
Ps	58:8	As a snail **w.** melteth, let every one of	
Ps	59:12	for cursing and lying **w.** they speak	
Ps	60:10	not thou, O God, **w.** hadst cast us off?	
Ps	60:10	**w.** didst not go out with our armies?	
Ps	61:7	and truth, **w.** may preserve him	
Ps	65:6	**W.** by his strength setteth fast the	
Ps	65:7	**W.** stilleth the noise of the seas, the	
Ps	65:9	the river of God, **w.** is full of water:	
Ps	66:9	**W.** holdeth our soul in life, and	
Ps	66:14	**W.** my lips have uttered, and my	834
Ps	66:20	God, **w.** hath not turned away my	834
Ps	68:6	he bringeth out those **w.** are bound	
Ps	68:16	the hill **w.** God desireth to dwell in;	
Ps	68:28	**w.** thou hast wrought for us	2098
Ps	68:33	heavens of heavens, **w.** were of old;	
Ps	69:4	restored that **w.** I took not away	834
Ps	69:22	**w.** should have been for their welfare,	
Ps	71:20	**w.** hast shewed me great and sore	834
Ps	71:23	my soul, **w.** thou hast redeemed	834
Ps	74:2	**w.** thou hast purchased of old;	
Ps	74:2	inheritance, **w.** thou hast redeemed;	
Ps	78:3	**W.** we have heard and known,	834
Ps	78:5	**w.** he commanded our fathers,	834
Ps	78:6	even the children **w.** should be born;	
Ps	78:45	flies among them, **w.** devoured them;	
Ps	78:45	and frogs, **w.** destroyed them	
Ps	78:54	**w.** his right hand had purchased	
Ps	78:60	the tent **w.** he placed among men;	
Ps	78:68	Judah, the mount Zion **w.** he loved	834
Ps	78:69	like the earth **w.** he hath established	
Ps	79:10	the blood of thy servants **w.** is shed	
Ps	80:12	they **w.** pass by the way do pluck her?	
Ps	80:15	vineyard **w.** thy right hand hath	834
Ps	81:10	God, **w.** brought thee out of the land	
Ps	83:10	**W.** perished at En-dor: they became	
Ps	85:12	Lord shall give that **w.** is good; and	
Ps	86:17	that they **w.** hate me may see it,	
Ps	89:49	**w.** thou swarest unto David in thy	
Ps	90:5	they are like the grass **w.** groweth up	
Ps	91:9	hast made the Lord, **w.** is my refuge,	
Ps	94:20	thee, **w.** frameth mischief by a law?	
Ps	102:18	the people **w.** shall be created shall	
Ps	104:8	place **w.** thou hast founded for	2088
Ps	104:10	the valleys, **w.** run among the hills	
Ps	104:12	fowls…**w.** sing among the branches	
Ps	104:15	and bread **w.** strengtheneth man's	
Ps	104:16	of Lebanon, **w.** he hath planted;	834
Ps	105:8	the word **w.** he commanded to a	
Ps	105:9	**W.** covenant he made with	834
Ps	106:21	**w.** had done great things in Egypt;	
Ps	106:36	idols: **w.** were a snare unto them	
Ps	107:25	wind, **w.** lifteth up the waves thereof	
Ps	107:37	**w.** may yield fruits of increase	
Ps	109:19	him as the garment **w.** covereth him,	
Ps	114:8	**W.** turned the rock into a standing	
Ps	115:15	the Lord **w.** made heaven and earth	
Ps	118:20	into **w.** the righteous shall enter	
Ps	118:22	The stone **w.** the builders refused is	
Ps	118:24	is the day **w.** the Lord hath made;	
Ps	118:27	is the Lord, **w.** hath shewed us light:	
Ps	119:21	**w.** do err from thy commandments	
Ps	119:39	Turn away my reproach **w.** I fear:	834
Ps	119:47	commandments, **w.** I have loved	834
Ps	119:48	commandments, **w.** I have loved;	834
Ps	119:49	**w.** thou hast caused me to hope	834
Ps	119:85	for me, **w.** are not after thy law	834
Ps	119:165	peace have they **w.** love thy law:	
Ps	121:2	the Lord, **w.** made heaven and earth	
Ps	125:1	as mount Zion, **w.** cannot be moved,	
Ps	129:6	**w.** withereth afore it groweth up:	
Ps	129:8	Neither do they **w.** go by say, The	
Ps	134:1	**w.** by night stand in the house of the	
Ps	135:21	of Zion, **w.** dwelleth at Jerusalem	
Ps	136:13	To him **w.** divided the Red sea into	
Ps	136:16	To him **w.** led his people through the	
Ps	136:17	To him **w.** smote great kings: for his	
Ps	138:8	will perfect that **w.** concerneth me:	
Ps	139:16	**w.** in continuance were fashioned,	
Ps	140:2	**W.** imagine mischiefs in their	834
Ps	141:5	oil, **w.** shall not break my head:	
Ps	141:9	the snares **w.** they have laid for me,	
Ps	144:1	**w.** teacheth my hands to war,	
Ps	146:6	**W.** made heaven, and earth, the sea,	
Ps	146:6	therein is: **w.** keepeth truth for ever:	
Ps	146:7	**W.** executeth judgment for the	
Ps	146:7	**w.** giveth food to the hungry	
Ps	147:9	and to the young ravens **w.** cry	834
Ps	148:6	hath made a decree **w.** shall not pass	
Pr	1:19	**w.** taketh away the life of the owners	
Pr	2:16	stranger **w.** flattereth with her words;	
Pr	2:17	**W.** forsaketh the guide of her youth,	
Pr	6:7	**W.** having no guide, overseer, or	834
Pr	7:5	stranger **w.** flattereth with her words	
Pr	9:5	drink of the wine **w.** I have mingled	
Pr	11:22	fair woman **w.** is without discretion	
Pr	12:27	not that **w.** he took in hunting:	
Pr	14:12	is a way **w.** seemeth right unto a man,	
Pr	14:33	that **w.** is in the midst of fools is made	
Pr	19:17	that **w.** he hath given will he pay him	
Pr	20:25	man who devoureth that **w.** is holy,	
Pr	22:28	landmark, **w.** thy fathers have set	834
Pr	23:5	set thine eyes upon that **w.** is not?	
Pr	23:8	morsel **w.** thou hast eaten shalt thou	
Pr	24:13	honeycomb, **w.** is sweet to thy taste:	
Pr	25:1	**w.** the men of Hezekiah king of	834
Pr	27:16	of his right hand, **w.** bewrayeth itself	
Pr	28:3	a sweeping rain **w.** leaveth no food	
Pr	30:18	be three things **w.** are too wonderful	
Pr	30:21	and for four **w.** it cannot bear:	
Pr	30:24	things **w.** are little upon the earth,	
Pr	30:29	There be three things **w.** go well, yea,	
Pr	30:30	A lion **w.** is strongest among beasts,	
Pr	31:3	thy ways to that **w.** destroyeth kings	
Ec	1:3	his labour **w.** he taketh under the sun?	
Ec	1:9	that hath been, it is that **w.** shall be;	
Ec	1:9	**w.** is done is that **w.** shall be done:	
Ec	1:10	of old time, **w.** was before us	834
Ec	1:15	That **w.** is crooked cannot be made	
Ec	1:15	and that **w.** is wanting cannot be	
Ec	2:3	**w.** they should do under the heaven	834
Ec	2:12	that **w.** hath been already done,	834
Ec	2:16	seeing that **w.** now is in the days to	
Ec	2:18	hated all my labour **w.** I had taken	
Ec	2:20	despair of all the labour **w.** I took	
Ec	3:2	a time to pluck up that **w.** is planted;	
Ec	3:10	**w.** God hath given to the sons of	834
Ec	3:15	That **w.** hath been is now; and that	
Ec	3:15	that **w.** is to be hath already been;	834
Ec	3:15	and God requireth that **w.** is past	
Ec	3:19	For that **w.** befalleth the sons of men	
Ec	4:2	praised the dead **w.** are already dead	
Ec	4:2	than the living **w.** are yet alive	834
Ec	4:3	**w.** hath not yet been, who hath not	834
Ec	4:15	all the living **w.** walk under the sun,	
Ec	5:4	pay that **w.** thou hast vowed	834
Ec	5:13	evil **w.** I have seen under the sun,	
Ec	5:15	**w.** he may carry away in his hand	
Ec	5:18	Behold that **w.** I have seen: it is	834
Ec	5:18	days of his life, **w.** God giveth him:	834
Ec	6:1	There is an evil **w.** I have seen	834
Ec	6:10	That **w.** hath been is named already,	
Ec	6:12	vain life **w.** he spendeth as a shadow?	
Ec	7:13	**w.** he hath made crooked?	834
Ec	7:19	ten mighty men **w.** are in the city	834
Ec	7:24	That **w.** is far off, and exceeding	4100
Ec	7:28	**W.** yet my soul seeketh, but I find	834
Ec	8:7	he knoweth not that **w.** shall be:	4100
Ec	8:12	that fear God, **w.** fear before him	834
Ec	8:13	prolong his days, **w.** are as a shadow;	
Ec	8:14	vanity **w.** is done upon the earth;	834
Ec	8:15	**w.** God giveth him under the sun	834
Ec	9:9	**w.** he hath given thee under the sun,	834
Ec	9:9	in thy labour **w.** thou takest under	
Ec	10:5	an evil **w.** I have seen under the sun,	
Ec	10:5	error **w.** proceedeth from the ruler:	
Ec	10:20	and that **w.** hath wings shall tell	
Ec	12:5	shall be afraid of that **w.** is high,	
Ec	12:10	and that **w.** was written was upright,	
Ec	12:11	**w.** are given from one shepherd	
Ca	1:1	song of songs, **w.** is Solomon's	834
Ca	3:7	Behold his bed, **w.** is Solomon's;	
Ca	4:2	**w.** came up from the washing;	
Ca	4:5	are twins, **w.** feed among the lilies	
Ca	6:6	of sheep **w.** go up from the washing,	
Ca	7:2	goblet, **w.** wanteth not liquor:	
Ca	7:4	Lebanon **w.** looketh toward Damascus	
Ca	7:13	and old, **w.** I have laid up for thee,	
Ca	8:6	**w.** hath a most vehement flame	
Ca	8:12	My vineyard, **w.** is mine, is before	
Isa	1:1	**w.** he saw concerning Judah and	834
Isa	1:29	of the oaks **w.** ye have desired,	834
Isa	2:8	**w.** their own fingers have made:	834
Isa	2:20	**w.** they made each for himself to	834
Isa	3:12	they **w.** lead thee cause thee to err,	
Isa	5:23	**W.** justify the wicked for reward,	
Isa	6:6	**w.** he had taken with the tongs	
Isa	8:18	of hosts, **w.** dwelleth in mount Zion	
Isa	10:1	grievousness **w.** they have prescribed;	
Isa	10:3	the desolation **w.** shall come from far?	
Isa	11:10	**w.** shall stand for an ensign of the	834
Isa	11:11,	16 of his people, **w.** shall be left,	834
Isa	13:1	**w.** Isaiah the son of Amoz did see	834
Isa	13:17	them, **w.** shall not regard silver;	834
Isa	14:12	ground, **w.** didst weaken the nations!	
Isa	15:7	and that **w.** they have laid up,	
Isa	17:2	shall be for flocks, **w.** shall lie down,	
Isa	17:8	that **w.** his fingers have made,	834
Isa	17:9	**w.** they left because of the children	834
Isa	17:12	**w.** make a noise like the noise of the	
Isa	18:1	**w.** is beyond the rivers of Ethiopia:	834
Isa	19:15	**w.** the head or tail, branch or rush,	
Isa	19:16	of hosts, **w.** he shaketh over it	834
Isa	19:17	**w.** he hath determined against it	834
Isa	21:10	that **w.** I have heard of the Lord of	834
Isa	22:3	together, **w.** have fled from far	
Isa	22:15	unto Shebna, **w.** is over the house,	834
Isa	26:2	**w.** keepeth the truth may enter in	
Isa	27:13	shall come **w.** were ready to perish	
Isa	28:1	**w.** are on the head of the fat	834
Isa	28:2	**w.** as a tempest of hail and a	
Isa	28:4	**w.** is on the head of the fat valley,	834
Isa	28:4	**w.** when he that looketh upon it	834
Isa	28:14	this people **w.** is in Jerusalem	834
Isa	28:29	hosts, **w.** is wonderful in counsel,	
Isa	29:11	**w.** men deliver to one that is	834
Isa	30:10	**W.** say to the seers, See not; and	834
Isa	30:24	**w.** hath been winnowed with the	834
Isa	30:31	be beaten down, **w.** smote with a rod	
Isa	30:32	**w.** the Lord shall lay upon him,	834
Isa	31:7	**w.** your own hands have made unto	834
Isa	36:3	son, **w.** was over the house, and	834
Isa	37:4	**w.** the Lord thy God hath heard:	834
Isa	37:12	delivered them **w.** my fathers have	834
Isa	37:12	of Eden **w.** were in Telassar?	834
Isa	37:17	**w.** hath sent to reproach the living	834
Isa	37:22	word **w.** the Lord hath spoken	834
Isa	37:29	back by the way **w.** thou camest	834
Isa	37:30	year that **w.** springeth of the same:	
Isa	38:3	have done that **w.** is good in thy sight	
Isa	38:8	**w.** is gone down in the sun dial of	834
Isa	38:8	by **w.** degrees it was gone down	
Isa	39:6	that **w.** thy fathers have laid up in	834
Isa	39:7	**w.** thou shalt beget, shall they take	834
Isa	39:8	of the Lord **w.** thou hast spoken	834
Isa	42:5	earth, and that **w.** cometh out of it;	
Isa	43:16	the Lord, **w.** maketh a way in the sea,	
Isa	43:17	**W.** bringeth forth the chariot and	
Isa	44:2	thee from the womb, **w.** will help thee;	
Isa	44:14	**w.** he strengtheneth for himself	
Isa	45:3	the Lord, **w.** call thee by thy name,	
Isa	46:3	**w.** are borne by me from the belly,	
Isa	46:3	belly, **w.** are carried from the womb:	
Isa	47:11	thee suddenly, **w.** thou shalt not know	
Isa	48:1	**w.** are called by the name of Israel,	
Isa	48:1	**w.** swear by the name of the Lord,	
Isa	48:14	**w.** among them hath declared	4310

Book	Ref	Context	No.
Isa	48:17	thy God w. teacheth thee to profit,	
Isa	48:17	w. leadeth thee by the way that thou	
Isa	49:20	The children w. thou shalt have, after	
Isa	50:1	w. of my creditors is it to whom	4310
Isa	51:10	Art thou not it w. hath dried the sea,	
Isa	51:12	son of man w. shall be made as grass;	
Isa	51:17	w. hast drunk at the hand of the	834
Isa	51:23	w. have said to my soul, Bow down,	834
Isa	52:15	w. had not been told them shall	834
Isa	52:15	that w. they had not heard shall they	834
Isa	55:2	spend money for that w. is not bread?	
Isa	55:2	your labour for that w. satisfieth not?	
Isa	55:2	eat ye that w. is good, and let your	
Isa	55:11	it shall accomplish that w. I please,	834
Isa	56:8	Lord God w. gathereth the outcasts	
Isa	56:11	dogs w. can never have enough,	
Isa	57:16	me, and the souls w. I have made	
Isa	59:5	that w. is crushed breaketh out into a	
Isa	59:21	words w. I have put in thy mouth,	834
Isa	61:9	the seed w. the Lord hath blessed.	
Isa	62:2	w. the mouth of the Lord shall	834
Isa	62:6	w. shall never hold their peace day	
Isa	62:8	for the w. thou hast laboured:	834
Isa	63:7	w. he hath bestowed on them	834
Isa	64:3	terrible things w. we looked not for,	
Isa	65:2	w. walketh in a way that was not	
Isa	65:4	W. remain among the graves, and	
Isa	65:4	w. eat swine's flesh, and broth of	
Isa	65:5	W. say, Stand by thyself, come not	
Isa	65:7	w. have burned incense upon the	834
Isa	65:18	for ever in that w. I create:	834
Isa	66:4	and chose that in w. I delighted not.	834
Isa	66:22	the new earth, w. I will make, shall	834
Jer	2:11	their gods, w. are yet no gods?	1992
Jer	2:11	glory for that w. did not profit.	1992
Jer	3:6	seen that w. backsliding Israel	834
Jer	3:15	w. shall feed you with knowledge and	
Jer	5:17	w. thy sons and thy daughters should	
Jer	5:21	w. have eyes, and see not;	
Jer	5:21	w. have ears, and hear not:	
Jer	5:22	w. have placed the sand for the	834
Jer	7:10	w. is called by my name, and say,	834
Jer	7:11	w. is called by my name, become	834
Jer	7:12	unto my place w. was in Shiloh,	834
Jer	7:14	house, w. is called by my name,	834
Jer	7:14	the place w. I gave to you and to	834
Jer	7:30	the house w. I called by my name,	834
Jer	7:31	w. is in the valley of the son of	834
Jer	7:31	w. I commanded them not, neither	834
Jer	8:3	w. remain in all the places whither I	
Jer	8:17	among you, w. will not be charmed,	834
Jer	9:13	my law w. I set before them,	834
Jer	9:14	w. their fathers taught them:	834
Jer	9:24	the Lord w. exercise lovingkindness,	
Jer	9:25	punish all them w. are circumcised	
Jer	10:1	word w. the Lord speaketh unto	834
Jer	11:4	W. I commanded your fathers in	834
Jer	11:4	to all w. I commanded you:	834
Jer	11:5	oath w. I have sworn unto your	834
Jer	11:8	w. I commanded them to do;	834
Jer	11:10	w. refused to hear my words; and	834
Jer	11:10	w. I made with their fathers.	834
Jer	11:11	w. they shall not be able to escape;	834
Jer	11:17	w. they have done against	834
Jer	12:14	w. I have caused my people Israel to	834
Jer	13:4	thou hast got, w. is upon thy loins,	834
Jer	13:6	w. I commanded thee to hide there.	834
Jer	13:10	people, w. refuse to hear my words,	
Jer	13:10	w. walk in the imagination of their	
Jer	13:10	this girdle, w. is good for nothing.	834
Jer	15:4	for that w. he did in Jerusalem.	834
Jer	15:14	into a land w. thou knowest not:	
Jer	15:14	mine anger, w. shall burn upon you.	
Jer	15:18	incurable, w. refuseth to be healed?	
Jer	17:4	in the land w. thou knowest not:	834
Jer	17:4	in mine anger, w. shall burn for ever.	
Jer	17:16	that w. came out of my lips was right	
Jer	17:19	by the w. they go out, and in all	834
Jer	18:1	The word w. came to Jeremiah	834
Jer	18:14	snow of Lebanon w. cometh from the	
Jer	19:2	w. is by the entry of the east gate,	834
Jer	19:3	the w. whosoever heareth, his ears	834
Jer	19:5	w. I commanded not, nor spake it,	834
Jer	20:2	w. was by the house of the Lord	834
Jer	20:5	w. shall spoil them, and take them,	834
Jer	20:16	the cities w. the Lord overthrew,	834
Jer	21:1	word w. came unto Jeremiah from	834
Jer	21:4	w. besiege you without the walls,	
Jer	21:13	w. say, Who shall come down against	
Jer	22:6	and cities w. are not inhabited.	
Jer	22:11	w. reigned instead of Josiah his	
Jer	22:11	w. went forth out of this place; He	834
Jer	22:28	cast into a land w. they know not?	834
Jer	23:4	over them w. shall feed them:	
Jer	23:7	w. brought up the children of	834
Jer	23:8	w. brought up and w. led the seed of	834
Jer	23:27	W. think to cause my people to forget	
Jer	23:27	w. they tell every man to his	834
Jer	23:40	shame, w. shall not be forgotten.	834
Jer	24:2	naughty figs, w. could not be eaten,	834
Jer	24:8	as the evil figs, w. cannot be eaten,	834
Jer	25:2	The w. Jeremiah the prophet spake	834
Jer	25:13	words w. I have pronounced against	834
Jer	25:13	w. Jeremiah hath prophesied	834
Jer	25:22	of the isles w. are beyond the sea,	834
Jer	25:26	w. are upon the face of the earth:	834
Jer	25:27	sword w. I will send among you.	834
Jer	25:29	on the city w. is called by my name,	834
Jer	26:2	w. come to worship in the Lord's	
Jer	26:3	evil w. I purpose to do unto them	834
Jer	26:4	in my law w. I have set before you,	834
Jer	26:19	of the evil w. he had pronounced	834
Jer	27:3	the messengers w. come to Jerusalem	
Jer	27:8	kingdom w. will not serve the	834
Jer	27:9	your sorcerers, w. speak unto you,	834
Jer	27:18	w. are left in the house of the Lord,	
Jer	27:20	W. Nebuchadnezzar king of	834
Jer	28:1	Azur the prophet, w. was of Gibeon,	834
Jer	28:6	thy words w. thou hast prophesied,	834
Jer	28:9	prophet w. prophesieth of peace,	834
Jer	29:1	elders w. were carried away captives,	
Jer	29:8	dreams w. ye caused to be dreamed.	834
Jer	29:19	w. I sent unto them by my servants	834
Jer	29:21	w. prophesy a lie unto you in my	
Jer	29:22	of Judah w. are in Babylon,	834
Jer	29:23	w. I have not commanded them;	834
Jer	29:27	w. maketh himself a prophet to you?	
Jer	31:2	The people w. were left of the sword	
Jer	31:21	even the way w. thou wentest:	
Jer	31:32	w. my covenant they brake,	834
Jer	31:35	w. giveth the sun for a light by day,	
Jer	31:35	w. divideth the sea when the waves	
Jer	32:1	w. was the eighteenth year of	1958
Jer	32:2	w. was in the king of Judah's	834
Jer	32:8	w. is in the country of Benjamin:	834
Jer	32:11	both that w. was sealed according to	
Jer	32:11	and custom, and that w. was open:	
Jer	32:14	of the purchase, both w. is sealed,	
Jer	32:14	and this evidence w. is open; and put	
Jer	32:20	W. hast set signs and wonders in	834
Jer	32:22	w. thou didst swear to their fathers	834
Jer	32:32	w. they have done to provoke me to	834
Jer	32:34	w. is called by my name, to defile it	834
Jer	32:35	w. are in the valley of the son of	834
Jer	32:35	w. I commanded them not, neither	834
Jer	33:3	mighty things, w. thou knowest not.	
Jer	33:4	w. are thrown down by the mounts,	
Jer	33:9	w. shall hear all the good that I do	834
Jer	33:10	w. ye say shall be desolate without	834
Jer	33:12	w. is desolate without man and	
Jer	33:14	good thing w. I have promised	834
Jer	33:24	families w. the Lord hath chosen,	834
Jer	34:1	The word w. came unto Jeremiah	834
Jer	34:5	former kings w. were before thee,	834
Jer	34:8	all the people w. were at Jerusalem,	834
Jer	34:10	w. had entered into the covenant,	834
Jer	34:14	w. hath been sold unto thee;	834
Jer	34:15	the house w. is called by my name:	834
Jer	34:18	w. have not performed the words of	834
Jer	34:18	covenant w. they had made before	834
Jer	34:19	w. passed between the parts of the	
Jer	34:21	army, w. are gone up from you.	
Jer	35:1	The word w. came unto Jeremiah	834
Jer	35:4	w. was by the chamber of the	834
Jer	35:4	w. was above the chamber of	834
Jer	35:15	in the land w. I have given to you	834
Jer	35:16	father, w. he commanded them;	834
Jer	36:3	evil w. I purpose to do unto them;	834
Jer	36:4	w. he had spoken unto him, upon a	834
Jer	36:6	w. thou hast written from my	834
Jer	36:21	the princes w. stood beside the king	
Jer	36:27	w. Baruch wrote at the mouth of	834
Jer	36:28	w. Jehoiakim the king of Judah hath	834
Jer	36:32	w. Jehoiakim king of Judah had	834
Jer	37:2	Lord, w. he spake by the prophet	834
Jer	37:7	army, w. is come forth to help you,	
Jer	37:19	prophets w. prophesied unto you,	834
Jer	38:3	of Babylon's army, w. shall take it	
Jer	38:7	w. was in the king's house, heard	1931
Jer	38:20	of the Lord, w. I speak unto thee:	834
Jer	39:10	of the people, w. had nothing,	834
Jer	40:1	The word w. came to Jeremiah from	
Jer	40:1	w. were carried away captive unto	
Jer	40:4	chains w. were upon thine hand	834
Jer	40:7	of the forces w. were in the field,	834
Jer	40:10	Chaldeans w. will come unto us:	834
Jer	40:15	all the Jews w. are gathered unto thee	
Jer	41:9	was it w. Asa the king had made for	834
Jer	41:13	the people w. were with Ishmael	834
Jer	41:17	of Chimham, w. is by Beth-lehem,	834
Jer	42:5	for the w. the Lord thy God shall	834
Jer	42:8	of the forces w. were with him,	834
Jer	42:16	sword, w. ye feared, shall overtake	834
Jer	42:21	for the w. he hath sent me unto you.	834
Jer	43:1	for w. the Lord their God had sent	834
Jer	43:9	w. is at the entry of Pharaoh's	834
Jer	44:1	Jews w. dwell in the land of Egypt,	
Jer	44:1	w. dwell at Migdol, and at Tahpanhes,	
Jer	44:3	w. they have committed to provoke	834
Jer	44:9	w. they have committed in the land	834
Jer	44:14	w. are gone into the land of Egypt to	
Jer	44:14	to the w. they...desire to return	834
Jer	44:15	men w. knew that their wives had	
Jer	44:20	people w. had given him that answer,	
Jer	44:22	of the abominations w. ye have	834
Jer	45:4	that w. I have built will I break	834
Jer	45:4	that w. I have planted I will pluck	834
Jer	46:1	The word...w. came to Jeremiah	834
Jer	46:2	w. was by the river Euphrates in	834
Jer	46:2	w. Nebuchadrezzar king of Babylon	834
Jer	49:28	w. Nebuchadrezzar king of Babylon	834
Jer	49:31	nations,...w. have neither gates nor	
Jer	49:31	neither gates nor bars w. dwell alone.	
Jer	50:3	w. shall make her land desolate,	1931
Jer	51:12	and done that w. he spake against	834
Jer	51:25	the Lord, w. destroyest all the earth:	
Jer	51:44	mouth that w. he hath swallowed up:	
Jer	51:59	The word w. Jeremiah the prophet	834
Jer	52:2	that w. was evil in the eyes of the	
Jer	52:7	walls, w. was by the king's garden:	834
Jer	52:12	w. was the nineteenth year of	1958
Jer	52:12	guard, w. served the king of Babylon,	
Jer	52:19	that w. was of gold in gold, and	834
Jer	52:19	and that w. was of silver in silver,	834
Jer	52:20	w. king Solomon had made in the	834
Jer	52:25	w. had...charge of the men of war;	834
Jer	52:25	person, w. were found in the city;	834
La	1:12	my sorrow, w. is done unto me,	834
La	2:3	fire, w. devoureth round about	
La	2:17	hath done that w. he had devised;	834
La	5:18	the mountain of Zion, w. is desolate,	
Eze	1:2	w. was the fifth year of king	1958
Eze	1:23	one had two, w. covered on this side,	
Eze	1:23	one had two, w. covered on that side,	
Eze	3:20	his righteousness w. he hath done	834
Eze	3:23	glory w. I saw by the river of Chebar:	834
Eze	4:10	And the meat w. thou shalt eat shall	834
Eze	4:14	I not eaten of that w. dieth of itself,	
Eze	5:9	do in thee that w. I have not done,	834
Eze	5:16	w. shall be for their destruction,	834
Eze	5:16	and w. I will send to destroy you:	834
Eze	6:9	heart, w. hath departed from me,	834
Eze	6:9	eyes, w. go a whoring after their idols:	
Eze	6:9	evils w. they have committed in all	834
Eze	7:13	shall not return to that w. is sold,	
Eze	7:13	multitude thereof, w. shall not return;	
Eze	8:3	of jealousy, w. provoketh to jealousy.	
Eze	8:14	house w. was toward the north;	834
Eze	8:17	abominations w. they commit here?	834
Eze	9:2	gate, w. lieth toward the north,	834
Eze	9:3	w. had the writer's inkhorn by his	834
Eze	9:6	men w. were before the house	834
Eze	9:11	w. had the inkhorn by his side,	834
Eze	10:22	w. I saw by the river of Chebar,	834
Eze	11:1	Lord's house, w. looketh eastward:	
Eze	11:3	W. say, It is not near; let us build	
Eze	11:23	w. is on the east side of the city.	834
Eze	12:2	w. have eyes to see, and see not;	834

Eze 12:28 word w. I have spoken shall be done,... 834
Eze 13:11 w. daub it with untempered morter,..........
Eze 13:16 w. prophesy concerning Jerusalem, ...
Eze 13:16 and w. see visions of peace for her, ...
Eze 13:17 w. prophesy out of their own heart;..........
Eze 14:7 w. separateth himself from me,................
Eze 15:2 w. is among the trees of the forest?..... 834
Eze 15:6 w. I have given to the fire for fuel, ... 834
Eze 16:14 comeliness, w. I had put upon thee, ... 834
Eze 16:17 of my silver, w. I had given thee,........ 834
Eze 16:19 My meat also w. I gave thee, fine 834
Eze 16:27 w. are ashamed of thy lewd way; ....
Eze 16:32 w. taketh strangers instead of her............
Eze 16:36 w. thou didst give unto them; 834
Eze 16:45 w. lothed their husbands and their 834
Eze 16:51 abominations w. thou hast done........... 834
Eze 16:52 also, w. hast judged thy sisters, ... 834
Eze 16:57 Philistines w. despised thee round...........
Eze 16:59 w. hast despised the oath in 834
Eze 17:3 of feathers, w. had divers colours, ... 834
Eze 18:5 and do that w. is lawful and right, ...
Eze 18:14 his father's sins w. he hath done, ... 834
Eze 18:18 w. is not good among his people,......... 834
Eze 18:19 the son hath done that w. is lawful..........
Eze 18:21 and do that w. is lawful and right, he........
Eze 18:27 doeth that w. is lawful and right, he..........
Eze 19:14 w. hath devoured her fruit, so that she .....
Eze 20:6 honey, w. is the glory of all lands:...... 1958
Eze 20:11, 13 w. if a man do, he shall even live 834
Eze 20:15 into the land w. I have given them,...... 834
Eze 20:15 honey, w. is the glory of all lands;...... 1958
Eze 20:21 w. if a man do, he shall even live in..... 834
Eze 20:28 w. I lifted up mine hand to give it to.... 834
Eze 20:32 that w. cometh into your mind shall..........
Eze 20:42 for the w. I lifted up mine hand........... 834
Eze 21:14 w. entereth into their privy chambers........
Eze 22:4 in thine idols w. thou hast made; 834
Eze 22:5 w. art infamous and much vexed...........
Eze 22:13 dishonest gain w. thou hast made, ... 834
Eze 22:13 thy blood w. hath been in the midst 834
Eze 23:6 W. were clothed with blue, captains..........
Eze 23:24 w. shall set against thee buckler and.........
Eze 23:42 w. put bracelets upon their hands,.............
Eze 24:21 eyes, and that w. your soul pitieth; ....
Eze 24:27 mouth be opened to him w. is escaped, ...
Eze 25:9 from his cities w. are on his frontiers,.......
Eze 26:6 her daughters w. are in the field.......... 834
Eze 26:17 w. wast strong in the sea, she and 834
Eze 26:17 w. cause their terror to be on all......... 834
Eze 27:3 w. art a merchant for the people on..........
Eze 27:7 that w. thou spreadest forth to be thy.......
Eze 27:7 of Elishah was that w. covered thee. ....
Eze 27:27 company w. is in the midst of thee, ... 834
Eze 29:3 w. hath said, My river is mine own, ...
Eze 29:16 Israel w. bringeth their iniquity to ....
Eze 30:22 the strong, and that w. was broken; ....
Eze 32:9 countries w. thou hast not known. 834
Eze 32:23 w. caused terror in the land of the....... 834
Eze 32:24 w. are gone down uncircumcised 834
Eze 32:24 w. caused their terror in the land of..... 834
Eze 32:27 w. are gone down to hell with their...... 834
Eze 32:29 w. with their might are laid by them..... 834
Eze 32:30 w. are gone down with the slain;......... 834
Eze 33:14 and do that w. is lawful and right; ....
Eze 33:16 he hath done that w. is lawful and............
Eze 33:19 do that w. is lawful and right, he shall.......
Eze 33:29 all their abominations w. they have....... 834
Eze 34:4 have ye healed that w. was sick,..............
Eze 34:4 have ye bound up that w. was broken, ...
Eze 34:4 ye brought again that w. was driven ....
Eze 34:4 have ye sought that w. was lost;..............
Eze 34:16 I will seek that w. was lost, and bring.......
Eze 34:16 bring again that w. was driven away, ...
Eze 34:16 and will bind up that w. was broken,.........
Eze 34:16 and will strengthen that w. was sick: ....
Eze 34:19 eat that w. ye have trodden with your.......
Eze 34:19 they drink that w. ye have fouled with ......
Eze 35:11 w. thou hast used out of thy hatred 834
Eze 35:12 blasphemies w. thou hast spoken......... 834
Eze 36:4 w. became a prey and derision to 834
Eze 36:5 w. have appointed my land into 834
Eze 36:21 w. the house of Israel had profaned...... 834
Eze 36:22 w. ye have profaned among the........... 834
Eze 36:23 w. was profaned among the heathen, ...
Eze 36:23 w. ye have profaned in the midst of 834
Eze 37:1 of the valley w. was full of bones, ... 1958
Eze 37:19 w. is in the land of Ephraim,.............. 834
Eze 38:8 Israel, w. have been always waste: 834
Eze 38:12 w. have gotten cattle and goods,............
Eze 38:17 w. prophesied in those days many............
Eze 39:19 of my sacrifice w. I have sacrificed....... 834
Eze 39:28 w. caused them to be led into ....
Eze 40:2 w. was as the frame of a city on the.........
Eze 40:6 gate, w. looketh toward the east, ... 834
Eze 40:6 of the gate, w. was one reed broad; ....
Eze 40:6 of the gate, w. was one reed broad. ....
Eze 40:40 w. was at the porch of the gate, ... 834
Eze 40:44 w. was at the side of the north gate;.... 834
Eze 40:46 w. come near to the Lord to minister ....
Eze 41:1 w. was the breadth of the tabernacle. ....
Eze 41:6 into the wall w. was of the house 834
Eze 41:9 w. was for the side chamber without 834
Eze 41:9 that w. was left was the place of the.........
Eze 41:15 separate place w. was behind it, ... 834
Eze 42:1 w. was before the building toward........ 834
Eze 42:3 cubits w. were for the inner court, ... 834
Eze 42:3 the pavement w. was for the utter........ 834
Eze 42:11 chambers w. were toward the north,.... 834
Eze 42:13 w. are before the separate place,......... 834
Eze 42:14 to those things w. are for the people.... 834
Eze 43:3 appearance of the vision w. I saw,....... 834
Eze 43:19 seed of Zadok, w. approach unto me,.........
Eze 44:1 sanctuary w. looketh toward the east;.......
Eze 44:10 w. went astray away from me after...... 834
Eze 44:13 their abominations w. they have 834
Eze 45:4 w. shall come near to minister unto ....
Eze 45:14 cor, w. is an homer of ten baths;....... 4480
Eze 46:19 w. was at the side of the gate,........... 834
Eze 46:19 priests, w. looked toward the north: ....
Eze 47:8 w. being brought forth into the sea,..........
Eze 47:9 every thing that liveth, w. moveth, ... 834
Eze 47:14 concerning the w. I lifted up mine........ 834
Eze 47:16 w. is between the border of 834
Eze 47:16 w. is by the coast of Hauran............... 834
Eze 47:22 w. shall beget children among you:....... 834
Eze 48:8 be the offering w. ye shall offer........... 834
Eze 48:11 of Zadok; w. have kept my charge, ... 834
Eze 48:11 w. went not astray when the 834
Eze 48:22 the midst of that w. is the prince's,...... 834
Eze 48:29 This is the land w. ye shall divide........ 834
Da 1:2 w. he carried into the land of Shinar ....
Da 1:5 meat, and of the wine w. he drank: ....
Da 1:8 meat, nor with the wine w. he drank: ....
Da 1:10 the children w. are of your sort? 834
Da 1:15 w. did eat the portion of the king's...........
Da 2:14 w. was gone forth to slay the wise..... 1768
Da 2:26 unto me the dream w. I have seen, ... 1768
Da 2:27 secret w. the king hath demanded......... 1768
Da 2:34 w. smote the image upon his feet that.......
Da 2:39 w. shall bear rule over all the........... 1768
Da 2:44 w. shall never be destroyed: 1768
Da 3:2 image w. Nebuchadnezzar the king..... 1768
Da 3:12 golden image w. thou hast set up....... 1768
Da 3:14 the golden image w. I have set up? 1768
Da 3:15 worship the image w. I have made; 1768
Da 3:18 golden image w. thou hast set up........ 1768
Da 3:29 w. speak any thing amiss against........ 1768
Da 4:5 I saw a dream w. made me afraid,............
Da 4:20 tree that thou sawest, w. grew,.......... 1768
Da 4:21 under w. the beasts of the field dwelt, ...
Da 4:24 w. is come upon my lord the king: 1768
Da 5:2 w. his father Nebuchadnezzar had....... 1768
Da 5:2 of the temple w. was in Jerusalem;...... 1768
Da 5:3 house of God w. was at Jerusalem;...... 1768
Da 5:13 Daniel, w. art of the children of the.... 1768
Da 5:23 w. see not, nor hear, nor know: 1768
Da 6:1 w. should be over the whole kingdom; ......
Da 6:8, 12 Medes and Persians, w. altereth.... 1768
Da 6:13 Daniel, w. is of the children of the 1768
Da 6:15 statute w. the king established........... 1768
Da 6:24 those men w. had accused Daniel,...... 1768
Da 6:26 that w. shall not be destroyed, ... 1768
Da 7:6 w. had upon the back of it four.......... 1768
Da 7:11 the great words w. the horn spake:...... 1768
Da 7:14 dominion, w. shall not pass away,....... 1768
Da 7:14 that w. shall not be destroyed. 1768
Da 7:17 These great beasts, w. are four, are... 1768
Da 7:17 w. shall arise out of the earth.................
Da 7:19 w. was diverse from all the others, ... 1768
Da 7:19 w. devoured, brake in pieces, and...........
Da 7:20 and of the other w. came up, and....... 1768
Da 7:23 earth, w. shall be diverse from all 1768
Da 8:1 that w. appeared unto me at the first........
Da 8:2 w. is in the province of Elam; and 834
Da 8:3 the river a ram w. had two horns:...........
Da 8:6 w. I had seen standing before the........ 834
Da 8:9 horn, w. waxed exceeding great,.............
Da 8:13 said unto that certain saint w. spake, ...
Da 8:16 w. called, and said, Gabriel, make this.......
Da 8:20 The ram w. thou sawest having........... 834
Da 8:26 the vision...w. was told is true:........... 834
Da 9:1 w. was made king over the realm of..... 834
Da 9:6 w. spake in thy name to our kings, ... 834
Da 9:10 w. he set before us by his servants 834
Da 9:12 his words, w. he spake against us,....... 834
Da 9:14 in all his works w. he doeth: for we..... 834
Da 9:18 the city w. is called by thy name: 834
Da 10:4 of the great river, w. is Hiddekel; 1931
Da 10:10 touched me, w. set me upon my knees, ...
Da 10:21 that w. is noted in the scripture of ....
Da 11:4 to his dominion w. he ruled: 834
Da 11:7 estate, w. shall come with an army,..........
Da 11:16 w. by his hand shall be consumed...........
Da 11:24 that w. his fathers have not done,........ 834
Da 12:1 prince w. standeth for the children ....
Da 12:6, 7 w. was upon the waters of the......... 834
Ho 1:3 w. conceived, and bare him a son............
Ho 1:10 the sand...w. cannot be measured........ 834
Ho 2:8 and gold, w. they prepared for Baal..........
Ho 2:23 will say to them w. are not my people, ...
Ho 5:9 made known that w. shall surely be..........
Joe 1:4 That w. the palmerworm hath left ....
Joe 1:4 and that w. the locust hath left hath.........
Joe 1:4 and that w. the cankerworm hath left.........
Joe 2:25 great army w. I sent among you.......... 834
Am 1:1 w. he saw concerning Israel in the....... 834
Am 1:4 w. shall devour the palaces of.................
Am 1:7 w. shall devour the palaces thereof: ....
Am 1:10 w. shall devour the palaces thereof...........
Am 1:12 w. shall devour the palaces of.................
Am 2:4 the w. their fathers have walked:......... 834
Am 3:1 w. I brought up from the land of 834
Am 4:1 of Bashan,...w. oppress the poor, ...
Am 4:1 the poor, w. crush the needy, ...
Am 4:1 w. say to their masters, Bring, and let.......
Am 4:3 every cow at that w. is before her; ....
Am 5:1 word w. I take up against you,............ 834
Am 5:3 and that w. went forth by an hundred ....
Am 5:26 god, w. ye made for yourselves. 834
Am 6:1 w. are named chief of the nations,............
Am 6:13 Ye w. rejoice in a thing of nought,............
Am 6:13 w. say, Have we not taken to us horns .....
Am 9:10 w. say, The evil shall not overtake nor......
Am 9:12 heathen, w. are called by my name, ... 834
Am 9:15 of their land w. I have given them, ... 834
Ob 20 of Jerusalem, w. is in Sepharad, ... 834
Jon 1:9 w. hath made the sea and the dry........ 834
Jon 4:10 for the w. thou hast not laboured,........ 834
Jon 4:10 w. came up in a night, and perished in ......
Mic 1:1 w. he saw concerning Samaria and....... 834
Mic 2:3 evil, from w. ye shall not remove 834
Mic 5:3 time that she w. travaileth hath................
Mic 6:14 and that w. thou deliverest will I 834
Mic 7:10 shame shall cover her w. said unto...........
Mic 7:14 w. dwell solitarily in the wood, ...
Mic 7:20 w. thou hast sworn unto our............... 834
Na 3:17 w. camp in the hedges in the cold day,......
Hab 1:1 The burden w. Habakkuk the............... 834
Hab 1:5 w. ye will not believe, though it ....
Hab 1:6 w. shall march through the breadth...........
Hab 2:4 his soul w. is lifted up is not upright.........
Hab 2:6 him that increaseth that w. is not his! ....
Hab 2:17 spoil of beasts, w. made them afraid, ...
Zep 1:1 the Lord w. came unto Zephaniah........ 834
Zep 1:9 w. fill their masters' houses with............
Zep 2:3 w. have wrought his judgment;............ 834
Hag 1:11 that w. the ground bringeth forth,......... 834
Hag 2:14 that w. they offer there is unclean. 834
Zec 1:6 w. I commanded my servants the 834
Zec 1:7 month, w. is the month Sebat, ... 1931
Zec 1:12 Judah, against w. thou hast had 834
Zec 1:19, 21 horns w. have scattered Judah, ... 834
Zec 1:21 w. lifted up their horn over the land of......
Zec 2:8 me unto the nations w. spoiled you:..........
Zec 4:2 lamps, w. are upon the top thereof:..........
Zec 4:10 w. run to and fro through the whole ....
Zec 4:12 w. through the two golden pipes.......... 834
Zec 6:5 w. go forth from standing before the.........

Book	Ref	Context	No.
Zec	6:6	The black horses w. are therein go	834
Zec	6:10	w. are come from Babylon, and	834
Zec	7:3	the priests w. were in the house	834
Zec	7:7	the words w. the Lord hath cried	834
Zec	7:12	and the words w. the Lord of hosts	834
Zec	8:9	w. were in the day that the	834
Zec	10:5	w. tread down their enemies in the	
Zec	11:10	w. I had made with all the people.	834
Zec	11:16	w. shall not visit those that be cut off,	
Zec	12:1	Lord, w. stretcheth forth the heavens,	
Zec	13:6	Those with w. I was wounded in	834
Zec	14:4	w. is before Jerusalem on the east,	834
Zec	14:7	day w. shall be known to the Lord,	1931
Zec	14:16	of all the nations w. came against	
Mal	1:13	and ye brought that w. was torn, and	
Mal	1:14	w. hath in his flock a male,	3426
Mal	2:11	holiness of the Lord w. he loved,	834
Mal	4:4	w. I commanded unto him in	834
Mt	1:20	w. is conceived in her is of the Holy	
Mt	1:22	fulfilled w. was spoken of the Lord	3588
Mt	1:23	Emmanuel, w. being interpreted	3739
Mt	2:9	lo, the star w. they saw in the east,	3739
Mt	2:15	fulfilled w. was spoken of the	3588
Mt	2:16	the time w. he had diligently	3739
Mt	2:17	that w. was spoken by Jeremy	3588
Mt	2:20	w. sought the young child's life.	3588
Mt	2:23	w. was spoken by the prophets,	3588
Mt	3:10	tree w. bringeth not forth good fruit	
Mt	4:13	in Capernaum, w. is upon the sea	3588
Mt	4:14	fulfilled w. was spoken by Esaias	3588
Mt	4:16	people w. sat in darkness saw	3588
Mt	4:16	w. sat in the region and shadow	3588
Mt	4:24	those w. were possessed with devils,	
Mt	4:24	and those w. were lunatick, and those	
Mt	5:6	**Blessed are they w. do hunger**	3588
Mt	5:10	**w. are persecuted for righteousness'**	
Mt	5:12	**the prophets w. were before you**	3588
Mt	5:16	**glorify your Father w. is in heaven.**	3588
Mt	5:44	**pray for them w. despitefully use**	3588
Mt	5:45	**the children of your Father w. is in**	3588
Mt	5:46	**For if ye love them w. love you,**	3588
Mt	5:48	**Father w. is in heaven is perfect**	3588
Mt	6:1	**of your Father w. is in heaven**	3588
Mt	6:4	**Father w. seeth in secret himself**	3588
Mt	6:6	**pray to thy Father w. is in secret;**	3588
Mt	6:6	**Father w. seeth in secret shall**	3588
Mt	6:9	**Our Father w. art in heaven,**	3588
Mt	6:18	**unto thy Father w. is in secret:**	3588
Mt	6:18	**and thy Father, w. seeth in secret,**	3588
Mt	6:27	**W. of you by taking thought can**	5101
Mt	6:30	**w. to day is, and to morrow is cast**	
Mt	7:6	**not that w. is holy unto the dogs,**	3588
Mt	7:11	**w. is in heaven give good things**	3588
Mt	7:13	**and many there be w. go in thereat:**	3588
Mt	7:14	**narrow is the way, w. leadeth**	3588
Mt	7:15	**w. come to you in sheep's**	3748
Mt	7:21	**will of my Father w. is in heaven**	3588
Mt	7:24	**w. built his house upon a rock:**	3748
Mt	7:26	**w. built his house upon the sand:**	3748
Mt	8:17	w. was spoken by Esaias the	3588
Mt	9:8	w. had given such power unto men.	3588
Mt	9:16	**that w. is put in to fill it up taketh**	
Mt	9:20	w. was diseased with an issue of	
Mt	10:20	**your Father w. speaketh in you**	3588
Mt	10:28	**And fear not them w. kill the body,**	3588
Mt	10:28	**fear him w. is able to destroy**	3588
Mt	10:32, 33	**before my Father w. is in heaven.**	3588
Mt	11:4	**those things w. ye do hear and**	3739
Mt	11:10	**w. shall prepare thy way before**	3739
Mt	11:14	**this is Elias, w. was for to come**	3588
Mt	11:21	**works, w. were done in you, had**	3588
Mt	11:23	**w. art exalted unto heaven,**	3588
Mt	11:23	**works, w. have been done in thee,**	3588
Mt	12:2	do that w. is not lawful to do upon	3739
Mt	12:4	**w. was not lawful for him to eat,**	3739
Mt	12:4	**neither for them w. were with him,**	
Mt	12:10	was a man w. had his hand withered.	
Mt	12:17	w. was spoken by Esaias the	3588
Mt	12:50	**will of my Father w. is in heaven,**	3588
Mt	13:14	**w. saith, By hearing ye shall hear,**	3588
Mt	13:17	**to see those things w. ye see,**	3739
Mt	13:17	**to hear those things w. ye hear,**	3739
Mt	13:19	**that w. was sown in his heart**	3588
Mt	13:19	**is he w. received by the way side**	3588
Mt	13:23	**w. also beareth fruit, and bringeth**	3739
Mt	13:24	**unto a man w. sowed good seed in**	

Book	Ref	Context	No.
Mt	13:31	**w. a man took, and sowed in his**	3739
Mt	13:32	**W. indeed is the least of all seeds;**	3739
Mt	13:33	**w. a woman took, and hid in three**	3739
Mt	13:35	w. was spoken by the prophet,	3588
Mt	13:35	I will utter things w. have been kept	
Mt	13:41	**offend, and them w. do iniquity;**	
Mt	13:44	**w. when a man hath found, he**	3739
Mt	13:48	**W., when it was full, they drew to**	3739
Mt	13:52	**w. is instructed unto the kingdom**	
Mt	13:52	**w. bringeth forth out of his**	3748
Mt	14:9	and them w. sat with him at meat,	
Mt	15:1	Pharisees, w. were of Jerusalem,	3588
Mt	15:11	**Not that w. goeth into the mouth**	
Mt	15:11	**that w. cometh out of the mouth,**	
Mt	15:13	**w. my heavenly Father hath not**	3739
Mt	15:18	**w. proceed out of the mouth**	3588
Mt	15:20	**are the things w. defile a man:**	3588
Mt	15:27	crumbs w. fall from their masters'	3588
Mt	16:8	W. when Jesus perceived, he said	
Mt	16:17	**but my Father w. is in heaven.**	3588
Mt	16:28	**w. shall not taste of death, till**	3748
Mt	17:5	a voice out of the cloud, w. said,	
Mt	18:6	**these little ones w. believe in me,**	3588
Mt	18:10	**face of my Father w. is in heaven**	3588
Mt	18:11	**is come to save that w. was lost**	3588
Mt	18:12	**seeketh that w. is gone astray?**	3588
Mt	18:13	**ninety and nine w. went not astray**	3588
Mt	18:14	**will of your Father w. is in heaven,**	3588
Mt	18:19	**them of my Father w. is in heaven**	3588
Mt	18:23	**w. would take account of his**	3739
Mt	18:24	**w. owed him ten thousand talents**	
Mt	18:28	**w. owed him an hundred pence:**	3739
Mt	19:4	**w. made them at the beginning**	3588
Mt	19:9	**marrieth her w. is put away doth**	3588
Mt	19:12	**w. were so born from their**	3748
Mt	19:12	**w. were made eunuchs of men:**	3748
Mt	19:12	**w. have made themselves eunuchs**	3748
Mt	19:18	He saith unto him, W.? Jesus	4169
Mt	19:28	**That ye w. have followed me, in**	3588
Mt	20:1	**w. went out early in the morning**	3748
Mt	20:12	**w. have borne the burden and**	3588
Mt	21:4	w. was spoken by the prophet,	3588
Mt	21:21	**do this w. is done to the fig tree,**	
Mt	21:24	**w. if ye tell me, I in like wise will**	3739
Mt	21:33	**householder, w. planted a**	3748
Mt	21:41	w. shall render him the fruits in	3748
Mt	21:42	**The stone w. the builders rejected,**	3739
Mt	22:2	**w. made a marriage for his son,**	3748
Mt	22:4	**Tell them w. are bidden, Behold, I**	
Mt	22:8	**w. were bidden were not worthy**	
Mt	22:11	**w. had not on a wedding garment:**	
Mt	22:21	**Caesar the things w. are Caesar's**	
Mt	22:23	w. say that there is no resurrection,	3588
Mt	22:31	**w. was spoken unto you by God,**	3588
Mt	22:35	Then one of them, w. was a lawyer,	
Mt	22:36	**w. is the great commandment in**	4169
Mt	23:9	**is your Father, w. is in heaven.**	3588
Mt	23:16	**unto you, ye blind guides, w. say,**	3588
Mt	23:24	**blind guides, w. strain at a gnat,**	3588
Mt	23:26	**first that w. is within the cup and**	3588
Mt	23:27	**w. indeed appear beautiful**	3748
Mt	23:31	**of them w. killed the prophets.**	
Mt	23:37	**stonest them w. are sent unto thee,**	
Mt	24:16	**Then let them w. be in Judaea flee**	
Mt	24:17	**Let him w. is on the housetop not**	
Mt	24:18	**Neither let him w. is in the field**	
Mt	25:1	**ten virgins, w. took their lamps,**	3748
Mt	25:24	**Then he w. had received the one**	
Mt	25:28	**give it unto him w. hath ten talents**	
Mt	25:29	**be taken away even that w. he hath.**	
Mt	26:25	Then Judas, w. betrayed him,	3588
Mt	26:28	**w. is shed for many for the**	3588
Mt	26:51	one of them w. were with Jesus	
Mt	26:62	is it w. these witness against thee?	
Mt	26:75	word of Jesus, w. said unto him,	3588
Mt	27:3	Then Judas, w. had betrayed him,	3588
Mt	27:9	that w. was spoken by Jeremy	3588
Mt	27:17	or Jesus w. is called Christ?	3588
Mt	27:22	then with Jesus w. is called Christ?	3588
Mt	27:35	w. was spoken by the prophet,	3588
Mt	27:44	also, w. were crucified with him,	3588
Mt	27:52	bodies of the saints w. slept arose,	3588
Mt	27:55	w. followed Jesus from Galilee,	3748
Mt	27:56	Among w. was Mary Magdalene,	3739
Mt	27:60	w. he had hewn out in the rock	3739
Mt	28:5	ye seek Jesus, w. was crucified.	3588

Book	Ref	Context	No.
Mk	1:2	**w. shall prepare thy way before**	3739
Mk	1:44	**those things w. Moses commanded,**	3739
Mk	2:3	sick of the palsy, w. was borne of	
Mk	2:24	sabbath day that w. is not lawful?	3739
Mk	2:26	**w. is not lawful to eat but for the**	3739
Mk	2:26	**also to them w. were with him?**	
Mk	3:1	a man there w. had a withered hand.	
Mk	3:3	unto the man w. had the withered	
Mk	3:17	Boanerges, w. is, The sons of	3739
Mk	3:19	Judas Iscariot, w. also betrayed	2076
Mk	3:22	the scribes w. came down from	3588
Mk	3:34	about on them w. sat about him,	3588
Mk	4:16	**likewise w. are sown on stony**	
Mk	4:18	**are they w. are sown among**	
Mk	4:20	**they w. are sown on good ground;**	
Mk	4:22	**hid, w. shall not be manifested;**	3739
Mk	4:25	**be taken even that w. he hath**	3739
Mk	4:31	**w., when it is sown in the earth,**	3739
Mk	5:25	w. had an issue of blood twelve years,	
Mk	5:35	w. said, Thy daughter is dead:	
Mk	5:41	w. is, being interpreted, Damsel,	3739
Mk	6:2	wisdom is this w. is given unto him,	
Mk	6:26	for their sakes w. sat with him,	3588
Mk	7:1	the scribes w. came from Jerusalem.	
Mk	7:4	be, w. they have received to hold,	3739
Mk	7:13	**tradition, w. ye have delivered:**	3739
Mk	7:15	**but the things w. come out of him,**	
Mk	7:20	**That w. cometh out of the man,**	
Mk	9:1	**here, w. shall not taste of death,**	3748
Mk	9:17	thee my son, w. hath a dumb spirit;	
Mk	9:39	**man w. shall do a miracle in my**	3739
Mk	10:42	**that they w. are accounted to rule**	
Mk	11:21	the fig tree w. thou cursedst is	3739
Mk	11:23	**w. he saith shall come to pass;**	3739
Mk	11:25	**your Father also w. is in heaven**	3588
Mk	11:26	**Father w. is in heaven forgive**	3588
Mk	12:10	**The stone w. the builders rejected**	3739
Mk	12:18	w. say there is no resurrection;	3748
Mk	12:25	**as the angels w. are in heaven.**	3588
Mk	12:28	**W. is the first commandment of**	4169
Mk	12:38	**w. love to go in long clothing,**	3588
Mk	12:40	**W. devour widows' houses, and**	3739
Mk	12:42	in two mites, w. make a farthing.	2076
Mk	12:43	**they w. have cast into the treasury:**	
Mk	13:19	**the creation w. God created unto**	3739
Mk	13:32	**not the angels w. are in heaven,**	3588
Mk	14:18	**One of you w. eateth with me**	3588
Mk	14:24	**testament, w. is shed for many.**	3588
Mk	14:32	a place w. was named Gethsemane:	
Mk	14:60	what is it w. these witness against	
Mk	15:7	w. lay bound with them that had	
Mk	15:22	w. is, being interpreted, The place	3739
Mk	15:28	scripture was fulfilled, w. saith,	3588
Mk	15:34	w. is, being interpreted, My God,	3739
Mk	15:39	centurion, w. stood over against	3588
Mk	15:41	women w. came up with him unto	3588
Mk	15:43	w....waited for the kingdom.	3739,846
Mk	15:46	sepulchre w. was hewn out of a	3739
Mk	16:6	Jesus...Nazareth, w. was crucified:	3588
Mk	16:14	w. had seen him after he was risen.	
Lu	1:1	things w. are most surely believed	
Lu	1:2	w. from the beginning were	3588
Lu	1:20	w. shall be fulfilled in their	3748
Lu	1:35	holy thing w. shall be born of thee	
Lu	1:45	things w. were told her from the Lord.	
Lu	1:70	w. have been since the world	3588
Lu	1:73	oath w. he sware to our father	3739
Lu	2:4	of David, w. is called Bethlehem;	3748
Lu	2:10	great joy, w. shall be to all people.	3748
Lu	2:11	a Saviour, w. is Christ the Lord.	3739
Lu	2:15	see this thing w. is come to pass,	3588
Lu	2:15	w. the Lord hath made known unto	3588
Lu	2:17	w. was told them concerning the	3588
Lu	2:18	things w. were told them by the	3588
Lu	2:21	w. was so named of the angel	3588
Lu	2:24	that w. is said in the law of the Lord,	
Lu	2:31	W. thou hast prepared before the	3739
Lu	2:33	those things w. were spoken of him.	
Lu	2:34	and for a sign w. shall be spoken	
Lu	2:37	w. departed not from the temple,	3739
Lu	2:50	the saying w. he spake unto them.	3739
Lu	3:9	w. bringeth not forth good fruit is	
Lu	3:13	more than that w. is appointed you.	
Lu	3:19	all the evils w. Herod had done,	3739
Lu	3:22	a voice came from heaven, w. said,	
Lu	3:23	son of Joseph, w. was the son of Heli,	

Lu 3:24 W. was the son of Matthat,
Lu 3:24 of Matthat, w. was the son of Levi,
Lu 3:24 son of Levi, w. was the son of Melchi,
Lu 3:24 of Melchi, w. was the son of Janna,
Lu 3:24 of Janna, w. was the son of Joseph,
Lu 3:25 W. was the son of Mattathias,
Lu 3:25 Mattathias, w. was the son of Amos,
Lu 3:25 son of Amos, w. was the son of Naum,
Lu 3:25 son of Naum, w. was the son of Esli,
Lu 3:25 son of Esli, w. was the son of Nagge,
Lu 3:26 W. was the son of Maath,
Lu 3:26 Maath, w. was the son of Mattathias,
Lu 3:26 Mattathias, w. was the son of Semei,
Lu 3:26 of Semei, w. was the son of Joseph,
Lu 3:26 son of Joseph, w. was the son of Juda,
Lu 3:27 W. was the son of Joanna,
Lu 3:27 of Joanna, w. was the son of Rhesa,
Lu 3:27 of Rhesa, w. was the son of Zorobabel,
Lu 3:27 Zorobabel, w. was the son of Salathiel,
Lu 3:27 of Salathiel, w. was the son of Neri,
Lu 3:28 W. was the son of Melchi,
Lu 3:28 son of Melchi, w. was the son of Addi,
Lu 3:28 son of Addi, w. was the son of Cosam,
Lu 3:28 Cosam, w. was the son of Elmodam,
Lu 3:28 son of Elmodam, w. was the son of Er,
Lu 3:29 W. was the son of Jose,
Lu 3:29 son of Jose, w. was the son of Eliezer,
Lu 3:29 of Eliezer, w. was the son of Jorim,
Lu 3:29 of Jorim, w. was the son of Matthat,
Lu 3:29 of Matthat, w. was the son of Levi,
Lu 3:30 W. was the son of Simeon,
Lu 3:30 son of Simeon, w. was the son of Juda,
Lu 3:30 son of Juda, w. was the son of Joseph,
Lu 3:30 of Joseph, w. was the son of Jonan,
Lu 3:30 of Jonan, w. was the son of Eliakim,
Lu 3:31 W. was the son of Melea,
Lu 3:31 son of Melea, w. was the son of Menan,
Lu 3:31 Menan, w. was the son of Mattatha,
Lu 3:31 Mattatha, w. was the son of Nathan,
Lu 3:31 of Nathan, w. was the son of David,
Lu 3:32 W. was the son of Jesse,
Lu 3:32 son of Jesse, w. was the son of Obed,
Lu 3:32 son of Obed, w. was the son of Booz,
Lu 3:32 of Booz, w. was the son of Salmon,
Lu 3:32 of Salmon, w. was the son of Naasson,
Lu 3:33 W. was the son of Aminadab,
Lu 3:33 w. was the son of Aram,
Lu 3:33 w. was the son of Esrom,
Lu 3:33 w. was the son of Phares,
Lu 3:33 of Phares, w. was the son of Juda,
Lu 3:34 W. was the son of Jacob,
Lu 3:34 w. was the son of Isaac,
Lu 3:34 w. was the son of Abraham,
Lu 3:34 w. was the son of Thara,
Lu 3:34 of Thara, w. was the son of Nachor,
Lu 3:35 W. was the son of Saruch,
Lu 3:35 w. was the son of Ragau,
Lu 3:35 w. was the son of Phalec,
Lu 3:35 w. was the son of Heber,
Lu 3:35 of Heber, w. was the son of Sala,
Lu 3:36 W. was the son of Cainan,
Lu 3:36 w. was the son of Arphaxad,
Lu 3:36 w. was the son of Sem,
Lu 3:36 w. was the son of Noe,
Lu 3:36 of Noe, w. was the son of Lamech,
Lu 3:37 W. was the son of Mathusala,
Lu 3:37 w. was the son of Enoch,
Lu 3:37 w. was the son of Jared,
Lu 3:37 w. was the son of Maleleel,
Lu 3:37 of Maleleel, w. was the son of Cainan,
Lu 3:38 W. was the son of Enos,
Lu 3:38 w. was the son of Seth,
Lu 3:38 w. was the son of Adam,
Lu 3:38 w. was the son of God.
Lu 4:22 w. proceeded out of his mouth. 3588
Lu 4:33 man, w. had a spirit of an unclean
Lu 5:3 one of the ships, w. was Simon's, 3739
Lu 5:7 w. were in the other ship, 3588
Lu 5:9 of fishes w. they had taken: 3739
Lu 5:10 Zebedee, w. were partners with 3739
Lu 5:17 w. were come out of every town of 3739
Lu 5:18 a man w. was taken with a palsy: 3739
Lu 5:21 is this w. speaketh blasphemies? 3739
Lu 6:2 do ye that w. is not lawful to do on 3739
Lu 6:3 hungred, and they w. were with 3739
Lu 6:4 w. it is not lawful to eat but for
Lu 6:8 man w. had the withered hand, 3739
Lu 6:16 Judas Iscariot, w. also was the 3739
Lu 6:17 w. came to hear him, and to be 3739
Lu 6:27 I saw unto you w. hear, Love your
Lu 6:27 do good to them w. hate you, 3588
Lu 6:28 for them w. despitefully use you.
Lu 6:32 if ye love them w. love you, what
Lu 6:33 ye do good to them w. do good to
Lu 6:45 heart bringeth forth that w. is good;
Lu 6:45 heart bringeth forth that w. is evil:
Lu 6:46 and do not the things w. I say? 3739
Lu 6:48 is like a man w. built a house, 3739
Lu 6:49 against w. the stream did beat 3739
Lu 7:25 they w. are gorgeously apparelled,
Lu 7:27 w. shall prepare thy way before 3739
Lu 7:37 woman in the city, w. was a 3748
Lu 7:39 w. had bidden him saw it, he 3588
Lu 7:41 certain creditor w. had two debtors:
Lu 7:42 w. of them will love him most? 5101
Lu 7:47 Her sins, w. are many, are 3588
Lu 8:2 w. had been healed of evil spirits 3739
Lu 8:3 w. ministered unto him of their 3748
Lu 8:13 w., when they hear, receive the 3739
Lu 8:13 no root, w. for a while, believe, 3739
Lu 8:14 that w. fell among thorns are they,
Lu 8:14 w., when they have heard, go forth,
Lu 8:15 w. in an honest and good heart, 3748
Lu 8:16 they w. enter in may see the light
Lu 8:18 even that w. he seemeth to have 3739
Lu 8:20 was told him by certain w. said, Thy
Lu 8:21 these w. hear the word of God, 3588
Lu 8:26 w. is over against Galilee. 3748
Lu 8:27 man w. had devils long time, and 3739
Lu 8:36 They also w. saw it told them by what
Lu 8:43 w. had spent all her living upon 3748
Lu 9:27 w. shall not taste of death, till 3739
Lu 9:30 men, w. were Moses and Elias: 3748
Lu 9:31 w. he should accomplish at 3739
Lu 9:36 of those things w. they had seen. 3739
Lu 9:43 every one at all things w. Jesus did, 3739
Lu 9:46 w. of them should be greatest. 5101
Lu 9:61 farewell, w. are at home at my house,
Lu 10:11 dust of your city, w. cleaveth on 3588
Lu 10:13 Sidon, w. have been done in you, 3739
Lu 10:15 w. are exalted to heaven, shalt 3588
Lu 10:23 eyes w. see the things that ye see: 3588
Lu 10:24 desired to see those things w. ye 3739
Lu 10:24 to hear those things w. ye hear, 3739
Lu 10:30 w. stripped him of his raiment, 3739
Lu 10:36 W. now of these three, thinkest 5101
Lu 10:39 w. also sat at Jesus' feet, and heard
Lu 10:42 w. shall not be taken away from 3748
Lu 11:2 Our Father w. art in heaven, 3588
Lu 11:5 W. of you shall have a friend, 5101
Lu 11:27 and the paps w. thou hast sucked. 3739
Lu 11:33 w. come in may see the light. 3588
Lu 11:35 light w. is in thee be not darkness 3588
Lu 11:40 he, that made that w. is without 3588
Lu 11:40 make that w. is within also?
Lu 11:44 ye are as graves w. appear not, 3588
Lu 11:50 prophets, w. was shed from the 3588
Lu 11:51 w. perished between the altar and 3588
Lu 12:1 the Pharisees, w. is hypocrisy 3748
Lu 12:3 w. ye have spoken in the ear, in 3739
Lu 12:5 w. after he hath killed hath power
Lu 12:15 abundance of the things w. he
Lu 12:20 things be, w. thou hast provided? 3739
Lu 12:24 w. neither have storehouse nor 3739
Lu 12:25 And w. of you with taking thought 5101
Lu 12:26 able to do that thing w. is least,
Lu 12:28 the grass, w. is to day in the field,
Lu 12:33 yourselves bags w. wax not old,
Lu 12:47 servant, w. knew his lord's will, 3588
Lu 13:11 a woman w. had a spirit of infirmity
Lu 13:14 six days in w. men ought to work: 3739
Lu 13:19 of mustard seed, w. a man took, 3739
Lu 13:21 leaven, w. a woman took and hid 3739
Lu 13:30 there are last w. shall be first; 3739
Lu 13:30 and there are first w. shall be last 3739
Lu 13:34 Jerusalem, w. killest the prophets, 3588
Lu 14:2 man before him w. had the dropsy.
Lu 14:5 W. of you shall have an ass or an 5101
Lu 14:7 a parable to those w. were bidden,
Lu 14:24 men w. were bidden shall taste 3588
Lu 14:28 w. of you, intending to build a 5101
Lu 15:4 after that w. is lost, until he find it?
Lu 15:6 have found my sheep w. was lost 3588
Lu 15:7 persons w. need no repentance 3748
Lu 15:9 have found the piece w. I had lost 3739
Lu 15:30 w. have devoured thy living with 3588
Lu 16:1 rich man, w. had a steward; 3739
Lu 16:10 faithful in that w. is least is faithful
Lu 16:12 faithful in that w. is another man's,
Lu 16:12 shall give you that w. is your own?
Lu 16:15 they w. justify yourselves before 3588
Lu 16:15 that w. is highly esteemed among
Lu 16:19 man w. was clothed in purple and 2532
Lu 16:20 Lazarus, w. was laid at his gate, 3739
Lu 16:21 crumbs w. fell from the rich 3588
Lu 16:26 they w. would pass from hence to
Lu 17:7 w. of you, having a servant 5101
Lu 17:10 those things w. are commanded you,
Lu 17:10 done that w. was our duty to do 3739
Lu 17:12 that were lepers, w. stood afar off: 3739
Lu 17:31 he w. shall be upon the housetop, 3739
Lu 18:2 a judge, w. feared not God, neither
Lu 18:7 own elect, w. cry day and night 3588
Lu 18:9 certain w. trusted in themselves 3588
Lu 18:27 things w. are impossible with men
Lu 18:34 knew they the things w. were spoken.
Lu 18:39 they w. went before rebuked him,
Lu 19:2 w. was the chief among the 2532,846
Lu 19:10 to seek and to save that w. was lost.
Lu 19:20 w. I have kept laid up in a napkin: 3739
Lu 19:26 every one w. hath shall be given; 3588
Lu 19:27 w. would not that I should reign 3588
Lu 19:30 in the w. at your entering ye shall 3739
Lu 19:42 the things w. belong unto thy peace!
Lu 20:17 The stone w. the builders rejected, 3739
Lu 20:20 w. should feign themselves just men,
Lu 20:25 unto Caesar the things w. be Caesar's,
Lu 20:25 and unto God the things w. be God's
Lu 20:27 w. deny that there is any 3588
Lu 20:35 they w. shall be accounted worthy to
Lu 20:46 w. desire to walk in long robes, 3588
Lu 20:47 W. devour widows' houses, and 3739
Lu 21:6 As for these things w. ye behold, 3739
Lu 21:6 in the w. there shall not be left one 3739
Lu 21:15 w. all your adversaries shall not be 3739
Lu 21:21 them w. are in Judaea flee to the
Lu 21:21 let them w. are in the midst of it
Lu 21:22 that all things w. are written 3588
Lu 21:26 those things w. are coming on the
Lu 22:1 drew nigh, w. is called the Passover.
Lu 22:19 is my body w. is given for you: 3588
Lu 22:20 in my blood, w. is shed for you 3588
Lu 22:23 w. of them it was that should do 5101
Lu 22:24 w. of them should be accounted 5101
Lu 22:28 w. have continued with me in my
Lu 22:49 w. were about him saw what would
Lu 22:52 the elders, w. were come to him,
Lu 23:27 w. also bewailed and lamented 3739
Lu 23:29 in the w. they shall say, Blessed 3739
Lu 23:29 and the paps w. never gave suck, 3739
Lu 23:33 to the place w. is called Calvary, 3588
Lu 23:39 malefactors w. were hanged railed on
Lu 23:48 beholding the things w. were done,
Lu 23:55 w. came with him from Galilee, 3748
Lu 24:1 the spices w. they had prepared, 3739
Lu 24:10 w. told these things unto the 3739
Lu 24:12 himself at that w. was come to pass.
Lu 24:13 w. was from Jerusalem about
Lu 24:14 of all these things w. had happened.
Lu 24:18 known the things w. are come to pass
Lu 24:19 w. was a prophet mighty in deed 3739
Lu 24:21 he w. should have redeemed Israel:
Lu 24:22 w. were early at the sepulchre;
Lu 24:23 angels, w. said that he was alive. 3739
Lu 24:24 w. were with us went to the sepulchre,
Lu 24:44 the words w. I spake unto you, 3739
Lu 24:44 w. were written in the law of 3588
Joh 1:9 w. lighteth every man that cometh 3739
Joh 1:13 W. were born, not of blood, nor of 3739
Joh 1:18 w. is in the bosom of the Father, 3588
Joh 1:24 w. were sent were of the Pharisees. 3588
Joh 1:29 w. taketh away the sin of the 3588
Joh 1:30 a man w. is preferred before me; 3739
Joh 1:33 he w. baptizeth with the Holy Ghost.
Joh 1:38 (w. is to say, being interpreted, 3739
Joh 1:40 One of the two w. heard John 3588
Joh 1:41 w. is, being interpreted, the Christ. 3739
Joh 1:42 w. is by interpretation, A stone, 3739

Joh 2:9 servants w. drew the water knew; 3588
Joh 2:10 well drunk then that w. is worse:
Joh 2:22 and the word w. Jesus had said. 3739
Joh 2:23 they saw the miracles w. he did 3739
Joh 3:6 That w. is born of the flesh is flesh;
Joh 3:6 that w. is born of the Spirit is spirit
Joh 3:13 the Son of man w. is in heaven 3588
Joh 3:29 w. standeth and heareth him, 3588
Joh 4:5 city of Samaria, w. is called Sychar,
Joh 4:9 of me, w. am a woman of Samaria?
Joh 4:12 Jacob, w. gave us the well, 3739
Joh 4:25 Messias cometh, w. is called 3588
Joh 4:29 w. told me all things that ever I 3739
Joh 4:39 w. testified, He told me all that ever I
Joh 4:53 in the w. Jesus said unto him, 3739
Joh 5:2 w. is called in the Hebrew tongue 3588
Joh 5:5 w. had an infirmity thirty and eight
Joh 5:12 w. said unto thee, Take up thy 3588
Joh 5:15 Jesus, w. had made him whole 3588
Joh 5:23 not the Father w. hath sent him 3588
Joh 5:28 in the w. all that are in the graves 3739
Joh 5:30 will of the Father w. hath sent me 3739
Joh 5:32 witness w. he witnesseth of me is 3739
Joh 5:36 works w. the Father hath given 3739
Joh 5:37 Father himself, w. hath sent me,
Joh 5:39 and they are they w. testify of me
Joh 5:44 w. receive honour one of another,
Joh 6:1 of Galilee, w. is the sea of Tiberias.
Joh 6:2 miracles w. he did on them that 3739
Joh 6:9 lad here, w. hath five barley loaves, 3739
Joh 6:13 w. remained over and above unto 3739
Joh 6:22 people w. stood on the other side 3588
Joh 6:27 not for the meat w. perisheth, but 3588
Joh 6:27 meat w. endureth unto everlasting 3588
Joh 6:27 w. the Son of man shall give unto 3739
Joh 6:33 is he w. cometh down from heaven, 3588
Joh 6:39 the Father's will w. hath sent me, 3588
Joh 6:39 w. he hath given me I should lose 3739
Joh 6:40 that every one w. seeth the Son, 3588
Joh 6:41 bread w. came down from heaven. 3588
Joh 6:44 except the Father w. hath sent me 3588
Joh 6:46 save he w. is of God, he hath seen 3588
Joh 6:50 bread w. cometh down from heaven, 3588
Joh 6:51 bread w. came down from heaven: 3588
Joh 6:51 w. I will give for the life of the 3739
Joh 6:58 bread w. came down from heaven: 3588
Joh 7:31 than these w. this man hath done? 3739
Joh 7:39 w. they that believe on him should 3739
Joh 8:9 And they w. heard it, being convicted
Joh 8:26 those things w. I have heard of him 3739
Joh 8:31 to those Jews w. believed on him, 3588
Joh 8:38 I speak that w. I have seen with 3739
Joh 8:38 ye do that w. ye have seen with 3739
Joh 8:40 the truth, w. I have heard of God: 3739
Joh 8:46 W. of you convinceth me of sin? 5101
Joh 8:53 our father Abraham, w. is dead? 3748
Joh 9:1 a man w. was blind from his birth
Joh 9:7 (w. is by interpretation, Sent.) 3739
Joh 9:8 w. before had seen him that he was
Joh 9:39 world, that they w. see not might see;
Joh 9:39 that they w. see might be made blind.
Joh 9:40 Pharisees w. were with him heard 3588
Joh 10:6 things they were w. he spake 3739
Joh 10:16 sheep I have, w. are not of this fold: 3739
Joh 10:29 My Father, w. gave them me, is 3739
Joh 10:32 w. of those works do ye stone me? 4169
Joh 11:2 Mary w. anointed the Lord with 3588
Joh 11:16 said Thomas, w. is called Didymus, 3588
Joh 11:27 God, w. should come into the world. 3588
Joh 11:31 Jews then w. were with her in the 3588
Joh 11:33 Jews also weeping w. came with her
Joh 11:37 w. opened the eyes of the blind, 3588
Joh 11:42 because of the people w. stand by 3588
Joh 11:45 many of the Jews w. came to Mary, 3588
Joh 11:45 the things w. Jesus did, believed 3739
Joh 12:1 where Lazarus was w. had been 3588
Joh 12:4 Simon's son, w. should betray him, 3588
Joh 12:21 Philip, w. was of Bethsaida of Galilee,
Joh 12:38 w. he spake, Lord, who hath 3739
Joh 12:49 but the Father w. sent me, he 3588
Joh 13:1 loved his own w. were in the world, 3588
Joh 14:24 the word w. ye hear is not mine, 3739
Joh 14:24 mine, but the Father's w. sent me 3588
Joh 14:26 the Comforter, w. is the Holy Ghost,
Joh 15:3 the word w. I have spoken unto 3739
Joh 15:24 the works w. none other man did, 3739
Joh 15:26 w. proceedeth from the Father, 3739
Joh 17:4 the work w. thou gavest me to do. 3739
Joh 17:5 w. I had with thee before the world 3739
Joh 17:6 men w. thou gavest me out of the 3739
Joh 17:8 them the words w. thou gavest me; 3739
Joh 17:9 for them w. thou hast given me; 3739
Joh 17:20 w. shall believe on me through their
Joh 17:22 glory w. thou gavest me I have 3739
Joh 17:24 my glory, w. thou hast given me: 3739
Joh 18:1 a garden, into the w. he entered, 3739
Joh 18:2 Judas also, w. betrayed him, knew 3588
Joh 18:5 w. betrayed him, stood with them. 3588
Joh 18:9 might be fulfilled, w. he spake, 3739
Joh 18:9 Of them w. thou gavest me have I 3739
Joh 18:11 cup w. my Father hath given me, 3739
Joh 18:13 Caiaphas, w. was the high priest 3739
Joh 18:14 he, w. gave counsel to the Jews, 3588
Joh 18:16 w. was known unto the high priest, 3739
Joh 18:21 ask them w. heard me, what I have
Joh 18:22 the officers w. stood by struck Jesus
Joh 18:32 w. he spake signifying what death 3739
Joh 19:17 w. is called in the Hebrew Golgotha: 3739
Joh 19:24 w. saith, They parted my raiment 3588
Joh 19:32 the other w. was crucified with him. 3588
Joh 19:39 w. at the first came to Jesus by 3588
Joh 20:8 w. came first to the sepulchre, 3588
Joh 20:16 him, Rabboni; w. is to say, Master. 3739
Joh 20:30 w. are not written in this book: 3739
Joh 21:10 of the fish w. ye have now caught. 3739
Joh 21:20 w. also leaned on his breast at 3739
Joh 21:20 Lord, w. is he that betrayeth thee? 5101
Joh 21:24 w. testifieth of these things, 3588
Joh 21:25 many other things w. Jesus did, 3745
Joh 21:25 w., if they should be written every 3748
Ac 1:2 the day in w. he was taken up, 3739
Ac 1:4 w., saith he, ye have heard of me. 3739
Ac 1:7 w. the Father hath put in his own. 3739
Ac 1:11 W. also said, Ye men of Galilee, 3739
Ac 1:11 w. is taken up from you, into 3588
Ac 1:12 w. is from Jerusalem a sabbath 3739
Ac 1:16 w. the Holy Ghost by the mouth of 3739
Ac 1:16 w. was guide to them that took 3588
Ac 1:21 these men w. have companied with us
Ac 1:24 Lord, w. knowest the hearts of all men,
Ac 1:25 w. Judas by transgression fell, and 3739
Ac 2:7 not all these w. speak Galilaeans? 3588
Ac 2:16 w. was spoken by the prophet Joel;
Ac 2:22 w. God did by him in the midst of 3739
Ac 2:33 forth this, w. ye now see and hear. 3739
Ac 3:2 the temple w. is called Beautiful, 3588
Ac 3:10 he w. sat for alms at the Beautiful 3588
Ac 3:10 at that w. had happened unto him
Ac 3:11 as the lame man w. was healed held
Ac 3:16 the faith w. is by him hath given him
Ac 3:18 w. God before had shewed by the 3739
Ac 3:20 w. before was preached unto you:
Ac 3:21 w. God hath spoken by the mouth 3739
Ac 3:23 soul, w. will not hear that 3748,302
Ac 3:25 covenant w. God made with our 3739
Ac 4:4 many of them w. heard the word
Ac 4:11 stone w. was set at nought of you 3588
Ac 4:11 w. is become the head of the corner 3588
Ac 4:14 man w. was healed standing with
Ac 4:20 the things w. we have seen and 3739
Ac 4:21 glorified god for that w. was done.
Ac 4:24 w. hast made heaven, and earth, 3588
Ac 4:32 things w. he possessed was his own;
Ac 4:36 (w. is, being interpreted, The son 3739
Ac 5:9 feet of them w. have buried thy
Ac 5:16 them w. were vexed with unclean
Ac 5:17 (w. is the sect of the Sadducees.) 3588
Ac 6:9 w. is called the synagogue of the 3588
Ac 6:10 and the spirit by w. he spake. 3739
Ac 6:11 they suborned men, w. said, We have
Ac 6:13 set up false witnesses, w. said, This
Ac 6:14 the customs w. Moses delivered us. 3739
Ac 7:3 into the land w. I shall shew thee. 3739
Ac 7:17 w. God had sworn to Abraham, 3739
Ac 7:18 king arose, w. knew not Joseph. 3739
Ac 7:20 In w. time Moses was born, and 3739
Ac 7:34 of my people w. is in Egypt, 3588
Ac 7:35 of the angel w. appeared to him in 3558
Ac 7:37 w. said unto the children of Israel, 3558
Ac 7:38 angel w. spake to him in the mount 3558
Ac 7:40 w. brought us out of the land of 3739
Ac 7:43 figures w. ye made to worship 3739
Ac 7:45 W. also our fathers that came after 3739
Ac 7:52 W. of the prophets have not your 5101
Ac 7:52 slain them w. shewed before of the 3558
Ac 8:1 the church w. was at Jerusalem; 3558
Ac 8:6 unto those things w. Philip spake,
Ac 8:6 and seeing the miracles w. he did
Ac 8:9 w. beforetime in the same city used
Ac 8:13 the miracles and signs w. were done
Ac 8:14 apostles w. were at Jerusalem 3558
Ac 8:24 of these things w. ye have spoken 3739
Ac 8:26 Jerusalem unto Gaza, w. is desert. 3778
Ac 8:32 of the scripture w. he read was this,
Ac 9:7 men w. journeyed with him stood 3588
Ac 9:11 the street w. is called Straight, 3588
Ac 9:19 the disciples w. were at Damascus.
Ac 9:21 them w. called on this name in 3588
Ac 9:22 the Jews w. dwelt at Damascus, 3588
Ac 9:30 W. when the brethren knew, they
Ac 9:32 to the saints w. dwelt at Lydda. 3588
Ac 9:33 w. had kept his bed eight years,
Ac 9:36 w. by interpretation is called 3739
Ac 9:36 works and almsdeeds w. she did. 3739
Ac 9:39 and garments w. Dorcas made, 3745
Ac 10:2 w. gave much alms to the people, and
Ac 10:7 the angel w. spake unto Cornelius 3588
Ac 10:17 vision w. he had seen should mean, 3739
Ac 10:17 men w. were sent from Cornelius 3588
Ac 10:18 Simon, w. was surnamed Peter, 3588
Ac 10:21 to the men w. were sent unto him 3588
Ac 10:36 word w. God sent unto the children 3739
Ac 10:37 w. was published throughout all
Ac 10:37 after the baptism w. John 3739
Ac 10:39 things w. he did both in the land 3739
Ac 10:42 w. was ordained of God to be the 3588
Ac 10:44 fell on all them w. heard the word
Ac 10:45 w. believed were astonished,
Ac 10:47 w. have received the Holy Ghost 3748
Ac 11:6 the w. when I had fastened mine 3739
Ac 11:13 w. stood and said unto him, Send men
Ac 11:19 they w. were scattered abroad upon
Ac 11:20 w., when they were come to 3748
Ac 11:22 the church w. was in Jerusalem: 3588
Ac 11:28 w. came to pass in the days of 3748
Ac 11:29 unto the brethren w. dwelt in Judaea:
Ac 11:30 W. also they did, and sent it to 3739
Ac 12:9 true w. was done by the angel; 3588
Ac 12:10 w. opened to them of his own 3748
Ac 13:1 w. had been brought up with Herod
Ac 13:7 W. was with the deputy of the 3739
Ac 13:22 heart, w. shall fulfil all my will, 3739
Ac 13:27 the prophets w. are read every 3588
Ac 13:31 of them w. came up with him from
Ac 13:32 the promise w. was made unto the
Ac 13:39 from w. ye could not be justified 3739
Ac 13:40 you, w. is spoken of in the prophets;
Ac 13:41 work w. ye shall in no wise believe,
Ac 13:45 those things w. were spoken by Paul,
Ac 14:3 w. gave testimony unto the word 3588
Ac 14:13 of Jupiter, w. was before their city, 3588
Ac 14:14 W. when the apostles, Barnabas and
Ac 14:15 the living God, w. made heaven, 3739
Ac 14:26 God for the work w. they fulfilled 3739
Ac 15:1 certain men w. came down from
Ac 15:5 the sect of the Pharisees w. believed,
Ac 15:8 And God, w. knoweth the hearts,
Ac 15:10 w. neither our fathers nor we 3739
Ac 15:16 of David, w. is fallen down; 3588
Ac 15:19 w. from among the Gentiles are 3588
Ac 15:23 brethren w. are of the Gentiles in 3588
Ac 15:24 certain w. went out from us have
Ac 15:29 from w. if ye keep yourselves, ye 3739
Ac 15:31 W. when they had read, they rejoiced
Ac 16:1 of a certain woman, w. was a Jewess,
Ac 16:2 W. was well reported of by the 3739
Ac 16:3 Jews w. were in those quarters: 3588
Ac 16:4 and elders w. were at Jerusalem. 3588
Ac 16:12 w. is the chief city of that part of 3748
Ac 16:13 unto the women w. resorted thither
Ac 16:14 Thyatira, w. worshipped God, heard
Ac 16:14 the things w. were spoken of Paul
Ac 16:16 w. brought her masters much gain 3748
Ac 16:17 God, w. shew unto us the way of 3748
Ac 16:21 w. are not lawful for us to receive, 3739
Ac 17:5 But the Jews w. believed not, moved
Ac 17:12 of honourable women w. were 3588

Ac 17:21 strangers **w.** were there, spent.......... *3588*
Ac 17:31 in the **w.** he will judge the world........ *3739*
Ac 17:34 among the **w.** was Dionysius the........ *3739*
Ac 18:27 much **w.** had believed through grace: ....
Ac 19:4 on him **w.** should come after him,............
Ac 19:10 they **w.** dwelt in Asia heard the word.......
Ac 19:13 to call over them **w.** had evil spirits.........
Ac 19:14 and chief of the priests, **w.** did so. ....
Ac 19:19 of them also **w.** used curious arts............
Ac 19:24 **w.** made silver shrines for Diana, ...
Ac 19:26 no gods, **w.** are made with hands:...... *3588*
Ac 19:31 chief of Asia, **w.** were his friends, sent......
Ac 19:35 the image **w.** fell down from Jupiter?.........
Ac 19:37 **w.** are neither robbers of churches, ...
Ac 19:38 and the craftsmen **w.** are with him, ...
Ac 20:19 **w.** befell me by the lying in wait........ *3588*
Ac 20:24 **w.** I have received of the Lord.......... *3739*
Ac 20:28 **w.** the Holy Ghost hath made you...... *3739*
Ac 20:28 **w.** he hath purchased with his own..... *3739*
Ac 20:32 grace, **w.** is able to build you up, ... *3588*
Ac 20:32 among all them **w.** are sanctified. ....
Ac 20:38 most of all for the words **w.** he *3739*
Ac 21:8 evangelist, **w.** was one of the seven; ....
Ac 21:9 daughters, virgins, **w.** did prophesy. ....
Ac 21:20 of Jews there are **w.** believe; and....... *3588*
Ac 21:21 the Jews **w.** are among the Gentiles ....
Ac 21:23 four men **w.** have a vow on them; ....
Ac 21:25 As touching the Gentiles **w.** believe, ...
Ac 21:27 the Jews **w.** were of Asia, when they........
Ac 21:38 **w.** before these days madest an..............
Ac 21:39 I am a man **w.** am a Jew of Tarsus, a ....
Ac 22:1 my defence **w.** I make now unto you. ....
Ac 22:3 a man **w.** am a Jew, born in Tarsus, ...
Ac 22:5 bring them **w.** were there bound unto ....
Ac 22:10 **things w. are appointed for thee**.... *3739*
Ac 22:12 report of all the Jews **w.** dwelt there, ...
Ac 22:29 **w.** should have examined him: *3588*
Ac 23:13 forty **w.** had made this conspiracy. *3588*
Ac 23:21 **w.** have bound themselves with *3748*
Ac 24:14 after the way **w.** they call heresy, ... *3739*
Ac 24:14 all things **w.** are written in the.......... *3588*
Ac 24:15 **w.** they themselves also allow, ... *3739*
Ac 24:24 his wife Drusilla, **w.** was a Jewess, ...
Ac 25:5 **w.** among you are able, go down..............
Ac 25:7 Jews **w.** came down from Jerusalem..........
Ac 25:7 Paul, **w.** they could not prove............ *3588*
Ac 25:16 **w.** is accused have the accusers face ....
Ac 25:19 and of one Jesus, **w.** was dead, whom.......
Ac 25:24 all men **w.** are here present with *3588*
Ac 26:3 and questions **w.** are among the Jews:.......
Ac 26:4 **w.** was at first among mine own *3588*
Ac 26:5 **W.** knew me from the beginning, if...........
Ac 26:7 **w.** promise our twelve tribes,............ *3739*
Ac 26:7 **w.** hope's sake, king Agrippa, I am..... *3739*
Ac 26:10 **W.** thing I also did in Jerusalem: *3739*
Ac 26:13 me and them **w.** journeyed with me. ....
Ac 26:16 **of these things w. thou hast seen,** ..*3739*
Ac 26:16 **in the w. I will appear unto thee;**.. *3739*
Ac 26:18 **among them w. are sanctified by**........
Ac 26:22 **w.** the prophets and Moses did say *3739*
Ac 27:8 a place **w.** is called The fair havens; ....
Ac 27:11 those things **w.** were spoken of by............
Ac 27:12 **w.** is an haven of Crete, and lieth.............
Ac 27:16 a certain island **w.** is called Clauda, ...
Ac 27:17 **W.** when they had taken up, they *3739*
Ac 27:39 into the **w.** they were minded,........... *3739*
Ac 27:43 **w.** could swim should cast themselves.......
Ac 28:9 **w.** had diseases in the island, ... *3588*
Ac 28:11 **w.** had wintered in the isle,.......................
Ac 28:24 some believed the things **w.** were ....
Ac 28:31 those things **w.** concern the Lord............
Ro 1:2 (**W.** he had promised afore by his....... *3739*
Ro 1:3 **w.** was made of the seed of David...... *3588*
Ro 1:19 **w.** may be known of God is manifest ....
Ro 1:26 into that **w.** is against nature: ....
Ro 1:27 men working that **w.** is unseemly, ...
Ro 1:27 recompence of their error **w.** was *3739*
Ro 1:28 those things **w.** are not convenient; ....
Ro 1:32 **w.** commit such things are worthy of ....
Ro 2:2 against them **w.** commit such things..........
Ro 2:3 that judgest them **w.** do such things,.........
Ro 2:14 the Gentiles, **w.** have not the law,...... *3588*
Ro 2:15 **W.** shew the work of the law........... *3748*
Ro 2:19 a light of them **w.** are in darkness, ...
Ro 2:20 **w.** hast the form of knowledge and of ....
Ro 2:21 Thou therefore **w.** teachest.............. *3588*

Ro 2:27 not uncircumcision **w.** is by nature,..........
Ro 2:28 he is not a Jew, **w.** is one outwardly;........
Ro 2:28 **w.** is outward in the flesh: ....
Ro 2:29 But he is a Jew, **w.** is one inwardly; ....
Ro 3:22 **w.** is by faith of Jesus Christ unto all........
Ro 3:26 justifier of him **w.** believeth in Jesus.........
Ro 3:30 **w.** shall justify the circumcision.......... *3739*
Ro 4:11 of the faith **w.** he had yet being *3588*
Ro 4:12 that faith...**w.** he had being yet................
Ro 4:14 For if they **w.** are of the law be heirs, ...
Ro 4:16 seed; not to that only **w.** is of the law,......
Ro 4:16 also **w.** is of the faith of Abraham;............
Ro 4:17 things **w.** be not as though they were. ......
Ro 4:18 according to that **w.** was spoken, ...
Ro 5:5 Holy Ghost **w.** is given unto us.......... *3588*
Ro 5:15 **w.** is by one man, Jesus Christ, ... *3588*
Ro 5:17 much more they **w.** receive abundance ....
Ro 6:17 form of doctrine **w.** was delivered *3739*
Ro 7:2 For the woman **w.** hath an husband is ....
Ro 7:5 sins, **w.** were by the law, did work *3588*
Ro 7:10 **w.** was ordained to life, I found *3588*
Ro 7:13 that **w.** is good made death unto me?........
Ro 7:13 death in me by that **w.** is good; ....
Ro 7:15 For that **w.** I do I allow not: for......... *3739*
Ro 7:16 If then I do that **w.** I would not, I...... *3739*
Ro 7:18 but how to perform that **w.** is good I........
Ro 7:19 not: but the evil **w.** I would not, ... *3739*
Ro 7:23 law of sin **w.** is in my members. *3588*
Ro 8:1 to them **w.** are in Christ Jesus,...............
Ro 8:18 the glory **w.** shall be revealed in ....
Ro 8:23 **w.** have the firstfruits of the Spirit,...........
Ro 8:26 with groanings **w.** cannot be uttered. ....
Ro 8:39 the love of God, **w.** is in Christ *3588*
Ro 9:6 are not all Israel, **w.** are of Israel:..... *3588*
Ro 9:8 They **w.** are the children of the flesh, ...
Ro 9:23 **w.** he had afore prepared unto........... *3739*
Ro 9:25 my people, **w.** were not my people;..........
Ro 9:25 and her beloved, **w.** was not beloved. ....
Ro 9:30 **w.** followed not...righteousness, ... *3588*
Ro 9:30 the righteousness **w.** is of faith. *3588*
Ro 9:31 Israel, **w.** followed after the law of...........
Ro 10:5 the righteousness **w.** is of the law,..... *3588*
Ro 10:5 man **w.** doeth those things shall live..........
Ro 10:6 **w.** is of faith speaketh on this wise,...........
Ro 10:8 the word of faith, **w.** we preach;.......... *3739*
Ro 11:2 away his people **w.** he foreknew. *3739*
Ro 11:7 not obtained that **w.** he seeketh......... *3739*
Ro 11:14 to emulation them **w.** are my flesh, ...
Ro 11:22 on them **w.** fell, severity; but toward.........
Ro 11:24 cut out of the olive tree **w.** is wild...........
Ro 11:24 **w.** be the natural branches, be graffed.......
Ro 12:1 God, **w.** is your reasonable service. ....
Ro 12:9 dissimulation. Abhor that **w.** is evil; ....
Ro 12:9 cleave to that **w.** is good. ....
Ro 12:14 Bless them **w.** persecute you: bless,.........
Ro 13:3 do that **w.** is good, and thou shalt ....
Ro 13:4 But if thou do that **w.** is evil, be..............
Ro 14:3 and let not him **w.** eateth not judge ....
Ro 14:19 after the things **w.** make for peace, ...
Ro 14:22 in that thing **w.** he alloweth............... *3739*
Ro 15:17 in those things **w.** pertain to God. ....
Ro 15:18 those things **w.** Christ hath not.......... *3739*
Ro 15:22 **w.** cause also I have been much......... *1352*
Ro 15:26 poor saints **w.** are at Jerusalem.......... *3588*
Ro 15:31 service **w.** I have for Jerusalem *3588*
Ro 16:1 you Phebe our sister, **w.** is a servant........
Ro 16:1 of the church **w.** is at Cenchrea: *3588*
Ro 16:10 Salute them **w.** are of Aristobulus'...........
Ro 16:11 of Narcissus, **w.** are in the Lord. 3588
Ro 16:12 Persis, **w.** laboured much in the......... *3748*
Ro 16:14 and the brethren **w.** are with them. ....
Ro 16:15 and all the saints **w.** are with them. ....
Ro 16:17 them **w.** cause divisions and offences ....
Ro 16:17 the doctrine **w.** ye have learned;........ *3739*
Ro 16:19 have you wise unto that **w.** is good, ...
Ro 16:25 **w.** was kept secret since the world ....
1Co 1:2 the church of God **w.** is at Corinth, ... *3588*
1Co 1:4 the grace of God **w.** is given you by... *3588*
1Co 1:11 by them **w.** are of the house of Chloe, ...
1Co 1:18 unto us **w.** are saved it is the power.........
1Co 1:24 them **w.** are called, both Jews and...... *3588*
1Co 1:27 confound the things **w.** are mighty;............
1Co 1:28 things **w.** are despised, hath God ....
1Co 1:28 things **w.** are not, to bring to............ *3588*
1Co 2:7 **w.** God ordained before the world...... *3739*
1Co 2:8 **W.** none of the princes of this........... *3739*

1Co 2:9 things **w.** God hath prepared for *3739*
1Co 2:11 the spirit of man **w.** is in him?........... 3588
1Co 2:12 world, but the spirit **w.** is of God;...... 3588
1Co 2:13 **W.** things also we spake, not in......... *3739*
1Co 2:13 the words **w.** man's wisdom teacheth. ....
1Co 2:13 but **w.** the Holy Ghost teacheth; ....
1Co 3:10 to the grace of God **w.** is given *3588*
1Co 3:11 that is laid, **w.** is Jesus Christ............ *3739*
1Co 3:14 man's work abide **w.** he hath built *3739*
1Co 3:17 of God is holy, **w.** temple ye are......... *3748*
1Co 4:6 of men above that **w.** is written, ... *3789*
1Co 4:17 of my ways **w.** be in Christ,.............. *3588*
1Co 4:19 the speech of them **w.** are puffed up,.........
1Co 6:16 that he **w.** is joined to a harlot is one........
1Co 6:19 of the Holy Ghost **w.** is in you,................
1Co 6:19 **w.** ye have of God, and ye are not..... *3739*
1Co 6:20 and in your spirit, **w.** are God's, ... *3748*
1Co 7:13 woman **w.** hath an husband that......... *3748*
1Co 7:35 upon you, but for that **w.** is comely, ...
1Co 8:10 man see thee **w.** hast knowledge......... *3588*
1Co 8:10 conscience of him **w.** is weak be ....
1Co 8:10 those things **w.** are offered to idols;..........
1Co 9:13 they **w.** minister about holy things...........
1Co 9:13 and they **w.** wait at the altar are..............
1Co 9:14 that they **w.** preach the gospel should ....
1Co 9:24 that they **w.** run in a race run all,............
1Co 10:16 The cup of blessing **w.** we bless, is.... *3739*
1Co 10:16 bread **w.** we break, is it not............. *3739*
1Co 10:18 not they **w.** eat of the sacrifices..............
1Co 10:19 or that **w.** is offered in sacrifice to............
1Co 10:20 that the things **w.** the Gentiles *3739*
1Co 10:30 of for that for **w.** I give thanks? *3739*
1Co 11:19 they **w.** are approved may be made ....
1Co 11:23 of the Lord that **w.** also I delivered *3739*
1Co 11:23 same night in **w.** he was betrayed, ... *3739*
1Co 11:24 **this is my body, w. is broken for**... *3588*
1Co 12:6 the same God **w.** worketh all in all. *3588*
1Co 12:22 of the body, **w.** seem to be more feeble, ...
1Co 12:23 **w.** we think to be less honourable, ... *3739*
1Co 12:24 honour to that part **w.** lacked: ....
1Co 13:10 But when that **w.** is perfect is come, ...
1Co 13:10 that **w.** is in part shall be done away.........
1Co 14:22 believe not, but for them **w.** believe. ....
1Co 15:1 the gospel **w.** I preached unto you,..... *3739*
1Co 15:1 **w.** also ye have received, and *3739*
1Co 15:2 **w.** also ye are saved, if ye keep in..... *3739*
1Co 15:3 first of all that **w.** I also received, ... *3739*
1Co 15:10 his grace **w.** was bestowed upon me.........
1Co 15:10 but the grace of God **w.** was with...... *3588*
1Co 15:18 also **w.** are fallen asleep in Christ are........
1Co 15:27 **w.** did put all things under him.................
1Co 15:29 they do **w.** are baptized for the dead,........
1Co 15:31 **w.** I have in Christ Jesus our Lord, ... *3739*
1Co 15:36 fool, that **w.** thou sowest is not *3739*
1Co 15:37 And that **w.** thou sowest, thou *3739*
1Co 15:46 that was not first **w.** is spiritual,...............
1Co 15:46 but that **w.** is natural; and afterward ....
1Co 15:46 and afterward that **w.** is spiritual. ....
1Co 15:57 **w.** giveth us the victory through *3588*
1Co 16:17 that **w.** was lacking on your part they ....
2Co 1:1 church of God **w.** is at Corinth, ... *3588*
2Co 1:1 all the saints **w.** are in all Achaia: *3588*
2Co 1:4 comfort them **w.** are in any trouble,...........
2Co 1:6 **w.** is effectual in the enduring of.......... *3588*
2Co 1:6 same sufferings **w.** ye also suffer: *3588*
2Co 1:8 our trouble **w.** came to us in Asia, ... *3588*
2Co 1:9 but in God **w.** raiseth the dead: *3588*
2Co 1:21 Now he **w.** stablisheth us with you in........
2Co 2:2 the same **w.** is made sorry by me?............
2Co 2:4 ye might know the love **w.** I have *3739*
2Co 2:6 this punishment, **w.** was inflicted........ *3588*
2Co 2:14 **w.** always causeth us to triumph in...........
2Co 2:17 not as many, **w.** corrupt the word of...........
2Co 3:7 **w.** glory was to be done away: *3588*
2Co 3:10 **w.** was made glorious had no glory in........
2Co 3:11 that **w.** is done away was glorious, ...
2Co 3:11 more that **w.** remaineth is glorious. ....
2Co 3:13 as Moses, **w.** put a vail over his face, ...
2Co 3:13 to the end of that **w.** is abolished: ....
2Co 3:14 **w.** vail is done away in Christ............ *3748*
2Co 4:4 the minds of them **w.** believe not, ...
2Co 4:11 we **w.** live are alway delivered........... *3588*
2Co 4:14 he **w.** raised up the Lord Jesus shall..........
2Co 4:16 For **w.** cause we faint not; but *1352*
2Co 4:17 affliction, **w.** is but for a moment,....... *3588*
2Co 4:18 we look not at the things **w.** are seen, ...

2Co 4:18 but at the things **w.** are not seen: ....
2Co 4:18 the things **w.** are seen are temporal; ....
2Co 4:18 things **w.** are not seen are eternal. ....
2Co 5:2 with our house **w.** is from heaven: 3588
2Co 5:12 them **w.** glory in appearance, ...
2Co 5:15 they **w.** live should not henceforth ....
2Co 5:15 unto him **w.** died for them, and rose ....
2Co 7:14 **w.** I made before Titus, is found a 3588
2Co 8:11 performance also...of that **w.** ye have ....
2Co 8:16 **w.** put the same earnest care into 3588
2Co 8:19 **w.** is administered by us to the 3588
2Co 8:20 abundance **w.** is administered by us: 3588
2Co 8:22 great confidence **w.** I have in you. 3588
2Co 9:2 for **w.** I boast of you to them of 3739
2Co 9:6 he **w.** soweth bountifully shall reap ....
2Co 9:6 He **w.** soweth sparingly shall reap ....
2Co 9:11 **w.** causeth...us thanksgiving 3748
2Co 9:14 **w.** long after you for the exceeding ....
2Co 10:2 **w.** think of us as if we walked 3588
2Co 10:8 **w.** the Lord hath given us for 3739
2Co 10:13 rule **w.** God hath distributed to us, ... 3739
2Co 11:4 spirit, **w.** ye have not received, ... 3739
2Co 11:4 gospel, **w.** ye have not accepted, ...
2Co 11:9 for that **w.** was lacking to me, the ....
2Co 11:9 brethren **w.** came from Macedonia ....
2Co 11:12 from them **w.** desire occasion; ....
2Co 11:17 That **w.** I speak, I speak it not 3739
2Co 11:28 that **w.** cometh upon me daily, the 3588
2Co 11:30 glory of the things **w.** concern mine ....
2Co 11:31 Christ, **w.** is blessed for evermore, ... 3588
2Co 12:4 **w.** it is not lawful for a man to 3739
2Co 12:6 above that **w.** he seeth me to be, ... 3739
2Co 12:21 bewail many **w.** have sinned 3588
2Co 12:21 and lasciviousness **w.** they have 3739
2Co 13:2 to them **w.** heretofore have sinned, ...
2Co 13:3 **w.** to you-ward is not weak, but 3739
2Co 13:7 that ye should do that **w.** is honest, ...
2Co 13:10 the power **w.** the Lord hath given 3739
Ga 1:2 And all the brethren **w.** are with me, ...
Ga 1:7 **W.** is not another; but there be 3739
Ga 1:8 you than that **w.** we have preached 3739
Ga 1:11 the gospel **w.** was preached of me 3588
Ga 1:17 to them **w.** are apostles before me; ....
Ga 1:20 Now the things **w.** I write unto 3739
Ga 1:22 of Judaea **w.** were in Christ: 3588
Ga 1:23 he **w.** persecuted us in times past now ....
Ga 1:23 the faith **w.** once he destroyed. 3739
Ga 2:2 that gospel **w.** I preach among the 3739
Ga 2:2 but privately to them **w.** were of ....
Ga 2:4 liberty **w.** we have in Christ Jesus, ... 3739
Ga 2:10 same **w.** I also was forward to do. 3739
Ga 2:12 them **w.** were of the circumcision. ....
Ga 2:18 again the things **w.** I destroyed, ... 3739
Ga 2:20 the life **w.** I now live in the flesh I 3739
Ga 3:7 ye therefore that they **w.** are of faith, ...
Ga 3:9 So then they **w.** be of faith are ....
Ga 3:10 **w.** are written in the book of the 3588
Ga 3:16 And to thy seed, **w.** is Christ. 3739
Ga 3:17 **w.** was four hundred and thirty years ....
Ga 3:21 been a law given **w.** could have 3588
Ga 3:23 faith **w.** should afterward be revealed. ....
Ga 4:8 unto them **w.** by nature are no gods. ....
Ga 4:14 my temptation **w.** was in my flesh ye ....
Ga 4:24 **W.** things are an allegory: for 3748
Ga 4:24 Sinai **w.** gendereth to bondage, ...
Ga 4:24 to bondage, **w.** is Agar 3748
Ga 4:25 answereth to Jerusalem, **w.** now 3588
Ga 4:26 But Jerusalem **w.** is above is free, ...
Ga 4:26 is free, **w.** is the mother of us all. 3748
Ga 4:27 more children than she **w.** hath an ....
Ga 5:6 but faith **w.** worketh by love. ....
Ga 5:12 were even cut off **w.** trouble you. ....
Ga 5:19 manifest, **w.** are these; Adultery, ... 3748
Ga 5:21 of the **w.** I tell you before, as I 3739
Ga 5:21 **w.** do such things shall not inherit ....
Ga 6:1 **w.** are spiritual, restore such an 3588
Eph 1:1 to the saints **w.** are at Ephesus, ... 3588
Eph 1:9 good pleasure **w.** he hath 3739
Eph 1:10 **w.** are in heaven, and **w.** are on 3588
Eph 1:14 **W.** is the earnest of our 3739
Eph 1:20 **W.** he wrought in Christ, when he 3739
Eph 1:21 world, but also in that **w.** is to come: ....
Eph 1:23 **W.** is his body, the fulness of him 3748
Eph 2:10 **w.** God hath before ordained that 3739
Eph 2:11 **w.** is called the Circumcision in 3588
Eph 2:17 peace to you **w.** were afar off, ... 3588
Eph 3:2 of God **w.** is given me to you-ward: 3588
Eph 3:5 **W.** in other ages was not made 3739
Eph 3:9 **w.** from the beginning of the 3588
Eph 3:11 **w.** he purposed in Christ Jesus our 3739
Eph 3:13 my tribulations for you, **w.** is your 3748
Eph 3:19 love of Christ, **w.** passeth knowledge, ...
Eph 4:15 him in all things **w.** is the head, ... 3739
Eph 4:16 by that **w.** evey joint supplieth, ...
Eph 4:22 **w.** is corrupt according to the 3588
Eph 4:24 man, **w.** after God is created in 3588
Eph 4:28 with his hands the thing **w.** is good, ...
Eph 4:29 **w.** is good to the use of edifying, ... 1536
Eph 5:4 nor jesting, **w.** are not convenient: 3588
Eph 5:12 things **w.** are done of them in secret ....
Eph 6:2 **w.** is the first commandment with 3748
Eph 6:17 of the Spirit, **w.** is the work of God: 3739
Eph 6:20 **w.** I am an ambassador in bonds: 3739
Php 1:1 in Christ Jesus **w.** are at Philippi, ... 3588
Php 1:6 **w.** hath begun a good work in you ....
Php 1:11 **w.** are by Jesus Christ, unto the 3588
Php 1:12 things **w.** happened unto me have ....
Php 1:23 to be with Christ; **w.** is far better: ....
Php 1:28 **w.** is to them an evident token of 3748
Php 1:30 the same conflict **w.** ye saw in me, ... 3634
Php 2:5 you, **w.** was also in Christ Jesus: 3739
Php 2:9 a name **w.** is above every name: 3588
Php 2:13 it is God **w.** worketh in you both 3588
Php 2:21 not the things **w.** are Jesus Christ's. ....
Php 3:3 **w.** worship God in the spirit, and 3588
Php 3:6 the righteousness **w.** is in the law, ... 3588
Php 3:9 own righteousness **w.** is of the law, ... 3588
Php 3:9 but that **w.** is the faith of Christ 3588
Php 3:9 righteousness **w.** is of God by faith: 3588
Php 3:12 that for **w.** also I am apprehended 3739
Php 3:13 forgetting those things **w.** are behind, ...
Php 3:13 unto those things **w.** are before, ...
Php 3:17 and mark them **w.** walk so as ye have ....
Php 4:3 women **w.** laboured with me in 3748
Php 4:7 God, **w.** passeth all understanding, ... 3588
Php 4:9 things **w.** ye have both learned 3739
Php 4:13 through Christ **w.** strengtheneth 3588
Php 4:18 the things **w.** were sent from you, ...
Php 4:21 The brethren **w.** are with me greet ....
Col 1:2 brethren in Christ **w.** are at Colosse: ....
Col 1:4 love **w.** ye have to all the saints, ... 3588
Col 1:5 For the hope **w.** is laid up for you 3588
Col 1:6 **W.** is come unto you, as it is in all 3588
Col 1:12 **w.** hath made us meet to be 3588
Col 1:23 hope of the gospel, **w.** ye have heard, ...
Col 1:23 **w.** was preached to every creature 3558
Col 1:23 to every creature **w.** is under heaven; ....
Col 1:24 that **w.** is behind of the afflictions of ....
Col 1:24 his body's sake, **w.** is the church: 3739
Col 1:25 of God **w.** is given to me for you, ... 3588
Col 1:26 Even the mystery **w.** hath been 3588
Col 1:27 **w.** is Christ in you, the hope of 3739
Col 1:29 **w.** worketh in me mightily. 3588
Col 2:10 **w.** is the head of all principality 3739
Col 2:14 against us, **w.** was contrary to us, ... 3739
Col 2:17 **W.** are a shadow of things to 3739
Col 2:18 those things **w.** he hath not seen, ... 3739
Col 2:19 **w.** all the body by joints and bands 3739
Col 2:22 **W.** all are to perish with the using;) 3739
Col 2:23 **W.** things have indeed a shew of 3748
Col 3:1 seek those things **w.** are above, ...
Col 3:5 members **w.** are upon the earth; 3588
Col 3:5 and covetousness, **w.** is idolatry: 3748
Col 3:6 **w.** things' sake the wrath of God 3739
Col 3:7 the **w.** ye also walked some time, ... 3739
Col 3:10 **w.** is renewed in knowledge after 3588
Col 3:14 **w.** is the bond of perfectness. 3748
Col 3:15 **w.** also ye are called in one body; 3739
Col 3:25 for the wrong **w.** he hath done: 3739
Col 4:1 unto your servants that **w.** is just and ....
Col 4:3 Christ, for **w.** I am also in bonds: 3739
Col 4:9 you all things **w.** are done here 3588
Col 4:11 Jesus, **w.** is called Justus, who are 3588
Col 4:11 **w.** have been a comfort unto me 3748
Col 4:15 the brethren **w.** ar in Laodicea, ...
Col 4:15 and the church **w.** is in his house. ....
Col 4:17 ministry **w.** thou hast received in 3739
1Th 1:1 **w.** is in God the Father, and in ....
1Th 1:10 **w.** delivered us from the wrath 3588
1Th 2:4 but God **w.** trieth our hearts. ....
1Th 2:13 the word of God **w.** ye heard of us, ye ....
1Th 2:13 **w.** effectually worketh also in you 3739
1Th 2:14 God **w.** in Judaea are in Christ: 3588
1Th 3:10 that **w.** is lacking in your faith? ....
1Th 4:5 the Gentiles **w.** knew not God: 3588
1Th 4:10 brethren **w.** are in all Macedonia: 3588
1Th 4:13 concerning them **w.** are asleep, ...
1Th 4:13 even as others **w.** have no hope. 3588
1Th 4:14 them also **w.** sleep in Jesus will God ....
1Th 4:15 **w.** are alive and remain unto the 3588
1Th 4:15 not prevent them **w.** are asleep. 3588
1Th 4:17 **w.** are alive and remain shall be 3588
1Th 5:12 know them **w.** labour among you, ... 3588
1Th 5:15 but ever follow that **w.** is good, ... 3588
1Th 5:21 things; hold fast that **w.** is good. 3588
1Ti 6:21 **W.** some professing have erred 3739
2Th 1:5 **W.** is a manifest token of the ....
2Th 1:5 of God, for **w.** ye also suffer: 3739
2Th 2:15 traditions **w.** ye have been taught, ... 3739
2Th 2:16 our Father, **w.** hath loved us, ... 3588
2Th 3:4 do the things **w.** we command you. 3739
2Th 3:6 the tradition **w.** he received of us. 3739
2Th 3:11 there are some **w.** walk among you ....
2Th 3:17 **w.** is the token in every epistle: 3739
1Ti 1:1 Lord Jesus Christ, **w.** is our hope: 3588
1Ti 1:4 endless genealogies, **w.** minister 3748
1Ti 1:4 than godly edifying **w.** is in faith: 3588
1Ti 1:6 From **w.** some having swerved 3739
1Ti 1:11 **w.** was committed to my trust. 3739
1Ti 1:14 faith and love **w.** is in Christ 3588
1Ti 1:16 to them **w.** should hereafter believe ....
1Ti 1:18 prophecies **w.** went before on thee, ...
1Ti 1:19 **w.** some having put away 3739
1Ti 2:10 (**w.** becometh women professing 3739
1Ti 3:7 good report of them **w.** are without ....
1Ti 3:13 in the faith **w.** is in Christ Jesus. 3588
1Ti 3:15 **w.** is the church of the living 3748
1Ti 4:3 **w.** God hath created to be received 3739
1Ti 4:3 **w.** believe and know the truth. ....
1Ti 4:8 now is, and of that **w.** is to come, ...
1Ti 4:14 **w.** was given thee by prophecy, ... 3739
1Ti 5:13 speaking things **w.** they ought not. 3588
1Ti 6:3 to the doctrine **w.** is according to ....
1Ti 6:9 **w.** drown men in destruction and 3748
1Ti 6:10 **w.** while some coveted after, they 3739
1Ti 6:15 **W.** in his times he shall shew, ... 3739
1Ti 6:16 light **w.** no man can approach unto; 3739
1Ti 6:20 that **w.** is committed to thy trust, ...
1Ti 6:21 **W.** some professing have erred 3739
1Ti *subscr.* **w.** is the chiefest city of 3748
2Ti 1:1 of life **w.** is in Christ Jesus, ... 3588
2Ti 1:5 **w.** dwelt first in thy grandmother, ... 3748
2Ti 1:6 **w.** is in thee by the putting on of 3739
2Ti 1:9 **w.** was given us in Christ Jesus 3588
2Ti 1:12 **w.** cause I also suffer these things: 3739
2Ti 1:12 **w.** I have committed unto him ....
2Ti 1:13 words **w.** thou hast heard of me, ... 3739
2Ti 1:13 and love **w.** is in Christ Jesus. 3588
2Ti 1:14 thing **w.** was committed unto thee ....
2Ti 1:14 the Holy Ghost **w.** dwelleth in us. 3588
2Ti 1:15 **w.** are in Asia be turned away ....
2Ti 2:10 the salvation **w.** is in Christ Jesus. 3588
2Ti 3:6 sort are they **w.** creep into houses, ...
2Ti 3:11 **w.** came unto me at Antioch, ... 3634
2Ti 3:14 thou in the things **w.** thou hast 3739
2Ti 3:15 **w.** are able to make thee wise 3588
2Ti 3:15 through faith **w.** is in Christ Jesus. 3588
2Ti 4:8 **w.** the Lord, the righteous judge, ... 3739
Tit 1:1 the truth **w.** is after godliness; 3588
Tit 1:2 **w.** God, that cannot lie, promised 3739
Tit 1:3 **w.** is committed unto me 3739
Tit 1:11 teaching things **w.** they ought not 3739
Tit 2:1 things **w.** become sound doctrine: 3739
Tit 3:5 righteousness **w.** we have done, ... 3739
Tit 3:6 **W.** he shed on us abundantly 3739
Tit 3:8 they **w.** have believed in God might be ....
Phm 5 **w.** thou hast toward the Lord 3739
Phm 6 good thing **w.** is in you in Christ 3588
Phm 8 enjoin thee that **w.** is convenient, ...
Phm 11 **W.** in time past was to thee 3588
Heb 1:5 **w.** of the angels said he at any 5101
Heb 1:13 to **w.** of the angels said he at any 5101
Heb 2:1 to the things **w.** we have heard, ...
Heb 2:3 **w.** at the first began to be spoken 3748
Heb 2:11 for **w.** cause he is not ashamed 3739
Heb 2:13 children **w.** God hath given me. 3739
Heb 3:5 things **w.** were to be spoken after; ....
Heb 4:3 we **w.** have believed do enter into 3583
Heb 4:15 not an high priest **w.** cannot be ....

Book	Ref.	Text	No.
Heb	5:8	by the things w. he suffered;	3739
Heb	5:12	w. be the first principles of the	5101
Heb	6:7	earth w. drinketh in the rain that	3588
Heb	6:8	that w. beareth thorns and briers	
Heb	6:10	w. ye have shewed toward his	3739
Heb	6:18	in w. it was impossible for God	3739
Heb	6:19	W. hope we have as an anchor of	3739
Heb	6:19	w. entereth into that within the veil;	
Heb	7:2	of Salem, w. is, King of peace;	3739
Heb	7:13	of w. no man gave attendance at	3739
Heb	7:14	of w. tribe Moses spake nothing	3739
Heb	7:19	by the w. we draw nigh unto God.	3739
Heb	7:28	men high priests w. have infirmity;	
Heb	7:28	of the oath, w. was since the law,	3588
Heb	8:1	things w. we have spoken this is	
Heb	8:2	the true tabernacle, w. the Lord	3739
Heb	8:6	w. was established upon better	3748
Heb	8:13	Now that w. decayeth and waxeth old	
Heb	9:2	the shewbread; w. is called the	3748
Heb	9:3	the tabernacle w. is called the	3588
Heb	9:4	W. had the golden censer, and the	
Heb	9:5	seat; of w. we cannot now speak	3739
Heb	9:7	blood, w. he offered for himself	3739
Heb	9:9	W. was a figure for the time then	3748
Heb	9:9	in w. were offered both gifts and	3739
Heb	9:10	W. stood only in meat and	
Heb	9:15	they w. are called might receive the	
Heb	9:20	testament w. God hath enjoined	3739
Heb	9:24	w. are the figures of the true;	
Heb	10:1	w. they offered year by year	3739
Heb	10:8	w. are offered by the law;	3748
Heb	10:10	By the w. will we are sanctified	3739
Heb	10:11	sacrifices, w. can never take away	3748
Heb	10:20	w. he hath consecrated for us,	3739
Heb	10:27	w. shall devour the adversaries.	
Heb	10:32	in w., after ye were illuminated,	3739
Heb	10:35	w. hath great recompense of	3748
Heb	11:3	things w. are seen were not made	3588
Heb	11:3	were not made of things w. do appear	
Heb	11:4	by w. he obtained witness that he	3739
Heb	11:7	by the w. he condemned the world,	3739
Heb	11:7	of the righteousness w. is by faith.	
Heb	11:8	place w. he should after receive	3739
Heb	11:10	looked for a city w. hath foundations,	
Heb	11:12	as the sand w. is by the sea shore	3588
Heb	11:29	w. the Egyptians assaying to do	3739
Heb	12:1	the sin w. doth so easily beset us, and	
Heb	12:5	w. speaketh unto you as unto	3748
Heb	12:9	fathers of our flesh w. corrected us,	
Heb	12:11	unto them w. are exercised thereby	
Heb	12:12	lift up the hands w. hang down, and	
Heb	12:13	lest that w. is lame be turned out of	
Heb	12:14	w. no man shall see the Lord:	3739
Heb	12:19	words, w. voice they that had heard	3739
Heb	12:20	not endure that w. was commanded,	
Heb	12:23	firstborn, w. are written in heaven,	
Heb	12:27	those things w. cannot be shaken may	
Heb	12:28	a kingdom w. cannot be moved,	
Heb	13:3	and them w. suffer adversity, as being	
Heb	13:7	Remember them w. have the rule over	
Heb	13:9	w. have not profited them that	3739
Heb	13:10	right to eat w. serve the tabernacle.	
Heb	13:21	that w. is wellpleasing in his sight,	
Jas	1:1	twelve tribes w. are scattered	3739
Jas	1:12	w. the Lord hath promised to them	3739
Jas	1:21	word, w. is able to save your souls.	3588
Jas	2:5	w. he hath promised to them that	3735
Jas	2:7	name by the w. ye are called?	3588
Jas	2:16	things w. are needful to the body;	
Jas	2:23	was fulfilled w. saith, Abraham	3588
Jas	3:4	the ships, w. though they be so great,	
Jas	3:9	w. are made after the similitude	3588
Jas	5:4	w. is of you kept back by fraud,	3588
Jas	5:4	the cries of them w. have reaped are	
Jas	5:11	we count them happy w. endure.	
Jas	5:20	that he w. converteth the sinner from	
1Pe	1:3	w. according to his abundant	3588
1Pe	1:10	Of w. salvation the prophets have	3739
1Pe	1:11	Spirit of Christ w. was in them did	3588
1Pe	1:12	w. are now reported unto you by	3739
1Pe	1:12	w. things the angels desire to look	3739
1Pe	1:15	But as he w. hath called you is holy,	
1Pe	1:23	of God, w. liveth and abideth for ever.	
1Pe	1:25	word w. by the gospel is preached	3588
1Pe	2:7	therefore w. believe he is precious:	3588
1Pe	2:7	but unto them w. be disobedient	
1Pe	2:7	the stone w. the builders disallowed,	
1Pe	2:8	to them w. stumble at the word,	3739
1Pe	2:10	W. in time past were not a people,	3588
1Pe	2:10	w. had not obtained mercy, but	3588
1Pe	2:11	lusts, w. war against the soul;	3748
1Pe	2:12	your good works, w. they shall behold,	
1Pe	3:4	heart, in that w. is not corruptible,	
1Pe	3:4	w. is in the sight of God of great	3739
1Pe	3:13	if ye be followers of that w. is good?	
1Pe	3:19	By w. also he went and preached	3739
1Pe	3:20	W. sometime were disobedient, when	
1Pe	4:11	as of the ability w. God giveth:	3739
1Pe	4:12	the fiery trial w. is to try you,	
1Pe	5:1	The elders w. are among you I exhort,	
1Pe	5:2	the flock of God w. is among you,	
2Pe	1:18	this voice w. came from heaven we	
2Pe	2:11	w. are greater in power and might,	
2Pe	2:15	W. have forsaken the right way, and	
2Pe	3:1	in both w. I stir up your pure	3739
2Pe	3:2	of the words w. were spoken before	
2Pe	3:7	heavens and the earth, w. are now,	
2Pe	3:10	w. the heavens shall pass away	3739
2Pe	3:16	in w. are some things hard to be	3739
2Pe	3:16	w. they that are unlearned and	3739
1Jo	1:1	That w. was from the beginning,	3739
1Jo	1:1	w. we have heard, w. we have seen	3739
1Jo	1:1	w. we have looked upon, and our	3739
1Jo	1:2	life, w. was with the Father, and	3748
1Jo	1:3	That w. we have seen and heard	3739
1Jo	1:5	message w. we have heard of him	3739
1Jo	2:7	w. ye had from the beginning.	3739
1Jo	2:7	the word w. ye have heard	3739
1Jo	2:8	w. thing is true in him and in you:	3739
1Jo	2:24	in you, w. ye have heard from the	3739
1Jo	2:24	If that w. ye have heard from the	3739
1Jo	2:27	w. ye have received of him abideth	3739
1Jo	3:24	by the Spirit w. he hath given us.	3739
1Jo	5:9	God, w. he hath testified of his Son.	3739
1Jo	5:16	sin a sin w. is not unto death,	
2Jo	2	the truth's sake, w. dwelleth in us,	3588
2Jo	5	w. we had from the beginning,	3739
2Jo	8	those things w. we have wrought,	3739
3Jo	6	W. have borne witness of thy	3739
3Jo	10	remember his deeds w. he doeth,	
3Jo	11	Beloved, follow not that w. is evil,	
3Jo	11	but that w. is good. He that doeth	
Jude	3	faith w. was once delivered unto the	
Jude	6	angels w. kept not their first estate,	
Jude	10	evil of those things w. they know	3745
Jude	15	w. they have ungodly committed,	3739
Jude	15	w. ungodly sinners have spoken	3739
Jude	17	the words w. were spoken before	3588
Re	1:1	w. God gave unto him, to shew	3739
Re	1:1	things w. must shortly come to	3739
Re	1:3	those things w. are written therein:	
Re	1:4	the seven churches w. are in Asia:	3588
Re	1:4	w. is, and w. was, and w. is to come;	3588
Re	1:4	the seven Spirits w. are before	3739
Re	1:7	and they also w. pierced him:	3748
Re	1:8	w. is, and w. was, and w. is to come,	3588
Re	1:11	the seven churches w. are in	3588
Re	1:19	Write the things w. thou hast	3739
Re	1:19	hast seen, and the things w. are,	3739
Re	1:19	the things w. shall be hereafter;	3739
Re	1:20	w. thou sawest in my right hand,	3739
Re	1:20	w. thou sawest are the seven	3739
Re	2:2	thou canst not bear them w. are	
Re	2:2	tried them w. say they are apostles,	
Re	2:6	the Nicolaitanes, w. I also hate	3739
Re	2:7	w. is in the midst of the paradise	3739
Re	2:8	first and the last, w. was dead,	3739
Re	2:9	of them w. say they are Jews,	3588
Re	2:10	those things w. thou shalt suffer:	3739
Re	2:12	saith he w. hath the sharp sword	
Re	2:15	the Nicolaitanes, w. thing I hate	3739
Re	2:17	w. no man knoweth saving he	3739
Re	2:20	Jezebel, w. calleth herself a	3588
Re	2:23	he w. searcheth the reins and	3739
Re	2:24	w. have not known the depths of	3748
Re	2:25	that w. ye have already hold fast	
Re	3:2	strengthen the things w. remain,	
Re	3:4	Sardis w. have not defiled their	3739
Re	3:9	w. say they are Jews, and are	3588
Re	3:10	w. shall come upon all the world,	3588
Re	3:11	hold that fast w. thou hast, that	3739
Re	3:12	of my God, w. is new Jerusalem,	3588
Re	3:12	w. cometh down out of heaven	3588
Re	4:1	first voice w. I heard was as it	3739
Re	4:1	w. said, Come up hither, and I will	
Re	4:1	thee things w. must be hereafter.	3739
Re	4:5	w. are the seven Spirits of God.	3739
Re	4:8	w. was, and is, and is to come.	3588
Re	5:6	w. are the seven Spirits of God	3739
Re	5:8	odours, w. are the prayers of saints.	3739
Re	5:13	And every creature w. is in heaven,	3739
Re	6:9	and for the testimony w. they held:	3739
Re	7:4	the number of them w. were sealed:	
Re	7:9	w. no man could number, of all	3739
Re	7:10	God w. sitteth upon the throne,	3588
Re	7:13	w. are arrayed in white robes?	3588
Re	7:14	These are they w. came out of great	
Re	7:17	For the Lamb w. is in the midst of	3588
Re	8:2	the seven angels w. stood before	3739
Re	8:3	golden altar w. was before the	3588
Re	8:4	w. came with the prayers of the	
Re	8:6	seven angels w. had the seven	3588
Re	8:9	of the creatures w. are in the sea,	3588
Re	8:13	three angels w. are yet to sound!	3588
Re	9:4	men w. have not the seal of God	3748
Re	9:11	w. is the angel of the bottomless pit,	
Re	9:13	the golden altar w. is before God.	3588
Re	9:14	sixth angel w. had the trumpet,	3739
Re	9:14	w. are bound in the great river	3588
Re	9:15	w. are prepared for an hour, and a	3588
Re	9:18	w. issued out of their mouths.	3588
Re	9:20	rest of the men w. were not killed	3739
Re	9:20	w. neither can see, nor hear, nor	3739
Re	10:4	things w. the seven thunders	3739
Re	10:5	the angel w. I saw stand upon the	3739
Re	10:6	sea, and the things w. are therein,	
Re	10:8	the voice w. I heard from heaven	3739
Re	10:8	book w. is open in the hand of the	3588
Re	10:8	angel w. standeth upon the sea	3588
Re	11:2	the court w. is without the temple,	3588
Re	11:8	w. spiritually is called Sodom and	3748
Re	11:11	fear fell upon them w. saw them.	
Re	11:16	w. sat before God on their seats,	3588
Re	11:17	w. art, and wast, and art to come:	3588
Re	11:18	destroy them w. destroy the earth.	
Re	12:4	w. was ready to be delivered,	3588
Re	12:9	w. deceiveth the whole world:	3588
Re	12:10	w. accused them before our God	3588
Re	12:13	w. brought forth the man child	3748
Re	12:16	the flood w. the dragon cast out	3739
Re	12:17	w. keep the commandments of	3588
Re	13:2	beast w. I saw was like unto a	3739
Re	13:4	dragon w. gave power unto the	3739
Re	13:12	and them w. dwell therein to worship	
Re	13:14	miracles w. he had power to do	3739
Re	13:14	w. had the wound by a sword	3739
Re	14:3	w. were redeemed from the earth	3588
Re	14:4	These are they w. are not defiled	3739
Re	14:4	are they w. follow the Lamb	3588
Re	14:10	w. is poured out without mixture	3588
Re	14:13	the dead w. die in the Lord from	3588
Re	14:17	out of the temple w. is in heaven,	3588
Re	14:18	from the altar w. had power over fire,	
Re	16:2	w. had the mark of the beast,	3588
Re	16:2	upon them w. worshipped his image	
Re	16:5	O Lord, w. art, and wast, and	3588
Re	16:9	w. hath power over these plagues:	3588
Re	16:14	w. go forth unto the kings of the	
Re	17:1	seven angels w. had the seven	3588
Re	17:7	w. hath the seven heads and ten	3588
Re	17:9	here is the mind w. hath wisdom.	3588
Re	17:9	on w. the woman sitteth.	3699,846
Re	17:12	ten horns w. thou sawest are	3739
Re	17:12	w. have received no kingdom as	3748
Re	17:15	The waters w. thou sawest, where	3739
Re	17:16	ten horns w. thou sawest upon	3739
Re	17:18	woman w. thou sawest is that	3739
Re	17:18	w. reigneth over the kings of the	3588
Re	18:6	in the cup w. she hath filled fill	3739
Re	18:14	things w. were dainty and godly	3588
Re	18:15	w. were made rich by her, shall	3588
Re	19:2	w. did corrupt the earth with her	3748
Re	19:9	they w. are called unto the marriage	
Re	19:14	And the armies w. were in heaven	3588
Re	19:20	with w. he deceived them that	3739
Re	19:21	w. sword proceeded out of his	3588
Re	20:2	that old serpent, w. is the Devil,	3739
Re	20:4	w. had not worshipped the beast,	3748

Re 20:8 nations w. are in the four quarters *3588*
Re 20:12 opened, w. is the book of life: *3739*
Re 20:12 those things w. were written in the ....
Re 20:13 gave up, the dead w. were in it; *3588*
Re 20:13 up the dead w. were in them: *3588*
Re 21:8 in the lake w. burneth with fire.......... *3739*
Re 21:8 brimstone: w. is the second death....... *3739*
Re 21:9 seven angels w. had the seven *3588*
Re 21:12 w. are the names of the twelve *3739*
Re 21:24 them w. are saved shall walk in the..........
Re 21:27 w. are written in the Lamb's book of.........
Re 22:2 life, w. bare twelve manner of fruits, ...
Re 22:6 the things w. must shortly be done...... *3739*
Re 22:8 angel, w. shewed me these things...... *3588*
Re 22:9 w. keep the sayings of this book: ....
Re 22:11 and he w. is filthy, let him be filthy ....
Re 22:19 the things w. are written in this book.........
Re 22:20 He w. testifieth these things saith, ...

WHILE See also WHILES; WHILST.

Ge 8:22 W. the earth remaineth, seedtime 5750
Ge 19:16 w. he lingered, the men laid hold upon......
Ge 25:6 from Isaac his son, w. he yet lived,..........
Ge 29:9 w. he yet spake with them, Rachel...........
Ge 45:1 w. Joseph made himself known unto..........
Ge 46:29 and wept on his neck a good w.......... 5750
Ex 33:22 w. my glory passeth by, that I will..... 5704
Ex 33:22 thee with my hand w. I pass by:........ 5704
Ex 34:29 his face shone w. he talked with him.........
Le 4:27 ignorance, w. he doeth somewhat.............
Le 14:46 the house all the w. that is shut up...........
Le 26:43 w. she lieth desolate without them: ....
Nu 11:33 w. the flesh was yet between their..........
Nu 15:32 w. the children of Israel were in the ....
Nu 23:15 offering, w. I meet the Lord yonder. ....
Nu 25:11 w. he was zealous for my sake among.......
De 19:6 pursue the slayer, w. his heart is....... 3588
De 31:27 w. I am yet alive with you this day,..........
Jos 14:10 w. the children of Israel wandered....... 834
Jg 3:26 And Ehud escaped w. they tarried,...... 5704
Jg 11:26 W. Israel dwelt in Heshbon and her..........
Jg 14:17 seven days, w. their feast lasted; ....
Jg 15:1 a w. after, in the time of the wheat..........
Jg 16:27 that beheld w. Samson made sport. ....
1Sa 2:13 came w. the flesh was in seething, ...
1Sa 7:2 to pass, w. the ark abode in.............. 3117
1Sa 9:27 but stand thou still a w., that I.......... 3117
1Sa 14:19 w. Saul talked unto the priest,........... 5704
1Sa 20:14 w. yet I live shew me the kindness...... 518
1Sa 22:4 the w. that David was in the hold....... 3117
1Sa 25:7 all the w. they were in Carmel. 3117
1Sa 25:16 w. we were with them keeping the...... 3117
1Sa 27:11 the w. he dwelleth in the country....... 3117
2Sa 3:6 w. there was war between the house........
2Sa 3:35 David to eat meat w. it was yet day, ...
2Sa 7:19 house for a great w. to come. 7350
2Sa 12:18 w. the child was yet alive, I fasted...........
2Sa 12:21 weep for the child, w. it was alive;..........
2Sa 12:22 W. the child was yet alive, I fasted..........
2Sa 13:30 w. they were in the way, that tidings.........
2Sa 15:8 vow w. I abode at Geshur in Syria, ...
2Sa 15:12 from Giloh, w. he offered sacrifices. ....
2Sa 17:2 upon him w. he is weary and weak............
2Sa 18:14 w. he was yet alive in the midst of..... 5750
2Sa 19:32 sustenance w. he lay at Mahanaim;...........
2Sa 24:13 thine enemies, w. they pursue thee?.........
1Ki 1:14 w. thou yet talkest there with the...........
1Ki 1:22 lo, w. she yet talked with the king, ...
2Sa 1:42 w. he yet spake, behold, Jonathan.............
1Ki 3:20 beside me, w. thine handmaid slept, ...
1Ki 6:7 in the house, w. it was in building. ....
1Ki 12:6 Solomon his father w. he yet lived,...........
1Ki 17:7 after a w., that the brook dried 3117
1Ki 18:45 the mean w., that the heaven was...... 3541
2Ki 6:33 And w. he yet talked with them,..............
1Ch 12:1 Ziklag, w. he yet kept himself close..........
1Ch 17:17 servant's house for a great w. to come,.....
1Ch 21:12 w. that the sword of thine enemies...........
2Ch 10:6 Solomon his father w. he yet lived,...........
2Ch 14:7 bars, w. the land is yet before us;............
2Ch 15:2 Lord is with you, w. ye be with him; ....
2Ch 26:19 w. he was wroth with the priests, the.......
2Ch 34:3 w. he was yet young, he began to...........
Ne 7:3 w. they stand by, let them shut......... 5704
Es 2:21 w. Mordecai sat in the king's gate, two.....
Es 6:14 w. they were yet talking with him, ...
Job 1:16, 17,18 W. he was yet speaking,.................
Job 20:23 shall rain it upon him w. he is eating.........
Job 24:24 They are exalted for a little w., but..........
Job 27:3 All the w. my breath is in me,............ 5750
Ps 7:2 in pieces, w. there is none to deliver. ....
Ps 31:13 w. they took counsel together against ....
Ps 37:10 yet a little w., and the wicked shall...........
Ps 39:1 bridle, w. the wicked is before me. 5750
Ps 39:3 me, w. I was musing the fire burned: ....
Ps 42:3 w. they continually say unto me, ...
Ps 42:10 w. they say daily unto me, Where is.........
Ps 49:18 Though w. he lived he blest his soul: ....
Ps 63:4 Thus will I bless thee w. I live: I will........
Ps 69:3 mine eyes fail w. I wait for my God..........
Ps 78:30 w. their meat was yet in their ....
Ps 88:15 w. I suffer thy terrors I am distracted.......
Ps 104:33 to my God w. I have my being. 5750
Ps 146:2 W. I live will I praise the Lord: I.............
Ps 146:2 unto my God w. I have any being. 5750
Pr 8:26 W. as yet he had not made the...............
Pr 19:18 Chasten thy son w. there is hope,...... 3588
Pr 31:15 She riseth also w. it is yet night, ...
Ec 9:3 madness is in their heart w. they live,.......
Ec 12:1 w. the evil days come not, nor the..... 5704
Ec 12:2 W. the sun or the light or the 5704
Ca 1:12 W. the king sitteth at his table, ... 5704
Isa 10:25 For yet a very little w., and the..............
Isa 28:4 w. it is yet in his hand he eateth it..........
Isa 29:17 Is it not yet a very little w., and.............
Isa 55:6 Seek ye the Lord w. he may be found, ...
Isa 55:6 call ye upon him w. he is near: ....
Isa 63:18 have possessed it but a little w.:........ 4705
Isa 65:24 w. they are yet speaking, I will...............
Jer 13:16 w. ye look for light, he turn it into the......
Jer 15:9 is gone down w. it was yet day: ....
Jer 33:1 w. he was yet shut up in the court...........
Jer 39:15 w. he was shut up in the court of the ....
Jer 40:5 now w. he was not yet gone back, ...
Jer 51:33 yet a little w., and the time of her...........
La 1:19 w. they sought their meat to............ 3588
Eze 9:8 to pass, w. they were slaying them, ...
Da 4:31 W. the word was in the king's........... 5751
Ho 1:4 for yet a little w., and I will avenge..........
Na 1:10 For w. they be folden together as...... 5704
Na 1:10 w. they are drunken as drunkards, ...
Hag 2:6 it is a little w., and I will shake the ....
Zec 14:12 away w. they stand upon their feet,..........
Mt 1:20 But w. he thought on these things,...........
Mt 9:18 W. he spake these things unto them, ...
Mt 12:46 W. he yet talked to the people, ...
Mt 13:21 **in himself, but dureth for a w.**...... *4340*
Mt 13:25 **w. men slept his enemy came.**.*1722,3588*
Mt 13:29 **Nay; lest w. ye gather up the tares,**.......
Mt 14:22 w. he sent the multitudes away. *2193*
Mt 17:5 W. he yet spake, behold, a bright ....
Mt 17:22 And w. they abode in Galilee, Jesus..........
Mt 22:41 W. the Pharisees were gathered ....
Mt 25:5 **W. the bridegroom tarried they all**......
Mt 25:10 **w. they went to buy, the bridegroom**...
Mt 26:36 **ye here, w. I go and pray yonder**... *2193*
Mt 26:47 w. he yet spake, lo, Judas, one of the.......
Mt 26:73 after a w. came unto him they that..... *3397*
Mt 27:63 deceiver said, w. he was yet alive, ...
Mt 28:13 and stole him away w. we slept. ....
Mk 1:35 rising up a great w. before day, he...........
Mk 2:19 **w. the bridgroom is with**....... *1722,3739*
Mk 5:35 W. he yet spake, there came from the......
Mk 6:31 **a desert place, and a rest a w.:**..... *3641*
Mk 6:45 w. he sent away the people. *2193*
Mk 12:35 and said, w. he taught in the temple, ...
Mk 14:32 **Sit ye here, w. I shall pray**........... *2193*
Mk 14:43 w. he yet spake cometh Judas, one of.......
Mk 15:44 whether he had been any w. dead. *3819*
Lu 1:8 w. he executed...priest's office ... *1722,3588*
Lu 2:6 w. they were there, the days were ....
Lu 5:34 **w. the bridegroom is with**...... *1722,3739*
Lu 8:13 **for a w. believe, and in time of**..... *2540*
Lu 8:49 W. he yet spake, there come one ....
Lu 9:34 W. he thus spake, there came a cloud,......
Lu 9:43 w. they wondered every one at all............
Lu 10:13 **they had a great w. ago repented,** ....
Lu 14:32 **w. the other is yet a great way**............
Lu 18:4 **And he would not for a w.: but**..... *5550*
Lu 22:47 w. he yet spake, behold a multitude,.........
Lu 22:58 And after a little w. another saw him, ...
Lu 22:60 w. he yet spake, the cock crew. ....
Lu 24:15 w. they communed together....... *1722,3588*
Lu 24:32 w. he talked with us by the way, ... *5613*
Lu 24:32 w. he opened to us the scriptures?..... *5613*
Lu 24:41 w. they yet believed not for joy, and ....
Lu 24:44 **w. I was yet with you, that all**.........
Lu 24:51 w. he blessed them, he was....... *1722,3588*
Joh 4:31 mean w. his disciples prayed him, ...
Joh 5:7 but w. I am coming, another...... *1722,3739*
Joh 7:33 **Yet a little w. am I with you,**....... *5550*
Joh 9:4 **of him that sent me, w. it is day:**.. *2193*
Joh 12:35 **Yet a little w. is the light with**..... *5550*
Joh 12:35 **w. ye have the light, lest**............ *2193*
Joh 12:36 **W. ye have light, believe in the**..... *2193*
Joh 13:33 **children, yet a little w. I am with**.......
Joh 14:19 **Yet a little w., and the world seeth**.....
Joh 16:16 **A little w., and ye shall not see me:**....
Joh 16:16 **again, a little w., and ye shall see**.......
Joh 16:17 A little w., and ye shall not see me: ....
Joh 16:17 again, a little w., and ye shall see me: .....,
Joh 16:18 What is this that he saith, A little w.? ......,
Joh 16:19 **A little w., and ye shall not see me:**....
Joh 16:19 **again, a little w., and ye shall see**.......
Joh 17:12 **W. I was with them in the world,**.. *3153*
Ac 1:9 w. they beheld, he was taken up;............
Ac 1:10 w. they looked stedfastly toward........ *5613*
Ac 9:39 Dorcas made, w. she was with them..........
Ac 10:10 but w. they made ready, he fell into a.......
Ac 10:17 w. Peter doubted in himself what....... *5613*
Ac 10:19 W. Peter thought on the vision, the..........
Ac 10:44 W. Peter yet spake these words, the........
Ac 15:7 that a good w. ago God made............ *2250*
Ac 17:16 w. Paul waited for them at Athens, ...
Ac 18:18 this tarried there yet a good w., ... *2250*
Ac 19:1 w. Apollos was at Corinth,......... *1722,3588*
Ac 20:11 talked a long w., even till break of............
Ac 22:17 w. I prayed in the temple, I was in a.........
Ac 24:20 in me, w. I stood before the council, ...
Ac 25:8 W. he answered for himself, neither ....
Ac 27:33 w. the day was coming on,.......... *891,3739*
Ac 28:6 but after they had looked a great w., ...
Ro 2:15 their thoughts the mean w. accusing ....
Ro 5:8 w. we were yet sinners, Christ died for ....
Ro 7:3 So then if, w. her husband liveth, she ....
1Co 3:4 For w. one saith, I am of Paul:.......... *3752*
1Co 8:13 eat no flesh w. the world standeth,............
1Co 16:7 I trust to tarry a w. with you, ... *5550,5099*
2Co 4:18 W. we look not at the things which ....
Ga 2:17 w. we seek to be justified by Christ, ...
1Ti 5:6 in pleasure is dead w. she liveth. ....
1Ti 6:10 which w. some coveted after, they ....
Heb 3:13 daily, w. it is called To day; *891,3739*
Heb 3:15 W. it is said, To day if ye will.... *1722,3588*
Heb 9:8 w. as the first tabernacle was yet.............
Heb 9:17 at all w. the testator liveth................ *3753*
Heb 10:37 For yet a little w., and he that *3397*
1Pe 3:2 W. they behold your chaste ....
1Pe 3:20 w. the ark was preparing, wherein ....
1Pe 5:10 after that ye have suffered a w., ... *3641*
2Pe 2:13 deceivings w. they feast with you;.............
2Pe 2:19 W. they promise them liberty, they...........

WHILES See also WHILE; WHILST.

Eze 21:29 W. they see vanity unto thee, ...
Eze 21:29 w. they divine a lie unto thee, ...
Eze 44:17 w. they minister in the gates of the..........
Da 5:2 Belshazzar, w. he tasted the wine, ...
Da 9:20 w. I was speaking and praying, ... 5750
Da 9:21 Yea, w. I was speaking in prayer, ... 5750
Ho 7:6 like an oven, w. they lie in wait: ....
Mt 5:25 **w. thou art in the way with**... *2193,3755*
Ac 5:4 W. it remained, was it not thine own?.......
2Co 9:13 W. by the experiment of this....................

WHILST See also WHILE.

Jg 6:31 put to death w. it is yet morning:........ 5704
Ne 6:3 the work cease, w. I leave it, ... 834
Job 8:12 W. it is yet in his greenness, and not ....
Job 32:11 w. ye searched out what to say. 5704
Ps 141:10 own nets, w. that I withal escape....... 5704
Jer 17:2 W. their children remember their ....
2Co 5:6 w. we are at home in the body, we are.....
2Co 7:15 w. he remembereth the obedience..............
Heb 10:33 w. ye were made a gazingstock both.........
Heb 10:33 w. ye became companions of them ....

WHIP See also WHIPS.

Pr 26:3 A w. for the horse, a bridle for the 7752
Na 3:2 The noise of a w., and the noise of 7752

WHIPS

1Ki 12:11 father hath chastised you with w., ... 7752

1Ki 12:14 father also chastised you with w. 7752
2Ch 10:11, 14 my father chastised you with w., 7752

WHIRLETH

Ec 1:6 it w. about continually, and 1980

WHIRLWIND See also WHIRLWINDS.

2Ki 2:1 up Elijah into heaven by a w., 5591
2Ki 2:11 Elijah went up by a w. into heaven. 5591
Job 37:9 Out of the south cometh the w. 5492
Job 38:1 Lord answered Job out of the w., 5591
Job 40:6 the Lord unto Job out of the w., 5591
Ps 58:9 shall take them away as with a w., 8175
Pr 1:27 your destruction cometh as a w.; 5492
Pr 10:25 As the w. passeth, so is the wicked 5492
Isa 5:28 flint, and their wheels like a w. 5492
Isa 17:13 like a rolling thing before the w. 5492
Isa 40:24 the w. shall take them away as 5591
Isa 41:16 and the w. shall scatter them: 5591
Isa 66:15 and with his chariots like a w., 5492
Jer 4:13 and his chariots shall be as a w. 5492
Jer 23:19 a w. of the Lord is gone forth in 5591
Jer 23:19 forth in fury, even a grievous w. 5591
Jer 25:32 great w. shall be raised up from 5591
Jer 30:23 w. of the Lord goeth forth with fury, 5591
Jer 30:23 forth with fury, a continuing w. 5591
Eze 1:4 a w. came out of the north, a 7307,5591
Da 11:40 shall come against him like a w., 8175
Ho 8:7 wind, and they shall reap the w. 5492
Ho 13:3 chaff that is driven with the w. 5590
Am 1:14 a tempest in the day of the w. 5492
Na 1:3 the Lord hath his way in the w. 5492
Hab 3:14 came out as a w. to scatter me: 5590
Zec 7:14 But I scattered them with a w. 5590

WHIRLWINDS

Isa 21:1 As w. in the south pass through; 5492
Zec 9:14 and shall go with w. of the south. 5591

WHISPER See also WHISPERED; WHISPERINGS.

Ps 41:7 All that hate me w. together 3907
Isa 29:4 and thy speech shall w. out of the 6850

WHISPERED

2Sa 12:19 David saw that his servants w., 3907

WHISPERER See also WHISPERERS.

Pr 16:28 and a w. separateth chief friends. 5372

WHISPERERS

Ro 1:29 debate, deceit, malignity; w., *5588*

WHISPERINGS

2Co 12:20 w., swellings, tumults: *5587*

WHIT

De 13:16 and all the spoil thereof every w., 3632
1Sa 3:18 And Samuel told him every w., 1697
Joh 7:23 **I have made a man every w.** *3650*
Joh 13:10 **his feet, but is clean every w.:** *3650*
Co 11:5 not a w. behind the very chiefest *3367*

WHITE See also WHITED; WHITER.

Ge 30:35 every one that had some w. in it, 3836
Ge 30:37 and pilled w. strakes in them, and 3836
Ge 30:37 w. appear which was in the rods. 3836
Ge 40:16 had three w. baskets on my head: 2751
Ge 49:12 wine, and his teeth w. with milk. 3836
Ex 16:31 and it was like coriander seed, w.; 3836
Le 13:3 the hair in the plague is turned w., 3836
Le 13:4 If the bright spot be w. in the skin 3836
Le 13:4 the hair thereof be not turned w.; 3836
Le 13:10 if the rising be w. in the skin, 3836
Le 13:10 and it have turned the hair w., and 3836
Le 13:13 hath the plague: it is all turned w.: 3836
Le 13:16 again, and be changed unto w. 3836
Le 13:17 if the plague be turned into w.: 3836
Le 13:19 place of boil there be a w. rising, 3836
Le 13:19 or a bright spot, w., and somewhat 3836
Le 13:20 and the hair thereof be turned w.; 3836
Le 13:21 there be no w. hairs therein, and 3836
Le 13:24 that burneth have a w. bright spot, 3836
Le 13:24 spot, somewhat reddish, or w.; 3836
Le 13:25 in the bright spot be turned w., 3836
Le 13:26 there be no w. hair in the bright 3836
Le 13:38 bright spots, even w. bright spots; 3836
Le 13:39 skin of their flesh be darkish w.; 3836
Le 13:42 or bald forehead, a w. reddish sore; 3836
Le 13:43 rising of the sore be w. reddish in 3836
Nu 12:10 Miriam became leprous, w. as snow:
Jg 5:10 Speak, ye that ride on w. asses, 6715
2Ki 5:27 his presence a leper as w. as snow.
2Ch 5:12 brethren, being arrayed in w. linen,
Es 1:6 Where were w., green, and blue, 2353
Es 1:6 and blue, and w., and black, marble 1858
Es 8:15 king in royal apparel of blue and w., 2353
Job 6:6 any taste in the w. of an egg? 7388
Ps 68:14 in it, it was w. as snow in Salmon.
Ec 9:8 Let thy garments be always w.; 3836
Ca 5:10 My beloved is w. and ruddy, the 6703
Isa 1:18 they shall be as w. as snow; 3835
Eze 27:18 the wine of Helbon, and w. wool. 6713
Da 7:9 whose garment was w. as snow, and
Da 11:35 to purge, and to make them w., 3835
Da 12:10 shall be purified, and made w., and 3835
Joe 1:7 the branches thereof are made w. 3835
Zec 1:8 there red horses, speckled, and w. 3836
Zec 6:3 And in the third chariot w. horses; 3836
Zec 6:6 and the w. go forth after them; 3836
Mt 5:36 **not make one hair w. or black.** *3022*
Mt 17:2 his raiment was w. as the light. *3022*
Mt 28:3 and his raiment w. as snow: *3022*
Mk 9:3 shining, exceeding w. as snow; *3022*
Mk 9:3 as no fuller on earth can w. them. *3021*
Mk 16:5 side, clothed in a long w. garment; *3022*
Lu 9:29 his raiment was w. and glistering. *3022*
Joh 4:35 **for they are w. already to harvest.** *3022*
Joh 20:12 And seeth two angels in w. sitting, *3022*
Ac 1:10 two men stood by them in w. *3022*
Re 1:14 His head and his hairs were w. like *3022*
Re 1:14 as w. as snow; and his eyes were as *3022*
Re 2:17 **will give him a w. stone, and in** *3022*
Re 3:4 **they shall walk with me in w.:** *3022*
Re 3:5 **shall be clothed in w. raiment;** *3022*
Re 3:18 **w. raiment, that thou mayest be** *3022*
Re 4:4 sitting, clothed in w. raiment; and *3022*
Re 6:2 And I saw, and behold a w. horse: *3022*
Re 6:11 w. robes were given unto every one *3022*
Re 7:9 clothed with w. robes, and palms *3022*
Re 7:13 which are arrayed in w. robes? *3022*
Re 7:14 make them w. in the blood of the *3021*
Re 14:14 I looked, and behold a w. cloud, *3022*
Re 15:6 clothed in pure and w. linen, *2986*
Re 19:8 arrayed in fine linen, clean and w.: *2986*
Re 19:11 opened and behold a w. horse; *3022*
Re 19:14 followed him upon w. horses, *3022*
Re 19:14 clothed in fine linen, w. and clean. *3022*
Re 20:11 I saw a great w. throne, and him *3022*

WHITED

Mt 23:27 **for ye are like unto w. sepulchres,** *2867*
Ac 23:3 God shall smite thee, thou w. wall: *2867*

WHITER

Ps 51:7 me, and I shall be w. than snow. 3835
La 4:7 snow, they were w. than milk, 6705

WHITHER See also WHITHERSOEVER.

Ge 16:8 camest thou? and w. wilt thou go? 575
Ge 20:13 every place w. we shall come, 834,8033
Ge 28:15 thee in all places w. thou goest, 834
Ge 32:17 Whoso art thou? and w. goest thou? 575
Ge 37:30 child is not; and I w. shall I go? 575
Ex 21:13 a place w. he shall flee. 834,8033
Ex 34:12 inhabitants of the land w. thou 834,5921
Le 18:3 w. I bring you, shall ye not do: 834,8033
Le 20:22 w. I bring you to dwell therein, 834,8033
Nu 13:27 unto the land w. thou sentest us, 834
Nu 15:18 into the land w. I bring you, 834,8033
Nu 35:25 of his refuge, w. he was fled: 834,8033
Nu 35:26 of his refuge, w. he was fled; 834,8033
De 1:28 W. shall we go up? our brethren 575
De 3:21 unto all the kingdoms w. thou 834,8033
De 4:5 the land w. ye go to possess it. 834,8033
De 4:14 w. ye go over to possess it. 834,8033
De 4:27 w. the Lord shall lead you. 834,8033
De 6:1 the land w. ye go to possess it: 834,8033
De 7:1 land w. thou goest to possess 834,8033
De 11:8 the land, w. ye go to possess it; 834,8033
De 11:10 w. thou goest in to possess it, 834,8033
De 11:11 the land, w. ye go to possess it, 834,8033
De 11:29 land w. thou goest to possess 834,8033
De 12:29 w. thou goest to possess them, 834,8033
De 21:14 then thou shalt let her go w. she will;
De 23:12 w. thou shalt go forth abroad: 8033
De 23:20 land w. thou goest to possess 834,8033
De 28:21 w. thou goest to possess it. 834,8033
De 28:37 nations w. the Lord shall lead 834,8033
De 28:63 land w. thou goest to possess 834,8033
De 30:1,3 w. the Lord thy God hath 834,8033
De 30:16 land w. thou goest to possess 834,8033
De 30:18 w. thou passest over Jordan to 834,8033
De 31:13 w. ye go over Jordan to possess 834,8033
De 31:16 w. they go to be among them, 834,8033
De 32:47 w. ye go over Jordan to possess 834,8033
De 32:50 in the mount w. thou goest up, 834,8033
Jos 2:5 out: w. the men went I wot not: 575
Jg 19:17 W. goest thou? and whence comest 575
Ru 1:16 for w. thou goest, I will go: 413,834
1Sa 10:14 and to his servant, W. went ye? 575
1Sa 27:10 W. have ye made a road to day? 413
2Sa 2:1 And David said, W. shall I go up? 575
2Sa 13:13 w. shall I cause my shame to go? 575
2Sa 15:20 seeing I go w. I may, return 5921,834
2Sa 17:18 in his court; w. they went down. 8033
1Ki 2:36 and go not forth thence any w. 575
1Ki 2:42 out, and walkest abroad any w., 575
1Ki 8:47 the land w. they were carried 834,8033
1Ki 18:10 w. my lord hath not sent to 834,8033
1Ki 18:12 shall carry thee w. I know 5921,834
1Ki 21:18 w. he is gone down to possess 834,8033
2Ki 5:25 he said, Thy servant went no w. 575
2Ch 6:37 the land w. they are carried 834,8033
2Ch 6:38 w. they have carried them captives, 834
2Ch 10:2 w. he had fled from the presence of 834
Ne 2:16 And the rulers knew not w. I went, 575
Ps 122:4 W. the tribes go up, the tribes of 8033
Ps 139:7 W. shall I go from thy spirit? 575
Ps 139:7 or w. shall I flee from thy presence? 575
Ec 9:10 in the grave, w. thou goest. 834,8033
Ca 6:1 W. is thy beloved gone, O thou 575
Ca 6:1 w. is thy beloved turned aside? that 575
Isa 20:6 w. we flee for help to be 834,8033
Jer 8:3 places w. I have driven them, 834,8033
Jer 15:2 unto thee, W. shall we go forth? 575
Jer 16:15 lands w. he had driven them: 834,8033
Jer 19:14 Tophet, w. the Lord had sent him 834
Jer 22:12 the place w. they have led him 834,8033
Jer 23:3 countries w. I have driven them, 834,8033
Jer 23:8 countries w. I had driven them; 834,8033
Jer 24:9 all places w. I shall drive them. 834,8033
Jer 29:7 city w. I have caused you to be 834,8033
Jer 29:14 the places w. I have driven you, 834,8033
Jer 29:18 nations w. I have driven them: 834,8033
Jer 30:11 nations w. I have driven them: 834,8033
Jer 32:37 w. I have driven them in mine 834,8033
Jer 40:4 w. it seemeth good and convenient 413
Jer 40:12 all places w. they were driven, 834,8033
Jer 42:22 in the place w. ye desire to go 834,8033
Jer 43:5 nations, w. they had been driven, 834,8033
Jer 44:8 Egypt, w. ye be gone to dwell, 834,8033
Jer 45:5 in all places w. thou goest. 834,8033
Jer 46:28 nations w. I have driven thee: 834,8033
Jer 49:36 nation w. the outcasts of Elam 834,8033
Eze 1:12 w. the spirit was to go, they 834,8033
Eze 4:13 Gentiles, w. I will drive them. 834,8033
Eze 6:9 nations w. they shall be carried 834,8033
Eze 10:11 to the place w. the head looked 834
Eze 12:16 among the heathen w. they 834,8033
Eze 29:13 people w. they were scattered: 834,8033
Eze 36:20 unto the heathen, w. they went, 834,8033
Eze 36:21, 22 the heathen, w. they went. 834,8033
Eze 37:21 the heathen, w. they be gone, 834,8033
Eze 47:9 live w. the river cometh. 413,834,8033
Da 9:7 w. thou hast driven them, 834,8033
Joe 3:7 the place w. ye have sold them, 834,8033
Zec 2:2 Then said I, W. goest thou? And 575
Zec 5:10 me, W. do these bear the ephah? 575
Lu 10:1 place, w. he himself would come. *3757*
Lu 24:28 nigh unto the village, w. they went: *3757*
Joh 3:8 **whence it cometh, and w. it** *4226*
Joh 6:21 was at the land w. they went. *1519,3739*
Joh 7:35 W. will he go, that we shall not *4226*
Joh 8:14 **I know whence I came, and w. I** *4226*
Joh 8:14 **tell whence I come, and w. I go;** *4226*
Joh 8:21 **sins: w. I go, ye cannot come.** *3699*
Joh 8:22 he saith, W. I go, ye cannot come. *3699*
Joh 12:35 **darkness knoweth not w. he.** *4226*
Joh 13:33 **Jews, W. I go, ye cannot come;** *3699*
Joh 13:36 said unto him, Lord, w. goest thou? *4226*
Joh 13:36 **W. I go, thou canst not follow me.** *3699*
Joh 14:4 **w. I go ye know, and the way ye** *3699*
Joh 14:5 we know not w. thou goest; and *4226*
Joh 16:5 **of you asketh me, W. goest thou?** *4226*
Joh 18:20 **temple, w. the Jews always** *3699*

Joh 21:18 **and walkedst w. thou wouldest:** *3699*
Joh 21:18 **carry thee w. thou wouldest not** *3699*
Heb 6:20 W. the forerunner is...entered, ... *3699*
Heb 11:8 went out, not knowing w. he went. *4226*
1Jo 2:11 and knoweth not w. he goeth, ... *4226*

WHITHERSOEVER
Jos 1:7 mayest prosper w. thou goest...... 3605,834
Jos 1:9 God is with thee w. thou goest. ... 3605,834
Jos 1:16 w. thou sendest us, we will ... 413,3605,834
Jg 2:15 W. they went out, the hand of..... 3605,834
1Sa 14:47 w. he turned himself, he vexed.... 3605,834
1Sa 18:5 David went out w. Saul sent him, ..3605,834
1Sa 23:13 Keilah, and went w. they could go. 834
2Sa 7:9 was with thee w. thou wentest, ... 3605,834
2Sa 8:6, 14 preserved David w. he went.... 3605,834
1Ki 2:3 w. thou turnest thyself: 3605,834,8033
1Ki 8:44 w. thou shalt send them, ... 1870,834
2Ki 18:7 he prospered w. he went forth:.... 3605,834
1Ch 17:8 with thee w. thou hast walked, ... 3605,834
1Ch 18:6, 13 preserved David w. he went.... 3605,834
Es 4:3 w. the king's commandment......... 4725,834
Es 8:17 w. the king's commandment and... 4725,834
Pr 17:8 w. it turneth, it prospereth. ... 413,3605,834
Pr 21:1 he turneth it w. he will........ 5921,3605,834
Eze 1:20 W. the spirit was to go, ... 5921,834,8033
Eze 21:16 or on the left, w. thy face is set........... 575
Eze 47:9 w. the rivers...come, ... 413,3605,834,8033
Mt 8:19 will follow thee w. thou goest..... *3699,1437*
Mk 6:56 And w. he entered, into *3699,302*
Lu 9:57 I will follow thee w. thou goest. ... *3699,302*
1Co 16:6 me on my journey w. I go......... *3757,1437*
Jas 3:4 helm, w. the governor listeth,...... *3699,302*
Re 14:4 follow the Lamb w. he goeth. *3699,302*

WHO See also WHICH; WHOM; WHOSE; WHOSOEVER.
Ge 3:11 W. told thee that thou wast.............. 4310
Ge 12:7 unto the Lord, w. appeared unto him. ....
Ge 14:12 brother's son, w. dwelt in Sodom,...... 1931
Ge 21:7 W. would have said unto 4310
Ge 21:26 I wot not w. hath done this thing: 4310
Ge 24:15 w. was born to Bethuel, son of........... 834
Ge 24:27 w. hath left destitute my master.......... 834
Ge 27:18 Here am I; w. art thou, my son? 4310
Ge 27:32 said unto him, W. art thou? 4310
Ge 27:33 Isaac trembled...and said, W.?........... 4310
Ge 30:2 w. hath withheld from thee the 834
Ge 33:5 and said, W. are those with thee?...... 4310
Ge 35:3 w. answered me in the day of my ....
Ge 36:1 generations of Esau, w. is Edom........ 1931
Ge 36:19 are the sons of Esau, w. is Edom, ...
Ge 36:20 Seir, the Horite, w. inhabited the land;......
Ge 36:35 w. smote Midian in the field of Moab, ...
Ge 42:30 The man, w. is the lord of the land, ...
Ge 43:22 tell w. put our money in our sacks. 4310
Ge 48:8 sons, and said, W. are these? 4310
Ge 48:14 Ephraim's head, w. was...younger, ... 1931
Ge 49:9 old lion, w. shall rouse him up?.......... 4310
Ge 49:25 God of thy father, w. shall help thee..........
Ge 49:25 w. shall bless thee with blessings of..........
Ex 2:14 W. made thee a prince and a judge..... 4310
Ex 3:11 And Moses said unto God, W. am I,.... 4310
Ex 4:11 him, w. hath made man's mouth? 4310
Ex 4:11 or w. maketh the dumb, or deaf, or.... 4310
Ex 4:28 words of the Lord w. had sent him, ... 834
Ex 5:2 and Pharaoh said, W. is the Lord,...... 4310
Ex 5:20 Moses and Aaron, w. stood in the way,.....
Ex 6:12 me, w. am of uncircumcised lips?......... 589
Ex 10:8 God: but w. are they that shall go? 4310
Ex 12:27 w. passed over the houses of............. 834
Ex 12:40 of Israel w. dwelt in Egypt, was.......... 834
Ex 15:11 W. is like unto thee, O Lord,............ 4310
Ex 15:11 w. is like thee, glorious in holiness, ... 4310
Ex 18:10 w. hath delivered you out of the.......... 834
Ex 18:10 w. hath delivered the people from........ 834
Ex 21:8 w. hath betrothed her to himself,.......... 834
Ex 32:26 said, W. is on the Lord's side? 4310
Le 5:8 w. shall offer that which is for the sin ....
Le 12:7 W. shall offer it before the Lord, and.........
Le 27:12 as thou valuest it, w. art the priest, ...
Nu 6:21 law of the Nazarite w. hath vowed,...... 834
Nu 7:2 w. were the princes of the tribes, ... 1992
Nu 9:6 w. were defiled by the dead body of...... 834
Nu 11:4 said, W. shall give us flesh to eat? 4310
Nu 11:18 saying, W. shall give us flesh to eat? .. 4310
Nu 12:7 so, w. is faithful in all mine house. 1931
Nu 14:36 w. returned, and made all the..................
Nu 16:5 the Lord will shew w. are his,....... 853,834
Nu 16:5 and w. is holy; and will cause him........ 853
Nu 21:26 w. had fought against the former......... 1931
Nu 23:10 W. can count the dust of Jacob,........ 4310
Nu 24:9 as a great lion: w. shall stir him up? ... 4310
Nu 24:23 w. shall live when God doeth this!...... 4310
Nu 25:6 w. were weeping before the door....... 1992
Nu 26:9 w. strove against Moses and against..... 834
Nu 26:47 w. were fifty and three thousand and ....
Nu 26:63 w. numbered the children of Israel....... 834
Nu 27:21 w. shall ask council for him after the.........
Nu 31:27 was upon them, w. went out to battle, ...
De 1:33 W. went in the way before you, to...........
De 2:25 w. shall hear report of thee and 834
De 4:7 w. hath God so nigh unto them, ... 834
De 4:46 the Amorites, w. dwelt at Heshbon, ... 834
De 5:3 w. are all of us here alive this day. 428
De 5:26 w. is thee of all flesh, that hath 4310
De 8:15 W. led thee through that great and...........
De 8:15 w. brought thee forth water out of the ......
De 8:16 W. fed thee in the wilderness with ....
De 9:2 W. can stand before the children........ 4310
De 21:1 it be not known w. had slain him:....... 4310
De 30:12 W. shall go up for us to heaven, ... 4310
De 30:13 W. shall go over the sea for us, ... 4310
De 33:9 W. said unto his father and to his............
De 33:26 w. rideth upon the heaven in thy help, ...
De 33:29 w. is like unto thee. O people 4310
De 33:29 w. is the sword of thy excellency? 834
Jos 9:8 W. are ye? and from whence 4310
Jos 11:8 the hand of Israel, w. smote them,...........
Jos 12:2 of the Amorites, w. dwelt in Heshbon, ...
Jos 13:12 w. remained of the remnant of the 1931
Jos 15:19 W. answered, Give me a blessing; ....
Jos 17:16 they w. are of Beth-shean and her....... 834
Jos 17:16 they w. are of the valley of Jezreel. 834
Jos 21:10 w. were of the children of Levi, had: ....
Jg 1:1 W. shall go up for us against the......... 4310
Jg 2:7 w. had seen all the great works of....... 834
Jg 3:9 up a deliverer..w. delivered them, ...
Jg 3:19 thee, O King: w. said, Keep silence. ....
Jg 6:29 another, W. hath done this thing?....... 4310
Jg 6:35 w. also was gathered after him: ....
Jg 7:1 Then Jerubbaal, w. is Gideon, and...... 1931
Jg 8:34 w. had delivered them out of the hands .....
Jg 9:28 Gaal...said, W. is Abimelech, and....... 4310
Jg 9:28 w. is Shechem, that we shall............ 4310
Jg 9:38 W. is Abimelech, that we should......... 4310
Jg 11:39 w. did with her according to his vow.........
Jg 15:6 said, W. hath done this?.................... 4310
Jg 17:4 w. made thereof a graven image and a ......
Jg 17:5 one of his sons, w. became his priest..........
Jg 17:7 a young man...w. was a Levite,.......... 1931
Jg 18:2 w. when they came to mount ....
Jg 18:3 him, W. brought thee hither? 4310
Jg 18:29 father, w. was born unto Israel: 834
Jg 19:1 w. took to him a concubine out of ....
Jg 21:5 W. is there among all the tribes.......... 4310
Ru 2:3 w. was of the kindred of Elimelech. 834
Ru 2:20 w. hath not left off his kindness to....... 834
Ru 3:9 And he said, W. art thou? And.......... 4310
Ru 3:16 said, W. art thou, my daughter? 4310
1Sa 2:25 the Lord, w. shall intreat for him?...... 4310
1Sa 4:8 w. shall deliver us out of the hand...... 4310
1Sa 6:20 W. is able to stand before this holy 4310
1Sa 10:12 and said, But w. is their father?......... 4310
1Sa 10:19 w. himself saved you out of all........... 834
1Sa 11:12 W. is he that said, Shall Saul............. 4310
1Sa 14:17 now and see w. is gone from us. 4310
1Sa 14:45 w. hath wrought this great 834
1Sa 16:16 man, w. is a cunning player on an harp:.....
1Sa 17:25 be, that the man w. killeth him, ... 834
1Sa 17:26 for w. is this uncircumcised............. 4310
1Sa 18:18 David said unto Saul, W. am I?.......... 4310
1Sa 20:10 to Jonathan, W. shall tell me?........... 4310
1Sa 22:14 w. is so faithful among all thy............ 4310
1Sa 23:22 is, and w. hath seen him there: 4310
1Sa 25:10 W. is David? and w. is the son of........ 4310
1Sa 26:6 W. will go down with me to Saul to.... 4310
1Sa 26:9 for w. can stretch forth his hand........ 4310
1Sa 26:14 W. art thou that criest to the king? 4310
1Sa 26:15 and w. is like to thee in Israel?.......... 4310
1Sa 30:23 w. hath preserved us, and delivered ....
1Sa 30:24 w. will hearken unto you in this......... 4310
2Sa 1:8 And he said unto me, W. art thou?..... 4310
2Sa 1:24 w. clothed you in scarlet, with other.........
2Sa 1:24 w. put on ornaments of gold....................
2Sa 4:5 Ish-bosheth, w. lay on a bed at.......... 1931
2Sa 4:9 w. hath redeemed my soul out of 834
2Sa 4:10 w. thought that I would have given 834
2Sa 6:20 w. uncovered himself to day in the....... 834
2Sa 7:18 W. am I, O Lord God? and what is 4310
2Sa 10:18 the captain of their host, w. died there,.....
2Sa 11:21 W. smote Abimelech the son of......... 4310
2Sa 12:22 W. can tell whether God will be......... 4310
2Sa 16:10 W. shall then say, Wherefore hast....... 4310
2Sa 22:4 the Lord, w. is worthy to be praised: ....
2Sa 22:32 For w. is God, save the Lord? 4310
2Sa 22:32 and w. is a rock, save our God? ....
2Sa 23:1 and the man w. was raised up on high,......
2Sa 23:20 Benaiah...w. had done many acts, ...
1Ki 1:20, 27 w. shall sit on the throne of.......... 4310
1Ki 2:24 and w. hath made me an house, ... 834
1Ki 2:32 w. fell upon two men more................. 834
1Ki 3:9 for w. is able to judge this thy so....... 4310
1Ki 8:23 w. keepest covenant and mercy with.........
1Ki 8:24 W. hast kept with thy servant............. 834
1Ki 8:50 before them w. carried them captive, ...
1Ki 9:9 w. brought forth their fathers out 834
1Ki 12:2 Jeroboam...w. was yet in Egypt, ... 1931
1Ki 12:9 w. have spoken to me, saying,............ 834
1Ki 12:18 Adoram, w. was over the tribute:........ 834
1Ki 13:26 w. was disobedient unto the word of 834
1Ki 14:8 David, w. kept my commandments,...... 834
1Ki 14:8 w. followed me with all his heart, to..... 834
1Ki 14:14 w. shall cut off the house of 834
1Ki 14:16 w. did sin, and w. made Israel to 834
1Ki 17:1 w. was of the inhabitants of Gilead, ...
1Ki 19:19 w. was plowing with twelve yoke 1931
1Ki 20:14 he said, W. shall order the battle?...... 4310
1Ki 21:11 the nobles w. were the inhabitants....... 834
1Ki 22:20 W. shall persuade Ahab, that he 4310
1Ki 22:52 of Nebat, w. made Israel to sin:........... 834
2Ki 4:5 w. brought the vessels to her;........... 1992
2Ki 7:17 w. spake when the king came 834
2Ki 8:14 came to his master; w. said to him..........
2Ki 9:31 Had Zimri peace, w. slew his master? ....
2Ki 9:32 and said, W. is on my side? w.? 4310
2Ki 10:9 slew him: but w. slew all these? 4310
2Ki 10:13 king of Judah, and said, W. are ye? 4310
2Ki 10:29 of Nebat, w. made Israel to sin,........... 834
2Ki 13:6 Jeroboam, w. made Israel sin,............. 834
2Ki 13:11 son of Nebat, w. made Israel to sin: 834
2Ki 14:24 son of Nebat, w. made Israel to sin. 834
2Ki 15:9, 18,24,28 w. made Israel to sin. 834
2Ki 17:36 w. brought you up out of the land of 834
2Ki 18:35 W. are they among all the gods......... 4310
2Ki 23:15 son of Nebat, w. made Israel to sin, ... 834
2Ki 23:16 w. proclaimed these words................. 834
1Ch 2:7 w. transgressed in the thing 834
1Ch 2:22 w. had three and twenty cities in the........
1Ch 4:22 w. had the dominion in Moab, and 834
1Ch 5:8 w. dwelt in Aroer, even unto Nebo 1931
1Ch 5:10 the Hagarites, w. fell by their hand:..........
1Ch 6:39 Asaph, w. stood on his right hand, ...
1Ch 7:24 w. built Beth-horon the nether,................
1Ch 7:31 w. is the father of Birzavith, ... 1931
1Ch 8:12 and Shamed, w. built Ono, and.......... 1931
1Ch 8:13 w. were heads of the fathers of......... 1992
1Ch 8:13 w. drove away the inhabitants of........ 1992
1Ch 9:1 w. were carried away to Babylon for.........
1Ch 9:18 W. hitherto waited in the king's gate.........
1Ch 9:31 w. was the first born of Shallum 1931
1Ch 9:33 w. remaining in the chambers were ....
1Ch 11:10 w. strengthened themselves with him........
1Ch 11:12 w. was one of the three mighties. 1931
1Ch 11:22 Benaiah...w. had done many acts; ....
1Ch 12:18 Amasai, w. was chief of the captains,........
1Ch 16:41 chosen, w. were expressed by name, ... 834
1Ch 17:16 W. am I, O Lord God, and what is..... 4310
1Ch 19:7 w. came and pitched before Medeba. ....
1Ch 21:16 Israel, w. were clothed in sackcloth, ...
1Ch 22:9 to thee, w. shall be a man of rest; 1931
1Ch 24:28 Mahli came Eleazar, w. had no sons. ....
1Ch 25:1 w. should prophesy with harps,................
1Ch 25:3 Jeduthun, w. prophesied with a harp, ...
1Ch 25:9 w. with his brethren and sons 1931
1Ch 27:6 w. was mighty among the thirty,..............
1Ch 29:5 w. then is willing to consecrate.......... 4310
1Ch 29:14 w. am I, and what is my people,........ 4310
2Ch 1:10 for w. can judge this thy people, ... 4310
2Ch 2:6 w. is able to build him an house,......... 4310
2Ch 2:6 w. am I then, that I should build........ 4310

2Ch 2:12 w. hath given to David the king a........ 834
2Ch 6:4 w. hath with his hands fulfilled that.........
2Ch 8:8 w. were left after them in the land,........ 834
2Ch 10:2 the son of Nebat, w. was in Egypt, ... 1931
2Ch 17:16 w. willingly offered himself unto the..........
2Ch 18:19 W. shall entice Ahab king of............. 4310
2Ch 19:6 Lord, w. is with you in the judgment. ....
2Ch 20:7 w. didst drive out the inhabitants of..........
2Ch 20:34 w. is mentioned in the book of........... 834
2Ch 20:35 of Israel, w. did very wickedly:......... 1931
2Ch 22:9 w. sought the Lord with all his........... 834
2Ch 26:1 Uzziah, w. was sixteen years old, ... 1931
2Ch 26:5 w. had understanding in the visions...........
2Ch 28:5 w. smote him with a great slaughter.........
2Ch 30:7 w. therefore gave them up to.................
2Ch 32:4 together, w. stopped all the fountains,.......
2Ch 32:14 W. was there among all the gods....... 4310
2Ch 32:31 w. sent unto him to enquire of the ....
2Ch 34:26 w. sent you to enquire of the Lord,...........
2Ch 35:21 w. is with me, that he destroy thee 834
2Ch 36:13 w. had made him swear by God: 834
2Ch 36:17 w. slew their young men with the ....
2Ch 36:23 W. is there among you of all his 4310
Ezr 1:3 W. is there among you of all his 4310
Ezr 3:12 of the fathers, w. were ancient men, ...
Ezr 5:3 W. hath commanded you to.............. 4479
Ezr 5:9 W. commanded you to build this 4479
Ezr 5:12 Chaldean, w. destroyed this house,...........
Ne 1:11 servants, w. desire to fear thy name:........
Ne 3:3 w. also laid the beams thereof, ... 1992
Ne 6:10 of Mehetabeel, w. was shut up;......... 1931
Ne 6:11 w. is there, that, being as I am, ... 4310
Ne 7:7 W. came with Zerubbabel, Jeshua,............
Ne 9:7 the God, w. didst choose Abram, ... 834
Ne 9:27 hand of their enemies, w. vexed them:......
Ne 9:27 w. saved them out of the hand of their......
Ne 9:32 God, w. keepest covenant and mercy,.......
Ne 13:26 like him, w. was beloved of his God, ...
Es 2:6 W. had been carried away from.......... 834
Es 2:15 w. had taken her for his daughter,......... 834
Es 2:22 w. told it unto Esther the queen: ....
Es 4:11 the inner court, w. is not called........... 834
Es 4:14 w. knoweth whether thou art 4310
Es 6:2 w. sought to lay hand on the king........ 834
Es 6:4 the king said, W. is in the court? 4310
Es 7:5 W. is he, and where is he, that 4310
Es 7:9 w. had spoken good for the king,......... 834
Job 3:8 day, w. are ready to raise up their...........
Job 3:15 gold, w. filled their houses with silver: ......
Job 4:2 but w. can withhold himself from........ 4310
Job 4:7 w. ever perished, being innocent? 4310
Job 5:10 W. giveth rain upon the earth, and...........
Job 9:4 w. hath hardened himself against........ 4310
Job 9:12 taketh away, w. can hinder him?........ 4310
Job 9:12 w. will say unto him, What doest 4310
Job 9:19 w. shall set me a time to plead? 4310
Job 9:24 thereof; if not, where, and w. is he?... 4310
Job 11:10 together, then w. can hinder him?...... 4310
Job 12:3 w. knoweth not such things as........... 4310
Job 12:4 w. calleth upon God, and he....................
Job 12:9 W. knoweth not in all these that 4310
Job 13:19 W. is he that will plead with me? 4310
Job 14:4 W. can bring a clean thing out of 4310
Job 16:9 me in his wrath, w. hateth me:..................
Job 17:3 w. is he that will strike hands........... 4310
Job 17:15 as for my hope, w. shall see it? 4310
Job 21:31 W. shall declare his way to his 4310
Job 21:31 w. shall repay him what he hath......... 4310
Job 23:13 one mind, and w. can turn him? 4310
Job 24:25 so now, w. will make me a liar, ... 4310
Job 26:14 of his power w. can understand? 4310
Job 27:2 w. hath taken away my judgment; ....
Job 27:2 the Almighty, w. hath vexed my soul: ....
Job 30:4 W. cut up mallows by the bushes,..............
Job 34:7 w. drinketh up scorning like water? ....
Job 34:13 W. hath given him a charge over 4310
Job 34:13 w. hath disposed the whole world? 4310
Job 34:29 w. then can make trouble?................ 4310
Job 34:29 his face, w. then can behold him?....... 4310
Job 35:10 maker, w. giveth songs in the night; ....
Job 35:11 W. teacheth us more than the beasts........
Job 36:22 his power: w. teacheth like him?........ 4310
Job 36:23 W. hath enjoined him this way? 4310
Job 36:23 or w. can say, Thou hast wrought....... 4310
Job 38:2 W. is this that darkeneth counsel....... 4310
Job 38:5 W. hath laid the measures thereof, ... 4310
Job 38:5 w. hath stretched the line upon it? 4310
Job 38:6 or w. laid the corner stone thereof, ... 4310
Job 38:8 Or w. shut up the sea with doors,............
Job 38:25 W. hath divided a watercourse........... 4310
Job 38:28 w. hath begotten the drop of dew? 4310
Job 38:29 of heaven, w. hath gendered it? 4310
Job 38:36 W. hath put wisdom in the inward...... 4310
Job 38:36 or w. hath given understanding to 4310
Job 38:37 W. can number the clouds in............ 4310
Job 38:37 w. can stay the bottles of heaven, ... 4310
Job 38:41 W. provideth for the raven his.......... 4310
Job 39:5 W. hath sent out the wild ass free? 4310
Job 39:5 w. hath loosed the bands of the 4310
Job 41:10 w. then is able to stand before me? 4310
Job 41:11 W. hath prevented me, that I........... 4310
Job 41:13 W. can discover the face of his.......... 4310
Job 41:13 w. can come to him with his double.... 4310
Job 41:14 W. can open the doors of his face?..... 4310
Job 41:33 not his like, w. is made without fear.........
Job 42:3 W. is he that hideth counsel............. 4310
Ps 4:6 say, W. will shew us any good?........... 4310
Ps 6:5 grave w. shall give thee thanks? 4310
Ps 8:1 w. hast set thy glory above the.......... 834
Ps 12:4 W. have said, With our tongue will 834
Ps 12:4 are our own: w. is lord over us?........ 4310
Ps 14:4 w. eat up my people as they eat ....
Ps 15:1 w. shall abide in thy tabernacle?......... 4310
Ps 15:1 w. shall dwell in thy holy hill?............ 4310
Ps 16:7 Lord, w. hath given me counsel: 834
Ps 17:9 enemies, w. compass me about................
Ps 18:*title* w. spake unto the Lord the 834
Ps 18:3 the Lord, w. is worthy to be praised: ....
Ps 18:31 For w. is God save the Lord? 4310
Ps 18:31 or w. is a rock save our God?........... 4310
Ps 19:12 W. can understand his errors?............ 4310
Ps 24:3 W. shall ascend into the hill of the...... 4310
Ps 24:3 w. shall stand in his holy place? 4310
Ps 24:4 w. hath not lifted up his soul unto........ 834
Ps 24:8, 10 W. is this King of glory? The.......... 4310
Ps 34:*title* w. drove him away, and he departed.........
Ps 35:10 say, Lord, w. is like unto thee, ... 4310
Ps 37:7 of him w. prospereth in his way,...............
Ps 37:7 the man w. bringeth wicked devices..........
Ps 39:6 knoweth not w. shall gather them........ 4310
Ps 42:11 w. is the health of my countenance,..........
Ps 43:5 w. is the health of my countenance,..........
Ps 53:4 w. eat up my people as they eat..............
Ps 59:7 lips: for w., say they, doth hear? 4310
Ps 60:9 W. will bring me into the strong 4310
Ps 60:9 city? w. will lead me into Edom?........ 4310
Ps 64:3 W. whet their tongue like a sword, ... 834
Ps 64:5 they say, W. shall see them? 4310
Ps 65:5 w. art the confidence of all the ends of......
Ps 68:19 w. daily loadeth us with benefits,..............
Ps 71:19 high, w. hast done great things: 834
Ps 71:19 O God, w. is like unto thee! 4310
Ps 72:18 w. only doeth wondrous things.................
Ps 73:12 the ungodly, w. prosper in the world; ....
Ps 76:7 w. may stand in thy sight when 4310
Ps 77:13 w. is so great a God as our God? 4310
Ps 78:6 w. should arise and declare them to..........
Ps 83:12 W. said, Let us take to ourselves........ 834
Ps 84:6 W. passing through the valley of..............
Ps 89:6 w. in the heaven can be compared...... 4310
Ps 89:6 w. among the sons of the mighty can........
Ps 89:8 w. is a strong Lord like unto thee?..... 4310
Ps 90:11 W. knoweth the power of thine 4310
Ps 94:16 W. will rise up for me against the 4310
Ps 94:16 w. will stand up for me against the..... 4310
Ps 103:3 W. forgiveth all thine iniquities;...............
Ps 103:3 iniquities; w. healeth all thy diseases.........
Ps 103:4 W. redeemeth thy life from......................
Ps 103:4 w. crowneth thee with lovingkindness........
Ps 103:5 W. satisfieth thy mouth with good ....
Ps 104:2 W. coverest thyself with light as with ....
Ps 104:2 w. stretchest out the heavens like a ....
Ps 104:3 W. layeth the beams of his chambers........
Ps 104:3 w. maketh the clouds his chariot: ....
Ps 104:3 w. walketh upon the wings of the..............
Ps 104:4 W. maketh his angels spirits; his.............
Ps 104:5 W. laid the foundations of the earth, ...
Ps 105:17 Joseph, w. was sold for a servant:...........
Ps 106:2 W. can utter the mighty acts of......... 4310
Ps 106:2 w. can shew forth all his praise? ....
Ps 108:10 W. will bring me into the strong 4310
Ps 108:10 city? w. will lead me into Edom?........ 4310
Ps 108:11 not thou, O God, w. hast cast us off? ....
Ps 113:5 W. is like unto the Lord our God,...... 4310
Ps 113:5 Lord our God, w. dwelleth on high,..........
Ps 113:6 W. humbleth himself to behold the ....
Ps 119:1 way, w. walk in the law of the Lord. ....
Ps 119:38 servant, w. is devoted to thy fear........ 834
Ps 124:1,2 been the Lord w. was on our side,...........
Ps 124:6 w. hath not given us as a prey to their......
Ps 124:8 the Lord, w. made heaven and earth.........
Ps 130:3 iniquities, O Lord, w. shall stand? 4310
Ps 135:8 W. smote the firstborn of Egypt, both......
Ps 135:9 W. sent tokens and wonders into the........
Ps 135:10 W. smote great nations, and slew ....
Ps 136:4 To him w. alone doeth great wonders: ......
Ps 136:23 W. remembered us in our low estate: ....
Ps 136:25 W. giveth food to all flesh: for his ....
Ps 137:7 w. said, Rase it, rase it, even to the.........
Ps 137:8 of Babylon, w. art to be destroyed; ....
Ps 140:4 w. have purposed to overthrow my...... 834
Ps 144:2 w. subdueth my people under me...............
Ps 144:10 w. delivereth David his servant from.........
Ps 147:8 W. covereth the heaven with clouds, ...
Ps 147:8 w. prepareth rain for the earth, ...
Ps 147:8 w. maketh grass to grow upon the ....
Ps 147:17 w. can stand before his cold? 4310
Pr 2:13 W. leave the paths of uprightness, to........
Pr 2:14 W. rejoice to do evil, and delight in..........
Pr 9:15 passengers w. go right on their ways:.......
Pr 18:14 a wounded spirit w. can bear? 4310
Pr 20:6 but a faithful man w. can find? 4310
Pr 20:9 W. can say, I have made my heart..... 4310
Pr 20:25 man w. devoureth that which is holy,........
Pr 21:24 his name w. dealeth in proud wrath. ....
Pr 23:29 W. hath woe? w. hath sorrow?............ 4310
Pr 23:29 w. hath contentions? w. hath............. 4310
Pr 23:29 w. hath wounds without cause?.......... 4310
Pr 23:29 w. hath redness of eyes?................. 4310
Pr 24:22 w. knoweth the ruin of them both?..... 4310
Pr 26:18 As a mad man w. casteth firebands,..........
Pr 27:4 w. is able to stand before envy? 4310
Pr 30:4 W. hath ascended up into heaven, ... 4310
Pr 30:4 w. hath gathered the wind in his 4310
Pr 30:4 w. hath bound the waters in a 4310
Pr 30:4 w. hath established all the ends of...... 4310
Pr 30:9 thee, and say, W. is the Lord?........... 4310
Pr 31:10 W. can find a virtuous woman? 4310
Ec 2:19 And w. knoweth whether he shall....... 4310
Ec 2:25 w. can eat, or w. else can hasten 4310
Ec 3:21 W. knoweth the spirit of man that....... 4310
Ec 3:22 w. shall bring him to see what shall.... 4310
Ec 4:3 w. hath not seen the evil work............ 834
Ec 4:13 w. will no more be admonished. 834
Ec 6:12 for w. can tell a man what shall be 4310
Ec 6:12 w. knoweth what is good for man........ 4310
Ec 7:13 for w. can make that straight, ... 4310
Ec 7:24 exceeding deep, w. can find it out?..... 4310
Ec 8:1 W. is as the wise man? and............. 4310
Ec 8:1 w. knoweth the interpretation of a....... 4310
Ec 8:4 w. may say unto him, What doest?..... 4310
Ec 8:7 w. can tell him when it shall be? ....
Ec 8:10 w. had come and gone from the place ....
Ec 10:14 be after him, w. can tell him?............ 4310
Ec 11:5 the works of God w. maketh all. 834
Ec 12:7 shall return unto God w. gave it.......... 834
Ca 3:6 W. is this that cometh out of the 4310
Ca 6:10 W. is she that looketh forth as the..... 4310
Ca 8:2 mother's house, w. would instruct me: ......
Ca 8:5 W. is this that cometh up from.......... 4310
Isa 1:12 w. hath required this at your............. 4310
Isa 6:8 shall I send, and w. will go for us? 4310
Isa 14:6 He w. smote the people in wrath.............
Isa 14:27 purposed, and w. shall disannul it?...... 4310
Isa 14:27 out, and w. shall turn it back? 4310
Isa 23:8 W. hath taken this counsel against...... 4310
Isa 24:18 w. fleeth from the noise of the fear ....
Isa 27:4 w. would set the briers and thorns..... 4310
Isa 29:15 W. seeth us? and w. knoweth us?....... 4310
Isa 29:22 the Lord, w. redeemed Abraham, ... 834
Isa 33:14 W. among us shall dwell with the....... 4310
Isa 33:14 w. among us shall dwell with............ 4310
Isa 36:20 W. are they among all the gods of....... 4310
Isa 37:2 w. was over the household,................ 834
Isa 40:12 W. hath measured the waters in 4310
Isa 40:13 W. hath directed the Spirit of the....... 4310
Isa 40:14 w. instructed him, and taught him in.........
Isa 40:26 and behold w. hath created these 4310
Isa 41:2 W. raised up the righteous man......... 4310
Isa 41:4 W. hath wrought and done it,............ 4310

Book	Ref	Context	No.
Isa	41:26	**W.** hath declared from the	4310
Isa	42:19	**W.** is blind, but my servant? or	4310
Isa	42:19	**w.** is blind as he that is perfect,	4310
Isa	42:23	**W.** among you will give ear to	4310
Isa	42:23	**w.** will hearken and hear for the time	
Isa	42:24	**W.** gave Jacob for a spoil, and	4310
Isa	43:9	**w.** among them can declare this,	4310
Isa	43:13	I will work, and **w.** shall let it?	4310
Isa	44:7	And **w.**, as I, shall call, and shall	4310
Isa	44:10	**W.** hath formed a god, or molten	4310
Isa	45:21	**w.** hath declared this from ancient	4310
Isa	45:21	**w.** hath told it from that time?	
Isa	49:21	**W.** hath begotten me these,	4310
Isa	50:8	**w.** will contend with me? let us	4310
Isa	50:8	**w.** is mine adversary? let him come	4310
Isa	50:9	**w.** is he that shall condemn me?	4310
Isa	50:10	**W.** is among you that feareth the	4310
Isa	51:12	**w.** art thou, that thou shouldest be	4310
Isa	51:19	thee; **w.** shall be sorry for thee?	4310
Isa	53:1	**W.** hath believed our report? and	4310
Isa	53:8	**w.** shall declare his generation?	4310
Isa	60:8	**W.** are these that fly as a cloud,	4310
Isa	63:1	**W.** is this that cometh from Edom,	4310
Isa	65:16	That he **w.** blesseth himself in the	834
Isa	66:8	**W.** hath heard such a thing?	4310
Isa	66:8	**w.** hath seen such things? Shall	834
Jer	1:16	**w.** have forsaken me, and have	
Jer	2:24	occasion **w.** can turn her away?	4310
Jer	9:12	**W.** is the wise man, that may	4310
Jer	9:12	**w.** is he to whom the mouth of the	
Jer	10:7	**W.** should not fear thee, O king	4310
Jer	15:5	For **w.** shall have pity upon thee,	4310
Jer	15:5	or **w.** shall bemoan thee?	4310
Jer	15:5	or **w.** shall go aside to ask how thou	
Jer	17:9	desperately wicked: **w.** can know	4310
Jer	18:13	**w.** hath heard such things:	4310
Jer	20:1	**w.** was also chief governor in the	1931
Jer	20:15	**w.** brought tidings to my father,	834
Jer	21:13	**W.** shall come down against us?	4310
Jer	21:13	**w.** shall enter into our habitations?	4310
Jer	23:18	**w.** hath stood in the counsel of the	4310
Jer	23:18	**w.** hath marked his word, and	4310
Jer	26:20	**w.** prophesied against this city and	
Jer	26:23	**w.** slew him with the sword, and cast	
Jer	30:21	**w.** is this that engaged his heart	4310
Jer	36:32	**w.** wrote therein from the mouth of	
Jer	46:7	**W.** is this that cometh up as a	4310
Jer	49:4	saying, **W.** shall come unto me?	4310
Jer	49:19	and **w.** is a chosen man, that I may	4310
Jer	49:19	**w.** is like me? and **w.** will appoint	4310
Jer	49:19	**w.** is that shepherd that will stand	4310
Jer	50:44	and **w.** is a chosen man, that I may	4310
Jer	50:44	**w.** is like me? and **w.** will appoint	4310
Jer	50:44	**w.** is that shepherd that will stand	4310
Jer	52:25	**w.** mustered the people of the land;	
La	2:13	like the sea: **w.** can heal thee?	4310
La	3:37	**W.** is he that saith, and it cometh	4310
Eze	10:7	with linen: **w.** took it, and went out	
Da	1:10	**w.** hath appointed your meat and	834
Da	2:23	**w.** hast given me wisdom and	1768
Da	3:15	**w.** is that God that shall deliver	4479
Da	3:28	**w.** hath sent his angel, and	1768
Da	6:27	**w.** hath delivered Daniel from the	1768
Ho	3:1	**w.** look to other gods, and love	1992
Ho	7:4	**w.** ceaseth from raising after he hath	
Ho	14:9	**W.** is wise, and he shall	4310
Joe	2:11	very terrible; and **w.** can abide it?	4310
Joe	2:14	**W.** knoweth if he will return and	4310
Am	1:1	**w.** was among the herdmen of	834
Am	3:8	lion hath roared, **w.** will not fear?	4310
Am	3:8	hath spoken, **w.** can but prophesy?	4310
Am	3:10	**w.** store up violence and robbery in	
Am	5:7	Ye **w.** turn judgment to wormwood,	
Ob	3	**W.** shall bring me down to the	4310
Jon	3:9	**W.** can tell if God will turn and	4310
Mic	3:2	**W.** hate the good, and love the evil;	
Mic	3:2	**w.** pluck off their skin from off	
Mic	3:3	**W.** also eat the flesh of my people,	834
Mic	5:8	**w.**, if he go through, both treadeth	834
Mic	6:9	the rod, and **w.** hath appointed it.	4310
Mic	7:18	**W.** is a God like unto thee, that	4310
Na	1:6	**W.** can stand before his	4310
Na	1:6	**w.** can abide in the fierceness of his	4310
Na	3:7	is laid waste: **w.** will bemoan her?	4310
Hab	2:5	**w.** enlargeth his desire as hell,	834
Zep	3:18	the solemn assembly, **w.** are of thee,	
Hag	2:3	**W.** is left among you that saw	4310
Zec	4:7	**W.** art thou, O great mountain?	4310
Zec	4:10	**w.** hath despised the day of small	4310
Mal	1:10	**W.** is there even among you that	4310
Mal	3:2	But **w.** may abide the day of his	4310
Mal	3:2	**w.** shall stand when he appeareth?	4310
Mt	1:16	born Jesus, **w.** is called Christ.	*3588*
Mt	3:7	**w.** hath warned you to flee from	*5101*
Mt	10:2	first, Simon, **w.** is called Peter,	*3588*
Mt	10:4	Judas Iscariot, **w.** also betrayed	*3588*
Mt	10:11	**enter, enquire w. in it is worthy;**	*5101*
Mt	12:48	said unto him...**W. is my mother?**	*5101*
Mt	12:48	**and w. are my brethren?**	*5101*
Mt	13:9,	**43 W. hath ears to hear, let him**	*3588*
Mt	13:46	**W., when he had found one pearl**	*3739*
Mt	18:1	**W.** is the greatest in the kingdom	*5101*
Mt	19:25	saying, **W.** then can be saved?	*5101*
Mt	21:10	city was moved, saying, **W.** is this?	*5101*
Mt	21:23	and **w.** gave thee this authority?	*5101*
Mt	24:45	**W. then is a faithful and wise**	*5101*
Mt	25:14	**w. called his own servants, and**	
Mt	26:3	priest, **w.** was called Caiaphas,	*3588*
Mt	26:68	Christ, **W.** is he that smote thee?	*5101*
Mt	27:57	**w.**...himself was Jesus' disciple:	*3739*
Mk	1:19	**w.** also were in the ship mending	*841*
Mk	1:24	I know thee **w.** thou art, the Holy	*5101*
Mk	2:7	**w.** can forgive sins but God only?	*5101*
Mk	3:33	**W. is my mother, or my**	*5101*
Mk	4:16	**w., when they have heard the**	*3739*
Mk	5:3	**W.** had his dwelling among the	*3739*
Mk	5:30	and said, **W. touched my clothes?**	*5101*
Mk	5:31	and sayest thou, **W.** touched me?	*5101*
Mk	9:34	**w.** should be the greatest.	*5101*
Mk	10:26	themselves, **W.** then can be saved?	*5101*
Mk	11:28	**w.** gave thee this authority to do	*5101*
Mk	13:34	**w. left his house, and gave**	
Mk	15:7	**w.** had committed murder in the	*3748*
Mk	15:21	one Simon a Cyrenian, **w.** passed by,	
Mk	15:41	**W.** also, when he was in Galilee,	*3739*
Mk	16:3	**W.** shall roll us away the stone	*5101*
Lu	1:36	with her, **w.** was called barren	*3588*
Lu	3:7	**w.** hath warned you to flee from	*5101*
Lu	4:34	I know thee **w.** thou art; the Holy	*5101*
Lu	5:12	**w.** seeing Jesus fell on his face,	*2532*
Lu	5:21	saying, **W.** is this which speaketh	*5101*
Lu	5:21	**W.** can forgive sins, but God alone?	*5101*
Lu	7:2	servant, **w.** was dear unto him,	*3739*
Lu	7:39	**w.** and what manner of woman	*5101*
Lu	7:49	**W.** is this that forgiveth sins also?	*5101*
Lu	8:45	And Jesus said, **W. touched me?**	*5101*
Lu	8:45	and sayest thou, **W.** touched me?	*5101*
Lu	9:9	but **w.** is this, of whom I hear such	*5101*
Lu	9:31	**W.** appeared in glory, and spake	*3739*
Lu	10:22	**no man knoweth w. the Son is,**	*5101*
Lu	10:22	**and w. the Father is, but the Son,**	*5101*
Lu	10:29	Jesus, And **w.** is my neighbour?	*5101*
Lu	12:14	**w. made me a judge or a divider**	*5101*
Lu	12:42	**W. then is that faithful and wise**	*5101*
Lu	16:11	**w. will commit to your trust the**	*5101*
Lu	16:12	**w. shall give you that which is**	*5101*
Lu	16:14	the Pharisees also, **w.** were covetous,	
Lu	18:26	it said, **W.** then can be saved?	*5101*
Lu	18:30	**W. shall not receive manifold**	*3739*
Lu	19:3	he sought to see Jesus **w.** he was;	*5101*
Lu	20:2	or **w.** is he that gave thee this	*5101*
Lu	22:64	Prophesy, **w.** is it that smote thee?	*5101*
Lu	23:7	**w.** himself also was at Jerusalem	
Lu	23:19	(**W.** for a certain sedition made in	*3748*
Lu	23:51	**w.** also himself waited for the	*3739*
Joh	1:19	to ask him, **W.** art thou?	*5101*
Joh	1:22	said they unto them, **W.** art thou?	*5101*
Joh	1:27	**w.** coming after me is preferred	*3588*
Joh	4:10	**and w. it is that saith to thee,**	*5101*
Joh	5:13	that was healed wist not **w.** it was:	*5101*
Joh	6:60	is an hard saying; **w.** can hear it?	*5101*
Joh	6:64	**w.** they were that believed not,	*5101*
Joh	6:64	and **w.** should betray him.	*5101*
Joh	7:20	a devil: **w.** goeth about to kill thee?	*5101*
Joh	7:49	people **w.** knoweth not the law	*3588*
Joh	8:25	said they unto him, **W.** art thou?	*5101*
Joh	9:2	**w.** did sin, this man, or his parents,	*5101*
Joh	9:19	son, **w.** ye say was born blind?	*3739*
Joh	9:21	**w.** hath opened his eyes, we know	*5101*
Joh	9:36	**W.** is he, Lord, that I might	*5101*
Joh	12:34	be lifted up? **w.** is this Son of man?	*5101*
Joh	12:38	Lord, **w.** hath believed our report?	*5101*
Joh	13:11	he knew **w.** should betray him:	*3588*
Joh	13:24	**w.** it should be of whom he spake.	*5101*
Joh	13:25	saith unto him, Lord, **w.** is it?	*5101*
Joh	18:18	**w.** had made a fire of coals; for it was	
Joh	21:12	durst ask him, **W.** art thou?	*5101*
Ac	1:23	**w.** was surnamed Justus, and	*3739*
Ac	3:3	**W.** seeing Peter and John about	*3739*
Ac	4:25	**W.** by the mouth of thy servant	*3588*
Ac	4:36	**w.** by the apostles was surnamed	*3588*
Ac	5:36	rose up Theudas,...**w.** was slain;	*3739*
Ac	7:27	**W.** made thee a ruler and a judge	*5101*
Ac	7:35	**W.** made thee a ruler and a judge?	*5101*
Ac	7:38	**w.** received the lively oracles to	*3739*
Ac	7:46	**W.** found favour before God, and	*3739*
Ac	7:53	**W.** have received the law by the	*3748*
Ac	8:15	**W.**, when they were come down,	*3748*
Ac	8:27	**w.** had the charge of all her	*3739*
Ac	8:33	**w.** shall declare his generation?	*5101*
Ac	9:5	And he said, **W.** art thou, Lord?	*5101*
Ac	10:32	**w.**, when he cometh, shall speak	*3739*
Ac	10:38	**w.** went about doing good, and	*3739*
Ac	10:41	**w.** did eat and drink with him	*3748*
Ac	11:14	**W.** shall tell thee words, where by	*3739*
Ac	11:17	**w.** believed on the Lord Jesus	
Ac	11:23	**W.**, when he came, and had seen	*3739*
Ac	13:7	**w.** called for Barnabas and Saul,	*3778*
Ac	13:9	Then Saul, (**w.** is also called Paul,)	*3739*
Ac	13:31	**w.** are his witnesses unto the	*3748*
Ac	13:43	**w.**, speaking to them, persuaded	*3748*
Ac	14:8	a cripple...**w.** never had walked:	*3739*
Ac	14:9	**w.** stedfastly beholding him, and	*3739*
Ac	14:16	**W.** in times past suffered all nations	*3739*
Ac	14:19	**w.** persuaded the people, and,	*2532*
Ac	15:17	Lord, **w.** doeth all these things.	*3588*
Ac	15:27	**w.** shall also tell you the same	*846*
Ac	15:38	**w.** departed from them from	*3588*
Ac	16:24	**W.**, having received such a	*3739*
Ac	17:10	**w.** coming thither went into the	*3748*
Ac	18:27	**w.**, when he was come, helped	*3739*
Ac	19:15	and Paul I know; but **w.** are ye?	*5101*
Ac	21:4	**w.** said to Paul through the	*3748*
Ac	21:32	**W.** immediately took soldiers and	*3739*
Ac	21:33	demanded **w.** he was, and what	*5101*
Ac	21:37	**W.** said, Canst thou speak Greek?	*3588*
Ac	22:8	I answered, **W.** art thou, Lord?	*5101*
Ac	23:18	**w.** hath something to say unto thee.	
Ac	23:33	**W.**, when they came to Caesarea,	*3748*
Ac	24:1	**w.** informed the governor against	*3748*
Ac	24:6	**W.** also hath gone about to	*3739*
Ac	24:19	**W.** ought to have been here before	*3739*
Ac	26:15	And I said, **W.** art thou, Lord?	*5101*
Ac	28:7	**w.** received us, and lodged us	*3739*
Ac	28:10	**W.** also honoured us with many	*3739*
Ac	28:18	**W.**, when they had examined me,	*3748*
Ro	1:18	**w.** hold...truth in unrighteousness;	*3588*
Ro	1:25	**W.** changed the truth of God into	*3748*
Ro	1:25	the Creator, **w.** is blessed for ever	*3739*
Ro	1:32	**W.** knowing the judgment of God,	*3748*
Ro	2:6	**W.** will render to every man	*3739*
Ro	2:7	To them **w.** by patient continuance	
Ro	2:27	**w.** by the letter and circumcision	*3588*
Ro	3:5	unrighteous **w.** taketh vengeance?	*3588*
Ro	3:19	it saith to them **w.** are under the law:	
Ro	4:12	**w.** are not of the circumcision	*3588*
Ro	4:12	**w.** also walk in the steps of that	*3588*
Ro	4:16	of Abraham; **w.** is father of us all,	*3739*
Ro	4:17	God, **w.** quickeneth the dead,	*3588*
Ro	4:18	**W.** against hope believed in hope,	*3739*
Ro	4:25	**W.** was delivered for our offences,	*3739*
Ro	5:14	**w.** is the figure of him that is to	*3739*
Ro	7:4	to him **w.** is raised from the dead,	
Ro	7:24	**w.** shall deliver me from the body	*5101*
Ro	8:1	**w.** walk not after the flesh, but after	
Ro	8:4	**w.** walk not after the flesh, but after	
Ro	8:20	**w.** hath subjected the same in hope;	
Ro	8:28	**w.** are the called according to his	
Ro	8:31	be for us, **w.** can be against us?	*5101*
Ro	8:33	**W.** shall lay any thing to the	*5101*
Ro	8:34	**W.** is he that condemneth? It is	*5101*
Ro	8:34	**w.** is even at the right hand of	*3739*
Ro	8:34	**w.** also maketh intercession for us	*3739*
Ro	8:35	**W.** shall separate us from the	*5101*
Ro	9:4	**W.** are Israelites; to whom	*3748*
Ro	9:5	**w.** is over all, God blessed for ever	*3588*
Ro	9:19	For **w.** hath resisted his will?	*5101*
Ro	9:20	**w.** art thou that repliest against	*5101*
Ro	10:6	**W.** shall ascend into heaven?	*5101*
Ro	10:7	Or, **W.** shall descend into the deep?	*5101*

Ro 10:16 Lord, w. hath believed our report? 5101
Ro 11:4 w. have not bowed the knee to the 3748
Ro 11:34 w. hath known the mind of the 5101
Ro 11:34 or w. hath been his counsellor? 5101
Ro 11:35 Or w. hath first given to him, and it ... 5101
Ro 14:2 another, w. is weak, eateth herbs. 3588
Ro 14:4 W. art thou that judgest another 5101
Ro 14:20 that man w. eateth with offence. 3588
Ro 16:4 W. have for my life laid down 3748
Ro 16:5 w. is the firstfruits of Achaia unto 3739
Ro 16:6 w. bestowed much labour on us. 3748
Ro 16:7 w. are of note among the apostles, ... 3748
Ro 16:7 w. also were in Christ before me. 3739
Ro 16:12 Tryphosa, w. labour in the Lord, ... 3588
Ro 16:22 I Tertius, w. wrote this epistle, ... 3588
1Co 1:8 W. shall also confirm you unto 3739
1Co 1:30 w. of God is made unto us wisdom, ... 3739
1Co 2:16 w. hath known the mind of the 5101
1Co 3:5 W. then is Paul, and w. is Apollos, ... 5101
1Co 4:5 w. both will bring to light the 3739
1Co 4:7 w. maketh thee to differ from 5101
1Co 4:17 w. is my beloved son, and faithful 3739
1Co 4:17 the Lord, w. shall bring you into 3739
1Co 6:4 to judge w. are least esteemed in the ....
1Co 9:7 W. goeth a warfare any time at 5100
1Co 9:7 w. planteth a vineyard, and eateth 5100
1Co 9:7 w. feedeth a flock, and eateth not 5100
1Co 10:13 w. will not suffer you to be 3739
1Co 14:8 w., shall prepare himself to the 5101
2Co 1:4 W. comforteth us in all our 3588
2Co 1:10 W. delivered us from so great a ....
2Co 1:19 w. was preached among you by 3588
2Co 1:22 W. hath also sealed us, and given 3588
2Co 2:2 w. is he then that maketh me 5101
2Co 2:16 w. is sufficient for these things? 5101
2Co 3:6 W. also hath made us able 3739
2Co 4:4 w. is the image of God, should 3739
2Co 4:6 w. commanded the light to shine 3588
2Co 5:5 w. also hath given unto us the 3588
2Co 5:18 w. hath reconciled us to himself by 3588
2Co 5:21 him to be sin for us, w. knew no sin; ....
2Co 8:10 for you, w. have begun before, ... 3748
2Co 8:19 w. was also chosen of the churches ....
2Co 10:1 w. in presence am base among 3739
2Co 11:29 W. is weak, and I am not weak? 5101
2Co 11:29 w. is offended, and I burn not? 5101
Ga 1:1 w. raised him from the dead;) 3588
Ga 1:4 W. gave himself for our sins, that 3588
Ga 1:15 w. separated me from my mother's 3588
Ga 2:3 neither Titus, w. was with me, ... 3588
Ga 2:4 w. came in privily to spy out our 3748
Ga 2:6 of these w. seemed to be somewhat, ...
Ga 2:6 for they w. seemed to be somewhat ....
Ga 2:9 and John, w. seemed to be pillars, ... 3588
Ga 2:15 We w. are Jews by nature, and not ....
Ga 2:20 w. loved me, and gave himself for 3588
Ga 3:1 Galatians, w. hath beweitched you, ... 5101
Ga 4:23 he w. was of the bondwoman was born .....
Ga 5:7 w. did hinder you that ye should 5101
Ga 6:10 them w. are of the household of faith, ...
Ga 6:13 they themselves w. are circumcised ....
Eph 1:3 Jesus Christ, w. hath blessed us 3588
Eph 1:11 purpose of him w. worketh all things ....
Eph 1:12 glory, w. first trusted in Christ. 3588
Eph 1:19 of his power to us-ward w. believe, ... 3588
Eph 2:1 w. were dead in trespasses and sins, ...
Eph 2:4 But God, w. is rich in mercy, for his ....
Eph 2:11 w. are called Uncircumcision by 3588
Eph 2:13 ye w. sometimes were far off are 3739
Eph 2:14 our peace, w. hath made both 3739
Eph 3:8 w. am less than the least of all ....
Eph 3:9 w. created all things by Jesus 3588
Eph 4:6 and Father of all, w. is above all, ... 3588
Eph 4:19 W. being past feeling have given 3748
Eph 5:5 covetous man, w. is an idolater, ... 3739
Php 2:6 W., being in the form of God, ...
Php 2:20 w. will naturally care for your 3748
Php 3:19 shame, w. mind earthly things.) 3588
Php 3:21 W. shall change our vile body, ...
Col 1:7 w. is for you a faithful minister of 3739
Col 1:8 W. also declared unto us your love 3588
Col 1:13 W. hath delivered us from the 3739
Col 1:15 W. is the image of the invisible 3739
Col 1:18 w. is the beginning, the firstborn 3739
Col 1:24 W. now rejoice in my sufferings ....
Col 2:12 w. hath raised him from the dead. 3588
Col 3:4 When Christ, w. is our life, shall ....
Col 4:7 w. is a beloved brother, and a ....
Col 4:9 beloved brother, w. is one of you 3739
Col 4:11 w. are of the circumcision 3588
Col 4:12 Epaphras, w. is one of you, a 3588
1Th 2:12 of God, w. hath called you unto his 3588
1Th 2:15 W. both killed the Lord Jesus, ... 3588
1Th 4:8 God, w. hath also given unto us ....
1Th 5:8 But let us, w. are of the day, be sober, ...
1Th 5:10 W. died for us, that, whether we 3588
1Th 5:24 that calleth you, w. also will do it. 3739
2Th 1:7 to you w. are troubled rest with us, ...
2Th 1:9 W. shall be punished with 3748
2Th 2:4 W. opposeth and exalteth himself 3588
2Th 2:7 only he w. now letteth will let, until he .....
2Th 2:12 all might be damned w. believed 3588
2Th 3:3 W. shall stablish you, and keep 3739
1Ti 1:12 our Lord, w. hath enabled me, ... 3588
1Ti 1:13 W. was before a blasphemer, and 3588
1Ti 2:4 W. will have all men to be saved 3739
1Ti 2:6 W. gave himself a ransom for all, ... 3588
1Ti 4:10 God, w. is the Saviour of all men, ... 3739
1Ti 5:17 w. labour in the word and doctrine. ....
1Ti 6:13 of God, w. quickeneth all things, ... 3588
1Ti 6:13 w. before Pontius Pilate witnessed 3588
1Ti 6:15 w. is the...only Potentate, ... 3588
1Ti 6:16 W. only hath immortality, ... 3588
1Ti 6:17 w. giveth us richly all things to 3588
2Ti 1:9 W. hath saved us, and called us 3588
2Ti 1:10 Christ, w. hath abolished death, ...
2Ti 2:2 w. shall be able to teach others 3748
2Ti 2:4 w. hath chosen him to be a soldier. ....
2Ti 2:18 W. concerning the truth have 3748
2Ti 2:26 w. are taken captive by him at his ....
2Ti 4:1 w. shall judge the quick and the 3588
Tit 1:11 w. subvert whole houses, teaching 3748
Tit 2:14 W. gave himself for us, that he 3739
Heb 1:1 W. at sundry times and in divers ....
Heb 1:3 W. being the brightness of his ....
Heb 1:7 W. maketh his angels spirits, ... 3739
Heb 1:14 them w. shall be heirs of salvation? ....
Heb 2:9 w. was made a little lower than 3588
Heb 2:11 sanctifieth and they w. are sanctified ....
Heb 2:15 them w. through fear of death 3745
Heb 3:2 W. was faithful to him that appointed ....
Heb 3:3 as he w. hath builded the house ....
Heb 5:2 W. can have compassion on the ....
Heb 5:7 W. in the days of his flesh, when 3739
Heb 5:14 w. by reason of use have their senses ....
Heb 6:4 for those w. were once enlightened, ...
Heb 6:12 w. through faith and patience inherit ....
Heb 6:18 w. have fled for refuge to lay hold 3588
Heb 7:1 w. met Abraham returning from 3588
Heb 7:5 Levi, w. receive the office of the 3588
Heb 7:9 Levi also, w. receiveth tithes, ... 3588
Heb 7:16 W. is made, not after the law of a 3739
Heb 7:26 w. is holy, harmless, undefiled, ...
Heb 7:27 W. needeth not daily, as those 3739
Heb 7:28 Son, w. is consecrated for evermore. ....
Heb 8:1 w. is set on the right hand of the 3739
Heb 8:5 W. serve unto the example and 3748
Heb 9:14 w. through the eternal Spirit 3739
Heb 10:29 w. hath trodden under foot the 3588
Heb 10:39 of them w. draw back unto perdition; ....
Heb 11:11 judge him faithful w. had promised. ....
Heb 11:27 endured, as seeing him w. is invisible. ....
Heb 11:33 W. through faith subdued 3739
Heb 12:2 w. for the joy that was set before 3739
Heb 12:16 w. for one morsel of meat sold his 3739
Heb 12:25 w. refused him that spake on earth, ...
Heb 13:7 w. have spoken unto you the word 3748
Jas 3:13 W. is a wise man and endued 5101
Jas 4:12 w. is able to save and to destroy: 3588
Jas 4:12 destroy: w. art thou that judgest 5101
Jas 5:4 w. have reaped down your fields, ... 3588
Jas 5:10 w. have spoken in the name of the 3739
1Pe 1:5 W. are kept by the power of God 3588
1Pe 1:10 w. prophesied of the grace that 3588
1Pe 1:17 w. without respect of persons 3588
1Pe 1:20 W. verily was foreordained before the ....
1Pe 1:21 W. by him do believe in God, that 3588
1Pe 2:9 w. hath called you out of darkness ....
1Pe 2:22 W. did no sin, neither was guile 3739
1Pe 2:23 W. when he was reviled, reviled 3739
1Pe 2:24 W. his own self bare our sins in 3739
1Pe 3:5 women also, w. trusted in God, ... 3588
1Pe 3:13 w. is he that will harm you, if ye 5101
1Pe 3:22 W. is gone into heaven, and is on 3739
1Pe 4:5 W. shall give account to him that 3739
1Pe 5:1 w. am also an elder, and a witness 3588
1Pe 5:10 w. hath called us into his eternal 3588
2Pe 2:1 w. privily shall bring in damnable 3748
2Pe 2:15 w. loved the wages of 3739
2Pe 2:18 escaped from them w. live in error. ....
1Jo 2:22 W. is a liar but he that denieth 5101
1Jo 3:12 as Cain, w. was of that wicked one, ...
1Jo 4:21 he w. loveth God love his brother ....
1Jo 5:5 W. is he that overcometh the 5101
2Jo 7 w. confess not that Jesus Christ 3588
3Jo 9 w. loveth to have the preeminence 3588
Jude 4 w. were before of old ordained to 3588
Jude 18 w. should walk after their own ....
Jude 19 These be they w. separate themselves, ...
Re 1:2 W. bare record of the word of 3739
Re 1:5 Christ, w. is the faithful witness, ...
Re 1:9 John, w. am also your brother, ... 3588
Re 2:1 w. walketh in the midst of the 3588
Re 2:13 martyr, w. was slain among you, .. 3739
Re 2:14 w. taught Balac to cast a 3739
Re 2:18 w. hath his eyes like unto a flame .3588
Re 4:9 throne, w. liveth for ever and ever, ... 3588
Re 5:2 W. is worthy to open the book, ... 5101
Re 6:17 and w. shall be able to stand? 5101
Re 10:6 w. created heaven, and the things ....
Re 12:5 w. was to rule all nations with 3739
Re 13:4 W. is like unto the beast? 5101
Re 13:4 w. is able to make war with him? 5101
Re 14:11 w. worship the beast and his 3588
Re 15:4 W. shall not fear thee, O Lord, ... 5101
Re 15:7 God w. liveth for ever and ever. 3588
Re 18:8 is the Lord God w. judgeth her. 3588
Re 18:9 w. have committed fornication 3588

WHOLE See also WHOLESOME.

Ge 2:6 and watered the w. face of the 854,3605
Ge 2:11 the w. land of Havilah, ... 854,3605
Ge 2:13 the w. land of Ethiopia. 854,3605
Ge 7:19 that were under the w. heaven, ... 3605
Ge 8:9 were on the face of the w. earth: 3605
Ge 9:19 them was the w. earth overspread. 3605
Ge 11:1 the w. earth was of one language, ... 3605
Ge 11:4 upon the face of the w. earth. 3605
Ge 13:9 Is not the w. land before thee? 3605
Ge 47:28 the w. age of Jacob was an hundred ....
Ex 10:15 covered the face of the w. earth, ... 3605
Ex 12:6 w. assembly of the congregation 3605
Ex 16:2 the w. congregation of the children 3605
Ex 16:3 to kill this w. assembly 854,3605
Ex 16:10 the w. congregation of the children 3605
Ex 19:18 and the w. mount quaked greatly. 3605
Ex 29:18 thou shalt burn the w. ram 854,3605
Le 3:9 the fat thereof, and the w. rump, ... 8549
Le 4:12 Even the w. bullock shall he 854,3605
Le 4:13 the w. congregation of Israel sin 3605
Le 7:14 shall offer one out of the w. oblation ... 3605
Le 8:21 and Moses burnt the w. ram 854,3605
Le 10:6 the w. house of Israel, bewail the 3605
Le 25:29 may redeem it within a w. year 8552
Nu 3:7 charge of the w. congregation. 3605
Nu 8:9 shalt gather the w. assembly 854,3605
Nu 10:2 of a w. piece shalt thou make 4749
Nu 11:20 But even a w. month, until it 3117
Nu 11:21 that they may eat a w. month, ... 3117
Nu 14:2 the w. congregation said unto 3605
Nu 14:29 according to your w. number, from 3605
Nu 20:1 w. congregation, into the desert of 3605
Nu 20:22 the w. congregation, journeyed 3605
De 2:25 that are under the w. heaven, ... 3605
De 4:19 all nations under the w. heaven. 3605
De 27:6 of the Lord thy God of w. stones: 8003
De 29:23 the w. land thereof is brimstone, ... 3605
De 33:10 w. burnt sacrifice upon thine 3632
Jos 5:8 in the camp, till they were w. 2421
Jos 8:31 an altar of w. stones, over which 8003
Jos 10:13 not to go down about a w. day. 8549
Jos 11:23 So Joshua took the w. land, ... 854,3605
Jos 18:1 w. congregation of the children of 3605
Jos 22:12 w. congregation of the children of 3605
Jos 22:16 the w. congregation of the Lord, ... 3605
Jos 22:18 with the w. congregation of Israel 3605
Jg 19:2 and was there four w. months. 3117
Jg 21:13 w. congregation sent some to 3605
2Sa 1:9 because my life is yet w. in me. 3605

2Sa 3:19 good to the w. house of Benjamin...... 3605
2Sa 6:19 among the w. multitude of Israel,...... 3605
2Sa 14:7 w. family is risen against thine.......... 3605
1Ki 6:22 w. house be overlaid with gold, ... 3605
1Ki 6:22 the w. altar that was by the oracle..... 3605
1Ki 11:34 w. kingdom out of his hand. 854,3605
2Ki 9:8 the w. house of Ahab shall perish:...... 3605
2Ch 6:3 blessed the w. congregation of..... 854,3605
2Ch 15:15 sought him with their w. desire; 3605
2Ch 16:9 run to and fro through the w. earth, ... 3605
2Ch 26:12 w. number of the chief of the fathers.. 3605
2Ch 30:23 w. assembly took counsel to keep...... 3605
2Ch 33:8 according to the law and the.......... 3605
Ezr 2:64 w. congregation together was forty..... 3605
Ne 7:66 w. congregation together was forty..... 3605
Es 3:6 the w. kingdom of Ahasuerus, ... 3605
Job 5:18 woundeth, and his hands make w.. 7495
Job 28:24 and seeth under the w. heaven; 3605
Job 34:13 who hath disposed the w. world? 3605
Job 37:3 directeth it under the w. heaven, ... 3605
Job 41:11 is under the w. heaven is mine.......... 3605
Ps 9:1 thee, O Lord, with my w. heart;........ 3605
Ps 48:2 joy of the w. earth, is mount Zion, ... 3605
Ps 51:19 offering and w. burnt offering: 3632
Ps 72:19 w. earth be filled with his glory;... 854,3605
Ps 97:5 presence of the Lord of the w. earth. ..3605
Ps 105:16 he brake the w. staff of bread. 3605
Ps 111:1 praise the Lord with my w. heart,...... 3605
Ps 119:2 that seek him with the w. heart......... 3605
Ps 119:10 my w. heart have I sought thee:........ 3605
Ps 119:34 shall observe it with my w. heart. 3605
Ps 119:58 thy favour with my w. heart:............ 3605
Ps 119:69 thy precepts with my w. heart.......... 3605
Ps 119:145 I cried with my w. heart; hear me, O ....
Ps 138:1 I will praise thee with my w. heart:.... 3605
Pr 1:12 w., as those that go down into 8549
Pr 16:33 the w. disposing thereof is of the 3605
Pr 26:26 be shewed before the w. congregation......
Ec 12:13 the conclusion of the w. matter:......... 3605
Ec 12:13 for this is the w. duty of man........... 3605
Isa 1:5 w. head is sick, and the w. heart......... 3605
Isa 3:1 the staff, the w. stay of bread, ... 3605
Isa 3:1 and the w. stay of water, ... 3605
Isa 6:3 the w. earth is full of his glory. 3605
Isa 10:12 his w. work upon mount Zion....... 854,3605
Isa 13:5 indignation, to destroy the w. land...... 3605
Isa 14:7 The w. earth is at rest, and is quiet: .. 3605
Isa 14:26 is purposed upon the w. earth: 3605
Isa 14:29 Rejoice not thou, w. Palestina, ... 3605
Isa 14:31 thou, w. Palestina, art dissolved:........ 3605
Isa 21:8 I am set in my ward w. nights:.......... 3605
Isa 28:22 even determined upon the w. earth. ... 3605
Isa 54:5 God of the w. earth shall he be 3605
Jer 1:18 brasen walls against the w. land,........ 3605
Jer 3:10 turned unto me with her w. heart, ... 3605
Jer 4:20 cried; for the w. land is spoiled:......... 3605
Jer 4:27 The w. land shall be desolate; 3605
Jer 4:29 The w. city shall flee for the noise 3605
Jer 7:15 even the w. seed of Ephraim. 3605
Jer 8:16 the w. land trembled at the sound...... 3605
Jer 12:11 the w. land is made desolate, ... 3605
Jer 13:11 unto me the w. house of Israel........... 3605
Jer 13:11 Israel and the w. house of Judah, ... 3605
Jer 15:10 man of contention to the w. earth! 3605
Jer 19:11 that cannot be made w. again: 7495
Jer 24:7 unto me with their w. heart. 3605
Jer 25:11 this w. land shall be a desolation, ... 3605
Jer 31:40 the w. valley of the dead bodies,........ 3605
Jer 32:41 my w. heart and with my w. soul....... 3605
Jer 35:3 the w. house of the Rechabites;......... 3605
Jer 37:10 had smitten the w. army of the.......... 3605
Jer 45:4 I will pluck up, even the w. land. 3605
Jer 50:23 hammer of the w. earth cut asunder ... 3605
Jer 51:41 praise of the w. earth surprised! 3605
Jer 51:47 her w. land shall be confounded, ... 3605
La 2:15 of beauty, The joy of the w. earth? 3605
Eze 5:10 the w. remnant of thee will I............ 3605
Eze 7:13 touching the w. multitude thereof, ... 3605
Eze 10:12 their w. body, and their backs, and..... 3605
Eze 15:5 when it was w., it was meet for no 8549
Eze 32:4 beasts of the w. earth with thee. 3605
Eze 35:14 When the w. earth rejoiceth, I will..... 3605
Eze 37:11 bones are the w. house of Israel: 3605
Eze 39:25 mercy upon the w. house of Israel, ... 3605
Eze 43:11 may keep the w. form thereof, ... 3605
Eze 43:12 the w. limit thereof round about......... 3605
Eze 45:6 shall be for the w. house of Israel...... 3605
Da 2:35 mountain, and filled the w. earth. 3606
Da 2:48 him ruler over the w. province 3606
Da 6:1 should be over the w. kingdom; 3606
Da 6:3 to set him over the w. realm............ 3606
Da 7:23 and shall devour the w. earth, ... 3606
Da 7:27 the kingdom under the w. heaven,...... 3606
Da 8:5 west on the face of the w. earth, ... 3605
Da 9:12 for under the w. heaven hath not....... 3605
Da 10:3 three w. weeks were fulfilled. 3117
Da 11:17 the strength of his w. kingdom, ... 3605
Am 1:6 away captive the w. captivity,............ 8003
Am 1:9 they delivered up the w. captivity....... 8003
Am 3:1 against the w. family which I............ 3605
Mic 4:13 unto the Lord of the w. earth............ 3605
Zep 1:18 w. land shall be devoured by the........ 3605
Zec 4:10 to and fro through the w. earth. 3605
Zec 4:14 stand by the Lord of the w. earth. 3605
Zec 5:3 forth over the face of the w. earth: 3605
Mal 3:9 robbed me, even the w. nation. 3605
Mt 5:29, 30 thy w. body should be cast *3650*
Mt 6:22 thy w. body shall be full of light... *3650*
Mt 6:23 w. body shall be full of darkness... *3650*
Mt 8:32 the w. herd of swine ran violently *3956*
Mt 8:34 the w. city came out to meet Jesus: *3956*
Mt 9:12 that be w. need not a physician,.... *2480*
Mt 9:21 touch his garment, I shall be w......... *4982*
Mt 9:22 thy faith hath made thee w.......... *4982*
Mt 9:22 woman was made w. from that.......... *4982*
Mt 12:13 it was restored w., like as the.......... *5199*
Mt 13:2 w. multitude stood on the shore......... *3956*
Mt 13:33 of meal, till the w. was leavened... *3650*
Mt 14:36 as touched were made perfectly w....... *1295*
Mt 15:28 was made w. from that very hour. *3390*
Mt 15:31 the maimed to be w., the lame to *5199*
Mt 16:26 if he shall gain the w. world, and.. *3650*
Mt 26:13 be preached in the w. world, ... *3650*
Mt 27:27 unto him the w. band of soldiers. *3650*
Mk 2:17 They that are w. have no need of .. *2480*
Mk 3:5 hand was restored w. as the other. *5199*
Mk 4:1 the w. multitude was by the sea *3956*
Mk 5:28 but his clothes, I shall be w.. .... *4982*
Mk 5:34 thy faith hath made thee w.;........ *4982*
Mk 5:34 peace, and be w. of thy plague...... *5199*
Mk 6:55 ran through that w. region round........ *3650*
Mk 6:56 as touch him were made w.. .... *4982*
Mk 8:36 if he shall gain the w. world, and.. *3650*
Mk 10:52 thy faith hath made thee w.......... *4982*
Mk 12:33 is more than all w. burnt offerings....... *3646*
Mk 14:9 preached throughout the w. *3650*
Mk 15:1 scribes and the w. council, and.......... *3650*
Mk 15:16 and they call together the w. band...... *3650*
Mk 15:33 was darkness over the w. land until.... *3650*
Lu 1:10 the w. multitude of the people *3956*
Lu 5:31 that are w. need not a physician; .. *5198*
Lu 6:10 hand was restored w. as the other. *5199*
Lu 6:19 w. multitude sought to touch him: *3956*
Lu 7:10 servant w. that had been sick........... *5198*
Lu 8:37 the w. multitude of the country *537*
Lu 8:39 published throughout the w. city *3650*
Lu 8:48 thy faith hath made thee w.; go *4982*
Lu 8:50 only, and she shall be made w.. ..... *4982*
Lu 9:25 if he gain the w. world, and lose... *3650*
Lu 11:34 thy w. body also is full of light;.... *3650*
Lu 11:36 w. body therefore be full of light,.. *3650*
Lu 11:36 dark, the w. shall be full of light, ..*3650*
Lu 13:21 of meal, till the w. was leavened... *3650*
Lu 17:19 thy faith hath made thee w.......... *4982*
Lu 19:37 w. multitude of the disciples began....... *537*
Lu 21:35 dwell on the face of the w. earth... *3956*
Lu 23:1 the w. multitude of them arose, ... *537*
Joh 4:53 believed, and his w. house............... *3650*
Joh 5:4 w. of whatsoever disease he had......... *5199*
Joh 5:6 unto him, Wilt thou be made w.? *5199*
Joh 5:9 immediately the man was made w., ... *5199*
Joh 5:11 He that made me w., the same said ... *5199*
Joh 5:14 him, Behold, thou art made w. *5199*
Joh 5:15 was Jesus, which had made him w....... *5199*
Joh 7:23 every whit w. on the sabbath day?. *5199*
Joh 11:50 and that the w. nation perish not........ *3650*
Ac 4:9 by what means he is made w.; *4982*
Ac 4:10 this man stand here before you w.. ...... *5199*
Ac 6:5 saying pleased the w. multitude: *3956*
Ac 9:34 Jesus Christ maketh thee w.: *2390*
Ac 11:26 that a w. year they assembled........... *3650*
Ac 13:44 came almost the w. city together *3956*
Ac 15:22 and elders, with the w. church, ... *3650*
Ac 19:29 w. city was filled with confusion:........ *3650*
Ac 28:30 two w. years in his own hired........... *3650*
Ro 1:8 spoken of throughout the w. world. *3650*
Ro 8:22 that the w. creation groaneth *3956*
Ro 16:23 of the w. church, saluteth you. *3650*
1Co 5:6 little leaven leaveneth the w. lump? *3650*
1Co 12:17 If the w. body were an eye,.............. *3650*
1Co 12:17 If the w. were hearing, ... *3650*
1Co 14:23 w. church become together into one ... *3650*
Ga 5:3 he is a debtor to do the w. law.......... *3650*
Ga 5:9 little leaven leaveneth the w. lump...... *3650*
Eph 3:15 w. family in heaven and earth is......... *3958*
Eph 4:16 the w. body fitly joined together *3958*
Eph 6:11 Put on the w. armour of God, that ye.......
Eph 6:13 take unto you the w. armour of God, ...
1Th 5:23 your w. spirit and soul and body *3648*
Tit 1:11 who subvert w. houses, teaching......... *3650*
Jas 2:10 whosoever shall keep the w. law,........ *3650*
Jas 3:2 able also to bridle the w. body........... *3650*
Jas 3:3 and we turn about their w. body. *3650*
Jas 3:6 that it defileth the w. body, and......... *3650*
1Jo 2:2 also for the sins of the w. world. *3650*
1Jo 5:19 the w. world lieth in wickedness. *3650*
Re 12:9 which deceiveth the w. world: *3650*
Re 16:14 of the earth and of the w. world, ... *3650*

WHOLESOME

Pr 15:4 A w. tongue is a tree of life: but........ 4832
1Ti 6:3 and consent not to w. words, even..... *5198*

WHOLLY

Le 6:22 the Lord; it shall be w. burnt. 3632
Le 6:23 offering...shall be w. burnt................ 3632
Le 19:9 not w. reap the corners of thy field 3615
Nu 3:9 they are w. given unto him out of ....
Nu 4:6 spread over it a cloth w. of blue, ... 3632
Nu 8:16 For they are w. given unto me from.........
Nu 32:11 they have not w. followed me:........... 4390
Nu 32:12 they have w. followed the Lord. 4390
De 1:36 he hath w. followed the Lord. 4390
Jos 14:8 I w. followed the Lord my God.......... 4390
Jos 14:9 hast w. followed the Lord my God. 4390
Jos 14:14 that he w. followed the Lord God....... 4390
Jg 17:3 w. dedicated the silver unto the......... 6942
1Sa 7:9 a burnt offering w. unto the Lord:...... 3632
1Ch 28:21 people...w. at thy commandment........ 3605
Job 21:23 full strength, being w. at ease and...... 3605
Isa 22:1 art w. gone up to the housetops?....... 3605
Jer 2:21 thee a noble vine, w. a right seed: 3605
Jer 6:6 is w. oppression in the midst of her.... 3605
Jer 13:19 it shall be w. carried away captive...... 7965
Jer 42:15 ye w. set your faces to enter into 7760
Jer 46:28 I not leave thee w. unpunished. 5352
Jer 50:13 but it shall be w. desolate:................ 3605
Eze 11:15 and all the house of Israel w., ... 3605
Am 8:8 and it shall rise up w. as a flood; 3605
Am 9:5 and it shall rise up w. like a flood; 3605
Ac 17:16 he saw the city w. given to idolatry..........
1Th 5:23 very God of peace sanctify you w.;...... *3651*
1Ti 4:15 give thyself w. to them; that...... *1510,1722*

WHOM See also WHOMSOEVER.

Ge 2:8 he put the man w. he had formed........ 834
Ge 3:12 The woman w. thou gavest to be 834
Ge 4:25 seed instead of Abel, w. Cain slew. 3588
Ge 6:7 will destroy man w. I have created 834
Ge 10:14 (out of w. came Philistim,) and........... 834
Ge 15:14 w. they shall serve, will I judge:.......... 834
Ge 21:3 him, w. Sarah bare to him, Isaac. 834
Ge 22:2 only son Isaac, w. thou lovest,........... 834
Ge 24:3 the Canaanites, among w. I dwell; 834
Ge 24:14 the damsel to w. I shall say, Let 834
Ge 24:40 before w. I walk, will send his angel..... 834
Ge 24:44 woman w. the Lord hath appointed 834
Ge 24:44 Nahor's son, w. Milcah bare unto 834
Ge 25:12 w. Hagar the Egyptian, Sarah's 834
Ge 30:26 children, for w. I have served thee, ... 834
Ge 41:38 is, a man in w. the Spirit of God is?..... 834
Ge 43:27 well, the old man of w. ye spake?........ 834
Ge 43:29 younger brother, of w. ye spake.......... 834
Ge 44:10 w. it is found shall be my servant; 834
Ge 44:16 he also with w. the cup is found. 834
Ge 45:4 your brother, w. ye sold into Egypt. 834
Ge 46:18 w. Laban gave to Leah his daughter,.... 834
Ge 48:9 w. God hath given me in this place. 834
Ge 48:15 my fathers Abraham and Isaac............. 834
Ge 49:8 art he w. thy brethren shall praise:...........
Ex 4:13 by the hand of him w. thou wilt send. ....
Ex 6:5 w. the Egyptians keep in bondage;....... 834

Ex 6:26 and Moses, to **w.** the Lord said, 834
Ex 14:13 Egyptians **w.** ye have seen to day, 834
Ex 18:9 **w.** he had delivered out of the land 834
Ex 22:9 **w.** the judges shall condemn, he 834
Ex 23:27 the people to **w.** thou shalt come, 834
Ex 28:3 **w.** I have filled with the spirit of 834
Ex 32:13 **w.** thou swarest by thine own self, 834
Ex 33:12 know **w.** thou wilt send with me. 853,834
Ex 33:19 gracious to **w.** I will be gracious, 853,834
Ex 33:19 mercy on **w.** I will shew mercy. 853,834
Ex 35:21 every one **w.** his spirit made willing, 834
Ex 35:23 every man, with **w.** was found blue, 834
Ex 35:24 with **w.** was found shittim wood 834
Ex 36:1 in **w.** the Lord put wisdom 834,1992
Le 6:5 it unto him to **w.** it appertaineth, 834
Le 13:45 And the leper in **w.** the plague is, 834
Le 14:32 him in **w.** is the plague of leprosy, 834
Le 15:18 woman also with **w.** man shall lie 834
Le 16:32 And the priest, **w.** he shall anoint, 834
Le 16:32 **w.** he shall consecrate to minister 834
Le 17:7 after **w.** they have gone a 834,1992
Le 22:5 of **w.** he may take uncleanness, 834
Le 25:27 unto the man to **w.** he sold it; 834
Le 25:55 my servants **w.** I brought forth 834,853
Le 26:45 **w.** I brought forth out of the 834,853
Le 27:24 unto him of **w.** it was bought, 834,853
Le 27:24 **w.**...possession of the land...belong. 834
Nu 3:3 **w.** he consecrated to minister in 834
Nu 4:41 **w.** Moses and Aaron did number 834
Nu 4:45 **w.** Moses and Aaron numbered 834
Nu 4:46 **w.** Moses and Aaron and the chief of 834
Nu 5:7 him against **w.** he hath trespassed, 834
Nu 11:16 **w.** thou knowest to be the elders of 834
Nu 11:21 The people, among **w.** I am, are six 834
Nu 12:1 woman **w.** he had married: 834
Nu 12:12 of **w.** the flesh is half consumed when
Nu 16:5 even him **w.** he hath chosen will 834
Nu 16:7 the man **w.** the Lord doth choose, 834
Nu 17:5 **w.** I shall choose, shall blossom: 834
Nu 22:6 that he **w.** thou blessest is blessed, 834
Nu 22:6 and he **w.** thou cursest is cursed. 834
Nu 23:8 shall I curse, **w.** God hath not cursed?
Nu 23:8 I defy, **w.** the Lord hath not defiled?
Nu 26:5 of **w.** cometh the family of the
Nu 26:59 **w.** her mother bare to Levi in 834,853
Nu 26:64 **w.** Moses and Aaron the priest
Nu 27:18 of Nun, a man in **w.** is the spirit, 834
Nu 34:29 are they **w.** the Lord commanded to 834
Nu 36:6 Let them marry to **w.** they think best;
De 4:46 **w.** Moses and the children of Israel 834
De 7:19 people of **w.** thou art afraid. 834,6440
De 9:2 of the Anakims, **w.** thou knowest, 834
De 9:2 and of **w.** thou hast heard say, 834
De 17:15 **w.** the Lord thy God shall choose: 834
De 19:4 **w.** he hated not in time past;
De 19:17 between **w.** the controversy is, 834,1992
De 21:8 Israel, **w.** thou hast redeemed, 834
De 24:11 man to **w.** thou dost lend shall bring 834
De 28:55 flesh of his children **w.** he shall eat: 834
De 29:26 them, gods **w.** they knew not, 834
De 29:26 and **w.** he had not given unto them: 834
De 31:4 land of them, **w.** he destroyed. 834,853
De 32:17 to gods **w.** they knew not, to new gods
De 32:17 newly up, **w.** your fathers feared not.
De 32:20 generation, children in **w.** is no faith.
De 32:37 gods, their rock in **w.** they trusted,
De 33:8 one, **w.** thou didst prove at Massah, 834
De 33:8 with **w.** thou didst strive at the waters
De 34:10 **w.** the Lord knew face to face, 834
Jos 2:10 and Og, **w.** ye utterly destroyed. 834,853
Jos 4:4 **w.** he had prepared of the children 834
Jos 5:6 **w.** the Lord sware that he 834,1992
Jos 5:7 **w.** he raised up in their stead,
Jos 10:11 **w.** the children of Israel slew with 834
Jos 10:25 enemies against **w.** ye fight 834,853
Jos 13:8 With **w.** the Reubenites and the 5973
Jos 13:21 **w.** Moses smote with the princes 834
Jos 24:15 you this day **w.** ye will serve; 4310
Jos 24:17 the people through **w.** we passed: 834
Jg 4:22 shew thee the man **w.** thou seekest. 834
Jg 7:4 shall be, that of **w.** I say unto thee, 834
Jg 8:15 with **w.** ye did upbraid me, saying, 834
Jg 8:18 men were they **w.** ye slew at Tabor? 834
Jg 12:9 thirty daughters, **w.** he sent abroad,
Jg 14:20 **w.** he had used as his friend. 834
Jg 21:23 them that danced, **w.** they caught: 834

Ru 2:19 with **w.** she had wrought, and 834,5973
Ru 2:19 **w.** I wrought to day is Boaz. 834,5973
Ru 4:1 kinsman of **w.** Boaz spake came by; 834
Ru 4:1 unto **w.** he said, Ho, such a one!
Ru 4:12 **w.** Tamar bare unto Judah, of the 834
1Sa 2:33 **w.** I shall not cut off from mine altar,
1Sa 6:20 and to **w.** shall he go up from us? 4310
1Sa 9:17 Behold the man **w.** I spake to thee 834
1Sa 9:20 on **w.** is all the desire of Israel? 4310
1Sa 10:24 See ye him **w.** the Lord hath 834
1Sa 12:3 I taken? or **w.** have I defrauded? 4310
1Sa 12:3 **w.** have I oppressed? or of whose
1Sa 12:13 the king **w.** ye have chosen, 4310
1Sa 12:13 chosen, and **w.** ye have desired! 4310
1Sa 16:3 unto me him **w.** I name unto thee. 834
1Sa 17:28 **w.** hast thou left those few sheep 4310
1Sa 17:45 of Israel, **w.** thou hast defied. 834
1Sa 21:9 **w.** thou slewest in the valley of 834
1Sa 24:14 After **w.** is the king of Israel come 4310
1Sa 24:14 after **w.** dost thou pursue? after a 4310
1Sa 25:11 **w.** I know not whence they be? 834
1Sa 25:25 men of my lord, **w.** thou didst send 834
1Sa 28:8 up, **w.** I shall name unto thee. 853,834
1Sa 28:11 **W.** shall I bring up unto thee? 853,4310
1Sa 29:5 of **w.** they sang one to another 834
1Sa 30:13 unto him, To **w.** belongest thou? 4310
1Sa 30:21 **w.** they had made also to abide at the
2Sa 7:7 **w.** I commanded to feed my people 834
2Sa 7:15 Saul, **w.** I put away before thee. 834
2Sa 7:23 **w.** God went to redeem for a people 834
2Sa 14:7 the life of his brother **w.** he slew; 834
2Sa 15:33 Unto **w.** David said, If thou passest
2Sa 16:18 but **w.** the Lord, and this people, 834
2Sa 16:19 And again, **w.** should I serve? 4310
2Sa 17:3 man **w.** thou seekest is as if all 834
2Sa 19:10 Absalom, **w.** we anointed over us, 834
2Sa 20:3 **w.** he had left to keep the house, and 834
2Sa 21:6 of Saul, **w.** the Lord did choose.
2Sa 21:8 **w.** she bare unto Saul, Armoni and 834
2Sa 21:8 **w.** she brought up for Adriel the son
2Sa 23:8 of the mighty men **w.** David had: 834
2Sa 23:8 hundred, **w.** he slew at one time.
1Ki 2:5 Amasa the son of Jether, **w.** he slew,
1Ki 5:5 son, **w.** I will set upon thy throne 834
1Ki 7:8 daughter, **w.** he had taken to wife, 834
1Ki 9:21 **w.** the children of Israel also were not
1Ki 10:26 **w.** he bestowed in the cities for
1Ki 11:20 **w.** Tahpenes weaned in Pharaoh's
1Ki 11:34 **w.** I chose, because he kept my 834
1Ki 13:23 prophet **w.** he had brought back. 834
1Ki 17:1 of Israel liveth, before **w.** I stand, 834
1Ki 17:20 upon the widow with **w.** I sojourn, 834
1Ki 18:15 of hosts liveth, before **w.** I stand, 834
1Ki 18:31 unto **w.** the word of the Lord came, 834
1Ki 20:14 And Ahab said, By **w.**? And he 4310
1Ki 20:42 **w.** I appointed to utter destruction,
1Ki 21:25 **w.** Jezebel his wife stirred up 834
1Ki 21:26 the Amorites, **w.** the Lord cast out 834
1Ki 22:8 by **w.** we may enquire of the Lord:
2Ki 3:14 of hosts liveth, before **w.** I stand, 834
2Ki 5:16 As the Lord liveth, before **w.** I stand, 834
2Ki 6:19 bring you to the man **w.** ye seek. 834
2Ki 6:22 those **w.** thou hast taken captive 834
2Ki 8:5 her son, **w.** Elisha restored to life 834
2Ki 10:24 of the men **w.** I have brought into 834
2Ki 16:3 **w.** the Lord cast out from before 834
2Ki 17:8 **w.** the Lord cast out from before 834
2Ki 17:11 heathen **w.** the Lord carried away 834
2Ki 17:15 **w.** the Lord had charged them, 834
2Ki 17:27 priests **w.** ye brought from thence; 834
2Ki 17:28 priests **w.** they had carried away 834
2Ki 17:33 the nations **w.** they carried away 834
2Ki 17:34 of Jacob, **w.** he named Israel; 834
2Ki 17:35 **w.** the Lord had made a covenant,
2Ki 18:20 Now on **w.** dost thou trust, that 4310
2Ki 19:4 **w.** the king of Assyria his master 834
2Ki 19:10 thy God in **w.** thou trustest deceive 834
2Ki 19:22 **W.** hast thou reproached and 853,4310
2Ki 19:22 against **w.** hast thou exalted thy 4310
2Ki 21:2 **w.** the Lord cast out before the 834
2Ki 21:9 the nations **w.** the Lord destroyed 834
2Ki 23:5 priests, **w.** the kings of Judah had 834
2Ki 25:22 **w.** Nebuchadnezzar king of 834
1Ch 1:12 (of **w.** came the Philistines,) 834
1Ch 2:21 **w.** he married when he was
1Ch 5:6 **w.** Tilgath-pilneser...carried 834

1Ch 5:25 **w.** God destroyed before them. 834
1Ch 6:31 they **w.** David set over the service 834
1Ch 7:14 of Manasseh; Ashriel, **w.** she bare: 834
1Ch 7:21 **w.** the men of Gath that were born
1Ch 9:22 **w.** David and Samuel the seer 834,1922
1Ch 11:10 of the mighty men **w.** David had, 834
1Ch 11:11 of the mighty men **w.** David had; 834
1Ch 17:6 **w.** I commanded to feed my people, 834
1Ch 17:21 **w.** God went to redeem to be his 834
1Ch 17:21 **w.** thou hast redeemed out of 834
1Ch 26:32 **w.** king David made rulers over the
1Ch 29:1 my son, **w.** alone God hath chosen,
1Ch 29:8 **w.** precious stones were found 834
2Ch 1:11 **w.** I have made thee king: 834,5921
2Ch 2:7 **w.** David my father did provide. 834
2Ch 8:8 **w.** the children of Israel consumed 834
2Ch 9:25 **w.** he bestowed in the chariot cities,
2Ch 17:19 **w.** the king put in fenced cities 834
2Ch 18:7 by **w.** we may enquire of the Lord:
2Ch 20:10 **w.** thou wouldest not let Israel 834
2Ch 22:7 **w.** the Lord had anointed to cut off 834
2Ch 23:18 **w.** David had distributed in the 834
2Ch 28:3 **w.** the Lord had cast out before the 834
2Ch 33:2 **w.** the Lord had cast out before the 834
2Ch 33:9 heathen, **w.** the Lord had destroyed 834
Ezr 2:1 **w.** Nebuchadnezzar the king of 834
Ezr 2:65 of **w.** there were seven thousand 428
Ezr 4:10 **w.** the great and noble Asnapper 1768
Ezr 5:14 **w.** he had made governor; 1768
Ezr 8:20 **w.** David and the princes had
Ezr 10:44 had wives by **w.** they had children.
Ne 1:10 **w.** thou hast redeemed by thy 834
Ne 7:6 **w.** Nebuchadnezzar the king of 834
Ne 7:67 of **w.** there were seven thousand 428
Ne 8:10 them for **w.** nothing is prepared:
Ne 9:37 kings **w.** thou hast set over us 834
Es 2:6 **w.** Nebuchadnezzar the king of 834
Es 2:7 **w.** Mordecai, when her father and
Es 4:5 **w.** he had appointed to attend 834
Es 4:11 to **w.** the king shall hold out the 834
Es 6:6 man **w.** the king delighteth to honour?
Es 6:6 To **w.** would the king delight to do
Es 6:7 **w.** the king delighteth to honour 4310
Es 6:9 **w.** the king delighteth to honour, 834
Es 6:9, 11 **w.** the king delighteth to honour. 834
Es 6:13 before **w.** thou hast begun to fall, 834
Job 3:23 is hid, and **w.** God hath hedged in?
Job 5:17 happy is the man **w.** God correcteth:
Job 9:15 **W.**, though I were righteous, yet 834
Job 15:19 **w.** alone the earth was given, 1992
Job 19:19 **w.** I loved are turned against me.
Job 19:27 **w.** I shall see for myself, and mine 834
Job 25:3 upon **w.** doth not his light arise? 4310
Job 26:4 To **w.** hast thou uttered words? 4310
Job 30:2 me, in **w.** old age was perished? 5921
Ps 10:3 the covetous, **w.** the Lord abhorreth.
Ps 16:3 the excellent, in **w.** is all my delight.
Ps 18:2 God, my strength, in **w.** I will trust;
Ps 18:43 **w.** I have not known shall serve me.
Ps 27:1 my salvation; **w.** shall I fear? 4310
Ps 27:1 of my life; of **w.** shall I be afraid? 4310
Ps 32:2 **w.** the Lord imputeth not iniquity,
Ps 33:12 people **w.** he hath chosen for his own
Ps 41:9 familiar friend, in **w.** I trusted, 834
Ps 45:16 **w.** thou mayest make princes in all
Ps 47:4 excellency of Jacob **w.** he loved. 834
Ps 65:4 Blessed is the man **w.** thou choosest
Ps 69:26 him **w.** thou hast smitten; 834
Ps 69:26 grief of those **w.** thou hast wounded.
Ps 73:25 **W.** have I in heaven but thee? 4310
Ps 80:17 **w.** thou madest strong for thyself.
Ps 86:9 All nations **w.** thou hast made 834
Ps 88:5 **w.** thou rememberest no more: 834
Ps 89:21 With **w.** my hand...be established: 834
Ps 94:1 God, to **w.** vengeance belongeth;
Ps 94:1 O God, to **w.** vengeance belongeth,
Ps 94:12 is the man **w.** thou chastenest, O 834
Ps 95:11 Unto **w.** I sware in my wrath that 834
Ps 104:26 **w.** thou hast made to play therein.
Ps 105:26 and Aaron **w.** he had chosen. 834
Ps 106:34 **w.** the Lord commanded them: 834
Ps 106:38 **w.** they sacrificed unto the idols of 834
Ps 107:2 **w.** he hath redeemed from the hand 834
Ps 144:2 my shield, and he in **w.** I trust;
Ps 146:3 the son of man, in **w.** there is no help.
Pr 3:12 For **w.** the Lord loveth he 853,834

Book	Ref	Context	No.
Pr	3:12	a father the son in w. he delighteth.	
Pr	3:27	not good from them to w. it is due,	
Pr	25:7	prince w. thine eyes have seen.	834
Pr	30:31	against w. there is no rising up.	5973
Ec	4:8	For w. do I labour, and bereave	4310
Ec	5:19	man also to w. God hath given	834
Ec	6:2	A man to w. God hath given riches,	834
Ec	8:14	just men, unto w. it happeneth	413
Ec	8:14	to w. it happeneth according to the	413
Ec	9:9	with the wife w. thou lovest all the	834
Ca	1:7	tell me, O thou w. my soul loveth,	
Ca	3:1	I sought him w. my soul loveth:	
Ca	3:2	I will seek him w. my soul loveth:	
Ca	3:3	the city found me: to w. I said,	
Ca	3:3	Saw ye him w. my soul loveth?	853
Ca	3:4	I found him w. my soul loveth: I held	
Isa	6:8	W. shall I send, and who will	853,4310
Isa	8:12	them to w. this people shall say,	834
Isa	8:18	children w. the Lord hath give me	834
Isa	10:3	to w. will ye flee for help? and	4310
Isa	19:25	W. the Lord of hosts shall bless,	834
Isa	22:16	w. hast thou here, that thou hast	4310
Isa	23:2	thou w. the merchants of Zidon, that	
Isa	28:9	W. shall he teach knowledge?	853,4310
Isa	28:9	and w. shall he make to	834,413
Isa	28:12	To w. he said, This is the rest	
Isa	31:6	unto him from w. the children	834
Isa	36:5	now on w. dost thou trust, that	4310
Isa	37:4	w. the king of Assyria his master	834
Isa	37:10	not thy God, in w. thou trustest,	834
Isa	37:23	w. hast thou reproached and	853,4310
Isa	37:23	against w. hast thou exalted thy	4310
Isa	40:14	With w. took he counsel, and who	4310
Isa	40:18	to w. then will ye liken God? or	4310
Isa	40:25	To w. then will ye liken me, or	4310
Isa	41:8	servant, Jacob w. I have chosen,	834
Isa	41:9	Thou w. I have taken from the	834
Isa	42:1	Behold my servant, w. I uphold;	
Isa	42:1	mine elect, in w. my soul delighteth;	
Isa	42:24	he against w. we have sinned?	2098
Isa	43:10	and my servant w. I have chosen:	834
Isa	44:1	and Israel, w. I have chosen:	
Isa	44:2	and thou, Jesurun, w. I have chosen.	
Isa	46:5	To w. will ye liken me, and make	4310
Isa	47:15	thee with w. thou hast laboured,	834
Isa	49:3	O Israel, in w. I will be glorified.	834
Isa	49:7	Holy One, to him w. man despiseth,	
Isa	49:7	to him w. the nation abhorreth,	
Isa	50:1	divorcement, w. I have put away?	834
Isa	50:1	creditors is it to w. I have sold you?	834
Isa	51:18	the sons w. she hath brought forth;	
Isa	51:19	by w. shall I comfort thee?	4310
Isa	53:1	and to w. is the arm of the Lord	4310
Isa	57:4	Against w. do ye sport yourselves?	4310
Isa	57:4	against w. make ye a wide mouth,	4310
Isa	57:11	And of w. hast thou been afraid or	4310
Isa	66:13	As one w. his mother comforteth,	834
Jer	1:12	w. the word of the Lord came in the	834
Jer	6:10	To w. shall I speak, and give	4310
Jer	7:9	after other gods w. ye know not;	834
Jer	8:2	w. they have loved, and w. they	834
Jer	8:2	and after w. they have walked,	834
Jer	8:2	and w. they have sought, and	
Jer	8:2	w. they have worshipped: they	834
Jer	9:12	who is he to w. the mouth of the	834
Jer	9:16	neither they nor their fathers	834
Jer	11:12	unto w. they offer incense:	834,1992
Jer	14:16	people to w. they prophesy	834,1992
Jer	18:8	against w. I have pronounced,	834
Jer	19:4	w. neither they nor their fathers	834
Jer	20:6	to w. thou hast prophesied	834,1992
Jer	23:9	like a man w. wine hath overcome,	
Jer	24:5	w. I have sent out of this place	834
Jer	25:15	to w. I send thee, to drink it.	834,413
Jer	25:17	unto w. the Lord hath sent me:	834,413
Jer	26:5	the prophets, w. I sent unto you,	834
Jer	27:5	unto w. it seemed meet unto me.	834
Jer	29:1	w. Nebuchadnezzar had carried	834
Jer	29:3	(w. Zedekiah king of Judah sent	834
Jer	29:4	w. I have caused to be carried away	834
Jer	29:20	w. I have sent from Jerusalem to	834
Jer	29:22	w. the king of Babylon roasted in	834
Jer	30:9	king, w. I will raise up unto them.	834
Jer	30:17	is Zion, w. no man seeketh after.	
Jer	33:5	w. I have slain in mine anger and	834
Jer	34:11	handmaids, w. they had let go free,	834
Jer	34:16	w. he had set a liberty at their	834
Jer	37:1	w. Nebuchadrezzar king of Babylon	834
Jer	38:9	w. they have cast into the	853,834
Jer	39:17	men of w. thou art afraid.	834,6440
Jer	40:5	w. the king of Babylon hath made	834
Jer	41:2	w. the king of Babylon had made	834
Jer	41:9	w. he had slain because of	834
Jer	41:10	w. Nebuzar-adan the captain of the	834
Jer	41:16	w. he had recovered from Ishmael	834
Jer	41:16	w. he had brought again from	834
Jer	41:18	w. the king of Babylon made	834
Jer	42:6	Lord our God, to w. we send thee;	
Jer	42:9	w. ye sent me to present your	834,413
Jer	42:11	Babylon, of w. ye are afraid;	834,6440
Jer	44:3	other gods, w. they knew not,	834
Jer	50:20	I will pardon them w. I reserve.	834
Jer	52:28	people w. Nebuchadrezzar carried	834
La	1:10	w. thou didst command that they	834
La	1:14	from w. I am not able to rise up.	
La	2:20	consider to w. thou hast done	4310
La	4:20	w. we said, Under his shadow we	834
Eze	9:6	any man upon w. is the mark;	834
Eze	11:1	among w. I saw Jaazaniah the son of	
Eze	11:7	Your slain w. ye have laid in the	834
Eze	11:15	w. the inhabitants of Jerusalem	834
Eze	13:22	sad, w. I have not made sad;	
Eze	16:20	w. thou hast borne unto me,	834
Eze	16:37	with w. thou hast taken pleasure,	834
Eze	20:9	the heathen, among w. they were,	834
Eze	23:7	and with all on w. she doted:	834
Eze	23:9	the Assyrians, upon w. she doted.	834
Eze	23:22	from w. thy mind is alienated,	834,1992
Eze	23:28	the hand of them w. thou hatest,	834
Eze	23:28	from w. thy mind is alienated:	834
Eze	23:37	their sons, w. they bare unto me,	834
Eze	23:40	unto w. a messenger was sent;	834,413
Eze	23:40	for w. thou didst wash thyself,	834
Eze	24:21	daughters w. ye have left shall fall	834
Eze	28:25	people among w. they are scattered,	834
Eze	31:2	W. art thou like in thy	413,4310
Eze	31:18	To w. art thou thus like in glory	4310
Eze	32:19	W. dost thou pass in beauty? go	4310
Eze	38:17	Art thou he of w. I have spoken in	834
Da	1:4	Children in w. was no blemish,	834,1992
Da	1:4	w. they might teach the learning	
Da	1:7	Unto w. the prince of the eunuchs	1992
Da	1:11	w. the prince of the eunuchs had	834
Da	2:24	w. the king had ordained to	1768
Da	3:12	Jews w. thou hast set over the	3487
Da	3:17	God w. we serve is able to deliver	1768
Da	4:8	in w. is the spirit of the holy gods:	1768
Da	5:11	in w. is the spirit of the holy gods;	1768
Da	5:11	w. the king Nebuchadnezzar thy	
Da	5:12	w. the king named Belteshazzar:	1768
Da	5:13	w. the king my father brought	1768
Da	5:19	before him: w. he would he slew;	1768
Da	5:19	and w. he would he kept alive;	1768
Da	5:19	alive; and w. he would he set up;	1768
Da	5:19	up; and w. he would he put down.	
Da	6:2	of w. Daniel was first:	1768,2006
Da	6:16	God w. thou servest continually,	1768
Da	6:20	God, w. thou servest continually,	1768
Da	7:8	before w. there were three of the	
Da	7:20	came up, and before w. three fell;	4479
Da	9:21	w. I had seen in the vision at the	834
Da	11:21	w. they shall not give the honour	5921
Da	11:38	a god w. his fathers knew not	834
Da	11:39	w. he shall acknowledge and	834
Ho	13:10	and thy judges of w. thou saidst,	834
Joe	2:32	the remnant w. the Lord shall call	834
Joe	3:2	w. they have scattered among the	834
Am	6:1	to w. the house of Israel came!	1992
Am	7:2,5	by w. shall Jacob arise? for he	4310
Na	3:19	w. hath not thy wickedness passed	4310
Zep	3:18	to w. the reproach...was a burden	5921
Zec	1:4	w. the former prophets have	834,413
Zec	1:10	These are they w. the Lord hath	834
Zec	7:14	all the nations w. they knew not.	834
Zec	12:10	look upon me w. they...pierced,	854,834
Mal	1:4	people against w. the Lord hath	834
Mal	2:14	w. thou hast dealt treacherously:	834
Mal	3:1	w. ye seek, shall suddenly come	834
Mal	3:1	of the covenant, w. ye delight in:	834
Mt	1:16	of Mary, of w. was born Jesus,	*3739*
Mt	3:17	Son, in w. I am well pleased.	*3739*
Mt	7:9	w. if his son ask bread, will he	*3739*
Mt	11:10	he, of w. it is written, Behold, I	*3739*
Mt	12:18	my servant, w. I have chosen;	*3739*
Mt	12:18	in w. my soul is well pleased:	*3739*
Mt	12:27	w. do your children cast them	*5101*
Mt	16:13	W. do men say that I the Son of	*5101*
Mt	16:15	them, But w. say ye that I am?	*5101*
Mt	17:5	Son, in w. I am well pleased;	*3939*
Mt	17:25	w. do the kings of the earth take	*5101*
Mt	18:7	that man by w. the offence	*3739*
Mt	19:11	saying, save they to w. it is given	*3739*
Mt	20:23	for w. it is prepared of my	*3739*
Mt	23:35	w. ye slew between the temple	*3739*
Mt	24:45	w. his lord hath made ruler over	*3739*
Mt	24:46	w. his lord when he cometh shall	*3739*
Mt	26:24	by w. the Son of man is betrayed!	*3739*
Mt	27:9	w....the children of Israel did value;	*3739*
Mt	27:15	people a prisoner, w. they would.	*3739*
Mt	27:17	W. will ye that I release unto you?	*5101*
Mk	1:11	Son, in w. I am well pleased.	*3739*
Mk	3:13	and calleth unto him w. he would:	*3739*
Mk	6:16	he said, It is John, w. I beheaded:	*3739*
Mk	8:27	them, W. do men say that I am?	*5101*
Mk	8:29	them, But w. say ye that I am?	*5101*
Mk	10:40	to them for w. it is prepared	*3739*
Mk	13:20	the elect's sake, w. he hath	*3739*
Mk	14:21	by w. the Son of man is betrayed!	*3739*
Mk	14:71	I know not this man of w. ye speak.	*3739*
Mk	15:12	him w. ye call the King of the Jews?	*3739*
Mk	15:40	among w. was Mary Magdalene,	*3739*
Mk	16:9	out of w. he had cast seven devils.	*3739*
Lu	6:13	twelve, w. also he named apostles;	*3739*
Lu	6:14	Simon, (w. he also named Peter,)	*3739*
Lu	6:34	to them of w. ye hope to receive,	*3739*
Lu	6:47	I will shew you to w. he is like:	*5101*
Lu	7:4	worthy for w. he should do this:	*3739*
Lu	7:27	This is he, of w. it is written,	*3739*
Lu	7:43	that he, to w. he forgave most.	*3739*
Lu	7:47	to w. little is given, the same	*3739*
Lu	8:2	out of w. went seven devils,	*3739*
Lu	8:35	out of w. the devils were departed,	*3739*
Lu	8:38	out of w. the devils were departed	*3739*
Lu	9:9	is this, of w. I hear such things?	*3739*
Lu	9:18	W. say the people that I am?	*5101*
Lu	9:20	them, But w. say ye that I am?	*5101*
Lu	10:22	he to w. the Son will reveal him.	*3739*
Lu	11:19	by w. do your sons cast them out?	*5101*
Lu	12:5	will forewarn you w. ye shall	*5101*
Lu	12:37	w. the lord when he cometh shall	*3739*
Lu	12:42	w. his lord shall make ruler over	*3739*
Lu	12:43	w. his lord when he cometh shall	*3739*
Lu	12:48	to w. men have committed much,	*3739*
Lu	13:4	upon w. the tower in Siloam fell,	*3739*
Lu	13:16	w. Satan hath bound, lo, these	*3739*
Lu	17:1	unto him, through w. they come!	*3739*
Lu	19:15	to w. he had given the money,	*3739*
Lu	22:22	that man by w. he is betrayed!	*3739*
Lu	23:25	into prison, w. they had desired;	*3739*
Joh	1:15	This was he of w. I spake, He that	*3739*
Joh	1:26	one among you, w. ye know not;	*3739*
Joh	1:30	This is he of w. I said, After me	*3739*
Joh	1:33	Upon w. thou shalt see the Spirit	*3739*
Joh	1:45	of w. Moses in the law, and the	*3739*
Joh	1:47	Israelite indeed, in w. is no guile!	*3739*
Joh	3:26	to w. thou barest witness, behold,	*3739*
Joh	3:34	For he w. God hath sent speaketh	*3739*
Joh	4:18	he w. thou now hast is not thy	*3739*
Joh	5:21	so the Son quickeneth w. he will	*3739*
Joh	5:38	w. he...sent, him ye believed not	*3739*
Joh	5:45	you, even Moses, in w. ye trust.	*3739*
Joh	6:29	ye believe on him w. he hath	*3739*
Joh	6:68	him, Lord, to w. shall we go?	*5101*
Joh	7:25	Is not this he, w. they seek to kill?	*3739*
Joh	7:28	sent me is true, w. ye know not.	*3739*
Joh	8:53	dead: w. makest thou thyself?	*5101*
Joh	8:54	of w. ye say, that he is your	*3739*
Joh	10:35	unto w. the word of God came,	*3739*
Joh	10:36	him, w. the Father hath	*3739*
Joh	11:3	behold, he w. thou lovest is sick.	*3739*
Joh	12:1	dead, w. he raised from the dead.	*3739*
Joh	12:9	w. he had raised from the dead,	*3739*
Joh	12:38	to w. hath the arm of the Lord	*5101*
Joh	13:18	I know w. I have chosen: but that	*3739*
Joh	13:22	another, doubting of w. he spake.	*5101*
Joh	13:23	one of his disciples, w. Jesus loved.	*3739*
Joh	13:24	who it should be of w. he spake.	*3739*
Joh	13:26	He it is, to w. I shall give a sop,	*3739*
Joh	14:17	w. the world cannot receive,	*3739*
Joh	14:26	w....Father will send in my name,	*3739*

Joh 15:26 **w. I will send unto you from the** *3739*
Joh 17:3 **Jesus Christ, w. thou hast sent** *3739*
Joh 17:11 **name those w. thou hast given** *3739*
Joh 17:24 **w. thou hast given me, be with** *3739*
Joh 18:4 and said unto them, **W. seek ye?** *5101*
Joh 18:7 asked he them again, **W. seek ye?** *5101*
Joh 19:26 disciple standing by, w. he loved, *3739*
Joh 19:37 shall look on him w. they pierced. *3739*
Joh 20:2 the other disciple, w. Jesus loved, *3739*
Joh 20:15 **weepest thou? w. seekest thou** *5101*
Joh 21:7 disciple w. Jesus loved saith unto *3739*
Joh 21:20 seeth the disciple w. Jesus loved *3739*
Ac 1:2 unto the apostles w. he had chosen: *3739*
Ac 1:3 To w. also he shewed himself alive *3739*
Ac 2:24 W. God hath raised up, having *3739*
Ac 2:36 same Jesus, w. ye have crucified *3739*
Ac 3:2 w. they laid daily at the gate of the *3739*
Ac 3:13 w. ye delivered up, and denied him *3739*
Ac 3:15 w. God hath raised from the dead; *3739*
Ac 3:16 made this man strong, w. ye see *3739*
Ac 3:21 W. the heaven must receive until *3739*
Ac 4:10 Christ of Nazareth, w. ye crucified, *3739*
Ac 4:10 w. God raised from the dead, *3739*
Ac 4:22 on w. this miracle of healing was *3739*
Ac 4:27 child Jesus, w. thou hast anointed, *3739*
Ac 5:25 the men w. ye put in prison are *3739*
Ac 5:30 w. ye slew and hanged on a tree. *3739*
Ac 5:32 w. God hath given to them that *3739*
Ac 5:36 to w. a number of men, about four *3739*
Ac 6:3 w. we may appoint over this *3739*
Ac 6:6 W. they set before the apostles: *3739*
Ac 7:7 to w. they shall be in bondage *3739*
Ac 7:35 This Moses w. they refused, saying, *3739*
Ac 7:39 To w. our fathers would not obey, *3739*
Ac 7:45 w. God drave out before the face of *3739*
Ac 7:52 of w. ye have been...the betrayers *3739*
Ac 8:10 To w. they all gave heed, from the *3739*
Ac 8:34 of w. speakest the prophet this? *5101*
Ac 9:5 **I am Jesus w. thou persecutest:** *3739*
Ac 9:37 w. when they had washed, they
Ac 10:21 said, Behold, I am he w. ye seek: *3739*
Ac 10:39 w. they slew and hanged on a tree: *3739*
Ac 13:22 to w. also he gave testimony, *3739*
Ac 13:25 w. think ye that I am? I am not *5101*
Ac 13:37 But he, w. God raised again, saw *3739*
Ac 14:23 to the Lord, on w. they believed *3739*
Ac 15:17 upon w. my name is called, *3739*
Ac 15:24 to w. we gave no...commandment: *3739*
Ac 17:3 Jesus, w. I preach unto you, is *3739*
Ac 17:7 W. Jason hath received: and these *3739*
Ac 17:23 W....ye ignorantly worship, *3739*
Ac 17:31 by that man w. he hath ordained; *3739*
Ac 18:26 w. when Aquila and Priscilla had *846*
Ac 19:13 you by Jesus w. Paul preacheth. *3739*
Ac 19:16 the man in w. the evil spirit was *3739*
Ac 19:25 W. he called together with the *3739*
Ac 19:27 w. all Asia and...world worshippeth. *3739*
Ac 20:25 among w. I have gone preaching *3739*
Ac 21:16 disciple, with w. we should lodge. *3739*
Ac 21:29 w. they supposed that Paul had *3739*
Ac 22:5 from w. also I received letters unto *3739*
Ac 22:8 **of Nazareth, w. thou persecutest** *3739*
Ac 23:29 W. I perceived to be accused of *3739*
Ac 24:6 w. we took, and would have judged *3739*
Ac 24:8 w. thyself mayest take knowledge *3739*
Ac 25:15 About w., when I was at *3739*
Ac 25:16 w. I answered, It is not the manner *3739*
Ac 25:18 w. when the accusers stood up, *3739*
Ac 25:19 dead, w. Paul affirmed to be alive. *3739*
Ac 25:24 w. all the multitude of the Jews *3739*
Ac 25:26 w. I have no certain thing to write *3739*
Ac 26:15 **I am Jesus w. thou persecutest** *3739*
Ac 26:17 **Gentiles, unto w. now I send** *3739*
Ac 26:26 before w. also I speak freely: *3739*
Ac 27:23 God, whose I am, and w. I serve, *3739*
Ac 28:4 w., though he hath escaped the sea, *3739*
Ac 28:8 to w. Paul entered in, and prayed, *3739*
Ac 28:15 w. when Paul saw, he thanked God, *3739*
Ac 28:23 to w. he expounded and testified *3739*
Ro 1:5 by w. we have received grace and *3739*
Ro 1:6 Among w. are ye also the called of *3739*
Ro 1:9 w. I serve with my spirit in the *3739*
Ro 3:25 W. God had set forth to be a *3739*
Ro 4:6 unto w. God imputed righteousness *3739*
Ro 4:8 to w. the Lord will not impute sin. *3739*
Ro 4:17 before him w. he believed, even *3739*
Ro 4:24 us also, to w. it shall be imputed, *3739*
Ro 5:2 By w. also we have access by faith *3739*
Ro 5:11 by w. we have now received the *3739*
Ro 6:16 to w. ye yield yourselves servants *3739*
Ro 6:16 his servants ye are to w. ye obey; *3739*
Ro 8:29 For w. he did foreknow, he also did *3739*
Ro 8:30 Moreover w. he did predestinate, *3739*
Ro 8:30 w. he called, them he also *3739*
Ro 8:30 w. he justified, them he also *3739*
Ro 9:4 to w. pertaineth the adoption, and *3739*
Ro 9:5 of w. as concerning the flesh *3739*
Ro 9:15 have mercy on w. I will have mercy, *3739*
Ro 9:15 on w. I will have compassion *3739*
Ro 9:18 he mercy on w. he will have mercy, *3739*
Ro 9:18 mercy, and w. he will hardeneth. *3739*
Ro 9:24 Even us, w. he hath called, not of *3739*
Ro 10:14 him in w. they have not believed? *3739*
Ro 10:14 in him of w. they have not heard? *3739*
Ro 11:36 things to w. be glory for ever. *846*
Ro 13:7 dues: tribute to w. tribute is due; *3588*
Ro 13:7 custom to w. custom; *3588*
Ro 13:9 fear to w. fear; *3588*
Ro 13:9 honour to w. honour. *3588*
Ro 14:15 with thy meat, for w. Christ died. *3739*
Ro 15:21 To w. he was not spoken of, they *3739*
Ro 16:4 unto w. not only I give thanks, but *3739*
1Co 1:9 by w. ye were called unto the *3739*
1Co 3:5 but ministers by w. ye believed, *3739*
1Co 7:39 to be married to w. she will; *3739*
1Co 8:6 of w. are all things, and we in him; *3739*
1Co 8:6 by w. are all things, and we by *3739*
1Co 8:11 brother perish, for w. Christ died? *3739*
1Co 10:11 upon w. the ends of the world are *3739*
1Co 15:6 of w. the greater part remain unto *3739*
1Co 15:15 w. he raised not up, if so be that *3739*
2Co 1:10 in w. we trust that he will yet *3739*
2Co 2:3 from them of w. I ought to rejoice; *3739*
2Co 2:10 To w. ye forgive any thing, I forgive *3739*
2Co 2:10 forgave any thing, to w. I forgave it, *3739*
2Co 4:4 In w. the god of this world hath *3739*
2Co 8:22 w. we have oftentimes proved *3739*
2Co 10:18 but w. the Lord commendeth. *3739*
2Co 11:4 another Jesus, w. we have not *3739*
2Co 12:17 any of them w. I sent unto you? *3739*
Ga 1:5 To w. be glory for ever and ever. *3739*
Ga 2:5 To w. we gave place by subjection, *3739*
Ga 3:19 come to w. the promise was made; *3739*
Ga 4:19 of w. I travail in birth again *3739*
Ga 6:14 by w. the world is crucified unto *3739*
Eph 1:7 in w. we have redemption through *3739*
Eph 1:11 In w. also we have obtained an *3739*
Eph 1:13 in w. also after that ye believed, *3739*
Eph 1:13 In w. ye also trusted, after that ye *3739*
Eph 2:3 Among w. also we all had our *3739*
Eph 2:21 In w. all the building fitly framed *3739*
Eph 2:22 In w. ye also are builded together *3739*
Eph 3:12 In w. we have boldness and access *3739*
Eph 3:15 Of w. the whole family in heaven *3739*
Eph 4:16 w. the whole body fitly joined *3739*
Eph 6:22 W. I have sent unto you for the *3739*
Php 2:15 among w. ye shine as lights in the *3739*
Php 3:8 for w. I have suffered the loss of *3739*
Php 3:18 walk, of w. I have told you often, *3739*
Col 1:14 In w. we have redemption through *3739*
Col 1:27 To w. God would make known what *3739*
Col 1:28 W. we preach, warning every man, *3739*
Col 2:3 In w. are hid all the treasures of *3739*
Col 2:11 In w. also ye are circumcised with *3739*
Col 4:8 W. I have sent unto you for the *3739*
Col 4:10 w. ye received commandments: *3739*
1Th 1:10 w. he raised from the dead, even *3739*
2Th 2:8 w. the Lord shall consume with the *3739*
1Ti 1:15 save sinners; of w. I am chief. *3739*
1Ti 1:20 w. is Hymenaeus and Alexander; *3739*
1Ti 1:20 w. I have delivered unto Satan, *3739*
1Ti 6:16 w. no man hath seen, nor can see: *3739*
1Ti 6:16 to w. be honour and power *3739*
2Ti 1:3 w. I serve from my forefathers *3739*
2Ti 1:12 I know w. I have believed, and am *3739*
2Ti 1:15 w. are Phygellus and Hermogenes. *3739*
2Ti 2:17 of w. is Hymenaeus and Philetus; *3739*
2Ti 3:14 of w. thou hast learned them; *5101*
2Ti 4:15 Of w. be thou ware also; for he *3739*
2Ti 4:18 to w. be glory for ever and ever. *3739*
Phm 10 w. I have begotten in my bonds: *3739*
Phm 12 W. I have sent again: thou *3739*
Phm 13 W. I would have retained with me, *3739*
Heb 1:2 w. he hath appointed heir of all *3739*
Heb 1:2 by w. also he made the worlds; *3739*
Heb 2:10 became him, for w. are all things, *3739*
Heb 2:10 and by w. are all things, in *3739*
Heb 3:17 with w. was he grieved forty years? *5101*
Heb 3:18 to w. sware he that they should not *5101*
Heb 4:6 they to w. it was first preached
Heb 4:13 eyes of him with w. we have to do. *3739*
Heb 5:11 Of w. we have many things to say, *3739*
Heb 6:7 meet for them by w. it is dressed, *3739*
Heb 7:2 To w. also Abraham gave a tenth *3739*
Heb 7:4 w. even the patriarch Abraham *3739*
Heb 7:8 of w. it is witnessed that he liveth
Heb 7:13 he of w. these things are spoken *3739*
Heb 11:18 Of w. it was said, That in Isaac *3739*
Heb 11:38 (Of w. the world was not worthy:) *3739*
Heb 12:6 w. the Lord loveth he chasteneth, *3739*
Heb 12:6 and scourgeth every son w. he *3739*
Heb 12:7 what son is he w. the father *3739*
Heb 13:21 to w. be glory for ever and ever. *3739*
Heb 13:23 with w., if he come shortly, I will *3739*
Jas 1:17 lights, with w. is no variableness, *3739*
1Pe 1:8 W. having not seen, ye love; *3739*
1Pe 1:8 w., though now ye see him not, yet
1Pe 1:12 Unto w. it was revealed, that not *3739*
1Pe 2:4 To w. coming, as unto a living *3739*
1Pe 4:11 w. be praise and dominion for ever. *3739*
1Pe 5:8 about, seeking w. he may devour: *5101*
1Pe 5:9 W. resist stedfast in the faith, *3739*
2Pe 1:17 son, in w. I am well pleased. *3739*
2Pe 2:2 by reason of w. the way of truth *3739*
2Pe 2:17 w. the mist of darkness is reserved *3739*
2Pe 2:19 for of w. a man is overcome, of the *3739*
1Jo 4:20 not his brother w. he hath seen, *3739*
1Jo 4:20 he love God w. he hath not seen? *3739*
2Jo 1 her children, w. I love in the truth; *3739*
3Jo 1 Gaius, w. I love in the truth. *3739*
3Jo 6 w. if thou bring forward on their *3739*
Jude 13 to w. is reserved the blackness of *3739*
Re 7:2 to w. it was given to hurt the earth *3739*
Re 17:2 With w. the kings of the earth have *3739*
Re 20:8 the number of w. is as the sand of *3739*

WHOMSOEVER

Ge 31:32 With w. thou findest thy gods, 834
Ge 44:9 With w. of thy servants it be found, 834
Le 15:11 w. he toucheth that hath the 3605,834
Jg 7:4 w. I say unto thee, this shall not go 834
Jg 11:24 w. the Lord our God shall drive 3605,834
Da 4:17 giveth it to w. he will, and setteth 4479
Da 4:25, 32 men, and giveth it to w. he will. 4479
Da 5:21 appointeth over it w. he will 4479,1768
Mt 11:27 **to w. the Son will reveal** *3739,1437*
Mt 21:44 **but on w. it shall fall, it will** *3739,302*
Mt 26:48 W. I shall kiss, that same is he: *3739,302*
Mk 14:44 W. I shall kiss, that same is he; *3739,302*
Mk 15:6 one prisoner, w. they desired. *3746*
Lu 4:6 me; and to w. I will I give it. *3739,1437*
Lu 12:48 **For unto w. much is given,** *3956,3739*
Lu 20:18 **w. it shall fall, it shall grind** *3739,302*
Joh 13:20 **receiveth w. I send receiveth** *1437,5100*
Ac 8:19 that on w. I lay hands, he may *3739,302*
1Co 16:3 w. ye shall approve by your *3739,1437*

WHORE See also WHOREMONGER; WHORE'S; WHORES; WHORING; WHORISH.

Le 19:29 daughter, to cause her to be a w.; 2181
Le 21:7 shall not take a wife that is a w., 2181
Le 21:9 profane herself by playing the w., 2181
De 22:21 to play the w. in her father's house: 2181
De 23:17 no w. of the daughters of Israel, 6948
De 23:18 shalt not bring the hire of a w., 2181
Jg 19:2 And his concubine played the w. 2181
Pr 23:27 For a w. is a deep ditch; and a 2181
Isa 57:3 seed of the adulterer and the w. 2181
Eze 16:28 hast played the w. also with the 2181
Re 17:1 judgment of the great w. that *4204*
Re 17:15 where the w. sitteth, are peoples, *4204*
Re 17:16 these shall hate the w., and shall *4204*
Re 19:2 for he hath judged the great w., *4204*

WHOREDOM See also WHOREDOMS.

Ge 38:24 behold, she is with child by w. 2183
Le 19:29 lest the land fall to w., and the 2181
Le 20:5 to commit w. with Molech, from 2181
Nu 25:1 people began to commit w. with 2181
Jer 3:9 through the lightness of her w., 2184
Jer 13:27 the lewdness of thy w., and thine 2184

Eze 16:17 and didst commit **w.** with them, ... 2181
Eze 16:33 unto thee on every side for thy **w.** ... 8457
Eze 20:30 commit ye **w.** after their ... 2181
Eze 23:8 and poured their **w.** upon her. ... 8457
Eze 23:17 and they defiled her with their **w.**, ... 8457
Eze 23:27 thy **w.** brought from the land of ... 2184
Eze 43:7 they, nor their kings, by their **w.**, ... 2184
Eze 43:9 Now let them put away their **w.**, ... 2184
Ho 1:2 land hath committed great **w.**, ... 2181
Ho 4:10 they shall commit **w.**, and shall not ... 2181
Ho 4:11 **W.** and wine and new wine take ... 2184
Ho 4:13 your daughters shall commit **w.**, ... 2181
Ho 4:14 daughters when they commit **w.**, ... 2181
Ho 4:18 have committed **w.** continually: ... 2181
Ho 5:3 O Ephraim, thou committest **w.**, ... 2181
Ho 6:10 there is the **w.** of Ephraim, Israel ... 2184

WHOREDOMS
Nu 14:33 and bear your **w.**, until your ... 2184
2Ki 9:22 as the **w.** of thy mother Jezebel ... 2183
2Ch 21:13 to the **w.** of the house of Ahab, ... 2181
Jer 3:2 hast polluted the land with thy **w.** ... 2184
Eze 16:20 Is this of thy **w.** a small matter, ... 8457
Eze 16:22 thy **w.** thou hast not remembered ... 8457
Eze 16:25 that past by, and multiplied thy **w.** ... 8457
Eze 16:26 hast increased thy **w.**, to provoke ... 8457
Eze 16:34 thee from other women in thy **w.**, ... 8457
Eze 16:34 none followeth thee to commit **w.**: ... 2181
Eze 16:36 discovered through thy **w.** with ... 8457
Eze 23:3 And they committed **w.** in Egypt; ...
Eze 23:3 they committed **w.** in their youth: ...
Eze 23:7 she committed her **w.** with them, ... 8457
Eze 23:8 left she her **w.** brought from Egypt: ... 8457
Eze 23:11 and in her **w.** more than her sister ... 8457
Eze 23:11 more than her sister in her **w.** ... 2183
Eze 23:14 And that she increased her **w.**: ... 8457
Eze 23:18 So she discovered her **w.**, and ... 8457
Eze 23:19 Yet she multiplied her **w.**, in ... 8457
Eze 23:29 of thy **w.** shall be discovered, ... 2183
Eze 23:29 both thy lewdness and thy **w.** ... 8457
Eze 23:35 thou also thy lewdness and thy **w.** ... 8457
Eze 23:43 Will they now commit **w.** with her, ... 8457
Ho 1:2 a wife of **w.** and children of **w.**: ... 2183
Ho 2:2 put away her **w.** out of her sight, ... 2183
Ho 2:4 for they be the children of **w.** ... 2183
Ho 4:12 of **w.** hath caused them to ere, ... 2183
Ho 5:4 spirit of **w.** is in the midst of them, ... 2183
Na 3:4 the **w.** of the wellfavoured harlot ... 2183
Na 3:4 that selleth nations through her **w.**, ... 2183

WHOREMONGER See also WHOREMONGERS.
Eph 5:5 we know, that no **w.**, nor unclean ... *4205*

WHOREMONGERS
1Ti 1:10 For **w.**, for them that defile ... *4205*
Heb 13:4 **w.** and adulterers God will judge. ... *4205*
Re 21:8 and **w.**, and sorcerers, and ... *4205*
Re 22:15 are dogs, and sorcerers, and **w.**, ... *4205*

WHORE'S
Jer 3:3 thou hadst a **w.** forehead, thou ... 2181

WHORES
Eze 16:33 They give gifts to all **w.**: but thou ... 2181
Ho 4:14 themselves are separated with **w.**, ... 2181

WHORING
Ex 34:15 and they go a **w.** after their gods, ... 2181
Ex 34:16 daughters go a **w.** after their gods, ... 2181
Ex 34:16 thy sons go a **w.** after their gods. ... 2181
Le 17:7 after whom they have gone a **w.** ... 2181
Le 20:5 off, and all that go a **w.** after him, ... 2181
Le 20:6 wizards, to go a **w.** after them, I ... 2181
Nu 15:39 after which ye used to go a **w.**: ... 2181
De 31:16 and go a **w.** after the gods of the ... 2181
Jg 2:17 but they went a **w.** after other gods, .. 2181
Jg 8:27 all Israel went thither a **w.** after it: ... 2181
Jg 8:33 again, and went a **w.** after Baalim, ... 2181
1Ch 5:25 and went a **w.** after the gods of the ... 2181
2Ch 21:13 inhabitants of Jerusalem...go a **w.**, ... 2181
Ps 73:27 all them that go a **w.** from thee. ... 2181
Ps 106:39 went a **w.** with their own inventions. .. 2181
Eze 6:9 which go a **w.** after their idols: ... 2181
Eze 23:30 hast gone a **w.** after the heathen, ... 2181
Ho 4:12 gone a **w.** from under their God ... 2181
Ho 9:1 thou hast gone a **w.** from thy God, ... 2181

WHORISH
Pr 6:26 by means of a **w.** woman a man is ... 2181
Eze 6:9 I am broken with their **w.** heart. ... 2181
Eze 16:30 work of an imperious **w.** woman; ... 2181

WHOSE See also WHOSOEVER.
Ge 1:11 **w.** seed is in itself, upon the earth: ... 834
Ge 1:12 **w.** seed was in itself, after his kind: ... 834
Ge 7:22 in **w.** nostrils was the breath of life, ... 834
Ge 11:4 tower, **w.** top may reach unto heaven; ...
Ge 16:1 an Egyptian, **w.** name was Hagar. ...
Ge 17:14 **w.** flesh of his foreskin is not ... 834
Ge 24:23 **W.** daughter art thou? tell me, I ... 4310
Ge 24:37 Canaanites, in **w.** land I dwell: ... 834
Ge 24:47 and said, **W.** daughter art thou? ... 4310
Ge 32:17 **W.** art thou? and whither goest ... 4310
Ge 32:17 thou? and **w.** are these before thee? ... 4310
Ge 38:1 Adullamite, **w.** name was Hirah. ...
Ge 38:2 Canaanite, **w.** name was Shuah; ...
Ge 38:6 Er his firstborn, **w.** name was Tamar. ...
Ge 38:25 man, **w.** these are, am I with child: ... 834
Ge 38:25 Discern, I pray thee, **w.** are these, ... 834
Ge 44:17 man in **w.** hand the cup is found. ...
Ge 49:22 well; **w.** branches run over the wall: ...
Ex 34:14 the Lord, **w.** name is Jealous, is a ...
Ex 35:21 every one **w.** heart stirred him up, ... 834
Ex 35:26 the women **w.** heart stirred them up ... 834
Ex 35:29 **w.** heart made them willing to bring ... 834
Ex 36:2 in **w.** heart the Lord had put wisdom, ... 834
Ex 36:2 one **w.** heart stirred him up to come ... 834
Le 13:40 man **w.** hair is fallen off his head, ... 3588
Le 14:32 **w.** hand is not able to get that ... 834
Le 15:32 and of him **w.** seed goeth from him, ... 834
Le 16:27 **w.** blood was brought in to make ... 834
Le 21:10 **w.** head the anointing oil was poured, ... 834
Le 22:4 or a man **w.** seed goeth from him; ... 834
Le 24:10 woman, **w.** father was an Egyptian, ...
Nu 24:3, 15 and the man **w.** eyes are open hath ...
De 8:9 a land **w.** stones are iron, and out ... 834
De 8:9 out of **w.** hills thou mayest dig brass. ...
De 19:1 **w.** land the Lord thy God giveth ... 834
De 28:49 a nation **w.** tongue thou shalt not ... 834
De 29:18 **w.** heart turneth away this day from ... 834
Jos 24:15 of the Amorites, in **w.** land ye dwell: ... 834
Jg 4:2 the captain of **w.** host was Sesira, ...
Jg 6:10 the Amorites, in **w.** land ye dwell: ... 834
Jg 8:31 son, **w.** name he called Abimelech. ... 853
Jg 13:2 of the Danites, **w.** name was Manoah; ...
Jg 16:4 valley of Sorek, **w.** name was Delilah. ...
Jg 17:1 mount Ephraim, **w.** name was Micah. ...
Ru 2:2 him in **w.** sight I shall find grace. ... 834
Ru 2:5 the reapers, **W.** damsel is this? ... 4310
Ru 2:12 under **w.** wings thou art come to ... 834
Ru 3:2 kindred, with **w.** maidens thou wast? ... 834
1Sa 9:1 **w.** name was Kish, the son of Abiel, ...
1Sa 9:2 And he had a son, **w.** name was Saul, ...
1Sa 10:26 of men, **w.** hearts God had touched. ... 834
1Sa 12:3 his anointed: **w.** ox have I taken? ... 4310
1Sa 12:3 or **w.** ass have I taken? ... 4310
1Sa 12:3 of **w.** hand have I receive any ... 4310
1Sa 17:4 **w.** height was six cubits and a span. ...
1Sa 17:12 **w.** name was Jesse; and he had ...
1Sa 17:55 host, Abner, **w.** son is this youth? ... 4310
1Sa 17:56 Enquire...**w.** son the stripling is. ... 4310
1Sa 17:58 **W.** son art thou, thou young man? ... 4310
1Sa 25:2 Maon, **w.** possessions were in Carmel; ...
2Sa 3:7 a concubine, **w.** name was Rizpah, ...
2Sa 3:12 his behalf, saying, **W.** is the land? ... 4310
2Sa 6:2 **w.** name is called by the name of ... 834
2Sa 9:2 of Saul a servant **w.** name was Ziba. ...
2Sa 9:12 had a young son, **w.** name was Micha. ...
2Sa 13:1 had a fair sister, **w.** name was Tamar; ...
2Sa 13:3 had a friend, **w.** name was Jonadab, ...
2Sa 14:27 one daughter, **w.** name was Tamar: ...
2Sa 16:5 **w.** name was Shimei, the son of Gera: ...
2Sa 16:8 Saul, in **w.** stead thou hast reigned; ... 834
2Sa 17:10 **w.** heart is as the heart of a lion, ... 834
2Sa 17:25 son, **w.** name was Ithra an Israelite, ...
2Sa 20:1 **w.** name was Sheba, the son of Bichri, ...
2Sa 21:16 weight of **w.** spear weighed three ...
2Sa 21:19 of **w.** spear was like a weaver's beam. ...
1Ki 3:26 woman **w.** the living child was unto ... 834
1Ki 8:39 to his ways, **w.** heart thou knowest; ... 834
1Ki 11:26 servant, **w.** mother's name was Zeruah, ...
2Ki 7:2 a lord on **w.** hand the king leaned ... 834
2Ki 7:17 the lord on **w.** hand he leaned to ... 834
2Ki 8:1,5 **w.** son he had restored to life, ... 834
2Ki 12:15 **w.** hand they delivered the money to ... 834
2Ki 18:22 is it not he, **w.** high places and ... 834,853
2Ki 18:22 and **w.** altars Hezekiah hath taken ... 853
1Ch 2:16 **W.** sisters were Zeruiah, and Abigail. ...
1Ch 2:26 another wife, **w.** name was Atarah; ...
1Ch 2:34 an Egyptian, **w.** name was Jarha. ...
1Ch 7:2 **w.** number was in the days of David ...
1Ch 7:15 **w.** sister's name was Maachah;) ...
1Ch 8:29 Gibeon; **w.** wife's name was Maachah: ...
1Ch 8:38 Azel had six sons, **w.** names are these, ...
1Ch 9:35 Jehiel, **w.** wife's name was Maachah: ...
1Ch 9:44 Azel had six sons, **w.** names are these, ...
1Ch 12:8 **w.** faces were like the faces of lions, ...
1Ch 13:6 cherubims, **w.** name is called on it. ... 834
1Ch 20:5 **w.** spear staff was like a weaver's beam. ...
1Ch 20:6 **w.** fingers and toes were four and ...
1Ch 26:7 **w.** brethren were strong men, Elihu, ...
2Ch 6:30 ways, **w.** heart thou knowest; ... 834,853
2Ch 16:9 them **w.** heart is perfect toward him. ...
2Ch 28:9 Lord was there, **w.** name was Obed: ...
Ezr 1:5 all them **w.** spirit God had raised, ... 853
Ezr 5:14 unto one, **w.** name was Sheshbazzar, ...
Ezr 7:15 **w.** habitation is in Jerusalem, ... 1768
Ezr 8:13 sons of Adonikam, **w.** names are ... 834
Es 2:5 a certain Jew, **w.** name was Mordecai, ...
Job 1:1 the land of Uz, **w.** name was Job; ...
Job 3:23 light given to a man **w.** way is hid, ... 834
Job 4:19 of clay, **w.** foundation is in the dust, ... 834
Job 5:5 **W.** harvest the hungry eateth up, ... 834
Job 8:14 **W.** hope shall be cut off, and ... 834
Job 8:14 and **w.** trust shall be a spider's web. ...
Job 12:6 **w.** hand God bringeth abundantly. ... 834
Job 12:10 In **w.** hand is the soul of every living ... 834
Job 22:16 **w.** foundation was overflown with a ...
Job 26:4 and **w.** spirit came from thee? ... 4310
Job 30:1 **w.** fathers I would have disdained ... 834
Job 38:29 Out of **w.** womb came the ice? and ... 4310
Job 39:6 **W.** house I have made the ... 834
Ps 15:4 In **w.** eyes a vile person is contemned; ...
Ps 17:14 **w.** belly thou fillest with thy hid ...
Ps 26:10 In **w.** hands is mischief, and their ... 834
Ps 32:1 Blessed is he **w.** transgression is ...
Ps 32:1 is forgiven, **w.** sin is covered. ...
Ps 32:2 and in **w.** spirit there is no guile. ...
Ps 32:9 **w.** mouth must be held in with bit and ...
Ps 33:12 is the nation **w.** God is the Lord; ... 834
Ps 38:14 not, and in **w.** mouths are no reproofs. ...
Ps 57:4 **w.** teeth are spears and arrows, and ...
Ps 78:8 **w.** spirit was not stedfast with God. ...
Ps 83:18 that thou, **w.** name alone is Jehovah, ...
Ps 84:5 is the man **w.** strength is in thee; ...
Ps 84:5 in **w.** heart are the ways of them. ...
Ps 105:18 **W.** feet they hurt with fetters: he was ...
Ps 144:8 **W.** mouth speaketh vanity, and ... 834
Ps 144:11 **w.** mouth speaketh vanity, and their ... 834
Ps 144:15 is that people, **w.** God is the Lord. ...
Ps 146:5 help, **w.** hope is in the Lord his God: ...
Pr 2:15 **W.** ways are crooked, and they ... 834
Pr 26:26 **W.** hatred is covered by deceit, his ...
Pr 30:14 a generation, **w.** teeth are as swords, ...
Ec 2:21 For there is a man **w.** labour is in ...
Ec 7:26 **w.** heart is snares and nets, ... 834,1931
Isa 1:30 shall be as an oak **w.** leaf fadeth, ...
Isa 2:22 man, **w.** breath is in his nostrils: ... 834
Isa 5:28 **W.** arrows are sharp, and all their ... 834
Isa 6:13 as an oak, **w.** substance is in them, ... 834
Isa 10:10 **w.** graven images did excel them of ...
Isa 14:2 them captives, **w.** captives they were; ...
Isa 18:2 **w.** land the rivers have spoiled! ... 834
Isa 18:7 **w.** land the rivers have spoiled, the ... 834
Isa 23:7 city, **w.** antiquity is of ancient days? ...
Isa 23:8 city, **w.** merchants are princes, ... 834
Isa 23:8 **w.** traffickers are the honourable of ...
Isa 26:3 peace, **w.** mind is stayed on thee: ...
Isa 28:1 **w.** glorious beauty is a fading flower, ...
Isa 30:13 **w.** breaking cometh suddenly at an ... 834
Isa 31:9 **w.** fire is in Zion, and his furnace in ... 834
Isa 36:7 is it not he, **w.** high places and ... 834,853
Isa 36:7 and **w.** altars Hezekiah hath taken ... 853
Isa 43:14 the Chaldeans, **w.** cry is in the ships. ...
Isa 45:1 **w.** right hand I have holden, ... 834
Isa 51:7 the people in **w.** heart is my law; ...
Isa 51:15 that divided the sea, **w.** waves roared: ...
Isa 57:15 **w.** name is Holy; I dwell in the ...
Isa 57:20 rest, **w.** waters cast up mire and dirt. ...
Isa 58:11 spring of water, **w.** waters fail not. ... 834
Jer 5:15 nation **w.** language thou knowest not, ...

Jer 17:5 and w. heart departed from the Lord........
Jer 17:7 the Lord, and w. hope the Lord is............
Jer 19:13 upon w. roofs they have burned 834
Jer 22:25 the hand of them w. face thou fearest, ...
Jer 32:29 w. roofs they have offered incense....... 834
Jer 33:5 w. wickedness I have hid my face........ 834
Jer 37:13 w. name was Irijah, the son of................
Jer 44:28 know w. words shall stand, mine,....... 4310
Jer 46:7 w. waters are moved as the rivers?..........
Jer 46:18 king, w. name is the Lord of hosts,..........
Jer 48:15 king, w. name is the Lord of hosts. ....
Jer 49:12 they w. judgment was not to drink....... 834
Jer 51:57 king, w. name is the Lord of hosts. ....
Eze 3:6 w. words...canst not understand.......... 834
Eze 11:21 w. heart walketh after the heart of...........
Eze 17:6 w. branches turned toward him,...............
Eze 17:16 him king, w. oath he despised, ... 834,853
Eze 17:16 w. covenant he brake, even with......... 853
Eze 20:9 w. sight I made myself known unto...... 853
Eze 20:14 in w. sight I brought them out. 834
Eze 20:22 in w. sight I brought them forth. 834
Eze 21:25 w. day is come, when iniquity shall 834
Eze 21:27 more, until he come w. right it is; 834
Eze 21:29 w. day is come, when their iniquity...... 834
Eze 23:20 w. flesh is as the flesh of asses, ...
Eze 23:20 w. issue is like the issue of horses. ....
Eze 24:6 city, to the pot w. scum is therein, ... 834
Eze 24:6 and w. scum is not gone out of it!............
Eze 32:23 W. graves are set in the sides of......... 834
Eze 40:3 w. appearance was like the appearance..........
Eze 40:45 w. prospect is toward the south, ... 834
Eze 40:46 w. prospect is toward the north 834
Eze 42:15 w. prospect is toward the east, ... 834
Eze 43:4 gate w. prospect is toward the east. 834
Eze 47:12 trees for meat, w. leaf shall not fade,........
Da 2:11 gods, w. dwelling is not with flesh...... 1768
Da 2:26 Daniel, w. name was Belteshazzar,..... 1768
Da 2:31 image, w. brightness was excellent,..........
Da 3:1 w. height was threescore cubits,........ 1768
Da 3:27 w. bodies the fire had no power,........ 1768
Da 4:8 w. name was Belteshazzar,............... 1768
Da 4:19 Daniel, w. name was Belteshazzar,..... 1768
Da 4:20 w. height reached unto the heaven, ...
Da 4:21 W. leaves were fair, and the fruit............
Da 4:21 upon w. branches the fowls of the............
Da 4:34 w. dominion is an everlasting............ 1768
Da 4:37 all w. works are truth, and all his....... 1768
Da 5:23 the God in w. hand thy breath is,....... 1768
Da 5:23 and w. are all thy ways, hast thou not.......
Da 7:9 sit, w. garment was white as snow,..........
Da 7:19 dreadful, w. teeth were of iron, ... 1768
Da 7:20 w. look was more stout than his ....
Da 7:27 w. kingdom is an everlasting kingdom,.......
Da 10:1 w. name was called Belteshazzar; 834
Da 10:5 w. loins were girded with fine gold of........
Joe 1:6 w. teeth are the teeth of a lion, and ....
Am 2:9 w. height was like the height of.......... 834
Am 5:27 Lord, w. name is The God of hosts. ....
Ob 3 of the rock, w. habitation is high;............
Jon 1:7 for w. cause this evil is upon us......... 4310
Jon 1:8 w. cause this evil is upon us;....... 834,4310
Mic 5:2 w. going forth have been from of old, ...
Na 3:8 w. rampart was the sea, and her 834
Zec 6:12 the man w. name is The Branch; ....
Zec 11:5 W. possessors slay them, and hold 834
Mt 3:11 w. shoes I am not worthy to bear; 3739
Mt 3:12 W. fan is in his hand, and he will 3739
Mt 10:3 w. surname was Thaddaeus; 3588
Mt 22:20 **W. is this image and**.................... 5101
Mt 22:28 W. wife shall she be of the seven? 5101
Mt 22:42 **think ye of Christ? w. son is he?**... 5101
Mk 1:7 latchet of w. shoes I am not worthy ... 3739
Mk 7:25 w. young daughter had an unclean......... 3739
Mk 12:16 them, **W. is this image and**........... 5101
Mk 12:23 w. wife shall she be of them? for 5101
Lu 1:27 to a man w. name was Joseph, ... 3739
Lu 2:25 Jerusalem, w. name was Simeon; 3739
Lu 3:16 w. shoes I am not worthy to............... 3739
Lu 3:17 W. fan is in his hand, and he will 3739
Lu 6:6 w. right hand was withered. 2532,846
Lu 12:20 **w. shall those things be, which**..... 5101
Lu 13:1 w. blood Pilate had mingled with........ 3739
Lu 20:24 **W. image and superscription**......... 5100
Lu 20:33 w. wife of them is.......................... 5100
Lu 24:18 w. name was Cleopas, answering 3739
Joh 1:6 sent from God, w. name was John. 846
Joh 1:27 w. shoe's latchet I am not worthy 3739
Joh 4:46 w. son was sick at Capernaum........... 3739
Joh 6:42 w. father and mother we know?.......... 3739
Joh 10:12 **w. own the sheep are not, seeth**.... 3739
Joh 11:2 hair, w. brother Lazarus was sick....... 3739
Joh 18:26 his kinsman w. ear Peter cut off, ... 3739
Joh 19:24 but cast lots for it, w. it shall be:....... 5101
Joh 20:23 **W. soever sins ye remit, they**....... 5100
Joh 20:23 **w. soever sins ye retain, they are**.. 5100
Ac 7:58 young man's feet, w. name was Saul.........
Ac 10:5 Simon, w. surname was Peter: 3739
Ac 10:6 tanner, w. house is by the sea side: ... 3739
Ac 10:32 Simon, w. surname is Peter;............. 3739
Ac 11:13 Simon, w. surname is Peter;............. 3588
Ac 12:12 of John, w. surname was Mark;............ 3588
Ac 12:25 them John, w. surname was Mark. 3588
Ac 13:6 a Jew, w. name was Bar-jesus:.......... 3739
Ac 13:25 w. shoes of his feet I am not 3739
Ac 15:37 them John, w. surname was Mark. 3588
Ac 16:14 w. heart the Lord opened, that she 3739
Ac 18:7 w. house joined hard to the.............. 3739
Ac 27:23 God, w. I am, and whom I serve, ... 3739
Ac 28:7 of the island, w. name was Publius;..........
Ac 28:11 isle, w. sign was Castor and Pollux...........
Ro 2:29 w. praise is not of men, but of God.... 3739
Ro 3:8 may come? w. damnation is just........... 3739
Ro 3:14 W. mouth is full of cursing and.......... 3739
Ro 4:7 are they w. iniquities are forgiven, ... 3739
Ro 4:7 forgiven, and w. sins are covered....... 3739
Ro 9:5 W. are the fathers, and of whom 3739
2Co 8:18 w. praise is in the gospel................ 3739
2Co 11:15 w. end shall be according to their....... 3739
Ga 3:1 before w. eyes Jesus Christ hath........ 3739
Php 3:19 W. end is destruction, w. God is 3739
Php 3:19 w. glory is in their shame, who 3588
Php 4:3 w. names are in the book of life.......... 3739
2Th 2:9 w. coming is after the working of....... 3739
Tit 1:11 W. mouths must be stopped, who...... 3739
Heb 3:6 w. house are we, if we hold fast the... 3739
Heb 3:17 w. carcases fell in the wilderness?...... 3739
Heb 6:8 cursing; w. end is to be burned. 3739
Heb 7:6 he w. descent is not counted from............
Heb 11:10 w. builder and maker is God. 3739
Heb 12:26 W. voice then shook the earth: but 3739
Heb 13:7 w. faith follow, considering the end..... 3739
Heb 13:11 w. blood is brought into the holy........ 3739
1Pe 2:24 by w. stripes ye were healed. 3739
1Pe 3:3 W. adorning, let it not be that........... 3739
1Pe 3:6 w. daughters ye are, as long as ye..... 3739
2Pe 2:3 w. judgment now of a long time......... 3739
Jude 12 trees w. fruit withereth, without ....
Re 9:11 w. name in the Hebrew tongue is 846
Re 13:8 w. names are not written in the......... 3739
Re 13:12 beast, w. deadly wound was healed. ... 3739
Re 17:8 w. names were not written in the 3739
Re 20:11 from w. face the earth and the 3739

WHOSO See also WHOSOEVER.

Ge 9:6 W. sheddeth man's blood, by man............
Le 11:27 w. toucheth their carcase shall be....... 3605
Le 22:4 w. toucheth any thing that is unclean ....
Nu 35:30 W. killeth any person, the 3605
De 19:4 W. killeth...neighbour ignorantly, ... 834
2Ch 23:14 w. followeth her, let him be slain with.......
Ps 50:23 W. offereth praise glorifieth me: and.........
Ps 101:5 W. privily slandereth his neighbour, ...
Ps 107:43 W. is wise, and will observe these 4310
Pr 1:33 But w. hearkeneth unto me shall dwell......
Pr 6:32 But w. committeth adultery with a............
Pr 8:35 For w. findeth me findeth life, and............
Pr 9:4, 16 W. is simple, let him turn in......... 4310
Pr 12:1 W. loveth instruction loveth ....
Pr 13:13 W. despiseth the word shall be...............
Pr 16:20 w. trusteth in the Lord, happy is he. ....
Pr 17:5 W. mocketh the poor reproacheth his........
Pr 17:13 W. rewardeth evil for good, evil shall........
Pr 18:22 W. findeth a wife findeth a good thing. ......
Pr 20:2 W. provoketh him to anger sinneth..........
Pr 20:20 W. curseth his father or his mother, ...
Pr 21:13 W. stoppeth his ears at the cry of the.......
Pr 21:23 W. keepeth his mouth and his ....
Pr 25:14 W. boasteth himself of a false........... 376,834
Pr 26:27 W. diggeth a pit shall fall therein:.............
Pr 27:18 W. keepeth the fig tree shall eat the.........
Pr 28:7 W. keepeth the law is a wise son:.............
Pr 28:10 W. causeth the righteous to go................
Pr 28:13 w. confesseth and forsaketh them.............
Pr 28:18 W. walketh uprightly shall be saved: ....
Pr 28:24 W. robbeth his father or his mother,.........
Pr 28:26 but w. walketh wisely, he shall be............
Pr 29:3 W. loveth wisdom rejoiceth his ....
Pr 29:24 W. is partner with a thief hateth his ....
Pr 29:25 but w. putteth his trust in the Lord ....
Ec 7:26 w. pleaseth God shall escape from............
Ec 8:5 W. keepeth the commandment shall..........
Ec 10:8 w. breaketh an hedge, a serpent shall ....
Ec 10:9 W. removeth stones shall be hurt.............
Da 3:6 w. falleth not...worshippeth........ 4479,1768
Da 3:11 w. falleth not...worshippeth,........ 4479,1768
Zec 14:17 that w. will not come up of all the 834
Mt 18:5 **w. shall receive one such**........ 3739,302
Mt 18:6 **w. shall offend one of these**........ 3739,302
Mt 19:9 **w. marrieth her which is put**........ 3588
Mt 23:20 **W. therefore shall swear by the**.... 3588
Mt 23:21 **w. shall swear by the temple,**........ 3588
Mt 24:15 **(w. readeth, let him understand:)**.. 3588
Mk 7:10 **W. curseth father or mother, let**... 3588
Joh 6:54 **W. eateth my flesh, and drinketh**.. 3588
Jas 1:25 w. looketh into the perfect law of....... 3588
1Jo 2:5 w. keepeth his word, in him........ 3739,302
1Jo 3:17 But w. hath this world's good, ... 3739,302

WHOSOEVER See also WHOSO.

Ge 4:15 W. slayeth Cain, vengeance shall........ 3605
Ex 12:15 for w. eateth leavened bread from...... 3605
Ex 12:19 w. eateth that which is leavened, ...
Ex 19:12 w. toucheth the mount shall be.......... 3605
Ex 22:19 w. lieth with a beast shall surely........ 3605
Ex 30:33 W. compoundeth any like it, ... 376
Ex 30:33 or w. putteth any of it upon a.............. 834
Ex 30:38 W. shall make like unto that, to..... 376,834
Ex 31:14 for w. doeth any work therein, that..........
Ex 31:15 w. doeth any work in the sabbath....... 3605
Ex 32:24 W. hath any gold, let them break....... 4310
Ex 32:33 W. hath sinned against me, ... 4310,834
Ex 35:2 w. doeth work therein shall be 3605
Ex 35:5 w. is of a willing heart, let him 3605
Le 7:25 For w. eateth the fat of the beast, ... 3605
Le 11:24 w. toucheth the carcase of them 3605
Le 11:25 w. beareth ought of the carcase of 3605
Le 11:31 w. doth touch them, when they be 3605
Le 15:5 w. toucheth his bed shall wash 376,834
Le 15:10 w. toucheth any thing that was.......... 3605
Le 15:19 w. toucheth her shall be unclean 3605
Le 15:21 w. toucheth her bed shall wash.......... 3605
Le 15:22 w. toucheth any thing that she sat...... 3605
Le 15:27 w. toucheth those things shall be 3605
Le 17:14 w. eateth it shall be cut off. 3605
Le 18:29 w. shall commit any of these 3605,834
Le 19:20 w. lieth carnally with a woman,...... 376,834
Le 20:2 W. he be of the children of Israel, ... 376
Le 21:17 W. he be of thy seed in their........ 376,834
Le 22:3 W. he be of all your seed............ 376,834
Le 22:5 w. toucheth any creeping thing, ... 376,834
Le 22:21 w. offereth a sacrifice of peace 376,834
Le 24:15 W. curseth his God shall bear 376,834
Nu 5:2 and w. is defiled by the dead:............ 3605
Nu 15:14 or w. be among you in your 834
Nu 17:13 W. cometh any thing near unto.......... 3605
Nu 19:13 W. toucheth the dead body of any...... 3605
Nu 19:16 w. toucheth one that is slain........ 3605,834
Nu 31:19 w. hath killed any person, and........... 3605
Nu 31:19 w. hath touched any slain, purify.......... 3605
De 18:19 w. will not hearken unto my.......... 376,834
Jos 1:18 W. he be that doth rebel............... 376,834
Jos 2:19 w. shall go out of the doors......... 3605,834
Jos 2:19 w. shall be with thee in the........... 3605,834
Jos 20:9 w. killeth any person at unawares........ 3605
Jg 7:3 W. is fearful and afraid, let him.......... 4310
1Sa 11:7 W. cometh not forth after Saul........... 834
2Sa 5:8 W. getteth up to the gutter, and.............
2Sa 14:10 W. saith ought unto thee, bring him..........
2Sa 17:9 w. heareth it will say, There is a ....
1Ki 13:33 w. would, he consecrated him,................
2Ki 10:19 w. shall be wanting, he shall........ 3605,834
2Ki 21:12 w. heareth of it, both his ears shall 3605
1Ch 11:6 w. smiteth the Jebusites first shall...... 3605
1Ch 26:28 and w. had dedicated any thing, ... 3605
2Ch 13:9 w. cometh to consecrate himself 3605
2Ch 15:13 w. would not seek the Lord God.......... 3605
2Ch 23:7 and w. else cometh into the house, he ......
Ezr 1:4 w. remaineth in any place where........ 3605
Ezr 6:11 that w. shall alter this word, ... 3605
Ezr 7:26 w. will not do the law of thy God,...... 3605

Ezr 10:8 w. would not come within three......... 3605
Es 4:11 that w., whether man or woman,......... 834
Pr 6:29 w. toucheth her shall not be.............. 3605
Pr 20:1 w. is deceived thereby is not wise...... 3605
Pr 27:16 W. hideth her hideth the wind, and..........
Isa 54:15 w. shall gather together against......... 4310
Isa 59:8 w. goeth therein shall not know......... 3605
Jer 19:3 which w. heareth, his ears shall......... 3605
Eze 33:4 Then w. heareth the sound of the............
Da 5:7 W. shall read this writing, and........... 3605
Da 6:7 w. shall ask a petition of any God....... 3605
Joe 2:32 w. shall call on the name of the........... 834
Mt 5:19 W. therefore shall break one.. 3739,1437
Mt 5:19 w. shall do and teach them, ... 3739,302
Mt 5:21 w. shall kill shall be in 3739,302
Mt 5:22 w. is angry with his brother... 3956,3588
Mt 5:22 w. shall say to his brother,......... 3739,302
Mt 5:22 but w. shall say, Thou fool,..... 3739,302
Mt 5:28 w. looketh on a woman to..... 3956,3588
Mt 5:31 W. shall put away his wife,..... 3739,302
Mt 5:32 w. shall put away his wife,...... 3739,302
Mt 5:32 w. shall marry her that is...... 3739,1437
Mt 5:39 w. shall smite thee on thy right.... 3748
Mt 5:41 w. shall compel thee to go a 3748
Mt 7:24 w. heareth these sayings of.... 3956,3748
Mt 10:14 And w. shall not receive 3739,1437
Mt 10:32 W. therefore shall confess......... 3956,3748
Mt 10:33 w. shall deny me before men, .. 3748,302
Mt 10:42 w. shall give to drink unto..... 3739,1437
Mt 11:6 w. shall not be offended in 3739,1437
Mt 12:32 w. speaketh a word against..... 3739,302
Mt 12:32 w. speaketh against the Holy .. 3739,302
Mt 12:50 w. shall do the will of my 3748,302
Mt 13:12 For w. hath, to him shall be......... 3748
Mt 13:12 w. hath not, from him shall be 3748
Mt 15:5 W. shall say to his father or.... 3739,302
Mt 16:25 w. will save his life shall lose.. 3739,302
Mt 16:25 w. will lose his life for my...... 3739,302
Mt 18:4 W. therefore shall humble 3748
Mt 19:9 W. shall put away his wife,...... 3739,302
Mt 20:26 w. will be great among you,... 3739,1437
Mt 20:27 w. will be chief among you,... 3739,1437
Mt 21:44 w. shall fall on this stone shall..... 3588
Mt 23:12 w. shall exalt himself shall be......... 3748
Mt 23:16 W. shall swear by the temple... 3739,302
Mt 23:16 w. shall swear by the gold of.... 3739,302
Mt 23:18 W. shall swear by the altar.... 3739,1437
Mt 23:18 w. sweareth by the gift that 3739,302
Mk 3:35 w. shall do the will of God,..... 3739,302
Mk 6:11 w. shall not receive you, nor... 3745,302
Mk 8:34 W. will come after me, let him 3748
Mk 8:35 w. will save his life shall lose.. 3736,302
Mk 8:35 w. shall lose his life for my..... 3736,302
Mk 8:38 W. therefore shall be ashamed..3736,302
Mk 9:37 W. shall receive one of such .. 3739,1437
Mk 9:37 w. shall receive me,............... 3739,1437
Mk 9:41 w. shall give you a cup of....... 3739,302
Mk 9:42 w. shall offend one of these..... 3739,302
Mk 10:11 W. shall put away his wife 3739,1437
Mk 10:15 W. shall not receive the.......... 3739,1437
Mk 10:43 w. will be great among you,... 3739,1437
Mk 10:44 w. of you will be the................ 3739,302
Mk 11:23 That w. shall say unto this...... 3739,302
Lu 6:47 W. cometh to me, and 3956,3588
Lu 7:23 w. shall not be offended in 3739,1437
Lu 8:18 w. hath, to him shall be.......... 3739,302
Lu 8:18 w. hath not, from him shall be.3739,302
Lu 9:5 And w. will not receive you,.... 3745,302
Lu 9:24 For w. will save his life shall .. 3739,302
Lu 9:24 w. will lose his life for my 3739,302
Lu 9:26 w. shall be ashamed of me 3739,302
Lu 9:48 W. shall receive this child...... 3739,1437
Lu 9:48 w. shall receive me.................. 3739,1437
Lu 12:8 W. shall confess me......... 3956,3739,302
Lu 12:10 w. shall speak a word.......... 3956,3739
Lu 14:11 w. exalted himself shall be..... 3956,3588
Lu 14:27 w. doth not bear his cross, and 3748
Lu 14:33 w. he be of you that forsaketh 3956
Lu 16:18 W. putteth away his wife,....... 3956,3588
Lu 16:18 w. marrieth her that is put.... 3956,3588
Lu 17:33 W. shall seek to save his life.. 3739,1437
Lu 17:33 w. shall lose his life shall...... 3739,1437
Lu 18:17 W. shall not receive the......... 3739,1437
Lu 20:18 W. shall fall upon that stone ..3956,3588
Joh 3:15, 16 w. believeth in him should..3956,3588
Joh 4:13 W. drinketh of this water......... 3956,3588
Joh 4:14 But w. drinketh of the water... 3739,302
Joh 5:4 w. then first after the troubling of...... 3588
Joh 8:34 W. committeth sin is the 3956,3588
Joh 11:26 w. liveth and believeth in me . 3956,3588
Joh 12:46 w. believeth on me should...... 3956,3588
Joh 16:2 w. killeth you will think that ..3956,3588
Joh 19:12 w. maketh himself a king........... 3956,3588
Ac 2:21 w. shall call on the name of the .. 3956,3739
Ac 10:43 w. believeth in him shall............ 3956,3588
Ac 13:26 w. among you feareth God, to you..... 3588
Ro 2:1 man, w. thou art that judgest: 3956,3588
Ro 9:33 w. believeth on him shall not...... 3956,3588
Ro 10:11 W. believeth on him shall not..... 3956,3588
Ro 10:13 w. shall call upon the 3956,3739,302
Ro 13:2 W. therefore resisteth the power, ... 3588
1Co 11:27 w. shall eat this bread, and 3739,302
Ga 5:4 w. of you are justified by the law; 3748
Ga 5:10 bear his judgment, w. he be. 3748,302
Jas 2:10 w. shall keep the whole law, and........ 3748
Jas 4:4 w. therefore will be a friend 3739,302
1Jo 2:23 W. denieth the Son, the same.... 3956,3588
1Jo 3:4 W. committeth sin 3956,3588
1Jo 3:6 W. abideth in him sinneth not:.... 3956,3588
1Jo 3:6 w. sinneth hath not seen him, ... 3956,3588
1Jo 3:9 W. is born of God doth not........ 3956,3588
1Jo 3:10 w. doeth not righteousness is..... 3956,3588
1Jo 3:15 W. hateth his brother is a 3956,3588
1Jo 4:15 W. shall confess that Jesus is....... 3739,302
1Jo 5:1 W. believeth that Jesus is.......... 3956,3588
1Jo 5:18 w. is born of God sinneth not;.... 3956,3588
2Jo 9 W. transgresseth, and abideth..... 3956,3588
Re 14:11 w. receiveth the mark of his name. 1536
Re 20:15 w. was not found written in the......... 1536
Re 22:15 w. loveth and maketh a lie.......... 3956,3588
Re 22:17 w. will, let him take the water of....... 3588

WHY

Ge 4:6 unto Cain, W. art thou wroth?.......... 4100
Ge 4:6 and w. is thy countenance fallen? 4100
Ge 12:18 w. didst thou not tell me that she 4100
Ge 12:19 W. saidst thou, She is my sister?....... 4100
Ge 25:22 she said, If it be so, w. am I thus?..... 4100
Ge 27:45 w. should I be deprived also of you 4100
Ge 42:1 W. do you look one upon another? 4100
Ge 47:15 w. should we die in thy presence?...... 4100
Ex 1:18 W. have ye done this thing, and 4069
Ex 2:20 w. is it that ye have left the man?...... 4100
Ex 3:3 this great sight, w. the bush is 4069
Ex 5:22 people? w. is it thou hast sent me? 4100
Ex 14:5 W. have we done this, that we.......... 4100
Ex 17:2 unto them, W. chide ye with me? 4100
Ex 18:14 w. sittest thou thyself alone, and.......... 4069
Ex 32:11 w. doth thy wrath wax hot against...... 4100
Nu 11:20 W. came we forth out of Egypt?......... 4100
Nu 20:4 And w. have ye brought up the 4100
Nu 27:4 W. should the name of our father....... 4100
De 5:25 Now therefore w. should we die?........ 4100
Jos 5:4 cause w. Joshua did circumcise:........... 834
Jos 7:25 W. hast thou troubled us? the 4100
Jos 17:14 W. hast thou given me but one.......... 4069
Jg 2:2 my voice: w. have ye done this?........ 4100
Jg 5:16 W. abodest thou among the 4100
Jg 5:17 and w. did Dan remain in ships?......... 4100
Jg 5:28 W. is his chariot so long in 4069
Jg 5:28 w. tarry the wheels of his chariot? 4069
Jg 6:13 w. then is all this befallen us?............ 4100
Jg 8:1 W. hast thou served us thus, that 4100
Jg 9:28 Shechem...w. should we serve him? ... 4100
Jg 11:7 w. are ye come unto me now when.... 4069
Jg 11:26 w. therefore did ye not recover......... 4069
Jg 13:18 W. askest thou thus after my............ 4100
Jg 15:10 W. are ye come up against us?.......... 4100
Jg 21:3 w. is this come to pass in Israel, ... 4100
Ru 1:11 w. will ye go with me? are there 4100
Ru 1:21 w. then call ye me Naomi, seeing....... 4100
Ru 2:10 W. have I found grace in thine 4069
1Sa 1:8 w. weepest thou? and w. eatest 4100
1Sa 1:8 w. is thy heart grieved? am I not......... 4100
1Sa 2:23 unto them, W. do ye such things?........ 4100
1Sa 6:3 you w. his hand is not removed.......... 4100
1Sa 17:8 W. are ye come out to set your 4100
1Sa 17:28 said, W. camest thou down hither?..... 4100
1Sa 19:17 W. hast thou deceived me so, and....... 4100
1Sa 19:17 Let me go; w. should I kill thee? 4100
1Sa 20:2 w. should my father hide this 4060
1Sa 20:8 for w. shouldest thou bring me to 4100
1Sa 21:1 W. art thou alone, and no man 4069
1Sa 22:13 W. have ye conspired against me, ... 4100
1Sa 27:5 for w. should thy servant dwell in 4100
1Sa 28:12 W. hast thou deceived me? for.......... 4100
1Sa 28:15 W. hast thou disquieted me, to.......... 4100
2Sa 3:24 w. is it that thou hast sent him.......... 4100
2Sa 7:7 W. build ye not me an house of......... 4100
2Sa 11:10 w. then didst thou not go down 4069
2Sa 11:21 w. went ye nigh the wall? then say..... 4100
2Sa 13:4 W. art thou, being the king's son, ... 4069
2Sa 13:26 him, W. should he go with thee?......... 4100
2Sa 16:9 W. should this dead dog curse my...... 4100
2Sa 16:17 w. wentest thou not with thy 4100
2Sa 18:11 w. didst thou not smite him there 4069
2Sa 19:10 w. speak ye not a word of bringing..... 4100
2Sa 19:11 W. are ye the last to bring the king.... 4100
2Sa 19:29 W. speakest thou any more of thy....... 4100
2Sa 19:36 w. should the king recompense it 4100
2Sa 19:41 W. have our brethren the men of....... 4069
2Sa 19:43 w. then did ye despise us, that our 4069
2Sa 20:19 w. wilt thou swallow up the 4100
2Sa 24:3 w. doth my lord the king delight 4100
1Ki 1:6 in saying, W. hast thou done so? 4069
1Ki 1:13 w. then doth Adonijah reign?............. 4069
1Ki 2:22 And w. dost thou ask Abishag the...... 4100
1Ki 2:43 W. then hast thou not kept the.......... 4100
1Ki 9:8 W. hath the Lord done thus....... 5921,4100
1Ki 14:6 w. feignest thou thyself to be........... 4100
1Ki 21:5 W. is thy spirit so sad, that thou 4100
2Ki 1:5 them, W. are ye now turned back? 4100
2Ki 7:3 W. sit we here until we die? 4100
2Ki 8:12 Hazael said, W. weepeth my lord?...... 4069
2Ki 12:7 W. repair ye not the breaches of 4069
2Ki 14:10 for w. shouldest thou meddle to.......... 4100
1Ch 17:6 W. have ye not built me an house...... 4100
1Ch 21:3 w. then doth my lord require this....... 4100
1Ch 21:3 w. will he be a cause of trespass to..........
2Ch 7:21 W. hath the Lord done thus unto 4100
2Ch 24:6 W. hast thou not required of the........ 4069
2Ch 24:20 W. transgress ye the.......................... 4100
2Ch 25:15 W. hast thou sought after the gods....... 4100
2Ch 25:16 w. shouldest thou be smitten? 4100
2Ch 25:19 w. shouldest thou meddle to thine 4100
2Ch 32:4 W. should the king of Assyria come,... 4100
Ezr 4:22 w. should damage grow to the........... 4101
Ezr 7:23 w. should there be wrath against......... 4101
Ne 2:2 W. is thy countenance sad, ... 4069
Ne 2:3 w. should not my countenance be....... 4069
Ne 6:3 w. should the work cease, whilst 4100
Ne 13:11 W. is the house of God forsaken? 4069
Ne 13:21 them, W. lodge ye about the wall? 4069
Es 3:3 W. transgressest thou the king's........ 4069
Es 4:5 know what it was, and w. it was......... 4100
Job 3:11 W. died I not from the womb? 4100
Job 3:11 w. did I not give up the ghost when I.......
Job 3:12 W. did the knees prevent me?............ 4069
Job 3:12 or w. the breasts that I should suck? .. 4069
Job 3:23 W. is light given to a man whose way.......
Job 7:20 w. hast thou set me as a mark.......... 4100
Job 7:21 And w. dost thou not pardon my......... 4100
Job 9:29 be wicked, w. then labour I in vain? ... 4100
Job 15:12 W. doth thine heart carry thee 4100
Job 19:22 W. do ye persecute me as God, ... 4100
Job 19:28 w. persecute we him, seeing the........ 4100
Job 21:4 so, w. should not my spirit be.......... 4069
Job 24:1 W., seeing times are not hidden 4069
Job 27:12 w. then are ye thus altogether........... 4100
Job 31:1 w. then should I think upon a............ 4100
Job 33:13 W. dost thou strive against him?........ 4069
Ps 2:1 W. do the heathen rage, and the.......... 4100
Ps 10:1 W. standest thou afar off, O Lord?..... 4100
Ps 10:1 w. hidest thou thyself in times of.............
Ps 22:1 My God, my God, w. hast thou.......... 4100
Ps 22:1 w. art thou so far from helping me, ...
Ps 42:5 W. art thou cast down, O my soul? 4100
Ps 42:5 w. art thou disquieted in me? ....
Ps 42:9 rock, W. hast thou forgotten me?....... 4100
Ps 42:9 w. go I mourning because of the........ 4100
Ps 42:11 W. art thou cast down, O my soul? 4100
Ps 42:11 w. art thou disquieted within me?...... 4100
Ps 43:2 strength: w. dost thou cast me off? 4100
Ps 43:2 w. go I mourning because of the........ 4100
Ps 43:5 W. art thou cast down, O my soul? 4100
Ps 43:5 w. art thou disquieted within me?....... 4100
Ps 44:23 Awake, w. sleepest thou, O Lord? 4100
Ps 52:1 W. boastest thou thyself in 4100
Ps 68:16 W. leap ye, ye high hills? this is 4100
Ps 74:1 w. hast thou cast us off for ever?....... 4100
Ps 74:1 w. doth thine anger smote against the.......

Ps 74:11 W. withdrawest thou thy hand, 4100
Ps 80:12 W. hast thou then broken down 4100
Ps 88:14 Lord, w. castest thou off my soul? 4100
Ps 88:14 w. hidest thou thy face from me?
Pr 5:20 w. wilt thou, my son, be ravished 4100
Pr 22:27 w. should he take away thy bed 4100
Ec 2:15 me; and w. was I then more wise? 4100
Ec 7:16 w. shouldest thou destroy thyself? 4100
Ec 7:17 w. shouldest thou die before thy 4100
Ca 1:7 w. should I be as one that turneth 4100
Isa 1:5 W. should ye be stricken any 5921,4100
Isa 40:27 W. sayest thou, O Jacob, and 4100
Isa 63:17 w. hast thou made us to err from 4100
Jer 2:14 homeborn slave? w. is he spoiled? 4069
Jer 2:33 W. trimmest thou thy way to 4100
Jer 2:36 W. gaddest thou about so much 4100
Jer 8:5 W. then is this people of 4069
Jer 8:14 W. do we sit still? assemble 5921,4100
Jer 8:19 W. have they provoked me to 4069
Jer 8:22 w. then is not the health of the 4069
Jer 14:8 w. shouldest thou be as a stranger 4100
Jer 14:9 W. shouldest thou be as a man 4100
Jer 14:19 w. hast thou smitten us, and 4069
Jer 15:18 W. is my pain perpetual, and my 4100
Jer 26:9 W. hast thou prophesied in the 4069
Jer 27:13 W. will ye die, thou and thy 4100
Jer 29:27 w. hast thou not reproved Jeremiah 4100
Jer 30:15 W. criest thou for thine affliction? 4100
Jer 36:29 W. hast thou written therein, 4069
Jer 46:15 W. are thy valiant men swept 4069
Jer 49:1 w. then doth their king inherit 4069
Eze 18:19 W.? doth not the son bear the 4069
Eze 18:31 w. will ye die, O house of Israel? 4100
Eze 33:11 w. will ye die, O house of Israel? 4100
Da 1:10 for w. should he see your faces 4100
Da 2:15 W. is the decree so hasty 5922,4101
Jon 1:10 him, W. hast thou done this? 4100
Mic 4:9 Now w. dost thou cry out aloud? 4100
Hab 1:3 W. dost thou show me iniquity, 4100
Hag 1:9 W.? saith the Lord of hosts. 3282,4100
Mal 2:10 w. do we deal treacherously 4069
Mt 6:28 **w. take ye thought for raiment?** *5101*
Mt 7:3 **w. beholdest thou the mote that** *5101*
Mt 8:26 **W. are ye fearful, O ye of little** *5101*
Mt 9:11 W. eateth your Master with *1302*
Mt 9:14 W. do we and the Pharisees fast *1302*
Mt 13:10 W. speakest thou unto them in *1302*
Mt 15:2 W. do thy disciples transgress the *1302*
Mt 15:3 **W. do ye also transgress the** *1302*
Mt 16:8 **w. reason ye among yourselves,** *5101*
Mt 17:10 W. then say the scribes that Elias *5101*
Mt 17:19 W. could not we cast him out? *1302*
Mt 19:7 W. did Moses then command to *5101*
Mt 19:17 **W. callest thou me good? there is** *5101*
Mt 20:6 **W. stand ye here all the day idle?** *5101*
Mt 21:25 us, **W. did ye not then believe him?** *1302*
Mt 22:18 **W. tempt ye me, ye hypocrites?** *5101*
Mt 26:10 **W. trouble ye the woman? for she** *5101*
Mt 27:23 said, W., what evil hath he done? *1063*
Mt 27:46 my God, w. hast thou forsaken me? *2444*
Mk 2:7 W. doth this man thus speak *5101*
Mk 2:8 **W. reason ye these things in your** *5101*
Mk 2:18 W. do the disciples of John and *1302*
Mk 2:24 w. do they on the sabbath day *5101*
Mk 4:40 **W. are ye so fearful? how is it** *5101*
Mk 5:35 w. troublest thou the Master any *5101*
Mk 5:39 **W. make ye this ado, and weep?** *5101*
Mk 7:5 W. walk not thy disciples *1302*
Mk 8:12 **W. doth this generation seek** *5101*
Mk 8:17 **W. reason ye, because ye have no** *5101*
Mk 9:11 W. say the scribes that Elias *3754*
Mk 9:28 W. could not we cast him out? *3754*
Mk 10:18 **W. callest thou me good? there is** *5101*
Mk 11:3 **man say unto you, W. do ye this?** *5101*
Mk 11:31 W. then did ye not believe him? *1302*
Mk 12:15 said unto them, **W. tempt ye me?** *5101*
Mk 14:4 W. was this waste of the *1519,5101*
Mk 14:6 **Let her alone; w. trouble ye her?** *5101*
Mk 15:14 them, W., what evil hath he done? *1063*
Mk 15:34 my God, w. hast thou forsaken *1519,5101*
Lu 2:48 W. hast thou thus dealt with us? *5101*
Lu 5:30 W. do ye eat and drink with *1302*
Lu 5:33 W. do the disciples of John fast *1302*
Lu 6:2 W. do ye that which is not lawful *5101*
Lu 6:41 **w. beholdest thou the mote that** *5101*
Lu 6:46 **w. call ye me, Lord, Lord, and** *5101*
Lu 12:26 **w. take ye thought for the rest?** *5101*
Lu 12:57 **w. even of yourselves judge ye** *5101*
Lu 13:7 **down; w. cumbereth it the** *2444*
Lu 18:19 him, **W. callest thou me good?** *5101*
Lu 19:31 **man ask you, W. do ye loose** *1302*
Lu 19:33 unto them, W. loose ye the colt? *5101*
Lu 20:5 say, W. then believed ye him not? *1302*
Lu 20:23 said unto them, **W. tempt ye me?** *5101*
Lu 22:46 them, **W. sleep ye? rise and pray,** *5101*
Lu 23:22 time, W., what evil hath he done? *1063*
Lu 24:5 W. seek ye the living among the *5101*
Lu 24:38 unto them, **W. are ye troubled?** *5101*
Lu 24:38 **w. do thoughts arise in...hearts?** *1302*
Joh 1:25 W. baptizest thou then, if thou be *5101*
Joh 4:27 thou? or, W. talkest thou with her? *5101*
Joh 7:19 **the law? W. go ye about to kill** *5101*
Joh 7:45 them, W. have ye not brought him? *1302*
Joh 8:43 **W. do ye not understand my** *1302*
Joh 8:46 **truth, w. do ye not believe me?** *1302*
Joh 9:30 W. herein is a marvellous thing, *1063*
Joh 10:20 devil, and is made; w. hear ye him? *5101*
Joh 12:5 W. was not this ointment sold *1302*
Joh 13:37 Lord, w. cannot I follow thee now? *1302*
Joh 18:21 **W. askest thou me? ask them** *5101*
Joh 18:23 **but if well, w. smitest thou me?** *5101*
Joh 20:13 **Woman, w. weepest thou?**
Joh 20:15 her, **Woman, w. weepest thou?** *5101*
Ac 1:11 w. stand ye gazing up into heaven? *5101*
Ac 3:12 w. marvel ye at this? or w. look ye *5101*
Ac 4:25 W. did the heathen rage, and the *2444*
Ac 5:3 w. hath Satan filled thine heart to *1302*
Ac 5:4 w. hast thou conceived this thing *5101*
Ac 7:26 w. do ye wrong one to another? *2444*
Ac 9:4 **Saul, w. persecutest thou me?** *5101*
Ac 14:15 Sirs, w. do ye these things? *5101*
Ac 15:10 Now therefore w. tempt ye God, to *5101*
Ac 22:7 **Saul, Saul, w. persecutest thou** *5101*
Ac 22:16 And now w. tarriest thou? arise, *5101*
Ac 26:8 W. should it be thought a thing *5101*
Ac 26:14 **Saul, Saul, w. persecutest thou** *5101*
Ro 3:7 w. yet am I also judged as a sinner? *5101*
Ro 8:24 man seeth, w. doth he yet hope for? *5101*
Ro 9:19 unto me, W. doth he yet find fault? *5101*
Ro 9:20 it, W. hast thou made me thus? *5101*
Ro 14:10 But w. dost thou judge thy brother? *5101*
Ro 14:10 w. dost thou set at nought thy *5101*
1Co 4:7 w. dost thou glory, as if thou hadst *5101*
1Co 6:7 W. do ye not rather take wrong? *1302*
1Co 6:7 w. do ye not rather suffer *1302*
1Co 10:29 w. is my liberty judged of *2444,5101*
1Co 10:30 w. am I evil spoken of for that *5101*
1Co 15:29 w. are they then baptized for the *5101*
1Co 15:30 w. stand ye in jeopardy every hour? *5101*
Ga 2:14 w. compellest thou the Gentiles to *5101*
Ga 5:11 w. do I yet suffer persecution? *5101*
Col 2:20 w., as though living in the world, *5101*

WICKED

Ge 13:13 the men of Sodom were w. and 7451
Ge 18:23 destroy the righteous with the w.? 7563
Ge 18:25 slay the righteous with the w. 7563
Ge 18:25 the righteous should be as the w., 7563
Ge 38:7 was w. in the sight of the Lord; 7451
Ex 9:27 and I and my people are w.. 7563
Ex 23:1 put not thine hand with the w. to 7563
Ex 23:7 not: for I will not justify the w. 7563
Le 20:17 it is a w. thing; and they shall 2617
Nu 16:26 from the tents of these w. men, 7563
De 15:9 be not a thought in thy w. heart, 1100
De 17:5 have committed that w. thing, 7451
De 23:9 keep thee from every w. thing. 7451
De 25:1 righteous, and condemn the w.. 7563
De 25:2 w. man be worthy to be beaten, 7563
1Sa 2:9 the w. shall be silent in darkness; 7563
1Sa 24:13 proceedeth from the w.: 7563
1Sa 30:22 answered all the w. men and 7451
2Sa 3:34 as a man falleth before w. men, 5766
2Sa 4:11 w. men have slain a righteous 7563
1Ki 8:32 thy servants, condemning the w., 7563
2Ki 17:11 wrought w. things to provoke 7451
2Ch 6:23 thy servants, by requiting the w., 7563
2Ch 7:14 face, and turn from their w. ways; 7451
2Ch 24:7 sons of Athaliah, that w. woman, 4849
Ne 9:35 turned they from their w. works. 7451
Es 7:6 and enemy is this w. Haman. 7451
Es 9:25 by letters that his w. device, 7451
Job 3:17 the w. cease from troubling: 7563
Job 8:22 of the w. shall come to nought. 7563
Job 9:22 destroyeth the perfect and the w.. 7563
Job 9:24 is given into the hand of the w.: 7563
Job 9:29 If I be w., why then labour I in 7561
Job 10:3 shine upon the counsel of the w.? 7563
Job 10:7 Thou knowest that I am not w.; 7561
Job 10:15 If I be w., woe unto me; and if I be 7561
Job 11:20 But the eyes of the w. shall fail, 7563
Job 15:20 The w. man travaileth with pain 7563
Job 16:11 me over into the hands of the w.. 7563
Job 18:5 the light of the w. shall be put out, 7563
Job 18:21 such are the dwellings of the w., 5767
Job 20:5 the triumphing of the w. is short, 7563
Job 20:22 hand of the w. shall come upon 6001
Job 20:29 This is the portion of the w. man 7563
Job 21:7 Wherefore do the w. live, become 7563
Job 21:16 counsel of the w. is far from me. 7563
Job 21:17 oft is the candle of the w. put out! 7563
Job 21:28 are the dwelling places of the w.? 7563
Job 21:30 the w. is reserved to the day of 7451
Job 22:15 way which w. men have trodden? 205
Job 22:18 counsel of the w. is far from me. 7563
Job 24:6 they gather the vintage of the w.. 7563
Job 27:7 Let mine enemy be as the w., and 7563
Job 27:13 the portion of a w. man with God, 7563
Job 29:17 And I brake the jaws of the w., 5767
Job 31:3 Is not destruction to the w.? and 5767
Job 34:8 and walketh with w. men. 7562
Job 34:18 fit to say to a king, Thou art w.? 1100
Job 34:26 He striketh them as w. men in the 7563
Job 34:36 because of his answers for w. men. 205
Job 36:6 preserveth not the life of the w.: 7563
Job 36:17 fulfilled the judgment of the w.: 7563
Job 38:13 the w. might be shaken out of it? 7563
Job 38:15 from the w. their light is withholden, 7563
Job 40:12 tread down the w. in their place. 7563
Ps 7:9 wickedness of the w. come to an 7563
Ps 7:11 God is angry with the w. every day.
Ps 9:5 thou hast destroyed the w., thou 7563
Ps 9:16 the w. is snared in the work of his 7563
Ps 9:17 w. shall be turned into hell, and 7563
Ps 10:2 w. in his pride doth persecute the 7563
Ps 10:3 w. boasteth of his heart's desire, 7563
Ps 10:4 The w., through the pride of his 7563
Ps 10:13 doth the w. contemn God? 7563
Ps 10:15 Break thou the arm of the w. and 7563
Ps 11:2 For, lo, the w. bend their bow, they 7563
Ps 11:5 the w. and him that loveth violence 7563
Ps 11:6 Upon the w. he shall rain snares, 7563
Ps 12:8 The w. walk on every side, when 7563
Ps 17:9 the w. that oppress me, from my 7563
Ps 17:13 deliver my soul from the w., which 7563
Ps 22:16 assembly of the w. have inclosed 7489
Ps 26:5 doers; and will not sit with the w.. 7563
Ps 27:2 When the w., even mine enemies 7489
Ps 28:3 Draw me not away with the w., 7563
Ps 31:17 let the w. be ashamed, and let 7563
Ps 32:10 Many sorrows shall be to the w.: 7563
Ps 34:21 Evil shall slay the w.: and they 7563
Ps 36:1 transgression of the w. saith 7563
Ps 36:11 not the hand of the w. remove me. 7563
Ps 37:7 who bringeth w. devices to pass. 4209
Ps 37:10 while, and the w. shall not be: 7563
Ps 37:12 the w. plotteth against the just, 7563
Ps 37:14 The w. have drawn out the sword, 7563
Ps 37:16 better than the riches of many w. 7563
Ps 37:17 the arms of the w. shall be broken: 7563
Ps 37:20 But the w. shall perish, and the 7563
Ps 37:21 the w. borroweth, and payeth not 7563
Ps 37:28 the seed of the w. shall be cut off. 7563
Ps 37:32 The w. watcheth the righteous, 7563
Ps 37:34 when the w. are cut off, thou shalt 7563
Ps 37:35 I have seen the w. in great power, 7563
Ps 37:38 the end of the w. shall be cut off. 7563
Ps 37:40 shall deliver them from the w., and 7563
Ps 39:1 bridle, while the w. is before me. 7563
Ps 50:16 But unto the w. God saith, What 7563
Ps 55:3 of the oppression of the w.: 7563
Ps 58:3 w. are estranged from the womb: 7563
Ps 58:10 wash his feet in the blood of the w. 7563
Ps 59:5 merciful to any w. transgressors. 205
Ps 64:2 from the secret counsel of the w.; 7489
Ps 68:2 w. perish at the presence of God. 7563
Ps 71:4 my God, out of the hand of the w., 7563
Ps 73:3 I saw the prosperity of the w.. 7563

Ps 74:19 unto the multitude of the **w.**:
Ps 75:4 and to the **w.**, Lift not up the horn: 7563
Ps 75:8 all the **w.** of the earth shall wring 7563
Ps 75:10 horns of the **w.** also will I cut off; 7563
Ps 82:2 and accept the persons of the **w.**? 7563
Ps 82:4 rid them out of the hand of the **w.**. 7563
Ps 91:8 and see the reward of the **w.**. 7563
Ps 92:7 When the **w.** spring as the grass, 7563
Ps 92:11 my desire of the **w.** that rise up 7489
Ps 94:3 Lord, how long shall the **w.**, how 7563
Ps 94:3 how long shall the **w.** triumph? 7563
Ps 94:13 until the pit be digged for the **w.** 7563
Ps 97:10 them out of the hand of the **w.**. 7563
Ps 101:3 set no **w.** thing before mine eyes: 1100
Ps 101:4 me: I will not know a **w.** person. 7451
Ps 101:8 destroy all the **w.** of the land; 7563
Ps 101:8 that I may cut off all the **w.** doers 205
Ps 104:35 earth, and let the **w.** be no more. 7563
Ps 106:18 the flame burned up the **w.**. 7563
Ps 109:2 the mouth of the **w.** and the mouth 7563
Ps 109:6 Set thou a **w.** man over him: and 7563
Ps 112:10 The **w.** shall see it, and be grieved; 7563
Ps 112:10 the desire of the **w.** shall perish. 7563
Ps 119:53 of the **w.** that forsake thy law. 7563
Ps 119:61 bands of the **w.** have robbed me: 7563
Ps 119:95 **w.** have waited for me to destroy 7563
Ps 119:110 The **w.** have laid a snare for me: 7563
Ps 119:119 puttest away all the **w.** of the earth 7563
Ps 119:155 Salvation is far from the **w.**: for 7563
Ps 125:3 the rod of the **w.** shall not rest 7562
Ps 129:4 cut asunder the cords of the **w.**. 7563
Ps 139:19 Surely thou wilt slay the **w.**, O God: 7563
Ps 139:24 see if there be any **w.** way in me, 6090
Ps 140:4 O Lord, from the hands of the **w.**; 7563
Ps 140:8 not, O Lord, the desires of the **w.**: 7563
Ps 140:8 further not his **w.** device; lest 2162
Ps 141:4 to practise **w.** works with men 7562
Ps 141:10 Let the **w.** fall into their own nets, 7563
Ps 145:20 him: but all the **w.** will he destroy. 7563
Ps 146:9 the way of the **w.** he turneth upside 7563
Ps 147:6 casteth the **w.** down to the ground. 7563
Pr 2:14 in the frowardness of the **w.**; 7451
Pr 2:22 **w.** shall be cut off from the earth, 7563
Pr 3:25 neither of the desolation of the **w.**, 7563
Pr 3:33 the Lord is in the house of the **w.**: 7563
Pr 4:14 Enter not into the path of the **w.**, 7563
Pr 4:19 The way of the **w.** is as darkness: 7563
Pr 5:22 iniquity shall take the **w.** himself, 7563
Pr 6:12 **w.** man, walketh with a froward 205
Pr 6:18 heart that deviseth **w.** imaginations, 205
Pr 9:7 he that rebuketh a **w.** man getteth 7563
Pr 10:3 away the substance of the **w.**. 7563
Pr 10:6 covereth the mouth of the **w.**. 7563
Pr 10:7 but the name of the **w.** shall rot 7563
Pr 10:11 violence covereth...mouth of the **w.**. 7563
Pr 10:16 to life: the fruit of the **w.** to sin. 7563
Pr 10:20 the heart of the **w.** is little worth. 7563
Pr 10:24 The fear of the **w.**, it shall come 7563
Pr 10:25 passeth, so is the **w.** no more: 7563
Pr 10:27 years of the **w.** shall be shortened. 7563
Pr 10:28 expectation of the **w.** shall perish. 7563
Pr 10:30 the **w.** shall not inhabit the earth. 7563
Pr 10:32 of the **w.** speaketh frowardness. 7563
Pr 11:5 **w.** shall fall by his own wickedness. 7563
Pr 11:7 When a **w.** man dieth, his 7563
Pr 11:8 and the **w.** cometh in his stead. 7563
Pr 11:10 the **w.** perish, there is shouting. 7563
Pr 11:11 overthrown by the mouth of the **w.**. 7563
Pr 11:18 The **w.** worketh a deceitful work: 7563
Pr 11:21 the **w.** shall not be unpunished: 7451
Pr 11:23 the expectation of the **w.** is wrath. 7563
Pr 11:31 much more the **w.** and the sinner. 7563
Pr 12:2 man of **w.** devices will...condemn. 4209
Pr 12:5 the counsels of the **w.** are deceit. 7563
Pr 12:6 words of the **w.** are to lie in wait 7563
Pr 12:7 **w.** are overthrown, and are not: 7563
Pr 12:10 tender mercies of the **w.** are cruel. 7563
Pr 12:12 The **w.** desireth the net of evil men: 7563
Pr 12:13 **w.** is snared by the transgression 7451
Pr 12:21 **w.** shall be filled with mischief. 7563
Pr 12:26 the way of the **w.** seduceth them. 7563
Pr 13:5 a **w.** man is loathsome, and cometh 7563
Pr 13:9 the lamp of the **w.** shall be put out. 7563
Pr 13:17 **w.** messenger falleth into mischief: 7563
Pr 13:25 but the belly of the **w.** shall want. 7563
Pr 14:11 The house of the **w.** shall be 7563
Pr 14:17 and a man of **w.** devices is hated. 4209
Pr 14:19 **w.** at the gates of the righteous. 7563
Pr 14:32 The **w.** is driven away in his 7563
Pr 15:6 in the revenues of the **w.** is trouble. 7563
Pr 15:8 sacrifice of the **w.** is an abomination. 7563
Pr 15:9 way of the **w.** is an abomination 7563
Pr 15:26 The thoughts of the **w.** are an 7451
Pr 15:28 mouth of the **w.** poureth out evil 7563
Pr 15:29 The Lord is far from the **w.**: but he 7563
Pr 16:4 yea, even the **w.** for the day of evil. 7563
Pr 17:4 A **w.** doer giveth heed to false lips; 7489
Pr 17:15 He that justifieth the **w.**, and he 7563
Pr 17:23 A **w.** man taketh a gift out of the 7563
Pr 18:3 When the **w.** cometh, then cometh 7563
Pr 18:5 good to accept the person of the **w.**, 7563
Pr 19:28 mouth of the **w.** devoureth iniquity. 7563
Pr 20:26 A wise king scattereth the **w.**, and 7563
Pr 21:4 and the plowing of the **w.**, is sin. 7563
Pr 21:7 The robbery of the **w.** shall destroy. 7563
Pr 21:10 the soul of the **w.** desireth evil: 7563
Pr 21:12 considereth the house of the **w.**: 7563
Pr 21:12 God overthroweth the **w.** for their 7563
Pr 21:18 The **w.** shall be a ransom for the 7563
Pr 21:27 sacrifice of the **w.** is abomination: 7563
Pr 21:27 he bringeth it with a **w.** mind? 2154
Pr 21:29 A **w.** man hardeneth his face: but 7563
Pr 24:15 Lay not wait, O **w.** man, against the 7563
Pr 24:16 but the **w.** shall fall into mischief. 7563
Pr 24:19 neither be thou envious at the **w.**; 7563
Pr 24:20 candle of the **w.** shall be put out. 7563
Pr 24:24 He that saith unto the **w.**, Thou art 7563
Pr 25:5 Take...the **w.** from before the king, 7563
Pr 25:26 man falling down before the **w.** 7563
Pr 26:23 Burning lips and a **w.** heart are 7451
Pr 28:1 **w.** flee when no man pursueth: 7563
Pr 28:4 that forsake the law praise the **w.**: 7563
Pr 28:12 when the **w.** rise, a man is hidden. 7563
Pr 28:15 is a **w.** ruler over the poor people. 7563
Pr 28:28 the **w.** rise, men hid themselves: 7563
Pr 29:2 but when the **w.** beareth rule, the 7563
Pr 29:7 the **w.** regardeth not to know it. 7563
Pr 29:12 to lies, all his servants are **w.**. 7563
Pr 29:16 When the **w.** are multiplied, 7563
Pr 29:27 the way is abomination to the **w.** 7563
Ec 3:17 judge the righteous and the **w.**: 7563
Ec 7:15 a **w.** man that prolongeth his life 7563
Ec 7:17 Be not over much **w.**, neither be 7561
Ec 8:10 And so I saw the **w.** buried, who 7563
Ec 8:13 it shall not be well with the **w.**, 7563
Ec 8:14 according to the work of the **w.**; 7563
Ec 8:14 again, there be **w.** men, to whom it 7563
Ec 9:2 to the righteous, and to the **w.**; 7563
Isa 3:11 Woe unto the **w.**! it shall be ill 7563
Isa 5:23 Which justify the **w.** for reward, 7563
Isa 11:4 of his lips shall he slay the **w.** 7563
Isa 13:11 evil, and the **w.** for their iniquity; 7563
Isa 14:5 Lord...broken the staff of the **w.**, 7563
Isa 26:10 Let favour be shewed to the **w.**, yet 7563
Isa 32:7 he deviseth **w.** devices to destroy 2154
Isa 48:22 peace, saith the Lord, unto the **w.**. 7563
Isa 53:9 And he made his grave with the **w.**, 7563
Isa 55:7 Let the **w.** forsake his way, and the 7563
Isa 57:20 the **w.** are like the troubled sea, 7563
Isa 57:21 no peace, saith my God, to the **w.**. 7563
Jer 2:33 also taught the **w.** ones thy ways. 7451
Jer 5:26 among my people are...**w.** men: 7563
Jer 5:28 they overpass the deeds of the **w.** 7451
Jer 6:29 for the **w.** are not plucked away 7451
Jer 12:1 doth the way of the **w.** prosper? 7563
Jer 15:21 thee out of the hand of the **w.**, 7451
Jer 17:9 all things, and desperately **w.** 605
Jer 23:19 upon the head of the **w.**. 7563
Jer 25:31 give them that are **w.** to the sword, 7563
Jer 30:23 with pain upon the head of the **w.**. 7563
Eze 3:18 When I say unto the **w.**, Thou shalt 7563
Eze 3:18 to warn the **w.** from his **w.** way, 7563
Eze 3:18 **w.** man shall die in his iniquity; 7563
Eze 3:19 if thou warn the **w.**, and he turn 7563
Eze 3:19 wickedness, nor from his **w.** way, 7563
Eze 7:21 to the **w.** of the earth for a spoil; 7563
Eze 8:9 the **w.** abominations that they do 7451
Eze 11:2 and give **w.** counsel in this city: 7451
Eze 13:22 the hands of the **w.**, that he should 7563
Eze 13:22 should not return from his **w.** way, 7563
Eze 18:20 wickedness of the **w.** shall be upon 7563
Eze 18:21 if the **w.** will turn from all his sins 7563
Eze 18:23 pleasure...that the **w.** should die? 7563
Eze 18:24 abominations...the **w.** man doeth, 7563
Eze 18:27 **w.** man turneth away from his 7563
Eze 20:44 not according to your **w.** ways, 7451
Eze 21:3 from thee the righteous and the **w.** 7563
Eze 21:4 from thee the righteous and the **w.**, 7563
Eze 21:25 thou, profane **w.** prince of Israel, 7563
Eze 21:29 of the **w.**, whose day is come, when 7563
Eze 30:12 the land into the hand of the **w.**: 7451
Eze 33:8 When I say unto the **w.**, O **w.** man, 7563
Eze 33:8 speak to warn the **w.** from his way, 7563
Eze 33:8 **w.** man shall die in his iniquity; 7563
Eze 33:9 warn the **w.** of his way to turn from 7563
Eze 33:11 no pleasure in the death of the **w.**; 7563
Eze 33:11 the **w.** turn from his way and live: 7563
Eze 33:12 as for the wickedness of the **w.**, he 7563
Eze 33:14 when I say unto the **w.**, Thou shalt 7563
Eze 33:15 If the **w.** restore the pledge, give 7563
Eze 33:19 if the **w.** turn from his wickedness, 7563
Da 12:10 tried; but the **w.** shall do wickedly: 7563
Da 12:10 none of the **w.** shall understand; 7563
Mic 6:10 wickedness in the house of the **w.**, 7563
Mic 6:11 them pure with the **w.** balances, 7562
Na 1:3 and will not at all acquit the **w.**:
Na 1:11 against the Lord, a **w.** counsellor. 1100
Na 1:15 **w.** shall no more pass through thee; 1100
Hab 1:4 **w.** doth compass about the 7563
Hab 1:13 when the **w.** devoureth the man 7563
Hab 3:13 the head out of the house of the **w.**, 7563
Zep 1:3 the stumbling blocks with the **w.**; 7563
Mal 3:18 between the righteous and the **w.**, 7563
Mal 4:3 And ye shall tread down the **w.**; 7563
Mt 12:45 **other spirits more w. than** *4191*
Mt 12:45 **be also unto this w. generation.** *4190*
Mt 13:19 **then cometh the w. one, and** *4190*
Mt 13:38 **are the children of the w. one;** *4190*
Mt 13:49 **sever the w. from among the just,** *4190*
Mt 16:4 **A w. and adulterous generation** *4190*
Mt 18:32 **O thou w. servant, I forgave thee** *4190*
Mt 21:41 miserably destroy those **w.** men, *2556*
Mt 25:26 **Thou w. and slothful servant,** *4190*
Lu 11:26 **other spirits more w. than** *4191*
Lu 19:22 **I judge thee, thou w. servant.** *4190*
Ac 2:23 **w.** hands have crucified and slain: *459*
Ac 18:14 a matter of wrong or **w.** lewdness, *4190*
1Co 5:13 among yourselves that **w.** person. *4190*
Eph 6:16 quench all the fiery darts of the **w.** *4190*
Col 1:21 enemies in your mind by **w.** works, *4190*
2Th 2:8 then shall that **W.** be revealed, *459*
2Th 3:2 from unreasonable and **w.** men: *4190*
2Pe 2:7 the filthy conversation of the **w.** *113*
2Pe 3:17 led away with the error of the **w.**, *113*
1Jo 2:13 ye have overcome the **w.** one. *4190*
1Jo 2:14 and ye have overcome the **w.** one. *4190*
1Jo 3:12 as Cain, who was of that **w.** one, *4190*
1Jo 5:18 and that **w.** one toucheth him not. *4190*

WICKEDLY

Ge 19:7 I pray you, brethren, do not so **w.**. 7489
De 9:18 doing **w.** in the sight of the Lord, 7451
Jg 19:23 nay, I pray you, do not so **w.**; 7489
1Sa 12:25 if ye shall still do **w.**, ye shall be 7489
2Sa 22:22 have not **w.** departed from my God. 7561
2Sa 24:17 have sinned, and I have done **w.** 5753
2Ki 21:11 done **w.** above all...the Amorites 7489
2Ch 6:37 done amiss, and have dealt **w.**; 7561
2Ch 20:35 king of Israel, who did very **w.** 7561
2Ch 22:3 mother was his counsellor to do **w.**. 7561
Ne 9:33 done right, but we have done **w.**: 7561
Job 13:7 Will ye speak **w.** for God? and 5766
Job 34:12 Yea, surely God will not do **w.**, 7561
Ps 18:21 have not **w.** departed from my God. 7561
Ps 73:8 speak **w.** concerning oppression: 7451
Ps 74:3 hath done **w.** in the sanctuary 7489
Ps 106:6 iniquity, we have done **w.** 7561
Ps 139:20 For they speak against thee **w.**, 4209
Da 9:5 have done **w.**, and have rebelled, 7561
Da 9:15 we have sinned, we have done **w.** 7561
Da 11:32 such as do **w.** against the covenant 7561
Da 12:10 tried; but the wicked shall do **w.** 7561
Mal 4:1 all that do **w.**, shall be stubble: 7564

WICKEDNESS

Ge 6:5 saw that the **w.** of man was great 7451
Ge 39:9 then can I do this great **w.**, and sin 7451
Le 18:17 are her near kinswomen: it is **w.** 2154
Le 19:29 and the land became full of **w.**. 2154
Le 20:14 a wife and her mother, it is **w.** 2154
Le 20:14 that there be no **w.** among you. 2154

De 9:4,5 but for the w. of these nations 7564
De 9:27 nor to their w., nor to their sin: 7562
De 13:11 do no more any such w. as this is 7451
De 17:2 wrought w. in the sight of the Lord 7451
De 28:20 because of the w. of thy doings, 7455
Jg 9:56 God rendered the w. of Abimelech, 7451
Jg 20:3 Israel, Tell us, how was this w.? 7451
Jg 20:12 What w. is this that is done among 7451
1Sa 12:17 and see that your w. is great, 7451
1Sa 12:20 Fear not: ye have done all this w. 7451
1Sa 24:13 W. proceedeth from the wicked: 7562
1Sa 25:39 hath returned the w. of Nabel 7451
2Sa 3:39 the doer of evil according to his w. 7451
2Sa 7:10 children of w. afflict them any 5766
1Ki 1:52 but if w. shall be found in him, 7451
1Ki 2:44 w. which thine heart is privy to, 7451
1Ki 2:44 return thy w. upon thine own head; 7451
1Ki 8:47 perversely, we...committed w.; 7561
1Ki 21:25 which did sell himself to work w. 7451
2Ki 21:6 wrought much w. in the sight of 7451
1Ch 17:9 the children of w. waste them 5766
Job 4:8 that plow iniquity, and sow w., 5999
Job 11:11 he seeth w. also; will he not then 205
Job 11:14 not w. dwell in thy tabernacles. 5766
Job 20:12 Though w. be sweet in his mouth, 7451
Job 22:5 Is not thy w. great? and thine 7451
Job 24:20 and w. shall be broken as a tree. 5766
Job 27:4 My lips shall not speak w., nor my 5766
Job 34:10 from God, that he should do w.; 7562
Job 35:8 Thy w. may hurt a man as thou art; 7562
Ps 5:4 not a God that hath pleasure in w. 7562
Ps 5:9 their inward part is very w.; their 1942
Ps 7:9 Oh let the w. of the wicked come 7451
Ps 10:15 seek out his w. till thou find none. 7562
Ps 28:4 according to the w. of their 7455
Ps 45:7 righteousness, and hatest w. 7562
Ps 52:7 strengthened himself in his w.. 1942
Ps 55:11 W. is in the midst thereof: deceit 1942
Ps 55:15 for w. is in their dwellings, and 7451
Ps 58:2 Yea, in heart ye work w.; ye 5766
Ps 84:10 than to dwell in the tents of w. 7562
Ps 89:22 him; nor the son of w. afflict him. 5766
Ps 94:23 shall cut them off in their own w. 7451
Ps 107:34 the w. of them that dwell therein. 7451
Pr 4:17 For they eat the bread of w., and 7562
Pr 8:7 w. is an abomination to my lips. 7562
Pr 10:2 Treasurers of w. profit nothing: 7562
Pr 11:5 wicked shall fall by his own w. 7564
Pr 12:3 shall not be established by w. 7562
Pr 13:6 but w. overthroweth the sinner. 7564
Pr 14:32 wicked is driven away in his w. 7451
Pr 16:12 abomination...kings to commit w. 7562
Pr 21:12 the wicked for their w.. 7451
Pr 26:26 his w. shall be shewed before the 7451
Pr 30:20 and saith, I have done no w. 205
Ec 3:16 of judgment, that w. was there; 7562
Ec 7:15 that prolongeth his life in his w. 7451
Ec 7:25 and to know the w. of folly, even 7562
Ec 8:8 neither shall w. deliver those that 7562
Isa 9:18 For w. burneth as the fire: it shall 7564
Isa 47:10 For thou hast trusted in thy w. 7451
Isa 58:4 and to smite with the fist of w. 7562
Isa 58:6 to loose the bands of w., to undo 7562
Jer 1:16 against them touching all their w., 7451
Jer 2:19 Thine own w. shall correct thee, 7451
Jer 3:2 thy whoredoms and with thy w. 7451
Jer 4:14 wash thine heart from w., that 7451
Jer 4:18 this is thy w., because it is bitter, 7451
Jer 6:7 waters, so she casteth out her w.: 7451
Jer 7:12 to it for the w. of my people Israel. 7451
Jer 8:6 no man repented him of his w., 7451
Jer 12:4 the w. of them that dwell therein? 7451
Jer 14:16 I will pour their w. upon them. 7451
Jer 14:20 We acknowledge, O Lord, our w., 7562
Jer 22:22 and confounded for all thy w. 7451
Jer 23:11 in my house have I found their w., 7451
Jer 23:14 that none doth return from his w. 7451
Jer 33:5 for all whose w. I have hid my face 7451
Jer 44:3 of their w....they have committed 7451
Jer 44:5 their ear to turn from their w., 7451
Jer 44:9 ye forgotten the w. of your fathers, 7451
Jer 44:9 and the w. of the kings of Judah, 7451
Jer 44:9 and the w. of their wives, 7451
Jer 44:9 of their wives, and your own w., 7451
Jer 44:9 and the w. of your wives, which 7451
La 1:22 Let all their w. come before thee; 7451
Eze 3:19 and he turn not from his w., nor 7562
Eze 5:6 changed my judgments into w. 7564
Eze 7:11 is risen up into a rod of w.: 7562
Eze 16:23 it came to pass after all thy w., 7451
Eze 16:57 Before thy w. was discovered, as at 7451
Eze 18:20 the w. of the wicked shall be upon 7564
Eze 18:27 wicked...turneth away from his w. 7564
Eze 31:11 I have driven him out for his w. 7562
Eze 33:12 as for the w. of the wicked, he 7564
Eze 33:12 day that he turneth from his w.; 7562
Eze 33:19 But if the wicked turn from his w., 7564
Ho 7:1 discovered, and the w. of Samaria: 7451
Ho 7:2 hearts that I remember all their w.: 7451
Ho 7:3 make the king glad with their w., 7451
Ho 9:15 All their w. is in Gilgal: for there I 7451
Ho 9:15 for the w. of their doings I will 7455
Ho 10:13 Ye have plowed w., ye have reaped 7562
Ho 10:15 unto you because of your great w.: 7451
Joe 3:13 fats overflow; for their w. is great. 7451
Jon 1:2 for their w. is come up before me. 7451
Mic 6:10 treasures of w. in the house of the 7562
Na 3:19 not thy w. passed continually? 7451
Zec 5:8 And he said, this is w.. And he 7564
Mal 1:4 shall call them, The border of w., 7564
Mal 3:15 yea, they that work w. are set up; 7564
Mt 22:18 but Jesus perceived their w., and *4189*
Mk 7:22 **Thefts, covetousness, w., deceit,** *4189*
Lu 11:39 **part is full of ravening and w..** *4189*
Ac 8:22 Repent therefore of this thy w., *2549*
Ac 25:5 man, if there be any w. in him. *5129,824*
Ro 1:29 w., covetousness, maliciousness; *4189*
1Co 5:8 with the leaven of malice and w.; *4189*
Eph 6:12 against spiritual w. in high places, *4189*
1Jo 5:19 and the whole world lieth in w. *4190*

WIDE
De 15:8 open thine hand w. unto him, 6605
De 15:11 thine hand w. unto thy brother, 6605
1Ch 4:40 the land was w., and quiet, 7342,3027
Job 29:23 opened their mouth w. as for the latter
Job 30:14 as a w. breaking in of waters: 7342
Ps 35:21 opened their mouth w. against 7337
Ps 81:10 open thy mouth w., and I will fill 7337
Ps 104:25 So is this great and w. sea, 7342,3027
Pr 13:3 he that openeth w. his lips shall have
Pr 21:9 a brawling woman in a w. house. 2267
Pr 25:24 brawling woman and in a w. house. 2267
Isa 57:4 against whom make ye a w. mouth, 7337
Jer 22:14 I will build me a w. house and 4060
Na 3:13 the gates...shall be set w. open 6605
Mt 7:13 **for w. is the gate, and broad is** *4116*

WIDENESS
Eze 41:10 the w. of twenty cubits round 7341

WIDOW See also WIDOW'S; WIDOWS.
Ge 38:11 Remain a w. at thy father's house, 490
Ex 22:22 Ye shall not afflict any w., or 490
Le 21:14 A w., or a divorced woman, or 490
Le 22:13 But if the priest's daughter be a w., 490
Nu 30:9 But every vow of a w., and of her 490
De 10:18 judgment of the fatherless and w., 490
De 14:29 and the fatherless, and the w., 490
De 16:11, 14 and the fatherless, and the w., 490
De 24:19 for the fatherless, and for the w.: 490
De 24:20, 21 for the fatherless, and for the w. 490
De 26:12 stranger, the fatherless, and the w., 490
De 26:13 to the fatherless, and to the w., 490
De 27:19 of the stranger, fatherless, and w. 490
2Sa 14:5 answered, I am indeed a w. woman, 490
1Ki 11:26 name was Zeruah, a w. woman, 490
1Ki 17:9 commanded a w. woman there to 490
1Ki 17:10 the w. woman was there gathering 490
1Ki 17:20 evil upon the w. with whom I 490
Job 24:21 not: and doeth not good to the w.. 490
Job 31:16 caused the eyes of the w. to fail; 490
Ps 94:6 They slay the w. and the stranger, 490
Ps 109:9 be fatherless, and his wife a w.. 490
Ps 146:9 he relieveth the fatherless and w.: 490
Pr 15:25 will establish the border of the w. 490
Isa 1:17 the fatherless, plead for the w.. 490
Isa 1:23 the cause of the w. come unto them. 490
Isa 47:8 I shall not sit as a w., neither shall I 490
Jer 7:6 stranger, the fatherless, and the w., 490
Jer 22:3 stranger, the fatherless, nor the w., 490
La 1:1 how is she become as a w.! she that 490
Eze 22:7 they vexed the fatherless and the w. 490
Eze 44:22 shall they take for their wives a w., 490
Eze 44:22 or a w. that had a priest before 490
Zec 7:10 And oppress not the w., nor the 490
Mal 3:5 the hireling in his wages, the w., 490
Mk 12:42 And there came a certain poor w., *5503*
Mk 12:43 **That this poor w. hath cast more** *5503*
Lu 2:37 a w. of about fourscore and four *5503*
Lu 4:26 **unto a woman that was a w.** *5503*
Lu 7:12 of his mother, and she was a w.: *5503*
Lu 18:3 **And there was a w. in that city;** *5503*
Lu 18:5 **Yet because this w. troubleth** *5503*
Lu 21:2 w. casting in thither two mites. *5503*
Lu 21:3 **w. hath cast in more than they** *5503*
1Ti 5:4 if any w. have children or nephews, *5503*
1Ti 5:5 that is a w. indeed, and desolate, *5503*
1Ti 5:9 not a w. be taken into the number *5503*
Re 18:7 I sit a queen, and am no w., and *5503*

WIDOWHOOD
Ge 38:19 and put on the garments of her w. 491
2Sa 20:3 the day of their death, living in w. 491
Isa 47:9 day, the loss of children, and w.: 489
Isa 54:4 remember the reproach of thy w. 491

WIDOW'S
Ge 38:14 And she put her w. garments off 491
De 24:17 nor take the w. raiment to pledge: 490
1Ki 7:14 was a w. son of the tribe of Naphtali, 490
Job 24:3 they take the w. ox for a pledge. 490
Job 29:13 I caused the w. heart to sing for joy. 490

WIDOWS See also WIDOWS'.
Ex 22:24 and your wives shall be w., and 490
Job 22:9 Thou hast sent w. away empty, and 490
Job 27:15 in death: and his w. shall not weep. 490
Ps 68:5 the fatherless, and a judge of the w., 490
Ps 78:64 and their w. made no lamentation. 490
Isa 9:17 mercy on their fatherless and w. 490
Isa 10:2 people, that w. may be their prey, 490
Jer 15:8 Their w. are increased to me above 490
Jer 18:21 bereaved of their children, and be w.; 490
Jer 49:11 alive; and let thy w. trust in me. 490
La 5:3 fatherless, our mothers are as w.. 490
Eze 22:25 made her many w. in the midst 490
Lu 4:25 **many w. were in Israel in the** *5503*
Ac 6:1 their w. were neglected in the daily *5503*
Ac 9:39 all the w. stood by him weeping, *5503*
Ac 9:41 he had called the saints and w., *5503*
1Co 7:8 therefore to the unmarried and w., *5503*
1Ti 5:3 Honour w. that are w. indeed. *5503*
1Ti 5:11 But the younger w. refuse: for *5503*
1Ti 5:16 or woman that believeth have w., *5503*
1Ti 5:16 relieve them that are w. indeed. *5503*
Jas 1:27 fatherless and w. in their affliction, *5503*

WIDOWS'
Mt 23:14 **for ye devour w. houses, and for** *5503*
Mk 12:40 **Which devour w. houses, and for** *5503*
Lu 20:47 **Which devour w. houses, and for** *5503*

WIDTH See WIDENESS.

WIFE See also MIDWFE; WIFE'S; WIVES.
Ge 2:24 and shall cleave unto his w. 802
Ge 2:25 both naked, the man and his w., 802
Ge 3:8 Adam and his w. hid themselves 802
Ge 3:17 hearkened unto the voice of thy w., 802
Ge 3:21 Unto Adam also and to his w. did 802
Ge 4:1 Adam knew Eve his w.; and she 802
Ge 4:17 Cain knew his w.; and she conceived, 802
Ge 4:25 Adam knew his w. again; and she 802
Ge 6:18 ark, thou, and thy sons, and thy w., 802
Ge 7:7 Noah went in,...his sons, and his w., 802
Ge 7:13 the sons of Noah, and Noah's w., and 802
Ge 8:16 Go forth of the ark, thou, and thy w., 802
Ge 8:18 went forth, and his sons, and his w. 802
Ge 11:29 the name of Abram's w. was Sarai; 802
Ge 11:29 the name of Nahor's w., Milcah, the 802
Ge 11:31 daughter in law, his son Abram's w.; 802
Ge 12:5 Abram took Sarai his w., and Lot 802
Ge 12:11 he said unto Sarai his w., Behold 802
Ge 12:12 that they shall say, This is his w. 802
Ge 12:17 plagues because of Sarai Abram's w. 802
Ge 12:18 thou not tell me that she was thy w.? 802
Ge 12:19 I might have taken her to me to w.: 802
Ge 12:19 behold thy w., take her, and go thy 802
Ge 12:20 and they sent him away, and his w., 802
Ge 13:1 went up out of Egypt, he, and his w., 802
Ge 16:1 Abram's w. bare him no children: 802

Book	Ref	Context	No.
Ge	16:3	Abram's w. took Hagar her maid	802
Ge	16:3	to her husband Abram to be his w.	802
Ge	17:15	As for Sarai thy w., thou shalt not	802
Ge	17:19	Sarah thy w. shall bare thee a son	802
Ge	18:9	unto him, where is Sarah thy w.?	802
Ge	18:10	lo, Sarah thy w. shall have a son.	802
Ge	19:15	take thy w., and thy two daughters,	802
Ge	19:16	hand, and upon the hand of his w.,	802
Ge	19:26	his w. looked back from behind him,	802
Ge	20:2	Abraham said of Sarah his w., She	802
Ge	20:3	hast taken; for she is a man's w.	1166
Ge	20:7	therefore restore the man his w.;	802
Ge	20:12	my mother; and she became my w.	802
Ge	20:14	and restored him Sarah his w.	802
Ge	20:17	God healed Abimelech, and his w.,	802
Ge	20:18	because of Sarah Abraham's w.	802
Ge	21:21	him a w. out of the land of Egypt.	802
Ge	23:19	Abraham buried Sarah his w. in	802
Ge	24:3	thou shalt not take a w. unto my son	802
Ge	24:4	and take a w. unto my son Isaac.	802
Ge	24:7	thou shalt take a w. unto my son	802
Ge	24:15	the w. of Nahor, Abraham's brother,	802
Ge	24:36	Sarah my master's w. bare a son to	802
Ge	24:37	Thou shalt not take a w. to my son	802
Ge	24:38	kindred, and take a w. unto my son.	802
Ge	24:40	take a w. for my son of my kindred,	802
Ge	24:51	and let her be thy master's son's w.,	802
Ge	24:67	Rebekah, and she became his w.;	802
Ge	25:1	Then again Abraham took a w.,	802
Ge	25:10	Abraham buried, and Sarah his w.,	802
Ge	25:20	old when he took Rebekah to w.,	802
Ge	25:21	Isaac intreated the Lord for his w.,	802
Ge	25:21	him, and Rebekah his w. conceived.	802
Ge	26:7	men of the place asked him of his w.;	802
Ge	26:7	for he feared to say, She is my w.;	802
Ge	26:8	was sporting with Rebekah his w.	802
Ge	26:9	Behold, of a surety she is thy w.	802
Ge	26:10	might lightly have lien with thy w.,	802
Ge	26:11	He that toucheth this man or his w.	802
Ge	26:34	he took to w. Judith the daughter of	802
Ge	27:46	if Jacob take a w. of the daughters	802
Ge	28:1	shalt not take a w. of the daughters	802
Ge	28:2	take thee a w. from thence of the	802
Ge	28:6	to take him a w. from thence; and	802
Ge	28:6	shalt not take a w. of the daughters	802
Ge	28:9	the sister of Nebajoth, to be his w.	802
Ge	29:21	Give me my w., for my days are	802
Ge	29:28	gave him Rachel his daughter to w.	802
Ge	30:4	gave him Bilhah her handmaid to w.	802
Ge	30:9	her maid, and gave her Jacob to w.	802
Ge	34:4	saying, Get me this damsel to w.	802
Ge	34:8	I pray you give her him to w.	802
Ge	34:12	me: but give me the damsel to w.	802
Ge	36:10	the son of Adah the w. of Esau,	802
Ge	36:10	son of Bashemath the w. of Esau.	802
Ge	36:12	were the sons of Adah Esau's w.	802
Ge	36:13	the sons of Bashemath Esau's w.	802
Ge	36:14	the daughter of Zibeon, Esau's w.	802
Ge	36:17	the sons of Bashemath Esau's w.	802
Ge	36:18	the sons of Aholibamah Esau's w.;	802
Ge	36:18	the daughter of Anah, Esau's w.	802
Ge	38:6	Judah took a w. for Er his firstborn,	802
Ge	38:8	Go in unto thy brother's w., and	802
Ge	38:9	he went in unto his brother's w.,	802
Ge	38:12	daughter of Shuah Judah's w. died;	802
Ge	38:14	she was not given unto him to w.	802
Ge	39:7	his master's w. cast her eyes upon	802
Ge	39:8	and said unto his master's w.,	802
Ge	39:9	but thee, because thou art his w.	802
Ge	39:19	his master heard the words of his w.,	802
Ge	41:45	gave him to w. Asenath the daughter	802
Ge	44:27	know that my w. bare me two sons:	802
Ge	46:19	The sons of Rachel Jacob's w.;	802
Ge	49:31	buried Abraham and Sarah his w.;	802
Ge	49:31	buried Isaac and Rebekah his w.;	802
Ex	2:1	Levi, and took to w. a daughter of Levi.	
Ex	4:20	And Moses took his w. and his sons,	802
Ex	6:20	Jochebed his father's sister to w.;	802
Ex	6:23	Amminadab, sister of Naashon, to w.;	802
Ex	6:25	one of the daughters of Putiel to w.;	802
Ex	18:2	in law took Zipporah, Moses' w.,	802
Ex	18:5	with his sons and his w. unto Moses	802
Ex	18:6	and thy w., and her two sons with	802
Ex	20:17	shalt not covet thy neighbour's w.,	802
Ex	21:3	then his w. shall go out with him.	802
Ex	21:4	If his master have given him a w.,	802
Ex	21:4	the w. and her children shall be her	802
Ex	21:5	I love my master, my w., and my	802
Ex	21:10	If he take him another w.; her food,	
Ex	22:16	shall surely endow her to be his w.	802
Le	18:8	father's w. shalt thou not uncover:	802
Le	18:14	thou shalt not approach to his w.	802
Le	18:15	she is thy son's w.; thou shalt not	802
Le	18:16	the nakedness of thy brother's w.	802
Le	18:18	shalt thou take a w. to her sister,	802
Le	18:20	lie carnally with thy neighbour's w.,	802
Le	20:10	adultery with another man's w.,	802
Le	20:10	adultery with his neighbour's w.,	802
Le	20:11	man that lieth with his father's w.	802
Le	20:14	if a man take a w. and her mother,	802
Le	20:20	a man shall lie with his uncle's w.,	1753
Le	20:21	if a man shall take his brother's w.	802
Le	21:7	shall not take a w. that is a whore,	802
Le	21:13	he shall take a w. in her virginity	802
Le	21:14	take a virgin of his own people to w.	802
Nu	5:12	If any man's w. go aside, and commit	802
Nu	5:14,	14 and he be jealous of his w., and	802
Nu	5:15	the man bring his w. unto the priest,	802
Nu	5:29	when a w. goeth aside to another	802
Nu	5:30	him, and he be jealous over his w.,	802
Nu	26:59	name of Amram's w. was Jochebed,	802
Nu	30:16	between a man and his w., between	802
Nu	36:8	shall be w. unto one of the family of	802
De	5:21	shalt thou desire thy neighbour's w.,	802
De	13:6	or the w. of thy bosom, or thy friend,	802
De	20:7	is there that hath betrothed a w.,	802
De	21:11	thou wouldest have her to thy w.;	802
De	21:13	her husband, and she shall be thy w.	802
De	22:13	If a man take a w., and go in unto	802
De	22:16	my daughter unto this man to w.,	802
De	22:19	and she shall be his w.; he may not	802
De	22:24	he hath humbled his neighbour's w.	802
De	22:29	of silver, and she shall be his w.	802
De	22:30	A man shall not take his father's w.,	802
De	24:1	When a man hath taken a w., and	802
De	24:2	she may go and be another man's w.	
De	24:3	die, which took her to be his w.;	802
De	24:4	may not take her again to be his w.,	802
De	24:5	When a man hath taken a new w.,	802
De	24:5	shall cheer up his w. which he hath	802
De	25:5	the w. of the dead shall not marry	802
De	25:5	take her to him to w., and perform	802
De	25:7	like not to take his brother's w.,	2994
De	25:7	his brother's w. go up to the gate	2994
De	25:9	his brother's w. come unto him	2994
De	25:11	and the w. of the one draweth near	802
De	27:20	he that lieth with his father's w.;	802
De	28:30	Thou shalt betroth a w., and another	802
De	28:54	and toward the w. of his bosom,	802
Jos	15:16	I give Achsah my daughter to w.	802
Jos	15:17	gave him Achsah his daughter to w.	802
Jg	1:12	I give Achsah my daughter to w.	802
Jg	1:13	gave him Achsah his daughter to w.	802
Jg	4:4	a prophetess, the w. of Lapidoth.	802
Jg	4:17	to the tent of Jael the w. of Heber	802
Jg	4:21	Then Jael Heber's w. took a nail of	802
Jg	5:24	Jael the w. of Heber the Kenite be,	802
Jg	11:2	Gilead's w. bare him sons; and his	802
Jg	13:2	and his w. was barren, and bare not	802
Jg	13:11	Manoah arose, and went after his w.,	802
Jg	13:19	and Manoah and his w. looked on.	802
Jg	13:20	And Manoah and his w. looked on it,	802
Jg	13:21	appear to Manoah and to his w.	802
Jg	13:22	Manoah said unto his w., We shall	802
Jg	13:23	But his w. said unto him, If the Lord	802
Jg	14:2	now therefore get her for me to w.	802
Jg	14:3	to take a w. of the uncircumcised	802
Jg	14:15	that they said unto Samson's w.,	802
Jg	14:16	And Samson's w. wept before him,	802
Jg	14:20	But Samson's w. was given to his	802
Jg	15:1	Samson visited his w. with a kid;	802
Jg	15:1	will go in to my w. into the chamber.	802
Jg	15:6	because he had taken his w., and	802
Jg	21:1	his daughter unto Benjamin to w.	802
Jg	21:18	be he that giveth a w. to Benjamin.	802
Jg	21:21	catch you every man his w. of the	802
Jg	21:22	we reserved not to each man his w.	802
Ru	1:1	the country of Moab, he, and his w.,	802
Ru	1:2	and the name of his w. Naomi,	802
Ru	4:5	the Moabitess, the w. of the dead,	802
Ru	4:10	Ruth the Moabitess,...w. of Mahlon,	802
Ru	4:10	have I purchased to be my w., to	802
Ru	4:13	Boaz took Ruth, and she was his w.	802
1Sa	1:4	offered, he gave to Peninnah his w.,	802
1Sa	1:19	and Elkanah knew Hannah his w.;	802
1Sa	2:20	And Eli blessed Elkanah and his w.,	802
1Sa	4:19	his daughter in law, Phinehas' w.,	802
1Sa	14:50	the name of Saul's w. was Ahinoam,	802
1Sa	18:17	Merab, her will I give thee to w.	802
1Sa	18:19	unto Adriel the Meholathite to w.	802
1Sa	18:27	gave him Michal his daughter to w.	802
1Sa	19:11	and Michal David's w. told him,	802
1Sa	25:3	and the name of his w. Abigail:	802
1Sa	25:14	young men told Abigail, Nabal's w.,	802
1Sa	25:37	his w. had told him these things,	802
1Sa	25:39	with Abigail, to take her to him to w.	802
1Sa	25:40	unto thee, to take thee to him to w.	802
1Sa	25:42	of David, and became his w.	802
1Sa	25:44	Michal his daughter, David's w., to	802
1Sa	27:3	Abigail the Carmelitess, Nabal's w.	802
1Sa	30:5	Abigail...w. of Nabal the Carmelite.	802
1Sa	30:22	save to every man his w. and his	802
2Sa	2:2	Abigail Nabal's w. the Carmelite.	802
2Sa	3:3	Abigail...w. of Nabal the Carmelite;	802
2Sa	3:5	Ithream, by Eglah David's w.	802
2Sa	3:14	Deliver me my w. Michal, which I	802
2Sa	11:3	Eliam, the w. of Uriah the Hittite?	802
2Sa	11:11	and to drink, and to lie with my w.?	802
2Sa	11:26	when the w. of Uriah heard that	802
2Sa	11:27	she became his w., and bare him a	802
2Sa	12:9	and hast taken his w. to be thy w.	802
2Sa	12:10	me, and hast taken the w. of Uriah	802
2Sa	12:10	of Uriah the Hittite to be thy w.	802
2Sa	12:15	which Uriah's w. bare unto David,	802
2Sa	12:24	David comforted Bath-sheba his w.,	802
1Ki	2:17	me Abishag the Shunammite to w.	802
1Ki	2:21	given to Adonijah thy brother to w.	802
1Ki	4:11,	15 the daughter of Solomon to w.	802
1Ki	7:8	daughter, whom he had taken to w.	802
1Ki	9:16	unto his daughter, Solomon's w.	802
1Ki	11:19	him to w. the sister of his own w.,	802
1Ki	14:2	And Jeroboam said to his w., Arise,	802
1Ki	14:2	not known to be the w. of Jeroboam;	802
1Ki	14:4	Jeroboam's w. did so, and arose,	802
1Ki	14:5	the w. of Jeroboam cometh to ask a	802
1Ki	14:6	said, Come in, thou w. of Jeroboam;	802
1Ki	14:17	Jeroboam's w. arose, and departed,	802
1Ki	16:31	he took to w. Jezebel the daughter	802
1Ki	21:5	But Jezebel his w. came to him, and	802
1Ki	21:7	Jezebel his w. said unto him, Dost	802
1Ki	21:25	whom Jezebel his w. stirred up.	802
2Ki	5:2	and she waited on Naaman's w.	802
2Ki	8:18	for the daughter of Ahab was his w.	802
2Ki	14:9	Give thy daughter to my son to w.	802
2Ki	22:14	the prophetess, the w. of Shallum	802
1Ch	2:18	begat children of Azubah his w.,	802
1Ch	2:24	Abiah Hezron's w. bare him Ashur	802
1Ch	2:26	Jerahmeel had also another w.,	802
1Ch	2:29	of the w. of Abishur was Abihail,	802
1Ch	2:35	daughter to Jarha his servant to w.	802
1Ch	3:3	the sixth, Ithream by Eglah his w.	802
1Ch	4:18	and his w. Jehudijah bare Jered the	802
1Ch	4:19	the sons of his w. Hodiah the sister	802
1Ch	7:15	And Machir took to w. the sister of	802
1Ch	7:16	Maachah the w. of Machir bare a	802
1Ch	7:23	And when he went in to his w., she	802
1Ch	8:9	he begat of Hodesh his w., Jobab,	802
2Ch	8:11	My w. shall not dwell in the house	802
2Ch	11:18	of Jerimoth the son of David to w.,	802
2Ch	21:6	he had the daughter of Ahab to w.	802
2Ch	22:11	the w. of Jehoiada the priest,	802
2Ch	25:18	Give thy daughter to my son to w.	802
2Ch	34:22	the prophetess, the w. of Shallum	802
Ezr	2:61	a w. of the daughters of Barzillai	802
Ne	7:63	of Barzillai the Gileadite to w.,	802
Es	5:10	for his friends, and Zeresh his w.	802
Es	5:14	Then said Zeresh his w. and all his	802
Es	6:13	Haman told Zeresh his w. and all his	802
Es	6:13	his wise men and Zeresh his w.	802
Job	2:9	Then said his w. unto him, Dost	802
Job	19:17	My breath is strange to my w.,	802
Job	31:10	Then let my w. grind unto another,	802
Ps	109:9	be fatherless, and his w. a widow.	802
Ps	128:3	thy w. shall be as a fruitful vine by	802
Pr	5:18	and rejoice with the w. of thy youth.	802
Pr	6:29	that goeth in to his neighbour's w.;	802
Pr	18:22	Whoso findeth a w. findeth a good	802
Pr	19:13	contentions of a w. are a continual	802

Pr 19:14 and a prudent w. is from the Lord....... 802
Ec 9:9 Live joyfully with the w. whom thou..... 802
Isa 54:1 the children of the married w.,........... 802
Isa 54:6 and a w. of youth, when thou wast...... 802
Jer 3:1 If a man put away his w., and she....... 802
Jer 3:20 as a w. treacherously departeth.......... 802
Jer 5:8 one neighed after his neighbour's w...... 802
Jer 6:11 husband with the w. shall be taken,...... 802
Jer 16:2 Thou shalt not take thee a w.,............ 802
Eze 16:32 as a w. that committeth adultery, ... 802
Eze 18:6 hath defiled his neighbour's w., ... 802
Eze 18:11 and defiled his neighbour's w., ... 802
Eze 18:15 hath not defiled his neighbour's w., ... 802
Eze 22:11 abomination with his neighbour's w.;..... 802
Eze 24:18 at even my w. died; and I did in the 802
Eze 33:26 defile every one his neighbour's w. 802
Ho 1:2 take unto thee a w. of whoredoms......... 802
Ho 2:2 she is not my w., neither am I her 802
Ho 12:12 of Syria, and Israel served for a w.,..... 802
Ho 12:12 and for a w. he kept sheep................ 802
Am 7:17 Thy w. shall be an harlot in the city, ... 802
Mal 2:14 between thee and...w. of thy youth,..... 802
Mal 2:14 and the w. of thy covenant.................. 802
Mal 2:15 deal treacherously against the w. of...... 802
Mt 1:6 of her that had been the w. of Urias;........
Mt 1:20 not to take unto thee Mary thy w...... *1135*
Mt 1:24 him, and took unto him his w........... *1135*
Mt 5:31 **Whosoever shall put away his w.,**.. *1135*
Mt 5:32 **whosoever shall put away his w.,**.. *1135*
Mt 14:3 sake, his brother Philip's w............... *1135*
Mt 18:25 **to be sold, and his w., and**........... *1135*
Mt 19:3 lawful for a man to put away his w..... *1135*
Mt 19:5 **and shall cleave to his w.:**........... *1135*
Mt 19:9 **Whosoever shall put away his w.,**.. *1135*
Mt 19:10 case of the man be so with his w.,...... *1135*
Mt 19:29 **or father, or mother, or w., or**...... *1135*
Mt 22:24 his brother shall marry his w., and..... *1135*
Mt 22:25 first, when he had married a w.,.............
Mt 22:25 issue, left his w. unto his brother:........ *1135*
Mt 22:28 whose w. shall she be of the seven?... *1135*
Mt 27:19 seat, his w. sent unto him, saying, ... *1135*
Mk 6:17 sake, his brother Philip's w.:.............. *1135*
Mk 6:18 for thee to have thy brother's w........ *1135*
Mk 10:2 for a man to put away his w.?........... *1135*
Mk 10:7 **and mother, and cleave to his w.;**.. *1135*
Mk 10:11 **Whosoever shall put away his w.,**.. *1135*
Mk 10:29 **or father, or mother, or w., or**...... *1135*
Mk 12:19 die, and leave his w. behind him,........ *1135*
Mk 12:19 that his brother should take his w., ... *1135*
Mk 12:20 the first took a w., and dying left....... *1135*
Mk 12:23 rise, whose w. shall she be of them? .. *1135*
Mk 12:23 for the seven had her to w................ *1135*
Lu 1:5 his w. was of the daughters of........... *1135*
Lu 1:13 w. Elisabeth shall bear thee a son, ... *1135*
Lu 1:18 and my w. well stricken in years........ *1135*
Lu 1:24 days his w. Elisabeth conceived, ... *1135*
Lu 2:5 taxed with Mary his espoused w., ... *1135*
Lu 3:19 Herodias his brother Philip's w., ... *1135*
Lu 8:3 the w. of Chuza Herod's steward, ... *1135*
Lu 14:20 **I have married a w., and**............. *1135*
Lu 14:26 **his father, and mother, and w.,**..... *1135*
Lu 16:18 **Whosoever putteth away his w.,**..... *1135*
Lu 17:32 **Remember Lot's w.**...................... *1135*
Lu 18:29 **or parents, or brethren, or w.,**...... *1135*
Lu 20:28 any man's brother die, having a w.,..... *1135*
Lu 20:28 that his brother should take his w., ... *1135*
Lu 20:29 the first took a w., and died without... *1135*
Lu 20:30 the second took her to w., and he...... *1135*
Lu 20:33 whose w. of them is she?................. *1135*
Lu 20:33 for seven had her to w.................... *1135*
Joh 19:25 sister, Mary the w. of Cleophas, ...
Ac 5:1 Ananias, with Sapphira his w., ... *1135*
Ac 5:2 price, his w. also being privy to it, ... *1135*
Ac 5:7 his w., not knowing what was done, ... *1135*
Ac 18:2 from Italy, with his w. Priscilla; *1135*
Ac 24:24 Felix came with his w. Drusilla, ... *1135*
1Co 5:1 one should have his father's w.......... *1135*
1Co 7:2 let every man have his own w., and ... *1135*
1Co 7:3 husband render unto the w. due........ *1135*
1Co 7:3 also the w. unto the husband............ *1135*
1Co 7:4 w. hath not power of her own body,... *1135*
1Co 7:4 power of his own body, but the w...... *1135*
1Co 7:10 Let not the w. depart from her.......... *1135*
1Co 7:11 not the husband put away his w........ *1135*
1Co 7:12 brother hath a w. that believeth........ *1135*
1Co 7:14 husband is sanctified by the w., ... *1135*
1Co 7:14 w. is sanctified by the husband: *1135*
1Co 7:16 For what knowest thou, O w., ... *1135*
1Co 7:16 whether thou shalt save thy w.? *1135*
1Co 7:27 Art thou bound unto a w.? seek not.... *1135*
1Co 7:27 loosed from a w.? seek not a w......... *1135*
1Co 7:33 world, how he may please his w........ *1135*
1Co 7:34 is difference also between a w. and *1135*
1Co 7:39 The w. is bound by the law as long.... *1135*
1Co 9:5 power to lead about a sister, a w.,..... *1135*
Eph 5:23 the husband is the head of the w., ... *1135*
Eph 5:28 that loveth his w. loveth himself......... *1135*
Eph 5:31 and shall be joined unto his w.,......... *1135*
Eph 5:33 so love his w. even as himself; and *1135*
Eph 5:33 the w. see that she reverence her...... *1135*
1Ti 3:2 the husband of one w., vigilant, ... *1135*
1Ti 3:12 deacons be the husbands of one w.,..... *1135*
1Ti 5:9 having been the w. of one man, ... *1135*
Tit 1:6 the husband of one w., having........... *1135*
1Pe 3:7 giving honour unto the w., as unto..... *1134*
Re 19:7 his w. hath made herself ready.......... *1135*
Re 21:9 shew thee the bride, the Lamb's w..... *1135*

WIFE'S

Ge 3:20 And Adam called his w. name Eve; 802
Ge 20:11 they will slay me for my w. sake......... 802
Ge 36:39 and his w. name was Mehetabel, ... 802
Le 18:11 The nakedness of thy father's w......... 802
Jg 11:2 and his w. sons grew up, and they....... 802
1Ch 1:50 and his w. name was Mehetabel, ... 802
1Ch 8:29 whose w. name was Maachah: 802
1Ch 9:35 whose w. name was Maachah: 802
Mt 8:14 house, he saw his w. mother laid, ... *3994*
Mk 1:30 Simon's w. mother lay sick of a *3994*
Lu 4:38 And Simon's w. mother was taken...... *3994*

WILD

Ge 16:12 And he will be a w. man; his hand...... 6501
Le 26:22 also send w. beasts among you,.......... 7704
De 14:5 the fallow deer, and the w. goat,......... 689
De 14:5 the pygarg, and the w. ox, and the..... 8377
1Sa 17:46 and to the w. beasts of the earth; 2416
1Sa 24:2 upon the rocks of the w. goats. 3277
2Sa 2:18 was as light of foot as a w. roe......... 7704
2Ki 4:39 gather herbs, and found a w. vine,...... 7704
2Ki 4:39 gathered thereof w. gourds his lap...... 7704
2Ki 14:9 a w. beast that was in Lebanon, ... 7704
2Ch 25:18 a w. beast that was in Lebanon, ... 7704
Job 6:5 w. ass bray when he hath grass? 6501
Job 11:12 may be born like a w. ass's colt......... 6501
Job 24:5 as w. asses in the desert, go they....... 6501
Job 39:1 w. goats of the rock bring forth?........ 3277
Job 39:5 Who hath sent out the w. ass free? ... 6501
Job 39:5 loosed the bands of the w. ass? 6171
Job 39:15 that the w. beast may break them....... 7704
Ps 50:11 the w. beasts of the field are mine. 2123
Ps 80:13 w. beasts of the field doth devour it. .. 2123
Ps 104:11 the w. asses quench their thirst. 6501
Ps 104:18 hills are a refuge for the w. goats; 3277
Isa 5:2 and it brought forth w. grapes............. 891
Isa 5:4 grapes, brought it forth w. grapes?...... 891
Isa 13:21 w. beasts of the desert shall lie 6728
Isa 13:22 w. beasts of the islands shall cry 338
Isa 32:14 a joy of w. asses, a pasture of........... 6501
Isa 34:14 w. beasts of the desert shall also 6728
Isa 34:14 also meet with the w. beasts of the 338
Isa 51:20 the streets, as a w. bull in a net:....... 8377
Jer 2:24 A w. ass used to the wilderness, ... 6501
Jer 14:6 w. asses did stand in the high............ 6501
Jer 50:39 the w. beasts of the desert with 6728
Jer 50:39 w. beasts of the islands shall dwell....... 338
Da 5:21 dwelling was with the w. asses: 6167
Ho 8:9 Assyria, a w. ass alone by himself: 6501
Ho 13:8 the w. beast shall tear them.............. 7704
Mt 3:4 his meat was locusts and w. honey......... *66*
Mk 1:6 he did eat locusts and w. honey;........... *66*
Mk 1:13 and was with the w. beasts;.............. *2342*
Ac 10:12 w. beasts, and creeping things,.......... *2342*
Ac 11:6 w. beasts, and creeping things, and *2342*
Ro 11:17 being a w. olive tree, wert graffed *65*
Ro 11:24 the olive tree which is w. by nature,...... *65*

WILD-ASS See WILD and ASS.

WILDERNESS

Ge 14:6 El-paran, which is by the w............. 4057
Ge 16:7 by a fountain of water in the w.,......... 4057
Ge 21:14 wandered in the w. of Beer-sheba. 4057
Ge 21:20 and he grew, and dwelt in the w.,...... 4057
Ge 21:21 And he dwelt in the w. of Paran: 4057
Ge 36:24 that found the mules in the w.,.......... 4057
Ge 37:22 him into his pit that is in the w.,........ 4057
Ex 3:18 three days' journey into the w., that... 4057
Ex 4:27 Go into the w. to meet Moses. 4057
Ex 5:1 may hold a feast unto me in the w. 4057
Ex 7:16 that they may serve me in the w. 4057
Ex 8:27 go three days' journey into the w.,..... 4057
Ex 8:28 to the Lord your God in the w.; 4057
Ex 13:18 the way of the w. of the Red sea:...... 4057
Ex 13:20 in Etham, in the edge of the w. 4057
Ex 14:3 the land, the w. hath shut them in...... 4057
Ex 14:3 taken us away to die in the w.? 4057
Ex 14:12 than that we should die in the w.. 4057
Ex 15:22 they went out into the w. of Shur;...... 4057
Ex 15:22 and they went three days in the w., .. 4057
Ex 16:1 of Israel came unto the w. of Sin, ... 4057
Ex 16:2 against Moses and Aaron in the w....... 4057
Ex 16:3 have brought us forth into this w., ... 4057
Ex 16:10 that they looked toward the w.,.......... 4057
Ex 16:14 upon the face of the w. there lay a...... 4057
Ex 16:32 wherewith I have fed you in the w., ... 4057
Ex 17:1 Israel journeyed from the w. of Sin,.... 4057
Ex 18:5 his wife unto Moses into the w.,......... 4057
Ex 19:1 came they into the w. of Sinai, ... 4057
Ex 19:2 Sinai, and had pitched in the w.; 4057
Le 7:38 unto the Lord, in the w. of Sinai. 4057
Le 16:10 him go for a scapegoat into the w.. 4057
Le 16:21 the hand of a fit man into the w......... 4057
Le 16:22 he shall let go the goat in the w.. 4057
Nu 1:1 spake unto Moses in the w. of Sinai, .. 4057
Nu 1:19 numbered them in the w. of Sinai....... 4057
Nu 3:4 before the Lord, in the w. of Sinai, ... 4057
Nu 3:14 unto Moses in the w. of Sinai,........... 4057
Nu 9:1 unto Moses in the w. of Sinai,........... 4057
Nu 9:5 month at even in the w. of Sinai: 4057
Nu 10:12 journeys out of the w. of Sinai;.......... 4057
Nu 10:12 cloud rested in the w. of Paran........... 4057
Nu 10:31 how we are to encamp in the w.,......... 4057
Nu 12:16 and pitched in the w. of Paran. 4057
Nu 13:3 sent them from the w. of Paran: 4057
Nu 13:21 from the w. of Zin unto Rehob, ... 4057
Nu 13:26 unto the w. of Paran, to Kadesh; 4057
Nu 14:2 would God we had died in this w.! 4057
Nu 14:16 he hath slain them in the w............... 4057
Nu 14:22 which I did in Egypt and in the w.,...... 4057
Nu 14:25 into the w. by the way of the Red...... 4057
Nu 14:29 Your carcases shall fall in this w.;....... 4057
Nu 14:32 carcases, they shall fall in this w.. 4057
Nu 14:33 shall wander in the w. forty years, ... 4057
Nu 14:33 your carcases be wasted in the w........ 4057
Nu 14:35 in this w. they shall be consumed,...... 4057
Nu 15:32 children of Israel were in the w., ... 4057
Nu 16:13 to kill us in the w., except thou......... 4057
Nu 20:4 of the Lord into this w.,.................... 4057
Nu 21:5 us up out of Egypt to die in the w.? ... 4057
Nu 21:11 in the w. which is before Moab,.......... 4057
Nu 21:13 which is in the w. that cometh out 4057
Nu 21:18 the w. they went to Mattanah: 4057
Nu 21:23 went out against Israel into the w. 4057
Nu 24:1 but he set his face toward the w. 4057
Nu 26:64 of Israel in the w. of Sinai. 4057
Nu 26:65 They shall surely die in the w.. 4057
Nu 27:3 Our father died in the w., and he........ 4057
Nu 27:14 Meribah in Kadesh in the w. of Zin..... 4057
Nu 32:13 them wander in the w. forty years, ... 4057
Nu 32:15 he will yet leave them in the w.;........ 4057
Nu 33:6 which is in the edge of the w.. 4057
Nu 33:8 the midst of the sea into the w.,......... 4057
Nu 33:8 went three days' journey in the w. 4057
Nu 33:11 and encamped in the w. of Sin........... 4057
Nu 33:12 their journey out of the w. of Sin, ... 4057
Nu 33:15 and pitched in the w. of Sinai. 4057
Nu 33:36 pitched in the w. of Zin, which is 4057
Nu 34:3 w. of Zin along by the coast of Edom,..4057
De 1:1 Israel on this side Jordan in the w., ... 4057
De 1:19 all that great and terrible w.,............ 4057
De 1:31 and in the w., where thou hast.......... 4057
De 1:40 take your journey into the w. by........ 4057
De 2:1 took our journey into the w. by the 4057
De 2:7 thy walking through this great w......... 4057
De 2:8 by the way of the w. of Moab. 4057
De 2:26 I sent messengers out of the w. of....... 4057
De 4:43 Bezer in the w., in the plain............. 4057
De 8:2 thee these forty years in the w.,......... 4057
De 8:15 through that great and terrible w.,...... 4057

De 8:16 who fed thee in the w. with manna, 4057
De 9:7 Lord thy God to wrath in the w. 4057
De 9:28 them out to slay them in the w. 4057
De 11:5 what he did unto you in the w., 4057
De 11:24 from the w. and Lebanon, from the 4057
De 29:5 have led you forty years in the w. 4057
De 32:10 and in the waste howling w.; 3452
De 32:51 Meribah-Kadesh, in the w. of Zin; 4057
Jos 1:4 From the w. and this Lebanon even 4057
Jos 5:4 of war, died in the w. by the way, 4057
Jos 5:5 that were born in the w. by the way 4057
Jos 5:6 Israel walked forty years in the w., 4057
Jos 8:15 and fled by the way of the w. 4057
Jos 8:20 people that fled to the w. turned 4057
Jos 8:24 in the w. wherein they chased them, 4057
Jos 12:8 in the w., and in the south country; 4057
Jos 14:10 of Israel wandered in the w. 4057
Jos 15:1 of Edom the w. of Zin southward 4057
Jos 15:61 In the w., Beth-arabah, Middin, 4057
Jos 16:1 the w. that goeth up from Jericho 4057
Jos 18:12 were at the w. of Beth-aven. 4057
Jos 20:8 assigned Bezer in the w. upon the 4057
Jos 24:7 ye dwelt in the w. a long season. 4057
Jg 1:16 of Judah into the w. of Judah, 4057
Jg 8:7 your flesh with the thorns of the w. 4057
Jg 8:16 and thorns of the w. and briers, 4057
Jg 11:16 walked through the w. unto the 4057
Jg 11:18 they went along through the w., 4057
Jg 11:22 and from the w. even unto Jordan. 4057
Jg 20:42 of Israel unto the way of the w.; 4057
Jg 20:45 fled toward the w. unto the rock of 4057
Jg 20:47 fled to the w. unto the rock 4057
1Sa 4:8 with all the plagues in the w. 4057
1Sa 13:18 valley of Zeboim toward the w. 4057
1Sa 17:28 thou left those few sheep in the w.? 4057
1Sa 23:14 David abode in the w. in strong 4057
1Sa 23:14 in a mountain in the w. of Ziph. 4057
1Sa 23:15 David was in the w. of Ziph in a 4057
1Sa 23:24 his men were in the w. of Maon, 4057
1Sa 23:25 rock, and abode in the w. of Maon. 4057
1Sa 23:25 after David in the w. of Maon. 4057
1Sa 24:1 David is in the w. of En-gedi. 4057
1Sa 25:1 and went down to the w. of Paran 4057
1Sa 25:4 David heard int he w. that Nabal 4057
1Sa 25:14 sent messengers out of the w. to 4057
1Sa 25:21 all that this fellow hath in the w., 4057
1Sa 26:2 and went down to the w. of Ziph, 4057
1Sa 26:2 to seek David in the w. of Ziph. 4057
1Sa 26:3 But David abode in the w., and he 4057
1Sa 26:3 Saul came after him into the w. 4057
2Sa 2:24 by the way of the w. of Gibeon. 4057
2Sa 15:23 over, toward the way of the w. 4057
2Sa 15:28 I will tarry in the plain of the w., 4057
2Sa 16:2 as be faint in the w. may drink. 4057
2Sa 17:16 this night in the plains of the w., 4057
2Sa 17:29 and weary, and thirsty, in the w. 4057
1Ki 2:34 buried in his own house in the w. 4057
1Ki 9:18 Baalath, and Tadmor in the w., 4057
1Ki 19:4 went a day's journey into the w., 4057
1Ki 19:15 on thy way to the w. of Damascus: 4057
2Ki 3:8 The way through the w. of Edom 4057
1Ch 5:9 unto the entering in of the w. 4057
1Ch 6:78 Bezer in the w. with her suburbs, 4057
1Ch 12:8 unto David into the hold to the w. 4057
1Ch 21:29 Lord, which Moses made in the w., 4057
2Ch 1:3 of the Lord had made in the w. 4057
2Ch 8:4 And he built Tadmor in the w., 4057
2Ch 20:16 the brook, before the w. of Jeruel. 4057
2Ch 20:20 went forth into the w. of Tekoa: 4057
2Ch 20:24 toward the watch tower in the w., 4057
2Ch 24:9 of God laid upon Israel in the w. 4057
Ne 9:19 forsookest them not in the w. 4057
Ne 9:21 didst thou sustain them in the w., 4057
Job 1:19 came a great wind from the w., 4057
Job 12:24 causeth them to wander in a w. 8414
Job 24:5 the w. yieldeth food for them and 6160
Job 30:3 fleeing into the w. in former time 6723
Job 38:26 the w., wherein there is no man; 4057
Job 39:6 whose house I have made the w., 6160
Ps 29:8 voice of the Lord shaketh the w.; 4057
Ps 29:8 Lord shaketh the w. of Kadesh. 4057
Ps 55:7 far off, and remain in the w. 4057
Ps 63:*title* when he was in the w. of Judah. 4057
Ps 65:12 drop upon the pastures of the w. 4057
Ps 68:7 thou didst march through the w.; 3452
Ps 72:9 They that dwell in the w. shall 6728
Ps 74:14 to the people inhabiting the w. 6728
Ps 78:15 He clave the rocks in the w., and 4057
Ps 78:17 provoking...most High in the w. 6723
Ps 78:19 Can God furnish a table in the w.? 4057
Ps 78:40 oft did they provoke him in the w., 4057
Ps 78:52 guided them in the w. like a flock 4057
Ps 95:8 in the day of temptation in the w. 4057
Ps 102:6 I am like a pelican of the w.: I am 4057
Ps 106:9 the depths, as through the w. 4057
Ps 106:14 But lusted exceedingly in the w., 4057
Ps 106:26 them, to overthrow them in the w. 4057
Ps 107:4 wandered in...w. in a solitary way; 4057
Ps 107:33 He turneth rivers into a w., and the 4057
Ps 107:35 turneth the w. into a standing 4057
Ps 107:40 causeth them to wander in the w. 8414
Ps 136:16 led his people through the w. 4057
Pr 21:19 It is better to dwell in the w., than 4057
Ca 3:6 is this that cometh out of the w. 4057
Ca 8:5 is this that cometh up from the w., 4057
Isa 14:17 that made the world a w., and 4057
Isa 16:1 of the land from Sela to the w., 4057
Isa 16:8 they wandered through the w. 4057
Isa 23:13 it for them that dwell in the w. 6728
Isa 27:10 forsaken, and left like a w.: 4057
Isa 32:15 high, and the w. be a fruitful field, 4057
Isa 32:16 judgment shall dwell in the w., 4057
Isa 33:9 Sharon is like a w.; and Bashan 6160
Isa 35:1 w. and the solitary place...be glad 4057
Isa 35:6 in the w. shall waters break out, 4057
Isa 40:3 voice of him that crieth in the w., 4057
Isa 41:18 I will make the w. a pool of water, 4057
Isa 41:19 I will plant in the w. the cedar, 4057
Isa 42:11 Let the w. and the cities thereof 4057
Isa 43:19 I will even made a way in the w., 4057
Isa 43:20 because I give waters in the w., 4057
Isa 50:2 the sea, I make the rivers a w. 4057
Isa 51:3 and he will make her w. like Eden, 4057
Isa 63:13 the deep, as an horse in the w., 4057
Isa 64:10 thy holy cities are a w., Zion is a 4057
Isa 64:10 Zion is a w., Jerusalem a 4057
Jer 2:2 thou wentest after me in the w., 4057
Jer 2:6 Egypt, that led us through the w., 4057
Jer 2:24 A wild ass used to the w., that 4057
Jer 2:31 Have I been a w. unto Israel? 4057
Jer 3:2 for them, as the Arabian in the w.; 4057
Jer 4:11 wind of the high places in the w. 4057
Jer 4:26 and, lo, the fruitful place was a w., 4057
Jer 9:2 that I had in the w. a lodging place 4057
Jer 9:10 and for the habitations of the w. 4057
Jer 9:12 and is burned up like a w., 4057
Jer 9:26 corners, that dwell in the w. 4057
Jer 12:10 my pleasant portion a desolate w. 4057
Jer 12:12 all high places through the w. 4057
Jer 13:24 passeth away by the wind of the w. 4057
Jer 17:6 the parched places in the w., 4057
Jer 22:6 yet surely I will make thee a w., 4057
Jer 23:10 places of the w. are dried up, 4057
Jer 31:2 of the sword found grace in the w.; 4057
Jer 48:6 and be like the heath in the w. 4057
Jer 50:12 of the nations shall be a w., 4057
Jer 51:43 a desolation, a dry land, and a w., 6160
La 4:3 cruel, like the ostriches in the w. 4057
La 4:19 they laid wait for us in the w. 4057
La 5:9 because of the sword of the w. 4057
Eze 6:14 than the w. toward Diblath, 4057
Eze 19:13 And now she is planted in the w., 4057
Eze 20:10 and brought them into the w. 4057
Eze 20:13 rebelled against me in the w.: 4057
Eze 20:13 out my fury upon them in the w., 4057
Eze 20:15 up my hand unto them in the w., 4057
Eze 20:17 I made an end of them in the w. 4057
Eze 20:18 said unto their children in the w., 4057
Eze 20:21 my anger against them in the w. 4057
Eze 20:23 mine hand unto them also in the w., 4057
Eze 20:35 bring you into the w. of the people, 4057
Eze 20:36 pleaded with your fathers in the w. 4057
Eze 23:42 were brought Sabeans from the w., 4057
Eze 29:5 will leave thee thrown into the w., 4057
Eze 34:25 they shall dwell safely in the w., 4057
Ho 2:3 and make her as a w., and set her 4057
Ho 2:14 her, and bring her into the w., 4057
Ho 9:10 found Israel like grapes in the w.; 4057
Ho 13:5 I did know thee in the w., in the land 4057
Ho 13:15 Lord shall come up from the w. 4057
Joe 1:19 devoured the pastures of the w., 4057
Joe 1:20 devoured the pastures of the w. 4057
Joe 2:3 and behind them a desolate w., 4057
Joe 2:22 for the pastures of the w. do spring, 4057
Joe 3:19 and Edom shall be a desolate w., 4057
Am 2:10 led you forty years through the w., 4057
Am 5:25 and offerings in the w. forty years, 4057
Am 6:14 Hemath unto the river of the w. 6166
Zep 2:13 a desolation, and dry like a w. 4057
Mal 1:3 waste for the dragons of the w. 4057
Mt 3:1 preaching in the w. of Judaea, *2048*
Mt 3:3 the voice of one crying in the w., *2048*
Mt 4:1 Jesus led up of the spirit in the w. *2048*
Mt 11:7 **went ye out into the w. to see?** *2048*
Mt 15:33 we have so much bread in the w., *2047*
Mk 1:3 the voice of one crying in the w., *2048*
Mk 1:4 John did baptize in the w., and *2048*
Mk 1:12 the spirit driveth him into the w. *2048*
Mk 1:13 he was there in the w. forty days, *2048*
Mk 8:4 men with bread here in the w.? *2047*
Lu 3:2 the son of Zacharias in the w. *2048*
Lu 3:4 The voice of one crying in the w., *2048*
Lu 4:1 was led by the Spirit into the w., *2048*
Lu 5:16 he withdrew himself into the w., *2048*
Lu 7:24 **went ye out into the w. for to see?** *2048*
Lu 8:29 was driven of the devil into the w.) *2048*
Lu 15:4 **leave the ninety and nine in the w.,** *2048*
Joh 1:23 the voice of one crying in the w., *2048*
Joh 3:14 **lifted up the serpent in the w.,** *2048*
Joh 6:49 **fathers did eat manna in the w.,** *2048*
Joh 11:54 unto a country near to the w., *2048*
Ac 7:30 in the w. of mount Sina an angel *2048*
Ac 7:36 Red sea, and in the w. forty years. *2048*
Ac 7:38 he, that was in the church in the w. *2048*
Ac 7:42 the space of forty years in the w.? *2048*
Ac 7:44 the tabernacle of witness in the w., *2048*
Ac 13:18 suffered he their manners in the w. *2048*
Ac 21:38 leddest out into the w. four *2048*
1Co 10:5 for they were overthrown in the w. *2048*
2Co 11:26 in the city, in perils in the w. *2047*
Heb 3:8 in the day of temptation in the w. *2048*
Heb 3:17 whose carcases fell in the w.? *2048*
Re 12:6 And the woman fled into the w., *2048*
Re 12:14 that she might fly into the w., *2048*
Re 17:3 me away in the spirit into the w. *2048*

WILD-GOAT See WILD and GOAT.

WILD-OX See WILD and OX.

WILES
Nu 25:18 For they vex you with their w., 5231
Eph 6:11 stand against the w. of the devil. *3180*

WILFULLY
Heb 10:26 For if we sin w. after that we have *1596*

WILILY
Jos 9:4 They did work w., and went and 6195

WILL See also FREEWILL; SELFWILL; WILFULLY; WILLETH; WILLING; WILT; WOULD.
Ge 2:18 I w. make him a help meet for him.
Ge 3:15 I w. put enmity between thee and the
Ge 3:16 I w. greatly multiply thy sorrow and
Ge 6:7 I w. destroy man whom I have
Ge 6:13 I w. destroy them with the earth.
Ge 6:18 with thee w. I establish my covenant;
Ge 7:4 I w. cause it to rain upon the earth
Ge 7:4 that I have made w. I destroy from
Ge 8:21 I w. not again curse the ground any
Ge 8:21 neither w. I again smite any more
Ge 9:5 your blood of your lives w. I require;
Ge 9:5 hand of every beast w. I require it,
Ge 9:5 every man's brother w. I require the
Ge 9:11 I w. establish my covenant with you;
Ge 9:15 I w. remember my covenant, which is
Ge 9:16 I w. look upon it, that I may remember
Ge 11:6 nothing w. be restrained from them,
Ge 12:1 house, unto a land that I w. show thee:
Ge 12:2 I w. make of thee a great nation.
Ge 12:2 I w. bless thee, and make thy name
Ge 12:3 And I w. bless them that bless thee,
Ge 12:7 Unto thy seed w. I give this land:
Ge 12:12 w. kill me, but they w. save thee alive
Ge 13:9 left hand, then I w. go to the right;
Ge 13:9 right hand, then I w. go to the left.
Ge 13:15 to thee w. I give it, and to thy seed for
Ge 13:16 I w. make thy seed as the dust of the
Ge 13:17 breadth of it; for I w. give it unto thee
Ge 14:23 I w. not take from a thread even to a

Ge	14:23	I **w.** not take any thing that is thine,
Ge	15:14	whom they shall serve, **w.** I judge:
Ge	16:10	I **w.** multiply thy seed exceedingly,
Ge	16:12	And he **w.** be a wild man; his hand
Ge	16:12	his hand **w.** be against every man, and
Ge	17:2	I **w.** make my covenant between me
Ge	17:2	and **w.** multiply thee exceedingly.
Ge	17:6	I **w.** make thee exceeding fruitful,
Ge	17:6	and I **w.** make nations of thee, and
Ge	17:7	I **w.** establish my covenant between
Ge	17:8	I **w.** give unto thee, and unto thy
Ge	17:8	possession; and I **w.** be their God.
Ge	17:16	I **w.** bless her, and give thee a son
Ge	17:16	I **w.** bless her, and she shall be a
Ge	17:19	I **w.** establish my covenant with him
Ge	17:20	blessed him, and **w.** make him fruitful.
Ge	17:20	and **w.** multiply him exceedingly;
Ge	17:20	and I **w.** make him a great nation.
Ge	17:21	But my covenant **w.** I establish with
Ge	18:5	I **w.** fetch a morsel of bread and
Ge	18:10	said, I **w.** certainly return unto thee
Ge	18:14	At the time appointed I **w.** return
Ge	18:19	he **w.** command his children and his
Ge	18:21	I **w.** go down now, and see whether
Ge	18:21	come unto me; and if not, I **w.** know.
Ge	18:26	I **w.** spare all the place for their sakes.
Ge	18:28	forty and five, I **w.** not destroy it.
Ge	18:29	he said, I **w.** not do it for forty's sake.
Ge	18:30	not the Lord be angry, and I **w.** speak:
Ge	18:30	he said, I **w.** not do it, if I find thirty
Ge	18:31	I **w.** not destroy it for twenty's sake.
Ge	18:32	and I **w.** speak yet but this once.
Ge	18:32	said, I **w.** not destroy it for ten's sake.
Ge	19:2	we **w.** abide in the street all night.
Ge	19:9	sojourn, and he **w.** needs to be judge:
Ge	19:9	**w.** we deal worse with thee, than with
Ge	19:13	for we **w.** destroy this place, because
Ge	19:14	for the Lord **w.** destroy this city.
Ge	19:21	that I **w.** not overthrow this city, for
Ge	19:32	and we **w.** lie with him, that we may
Ge	20:11	and they **w.** slay me for my wife's sake.
Ge	21:6	that all that hear **w.** laugh with me.
Ge	21:13	of the bondwoman **w.** I make a nation,
Ge	21:18	for I **w.** make him a great nation.
Ge	21:24	and Abraham said, I **w.** swear.
Ge	22:2	mountains which I **w.** tell thee of.
Ge	22:5	and I and the lad **w.** go yonder and
Ge	22:8	son, God **w.** provide himself a lamb
Ge	22:17	That in blessing I **w.** bless thee,
Ge	22:17	multiplying I **w.** multiply thy seed as
Ge	23:13	and I **w.** bury my dead there.
Ge	23:13	I **w.** give thee money for the field;
Ge	24:3	I **w.** make thee swear by the Lord,
Ge	24:5	woman **w.** not be willing to follow
Ge	24:7	Unto thy seed **w.** I give this land;
Ge	24:8	woman **w.** not be willing to follow
Ge	24:14	and I **w.** give thy camels drink also:
Ge	24:19	**w.** draw water for thy camels also,
Ge	24:33	I **w.** not eat, until I have told mine
Ge	24:39	the woman **w.** not follow me.
Ge	24:40	**w.** send his angel with thee, and
Ge	24:44	and I **w.** also draw for thy camels:
Ge	24:46	and I **w.** give thy camels drink also:
Ge	24:49	if ye **w.** deal kindly and truly with my
Ge	24:57	We **w.** call the damsel, and enquire at
Ge	24:58	with this man? And she said, I **w.** go.
Ge	26:3	I **w.** be with thee, and **w.** bless thee;
Ge	26:3	thy seed, I **w.** give all these countries,
Ge	26:3	I **w.** perform the oath which I sware
Ge	26:4	I **w.** make thy seed to multiply as the
Ge	26:4	and **w.** give unto thy seed all these
Ge	26:24	for I am with thee, and **w.** bless thee,
Ge	27:9	I **w.** make them savoury meat for thy
Ge	27:12	My father peradventure **w.** feel me,
Ge	27:25	me, and I **w.** eat of my son's venison,
Ge	27:41	then **w.** I slay my brother Jacob.
Ge	27:45	then **w.** I send, and fetch thee from
Ge	28:13	thou liest, to thee **w.** I give it,
Ge	28:15	**w.** keep thee in all places whither thou
Ge	28:15	and **w.** bring thee again into this land;
Ge	28:15	for I **w.** not leave thee, until I have
Ge	28:20	a vow, saying, If God **w.** be with me,
Ge	28:20	and **w.** keep me in this way that I go,
Ge	28:20	**w.** give me bread to eat, and raiment
Ge	28:22	I **w.** surely give the tenth unto thee.
Ge	29:18	I **w.** serve thee seven years for Rachel
Ge	29:27	and we **w.** give thee this also for the
Ge	29:32	now therefore my husband **w.** love me.
Ge	29:34	this time **w.** my husband be joined
Ge	29:35	she said, Now **w.** I praise the Lord:
Ge	30:13	for the daughters **w.** call me blessed:
Ge	30:20	now **w.** my husband dwell with me,
Ge	30:28	me thy wages, and I **w.** give it.
Ge	30:31	I **w.** again feed and keep thy flock.
Ge	30:32	I **w.** pass through all thy flock to day,
Ge	31:3	to thy kindred; and I **w.** be with thee.
Ge	31:52	I **w.** not pass over this heap to thee,
Ge	32:9	and I **w.** deal well with thee:
Ge	32:11	him, lest he **w.** come and smite me,
Ge	32:12	thou saidst, I **w.** surely do thee good,
Ge	32:20	I **w.** appease him with the present
Ge	32:20	me, and afterward I **w.** see his face;
Ge	32:20	peradventure he **w.** accept of me.
Ge	32:26	said, I **w.** not let thee go, except thou
Ge	33:12	and let us go, and I **w.** go before thee.
Ge	33:13	them one day, all the flock **w.** die.
Ge	33:14	his servant; and I **w.** lead on softly,
Ge	34:11	what ye shall say unto me I **w.** give.
Ge	34:12	I **w.** give according as ye shall say
Ge	34:15	But in this **w.** we consent unto you:
Ge	34:15	If ye **w.** be as we be, that every male
Ge	34:16	Then **w.** we give our daughters unto
Ge	34:16	and we **w.** take your daughters to us,
Ge	34:16	and we **w.** dwell with you,
Ge	34:16	and we **w.** become one people.
Ge	34:17	But if ye **w.** not hearken unto us, to
Ge	34:17	then **w.** we take our daughter,
Ge	34:17	and we **w.** be gone.
Ge	34:22	herein **w.** the men consent unto us
Ge	34:23	unto them, and they **w.** dwell with us
Ge	35:3	I **w.** make there an altar unto God
Ge	35:12	to thee I **w.** give it, and to thy seed
Ge	35:12	seed after thee **w.** I give the land.
Ge	37:13	come, and I **w.** send thee unto them.
Ge	37:20	and we **w.** say, Some evil beast hath
Ge	37:20	see what **w.** become of his dreams.
Ge	37:35	I **w.** go down into the grave unto my
Ge	38:17	I **w.** send thee a kid from the flock.
Ge	41:32	and God **w.** shortly bring it to pass.
Ge	41:40	the throne **w.** I be greater than thou.
Ge	42:34	**w.** I deliver you your brother, and ye
Ge	42:36	and ye **w.** take Benjamin away:
Ge	42:37	and I **w.** bring him to thee again.
Ge	43:4	us, we **w.** go down and buy thee food:
Ge	43:5	wilt not send him, we **w.** not go down:
Ge	43:8	lad with me, and we **w.** arise and go;
Ge	43:9	I **w.** be surety for him; of my hand
Ge	44:9	and we also **w.** be my lord's bondmen.
Ge	44:26	be with us, then **w.** we go down:
Ge	44:31	the lad is not with us, that he **w.** die:
Ge	45:11	And there **w.** I nourish thee; for yet
Ge	45:18	I **w.** give you the good of the land of
Ge	45:28	I **w.** go and see him before I die.
Ge	46:3	for I **w.** there make of thee a great
Ge	46:4	I **w.** go down with thee into Egypt;
Ge	46:4	I **w.** also surely bring thee up again:
Ge	46:31	I **w.** go up, and shew Pharaoh, and say
Ge	47:16	I **w.** give you for your cattle, if money
Ge	47:18	We **w.** not hide it from my lord, how
Ge	47:19	and we and our land **w.** be servants
Ge	47:25	and we **w.** be Pharaoh's servants.
Ge	47:30	But I **w.** lie with my fathers, and thou
Ge	47:30	And he said, I **w.** do as thou hast said.
Ge	48:4	I **w.** make thee fruitful, and multiply
Ge	48:4	and I **w.** make of thee a multitude of
Ge	48:4	**w.** give this land to thy seed after thee
Ge	48:9	thee, unto me, and I **w.** bless them.
Ge	49:7	I **w.** divide them in Jacob, and scatter
Ge	50:5	bury my father, and I **w.** come again.
Ge	50:15	said, Joseph **w.** peradventure hate us,
Ge	50:15	**w.** certainly requite all the evil which
Ge	50:21	I **w.** nourish you, and your little ones.
Ge	50:24	and God **w.** surely visit you, and bring
Ge	50:25	God **w.** surely visit you, and ye shall
Ex	2:9	it for me, and I **w.** give thee thy wages.
Ex	3:3	Moses said, I **w.** now turn aside, and
Ex	3:10	and I **w.** send thee unto Pharaoh, that
Ex	3:12	he said, Certainly I **w.** be with thee;
Ex	3:17	I **w.** bring you up out of the affliction
Ex	3:19	the king of Egypt **w.** not let you go,
Ex	3:20	and I **w.** stretch out my hand, and
Ex	3:20	which I **w.** do in the midst thereof:
Ex	3:20	and after that he **w.** let you go.
Ex	3:21	I **w.** give this people favour in the
Ex	4:1	they **w.** not believe me, nor hearken
Ex	4:1	for they **w.** say, The Lord hath not
Ex	4:8	if they **w.** not believe thee, neither
Ex	4:8	**w.** believe the voice of the latter sign.
Ex	4:9	**w.** not believe also these two signs,
Ex	4:12	and I **w.** be with thy mouth, and
Ex	4:14	thee, he **w.** be glad in his heart.
Ex	4:15	and I **w.** be with they mouth, and with
Ex	4:15	and **w.** teach you what ye shall do.
Ex	4:21	but I **w.** harden his heart, that he
Ex	4:23	behold, I **w.** slay thy son, even thy
Ex	5:2	the Lord, neither **w.** I let Israel go.
Ex	5:10	Pharaoh, I **w.** not give you straw.
Ex	6:1	thou see what I **w.** do to Pharaoh:
Ex	6:6	I **w.** bring you out from under the
Ex	6:6	and I **w.** rid you out of their bondage,
Ex	6:6	I **w.** redeem you with a stretched out
Ex	6:7	I **w.** take you to me for a people, and I
Ex	6:7	I **w.** be to you a God: and ye shall
Ex	6:8	And I **w.** bring you unto the land,
Ex	6:8	and I **w.** give it you for an heritage:
Ex	7:3	I **w.** harden Pharaoh's heart, and
Ex	7:17	I **w.** smite with the rod that is in mine
Ex	8:2	I **w.** smite all thy borders with frogs:
Ex	8:8	I **w.** let the people go, that they may
Ex	8:21	I **w.** send swarms of flies upon thee,
Ex	8:22	And I **w.** sever in that day the land of
Ex	8:23	I **w.** put a division between my people
Ex	8:26	their eyes, and **w.** they not stone us?
Ex	8:27	We **w.** go three day's journey into the
Ex	8:28	Pharaoh said, I **w.** let you go, that ye
Ex	8:29	I **w.** entreat the Lord that the swarms
Ex	9:14	I **w.** send at this time all my plagues
Ex	9:15	I **w.** stretch out my hand, that I may
Ex	9:18	I **w.** cause it to rain a very grievous
Ex	9:28	and I **w.** let you go,
Ex	9:29	I **w.** spread abroad my hands unto the
Ex	9:30	I know that ye **w.** not yet fear the Lord
Ex	10:4	**w.** I bring the locusts into thy coast:
Ex	10:9	We **w.** go with our young and with our
Ex	10:9	flocks and with our herds **w.** we go;
Ex	10:10	I **w.** let you go, and your little ones:
Ex	10:29	well, I **w.** see thy face again no more.
Ex	11:1	Yet **w.** I bring one plague more upon
Ex	11:1	afterwards he **w.** let you go hence:
Ex	11:4	About midnight **w.** I go out into the
Ex	11:8	thee: and after that I **w.** go out.
Ex	12:12	I **w.** pass through the land of Egypt
Ex	12:12	**w.** smite all the firstborn in the land
Ex	12:12	gods of Egypt I **w.** execute judgment:
Ex	12:13	I **w.** pass over you, and the plague
Ex	12:23	the Lord **w.** pass through to smite the
Ex	12:23	posts, the Lord **w.** pass over the door,
Ex	12:23	**w.** not suffer the destroyer to come in
Ex	12:25	the land which the Lord **w.** give you,
Ex	12:48	and **w.** keep the passover to the Lord,
Ex	13:19	saying, God **w.** surely visit you;
Ex	14:3	Pharaoh **w.** say of the children of
Ex	14:4	And I **w.** harden Pharaoh's heart, that
Ex	14:4	and I **w.** be honoured upon Pharaoh,
Ex	14:13	Lord, which he **w.** shew to you to day:
Ex	14:17	I **w.** harden the hearts of the
Ex	14:17	I **w.** get me honour upon Pharaoh,
Ex	15:1	I **w.** sing unto the Lord, for he hath
Ex	15:2	and I **w.** prepare him an habitation;
Ex	15:2	my father's God, and I **w.** exalt him.
Ex	15:9	said, I **w.** pursue, I **w.** overtake,
Ex	15:9	I **w.** divide the spoil; my lust shall be
Ex	15:9	I **w.** draw my sword, my hand shall
Ex	15:26	I **w.** put none of these diseases upon
Ex	16:4	I **w.** rain bread from heaven for you;
Ex	16:4	they **w.** walk in my law, or no.
Ex	16:23	bake that which ye **w.** bake to day,
Ex	16:23	to day, and seethe that ye **w.** seethe;
Ex	17:6	I **w.** stand before thee there upon the
Ex	17:9	I **w.** stand on the top of the hill
Ex	17:14	I **w.** utterly put out the remembrance
Ex	17:16	the Lord **w.** have war with Amalek
Ex	18:19	I **w.** give thee counsel, and God shall
Ex	19:5	If ye **w.** obey my voice indeed,
Ex	19:8	that the Lord hath spoken we **w.** do.
Ex	19:11	Lord **w.** come down in the sight of all
Ex	20:7	for the Lord **w.** not hold him guiltless
Ex	20:19	speak thou with us, and we **w.** hear:
Ex	20:24	record my name I **w.** come unto thee,
Ex	20:24	come unto thee, and I **w.** bless thee.
Ex	21:5	my children; I **w.** not go out free:

Ex 21:13 I **w.** appoint thee a place whither he
Ex 21:22 woman's husband **w.** lay upon him;
Ex 22:23 all unto me. I **w.** surely hear their cry;
Ex 22:24 and I **w.** kill you with the sword;
Ex 22:27 he crieth unto me, that I **w.** hear;
Ex 23:7 not: for I **w.** not justify the wicked.
Ex 23:21 he **w.** not pardon your transgressions:
Ex 23:22 I **w.** be an enemy unto thy enemies,
Ex 23:23 the Jebusites: and I **w.** cut them off.
Ex 23:25 I **w.** take sickness away from the
Ex 23:26 the number of thy days I **w.** fulfil.
Ex 23:27 I **w.** send my fear before thee, and
Ex 23:27 and **w.** destroy all the people to whom
Ex 23:27 and I **w.** make all thine enemies turn
Ex 23:28 And I **w.** send hornets before thee,
Ex 23:29 I **w.** not drive them out from before
Ex 23:30 I **w.** drive them out from before thee,
Ex 23:31 I **w.** set thy bounds from the Red sea
Ex 23:31 I **w.** deliver the inhabitants of the land
Ex 23:33 it **w.** surely be a snare unto thee.
Ex 24:3 which the Lord hath said **w.** we do.
Ex 24:7 that the Lord hath said **w.** we do,
Ex 24:12 and I **w.** give thee tables of stone.
Ex 25:22 And there I **w.** meet with thee, and
Ex 25:22 I **w.** commune with thee from above
Ex 25:22 I **w.** give thee in commandment
Ex 29:42 I **w.** meet you, to speak there unto
Ex 29:43 I **w.** meet with the children of Israel.
Ex 29:44 And I **w.** sanctify the tabernacle
Ex 29:44 I **w.** sanctify also both Aaron and his
Ex 29:45 And I **w.** dwell among the children
Ex 29:45 of Israel, and **w.** be their God.
Ex 30:6 testimony, where I **w.** meet with thee
Ex 30:36 where I **w.** meet with thee:
Ex 32:10 and I **w.** make of thee a great nation.
Ex 32:13 I **w.** multiply your seed as the stars
Ex 32:13 spoken of **w.** I give unto your seed,
Ex 32:30 and now I **w.** go up unto the Lord;
Ex 32:33 me, him **w.** I blot out of my book
Ex 32:34 I visit I **w.** visit their sin upon them
Ex 33:1 saying, Unto thy seed **w.** I give it:
Ex 33:2 And I **w.** send an angel before thee;
Ex 33:2 and I **w.** drive out the Canaanite
Ex 33:3 I **w.** not go up in the midst of thee;
Ex 33:5 I **w.** come up into the midst of thee
Ex 33:14 with thee, and I **w.** give thee rest.
Ex 33:17 I **w.** do this thing also that thou hast
Ex 33:19 I **w.** make all my goodness pass
Ex 33:19 I **w.** proclaim the name of the Lord
Ex 33:19 and **w.** be gracious unto whom I **w.** be
Ex 33:19 **w.** shew mercy to whom I **w.** shew
Ex 33:22 that I **w.** put thee in a clift of a rock
Ex 33:22 **w.** cover thee with my hand while I
Ex 33:23 I **w.** take away mine hand, and thou
Ex 34:1 I **w.** write upon these tables the words
Ex 34:7 that **w.** by no means clear the guilty;
Ex 34:10 before all thy people I **w.** do marvels,
Ex 34:10 for it is a terrible thing that I **w.** do
Ex 34:24 I **w.** cast out the nations before thee.
Le 1:3 offer it of his own voluntary **w.** 7522
Le 2:1 when any **w.** offer a meat offering
Le 9:4 for to day the Lord **w.** appear unto
Le 10:3 I **w.** be sanctified in them that come
Le 10:3 before all the people I **w.** be glorified.
Le 16:2 for I **w.** appear in a cloud upon the
Le 17:10 I **w.** even set my face against that
Le 17:10 and **w.** cut him off from among his
Le 19:5 ye shall offer it at your own **w.** 7522
Le 20:3 I **w.** set my face against that man,
Le 20:3 and **w.** cut him off from among his people;
Le 20:5 and **w.** cut him off, and all that
Le 20:5 I **w.** set my face against that man,
Le 20:6 I **w.** even set my face against that
Le 20:6 and **w.** cut him off from among his
Le 20:24 I **w.** give it unto you to possess it,
Le 22:18 **w.** offer his oblation for all his vows,
Le 22:18 which they **w.** offer unto the Lord
Le 22:19 at your own **w.** a male without 7522
Le 22:29 And when ye **w.** offer a sacrifice
Le 22:29 the Lord, offer it at your own **w.** 7522
Le 22:32 I **w.** be hallowed among the children
Le 23:30 **w.** I destroy from among his people.
Le 25:21 I **w.** command my blessing upon you
Le 26:4 I **w.** give you rain in due season,
Le 26:6 I **w.** give peace in the land, and ye
Le 26:6 I **w.** rid evil beasts out of the land,
Le 26:9 I **w.** have respect unto you, and make
Le 26:11 I **w.** set my tabernacle among you:
Le 26:12 I **w.** walk among you,
Le 26:12 and **w.** be your God, and ye shall
Le 26:14 But if ye **w.** not hearken unto me,
Le 26:14 **w.** not do all these commandments;
Le 26:15 Ye **w.** not do all my commandments,
Le 26:16 I also **w.** do this unto you;
Le 26:16 I **w.** even appoint over you terror,
Le 26:17 I **w.** set my face against you, and ye
Le 26:18 if ye **w.** not yet for all this hearken
Le 26:18 I **w.** punish you seven times more for
Le 26:19 I **w.** break the pride of your power;
Le 26:19 and I **w.** make your heaven as iron,
Le 26:21 me, and **w.** not hearken unto me; 14
Le 26:21 I **w.** bring seven times more plagues
Le 26:22 I **w.** also send wild beasts among
Le 26:23 And if ye **w.** not be reformed by me
Le 26:23 but **w.** walk contrary unto me;
Le 26:24 Then **w.** I also walk contrary unto
Le 26:24 **w.** punish you yet seven times for
Le 26:25 And I **w.** bring a sword upon you,
Le 26:25 I **w.** send the pestilence among you;
Le 26:27 if ye **w.** not for all this hearken unto
Le 26:28 Then I **w.** walk contrary unto you
Le 26:28 I, **w.** chastise you seven times for
Le 26:30 I **w.** destroy your high places, and cut
Le 26:31 I **w.** make your cities waste, and bring
Le 26:31 I **w.** not smell the savour of your
Le 26:32 I **w.** bring the land into desolation:
Le 26:33 I **w.** scatter you among the heathen,
Le 26:33 and **w.** draw out a sword after you:
Le 26:36 I **w.** send a faintness into their hearts
Le 26:42 Then **w.** I remember my covenant
Le 26:42 with Abraham **w.** I remember;
Le 26:42 and I **w.** remember the land.
Le 26:44 I **w.** not cast them away, neither
Le 26:44 neither **w.** I abhor them, to destroy
Le 26:45 I **w.** for their sakes remember the
Le 27:13 if he **w.** at all redeem it, then he shall
Le 27:15 that sanctified it **w.** redeem his house,
Le 27:19 the field **w.** in any wise redeem it,
Le 27:20 And if he **w.** not redeem the field,
Le 27:31 if a man **w.** at all redeem ought of
Nu 6:27 of Israel; and I **w.** bless them.
Nu 9:8 and I **w.** hear what the Lord
Nu 9:8 Lord **w.** command concerning you.
Nu 9:14 **w.** keep the passover unto the Lord;
Nu 10:29 which the Lord said, I **w.** give it you:
Nu 10:29 thou with us, and we **w.** do thee good:
Nu 10:30 And he said unto him, I **w.** not go;
Nu 10:30 I **w.** depart to mine own land, and to
Nu 10:32 unto us, the same **w.** we do unto thee.
Nu 11:17 I **w.** come down and talk with thee
Nu 11:17 I **w.** take of the spirit which is upon
Nu 11:17 **w.** put it upon them; and they shall
Nu 11:18 therefore the Lord **w.** give you flesh,
Nu 11:21 I **w.** give them flesh, that they may eat
Nu 12:6 I the lord **w.** make myself known unto
Nu 12:6 and **w.** speak unto you in a dream.
Nu 12:8 With him **w.** I speak mouth to mouth,
Nu 14:8 he **w.** bring us into this land, and give
Nu 14:11 How long **w.** this people provoke me?
Nu 14:11 how long **w.** it be ere they believe me,
Nu 14:12 I **w.** smite them with the pestilence,
Nu 14:12 and **w.** make of thee a greater nation
Nu 14:14 they **w.** tell it to the inhabitants of this
Nu 14:15 the fame of thee **w.** speak, saying,
Nu 14:24 him **w.** I bring into the land whereunto
Nu 14:28 spoken in mine ears, so **w.** I do to you:
Nu 14:31 them **w.** I bring in, and they shall
Nu 14:35 I **w.** surely do it unto all this evil
Nu 14:40 and **w.** go up unto the place which the
Nu 14:43 therefore the Lord **w.** not be with you.
Nu 15:3 **w.** make an offering by fire unto the
Nu 15:14 and **w.** offer an offering made by fire,
Nu 16:5 morrow the Lord **w.** show who are his,
Nu 16:5 **w.** cause him to come near unto him:
Nu 16:5 chosen **w.** he cause to come near unto
Nu 16:12 Eliab: which said, We **w.** not come up:
Nu 16:14 we **w.** not come up.
Nu 17:4 testimony, where I **w.** meet with you.
Nu 17:5 I **w.** make to cease from me the
Nu 20:17 we **w.** not pass through the fields,
Nu 20:17 **w.** we drink of the water of the wells:
Nu 20:17 we **w.** go by the king's high way,
Nu 20:17 we **w.** not turn to the right hand nor to
Nu 20:19 unto him, We **w.** go by the high way:
Nu 20:19 of thy water, then **w.** I pay for it:
Nu 20:19 I **w.** only, without doing any thing else,
Nu 21:2 then I **w.** utterly destroy their cities.
Nu 21:16 together, and I **w.** give them water.
Nu 21:22 we **w.** not turn into the fields, or into
Nu 21:22 **w.** not drink of the waters of the well:
Nu 21:22 we **w.** go along by the king's high way,
Nu 22:8 I **w.** bring you word again, as the Lord
Nu 22:17 For I **w.** promote thee unto very great
Nu 22:17 I **w.** do whatsoever thou sayest unto
Nu 22:19 what the Lord **w.** say unto me more.
Nu 22:34 displease thee, I **w.** get me back again.
Nu 23:3 Stand by thy burnt offering, and I **w.** go:
Nu 23:3 the Lord **w.** come to meet me:
Nu 23:3 whatever he sheweth me I **w.** tell thee.
Nu 23:27 I **w.** bring thee unto another place;
Nu 23:27 it **w.** please God that thou mayest
Nu 24:13 what the Lord saith, that **w.** I speak?
Nu 24:14 I **w.** advertise thee what this people
Nu 32:15 he **w.** yet again leave them in the
Nu 32:16 We **w.** build sheepfolds here for our
Nu 32:17 But we ourselves **w.** go ready armed
Nu 32:18 We **w.** not return unto our houses,
Nu 32:19 For we **w.** not inherit with them on
Nu 32:20 said unto them, If ye **w.** do this thing,
Nu 32:20 ye **w.** go armed before the Lord to war,
Nu 32:21 **w.** go all of you armed over Jordan
Nu 32:23 But if ye **w.** not do so, behold, ye have
Nu 32:23 and be sure your sin **w.** find you out.
Nu 32:25 **w.** do as my lord commandeth.
Nu 32:27 thy servants **w.** pass over, every man
Nu 32:29 Reuben **w.** pass with you over Jordan,
Nu 32:30 But if they **w.** not pass over with you
Nu 32:31 said unto thy servants, so **w.** we do.
Nu 32:32 **w.** pass over armed before the Lord
Nu 33:55 if ye **w.** not drive out the inhabitants
De 1:13 and I **w.** make them rulers over you.
De 1:17 you, bring it unto me, and I **w.** hear it.
De 1:22 We **w.** send men before us, and they
De 1:36 to him **w.** I give the land that he hath
De 1:39 and unto them **w.** I give it, and they
De 1:41 we **w.** go up and fight, according to all
De 2:5 for I **w.** not give you of their land, no,
De 2:9 for I **w.** not give thee of their land
De 2:19 for I **w.** not give thee of the land of the
De 2:25 this day **w.** I begin to put the dread
De 2:27 land: I **w.** go along by the high way,
De 2:27 I **w.** neither turn unto the right hand
De 2:28 only I **w.** pass through on my feet;
De 3:2 for I **w.** deliver him, and all his people,
De 4:10 I **w.** make them; hear my words, that
De 4:31 he **w.** not forsake thee, neither destroy
De 5:11 Lord **w.** not hold them guiltless that
De 5:25 for this great fire **w.** consume us: if we
De 5:27 unto thee; and we **w.** hear it, and do it.
De 5:31 and I **w.** speak unto thee all the
De 7:4 For they **w.** turn away thy son from
De 7:4 so **w.** the anger of the Lord be kindled
De 7:10 he **w.** not be slack to him that hateth
De 7:10 him, he **w.** repay him to his face.
De 7:13 and he **w.** love thee, and bless thee,
De 7:13 he **w.** also bless the fruit of thy womb,
De 7:15 the Lord **w.** take away from thee all
De 7:15 and **w.** put none of the evil diseases
De 7:15 **w.** lay them upon all them that hate
De 7:16 for that **w.** be a snare unto thee.
De 7:20 God **w.** send the hornet among them,
De 7:22 thy God **w.** put out those nations
De 9:14 I **w.** make of thee a nation mightier
De 10:2 I **w.** write on the tables the words
De 11:14 I **w.** give you the rain of your land
De 11:15 I **w.** send grass in thy fields for thy
De 11:23 **w.** the Lord drive out all these
De 11:28 if ye **w.** not obey the commandments
De 12:20 I **w.** eat flesh, because thy soul
De 12:30 their gods? even so **w.** I do likewise
De 15:16 I **w.** not go away from thee; because
De 17:12 man that **w.** do presumptuously, and
De 17:12 **w.** not hearken unto the priest that
De 17:14 I **w.** set a king over me, like as all the
De 18:15 God **w.** raise up unto thee a Prophet
De 18:18 I **w.** raise them up a Prophet from
De 18:18 and **w.** put my words in his mouth;
De 18:19 **w.** not hearken unto my words

De 18:19 in my name, I w. require it of him
De 20:12 if it w. make no peace with thee,
De 20:12 w. make war against thee, then thou
De 21:14 shalt let her go whither she w.; 5315
De 21:18 w. not obey the voice of his father,
De 21:18 him, w. not hearken unto them.
De 21:20 rebellious, he w. not obey our voice;
De 23:21 thy God w. surely require it of thee;
De 25:7 w. not perform the duty of my 14
De 25:9 w. not build up his brother's house.
De 28:1 thy God w. set thee on high above all
De 28:27 w. smite thee with the botch of Egypt,
De 28:55 that he w. not give to any of them
De 28:59 Lord w. make thy plagues wonderful,
De 28:60 he w. bring upon thee all the diseases
De 28:61 them w. the Lord bring upon thee,
De 28:63 so the Lord w. rejoice over you
De 29:20 The Lord w. not spare him, but then
De 30:3 Lord thy God w. turn thy captivity,
De 30:3 w. return and gather thee from all
De 30:4 from thence w. the Lord thy God
De 30:4 and from thence w. he fetch thee:
De 30:5 thy God w. bring thee into the land
De 30:5 he w. do thee good, and multiply thee
De 30:6 the Lord...w. circumcise thine heart,
De 30:7 God w. put all these curses upon thine
De 30:9 Lord thy God w. make thee plenteous
De 30:9 for the Lord w. again rejoice over thee
De 31:3 thy God, he w. go over before thee,
De 31:3 and he w. destroy these nations from
De 31:6 he w. not fail thee, nor forsake thee.
De 31:8 he w. be with thee, he w. not fail thee,
De 31:16 and this people w. rise up, and go
De 31:16 and w. forsake me, and break my
De 31:17 I w. forsake them, and I w. hide my
De 31:17 so that they w. say in that day, Are
De 31:18 I w. surely hide my face in that day
De 31:20 then w. they turn unto other gods,
De 31:23 unto them: and I w. be with thee.
De 31:29 after my death ye w. utterly corrupt
De 31:29 evil w. befall you in the latter days;
De 31:29 because ye w. do evil in the sight of
De 32:1 ear, O ye heavens, and I w. speak;
De 32:3 I w. publish the name of the Lord:
De 32:7 ask thy father, and he w. shew thee;
De 32:7 thy elders, and they w. tell thee.
De 32:20 he said, I w. hide my face from them,
De 32:20 I w. see what their end shall be:
De 32:21 I w. move them to jealousy with those
De 32:21 I w. provoke them to anger with a
De 32:23 I w. heap mischiefs upon them;
De 32:23 I w. spend mine arrows upon them.
De 32:24 I w. also send the teeth of beasts upon
De 32:41 I w. render vengeance to mine
De 32:41 and w. reward them that hate me.
De 32:42 I w. make mine arrows drunk with
De 32:43 for he w. avenge the blood of his
De 32:43 and w. render vengeance to his
De 32:43 w. be merciful unto his land, and to
De 33:16 for the good w. of him that dwell in.... 7522
De 34:4 saying, I w. give it unto thy seed: I
Jos 1:5 was with Moses, so I w. be with thee:
Jos 1:5 I w. not fail thee, nor forsake thee.
Jos 1:16 that thou commandest us we w. do,
Jos 1:16 thou sendest us, we w. go.
Jos 1:17 things, so w. we hearken unto thee:
Jos 1:18 and w. not hearken unto thy words
Jos 2:12 that ye w. also shew kindness unto
Jos 2:13 that ye w. save alive my father, and
Jos 2:14 we w. deal kindly and truly with thee.
Jos 2:17 we w. be blameless of this thine oath
Jos 2:19 upon his head, and we w. be guiltless:
Jos 2:20 then we w. be quit of thine oath
Jos 3:5 the Lord w. do wonders among you.
Jos 3:7 This day w. I begin to magnify thee in
Jos 3:7 I was with Moses, so I w. be with thee.
Jos 3:10 and that he w. without fail drive out
Jos 7:12 neither w. I be with you any more,
Jos 8:5 with me, w. approach unto the city:
Jos 8:5 the first, that we w. flee before them,
Jos 8:6 (For they w. come out after us) till we
Jos 8:6 for they w. say, They flee before us, as
Jos 8:6 first: therefore we w. flee before them.
Jos 8:7 the Lord your God w. deliver it into
Jos 8:18 Ai; for I w. give it into thy hand.
Jos 9:20 This we w. do to them;
Jos 9:20 we w. even let them live, lest
Jos 11:6 about this time w. I deliver them up
Jos 13:6 w. I drive out before the children
Jos 14:12 if so be the Lord w. be with me, then I
Jos 15:16 w. I give Achsah my daughter to wife.
Jos 18:4 I w. send them, and they shall rise,
Jos 22:18 it w. be, seeing ye rebel to day against
Jos 22:18 to morrow he w. be wroth with the
Jos 23:13 Lord your God w. no more drive out
Jos 24:15 choose you this day whom ye w. serve;
Jos 24:15 and my house, we w. serve the Lord.
Jos 24:18 therefore w. we serve the Lord;
Jos 24:19 he w. not forgive your transgressions
Jos 24:20 then he w. turn and do you hurt, and
Jos 24:21 Nay; but we w. serve the Lord.
Jos 24:24 God w. we serve, and his voice w. we
Jg 1:3 I likewise w. go with thee unto thy lot
Jg 1:12 to him w. I give Achsah my daughter
Jg 1:24 the city, and we w. shew thee mercy.
Jg 2:1 I w. never break my covenant with
Jg 2:3 I w. not drive them out from before
Jg 2:21 w. not henceforth drive out any from
Jg 2:22 they w. keep the way of the Lord
Jg 4:7 And I w. draw unto thee to the river
Jg 4:7 and I w. deliver him into thine hand.
Jg 4:8 If thou wilt go with me, then I w. go:
Jg 4:8 wilt not go with me, then I w. not go.
Jg 4:9 And she said, I w. surely go with thee:
Jg 4:22 I w. shew thee the man whom thou
Jg 5:3 I, even I, w. sing unto the Lord;
Jg 5:3 I w. sing praise to the Lord God of
Jg 6:16 Surely I w. be with thee, and thou
Jg 6:18 said, I w. tarry until thou come again.
Jg 6:31 W. ye plead for Baal? w. ye save him?
Jg 6:31 he that w. plead for him, let him be put
Jg 6:37 I w. put a fleece of wool in the floor;
Jg 6:39 me, and I w. speak but this once:
Jg 7:4 and I w. try them for thee there:
Jg 7:7 men that lapped w. I save you,
Jg 8:7 I w. tear your flesh with the thorns of
Jg 8:9 in peace, I w. break down this tower.
Jg 8:23 unto them, I w. not rule over you,
Jg 8:25 answered, We w. willingly give
Jg 10:13 wherefore I w. deliver you no more.
Jg 10:18 What man is he that w. begin to fight
Jg 11:24 from before us, them w. we possess.
Jg 11:31 I w. offer it up for a burnt offering.
Jg 12:1 w. burn thine house upon thee with
Jg 13:16 detain me, I w. not eat of thy bread:
Jg 14:12 I w. now put forth a riddle unto you:
Jg 14:12 I w. give you thirty sheets and thirty
Jg 15:1 I w. go in to my wife into the chamber.
Jg 15:7 done this, yet w. I be avenged of you,
Jg 15:7 avenged of you, and after...I w. cease.
Jg 15:12 ye w. not fall upon me yourselves.
Jg 15:13 but we w. bind thee fast, and deliver
Jg 15:13 hand: but surely we w. not kill thee.
Jg 16:5 we w. give thee every one of us eleven
Jg 16:17 then my strength w. go from me,
Jg 16:20 I w. go out as at other times before,
Jg 17:3 therefore I w. restore it unto thee.
Jg 17:10 I w. give thee ten shekels of silver by
Jg 17:13 know I that the Lord w. do me good,
Jg 19:12 We w. not turn aside hither into the
Jg 19:12 of Israel; we w. pass over to Gibeah.
Jg 19:24 them I w. bring out now, and humble
Jg 20:8 We w. not any of us go to his tent,
Jg 20:8 neither w. we any of us turn into his
Jg 20:9 the thing which we w. do to Gibeah;
Jg 20:9 Gibeah; we w. go up by lot against it;
Jg 20:10 And we w. take ten men of an hundred
Jg 20:28 I w. deliver them into thy hand.
Jg 21:7 we w. not give them of our daughters
Jg 21:22 complain, that we w. say unto them,
Ru 1:10 we w. return with thee unto thy people.
Ru 1:11 my daughters: why w. ye go with me?
Ru 1:16 for whither thou goest, I w. go: and
Ru 1:16 and where thou lodgest, I w. lodge:
Ru 1:17 w. I die, and there w. I be buried:
Ru 3:4 and he w. tell thee what thou shalt do.
Ru 3:5 All that thou sayest unto me I w. do.
Ru 3:11 I w. do to thee all that thou requirest:
Ru 3:13 if he w. perform unto thee the
Ru 3:13 but if he w. not do the part of a 2654
Ru 3:13 then w. I do the part of a kinsman to
Ru 3:18 thou know how the matter w. fall:
Ru 3:18 for the man w. not be in rest, until he
Ru 4:4 thee. And he said, I w. redeem it.
1Sa 1:11 then I w. give him unto the Lord all
1Sa 1:22 I w. not go up until the child be
1Sa 1:22 and then I w. bring him, that he may
1Sa 2:9 He w. keep the feet of his saints, and
1Sa 2:15 he w. not have sodden flesh of thee,
1Sa 2:16 now: and if not, I w. take it by force.
1Sa 2:30 for them that honour me I w. honour.
1Sa 2:31 days come, that I w. cut off thine arm,
1Sa 2:35 And I w. raise me up a faithful priest,
1Sa 2:35 I w. build him a sure house; and he
1Sa 3:11 Behold, I w. do a thing in Israel,
1Sa 3:12 I w. perform against Eli all things
1Sa 3:12 when I begin, I w. also make an end.
1Sa 3:13 him that I w. judge his house for ever
1Sa 6:5 peradventure he w. lighten his hand
1Sa 7:3 he w. deliver you out of the hand of the
1Sa 7:5 and I w. pray for you unto the Lord.
1Sa 7:8 he w. save us out of the hand of the
1Sa 8:11 This w. be the manner of the king that
1Sa 8:11 w. take your sons, and appoint them
1Sa 8:12 he w. appoint him captains over
1Sa 8:12 w. set them to ear his ground, and to
1Sa 8:13 he w. take your daughters to be
1Sa 8:14 And he w. take your fields, and your
1Sa 8:15 And he w. take the tenth of your seed,
1Sa 8:16 And he w. take your menservants,
1Sa 8:17 He w. take the tenth of your sheep:
1Sa 8:18 the Lord w. not hear you in that day.
1Sa 8:19 Nay; but we w. have a king over us;
1Sa 9:8 w. I give to the man of God, to tell us
1Sa 9:13 the people w. not eat until he come,
1Sa 9:16 I w. send thee a man out of the land of
1Sa 9:19 to day, and to morrow I w. let thee go,
1Sa 9:19 w. tell thee all that is in thine heart.
1Sa 10:2 and they w. say unto thee, The asses
1Sa 10:4 they w. salute thee, and give thee two
1Sa 10:6 Spirit of the Lord w. come upon thee,
1Sa 10:8 I w. come down unto thee, to offer
1Sa 11:1 with us, and we w. serve thee.
1Sa 11:2 condition w. I make a covenant with
1Sa 11:3 to save us, we w. come out to thee.
1Sa 11:10 To morrow we w. come out unto you,
1Sa 12:3 there with? and I w. restore it you.
1Sa 12:10 of our enemies, and we w. serve thee.
1Sa 12:14 If ye w. fear the Lord, and serve him,
1Sa 12:15 ye w. not obey the voice of the Lord,
1Sa 12:16 the Lord w. do before your eyes.
1Sa 12:17 I w. call unto the Lord, and he shall
1Sa 12:22 the Lord w. not forsake his people
1Sa 12:23 I w. teach you the good and the right
1Sa 13:12 the Philistines w. come down now
1Sa 14:6 may be that the Lord w. work for us:
1Sa 14:8 we w. pass over unto these men,
1Sa 14:8 we w. discover ourselves unto them.
1Sa 14:9 then we w. stand still in our place,
1Sa 14:9 and w. not go up unto them.
1Sa 14:10 come up unto us: then we w. go up;
1Sa 14:12 up to us, and we w. shew you a thing.
1Sa 14:40 my son w. be on the other side.
1Sa 15:16 I w. tell thee what the Lord hath said
1Sa 15:26 unto Saul, I w. not return with thee:
1Sa 15:29 also the Strength of Israel w. not lie
1Sa 16:1 go, I w. send thee to Jesse the
1Sa 16:2 can I go? If Saul hear it, he w. kill me.
1Sa 16:3 I w. shew thee what thou shalt do:
1Sa 16:11 for we w. not sit down till he come
1Sa 17:9 kill me, then w. we be your servants:
1Sa 17:25 the king w. enrich him with great
1Sa 17:25 and w. give him his daughters,
1Sa 17:32 they servant w. go and fight with this
1Sa 17:37 he w. deliver me out of the hand of
1Sa 17:44 and I w. give thy flesh unto the fowls
1Sa 17:46 This day w. the Lord deliver thee into
1Sa 17:46 I w. smite thee, and take thine head
1Sa 17:46 and I w. give the carcases of the host
1Sa 17:47 and he w. give you into our hands.
1Sa 18:11 I w. smite David...to the wall with it.
1Sa 18:17 Merab, her w. I give thee to wife:
1Sa 18:21 I w. give him her, that she may be a
1Sa 19:3 I w. go out and stand beside my father
1Sa 19:3 I w. commune with my father of thee;
1Sa 19:3 and what I see, that w. tell thee.
1Sa 20:2 my father w. do nothing either great
1Sa 20:2 but that he w. shew it me: and why

1Sa	20:4	desireth, I **w.** even do it for thee.
1Sa	20:13	I **w.** shew it thee, and send thee away,
1Sa	20:18	missed, because thy seat **w.** be empty.
1Sa	20:20	I **w.** shoot three arrows on the side
1Sa	20:21	I **w.** send a lad, saying, Go, find out
1Sa	22:3	till I know what God **w.** do for me
1Sa	22:7	**w.** the son of Jesse give every one
1Sa	23:4	I **w.** deliver the Philistines into thine
1Sa	23:11	**W.** the men of Keilah deliver me up
1Sa	23:11	**w.** Saul come down, as thy servant
1Sa	23:11	And the Lord said, He **w.** come down.
1Sa	23:12	**W.** the men of Keilah deliver me and
1Sa	23:12	the Lord said, They **w.** deliver thee up.
1Sa	23:23	the certainty, and I **w.** go with you:
1Sa	23:23	I **w.** search him out throughout all the
1Sa	24:4	I **w.** deliver thine enemy into thine
1Sa	24:10	I **w.** not put forth mine hand against
1Sa	24:19	enemy, **w.** he let him go well away?
1Sa	25:8	young men, and they **w.** shew thee.
1Sa	25:28	**w.** certainly make my lord a sure
1Sa	26:6	Who **w.** go down with me to Saul
1Sa	26:6	Abishai said, I **w.** go down with thee.
1Sa	26:8	I **w.** not smite him the second time.
1Sa	26:21	for I **w.** no more do thee harm,
1Sa	27:11	and so **w.** be his manner all the while
1Sa	28:2	**w.** I make thee keeper of mine head
1Sa	28:29	the Lord **w.** also deliver Israel with
1Sa	28:23	he refused, and said, I **w.** not eat.
1Sa	30:15	I **w.** bring thee down to this company.
1Sa	30:22	we **w.** not give them ought of the spoil
1Sa	30:24	who **w.** hearken unto you in this
2Sa	2:6	I also **w.** requite you this kindness,
2Sa	2:26	it **w.** be bitterness in the latter end?
2Sa	3:13	Well; I **w.** make a league with thee:
2Sa	3:18	I **w.** save my people Israel out of the
2Sa	3:21	I **w.** arise and go, and **w.** gather all
2Sa	5:19	I **w.** doubtless deliver the Philistines
2Sa	6:21	therefore **w.** I play before the Lord.
2Sa	6:22	I **w.** yet be more vile than thus, and
2Sa	6:22	**w.** he base in mine own sight:
2Sa	7:10	I **w.** appoint a place for my people
2Sa	7:10	**w.** plant them, that they may dwell
2Sa	7:11	that he **w.** make thee an house.
2Sa	7:12	I **w.** set up thy seed after thee,
2Sa	7:12	and I **w.** establish his kingdom.
2Sa	7:13	and I **w.** stablish the throne of his
2Sa	7:14	I **w.** be his father, and he shall be my
2Sa	7:14	I **w.** chasten him with the rod of men,
2Sa	7:27	saying, I **w.** build thee an house:
2Sa	9:7	for I **w.** surely shew thee kindness
2Sa	9:7	**w.** restore thee all the land of Saul
2Sa	10:2	I **w.** shew kindness unto Hanun
2Sa	10:11	thee, then **w.** I come and help thee.
2Sa	11:11	soul liveth, I **w.** not do this thing.
2Sa	11:12	and to morrow I **w.** let thee depart.
2Sa	12:11	I **w.** raise up evil against thee out of
2Sa	12:11	I **w.** take thy wives before thine eyes,
2Sa	12:12	I **w.** do this thing before all Israel,
2Sa	12:18	how **w.** he then vex himself, if we tell
2Sa	12:22	whether God **w.** be gracious to me,
2Sa	13:13	for he **w.** not withhold me from thee.
2Sa	14:7	and we **w.** destroy the heir also:
2Sa	14:8	and I **w.** give charge concerning thee.
2Sa	14:15	said, I will now speak unto the king;
2Sa	14:15	that the king **w.** perform the request
2Sa	14:16	For the king **w.** hear, to deliver his
2Sa	14:17	the Lord thy God **w.** be with thee.
2Sa	15:8	Jerusalem, then **w.** I serve the Lord.
2Sa	15:21	even there also **w.** thy servant be.
2Sa	15:25	he **w.** bring me again, and shew me
2Sa	15:28	I **w.** tarry in the plain of the
2Sa	15:34	Absalom, I **w.** be thy servant, O king;
2Sa	15:34	so **w.** I now also be thy servant:
2Sa	16:12	that the Lord **w.** look on my affliction,
2Sa	16:12	that the Lord **w.** requite me good
2Sa	16:18	his **w.** I be, and with him **w.** I abide.
2Sa	16:19	presence, so **w.** I be in thy presence.
2Sa	17:1	and I **w.** arise and pursue after David
2Sa	17:2	**w.** come upon him while he is weary
2Sa	17:2	handed, and **w.** make him afraid:
2Sa	17:2	flee; and I **w.** smite the king only:
2Sa	17:3	and I **w.** bring back all the people
2Sa	17:3	and **w.** not lodge with the people
2Sa	17:9	and it **w.** come to pass, when some of
2Sa	17:9	that whosoever heareth it **w.** say,
2Sa	17:12	and we **w.** light upon him as the dew
2Sa	17:13	and we **w.** draw it into the river,
2Sa	18:2	I **w.** surely go forth with you myself
2Sa	18:3	we flee away, they **w.** not care for us;
2Sa	18:3	if half of us die, **w.** they care for us:
2Sa	18:4	them, what seemeth you best I **w.** do.
2Sa	19:7	**w.** not tarry one with thee this night:
2Sa	19:7	**w.** be worse unto thee than all the evil
2Sa	19:26	I **w.** saddle me an ass, that I may ride
2Sa	19:33	I **w.** feed thee with me in Jerusalem.
2Sa	19:36	servant **w.** go a little way over Jordan
2Sa	19:38	I **w.** do to him that which shall seem
2Sa	19:38	require of me, that **w.** I do for thee.
2Sa	20:21	only, I **w.** depart from the city
2Sa	21:4	We **w.** have no silver nor gold of Saul,
2Sa	21:4	ye shall say, that **w.** I do for you.
2Sa	21:6	we **w.** hang them up unto the Lord
2Sa	21:6	And the king said, I **w.** give them.
2Sa	22:3	God of my rock; in him **w.** I trust:
2Sa	22:4	I **w.** call on the Lord, who is worthy
2Sa	22:29	and the Lord **w.** lighten my darkness.
2Sa	22:50	therefore I **w.** give thanks unto thee,
2Sa	22:50	and I **w.** sing praises unto thy name.
2Sa	24:24	I **w.** surely buy it of thee at a price:
2Sa	24:24	neither **w.** I offer burnt offerings
1Ki	1:5	himself, saying, I **w.** be a king:
1Ki	1:14	I also **w.** come in after thee,
1Ki	1:30	even so **w.** I certainly do this day
1Ki	1:51	that he **w.** not slay his servant with
1Ki	1:52	If he **w.** shew himself a worthy man,
1Ki	2:8	I **w.** not put thee to death with the
1Ki	2:17	king, (for he **w.** not say thee nay,)
1Ki	2:18	I **w.** speak for thee unto the king.
1Ki	2:20	mother: for I **w.** not say thee nay.
1Ki	2:26	I **w.** not at this time put thee to death,
1Ki	2:30	And he said, Nay; but I **w.** die here.
1Ki	2:38	king hath said, so **w.** thy servant do.
1Ki	3:14	did walk, then I **w.** lengthen thy days.
1Ki	5:5	whom I **w.** set upon thy throne in thy
1Ki	5:6	thee **w.** I give hire for thy servants
1Ki	5:8	I **w.** do all thy desire concerning
1Ki	5:9	I **w.** convey them by sea in floats unto
1Ki	5:9	**w.** cause them to be discharged there,
1Ki	6:12	**w.** I perform my word with thee,
1Ki	6:13	**w.** dwell among the children of Israel,
1Ki	6:13	and **w.** not forsake my people Israel.
1Ki	8:27	**w.** God indeed dwell on the earth?
1Ki	9:5	I **w.** establish the throne of thy
1Ki	9:6	**w.** not keep my commandments and
1Ki	9:7	**w.** I cut off Israel out of the land
1Ki	9:7	my name, **w.** I cast out of my sight;
1Ki	11:2	**w.** turn away your heart after their
1Ki	11:11	I **w.** surely rend the kingdom from
1Ki	11:11	thee, and **w.** give it to thy servant.
1Ki	11:12	I **w.** not do it for David thy father's
1Ki	11:12	I **w.** rend it out of the hand of thy son.
1Ki	11:13	I **w.** not rend away all the kingdom;
1Ki	11:13	**w.** give one tribe to thy son for David
1Ki	11:31	I **w.** rend the kingdom out of the hand
1Ki	11:31	and **w.** give ten tribes to thee.
1Ki	11:34	I **w.** not take the whole kingdom out
1Ki	11:34	I **w.** make him prince all the days of
1Ki	11:35	I **w.** take the kingdom out of his son's
1Ki	11:35	**w.** give it unto thee, even ten tribes.
1Ki	11:36	And unto his son **w.** I give one tribe,
1Ki	11:37	I **w.** take thee, and thou shalt reign
1Ki	11:38	I **w.** be with thee, and build thee a
1Ki	11:38	David, and **w.** give Israel unto thee.
1Ki	11:39	I **w.** for this afflict the seed of David,
1Ki	12:4	us, lighter, and we **w.** serve thee.
1Ki	12:7	they **w.** be thy servants for ever.
1Ki	12:11	heavy yoke, I **w.** add to your yoke:
1Ki	12:11	but I **w.** chastise you with scorpions.
1Ki	12:14	heavy, and I **w.** add to your yoke:
1Ki	12:14	but I **w.** chastise you with scorpions.
1Ki	13:7	thyself, and I **w.** give thee a reward.
1Ki	13:8	thine house, I **w.** not go with thee,
1Ki	13:8,	16 neither **w.** I eat bread nor drink
1Ki	14:10	I **w.** bring evil upon the house of
1Ki	14:10	**w.** cut off from Jeroboam him that
1Ki	14:10	**w.** take away the remnant of the
1Ki	16:3	**w.** take away the posterity of Baasha,
1Ki	16:3	**w.** make thy house like the house
1Ki	18:1	and I **w.** send rain upon the earth.
1Ki	18:15	I **w.** surely shew myself unto him to
1Ki	18:23	I **w.** dress the other bullock, and lay
1Ki	18:24	I **w.** call on the name of the Lord:
1Ki	19:20	mother, and then I **w.** follow thee.
1Ki	20:6	I **w.** send my servants unto thee to
1Ki	20:9	for to thy sevants as first I **w.** do:
1Ki	20:13	I **w.** deliver it into thine hand this day;
1Ki	20:22	king of Syria **w.** come up against thee.
1Ki	20:25	we **w.** fight against them in the plain,
1Ki	20:28	**w.** I deliver all this great multitude
1Ki	20:31	peradventure he **w.** save thy life.
1Ki	20:34	took from thy father, I **w.** restore;
1Ki	20:34	**w.** send thee away with this covenant.
1Ki	21:2	I **w.** give thee for it a better vineyard
1Ki	21:2	**w.** give thee the worth of it in money.
1Ki	21:4	I **w.** not give thee the inheritance of
1Ki	21:6	I **w.** give thee another vineyard for it:
1Ki	21:6	I **w.** not give thee my vineyard.
1Ki	21:7	I **w.** give thee the vineyard if Naboth
1Ki	21:21	Behold, I **w.** bring evil upon thee,
1Ki	21:21	and **w.** take thy posterity, and
1Ki	21:21	and **w.** cut off from Ahab him that
1Ki	21:22	**w.** make thine house like the house
1Ki	21:29	I **w.** not bring the evil in his days:
1Ki	21:29	in his son's day **w.** bring the evil
1Ki	22:14	the Lord saith to me, that **w.** I speak.
1Ki	22:21	Lord, and said, I **w.** persuade him.
1Ki	22:22	I **w.** go forth, and I **w.** be a lying spirit
1Ki	22:30	I **w.** disguise myself, and enter into
2Ki	2:2	thy soul liveth, I **w.** not leave thee.
2Ki	2:3	Lord **w.** take away thy master from
2Ki	2:4	as thy soul liveth, I **w.** not leave thee.
2Ki	2:5	Lord **w.** take away thy master from
2Ki	2:6	as thy soul liveth, I **w.** not leave thee.
2Ki	3:7	he said, I **w.** go up: I am as thou art,
2Ki	3:18	**w.** deliver the Moabites also into your
2Ki	4:30	as thy soul liveth, I **w.** not leave thee.
2Ki	5:5	I **w.** send a letter unto the king of
2Ki	5:11	He **w.** surely come out to me, and
2Ki	5:16	whom I stand, I **w.** receive none.
2Ki	5:17	servant **w.** henceforth offer neither
2Ki	5:20	I **w.** run after him, and take somewhat
2Ki	6:3	And he answered, I will go.
2Ki	6:11	**W.** ye not shew me which of us is for
2Ki	6:19	I **w.** bring you to the man whom ye
2Ki	6:28	and we **w.** eat my son to morrow.
2Ki	7:4	We **w.** enter into the city, then the
2Ki	7:9	light, some mischief **w.** come upon us:
2Ki	7:12	I **w.** now shew you what the Syrians
2Ki	9:8	I **w.** cut off from Ahab him that
2Ki	9:9	I **w.** make the house of Ahab like the
2Ki	9:26	I **w.** requite thee in this plat, saith
2Ki	10:5	and **w.** do all that thou shalt bid us;
2Ki	10:5	we **w.** not make any king: do thou
2Ki	10:6	if ye **w.** hearken unto my voice, take
2Ki	18:14	which thou puttest on me **w.** I bear.
2Ki	18:21	**w.** go into his hand, and pierce it:
2Ki	18:23	I **w.** deliver thee two thousand horses,
2Ki	18:30	The Lord **w.** surely deliver us, and
2Ki	18:32	you saying, the Lord **w.** deliver us.
2Ki	19:4	thy God **w.** hear all the words of
2Ki	19:4	**w.** reprove the words which the Lord
2Ki	19:7	I **w.** send a blast upon him, and he
2Ki	19:7	I **w.** cause him to fall by the sword in
2Ki	19:23	and **w.** cut down the tall cedar trees
2Ki	19:23	I **w.** enter into the lodgings of his
2Ki	19:28	I **w.** put my hook in thy nose,
2Ki	19:28	I **w.** turn thee back by the way by
2Ki	19:34	For I **w.** defend this city, to save it,
2Ki	20:5	thy tears: behold, I **w.** heal thee:
2Ki	20:6	I **w.** add unto thy days fifteen years;
2Ki	20:6	I **w.** deliver thee and this city out of
2Ki	20:6	I **w.** defend this city for mine own
2Ki	20:8	be the sign that the Lord **w.** heal me,
2Ki	20:9	Lord **w.** do the thing he hath spoken:
2Ki	21:4	In Jerusalem **w.** I put my name.
2Ki	21:7	of Israel, **w.** I put my name for ever:
2Ki	21:8	Neither **w.** I make the feet of Israel
2Ki	21:8	if they **w.** observe to do according to
2Ki	21:13	I **w.** stretch over Jerusalem the line of
2Ki	21:13	I **w.** wipe Jerusalem as a man wipeth
2Ki	21:14	I **w.** forsake the remnant of mine
2Ki	22:16	I **w.** bring evil upon this place, and
2Ki	22:20	I **w.** gather thee unto thy fathers,
2Ki	22:20	evil which I **w.** bring upon this place.
2Ki	23:27	I **w.** remove Judah also out of my
2Ki	23:27	**w.** cast off this city Jerusalem which
1Ch	12:19	He **w.** fall to his master Saul to the
1Ch	14:10	I **w.** deliver them into thine hand.
1Ch	16:18	Unto thee **w.** I give the land of Canaan,
1Ch	17:9	I **w.** ordain a place for my people
1Ch	17:9	and **w.** plant them, and they shall

1Ch 17:10 I **w.** subdue all thine enemies.
1Ch 17:10 that the Lord **w.** build thee an house.
1Ch 17:11 that I **w.** raise up thy seed after thee,
1Ch 17:11 and I **w.** establish his kingdom.
1Ch 17:12 and I **w.** stablish his throne for ever.
1Ch 17:13 I **w.** be his father, and he shall be my
1Ch 17:13 I **w.** not take my mercy away from
1Ch 17:14 I **w.** settle him in mine house and in
1Ch 19:2 I **w.** shew kindness unto Hanun the
1Ch 19:12 strong for thee, then I **w.** help thee.
1Ch 21:3 **w.** he be a cause of trespass to Israel?
1Ch 21:24 I **w.** verily buy it for the full price:
1Ch 21:24 I **w.** not take that which is thine for
1Ch 22:5 I **w.** therefore now make preparation
1Ch 22:9 I **w.** give him rest from all his enemies
1Ch 22:9 I **w.** give peace and quietness unto
1Ch 22:10 be my son, and I **w.** be his father;
1Ch 22:10 and I **w.** establish the throne of his
1Ch 28:6 to be my son, and I **w.** be his father.
1Ch 28:7 I **w.** establish his kingdom for ever,
1Ch 28:9 seek him, he **w.** be found of thee;
1Ch 28:9 forsake him, he **w.** cast thee off for
1Ch 28:20 God, even my God **w.** be with thee;
1Ch 28:20 he **w.** not fail thee, nor forsake thee,
1Ch 28:21 **w.** be wholly at thy commandment.
2Ch 1:12 I **w.** give thee riches, and wealth, and
2Ch 2:10 I **w.** give to thy servants, the hewers
2Ch 2:16 **w.** cut wood out of Lebanon, as much
2Ch 2:16 **w.** bring it to thee in floats by sea
2Ch 6:18 **w.** God in every deed dwell with men
2Ch 7:14 ways, then **w.** I hear from heaven.
2Ch 7:14 and **w.** forgive their sin,
2Ch 7:14 and **w.** heal their land.
2Ch 7:18 **w.** I stablish the throne of thy
2Ch 7:20 **w.** I pluck them up by the roots out of
2Ch 7:20 my name, **w.** I cast out of my sight,
2Ch 7:20 and **w.** make it to be a proverb and a
2Ch 10:4 he put upon us, and we **w.** serve thee.
2Ch 10:7 them, they **w.** be thy servants for ever.
2Ch 10:11 upon you, I **w.** put more to your yoke:
2Ch 10:11 but I **w.** chastise you with scorpions.
2Ch 10:14 your yoke heavy, but I **w.** add thereto:
2Ch 10:14 but I **w.** chastise you with scorpions.
2Ch 12:7 therefore I **w.** not destroy them,
2Ch 12:7 I **w.** grant them some deliverance;
2Ch 15:2 if ye seek him, he **w.** be found of you;
2Ch 15:2 if ye forsake him, he **w.** forsake you.
2Ch 18:3 and **w.** be with thee in the war.
2Ch 18:5 for God **w.** deliver it into the king's
2Ch 18:13 what my God saith, that **w.** I speak.
2Ch 18:20 the Lord, and said, I **w.** entice him.
2Ch 18:21 I **w.** go out, and be a lying spirit
2Ch 18:29 Jehoshaphat, I **w.** disguise myself,
2Ch 18:29 and **w.** go to the battle; but put thou
2Ch 20:17 them: for the Lord **w.** be with you.
2Ch 21:14 a great plague **w.** the Lord smite thy
2Ch 28:23 them, therefore **w.** I sacrifice to them,
2Ch 30:6 he **w.** return to the remnant of you,
2Ch 30:9 **w.** not turn away his face from you,
2Ch 33:7 of Israel, **w.** I put my name for ever:
2Ch 33:8 Neither **w.** I any more remove the foot
2Ch 33:8 so that they **w.** take heed to do all that
2Ch 34:24 I **w.** bring evil upon this place,
2Ch 34:28 I **w.** gather thee to thy fathers,
2Ch 34:28 evil that I **w.** bring upon this place,
Ezr 4:3 together **w.** build unto the Lord God
Ezr 4:13 then **w.** they not pay toll, tribute,
Ezr 7:18 that do after the **w.** of your God. 7470
Ezr 7:26 And whosoever **w.** not do the law of
Ezr 10:4 we also **w.** be with thee: be of good
Ne 1:8 I **w.** scatter you abroad among the
Ne 1:9 yet **w.** I gather them from thence,
Ne 1:9 **w.** bring them unto the place that
Ne 2:19 ye do? **w.** ye rebel against the king?
Ne 2:20 The God of heaven, he **w.** prosper us;
Ne 2:20 we his servants **w.** arise and build:
Ne 4:2 Jews? **w.** they fortify themselves?
Ne 4:2 **w.** they sacrifice? **w.** they make an
Ne 4:2 **w.** they revive the stones out of the
Ne 4:12 return unto us they **w.** be upon you.
Ne 5:8 **w.** ye even sell your brethren? or shall
Ne 5:12 We **w.** restore them, and **w.** require
Ne 5:12 of them; so **w.** we do as thou sayest.
Ne 6:10 temple: for they **w.** come to slay thee;
Ne 6:10 in the night **w.** they come to slay thee.
Ne 6:11 save his life? I **w.** not go in.
Ne 10:39 **w.** not forsake the house of our God.
Ne 13:21 ye do so again, I **w.** lay hands on you.
Es 3:9 I **w.** pay ten thousand talents of silver
Es 4:16 and my maidens **w.** fast likewise;
Es 4:16 so **w.** I go in unto the king, which is not
Es 5:8 **w.** do to morrow as the king hath said.
Es 7:8 **W.** he force the queen also before me
Job 1:11 hath, and he **w.** curse thee to thy face.
Job 2:4 that a man hath **w.** he give for his life.
Job 2:5 flesh, and he **w.** curse thee to thy face.
Job 5:1 if there be any that **w.** answer thee;
Job 6:24 Teach me, and I **w.** hold my tongue:
Job 7:11 Therefore I **w.** not refrain my mouth;
Job 7:11 I **w.** speak in the anguish of my spirit;
Job 7:11 I **w.** complain in the bitterness of my
Job 8:20 God **w.** not cast away a perfect man,
Job 8:20 neither **w.** he help the evil doers:
Job 9:3 If he **w.** contend with him, he cannot
Job 9:12 who **w.** say unto him, What doest
Job 9:13 If God **w.** not withdraw his anger,
Job 9:18 **w.** not suffer me to take my breath,
Job 9:23 **w.** laugh at the trial of the innocent.
Job 9:27 If I say, I **w.** forget my complaint,
Job 9:27 I **w.** leave off my heaviness,
Job 10:1 I **w.** leave my complaint upon myself:
Job 10:1 I **w.** speak in the bitterness of my soul.
Job 10:2 I **w.** say unto God, Do not condemn
Job 10:15 righteous, yet **w.** I not lift up my head.
Job 11:11 also; **w.** he not then consider it?
Job 13:7 **W.** ye speak wickedly for God?
Job 13:8 **W.** ye accept his person? **w.** ye
Job 13:10 He **w.** surely reprove you, if ye do
Job 13:13 speak, and let come on me what **w.**
Job 13:15 Though he slay me, yet **w.** I trust him:
Job 13:15 but I **w.** maintain mine own ways
Job 13:19 Who is he that **w.** plead with me?
Job 13:20 then **w.** I not hide myself from thee.
Job 13:22 Then call thou, and I **w.** answer:
Job 14:7 be cut down, that it **w.** sprout again,
Job 14:7 tender branch thereof **w.** not cease.
Job 14:9 through the scent of water it **w.** bud,
Job 14:14 days of my appointed time **w.** I wait,
Job 14:15 Thou shalt call, and I **w.** answer thee:
Job 15:17 I **w.** shew thee, hear me; and that
Job 15:17 that which I have seen I **w.** declare;
Job 17:3 is he that **w.** strike hands with me?
Job 18:2 How long **w.** it be ere ye make an end
Job 18:2 mark, and afterwards we **w.** speak.
Job 19:2 How long **w.** ye vex my soul,
Job 19:5 If indeed ye **w.** magnify yourselves
Job 22:4 **W.** he reprove thee for fear of thee?
Job 22:4 **w.** he enter with thee into judgment?
Job 23:6 **W.** he plead against me with his great
Job 24:25 who **w.** make me a liar, and make my
Job 27:5 **w.** not remove mine integrity from me.
Job 27:6 I hold fast, and **w.** not let it go:
Job 27:9 **W.** God hear his cry when trouble
Job 27:10 **W.** he delight himself in the Almighty?
Job 27:10 **w.** he always call upon God?
Job 27:11 I **w.** teach you by the hand of God:
Job 27:11 with the Almighty **w.** I not conceal.
Job 30:24 he **w.** not stretch out his hand to the
Job 32:10 to me; I also **w.** shew mine opinion.
Job 32:14 neither **w.** I answer him with your
Job 32:17 I said, I **w.** answer my part, I also
Job 32:17 part, I also **w.** shew mine opinion.
Job 32:20 I **w.** speak, that I may be refreshed:
Job 32:20 I **w.** open my lips and answer.
Job 33:12 I **w.** answer thee, that God is greater
Job 33:26 and he **w.** be favourable unto him:
Job 33:26 **w.** render...man his righteousness.
Job 33:28 He **w.** deliver his soul from going
Job 33:31 hold thy peace, and I **w.** speak.
Job 34:12 Yea, surely God **w.** not do wickedly,
Job 34:12 **w.** the Almighty pervert judgment.
Job 34:23 For ye **w.** not lay upon man more than
Job 34:31 I **w.** not offend any more:
Job 34:32 I have done iniquity, I **w.** do no more.
Job 34:33 he **w.** recompense it, whether thou
Job 35:3 What advantage **w.** it be unto thee?
Job 35:4 I **w.** answer thee, and thy companions
Job 35:13 Surely God **w.** not hear vanity,
Job 35:13 neither **w.** the Almighty regard it.
Job 36:2 and I **w.** shew thee that I have yet to
Job 36:3 I **w.** fetch my knowledge from afar,
Job 36:3 **w.** ascribe righteousness to my Maker.
Job 36:19 **W.** he esteem thy riches? no, not gold,
Job 37:4 he **w.** not stay them when his voice is
Job 37:23 in plenty of justice: he **w.** not afflict.
Job 38:3 for I **w.** demand of thee, and answer
Job 39:9 **W.** the unicorn be willing to serve
Job 39:10 or **w.** he harrow the valleys after thee?
Job 39:12 that he **w.** bring home thy seed,
Job 40:4 I **w.** lay mine hand upon my mouth.
Job 40:5 have I spoken; but I **w.** not answer:
Job 40:5 twice; but I **w.** proceed no further.
Job 40:7 I **w.** demand of thee, and declare thou
Job 40:14 Then **w.** I also confess unto thee that
Job 41:3 **W.** he make many supplications unto
Job 41:3 **w.** he speak soft words unto thee?
Job 41:4 **W.** he make a covenant with thee?
Job 41:12 I **w.** not conceal his parts, nor his
Job 42:4 Hear, I beseech thee, and I **w.** speak:
Job 42:4 I **w.** demand of thee, and declare thou
Job 42:8 for him **w.** I accept: lest I deal with
Ps 2:7 I **w.** declare the decree: the Lord hath
Ps 3:6 I **w.** not be afraid of ten thousands of
Ps 4:2 **w.** ye turn my glory into shame?
Ps 4:2 how long **w.** ye love vanity, and seek
Ps 4:3 the Lord **w.** hear when I call unto him.
Ps 4:6 that say, Who **w.** shew us any good?
Ps 4:8 I **w.** both lay me down in peace,
Ps 5:2 and my God: for unto thee **w.** I pray.
Ps 5:3 in the morning **w.** direct my prayer
Ps 5:3 my prayer unto thee, and **w.** look up.
Ps 5:6 the Lord **w.** abhor the bloody and
Ps 5:7 I **w.** come unto thy house in the
Ps 5:7 and in thy fear **w.** I worship toward
Ps 6:9 the Lord **w.** receive my prayer.
Ps 7:12 If he turn not, he **w.** whet his sword;
Ps 7:17 I **w.** praise the Lord according to his
Ps 7:17 **w.** sing praise to the name of the Lord
Ps 9:1 I **w.** praise thee, O Lord, with my
Ps 9:1 I **w.** shew forth all thy marvellous
Ps 9:2 I **w.** be glad and rejoice in thee:
Ps 9:2 I **w.** sing praise to thy name, O thou
Ps 9:9 The Lord also **w.** be a refuge for the
Ps 9:10 thy name **w.** put their trust in thee:
Ps 9:14 Zion: I **w.** rejoice in thy salvation.
Ps 10:4 countenance, **w.** not seek after God:
Ps 10:11 hideth his face; he **w.** never see it.
Ps 12:4 said, With our tongue **w.** we prevail;
Ps 12:5 needy, now **w.** I arise, saith the Lord;
Ps 12:5 I **w.** set him in safety from him that
Ps 13:6 I **w.** sing unto the Lord, because he
Ps 16:4 offerings of blood **w.** I not offer,
Ps 16:7 I **w.** bless the Lord, who hath given
Ps 17:15 I **w.** behold thy face in righteousness:
Ps 18:1 I **w.** love thee, O Lord, my strength.
Ps 18:2 my strength, in whom I **w.** trust;
Ps 18:3 I **w.** call upon the Lord, who is worthy
Ps 18:28 my God **w.** enlighten my darkness.
Ps 18:49 Therefore **w.** I give thanks unto thee,
Ps 20:5 We **w.** rejoice in thy salvation, and in
Ps 20:5 name of our God we **w.** set up our
Ps 20:6 **w.** hear him from his holy heaven
Ps 20:7 **w.** remember the name of the Lord
Ps 21:13 so **w.** we sing and praise thy power.
Ps 22:22 I **w.** declare thy name unto my
Ps 22:22 of the congregation **w.** I praise thee.
Ps 22:25 I **w.** pay my vows before them that
Ps 23:4 shadow of death, I **w.** fear no evil:
Ps 23:6 I **w.** dwell in the house of the Lord for
Ps 25:8 **w.** he teach sinners in the way.
Ps 25:9 the meek **w.** he guide in judgment:
Ps 25:9 and the meek **w.** he teach his way.
Ps 25:14 and he **w.** shew them his covenant.
Ps 26:4 neither **w.** I go in with dissemblers.
Ps 26:5 doers; and **w.** not sit with the wicked.
Ps 26:6 I **w.** wash mine hands in innocency:
Ps 26:6 so **w.** I compass thine altar, O Lord:
Ps 26:11 for me, I **w.** walk in mine integrity:
Ps 26:12 the congregations **w.** I bless the Lord.
Ps 27:3 against me, in this **w.** I be confident.
Ps 27:4 of the Lord, that **w.** I seek after;
Ps 27:6 therefore **w.** I offer in his tabernacle
Ps 27:6 I **w.** sing, yea, I **w.** sing praises unto
Ps 27:8 unto thee, Thy face, Lord, **w.** I seek.
Ps 27:10 me, then the Lord **w.** take me up.
Ps 27:12 over unto the **w.** of mine enemies: 5315
Ps 28:1 Unto thee **w.** I cry, O Lord my rock;
Ps 28:7 and with my song **w.** I praise him.

Ps 29:11 The Lord w. give strength unto his
Ps 29:11 Lord w. bless his people with peace.
Ps 30:1 I w. extol thee, O Lord; for thou hast
Ps 30:12 I w. give thanks unto thee for ever.
Ps 31:7 I w. be glad and rejoice in thy mercy:
Ps 32:5 I w. confess my transgressions unto
Ps 32:8 I w. instruct thee and teach thee in
Ps 32:8 go: I w. guide thee with mine eye.
Ps 34:1 I w. bless the Lord at all times: his
Ps 34:11 I w. teach you the fear of the Lord.
Ps 35:18 I w. give thee thanks in the great
Ps 35:18 I w. praise thee among much people.
Ps 37:33 Lord w. not leave him in his hand,
Ps 38:18 For I w. declare mine iniquity;
Ps 38:18 iniquity; I w. be sorry for my sin.
Ps 39:1 I said, I w. take heed to my ways, that
Ps 39:1 I w. keep my mouth with a bridle,
Ps 40:8 I delight to do thy w., O my God: 7522
Ps 41:1 the Lord w. deliver him in time of
Ps 41:2 The Lord w. preserve him, and
Ps 41:2 him unto the w. of his enemies. 5315
Ps 41:3 Lord w. strengthen him upon the bed
Ps 42:6 w. I remember thee from the land of
Ps 42:8 Lord w. command his lovingkindness
Ps 42:9 I w. say unto god my rock, Why hast
Ps 43:4 Then w. I go unto the altar of God,
Ps 43:4 upon the harp w. I praise thee, O God
Ps 44:5 Through thee w. we push down our
Ps 44:5 through thy name w. we tread them
Ps 44:6 For I w. not trust in my bow, neither
Ps 45:17 w. make thy name to be remembered
Ps 46:2 Therefore w. not we fear, though the
Ps 46:10 I w. be exalted among the heathen,
Ps 46:10 heathen, I w. be exalted in the earth.
Ps 48:8 God w. establish it for ever. Selah.
Ps 48:14 he w. be our guide even unto death.
Ps 49:4 I w. incline mine ear to a parable:
Ps 49:4 I w. open my dark saying upon the
Ps 49:15 But God w. redeem my soul from
Ps 49:18 and men w. praise thee, when thou
Ps 50:7 Hear, O my people, and I w. speak;
Ps 50:7 Israel, and I w. testify against thee:
Ps 50:8 I w. not reprove thee for thy sacrifices
Ps 50:9 I w. take no bullock out of thy house,
Ps 50:13 W. I eat the flesh of bulls, or drink
Ps 50:15 w. deliver thee, and thou shalt glorify
Ps 50:21 but I w. reprove thee, and set them in
Ps 50:23 aright w. I shew the salvation of God.
Ps 51:13 w. I teach transgressors thy ways;
Ps 52:9 I w. praise thee for ever, because thou
Ps 52:9 and I w. wait on thy name; for it is
Ps 54:6 w. freely sacrifice unto thee:
Ps 54:6 I w. praise thy name, O Lord;
Ps 55:16 As for me, I w. call upon God; and the
Ps 55:17 at noon, w. I pray, and cry aloud:
Ps 55:23 their days; but I w. trust in thee.
Ps 56:3 time I am afraid, I w. trust in thee.
Ps 56:4 In God I w. praise his word, in God I
Ps 56:4 I w. not fear what flesh can do unto
Ps 56:10 In God w. I praise his word:
Ps 56:10 in the Lord w. I praise his word.
Ps 56:11 I w. not be afraid what man can do.
Ps 56:12 God: I w. render praises unto thee.
Ps 57:1 of thy wings w. I make my refuge,
Ps 57:2 I w. cry unto God most high; unto
Ps 57:7 is fixed: I w. sing and give praise.
Ps 57:8 and harp: I myself w. awake early.
Ps 57:9 I w. praise thee, O Lord, among the
Ps 57:9 I w. sing unto thee among the nations.
Ps 58:5 w. not hearken to the voice of
Ps 59:9 of his strength w. I wait upon thee:
Ps 59:16 but I w. sing of thy power: yea,
Ps 59:16 I w. sing aloud of thy mercy in the
Ps 59:17 Unto thee, O my strength, w. I sing:
Ps 60:6 I w. rejoice, I w. divide Shechem, and
Ps 60:8 over Edom w. I cast out my shoe:
Ps 60:9 Who w. bring me into the strong city?
Ps 60:9 city? who w. lead me unto Edom?
Ps 61:2 end of the earth w. I cry unto thee,
Ps 61:4 I w. abide in thy tabernacle for ever:
Ps 61:4 I w. trust in the covert of thy wings.
Ps 61:8 So w. I sing praise unto thy name for
Ps 62:3 How long w. ye imagine mischief
Ps 63:1 art my god; early w. I seek thee:
Ps 63:4 Thus w. I bless thee while I live:
Ps 63:4 I w. lift up my hands in thy name.
Ps 63:7 the shadow of thy wings w. I rejoice.
Ps 66:13 I w. go into thy house with burnt
Ps 66:13 offerings: I w. pay thee my vows,
Ps 66:15 I w. offer unto thee burnt sacrifices of
Ps 66:15 rams: I w. offer bullocks with goats.
Ps 66:16 and I w. declare what he hath done
Ps 66:18 my heart, the Lord w. not hear me.
Ps 68:16 yea, the Lord w. dwell in it for ever.
Ps 68:22 said, I w. bring again from Bashan,
Ps 68:22 I w. bring my people again from the
Ps 69:30 I w. praise the name of God with a
Ps 69:30 w. magnify him with thanksgiving.
Ps 69:35 For God w. save Zion, and w. build
Ps 71:14 But I w. hope continually, and
Ps 71:14 and w. yet praise thee more and more.
Ps 71:16 I w. go in the strength of the Lord
Ps 71:16 I w....mention of thy righteousness,
Ps 71:22 I w. also praise thee with the psaltery,
Ps 71:22 unto thee w. I sing with the harp,
Ps 73:15 If I say, I w. speak thus; behold, I
Ps 75:2 the congregation I w. judge uprightly.
Ps 75:9 I w. declare for ever; I w. sing praises
Ps 75:10 horns of the wicked also w. I cut off;
Ps 77:7 W. the Lord cast off for ever? and
Ps 77:7 w. he be favourable no more?
Ps 77:10 I w. remember the years of the right
Ps 77:11 I w. remember the works of the Lord:
Ps 77:11 I w. remember thy wonders of old.
Ps 77:12 I w. meditate also of all thy work,
Ps 78:2 I w. open my mouth in a parable:
Ps 78:2 I w. utter dark sayings of old:
Ps 78:4 We w. not hide them from their
Ps 79:13 pasture w. give thee thanks for ever:
Ps 79:13 we w. shew forth thy praise to all
Ps 80:18 So w. not we go back from thee:
Ps 80:18 us, and we w. call upon thy name.
Ps 81:8 people, and I w. testify unto thee:
Ps 81:10 open thy mouth wide, and I w. fill it.
Ps 82:2 How long w. ye judge unjustly,
Ps 82:5 know not, neither w. they understand;
Ps 84:4 house; they w. be still praising thee.
Ps 84:11 the Lord w. give grace and glory:
Ps 84:11 no good thing w. he withhold from
Ps 85:8 I w. hear what God the Lord w. speak:
Ps 85:8 for he w. speak peace unto his people,
Ps 86:7 day of my trouble I w. call upon thee:
Ps 86:11 way, O Lord; I w. walk in thy truth:
Ps 86:12 I w. praise thee, O Lord my God,
Ps 86:12 I w. glorify thy name for evermore.
Ps 87:4 I w. make mention of Rahab and
Ps 89:1 I w. sing of the mercies of the Lord
Ps 89:1 w. I make known thy faithfulness
Ps 89:4 Thy seed w. I establish for ever,
Ps 89:23 And I w. beat down his foes before his
Ps 89:25 I w. set his hand also in the sea,
Ps 89:27 Also I w. make him my firstborn,
Ps 89:28 My mercy w. I keep for him for
Ps 89:29 His seed also w. I make to endure
Ps 89:32 Then w. I visit their transgression
Ps 89:33 my lovingkindness w. I not utterly
Ps 89:34 My covenant w. I not break,
Ps 89:35 holiness that I w. not lie unto David.
Ps 91:2 I w. say of the Lord, He is my refuge
Ps 91:2 my God; in him w. I trust.
Ps 91:14 upon me, therefore w. I deliver him:
Ps 91:14 I w. set him on high, because he hath
Ps 91:15 call upon me, and I w. answer him:
Ps 91:15 I w. be with him in trouble;
Ps 91:15 I w. deliver him, and honour him.
Ps 91:16 With long life w. I satisfy him,
Ps 92:4 w. triumph in the works of thy hands.
Ps 94:8 and ye fools, when w. ye be wise?
Ps 94:14 For the Lord w. not cast off his people,
Ps 94:14 neither w. he forsake his interitance.
Ps 94:16 Who w. rise up for me against the
Ps 94:16 or who w. stand up for me against
Ps 95:7 To day if ye w. hear his voice,
Ps 101:1 I w. sing of mercy and judgment:
Ps 101:1 unto thee, O Lord, w. I sing.
Ps 101:2 I w. behave myself wisely in a perfect
Ps 101:2 I w. walk within my house with a
Ps 101:3 I w. set no wicked thing before mine
Ps 101:4 I w. not know a wicked person.
Ps 101:5 his neighbour, him w. I cut off:
Ps 101:5 and a proud heart w. not I suffer.
Ps 101:8 I w. early destroy all the wicked
Ps 102:17 He w. regard the prayer of the
Ps 103:9 He w. not always chide: neither
Ps 103:9 neither w. he keep his anger for ever.
Ps 104:33 w. sing unto the Lord as long as I live:
Ps 104:33 I w. sing praise to my God while I have
Ps 104:34 be sweet: I w. be glad in the Lord.
Ps 105:11 Unto thee w. I give the land of Canaan,
Ps 107:43 is wise, and w. observe these things,
Ps 108:1 I w. sing and give priase, even with
Ps 108:2 and harp: I myself w. awake early.
Ps 108:3 I w. praise thee, O Lord, among the
Ps 108:3 and I w. sing priases unto thee
Ps 108:7 I w. rejoice, I w. divide Shechem,
Ps 108:9 over Edom w. I cast out my shoe;
Ps 108:9 my shoe: over Philistia w. I triumph.
Ps 108:10 Who w. bring me into the strong city?
Ps 108:10 who w. lead me into Edom?
Ps 109:30 I w. greatly praise the Lord with my
Ps 109:30 I w. praise him among the multitude.
Ps 110:4 Lord hath sworn, and w. not repent,
Ps 111:1 I w. praise the Lord with my whole
Ps 111:5 w. ever be mindful of his covenant.
Ps 112:5 he w. guide his affairs with discretion.
Ps 115:12 he w. bless us; he w. bless the house
Ps 115:12 he w. bless the house of Aaron.
Ps 115:13 He w. bless them that fear the Lord,
Ps 115:18 But we w. bless the Lord from this
Ps 116:2 therefore w. I call upon him as long
Ps 116:9 I w. walk before the Lord in the land.
Ps 116:13 I w. take the cup of salvation, and call
Ps 116:14 I w. pay my vows unto the Lord now
Ps 116:17 I w. offer to thee the sacrifice of
Ps 116:17 and w. call upon the name of the Lord.
Ps 116:18 I w. pay my vows unto the Lord now
Ps 118:6 The Lord is on my side; I w. not fear:
Ps 118:10 name of the Lord w. I destroy them.
Ps 118:11, 12 name of the Lord I w. destroy them.
Ps 118:19 I w. go into them, and I w. praise the
Ps 118:21 I w. praise thee: for thou hast heard
Ps 118:24 made; we w. rejoice and be glad in it.
Ps 118:28 Thou art my God, and I w. praise thee:
Ps 118:28 thou art my god, I w. exalt thee.
Ps 119:7 I w. praise thee with uprightness
Ps 119:8 I w. keep thy statutes: O forsake me
Ps 119:15 I w. meditate in thy precepts,
Ps 119:16 I w. delight myself in thy statutes:
Ps 119:16 statutes: I w. not forget thy word.
Ps 119:32 I w. run the way of...commandments,
Ps 119:45 And I w. walk at liberty; for I seek
Ps 119:46 I w. speak of thy testimonies also
Ps 119:46 kings, and w. not be ashamed.
Ps 119:47 And I w. delight myself in thy
Ps 119:48 My hands also w. I lift up unto thy
Ps 119:48 and I w. meditate in thy statutes.
Ps 119:62 At midnight I w. rise to give thanks
Ps 119:69 but I w. keep thy precepts with my
Ps 119:74 They that fear thee w. be glad when
Ps 119:78 but I w. meditate in thy precepts.
Ps 119:93 I w. never forget thy precepts:
Ps 119:95 but I w. consider thy testimonies.
Ps 119:106 I have sworn, and I w. perform it,
Ps 119:106 w. keep thy righteous judgments.
Ps 119:115 for I w. keep thy commandments of
Ps 119:117 I w. have respect unto thy statutes
Ps 119:134 of man: so w. I keep thy precepts.
Ps 119:145 me, O Lord: I w. keep thy statutes.
Ps 121:1 I w. lift up mine eyes unto the hills,
Ps 121:3 He w. not suffer thy foot to be moved:
Ps 121:3 he that keepeth thee w. not slumber.
Ps 122:8 I w. now say, Peace be within thee.
Ps 122:9 the Lord our God I w. seek thy good.
Ps 132:3 I w. not come into the tabernacle
Ps 132:4 I w. not give sleep to mine eyes,
Ps 132:7 We w. go into his tabernacles:
Ps 132:7 we w. worship at his footstool.
Ps 132:11 unto David; he w. not turn from it;
Ps 132:11 of thy body w. I set upon thy throne.
Ps 132:12 If thy children w. keep my covenant
Ps 132:14 here w. I dwell; for I have desired it.
Ps 132:15 I w. abundantly bless her provision:
Ps 132:15 I w. satisfy her poor with bread.
Ps 132:16 I w. also clothe her priest with
Ps 132:17 There w. I make the home of David
Ps 132:18 His enemies w. I clothe with shame:
Ps 135:14 For the Lord w. judge his people,
Ps 135:14 w. repent himself concerning his
Ps 138:1 I w. praise thee with my whole heart:
Ps 138:1 before the gods w. I sing praise unto

Ps	138:2	I w. worship toward thy holy temple,
Ps	138:8	Lord w. perfect that which concerneth
Ps	139:14	I w. praise thee; for I am fearfully
Ps	140:12	that the Lord w. maintain the cause
Ps	143:10	Teach me to do thy w.; for thou 7522
Ps	144:9	I w. sing a new song unto thee, O God
Ps	144:9	ten strings w. I sing praises unto thee.
Ps	145:1	I w. extol thee, my God, O king;
Ps	145:1	and I w. bless thy name for ever and
Ps	145:2	Every day w. I bless thee; and I
Ps	145:2	and I w. praise thy name for ever and
Ps	145:5	I w. speak of the glorious honour
Ps	145:6	acts: and I w. declare thy greatness.
Ps	145:19	He w. fulfill the desire of them that
Ps	145:19	w. hear their cry, and w. save them.
Ps	145:20	but all the wicked w. he destroy.
Ps	146:2	While I live w. I praise the Lord:
Ps	146:2	I w. sing praises unto my God while I
Ps	149:4	w. beautify the meek with salvation.
Pr	1:5	A wise man w. hear,
Pr	1:5	and w. increase learning;
Pr	1:22	ye simple ones, w. ye love simplicity?
Pr	1:23	I w. pour out my spirit unto you,
Pr	1:23	I w. make known my words unto you.
Pr	1:26	I also w. laugh at your calamity;
Pr	1:26	I w. mock when your face cometh;
Pr	1:28	call upon me, but I w. not answer;
Pr	3:28	come again, and to mrrow I w. give;
Pr	6:26	adulteress w. hunt for...precious life.
Pr	6:34	w. not spare in the day for vengeance.
Pr	6:35	He w. not regard any ransom;
Pr	6:35	neither w. he rest content,
Pr	7:20	w. come home at the day appointed.
Pr	8:6	for I w. speak of excellent things;
Pr	8:21	and I w. fill their treasures.
Pr	9:8	a wise man, and he w. love thee.
Pr	9:9	to a wise man, and he w. be yet wiser:
Pr	9:9	man, and he w. increase in learning.
Pr	10:3	The Lord w. not suffer the soul of the
Pr	10:8	in heart w. receive commandments:
Pr	12:2	man of wicked devices w. he condemn.
Pr	14:5	A faithful witness w. not lie:
Pr	14:5	but a false witness w. utter lies.
Pr	15:12	neither w. he go unto the wise.
Pr	15:25	The Lord w. destroy the house of the
Pr	15:25	w. establish the border of the widow.
Pr	16:14	of death: but a wise man w. pacify it.
Pr	18:14	a man w. sustain his infirmity:
Pr	19:6	w. intreat the favour of the prince:
Pr	19:17	he hath given w. he pay him again.
Pr	19:24	and w. not so much as bring it to his
Pr	19:25	a scorner, and the simple w. beware:
Pr	19:25	and he w. understand knowledge.
Pr	20:3	strife: but every fool w. be meddling.
Pr	20:4	The sluggard w. not plow by reason of
Pr	20:5	man of understanding w. draw it out.
Pr	20:6	Most men w. proclaim every one his
Pr	20:22	Say not thou, I w. recompense evil;
Pr	21:1	he turneth it whithersoever he w. 2654
Pr	22:6	he is old, he w. not depart from it.
Pr	22:23	For the Lord w. plead their cause,
Pr	23:9	he w. despise the wisdom of thy words,
Pr	23:35	shall I awake? I w. seek it yet again.
Pr	24:29	w. do so to him as he hath done to me:
Pr	24:29	I w. render to the man according to
Pr	26:27	rolleth a stone, it w. return upon him.
Pr	27:22	yet w. not his foolishness depart
Pr	28:8	gather it for him that w. pity the poor.
Pr	28:21	piece of bread that man w. transgress.
Pr	29:19	servant w. not be corrected by words:
Pr	29:19	he understand he w. not answer.
Pr	31:12	She w. do him good and not evil all
Ec	2:1	Go to now, I w. prove thee with mirth,
Ec	4:10	fall, the one w. lift up his fellow:
Ec	4:13	who w. no more be admonished. 3045
Ec	5:12	abundance of the rich w. not suffer
Ec	7:2	and the living w. lay it to his heart.
Ec	7:23	I w. be wise; but it was far from me.
Ec	10:11	Surely the serpent w. bite without
Ec	10:12	lips of a fool w. swallow up himself.
Ec	11:9	God w. bring thee into judgment.
Ca	1:4	Draw me, we w. run after thee: the
Ca	1:4	we w. be glad and rejoice in thee,
Ca	1:4	w. remember thy love more than wine:
Ca	1:11	We w. make thee borders of gold with
Ca	3:2	I w. rise now, and go about the city in
Ca	3:2	I w. seek him whom my soul loveth:
Ca	4:6	I w. get me to the mountain of myrrh,
Ca	6:13	What w. ye see in the Shulamite?
Ca	7:8	I said, I w. go up to the palm tree,
Ca	7:8	I w. take hold of the boughs thereof:
Ca	7:12	forth: there w. I give thee my loves.
Ca	8:9	wall, we w. build upon her a palace of
Ca	8:9	w. inclose her with boards of cedar.
Isa	1:5	ye w. revolt more and more: the
Isa	1:15	hands, I w. hide mine eyes from you;
Isa	1:15	ye make many prayers, I w. not hear;
Isa	1:24	Ah, I w. ease me of mine adversaries,
Isa	1:25	I w. turn my hand upon thee, and
Isa	1:26	And I w. restore thy judges as at the
Isa	2:3	and he w. teach us of his ways,
Isa	2:3	and we w. walk in his paths: for out
Isa	3:4	I w. give children to be their princes,
Isa	3:7	swear, saying, I w. not be an healer;
Isa	3:14	Lord w. enter into judgment with the
Isa	3:17	the Lord w. smite with a scab the
Isa	3:17	and the Lord w. discover their secret
Isa	3:18	Lord w. take away the bravery of their
Isa	4:1	We w. eat our own bread, and wear
Isa	4:5	And the Lord w. create upon every
Isa	5:1	Now w. I sing my wellbeloved a song
Isa	5:5	I w. tell you what I w. do to my
Isa	5:5	I w. take away the hedge thereof, and
Isa	5:6	And I w. lay it waste: it shall not be
Isa	5:6	I w. also command the clouds that
Isa	5:26	And he w. lift up an ensign to the
Isa	5:26	and w. hiss unto them from the end of
Isa	6:8	shall I send, and who w. go for us?
Isa	7:9	If ye w. not believe, surely ye shall
Isa	7:12	I w. not ask, neither w. I tempt,
Isa	7:13	men, but w. ye weary my God also?
Isa	8:17	I w. wait upon the Lord, that hideth
Isa	8:17	house of Jacob, and I w. look for him.
Isa	9:7	of the Lord of hosts w. perform this.
Isa	9:10	but we w. build with hewn stones:
Isa	9:10	but we w. change them into cedars.
Isa	9:14	the Lord w. cut off from Israel head
Isa	10:3	And what w. ye do in the day of
Isa	10:3	from far? to whom w. ye flee for help?
Isa	10:3	and where w. ye leave your glory?
Isa	10:6	I w. send him against an hypocritical
Isa	10:6	of my wrath w. I give him a charge,
Isa	10:12	I w. punish the fruit of the stout heart
Isa	12:1	shalt say, O Lord, I w. praise thee:
Isa	12:2	I w. trust, and not be afraid:
Isa	13:11	And I w. punish the world for their
Isa	13:11	I w. cause the arrogancy of the proud
Isa	13:11	and w. lay low the haughtiness of the
Isa	13:12	I w. make a man more precious than
Isa	13:13	Therefore I w. shake the heavens, and
Isa	13:17	I w. stir up the Medes against them,
Isa	14:1	For the Lord w. have mercy on Jacob,
Isa	14:1	and w. yet choose Israel, and set
Isa	14:13	thine heart, I w. ascend into heaven,
Isa	14:13	I w. exalt my throne above the stars of
Isa	14:13	I w. sit also upon the mount of the
Isa	14:14	I w. ascend above the heights of the
Isa	14:14	I w. be like the most High.
Isa	14:22	For I w. rise up against them, saith
Isa	14:23	I w. also make it a possession for the
Isa	14:23	I w. sweep it with the besom of
Isa	14:25	That I w. break the Assyrian in my
Isa	14:30	I w. kill thy root with famine, and he
Isa	15:9	for I w. bring more upon Dimon, lions
Isa	16:9	I w. bewail with the weeping of Jazer
Isa	16:9	I w. water thee with my tears, O
Isa	18:4	Lord said unto me, I w. take my rest,
Isa	18:4	and I w. consider in my dwelling place
Isa	19:2	I w. set the Egyptians against the
Isa	19:3	and I w. destroy the counsel thereof:
Isa	19:4	And the Egyptians w. I give over into
Isa	21:12	if ye w. enquire, enquire ye: return,
Isa	22:4	I w. weep bitterly, labour not to
Isa	22:17	Lord w. carry thee away with a
Isa	22:17	and w. surely cover thee.
Isa	22:18	He w. surely violently turn and toss
Isa	22:19	And I w. drive thee from thy station,
Isa	22:20	I w. call my servant Eliakim the son
Isa	22:21	I w. clothe him with thy robe, and
Isa	22:21	I w. commit thy government into his
Isa	22:22	the key...w. I lay upon his shoulder;
Isa	22:23	And I w. fasten him as a nail in a sure
Isa	23:17	that the Lord w. visit Tyre, and she
Isa	25:1	I w. exalt thee, I w. praise thy name;
Isa	25:7	he w. destroy in this mountain the
Isa	25:8	He w. swallow up death in victory;
Isa	25:8	Lord God w. wipe away tears from off
Isa	25:9	waited for him, and he w. save us:
Isa	25:9	him, he w. be glad and rejoice in his
Isa	26:1	salvation w. God appoint for walls and
Isa	26:9	spirit within me w. I seek thee early:
Isa	26:9	of the world w. learn righteousness.
Isa	26:10	yet w. he not learn righteousness:
Isa	26:10	of uprightness w. he deal unjustly,
Isa	26:10	w. not behold the majesty of the Lord.
Isa	26:11	thy hand is lifted up, they w. not see:
Isa	26:13	by thee only w. we make mention of
Isa	27:3	keep it; I w. water it every moment:
Isa	27:3	hurt it, I w. keep it night and day.
Isa	27:11	them w. not have mercy on them,
Isa	27:11	formed them w. shew them no favour.
Isa	28:11	another tongue w. he speak to this
Isa	28:17	Judgment also w. I lay to the line, and
Isa	28:28	he w. not ever be threshing it, nor
Isa	29:2	Yet I w. distress Ariel, and there shall
Isa	29:3	I w. camp against thee round about,
Isa	29:3	and w. lay siege against thee with a
Isa	29:3	and I w. raise forts against thee.
Isa	29:14	I w. proceed to do a marvellous work
Isa	30:6	they w. carry their riches upon the
Isa	30:9	children that w. not hear the law of 14
Isa	30:16	said, No; for we w. flee upon horses;
Isa	30:16	We w. ride upon the swift; therefore;
Isa	30:18	And therefore w. the Lord wait, that
Isa	30:18	you, and therefore w. he be exalted,
Isa	30:19	he w. be very gracious unto thee at
Isa	30:19	he shall hear it, he w. answer thee.
Isa	30:32	and in battles of shaking w. he fight
Isa	31:2	yet he also is wise, and w. bring evil,
Isa	31:2	evil, and w. not call back his words:
Isa	31:2	but w. arise against the house of the
Isa	31:4	he w. not be afraid of their voice, nor
Isa	31:5	so w. the Lord of hosts defend
Isa	31:5	defending also he w. deliver it; and
Isa	31:5	and passing over he w. preserve it.
Isa	32:6	For the vile person w. speak villany,
Isa	32:6	and his heart w. work iniquity, to
Isa	32:6	he w. cause the drink of the thirsty to
Isa	33:10	Now w. I arise, saith the Lord; now
Isa	33:10	w. I be exalted; now w. I lift up
Isa	33:21	Lord w. be unto us a place of broad
Isa	33:22	the Lord is our king; he w. save us.
Isa	35:4	your God w. come with vengeance,
Isa	35:4	recompence; he w. come and save you.
Isa	36:6	it w. go into his hand, and pierce it:
Isa	36:8	I w. give thee two thousand horses,
Isa	36:15	saying, The Lord w. surely deliver us;
Isa	36:18	you, saying, The Lord w. deliver us.
Isa	37:4	Lord thy God w. hear the words of
Isa	37:4	and w. reprove the words which the
Isa	37:7	I w. send a blast upon him, and he shall
Isa	37:7	I w. cause him to fall by the sword in
Isa	37:24	I w. cut down the tall cedars thereof,
Isa	37:24	I w. enter into the height of his border,
Isa	37:29	w. I put my hook in thy nose,
Isa	37:29	I w. turn thee back by the way by
Isa	37:35	For I w. defend this city to save it for
Isa	38:5	I w. add unto thy days fifteen years.
Isa	38:6	And I w. deliver thee and this city
Isa	38:6	Assyria: and I w. defend this city,
Isa	38:7	Lord w. do this thing that he hath
Isa	38:8	I w. bring again the shadow of the
Isa	38:12	he w. cut me off with pining sickness:
Isa	38:13	as a lion, so w. he break all my bones:
Isa	38:20	we w. sing my songs to the stringed
Isa	40:10	the Lord God w. come with strong
Isa	40:18	To whom then w. ye liken God? or
Isa	40:18	or what likeness w. ye compare unto
Isa	40:20	chooseth a tree that w. not rot;
Isa	40:25	To whom then w. he liken me, or shall
Isa	41:10	I w. strengthen thee;
Isa	41:10	yea, I w. help thee;
Isa	41:10	I w. uphold thee with the right hand of
Isa	41:13	Lord thy God w. hold thy right hand,
Isa	41:13	unto thee, Fear not; I w. help thee.
Isa	41:14	I w. help thee, saith the Lord, and thy
Isa	41:15	I w. make thee a new sharp threshing
Isa	41:17	I the Lord w. hear them, I the God of

Isa	41:17	God of Israel **w.** not forsake them.
Isa	41:18	I **w.** open rivers in high places, and
Isa	41:18	I **w.** make the wilderness a pool of
Isa	41:19	I **w.** plant in the wilderness the cedar,
Isa	41:19	I **w.** set in the desert the fir tree, and
Isa	41:27	I **w.** give to Jerusalem one that
Isa	42:6	**w.** hold thine hand, and **w.** keep thee,
Isa	42:8	my glory **w.** I not give to another,
Isa	42:14	now **w.** I cry like a travailing woman;
Isa	42:14	I **w.** destroy and devour at once.
Isa	42:15	I **w.** make waste mountains and hills,
Isa	42:15	and I **w.** make the rivers islands, and
Isa	42:15	islands, and I **w.** dry up the pools
Isa	42:16	I **w.** bring the blind by a way that
Isa	42:16	I **w.** lead them in paths that they have
Isa	42:16	I **w.** make darkness light before them,
Isa	42:16	These things **w.** I do unto them, and
Isa	42:21	he **w.** magnify the law, and make it
Isa	42:23	Who among you **w.** give ear to this?
Isa	42:23	who **w.** hearken and hear for the time
Isa	43:2	the waters, I **w.** be with thee;
Isa	43:4	therefore **w.** I give men for thee, and
Isa	43:5	I **w.** bring thy seed from the east,
Isa	43:6	I **w.** say to the north, Give up; and to
Isa	43:13	hand: I **w.** work, and who shall let it?
Isa	43:19	Behold, I **w.** do a new thing; now it
Isa	43:19	I **w.**...make a way in the wilderness,
Isa	43:25	sake, and **w.** not remember thy sins.
Isa	44:2	from the womb, which **w.** help thee;
Isa	44:3	For I **w.** our water upon him that
Isa	44:3	I **w.** pour my spirit upon thy seed,
Isa	44:15	for he **w.** take thereof, and warm
Isa	44:26	and I **w.** raise up the decayed places
Isa	44:27	Be dry, and I **w.** dry up thy rivers:
Isa	45:1	and I **w.** loose the loins of kings,
Isa	45:2	I **w.** go before thee, and make the
Isa	45:2	I **w.** break in pieces the gates of brass,
Isa	45:3	**w.** give thee the treasures of darkness,
Isa	45:13	and I **w.** direct all his ways:
Isa	46:4	and even to hoar hairs **w.** I carry you:
Isa	46:4	carry you: I have made, and I **w.** bear;
Isa	46:4	even I **w.** carry, and **w.** deliver you.
Isa	46:5	To whom **w.** ye liken me, and make
Isa	46:10	stand, and I **w.** do all my pleasure:
Isa	46:11	spoken it, I **w.** also bring it to pass;
Isa	46:11	I have purposed it, I **w.** also do it.
Isa	46:13	**w.** place salvation in Zion for Israel
Isa	47:3	shall be seen: I **w.** take vengeance,
Isa	47:3	and I **w.** not meet thee as a man.
Isa	48:6	see all this; and **w.** not ye declare it?
Isa	48:9	name's sake **w.** I defer mine anger,
Isa	48:9	for my praise **w.** I refrain for thee,
Isa	48:11	even for mine own sake, **w.** I do it:
Isa	48:11	I **w.** not give my glory unto another.
Isa	48:14	he **w.** do his pleasure on Babylon,
Isa	49:3	O Israel, in whom I **w.** be glorified.
Isa	49:6	I **w.** also give thee for a light to the
Isa	49:8	and I **w.** preserve thee, and give thee
Isa	49:11	I **w.** make all my mountains a way,
Isa	49:13	**w.** have mercy upon his afflicted.
Isa	49:15	may forget, yet **w.** I not forget thee.
Isa	49:22	I **w.** lift up mine hand to the Gentiles,
Isa	49:25	**w.** contend with him that contendeth
Isa	49:25	with thee, and I **w.** save thy children.
Isa	49:26	And I **w.** feed them that oppress thee
Isa	50:7	For the Lord God **w.** help me;
Isa	50:8	me; who **w.** contend with thee?
Isa	50:9	Behold, the Lord God **w.** help me;
Isa	51:3	he **w.** comfort all her desolate places;
Isa	51:3	**w.** make her wilderness like Eden,
Isa	51:4	and I **w.** make my judgment to rest
Isa	51:23	But I **w.** put it into the hand of them
Isa	52:12	for the Lord God **w.** go before you;
Isa	52:12	God of Israel **w.** be your rereward.
Isa	53:12	Therefore **w.** I divide him a portion
Isa	54:7	with great mercies **w.** I gather thee.
Isa	54:8	everlasting kindness **w.** I have mercy
Isa	54:11	I **w.** lay thy stones with fair colours,
Isa	54:12	And I **w.** make thy windows of agates,
Isa	55:3	and I **w.** make an everlasting covenant
Isa	55:7	Lord, and he **w.** have mercy upon him;
Isa	55:7	our God, for he **w.** abundantly pardon.
Isa	56:5	unto them **w.** I give in mine house
Isa	56:5	I **w.** give them an everlasting name,
Isa	56:7	**w.** I bring to my holy mountain,
Isa	56:8	Yet **w.** I gather others to him, besides
Isa	56:12	Come ye, say they, I **w.** fetch wine,
Isa	56:12	we **w.** fill ourselves with strong drink;
Isa	57:12	I **w.** declare thy righteousness,
Isa	57:16	For I **w.** not contend for ever, neither
Isa	57:16	neither **w.** I be always wroth: for the
Isa	57:18	have seen his ways, and **w.** heal him:
Isa	57:18	I **w.** lead him also, and restore
Isa	57:19	saith the Lord; and I **w.** heal him.
Isa	58:14	and I **w.** cause thee to ride upon the
Isa	59:2	his face from you, that he **w.** not hear.
Isa	59:18	he **w.** repay, fury to his adversaries,
Isa	59:18	to the islands he **w.** repay recompence.
Isa	60:7	and I **w.** glorify the house of my glory,
Isa	60:12	and kingdom that **w.** not serve thee
Isa	60:13	**w.** make the place of my feet glorious.
Isa	60:15	I **w.** make thee an eternal excellency,
Isa	60:17	For brass I **w.** bring gold, and for iron
Isa	60:17	and for iron I **w.** bring silver, and for
Isa	60:17	I **w.** also make thy officers peace,
Isa	60:22	I the Lord **w.** hasten it in his time.
Isa	61:8	and I **w.** direct their work in truth,
Isa	61:8	I **w.** make an everlasting covenant
Isa	61:10	I **w.** greatly rejoice in the Lord,
Isa	61:11	the Lord God **w.** cause righteousness
Isa	62:1	For Zion's sake I **w.** not hold my peace,
Isa	62:1	and for Jerusalem's sake I **w.** not rest,
Isa	62:8	Surely I **w.** no more give thy corn to
Isa	63:3	for I **w.** tread them in mine anger,
Isa	63:3	and I **w.** stain all my raiment.
Isa	63:6	I **w.** tread down the people of mine
Isa	63:6	I **w.** bring down their strength to the
Isa	63:7	I **w.** mention the lovingkindnesses
Isa	63:8	my people, children that **w.** not lie:
Isa	65:6	I **w.** not...silence, but **w.** recompense
Isa	65:7	therefore **w.** I measure their former
Isa	65:8	so **w.** I do for my servants' sakes, that
Isa	65:9	I **w.** bring forth a seed out of Jacob,
Isa	65:12	**w.** I number you to the sword,
Isa	65:19	And I **w.** rejoice in Jerusalem,
Isa	65:24	that before they call, I **w.** answer;
Isa	65:24	they are yet speaking, I **w.** hear.
Isa	66:2	but to this man **w.** I look, even to him
Isa	66:4	I also **w.** choose their delusions,
Isa	66:4	and **w.** bring their fears upon them;
Isa	66:12	I **w.** extend peace to her like a river,
Isa	66:13	comforteth, so **w.** I comfort you;
Isa	66:15	the Lord **w.** come with fire, and with
Isa	66:16	and by his sword **w.** the Lord plead
Isa	66:18	I **w.** gather all nations and tongues;
Isa	66:19	And I **w.** set a sign among them,
Isa	66:19	I **w.** send those that escape of them
Isa	66:21	And I **w.** also take of them for priests
Isa	66:22	and the new earth, which I **w.** make.
Jer	1:12	for I **w.** hasten my word to perform it.
Jer	1:15	I **w.** call al the families of the
Jer	1:16	And I **w.** utter my judgments against
Jer	2:9	Wherefore I **w.** yet plead with you,
Jer	2:9	your children's children **w.** I plead.
Jer	2:20	and thou saidst, I **w.** not transgress;
Jer	2:24	all they that seek her **w.** not weary
Jer	2:25	strangers, and after them **w.** I go.
Jer	2:27	of their trouble they **w.** say, Arise,
Jer	2:29	Wherefore **w.** ye plead with me? ye all
Jer	2:31	lords; we **w.** come no more unto thee?
Jer	2:35	Behold, I **w.** plead with thee, because
Jer	3:5	**W.** he reserve his anger for ever?
Jer	3:5	**w.** he keep it to the end? Behold, thou
Jer	3:12	I **w.** not cause mine anger to fall upon
Jer	3:12	Lord, and I **w.** not keep anger for ever.
Jer	3:14	I **w.** take you one of a city, and two of
Jer	3:14	a family, and I **w.** bring you to Zion.
Jer	3:15	I **w.** give you pastors according to
Jer	3:22	and I **w.** heal your backslidings,
Jer	4:6	for I **w.** bring evil from the north,
Jer	4:12	also **w.** I give sentence against them.
Jer	4:27	desolate; yet **w.** I make a full end.
Jer	4:28	have purposed it, and **w.** not repent,
Jer	4:28	neither **w.** I turn back from it.
Jer	4:30	fair; thy lovers **w.** despise thee,
Jer	4:30	despise thee, they **w.** seek thy life.
Jer	5:1	seeketh the truth; and I **w.** pardon it.
Jer	5:5	I **w.** get me unto the great men,
Jer	5:5	and **w.** speak unto them; for they
Jer	5:14	I **w.** make my words in thy mouth
Jer	5:15	**w.** bring a nation upon you from far,
Jer	5:18	I **w.** not make a full end with you.
Jer	5:22	**w.** ye not tremble at my presence,
Jer	5:31	and what **w.** ye do in the end thereof?
Jer	6:11	I **w.** pour it out upon the children
Jer	6:12	for I **w.** stretch out my hand upon the
Jer	6:16	But they said, We **w.** not walk therein.
Jer	6:17	But they said, We **w.** not hearken.
Jer	6:19	I **w.** bring evil upon this people,
Jer	6:21	I **w.** lay stumblingblocks before this
Jer	7:3	I **w.** cause you to dwell in this place.
Jer	7:7	**w.** I cause you to dwell in this place,
Jer	7:9	**W.** ye steal, murder, and commit
Jer	7:14	Therefore **w.** I do unto this house,
Jer	7:15	And I **w.** cast you out of my sight,
Jer	7:16	to me: for I **w.** not hear thee.
Jer	7:23	Obey my voice, and I **w.** be your God,
Jer	7:27	but they **w.** not hearken to thee:
Jer	7:27	them; but they **w.** not answer thee.
Jer	7:34	**w.** I cause to cease from the cities
Jer	8:10	**w.** I give their wives unto others,
Jer	8:13	I **w.** surely consume them, saith the
Jer	8:17	I **w.** send serpents, cockatrices,
Jer	8:17	which **w.** not be charmed, and they
Jer	9:4	for every brother **w.** utterly supplant,
Jer	9:4	neighbour **w.** walk with slanders.
Jer	9:5	**w.** deceive every one his neighbour,
Jer	9:5	**w.** not speak the truth: they have
Jer	9:7	I **w.** melt them, and try them; for
Jer	9:10	For the mountains **w.** I take up a
Jer	9:11	I **w.** make Jerusalem heaps, and a
Jer	9:11	I **w.** make the cities of Judah desolate,
Jer	9:15	I **w.** feed them, even this people,
Jer	9:16	I **w.** scatter them also among the
Jer	9:16	I **w.** send a sword after them, till I
Jer	9:25	that I **w.** punish all them that are
Jer	10:18	I **w.** sling out the inhabitants of the
Jer	10:18	**w.** distress them, that they may find it
Jer	11:4	be my people, and I **w.** be your God:
Jer	11:8	I **w.** bring upon them all the words
Jer	11:11	I **w.** bring evil upon them, which they
Jer	11:11	unto me, I **w.** not hearken unto them.
Jer	11:14	for I **w.** not hear them in the time
Jer	11:22	of hosts, Behold, I **w.** punish them:
Jer	11:23	for I **w.** bring evil upon the men of
Jer	12:14	I **w.** pluck them out of their land,
Jer	12:15	I have plucked them out I **w.** return,
Jer	12:15	**w.** bring them again, every man to his
Jer	12:16	if they **w.** diligently learn the ways of
Jer	12:17	But if they **w.** not obey,
Jer	12:17	I **w.** utterly pluck and destroy
Jer	13:9	After this manner **w.** I mar the pride
Jer	13:13	I **w.** fill all the inhabitants of this
Jer	13:14	I **w.** dash them one against another,
Jer	13:14	I **w.** not pity, nor spare, nor have
Jer	13:17	But if ye **w.** not hear it, my soul shall
Jer	13:24	**w.** I scatter them as the stubble
Jer	13:26	**w.** I discover thy skirts upon thy face,
Jer	14:10	he **w.** now remember their iniquity,
Jer	14:12	they fast, I **w.** not hear their cry;
Jer	14:12	and an oblation, I **w.** not accept them:
Jer	14:12	I **w.** consume them by the sword, and
Jer	14:13	but I **w.** give you assured peace in
Jer	14:16	I **w.** pour their wickedness upon them.
Jer	14:22	God? therefore we **w.** wait upon thee:
Jer	15:3	I **w.** appoint over them four kinds,
Jer	15:4	I **w.** cause them to be removed into
Jer	15:6	therefore **w.** I stretch out my hand
Jer	15:7	I **w.** fan them with a fan in the gates
Jer	15:7	I **w.** bereave them of children,
Jer	15:7	I **w.** destroy my people, since they
Jer	15:9	residue of them **w.** I deliver to the
Jer	15:11	verily I **w.** cause the enemy to entreat
Jer	15:13	treasures **w.** I give to the spoil
Jer	15:14	I **w.** make thee to pass with thine
Jer	15:19	return, then **w.** I bring thee again,
Jer	15:20	I **w.** make thee unto this people as
Jer	15:21	I **w.** deliver thee out of the hand of
Jer	15:21	I **w.** redeem thee out of the hand of
Jer	16:9	I **w.** cause to cease out of this place
Jer	16:13	**w.** I cast you out of this land into
Jer	16:13	where I **w.** not shew you favour.
Jer	16:15	I **w.** bring them again into their land
Jer	16:16	I **w.** send for many fishers, saith the
Jer	16:16	after **w.** I send for many hunters, and
Jer	16:18	first I **w.** recompense their iniquity
Jer	16:21	I **w.** this once cause them to know,
Jer	16:21	I **w.** cause them to know mine hand

Jer 17:3 I w. give thy substance and all thy
Jer 17:4 I w. cause thee to serve thine enemies
Jer 17:27 But if ye w. not hearken unto me
Jer 17:27 then w. I kindle a fire in the gates
Jer 18:2 and there w. I cause thee to hear my
Jer 18:8 I w. repent of the evil that I thought
Jer 18:10 then w. I repent of the good,
Jer 18:12 but we w. walk after our own devices,
Jer 18:12 we w. every one do the imagination of
Jer 18:14 W. a man leave the snow of Lebanon
Jer 18:17 I w. scatter them as with an east wind
Jer 18:17 I w. shew them the back, and not the
Jer 19:3 I w. bring evil upon this place, the
Jer 19:7 I w. make void the counsel of Judah
Jer 19:7 I w. cause them to fall by the sword
Jer 19:7 their carcases w. I give to be meat for
Jer 19:8 I w. make this city desolate, and a
Jer 19:9 I w. cause them to eat the flesh of
Jer 19:11 Even so w. I break this people and
Jer 19:12 Thus w. I do unto this place, saith the
Jer 19:15 I w. bring upon this city and upon all
Jer 20:4 I w. make thee a terror to thyself,
Jer 20:4 I w. give all Judah into the hand of
Jer 20:5 I w. deliver all the strength of this
Jer 20:5 w. I give into the hand of their enemies,
Jer 20:9 I w. not make mention of him, nor
Jer 20:10 Report, say they, and we w. report it.
Jer 20:10 Peradventure he w. be enticed, and
Jer 21:2 if so be that the Lord w. deal with us
Jer 21:4 I w. turn back the weapons of war
Jer 21:4 I w. assemble them into the midst of
Jer 21:5 And I myself w. fight against you
Jer 21:6 I w. smite the inhabitants of this city,
Jer 21:7 I w. deliver Zedekiah king of Judah,
Jer 21:14 I w. punish you according to the fruit
Jer 21:14 and I w. kindle a fire in the forest
Jer 22:5 But if ye w. not hear these words, I
Jer 22:6 surely I w. make thee a wilderness,
Jer 22:7 I w. prepare destroyers against thee,
Jer 22:14 I w. build me a wide house and large
Jer 22:21 but thou saidst, I w. not hear.
Jer 22:25 And I w. give thee in the hand of them
Jer 22:26 I w. cast thee out, and thy mother
Jer 23:2 I w. visit upon you the evil of your
Jer 23:3 I w. gather the remnant of my flock
Jer 23:3 w. bring them again to their folds;
Jer 23:4 And I w. set up shepherds over them
Jer 23:5 that I w. raise unto David a righteous
Jer 23:12 for I w. bring evil upon them, even the
Jer 23:15 I w. feed them with wormwood, and
Jer 23:33 I w. even forsake you, saith the Lord.
Jer 23:34 w. even punish that man and his house
Jer 23:39 I, even I, w. utterly forget you,
Jer 23:39 and I w. forsake you, and the city that
Jer 23:40 I w. bring an everlasting reproach
Jer 24:5 so w. I acknowledge them that are
Jer 24:6 I w. set mine eyes upon them for
Jer 24:6 I w. bring them again to this land:
Jer 24:6 I w. build them, and not pull them
Jer 24:6 I w. plant them, and not pluck them
Jer 24:7 I w. give them an heart to know me,
Jer 24:7 be my people, and I w. be their God:
Jer 24:8 So w. I give Zedekiah the king of
Jer 24:9 I w. deliver them to be removed into
Jer 24:10 And I w. send the sword, the famine,
Jer 25:6 your hands; and I w. do you no hurt.
Jer 25:9 I w. send and take all the families
Jer 25:9 and w. bring them against this land,
Jer 25:9 and w. utterly destroy them, and
Jer 25:10 I w. take from them the voice of mirth,
Jer 25:12 that I w. punish the king of Babylon,
Jer 25:12 and w. make it perpetual desolations.
Jer 25:13 I w. bring upon that land all my words
Jer 25:14 I w. recompense them according to
Jer 25:16 sword that I w. send among them.
Jer 25:26 the sword which I w. send among you.
Jer 25:29 I w. call for a sword upon all the
Jer 25:31 nations: he w. plead with all flesh;
Jer 25:31 w. give them that are wicked to the
Jer 26:3 so be they w. hearken, and turn every
Jer 26:4 If ye w. not hearken to me, to walk
Jer 26:6 w. I make this house like Shiloh,
Jer 26:6 w. make this city a curse to all the
Jer 26:13 and the Lord w. repent him of the evil
Jer 27:8 w. not serve the same Nebuchadnezzar

Jer 27:8 w. not put their neck under the yoke
Jer 27:8 that nation w. I punish, saith the Lord,
Jer 27:11 those w. I let remain still in their own
Jer 27:13 Why w. ye die, thou and thy people,
Jer 27:13 that w. not serve the king of Babylon?
Jer 27:22 then w. I bring them up, and restore
Jer 28:3 w. I bring again into this place all
Jer 28:4 w. bring again to this place Jeconiah
Jer 28:4 for I w. break the yoke of the king of
Jer 28:11 Even so w. I break the yoke of
Jer 28:16 I w. cast thee from off the face of the
Jer 29:10 be accomplished at Babylon I w. visit
Jer 29:12 unto me, and I w. hearken unto you.
Jer 29:14 And I w. be found of you, saith the
Jer 29:14 and I w. turn away your captivity,
Jer 29:14 I w. gather you from all the nations,
Jer 29:14 I w. bring you again into the place
Jer 29:17 I w. send upon them the sword, the
Jer 29:17 and w. make them like vile figs, that
Jer 29:18 I w. persecute them with the sword,
Jer 29:18 w. deliver them to be removed to all
Jer 29:21 I w. deliver them into the hand of
Jer 29:32 w. punish Shemaiah the Nehelamite,
Jer 29:32 the good that I w. do for my people,
Jer 30:3 I w. bring again the captivity of my
Jer 30:3 I w. cause them to return to the land
Jer 30:8 I w. break his yoke from off thy neck,
Jer 30:8 w. burst thy bonds, and strangers
Jer 30:9 king, whom I w. raise up unto them.
Jer 30:10 I w. save thee from afar, and thy
Jer 30:11 yet w. I not make a full end of thee:
Jer 30:11 I w. correct thee in measure, and
Jer 30:11 and w. not leave thee altogether
Jer 30:16 prey upon thee w. I give for a prey.
Jer 30:17 For I w. restore health unto thee,
Jer 30:17 I w. heal thee of thy wounds, saith
Jer 30:18 w. bring again the captivity of Jacob's
Jer 30:19 I w. multiply them, and they shall
Jer 30:19 I w. also glorify them, and they shall
Jer 30:20 I w. punish all that oppress them.
Jer 30:21 and I w. cause him to draw near,
Jer 30:22 be my people, and I w. be your God.
Jer 31:1 w. I be the God of all the families of
Jer 31:4 I w. build thee, and thou shalt be
Jer 31:8 I w. bring them from the north
Jer 31:9 and with supplications w. I lead them:
Jer 31:9 I w. cause them to walk by the rivers
Jer 31:10 that scattered Israel w. gather him,
Jer 31:13 for I w. turn their mourning into joy,
Jer 31:13 and w. comfort them, and make them
Jer 31:14 I w. satiate the soul of the priests
Jer 31:20 I w. surely have mercy upon him,
Jer 31:27 I w. sow the house of Israel and the
Jer 31:28 so w. I watch over them, to build, and
Jer 31:31 I w. make a new covenant with the
Jer 31:33 that I w. make with the house of
Jer 31:33 I w. put my law in their inward parts,
Jer 31:33 and w. be their God, and they shall be
Jer 31:34 for I w. forgive them their iniquity,
Jer 31:34 I w. remember their sin no more.
Jer 31:37 I w. also cast off all the seed of Israel
Jer 32:3, 28 I w. give this city into the hand of
Jer 32:37 I w. gather them out of all countries,
Jer 32:37 I w. bring them again unto this place,
Jer 32:37 and I w. cause them to dwell safely:
Jer 32:38 be my people, and I w. be their God:
Jer 32:39 And I w. give them one heart, and
Jer 32:40 I w. make an everlasting covenant
Jer 32:40 that I w. not turn away from them,
Jer 32:40 but I w. put my fear in their hearts,
Jer 32:41 I w. rejoice over them to do them
Jer 32:41 I w. plant them in this land assuredly
Jer 32:42 so w. I bring upon them all the good
Jer 32:44 I w. cause their captivity to return.
Jer 33:3 I w. answer thee, and shew thee great
Jer 33:6 I w. bring it health and cure, and
Jer 33:6 I w. cure them, and w. reveal unto
Jer 33:7 And I w. cause the captivity of Judah
Jer 33:7 and w. build them, as at the first.
Jer 33:8 I w. cleanse them from all their
Jer 33:8 and I w. pardon all their iniquities,
Jer 33:11 I w. cause to return the captivity of
Jer 33:14 I w. perform that good thing which I
Jer 33:15 w. I cause the Branch of righteousness
Jer 33:22 so w. I multiply the seed of David my
Jer 33:26 Then w. I cast away the seed of Jacob,

Jer 33:26 so that I w. not take any of his seed
Jer 33:26 for I w. cause their captivity to return,
Jer 34:2 I w. give this city into the hand of
Jer 34:5 and they w. lament thee, saying, Ah
Jer 34:17 I w. make you to be removed into all
Jer 34:18 And I w. give the men that have
Jer 34:20 I w. even give them into the hand of
Jer 34:21 his princes w. I give into the hand of
Jer 34:22 I w. command, saith the Lord,
Jer 34:22 and I w. make the cities of Judah a
Jer 35:6 But they said, We w. drink no wine:
Jer 35:13 W. ye not receive instruction to
Jer 35:17 I w. bring upon Judah and upon all
Jer 36:3 house of Judah w. hear all the evil
Jer 36:7 they w. present their supplication
Jer 36:7 w. return every one from his evil way:
Jer 36:16 We w. surely tell the king all these
Jer 36:31 I w. punish him and his seed and his
Jer 36:31 and I w. bring upon them, and upon
Jer 38:14 unto Jeremiah, I w. ask thee a thing;
Jer 38:16 this soul, I w. not put thee to death,
Jer 38:16 neither w. I give thee into the hand
Jer 38:25 and we w. not put thee to death;
Jer 39:16 I w. bring my words upon this city
Jer 39:17 But I w. deliver thee in that day,
Jer 39:18 For I w. surely deliver thee, and thou
Jer 40:4 and I w. look well unto thee: but if it
Jer 40:10 I w. dwell at Mizpah, to serve the
Jer 40:10 which w. come unto us: but ye,
Jer 40:15 w. slay Ishmael the son of Nethaniah,
Jer 42:4 I w. pray unto the Lord your God
Jer 42:4 answer you, I w. declare it unto you;
Jer 42:4 I w. keep nothing back from you.
Jer 42:6 we w. obey the voice of the Lord our
Jer 42:10 If ye w. still abide in this land, then
Jer 42:10 then w. I build you, and not pull you
Jer 42:10 I w. plant you, and not pluck you up:
Jer 42:12 And I w. shew mercies unto you,
Jer 42:13 say, We w. not dwell in this land,
Jer 42:14 but we w. go into the land of Egypt,
Jer 42:14 of bread; and there w. we dwell:
Jer 42:17 the evil that I w. bring upon them.
Jer 42:20 so declare unto us, and we w. do it.
Jer 43:10 I w. send and take Nebuchadrezzar
Jer 43:10 and w. set his throne upon these stones
Jer 43:12 I w. kindle a fire in the houses of the
Jer 44:11 I w. set my face against you for evil,
Jer 44:12 And I w. take the remnant of Judah,
Jer 44:13 For I w. punish them that dwell in the
Jer 44:16 Lord, we w. not hearken unto thee.
Jer 44:17 But we w. certainly do whatsoever
Jer 44:25 We w. surely perform our vows that
Jer 44:25 ye w. surely accomplish your vows,
Jer 44:27 Behold, I w. watch over them for evil,
Jer 44:29 that I w. punish you in this place,
Jer 44:30 I w. give Pharaoh-hophra king of
Jer 45:4 which I have built, we I break down,
Jer 45:4 which I have planted I w. pluck up,
Jer 45:5 I w. bring evil upon all flesh, saith
Jer 45:5 thy life w. I give unto thee for a prey
Jer 46:8 I w. go up, and w. cover the earth;
Jer 46:8 I w. destroy the city and the
Jer 46:25 I w. punish the multitude of No, and
Jer 46:26 And I w. deliver them into the hand
Jer 46:27 behold, I w. save thee from afar off,
Jer 46:28 for I w. make a full end of all the
Jer 46:28 but I w. not make a full end of thee,
Jer 46:28 yet w. I not leave thee wholly
Jer 47:4 for the Lord w. spoil the Philistines,
Jer 47:6 how long w. it be ere thou be quiet?
Jer 48:12 that I w. send unto him wanderers,
Jer 48:31 Therefore w. I howl for Moab, and
Jer 48:31 and I w. cry out for all Moab; mine
Jer 48:32 I w. weep for thee with the weeping
Jer 48:35 I w. cause to cease in Moab, saith
Jer 48:44 I w. bring upon it, even upon Moab,
Jer 48:47 w. I bring again the captivity of Moab
Jer 49:2 that I w. cause an alarm of war to be
Jer 49:5 I w. bring fear upon thee, saith the
Jer 49:6 I w. bring again the captivity
Jer 49:8 I w. bring the calamity of Esau upon
Jer 49:8 him, the time that I w. visit him.
Jer 49:9 they w. destroy till they have enough
Jer 49:11 I w. preserve them alive; and let thy
Jer 49:15 I w. make thee small among the
Jer 49:16 I w. bring thee down from thence,

Jer 49:19 I w. suddenly make him run away
Jer 49:19 and who w. appoint me the time?
Jer 49:19 who is that shepherd that w. stand
Jer 49:27 And I w. kindle a fire in the wall of
Jer 49:32 I w. scatter into all winds them that
Jer 49:32 I w. bring their calamity from all
Jer 49:35 I w. break the bow of Elam, the chief
Jer 49:36 upon Elam, w. I bring the four winds
Jer 49:36 w. scatter them towards all those
Jer 49:37 For I w. cause Elam to be dismayed
Jer 49:37 I w. bring evil upon them, even my
Jer 49:37 and I w. send the sword after them,
Jer 49:38 And I w. set my throne in Elam, and
Jer 49:38 w. destroy from thence the king and
Jer 49:39 I w. bring again the captivity of Elam,
Jer 50:9 I w. raise and cause to come up
Jer 50:18 I w. punish the king of Babylon and
Jer 50:19 And I w. bring Israel again to his
Jer 50:20 I w. pardon them whom I reserve.
Jer 50:31 is come, the time that I w. visit thee.
Jer 50:32 I w. kindle a fire in his cities, and it
Jer 50:42 are cruel, and w. not shew mercy:
Jer 50:44 I w. make them suddenly run away
Jer 50:44 and who w. appoint me the time?
Jer 50:44 shepherd that w. stand before me?
Jer 51:1 I w. raise up against Babylon, and
Jer 51:2 And w. send unto Babylon fanners,
Jer 51:6 he w. render unto her a recompense.
Jer 51:14 Surely I w. fill thee with men,
Jer 51:20 w. I break in pieces the nations,
Jer 51:20 and with thee w. I destroy kingdoms:
Jer 51:21 thee w. I break in pieces the horse
Jer 51:21 thee w. I break in pieces the chariot
Jer 51:22 w. I break in pieces man and woman.
Jer 51:22 w. I break in pieces old and young;
Jer 51:22 w. I break in pieces the young man and
Jer 51:23 I w. also break in pieces with thee
Jer 51:23 w. I break in pieces the husbandman
Jer 51:23 w. I break in pieces captains and
Jer 51:24 I w. render unto Babylon and to all
Jer 51:25 I w. stretch out mine hand upon thee,
Jer 51:25 and w. make thee a burnt mountain.
Jer 51:36 I w. plead thy cause, and take
Jer 51:36 I w. dry up her sea, and make her
Jer 51:39 In their heat I w. make their feasts,
Jer 51:39 I w. make them drunken, that they
Jer 51:40 I w. bring them down like lambs
Jer 51:44 And I w. punish Bel in Babylon,
Jer 51:44 I w. bring forth out of his mouth that
Jer 51:47 I w. do judgment upon the graven
Jer 51:52 I w. do judgment upon her graven
Jer 51:57 I w. make drunk her princes, and her
Jer 51:64 the evil that I w. bring upon her:
La 3:24 my soul: therefore w. I hope in him.
La 3:31 For he Lord w. not cast off for ever:
La 3:32 yet w. he have compassion
La 4:16 them; he w. no more regard them:
La 4:22 he w. no more carry thee away into
La 4:22 he w. visit thine iniquity, O daughter
La 4:22 of Edom; he w. discover thy sins.
Eze 2:1 thy feet, and I w. speak unto thee.
Eze 2:5 whether they w. hear, or whether they
Eze 2:5 or whether they w. forbear, (for they
Eze 2:7 unto them, whether they w. hear,
Eze 2:7 or whether they w. forbear: for they
Eze 3:7 house of Israel w. not hearken unto 14
Eze 3:7 for they w. not hearken unto me: 14
Eze 3:11 saith the Lord; whether they w. hear,
Eze 3:11 or whether they w. forbear.
Eze 3:18, 20 blood w. I require at thine hand.
Eze 3:22 plain, and I w. there talk with thee.
Eze 3:26 I w. make thy tongue cleave to the
Eze 3:27 with thee, I w. open thy mouth,
Eze 4:8 I w. lay hands upon thee, and thou
Eze 4:13 the Gentiles, whither I w. drive them.
Eze 4:16 I w. break the staff of bread in
Eze 5:2 and I w. draw out a sword after them.
Eze 5:8 w. execute judgments in the midst of
Eze 5:9 I w. do in thee that which I have not
Eze 5:9 I w. not do any more the like,
Eze 5:10 and I w. execute judgments in thee,
Eze 5:10 thee w. I scatter unto all the winds.
Eze 5:11 therefore w. I also diminish thee;
Eze 5:11 eye spare, neither w. I have any pity.
Eze 5:12 I w. scatter a third part into all
Eze 5:12 and I w. draw out a sword after them.

Eze 5:13 I w. cause my fury to rest upon them,
Eze 5:13 and I w. be comforted: and they shall
Eze 5:13 I w. make thee waste, and a reproach
Eze 5:16 which I w. send to destroy you:
Eze 5:16 I w. increase the famine upon you,
Eze 5:16 and w. break your staff of bread:
Eze 5:17 w. I send upon you famine and evil
Eze 5:17 and I w. bring the sword upon thee.
Eze 6:3 I, even I, w. bring a sword upon you,
Eze 6:3 and I w. destroy your high places.
Eze 6:4 I w. cast down your slain men before
Eze 6:5 And I w. lay the dead carcases of the
Eze 6:5 I w. scatter your bones round about
Eze 6:8 Yet w. I leave a remnant, that ye may
Eze 6:12 w. I accomplish my fury upon them.
Eze 6:14 So w. I stretch out my hand upon
Eze 7:3 and I w. send mine anger upon thee,
Eze 7:3 w. judge thee according to thy ways,
Eze 7:3 w. recompense upon thee all thine
Eze 7:4 not spare thee, neither w. I have pity:
Eze 7:4 w. recompense thy ways upon thee,
Eze 7:8 Now w. I shortly pour out my fury
Eze 7:8 w. judge thee according to thy ways,
Eze 7:8 w. recompense thee for all thine
Eze 7:9 not spare, neither w. I have pity:
Eze 7:9 I w. recompense thee according to thy
Eze 7:21 I w. give it into the hands of the
Eze 7:22 My face w. I turn also from them.
Eze 7:24 I w. bring the worst of the heathen,
Eze 7:24 I w. also make the pomp of the strong
Eze 7:27 I w. do unto them after their way,
Eze 7:27 to their deserts w. I judge them;
Eze 8:18 Therefore w. I also deal in fury: mine
Eze 8:18 not spare, neither w. I have pity:
Eze 8:18 a loud voice, yet w. I not hear them.
Eze 9:10 not spare, neither w. I have pity,
Eze 9:10 but I w. recompense their way upon
Eze 11:7 But I w. bring you forth out of the
Eze 11:8 I w. bring a sword upon you, saith the
Eze 11:9 And I w. bring you out of the midst
Eze 11:9 and w. execute judgment among you.
Eze 11:10 I w. judge you in the border of Israel;
Eze 11:11 I w. judge you in the border of Israel:
Eze 11:16 yet w. I be to them as a little
Eze 11:17 I w. even gather you from the people,
Eze 11:17 and I w. give you the land of Israel.
Eze 11:19 And I w. give them one heart,
Eze 11:19 and I w. put a new spirit within you;
Eze 11:19 I w. take the stony heart out of their
Eze 11:19 and w. give them a heart of flesh:
Eze 11:20 by my people, and I w. be their God.
Eze 11:21 I w. recompense their way upon their
Eze 12:3 it may be they w. consider, though
Eze 12:13 My net also w. I spread upon him,
Eze 12:13 I w. bring him to Babylon to the land
Eze 12:14 I w. scatter toward every wind all that
Eze 12:14 I w. draw out the sword after them.
Eze 12:16 I w. leave a few men of them from the
Eze 12:23 I w. make this proverb to cease,
Eze 12:25 I w. speak, and the word that I shall
Eze 12:25 O rebellious house, w. I say the word,
Eze 12:25 and w. perform it, saith the Lord God.
Eze 13:13 I w. even rend it with a stormy wind
Eze 13:14 w. I break down the wall that ye have
Eze 13:15 w. I accomplish my wrath upon the
Eze 13:15 w. say unto you, The wall is no more,
Eze 13:18 W. ye hunt the souls of my people,
Eze 13:18 w. ye save the souls alive that come
Eze 13:19 w. ye pollute me among my people for
Eze 13:20 and I w. tear them from your arms,
Eze 13:20 w. let the souls go, even the souls that
Eze 13:21 Your kerchiefs also w. I tear, and
Eze 13:23 w. deliver my people out of your hand:
Eze 14:4 I the Lord w. answer him that cometh
Eze 14:7 I the Lord w. answer him by myself:
Eze 14:8 I w. set my face against that man,
Eze 14:8 w. make him a sign and a proverb,
Eze 14:8 I w. cut him off from the midst of my
Eze 14:9 I w. stretch out my hand upon him,
Eze 14:9 w. destroy him from the midst of my
Eze 14:13 w. I stretch out mine hand upon it,
Eze 14:13 and w. break the staff of the bread
Eze 14:13 and w. send famine upon it, and
Eze 14:13 and w. cut off man and beast from it:
Eze 15:3 or w. men take a pin of it to hang any
Eze 15:6 fuel, so w. I give the inhabitants of

Eze 15:7 And I w. set my face against them;
Eze 15:8 And I w. make the land desolate,
Eze 16:27 delivered thee unto the w. of them 5314
Eze 16:37 therefore I w. gather all thy lovers,
Eze 16:37 I w. even gather them round about
Eze 16:37 w. discover thy nakedness unto them,
Eze 16:38 And I w. judge thee, as women that
Eze 16:38 and I w. give thee blood in fury and
Eze 16:39 I w. also give thee into their hand,
Eze 16:41 I w. cause thee to cease from playing
Eze 16:42 So w. I make my fury toward thee
Eze 16:42 and I w. be quiet, and w. be no more
Eze 16:43 I also w. recompense thy way upon
Eze 16:53 then w. I bring again thy captivity
Eze 16:59 I w. even deal with thee as thou hast
Eze 16:60 I w. remember my covenant with thee
Eze 16:60 I w. establish unto thee an everlasting
Eze 16:61 w. give them unto thee for daughters,
Eze 16:62 I w. establish my covenant with thee;
Eze 17:19 even it w. I recompense upon his own
Eze 17:20 And I w. spread my net upon him,
Eze 17:20 snare, and I w. bring him to Babylon,
Eze 17:20 and w. plead with him there for his
Eze 17:22 I w. also take of the highest branch
Eze 17:22 branch of the high cedar, and w. set it;
Eze 17:22 I w. crop off from the top of his young
Eze 17:22 and w. plant it upon an high mountain
Eze 17:23 of the height of Israel w. I plant it:
Eze 18:21 if the wicked w. turn from all his sins
Eze 18:30 Therefore I w. judge you, O house of
Eze 18:31 for why w. ye die, O house of Israel?
Eze 20:3 God, I w. not be enquired of by you.
Eze 20:8 I w. pour out my fury upon them,
Eze 20:31 God, I w. not be enquired of by you.
Eze 20:32 w. be as the heathen, as the families
Eze 20:33 fury poured out, w. I rule over you:
Eze 20:34 I w. bring you out from the people,
Eze 20:34 w. gather you out of the countries wherein
Eze 20:35 I w. bring you into the wilderness
Eze 20:35 there w. I plead with you face to face.
Eze 20:36 so w. I plead with you, saith the Lord
Eze 20:37 I w. cause you to pass under the rod,
Eze 20:37 I w. bring you into the bond of the
Eze 20:38 I w. purge out from among you the
Eze 20:38 I w. bring them forth out of the
Eze 20:39 also, if ye w. not hearken unto me:
Eze 20:40 serve me: there w. I accept them,
Eze 20:40 there w. I require your offerings,
Eze 20:41 I w. accept you with your sweet
Eze 20:41 I w. be sanctified in you before the
Eze 20:47 I w. kindle a fire in thee, and it shall
Eze 21:3 w. draw forth my sword out of the
Eze 21:3, 4 w. cut off from thee the righteous
Eze 21:17 I w. also smite mine hands together,
Eze 21:17 I w. cause my fury to rest: I the Lord
Eze 21:23 but he w. call to remembrance the
Eze 21:27 I w. overturn, overturn, overturn, it:
Eze 21:27 right it is; and I w. give it him.
Eze 21:30 I w. judge thee in the place where
Eze 21:31 I w. pour out mine indignation upon
Eze 21:31 I w. blow against thee in the fire of my
Eze 22:14 the Lord have spoken it, and w. do it.
Eze 22:15 I w. scatter thee among the heathen,
Eze 22:15 w. consume thy filthiness out of thee.
Eze 22:19 I w. gather you into the midst of
Eze 22:20 so w. I gather you in mine anger and
Eze 22:20 I w. leave you there, and melt you.
Eze 22:21 I w. gather you, and blow upon you
Eze 23:22 I w. raise up thy lovers against thee,
Eze 23:22 I w. bring them against thee on every
Eze 23:24 and I w. set judgment before them,
Eze 23:25 And I w. set my jealousy against thee,
Eze 23:27 Thus w. I make thy lewdness to cease
Eze 23:28 I w. deliver thee into the hand of them
Eze 23:30 I w. do these things unto thee,
Eze 23:31 w. I give her cup into thine hand.
Eze 23:43 W. they now commit whoredoms with
Eze 23:46 I w. bring up a company upon them,
Eze 23:46 and w. give them to be removed and
Eze 23:48 Thus w. I cause lewdness to cease.
Eze 24:9 I w. even make the pile for fire great.
Eze 24:14 and I w. do it; I w. not go back,
Eze 24:14 neither w. I spare, neither w. I repent;
Eze 24:21 Behold, I w. profane my sanctuary,
Eze 25:4 I w. deliver thee to the men of the east
Eze 25:5 w. make Rabbah a stable for camels,

Eze 25:7 I **w.** stretch out mine hand upon thee,
Eze 25:7 and **w.** deliver thee for a spoil to the
Eze 25:7 and I **w.** cut off from the people,
Eze 25:7 and I **w.** cause thee to perish out of
Eze 25:7 I **w.** destroy thee; and thou shalt
Eze 25:9 I **w.** open the side of Moab from the
Eze 25:10 and **w.** give them in possession, that
Eze 25:11 I **w.** execute judgments upon Moab;
Eze 25:13 I **w.** also stretch out mine hand upon
Eze 25:13 and **w.** cut off man and beast from it;
Eze 25:13 I **w.** make it desolate from Teman;
Eze 25:14 I **w.** lay my vengeance upon Edom by
Eze 25:16 I **w.** stretch out mine hand upon the
Eze 25:16 and I **w.** cut off the Cherethims, and
Eze 25:17 I **w.** execute great vengeance upon
Eze 26:3 **w.** cause many nations to come up
Eze 26:4 I **w.** also scrape her dust from her,
Eze 26:7 Behold, I **w.** bring upon Tyrus
Eze 26:13 I **w.** cause the noise of thy songs to
Eze 26:14 I **w.** make thee like the top of a rock:
Eze 26:21 I **w.** make thee a terror, and thou shalt
Eze 28:7 I **w.** bring strangers upon thee,
Eze 28:16 I **w.** cast thee as profane out of the
Eze 28:16 I **w.** destroy thee, O covering cherub,
Eze 28:17 I **w.** cast thee to the ground,
Eze 28:17 I **w.** lay thee before kings, that they
Eze 28:18 **w.** I bring forth a fire from the
Eze 28:18 and I **w.** bring thee to ashes upon the
Eze 28:22 I **w.** be glorified in the midst of thee:
Eze 28:23 For I **w.** send into her pestilence, and
Eze 29:4 But I **w.** put hooks in thy jaws, and
Eze 29:4 I **w.** cause the fish of the rivers to
Eze 29:4 I **w.** bring thee up out of the midst of
Eze 29:5 And I **w.** leave thee thrown into the
Eze 29:8 I **w.** bring a sword upon thee, and
Eze 29:10 I **w.** make the land of Egypt utterly
Eze 29:12 I **w.** make the land of Egypt desolate
Eze 29:12 I **w.** scatter the Egyptians among the
Eze 29:12 and **w.** disperse them through the
Eze 29:13 forty years **w.** I gather the Egyptians
Eze 29:14 I **w.** bring the captivity of Egypt,
Eze 29:14 **w.** cause them to return into the land
Eze 29:15 for I **w.** diminish them, that they shall
Eze 29:19 I **w.** give the land of Egypt unto
Eze 29:21 day **w.** I cause the horn of the house
Eze 29:21 I **w.** give thee the opening of the
Eze 30:10 I **w.** also make the multitude of Egypt
Eze 30:12 And I **w.** make the rivers dry, and sell
Eze 30:12 I **w.** make the land waste, and all that
Eze 30:13 I **w.** also destroy the idols, and I
Eze 30:13 I **w.** cause their images to cease out
Eze 30:13 I **w.** put a fear in the land of Egypt.
Eze 30:14 And I **w.** make Pathros desolate, and
Eze 30:14 desolate, and **w.** set fire in Zoan,
Eze 30:14 Zoan, and **w.** execute judgments in No.
Eze 30:15 And I **w.** pour my fury upon Sin,
Eze 30:15 and I **w.** cut off the multitude of No.
Eze 30:16 And I **w.** set fire in Egypt: Sin shall
Eze 30:19 **w.** I execute judgments in Egypt:
Eze 30:22 king of Egypt, and **w.** break his arms,
Eze 30:22 I **w.** cause the sword to fall out of his
Eze 30:23 I **w.** scatter the Egyptians among the
Eze 30:23 and **w.** disperse them through the
Eze 30:24 I **w.** strengthen the arms of the king
Eze 30:24 I **w.** break Pharaoh's arms, and he
Eze 30:25 I **w.** strengthen the arms of the king
Eze 30:26 I **w.** scatter the Egyptians among the
Eze 32:3 I **w.** therefore spread out my net over
Eze 32:4 Then **w.** I leave thee upon the land,
Eze 32:4 I **w.** cast thee forth upon the open
Eze 32:4 **w.** cause all the fowls of the heaven to
Eze 32:4 I **w.** fill the beasts of the whole earth
Eze 32:5 I **w.** lay thy flesh upon the mountains,
Eze 32:6 I **w.** also water with thy blood the
Eze 32:7 I **w.** cover the heaven, and make the
Eze 32:7 I **w.** cover the sun with a cloud, and
Eze 32:8 lights of heaven **w.** I make dark over
Eze 32:9 I **w.** also vex the hearts of many
Eze 32:10 I **w.** make many people amazed at thee,
Eze 32:12 **w.** I cause thy multitude to fall,
Eze 32:13 I **w.** destroy also all the beasts thereof
Eze 32:14 Then **w.** I make their waters deep, and
Eze 33:6 but his blood **w.** I require at the
Eze 33:8 his blood **w.** I require at thine hand.
Eze 33:11 for why **w.** ye die, O house of Israel?
Eze 33:20 I **w.** judge you every one after his

Eze 33:27 in the open field **w.** I give to the beasts
Eze 33:28 For I **w.** lay the land most desolate,
Eze 33:31 thy words, but they **w.** not do them:
Eze 33:33 this cometh to pass, (lo, it **w.** come,)
Eze 34:10 I **w.** require my flock at their hand,
Eze 34:10 for I **w.** deliver my flock from their
Eze 34:11 I, **w.** both search my sheep, and seek
Eze 34:12 **w.** I seek out my sheep, and **w.** deliver
Eze 34:13 I **w.** bring them out from the people,
Eze 34:13 **w.** bring them to their own land, and
Eze 34:14 I **w.** feed them in a good pasture, and
Eze 34:15 I **w.** feed my flock, and
Eze 34:15 I **w.** cause them to lie down,
Eze 34:16 I **w.** seek that which was lost, and
Eze 34:16 **w.** bind up that which was broken,
Eze 34:16 **w.** strengthen that which was sick:
Eze 34:16 I **w.** destroy the fat and the strong;
Eze 34:16 I **w.** feed them with judgment.
Eze 34:20 even I, **w.** judge between the fat cattle
Eze 34:22 **w.** I save my flock, and they shall
Eze 34:22 I **w.** judge between cattle and cattle.
Eze 34:23 I **w.** set up one shepherd over them,
Eze 34:24 I the Lord **w.** be their God, and my
Eze 34:25 I **w.** make with them a covenant of
Eze 34:25 **w.** cause the evil beast to cease out of
Eze 34:26 I **w.** make them and the places round
Eze 34:26 I **w.** cause the shower to come down in
Eze 34:29 I **w.** raise up for them a plant of
Eze 35:3 I **w.** stretch out mine hand against
Eze 35:3 and I **w.** make thee most desolate,
Eze 35:4 I **w.** lay thy cities waste, and thou
Eze 35:6 I **w.** prepare thee unto blood, and
Eze 35:7 **w.** I make mount Seir most desolate,
Eze 35:8 I **w.** fill his mountains with his slain
Eze 35:9 I **w.** make thee perpetual desolations,
Eze 35:10 shall be mine, and we **w.** possess it;
Eze 35:11 I **w.** even do according to thine anger,
Eze 35:11 I **w.** make myself known among them,
Eze 35:14 rejoiceth, I **w.** make thee desolate.
Eze 35:15 it was desolate, so **w.** I do unto thee:
Eze 36:9 and I **w.** turn unto you, and ye shall
Eze 36:10 I **w.** multiply men upon you, all the
Eze 36:11 And I **w.** multiply upon you man and
Eze 36:11 I **w.** settle you after your old estates,
Eze 36:11 **w.** do better unto you than at your
Eze 36:12 I **w.** cause men to walk upon you,
Eze 36:15 **w.** I cause men to hear in thee the
Eze 36:23 I **w.** sanctify my great name, which
Eze 36:24 For I **w.** take you from among the
Eze 36:24 and **w.** bring you into your own land.
Eze 36:25 **w.** I sprinkle clean water upon you,
Eze 36:25 from all your idols, **w.** I cleanse you.
Eze 36:26 A new heart also **w.** I give you,
Eze 36:26 and a new spirit **w.** I put within you:
Eze 36:26 I **w.** take away the stony heart out of
Eze 36:26 and I **w.** give you an heart of flesh,
Eze 36:27 I **w.** put my spirit within you, and
Eze 36:28 be my people, and I **w.** be your God.
Eze 36:29 I **w.** also save you from all your
Eze 36:29 I **w.** call for the corn, and **w.** increase
Eze 36:30 I **w.** multiply the fruit of the tree, and
Eze 36:33 I **w.** also cause you to dwell in the
Eze 36:36 Lord have spoken it, and I **w.** do it.
Eze 36:37 I **w.** yet for this be enquired of by the
Eze 36:37 I **w.** increase them with men like a
Eze 37:5 I **w.** cause breath to enter into you,
Eze 37:6 And I **w.** lay sinews upon you, and
Eze 37:6 **w.** bring up flesh from you, and cover
Eze 37:12 I **w.** open your graves, and cause
Eze 37:19 I **w.** take the stick of Joseph, which is
Eze 37:19 **w.** put them with him, even with the
Eze 37:21 I **w.** take the children of Israel from
Eze 37:21 **w.** gather them on every side, and
Eze 37:22 I **w.** make them one nation in the
Eze 37:23 but I **w.** save them out of all their
Eze 37:23 have sinned, and **w.** cleanse them:
Eze 37:23 be my people, and I **w.** be their God.
Eze 37:26 I **w.** make a covenant of peace with
Eze 37:26 I **w.** place them, and multiply them,
Eze 37:26 **w.** set my sanctuary in the midst of
Eze 37:27 I **w.** be their God, and they shall be
Eze 38:4 I **w.** turn thee back, and put hooks
Eze 38:4 I **w.** bring thee forth, and all thine
Eze 38:11 I **w.** go up to the land of unwalled
Eze 38:11 I **w.** go to them that are at rest, that
Eze 38:16 I **w.** bring thee against my land, that

Eze 38:21 And I **w.** call for a sword against him
Eze 38:22 I **w.** plead against him with pestilence
Eze 38:22 and I **w.** rain upon him, and upon his
Eze 38:23 **w.** I magnify myself, and sanctify
Eze 38:23 and I **w.** be known in the eyes of many
Eze 39:2 I **w.** turn thee back, and leave but the
Eze 39:2 **w.** cause thee to come up from the
Eze 39:2 **w.** bring thee upon the mountain of
Eze 39:3 and I **w.** smite thy bow out of thy left
Eze 39:3 and **w.** cause thine arrows to fall out
Eze 39:4 I **w.** give thee unto the ravenous birds
Eze 39:6 I **w.** send a fire on Magog, and among
Eze 39:7 So **w.** I make my holy name known in
Eze 39:7 and I **w.** not let them pollute my holy
Eze 39:11 I **w.** give unto Gog a place there of
Eze 39:21 I **w.** set my glory among the heathen,
Eze 39:25 Now **w.** I bring again the captivity of
Eze 39:25 and **w.** be jealous for my holy name;
Eze 39:29 **w.** I hide my face any more from
Eze 43:7 I **w.** dwell in the midst of the children
Eze 43:9 I **w.** dwell in the midst of them for
Eze 43:27 I **w.** accept you, saith the Lord God.
Eze 44:14 But I **w.** make them keepers of the
Da 2:4 and we **w.** shew the interpretation
Da 2:5 if ye **w.** not make known unto me the
Da 2:7 we **w.** shew the interpretation of it
Da 2:9 if ye **w.** not make known unto me the
Da 2:24 I **w.** shew unto the king the
Da 2:25 **w.** make known unto the king the
Da 2:36 we **w.** tell the interpretation thereof
Da 3:17 he **w.** deliver us out of thine hand, O
Da 3:18 king, that we **w.** not serve thy gods,
Da 4:17 and giveth it to whomsoever he **w.**, 6634
Da 4:25, 32 giveth it to whomsoever he **w.**. 6634
Da 4:35 to his **w.** in the army of heaven, 6634
Da 5:12 and he **w.** shew the interpretation.
Da 5:17 I **w.** read the writing unto the king,
Da 5:21 over it whomsoever he **w.** 6634
Da 6:16 servest continually, he **w.** deliver thee
Da 8:4 but he did according to his **w.**, and 7522
Da 8:19 I **w.** make thee known what shall be in
Da 10:20 I **w.** return to fight with the prince
Da 10:21 I **w.** shew thee that which is noted in
Da 11:2 And now **w.** I shew thee the truth
Da 11:3 and do according to his **w.** 7522
Da 11:16 shall do according to his own **w.**, 7522
Da 11:36 king shall do according to his **w.**; 7522
Ho 1:4 I **w.** avenge the blood of Jezreel upon
Ho 1:4 **w.** cause to cease the kingdom of the
Ho 1:5 I **w.** break the bow of Israel in the
Ho 1:6 I **w.** no more have mercy upon the
Ho 1:6 but I **w.** utterly take them away
Ho 1:7 I **w.** have mercy upon the house
Ho 1:7 **w.** save them by the Lord their God,
Ho 1:7 **w.** not save them by bow, nor by
Ho 1:9 my people, and I **w.** not be your God.
Ho 2:4 **w.** not have mercy upon her children;
Ho 2:5 I **w.** go after my lovers, that give me
Ho 2:6 I **w.** hedge up thy way with thorns,
Ho 2:7 **w.** go and return to my first husband;
Ho 2:9 **w.** I return, and take away my corn
Ho 2:9 **w.** recover my wool and my flax given
Ho 2:10 And now **w.** I discover her lewdness in
Ho 2:11 I **w.** also cause all her mirth to cease,
Ho 2:12 I **w.** destroy her vines and her fig
Ho 2:12 and I **w.** make them a forest, and
Ho 2:13 And I **w.** visit upon her the days of
Ho 2:14 I **w.** allure her, and bring her into
Ho 2:15 I **w.** give her her vineyards from
Ho 2:17 I **w.** take away the names of Baalim
Ho 2:18 day **w.** I make a covenant for them
Ho 2:18 I **w.** break the bow and the sword
Ho 2:18 and **w.** make them to lie down safely.
Ho 2:19 I **w.** betroth thee unto me for ever;
Ho 2:19 yea, I **w.** betroth thee unto me in
Ho 2:20 I **w.** even betroth thee unto me in
Ho 2:21 in that day, I **w.** hear, saith the Lord,
Ho 2:21 I **w.** hear the heavens, and they
Ho 2:23 I **w.** sow her unto me in the earth;
Ho 2:23 I **w.** have mercy upon her that had
Ho 2:23 I **w.** say to them which were not my
Ho 3:3 another man: so **w.** I also be for thee.
Ho 4:5 night, and I **w.** destroy thy mother.
Ho 4:6 I **w.** also reject thee, that thou shalt
Ho 4:6 God, I **w.** also forget thy children.
Ho 4:7 **w.** I change their glory into shame.

Ho 4:9 I **w.** punish them for their ways,
Ho 4:14 I **w.** not punish your daughters when
Ho 4:16 now the Lord **w.** feed them as a lamb
Ho 5:4 **w.** not frame their doings to turn
Ho 5:10 I **w.** pour out my wrath upon them
Ho 5:12 **w.** I be unto Ephraim as a moth,
Ho 5:14 For I **w.** be unto Ephraim as a lion,
Ho 5:14 **w.** tear and go away; I **w.** take away,
Ho 5:15 I **w.** go and return to my place, till
Ho 5:15 their affliction they **w.** seek me early.
Ho 6:1 he hath torn us, and he **w.** heal us:
Ho 6:1 hath smitten, and he **w.** bind us up.
Ho 6:2 After two days **w.** he revive us;
Ho 6:2 in the third day he **w.** raise us up,
Ho 7:12 go, I **w.** spread my net upon them;
Ho 7:12 I **w.** bring them down as the fowls of
Ho 7:12 I **w.** chastise them, as their
Ho 8:5 how long **w.** it be ere they attain to
Ho 8:10 now **w.** I gather them, and they shall
Ho 8:13 now **w.** he remember their iniquity,
Ho 8:14 but I **w.** send a fire upon his cities,
Ho 9:5 What **w.** ye do in the solemn day,
Ho 9:9 he **w.** remember their iniquity,
Ho 9:9 he **w.** visit their sins.
Ho 9:12 yet **w.** I bereave them, that there shall
Ho 9:15 I **w.** drive them out of mine house,
Ho 9:15 mine house, I **w.** love them no more:
Ho 9:16 yet **w.** I slay even the beloved fruit
Ho 9:17 My God **w.** cast them away, because
Ho 10:11 I **w.** make Ephraim to ride; Judah
Ho 11:9 I **w.** not execute the fierceness of
Ho 11:9 I **w.** not return to destroy Ephraim:
Ho 11:9 and I **w.** not enter into the city.
Ho 11:11 I **w.** place them in their houses,
Ho 12:2 and **w.** punish Jacob according to his
Ho 12:2 to his doings **w.** he recompense him.
Ho 12:9 of Egypt **w.** yet make thee to dwell
Ho 13:7 Therefore I **w.** be unto them as a lion:
Ho 13:7 leopard by the way **w.** I observe them:
Ho 13:8 I **w.** meet them as a bear that is
Ho 13:8 and **w.** rend the caul of their heart,
Ho 13:8 there **w.** I devour them like a lion:
Ho 13:10 I **w.** be thy king: where is any 165
Ho 13:14 I **w.** ransom them from the power
Ho 13:14 I **w.** redeem them from death:
Ho 13:14 O death, I **w.** be thy plagues; 165
Ho 13:14 O grave, I **w.** be thy destruction: 165
Ho 14:2 so **w.** we render the calves of our lips.
Ho 14:3 save us; we **w.** not ride upon horses:
Ho 14:3 neither **w.** we say any more to the
Ho 14:4 I **w.** heal their backsliding,
Ho 14:4 I **w.** love them freely: for mine anger
Ho 14:5 I **w.** be as the dew unto Israel:
Joe 1:19 O Lord, to thee **w.** I cry: for the fire
Joe 2:14 Who knoweth if he **w.** return and
Joe 2:18 **w.** the Lord be jealous for his land,
Joe 2:19 Lord **w.** answer and say unto his
Joe 2:19 I **w.** send you corn, and wine, and oil,
Joe 2:19 I **w.** no more make you a reproach
Joe 2:20 But I **w.** remove far off from you the
Joe 2:20 and **w.** drive him into a land barren
Joe 2:21 for the Lord **w.** do great things
Joe 2:23 he **w.** cause to come down for you the
Joe 2:25 And I **w.** restore to you the years that
Joe 2:28 I **w.** pour out my Spirit upon all flesh;
Joe 2:29 In those days **w.** I pour out my spirit
Joe 2:30 I **w.** shew wonders in the heavens
Joe 3:2 I **w.** also gather all nations, and
Joe 3:2 **w.** bring them down into the valley
Joe 3:2 and **w.** plead with them there for my
Joe 3:4 **w.** ye render me a recompence?
Joe 3:4 speedily **w.** I return your recompence
Joe 3:7 I **w.** raise them out of the place
Joe 3:7 **w.** return your recompence upon your
Joe 3:8 I **w.** sell your sons and your daughters
Joe 3:12 there **w.** I sit to judge all the heathen
Joe 3:16 the Lord **w.** be the hope of his people,
Joe 3:21 I **w.** cleanse their blood that I have
Am 1:2 The Lord **w.** roar from Zion, and utter
Am 1:3 I **w.** not turn away the punishment
Am 1:4 I **w.** send a fire into the house of
Am 1:5 I **w.** break also the bar of Damascus,
Am 1:6 I **w.** not turn away the punishment
Am 1:7 I **w.** send a fire on the wall of Gaza,
Am 1:8 And I **w.** cut off the inhabitant from
Am 1:8 I **w.** turn mine hand against Ekron:
Am 1:9 I **w.** not turn away the punishment
Am 1:10 I **w.** send a fire on the wall of Tyrus,
Am 1:11 I **w.** not turn away the punishment
Am 1:12 But I **w.** send a fire upon Teman,
Am 1:13 I **w.** not turn away the punishment
Am 1:14 But I **w.** kindle a fire in the wall of
Am 2:1 I **w.** not turn away the punishment
Am 2:2 But I **w.** send a fire upon Moab,
Am 2:3 I **w.** cut off the judge from the midst
Am 2:3 **w.** slay all the princes thereof with
Am 2:4 I **w.** not turn away the punishment
Am 2:5 But I **w.** send a fire upon Judah,
Am 2:6 I **w.** not turn away the punishment
Am 2:7 father **w.** go in unto the same maid,
Am 3:2 I **w.** punish you for all your iniquities.
Am 3:4 **W.** a lion roar in the forest, when he
Am 3:4 **w.** a young lion cry out of his den,
Am 3:7 Surely the Lord God **w.** do nothing,
Am 3:8 lion hath roared, who **w.** not fear?
Am 3:14 I **w.** also visit the altars of Beth-el:
Am 3:15 I **w.** smite the winter house with the
Am 4:2 that he **w.** take you away with hooks,
Am 4:12 thus **w.** I do unto thee, O Israel:
Am 4:12 because I **w.** do this unto thee,
Am 5:15 **w.** be gracious unto the remnant of
Am 5:17 **w.** pass through thee, saith the Lord.
Am 5:21 and I **w.** not smell in your solemn
Am 5:22 meat offerings, I **w.** not accept them:
Am 5:22 neither **w.** I regard the peace offerings
Am 5:23 I **w.** not hear the melody of thy viols.
Am 5:27 **w.** I cause you to go into captivity
Am 6:8 **w.** I deliver up the city with all that
Am 6:11 he **w.** smite the great house with
Am 6:12 rock? **w.** one plow there with oxen?
Am 6:14 I **w.** raise up against you a nation,
Am 7:8 I **w.** set a plumbline in the midst
Am 7:8 I **w.** not again pass by them any more:
Am 7:9 **w.** rise against the house of Jeroboam
Am 8:2 I **w.** not again pass by them any more.
Am 8:5 When **w.** the new moon be gone,
Am 8:7 I **w.** never forget any of their works.
Am 8:9 I **w.** cause the sun to go down at noon.
Am 8:9 I **w.** darken the earth in the clear day:
Am 8:10 I **w.** turn your feasts into mourning,
Am 8:10 I **w.** bring up sackcloth upon all loins,
Am 8:10 I **w.** make it as the mourning of an
Am 8:11 that I **w.** send a famine in the land.
Am 9:1 I **w.** slay the last of them with the
Am 9:2 thence **w.** I bring them down:
Am 9:3 I **w.** search and take them out thence;
Am 9:3 thence **w.** I command the serpent,
Am 9:4 thence **w.** I command the sword,
Am 9:4 **w.** set mine eyes upon them for evil,
Am 9:8 I **w.** destroy it from off the face of the
Am 9:8 I **w.** not utterly destroy the house of
Am 9:9 I **w.** command, and I **w.** sift the house
Am 9:11 that day **w.** I raise up the tabernacle
Am 9:11 and I **w.** raise up his ruins,
Am 9:11 I **w.** build it as in the days of old:
Am 9:14 I **w.** bring again the captivity of my
Am 9:15 And I **w.** plant them upon their land,
Ob 4 thence **w.** I bring thee down, saith the
Jon 1:6 if so be that God **w.** think upon us,
Jon 2:4 yet I **w.** look again toward thy holy
Jon 2:9 I **w.** sacrifice unto thee with the voice
Jon 2:9 I **w.** pay that that I have vowed.
Jon 3:9 can tell if God **w.** turn and repent,
Mic 1:3 **w.** come down, and tread upon the
Mic 1:6 I **w.** make Samaria as an heap of the
Mic 1:6 and I **w.** pour down the stones thereof
Mic 1:6 I **w.** discover the foundations thereof.
Mic 1:7 all the idols thereof **w.** I lay desolate:
Mic 1:8 Therefore I **w.** wail and howl,
Mic 1:8 and howl, I **w.** go stripped and naked:
Mic 1:8 I **w.** make a wailing like the dragons,
Mic 1:15 Yet **w.** I bring an heir unto thee,
Mic 2:11 I **w.** prophesy unto thee of wine
Mic 2:12 I **w.** surely assemble, O Jacob, all of
Mic 2:12 I **w.** surely gather the remnant of
Mic 2:12 I **w.** put them together as the sheep
Mic 3:4 the Lord, but he **w.** not hear them:
Mic 3:4 he **w.** even hide his face from them
Mic 3:11 **w.** they lean upon the Lord, and say,
Mic 4:2 and he **w.** teach us of his ways,
Mic 4:2 ways, and we **w.** walk in his paths:
Mic 4:5 **w.** walk every one in the name of his
Mic 4:5 we **w.** walk in the name of the Lord
Mic 4:6 **w.** I assemble her that halteth,
Mic 4:6 and I **w.** gather her that is driven out,
Mic 4:7 I **w.** make her that halted a remnant,
Mic 4:13 for I **w.** make thine horn iron, and I
Mic 4:13 iron, and I **w.** make thy hoofs brass:
Mic 4:13 I **w.** consecrate their gain unto the
Mic 5:3 Therefore **w.** he give them up, until
Mic 5:10 I **w.** cut off thy horses out of the midst
Mic 5:10 of thee, and I **w.** destroy thy chariots:
Mic 5:11 And I **w.** cut off the cities of thy land,
Mic 5:12 I **w.** cut off witchcrafts out of thine
Mic 5:13 Thy graven images also **w.** I cut off,
Mic 5:14 I **w.** pluck up thy groves out of the
Mic 5:14 of thee: so **w.** I destroy thy cities.
Mic 5:15 I **w.** execute vengeance in anger
Mic 6:2 people, and he **w.** plead with Israel.
Mic 6:7 **W.** the Lord be pleased with
Mic 6:13 **w.** I make thee sick in smiting thee,
Mic 6:14 which thou deliverest **w.** I give up
Mic 8:7 Therefore I **w.** look unto the Lord;
Mic 8:7 I **w.** wait for the God of my salvation:
Mic 8:7 of my salvation: My God **w.** hear me.
Mic 8:9 I **w.** bear the indignation of the Lord,
Mic 8:9 he **w.** bring me forth to the light,
Mic 8:15 **w.** I show unto him marvellous things.
Mic 8:19 He **w.** turn again, he
Mic 8:19 he **w.** have compassion upon us;
Mic 8:19 he **w.** subdue our iniquities; and thou
Na 1:2 Lord **w.** take vengeance on his
Na 1:3 and **w.** not all acquit the wicked:
Na 1:8 he **w.** make an utter end of the place
Na 1:9 **w.** make an utter end: affliction shall
Na 1:12 thee, I **w.** afflict thee no more.
Na 1:13 now **w.** I break his yoke from off thee,
Na 1:13 and **w.** burst thy bonds in sunder.
Na 1:14 gods **w.** I cut off the graven image
Na 1:14 I **w.** make thy grave; for thou art vile.
Na 2:13 I **w.** burn her chariots in the smoke,
Na 2:13 I **w.** cut off thy prey from the earth,
Na 3:5 **w.** discover thy skirts upon thy face,
Na 3:5 I **w.** shew the nations thy nakedness,
Na 3:6 **w.** cast abominable filth upon thee,
Na 3:6 and **w.** set thee as a gazingstock.
Na 3:7 is laid waste: who **w.** bemoan her?
Hab 1:5 for I **w.** work a work in your days,
Hab 1:5 which ye **w.** not believe, though it be
Hab 2:1 I **w.** stand upon my watch, and set
Hab 2:1 and **w.** watch to see what he **w.** say
Hab 2:3 it **w.** surely come, it **w.** not tarry.
Hab 3:16 he **w.** invade them with his troops.
Hab 3:18 Yet I **w.** rejoice in the Lord,
Hab 3:18 I **w.** joy in the God of my salvation.
Hab 3:19 and he **w.** make my feet like hind's
Hab 3:19 he **w.** make me to walk upon mine
Zep 1:2 I **w.** utterly consume all things from
Zep 1:3 I **w.** consume man and beast;
Zep 1:3 I **w.** consume the fowls of the heaven.
Zep 1:3 I **w.** cut off man from off the land,
Zep 1:4 I **w.** also stretch out mine hand upon
Zep 1:4 and I **w.** cut off the remnant of Baal
Zep 1:8 that I **w.** punish the princes, and the
Zep 1:9 same day also **w.** I punish all those
Zep 1:12 I **w.** search Jerusalem with candles,
Zep 1:12 The Lord **w.** not do good,
Zep 1:12 neither **w.** he do evil.
Zep 1:17 And I **w.** bring distress upon men,
Zep 2:5 Philistines, I **w.** even destroy thee,
Zep 2:11 The Lord **w.** be terrible unto them:
Zep 2:11 he **w.** famish all the gods of the earth;
Zep 2:13 he **w.** stretch out his hand against the
Zep 2:13 and **w.** make Nineveh a desolation,
Zep 3:5 midst thereof; he **w.** not do iniquity:
Zep 3:9 then **w.** I turn to the people a pure
Zep 3:11 **w.** take away out of the midst of thee
Zep 3:12 I **w.** also leave in the midst of thee
Zep 3:17 he **w.** save, he **w.** rejoice over thee
Zep 3:17 he **w.** rest in his love, he **w.** joy over
Zep 3:18 I **w.** gather them that are sorrowful
Zep 3:19 time I **w.** undo all that afflict thee:
Zep 3:19 I **w.** save her that halteth, and gather
Zep 3:19 I **w.** get them praise and fame in
Zep 3:20 At that time **w.** I bring you again,
Zep 3:20 I **w.** make you a name and a praise
Hag 1:8 house: and I **w.** take pleasure in it,
Hag 1:8 and I **w.** be glorified, saith the Lord.
Hag 2:6 I **w.** shake the heavens, and the earth,
Hag 2:7 I **w.** shake all nations, and the desire
Hag 2:7 I **w.** fill this house with glory, saith

Hag 2:9 in this place w. I give peace, saith the
Hag 2:19 from this day w. I bless you
Hag 2:21 I w. shake the heavens and the earth;
Hag 2:22 I w. overthrow the throne of
Hag 2:22 I w. destroy the strength of the
Hag 2:22 and I w. overthrow the chariots,
Hag 2:23 w. I take thee, O Zerubbabel, my
Hag 2:23 Lord, and w. make thee as a signet:
Zec 1:3 I w. turn unto you, saith the Lord
Zec 1:9 me, I w. shew thee what these be.
Zec 2:5 w. be unto her a wall of fire round
Zec 2:5 and w. be glory in the midst of her
Zec 2:9 I w. shake mine hand upon them,
Zec 2:10, 11 and I w. dwell in the midst of thee,
Zec 3:4 I w. clothe thee with change of
Zec 3:7 I w. give thee places to walk among
Zec 3:8 I w. bring forth my servant the
Zec 3:9 I w. engrave the graving thereof,
Zec 3:9 I w. remove the iniquity of that land
Zec 5:4 I w. bring it forth, saith the Lord of
Zec 6:15 if ye w. diligently obey the voice of the
Zec 8:3 w. dwell in the midst of Jerusalem:
Zec 8:7 I w. save my people from the east
Zec 8:8 And I w. bring them, and they shall
Zec 8:8 be my people, and I w. be their God,
Zec 8:11 I w. not be unto the residue of this
Zec 8:12 I w. cause the remnant of this people
Zec 8:13 so w. I save you, and ye shall be a
Zec 8:21 seek the Lord of hosts: I w. go also.
Zec 8:23 is a Jew, saying, We w. go with you:
Zec 9:4 Behold, the Lord w. cast her out,
Zec 9:4 and he w. smite her power in the sea;
Zec 9:6 and I w. cut off the pride of the
Zec 9:7 And I w. take away his blood out of
Zec 9:8 And I w. encamp about mine house
Zec 9:10 I w. cut off the chariot from Ephraim,
Zec 9:12 that I w. render double unto thee;
Zec 10:6 I w. strengthen the house of Judah,
Zec 10:6 and I w. save the house of Joseph,
Zec 10:6 I w. bring them again to place them;
Zec 10:6 the Lord their God, and w. hear them
Zec 10:8 I w. hiss for them, and gather them;
Zec 10:9 I w. sow them among the people:
Zec 10:10 I w. bring them again also out of the
Zec 10:10 w. bring them into the land of Gilead
Zec 10:12 I w. strengthen them in the Lord;
Zec 11:6 For I w. no more pity the inhabitants
Zec 11:6 I w. deliver the men every one into his
Zec 11:6 of their hand I w. not deliver them.
Zec 11:7 And I w. feed the flock of slaughter,
Zec 11:9 Then said I, I w. not feed you: that
Zec 11:16 I w. raise up a shepherd in the land,
Zec 12:2 I w. make Jerusalem a cup of
Zec 12:3 w. I make Jerusalem a burdensome
Zec 12:4 I w. smite every horse with
Zec 12:4 I w. open mine eyes upon the house
Zec 12:4 and w. smite every horse of the
Zec 12:6 In that day w. I make the governors
Zec 12:9 I w. seek to destroy all the nations
Zec 12:10 I w. pour upon the house of David,
Zec 13:2 I w. cut off the names of the idols
Zec 13:2 and also I w. cause the prophets and
Zec 13:7 I w. turn mine hand upon the ones.
Zec 13:9 And I w. bring the third part through
Zec 13:9 and w. refine them as silver is refined,
Zec 13:9 and w. try them as gold is tried:
Zec 13:9 on my name, and I w. hear them:
Zec 13:9 I w. say, It is my people: and they
Zec 14:2 For I w. gather all nations against
Zec 14:12 the Lord w. smite all the people
Zec 14:17 that whoso w. not come up of all the
Zec 14:18 the Lord w. smite the heathen
Mal 1:4 we w. return and build the desolate
Mal 1:4 shall build, but I w. throw down;
Mal 1:5 The Lord w. be magnified from the
Mal 1:8 w. he be pleased with thee, or accept
Mal 1:9 God that he w. be gracious unto us:
Mal 1:9 w. he regard your persons? saith the
Mal 1:10 neither w. I accept an offering at your
Mal 2:2 w. not hear, and...w. not lay it to heart,
Mal 2:2 I w. even send a curse upon you,
Mal 2:2 you, and I w. curse your blessings:
Mal 2:3 Behold, I w. corrupt your seed, and
Mal 2:12 The Lord w. cut off the man that
Mal 2:13 or receiveth it with good w. at 7522
Mal 3:1 Behold, I w. send my messenger,
Mal 3:5 I w. come near to you to judgment;
Mal 3:5 I w. be a swift witness against the
Mal 3:7 unto me, and I w. return unto you,
Mal 3:8 W. a man rob God? Yet ye have
Mal 3:10 if I w. not open you the windows of
Mal 3:11 I w. rebuke the devourer for your
Mal 3:17 I w. spare them, as a man spareth
Mal 4:5 I w. send you Elijah the prophet
Mt 2:13 Herod w. seek the young child to 3195
Mt 3:12 and he w. throughly purge his floor,
Mt 3:12 but he w. burn up the chaff with
Mt 4:9 All these things w. I give thee, if thou
Mt 4:19 and I w. make you fishers of men,
Mt 5:40 if any man w. sue thee at the law, 2309
Mt 6:10 Thy w. be done in earth, as it is 2307
Mt 6:14 heavenly Father w. also forgive you:
Mt 6:15 neither w. your Father forgive your
Mt 6:21 is, there w. your heart be also
Mt 6:24 for either he w. hate the one, and love
Mt 6:24 or else he w. hold to the one, and
Mt 7:9 ask bread, w. he give him a stone?
Mt 7:10 ask a fish, w. he give him a serpent?
Mt 7:21 he that doeth the w. of my Father 2307
Mt 7:22 w. say to them in that day, Lord,
Mt 7:23 And then w. I profess unto them, I
Mt 7:24 I w. liken him unto a wise man,
Mt 8:3 him, saying, I w.; be thou clean. 2309
Mt 8:7 unto him, I w. come and heal him.
Mt 8:19 I w. follow thee whithersoever thou
Mt 9:13 I w. have mercy, and not sacrifice: 2309
Mt 9:15 but the days w. come, when the
Mt 9:38 he w. send forth labourers into his
Mt 10:17 w. deliver you up to the councils,
Mt 10:17 and they w. scourge you in their
Mt 10:32 w. I confess also before my Father
Mt 10:33 him w. I also deny before my Father
Mt 11:14 And if ye w. receive it, this is 2309
Mt 11:27 whomsoever the Son w. reveal him. 1014
Mt 11:28 heavy laden, and I w. give you rest.
Mt 12:7 I w. have mercy, and not sacrifice, 2309
Mt 12:11 w. he not lay hold on it, and lift it
Mt 12:18 I w. put my spirit upon him, and he
Mt 12:29 man? and then he w. spoil his house.
Mt 12:44 I w. return into my house from
Mt 12:50 do the w. of my Father which is 2307
Mt 13:30 of harvest I w. say to the reapers,
Mt 13:35 I w. open my mouth in parables;
Mt 13:35 I w. utter things which have been
Mt 15:32 I w. not send them away fasting, 2309
Mt 16:2 It w. be fair weather: for the sky is
Mt 16:3 It w. be foul weather to day: for the
Mt 16:18 upon this rock I w. build my church;
Mt 16:19 And I w. give unto thee the keys of
Mt 16:24 If any man w. come after me, let 2309
Mt 16:25 w. save his life shall lose it: 2309
Mt 16:25 w. lose his life for my sake shall find
Mt 18:14 so it is not the w. of your Father 2307
Mt 18:16 But if he w. not hear thee, then take
Mt 18:26, 29 with me, and I w. pay thee all
Mt 20:4 and whatsoever is right I w. give you
Mt 20:14 I w. give unto this last, even as 2309
Mt 20:15 to do what I w. with mine own? 2309
Mt 20:26 whosoever w. be great among you, 2309
Mt 20:27 whosoever w. be chief among you, 2309
Mt 20:32 What w. ye that I shall do unto 2309
Mt 21:3 and straightway he w. send them.
Mt 21:24 I also w. ask you one thing, which if
Mt 21:24 I in like wise w. tell you by what
Mt 21:25 he w. say unto us, Why did ye not then
Mt 21:29 He answered and said, I w. not: 2309
Mt 21:31 twain did the w. of his father? 2307
Mt 21:37 saying, They w. reverence my son.
Mt 21:40 what w. he do unto those husbandmen?
Mt 21:41 He w. miserably destroy those wicked
Mt 21:41 and w. let out his vineyard unto other
Mt 21:44 shall fall, it w. grind him to powder.
Mt 23:4 themselves w. not move from 2309
Mt 24:28 there w. the eagles be gathered
Mt 25:21, 23 I w. make thee ruler over many
Mt 26:15 unto them, What w. ye give me, 2309
Mt 26:15 and I w. deliver him unto you?
Mt 26:18 I w. keep the passover at thy house
Mt 26:29 I w. not drink henceforth of this fruit
Mt 26:31 it is written, I w. smite the shepherd,
Mt 26:32 again, I w. go before you into Galilee
Mt 26:33 of thee, yet w. I never be offended.
Mt 26:35 die with thee, yet w. I not deny thee
Mt 26:39 nevertheless not as I w., but as 2309
Mt 26:42 except I drink it, thy w. be done 2307
Mt 27:17 Whom w. ye that I release unto 2309
Mt 27:21 of the twain w. ye that I release 2309
Mt 27:42 from the cross, and we w. believe him.
Mt 27:43 deliver him...if he w. have him; 2309
Mt 27:49 whether Elias w. come to save him.
Mt 27:63 alive, After three days I w. rise again.
Mt 28:14 we w. persuade him, and secure you.
Mk 1:17 w. make you to become fishers of men.
Mk 1:41 saith unto him, I w.; be thou clean. 2309
Mk 2:20 But the days w. come, when the
Mk 2:22 spilled, and the bottles w. be marred:
Mk 3:27 except he w. first bind the strong
Mk 3:27 and then he w. spoil his house.
Mk 3:35 whosoever shall do the w. of God, 2307
Mk 4:13 then w. ye know all the parables?
Mk 6:22 thou wilt, and I w. give it thee.
Mk 6:23 I w. give it thee, unto the half of my
Mk 6:25 I w. that thou give me by and by 2309
Mk 8:3 houses, they w. faint by the way:
Mk 8:34 Whosoever w. come after me, let 2309
Mk 8:35 whosoever w. save his life shall 2309
Mk 9:50 saltness, wherewith w. ye season it?
Mk 10:43 whosoever w. be great among you, 2309
Mk 10:44 whosoever of you w. be...chiefest, 2309
Mk 11:3 straightway, he w. send him hither.
Mk 11:26 neither w. your Father which is in
Mk 11:29 I w. also ask of you one question,
Mk 11:29 I w. tell you by what authority I do
Mk 11:31 he w. say, Why then did ye not believe
Mk 12:6 saying, They w. reverence my son.
Mk 12:9 w. come and destroy the husbandmen,
Mk 12:9 w. give the vineyard unto others.
Mk 14:7 whensoever ye w. ye may do them. 2309
Mk 14:15 he w. shew you a large upper room
Mk 14:25 I w. drink no more of the fruit of the
Mk 14:27 is written, I w. smite the shepherd,
Mk 14:28 risen, I w. go before you into Galilee.
Mk 14:29 all shall be offended, yet w. not I.
Mk 14:31 thee, I w. not deny thee in any wise.
Mk 14:36 nevertheless not what I w., but 2309
Mk 14:58 I w. destroy this temple that is made
Mk 14:58 and within three days I w. build
Mk 15:9 W. ye that I release unto you the 2309
Mk 15:12 What w. ye then that I shall do 2309
Mk 15:36 whether Elias w. come to take him
Lu 2:14 peace, good w. toward men. 2107
Lu 3:17 and he w. throughly purge his floor,
Lu 3:17 w. gather the wheat into his garner;
Lu 3:17 but the chaff he w. burn with fire
Lu 4:6 power w. I give thee, and the glory
Lu 4:6 and to whomsoever I w. I give it. 2309
Lu 4:23 w. surely say unto me this proverb,
Lu 5:5 at thy word I w. let down the net.
Lu 5:13 him, saying, I w.: be thou clean. 2309
Lu 5:35 days w. come, when the bridegroom
Lu 5:37 else the new wine w. burst the bottles,
Lu 6:9 unto them, I w. ask you one thing;
Lu 6:47 I w. shew you to whom he is like:
Lu 7:42 which of them w. love him most?
Lu 9:5 And whosoever w. not receive you,
Lu 9:23 If any man w. come after me, let 2309
Lu 9:24 whosoever w. save his life shall 2309
Lu 9:24 whosoever w. lose his life for my sake,
Lu 9:57 I w. follow thee whithersoever thou
Lu 9:61 also said, Lord, I w. follow thee;
Lu 10:22 he to whom the Son w. reveal him. 1014
Lu 10:35 when I come again, I w. repay thee.
Lu 11:2 Thy w. be done, as in heaven, so 2307
Lu 11:8 Though he w. not rise and give him,
Lu 11:8 because of his importunity he w. rise
Lu 11:11 that is a father, w. he give him stone?
Lu 11:11 w. he for a fish give him a serpent?
Lu 11:12 an egg, w. he offer him a scorpion?
Lu 11:24 I w. return unto my house whence I
Lu 11:49 I w. send them prophets and apostles,
Lu 12:5 I w. forward you whom ye shall fear:
Lu 12:18 And he said, This w. I do:
Lu 12:18 I w. pull down my barns, and build
Lu 12:18 there w. I bestow all my fruits and
Lu 12:19 I w. say to my soul, Soul, thou hast
Lu 12:28 how much more w. he clothe you,
Lu 12:34 there w. your heart be also.
Lu 12:36 when he w. return from the wedding;

Lu 12:37 and w. come forth and serve them
Lu 12:44 he w. make him ruler over all that he
Lu 12:46 lord of that servant w. come in a day
Lu 12:46 not aware, and w. cut him in sunder,
Lu 12:46 w. appoint him his portion with the
Lu 12:47 knew his lord's w., and prepared 2307
Lu 12:47 neither did according to his w., 2307
Lu 12:48 much, of him they w. ask the more
Lu 12:49 w. I, if it, be already kindled? 2309
Lu 12:55 wind blow, ye say, There w. be heat;
Lu 13:24 I say unto you, w. seek to enter in,
Lu 13:31 hence: for Herod w. kill thee. 2309
Lu 14:5 w. not straightway pull him out on the.
Lu 15:18 I w. arise and go to my father,
Lu 15:18 w. say unto him, Father, I have sinned
Lu 16:11 who w. commit to your trust the true
Lu 16:13 for either he w. hate the one, and love
Lu 16:13 or else he w. hold to the one, and
Lu 16:30 them from the dead, they w. repent
Lu 16:31 neither w. they be persuaded, though
Lu 17:1 impossible but that offences w. come:
Lu 17:7 w. say unto him by and by, when he is.
Lu 17:8 And w. not rather say unto him,
Lu 17:22 The days w. come, when ye shall
Lu 17:37 thither w. the eagles be gathered
Lu 18:5 I w. avenge her, lest by her continual
Lu 18:8 that he w. avenge them speedily
Lu 19:14 We w. not have this man to reign 2309
Lu 19:22 of thine own mouth w. I judge thee,
Lu 20:3 I w. ask you one thing; and answer
Lu 20:5 he w. say, Why then believed ye him
Lu 20:6 Of men; all the people w. stone us:
Lu 20:13 I w. send my beloved son: it may be
Lu 20:13 may be they w. reverence him when
Lu 20:18 shall fall, it w. grind him to powder
Lu 21:6 the days w. come, in the which there
Lu 21:7 what sign w. there be when these
Lu 21:15 For I w. give you a mouth and
Lu 22:16 you, I w. not any more eat thereof,
Lu 22:18 I w. not drink of the fruit of the vine
Lu 22:42 nevertheless not my w., but thine, 2307
Lu 22:67 If I tell you, ye w. not believe:
Lu 22:68 ye w. not answer me, nor let me go
Lu 23:16 I w. therefore chastise him, and
Lu 23:22 I w. therefore chastise him, and let
Lu 23:25 but he delivered Jesus to their w. 2307
Joh 1:13 w. of the flesh, nor of the w. of man, 2307
Joh 2:19 and in three days I w. raise it up
Joh 4:25 he is come, he w. tell us all things.
Joh 4:34 is to do the w. of him that sent me 2307
Joh 4:48 signs and wonders, ye w. not believe.
Joh 5:20 and he w. shew him greater works
Joh 5:21 the Son quickeneth whom he w. 2309
Joh 5:30 because I seek not mine own w., 2307
Joh 5:30 w. of the Father which...sent me, 2307
Joh 5:40 and ye w. not come to me, that ye 2309
Joh 5:43 in his own name, him ye w. receive
Joh 5:45 Do not think that I w. accuse you
Joh 6:37 cometh to me I w. in no wise cast out
Joh 6:38 heaven, not to do mine own w., 2307
Joh 6:38 but the w. of him that sent me. 2307
Joh 6:39 Father's w. which hath sent me 2307
Joh 6:40 this is the w. of him that sent me, 2307
Joh 6:40, 44 I w. raise him up at the last day
Joh 6:51 the bread that I w. give is my flesh,
Joh 6:51 I w. give for the life of the world
Joh 6:54 and I w. raise him up at the last day
Joh 6:67 the twelve, W. ye also go away? 2309
Joh 7:17 If any man w....he shall know 2309
Joh 7:17 If any man...do his w., he shall 2307
Joh 7:31 w. he do more miracles than these
Joh 7:35 Whither w. he go, that we shall not 3195
Joh 7:35 w. he go unto the dispersed among 3195
Joh 8:22 said the Jews, W. he kill himself?
Joh 8:44 the lusts of your father ye w. do, 2309
Joh 9:27 w. ye also be his disciples? 2309
Joh 9:31 and doeth his w., him he heareth. 2307
Joh 10:5 And a stranger w. they not follow,
Joh 10:5 w. flee from him: for they know not
Joh 11:22 wilt ask of God, God w. give it thee.
Joh 11:48 thus alone, all men w. belive on him:
Joh 11:56 that he w. not come to the feast?
Joh 12:26 serve me, him w. my Father honour
Joh 12:28 glorified it, and w. glorify it again.
Joh 12:32 the earth, w. draw all men unto me.
Joh 13:37 I w. lay down my life for thy sake.
Joh 14:3 I w. come again, and receive you unto
Joh 14:13 that w. I do, that the Father may be
Joh 14:14 ask any thing in my name, I w. do it.
Joh 14:16 I w. pray the Father, and he shall give.
Joh 14:18 I w. not leave you comfortless:
Joh 14:18 you comfortless: I w. come to you
Joh 14:21 I w. love him, and w. manifest myself.
Joh 14:23 a man love me, he w. keep my words:
Joh 14:23 w. love him, and we w. come unto him,
Joh 14:26 whom the Father w. send in my name,
Joh 14:30 Hereafter I w. not talk much with you:
Joh 15:7 ye shall ask what ye w., and it 2309
Joh 15:20 me, they w. also persecute you;
Joh 15:20 my sayings, they w. keep yours also
Joh 15:21 all these things w. they do unto you
Joh 15:26 I w. send unto you from the Father,
Joh 16:2 w. think that he doeth God sevice.
Joh 16:3 And these things w. they do unto you,
Joh 16:7 the Comforter w. not come unto you;
Joh 16:7 if I depart, I w. send him unto you.
Joh 16:8 he w. reprove the world of sin, and of
Joh 16:13 come, he w. guide you into all truth:
Joh 16:13 and he w. shew you things to come.
Joh 16:22 but I w. see you again, and your
Joh 16:23 Father in my name, he w. give it you
Joh 16:26 that I w. pray the Father for you:
Joh 17:24 Father, I w. that they also, whom. 2309
Joh 17:26 unto them thy name, and w. declare it:
Joh 18:39 w. ye therefore that I release unto 1014
Joh 20:15 hast laid him, and I w. take him away.
Joh 20:25 hand into his side, I w. not believe.
Joh 21:22 If I w. that he tarry till I come, 2309
Joh 21:23 If I w. that he tarry till
Ac 2:17 God, I w. pour out my Spirit upon all
Ac 2:18 I w. pour out in those days of my
Ac 2:19 I w. shew wonders in heaven above,
Ac 3:23 soul, which w. not hear that prophet,
Ac 5:38 be of men, it w. come to nought:
Ac 6:4 we w. give ourselves continually to
Ac 7:7 they shall be in bondage w. I judge,
Ac 7:34 now come, I w. send thee into Egypt.
Ac 7:43 w. carry you away beyond Babylon.
Ac 7:49 what house w. ye build me? saith the
Ac 9:16 I w. shew him how great things he
Ac 13:22 heart, which shall fulfill all my w. 2307
Ac 13:34 I w. give you the sure mercies of
Ac 13:36 own generation by the w. of God, 1012
Ac 15:16 After this I w. return, and w. build
Ac 15:16 w. build again the ruins thereof, and I
Ac 15:16 the ruins thereof, and I w. set it up:
Ac 17:18 said, What w. this babbler say? 2309
Ac 17:31 which he w. judge the world in 3195
Ac 17:32 w. hear thee again of this matter
Ac 18:6 henceforth I w. go unto the Gentiles.
Ac 18:15 I w. be no judge of such matters. 1014
Ac 18:21 but I w. return again unto you,
Ac 18:21 again unto you, if God w. 2309
Ac 21:14 The w. of the Lord be done. 2307
Ac 21:22 for they w. hear that thou art come.
Ac 22:14 that thou shouldest know his w., 2307
Ac 22:18 for they w. not receive thy testimony
Ac 22:21 I w. send thee far hence unto the
Ac 23:14 we w. eat nothing until we have slain
Ac 23:21 they w. neither eat nor drink till they
Ac 23:35 I w. hear thee, said he, when thine
Ac 24:22 I w. know the uttermost of your
Ac 24:25 convenient season, I w. call for thee.
Ac 26:16 in the which I w. appear unto thee;
Ac 27:10 that this voyage w. be with hurt 3195
Ac 28:28 the Gentiles, and that they w. hear it
Ro 1:10 by the w. of God to come unto you. 2307
Ro 2:6 Who w. render to every man according
Ro 2:18 knowest his w., and approvest the 2307
Ro 4:8 to whom the Lord w. not impute sin.
Ro 5:7 for a righteous man w. one die:
Ro 7:18 for to w. is present with me; but 2309
Ro 8:27 the saints according to the w. of God.
Ro 9:9 At this time w. I come, and Sarah
Ro 9:15 I w. have mercy on whom I...have
Ro 9:15 mercy on whom I w. have mercy,
Ro 9:15 I w. have compassion on whom I
Ro 9:15 on whom I w. have compassion.
Ro 9:18 mercy on whom he w. have mercy, 2309
Ro 9:18 and whom he w. he hardeneth. 2309
Ro 9:19 For who hath resisted his w.? 1013
Ro 9:25 I w. call them my people, which were
Ro 9:28 For he w. finish the work, and cut it
Ro 9:28 a short work w. the Lord make upon
Ro 10:19 I w. provoke you to jealousy by them
Ro 10:19 by a foolish nation I w. anger you.
Ro 12:2 acceptable, and perfect, w. of God. 2307
Ro 12:19 Vengeance is mine; I w. repay, saith
Ro 15:9 For this cause I w. confess to thee.
Ro 15:18 I w. not dare to speak of any of those
Ro 15:24 journey into Spain, I w. come to you:
Ro 15:28 fruit, I w. come by you into Spain.
Ro 15:32 you with joy by the w. of God, 2307
1Co 1:1 Jesus Christ through the w. of God, 2307
1Co 1:19 I w. destroy the wisdom of the wise,
1Co 1:19 w. bring to nothing the understanding
1Co 4:5 who both w. bring to light the hidden
1Co 4:5 and w. make manifest the counsels
1Co 4:19 But I w. come to you shortly,
1Co 4:19 if the Lord w., 2309
1Co 4:19 w. know, not the speech of them
1Co 4:21 What w. ye? shall I come unto you 2309
1Co 6:12 I w. not be brought under the power
1Co 6:14 w. also raise up us by his own power.
1Co 7:36 let him do what he w., he sinneth 2309
1Co 7:37 but hath power over his own w., 2307
1Co 7:37 heart that he w. keep his virgin,
1Co 7:39 to be married to whom she w.; 2309
1Co 8:13 I w. eat no flesh while the world
1Co 9:17 but if against my w., a dispensation 210
1Co 10:13 who w. not suffer you to be tempted
1Co 10:13 w. with the temptation also make a
1Co 11:34 rest w. I set in order when I come.
1Co 12:11 to every man severally as he w. 1014
1Co 14:15 is it then? I w. pray with the spirit,
1Co 14:15 and I w. pray with the understanding
1Co 14:15 I w. sing with the spirit,
1Co 14:15 and I w. sing with the understanding
1Co 14:21 other lips w. I speak unto this people;
1Co 14:21 yet for all that w. they not hear me,
1Co 14:23 w. they not say that ye are mad?
1Co 14:25 down on his face he w. worship God,
1Co 14:35 And if they w. learn any thing, 2309
1Co 15:35 some man w. say, How are the dead
1Co 16:3 them w. I send to bring your liberality
1Co 16:5 Now I w. come unto you, when I shall
1Co 16:6 And it may be that I w. abide, yea,
1Co 16:7 I w. not see you now by the way; 2309
1Co 16:8 I w. tarry at Ephesus until Pentecost.
1Co 16:12 his w. was not at all to come at 2307
1Co 16:12 but he w. come when he shall have
2Co 1:1 of Jesus Christ by the w. of God, 2307
2Co 1:10 we trust that he w. yet deliver us;
2Co 6:16 I w. dwell in them, and walk in them,
2Co 6:16 and I w. be their God, and they shall
2Co 6:17 unclean thing; and I w. receive you,
2Co 6:18 And w. be a Father unto you, and ye
2Co 8:5 and unto us by the w. of God. 2307
2Co 8:11 as there was a readiness to w., 2309
2Co 10:11 such w. we be also in deed when we
2Co 10:13 we w. not boast of things without our
2Co 11:9 unto you, and so w. I keep myself.
2Co 11:12 But what I do, that I w. do, that I may
2Co 11:18 glory after the flesh, I w. glory also.
2Co 11:30 I w. glory of the things which concern
2Co 12:1 I w. come to visions and revelations of
2Co 12:5 Of such an one w. I glory: yet of
2Co 12:5 of myself I w. not glory, but in mine
2Co 12:6 not be a fool; for I w. say the truth:
2Co 12:9 w. I rather glory in mine infirmities,
2Co 12:14 and I w. not be burdensome to you:
2Co 12:15 I w. very gladly spend and be spent
2Co 12:21 my God w. humble me among you,
2Co 13:2 that, if I come again, I w. not spare:
Ga 1:4 according to the w. of God and our 2307
Ga 5:10 that ye w. be none otherwise minded:
Eph 1:1 of Jesus Christ by the w. of God, 2307
Eph 1:5 to the good pleasure of his w., 2307
Eph 1:9 unto us the mystery of his w., 2307
Eph 1:11 after the counsel of his own w. 2307
Eph 5:17 but...what the w. of the Lord is. 2307
Eph 6:6 doing the w. of God from the heart; 2307
Eph 6:7 With good w. doing service, as 2133
Php 1:6 w. I perform it until the day of Jesus
Php 1:15 strife; and some also of good w. 2107
Php 1:18 therein do rejoice, yea, and w. rejoice.

Book	Ref	Context	No.
Php	2:13	both to w. and to do of his good	*2309*
Php	2:20	who w. naturally care for your state.	
Php	2:23	as I shall see how it w. go with me.	
Col	1:1	of Jesus Christ by the w. of God,	*2307*
Col	1:9	filled with the knowledge of his w.	*2307*
Col	2:23	a shew of wisdom in w. worship,	*1479*
Col	4:12	and complete in all the w. of God.	*2307*
1Th	4:3	w. of God, even your sanctification,	*2307*
1Th	4:14	which sleep in Jesus w. God bring	
1Th	5:18	for this is the w. of God in Christ	*2307*
1Th	5:24	that calleth you, who also w. do it.	
2Th	2:7	only he who now letteth w. let, until	
2Th	3:4	w. do the things which we command	
1Ti	2:4	Who w. have all men to be saved,	*2309*
1Ti	2:8	I w. therefore that men pray	*1014*
1Ti	5:11	against Christ, they w. marry;	*2309*
1Ti	5:14	I w. therefore that the younger	*1014*
1Ti	6:9	that w. be rich fall into temptation	*1014*
2Ti	1:1	of Jesus Christ by the w. of God,	*2307*
2Ti	2:12	if we deny him, he also w. deny us:	
2Ti	2:16	w. increase unto more ungodliness.	
2Ti	2:17	their word w. eat as doth a canker:	
2Ti	2:25	if God...w. give them repentance	
2Ti	2:26	are taken captive by him at his w.	*2307*
2Ti	3:12	and all that w. live godly in Christ	*2309*
2Ti	4:3	time w. come when they w. not endure	
2Ti	4:18	and w. preserve me unto his heavenly	
Tit	3:8	these things I w. that thou affirm	*1014*
Phm	19	with mine own hand, I w. repay it:	
Heb	1:5	I w. be to him a Father, and he shall	
Heb	2:4	Ghost, according to his own w.?	*2308*
Heb	2:12	I w. declare thy name unto my	
Heb	2:12	the church w. I sing praise unto thee.	
Heb	2:13	And again, I w. put my trust in him.	
Heb	3:7	saith, To day if ye w. hear his voice,	
Heb	3:15	To day if ye w. hear his voice,	
Heb	4:7	To day if ye w. hear his voice, harden	
Heb	6:3	And this w. we do, if God permit.	
Heb	6:14	Saying, Surely blessing I w. bless thee,	
Heb	6:14	and multiplying I w. multiply thee.	
Heb	7:21	The Lord sware and w. not repent,	
Heb	8:8	when I w. make a new covenant	
Heb	8:10	I w. make with the house of Israel	
Heb	8:10	I w. put my laws into their mind,	
Heb	8:10	and I w. be to them a God, and they	
Heb	8:12	For I w. be merciful to their	
Heb	8:12	iniquities w. I remember no more.	
Heb	10:7	written of me,) to do thy w., O God,	*2307*
Heb	10:9	he, Lo, I come to do thy w., O God	*2307*
Heb	10:10	By the which w. we are sanctified	*2307*
Heb	10:16	covenant that I w. make with them	
Heb	10:16	I w. put my laws into their hearts,	
Heb	10:16	and in their minds w. I write them;	
Heb	10:17	and iniquities w. I remember no more.	
Heb	10:30	me, I w. recompense, saith the Lord.	
Heb	10:36	after ye have done the w. of God,	2307
Heb	10:37	shall come w. come, and w. not tarry.	
Heb	13:4	and adulterers God w. judge.	
Heb	13:5	I w. never leave thee, nor forsake	
Heb	13:6	I w. not fear what man shall do unto	
Heb	13:21	in every good work to do his w.,	*2307*
Heb	13:23	if he come shortly, I w. see you.	
Jas	1:18	Of his own w. begat he us with the	*1014*
Jas	2:18	I w. shew thee my faith by my works.	
Jas	4:4	therefore w. be a friend of the	*1014*
Jas	4:7	Resist the devil, and he w. flee from	
Jas	4:8	to God, and he w. draw nigh to you.	
Jas	4:13	to morrow we w. go into such a city,	
Jas	4:15	If the Lord w., we shall live, and	*2309*
1Pe	2:15	For so is the w. of God, that with	*2307*
1Pe	3:10	For he that w. love life, and see	*2309*
1Pe	3:13	And who is he that w. harm you, if ye	
1Pe	3:17	it is better, if the w. of God be so,	*2307*
1Pe	4:2	lusts of men, but to the w. of God.	*2307*
1Pe	4:3	wrought the w. of the Gentiles,	*2307*
1Pe	4:19	suffer according to the w. of God	*2307*
2Pe	1:12	I w. not be negligent to put you	
2Pe	1:15	I w. endeavour that ye may be able	
2Pe	1:21	not in old time by the w. of man:	*2307*
2Pe	3:10	day of the Lord w. come as a thief	
1Jo	2:17	he that doeth the w. of God abideth	*2307*
1Jo	5:14	according to his w., he heareth us:	*2307*
3Jo	10	I w. remember to his deeds which he	
3Jo	13	I w. not with ink and pen write	*2309*
Jude	5	I w....put you in remembrance,	*1014*
Re	2:5	**or else I w. come unto thee quickly,**	
Re	2:5	**w. remove thy candlestick out of his**	
Re	2:7	**To him that overcometh w. I give to**	
Re	2:10	**and I w. give thee a crown of life.**	
Re	2:16	**or else I w. come unto thee quickly,**	
Re	2:16	**w. fight against them with the sword**	
Re	2:17	**To him that overcometh w. I give to**	
Re	2:17	**and w. give him a white stone, and in**	
Re	2:22	**Behold, I w. cast her into a bed, and**	
Re	2:23	**I w. kill her children with death;**	
Re	2:23	**and I w. give unto every one of you**	
Re	2:24	**I w. put upon you none other burden.**	
Re	2:26	**to whom w. I give power over the**	
Re	2:28	**And I w. give him the morning star.**	
Re	3:3	**I w. come on thee as a thief, and**	
Re	3:3	**know what hour I w. come upon thee**	
Re	3:5	**I w. not blot out his name out of the**	
Re	3:5	**but I w. confess his name before my**	
Re	3:9	**I w. make them of the synagogue of**	
Re	3:9	**I w. make them to come and worship**	
Re	3:10	**I also w. keep thee from the hour of**	
Re	3:12	**Him that overcometh w. I make a**	
Re	3:12	**I w. write upon him the name of my**	
Re	3:12	**I w. write upon him my new name.**	
Re	3:16	**I w. spue thee out of my mouth.**	*3195*
Re	3:20	**I w. come in to him, and w. sup with**	
Re	3:21	**To him that overcometh w. I grant to**	
Re	4:1	I w. shew thee things which must be	
Re	11:3	w. give power unto my two witnesses,	
Re	11:5	And if any man w. hurt them,	*2309*
Re	11:5	and if any man w. hurt them, he	*2309*
Re	11:6	all plagues, as often as they w.	*2309*
Re	17:1	I w. shew unto thee the judgment of	
Re	17:7	I w. tell thee the mystery of the	
Re	17:17	put in their hearts to fulfill his w.,	*1106*
Re	21:3	and he w. dwell with them, and they	
Re	21:6	I w. give unto him that is athirst of	
Re	21:7	and I w. be of God, and he shall be	
Re	21:9	hither, I w. shew thee the bride, the	
Re	22:17	whosoever w., let him take the	*2309*

WILLETH

Book	Ref	Context	No.
Ro	9:16	So then it is not of him that w.,	*2309*

WILLING

Book	Ref	Context	No.
Ge	24:5	the woman will not be w. to follow	14
Ge	24:8	woman will not be w. to follow thee,	14
Ex	35:5	whosoever is of a w. heart, let him	5081
Ex	35:21	one whom his spirit made w.,	5068
Ex	35:22	as many as were w. hearted,	5081
Ex	35:29	of Israel brought a w. offering	5071
Ex	35:29	whose heart made them w. to	5068
1Ch	28:9	perfect heart and with a w. mind:	2655
1Ch	28:21	workmanship every w. skilful	5081
1Ch	29:5	who then is w. to consecrate his	5068
Job	39:9	Will the unicorn be w. to serve thee,	14
Ps	110:3	Thy people shall be w. in the day	5071
Isa	1:19	If ye be w. and obedient, ye shall eat	14
Mt	1:19	w. to make her a publick example,	*2309*
Mt	26:41	**the spirit indeed is w., but the**	*4289*
Mk	15:15	Pilate, w. to content the people,	*1014*
Lu	10:29	But he, w. to justify himself, said	*2309*
Lu	22:42	**Father, if thou be w., remove this**	*1014*
Lu	23:20	Pilate...w. to release Jesus, spake	*2309*
Joh	5:35	**ye were w. for a season to rejoice**	*2309*
Ac	24:27	w. to shew the Jews a pleasure,	*2309*
Ac	25:9	w. to do the Jews a pleasure,	*2309*
Ac	27:43	But the centurion, w. to save Paul,	*1014*
Ro	9:22	if God, w. to show his wrath, and	*2309*
2Co	5:8	w. rather to be absent from the	*2106*
2Co	8:3	power they were w. of themselves;	*830*
2Co	8:12	For if there be first a w. mind,	*4288*
1Th	2:8	were w. to have imparted unto you,	*2106*
1Ti	6:18	to distribute, w. to communicate;	*2843*
Heb	6:17	w. more abundantly to shew unto	*1014*
Heb	13:18	in all things w. to live honestly.	*2309*
2Pe	3:9	not w. that any should perish,	*1014*

WILLINGLY

Book	Ref	Context	No.
Ex	25:2	every man that giveth it w. with	5068
Jg	5:2	the people w. offered themselves.	5068
Jg	5:9	that offered themselves w. among	5068
Jg	8:25	answered, We will w. give them.	5414
1Ch	29:6	of the king's work, offered w.,	5068
1Ch	29:9	rejoiced, for that they offered w.,	5068
1Ch	29:9	with perfect heart they offered w.	5068
1Ch	29:14	should be able to offer so w. after	5068
1Ch	29:17	I have w. offered all these things:	5068
1Ch	29:17	present here, to offer w. unto thee.	5068
2Ch	17:16	w. offered himself unto the Lord;	5068
2Ch	35:8	princes gave w. unto the people,	5071
Ezr	1:6	beside all that was w. offered.	5068
Ezr	3:5	that w. offered a freewill offering	5068
Ezr	7:16	offering w. for the house of their God.	5068
Ne	11:2	that w. offered themselves to dwell at	
Pr	31:13	and worketh w. with her hands.	2656
La	3:33	For he doth not afflict w., nor	3820
Ho	5:11	because he w. walked after the	2974
Joh	6:21	they w. received him into the ship:	*2309*
Ro	8:20	subject to vanity, not w., but	*1635*
1Co	9:17	For if I do this thing w., I	*1635*
Phm	14	it were of necessity, but w.	*2596,1595*
1Pe	5:2	thereof, not by constraint, but w.;	*1596*
2Pe	3:5	For this they w. are ignorant of,	*2309*

WILLOW See also WILLOWS.

Book	Ref	Context	No.
Eze	17:5	waters, and set it as a w. tree.	6851

WILLOWS

Book	Ref	Context	No.
Le	23:40	thick trees, and w. of the brook;	6155
Job	40:22	the w. of the brook compass him	6155
Ps	137:2	We hanged our harps upon the w.	6155
Isa	15:7	carry away to the brook of the w.	6155
Isa	44:4	grass, as w. by the water courses.	6155

WILL-WORSHIP See WILL and WORSHIP.

WILT

Book	Ref	Context	No.
Ge	13:9	if thou w. take the left hand, then I	
Ge	15:2	what w. thou give me, seeing I go	
Ge	16:8	thou? and whither w. thou go?	
Ge	18:23	W. thou also destroy the righteous	
Ge	18:24	w. thou also destroy and not spare	
Ge	18:28	w. thou destroy all the city for lack of	
Ge	20:4	w. thou slay also a righteous nation?	
Ge	21:23	that thou w. not deal falsely with me,	
Ge	23:13	But if thou w. give it, I pray thee,	
Ge	24:58	unto her, W. thou go with this man?	
Ge	26:29	That thou w. do us no hurt,	
Ge	30:31	if thou w. do this thing for me, I will	
Ge	38:16	What w. thou give me, that thou	
Ge	38:17	W. thou give me a pledge, till thou	
Ge	43:4	If thou w. send our brother with us,	
Ge	43:5	But if thou w. not send him, we will	
Ex	4:13	the hand of him whom thou w. send.	
Ex	8:21	if thou w. not let my people go,	
Ex	9:2	let them go, and w. hold them still,	
Ex	9:17	people, that thou w. not let them go?	
Ex	10:3	long w. thou refuse to humble thyself	
Ex	13:13	and if thou w. redeem it, then thou	
Ex	15:26	w. diligently hearken to the voice	
Ex	15:26	and w. do that which is right in his	
Ex	15:26	w. give ear to his commandments,	
Ex	18:18	Thou w. surely wear away, both thou	
Ex	20:25	And if thou w. make an altar of stone,	
Ex	32:32	now, if thou w. forgive their sin—;	
Ex	33:12	know whom thou w. send with me.	
Nu	16:14	w. thou put out the eyes of these men?	
Nu	16:22	and w. thou be wroth with all the	
Nu	21:2	If thou w. indeed deliver this people	
De	23:13	when thou w. ease thyself abroad,	
De	28:15	if thou w. not hearken unto the voice	
De	28:58	If thou w. not observe to do all	
De	30:17	so that thou w. not hear, but shall be	
Jos	7:9	what w. thou do unto thy great name?	
Jg	1:14	Caleb said unto her, What w. thou?	
Jg	4:8	If thou w. go with me, then I will go:	
Jg	4:8	but if thou w. not go with me, then I	
Jg	6:36	If thou w. save Israel by mine hand,	
Jg	6:37	thou w. save Israel by mine hand,	
Jg	11:24	W. not thou possess that which	
Jg	13:16	and if thou w. offer a burnt offering,	
Ru	4:4	If thou w. redeem it, redeem it:	
Ru	4:4	but if thou w. not redeem it, then tell	
1Sa	1:11	thou w. indeed look on the affliction	
1Sa	1:11	but w. give unto thine handmaid a	
1Sa	1:14	How long w. thou be drunken?	
1Sa	14:37	w. thou deliver them into the hand	
1Sa	16:1	How long w. thou mourn for Saul,	
1Sa	19:5	then w. thou sin against innocent	
1Sa	21:9	if thou w. take that, take it: for there	
1Sa	24:21	thou w. not cut off my seed after me,	
1Sa	24:21	that thou w. not destroy my name	
1Sa	25:17	know and consider what thou w. do;	
1Sa	30:15	by God; that thou w. neither kill me,	
2Sa	5:19	w. thou deliver them into mine hand?	
2Sa	13:4	w. thou not tell me? And Amnon said	

2Sa 18:22 Wherefore w. thou run, my son,
2Sa 20:19 why w. thou swallow up the
2Sa 22:26 thou w. shew thyself merciful,
2Sa 22:26 man thou w. shew thyself upright
2Sa 22:27 the pure thou w. shew thyself pure;
2Sa 22:27 thou w. shew thyself unsavoury.
2Sa 22:28 And the afflicted people thou w. save:
2Sa 24:13 or w. thou flee three months before
1Ki 3:14 And if thou w. walk in my ways,
1Ki 6:12 if thou w. walk in my statutes,
1Ki 9:4 And if thou w. walk before me,
1Ki 9:4 and w. keep my statutes and my
1Ki 11:38 w. hearken unto all that I command
1Ki 11:38 and w. walk in my ways, and do that
1Ki 12:7 If thou w. be a servant unto this
1Ki 12:7 and w. serve them, and answer them,
1Ki 13:8 If thou w. give me half thine house,
1Ki 22:4 W. thou go with me to battle to
2Ki 3:7 w. thou go with me against Moab to
2Ki 4:23 Wherefore w. thou go to him to day?
2Ki 8:12 the evil that thou w. do unto the
2Ki 8:12 their strong holds w. thou set on fire,
2Ki 8:12 men w. thou slay with the sword,
2Ki 8:12 and w. dash their children, and rip up
2Ki 18:24 How then w. thou turn away the face
1Ch 14:10 w. thou deliver them into mine hand?
1Ch 17:25 that thou w. build him an house:
2Ch 7:17 if thou w. walk before me, as David
2Ch 18:3 king of Judah, W. thou go with me
2Ch 20:9 affliction, then thou w. hear and help
2Ch 20:12 O our God, w. thou not judge them?
2Ch 25:8 But if thou w. go, do it, be strong for
Ne 2:6 and when thou w. return?
Es 5:3 unto her, What w. thou, queen Esther?
Job 4:2 with thee, w. thou be grieved?
Job 5:1 to which of the saints w. thou turn?
Job 7:19 How long w. thou not depart from me,
Job 8:2 How long w. thou not speak these
Job 9:28 that thou w. not hold me innocent.
Job 10:9 and w. thou bring me into dust again?
Job 10:14 and thou w. not acquit me from mine
Job 13:25 W. thou break a leaf driven to and
Job 13:25 and w. thou pursue the dry stubble?
Job 14:15 w. have a desire to the work of thine
Job 30:23 I know that thou w. bring me to death,
Job 34:17 w. thou condemn him that is most
Job 38:39 W. thou hunt the prey for the lion?
Job 39:11 W. thou trust him, because his
Job 39:11 or w. thou leave thy labour to him?
Job 39:12 W. thou believe him, that he will
Job 40:8 W. thou also disannul my
Job 40:8 w. thou condemn me, that thou
Job 41:4 w. thou take him for a servant for
Job 41:5 W. thou play with him as with a bird,
Job 41:5 or w. thou bind him for thy maidens?
Ps 5:12 Lord, w. thou bless the righteous;
Ps 5:12 with favour w. thou compass him as
Ps 10:13 in his heart, Thou w. not require it.
Ps 10:17 w. prepare their heart, thou w. cause
Ps 13:1 How long w. thou forget me, O Lord?
Ps 13:1 long w. thou hide thy face from me?
Ps 16:10 For thou w. not leave my soul in hell;
Ps 16:10 w. thou suffer thine Holy One to see
Ps 16:11 Thou w. shew me the path of life:
Ps 17:6 thee, for thou w. hear me, O God:
Ps 18:25 thou w. shew thyself merciful;
Ps 18:25 man thou w. shew thyself upright;
Ps 18:26 the pure thou w. shew thyself pure;
Ps 18:26 thou w. shew thyself froward.
Ps 18:27 For thou w. save the afflicted people;
Ps 18:27 but w. bring down high looks
Ps 18:28 thou w. light my candle: the Lord my
Ps 35:17 Lord, how long w. thou look on?
Ps 38:15 thou w. hear, O Lord my God
Ps 41:2 thou w. not deliver him unto the will
Ps 41:3 w. make all his bed in his sickness.
Ps 51:17 heart, O God, thou w. not despise.
Ps 56:13 w. not thou deliver my feet from
Ps 60:10 W. not thou, O God, which hadst
Ps 61:6 Thou w. prolong the king's life: and
Ps 65:5 in righteousness w. thou answer us,
Ps 79:5 Lord? w. thou be angry for ever?
Ps 80:4 how long w. thou be angry against
Ps 81:8 O Israel, if thou w. hearken unto me;
Ps 85:5 W. thou be angry with us for ever?
Ps 85:5 w. thou draw out thine anger to all
Ps 85:6 W. thou not revive us again: that thy
Ps 86:7 upon thee: for thou w. answer me
Ps 88:10 W. thou shew wonders to the dead?
Ps 89:46 Lord? w. thou hide thyself for ever?
Ps 101:2 O when w. thou come unto me? I will
Ps 108:11 W. not thou, O God, who hast cast
Ps 108:11 w. not thou, O God, go forth with our
Ps 119:82 saying, When w. thou comfort me?
Ps 119:84 w. thou execute judgment on them
Ps 138:7 midst of trouble, thou w. revive me:
Ps 139:19 Surely thou w. slay the wicked, O God:
Pr 2:1 My son, if thou w. receive my words,
Pr 5:20 why w. thou, my son, be ravished
Pr 6:9 How long w. thou sleep, O sluggard?
Pr 6:9 when w. thou arise out of thy sleep?
Pr 23:5 W. thou set thine eyes upon that
Isa 26:3 Thou w. keep him in perfect peace,
Isa 26:12 Lord, thou w. ordain peace for us:
Isa 27:8 shooteth forth, thou w. debate with it:
Isa 36:9 How then w. thou turn away the face
Isa 38:12, 13 w. thou make an end of me.
Isa 38:16 so w. thou recover me, and make
Isa 58:5 w. thou call this a fast, and an
Isa 64:12 W. thou refrain thyself for these
Isa 64:12 w. thou hold thy peace, and afflict us
Jer 3:4 W. thou not from this time cry unto
Jer 4:1 If thou w. return, O Israel, saith the
Jer 4:1 and if thou w. put away thine
Jer 4:30 thou art spoiled, what w. thou do?
Jer 12:5 w. thou do in the swelling of Jordan?
Jer 13:21 What w. thou say when he shall
Jer 13:27 w. thou not be made clean?
Jer 15:18 w. thou be...unto me as a liar,
Jer 31:22 How long w. thou go about, O thou
Jer 38:15 w. thou not surely put me to death?
Jer 38:15 w. thou not hearken unto me?
Jer 38:17 If thou w. assuredly go forth unto the
Jer 38:18 But if thou w. not go forth to the
Jer 47:5 valley: how long w. thou cut thyself?
La 1:21 thou w. bring the day that thou hast
Eze 9:8 w. thou destroy all the residue of
Eze 11:13 w. thou make a full end of the
Eze 20:4 W. thou judge them, son of man,
Eze 20:4 w. thou judge them? cause them to
Eze 22:2 thou son of man, w. thou judge,
Eze 22:2 w. thou judge the bloody city?
Eze 23:36 w. thou judge Aholah and Aholibah?
Eze 24:19 W. thou not tell us these things are
Eze 28:9 W. thou yet say before him that
Eze 37:18 W. thou not shew us what thou
Ho 9:14 O Lord: what w. thou give? give them
Mic 7:19 w. cast all their sins into the depths of
Mic 7:20 Thou w. perform the truth to Jacob,
Hab 1:2 shall I cry, and thou w. not hear!
Hab 1:2 out of violence, and thou w. not save!
Zep 3:7 I said, Surely thou w. fear me,
Zep 3:7 thou w. receive instruction; so their
Zec 1:12 how long w. thou not have mercy on
Zec 3:7 If thou w. walk in my ways, and if
Zec 3:7 and if thou w. keep my charge,
Mt 4:9 if thou w. fall down and worship me
Mt 7:4 **w. thou say to thy brother, Let me**
Mt 8:2 Lord, if thou w., thou canst make 2309
Mt 13:28 **W. thou then that we go and** 2309
Mt 15:28 **be it unto thee even as thou w.** 2309
Mt 17:4 if thou w., let us make here three 2309
Mt 19:17 **but if thou w. enter into life, keep** 2309
Mt 19:21 **If thou w. be perfect, go and sell** 2309
Mt 20:21 he said unto her, **What w. thou?** 2309
Mt 26:17 Where w. thou that we prepare for 2309
Mt 26:39 **not as I will, but as thou w.**
Mk 1:40 If thou w., thou canst make me 2309
Mk 6:22 Ask of me whatsoever thou w., and 2309
Mk 10:51 **What w. thou that I should do** 2309
Mk 14:12 Where w. thou that we go and 2309
Mk 14:36 **not what I will, but what thou w.** 2309
Lu 4:7 If thou therefore w. worship me, all
Lu 5:12 Lord, if thou w., thou canst make 2309
Lu 9:54 w. thou that we command fire to 2309
Lu 18:41 **What w. thou that I shall do unto** 2309
Lu 22:9 Where w. thou that we prepare? 2309
Joh 2:20 and w. thou rear it up in three days?
Joh 5:6 him, **W. thou be made whole?** 2309
Joh 11:22 whatsoever thou w. ask of God,
Joh 13:38 **W. thou lay down thy life for my**
Joh 14:22 that thou w. manifest thyself unto us,
Ac 1:6 w. thou at this time restore again the
Ac 2:27 thou w. not leave my soul in hell,
Ac 2:27 neither w. thou suffer thine Holy One
Ac 7:28 W. thou kill me as thou diddest 2309
Ac 9:6 Lord, what w. thou have me to do? 2309
Ac 13:10 w. thou not cease to pervert the
Ac 25:9 W. thou go up to Jerusalem, and
Ro 9:19 Thou w. say then unto me, Why doth
Ro 11:19 Thou w. say then, The branches were
Ro 13:3 W. not then not be afraid of the 2309
Phm 21 thou w. also do more than I say
Jas 2:20 But w. thou know, O vain man, 2309

WIMPLES

Isa 3:22 and the w., and the crisping pins, 4304

WIN See also WINNETH; WON.

2Ch 32:1 thought to w. them for himself. 1234
Php 3:8 but dung, that I may w. Christ. 2770

WIND See also WHIRLWIND; WINDING; WINDS; WOUND.

Ge 8:1 God made a w. to pass over the 7307
Ge 41:6 blasted with the east w. sprung up
Ge 41:23 blasted with the east w., sprung up
Ge 41:27 empty ears blasted with the east w.
Ex 10:13 Lord brought an east w. upon the 7307
Ex 10:13 the east w. brought the locusts 7307
Ex 10:19 turned a mighty strong west w., 7307
Ex 14:21 sea to go back by a strong east w. 7307
Ex 15:10 Thou didst blow with thy w., the 7307
Nu 11:31 went forth a w. from the Lord, and 7307
2Sa 22:11 was seen upon the wings of the w. 7307
1Ki 18:45 was black with clouds and w., 7307
1Ki 19:11 and strong w. rent the mountains, 7307
1Ki 19:11 but the Lord was not in the w. 7307
1Ki 19:11 and after the w. an earthquake; 7307
2Ki 3:17 Ye shall not see w., neither shall 7307
Job 1:19 a great w. from the wilderness, 7307
Job 6:26 is desperate, which are as w.? 7307
Job 7:7 O remember that my life is w. 7307
Job 8:2 of thy mouth be like a strong w.? 7307
Job 15:2 and fill his belly with the east w.? 7307
Job 21:18 They are as stubble before the w., 7307
Job 27:21 The east w. carrieth him away, and
Job 30:15 they pursue my soul as the w. 7307
Job 30:22 Thou liftest me up to the w.; thou 7307
Job 37:17 quieteth the earth by the south w.?
Job 37:21 but the w. passeth, and cleanseth 7307
Job 38:24 scattereth the east w. upon the earth?
Ps 1:4 chaff which the w. driveth away. 7307
Ps 18:10 he did fly upon the wings of the w. 7307
Ps 18:42 small as the dust before the w. 7307
Ps 35:5 Let them be as chaff before the w. 7307
Ps 48:7 ships of Tarshish with an east w. 7307
Ps 78:26 He caused an east w. to blow in the
Ps 78:26 power he brought in the south w.
Ps 78:39 a w. that passeth away, and 7307
Ps 83:13 wheel; as the stubble before the w. 7307
Ps 103:16 For the w. passeth over it, and it is 7307
Ps 104:3 walketh upon the wings of the w. 7307
Ps 107:25 and raiseth the stormy w., 7307
Ps 135:7 bringeth the w. out of his treasuries. 7307
Ps 147:18 he caused his w. to blow, and the 7307
Ps 148:8 stormy w. fulfilling his word: 7307
Pr 11:29 his own house shall inherit the w. 7307
Pr 25:14 like clouds and w. without rain. 7307
Pr 25:23 The north w. driveth away rain: 7307
Pr 27:16 hideth her hideth the w., and 7307
Pr 30:4 hath gathered the w. in his fists? 7307
Ec 1:6 w. goeth toward the south, and 7307
Ec 1:6 w. returneth again according to the 7307
Ec 5:16 he that hath laboured for the w.? 7307
Ec 11:4 observeth the w. shall not sow; 7307
Ca 4:16 Awake, O north w.; and come, thou
Isa 7:2 the wood are moved with the w. 7307
Isa 11:15 with his mighty w. shall he shake 7307
Isa 17:13 of the mountains before the w., 7307
Isa 26:18 have as it were brought forth w.; 7307
Isa 27:8 he stayeth his rough w. 7307
Isa 27:8 in the day of the east w.
Isa 32:2 be as an hiding place from the w., 7307
Isa 41:16 and the w. shall carry them away, 7307
Isa 41:29 molten images are w. and confusion. 7307
Isa 57:13 the w. shall carry them all away; 7307
Isa 64:6 iniquities, like the w., have taken 7307
Jer 2:24 snuffeth up the w. at her pleasure; 7307
Jer 4:11 A dry w. of the high places in the 7307
Jer 4:12 w. from those places shall come 7307

Jer 5:13 And the prophets shall become w., 7307
Jer 10:13 forth the w. out of his treasures. 7307
Jer 13:24 away by the w. of the wilderness. 7307
Jer 14:6 snuffed up the w. like dragons; 7307
Jer 18:17 will scatter them as with an east w. 7307
Jer 22:22 The w. shall eat up all thy pastors, 7307
Jer 51:1 up against me, a destroying w.; 7307
Jer 51:16 forth the w. out of his treasures. 7307
Eze 5:2 part thou shalt scatter in the w.; 7307
Eze 12:14 scatter toward every w. all that are 7307
Eze 13:11 fall; and a stormy w. shall rend it. 7307
Eze 13:13 rend it with a stormy w. in my fury; 7307
Eze 17:10 when the east w. toucheth it? 7307
Eze 19:12 and the east w. dried up her fruit: 7307
Eze 27:26 the east w. hath broken thee in 7307
Eze 37:9 he unto me, Prophesy unto the w., 7307
Eze 37:9 son of man, and say to the w., 7307
Da 2:35 and the w. carried them away, that 7308
Ho 4:19 The w. hath bound her up in her 7307
Ho 8:7 they have sown the w., and they 7307
Ho 12:1 Ephraim feedeth on w., 7307
Ho 12:1 and followeth after the east w.
Ho 13:15 brethren, an east w. shall come,
Ho 13:15 the w. of the Lord shall come up 7307
Am 4:13 mountains, and createth the w., 7307
Jon 1:4 sent out a great w. into the sea 7307
Jon 4:8 God prepared a vehement east w.; 7307
Hab 1:9 their faces shall sup up as the east w.,
Zec 5:9 and the w. was in their wings; 7307
Mt 11:7 **to see. A reed shaken with the w.?** *417*
Mt 14:24 with waves: for the w. was contrary. *417*
Mt 14:30 But when he saw the w. boisterous, *417*
Mt 14:32 come into the ship, the w. ceased. *417*
Mk 4:37 And there arose a great storm of w., *417*
Mk 4:39 And he arose, and rebuked the w., *417*
Mk 4:39 the w. ceased, and there was a great *417*
Mk 4:41 even the w. and the sea obey him? *417*
Mk 6:48 for the w. was contrary unto them: *417*
Mk 6:51 into the ship; and the w. ceased: *417*
Lu 7:24 **to see? A reed shaken with the w.?** *417*
Lu 8:23 down a storm of w. on the lake; *417*
Lu 8:24 rebuked the w. and the raging of *417*
Lu 12:55 **And when ye see the south w. blow,**
Joh 3:8 **The w. bloweth where it listeth,** *4151*
Joh 6:18 by reason of the great w. that blew. *417*
Ac 2:2 heaven as of a rushing mighty w., *4157*
Ac 27:7 the w. not suffering us, we sailed *417*
Ac 27:13 And when the south w. blew softly,
Ac 27:14 arose against it a tempestous w., *417*
Ac 27:15 and could not bear up into the w., *417*
Ac 27:40 hoised up the mainsail to the w., *4154*
Ac 28:13 and after one day the south w. blew,
Eph 4:14 about with every w. of doctrine, *417*
Jas 1:6 wave of the sea driven with the w. *416*
Re 6:13 when she is shaken of a mighty w. *417*
Re 7:1 the w. should not blow on the earth, *417*

WINDING

1Ki 6:8 and they went up with w. stairs 3583
Eze 41:7 a w. about still upward to the side. 5437
Eze 41:7 w. about the house went still 4141

WINDOW See also WINDOWS.

Ge 6:16 A w. shalt thou make to the ark, 6672
Ge 8:6 Noah opened the w. of the ark 2474
Ge 26:8 the Philistines looked out at a w., 2474
Jos 2:15 down by a cord through the w. 2474
Jos 2:18 bind this line of...thread in the w. 2474
Jos 2:21 she bound the scarlet line in the w. 2474
Jg 5:28 of Sisera looked out at a w., 2474
1Sa 19:12 let David down through a w. 2474
2Sa 6:16 daughter looked through a w., 2474
2Ki 9:30 her head, and looked out at a w. 2474
2Ki 9:32 And he lifted up his face to the w., 2474
2Ki 13:17 And he said, Open the w. eastward. 2474
1Ch 15:29 looking out at a w. saw king David 2474
Pr 7:6 at the w. of my house I looked 2474
Ac 20:9 sat in a w. a certain young man *2376*
2Co 11:33 through a w. in a basket was I let *2376*

WINDOWS

Ge 7:11 and the w. of heaven were opened. 699
Ge 8:2 and the w. of heaven were stopped, 699
2Ki 6:4 he made w. of narrow lights. 2474
2Ki 7:4 And there were w. in three rows, 8261
2Ki 7:5 posts were square, with the w. 8260
2Ki 7:2 Lord would make w. in heaven, 699
2Ki 7:19 Lord should make w. in heaven, 699
Ec 12:3 that look out of the w. be darkened, 699
Ca 2:9 he looketh forth at the w., 2474
Isa 24:18 for the w. from on high are opened, 699
Isa 54:12 I will make thy w. of agates, and 8121
Isa 60:8 and as the doves to their w.? 699
Jer 9:21 For death is come up into our w., 2474
Jer 22:14 chambers, and cutteth him out w.; 2474
Eze 40:16 narrow w. to the little chambers, 2474
Eze 40:16 and w. were round about inward: 2474
Eze 40:22 And their w., and their arches, and 2474
Eze 40:25 were w. in it and in the arches 2474
Eze 40:25 thereof round about, like those w. 2474
Eze 40:29 were w. in it and in the arches 2474
Eze 40:33 were w. therein and in the arches 2474
Eze 40:36 and the w. to it round about: 2474
Eze 41:16 The door posts, and the narrow w., 2474
Eze 41:16 and from the ground up to the w., 2474
Eze 41:16 and the w. were covered; 2474
Eze 41:26 were narrow w. and palm trees 2474
Da 6:10 his w. being open in his chamber 3551
Joe 2:9 shall enter in at the w. like a thief. 2474
Zep 2:14 their voice shall sing in the w.; 2474
Mal 3:10 will not open you the w. of heaven, 699

WINDS See also WHIRLWINDS.

Job 28:25 To make the weight for the w.; 7307
Jer 49:32 I will scatter into all w. them that 7307
Jer 49:36 upon Elam will I bring the four w. 7307
Jer 49:36 scatter them toward all those w.; 7307
Eze 5:10 of thee will I scatter into all the w. 7307
Eze 5:12 scatter a third part into all the w., 7307
Eze 17:21 shall be scattered toward all w. 7307
Eze 37:9 Come from the four w., O breath, 7307
Da 7:2 the four w. of the heaven strove 7308
Da 8:8 ones toward the four w. of heaven. 7307
Da 11:4 toward the four w. of heaven; 7307
Zec 2:6 as the four w. of the heaven, 7307
Mt 7:25, **27 the floods came, and the w.** *417*
Mt 8:26 and rebuked the w. and the sea; *417*
Mt 8:27 even the w. and the sea obey him! *417*
Mt 24:31 **together his elect from the four w.,** *417*
Mk 13:27 **together his elect from the four w.,** *417*
Lu 8:25 commandeth even the w. and water, *417*
Ac 27:4 because the w. were contrary. *417*
Jas 3:4 are driven of fierce w., yet are they *417*
Jude 12 without water, carried about of w.; *417*
Re 7:1 holding the four w. of the earth, *417*

WINDY

Ps 55:8 my escape from the w. storm 7307

WINE See also WINEBIBBER; WINEFAT; WINEPRESS; WINES.

Ge 9:21 And he drank of the w., and was 3196
Ge 9:24 Noah awoke from his w., and knew 3196
Ge 14:18 Salem brought forth bread and w. 3196
Ge 19:32 let us make our father drink w., 3196
Ge 19:33 they made their father drink w. 3196
Ge 19:34 make him drink w. this night also; 3196
Ge 19:35 they made their father drink w. 3196
Ge 27:25 he brought him w., and he drank. 3196
Ge 27:28 earth, and plenty of corn, and w. 8492
Ge 27:37 corn and w. have I sustained him: 8492
Ge 49:11 he washed his garments in w., 3196
Ge 49:12 His eyes shall be red with w., 3196
Ex 29:40 the fourth part of an hin of w. 3196
Le 10:9 Do not drink w. nor strong drink, 3196
Le 23:13 drink offering thereof shall be of w., 3196
Nu 6:3 He shall separate himself from w. 3196
Nu 6:3 and shall drink no vinegar of w., 3196
Nu 6:20 that the Nazarite may drink w. 3196
Nu 15:5 the fourth part of an hin of w. 3196
Nu 15:7 offer the third part of an hin of w., 3196
Nu 15:10 a drink offering half an hin of w., 3196
Nu 18:12 all the best of the w., and of the 8492
Nu 28:7 cause the strong w. to be poured 7941
Nu 28:14 offerings shall be half an hin of w. 3196
De 7:13 of thy land, thy corn, and thy w., 8492
De 11:14 gather in thy corn, and thy w. 8492
De 12:17 the tithe of thy corn, or of thy w., 8492
De 14:23 the tithe of thy corn, of thy w., 8492
De 14:26 for sheep, or for w., or for strong 3196
De 16:13 gathered in thy corn and thy w. 3342
De 18:4 also of the corn, of thy w., and of 8492
De 28:39 but shalt neither drink of the w., 3196
De 28:51 leave thee either corn, w., or oil, 8492
De 29:6 neither have ye drunk w. or strong 3196
De 32:33 Their w. is the poison of dragons, 3196
De 32:38 and drank the w. of their drink 3196
De 33:28 be upon a land of corn and w.; 8492
Jos 9:4 and w. bottles, old, and rent, and 3196
Jos 9:13 these bottles of w., which we filled, 3196
Jg 9:13 Should I leave my w., which 8492
Jg 13:4 and drink not w. nor strong drink, 3196
Jg 13:7 now drink no w. nor strong drink, 3196
Jg 13:14 let her drink w. or strong drink, 3196
Jg 19:19 there is bread and w. also for me, 3196
1Sa 1:14 put away thy w. from thee. 3196
1Sa 1:15 drunk neither w. nor strong drink, 3196
1Sa 1:24 ephah of flour, and a bottle of w., 3196
1Sa 10:3 another carrying a bottle of w. 3196
1Sa 16:20 with bread, and a bottle of w., 3196
1Sa 25:18 hundred loaves, two bottles of w., 3196
1Sa 25:37 when the w. was gone out of Nabal, 3196
2Sa 6:19 piece of flesh, and a flagon of w. 3196
2Sa 13:28 Amnon's heart is merry with w., 3196
2Sa 16:1 summer fruits, and a bottle of w. 3196
2Sa 16:2 and the w., that such as be faint 3196
2Ki 18:32 own land, a land of corn and w., 8492
1Ch 9:29 fine flour, and the w., and the oil, 3196
1Ch 12:40 bunches of raisins, and w., and oil, 3196
1Ch 16:3 good piece of flesh, and a flagon of w.
1Ch 27:27 of the vineyards for the w. cellars 3196
2Ch 2:10 and twenty thousand baths of w., 3196
2Ch 2:15 and the w., which my lord hath 3196
2Ch 11:11 store of victual, and of oil and w. 3196
2Ch 31:5 the firstfruits of corn, w., and oil, 8492
2Ch 32:28 increase of corn, and w., and oil; 8492
Ezr 6:9 God of heaven, wheat, salt, w., 2562
Ezr 7:22 and to an hundred baths of w., 2562
Ne 2:1 the king, that w. was before him: 3196
Ne 2:1 and I took up the w., and gave it 3196
Ne 5:11 the w., and the oil, that ye exact 8492
Ne 5:15 had taken of them bread and w., 3196
Ne 5:18 ten days store of all sorts of w. 3196
Ne 10:37 of w. and of oil, unto the priests, 8492
Ne 10:39 offering of the corn, of the new w., 8492
Ne 13:5 tithes of the corn, the new w., 8492
Ne 13:12 the new w. and the oil unto the 8492
Ne 13:15 some treading w. presses on the 1660
Ne 13:15 as also w., grapes, and figs, and 3196
Es 1:7 and royal w. in abundance, 3196
Es 1:10 of the king was merry with w., 3196
Es 5:6 unto Esther at the banquet of w., 3196
Es 7:2 second day at the banquet of w., 3196
Es 7:7 arising from the banquet of w. in 3196
Es 7:8 into the place of the banquet of w.; 3196
Job 1:13, 18 and drinking w. in their eldest 3196
Job 32:19 belly is as w. which hath no vent; 3196
Ps 4:7 their corn and their w. increased 8492
Ps 60:3 to drink the w. of astonishment. 3196
Ps 75:8 there is a cup, and the w. is red; 3196
Ps 78:65 man that shouteth by reason of w. 3196
Ps 104:15 w. that maketh glad the heart of 3196
Pr 3:10 shall burst out with new w. 8492
Pr 4:17 and drink the w. of violence. 3196
Pr 9:2 beasts; she hath mingled her w.; 3196
Pr 9:5 and drink of the w. which I have 3196
Pr 20:1 W. is a mocker, strong drink is 3196
Pr 21:17 he that loveth w. and oil shall not 3196
Pr 23:30 They that tarry long at the w.; 3196
Pr 23:30 they that go to seek mixed w. 4469
Pr 23:31 Look not thou upon the w. when 3196
Pr 31:4 it is not for kings to drink w.; 3196
Pr 31:6 and w. unto those that be of heavy 3196
Ec 2:3 mine heart to give myself unto w., 3196
Ec 9:7 drink thy w. with a merry heart; 3196
Ec 10:19 for laughter, and w. maketh merry: 3196
Ca 1:2 for thy love is better than w. 3196
Ca 1:4 remember thy love more than w. 3196
Ca 4:10 much better is thy love than w.! 3196
Ca 5:1 I have drunk my w. with my milk: 3196
Ca 7:9 like the best w. for my beloved, 3196
Ca 8:2 cause thee to drink of spiced w. 3196
Isa 1:22 dross, thy w. mixed with water 5435
Isa 5:11 until night, till w. inflame them! 3196
Isa 5:12 pipe, and w., are in their feasts: 3196
Isa 5:22 them that are mighty to drink w., 3196
Isa 16:10 tread out no w. in their presses; 3196
Isa 22:13 eating flesh, and drinking w. 3196
Isa 24:7 The new w. mourneth, the vine 8492
Isa 24:9 shall not drink w. with a song; 3196
Isa 24:11 is a crying for w. in the streets; 3196
Isa 27:2 ye unto her, A vineyard of red w. 2561
Isa 28:1 them that are overcome with w.! 3196

Isa 28:7 they also have erred through w., ... 3196
Isa 28:7 drink, they are swallowed up of w., ... 3196
Isa 29:9 they are drunken, but not with w.; 3196
Isa 36:17 own land, a land of corn and w., ... 8492
Isa 49:26 their own blood, as with sweet w....... 6071
Isa 51:21 and drunken, but not with w. 3196
Isa 55:1 buy w. and milk without money 3196
Isa 56:12 Come ye, say they, I will fetch w., ... 3196
Isa 62:8 the stranger shall not drink thy w.,..... 8492
Isa 65:8 new w. is found in the cluster, ... 8492
Jer 13:12 bottle shall be filled with w. 3196
Jer 13:12 every bottle shall be filled with w.?..... 3196
Jer 23:9 like a man whom w. hath overcome, ... 3196
Jer 25:15 Take the w. cup of this fury at my 3196
Jer 31:12 for wheat, and for w., and for oil, ... 8492
Jer 35:2 chambers, and give them w. to drink. ..3196
Jer 35:5 of the Rechabites pots full of w., ... 3196
Jer 35:5 and I said unto them, Drink ye w. 3196
Jer 35:6 they said, We will drink no w. 3196
Jer 35:6 Ye shall drink no w., neither ye, ... 3196
Jer 35:8 us, to drink no w. all our days, ... 3196
Jer 35:14 his sons not to drink w., ... 3196
Jer 40:10 gather ye w., and summer fruits, ... 3196
Jer 40:12 gathered w. and summer fruits very ... 3196
Jer 48:33 w. to fail from the winepresses: 3196
Jer 51:7 the nations have drunken of her w.; 3196
La 2:12 mothers, Where is corn and w.? 3196
Eze 27:18 in the w. of Helbon, and white wool. .. 3196
Eze 44:21 Neither shall any priest drink w., ... 3196
Da 1:5 meat, and of the w. which he drank: ... 3196
Da 1:8 nor with the w. which he drank: 3196
Da 1:16 and the w. that they should drink; 3196
Da 5:1 and drank w. before the thousand 2562
Da 5:2 Belshazzar, whiles he tasted the w., ... 2562
Da 5:4 They drank w., and praised the 2562
Da 5:23 concubines, have drunk w. in them; 2562
Da 10:3 came flesh nor w. in my mouth, ... 3196
Ho 2:8 know that I gave her corn, and w., ... 8492
Ho 2:9 and my w. in the season thereof, ... 8492
Ho 2:22 shall hear the corn, and the w., ... 8492
Ho 3:1 other gods, and love flagons of w., ... 6025
Ho 4:11 Whoredom and w. and new 3196
Ho 4:11 and new w. take away the heart. 8492
Ho 7:5 made him sick with bottles of w.; 3196
Ho 7:14 themselves for corn and w., ... 8492
Ho 9:2 and the new w. shall fail in her. 8492
Ho 9:4 They shall not offer w. offerings 8492
Ho 14:7 shall be as the w. of Lebanon. 8492
Joe 1:5 and howl, all ye drinkers of w., ... 3196
Joe 1:5 because of the new w.; for it is cut 6071
Joe 1:10 the new w. is dried up, the oil. 8492
Joe 2:19 I will send you corn, and w., and 8492
Joe 2:24 fats shall overflow with w. and oil. 8492
Joe 3:3 sold a girl for w., that they might 3196
Joe 3:18 shall drop down new w., ... 6071
Am 2:8 drink the w. of the condemned in 3196
Am 2:12 ye gave the Nazarites w. to drink; 3196
Am 5:11 but ye shall not drink w. of them. 3196
Am 6:6 That drink w. in bowls, and anoint 3196
Am 9:13 the mountains shall drop sweet w., ... 6071
Am 9:14 plant vineyards, and drink the w. 3196
Mic 2:11 I will prophesy unto thee of w. 3196
Mic 6:15 anoint thee with oil; and sweet w., ... 8492
Mic 6:15 but shalt not drink w. 3196
Hab 2:5 because he transgresseth by w., ... 3196
Zep 1:13 but not drink the w. thereof. 3196
Hag 1:11 upon the new w., and upon the oil, ... 8492
Hag 2:12 do touch bread, or pottage, or w., ... 3196
Zec 9:15 and make a noise as through w.; 3196
Zec 9:17 cheerful, and new w. the maids. 8492
Zec 10:7 heart shall rejoice as through w. 3196
Mt 9:17 **men put new w. into old bottles:** ... *3631*
Mt 9:17 **and the w. runneth out, and the** *3631*
Mt 9:17 **they put new w. into new bottles,** .. *3631*
Mk 2:22 **putteth new w. into old bottles;** *3631*
Mk 2:22 **the new w. doth burst the bottles,** ..*3631*
Mk 2:22 **and the w. is spilled, and the** *3631*
Mk 2:22 **but new w. must be put into new** .. *3631*
Mk 15:23 to drink w. mingled with myrrh: *3631*
Lu 1:15 drink neither w. nor strong drink; *3631*
Lu 5:37 **putteth new w. into old bottles;** *3631*
Lu 5:37 **the new w. will burst the bottles,** .. *3631*
Lu 5:38 **But new w. must be put into new** .. *3631*
Lu 5:39 **also having drunk old w. straightway** ..
Lu 7:33 **eating bread nor drinking w.;** *3631*
Lu 10:34 his wounds, pouring in oil and w., .*3631*
Joh 2:3 when they wanted w., the mother *3631*
Joh 2:3 saith unto him, They have no w. *3631*
Joh 2:9 tasted the water that was made w., ... *3631*
Joh 2:10 beginning doth set forth good w.; *3631*
Joh 2:10 hast kept the good w. until now. *3631*
Joh 4:46 where he made the water w. *3631*
Ac 2:13 said, These men are full of new w. *1098*
Ro 14:21 to eat flesh, nor to drink w., ... *3631*
Eph 5:18 And be not drunk with w., wherein *3631*
1Ti 3:3 Not given to w., no striker, not *3943*
1Ti 3:8 not given to much w., not greedy *3631*
1Ti 5:23 use a little w. for thy stomach's *3631*
Tit 1:7 not given to w., no striker, not *3943*
Tit 2:3 not given to much w., teachers of *3631*
1Pe 4:3 lusts, excess of w., revellings, ... *3632*
Re 6:6 thou hurt not the oil and the w. *3631*
Re 14:8 drink of the w. of the wrath of her *3631*
Re 14:10 drink of the w. of the wrath of God, ... *3631*
Re 16:19 the cup of the w. of the fierceness *3631*
Re 17:2 drunk with the w. of her fornication. ... *3631*
Re 18:3 have drunk of the w. of the wrath *3631*
Re 18:13 and w., and oil, and fine flour, and *3631*

WINEBIBBER See also WINEBIBBERS.
Mt 11:19 **and a w., a friend of publicans** *3630*
Lu 7:34 **and a w., a friend of publicans** *3630*

WINEBIBBERS
Pr 23:20 Be not among w.; among 5433,3196

WINE-CELLARS See WINE and CELLARS.

WINE-CUP See WINE and CUP.

WINEFAT
Isa 63:2 like him that treadeth in the w.? 1660
Mk 12:1 **and digged a place for the w., and** ..*5276*

WINE-OFFERINGS See WINE and OFFERINGS.

WINEPRESS See also WINEPRESSES.
Nu 18:27 and as the fulness of the w. 3342
Nu 18:30 and as the increase of the w. 3342
De 15:14 out of thy floor, and out of thy w. 3342
Jg 6:11 Gideon threshed wheat by the w., ... 1660
Jg 7:25 Zeeb they slew at the w. of Zeeb, ... 3342
2Ki 6:27 of the barnfloor, or out of the w.? 3342
Isa 5:2 of it, and also made a w. therein: 3342
Isa 63:3 I have trodden the w. alone; and 6333
La 1:15 the daughter of Judah, as in a w. 1660
Ho 9:2 The floor and the w. shall not feed 3342
Mt 21:33 **and digged a w. in it, and built a** .. *3025*
Re 14:19 great w. of the wrath of God. *3025*
Re 14:20 w. was trodden without the city, ... *3025*
Re 14:20 and blood came out of the w., even *3025*
Re 19:15 treadeth the w. of the fierceness .*3025,3631*

WINEPRESSES See also WINE and PRESSES.
Job 24:11 tread their w., and suffer thirst 3342
Jer 48:33 caused wine to fail from the w. 3342
Zec 14:10 of Hananeel unto the king's w. 3342

WINES
Isa 25:6 a feast of w. on the lees, of fat 8105
Isa 25:6 of w. on the lees well refined. 8105

WING See also LAPWING; WINGED; WINGS.
1Ki 6:24 was the one w. of the cherub, ... 3671
1Ki 6:24 cubits the other w. of the cherub: 3671
1Ki 6:24 uttermost part of the one w. unto 3671
1Ki 6:27 w. of the one touched the one wall, ... 3671
1Ki 6:27 w. of the other cherub touched the 3671
2Ch 3:11 one w. of the one cherub was five 3671
2Ch 3:11 other w. was likewise five cubits, ... 3671
2Ch 3:11 reaching to the w. of the other 3671
2Ch 3:12 one w. of the other cherub was five ... 3671
2Ch 3:12 and the other w. was five cubits 3671
2Ch 3:12 joining to...w. of the other cherub. 3671
Isa 10:14 there was none that moved the w., ... 3671
Eze 17:23 it shall dwell all fowl of every w.; 3671

WINGED See also LONGWINGED.
Ge 1:21 and every w. fowl after his kind: 3671
De 4:17 likeness of any w. fowl that flieth in 3671

WINGS
Ex 19:4 and how I bare you on eagles' w., ... 3671
Ex 25:20 cherubims...stretch forth their w. 3671
Ex 25:20 the mercy seat with their w., ... 3671
Ex 37:9 the cherubims spread out their w. 3671
Ex 37:9 and covered with their w. over the 3671
Le 1:17 shall cleave it with the w. thereof, ... 3671
De 32:11 her young, spreadeth abroad her w., ... 3671
De 32:11 them, beareth them on her w. 84
Ru 2:12 under whose w. thou art come to 3671
2Sa 22:11 was seen upon the w. of the wind. 3671
1Ki 6:27 they stretched forth the w. of 3671
1Ki 6:27 their w. touched one another in the 3671
1Ki 8:6 even under the w. of the cherubims 3671
1Ki 8:7 spread forth their two w. over the 3671
1Ch 28:18 cherubims, that spread out their w., ...
2Ch 3:11 w. of the cherubims were twenty 3671
2Ch 3:13 The w. of these cherubims spread 3671
2Ch 5:7 even under the w. of the cherubims; ... 3671
2Ch 5:8 cherubims spread forth their w. 3671
Job 39:13 the goodly w. unto the peacocks? 3671
Job 39:13 or w. and feathers unto the ostrich? 84
Job 39:26 stretch her w. toward the south? 3671
Ps 17:8 hide me under the shadow of thy w., .. 3671
Ps 18:10 he did fly upon the w. of the wind. 3671
Ps 36:7 trust under the shadow of thy w. 3671
Ps 55:6 said, Oh that I had w. like a dove! 83
Ps 57:1 in the shadow of thy w. will I 3671
Ps 61:4 I will trust in the covert of thy w. 3671
Ps 63:7 the shadow of thy w. will I rejoice. 3671
Ps 68:13 w. of a dove covered with silver, ... 3671
Ps 91:4 and under his w. shalt thou trust: 3671
Ps 104:3 walketh upon the w. of the wind: 3671
Ps 139:9 If I take the w. of the morning, and 3671
Pr 23:5 for riches...make themselves w.; 3671
Ec 10:20 which hath w. shall tell the matter. 3671
Isa 6:2 the seraphims: each one had six w.; ... 3671
Isa 8:8 the stretching out of his w. shall 3671
Isa 18:1 Woe to the land shadowing with w., ... 3671
Isa 40:31 shall mount up with w. as eagles; 83
Jer 48:9 Give w. unto Moab, that it may 6731
Jer 48:40 and shall spread his w. over Moab 3671
Jer 49:22 and spread his w. over Bozrah: and 3671
Eze 1:6 faces, and every one had four w. 3671
Eze 1:8 the hands of a man under their w. 3671
Eze 1:8 four had their faces and their w. 3671
Eze 1:9 Their w. were joined one to 3671
Eze 1:11 their w. were stretched upward; 3671
Eze 1:11 two w. of every one were joined one to ....
Eze 1:23 firmament were their w. straight, ... 3671
Eze 1:24 I heard the noise of their w., like 3671
Eze 1:24 they stood, they let down their w. 3671
Eze 1:25 stood, and had let down their w. 3671
Eze 3:13 of the w. of the living creatures 3671
Eze 10:5 the sound of the cherubims w. was 3671
Eze 10:8 of a man's hand under their w. 3671
Eze 10:12 and their hands, and their w., and 3671
Eze 10:16 the cherubims lifted up their w. to 3671
Eze 10:19 the cherubims lifted up their w., ... 3671
Eze 10:21 apiece, and every one four w.; and 3671
Eze 10:21 hands of a man was under their w. 3671
Eze 11:22 did the cherubims lift up their w., ... 3671
Eze 17:3 A great eagle with great w., ... 3671
Eze 17:7 another great eagle with great w. 3671
Da 7:4 was like a lion, and had eagle's w. 1611
Da 7:4 till the w. thereof were plucked, ... 1611
Da 7:6 the back of it four w. of a fowl; 1611
Ho 4:19 wind hath bound her up in her w., ... 3671
Zec 5:9 and the wind was in their w.; for 3671
Zec 5:9 they had w. like the w. of a stork: 3671
Mal 4:2 arise with healing in his w.; 3671
Mt 23:37 **her chickens under her w.,** *4420*
Lu 13:34 **gather her brood under her w.,** *4420*
Re 4:8 four beasts had each of them six w. *4420*
Re 9:9 sound of their w. was as the sound *4420*
Re 12:14 given two w. of a great eagle, ... *4420*

WINK See also WINKED; WINKETH.
Job 15:12 away? and what do thy eyes w. at, ... 7335
Ps 35:19 them w. with the eye that hate me. 7169

WINKED
Ac 17:30 times of this ignorance God w. at; *5237*

WINKETH
Pr 6:13 He w. with his eyes, he speaketh 7169
Pr 10:10 He that w. with the eye causeth 7169

WINNETH
Pr 11:30 life; and he that w. souls is wise. 3947

WINNOWED
Isa 30:24 hath been **w.** with the shovel and....... 2219

WINNOWETH
Ru 3:2 he **w.** barley to night in the.............. 2219

WINTER See also WINTERED; WINTERHOUSE.
Ge 8:22 cold and heat, and summer and **w.**, ... 2779
Ps 74:17 thou hast made summer and **w.**........ 2779
Ca 2:11 the **w.** is past, the rain is over and..... 5638
Isa 18:6 the beasts...shall **w.** upon them. 2778
Am 3:15 I will smite the **w.** house with the...... 2779
Zec 14:8 in summer and in **w.** shall it be.......... 2778
Mt 24:20 **that your flight may not be in w.**,.. *5494*
Mk 13:18 **that your flight may not be in w.**.. *5494*
Joh 10:22 of the dedication, and it was in **w.**..... *5494*
Ac 27:12 haven was not commodious to **w.** in,... *3915*
Ac 27:12 attain to Phenice, and there to **w.**; *3914*
1Co 16:6 I will abide, yea, and **w.** with you,...... *3914*
2Ti 4:21 thy diligence to come before **w.**......... *5494*
Tit 3:12 for I have determined there to **w.**...... *3914*

WINTERED
Ac 28:11 which had **w.** in the isle, whose......... *3916*

WINTERHOUSE See also WINTER and HOUSE.
Jer 36:22 the king sat in the **w.** in the ninth...... 2779

WIPE See also WIPED; WIPETH; WIPING.
2Ki 21:13 and I will **w.** Jerusalem as a man........ 4229
Ne 13:14 **w.** not out my good deeds that I......... 4229
Isa 25:8 Lord God will **w.** away tears from....... 4229
Lu 7:38 did **w.** them with the hairs of her....... *1591*
Lu 10:11 **on us, we do w. off against you:**..... *631*
Joh 13:5 and to **w.** them with the towel........... *1591*
Re 7:17 God shall **w.** away all tears from........ *1813*
Re 21:4 God shall **w.** away all tears from........ *1813*

WIPED
Pr 6:33 his reproach shall not be **w.** away....... 4229
Lu 7:44 **w. them with the hairs of her**........ *1591*
Joh 11:2 and **w.** his feet with her hair,............ *1591*
Joh 12:3 and **w.** his feet with her hair: *1591*

WIPETH
2Ki 21:13 Jerusalem as a man **w.** a dish, ... 4229
Pr 30:20 she eateth, and **w.** her mouth, and..... 4229

WIPING
2Ki 21:13 **w.** it, and turning it upside down........ 4229

WIRES
Ex 39:3 into thin plates, and cut it into **w.**,....... 6616

WISDOM
Ex 28:3 I have filled with the spirit of **w.**, ... 2451
Ex 31:3 with the spirit of God, in **w.**,............ 2451
Ex 31:6 are wise hearted I have put **w.**,.......... 2451
Ex 35:26 whose heart stirred them up in **w.**....... 2451
Ex 35:31 with the spirit of God, in **w.**,............ 2451
Ex 35:35 hath he filled with **w.** of heart,.......... 2451
Ex 36:1 in whom the Lord put **w.** and............ 2451
Ex 36:2 in whose heart the Lord had put **w.**,..... 2451
De 4:6 is your **w.** and your understanding...... 2451
De 34:9 of Nun was full of the spirit of **w.**;...... 2451
2Sa 14:20 according to the **w.** of an angel of 2451
2Sa 20:22 went unto all the people in her **w.**...... 2451
1Ki 2:6 Do therefore according to thy **w.**, ... 2451
1Ki 3:28 saw that the **w.** of God was in him,...... 2451
1Ki 4:29 And God gave Solomon **w.** and.......... 2451
1Ki 4:30 Solomon's **w.** excelled the **w.** of all..... 2451
1Ki 4:30 country, and all the **w.** of Egypt.......... 2451
1Ki 4:34 people to hear the **w.** of Solomon,....... 2451
1Ki 4:34 earth, which had heard of his **w.**......... 2451
1Ki 5:12 And the Lord gave Solomon **w.**,........... 2451
1Ki 7:14 filled with **w.**, and understanding, ... 2451
1Ki 10:4 Sheba had seen all Solomon's **w.**,....... 2451
1Ki 10:6 own land of thy acts and of thy **w.**.. 2451
1Ki 10:7 thy **w.** and prosperity exceedeth 2451
1Ki 10:8 before thee, and that hear thy **w.**......... 2451
1Ki 10:23 of the earth for riches and for **w.** 2451
1Ki 10:24 sought to Solomon, to hear his **w.**,...... 2451
1Ki 11:41 and his **w.**, are they not written.......... 2451
1Ch 22:12 Only the Lord give thee **w.** and.......... 7922
2Ch 1:10 Give me now **w.** and knowledge,......... 2451
2Ch 1:11 but hast asked **w.** and knowledge........ 2451
2Ch 1:12 **W.** and knowledge is granted unto........ 2451
2Ch 9:3 Sheba had seen the **w.** of Solomon, ... 2451
2Ch 9:5 land of thine acts, and of thy **w.**......... 2451
2Ch 9:6 greatness of thy **w.** was not told......... 2451
2Ch 9:7 before thee, and hear thy **w.**............. 2451
2Ch 9:22 kings of the earth in riches and **w.**. 2451
2Ch 9:23 of Solomon, to hear his **w.**,.............. 2451
Ezr 7:25 thou, Ezra, after the **w.** of thy God, ... 2452
Job 4:21 go away? they die, even without **w.**.... 2451
Job 6:13 and is **w.** driven quite from me?......... 8454
Job 11:6 would shew thee the secrets of **w.**, ... 2451
Job 12:2 people, and **w.** shall die with you. 2451
Job 12:12 With the ancient is **w.**; and in........... 2451
Job 12:13 With him is **w.** and strength, he......... 2451
Job 12:16 With him is strength and **w.**: the........ 8454
Job 13:5 peace! and it should be your **w.**......... 2451
Job 15:8 dost thou restrain **w.** to thyself? 2451
Job 26:3 counselled him that hath no **w.**? 2451
Job 28:12 But where shall **w.** be found? 2451
Job 28:18 for the price of **w.** is above rubies...... 2451
Job 28:20 Whence then cometh **w.**? and............ 2451
Job 28:28 the fear of the Lord, that is **w.**;......... 2451
Job 32:7 multitude of years shall teach **w.**......... 2451
Job 32:13 should say, We have found out **w.**....... 2451
Job 33:33 peace, and I shall teach thee **w.**......... 2451
Job 34:35 and his words were without **w.**........... 7919
Job 36:5 he is mighty in strength and **w.**. 3820
Job 38:36 hath put **w.** in the inward parts? 2451
Job 38:37 Who can number the clouds in **w.**? 2451
Job 39:17 God hath deprived her of **w.**, ... 2451
Job 39:26 Doth the hawk fly by the **w.**, and 998
Ps 37:30 of the righteous speaketh **w.**, ... 2451
Ps 49:3 My mouth shall speak of **w.**; and......... 2454
Ps 51:6 thou shalt make me to know **w.**........... 2451
Ps 90:12 we may apply our hearts unto **w.**. 2451
Ps 104:24 in **w.** hast thou made them all: 2451
Ps 105:22 and teach his senators **w.**. 2449
Ps 111:10 the Lord is the beginning of **w.**........... 2451
Ps 136:5 him that by **w.** made the heavens:...... 8394
Pr 1:2 To know **w.** and instruction:.............. 2451
Pr 1:3 To receive the instruction of **w.**, ... 7919
Pr 1:7 fools despise **w.** and instruction.......... 2451
Pr 1:20 **W.** crieth without; she uttereth........... 2454
Pr 2:2 thou incline thine ear unto **w.**, ... 2451
Pr 2:6 For the Lord giveth **w.**: out of his...... 2451
Pr 2:7 He layeth up sound **w.** for the........... 8454
Pr 2:10 **w.** entereth into thine heart, and........ 2451
Pr 3:13 Happy is the man that findeth **w.**,....... 2451
Pr 3:19 Lord by **w.** hath founded the earth; 2451
Pr 3:21 keep sound **w.** and discretion: 8454
Pr 4:5 Get **w.**, get understanding: forget........ 2451
Pr 4:7 **W.** is the principal thing; 2451
Pr 4:7 principal thing; therefore get **w.**......... 2451
Pr 4:11 have taught thee in the way of **w.**; 2451
Pr 5:1 My son, attend unto my **w.**, and......... 2451
Pr 7:4 Say unto **w.**, Thou art my sister; 2451
Pr 8:1 Doth not **w.** cry? and understanding..... 2451
Pr 8:5 O ye simple, understand **w.**: and,........ 6195
Pr 8:11 For **w.** is better than rubies; and 2451
Pr 8:12 I **w.** dwell with prudence, and find....... 2451
Pr 8:14 Counsel is mine, and sound **w.** 8454
Pr 9:1 **W.** hath builded her house, she 2454
Pr 9:10 of the Lord is the beginning of **w.** 2451
Pr 10:13 hath understanding **w.** is found:.......... 2451
Pr 10:21 but fools die for want of **w.**.............. 3820
Pr 10:23 man of understanding hath **w.**............ 2451
Pr 10:31 mouth of the just bringeth forth **w.**...... 2451
Pr 11:2 shame: but with the lowly is **w.**.......... 2451
Pr 11:12 He that is void of **w.** despiseth his 3820
Pr 12:8 commended according to his **w.** 7922
Pr 13:10 but with the well advised is **w.**........... 2451
Pr 14:6 A scorner seeketh **w.**, and findeth...... 2451
Pr 14:8 **w.** of the prudent is to understand....... 2451
Pr 14:33 **W.** resteth in the heart of him that..... 2451
Pr 15:21 joy to him that is destitute of **w.**........ 3820
Pr 15:33 the Lord is the instruction of **w.**; 2451
Pr 16:16 better is it to get **w.** than gold! 2451
Pr 17:16 price in the hand of a fool to get **w.**,... 2451
Pr 17:24 **W.** is before him that hath................ 2451
Pr 18:1 and intermeddleth with all **w.**.............. 8454
Pr 18:4 wellspring of **w.** as a flowing 2451
Pr 19:8 getteth **w.** loveth his own soul:.......... 3820
Pr 21:30 There is no **w.** nor understanding......... 2451
Pr 23:4 be rich: cease from thine own **w.**......... 998
Pr 23:9 will despise the **w.** of thy words. 7922
Pr 23:23 also **w.**, and instruction, and.............. 2451
Pr 24:3 Through **w.** is an house builded; 2451
Pr 24:7 **W.** is too high for a fool: he.............. 2454
Pr 24:14 knowledge of **w.** be unto thy soul:...... 2451
Pr 29:3 Whoso loveth **w.** rejoiceth his............ 2451
Pr 29:15 The rod and reproof give **w.**: but........ 2451
Pr 30:3 I neither learned **w.**, nor have the...... 2451
Pr 31:26 She openeth her mouth with **w.**; 2451
Ec 1:13 search out by **w.** concerning all.......... 2451
Ec 1:16 have gotten more **w.** than all they 2451
Ec 1:16 my heart had great experience of **w.**.... 2451
Ec 1:17 And I gave my heart to know **w.**, ... 2451
Ec 1:18 For in much **w.** is much grief: 2451
Ec 2:3 acquainting mine heart with **w.**;.......... 2451
Ec 2:9 also my **w.** remained with me............. 2451
Ec 2:12 And I turned myself to behold **w.**,...... 2451
Ec 2:13 Then I saw that **w.** excelleth folly, ... 2451
Ec 2:21 is a man whose labour is in **w.**, ... 2451
Ec 2:26 a man that is good in his sight **w.**,...... 2451
Ec 7:11 **W.** is good with an inheritance:........... 2451
Ec 7:12 For **w.** is a defence, and money is a... 2451
Ec 7:12 **w.** giveth life to them that have it. 2451
Ec 7:19 **W.** strengtheneth the wise more........ 2451
Ec 7:23 All this have I proved by **w.**............... 2451
Ec 7:25 to seek out **w.**, and the reason of 2451
Ec 8:1 a man's **w.** maketh his face to 2451
Ec 8:16 I applied mine heart to know **w.**,......... 2451
Ec 9:10 nor device, nor knowledge, nor **w.**, ... 2451
Ec 9:13 This **w.** have I seen also under the...... 2451
Ec 9:15 he by his **w.** delivered the city; 2451
Ec 9:16 said I, **W.** is better than strength: 2451
Ec 9:16 the poor man's **w.** is despised, ... 2451
Ec 9:18 **W.** is better than weapons of war: 2451
Ec 10:1 in reputation for **w.** and honour.......... 2451
Ec 10:3 his **w.** faileth him, and he saith 3820
Ec 10:10 but **w.** is profitable to direct............. 2451
Isa 10:13 hand I have done it, and by my **w.**; 2451
Isa 11:2 the spirit of **w.** and understanding,...... 2451
Isa 29:14 **w.** of their wise men shall perish,....... 2451
Isa 33:6 **w.** and knowledge shall be the........... 2451
Isa 47:10 Thy **w.** and thy knowledge, it hath 2451
Jer 8:9 the Lord; and what **w.** is in them?...... 2451
Jer 9:23 not the wise man glory in his **w.**, ... 2451
Jer 10:12 hath established the world by his **w.**, .. 2451
Jer 49:7 Is **w.** no more in Teman? is counsel ... 2451
Jer 49:7 the prudent? is their **w.** vanished? 2451
Jer 51:15 hath established the world by his **w.**, .. 2451
Eze 28:4 With thy **w.** and with thine................ 2451
Eze 28:5 By thy great **w.** and by thy traffick..... 2451
Eze 28:7 swords against the beauth of thy **w.**,... 2451
Eze 28:12 Thou sealest up the sum, full of **w.**, ... 2451
Eze 28:17 thou hast corrupted thy **w.** by........... 2451
Da 1:4 and skilful in all **w.**, and cunning......... 2451
Da 1:17 and skill in all learning and **w.**.......... 2451
Da 1:20 matters of **w.** and understanding. 2451
Da 2:14 answered with counsel and **w.** to........ 2942
Da 2:20 ever: for **w.** and might are his:.......... 2452
Da 2:21 he giveth **w.** unto the wise, and......... 2452
Da 2:23 who hast given me **w.** and might,........ 2452
Da 2:30 is not revealed to me for any **w.**......... 2452
Da 5:11 light and understanding and **w.**,.......... 2452
Da 5:11 like the **w.** of the gods, was found....... 2452
Da 5:14 and excellent **w.** is found in thee........ 2452
Mic 6:9 the man of **w.** shall see thy name:....... 8454
Mt 11:19 **But w. is justified of her children.** *4678*
Mt 12:42 **earth to hear the w. of Solomon;**... *4678*
Mt 13:54 Whence hath this man this **w.**, and..... *4678*
Mk 6:2 **w.** is this which is given unto him, ... *4678*
Lu 1:17 disobedient to the **w.** of the just; *5428*
Lu 2:40 strong in spirit, filled with **w.** *4678*
Lu 2:52 Jesus increased in **w.** and stature, ... *4678*
Lu 7:35 **w. is justified of all her children**..... *4678*
Lu 11:31 **earth to hear the w. of Solomon;**... *4678*
Lu 11:49 **Therefore also said the w. of God,**. *4678*
Lu 21:15 **I will give you a mouth and w.,** *4678*
Ac 6:3 full of the Holy Ghost and **w.**, ... *4678*
Ac 6:10 they were not able to resist the **w.** *4678*
Ac 7:10 gave him favour and **w.** in the sight.... *4678*
Ac 7:22 in all the **w.** of the Egyptians,........... *4678*
Ro 11:33 depth of the riches both of the **w.**........ *4678*
1Co 1:17 not with **w.** of words, lest the cross ... *4678*
1Co 1:19 I will destroy the **w.** of the wise, ... *4678*
1Co 1:20 made foolish the **w.** of this world? *4678*
1Co 1:21 For after that in the **w.** of God.......... *4678*
1Co 1:21 the world by **w.** knew not God, ... *4678*
1Co 1:22 sign, and the Greeks seek after **w.**...... *4678*
1Co 1:24 the power of God, and the **w.** of God. *4678*
1Co 1:30 who of God is made unto us **w.**,......... *4678*
1Co 2:1 with excellency of speech or of **w.**,....... *4678*
1Co 2:4 with enticing words of man's **w.**, ... *4678*
1Co 2:5 should not stand in the **w.** of men, ... *4678*
1Co 2:6 **w.** speak we among them that are...... *4678*

1Co 2:6 yet not the **w.** of this world, nor of.... *4678*
1Co 2:7 we speak the **w.** of God in a........... *4678*
1Co 2:7 even the hidden **w.**, which God...............
1Co 2:13 words which man's **w.** teacheth,........ *4678*
1Co 3:19 **w.** of this world is foolishness with..... *4678*
1Co 12:8 given by the Spirit the word of **w.**;..... *4678*
2Co 1:12 not with fleshly **w.**, but by the grace... *4678*
Eph 1:8 hath abounded toward us in all **w.** *4678*
Eph 1:17 you the spirit of **w.** and revelation...... *4678*
Eph 3:10 the church the manifold **w.** of God,..... *4678*
Col 1:9 the knowledge of his will in all **w.**........ *4678*
Col 1:28 and teaching every man in all **w.**;....... *4678*
Col 2:3 whom are hid all the treasures of **w.**... *4678*
Col 2:23 indeed a shew of **w.** in will worship, ... *4678*
Col 3:16 Christ dwell in you richly in all **w.**; *4678*
Col 4:5 Walk in **w.** toward them that are....... *4678*
Jas 1:5 If any of you lack **w.**, let him ask....... *4678*
Jas 3:13 his works with meekness of **w.**.......... *4678*
Jas 3:15 This **w.** descendeth not from above, ... *4678*
Jas 3:17 But the **w.** that is from above is *4678*
2Pe 3:15 according to the **w.** given unto him...... *4678*
Re 5:12 and **w.**, and strength, and honour,...... *4678*
Re 7:12 Blessing, and glory, and **w.**, and *4678*
Re 13:18 Here is **w.**. Let him that hath........... *4678*
Re 17:9 here is the mind which hath **w.**.......... *4678*

WISE See also CONTRARIWISE; LIKEWISE; OTHERWISE; UNWISE; WISER.

Ge 3:6 tree to be desired to make one **w.**, ... 7919
Ge 41:8 and all the **w.** men thereof:............... 2450
Ge 41:33 look out a man discreet and **w.**,.......... 2450
Ge 41:39 so discreet and **w.** as thou art: 2450
Ex 7:11 Pharaoh also called the **w.** men.......... 2450
Ex 22:23 If thou afflict them in any **w.**, and....... 6031
Ex 23:8 the gift blindeth the **w.**, and.............. 6493
Ex 28:3 speak unto all that are **w.** hearted, ... 2450
Ex 31:6 the hearts of all that are **w.** hearted.... 2450
Ex 35:10 every **w.** hearted among you shall...... 2450
Ex 35:25 the women that were **w.** hearted........ 2450
Ex 36:1 every **w.** hearted man, in whom.......... 2450
Ex 36:2 every **w.** hearted man, in whose 2450
Ex 36:4 And all the **w.** men, that wrought....... 2450
Ex 36:8 every **w.** hearted man among them..... 2450
Le 7:24 use: but ye shall in no **w.** eat of it...........
Le 19:17 thou shalt in any **w.** rebuke thy 3198
Le 27:19 the field will in any **w.** redeem it.............
Nu 6:23 On this **w.** ye shall bless the children........
De 1:13 Take you **w.** men, and..................... 2450
De 1:15 the chief of your tribes, **w.** men,........ 2450
De 4:6 is a **w.** and understanding people......... 2450
De 16:19 a gift doth blind the eyes of the **w.**,.... 2450
De 17:15 shalt in any **w.** set him king over ....
De 21:23 shalt in any **w.** bury him that day; ....
De 22:7 thou shalt in any **w.** let the dam go,..........
De 32:29 O that they were **w.**, that they.......... 2449
Jos 6:18 in any **w.** keep yourselves from the ....
Jos 23:12 if ye do in any **w.** go back, and cleave.......
Jg 5:29 Her **w.** ladies answered her, yea,....... 2450
1Sa 6:3 any **w.** return him a trespass offering:.......
2Sa 14:2 and fetched thence a **w.** woman, ... 2450
2Sa 14:20 and my lord is **w.**, according to the 2450
2Sa 20:16 Then cried a **w.** woman out of the....... 2450
1Ki 2:9 for thou art a **w.** man, and knowest.... 2450
1Ki 3:12 a **w.** and an understanding heart;........ 2450
1Ki 3:26 the living child, and in no **w.** slay it. ... 2450
1Ki 3:27 the living child, and in no **w.** slay it: ... 2450
1Ki 5:7 hath given unto David a **w.** son.......... 2450
1Ki 11:22 Nothing: howbeit let me go in any **w.**........
1Ch 26:14 Zechariah his son, a **w.** counseller, ... 7922
1Ch 27:32 counseller, a **w.** man, and a scribe: 995
2Ch 2:12 given to David the king a **w.** son,........ 2450
Es 1:13 Then the king said to the **w.** men,...... 2450
Es 6:13 Then said his **w.** men and Zeresh....... 2450
Job 5:13 He taketh the **w.** in their own 2450
Job 9:4 He is **w.** in heart, and mighty in 2450
Job 11:12 vain man would be **w.**, though.......... 3823
Job 15:2 a **w.** man utter vain knowledge,......... 2450
Job 15:18 **w.** men have told from their fathers,... 2450
Job 17:10 cannot find one **w.** man among you. 2450
Job 22:2 he that is **w.** may be profitable 7919
Job 32:9 Great men are not always **w.** 2449
Job 34:2 Hear my words, O ye **w.** men;........... 2450
Job 34:34 and let a **w.** man hearken unto me. 2450
Job 37:24 not any that are **w.** of heart............. 2450
Ps 2:10 Be **w.** now therefore, O ye kings:...... 7919
Ps 19:7 is sure, making **w.** the simple........... 2449
Ps 36:3 he hath left off to be **w.**, and to do..... 7919
Ps 37:8 fret not thyself in any **w.** to do evil..........
Ps 49:10 For he seeth that **w.** men die,............ 2450
Ps 94:8 and ye fools, when will ye be **w.**? 7919
Ps 107:43 Whoso is **w.**, and will observe........... 2450
Pr 1:5 **w.** man will hear, and will increase..... 2450
Pr 1:5 man...shall attain unto **w.** counsels:...........
Pr 1:6 the words of the **w.**, and their dark.... 2450
Pr 3:7 Be not **w.** in thine own eyes: fear...... 2450
Pr 3:35 The **w.** shall inherit glory: but 2450
Pr 6:6 consider her ways, and be **w.**............ 2449
Pr 8:33 Hear instruction, and be **w.**, and........ 2449
Pr 9:8 rebuke a **w.** man, and he will love....... 2450
Pr 9:9 Give instruction to a **w.** man, and....... 2450
Pr 9:12 If thou be **w.**, thou shalt be **w.** for..... 2449
Pr 10:1 A **w.** son maketh a glad father:.......... 2450
Pr 10:5 gathereth in summer is a **w.** son:........ 7919
Pr 10:8 The **w.** in heart will receive.............. 2450
Pr 10:14 **W.** men lay up knowledge: but.......... 2450
Pr 10:19 he that refraineth his lips is **w.**.. 7919
Pr 11:29 be servant to the **w.** of heart............ 2450
Pr 11:30 and he that winneth souls is **w.**.......... 2450
Pr 12:15 hearkeneth unto counsel is **w.**. 2450
Pr 12:18 but the tongue of the **w.** is health. 2450
Pr 13:1 A **w.** son heareth his father's 2450
Pr 13:14 law of the **w.** is a fountain of life,....... 2450
Pr 13:20 He that walketh with **w.** men shall...... 2450
Pr 13:20 shall be **w.**: but a companion of.......... 2449
Pr 14:1 Every **w.** woman buildeth her............ 2454
Pr 14:3 the lips of the **w.** shall preserve......... 2450
Pr 14:16 A **w.** man feareth, and departeth........ 2450
Pr 14:24 The crown of the **w.** is their riches: ... 2450
Pr 14:35 favour is toward a **w.** servant:........... 7919
Pr 15:2 the **w.** useth knowledge aright:........... 2450
Pr 15:7 lips of the **w.** disperse knowledge:....... 2450
Pr 15:12 neither will he go unto the **w.**. 2450
Pr 15:20 A **w.** son maketh a glad father: but..... 2450
Pr 15:24 The way of life is above to the **w.**,..... 7919
Pr 15:31 of life abideth among the **w.**. 2450
Pr 16:14 death: but a **w.** man will pacify it. 2450
Pr 16:21 **w.** in heart shall be called prudent: 2450
Pr 16:23 heart of the **w.** teacheth his mouth,..... 2450
Pr 17:2 A **w.** servant shall have rule over....... 7919
Pr 17:10 A reproof entereth more into a **w.**........ 995
Pr 17:28 holdeth his peace, is counted **w.** 2450
Pr 18:15 the ear of the **w.** seeketh knowledge. . 2450
Pr 19:20 that thou mayest be **w.** in thy........... 2449
Pr 20:1 is deceived thereby is not **w.** 2449
Pr 20:26 A **w.** king scattereth the wicked,........ 2450
Pr 21:11 punished, the simple is made **w.** 2449
Pr 21:11 and when the **w.** is instructed, he 2450
Pr 21:20 and oil in the dwelling of the **w.**;........ 2450
Pr 21:22 A **w.** man scaleth the city of the........ 2450
Pr 22:17 and hear the words of the **w.**, and...... 2450
Pr 23:15 My son, if thine heart be **w.**, my 2449
Pr 23:19 Hear thou, my son, and be **w.**, and 2449
Pr 23:24 he that begetteth a **w.** child shall....... 2450
Pr 24:5 A **w.** man is strong; yea, a man of..... 2450
Pr 24:6 by **w.** counsel thou shalt make thy...........
Pr 24:23 These things also belong to the **w.**. 2450
Pr 25:12 a **w.** reprover upon an obedient ear. ... 2450
Pr 26:5 lest he be **w.** in his own conceit......... 2450
Pr 26:12 thou a man **w.** in his own conceit?...... 2450
Pr 27:11 be **w.**, and make my heart glad,......... 2449
Pr 28:7 Whoso keepeth the law is a **w.** son:..... 995
Pr 28:11 rich man is **w.** in his own conceit;....... 2450
Pr 29:8 snare: but **w.** men turn away wrath. ... 2450
Pr 29:9 a **w.** man contendeth with a foolish..... 2450
Pr 29:11 but a **w.** man keepeth it in till............ 2450
Pr 30:24 earth, but they are exceeding **w.**......... 2450
Ec 2:14 The **w.** man's eyes are in his head; 2450
Ec 2:15 me; and why was I then more **w.**? 2449
Ec 2:16 no remembrance of the **w.** more 2450
Ec 2:16 how dieth the **w.** man? as the fool...... 2450
Ec 2:19 he shall be a **w.** man or a fool?.......... 2450
Ec 2:19 wherein I have shewed myself **w.**........ 2449
Ec 4:13 Better is a poor and a **w.** child, ... 2450
Ec 6:8 hath the **w.** more than the fool? 2450
Ec 7:4 heart of the **w.** is in the house of....... 2450
Ec 7:5 better to hear the rebuke of the **w.**, ... 2450
Ec 7:7 oppression maketh a **w.** man mad;...... 2450
Ec 7:16 neither make thyself over **w.**............ 2449
Ec 7:19 Wisdom strengtheneth the **w.**............ 2450
Ec 7:23 I said, I will be **w.**; but it was far....... 2449
Ec 8:1 Who is as the **w.** man? and who 2450
Ec 8:5 a **w.** man's heart discerneth both........ 2450
Ec 8:17 though a **w.** man think to know it,...... 2450
Ec 9:1 that the righteous, and the **w.**, and..... 2450
Ec 9:11 neither yet bread to the **w.**, nor 2450
Ec 9:15 there was found in it a poor **w.** man, .. 2450
Ec 9:17 The words of **w.** men are heard in..... 2450
Ec 10:2 A **w.** man's heart is at his right 2450
Ec 10:12 of a **w.** man's mouth are gracious;...... 2450
Ec 12:9 because the preacher was **w.**, he 2450
Ec 12:11 The words of the **w.** are as goads,..... 2450
Isa 5:21 unto them that are **w.** in their own..... 2450
Isa 19:11 the **w.** counsellers of Pharaoh is......... 2450
Isa 19:11 I am the son of the **w.**, the son of..... 2450
Isa 19:12 are they? where are thy **w.** men?....... 2450
Isa 29:14 the wisdom of their **w.** men shall 2450
Isa 31:2 Yet he also is **w.**, and will bring.......... 2450
Isa 44:25 that turneth **w.** men backward,.......... 2450
Jer 4:22 they are **w.** to do evil, but to do........ 2450
Jer 8:8 We are **w.**, and the law of the Lord.... 2450
Jer 8:9 **w.** men are ashamed, they are 2450
Jer 9:12 Who is the **w.** man, that may 2450
Jer 9:23 the **w.** man glory in his wisdom, ... 2450
Jer 10:7 among all the **w.** men of the nations ... 2450
Jer 18:18 nor counsel from the **w.**, nor the 2450
Jer 50:35 her princes, and upon her **w.** men...... 2450
Jer 51:57 drunk her princes, and her **w.** men,.... 2450
Eze 27:8 thy **w.** men, O Tyrus, that were in 2450
Eze 27:9 Gebal and the **w.** men thereof were.... 2450
Da 2:12 destroy all the **w.** men of Babylon. 2445
Da 2:13 that the **w.** men should be slain; 2445
Da 2:14 to slay the **w.** men of Babylon:.......... 2445
Da 2:18 the rest of the **w.** men of Babylon...... 2445
Da 2:21 he giveth wisdom unto the **w.**, and..... 2445
Da 2:24 to destroy the **w.** men of Babylon: 2445
Da 2:24 Destroy not the **w.** men of Babylon: ... 2445
Da 2:27 hath demanded cannot the **w.** men,..... 2445
Da 2:48 over all the **w.** men of Babylon.......... 2445
Da 4:6 bring in all the **w.** men of Babylon...... 2445
Da 4:18 **w.** men of my kingdom are not able.... 2445
Da 5:7 and said to the **w.** men of Babylon, ... 2445
Da 5:8 Then came in all the king's **w.** men: ... 2445
Da 5:15 now the **w.** men, the astrologers,....... 2445
Da 12:3 And they that be **w.** shall shine.......... 7919
Da 12:10 but the **w.** shall understand.............. 7919
Ho 14:9 Who is **w.**, and he shall understand..... 2450
Ob 8 destroy the **w.** men out of Edom, ... 2450
Zec 9:2 and Zidon, though it be very **w.**......... 2449
Mt 1:18 of Jesus Christ was on this **w.**.......... *3779*
Mt 2:1 there came **w.** men from the east *3097*
Mt 2:7 he had privily called the **w.** men,........ *3097*
Mt 2:16 that he was mocked of the **w.** men,.... *3097*
Mt 2:16 diligently enquired of the **w.** men. *3097*
Mt 5:18 **one tittle shall in no w. pass from........**
Mt 7:24 **I will liken him unto a w. man,**.... *5429*
Mt 10:16 **be ye therefore w. as serpents,**...... *5429*
Mt 10:42 **he shall in no w. lose his reward.........**
Mt 11:25 **hast hid these things from the w.**.... *4680*
Mt 21:24 **I in like w. will tell you by what.........**
Mt 23:34 **unto you prophets, and w. men,**.... *4680*
Mt 24:45 **then is a faithful and w. servant,**.. *5429*
Mt 25:2 **And five of them were w., and five.***5429*
Mt 25:4 **But the w. took oil in their vessels.***5429*
Mt 25:8 **And the foolish said unto the w.,**.. *5429*
Mt 25:9 **the w. answered, saying, Not so;**... *5429*
Mk 14:31 thee, I will not deny thee in any **w.**..........
Lu 10:21 **hast hid these things from the w.**.. *4680*
Lu 12:42 **is that faithful and w. steward,**...... *5429*
Lu 13:11 could in no **w.** lift up herself....... *3588,3838*
Lu 18:17 **child shall in no w. enter therein.**.......
Joh 6:37 **cometh to me I will in no w. cast out..**
Joh 21:1 and on this **w.** shewed he himself....... *3779*
Ac 7:6 And God spake on this **w.**, that his..... *3779*
Ac 13:34 he said on this **w.**, I will give you *3779*
Ac 13:41 work which ye shall in no **w.** believe,........
Ro 1:14 both to the **w.**, and to the unwise. *4680*
Ro 1:22 Professing themselves to be **w.**, ... *4680*
Ro 3:9 No, in no **w.**: for we have before....... *3843*
Ro 10:6 is of faith speaketh on this **w.**,........... *3779*
Ro 11:25 should be **w.** in your own conceits;...... *5429*
Ro 12:16 Be not **w.** in your own conceits. *5429*
Ro 16:19 you **w.** unto that which is good,........ *4680*
Ro 16:27 To God only **w.**, be glory through....... *4680*
1Co 1:19 I will destroy the wisdom of the **w.**, ... *4680*
1Co 1:20 Where is the **w.**? where is the scribe.. *4680*
1Co 1:26 not many **w.** men after the flesh, ... *4680*
1Co 1:27 of the world to confound the **w.**;........ *4680*
1Co 3:10 as a **w.** masterbuilder, I have laid....... *4680*

1Co 3:18 you seemeth to be w. in this world, ... *4680*
1Co 3:18 become a fool, that he may be w.. ..... *4680*
1Co 3:19 He taketh the w. in their own *4680*
1Co 3:20 knoweth the thoughts of the w., ... *4680*
1Co 4:10 sake, but ye are w. in Christ;........... *5429*
1Co 6:5 there is not a w. man among you?...... *4680*
1Co 10:15 I speak as to w. men; judge ye *5429*
2Co 10:12 among themselves, are not w............ *4920*
2Co 11:19 seeing ye yourselves are w.............. *5429*
Eph 5:15 not as fools, but as w., ... *4680*
1Ti 1:17 the only w. God, be honour and......... *4680*
2Ti 3:15 to make thee w. unto salvation *4679*
Heb 4:4 of the seventh day on this w., ... *3779*
Jas 3:13 Who is a w. man and endued with....... *4680*
Jude 25 To the only w. God our Saviour,........ *4680*
Re 21:27 there shall in no w. enter into it any.........

WISE-HEARTED See WISE and HEARTED.

WISELY
Ex 1:10 Come on, let us deal w. with them;.... 2449
1Sa 18:5 sent him, and behaved himself w........ 7919
1Sa 18:14 And David behaved himself w........... 7919
1Sa 18:15 that he behaved himself very w., ... 7919
1Sa 18:30 David behaved himself more w. 7919
2Ch 11:23 And he dealt w., and dispersed of....... 995
Ps 58:5 charmers, charming never so w.. 2449
Ps 64:9 they shall w. consider of his doing...... 7919
Ps 101:2 behave myself w. in a perfect way...... 7919
Pr 19:20 He that handeth a matter w. shall 7919
Pr 21:12 The righteous man w. considereth...... 7919
Pr 28:26 but whoso walketh w., he shall be...... 2451
Ec 7:10 for thou dost not enquire w.............. 2451
Lu 16:8 **steward, because he had done w....** *5430*

WISE-MEN See WISE and MEN.

WISER
1Ki 4:31 For he was w. than all men; than....... 2449
Job 35:11 and maketh us w. than the fowls........ 2449
Ps 119:98 commandments hast made me w........ 2449
Pr 9:9 a wise man, and he will be yet w........ 2449
Pr 26:16 sluggard is w. in his own conceit........ 2450
Eze 28:3 Behold, thou art w. than Daniel; 2450
Lu 16:8 **w. than the children of light.........** *5429*
1Co 1:25 foolishness of God is w. than men; *4680*

WISE-WOMAN See WISE and WOMAN.

WISH See also WISHED; WISHING.
Job 33:6 I am according to thy w. in God's 6310
Ps 40:14 and put to shame that w. me evil....... 2655
Ps 73:7 have more than heart could w.. 4906
Ro 9:3 could w. that myself were accursed....... *2172*
2Co 13:9 and this also we w., even your.......... *2172*
3Jo 2 I w. above all things that thou *2172*

WISHED
Jon 4:8 and w. in himself to die, and said, ... 7592
Ac 27:29 of the stern, and w. for the day......... *2172*

WISHING
Job 31:30 to sin by w. a curse to his soul.......... 7592

WIST See also WIT; WOT.
Ex 16:15 for they w. not what it was.............. 3045
Ex 34:29 Moses w. not that the skin of his....... 3045
Le 5:17 though he w. it not, yet is he guilty,... 3045
Le 5:18 wherein he erred and w. it not........... 3045
Jos 2:4 me, but I w. not whence they were:.... 3045
Jos 8:14 he w. not that there were liers in 3045
Jg 16:20 w. not that the Lord was departed..... 3045
Mk 9:6 For he w. not what to say: for they .. *1492*
Mk 14:40 neither w. they what to answer......... 1492
Lu 2:49 **w. ye not that I must be about my.**1492
Joh 5:13 that was healed w. not who it was: 1492
Ac 12:9 w. not that it was true which was 1492
Ac 23:5 Then said Paul, I w. not, brethren, ... 1492

WIT See also WIST; WIT'S; WITTINGLY; WOT.
Ge 24:21 to w. whether the Lord had made....... 3045
Ex 2:4 to w. what would be done to him........ 3045
Jos 17:1 to w., for Machir the firstborn of............
1Ki 2:32 to w., Abner the son of Ner, captain of.....
1Ki 7:50 doors of the house, to w., of the temple....
1Ki 13:23 to w., for the prophet whom he had.........
2Ki 10:29 to w., the golden calves that were in.........
1Ch 7:2 of their father's house, to w., of Tola:........
1Ch 27:1 to w., the chief fathers and.....................
2Ch 4:12 To w., the two pillars, and the ....
2Ch 25:7 Israel, to w., with all the children of.........
2Ch 25:10 to w., the army that was come...............
2Ch 31:3 to w., for the morning and evening...........
Ne 11:3 cities, to w., Israel, the priests, and the....
Es 2:12 to w. six months with oil of myrrh,...........
Jer 25:18 To w., Jerusalem, and the cities of...........
Jer 34:9 of them, to w., of a Jew his brother. ....
Eze 13:16 To w., the prophets of Israel which..........
Ro 8:23 to w., the redemption of our body............
2Co 5:19 To w., that God was in Christ,........... *5613*
2Co 8:1 do you to w. of the grace of God....... *1107*

WITCH See also BEWITCH; WITCHCRAFT.
Ex 22:18 Thou shalt not suffer a w. to live. 3784
De 18:10 of times, or an enchanter, or a w.,..... 3784

WITCHCRAFT See also WITCHCRAFTS.
1Sa 15:23 For rebellion is as the sin of w., ... 7081
2Ch 33:6 used enchantments, and used w.,....... 3784
Ga 5:20 Idolatry, w., hatred, variance, ... *5331*

WITCHCRAFTS
2Ki 9:22 Jezebel and her w. are so many?........ 3785
Mic 5:12 will cut off w. out of thine hand; 3785
Na 3:4 the mistress of w., that selleth.......... 3785
Na 3:4 and families through her w................ 3785

WITH See in the APPENDIX; also HEREWITH; THEREWITH; WHEREWITH; WITHAL; WITHDRAW; WITHHOLD; WITHIN; WITHOUT; WITHS; WITHSTAND.

WITHAL See also WHEREWITHAL.
Ex 25:29 and bowls thereof, to cover w........... 2004
Ex 30:4 places for the staves to bear it w....... 1992
Ex 30:18 and his foot also of brass, to wash w. ....
Ex 36:3 of the sanctuary, to make it w.................
Ex 37:16 covers to cover w., of pure gold......... 2004
Ex 37:27 places for the staves to bear it w............
Ex 38:7 the sides of the altar, to bear it w.;..........
Ex 40:30 and put water there, to wash w..............
Le 5:3 it be that a man shall be defiled w., ...
Le 6:30 to reconcile w. in the holy place,..............
Le 11:21 feet, to leap w. upon the earth; 2004
Le 19:24 shall be holy to praise the Lord w. ....
Nu 4:7 the bowls, and covers to cover w............
Jg 7:20 in their right hands to blow w..................
1Sa 16:12 w. of a beautiful countenance,............ 5973
1Ki 19:1 w. how he had slain all the.......... 834,3605
2Ki 23:26 that Manasseh had provoked him w. ....
1Ch 29:4 to overlay the walls of the houses w.........
2Ch 24:14 vessels to minister, and to offer w., ...
2Ch 26:15 to shoot arrows and great stones w..........
Es 6:9 array the man w. whom the king................
Job 2:8 him a potsherd to scrape himself w...........
Ps 141:10 own nets, whilst that I w. escape....... 3162
Pr 22:18 they shall w. be fitted in thy lips. 3162
Isa 30:14 or to take water w. out of the pit............
Isa 30:23 that thou shalt sow the ground w.;............
Mk 10:39 **I am baptized w. shall ye be baptized:..**
Lu 6:38 **that ye mete w. it shall be measured...**
Ac 25:27 not w. to signify the crimes laid..............
1Co 12:7 is given to every man to profit w. ....
Col 4:3 W. praying also for us, that God *260*
1Ti 5:13 w. they learn to be idle, wandering....... *260*
Phm 22 But w. prepare me also a lodging: *260*

WITHDRAW See also WITHDRAWEST; WITHDRAWETH; WITHDRAWN; WITHDREW.
1Sa 14:19 unto the priest, W. thine hand. 622
Job 9:13 If God will not w. his anger, the 7725
Job 13:21 W. thine hand far from me: and......... 7368
Job 33:17 he may w. man from his purpose, ... 5493
Pr 25:17 W. thy foot from thy neighbour's 3365
Ec 7:18 also from this w. not thine hand;........ 3240
Isa 60:20 neither shall thy moon w. itself: 622
Joe 2:10 and the stars shall w. their shining:...... 622
Joe 3:15 and the stars shall w. their shining....... 622
2Th 3:6 w. yourselves from every brother *4724*
1Ti 6:5 godliness: from such w. thyself. *868*

WITHDRAWEST
Ps 74:11 Why w. thou thy hand, even thy........ 7725

WITHDRAWETH
Job 36:7 He w. not his eyes from the 1639

WITHDRAWN
De 13:13 w. the inhabitants of their city, ... 5080
Ca 5:6 but my beloved had w. himself, ... 2559
La 2:8 not w. his hand from destroying:........ 7725
Eze 18:8 hath w. his hand from iniquity,........... 7725
Ho 5:6 he hath w. himself from them............ 2502
Lu 22:41 And he was w. from them about a....... *645*

WITHDREW
Ne 9:29 and w. the shoulder, and.......... 5414,5437
Eze 20:22 Nevertheless I w. mine hand,............ 7725
Mt 12:15 it, he w. himself from thence:............ *402*
Mk 3:7 Jesus w. himself with his disciples........ *402*
Lu 5:16 he w. himself into the wilderness, ... *5298*
Ga 2:12 he w. and separated himself, ... *5288*

WITHER See also WITHERED; WITHERETH.
Ps 1:3 his leaf also shall not w.; and............ 5034
Ps 37:2 grass, and w. as the green herb. 5034
Isa 19:6 up: the reeds and flags shall w. 7060
Isa 19:7 sown by the brooks, shall w.,............ 3001
Isa 40:24 blow upon them, and they shall w., ... 3001
Jer 12:4 and the herbs of every field w.,.......... 3001
Eze 17:9 cut off the fruit thereof, that it w.?..... 3001
Eze 17:9 w. in all the leaves of her spring,........ 3001
Eze 17:10 shall it not utterly w., when the........ 3001
Eze 17:10 w. in the furrows where it grew. 3001
Am 1:2 and the top of Carmel shall w............ 3001

WITHERED
Ge 41:23 seven ears, w., thin, and blasted........ 6798
Ps 102:4 heart is smitten, and w. like grass;..... 3001
Ps 102:11 and I am w. like grass. 3001
Isa 15:6 for the hay is w. away, the grass....... 3001
Isa 27:11 When the boughs thereof are w., ... 3001
La 4:8 it is w., it is become like a stick. 3001
Eze 19:12 strong rods were broken and w.; 3001
Joe 1:12 all the trees of the field, are w. 3001
Joe 1:12 joy is w. away from the sons of men. ..3001
Joe 1:17 broken down; for the corn is w.......... 3001
Am 4:7 piece whereupon it rained not w. 3001
Jon 4:7 and it smote the gourd that it w. 3001
Mt 12:10 a man which had his hand w............. *3584*
Mt 13:6 **they had no root, they w. away.....** *3583*
Mt 21:19 And presently the fig tre w. away. *3583*
Mt 21:20 How soon is the fig tre w. away! *3583*
Mk 3:1 man there which had a w. hand. *3583*
Mk 3:3 the man which had the w. hand, ... *3583*
Mk 4:6 **because it had no root, it w. away..***3583*
Mk 11:21 which thou cursedst is w. away. *3583*
Lu 6:6 a man whose right hand was w. *3584*
Lu 6:8 man which had the w. hand, **Rise**...... *3584*
Lu 8:6 **it w....because it lacked moisture..** *3583*
Joh 5:3 halt, w., waiting for the moving of...... *3584*
Joh 15:6 **cast forth as a branch, and is w.;..** *3583*

WITHERETH
Job 8:12 down, it w. before any other herb...... 3001
Ps 90:6 the evening it is cut down, and w....... 3001
Ps 129:6 which w. afore it groweth up:............ 3001
Isa 40:7,8 The grass w.,the flowers fadeth:........ 3001
Jas 1:11 burning heat, but it w. the grass,....... *3583*
1Pe 1:24 The grass w., and the flower *3583*
Jude 12 trees whose fruit w., without fruit,..... *5352*

WITHHELD See also WITHHELDEST; WITHHOLDEN.
Ge 20:6 I also w. thee from sinning 2820
Ge 22:12 seeing thou hast not w. thy son, ... 2820
Ge 22:16 hast not w. thy son, thine only son:.... 2820
Ge 30:2 who hath w. from thee the fruit of 4513
Job 31:16 If I have w. the poor from their......... 4513
Ec 2:10 I w. not my heart from any joy;......... 4513

WITHHELDEST
Ne 9:20 w. not thy manna from their.............. 4513

WITHHOLD See also WITHHELD; WITHHOLDEN; WITHHOLDETH.
Ge 23:6 shall w. from thee his sepulchre,........ 3607
2Sa 13:13 for he will not w. me from thee.......... 4513
Job 4:2 can w. himself from speaking? 6113
Ps 40:11 W. not thou thy tender mercies......... 3607
Ps 84:11 good thing will he w. from them 4513
Pr 3:27 W. not good from them to whom it 4513
Pr 23:13 W. not correction from a child:......... 4513
Ec 11:6 in the evening w. not thine hand: 3240
Jer 2:25 W. thy foot from being unshod, ... 4513

WITHHOLDEN See also WITHHELD.
1Sa 25:26 w. thee from coming to shed............ 4513
Job 22:7 hast w. bread from the hungry. 4513
Job 38:15 from the wicked their light is w., ... 4513
Job 42:2 no thought can be w. from thee. 1219
Ps 21:2 hast not w. the request of his lips. 4513
Jer 3:3 the showers have been w., ... 4513
Jer 5:25 your sins have w. good things from 4513
Eze 18:16 hath not w. the pledge, neither.......... 2254

Joe 1:13 drink offering is **w.** from the............. 4513
Am 4:7 also I have **w.** the rain from you, ... 4513

WITHHOLDETH

Job 12:15 he **w.** the waters, and they dry up: 6113
Pr 11:24 is that **w.** more than is meet, ... 2820
Pr 11:26 He that **w.** corn, the people shall 4513
2Th 2:6 what **w.** that he might be revealed *2722*

WITHIN

Ge 6:14 pitch it **w.** and without with pitch. 1004
Ge 9:21 and he was uncovered **w.** his tent. 8432
Ge 18:12 Sarah laughed **w.** herself, saying, ... 7130
Ge 18:24 be fifty righteous **w.** the city: 8432
Ge 18:26 Sodom fifty righteous **w.** the city,....... 8432
Ge 25:22 children struggled together **w.** 7130
Ge 39:11 of the men of the house there **w.**....... 1004
Ge 40:13, 19 Yet **w.** three days shall Pharaoh..........
Ex 20:10 nor thy stranger that is **w.** thy gates:........
Ex 25:11 **w.** and without shalt thou overlay 1004
Ex 26:33 in thither **w.** the vail of the ark of 1004
Ex 37:2 it with pure gold **w.** and without, ... 1004
Le 10:18 not brought in **w.** the holy place:........ 6441
Le 13:55 whether it be bare **w.** or without. 7146
Le 14:41 caused the house to be scraped **w.**...... 1004
Le 16:2 holy place **w.** the vail before the 1004
Le 16:12 small, and bring it within the vail: 1004
Le 16:15 and bring his blood **w.** the vail, ... 1004
Le 25:29 it **w.** a whole year after it is sold; 5704
Le 25:29 **w.** a full year may he redeem it. 8537
Le 25:30 redeemed **w.** the space of a...year, ... 5704
Le 26:25 gathered together **w.** your cities, ... 413
Nu 4:10 **w.** a covering of badgers' skins, ... 413
Nu 18:7 of the altar, and **w.** the vail;............. 1004
De 5:14 thy stranger that is **w.** thy gates;............
De 12:12 the Levite that is **w.** your gates;............
De 12:17 Thou mayest not eat **w.** thy gates the.......
De 12:18 and the Levite that is **w.** thy gates: ....
De 14:27 And the Levite that is **w.** thy gates; ....
De 14:28 and shalt lay it up **w.** thy gates: ....
De 14:29 the widow, which are **w.** thy gates, ...
De 15:7 of thy brethren **w.** any of thy gates ....
De 15:22 Thou shalt eat it **w.** thy gates: the ....
De 16:5 the passover **w.** any of thy gates,............
De 16:11 and the Levite that is **w.** thy gates ....
De 16:14 the widow, that are **w.** thy gates,............
De 17:2 **w.** any of thy gates which the Lord ....
De 17:8 matters of controversy **w.** thy gates: ....
De 23:10 he shall not come **w.** the camp: 8432
De 24:14 that are in thy land **w.** thy gates: ....
De 26:12 that they may eat **w.** thy gates, and ....
De 28:43 stranger that is **w.** thee shall get......... 7130
De 31:12 thy stranger that is **w.** thy gates, ...
De 32:25 The sword without, and terror **w.**, ... 2315
Jos 1:11 **w.** three days ye shall pass over........ 5750
Jos 19:1 **w.** the inheritance of the children 8432
Jos 19:9 inheritance **w.** the inheritance of......... 8432
Jos 21:41 **w.** the possession of the children 8432
Jg 7:16 and lamps **w.** the pitchers................. 8432
Jg 9:51 was a strong tower **w.** the city, ... 8432
Jg 11:18 came not **w.** the border of Moab: ....
Jg 11:26 ye not recover them **w.** that time? ....
Jg 14:12 declare it me **w.** the seven days..............
Jg 15:1 But it came to pass **w.** a while after, ...
1Sa 13:11 camest not **w.** the days appointed,............
1Sa 14:14 **w.** as it were an half acre of land, ...
1Sa 25:36 Nabal's heart was merry **w.** him,........ 5921
1Sa 25:37 that his heart died **w.** him, and 7130
1Sa 26:7 Saul lay sleeping **w.** the trench, ...
2Sa 7:2 ark of God dwelleth **w.** curtains. 8432
2Sa 20:4 me the men of Judah **w.** three days, ...
1Ki 6:15 house **w.** with boards of cedar, ... 1004
1Ki 6:16 he even built them for it **w.**, even...... 1004
1Ki 6:18 cedar of the house **w.** was carved 6441
1Ki 6:19 oracle he prepared in the house **w.**,.... 6441
1Ki 6:21 the house **w.** with pure gold:............. 6441
1Ki 6:23 **w.** the oracle he made two cherubims ....
1Ki 6:27 cherubims **w.** the inner house:........... 8432
1Ki 6:29 and open flowers, **w.** and without. 6441
1Ki 6:30 overlaid with gold, **w.** and without. 6441
1Ki 7:8 had another court **w.** the porch,......... 1004
1Ki 7:9 sawed with saws, **w.** and without, ... 1004
1Ki 7:31 mouth of it **w.** the chapiter and.......... 1004
2Ki 4:27 alone; for her soul is vexed **w.** her...........
2Ki 6:30 had sackcloth **w.** upon his flesh. 1004
2Ki 7:11 they told it to the king's house **w.**....... 6441
2Ki 11:8 and he that cometh **w.** the ranges, ...
2Ch 3:4 he overlaid it **w.** with pure gold. 6441
Ezr 4:15 sedition **w.** the same of old time: 4481
Ezr 10:8 would not come **w.** three days,...............
Ezr 10:9 unto Jerusalem **w.** three days. ....
Ne 4:22 his servant lodge **w.** Jerusalem, ... 8432
Ne 6:10 the house of God, **w.** the temple,....... 8432
Job 6:4 arrows of the Almighty are **w.** me,..... 5978
Job 14:22 and his soul **w.** him shall mourn. 5921
Job 19:27 my reins be consumed **w.** me............ 2436
Job 20:13 but keep it still **w.** his mouth;............ 8432
Job 20:14 it is the gall of asps **w.** him.............. 7130
Job 24:11 Which make oil **w.** their walls, and....... 996
Job 32:18 the spirit **w.** me constraineth me. 990
Ps 36:1 of the wicked saith **w.** my heart,........ 7130
Ps 39:3 My heart was hot **w.** me, while I........ 7130
Ps 40:8 God: yea, thy law is **w.** my heart....... 8432
Ps 40:10 hid thy righteousness **w.** my heart;..... 8432
Ps 42:6 God, my soul is cast down **w.** me: 5921
Ps 42:11 why art thou disquieted **w.** me? 5921
Ps 43:5 why art thou disquieted **w.** me? 5921
Ps 45:13 king's daughter is all glorious **w.** 6441
Ps 51:10 and renew a right spirit **w.** me. 7130
Ps 55:4 My heart is sore pained **w.** me:......... 7130
Ps 94:19 multitude of my thoughts **w.** me......... 7130
Ps 101:2 walk **w.** my house with a perfect......... 7130
Ps 101:7 deceit shall not dwell **w.** my house: 7130
Ps 103:1 all that is **w.** me, bless his holy 7130
Ps 109:22 and my heart is wounded **w.** me. 7130
Ps 122:2 Our feet shall stand **w.** thy gates, ... 7130
Ps 122:7 Peace be **w.** thy walls, and prosperity.......
Ps 122:7 walls, and prosperity **w.** thy palaces..........
Ps 122:8 I will now say, Peace be **w.** thee. ....
Ps 142:3 my spirit was overwhelmed **w.** me, ... 5921
Ps 143:4 is my spirit overwhelmed **w.** me; 5921
Ps 143:4 my heart **w.** me is desolate............. 8432
Ps 147:13 hath blessed thy children **w.** thee. 7130
Pr 22:18 thing if thou keep them **w.** thee; 990
Pr 26:24 lips, and layeth up deceit **w.** him;........ 7130
Ec 9:14 was a little city, and a few men **w.** it; ....
Ca 4:1 thou hast doves' eyes **w.** thy locks: 1157
Ca 4:3 of a pomegranate **w.** thy locks. 1157
Ca 6:7 are thy temples **w.** thy locks............. 1157
Isa 7:8 **w.** threescore and five years shall ....
Isa 16:14 **W.** three years, as the years of an...........
Isa 21:16 **W.** a year, according to the years 5750
Isa 26:9 my spirit **w.** me will I seek thee 7130
Isa 56:5 mine house and **w.** my walls a place ....
Isa 60:18 nor destruction **w.** thy borders;...............
Isa 63:11 he that put his holy Spirit **w.** him?...... 7130
Jer 4:14 thy vain thoughts lodge **w.** thee?......... 7130
Jer 23:9 Mine heart **w.** me is broken because... 7130
Jer 28:3 **W.** two full years will I bring............ 5750
Jer 28:11 **w.** the space of two full years. 5750
La 1:20 mine heart is turned **w.** me; for I....... 7130
Eze 1:27 of fire round about **w.** it,................... 1004
Eze 2:10 it was written **w.** and without: 6440
Eze 3:24 Go, shut thyself **w.** thine house. 8432
Eze 7:15 the pestilence and the famine **w.**........ 1004
Eze 11:19 and I will put a new spirit **w.** you;...... 7130
Eze 12:24 divination **w.** the house of Israel......... 8432
Eze 36:26 and a new spirit will I put **w.** you:...... 7130
Eze 36:27 And I will put my spirit **w.** you, ... 7130
Eze 40:7 porch of the gate **w.** was one reed. 1004
Eze 40:8 also the porch of the gate **w.**,........... 1004
Eze 40:16 posts **w.** the gate round about, ... 6441
Eze 40:43 **w.** were hooks, an hand broad, ... 1004
Eze 41:9 of the side chambers that were **w.** 1004
Eze 41:17 wall round about **w.** and without,......... 6442
Eze 44:17 gates of the inner court, and **w.**......... 1004
Da 6:12 of any God or man **w.** thirty days,....... 5705
Da 11:20 but **w.** few days he shall be destroyed,......
Ho 11:8 mine heart is turned **w.** me, my..............
Jon 2:7 When my soul fainteth **w.** me I.......... 5921
Mic 3:3 pot, and as flesh **w.** the caldron. 8432
Mic 5:6 and when he treadeth **w.** our borders........
Zep 3:3 princes **w.** her are roaring lions; 7130
Zec 12:1 formeth the spirit of man **w.** him. 7130
Mt 3:9 think not to say **w.** yourselves,.......... *1722*
Mt 9:3 of the scribes said **w.** themselves, ... *1722*
Mt 9:21 For she said **w.** herself, If I may........ *1722*
Mt 23:25 **w. they are full of extortion and** ... *2081*
Mt 23:26 **first that which is w. the cup and** ... *1787*
Mt 23:27 **are w. full of dead men's bones,** *2081*
Mt 23:28 **but w. ye are full of hypocrisy** *2081*
Mk 2:8 they so reasoned **w.** themselves, ... *1722*
Mk 7:21 **from w., out of the heart of men,**.. *2081*
Mk 7:23 **All these evil things come from w.,** *2081*
Mk 14:4 had indignation **w.** themselves,........... *4314*
Mk 14:58 **w. three days I will build another** *1223*
Lu 3:8 begin not to say **w.** yourselves, We.... *1722*
Lu 7:39 he spake **w.** himself, saying, This.... *1722*
Lu 7:49 him began to say **w.** themselves, ... *1722*
Lu 11:7 **he from w. shall answer and say,** .. *2081*
Lu 11:40 **make that which is w. also?** *2081*
Lu 12:17 **And he thought w. himself, saying,** *1722*
Lu 16:3 **Then the steward said w. himself,** . *1722*
Lu 17:21 **the kingdom of God is w. you.**...... *1787*
Lu 18:4 **but afterward he said w. himself,** .. *1722*
Lu 19:44 **ground, and thy children w. thee;** ..*1722*
Lu 24:32 Did not our heart burn **w.** us, while.... *1722*
Joh 20:26 days again his disciples were **w.**,........ *2080*
Ac 5:23 had opened, we found no man **w.**....... *2080*
Ro 8:23 we ourselves groan **w.** ourselves,....... *1722*
1Co 5:12 do not ye judge them that are **w.**?...... *2080*
2Co 7:5 were fightings, **w.** were fears............ *2081*
Heb 6:19 entereth into that **w.** the vail;........... *2082*
Re 4:8 and they were full of eyes **w.**............ *2081*
Re 5:1 on the throne a book written **w.** *2081*

WITHOUT

Ge 1:2 earth was **w.** form, and void; 8414
Ge 6:14 pitch it within and **w.** with pitch. 2351
Ge 9:22 and told his two brethren **w.**.............. 2351
Ge 19:16 him forth, and set him **w.** the city...... 2351
Ge 24:11 camels to kneel down **w.** the city by.... 2351
Ge 24:31 wherefore standeth thou **w.**? for I 2351
Ge 37:33 Joseph is **w.** doubt rent in pieces. 2963
Ge 41:44 **w.** thee shall no man lift up his.......... 1107
Ge 41:49 numbering; for it was **w.** number......... 369
Ex 12:5 Your lamb shall be **w.** blemish, ... 8549
Ex 21:11 then shall she go out free **w.** money..... 369
Ex 25:11 and **w.** shalt thou overlay it,............. 2351
Ex 26:35 thou shalt set the table **w.** the vail, ... 2351
Ex 27:21 of the congregation **w.** the vail,.......... 2351
Ex 29:1 bullock and two rams **w.** blemish,....... 8549
Ex 29:14 thou burn with fire **w.** the camp:......... 2351
Ex 33:7 and pitched it **w.** the camp,............... 2351
Ex 33:7 which was **w.** the camp..................... 2351
Ex 37:2 it with pure gold within and **w.**, ... 2351
Ex 40:22 tabernacle northward, **w.** the vail. 2351
Le 1:3 let him offer a male **w.** blemish:......... 8549
Le 1:10 he shall bring it a male **w.** blemish...... 8549
Le 3:1 he shall offer it **w.** blemish before 8549
Le 3:6 female, he shall offer it **w.** blemish. 8549
Le 4:3 a young bullock **w.** blemish unto.......... 8549
Le 4:12 shall he carry forth **w.** the camp 2351
Le 4:21 forth the bullock **w.** the camp,........... 2351
Le 4:23 of the goats, a male **w.** blemish: 8549
Le 4:28 of the goats, a female **w.** blemish,....... 8549
Le 4:32 shall bring it a female **w.** blemish. 8549
Le 5:15 a ram **w.** blemish out of the flocks,..... 8549
Le 5:18 a ram **w.** blemish out of the flock,....... 8549
Le 6:6 a ram **w.** blemish out of the flock,....... 8549
Le 6:11 carry forth the ashes **w.** the camp...... 2351
Le 8:17 he burnt with fire **w.** the camp; 2351
Le 9:2 for a burnt offering, **w.** blemish,......... 8549
Le 9:3 both of the first year, **w.** blemish, ... 8549
Le 9:11 he burnt with fire **w.** he camp. 2351
Le 10:12 eat it **w.** leaven beside the altar: 4682
Le 13:46 **w.** the camp shall his habitation......... 2351
Le 13:55 whether it be bare within or **w.**, ... 1372
Le 14:10 take two he lambs **w.** blemish, ... 8549
Le 14:10 lamb of the first year **w.** blemish,....... 8549
Le 14:40 into an unclean place **w.** the city: 2351
Le 14:41 **w.** the city into an unclean place: 2351
Le 16:27 shall one carry forth **w.** the camp;...... 2351
Le 22:19 your own will a male **w.** blemish, ... 8549
Le 23:12 an he lamb **w.** blemish of the first 8549
Le 23:18 seven lambs **w.** blemish of the first..... 8549
Le 24:3 **W.** the vail of the testimony, in 2351
Le 24:14 him that hath cursed **w.** the camp; 2351
Le 26:43 while she lieth desolate **w.** them: ....
Nu 5:3 **w.** the camp shall ye put them;........... 2351
Nu 5:4 so, and put them out **w.** the camp:....... 2351
Nu 6:14, 14 lamb of the first year **w.** blemish.... 8549
Nu 6:14 and one ram **w.** blemish for peace 8549
Nu 15:24 **w.** the knowledge of the congregation, ...
Nu 15:35 him with stones **w.** the camp............ 2351
Nu 15:36 brought him **w.** the camp,................. 2351
Nu 19:2 bring thee a red heifer **w.** spot, ... 8549
Nu 19:3 may bring her forth **w.** the camp,........ 2351
Nu 19:9 up **w.** the camp in a clean place, ... 2351
Nu 20:19 **w.** doing any thing else, go through...... 369

Nu 28:3 two lambs of the first year w. spot..... 8549
Nu 28:9 two lambs of the first year w. spot,.... 8549
Nu 28:11 lambs of the first year w. spot;......... 8549
Nu 28:19 they shall be unto you w. blemish: 8549
Nu 28:31 they shall be unto you w. blemish) 8549
Nu 29:2 lambs of the first year w. blemish: 8549
Nu 29:8 they shall be unto you w. blemish: 8549
Nu 29:13 first year; they shall be w. blemish:.... 8549
Nu 29:17 lambs of the first year w. spot:.......... 8549
Nu 29:20 lambs of the first year w. blemish; 8549
Nu 29:23 lambs of the first year w. blemish: 8549
Nu 29:26 lambs of the first year w. spot:.......... 8549
Nu 29:29, 32,36 of the first year w. blemish:...... 8549
Nu 31:13 forth to meet them w. the camp. 2351
Nu 31:19 ye abide w. the camp seven days: 2351
Nu 35:5 shall measure from w. the city on 2351
Nu 35:22 thrust him suddenly w. enmity,.......... 3808
Nu 35:22 him any thing w. laying of wait, ... 3808
Nu 35:26 time come w. the border of the city ....
Nu 35:27 find him w. the borders of the city 2351
De 8:9 thou shalt eat bread w. scarceness, ... 3808
De 23:12 have a place also w. the camp, ... 2351
De 25:5 shall not marry w. unto a stranger:..... 2351
De 32:4 a God of truth and w. iniquity, ... 369
De 32:25 The sword w., and terror within 2351
Jos 3:10 he will w. fail drive out from before..........
Jos 6:23 left them w. the camp of Israel.......... 2351
Jg 2:23 w. driving them out hastily;................ 1115
Jg 6:5 and their camels were w. number: 369
Jg 7:12 and their camels were w. number, ... 369
Jg 11:30 thou shalt w. fail deliver the children.........
Ru 4:14 left thee this day w. a kinsman, ...
1Sa 19:5 blood, to stay David w. a cause?......... 2600
1Sa 30:8 overtake them, and w. fail recover all. ......
2Sa 23:4 riseth, even a morning w. clouds;....... 3808
1Ki 6:6 for w. in the wall of the house he 2351
1Ki 6:29 and open flowers, within and w.......... 2435
1Ki 6:30 overlaid with gold, within and w.......... 2435
1Ki 7:9 sawed with saws, within and w., ... 2351
1Ki 8:8 oracle, and they were not seen w. 2351
1Ki 22:1 three years w. war between Syria and.. 369
2Ki 10:24 Jehu appointed fourscore men w.,........ 2351
2Ki 11:15 Have her forth w. the ranges:...... 413,1004
2Ki 16:18 the king's entry w., turned he.......... 2435
2Ki 18:25 come up w. the Lord against............. 1107
2Ki 23:4 he burned them w. Jerusalem in......... 2351
2Ki 23:6 w. Jerusalem, unto the brook 2351
2Ki 25:16 all these vessels was w. weight. 3808
1Ch 2:30 but Seled died w. children............... 3808
1Ch 2:32 and Jether died w. children. 3808
1Ch 21:24 nor offer burnt offerings w. cost. 2600
1Ch 22:3 and brass in abundance w. weight;...........
1Ch 22:14 and of brass and of iron w. weight;......... 369
2Ch 5:9 oracle; but they were not sen w.......... 2351
2Ch 12:3 people were w. number that came 369
2Ch 15:3 Israel hath been w. the true God, ... 3808
2Ch 15:3 w. a teaching priest, and w. law. 3808
2Ch 21:20 and departed w. being desired. 3808
2Ch 24:8 set it w. at the gate of the house....... 2351
2Ch 32:3 fountains which were w. the city:....... 2351
2Ch 32:5 the towers, and another wall w.,......... 2351
2Ch 33:14 built a wall w. the city of David, ... 2435
Ezr 6:9 it be given them day by day w. fail:..........
Ezr 7:22 salt w. prescribing how much. 3809
Ezr 10:13 and we are not able to stand w.,......... 2351
Ne 13:20 ware lodged w. Jerusalem once or...... 2351
Job 2:3 him, to destroy him w. cause. 2600
Job 4:20 perish forever w. any regarding it. ....
Job 4:21 away? they die, even w. wisdom......... 3808
Job 5:9 marvellous things w. number: 5704,369
Job 6:6 is unsavoury be eaten w. salt?........... 1097
Job 7:6 shuttle, and are spent w. hope............ 657
Job 8:11 Can the rush grow up w. mire? 3808
Job 8:11 can the flag grow w. water? 1097
Job 9:10 yea, and wonders w. number....... 5704,369
Job 9:17 multiplieth my wounds w. cause. 2600
Job 10:22 shadow of death, w. any order, ... 3808
Job 11:15 shalt thou lift up thy faces w. spot;..........
Job 12:25 They grope in the dark w. light, ... 3808
Job 24:7 the naked to lodge w. clothing, ... 1097
Job 24:10 him to go naked w. clothing, ... 1097
Job 26:2 thou helped him that is w. power?...... 3808
Job 30:28 I went mourning w. the sun:.............. 3808
Job 31:19 clothing, or any poor w. covering;........... 369
Job 31:39 eaten the fruits thereof w. money, ... 1097
Job 33:9 I am clean w. transgression, I am 1097
Job 34:6 is incurable w. transgression. 1097
Job 34:20 shall be taken away w. hand............. 3808
Job 34:24 in pieces mighty men w. number,....... 3808
Job 34:35 Job hath spoken w. knowledge,.......... 3808
Job 34:35 and his words were w. wisdom........... 3808
Job 35:16 multiplieth words w. knowledge. 1097
Job 36:12 and they shall die w. knowledge......... 1097
Job 38:2 counsel by words w. knowledge?........ 1097
Job 39:16 her labour is in vain w. fear; 1097
Job 41:33 not his like, who is made w. fear. 1097
Job 42:3 that hideth counsel w. knowledge?....... 1097
Ps 7:4 him that w. cause is mine enemy:) 7387
Ps 25:3 which transgress w. cause. 7387
Ps 31:11 that did see me w. fled from me. 2351
Ps 35:7 w. cause have they hid for me........... 2600
Ps 35:7 w. cause they have digged for my...... 2600
Ps 35:19 the eye that hate me w. a cause........ 2600
Ps 59:4 prepare themselves w. my fault: 1097
Ps 69:4 They that hate me w. a cause are...... 2600
Ps 105:34 caterpillers, and that w. number, ... 369
Ps 109:3 and fought against me w. a cause. 2600
Ps 119:78 perversely with me w. a cause: 8267
Ps 119:161 have persecuted me w. a cause: 2600
Pr 1:11 privily for the innocent w. cause: 2600
Pr 1:20 Wisdom crieth w.; she uttereth.......... 2351
Pr 3:30 Strive not with a man w. cause,......... 2600
Pr 5:23 He shall die w. instruction; and 369
Pr 6:15 shall he be broken w. remedy............. 369
Pr 7:12 Now is she w., now in the streets, ... 2351
Pr 11:22 fair woman which is w. discretion....... 5493
Pr 15:22 W. counsel purposes are..................... 369
Pr 16:8 than great revenues w. right. 3808
Pr 19:2 that the soul be w. knowledge, ... 3808
Pr 22:13 There is a lion w., I shall be slain 2351
Pr 23:29 who hath wounds w. cause? 2600
Pr 24:27 Prepare thy work w., and make it...... 2351
Pr 24:28 against thy neighbour w. cause; 2600
Pr 25:14 gift is like clouds and wind w. rain. 369
Pr 25:28 that is broken down, and w. walls......... 369
Pr 29:1 be destroyed, and that w. remedy. 369
Ec 10:11 serpent will bite w. enchantment;....... 3808
Ca 6:8 concubines, and virgins w. number....... 369
Ca 8:1 when I should find thee w., I 2351
Isa 5:9 even great and fair, w. inhabitant. 369
Isa 5:14 opened her mouth w. measure:.......... 1097
Isa 6:11 the cities be wasted w. inhabitant, ... 369
Isa 6:11 and the houses w. man, and the.......... 369
Isa 10:4 W. me they shall bow down under 1115
Isa 33:7 their valiant ones shall cry w............. 2351
Isa 36:10 now come up w. the Lord against 1107
Isa 45:17 confounded world w. end.......... 5769,5703
Isa 52:3 ye shall be redeemed w. money......... 3808
Isa 52:4 oppressed them w. cause..................... 657
Isa 55:1 and mild w. money and w. price. 3808
Jer 2:15 cities are burned w. inhabitant............ 1097
Jer 2:32 have forgotten me days w. number. 369
Jer 4:7 be laid waste, w. an inhabitant. 369
Jer 4:23 the earth, and, lo, it was w. form, ... 8414
Jer 5:21 people, and w. understanding; 369
Jer 9:11 Judah desolate, w. an inhabitant. 1097
Jer 9:21 to cut off the children from w.,........... 2351
Jer 15:13 will I give to the spoil w. price, ... 3808
Jer 21:4 which besiege you w. the walls, ... 2351
Jer 22:13 his neighbour's service w. wages,........ 2600
Jer 26:9 shall be desolate w. an inhabitant?........ 369
Jer 32:43 say, it is desolate w. man or beast....... 369
Jer 33:10 be desolate w. man and w. beast,........ 369
Jer 33:10 that are desolate, w. man,.................. 369
Jer 33:10 and w. inhabitant, and w. beast.......... 369
Jer 33:12 desolate w. man and w. beast,..... 369,5704
Jer 34:22 Judah a desolation w.... inhabitant. 369
Jer 44:19 offerings unto her, w. our men?......... 1107
Jer 44:22 and a curse, w. an inhabitant, ... 369
Jer 46:19 and desolate w. an inhabitant. 369
Jer 48:9 desolate, w. any to dwell therein. 369
Jer 49:31 nation, that dwelleth w. care, ...
Jer 51:29 a desolation w. an inhabitant. 369
Jer 51:37 and an hissing, w. an inhabitant. 369
Jer 52:20 of all these vessels was w. weight...... 3808
La 1:6 w. strength before the pursuer. 3808
La 3:49 ceaseth not, w. any intermission,.......... 369
La 3:52 me sore, like a bird, w. cause. 2600
Eze 2:10 and it was written within and w.......... 268
Eze 7:15 sword is w., and the pestilence.......... 2351
Eze 14:23 w. cause all that I have done in it, ... 2600
Eze 17:9 w. great power or many people to....... 3808
Eze 33:15 of life, w. committing iniquity; 1115
Eze 38:11 all of them dwelling w. walls, ... 369
Eze 40:19 the forefront of the inner court w.,...... 2351
Eze 40:40 at the side w., as one goeth up to...... 2351
Eze 40:44 w. the inner gate were the 2351
Eze 41:9 which was for the side chamber w.,..... 2351
Eze 41:17 even unto the inner house, and w., ... 2351
Eze 41:17 wall round about within and w., ... 2435
Eze 41:25 upon the face of the porch w............ 2351
Eze 42:7 wall that was w. over aganst the........ 2351
Eze 43:21 of the house, w. the sanctuary. 2351
Eze 43:22 offer a kid of the goats w. blemish 8549
Eze 43:23 offer a young bullock w. blemish, ... 8549
Eze 43:23 a ram out of the flock w. blemish....... 8549
Eze 43:25 a ram out of the flock, w. blemish. 8549
Eze 45:18 take a young bullock w. blemish, ... 8549
Eze 45:23 and seven rams w. blemish daily 8549
Eze 46:2 way of the porch of that gate w., ... 2351
Eze 46:4 shall be six lambs w. blemish, ... 8549
Eze 46:4 and a ram w. blemish. 8549
Eze 46:6 be a young bullock w. blemish, ... 8549
Eze 46:6 a ram: they shall be w. blemish. 8549
Eze 46:13 a lamb of the first year w. blemish: 8549
Eze 47:2 led me about the way w. unto 2351
Da 2:34 a stone was cut out w. hands,.... 1768,3809
Da 2:45 out of the mountain w. hands, ... 1768,3809
Da 8:25 but he shall be broken w. hand. 657
Da 11:18 w. his own reproach he shall............ 1115
Ho 3:4 days w. a king, and w. a prince, ... 369
Ho 3:4 w. a sacrifice, and w. an image, ... 369
Ho 3:4 w. [369] an ephod, and w. teraphim: ....
Ho 7:1 the troop of robbers spoileth w.......... 2351
Ho 7:11 also is like a silly dove w. heart: 369
Joe 1:6 my land, strong, and w. number, ... 369
Zec 2:4 shall be inhabited as towns w. walls..........
Mt 5:22 **angry with his brother w. a cause** ..*1500*
Mt 10:29 **fall on the ground w. your Father.** ..*427*
Mt 12:46 mother and his brethren stood w., ... *1854*
Mt 12:47 mother and thy brethren stood w., ... *1854*
Mt 13:34 w. a parable spake he not unto *5565*
Mt 13:57 **A prophet is not w. honour, save** *820*
Mt 15:16 **Are ye also yet w. understanding?**... *801*
Mt 26:69 Peter sat w. in the palace: and a........ *1854*
Mk 1:45 city, but was w. in desert places:......... *1854*
Mk 3:31 and, standing w., sent unto him, ... *1854*
Mk 3:32 and thy brethren w. seek for thee...... *1854*
Mk 4:11 **unto them that are w., all these** *1854*
Mk 4:34 w. a parable spake he not unto *5565*
Mk 6:4 **A prophet is not w. honour, but**...... *820*
Mk 7:15 **There is nothing from w. a man,**... *1855*
Mk 7:18 **Are ye so w. understanding also?** *801*
Mk 7:18 **from w. entereth into the man,** *1855*
Mk 11:4 the colt tied by the door w. in a *1854*
Mk 14:58 will build another made w. hands. *886*
Lu 1:10 praying w. at the time of incense. *1854*
Lu 1:74 enemies might serve him w. fear, ... *870*
Lu 6:49 **a man that w. a foundation built** .. *5565*
Lu 8:20 mother and thy brethren stand w., ... *1854*
Lu 11:40 **he that made that which is w.**........ *1855*
Lu 13:25 **begin to stand w., and to knock** *1854*
Lu 20:28 a wife, and he die w. children, ... *815*
Lu 20:29 took a wife, and died w. children. *815*
Lu 22:35 **When I sent you w. purse, and**...... *817*
Joh 1:3 w. him was not any thing made *5565*
Joh 8:7 **He that is w. sin among you, let**..... *361*
Joh 15:5 **for w. me ye can do nothing.** *5565*
Joh 15:25 **law, They hated me w. a cause.** *1432*
Joh 18:16 But Peter stood at the door w........... *1854*
Joh 19:23 now the coat was w. seam, woven........ *729*
Joh 20:11 Mary stood w. at the sepulchre *1854*
Ac 5:23 the keepers standing w. before the..... *1854*
Ac 5:26 and brought them w. violence:.... *3756,3326*
Ac 9:9 And he was three days w. sight,......... *3361*
Ac 10:29 came I unto you w. gainsaying, ... *369*
Ac 12:5 prayer was made w. ceasing of.......... *1618*
Ac 14:17 he left not himself w. witness, ... *267*
Ac 25:17 w. any delay on the morrow I.... *3367,4160*
Ro 1:9 w. ceasing I make mention of you *89*
Ro 1:20 so that they are w. excuse:................ *379*
Ro 1:31 W. understanding, ... *801*
Ro 1:31 w. natural affection, implacable, ... *794*
Ro 2:12 For as many as have sinned w. law...... *460*
Ro 2:12 shall also perish w. law; and as *460*
Ro 3:3 make the faith of God w. effect? *2673*
Ro 3:21 righteousness of God w. the law *5565*
Ro 3:28 by faith w. the deeds of the law......... *5565*
Ro 4:6 inputeth righteousness w. works, ... *5565*

Ro 5:6 For when we were yet w. strength, *772*
Ro 7:8 For w. the law sin was dead. *5565*
Ro 7:9 I was alive w. the law once: but *5565*
Ro 10:14 how shall they hear w. a preacher? *5565*
Ro 11:29 calling of god are w. repentance. *278*
Ro 12:9 Let love be w. dissimulation. *505*
1Co 4:8 ye have reigned as kings w. us: *5565*
1Co 5:12 do to judge them also that are w.? *1854*
1Co 5:13 But them that are w. God judgeth. *1854*
1Co 6:18 that a man doeth is w. the body; *1622*
1Co 7:32 I would have you w. carefulness. *275*
1Co 7:35 attend upon the Lord w. distraction. *563*
1Co 9:18 the gospel of Christ w. charge, *77*
1Co 9:21 To them that are w. law, as w. law, *459*
1Co 9:21 not w. law to God, but under the law *459*
1Co 9:21 I might gain them that are w. law. *459*
1Co 11:11 neither is the man w. the woman, *5565*
1Co 11:11 neither the woman w. the man, in *5565*
1Co 14:7 even things w. life giving sound, *895*
1Co 14:10 none of them is w. signification. *880*
1Co 16:10 that he may be with you w. fear: *870*
2Co 7:5 w. were fightings, within were *1855*
2Co 10:13 boast of things w. our measure, *280*
2Co 10:15 boasting of things w. our measure, *280*
2Co 11:28 Beside those things that are w., *8924*
Eph 1:4 and w. blame before him in love: *299*
Eph 2:12 at that time ye were w. Christ, *5565*
Eph 2:12 no hope, and w. God in the world: *112*
Eph 3:21 throughout all ages, world w. end.
Eph 5:27 it should be holy and w. blemish. *299*
Php 1:10 w. offence till the day of Christ, *677*
Php 1:14 bold to speak the word w. fear. *870*
Php 2:14 Do all things w. murmurings *5565*
Php 2:15 the sons of God, w. rebuke, in the *298*
Col 2:11 the circumcision made w. hands, *886*
Col 4:5 wisdom toward them that are w., *1854*
1Th 1:3 Remembering w. ceasing your work *89*
1Th 2:13 also thank we God w. ceasing, *89*
1Th 4:12 honestly toward them that are w., *1854*
1Th 5:17 Pray w. ceasing. *89*
1Ti 2:8 hands, w. wrath and doubting. *5565*
1Ti 3:7 good report of them which are w.; *1855*
1Ti 3:16 w. controversy great is the mystery *3672*
1Ti 5:21 w. preferring one before another, *5565*
1Ti 6:14 keep this commandment w. spot, *784*
2Ti 1:3 w. ceasing I have remembrance of *88*
2Ti 3:3 W....affection, trucebreakers, *794*
Phm 14 w. thy mind would I do nothing; *5565*
Heb 4:15 tempted like as we are, yet w. sin. *5565*
Heb 7:3 W. father, [*540*] w. mother *282*
Heb 7:3 w. descent, having neither *35*
Heb 7:7 w. all contradiction the less is *5565*
Heb 7:20 not w. an oath he was made priest: *5565*
Heb 7:21 priests were made w. an oath; *5565*
Heb 9:7 not w. blood, which he offered for *5565*
Heb 9:14 offered himself w. spot to God, *299*
Heb 9:18 testament was dedicated w. blood. *5565*
Heb 9:22 and w. shedding of blood is no *5565*
Heb 9:28 second time w. sin unto salvation. *5565*
Heb 10:23 profession of our faith w. wavering; *186*
Heb 10:28 despised Moses' law died w. mercy *5565*
Heb 11:6 w. faith it is impossible to please *5565*
Heb 11:40 w. us should not be made perfect. *5565*
Heb 12:8 But if ye be w. chastisement, *5565*
Heb 12:14 w. which no man shall see the *5565*
Heb 13:5 conversation be w. covetousness; *866*
Heb 13:11 for sin, are burned w. the camp. *1854*
Heb 13:12 own blood, suffered w. the gate. *1854*
Heb 13:13 therefore unto him w. the camp, *1854*
Jas 2:13 he shall have judgment w. mercy, *448*
Jas 2:18 shew me thy faith w. thy works. *5565*
Jas 2:20 man, that faith w. works is dead? *5565*
Jas 2:26 as the body w. the spirit is dead, *5565*
Jas 2:26 so faith w. works is deal also. *5565*
Jas 3:17 w. partiality, [*87*] and w. hypocrisy. *505*
1Pe 1:17 who w. respect of persons judgeth *678*
1Pe 1:19 lamb w. blemish [*299*] and w. spot: *784*
1Pe 3:1 they also may w. the word be won *427*
1Pe 4:9 one to another w. grudging *427*
2Pe 2:17 These are wells w. water, clouds *504*
2Pe 3:14 in peace, w. spot, and blameless. *784*
Jude 12 you, feeding themselves w. fear: *870*
Jude 12 clouds they are w. water, carried *504*
Jude 12 w. fruit, twice dead, plucked up *175*
Re 11:2 court which is w. the temple leave *1855*
Re 14:5 w. fault before the throne of God. *299*
Re 14:10 poured out w. mixture into the cup *194*
Re 14:20 winepress was trodden w. the city. *1854*
Re 22:15 For w. are dogs, and sorcerers, *1854*

WITHS

Jg 16:7 they bind me with seven green w. 3499
Jg 16:8 brought up to her seven green w. 3499
Jg 16:9 he brake the w., as a thread of tow 3499

WITHSTAND See also NOTWITHSTANDING; WITHSTOOD.

Nu 22:32 I went out to w. thee, because thy 7854
2Ch 13:7 an could not w. them. 2388
2Ch 13:8 to w. the kingdom of the Lord 2388
2Ch 20:6 so that none is able to w. thee? 3320
Es 9:2 and no man could w. them; for 5975
Ec 4:12 against him, two shall w. him; 5975
Da 1:15 the arms of the south shall not w., 5975
Da 1:15 shall there be any strength to w. 5975
Ac 11:17 what was I, that I could w. God? *2967*
Eph 6:13 ye may be able to w. in the evil day, *436*

WITHSTOOD

2Ch 26:18 And they w. Uzziah the king, and 5975
Da 10:13 of the kingdom of Persia w. me 5975
Ac 13:8 w. them seeking to turn away the *436*
Ga 2:11 I w. him to the face, because he was *436*
2Ti 3:8 as Jannes and Jambres w. Moses, *436*
2Ti 4:15 for he hath greatly w. our words. *436*

WITNESS See also EYEWITNESS; WITNESSED; WITNESSES; WITNESSETH; WITNESSING.

Ge 21:30 that they may be a w. unto me, 5713
Ge 31:44 be for a w. between me and thee. 5707
Ge 31:48 heap is a w. between me and thee 5707
Ge 31:50 see, God is w. betwixt me and thee. 5707
Ge 31:52 This heap be w., and this pillar 5707
Ge 31:52 and this pillar be w., that I will 5711
Ex 20:16 shalt not bear false w. against thy 5707
Ex 22:13 then let him bring it for w., and he 5707
Ex 23:1 the wicked to be an unrighteous w. 5707
Le 5:1 the voice of swearing, and is a w., 5707
Nu 5:13 and there be no w. against her, 5707
Nu 17:7 the Lord in the tabernacle of w. 5715
Nu 17:8 went into the tabernacle of w.; 5715
Nu 18:2 before the tabernacle of w. 5715
Nu 35:30 but one w. shall not testify against 5707
De 4:26 I call heaven and earth to w. 5749
De 5:20 shalt thou bear false w. against 5707
De 17:6 at the mouth of one w. he shall not 5707
De 19:15 One w. shall not rise up against a 5707
De 19:16 a false w. rise up against any man 5707
De 19:18 if the w. be a false w., and hath 5707
De 31:19 that this song may be a w. for me 5707
De 31:21 shall testify against them as a w.; 5707
De 31:26 may be there for a w. against thee. 5707
Jos 22:27 But that it may be a w. between us, 5707
Jos 22:28 but it is a w. between us and you. 5707
Jos 22:34 be a w. between us that the Lord is 5707
Jos 24:27 this stone shall be a w. unto us; 5713
Jos 24:27 it shall be therefore a w. unto you, 5713
Jg 11:10 The Lord be w. between us, if we 8085
1Sa 12:3 w. against me before the Lord, 6030
1Sa 12:5 The Lord is w. against you, and 5707
1Sa 12:5 and his anointed is w. this day, 5707
1Sa 12:5 And they answered, He is w. 5707
1Ki 21:10 to bare w. against him, saying, 5749
2Ch 24:6 Israel, for the tabernacle of w.? 5715
Job 16:8 which is a w. against me: 5707
Job 16:8 up in me beareth w. to my face 6030
Job 16:19 my w. is in heaven, and my record 5707
Job 29:11 the eye saw me, it gave w. to me: 5749
Ps 89:37 and as a faithful w. in heaven. 5707
Pr 6:19 A false w. that speaketh lies, and 5707
Pr 12:17 righteous: but a false w. deceit. 5707
Pr 14:5 A faithful w. will not lie: but a false 5707
Pr 14:5 lie: but a false w. will utter lies. 5707
Pr 14:25 A true w. delivereth souls: but a 5707
Pr 14:25 but a deceitful w. speaketh lies.
Pr 19:5,9 A false w. shall not be 5707
Pr 19:28 An ungodly w. scorneth judgment: 5707
Pr 21:28 A false w. shall perish: but the 5707
Pr 24:28 Be not a w. against thy neighbour 5707
Pr 25:18 that beareth false w. against his 5707
Isa 3:9 countenance doth w. against them; 5707
Isa 19:20 it shall be for a sign and for a w. 5707
Isa 55:4 given him for a w. to the people, 5707
Jer 29:23 I know, and am a w., saith the Lord 5707
Jer 42:5 The Lord be a true and faithful w. 5707
La 2:13 thing shall I take to w. for thee? 5749
Mic 1:2 the Lord God be w. against you, 5707
Mal 2:14 the Lord hath been w. between 5749
Mal 3:5 a swift w. against the sorcerers, 5707
Mt 15:19 **thefts, false w., blasphemies:** *5577*
Mt 19:18 **steal, Thou shalt not bare false w.,** *5576*
Mt 24:14 **preached in all the world for a w.** *3142*
Mt 26:59 sought false w. against Jesus, *5577*
Mt 26:62 is it which these w. against thee? *2649*
Mt 27:13 many things they w. against thee? *2649*
Mk 10:19 **Do not bare false w., Defraud not,** *5576*
Mk 14:55 sought for w. against Jesus *3141*
Mk 14:56 many bare false w. against him, *5576*
Mk 14:56 but their w. agreed not together. *3141*
Mk 14:57 an bare false w. against him, *5576*
Mk 14:59 neither so did their w. agree *3141*
Mk 14:60 is it which these w. against thee? *2649*
Mk 15:4 many things they w. against thee. *2649*
Lu 4:22 all bare him w., and wondered at *3140*
Lu 11:48 **Truly ye bare w. that ye allow** *3140*
Lu 18:20 **Do not bare false w., Honour thy** *5576*
Lu 22:71 What need we any further w.? *3141*
Joh 1:7 The same came for a w., to bear *3141*
Joh 1:7 to bear w. of the Light, that all *3140*
Joh 1:8 was sent to bear w. of that Light. *3140*
Joh 1:15 John bare w. of him, and cried, *3140*
Joh 3:11 **seen; and ye receive not our w.** *3141*
Joh 3:26 Jordan, to whom thou barest w. *3140*
Joh 3:28 Ye yourselves bear me w., that I *3140*
Joh 5:31 **If I bear w. of myself,** *3140*
Joh 5:31 **my w. is not true,** *3141*
Joh 5:32 **is another that beareth w. of me;** *3140*
Joh 5:32 **I know that the w. which he** *3141*
Joh 5:33 **and he bare w. unto the truth.** *3140*
Joh 5:36 **have greater w. than that of John:** *3141*
Joh 5:36 **works that I do, bear w. of me,** *3140*
Joh 5:37 **hath sent me, hath borne w. of me.** *3140*
Joh 8:18 **I am one that bear w. of myself,** *3140*
Joh 8:18 **that sent me beareth w. of me.** *3140*
Joh 10:25 **Father's name, they bear w. of me.** *3140*
Joh 15:27 **ye also shall bear w., because ye** *3140*
Joh 18:23 **spoken evil, bear w. of the evil:** *3140*
Joh 18:37 **I should bear w. unto the truth.** *3140*
Ac 1:22 be a w. with us of his resurrection. *3144*
Ac 4:33 the apostles w. of the resurrection *3142*
Ac 7:44 tabernacle of w. in the wilderness, *3142*
Ac 10:43 To him give all the prophets w., *3140*
Ac 14:17 he left not himself without w., *267*
Ac 15:8 knoweth the hearts, bare them w., *3140*
Ac 22:5 the high priest doth bear me w., *3140*
Ac 22:15 thou shalt be his w. unto all men *3144*
Ac 23:11 must thou bear w. also at Rome. *3140*
Ac 26:16 **and a w. both of these things** *3144*
Ro 1:9 For God is my w., whom I serve *3144*
Ro 2:15 their conscience also bearing w., *4828*
Ro 8:16 itself beareth w. with our spirit, *4828*
Ro 9:1 not, my conscience bearing me w. *4828*
Ro 13:9 Thou shalt not bear false w., 5576
1Th 2:5 a cloke of covetousness; God is w. *3144*
Tit 1:13 This w. is true. Wherefore rebuke *3141*
Heb 2:4 God also bearing them w., both *4901*
Heb 10:15 the Holy Ghost also is a w. to us: *3140*
Heb 11:4 obtained w. that he was righteous, *3140*
Jas 5:3 the rust of them shall be a w. *3142*
1Pe 5:1 a w. of the sufferings of Christ, *3144*
1Jo 1:2 we have seen it, and bear w., *3140*
1Jo 5:6 And it is the Spirit that beareth w., *3140*
1Jo 5:8 are three that bear w. in earth, *3140*
1Jo 5:9 If we receive the w. of men, *3141*
1Jo 5:9 the w. of God is greater: *3141*
1Jo 5:9 this is the w. of God whch he hath *3141*
1Jo 5:10 Son of God hath the w. in himself: *3141*
3Jo 6 have borne w. of thy charity *3140*
Re 1:5 Christ, who is the faithful w., *3144*
Re 3:14 **the faithful and the true w., the** *3144*
Re 20:4 beheaded for the w. of Jesus, *3141*

WITNESSED

1Ki 21:13 the men of Belial w. against him, 579
Ro 3:21 being w. by the law and the *3140*
1Ti 6:13 Pontius Pilate w. a good confession; *3140*
Heb 7:8 them of whom it w. that he liveth, *3140*

WITNESSES See also EYEWITNESSES.

Nu 35:30 be put to death by the mouth of w. 5707
De 17:6 At the mouth of two w., 5707
De 17:6 or three w., shall he that is worthy 5707
De 17:7 The hands of the w. shall be first 5707

De 19:15 sinneth: at the mouth of two w.,........ 5707
De 19:15 or at the mouth of three w., shall...... 5707
Jos 24:22 Ye are w. against yourselves that........ 5707
Jos 24:22 him. And they said, we are w.. 5707
Ru 4:9 Ye are w. this day, that I have.......... 5707
Ru 4:10 of his place: ye are w. this day......... 5707
Ru 4:11 and the elders, said, We are w.. 5707
Job 10:17 Thou renewest thy w. against me, ... 5707
Ps 27:12 false w. are risen up against me,....... 5707
Ps 35:11 False w. did rise up; they laid to........ 5707
Isa 8:2 took unto me faithful w. to record,..... 5707
Isa 43:9 let them bring forth their w., that...... 5707
Isa 43:10 Ye are my w., saith the Lord, and 5707
Isa 43:12 ye are my w., saith the Lord, that I... 5707
Isa 44:8 declared it? ye are even my w........... 5707
Isa 44:9 and they are their own w.; they......... 5707
Jer 32:10 evidence, and sealed it, and took w.... 5707
Jer 32:12 presence of the w. that subscribed..... 5707
Jer 32:25 the field for money, and take w.; 5707
Jer 32:44 take w. in the land of Benjamin,........ 5707
Mt 18:16 **in the mouth of two or three w.**..... *3144*
Mt 23:31 **ye be w. unto yourselves, that**....... *3140*
Mt 26:60 though many false w. came, yet......... *5575*
Mt 26:60 At the last came two false w.,........... *5575*
Mt 26:65 what further need have we of w.?........ *3144*
Mk 14:63 What need we any further w.?........... *3144*
Lu 24:48 **And ye are w. of these things**........ *3144*
Ac 1:8 **and ye shall be w. unto me both**... *3144*
Ac 2:32 raised up, whereof we all are w.......... *3144*
Ac 3:15 from the dead; whereof we are w.. ...... *3144*
Ac 5:32 And we are his w. of these things;..... *3144*
Ac 6:13 And set us false w., which said,......... *3144*
Ac 7:58 and the w. laid down their clothes...... *3144*
Ac 10:39 we are w. of al things which he did.... *3144*
Ac 10:41 but unto w. chosen before of God, ... *3144*
Ac 13:31 who are his w. unto the people........... *3144*
1Co 15:15 and we are found false w. of God;....... *5575*
2Co 13:1 In the mouth of two or three w.......... *3144*
1Th 2:10 Ye are w., and God also, how holily... *3144*
1Ti 5:19 but before two or three w.. .... *3144*
1Ti 6:12 a good profession before many w.. .... *3144*
2Ti 2:2 hast heard of me among many w.,........ *3144*
Heb 10:28 mercy under two or three w.............. *3144*
Heb 12:1 about with so great a cloud of w., ... *3144*
Re 11:3 I will give power unto my two w.,...... *3144*

WITNESSETH
Joh 5:32 **witness which he w. of me is true**. *3140*
Ac 20:23 the Holy Ghost w. in every city,......... *1263*

WITNESSING
Ac 26:22 w. both to small and great, saying...... *3140*

WIT'S
Ps 107:27 man, and are at their w. end............. 2451

WITTINGLY
Ge 48:14 head, guiding his hands w.;............... 7919

WITTY
Pr 8:12 find out knowledge of w. inventions. ....

WIVES See also MIDWIVES; WIVES'.
Ge 4:19 Lamech took unto him two w.: the 802
Ge 4:23 And Lamech said unto his w., Adah 802
Ge 4:23 ye w. of Lamech, hearken unto my...... 802
Ge 6:2 them w. of all which they chose. 802
Ge 6:18 wife, and hy sons' w. with thee........... 802
Ge 7:7 his sons' w. with him, into the ark,....... 802
Ge 7:13 the three w. of his sons with them, ... 802
Ge 8:16 thy sons, and thy sons' w. with thee. ... 802
Ge 8:18 his wife, and his sons' w. with him:...... 802
Ge 11:29 Abram and Nahor took them w. 802
Ge 28:9 and took unto the w. which he had 802
Ge 30:26 Give me my w. and my children,.......... 802
Ge 31:17 set his sons and his w. upon camels;.... 802
Ge 31:50 take other w. beside my daughters, ... 802
Ge 32:22 up that night, and took his two w., ... 802
Ge 34:21 us take their daughters to us for w.,.... 802
Ge 34:29 ones, and their w. took they captive,.... 802
Ge 36:2 Esau took his w. of the daughters of.... 802
Ge 36:6 And Esau took his w., and his sons,..... 802
Ge 37:2 the sons of Zilpah, his father's w. 802
Ge 45:19 for your little ones, and for your w., ... 802
Ge 46:5 and their little ones, and their w.,........ 802
Ge 46:26 besides Jacob's sons; w., all the souls... 802
Ex 19:15 the third day: come not at your w.. 802
Ex 22:24 your w. shall be widows, and your....... 802
Ex 32:2 which are in the ears of your w.,......... 802
Nu 14:3 that our w. and our children should...... 802
Nu 16:27 and their w., and their sons, and......... 802
Nu 32:26 Our little ones, our w., our flocks,....... 802
De 3:19 But your w., and your little ones,........ 802
De 17:17 Neither shall he multiply w. to........... 802
De 21:15 If a man have two w., one beloved, ... 802
De 29:11 Your little ones, your w., and thy........ 802
Jos 1:14 Your w., your little ones, and your 802
Jg 3:6 took their daughters to be their w., ... 802
Jg 8:30 body begotten: for he had many w.. 802
Jg 21:7 How shall we do for w. for them that... 802
Jg 21:7 give them of our daughters to w.? 802
Jg 21:14 gave them w. which they had saved..... 802
Jg 21:16 How shall we do for w. for them that... 802
Jg 21:18 not give them w. of our daughters: 802
Jg 21:23 and took them w. according to............ 802
Ru 1:4 them w. of the women of Moab; 802
1Sa 1:2 And he had two w.; the name of the.... 802
1Sa 25:43 they were also both of them his w.. 802
1Sa 27:3 even David with his two w., ... 802
1Sa 30:3 and their w., and their sons, and.......... 802
1Sa 30:5 David's two w. were taken captives, ... 802
1Sa 30:18 away: and David rescued his two w...... 802
2Sa 2:2 up thither, and his two w. also,........... 802
2Sa 5:13 took him more concubines and w.,........ 802
2Sa 12:8 and thy master's w. into thy bosom,..... 802
2Sa 12:11 I will take thy w. before thine eyes,..... 802
2Sa 12:11 he shall lie with thy w. in the sight 802
2Sa 19:5 daughters, and the lives of thy w.,........ 802
1Ki 11:3 And he had seven hundred w.,............ 802
1Ki 11:3 and his w. turned away his heart. 802
1Ki 11:4 his w. turned away his heart after........ 802
1Ki 11:8 did he for all his strange w., which 802
1Ki 20:3 thy w. also and thy children, even 802
1Ki 20:5 gold, and thy w., and thy children;....... 802
1Ki 20:7 for he sent unto me for my w.,............ 802
2Ki 4:1 certain woman of the w. of the sons....... 802
2Ki 24:15 and the king's w., and his officers,........ 802
1Ch 4:5 the father of Tekoa had two w.,.......... 802
1Ch 7:4 for they had many w. and sons. 802
1Ch 8:8 Hushim and Baara were his w.............. 802
1Ch 14:3 And David took more w. at................. 802
2Ch 11:21 of Absalom above all his w. and........... 802
2Ch 11:21 (for he took eighteen w., and.............. 802
2Ch 11:23 And he desired many w.. 802
2Ch 13:21 mighty, and married fourteen w.,......... 802
2Ch 20:13 ones, their w., and their children.......... 802
2Ch 21:14 and thy children, and thy w., and.......... 802
2Ch 21:17 and his sons also, and his w.; 802
2Ch 24:3 And Jehoiada took for him two w.;........ 802
2Ch 29:9 and our w. are in captivity for this. 802
2Ch 31:18 their w., and their sons, and their......... 802
Ezr 10:2 have taken strange w. of the people..... 802
Ezr 10:3 with our God to put away all the w.,.... 802
Ezr 10:10 and have taken strange w., to............. 802
Ezr 10:11 the land, and from the strange w.......... 802
Ezr 10:14 have taken strange w. in our cities........ 802
Ezr 10:17 the men that had taken strange w......... 802
Ezr 10:18 found that had taken strange w. 802
Ezr 10:19 that they would put away their w.;......... 802
Ezr 10:44 All these had taken strange w.: and 802
Ezr 10:44 some of them had w. by whom they....... 802
Ne 4:14 daughters, your w., and your houses.... 802
Ne 5:1 of their w. against their brethren......... 802
Ne 10:28 their w., and their sons, and their......... 802
Ne 12:43 w. also and the children rejoiced:......... 802
Ne 13:23 Jews that had married w. of Ashdod,.... 802
Ne 13:27 our God in marrying strange w.? 802
Es 1:20 w. shall give to their husbands............ 802
Isa 13:16 be spoiled, and their w. ravished. 802
Jer 6:12 with their fields and w. together:.......... 802
Jer 8:10 will I give their w. unto others,............ 802
Jer 14:16 none to bury them, their w., ... 802
Jer 18:21 let their w. be bereaved of their.......... 802
Jer 29:6 Take ye w., and begat sons and........... 802
Jer 29:6 take w. for your sons, and give your.... 802
Jer 29:23 adultery with their neighbours' w.,........ 802
Jer 35:8 our w., our sons, nor our daughters;.... 802
Jer 38:23 So they shall bring out all thy w. 802
Jer 44:9 and the wickedness of their w.,........... 802
Jer 44:9 and the wickedness of your w.,............ 802
Jer 44:15 that their w. had burned incense........... 802
Jer 44:25 Ye and your w. have both spoken........ 802
Eze 44:22 shall they take for their w. a widow, ... 802
Da 5:2 his w., and his concubines, might....... 7695
Da 5:3 his w., and his concubines, drank....... 7695
Da 5:23 thy w., and thy concubines, have 7695
Da 6:24 them, their children, and their w.;....... 5389
Zec 12:12 of David apart, and their w. apart;........ 802
Zec 12:12 of Nathan apart, and their w. apart; 802
Zec 12:13 of Levi apart, and their w. apart;......... 802
Zec 12:13 of Shimei apart, and their w............... 802
Zec 12:14 family apart, and their w. apart. 802
Mt 19:8 **suffered you to put away your w**... *1135*
Lu 17:27 **they drank, they married w., they**......
Ac 21:5 on our way, with w. and children, ... *1135*
1Co 7:29 have w. be as though they had none;.. *1135*
Eph 5:22 W., submit yourselves unto your........ *1135*
Eph 5:24 let the w. be to their own husbands.... *1135*
Eph 5:25 Husbands, love your w., even as *1135*
Eph 5:28 to love their w. as their own bodies..... *1135*
Col 3:18 W., submit yourselves unto your........ *1135*
Col 3:19 Husbands, love your w., and be not.... *1135*
1Ti 3:11 Even so must their w. be grave,......... *1135*
1Pe 3:1 ye w., be in subjection to your own.... *1135*
1Pe 3:1 won by the conversation of the w.;...... *1135*

WIVES'
1Ti 4:7 refuse profane and old w. fables,......... *1126*

WIZARD See also WIZARDS.
Le 20:27 or that is a w., shall surely be put...... 3049
De 18:11 spirits, or a w., or a necromancer. 3049

WIZARDS
Le 19:31 neither seek after w., to be defiled..... 3049
Le 20:6 and after w., to go a whoring after..... 3049
1Sa 28:3 spirits, and the w., out of the land. 3049
1Sa 28:9 spirits, and the w., out of the land: 3049
2Ki 21:6 dealt with familiar spirits and w.......... 3049
2Ki 23:24 with familiar spirits, and the w.,......... 3049
2Ch 33:6 with a familiar spirit, and with w. 3049
Isa 8:19 unto w. that peep, and that mutter:.... 3049
Isa 19:3 have familiar spirits, and to the w....... 3049

WOE See also WOEFUL; WOES.
Nu 21:29 W. to thee, Moab! thou art undone,..... 188
1Sa 4:7 W. unto us! for there hath not............ 188
1Sa 4:8 W. unto us! who shall deliver us 188
Job 10:15 If I be wicked, w. unto me; and if I..... 480
Ps 120:5 W. is me, that I sojourn in Mesech,..... 190
Pr 23:29 Who hath w.? who hath sorrow?.......... 188
Ec 4:10 but w. to him that is alone when 337
Ec 10:16 W. to thee, O land, when thy king....... 337
Isa 3:9 W. unto their soul! for they have......... 188
Isa 3:11 W. unto the wicked! it shall be ill 188
Isa 5:8 W. unto them that join house to 1945
Isa 5:11 W. unto them that rise up early in 1945
Isa 5:18 W. unto them that draw iniquity......... 1945
Isa 5:20 W. unto them that call evil good, ... 1945
Isa 5:21 W. unto them that are wise in........... 1945
Isa 5:22 W. unto them that are mighty to........ 1945
Isa 6:5 said I, W. is me! for I am undone:........ 188
Isa 10:1 W. unto them that decree................. 1945
Isa 17:12 W. to the multitude of many 1945
Isa 18:1 W. to the land shadowing with........... 1945
Isa 24:16 leanness, my leanness, w. unto me! 188
Isa 28:1 W. to the crown of pride, to the........ 1945
Isa 29:1 W. to Ariel, to Ariel, the city 1945
Isa 29:15 W. unto them that seek deep to 1945
Isa 30:1 W. to the rebellious children, saith 1945
Isa 31:1 W. to them that go down to Egypt...... 1945
Isa 33:1 W. to thee that spoilest, and thou 1945
Isa 45:9 W. unto him that striveth with his...... 1945
Isa 45:10 W. unto him that saith unto his.......... 1945
Jer 4:13 W. unto us! for we are spoiled............ 188
Jer 4:31 W. is me now! for my soul is 188
Jer 6:4 W. unto us! for the day goeth away, ... 188
Jer 10:19 W. is me for my hurt! my wound 188
Jer 13:27 W. unto thee, O Jerusalem! wilt.......... 188
Jer 15:10 W. is me, my mother, that thou.......... 188
Jer 22:13 W. unto him that buildeth his 1945
Jer 23:1 W. be unto the pastors that.............. 1945
Jer 45:3 Thou didst say, W. is me now! 188
Jer 48:1 W. unto Nebo! for it is spoiled: 1945
Jer 48:46 W. be unto thee, O Moab! the........... 188
Jer 50:27 w. unto them! for their day is............ 1945
La 5:16 w. unto us, that we have sinned!......... 188
Eze 2:10 and mourning, and w.. 1958
Eze 13:3 W. unto the foolish prophets, ... 1945
Eze 13:18 W. to the women that sew pillows 1945
Eze 16:23 (w., w. unto thee! saith the Lord 188
Eze 24:6 W. to the bloody city, to the pot 188
Eze 24:9 W. to the bloody city! I will even 188

Eze 30:2 God; Howl ye, W. worth the day!...... 1929
Eze 34:2 W. be to the shepherds of Israel........ 1945
Ho 7:13 W. unto them! for they have fled......... 188
Ho 9:12 w. also to them when I depart........... 188
Am 5:18 W. unto you that desire the day 1945
Am 6:1 W. to them that are at ease in 1945
Mic 2:1 W. to them that devise iniquity,......... 1945
Mic 7:1 W. is me! for I am as when they......... 480
Na 3:1 W. to the bloody city! it is all full....... 1945
Hab 2:6 W. to him that increaseth that.......... 1945
Hab 2:9 W. to him that coveteth an evil 1945
Hab 2:12 W. to him that buildeth a town 1945
Hab 2:15 W. unto him that giveth his............... 1945
Hab 2:19 W. unto him that saith to the wood, ... 1945
Zep 2:5 W. unto the inhabitants of the sea...... 1945
Zep 3:1 W. to her that is filthy and 1945
Zec 11:17 W. to the idol shepherd that............. 1945
Mt 11:21 W. unto thee, Chorazin! *3759*
Mt 11:21 w. unto thee, Bethsaida! for if...... *3759*
Mt 18:7 W. unto the world because of............ *3759*
Mt 18:7 but w. to that man by whom the... *3759*
Mt 23:13 w. unto you, scribes and.............. *3759*
Mt 23:14 W. unto you, scribes and *3759*
Mt 23:15 W. unto you, scribes and *3759*
Mt 23:16 W. unto you, ye blind guides, ... *3759*
Mt 23:23, 25,27,29 W. unto you, scribes and.. *3759*
Mt 24:19 w. unto them that are with child,.. *3759*
Mt 26:24 w. unto that man by whom the..... *3759*
Mk 13:17 w. to them that are with child, ... *3759*
Mk 14:21 w. to that man by whom the Son .. *3759*
Lu 6:24 But w. unto you that are rich!......... *3759*
Lu 6:25 W. unto you that are full! for ye... *3759*
Lu 6:25 W. unto you that laugh now! for... *3759*
Lu 6:26 W. unto you, when all men shall... *3759*
Lu 10:13 W. unto thee, Chorazin! *3759*
Lu 10:13 w. unto thee, Bethsaida! for if...... *3759*
Lu 11:42 But w. unto you, Pharisees!........... *3759*
Lu 11:43 W. unto you, Pharisees! for ye...... *3759*
Lu 11:44 W. unto you, scribes and.............. *3759*
Lu 11:46 W. unto you also, ye lawyers! *3759*
Lu 11:47 W. unto you! for ye build the....... *3759*
Lu 11:52 W. unto you, lawyers! for ye have. *3759*
Lu 17:1 w. unto him, through whom they .. *3759*
Lu 21:23 w. unto them that are with child,.. *3759*
Lu 22:22 w. unto that man by whom he is.... *3759*
1Co 9:16 w. is unto me, if I preach not the *3759*
Jude 11 W. unto them! for they have gone...... *3759*
Re 8:13 W., w., w., to the inhabiters of the ... *3759*
Re 9:12 One w. is past; and, behold, there *3759*
Re 11:14 The second w. is past; and,............... *3759*
Re 11:14 behold, the third w. cometh quickly. ... *3759*
Re 12:12 W. to the inhabiters of the earth........ *3759*

WOEFUL

Jer 17:16 neither have I desired the w. day; 605

WOES

Re 9:12 there come two w. more hereafter. *3759*

WOLF See also WOLVES.

Ge 49:27 Benjamin shall ravin as a w............... 2061
Isa 11:6 w. also shall dwell with the lamb,........ 2061
Isa 65:25 The w. and the lamb shall feed.......... 2061
Jer 5:6 and a w. of the evenings shall spoil..... 2061
Joh 10:12 seeth the w. coming, and leaveth... *3074*
Joh 10:12 and the w. catcheth them, and...... *3074*

WOLVES

Eze 22:27 are like w. ravening the prey, ... 2061
Hab 1:8 more fierce than the evening w.......... 2061
Zep 3:3 her judges are evening w.; they......... 2061
Mt 7:15 but inwardly they are ravening w...*3074*
Mt 10:16 forth as sheep in the midst of w.... *3074*
Lu 10:3 send you forth as lambs among w. .*3074*
Ac 20:29 grievous w. enter in among you, ... *3074*

WOMAN See also BONDWOMAN; FREEWOMAN; KINSWOMAN; WOMANKIND; WOMAN'S; WOMEN.

Ge 2:22 made he a w., and brought her 802
Ge 2:23 she shall be called W., because she....... 802
Ge 3:1 he said unto the w., Yea, hath God...... 802
Ge 3:2 w. said unto the serpent, We may 802
Ge 3:4 serpent said unto the w., Ye shall........ 802
Ge 3:6 the w. saw that the tree was good....... 802
Ge 3:12 The w. whom thou gavest to be........... 802
Ge 3:13 Lord God said unto the w., what is...... 802
Ge 3:13 w. said, The serpent beguiled me, ... 802
Ge 3:15 put enmity between thee and the w., ... 802
Ge 3:16 Unto the w. he said, I will greatly 802
Ge 12:11 that thou art a fair w. to look upon: 802
Ge 12:14 the Egyptians beheld the w. that she.... 802
Ge 12:15 w. was taken into Pharaoh's house....... 802
Ge 20:3 for the w. which thou hast taken; 802
Ge 24:5 w. will not be willing to follow me........ 802
Ge 24:8 if the w. will not be willing to follow..... 802
Ge 24:39 Peradventure the w. will not follow...... 802
Ge 24:44 same be the w. whom the Lord 802
Ge 46:10 and Shaul the son of a Canaanitish w.........
Ex 2:2 the w. conceived and bare a son:......... 802
Ex 2:9 w. took the child, and nursed it........... 802
Ex 3:22 But every w. shall borrow of her......... 802
Ex 6:15 and Shaul the son of a Canaanitish w.........
Ex 11:2 every w. of her neighbour, jewels........ 802
Ex 21:22 men strive, and hurt a w. with child,.... 802
Ex 21:28 If an ox gore a man or a w., that 802
Ex 21:29 that he hath killed a man or a w.......... 802
Ex 35:29 every man and w., whose heart 802
Ex 36:6 neither man nor w. make any more...... 802
Le 12:2 If a w. have conceived seed, and......... 802
Le 13:29 If a man or w. have a plague upon...... 802
Le 13:38 a man also or a w. have in the skin...... 802
Le 15:18 The w. also with whom man shall........ 802
Le 15:19 And if a w. have an issue, and her....... 802
Le 15:25 if a w. have an issue of her blood........ 802
Le 15:33 issue, of the man, and of the w.. 5347
Le 18:17 not uncover the nakedness of a w......... 802
Le 18:19 not approach unto a w. to uncover....... 802
Le 18:23 neither shall any w. stand before a....... 802
Le 19:20 whosoever lieth carnally with a w., ... 802
Le 20:13 as he lieth with a w., both of them....... 802
Le 20:16 And if a w. approach unto any beast,..... 802
Le 20:16 thou shalt kill the w., and the beast: 802
Le 20:18 lie with a w. having her sickness, ... 802
Le 20:27 or w. that hath a familiar spirit, ... 802
Le 21:7 neither shall they take a w. put away ... 802
Le 21:14 A widow, or a divorced w., or profane. .....
Le 24:10 And the son of an Israelitish w.,......... 802
Le 24:10 and this son of the Israelitish w. ....
Nu 5:6 man or w. shall commit any sin........... 802
Nu 5:18 shall set the w. before the Lord,......... 802
Nu 5:19 say unto the w., If no man have lain 802
Nu 5:21 shall charge the w. with an oath of........ 802
Nu 5:21 and the priest shall say unto the w.,...... 802
Nu 5:22 And the w. shall say, Amen, amen....... 802
Nu 5:24 cause the w. to drink the bitter........... 802
Nu 5:26 cause the w. to drink the water........... 802
Nu 5:27 the w. shall be a curse among her 802
Nu 5:28 And if the w. be not defiled, but be 802
Nu 5:30 and shall set the w. before the Lord,.... 802
Nu 5:31 and this w. shall bear her iniquity. 802
Nu 6:2 either man or w. shall separate 802
Nu 12:1 Ethiopian w. whom he had married: 802
Nu 12:1 for he had married an Ethiopian w.. 802
Nu 25:6 a Midianitish w. in the sight of Moses, ...
Nu 25:8 and the w. through her belly.............. 802
Nu 25:14 was slain with the Midianitish w.,.............
Nu 25:15 Midianitish w. that was slain was......... 802
Nu 30:3 a w. also vow a vow unto the Lord,..... 802
Nu 31:17 kill every w. that hath known man....... 802
De 15:12 or an Hebrew w., be sold unto thee, ...
De 17:2 man or w., that hath wrought............ 802
De 17:5 bring forth that man or that w.,........... 802
De 17:5 gates, even that man or that w., ... 802
De 21:11 among the captives a beautiful w.,........ 802
De 22:5 The w. shall not wear that which......... 802
De 22:14 I took this w., and when I came to...... 802
De 22:22 found lying with a w. married to an...... 802
De 22:22 both the man that lay with the w., ... 802
De 22:22 and the w.: so shalt thou put away...... 802
De 28:56 The tender and delicate w. among you, ...
De 29:18 should be among you man, or w., ... 802
Jos 2:4 w. took the two men, and hid them, ... 802
Jos 6:21 both man and w., young and old,......... 802
Jos 6:22 house, and bring out thence the w., ... 802
Jg 4:9 shall sell Sisera into the hand of a w..... 802
Jg 9:53 And a certain w. cast a piece of a........ 802
Jg 9:54 men say not of me, A w. slew him. 802
Jg 11:2 for thou art the son of a strange w.. 802
Jg 13:3 of the Lord appeared unto the w.. 802
Jg 13:6 the w. came and told her husband,....... 802
Jg 13:9 angel of God came again unto the w..... 802
Jg 13:10 w. made haste, and ran, and told......... 802
Jg 13:11 the man that spakest unto the w.? 802
Jg 13:13 I said unto the w. let her beware. 802
Jg 13:24 And the w. bare a son, and called........ 802
Jg 14:1 and saw a w. in Timnath of the........... 802
Jg 14:2 I have seen a w. in Timnath of the 802
Jg 14:3 never a w. among the daughters.......... 802
Jg 14:7 went down, and talked with the w.; 802
Jg 14:10 So his father went down unto the w..... 802
Jg 16:4 loved a w. in the valley of Sorek, ... 802
Jg 19:26 came the w. in the dawning of the 802
Jg 19:27 the w. his concubine was fallen 802
Jg 20:4 husband of the w. that was slain,......... 802
Jg 21:11 and every w. that hath lain by man. 802
Ru 1:5 and the w. was left of her two sons 802
Ru 3:8 and, behold, a w. lay at his feet. 802
Ru 3:11 know that thou art a virtuous w.. 802
Ru 3:14 not be known that a w. came into......... 802
Ru 4:11 The Lord make the w. that is come..... 802
Ru 4:12 Lord shall give thee of this young w.. ..5291
1Sa 1:15 lord, I am a w. of a sorrowful spirit: 802
1Sa 1:18 So the w. went her way, and did eat,... 802
1Sa 1:23 So the w. abode, and gave her son...... 802
1Sa 1:26 I am the w. that stood by thee here,.... 802
1Sa 2:20 The Lord give thee seed of this w....... 802
1Sa 15:3 but slay both man and w., infant and.... 802
1Sa 20:30 Thou son of the perverse rebellious w.,.....
1Sa 25:3 she was a w. of good understanding, ... 802
1Sa 27:9 and left neither man nor w. alive, ... 802
1Sa 27:11 And David saved neither man nor w..... 802
1Sa 28:7 a w. that hath a familiar spirit. 802
1Sa 28:7 is a w. that hath a familiar spirit........... 802
1Sa 28:8 and they came to the w. by night: 802
1Sa 28:9 the w. said unto him, Behold, thou 802
1Sa 28:11 said the w., Whom shall I bring.......... 802
1Sa 28:11 when the w. saw Samuel, she cried 802
1Sa 28:12 and the w. spake to Saul, saying, ... 802
1Sa 28:13 the w. said unto Saul, I saw gods 802
1Sa 28:21 the w. came unto Saul, and saw that.... 802
1Sa 28:23 together with the w., compelled him;.... 802
1Sa 28:24 the w. had a fat calf in the house;........ 802
2Sa 3:8 day with a fault concerning this w.?...... 802
2Sa 11:2 roof he saw a w. washing herself;....... 802
2Sa 11:2 w. was very beautiful to look upon....... 802
2Sa 11:3 David sent and enquired after the w.... 802
2Sa 11:5 the w. conceived, and sent and told 802
2Sa 11:21 did not a w. cast a piece of a............. 802
2Sa 13:17 put now this w. out from me, and bolt ......
2Sa 14:2 and fetched thence a wise w.,............ 802
2Sa 14:2 be as a w. that had a long time........... 802
2Sa 14:4 when the w. of Tekoah spake to 802
2Sa 14:5 answered, I am indeed a widow w., ... 802
2Sa 14:8 king said unto the w., Go to thine 802
2Sa 14:9 w. of Tekoah said unto the king, ... 802
2Sa 14:12 the w. said, Let thine handmaid,.......... 802
2Sa 14:13 the w. said, Wherefore then hast......... 802
2Sa 14:18 king answered and said unto the w.,....... 802
2Sa 14:18 the w. said, Let my lord the king 802
2Sa 14:19 the w. answered and said, As thy........ 802
2Sa 14:27 she was a w. of a fair countenance....... 802
2Sa 17:19 the w. took and spread a covering 802
2Sa 17:20 Absalom's servants came to the w........ 802
2Sa 17:20 And the w. said unto them, They be.... 802
2Sa 20:16 Then cried a wise w. out of the city,.... 802
2Sa 20:17 unto her, the w. said, Art thou Joab? ... 802
2Sa 20:21 And the w. said unto Joab, Behold, ... 802
2Sa 20:22 the w. went unto all the people............ 802
1Ki 3:17 And the one w. said, O my lord, I....... 802
1Ki 3:17 I and this w. dwell in one house;......... 802
1Ki 3:18 that this w. was delivered also: 802
1Ki 3:22 the other w. said, Nay; but the............ 802
1Ki 3:26 Then spake the w. whose the living..... 802
1Ki 11:26 name was Zeruah, a widow w.. 802
1Ki 14:5 shall feign herself to be another w.. ....
1Ki 17:9 a widow w. there to sustain thee......... 802
1Ki 17:10 widow w. was...gathering of sticks:...... 802
1Ki 17:17 that the son of the w., the mistress...... 802
1Ki 17:24 the w. said to Elijah, Now by this...... 802
2Ki 4:1 Now there cried a certain w. of the 802
2Ki 4:8 to Shunem, where was a great w.; 802
2Ki 4:17 the w. conceived, and bare a son.......... 802
2Ki 6:26 there cried a w. unto him, saying, ... 802
2Ki 6:28 This w. said unto me, Give thy son, ... 802
2Ki 6:30 the king heard the words of the w., ... 802
2Ki 8:1 Then spake Elisha unto the w.,.......... 802
2Ki 8:2 And the w. arose, and did after the...... 802
2Ki 8:3 the w. returned out of the land of......... 802
2Ki 8:5 the w., whose son he had restored 802
2Ki 8:5 O king, this is the w., and this is......... 802
2Ki 8:6 when the king asked the w., she 802

2Ki 9:34 see now this cursed w., and bury her: ......
1Ch 16:3 both man and w., to every one a......... 802
2Ch 2:14 son of a w. of the daughters of Dan, ... 802
2Ch 15:13 small or great, whether man or w......... 802
2Ch 24:7 sons of Athaliah, that wicked w.,.............
Es 4:11 whether man or w., shall come 802
Job 14:1 Man that is born of a w. is of few........ 802
Job 15:14 he which is born of a w., that he......... 802
Job 25:4 can he be clean that is born of a w.?.... 802
Job 31:9 heart have been deceived by a w.,....... 802
Ps 48:6 and pain, as of a w. in travail. ....
Ps 58:8 like the untimely birth of a w.............. 802
Ps 113:9 maketh the barren w. to keep house,........
Pr 2:16 deliver thee from the strange w., ... 802
Pr 5:3 For the lips of a strange w. drop as an.......
Pr 5:20 my son, be ravished with a strange w.......
Pr 6:24 To keep thee from the evil w., ... 802
Pr 6:24 of the tongue of a strange w.. ....
Pr 6:26 by means of a whorish w. a man is...... 802
Pr 6:32 committeth adultery with a w............. 802
Pr 7:5 may keep thee from the strange w.,..... 802
Pr 7:10 met him a w. with the attire of a......... 802
Pr 9:13 A foolish w. is clamorous: she is 802
Pr 11:16 A gracious w. retaineth honour:........... 802
Pr 11:22 fair w. which is without discretion........ 802
Pr 12:4 A virtuous w. is a crown to her........... 802
Pr 14:1 Every wise w. buildeth her house:........ 802
Pr 20:16 a pledge of him for a strange w.. ....
Pr 21:9 with a brawling w. in a wide house. 802
Pr 21:19 a contentious and an angry w............ 802
Pr 23:27 and a strange w. is a narrow pit..................
Pr 25:24 a brawling w. in a wide house............ 802
Pr 27:13 a pledge of him for a strange w.. ....
Pr 27:15 and a contentious w. are alike............. 802
Pr 30:20 Such is the way of an adulterous w.; 802
Pr 30:23 an odious w. when she is married;............
Pr 31:10 Who can find a virtuous w.? for........... 802
Pr 31:30 a w. that feareth the Lord, she............ 802
Ec 7:26 find more bitter than death the w., ... 802
Ec 7:28 a w. among all those have I not........... 802
Isa 13:8 be in pain as a w. that travaileth: ....
Isa 21:3 as the pangs of a w. that travaileth:..........
Isa 26:17 Like as a w. with child, that draweth ....
Isa 42:14 now will I cry like a travailing w.;............
Isa 45:10 or to the w., What hast thou 802
Isa 49:15 Can a w. forget her sucking child,........ 802
Isa 54:6 as a w. forsaken and grieved in........... 802
Jer 4:31 heard a voice as of a w. in travail,............
Jer 6:2 of Zion to a comely and delicate w...........
Jer 6:24 of us, and pain, as of a w. in travail. ....
Jer 13:21 take thee, as a w. in travail?............... 802
Jer 22:23 thee, the pain as of a w. in travail! ....
Jer 30:6 hands on his loins, as a w. in travail,.........
Jer 31:8 lame, the w. with child and her that..........
Jer 31:22 earth, A w. shall compass a man........ 5347
Jer 44:7 to cut off from you man and w.. 802
Jer 48:41 be as the heart of a w. in her pangs..... 802
Jer 49:22 be as the heart of a w. in her pangs..... 802
Jer 49:24 have taken her, as a w. in travail. ....
Jer 50:43 him, and pangs as of a w. in travail..........
Jer 51:22 will I break in pieces man and w.;......... 802
La 1:17 Jerusalem is as a menstruous w....................
Eze 16:30 work of an imperious whorish w.;.......... 802
Eze 18:6 hath come near to a menstruous w., ... 802
Eze 23:44 unto a w. that playeth the harlot:......... 802
Eze 23:44 unto Aholibah, the lewd w................... 802
Eze 36:17 as the uncleanness of a removed w...........
Ho 3:1 love a w. beloved of her friend,............ 802
Ho 13:13 sorrows of a travailing w. shall come.........
Mic 4:9 have taken thee as a w. in travail. ....
Mic 4:10 daughter of Zion, like a w. in travail;.........
Zec 5:7 this is a w. that sitteth in the midst 802
Mt 5:28 **whosoever looketh on a w. to lust**..1135
Mt 9:20 a w., which was diseased with an......... 1135
Mt 9:22 the w. was made whole from that 1135
Mt 13:33 **like unto leaven, which a w. took,** .1135
Mt 15:22 a w. of Canaan came out of the 1135
Mt 15:28 unto her, **O w., great is thy faith**:.. 1135
Mt 22:27 And last of all the w. died also. 1135
Mt 26:7 him a w. having an alabaster box of.... 1135
Mt 26:10 unto them, **Why trouble ye the w.?** . 1135
Mt 26:13 **that this w. hath done, be told for**........
Mk 5:25 certain w., which had an issue of 1135
Mk 5:33 But the w. fearing and trembling,....... 1135
Mk 7:25 a certain w., whose young daughter.... 1135
Mk 7:26 The w. was a Greek, a................... 1135

Mk 10:12 **a w. shall put away her husband**,.. 1135
Mk 12:22 seed: last of all the w. died also......... 1135
Mk 14:3 came a w. having an alabaster box...... 1135
Lu 4:26 **unto a w. that was a widow**.............. 1135
Lu 7:37 behold, a w. in the city, which was..... 1135
Lu 7:39 what manner of w. this is that.......... 1135
Lu 7:44 he turned to the w., and said unto 1135
Lu 7:44 said unto Simon, **Seest thou this w.?** 1135
Lu 7:45 **this w. since the time I came in**..........
Lu 7:46 **this w. hath anointed my feet with**......
Lu 7:50 he said to the w., **Thy faith hath**..... 1135
Lu 8:43 a w. having an issue of blood............ 1135
Lu 8:47 the w. saw that she was not hid, ... 1135
Lu 10:38 a certain w. named Martha 1135
Lu 11:27 certain w. of the company lifted up..... 1135
Lu 13:11 there was a w. which had a spirit....... 1135
Lu 13:12 **W., thou art loosed from thine**...... 1135
Lu 13:16 **And ought not this w., being a**...... 1135
Lu 13:21 **which a w. took and hid in three** .. 1135
Lu 15:8 **what w. having ten pieces of silver**,1135
Lu 20:32 Last of all the w. died also................ 1135
Lu 22:57 him, saying, W., I know him not......... 1135
Joh 2:4 **W., what have I to do with thee?** .. 1135
Joh 4:7 a w. of Samaria to draw water:.......... 1135
Joh 4:9 saith the w. of Samaria unto him. 1135
Joh 4:9 of me, which am a w. of Samaria?....... 1135
Joh 4:11 w. saith unto him, Sir, Thou hast........ 1135
Joh 4:15 The w. saith unto him, Sir, give 1135
Joh 4:17 The w. answered and said, I have...... 1135
Joh 4:19 The w. saith unto him, Sir, I.............. 1135
Joh 4:21 **W., believe me, the hour cometh**,.. 1135
Joh 4:25 The w. saith unto him, I know that 1135
Joh 4:27 that he talked with the w................... 1135
Joh 4:28 The w. then left her waterpot, and..... 1135
Joh 4:39 on him for the saying of the w.,......... 1135
Joh 4:42 said unto the w., Now we believe, ... 1135
Joh 8:3 brought unto him a w. taken in.......... 1135
Joh 8:4 this w. was taken in adultery,............ 1135
Joh 8:9 and the w. standing in the midst. 1135
Joh 8:10 saw none but the w., he said unto...... 1135
Joh 8:10 **W., where are...thine accusers?**.... 1135
Joh 16:21 **A w. when she is in travail hath** ... 1135
Joh 19:26 his mother, **W., behold thy son!**..... 1135
Joh 20:13 **W., why weepest thou?** ....
Joh 20:15 unto her, **W., why weepest thou?**.... 1135
Ac 9:36 this w. was full of good works ....
Ac 16:1 Timotheus, the son of a certain w., ... 1135
Ac 16:14 a certain w. named Lydia, a seller...... 1135
Ac 17:34 a w. named Damaris, and others....... 1135
Ro 1:27 leaving the natural use of the w., ... 2338
Ro 7:2 w. which hath an husband is bound..... 1135
1Co 7:1 good for a man not to touch a w.. 1135
1Co 7:2 every w. have her own husband...............
1Co 7:13 the w. which hath an husband.................
1Co 7:34 w. careth for the things of the Lord,.........
1Co 11:3 the head of the w. is the man:...................
1Co 11:5 w. that prayeth or prophesieth.................
1Co 11:6 if the w. be not covered, let her..............
1Co 11:6 it be a shame for a w. to be shorn ....
1Co 11:7 but the w. is the glory of the man............
1Co 11:8 For the man is not of the w.;.....................
1Co 11:8 but the w. of the man...........................
1Co 11:9 was the man created for the w.; ....
1Co 11:9 but the w. for the man..............................
1Co 11:10 cause ought the w. to have power............
1Co 11:11 neither is the man without the w.,.............
1Co 11:11 neither the w. without the man, ...
1Co 11:12 For as the w. is of the man, even so........
1Co 11:12 even so is the man also by the w.;.............
1Co 11:13 a w. pray unto God uncovered? ....
1Co 11:15 if a w. have long hair, it is a glory...........
Ga 4:4 sent forth his Son, made of a w., ...
1Th 5:3 as travail upon a w. with child; ....
1Ti 2:11 Let the w. learn in silence with 1135
1Ti 2:12 I suffer not a w. to teach, nor to 1135
1Ti 2:14 but the w. being deceived was in....... 1135
1Ti 5:16 If any man or w. that believeth have.........
Re 2:20 **thou sufferest that w. Jezebel**. 1135
Re 12:1 a w. clothed with the sun, and the 1135
Re 12:4 w. which was ready to be delivered, ... 1135
Re 12:6 w. fled into the wilderness, where...... 1135
Re 12:13 w. which brought forth the man.......... 1135
Re 12:14 to the w. were given two wings.......... 1135
Re 12:15 mouth water as a flood after the w.,... 1135
Re 12:16 the earth helped the w., and the........ 1135
Re 12:17 the dragon was wroth with the w.,..... 1135

Re 17:3 a w. sit upon a scarlet coloured 1135
Re 17:4 w. was arrayed in purple and 1135
Re 17:6 I saw the w. drunken with the........... 1135
Re 17:7 tell thee the mystery of the w., ... 1135
Re 17:9 mountains, on which the w. sitteth. 1135
Re 17:18 w. which thou sawest is that great..... 1135

WOMANKIND
Le 18:22 not lie with mankind, as with w........... 802

WOMAN'S
Ge 38:20 his pledge from the w. hand: 802
Ex 21:22 according as the w. husband will.......... 802
Le 24:11 Israelitish w. son blasphemed the......... 802
Nu 5:18 uncover the w. head, and put the 802
Nu 5:25 jealousy offering out of the w. hand,..... 802
De 22:5 shall a man put on a w. garment:......... 802
1Ki 3:19 And this w. child died in the night;........ 802

WOMB See also WOMBS.
Ge 25:23 Two nations are in thy w., and two...... 990
Ge 25:24 behold, there were twins in her w.. 990
Ge 29:31 Leah was hated, he opened her w.:.... 7358
Ge 30:2 from thee the fruit of the w.? 990
Ge 30:22 to her, and opened her w.. 7358
Ge 38:27 that, behold, twins were in her w.. 990
Ge 49:25 of the breasts, and of the w.: 7356
Ex 13:2 whatsoever openeth the w. among...... 7358
Nu 8:16 instead of such as open every w.. 7358
Nu 12:12 he cometh out of his mother's w....... 7358
De 7:13 will also bless the fruit of thy w., ... 990
Jg 13:5 be a Nazarite unto God from the w.: 990
Jg 13:7 be a Nazarite to God from the w......... 990
Jg 16:17 unto God from my mother's w.: 990
Ru 1:11 there yet any more sons in my w.,...... 4578
1Sa 1:5 but the Lord had shut up her w.. 7358
1Sa 1:6 the Lord had shut up her w.. 7358
Job 1:21 came I out of my mother's w., and...... 990
Job 3:10 not up the doors of my mother's w.,..... 990
Job 3:11 Why died I not from the w.? why....... 7358
Job 10:18 brought me forth out of the w.?......... 7358
Job 10:19 carried from the w. to the grave. 990
Job 24:20 The w. shall forget him; the worm..... 7358
Job 31:15 that made me in the w. make him? 990
Job 31:15 did not one fashion us in the w.?....... 7358
Job 31:18 guided her from my mother's w.;)......... 990
Job 38:8 as if it had issued out of the w.? 7358
Job 38:29 Out of whose w. came the ice? 990
Ps 22:9 art he that took me out of the w.: 990
Ps 22:10 I was cast upon thee from the w.:...... 7358
Ps 58:3 wicked are estranged from the w.: 7358
Ps 71:6 have I been holden up from the w.: 990
Ps 110:3 from the w. of the morning:............... 7358
Ps 127:3 the fruit of the w. is his reward. 990
Ps 139:13 hast covered me in my mother's w.. 990
Pr 30:16 The grave; and the barren w.;........... 7356
Pr 31:2 son? and what, the son of my w.? 990
Ec 5:15 As he came forth of his mother's w.,..... 990
Ec 11:5 the bones do grow in the w. of her...... 990
Isa 13:18 have no pity on the fruit of the w.; 990
Isa 44:2 thee, and formed thee from the w., ... 990
Isa 44:24 he that formed thee from the w., ... 990
Isa 46:3 which are carried from the w.: 7356
Isa 48:8 called a transgressor from the w.......... 990
Isa 49:1 Lord hath called me from the w.; 990
Isa 49:5 formed me from the w. to be his......... 990
Isa 49:15 compassion on the son of her w.? 990
Isa 66:9 cause to bring forth, and shut the w.? ....
Jer 1:5 thou camest forth out of the w. I....... 7358
Jer 20:17 he slew me not from the w.:.............. 7358
Jer 20:17 her w. to be always great with me. 7358
Jer 20:18 I forth out of the w. to see labour...... 7358
Eze 20:26 the fire all that openeth the w., ... 7356
Ho 9:11 from the birth, and from the w........... 990
Ho 9:14 give them a miscarrying w. and 7358
Ho 9:16 even the beloved fruit of their w.. 990
Ho 12:3 his brother by the heel in the w., ... 990
Mt 19:12 **so born from their mother's w**....... 2836
Lu 1:15 Ghost, even from his mother's w.. 2836
Lu 1:31 thou shalt conceive in thy w., and....... 1064
Lu 1:41 the babe leaped in her w.: and 2836
Lu 1:42 and blessed is the fruit of thy w......... 2836
Lu 1:44 the babe leaped in my w. for joy......... 2836
Lu 2:21 before he was conceived in the w....... 2836
Lu 2:23 Every male that openeth the w.......... 3388
Lu 11:27 Blessed is the w. that bare thee, ... 2836
Joh 3:4 second time into his mother's w.,........ 2836
Ac 3:2 man lame from his mother's w. was.... 2836

Ac 14:8 a cripple from his mother's w., ... *2836*
Ro 4:19 yet the deadness of Sarah's w.: ... *3388*
Ga 1:15 me from my mother's w., and ... *2836*

WOMBS

Ge 20:18 Lord had fast closed up all the w. ... 7358
Lu 23:29 **and the w. that never bare, and** ... *2836*

WOMEN See also BONDWOMEN; KINSWOMEN; WOMEN'S; WOMENSERVANTS.

Ge 14::16 and the w. also, and the people... 802
Ge 18:11 with Sarah after the manner of w... 802
Ge 24:11 the time that w. go out to draw water. ...
Ge 31:35 for the custom of w. is upon me... 802
Ge 33:5 and saw the w. and the children; ... 802
Ex 1:16 office of a midwife to the Hebrew w., ...
Ex 1:19 w. are not as the Egyptian w... 802
Ex 2:7 call to thee a nurse of the Hebrew w., ...
Ex 15:20 all the w. went out after her with... 802
Ex 35:22 And they came, both men and w., ... 802
Ex 35:25 all the w. that were wise hearted ... 802
Ex 35:26 all the w. whose heart stirred them... 802
Ex 38:8 lookingglasses of the w. assembling, ...
Le 26:26 ten w. shall bake your bread in one... 802
Nu 31:9 took all the w. of Midian captives, ... 802
Nu 31:15 Have ye saved all the w. alive?... 5347
Nu 31:18 all the w. children, that have not ... 802
Nu 31:35 of w. that had not known man by ... 802
De 2:34 destroyed the men, and the w., and... 802
De 3:6 utterly destroying the men, w., and ... 802
De 20:14 But the w., and the little ones, and... 802
De 31:12 the people together, men, and w., ... 802
Jos 8:25 fell that day, both of men and w., ... 802
Jos 8:35 congregation of Israel, with the w... 802
Jg 5:24 Blessed above w. shall Jael the wife ... 802
Jg 5:24 blessed shall she be above w. in the... 802
Jg 9:49 also, about a thousand men and w... 802
Jg 9:51 and thither fled all the men and w., ... 802
Jg 16:27 the house was full of men and w.; ... 802
Jg 16:27 about three thousand men and w., ... 802
Jg 21:10 sword, with the w., and the children. ... 802
Jg 21:14 alive of the w. of Jabesh-gilead: ... 802
Jg 21:16 w. are destroyed out of Benjamin? ... 802
Ru 1:4 took them wives of the w. of Moab;... 802
Ru 4:1 w. said unto Naomi, Blessed be ... 802
Ru 4:17 the w. her neighbours gave it a name, ...
1Sa 2:22 how they lay with the w. that... 802
1Sa 4:20 time of her death the w. that stood by ...
1Sa 15:33 thy sword hath made w. childless, ... 802
1Sa 15:33 thy mother be childless among w... 802
1Sa 18:6 w. came out of all cities of Israel, ... 802
1Sa 18:7 w. answered one another as they ... 802
1Sa 21:4 kept themselves at least from w... 802
1Sa 21:5 Of a truth w. have been kept from us... 802
1Sa 22:19 edge of the sword, both men and w., ... 802
1Sa 30:2 had taken the w. captives, that were... 802
2Sa 1:26 wonderful, passing the love of w... 802
2Sa 6:19 as well to the w. as men, to every ... 802
2Sa 15:16 the king left ten w., which were... 802
2Sa 19:35 voice of singing men and singing w.? ...
2Sa 20:3 and the king took the ten w. his... 802
1Ki 3:16 Then came there two w., that were... 802
1Ki 11:1 Solomon loved many strange w., ... 802
1Ki 11:1 w. of the Moabites, Ammonites, ...
2Ki 8:12 and rip up their w. with child...
2Ki 15:16 w. therein that were with child he ...
2Ki 23:7 the w. wove hangings for the grove. ... 802
2Ch 28:8 thousand, w., sons, and daughters, ... 802
2Ch 35:25 singing w. spake of Josiah in their...
Ezr 2:65 hundred singing men and singing w.. ...
Ezr 10:1 great congregation of men and w... 802
Ne 7:67 and five singing men and singing w.. ...
Ne 8:2 congregation both of men and w., ... 802
Ne 8:3 before the men and the w., and ... 802
Ne 13:26 him did outlandish w. cause to sin... 802
Es 1:9 the queen made a feast for the w. ... 802
Es 1:17 queen shall come abroad unto all w., ... 802
Es 2:3 the palace, to the house of the w., ... 802
Es 2:3 chamberlain, keeper of the w.; ... 802
Es 2:8 custody of Hegai, keeper of the w.. ... 802
Es 2:9 best place of the house of the w.. ... 802
Es 2:12 according to the manner of the w., ... 802
Es 2:12 things for the purifying of the w.; ... 802
Es 2:13 house of the w. unto the king's house... 802
Es 2:14 into the second house of the w., ... 802
Es 2:15 chamberlain, the keeper of the w., ... 802
Es 2:17 king loved Esther above all the w., ... 802
Es 3:13 young and old, little children and w., ... 802
Es 8:11 both little ones and w., and to take ... 802
Job 2:10 as one of the foolish w. speaketh. ...
Job 42:15 all the land were no w. found so fair ... 802
Ps 45:9 were among thy honourable w.: ...
Pr 22:14 mouth of strange w. is a deep pit: ...
Pr 23:33 Thine eyes shall behold strange w., ...
Pr 31:3 Give not thy strength unto w., nor ... 802
Ec 2:8 I gat me men singers and w. singers, ...
Ca 1:8 know not, O thou fairest among w., ... 802
Ca 5:9 beloved, O thou fairest among w.? ... 802
Ca 6:1 gone, O thou fairest among w.? ... 802
Isa 3:12 oppressors, and w. rule over them... 802
Isa 4:1 seven w. shall take hold of one man, ... 802
Isa 19:16 day shall Egypt be like unto w.: ... 802
Isa 27:11 the w. come, and set them on fire: ... 802
Isa 32:9 Rise up, ye w. that are at ease; hear ... 802
Isa 32:10 shall ye be troubled, ye careless w.; ...
Isa 32:11 Tremble, ye w. that are at ease; be ...
Jer 7:18 the w. knead their dough, to make... 802
Jer 9:17 ye, and call for the mourning w., ...
Jer 9:17 send for cunning w., that they may...
Jer 9:20 hear the word of the Lord, O ye w., ... 802
Jer 38:22 all the w. that are left in the king ... 802
Jer 38:22 and those w. shall say, Thy friends...
Jer 40:7 committed unto him men, and w., ... 802
Jer 41:16 and the w., and the children, and... 802
Jer 43:6 Even men, and w., and children, ... 802
Jer 44:15 and all the w. that stood by, a great... 802
Jer 44:20 to the men, and to the w., and to all... 802
Jer 44:24 and to all the w., Hear the word ... 802
Jer 50:37 her; and they shall become as w.: ... 802
Jer 51:30 hath failed; they became as w.: ... 802
La 2:20 Shall the w. eat their fruit, and... 802
La 4:10 pitiful w. have sodden their own ... 802
La 5:11 They ravished the w. in Zion, and... 802
Eze 8:14 there sat w. weeping for Tammuz... 802
Eze 9:6 maids, and little children, and w.: ... 802
Eze 13:18 Woe to the w. that sew pillows to all...
Eze 16:34 from other w. in thy whoredoms, ... 802
Eze 16:38 judge thee, as w. that break wedlock...
Eze 16:41 upon thee in the sight of many w.: ... 802
Eze 23:2 there were two w., the daughters... 802
Eze 23:10 and she became famous among w.: ... 802
Eze 23:44 and unto Aholibah, the lewd w.. ... 802
Eze 23:45 after the manner of w. that shed blood; ...
Eze 23:48 that all w. may be taught not to do ... 802
Da 11:17 shall give him the daughter of w., ... 802
Da 11:37 nor the desire of w., nor regard any ... 802
Ho 13:16 their w. with child shall be ripped up...
Am 1:13 they have ripped up the w. with child...
Mic 2:9 w. of my people have ye cast out ... 802
Na 3:13 people in the midst of thee are w.: ... 802
Zec 5:9 behold, there came out two w., ... 802
Zec 8:4 men and old w. dwell in the streets...
Zec 14:2 houses rifled, and the w. ravished; ... 802
Mt 11:11 **Among them that are born of w** ... *1135*
Mt 14:21 five thousand men, beside w. and... *1135*
Mt 15:38 four thousand men, beside w. and ... *1135*
Mt 24:41 **Two w. shall be grinding at the** ... *1135*
Mt 27:55 many w. were there beholding... *1135*
Mt 28:5 answered and said unto the w., ... *1135*
Mk 15:40 were also w. looking on afar off: ... *1135*
Mk 15:41 other w. which came up with him...
Lu 1:28 blessed art thou among w.. ... *1135*
Lu 1:42 said, Blessed art thou among w., ... *1135*
Lu 7:28 **Among those that are born of w** ... *1135*
Lu 8:2 certain w., which had been healed ... *1135*
Lu 17:35 **Two w. shall be grinding together;** ...
Lu 23:27 company of people, and of w., ... *1135*
Lu 23:49 w. that followed him from Galilee, ... *1135*
Lu 23:55 the w. also, which came with him... *1135*
Lu 24:10 and other w. that were with them, ...
Lu 24:22 and certain w. also of our company... *1135*
Lu 24:24 it even so as the w. had said: ... *1135*
Ac 1:14 and supplication, with the w., ... *1135*
Ac 5:14 multitudes both of men and w., ... *1135*
Ac 8:3 haling men and w. committed them... *1135*
Ac 8:12 were baptized, both men and w.. ... *1135*
Ac 9:2 whether they were men or w., he... *1135*
Ac 13:50 the devout and honourable w., ... *1135*
Ac 16:13 spake unto the w. which resorted... *1135*
Ac 17:4 and of the chief w. not a few... *1135*
Ac 17:12 honourable w. which were Greeks, ... *1135*
Ac 22:4 into prisons both men and w.. ... *1135*
Ro 1:26 their w. did change the natural use ... *2338*
1Co 14:34 w. keep silence in the churches: ... *1135*
1Co 14:35 for w. to speak in the church. ... *1135*
Php 4:3 help those w. which laboured with me ...
1Ti 2:9 w. adorn themselves in modest... *1135*
1Ti 2:10 (which becometh w. professing ... *1135*
1Ti 5:2 The elder w. as mothers; the younger ...
1Ti 5:14 therefore that the younger w. marry, ...
2Ti 3:6 captive silly w. laden with sins, ... *1133*
Tit 2:3 The aged w. likewise, that they be... *4247*
Tit 2:4 may teach the young w. to be sober, ...
Heb 11:35 W. received their dead raised to ... *1135*
1Pe 3:5 in the old time the holy w. also, ... 1135
Re 9:8 they had hair as the hair of w... 1135
Re 14:4 which were not defiled with w.; ... 1135

WOMEN'S

Es 2:11 before the court of the w. house, ... 802

WOMENSERVANTS

Ge 20:14 and w., and gave them unto... 8198
Ge 32:5 flocks, and menservants, and w.: ... 8198
Ge 32:22 his two w., and his eleven sons, ... 8198

WON

1Ch 26:27 Out of the spoils w. in battles did they ...
Pr 18:19 brother offended is harder to be w. ...
1Pe 3:1 may without the word be w. ... *2770*

WONDER See also WONDERED; WONDERFUL; WONDERING; WONDERS.

De 13:1 and giveth thee a sign of a w., ... 4159
De 13:2 the sign or the w. come to pass, ... 4159
De 28:46 upon thee for a sign and for a w., ... 4159
2Ch 32:31 enquire of the w. that was done... 4159
Ps 71:7 I am as a w. unto many; but thou ... 4159
Isa 20:3 for a sign and w. upon Egypt ... 4159
Isa 29:9 Stay yourselves,and w.; cry ye... 8539
Isa 29:14 even a marvellous work and a w.: ... 6382
Jer 4:9 and the prophets shall w... 8539
Hab 1:5 and regard, and w. marvellously: ... 8539
Ac 3:10 and they were filled with w. and ... *2285*
Ac 13:41 Behold, ye despisers, and w., ... *2296*
Re 12:1 appeared a great w. in heaven; ... *4592*
Re 12:3 appeared another w. in heaven; ... *4592*
Re 17:8 that dwell on the earth shall w., ... *2296*

WONDERED

Isa 59:16 w. that there was no intercessor: ... 8074
Isa 63:5 w. that there was none to uphold: ... 8074
Zec 3:8 thee: for they are men w. at: ... 4159
Mt 15:31 Insomuch that the multitude w., ... *2296*
Mk 6:51 beyond measure, and w... *2296*
Lu 2:18 that heard it w. at those things... *2296*
Lu 4:22 and w. at the gracious words which ... *2296*
Lu 8:25 they being afraid w., saying one to ... *2296*
Lu 9:43 they w. every one at all things ... *2296*
Lu 11:14 dumb spake; and the people w... *2296*
Lu 24:41 they yet believed not for joy, and w., ..*2296*
Ac 7:31 Moses saw it, he w. at the sight: ... *2296*
Ac 8:13 and w., beholding the miracles... *1839*
Re 13:3 and all the world w. ater the beast ... *2296*
Re 17:6 her, I w. with great admiration. ... *2296*

WONDERFUL

De 28:59 the Lord will make thy plagues w., ... 6381
2Sa 1:26 thy love to me was w., passing the ... 6381
2Ch 2:9 am about to build shall be w. great. ... 6381
Job 42:3 things too w. for me, which I knew ... 6381
Ps 40:5 thy w. works which thou hast done. ... 6381
Ps 78:4 and his w. works that he hath done. ... 6381
Ps 107:8, 15,21,31 w. works to the children of... 6381
Ps 111:4 his w. works to be remembered: ... 6381
Ps 119:129 Thy testimonies are w.: ... 6382
Ps 139:6 Such knowledge is too w. for me; ... 6383
Pr 30:18 be three things which are too w... 6381
Isa 9:6 and his name shall be called W., ... 6382
Isa 25:1 for thou hast done w. things; thy ... 6382
Isa 28:29 which is w. in counsel, and ... 6381
Jer 5:30 w. and horrible thing is committed... 8047
Mt 7:22 **name done many w. works?** ... *1411*
Mt 21:15 saw the w. things that he did, ... *2297*
Ac 2:11 our tongues the w. works of God. ... *3167*

WONDERFULLY

1Sa 6:6 he had wrought w. among them, ... 5953
Ps 139:14 for I am fearfully and w. made: ... 6395
La 1:9 therefore she came down w.: she... 6382
Da 8:24 and he shall destroy w., and shall... 6381

WONDERING

Ge 24:21 the man w. at her held his peace, ... 7583

Lu 24:12 w. in himself at that which was *2296*
Ac 3:11 is called Solomon's, greatly w. *1569*

WONDEROUSLY See also WONDROUSLY.
Jg 13:19 and the angel did w.; and Manaoh 6381

WONDERS
Ex 3:20 smite Egypt with all my w. which 6381
Ex 4:21 do all those w. before Pharaoh, 4159
Ex 7:3 and my w. in the land of Egypt 4159
Ex 11:9 that my w. may be multiplied in 4159
Ex 11:10 did all these w. before Pharaoh: 4159
Ex 15:11 fearful in praises, doing w.? 6382
De 4:34 by signs, and by w., and by war, 4159
De 6:22 And the Lord shewed signs and w., 4159
De 7:19 and the w., and the mighty hand, 4159
De 26:8 and with signs and with w.: 4159
De 34:11 the w., which the Lord sent him to 4159
Jos 3:5 the Lord will do w. among you. 6381
1Ch 16:12 his w., and the judgments of his 4159
Ne 9:10 signs and w. upon Pharaoh, 4159
Ne 9:17 neither were mindful of thy w. 6381
Job 9:10 out; yea, and w. without number. 6381
Ps 77:11 I will remember thy w. of old. 6382
Ps 77:14 Thou art the God that doest w.: 6382
Ps 78:11 his w. that he had shewed them. 6381
Ps 78:43 and his w. in the field of Zoan: 4159
Ps 88:10 Wilt thou shew w. to the dead? 6382
Ps 88:12 Shall thy w. be known in the dark? 6382
Ps 89:5 And the heavens shall praise thy w., 6382
Ps 96:3 heathen, his w. among all people. 6381
Ps 105:5 his w., and the judgments of his 4159
Ps 105:27 them, and w. in the land of Ham. 4159
Ps 106:7 Our fathers understood not thy w. 6381
Ps 107:24 the Lord, and his w. in the deep. 6381
Ps 135:9 Who sent tokens and w. into the 4159
Ps 136:4 To him who alone doeth great w.: 6381
Isa 8:18 for w. in Israel from the Lord 4159
Jer 32:20 signs and w. in the land of Egypt, 4159
Jer 32:21 with signs, and with w., and with a 4159
Da 4:2 w. that the high God hath wrought 8540
Da 4:3 and how mighty are his w.! 8540
Da 6:27 he worketh signs and w. in heaven 8540
Da 12:6 shall it be to the end of these w. 6382
Joe 2:30 And I will shew w. in the heavens 4159
Mt 24:24 **and shall shew great signs and w.** *5059*
Mk 13:22 **rise, and shall shew signs and w.** *5059*
Joh 4:48 **Except ye see signs and w., ye** *5059*
Ac 2:19 And I will shew w. in heaven above, *5059*
Ac 2:22 you by miracles and w. and signs, *5059*
Ac 2:43 and many w. and signs were done *5059*
Ac 4:30 and that signs and w. may be done *5059*
Ac 5:12 were many signs and w. wrought *5059*
Ac 6:8 did great w. and miracles among *5059*
Ac 7:36 that he had shewed w. and signs *5059*
Ac 14:3 granted signs and w. to be done *5059*
Ac 15:12 declaring what miracles and w. God *5059*
Ro 15:19 Through mighty signs and w., by *5059*
2Co 12:12 signs, and w., and mighty deeds. *5059*
2Th 2:9 all power and signs and lying w., *5059*
Heb 2:4 witness, both with signs and w., *5059*
Re 13:13 And he doeth great w., so that he *4592*

WONDROUS
1Ch 16:9 him, talk ye of all his w. works. 6381
Job 37:14 and consider the w. works of God. 6381
Job 37:16 w. work of him which is perfect 4652
Ps 26:7 and tell of all thy w. works. 6381
Ps 71:17 have I declared thy w. works. 6381
Ps 72:18 of Israel, who only doeth w. things. 6381
Ps 75:1 name is near thy w. works declare. 6381
Ps 78:32 and believed not for his w. works. 6381
Ps 86:10 thou art great, and doest w. things: 6381
Ps 105:2 him: talk ye of all his w. works 6381
Ps 106:22 W. works in the land of Ham, and 6381
Ps 119:18 behold w. things out of thy law. 6381
Ps 119:27 so shall I talk of thy w. works. 6381
Ps 145:5 of thy majesty, and of thy w. works. 6381
Jer 21:2 us according to all his w. works, 6381

WONDROUSLY See also WONDEROUSLY.
Joe 2:26 God, that hath dealt w. with you: 6381

WONT
Ex 21:29 ox were w. to push with his horn 5056
Nu 22:30 was I ever w. to do so unto thee? 5532
1Sa 30:31 and his men were w. to haunt. 1980
2Sa 20:18 They were w. to speak in old time, 1696
Da 3:19 seven times more than it was w. 2370
Mt 27:15 governor was w. to release unto *1486*
Mk 10:1 and, as he was w., he taught them *1486*
Lu 22:39 and went, as he was w., to *2596,1485*
Ac 16:13 where prayer was w. to be made; *3543*

WOOD See also WOODS; WORMWOOD.
Ge 6:14 Make thee an ark of gopher w.; 6086
Ge 22:3 clave the w. for the burnt offering, 6086
Ge 22:6 took the w. of the burnt offering, 6086
Ge 22:7 he said, Behold the fire and the w.: 6086
Ge 22:9 and laid the w. in order, and bound 6086
Ge 22:9 laid him on the altar upon the w. 6086
Ex 7:19 both in vessels of w., and in vessels 6086
Ex 25:5 and badgers' skins, and shittim w., 6086
Ex 25:10 shall make an ark of shittim w.: 6086
Ex 25:13 shalt make staves of shittim w., 6086
Ex 25:23 also make a table of shittim w.: 6086
Ex 25:28 shalt make the staves of shittim w., 6086
Ex 26:15 for the tabernacle of shittim w. 6086
Ex 26:26 thou shalt make bars of shittim w.; 6086
Ex 26:32 four pillars of shittim w. overlaid
Ex 26:37 the hanging five pillars of shittim w.,
Ex 27:1 shalt make an altar of shittim w., 6086
Ex 27:6 staves of shittim w., and overlay 6086
Ex 30:1 of shittim w. shalt thou make it. 6086
Ex 30:5 shalt make the staves of shittim w., 6086
Ex 35:7 and badgers' skins, and shittim w., 6086
Ex 35:24 with whom was found shittim w. 6086
Ex 35:33 and in carving of w., to make any 6086
Ex 36:20 for the tabernacle of shittim w., 6086
Ex 36:31 and he made bars of shittim w.; five 6086
Ex 36:36 thereunto four pillars of shittim w.,
Ex 37:1 made the ark of shittim w.: 6086
Ex 37:4 And he made staves of shittim w., 6086
Ex 37:10 he made the table of shittim w.: 6086
Ex 37:15 he made the staves of shittim w., 6086
Ex 37:25 made the incense altar of shittim w.: 6086
Ex 37:28 he made the staves of shittim w., 6086
Ex 38:1 altar of burnt offering of shittim w.: 6086
Ex 38:6 he made the staves of shittim w., 6086
Le 1:7 lay the w. in order upon the fire: 6086
Le 1:8 order upon the w. that is on the fire 6086
Le 1:12 order on the w. that is on the fire 6086
Le 1:17 upon the w. that is upon the fire: 6086
Le 3:5 is upon the w. that is on the fire: 6086
Le 4:12 and burn him on the w. with fire: 6086
Le 6:12 the priest shall burn w. on it every 6086
Le 11:32 whether it be any vessel of w., or 6086
Le 14:4 and cedar w., and scarlet, and 6086
Le 14:6 and the cedar w., and the scarlet, 6086
Le 14:49 and cedar w., and scarlet, and 6086
Le 14:51 the cedar w., and the hyssop, 6086
Le 14:52 with the cedar w., and with the 6086
Le 15:12 every vessel of w. shall be rinsed 6086
Nu 13:20 whether there be w. therein, 6086
Nu 19:6 shall take cedar w., and hyssop, 6086
Nu 31:20 hair, and all things made of w. 6086
Nu 35:18 him with an hand weapon of w., 6086
De 4:28 work of men's hands, w. and stone, 6086
De 10:1 mount, and make thee an ark of w. 6086
De 10:3 And I made an ark of shittim w., 6086
De 19:5 As when a man goeth into the w. 3293
De 19:5 with his neighbour to hew w., 6086
De 28:36 thou serve other gods, w. and stone 6086
De 28:64 have known, even w. and stone. 6086
De 29:11 hewer of thy w. unto the drawer 6086
De 29:17 and their idols, w. and stone, silver 6086
Jos 9:21 but let them be hewers of w. and 6086
Jos 9:23, 27 hewers of w....drawers of water 6086
Jos 17:15 then get thee up to the w. country, 3293
Jos 17:18 for it is a w., and thou shalt cut it 3293
Jg 6:26 sacrifice with the w. of the grove 6086
1Sa 6:14 and they clave the w. of the cart, 6086
1Sa 14:25 all they of the land came to a w.; 3293
1Sa 14:26 the people were come into the w., 3293
1Sa 23:15 in the wilderness of Ziph in a w. 2793
1Sa 23:16 and went to David into the w., and 2793
1Sa 23:18 and David abode in the w., and 2793
1Sa 23:19 with us in strong holds in the w., 2793
2Sa 6:5 of instruments made of fir w., 6086
2Sa 18:6 battle was in the w. of Ephraim; 3293
2Sa 18:8 the w. devoured more people that 3293
2Sa 18:17 cast him into a great pit in the w., 3293
2Sa 24:22 instruments of the oxen for w. 6086
1Ki 6:15 covered them on the inside with w., 6086
1Ki 18:23, 23 and lay it on w., and put no fire 6086
1Ki 18:33 And he put the w. in order, and cut 6086
1Ki 18:33 in pieces, and laid him on the w., 6086
1Ki 18:33 the burnt sacrifice, and on the w. 6086
1Ki 18:38 the burnt sacrifice, and the w., 6086
2Ki 2:24 forth two she bears out of the w., 3293
2Ki 6:4 came to Jordan, they cut down w. 6086
2Ki 19:18 work of men's hands, w. and stone: 6086
1Ch 16:33 shall the trees of the w. sing out 3293
1Ch 21:23 the threshing instruments for w., 6086
1Ch 22:4 of Tyre brought much cedar w. to 6086
1Ch 29:2 of iron, and w. for things of w.; 6086
2Ch 2:16 And we will cut w. out of Lebanon, 6086
Ne 8:4 the scribe stood upon a pulpit of w., 6086
Ne 10:34 and the people, for the w. offering, 6086
Ne 13:31 And for the w. offering, at times 6086
Job 41:27 as straw, and brass as rotten w. 6086
Ps 80:13 boar out of the w. doth waste it, 3293
Ps 83:14 As the fire burneth a w., and as 3293
Ps 96:12 shall all the trees of the w. rejoice. 3293
Ps 132:6 we found it in the fields of the w. 3293
Ps 141:7 and cleaveth w. upon the earth.
Pr 26:20 Where no w. is, there the fire 6086
Pr 26:21 to burning coals, and w. to fire; 6086
Ec 2:6 the w. that bringeth forth trees: 3293
Ec 10:9 and he that cleaveth w. shall be 6086
Ca 2:3 tree among the trees of the w., 3293
Ca 3:9 a chariot of the w. of Lebanon. 6086
Isa 7:2 as the trees of the w. are moved 3293
Isa 10:15 lift up itself, as if it were no w. 6086
Isa 30:33 pile thereof is fire and much w.; 6086
Isa 37:19 work of men's hands, w. and stone: 6086
Isa 45:20 set up the w. of their graven image. 6086
Isa 60:17 for w. brass, and for stones iron: 6086
Jer 5:14 thy mouth fire, and this people w., 6086
Jer 7:18 The children gather w., and the 6086
Jer 28:13 Thou hast broken the yokes of w.; 6086
Jer 46:22 her with axes, as hewers of w. 6086
La 5:4 for money; our w. is sold unto us. 6086
La 5:13 and the children fell under the w. 6086
Eze 15:3 w. be taken thereof to do any work? 6086
Eze 20:32 countries, to serve w. and stone. 6086
Eze 24:10 Heap on w., kindle the fire, 6086
Eze 39:10 shall take no w. out of the field, 6086
Eze 41:16 door, cieled with w. round about, 6086
Eze 41:22 altar of w. was three cubits high, 6086
Eze 41:22 and the walls thereof, were of w.: 6086
Da 5:4 brass, of iron, of w., and of stone. 636
Da 5:23 gold, of brass, iron, w., and stone, 636
Mic 7:14 which dwell solitarily in the w., 3293
Hab 2:19 him that saith to the w., Awake; 6086
Hag 1:8 up to the mountain, and bring w., 6086
Zec 12:6 an hearth of fire among the w., 6086
1Co 3:12 precious stones, w., hay, stubble; *3586*
2Ti 2:20 silver, but also of w. and of earth; *3585*
Re 9:20 and brass, and stone, and of w.: *3585*
Re 18:12 and scarlet, and all thyine w., *3586*
Re 18:12 manner vessels of most precious w., *3586*

WOOD-OFFERING See WOOD and OFFERING.

WOODS
Eze 34:25 wilderness, and sleep in the w. 3264

WOOF
Le 13:48 Whether it e in the warp, or w.; 6154
Le 13:49, 51 either in the warp, or in the w., 6154
Le 13:52 whether warp or w., in woollen or 6154
Le 13:53 either in the warp, or in the w., or 6154
Le 13:56 or out of the warp, or out of the w.: 6154
Le 13:57 either in the warp, or in the w., 6154
Le 13:58 the garment, either warp, or w., 6154
Le 13:59 either in the warp, or w., or any 6154

WOOL
Jg 6:37 will put a fleece of w. in the floor; 6785
2Ki 3:4 thousand rams, with the w. 6785
Ps 147:16 He giveth snow like w.: he 6785
Pr 31:13 She seeketh w., and flax, and 6785
Isa 1:18 like crimson, they shall be as w. 6785
Isa 51:8 the worm shall eat them like w.: 6785
Eze 27:18 the wine of Helbon, and white w. 6785
Eze 34:3 fat, and ye clothe you with the w., 6785
Eze 44:17 and no w. shall come upon them, 6785
Da 7:9 hair of his head like the pure w.: 6015
Ho 2:5 my w. and my flax, mine oil and 6785
Ho 2:9 will recover my w. and my flax 6785
Heb 9:19 and scarlet w. and hyssop, and *2053*
Re 1:14 and his hairs were white like w., *2053*

WOOLLEN

Le	13:47	whether it be a **w.** garment, or a	6785
Le	13:48	warp, or woof; of linen, or of **w.**;	6785
Le	13:52	warp or woof, in **w.** or in linen,	6785
Le	13:59	leprosy in a garment of **w.** or linen,	6785
Le	19:19	garment mingled of linen and **w.**	8162
De	22:11	sorts, as of **w.** and linen together.	6785

WORD See also WORD'S; WORDS.

Ge	15:1	**w.** of the Lord came unto Abram	1697
Ge	15:4	the **w.** of the Lord came unto him,	1697
Ge	30:34	it might be according to thy **w.**.	1697
Ge	37:14	the flocks; and bring me **w.** again.	1697
Ge	41:40	according unto thy **w.** shall all my	6310
Ge	44:2	to the **w.** that Joseph had spoken.	1697
Ge	44:18	thee, speak a **w.** in my lord's ears,	1697
Ex	8:10	he said, Be it according to thy **w.**:	1697
Ex	8:13	did according to the **w.** of Moses;	1697
Ex	8:31	Lord according to the **w.** of Moses;	1697
Ex	9:20	He that feared the **w.** of the Lord	1697
Ex	9:21	regarded not the **w.** of the Lord	1697
Ex	12:35	did according to the **w.** of Moses;	1697
Ex	14:12	the **w.** that we did tell thee in Egypt,	1697
Ex	32:28	did according to the **w.** of Moses:	1697
Le	10:7	did according to the **w.** of Moses.	1697
Nu	3:16,	51 according to the **w.** of the Lord,	6310
Nu	4:45	according to the **w.** of the Lord	6310
Nu	11:23	whether my **w.** shall come to pass	1697
Nu	13:26	and brought back **w.** unto them,	1697
Nu	14:20	have pardoned according to thy **w.**:	1697
Nu	15:31	hath despised the **w.** of the Lord,	1697
Nu	20:24	rebelled against my **w.** at the	6310
Nu	22:8	I will bring you **w.** again, as the	1697
Nu	22:18	go beyond the **w.** of the Lord	6310
Nu	22:20	the **w.** which I shall say unto thee,	1697
Nu	22:35	the **w.** that I shall speak unto thee,	1697
Nu	22:38	**w.** that God putteth in my mouth,	1697
Nu	23:5	Lord put a **w.** in Balaam's mouth,	1697
Nu	23:16	Balaam, and put a **w.** in his mouth,	1697
Nu	27:21	Lord: at his **w.** shall they go out,	6310
Nu	27:21	and at his **w.** they shall come in,	6310
Nu	30:2	he shall not break his **w.**, he shall	1697
Nu	36:5	according to the **w.** of the Lord,	6310
De	1:22	bring us **w.** again by what way we	1697
De	1:22	and brought us **w.** again, and said,	1697
De	4:2	add unto the **w.** which I command	1697
De	5:5	to shew you the **w.** of the Lord:	1697
De	8:3	but by every **w.** that proceedeth out	
De	9:5	the **w.** which the Lord sware unto	1697
De	18:20	presume to speak a **w.** in my name,	1697
De	18:21	know the **w.** which the Lord hath	1697
De	21:5	by their **w.** shall every controversy	6310
De	30:14	But the **w.** is very nigh unto thee,	1697
De	33:9	for they have observed thy **w.**, and	565
De	34:5	according to the **w.** of the Lord.	6310
Jos	1:13	Remember the **w.** which Moses	1697
Jos	6:10	neither shall any **w.** proceed out	1697
Jos	8:27	according unto the **w.** of the Lord	1697
Jos	8:35	was not a **w.** of all that Moses	1697
Jos	14:7	I brought him **w.** again as it was	1697
Jos	14:10	the Lord spake this **w.** unto Moses,	1697
Jos	19:50	According to the **w.** of the Lord	6310
Jos	22:9	according to the **w.** of the Lord by	6310
Jos	22:32	and brought them **w.** again.	1697
1Sa	1:23	him; only the Lord establish his **w.**	1697
1Sa	3:1	the **w.** of the Lord was precious	1697
1Sa	3:7	neither was the **w.** of the Lord yet	1697
1Sa	3:21	in Shiloh by the **w.** of the Lord.	1697
1Sa	4:1	**w.** of Samuel came to all Israel.	1697
1Sa	9:27	that I may shew thee the **w.** of God.	1697
1Sa	15:10	the **w.** of the Lord unto Samuel,	1697
1Sa	15:23,	26 hast rejected the **w.** of the Lord,	1697
2Sa	3:11	could not answer Abner a **w.** again,	1697
2Sa	7:4	**w.** of the Lord came unto Nathan,	1697
2Sa	7:7	spake I a **w.** with any of the tribes	1697
2Sa	7:25	the **w.** that thou hast spoken	1697
2Sa	14:12	speak one **w.** unto my lord the king.	1697
2Sa	14:17	The **w.** of my lord the king shall	1697
2Sa	15:28	until there come **w.** from you to	1697
2Sa	19:10	speak ye not a **w.** of bringing the king	
2Sa	19:14	that they sent this **w.** unto the king,	
2Sa	22:31	perfect; the **w.** of the Lord is tried:	565
2Sa	23:2	me, and his **w.** was in my tongue.	4405
2Sa	24:4	king's **w.** prevailed against Joab,	1697
2Sa	24:11	the **w.** of the Lord came unto the	1697
1Ki	2:4	Lord may continue his **w.** which he	1697
1Ki	2:23	spoken this **w.** against his own life	1697
1Ki	2:27	he might fulfil the **w.** of the Lord,	1697
1Ki	2:30	Benaiah brought the king **w.** again,	1697
1Ki	2:42	The **w.** that I have heard is good.	1697
1Ki	6:11	**w.** of the Lord came to Solomon,	1697
1Ki	6:12	will I perform my **w.** with thee,	1697
1Ki	8:20	Lord hath performed his **w.** that he	1697
1Ki	8:26	let thy **w.**, I pray thee, be verified,	1697
1Ki	8:56	hath not failed one **w.** of all his	1697
1Ki	12:22	the **w.** of God came unto Shemaiah.	1697
1Ki	12:24	therefore to the **w.** of the Lord,	1697
1Ki	12:24	according to the **w.** of the Lord.	1697
1Ki	13:1	by the **w.** of the Lord unto Beth-el:	1697
1Ki	13:2	the altar in the **w.** of the Lord,	1697
1Ki	13:5	had given by the **w.** of the Lord.	1697
1Ki	13:9	charged me by the **w.** of the Lord,	1697
1Ki	13:17	said to me by the **w.** of the Lord,	1697
1Ki	13:18	unto me by the **w.** of the Lord,	1697
1Ki	13:20	the **w.** of the Lord came unto the	1697
1Ki	13:26	disobedient unto the **w.** of the	6310
1Ki	13:26	according to the **w.** of the Lord.	1697
1Ki	13:32	he cried by the **w.** of the Lord	1697
1Ki	14:18	according to the **w.** of the Lord,	1697
1Ki	16:1	the **w.** of the Lord came to Jehu	1697
1Ki	16:7	**w.** of the Lord against Baasha,	1697
1Ki	16:12,	34 according to the **w.** of the Lord,	1697
1Ki	17:1	years, but according to my **w.**	1697
1Ki	17:2	the **w.** of the Lord came unto him,	1697
1Ki	17:5	according unto the **w.** of the Lord:	1697
1Ki	17:8	the **w.** of the Lord came unto him,	1697
1Ki	17:16	according to the **w.** of the Lord,	1697
1Ki	17:24	the **w.** of the Lord in thy mouth	1697
1Ki	18:1	**w.** of the Lord came to Elijah	1697
1Ki	18:21	the people answered him not a **w.**.	1697
1Ki	18:31	unto whom the **w.** of the Lord came,	1697
1Ki	18:36	have done all these things at thy **w.**	1697
1Ki	19:9	the **w.** of the Lord came to him,	1697
1Ki	20:9	departed, and brought him **w.** again.	1697
1Ki	20:35	neighbour in the **w.** of the Lord,	1697
1Ki	21:4	**w.** which Naboth the Jazreelite had	1697
1Ki	21:17,	28 **w.** of the Lord came to Elijah	1697
1Ki	22:5	thee, at the **w.** of the Lord to day.	1697
1Ki	22:13	one mouth: let thy **w.**, I pray thee,	1697
1Ki	22:13	be like the **w.** of one of them, and	1697
1Ki	22:19	thou therefore the **w.** of the Lord:	1697
1Ki	22:38	according unto the **w.** of the Lord	1697
2Ki	1:16	God in Israel to enquire of his **w.**?	1697
2Ki	1:17	according to the **w.** of the Lord	1697
2Ki	3:12	The **w.** of the Lord is with him.	1697
2Ki	4:44	according to the **w.** of the Lord.	1697
2Ki	6:18	according to the **w.** of Elisha.	1697
2Ki	7:1	said, Hear ye the **w.** of the Lord;	1697
2Ki	7:16	according to the **w.** of the Lord.	1697
2Ki	9:26	according to the **w.** of the Lord.	1697
2Ki	9:36	This is the **w.** of the Lord, which he	1697
2Ki	10:10	earth nothing of the **w.** of the Lord,	1697
2Ki	14:25	according to the **w.** of the Lord God	1697
2Ki	15:12	This was the **w.** of the Lord which	1697
2Ki	18:28	Hear the **w.** of the great king, the	1697
2Ki	18:36	peace, and answered him not a **w.**:	1697
2Ki	19:21	the **w.** that the Lord hath spoken	1697
2Ki	20:4	the **w.** of the Lord came to him,	1697
2Ki	20:16	Hezekiah, hear the **w.** of the Lord.	1697
2Ki	20:19	Good is the **w.** of the Lord which	1697
2Ki	22:9	and brought the king **w.** again,	1697
2Ki	22:20	they brought the king **w.** again.	1697
2Ki	23:16	according to the **w.** of the Lord	1697
2Ki	24:2	according to the **w.** of the Lord,	1697
1Ch	10:13	even against the **w.** of the Lord,	1697
1Ch	11:3,	10 according to the **w.** of the Lord.	1697
1Ch	12:23	according to the **w.** of the Lord.	6310
1Ch	15:15	according to the **w.** of the Lord.	1697
1Ch	16:15	the **w.** which he commanded to a	1697
1Ch	17:3	the **w.** of God came to Nathan,	1697
1Ch	17:6	spake I a **w.** to any of the judges of	1697
1Ch	21:4	king's **w.** prevailed against Joab.	1697
1Ch	21:6	king's **w.** was abominable to Joab.	1697
1Ch	21:12	what **w.** I shall bring again to him.	1697
1Ch	22:8	but the **w.** of the Lord came to me,	1697
2Ch	6:10	hath performed his **w.** that he hath	1697
2Ch	6:17	God of Israel, let thy **w.** be verified,	1697
2Ch	10:15	the Lord might perform his **w.**,	1697
2Ch	11:2	**w.** of the Lord came to Shemaiah	1697
2Ch	12:7	**w.** of the Lord came to Shemaiah,	1697
2Ch	18:4	thee, at the **w.** of the Lord to day.	1697
2Ch	18:12	let thy **w.** therefore, I pray thee, be	1697
2Ch	18:18	Therefore hear the **w.** of the Lord;	1697
2Ch	30:12	the princes, by the **w.** of the Lord.	1697
2Ch	34:16	brought the king **w.** back again,	1697
2Ch	34:21	have not kept the **w.** of the Lord,	1697
2Ch	34:28	So they brought the king **w.** again.	1697
2Ch	35:6	do according to the **w.** of the Lord	1697
2Ch	36:21	To fulfil the **w.** of the Lord by the	1697
2Ch	36:22	that the **w.** of the Lord spoken by	1697
Ezr	1:1	**w.** of the lord by the mouth of	1697
Ezr	6:11	that whosoever shall alter this **w.**,	6600
Ezr	10:5	should do according to this **w.**.	1697
Ne	1:8	**w.** that thou commandest thy	1697
Es	1:21	according to the **w.** of Memucan:	1697
Es	7:8	**w.** went out of the king's mouth,	1697
Job	2:13	and none spake a **w.** unto him:	1697
Ps	17:4	**w.** of thy lips I have kept me from	1697
Ps	18:30	the **w.** of the Lord is tried: he is a	565
Ps	33:4	For the **w.** of the Lord is right;	1697
Ps	33:6	By the **w.** of the Lord were the	1697
Ps	56:4	In God I will praise his **w.**, in God I	1697
Ps	56:10	In God will I praise his **w.**:	1697
Ps	56:10	in the Lord will I praise his **w.**.	1697
Ps	68:11	The Lord gave the **w.**: great was	562
Ps	103:20	unto the voice of his **w.**.	1697
Ps	105:8	the **w.** which he commanded to a	1697
Ps	105:19	Until the time that his **w.** came:	1697
Ps	105:19	the **w.** of the Lord tried him.	565
Ps	105:28	they rebelled not against his **w.**.	1697
Ps	106:24	land, they believed not his **w.**:	1697
Ps	107:20	He sent his **w.**, and healed them,	1697
Ps	119:9	heed thereto according to thy **w.**	1697
Ps	119:11	Thy **w.** have I hid in mine heart,	565
Ps	119:16	statutes: I will not forget thy **w.**.	1697
Ps	119:17	that I may live, and keep thy **w.**.	1697
Ps	119:25	quicken...me according to thy **w.**	1697
Ps	119:28	thou me according unto thy **w.**.	1697
Ps	119:38	Stablish thy **w.** unto thy servant,	565
Ps	119:41	thy salvation, according to thy **w.**.	565
Ps	119:42	me: for I trust in thy **w.**	1697
Ps	119:43	take not the **w.** of truth utterly out	1697
Ps	119:49	Remember the **w.** unto thy servant,	1697
Ps	119:50	for thy **w.** hath quickened me.	565
Ps	119:58	unto me according to thy **w.**.	565
Ps	119:65	O Lord, according unto thy **w.**	1697
Ps	119:67	astray: but now have I kept thy **w.**.	565
Ps	119:74	because I have hoped in thy **w.**.	1697
Ps	119:76	to thy **w.** unto thy servant.	565
Ps	119:81	salvation: but I hope in thy **w.**.	1697
Ps	119:82	Mine eyes fail for thy **w.**, saying,	565
Ps	119:89	Lord, thy **w.** is settled in heaven.	1697
Ps	119:101	evil way, that I might keep thy **w.**	1697
Ps	119:105	Thy **w.** is a lamp unto my feet, and	1697
Ps	119:107	O Lord, according unto thy **w.**	1697
Ps	119:114	and my shield: I hope in thy **w.**.	1697
Ps	119:116	Uphold me according unto thy **w.**,	565
Ps	119:123	and for the **w.** of thy righteousness.	565
Ps	119:133	Order my steps in thy **w.**: and let not	565
Ps	119:140	Thy **w.** is very pure: therefore thy	565
Ps	119:147	and cried: I hoped in thy **w.**.	1697
Ps	119:148	that I might meditate in thy **w.**	565
Ps	119:154	quicken me according to thy **w.**.	565
Ps	119:158	because they kept not thy **w.**	565
Ps	119:160	Thy **w.** is true from the beginning:	1697
Ps	119:161	heart standeth in awe of thy **w.**.	1697
Ps	119:162	I rejoice at thy **w.**, as one that	565
Ps	119:169	according to thy **w.**,	1697
Ps	119:170	deliver me according to thy **w.**.	565
Ps	119:172	My tongue shall speak of thy **w.**:	565
Ps	130:5	doth wait, and in his **w.** do I hope.	1697
Ps	138:2	hast magnified thy **w.** above all	565
Ps	139:4	there is not a **w.** in my tongue,	4405
Ps	147:15	earth: his **w.** runneth very swiftly	1697
Ps	147:18	He sendeth out his **w.**, and melteth	1697
Ps	147:19	He sheweth his **w.** unto Jacob,	1697
Ps	148:8	stormy wind fulfilling his **w.**:	1697
Pr	12:25	but a good **w.** maketh it glad.	1697
Pr	13:13	despiseth the **w.** shall be destroyed:	1697
Pr	14:15	The simple believeth every **w.**:	1697
Pr	15:23	and a **w.** spoken in due season,	1697
Pr	25:11	A **w.** fitly spoken is like apples of	1697
Pr	30:5	Every **w.** of God is pure: he is a	565
Ec	8:4	Where the **w.** of a king is, there is	1697
Isa	1:10	Hear the **w.** of the Lord, ye rulers	1697
Isa	2:1	The **w.** that Isaiah the son of Amoz	1697
Isa	2:3	the **w.** of the Lord from Jerusalem.	1697
Isa	5:24	despised the **w.** of the Holy One of	565
Isa	8:10	speak the **w.**, and it shall not	1697

Isa 8:20 speak not according to this w., ... 1697
Isa 9:8 The Lord sent a w. into Jacob, and ... 1697
Isa 16:13 is the w. that the Lord hath spoken ... 1697
Isa 24:3 for the Lord hath spoken this w. ... 1697
Isa 28:13 the w. of the Lord was unto them ... 1697
Isa 28:14 Wherefore hear the w. of the Lord ... 1697
Isa 29:21 make a man an offender for a w., ... 1697
Isa 30:12 Because ye despise this w., and ... 1697
Isa 30:21 ears shall hear a w. behind thee, ... 1697
Isa 36:21 peace, and answered him not a w.: ... 1697
Isa 37:22 the w. which the Lord hath spoken ... 1697
Isa 38:4 came the w. of the Lord to Isaiah, ... 1697
Isa 39:5 Hear the w. of the Lord of hosts: ... 1697
Isa 39:8 Good is the w. of the Lord which ... 1697
Isa 40:8 w. of our God shall stand for ever ... 1697
Isa 41:28 I asked of them, could answer a w. ... 1697
Isa 44:26 confirmeth the w. of his servant, ... 1697
Isa 45:23 the w. is gone out of my mouth in ... 1697
Isa 50:4 speak a w. in season to him that is ... 1697
Isa 55:11 So shall my w. be that goeth forth ... 1697
Isa 66:2 spirit, and trembleth at my w. ... 1697
Isa 66:5 Hear the w. of the Lord, ye that ... 1697
Isa 66:5 ye that tremble at his w.; Your ... 1697
Jer 1:2 To whom the w. of the Lord came ... 1697
Jer 1:4, 11 the w. of the Lord came unto me, ... 1697
Jer 1:12 I will hasten my w. to perform it. ... 1697
Jer 1:13 the w. of the Lord came unto me ... 1697
Jer 2:1 the w. of the Lord came to me, ... 1697
Jer 2:4 Hear ye the w. of the Lord, O ... 1697
Jer 2:31 see ye the w. of the Lord. ... 1697
Jer 5:13 wind, and the w. is not in them: ... 1699
Jer 5:14 Because ye speak this w., behold, ... 1697
Jer 6:10 the w. of the Lord is unto them a ... 1697
Jer 7:1 w. that came to Jeremiah from the ... 1697
Jer 7:2 house, and proclaim there this w., ... 1697
Jer 7:2 Hear ye the w. of the Lord, all ye ... 1697
Jer 8:9 have rejected the w. of the Lord: ... 1697
Jer 9:20 Yet hear the w. of the Lord, O ye ... 1697
Jer 9:20 ear receive the w. of his mouth, ... 1697
Jer 10:1 Hear ye the w. which the Lord ... 1697
Jer 11:1 The w. that came to Jeremiah ... 1697
Jer 13:2 according to the w. of the Lord, ... 1697
Jer 13:3 the w. of the Lord came unto me ... 1697
Jer 13:8 the w. of the Lord came unto me, ... 1697
Jer 13:12 thou shalt speak unto them this w.; ... 1697
Jer 14:1 The w. of the Lord that came to ... 1697
Jer 14:17 thou shalt say this w. unto them; ... 1697
Jer 15:16 and thy w. was unto me the joy ... 1697
Jer 16:1 w. of the Lord came also unto me, ... 1697
Jer 17:15 Where is the w. of the Lord? let it ... 1697
Jer 17:20 Hear ye the w. of the Lord, ye ... 1697
Jer 18:1 w. which came to Jeremiah from ... 1697
Jer 18:5 the w. of the Lord came to me, ... 1697
Jer 18:18 wise, nor the w. from the prophet ... 1697
Jer 19:3 Hear ye the w. of the Lord, O kings ... 1697
Jer 20:8 the w. of the Lord was made a ... 1697
Jer 20:9 w. was in mine heart as a burning ...
Jer 21:1 w. which came unto Jeremiah ... 1697
Jer 21:11 say, Hear ye the w. of the Lord; ... 1697
Jer 22:1 of Judah, and speak there this w., ... 1697
Jer 22:2 Hear the w. of the Lord, O king of ... 1697
Jer 22:29 earth, hear the w. of the Lord ... 1697
Jer 23:18 hath perceived and heard his w.? ... 1697
Jer 23:18 who hath marked his w., and heard ... 1697
Jer 23:28 and he that hath my w., ... 1697
Jer 23:28 let him speak my w. faithfully ... 1697
Jer 23:29 Is not my w. like as a fire? saith the ... 1697
Jer 23:36 every man's w. shall be his burden; ... 1697
Jer 23:38 Because ye say this w., the burden ... 1697
Jer 24:4 the w. of the Lord came unto me, ... 1697
Jer 25:1 The w. that came to Jeremiah ... 1697
Jer 25:3 w. of the Lord hath come unto me, ... 1697
Jer 26:1 Judah came this w. from the Lord, ... 1697
Jer 26:2 unto them; diminish not a w.: ... 1697
Jer 27:1 w. unto Jeremiah from the Lord, ... 1697
Jer 27:18 if the w. of the Lord be with them, ... 1697
Jer 28:7 hear thou now this w. that I speak ... 1697
Jer 28:9 the w. of the prophet shall come to ... 1697
Jer 28:12 the w. of the Lord came unto ... 1697
Jer 29:10 perform my good w. toward you, ... 1697
Jer 29:20 Hear ye...the w. of the Lord, ... 1697
Jer 29:30 the w. of the Lord unto Jeremiah, ... 1697
Jer 30:1 w. that came to Jeremiah from the ... 1697
Jer 31:10 Hear the w. of the Lord, O ye ... 1697
Jer 32:1 The w. that came to Jeremiah ... 1697
Jer 32:6 The w. of the Lord came unto me, ... 1697
Jer 32:8 according to the w. of the Lord, ... 1697
Jer 32:8 that this was the w. of the Lord. ... 1697
Jer 32:26 the w. of the Lord unto Jeremiah, ... 1697
Jer 33:1, 19 the w. of the Lord came unto ... 1697
Jer 33:23 the w. of the Lord came to ... 1697
Jer 34:1 The w. which came unto Jeremiah ... 1697
Jer 34:4 Yet hear the w. of the Lord, O ... 1697
Jer 34:5 for I have pronounced the w., ... 1697
Jer 34:8 w. that came unto Jeremiah from ... 1697
Jer 34:12 the w. of the Lord came to ... 1697
Jer 35:1 w. which came unto Jeremiah from ... 1697
Jer 35:12 the w. of the Lord unto Jeremiah, ... 1697
Jer 36:1 that this w. came unto Jeremiah ... 1697
Jer 36:27 the w. of the Lord came to ... 1697
Jer 37:6 w. of the Lord unto the prophet ... 1697
Jer 37:17 Is there any w. from the Lord? ... 1697
Jer 38:21 w. that the Lord hath shewed me: ... 1697
Jer 39:15 the w. of the Lord came unto ... 1697
Jer 40:1 The w. that came to Jeremiah from ... 1697
Jer 2:7 that the w. of the Lord came unto ... 1697
Jer 2:15 therefore hear the w. of the Lord, ... 1697
Jer 43:8 the w. of the Lord unto Jeremiah ... 1697
Jer 44:1 The w. that came to Jeremiah ... 1697
Jer 44:16 w. that thou hast spoken unto us ... 1697
Jer 44:24 Hear the w. of the Lord, all Judah ... 1697
Jer 44:26 hear ye the w. of the Lord, all ... 1697
Jer 45:1 The w. that Jeremiah the prophet ... 1697
Jer 46:1 The w. of the Lord which came to ... 1697
Jer 46:13 The w. that the Lord spake to ... 1697
Jer 47:1 The w. of the Lord that came to ... 1697
Jer 49:34 The w. of the Lord that came to ... 1697
Jer 50:1 w. that the Lord spake against ... 1697
Jer 51:59 w. which Jeremiah the prophet ... 1697
La 2:17 he hath fulfilled his w. that he had ... 565
Eze 1:3 w. of the Lord came expressly ... 1697
Eze 3:16 the w. of the Lord came unto me, ... 1697
Eze 3:17 hear the w. at my mouth, and give ... 1697
Eze 6:1 the w. of the Lord came unto me, ... 1697
Eze 6:3 hear the w. of the Lord God; ... 1697
Eze 7:1 the w. of the Lord came unto me, ... 1697
Eze 11:14 the w. of the Lord came unto me, ... 1697
Eze 12:1 w. of the Lord also came unto me, ... 1697
Eze 12:8 came the w. of the Lord unto me, ... 1697
Eze 12:17 the w. of the Lord came to me, ... 1697
Eze 12:21 the w. of the Lord came unto me, ... 1697
Eze 12:25 w. that I shall speak shall come to ... 1697
Eze 12:25 will I say the w., and will perform ... 1697
Eze 12:26 the w. of the Lord came to me, ... 1697
Eze 12:28 w. which I have spoken shall be ... 1697
Eze 13:1 the w. of the Lord came unto me, ... 1697
Eze 13:2 hearts, Hear ye the w. of the Lord; ... 1697
Eze 13:6 that they would confirm the w. ... 1697
Eze 14:2 the w. of the Lord came unto me, ... 1697
Eze 14:12 The w. of the Lord came unto me, ... 1697
Eze 15:1 the w. of the Lord came unto me, ... 1697
Eze 16:1 the w. of the Lord came unto me, ... 1697
Eze 16:35 O harlot, hear the w. of the Lord: ... 1697
Eze 17:1, 11 the w. of the Lord came unto me, ... 1697
Eze 18:1 The w. of the Lord came unto me ... 1697
Eze 20:2 came the w. of the Lord unto me, ... 1697
Eze 20:45 the w. of the Lord came unto me, ... 1697
Eze 20:46 and drop thy w. toward the south, ...
Eze 20:47 south, Hear the w. of the Lord; ... 1697
Eze 21:1 the w. of the Lord came unto me, ... 1697
Eze 21:2 drop thy w. toward the holy places, ...
Eze 21:8 the w. of the Lord came unto me, ... 1697
Eze 21:18 The w. of the Lord came unto me ... 1697
Eze 22:1, 17,23 the w. of the Lord came ... 1697
Eze 23:1 w. of the Lord came again unto me, ... 1697
Eze 24:1, 15 the w. of the Lord came unto me, ... 1697
Eze 24:20 The w. of the Lord came unto me, ... 1697
Eze 25:1 w. of the Lord came again unto me, ... 1697
Eze 25:3 Hear the w. of the Lord God; ... 1697
Eze 26:1 the w. of the Lord came unto me, ... 1697
Eze 27:1 w. of the Lord came again unto me, ... 1697
Eze 28:1 w. of the Lord came again unto me, ... 1697
Eze 28:11, 20 w. of the Lord came unto me, ... 1697
Eze 29:1, 17 w. of the Lord came unto me, ... 1697
Eze 30:1 w. of the Lord came again unto me, ... 1697
Eze 30:20 the w. of the Lord came unto me, ... 1697
Eze 31:1 the w. of the Lord came unto me, ... 1697
Eze 32:1, 17 w. of the Lord came unto me, ... 1697
Eze 33:1 the w. of the Lord came unto me, ... 1697
Eze 33:7 shalt hear the w. at my mouth, ... 1697
Eze 33:23 the w. of the Lord came unto me, ... 1697
Eze 33:30 what is the w. that cometh forth ... 1697
Eze 34:1 the w. of the Lord came unto me, ... 1697
Eze 34:7, 9 hear the w. of the Lord: ... 1697
Eze 35:1 the w. of the Lord came unto me, ... 1697
Eze 36:1 Israel, hear the w. of the Lord: ... 1697
Eze 36:4 Israel, hear the w. of the Lord God; ... 1697
Eze 36:16 the w. of the Lord came unto me, ... 1697
Eze 37:4 dry bones, hear the w. of the Lord. ... 1697
Eze 37:15 w. of the Lord came again unto me, ... 1697
Eze 38:1 the w. of the Lord came unto me, ... 1697
Da 3:28 and have changed the king's w., ... 4406
Da 4:17 demand by the w. of the holy ones: ... 3983
Da 4:31 the w. was in the king's mouth, ... 4406
Da 9:2 w. of the Lord came to Jeremiah ... 1697
Da 10:11 he had spoken this w. unto me, ... 1697
Ho 1:1 The w. of the Lord that came unto ... 1697
Ho 1:2 of the w. of the Lord by Hosea. ... 1699
Ho 4:1 Hear the w. of the Lord, ye ... 1697
Joe 1:1 w. of the Lord that came to Joel ... 1697
Joe 2:11 he is strong that executeth his w.: ... 1697
Am 3:1 Hear this w. that the Lord hath ... 1697
Am 4:1 Hear this w., ye kine of Bashan, ... 1697
Am 5:1 Hear ye this w. which I take up ... 1697
Am 7:16 hear thou the w. of the Lord: ... 1697
Am 7:16 not thy w. against the house of Isaac. ...
Am 8:12 and fro to seek the w. of the Lord ... ,1697
Jon 1:1 the w. of the Lord came unto Jonah ... ,1697
Jon 3:1 the w. of the Lord came unto Jonah ... ,1697
Jon 3:3 according to the w. of the Lord. ... ,1697
Jon 3:6 w. came unto the king of Nineveh, ... ,1697
Mic 1:1 w. of the Lord that came to Micah ... ,1697
Mic 4:2 the w. of the Lord from Jerusalem. ... ,1697
Hab 3:9 the oaths of the tribes, even thy w. ... 562
Zep 1:1 w. of the Lord which came unto ... 1697
Zep 2:5 the w. of the Lord is against you; ... 1697
Hag 1:1,3 came the w. of the Lord by Haggai ... 1697
Hag 2:1 the w. of the Lord by the prophet ... 1697
Hag 2:5 the w. that I covenanted with you ... 1697
Hag 2:10 came the w. of the Lord by Haggai ... 1697
Hag 2:20 w. of the Lord came unto Haggai ... 1697
Zec 1:1,7 w. of the Lord unto Zechariah, ... 1697
Zec 4:6 w. of the Lord unto Zerubbabel, ... 1697
Zec 4:8 the w. of the Lord came unto me, ... 1697
Zec 6:9 the w. of the Lord came unto me, ... 1697
Zec 7:1 that the w. of the Lord came unto ... 1697
Zec 7:4 came the w. of the Lord of hosts ... 1697
Zec 7:8 And the w. of the Lord came unto ... 1697
Zec 8:1,18 w. of the Lord of hosts came to me, ... 1697
Zec 9:1 The burden of the w. of the Lord ... 1697
Zec 11:11 knew that it was the w. of the Lord. ... 1697
Zec 12:1 The burden of the w. of the Lord ... 1697
Mal 1:1 The burden of the w. of the Lord ... 1697
Mt 2:8 bring me w. again, that I may ... 518
Mt 2:13 thou there until I bring thee w.: ... 2036
Mt 4:4 **by every w. that proceedeth out** ... 4487
Mt 8:8 but speak the w. only, and my ... 3056
Mt 8:16 he cast out the spirits with his w., ... 3056
Mt 12:32 **speaketh a w. against the Son of** ... 3056
Mt 12:36 **every idle w. that men shall speak,** 4487
Mt 13:19 **one heareth the w. of the kingdom,** 3056
Mt 13:20 **the same is he that heareth the w.,** 3056
Mt 13:21 **ariseth because of the w.,** ... 3056
Mt 13:22 **thorns is he that heareth the w.;** ... 3056
Mt 13:22 **choke the w., and he becometh** ... 3056
Mt 13:23 **ground is he that heareth the w.,** ... 3056
Mt 15:23 But he answered her not a w. ... 3056
Mt 18:16 **every w. may be established** ... 4487
Mt 22:46 man was able to answer him a w., ... 3056
Mt 26:75 remembered the w. of Jesus, ... 4487
Mt 27:14 he answered him to never a w.: ... 4487
Mt 28:8 did run to bring his disciples w. ... 518
Mk 2:2 he preached the w. unto them ... 3056
Mk 4:14 **The sower soweth the w.** ... 3056
Mk 4:15 **way side, where the w. is sown;** ... 3056
Mk 4:15 **taketh away the w. that was sown** 3056
Mk 4:16 **when they have heard the w.,** ... 3056
Mk 4:18 **thorns: such as hear the w.,** ... 3056
Mk 4:19 **choke the w., and it becometh** ... 3056
Mk 4:20 **such as hear the w., and receive it,** 3056
Mk 4:33 parables spake he the w. unto them, ... 3056
Mk 5:36 Jesus heard the w. that was spoken, ... 3056
Mk 7:13 **Making the w. of God of none** ... 3056
Mk 14:72 the w. that Jesus said unto him, ... 4487
Mk 16:20 and confirming the w. with signs ... 3056
Lu 1:2 and ministers of the w.; ... 3056
Lu 1:38 be it unto me according to thy w. ... 4487
Lu 2:29 in peace, according to thy w.: ... 4487

Lu 3:2 the w. of God came unto John the...... 4487
Lu 4:4 **alone, but by every w. of God.** 4487
Lu 4:32 for his w. was with power. 3056
Lu 4:36 saying, What a w. is this! for with...... 3056
Lu 5:1 upon him to hear the w. of God,........ 3056
Lu 5:5 at thy w. I will let down the net. 4487
Lu 7:7 but say in a w., and my servant......... 3056
Lu 8:11 **is this: The seed is the w. of God.**. 3056
Lu 8:12 **away the w. out of their hearts,**.... 3056
Lu 8:13 **they hear, receive the w. with joy;** .3056
Lu 8:15 **heart, having heard the w., keep it,**3056
Lu 8:21 **these which hear the w. of God**..... 3056
Lu 10:39 sat at Jesus' feet, and heard his w...... 3056
Lu 11:28 **hear the w. of God, and keep it**..... 3056
Lu 12:10 **speak a w. against the Son of man,**3056
Lu 22:61 remembered the w. of the Lord,........ 3056
Lu 24:19 mighty in deed and w. before God...... 3056
Joh 1:1 In the beginning was the W., ... 3056
Joh 1:1 and the W. was with God, ... 3056
Joh 1:1 and the W. was God. 3056
Joh 1:14 the W. was made flesh, and dwelt...... 3056
Joh 2:22 and the w. which Jesus had said......... 3056
Joh 4:41 believed because of his own w.;......... 3056
Joh 4:50 man believed the w. that Jesus had..... 3056
Joh 5:24 **He that heareth my w., and** 3056
Joh 5:38 **ye have not his w. abiding in you:**..3056
Joh 8:31 **If ye continue in my w., then are**.. 3056
Joh 8:37 **my w. hath no place in you,** 3056
Joh 8:43 **because ye cannot hear my w.**....... 3056
Joh 10:35 **unto whom the w. of God came,**.... 3056
Joh 12:48 **w. that I have spoken, the same**.... 3056
Joh 14:24 **the w. which ye hear is not mine,** ..3056
Joh 15:3 **w. which I have spoken unto you**...3056
Joh 15:20 **Remember the w. that I said**........ 3056
Joh 15:25 **that the w. might be fulfilled**........ 3056
Joh 17:6 **me; and they have kept thy w.** 3056
Joh 17:14 **I have given them thy w.; and**....... 3056
Joh 17:17 **through thy truth: thy w. is**......... 3056
Joh 17:20 **believe on me through their w.;**..... 3056
Ac 2:41 received his w. were baptized: 3056
Ac 4:4 them which heard the w. believed; 3056
Ac 4:29 boldness they may speak thy w., ... 3056
Ac 4:31 spake the w. of God with boldness. 3056
Ac 6:2 that we should leave the w. of God, ... 3056
Ac 6:4 and to the ministry of the w............. 3056
Ac 6:7 And the w. of God increased; and....... 3056
Ac 8:4 went every where preaching the w...... 3056
Ac 8:14 had received the w. of God, they....... 3056
Ac 8:25 and preached the w. of the Lord, ... 3056
Ac 10:36 The w. which God sent unto the........ 3056
Ac 10:37 That w., I say, ye know, which......... 4487
Ac 10:44 on all them which heard the w.......... 3056
Ac 11:1 had also received the w. of God......... 3056
Ac 11:16 remembered I the w. of the Lord,....... 4487
Ac 11:19 preaching the w. to none but unto...... 3056
Ac 12:24 the w. of God grew and multiplied...... 3056
Ac 13:5 they preached the w. of God in the 3056
Ac 13:7 and desired to hear the w. of God...... 3056
Ac 13:15 if ye have any w. of exhortation for.... 3056
Ac 13:26 to you is the w. of this salvation........ 3056
Ac 13:44 together to hear the w. of God........... 3056
Ac 13:46 It was necessary that the w. of God... 3056
Ac 13:48 and glorified the w. of the Lord: 3056
Ac 13:49 the w. of the Lord was published........ 3056
Ac 14:3 which gave testimony unto the w. 3056
Ac 14:25 they had preached the w. in Perga, ... 3056
Ac 15:7 should hear the w. of the gospel, ... 3056
Ac 15:35 and preaching the w. of the Lord, ... 3056
Ac 15:36 have preached the w. of the Lord, ... 3056
Ac 16:6 of the Holy Ghost to preach the w..... 3056
Ac 16:32 spake unto him the w. of the Lord, ... 3056
Ac 17:11 received the w. with all readiness....... 3056
Ac 17:13 w. of God was preached of Paul........ 3056
Ac 18:11 teaching the w. of God among them.... 3056
Ac 19:10 in Asia heard the w. of the Lord........ 3056
Ac 19:20 So mightily grew the w. of God and.... 3056
Ac 20:32 to God, and to the w. of his grace, ... 3056
Ac 22:22 gave him audience unto this w., ... 3056
Ac 28:25 after that Paul had spoken one w., ... 4487
Ro 9:6 Not as though the w. of God hath...... 3056
Ro 9:9 For this is the w. of promise, At 3056
Ro 10:8 w. is nigh thee, even in thy mouth, ... 4487
Ro 10:8 the w. of faith, which we preach; 4487
Ro 10:17 and hearing by the w. of God. 4487
Ro 15:18 obedient, by w. and deed, ... 3056
1Co 4:20 the kingdom of God is not in w.,........ 3056
1Co 12:8 given by the Spirit the w. of wisdom;.. 3056
1Co 12:8 to another the w. of knowledge by 3056
1Co 14:36 came the w. of God out from you? 3056
2Co 1:18 our w. toward you was not yea and.... 3056
2Co 2:17 many, which corrupt the w. of God: ... 3056
2Co 4:2 the w. of God deceitfully; 3056
2Co 5:19 unto us the w. of reconciliation. 3056
2Co 6:7 By the w. of truth, by the power of ... 3056
2Co 10:11 such as we are in w. by letters when.. 3056
2Co 13:1 shall every w. be established............ 4487
Ga 5:14 all the law is fulfilled in one w., ... 4487
Ga 6:6 Let him that is taught in the w. 4487
Eph 1:13 after that ye heard the w. of truth,..... 4487
Eph 5:26 the washing of water by the w., ... 4487
Eph 6:17 the Spirit, which is the w. of God: 4487
Php 1:14 bold to speak the w. without fear. 3056
Php 2:16 Holding forth the w. of life; that I 3056
Col 1:5 heard before in the w. of the truth..... 3056
Col 1:25 me for you, to fulfil the w. of God;..... 3056
Col 3:16 Let the w. of Christ dwell in you 3056
Col 3:17 whatsoever ye do in w. or deed, do ... 3056
1Th 1:5 came not unto you in w. only, ... 3056
1Th 1:6 received the w. in much affliction, ... 3056
1Th 1:8 you sounded out the w. of the Lord.... 3056
1Th 2:13 w. of God which ye heard of us,......... 3056
1Th 2:13 ye received it not as the w. of men, ... 3056
1Th 2:13 but as it is in truth, the w. of God, ... 3056
1Th 4:15 say unto you by the w. of the Lord, ... 3056
2Th 2:2 neither by spirit, nor by w.,.............. 3056
2Th 2:15 whether by w., or our epistle............ 3056
2Th 2:17 and stablish you in every good w. 3056
2Th 3:1 the w. o the Lord may have free 3056
2Th 3:14 obey not our w. by this epistle, ... 3056
1Ti 4:5 is sanctified by the w. of God and 3056
1Ti 4:12 an example of the believers, in w., ... 3056
1Ti 5:17 they who labour in the w. and........... 3056
2Ti 2:9 but the w. of God is not bound. 3056
2Ti 2:15 rightly divding the w. of truth. 3056
2Ti 2:17 their w. will eat as doth a canker: 3056
2Ti 4:2 Preach the w.; be instant in.............. 3056
Tit 1:3 in due times manifested his w. 3056
Tit 1:9 Holding fast the faithful w. as he........ 3056
Tit 2:5 the w. of God be not blasphemed. 3056
Heb 1:3 all things by the w. of his power, ... 4487
Heb 2:2 For if the w. spoken by angels was 3056
Heb 4:2 w. preached did not profit them, ... 3056
Heb 4:12 For the w. of God is quick, and........ 3056
Heb 5:13 unskilful in the w. of righteousness: 3056
Heb 6:5 have tasted the good w. of God, ... 4487
Heb 7:28 but the w. of the oath, which was...... 3056
Heb 11:3 were framed by the w. of God, ... 4487
Heb 12:19 that the w. should not be spoken 3056
Heb 12:27 this w., Yet once more, signifieth............
Heb 13:7 spoken unto you the w. of God:.......... 3056
Heb 13:22 suffer the w. of exhortation:.............. 3056
Jas 1:18 begat he us with the w. of truth, ... 3056
Jas 1:21 with meekness the engrafted w.,........ 3056
Jas 1:22 But be ye doers of the w., and not 3056
Jas 1:23 For if any be a hearer of the w., ... 3056
Jas 3:2 If any man offend not in w., the......... 3056
1Pe 1:23 by the w. of God, which liveth and..... 3056
1Pe 1:25 w. of the Lord endureth for ever. 4487
1Pe 1:25 w. which by the gospel is preached 4487
1Pe 2:2 desire the sincere milk of the w., ... 3050
1Pe 2:8 to them which stumble at the w.,........ 3056
1Pe 3:1 that, if any obey not the w., they....... 3056
1Pe 3:1 also may without the w. be won 3056
2Pe 1:19 also a more sure w. of prophecy;....... 3056
2Pe 3:5 by the w. of God the heavens were.... 3056
2Pe 3:7 by the same w. are kept in store, ... 3056
1Jo 1:1 have handled, of the W. of life;.......... 3056
1Jo 1:10 him a liar, and his w. is not in us. 3056
1Jo 2:5 But whoso keepeth his w., in him 3056
1Jo 2:7 the w. which ye have heard from 3056
1Jo 2:14 and the w. of God abideth in you. 3056
1Jo 3:18 children, let us not love in w.,........... 3056
1Jo 5:7 the Father, the W., and the Holy........ 3056
Re 1:2 Who bare record of the w. of God,..... 3056
Re 1:9 for the w. of God, and for the........... 3056
Re 3:8 **and hast kept my w., and hast not** .3056
Re 3:10 **hast kept the w. of my patience,**.... 3056
Re 6:9 that were slain for the w. of God, ... 3056
Re 12:11 and by the w. of their testimony; 3056
Re 19:13 his name is called The W. of God, ... 3056
Re 20:4 and for the w. of God, and which....... 3056

WORD'S

2Sa 7:21 For thy w. sake, and according to...... 1697
Mk 4:17 **persecution ariseth for...w. sake,**... 3056

WORDS

Ge 24:30 when he heard the w. of Rebekah...... 1697
Ge 24:52 Abraham's servant heard their w.,...... 1697
Ge 27:34 Esau heard the w. of his father,......... 1697
Ge 27:42 w. of Esau her elder son were told 1697
Ge 31:1 he heard the w. of Laban's sons, ... 1697
Ge 34:18 And their w. pleased Hamor, and...... 1697
Ge 37:8 more for his dreams, and for his w..... 1697
Ge 39:17 unto him according to these w., ... 1697
Ge 39:19 master heard the w. of his wife, ... 1697
Ge 42:16 prison, that your w. may be proved,... 1697
Ge 42:20 so shall your w. be verified, and ye.... 1697
Ge 43:7 according to the tenor of these w.:..... 1697
Ge 44:6 he spake unto them these same w....... 1697
Ge 44:7 Wherefore saith my lord these w. 1697
Ge 44:10 let it be according unto your w. 1697
Ge 44:24 we told him the w. of my lord. 1697
Ge 45:27 they told him all the w. of Joseph,...... 1697
Ge 49:21 hind let loose: he giveth goodly w....... 561
Ex 4:15 him, and put w. in his mouth:........... 1697
Ex 4:28 told Aaron all the w. of the Lord........ 1697
Ex 4:30 spake all the w. which the Lord......... 1697
Ex 5:9 and let them not regard vain w. 1697
Ex 19:6 are the w. which thou shalt speak 1697
Ex 19:7 w. which the Lord commanded him..... 1697
Ex 19:8 Moses returned the w. of the people .. 1697
Ex 19:9 Moses told the w. of the people 1697
Ex 20:1 God spake all these w., saying, ... 1697
Ex 23:8 perverteth the w. of the righteous...... 1697
Ex 24:3 the people all the w. of the Lord,....... 1697
Ex 24:3 w. which the Lord hath said will 1697
Ex 24:4 Moses wrote all the w. of the Lord, ... 1697
Ex 24:8 with you concerning all these w.. 1697
Ex 34:1 the w. that were in the first tables, ... 1697
Ex 34:27 unto Moses, Write thou these w.: 1697
Ex 34:27 after the tenor of these w. I have 1697
Ex 34:28 the tables the w. of the covenant, ... 1697
Ex 35:1 are the w. which the Lord hath 1697
Nu 11:24 told the people the w. of the Lord,..... 1697
Nu 12:6 And he said, Hear now my w.: If........ 1697
Nu 16:31 an end of speaking all these w.,......... 1697
Nu 22:7 and spake unto him the w. of Balak. ... 1697
Nu 24:4, 16 which heard the w. of God,............ 561
De 1:1 the w. which Moses spake unto all..... 1697
De 1:34 the Lord heard the voice of your w., .. 1697
De 2:26 king of Heshbon with w. of peace,...... 1697
De 4:10 and I will make them hear my w.,...... 1697
De 4:12 ye heard the voice of the w., but....... 1697
De 4:36 heardest his w. out of the midst 1697
De 5:22 w. the Lord spake unto all your......... 1697
De 5:28 Lord heard the voice of your w., ... 1697
De 5:28 the voice of the w. of this people, ... 1697
De 6:6 these w., which I command thee......... 1697
De 9:10 written according to all the w., ... 1697
De 10:2 the w. that were in the first tables..... 1697
De 11:18 lay up these my w. in your heart 1697
De 12:28 hear all these w. which I command.... 1697
De 13:3 hearken unto the w. of that prophet,... 1697
De 16:19 and pervert the w. of the righteous. ... 1697
De 17:19 to keep all the w. of this law and....... 1697
De 18:18 and will put my w. in his mouth;........ 1697
De 18:19 w. which he shall speak in my name, .. 1697
De 27:3 upon them all the w. of this law,........ 1697
De 27:8 upon the stones all the w. of this law.. 1697
De 27:26 not all the w. of this law to do them... 1697
De 28:14 w. which I command thee this day,..... 1697
De 28:58 w. of this law that are written in........ 1697
De 29:1 These are the w. of the covenant,....... 1697
De 29:9 therefore the w. of this covenant, ... 1697
De 29:19 he heareth the w. of this curse,......... 1697
De 29:29 we may do all the w. of this law. 1697
De 31:1 and spake these w. unto all Israel. 1697
De 31:12 observe to do all the w. of this law: 1697
De 31:24 an end of writing the w. of this law ... 1697
De 31:28 I may speak these w. in their ears, ... 1697
De 31:30 of Israel the w. of this song, ... 1697
De 32:1 hear, O earth, the w. of my mouth. 561
De 32:44 and spake all the w. of this song........ 1697
De 32:45 end of speaking all these w. to all 1697
De 32:46 hearts unto all the w. which I testify... 1697
De 32:46 observe to do, all the w. of this law. .. 1697
De 33:3 every one shall receive of thy w.. 1703

Jos 1:18 and will not hearken unto thy w. 1697
Jos 2:21 According unto your w., so be it. 1697
Jos 3:9 hear the w. of the Lord your God. 1697
Jos 8:34 he read all the w. of the law, 1697
Jos 22:30 the w. that the children of Reuben 1697
Jos 24:26 Joshua wrote these w. in the book 1697
Jos 24:27 it hath heard all the w. of the Lord 561
Jg 2:4 angel of the Lord spake these w. 1697
Jg 9:3 all the men of Shechem all these w.: 1697
Jg 9:30 of the city heard the w. of Gaal 1697
Jg 11:10 we do not so according to thy w. 1697
Jg 11:11 Jephthah uttered all his w. before 1697
Jg 11:28 not unto the w. of Jephthah. 1697
Jg 13:12 said, Now let thy w. come to pass. 1697
Jg 16:16 she pressed him daily with her w., 1697
1Sa 3:19 none of his w. fall to the ground. 1697
1Sa 8:10 Samuel told all the w. of the Lord 1697
1Sa 8:21 heard all the w. of the people, 1697
1Sa 15:1 unto the voice of the w. of the Lord. 1697
1Sa 15:24 of the Lord, and thy w.: 1697
1Sa 17:11 heard those w. of the Philistine, 1697
1Sa 17:23 spake according to the same w.: 1697
1Sa 17:31 w. were heard which David spake, 1697
1Sa 18:23 Saul's servants spake those w. in 1697
1Sa 18:26 his servants told David these w., 1697
1Sa 21:12 And David laid up these w. in his 1697
1Sa 24:7 stayed his servants with these w., 1697
1Sa 24:9 Wherefore hearest thou men's w., 1697
1Sa 24:16 made an end of speaking these w. 1697
1Sa 25:9 according to all those w. in the 1697
1Sa 25:24 and hear the w. of thine handmaid. 1697
1Sa 26:19 the king hear the w. of his servant. 1697
1Sa 28:20 afraid, because of the w. of Samuel: 1697
1Sa 28:21 hearkened unto the w. which thou 1697
2Sa 3:8 wroth for the w. of Ish-bosheth, 1697
2Sa 7:17 According to all these w., and 1697
2Sa 7:28 and thy w. be true, and thou hast 1697
2Sa 14:3 So Joab put the w. in her mouth. 1697
2Sa 14:19 w. in the mouth of thine handmaid: 1697
2Sa 19:43 w. of the men of Judah were fiercer 1697
2Sa 19:43 than the w. of the men of Israel. 1697
2Sa 20:17 Hear the w. of thine handmaid. 1697
2Sa 22:1 unto the Lord the w. of this song 1697
2Sa 23:1 Now these be the last w. of David 1697
1Ki 1:14 in after thee, and confirm thy w. 1697
1Ki 3:12 I have done according to thy w.: 1697
1Ki 5:7 Hiram heard the w. of Solomon, 1697
1Ki 8:59 And let these my w., wherewith 1697
1Ki 10:7 Howbeit I believed not the w., 1697
1Ki 12:7 speak good w. to them, that they 1697
1Ki 13:11 w. which he had spoken unto the 1697
1Ki 21:27 when Ahab heard those w., that he 1697
1Ki 22:13 w. of the prophets declare good 1697
2Ki 1:7 to meet you, and told you these w.? 1697
2Ki 6:12 the w. that thou speakest in thy 1697
2Ki 6:30 king heard the w. of the woman, 1697
2Ki 18:20 (but they are but vain w.,) I have 1697
2Ki 18:27 and to thee, to speak these w.? 1697
2Ki 18:37 told him the w. of Rab-shakeh. 1697
2Ki 19:4 will hear all the w. of Rab-shakeh, 1697
2Ki 19:4 reprove the w. which the Lord thy 1697
2Ki 19:6 of the w. which thou hast heard, 1697
2Ki 19:16 hear the w. of Sennacherib, which 1697
2Ki 22:11 king had heard the w. of the book 1697
2Ki 22:13 the w. of this book that is found: 1697
2Ki 22:13 hearkened unto the w. of this book, 1697
2Ki 22:16 the w. of the book which the king 1697
2Ki 22:18 the w. which thou hast heard; 1697
2Ki 23:2 the w. of the book of the covenant 1697
2Ki 23:3 to perform the w. of this covenant 1697
2Ki 23:16 who proclaimed these w. 1697
2Ki 23:24 might perform the w. of the law 1697
1Ch 17:15 According to these w., and 1697
1Ch 23:27 by the last w. of David the Levites 1697
1Ch 25:5 the king's seer in the w. of God, 1697
2Ch 9:6 I believed not their w., until I came, 1697
2Ch 10:7 speak good w. to them, they will 1697
2Ch 11:4 they obeyed the w. of the Lord, 1697
2Ch 15:8 And when Asa heard these w., and 1697
2Ch 18:12 the w. of the prophets declare good 1697
2Ch 29:15 of the king by the w. of the Lord, 1697
2Ch 29:30 unto the Lord with the w. of David, 1697
2Ch 32:8 the w. of Hezekiah king of Judah. 1697
2Ch 33:18 w. of the seers that spake to him 1697
2Ch 34:19 king had heard the w. of the law, 1697
2Ch 34:21 the w. of the book that is found: 1697
2Ch 34:26 the w. which thou hast heard; 1697
2Ch 34:27 heardest his w. against this place, 1697
2Ch 34:30 the w. of the book of the covenant 1697
2Ch 34:31 to perform the w. of the covenant 1697
2Ch 35:22 hearkened not unto the w. of Necho 1697
2Ch 36:16 despised his w., and misused his 1697
Ezr 7:11 of the w. of the commandments 1697
Ezr 9:4 trembled at the w. of the God of 1697
Ne 1:1 The w. of Nehemiah the son of 1697
Ne 1:4 when I heard these w., that I sat 1697
Ne 2:18 king's w. that he had spoken unto 1697
Ne 5:6 when I heard their cry and these w. 1697
Ne 6:6 be their king, according to these w. 1697
Ne 6:7 to the king, according to these w. 1697
Ne 6:19 me, and uttered my w. to him. 1697
Ne 8:9 when they heard the w. of the law. 1697
Ne 8:12 the w. that were declared unto 1697
Ne 8:13 to understand the w. of the law. 1697
Ne 9:8 seed, and hast performed thy w.; 1697
Es 4:9 and told Esther the w. of Mordecai. 1697
Es 4:12 they told to Mordecai Esther's w. 1697
Es 9:26 for all the w. of this letter. 1697
Es 9:30 with w. of peace and truth, 1697
Job 4:4 Thy w. have upholden him that 4405
Job 6:3 therefore my w. are swallowed up. 1697
Job 6:10 concealed the w. of the Holy One. 561
Job 6:25 How forcible are right w.! but what 561
Job 6:26 Do ye imagine to reprove w., and 4405
Job 8:2 w. of thy mouth be like a strong 561
Job 8:10 and utter w. out of their heart? 4405
Job 9:14 out my w. to reason with him? 1697
Job 11:2 the multitude of w. be answered? 1697
Job 12:11 Doth not the ear try w.? and the 4405
Job 15:13 lettest such w. go out of thy mouth? 4405
Job 16:3 Shall vain w. have an end? 1697
Job 16:4 I could heap up w. against you, 4405
Job 18:2 will it be ere ye make an end of w.? 4405
Job 19:2 and break me in pieces with w.? 4405
Job 19:23 Oh that my w. were now written! 4405
Job 22:22 and lay up his w. in thine heart. 561
Job 23:5 w. which he would answer me, 4405
Job 23:12 have esteemed the w. of his mouth 561
Job 26:4 To whom hast thou uttered w.? 4405
Job 29:22 After my w. they spake not again; 1697
Job 31:40 The w. of Job are ended. 1697
Job 32:11 I waited for your w.; I gave ear 1697
Job 32:12 Job, or that answered his w.: 561
Job 32:14 not directed his w. against me: 4405
Job 33:1 and hearken to all my w. 1697
Job 33:3 My w. shall be of the uprightness 561
Job 33:5 me, set thy w. in order before me,
Job 33:8 I have heard the voice of thy w., 4405
Job 34:2 Hear my w., O ye wise men; and 4405
Job 34:3 For the ear trieth w., as the mouth 4405
Job 34:16 hearken to the voice of my w. 4405
Job 34:35 and his w. were without wisdom. 1697
Job 34:37 and multiplieth his w. against God. 561
Job 35:16 he multiplieth w. with knowledge 4405
Job 36:4 For truly my w. shall not be false: 4405
Job 38:2 counsel by w. without knowledge? 4405
Job 41:3 will he speak soft w. unto thee?
Job 42:7 had spoken these w. unto Job, 1697
Ps 5:1 Give ear to my w., O Lord, consider 561
Ps 7:*title* concerning the w. of Cush 1697
Ps 12:6 The w. of the Lord are pure w. 565
Ps 18:*title* unto the Lord the w. of this song 1697
Ps 19:4 their w. to the end of the world. 4405
Ps 19:14 Let the w. of my mouth, and the 561
Ps 22:1 and from the w. of my roaring? 1697
Ps 36:3 The w. of his mouth are iniquity 1697
Ps 50:17 and castest my w. behind thee. 1697
Ps 52:4 Thou lovest all devouring w., 1697
Ps 54:2 give ear to the w. of my mouth. 561
Ps 55:21 w. of his mouth were smoother
Ps 55:21 his w. were softer than oil, yet were 1697
Ps 56:5 Every day they wrest my w.: all 1697
Ps 59:12 the w. of their lips let them even 1697
Ps 64:3 shoot their arrows, even bitter w.: 1697
Ps 78:1 your ears to the w. of my mouth. 561
Ps 106:12 Then believed they his w.; they 1697
Ps 107:11 rebelled against the w. of God, 561
Ps 109:3 me about also with w. of hatred; 1697
Ps 119:57 have said that I would keep thy w. 1697
Ps 119:103 sweet are thy w. unto my taste! 565
Ps 119:130 entrance of thy w. giveth light; 1697
Ps 119:139 mine enemies have forgotten thy w. 1697
Ps 138:4 they hear the w. of thy mouth. 561
Ps 141:6 they shall hear my w.; for they are 561
Pr 1:2 to perceive the w. of understanding; 561
Pr 1:6 the w. of the wise, and their dark 1697
Pr 1:21 in the city she uttereth her w., 561
Pr 1:23 will make known my w. unto you. 1697
Pr 2:1 My son, if thou wilt receive my w., 561
Pr 2:16 which flattereth with her w.; 561
Pr 4:4 Let thine heart retain my w.: 1697
Pr 4:5 decline from the w. of my mouth. 561
Pr 4:20 My son, attend to my w.; incline 1697
Pr 5:7 not from the w. of my mouth. 561
Pr 6:2 snared with the w. of thy mouth, 561
Pr 6:2 are taken with the w. of thy mouth. 561
Pr 7:1 My son, keep my w., and lay up my 561
Pr 7:5 which flattereth with her w. 561
Pr 7:24 and attend to the w. of my mouth. 561
Pr 8:8 All the w. of my mouth are in 561
Pr 10:19 multitude of w. there wanteth not 1697
Pr 12:6 w. of the wicked are to lie in wait 1697
Pr 15:1 but grievous w. stir up anger. 1697
Pr 15:26 the w. of the pure are pleasant w.
Pr 16:24 Pleasant w. are as an honeycomb, 561
Pr 17:27 that hath knowledge spareth his w.: 561
Pr 18:4 The w. of the man's mouth are as 1697
Pr 18:8 w. of a talebearer are as wounds, 1697
Pr 19:7 he pursueth them with w., yet they 561
Pr 19:27 to err from the w. of knowledge. 561
Pr 22:12 the w. of the transgressor. 1697
Pr 22:17 hear the w. of the wise, and apply 1697
Pr 22:21 the certainty of the w. of truth; 561
Pr 22:21 mightest answer the w. of truth 561
Pr 23:8 vomit up, and lose thy sweet w. 1697
Pr 23:9 will despise the wisdom of thy w. 4405
Pr 23:12 thine ears to the w. of knowledge. 561
Pr 26:22 w. of a talebearer are as wounds, 1697
Pr 29:19 servant will not be corrected by w.: 1697
Pr 29:20 thou a man that is hasty in his w.? 1697
Pr 30:1 the w. of Agur the son of Jakeh, 1697
Pr 30:6 Add thou not unto his w., lest he 1697
Pr 31:1 The w. of king Lemuel, the 1697
Ec 1:1 The w. of the Preacher, the son of 1697
Ec 5:2 earth: therefore let thy w. be few. 1697
Ec 5:3 voice is known by multitude of w. 1697
Ec 5:7 and many w. there are also divers 1697
Ec 7:21 heed unto all w. that are spoken; 1697
Ec 9:16 despised, and his w. are not heard. 1697
Ec 9:17 w. of wise men are heard in quiet 1697
Ec 10:12 The w. of a wise man's mouth are 1697
Ec 10:13 beginning of the w. of his mouth 1697
Ec 10:14 A fool also is full of w. a man 1697
Ec 12:10 sought to find out acceptable w.: 1697
Ec 12:10 was upright, even w. of truth. 1697
Ec 12:11 The w. of the wise are as goads, 1697
Isa 29:11 as the w. of a book that is sealed, 1697
Isa 29:18 the deaf hear the w. of the book, 1697
Isa 31:2 evil, and will not call back his w.: 1697
Isa 32:7 to destroy the poor with lying w., 561
Isa 36:5 thou, (but they are but vain w.) I 1697
Isa 36:12 and to thee to speak these w.? 1697
Isa 36:13 Hear ye the w. of the great king, 1697
Isa 36:22 and told him the w. of Rabshakeh. 1697
Isa 37:4 God will hear the w. of Rabshakeh, 1697
Isa 37:4 will reprove the w. which the Lord 1697
Isa 37:6 of the w. that thou hast heard, 1697
Isa 37:17 and hear all the w. of Sennacherib, 1697
Isa 41:26 there is none that heareth your w. 561
Isa 51:16 I have put my w. in thy mouth, 1697
Isa 58:13 nor speaking thine own w.: 1697
Isa 59:13 from the heart w. of falsehood. 1697
Isa 59:21 w. which I have put in thy mouth, 1697
Jer 1:1 w. of Jeremiah the son of Hilkiah, 1697
Jer 1:9 I have put my w. in my mouth. 1697
Jer 3:12 Go and proclaim these w. toward 1697
Jer 5:14 I will make my w. in thy mouth fire, 1697
Jer 6:19 have not hearkened into my w., 1697
Jer 7:4 Trust ye not in lying, saying, 1697
Jer 7:8 Behold, ye trust in long w., that 1697
Jer 7:27 shalt speak all these w. unto them; 1697
Jer 11:2 Hear ye the w. of this covenant, 1697
Jer 11:3 obeyeth not the w. of this covenant, 1697
Jer 11:6 Proclaim all these w. in the cities 1697
Jer 11:6 Hear ye the w. of this covenant, 1697
Jer 11:8 them all the w. of the covenant, 1697
Jer 11:10 which refused to her my w.; 1697
Jer 12:6 though they speak far w. unto thee.

Jer 13:10 which refuse to hear any w., which 1697
Jer 15:16 Thy w. were found and I did eat........ 1697
Jer 16:10 shalt shew this people all these w., ... 1697
Jer 18:2 I will cause thee to hear my w.. 1697
Jer 18:18 us not give heed to my of his w.. 1697
Jer 19:2 there the w. that I shall tell thee, ... 1697
Jer 19:15 that they might not hear my w.. 1697
Jer 22:5 But if ye will not hear these w., I...... 1697
Jer 23:9 because of the w. of his holiness....... 1697
Jer 23:16 not unto the w. of the prophets 1697
Jer 23:22 caused my people to hear my w.,........ 1697
Jer 23:30 steal my w. every one from his 1697
Jer 23:36 perverted the w. of the living God,..... 1697
Jer 25:8 Because ye have not heard my w.,..... 1697
Jer 25:13 my w. which I have announced 1697
Jer 25:30 thou against them all these w., ... 1697
Jer 26:2 w. that I command thee to speak 1697
Jer 26:5 hearken to the w. of my servants....... 1697
Jer 26:7 Jeremiah speaking these w. in the 1697
Jer 26:12 city all the w. that ye have heard....... 1697
Jer 26:15 to speak all these w. in your ears. 1697
Jer 26:20 according to all the w. of Jeremiah:..... 1697
Jer 26:21 and all the princes heard his w., ... 1697
Jer 27:12 of Judah according all these w.,.......... 1697
Jer 27:14 not unto the w. of the prophets 1697
Jer 27:16 not to the w. of your prophets 1697
Jer 28:6 perform thy w. which thou hast 1697
Jer 29:1 w. of the letter that Jeremiah 1697
Jer 29:19 they have not hearkened to my w., ... 1697
Jer 29:23 have spoken lying w. in my name,..... 1697
Jer 30:2 all the w. that I have spoken unto 1697
Jer 30:4 are the w. that the Lord spake.......... 1697
Jer 34:6 spake all these w. unto Zedekiah........ 1697
Jer 34:18 w. of the covenant which they had 1697
Jer 35:13 instruction to hearken to my w.?........ 1697
Jer 35:14 w. of Jonadab the son of Rechab,....... 1697
Jer 36:2 write...all the w. that I have spoken ... 1697
Jer 36:4 of Jeremiah all the w. of the Lord, ... 1697
Jer 36:6 the w. of the Lord in the ears of the .. 1697
Jer 36:8 in the book the w. of the Lord 1697
Jer 36:10 in the book the w. of Jeremiah 1697
Jer 36:11 of the book all the w. of the Lord, ... 1697
Jer 36:13 them all the w. that he had heard,..... 1697
Jer 36:16 when they had heard all the w.,......... 1697
Jer 36:16 surely tell the king of all these w.. 1697
Jer 36:17 write all these w. at his mouth?......... 1697
Jer 36:18 pronounced all these w. unto me......... 1697
Jer 36:20 all the w. in the ears of the king......... 1697
Jer 36:24 servants that heard all these w.. 1697
Jer 36:27 w. which Baruch wrote at the 1697
Jer 36:28 the former w. that were in the first.... 1697
Jer 36:32 w. of the book which Jehoiakim.......... 1697
Jer 36:32 besides unto them many like w.. 1697
Jer 37:2 hearken unto the w. of the Lord, ... 1697
Jer 38:1 the w. that Jeremiah had spoken......... 1697
Jer 38:4 in speaking such w. unto them:......... 1697
Jer 38:24 Let no man know of these w., and..... 1697
Jer 38:27 w. that the king had commanded........ 1697
Jer 39:16 bring my w. upon this city for evil,..... 1697
Jer 42:4 your God according to your w.; 1697
Jer 43:1 the people all the w. of the Lord........ 1697
Jer 43:1 him to them, even all these w., ... 1697
Jer 44:28 shall know whose w. shall stand,......... 1697
Jer 44:29 know that my w. shall surely stand..... 1697
Jer 45:1 he had written these w. in a book...... 1697
Jer 51:60 all these w. that are written against.... 1697
Jer 51:61 see, and shalt read all these w.; 1697
Jer 51:64 Thus far are the w. of Jeremiah. 1697
Eze 2:6 them, neither be afraid of their w.,..... 1697
Eze 2:6 be not afraid of their w., nor be......... 1697
Eze 2:7 thou shalt speak my w. unto them,..... 1697
Eze 3:4 and speak with my w. unto them. 1697
Eze 3:6 w. thou canst not understand. 1697
Eze 3:10 my w. that I shall speak unto thee 1697
Eze 12:28 shall none of my w. be prolonged....... 1697
Eze 33:31 they hear thy w., but they will not 1697
Eze 33:32 for they hear thy w., but they do....... 1697
Eze 35:13 have multiplied your w. against me: 1697
Da 2:9 corrupt w. to speak before me, ... 4406
Da 5:10 by reason of the w. of the king and 4406
Da 6:14 the king, when he heard these w., ... 4406
Da 7:11 great w. which the horn spake:......... 4406
Da 7:25 great w. against the most High,......... 4406
Da 9:12 And he hath confirmed his w.,........... 1697
Da 10:6 his w. like the voice of a multitude. 1697
Da 10:9 Yet heard I the voice of his w.: 1697
Da 10:9 when I heard the voice of his w.,....... 1697
Da 10:11 understand the w. that I speak 1697
Da 10:12 before thy God, thy w. were heard, ... 1697
Da 10:12 heard, and I am come for thy w.......... 1697
Da 10:15 he had spoken such w. unto me,........ 1697
Da 12:4 O Daniel, shut up the w., and seal..... 1697
Da 12:9 for the w. are closed up and sealed 1697
Ho 6:5 slain them by the w. of my mouth: 561
Ho 10:4 They have spoken w., swearing.......... 1697
Ho 14:2 Take with you w., and turn to the...... 1697
Am 1:1 The w. of Amos, who was among 1697
Am 7:10 land is not able to bear all his w.. 1697
Am 8:11 but of hearing the w. of the Lord:...... 1697
Mic 2:7 do not my w. do good to him that...... 1697
Hag 1:12 and the w. of Haggai the prophet, ... 1697
Zec 1:6 But my w. and my statutes, which 1697
Zec 1:13 with good w. and comfortable w.. 1697
Zec 7:7 the w. which the Lord hath cried 1697
Zec 7:12 w. which the Lord of hosts hath 1697
Zec 8:9 w. by the mouth of the prophets,....... 1697
Mal 2:17 wearied the Lord with your w.. 1697
Mal 3:13 Your w. have been stout against 1697
Mt 10:14 **nor hear your w., when ye depart..** *3056*
Mt 12:37 **by thy w. thou shalt be justified,...** *3056*
Mt 12:37 **thy w. thou shalt be condemned....** *3056*
Mt 22:22 When they had heard these w., ...
Mt 24:35 **but my w. shall not pass away......** *3056*
Mt 26:44 third time, saying the same w.. .... *3056*
Mk 8:38 **be ashamed of me and of my w.....** *3056*
Mk 10:24 disciples were astonished at his w.. .... *3056*
Mk 12:13 Herodians, to catch him in his w......... *3056*
Mk 13:31 **but my w. shall not pass away......** *3056*
Mk 14:39 prayed, and spake the same w........... *3056*
Lu 1:20 because thou believest not my w.,...... *3056*
Lu 3:4 in the book of the w. of Esaias.......... *3056*
Lu 4:22 wondered at the gracious w. which..... *3056*
Lu 9:26 **be ashamed of me and of my w.,...** *3056*
Lu 20:20 they might take hold of his w., ... *3056*
Lu 20:26 they could not take hold of his w. *4487*
Lu 21:33 **but my w. shall not pass away......** *3056*
Lu 23:9 questioned with him in many w.; *3056*
Lu 24:8 And they remembered his w., ... *4487*
Lu 24:11 their w. seemed to them as idle......... *4487*
Lu 24:44 **These are the w. which I spake ....** *3056*
Joh 3:34 hath sent speaketh the w. of God:...... *4487*
Joh 5:47 **how shall ye believe my w.?.........** *4487*
Joh 6:63 **the w. that I speak unto you,.........** *4487*
Joh 6:68 go? thou hast the w. of eternal life. *4487*
Joh 7:9 he had said these w. unto them, ...
Joh 8:20 w. spake Jesus in the treasury,.......... *4487*
Joh 8:30 As he spake these w., many believed........
Joh 8:47 **that is of God heareth God's w.:.....** *4487*
Joh 9:22 These w. spake his parents, because ....
Joh 9:40 which were with him heard these w.,........
Joh 10:21 the w. of him that hath a devil.......... *4487*
Joh 12:47 **And if any man hear my w., and....** *4487*
Joh 12:48 **and receiveth not my w., hath......** *4487*
Joh 14:10 **w. that I speak unto you I speak...** *4487*
Joh 14:23 **man love me, he will keep my w.: ..** *3056*
Joh 15:7 **my w. abide in you, ye shall ask ...** *4487*
Joh 17:1 These w. spake Jesus, and lifted up..........
Joh 17:8 **them the w. which thou gavest me;** *4487*
Joh 18:1 When Jesus had spoken these w., he ....
Ac 2:14 unto you, and hearken to my w.: *4487*
Ac 2:22 Ye men of Israel, hear these w.:......... *3056*
Ac 2:40 with many other w. did he testify....... *3056*
Ac 5:5 Ananias hearing these w. fell down,..... *3056*
Ac 5:20 to the people all the w. of this life...... *4487*
Ac 6:11 blasphemous w. against Moses, ... *4487*
Ac 6:13 blasphemous w. against this holy......... *4487*
Ac 7:22 was mighty in w. and in deeds........... *3056*
Ac 10:22 his house, and to hear w. of thee....... *4487*
Ac 10:44 While Peter yet spake these w., ... *4487*
Ac 11:14 Who shall tell thee w., whereby......... *4487*
Ac 13:42 that these w. might be preached......... *4487*
Ac 15:15 this agree the w. of the prophets; *3056*
Ac 15:24 from us have troubled you with w., ... *3056*
Ac 15:32 exhorted...brethren with many w.. ..... *3056*
Ac 16:38 told these w. unto the magistrates:..... *4487*
Ac 18:15 it be a question of w. and names,....... *3056*
Ac 20:35 remember the w. of the Lord Jesus, ... *3056*
Ac 20:38 of all for the w. which he spake,......... *3056*
Ac 24:4 hear us of thy clemency a few w...........
Ac 26:25 but speak forth the w. of truth *4487*
Ac 28:29 And when he had said these w., ...
Ro 10:18 w. unto the ends of the world. *4487*
Ro 16:18 good w. and fair speeches deceive...... *5542*
1Co 1:17 not with wisdom of w., lest the *3056*
1Co 2:4 with enticing w. of man's wisdom, ... *3056*
1Co 2:13 w. which man's wisdom teacheth,....... *3056*
1Co 14:9 tongue w. easy to be understood, ... *3056*
1Co 14:9 five w. with my understanding, ... *3056*
1Co 14:9 thousand w. in an unknown tongue. *3056*
2Co 12:4 and heard unspeakable w., which........ *4487*
Eph 3:3 mystery; (as I wrote afore in few w., ...
Eph 5:6 no man deceive you with vain w.: *3056*
Col 2:4 beguile you with enticing w.............. *4086*
1Th 2:5 any time used we flattering w.,........... *3056*
1Th 4:18 comfort one another with these w.. .... *3056*
1Ti 4:6 nourished up in the w. of faith and *3056*
1Ti 6:3 and consent not to wholesome w.,...... *3056*
1Ti 6:3 the w. of our Lord Jesus Christ, ...
1Ti 6:4 about questions and strifes of w.,........ *3055*
2Ti 1:13 Hold fast the form of sound w., ... *3056*
2Ti 2:14 strive not about w. to no profit,......... *3054*
2Ti 4:15 he hath greatly withstood our w.......... *3056*
Heb 12:19 a trumpet, and the voice of w.; *4487*
Heb 13:22 a letter unto you in a few w...................
2Pe 2:3 with feigned w. make merchandise...... *3056*
2Pe 2:18 speak great swelling w. of vanity,.............
2Pe 3:2 of the w. which were spoken *4487*
3Jo 10 against us with malicious w.: *3056*
Jude 16 mouth speaketh great swelling w.,............
Jude 17 the w. which were spoken before....... *4487*
Re 1:3 that hear the w. of this prophecy, ... *3056*
Re 17:17 the w. of God shall be fulfilled. *4487*
Re 21:5 for these w. are true and faithful. *3056*
Re 22:18 w. of the prophecy of this book, ... *3056*
Re 22:19 w. of the book of this prophecy, ... *3056*

WORE See WARE.

WORK See also HANDYWORK; NETWORK; WORKETH; WORKFELLOW; WORKING; WORKMAN; WORK'S; WORKS; WROUGHT.

Ge 2:2 the seventh day God ended his w....... 4399
Ge 2:2 on the seventh day from all his w....... 4399
Ge 2:3 in it he had rested from all his w. 4399
Ge 5:29 comfort us concerning our w. 4639
Ex 5:9 more w. be laid upon the men, ... 5656
Ex 5:11 of your w. shall be diminished. 5656
Ex 5:18 Go therefore now, and w.; for........... 5647
Ex 12:16 no manner of w. shall be done in 4399
Ex 14:31 saw that great w. which the Lord....... 3027
Ex 18:20 and the w. that they must do. 4640
Ex 20:9 thou labour, and do all thy w.:........... 4399
Ex 20:10 in it thou shalt not do any w., thou..... 4399
Ex 23:12 Six days thou shalt do thy w., and...... 4639
Ex 24:10 a paved w. of a sapphire stone, ... 4639
Ex 25:18 beaten w. shalt thou make them, ... 4749
Ex 25:31 of beaten w. shall the candlestick 4749
Ex 25:36 shall be one beaten w. of pure gold. ... 4749
Ex 26:1 cherubims of cunning w. shalt............ 4639
Ex 26:31 fine twined linen of cunning w.:........... 4639
Ex 28:6 fine twined linen, with cunning w.......... 4639
Ex 28:8 same, according to the w. thereof; 4639
Ex 28:11 the w. of an engraver in stone, like 4639
Ex 28:14 wreathen w. shalt thou make them,...... 4639
Ex 28:15 of judgment with cunning w.;............. 4639
Ex 28:15 after the w. of the ephod thou shalt.... 4639
Ex 28:22 ends of wreathen w. of pure gold........ 4639
Ex 28:32 a binding of woven w. round about 4639
Ex 31:4 to w. in gold, and in silver, and in...... 6213
Ex 31:5 w. in all manner of workmanship. 6213
Ex 31:14 whosoever doeth any w. therein, ... 4399
Ex 31:15 Six days may w. be done; but in........ 4399
Ex 31:15 doeth any w. in the sabbath day,........ 4399
Ex 32:16 the tables were the w. of God, and 4639
Ex 34:10 art shall see the w. of the Lord: 4639
Ex 34:21 Six days thou shalt w., but on........... 5627
Ex 35:2 Six days shall w. be done, but on......... 4399
Ex 35:2 whosoever doeth w. therein shall be ... 4399
Ex 35:21 offering to the w. of the tabernacle..... 4399
Ex 35:24 wood for any w. of the service, ... 4399
Ex 35:29 to bring for all manner of w., ... 4399
Ex 35:32 to w. in gold, and in silver, and in...... 6213
Ex 35:33 make any manner of cunning w.. 4399
Ex 35:35 wisdom of heart, to w. all manner 6213
Ex 35:35 manner of w., of the engraver, ... 4399
Ex 35:35 even of them that do any w., ... 4399
Ex 35:35 of those that devise cunning w...............
Ex 36:1 understanding to know how to w......... 6213
Ex 36:1 all manner of w. for the service 4399
Ex 36:2 up to come unto the w. to do it:........ 4399

Ex 36:3 brought for the **w.** of the service 4399
Ex 36:4 wrought all the **w.** of the sanctuary, 4399
Ex 36:4 came every man from his **w.** which 4399
Ex 36:5 enough for the service of the **w.**, 4399
Ex 36:6 man nor woman make any more **w.** 4399
Ex 36:7 had was sufficient for all the **w.** 4399
Ex 36:8 wrought the **w.** of the tabernacle 4399
Ex 36:8 cherubims of cunning **w.** made he 4639
Ex 36:35 made he it of cunning **w.** 4639
Ex 37:17 beaten **w.** made he the candlestick; 4749
Ex 37:22 it was one beaten **w.** of pure gold. 4749
Ex 37:29 to the **w.** of the apothecary. 4639
Ex 38:24 gold that was occupied for the **w.** 4399
Ex 38:24 all the **w.** of the holy place, even 4399
Ex 39:3 **w.** it in the blue, and in the purple, 6213
Ex 39:3 in the fine linen, with cunning **w.** 4639
Ex 39:5 same, according to the **w.** thereof; 4639
Ex 39:8 the breastplate of cunning **w.**, 4639
Ex 39:8 like the **w.** of the ephod; of gold, 4639
Ex 39:15 ends, of wreathen **w.** of pure gold. 4639
Ex 39:22 the robe of the ephod of woven **w.**, 4639
Ex 39:27 of fine linen of woven **w.** for Aaron, 4639
Ex 39:32 was all the **w.** of the tabernacle 5656
Ex 39:42 children of Israel made all the **w.** 5656
Ex 39:43 Moses did look upon all the **w.**, 4399
Ex 40:33 gate. So Moses finished the **w.** 4399
Le 11:32 wherein any **w.** is done, it must be 4399
Le 13:51 or in any **w.** that is made of skin; 4399
Le 16:29 and do no **w.** at all, whether it be 4399
Le 23:3 Six days shall **w.** be done: but the 4399
Le 23:3 ye shall do no **w.** therein: it is the 4399
Le 23:7, 8 ye shall do no servile **w.** therein. 4399
Le 23:21 ye shall do no servile **w.** therein: 4399
Le 23:25 Ye shall do no servile **w.** therein: 4399
Le 23:28 ye shall do no **w.** in that same day: 4399
Le 23:30 that doeth any **w.** in that same day, 4399
Le 23:31 Ye shall do no manner of **w.**: it 4399
Le 23:35, 36 ye shall do no servile **w.** therein. 4399
Nu 4:3 to do the **w.** in the tabernacle of 4399
Nu 4:23 to do the **w.** in the tabernacle of 5656
Nu 4:30 to do the **w.** of the tabernacle of 5656
Nu 4:35, 39,43 for the **w.** in the tabernacle of 5656
Nu 8:4 this **w.** of the candlestick was of 4639
Nu 8:4 flowers thereof, was beaten **w.**:
Nu 28:18 shall do no manner of servile **w.** 4399
Nu 28:25 ye shall do no servile **w.** 4399
Nu 28:26 ye shall do no servile **w.**: 4399
Nu 29:1 ye shall do no servile **w.**: 4399
Nu 29:7 ye shall not do any **w.** therein: 4399
Nu 29:12 ye shall do no servile **w.**, and ye 4399
Nu 29:35 ye shall do no servile **w.** therein: 4399
Nu 31:20 of skins, and all **w.** of goats' hair, 4639
De 4:28 serve gods, the **w.** of men's hands, 4639
De 5:13 shalt labour, and do all thy **w.**: 4399
De 5:14 in it thou shalt not do any **w.**, thou, 4399
De 14:29 thee in all the **w.** of thine hand 4639
De 15:19 shalt do no **w.** with the firstling 5647
De 16:8 God: thou shalt do no **w.** therein 4399
De 24:19 thee in all the **w.** of thine hands. 4639
De 27:15 **w.** of the hands of the craftsman, 4639
De 28:12 to bless all the **w.** of thine hand: 4639
De 30:9 plenteous in every **w.** of thine hand, 4639
De 31:29 through the **w.** of your hands. 4639
De 32:4 He is the Rock, his **w.** is perfect: 6467
De 33:11 and accept the **w.** of his hands: 6467
Jos 9:4 They did **w.** wilily, and went and 6213
Jg 19:16 came an old man from his **w.** out 4639
Ru 2:12 The Lord recompense thy **w.**, and 6467
1Sa 8:16 asses, and put them to his **w.** 4399
1Sa 14:6 be that the Lord will **w.** for us: 6213
1Ki 5:16 officers which were over the **w.**, 4399
1Ki 5:16 the people that wrought in the **w.** 4399
1Ki 6:35 with gold fitted upon the carved **w.**
1Ki 7:8 porch, which was of the like **w.** 4649
1Ki 7:14 cunning to **w.** all works in brass. 6213
1Ki 7:14 Solomon, and wrought all his **w.** 4399
1Ki 7:17 And nets of checker **w.**, 4639
1Ki 7:17 and wreaths of chain **w.**, 4639
1Ki 7:9 pillars were of lily **w.** in the porch, 4639
1Ki 7:22 the top of the pillars was lily **w.**: 4639
1Ki 7:22 was the **w.** of the pillars finished. 4399
1Ki 7:28 the **w.** of the bases was on this 4639
1Ki 7:29 certain additions made of thin **w.** 4639
1Ki 7:31 was round after the **w.** of the base, 4639
1Ki 7:33 And the **w.** of the wheels was like 4639
1Ki 7:33 was like the **w.** of a chariot wheel: 4639
1Ki 7:40 made an end of doing all the **w.** 4399
1Ki 7:51 ended all the **w.** that king Solomon 4399
1Ki 9:23 that were over Solomon's **w.**, 4399
1Ki 9:23 the people that wrought in the **w.** 4399
1Ki 16:7 to anger with the **w.** of his hands, 4639
1Ki 21:20 **w.** evil in the sight of the Lord. 6213
1Ki 21:25 did sell himself to **w.** wickedness 6213
2Ki 12:11 the hands of them that did the **w.**, 4399
2Ki 19:18 but the **w.** of men's hands, wood 4639
2Ki 22:5 the hand of the doers of the **w.**, 4399
2Ki 22:5 them give it to the doers of the **w.**, 4399
2Ki 22:9 the hand of them that do the **w.**, 4399
2Ki 25:17 and the wreathen **w.**, and 7639
2Ki 25:17 second pillar with wreathen **w.** 7639
1Ch 4:23 dwelt with the king for his **w.** 4399
1Ch 6:49 all the **w.** of the place most holy, 4399
1Ch 9:13 able men for the **w.** of the service 4399
1Ch 9:19 were over the **w.** of the service, 4399
1Ch 9:33 employed in that **w.** day and night. 4399
1Ch 16:37 as every day's **w.** required: 1697
1Ch 22:15 men for every manner of **w.** 4399
1Ch 23:4 the **w.** of the house of the Lord; 4399
1Ch 23:24 the **w.** for the service of the house 4399
1Ch 23:28 the **w.** of the service of the house 4639
1Ch 27:26 did the **w.** of the field for tillage 4399
1Ch 28:13 the **w.** of the service of the house 4399
1Ch 28:20 the **w.** for the service of the house 4399
1Ch 29:1 and tender, and the **w.** is great: 4399
1Ch 29:5 of **w.** to be made by the hands 4399
1Ch 29:6 with the rulers of the king's **w.**, 4399
2Ch 2:7 a man cunning to **w.** in gold, 6213
2Ch 2:14 man of Tyre, skilful to **w.** in gold, 6213
2Ch 2:18 overseers to set the people a **w.** 5647
2Ch 3:10 made two cherubims of image **w.**, 4639
2Ch 4:5 it like the **w.** of the brim of a cup, 4639
2Ch 4:11 Huram finished the **w.** that he 4399
2Ch 5:1 all the **w.** that Solomon made for 4399
2Ch 8:9 make no servants for his **w.**; 4399
2Ch 8:16 all the **w.** of Solomon was prepared 4399
2Ch 15:7 for your **w.** shall be rewarded. 6468
2Ch 16:5 of Ramah, and let his **w.** cease. 4399
2Ch 24:12 such as did the **w.** of the service 4399
2Ch 24:13 and the **w.** was perfected by them, 4399
2Ch 29:34 till the **w.** was ended, and until the 4399
2Ch 31:21 in every **w.** that he began in the 4639
2Ch 32:19 were the **w.** of the hands of man. 4639
2Ch 34:12 the men did the **w.** faithfully: 4399
2Ch 34:13 of all that wrought the **w.** in any 4399
Ezr 2:69 ability unto the treasure of the **w.** 4399
Ezr 3:8 to set forward the **w.** of the house 4399
Ezr 4:24 ceased the **w.** of the house of God 5673
Ezr 5:8 and this **w.** goeth fast on, and 5673
Ezr 6:7 Let the **w.** of this house of God 5673
Ezr 6:22 in the **w.** of the house of God, 4399
Ezr 10:13 is this a **w.** of one day or two: 4399
Ne 2:16 nor to the rest that did the **w.** 4399
Ne 2:18 their hands for this good **w.**
Ne 3:5 necks to the **w.** of their Lord. 5656
Ne 4:6 for the people had a mind to **w.** 6213
Ne 4:11 them, and cause the **w.** to cease. 4399
Ne 4:15 to the wall, every one unto his **w.** 4399
Ne 4:16 of my servants wrought in the **w.**, 4399
Ne 4:17 one of his hands wrought in the **w.**, 4399
Ne 4:19 The **w.** is great and large, and we 4399
Ne 4:21 So we laboured in the **w.**: and half 4399
Ne 5:16 continued in the **w.** of this wall, 4399
Ne 5:16 were gathered thither unto the **w.** 4399
Ne 6:3 I am doing a great **w.**, so that I 4399
Ne 6:3 why should the **w.** cease, whilst I 4399
Ne 6:9 shall be weakened from the **w.**, 4399
Ne 6:16 this **w.** was wrought of our God. 4399
Ne 7:70 of the fathers gave unto the **w.** 4399
Ne 7:71 gave to the treasure of the **w.** 4399
Ne 10:33 all the **w.** of the house of our God 4399
Ne 11:12 that did the **w.** of the house 4399
Ne 13:10 and the singers, that did the **w.**, 4399
Job 1:10 hast blessed the **w.** of his hands, 4639
Job 7:2 looketh for the reward of his **w.**: 6467
Job 10:3 despise the **w.** of thine hands, 3018
Job 14:15 a desire to the **w.** of thine hands. 4639
Job 23:9 the left hand, where he doth **w.**, 6213
Job 24:5 desert, go they forth to their **w.**; 6467
Job 34:11 the **w.** of a man shall he render 6467
Job 34:19 they all are the **w.** of his hands. 4639
Job 36:9 Then he sheweth them their **w.**, 6467
Job 36:24 that thou magnify his **w.** 6467
Job 37:7 that all men may know his **w.** 4639
Ps 8:3 thy heavens, the **w.** of thy fingers, 4639
Ps 9:16 snared in the **w.** of his own hands. 6467
Ps 28:4 them after the **w.** of their hands, 4639
Ps 44:1 what **w.** thou didst in their days, 6467
Ps 58:2 Yea, in heart ye **w.** wickedness; 6466
Ps 62:12 to every man according to his **w.** 4639
Ps 64:9 and shall declare the **w.** of God; 6467
Ps 74:6 they break down the carved **w.** 6603
Ps 77:12 I will meditate also of all thy **w.**, 6467
Ps 90:16 thy **w.** appear unto thy servants, 6467
Ps 90:17 establish thou the **w.** of our hands 4639
Ps 90:17 **w.** of our hands establish thou it. 4639
Ps 92:4 made me glad through thy **w.**: 6467
Ps 95:9 me, proved me, and saw my **w.** 6467
Ps 101:3 I hate the **w.** of them that turn 6213
Ps 102:25 heavens are the **w.** of thy hands. 4639
Ps 104:23 Man goeth forth unto his **w.** and 6467
Ps 111:3 His **w.** is honourable and glorious: 6467
Ps 115:4 and gold, the **w.** of men's hands. 4639
Ps 119:126 It is time for thee, Lord, to **w.**: 6213
Ps 135:15 and gold, the **w.** of men's hands. 4639
Ps 141:4 works with men that **w.** iniquity: 5950
Ps 143:5 I muse on the **w.** of thy hands. 4639
Pr 11:18 wicked worketh a deceitful **w.**: 6468
Pr 16:11 the weights of the bag are his **w.** 4639
Pr 18:9 He also that is slothful in his **w.** 4399
Pr 20:11 doings, whether his **w.** be pure, 6467
Pr 21:8 as for the pure, his **w.** is right. 6467
Pr 24:27 Prepare thy **w.** without, and make 4399
Pr 24:29 to the man according to his **w.** 6467
Ec 2:17 **w.** that is wrought under the sun 4639
Ec 3:11 find out the **w.** that God maketh 4639
Ec 3:17 every purpose and for every **w.** 4639
Ec 4:3 not seen the evil **w.** that is done 4639
Ec 4:4 all travail, and every right **w.**, 4639
Ec 5:6 and destroy the **w.** of thine hands? 4639
Ec 7:13 Consider the **w.** of God: for who 4639
Ec 8:9 applied my heart unto every **w.** 4639
Ec 8:11 sentence against an evil **w.** is not 4639
Ec 8:14 according to the **w.** of the wicked; 4639
Ec 8:14 to the **w.** of the righteous: 4639
Ec 8:17 Then I beheld all the **w.** of God, 4639
Ec 8:17 cannot find out the **w.** that is done 4639
Ec 9:10 for there is no **w.**, nor device, nor 4639
Ec 12:14 bring every **w.** into judgment, 4639
Ca 7:1 **w.** of the hands of a cunning 4639
Isa 2:8 worship the **w.** of their own hands, 4639
Isa 5:12 regard not the **w.** of the Lord, 6467
Isa 5:19 make speed, and hasten his **w.**, 4639
Isa 10:12 Lord hath performed his whole **w.** 4639
Isa 17:8 to the altars, the **w.** of his hands, 4639
Isa 19:9 Moreover they that **w.** in fine flax, 5647
Isa 19:14 Egypt to err in every **w.** thereof, 4639
Isa 19:15 shall there be any **w.** for Egypt, 4639
Isa 19:25 and Assyria the **w.** of my hands, 4639
Isa 28:21 he may do his **w.**, his strange **w.**; 4639
Isa 29:14 marvellous **w.** among this people, 6381
Isa 29:14 a marvellous **w.** and a wonder: 6381
Isa 29:16 the **w.** say of him that made it, 4639
Isa 29:23 his children, the **w.** of mine hands, 4639
Isa 31:2 the help of them that **w.** iniquity. 6213
Isa 32:6 and his heart will **w.** iniquity, to 6213
Isa 32:17 the **w.** of righteousness shall be 4639
Isa 37:19 the **w.** of men's hands, wood and 4639
Isa 40:10 with him, and his **w.** before him. 6468
Isa 41:24 nothing, and your **w.** of nought: 6467
Isa 43:13 I will **w.**, and who shall let it? 6466
Isa 45:9 What makest thou? or thy **w.**, 6467
Isa 45:11 concerning the **w.** of my hands 6467
Isa 49:4 Lord, and my **w.** with my God. 6468
Isa 54:16 forth an instrument for his **w.**; 4639
Isa 60:21 my planting, the **w.** of my hands, 4639
Isa 61:8 and I will direct their **w.** in truth, 6468
Isa 62:11 with him, and his **w.** before him. 6468
Isa 64:8 and we all are the **w.** of thine hand. 4639
Isa 65:7 will I measure their former **w.** 6468
Isa 65:22 long enjoy the **w.** of their hands. 4639
Jer 10:3 **w.** of the hands of the workman, 4639
Jer 10:9 the **w.** of the workman, and of 4639
Jer 10:9 are all the **w.** of cunning men. 4639
Jer 10:15 are vanity, and the **w.** of errors: 4639
Jer 17:22 neither do ye any **w.**, but hallow 4399
Jer 17:24 sabbath day, to do no **w.** therein: 4399
Jer 18:3 he wrought a **w.** on the wheels. 4399
Jer 22:13 and giveth him not for his **w.**; 6467

Jer	31:16	for thy **w.** shall be rewarded, saith	6468
Jer	32:19	in counsel, and mighty in **w.**:	5950
Jer	32:30	anger with the **w.** of their hands,	4639
Jer	48:10	the **w.** of the Lord deceitfully,	4399
Jer	50:25	this is the **w.** of the Lord God of	4399
Jer	50:29	her according to her **w.**;	6467
Jer	51:10	declare in Zion the **w.** of the Lord	4639
Jer	51:18	They are vanity, the **w.** of errors:	4639
La	3:64	according to the **w.** of their hands.	4639
La	4:2	the **w.** of the hands of the potter!	4639
Eze	1:16	their **w.** was like unto the colour	4639
Eze	1:16	and their **w.** was as it were a wheel	4639
Eze	15:3	be taken thereof to do any **w.**?	4399
Eze	15:4	is burned. It is meet for any **w.**?	4399
Eze	15:5	was whole, it was meet for no **w.**:	4399
Eze	15:5	less shall it be meet for any **w.**,	4399
Eze	16:10	thee also with broidered **w.**,	7553
Eze	16:13	linen, and silk, and broidered **w.**;	7553
Eze	16:30	the **w.** of an imperious whorish	4639
Eze	27:7	Fine linen with broidered **w.**	7553
Eze	27:16	and broidered **w.**, and fine linen,	7553
Eze	27:24	in blue clothes, and broidered **w.**,	7553
Eze	33:26	ye **w.** abomination, and ye defile	6213
Da	11:23	with him he shall **w.** deceitfully:	6213
Ho	6:8	a city of them that **w.** iniquity,	6466
Ho	13:2	all of it the **w.** of the craftsman:	4639
Ho	14:3	any more to the **w.** of our hands,	4639
Mic	2:1	and **w.** evil upon their beds!	6466
Mic	5:13	worship the **w.** of thine hands.	4639
Hab	1:5	marvellously: for I will **w.**	6466
Hab	1:5	a **w.** in your days, which ye will	6467
Hab	2:18	maker of his **w.** trusteth therein,	3336
Hab	3:2	revive thy **w.** in the midst of the	6467
Zep	2:14	for he shall uncover the cedar **w.**	731
Hag	1:14	did **w.** in the house of the Lord	4399
Hag	2:4	the land, saith the Lord, and **w.**:	6213
Hag	2:14	and so is every **w.** of their hands;	4639
Mal	3:15	that **w.** wickedness are set up;	6213
Mt	7:23	**from me, ye that w. iniquity**	*2038*
Mt	21:28	**Son, go w. to day in my vineyard.**	*2038*
Mt	26:10	**hath wrought a good w. upon me.**	*2041*
Mk	6:5	he could there do no mighty **w.**,	*1411*
Mk	13:34	**servants, and to every man his w.,**	*2041*
Mk	14:6	she hath wrought a good **w.** on me.	*2041*
Lu	13:14	days in which men ought to **w.**:	*2038*
Joh	4:34	**that sent me, and to finish his w.**	*2041*
Joh	5:17	**worketh hitherto, and I w.**	*2038*
Joh	6:28	that we might **w.** the works of God?	*2038*
Joh	6:29	**This is the w. of God, that ye**	*2041*
Joh	6:30	believe thee? what dost thou **w.**?	*2038*
Joh	7:21	**I have done one w., and ye all**	*2041*
Joh	9:4	**I must w. the works of him that**	*2038*
Joh	9:4	**cometh, when no man can w.**	*2038*
Joh	10:33	For a good **w.** we stone thee not;	*2041*
Joh	17:4	**finished the w. which thou gavest**	*2041*
Ac	5:38	or this **w.** be of men, it will come	*2041*
Ac	13:2	for the **w.** whereunto I have called	*2041*
Ac	13:41	for I **w.** [*2038*] a **w.** in your days,	*2040*
Ac	13:41	a **w.** which ye shall in no wise	*2041*
Ac	14:26	for the **w.** which they fulfilled.	*2041*
Ac	15:38	and went not with them to the **w.**	*2041*
Ac	27:16	we had much **w.** to come by	*3433,2480*
Ro	2:15	shew the **w.** of the law written in	*2041*
Ro	7:5	did **w.** in our members to bring	*1754*
Ro	8:28	all things **w.** together for good to	*4903*
Ro	9:28	For he will finish the **w.**, and cut	*3056*
Ro	9:28	short **w.** will the Lord make upon	*3056*
Ro	11:6	otherwise **w.** is no more **w.**	*2041*
Ro	14:20	meat destroy not the **w.** of God.	*2041*
1Co	3:13	man's **w.** shall be made manifest:	*2041*
1Co	3:13	fire shall try every man's **w.**	*2041*
1Co	3:14	If any man's **w.** abide which he	*2041*
1Co	3:15	If any man's **w.** shall be burned, he	*2041*
1Co	9:1	are not ye my **w.** in the Lord?	*2041*
1Co	15:58	abounding in the **w.** of the Lord,	*2041*
1Co	16:10	for he worketh the **w.** of the Lord,	*2041*
2Co	9:8	may abound to every good **w.**:	*2041*
Ga	6:4	But let every man prove his own **w.**,	*2041*
Eph	4:12	for the **w.** of the ministry, for the	*2041*
Eph	4:19	to **w.** all uncleanness with	*2039*
Php	1:6	which hath begun a good **w.** in you.	*2041*
Php	2:12	**w.** out your own salvation with	*2716*
Php	2:30	for the **w.** of Christ he was nigh	*2041*
Col	1:10	being fruitful in every good **w.**, and	*2041*
1Th	1:3	without ceasing your **w.** of faith,	*2041*
1Th	4:11	and to **w.** with your own hands,	*2038*
2Th	1:11	and the **w.** of faith with power:	*2041*
2Th	2:7	of iniquity doth already **w.**:	*1754*
2Th	2:17	you in every good word and **w.**	*2041*
2Th	3:10	that if any would not **w.**, neither	*2038*
2Th	3:12	that with quietness they **w.**, and	*2038*
1Ti	3:1	of a bishop, he desireth a good **w.**	*2041*
1Ti	5:10	diligently followed every good **w.**	*2041*
2Ti	2:21	and prepared unto every good **w.**	*2041*
2Ti	4:5	do the **w.** of an evangelist, make	*2041*
2Ti	4:18	shall deliver me from every evil **w.**,	*2041*
Tit	1:16	and unto every good **w.** reprobate.	*2041*
Tit	3:1	to be ready to every good **w.**,	*2041*
Heb	6:10	forget your **w.** and labour of love,	*2041*
Heb	13:21	Make you perfect in every good **w.**	*2041*
Jas	1:4	let patience have her perfect **w.**,	*2041*
Jas	1:25	but a doer of the **w.**, this man shall	*2041*
Jas	3:16	is confusion and every evil **w.**	*4229*
1Pe	1:17	according to every man's **w.**,	*2041*
Re	22:12	**man according as his w. shall be**	*2041*

WORKED See WROUGHT.

WORKER See also WORKERS.

1Ki	17:14	was a man of Tyre, a **w.** in brass:	2790

WORKERS See also FELLOWWORKERS.

2Ki	23:24	Moreover the **w.** with familiar spirits,	
1Ch	22:15	and **w.** of stone and timber, and	2796
Job	31:3	punishment to the **w.** of iniquity?	6466
Job	34:8	in company with the **w.** of iniquity,	6466
Job	34:22	where the **w.** of iniquity may hide	6466
Ps	5:5	thou hateth all **w.** of iniquity.	6466
Ps	6:8	from me, all ye **w.** of iniquity;	6466
Ps	14:4	the **w.** of iniquity no knowledge?	6466
Ps	28:3	with the **w.** of iniquity, which speak	6466
Ps	36:12	There are the **w.** of iniquity fallen:	6466
Ps	37:1	against the **w.** of iniquity.	6213
Ps	53:4	the **w.** of iniquity no knowledge?	6466
Ps	59:2	Deliver me from the **w.** of iniquity,	6466
Ps	64:2	insurrection of the **w.** of iniquity:	6466
Ps	92:7	all the **w.** of iniquity do flourish;	6466
Ps	92:9	**w.** of iniquity shall be scattered.	6466
Ps	94:4	**w.** of iniquity boast themselves?	6466
Ps	94:16	for me against the **w.** of iniquity?	6466
Ps	125:5	them forth with the **w.** of iniquity:	6466
Ps	141:9	and the gins of the **w.** of iniquity.	6466
Pr	10:29	shall be to the **w.** of iniquity.	6466
Pr	21:15	shall be to the **w.** of iniquity.	6466
Lu	13:27	**from me, all ye w. of iniquity.**	*2040*
1Co	12:29	teachers? are all **w.** of miracles?	*1411*
2Co	6:1	We then, as **w.** together with him,	*4903*
2Co	11:13	are false apostles, deceitful **w.**	*2040*
Php	3:2	Beware of dogs, beware of evil **w.**,	*2040*

WORKETH

Job	33:29	these things **w.** God oftentimes	6466
Ps	15:2	and **w.** righteousness, and speaketh	6466
Ps	101:7	He that **w.** deceit shall not dwell	6213
Pr	11:18	The wicked **w.** a deceitful work:	6213
Pr	26:28	and a flattering mouth **w.** ruin.	6213
Pr	31:13	and **w.** willingly with her hands.	6213
Ec	3:9	What profit hath he that **w.** in that	6213
Isa	44:12	with the tongs both **w.** in the coals,	6466
Isa	44:12	**w.** it with the strength of his arms:	6466
Isa	64:5	rejoiceth and **w.** righteousness,	6213
Da	6:27	**w.** signs and wonders in heaven	5648
Joh	5:17	**Father w. hitherto, and I work.**	*2038*
Ac	10:35	**w.** righteousness, is accepted with	*2038*
Ro	2:10	peace, to every man that **w.** good,	*2038*
Ro	4:4	to him that **w.** is the reward not	*2038*
Ro	4:5	But to him that **w.** not, but	*2038*
Ro	4:15	Because the law **w.** wrath: for	*2716*
Ro	5:3	knowing...tribulation **w.** patience;	*2716*
Ro	13:10	Love **w.** no ill to his neighbour:	*2038*
1Co	12:6	the same God which **w.** all in all.	*1754*
1Co	12:11	**w.** that one and the selfsame Spirit,	*1754*
1Co	16:10	he **w.** the work of the Lord, as I	*2038*
2Co	4:12	So then death **w.** in us, but life in	*1754*
2Co	4:17	**w.** for us a far more exceeding	*2716*
2Co	7:10	godly sorrow **w.** repentance unto	*2716*
2Co	7:10	the sorrow of the world **w.** death.	*2716*
Ga	3:5	Spirit, and **w.** miracles among you,	*1754*
Ga	5:6	but faith which **w.** by love.	*1754*
Eph	1:11	purpose of him who **w.** all things	*1754*
Eph	2:2	spirit that now **w.** in the children	*1754*
Eph	3:20	to the power that **w.** in us,	*1754*
Php	2:13	is God which **w.** in you both to will	*1754*
Col	1:29	working, which **w.** in me mightily.	*1754*
1Th	2:13	which effectually **w.** also in you	*1754*
Jas	1:3	trying of your faith **w.** patience.	*2716*
Jas	1:20	**w.** not the righteousness of God.	*2716*
Re	21:27	whatsoever **w.** abomination, or	*4160*

WORKFELLOW See also FELLOWWORKERS.

Ro	16:21	Timotheus my **w.**, and Lucius,	*4904*

WORKING

Ps	52:2	like a sharp rasor, **w.** deceitfully.	6213
Ps	74:12	**w.** salvation in the midst of the	6466
Isa	28:29	in counsel, and excellent in **w.**	8454
Eze	46:1	east shall be shut the six **w.** days;	4639
Mk	16:20	the Lord **w.** with them, and	*4903*
Ro	1:27	men **w.** that which is unseemly,	*2716*
Ro	7:13	**w.** death in me by that which is	*2716*
1Co	4:12	labour, **w.** with our own hands:	*2038*
1Co	9:6	have not we power to forbear **w.**?	*2038*
1Co	12:10	To another the **w.** of miracles;	*1755*
Eph	1:19	to the **w.** of his mighty power,	*1753*
Eph	3:7	me by the effectual **w.** of his power.	*1753*
Eph	4:16	to the effectual **w.** in the measure	*1753*
Eph	4:28	**w.** with his hands the thing which	*2038*
Php	3:21	according to the **w.** whereby he is	*1753*
Col	1:29	striving according to his **w.**, which	*1753*
2Th	2:9	coming is after the **w.** of Satan	*1753*
2Th	3:11	**w.** not at all, but are busybodies.	*2038*
Heb	13:21	his will, **w.** in you that which is	*4160*
Re	16:14	the spirits of devils, **w.** miracles,	*4160*

WORKMAN See also WORKMANSHIP; WORKMEN.

Ex	35:35	engraver, and of the cunning **w.**,	2803
Ex	38:23	an engraver, and a cunning **w.**,	2803
Ca	7:1	work of the hands of a cunning **w.**	542
Isa	40:19	The **w.** melteth a graven image,	2796
Isa	40:20	seeketh unto him a cunning **w.** to	2796
Jer	10:3	the work of the hands of the **w.**,	2796
Jer	10:9	from Uphaz, the work of the **w.**,	2796
Ho	8:6	the **w.** made it; therefore it is not	2796
Mt	10:10	**for the w. is worthy of his meat.**	*2040*
2Ti	2:15	a **w.** that needeth not to be	*2040*

WORKMANSHIP

Ex	31:3	and in all manner of **w.**,	4399
Ex	31:5	to work in all manner of **w.**,	4399
Ex	35:31	and in all manner of **w.**;	4399
2Ki	16:10	according to all the **w.** thereof.	4639
1Ch	28:21	be with thee for all manner of **w.**	4399
Eze	28:13	**w.** of thy tabrets and of thy pipes	4399
Eph	2:10	For we are his **w.**, created in	*4161*

WORKMEN See also WORKMEN'S.

2Ki	12:14	But they gave that to the **w.**,	6213,4399
2Ki	12:15	money to be bestowed on **w.**	6213,4399
1Ch	22:15	are **w.** with thee in abundance.	6213,4399
1Ch	25:1	number of the **w.** according	582,4399
2Ch	24:13	So the **w.** wrought, and the	6213,4399
2Ch	34:10	**w.** that had the oversight	6213,4399
2Ch	34:10	**w.** that wrought in the house	6213,4399
2Ch	34:17	and to the hand of the **w.**	6213,4399
Ezr	3:9	the **w.** in the house of God:	6213,4399
Isa	44:11	and the **w.**, they are of men:	2796
Ac	19:25	with the **w.** of like occupation,	*2040*

WORKMEN'S

Jg	5:26	her right hand to the **w.** hammer;	6001

WORK'S

1Th	5:13	highly in love for their **w.** sake.	*2041*

WORKS See also NETWORKS.

Ex	5:4	let the people from their **w.**?	4639
Ex	5:13	Fulfil your **w.**, your daily tasks,	4639
Ex	23:24	serve them, nor do after their **w.**	4639
Ex	31:4	To devise cunning **w.**, to work in	
Ex	35:32	And to devise curious **w.**, to work	
Nu	16:28	hath sent me to do all these **w.**;	4639
De	2:7	thee in all the **w.** of thy hand:	4639
De	3:24	that can do according to thy **w.**,	4639
De	15:10	God shall bless thee in all thy **w.**,	4639
De	16:15	and in all the **w.** of thine hands,	4639
Jos	24:31	had known all the **w.** of the Lord,	4639
Jg	2:7	seen all the great **w.** of the Lord,	4639
Jg	2:10	**w.** which he had done for Israel.	4639
1Sa	8:8	to all the **w.** which they have done	4639
1Sa	19:4	his **w.** have been to thee-ward	4639
1Ki	7:14	cunning to work all **w.** in brass.	4399
1Ki	13:11	**w.** that the man of God had done	4639
2Ki	22:17	with all the **w.** of their hands;	4639
1Ch	16:9	talk ye of all his wondrous **w.**	

1Ch 16:12 Remember his marvellous w. that he
1Ch 16:24 his marvellous w. among all nations
1Ch 28:19 even all the w. of this pattern. 4399
2Ch 20:37 the Lord hath broken thy w. 4639
2Ch 32:30 Hezekiah prospered in all his w. 4639
2Ch 34:25 with all the w. of their hands; 4639
Ne 6:14 according to these their w., 4639
Ne 9:35 turned they from their wicked w. 4611
Job 34:25 Therefore he knoweth their w., 4566
Job 37:14 consider the wondrous w. of God.
Job 37:16 wondrous w. of him which is perfect
Ps 8:6 dominion over the w. of thy hands 4639
Ps 9:1 shew forth all thy marvellous w.
Ps 14:1 they have done abominable w. 5949
Ps 17:4 Concerning the w. of men, by the 6468
Ps 26:7 and tell of all thy wondrous w.
Ps 28:5 regard not the w. of the Lord, 6468
Ps 33:4 and all his w. are done in truth. 4640
Ps 33:15 alike; he considereth all their w. 4640
Ps 40:5 wonderful w. which thou hast done,
Ps 46:8 Come, behold the w. of the Lord, 4659
Ps 66:3 How terrible art thou in thy w.! 4639
Ps 66:5 Come and see the w. of God: he is 4659
Ps 71:17 have I declared thy wondrous w.
Ps 73:28 God, that I may declare all thy w. 4399
Ps 75:1 is near thy wondrous w. declare
Ps 77:11 remember the w. of the Lord: 4611
Ps 78:4 wonderful w. that he hath done.
Ps 78:7 God, and not forget the w. of God, 4611
Ps 78:11 forgat his w., and his wonders 5949
Ps 78:32 believed not for his wondrous w.
Ps 86:8 neither are there any w. like unto
Ps 86:8 are there any...like unto thy w. 4639
Ps 92:4 triumph in the w. of thy hands. 4639
Ps 92:5 O Lord, how great are thy w.! 4639
Ps 103:22 his w. in all places of his dominion: 4639
Ps 104:13 is satisfied with the fruit of thy w. 4639
Ps 104:24 O Lord, how manifold are thy w.! 4639
Ps 104:31 the Lord shall rejoice in his w. 4639
Ps 105:2 talk ye of all his wondrous w.
Ps 105:5 Remember his marvellous w. that
Ps 106:13 They soon forgat his w.: they 4639
Ps 106:22 Wondrous w. in the land of Ham,
Ps 106:35 the heathen, and learned their w. 4639
Ps 106:39 they defiled with their own w., 4639
Ps 107:8, 15,21 for his wonderful w. to the
Ps 107:22 and declare his w. with rejoicing. 4639
Ps 107:24 These see the w. of the Lord, and 4639
Ps 107:31 his wonderful w. to the children
Ps 111:2 The w. of the Lord are great, 4639
Ps 111:4 wonderful w. to be remembered:
Ps 111:6 his people the power of his w., 4639
Ps 111:7 The w. of his hands are verity 4639
Ps 118:17 and declare the w. of the Lord. 4639
Ps 119:27 so shall I talk of thy wondrous w.
Ps 138:8 not the w. of thine own hands, 4639
Ps 139:14 marvellous are thy w.: and that 4639
Ps 141:4 practise wicked w. with men that 5949
Ps 143:5 I meditate on all thy w.; I muse 6467
Ps 145:4 shall praise thy w. to another, 4639
Ps 145:5 and of thy wondrous w. 1697
Ps 145:9 tender mercies are over all his w. 4639
Ps 145:10 All thy w. shall praise thee, O 4639
Ps 145:17 all his ways, and holy in all his w. 4639
Pr 7:16 with carved w., with fine linen
Pr 8:22 of his way, before his w. of old. 4659
Pr 16:3 Commit thy w. unto the Lord, 4639
Pr 24:12 every man according to his w.? 6467
Pr 31:31 her own w. praise her in the gates. 4639
Ec 1:14 have seen all the w. that are done 4639
Ec 2:4 I made me great w.; I builded me 4639
Ec 2:11 w. that my hands had wrought, 4639
Ec 3:22 man should rejoice in his own w.; 4639
Ec 9:1 and their w., are in the hand of 5652
Ec 9:7 for God now accepteth thy w. 4639
Ec 11:5 thou knowest not the w. of God 4639
Isa 26:12 hast wrought all our w. in us. 4639
Isa 29:15 their w. are in the dark, and they 4639
Isa 41:29 all vanity; their w. are nothing: 4639
Isa 57:12 thy righteousness, and thy w.; 4639
Isa 59:6 cover themselves with their w. 4639
Isa 59:6 their w. are w. of iniquity, and the 4639
Isa 66:18 know their w. and their thoughts: 4639
Jer 1:16 the w. of their own hands. 4639
Jer 7:13 because ye have done all these w., 4639
Jer 21:2 according to all his wondrous w.
Jer 25:6 anger with the w. of your hands; 4639
Jer 25:7 to anger with the w. of your hands 4639
Jer 25:14 to the w. of their own hands. 4639
Jer 44:8 wrath with the w. of your hands, 4639
Jer 48:7 thou hast trusted in thy w. and in 4639
Eze 6:6 and your w. may be abolished. 4639
Da 4:37 heaven, all whose w. are truth, 4567
Da 9:14 our God is righteous in all his w. 4639
Am 8:7 I will never forget any of their w. 4639
Jon 3:10 And God saw their w., that they 4639
Mic 6:16 and all the w. of the house of Ahab, 4639
Mt 5:16 **that they may see your good w.,** 2041
Mt 7:22 **name done many wonderful w.?**
Mt 11:2 in the prison the w. of Christ, 2041
Mt 11:20 most of his mighty w. were done,
Mt 11:21 **if the mighty w., which were done**
Mt 11:23 **if the mighty w., which have been**
Mt 13:54 this wisdom, and these mighty w.?
Mt 13:58 he did not many mighty w. there
Mt 14:2 therefore mighty w. do shew forth
Mt 16:27 **every man according to his w.** 4234
Mt 23:3 **but do not ye after their w.:** 2041
Mt 23:5 **w. they do for to be seen of men:** 2041
Mk 6:2 even such mighty w. are wrought
Mk 6:14 mighty w. do shew forth...in him.
Lu 10:13 **mighty w., had been done in Tyre**
Lu 19:37 the mighty w. that they had seen;
Joh 5:20 **shew him greater w. than these,** 2041
Joh 5:36 **w. which the Father hath given** 2041
Joh 5:36 **same w. that I do, bear witness** 2041
Joh 6:28 that we might work the w. of God? 2041
Joh 7:3 may see the w. that thou doest. 2041
Joh 7:7 **of it, that the w. thereof are evil.** 2041
Joh 8:39 **ye would do the w. of Abraham.** 2041
Joh 9:3 **w. of God should be made** 2041
Joh 9:4 **work the w. of him that sent me.** 2041
Joh 10:25 **w. that I do in my Father's name,** 2041
Joh 10:32 **Many good w. have I shewed you** 2041
Joh 10:32 **which of those w. do ye stone me?** 2041
Joh 10:37 **If I do not the w. of my Father,** 2041
Joh 10:38 **ye believe not me, believe the w.** 2041
Joh 14:10 **dwelleth in me, he doeth the w.** 2041
Joh 14:12 **the w. that I do shall he do also;** 2041
Joh 14:12 **greater w. than these shall he do;** 2041
Joh 15:24 **the w. which none other man did,** 2041
Ac 2:11 tongues the wonderful w. of God.
Ac 7:41 in the w. of their own hands. 2041
Ac 9:36 this woman was full of good w. and 2041
Ac 15:18 Known unto God are all his w. 2041
Ac 26:20 and do w. meet for repentance. 2041
Ro 3:27 By what law? of w.? Nay: but by 2041
Ro 4:2 if Abraham were justified by w., 2041
Ro 4:6 imputeth righteousness without w., 2041
Ro 9:11 not of w., but of him that calleth;) 2041
Ro 9:32 but as it were by the w. of the law. 2041
Ro 11:6 by grace, then is it no more of w. 2041
Ro 11:6 But if it be of w., then is it no more 2041
Ro 13:3 rulers are not a terror to good w., 2041
Ro 13:12 cast off the w. of darkness, and 2041
2Co 11:15 end shall be according to their w. 2041
Ga 2:16 not justified by the w. of the law, 2041
Ga 2:16 and not by the w. of the law: 2041
Ga 2:16 by the w. of the law shall no flesh 2041
Ga 3:2 Received ye the Spirit by the w. of 2041
Ga 3:5 doeth he it by the w. of the law, 2041
Ga 3:10 many as are of the w. of the law 2041
Ga 5:19 the w. of the flesh are manifest, 2041
Eph 2:9 Not of w., lest any man should 2041
Eph 2:10 in Christ Jesus unto good w., 2041
Eph 5:11 with the unfruitful w. of darkness, 2041
Col 1:21 enemies in your mind by wicked w., 2041
1Ti 2:10 godliness) with good w. 2041
1Ti 5:10 Well reported of for good w.; if she 2041
1Ti 5:25 the good w. of some are manifest 2041
1Ti 6:18 that they be rich in good w., ready 2041
2Ti 1:9 calling, not according to our w., 2041
2Ti 3:17 furnished unto all good w. 2041
2Ti 4:14 reward him according to his w. 2041
Tit 1:16 but in w. they deny him, being 2041
Tit 2:7 thyself a pattern of good w. 2041
Tit 2:14 peculiar people, zealous of good w. 2041
Tit 3:5 Not by w. of righteousness which 2041
Tit 3:8 be careful to maintain good w. 2041
Tit 3:14 to maintain good w. for necessary 2041
Heb 1:10 heavens are the w. of thine hands: 2041
Heb 2:7 set him over the w. of thy hands: 2041
Heb 3:9 me, and saw my w. forty years. 2041
Heb 4:3 the w. were finished from the 2041
Heb 4:4 the seventh day from all his w. 2041
Heb 4:10 also hath ceased from his own w., 2041
Heb 6:1 of repentance from dead w., and of 2041
Heb 9:14 purge your conscience from dead w. 2041
Heb 10:24 provoke unto love and to good w.; 2041
Jas 2:14 say he hath faith, and have not w.? 2041
Jas 2:17 so faith, if it hath not w., is dead, 2041
Jas 2:18 say, Thou hast faith, and I have w. 2041
Jas 2:18 shew me thy faith without thy w., 2041
Jas 2:18 I will shew thee my faith by my w. 2041
Jas 2:20 man, that faith without w. is dead? 2041
Jas 2:21 Abraham our father justified by w. 2041
Jas 2:22 how faith wrought with his w. 2041
Jas 2:22 and by w. was faith made perfect? 2041
Jas 2:24 how that by w. a man is justified, 2041
Jas 2:25 Rahab the harlot justified by w., 2041
Jas 2:26 so faith without w. is dead also. 2041
Jas 3:13 out of a good conversation his w. 2041
1Pe 2:12 they may by your good w., which 2041
2Pe 3:10 w. that are therein shall be burned 2041
1Jo 3:8 might destroy the w. of the devil. 2041
1Jo 3:12 Because his own w. were evil, and 2041
Re 2:2 **I know thy w., and thy labour,** 2041
Re 2:5 **and repent, and do the first w.;** 2041
Re 2:9 **I know thy w., and tribulation,** 2041
Re 2:13 **I know thy w., and where thou** 2041
Re 2:19 **I know thy w., and charity, and** 2041
Re 2:19 **and thy patience, and thy w.;** 2041
Re 2:23 **one of you according to your w.** 2041
Re 2:26 **and keepeth my w. unto the end,** 2041
Re 3:1 **I know thy w., that thou hast a** 2041
Re 3:2 **for I have not found thy w.** 2041
Re 3:8 **I know thy w.: behold, I have set** 2041
Re 3:15 **I know thy w., that thou art** 2041
Re 9:20 yet repented not of the w. of their 2041
Re 14:13 and their w. do follow them. 2041
Re 15:3 Great and marvellous are thy w., 2041
Re 18:6 her double according to her w.: 2041
Re 20:12 in the books, according to their w. 2041
Re 20:13 every man according to their w. 2041

WORKS'

Joh 14:11 **believe me for the very w. sake.** 2041

WORLD See also WORLD'S; WORLDS.

1Sa 2:8 and he hath set the w. upon them. 8398
2Sa 22:16 the foundations of the w. were 8398
1Ch 16:30 the w. also shall be stable, that it 8398
Job 18:18 darkness, and chased out of the w. 8398
Job 34:13 or who hath disposed the whole w.? 8398
Job 37:12 upon the face of the w. in the earth. 8398
Ps 9:8 shall judge the w. in righteousness. 8398
Ps 17:14 from men of the w., which have 2465
Ps 18:15 the foundations of the w. were 8398
Ps 19:4 their words to the end of the w. 8398
Ps 22:27 ends of the w. shall remember 776
Ps 24:1 the w., and they that dwell therein. 8398
Ps 33:8 inhabitants of the w. stand in awe 8398
Ps 49:1 ear, all ye inhabitants of the w. 2465
Ps 50:12 for the w. is mine, and the fulness 8398
Ps 73:12 ungodly, who prosper in the w.; 5769
Ps 77:18 the lightnings lightened the w. 8398
Ps 89:11 for the w. and the fulness thereof, 8398
Ps 90:2 hadst formed the earth and the w., 8398
Ps 93:1 the w. also is stablished, that it 8398
Ps 96:10 the w. also shall be established that 8398
Ps 96:13 judge the w. with righteousness, 8398
Ps 97:4 His lightnings enlightened the w. 8398
Ps 98:7 the w., and they that dwell therein. 8398
Ps 98:9 righteousness shall he judge the w., 8398
Pr 8:26 highest part of the dust of the w. 8398
Ec 3:11 he hath set the w. in their heart, 5769
Isa 13:11 I will punish the w. for their evil, 8398
Isa 14:17 That made the w. as a wilderness, 8398
Isa 14:21 fill the face of the w. with cities. 8398
Isa 18:3 All ye inhabitants of the w., and 8398
Isa 23:17 with all the kingdoms of the w. 776
Isa 24:4 w. languisheth and fadeth away, 8398
Isa 26:9 of the w. will learn righteousness. 8398
Isa 26:18 the inhabitants of the w. fallen. 8398
Isa 27:6 and fill the face of the w. with fruit. 8398
Isa 34:1 the w., and all things that come 8398
Isa 38:11 with the inhabitants of the w. 2309
Isa 45:17 nor confounded w. without end. 5769
Isa 62:11 proclaimed unto the end of the w., 776

Isa 64:4 since the beginning of the w. men 5769
Jer 10:12 established the w. by his wisdom, 8398
Jer 25:26 and all the kingdoms of the w., 776
Jer 51:15 established the w. by his wisdom, 8398
La 4:12 and all the inhabitants of the w., 8398
Na 1:5 the w., and all that dwell therein. 8398
Mt 4:8 him all the kingdoms of the w., 2889
Mt 5:14 Ye are the light of the w.. A city 2889
Mt 12:32 forgiven him, neither in this w., 165
Mt 12:32 neither in the w. to come.
Mt 13:22 the word; and the care of this w., 165
Mt 13:35 from the foundation of the w. 2889
Mt 13:38 The field is the w.; the good seed 2889
Mt 13:39 the harvest is the end of the w.; 165
Mt 13:40 so shall it be in the end of this w. 165
Mt 13:49 So shall it be at the end of the w. 165
Mt 16:26 if he shall gain the whole w., and 2889
Mt 18:7 Woe unto the w. because of 2889
Mt 24:3 coming, and of the end of the w.? 165
Mt 24:14 shall be preached in all the w. for. 3625
Mt 24:21 not since the beginning of the w. 2889
Mt 25:34 you from the foundation of the w. 2889
Mt 26:13 shall be preached in the whole w., 2889
Mt 28:20 alway, even unto the end of the w. 165
Mk 4:19 And the cares of this w., and the 165
Mk 8:36 if he shall gain the whole w., and 2889
Mk 10:30 and in the w. to come eternal life 165
Mk 14:9 preached throughout the whole w., 2889
Mk 16:15 Go ye into all the w., and preach 2889
Lu 1:70 have been since the w. began: 165
Lu 2:1 that all the w. should be taxed. 3625
Lu 4:5 unto him all the kingdoms of the w. 3625
Lu 9:25 if he gain the whole w., and lose 2889
Lu 11:50 from the foundation of the w., 2889
Lu 12:30 do the nations of the w. seek 2889
Lu 16:8 the children of this w. are in their 165
Lu 18:30 in the w. to come life everlasting. 165
Lu 20:34 The children of this w. marry, and 165
Lu 20:35 accounted worthy to obtain that w., 165
Joh 1:9 every man that cometh into the w. 2889
Joh 1:10 He was in the w., 2889
Joh 1:10 and the w. was made by him, 2889
Joh 1:10 and the w. knew him not. 2889
Joh 1:29 which taketh away the sin of the w. 2889
Joh 3:16 For God so loved the w., that he 2889
Joh 3:17 Son into the w. to condemn the w.; 2889
Joh 3:17 w. through him might be saved. 2889
Joh 3:19 that light is come into the w., 2889
Joh 4:42 the Christ, the Saviour of the w. 2889
Joh 6:14 that should come into the w. 2889
Joh 6:33 and giveth light unto the w. 2889
Joh 6:51 I will give for the life of the w. 2889
Joh 7:4 these things, shew thyself to the w. 2889
Joh 7:7 The w. cannot hate you; but me 2889
Joh 8:12 saying, I am the light of the w. 2889
Joh 8:23 am from above: ye are of this w.; 2889
Joh 8:23 I am not of this w. 2889
Joh 8:26 I speak to the w. those things 2889
Joh 9:5 As long as I am in the w., 2889
Joh 9:5 I am the light of the w. 2889
Joh 9:32 Since the w. began was it not heard 165
Joh 9:39 Judgment I am come into this w., 2889
Joh 10:36 sanctified, and sent into the w., 2889
Joh 1:19 he seeth the light of this w. 2889
Joh 1:27 God, which should come into the w. 2889
Joh 12:19 behold, the w. is gone after him. 2889
Joh 12:25 that hateth his life in this w. 2889
Joh 12:31 Now is the judgment of this w.: 2889
Joh 12:31 the prince of this w. be cast out. 2889
Joh 12:46 I am come a light into the w., 2889
Joh 12:47 to judge the w., but to save the w. 2889
Joh 13:1 he should depart out of this w. unto 2889
Joh 13:1 loved his own which were in the w., 2889
Joh 14:17 whom the w. cannot receive, 2889
Joh 14:19 while, and the w. seeth me no more;
Joh 14:22 unto us, and not unto the w.?
Joh 14:27 not as the w. giveth, give I unto you
Joh 14:30 for the prince of this w. cometh,
Joh 14:31 w. may know that I love the Father;
Joh 15:18 If the w. hate you, ye know that it
Joh 15:19 of the w., the w. would love his own:
Joh 15:19 but because ye are not of the w.,
Joh 15:19 I have chosen you out of the w.,
Joh 15:19 therefore the w. hateth you.
Joh 16:8 he will reprove the w. of sin, and of
Joh 16:11 the prince of this w. is judged.
Joh 16:20 lament, but the w. shall rejoice:
Joh 16:21 joy that a man is born into the w.
Joh 16:28 Father, and am come into the w.:
Joh 16:28 I leave the w., and go to the Father.
Joh 16:33 In the w. ye shall have tribulation:
Joh 16:33 cheer; I have overcome the w.
Joh 17:5 I had with thee before the w. was.
Joh 17:6 thou gavest me out of the w.:
Joh 17:9 I pray not for the w., but for them
Joh 17:11 And now I am no more in the w.,
Joh 17:11 but these are in the w., and I come
Joh 17:12 While I was with them in the w.,
Joh 17:13 and these things I speak in the w.,
Joh 17:14 word; and the w. hath hated them,
Joh 17:14 because they are not of the w.,
Joh 17:14 even as I am not of the w.
Joh 17:15 shouldest take them out of the w.,
Joh 17:16 They are not of the w.,
Joh 17:16 even as I am not of the w.
Joh 17:18 As thou hast sent me into the w.,
Joh 17:18 so have I also sent them into the w.
Joh 17:21 w. may believe...thou hast sent me.
Joh 17:23 w. may know...thou hast sent me,
Joh 17:24 me before the foundation of the w.
Joh 17:25 the w. hath not known thee: but I
Joh 18:20 I spake openly to the w.; I ever
Joh 18:36 My kingdom is not of this w.
Joh 18:36 if my kingdom were of this w., then
Joh 18:37 for this cause came I into the w.,
Joh 21:25 even the w. itself could not contain.
Ac 3:21 holy prophets since the w. began. 165
Ac 11:28 dearth throughout all the w.: 3625
Ac 15:18 from the beginning of the w. 165
Ac 17:6 have turned the w. upside down 3625
Ac 17:24 God that made the w. and all 2889
Ac 17:31 will judge the w. in righteousness 3625
Ac 19:27 all Asia and the w. worshippeth. 3625
Ac 24:5 all the Jews throughout the w., 3625
Ro 1:8 spoken of throughout the whole w. 2889
Ro 1:20 from the creation of the w. are 2889
Ro 3:6 then how shall God judge the w.? 2889
Ro 3:19 all the w. may become guilty before 2889
Ro 4:13 that he should be the heir of the w., 2889
Ro 5:12 by one man sin entered into the w., 2889
Ro 5:13 (For until the law sin was in the w.: 2889
Ro 10:18 words unto the ends of the w. 3625
Ro 11:12 of them be the riches of the w. 2889
Ro 11:15 them be the reconciling of the w., 2889
Ro 12:2 And be not conformed to this w. 165
Ro 16:25 kept secret since the w. began. 166
1Co 1:20 where is the disputer of this w.? 165
1Co 1:20 foolish the wisdom of this w.? 2889
1Co 1:21 the w. by wisdom knew not God, 2889
1Co 1:27 chosen the foolish things of the w. 2889
1Co 1:27 chosen the weak things of the w. 2889
1Co 1:28 And base things of the w., and 2889
1Co 2:6 yet not the wisdom of this w. 165
1Co 2:6 nor of the princes of this w., that 165
1Co 2:7 God ordained before the w. unto 165
1Co 2:8 of the princes of this w. knew: 165
1Co 2:12 received, not the spirit of the w., 2889
1Co 3:18 you seemeth to be wise in this w., 165
1Co 3:19 wisdom of this w. is foolishness 2889
1Co 3:22 or the w., or life, or death, or 2889
1Co 4:9 are made a spectacle unto the w., 2889
1Co 4:13 we are made as the filth of the w., 2889
1Co 5:10 with the fornicators of this w., 2889
1Co 5:10 must ye needs go out of the w. 2889
1Co 6:2 that the saints shall judge the w.? 2889
1Co 6:2 if the w. shall be judged by you, 2889
1Co 7:31 And they that use this w., as not 2889
1Co 7:31 fashion of this w. passeth away 2889
1Co 7:33 for the things that are of the w., 2889
1Co 7:34 careth for the things of the w., 2889
1Co 8:4 that an idol is nothing in the w. 2889
1Co 8:13 no flesh while the w. standeth, 165
1Co 10:11 whom the ends of the w. are come. 165
1Co 11:32 not be condemned with the w. 2889
1Co 14:10 so many kinds of voices in the w., 2889
2Co 1:12 had our conversation in the w., 2889
2Co 4:4 the god of this w. hath blinded the 165
2Co 5:19 reconciling the w. unto himself, 2889
2Co 7:10 sorrow of the w. worketh death. 2889
Ga 1:4 deliver us from the present evil w., 165
Ga 4:3 under the elements of the w. 2889
Ga 6:14 whom the w. is crucified unto me, 2889
Ga 6:14 and I unto the w., 2889
Eph 1:4 before the foundation of the w., 2889
Eph 1:21 that is named, not only in this w., 165
Eph 2:2 according to the course of this w., 2889
Eph 2:12 hope, and without God in the w. 2889
Eph 3:9 the beginning of the w. hath been 165
Eph 3:21 throughout all ages, w. without end. 165
Eph 6:12 rulers of the darkness of this w., 165
Php 2:15 whom ye shine as lights in the w.; 2889
Col 1:6 come unto you, as it is in all the w.; 2889
Col 2:8 after the rudiments of the w., and 2889
Col 2:20 from the rudiments of the w., why, 2889
Col 2:20 as though living in the w., are ye 2889
1Ti 1:15 came into the w. to save sinners; 2889
1Ti 3:16 believed on in the w., received up 2889
1Ti 6:7 we brought nothing into this w., 2889
1Ti 6:17 them that are rich in this w., 165
2Ti 1:9 Christ Jesus before the w. began, 166
2Ti 4:10 me, having loved this present w., 165
Tit 1:2 promised before the w. began; 166
Tit 2:12 and godly, in this present w.; 165
Heb 1:6 in the firstbegotten into the w., 3625
Heb 2:5 put in subjection the w. to come, 3625
Heb 4:3 from the foundation of the w. 2889
Heb 6:5 and the powers of the w. to come, 165
Heb 9:26 since the foundation of the w. 2889
Heb 9:26 but now once in the end of the w. 165
Heb 10:5 when he cometh into the w., he 2889
Heb 11:7 by the which he condemned the w., 2889
Heb 11:38 (Of whom the w. was not worthy:) 2889
Jas 1:27 himself unspotted from the w. 2889
Jas 2:5 the poor of this w. rich in faith, 2889
Jas 3:6 tongue is a fire, a w. of iniquity: 2889
Jas 4:4 the friendship of the w. is enmity 2889
Jas 4:4 be a friend of the w. is the enemy 2889
1Pe 1:20 before the foundation of the w. 2889
1Pe 5:9 your brethren that are in the w. 2889
2Pe 1:4 the corruption that is in the w. 2889
2Pe 2:5 And spared not the old w., but 2889
2Pe 2:5 flood upon the w. of the ungodly; 2889
2Pe 2:20 escaped the pollutions of the w. 2889
2Pe 3:6 Whereby the w. that then was, 2889
1Jo 2:2 also for the sins of the whole w. 2889
1Jo 2:15 Love not the w., neither 2889
1Jo 2:15 the things that are in the w. 2889
1Jo 2:15 If any man love the w., the love of 2889
1Jo 2:16 For all that is in the w., the lust of 2889
1Jo 2:16 not of the Father, but is of the w. 2889
1Jo 2:17 And the w. passeth away, and the 2889
1Jo 3:1 therefore the w. knoweth us not, 2889
1Jo 3:13 my brethren, if the w. hate you. 2889
1Jo 4:1 prophets are gone out into the w. 2889
1Jo 4:3 even now already is it in the w. 2889
1Jo 4:4 is in you, than he that is in the w. 2889
1Jo 4:5 They are of the w.: therefore 2889
1Jo 4:5 therefore speak they of the w., 2889
1Jo 4:5 and the w. heareth them. 2889
1Jo 4:9 his only begotten Son into the w. 2889
1Jo 4:14 Son to be the Saviour of the w. 2889
1Jo 4:17 as he is, so are we in this w. 2889
1Jo 5:4 born of God overcometh the w.: 2889
1Jo 5:4 the victory that overcometh the w., 2889
1Jo 5:5 Who is he that overcometh the w., 2889
1Jo 5:19 the whole w. lieth in wickedness. 2889
2Jo 7 deceivers are entered into the w., 2889
Re 3:10 which shall come upon all the w., 3625
Re 11:15 kingdoms of this w. are become 2889
Re 12:9 which deceiveth the whole w.: 3625
Re 13:3 the w. wondered after the beast. 1093
Re 13:8 from the foundation of the w. 2889
Re 16:14 of the earth and of the whole w., 3625
Re 17:8 from the foundation of the w., 2889

WORLDLY
Tit 2:12 denying ungodliness and w. lusts, 2886
Heb 9:1 service, and a w. sanctuary. 2886

WORLD'S
1Jo 3:17 But whoso hath this w. good, 2889

WORLDS
Heb 1:2 by whom also he made the w.; 165
Heb 11:3 the w. were framed by the word of 165

WORM See also CANKERWORM; PALMERWORM; WORMS; WORMWOOD.
Ex 16:24 neither was there any w. therein. 7415
Job 17:14 to the w., Thou art my mother, 7415

Job 24:20 the w. shall feed sweetly on him;....... 7415
Job 25:6 How much less man, that is a w.?...... 7415
Job 25:6 the son of man, which is a w.?.......... 8438
Ps 22:6 But I am a w., and no man;............... 8438
Isa 14:11 the w. is spread under thee, and........ 7415
Isa 41:14 Fear not, thou w. Jacob, and ye......... 8438
Isa 51:8 the w. shall eat them like wool:......... 5580
Isa 66:24 for their w. shall not die, neither........ 8438
Jon 4:7 But God prepared a w. when the....... 8438
Mk 9:44, 46 **Where their w. dieth not,**.......... *4663*
Mk 9:48 **Where their w. dieth not,**.......... *4663*

WORMS

Ex 16:20 and it bred w., and stank:................. 8438
De 28:39 grapes; for the w. shall eat them....... 8438
Job 7:5 My flesh is clothed with w. and......... 7415
Job 19:26 after my skin w. shall destroy this............
Job 21:26 dust, and the w. shall cover them...... 7415
Isa 14:11 under thee, and the w. cover thee..... 8438
Mic 7:17 of their holes like w. of the earth:...... 2119
Ac 12:23 he was eaten of w., and gave up......... *4662*

WORMWOOD

De 29:18 a root that beareth gall and w.;........... 3939
Pr 5:4 But her end is bitter as w., sharp...... 3939
Jer 9:15 them, even this people, with w.,......... 3939
Jer 23:15 I will feed them with w., and make..... 3939
La 3:15 hath made me drunken with w............ 3939
La 3:19 my misery, the w. and the gall.......... 3939
Am 5:7 Ye who turn judgment to w., and........ 3939
Re 8:11 the name of the star is called W.:........ *894*
Re 8:11 part of the waters became w.;............ *894*

WORSE

Ge 19:9 now will we deal w. with thee,.......... 7489
2Sa 19:7 that will be w. unto thee than all....... 7489
1Ki 16:25 did w. than all that were before......... 7489
2Ki 14:12 Judah was put to the w. before.......... 5062
1Ch 19:16, 19 were put to the w. before Israel,... 5062
2Ch 6:24 thy people Israel be put to the w....... 5062
2Ch 25:22 Judah was put to the w. before.......... 5062
2Ch 33:9 to do w. than the heathen, whom......... 7451
Jer 7:26 they did w. than their fathers............ 7489
Jer 16:12 have done w. than your fathers;.......... 7489
Da 1:10 faces w. liking than the children......... 2196
Mt 9:16 **garment, and the rent is made w...** *5501*
Mt 12:45 **of that man is w. than the first**.... *5501*
Mt 27:64 last error shall be w. than the first..... *5501*
Mk 2:21 **the old, and the rent is made w**..... *5501*
Mk 5:26 bettered, but rather grew w.,............ *5501*
Lu 11:26 **of that man is w. than the first**.... *5501*
Joh 2:10 well drunk, then that which is w.:....... *1640*
Joh 5:14 **lest a w. thing come unto thee**,....... *5501*
1Co 8:8 if we eat not, are we the w............... *5302*
1Co 11:17 not for the better, but for the w......... *2276*
1Ti 5:8 faith, and is w. than an infidel........... *5501*
2Ti 3:13 and seducers shall wax w. and w.,...... *5501*
2Pe 2:20 the latter end is w. with them than..... *5501*

WORSHIP See also WORSHIPPED; WORSHIPPETH; WORSHIPPING.

Ge 22:5 and the lad will go yonder and w.,....... 7812
Ex 24:1 of Israel; and w. ye afar off............... 7812
Ex 34:14 For thou shalt w. no other god:.......... 7812
De 4:19 shouldest be driven to w. them,........... 7812
De 8:19 and serve them, and w. them,............. 7812
De 11:16 and serve other gods, and w. them;... 7812
De 26:10 and w. before the Lord thy God:....... 7812
De 30:17 w. other gods, and serve them;.......... 7812
Jos 5:14 on his face to the earth, and did w.,... 7812
1Sa 1:3 went up out of his city yearly to w.... 7812
1Sa 15:25 with me, that I may w. the Lord,........ 7812
1Sa 15:30 that I may w. the Lord thy God......... 7812
1Ki 9:6 and serve other gods, and w. them:... 7812
1Ki 12:30 the people went to w. before the one, ...
2Ki 5:18 the house of Rimmon to w. there,....... 7812
2Ki 17:36 shall ye fear, and him shall ye w.,...... 7812
2Ki 18:22 w. before the altar in Jerusalem?........ 7812
1Ch 16:29 w. the Lord in the beauty of............. 7812
2Ch 7:19 and serve other gods, and w. them;... 7812
2Ch 32:12 Ye shall w. before one altar, and......... 7812
Ps 5:7 will I w. toward thy holy temple......... 7812
Ps 22:27 the nations shall w. before thee......... 7812
Ps 22:29 fat upon earth shall eat and w.:......... 7812
Ps 29:2 w. the Lord in the beauty of............. 7812
Ps 45:11 he is thy Lord; and w. thou him......... 7812
Ps 66:4 All the earth shall w. thee, and.......... 7812
Ps 81:9 shalt thou w. any strange god............ 7812
Ps 86:9 shall come and w. before thee;.......... 7812
Ps 95:6 O come, let us w. and bow down:...... 7812
Ps 96:9 O w. the Lord in the beauty of.......... 7812
Ps 97:7 of idols: w. him, all ye gods............. 7812
Ps 99:5 our God, and w. at his footstool;........ 7812
Ps 99:9 our God, and w. at his holy hill;......... 7812
Ps 132:7 we will w. at his footstool................. 7812
Ps 138:2 I will w. toward thy holy temple,....... 7812
Isa 2:8 w. the work of their own hands,......... 7812
Isa 2:20 made each one for himself to w.,........ 7812
Isa 27:13 shall w. the Lord in the holy mount.... 7812
Isa 36:7 Ye shall w. before this altar?............ 7812
Isa 46:6 a god: they fall down, yea, they w..... 7812
Isa 49:7 see and arise, princes also shall w.,.... 7812
Isa 66:23 all flesh come to w. before me,......... 7812
Jer 7:2 in at these gates to w. the Lord......... 7812
Jer 13:10 gods, to serve them, and to w. them,. 7812
Jer 25:6 gods to serve them, and to w. them,.. 7812
Jer 26:2 come to w. in the Lord's house,......... 7812
Jer 44:19 did we make her cakes to w. her,...... 6087
Eze 46:2 w. at the threshold of the gate:......... 7812
Eze 46:3 shall w. at the door of this gate........ 7812
Eze 46:9 by the way of the north gate to w...... 7812
Da 3:5 fall down and w. the golden image...... 5457
Da 3:10 fall down and w. the golden image:..... 5457
Da 3:12 nor w. the golden image which thou.... 5457
Da 3:14 nor w. the golden image which I........ 5457
Da 3:15 ye fall down and w. the image.......... 5457
Da 3:15 but if ye w. not, ye shall be cast........ 5457
Da 3:18 nor w. the golden image which thou.... 5457
Da 3:28 might not serve nor w. any god,........ 5457
Mic 5:13 more w. the work of thine hands........ 7812
Zep 1:5 them that w. the host of heaven........ 7812
Zep 1:5 w. and that swear by the Lord,........... 7812
Zep 2:11 and men shall w. him, every one........ 7812
Zec 14:16 from year to year to w. the King,....... 7812
Zec 14:17 unto Jerusalem to w. the King,.......... 7812
Mt 2:2 the east, and are come to w. him......... *4352*
Mt 2:8 that I may come and w. him also........ *4352*
Mt 4:9 if thou wilt fall down and w. me......... *4352*
Mt 4:10 **Thou shalt w. the Lord thy God,**... *4352*
Mt 15:9 **But in vain do they w. me,**........... *4576*
Mk 7:7 **Howbeit in vain do they w. me,**...... *4576*
Lu 4:7 If thou therefore wilt w. me,...... *4352,1799*
Lu 4:8 **Thou shalt w. the Lord thy God,**... *4352*
Lu 14:10 **have w. in the presence** of them..... *1391*
Joh 4:20 the place where men ought to w......... *4352*
Joh 4:21 yet at Jerusalem, w. the Father......... *4352*
Joh 4:22 **Ye w. ye know not what:**............. 4352
Joh 4:22 **know what we w.: for salvation**..... 4352
Joh 4:23 **shall w. the Father in Spirit and**... 4352
Joh 4:23 **the Father seeketh such to w. him**. 4352
Joh 4:24 **is a Spirit: and they that w. him**... 4352
Joh 4:24 **w. him in spirit and in truth**......... 4352
Joh 12:20 that came up to w. at the feast:......... 4352
Ac 7:42 them up to w. the host of heaven;..... *3000*
Ac 7:43 which ye made to w. them:............... *4352*
Ac 8:27 had come to Jerusalem for to w.,........ *4352*
Ac 17:23 Whom therefore ye ignorantly w.,...... *2151*
Ac 18:13 fellow persuadeth men to w. God........ *4576*
Ac 24:11 I went up to Jerusalem for to w......... *4352*
Ac 24:14 so w. I the God of my fathers,........... *3000*
1Co 14:25 down on his face he will w. God,......... *4352*
Php 3:3 which w. God in the spirit, and........... *3000*
Col 2:23 indeed a shew of wisdom in will w.,..... *1479*
Heb 1:6 let all the angels of God w. him........... *4352*
Re 3:9 **to come and w. before thy feet,**...... *4352*
Re 4:10 and w. him that liveth for ever and..... *4352*
Re 9:20 that they should not w. devils, and..... *4352*
Re 11:1 altar, and them that w. therein........... *4352*
Re 13:8 dwell upon the earth shall w. him,....... *4352*
Re 13:12 dwell therein to w. the first beast,...... *4352*
Re 13:15 not w. the image of the beast............ *4352*
Re 14:7 and w. him that made heaven, and..... *4352*
Re 14:9 If any man w. the beast and his......... *4352*
Re 14:11 who w. the beast and his image,.......... *4352*
Re 15:4 shall come and w. before thee;.......... *4352*
Re 19:10 And I fell at his feet to w. him.......... *4352*
Re 19:10 w. God: for the testimony of Jesus..... *4352*
Re 22:8 I fell down to w. before the feet of..... *4352*
Re 22:9 the sayings of this book: w. God........ *4352*

WORSHIPPED

Ge 24:26 down his head, and w. the Lord........ 7812
Ge 24:48 down my head, and w. the Lord,........ 7812
Ge 24:52 heard their words, he w. the Lord,...... 7812
Ex 4:31 they bowed their heads and w............ 7812
Ex 12:27 the people bowed the head and w....... 7812
Ex 32:8 them a molten calf, and have w. it...... 7812
Ex 33:10 and all the people rose up and w.,....... 7812
Ex 34:8 his head toward the earth, and w....... 7812
De 17:3 and served other gods, and w. them,.. 7812
De 29:26 and served other gods, and w. them,.. 7812
Jg 7:15 interpretation thereof, that he w.,...... 7812
1Sa 1:19 w. before the Lord, and returned,....... 7812
1Sa 1:28 Lord. And he w. the Lord there........ 7812
1Sa 15:31 after Saul; and Saul w. the Lord........ 7812
2Sa 12:20 into the house of the Lord, and w.:..... 7812
2Sa 15:32 top of the mount, where he w. God,... 7812
1Ki 9:9 upon other gods, and have w. them,... 7812
1Ki 11:33 have w. Ashtoreth the goddess of...... 7812
1Ki 16:31 went and served Baal, and w. him...... 7812
1Ki 22:53 For he served Baal, and w. him,......... 7812
2Ki 17:16 and w. all the host of heaven, and...... 7812
2Ki 21:3 and w. all the host of heaven, and...... 7812
2Ki 21:21 that his father served, and w. them:... 7812
1Ch 29:20 down their heads, and w. the Lord,.... 7812
2Ch 7:3 and w., and praised the Lord,........... 7812
2Ch 7:22 hold on other gods, and w. them,......... 7812
2Ch 29:28 And all the congregation w., and......... 7812
2Ch 29:29 him bowed themselves, and w........... 7812
2Ch 29:30 and they bowed their heads and w...... 7812
2Ch 33:3 and w. all the host of heaven,............. 7812
Ne 8:6 and w. the Lord with their faces to.... 7812
Ne 9:3 and w. the Lord their God................ 7812
Job 1:20 fell down upon the ground, and w.,..... 7812
Ps 106:19 in Horeb, and w. the molten image..... 7812
Jer 1:16 w. the works of their own hands......... 7812
Jer 8:2 sought, and whom they have w.:......... 7812
Jer 16:11 served them, and have w. them,......... 7812
Jer 22:9 w. other gods, and served them.......... 7812
Eze 8:16 they w. the sun toward the east.......... 7812
Da 2:46 and w. Daniel, and commanded........... 5457
Da 3:7 fell down and w. the golden image...... 5457
Mt 2:11 mother, and fell down and w. him:..... *4352*
Mt 8:2 there came a leper and w. him,.......... *4352*
Mt 9:18 came a certain ruler, and w. him,........ *4352*
Mt 14:33 were in the ship came and w. him,...... *4352*
Mt 15:25 Then came she and w. him, saying,..... *4352*
Mt 18:26 **down, and w. him, saying, Lord,**... *4352*
Mt 28:9 held him by the feet, and w. him........ *4352*
Mt 28:17 they w. him: but some doubted.......... *4352*
Mk 5:6 Jesus afar off, he ran and w. him,....... *4352*
Mk 15:19 and bowing their knees w. him.......... *4352*
Lu 24:52 And they w. him, and returned to...... *4352*
Joh 4:20 Our fathers w. in this mountain;......... *4352*
Joh 9:38 Lord, I believe. And he w. him.......... *4352*
Ac 10:25 fell down at his feet, and w. him......... *4352*
Ac 16:14 Thyatira, which w. God, heard us;...... *4576*
Ac 17:25 Neither is w. with men's hands,.......... *2323*
Ac 18:7 named Justus, one that w. God,.......... *4576*
Ro 1:25 and w. and served the creature.......... *4573*
2Th 2:4 all that is called God, or that is w.;.... *4574*
Heb 11:21 and w., leaning upon the top of.......... *4352*
Re 5:14 and w. him that liveth for ever and..... *4352*
Re 7:11 throne on their faces, and w. God,...... *4352*
Re 11:16 fell upon their faces, and w. God,........ *4352*
Re 13:4 w. the dragon which gave power.......... *4352*
Re 13:4 and they w. the beast, saying, Who.... *4352*
Re 16:2 and upon them which w. his image...... *4352*
Re 19:4 four beasts fell down and w. God....... *4352*
Re 19:20 beast, and them that w. his image...... *4352*
Re 20:4 which had not w. the beast, neither..... *4352*

WORSHIPPER See also WORSHIPPERS.

Joh 9:31 but if any man be a w. of God, and.... *2318*
Ac 19:35 a w. of the great goddess Diana,......... *3511*

WORSHIPPERS

2Ki 10:19 he might destroy the w. of Baal......... 5647
2Ki 10:21 all the w. of Baal came, so that.......... 5647
2Ki 10:22 vestments for all the w. of Baal......... 5647
2Ki 10:23 said unto the w. of Baal, Search,........ 5647
2Ki 10:23 the Lord, but the w. of Baal only........ 5647
Joh 4:23 **true w. shall worship the Father**... *4353*
Heb 10:2 the w. once purged should have.......... *3000*

WORSHIPPETH

Ne 9:6 and the host of heaven w. thee.......... 7812
Isa 44:15 yea, he maketh a god, and w. it;....... 7812
Isa 44:17 he falleth down into it, and w. it,....... 7812
Da 3:6 whoso falleth not down and w.......... 5457
Da 3:11 And whoso falleth not down and w.,... 5457
Ac 19:27 whom all Asia and the world w.......... *4576*

WORSHIPPING

2Ki 9:37 w. in the house of Nisroch his god,.... 7812

2Ch 20:18 fell before the Lord, w. the Lord. 7812
Isa 37:38 w. in the house of Nisroch his god, 7812
Mt 20:20 w. him, and desiring a certain *4352*
Col 2:18 humility and w. of angels, *2356*

WORST
Eze 7:24 I will bring the w. of the heathen, 7451

WORTH See also PENNYWORTH.
Ge 23:9 money as it is w. he shall give it 4392
Ge 23:15 is w. four hundred shekels of silver;
Le 27:23 unto him the w. of thy estimation, 4373
De 15:18 been w. a double hired servant 7939
2Sa 18:3 thou art w. ten thousand of us: 3644
1Ki 21:2 give thee the w. of it in money 4242
Job 24:25 and make my speech nothing w.?
Pr 10:20 the heart of the wicked is little w..
Eze 30:2 God; Howl ye, Woe w. the day!

WORTHIES
Na 2:5 He shall recount his w.: they shall 117

WORTHILY See also UNWORTHILY.
Ru 4:11 do thou w. in Ephratah, and be 2428

WORTHY See also THANKWORTHY; UNWORTHY; WORTHIES.
Ge 32:10 I am not w. of the least of all the 6994
De 17:6 is w. of death to be put ot death;
De 19:6 whereas he was not w. of death,
De 21:22 have committed a sin w. of death,
De 22:26 is in the damsel no sin w. of death:
De 25:2 wicked man be w. to be beaten, 1121
1Sa 1:5 unto Hannah he gave a w. portion; 639
1Sa 26:16 ye are w. to die, because ye have 1121
2Sa 22:4 the Lord, who is w. to be praised:
1Ki 1:52 will shew himself a w. man, 2428
1Ki 2:26 fields; for thou art w. of death: 376
Ps 18:3 the Lord, who is w. to be praised:
Jer 26:11 saying, this man is w. to die;
Jer 26:16 This man is not w. to die: for he
Mt 3:11 whose shoes I am not w. to bear: *2425*
Mt 8:8 I am not w. that thou shouldest *2425*
Mt 10:10 **for the workman is w. of his meat** *514*
Mt 10:11 **shall enter, enquire who in it is w.;** *514*
Mt 10:13 **if the house be w., let your peace** *514*
Mt 10:13 **it be not w., let your peace return** *514*
Mt 10:37 **more than me is not w. of me:** *514*
Mt 10:37 **more than me is not w. of me.** *514*
Mt 10:38 **followeth after me, is not w. of** *514*
Mt 22:8 **which were bidden were not w.** *514*
Mk 1:7 shoes I am not w. to stoop down *2425*
Lu 3:8 therefore fruits w. of repentance, *514*
Lu 3:16 shoes I am not w. to unloose: *2425*
Lu 7:4 he was w. for whom he should do *514*
Lu 7:6 I am not w. that thou shouldest *2425*
Lu 7:7 thought I myself w. to come *515*
Lu 10:7 **for the labourer is w. of his hire** *514*
Lu 12:48 **did commit things w. of stripes,** *514*
Lu 15:19 **no more w. to be called thy son:** *514*
Lu 15:21 **am no more w. to be called thy** *514*
Lu 20:35 **accounted w. to obtain that world,** *2661*
Lu 21:36 **accounted w. to escape all these** *2661*
Lu 23:15 nothing w. of death is done unto *514*
Joh 1:27 latchet I am not w. to unloose *514*
Ac 5:41 were counted w. to suffer shame *2661*
Ac 13:25 of his feet I am not w. to loose *514*
Ac 23:29 laid to his charge w. of death *514*
Ac 24:2 very w. deeds are done unto this *2735*
Ac 25:11 committed any thing w. of death, *514*
Ac 25:25 had committed nothing w. of death, *514*
Ac 26:31 nothing w. of death or of bonds *514*
Ro 1:32 such things are w. of death, *514*
Ro 8:18 time are not w. to be compared *514*
Eph 4:1 that ye walk w. of the vocation *516*
Col 1:10 might walk w. of the Lord unto *516*
1Th 2:12 That ye would walk w. of God, who *516*
2Th 1:5 may be counted w. of the kingdom *2661*
2Th 1:11 count you w. of this calling, *515*
1Ti 1:15 saying, and w. of all acceptation, *514*
1Ti 4:9 saying and w. of all acceptation. *514*
1Ti 5:17 be counted w. of double honour, *515*
1Ti 5:18 The labourer is w. of his reward. *514*
1Ti 6:1 their own masters w. of all honour, *514*
Heb 3:3 man was counted w. of more glory *515*
Heb 10:29 shall he be thought w., who hath *515*
Heb 11:38 (Of whom the world was not w.:) *514*
Jas 2:7 they blaspheme that w. name *2570*
Re 3:4 **with me in white: for they are w..** *514*
Re 4:11 Thou art w., O Lord, to receive *514*
Re 5:2 Who is w. to open the book, and to *514*
Re 5:4 no man was found w. to open and *514*
Re 5:9 Thou art w. to take the book, and *514*
Re 5:12 W. is the lamb that was slain to *514*
Re 16:6 blood to drink; for they are w.. *514*

WOT See also WIST; WIT; WOTTETH.
Ge 21:26 I w. not who hath done this thing: 3045
Ge 44:15 w. ye not that such a man as I can 3045
Ex 32:1, 23 w. not what is become of him 3045
Nu 22:6 I w. that he whom thou blessest is 3045
Jos 2:5 whither the men went I w. not; 3045
Ac 3:17 I w. that through ignorance ye did *1492*
Ac 7:40 we w. not what is become of him *1492*
Ro 11:2 W. ye not what the scripture saith *1492*
Php 1:22 yet what I shall choose I w. not *1107*

WOTTETH
Ge 39:8 my master w. not what is with me 3045

WOULD See also WOULDEST.
Ge 2:19 Adam to see what he w. call them:
Ge 21:7 Who w. have said unto Abraham, that
Ge 30:34 I w. that it might be according 3863
Ge 42:21 he besought us, and we w. not hear;
Ge 42:22 and ye w. not hear? therefore, behold,
Ge 43:7 certainly know that he w. say, Bring
Ge 44:2 leave his father, his father w. die.
Ex 2:4 afar off, to wit what w. be done to him.
Ex 8:32 neither w. he let the people go.
Ex 9:35 neither w. he let the children of
Ex 10:20 he w. not let the children of Israel.
Ex 10:27 heart, and he w. not let them go. 14
Ex 11:10 he w. not let the children of Israel.
Ex 13:15 when Pharaoh w. hardly let us go,
Ex 16:3 W. to God we had died by 4310,5414
Nu 11:29 w. God that all the Lord's 4310,5414
Nu 11:29 Lord w. put his spirit upon them! 4310,5414
Nu 14:2 W. God that we had died in the 3863
Nu 14:2 w. God we...died in the wilderness! 3863
Nu 20:3 W. God that we had died when 3863
Nu 21:23 And Sihon w. not suffer Israel to pass
Nu 22:18 If Balak w. give me his house full of
Nu 22:29 I w. there were a sword in mine 3863
Nu 22:29 in mine hand, for now I w. kill thee.
Nu 24:13 If Balak w. give me his house full of
De 1:26 Notwithstanding ye w. not go up, 14
De 1:43 and ye w. not hear, but rebelled
De 1:45 Lord w. not hearken to your voice,
De 2:30 king of Heshbon w. not let us pass 14
De 3:26 for your sakes, and w. not hear me:
De 5:29 a heart in them, that they w. fear me,
De 7:8 because he w. keep the oath which he
De 8:20 ye w. not be obedient unto the voice
De 9:25 the Lord had said he w. destroy you.
De 10:10 and the Lord w. not destroy thee. 14
De 23:5 God w. not hearken unto Balaam; 14
De 23:21 it of thee; and it w. be sin in thee.
De 28:56 w. not adventure to set the sole of
De 28:67 say, W. God it were even! 4310,5414
De 28:67 say, W. God it were morning! 4310,5414
De 32:26 I said, I w. scatter them into corners,
De 32:26 I w. make the remembrance of them
De 32:29 they w. consider their latter end!
Jos 5:6 that he w. not shew them the land,
Jos 5:6 unto their fathers that he w. give us,
Jos 7:7 w. to God we had been content, 3863
Jos 17:12 Canaanites w. dwell in that land. 2974
Jos 24:10 But I w. not hearken unto Balaam; 14
Jg 1:27 Canaanites w. dwell in that land. 2974
Jg 1:34 for they w. not suffer them to come
Jg 1:35 Amorites w. dwell in mount Heres 2974
Jg 2:17 w. not hearken unto their judges,
Jg 3:4 to know whether they w. hearken
Jg 8:19 saved them alive, I w. not slay you
Jg 8:24 them, I w. desire a request from you,
Jg 8:24 w. give me every man the earrings
Jg 9:29 w. to God this people were 4310,5414
Jg 9:29 then w. I remove Abimelech. And he
Jg 11:17 the king of Edom w. not hearken
Jg 11:17 king of Moab: but he w. not consent: 14
Jg 13:23 he w. not have received a burnt
Jg 13:23 neither w. he have shewed us all
Jg 13:23 nor w. as at this time have told us
Jg 14:6 he rent him as he w. have rent a kid,
Jg 15:1 her father w. not suffer him to go in.
Jg 19:10 But the man w. not tarry that night, 14
Jg 19:25 the men w. not hearken to him: 14
Jg 20:13 of Benjamin w. not hearken to the 14
Ru 1:13 W. ye tarry for them till they were
Ru 1:13 w. ye stay for them from having
1Sa 2:16 then he w. answer him, Nay; but
1Sa 2:25 because the Lord w. slay them. 2654
1Sa 13:13 for now w. the Lord have established
1Sa 15:9 and w. not utterly destroy them: 14
1Sa 18:2 and w. let him go no more home to his
1Sa 20:9 come upon thee, then w. not I tell it
1Sa 22:17 servants of the king w. not put forth 14
1Sa 22:22 was there, that he w. surely tell Saul:
1Sa 26:23 but I w. not stretch forth mine hand 14
1Sa 31:4 But his armourbearer w. not; for he 14
2Sa 2:21 But Asahel w. not turn aside from 14
2Sa 4:6 through they w. have fetched wheat;
2Sa 4:10 that I w. have given him a reward
2Sa 6:10 So David w. not remove the ark of 14
2Sa 11:20 knew ye not that they w. shoot from
2Sa 12:8 I w. moreover have given unto thee
2Sa 12:17 but he w. not, neither did he eat 14
2Sa 12:18 he w. not hearken unto our voice:
2Sa 13:14 he w. not hearken unto her voice: 14
2Sa 13:16 me. But he w. not hearken unto her 14
2Sa 13:25 howbeit he w. not go, but blessed 14
2Sa 14:16 man that w. destroy me and my son
2Sa 14:29 king; but he w. not come to him: 14
2Sa 14:29 second time, he w. not come. 14
2Sa 15:4 unto me, and I w. do him justice!
2Sa 18:11 I w. have given thee ten shekels of
2Sa 18:12 yet w. I not put forth mine hand
2Sa 18:33 w. God I had died for thee, O 4310,5414
2Sa 23:15 that one w. give me drink of the water
2Sa 23:16 nevertheless he w. not drink 14
2Sa 23:17 therefore he w. not drink it. These 14
1Ki 8:12 he w. dwell in the thick darkness.
1Ki 13:33 whosoever w., he consecrated him, 2655
1Ki 18:32 as great as w. contain two measures of
1Ki 20:33 whether any thing w. come from him,
1Ki 21:4 away his face, and w. eat no bread.
1Ki 22:18 w. prophesy no good concerning me,
1Ki 22:49 the ships. But Jehoshaphat w. not. 14
2Ki 2:1 when the Lord w. take up Elijah into
2Ki 3:14 I w. not look toward thee, nor see
2Ki 5:3 W. God my lord were with the 305
2Ki 5:3 for he w. recover him of his leprosy.
2Ki 7:2 the Lord w. make windows in heaven,
2Ki 8:19 Yet the Lord w. not destroy Judah 14
2Ki 13:23 and w. not destroy them, neither 14
2Ki 14:11 But Amaziah w. not hear. Therefore
2Ki 14:27 that he w. blot out the name of Israel
2Ki 17:14 Notwithstanding they w. not hear,
2Ki 18:12 and w. not hear them, nor do them.
2Ki 24:4 which the Lord w. not pardon. 14
1Ch 10:4 But his armourbearer w. not; for he 14
1Ch 11:17 that one w. give me drink of the water
1Ch 11:18 but David w. not drink of it, but 14
1Ch 11:19 Therefore he w. not drink it. 14
1Ch 13:4 congregation said that they w. do so:
1Ch 19:19 neither w. the Syrians help the 14
1Ch 27:23 he w. increase Israel like to the stars
2Ch 6:1 that he w. dwell in the thick darkness.
2Ch 10:16 saw that the king w. not hearken
2Ch 12:12 that he w. not destroy him altogether:
2Ch 15:13 whosoever w. not seek the Lord God of
2Ch 18:17 that he w. not prophesy good unto me,
2Ch 21:7 w. not destroy the house of David, 14
2Ch 24:19 them: but they w. not give ear.
2Ch 25:20 But Amaziah w. not hear; for it came
2Ch 33:10 his people: but they w. not hearken.
2Ch 35:22 Josiah w. not turn his face from him,
Ezr 10:8 w. not come within three days,
Ezr 10:19 that they w. put away their wives;
Ne 6:11 w. go into the temple to save his life?
Ne 6:14 prophets, that w. have put me in fear.
Ne 9:24 they might do with them as they w..
Ne 9:29 hardened their neck, and w. not hear.
Ne 9:30 yet w. they not give ear: therefore
Ne 10:30 we w. not give our daughters unto the
Ne 10:31 w. not buy it of them on the sabbath,
Ne 10:31 that we w. leave the seventh year,
Es 3:4 whether Mordecai's matters w. stand:
Es 6:6 To whom w. the king delight to do
Es 8:11 and province that w. assault them,
Es 9:5 what they w. unto those that hated
Es 9:27 that they w. keep these two days

Job 5:8 I w. seek unto God,
Job 5:8 and unto God w. I commit my cause:
Job 6:3 it w. be heavier than the sand of the
Job 6:8 that God w. grant me the thing that
Job 6:9 that it w. please God to destroy me;
Job 6:9 that he w. let loose his hand, and cut
Job 6:10 I w. harden myself in sorrow: let
Job 7:16 I loathe it, I w. not live alway: let me
Job 8:6 surely now he w. awake for thee, and
Job 9:15 I were righteous, yet w. I not answer,
Job 9:15 I w. make supplication to my judge.
Job 9:16 w. I not believe that he had hearkened
Job 9:21 perfect, yet w. I not know my soul:
Job 9:21 I w. despise my life.
Job 9:35 Then w. I speak, and not fear him;
Job 11:5 But oh that God w. speak, and open
Job 11:6 he w. shew thee the secrets of wisdom,
Job 11:12 For vain man w. be wise, though man
Job 13:3 Surely I w. speak to the Almighty, and
Job 13:5 ye w. altogether hold your peace!
Job 16:5 I w. strengthen you with my mouth,
Job 23:4 I w. order my cause before him, and
Job 23:5 I w. know the words which
Job 23:5 he w. answer me, and understand
Job 23:5 understand what he w. say unto me.
Job 23:6 No; but he w. put strength in me.
Job 27:22 spare: he w. fain flee out of his hand.
Job 30:1 whose fathers I w. have disdained to
Job 31:12 and w. root out all mine increase.
Job 31:35 Oh that one w. hear me! behold, my
Job 31:35 that the Almighty w. answer me, and
Job 31:36 Surely I w. take it upon my shoulder,
Job 31:37 I w. declare unto him the number of
Job 31:37 as a prince w. I go near unto him.
Job 32:22 in so doing my maker w. soon take me
Job 34:27 and w. not consider any of his ways:
Job 36:16 Even so w. he have removed thee out
Job 41:32 one w. think the deep to be hoary.
Ps 22:8 on the Lord that he w. deliver him:
Ps 35:25 their hearts, Ah, so w. we have it: 5315
Ps 40:5 if I w. declare and speak of them,
Ps 50:12 If I were hungry, I w. not tell thee:
Ps 51:16 not sacrifice; else w. I give it: thou
Ps 55:6 for then w. I fly away, and be at rest.
Ps 55:7 Lo, then w. I wander far off, and
Ps 55:8 I w. hasten my escape from the
Ps 55:12 then I w. have hid myself from him:
Ps 56:1 O God: for man w. swallow me up;
Ps 56:2 Mine enemies w. daily swallow me up:
Ps 57:3 reproach of him that w. swallow me
Ps 69:4 w. destroy me, being mine enemies
Ps 81:11 people w. not hearken to my voice;
Ps 81:11 and Israel w. none of me. 14
Ps 106:23 he said that he w. destroy them,
Ps 107:8, 15,21,31 men w. praise the Lord for
Ps 119:57 I have said that I w. keep thy words.
Ps 142:4 there was no man that w. know me:
Pr 1:25 counsel, and w. none of my reproof: 14
Pr 1:30 They w. none of my counsel: they 14
Ca 3:4 I held him, and w. not let him go,
Ca 8:1 find thee without, I w. kiss thee;
Ca 8:2 I w. lead thee, and bring thee into
Ca 8:2 mother's house, who w. instruct me:
Ca 8:2 w. cause thee to drink of spiced wine
Ca 8:7 if a man w. give all the substance of
Ca 8:7 for love, it w. utterly be contemned.
Isa 27:4 who w. set the briers and thorns
Isa 27:4 I w. go through them,
Isa 27:4 I w. burn them together
Isa 28:12 refreshing: yet they w. not hear 14
Isa 30:15 be your strength: and ye w. not 14
Isa 42:24 for they w. not walk in his ways, 14
Isa 54:9 that I w. not be wroth with thee,
Jer 8:18 I w. comfort myself against sorrow,
Jer 10:7 Who w. not fear thee, O King of
Jer 13:11 for a glory: but they w. not hear.
Jer 18:10 wherewith I said I w. benefit them.
Jer 22:24 hand, yet w. I pluck thee hence;
Jer 29:19 but ye w. not hear, saith the Lord.
Jer 36:25 the king that he w. not burn the roll:
Jer 36:25 but he w. not hear them.
Jer 38:26 that he w. not cause me to return to
Jer 49:9 w. they not leave some gleaning
Jer 51:9 We w. have healed Babylon, but she
La 4:12 w. not have believed that the
Eze 3:6 they w. have hearkened unto thee.
Eze 6:10 that I w. do this evil unto them.
Eze 13:6 hope that they w. confirm the word.
Eze 20:8 me, and w. not hearken unto me: 14
Eze 20:13 I w. pour out my fury upon them
Eze 20:15 I w. not bring into the land which I
Eze 20:21 I w. pour out my fury upon them.
Eze 20:23 I w. scatter them among the heathen,
Eze 38:17 that I w. bring thee against them?
Da 1:8 heart that he w. not defile himself
Da 2:8 of certainty that ye w. gain the time,
Da 2:16 of the king that he w. give him time,
Da 2:16 w. shew the king the interpretation.
Da 2:18 they w. desire mercies of the God of
Da 5:19 before him: whom he w. he slew; 6634
Da 5:19 and whom he w. he kept alive; 6634
Da 5:19 and whom he w. he set up; 6634
Da 5:19 and whom he w. he put down. 6634
Da 7:19 I w. know the truth of the fourth 6634
Da 9:2 that he w. accomplish seventy years
Ho 7:1 When I w. have healed Israel, then
Ho 11:7 most High, none at all w. exalt him.
Ob 5 w. they not have stolen till they had
Ob 5 w. they not leave some grapes?
Jon 3:10 he had said that he w. do unto them;
Jon 4:5 see what w. become of the city.
Zec 7:13 as he cried, and they w. not hear;
Zec 7:13 so they cried, and I w. not hear,
Mal 1:10 that w. shut the doors for nought?
Mt 2:18 children, and w. not be comforted, 2309
Mt 5:42 **that w. borrow of thee turn not** 2309
Mt 7:12 **ye w. that men should do to you,** 2309
Mt 8:34 he w. depart out of their coasts.
Mt 11:21 **they w. have repented long ago in**
Mt 11:23 **it w. have remained until this day.**
Mt 12:7 **ye w. not have condemned the**
Mt 12:38 we w. see a sign from thee. 2309
Mt 14:5 when he w. have put him to death, 2309
Mt 14:7 to give her whatsoever she w. ask.
Mt 16:1 he w. shew them a sign from heaven.
Mt 18:23 **w. take account of his servants.** 2309
Mt 18:30 **he w. not: but went and cast him** 2309
Mt 22:3 **wedding: and they w. not come.** 2309
Mt 23:30 **we w. not have been partakers with**
Mt 23:37 **w. I have gathered thy children** 2309
Mt 23:37 **under her wings, and ye w. not!** 2309
Mt 24:43 **in what watch the thief w. come,**
Mt 24:43 **come, he w. have watched, and**
Mt 24:43 **w. not have suffered his house to be**
Mt 27:15 people a prisoner, whom they w. 2309
Mt 27:34 tasted thereof, he w. not drink. 2309
Mk 3:2 whether he w. heal on the sabbath
Mk 3:13 and calleth unto him whom he w.: 2309
Mk 5:10 that he w. not send them away out
Mk 6:19 and w. have killed him; but she 2309
Mk 6:26 sat with him, he w. not reject her. 2309
Mk 6:48 sea, and w. have passed by them. 2309
Mk 7:24 and w. have no man know it: 2309
Mk 7:26 that he w. cast forth the devil out of
Mk 9:30 he w. not that any man should 2309
Mk 10:35 Master, we w. that thou shouldest 2309
Mk 10:36 **w. ye that I should do for you?** 2309
Mk 11:16 And w. not suffer that any man should
Lu 1:62 father, how he w. have him called. 2309
Lu 1:74 That he w. grant unto us, that we
Lu 5:3 w. thrust out a little from the land.
Lu 6:7 whether he w. heal on the sabbath
Lu 6:31 **ye w. that men should do to you,** 2309
Lu 7:3 that he w. come and heal his servant.
Lu 7:36 desired him that he w. eat with him.
Lu 7:39 w. have known who and what manner
Lu 8:31 he w. not command them to go out
Lu 8:32 that he w. suffer them to enter into
Lu 8:41 him that he w. come into his house:
Lu 9:53 as though he w. go to Jerusalem.
Lu 10:1 whither he himself w. come. 3195
Lu 10:2 **that he w. send forth labourers**
Lu 12:39 **known what hour the thief w. come,**
Lu 12:39 **he w. have watched, and not have**
Lu 13:34 **w. I have gathered thy children** 2309
Lu 13:34 **under her wings, and ye w. not!** 2309
Lu 15:16 **he w. fain have filled his belly with**
Lu 15:28 **he was angry, and w. not go in:** 2309
Lu 16:26 **which w. pass from hence to you** 2309
Lu 16:26 **to us, that w. come from thence.**
Lu 18:4 **And he w. not for a while: but** 2309
Lu 18:13 **w. not life up so much as his eyes** 2309
Lu 18:15 infants, that he w. touch them:
Lu 19:27 **which w. not that I should reign** 2309
Lu 19:40 **the stones w. immediately cry out.**
Lu 22:49 were about him saw what w. follow,
Lu 24:28 as though he w. have gone further.
Joh 1:43 Jesus w. go forth into Galilee, 2309
Joh 4:10 **he w. have given thee living water.**
Joh 4:40 him that he w. tarry with them:
Joh 4:47 besought him that he w. come down,
Joh 5:46 Moses, ye w. have believed me:
Joh 6:6 he himself knew what he w. do 3195
Joh 6:11 of the fishes as much as they w. 2309
Joh 6:15 w. come and take him by force, 3195
Joh 7:1 for he w. not walk in Jewry, 2309
Joh 7:44 some of them w. have taken him; 2309
Joh 8:39 **ye w. do the works of Abraham.**
Joh 8:42 **God were your Father, ye w. love me:**
Joh 9:27 wherefore w. ye hear it again? 2309
Joh 12:21 him, saying, Sir, we w. see Jesus. 2309
Joh 14:2 **if it were not so, I w. have told you.**
Joh 14:28 **If ye loved me, ye w. rejoice, because**
Joh 15:19 **the world, the world w. love his own;**
Joh 18:30 we w. not have delivered him up
Joh 18:36 **then w. my servants fight, that I**
Ac 2:30 he w. raise up Christ to sit on his
Ac 5:24 of them whereunto this w. grow.
Ac 7:5 he w. give it to him for a possession,
Ac 7:25 brethren w. have understood that God
Ac 7:25 that God by his hand w. deliver them:
Ac 7:26 w. have set them at one again, saying,
Ac 7:39 To whom our fathers w. not obey, 2309
Ac 8:31 that he w. come up and sit with him.
Ac 9:38 he w. not delay to come to them.
Ac 10:10 very hungry, and w. have eaten: 2309
Ac 11:23 heart that w. cleave unto the Lord.
Ac 12:6 Herod w. have brought him forth, 3195
Ac 14:13 w. have done sacrifice with the 2309
Ac 16:3 Him w. Paul have to go forth with 2309
Ac 16:27 sword, and w. have killed himself, 3195
Ac 17:20 w. know therefore what these things
Ac 18:14 reason w. that I should bear with you:
Ac 19:30 when Paul w. have entered in unto
Ac 19:31 that he w. not adventure himself into
Ac 19:33 w. have made his defence unto the 2309
Ac 20:16 he w. not spend the time in Asia: 1096
Ac 21:14 And when he w. not be persuaded,
Ac 22:30 he w. have known the certainty
Ac 23:12 w. neither eat nor drink till they had
Ac 23:15 ye w. enquire something more 3195
Ac 23:20 they w. enquire somewhat of him 3195
Ac 23:28 when I w. have known the cause
Ac 24:6 w. have judged according to our 2309
Ac 25:3 he w. send for him to Jerusalem,
Ac 25:4 that he himself w. depart shortly 3195
Ac 25:20 him whether he w. go to Jerusalem,
Ac 25:22 I w. also hear the man myself.
Ac 26:5 the beginning, if they w. testify, 2309
Ac 26:29 I w. to God, that not only thou, 2172
Ac 27:30 though they w. have cast anchors 3195
Ac 28:18 examined me, w. have let me go,
Ro 1:13 Now I w. not have you ignorant, 2309
Ro 5:7 good man some w. even dare to die.
Ro 7:15 for what I w., that I do not; but 2309
Ro 7:16 If then I do that which I w. not, 2309
Ro 7:19 For the good that I w. I do not: 2309
Ro 7:19 the evil which I w. not, that I do. 2309
Ro 7:20 Now if I do that I w. not, it is no 2309
Ro 7:21 when I w. do good, evil is present 2309
Ro 11:25 For I w. not, brethren, that ye 2309
Ro 16:19 yet I w. have you wise unto that 2309
1Co 2:8 they w. not have crucified the Lord of
1Co 4:8 and I w. to God ye did reign, that 3785
1Co 4:18 up, as though I w. not come to you.
1Co 7:7 I w. that all men were even as I 2309
1Co 7:32 I w. have you without carefulness. 2309
1Co 10:1 I w. not that ye should be ignorant, 2309
1Co 10:20 and I w. not that ye should have 2309
1Co 11:3 I w. have you know, that the head 2309
1Co 11:31 For if we w. judge ourselves, we
1Co 12:1 I w. not have you ignorant. 2309
1Co 14:5 I w. that ye all spake with tongues, 2309
2Co 1:8 For we w. not, brethren, have you 2309
2Co 2:1 that I w. not come again to you in
2Co 2:8 you that ye w. confirm your love.
2Co 5:4 not for that we w. be unclothed, 2309
2Co 8:4 intreaty that we w. receive the gift,

2Co 8:6 so he w. also finish in you the same
2Co 9:5 that they w. go before unto you;
2Co 10:9 seem as if I w. terrify you by letters.
2Co 11:1 W. to God ye could bear with me *3785*
2Co 12:6 For though I w. desire to glory,
2Co 12:20 I shall not find you such as I w., ... *2309*
2Co 12:20 found unto you such as ye w. not: *2309*
Ga 1:7 and w. pervert the gospel of Christ. ... *2309*
Ga 2:10 they w. that we should remember the
Ga 3:2 This only w. I learn of you, ... *2309*
Ga 3:8 foreseeing that God w. justify the
Ga 4:15 w. have plucked out your own eyes,
Ga 4:17 they w. exclude you, that ye *2309*
Ga 5:12 I w. they were even cut off which *3785*
Ga 5:17 cannot do the things that ye w.. .... *2309*
Eph 3:16 That he w. grant you, according to
Php 1:12 But I w. ye should understand,
Col 1:27 To whom God w. make known *2309*
Col 2:1 For I w. that ye knew what great *2309*
Col 4:3 that God w. open unto us a door of
1Th 2:9 we w. not be chargeable unto any
1Th 2:12 That ye w. walk worthy of God, who
1Th 2:18 we w. have come unto you, ... *2309*
1Th 4:1 God, so ye w. abound more and more
1Th 4:13 I w. not have you to be ignorant, ... *2309*
2Th 1:11 our God w. count you worthy of this
2Th 3:10 that if any w. not work, neither *2309*
Phm 13 Whom I w. have retained with me,
Phm 14 without thy mind w. I do nothing; *2309*
Heb 4:8 then w. he not afterward have spoken
Heb 10:2 For then w. they not have ceased to be
Heb 11:32 the time w. fail me to tell of Gideon,
Heb 12:17 he w. have inherited the blessing, ... *2309*
1Jo 2:19 w. no doubt have continued with us:
2Jo 12 I w. not write with paper and ink: *1014*
3Jo 10 forbiddeth them that w., and casteth ... *1014*
Re 3:15 **hot: I w. thou wert cold or hot.** *3785*
Re 13:15 as many as w. not worship the image

WOULDEST
Ge 30:15 and w. thou take away my son's
Ge 31:30 now, though thou w. needs be gone,
Ge 31:31 thou w. take by force thy daughters
Ex 7:16 behold, hitherto thou w. not hear.
Ex 23:5 burden, and w. forbear to help him,
De 8:2 thou w. keep his commandments,
De 21:11 her, that thou w. have her to thy wife;
De 28:62 w. not obey the voice of the Lord thy
Jos 15:18 Caleb said unto her, What w. thou?
2Sa 14:11 w. not suffer the revengers of blood
2Sa 18:13 thyself w. have set thyself against me.
1Ki 1:16 And the king said, What w. thou?
1Ki 18:9 w. deliver thy servant into the hand of
2Ki 4:13 w. thou be spoken for to the king, ... 3426
2Ki 5:13 great thing, w. thou not have done it?
2Ki 6:22 w. thou smite those whom thou hast
1Ch 4:10 Oh that thou w. bless me indeed, and
1Ch 4:10 and that thou w. keep me from evil,
2Ch 6:20 that thou w. put thy name there;
2Ch 20:10 whom thou w. not let Israel invade,
Ezr 9:14 w. not thou be angry with us till thou
Ne 2:5 that thou w. send me unto Judah,
Job 8:5 If thou w. seek unto God betimes, and
Job 14:13 O that thou w. hide me in the grave,
Job 14:13 that thou w. keep me secret, until thy
Job 14:13 that thou w. appoint me a set time,
Isa 48:8 that thou w. deal very treacherously,
Isa 64:1 Oh that thou w. rend the heavens,
Isa 64:1 that thou w. come down, that the
Lu 16:27 **w. send him to my father's house:**
Joh 4:10 **w. have asked of him, and he would**
Joh 11:40 if thou w. believe, thou shouldest see
Joh 21:18 **and walkedst whither thou w.** *2309*
Joh 21:18 **carry thee whither thou w. not.** *2309*
Ac 23:20 thee that thou w. bring down Paul
Ac 24:4 thou w. hear us of thy clemency
Heb 10:5 Sacrifice and offering thou w. not, ... *2309*
Heb 10:8 and offering for sin thou w. not, ... *2309*

WOULDST See WOULDEST.

WOUND See also WOUNDED; WOUNDETH; WOUNDING; WOUNDS.
Ex 21:25 burning, w. for w., stripe for stripe. ... 6482
De 32:39 I make alive; I w., and I heal: 4272
1Ki 22:35 the blood ran out of the w. into 4347
Job 34:6 my w. is incurable without 2671
Ps 68:21 But God shall w. the head of his 4272
Ps 110:6 he shall w. the heads over many 4272
Pr 6:33 A w. and dishonour shall he get; 5061
Pr 20:30 blueness of a w. cleanseth...evil: 6482
Isa 30:26 and healeth the stroke of their w.. 4347
Jer 10:19 me for my hurt! my w. is grievous: 4347
Jer 15:18 perpetual, and my w. incurable, ... 4347
Jer 30:12 incurable, and thy w. is grievous. 4347
Jer 30:14 thee with the w. of an enemy, ... 4347
Ho 5:13 sickness, and Judah saw his w., ... 4205
Ho 5:13 heal you, nor cure you of your w.. 4205
Ob 7 bread have laid a w. under thee: 4204
Mic 1:9 her w. is incurable; for it is come 4347
Na 3:19 of thy bruise; thy w. is grievous: 4347
Joh 19:40 and w. it in linen clothes with the *1210*
Ac 5:6 the young men arose, w. him up, ... *4958*
1Co 8:12 and w. their weak conscience, ye *5180*
Re 13:3 and his deadly w. was healed: *4127*
Re 13:12 beast, whose deadly w. was healed *4127*
Re 13:14 which had the w. by a sword, and *4127*

WOUNDED See also WOUNDEDST.
De 23:1 He that is w. in the stones, ... 1795
Jg 9:40 many were overthrown and w., ... 2491
1Sa 17:52 the w. of the Philistines fell down 2491
1Sa 31:3 he was sore w. of the archers. 2342
2Sa 22:39 consumed them, and w. them. 4272
1Ki 20:37 so that in smiting he w. him. 6481
1Ki 22:34 me out of the host; for I w. 2470
2Ki 8:28 and the Syrians w. Joram. 5221
1Ch 10:3 and he was w. of the archers. 2342
2Ch 18:33 out of the host; for I am sore w.. 2470
2Ch 35:23 Have me away; for I am sore w.. 2470
Job 24:12 and the soul of the w. crieth out: 2491
Ps 18:38 w. them that they were not able 4272
Ps 64:7 arrow; suddenly shall they be w. 4347
Ps 69:26 grief of those whom thou hast w.. 2491
Ps 109:22 and my heart is w. within me. 2490
Pr 7:26 For she hath cast down many w. 2491
Pr 18:14 but a w. spirit who can bear? 5218
Ca 5:7 me, they smote me, they w. me; 6481
Isa 51:9 cut Rahab, and w. the dragon? 2490
Isa 53:5 he was w. for our transgressions, ... 2490
Jer 30:14 I have w. thee with the wound of 5221
Jer 37:10 there remained but w. men among 1856
Jer 51:52 all her land the w. shall groan. 2491
La 2:12 swooned as the w. in the streets 2491
Eze 26:15 sound of thy fall, when the w. cry, ... 2491
Eze 28:23 the w. shall be judged in the midst 2491
Eze 30:24 groanings of a deadly w. man. 2491
Joe 2:8 the sword, they shall not be w.. 1214
Zec 13:6 was w. in the house of my friends. 5221
Mk 12:4 **and w. him in the head, and sent him**
Lu 10:30 **w. him, and departed, leaving** .*4127,2007*
Lu 20:12 **and they w. him also, and cast** *5135*
Ac 19:16 fled out of that house naked and w.. ... *5135*
Re 13:3 his heads as it were w. to death; *4969*

WOUNDEDST
Hab 3:13 thou w. the head out of the house 4272

WOUNDETH
Job 5:18 he w., and his hands make whole. 4272

WOUNDING
Ge 4:23 for I have slain a man to my w., ... 6482

WOUNDS
2Ki 8:29 to be healed in Jezreel of the w. 4347
2Ki 9:15 to be healed in Jezreel of the w. 4347
2Ch 22:6 healed in Jezreel because of the w. 4347
Job 9:17 multiplieth my w. without cause. 6482
Ps 38:5 My w. stink and are corrupt 2250
Ps 147:3 in heart, and bindeth up their w.. 6094
Pr 18:8 words of a talebearer are as w., ... 3859
Pr 23:29 who hath w. without cause? who 6482
Pr 26:22 words of a talebearer are as w., ... 3859
Pr 27:6 Faithful are the w. of a friend; 6482
Isa 1:6 but w., and bruises, and putrifying 6482
Jer 6:7 me continually is grief and w. 4347
Jer 30:17 and I will heal thee of thy w., saith 4347
Zec 13:6 What are these w. in thine hands? 4347
Lu 10:34 **went to him, and bound up his w.,** .*5134*

WOVE See also WOVEN.
2Ki 23:7 women w. hangings for the grove. 707

WOVEN
Ex 28:32 it shall have a binding to w. work 707
Ex 39:22 the robe of the ephod of w. work, ... 707
Ex 39:27 of fine linen of w. work for Aaron, ... 707
Joh 19:23 seam, w. from the top throughout. *5307*

WRAP See also WRAPPED.
Isa 28:20 than that he can w. himself in it. 3664
Mic 7:3 desire: so they w. it up 5686

WRAPPED
Ge 38:14 her with a vail and w. herself, ... 5968
1Sa 21:9 w. in a cloth behind the ephod: 3874
1Ki 19:13 that he w. his face in his mantle, ... 3874
2Ki 2:8 his mantle, and w. it together, ... 1563
Job 8:17 His roots are w. about the heap, ... 5440
Job 40:17 the sinews of his stones are w. 8276
Eze 21:15 it is w. up for the slaughter. 4593
Jon 2:5 the weeds were w. about my head. 2280
Mt 27:59 he w. it in a clean linen cloth, ... *1794*
Mk 15:46 him down, and w. him in the linen, ... *1750*
Lu 2:7 and w. him in swaddling clothes, ... *4683*
Lu 2:12 the babe w. in swadding clothes, ... *4683*
Lu 23:53 it down, and w. it in linen, ... *1794*
Joh 20:7 but w. together in a place by itself. *1794*

WRATH See also WRATHFUL; WRATHS.
Ge 39:19 to me; that his w. was kindled. 639
Ge 49:7 and their w., for it was cruel: 5678
Ex 15:7 thou sentest forth thy w., which 2740
Ex 22:24 And my w. shall wax hot, and I 639
Ex 32:10 my w. may wax hot against them, ... 639
Ex 32:11 thy w. wax hot against thy people, ... 639
Ex 32:12 Turn from thy fierce w., and repent 639
Le 10:6 lest w. come upon all the people: 7107
Nu 1:53 be no w. upon the congregation 7110
Nu 11:33 w. of the Lord was kindled against 639
Nu 16:46 is w. gone out from the Lord; 7110
Nu 18:5 no w. any more upon the children 7110
Nu 25:11 my w. away from the children 2534
De 9:7 provokedst the Lord thy God to w. 7107
De 9:8 Horeb ye provoked the Lord to w., ... 7107
De 9:22 ye provoked the Lord to w.. 7107
De 11:17 Lord's w. be kindled against you, ... 639
De 29:23 in his anger, and in his w.: 2534
De 29:28 and in w., and in great indignation, ... 2534
De 32:27 that I feared the w. of the enemy, ... 3708
Jos 9:20 let them live, lest w. be upon us, ... 7110
Jos 22:20 w. fell on all the congregation of 7110
1Sa 28:18 his fierce w. upon Amalek, ... 639
2Sa 11:20 if so be that the king's w. arise, ... 2534
2Ki 22:13 great is the w. of the Lord that is 2534
2Ki 22:17 my w. shall be kindled against this 2534
2Ki 23:26 from the fierceness of his great w., ... 639
1Ch 27:24 there fell w. for it against Israel; 7110
2Ch 12:7 my w. shall not be poured out 2534
2Ch 12:12 w. of the Lord turned from him, ... 639
2Ch 19:2 therefore is w. upon thee from 7110
2Ch 19:10 and so w. come upon you, and 7110
2Ch 24:18 w. came upon Judah and Jerusalem 7110
2Ch 28:11 fierce w. of the Lord is upon you. 639
2Ch 28:13 there is fierce w. against Israel. 639
2Ch 29:8 w. of the Lord was upon Judah 7110
2Ch 29:10 fierce w. may turn away from us. 639
2Ch 30:8 fierceness of his w. may turn away 639
2Ch 32:25 therefore there was w. upon him, ... 7110
2Ch 32:26 the w. of the Lord came not upon 7110
2Ch 34:21 great is the w. of the Lord that is 2534
2Ch 34:25 my w. shall be poured out upon 2534
2Ch 36:16 the w. of the Lord arose against 2534
Ezr 5:12 the God of heaven unto w., ... 7265
Ezr 7:23 there be w. against the realm 7109
Ezr 8:22 his power and his w. is against all 639
Ezr 10:14 fierce w. of our God for this matter 639
Ne 13:18 yet ye bring more w. upon Israel 2740
Es 1:18 arise too much contempt and w.. 7110
Es 2:1 the w. of king Ahasuerus was 2534
Es 3:5 then was Haman full of w.. 2534
Es 7:7 in his w. went into the palace 2534
Es 7:10 Then was the king's w. pacified. 2534
Job 5:2 For w. killeth the foolish man, ... 3708
Job 14:13 me secret, until thy w. be past, ... 639
Job 16:9 He teareth me in his w., who hateth 639
Job 19:11 hath also kindled his w. against me, ... 639
Job 19:29 for w. bringeth the punishments 2534
Job 20:23 cast the fury of his w. upon him, ... 639
Job 20:28 shall flow away in the day of his w. 639
Job 21:20 drink of the w. of the Almighty. 2534
Job 21:30 be brought forth to the day of w.. 5678
Job 32:2 kindled the w. of Elihu the son 639
Job 32:2 against Job was his w. kindled, ... 639

Job 32:3 his three friends was his **w.** kindled, 639
Job 32:5 three men, then his **w.** was kindled. 639
Job 36:13 hypocrites in heart heap up **w.**: 639
Job 36:18 Because there is **w.**, beware lest 2534
Job 40:11 Cast abroad the rage of thy **w.**: 639
Job 42:7 My **w.** is kindled against thee, and 639
Ps 2:5 shall he speak unto them in his **w**, 639
Ps 2:12 when his **w.** is kindled but a little. 639
Ps 21:9 shall swallow them up in his **w.**, 639
Ps 37:8 Cease from anger, and forsake **w.**: 2534
Ps 38:1 O Lord, rebuke me not in thy **w.**: 7110
Ps 55:3 upon, me, and in **w.** they hate me. 639
Ps 58:9 both living, and in his **w.**. 2740
Ps 59:13 Consume them in **w.**, consume 2534
Ps 76:10 the **w.** of man shall praise thee: 2534
Ps 76:10 remainder of **w.** shalt thou restrain. 2534
Ps 78:31 The **w.** of God came upon them, 639
Ps 78:38 and did not stir up all his **w.** 2534
Ps 78:49 the fierceness of his anger, **w.**, 5678
Ps 79:6 Pour out thy **w.** upon the heathen 2534
Ps 85:3 Thou hast taken away all thy **w.**: 5678
Ps 88:7 Thy **w.** lieth hard upon me, and 2534
Ps 88:16 Thy fierce **w.** goeth over me; thy 2740
Ps 89:46 ever? shall thy **w.** burn like fire? 2534
Ps 90:7 and by thy **w.** are we troubled. 2534
Ps 90:9 days are passed away in thy **w.**: 5678
Ps 90:11 according to thy fear, so is thy **w.** 5678
Ps 95:11 Unto whom I sware in my **w.** that 639
Ps 102:10 of thine indignation and thy **w.**: 7110
Ps 106:23 to turn away his **w.**, lest he should 2534
Ps 106:40 the **w.** of the Lord kindleth against 639
Ps 110:5 through kings in the day of his **w.** 639
Ps 124:3 their **w.** was kindled against us: 639
Ps 138:7 against the **w.** of mine enemies, 639
Pr 11:4 Riches profit not in the day of **w.**: 5678
Pr 11:23 expectation of the wicked is **w.** 5678
Pr 12:16 A fool's **w.** is presently known: 3708
Pr 14:29 He that is slow to **w.** is of great 639
Pr 14:35 his **w.** is against him that causeth 5678
Pr 15:1 A soft answer turneth away **w.**: 2534
Pr 16:14 The **w.** of a king is as messengers 2534
Pr 19:12 The king's **w.** is as the roaring of 2197
Pr 19:19 A man of great **w.** shall suffer 2534
Pr 21:14 a reward in the bosom strong **w.** 2534
Pr 21:24 name, who dealeth in proud **w.** 5678
Pr 24:18 and he turn away his **w.** from him. 639
Pr 27:3 a fool's **w.** is heavier than them 3708
Pr 27:4 **w.** is cruel, and anger is 2534
Pr 29:8 snare: but wise men turn away **w.** 639
Pr 30:33 forcing of **w.** bringeth forth strife. 639
Ec 5:17 he hath much sorrow and **w.** with 7110
Isa 9:19 Through the **w.** of the Lord of 5678
Isa 10:6 against the people of my **w.** will I. 5678
Isa 13:9 cruel both with **w.** and fierce anger, 5678
Isa 13:13 in the **w.** of the Lord of hosts, and 5678
Isa 14:6 He who smote the people in **w.** 5678
Isa 16:6 and his pride, and his **w.**: 5678
Isa 54:8 In a little **w.** I hid my face from 7110
Isa 60:10 in my **w.** I smote thee, but in my 7110
Jer 7:29 forsaken the generation of his **w.** 5678
Jer 10:10 at his **w.** the earth shall tremble, 7110
Jer 18:20 to turn away thy **w.** from them. 2534
Jer 21:5 and in fury, and in great **w.** 7110
Jer 32:37 and in my fury, and in great **w.**; 7110
Jer 44:8 me unto **w.** with the works 3707
Jer 48:30 I know his **w.**, saith the Lord; 5678
Jer 50:13 Because of the **w.** of the Lord it 7110
La 2:2 down in his **w.** the strong holds 5678
La 3:1 seen affliction by the rod of his **w.** 5678
Eze 7:12, 14 **w.** is upon all the multitude 2740
Eze 7:19 in the day of the **w.** of the Lord: 5678
Eze 13:15 accomplish my **w.** upon the wall, 2534
Eze 21:31 against thee in the fire of my **w.**, 5678
Eze 22:21 blow upon you in the fire of my **w.**, 5678
Eze 22:31 them with the fire of my **w.**: 5678
Eze 38:19 in the fire of my **w.** have I spoken, 5678
Ho 5:10 I will pour out my **w.** upon them 5678
Ho 13:11 and took him away in my **w.** 5678
Am 1:11 and he kept his **w.** for ever: 5678
Na 1:2 and he reserveth **w.** for his enemies.
Hab 3:2 known; in **w.** remember mercy. 7267
Hab 3:8 was thy **w.** against the sea, that 5678
Zep 1:15 That day is a day of **w.**, a day of 5678
Zep 1:18 them in the day of the Lord's **w.**; 5678
Zec 7:12 came a great **w.** from the Lord of 7110
Zec 8:14 your fathers provoked me to **w.**, 7107

Mt 3:7 you to flee from the **w.** to come? *3709*
Lu 3:7 you to flee from the **w.** to come? *3709*
Lu 4:28 these things, were filled **w.** *2372*
Lu 21:23 **the land, and w. upon his people.** *3709*
Joh 3:36 but the **w.** of God abideth on him. *3709*
Ac 19:28 these sayings, they were full of **w.**, *2372*
Ro 1:18 For the **w.** of God is revealed from *3709*
Ro 2:5 heart treasurest up unto thyself **w.** *3709*
Ro 2:5 against the day of **w.** and *3709*
Ro 2:8 unrighteousness, indignation...**w.**, *3709*
Ro 4:15 Because the law worketh **w.**: for *3709*
Ro 5:9 be saved from **w.** through him. *3709*
Ro 9:22 What if God, willing to shew his **w.**, *3709*
Ro 9:22 vessels of **w.** fitted to destruction: *3709*
Ro 12:19 but rather give place unto **w.**: *3709*
Ro 13:4 to execute **w.** upon him that doeth *3709*
Ro 13:5 needs be subject, not only for **w.**, *3709*
Ga 5:20 hatred, variance, emulations, **w.**, *2372*
Eph 2:3 were by nature the children of **w.**, *3709*
Eph 4:26 the sun go down upon your **w.**: *3950*
Eph 4:31 and **w.**, and anger, and clamour, *2372*
Eph 5:6 things cometh the **w.** of God *3709*
Eph 6:4 provoke not your children to **w.**: *3949*
Col 3:6 things' sake the **w.** of God cometh *3709*
Col 3:8 anger, **w.**, malice, blasphemy, *2372*
1Th 1:10 delivered us from the **w.** to come. *3709*
1Th 2:16 for the **w.** is come upon them to *3709*
1Th 5:9 God hath not appointed us to **w.**, *3709*
1Ti 2:8 hands, without **w.** and doubting. *3709*
Heb 3:11 So I sware in my **w.**, They shall *3709*
Heb 4:3 As I have sworn in my **w.**, If they *3709*
Heb 11:27 not fearing the **w.** of the king: *2372*
Jas 1:19 hear, slow to speak, slow to **w.** *3709*
Jas 1:20 For the **w.** of man worketh not the *3709*
Re 6:16 and from the **w.** of the Lamb: *3709*
Re 6:17 the great day of his **w.** has come; *3709*
Re 11:18 were angry, and thy **w.** is come, *3709*
Re 12:12 having great **w.**, because he *2372*
Re 14:8 wine of the **w.** of her fornication. *2372*
Re 14:10 drink of the wine of the **w.** of God, *2372*
Re 14:19 great winepress of the **w.** of God. *2372*
Re 15:1 in them is filled up the **w.** of God. *2372*
Re 15:7 golden vials full of the **w.** of God, *2372*
Re 16:1 pour out the vials of the **w.** of God. *2372*
Re 16:19 wine of the fierceness of his **w.** *3709*
Re 18:3 wine of the **w.** of her fornication, *2372*
Re 19:15 fierceness and **w.** of Almighty God. *3709*

WRATHFUL See also WROTH.
Ps 69:24 thy **w.** anger take hold of them. 2740
Pr 15:18 A **w.** man stirreth up strife: but 2534

WRATHS
2Co 12:20 debates, envyings, **w.**, strifes, *2372*

WREATH See also WREATHED; WREATHS.
2Ch 4:13 rows of pomegranates on each **w.**, 7639

WREATHED See also WREATHEN.
La 1:14 they are **w.**, and come up upon 8276

WREATHEN See also WREATHED.
Ex 28:14 of **w.** work shalt thou make them, 5688
Ex 28:14 fasten the **w.** chains to the ouches. 5688
Ex 28:22 the ends of **w.** work of pure gold. 5688
Ex 28:24 shalt put the two **w.** chains of gold 5688
Ex 28:25 of the two **w.** chains thou shalt 5688
Ex 39:15 the ends, of **w.** work of pure gold. 5688
Ex 39:17 they put the two **w.** chains of gold 5688
Ex 39:18 of the two **w.** chains they fastened 5688
2Ki 25:17 the **w.** work, and pomegranates 7639
2Ki 25:17 had the second pillar with **w.** work. 7639

WREATHS
1Ki 7:17 **w.** of chain work, for the chapiters 1434
2Ch 4:12 two **w.** to cover the two pommels 7639
2Ch 4:13 hundred pomegranates on...two **w.**; 7639

WRECK See SHIPWRECK.

WREST
Ex 23:2 after many to **w.** judgment: 5186
Ex 23:6 shalt not **w.** the judgment of thy 5186
De 16:19 Thou shalt not **w.** judgment; thou 5186
Ps 56:5 Every day they **w.** my words: 6087
2Pe 3:16 are unlearned and unstable **w.**, *4761*

WRESTLE See also WRESTLED; WRESTLINGS.
Eph 6:12 For we **w.** not against flesh *2076,3823*

WRESTLED
Ge 30:8 have I **w.** with my sister,and I 6617
Ge 32:24 there **w.** a man with him until the 79
Ge 32:25 was out of joint, as he **w.** with him. 79

WRESTLINGS
Ge 30:8 With great **w.** have I wrestled 5319

WRETCHED
Ro 7:24 O **w.** man that I am! who shall *5005*
Re 3:17 **and knowest not that thou art w.,** *5005*

WRETCHEDNESS
Nu 11:15 sight; and let me not see my **w.**. 7451

WRING See also WRINGED; WRINGING; WRUNG.
Le 1:15 **w.** off his head, and burn it on the 4454
Le 5:8 and **w.** off his head from his neck, 4454
Ps 75:8 of the earth shall **w.** them out, 4680

WRINGED See also WRUNG.
Jg 6:38 and **w.** the dew out of the fleece, 4680

WRINGING
Pr 30:33 the **w.** of the nose bringeth forth 4330

WRINKLE See also WRINKLES.
Eph 5:27 spot, or **w.**, or any such thing; *4512*

WRINKLES
Job 16:8 And thou hast filled me with **w.**, 7059

WRITE See also WRITEST; WRITETH; WRITING; WRITTEN; WROTE.
Ex 17:14 **W.** this for a memorial in a book, 3789
Ex 34:1 will **w.** upon these tables the words 3789
Ex 34:27 unto Moses, **W.** thou these words: 3789
Nu 5:23 priest shall **w.** these curses in a 3789
Nu 17:2 **w.** thou every man's name upon 3789
Nu 17:3 **w.** Aaron's name upon the rod of 3789
De 6:9 thou shalt **w.** them upon the posts 3789
De 10:2 I will **w.** on the tables the words 3789
De 11:20 shalt **w.** them upon the door posts 3789
De 17:18 he shall **w.** him a copy of this law 3789
De 24:1, 3 **w.** her a bill of divorcement, 3789
De 27:3 shalt **w.** upon them all the words 3789
De 27:8 **w.** upon the stones all the words 3789
De 31:19 therefore **w.** ye this song for you, 3789
2Ch 26:22 the prophet, the son of Amoz, **w.** 3789
Ezr 5:10 we might **w.** the names of the men 3790
Ne 9:38 make a sure covenant, and **w.** it; 3789
Es 8:8 **W.** ye also for the Jews, as it 3789
Pr 3:3 **w.** them upon the table of thine 3789
Pr 7:3 **w.** them upon the table of thine 3789
Isa 8:1 and **w.** in it with a man's pen 3789
Isa 10:1 that **w.** grievousness which they 3789
Isa 10:19 be few, that a child may **w.** them. 3789
Isa 30:8 go, **w.** it before them in a table, 3789
Jer 22:30 **W.** ye this man childless, a man 3789
Jer 30:2 **W.** thee all the words that I have 3789
Jer 31:33 parts, and **w.** it in their hearts; 3789
Jer 36:2 **w.** therein all the words that I have 3789
Jer 36:17 How didst thou **w.** all these words 3789
Jer 36:28 **w.** in it all the former words that 3789
Eze 24:2 man, **w.** thee the name of the day, 3789
Eze 37:16 take thee one stick, and **w.** upon it, 3789
Eze 37:16 take another stick, and **w.** upon it, 3789
Eze 43:11 **w.** it in their sight, that they may 3789
Hab 2:2 **W.** the vision, and make it plain 3789
Mk 10:4 to **w.** a bill of divorcement, *1125*
Lu 1:3 very first, to **w.** unto thee in order, *1125*
Lu 16:6 **and sit down quickly, and w. fifty** *1125*
Lu 16:7 **Take thy bill, and w. fourscore.** *1125*
Joh 1:45 in the law, and the prophets, did **w.**, *1125*
Joh 19:21 **W.** not, The King of the Jews; *1125*
Ac 15:20 But that we **w.** unto them, that *1989*
Ac 25:26 I have no certain thing to **w.** unto *1125*
Ac 25:26 had, I might have somewhat to **w.** *1125*
1Co 4:14 I **w.** not these things to shame you, *1125*
1Co 14:37 that the things that I **w.** unto you. *1125*
2Co 1:13 we **w.** none other things unto you, *1125*
2Co 2:9 For to this end also did I **w.**, that I *1125*
2Co 9:1 is superfluous for me to **w.** to you: *1125*
2Co 13:2 I **w.** to them which heretofore have *1125*
2Co 13:10 I **w.** these thigs being absent, lest *1125*
Ga 1:20 the things which I **w.** unto you, *1125*
Php 3:1 To **w.** the same things to you, *1125*
1Th 4:9 ye need not that I **w.** unto you: *1125*
1Th 5:1 have no need that I **w.** unto you. *1125*
2Th 3:17 token in every epistle: so I **w.** *1125*
1Ti 3:14 These things **w.** I unto thee, *1125*
Heb 8:10 mind, and **w.** them in their hearts: *1924*
Heb 10:16 and in their minds will I **w.** them; *1924*

2Pe 3:1 beloved, I now w. unto you; *1125*
1Jo 1:4 And these things w. we unto you, *1125*
1Jo 2:1 these things w. I unto you, that ye *1125*
1Jo 2:7 I w. no new commandment unto *1125*
1Jo 2:8 new commandment I w. unto you, *1125*
1Jo 2:12 I w. unto you, little children, *1125*
1Jo 2:13 I w. unto you, fathers, because ye *1125*
1Jo 2:13 I w. unto you, young men, because *1125*
1Jo 2:13 I w. unto you, little children, *1125*
2Jo 12 Having many things to w. unto you, *1125*
2Jo 12 I would not w. with paper and ink:
3Jo 13 I had many things to w., but I will *1125*
3Jo 13 not with ink and pen w. unto thee: *1125*
Jude 3 to w. unto you of the common *1125*
Jude 3 needful for me to w. unto you, *1125*
Re 1:11 **What thou seest, w. in a book,** *1125*
Re 1:19 **W. the things which thou hast** *1125*
Re 2:1 **angel of the church of Ephesus w.;** *1125*
Re 2:8 **angel of the church in Smyrna w.;** *1125*
Re 2:12 **of the church in Pergamos w.;** *1125*
Re 2:18 **angel of the church in Thyatira w.;** *1125*
Re 3:1 **angel of the church in Sardis w.;** *1125*
Re 3:7 **of the church in Philadelphia w.;** *1125*
Re 3:12 **I will w. upon him the name of my** *1125*
Re 3:12 **I will w. upon him my new name.**
Re 3:14 **the church of the Laodiceans w.;** *1125*
Re 10:4 their voices, I was about to w.: *1125*
Re 10:4 thunders uttered, and w. them not. *1125*
Re 14:13 W., Blessed are the dead which die *1125*
Re 19:9 W., Blessed are they which are *1125*
Re 21:5 W.: for these words are true *1125*

WRITER See also WRITER'S.
Jg 5:14 they that handle the pen of the w. 5608
Ps 45:1 my tongue is the pen of a ready w. 5608

WRITER'S
Eze 9:2 with a w. inkhorn by his side: 5608
Eze 9:3 had the w. inkhorn by his side; 5608

WRITEST
Job 13:26 thou w. bitter things against me, 3789
Eze 37:20 sticks whereon thou w. shall be in 3789

WRITETH
Ps 87:6 count, when he w. up the people, 3789

WRITING See also HANDWRITING; WRITINGS.
Ex 32:16 the w. was the w. of God, graven 4385
Ex 39:30 pure gold, and wrote upon it a w., 4385
De 10:4 according to the first w., the ten 4385
De 31:24 an end of w. the words of this law 3789
1Ch 28:19 Lord made me understand in w. 3791
2Ch 2:11 the king of Tyre answered in w., 3791
2Ch 21:12 came a w. to him from Elijah the 4385
2Ch 35:4 to the w. of David king of Israel, 3791
2Ch 35:4 to the w. of Solomon his son. 4385
2Ch 36:22 his kingdom, and put it also in w., 4385
Ezr 1:1 his kingdom, and put it also in w., 4385
Ezr 4:7 w. of the letter was written in the 3791
Es 1:22 every province according to the w. 3791
Es 3:12 every province according to the w. 3791
Es 3:14 copy of the w. for a commandment 3791
Es 4:8 the copy of the w. of the decree 3791
Es 8:8 w. which is written in the king's 3791
Es 8:9 every province according to the w. 3791
Es 8:9 to the Jews according to their w., 3791
Es 8:13 copy of the w. for a commandment 3791
Es 9:27 two days according to their w., 3791
Isa 38:9 w. of Hezekiah king of Judah, 4385
Eze 13:9 in the w. of the house of Israel, 3791
Da 5:7 Whosoever shall read this w., 3792
Da 5:8 but they could not read the w., 3792
Da 5:15 that they should read this w., 3792
Da 5:16 now if thou canst read the w., 3792
Da 5:17 I will read the w. unto the king, 3792
Da 5:24 from him; and this w. was written. 3792
Da 5:25 And this is the w. that was written, 3792
Da 6:8 the decree, and sign the w., 3792
Da 6:9 king Darius signed the w. and the 3792
Da 6:10 Daniel knew that the w. was signed, 3792
Mt 5:31 **let him give her a w. of divorcement:**
Mt 19:7 to give a w. of divorcement, and to *975*
Lu 1:63 And he asked for a w. table, and *4098*
Joh 19:19 And the w. was, Jesus Of Nazareth *1125*

WRITINGS
Joh 5:47 **if ye believe not his w., how shall** *1121*

WRITING-TABLE See WRITING and TABLE.

WRITTEN
Ex 24:12 commandments which I have w.; 3789
Ex 31:18 stone, w. with the finger of God 3789
Ex 32:15 tables were w. on both their sides; 3789
Ex 32:15 and on the other were they w. 3789
Ex 32:32 out of thy book which thou hast w. 3789
Nu 11:26 they were of them that were w., 3789
De 9:10 stone w. with the finger of God; 3789
De 9:10 was w. according to all the words,
De 28:58 this law that are w. in this book, 3789
De 28:61 is not w. in the book of this law, 3789
De 29:20 the curses that are w. in this book 3789
De 29:21 covenant that are w. in this book 3789
De 29:27 the curses that are w. in this book: 3789
De 30:10 statutes which are w. in this book 3789
Jos 1:8 according to all that is w. therein: 3789
Jos 8:31 as it is w. in the book of the law of 3789
Jos 8:34 all that is w. in the book of the law. 3789
Jos 10:13 not this w. in the book of Jasher? 3789
Jos 23:6 all that is w. in the book of the law 3789
2Sa 1:18 it is w. in the book of Jasher.) 3789
1Ki 2:3 as it is w. in the law of Moses, 3789
1Ki 11:41 not w. in the book of the acts of 3789
1Ki 14:19, 29 w. in the book of the chronicles 3789
1Ki 15:7, 23,31 not w. in the book of the 3789
1Ki 16:5, 14,20,27 not w. in the book of the 3789
1Ki 21:11 as it was w. in the letters which 3789
1Ki 22:39, 45 w. in the book of the chronicles 3789
2Ki 1:18 not w. in the book of the chronicles 3789
2Ki 8:23 not w. in the book of the chronicles 3789
2Ki 10:34 not w. in the book of the chronicles 3789
2Ki 12:19 not w. in the book of the chronicles 3789
2Ki 13:8, 12 w. in the book of the chronicles 3789
2Ki 14:6 which is w. in the book of the law 3789
2Ki 14:15, 18,28 not w. in the book of the 3789
2Ki 15:6, 11,15,21,26,31,36 not w. in the book 3789
2Ki 16:19 not w. in the book of the chronicles 3789
2Ki 20:20 not w. in the book of the chronicles 3789
2Ki 21:17, 25 w. in the book of the chronicles 3789
2Ki 22:13 all that which is w. concerning us 3789
2Ki 23:3 covenant that were w. in this book 3789
2Ki 23:21 w. in the book of this covenant 3789
2Ki 23:24 which were w. in the book of Hilkiah 3789
2Ki 23:28 not w. in the book of the chronicles 3789
2Ki 24:5 not w. in the book of the chronicles 3789
1Ch 4:41 these w. by name came in the days 3789
1Ch 9:1 were w. in the book of the kings of 3789
1Ch 16:40 that is w. in the law of the Lord, 3789
1Ch 29:29 w. in the book of Samuel the seer, 3789
2Ch 9:29 not w. in the book of Nathan the 3789
2Ch 12:15 not w. in the book of Shemaiah the 3789
2Ch 13:22 w. in the story of the prophet Iddo 3789
2Ch 16:11 w. in the book of the kings of Judah 3789
2Ch 20:34 they are w. in the book of Jehu 3789
2Ch 23:18 as it is w. in the law of Moses, 3789
2Ch 24:27 are w. in the story of the book 3789
2Ch 25:4 w. in the law in the book of Moses, 3789
2Ch 25:26 w. in the book of the kings of Judah 3789
2Ch 27:7 w. in the book of the kings of Israel 3789
2Ch 28:26 w. in the book of the kings of Judah 3789
2Ch 30:5 long time in such sort as it was w. 3789
2Ch 30:18 passover otherwise than it was w. 3789
2Ch 31:3 as it is w. in the law of the Lord. 3789
2Ch 32:32 they are w. in the vision of Isaiah 3789
2Ch 33:18 w. in the book of the kings of Israel.
2Ch 33:19 w. among the sayings of the seers. 3789
2Ch 34:21 do after all that is w. in this book 3789
2Ch 34:24 the curses that are w. in the book 3789
2Ch 34:31 covenant which are w. in this book 3789
2Ch 35:12 as it is w. in the book of Moses. 3789
2Ch 35:25 they are w. in the lamentations. 3789
2Ch 35:26 was w. in the law of the Lord, 3789
2Ch 35:27 w. in the book of the kings of Israel 3789
2Ch 36:8 w. in the book of the kings of Israel 3789
Ezr 3:2 as it is w. in the law of Moses 3789
Ezr 3:4 feast of tabernacles, as it is w., 3789
Ezr 4:7 letter was w. in the Syrian tongue, 3789
Ezr 5:7 was w. thus; Unto Darius the 3790
Ezr 6:2 a roll, and therein was a record w.: 3790
Ezr 6:18 as it is w. in the book of Moses. 3792
Ezr 8:34 the weight was w. at that time. 3789
Ne 6:6 Wherein was w., It is reported 3789
Ne 7:5 at the first, and found w. therein, 3789
Ne 8:14 found w. in the law which the Lord 3789
Ne 8:15 trees, to make booths, as it is w. 3789
Ne 10:34 Lord our God, as it is w. in the law: 3789
Ne 10:36 of our cattle, as it is w. in the law, 3789
Ne 12:23 w. in the book of the chronicles, 3789
Ne 13:1 and therein was found w., that the 3789
Es 1:19 w. among the laws of the Persians 3789
Es 2:23 w. in the book of the chronicles 3789
Es 3:9 it be w. that they may be destroyed: 3789
Es 3:12 w. according to all that Haman had 3789
Es 3:12 name of king Ahasuerus was it w., 3789
Es 6:2 it was found w., that Mordecai had 3789
Es 8:5 let it be w. to reverse the letters 3789
Es 8:8 which is w. in the king's name, 3789
Es 8:9 w. according to all that Mordecai 3789
Es 9:23 as Mordecai had w. unto them; 3789
Es 9:32 Purim; and it was w. in the book. 3789
Es 10:2 not w. in the book of the chronicles 3789
Job 19:23 Oh that my words were now w.! 3789
Job 31:35 that mine adversary had w. a book. 3789
Ps 40:7 volume of the book it is w. of me, 3789
Ps 69:28 and not be w. with the righteous. 3789
Ps 102:18 be w. for the generation to come: 3789
Ps 139:16 thy book all my members were w., 3789
Ps 149:9 upon them the judgment w.: 3789
Pr 22:20 not I w. to thee excellent things 3789
Ec 12:10 that which was w. was upright, 3789
Isa 4:3 one that is w. among the living 3789
Isa 65:6 it is w. before me: I will not keep 3789
Jer 17:1 sin of Judah is w. with a pen of 3789
Jer 17:13 from me shall be w. in the earth, 3789
Jer 25:13 even all that is w. in this book, 3789
Jer 36:6 thou hast w. from my mouth, 3789
Jer 36:29 saying, Why hast thou w. therein, 3789
Jer 45:1 when he had w. these words in a 3789
Jer 51:60 words that are w. against Babylon 3789
Eze 2:10 and it was w. within and without: 3789
Eze 2:10 there was w. therein lamentations, 3789
Eze 13:9 neither shall they be w. in the 3789
Da 5:24 him; and this writing was w. 7560
Da 5:25 And this is the writing that was w., 7560
Da 9:11 oath that is w. in the law of Moses 3789
Da 9:13 As it is w. in the law of Moses, all 3789
Da 12:1 that shall be found w. in the book 3789
Ho 8:12 I have w. to him the great things 3789
Mal 3:16 and a book of remembrance was w. 3789
Mt 2:5 for thus it is w. by the prophet, *1125*
Mt 4:4 **It is w., Man shall not live by** *1125*
Mt 4:6 for it is w., He shall give his angels *1125*
Mt 4:7 **It is w. again, Thou shalt not** *1125*
Mt 4:10 **for it is w., Thou shalt worship** *1125*
Mt 11:10 **For this is he, of whom it is w.,** *1125*
Mt 21:13 **It is w., My house shall be called** *1125*
Mt 26:24 **Son of man goeth as it is w. of** *1125*
Mt 26:31 **it is w., I will smite the shepherd,** *1125*
Mt 27:37 up over his head his accusation w., *1125*
Mk 1:2 As it is w. in the prophets, Behold, *1125*
Mk 7:6 **it is w., This people honoureth me** *1125*
Mk 9:12 **how it is w. of the Son of man,** *1125*
Mk 9:13 **they listed, as it is w. of him.** *1125*
Mk 11:17 **it is w., My house shall be called** *1125*
Mk 14:21 **indeed goeth, as it is w. of him:** *1125*
Mk 14:27 **it is w., I will smite the shepherd,** *1125*
Mk 15:26 of his accusation was w. over, *1924*
Lu 2:23 (As it is w. in the law of the Lord, *1125*
Lu 3:4 As it is w. in the book of the words *1125*
Lu 4:4 **It is w., That man shall not live by** *1125*
Lu 4:8 **it is w., Thou shalt worship the** *1125*
Lu 4:10 it is w., He shall give his angels *1125*
Lu 4:17 he found the place where it was w., *1125*
Lu 7:27 **is he, of whom it is w., Behold,** *1125*
Lu 10:20 **your names are w. in heaven.** *1125*
Lu 10:26 **What is w. in the law? how readest** *1125*
Lu 18:31 **things that are w. by the prophets.** *1125*
Lu 19:46 **It is w., My house is the house of.** *1125*
Lu 20:17 said, **what is this then that is w.,** *1125*
Lu 21:22 **all things...w. may be fulfilled.** *1125*
Lu 22:37 **is w. must yet be accomplished** *1125*
Lu 23:38 a superscription...was w. over him *1125*
Lu 24:44 **which were w. in the law of Moses,** *1125*
Lu 24:46 **is w., and thus it behoved Christ** *1125*
Joh 2:17 remembered that it was w., *1125*
Joh 6:31 as it is w., He gave them bread *1125*
Joh 6:45 **It is w. in the prophets, And they** *1125*
Joh 8:17 **It is also w. in your law, that the** *1125*
Joh 10:34 **is it not w. in your law, I said, Ye** *1125*
Joh 12:14 young ass, sat thereon; as it is w., *1125*
Joh 12:16 that these things were w. of him, *1125*
Joh 15:25 **be fulfilled that is w. in their law,** *1125*

Joh 19:20 it was w. in Hebrew, and Greek, ... 1125
Joh 19:22 What I have w. I have w................. 1125
Joh 20:30 which are not w. in this book: 1125
Joh 20:31 these are w., that ye might believe 1125
Joh 21:25 if they should be w. every one, I 1125
Joh 21:25 the books that should be w., ... 1125
Ac 1:20 it is w. in the book of Psalms, ... 1125
Ac 7:42 it is w. in the book of the prophets, ... 1125
Ac 13:29 had fulfilled all that was w. of him, ... 1125
Ac 13:33 it is also w. in the second psalm, ... 1125
Ac 15:15 words of the prophets; as it is w., ... 1125
Ac 21:25 we have w. and concluded that 1989
Ac 23:5 for it is w., Thou shalt not speak 1125
Ac 24:14 all things which are w. in the law 1125
Ro 1:17 as it is w., The just shall live by 1125
Ro 2:15 work of the law w. in their hearts, ... 1123
Ro 2:24 Gentiles through you, as it is w. 1125
Ro 3:4 but every man a liar; as it is w., ... 1125
Ro 3:10 it is w., There is none righteous, ... 1125
Ro 4:17 As it is w., I have made thee a 1125
Ro 4:23 it was not w. for his sake alone, ... 1125
Ro 8:36 As it is w., For thy sake we are 1125
Ro 9:13 As it is w., Jacob have I loved, but 1125
Ro 9:33 As it is w., Behold, I lay in Sion a 1125
Ro 10:15 it is w., How beautiful are the feet 1125
Ro 11:8 (According as it is w., God hath 1125
Ro 11:26 as it is w., There shall come out of 1125
Ro 12:19 for it is w., Vengeance is mine; 1125
Ro 14:11 For it is w., As I live, saith the 1125
Ro 15:3 as it is w., The reproaches of them 1125
Ro 15:4 For whatsoever things were w. 4270
Ro 15:4 were w. for our learning, that we 4270
Ro 15:9 as it is w., For this cause I will 1125
Ro 15:15 I have w. the more boldly unto you 1125
Ro 15:21 But as it is w., To whom he was not.. 1125
Ro *subscr.* W. to the Romans from Corinthus, ... 1125
1Co 1:19 it is w., I will destroy the wisdom 1125
1Co 1:31 as it is w., He that glorieth, ... 1125
1Co 2:9 But as it is w., Eye hath not seen, ... 1125
1Co 3:19 For it is w., He taketh the wise in 1125
1Co 4:6 of men above that which is w., ... 1125
1Co 5:11 w. unto you not to keep company, ... 1125
1Co 9:9 For it is w. in the law of Moses, ... 1125
1Co 9:10 For our sakes, no doubt, this is w.: 1125
1Co 9:15 neither have I w. these things, ... 1125
1Co 10:7 as it is w., The people sat down to 1125
1Co 10:11 they are w. for our admonition, ... 1125
1Co 14:21 In the law it is w., With men of 1125
1Co 15:45 so it is w., The first man Adam was ... 1125
1Co 15:54 to pass the saying that is w., ... 1125
1Co *subscr.* to the Corinthians was w. 1125
2Co 3:2 Ye are our epistle w. in our hearts, ... 1449
2Co 3:3 ministered by us, w. not with ink, ... 1449
2Co 3:7 w. and engraven in stones, ... 1722,1121
2Co 4:13 according as it is w., I believed, ... 1125
2Co 8:15 As it is w., He that had gathered 1125
2Co 9:9 (As it is w., He hath dispersed 1125
2Co *subscr.* to the Corinthians was w. 1125
Ga 3:10 for it is w., Cursed is every one 1125
Ga 3:10 which are w. in the book of the law 1125
Ga 3:13 for it is w., Cursed is every one 1125
Ga 4:22 is w., that Abraham had two sons, ... 1125
Ga 4:27 For it is w., Rejoice, thou barren 1125
Ga 6:11 large a letter I have w. unto you 1125
Ga *subscr.* Unto the Galatians w. from Rome. 1125
Eph *subscr.* W. from Rome unto...Ephesians 1125
Php *subscr.* It was w. to the Philippians 1125
Col *subscr.* W. from Rome to the Colossians 1125
1Th *subscr.* unto the Thessalonians was w. 1125
2Th *subscr.* to the Thessalonians was w. 1125
1Ti *subscr.* The first to Timothy was w. from 1125
2Ti *subscr.* Ephesians, was w. from Rome, ... 1125
Tit *subscr.* It was w. to Titus, ordained the 1125
Phm 19 I Paul have w. it with mine own 1125
Phm *subscr.* W. from Rome to Philemon, by 1125
Heb 10:7 volume of the book it is w. of me,) 1125
Heb 12:23 firstborn, which are w. in heaven, ... 583
Heb 13:22 w. a letter unto you in few words. 1989
Heb *subscr.* W. to the Hebrews from Italy 1125
1Pe 1:16 Because it is w., Be ye holy; 1125
1Pe 5:12 I have w. briefly, exhorting, and 1125
2Pe 3:15 given unto him hath w. unto you; 1125
1Jo 2:14 I have w. unto you, fathers, ... 1125
1Jo 2:14 I have w. unto you, young men, ... 1125
1Jo 2:21 I have not w. unto you because ye 1125
1Jo 2:26 These things have I w. unto you 1125
1Jo 5:13 These things have I w. unto you 1125
Re 1:3 those things which are w. therein: 1125
Re 2:17 **and in the stone a new name w.,** ... 1125
Re 5:1 book w. within and on the backside, ... 1125
Re 13:8 names are not w. in the book of life 1125
Re 14:1 Father's name w. in their foreheads 1125
Re 17:5 upon her forehead was a name w., ... 1125
Re 17:8 names...not w. in the book of life 1125
Re 19:12 had a name w., that no man knew, ... 1125
Re 19:16 and on his thigh a name w., ... 1125
Re 20:12 things which were w. in the books, ... 1125
Re 20:15 was not found w. in the book of life 1125
Re 21:12 and names w. thereon, which are 1924
Re 21:27 are w. in the Lamb's book of life 1125
Re 22:18 plagues that are w. in this book: 1125
Re 22:19 things which are w. in this book 1125

WRONG See also WRONGED; WRONGETH; WRONGFULLY.

Ge 16:5 unto Abram, My w. be upon thee: 2555
Ex 2:13 he said to him that did the w., ... 7563
De 19:16 against him that which is w.; 5627
Jg 11:27 doest me w. to war against me: 7451
1Ch 12:17 there is no w. in mine hands, ... 2555
1Ch 16:21 suffered no man to do them w. 6231
Es 1:16 the queen hath not done w. to the 5753
Job 19:7 Behold, I cry out of w., but I am 2555
Ps 105:14 suffered no man to do them w. 6231
Jer 22:3 and do no w., do no violence 3238
Jer 22:13 and his chambers by w.; 3808,4941
La 3:59 O Lord, thou hast seen my w. 5792
Hab 1:4 w. judgment proceedeth. 6127
Mt 20:13 **Friend, I do thee no w.: didst not** 91
Ac 7:24 And seeing one of them suffer w., ... 91
Ac 7:26 why do ye w. one to another? 91
Ac 7:27 he that did his neighbour w. thrust 91
Ac 18:14 matter of w. or wicked lewdness, ... 92
Ac 25:10 to the Jews have I done no w., ... 91
1Co 6:7 Why do ye not rather take w.? why 91
1Co 6:8 Nay, ye do w., and defraud, and that 91
2Co 7:12 for his cause that had done the w., ... 91
2Co 7:12 for his cause that suffered w., but 91
2Co 12:13 to you? forgive me this w. 93
Col 3:25 But he that doeth w. shall receive 91
Col 3:25 for the w. which he hath done: 91

WRONGED

2Co 7:2 we have w. no man, we have 91
Phm 18 If he hath w. thee, or oweth thee 91

WRONGETH

Pr 8:36 against me w. his own soul: 2554

WRONGFULLY

Job 21:27 which ye w. imagine against me. 2554
Ps 35:19 mine enemies w. rejoice over me: 8267
Ps 38:19 that hate me w. are multiplied. 8267
Ps 69:4 being mine enemies w., are 8267
Ps 119:86 they persecute me w.; help thou 8267
Eze 22:29 oppressed the stranger w. 3808,4941
1Pe 2:19 God endure grief, suffering w. 95

WROTE

Ex 24:4 Moses w. all the words of the 3789
Ex 34:28 he w. upon the tables the words of 3789
Ex 39:30 pure gold, and w. upon it a writing, ... 3789
Nu 33:2 And Moses w. their goings out 3789
De 4:13 w. them upon two tables of stone. 3789
De 5:22 he w. them in two tables of stone, ... 3789
De 10:4 he w. on the tables, according to 3789
De 31:9 Moses w. this law, and delivered it 3789
De 31:22 Moses therefore w. this song the 3789
Jos 8:32 he w. there upon the stones a copy 3789
Jos 8:32 which he w. in the presence of the 3789
Jos 24:26 Joshua w. these words in the book 3789
1Sa 10:25 and w. it in a book, and laid it up 3789
2Sa 11:14 that David w. a letter to Joab, and 3789
2Sa 11:15 he w. in the letter, saying, Set ye 3789
1Ki 21:8 So she w. letters in Ahab's name, ... 3789
1Ki 21:9 And she w. in the letters, saying, ... 3789
2Ki 10:1 And Jehu w. letters, and sent to 3789
2Ki 10:6 Then he w. a letter the second time ... 3789
2Ki 17:37 commandment, which he w. for you, ... 3789
1Ch 24:6 Levites, w. them before the king, ... 3789
2Ch 30:1 w. letters also to Ephraim and 3789
2Ch 32:17 w. also letters to rail on the Lord 3789
Ezr 4:6 w. they unto him an accusation 3789
Ezr 4:7 days of Artaxerxes w. Bishlam, ... 3789
Ezr 4:8 Shimshai the scribe w. a letter 3790
Ezr 4:9 Then w. Rehum the chancellor, and ....
Es 8:5 which he w. to destroy the Jews 3789
Es 8:10 w. in the king Ahasuerus' name, ... 3789
Es 9:20 And Mordecai w. these things, and 3789
Es 9:29 Mordecai...w. with all authority, ... 3789
Jer 36:4 w. from the mouth of Jeremiah 3789
Jer 36:18 I w. them with ink in the book. 3789
Jer 36:27 w. at the mouth of Jeremiah, ... 3789
Jer 36:32 w....from the mouth of Jeremiah 3789
Jer 51:60 Jeremiah w. in a book all the evil 3789
Da 5:5 w. over against the candlestick 3790
Da 5:5 saw the part of the hand that w. 3790
Da 6:25 king Darius w. unto all people, ... 3790
Da 7:1 he w. the dream, and told the sum 3790
Mk 10:5 **your heart he w. you this precept** .. 1125
Mk 12:19 Master, Moses w. unto us, If a 1125
Lu 1:63 and w., saying, His name is John. 1125
Lu 20:28 Master, Moses w. unto us, If any 1125
Joh 5:46 **have believed me: for he w. of me.** .1125
Joh 8:6 with his finger w. on the ground, ... 1125
Joh 8:8 down, and w. on the ground. 1125
Joh 19:19 And Pilate w. a title, and put it on 1125
Joh 21:24 these things, and w. these things: 1125
Ac 15:23 they w. letters by them after this 1125
Ac 18:27 the brethren w., exhorting the 1125
Ac 23:25 he w. a letter after this manner: 1125
Ro 16:22 I Tertius, who w. this epistle, ... 1125
1Co 5:9 I w. unto you in an epistle not to 1125
1Co 7:1 the things whereof ye w. unto me: 1125
2Co 2:3 And I w. this same unto you, lest, ... 1125
2Co 2:4 I w. unto you with many tears; 1125
2Co 7:12 though I w. unto you, I did it not 1125
Eph 3:3 (as I w. afore in few words, ... 4270
Phm 21 in thy obedience I w. unto thee, ... 1125
2Jo 5 though I w. a new commandment 1125
3Jo 9 I w. unto the church: but 1125

WROTH See also WRATHFUL.

Ge 4:5 And Cain was very w., and his 2734
Ge 4:6 said unto Cain, Why art thou w.? 2734
Ge 31:36 Jacob was w., and chode with 2734
Ge 34:7 and they were very w., because he 2734
Ge 40:2 Pharaoh was w. against two of his 7107
Ge 41:10 Pharaoh was w. with his servants, ... 7107
Ex 16:20 and Moses was w. with them. 7107
Nu 16:15 And Moses was very w., and said 2734
Nu 16:22 be w. with all the congregation? 7107
Nu 31:14 Moses was w. with the officers of 7107
De 1:34 words, and was w., and sware, ... 7107
De 3:26 the Lord was w. with me for your 5674
De 9:19 the Lord was w. against you to 7107
Jos 22:18 he will be w. with the whole 7107
1Sa 18:8 Saul was very w., and the saying 2734
1Sa 20:7 but if he be very w., then be sure 2734
1Sa 29:4 the Philistines were w. with him; 7107
2Sa 3:8 was Abner very w. for the words 2734
2Sa 13:21 all these things, he was very w. 2734
2Sa 22:8 and shook, because he was w. 2734
2Ki 5:11 Naaman was w., and went away, ... 7107
2Ki 13:19 the man of God was w. with him, ... 7107
2Ch 16:10 Then Asa was w. with the seer, ... 3707
2Ch 26:19 Then Uzziah was w., and had a 2196
2Ch 26:19 while he was w. with the priests, ... 2196
2Ch 28:9 of your fathers was w. with Judah, ... 2534
Ne 4:1 we builded the wall, he was w., ... 2734
Ne 4:7 be stopped, then they were very w., .. 2734
Es 1:12 therefore was the king very w., ... 7107
Es 2:21 were w., and sought to lay hand on 7107
Ps 18:7 were shaken, because he was w. 2734
Ps 78:21 the Lord heard this, and was w. 5674
Ps 78:59 When God heard this, he was w., ... 5674
Ps 78:62 and was w. with his inheritance. 5674
Ps 89:38 hast been w. with thine anointed. 5674
Isa 28:21 he shall be w. as in the valley of 7264
Isa 47:6 I was w. with my people, I have 7107
Isa 54:9 that I would not be w. with thee, ... 7107
Isa 57:16 ever, neither will I be always w. 7107
Isa 57:17 of his covetousness was I w., ... 7107
Isa 57:17 I hid me, and was w., and he went 7107
Isa 64:5 thou art w.; for we have sinned: 7107
Isa 64:9 Be not w. very sore, O Lord, ... 7107
Jer 37:15 the princes were w. with Jeremiah, ... 7107
La 5:22 thou art very w. against us. 7107
Mt 2:16 was exceeding w., and sent forth, ... 2373
Mt 18:34 **his lord was w., and delivered** 3710
Mt 22:7 **the king heard thereof, he was w.** .3710
Re 12:17 dragon was w. with the woman, ... 3710

WROUGHT See also WROUGHTEST.
Ge 34:7 because he had **w.** folly in Israel ... 6213
Ez 10:2 what things I have **w.** in Egypt, ... 5953
Ex 26:36 twined linen, **w.** with needlework. ... 4639
Ex 27:16 twined linen, **w.** with needlework: ...
Ex 36:1 Then **w.** Bezaleel and Aholiab, ... 6213
Ex 36:4 **w.** all the work of the sanctuary, ... 6213
Ex 36:8 **w.** the work of the tabernacle ... 6213
Ex 39:6 **w.** onyx stones inclosed in ouches ... 6213
Le 20:12 they have **w.** confusion; their blood ... 6213
Nu 23:23 and of Israel, what hath God **w.**! ... 6466
Nu 31:51 gold of them, even all **w.** jewels ... 4639
De 13:14 abomination is **w.** among you; ... 6213
De 17:2 hath **w.** wickedness in the sight ... 6213
De 17:4 such abomination is **w.** in Israel: ... 6213
De 21:3 which hath not been **w.** with, ... 5647
De 22:21 she hath **w.** folly in Israel, to play ... 6213
De 31:18 the evils which they shall have **w.**, ... 6213
Jos 7:15 because he hath **w.** folly in Israel. ... 6213
Jg 20:10 folly that they have **w.** in Israel. ... 6213
Ru 2:19 in law with whom she had **w.**, and ... 6213
Ru 2:19 with whom I **w.** to day is Boaz. ... 6213
1Sa 6:6 **w.** wonderfully among them, ... 5953
1Sa 11:13 Lord hath **w.** salvation in Israel. ... 6213
1Sa 14:45 **w.** this great salvation in Israel? ... 6213
1Sa 14:45 for he hath **w.** with God this day. ... 6213
1Sa 19:5 the Lord **w.** a great salvation for all ... 6213
2Sa 18:13 I should have **w.** falsehood against ... 6213
2Sa 23:10 Lord **w.** a great victory that day; ... 6213
2Sa 23:12 and the Lord **w.** a great victory. ... 6213
1Ki 5:16 over the people that **w.** in the work. ... 6213
1Ki 7:14 king Solomon, and **w.** all his work. ... 6213
1Ki 7:26 was **w.** like the brim of a cup, ... 4639
1Ki 9:23 the people that **w.** in the work. ... 6213
1Ki 16:20 his treason that he **w.**, are they ... 7194
1Ki 16:25 But Omri **w.** evil in the eyes of the ... 6213
2Ki 3:2 he **w.** evil in the sight of the Lord; ... 6213
2Ki 12:11 that **w.** upon the house of the Lord, ... 6213
2Ki 17:11 **w.** wicked things to provoke the ... 6213
2Ki 21:6 he **w.** much wickedness in the ... 6213
1Ch 4:21 house of them that **w.** fine linen, ... 5656
1Ch 22:2 set masons to hew **w.** stones to ... 1496
2Ch 3:14 linen, and **w.** cherubims thereon. ... 5927
2Ch 21:6 and he **w.** that which was evil in ... 6213
2Ch 24:12 such as **w.** iron and brass to mend ... 2790
2Ch 24:13 So the workmen **w.**, and the work ... 6213
2Ch 31:20 **w.** that which was good and right ... 6213
2Ch 33:6 he **w.** much evil in the sight of the ... 6213
2Ch 34:10 workmen that **w.** in the house of ... 6213
2Ch 34:13 all that **w.** the work in any manner ... 6213
Ne 4:16 half of my servants **w.** in the work, ... 6213
Ne 4:17 one of his hands **w.** in the work, ... 6213
Ne 6:16 that this work was **w.** of our God. ... 6213
Ne 9:18 and had **w.** great provocations; ... 6213
Ne 9:26 and they **w.** great provocations. ... 6213
Job 12:9 the hand of the Lord hath **w.** this? ... 6213
Job 36:23 can say, Thou hast **w.** iniquity? ... 6466
Ps 31:19 thou hast **w.** for them that trust in ... 6466
Ps 45:13 within: her clothing is of **w.** gold ... 4865
Ps 68:28 that which thou hast **w.** for us. ... 6466
Ps 78:43 How he had **w.** his signs in Egypt, ... 7760
Ps 139:15 curiously **w.** in the lowest parts of ... 7551
Ec 2:11 the works that my hands had **w.**, ... 6213
Ec 2:17 the work that is **w.** under the sun is ... 6213
Isa 26:12 also hast **w.** all our works in us. ... 6466
Isa 26:18 we have not **w.** any deliverance in ... 6213
Isa 41:4 Who hath **w.** and done it, calling ... 6466
Jer 11:15 she hath **w.** lewdness with many, ... 6213
Jer 18:3 he **w.** a work on the wheels. ... 6213
Eze 2:9, 14,22 **w.** for my name's sake, ... 6213
Eze 2:44 **w.** with you for my name's sake, ... 6213
Eze 29:20 because they **w.** for me, saith the ... 6213
Da 4:2 the high God hath **w.** toward me. ... 5648
Jon 1:11 unto us, for the sea **w.**, and was ... 1980
Jon 1:13 sea **w.**, and was tempestuous. ... 1980
Zep 2:3 which have **w.** his judgment; ... 6466
Mt 20:12 **These last have w. but one hour,** ... *4160*
Mt 26:10 **she hath w. a good work upon me.** *2038*
Mk 6:2 mighty works are **w.** by his hands? ... *1096*
Mk 14:6 **she hath w. a good work on me.** ... *2038*
Joh 3:21 **manifest, that they are w. in God.** *2038*
Ac 5:12 and wonders **w.** among the people; ... *1096*
Ac 15:12 God had **w.** among the Gentiles ... *4160*
Ac 18:3 he abode with them, and **w.**: ... *2038*
Ac 19:11 God **w.** special miracles by the ... *4160*
Ac 21:19 God had **w.** among the Gentiles by ... *4160*
Ro 7:8 **w.** in me all manner of ... *2716*
Ro 15:18 which Christ hath not **w.** by me, ... *2716*
2Co 5:5 that hath **w.** us for the selfsame ... *2716*
2Co 7:11 what carefulness it **w.** in you, yea, ... *2716*
2Co 12:12 signs of an apostle were **w.** among ... *2716*
Ga 2:8 (For he that **w.** effectually in ... *1754*
Eph 1:20 Which he **w.** in Christ, when he ... *1754*
2Th 3:8 **w.** with labour and travail night ... *2038*
Heb 11:33 **w.** righteousnes, obtained ... *2038*
Jas 2:22 thou how faith **w.** with his works, ... *4903*
1Pe 4:3 have **w.** the will of the Gentiles, ... *2716*
2Jo 8 not those things which we have **w.**, ... *2038*
Re 19:20 the false prophet that **w.** miracles. ... *4160*

WROUGHTEST
Ru 2:19 to day? and where **w.** thou? ... 6213

WRUNG See also WRINGED.
Le 1:15 the blood thereof shall be **w.** out ... 4680
Le 5:9 rest of the blood shall be **w.** out ... 4680
Ps 73:10 of a full cup are **w.** out to them. ... 4680
Isa 51:17 cup of trembling, and **w.** them out. ... 4680

Y.

YARD See METEYARD; OLIVEYARD; VINEYARD.

YARN
1Ki 10:28 out of Egypt, and linen **y.** ... 4723
1Ki 10:28 received the linen **y.** at a price. ... 4723
2Ch 1:16 out of Egypt, and linen **y.** ... 4723
2Ch 1:16 received the linen **y.** at a price. ... 4723

YE See in the APPENDIX; also YOU.

YEA See also YES.
Ge 3:1 **Y.**, hath God said, Ye shall ... 637,3588
Ge 17:16 **y.**, I will bless her, and she shall be a ...
Ge 20:6 **Y.**, I know that thou didst this in ... 1571
Ge 27:33 him? **y.**, and he shall be blessed. ... 1571
Le 25:35 **y.**, though he be a stranger, or a ...
Nu 10:32 **y.**, it shall be, that what goodness the ...
De 33:3 **Y.**, he loved the people; all his ... 637
Jg 5:29 **y.**, she returned answer to herself, ... 637
1Sa 17:20 **Y.**, I have obeyed the voice of the ... 834
1Sa 21:5 **y.**, though it were sanctified this ... 637
1Sa 24:11 **y.**, see the skirts of thy robe in my ... 637
2Sa 19:30 unto the king, **Y.**, let him take all, ... 637
2Sa 22:39 **y.**, they are fallen under my feet. ...
2Ki 2:3,5 **Y.**, I know it; hold...your peace. ... 1571
2Ki 16:3 **y.**, and made his son to pass ... 1571
1Ch 16:21 **y.**, he reproved kings for their sakes. ...
2Ch 26:20 **y.**, himself hasted also to go out, because ..
Ezr 9:2 **y.**, the hand of the princes and rulers ...
Ne 5:15 **y.**, even their servants bare rule ... 1571
Ne 5:16 **Y.**, also I continued in the work ... 1571
Ne 6:10 **y.**, in the night will they come to slay ...
Ne 9:18 **Y.**, when they had made them a ... 637
Ne 9:21 **Y.**, forty years didst thou sustain ...
Es 5:12 **Y.**, Esther the queen did let no man ...
Job 1:15 **y.**, they have slain the servants ...
Job 1:17 **y.**, and slain the servants with the ...
Job 2:4 **y.**, all that man hath will he give ...
Job 5:19 **y.**, in seven there shall no evil touch ...
Job 6:10 **y.**, I would harden myself in sorrow: ...
Job 6:27 **Y.**, ye overwhelm the fatherless, ... 637
Job 6:29 **y.**, return again, my righteousness is ...
Job 9:10 out; **y.**, and wonders without number. ...
Job 11:15 **y.**, thou shalt be stedfast, and shalt ...
Job 11:18 **y.**, thou shalt dig about thee, and thou ...
Job 11:19 **y.**, many shall make suit unto thee. ...
Job 12:3 **y.**, who knoweth not such things as ...
Job 14:10 **y.**, man giveth up the ghost, and where ...
Job 15:4 **Y.**, thou castest off fear, and ... 637
Job 15:6 **y.**, thine own lips testify against thee. ...
Job 15:15 **y.**, the heavens are not clean in his ...
Job 18:5 **Y.**, the light of the wicked shall ... 1571
Job 19:18 **Y.**, young children despised me; ... 1571
Job 20:8 **y.**, he shall be chased away as a ...
Job 20:25 **y.**, the glittering sword cometh out ...
Job 21:7 old, **y.**, are mighty in power? ... 1571
Job 22:25 **Y.**, the Almighty shall be thy ...
Job 25:5 **y.**, the stars are not pure in his sight. ...
Job 28:27 he prepared it, **y.**, and searched it. ... 1571
Job 30:2 **Y.**, whereto might the strength ... 1571
Job 30:8 of fools, **y.**, children of base men: ... 1571
Job 30:9 I their song, **y.**, I am their byword. ...
Job 31:8 **y.**, let my offspring be rooted out. ...
Job 31:11 **y.**, it is an iniquity to be punished ...
Job 32:12 **Y.**, I attended unto you, and, behold, ...
Job 33:14 For God speaketh once, **y.** twice, yet ...
Job 33:22 **Y.**, his soul draweth near unto the ...
Job 34:12 **Y.**, surely God will not do ... 637
Job 36:7 **y.**, he doth establish them for ever, ...
Job 40:5 not answer: **y.**, twice; but I will ...
Job 41:24 **y.**, as hard as a piece of the nether ...
Ps 7:4 (**y.**, I have delivered him that without ...
Ps 7:5 **y.**, let him tread down my life upon ...
Ps 8:7 **y.**, and the beasts of the field; ... 1571
Ps 16:6 **y.**, I have a goodly heritage. ... 637
Ps 18:10 **y.**, he did fly upon the wings of the ...
Ps 18:14 **Y.**, he sent out his arrows, and ...
Ps 18:48 **y.**, thou liftest me up above those ... 637
Ps 19:10 than gold, **y.**, than much fine gold: ...
Ps 23:4 **Y.**, though I walk through the valley ... 1571
Ps 25:3 **Y.**, let none that wait on thee be ... 1571
Ps 27:6 **y.**, I will sing praises unto the Lord. ...
Ps 29:5 **y.**, the Lord breaketh the cedars of ...
Ps 29:10 **y.**, the Lord sitteth King for ever. ...
Ps 31:9 with grief, **y.**, my soul and my belly. ...
Ps 35:10 **y.**, the poor and the needy from him ...
Ps 35:15 **y.**, the abjects gathered themselves ...
Ps 35:21 **Y.**, they opened their mouth wide ...
Ps 35:27 **y.**, let them say continually, Let the ...
Ps 37:10 **y.**, thou shalt diligently consider his ...
Ps 37:36 **y.**, I sought him, but he could not ...
Ps 40:8 God: **y.**, thy law is within my heart. ...
Ps 41:9 **Y.**, mine own familiar friend, ... 1571
Ps 43:4 **y.**, upon the harp will I praise thee, O ...
Ps 44:22 **Y.**, for thy sake are we killed all ... 3588
Ps 57:1 **y.**, in the shadow of thy wings will I ...
Ps 58:2 **Y.**, in heart ye work wickedness; ... 637
Ps 59:16 **y.**, I will sing aloud of thy mercy ...
Ps 68:3 God: **y.**, let them exceedingly rejoice. ...
Ps 68:16 **y.**, the Lord will dwell in it for ever. ... 637
Ps 68:18 for men: **y.**, for the rebellious also, ... 637
Ps 72:11 **Y.**, all kings shall fall down before ...
Ps 78:19 **Y.**, they spake against God; they ...
Ps 78:38 **y.**, many a time turned he his anger ...
Ps 78:41 **Y.**, they turned back and tempted ...
Ps 83:11 Zeeb: **y.**, all their princes as Zebah, ...
Ps 83:17 **y.**, let them be put to shame, and ...
Ps 84:2 My soul longeth, **y.**, even fainteth ... 1571
Ps 84:3 **Y.**, the sparrow hath found an ... 1571
Ps 85:12 **Y.**, the Lord shall give that which ... 1571
Ps 90:17 **y.**, the work of our hands establish ...
Ps 93:4 **y.**, than the mighty waves of the sea. ...
Ps 94:23 **y.**, the Lord our God shall cut them ...
Ps 102:13 her, **y.**, the set time, is come. ... 3588
Ps 102:26 **y.**, all of them shall wax old like a ...
Ps 105:12 **y.**, very few, and strangers in it. ...
Ps 105:14 **y.**, he reproved kings for their sakes; ...
Ps 106:24 **Y.**, they despised the pleasant land, ...
Ps 106:37 **Y.**, they sacrificed their sons and ...
Ps 109:30 **y.**, I will praise him among the ...
Ps 116:5 righteous; **y.**, our God is merciful. ...
Ps 118:11 **y.**, they compassed me about: ... 1571
Ps 119:34 **y.**, I shall observe it with my...heart. ...
Ps 119:103 **y.**, sweeter than honey to my mouth. ...
Ps 119:127 above gold; **y.**, above fine gold. ...
Ps 128:6 **Y.**, thou shalt see thy children's ...
Ps 137:1 **y.**, we wept, when we remembered. ... 1571
Ps 138:5 **Y.**, they shall sing in the ways of the ...
Ps 139:12 **Y.**, the darkness hideth not from ... 1571
Ps 144:15 **y.**, happy is that people, whose God ...
Pr 2:3 **Y.**, if thou criest after knowledge, ... 3588
Pr 2:9 and equity; **y.**, every good path. ...
Pr 3:24 **y.**, thou shalt lie down, and thy sleep ...
Pr 6:16 **y.**, seven are an abomination unto ...

Pr 7:26 **y.**, many strong men have been slain
Pr 8:18 **y.**, durable riches and righteousness
Pr 8:19 better than gold, **y.**, than fine gold;
Pr 16:4 **y.**, even the wicked for the day of 1571
Pr 22:10 **y.**, strife and reproach shall cease.
Pr 23:16 **Y.**, my reins shall rejoice, when thy
Pr 23:34 **Y.**, thou shalt be as he that lieth
Pr 24:5 **y.**, a man of knowledge increaseth
Pr 29:17 **y.**, he shall give delight unto thy soul.
Pr 30:15 **y.**, four things say not, It is enough:
Pr 30:18 for me, **y.**, four which I know not:
Pr 30:29 go well, **y.**, four are comely in going.
Pr 31:20 **y.**, she reacheth forth her hands to the
Ec 1:16 **y.**, my heart had great experience of
Ec 2:18 **Y.**, I hated all my labour which I had
Ec 2:23 **y.**, his heart taketh not rest in the 1571
Ec 3:19 **y.**, they have all one breath; so that
Ec 4:3 **Y.**, better is he than both they, which
Ec 4:8 **y.**, he hath neither child nor 1571
Ec 4:8 is also vanity, **y.**, it is a sore travail.
Ec 6:6 **Y.**, though he live a thousand years 432
Ec 7:18 **y.**, also from this withdraw not 1571
Ec 8:17 **y.** farther; though a wise man 1571
Ec 9:3 **y.**, also the heart of the sons of men 1571
Ec 10:3 **Y.** also, when he that is a fool 1571
Ec 12:9 **y.**, he gave good heed, and sought out
Ca 1:16 art fair, my beloved, **y.**, pleasant: 637
Ca 5:1 **y.**, drink abundantly, O beloved
Ca 5:16 most sweet; **y.**, he is altogether lovely
Ca 6:9 **y.**, the queens and the concubines,
Ca 8:1 **y.**, I should not be despised. 1571
Isa 1:15 **y.**, when ye make many prayers, 1571
Isa 5:10 **Y.**, ten acres of vineyard shall 3588
Isa 5:29 **y.**, they shall roar, and lay hold of the
Isa 14:8 **Y.**, the fir trees rejoice at thee, 1571
Isa 19:21 **y.**, they shall vow a vow unto the
Isa 24:16 **y.**, the treacherous dealers have dealt
Isa 26:8 **Y.**, in the way of thy judgments, 687
Isa 26:9 **y.**, with my spirit within me will I 687
Isa 26:11 **y.**, the fire of thine enemies shall 687
Isa 29:5 **y.**, it shall be at an instant suddenly.
Isa 30:33 **y.**, for the king it is prepared; 1571
Isa 32:13 **y.**, upon all the houses of joy in 3588
Isa 40:24 **Y.**, they shall not be planted; 637
Isa 40:24 **y.**, they shall not be sown: 637
Isa 40:24 **y.**, their stock shall not take root in 637
Isa 41:10 **y.**, I will help thee; **y.**, I will uphold 637
Isa 41:23 **y.**, do good, or do evil, that we may 637
Isa 41:26 **y.**, there is none that sheweth, 637
Isa 41:26 **y.**, there is none that declareth, 637
Isa 41:26 **y.**, there is none that heareth your 637
Isa 42:13 he shall cry, **y.**, roar; he shall 637
Isa 43:7 formed him; **y.**, I have made him. 637
Isa 43:13 **Y.**, before the day was I am he; and 1571
Isa 44:8 **y.**, there is no God; I know not any
Isa 44:12 **y.**, he is hungry, and his strength 1571
Isa 44:15 **y.**, he kindleth it, and baketh 637
Isa 44:15 **y.**, he maketh a god, and 637
Isa 44:16 **y.**, he warmeth himself, and saith, 637
Isa 44:19 **y.**, also I have baked bread upon 637
Isa 45:21 **y.**, let them take counsel together: 637
Isa 46:6 they fall down, **y.**, they worship. 637
Isa 46:7 **y.**, one shall cry unto him, yet can 637
Isa 46:11 **y.**, I have spoken it, I will also bring 637
Isa 47:3 **y.**, thy shame shall be seen: I will 1571
Isa 48:8 **Y.**, thou heardest not; **y.**, thou 1571
Isa 48:8 **y.**, from that time that thine ear 1571
Isa 48:15 have spoken; **y.**, I have called him: 637
Isa 49:15 **y.**, they may forget, yet will I not 1571
Isa 55:1 **y.**, come, buy wine and milk without
Isa 56:9 devour, **y.**, all ye beasts in the forest
Isa 56:11 **y.**, they are greedy dogs which can
Isa 59:15 **Y.**, truth faileth; and he that
Isa 60:12 **y.**, these nations shall be utterly
Isa 66:3 **Y.**, they have chosen their own 1571
Jer 2:37 **y.**, thou shalt go forth from him, 1571
Jer 5:28 **y.**, they overpass the deeds of the 1571
Jer 8:7 **Y.**, the stork in the heaven 1571
Jer 12:2 them, **y.**, they have taken root: 1571
Jer 12:2 grow, **y.**, they bring forth fruit: 1571
Jer 12:6 **y.**, they have called a multitude 1571
Jer 14:5 **Y.**, the hind also calved in 3588, 1571
Jer 14:18 **y.**, both the prophet and the 3588, 1571
Jer 23:11 **y.**, in my house have I found their 1571
Jer 23:26 **y.**, they are prophets of the deceit of
Jer 27:21 **Y.**, thus saith the Lord of hosts, 3588
Jer 31:3 **Y.**, I have loved thee with an
Jer 31:19 was ashamed, **y.**, even confounded, 1571
Jer 32:41 **Y.**, I will rejoice over them to do
Jer 46:16 many to fall, **y.**, one fell upon another:
Jer 51:44 **y.**, the wall of Babylon shall fall. 1571
La 1:8 **y.**, she sigheth, and turneth 1571
Eze 6:14 desolate, **y.**, more desolate than the
Eze 16:6 **y.**, I said unto thee when thou wast in
Eze 16:8 **y.**, I sware unto thee, and entered
Eze 16:9 **y.**, I throughly washed away thy
Eze 16:28 **y.**, thou hast played the harlot with
Eze 16:52 **y.**, be thou confounded also, and 1571
Eze 17:10 **Y.**, behold, being planted, shall it
Eze 22:2 **y.**, thou shalt shew her all her
Eze 22:21 **Y.**, I will gather you, and blow upon
Eze 22:29 **y.**, they have oppressed the stranger
Eze 23:36 Aholibah? **y.**, decare unto them
Eze 26:18 **y.**, the isles that are in the sea shall be
Eze 28:26 **y.**, they shall dwell with confidence,
Eze 32:10 **Y.**, I will make many people amazed
Eze 32:28 **Y.**, thou shalt be broken in the midst
Eze 34:6 **y.**, my flock was scattered upon all
Eze 36:12 **Y.**, I will cause men to walk upon
Eze 37:27 **y.**, I will be their God, and they
Eze 39:13 **Y.**, all the people of the land shall
Da 8:11 **Y.**, he magnified himself even to the
Da 9:11 **Y.**, all Israel have transgressed thy
Da 9:21 **Y.**, whiles I was speaking in prayer,
Da 10:19 be unto thee; be strong, **y.**, be strong.
Da 11:22 **y.**, also the prince of the covenant 1571
Da 11:24 **y.**, and he shall forecast his devices
Da 11:26 **Y.**, they that feed of the portion of
Ho 2:19 **y.**, I will betroth thee unto me in
Ho 4:3 **y.**, the fishes of the sea also shall 1571
Ho 7:9 **y.**, gray hairs are here and there 1571
Ho 8:10 **Y.**, though they have hired among 1571
Ho 9:12 **y.**, woe also to them when I 3588
Ho 9:16 **y.**, though they bring forth, yet will 1571
Ho 12:4 **Y.**, he had power over the angel, and
Ho 12:11 **y.**, their altars are as heaps in the 1571
Joe 1:16 **y.**, joy and gladness from the house of
Joe 1:18 **y.**, the flocks of sheep are made 1571
Joe 2:3 **y.**, and nothing shall escape them. 1571
Joe 2:19 **Y.**, the Lord will answer and say
Joe 3:4 **Y.**, and what have ye to do with 1571
Am 8:6 **y.**, and sell the refuse of the wheat!
Ob 13 **y.**, thou shouldest not have looked 1571
Ob 16 **y.**, they shall drink, and they shall
Jon 3:8 **y.**, let them turn every one from his
Mic 3:7 **y.**, they shall all cover their lips;
Na 1:5 **y.**, the world, and all that dwell
Hab 2:5 **Y.** also, because he transgresseth 637
Zep 2:1 **y.**, gather together, O nation not
Hag 2:19 **y.**, as yet the vine, and the fig tree,
Zec 7:12 **Y.**, they made their hearts as an
Zec 8:22 **Y.**, many people and strong nations
Zec 10:7 **y.**, their children shall see it, and be
Zec 14:5 **y.**, ye shall flee, like as ye fled from
Zec 14:21 **Y.**, every pot in Jerusalem and in
Mal 2:2 **y.**, I have cursed them already, 1571
Mal 3:15 **y.**, they that work wickedness are 1571
Mal 3:15 **y.**, they that tempt God are even 1571
Mal 4:1 proud, **y.**, and all that do wickedly,
Mt 5:37 let your communication be, **Y.**, **y.**; *3483*
Mt 9:28 They said unto him, **Y.**, Lord. *3483*
Mt 11:9 A prophet? **y.**, I say unto you, and *3483*
Mt 13:51 They say unto him, **Y.**, Lord. *3483*
Mt 21:16 **Y.**; have ye never read, Out of the *3483*
Mt 26:60 **y.**, though many false witnesses *2532*
Lu 2:35 (**Y.**, a sword shall pierce through *1161*
Lu 7:26 A prophet? **Y.**, I say unto you, *3483*
Lu 11:28 **Y.** rather, blessed are they that *3304*
Lu 12:5 hell; **y.**, I say unto you, Fear him. *3483*
Lu 12:57 **Y.**, and why even of yourselves judge
Lu 14:26 **y., and his own life also, he** *2089*
Lu 24:22 **Y.**, and certain women also of our *235*
Joh 11:27 **Y.**, Lord: I believe that thou art *3483*
Joh 16:2 **y.**, the time cometh, that whosoever *235*
Joh 16:32 the hour cometh, **y.**, is now come, *2532*
Joh 21:15, 16 **Y.**, Lord: thou knowest that I *3483*
Ac 3:16 **y.**, the faith which is by him hath *2532*
Ac 3:24 **Y.**, and all the prophets from *1161*
Ac 5:8 And she said, **Y.**, for so much *3483*
Ac 7:43 **Y.**, ye took up the tabernacle of *2532*
Ac 20:34 **Y.**, ye yourselves know, that these *1161*
Ac 22:27 art thou a Roman? He said, **Y.** *3483*
Ro 3:4 **y.**, let God be true, but every man a *1161*
Ro 3:31 forbid: **y.**, we establish the law. *235*
Ro 8:34 died, **y.** rather, that is risen again, *1161*
Ro 14:4 **Y.**, he shall be holden up: for God *235*
Ro 15:20 **Y.**, so have I strived to preach the *235*
1Co 1:28 chosen, **y.**, and things which are not,
1Co 2:10 things, **y.**, the deep things of God. *2532*
1Co 4:3 **y.**, I judge not mine own self. *235*
1Co 9:16 **y.**, woe is unto me, if I preach not *1161*
1Co 15:15 **Y.**, and we are found false witnesses *1161*
1Co 16:6 will abide, **y.**, and winter with you, *2228*
2Co 1:17 that with me there should be **y. y.**, *3483*
2Co 1:18 toward you was not **y.** and nay. *3483*
2Co 1:19 not **y.** and nay, but in him was **y.** *3483*
2Co 1:20 the promises of God in him are **y.**, *3483*
2Co 5:16 **y.**, though we have known Christ *1161*
2Co 7:11 **y.**, what clearing of yourselves, *235*
2Co 7:11 **y.**, what indignation, **y.**, what fear, *235*
2Co 7:11 **y.**, what vehement desire, *235*
2Co 7:11 **y.**, what zeal, **y.**, what revenge! *235*
2Co 7:13 **y.**, and exceedingly the more joyed we
2Co 8:3 **y.**, and beyond their power they were
Ga 4:17 **y.**, they would exclude you, that ye *235*
Php 1:18 do rejoice, **y.**, and will rejoice. *235*
Php 2:17 **Y.**, and if I be offered upon the *235*
Php 3:8 **Y.** doubtless, and I count all *235*
2Ti 3:12 **Y.**, and all that will live godly in *1161*
Phm 20 **Y.**, brother, let me have joy of *3483*
Heb 11:36 **y.**, moreover of bonds and *1161*
Jas 2:18 **Y.**, a man may say, Thou hast *235*
Jas 5:12 your **y.** be **y.**, and your nay, nay; *3483*
1Pe 5:5 **Y.**, all of you be subject one to *1161*
2Pe 1:13 **Y.**, I think it meet, as long as I am *1161*
3Jo 12 **y.**, and we also bear record; and ye *1161*
Re 14:13 **Y.**, saith the Spirit, that they may *3483*

YEAR See also YEAR'S; YEARS.
Ge 7:11 six hundredth **y.** of Noah's life, 8141
Ge 8:13 in the six hundredth and first **y.**, 8141
Ge 14:4 in the thirteenth **y.** they rebelled. 8141
Ge 14:5 fourteenth **y.** came Chedorlaomer, 8141
Ge 17:21 thee at this set time in the next **y.** 8141
Ge 26:12 in the same **y.** an hundredfold: 8141
Ge 47:17 bread for all their cattle for that **y.** 8141
Ge 47:18 when that **y.** was ended, they came 8141
Ge 47:18 they came unto him the second **y.** 8141
Ex 12:2 be the first month of the **y.** to you. 8141
Ex 12:5 blemish, a male of the first **y.** 8141
Ex 13:10 in his season from **y.** to **y.** 3117
Ex 23:11 the seventh **y.** thou shalt let it rest
Ex 23:14 keep a feast unto me in the **y.** 8141
Ex 23:16 which is in the end of the **y.**, when 8141
Ex 23:17 Three times in the **y.** all thy males 8141
Ex 23:29 out from before thee in one **y.**; 8141
Ex 29:38 two lambs of the first **y.** day by day 8141
Ex 30:10 upon the horns of it once in a **y.** 8141
Ex 30:10 once in the **y.** shall he make 8141
Ex 34:23 Thrice in the **y.** shall all your 8141
Ex 34:24 the Lord thy God thrice in the **y.** 8141
Ex 40:17 in the first month in the second **y.** 8141
Le 9:3 calf and a lamb, both of the first **y.**, 8141
Le 12:6 shall bring a lamb of the first **y.** 8141
Le 14:10 one ewe lamb of the first **y.** without 8141
Le 16:34 of Israel for all their sins once a **y.** 8141
Le 19:24 in the fourth **y.** all the fruit thereof 8141
Le 19:25 the fifth **y.** shall ye eat of the fruit 8141
Le 23:12 lamb without blemish of the first **y.** 8141
Le 23:18 without blemish of the first **y.**, 8141
Le 23:19 two lambs of the first **y.** for a 8141
Le 23:41 unto the Lord seven days in the **y.** 8141
Le 25:4 the seventh **y.** shall be a sabbath 8141
Le 25:5 it is a **y.** of rest unto the land 8141
Le 25:10 And ye shall hallow the fiftieth **y.**, 8141
Le 25:11 A jubile shall that fiftieth **y.** be 8141
Le 25:13 In the **y.** of this jubile ye shall 8141
Le 25:20 What shall we eat the seventh **y.**? 8141
Le 25:21 blessing upon you in the sixth **y.**, 8141
Le 25:22 ye shall sow the eight **y.**, and eat 8141
Le 25:22 yet of old fruit until the ninth **y.**; 8141
Le 25:28 bought it until the **y.** of jubile: 8141
Le 25:29 within a whole **y.** after it is sold; 8141
Le 25:29 within a full **y.** may he redeem it. 3117
Le 25:30 within the space of a full **y.**, 8141
Le 25:33 shall go out in the **y.** of jubile:
Le 25:40 serve thee unto the **y.** of jubile: 8141
Le 25:50 him that bought him from the **y.** 8141

Le 25:50 sold him unto the **y.** of jubile............ 8141
Le 25:52 but few years unto the **y.** of jubile,..... 8141
Le 25:54 he shall go out in the **y.** of jubile,....... 8141
Le 27:17 his field from the **y.** of jubile, ... 8141
Le 27:18 even unto the **y.** of the jubile, ... 8141
Le 27:23 even unto the **y.** of the jubile: 8141
Le 27:24 In the **y.** of the jubile the field shall.... 8141
Nu 1:1 in the second **y.** after they were........ 8141
Nu 6:12 bring a lamb of the first **y.** for a......... 8141
Nu 6:14 one he lamb of the first **y.** without 8141
Nu 6:14 one ewe lamb of the first **y.** without... 8141
Nu 7:15 one ram, one lamb of the first **y.**, ... 8141
Nu 7:17 he goats, five lambs of the first **y.**...... 8141
Nu 7:21 one ram, one lamb of the first **y.**, ... 8141
Nu 7:23 he goats, five lambs of the first **y.**...... 8141
Nu 7:27 one ram, one lamb of the first **y.**, ... 8141
Nu 7:29 he goats, five lambs of the first **y.**...... 8141
Nu 7:33 one ram, one lamb of the first **y.**, ... 8141
Nu 7:35 he goats, five lambs of the first **y.**...... 8141
Nu 7:39 one ram, one lamb of the first **y.**, ... 8141
Nu 7:41 he goats, five lambs of the first **y.**...... 8141
Nu 7:45 one ram, one lamb of the first **y.**, ... 8141
Nu 7:47 he goats, five lambs of the first **y.**...... 8141
Nu 7:51 one ram, one lamb of the first **y.**, ... 8141
Nu 7:53 he goats, five lambs of the first **y.**...... 8141
Nu 7:57 one ram, one lamb of the first **y.**, ... 8141
Nu 7:59 he goats, five lambs of the first **y.**...... 8141
Nu 7:63 one ram, one lamb of the first **y.**, ... 8141
Nu 7:65 he goats, five lambs of the first **y.**...... 8141
Nu 7:69 one ram, one lamb of the first **y.**, ... 8141
Nu 7:71 he goats, five lambs of the first **y.**...... 8141
Nu 7:75 one ram, one lamb of the first **y.**, ... 8141
Nu 7:77 he goats, five lambs of the first **y.**...... 8141
Nu 7:81 one ram, one lamb of the first **y.**, ... 8141
Nu 7:83 he goats, five lambs of the first **y.**...... 8141
Nu 7:87 the lambs of the first **y.** twelve,......... 8141
Nu 7:88 the lambs of the first **y.** sixty. 8141
Nu 9:1 of the second **y.** after they were........ 8141
Nu 9:22 month, or a **y.**, that the cloud........... 3117
Nu 10:11 in the second **y.**, that the cloud 8141
Nu 14:34 each day for a **y.**, shall ye bear your... 8141
Nu 15:27 shall bring a she goat of the first **y.**.... 8141
Nu 28:3 lambs of the first **y.** without spot 8141
Nu 28:9 lambs of the first **y.** without spot, ... 8141
Nu 28:11 lambs of the first **y.** without spot; 8141
Nu 28:14 throughout the months of the **y.**......... 8141
Nu 28:19 and seven lambs of the first **y.** 8141
Nu 28:27 ram, seven lambs of the first **y.**;......... 8141
Nu 29:2 seven lambs of the first **y.** without 8141
Nu 29:8 and seven lambs of the first **y.**: 8141
Nu 29:13 and fourteen lambs of the first **y.**; 8141
Nu 29:17, 20,23,26,29,32 fourteen lambs
of the first **y.** without 8141
Nu 29:36 seven lambs of the first **y.** without 8141
Nu 33:38 the fortieth **y.** after the children......... 8141
De 1:3 it came to pass in the fortieth **y.**, ... 8141
De 11:12 from the beginning of the **y.**.............. 8141
De 11:12 even unto the end of the **y.**, ... 8141
De 14:22 the field bringeth forth **y.** by **y.**. 8141
De 14:28 tithe of thine increase the same **y.**,..... 8141
De 15:9 The seventh **y.**, the **y.** of release,...... 8141
De 15:12 the seventh **y.** thou shall let him go.... 8141
De 15:20 before the Lord thy God **y.** by **y.**....... 8141
De 16:16 Three times in a **y.** shall all thy 8141
De 24:5 but he shall be free at home one **y.**, ... 8141
De 26:12 tithes of thine increase the third **y.**,.... 8141
De 26:12 which is the **y.** of tithing, and hast...... 8141
De 31:10 in the solemnity of the **y.** of release,... 8141
Jos 5:12 fruit of the land of Canann that **y.**........ 8141
Jg 10:8 that **y.** they vexed and oppressed....... 8141
Jg 11:40 the Gileadite four days in a **y.**. 8141
Jg 17:10 ten shekels of silver by the **y.**, ... 3117
1Sa 1:7 And as he did so **y.** by **y.**, when she .. 8141
1Sa 2:19 brought it to him from **y.** to **y.**, ... 3117
1Sa 7:16 he went from **y.** to **y.** in circuit to...... 8141
1Sa 13:1 Saul reigned one **y.**; and when he....... 8141
1Sa 27:7 of the Philistines was a full **y.**..................
2Sa 11:1 after the **y.** was expired, at the 8141
2Sa 21:1 of David three years, **y.** after **y.**; 8141
1Ki 4:7 each man his month in a **y.** made 8141
1Ki 5:11 gave Solomon to Hiram **y.** by **y.**. 8141
1Ki 6:1 and eightieth **y.** after the children...... 8141
1Ki 6:1 in the fourth **y.** of Solomon's reign...... 8141
1Ki 6:37 In the fourth **y.** was the foundation..... 8141
1Ki 6:38 in the eleventh **y.**, in the month......... 8141
1Ki 9:25 three times in a **y.** did Solomon 8141
1Ki 10:14 that came to Solomon in one **y.** 8141
1Ki 10:25 horses, and mules, a rate **y.** by **y.**. 8141
1Ki 14:25 in the fifty **y.** of king Rehoboam,........ 8141
1Ki 15:1 the eighteenth **y.** of king Jeroboam..... 8141
1Ki 15:9 in the twentieth **y.** of Jeroboam........... 8141
1Ki 15:25 the second **y.** of Asa king of Judah, ... 8141
1Ki 15:28, 33 the third **y.** of Asa king of Judah.... 8141
1Ki 16:8 twenty and sixth **y.** of Asa king 8141
1Ki 16:10, 15 twenty and seventh **y.** of Asa king ..8141
1Ki 16:23 thirty and first **y.** of Asa king of......... 8141
1Ki 16:29 thirty and eighth **y.** of Asa king of...... 8141
1Ki 18:1 Lord came to Elijah in the third **y.**,..... 8141
1Ki 20:22 at the return of the **y.** the king.......... 8141
1Ki 20:26 to pass at the return of the **y.**,........... 8141
1Ki 22:2 And it came to pass in the third **y.**, ... 8141
1Ki 22:41 the fourth **y.** of Ahab king of Israel..... 8141
1Ki 22:51 the seventeeth **y.** of Jehoshaphat........ 8141
2Ki 1:17 in the second **y.** of Jehoram the son.... 8141
2Ki 3:1 the eighteenth **y.** of Jehoshaphat 8141
2Ki 8:16 fifth **y.** of Joram the son of Ahab........ 8141
2Ki 8:25 twelfth **y.** of Joram the son of Ahab.... 8141
2Ki 8:26 he reigned one **y.** in Jerusalem. 8141
2Ki 9:29 the eleventh **y.** of Joram the son of 8141
2Ki 11:4 the seventh **y.** of Jehoiada sent and 8141
2Ki 12:1 In the seventh **y.** of Jehu Jehoash....... 8141
2Ki 12:6 three and twentieth **y.** of...Jehoash..... 8141
2Ki 13:1 three and twentieth **y.** of Joash.......... 8141
2Ki 13:10 thirty and seventh **y.** of Joash king 8141
2Ki 13:20 the land at the coming in of the **y.**....... 8141
2Ki 14:1 second **y.** of Joash son of Jehoahaz 8141
2Ki 14:23 fifteenth **y.** of Amaziah the son of........ 8141
2Ki 15:1 twenty and seventh **y.** of Jeroboam..... 8141
2Ki 15:8 thirty and eighth **y.** of Azariah king..... 8141
2Ki 15:13 nine and thirtieth **y.** of Uzziah........... 8141
2Ki 15:17 nine and thirtieth **y.** of Azariah........... 8141
2Ki 15:23 fiftieth **y.** of Azariah king of Judah....... 8141
2Ki 15:27 two and fiftieth **y.** of Azariah king....... 8141
2Ki 15:30 twentieth **y.** of Jotham the son of......... 8141
2Ki 15:32 the second **y.** of Pekah the son of...... 8141
2Ki 16:1 seventeenth **y.** of Pekah the son of..... 8141
2Ki 17:1 twelfth **y.** of Ahaz king of Judah......... 8141
2Ki 17:4 of Assyria, as he had done **y.** by **y.**.... 8141
2Ki 17:6 the ninth **y.** of Hoshea the king of........ 8141
2Ki 18:1 to pass in the third **y.** of Hoshea......... 8141
2Ki 18:9 the fourth **y.** of king Hezekiah, ... 8141
2Ki 18:9 which was the seventh **y.** of Hoshea... 8141
2Ki 18:10 even in the sixth **y.** of Hezekiah,......... 8141
2Ki 18:10 that is the ninth **y.** of Hoshea king...... 8141
2Ki 18:13 the fourteenth **y.** of king Hezekiah...... 8141
2Ki 19:29 eat this **y.** such things as grow 8141
2Ki 19:29 the second **y.** that which springeth 8141
2Ki 19:29 in the third **y.** sow ye, and reap,........ 8141
2Ki 22:3 in the eighteenth **y.** of king Josiah, ... 8141
2Ki 23:23 in the eighteenth **y.** of king Josiah, ... 8141
2Ki 24:12 him in the eighth **y.** of his reign. 8141
2Ki 25:1 to pass in the ninth **y.** of his reign,..... 8141
2Ki 25:2 the eleventh **y.** of king Hezekiah. 8141
2Ki 25:8 which is the nineteenth **y.** of king......... 8141
2Ki 25:27 and thirtieth **y.** of the captivity........... 8141
2Ki 25:27 in the **y.** that he began to reign 8141
1Ch 20:1 pass, that after the **y.** was expired, ... 8141
1Ch 26:31 fortieth **y.** of the reign of David 8141
1Ch 27:1 throughout all the months of the **y.**,...... 8141
2Ch 3:2 month, in the fourth **y.** of his reign..... 8141
2Ch 8:13 solemn feasts, three times in the **y.**,... 8141
2Ch 9:13 that came to Solomon in one **y.** 8141
2Ch 9:24 horses, and mules, a rate **y.** by **y.**. 8141
2Ch 12:2 in the fifth **y.** of king Rehoboam......... 8141
2Ch 13:1 the eighteenth **y.** of king Jeroboam 8141
2Ch 15:10 the fifteenth **y.** of the reign of Asa. 8141
2Ch 15:19 thirtieth **y.** of the reign of Asa. 8141
2Ch 16:1 and thirtieth **y.** of the reign of Asa 8141
2Ch 16:12 Asa in the thirty and ninth **y.** of his 8141
2Ch 16:13 the one and fortieth **y.** of his reign. 8141
2Ch 17:7 third **y.** of his reign he sent to his...... 8141
2Ch 22:2 he reigned one **y.** in Jerusalem. 8141
2Ch 23:1 And in the seventh **y.** Jehoiada 8141
2Ch 24:5 the house of your God from **y.** to **y.**,... 8141
2Ch 24:23 it came to pass at the end of the **y.**,... 8141
2Ch 27:5 the same **y.** an hundred talents of 8141
2Ch 27:5 pay unto him, both the second **y.**, ... 8141
2Ch 29:3 He in the first **y.** of his reign,........... 8141
2Ch 34:3 For in the eighth **y.** of his reign, ... 8141
2Ch 34:3 in the twelfth **y.** he began to purge..... 8141
2Ch 34:8 in the eighteenth **y.** of his reign, ... 8141
2Ch 35:19 In the eighteenth **y.** of the reign of..... 8141
2Ch 36:10 when the **y.** was expired, king.......... 8141
2Ch 36:22 the first **y.** of Cyrus king of Persia, ... 8141
Ezr 1:1 the first **y.** of Cyrus king of Persia, ... 8141
Ezr 3:8 in the second **y.** of their coming......... 8141
Ezr 4:24 unto the second **y.** of the reign......... 8140
Ezr 5:13 in the first **y.** of Cyrus the king of...... 8140
Ezr 6:3 In the first **y.** of Cyrus the king......... 8140
Ezr 6:15 the sixty **y.** of the reign of Darius 8140
Ezr 7:7 in the seventh **y.** of Artaxerxes 8141
Ezr 7:8 was in the seventh **y.** of the king. 8141
Ne 1:1 month Chisleu, in the twentieth **y.**,..... 8141
Ne 2:1 the twentieth **y.** of Artaxerxes the...... 8141
Ne 5:14 the twentieth **y.** even unto the two..... 8141
Ne 5:14 two and thirtieth **y.** of Artaxerxes 8141
Ne 10:31 we would leave the seventh **y.**, ... 8141
Ne 10:34 at times appointed **y.** by **y.**, to burn ... 8141
Ne 10:35 of all fruit of all trees, **y.** by **y.**, ... 8141
Ne 13:6 two and thirtieth **y.** of Artaxerxes 8141
Es 1:3 In the third **y.** of his reign, he made... 8141
Es 2:16 in the seventh **y.** of his reign............ 8141
Es 3:7 in the twelfth **y.** of king Ahasuerus, ... 8141
Es 9:27 to their appointed time every **y.**;......... 8141
Job 3:6 be joined unto the days of the **y.**,........ 8141
Ps 65:11 crownest the **y.** with thy goodness; 8141
Isa 6:1 In the **y.** that king Uzziah died I 8141
Isa 14:28 In the **y.** that king Ahaz died was........ 8141
Isa 20:1 **y.** that Tartan came unto Ashdod, ... 8141
Isa 21:16 Within a **y.**, according to the years..... 8141
Isa 29:1 add ye **y.** to **y.**; let them kill............ 8141
Isa 34:8 and the **y.** of recompences for the...... 8141
Isa 36:1 the fourteenth **y.** of king Hezekiah,..... 8141
Isa 37:30 Ye shall eat this **y.** such as groweth..... 8141
Isa 37:30 the second **y.** that which springeth 8141
Isa 37:30 in the third **y.** sow ye, and reap,........ 8141
Isa 61:2 the acceptable **y.** of the Lord, ... 8141
Isa 63:4 and the **y.** of my redeemed is come.... 8141
Jer 1:2 in the thirteenth **y.** of his reign. 8141
Jer 1:3 end of the eleventh **y.** of Zedekiah...... 8141
Jer 11:23 even the **y.** of their visitation. 8141
Jer 17:8 not be careful in the **y.** of drought, ... 8141
Jer 23:12 even the **y.** of their visitation, said 8141
Jer 25:1 fourth **y.** of Jehoiakim the son of 8141
Jer 25:1 was the first **y.** of Nebuchadrezzar 8141
Jer 25:3 thirteenth **y.** of Josiah the son of........ 8141
Jer 25:3 that is the three and twentieth **y.**,...... 8141
Jer 28:1 And it came to pass the same **y.**,........ 8141
Jer 28:1 in the fourth **y.**, and in the fifth 8141
Jer 28:16 this **y.** thou shalt die, because thou..... 8141
Jer 28:17 the prophet died the same **y.** 8141
Jer 32:1 in the tenth **y.** of Zedekiah king of...... 8141
Jer 32:1 eighteenth **y.** of Nebuchadrezzar 8141
Jer 36:1 pass in the fourth **y.** of Jehoiakim 8141
Jer 36:9 to pass in the fifth **y.** of Jehoiakim....... 8141
Jer 39:1 In the ninth **y.** of Zedekiah king of...... 8141
Jer 39:2 And in the eleventh **y.** of Zedekiah, ... 8141
Jer 45:1 in the fourth **y.** of Jehoiakim the......... 8141
Jer 46:2 smote in the fourth **y.** of Jehoiakim..... 8141
Jer 48:44 Moab, the **y.** of their visitation, ... 8141
Jer 51:46 a rumour shall both come one **y.**, ... 8141
Jer 51:46 in another **y.** shall come a rumour, ... 8141
Jer 51:59 in the fourth **y.** of his reign. 8141
Jer 52:4 to pass in the ninth **y.** of his reign,..... 8141
Jer 52:5 the eleventh **y.** of king Zedekiah. 8141
Jer 52:12 the nineteenth **y.** of Nebuchadrezzar ... 8141
Jer 52:28 the seventh **y.** three thousand Jews.... 8141
Jer 52:29 eighteenth **y.** of Nebuchadrezzar 8141
Jer 52:30 and twentieth **y.** of Nebuchadrezzar.... 8141
Jer 52:31 and thirtieth **y.** of the captivity.......... 8141
Jer 52:31 in the first **y.** of his reign lifted up...... 8141
Eze 1:1 it came to pass in the thirtieth **y.**, ... 8141
Eze 1:2 the fifth **y.** of king Jehoiachin's........... 8141
Eze 4:6 appointed thee each day for a **y.**. 8141
Eze 8:1 it came to pass in the sixth **y.**, ... 8141
Eze 20:1 it came to pass in the seventh **y.**, ... 8141
Eze 24:1 in the ninth **y.**, in the tenth month,..... 8141
Eze 26:1 came to pass in the eleventh **y.**, ... 8141
Eze 29:1 In the tenth **y.**, in the tenth month, ... 8141
Eze 29:17 pass in the seven and twentieth **y.**, ... 8141
Eze 30:20 it came to pass in the eleventh **y.**, ... 8141
Eze 31:1 it came to pass in the eleventh **y.**, ... 8141
Eze 32:1 it came to pass in the twelfth **y.**, ... 8141
Eze 32:17 came to pass also in the twelfth **y.**, ... 8141
Eze 33:21 in the twelfth **y.** of our captivity,........ 8141
Eze 40:1 and twentieth **y.** of our captivity,......... 8141
Eze 40:1 in the beginning of the **y.**, in the........ 8141
Eze 40:1 fourteenth **y.** after that the city.......... 8141

Eze 46:13 of a lamb of the first y. without 8141
Eze 46:17 it shall be his to the y. of liberty; 8141
Da 1:1 third y. of the reign of Jehoiakim 8141
Da 1:21 even unto the first y. of king Cyrus ... 8141
Da 2:1 in the second y. of the reign of 8141
Da 7:1 In the first y. of Belshazzar king 8140
Da 8:1 In the third y. of the reign of king 8141
Da 9:1 In the first y. of Darius the son of 8141
Da 9:2 In the first y. of his reign I Daniel 8141
Da 10:1 the third y. of Cyrus king of Persia 8141
Da 11:1 I in the first y. of Darius the Mede, ... 8141
Mic 6:6 offerings, with calves of a y. old? 8141
Hag 1:1 the second y. of Darius the king, ... 8141
Hag 1:15 the second y. of Darius the king. 8141
Hag 2:10 in the second y. of Darius, came 8141
Zec 1:1,7 in the second y. of Darius, came 8141
Zec 7:1 pass in the fourth y. of king Darius, ... 8141
Zec 14:16 even go up from y. to y. to worship ... 8141
Lu 2:41 parents went to Jerusalem every y. *2094*
Lu 3:1 fifteenth y. of the reign of Tiberius *2094*
Lu 4:19 **the acceptable y. of the Lord** *1763*
Lu 13:8 **Lord, let it alone this y. also, till** .. *2094*
Joh 11:49 being the high priest that same y., ... *1763*
Joh 11:51 but being high priest that y., he *1763*
Joh 18:13 was the high priest that same y. *1763*
Ac 11:26 that a whole y. they assembled *1763*
Ac 18:11 he continued there a y. and six *1763*
2Co 8:10 but also to be forward a y. ago *4070*
2Co 9:2 Achaia was ready a y. ago; *4070*
Heb 9:7 the high priest alone once every y., ... *1763*
Heb 9:25 into the holy place every y. with *1763*
Heb 10:1 they offered y. by y. continually, ... *1763*
Heb 10:3 again made of sins every y. *1763*
Jas 4:13 and continue there a y., and buy *1763*
Re 9:15 and a day, and a month, and a y., ... *1763*

YEARLY
Le 25:53 as a y. hired servant shall he be 8141
Jg 11:40 of Israel went y. to lament 3117
Jg 21:19 is a feast of the Lord in Shiloh y. 3117
1Sa 1:3 up out of his city y. to worship 3117
1Sa 1:21 offer unto the Lord the y. sacrifice, ... 3117
1Sa 2:19 husband to offer the y. sacrifice. 3117
1Sa 20:6 there is a y. sacrifice there for all 3117
Ne 10:32 charge ourselves y. with the third 8141
Es 9:21 the fifteenth day of the same, y., ... 8141

YEARN See also YEARNED.
Ge 43:30 bowels did y. upon his brother: 3648

YEARNED
1Ki 3:26 for her bowels y. upon her son, ... 3648

YEAR'S
Ex 34:22 feast of ingathering at the y. end 8141
2Sa 14:26 at every y. end that he polled it: 3117

YEARS
Ge 1:14 for seasons, and for days, and y. 8141
Ge 5:3 lived an hundred and thirty y., ... 8141
Ge 5:4 Seth were eight hundred y. 8141
Ge 5:5 were nine hundred and thirty y. 8141
Ge 5:6 Seth lived an hundred and five y., ... 8141
Ge 5:7 Enos eight hundred and seven y., ... 8141
Ge 5:8 were nine hundred and twelve y. 8141
Ge 5:9 Enos lived ninety y., and begat 8141
Ge 5:10 eight hundred and fifteen y., ... 8141
Ge 5:11 were nine hundred and five y. 8141
Ge 5:12 Cainan lived seventy y., and begat 8141
Ge 5:13 eight hundred and forty y., and 8141
Ge 5:14 were nine hundred and ten y. 8141
Ge 5:15 Mahalaleel lived sixty and five y., ... 8141
Ge 5:16 Jared eight hundred and thirty y., ... 8141
Ge 5:17 eight hundred ninety and five y. 8141
Ge 5:18 lived an hundred sixty and two y., ... 8141
Ge 5:19 he begat Enoch eight hundred y., ... 8141
Ge 5:20 nine hundred sixty and two y. 8141
Ge 5:21 Enoch lived sixty and five y., and 8141
Ge 5:22 Methuselah three hundred y., ... 8141
Ge 5:23 three hundred sixty and five y. 8141
Ge 5:25 an hundred eighty and seven y., ... 8141
Ge 5:26 seven hundred eighty and two y., ... 8141
Ge 5:27 nine hundred sixty and nine y. 8141
Ge 5:28 an hundred eighty and two y., ... 8141
Ge 5:30 five hundred ninety and five y., ... 8141
Ge 5:31 hundred seventy and seven y.: 8141
Ge 5:32 Noah was five hundred y. old 8141
Ge 6:3 shall be an hundred and twenty y. 8141
Ge 7:6 Noah was six hundred y. old when 8141
Ge 9:28 flood three hundred and fifty y. 8141
Ge 9:29 were nine hundred and fifty y. 8141
Ge 11:10 Shem was an hundred y. old, ... 8141
Ge 11:10 Arphaxad two y. after the flood: 8141
Ge 11:11 begat Arphaxad five hundred y., ... 8141
Ge 11:12 Arphaxad lived five and thirty y., ... 8141
Ge 11:13 Salah four hundred and three y., ... 8141
Ge 11:14 Salah lived thirty y., and begat 8141
Ge 11:15 Eber four hundred and three y., ... 8141
Ge 11:16 And Eber lived four and thirty y., ... 8141
Ge 11:17 Peleg four hundred and thirty y., ... 8141
Ge 11:18 Peleg lived thirty y., and begat 8141
Ge 11:19 begat Reu two hundred and nine y., ... 8141
Ge 11:20 And Reu lived two and thirty y., ... 8141
Ge 11:21 Serug two hundred and seven y., ... 8141
Ge 11:22 Serug lived thirty y., and begat 8141
Ge 11:23 he begat Nahor two hundred y., ... 8141
Ge 11:24 Nahor lived nine and twenty y., ... 8141
Ge 11:25 Terah an hundred and nineteen y., ... 8141
Ge 11:26 Terah lived seventy y., and begat 8141
Ge 11:32 were two hundred and five y. 8141
Ge 12:4 Abram was seventy and five y. old 8141
Ge 14:4 Twelve y. they served 8141
Ge 15:9 Take me an heifer of three y. old, ... 8027
Ge 15:9 and a she goat of three y. old, ... 8027
Ge 15:9 and a ram of three y. old, and a 8027
Ge 15:13 shall afflict them four hundred y.; 8141
Ge 16:3 Abram had dwelt ten y. in the land 8141
Ge 16:16 Abram was fourscore and six y. old, ... 8141
Ge 17:1 Abram was ninety y. old and nine, ... 8141
Ge 17:17 unto him that is an hundred y. old? 8141
Ge 17:17 Sarah, that is ninety y. old, bear? 8141
Ge 17:24 Abraham was ninety y. old and 8141
Ge 17:25 his son was thirteen y. old, ... 8141
Ge 21:5 Abraham was an hundred y. old, ... 8141
Ge 23:1 and seven and twenty y. old: 8141
Ge 23:1 were the y. of the life of Sarah 8141
Ge 25:7 days of the y. of Abraham's life 8141
Ge 25:7 hundred threescore and fifteen y. 8141
Ge 25:8 old age, an old man, and full of y.; ....
Ge 25:17 are the y. of the life of Ishmael, ... 8141
Ge 25:17 hundred and thirty and seven y., ... 8141
Ge 25:20 Isaac was forty y. old when he took ... 8141
Ge 25:26 Isaac was threescore y. old when 8141
Ge 26:34 Esau was forty y. old when he took 8141
Ge 29:18 will serve thee seven y. for Rachel 8141
Ge 29:20 Jacob served seven y. for Rachel; 8141
Ge 29:27 serve with me yet seven other y. 8141
Ge 29:30 served with him yet seven other y. 8141
Ge 31:38 twenty y. have I been with thee; 8141
Ge 31:41 have I been twenty y. in thy house; ... 8141
Ge 31:41 I served thee fourteen y. for thy 8141
Ge 31:41 six y. for thy cattle: and thou hast 8141
Ge 35:28 were an hundred and fourscore y. 8141
Ge 37:2 Joseph, being seventeen y. old, was ... 8141
Ge 41:1 to pass at the end of two full y., ... 8141
Ge 41:26 The seven good kine are seven y.; 8141
Ge 41:26 the seven good ears are seven y. 8141
Ge 41:27 came up after them are seven y.; 8141
Ge 41:27 wind shall be seven y. of famine. 8141
Ge 41:29 there came seven y. of great plenty 8141
Ge 41:30 after them seven y. of famine; 8141
Ge 41:34 of Egypt in the seven plenteous y. 8141
Ge 41:35 food of those good y. that come, ... 8141
Ge 41:36 against the seven y. of famine, ... 8141
Ge 41:46 Joseph was thirty y. old when he 8141
Ge 41:47 in the seven plenteous y. the earth 8141
Ge 41:48 up all the food of the seven y., ... 8141
Ge 41:50 sons before the y. of famine came, ... 8141
Ge 41:53 And the seven y. of plenteousness, ... 8141
Ge 41:54 seven y. of dearth began to come, ... 8141
Ge 45:6 these two y. hath the famine been 8141
Ge 45:6 and yet there are five y., in which 8141
Ge 45:11 for yet there are five y. of famine; 8141
Ge 47:9 days of the y. of my pilgrimage are 8141
Ge 47:9 are an hundred and thirty y. 8141
Ge 47:9 the days of the y. of my life been, ... 8141
Ge 47:9 of the y. of the life of my fathers 8141
Ge 47:28 in the land of Egypt seventeen y. 8141
Ge 47:28 was an hundred forty and seven y. 8141
Ge 50:22 lived an hundred and ten y. 8141
Ge 50:26 being an hundred and ten y. old: 8141
Ex 6:16 the y. of the life of Levi were an 8141
Ex 6:16 an hundred thirty and seven y. 8141
Ex 6:18 the y. of the life of Kohath were an 8141
Ex 6:18 an hundred thirty and three y. 8141
Ex 6:20 the y. of the life of Amram were an 8141
Ex 6:20 hundred and thirty and seven y. 8141
Ex 7:7 Moses was fourscore y. old, ... 8141
Ex 7:7 Aaron fourscore and three y. old, ... 8141
Ex 12:40 was four hundred and thirty y. 8141
Ex 12:41 of the four hundred and thirty y., ... 8141
Ex 16:35 of Israel did eat manna forty y., ... 8141
Ex 21:2 servant, six y. he shall serve: 8141
Ex 23:10 And six y. thou shalt sow thy land, ... 8141
Ex 30:14 from twenty y. old and above, shall 8141
Ex 38:26 from twenty y. old and upward, ... 8141
Le 19:23 three y. shall it be as 8141
Le 25:3 Six y. thou shalt sow thy field, ... 8141
Le 25:3 y. thou shalt prune thy vineyard, ... 8141
Le 25:8 number seven sabbaths of y. unto 8141
Le 25:8 unto thee, seven times seven y.; 8141
Le 25:8 space of the seven sabbaths of y. 8141
Le 25:8 be unto thee forty and nine y. 8141
Le 25:15 the number of y. after the jubile 8141
Le 25:15 the number of y. of the fruits 8141
Le 25:16 According to the multitude of y. 8141
Le 25:16 according to the fewness of y. thou 8141
Le 25:16 according to the number of the y. 8141
Le 25:21 shall bring forth fruit for thee y. 8141
Le 25:27 let him count the y. of the sale 8141
Le 25:50 according unto the number of y., ... 8141
Le 25:51 If there be yet many y. behind, ... 8141
Le 25:52 but few y. unto the year of jubile, ... 8141
Le 25:52 according unto his y. shall he give 8141
Le 25:54 if he be not redeemed in these y., ... 8141
Le 27:3 twenty y. old even unto sixty y. old, .. 8141
Le 27:5 five y. old even unto twenty y. old, ... 8141
Le 27:6 a month old even unto five y. old, ... 8141
Le 27:7 if it be from sixty y. old and above; 8141
Le 27:18 according to the y. that remain, ... 8141
Nu 1:3 From twenty y. old and upward, ... 8141
Nu 1:18, 20,22,24,26,28,30,32,34,36,38,40,42,
45 from twenty y. old and 8141
Nu 4:3 thirty y. old...until fifty y. old, ... 8141
Nu 4:23 thirty y. old...until fifty y. old 8141
Nu 4:30 thirty y. old...unto fifty y. old 8141
Nu 4:35, 39,43,47 thirty y. old...until fifty y. 8141
Nu 8:24 twenty and five y. old and upward 8141
Nu 8:25 the age of fifty y. they shall cease 8141
Nu 13:22 Hebron was built seven y. before 8141
Nu 14:29 from twenty y. old and upward, ... 8141
Nu 14:33 wander in the wilderness forty y., ... 8141
Nu 14:34 even forty y., and ye shall know 8141
Nu 26:2 from twenty y. old and upward, ... 8141
Nu 26:4 from twenty y. old and upward; 8141
Nu 32:11 from twenty y. old and upward, ... 8141
Nu 32:13 wander in the wilderness forty y. 8141
Nu 33:39 and twenty and three y. old 8141
De 2:7 these forty y. the Lord thy God 8141
De 2:14 Zered, was thirty and eight y.; 8141
De 8:2 thy God led thee these forty y. 8141
De 8:4 did thy foot swell, these forty y. 8141
De 14:28 end of three y. thou shalt bring 8141
De 15:1 end of every seven y. thou shalt 8141
De 15:12 unto thee, and serve thee six y.; 8141
De 15:18 to thee, in serving thee six y.: 8141
De 29:5 And I have led you forty y. in the 8141
De 31:2 hundred and twenty y. old this day; 8141
De 31:10 At the end of every seven y., ... 8141
De 32:7 the y. of many generations: 8141
De 34:7 was an hundred and twenty y. old 8141
Jos 5:6 children of Israel walked forty y. 8141
Jos 13:1 Joshua was old and stricken in y.; 8141
Jos 13:1 Thou art old and stricken in y., ... 8141
Jos 14:7 Forty y. old was I when Moses the 8141
Jos 14:10 these forty and five y., even since 8141
Jos 14:10 this day fourscore and five y. old. 8141
Jos 24:29 being an hundred and ten y. old. 8141
Jg 2:8 being an hundred and ten y. old. 8141
Jg 3:8 Chushan-rishathaim eight y. 8141
Jg 3:11 And the land had rest forty y. 8141
Jg 3:14 the king of Moab eighteen y. 8141
Jg 3:30 And the land had rest fourscore y. 8141
Jg 4:3 twenty y. he mightily oppressed 8141
Jg 5:31 And the land had rest forty y. 8141
Jg 6:1 into the hand of Midian seven y. 8141
Jg 6:25 the second bullock of seven y. old, ... 8141
Jg 8:28 country was in quietness forty y. 8141
Jg 9:22 Abimelech had reigned three y. 8141
Jg 10:2 judged Israel twenty and three y., ... 8141
Jg 10:3 judged Israel twenty and two y. 8141

Book	Ref	Context	Number
Jg	10:8	eighteen **y.**, all the children of	8141
Jg	11:26	coasts of Arnon, three hundred **y.**?	8141
Jg	12:7	and Jephthah judged Israel six **y.**.	8141
Jg	12:9	And he judged Israel seven **y.**.	8141
Jg	12:11	Israel; and he judged Israel ten **y.**.	8141
Jg	12:14	and he judged Israel eight **y.**.	8141
Jg	13:1	the hand of the Philistines forty **y.**.	8141
Jg	15:20	days of the Philistines twenty **y.**.	8141
Jg	16:31	And he judged Israel twenty **y.**.	8141
Ru	1:4	they dwelled there about ten **y.**.	8141
1Sa	4:15	Eli was ninety and eight **y.** old;	8141
1Sa	4:18	And he had judged Israel forty **y.**.	8141
1Sa	7:2	time was long; for it was twenty **y.**	8141
1Sa	13:1	he had reigned two **y.** over Israel,	8141
1Sa	29:3	with me these days, or these **y.**,	8141
2Sa	2:10	Saul's son was forty **y.** old when	8141
2Sa	2:10	over Israel, and reigned two **y.**	8141
2Sa	2:11	Judah was seven **y.** and six	8141
2Sa	4:4	He was five **y.** old when the tidings	8141
2Sa	5:4	David was thirty **y.** old when he	8141
2Sa	5:4	to reign, and he reigned forty **y.**	8141
2Sa	5:5	he reigned over Judah seven **y.** and	8141
2Sa	5:5	thirty and three **y.** over all Israel	8141
2Sa	13:23	it came to pass after two full **y.**,	8141
2Sa	13:38	to Geshur, and was there three **y.**.	8141
2Sa	14:28	So Absalom dwelt two full **y.** in	8141
2Sa	15:7	And it came to pass after forty **y.**,	8141
2Sa	19:32	aged man, even fourscore **y.** old:	8141
2Sa	19:35	I am this day fourscore **y.** old:	8141
2Sa	21:1	famine in the days of David three **y.**,	8141
2Sa	24:13	Shall seven **y.** of famine come unto	8141
1Ki	1:1	David was old and stricken in **y.**	3117
1Ki	2:11	reigned over Israel were forty **y.**	8141
1Ki	2:11	seven **y.** reigned he in Hebron,	8141
1Ki	2:11	thirty and three **y.** reigned he in	8141
1Ki	2:39	came to pass at the end of three **y.**,	8141
1Ki	6:38	so was he seven **y.** in building it.	8141
1Ki	7:1	building his own house thirteen **y.**,	8141
1Ki	9:10	to pass at the end of twenty **y.**,	8141
1Ki	10:22	once in three **y.** came the navy of	8141
1Ki	11:42	over all Israel was forty **y.**	8141
1Ki	14:20	reigned were two and twenty **y.**	8141
1Ki	14:21	Rehoboam was forty and one **y.** old	8141
1Ki	14:21	reigned seventeen **y.** in Jerusalem,	8141
1Ki	15:2	Three **y.** reigned he in Jerusalem.	8141
1Ki	15:10	And forty and one **y.** reigned he in	8141
1Ki	15:25	and reigned over Israel two **y.**	8141
1Ki	15:33	Israel in Tirzah, twenty and four **y.**	8141
1Ki	16:8	reign over Israel in Tirzah, two **y.**	8141
1Ki	16:23	to reign over Israel, twelve **y.**	8141
1Ki	16:23	six **y.** reigned he in Tirzah.	8141
1Ki	16:29	in Samaria twenty and two **y.**	8141
1Ki	17:1	shall not be dew nor rain these **y.**,	8141
1Ki	22:1	they continued three **y.** without war	8141
1Ki	22:42	thirty and five **y.** old when he	8141
1Ki	22:42	he reigned twenty and five **y.** in	8141
1Ki	22:51	and reigned two **y.** over Israel.	8141
2Ki	3:1	of Judah, and reigned twelve **y.**	8141
2Ki	8:1	also come upon the land seven **y.**	8141
2Ki	8:2	land of the Philistines seven **y.**.	8141
2Ki	8:17	Thirty and two **y.** old was he when	8141
2Ki	8:17	he reigned eight **y.** in Jerusalem.	8141
2Ki	8:26	Two and twenty **y.** old was Ahaziah	8141
2Ki	10:36	Samaria was twenty and eight **y.**	8141
2Ki	11:3	hid in the house of the Lord six **y.**.	8141
2Ki	11:21	Seven **y.** old was Jehoash when he	8141
2Ki	12:1	forty **y.** reigned he in Jerusalem.	8141
2Ki	13:1	Samaria, and reigned seventeen **y.**	8141
2Ki	13:10	Samaria, and reigned sixteen **y.**	8141
2Ki	14:2	twenty and five **y.** old when he	8141
2Ki	14:2	twenty and nine **y.** in Jerusalem.	8141
2Ki	14:17	Jehoahaz king of Israel fifteen **y.**.	8141
2Ki	14:21	which was sixteen **y.** old, and made	8141
2Ki	14:23	and reigned forty and one **y.**	8141
2Ki	15:2	Sixteen **y.** old was he when he	8141
2Ki	15:2	two and fifty **y.** in Jerusalem.	8141
2Ki	15:17	and reigned ten **y.** in Samaria.	8141
2Ki	15:23	in Samaria, and reigned two **y.**.	8141
2Ki	15:27	in Samaria, and reigned twenty **y.**.	8141
2Ki	15:33	Five and twenty **y.** old was he when	8141
2Ki	15:33	he reigned sixteen **y.** in Jerusalem.	8141
2Ki	16:2	Twenty **y.** old was Ahaz when he	8141
2Ki	16:2	reigned sixteen **y.** in Jerusalem,	8141
2Ki	17:1	in Samaria over Israel nine **y.**	8141
2Ki	17:5	Samaria, and besieged it three **y.**.	8141
2Ki	18:2	Twenty and five **y.** old was he when	8141
2Ki	18:2	twenty and nine **y.** in Jerusalem.	8141
2Ki	18:10	at the end of three **y.** they took it:	8141
2Ki	20:6	will add unto thy days fifteen **y.**;	8141
2Ki	21:1	Manasseh was twelve **y.** old when	8141
2Ki	21:1	fifty and five **y.** in Jerusalem.	8141
2Ki	21:19	Amon was twenty and two **y.** old	8141
2Ki	21:19	he reigned two **y.** in Jerusalem.	8141
2Ki	22:1	Josiah was eight **y.** old when he	8141
2Ki	22:1	thirty and one **y.** in Jerusalem.	8141
2Ki	23:31	Jehoahaz was twenty and three **y.**	8141
2Ki	23:36	Jehoiakim was twenty and five **y.**	8141
2Ki	23:36	reigned eleven **y.** in Jerusalem.	8141
2Ki	24:1	became his servant three **y.**	8141
2Ki	24:8	Jehoiachin was eighteen **y.** old	8141
2Ki	24:18	Zedekiah was twenty and one **y.** old	8141
2Ki	24:18	he reigned eleven **y.** in Jerusalem.	8141
1Ch	2:21	when he was threescore **y.** old;	8141
1Ch	3:4	reigned seven **y.** and six months:	8141
1Ch	3:4	he reigned thirty and three **y.**	8141
1Ch	23:3	the age of thirty **y.** and upward:	8141
1Ch	23:24	the age of twenty **y.** and upward	8141
1Ch	23:27	from twenty **y.** old and above:	8141
1Ch	27:23	from twenty **y.** old and under:	8141
1Ch	29:27	he reigned over Israel was forty **y.**;	8141
1Ch	29:27	seven **y.** reigned he in Hebron,	8141
1Ch	29:27	and thirty and three **y.** reigned he	8141
2Ch	8:1	to pass at the end of twenty **y.**,	8141
2Ch	9:21	every three **y.** once came the ships	8141
2Ch	9:30	Jerusalem over all Israel forty **y.**	8141
2Ch	11:17	son of Solomon strong, three **y.**	8141
2Ch	11:17	three **y.** they walked in the way of	8141
2Ch	12:13	Rehoboam was one and forty **y.** old	8141
2Ch	12:13	reigned seventeen **y.** in Jerusalem,	8141
2Ch	13:2	He reigned three **y.** in Jerusalem.	8141
2Ch	14:1	his days the land was quiet ten **y.**.	8141
2Ch	14:6	rest, and he had no war in those **y.**;	8141
2Ch	18:2	after certain **y.** he went down to	8141
2Ch	20:31	he was thirty and five **y.** old when	8141
2Ch	20:31	he reigned twenty and five **y.** in	8141
2Ch	21:5	Jehoram was thirty and two **y.** old	8141
2Ch	21:5	he reigned eight **y.** in Jerusalem.	8141
2Ch	21:19	of time, after the end of two **y.**,	3117
2Ch	21:20	Thirty and two **y.** old was he	
2Ch	21:20	he reigned in Jerusalem eight **y.**,	8141
2Ch	22:2	Forty and two **y.** old was Ahaziah	8141
2Ch	22:12	them hid in the house of God six **y.**	8141
2Ch	24:1	Joash was seven **y.** old when he	8141
2Ch	24:1	he reigned forty **y.** in Jerusalem.	8141
2Ch	24:15	an hundred and thirty **y.** old was he	8141
2Ch	25:1	Amaziah was twenty and five **y.** old	8141
2Ch	25:1	he reigned twenty and nine **y.** in	8141
2Ch	25:5	from twenty **y.** old and above,	8141
2Ch	25:25	Jehoahaz king of Israel fifteen **y.**.	8141
2Ch	26:1	Uzziah, who was sixteen **y.** old,	8141
2Ch	26:3	Sixteen **y.** old was Uzziah when he	8141
2Ch	26:3	and he reigned fifty and two **y.** in	8141
2Ch	27:1	Jotham was twenty and five **y.** old	8141
2Ch	27:1	he reigned sixteen **y.** in Jerusalem.	8141
2Ch	27:8	He was five and twenty **y.** old	8141
2Ch	27:8	reigned sixteen **y.** in Jerusalem.	8141
2Ch	28:1	Ahaz was twenty **y.** old when he	8141
2Ch	28:1	he reigned sixteen **y.** in Jerusalem:	8141
2Ch	29:1	when he was five and twenty **y.** old,	8141
2Ch	29:1	he reigned nine and twenty **y.** in	8141
2Ch	31:16	from three **y.** old and upward, even	8141
2Ch	31:17	from twenty **y.** old and upward,	8141
2Ch	33:1	Manasseh was twelve **y.** old when	8141
2Ch	33:1	and he reigned fifty and five **y.** in	8141
2Ch	33:21	Amon was two and twenty **y.** old	8141
2Ch	33:21	and reigned two **y.** in Jerusalem.	8141
2Ch	34:1	Josiah was eight **y.** old when he	8141
2Ch	34:1	in Jerusalem one and thirty **y.**	8141
2Ch	36:2	Jehoahaz was twenty and three **y.**	8141
2Ch	36:5	Jehoiakim was twenty and five **y.**	8141
2Ch	36:5	he reigned eleven **y.** in Jerusalem:	8141
2Ch	36:9	Jehoiachin was eight **y.** old when	8141
2Ch	36:11	Zedekiah was one and twenty **y.** old	8141
2Ch	36:11	reigned eleven **y.** in Jerusalem.	8141
2Ch	36:21	to fulfill threescore and ten **y.**	8141
Ezr	3:8	from twenty **y.** old and upward,	8141
Ezr	5:11	was builded these many **y.** ago.	8140
Ne	5:14	twelve **y.**, I and my brethren have	8141
Ne	9:21	forty **y.** didst thou sustain them in	8141
Ne	9:30	Yet many **y.** didst thou forbear	8141
Job	10:5	of man? are thy **y.** as man's days,	8141
Job	15:20	the number of **y.** is hidden to the	8141
Job	16:22	When a few **y.** are come, then I	8141
Job	32:7	and multitude of **y.** should teach	8141
Job	36:11	and their **y.** in pleasures.	8141
Job	36:26	number of his **y.** be searched out.	8141
Job	42:16	lived Job an hundred and forty **y.**,	8141
Ps	31:10	with grief, and my **y.** with sighing:	8141
Ps	61:6	and his **y.** as many generations.	8141
Ps	77:5	days of old, the **y.** of ancient times.	8141
Ps	77:10	remember the **y.** of the right hand.	8141
Ps	78:33	in vanity, and their **y.** in trouble.	8141
Ps	90:4	For a thousand **y.** in thy sight are	8141
Ps	90:9	we spend our **y.** as a tale that is	8141
Ps	90:10	The days of our **y.** are threescore **y.**	8141
Ps	90:10	of strength they be fourscore **y.**,	8141
Ps	90:15	the **y.** wherein we have seen evil.	8141
Ps	95:10	Forty **y.** long was I grieved with	8141
Ps	102:24	**y.** are throughout all generations.	8141
Ps	102:27	same, and thy **y.** shall have no end.	8141
Pr	4:10	and the **y.** of thy life shall be many.	8141
Pr	5:9	others, and thy **y.** unto the cruel:	8141
Pr	9:11	the **y.** of thy life shall be increased.	8141
Pr	10:27	**y.** of the wicked shall be shortened.	8141
Ec	6:3	hundred children, and live may **y.**,	8141
Ec	6:3	so that the days of his **y.** be many,	8141
Ec	6:6	though he live a thousand **y.** twice	8141
Ec	11:8	But if a man live many **y.**, and	8141
Ec	12:1	nor the **y.** draw nigh, when thou	8141
Isa	7:8	within threescore and five **y.** shall	8141
Isa	15:5	unto Zoar, an heifer of three **y.** old:	
Isa	16:4	Within three **y.**, as the **y.** of an	8141
Isa	20:3	walked naked and barefoot three **y.**	8141
Isa	21:16	according to the **y.** of an hireling,	8141
Isa	23:15	Tyre shall be forgotten seventy **y.**,	8141
Isa	23:15	end of seventy **y.** shall Tyre sing	8141
Isa	23:17	to pass after the end of seventy **y.**,	8141
Isa	32:10	days and **y.** shall ye be troubled,	8141
Isa	38:5	I will add unto thy days fifteen **y.**	8141
Isa	38:10	deprived of the residue of my **y.**	8141
Isa	38:15	I shall go softly all my **y.** in the	8141
Isa	65:20	child shall die an hundred **y.** old;	8141
Isa	65:20	the sinner being an hundred **y.** old.	8141
Jer	25:11	the king of Babylon seventy **y.**.	8141
Jer	25:12	when seventy **y.** are accomplished,	8141
Jer	28:3	Within two full **y.** will I bring	8141
Jer	28:11	within the space of two full **y.**.	8141
Jer	29:10	after seventy **y.** be accomplished	8141
Jer	34:14	at the end of seven **y.** let ye go	8141
Jer	34:14	when he hath served thee six **y.**,	8141
Jer	48:34	as an heifer of three **y.** old:	
Jer	52:1	Zedekiah was one and twenty **y.**	8141
Jer	52:1	he reigned eleven **y.** in Jerusalem.	8141
Eze	4:5	upon thee the **y.** of their iniquity,	8141
Eze	22:4	and art come even unto thy **y.**	8141
Eze	29:11	shall it be inhabited forty **y.**	8141
Eze	29:12	waste shall be desolate forty **y.**	8141
Eze	29:13	At the end of forty **y.** will I gather	8141
Eze	38:8	in the latter **y.** thou shalt come	8141
Eze	38:17	in those days many **y.** that I would	8141
Eze	39:9	shall burn them with fire seven **y.**	8141
Da	1:5	so nourishing them three **y.**, that at	8141
Da	5:31	about threescore and two **y.** old.	8140
Da	9:2	by books the number of the **y.**,	8141
Da	9:2	he would accomplish seventy **y.** in	8141
Da	11:6	and in the end of **y.** they shall join	8141
Da	11:8	continue more **y.** than the king	8141
Da	11:13	come after certain **y.** with a great	8141
Joe	2:2	after it, even to the **y.** of many	8141
Joe	2:25	restore to you the **y.** that the locust	8141
Am	1:1	two **y.** before the earthquake.	8141
Am	2:10	led you forty **y.** through the	8141
Am	4:4	and your tithes after three **y.**	3117
Am	5:25	in the wilderness forty **y.**,	8141
Hab	3:2	thy work in the midst of the **y.**,	8141
Hab	3:2	in the midst of the **y.** make known;	8141
Zec	1:12	these threescore and ten **y.**?	8141
Zec	7:3	as I have done these so many **y.**?	8141
Zec	7:5	even those seventy **y.**, did ye all	8141
Mal	3:4	the days of old, and as in former **y.**	8141
Mt	2:16	from two **y.** old and under,	*1332*
Mt	9:20	with an issue of blood twelve **y.**,	*2094*
Mk	5:25	had an issue of blood twelve **y.**,	*2094*
Mk	5:42	for she was of the age of twelve **y.**.	*2094*
Lu	1:7	both were now well stricken in **y.**.	*2250*
Lu	1:18	and my wife well stricken in **y.**.	*2250*
Lu	2:36	had lived with an husband seven **y.**	*2094*
Lu	2:37	of about fourscore and four **y.**,	*2094*

Lu 2:42 when he was twelve **y.** old, they........ *2094*
Lu 3:23 began to be about thirty **y.** of age, ... *2094*
Lu 4:25 shut up three **y.** and six months,... *2094*
Lu 8:42 daughter, about twelve **y.** of age,....... *2094*
Lu 8:43 having an issue of blood twelve **y.**, ... *2094*
Lu 12:19 much goods laid up for many **y.**;... *2094*
Lu 13:7 these three **y.** I come seeking fruit.*2094*
Lu 13:11 had a spirit of infirmity eighteen **y.**, ... *2094*
Lu 13:16 hath bound, lo, these eighteen **y.**,..*2094*
Lu 15:29 Lo, these many **y.** do I serve thee,.*2094*
Joh 2:20 Forty and six **y.** was this temple in..... *2094*
Joh 5:5 had an infirmity thirty and eight **y.**..... *2094*
Joh 8:57 Thou art not yet fifty **y.** old, and........ *2094*
Ac 4:22 the man was above forty **y.** old,........ *2094*
Ac 7:6 entreat them evil four hundred **y.**....... *2094*
Ac 7:23 And when he was full forty **y.** old,...... *5063*
Ac 7:30 And when forty **y.** were expired, ... *2094*
Ac 7:36 and in the wilderness forty **y.**........... *2094*
Ac 7:42 space of forty **y.** in the wilderness? *2094*
Ac 9:33 which had kept his bed eight **y.**, ... *2094*
Ac 13:18 And about the time of forty **y.**.......... *5063*
Ac 13:20 space of four hundred and fifty **y.**,....... *2094*
Ac 13:21 Benjamin, by the space of forty **y.**......... *2094*
Ac 19:10 continued by the space of two **y.**;......... *2094*
Ac 20:31 the space of three **y.** I ceased not...... *5148*
Ac 24:10 thou hast been of many **y.** a judge...... *2094*
Ac 24:17 after many **y.** I came to bring alms..... *2094*
Ac 24:27 after two **y.** Porcius Festus came....... *1333*
Ac 28:30 Paul dwelt two whole **y.** in his own *1333*
Ro 4:19 he was about an hundred **y.** old, ... *1541*
Ro 15:23 a great desire these many **y.** to *2094*
2Co 12:2 in Christ above fourteen **y.** ago,.......... *2094*
Ga 1:18 Then after three **y.** I went up to......... *2094*
Ga 2:1 fourteen **y.** after I went up again......... *2094*
Ga 3:17 four hundred and thirty **y.** after,.......... *2094*
Ga 4:10 and months, and times, and **y.**.......... *1763*
1Ti 5:9 number under threescore **y.** old, ... *2094*
Heb 1:12 the same, and thy **y.** shall not fail....... *2094*
Heb 3:9 me, and saw my works forty **y.**.......... *2094*
Heb 3:17 whom was he grieved forty **y.**?.......... *2094*
Heb 11:24 when he was come to **y.**, ...*1096,3173*
Jas 5:17 earth by the space of three **y.** and...... *1763*
2Pe 3:8 is with the Lord as a thousand **y.**,...... *2094*
2Pe 3:8 and a thousand **y.** as one day. *2094*
Re 20:2 and bound him a thousand **y.**,........... *2094*
Re 20:3 the thousand **y.** should be fulfilled:...... *2094*
Re 20:4 reigned with Christ a thousand **y.**......... *2094*
Re 20:5 until the thousand **y.** were finished. *2094*
Re 20:6 shall reign with him a thousand **y.**. *2094*
Re 20:7 when the thousand **y.** are expired,....... *2094*

YEARS'
2Ki 8:3 came to pass at the seven **y.** end,...... 8141
1Ch 21:12 Either three **y.** famine; or three......... 8141

YELL See also YELLED.
Jer 51:38 they shall **y.** as lions' whelps. 5286

YELLED
Jer 2:15 lions roared upon him, and **y.**,.... 5414,6963

YELLOW
Le 13:30 and there be in it a **y.** thin hair;......... 6669
Le 13:32 and there be in it no **y.** hair, ... 6669
Le 13:36 the priest shall not seek for **y.** hair;.... 6669
Ps 68:13 and her feathers were **y.** gold............ 3422

YES See also YEA.
Mt 17:35 He saith, **Y.**. And when he was......... *3483*
Mk 7:38 and said unto him, **Y.**, Lord:.............. *3483*
Re 3:29 Gentiles? **Y.**, of the Gentiles also:...... *3483*
Re 10:18 **Y.**, verily, their sound went into........ *3304*

YESTERDAY
Ex 5:14 task in making brick both **y.**.............. 8543
1Sa 20:27 to meat, neither **y.**, nor to day?.......... 8543
2Sa 15:20 Whereas thou camest but **y.**,............. 8543
2Ki 9:26 I have seen **y.** the blood of Naboth, ... 570
Job 8:9 (For we are but of **y.**, and know........ 8543
Ps 90:4 years in thy sight are but as **y.** 865
Joh 4:52 **Y.** at the seventh hour the fever.......... *5504*
Ac 7:28 as thou diddest the Egyptian **y.**? *5504*
Heb 13:8 Jesus Christ the same **y.**, and to day, ..*5504*

YESTERNIGHT
Ge 19:34 Behold, I lay **y.** with my father: 570
Ge 31:29 God of your father spake unto me **y.**,.... 570
Ge 31:42 of my hands, and rebuked thee **y.**........ 570

YET
Ge 6:3 **y.** his days shall be an hundred and..........
Ge 7:4 **y.** seven days, and I will cause it 5750
Ge 8:10, 12 And he stayed **y.** other seven days:......
Ge 15:16 of the Amorites is not **y.** full. 5704,2008
Ge 18:22 but Abraham stood **y.** before the........ 5750
Ge 18:29 And he spake unto him **y.** again, ... 5750
Ge 18:32 and I will speak **y.** but this once: 389
Ge 20:12 And **y.** indeed she is my sister; 1571
Ge 21:26 neither **y.** heard I of it, but to day...... 1571
Ge 25:6 Isaac his son, while he **y.** lived, ...
Ge 27:30 Jacob was **y.** scarce gone out from....... 389
Ge 29:7 And he said, Lo, it is **y.** high day, ... 5750
Ge 29:9 And while he **y.** spake with them,....... 5750
Ge 29:27 serve with me **y.** seven other years.... 5750
Ge 29:30 with him **y.** other seven years. 5750
Ge 31:14 Is there **y.** any portion or.................. 5750
Ge 31:30 **y.** wherefore hast...stolen my gods? ....
Ge 37:5 and they hated him **y.** the more........... 5750
Ge 37:8 And they hated him **y.** the more 5750
Ge 37:9 And he dreamed **y.** another dream,...... 5750
Ge 38:5 And she **y.** again conceived, and 5750
Ge 40:13, 19 **Y.** within three days shall............. 5750
Ge 40:23 **Y.** did not the chief butler remember ....
Ge 43:6 man whether ye had **y.** a brother?...... 5750
Ge 43:7 saying, Is your father **y.** alive?..................
Ge 43:27 of whom ye spake? Is he **y.** alive?...... 5750
Ge 43:28 is in good health, he is **y.** alive......... 5750
Ge 44:4 gone out of the city, and not **y.** far off, ...
Ge 44:14 house; for he was **y.** there:............... 5750
Ge 45:3 am Joseph; doth my father **y.** live? 5750
Ge 45:6 **y.** there are five years, in the which... 5750
Ge 45:11 for **y.** there are five years of famine; .. 5750
Ge 45:26 told him, saying, Joseph is **y.** alive,..... 5750
Ge 45:28 Joseph my son is **y.** alive: I will go...... 5750
Ge 46:30 thy face, because thou art **y.** alive...... 5750
Ge 48:7 when **y.** there was but a little way 5750
Ex 4:18 and see whether they be **y.** alive........ 5750
Ex 5:11 **y.** not ought of your work shall........... 3588
Ex 5:18 **y.** shall ye deliver the tale of bricks. ....
Ex 9:17 **y.** exaltest thou thyself against............ 5750
Ex 9:30 ye will not **y.** fear the Lord God. 2962
Ex 9:34 he sinned **y.** more, and hardened...................
Ex 10:7 knowest thou not **y.** that Egypt is 2962
Ex 11:1 **Y.** will I bring one plague more 5750
Ex 21:22 from her, and **y.** no mischief follow: ....
Ex 32:32 **Y.** now, if thou wilt forgive their sin-; ....
Ex 33:12 **Y.** thou hast said, I know thee by ....
Ex 36:3 brought **y.** unto him free offerings 5750
Le 5:17 though he wist it not, **y.** is he guilty, ...
Le 11:7 **y.** he cheweth not the cud; ....
Le 11:21 **Y.** these may ye eat of every flying 389
Le 13:40 his head, he is bald; **y.** is he clean. ....
Le 13:41 he is forehead bald; **y.** is he clean. ....
Le 25:22 eat **y.** of old fruit until the ninth year; ....
Le 25:51 If there be **y.** many years behind, ... 5750
Le 26:18 ye will not **y.** for all this hearken......... 5704
Le 26:24 you **y.** seven times for your sins. ....
Le 26:44 **y.** for all that, when they be in the 637
Nu 9:10 **y.** he shall keep the passover unto............
Nu 11:33 flesh was **y.** between their teeth, ... 5750
Nu 19:13 his uncleanness is **y.** upon him........... 5750
Nu 22:15 and Balak sent **y.** again princes,........ 5750
Nu 22:20 **y.** the word which I shall say unto......... 389
Nu 30:16 **y.** in her youth in her father's house. ....
Nu 32:14 to augment **y.** the fierce anger of........ 5750
Nu 32:15 he will **y.** again leave them in the 5750
De 1:32 **Y.** in this thing ye did not believe the ....
De 9:29 **Y.** they are thy people and thine................
De 12:9 not as **y.** come to the rest......... 5704,6258
De 14:8 the hoof, **y.** cheweth not the cud,...............
De 20:6 vineyard, and hath not **y.** eaten of it?........
De 22:17 and **y.** these are the tokens of my.............
De 29:4 **Y.** the Lord hath not given you..................
De 31:27 while I am **y.** alive with you this 5750
De 32:52 **Y.** thou shalt see the land before 3588
Jos 3:4 **Y.** there shall be a place between........ 389
Jos 13:1 there remaineth **y.** very much land ....
Jos 13:2 This is the land that **y.** remaineth:............
Jos 14:11 As **y.** I am as strong this day as I...... 5750
Jos 17:12 **Y.** the children of Manasseh could ....
Jos 17:13 **Y.** it came to pass, when the children ....
Jos 18:2 had not **y.** received their inheritance. ....
Jg 1:35 **y.** the hand of the house of Joseph ....
Jg 2:10 nor **y.** the works which he had 1571
Jg 2:17 **y.** they would not hearken unto 1571
Jg 6:24 is **y.** in Ophrah of the Abi-ezrites. 5750
Jg 6:31 to death whilst it is **y.** morning: ....
Jg 7:4 The people are **y.** too many;............. 5750
Jg 8:4 with him, faint, **y.** pursuing them. ....
Jg 8:20 feared, because he was **y.** a youth...... 5750
Jg 9:5 **y.** Jotham the youngest son of....................
Jg 10:13 **Y.** ye have forsaken me, and served...........
Jg 15:7 **y.** will I be avenged of you,........... 3588,518
Jg 17:4 **Y.** he restored the money unto his...............
Jg 19:19 **Y.** there is both straw and................... 1571
Jg 20:28 Shall I **y.** again go out to battle.......... 5750
Jg 21:14 and **y.** so they sufficed them not. ....
Ru 1:11 are there **y.** any more sons in my 5750
1Sa 3:6 the Lord called **y.** again, Samuel. 5750
1Sa 3:7 Samuel did not **y.** know the Lord, ... 2962
1Sa 3:7 word of the Lord **y.** revealed unto....... 2962
1Sa 8:9 **y.** protest solemnly unto them, ... 3588
1Sa 10:22 if the man shall **y.** come thither. 5750
1Sa 12:20 **y.** turn not aside from following........... 389
1Sa 13:7 As for Saul, he was **y.** in Gilgal, ... 5750
1Sa 13:21 **Y.** they had a file for the mattocks, ...
1Sa 15:30 I have sinned: **y.** honour me now, ...
1Sa 16:11 There remaineth **y.** the youngest, ... 5750
1Sa 18:29 Saul was **y.** the more afraid of.................
1Sa 20:14 not only while **y.** I live shew me 5750
1Sa 23:4 enquired of the Lord **y.** again. 5750
1Sa 23:22 Go, I pray you, prepare **y.**, and know ....
1Sa 24:11 **y.** thou huntest my soul to take it. ....
1Sa 25:29 **Y.** a man is risen to pursue thee,.............
2Sa 1:9 because my life is **y.** whole in me......... 5750
2Sa 3:35 to eat meat while it was **y.** day,......... 5750
2Sa 5:13 were **y.** sons and daughters born 5750
2Sa 5:22 the Philistines came up **y.** again, ... 5750
2Sa 6:22 I will **y.** be more vile than thus,......... 5750
2Sa 7:19 was **y.** a small thing in thy sight,........ 5750
2Sa 9:1 there **y.** any that is left of the house... 5750
2Sa 9:3 not **y.** any of the house of Saul, ... 5750
2Sa 9:3 Jonathan hath **y.** a son, which is......... 5750
2Sa 12:18 while the child was **y.** alive, we ....
2Sa 12:22 While the child was **y.** alive, I fasted... 5750
2Sa 14:14 **y.** doth he devise means, that his...............
2Sa 18:12 **y.** would I not put forth mine hand ....
2Sa 18:14 was **y.** alive in the midst of the oak. ....
2Sa 18:22 the son of Zadok **y.** again 5750
2Sa 19:28 **y.** didst thou set thy servant among............
2Sa 19:28 What right therefore have I **y.** to cry ....
2Sa 19:35 servant be **y.** a burden unto my......... 5750
2Sa 21:15 the Philistines had **y.** war again.......... 5750
2Sa 21:20 there was **y.** a battle in Gath,............ 5750
2Sa 23:5 **y.** he hath made with me an................ 3588
1Ki 1:14 **y.** talkest there with the king,............. 5750
1Ki 1:22 while she **y.** talked with the king,........ 5750
1Ki 1:42 And while he **y.** spake, behold,.......... 5750
1Ki 8:28 **Y.** have thou respect unto the prayer.........
1Ki 8:47 **Y.** if they shall bethink themselves ....
1Ki 11:17 Egypt; Hadad being **y.** a little child. ....
1Ki 12:2 Nebat, who was **y.** in Egypt, heard 5750
1Ki 12:5 Depart **y.** for three days, then........... 5750
1Ki 12:6 Solomon his father while he **y.** lived, ...
1Ki 14:8 **y.** thou hast not been as my servant ....
1Ki 19:18 **Y.** I have left me seven thousand in ....
1Ki 20:6 **Y.** I will send my servants unto.......... 3588
1Ki 20:32 And he said, Is he **y.** alive? he is 3588
1Ki 22:8 There is **y.** one man, Micaiah the......... 3588
1Ki 22:43 burn incense **y.** in the high places,....... 3588
2Ki 3:17 **y.** that valley shall be filled with water,......
2Ki 4:6 unto her son, bring me **y.** a vessel. ....
2Ki 6:33 And while he **y.** talked with them,....... 5750
2Ki 8:19 **Y.** the Lord would not destroy Judah ....
2Ki 8:22 **Y.** Edom revolted from under the ....
2Ki 13:23 them from his presence as **y.**...... 5704,6258
2Ki 14:3 **y.** not like David his father:................ 7535
2Ki 14:4 as **y.** the people did sacrifice 5750
2Ki 17:13 **Y.** the Lord testified against Israel, ...
2Ki 19:30 Judah shall **y.** again take root..................
1Ch 12:1 while he **y.** kept himself close............. 5750
1Ch 14:13 the Philistines **y.** again spread............. 5750
1Ch 17:17 **y.** this was a small thing in thine ....
1Ch 20:6 **y.** again there was war at Gath,......... 5750
1Ch 26:10 **y.** his father made him the chief;) ....
1Ch 29:1 hath chosen, is **y.** young and tender,..........
2Ch 1:11 neither **y.** hast asked long life;............ 1571
2Ch 6:16 **y.** so that thy children take heed......... 7535
2Ch 6:26 **y.** if they pray toward this place, and.........
2Ch 6:37 **Y.** if they bethink themselves in the ....
2Ch 10:6 Solomon his father while he **y.** lived,.........
2Ch 13:6 **Y.** Jeroboam the son of Nebat, ...
2Ch 14:7 while the land is **y.** before us; 5750

2Ch 16:8 **y.**, because thou didst rely on the ....
2Ch 16:12 **y.** in his disease he sought not to....... 1571
2Ch 18:7 There is **y.** one man, by whom we..... 5750
2Ch 20:33 as **y.** the people had not prepared 5750
2Ch 24:19 **Y.** he sent prophets to them, to bring.......
2Ch 27:2 And the people did **y.** corruptly.......... 5750
2Ch 28:22 trespass **y.** more against the Lord: ....
2Ch 30:18 **y.** did they eat the passover............. 3588
2Ch 32:15 this manner, neither **y.** believe him:.........
2Ch 32:16 And his servants spake **y.** more........ 5750
2Ch 33:17 **y.** unto the Lord their God only.............
2Ch 34:3 while he was **y.** young, he began 5750
Ezr 3:6 the temple of the Lord was not **y.** laid. .....
Ezr 5:16 in building, and **y.** it is not finished. ....
Ezr 9:9 **y.** our God hath not forsaken us in ....
Ezr 9:15 for we remain **y.** escaped, as it is this......
Ezr 10:2 **y.** now there is hope in Israel.................
Ne 1:9 **y.** will I gather them from thence, ...
Ne 2:16 neither had I as **y.** told it to....... 5704,3651
Ne 5:5 **Y.** now our flesh is as the flesh of our ......
Ne 5:18 **y.** for all this required not I the bread.......
Ne 6:4 **Y.** they sent unto me four times..............
Ne 9:19 **Y.** thou in thy manifold mercies ....
Ne 9:28 **y.** when they returned, and cried unto.......
Ne 9:29 **y.** they dealt proudly, and hearkened.........
Ne 9:30 **Y.** many years didst thou forbear ....
Ne 9:30 prophets: **y.** would they not give ear:........
Ne 13:18 **y.** ye bring more wrath upon Israel by ......
Ne 13:26 **y.** among many nations was there no ....
Es 2:20 Esther had not **y.** shewed her ....
Es 5:13 **Y.** all this availeth me nothing,.................
Es 6:14 they were **y.** talking with him, ... 5750
Es 8:3 Esther spake **y.** again before the...............
Job 1:16, 17,18 While he was **y.** speaking, ...
Job 3:26 neither was I quiet; **y.** trouble came. ....
Job 5:7 **Y.** man is born to trouble, as the....... 3588
Job 6:10 Then should I **y.** have comfort;.......... 5750
Job 8:7 **y.** thy latter end should greatly ....
Job 8:12 Whilst it is **y.** in his greenness,.......... 5750
Job 9:15 righteous, **y.** would I not answer,.............
Job 9:16 **y.** would I not believe that he had...........
Job 9:21 **y.** would I not know my soul: ....
Job 9:31 **Y.** shalt thou plunge me in the........... 227
Job 10:8 about; **y.** thou dost destroy me...............
Job 10:15 **y.** will I not lift up my head....................
Job 13:15 he slay me, **y.** will I trust in him:............
Job 14:9 **Y.** through the scent of water it will.........
Job 19:26 body, **y.** in my flesh shall I see God:.........
Job 20:7 **Y.** he shall perish for ever like his............
Job 20:14 **Y.** his meat in his bowels is turned,..........
Job 21:32 **Y.** shall he be brought to the grave, ...
Job 22:18 **Y.** he filled their houses with good...........
Job 24:12 **y.** God layeth not folly to them. ....
Job 24:23 **y.** his eyes are upon their ways. ....
Job 29:5 the Almighty was **y.** with me,............ 5750
Job 32:3 answer, and **y.** had condemned Job. ....
Job 33:14 yea twice, **y.** man perceiveth it not..........
Job 35:14 **y.** judgment is before him; ....
Job 35:15 anger; **y.** he knoweth it not in great ....
Job 36:2 have **y.** to speak on God's behalf........ 5750
Ps 2:6 **Y.** have I set my king upon my holy.........
Ps 37:10 For **y.** a little while, and the............. 5750
Ps 37:25 **y.** have I not seen the righteous ....
Ps 37:36 **Y.** he passed away, and, lo, he was..........
Ps 40:17 needy; **y.** the Lord thinketh upon me: ....
Ps 42:5 I shall **y.** praise him for the help 5750
Ps 42:8 **Y.** the Lord will command his.................
Ps 42:11 for I shall **y.** praise him, who is 5750
Ps 43:5 for I shall **y.** praise him, who is 5750
Ps 44:17 **y.** have we not forgotten thee, neither ......
Ps 49:13 **y.** their posterity approve their ....
Ps 55:21 than oil, **y.** were they drawn swords. ....
Ps 68:13 **y.** shall ye be as the wings of a dove ....
Ps 71:14 will **y.** praise thee more and more. ....
Ps 78:17 sinned **y.** more against him 5750
Ps 78:30 their meat was **y.** in their mouths,...... 5750
Ps 78:56 **Y.** they tempted and provoked the ....
Ps 90:10 years, **y.** is their strength labour and ......
Ps 94:7 **Y.** they say, The Lord shall not see, ...
Ps 107:41 **Y.** setteth he the poor on high from ....
Ps 119:51 **y.** have I not declined from thy law. ....
Ps 119:83 smoke; **y.** do I not forget thy statutes. ......
Ps 119:109 my hand: **y.** do I not forget thy law. ....
Ps 119:110 me: **y.** I erred not from thy precepts. ....
Ps 119:141 **y.** do not I forget thy precepts. ....
Ps 119:143 me: **y.** thy commandments are my...........
Ps 119:157 **y.** do not I decline from thy ....
Ps 129:2 **y.** they have not prevailed 1571
Ps 138:6 **y.** hath he respect unto the lowly: ....
Ps 139:16 my substance, **y.** being unperfect; ....
Ps 139:16 when as **y.** there was none of them. ....
Ps 141:5 for **y.** my prayer also shall be in 5750
Pr 6:10 **Y.** a little sleep, a little slumber, ...
Pr 8:26 While as **y.** he had not made the........ 5704
Pr 9:9 man, and he will be **y.** wiser: 5750
Pr 11:24 that scattereth, and **y.** increaseth; 5750
Pr 13:7 maketh himself rich, **y.** hath nothing: ....
Pr 13:7 himself poor, **y.** hath great riches. ....
Pr 19:7 words, **y.** they are wanting to him. ....
Pr 19:19 him, **y.** thou must do it again............. 5750
Pr 23:35 awake? I will seek it **y.** again. ....
Pr 24:33 **Y.** a little sleep, a little slumber, ...
Pr 27:22 **y.** will not his foolishness depart from ....
Pr 30:12 **y.** is not washed from their filthiness.........
Pr 30:25 **y.** they prepare...meat in the summer; ......
Pr 30:26 **y.** make they...houses in the rocks; ....
Pr 30:27 **y.** go they forth all of them by bands; ....
Pr 31:15 riseth also while it is **y.** night, ... 5750
Ec 1:7 run into the sea; **y.** the sea is not full; ......
Ec 2:3 **y.** acquainting mine heart with ....
Ec 2:19 **y.** shall he have rule over all my ....
Ec 2:21 **y.** to a man that hath not laboured...........
Ec 4:2 than the living which are **y.** alive. 5728
Ec 4:3 both they, which have not **y.** been,..... 5728
Ec 4:8 **y.** is there no end of all his labour; ....
Ec 6:2 **y.** God giveth him not power to eat..........
Ec 6:6 twice told, **y.** hath he seen no good: ....
Ec 6:7 and **y.** the appetite is not filled. 1571
Ec 7:28 Which **y.** my soul seeketh, but I 5750
Ec 8:12 **y.** surely I know that it shall be 3588
Ec 8:17 to seek it out, **y.** he shall not find it;.........
Ec 8:17 **y.** shall he not be able to find it. ....
Ec 9:11 neither **y.** bread to the wise,............. 1571
Ec 9:11 **y.** riches to men of understanding,...... 1571
Ec 9:11 nor **y.** favour to men of skill;............. 1571
Ec 9:15 **y.** no man remembered that same ....
Ec 11:8 **y.** let him remember the days of..............
Isa 6:13 But **y.** it shall be a tenth, and it......... 5750
Isa 10:22 **y.** a remnant of them shall return: ....
Isa 10:25 For **y.** a very little while, and the...... 5750
Isa 10:32 **y.** shall he remain at Nob that day:..... 5750
Isa 14:1 and will **y.** choose Israel, and set 5750
Isa 14:15 **Y.** thou shalt be brought down to........ 389
Isa 17:6 **Y.** gleaning grapes shall be left in it, ...
Isa 26:10 **y.** will he not learn righteousness; ....
Isa 27:10 **Y.** the defenced city shall be desolate, ...
Isa 28:4 is **y.** in his hand he eateth it up. 5750
Isa 28:12 refreshing: **y.** they would not hear............
Isa 29:2 **Y.** I will distress Ariel, and there ....
Isa 29:17 Is it not **y.** a very little while, and...... 5750
Isa 30:20 **y.** shall not thy teachers be removed ....
Isa 31:2 **Y.** he also is wise, and will bring evil, ...
Isa 42:25 fire round about, **y.** he knew not; ....
Isa 42:25 burned him, **y.** he laid it not to heart. ....
Isa 44:1 **Y.** now hear, O Jacob my servant; ....
Isa 44:11 **y.** they shall fear, and they shall be ....
Isa 46:7 **y.** can he not answer, nor save him..........
Isa 46:10 the things that are not **y.** done, ...
Isa 49:4 **y.** surely my judgment is with the ....
Isa 49:5 **y.** shall I be glorious in the eyes of..........
Isa 49:15 may forget, **y.** will I not forget thee..........
Isa 53:4 **y.** we did esteem him stricken, ...
Isa 53:7 afflicted, **y.** he opened not his mouth:........
Isa 53:10 **Y.** it pleased the Lord to bruise him: ....
Isa 56:8 **Y.** will I gather others to him, ... 5750
Isa 57:10 **y.** saidst thou not, There is no hope: ....
Isa 58:2 **Y.** they seek me daily, and delight to........
Isa 65:24 while they are **y.** speaking, I will........ 5750
Jer 2:9 Wherefore I will **y.** plead with you,..... 5750
Jer 2:11 their gods, which are **y.** no gods.? ....
Jer 2:21 **Y.** I had planted thee a noble vine, ...
Jer 2:22 **y.** thine iniquity is marked before me, ...
Jer 2:32 **y.** my people have forgotten me days.........
Jer 2:35 **Y.** thou sayest, Because I am..................
Jer 3:1 **y.** return again to me, saith the Lord. ....
Jer 3:8 **y.** her treacherous sister Judah ....
Jer 3:10 And **y.** for all this her treacherous ....
Jer 4:27 desolate; **y.** will I not make a full end........
Jer 5:22 themselves, **y.** can they not prevail; ....
Jer 5:22 roar, **y.** can they not pass over it? ....
Jer 5:28 of the fatherless, **y.** they prosper; ....
Jer 7:26 **Y.** they hearkened not unto me, nor.........
Jer 9:20 **Y.** hear the word of the Lord,........... 3588
Jer 11:8 **Y.** they obeyed not, nor inclined their.......
Jer 12:1 **y.** let me talk with thee of thy 389
Jer 14:9 **y.** thou, O Lord, art in the midst of..........
Jer 14:15 not, **y.** they say, Sword and famine ....
Jer 15:1 **y.** my mind could not be toward this ....
Jer 15:9 sun is gone down while it is **y.** day:.... 5750
Jer 15:10 **y.** every one of them doth curse me. ....
Jer 18:23 **Y.**, Lord, thou knowest all their...............
Jer 22:6 **y.** surely I will make thee a ....
Jer 22:24 hand, **y.** would I pluck thee hence; 3588
Jer 23:21 not sent these prophets, **y.** they ran: ....
Jer 23:21 spoken to them, **y.** they prophesied. ....
Jer 23:32 **y.** I sent them not, nor commanded..........
Jer 25:7 **Y.** ye have not hearkened unto me, ...
Jer 27:15 **y.** they prophesy a lie in my name;...........
Jer 30:11 **y.** will I not make a full end of............ 389
Jer 31:5 Thou shalt **y.** plant vines upon........... 5750
Jer 31:23 As **y.** they shall use this speech in 5750
Jer 31:39 the measuring line shall **y.** go forth...... 5750
Jer 32:33 **y.** they have not hearkened to receive.......
Jer 33:1 he was **y.** shut up in the court.......... 5750
Jer 34:4 **Y.** hear the word of the Lord, ... 389
Jer 36:24 **Y.** they were not afraid, nor rent............
Jer 37:10 **y.** should they rise up every man in..........
Jer 40:5 while he was not **y.** gone back,.......... 5750
Jer 44:28 **Y.** a small number that escape the............
Jer 46:28 **y.** will I not leave thee wholly..................
Jer 48:47 **Y.** will I bring again the captivity of..........
Jer 51:33 **y.** a little while, and the time of......... 5750
Jer 51:53 **y.** from me shall spoilers come ....
La 3:32 **y.** will he have compassion according..........
La 4:17 eyes are **y.** failed for our vain help: 5750
Eze 2:5 **y.** shall know that there hath been a ....
Eze 3:19 **Y.** if thou warn the wicked, and he...........
Eze 6:8 **Y.** will I leave a remnant, that ye may ......
Eze 7:13 sold, although they were **y.** alive:....... 5750
Eze 8:6 turn thee **y.** again, and thou shalt....... 5750
Eze 8:13 Turn thee **y.** again, and thou shalt...... 5750
Eze 8:15 turn thee **y.** again, and thou shalt....... 5750
Eze 8:18 a loud voice, **y.** will I not hear them. ....
Eze 11:16 **y.** will I be to them as a little.................
Eze 12:13 **y.** shall he not see it, though he shall........
Eze 14:22 **Y.**, behold, therein shall be left a ....
Eze 15:5 less it be meet **y.** for any work,..............
Eze 16:28 and **y.** couldest not be satisfied. ....
Eze 16:29 and **y.** thou wast not satisfied............ 1571
Eze 16:47 **Y.** hast thou not walked after their...........
Eze 18:19 **Y.** say ye, Why? doth not the son.............
Eze 18:25 **Y.** ye say, The way of the Lord is not......
Eze 18:29 **Y.** saith the house of Israel, The way ....
Eze 20:15 **Y.** also I lifted up my hand unto..............
Eze 20:27 **Y.** in this your fathers have 5750
Eze 23:19 **Y.** she multiplied her whoredoms, ...
Eze 23:44 **Y.** they went in unto her, as they ....
Eze 24:16 **y.** neither shalt thou mourn nor weep,........
Eze 26:21 **y.** shalt thou never be found again, ...
Eze 28:2 **y.** thou art a man, and not God,...............
Eze 28:9 Wilt thou **y.** say before him that.......... 559
Eze 29:13 **Y.** thus saith the Lord God; At.......... 3588
Eze 29:18 **y.** had he no wages, nor his army, ...
Eze 31:18 **y.** shalt thou be brought down with..........
Eze 32:24, 25 **y.** have they borne their shame ....
Eze 33:17 **Y.** the children of thy people say,............
Eze 33:20 **Y.** ye say, The way of the Lord is not......
Eze 36:37 I will **y.** for this be enquired of by...... 5750
Eze 44:11 **Y.** they shall be ministers in my.............
Da 4:23 **y.** leave the stump of the roots.......... 1297
Da 5:17 **y.** I will read the writing unto the....... 1297
Da 7:12 **y.** their lives were prolonged for a...........
Da 9:13 **y.** made we not our prayer before the.......
Da 10:9 **Y.** heard I the voice of his words: and ......
Da 10:14 for **y.** the vision is for many days:...... 5750
Da 11:2 stand up **y.** three kings in Persia;........ 5750
Da 11:27 for **y.** the end shall be at the time...... 5750
Da 11:33 **y.** they shall fall by the sword, and by.......
Da 11:35 it is **y.** for a time appointed.............. 5750
Da 11:45 **y.** he shall come to his end, and none ....
Ho 1:4 for **y.** a little while, and I will 5750
Ho 1:10 **Y.** the number of the children of.............
Ho 3:1 Go **y.**, love a woman beloved of......... 5750
Ho 3:1 of her friend, **y.** an adulteress,.................
Ho 4:4 **Y.** let no man strive, nor reprove........ 389
Ho 4:15 the harlot, **y.** let not Judah offend;............
Ho 5:13 **y.** could he not heal you, nor cure you......
Ho 7:9 there upon him, **y.** he knoweth not:..........

Ho 7:13 y. they have spoken lies against me
Ho 7:15 y. do they imagine mischief against
Ho 9:12 their children, y. will I bereave them,
Ho 9:16 y. will I slay even the beloved fruit of
Ho 11:12 but Judah y. ruleth with God, and 5750
Ho 12:8 Y. I am become rich, I have found 389
Ho 12:9 Egypt will y. make thee to dwell 5750
Ho 13:4 Y. I am the Lord thy God from the
Am 2:9 Y. destroyed I the Amorite before
Am 2:9 y. I destroyed his fruit from above.
Am 4:6 y. have ye not returned unto me, saith
Am 4:7 when there was y. three months 5750
Am 4:8, 9,10,11 y. have ye not returned unto
Am 6:10 the house, Is there y. any with thee?
Am 9:9 y. shall not the least grain fall upon
Jon 2:4 y. I will look again toward thy holy 389
Jon 2:6 y. hast thou brought up my life from
Jon 3:4 Y. forty days, and Nineveh shall 5750
Jon 4:2 when I was y. in my country? 5704
Mic 1:15 Y. will I bring an heir unto thee, 5750
Mic 3:11 y. will they lean upon the Lord, and
Mic 5:2 y. out of thee shall he come forth unto
Mic 6:10 Are there y. the treasures of 5750
Na 1:12 many, y. thus shall they be cut down,
Na 2:8 of water: y. they shall flee away.
Na 3:10 Y. was she carried away, she 1571
Hab 2:3 vision is y. for an appointed time, 5750
Hab 3:18 Y. I will rejoice in the Lord, I will
Hag 2:4 Y. now be strong, O Zerubbabel, saith
Hag 2:6 Y. once, it is a little while, and I 5750
Hag 2:17 y. ye turned not to me, saith the Lord.
Hag 2:19 Is the seed y. in the barn? yea, 5750
Hag 2:19 as y. the vine, and the fig tree, 5704
Zec 1:17 Cry y., saying, Thus saith the 5750
Zec 1:17 through prosperity shall y. be 5750
Zec 1:17 the Lord shall y. comfort Zion, 5750
Zec 1:17 and shall y. choose Jerusalem. 5750
Zec 8:4 shall y. old men and old women 5750
Zec 8:20 It shall y. come to pass, that there 5750
Zec 11:15 Take unto thee y. the instruments 5750
Zec 13:3 that when any shall y. prophesy, 5750
Mal 1:2 Y. ye say, Wherein hast thou loved
Mal 1:2 saith the Lord: y. I loved Jacob,
Mal 2:14 Y. ye say, Wherefore? Because the
Mal 2:14 y. is she thy companion, and the wife
Mal 2:15 Y. had he the residue of the spirit
Mal 2:17 Y. ye say, Wherein have we wearied
Mal 3:8 rob God? Y. have ye robbed me.
Mal 3:13 Y. ye say, What have we spoken so
Mt 6:25 y. for your body, what ye shall put
Mt 6:26 y. your heavenly Father feedeth them.
Mt 6:29 y. I say unto you, That even Solomon
Mt 10:10 coats, neither shoes, nor y. staves:
Mt 12:46 While he y. talked to the people, 2089
Mt 13:21 Y. hath he not root in himself, 1161
Mt 15:16 ye also y. without understanding? 188
Mt 15:17 Do ye not y. understand, that 3768
Mt 15:27 y. the dogs eat of the crumbs 1063
Mt 16:9 Do ye not y. understand, neither 3768
Mt 17:5 While he y. spake, behold, a bright 2089
Mt 19:20 from my youth up: what lack I y.? 2089
Mt 24:6 come to pass, but the end is not y. 3768
Mt 24:32 When his branch is y. tender, and 2236
Mt 26:33 of thee, y. will I never be offended.
Mt 26:35 die with thee, y. will I not deny 3364
Mt 26:47 And while he y. spake, lo, Judas, 2089
Mt 26:60 witnesses came, y. found they none.
Mt 27:63 said, while he was y. alive, 2089
Mk 5:35 While he y. spake, there came 2089
Mk 6:26 y. for his oath's sake, and for their
Mk 7:28 y. the dogs under the table eat 1063
Mk 8:17 perceive ye not y., neither 3768
Mk 8:17 have ye your heart y. hardened? 2089
Mk 11:13 for the time of figs was not y.
Mk 12:6 Having y. therefore one son, his 2089
Mk 13:7 be; but the end shall not be y. 3768
Mk 13:28 When her branch is y. tender, 2236
Mk 14:29 all shall be offended, y. will not I. 235
Mk 14:43 while he y. spake, cometh Judas, 2089
Mk 15:5 But Jesus y. answered nothing; 3765
Lu 3:20 Added y. this above all, that he 2596
Lu 8:49 While he y. spake, there cometh 2089
Lu 9:42 And as he was y. a coming, the 2089
Lu 11:8 y. because of his importunity he 1065
Lu 12:27 y. I say unto you, that Solomon in
Lu 14:22 commanded, and y. there is room. 2089
Lu 14:32 while the other is y. a great way 2089
Lu 14:35 the land, nor y. for the dunghill;
Lu 15:20 when he was y. a great way off, 2089
Lu 15:29 y. thou never gavest me a kid, that I
Lu 18:5 Y. because this widow troubleth 1065
Lu 18:22 him, Y. lackest thou one thing: 2089
Lu 19:30 colt tied, whereon y. never man sat:
Lu 22:37 written must y. be accomplished 2089
Lu 22:47 And while he y. spake, behold a 2089
Lu 22:60 while he y. spake, the cock crew. 2089
Lu 23:15 No, nor y. Herod: for I sent you to
Lu 24:6 you when he was y. in Galilee, 2089
Lu 24:41 while they y. believed not for joy, 2089
Lu 24:44 unto you, while I was y. with you, 2089
Joh 2:4 thee? mine hour is not y. come. 3768
Joh 3:24 John was not y. cast into prison. 3768
Joh 4:21 mountain, nor y. at Jerusalem,
Joh 4:27 y. no man said, What seekest 3305
Joh 4:35 There are y. four months, and 2089
Joh 7:6 unto them, My time is not y. come: 3768
Joh 7:8 I go not up y. unto this feast; 3768
Joh 7:8 for my time is not y. full come. 3768
Joh 7:19 y. none of you keepeth the law?
Joh 7:30 because his hour was not y. come. 3768
Joh 7:33 Y. a little while am I with you, 2089
Joh 7:39 the Holy Ghost was not y. given; 3768
Joh 7:39 that Jesus was not y. glorified.) 3764
Joh 8:14 record of myself, y. my record is true:
Joh 8:16 y. if I judge, my judgment is true:
Joh 8:20 him; for his hour was not y. come. 3768
Joh 8:55 Y. ye have not known him; but I
Joh 8:57 Thou art not y. fifty years old, and 2532
Joh 9:30 and y. he hath opened mine eyes.
Joh 11:25 though he were dead, y. shall he live:
Joh 11:30 Jesus was not y. come into the 3768
Joh 12:35 Y. a little while is the light with 2089
Joh 12:37 them, y. they believed not on him:
Joh 13:33 y. a little while I am with you. 2089
Joh 14:9 y. hast thou not known me, Phillip?
Joh 14:19 Y. a little while, and the world 2089
Joh 14:25 unto you, being y. present with you.
Joh 16:12 I have y. many things to say unto 2089
Joh 16:32 y. I am not alone, because the Father
Joh 19:41 wherein was never man y. laid. 3764
Joh 20:1 when it was y. dark, unto the 2089
Joh 20:5 clothes lying; y. went they not in. 3305
Joh 20:9 as y. they knew not the scripture, 3764
Joh 20:17 am not y. ascended to my Father: 3768
Joh 20:29 have not seen, and y. have believed.
Joh 21:11 so many, y. was not the net broken.
Joh 21:23 y. Jesus said not unto him, He shall 2532
Ac 7:5 y. he promised that he would give 2532
Ac 7:5 him, when as y. he had no child
Ac 8:16 as y. he was fallen upon none of 3768
Ac 9:1 y. breathing out threatenings and 2089
Ac 10:44 While Peter y. spake these words, 2089
Ac 13:27 nor y. the voices of the prophets
Ac 13:28 y. desired they Pilate that he should
Ac 18:18 this tarried there y. a good while, 2089
Ac 19:37 nor y. blasphemers of your
Ac 22:3 y. brought up in this city at the feet
Ac 24:11 there are y. but twelve days since
Ac 25:8 the temple, nor y. against Caesar,
Ac 28:4 y. vengeance suffereth not to live.
Ac 28:17 y. was I delivered prisoner from
Ro 3:7 why y. am I also judged as a 2089
Ro 4:11 which he had y. being uncircumcised:
Ro 4:12 which he had being y. uncircumcised.
Ro 4:29 y. the deadness of Sarah's womb:
Ro 5:6 we were y. without strength, 2089
Ro 5:7 y. peradventure for a good man 1063
Ro 5:8 while we were y. sinners, Christ 2089
Ro 8:24 man seeth, why doth he y. hope for?
Ro 9:11 (For the children being not y. born, 3380
Ro 9:19 me, Why doth he y. find fault? 2089
Ro 11:30 y. have now obtained mercy through
Ro 16:19 y. I would have you wise unto that 1161
1Co 2:6 y. not the wisdom of this world, nor 1161
1Co 2:15 y. he himself is judged of no man. 1161
1Co 3:2 bear it, neither y. now are ye able. 2089
1Co 3:3 For ye are y. carnal: for whereas 2089
1Co 3:15 shall be saved: y. so as by fire. 1161
1Co 4:4 y. am I not hereby justified: but he 235
1Co 4:15 Christ, y. have ye not many fathers: 235
1Co 5:10 Y. not altogether with the 2532
1Co 7:10 y. not I, but the Lord, Let not the wife
1Co 7:25 y. I give my judgment, as one that 1161
1Co 8:2 knoweth nothing y. as he ought 3764
1Co 9:2 others, y. doubtless I am to you: 235
1Co 9:19 y. have I made myself servant unto
1Co 12:20 many members, y. but one body. 1161
1Co 12:31 and y. shew I unto you a more 2089
1Co 14:19 Y. in the church I had rather 235
1Co 14:21 y. for all that will they not hear me,
1Co 15:10 y. not I, but the grace of God which 1161
1Co 15:17 is vain; ye are y. in your sins. 2089
2Co 1:10 we trust that he will y. deliver us; 2089
2Co 1:23 you I came not as y. unto Corinth. 3765
2Co 4:8 on every side, y. not distressed; 235
2Co 4:16 y. the inward man is renewed day 235
2Co 5:16 y. now henceforth know we him 235
2Co 6:8 good report: as deceivers, and y. true;
2Co 6:9 As unknown, and y. well known;
2Co 6:10 As sorrowful, y. alway rejoicing; 1161
2Co 6:10 as poor, y. making many rich; 1161
2Co 6:10 nothing, and y. possessing all things.
2Co 8:9 y. for your sakes he became poor,
2Co 9:3 Y. have I sent the brethren, lest 1161
2Co 11:6 in speech, y. not in knowledge; 235
2Co 11:16 y. as a fool receive me, that I may 2579
2Co 12:5 y. of myself I will not glory, but in 1161
2Co 13:4 y. he liveth by the power of God. 235
Ga 1:10 for if I y. pleased men, I should 2089
Ga 2:20 y. not I, but Christ liveth in me: 3765
Ga 3:4 things in vain? if it be y. in vain. 2596
Ga 3:15 y. if it be confirmed, no man
Ga 5:11 if I y. preach circumcision, 2089
Ga 5:11 why do I y. suffer persecution? 2089
Eph 5:29 no man ever y. hated his own flesh;
Php 1:9 love may abound y. more and 2089
Php 1:22 y. what I shall choose I wot not. 2532
Php 2:25 Y. I supposed it necessary to send 1161
Col 1:21 works, y. now hath he reconciled 1161
Col 2:5 y. am I with you in the spirit, 235
1Th 2:6 nor y. of others, when we might have
2Th 2:5 when I was y. with you, I told you 2089
2Th 3:15 Y. count him not as an enemy, but 2532
2Ti 2:5 for masteries, y. is he not crowned,
2Ti 2:13 we believe not, y. he abideth faithful:
Phm 9 Y. for love's sake I rather beseech
Heb 2:8 not y. all things put under him. 3768
Heb 4:15 tempted like as we are, y. without sin.
Heb 5:8 y. learned he obedience by the things
Heb 7:10 he was y. in the loins of his father, 2089
Heb 7:15 And it is y. far more evident: 2089
Heb 9:8 of all was not y. made manifest, 2089
Heb 9:8 first tabernacle was y. standing: 2089
Heb 9:25 Nor y. that he should offer himself
Heb 10:37 For y. a little while, and he that 2089
Heb 11:4 by it he being dead y. speaketh. 2089
Heb 11:7 of God of things not seen as y., 3369
Heb 12:4 Ye have not y. resisted unto blood, 3768
Heb 12:26 Y. once more I shake not the 2089
Heb 12:27 word, Y. once more, signifieth the 2089
Jas 2:10 y. offend in one point, he is guilty of
Jas 2:11 commit no adultery, y. if thou kill, 1161
Jas 3:4 y. are they turned about with a very
Jas 4:2 y. ye have not, because ye ask not. 1161
1Pe 1:8 now ye see him not, y. believing, 1161
1Pe 4:16 Y. if any man suffer as a Christian, 1161
1Jo 3:2 not y. appear what we shall be: 3768
Jude 9 Y. Michael the archangel, when 1161
Re 6:11 should rest y. for a little season, 2089
Re 8:13 angels, which are y. to sound. 3195
Re 9:20 by these plagues y. repented not
Re 17:8 that was, and is not, and y. is. 2539
Re 17:10 one is, and the other is not y. come; 3768
Re 17:12 have received no kingdom as y.; 3768

YIELD See also YIELDED; YIELDETH; YIELDING.

Ge 4:12 not henceforth y. unto thee fruits. 5414
Ge 49:20 fat, and he shall y. royal dainties. 5414
Le 19:25 it may y. unto you the increase 3254
Le 25:19 And the land shall y. her fruit, 5414
Le 26:4 and the land shall y. her increase, 5414
Le 26:4 trees of the field shall y. their fruit. 5414
Le 26:20 your land shall not y. her increase, 5414
Le 26:20 the trees of the land y. their fruits. 5414
De 11:17 and that the land y. not her fruit; 5414
2Ch 30:8 y. yourselves unto the Lord, 5414,3027
Ps 67:6 shall the earth y. her increase; 5414
Ps 85:12 and our land shall y. her increase. 5414
Ps 107:37 which may y. fruits of increase. 6213

Pr 7:21 fair speech she caused him to y., 5186
Isa 5:10 of vineyard shall y. one bath, 6213
Isa 5:10 seed of an homer shall y. an ephah. 6213
Eze 34:27 tree of the field shall y. her fruit, 5414
Eze 34:27 and the earth shall y. her increase, 5414
Eze 36:8 and y. your fruit to my people of 5375
Ho 8:7 stalk: the bud shall y. no meal: 6213
Ho 8:7 if so be it y., the strangers shall 6213
Joe 2:22 and the vine do y. their strength. 5414
Hab 3:17 fail, and the field shall y. no meat; 6213
Mk 4:8 **and did y. fruit that sprang up** *1325*
Ac 23:21 But do not thou y. unto them: *3982*
Ro 6:13 Neither y. ye your members as *3936*
Ro 6:13 but y. yourselves unto God, as *3936*
Ro 6:16 ye y. yourselves servants to obey, *3936*
Ro 6:19 so now y. your members servants *3936*
Jas 3:12 no fountain both y. salt water and *4160*

YIELDED
Ge 49:33 y. up the ghost, and was gathered 1478
Nu 17:8 blossoms, and y. almonds. 1580
Da 3:28 king's word, and y. their bodies, 3052
Mt 27:50 with a loud voice, y. up the ghost. *863*
Mk 4:7 **and choked it, and it y. no fruit** *1325*
Ac 5:10 at his feet, and y. up the ghost: *1634*
Ro 6:19 have y. your members servants *3936*
Re 22:2 and y. her fruit every month: *591*

YIELDETH
Ne 9:37 it y. much increase unto the kings 7235
Job 24:5 the wilderness y. food for them and
Pr 12:12 the root of the righteous y. fruit. 5414
Heb 12:11 afterward it y. the peaceable fruit *591*

YIELDING
Ge 1:11 forth grass, the herb y. seed, 2232
Ge 1:11 fruit tree y. fruit after his kind, 6213
Ge 1:12 and herb y. seed after his kind, 2232
Ge 1:12 and the tree y. fruit, whose seed 6213
Ge 1:29 is the fruit of a tree y. seed; 2232
Ec 10:4 for y. pacifieth great offences. 4832
Jer 17:8 neither shall cease from y. fruit. 6213

YOKE See also YOKED; YOKEFELLOW; YOKES.
Ge 27:40 break his y. from off thy neck. 5923
Le 26:13 I have broken the bands of your y., 5923
Nu 19:2 and upon which never came y.: 5923
De 21:3 which hath not drawn in the y.; 5923
De 28:48 shall put a y. of iron upon thy neck, 5923
1Sa 6:7 on which there hath come no y., 5923
1Sa 11:7 And he took a y. of oxen, and 6776
1Sa 14:14 which a y. of oxen might plow 6776
1Ki 12:4 Thy father made our y. grievous: 5928
1Ki 12:4 his heavy y. which he put upon us, 5928
1Ki 12:9 y. which thy father did put upon us 5928
1Ki 12:10 Thy father made our y. heavy, but 5928
1Ki 12:11 father did lade you with a heavy y., 5928
1Ki 12:11 I will add to your y.: my father 5928
1Ki 12:14 My father made your y. heavy, and 5928
1Ki 12:14 and I will add to your y.: my 5928
1Ki 19:19 plowing with twelve y. of oxen 6776
1Ki 19:21 took a y. of oxen, and slew them, 6776
2Ch 10:4 Thy father made our y. grievous: 5923
2Ch 10:4 his heavy y. that he put upon us, 5923
2Ch 10:9 y. that thy father did put upon us? 5923
2Ch 10:10 Thy father made our y. heavy, 5923
2Ch 10:11 my father put a heavy y. upon you, 5923
2Ch 10:11 will put more to your y.: my father 5923
2Ch 10:14 My father made your y. heavy, 5923
Job 1:3 and five hundred y. of oxen, 6776
Job 42:12 and a thousand y. of oxen, and a 6776
Isa 9:4 hast broken the y. of his burden, 5923
Isa 10:27 and his y. from off thy neck, 5923
Isa 10:27 and the y. shall be destroyed 5923
Isa 14:25 shall his y. depart from off them, 5923
Isa 47:6 hast thou very heavily laid thy y.. 5923
Isa 58:6 free, and that ye brake every y.? 4133
Isa 58:9 away from the midst of thee the y., 4133
Jer 2:20 of old time I have broken thy y., 5923
Jer 5:5 have altogether broken the y., 5923
Jer 27:8, 11,12 the y. of the king of Babylon, 5923
Jer 28:2 the y. of the king of Babylon. 5923
Jer 28:4 brake the y. of the king of Babylon. 5923
Jer 28:10 took the y. from off the prophet 4133
Jer 28:11 I break the y. of Nebuchadnezzar 5923
Jer 28:12 the prophet had broken the y. 4133
Jer 28:14 a y. of iron upon the neck of all 5923
Jer 30:8 break his y. from off thy neck, 5923
Jer 31:18 as a bullock unaccustomed to the y.:
Jer 51:23 husbandman and his y. of oxen; 6776
La 1:14 The y. of my transgressions is 5923
La 3:27 that he bear the y. in his youth. 5923
Eze 34:27 have broken the bands of their y., 5923
Ho 11:4 that take off the y. on their jaws, 5923
Na 1:13 will I break his y. from off thee, 4132
Mt 11:29 **Take my y. upon you, and learn of** *2218*
Mt 11:30 **For my y. is easy, and my burden** *2218*
Lu 14:19 **I have bought five y. of oxen,** *2201*
Ac 15:10 y. upon the neck of the disciples, *2218*
Ga 5:1 again with the y. of bondage. *2218*
1Ti 6:1 many servants as are under the y. *2218*

YOKED
2Co 6:14 y. together with unbelievers: *2086*

YOKEFELLOW
Php 4:3 true y., help those women which *4805*

YOKES
Jer 27:2 Make thee bonds and y., and put 4133
Jer 28:13 Thou hast broken the y. of wood; 4133
Jer 28:13 shalt make for them y. of iron. 4133
Eze 30:18 shall break there the y. of Egypt: 4133

YONDER
Ge 22:5 lad will go y. and worship, 5704,3541
Nu 16:37 and scatter thou the fire y.; 1973
Nu 23:15 offering, while I meet the Lord y.. 3541
Nu 32:19 inherit with them on y. side Jordan, 5676
2Ki 4:25 Behold, y. is that Shunammite:
Mt 17:20 **Remove hence to y. place;** *1563*
Mt 26:36 **Sit ye here, while I go and pray y.** *1563*

YOU See in the APPENDIX; also YOUR; YOUWARD.

YOUNG See also YOUNGER; YOUNGEST.
Ge 4:23 and a y. man to my hurt. 3206
Ge 14:24 which the y. men have eaten, 5288
Ge 15:9 and a turtledove, and a y. pigeon. 1469
Ge 18:7 good, and gave it unto a y. man; 5288
Ge 19:4 the house round, both old and y., 5288
Ge 22:3 took two of his y. men with him, 5288
Ge 22:5 Abraham said unto his y. men, 5288
Ge 22:19 Abraham returned unto his y. men, 5288
Ge 31:38 thy she goats have not cast their y.,
Ge 33:13 and herds with y. are with me: 5763
Ge 34:19 y. man deferred not to do the 5288
Ge 41:12 there was there with us a y. man, 5288
Ex 10:9 go with our y. and with our old, 5288
Ex 23:26 There shall nothing cast their y., nor
Ex 24:5 y. men of the children of Israel, 5288
Ex 29:1 Take one y. bullock, and 1121,1241
Ex 33:11 Joshua, the son of Nun, a y. man, 5288
Le 1:14 of turtledoves, or of y. pigeons. 1121
Le 4:3 a y. bullock without blemish 1121,1241
Le 4:14 offer a y. bullock for the sin, 1121,1241
Le 5:7 or two y. pigeons, unto the Lord; 1121
Le 5:11 two y. pigeons, then he that sinned 1121
Le 9:2 a y. calf for a sin offering, 1121,1241
Le 12:6 a y. pigeon, or a turtledove, 1121
Le 12:8 two turtles, or two y. pigeons; 1121
Le 14:22 two y. pigeons, such as he is able 1121
Le 14:30 y. pigeons, such as he can get; 1121
Le 15:14 or two y. pigeons, and come before 1121
Le 15:29 or two y. pigeons, and bring them 1121
Le 16:3 a y. bullock for a sin offering, 1121,1241
Le 22:28 kill it and her y. both in one day. 1121
Le 23:18 one y. bullock, and two rams: 1121,1241
Nu 6:10 or two y. pigeons, to the priest, 1121
Nu 7:15, 21,27,33,39,45,51,57,63,69,75,
81 One y. bullock, one ram, one 1121,1241
Nu 8:8 Then let them take a y. bullock 1121,1241
Nu 8:8 y. bullock shalt thou take 1121,1241
Nu 11:27 ran a y. man, and told Moses, 5288
Nu 11:28 one of his y. men, answered 979
Nu 15:24 offer one y. bullock for a burnt 1121,1241
Nu 23:24 and lift up himself as a y. lion:
Nu 28:11, 19,27 y. bullocks, one ram, 1121,1241
Nu 29:2,8 one y. bullock, one ram, and 1121,1241
Nu 29:13 thirteen y. bullocks, two rams, 1121,1241
Nu 29:17 shall offer twelve y. bullocks, 1121,1241
De 22:6 whether they be y. ones, or eggs, 667
De 22:6 and the dam sitting upon the y., 667
De 22:6 not take the dam with the y.: 1121
De 22:7 dam go, and take the y. to thee; 1121
De 28:50 old, nor shew favour to the y.: 5288
De 28:57 toward her y. one that cometh out 7988
De 32:11 fluttereth over her y., spreadeth 1469
De 32:25 shall destroy both the y. man and 970
Jos 6:21 both man and woman, y. and old, 5288
Jos 6:23 y. men that were spies went in, 5288
Jg 6:25 Take thy father's y. bullock, even 6499
Jg 8:14 a y. man of the men of Succoth, 5288
Jg 9:54 unto the y. man his armourbearer, 5288
Jg 9:54 his y. man thrust him through, and 5288
Jg 14:5 a y. lion roared against him. 3715
Jg 14:10 feast; for so used the y. men to do. 970
Jg 17:7 a y. man out of Beth-lehem-judah 5288
Jg 17:11 y. man was unto him as one of his 5288
Jg 17:12 and the y. man became his priest, 5288
Jg 18:3 the voice of the y. man the Levite: 5288
Jg 18:15 the house of the y. man the Levite, 5288
Jg 19:19 y. man which is with thy servants: 5288
Jg 21:12 four hundred y. virgins, that had 5291
Ru 2:9 have I not charged the y. men 5288
Ru 2:9 that which the y. men have drawn. 5288
Ru 2:15 Boaz commanded his y. men, 5288
Ru 2:21 shalt keep fast by my y. men, 5288
Ru 3:10 as thou followedst not y. men, 970
Ru 4:12 shall give thee of this y. woman. 5291
1Sa 1:24 in Shiloh: and the child was y.. 5288
1Sa 2:17 the sin of the y. men was very great 5288
1Sa 8:16 your goodliest y. men, and your 970
1Sa 9:2 Saul, a choice y. man, and a goodly: 970
1Sa 9:11 y. maidens going out to draw 5291
1Sa 14:1 son of Saul said unto the y. man 5288
1Sa 14:6 Jonathan said to the y. man that 5288
1Sa 17:58 Whose son art thou, thou y. man? 5288
1Sa 20:22 But if I say thus unto the y. man, 5958
1Sa 21:4 if the y. men have kept themselves 5288
1Sa 21:5 vessels of the y. men are holy, 5288
1Sa 25:5 And David sent out ten y. men, 5288
1Sa 25:5 David said unto the y. men, Get 5288
1Sa 25:8 Ask thy y. men, and they will shew 5288
1Sa 25:8 let the y. men find favour in thine 5288
1Sa 25:9 And when David's y. men came, 5288
1Sa 25:12 So David's y. men turned their way, 5288
1Sa 25:14 But one of the y. men told Abigail, 5288
1Sa 25:25 thine handmaid saw not the y. men. 5288
1Sa 25:27 the y. men that follow my lord. 5288
1Sa 26:22 let one of the y. men come over and 5288
1Sa 30:13 he said, I am a y. man of Egypt, 5288
1Sa 30:17 save four hundred y. men, which 5288
2Sa 1:5 David said unto the y. man that 5288
2Sa 1:6 And the y. man that told him said, 5288
2Sa 1:13 And David said unto the y. man 5288
2Sa 1:15 David called one of the y. men, and 5288
2Sa 2:14 Let the y. men now arise, and 5288
2Sa 2:21 lay thee hold on one of the y. men, 5288
2Sa 4:12 And David commanded his y. men, 5288
2Sa 9:12 Mephibosheth had a y. son, whose 6996
2Sa 13:32 all the y. men the king's sons; 5288
2Sa 13:34 the y. man that kept the watch 5288
2Sa 14:21 bring the y. man Absalom again. 5288
2Sa 16:2 summer fruit for the y. men to eat; 5288
2Sa 18:5 gently for my sake with the y. man, 5288
2Sa 18:12 none touch the y. man Absalom. 5288
2Sa 18:15 y. men that bare Joab's armour 5288
2Sa 18:29 said, Is the y. man Absalom safe? 5288
2Sa 18:32 Is the y. man Absalom safe? And 5288
2Sa 18:32 do thee hurt, be as that y. man is. 5288
1Ki 1:2 for my lord the king a y. virgin: 5291
1Ki 11:28 Solomon seeing the y. man that 5288
1Ki 12:8 consulted with the y. men that 3206
1Ki 12:10 y. men that were grown up with 3206
1Ki 12:14 after the counsel of the y. men, 3206
1Ki 20:14, 15,17,19 y. men of the princes of 5288
2Ki 4:22 me, I pray thee, one of the y. men, 5288
2Ki 5:22 two y. men of the sons of the 5288
2Ki 6:17 Lord opened the eyes of the y. man; 5288
2Ki 8:12 their y. men wilt thou slay with 970
2Ki 9:4 So the y. man, even the 5288
2Ki 9:4 even the y. man the prophet, 5288
1Ch 12:28 Zadok, a y. man mighty of valour, 5288
1Ch 22:5 Solomon my son is y. and tender, 5288
1Ch 29:1 hath chosen, is yet y. and tender, 5288
2Ch 10:8 took counsel with the y. men that 3206
2Ch 10:10 y. men that were brought up with 3206
2Ch 10:14 after the advice of the y. men, 3206
2Ch 13:7 when Rehoboam was y. and 5288
2Ch 13:9 himself with a y. bullock 1121,1241
2Ch 34:3 while he was yet y., he began to 5288
2Ch 36:17 who slew their y. men with the 970

2Ch 36:17 had no compassion upon y. man or....... 970
Ezr 6:9 both y. bullocks, and rams,............... 1123
Es 2:2 there be fair y. virgins sought 5291
Es 2:3 together all the fair y. virgins........... 5291
Es 3:13 perish, all Jews, both y. and old,........ 5288
Es 8:10 camels, and y. dromedaries:............. 1121
Job 1:19 it fell upon the y. men, and they........ 5288
Job 4:10 and the teeth of the y. lions, are........ 3715
Job 19:18 Yea, y. children despised me;................
Job 29:8 The y. men saw me, and hid............. 5288
Job 32:6 I am y., and ye are very old; 6810,3117
Job 38:39 or fill the appetite of the y. lions, ... 3715
Job 38:41 when his y. ones cry unto God, ... 3206
Job 39:3 they bring forth their y. ones, ... 3206
Job 39:4 Their y. ones are in good liking, ... 1121
Job 39:16 is hardened against her y. ones,......... 1121
Job 39:30 Her y. ones also suck up blood: 667
Ps 17:12 a y. lion lurking in secret places......... 3715
Ps 29:6 and Sirion like a y. unicorn................ 1121
Ps 34:10 The y. lions do lack, and suffer.......... 3715
Ps 37:25 I have been y., and now am old;........ 5288
Ps 58:6 out the great teeth of the y. lions, ... 3715
Ps 78:63 The fire consumed their y. men; 970
Ps 78:71 following the ewes great with y. 5763
Ps 84:3 where she may lay her y., even.......... 667
Ps 91:13 y. lion and the dragon shalt thou 3715
Ps 104:21 The y. lions roar after their prey, ... 3715
Ps 119:9 shall a y. man cleanse his way?......... 5288
Ps 147:9 and to the y. ravens which cry. 1121
Ps 148:12 Both y. men, and maidens; old........... 970
Pr 1:4 y. man knowledge and discretion.......... 5288
Pr 7:7 a y. man void of understanding, ... 5288
Pr 20:29 glory of y. men is their strength:......... 970
Pr 30:17 out, and the y. eagles shall eat it. 1121
Ec 11:9 Rejoice, O y. man, in thy youth; 970
Ca 2:9 beloved is like a roe or a y. hart:....... 6082
Ca 2:17 roe or a y. hart upon the mountains..... 6082
Ca 4:5 are like two y. roes that are twins, ... 6082
Ca 7:3 are like two y. roes that are twins. 6082
Ca 8:14 be thou like to a roe or to a y. hart.... 6082
Isa 5:29 lion, they shall roar like y. lions: 3715
Isa 7:21 that a man shall nourish a y. cow,....... 1241
Isa 9:17 shall have no joy in their y. men,......... 970
Isa 11:6 and the y. lion and the fatling............ 3715
Isa 11:7 y. ones shall lie down together: 3206
Isa 13:18 shall dash the y. men to pieces;......... 5288
Isa 20:4 Ethiopians captives, y. and old,.......... 5288
Isa 23:4 neither do I nourish up y. men,.......... 970
Isa 30:6 whence come the y. and old lion, ... 3838
Isa 30:6 riches upon the shoulders of y. asses, ...
Isa 30:24 y. asses that ear the ground shall eat........
Isa 31:4 the y. lion roaring on his prey, ... 3715
Isa 31:8 his y. men shall be discomfited............ 970
Isa 40:11 gently lead those that are with y.......... 5763
Isa 40:30 the y. men shall utterly fall:......... 5288,970
Isa 62:5 For as a y. man marrieth a virgin, .5288,970
Jer 2:15 The y. lions roared upon him, and...... 3715
Jer 6:11 the assembly of y. men together: 970
Jer 9:21 and the y. men from the streets........... 970
Jer 11:22 the y. men shall die by the sword;....... 970
Jer 15:8 against the mother of the y. men......... 970
Jer 18:21 their y. men be slain by the sword....... 970
Jer 31:12 the y. of the flock and of the herd:..... 1121
Jer 31:13 both y. men and old together:............ 970
Jer 48:15 his chosen y. men are gone down to 970
Jer 49:26 her y. men shall fall in her streets, ... 970
Jer 50:30 shall her y. men fall in the streets, ... 970
Jer 51:3 spare ye not her y. men; destroy ye 970
Jer 51:22 will I break in pieces old and y.; 5288
Jer 51:22 in pieces the y. man and the maid;....... 970
La 1:15 against me to crush my y. men: 970
La 1:18 my y. men are gone into captivity........ 970
La 2:19 him for the life of thy y. children, ...
La 2:21 y. and the old lie on the ground in....... 5288
La 2:21 virgins and my y. men are fallen.......... 970
La 4:3 they give suck to their y. ones: 1482
La 4:4 the y. children ask bread, and no man.......
La 5:13 They took the y. men to grind, and 970
La 5:14 gate, the y. men from their musick, ... 970
Eze 9:6 Slay utterly old and y., both maids, ... 970
Eze 17:4 off the top of his y. twigs, and........... 3242
Eze 17:22 off from the top of his y. twigs.......... 3127
Eze 19:2 her whelps among y. lions. 3715
Eze 19:3 it became a y. lion, and it learned 3715
Eze 19:5 whelps, and made him a y. lion........... 3715
Eze 19:6 he became a y. lion, and learned........ 3715
Eze 23:6 all of them desirable y. men,.............. 970
Eze 23:12 all of them desirable y. men............... 970
Eze 23:23 them: all of them desirable y. men, ... 970
Eze 30:17 y. men of Aven and of Pi-beseth 970
Eze 31:6 of the field bring forth their y.,...............
Eze 32:2 art like a y. lion of the nations,........... 3715
Eze 38:13 of Tarshish, with all the y. lions......... 3715
Eze 41:19 face of a y. lion toward the palm........ 3715
Eze 43:19 y. bullock for a sin offering. 1121,1241
Eze 43:23 a y. bullock without blemish, ... 1121,1241
Eze 43:25 shall also prepare a y. bullock,.... 1121,1241
Eze 45:18 a y. bullock without blemish, ... 1121,1241
Eze 46:6 a y. bullock without blemish. 1121,1241
Ho 5:14 as a y. lion to the house of Judah: 3715
Joe 2:28 your y. men shall see visions:............ 970
Am 2:11 and of your y. men for Nazarites. 970
Am 3:4 will a y. lion cry out of his den, ... 3715
Am 4:10 your y. men have I slain with the 970
Am 8:13 virgins and y. men faint for thirst......... 970
Mic 5:8 as a y. lion among the flocks of 3715
Na 2:11 the feeding place of the y. lions, ... 3715
Na 2:13 sword shall devour thy y. lions: 3715
Na 3:10 her y. children also were dashed in..........
Zec 2:4 Run, speak to this y. man, saying, ... 5288
Zec 9:17 shall make the y. men cheerful,........... 970
Zec 11:3 a voice of the roaring of y. lions; 3715
Zec 11:16 neither shall seek the y. one,............ 5288
Mt 2:8 search diligently for the y. child; 3813
Mt 2:9 stood over where the y. child was...... 3813
Mt 2:11 the y. child with Mary his mother, ... 3813
Mt 2:13 take the y. child and his mother,........ 3813
Mt 2:13 seek the y. child to destroy him......... 3813
Mt 2:14 he took the y. child and his mother 3813
Mt 2:20 take the y. child and his mother,........ 3813
Mt 2:20 which sought the y. child's life........... 3813
Mt 2:21 took the y. child and his mother,........ 3813
Mt 19:20 The y. man saith unto him, All......... 3495
Mt 19:22 the y. man heard that saying, he......... 3495
Mk 7:25 y. daughter had an unclean spirit, ... 2365
Mk 10:13 they brought y. children to him,......... 3813
Mk 14:51 followed him a certain y. man, ... 3495
Mk 14:51 and the y. men laid hold on him: 3495
Mk 16:5 saw a y. man sitting on the right........ 3495
Lu 2:24 of turtledoves, or two y. pigeons. 3502
Lu 7:14 **Y. man, I say unto thee, Arise**...... 3495
Joh 12:14 when he had found a y. ass, sat.......... 3678
Joh 21:18 **When thou wast y., thou girdedst**.. 3501
Ac 2:17 and your y. men shall see visions,...... 3495
Ac 5:6 the y. men arose, wound him up,....... 3501
Ac 5:10 y. men came in, and found her 3495
Ac 7:19 they cast out their y. children,........... 1025
Ac 7:58 their clothes at a y. man's feet, ... 3494
Ac 20:9 a certain y. man named Eutychus,...... 3494
Ac 20:12 they brought the y. man alive,........... 3816
Ac 23:17 this y. man unto the chief captain:...... 3494
Ac 23:18 prayed me to bring this y. man........... 3494
Ac 23:22 then let the y. man depart, ... 3494
Tit 2:4 teach the y. women to be sober, ... 3501
Tit 2:6 Y. men likewise exhort to be 3501
1Jo 2:13 I write unto you, y. men, because...... 3495
1Jo 2:14 written unto you, y. men, because 3495

YOUNGER

Ge 9:24 knew what his y. son had done.......... 6996
Ge 19:31, 34 the firstborn said unto the y.,......... 6810
Ge 19:35 and the y. arose, and lay with him;..... 6810
Ge 19:38 And the y., she also bare a son, ... 6810
Ge 25:23 and the elder shall serve the y.. 6810
Ge 27:15 put them upon Jacob her y. son: 6996
Ge 27:42 sent and called Jacob her y. son, ... 6996
Ge 29:16 and the name of the y. was Rachel. 6996
Ge 29:18 years for Rachel the y. daughter. 6996
Ge 29:26 to give the y. before the firstborn. 6810
Ge 43:29 Is this your y. brother, of whom 6996
Ge 48:14 Ephraim's head, who was the y., ... 6810
Ge 48:19 his y. brother shall be greater 6996
Jg 1:13 Kenaz, Caleb's y. brother, took it: 6996
Jg 3:9 son of Kenaz, Caleb's y. brother. 6996
Jg 15:2 is not her y. sister fairer than she?...... 6996
1Sa 14:49 and the name of the y. Michal: 6996
1Ch 24:31 over against their y. brethren. 6996
Job 30:1 y. than I have me in derision,..... 6810,3117
Eze 16:46 thy y. sister, that dwelleth at thy......... 6996
Eze 16:61 thy sisters, thine elder and thy y.: 6996
Lu 15:12 **the y. of them said to his father,**... 3501
Lu 15:13 **the y. son gathered all together,**.... 3501
Lu 22:26 **among you, let him be as the y.;**... 3501
Ro 9:12 her, The elder shall serve the y......... 1640
1Ti 5:1 and the y. men as brethren;............... 3501
1Ti 5:2 the y. as sisters, with all purity. 3501
1Ti 5:11 But the y. widows refuse: for when.... 3501
1Ti 5:14 therefore that the y. women marry,..... 3501
1Pe 5:5 ye y., submit yourselves unto the 3501

YOUNGEST

Ge 42:13 the y. is this day with our father,....... 6996
Ge 42:15 your y. brother come hither............. 6996
Ge 42:20 bring your y. brother unto me;.......... 6996
Ge 42:32 the y. is this day with our father........ 6996
Ge 42:34 bring your y. brother unto me: 6996
Ge 43:33 and the y. according to his youth: 6810
Ge 44:2 cup, in the sack's mouth of the y., ... 6996
Ge 44:12 at the eldest, and left at the y.: 6996
Ge 44:23 Except your y. brother come down..... 6996
Ge 44:26 if our y. brother be with us, then........ 6996
Ge 44:26 except our y. brother be with us........ 6996
Jos 6:26 and in his y. son shall he set up......... 6810
Jg 9:5 the y. son of Jerubbaal was left;......... 3996
1Sa 16:11 said, There remaineth yet the y.,........ 3996
1Sa 17:14 And David was the y.: and the 3996
1Ki 16:34 gates thereof in his y. son Segub, ... 6810
2Ch 21:17 save Jehoahaz, the y. of his sons. 6996
2Ch 22:1 made Ahaziah his y. son king in......... 6996

YOUR See also YOURS; YOURSELVES.

Ge 3:5 thereof, then y. eyes shall be opened,.......
Ge 9:2 sea; into y. hand are they delivered.........
Ge 9:5 y. blood of y. lives will I require;............
Ge 9:9 with you, and with y. seed after you;........
Ge 17:11 circumcise the flesh of y. foreskin; ....
Ge 17:12 every man child in y. generations, he........
Ge 17:13 my covenant shall be in y. flesh for..........
Ge 18:4 you, be fetched, and wash y. feet,............
Ge 18:5 of bread, and comfort ye y. hearts; ....
Ge 18:5 therefore are ye come to y. servant. ....
Ge 19:2 I pray you, into y. servant's house, ...
Ge 19:2 and tarry all night, and wash y. feet,.........
Ge 19:2 rise up early, and go on y. ways...............
Ge 19:8 do ye to them as is good in y. eyes:.........
Ge 23:8 y. mind that I should bury my dead ....
Ge 31:5 I see y. father's countenance, that it........
Ge 31:6 my power I have served y. father. ....
Ge 31:7 And y. father hath deceived me, ...
Ge 31:9 taken away the cattle of y. father, ...
Ge 31:29 the God of y. father spake unto me ....
Ge 34:8 Shechem longeth for y. daughter: ....
Ge 34:9 give y. daughters unto us, and take ....
Ge 34:11 Let me find grace in y. eyes, and what .....
Ge 34:16 we will take y. daughters, and we ....
Ge 35:2 be clean, and change y. garments:............
Ge 37:7 y. sheaves stood round about, ...
Ge 42:15 except y. youngest brother come ....
Ge 42:16 of you, and let him fetch y. brother, ...
Ge 42:16 that y. words may be proved, whether......
Ge 42:19 true men, let one of y. brethren ....
Ge 42:19 bound in the house of y. prison:..............
Ge 42:19 corn for the famine of y. houses:..............
Ge 42:20 bring y. youngest brother unto me; ....
Ge 42:20 so shall y. words be verified, and ye.........
Ge 42:33 on of y. brethren here with me,................
Ge 42:33 food for the famine of y. households, ...
Ge 42:34 bring y. youngest brother unto me: ....
Ge 42:34 so will I deliver you y. brother, and..........
Ge 43:3,5 except y. brother be with you. ....
Ge 43:7 saying, Is y. father yet alive? ....
Ge 43:7 would say, Bring y. brother down? ....
Ge 43:11 best fruits in the land in y. vessels, ...
Ge 43:12 And take double money in y. hand;...........
Ge 43:12 again in the mouth of y. sacks, ...
Ge 43:12 carry it again in y. hand;.........................
Ge 43:13 Take also y. brother, and arise, go............
Ge 43:14 he may send away y. other brother, ...
Ge 43:23 y. God, and the God of y. father,.............
Ge 43:23 hath given you treasure in y. sacks:..........
Ge 43:23 I had y. money. And he brought ....
Ge 43:27 Is y. father well, the old man of whom......
Ge 43:29 Is this y. younger brother, of whom ....
Ge 44:10 let it be according unto y. words:.............
Ge 44:17 get you up in peace unto y. father............
Ge 44:23 Except y. youngest brother come...............
Ge 45:4 I am Joseph y. brother, whom ye sold.......
Ge 45:7 and to save y. lives by a great.................
Ge 45:12 y. eyes see, and the eyes of my brother ...
Ge 45:17 lade y. beasts, and go, get you unto.........

Ge 45:18 take **y.** father, and **y.** households,
Ge 45:19 the land of Egypt for **y.** little ones,
Ge 45:19 and for **y.** wives, and bring **y.** father,
Ge 45:20 Also regard not **y.** stuff; for the good
Ge 46:33 shall say, What is **y.** occupation?
Ge 47:3 his brethren, What is **y.** occupation?
Ge 47:16 And Joseph said, Give **y.** cattle;
Ge 47:16 I will give you for **y.** cattle, if money
Ge 47:23 I have bought you this day and **y.** land
Ge 47:24 and four parts shall be **y.** own, for seed
Ge 47:24 **y.** food, and for them of **y.** households,
Ge 47:24 and for food for **y.** little ones.
Ge 48:21 you again unto the land of **y.** fathers.
Ge 49:2 and hearken unto Israel **y.** father.
Ge 50:4 now I have found grace in **y.** eyes,
Ge 50:21 I will nourish you, and **y.** little ones.
Ex 3:13 God of **y.** fathers hath sent me unto
Ex 3:15, 16 the Lord God of **y.** fathers,
Ex 3:22 upon **y.** sons, and upon **y.** daughters;
Ex 5:4 works? get you unto **y.** burdens.
Ex 5:11 ought of **y.** work shall be diminished.
Ex 5:13 hasted them, saying, Fulfil **y.** works,
Ex 5:13 **y.** daily tasks, as when there was
Ex 5:14 have ye not fulfilled **y.** task
Ex 5:19 ought from **y.** bricks of **y.** daily task.
Ex 6:7 shall know that I am the Lord **y.** God,
Ex 8:25 Go ye, sacrifice to **y.** God in the land.
Ex 8:28 ye may sacrifice to the Lord **y.** God
Ex 10:8 unto them, Go, serve the Lord **y.** God:
Ex 10:10 I will let you go, and **y.** little ones:
Ex 10:16 have sinned against the Lord **y.** God,
Ex 10:17 and intreat the Lord **y.** God, that he
Ex 10:24 let **y.** flocks and **y.** herds be stayed:
Ex 10:24 let **y.** little ones also go with you.
Ex 12:4 to his eating shall make **y.** count
Ex 12:5 **Y.** lamb shall be without blemish,
Ex 12:11 **y.** loins girded, **y.** shoes on **y.** feet,
Ex 12:11 and **y.** staff in **y.** hand;
Ex 12:14 the Lord throughout **y.** generations;
Ex 12:15 put away leaven out of **y.** houses:
Ex 12:17 **y.** armies out of the land of Egypt:
Ex 12:17 ye observe this day in **y.** generations
Ex 12:19 there be no leaven found in **y.** houses:
Ex 12:20 in all **y.** habitations shall ye eat
Ex 12:21 you a lamb according to **y.** families,
Ex 12:23 destroyer to come in unto **y.** houses to
Ex 12:26 when **y.** children shall say unto you,
Ex 12:32 Also take **y.** flocks and **y.** herds,
Ex 14:14 for you, and ye shall hold **y.** peace.
Ex 16:7 he heareth **y.** murmurings against
Ex 16:8 **y.** murmurings which ye murmur
Ex 16:8 **y.** murmurings are not against us,
Ex 16:9 for he hath heard **y.** murmurings.
Ex 16:12 shall know that I am the Lord **y.** God.
Ex 16:16 to the number of **y.** persons;
Ex 16:32 of it to be kept for **y.** generations;
Ex 16:33 Lord, to be kept for **y.** generations.
Ex 19:15 the third day: come not at **y.** wives.
Ex 20:20 that his fear may be before **y.** faces,
Ex 22:24 and **y.** wives shall be widows,
Ex 22:24 and **y.** children fatherless.
Ex 23:21 he will not pardon **y.** transgressions:
Ex 23:25 And ye shall serve the Lord **y.** God,
Ex 23:31 inhabitants of the land unto **y.** hand;
Ex 29:42 offerings throughout **y.** generations
Ex 30:8 the Lord throughout **y.** generations.
Ex 30:10 upon it throughout **y.** generations:
Ex 30:15, 16 to make an atonement for **y.** souls.
Ex 30:31 unto me throughout **y.** generations.
Ex 31:13 and you throughout **y.** generations;
Ex 32:2 which are in the ears of **y.** wives,
Ex 32:2 of **y.** sons, and of **y.** daughters,
Ex 32:13 I will multiply **y.** seed as the stars of
Ex 32:13 spoken of will I give unto **y.** seed,
Ex 32:30 I shall make an atonement for **y.** sin.
Ex 34:23 all **y.** menchildren appear before the
Ex 35:3 no fire throught **y.** habitations
Le 1:2 ye shall bring **y.** offering of the cattle,
Le 3:17 a perpetual statute for **y.** generations
Le 3:17 throughout all **y.** dwellings, that ye
Le 6:18 a statute for ever in **y.** generations
Le 7:26 or of beast, in any of **y.** dwellings.
Le 7:32 of the sacrifices of **y.** peace offerings.
Le 8:33 until the days of **y.** consecration be
Le 10:4 carry **y.** brethren from before the
Le 10:6 his sons, Uncover not **y.** heads,
Le 10:6 neither rend **y.** clothes; lest ye die,
Le 10:6 but let **y.** brethren, the whole house
Le 10:9 for ever throughout **y.** generations:
Le 11:43 not make **y.** selves abominable? 5315
Le 11:44 For I am the Lord **y.** God: ye shall
Le 11:45 of the land of Egypt, to be **y.** God:
Le 14:34 a house of the land of **y.** possession;
Le 16:29 ye shall afflict **y.** souls, and do no
Le 16:29 whether it be one of **y.** own country,
Le 16:30 ye may be clean from all **y.** sins
Le 16:31 and ye shall afflict **y.** souls, by a
Le 17:11 to make an atonement for **y.** souls:
Le 17:15 whether it be one of **y.** own country,
Le 18:2 say unto them, I am the Lord **y.** God.
Le 18:4 walk therein: I am the Lord **y.** God.
Le 18:26 neither any of **y.** own nation, nor any
Le 18:30 I am the Lord **y.** God.
Le 26:28 chastise you seven times for **y.** sins.
Le 19:2 holy: for I the Lord **y.** God am holy.
Le 19:3 my sabbaths: I am the Lord **y.** God.
Le 19:4 molten gods: I am the Lord **y.** God.
Le 19:5 Lord, ye shall offer it at **y.** own will.
Le 19:9 when ye reap the harvest of **y.** land,
Le 19:10 and stranger: I am the Lord **y.** God.
Le 19:25 thereof: I am the Lord **y.** God.
Le 19:27 not round the corners of **y.** heads,
Le 19:28 not make any cuttings in **y.** flesh
Le 19:31 defiled by them: I am the Lord **y.** God.
Le 19:33 stranger sojourn with thee in **y.** land,
Le 19:34 land of Egypt: I am the Lord **y.** God.
Le 19:36 I am the Lord **y.** God, which brought
Le 20:7 be ye holy: for I am the Lord **y.** God.
Le 20:24 I am the Lord **y.** God, which have
Le 20:25 shall not make **y.** souls abominable
Le 22:3 of all **y.** seed among **y.** generations,
Le 22:19 Ye shall offer at **y.** own will a male
Le 22:24 make an offering thereof in **y.** land.
Le 22:25 offer the bread of **y.** God of any of
Le 22:29 unto the Lord, offer it at **y.** own will.
Le 22:33 of the land of Egypt, to be **y.** God:
Le 23:3 of the Lord in all **y.** dwellings.
Le 23:10 sheaf of the firstfruits of **y.** harvest
Le 23:14 brought an offering unto **y.** God:
Le 23:14 **y.** generations in all **y.** dwellings.
Le 23:17 Ye shall bring out of **y.** habitations
Le 23:21 statute for ever in all **y.** dwellings.
Le 23:21 throughout **y.** generations.
Le 23:22 when ye reap the harvest of **y.** land,
Le 23:22 the stranger: I am the Lord **y.** God.
Le 23:27 and ye shall afflict **y.** souls, and offer
Le 23:28 for you before the Lord **y.** God.
Le 23:31 **y.** generations in all **y.** dwellings.
Le 23:32 of rest, and ye shall afflict **y.** souls:
Le 23:32 even, shall ye celebrate **y.** sabbath.
Le 23:38 beside **y.** gifts, and beside all **y.** vows,
Le 23:38 and beside all **y.** freewill offerings,
Le 23:40 shall rejoice before the Lord **y.** God.
Le 23:41 a statute for ever in **y.** generations:
Le 23:43 That **y.** generations may know that I
Le 23:43 land of Egypt: I am the Lord **y.** God.
Le 24:3 a statute for ever in **y.** generations.
Le 24:22 as for one of **y.** own country:
Le 24:22 for I am the Lord **y.** God.
Le 25:9 sound throughout all **y.** land.
Le 25:17 thy God: for I am the Lord **y.** God.
Le 25:19 and ye shall eat **y.** fill, and dwell
Le 25:24 And in all the land of **y.** possession
Le 25:38 I am the Lord **y.** God, which brought
Le 25:38 the land of Canaan, and to be **y.** God.
Le 25:45 you, which they begat in **y.** land:
Le 25:45 and they shall be **y.** possession.
Le 25:46 inheritance for **y.** children after you,
Le 25:46 they shall be **y.** bondmen for ever:
Le 25:46 over **y.** brethren the children of Israel
Le 25:55 land of Egypt: I am the Lord **y.** God.
Le 26:1 set up any image of stone in **y.** land,
Le 26:1 unto it: for I am the Lord **y.** God.
Le 26:5 **y.** threshing shall reach unto the
Le 26:5 and ye shall eat **y.** bread to the full,
Le 26:5 to the full, and dwell in **y.** land safely.
Le 26:6 shall the sword go through **y.** land.
Le 26:7 And ye shall chase **y.** enemies, and
Le 26:8 and **y.** enemies shall fall before you
Le 26:12 walk among you, and will be **y.** God,
Le 26:13 I am the Lord **y.** God, which brought
Le 26:13 I have broken the bands of **y.** yoke,
Le 26:15 or if **y.** soul abhor my judgments, so
Le 26:16 and ye shall sow **y.** seed in vain,
Le 26:16 for **y.** enemies shall eat it.
Le 26:17 ye shall be slain before **y.** enemies:
Le 26:18 you seven times more for **y.** sins.
Le 26:19 I will break the pride of **y.** power;
Le 26:19 **y.** heaven…iron, and **y.** earth as brass:
Le 26:20 And **y.** strength shall be spent in vain:
Le 26:20 **y.** land shall not yield her increase,
Le 26:21 plagues upon you according to **y.** sins.
Le 26:22 of **y.** children, and destroy **y.** cattle,
Le 26:22 and **y.** high ways shall be desolate.
Le 26:24 you yet seven times for **y.** sins.
Le 26:25 are gathered together within **y.** cities,
Le 26:26 I have broken the staff of **y.** bread,
Le 26:26 ten women shall bake **y.** bread in one
Le 26:26 deliver you **y.** bread again by weight:
Le 26:29 And ye shall eat the flesh of **y.** sons,
Le 26:29 the flesh of **y.** daughters shall ye eat.
Le 26:30 I will destroy **y.** high places,
Le 26:30 and cut down **y.** images,
Le 26:30 cast **y.** carcases upon the carcases
Le 26:30 upon the carcases of **y.** idols,
Le 26:31 And I will make **y.** cities waste,
Le 26:31 bring **y.** sanctuaries unto desolation,
Le 26:31 smell the savour of **y.** sweet odours.
Le 26:32 and **y.** enemies which dwell therein.
Le 26:33 **y.** land shall be desolate, and **y.** cities
Le 26:34 and ye be in **y.** enemies' land;
Le 26:35 because it did not rest in **y.** sabbaths,
Le 26:37 no power to stand before **y.** enemies.
Le 26:38 land of **y.** enemies shall eat you up.
Le 26:39 in their iniquity in **y.** enemies' lands;
Nu 9:10 If any man of you or of **y.** posterity
Nu 10:8 for ever throughout **y.** generations.
Nu 10:9 And if ye go to war in **y.** land against
Nu 10:9 remembered before the Lord **y.** God,
Nu 10:9 ye shall be saved from **y.** enemies.
Nu 10:10 of **y.** gladness, and in **y.** solemn days,
Nu 10:10 and in the beginnings of **y.** months,
Nu 10:10 the trumpets over **y.** burnt offerings,
Nu 10:10 the sacrifices of **y.** peace offerings;
Nu 10:10 you for a memorial before **y.** God:
Nu 10:10 I am the Lord **y.** God.
Nu 11:20 until it come out at **y.** nostrils, and it
Nu 14:29 **Y.** carcases shall fall in this
Nu 14:29 you, according to **y.** whole number,
Nu 14:31 But **y.** little ones, which ye said
Nu 14:32 as for you, **y.** carcases, they shall
Nu 14:33 **y.** children shall wander in the
Nu 14:33 years; and bear **y.** whoredoms,
Nu 14:33 until **y.** carcases be wasted
Nu 14:34 shall ye bear **y.** iniquities, even forty
Nu 14:42 ye be not smitten before **y.** enemies.
Nu 15:2 come into the land of **y.** habitations,
Nu 15:3 offering, or in **y.** solemn feasts,
Nu 15:14 be among you in **y.** generations,
Nu 15:15 ordinance for ever in **y.** generations:
Nu 15:20 of **y.** dough for an heave offering:
Nu 15:21 Of the first of **y.** dough ye shall give
Nu 15:21 an heave offering in **y.** generations.
Nu 15:23 henceforward among **y.** generations;
Nu 15:39 after **y.** own heart and **y.** own eyes,
Nu 15:40 and be holy unto **y.** God.
Nu 15:41 I am the Lord **y.** God, which brought
Nu 15:41 to be **y.** God: I am the Lord **y.** God.
Nu 18:1 bear the iniquity of **y.** priesthood.
Nu 18:6 I have taken **y.** brethren the Levites
Nu 18:7 with thee shall keep **y.** priest's office
Nu 18:7 I have given **y.** priest's office unto
Nu 18:23 for ever throughout **y.** generations,
Nu 18:26 you from them for **y.** inheritance,
Nu 18:27 **y.** heave offering shall be reckoned
Nu 18:28 offering unto the Lord of all **y.** tithes,
Nu 18:29 Out of all **y.** gifts ye shall offer
Nu 18:31 every place, ye and **y.** households:
Nu 18:31 for it is **y.** reward for **y.** service in
Nu 22:13 get you into **y.** land: for the Lord
Nu 28:11 And in the beginning of **y.** months ye
Nu 28:26 unto the Lord, after **y.** weeks be out,
Nu 29:7 and ye shall afflict **y.** souls: ye shall
Nu 29:39 Lord in **y.** set feasts, beside **y.** vows,
Nu 29:39 **y.** freewill offerings, for **y.** burnt
Nu 29:39 **y.** meat offerings, and for **y.** drink
Nu 29:39 offerings, and for **y.** peace offerings.
Nu 31:19 both yourselves and **y.** captives.

Nu 31:20 And purify all **y.** raiment, and all
Nu 31:24 wash **y.** clothes on the seventh day,
Nu 32:6 Shall **y.** brethren go to war, and shall
Nu 32:8 Thus did **y.** fathers, when I sent
Nu 32:14 ye are risen up in **y.** fathers' stead,
Nu 32:22 and this land shall be **y.** possession
Nu 32:23 and be sure **y.** sin will find you out.
Nu 32:24 Build you cities for **y.** little ones,
Nu 32:24 and folds for **y.** sheep;
Nu 32:24 hath proceeded out of **y.** mouth.
Nu 33:54 for an inheritance among **y.** families:
Nu 33:54 to the tribes of **y.** fathers ye
Nu 33:55 in **y.** eyes, and thorns in **y.** sides,
Nu 34:3 Then **y.** south quarter shall be from
Nu 34:3 **y.** south border shall be the outmost
Nu 34:4 **y.** border shall turn from the south
Nu 34:6 border: this shall be **y.** west border.
Nu 34:7 And this shall be **y.** north border:
Nu 34:8 Hor ye shall point out **y.** border
Nu 34:9 this shall be **y.** north border.
Nu 34:10 ye shall point out **y.** east border from
Nu 34:12 this shall be **y.** land with the coasts
Nu 35:29 **y.** generations in all **y.** dwellings.
De 1:7 Turn you, and take **y.** journey, and go
De 1:8 the Lord sware unto **y.** fathers,
De 1:10 The Lord **y.** God hath multiplied you,
De 1:11 (The Lord God of **y.** fathers make you
De 1:12 I myself alone bear **y.** cumbrance,
De 1:12 and **y.** burden, and **y.** strife?
De 1:13 and known among **y.** tribes, and I
De 1:15 So I took the chief of **y.** tribes,
De 1:15 over tens, and officers among **y.** tribes.
De 1:16 and I charged **y.** judges at that time,
De 1:16 Hear the causes between **y.** brethren,
De 1:26 commandment of the Lord **y.** God:
De 1:27 And ye murmured in **y.** tents, and
De 1:30 Lord **y.** God which goeth before you,
De 1:30 did for you in Egypt before **y.** eyes;
De 1:32 ye did not believe the Lord **y.** God,
De 1:33 you out a place to pitch **y.** tents in,
De 1:34 the Lord heard the voice of **y.** words,
De 1:35 which I sware to give unto **y.** fathers,
De 1:37 was angry with me for **y.** sakes,
De 1:39 Moreover **y.** little ones, which ye said
De 1:39 **y.** children, which in that day had no
De 1:40 take **y.** journey into the wilderness
De 1:42 lest ye be smitten before **y.** enemies.
De 1:45 Lord would not hearken to **y.** voice,
De 2:4 pass through the coast of **y.** brethren
De 2:24 Rise ye up, take **y.** journey,
De 3:18 The Lord **y.** God hath given you this
De 3:18 pass over armed before **y.** brethren
De 3:19 But **y.** wives, and **y.** little ones,
De 3:19 and **y.** cattle, (for I know that ye have
De 3:19 shall abide in **y.** cities which I have
De 3:20 Lord have given rest unto **y.** brethren,
De 3:20 the Lord **y.** God hath given them
De 3:21 all that the Lord **y.** God hath done
De 3:22 Lord **y.** God he shall fight for you.
De 3:26 Lord was wroth with me for **y.** sakes,
De 4:1 Lord God of **y.** fathers giveth you.
De 4:2 commandments of the Lord **y.** God
De 4:3 **Y.** eyes have seen what the Lord did
De 4:4 that did cleave unto the Lord **y.** God
De 4:6 is **y.** wisdom and **y.** understanding
De 4:21 Lord was angry with me for **y.** sakes,
De 4:26 ye shall not prolong **y.** days upon it,
De 4:34 to all that the Lord **y.** God did
De 4:34 for you in Egypt before **y.** eyes?
De 5:1 which I speak in **y.** ears this day,
De 5:22 the Lord spake unto all **y.** assembly
De 5:23 even all the heads of **y.** tribes,
De 5:23 the heads of **y.** tribes, and **y.** elders;
De 5:28 the Lord heard the voice of **y.** words,
De 5:30 to them, Get you into **y.** tents again.
De 5:32 Lord **y.** God hath commanded you:
De 5:33 Lord **y.** God hath commanded you,
De 5:33 ye may prolong **y.** days in the land
De 6:1 the Lord **y.** God commanded to teach
De 6:16 Ye shall not tempt the Lord **y.** God,
De 6:17 commmandments of the Lord **y.** God,
De 7:8 which he had sworn unto **y.** fathers,
De 7:14 barren among you, or among **y.** cattle.
De 8:1 which the Lord sware unto **y.** fathers
De 8:20 the Lord destroyeth before **y.** face,
De 8:20 unto the voice of the Lord **y.** God.

De 9:16 sinned against the Lord **y.** God,
De 9:17 hands, and brake them before **y.** eyes.
De 9:18 of all **y.** sins which ye sinned,
De 9:21 And I took **y.** sin, the calf which ye
De 9:23 the commandment of the Lord **y.** God,
De 10:16 therefore the foreskin of **y.** heart,
De 10:17 For the Lord **y.** God is God of gods,
De 11:2 I speak not with **y.** children which
De 11:2 chastisement of the Lord **y.** God,
De 11:7 **y.** eyes have seen all the great acts
De 11:9 ye may prolong **y.** days in the land,
De 11:9 Lord sware unto **y.** fathers to give
De 11:13 this day, to love the Lord **y.** God,
De 11:13 with all **y.** heart and with all **y.** soul,
De 11:14 I will give you the rain of **y.** land
De 11:16 that **y.** heart be not deceived, and ye
De 11:18 my words in **y.** heart and in **y.** soul,
De 11:18 bind them for a sign upon **y.** hand,
De 11:18 may be as frontlets between **y.** eyes.
De 11:19 And ye shall teach them **y.** children,
De 11:21 That **y.** days may be multiplied,
De 11:21 and the days of **y.** children, in the
De 11:21 Lord sware unto **y.** fathers to give
De 11:22 to love the Lord **y.** God, to walk in all
De 11:24 the soles of **y.** feet shall tread shall be
De 11:24 the uttermost sea shall **y.** coast be.
De 11:25 the Lord **y.** God shall lay the fear of
De 11:27, 28 commandments of the Lord **y.** God,
De 11:31 which the Lord **y.** God giveth you,
De 12:4 shall not do so unto the Lord **y.** God.
De 12:5 **y.** God shall choose out of all **y.** tribes
De 12:6 **y.** burnt offerings, and **y.** sacrifices,
De 12:6 **y.** tithes, and heave offerings of **y.**
De 12:6 and **y.** vows, and **y.** freewill offerings,
De 12:6 firstlings of **y.** herds and of **y.** flocks,
De 12:7 ye shall eat before the Lord **y.** God,
De 12:7 rejoice in all that ye put **y.** hand unto,
De 12:7 ye and **y.** household, wherein the
De 12:9 which the Lord **y.** God giveth you.
De 12:10 which the Lord **y.** God giveth you
De 12:10 rest from all **y.** enemies round about,
De 12:11 which the Lord **y.** God shall choose
De 12:11 I command you; **y.** burnt offerings,
De 12:11 and **y.** sacrifices, **y.** tithes,
De 12:11 and the heave offering of **y.** hand,
De 12:11 and all **y.** choice vows which ye vow
De 12:12 shall rejoice before the Lord **y.** God,
De 12:12 ye, and **y.** sons, and **y.** daughters,
De 12:12 **y.** menservants, and **y.** maidservants,
De 12:12 the Levite that is within **y.** gates;
De 13:3 for the Lord **y.** God proveth you, to
De 13:3 whether ye love the Lord **y.** God,
De 13:3 with all **y.** heart and with all **y.** soul.
De 13:4 Ye shall walk after the Lord **y.** God,
De 13:5 turn you away from the Lord **y.** God,
De 14:1 are the children of the Lord **y.** God:
De 14:1 make any baldness between **y.** eyes
De 20:3 day unto battle against **y.** enemies:
De 20:3 let not **y.** hearts faint, fear not, and
De 20:4 **y.** God is he that goeth with you,
De 20:4 to fight for you against **y.** enemies,
De 20:18 should ye sin against the Lord **y.** God.
De 28:68 ye shall be sold unto **y.** enemies
De 29:2 did before **y.** eyes in the land of Egypt
De 29:5 **y.** clothes are not waxen old upon you,
De 29:6 know that I am the Lord **y.** God.
De 29:10 day all of you before the Lord **y.** God;
De 29:10 **y.** captains of **y.** tribes, **y.** elders,
De 29:10 **y.** officers, with all the men of Israel,
De 29:11 **Y.** little ones, **y.** wives, and thy
De 29:22 **y.** children that shall rise up after you,
De 30:18 not prolong **y.** days upon the land,
De 31:5 shall give them up before **y.** face,
De 31:12 may learn, and fear the Lord **y.** God,
De 31:13 and learn to fear the Lord **y.** God,
De 31:26 of the covenant of the Lord **y.** God,
De 31:28 elders of **y.** tribes, and **y.** officers,
De 31:29 anger through the work of **y.** hands.
De 32:17 up, whom **y.** fathers feared not.
De 32:38 and help you, and be **y.** protection.
De 32:46 Set **y.** hearts unto all the words
De 32:46 command **y.** children to observe
De 32:47 thing for you, because it is **y.** life:
De 32:47 shall prolong **y.** days in the land,
Jos 1:3 the sole of **y.** foot shall tread upon,
Jos 1:4 down of the sun, shall be **y.** coast.

Jos 1:11 Lord **y.** God giveth you to possess
Jos 1:13 The Lord **y.** God hath given you rest,
Jos 1:14 **Y.** wives, **y.** little ones, and **y.** cattle,
Jos 1:14 shall pass before **y.** brethren armed,
Jos 1:15 the Lord hath given **y.** brethren rest,
Jos 1:15 which the Lord **y.** God giveth them:
Jos 1:15 unto the land of **y.** possession,
Jos 2:9 and that **y.** terror is fallen upon us,
Jos 2:11 the Lord **y.** God, he is God in heaven
Jos 2:16 and afterward may ye go **y.** way.
Jos 2:21 According unto **y.** words, so be it
Jos 3:3 of the covenant of the Lord **y.** God,
Jos 3:3 then ye shall remove from **y.** place,
Jos 3:9 hear the words of the Lord **y.** God.
Jos 4:5 over before the ark of the Lord **y.** God
Jos 4:6 when **y.** children ask their fathers
Jos 4:21 **y.** children shall ask their fathers
Jos 4:22 Then ye shall let **y.** children know,
Jos 4:23 the Lord **y.** God dried up the waters
Jos 4:23 as the Lord **y.** God did to the Red sea,
Jos 4:24 that ye might fear the Lord **y.** God for
Jos 6:10 nor make any noise with **y.** voice,
Jos 6:10 any word proceed out of **y.** mouth,
Jos 7:14 be brought according to **y.** tribes:
Jos 8:7 **y.** God will deliver it unto **y.** hand.
Jos 9:11 say unto them, We are **y.** servants:
Jos 10:19 ye not, but pursue after **y.** enemies,
Jos 10:19 **y.** God...delivered them into **y.** hand
Jos 10:24 **y.** feet upon the necks of these kings.
Jos 10:25 shall the Lord do to all **y.** enemies
Jos 15:4 the sea: this shall be **y.** south coast.
Jos 18:3 Lord God of **y.** fathers hath given you?
Jos 20:3 shall be **y.** refuge from the avenger
Jos 22:3 Ye have not left **y.** brethren these
Jos 22:3 commandment of the Lord **y.** God.
Jos 22:4 the Lord **y.** God hath given rest
Jos 22:4 hath given rest unto **y.** brethren,
Jos 22:4 return ye, and get you unto **y.** tents,
Jos 22:4 and unto the land of **y.** possession,
Jos 22:5 to love the Lord **y.** God, and to walk
Jos 22:5 with all **y.** heart and with all **y.** soul.
Jos 22:8 with much riches unto **y.** tents,
Jos 22:8 spoil of **y.** enemies with **y.** brethren.
Jos 22:19 the land of **y.** possession be unclean,
Jos 22:24 time to come **y.** children might speak
Jos 22:25 **y.** children make our children cease
Jos 22:27 **y.** children may not say to our
Jos 23:3 all that the Lord **y.** God hath done
Jos 23:3 the Lord **y.** God is he that hath fought
Jos 23:4 to be an inheritance for **y.** tribes,
Jos 23:5 the Lord **y.** God, he shall expel them
Jos 23:5 and drive them from out of **y.** sight;
Jos 23:5 Lord **y.** God hath promised unto you.
Jos 23:8 But cleave unto the Lord **y.** God,
Jos 23:10 Lord **y.** God, he it is that fighteth for
Jos 23:11 heed therefore unto **y.** selves,
Jos 23:11 that ye love the Lord **y.** God.
Jos 23:13 Lord **y.** God will no more drive out
Jos 23:13 unto you, and scourges in **y.** sides,
Jos 23:13 and thorns in **y.** eyes, until ye perish
Jos 23:13 the Lord **y.** God hath given you.
Jos 23:14 in all **y.** hearts and in all **y.** souls,
Jos 23:14 things which the Lord **y.** God spake
Jos 23:15 the Lord **y.** God promised you;
Jos 23:15 the Lord **y.** God hath given you.
Jos 23:16 the covenant of the Lord **y.** God,
Jos 24:2 **Y.** fathers dwelt on the other side of
Jos 24:3 I took **y.** father Abraham from the
Jos 24:6 I brought **y.** fathers out of Egypt:
Jos 24:6 Egyptians pursued after **y.** fathers
Jos 24:7 **y.** eyes have seen what I have done in
Jos 24:8 and I gave them into **y.** hand,
Jos 24:11 and I delivered them into **y.** hand.
Jos 24:14, 15 the gods which **y.** fathers served
Jos 24:19 forgive **y.** transgressions nor **y.** sins.
Jos 24:23 incline **y.** heart unto the Lord God
Jos 24:27 unto you, lest ye deny **y.** God.
Jg 2:1 land which I sware unto **y.** fathers;
Jg 2:3 they shall be as thorns in **y.** sides,
Jg 3:28 **y.** enemies the Moabites into **y.** hand
Jg 6:10 said unto you, I am the Lord **y.** God;
Jg 7:15 delivered into **y.** hand the host of
Jg 8:3 delivered into **y.** hand the princes
Jg 8:7 I will tear **y.** flesh with the thorns
Jg 9:2 also that I am **y.** bone and **y.** flesh.
Jg 9:15 come and put **y.** trust in my shadow:

Jg 9:18 Shechem, because he is **y.** brother;)
Jg 10:14 you in the time of **y.** tribulation.
Jg 11:9 them before me, shall I be **y.** head?
Jg 18:6 the Lord is **y.** way wherein ye go.
Jg 18:10 for God hath given it into **y.** hands;
Jg 19:5 of bread, and afterward go **y.** way.
Jg 19:9 to morrow get you early on **y.** way,
Jg 19:30 take advice, and speak **y.** minds.
Jg 20:7 give here **y.** advice and counsel.
Ru 1:11 womb, that they may be **y.** husbands?
Ru 1:12 again, my daughters, go **y.** way;
Ru 1:13 for it grieveth me much for **y.** sakes
1Sa 2:3 not arrogancy come out of **y.** mouth:
1Sa 2:23 for I hear of **y.** evil dealings by all
1Sa 6:4 was on you all, and on **y.** lords.
1Sa 6:5 ye shall make images of **y.** emerods,
1Sa 6:5 images of **y.** mice that mar the land;
1Sa 6:5 from off **y.** gods, and from off **y.** land.
1Sa 6:6 then do ye harden **y.** hearts,
1Sa 7:3 unto the Lord with all **y.** hearts,
1Sa 7:3 and prepare **y.** hearts unto the Lord,
1Sa 8:11 He will take **y.** sons, and appoint
1Sa 8:13 **y.** daughters to be confectionaries,
1Sa 8:14 he will take **y.** fields, and **y.** vineyards,
1Sa 8:14 **y.** oliveyards, even the best of them,
1Sa 8:15 tenth of **y.** seed, and of **y.** vineyards,
1Sa 8:16 **y.** menservants, and **y.** maidservants,
1Sa 8:16 **y.** goodliest young men, and **y.** asses,
1Sa 8:17 He will take the tenth of **y.** sheep:
1Sa 8:18 cry out in that day because of **y.** king
1Sa 10:19 And ye have this day rejected **y.** God,
1Sa 10:19 all **y.** adversities and **y.** tribulations;
1Sa 10:19 by **y.** tribes, and by **y.** thousands.
1Sa 11:2 that I may thrust out all **y.** right eyes,
1Sa 12:1 I have hearkened unto **y.** voice
1Sa 12:6 brought **y.** fathers up out of the land.
1Sa 12:7 which he did to you and to **y.** fathers.
1Sa 12:8 and **y.** fathers cried unto the Lord,
1Sa 12:8 brought forth **y.** fathers out of Egypt,
1Sa 12:11 you out of the hand of **y.** enemies
1Sa 12:12 when the Lord **y.** God was **y.** king.
1Sa 12:14 continue following the Lord **y.** God:
1Sa 12:15 you, as it was against **y.** fathers.
1Sa 12:16 which the Lord will do before **y.** eyes.
1Sa 12:17 and see that **y.** wickedness is great,
1Sa 12:20 but serve the Lord with all **y.** heart;
1Sa 12:24 serve him in truth with all **y.** heart:
1Sa 12:25 be consumed, both ye and **y.** king.
1Sa 17:8 ye come out to set **y.** battle in array?
1Sa 17:9 kill me, then will we be **y.** servants:
1Sa 26:16 because ye have not kept **y.** master,
2Sa 1:24 on ornaments of gold upon **y.** apparel.
2Sa 2:5 shewed this kindness unto **y.** lord,
2Sa 2:7 now let **y.** hands be strengthened,
2Sa 2:7 for **y.** master Saul is dead, and also
2Sa 3:31 Rend **y.** clothes, and gird you with
2Sa 4:11 require his blood of **y.** hand, and take
2Sa 10:5 at Jericho until **y.** beards be grown,
2Sa 15:27 in peace, and **y.** two sons with you,
1Ki 1:33 take with you the servants of **y.** lord,
1Ki 8:61 Let **y.** heart therefore be perfect with
1Ki 9:6 from following me, ye or **y.** children,
1Ki 11:2 turn away **y.** heart after their gods:
1Ki 12:11 a heavy yoke, I will add to **y.** yoke:
1Ki 12:14 My father made **y.** yoke heavy, and I
1Ki 12:14 and I will add to **y.** yoke: my father
1Ki 12:16 to **y.** tents, O Israel: now see to thine
1Ki 12:24 nor fight against **y.** brethren the
1Ki 18:24 And call ye on the name of **y.** gods,
1Ki 18:25 call on the name of **y.** gods, but put
2Ki 2:3,5 Yea, I know it; hold ye **y.** peace.
2Ki 3:17 both ye, and **y.** cattle, and **y.** beasts.
2Ki 3:18 deliver the Moabites...into **y.** hand.
2Ki 9:15 If it be **y.** minds, then let none go
2Ki 10:2 seeing **y.** master's sons are with you,
2Ki 10:3 best and meetest of **y.** master's sons,
2Ki 10:3 throne, and fight for **y.** master's house.
2Ki 10:6 heads of the men **y.** master's sons,
2Ki 10:24 I have brought into **y.** hands escape,
2Ki 12:7 no more money of **y.** acquaintance,
2Ki 17:13 Turn ye from **y.** evil ways, and keep
2Ki 17:13 law which I commanded **y.** fathers,
2Ki 17:39 But the Lord **y.** God ye shall fear;
2Ki 17:39 you out of the hand of all **y.** enemies.
2Ki 18:32 you away to a land like **y.** own land,
2Ki 19:6 Thus shall ye say to **y.** master, Thus
2Ki 23:21 the passover unto the Lord **y.** God,
1Ch 15:12 yourselves, both ye and **y.** brethren,
1Ch 16:18 of Canaan, the lot of **y.** inheritance;
1Ch 19:5 at Jericho until **y.** beards be grown,
1Ch 22:18 Is not the Lord **y.** God with you? and
1Ch 22:19 Now set **y.** heart and **y.** soul to
1Ch 22:19 seek the Lord **y.** God; arise
1Ch 28:8 commandments of the Lord **y.** God:
1Ch 28:8 inheritance for **y.** children after you
1Ch 29:20 Now bless the Lord **y.** God. And all
2Ch 10:11 upon you, I will put more to **y.** yoke:
2Ch 10:14 My father made **y.** yoke heavy, but I
2Ch 10:16 every man to **y.** tents, O Israel: and
2Ch 11:4 go up, nor fight against **y.** brethren:
2Ch 13:12 against the Lord God of **y.** fathers;
2Ch 15:7 and let not **y.** hands be weak:
2Ch 15:7 for **y.** work shall be rewarded.
2Ch 18:14 they shall be delivered into **y.** hand.
2Ch 19:10 **y.** brethren that dwell in their cities,
2Ch 19:10 come upon you, and upon **y.** brethren:
2Ch 20:20 Believe in the Lord **y.** God, so shall
2Ch 24:5 repair the house of **y.** God from year
2Ch 28:9 the Lord God of **y.** fathers was wroth
2Ch 28:9 he hath delivered them into **y.** hand,
2Ch 28:10 you, sins against the Lord **y.** God?
2Ch 28:11 ye have taken captive of **y.** brethren:
2Ch 29:5 house of the Lord God of **y.** fathers,
2Ch 29:8 and to hissing, as ye see with **y.** eyes.
2Ch 30:7 like **y.** fathers, and like **y.** brethren,
2Ch 30:8 not stiffnecked, as **y.** fathers were,
2Ch 30:8 and serve the Lord **y.** God, that the
2Ch 30:9 **y.** brethren and **y.** children shall find
2Ch 30:9 the Lord **y.** God is gracious and
2Ch 32:14 **y.** God should be able to deliver you
2Ch 32:15 much less shall **y.** God deliver you.
2Ch 33:8 which I have appointed for **y.** fathers;
2Ch 35:3 not be a burden upon **y.** shoulders:
2Ch 35:3 serve now the Lord **y.** God, and his
2Ch 35:4 by the houses of **y.** fathers,
2Ch 35:4 after **y.** courses, according to the
2Ch 35:5 families of the fathers of **y.** brethren
2Ch 35:6 and prepare **y.** brethren, that they
Ezr 4:2 for we seek **y.** God, as ye do; and we
Ezr 6:6 **y.** companions the Apharsachites,
Ezr 7:17 altar of the house of **y.** God which is
Ezr 7:18 gold, that do after the will of **y.** God.
Ezr 8:28 unto the Lord God of **y.** fathers.
Ezr 9:12 not **y.** daughters unto their sons,
Ezr 9:12 take their daughters unto **y.** sons,
Ezr 9:12 an inheritance to **y.** children for ever.
Ezr 10:11 unto the Lord God of **y.** fathers,
Ne 4:14 and fight for **y.** brethren, **y.** sons, and
Ne 4:14 **y.** daughters, **y.** wives, and **y.** houses.
Ne 5:8 and will ye even sell **y.** brethren?
Ne 8:9 day is holy unto the Lord **y.** God;
Ne 8:10 Go **y.** way, eat the fat, and drink the
Ne 8:10 for the joy of the Lord is **y.** strength.
Ne 8:11 Hold **y.** peace, for the day is holy;
Ne 9:5 bless the Lord **y.** God for ever and
Ne 13:18 Did not **y.** fathers thus, and did not
Ne 13:25 give **y.** daughters unto their sons,
Ne 13:25 take their daughters unto **y.** sons,
Job 6:22 a reward for me of **y.** substance?
Job 6:25 but what doth **y.** arguing reprove?
Job 6:27 and ye dig a pit for **y.** friend.
Job 13:5 ye would altogether hold **y.** peace!
Job 13:5 and it should be **y.** wisdom.
Job 13:12 **Y.** remembrances are like unto
Job 13:12 ashes, **y.** bodies to bodies of clay.
Job 13:13 Hold **y.** peace, let me alone, that I
Job 13:17 and my declaration with **y.** ears.
Job 16:4 if **y.** souls were in my soul's stead,
Job 16:5 of my lips should asswage **y.** grief.
Job 18:3 beasts, and reputed vile in **y.** sight?
Job 21:2 and let this be **y.** consolations.
Job 21:5 and lay **y.** hand upon **y.** mouth.
Job 21:27 I know **y.** thoughts, and the devices
Job 21:34 seeing in **y.** answers there remaineth
Job 32:11 Behold, I waited for **y.** words;
Job 32:11 I gave ear to **y.** reasons, whilst ye
Job 32:14 will I answer him with **y.** speeches.
Job 42:8 lest I deal with you after **y.** folly,
Ps 4:4 with **y.** own heart upon **y.** bed,
Ps 4:5 and put **y.** trust in the Lord.
Ps 11:1 Flee as a bird to **y.** mountain?
Ps 22:26 seek him: **y.** heart shall live for ever.
Ps 24:7 Lift up **y.** heads, O ye gates; and be
Ps 24:9 Lift up **y.** heads, O ye gates; even lift
Ps 31:24 he shall strengthen **y.** heart, all ye
Ps 47:1 O clap **y.** hands, all ye people;
Ps 58:2 the violence of **y.** hands in the earth.
Ps 58:9 Before **y.** pots can feel the thorns,
Ps 62:8 people, pour out **y.** heart before him:
Ps 62:10 increase, set not **y.** heart upon them.
Ps 69:32 **y.** heart shall live that seek God.
Ps 75:5 Lift not up **y.** horn on high: speak
Ps 76:11 Vow, and pay unto the Lord **y.** God:
Ps 78:1 incline **y.** ears to the words of my
Ps 95:8 Harden not **y.** heart, as in the
Ps 95:9 When **y.** fathers tempted me, proved
Ps 105:11 of Canaan, the lot of **y.** inheritance:
Ps 115:14 more and more, you and **y.** children.
Ps 134:2 Lift up **y.** hands in the sanctuary,
Ps 146:3 Put not **y.** trust in princes, nor in
Pr 1:26 I also will laugh at **y.** calamity;
Pr 1:26 I will mock when **y.** fear cometh;
Pr 1:27 When **y.** fear cometh as desolation,
Pr 1:27 **y.** destruction cometh as a whirlwind;
Isa 1:7 **Y.** country is desolate, **y.** cities are
Isa 1:7 **y.** land, strangers devour it in **y.**
Isa 1:11 is the multitude of **y.** sacrifices
Isa 1:12 who hath required this at **y.** hand,
Isa 1:14 **Y.** new moons and **y.** appointed feasts
Isa 1:15 And when ye spread forth **y.** hands,
Isa 1:15 not hear: **y.** hands are full of blood.
Isa 1:16 put away the evil of **y.** doings from
Isa 1:18 though **y.** sins be as scarlet, they
Isa 3:14 the spoil of the poor is in **y.** houses.
Isa 8:13 be **y.** fear, and let him be **y.** dread.
Isa 10:3 and where will ye leave **y.** glory?
Isa 23:7 Is this **y.** joyous city, whose antiquity
Isa 23:14 for **y.** strength is laid waste.
Isa 28:18 **y.** covenant with death shall be
Isa 28:18 **y.** agreement with hell shall not stand;
Isa 28:22 lest **y.** bands be made strong:
Isa 29:10 deep sleep, and hath closed **y.** eyes:
Isa 29:10 the prophets and **y.** rulers, the seers
Isa 29:16 Surely **y.** turning of things upside
Isa 30:3 the strength of Pharaoh be **y.** shame,
Isa 30:3 in the shadow of Egypt **y.** confusion.
Isa 30:15 in confidence shall be **y.** strength:
Isa 31:7 which **y.** own hands have made unto
Isa 32:11 and gird sackcloth upon **y.** loins.
Isa 33:4 **y.** spoil shall be gathered like the
Isa 33:11 **y.** breath, as fire, shall devour you.
Isa 35:4 **y.** God will come with vengeance,
Isa 36:17 you away to a land like **y.** own land,
Isa 37:6 Thus shall ye say unto **y.** master,
Isa 40:1 comfort ye my people, saith **y.** God.
Isa 40:9 the cities of Judah, Behold **y.** God!
Isa 40:26 Lift up **y.** eyes on high, and behold
Isa 41:21 Produce **y.** cause, saith the Lord;
Isa 41:21 bring forth **y.** strong reasons, saith
Isa 41:24 of nothing, and **y.** work of nought:
Isa 41:26 there is none that heareth **y.** words.
Isa 43:14 Thus saith the Lord, **y.** redeemer,
Isa 43:14 For **y.** sake I have sent to Babylon,
Isa 43:15 I am the Lord, **y.** Holy One,
Isa 43:15 the creator of Israel, **y.** King.
Isa 46:1 **y.** carriages were heavy laden; they
Isa 46:4 And even to **y.** old age I am he;
Isa 50:1 the bill of **y.** mother's divorcement,
Isa 50:1 **y.** iniquities have ye sold yourselves,
Isa 50:1 for **y.** transgressions is **y.** mother put
Isa 50:11 walk in the light of **y.** fire, and in
Isa 51:2 Look unto Abraham **y.** father, and
Isa 51:6 Life us **y.** eyes to the heavens, and
Isa 52:12 the God of Israel with be **y.** rereward.
Isa 55:2 **y.** labour for that which satisfieth not?
Isa 55:2 let **y.** soul delight itself in fatness.
Isa 55:3 Incline **y.** ear, and come unto me:
Isa 55:3 hear, and **y.** soul shall live; and I
Isa 55:8 For my thoughts are not **y.** thoughts,
Isa 55:8 neither are **y.** ways my ways, saith
Isa 55:9 so are my ways higher than **y.** ways,
Isa 55:9 and my thoughts than **y.** thoughts.
Isa 58:3 in the day of **y.** fast ye find pleasure,
Isa 58:3 and exact all **y.** labours.
Isa 58:4 to make **y.** voice to be heard on high.
Isa 59:2 But **y.** iniquities have separated
Isa 59:2 **y.** God and **y.** sins have hid his face
Isa 59:3 For **y.** hands are defiled with blood,

Isa 59:3 and **y.** fingers with iniquity;
Isa 59:3 **y.** lips have spoken lies,
Isa 59:3 **y.** tongue hath muttered perverseness.
Isa 16:5 shall stand and feed **y.** flocks,
Isa 16:5 be **y.** plowmen and **y.** vinedressers.
Isa 16:7 For **y.** shame ye shall have double;
Isa 65:7 **Y.** iniquities, and the iniquities of
Isa 65:7 iniquities of **y.** fathers together,
Isa 65:15 ye shall leave **y.** name for a curse
Isa 66:5 **Y.** brethren that hated you, that cast
Isa 66:5 but he shall appear to **y.** joy, and
Isa 66:14 ye see this, **y.** heart shall rejoice,
Isa 66:14 **y.** bones shall flourish like an herb:
Isa 66:20 And they shall bring all **y.** brethren
Isa 66:22 so shall **y.** seed and **y.** name remain.
Jer 2:5 What iniquity...**y.** fathers found in me,
Jer 2:9 with **y.** children's children will I
Jer 2:30 In vain have I smitten **y.** children;
Jer 2:30 **y.** own sword...devoured **y.** prophets,
Jer 3:18 for an inheritance unto **y.** fathers.
Jer 3:22 and I will heal **y.** backslidings.
Jer 4:3 Break up **y.** fallow ground, and sow
Jer 4:4 take away the foreskins of **y.** heart,
Jer 4:4 it, because of the evil of **y.** doings.
Jer 5:19 and served strange gods in **y.** land,
Jer 5:25 **Y.** iniquities have turned away these
Jer 5:25 **y.** sins have withholden good things
Jer 6:16 and ye shall find rest for **y.** souls.
Jer 6:20 **y.** burnt offerings are not acceptable,
Jer 6:20 nor **y.** sacrifices sweet unto me,
Jer 7:3 Amend **y.** ways and **y.** doings, and I
Jer 7:5 amend **y.** ways and **y.** doings; if ye
Jer 7:6 walk after other gods to **y.** hurt:
Jer 7:7 in the land that I gave to **y.** fathers,
Jer 7:11 become a den of robbers in **y.** eyes?
Jer 7:14 which I gave to you and to **y.** fathers,
Jer 7:15 as I have cast out all **y.** brethren,
Jer 7:21 **y.** burnt offerings unto **y.** sacrifices,
Jer 7:22 For I spake not unto **y.** fathers,
Jer 7:23 Obey my voice, and I will be **y.** God,
Jer 7:25 Since the day that **y.** fathers came
Jer 9:20 let **y.** ear receive the word at his
Jer 9:20 and teach **y.** daughters wailing, and
Jer 11:4 I commanded **y.** fathers in the day
Jer 11:4 be my people, and I will be **y.** God:
Jer 11:5 which I have sworn unto **y.** fathers,
Jer 11:7 I earnestly protested unto **y.** fathers
Jer 12:13 they shall be ashamed of **y.** revenues
Jer 13:16 Give glory to the Lord **y.** God, before
Jer 13:16 before **y.** feet stumble upon the dark
Jer 13:17 weep in secret places for **y.** pride;
Jer 13:18 for **y.** principalities shall come down,
Jer 13:18 even the crown of **y.** glory.
Jer 13:20 Lift up **y.** eyes, and behold them that
Jer 16:9 this place in **y.** eyes, and in **y.** days,
Jer 16:11 Because **y.** fathers have forsaken me,
Jer 16:12 have done worse than **y.** fathers;
Jer 16:13 know not, neither ye nor **y.** fathers;
Jer 17:1 and upon the horns of **y.** altars;
Jer 17:22 carry forth a burden out of **y.** houses
Jer 17:22 day, as I commanded **y.** fathers.
Jer 18:11 and make **y.** ways and **y.** doings good.
Jer 21:4 weapons of war that are in **y.** hands,
Jer 21:12 it, because of the evil of **y.** doings.
Jer 21:14 according to the fruit of **y.** doings,
Jer 23:2 visit upon you the evil of **y.** doings,
Jer 23:39 city that I gave you and **y.** fathers,
Jer 25:4 hearkened, nor inclined **y.** ear to hear.
Jer 25:5 evil way, and the evil of **y.** doings,
Jer 25:5 unto you and to **y.** fathers for ever
Jer 25:6 to anger with the works of **y.** hands;
Jer 25:7 the works of **y.** hands to **y.** own hurt
Jer 25:34 for the days of **y.** slaughter and
Jer 25:34 of **y.** dispersions are accomplished;
Jer 26:11 city, as ye have heard with **y.** ears.
Jer 26:13 now amend **y.** ways and **y.** doings,
Jer 26:13 obey the voice of the Lord **y.** God;
Jer 26:14 As for me, behold, I am in **y.** hand:
Jer 26:15 to speak all these things in **y.** ears.
Jer 27:4 Thus shall ye say unto **y.** masters;
Jer 27:9 hearken not ye to **y.** prophets,
Jer 27:9 to **y.** diviners, nor to **y.** dreamers,
Jer 27:9 to **y.** enchanters, nor to **y.** sorcerers,
Jer 27:10 to remove you far from **y.** land;
Jer 27:12 Bring **y.** necks under the yoke of the
Jer 27:16 not to the words of **y.** prophets that
Jer 29:6 and take wives for **y.** sons,
Jer 29:6 and give **y.** daughters to husbands,
Jer 29:8 Let not **y.** prophets and **y.** diviners
Jer 29:8 hearken to **y.** dreams which ye
Jer 29:13 shall search for me with all **y.** heart.
Jer 29:14 and I will turn away **y.** captivity, and
Jer 29:16 **y.** brethren that are not gone forth
Jer 29:21 and he shall slay them before **y.** eyes,
Jer 30:22 be my people, and I will be **y.** God.
Jer 34:13 I made a covenant with **y.** fathers in
Jer 34:14 **y.** fathers hearkened not unto me,
Jer 35:6 wine, neither ye, nor **y.** sons for ever:
Jer 35:7 but all **y.** days ye shall dwell in tents;
Jer 35:15 amend **y.** doings, and go not after
Jer 35:15 I have given to you and to **y.** fathers:
Jer 35:15 but ye have not inclined **y.** ear, nor
Jer 35:18 commandment of Jonadab **y.** father,
Jer 37:19 now **y.** prophets which prophesied
Jer 38:5 king said, Behold, he is in **y.** hand:
Jer 40:10 and oil, and put them in **y.** vessels,
Jer 40:10 and dwell in **y.** cities that ye have
Jer 42:4 I will pray unto the Lord **y.** God
Jer 42:4 according to **y.** words; and it shall
Jer 42:9 present **y.** supplication before him;
Jer 42:12 cause you to return to **y.** own land.
Jer 42:13 obey the voice of the Lord **y.** God,
Jer 42:14 If ye wholly set **y.** faces to enter into
Jer 42:20 ye dissembled in **y.** hearts, when ye
Jer 42:20 ye sent me unto the Lord **y.** God,
Jer 42:21 obeyed the voice of the Lord **y.** God,
Jer 44:3 not, neither they, ye, nor **y.** fathers.
Jer 44:7 ye this great evil against **y.** souls,
Jer 44:8 wrath with the works of **y.** hands,
Jer 44:9 forgotten the wickedness of **y.** fathers,
Jer 44:9 of their wives, and **y.** own wickedness,
Jer 44:9 and the wickedness of **y.** wives,
Jer 44:10 I set before you and before **y.** fathers.
Jer 44:21 **y.** fathers, **y.** kings, and **y.** princes,
Jer 44:22 because of the evil of **y.** doings, and
Jer 44:22 therefore is **y.** land a desolation, and
Jer 44:25 Ye and **y.** wives have both spoken
Jer 44:25 **y.** mouths, and fulfilled with **y.** hand,
Jer 44:25 ye will surely accomplish **y.** vows,
Jer 44:25 and surely perform **y.** vows.
Jer 46:4 and stand forth with **y.** helmets;
Jer 48:6 Flee, save **y.** lives, and be like the
Jer 50:12 **Y.** mother shall be sore confounded;
Jer 51:24 they have done in Zion in **y.** sight,
Jer 51:46 And lest **y.** heart faint, and ye fear
Jer 51:50 and let Jerusalem come into **y.** mind.
Eze 5:16 you, and will break **y.** staff of bread:
Eze 6:3 you, and I will destroy **y.** high places.
Eze 6:4 And **y.** altars shall be desolate,
Eze 6:4 and **y.** images shall be broken: and I
Eze 6:4 down **y.** slain men before **y.** idols.
Eze 6:5 **y.** bones round about **y.** altars.
Eze 6:6 In all **y.** dwellingplaces the cities
Eze 6:6 that **y.** altars may be laid waste and
Eze 6:6 **y.** idols may be broken and cease,
Eze 6:6 and **y.** images may be cut down,
Eze 6:6 and **y.** works may be abolished.
Eze 9:5 let not **y.** eye spare, neither have ye
Eze 11:5 the things that come into **y.** mind,
Eze 11:6 have multiplied **y.** slain in this city,
Eze 11:7 **Y.** slain whom ye have laid in the
Eze 11:11 This city shall not be **y.** caldron,
Eze 12:11 Say, I am **y.** sign: like as I have done,
Eze 12:25 for in **y.** days, O rebellious house, will
Eze 13:19 by **y.** lying to my people that hear
Eze 13:19 to my people that hear **y.** lies?
Eze 13:20 Behold, I am against **y.** pillows,
Eze 13:20 and I will tear them from **y.** arms,
Eze 13:21 **Y.** kerchiefs also will I tear, and
Eze 13:21 and deliver my people out of **y.** hand,
Eze 13:21 be no more in **y.** hand to be hunted;
Eze 13:23 will deliver my people out of **y.** hand:
Eze 14:6 and turn yourselves from **y.** idols;
Eze 14:6 **y.** faces from all **y.** abominations.
Eze 16:45 **y.** mother was an Hittite,
Eze 16:45 and **y.** father an Amorite.
Eze 16:55 shall return to **y.** former estate.
Eze 18:25 way equal? are not **y.** ways unequal?
Eze 18:29 ways equal? are not **y.** ways unequal?
Eze 18:30 yourselves from all **y.** transgressions;
Eze 18:30 so iniquity shall not be **y.** ruin.
Eze 18:31 away from you all **y.** transgressions,
Eze 20:5 them, saying, I am the Lord **y.** God;
Eze 20:7 idols of Egypt: I am the Lord **y.** God.
Eze 20:18 ye not in the statutes of **y.** fathers,
Eze 20:19 I am the Lord **y.** God; walk in my
Eze 20:20 may know that I am the Lord **y.** God.
Eze 20:27 in this **y.** fathers have blasphemed
Eze 20:30 after the manner of **y.** fathers?
Eze 20:31 For when ye offer **y.** gifts, when ye
Eze 20:31 make **y.** sons to pass through the fire,
Eze 20:31 pollute yourselves with all **y.** idols,
Eze 20:32 And that which cometh into **y.** mind
Eze 20:36 Like as I pleaded with **y.** fathers
Eze 20:39 more with **y.** gifts, and with **y.** idols.
Eze 20:40 and there will I require **y.** offerings,
Eze 20:40 **y.** oblations, with all **y.** holy things.
Eze 20:41 will accept you with **y.** sweet savour,
Eze 20:42 up mine hand to give it to **y.** fathers.
Eze 20:43 And there shall ye remember **y.** ways,
Eze 20:43 and all **y.** doings, wherein ye have
Eze 20:43 shall lothe yourselves in **y.** own sight
Eze 20:43 all **y.** evils that ye have committed.
Eze 20:44 not according to **y.** wicked ways,
Eze 20:44 nor according to **y.** corrupt doings,
Eze 21:24 made **y.** iniquity to be remembered,
Eze 21:24 that **y.** transgressions are discovered,
Eze 21:24 that in all **y.** doings **y.** sins do appear;
Eze 23:48 be taught ot to do after **y.** lewdness.
Eze 23:49 they shall recompense **y.** lewdness
Eze 23:49 and ye shall bear the sins of **y.** idols:
Eze 24:21 of **y.** strength, the desire of **y.** eyes,
Eze 24:21 and that which **y.** soul pitieth;
Eze 24:21 and **y.** sons and **y.** daughters whom
Eze 24:22 ye shall not cover **y.** lips, nor eat the
Eze 24:23 And **y.** tires shall be upon **y.** heads,
Eze 24:23 and **y.** shoes upon **y.** feet: ye shall
Eze 24:23 ye shall pine away for **y.** iniquities,
Eze 33:11 turn ye from **y.** evil ways; for why will
Eze 33:25 and lift up **y.** eyes toward **y.** idols, and
Eze 33:26 Ye stand upon **y.** sword, ye work
Eze 34:18 with **y.** feet the residue of **y.** pastures?
Eze 34:18 ye must foul the residue with **y.** feet?
Eze 34:19 which ye have trodden with **y.** feet;
Eze 34:19 which ye have fouled with **y.** feet.
Eze 34:21 pushed all the diseased with **y.** horns,
Eze 34:31 men, and I am **y.** God, saith the Lord
Eze 35:13 Thus with **y.** mouth ye have boasted
Eze 35:13 have multiplied **y.** words against me:
Eze 36:8 ye shall shoot forth **y.** branches,
Eze 36:8 yield **y.** fruit to my people of Israel;
Eze 36:11 I will settle you after **y.** old estates,
Eze 36:11 unto you than at **y.** beginnings:
Eze 36:22 I do not this for **y.** sakes, O house of
Eze 36:24 and will bring you into **y.** own land.
Eze 36:25 all **y.** filthiness, and from all **y.** idols,
Eze 36:26 away the stony heart out of **y.** flesh,
Eze 36:28 in the land that I gave to **y.** fathers;
Eze 36:28 be my people, and I will be **y.** God.
Eze 36:29 save you from all **y.** uncleannesses:
Eze 36:31 shall ye remember **y.** own evil ways,
Eze 36:31 and **y.** doings that were not good,
Eze 36:31 lothe yourselves in **y.** own sight for
Eze 36:31 **y.** iniquities and for **y.** abominations.
Eze 36:32 Not for **y.** sakes do I this, saith the
Eze 36:32 and confounded for **y.** own ways,
Eze 36:33 cleansed you from all **y.** iniquities
Eze 37:12 O my people, I will open **y.** graves,
Eze 37:12 cause you to come up out of **y.** graves,
Eze 37:13 when I have opened **y.** graves, O my
Eze 37:13 and brought you up out of **y.** graves,
Eze 37:14 and I shall place you in **y.** own land:
Eze 37:25 wherein **y.** fathers have dwelt;
Eze 43:27 **y.** burnt offerings upon the altar,
Eze 43:27 and **y.** peace offerings; and I will
Eze 44:6 it suffice you of all **y.** abominations,
Eze 44:7 because of all **y.** abominations.
Eze 44:30 every sort of **y.** oblations, shall be
Eze 44:30 unto the priest the first of **y.** dough,
Eze 45:9 away **y.** exactions from my people,
Eze 45:12 fifteen shekels, shall be **y.** maneh.
Eze 47:14 mine hand to give it unto **y.** fathers:
Da 1:10 hath appointed **y.** meat and **y.** drink:
Da 1:10 for why should he see **y.** faces worse
Da 1:10 the children which are of **y.** sort?
Da 2:5 **y.** houses shall be made a dunghill.
Da 2:47 it is, that **y.** God is a God of gods,
Da 10:21 in these things, but Michael **y.** prince.

Ho	1:9	my people, and I will not be **y.** God.........	
Ho	2:1	Say ye unto **y.** brethren, Ammi;...............	
Ho	2:1	and to **y.** sisters, Ruhamah..................	
Ho	2:2	Plead with **y.** mother, plead: for she.........	
Ho	4:13	**y.** daughters shall commit..................	
Ho	4:13	**y.** spouses shall commit adultery.............	
Ho	4:14	I will not punish **y.** daughters when..........	
Ho	4:14	nor **y.** spouses when they commit.............	
Ho	5:13	heal you, nor cure you of **y.** wound..........	
Ho	6:4	**y.** goodness is as a morning cloud,...........	
Ho	9:10	I saw **y.** fathers as the firstripe in the.......	
Ho	10:12	in mercy, break up **y.** fallow ground:.........	
Ho	10:15	you because of **y.** great wickedness:.........	
Joe	1:2	the land. Hath this been in **y.** days,..........	
Joe	1:2	or even in the days of **y.** fathers?............	
Joe	1:3	Tell ye **y.** children of it, and let.............	
Joe	1:3	let **y.** children tell their children,.............	
Joe	1:5	wine; for it is cut off from **y.** mouth..........	
Joe	1:13	withholden from the house of **y.** God.........	
Joe	1:14	into the house of the Lord **y.** God,...........	
Joe	2:12	turn ye even to me with all **y.** heart,.........	
Joe	2:13	rend **y.** heart, and not **y.** garments,..........	
Joe	2:13	and turn unto the Lord **y.** God: for he.......	
Joe	2:14	drink offering unto the Lord **y.** God?.........	
Joe	2:23	Zion, and rejoice in the Lord **y.** God:........	
Joe	2:26	praise the name of the Lord **y.** God,.........	
Joe	2:27	and that I am the Lord **y.** God,...............	
Joe	2:28	and **y.** sons and **y.** daughters shall............	
Joe	2:28	**y.** old men shall dream dreams,...............	
Joe	2:28	**y.** young men shall see visions:...............	
Joe	3:4	**y.** recompence upon **y.** own head;............	
Joe	3:5	and have carried into **y.** temple my...........	
Joe	3:7	**y.** recompence upon **y.** own head:............	
Joe	3:8	I will sell **y.** sons and **y.** daughters...........	
Joe	3:10	Beat **y.** plowshares into swords,...............	
Joe	3:10	and **y.** pruninghooks into spears:..............	
Joe	3:17	ye know that I am the Lord **y.** God...........	
Am	2:11	I raised up of **y.** sons for prophets,...........	
Am	2:11	and of **y.** young men for Nazarites............	
Am	3:2	I will punish you for all **y.** iniquities..........	
Am	4:2	hooks, and **y.** posterity with fishhooks.......	
Am	4:4	and bring **y.** sacrifices every morning,.......	
Am	4:4	and **y.** tithes after three years:................	
Am	4:6	you cleanness of teeth in all **y.** cities,........	
Am	4:6	and want of bread in all **y.** places:...........	
Am	4:9	when **y.** gardens and **y.** vineyards............	
Am	4:9	and **y.** fig trees and **y.** olive trees...........	
Am	4:10	**y.** young men have I slain with the..........	
Am	4:10	and have taken away **y.** horses;...............	
Am	4:10	I have made the stink of **y.** camps............	
Am	4:10	to come up unto **y.** nostrils: yet have........	
Am	5:11	as **y.** treading is upon the poor,...............	
Am	5:12	I know **y.** manifold transgressions............	
Am	5:12	**y.** mighty sins: they afflict the just,...........	
Am	5:21	I hate, I despise **y.** feast days,................	
Am	5:21	will not smell in **y.** solemn assemblies.......	
Am	5:22	burnt offerings and **y.** meat offerings,........	
Am	5:22	the peace offerings of **y.** fat beasts...........	
Am	5:26	borne the tabernacle of **y.** Moloch............	
Am	5:26	Chiun **y.** images, the star of **y.** god,.........	
Am	6:2	or their border greater than **y.** border?......	
Am	8:10	I will turn **y.** feasts into mourning,...........	
Am	8:10	and all **y.** songs into lamentation;.............	
Mic	2:3	which ye shall not remove **y.** necks;..........	
Mic	2:10	and depart; for this is not **y.** rest:...........	
Mic	3:12	shall Zion for **y.** sake be plowed as...........	
Hab	1:5	for I will work a work in **y.** days,.............	
Zep	3:20	turn back **y.** captivity before **y.** eyes,........	
Hag	1:4	O ye, to dwell in **y.** cieled houses,...........	
Hag	1:5	the Lord of hosts; Consider **y.** ways..........	
Hag	1:7	Lord of hoss; consider **y.** ways...............	
Hag	2:3	is it not in **y.** eyes in comparison of it........	
Hag	2:17	hail in all the labours of **y.** hands;...........	
Zec	1:2	been sore displeased with **y.** fathers..........	
Zec	1:4	Be ye not as **y.** fathers, unto whom...........	
Zec	1:4	turn ye now from **y.** evil ways,................	
Zec	1:4	and from **y.** evil doings; but they did.........	
Zec	1:5	**Y.** fathers, where are they? and the..........	
Zec	1:6	did they not take hold of **y.** fathers?.........	
Zec	6:15	obey the voice of the Lord **y.** God...........	
Zec	7:10	evil against his brother in **y.** heart...........	
Zec	8:9	Let **y.** hands be strong, ye that hear..........	
Zec	8:13	fear not, but let **y.** hands be strong..........	
Zec	8:14	when **y.** fathers provoked me to wrath,.....	
Zec	8:16	of truth and peace in **y.** gates:...............	
Zec	8:17	none of you imagine evil in **y.** hearts.........	

Mal	1:5	And **y.** eyes shall see, and ye shall say,......	
Mal	1:9	unto us: this hath been by **y.** means:........	
Mal	1:9	will he regard **y.** persons? saith..............	
Mal	1:10	will I accept an offering at **y.** hand...........	
Mal	1:13	should I accept this of **y.** hand? saith.........	
Mal	2:2	I will curse **y.** blessings: yea, I have.........	
Mal	2:3	Behold I will corrupt **y.** seed,.................	
Mal	2:3	and spread dung upon **y.** faces,................	
Mal	2:3	even the dung of **y.** solemn feasts;...........	
Mal	2:13	it with good will at **y.** hand...................	
Mal	2:15	Therefore take heed to **y.** spirit, and........	
Mal	2:16	therefore take heed to **y.** spirit, that.........	
Mal	2:17	have wearied the Lord with **y.** words.........	
Mal	3:7	Even from the days of **y.** fathers.............	
Mal	3:11	will rebuke the devourer for **y.** sakes.........	
Mal	3:11	not destroy the fruits of **y.** ground;...........	
Mal	3:11	shall **y.** vine cast her fruit before the........	
Mal	3:13	**Y.** words have been stout against me........	
Mal	4:3	be ashes under the soles of **y.** feet...........	5216
Mt	5:12	for great is **y.** reward in heaven:..	5216
Mt	5:16	Let **y.** light so shine before men,...	5216
Mt	5:16	that they may see **y.** good works,..	5216
Mt	5:16	and glorify **y.** Father which is in...	5216
Mt	5:20	except **y.** righteousness exceed......	5216
Mt	5:37	But let **y.** communication be, Y....	5216
Mt	5:44	Love **y.** enemies, bless them that...	5216
Mt	5:45	may be the children of **y.** Father...	5216
Mt	5:47	And if ye salute **y.** brethren only,..	5216
Mt	5:48	as **y.** Father which is in heaven....	5216
Mt	6:1	that ye do not **y.** alms before........	5216
Mt	6:1	ye have no reward of **y.** Father.....	5216
Mt	6:8	for **y.** Father knoweth what..........	5216
Mt	6:14	**y.** heavenly Father will also..........	5216
Mt	6:15	**y.** Father forgive **y.** trespasses.......	5216
Mt	6:21	For where **y.** treasure is,.............	5216
Mt	6:21	there will **y.** heart be also............	5216
Mt	6:25	Take no thought for **y.** life, what..	5216
Mt	6:25	nor yet for **y.** body, what ye shall..	5216
Mt	6:26	**y.** heavenly Father feedeth them...	5216
Mt	6:32	for **y.** heavenly Father knoweth....	5216
Mt	7:6	cast ye **y.** pearls before swine,........	5216
Mt	7:11	give good gifts unto **y.** children,.....	5216
Mt	7:11	how much more shall **y.** Father....	5216
Mt	9:4	think ye evil in **y.** hearts?.............	5216
Mt	9:11	eateth **y.** Master with publicans.........	5216
Mt	9:29	According to **y.** faith be it unto.....	5216
Mt	10:9	nor silver, nor brass in **y.** purses,..	5216
Mt	10:10	Nor script for **y.** journey, neither........	
Mt	10:13	worthy, let **y.** peace come upon.....	5216
Mt	10:13	worthy, let **y.** peace return to you..	5216
Mt	10:14	not receive you, nor hear **y.**...........	5216
Mt	10:14	city, shake off the dust of **y.** feet...	5216
Mt	10:20	Spirit of **y.** Father which..............	5216
Mt	10:29	on the ground without **y.** Father...	5216
Mt	10:30	hairs of **y.** head are all numbered..	5216
Mt	11:29	ye shall find rest unto **y.** souls......	5216
Mt	12:27	whom do **y.** children cast them......	5216
Mt	12:27	therefore they shall be **y.** judges....	5216
Mt	13:16	blessed are **y.** eyes, for they see:...	5216
Mt	13:16	and **y.** ears, for they hear.............	5216
Mt	13:153	of God by **y.** tradition?................	5216
Mt	13:6	God of none effect by **y.**................	5216
Mt	17:20	Because of **y.** unbelief: for verily...	5216
Mt	17:24	Doth not **y.** master pay tribute?.........	5216
Mt	18:14	of **y.** Father which is in heaven,....	5216
Mt	18:35	ye from **y.** hearts forgive not........	5216
Mt	19:8	of the hardness of **y.** hearts..........	5216
Mt	19:8	suffered you to put away **y.**..........	5216
Mt	20:26	among you, let him be **y.**.............	5216
Mt	20:27	among you, let him be **y.** servant:..	5216
Mt	23:8	for one is **y.** Master, even Christ;..	5216
Mt	23:9	no man **y.** father upon the earth:..	5216
Mt	23:9	for one is **y.** Father, which is in....	5216
Mt	23:10	for one is **y.** Master, even Christ...	5216
Mt	23:11	among you shall be **y.** servant.......	5216
Mt	23:32	up then the measure of **y.** fathers..	5216
Mt	23:34	shall ye scourge in **y.** synagogues,..	5216
Mt	23:38	**y.** house is left unto you desolate...	5216
Mt	24:20	that **y.** flight be not in the winter,.	5216
Mt	24:42	not what hour **y.** Lord doth come..	5216
Mt	25:8	Give us of **y.** oil; for our lamps.....	5216
Mt	26:45	Sleep on now, and take **y.** rest:..........	
Mt	27:65	go **y.** way, make it as sure as you..........	
Mk	2:8	reason ye these things in **y.**..........	5216
Mk	6:11	shake off the dust under **y.** feet....	5216
Mk	7:9	that ye may keep **y.** own tradition..	5216

Mk	7:13	none effect through **y.** tradition,...	5216
Mk	8:17	have ye **y.** heart yet hardened?......	5216
Mk	10:5	For the hardness of **y.** heart be.....	5216
Mk	10:43	among you, shall be **y.** minister:...	5216
Mk	11:2	Go **y.** way into the village over...........	
Mk	11:25	**y.** Father also which is in heaven..	5216
Mk	11:25	may forgive you **y.** trespasses........	5216
Mk	11:26	neither will **y.** Father which is in..	5216
Mk	11:26	is in heaven forgive **y.** trespasses...	5216
Mk	13:18	that **y.** flight be not in the winter..	5216
Mk	14:41	Sleep on now, and take **y.** rest: it is....	
Mk	16:7	But go **y.** way, tell his disciples and..........	
Lu	3:14	and be content with **y.** wages..........	5216
Lu	4:21	this scripture fulfilled in **y.** ears....	5216
Lu	5:4	let down **y.** nets for a draught.......	5216
Lu	5:22	What reason ye in **y.** hearts?.........	5216
Lu	6:22	and cast out **y.** name as evil, for...	5216
Lu	6:23	**y.** reward is great in heaven:.........	5216
Lu	6:24	ye have received **y.** consolation.....	5216
Lu	6:27	Love **y.** enemies, do good to.........	5216
Lu	6:35	love ye **y.** enemies, and do good,...	5216
Lu	6:35	and **y.** reward shall be great, and..	5216
Lu	6:36	as **y.** Father also is merciful.........	5216
Lu	6:38	shall men give into **y.** bosom.........	5216
Lu	7:22	Go **y.** way, and tell John what things..	
Lu	8:25	unto them, Where is **y.** faith?.........	5216
Lu	9:3	Take nothing for **y.** journey,.........	3588
Lu	9:5	shake off the very dust from **y.**......	5216
Lu	9:44	sayings sink down into **y.** ears:.....	5216
Lu	10:3	Go **y.** ways: behold, I send you............	
Lu	10:6	there, **y.** peace shall rest upon it:.......	5216
Lu	10:10	go **y.** ways out into the streets of........	
Lu	10:11	Even the very dust of **y.** city,........	5216
Lu	10:20	**y.** names are written in heaven.....	5216
Lu	11:13	give good gifts unto **y.** children:....	5216
Lu	11:13	more shall **y.** heavenly Father.......	3588
Lu	11:19	whom do **y.** sons cast them out?....	5216
Lu	11:19	therefore shall they be **y.** judges....	5216
Lu	11:39	**y.** inward part is full of ravening..	5216
Lu	11:46	the burdens with one of **y.** fingers..	5216
Lu	11:47	prophets...**y.** fathers killed them....	5216
Lu	11:48	ye allow the deeds of **y.** fathers:....	5216
Lu	12:7	hairs of **y.** head are all numbered..	5216
Lu	12:22	Take no thought for **y.** life, what..	5216
Lu	12:30	**y.** Father knoweth that ye have....	5216
Lu	12:32	for it is **y.** Father's good pleasure..	5216
Lu	12:34	For where **y.** treasure is,.............	5216
Lu	12:34	there will **y.** heart be also............	5216
Lu	12:35	Let **y.** loins be girded about, and...	5216
Lu	12:35	and **y.** lights burning;..................	3588
Lu	13:35	**y.** house is left unto you desolate:..	5216
Lu	16:11	commit to **y.** trust the true..........	5213
Lu	16:12	give you that which is **y.** own?.......	5212
Lu	16:15	but God knoweth **y.** hearts: for.....	5216
Lu	19:30	at **y.** entering ye shall find a colt........	
Lu	21:14	Settle it therefore in **y.** hearts,......	5216
Lu	21:15	**y.** adversaries shall not be able......	5213
Lu	21:18	shall not an hair of **y.** head...........	5216
Lu	21:19	In **y.** patience possess ye **y.** souls..	5216
Lu	21:28	look up, and lift up **y.** heads;........	5216
Lu	21:28	for **y.** redemption draweth nigh.....	5216
Lu	21:30	ye see and know of **y.** own selves..	1438
Lu	21:34	any time **y.** hearts be overcharged..	5216
Lu	22:53	but this is **y.** hour, and the power..	5216
Lu	23:28	for yourselves, and for **y.** children..	5216
Lu	24:38	do thoughts arise in **y.** hearts?......	5216
Joh	4:35	Lift up **y.** eyes, and look on the.....	5216
Joh	6:49	**Y.** fathers did eat manna in the....	5216
Joh	6:58	not as **y.** fathers did eat manna,....	5216
Joh	7:6	but **y.** time is alway ready............	5212
Joh	8:17	It is also written in **y.** law, that....	5212
Joh	8:21	seek me, and shall die in **y.** sins:...	5216
Joh	8:24	you, that ye shall die in **y.** sins:....	5216
Joh	8:24	I am he, ye shall die in **y.** sins......	5216
Joh	8:38	which ye have seen with **y.** father..	5216
Joh	8:41	Ye do the deeds of **y.** father..........	5216
Joh	8:42	If God were **y.** Father, ye would....	5216
Joh	8:44	Ye are of **y.** father the devil,.........	5216
Joh	8:44	the lusts of **y.** father ye will do......	5216
Joh	8:54	whom ye say, that he is **y.** God:.....	5216
Joh	8:56	**Y.** father Abraham rejoiced to see..	5216
Joh	9:19	Is this **y.** son, who ye say was born...	5216
Joh	9:41	see; therefore **y.** sin remaineth......	5216
Joh	10:34	Is it not written in **y.** law, I said,..	5216
Joh	11:15	glad for **y.** sakes that I was not....	5209
Joh	12:30	not because of me, but for **y.**.........	5209

Joh 13:14 If I then, y. Lord and Master, 3588
Joh 13:14 washed y. feet; ye also ought 5216
Joh 14:1 Let not y. heart be troubled; 5216
Joh 14:26 all things to y. remembrance, 5209
Joh 14:27 Let not y. heart be troubled 5216
Joh 15:11 and that y. joy might be full 5216
Joh 15:16 and that y. fruit should remain: 5216
Joh 16:6 you, sorrow hath filled y. heart 5216
Joh 16:20 y. sorrow shall be turned into 5216
Joh 16:22 again, and y. heart shall rejoice, 5216
Joh 16:22 and y. joy no man taketh from 5216
Joh 16:24 receive, that y. joy may be full. 5216
Joh 18:31 and judge him according to y. law 5216
Joh 19:14 unto the Jews, Behold y. King! 5216
Joh 19:15 unto them, Shall I crucify y. King? 5216
Joh 20:17 unto my Father, and y. Father; 5216
Joh 20:17 and to my God, and y. God 5216
Ac 2:17 y. sons and y. daughters shall 5216
Ac 2:17 and y. young men shall see visions 5216
Ac 2:17 y. old men shall dream dreams: 5216
Ac 2:39 is unto you, and to y. children, 5216
Ac 3:17 ye did it, as did also y. rulers 5216
Ac 3:19 that y. sins may be blotted out, 5216
Ac 3:22 A prophet shall the Lord y. God 5216
Ac 3:22 raise up unto you of y. brethren, 5216
Ac 5:28 filled Jerusalem with y. doctrine, 5216
Ac 7:37 A prophet shall the Lord y. God 5216
Ac 7:37 raise up unto you of y. brethren, 5216
Ac 7:43 and the star of y. god Remphan, 5216
Ac 7:51 Ghost: as y. fathers did, so do ye. 5216
Ac 7:52 have not y. fathers persecuted? 5216
Ac 13:41 for I work a work in y. days, 5216
Ac 15:24 subverting y. souls, saying, Ye 5216
Ac 17:23 passed by, and beheld y. devotions, 5216
Ac 17:28 also of y. own poets have said, 2596,5209
Ac 18:6 Y. blood be upon y. own heads; 546
Ac 18:15 and names, and of y. law, 2596,5209
Ac 19:37 yet blasphemers of y. goddess. 5216
Ac 20:30 of y. own selves shall men arise, 5216
Ac 24:22 know...uttermost of y. matter. 2596,5209
Ac 27:34 meat: for this is for y. health: 5212
Ro 1:8 y. faith is spoken of throughout 5216
Ro 6:12 therefore reign in y. mortal body, 5216
Ro 6:13 yield ye y. members as instruments 5216
Ro 6:13 and y. members as instruments of 5216
Ro 6:19 because of the infirmity of y. flesh: 5216
Ro 6:19 have yielded y. members servants 5216
Ro 6:19 so now yield y. members servants 5216
Ro 6:22 ye have y. fruit unto holiness, and 5216
Ro 8:11 quicken y. mortal bodies by his 5216
Ro 11:25 be wise in y. own conceits; 3844,1438
Ro 11:28 they are enemies for y. sakes: 5209
Ro 11:31 through y. mercy they also may 5212
Ro 12:1 y. bodies a living sacrifice, 5216
Ro 12:1 which is y. reasonable service. 5216
Ro 12:2 by the renewing of y. mind, 5216
Ro 12:16 Be not wise in y. own conceits. 5216
Ro 14:16 then y. good be evil spoken of: 5216
Ro 15:24 somewhat filled with y. company. 5216
Ro 15:30 together with me in y. prayers 3588
Ro 16:19 For y. obedience is come abroad 5216
Ro 16:19 I am glad therefore on y. behalf: 5213
Ro 16:20 bruise Satan under y. feet shortly 5216
1Co 1:4 thank my God always on y. behalf, 5216
1Co 1:26 For ye see y. calling, brethren, 5216
1Co 2:5 That y. faith should not stand in 5216
1Co 4:6 myself and to Apollos for y. sakes; 5209
1Co 5:6 Y. glorifying is not good. Know 5216
1Co 6:5 I speak to y. shame. Is it so, that 5213
1Co 6:8 and defraud, and that y. brethren.
1Co 6:15 that y. bodies are the members of 5216
1Co 6:19 ye not that y. body is the temple 1438
1Co 6:19 of God, and ye are not y. own? 5216
1Co 6:20 therefore glorify God in y. body, 5216
1Co 6:20 and in y. spirit, which are God's. 5216
1Co 7:5 tempt you not for y. incontinency. 5216
1Co 7:14 else were y. children unclean; 5216
1Co 7:35 And this I speak for y. own profit; 5216
1Co 9:11 if we shall reap y. carnal things? 5216
1Co 14:34 Let y. women keep silence in the 5216
1Co 15:14 vain, and y. faith is also vain. 5216
1Co 15:17 be not raised, y. faith is vain; 5216
1Co 15:17 ye are yet in y. sins. 5216
1Co 15:31 I protest by y. rejoicing which I 5212
1Co 15:34 of God: I speak this to y. shame. 5213
1Co 15:58 ye know that y. labour is not 5216
1Co 16:3 ye shall approve by y. letters,
1Co 16:3 will I send to bring y. liberality 5216
1Co 16:14 y. things be done with charity. 5216
1Co 16:17 that which was lacking on y. part 5216
2Co 1:6,6 it is for y. consolation and 5216
2Co 1:14 that we are y. rejoicing, even as ye 5216
2Co 1:24 we have dominion over y. faith, 5216
2Co 1:24 are helpers of y. joy: for by faith 5216
2Co 2:8 would confirm y. love toward him.
2Co 2:10 for y. sakes forgave I it in the 5209
2Co 4:5 ourselves y. servants for Jesus' 5216
2Co 4:15 For all things are for y. sakes, 5209
2Co 5:11 made manifest in y. consciences. 5216
2Co 5:13 we be sober, it is for y. cause. 5213
2Co 6:12 ye are straitened in y. own bowels. 5216
2Co 7:7 when he told us y. earnest desire, 5216
2Co 7:7 y. mourning, y. fervent mind 5216
2Co 7:13 we were comforted in y. comfort: 5213
2Co 8:7 and in y. love to us, see that ye 5209
2Co 8:8 to prove the sincerity of y. love. 5212
2Co 8:9 yet for y. sakes he became poor, 5216
2Co 8:14 y. abundance may be a supply for 5216
2Co 8:14 also may be a supply for y. want: 5216
2Co 8:19 and declaration of y. ready mind: 5216
2Co 8:24 the churches, the proof of y. love, 5216
2Co 8:24 and of our boasting on y. behalf. 5216
2Co 9:2 know the forwardness of y. mind, 5216
2Co 9:2 y. zeal hath provoked very many. 5216
2Co 9:5 and make up beforehand y. bounty, 5216
2Co 9:10 both minister bread for y. food,
2Co 9:10 and multiply y. seed sown, 5216
2Co 9:10 the fruits of y. righteousness;) 5216
2Co 9:13 y. professed subjection unto the 5216
2Co 9:13 y. liberal distribution unto them, 3588
2Co 10:6 when y. obedience is fulfilled. 5216
2Co 10:8 and not for y. destruction, I should 5216
2Co 10:15 when y. faith is increased, that we 5216
2Co 11:3 so y. minds should be corrupted 5216
2Co 12:19 dearly beloved, for y. edifying. 5216
2Co 13:5 in the faith; prove y. own selves. 1438
2Co 13:5 Know ye not y. own selves, how 1438
2Co 13:9 we wish, even y. perfection. 5216
Ga 4:6 the Spirit of his Son into y. hearts, 5216
Ga 4:15 have plucked out y. own eyes, 5216
Ga 4:16 Am I therefore become y. enemy, 5216
Ga 6:13 that they may glory in y. flesh. 5212
Ga 6:18 Lord Jesus Christ be with y. spirit. 5212
Eph 1:13 truth, the gospel of y. salvation: 5216
Eph 1:15 of y. faith in the Lord Jesus, 5209
Eph 1:18 eyes of y. understanding being 5216
Eph 3:13 tribulations for you, which is y. glory.
Eph 3:17 that Christ may dwell in y. hearts 5216
Eph 4:4 are called in one hope of y. calling; 5216
Eph 4:23 renewed in the spirit of y. mind; 5216
Eph 4:26 the sun go down upon y. wrath: 5216
Eph 4:29 proceed out of y. mouth, 5216
Eph 5:19 melody in y. heart to the Lord; 5216
Eph 5:22 yourselves unto y. own husbands; 3588
Eph 5:25 Husbands, love y. wives, even as 1438
Eph 6:1 obey y. parents in the Lord: 5216
Eph 6:4 provoke not y. children to wrath: 5216
Eph 6:5 to them that are y. masters
Eph 6:5 in singleness of y. heart, as unto 5216
Eph 6:9 that y. Master also is in heaven; 5216
Eph 6:14 y. loins girt about with truth, 5216
Eph 6:15 y. feet shod with the preparation 3588
Eph 6:22 that he might comfort y. hearts. 5216
Php 1:5 For y. fellowship in the gospel 5216
Php 1:9 that y. love may abound yet more 5216
Php 1:19 my salvation through y. prayer, 5216
Php 1:25 with you all for y. furtherance and 5216
Php 1:26 y. rejoicing may be more abundant 5216
Php 1:27 y. conversation be as it becometh
Php 1:27 I may hear of y. affairs, that ye 5216
Php 1:28 nothing terrified by y. adversaries: 3588
Php 2:12 work out y. own salvation with fear 1438
Php 2:17 sacrifice and service of y. faith, 5216
Php 2:19 comfort, when I know y. state. 5216
Php 2:20 who will naturally care for y. state 5216
Php 2:25 but y. messenger, and he that 5216
Php 2:30 to supply y. lack of service toward 5216
Php 4:5 y. moderation be known unto all 5216
Php 4:6 let y. requests be made known unto 5216
Php 4:7 keep y. hearts and minds through 5216
Php 4:10 last y. care of me hath flourished 3588
Php 4:17 may abound unto y. account. 5216
Php 4:19 my God shall supply all y. need 5216
Col 1:4 Since we heard of y. faith in Christ 5216
Col 1:8 unto us y. love in the Spirit. 5216
Col 1:21 enemies in y. mind by wicked 3588
Col 2:5 joying and beholding y. order, 5216
Col 2:5 stedfastness of y. faith in Christ. 5216
Col 2:13 And you, being dead in y. sins and 5216
Col 2:13 and the uncircumcision of y. flesh, 5216
Col 2:18 no man beguile you of y. reward
Col 3:2 Set y. affection on things above, not
Col 3:3 y. life is hid with Christ in God. 5216
Col 3:5 Mortify therefore y. members 5216
Col 3:8 communication out of y. mouth. 5216
Col 3:15 the peace of God rule in y. hearts, 5216
Col 3:16 singing with grace in y. hearts to 5216
Col 3:18 yourselves unto y. own husbands, 2398
Col 3:19 Husbands, love y. wives, and be not 3588
Col 3:20 Children, obey y. parents in all 3588
Col 3:21 provoke not y. children to anger, 5216
Col 3:22 obey in all things y. masters 3588
Col 4:1 unto y. servants that which is just 3588
Col 4:6 y. speech be alway with grace, 5216
Col 4:8 that he might know y. estate, 5216
Col 4:8 and comfort y. hearts: 5216
1Th 1:3 ceasing y. work of faith, 5209
1Th 1:4 beloved, y. election of God. 5216
1Th 1:5 we were among you for y. sake. 5209
1Th 1:8 every place y. faith to God-ward 5216
1Th 2:14 like things of y. own countrymen, 2398
1Th 2:17 to see y. face with great desire. 5216
1Th 3:2 to comfort you concerning y. faith: 5216
1Th 3:5 I sent to know y. faith, lest by 5216
1Th 3:6 brought us good tidings of y. faith 5216
1Th 3:7 affliction and distress by y. faith: 5216
1Th 3:9 we joy for y. sakes before our God: 5209
1Th 3:10 that we might see y. face, and 5216
1Th 3:10 that which is lacking in y. faith? 5216
1Th 3:13 the end he may stablish y. hearts 5216
1Th 4:3 will of God, even y. sanctification, 5216
1Th 4:11 quiet, and to do y. own business, 2398
1Th 4:11 and to work with y. own hands, 2398
1Th 5:23 I pray God y. whole spirit and soul 3588
2Th 1:3 that y. faith groweth exceedingly, 5216
2Th 1:4 of God for y. patience and faith 5216
2Th 1:4 y. persecutions and tribulations 5216
2Th 2:17 Comfort y. hearts, and stablish you 5216
2Th 3:5 Lord direct y. hearts into the love 5216
Phm 22 for I trust that through y. prayers 5216
Phm 25 Lord Jesus Christ be with y. spirit 5216
Heb 3:8 Harden not y. hearts, as in the 5216
Heb 3:9 When y. fathers tempted me, 5216
Heb 3:15 hear his voice, harden not y. hearts, 5216
Heb 4:7 hear his voice, harden not y. hearts. 5216
Heb 6:10 forget y. work and labour of love, 5216
Heb 9:14 purge y. conscience from dead 5216
Heb 10:34 joyfully he spoiling of y. goods, 5216
Heb 10:35 not away therefore y. confidence, 5216
Heb 12:3 ye be wearied and faint in y. minds. 5216
Heb 12:13 make straight paths for y. feet, 5216
Heb 13:5 Let y. conversation be without 3588
Heb 13:17 for they watch for y. souls, 5216
Jas 1:3 trying of y. faith worketh patience. 5216
Jas 1:21 which is able to save y. souls. 5216
Jas 1:22 only, deceiving y. own selves. 1438
Jas 2:2 come unto y. assembly a man 5216
Jas 3:14 envying and strife in y. hearts, 5216
Jas 4:1 y. lusts that war in y. members? 5216
Jas 4:3 ye may consume it upon y. lusts. 5216
Jas 4:8 Cleanse y. hands, ye sinners;
Jas 4:8 and purify y. hearts, ye double minded.
Jas 4:9 y. laughter be turned to mourning, 5216
Jas 4:9 and y. joy to heaviness. 3588
Jas 4:14 For what is y. life? It is even a 5216
Jas 4:16 now ye rejoice in y. boastings: 5216
Jas 5:1 weep and howl for y. miseries that 5216
Jas 5:2 Y. riches are corrupted, and 5216
Jas 5:2 and y. garments are motheaten. 5216
Jas 5:3 Y. gold and silver is cankered; 5216
Jas 5:3 shall eat y. flesh as it were fire. 5216
Jas 5:4 who have reaped down y. fields, 5216
Jas 5:5 ye have nourished y. hearts, as in a 5216
Jas 5:8 ye also patient; stablish y. hearts: 5216
Jas 5:12 oath: but let y. yea be yea; 5216
Jas 5:12 and y. nay, nay; lest ye fall 3588
Jas 5:16 Confess y. faults one to another, 3588
1Pe 1:7 That the trial of y. faith, being 5216

1Pe 1:9 Receiving the end of **y.** faith, ... *5216*
1Pe 1:9 even the salvation of **y.** souls. ...
1Pe 1:13 gird up the loins of **y.** mind, ... *5216*
1Pe 1:14 to the former lusts in **y.** ignorance: ... *5216*
1Pe 1:17 time of **y.** sojourning here in fear: ... *5216*
1Pe 1:18 from **y.** vain conversation received ... *5216*
1Pe 1:18 by tradition from **y.** fathers; ... *5216*
1Pe 1:21 **y.** faith and hope might be in God. ... *5216*
1Pe 1:22 Seeing ye have purified **y.** souls in ... *5216*
1Pe 2:12 Having **y.** conversation honest ... *5216*
1Pe 2:12 they may be **y.** good works, which ... *3588*
1Pe 2:16 and not using **y.** liberty for a cloke ... *3588*
1Pe 2:18 subject to **y.** masters with all fear; ... *3588*
1Pe 2:20 when ye be buffeted for **y.** faults, ...
1Pe 2:25 Shepherd and Bishop of **y.** souls. ... *5216*
1Pe 3:1 in subjection to **y.** own husbands; ... *3588*
1Pe 3:2 behold **y.** chaste conversation ... *5216*
1Pe 3:7 that **y.** prayers be not hindered ... *5216*
1Pe 3:15 the Lord God in **y.** hearts: ... *5216*
1Pe 3:16 accuse **y.** good conversation ... *5216*
1Pe 4:14 of, but on **y.** part he is glorified. ... *5209*
1Pe 5:7 Casting all **y.** care upon him; for ... *5216*
1Pe 5:8 because **y.** adversary the devil, ... *5216*
1Pe 5:9 are accomplished in **y.** brethren ... *5216*
2Pe 1:5 add to **y.** faith virtue; and to ... *5216*
2Pe 1:10 give diligence to make **y.** calling ... *5216*
2Pe 1:19 the day star arise in **y.** hearts: ... *5216*
2Pe 3:1 both which I stir up **y.** pure minds ... *5216*
2Pe 3:17 fall from **y.** own stedfastness. ... *3588*
1Jo 1:4 unto you, that **y.** joy may be full. ... *5216*
1Jo 2:12 because **y.** sins are forgiven you for ... *3588*
2Jo 10 receive him not into **y.** house, neither ...
Jude 12 are spots in **y.** feasts of charity, ... *5216*
Jude 20 yourselves on **y.** most holy faith, ... *5216*
Re 1:9 I John, who also am **y.** brother, ... *5216*
Re 2:23 **one of you according to y. works** .. *5216*
Re 16:1 Go **y.** ways, and pour out the vials of ...

YOURS See also YOURSELVES.
Ge 45:20 the good of all the land of Egypt is **y.** ...
De 11:24 of your feet shall tread shall be **y.**: ...
Jos 2:14 Our life for **y.**, if ye utter not this our ...
2Ch 20:15 for the battle is not **y.**, but God's. ...
Jer 5:19 strangers in a land that is not **y.**. ...
Lu 6:20 **poor: for y. is the kingdom of** ... *5212*
Joh 15:20 **saying, they will keep y. also** ... *5212*
1Co 3:21 in men; for all things are **y.** ... *5216*
1Co 3:22 or things to come; all are **y.**; ... *5216*
1Co 8:9 means this liberty of **y.** become a ... *5216*
1Co 16:18 have refreshed my spirit and **y.**: ... *5216*
2Co 12:14 for I seek not **y.**, but you: for the ... *5216*

YOURSELVES See also YOUR and SELVES.
Ge 18:4 your feet, and rest **y.** under the tree: ...
Ge 45:5 be not grieved, nor angry with **y.**, ... 5869
Ge 49:1 Gather **y.** together, that I may tell ...
Ge 49:2 Gather **y.** together, and hear, ye ...
Ex 19:12 Take heed to **y.**, that ye go not up ...
Ex 30:37 ye shall not make to **y.** according to ...
Ex 32:29 Consecrate **y.** to day to the Lord, ... 3027
Le 11:43 neither shall ye make **y.** unclean ... 5315
Le 11:43 not make [*your selves*] abominable ... 5315
Le 11:44 ye shall therefore sanctify **y.**, and ... 5315
Le 11:44 neither shall ye defile **y.** with any ... 5315
Le 18:24 Defile not ye **y.** in any of these ...
Le 18:30 and that ye defile not **y.** therein: ...
Le 19:4 idols, nor make to **y.** molten gods: ...
Le 20:7 Sanctify **y.** therefore, and be ye ...
Nu 11:18 Sanctify **y.** against to morrow, and ye ...
Nu 16:3 lift ye up **y.** above the congregation ...
Nu 16:21 Separate **y.** from among this ...
Nu 31:3 Arm some of **y.** unto the war, and ... 853
Nu 31:18 lying with him, keep alive for **y.** ...
Nu 31:19 purify both **y.** and your captives on ...
De 2:4 take ye good heed unto **y.** therefore: ...
De 4:15 ye therefore good heed unto **y.**; ... 5315
De 4:16 Lest ye corrupt **y.**, and make you ...
De 4:23 Take heed unto **y.**, lest ye forget ...
De 4:25 corrupt **y.**, and make a graven image, ...
De 11:16 Take heed to **y.**, that your heart ...
De 11:23 greater nations and mightier than **y.** ...
De 14:1 ye shall not cut **y.**, nor make any ...
De 31:14 and present **y.** in the tabernacle of the ...
De 31:29 my death ye will utterly corrupt **y.**, ...
Jos 2:16 and hide **y.** there three days, until the ...
Jos 3:5 Sanctify **y.**: for to morrow the Lord ...
Jos 6:18 keep **y.** from the accursed thing, ...
Jos 6:18 lest ye make **y.** accursed, when ye ...
Jos 7:13 say, Sanctify **y.** against to morrow: ...
Jos 8:2 shall ye take for a prey unto **y.**: ...
Jos 23:7 serve them, nor bow **y.** unto them: ...
Jos 23:11 heed therefore unto [*your selves*], ... 5315
Jos 23:16 other gods, and bowed **y.** to them; ...
Jos 24:22 Ye are witnesses against **y.** that ye ...
Jg 15:12 that ye will not fall upon me **y.** ... 859
1Sa 2:29 to make **y.** fat with the chiefest of ...
1Sa 4:9 Be strong, and quit **y.** like men, ...
1Sa 4:9 to you: quit **y.** like men, and fight. ...
1Sa 10:19 therefore present **y.** before the Lord ...
1Sa 14:34 said, Disperse **y.** among the people, ...
1Sa 16:5 sanctify **y.**, and come with me to ...
1Ki 18:25 Choose you one bullock for **y.**, ...
1Ki 20:12 unto his servants Set **y.** in array. ...
2Ki 17:35 nor bow **y.** to them, nor serve them, ...
1Ch 15:12 sanctify **y.**, both ye and your brethren, ...
2Ch 20:17 set **y.**, stand ye still, and see the ...
2Ch 29:5 ye Levites, sanctify now **y.**, and ...
2Ch 29:31 have consecrated **y.** unto the Lord, ... 3027
2Ch 30:8 but yield **y.** unto the Lord, and ... 3027
2Ch 32:11 to give over **y.** to die by famine ...
2Ch 35:4 And prepare **y.** by the houses of ...
2Ch 35:6 So kill the passover, and sanctify **y.**, ...
Ezr 10:11 separate **y.** from the people of the ...
Ne 13:25 daughters unto your sons, or for **y.**. ...
Job 19:3 that ye make **y.** strange to me. ...
Job 19:5 ye will magnify **y.** against me. ...
Job 27:12 Behold, all ye **y.** have seen it; ...
Job 42:8 and offer up for **y.** a burnt offering; ...
Isa 8:9 Associate **y.**, O ye people, and ye ...
Isa 8:9, 9 gird **y.**, and ye shall be broken in ...
Isa 29:9 Stay **y.**, and wonder; cry ye out, ...
Isa 45:20 Assemble **y.** and come; draw near ...
Isa 46:8 Remember this, and shew **y.** men: ...
Isa 48:14 All ye, assemble **y.**, and hear; ...
Isa 49:9 them that are in darkness, Shew **y.** ...
Isa 50:1 for your iniquities have ye sold **y.**, ...
Isa 50:11 that compass **y.** about with sparks: ...
Isa 52:3 Ye have sold **y.** for nought; ...
Isa 57:4 Against whom do ye sport **y.**? ...
Isa 57:5 Enflaming **y.** with idols under every ...
Isa 61:6 and in their glory shall ye boast **y.** ...
Jer 4:4 Circumcise **y.** to the Lord, and take ...
Jer 4:5 Assemble **y.**, and let us go into the ...
Jer 6:1 gather **y.** to flee out of the midst of ...
Jer 8:14 assemble **y.**, and let us enter into ...
Jer 13:18 to the queen, Humble **y.**, sit down: ...
Jer 17:21 Take heed to **y.**, and bear no ... 5315
Jer 25:34 and wallow **y.** in the ashes, ye ...
Jer 26:15 surely bring innocent blood upon **y.**, ...
Jer 37:9 Deceive not **y.**, saying, The ... 5315
Jer 44:8 that ye might cut **y.** off, and that ...
Jer 50:14 Put **y.** in array against Babylon ...
Eze 14:6 and turn **y.** from your idols; ...
Eze 18:30 **y.** from all your transgressions; ...
Eze 18:32 wherefore turn **y.**, and live ye. ...
Eze 20:7 defile not **y.** with the idols of Egypt: ...
Eze 20:18 nor defile **y.** with their idols: ...
Eze 20:31 ye pollute **y.** with all your idols, ...
Eze 20:43 ye shall lothe **y.** in your own sight ...
Eze 36:31 and shall lothe **y.** in your own sight ...
Eze 39:17 of the field, Assemble **y.**, and come; ...
Eze 39:17 gather **y.** on every side to my ...
Eze 44:8 my charge in my sanctuary for **y.**. ...
Ho 10:12 Sow to **y.** in righteousness, reap ...
Joe 1:13 Gird **y.**, and lament, ye priests: ...
Joe 3:11 Assemble **y.**, and come, all ye ...
Joe 3:11 and gather **y.** together round about: ...
Am 3:9 Assemble **y.** upon the mountains of ...
Am 5:26 of your God, which ye made to **y.**. ...
Zep 2:1 Gather **y.** together, yea, gather ...
Zec 7:6 not ye eat for **y.**, and drink for **y.**? ...
Mt 3:9 And think not to say within **y.**, ... *1438*
Mt 6:19 **up for y. treasures upon earth,** ... *5213*
Mt 6:20 **lay up for y. treasures in heaven,** .. *5213*
Mt 16:8 **why reason ye among y., because** .. *1438*
Mt 23:13 **for ye neither go in y., neither suffer** ..
Mt 23:15 **more the child of hell than y.** ... *5216*
Mt 23:31 **Wherefore ye be witnesses unto y.,** .*1438*
Mt 25:9 **to them that sell, and buy for y.** .. *1438*
Mk 6:31 **come ye y. apart into a** ... *5210,846*
Mk 9:33 **ye disputed among y. by the way?** .*1438*
Mk 9:50 **Have salt in y., and have peace** ... *1438*
Mk 13:9 **But take heed to y.: for they** ... *1438*
Lu 3:8 to say within **y.**, We have Abraham ... *1438*
Lu 11:46 **and ye y. touch not the burdens** ... *846*
Lu 11:52 **ye entered not in y., and them** ... *846*
Lu 12:33 **provide y. bags which wax not old,** .*1438*
Lu 12:36 **And ye y. like unto men that wait** ...
Lu 12:57 **even of y. judge ye not what** ... *1438*
Lu 13:28 **of God, and you y. thrust out** ...
Lu 16:9 **to y. friends of the mammon of** ... *1438*
Lu 16:15 **they which justify y. before men;** .. *1438*
Lu 17:3 **Take heed to y.: If thy brother** ... *1438*
Lu 17:14 **Go shew y. unto the priests.** ... *1438*
Lu 21:34 **And take heed to y., lest at any** ... *1438*
Lu 22:17 **Take this, and divide it among y.:** ..*1438*
Lu 23:28 **weep not for me, but weep for y.,** .. *1438*
Joh 3:28 Ye **y.** bear me witness, that I ... *5210,846*
Joh 6:43 unto them, **Murmur not among y.,** ... *240*
Joh 16:19 **enquire among y. of that I said,** ... *240*
Ac 2:22 midst of you, as ye **y.** also know: ... *846*
Ac 2:40 **y.** from this untoward generation. ...
Ac 5:35 take heed to **y.** what ye intend to ... *1438*
Ac 13:46 **y.** unworthy of everlasting life, ... *1438*
Ac 15:29 from which if ye keep **y.**, ye shall ... *1438*
Ac 20:10 Trouble not **y.**; for his life is in him. ...
Ac 20:28 Take heed therefore unto **y.**, and ... *1438*
Ac 20:34 Yea, ye **y.** know, that these hands ... *846*
Ro 6:11 also **y.** to be dead indeed unto sin, ... *1438*
Ro 6:13 but yield **y.** unto God, as those ... *1438*
Ro 6:16 whom ye yield **y.** servants to obey, ... *1438*
Ro 12:19 Dearly beloved, avenge not **y.**, ... *1438*
1Co 5:13 from among **y.** that wicked ... *5216,846*
1Co 6:7 not rather suffer **y.** to be defrauded? ...
1Co 7:5 may give **y.** to fasting and prayer; ...
1Co 11:13 Judge in **y.**: is it comely that a ... *5213,846*
1Co 16:16 That ye submit **y.** unto such, and ...
2Co 7:11 in you, yea, what clearing of **y.**, ...
2Co 7:11 have approved **y.** to be clear in this ... *1438*
2Co 11:19 fools gladly, seeing ye **y.** are wise. ...
2Co 13:5 Examine **y.**, whether ye be in ... *1438*
Eph 2:8 and that not of **y.**: it is the gift of ... *5216*
Eph 5:19 Speaking to **y.** in psalms and ... *1438*
Eph 5:21 Submitting **y.** one to another ...
Eph 5:22 submit **y.** unto your own husbands, ...
Col 3:18 submit **y.** unto your own husbands, ...
1Th 2:1 For **y.**, brethren, know our entrance ... *846*
1Th 3:3 for **y.** know that we are appointed ... *846*
1Th 4:9 for ye **y.** are taught of God to love ... *846*
1Th 5:2 For **y.** know perfectly that the day ... *846*
1Th 5:11 Wherefore comfort **y.** together, ... *240*
1Th 5:13 And be at peace among **y.** ... *1438*
1Th 5:15 that which is good, both among **y.**, ... *1438*
2Th 3:6 ye withdraw **y.** from every brother ...
2Th 3:7 For **y.** know how ye ought to follow ... *846*
Heb 10:34 knowing in **y.** that ye have in ... *1438*
Heb 13:3 as being **y.** also in the body. ... *846*
Heb 13:17 the rule over you, and submit **y.**: ... *5216*
Jas 2:4 Are ye not then partial in **y.**, ... *1438*
Jas 4:7 Submit **y.** therefore to God. ...
Jas 4:10 Humble **y.** in the sight of the Lord, ...
1Pe 1:14 not fashioning **y.** according to the ...
1Pe 2:13 Submit **y.** to every ordinance ...
1Pe 4:1 arm **y.** likewise with the same mind: ...
1Pe 4:8 have fervent charity among **y.** ... *1438*
1Pe 5:5 ye younger, submit **y.** unto the elder. ...
1Pe 5:6 Humble **y.** therefore under the ...
1Jo 5:21 Little children, keep **y.** from idols ... *1438*
2Jo 8 Look to **y.**, that we lose not those ... *1438*
Jude 20 building up **y.** on your most holy ... *1438*
Jude 21 Keep **y.** in the love of God, looking ... *1438*
Re 19:17 gather **y.** together unto the supper ...

YOUTH See also YOUTHFUL; YOUTHS.
Ge 8:21 of man's heart is evil from his **y.**; ... 5271
Ge 43:33 the youngest according to his **y.** ... 6812
Ge 46:34 cattle from our **y.** even until now, ... 5271
Le 22:13 her father's house, as in her **y.**, ... 5271
Nu 30:3 in her father's house in her **y.**; ... 5271
Nu 30:16 yet in her **y.** in her father's house. ... 5271
Jg 8:20 But the **y.** drew not his sword: ... 5288
Jg 8:20 feared, because he was yet a **y.** ... 5288
1Sa 17:33 with him: for thou art but a **y.**, ... 5288
1Sa 17:33 and he a man of war from his **y.**. ... 5271
1Sa 17:42 for he was but a **y.**, and ruddy, ... 5288
1Sa 17:55 host, Abner, whose son is this **y.**? ... 5288
2Sa 19:7 evil that befell thee from thy **y.** ... 5271
1Ki 18:12 servant fear the Lord from my **y.** ... 5271
Job 13:26 possess the iniquities of my **y.** ... 5271

Job 20:11 bones are full of the sin of his **y.**,........ 5934
Job 29:4 As I was in the days of my **y.**.......... 2779
Job 30:12 Upon my right hand rise the **y.**;......... 6526
Job 31:18 from my **y.** he was brought up 5271
Job 33:25 shall return to the days of his **y.**........ 5934
Job 36:14 They die in **y.**, and their life is 5290
Ps 25:7 Remember not the sins of my **y.**,........ 5271
Ps 71:5 thou art my trust from my **y.**............ 5271
Ps 71:17 thou hast taught me from my **y.**.......... 5271
Ps 88:15 and ready to die from my **y.** up: 5290
Ps 89:45 The days of his **y.** hast thou.............. 5934
Ps 103:5 thy **y.** is renewed like the eagle's....... 5271
Ps 110:3 thou hast the dew of thy **y.**................ 3208
Ps 127:4 man; so are children of the **y.**.......... 5271
Ps 129:1 have they afflicted me from my **y.**,...... 5271
Ps 129:2 have they afflicted me from my **y.**....... 5271
Ps 144:12 be as plants grown up in their **y.**;......... 5271
Pr 2:17 forsaketh the guide of her **y.**,............. 5271
Pr 5:18 rejoice with the wife of thy **y.**............ 5271
Ec 11:9 Rejoice, O young man, in thy **y.**; 3208
Ec 11:9 cheer thee in the days of thy **y.**, ... 979
Ec 11:10 for childhood and **y.** are vanity........... 7839
Ec 12:1 thy Creator in the days of thy **y.**, ... 979
Isa 47:12 thou hast laboured from thy **y.**;.......... 5271
Isa 47:15 even thy merchants, from thy **y.**......... 5271
Isa 54:4 shalt forget the shame of thy **y.**,........ 5934
Isa 54:6 and a wife of **y.**, when thou wast 5271
Jer 2:2 the kindness of thy **y.**, the love 5271
Jer 3:4 father, thou art the guide of my **y.**?.... 5271
Jer 3:24 labour of our fathers from our **y.**;........ 5271
Jer 3:25 from our **y.** even unto this day, ... 5271
Jer 22:21 been thy manner from thy **y.**............. 5271
Jer 31:19 I did bear the reproach of my **y.**......... 5271
Jer 32:30 done evil before me from their **y.**....... 5271
Jer 48:11 hath been at ease from his **y.**,........... 5271
La 3:27 that he bear the yoke in his **y.**........... 5271
Eze 4:14 from my **y.** up even till now have I..... 5271
Eze 16:22, 43 remembered the days of thy **y.**,...... 5271
Eze 16:60 with thee in the days of thy **y.**,......... 5271
Eze 23:3 committed whoredoms in their **y.**........ 5271
Eze 23:8 for in her **y.** they lay with her,........... 5271
Eze 23:19 to remembrance the days of her **y.**,...... 5271
Eze 23:21 the lewdness of thy **y.**,.................... 5271
Eze 23:21 Egyptians for the paps of thy **y.**......... 5271
Ho 2:15 sing there, as in the days of her **y.**,..... 5271
Joe 1:8 for the husband of her **y.**.................. 5271
Zec 13:5 me to keep cattle from my **y.**.............. 5271
Mal 2:14 thee and the wife of thy **y.**, ... 5271
Mal 2:15 against the wife of his **y.**.................. 5271
Mt 19:20 have I kept from my **y.** up:............... *3503*
Mk 10:20 these have I observed from my **y.**....... *3503*
Lu 18:21 these have I kept from my **y.** up........ *3503*
Ac 26:4 My manner of life from my **y.**,............ *3503*
1Ti 4:12 Let no man despise thy **y.**; but be...... *3503*

YOUTHFUL
2Ti 2:22 Flee also **y.** lusts: but follow *3512*

YOUTHS
Pr 7:7 I discerned among the **y.**, a young...... 1121
Isa 40:30 the **y.** shall faint and be weary,.......... 5288

YOU-WARD
2Co 1:12 and more abundantly to **y.**......... *4314,5209*
2Co 13:3 which to **y.** is not weak, but is ... *1519,5209*
Eph 3:2 grace...which is given me to **y.**... *1519,5209*

Z.

ZAANAIM (za-an-a'-im) See also ZAANANNIM.
Jg 4:11 his tent unto the plain of **Z.**, ... 6815

ZAANAN (za'-an-an) See also ZENAN.
Mic 1:11 inhabitant of **Z.** came not forth........... 6630

ZAANANNIM (za-an-an'-nim) See also ZAANAIM.
Jos 19:33 from Heleph, from Allon to **Z.**, ... 6815

ZAAVAN (za'-av-an) See also ZAVAN.
Ge 36:27 of Ezer are these; Bilhan, and **Z.**,...... 2190

ZABAD (za'-bad) See also JOSABAD; JOZACHAR.
1Ch 2:36 Nathan, and Nathan begat **Z.**,........... 2066
1Ch 2:37 And **Z.** begat Ephlal, and Ephlal......... 2066
1Ch 7:21 And **Z.** his son, and Shuthelah............ 2066
1Ch 11:41 the Hittite, **Z.** the son of Ahlai, ... 2066
2Ch 24:26 **Z.** the son of Shimeath an................. 2066
Ezr 10:27 Mattaniah, and Jeremoth, and **Z.**,....... 2066
Ezr 10:33 Mattathah, **Z.**, Eliphelet, Jeremai,....... 2066
Ezr 10:43 Mattithiah, **Z.**, Zebina, Jadau, ... 2066

ZABBAI (zab'-bahee) See also ZACCAI.
Ezr 10:28 Hananiah, **Z.**, and Athlai.................. 2079
Ne 3:20 Baruch the son of **Z.** earnestly 2079

ZABBUD (zab'-bud) See also ZACCUR.
Ezr 8:14 Uthai, and **Z.**, and with them 2072

ZABDI (zab'-di) See also ZACCHUR; ZICHRI.
Jos 7:1 the son of Carmi, the son of **Z.**, ... 2067
Jos 7:17 man by man; and **Z.** was taken.......... 2067
Jos 7:18 the son of Carmi, the son of **Z.**, ... 2067
1Ch 8:19 And Jakim, and Zichri, and **Z.**,............ 2067
1Ch 27:27 wine cellars was **Z.** the Shiphmite: 2067
Ne 11:17 the son of **Z.**, the son of Asaph, ... 2067

ZABDIEL (zab'-de-el)
1Ch 27:2 was Jashobeam the son of **Z.**:............ 2068
Ne 11:14 and their overseer was **Z.**, the son..... 2068

ZABUD (za'-bud)
1Ki 4:5 **Z.** the son of Nathan was principal...... 2071

ZABULON (zab'-u-lon) See also ZEBULUN.
Mt 4:13 borders of **Z.** and Nephthalim:........... *2194*
Mt 4:15 The land of **Z.**, and the land of........... *2194*
Re 7:8 Of the tribe of **Z.** were sealed............ *2194*

ZACCAI (zac'-cahee) See also ZABBAI.
Ezr 2:9 The children of **Z.**, seven hundred...... 2140
Ne 7:14 The children of **Z.**, seven hundred...... 2140

ZACCHAEUS (zak-ke'-us)
Lu 19:2 there was a man named **Z.**, ... *2195*
Lu 19:5 and unto him, **Z., make haste,**......... *2195*
Lu 19:8 **Z.** stood, and said unto the Lord;....... *2195*

ZACCHUR (zac'-cur) See also ZACCUR.
1Ch 4:26 Hamuel his son, **Z.** his son, ... 2139

ZACCUR (zac'-cur) See also ZABBUD; ZABDI; ZACCHUR; ZICHRI.
Nu 13:4 Reuben, Shammua the son of **Z.**....... 2139
1Ch 24:27 and Shoham, and **Z.**, and Ibri. 2139
1Ch 25:2 **Z.**, and Joseph, and Nethaniah, ... 2139
1Ch 25:10 The third to **Z.**, he, his sons, and 2139
Ne 3:2 them builded **Z.** the son of Imri. 2139
Ne 10:12 **Z.**, Sherebiah, Shebaniah, ... 2139
Ne 12:35 the son of Michaiah, the son of **Z.**,..... 2139
Ne 13:13 to them was Hanan the son of **Z.**,....... 2139

ZACHARIAH (zak-a-ri'-ah) See also ZECHARIAH.
2Ki 14:29 **Z.**, his son reigned in his stead.......... 2148
2Ki 15:8 did **Z.** the son of Jeroboam reign........ 2148
2Ki 15:11 And the rest of the acts of **Z.**,........... 2148
2Ki 18:2 also was Abi, the daughter of **Z.**........ 2148

ZACHARIAS zak'-a-ri'-as) See also ZECHARIAH.
Mt 23:35 **blood of Z. son of Barachias,**........ *2197*
Lu 1:5 a certain priest named **Z.**, of the........ *2197*
Lu 1:12 And when **Z.** saw him, he was *2197*
Lu 1:13 angel said unto him, Fear not, **Z.** *2197*
Lu 1:18 And **Z.** said unto the angel,............... *2197*
Lu 1:21 And the people waited for **Z.**,............ *2197*
Lu 1:40 And entered into the house of **Z.**, ... *2197*
Lu 1:59 they called him **Z.**, after the name...... *2197*
Lu 1:67 And his father **Z.** was filled with *2197*
Lu 3:2 came unto John the son of **Z.**............ *2197*
Lu 11:51 **of Abel unto the blood of Z.**,.......... *2197*

ZACHER (za'-kur) See also ZECHARIAH.
1Ch 8:31 And Gedor, and Ahio, and **Z.** 2144

ZADOK (za'-dok) See also ZADOK'S.
2Sa 8:17 And **Z.** the son of Ahitub, and........... 6659
2Sa 15:24 And lo **Z.** also, and all the Levites...... 6659
2Sa 15:25 the king said unto **Z.**, Carry back....... 6659
2Sa 15:27 king said also unto **Z.** the priest,........ 6659
2Sa 15:29 **Z.** therefore and Abiathar carried 6659
2Sa 15:35 hast thou not there with thee **Z.**......... 6659
2Sa 15:35 thou shalt tell it to **Z.** and Abiathar..... 6659
2Sa 17:15 Then said Hushai unto **Z.** and to........ 6659
2Sa 18:19 Then said Ahimaaz the son of **Z.**,........ 6659
2Sa 18:22 Then said Ahimaaz the son of **Z.**......... 6659
2Sa 18:27 running of Ahimaaz the son of **Z.** 6659
2Sa 19:11 David sent to **Z.** and to Abiathar......... 6659
2Sa 20:25 **Z.** and Abiathar were the priests:........ 6659
1Ki 1:8,26 **Z.** the priet, and Benaiah...son 6659
1Ki 1:32 Call me **Z.** the priest, and Nathan 6659
1Ki 1:34 let **Z.** the priest, and Nathan the........ 6659
1Ki 1:38 So **Z.** the priest, and Nathan the........ 6659
1Ki 1:39 And **Z.** the priest took an horn of oil... 6659
1Ki 1:44 hath sent with him **Z.** the priest,........ 6659
1Ki 1:45 And **Z.** the priest and Nathan the........ 6659
1Ki 2:35 **Z.** the priest did the king put in.......... 6659
1Ki 4:2 Azariah the son of **Z.** the priest, ... 6659
1Ki 4:4 **Z.** and Abiathar were the priests:........ 6659
2Ki 15:33 was Jerusha, the daughter of **Z.**......... 6659
1Ch 6:8, 12 Ahitub begat **Z.**, and **Z.** begat 6659
1Ch 6:53 **Z.** his son, Ahimaaz his son. 6659
1Ch 9:11 son of Meshullam, the son of **Z.**, ... 6659
1Ch 12:28 And **Z.**, a young man mighty of 6659
1Ch 15:11 David called for **Z.** and Abiathar......... 6659
1Ch 16:39 And **Z.** the priest, and his brethren 6659
1Ch 18:16 And **Z.** the son of Ahitub, and............ 6659
1Ch 24:3 both **Z.** of the sons of Eleazar, ... 6659
1Ch 24:6 and the princes, and **Z.** the priest, ... 6659
1Ch 24:31 presence of David the king, and **Z.**,..... 6659
1Ch 27:17 of Kemuel: of the Aaronites, **Z.**.......... 6659
1Ch 29:22 chief governor, and **Z.** to be priest. 6659
2Ch 27:1 was Jerushah, the daughter of **Z.**........ 6659
2Ch 31:10 chief priest of the house of **Z.**........... 6659
Ezr 7:2 The son of Shallum, the son of **Z.**, ... 6659
Ne 3:4 repaired **Z.** the son of Baana............. 6659
Ne 3:29 repaired **Z.** the son of Immer............. 6659
Ne 10:21 Meshazabeel, **Z.**, Jaddua,.................. 6659
Ne 11:11 son of Meshullam, the son of **Z.**,......... 6659
Ne 13:13 the priest, and **Z.** the scribe, ... 6659
Eze 40:46 these are the sons of **Z.** among the 6659
Eze 43:19 Levites that be of the seed of **Z.**,........ 6659
Eze 44:15 the sons of **Z.**, that kept the charge 6659
Eze 48:11 are sanctified of the sons of **Z.**;.......... 6659

ZADOK'S (za'-doks)
2Sa 15:36 Ahimaaz **Z.** son, and Jonathan............ 6659

ZAHAM (za'-ham)
2Ch 11:19 Jeush, and Shamariah, and **Z.**............ 2093

ZAIN (zah'-yin)
Ps 119:49 *title* [ז] **Z.**...

ZAIR (za'-ur)
2Ki 8:21 So Joram went over to **Z.**, and all 6811

ZALAPH (za'-laf)
Ne 3:30 and Hanun the sixth son of **Z.**, ... 6764

ZALMON (zal'-mon) See also ILAI; SALMON.
Jg 9:48 got him up to mount **Z.**,.................... 6756
2Sa 23:28 **Z.** the Ahohite, Maharai the............... 6756

ZALMONAH (zal-mo'-nah)
Nu 33:41 mount Hor, and pitched in **Z.**............ 6758
Nu 33:42 And they departed from **Z.**, and......... 6758

ZALMUNNA (zal-mun'-nah)
Jg 8:5 am pursuing after Zebah and **Z.**,........ 6759
Jg 8:6 Are the hands of Zebah and **Z.** now..... 6759
Jg 8:7 Lord hath delivered Zebah and **Z.**........ 6759
Jg 8:10 Zebah and **Z.** were in Karkor, ... 6759
Jg 8:12 And when Zebah and **Z.** fled, he 6759
Jg 8:12 two kings of Midian, Zebah and **Z.**,....... 6759
Jg 8:15 Behold Zebah and **Z.**, with whom 6759
Jg 8:15 Are the hands of Zebah and **Z.** now...... 6759
Jg 8:18 Then said he unto Zebah and **Z.**,.......... 6759
Jg 8:21 Zebah and **Z.** said, Rise thou,............ 6759
Jg 8:21 arose, and slew Zebah and **Z.**,............ 6759
Ps 83:11 their princes as Zebah, and as **Z.**: 6759

ZAMZUMMIMS (zam-zum'-mims) See also ZUZIMS.
De 2:20 and the Ammonites call them **Z.**;........ 2157

ZANOAH (za-no'-ah)
Jos 15:34 **Z.**, and En-gannim, Tappuah, ... 2182

Jos 15:56 And Jezreel, and Jokdeam, and Z., 2182
2Ch 4:18 and Jekuthiel the father of Z. 2182
Ne 3:13 Hanun, and the inhabitants of Z.; 2182
Ne 11:30 Z., Adullam, and in their villages, 2182

ZAPHNATH-PAANEAH (zaf''-nath-pa-a-ne'-ah)
Ge 41:45 called Joseph's name Z.; 6847

ZAPHON (za'-fon)
Jos 13:27 and Z., the rest of the kingdom 6829

ZARA (za'-rah) See also ZARAH; ZERAH.
Mt 1:3 Judas begat Phares and Z. of *2196*

ZARAH (za'-rah) See also ZARA; ZERAH.
Ge 38:30 and his name was called Z.. 2226
Ge 46:12 and Shelah, and Pharez, and Z.: 2226

ZAREAH (za'-re-ah) See also ZAREATHITES; ZORAH.
Ne 11:29 And at En-rimmon, and at Z., 6881

ZAREATHITES (za'-re-ath-ites) See also ZORATHITES.
1Ch 2:53 of them came the Z., and the 6882

ZARED (za'-red) See also ZERED.
Nu 21:12 and pitched in the valley of Z.. 2218

ZAREPHATH (zar'-e-fath) See also SAREPTA.
1Ki 17:9 Arise, get thee to Z., which 6886
1Ki 17:10 So he arose and went to Z.. 6886
Ob 20 of the Canaanites, even unto Z.; 6886

ZARETAN (zar'-e-tans) See also ZARTANAH; ZEREDATHAH.
Jos 3:16 the city Adam, that is beside Z. 6891

ZARETH-SHAHAR (za''-reth-sha'-har)
Jos 13:19 and Z. in the mount of the valley, 6890

ZARHITES (zar'-hites)
Nu 26:13 Of Zerah, the family of Z. 2227
Nu 26:20 of Zerah, the family of Z.. 2227
Jos 7:17 and he took the family of the Z. 2227
Jos 7:17 he brought the family of the Z. 2227
1Ch 27:11 Sibbecai the Hushathite, of the Z. 2227
1Ch 27:13 the Netophathite, of the Z. 2227

ZARTANAH (zar'-ta-nah) See also ZARETAN; ZARTHAN
1Ki 4:12 which is by Z. beneath Jezreel, 6891

ZARTHAN (za' than) See also ZARETAN; ZARTHANAH.
1Ki 7:46 ground between Succoth and Z. 6891

ZATTHU (zath'-u) See also ZATTU.
Ne 10:14 Parosh, Pahath-moab, Elam, Z. 2240

ZATTU (zath'-u) See also ZATTHU.
Ezr 2:8 The children of Z., nine hundred 2240
Ezr 10:27 sons of Z.; Elioenai, Eliashib, 2240
Ne 7:13 The children of Ze, eight hundred 2240

ZAVAN (za'-van) See also ZAAVAN.
1Ch 1:42 Ezer; Bilhan, and Z., and Jakan. 2190

ZAZA (za'-zah)
1Ch 2:33 sons of Jonathan; Peleth and Z.. 2117

ZEAL
2Sa 21:2 slay them in his z. to the children 7065
2Ki 10:16 and see my z. for the Lord. 7068
2Ki 19:31 z. of the Lord of hosts shall do this. 7068
Ps 69:9 z. of thine house hath eaten me up; 7068
Ps 119:139 My z. hath consumed me, because 7068
Isa 9:7 The z. of the Lord of hosts will 7068
Isa 37:32 z. of the Lord of hosts shall do this. 7068
Isa 59:17 and was clad with z. as a cloke. 7068
Isa 63:15 where is thy z. and thy strength, 7068
Eze 5:13 I the Lord have spoken it in my z., 7068
Joh 2:17 z. of thine house hath eaten me *2205*
Ro 10:2 record that they have a z. of God, *2205*
2Co 7:11 yea, what z., yea, what revenge! *2205*
2Co 9:2 your z. hath provoked very many. *2205*
Php 3:6 Concerning z., persecuting the *2205*
Col 4:13 that he hath a great z. for you, *2205*

ZEALOUS
Nu 25:11 while he was z. for my sake 7065
Nu 25:13 because he was z. for his God, and 7065
Ac 21:20 and they are all z. of the law: *2207*
Ac 22:3 and was z. toward God, as ye all *2207*
1Co 14:12 as ye are z. of spiritual gifts, *2207*
Ga 1:14 z. of the traditions of my fathers. *2207*
Tit 2:14 a peculiar people, z. of good works. *2207*
Re 3:19 be z. therefore, and repent *2206*

ZEALOUSLY
Ga 4:17 They z. affect you, but not well; *2206*
Ga 4:18 good to be z. affected always in a *2206*

ZEBADIAH (zeb-ad-i'-ah)
1Ch 8:15 And Z., and Arad, and Ader, 2069
1Ch 8:17 And Z., and Meshullam, and 2069
1Ch 12:7 and Z., the sons of Jeroham 2069
1Ch 26:2 Jediael the second, Z. the third, 2069
1Ch 27:7 Joab, and Z. his son after him: 2069
2Ch 17:8 and Nethaniah, and Z., and Asahel, 2069
2Ch 19:11 Z. the son of Ishmael, the ruler 2069
Ezr 8:8 Z. the son of Michael, and with 2069
Ezr 10:20 sons of Immer; Hanani, and Z.. 2069

ZEBAH (ze'-bah)
Jg 8:5 and I am pursuing after Z. and 2078
Jg 8:6 Are the hands of Z. and Zalmunna 2078
Jg 8:7 when the Lord hath delivered Z. 2078
Jg 8:10 Now Z. and Zalmunna were in 2078
Jg 8:12 And when Z. and Zalmunna fled, 2078
Jg 8:12 kings of Midian, Z. and Zalmunna, 2078
Jg 8:15 Behold Z. and Zalmunna, with 2078
Jg 8:15 Are the hands of Z. and Zalmunna 2078
Jg 8:18 said he unto Z. and Zalmunna, 2078
Jg 8:21 Z. and Zalmunna said, Rise thou, 2078
Jg 8:21 slew Z. and Zalmunna, and took 2078
Ps 83:11 all their princes as Z., and as 2078

ZEBAIM (ze-ba'-im)
Ezr 2:57 the children of Pochereth of Z., 6380
Ne 7:59 the children of Pochereth of Z., 6380

ZEBEDEE (zeb'-e-dee) See also ZEBEDEE'S.
Mt 4:21 James the son of Z., and John his *2199*
Mt 4:21 in a ship with Z. their father, *2199*
Mt 10:2 James the son of Z., and John his *2199*
Mt 26:37 him Peter and the two sons of Z., *2199*
Mk 1:19 he saw James the son of Z., and *2199*
Mk 1:20 left their father Z. in the ship *2199*
Mk 3:17 And James the son of Z., and John *2199*
Mk 10:35 James and John, the sons of Z., *2199*
Lu 5:10 James, and John, the sons of Z.. *2199*
Joh 21:2 and the sons of Z., and two other *2199*

ZEBEDEE'S (zeb'-e-dees)
Mt 20:20 came...the mother of Z. children *2199*
Mt 27:56 and the mother of Z. children. *2199*

ZEBINA (ze-bi'-nah)
Ezr 10:43 Zabad, Z., Jadan, and Joel, 2081

ZEBOIIM (ze-boy'-im) See also ZEBOIM.
Ge 14:2 Shemeber king of Z., and the 6636
Ge 14:8 king of Z., and the king of Bela 6636

ZEBOIM (ze-bo'-im) See also ZEBOIIM.
Ge 10:19 Gomorrah, and Admah, and Z., 6636
De 29:23 and Gomorrah, Admah, and Z., 6636
1Sa 13:18 that looketh to the valley of Z. 6650
Ne 11:34 Hadid, Z., Neballat, 6650
Ho 11:8 how shall I set thee as Z.? 6636

ZEBUB See BAAL-ZEBUB.

ZEBUDAH (ze-bu'-dah)
2Ki 23:36 And his mother's name was Z., 2081

ZEBUL (ze'-bul)
Jg 9:28 And Z. his officer? serve the men 2083
Jg 9:30 when Z. the ruler of the city heard 2083
Jg 9:36 he said to Z., Behold, there come 2083
Jg 9:36 And Z. said unto him, Thou seest 2083
Jg 9:38 Then said Z. unto him, Where is 2083
Jg 9:41 Z. thrust out Gaal and his brethren, 2083

ZEBULONITE (zeb'-u-lon-ite) See also ZEBULUNITES.
Jg 12:11 after him Elon, a Z., judged 2075
Jg 12:12 And Elon the Z. died, and was 2075

ZEBULUN (zeb'-u-lun) See also ZABULON; ZEBULONITE; ZEBULUNITES.
Ge 30:20 and she called his name Z. 2074
Ge 35:23 and Judah, and Issachar, and Z. 2074
Ge 46:14 sons of Z.; Sered, and Elon, 2074
Ge 49:13 Z. shall dwell at the haven 2074
Ex 1:3 Issachar, Z., and Benjamin, 2074
Nu 1:9 Of Z.; Eliab the son of Helon. 2074
Nu 1:30 Of the children of Z., by their 2074
Nu 1:31 even of the tribe of Z., were fifty 2074
Nu 2:7 Then the tribe of Z.: and Eliab 2074
Nu 2:7 be captain of the children of Z.. 2074
Nu 7:24 Helon, prince of the children of Z., 2074
Nu 10:16 of the children of Z. was Eliab 2074
Nu 13:10 Of the tribe of Z., Gaddiel the 2074
Nu 26:26 sons of Z. after their families: 2074
Nu 34:25 of the tribe of the children of Z., 2074
De 27:13 Gad, and Asher, and Z., Dan, 2074
De 33:18 of Z. he said, Rejoice, Z., in thy 2074
Jos 19:10 came up for the children of Z. 2074
Jos 19:16 inheritance of the children of Z. 2074
Jos 19:27 reacheth to Z., and to the valley 2074
Jos 19:34 reacheth to Z. on the south side, 2074
Jos 21:7 out of the tribe of Z., twelve cities. 2074
Jos 21:34 out of the tribe of Z., Jokneam 2074
Jg 1:30 Z. drive out the inhabitants 2074
Jg 4:6 Naphtali and of the children of Z.? 2074
Jg 4:10 Barak called Z. and Naphtali to 2074
Jg 5:14 out of Z. they that handle the pen 2074
Jg 5:18 Z. and Naphtali were a people that 2074
Jg 6:35 and unto Z., and unto Naphtali; 2074
Jg 12:12 in Aijalon in the country of Z. 2074
1Ch 2:1 and Judah, Issachar, and Z., 2074
1Ch 6:63 out of the tribe of Z., twelve cities. 2074
1Ch 6:77 were given out of the tribe of Z., 2074
1Ch 12:33 Of Z., such as went forth to battle, 2074
1Ch 12:40 even unto Issachar and Z. and 2074
1Ch 27:19 Of Z., Ishmaiah the son of 2074
2Ch 30:10 and Manasseh even unto Z.: 2074
2Ch 30:11 and Manasseh and of Z. humbled 2074
2Ch 30:18 Issachar and Z., had not cleansed 2074
Ps 68:27 princes of Z., and the princes of 2074
Isa 9:1 he lightly afflicted the land of Z. 2074
Ezr 48:26 unto the west side, Z. a portion 2074
Ezr 48:27 And by the border of Z., from the 2074
Ezr 48:33 gate of Issachar, one gate of Z.. 2074

ZEBULUNITES (zeb'-u-lun-ites) See also ZEBULONITE.
Nu 26:27 These are the families of the Z. 2075

ZECHARIAH (zek-a-ri'-ah) See also ZACCUR; ZACHARIAH; ZACHARIAS; ZACHER.
1Ch 5:7 were the chief, Jeiel, and Z. 2148
1Ch 9:21 And Z. the son of Meshelemiah 2148
1Ch 9:37 And Gedor, and Ahio, and Z., 2148
1Ch 15:18 Z., Ben, and Jaaziel, and 2148
1Ch 15:20 And Z., and Aziel, and 2148
1Ch 15:24 and Z., and Benaiah, and Eliezer, 2148
1Ch 16:5 the chief, and next to him Z., 2148
1Ch 24:25 of the sons of Isshiah; Z. 2148
1Ch 26:2 Z. the firstborn, Jediael the 2148
1Ch 26:11 Tebaliah the third, Z. the fourth: 2148
1Ch 26:14 for Z. his son, a wise counsellor, 2148
1Ch 27:21 in Gilead, Iddo the son of Z. 2148
2Ch 17:7 and to Obadiah, and to Z., and 2148
2Ch 20:14 Then upon Jahaziel the son of Z., 2148
2Ch 21:2 and Jehiel, and Z., and Azariah, 2148
2Ch 24:20 Spirit of God came upon Z. the son 2148
2Ch 26:5 he sought God in the days of Z., 2148
2Ch 29:1 was Abijah, the daughter of Z. 2148
2Ch 29:13 sons of Asaph; Z., and Mattaniah: 2148
2Ch 34:12 and Z. and Meshullam, of the sons 2148
2Ch 35:8 Hilkiah and Z. and Jehiel, 2148
Ezr 5:1 prophet, and Z. the son of Iddo, 2148
Ezr 6:14 prophet and Z. the son of Iddo. 2148
Ezr 8:3 of the sons of Pharosh; Z.: 2148
Ezr 8:11 Z. the son of Bebai, and with him 2148
Ezr 8:16 for Z., and for Meshullam, chief 2148
Ezr 10:26 Mattaniah, Z., and Jehiel, and 2148
Ne 8:4 Hashbadana, Z., and Meshullam. 2148
Ne 11:4 the son of Z., the son of Amariah, 2148
Ne 11:5 the son of Joiarib, the son of Z., 2148
Ne 11:12 the son of Z., the son of Pashur, 2148
Ne 12:16 Of Iddo, Z.; of Ginnethon, 2148
Ne 12:35 namely, Z. the son of Jonathan, 2148
Ne 12:41 Z., and Hananiah, with trumpets; 2148
Isa 8:2 and Z. the son of Jeberechiah. 2148
Zec *general title* Z. 2148
Zec 1:1,7 came the word of the Lord unto Z., 2148
Zec 7:1 the word of the Lord came unto Z. 2148
Zec 7:8 the word of the Lord came unto Z., 2148

ZEDAD (ze'-dad)
Nu 34:8 forth of the border shall be to Z. 6657
Eze 47:15 way of Hethlon, as men go to Z.; 6657

ZEDEKIAH (zed-e-ki'-ah) See also MATTANIAH; ZEDEKIAH'S; ZIDKIJAH.
1Ki 22:11 Z. the son of Chenaanah made 6667

1Ki 22:24 **Z.** the son of Chenaanah went near, ... 6667
2Ki 24:17 stead, and changed his name to **Z.**. 6667
2Ki 24:18 **Z.** was twenty and one years old 6667
2Ki 24:20 that **Z.** rebelled against the king........ 6667
2Ki 25:2 unto the eleventh year of king **Z.**. 6667
2Ki 25:7 slew the sons of **Z.** before his eyes.... 6667
2Ki 25:7 put out the eyes of **Z.**, and bound...... 6667
1Ch 3:15 second Jehoiakim, the third **Z.**, ... 6667
1Ch 3:16 Jeconiah his son, **Z.** his son............. 6667
2Ch 18:10 **Z.** the son of Chenaanah had made..... 6667
2Ch 18:23 **Z.** the son of Chenaanah came.......... 6667
2Ch 36:10 made **Z.** his brother king over.......... 6667
2Ch 36:11 **Z.** was one and twenty years old 6667
Jer 1:3 eleventh year of **Z.** the son of.......... 6667
Jer 21:1 king **Z.** sent unto him Pashur the....... 6667
Jer 21:3 them, Thus shall ye say to **Z.**.......... 6667
Jer 21:7 I will deliver **Z.** king of Judah, ... 6667
Jer 24:8 will I give **Z.** the king of Judah, ... 6667
Jer 27:3 come to Jerusalem unto **Z.** king of...... 6667
Jer 27:12 I spake also to **Z.** king of Judah 6667
Jer 28:1 in the beginning of the reign of **Z.**. 6667
Jer 29:3 (whom **Z.** king of Judah sent unto......... 6667
Jer 29:21 and of **Z.** the son of Maaseiah, ... 6667
Jer 29:22 The Lord make thee like **Z.** and 6667
Jer 32:1 the Lord in the tenth year of **Z.**......... 6667
Jer 32:3 For **Z.** king of Judah had shut him...... 6667
Jer 32:4 **Z.** king of Judah shall not escape........ 6667
Jer 32:5 And he shall lead **Z.** to Babylon, ... 6667
Jer 34:2 Go and speak to **Z.** king of Judah, ... 6667
Jer 34:4 of the Lord, O **Z.** king of Judah; 6667
Jer 34:6 spake all these words unto **Z.** king 6667
Jer 34:8 the king of **Z.** had made a covenant.... 6667
Jer 34:21 **Z.** king of Judah and his princes......... 6667
Jer 36:12 and **Z.** the son of Hananiah, ... 6667
Jer 37:1 king **Z.** the son of Josiah reigned......... 6667
Jer 37:3 **Z.** the king sent Jehucal the son......... 6667
Jer 37:17 **Z.** the king sent, and took him out: 6667
Jer 37:18 Jeremiah said unto king **Z.**, What 6667
Jer 37:21 **Z.** the king commanded that they....... 6667
Jer 38:5 **Z.** the king said, Behold, he is in....... 6667
Jer 38:14 Then **Z.** the king sent, and took 6667
Jer 38:15 Jeremiah said unto **Z.**, If I declare...... 6667
Jer 38:16 So **Z.** the king sware secretly unto...... 6667
Jer 38:17 Then said Jeremiah unto **Z.**, Thus...... 6667
Jer 38:19 **Z.** the king said unto Jeremiah, I........ 6667
Jer 38:24 said **Z.** unto Jeremiah, Let no man 6667
Jer 39:1 ninth year of **Z.** king of Judah, ... 6667
Jer 39:2 And in the eleventh year of **Z.**,.......... 6667
Jer 39:4 when **Z.** the king of Judah saw 6667
Jer 39:5 and overtook **Z.** in the plains of......... 6667
Jer 39:6 king of Babylon slew the sons of **Z.**.... 6667
Jer 44:30 as I gave **Z.** king of Judah into........... 6667
Jer 49:34 in the beginning of the reign of **Z.**........ 6667
Jer 51:59 went with **Z.** the king of Judah 6667
Jer 52:1 **Z.** was one and twenty years old 6667
Jer 52:3 that **Z.** rebelled against the king......... 6667
Jer 52:5 unto the eleventh year of king **Z.**. 6667
Jer 52:8 and overtook **Z.** in the plains of......... 6667
Jer 52:10 slew the sons of **Z.** before his eyes: ... 6667
Jer 52:11 Then he put out the eyes of **Z.**; 6667

ZEDEKIAH'S (zed-e-ki'-ahs)
Jer 39:7 Moreover he put out **Z.** eyes 6667

ZEEB (ze'-eb)
Jg 7:25 of the Midianites, Oreb and **Z.**;.......... 2062
Jg 7:25 **Z.** they slew at the winepress of **Z.**,... 2062
Jg 7:25 heads of Oreb and **Z.** to Gideon......... 2062
Jg 8:3 princes of Midian, Oreb and **Z.**: 2062
Ps 83:11 nobles like Oreb, and like **Z.**: 2062

ZELAH (ze'-lah)
Jos 18:28 **Z.**, Eleph, and Jebusi, which is 6762
2Sa 21:14 in the country of Benjamin in **Z.**,......... 6762

ZELEK (ze'-lek)
2Sa 23:37 **Z.** the Ammonite, Nahari the............ 6768
1Ch 11:39 **Z.** the Ammonite, Naharai the 6768

ZELOPHEHAD (ze-lo'-fe-had)
Nu 26:33 **Z.** the son of Hepher had no sons, ... 6765
Nu 26:33 the names of the daughters of **Z.** 6765
Nu 27:1 Then came the daughters of **Z.**,.......... 6765
Nu 27:7 The daughters of **Z.** speak right:........ 6765
Nu 36:2 the inheritance of **Z.** our brother........ 6765
Nu 36:6 concerning the daughters of **Z.**, ... 6765
Nu 36:10 Moses, so did the daughters of **Z.**:..... 6765
Nu 36:11 the daughters of **Z.**, were married...... 6765
Jos 17:3 **Z.**, the son of Hepher, the son of 6765
1Ch 7:15 was **Z.**: and **Z.** had daughters.......... 6765

ZELOTES (ze-lo'-teze) See also CANAANITE; SIMON.
Lu 6:15 of Alphaeus, and Simon called **Z.**,....... *2208*
Ac 1:13 Simon **Z.**, and Judas the brother *2208*

ZELZAH (zel'-zah)
1Sa 10:2 in the border of Benjamin at **Z.**;......... 6766

ZEMARAIM (zem-a-ra'-im) See also ZEMARITE.
Jos 18:22 Beth-arabah, and **Z.**, and Beth-el,....... 6787
2Ch 13:4 Abijah stood up upon mount **Z.**,........ 6787

ZEMARITE (zem'-a-rite)
Ge 10:18 and the **Z.**, and the Hamathite:.......... 6786
1Ch 1:16 and the **Z.**, and the Hamathite........... 6786

ZEMIRA ze-mi'-rah)
1Ch 7:8 sons of Becher; **Z.**, and Joash, ... 2160

ZENAN (ze'-nan) See also ZAANAN.
Jos 15:37 **Z.**, and Hadashah, Migdal-gad,........... 6799

ZENAS (ze'-nas)
Tit 3:13 Bring **Z.** the lawyer and Apollos......... *2211*

ZEPHANIAH (zef-a-ni'-ah)
2Ki 25:18 priest, and **Z.** the second priest, ... 6846
1Ch 6:36 the son of Azariah, the son of **Z.**, ... 6846
Jer 21:1 **Z.** the son of Maaseiah the priest,...... 6846
Jer 29:25 to **Z.** the son of Maaseiah the priest, .. 6846
Jer 29:29 And **Z.** the priest read this letter....... 6846
Jer 37:3 **Z.** the son of Maaseiah the priest....... 6846
Jer 52:24 priest, and **Z.** the second priest, ... 6846
Zep *general title* **Z.**... 6846
Zep 1:1 came unto **Z.** the son of Cushi,........... 6846
Zec 6:10 the house of Josiah the son of **Z.**; 6846
Zec 6:14 Jedaiah, and to Hen the son of **Z.**,....... 6846

ZEPHATH (ze'-fath) See also HORMAH.
Jg 1:17 the Canaanites that inhabited **Z.**,......... 6857

ZEPHATHAH (zef'-a-thah)
2Ch 14:10 in the valley of **Z.** at Mareshah........... 6859

ZEPHI (ze'-fi) See also ZEPHO.
1Ch 1:36 Eliphaz; Teman, and Omar, **Z.**,.......... 6825

ZEPHO (ze'-fo) See also ZEPHI.
Ge 36:11 Eliphaz were Teman, Omar, **Z.**,.......... 6825
Ge 36:15 duke Omar, duke **Z.**, duke Kenaz,...... 6825

ZEPHON (ze'-fon) See also BAAL-ZEPHON; ZEPHONITES; ZIPHION.
Nu 26:15 families: of **Z.**, the family of the......... 6827

ZEPHONITES (zef'-on-ites)
Nu 26:15 of Zephon, the family of the **Z.** 6831

ZER (zur)
Jos 19:35 the fenced cities are Ziddim, **Z.**, ... 6863

ZERAH (ze'-rah) See also EZRAHITE; ZARAH; ZARHITES; ZOHAR.
Ge 36:13 sons of Reuel; Nahath, and **Z.**,........... 2226
Ge 36:17 Nahath, duke **Z.**, duke Shammah,....... 2226
Ge 36:33 and Jobab the son of **Z.** of Bozrah...... 2226
Nu 26:13 Of **Z.**, the family of the Zarhites: 2226
Nu 26:20 of **Z.**, the family of the Zarhites. 2226
Jos 7:1,18 the son of **Z.**, of the tribe of............ 2226
Jos 7:24 took Achan the son of **Z.**, and the........ 2226
Jos 22:20 Did not Achan the son of **Z.**.............. 2226
1Ch 1:37 of Reuel; Nahath, **Z.**, Shammah, ... 2226
1Ch 1:44 Jobab the son of **Z.** of Bozrah............ 2226
1Ch 2:4 in law bare him Pharez and **Z.**.......... 2226
1Ch 2:6 sons of **Z.**; Zimri, and Ethan, ... 2226
1Ch 4:24 and Jamin, Jarib, **Z.**, and Shaul:.......... 2226
1Ch 6:21 Iddo his son, **Z.** his son, Jeaterai........ 2226
1Ch 6:41 The son of Ethni, the son of **Z.**, ... 2226
1Ch 9:6 of the sons of **Z.**; Jeuel and their 2226
2Ch 14:9 out against them **Z.** the Ethiopian....... 2226
Ne 11:24 children of **Z.** the son of Judah,......... 2226

ZERAHIAH (zer-a-hi'-ah)
1Ch 6:6 Uzzi begat **Z.**, and **Z.** begat.............. 2228
1Ch 6:51 his son, Uzzi his son, **Z.** his son,........ 2228
Ezr 7:4 The son of **Z.**, the son of Uzzi, ... 2228
Ezr 8:4 Elihoenai the son of **Z.**, and with......... 2228

ZERED (ze'-red) See also ZARED.
De 2:13 and get you over the brook **Z.**............ 2218
De 2:13 And we went over the brook **Z.**........... 2218
De 2:14 we were come over the brook **Z.**,......... 2218

ZEREDA (zer'-e-dah)
1Ki 11:26 an Ephrathite of **Z.**; Solomon's........... 6868

ZEREDATHAH (ze-red'-a-thah) See also ZARTHAN; ZERERATH.
2Ch 4:17 ground between Succoth and **Z.**. 6868

ZERERATH (zer'-e-rath) See also ZARTHAN; ZEREDATHAH.
Jg 7:22 host fled to Beth-shittah in **Z.**,............ 6888

ZERESH (ze'-resh)
Es 5:10 for his friends, and **Z.** his wife........... 2238
Es 5:14 said **Z.** his wife and...his friends......... 2238
Es 6:13 Haman told **Z.** his wife, and all his...... 2238
Es 6:13 said his wise men and **Z.** his wife........ 2238

ZERETH (ze'-reth)
1Ch 4:7 And the sons of Helah were, **Z.**,........ 6889

ZERI (ze'-ri) See also IZRI.
1Ch 25:3 of Jeduthun; Gedaliah, and **Z.**, ... 6874

ZEROR (ze'-ror)
1Sa 9:1 the son of Abiel, the son of **Z.**, ... 6872

ZERUAH (ze-ru'-ah)
1Ki 11:26 whose mother's name was **Z.**, ... 6871

ZERUBBABEL (ze-rub'-ba-bel) See also SHESHBAZ-ZAR; ZOROBABEL.
1Ch 3:19 and the sons of Pedaiah were, **Z.**,....... 2216
1Ch 3:19 and the sons of **Z.**; Meshullam,.......... 2216
Ezr 2:2 Which came with **Z.**: Jeshua, ... 2216
Ezr 3:2 priests, and **Z.** the son of Shealtiel, ... 2216
Ezr 3:8 began **Z.** the son of Shealtiel, ... 2216
Ezr 4:2 Then they came to **Z.**, and to the 2216
Ezr 4:3 But **Z.**, and Jeshua, and the rest......... 2216
Ezr 5:2 rose up **Z.** the son of Shealtiel,........... 2217
Ne 7:7 Who came with **Z.**, Jeshua,................ 2216
Ne 12:1 the Levites that went up with **Z.**......... 2216
Ne 12:47 And all Israel in the days of **Z.**,......... 2216
Hag 1:1 by Haggai the prophet unto **Z.** the...... 2216
Hag 1:12 Then **Z.** the son of Shealtiel,.............. 2216
Hag 1:14 Lord stirred up the spirit of **Z.** 2216
Hag 2:2 Speak now to **Z.** the son of................ 2216
Hag 2:4 Yet now be strong, O **Z.**, saith............ 2216
Hag 2:21 Speak to **Z.**, governor of Judah,.......... 2216
Hag 2:23 will I take thee, O **Z.**, my servant,..... 2216
Zec 4:6 is the word of the Lord unto **Z.**,......... 2216
Zec 4:7 before **Z.** thou shalt become a........... 2216
Zec 4:9 The hands of **Z.** have laid the............ 2216
Zec 4:10 plummet the hand of **Z.** with............. 2216

ZERUIAH (ze-ru-i'-ah)
1Sa 26:6 Abishai the son of **Z.**, brother to......... 6870
2Sa 2:13 And Joab the son of **Z.**, and the.......... 6870
2Sa 2:18 were three sons of **Z.** there, Joab, ... 6870
2Sa 3:39 the sons of **Z.** be too hard for me: 6870
2Sa 8:16 the son of **Z.** was over the host;........ 6870
2Sa 14:1 the son of **Z.** perceived that the......... 6870
2Sa 16:9 Then said Abishai the son of **Z.** 6870
2Sa 16:10 I to do with you, ye sons of **Z.**? 6870
2Sa 17:25 sister to **Z.** Joab's mother................. 6870
2Sa 18:2 the hand of Abishai the son of **Z.**, ... 6870
2Sa 19:21 Abishai the son of **Z.** answered.......... 6870
2Sa 19:22 ye sons of **Z.**, that ye should this....... 6870
2Sa 21:17 the son of **Z.** succoured him,............. 6870
2Sa 23:18 son of **Z.**, was chief among three......... 6870
2Sa 23:37 armourbearer to Joab the son of **Z.**...... 6870
1Ki 1:7 conferred with Joab the son of **Z.**,....... 6870
1Ki 2:5 also what Joab the son of **Z.** did.......... 6870
1Ki 2:22 priest, and for Joab the son of **Z.**. 6870
1Ch 2:16 Whose sisters were **Z.**, and Abigail...... 6870
1Ch 2:16 sons of **Z.**; Abishai, and Joab, and 6870
1Ch 11:6 Joab the son of **Z.** went first up,......... 6870
1Ch 11:39 armourbearer to Joab the son of **Z.**,..... 6870
1Ch 18:12 son of **Z.** slew of the Edomites.......... 6870
1Ch 18:15 the son of **Z.** was over the host;......... 6870
1Ch 26:28 Joab the son of **Z.**, had dedicated; 6870
1Ch 27:24 the son of **Z.** began to number, ... 6870

ZETHAM (ze'-tham)
1Ch 23:8 the chief was Jehiel, and **Z.**, and........ 2241
1Ch 26:22 **Z.**, and Joel his brother, which 2241

ZETHAN (ze'-than)
1Ch 7:10 and Chenannah, and **Z.**, and.............. 2133

ZETHAR (ze'-thar)
Es 1:10 Bigtha, and Abagtha, **Z.**, and............ 2242

ZIA (zi'-ah)
1Ch 5:13 and Jorai, and Jachan, and **Z.**, 2127

ZIBA (zi'-bah)
2Sa 9:2 a servant whose name was **Z.**. 6717
2Sa 9:2 king said unto him, Art thou **Z.**? 6717
2Sa 9:3 **Z.** said unto the king, Jonathan 6717
2Sa 9:4 **Z.** said unto the king, Behold, he 6717
2Sa 9:9 Then the king called to **Z.**, Saul's 6717
2Sa 9:10 Now **Z.** had fifteen sons and 6717
2Sa 9:11 Then said **Z.** unto the king, 6717
2Sa 9:12 all that dwelt in the house of **Z.** 6717
2Sa 16:1 **Z.** the servant of Mephibosheth 6717
2Sa 16:2 king said unto **Z.**, What meanest 6717
2Sa 16:2 **Z.** said, The asses be for the king's 6717
2Sa 16:3 **Z.** said unto the king, Behold, 6717
2Sa 16:4 Then said the king to **Z.**, Behold, 6717
2Sa 16:4 **Z.** said, I humbly beseech thee 6717
2Sa 19:17 and **Z.** the servant of the house 6717
2Sa 19:29 said, Thou and **Z.** divide the land. 6717

ZIBEON (zib'-e-un)
Ge 36:2 the daughter of **Z.** the Hivite; 6649
Ge 36:14 the daughter of **Z.**, Esau's wife: 6649
Ge 36:20 and Shobal, and **Z.**, and Anah, 6649
Ge 36:24 And these are the children of **Z.**; 6649
Ge 36:24 as he fed the asses of **Z.** his father. 6649
Ge 36:29 duke Shobal, duke **Z.**, duke Anah, 6649
1Ch 1:38 and Shobal, and **Z.**, and Anah, 6649
1Ch 1:40 the sons of **Z.**; Aiah, and Anah. 6649

ZIBIA (zib'-e-ah)
1Ch 8:9 Hodesh his wife, Jobab, and **Z.**, 6644

ZIBIAH (zib'-e-ah)
2Ki 12:1 And his mother's name was **Z.** of 6645
2Ch 24:1 His mother's name also was **Z.** of 6645

ZICHRI (zik'-ri) See also ZITHRI.
Ex 6:21 Korah, and Nepheg, and **Z.** 2147
1Ch 8:19 And Jakim, and **Z.**, and Zabdi, 2147
1Ch 8:23 And Abdon, and **Z.**, and Hanan, 2147
1Ch 8:27 and **Z.**, the sons of Jeroham. 2147
1Ch 9:15 the son of Micah, the son of **Z.**, 2147
1Ch 26:25 and Joram his son, and **Z.** his son, 2147
1Ch 27:16 was Eliezer the son of **Z.**: 2147
2Ch 17:16 him was Amasiah the son of **Z.**, 2147
2Ch 23:1 and Elishaphat the son of **Z.**, 2147
2Ch 28:7 And **Z.**, a mighty man of Ephraim, 2147
Ne 11:9 the son of **Z.** was their overseer: 2147
Ne 12:17 Of Abijah, **Z.**; of Miniamin, of 2147

ZIDDIM (zid'-dim)
Jos 19:35 And the fenced cities are **Z.**, Zer, 6661

ZIDKIJAH (zid-ki'-jah) See also ZEDEKIAH.
Ne 10:1 the son of Hachaliah, and **Z.**, 6667

ZIDON (zi'-don) See also SIDON; ZIDONIANS.
Ge 49:13 and his border shall be unto **Z.** 6721
Jos 11:8 and chased them unto great **Z.**, 6721
Jos 19:28 and Kanah, even unto great **Z.**; 6721
Jg 1:31 Accho, nor the inhabitants of **Z.**, 6721
Jg 10:6 gods of Syria, and the gods of **Z.**, 6721
Jg 18:28 because it was far from **Z.**, 6721
2Sa 24:6 came to Dan-jaan, and about to **Z.**, 6721
1Ki 17:9 Zarephath, which belongeth to **Z.**, 6721
1Ch 1:13 And Canaan begat **Z.** his firstborn, 6721
Ezr 3:7 drink, and oil, unto them of **Z.**, 6722
Isa 23:2 thou whom the merchants of **Z.**, 6721
Isa 23:4 Be thou ashamed, O **Z.**: for the 6721
Isa 23:12 oppressed virgin, daughter of **Z.** 6721
Jer 25:22 of Tyrus, and all the kings of **Z.**, 6721
Jer 27:3 and to the king of **Z.**, by the hand 6721
Jer 47:4 to cut off from Tyrus and **Z.** every 6721
Eze 27:8 inhabitants of **Z.** and Arvad were 6721
Eze 28:21 Son of man, set thy face against **Z.**, 6721
Eze 28:22 Behold, I am against thee, O **Z.**; 6721
Joe 3:4 ye to do with me, O Tyre, and **Z.**, 6721
Zec 9:2 Tyrus, and **Z.**, though it be very 6721

ZIDONIANS (zi-do'-ne-uns) See also SIDONIANS.
Jg 10:12 The **Z.** also, and the Amalekites, 6722
Jg 18:7 after the manner of the **Z.**, quiet 6722
Jg 18:7 and they were far from the **Z.**, and 6722
1Ki 11:1 Ammonites, Edomites, **Z.**, and 6722
1Ki 11:5, 33 Ashtoreth the goddess of the **Z.**, 6722
1Ki 16:31 daughter of Ethbaal king of the **Z.**, 6722
2Ki 23:13 the abomination of the **Z.**, 6722
1Ch 22:4 for the **Z.**, and they of Tyre brought 6722
Eze 32:30 north, all of them, and all the **Z.**, 6722

ZIF (zif)
1Ki 6:1 reign over Israel, in the month **Z.**, 2099
1Ki 6:37 of the Lord laid, in the month **Z.** 2099

ZIHA (zi'-hah)
Ezr 2:43 children of **Z.**, the children of 6727
Ne 7:46 children of **Z.**, the children of 6727
Ne 11:21 and **Z.** and Gispa were over the 6727

ZIKLAG (zik'-lag)
Jos 15:31 And **Z.**, and Madmannah, and 6860
Jos 19:5 And **Z.**, and Beth-marcaboth, 6860
1Sa 27:6 Then Achish gave him **Z.** that day: 6860
1Sa 27:6 **Z.** pertaineth unto the kings of 6860
1Sa 30:1 and his men were come to **Z.** 6860
1Sa 30:1 had invaded the south, and **Z.**, 6860
1Sa 30:1 smitten **Z.**, and burnt it with fire; 6860
1Sa 30:14 Caleb; and we burned **Z.** with fire. 6860
1Sa 30:26 when David came to **Z.**, he sent of 6860
2Sa 1:1 David had abode two days in **Z.**; 6860
2Sa 4:10 hold of him, and slew him in **Z.**, 6860
1Ch 4:30 Bethuel, and at Hormah, and at **Z.**, 6860
1Ch 12:1 are they that came to David to **Z.**, 6860
1Ch 12:20 As he went to **Z.**, there fell to him 6860
Ne 11:28 And at **Z.**, and at Mekonah, and 6860

ZILLAH (zil'-lah)
Ge 4:19 and the name of the other **Z.** 6741
Ge 4:22 And **Z.**, she also bare Tubal-cain, 6741
Ge 4:23 said unto his wives, Adah and **Z.**, 6741

ZILPAH (zil'-pah)
Ge 29:24 gave unto his daughter Leah **Z.** 2153
Ge 30:9 she took **Z.** her maid, and gave 2153
Ge 30:10 **Z.** Leah's maid bare Jacob a son. 2153
Ge 30:12 And **Z.** Leah's maid bare Jacob a 2153
Ge 35:26 the sons of **Z.**, Leah's handmaid; 2153
Ge 37:2 with sons of **Z.**, his father's wives: 2153
Ge 46:18 These are the sons of **Z.**, whom 2153

ZILTHAI (zil'-thahee)
1Ch 8:20 And Elienai, and **Z.**, and Eliel, 6769
1Ch 12:20 and **Z.**, captains of the thousands 6769

ZIMMAH (zim'-mah)
1Ch 6:20 son, Jahath his son, **Z.** his son, 2155
1Ch 6:42 the son of **Z.**, the son of Shimei, 2155
2Ch 29:12 Joah the son of **Z.**, and Eden 2155

ZIMRAN (zim'-ran)
Ge 25:2 she bare him **Z.**, and Jokshan, 2175
1Ch 1:32 she bare **Z.**, and Jokshan, and 2175

ZIMRI (zim'-ri)
Nu 25:14 the Midianitish woman, was **Z.**, 2174
1Ki 16:9 And his servant **Z.**, captain of half 2174
1Ki 16:10 And **Z.** went in and smote him, 2174
1Ki 16:12 Thus did **Z.** destroy all the house 2174
1Ki 16:15 of Judah did **Z.** reign seven days 2174
1Ki 16:16 **Z.** hath conspired, and hath also 2174
1Ki 16:18 **Z.** saw that the city was taken, 2174
1Ki 16:20 the rest of the acts of **Z.**, and his 2174
2Ki 9:31 said, Had **Z.** peace, who slew his 2174
1Ch 2:6 sons of Zerah; **Z.**, and Ethan, and 2174
1Ch 8:36 and **Z.**; and **Z.** begat Moza; 2174
1Ch 9:42 and **Z.**; and **Z.** begat Moza; 2174
Jer 25:25 And all the kings of **Z.**, and all the 2174

ZIN (zin)
Nu 13:21 the wilderness of **Z.** unto Rehob, 6790
Nu 20:1 congregation, into the desert of **Z.** 6790
Nu 27:14 commandment in the desert of **Z.**, 6790
Nu 27:14 in Kadesh in the wilderness of **Z.** 6790
Nu 33:36 and pitched in the wilderness of **Z.**, 6790
Nu 34:3 shall be from the wilderness of **Z.** 6790
Nu 34:4 of Akrabbim, and pass on to **Z.** 6790
De 32:51 Kadesh, in the wilderness of **Z.**; 6790
Jos 15:1 of Edom the wilderness of **Z.** 6790
Jos 15:3 passed along to **Z.**, and ascended 6790

ZINA (zi'-nah) See also ZIZAH.
1Ch 23:10 sons of Shimei were, Jahath, **Z.**, 2126

ZION (zi'-un) See also SION; ZION'S.
2Sa 5:7 David took the strong hold of **Z.**; 6726
1Ki 8:1 of the city of David, which is **Z.** 6726
2Ki 19:21 daughter of **Z.** hath despised thee, 6726
2Ki 19:31 they that escape out of mount **Z.** 6726
1Ch 11:5 David took the castle of **Z.**, 6726
2Ch 5:2 of the city of David, which is **Z.** 6726
Ps 2:6 my king upon my holy hill of **Z.** 6726
Ps 9:11 to the Lord, which dwelleth in **Z.** 6726
Ps 9:14 in the gates of the daughter of **Z.** 6726
Ps 14:7 of Israel were come out of **Z.**! 6726
Ps 20:2 and strengthen thee out of **Z.**; 6726
Ps 48:2 of the whole earth, is mount **Z.**, 6726
Ps 48:11 Let mount **Z.** rejoice, let the 6726
Ps 48:12 Walk about **Z.**, and go round 6726
Ps 50:2 Out of **Z.** the perfection of beauty, 6726
Ps 51:18 good in thy good pleasure unto **Z.** 6726
Ps 53:6 of Israel were come out of **Z.**! 6726
Ps 69:35 For God will save **Z.**, and will 6726
Ps 74:2 this mount **Z.**, wherein thou hast 6726
Ps 76:2 and his dwelling place in **Z.** 6726
Ps 78:68 the mount **Z.** which he loved. 6726
Ps 84:7 every one of them in **Z.** appeareth 6726
Ps 87:2 The Lord loveth the gates of **Z.** 6726
Ps 87:5 And of **Z.** it shall be said, This and 6726
Ps 97:8 **Z.** heard, and was glad; and the 6726
Ps 99:2 The Lord is great in **Z.**; and he is 6726
Ps 102:13 arise, and have mercy upon **Z.** 6726
Ps 102:16 when the Lord shall build up **Z.**, 6726
Ps 102:21 declare the name of the Lord in **Z.**, 6726
Ps 110:2 the rod of thy strength out of **Z.**: 6726
Ps 125:1 in the Lord shall be as mount **Z.**, 6726
Ps 126:1 turned again the captivity of **Z.**, 6726
Ps 128:5 The Lord shall bless thee out of **Z.** 6726
Ps 129:5 and turned back that hate **Z.** 6726
Ps 132:13 For the Lord hath chosen **Z.**; 6726
Ps 133:3 upon the mountains of **Z.** 6726
Ps 134:3 and earth bless thee out of **Z.** 6726
Ps 135:21 Blessed be the Lord out of **Z.**, 6726
Ps 137:1 we wept, when we remembered **Z.** 6726
Ps 137:3 Sing us one of the songs of **Z.** 6726
Ps 146:10 reign for ever, even thy God, O **Z.**, 6726
Ps 147:12 O Jerusalem; praise thy God, O **Z.** 6726
Ps 149:2 let the children of **Z.** be joyful in 6726
Ca 3:11 Go forth, O ye daughters of **Z.**, and 6726
Isa 1:8 daughter of **Z.** if left as a cottage 6726
Isa 1:27 **Z.** shall be redeemed with 6726
Isa 2:3 for out of **Z.** shall go forth the law, 6726
Isa 3:16 the daughters of **Z.** are haughty, 6726
Isa 3:17 of the head of the daughters of **Z.**, 6726
Isa 4:3 to pass, that he that is left in **Z.**, 6726
Isa 4:4 the filth of the daughters of **Z.**, 6726
Isa 4:5 every dwelling place of mount **Z.**, 6726
Isa 8:18 hosts, which dwelleth in mount **Z.** 6726
Isa 10:12 his whole work upon mount **Z.** 6726
Isa 10:24 O my people that dwellest in **Z.**, 6726
Isa 10:32 the mount of the daughter of **Z.**, 6726
Isa 12:6 and shout, thou inhabitant of **Z.** 6726
Isa 14:32 That the Lord hath founded **Z.**, 6726
Isa 16:1 the mount of the daughter of **Z.** 6726
Isa 18:7 of the Lord of hosts, the mount **Z.** 6726
Isa 24:23 of hosts shall reign in mount **Z.**, 6726
Isa 28:16 I lay in **Z.** for a foundation a stone, 6726
Isa 29:8 be, that fight against mount **Z.** 6726
Isa 30:19 shall dwell in **Z.** at Jerusalem: 6726
Isa 31:4 come down to fight for mount **Z.**, 6726
Isa 31:9 the Lord, whose fire is in **Z.**, 6726
Isa 33:5 he hath filled **Z.** with judgment 6726
Isa 33:14 The sinners in **Z.** are afraid; 6726
Isa 33:20 Look upon **Z.**, the city of our 6726
Isa 34:8 for the controversy of **Z.** 6726
Isa 35:10 and come to **Z.** with songs and 6726
Isa 37:22 daughter of **Z.**, hath despised thee, 6726
Isa 37:32 they that escape out of mount **Z.** 6726
Isa 40:9 O **Z.**, that bringest good tidings, 6726
Isa 41:27 The first shall say to **Z.**, Behold, 6726
Isa 46:13 place salvation in **Z.** for Israel my 6726
Isa 49:14 **Z.** said, The Lord hath forsaken 6726
Isa 51:3 For the Lord shall comfort **Z.** 6726
Isa 51:11 and come with singing unto **Z.**; 6726
Isa 51:16 say unto **Z.**, Thou art my people, 6726
Isa 52:1 awake; put on thy strength, O **Z.**; 6726
Isa 52:2 thy neck, O captive daughter of **Z.** 6726
Isa 52:7 saith unto **Z.**, Thy God reigneth! 6726
Isa 52:8 the Lord shall bring again **Z.** 6726
Isa 59:20 the Redeemer shall come to **Z.**, 6726
Isa 60:14 The **Z.** of the Holy One of Israel. 6726
Isa 61:3 unto them that mourn in **Z.**, 6726
Isa 62:11 Say ye to the daughter of **Z.**, 6726
Isa 64:10 **Z.** is a wilderness, Jerusalem a 6726
Isa 66:8 for as soon as **Z.** travailed, she 6726
Jer 3:14 family, and I will bring you to **Z.** 6726
Jer 4:6 Set up the standard toward **Z.** 6726
Jer 4:31 the voice of the daughter of **Z.**, 6726

Jer 6:2 have likened the daughter of **Z.** to...... 6726
Jer 6:23 war against thee, O daughter of **Z.**..... 6726
Jer 8:19 Is not the Lord in **Z.**? is not her........ 6726
Jer 9:19 voice of wailing is heard out of **Z.**, ... 6726
Jer 14:19 Judah? hath thy soul lothed **Z.**?.......... 6726
Jer 26:18 **Z.** shall be plowed like a field, and...... 6726
Jer 30:17 This is **Z.**, whom no man seeketh...... 6726
Jer 31:6 let us go to up to **Z.** unto the Lord.... 6726
Jer 31:12 come and sing in the height of **Z.**,....... 6726
Jer 50:5 They shall ask the way to **Z.** with...... 6726
Jer 50:28 to declare in **Z.** the vengeance of the.. 6726
Jer 51:10 declare in **Z.** the work of the Lord..... 6726
Jer 51:24 evil that they have done in **Z.**............ 6726
Jer 51:35 shall the inhabitant of **Z.** say;............ 6726
La 1:4 The ways of **Z.** do mourn, because..... 6726
La 1:6 from the daughter of **Z.** all her.......... 6726
La 1:17 **Z.** spreadeth forth her hands, and...... 6726
La 2:1 covered the daughter of **Z.** with a...... 6726
La 2:4 tabernacle of the daughter of **Z.**.......... 6726
La 2:6 and sabbaths to be forgotten in **Z.**,..... 6726
La 2:8 the wall of the daughter of **Z.**............ 6726
La 2:10 The elders of the daughter of **Z.** sit.... 6726
La 2:13 thee, O virgin daughter of **Z.**?............ 6726
La 2:18 O wall of the daughter of **Z.**, let........ 6726
La 4:2 The precious sons of **Z.**,.................. 6726
La 4:11 and hath kindled a fire in **Z.**,............. 6726
La 4:22 is accomplished, O daughter of **Z.**;..... 6726
La 5:11 They ravished the women in **Z.**,........ 6726
La 5:18 Because of the mountain of **Z.**,.......... 6726
Joe 2:1 Blow ye the trumpet in **Z.**, and......... 6726
Joe 2:15 Blow the trumpet in **Z.**, sanctify........ 6726
Joe 2:23 Be glad then, ye children of **Z.**,......... 6726
Joe 2:32 for in mount **Z.** and in Jerusalem........ 6726
Joe 3:16 Lord also shall roar out of **Z.**,............ 6726
Joe 3:17 the Lord your God dwelling in **Z.**,...... 6726
Joe 3:21 for the Lord dwelleth in **Z.**.............. 6726
Am 1:2 The Lord will roar from **Z.**, and.......... 6726
Am 6:1 Woe to them that are at ease in **Z.**,... 6726
Ob 17 upon mount **Z.** shall be deliverance,.... 6726
Ob 21 come up on mount **Z.** to judge........... 6726
Mic 1:13 of the sin to the daughter of **Z.**:........ 6726
Mic 3:10 They build up **Z.** with blood, and........ 6726
Mic 3:12 shall **Z.** for your sake be plowed........ 6726
Mic 4:2 for the law shall go forth of **Z.**,.......... 6726
Mic 4:7 shall reign over them in mount **Z.**...... 6726
Mic 4:8 strong hold of the daughter of **Z.**,...... 6726
Mic 4:10 to bring forth, O daughter of **Z.**,........ 6726
Mic 4:11 and let our eye look upon **Z.**............. 6726
Mic 4:13 and thresh, O daughter of **Z.**............. 6726
Zep 3:14 Sing, O daughter of **Z.**; shout,........... 6726
Zep 3:16 and to **Z.**, Let not thine hands be....... 6726
Zec 1:14 jealous for Jerusalem and for **Z.**......... 6726
Zec 1:17 and the Lord shall yet comfort **Z.**,....... 6726
Zec 2:7 Deliver thyself, O **Z.**, that dwellest..... 6726
Zec 2:10 and rejoice, O daughter of **Z.**:........... 6726
Zec 8:2 jealous for **Z.** with great jealousy,....... 6726
Zec 8:3 I am returned unto **Z.**, and will.......... 6726
Zec 9:9 Rejoice greatly, O daughter of **Z.**;...... 6726
Zec 9:13 and raised up thy sons, O **Z.**,............ 6726

ZION'S (zi'-uns)
Isa 62:1 For **Z.** sake will I not hold my........... 6726

ZIOR (zi'-or)
Jos 15:54 which is Hebron, and **Z.**; nine........... 6730

ZIPH (zif) See also ZIPHITES.
Jos 15:24 **Z.**, and Telem, and Bealoth,............. 2128
Jos 15:55 Moan, Carmel, and **Z.**, and Juttah,..... 2128
1Sa 23:14 mountain in the wilderness of **Z.**....... 2128
1Sa 23:15 David was in the wilderness of **Z.**....... 2128
1Sa 23:24 arose, and went to **Z.** before Saul:..... 2128
1Sa 26:2 went down to the wilderness of **Z.**,.... 2128
1Sa 26:2 seek David in the wilderness of **Z.**..... 2128
1Ch 2:42 which was the father of **Z.**;.............. 2128
1Ch 4:16 **Z.**, and Ziphah, Tiria, and Asareel...... 2128
2Ch 11:8 And Gath, and Mareshah, and **Z.**,...... 2128

ZIPHAH (zi'-fah)
1Ch 4:16 Ziph, and **Z.**, Tiria, and Asareel......... 2129

ZIPHIMS (zif'-ims) See also ZIPHITES.
Ps 54:*title* the **Z.** came and said to Saul,............ 2130

ZIPHION (zif'-e-on) See also ZEPHON.
Ge 46:16 the sons of Gad; **Z.**, and Haggi,......... 6837

ZIPHITES (zif'-ites) See also ZIPHIMS.
1Sa 23:19 came up the **Z.** to Saul to Gibeah,...... 2130
1Sa 26:1 the **Z.** came unto Saul to Gibeah,....... 2130

ZIPHRON (zif'-ron)
Nu 34:9 And the border shall go on to **Z.**,....... 2202

ZIPPOR (zip'-por)
Nu 22:2 And Balak the son of **Z.** saw all......... 6834
Nu 22:4 Balak the son of **Z.** was king of......... 6834
Nu 22:10 Balak the son of **Z.**, king of Moab,..... 6834
Nu 22:16 Thus saith Balak the son of **Z.**,.......... 6834
Nu 23:18 hearken unto me, thou son of **Z.**......... 6834
Jos 24:9 Balak the son of **Z.**, king of Moab,..... 6834
Jg 11:25 Balak the son of **Z.**, king of Moab?..... 6834

ZIPPORAH (zip-po'-rah)
Ex 2:21 he gave Moses **Z.** his daughter.......... 6855
Ex 4:25 Then **Z.** took a sharp stone, and........ 6855
Ex 18:2 father in law, took **Z.**, Moses' wife,.... 6855

ZITHRI (zith'-ri) See also ZICHRI.
Ex 6:22 Mishael, and Elzaphan, and **Z.**........... 5644

ZIZ (ziz)
2Ch 20:16 they come up by the cliff of **Z.**;......... 6732

ZIZA (zi'-zah) See also ZIZAH.
1Ch 4:37 **Z.** the son of Shiphi, the son of......... 2124
2Ch 11:20 and Attai, and **Z.**, and Shelomith........ 2124

ZIZAH (zi'-zah) See also ZINA; ZIZA.
1Ch 23:11 was the chief, and **Z.** the second:....... 2125

ZOAN (zo'-an)
Nu 13:22 seven years before **Z.** in Egypt,......... 6814
Ps 78:12 the land of Egypt, in the field of **Z.**.... 6814
Ps 78:43 and his wonders in the field of **Z.**:...... 6814
Isa 19:11 Surely the princes of **Z.** are fools,...... 6814
Isa 19:13 The princes of **Z.** are become fools,... 6814
Isa 30:4 For his princes were at **Z.**, and his.... 6814
Eze 30:14 will set fire in **Z.**, and will execute..... 6814

ZOAR (zo'-ar)
Ge 13:10 of Egypt, as thou comest unto **Z.**....... 6820
Ge 14:2 and the king of Bela, which is **Z.**........ 6820
Ge 14:8 the king of Bela, (the same is **Z.**;)....... 6820
Ge 19:22 the name of the city was called **Z.**...... 6820
Ge 19:23 earth when Lot entered into **Z.**.......... 6820
Ge 19:30 Lot went up out of **Z.**, and dwelt....... 6820
Ge 19:30 for he feared to dwell in **Z.**: and........ 6820
De 34:3 the city of palm trees, unto **Z.**........... 6820
Isa 15:5 his fugitives shall flee unto **Z.**........... 6820
Jer 48:34 from **Z.** even unto Horoniam,............ 6820

ZOBA (zo'-bah) See also ZOBAH.
2Sa 10:6 and the Syrians of **Z.**, twenty............ 6678
2Sa 10:8 the Syrians of **Z.**, and of Rehob,........ 6678

ZOBAH (zo'-bah) See also ARM-ZOBAH; HAMATHZOBAH; ZOBA.
1Sa 14:47 and against the kings of **Z.**, and......... 6678
2Sa 8:3 the son of Rehob, king of **Z.**, as he.... 6678
2Sa 8:5 to succour Hadadezer king of **Z.**,....... 6678
2Sa 8:12 son of Rehob, king of **Z.**.................. 6678
2Sa 23:36 Igal the son of Nathan of **Z.**, Bani...... 6678
1Ki 11:23 his lord Hadadezer king of **Z.**:........... 6678
1Ki 11:24 hand, when David slew them of **Z.**:..........
1Ch 18:3 David smote Hadzrezer king of **Z.**....... 6678
1Ch 18:5 came to help Hadarezer king of **Z.**,...... 6678
1Ch 18:9 the host of Hadarezer king of **Z.**;....... 6678
1Ch 19:6 of Syria-maachah, and out of **Z.**........ 6678

ZOBEBAH (zo-be'-bah)
1Ch 4:8 And Coz begat Anub, and **Z.**, and...... 6637

ZOHAR (zo'-har) See also ZERAH; ZEROR.
Ge 23:8 for me to Ephron the son of **Z.**......... 6714
Ge 25:9 the field of Ephron the son of **Z.**......... 6714
Ge 46:10 and Ohad, Jachin, and **Z.**................ 6714
Ex 6:15 and Ohad, and Jachin, and **Z.**,............ 6714

ZOHELETH (zo'-he-leth)
1Ki 1:9 and fat cattle by the stone of **Z.**,........ 2120

ZOHETH (zo'-heth) See also BEN-ZOHETH.
1Ch 4:20 and the sons of Ishi were, **Z.**, and...... 2105

ZOPHAH (zo'-fah)
1Ch 7:35 **Z.**, and Imna, and Shelesh, and.......... 6690
1Ch 7:36 sons of **Z.**; Suah, and Harnepher,........ 6690

ZOPHAI (zo'-fahee) See also ZUPH.
1Ch 6:26 sons of Elkanah; **Z.** his son, and........ 6689

ZOPHAR (zo'-far)
Job 2:11 Shuhite, and **Z.** the Naamathite:......... 6691
Job 11:1 answered **Z.** the Naamathite, and....... 6691
Job 20:1 answered **Z.** the Naamathite, and....... 6691
Job 42:9 **Z.** the Naamathite went, and did........ 6691

ZOPHIM (zo'-fim) See also RAMATHAIM-ZOPHIM.
Nu 23:14 brought him into the field of **Z.**,......... 6839

ZORAH (zo-rah) See also ZAREAH; ZORATHITES; ZOREAH; ZORITES.
Jos 19:41 coast of their inheritance was **Z.**,....... 6881
Jg 13:2 there was a certain man of **Z.**,.......... 6881
Jg 13:25 the camp of Dan between **Z.** and....... 6881
Jg 16:31 and buried him between **Z.** and.......... 6881
Jg 18:2 men of valour, from **Z.**, and from....... 6881
Jg 18:8 came unto their brethren to **Z.**.......... 6881
Jg 18:11 family of the Danites, out of **Z.**.......... 6881
2Ch 11:10 And **Z.**, and Aijalon, and Hebron,....... 6881

ZORATHITES (zo'-rath-ites) See also ZAREATHITES; ZORITES.
1Ch 4:2 These are the families of the **Z.**......... 6882

ZOREAH (zo'-re-ah) See also ZORAH.
Jos 15:33 in the valley, Eshtaol, and **Z.**,........... 6881

ZORITES (zo'-rites) See also ZAREATHITES; ZORATHITES.
1Ch 2:54 half of the Manahethites, the **Z.**......... 6882

ZOROBABEL (zo-rob'-a-bel) See also ZERUBBABEL.
Mt 1:12 and Salathiel begat **Z.**; Salathiel;......... *2216*
Mt 1:13 And **Z.** begat Abiud; and Abiud.......... *2216*
Lu 3:27 which was the son of **Z.**, which........ *2216*

ZUAR (zu'-ar)
Nu 1:8 Issachar: Nethaneel the son of **Z.**........ 6686
Nu 2:5 Nethaneel the son of **Z.** shall be........ 6686
Nu 7:18 day Nethaneel the son of **z.**,............. 6686
Nu 7:23 of Nethaneel the son of **z.**,.............. 6686
Nu 10:15 was Nethaneel the son of **Z.**............ 6686

ZUPH (zuf) See also RAMATHAIM-ZOPHIM.
1Sa 1:1 the son of **Z.**, and Ephrathite:........... 6689
1Sa 9:5 they were come to the land of **Z.**,...... 6689
1Ch 6:35 The son of **Z.**, the son of Elkanah...... 6689

ZUR (zur) See also BETH-ZUR.
Nu 25:15 was Cozii, the daughter of **Z.**:........... 6698
Nu 31:8 namely, Evi, and Rekem, and **Z.**,....... 6698
Jos 13:21 Midian, Evi, and Rekem, and **Z.**,....... 6698
1Ch 8:30 his firstborn son Abdon, and **Z.**,....... 6698
1Ch 9:36 firstborn son Abdon, then **Z.**,............ 6698

ZURIEL (zu'-re-el)
Nu 3:35 of the families of Merari was **Z.**......... 6700

ZURISHADDAI (zu-re-shad'-da-i)
Nu 1:6 Simeon; Shelumiel the son of **Z.**......... 6701
Nu 2:12 shall be Shelumiel the son of **Z.**........ 6701
Nu 7:36 fifth day Shelumiel the son of **Z.**,....... 6701
Nu 7:41 of Shelumiel the son of **Z.**................. 6701
Nu 10:19 was Shelumiel the son of **Z.**............. 6701

ZUZIMS (zu'-zims) See also ZAMZUMMIMS.
Ge 14:5 the **Z.** in Ham, and the Emins in........ 2104

Appendix

Giving the Occurrences of the Forty-Seven Words Cited by Reference Only

APPENDIX

THE following forty-seven unimportant words of very frequent occurrence are cited here by reference to chapter and verse only, inasmuch as no one would think of searching out a text by means of them. The quotation in full of the passages where they are found would be nearly tantamount to reprinting the entire Bible under each of them:

a	as	for	him	is	not	out	that	them	to	us	with
an	be	from	his	it	O	shall	the	they	unto	was	ye
and	but	he	I	me	of	shalt	thee	thou	up	we	you
are	by	her	in	my	our	she	their	thy	upon	were	

The small superior figures (^{2}, ^{3}, ^{4}, etc.) denote the number of times the word occurs in the verses to which they are attached.

The Hebrew or Greek term, of which the words in this Appendix are respectively the proper or strict (but not uniform) translation (when such term exists), is indicated (by its appropriate number in the accompanying DICTIONARIES) once for all at the head of each. But (inasmuch as those terms are, as a rule, only expressed when more or less emphatic) the English words are usually the rendering merely of some inflection (such as by declension, conjugation, mood, tense, affix, etc.), construction, or implication of the principal word in the sentence (as an auxiliary, pronoun, preposition, etc.). They are frequently supplied (not always in *italics*) in the KJV merely for the sake of greater clearness or fullness of meaning. Many of them, moreover, often stand in the English text as renderings of various other words in the original, which are elsewhere represented by very different ones from those here indicated.

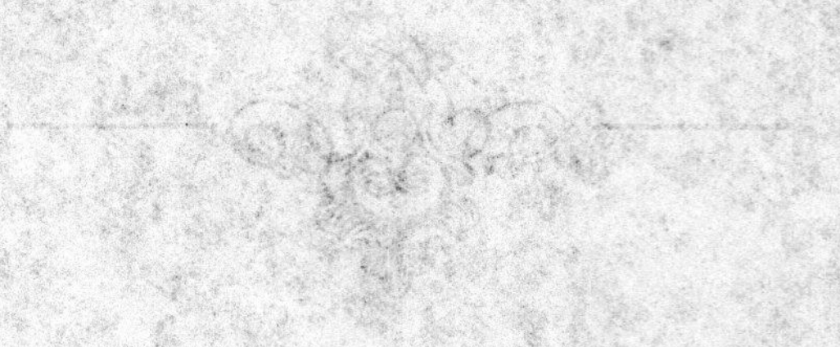

Appendix to the Main Concordance

A (See also AN)

GE

1:6 1:29 2:5 2:6 2:7 2:8 2:10 2:21 2:22 2:24 3:6 3:24 4:1 4:2^{2} 4:12^{2} 4:14^{2} 4:15 4:17 4:23^{2} 4:25 4:26 5:3 5:28 6:9 6:16^{2} 6:17 8:1 8:7 8:8 8:21 9:11^{2} 9:13^{2} 9:14 9:15 9:20 9:23 9:25 10:8 10:9 10:12 10:30 11:2 11:4^{3} 12:1 12:2^{2} 12:8 12:10 12:11 13:7 13:16 14:23^{2} 15:1 15:9^{4} 15:12 15:13^{3} 15:15 15:17^{2} 15:18 16:7 16:11 16:12 16:15 17:4 17:5 17:7 17:8 17:11 17:16^{2} 17:17 17:19 17:20 18:4 18:5 18:7^{2} 18:10 18:13^{2} 18:14 18:18 19:3 19:9 19:20^{2} 19:26 19:28 19:30 19:31 19:37 19:38 20:3^{3} 20:4 20:6 20:7 20:9 20:16^{2} 21:2 21:7 21:8 21:13 21:14 21:16^{2} 21:18 21:19 21:21 21:25 21:27 21:30 21:32 21:33 22:2 22:6 22:7 22:8 22:13^{3} 23:4^{4} 23:6 23:9^{2} 23:18 23:20^{2} 24:3 24:4 24:7 24:11 24:16 24:17 24:22^{2} 24:29 24:36 24:37 24:38 24:40 24:43 24:55 24:65 25:1 25:8 25:27^{3} 26:1 26:8^{2} 26:9 26:19 26:25 26:28 26:30 26:35 27:11^{2} 27:12^{3} 27:27 27:34 27:36 27:44 27:46 28:1 28:2 28:3 28:4 28:6^{3} 28:11 28:12 28:18 28:20 28:22 29:2^{2} 29:14 29:20 29:22 29:32 29:33 29:34 29:35 30:5 30:6 30:7 30:10 30:11 30:12 30:15 30:20 30:21 30:23 30:30 31:10 31:11 31:13 31:24 31:44^{2} 31:45^{2} 31:48 32:13 32:16 32:18 32:24 32:28 33:18 33:19^{2} 34:14 35:11^{2} 35:14^{3} 35:16 35:20 37:1 37:3 37:5 37:9 37:15 37:24 37:25 37:31 38:1 38:2^{2} 38:3 38:4 38:5 38:6 38:11 38:14 38:17^{2} 38:28 39:2 39:6 39:14 39:20 40:4 40:5 40:8 40:9 40:19 40:20 41:2 41:7 41:11 41:12 41:15^{2} 41:18 41:33 41:38^{2} 41:42 43:2 43:6 43:11^{3} 44:15 44:18 44:19^{2} 44:20^{3} 44:25 44:33 45:7^{2} 45:8^{2} 46:3 46:10 46:29 47:11 47:22 47:26 48:4 48:7 48:16 48:19^{2} 49:6^{2} 49:9^{2} 49:10 49:14 49:15 49:17 49:19 49:21 49:22^{3} 49:27 49:30^{2} 50:9 50:10^{2} 50:11 50:13^{2} 50:16 50:26

EX

1:8 1:16^{3} 2:1^{2} 2:2^{2} 2:7 2:14^{2} 2:15 2:22^{3} 3:2^{2} 3:8^{3} 3:12 3:17 3:19 4:2 4:3 4:4 4:10 4:16 4:25^{2} 4:26 5:1 5:21 6:1^{2} 6:6 6:7^{2} 6:13 6:15 7:1 7:9^{2} 7:10 7:15 8:23 8:24 9:3 9:5 9:9 9:10 9:18 9:24 10:7 10:9 10:19 10:22 11:6 11:7^{2} 11:8 12:3^{2} 12:5 12:13 12:14^{3} 12:19 12:21 12:22 12:30^{2} 12:38 12:42 12:45 12:46 12:48 13:5 13:6 13:9^{3} 13:12 13:13 13:16 13:21^{3} 14:20 14:21 14:22 14:29 15:3 15:5 15:16 15:20 15:25^{2} 16:4 16:14 16:25 16:33 16:35 17:12 17:14^{2} 18:3 18:12 18:16 19:5 19:6 19:9 19:16 19:18^{2} 19:19 20:5 21:4 21:7^{2} 21:8 21:12 21:13^{2} 21:14 21:16 21:18 21:20^{2} 21:21 21:22 21:26 21:28^{2} 21:29^{2} 21:30 21:31^{2} 21:32^{2} 21:33^{4} 22:1^{3} 22:2 22:5^{2} 22:7 22:10^{2} 22:14 22:16^{2} 22:18 22:19 22:21 22:25 23:1 23:2^{2} 23:3 23:7 23:9^{2} 23:14 23:19 23:33 24:10^{2} 24:12 24:15 25:8 25:10^{5} 25:11 25:17^{4} 25:23^{4} 25:24 25:25^{2} 25:31 25:33^{4} 25:35^{3} 25:39 26:7 26:13^{2} 26:14^{2} 26:16^{3} 26:31 27:4 27:21 28:4^{5} 28:11 28:12 28:16^{2} 28:17^{3} 28:18^{2} 28:19 28:20^{2} 28:21 28:28 28:29 28:32 28:34^{4} 28:36^{2} 28:37 28:43 29:9 29:10 29:14 29:18^{2} 29:22 29:24 29:25^{2} 29:26 29:28 29:33 29:36^{2} 29:40^{2} 29:41 29:42 30:2^{2} 30:3 30:8 30:10 30:12 30:13^{2} 30:15 30:16 30:18 30:21 30:33 30:34 30:35^{2} 31:13 31:16 31:17 32:4^{2} 32:5 32:8 32:9 32:10 32:11 32:17 32:21 32:29 32:30 32:31 33:3^{2} 33:5^{2} 33:11^{2} 33:21^{2} 33:22 34:9 34:10^{2} 34:12^{2} 34:14 34:15^{2} 34:16^{2} 34:20 34:26 34:27 34:33 35:2 35:5 35:29 36:19^{2} 36:21^{3} 36:35 37:1^{5} 37:2 37:6^{2} 37:10^{2} 37:11 37:12^{2} 37:19^{4} 37:21^{3} 37:24 37:25^{2} 37:26 38:4 38:23 38:25 38:26^{2} 38:27^{2} 39:7 39:9^{2} 39:10^{3} 39:11^{2} 39:12 39:13^{2} 39:14 39:21 39:23 39:26^{4} 39:28 39:29 39:30^{2} 39:31 40:34

LE

1:3^{2} 1:9^{2} 1:10^{2} 1:13^{2} 1:17^{2} 2:1 2:2 2:3 2:4 2:5^{2} 2:6 2:7 2:9^{2} 2:10 2:12 2:14 2:15 3:1^{2} 3:5 3:6 3:7 3:12 3:16 3:17 4:2 4:3^{2} 4:12 4:14 4:20 4:21 4:22 4:23^{2} 4:24 4:28^{2} 4:31 4:32^{3} 4:33 5:1^{2} 5:1^{2} 5:2^{3} 5:3 5:4^{2} 5:6^{4} 5:7^{3} 5:9 5:10 5:11^{2} 5:12^{2} 5:13 5:15^{4} 5:17 5:18^{2} 5:19 6:2^{3} 6:3 6:6^{2} 6:11 6:15 6:18 6:20 6:21^{2} 6:22 6:28 7:5 7:12 7:16^{2} 7:30 7:34 7:36 8:2^{2} 8:21^{2} 8:26 8:27 8:28 8:29 9:2^{4} 9:3^{5} 9:4^{2} 9:18 9:21 9:24 10:9 10:14 10:15^{2} 11:36 11:47 12:2^{2} 12:5 12:6^{7} 12:7^{2} 12:8^{2} 13:2^{3} 13:3 13:5 13:6 13:8 13:9 13:12 13:15 13:18 13:19^{2} 13:20 13:22 13:23 13:24^{2} 13:25 13:28 13:29^{2} 13:30^{3} 13:37 13:38^{2} 13:39 13:42^{2} 13:44 13:45 13:47^{2} 13:48 13:49 13:51^{2} 13:52 13:57 13:59 14:10 14:12^{2} 14:21^{3} 14:22^{2} 14:24 14:31^{2} 14:34^{2} 14:35 14:44 13:55^{2} 14:56^{3} 15:2 15:15^{2} 15:19 15:25 15:30^{2} 16:3^{4} 16:4 16:5^{2} 16:9 16:10 16:12 16:21 16:22 16:29^{2} 16:31^{2} 16:34 17:6 17:7^{2} 17:8 17:15 18:5 18:17 18:18 18:19 18:23 19:5 19:14 19:16 19:19^{2} 19:20^{3} 19:21^{2} 19:29 19:33 19:36^{2} 20:5 20:6 20:12 20:13^{2} 20:14^{2} 20:15^{2} 20:16 20:17^{2} 20:18^{2} 20:20 20:21 20:24 20:27^{3} 21:3 21:4 21:7^{3} 21:13 21:14^{3} 21:18^{4} 21:19 21:20^{2} 21:21^{2} 21:23 22:4^{3} 22:5 22:10 22:12 22:13 22:14 22:18 22:19 22:20 22:21^{2} 22:22 22:23^{4} 22:25 22:27^{3} 22:29 23:10 23:12 23:13 23:14 23:16 23:18 23:19^{2} 23:20 23:21 23:24^{2} 23:27 23:28 23:31 23:32 23:36 23:37^{3} 23:39^{3} 23:41^{2} 24:3 24:6 24:7 24:9 24:10 24:18 24:19^{2} 24:20^{2} 24:21^{2} 25:2 25:4^{2} 25:5 25:10 25:11 25:24 25:29^{5} 25:30 25:33 25:35^{2} 25:39 25:40 25:46 25:47 25:53 26:1 26:25 26:33 26:36^{2} 26:37 27:2^{2} 27:4 27:6 27:7 27:9 27:10^{4} 27:11 27:13 27:14 27:16^{2} 27:21 27:22^{2} 27:23 27:27 27:28 27:31

NU

1:4 3:15 3:22 3:28 3:34 3:39 3:40 3:43 3:50 4:6 4:7 4:8^{2} 4:9 4:10^{2} 4:11^{2} 4:12^{3} 4:13 4:14 5:6^{2} 5:12 5:13 5:21 5:23 5:27 5:29 6:2 6:11^{2} 6:12^{2} 6:14^{2} 6:15 6:17 6:20 7:3 7:13 7:15 7:16 7:17 7:19 7:21 7:22 7:23 7:25 7:27 7:28 7:29 7:31 7:33 7:34 7:35 7:37 7:39 7:40 7:41 7:43 7:45 7:46 7:47 7:49 7:51 7:52 7:53 7:55 7:57 7:58 7:59 7:61 7:63 7:64 7:65 7:67 7:69 7:70 7:71 7:73 7:75 7:76 7:77 7:79 7:81 7:82 7:83 8:8^{2} 8:12^{2} 8:19 9:6 9:7 9:10^{2} 9:13 9:14 9:20 9:22^{2} 10:2 10:10 10:33 11:4 11:8 11:12 11:20 11:21 11:25 11:27 11:31^{2} 11:33 12:6^{3} 13:2^{2} 13:23^{2} 13:32^{2} 14:3 14:4 14:8 14:12 14:14^{3} 14:31 14:34 14:36 15:3^{5} 15:4^{2} 15:5 15:6^{2} 15:7^{2} 15:8^{4} 15:9^{2} 15:10^{2} 15:11^{2} 15:13 15:14^{2} 15:20 15:24^{3} 15:25 15:27^{2} 15:30 15:32 15:38 15:39^{2} 16:9 16:13^{3} 16:14 16:21 16:30 16:35 16:38^{2} 16:39 16:40 16:45 16:46 17:2 17:6 17:10 18:4 18:6 18:7 18:11 18:16 18:17^{4} 18:19^{2} 18:23 18:26 19:2 19:^{4} 19:10 19:14^{2} 19:16^{5} 19:17 19:18^{3} 19:21 20:15 20:16 20:20 21:2 21:8^{2} 21:9^{3} 21:28^{2} 22:5 22:11 22:24^{3} 22:26 22:27 22:29 22:36 23:2 23:4^{2} 23:5 23:14^{2} 23:16 23:19 23:21 23:22 23:24^{2} 23:30^{2} 24:4 24:8 24:9^{2} 24:16 24:17^{2} 24:18^{2} 24:21 25:6 25:7 25:14^{2} 25:15^{2} 25:18 26:10 26:51 26:62 26:64 26:65 27:4 27:7 27:8 27:11 27:16 27:18 27:19 27:23 28:2 28:3 28:5^{2} 28:6^{3} 28:7 28:8^{2} 28:9 28:11 28:12^{2} 28:13^{5} 28:14^{4} 28:15 28:19^{2} 28:20^{2} 28:21 28:22 28:23 28:24 28:26 28:27 28:29 29:1 29:2^{2} 29:3^{2} 29:5 29:6^{2} 29:5 29:8^{2} 29:9 29:10 29:11 29:12 29:13^{3} 29:15 29:16 29:19 29:22 29:25 29:28 29:31 29:34 29:35 29:36^{3} 29:38 30:2^{3} 30:3^{3} 30:9 30:10 30:16 31:4 31:5 31:6 31:16 31:18 31:28 31:54 32:1^{2} 32:4 32:5 32:29 33:3 34:5 34:6 35:4 35:15 35:16 35:17^{2} 35:18 35:21 35:23 35:29 35:31

DE

1:11 1:23 1:25 1:31 1:33^{2} 1:39 2:5^{2} 2:9^{2} 2:10 2:19 2:20 2:21 2:35 3:4 3:5 3:7 3:11^{2} 4:6 4:12 4:16 4:20 4:23 4:24^{2} 4:25 4:31 4:34^{3} 5:2 5:9 5:15^{3} 5:22 6:8 6:15 6:21 7:6 7:8 7:9 7:16 7:21 7:23 7:26^{2} 8:5 8:7^{2} 8:8^{2} 8:9^{2} 9:2 9:3 9:6 9:12 9:13 9:14 9:16 9:26 10:7 10:15 10:17^{3} 11:9 11:10 11:11 11:12 11:18 11:26^{2} 11:27 11:28 12:11 13:1^{4} 14:2 14:21 15:1 15:3 15:7 15:9 15:15 15:18 16:8 16:10^{2} 16:12 16:15 16:16 16:19^{2} 16:21 17:8 17:14 17:15 17:18 18:3 18:6 18:10 18:11^{4} 18:15 18:18 18:20 18:22 19:3 19:5^{2} 19:15 19:16 19:18 20:1 20:5 20:6 20:7 20:10 20:19^{2} 21:4 21:11^{2} 21:13 21:15 21:17 21:18^{2} 21:20^{2} 21:22^{3} 22:5^{2} 22:6 22:8^{2} 22:11 22:13 22:14 22:17 22:19 22:22^{2} 22:23^{4} 22:25^{2} 22:26 22:28^{3} 22:30 23:2 23:5 23:7 23:12 23:13 23:17 23:18^{2} 23:20 23:21 23:23 23:25 24:1^{3} 24:3 24:5^{2} 24:6 24:7 24:17 24:18 24:19 24:22 25:1 25:2 25:7 25:13^{2} 25:14^{2} 25:15^{2} 26:2 26:5^{3} 26:8 26:9 26:15 27:3 27:14 27:15 28:22^{2} 28:30^{2} 28:33 28:35 28:36 28:37^{2} 28:46^{2} 28:48 28:49^{2} 28:50 28:65 29:13^{2} 29:18 29:22 31:6 31:7 31:14 31:15^{2} 31:16 31:19 31:21 31:23^{2} 31:24 31:26 32:4 32:5 32:10 32:20 32:21^{2} 32:22 32:28 32:30 32:47 32:49 33:2 33:4 33:20 33:21 33:22 33:28 34:6 34:10

JOS

1:6 1:9 1:18 2:12 2:15 3:4 3:12 4:2 4:4 4:5 4:6 4:7 5:6 5:13 6:5^{2} 6:18 6:20 7:1 7:21^{2} 7:26 8:2 8:11 8:14 8:17 8:27 8:28 8:29^{2} 8:32 8:35 9:6^{2} 9:7 9:9 9:11 9:15 9:16 10:2 10:8 10:10 10:13 10:14 10:16 10:17 10:20 11:14 11:18 11:19 12:6 12:7 14:15 15:3 15:13 15:18 15:19^{2} 17:1 17:2 17:14 17:15 17:17 17:18 18:9 18:14 20:4 21:13 21:21 21:27 21:32 21:38 21:44 22:10 22:14 22:17 22:20 22:25 22:27 22:28 22:34 23:1 23:10 23:13 24:7 24:13 24:19 24:25^{2} 24:26 24:27^{2} 24:32 24:33

JG

1:14 1:15^{2} 1:24 1:26 2:3 2:17 3:15^{4} 3:16^{2} 3:17 3:19 3:20^{2} 3:25 3:27 3:28 3:29 4:4 4:9 4:16 4:18 4:19^{2} 4:21 5:7 5:8 5:12 5:14 5:18 5:25 5:28

5:30[2]
6:8
6:17
6:19[3]
6:26
6:31
6:34
6:37
6:38
7:5
7:13[5]
7:14
7:16
7:18
8:14
8:18
8:20
8:24
8:25
8:26
8:27[2]
8:31
8:32
8:33
9:8[2]
9:48
9:49
9:51
9:53[2]
9:54
10:1
10:3
11:1
11:2
11:30
11:31
11:33
11:39
11:40
12:11
12:13
13:2
13:3
13:5[2]
13:6
13:7[2]
13:15
13:16
13:19[3]
13:23[2]
13:24
14:1
14:2
14:3[2]
14:5
14:6
14:8[2]
14:10
14:12
14:16
14:18
15:1[2]
15:3
15:4
15:8
15:15[2]
15:16
16:4
16:9
16:12
16:17[2]
16:19
16:23
17:1
17:3[2]
17:4[2]
17:7[2]
17:8
17:9[2]
17:10[3]
17:13
18:10[3]
18:14[2]
18:19[6]
18:22
18:23
18:27
18:28
19:1[2]
19:3
19:5
19:12
19:15
19:17
19:24[2]
19:29
20:10[2]
20:38
20:40
21:5
21:15
21:17
21:18
21:19[2]

RU

1:1[2]
2:1[2]
2:3
2:7
2:10
2:11
2:12
3:8
3:9
3:11
3:12
3:13[2]
3:14
4:1
4:3
4:7[2]
4:13
4:14
4:15[2]
4:17[2]

1 SA

1:1
1:5
1:9[2]
1:11[2]
1:15[2]
1:16
1:20
1:24
1:25
2:3
2:13
2:18[2]
2:19
2:25
2:27
2:34
2:35[2]
2:36[3]
3:11
3:20
4:5
4:7
4:10
4:12
4:13
4:17
4:20
5:9
5:11
6:3
6:7
6:8[2]
6:9
6:14[3]
6:17
6:19
7:9[2]
7:10
7:12
8:5
8:6
8:10
8:19
8:22
9:1[3]
9:2[4]
9:6
9:7
9:8
9:9[3]
9:12
9:15
9:16
9:21
9:27
10:1
10:3
10:5[3]
10:10
10:12
10:19
10:25
10:26
11:1
11:2[2]
11:7
11:13
12:10
12:12
12:13
12:17
12:19
13:2
13:4
13:6
13:9
13:12
13:14
13:21
14:1
14:2
14:4[2]
14:10
14:12
14:14
14:15
14:20
14:25
14:29
14:30
14:33
14:36
14:39
14:41
14:43
15:5
15:12
15:18
15:28
15:29
16:1
16:12
16:16[2]
16:17
16:18[4]
16:20[2]
17:3[3]
17:4[2]
17:5
17:6
17:7[2]
17:8[2]
17:10
17:20
17:29
17:33[2]
17:34[3]
17:38
17:40[2]
17:42[2]
17:43
17:45[3]
17:46
17:49
17:50[2]
18:3
18:10
18:13
18:21
18:23[3]
19:5[2]
19:8
19:12
19:13[2]
19:16
19:22
20:3
20:6
20:8
20:16
20:20
20:21
20:25
20:29
20:33
20:35
20:41
21:2[2]
21:5[2]
21:7
21:9
22:2
22:6
22:8
22:13
22:18
23:5
23:7
23:14
23:15
23:18
23:25
23:27
24:3
24:14[2]
24:19
25:2[2]
25:3[2]
25:8
25:10
25:16
25:17[2]
25:28
25:29[2]
25:36[2]
25:37
25:41
26:12
26:13
26:15
26:20[2]
27:5
27:7
27:10
28:7[4]
28:9
28:12
28:14
28:22
28:24
29:1
30:12[2]
30:13
30:17
30:25
30:26
31:4
31:13

2 SA

1:2
1:13
2:17
2:18
2:28
3:7
3:8[2]
3:11
3:13
3:21
3:22[2]
3:29[2]
3:33
3:34
3:38[2]
4:2
4:4
4:5
4:10
4:11
5:2
5:3
5:23
5:24
6:3
6:8
6:14
6:16
6:19[3]
7:6[2]
7:7
7:9
7:10[2]
7:19[2]
7:23[2]
7:24
8:2
8:4
8:13
9:2
9:3
9:8
9:12
10:6
11:2
11:8
11:14
11:16
11:21[3]
11:27
12:3
12:4
12:24
12:30
13:1
13:2
13:3[2]
13:6
13:9
13:18
14:2[4]
14:5
14:13
14:27[2]
15:2
15:8
15:13
15:17
15:19
15:23
15:27
15:33
16:1[3]
16:5
16:8
16:22
16:23
17:8[2]
17:9
17:10[2]
17:13
17:18[3]
17:19
17:25
18:2[3]
18:7
18:9[2]
18:10
18:11
18:12
18:17[2]
18:18
18:24
18:27
18:29
19:4
19:10
19:16
19:17
19:18
19:32[2]
19:35
19:36[2]
20:1[3]
20:8[6]
20:12
20:15
20:16
20:19[2]
20:21
20:22
20:26
21:1
21:16
21:18
21:19[2]
21:20[2]
22:9
22:11
22:20
22:30[2]
22:31
22:32
22:35
22:44
23:4
23:7
23:10
23:11[2]
23:12
23:20[3]
23:21[3]
23:29
24:14
24:15
24:23
24:24

1 KI

1:2
1:3[2]
1:6
1:42
1:52
2:2
2:4
2:8[2]
2:9
2:19
2:42
3:4
3:5
3:6
3:7
3:8
3:9
3:12
3:15[2]
3:17
3:24[2]
4:7
4:32
5:1
5:7
5:12
5:13
5:14[2]
6:21
6:31
6:33
6:36
7:3
7:6
7:7
7:12
7:14[3]
7:15
7:23[2]
7:24
7:26
7:29
7:31[2]
7:32[3]
7:33
7:35
8:9
8:13
8:21
8:25
8:41[2]
8:55
8:63
8:65[2]
9:5
9:7
9:16
9:21
9:25
9:26
10:6
10:18
10:22
10:25
10:25
10:26
10:28
10:29
11:17
11:24
11:26
11:28
11:29
11:36
11:38
12:7
12:11
12:30
12:32
12:33
13:1
13:2
13:3
13:7
13:18
13:24
14:3
14:5
14:10
14:14
14:15
15:4
15:13
15:19[2]
15:22
16:11
16:31
16:33
17:7
17:9
17:10[2]
17:11
17:12[4]
17:13
17:19
17:24
18:2
18:4
18:13
18:21
18:22
18:27[2]
18:32
18:41
18:44[2]
18:45
19:2
19:4[2]
19:5
19:6[2]
19:9
19:11
19:12[2]
19:13
19:21
20:13
20:21
20:28
20:30
20:34
20:35
20:36[2]
20:39[3]
20:42
21:1
21:2[2]
21:9
21:12
22:7
22:10
22:17
22:21
22:22
22:23
22:34[3]
22:36
22:47

2 KI

1:2
1:3
1:6[2]
1:8
1:9[2]
1:10
1:12
1:13
2:1
2:9
2:10
2:11[2]
2:20
3:4
3:9
3:11
3:15
3:18
3:27
4:1
4:2
4:3
4:6[2]
4:8[2]
4:10[5]
4:11
4:16
4:17
4:18
4:19
4:28
4:38
4:39
4:42
5:1[3]
5:2
5:5
5:7[2]
5:8
5:10
5:12
5:14
5:15
5:19
5:22
5:26
5:27
6:2[2]
6:5
6:6
6:8
6:9
6:14
6:25[2]
6:26
6:32[2]
7:1[3]
7:2
7:6[3]
7:9
7:16[3]
7:18[3]
7:19
8:1
8:5
8:6
8:8
8:9
8:13
8:15
8:19
8:20
9:16
9:17[2]
9:19
9:24
9:28
9:30
9:34
10:2
10:6
10:8
10:18
10:19
10:20
10:21
10:27
11:4
11:5
11:6[2]
11:14
11:17
12:9[2]
12:20
13:5
13:21[2]
14:9
14:19
15:5[2]
15:13
15:19
15:25
15:30
16:8
16:17
17:16
17:21
17:35
17:36
18:17
18:21
18:28
18:31
18:32[4]
18:36
19:3
19:7[2]
19:17
19:29
19:31
19:32
20:3
20:7
20:10
20:12
20:14
20:20[2]
21:3
21:7
21:13[2]
21:14[2]
22:10
22:12
22:19[2]
23:3[2]
23:8
23:22
23:30
22:33[2]
24:16
25:8
25:23
25:30[2]

1 CH

2:34
5:25
6:33
7:16
7:23
9:13
10:4
10:13
11:3
11:13
11:14
11:20
11:22[4]
11:23[4]
11:42
12:2
12:4
12:14
12:22
12:28
12:34
12:38
13:7
13:11
14:12
14:15
15:1[2]
15:13
15:27
15:28
15:29
16:3[3]
16:5
16:15
16:17
16:19
16:42
17:4
17:6
17:8
17:9
17:17[3]
17:21
17:24
18:4
19:6
20:2
20:5
20:6
21:3
21:5
21:13
21:16
22:9[2]
22:14
25:3
26:14
26:17[2]
26:30
27:5
27:32[3]
28:3
28:9[2]
29:15
29:19
29:21[3]
29:28

2 CH

1:4
1:6
1:9
1:14
1:16
1:17
2:7
2:12
2:13
2:14[2]
2:18
4:2[2]
4:3
4:5[2]
5:10
5:13
6:2
6:5
6:13
6:16
6:22
6:32
6:36
7:5
7:8
7:9
7:18
7:20[2]
8:13
9:1
9:5
9:17
9:18
9:24
10:11
13:5
13:8
13:9[2]
13:15
13:17
14:9
15:3[2]
15:12
15:14
15:16
16:3
16:8
16:10[2]
16:14
17:17
18:6
18:9
18:20
18:21
18:22
18:33[3]
19:9
20:2
20:3
20:8
20:14
20:19
21:7
21:8
21:12
21:13
21:14
21:17
22:11
23:3
23:4
23:5[2]
23:16
24:8
24:9
24:24[2]
24:26
25:2
25:7
25:15
25:18
25:27
26:19
26:21[3]
26:23
28:5[2]
28:7
28:9[2]
28:21
29:10
29:21
29:31
29:32
30:5[2]
30:13
30:18
30:24[3]
32:18
32:24
33:6
33:7
33:14[2]
34:14
34:18
34:20
34:31
35:1
35:3
35:18
36:3
36:22

EZR

1:1
1:9
1:10[2]
2:7
2:12
2:31
2:37
2:38
2:39
2:61
2:63
3:5
3:11
3:12
3:13
4:8
4:10
4:11
4:15
4:17
5:7
5:11
5:13
5:17
6:1
6:2[2]
6:3
6:4
6:8
6:11[2]
6:12
6:17
7:6
7:11
7:12[2]
7:13
7:21
7:27
8:18
8:21[2]
8:22
8:27
8:28
8:35[2]
9:7[2]
9:8[4]
9:9[2]
10:1
10:3
10:12
10:13[2]
10:19

NE

2:6
2:8
2:10
2:17
3:13
4:2
4:3
4:4
4:6
4:9
4:17
4:22
5:1
5:7
6:3
6:7
6:11
7:2
7:5
7:12
7:34
7:40
7:41
7:42
7:65
7:70
8:4
8:18
9:4
9:8
9:10
9:11
9:12[2]
9:17[2]
9:18
9:25
9:29
9:31
9:38
10:29
10:32
11:23
13:2
13:5
13:7

ES

1:3
1:5
1:6
1:9
1:19
2:5[2]
2:18[2]
2:23
3:4
3:8
3:13
3:14
4:1[2]
4:5
4:14
5:9
5:14
8:11
8:13
8:15[2]
8:17[2]
9:17
9:18
9:19[2]
9:22
10:1

JOB

1:1
1:3
1:6
1:8
1:13
1:14
1:19
2:1
2:3
2:4
2:8
2:13
3:3
3:5
3:23
4:12[2]
4:15
4:16
4:17
5:26[2]
6:15
6:22
6:27
7:1
7:2[2]
7:6
7:12[2]
7:20[2]
8:2
8:9
8:14
8:20
9:2
9:3
9:17
9:19
9:25
9:32
10:16
10:20
10:22
11:2
11:12
12:5
12:14
12:18
12:25
13:25
13:27
13:28[2]
14:1
14:2[2]
14:4
14:7
14:9
14:13
14:14
14:15
14:17
15:2
15:14
15:21
15:24
16:8
16:14
16:21[2]
16:22
17:3
17:6[2]
17:7
18:8[2]
18:10
19:10
19:15
19:23
19:29
20:5
20:8[2]
20:26
20:29
21:11
21:13
22:2
22:6
22:14
22:16
22:28
24:3
24:5
24:8
24:9
24:14
24:20
24:24
24:25
25:4
25:6[2]
26:14
27:13
27:18[2]
27:20
27:21
28:1[2]
28:7
28:26[2]
29:14[2]
29:16
29:25
30:5
30:14
30:15
30:29[2]
31:1[2]
31:3
31:9
31:12
31:18
31:23
31:30
31:34
31:35
31:36
31:37
32:8
33:15[2]
33:23[2]
33:24
33:25
34:9
34:11
34:13
34:18
34:20
34:29[2]
34:34
35:8
36:2
36:16
36:18
37:4
37:18
37:20
38:3
38:9
38:14
38:25[2]
38:28
38:30
39:20
40:7
40:9
40:17
40:23
41:1
41:2
41:4[2]
41:5
41:6
41:15
41:18
41:20
41:21
41:24[2]
41:29
41:31[2]
41:32
41:34
42:8
42:11
42:12[2]

PS

1:3
2:1
2:9[2]
2:12
3 *title*
3:3
4 *title*
5 *title*
5:4
5:12
6 *title*
7:2
7:15
8 *title*
8:5
9 *title*
9:6
9:9[2]
10:9
11 *title*
11:1
12 *title*
12:2
12:6
13 *title*
14 *title*
15 *title*
15:3
15:4
16:6
17 *title*
17:12[2]
18 *title*
18:8
18:10
18:19
18:29[2]
18:30
18:31
18:34
18:43
19 *title*
19:4
19:5[3]
20 *title*
21 *title*
21:3
21:9
21:11
22 *title*
22:6[2]
22:13[2]
22:15
22:30[2]
22:31
23 *title*
23:5
24 *title*
24:4
25 *title*
26 *title*
27 *title*
27:5
27:11
28 *title*
29 *title*
29:6[2]
30 *title*
30:5[2]
31 *title*
31:8
31:11[2]
31:12[2]
31:20
31:21
32 *title*
32:6
33:3[2]
33:16
33:17
34 *title*
34:18[2]
35 *title*
35:7
35:19
36 *title*
36:4
36:6
37 *title*
37:10
37:16[2]
37:23
37:35
38 *title*
38:7
38:13[2]
38:14
39 *title*
39:1
39:6
39:11
39:12[2]
40 *title*
40:2
40:3
40:15
41 *title*
42:4
42:10
44:3
44:13[2]
44:14[2]
44:20
45 *title*
45:1[2]
45:6
45:12
46 *title*
46:1
46:4
47 *title*
47:2
47:5[2]
48 *title*
48:3
48:6
49 *title*
49:4
49:7
50 *title*
50:3
50:5
50:10
50:18
51 *title*
51:10[2]
51:17[3]
52 *title*
52:2
52:8
53 *title*
54 *title*
55 *title*
55:2
55:6
55:13
56 *title*
57:4
57:6[2]
58:4
58:8[2]
58:9
58:11[2]
59:6[2]
59:14[2]
60:4
61 *title*
61:3[2]
62 *title*
62:3[2]
62:8
62:9
63 *title*
63:1
63:10
64 *title*
64:3
64:6
65 *title*
66 *title*
66:1
66:12
67 *title*
68 *title*
68:5[2]
68:6
68:9
68:13
68:33
69 *title*
69:4
69:8
69:11
69:22[2]
69:30
70 *title*
79:3
71:7
72 *title*
73 *title*
73:1
73:6[2]
73:10
73:19
73:20
73:22
73:27
74:5
75 *title*
75:5
75:8
76 *title*
76:6
77 *title*
77:13
77:17
77:20
78:2
78:5[2]
78:8[2]
78:14[2]
78:19
78:21
78:38
78:39
78:50
78:52
78:57
78:65
78:66
79 *title*
79:4[2]
80 *title*
80:1
80:6
80:8
81 *title*
81:1
81:2
81:4[2]
81:5[2]
82 *title*
83 *title*
83:2
83:4
83:13
83:14
84 *title*
84:3
84:6
84:10[3]
84:11
85 *title*
86 *title*
86:15
86:17
87 *title*
88 *title*
88:4
89:3
89:8
89:13
89:37
89:41
90 *title*
90:4[2]
90:5[2]
90:9
91:7
91:12
92 *title*
92:1
92:3
92:6[2]
92:12
94:2
94:20
95:1
95:2
95:3[2]
95:10
96:1
97:3
98 *title*
98:1
98:4[2]
98:5
98:6
99:8
100 *title*
100:1
101 *title*[2]
101:4[2]
101:5
101:6
102 *title*
102:6
102:7
102:11
102:26[2]
103 *title*
103:13
103:15
104:2[2]
104:4
104:6
104:9
104:18
105:8

105:10
105:12
105:16
105:17^{2}
105:39^{2}
105:41
106:18
106:19
106:36
106:39
107:4
107:7
107:27
107:29
107:33
107:34
107:35
107:36
107:41
108 *title*
109 *title*
109:2
109:3
109:6
109:9
109:19
109:25
109:29
110 *title*
110:4
111:10
112:5
113:9
114:1
114:8^{2}
118:5
119:19
119:63
119:69
119:78
119:83
119:105^{2}
119:110
119:161
119:164
119:176
120 *title*
120:2
121 *title*
122 *title*
122:3
123 *title*
123:2
124 *title*
124:6
124:7
125 *title*
126 *title*
127 *title*
127:4
128 *title*
128:3
129 *title*
129:1
129:2
130 *title*
131 *title*
131:2^{2}
132 *title*
132:5
132:17
133 *title*
134 *title*
135:12^{2}
136:12^{2}
137:3
137:4
138 *title*
139 *title*
139:4
140 *title*
140:3
140:5^{2}
141 *title*
141:3
141:5
142 *title*
142:3
141:5
142 *title*
142:3
143 *title*
143:6
144 *title*
144:4
144:8
144:9^{2}
144:11
144:12
144:15
147:10
148:6
148:14
149:1
149:6

PR

1:5^{2}
1:6
1:27
2:7
3:12
3:18
3:30
4:1
4:9
4:24
5:3
5:4
5:10
5:20^{2}
6:1
6:5^{2}
6:10^{2}
6:12^{3}
6:17^{2}
6:19
6:23
6:24
6:26^{2}
6:27
6:30
6:32
6:33
6:34
7:7
7:10
7:19
7:20
7:22
7:23^{2}
8:27
9:7^{2}
9:8^{2}
9:9^{2}
9:13
9:14
10:1^{3}
10:4
10:5^{2}
10:8
10:10
10:11^{2}
10:13
10:18^{2}
10:23^{2}
11:1^{2}
11:7
11:12
11:13^{2}
11:15
11:16
11:18^{2}
11:20
11:22^{3}
11:28
11:30
12:2^{2}
12:3
12:4^{2}
12:8^{2}
12:9
12:10
12:14^{2}
12:15
12:16^{2}
12:17
12:18
12:19^{2}
12:23
12:25
12:27
13:1^{2}
13:2
13:5^{2}
13:8
13:12
13:14
13:16
13:17^{2}
13:20
13:22
14:3
14:5^{2}
14:6
14:7
14:9
14:10
14:12^{2}
14:14
14:16
14:17
14:25^{2}
14:26
14:27
14:30
14:34^{2}
14:35
15:1
15:4^{3}
15:5
15:12
15:13^{2}
15:15^{2}
15:17^{3}
15:18
15:20^{3}
15:21
15:23^{2}
15:30
16:2
16:7
16:8
16:9
16:10
16:11
16:14^{2}
16:15
16:18
16:20
16:22
16:25^{2}
16:27
16:28^{2}
16:29
16:31
16:32
17:1
17:2^{2}
17:4^{3}
17:7^{2}
17:8^{2}
17:9^{2}
17:10^{3}
17:11
17:12^{3}
17:16^{2}
17:17^{2}
17:18
17:20^{2}
17:21^{2}
17:22^{3}
17:23^{3}
17:24
17:25^{2}
17:27
17:28^{2}
18:1
18:2
18:4^{2}
18:6
18:7
18:8
18:9
18:10
18:13
18:14^{2}
18:16
18:19^{3}
18:20
18:22^{2}
18:24^{3}
19:1
19:5
19:6
19:9
19:10^{2}
19:11^{2}
19:12
19:13^{3}
19:14
19:15
19:19
19:21
19:22^{3}
19:24
19:25
19:26
20:1
20:2^{3}
20:3
20:5
20:6
20:8
20:11
20:15^{2}
20:16^{3}
20:17
20:19
20:23
20:24
20:25
20:26
20:30
21:2
21:4
21:6^{2}
21:9^{3}
21:14^{2}
21:17
21:18
21:19
21:20
21:22
21:27
21:28
21:29
22:1
22:3
22:6
22:9
22:13
22:14
22:15
22:18
22:24
22:25
22:29
23:1
23:2^{2}
23:9
23:21
23:24
23:27^{4}
23:28
23:32
23:34
24:5^{2}
24:7
24:8
24:14
24:16
24:25
24:26
24:28
24:33^{3}
25:2^{2}
25:4
25:9
25:11
25:12
25:13
25:14
25:15^{2}
25:18^{4}
25:19^{2}
25:20
25:23
25:24^{2}
25:25^{2}
25:26^{3}
25:28
26:1
26:3^{3}
26:4
26:5
26:6^{2}
26:7
26:8^{3}
26:9^{3}
26:11^{2}
26:12^{2}
26:13^{2}
26:16
26:17
26:18
26:21
26:22
26:23^{2}
26:27^{2}
26:28^{2}
27:1
27:2
27:3^{2}
27:6
27:8^{2}
27:9
27:10^{2}
27:12
27:13^{3}
27:14^{2}
27:15^{3}
27:17
27:21
27:22^{3}
28:1
28:2^{2}
28:3^{2}
28:7^{2}
28:12
28:15^{3}
28:16
28:17
28:20
28:21
28:23
28:24
28:25
28:26
28:27
29:5^{2}
29:6
29:8^{2}
29:9^{2}
29:11^{2}
29:12
29:15
29:19
29:20^{2}
29:21
29:22
29:23
29:24
29:25
30:2
30:4
30:5
30:6
30:10
30:11
30:12
30:13
30:14
30:19^{5}
30:22^{2}
30:25
30:26
30:30
30:31^{2}
31:10
31:15
31:16^{2}
31:30

EC

1:3
2:19^{2}
2:21^{3}
2:24
2:26
3:1^{2}
3:2^{4}
3:3^{4}
3:4^{4}
3:5^{4}
3:6^{4}
3:7^{4}
3:8^{4}
3:12
3:17
3:19^{2}
19:22
4:4
4:8^{2}
4:9
4:12
4:13^{2}
5:3^{2}
5:4
5:8
5:12
5:13
5:14
5:16
6:2^{2}
6:3
6:6
6:12^{2}
7:1
7:5
7:6
7:7^{2}
7:8
7:8
7:12^{2}
7:15^{2}
7:20
7:28^{2}
8:1^{2}
8:4
8:5
8:9
8:12
8:13
8:14
8:15
8:17^{3}
9:4^{2}
9:5
9:6
9:7
9:14^{2}
9:15
10:1^{2}
10:2^{2}
10:3^{2}
10:8^{3}
10:11
10:12^{2}
10:14^{2}
10:16
10:19
10:20
11:2
11:7
11:8
12:5
12:12

CA

1:9
4:3^{3}
1:8
1:13
1:14
2:9^{2}
2:13
2:17^{2}
3:4
3:9
4:1
4:3^{3}
4:4
4:12^{3}
4:15^{2}
5:11
5:13
6:5
6:6
6:7^{2}
7:1
7:2
7:4
7:7
7:13
8:6^{2}
8:7
8:8
8:9^{3}
8:10
8:11^{2}
8:12
8:14^{2}

ISA

1:4^{2}
1:8^{5}
1:9
1:14
1:30
1:30
1:31
2:20
3:6
3:7
3:16
3:17
3:24^{4}
4:5^{3}
4:6^{4}
5:1^{3}
5:2^{2}
5:7
5:9
5:18
5:28
5:29
6:1
6:5^{2}
6:6
6:12
6:13^{2}
7:6^{2}
7:8
7:11
7:13
7:14^{3}
7:20
7:21^{2}
7:23^{2}
8:1^{2}
8:3
8:11
8:12^{2}
8:14^{5}
8:19
9:2
9:6^{2}
9:8
10:6
10:7
10:13
10:14
10:16^{2}
10:17^{2}
10:18
10:19
10:22
10:23
10:24
10:25
10:26
10:34
11:1^{2}
11:6
11:10
13:2
13:4^{3}
13:5
13:6
13:8
13:12^{2}
13:14
14:6
14:17
14:19^{2}
14:23
14:29^{2}
14:31
15:5
16:2
16:4
17:1^{2}
17:7
17:9
17:11
17:12^{2}
17:13
18:2^{3}
18:3
18:4^{2}
18:7^{2}
19:1
19:4^{2}
19:14^{2}
19:17
19:19
19:20^{4}
19:21
19:23
19:24
20:3
21:1
21:2
21:3
21:6
21:7^{4}
21:8
21:9^{2}
21:16
22:2^{2}
22:5
22:11
22:16^{2}
22:17
22:18^{2}
22:21
22:23^{2}
23:3
23:10
23:11
24:9
24:20^{2}
25:2^{4}
25:4^{5}
25:5^{2}
25:6^{2}
26:1
26:16
26:17
26:20
27:2
27:10
27:11
28:1
28:2^{4}
28:4
28:5^{2}
28:6
28:10^{2}
28:13^{2}
28:15
28:16^{5}
28:19
28:20
28:22
28:27^{4}
29:3
29:4
29:7^{2}
29:8
29:11
29:14^{3}
29:17^{3}
29:21^{4}
30:1
30:5^{3}
30:6
30:8^{2}
30:9
30:13^{2}
30:14
30:17^{2}
30:18
30:20
30:21
30:22
30:27
30:28
30:29^{3}
30:30
30:31
30:33
31:4
31:7
31:8^{2}
32:1
32:2^{5}
32:14^{2}
32:15^{2}
32:18
32:19
33:9
33:19^{4}
33:20^{2}
33:21
33:23
34:4^{2}
34:6^{2}
34:13
34:14
35:4^{2}
35:7
35:8
36:2
36:6
36:13
36:16
36:17^{3}
36:21
37:3
37:7^{2}
37:18
37:30
37:32
37:33
37:36
38:3
38:7
38:12^{2}
38:13
38:14^{2}
38:21^{3}
39:1
39:3
40:3
40:11
40:12^{3}
40:15^{3}
40:16
40:19
40:20^{3}
40:22^{2}
41:12
41:15
41:18
41:28
42:3
42:6^{2}
42:10
42:13^{2}
42:14
42:16
42:22^{3}
42:24
43:16^{2}
43:19^{2}
44:8
44:9
44:10^{2}
44:13^{3}
44:15^{3}
44:17
44:19
44:20^{2}
44:22^{2}
45:15
45:19
45:20
45:21^{2}
46:1
46:6^{2}
46:11^{2}
47:3
47:7
47:8
47:9
47:14
48:8
48:18
48:20
49:2^{2}
49:6^{2}
49:7
49:8^{2}
49:11
49:15
49:18
49:21
50:2
50:4
50:7
50:9
50:11
51:4^{2}
51:6
51:8
51:10
51:12
51:20^{2}
53:2^{3}
53:3
53:7^{2}
53:12
54:6^{2}
54:7
54:8^{2}
55:4^{2}
55:5
55:13
56:3
56:5^{2}
57:4^{2}
57:6^{2}
57:7
57:8
57:15
58:1
58:2
58:5^{5}
58:11^{3}
58:13
59:5
59:15
59:17^{2}
59:19^{2}
60:8
60:15
60:22^{4}
61:10^{2}
62:1
62:2
62:3^{2}
62:5^{2}
62:7
62:10
62:12
63:14^{2}
63:18
64:6
64:10^{3}
65:1
65:2^{2}
65:3
65:5^{2}
65:8
65:9
65:10^{2}
65:11
65:15
65:17
65:18^{2}
65:22
66:2
66:3^{3}
66:6^{3}
66:7
66:8^{2}
66:12^{2}
66:15
66:19
66:20

JER

1:5
1:6
1:7
1:11
1:13
1:18
2:2
2:6^{3}
2:7
2:10
2:11
2:14^{2}
2:21^{3}
2:23
2:24
2:27^{2}
2:30
2:31^{2}
2:32^{4}
3:1
3:3
3:8
3:14^{2}
3:19^{2}
3:20
3:21
4:6
4:11
4:12
4:13
4:15
4:16
4:17
4:19
4:20
4:26
4:27
4:29
4:31^{2}
5:1
5:3
5:6^{3}
5:9
5:10
5:15^{3}
5:18
5:19
5:22
5:23^{2}
5:26
5:27
5:29
5:30
6:1
6:2
6:6
6:7
6:8
6:9^{2}
6:10
6:20
6:22^{2}
6:24
6:27^{2}
7:5
7:11
7:28
7:29
8:5
8:15
8:19
9:1
9:2
9:9
9:10^{2}
9:11
9:12
9:16
9:18
9:19
10:3
10:8
10:13
10:19
10:22^{9}
11:5
11:9
11:14
11:16^{2}
11:19
12:6
12:8
12:9
12:10
13:1
13:2
13:4
13:11^{5}
13:21
14:8^{3}
14:9^{2}
14:14^{2}
14:17^{2}
14:18
15:7
15:8
15:10^{2}
15:14^{2}
15:18
15:20
16:2
16:13
16:20
17:1^{2}
17:4
17:6
17:8
17:11
17:12
17:16
17:22
17:27^{2}
18:3
18:7^{2}
18:9^{2}
18:11
18:13
18:14
18:15
18:16
18:20
18:22^{2}
19:1
19:11
20:4
20:8^{2}
20:9
20:11
20:15
21:5
21:6
21:9
21:14
22:5
22:6
22:14
22:23
22:28^{3}
22:30
23:5^{2}
23:9^{2}
23:16
23:19^{2}
23:23^{2}
23:28^{2}
23:29^{2}
23:33
23:40
25:9^{4}
25:11
25:18
25:29
25:30
25:31^{2}
25:32
25:34
25:36
26:2
26:6
26:15
26:18^{2}
26:20
27:10
27:14
27:15
27:16
28:14
28:15
29:18^{2}
29:21
29:22
29:23
29:26
29:27
29:31
29:32
30:2
30:5
30:6^{2}
30:11^{2}
30:14
30:16^{2}
30:23
31:6
31:8
31:9^{2}
31:10
31:12
31:15
31:18
31:20
31:22^{3}
31:29
31:31
31:35^{2}
31:36
32:20
32:21^{2}
32:22
32:31
33:9^{2}
33:17
33:18
33:21
33:24
34:8
34:9
34:13
34:15
34:17
34:22
35:4
35:19
36:2^{2}
36:4^{2}
36:9
36:22
37:13
37:21
38:2
38:14
39:18
40:5
40:8
40:11
42:2
42:5
42:18^{2}
43:12^{2}
44:2
44:8^{2}
44:12^{2}
44:12^{2}
44:14
44:15
44:22^{2}
44:28
44:29
45:1
45:5
46:7
46:8
46:10^{2}
46:17
46:20
46:22
46:28^{2}
47:7
48:2
48:3
48:4
48:5
48:27
48:38
48:39^{2}
48:41
48:42
48:45^{2}
49:2
49:5
49:13^{4}
49:14
49:17
49:18
49:19^{2}
49:22
49:24
49:27
49:30
49:32^{2}
49:33^{2}
50:2
50:3
50:5
50:9
50:10
50:12^{3}
50:17
50:22
50:23
50:24
50:32
50:35
50:36^{2}
50:37^{2}
50:38
50:41^{2}
50:42
50:43
50:44^{2}
51:1
51:6
51:7
51:14
51:16
51:25
51:26^{3}
51:27^{2}
51:29
51:33^{2}
51:34
51:37
51:39
51:43^{4}
51:46^{2}
51:54^{2}
51:55
51:57
51:59
51:60
51:63
52:21
52:22
52:23
52:34^{2}

LA

1:1
1:13
1:15
1:17
2:1
2:3
2:6
2:7^{2}
2:8
2:18
2:20
2:22
3:10^{2}
3:12
3:14
3:26
3:27
3:35
3:36
3:39^{2}
3:44
3:47
3:52
3:53
3:64
4:6
4:8^{2}
4:11
4:17

EZE

1:4^{4}
1:5
1:7
1:8
1:10^{2}
1:14
1:16^{2}
1:25
1:26^{3}
1:28
2:3
2:5^{2}
2:6
2:9
2:12^{2}
2:13^{2}
2:17
2:20^{2}
2:26^{2}
2:27
4:1
4:2^{2}
4:3^{2}
4:6
4:10
5:1^{2}
5:2^{5}
5:3
5:4
5:12^{4}
5:14
5:15^{2}
6:3
6:8
6:9
7:11
7:21^{2}
7:23
7:26
8:2
8:3
8:7
8:8
8:11
8:17
8:18
9:1
9:2^{2}
9:4
10:1^{2}
10:8
10:9
10:10^{2}
10:14^{3}
10:21
11:8
11:13^{2}
11:16
11:19
11:24
12:2^{2}
12:3
12:6
12:16
12:23
13:7^{2}
13:10
13:11
13:13
14:7
14:8^{2}
14:9
14:17
14:19
14:22
15:2
15:3
15:8
16:8
16:11
16:12^{2}
16:13
16:19
16:20
16:32
16:34
16:40
16:47
16:54
17:2^{2}
17:3
17:4^{2}
17:5^{2}
17:6^{2}
17:8^{2}
17:13
17:22
17:23
18:5
18:6
18:7
18:10^{3}
18:14
18:16
18:26
18:31^{2}
19:1
19:2
19:3
19:5
19:6
19:10
19:13
19:14^{4}
20:6
20:11
20:12
20:13
20:20
20:21
20:27
20:33^{2}
20:34^{2}
20:47
21:9^{2}
21:10
21:13
21:19
21:20
21:22^{2}
21:23
21:29
22:4^{2}
22:25^{2}
22:30
23:30
23:40
23:41^{2}
23:42^{2}
23:44
23:46
24:3^{2}
24:7
24:8
24:16
24:24
24:27
25:4
25:5^{2}
25:7
25:15
26:4
26:5^{2}
26:7
26:8^{2}
26:10^{2}
26:12^{2}
26:14^{2}
26:17
26:19
26:21
27:2
27:3
27:15
27:32
27:36
28:2^{2}
28:9
28:12
28:18
28:19
28:24
29:6
29:7
29:8
29:14
29:18
30:3
30:8
30:13^{2}
30:18
30:21
30:24
31:3^{2}
31:15
32:2^{3}
32:3
32:7
32:25
33:2^{2}
33:7
33:32^{2}
33:33
34:8
34:12
34:14^{3}
34:18
34:22
34:24
34:25
34:26
34:28
34:29
35:5
36:3
36:4
36:5
36:17
36:26^{2}
36:37
37:7^{2}
37:26
38:4
38:7
38:9^{2}
38:12^{2}
38:13^{3}
38:15^{2}
38:16
38:19
38:21
39:6
39:11
39:13
39:15^{2}
39:17
40:2^{2}
40:3^{3}
40:5^{2}
40:17
40:24
40:27
40:42^{2}
41:7
41:8
41:18^{3}
41:19^{2}
42:4^{2}
42:12
42:20^{2}
43:2
43:13^{4}
43:17^{2}
43:19^{2}
43:22^{2}
43:23^{2}
43:24
43:25^{4}
44:13
44:22^{3}
45:4
45:5
45:7
45:10^{2}
45:14
45:15^{2}
45:18
45:21
45:22^{2}
45:23^{3}
45:24^{3}
46:4
46:5
46:6^{2}
46:7^{3}
46:11^{2}
46:12
46:13^{2}
46:14^{3}
46:15
46:16
46:17
46:19
46:21
46:23
47:3
47:4^{2}
47:5^{3}
47:9
47:10
47:20
48:1
48:2
48:3
48:4
48:5
48:6
48:7
48:12
48:15
48:23
48:24
48:25
48:26
48:27

DA

1:5
2:3
2:5
2:10
2:11

2:19
2:25
2:28
2:31
2:34
2:35
2:37[2]
2:44
2:47[4]
2:48
3:6
3:10
3:11
3:15
3:29[2]
4:5
4:6
4:10
4:13
4:15
4:16
4:23[2]
4:27
4:31
5:1[2]
5:5
5:7
5:11
5:16
5:18
5:29[2]
6:7[3]
6:10
6:12[2]
6:13
6:17
6:20
6:26
7:1
7:4[3]
7:5[2]
7:6[2]
7:7
7:8
7:10
7:12
7:14
7:20
7:25
8:1
8:2[2]
8:3
8:5
8:9
8:15
8:16
8:18
8:23
9:12
9:15
9:16
9:26
10:1
10:5
10:6
10:7
10:9
10:11
10:18
11:3
11:7
11:10
11:11
11:13[2]
11:15
11:18
11:20
11:21
11:22
11:23
11:25[2]
11:34
11:35
11:38
11:39
11:40
12:1[2]
12:7
12:11

HO

1:2
1:3
1:4
1:6
1:8
2:3[2]
2:6
2:12
2:15
2:18
3:1
3:4[3]
4:1
4:12
4:16[3]
5:1[2]
5:2
5:7
5:12
5:14[2]
6:4
6:8
6:9
7:6
7:8
7:11
7:16
8:8
8:9
8:10
8:12
8:14
9:1[2]
9:7
9:8[2]
9:11
9:12
9:13
9:14
10:3
10:4
10:6
10:14
10:15
11:1
11:4
11:10
11:11[2]
12:1
12:2
12:7
12:12[2]
12:13[2]
13:7[2]
13:8[2]
13:10
13:11
13:13
14:8

JOE

1:6[2]
1:8
1:14[2]
1:15
2:2[4]
2:3[3]
2:5[2]
2:9
2:14[3]
2:15[2]
2:19
2:20
3:3[2]
3:4
3:8
3:18
3:19[2]

AM

1:4
1:7
1:10
1:12
1:14[2]
2:2
2:5
2:6
2:7
2:13
3:4[2]
3:5[2]
3:6[2]
3:12[3]
4:5
4:11
5:1
5:3
5:12
5:19[4]
5:24
6:10
6:13
6:14
7:4
7:7[3]
7:8[2]
7:14[2]
7:17
8:1
8:2
8:6
8:8
8:10
8:11[3]
9:5
9:9

OB

1
7
12
18[2]

JON

1:3
1:4[2]
1:16
1:17
3:4
3:5
4:2
4:5
4:6[2]
4:7
4:8
4:10[2]

MIC

1:4
1:6
1:8
1:14
2:2[2]
2:4[2]
2:5
2:10
2:11
3:6
3:12
4:3
4:7[2]
4:9
4:10
5:1
5:7
5:8[2]
6:2
6:6
6:16
7:2
7:3
7:4[2]
7:5[2]
7:6
7:8
7:17
7:18

NA

1:7
1:11
1:14
2:8
3:2
3:3[2]
3:6

HAB

1:5
1:10
2:5
2:6[2]
2:12[2]
2:18
3:1
3:14

ZEP

1:7
1:10[2]
1:13[2]
1:15[5]
1:16
1:18
2:4
2:9
2:13[2]
2:15[2]
3:9
3:13
3:18
3:20[2]

HAG

1:6
1:11
2:6
2:13
2:15[2]
2:23

ZEC

1:8[2]
1:14
1:15
1:16
2:1[2]
2:5
2:9
3:2
3:5[2]
4:1
4:2[2]
4:7
5:1
5:2
5:7[2]
5:9
6:13
6:14
7:12
7:14
8:3
8:13[2]
8:23
9:3
9:6
9:7[2]
9:9
9:13
9:15
9:16
10:2[2]
10:7
11:3[2]
11:13
11:15
11:16
12:2
12:3
12:6[2]
12:11
13:1
13:4
14:4
14:10
14:13

MAL

1:6[4]
1:11
1:13
1:14[3]
2:2
2:11
2:15
3:2
3:3
3:5
3:8
3:9
3:10
3:12
3:16
3:17
4:6

MT

1:19[2]
1:20
1:21
1:23[2]
2:6
2:12
2:13
2:18
2:19
2:22
2:23[2]
3:4
3:16
3:17
4:5
4:6
4:18
4:21
5:1
5:14
5:15[3]
5:22
5:28
5:31
5:38[2]
5:41
6:2
6:16
7:4
7:9
7:10[2]
7:17
7:18[2]
7:24[2]
7:25
7:26
8:2
8:4
8:5
8:14
8:19
8:23
8:24
8:26
8:30
8:32[2]
9:1
9:2[2]
9:9
9:12
9:16
9:18
9:20
9:23
9:32[2]
10:18
10:29
10:34
10:35
10:36
10:41[6]
10:42[2]
11:7
11:8
11:9[2]
11:11
11:18
11:19[3]
12:10
12:11
12:12[2]
12:14
12:20
12:22
12:29
12:32
12:35
12:38
12:39
12:41
12:42
12:43
13:2
13:3
13:21
13:24
13:31[2]
13:32
13:33
13:34
13:42
13:44[2]
13:45
13:47
13:52
13:57
14:5
14:8
14:11
14:13
14:14
14:15
14:22
14:23
14:26
14:33
15:5
15:11[2]
15:20[2]
15:22[2]
15:23
15:29
15:33
15:34
16:1
16:4[2]
16:26[2]
17:5[2]
17:14
17:20
17:27
18:2
18:6
18:12
18:17
18:23
19:3
19:5
19:7
19:23
19:24[3]
20:1
20:2[2]
20:9
20:10
20:13
20:20
20:28
20:29
21:2
21:5
21:8
21:13
21:19
21:26
21:28
21:33[5]
21:43
21:46
22:2[2]
22:11[2]
22:12
22:19
22:24
22:25
22:35[2]
22:46
23:14
23:16
23:24[2]
23:37
24:14
24:31[2]
24:32
24:45
24:50
25:6
25:14[2]
25:19
25:21
25:23
25:32
25:35
25:38
25:43
25:44
26:7
26:10
26:13
26:18
26:36
26:39
26:47
26:48
26:51
26:55
26:69
26:73
27:14
27:15
27:16
27:19
27:24
27:28
27:29[2]
27:32
27:33[3]
27:46
27:48[2]
27:50
27:57
27:59
27:60
27:65
27:66
28:2
28:16

MK

1:6[2]
1:10
1:11
1:16
1:19
1:23
1:26
1:30
1:35[2]
1:40
1:44
2:21
3:1[2]
3:7
3:8
3:9
3:13
3:24
3:25
3:27
4:1[2]
4:3
4:17
4:21[4]
4:26
4:31
4:34
4:37
4:38
4:39
5:2
5:7
5:11
5:13
5:25
5:42
6:4
6:5
6:8
6:10
6:11
6:15
6:19
6:20
6:21[2]
6:25
6:28
6:29
6:31[2]
6:32
6:34
6:35
6:46
6:49
7:11
7:15
7:26[2]
7:36
8:4
8:7
8:10
8:11
8:12
8:22
8:36
8:37
9:7[2]
9:14
9:17
9:21
9:36
9:39
9:41
9:42
10:2
10:4
10:7
10:12
10:15
10:25[3]
10:45
10:46
10:48
11:2
11:4
11:13
11:17
11:32
12:1[5]
12:2
12:15
12:19
12:20
12:40
12:42[2]
13:9
13:28
13:34[2]
14:3
14:6
14:9
14:13[2]
14:15
14:32
14:35
14:43
14:44
14:47[2]
14:48
14:51[2]
14:69
14:70[2]
15:1
15:17
15:19
15:21
15:22
15:34
15:36[2]
15:37
15:46[3]
16:5[2]

LU

1:1
1:5
1:13
1:17
1:22
1:26
1:27[2]
1:31
1:34
1:36
1:39
1:42
1:45
1:57
1:63
2:1
2:7
2:11
2:12[2]
2:13
2:16
2:24[2]
2:25
2:32
2:34
2:35
2:36[2]
2:37
2:44
3:22[3]
4:5
4:9
4:11
4:13
4:14
4:25
4:26[3]
4:31
4:33[3]
4:36
4:38
4:42
5:3
5:4
5:6
5:8
5:12[2]
5:14
5:15
5:17
5:18[3]
5:27
5:29[2]
5:31
5:36[4]
6:6
6:12
6:17
6:39
6:43[2]
6:44
6:45
6:48[3]
6:49[2]
7:2
7:5
7:7
7:8
7:11
7:12[2]
7:16[2]
7:24
7:25
7:26[2]
7:28
7:33
7:34[3]
7:37[2]
7:39[2]
7:41
8:4
8:5
8:6
8:13
8:16[4]
8:22[2]
8:23
8:24
8:27
8:28
8:33
8:41[2]
8:42
8:43
9:5
9:10
9:12
9:14
9:25
9:27
9:28
9:34
9:35
9:38
9:39
9:42
9:46
9:47
9:52
9:57
10:13
10:25
10:30
10:31
10:32
10:33
10:38[2]
10:39
11:1
11:5
11:6
11:11[6]
11:12
11:14
11:16
11:17[2]
11:21
11:22
11:24
11:27
11:29
11:30
11:31
11:32
11:33[4]
11:36
11:37
12:10
12:14[2]
12:15
12:16[2]
12:33
12:44
12:46
12:50
12:54[2]
13:6[2]
13:11[2]
13:16
13:19[3]
13:21
13:33
13:34
14:2
14:5
14:7
14:8[2]
14:12[3]
14:13
14:16[2]
14:18
14:20
14:28
14:32
15:8
15:11
15:13
15:14
15:15
15:20
15:22
15:29
16:1[2]
16:19
16:20
16:26
17:2
17:4[2]
17:6
17:7
17:12
17:15
17:16
18:1
18:2[2]
18:3
18:4
18:10[2]
18:13
18:17
18:18
18:25[3]
18:35
19:2
19:4
19:7[2]
19:9
19:11
19:12[3]
19:14
19:17
19:20
19:30
19:37
19:43
19:46
20:6
20:9[4]
20:10
20:12
20:24
20:28
20:29
20:38
20:47
21:2
21:3
21:13
21:15
21:27
21:29
21:35
22:10[2]
22:12
22:24
22:29
22:36
22:41
22:47
22:48
22:52
22:55
22:56
22:58
22:59[2]
23:2
23:6
23:8
23:11
23:19
23:26
23:27
23:31
23:38
23:44
23:47
23:50[4]
23:51
23:53
24:13
24:18
24:19
24:23
24:37
24:39
24:42[2]

JOH

1:6
1:7
1:30
1:32
1:42
2:1
2:15
3:1[2]
3:2
3:3
3:4
3:5
3:10
3:25
3:27
4:5
4:7
4:9[2]
4:14
4:19
4:24
4:29
4:44
4:46
5:1
5:2
5:3
5:4
5:5
5:6
5:13
5:14
5:35[3]
6:2
6:3
6:4
6:5
6:7
6:9
6:14
6:15[2]
6:17
6:18
6:50
6:70
7:12
7:20
7:22
7:23[2]
7:33
7:40
7:43
8:3
8:7
8:40
8:44[3]
8:48[2]
8:49
8:51
8:52[2]
8:55
9:1
9:11
9:16[3]
9:17
9:24
9:25
9:30
9:31
10:1[2]
10:5
10:19
10:20
10:21[2]
10:33[2]
11:1
11:10
11:38[2]
11:43
11:44
11:47
11:54[2]
11:57
12:2
12:3
12:6
12:14
12:24
12:28
12:35
12:46
12:49
13:4
13:5
13:26
13:33
13:34
14:2
14:3
14:19
14:23
15:6[2]
15:13
15:25
16:16[2]
16:17[2]
16:18
16:19[2]
16:21[2]
18:1
18:3
18:10
18:18
18:30
18:35
18:37[2]
18:39
18:40
19:2[2]
19:7
19:12
19:13
19:17[2]
19:19
19:23
19:29[2]
19:34
19:36
19:38
19:39
19:41[2]
20:7
21:3[2]
21:8
21:9

AC

1:9
1:12
1:18
1:22
2:2[2]
2:22
2:30
3:2
3:14
3:22
4:16
4:27
4:36
5:1[2]
5:2
5:16
5:30
5:31[2]
5:34[3]
5:36
6:1
6:5[2]
6:7
7:5
7:6
7:11
7:16
7:27[2]
7:29
7:30[2]
7:35[4]
7:37
7:41
7:46
7:57
7:58
7:60
8:1
8:9
8:27
8:32[2]
8:36
9:3
9:4
9:7
9:10[2]
9:12[2]
9:15
9:25
9:26
9:33
9:36
9:43
10:1[2]
10:2
10:3
10:4
10:6
10:7
10:10
10:11[2]
10:13
10:22
10:26
10:28[2]
10:30
10:32
10:34
10:39
11:5[4]
11:7
11:21
11:24
11:26
12:7
12:9
12:11
12:13
12:21
12:22[3]
13:6[3]
13:7
13:11[3]
13:21[2]
13:22
13:23
13:29
13:41[3]
13:47
14:1
14:8[2]
14:10
15:7
15:10
15:14
15:33
16:1[3]
16:3
16:9[2]
16:11
16:12
16:13
16:14[2]
16:16[2]
16:24
16:26
16:28
16:29
17:1
17:4[2]
17:5
17:12
17:15
17:18
17:31
17:34
18:2
18:7
18:9
18:11
18:14
18:15
18:18[2]
18:24
19:14
19:22
19:24[2]
19:34
19:35
19:38
19:39
20:9[3]
20:11
20:12
21:1
21:2
21:10
21:23
21:39[4]
21:40
22:3[3]
22:6
22:7
22:12
22:17
22:22
22:25[2]
22:26
22:27
22:28
22:29
23:6[2]
23:7
23:9[2]
23:10
23:12
23:14
23:17
23:21
23:25
23:27
24:1
24:4
24:5[3]
24:10
24:15
24:16
24:23
24:24
24:25
24:27
25:9
25:14
25:27
26:5
26:8
26:13
26:14
26:16[2]
26:24
26:26
26:28
27:1[2]
27:2[2]
27:5
27:6
27:8
27:14
27:16
27:18
27:26
27:28
27:39[2]
27:41
28:2
28:3[2]
28:4
28:6[2]
28:8[2]
28:11
28:13
28:16
28:23

RO

1:1
1:10
1:25
1:28
2:14
2:17
2:19[2]
2:20
2:21
2:22
2:25
2:28
2:29
3:4
3:5
3:7
3:25
3:28
4:11
4:17
5:7[2]
7:1
7:21
8:24
9:9
9:27
9:28
9:29
9:33
10:2
10:14
10:19
10:21
11:5
11:9[4]
11:17
11:24
12:1
13:3
13:4
14:13
15:8
15:12
15:23
15:26
16:1
16:2
16:23

1 CO

1:22
1:23
2:7
2:11
3:10
3:14
3:18
4:1
4:2
4:3
4:6
4:9
4:21
5:5
5:6
5:7
5:11[4]
6:1
6:5
6:7
6:18
6:20
7:1[2]
7:5
7:12
7:15[2]
7:21
7:22
7:23
7:26
7:27[3]
7:28
7:34[2]
7:35
8:7
8:9
9:5[2]
9:7[3]
9:8
9:11
9:17[2]
9:20
9:24
9:25
9:27
10:13
10:27
10:30
11:6[2]
11:7
11:13
11:14[2]
11:15[3]
11:28
12:31
13:1
13:11[5]
13:12
14:7
14:11[2]
14:22
14:25
14:26[4]
14:35
14:37
15:38
15:44[4]
15:45[2]
15:51
15:52
16:7
16:9

2 CO

1:10
1:15
1:23
2:6
2:7
2:12
2:15
3:13
3:18
4:17[2]
5:1
5:17
6:2
6:13
6:18
7:8[2]
7:9
7:11
7:14
8:2
8:10
8:11[2]
8:12[2]
8:14[2]
9:2
9:5
9:7
10:6
10:13
11:1
11:2
11:5
11:16[2]
11:20[5]
11:23
11:25[2]
11:32
11:33[2]
12:2
12:3
12:4
12:6
12:7
12:11
12:17
12:18[2]
13:3
subscr.

GA

2:3
2:14
2:16
2:18
3:13[2]
3:15
3:19
3:20[2]
3:21
3:25
4:1[2]
4:4
4:7[3]
4:18
4:22[2]
4:27
5:3
5:9
6:1[2]
6:3
6:7
6:11
6:12
6:15

EPH

3:7
4:13
5:2[2]
5:12
5:27
5:31
5:32
6:21

PHP

1:6
1:23[2]
2:7
2:8
2:9
2:15
2:22
3:5
4:17
4:18[2]

COL

1:7
1:23
1:25

2:15
2:17
2:18
2:23
3:13
4:1
4:3
4:7[2]
4:9
4:11
4:12
4:13

1 TH

2:5
2:7
2:11
2:17
4:16
5:2
5:3
5:4

2 TH

1:5
1:6
2:3
2:11
3:15

1 TI

1:5[2]
1:8
1:9
1:13[2]
1:15
1:16
1:18
1:19
2:2
2:6
2:7[2]
2:12
3:1[4]
3:2
3:3
3:5
3:6
3:7
3:9
3:10
3:13[2]
4:2
4:6
4:9
5:1
5:5
5:9
5:23
6:9
6:12
6:13
6:19

2 TI

1:7
1:11[2]
2:3
2:4
2:5
2:11
2:15
2:17
2:20
2:21[2]
2:22
3:5
3:15
4:7
4:8

TIT

1:1
1:7
1:8[2]
1:12
2:7
2:14
3:8
3:10

PHM

1
9
15
16[3]
17
22
subscr.

HEB

1:4
1:5[2]
1:7
1:8
1:11
1:12
2:2
2:6
2:7
2:9
2:17
3:5[2]
3:6
4:1
4:4
4:7[2]
4:9
4:12
4:14
5:6
5:8
5:13
6:18
7:2
7:3
7:5
7:12
7:16
7:17
7:18
7:19
7:21
7:22[2]
8:2
8:4
8:6[2]
8:8
8:10[2]
8:13
9:1
9:2
9:9
9:11
9:16
9:17
10:1
10:3
10:5
10:15
10:20
10:22
10:27
10:31
10:32
10:33
10:34
10:37
11:2
11:4
11:6
11:8
11:9
11:10
11:11
11:14
11:16[2]
11:19
11:21
11:23
11:25
11:35
11:39
12:1
12:10
12:19
12:20[2]
12:28
12:29
13:9
13:18
13:22

JAS

1:1
1:6
1:8
1:11
1:18
1:23[4]
1:25[2]
2:2[3]
2:3
2:11
2:14
2:15
2:18
2:24
3:2
3:4
3:5[3]
3:6[2]
3:11
3:12
3:13[2]
4:4
4:11[2]
4:13[2]
4:14[2]
5:3
5:5
5:16
5:17
5:20[2]

1 PE

1:3
1:6
1:19
1:22
2:4
2:5
2:6
2:8[2]
2:9[2]
2:10
2:16
2:19
3:4
3:9
3:15
3:16
3:20
3:21
4:15[3]
4:16
4:19
5:1[2]
5:2
5:4
5:8
5:10
5:12
5:14

2 PE

1:1
1:17
1:19[3]
2:3
2:5
2:17
2:19
3:8[2]
3:10[2]
3:13

1 JO

1:10
2:4
2:8
2:22
3:15
4:20[2]
5:10
5:16[2]
5:17

2 JO

4
5
7
8

3 JO

6

JUDE

9
22

RE

1:10[2]
1:11
1:13[2]
1:14
1:15
1:16
2:10
2:14
2:17[2]
2:18
2:20[2]
2:22
2:27[2]
3:1
3:3
3:4
3:8
3:12
4:1[2]
4:2
4:3[3]
4:6
4:7[5]
5:1
5:2[2]
5:6
5:9
5:12
6:2[3]
6:4
6:5[2]
6:6[4]
6:8
6:10
6:11
6:12
6:13[2]
6:14
7:2
7:9
7:10
8:3
8:8
8:10[2]
8:12
8:13
9:1
9:2[2]
9:5[2]
9:11
9:13
9:15[3]
10:1[2]
10:2
10:3[2]
10:4
11:1[2]
11:3
11:12[2]
11:13
12:1[3]
12:3
12:5[2]
12:6[2]
12:10
12:12
12:14[3]
12:15
13:1
13:2[3]
13:5
13:11[2]
13:14
13:16
13:18
14:1
14:2[2]
14:3
14:7
14:9
14:13
14:14[3]
14:15
14:17
14:18
14:20
15:2
16:1
16:2
16:3
16:15
16:16
16:17
16:18
16:21[2]
17:3[2]
17:4
17:5
17:10
18:2[6]
18:7
18:21[3]
18:22
18:23
19:1
19:5
19:6
19:11
19:12[2]
19:13
19:15[2]
19:16
19:17
19:20
20:1
20:2
20:3[2]
20:4
20:6[3]
20:11
21:1[2]
21:2
21:3
21:10
21:11[2]
21:12
21:15
21:17
21:19
21:20[2]
21:27
22:1
22:15

AN (See also A)

GE

2:18
2:20
4:3
4:22
5:3
5:6
5:18
5:25
5:28
6:3
6:14
7:24
8:11
8:20
9:20
11:10
11:25
12:7
12:8
13:18
15:9
15:12
16:1[2]
17:7
17:8
17:13
17:17
17:19
21:5
21:20
22:9
23:1
25:7
25:8
25:17
25:25
26:12
26:25
26:28
27:30
29:24
31:46
33:17
33:19
33:20
34:31
35:1
35:3
35:7
35:8
35:28
37:33
37:36
38:14
38:15
39:1[2]
39:14
41:12
41:16
42:23
43:12
43:32
44:20
46:34
47:9
47:28
48:4
49:9
49:13
49:17
49:33
50:22
50:25
50:26

EX

2:3
2:11[2]
2:19
4:20
6:8
6:16
6:18
6:20
10:13
10:26
12:3
12:14
12:16[2]
12:17
12:24
12:45
13:13
14:8
15:2
15:8
15:25
16:16
16:18
16:32
16:33
16:36[2]
17:15
18:3
19:6
19:13
20:24
20:25
21:2
21:6
21:28
21:33[2]
22:1[2]
22:10[2]
22:11
22:15
22:25
23:1
23:20
23:22[2]
24:4
25:2
25:10
25:25
26:36
27:1
27:9
27:11
27:16
27:18
28:4
28:11
28:18
28:19[2]
28:20
28:32[2]
29:18
29:25
29:28[2]
29:36
29:37[2]
29:40[2]
29:41
30:1
30:10
30:13
30:14
30:15[2]
30:16
30:24
30:25[3]
30:31
31:18
32:5
32:30
33:2
34:20
35:2
35:5[2]
35:22
35:24
36:37
37:12
38:9
38:11
38:23[2]
38:25
38:27
39:11
39:12[2]
39:13
39:23[2]
40:10
40:15

LE

1:2
1:9
1:13
1:17
2:2
2:4
2:9
2:16
3:3
3:5
3:9
3:14
4:20
4:26
4:31
4:35
5:2
5:4
5:6
5:10
5:11
5:13
5:16
5:18
6:7
6:20
7:5
7:14
7:18
7:25
7:32
8:21
8:28
8:33
8:34
9:7[2]
9:17
11:10
11:11
11:12
11:13
11:20
11:23
11:41
11:42
12:7
12:8
13:11
13:28
14:5
14:18
14:19
14:20
14:21
14:29
14:31
14:40
14:41
14:45
14:50
14:53
15:13
15:15
15:19
15:25
15:30
15:32
15:33
16:6
16:10
16:11
16:16
16:17[2]
16:18
16:20
16:24
16:30
16:33[2]
16:34[2]
17:3
17:4
17:11[2]
19:20
19:22
20:13
20:21
21:14
22:10
22:12
22:22
22:27
23:3
23:7
23:8[2]
23:12
23:13[2]
23:14
23:18
23:21
23:24
23:25
23:27[2]
23:28
23:35
23:36[2]
23:37
24:7
24:8
24:10[2]
25:40
25:46
25:50
26:8[2]
27:9
27:16
27:27

NU

2:9
2:16
2:24[2]
2:31
4:15
5:2
5:8
5:15[3]
5:17
5:19
5:21[2]
5:26
6:11
7:3
7:13
7:19
7:25
7:31
7:37
7:43
7:49
7:55
7:61
7:67
7:73
7:79
7:85
7:86
8:11
8:12
8:13
8:15
8:19
8:21[2]
9:7
10:5
10:6[2]
10:7
10:8
10:9
12:1
13:32
14:7
15:3
15:4
15:5
15:6
15:7
15:9
15:10[2]
15:13
15:14
15:15
15:19
15:20
15:21
15:25
15:28[2]
16:31
16:46
16:47
18:8
18:17
18:21
18:24
18:26
18:28
19:17
20:16
22:22
23:3
23:22
24:8
25:13[2]
26:53
27:7
28:5[2]
28:7
28:14[2]
28:18
28:22
28:25
28:26
28:30
29:1
29:5
29:7
29:12
30:2
30:6
30:10
31:29
31:50[2]
32:14
33:3
33:39
33:54
34:2
35:16
35:18
36:2
36:8

DE

4:21
4:38
5:29
7:6
7:25
7:26
10:1
10:3
13:16
14:2
14:21[2]
15:4
15:12[2]
15:17
17:1
18:10[2]
18:12
19:10
20:9
20:16
20:19
21:3
21:23
22:10[2]
22:14
22:19[2]
22:22
22:23
23:3
23:7[2]
24:4
24:14
25:5
25:16
25:19
26:1
26:8
26:12
26:19
27:5[2]
27:15
27:25
28:9
28:22[2]
28:30
28:37
29:4
29:8
31:2
31:24
32:11
32:45
33:7
34:7

JOS

1:6
2:1
3:13
3:16
7:13
8:2
8:24
8:28
8:30
8:31
10:20
11:23
13:6
13:7
14:3
14:13
17:4[2]
17:6
19:49[2]
19:51[2]
22:10
22:11
22:14
22:16
22:19
22:23
22:26
22:29
23:4
24:19
24:25
24:26
24:29
24:32

JG

2:1
2:8
3:18
3:31
4:21
6:11[2]
6:19
6:22[2]
6:24
6:26
8:10
8:27
9:23
9:46
9:48
11:1
12:5
13:6
13:16
13:21
14:4
15:15
15:16[2]
15:17
15:19
16:1
16:3
17:5[2]
18:1
18:14
19:9
19:16
19:28
20:10[2]
20:16
20:35
20:38
21:4
21:17

RU

1:12[2]
2:17

1 SA

1:1
2:28
2:31
2:32[2]
3:12
4:18
7:17
9:6
10:13
13:10
14:3
14:14
14:27
14:28
14:35
14:48
16:2
16:14
16:15
16:16
16:20
16:23
17:5
17:12
17:17
17:38
18:1
18:25
19:13
19:16
20:36
21:7
23:6
24:16
25:18
25:42
26:13
26:19
28:14
29:4
29:9
30:11
30:13
30:14
30:25

2 SA

1:8
1:13
2:25
3:14
3:29
5:11
6:18
7:2
7:5
7:7
7:11
7:13
7:27
8:4
11:2
11:19
13:36
14:17
14:20
15:19
16:1[2]
17:25
18:10
19:26
19:27
23:5
23:14
23:21
23:38[2]
24:3
24:18
24:21
24:25

1 KI

1:39
1:41[2]
1:52
2:24
2:36
3:1
3:9
3:12
4:23
5:3
5:5[2]
7:2
7:8
7:26
7:31
7:40
8:13
8:16
8:17
8:18
8:20
8:31
8:36
8:54
8:63
10:10
10:29[2]
11:7
11:14
11:18
11:25
11:26
12:21
12:31
13:11
13:14
13:18
14:21
14:31
15:13
16:32
17:12
18:4
18:10
18:13
18:32
19:5
19:11
20:20
20:25
20:29
20:30
22:9
22:25

2 KI

1:8
1:9
3:4[2]
4:9
4:24
4:43
6:15
6:25
9:2
9:5
9:17
10:25
11:4
16:10
16:11
18:31
19:32
19:35
23:33
25:19

1 CH

2:34
5:21
6:49
8:40
11:11
11:23
12:14
12:37
14:1
15:5
15:7
15:10
15:27
16:2
16:17
16:29
17:1
17:4
17:5
17:6
17:10
17:12
17:25
18:4
21:3
21:5
21:15
21:18
21:22
21:26
22:6
22:7
22:8
22:10
22:14
27:4
28:2
28:3
28:8
28:10
29:16

2 CH

1:17[2]
2:1[2]
2:3
2:4[2]
2:6[2]
2:12[2]
2:17
3:4
3:16
4:1
4:5
4:8
5:12
6:2
6:5
6:7
6:8
6:22
6:27
7:1
7:5
7:12
7:21
9:9
11:1
12:13
13:3
13:13
14:8
14:9
15:16
17:18
18:24
20:23
21:18
24:10
24:15
24:26
25:6[2]
26:11
26:13
27:5
28:6
29:17
29:24
29:29
29:32
32:8
32:21
35:25
36:3
36:23

EZR

1:2
2:3
2:18
2:21
2:23
2:27
2:30
2:41
2:42
4:3
4:6
4:17
6:17
7:22[4]
8:3
8:10
8:12
8:26[2]
9:11
9:12
10:17

NE

4:2
5:12
5:17
6:5
6:13
7:8
7:24
7:26
7:27
7:31
7:32
7:44
7:45
10:29
10:33
11:14
11:19

ES

1:1
1:4
8:9

JOB

1:8
1:10
2:3
2:11
3:16
4:16
6:6
7:1[2]
7:2
13:16
14:3
14:4
14:6
16:3
18:2
19:15
19:24
20:19
26:10
28:3
31:6
31:11[2]
31:28
33:23
40:9
40:15
41:1
41:2
42:11
42:16

PS

5:9
7:9
11:6
18:25
26:12
27:3
31:2
33:2
33:7
33:16
33:17
38:4
39:5
40:2
41:8
43:1
48:7
50:21
55:12
64:5
64:7
68:15
68:21
69:8
69:13
69:31
72:16
78:13
78:26
78:55
84:3
88:8
92:3
92:10
96:8
101:5
102:3
102:6
105:10
106:20
119:96
119:111
119:142
127:3
132:5
135:12[2]
136:21
136:22
140:11
141:5
144:9
145:13

PR

1:9
4:9
5:3
6:11
6:16
6:18
7:10
7:13
7:22
8:5
8:7
10:25
11:9
13:22
15:8
15:9
15:19
15:26
16:5
16:12
16:18
16:19
16:24
16:27
17:1
17:10
17:11
17:27
18:11
19:15
19:28
20:3
20:21
20:23
21:4
21:19
22:24
23:5
23:6
23:18
23:32
24:3
24:9
24:34
25:12[3]
25:19
25:20
25:23
27:6
27:7
28:10
28:22
29:6
29:22
29:27[2]
30:19
30:20
30:23[2]
30:31

EC

4:6
4:13
5:6
6:1
6:2
6:3[2]
7:11
8:3
8:11
8:12
9:2
9:3
9:12[2]
10:5[2]
10:8

CA

4:4
4:13
6:4
6:10
7:2

ISA

1:13
1:21
1:30
3:7
5:10[2]
5:26
6:13
9:17[2]
10:6

11:10 11:12 11:16 14:19 15:5 16:4 16:11 16:14 17:6 17:9 18:3 19:19 21:16 22:16 23:15 23:16 24:13 25:2 29:5 29:8 29:21 30:5 30:13 30:17^{2} 30:28 32:2 33:1 34:13 35:6 35:8 36:16 37:33 37:36 38:12 38:13 41:24 43:23 44:14 44:19

45:17 48:4 49:8 49:18 53:10 54:16 55:3 55:13 56:5 56:7 58:5 59:17 60:15 60:19 61:8 63:12 63:13 64:6 65:9 65:20^{4} 66:3^{3} 66:14 66:20^{2} 66:24

JER

1:11 1:14 1:18 2:7 2:19 3:18 4:7 5:15 5:16 6:26 9:2

9:8 9:11 10:10 11:19 14:12 18:17 19:8 21:5 22:19 23:14 23:40 24:7 25:9^{2} 25:11 25:18^{2} 25:36 26:8 26:9 29:11 29:18^{2} 30:14 30:17 31:3 31:32 32:14 32:40 33:9 33:12 34:9^{2} 34:14 34:22 42:18^{2} 43:1 44:12^{3} 44:22^{2} 44:27 46:19 46:22 47:2

48:34 48:40 49:2 49:14 50:9 51:29 51:34 51:37^{3} 51:41 51:63 52:23 52:25

LA

1:15 2:4^{2} 2:5 5:10

EZE

1:10^{2} 1:24 2:9 3:5 3:6 3:9 4:3 4:11 5:15^{2} 7:2 7:5^{2} 7:6 8:3 10:14 11:19 13:11

13:13 16:3^{2} 16:24^{2} 16:30 16:31 16:45^{2} 16:60 17:13 17:22 20:17 21:25 21:29 23:24 31:3 33:32 35:5 36:3 36:26 37:10 37:26 38:10 38:22 40:5 40:19 40:23 40:27 40:42^{2} 40:43 40:47^{2} 41:7 41:13^{2} 41:14 41:15 42:2 42:8 42:15 43:13 43:23 44:28

45:1^{2} 45:4 45:11^{2} 45:13^{4} 45:14^{2} 45:24^{4} 46:5^{3} 46:7^{4} 46:11^{4} 46:14^{2} 47:22

DA

2:46 3:1 3:4 3:27 4:3 4:13 4:23 4:34 5:12 6:1 6:3 7:14 7:27 8:5 8:12 9:24 10:10 11:6 11:7 12:7

HO

3:1 3:2^{2}

3:4^{2} 6:10 6:11 7:4 7:6 7:7 8:1 10:1 10:11 13:13 13:15

JOE

2:1 3:3

AM

3:11 3:12 3:15 5:3^{2} 5:13 7:2 7:14 7:17 8:10

OB

1

JON

1:9 3:3

MIC

1:6 1:7^{2} 1:15 2:3 2:8 6:16

NA

1:8^{2} 1:9

HAB

2:3 2:9

ZEP

1:10 3:12

HAG

2:16

ZEC

5:6 5:11 7:12 9:9^{2} 9:16 12:6 13:5

MAL

1:10 1:13 2:11 2:12 3:3 4:1

MT

2:19 4:2 4:8 5:14 5:38^{2} 8:30 9:16 9:20 10:12 11:1 12:1 12:3 12:35 12:39 13:8 13:23 13:28 13:52 14:7 16:23 17:1 17:27 18:12 18:17 18:28 19:29 20:1 21:2

21:5^{2} 24:44 24:50 25:24 25:35 25:37 25:42 25:44 26:5 26:7 26:30 26:72

MK

1:23 2:21 2:25 3:19 3:26 3:30 4:8 4:20 5:2 5:25 6:10 6:20 6:27 7:22 7:24 7:25 7:32 9:2 10:30 12:1 14:2 14:3 14:26 15:43

LU

1:11 1:18 1:69 2:36 4:5 4:33 5:36 6:3 6:7 6:45 6:48 6:49 7:37 8:8 8:15 8:32 8:43 9:28 10:34 11:12 11:29 12:1 12:40 12:46 14:5^{2} 14:32 15:4 16:2 16:6 16:7 19:21 19:22 21:18 22:37 22:43 22:44 24:42

JOH

1:22 1:47 2:16 5:4 5:5 6:60 10:12 10:13 12:15 12:29 13:15 19:31 19:39 21:11

AC

1:13 1:15 2:30 3:3 6:15 7:30 7:47 8:27 9:37 10:3 10:22 10:28 11:13 12:21 13:17 14:5 17:5 17:23 18:24 19:40

20:32 21:16 21:26 21:29 21:31 21:38 23:9 23:21 23:27 25:11 27:12 27:34

RO

1:1 1:23 2:20 3:13 4:19 7:2 7:3 11:1 14:13 16:16

1 CO

1:1 5:5 5:9 5:11^{3} 6:15 6:16 8:4 8:7 9:1 9:2 9:25

12:17 14:2 14:4 14:8 14:13 14:14 14:19 14:26 14:27 15:9 15:52 16:20

2 CO

1:1 2:11 5:1 6:15 8:14 10:11 11:7 11:14 12:2 12:5 12:12 13:13

GA

1:1 1:8 2:5 4:7 4:14 4:24 4:27 5:13 6:1

EPH

1:1 1:11 2:21 2:22 5:2 5:5 6:20

PHP

1:28 3:5 3:17 4:18

COL

1:1 2:16

1 TH

5:8 5:26

2 TH

3:9 3:15

1 TI

1:1 2:7 4:12 5:1

5:8 5:19^{2}

2 TI

1:1 1:9 1:11 2:9 4:5

TIT

1:1 3:10

PHM

9

HEB

3:12 4:15 5:5 5:10 6:6 6:16^{2} 6:17 6:19 6:20 7:16 7:20 7:21^{2} 7:24 7:26 8:1 9:11

9:13 10:21 10:22 10:29 10:34 11:7 11:8 11:16 12:22 13:10

JAS

3:8 5:10

1 PE

1:1 1:4 2:5 2:9 2:21 3:15 4:15 5:1

2 PE

1:1 1:11 2:6^{2} 2:14

1 JO

2:1 2:7

2:20 5:20

2 JO

7

JUDE

7

RE

2:7 2:11 2:17 2:29 3:6 3:8 3:13 3:22 4:3 7:4 8:1 8:5 8:13 9:15 11:9 11:11 11:19 13:9 13:14 14:1 16:18 19:17 20:1 21:17 21:19 21:20

AND

2532

GE

1:1 1:2^{4} 1:3^{2} 1:4^{2} 1:5^{4} 1:6^{3} 1:7^{3} 1:8^{3} 1:9^{3} 1:10^{3} 1:11^{3} 1:12^{4} 1:13^{2} 1:14^{5} 1:15^{2} 1:16^{2} 1:17 1:18^{4} 1:19^{2} 1:20^{2} 1:21^{4} 1:22^{4} 1:23^{2} 1:24^{4} 1:25^{4} 1:26^{6} 1:27 1:28^{3} 1:29^{2} 1:30^{4} 1:31^{4} 2:1^{2} 2:2^{2} 2:3^{3} 2:4^{2} 2:5^{3} 2:6 2:7^{3} 2:8^{2} 2:9^{4} 2:10^{3} 2:12^{2}

2:13 2:14^{2} 2:15^{3} 2:16 2:17 2:18 2:19^{4} 2:20^{3} 2:21^{4} 2:22^{2} 2:23^{2} 2:24^{3} 2:25^{2} 3:1 3:2 3:4 3:5^{2} 3:6^{6} 3:7^{4} 3:8^{3} 3:9^{2} 3:10^{3} 3:11 3:12^{2} 3:13^{3} 3:14^{3} 3:15^{5} 3:16^{3} 3:17^{2} 3:18^{2} 3:19 3:20 3:21^{2} 3:22^{6} 3:24^{2} 4:1^{4} 4:2^{2} 4:3 4:4^{4} 4:5^{3} 4:6^{2} 4:7^{3}

4:8^{3} 4:9^{2} 4:10 4:11 4:12 4:13 4:14^{3} 4:15^{2} 4:16^{2} 4:17^{5} 4:18^{4} 4:19^{2} 4:20^{2} 4:21^{2} 4:22^{3} 4:23^{3} 4:24 4:25^{3} 4:26^{2} 5:2^{3} 5:3^{4} 5:4^{3} 5:5^{3} 5:6^{3} 5:7^{4} 5:8^{3} 5:9^{2} 5:10^{4} 5:11^{3} 5:12^{2} 5:13^{4} 5:14^{3} 5:15^{3} 5:16^{4} 5:17^{3} 5:18^{3} 5:19^{3} 5:20^{3} 5:21^{3} 5:22^{3} 5:23^{2} 5:24^{2} 5:25^{3}

5:26^{4} 5:27^{3} 5:28 5:29 5:30^{4} 5:31^{3} 5:32^{3} 6:1^{2} 6:2 6:3^{2} 6:4^{2} 6:5^{2} 6:6^{2} 6:7^{4} 6:9^{2} 6:10^{2} 6:11 6:12^{2} 6:13^{2} 6:14^{2} 6:15 6:16^{3} 6:17^{2} 6:18^{4} 6:19^{2} 6:20 6:21^{4} 7:1^{2} 7:2^{3} 7:3 7:4^{3} 7:5 7:6 7:7^{4} 7:8^{3} 7:9^{2} 7:10 7:11 7:12^{2} 7:13^{5} 7:14^{4} 7:15^{2} 7:16^{3}

7:17^{4} 7:18^{3} 7:19^{2} 7:20 7:21^{5} 7:23^{7} 7:24^{2} 8:1^{5} 8:2^{2} 8:3^{3} 8:4 8:5 8:6 8:7^{2} 8:9^{3} 8:10^{2} 8:11^{2} 8:12^{2} 8:13^{5} 8:14^{2} 8:15 8:16^{3} 8:17^{4} 8:18^{4} 8:19^{2} 8:20^{4} 8:21^{2} 8:22^{7} 9:1^{5} 9:2^{4} 9:5^{2} 9:7^{3} 9:8^{2} 9:9^{2} 9:10^{2} 9:11 9:12^{3} 9:13^{2} 9:14 9:15^{4} 9:16^{3} 9:17^{2} 9:18^{4}

9:19 9:20^{2} 9:21^{3} 9:22^{2} 9:23^{7} 9:24^{2} 9:25 9:26^{2} 9:27^{2} 9:28^{2} 9:29^{3} 10:1^{2} 10:2^{6} 10:3^{3} 10:4^{3} 10:6^{4} 10:7^{7} 10:8 10:10^{4} 10:11^{3} 10:12^{2} 10:13^{4} 10:14^{3} 10:15^{2} 10:16^{3} 10:17^{1} 10:18^{4} 10:19^{4} 10:20 10:22^{4} 10:23^{4} 10:24^{2} 10:25^{2} 10:26^{4} 10:27^{3} 10:28^{3} 10:29^{3} 10:30 10:32 11:1^{2} 11:2^{2} 11:3^{4} 11:4^{3}

11:5^{2} 11:6^{4} 11:7 11:8 11:9 11:10 11:11^{3} 11:12^{3} 11:13^{4} 11:14^{2} 11:15^{4} 11:16^{3} 11:17^{4} 11:18^{2} 11:19^{4} 11:20^{3} 11:21^{4} 11:22^{2} 11:23^{3} 11:24^{3} 11:25^{4} 11:26^{3} 11:27^{2} 11:28 11:29^{4} 11:31^{6} 11:32^{3} 12:1^{2} 12:2^{4} 12:3^{3} 12:4^{3} 12:5^{6} 12:6^{2} 12:7^{3} 12:8^{5} 12:9 12:10^{3} 12:11 12:12 12:13 12:14 12:15^{2} 12:16^{8}

12:17^{2} 12:18^{2} 12:19 12:20^{4} 13:1^{4} 13:2^{2} 13:3^{2} 13:4 13:5^{3} 13:6 13:7^{4} 13:8^{4} 13:10^{3} 13:11^{2} 13:12^{2} 13:13^{2} 13:14^{5} 13:15 13:16 13:17 13:18^{4} 14:1^{2} 14:2^{3} 14:4 14:5^{5} 14:6 14:7^{4} 14:8^{6} 14:9^{3} 14:10^{5} 14:11^{4} 14:12^{3} 14:13^{4} 14:14^{3} 14:15^{4} 14:16^{5} 14:17^{2} 14:18^{3} 14:19^{3} 14:20^{2} 14:21^{2} 14:22^{2} 14:23

14:24^{2} 15:1 15:2^{2} 15:3^{2} 15:4 15:5^{4} 15:6^{2} 15:7 15:8 15:9^{5} 15:10^{3} 15:11 15:12^{2} 15:13^{3} 15:14^{2} 15:15 15:17^{3} 15:19^{2} 15:20^{3} 15:21^{4} 16:1 16:2^{3} 16:3 16:4^{3} 16:5^{3} 16:6 16:7 16:8^{3} 16:9^{2} 16:10 16:11^{2} 16:12^{3} 16:13 16:14 16:15^{2} 16:16^{2} 17:1^{4} 17:2^{3} 17:3^{2} 17:4 17:6^{3} 17:7^{4} 17:8^{3}

17:9^{2} 17:10^{2} 17:11^{3} 17:12 17:13^{2} 17:14 17:15 17:16^{3} 17:17^{3} 17:18 17:19^{4} 17:20^{4} 17:22^{2} 17:23^{4} 17:24^{2} 17:25 17:26 17:27^{2} 18:1^{2} 18:2^{5} 18:3 18:4^{2} 18:5^{3} 18:6^{3} 18:7^{5} 18:8^{6} 18:9^{2} 18:10^{3} 18:11^{3} 18:13 18:14 18:15 18:16^{3} 18:17 18:18^{2} 18:19^{3} 18:20^{3} 18:21^{2} 18:22^{2} 18:23^{2} 18:24 18:25 18:26

18:27^{3} 18:28^{2} 18:29^{3} 18:30^{3} 18:31^{2} 18:32^{3} 18:33^{2} 19:1^{4} 19:2^{6} 19:3^{6} 19:4 19:5^{2} 19:6^{2} 19:7 19:8 19:9^{5} 19:10^{2} 19:11^{2} 19:12^{4} 19:13 19:14^{3} 19:15^{2} 19:16^{5} 19:17 19:18 19:19^{3} 19:20^{3} 19:21 19:24^{2} 19:25^{4} 19:26 19:27 19:28^{5} 19:29^{2} 19:30^{5} 19:31^{2} 19:32 19:33^{4} 19:34^{3} 19:35^{4} 19:37^{4} 19:38^{2} 20:1^{4}

20:2^{3} 20:3 20:4 20:5^{2} 20:6 20:7^{4} 20:8^{3} 20:9^{3} 20:10 20:11^{2} 20:12^{2} 20:13 20:14^{6} 20:15 20:16^{2} 20:17^{4} 21:1^{2} 21:2 21:3 21:4 21:5 21:6 21:7 21:8^{3} 21:9 21:10 21:11 21:12^{2} 21:13 21:14^{8} 21:15^{2} 21:16^{5} 21:17^{3} 21:18 21:19^{5} 21:20^{4} 21:21^{2} 21:22^{2} 21:23 21:24 21:25 21:26 21:27^{4}

21:28 21:29 21:30 21:32^{2} 21:33^{2} 21:34 22:1^{3} 22:2^{3} 22:3^{7} 22:4 22:5^{5} 22:6^{6} 22:7^{8} 22:8 22:9^{5} 22:10^{2} 22:11^{3} 22:12 22:13^{6} 22:14 22:15 22:16 22:17^{3} 22:18 22:19^{3} 22:20 22:21^{2} 22:22^{5} 22:23 22:24^{4} 23:1^{3} 23:2^{3} 23:3^{2} 23:4 23:5 23:7^{2} 23:8^{2} 23:10^{2} 23:11 23:12 23:13^{2} 23:14 23:15

23:16^{2} 23:17^{3} 23:19 23:20^{2} 24:1^{3} 24:2 24:3^{2} 24:4^{2} 24:5 24:6 24:7^{3} 24:8 24:9^{2} 24:10^{4} 24:11 24:12^{2} 24:13 24:14^{3} 24:15 24:16^{4} 24:17^{2} 24:18^{4} 24:19 24:20^{4} 24:21 24:22^{2} 24:23 24:24 24:25^{2} 24:26^{2} 24:27^{2} 24:28^{2} 24:29^{3} 24:30^{4} 24:31^{2} 24:32^{6} 24:33^{2} 24:34 24:35^{10} 24:36^{2} 24:37 24:38^{2}

24:39 24:40^{4} 24:41 24:42^{2} 24:43^{4} 24:44^{2} 24:45^{4} 24:46^{5} 24:47^{5} 24:48^{3} 24:49^{3} 24:50^{2} 24:51^{2} 24:52 24:53^{5} 24:54^{6} 24:55^{2} 24:56 24:57^{2} 24:58^{3} 24:59^{4} 24:60^{3} 24:61^{6} 24:62 24:63^{4} 24:64^{2} 24:65^{2} 24:66 24:67^{5} 25:1 25:2^{6} 25:3^{5} 25:4^{5} 25:5 25:6 25:7^{2} 25:8^{3} 25:9^{2} 25:10 25:11^{2} 25:13^{4} 25:14^{3} 25:15^{2}

25:16^{2} 25:17^{6} 25:18^{2} 25:19 25:20 25:21^{3} 25:22^{3} 25:23^{4} 25:24 25:25^{2} 25:26^{4} 25:27^{3} 25:28 25:29^{3} 25:30 25:31 25:32^{2} 25:33^{3} 25:34^{5} 26:1^{2} 26:2^{2} 26:3^{4} 26:4^{3} 26:5^{2} 26:6 26:7^{2} 26:8^{3} 26:9^{4} 26:10^{2} 26:11 26:12^{2} 26:13^{3} 26:14^{3} 26:15 26:16 26:17^{3} 26:18^{2} 26:19^{2} 26:20^{2} 26:21^{3} 26:22^{6} 26:23 26:24^{4}

26:25^{4} 26:26^{2} 26:27^{2} 26:28^{4} 26:29^{2} 26:30^{3} 26:31^{4} 26:32^{3} 26:33 26:34^{2} 26:35 27:1^{4} 27:2 27:3^{3} 27:4^{2} 27:5^{3} 27:6 27:7^{2} 27:9^{2} 27:10^{2} 27:11^{2} 27:12^{3} 27:13^{2} 27:14^{4} 27:15^{2} 27:16^{2} 27:17^{2} 27:18^{3} 27:19^{2} 27:20^{2} 27:21 27:22^{3} 27:23 27:24^{2} 27:25^{6} 27:26^{2} 27:27^{5} 27:28^{3} 27:29^{3} 27:30^{2} 27:31^{4} 27:32^{2} 27:33^{6}

27:34^{3} 27:35^{2} 27:36^{3} 27:37^{6} 27:38^{3} 27:39^{3} 27:40^{3} 27:41^{2} 27:42^{4} 27:43 27:44 27:45^{3} 27:46 28:1^{4} 28:2 28:3^{3} 28:4^{2} 28:5^{3} 28:6^{2} 28:7^{3} 28:8 28:9 28:10^{2} 28:11^{5} 28:12^{5} 28:13^{4} 28:14^{7} 28:15^{3} 28:16^{3} 28:17^{3} 28:18^{4} 28:19 28:20^{4} 28:22^{2} 29:1 29:2^{4} 29:3^{4} 29:4^{2} 29:5^{2} 29:6^{3} 29:7^{3} 29:8^{2} 29:9

29:10[4] 29:11[3] 29:12[4] 29:13[5] 29:14[3] 29:15 29:16[2] 29:17 29:18[2] 29:19 29:20[2] 29:21 29:22[2] 29:23[3] 29:24 29:25[2] 29:26 29:27 29:28[3] 29:29 29:30[3] 29:31 29:32[3] 29:33[4] 29:34[3] 29:35[4] 30:1[2] 30:2[2] 30:3[2] 30:4[2] 30:5[2] 30:6[3] 30:7[2] 30:8[3] 30:9 30:10 30:11[2] 30:12 30:13[2] 30:14[3] 30:15[3] 30:16[4] 30:17[3] 30:18[2] 30:19[2] 30:20[2] 30:21[2] 30:22[3] 30:23[3] 30:24[2] 30:25[2] 30:26[2] 30:27 30:28[2] 30:29[2] 30:30[3] 30:31[3] 30:32[5] 30:33[2] 30:34 30:35[7] 30:36[3] 30:37[5] 30:38 30:39[3] 30:40[5] 30:41 30:42 30:43[6] 31:1[2] 31:2[2] 31:3[3] 31:4[3] 31:5 31:6 31:7[2] 31:8 31:9 31:10[4] 31:11[2] 31:12[3] 31:13[2] 31:14[3] 31:15 31:16 31:17[2] 31:18[2]

31:19[2] 31:20 31:21[3] 31:22 31:23[3] 31:24[2] 31:25 31:26[2] 31:27[4] 31:28[2] 31:30 31:31[2] 31:32 31:33[4] 31:34[3] 31:35[2] 31:36[4] 31:37 31:38[2] 31:40[2] 31:41[2] 31:42[3] 31:43[6] 31:44[3] 31:45[2] 31:46[4] 31:47 31:48[2] 31:49[2] 31:50 31:51[3] 31:52[3] 31:53[2] 31:54[3] 31:55[6] 32:1[2] 32:2[2] 32:3 32:4[2] 32:5[5] 32:6[3] 32:7[5] 32:8[2] 32:9[4] 32:10[2] 32:11[2] 32:12[2] 32:13[2] 32:14[2] 32:15[2] 32:16[4] 32:17[4] 32:18 32:19[3] 32:20[2] 32:21 32:22[5] 32:23[3] 32:24[2] 32:25[2] 32:26[2] 32:27[2] 32:28[3] 32:29[4] 32:30[2] 32:31[2] 33:1[7] 33:2[6] 33:3[2] 33:4[5] 33:5[5] 33:6[2] 33:7[5] 33:8[2] 33:9 33:10[2] 33:11[3] 33:12[3] 33:13[4] 33:14[2] 33:15[2] 33:17[3] 33:18[2] 33:19 33:20[2] 34:1 34:2[3]

34:3[3] 34:4 34:5[2] 34:6 34:7[3] 34:8 34:9[3] 34:10[4] 34:11[3] 34:12[3] 34:13[2] 34:14 34:16[3] 34:17 34:18[2] 34:19[2] 34:20[3] 34:21[2] 34:23[3] 34:24[3] 34:25[4] 34:26[4] 34:27 34:28[4] 34:29[4] 34:30[7] 34:31 35:1[3] 35:2[3] 35:3[4] 35:4[3] 35:5[3] 35:6 35:7[2] 35:8[2] 35:9[2] 35:10[2] 35:11[4] 35:12[3] 35:13 35:14[3] 35:15 35:16[4] 35:17 35:18 35:19[2] 35:20 35:21[2] 35:22[3] 35:23[5] 35:24 35:25[2] 35:26[2] 35:27[2] 35:28[2] 35:29[6] 36:2 36:3 36:4[2] 36:5[3] 36:6[8] 36:7 36:9 36:11[3] 36:12[2] 36:13[3] 36:14[4] 36:16 36:17 36:18 36:19 36:20[3] 36:21[3] 36:22[3] 36:23[4] 36:24[2] 36:25[2] 36:26[4] 36:27[2] 36:28 36:31 36:32[2] 36:33[2] 36:34[2] 36:35[3] 36:36[2] 36:37[2]

36:38[2] 36:39[4] 36:40 37:1 37:2[3] 37:3 37:4[2] 37:5[3] 37:6 37:7[4] 37:8[3] 37:9[6] 37:10[6] 37:11 37:12 37:13[3] 37:14[4] 37:15[3] 37:16 37:17[3] 37:18 37:19 37:20[4] 37:21[3] 37:22[2] 37:23 37:24[3] 37:25[6] 37:26[2] 37:27[4] 37:28[4] 37:29[3] 37:30[3] 37:31[3] 37:32[3] 37:33[2] 37:34[3] 37:35[3] 37:36 38:1[2] 38:2[3] 38:3[3] 38:4[3] 38:5[4] 38:6 38:7[2] 38:8[3] 38:9[2] 38:10 38:11[2] 38:12[4] 38:13 38:14[5] 38:16[3] 38:17[2] 38:18[7] 38:19[4] 38:20 38:21 38:22[3] 38:23[3] 38:24[4] 38:25[3] 38:26[3] 38:27 38:28[3] 38:29[2] 38:30[2] 39:1[2] 39:2[3] 39:3[2] 39:4[4] 39:5[4] 39:6[4] 39:7[2] 39:8[2] 39:9 39:10 39:11[2] 39:12[4] 39:13[2] 39:14[2] 39:15[4] 39:16 39:17 39:18[3] 39:19

39:20[3] 39:21[2] 39:22[2] 39:23 40:1[2] 40:2[2] 40:3 40:4[3] 40:5[2] 40:6[3] 40:7 40:8[3] 40:9[2] 40:10[4] 40:11[4] 40:12 40:13[2] 40:14[3] 40:15 40:16 40:17[2] 40:18[2] 40:19[2] 40:20[3] 40:21[2] 41:1[2] 41:2[3] 41:3[3] 41:4[3] 41:5[4] 41:6[2] 41:7[4] 41:8[5] 41:10[2] 41:11[2] 41:12[3] 41:13[2] 41:14[5] 41:15[3] 41:16 41:17 41:18[3] 41:19[3] 41:20[2] 41:21 41:22[3] 41:23[2] 41:24[2] 41:25 41:26 41:27[4] 41:30[3] 41:31 41:32[2] 41:33[2] 41:34[2] 41:35[3] 41:36 41:37[2] 41:38 41:39[2] 41:40 41:41 41:42[4] 41:43[3] 41:44[2] 41:45[3] 41:46[3] 41:47 41:48[2] 41:49 41:50 41:51[2] 41:52 41:53 41:54[2] 41:55[2] 41:56[4] 41:57 42:2[3] 42:3 42:5 42:6[4] 42:7[5] 42:8 42:9[2] 42:10

42:12 42:13[3] 42:14 42:16[2] 42:17 42:18[2] 42:20[2] 42:21[2] 42:22[2] 42:23 42:24[6] 42:25[3] 42:26[2] 42:27 42:28[4] 42:29[2] 42:30 42:31 42:32 42:33[3] 42:34[2] 42:35[3] 42:36[3] 42:37[2] 42:38[2] 43:1 43:2 43:3 43:4 43:6 43:7[3] 43:8[6] 43:9 43:11[5] 43:12[2] 43:13 43:14 43:15[6] 43:16[3] 43:17[2] 43:18[5] 43:19[2] 43:20 43:21[3] 43:22 43:23[3] 43:24[4] 43:25 43:26[2] 43:27[2] 43:28[3] 43:29[4] 43:30[4] 43:31[4] 43:32[3] 43:33[3] 43:34[4] 44:1[2] 44:2[3] 44:3 44:4[3] 44:5 44:6[2] 44:7 44:9 44:10[2] 44:11 44:12[4] 44:13[2] 44:14[3] 44:15 44:16[2] 44:17[2] 44:18[2] 44:20[5] 44:21 44:22 44:23 44:24 44:25[2] 44:26 44:27 44:28[3] 44:29[2] 44:30 44:31 44:33

44:34 45:1[2] 45:2[3] 45:3[2] 45:4[3] 45:6 45:7[2] 45:8[3] 45:9[2] 45:10[7] 45:11[3] 45:12[2] 45:13[4] 45:14[3] 45:15[2] 45:16[3] 45:17[2] 45:18[5] 45:19[3] 45:21[3] 45:22 45:23[4] 45:24[2] 45:25[2] 45:26[3] 45:27[2] 45:28[2] 46:1[3] 46:2[3] 46:3 46:4[2] 46:5[4] 46:6[4] 46:7[3] 46:8[2] 46:9[4] 46:10[6] 46:11[2] 46:12[9] 46:13[4] 46:14[3] 46:15[2] 46:16[5] 46:17[7] 46:18 46:19 46:20[2] 46:21[7] 46:22 46:23 46:24[4] 46:25 46:26 46:27[2] 46:28[2] 46:29[5] 46:30 46:31[5] 46:32[4] 46:33[2] 46:34 47:1[7] 47:2[2] 47:3[3] 47:5[2] 47:6[2] 47:7[3] 47:8 47:9[4] 47:10[2] 47:11[3] 47:12[3] 47:13[2] 47:14[3] 47:15[3] 47:16[2] 47:17[6] 47:18[2] 47:19[5] 47:20 47:21[2] 47:23[2] 47:24[5] 47:25[2] 47:26 47:27[4] 47:28[2]

47:29[5] 47:30[3] 47:31[3] 48:1[3] 48:2[4] 48:3[2] 48:4[4] 48:5[3] 48:6[2] 48:7[2] 48:8[2] 48:9 48:10[2] 48:11[2] 48:12[2] 48:13[3] 48:14[3] 48:15[3] 48:16[4] 48:17[2] 48:18 48:19[4] 48:20[3] 48:21[2] 48:22 49:1[2] 49:2[2] 49:3[2] 49:5 49:6 49:7[2] 49:9 49:10 49:11[2] 49:12 49:13[2] 49:15[4] 49:20 49:23[2] 49:24 49:25[2] 49:26 49:27 49:28[2] 49:29[2] 49:31[3] 49:32 49:33[3] 50:1[3] 50:2[2] 50:3[3] 50:4 50:5[2] 50:6[2] 50:7[3] 50:8[5] 50:9[3] 50:10[4] 50:11 50:12 50:13 50:14[3] 50:15[2] 50:16 50:17[3] 50:18[3] 50:19 50:21[3] 50:22[4] 50:23 50:24[4] 50:25[2] 50:26[3]

EX

1:1 1:2 1:3 1:4 1:5 1:6[3] 1:7[5] 1:9[2] 1:10 1:11[2]

1:12[2] 1:13 1:14[3] 1:15[2] 1:16[2] 1:17 1:18[3] 1:19[2] 1:20[2] 1:21 1:22[2] 2:1[2] 2:2[3] 2:3[5] 2:4 2:5[3] 2:6[4] 2:7 2:8[3] 2:9[5] 2:10[5] 2:11[3] 2:12[4] 2:13[2] 2:14[4] 2:15[2] 2:16[3] 2:17[4] 2:18 2:19[3] 2:20[2] 2:21[2] 2:22[2] 2:23[4] 2:24[3] 2:25[2] 3:1[2] 3:2[4] 3:3[2] 3:4[3] 3:5 3:6[2] 3:7[2] 3:8[9] 3:9 3:10 3:11[2] 3:12[2] 3:13[2] 3:14[2] 3:15[3] 3:16[4] 3:17[7] 3:18[5] 3:19 3:20[3] 3:21[2] 3:22[6] 4:1[2] 4:2[2] 4:3[4] 4:4[5] 4:5 4:6[3] 4:7[4] 4:8 4:9[3] 4:10[2] 4:11 4:12[2] 4:13 4:14[4] 4:15[5] 4:16[3] 4:17 4:18[6] 4:19 4:20[5] 4:21 4:22 4:23[2] 4:24[2] 4:25[2] 4:27[4] 4:28[2] 4:29[3] 4:30[2]

4:31[4] 5:1[3] 5:2 5:3[2] 5:4[2] 5:5[2] 5:6[2] 5:7 5:8[2] 5:9 5:10[3] 5:11 5:13 5:14[3] 5:15 5:16[2] 5:17 5:18 5:19 5:20[2] 5:21[3] 5:22[2] 6:1 6:2[2] 6:3[2] 6:4 6:5[2] 6:6[4] 6:7[3] 6:8[3] 6:9[2] 6:10 6:12 6:13[4] 6:14[2] 6:15[6] 6:16[5] 6:17 6:18[6] 6:19[2] 6:20[6] 6:21[3] 6:22[3] 6:23[4] 6:24[3] 6:25[2] 6:26 6:27 6:28 6:30[2] 7:1[2] 7:2 7:3[3] 7:4[2] 7:5[2] 7:6[2] 7:7[3] 7:8[2] 7:9[2] 7:10[6] 7:11 7:12 7:13 7:14 7:15[2] 7:16[2] 7:17 7:18[3] 7:19[6] 7:20[6] 7:21[4] 7:22[2] 7:23[2] 7:24 7:25 8:1[2] 8:2 8:3[8] 8:4[3] 8:5[3] 8:6[2] 8:7[2] 8:8[4] 8:9[4] 8:10[2] 8:11[4] 8:12[3]

8:13[3] 8:14[2] 8:15 8:16[2] 8:17[4] 8:18[2] 8:19[2] 8:20[3] 8:21[5] 8:22 8:23[2] 8:24[4] 8:25[2] 8:26[2] 8:27 8:28 8:29[3] 8:30[2] 8:31[3] 8:32 9:1 9:2 9:3 9:4[3] 9:5 9:6[2] 9:7[4] 9:8[3] 9:9[3] 9:10[5] 9:11[2] 9:12[2] 9:13[3] 9:14[2] 9:15[2] 9:16[2] 9:19[5] 9:20 9:21[2] 9:22[3] 9:23[5] 9:24 9:25[4] 9:27[6] 9:28[3] 9:29[2] 9:30 9:31[3] 9:32 9:33[5] 9:34[5] 9:35 10:1[2] 10:2[3] 10:3[3] 10:5[3] 10:6[5] 10:7 10:8[3] 10:9[4] 10:10[2] 10:11[2] 10:12[2] 10:13[4] 10:14[2] 10:15[3] 10:16[3] 10:17 10:18[2] 10:19[2] 10:21 10:22[2] 10:24[3] 10:25[2] 10:26 10:27 10:28 10:29 11:1[2] 11:2[3] 11:3[2] 11:4[1] 11:5[2] 11:6 11:7 11:8[5] 11:9

11:10[3] 12:1[2] 12:4[2] 12:6[2] 12:7[3] 12:8[3] 12:9 12:10[2] 12:11[3] 12:12[3] 12:13[3] 12:14[2] 12:16[2] 12:17 12:18 12:21[3] 12:22[5] 12:23[3] 12:24[2] 12:25 12:26 12:27[3] 12:28[3] 12:29[2] 12:30[4] 12:31[6] 12:32[3] 12:33 12:34 12:35[4] 12:36[2] 12:37 12:38[3] 12:39[2] 12:40 12:41[2] 12:43[2] 12:45 12:48[5] 12:49 12:50 12:51 13:1 13:2 13:3 13:5[6] 13:6 13:7 13:8 13:9[2] 13:11[3] 13:12 13:13[3] 13:14 13:15[2] 13:16[2] 13:17[2] 13:18 13:19[2] 13:20[2] 13:21[3] 14:1 14:2[2] 14:4[4] 14:5[4] 14:6[2] 14:7[3] 14:8[3] 14:9[4] 14:10[4] 14:11 14:13[2] 14:15 14:16[3] 14:17[5] 14:18[2] 14:19[4] 14:20[4] 14:21[4] 14:22[3] 14:23[3] 14:24[3] 14:25 14:26[2] 14:27[4] 14:28[4] 14:29[2]

14:30 14:31 15:1[3] 15:2[4] 15:4 15:7 15:8[2] 15:14 15:16 15:17 15:18 15:19[2] 15:20[3] 15:21[2] 15:22[3] 15:23 15:24 15:25[4] 15:26[4] 15:27[4] 16:1[3] 16:2[2] 16:3[2] 16:4[2] 16:5[2] 16:6[2] 16:7[2] 16:8[3] 16:9 16:10[2] 16:11 16:12[2] 16:13[3] 16:14 16:15[2] 16:17[2] 16:18[2] 16:19 16:20[3] 16:21[2] 16:22[3] 16:23[3] 16:24[2] 16:25 16:27[2] 16:28[2] 16:31[3] 16:32 16:33[3] 16:35 17:1[3] 17:2[2] 17:3[5] 17:4 17:5[4] 17:6[3] 17:7[3] 17:8 17:9[2] 17:10[3] 17:11[2] 17:12[7] 17:13[2] 17:14[2] 17:15[2] 18:1 18:2 18:3 18:4[2] 18:5[2] 18:6[3] 18:7[5] 18:8[4] 18:9 18:10[2] 18:12[4] 18:13[2] 18:14[2] 18:15 18:16[4] 18:17 18:18 18:19 18:20[4] 18:21[3] 18:22[3] 18:23[2]

18:24 18:25[3] 18:26 18:27[2] 19:2[3] 19:3[3] 19:4[2] 19:5 19:6[2] 19:7[3] 19:8[3] 19:9[3] 19:10[4] 19:11 19:12 19:14[3] 19:15 19:16[4] 19:17[2] 19:18[3] 19:19[4] 19:20[3] 19:21[2] 19:22 19:23[2] 19:24[4] 19:25 20:1 20:5 20:6[2] 20:9 20:11[4] 20:12 20:18[6] 20:19[2] 20:20 20:21[2] 20:22 20:24[4] 20:25 21:2 21:4[3] 21:5[2] 21:6[2] 21:7 21:9 21:10 21:11 21:13 21:15 21:16[2] 21:17 21:18[3] 21:19[2] 21:20[3] 21:22[3] 21:23 21:26 21:27 21:28 21:29[3] 21:32 21:33[3] 21:34[2] 21:35[3] 21:36[2] 22:1[2] 22:2 22:5[3] 22:6 22:7 22:9 22:10 22:11[2] 22:12 22:13 22:14[2] 22:16[2] 22:23 22:24[4] 22:27 22:29 22:30 22:31 23:5 23:7[2] 23:8[2]

23:10[2] 23:11[3] 23:12[4] 23:13[2] 23:15 23:16[2] 23:20 23:21 23:22[2] 23:23[6] 23:24 23:25[4] 23:27[2] 23:28[2] 23:29 23:30[2] 23:31[3] 24:1[5] 24:2 24:3[5] 24:4[4] 24:5[2] 24:6[3] 24:7[4] 24:8[3] 24:9[3] 24:10[3] 24:11[3] 24:12[5] 24:13[3] 24:14[3] 24:15[2] 24:16[3] 24:17 24:18[4] 25:1 25:3[3] 25:4[5] 25:5[3] 25:6 25:7[2] 25:8 25:9 25:10[6] 25:11[3] 25:12[4] 25:13[2] 25:14 25:16 25:17[4] 25:18 25:19[2] 25:20[2] 25:21[2] 25:22[2] 25:23[2] 25:24[2] 25:25[2] 25:26[2] 25:28[2] 25:29[3] 25:30 25:31 25:32[2] 25:33[3] 25:34[2] 25:35[3] 25:36 25:37[2] 25:38[2] 25:40 26:1[3] 26:2[3] 26:3 26:4[2] 26:5 26:6[3] 26:7 26:8[2] 26:9[3] 26:10[2] 26:11[3] 26:12 26:13[3] 26:14[2] 26:15 26:16[2]

26:18 26:19[2] 26:20 26:21[2] 26:22 26:23 26:24[2] 26:25[2] 26:26 26:27[2] 26:28 26:29[3] 26:31[4] 26:32 26:33[3] 26:34 26:35[2] 26:36[4] 26:37[4] 27:1[3] 27:2[2] 27:3[5] 27:4[2] 27:5 27:6[2] 27:7[2] 27:9 27:10[3] 27:11[4] 27:12[2] 27:13 27:14 27:15[2] 27:16[2] 27:17 27:18[3] 27:19[2] 27:20 27:21 28:1[4] 28:2[2] 28:3 28:4[7] 28:5[5] 28:6[3] 28:7 28:8[4] 28:9[2] 28:10 28:12[2] 28:13 28:14[2] 28:15[4] 28:16 28:17[2] 28:18[2] 28:19[2] 28:20[3] 28:21 28:22 28:23[2] 28:24 28:25[2] 28:26[2] 28:27[2] 28:28[2] 28:29 28:30[4] 28:31 28:32 28:33[4] 28:34[2] 28:35[3] 28:36[2] 28:37 28:38[2] 28:39[3] 28:40[4] 28:41[5] 28:42 28:43[4] 29:1[2] 29:2[2] 29:3[2] 29:4[2] 29:5[6] 29:6[2]

29:7[2] 29:8[2] 29:9[6] 29:10[3] 29:11 29:12[3] 29:13[5] 29:14[2] 29:15[2] 29:16[3] 29:17[5] 29:18 29:19[3] 29:20[6] 29:21[10] 29:22[6] 29:23[3] 29:24[3] 29:25[2] 29:26[3] 29:27[4] 29:28[3] 29:29[2] 29:30 29:31[2] 29:32[2] 29:33[2] 29:34 29:35[2] 29:36[3] 29:37[2] 29:39 29:40[2] 29:41[3] 29:43[2] 29:44[3] 29:45[2] 29:46 30:1 30:2[2] 30:3[4] 30:4[2] 30:5[2] 30:6 30:7 30:8 30:10 30:11 30:14 30:15 30:16[2] 30:17 30:18[4] 30:19[2] 30:21[3] 30:23[4] 30:24[2] 30:25 30:26[3] 30:27[5] 30:28[3] 30:29 30:30[3] 30:31 30:32 30:34[3] 30:35[2] 30:36[2] 30:37 31:1 31:3[4] 31:4[2] 31:5[2] 31:6[2] 31:7[3] 31:8[4] 31:9[3] 31:10[3] 31:11[2] 31:12 31:13 31:17[4] 31:18 32:1[2] 32:2[3] 32:3[2] 32:4[3]

32:5[3] 32:6[5] 32:7 32:8[3] 32:9[2] 32:10[2] 32:11[3] 32:12[3] 32:13[4] 32:14 32:15[4] 32:16[2] 32:17 32:18 32:19[5] 32:20[5] 32:21 32:22 32:24[2] 32:25 32:26[2] 32:27[6] 32:28[2] 32:29 32:30[2] 32:31[3] 32:32 32:33 32:35 33:1[4] 33:2[5] 33:3 33:4[2] 33:5 33:6 33:7[4] 33:8[3] 33:9[3] 33:10[3] 33:11[2] 33:12[3] 33:13 33:14[2] 33:15 33:16[2] 33:17[2] 33:18 33:19[4] 33:20[2] 33:21[2] 33:22[2] 33:23[2] 34:1[2] 34:2[3] 34:3 34:4[4] 34:5[3] 34:6[5] 34:7[5] 34:8[3] 34:9[4] 34:10[2] 34:11[5] 34:13 34:15[4] 34:16[3] 34:19 34:20[2] 34:21 34:22[2] 34:24 34:27[2] 34:28[3] 34:29 34:30[3] 34:31[4] 34:32[2] 34:33 34:34[2] 34:35[2] 35:1[2] 35:4 35:5[2] 35:6[5] 35:7[3] 35:8[3] 35:9[3]

35:10[2] 35:11[3] 35:12[2] 35:13[3] 35:14[2] 35:15[5] 35:16[2] 35:17[2] 35:18[2] 35:19 35:20 35:21[5] 35:22[7] 35:23[7] 35:24[2] 35:25[5] 35:26 35:27[3] 35:28[4] 35:29 35:30[2] 35:31[3] 35:32[3] 35:33[2] 35:34[2] 35:35[6] 36:1[3] 36:2[3] 36:3[2] 36:4 36:5 36:6[2] 36:7 36:8[4] 36:9[2] 36:10[2] 36:11 36:12 36:13[2] 36:14 36:15 36:16[2] 36:17[2] 36:18 36:19[2] 36:20 36:21[2] 36:23 36:24[2] 36:25 36:26[2] 36:27 36:28 36:29[2] 36:30[2] 36:31 36:32[2] 36:33 36:34[3] 36:35[4] 36:36[3] 36:37[4] 36:38[3] 37:1[6] 37:2[3] 37:3[2] 37:4[2] 37:5 37:6[4] 37:7 37:8 37:9[2] 37:10[4] 37:11[2] 37:12 37:13[2] 37:15[2] 37:16[4] 37:17[3] 37:18[2] 37:19[3] 37:20[2] 37:21[3] 37:22 37:23[3] 37:24 37:25[3]

37:26[3] 37:27 37:28[2] 37:29[2] 38:1[3] 38:2[2] 38:3[5] 38:4 38:5 38:6[2] 38:7 38:8[2] 38:9 38:10[2] 38:11[3] 38:12[3] 38:13 38:14 38:15[3] 38:17[4] 38:18[6] 38:19[4] 38:20[2] 38:22 38:23[6] 38:24[3] 38:25[4] 38:26[4] 38:27[2] 38:28[4] 38:29[2] 38:30[4] 38:31[4] 39:1[4] 39:2[4] 39:3[5] 39:5[4] 39:6 39:7 39:8[4] 39:9 39:10[2] 39:11[2] 39:12[2] 39:13[2] 39:14 39:15 39:16[3] 39:17 39:18[2] 39:19[2] 39:20[2] 39:21[2] 39:22 39:23 39:24[4] 39:25[2] 39:26[2] 39:27[2] 39:28[3] 39:29[4] 39:30[2] 39:31 39:32 39:33[4] 39:34[3] 39:35[2] 39:36[2] 39:37[2] 39:38[4] 39:39[3] 39:40[4] 39:41[2] 39:43[2] 40:1 40:3[2] 40:4[4] 40:5[2] 40:6 40:7[3] 40:8[2] 40:9[6] 40:10[4] 40:11[2] 40:12[3] 40:13[3] 40:14[2]

40:15 40:17 40:18[5] 40:19[2] 40:20[4] 40:21[3] 40:22 40:23 40:24 40:25 40:26 40:27 40:28 40:29[3] 40:30[3] 40:31[4] 40:32 40:33[3] 40:34 40:35[2] 40:36 40:38

LE

1:1[2] 1:2[3] 1:4[2] 1:5[3] 1:6[2] 1:7[2] 1:8[2] 1:9[2] 1:10 1:11[2] 1:12[3] 1:13[3] 1:14 1:15[4] 1:16[2] 1:17[2] 2:1[3] 2:2[4] 2:3[2] 2:4 2:5 2:6 2:7 2:8[2] 2:9[2] 2:10[2] 2:13 2:14 2:15 2:16[2] 3:1 3:2[3] 3:3[2] 3:4[3] 3:5 3:6 3:8[3] 3:9[4] 3:10[3] 3:11 3:12 3:13[3] 3:14[2] 3:15[3] 3:16 4:1 4:2 4:4[3] 4:5[2] 4:6[2] 4:7[2] 4:8[2] 4:9[3] 4:10 4:11[5] 4:12 4:13[4] 4:14 4:15[2] 4:16 4:17[2]

4:18[2] 4:19[2] 4:20[3] 4:21[2] 4:22[2] 4:24[2] 4:25[3] 4:26[3] 4:27[2] 4:29[2] 4:30[3] 4:31[4] 4:32 4:33[2] 4:34[3] 4:35[4] 5:1[3] 5:2[2] 5:3 5:4 5:5 5:6[2] 5:7[2] 5:8[2] 5:9[2] 5:10[3] 5:12[2] 5:13[3] 5:14 5:15 5:16[5] 5:17[3] 5:18[4] 6:1 6:2[2] 6:3[2] 6:4 6:5[2] 6:6 6:7 6:8 6:9[2] 6:10[4] 6:11[3] 6:12[4] 6:14 6:15[4] 6:16[2] 6:17 6:19 6:20[2] 6:21[2] 6:22 6:24 6:25 6:27 6:28[2] 6:30 7:2 7:3 7:4[2] 7:5 7:8 7:9[3] 7:10[2] 7:11 7:12[2] 7:14[2] 7:15 7:16 7:18[2] 7:19[2] 7:21 7:22 7:24[2] 7:28 7:31 7:32 7:33 7:34[3] 7:35 7:37[4] 8:1 8:2[6] 8:3 8:4[2] 8:5

8:6[3] 8:7[6] 8:8[2] 8:9 8:10[4] 8:11[4] 8:12[2] 8:13[4] 8:14[3] 8:15[6] 8:16[5] 8:17[2] 8:18[3] 8:19[2] 8:20[4] 8:21[4] 8:22[2] 8:23[4] 8:24[5] 8:25[7] 8:26[5] 8:27[3] 8:28[2] 8:29[2] 8:30[10] 8:31[4] 8:32[2] 8:33 8:35[2] 8:36 9:1[3] 9:2[3] 9:3[3] 9:4[2] 9:5[3] 9:6[2] 9:7[7] 9:8 9:9[4] 9:10[2] 9:11[2] 9:12[2] 9:13[3] 9:14[3] 9:15[4] 9:16[2] 9:17[3] 9:18[2] 9:19[5] 9:20[2] 9:21[2] 9:22[5] 9:23[5] 9:24[4] 10:1[5] 10:2[3] 10:3[2] 10:4[3] 10:5 10:6[4] 10:7[2] 10:8 10:10[4] 10:11 10:12[4] 10:13[2] 10:14[5] 10:15[3] 10:16[4] 10:17 10:19[4] 10:20 11:1[2] 11:3[2] 11:5 11:6 11:7[2] 11:8 11:9[2] 11:10[4] 11:13[3] 11:14[2] 11:16[4] 11:17[3] 11:18[3] 11:19[3] 11:22[3]

11:24 11:25[2] 11:26 11:27 11:28[2] 11:29[2] 11:30[5] 11:32[2] 11:33[2] 11:34 11:35[2] 11:37 11:38 11:39 11:40[3] 11:41 11:42 11:44 11:46[3] 11:47[3] 12:1 12:2 12:3 12:4[2] 12:5[2] 12:6[2] 12:7[2] 12:8[4] 13:1[2] 13:2 13:3[5] 13:4[2] 13:5[3] 13:6[5] 13:8 13:10[4] 13:11[2] 13:12[2] 13:13 13:15[2] 13:16 13:17[2] 13:18 13:19[3] 13:20[2] 13:21[2] 13:22 13:23[2] 13:24 13:25[2] 13:26[2] 13:27[2] 13:28[3] 13:30[2] 13:31[3] 13:32[4] 13:33 13:34[4] 13:36 13:37[2] 13:39 13:40 13:41 13:42 13:43 13:45[4] 13:49[2] 13:50[2] 13:51 13:53[2] 13:54 13:55[3] 13:56[2] 13:57 13:58[2] 14:1 14:3[3] 14:4[4] 14:5 14:6[5] 14:7[3] 14:8[5] 14:9[4] 14:10[4] 14:11[2] 14:12[4] 14:13[2]

14:14[4] 14:15[2] 14:16[2] 14:17[3] 14:18[2] 14:19[3] 14:20[4] 14:21[4] 14:22[3] 14:23 14:24[3] 14:25[5] 14:26 14:27 14:28[3] 14:29 14:30 14:31[2] 14:33[2] 14:34 14:35[2] 14:36 14:37[2] 14:38 14:39[3] 14:40 14:41[2] 14:42[4] 14:43[4] 14:44[2] 14:45[4] 14:47[2] 14:48[3] 14:49[4] 14:50 14:51[7] 14:52[6] 14:53[2] 14:54 14:55[2] 14:56[3] 14:57 15:1[2] 15:2 15:3 15:4 15:5[3] 15:6[3] 15:7[3] 15:8[3] 15:9 15:10[4] 15:11[4] 15:12[2] 15:13[4] 15:14[3] 15:15[3] 15:16[2] 15:17[3] 15:18 15:19[3] 15:20 15:21[3] 15:22[3] 15:23 15:24[3] 15:25 15:26 15:27[4] 15:28 15:29[2] 15:30[3] 15:32[2] 15:33[4] 16:1[2] 16:2 16:3 16:4[4] 16:5[2] 16:6[3] 16:7[2] 16:8[2] 16:9[2] 16:10 16:11[4] 16:12[3] 16:13

16:14[3] 16:15[4] 16:16[3] 16:17[4] 16:18[5] 16:19[3] 16:20[3] 16:21[4] 16:22[2] 16:23[3] 16:24[7] 16:25 16:26[3] 16:27[5] 16:28[3] 16:29[2] 16:31 16:32[3] 16:33[5] 16:34[2] 17:1 17:2[3] 17:4[2] 17:5 17:6[2] 17:7 17:8 17:9 17:10[2] 17:11 17:13[3] 17:15[3] 18:1 18:2 18:3 18:4 18:5 18:17 18:21 18:25[2] 18:26[2] 18:27 18:30 19:1 19:2 19:3[2] 19:5 19:6[2] 19:7 19:8 19:9 19:10[2] 19:12 19:16 19:17 19:19 19:20[2] 19:21 19:22[2] 19:23[2] 19:25 19:29 19:30 19:32[2] 19:33 19:34 19:36 19:37[2] 20:1 20:3[3] 20:4[2] 20:5[3] 20:6[3] 20:7 20:8[2] 20:10[2] 20:11 20:11 20:12 20:14[3] 20:15[2] 20:16[2] 20:17[4] 20:18[4] 20:19 20:21 20:22[2]

20:23[2] 20:24[2] 20:25[4] 20:26[2] 21:1[2] 21:2[4] 21:3 21:6[2] 21:9 21:10[2] 21:13 21:16 21:22 21:24[3] 22:1 22:2[2] 22:4 22:6 22:7[2] 22:9 22:11 22:13[2] 22:14[2] 22:15 22:17 22:18[4] 22:21 22:25 22:26 22:27[2] 22:28[2] 22:29 22:31 23:1 23:2 23:6 23:9 23:10[2] 23:11 23:12 23:13[2] 23:14 23:15 23:16 23:18[4] 23:19 23:20 23:21 23:22[2] 23:23 23:26 23:27[2] 23:28 23:30 23:32 23:33 23:36[2] 23:37[2] 23:38[3] 23:39 23:40[4] 23:41 23:44 24:1 24:5[2] 24:6 24:7 24:9[3] 24:10[3] 24:11[4] 24:12 24:13 24:14[2] 24:15 24:16[2] 24:17 24:18 24:19 24:21[2] 24:23[3] 25:1 25:2 25:3[2] 25:6[5] 25:7[2] 25:8[3] 25:10[4]

25:14 25:15 25:16 25:18[3] 25:19[3] 25:20 25:21 25:22[2] 25:23 25:24 25:25[2] 25:26[2] 25:27 25:28[2] 25:29 25:30 25:31 25:32 25:33[2] 25:35[2] 25:38 25:39[2] 25:40[2] 25:41[4] 25:44[2] 25:45[2] 25:46 25:47[3] 25:50[2] 25:52[2] 25:53[2] 25:54[2] 26:2 26:3[2] 26:4[2] 26:5[4] 26:6[4] 26:7[2] 26:8[3] 26:9[3] 26:10[2] 26:11[2] 26:12[3] 26:13[2] 26:14 26:15 26:16[3] 26:17[3] 26:18 26:19[3] 26:20 26:21[2] 26:22[3] 26:23 26:24 26:25[3] 26:26[4] 26:27 26:28 26:29[2] 26:30[4] 26:31[3] 26:32[2] 26:33[4] 26:34[2] 26:36[4] 26:37[2] 26:38[2] 26:39[2] 26:40[2] 26:41[3] 26:42[3] 26:43[3] 26:44[2] 26:46[3] 27:1 27:2 27:3 27:4 27:5[2] 27:6[2] 27:7[3] 27:8 27:9 27:10[2] 27:11 27:12

27:14 27:15[2] 27:16 27:18 27:19[2] 27:20 27:22 27:23 27:25 27:27[2] 27:28[2] 27:30 27:31 27:32 27:33[2]

NU

1:1 1:3[2] 1:4 1:5 1:17[2] 1:18[3] 1:20[2] 1:21[2] 1:22 1:23[2] 1:24 1:25[2] 1:26 1:27[2] 1:28 1:29[2] 1:30 1:31[2] 1:32 1:33 1:34 1:35[2] 1:36 1:37[2] 1:38 1:39[2] 1:40 1:41[2] 1:42 1:43[2] 1:44[2] 1:45 1:46[3] 1:50[5] 1:51[3] 1:52[2] 1:53 1:54 2:1[2] 2:3[2] 2:4[4] 2:5[2] 2:6[4] 2:7 2:8[4] 2:9[3] 2:10 2:11[4] 2:12[2] 2:13[4] 2:14 2:15[5] 2:16[5] 2:18 2:19[3] 2:20[2] 2:21[4] 2:22 2:23[4] 2:24[3] 2:25 2:26[4] 2:27[2] 2:28[4] 2:29 2:30[4] 2:31[3] 2:32[3]

2:34[2] 3:1 3:2[3] 3:4[5] 3:5 3:6 3:7[2] 3:8[2] 3:9[2] 3:10[4] 3:11 3:12 3:13 3:14 3:15 3:16 3:17[3] 3:18[2] 3:19[3] 3:20[2] 3:21 3:22[2] 3:24 3:25[3] 3:26[4] 3:27[4] 3:28 3:30 3:31[7] 3:32[2] 3:33 3:34[3] 3:35 3:36[7] 3:37[4] 3:38[3] 3:39[3] 3:40[3] 3:41[2] 3:42 3:43[5] 3:44 3:45[2] 3:46[3] 3:48[2] 3:49[2] 3:50[2] 3:51[2] 4:1[2] 4:3 4:5[4] 4:6[3] 4:7[6] 4:8[3] 4:9[6] 4:10[2] 4:11[3] 4:12[4] 4:13[2] 4:14[5] 4:15[3] 4:16[7] 4:17[2] 4:19[4] 4:21 4:23 4:24 4:25[4] 4:26[6] 4:27[3] 4:28 4:30 4:31[4] 4:32[6] 4:34[4] 4:35 4:36[2] 4:37 4:38[2] 4:39 4:40[2] 4:41 4:42 4:43 4:44 4:45 4:46[2]

4:47[2] 4:48[2] 4:49 5:1 5:2[2] 5:3 5:4[2] 5:5 5:6 5:7[3] 5:9 5:10 5:11 5:12[2] 5:13[5] 5:14[5] 5:15 5:16[2] 5:17[3] 5:18[4] 5:19[3] 5:20[2] 5:21[3] 5:22[3] 5:23[2] 5:24[3] 5:25[2] 5:26[3] 5:27[6] 5:28[2] 5:29 5:30[3] 5:31 6:1 6:2 6:3[2] 6:5 6:9[2] 6:10 6:11[4] 6:12[2] 6:13 6:14[3] 6:15[4] 6:16[3] 6:17[2] 6:18[3] 6:19[4] 6:20[3] 6:21 6:22 6:23 6:24 6:25 6:26 6:27[2] 7:1[7] 7:2 7:3[4] 7:4 7:5 7:6[3] 7:7 7:8[2] 7:10 7:11 7:12 7:13[2] 7:17 7:19 7:23 7:25 7:29 7:31 7:35 7:37 7:41 7:43 7:47 7:49 7:53 7:55 7:59 7:61 7:65 7:67 7:71

7:73 7:77 7:79 7:83 7:85[2] 7:86 7:87 7:88[2] 7:89[2] 8:1 8:2 8:3 8:4 8:5 8:6 8:7[4] 8:8 8:9[2] 8:10[2] 8:11 8:12[3] 8:13[3] 8:14 8:15[3] 8:17 8:18 8:19[3] 8:20[3] 8:21[4] 8:22[2] 8:23 8:24[2] 8:25[2] 8:26 9:1 9:3 9:4 9:5 9:6[3] 9:7 9:8[2] 9:9 9:11[2] 9:13[2] 9:14[4] 9:15[2] 9:16 9:17[2] 9:18 9:19[2] 9:20[2] 9:21[2] 9:22 9:23 10:1 10:2 10:3 10:4 10:8[2] 10:9[3] 10:10[3] 10:11 10:12[2] 10:13 10:14 10:15 10:16 10:17[3] 10:18[2] 10:19 10:20 10:21[2] 10:22[2] 10:23 10:24 10:25[2] 10:26 10:27 10:29[2] 10:30[2] 10:31[2] 10:32 10:33[2] 10:34 10:35[3] 10:36 11:1[5]

11:2[2] 11:3 11:4[3] 11:5[4] 11:7[2] 11:8[6] 11:9 11:10 11:11[2] 11:15[2] 11:16[3] 11:17[5] 11:18[3] 11:20[2] 11:21[2] 11:22 11:23 11:24[4] 11:25[6] 11:26[4] 11:27[4] 11:28[2] 11:29[2] 11:30[2] 11:31[5] 11:32[5] 11:33[2] 11:34 11:35[2] 12:1[2] 12:2[2] 12:4[4] 12:5[5] 12:6[2] 12:8[2] 12:9[2] 12:10[4] 12:11[2] 12:13 12:14[2] 12:15[2] 12:16[2] 13:1 13:3 13:4 13:16 13:17[3] 13:18[2] 13:19[2] 13:20[3] 13:21 13:22[3] 13:23[3] 13:25 13:26[7] 13:27[5] 13:28[3] 13:29[5] 13:30[3] 13:32[2] 13:33[3] 14:1[3] 14:2[3] 14:3[2] 14:4[2] 14:5 14:6[2] 14:7 14:8[2] 14:9 14:10 14:11[2] 14:12[3] 14:13 14:14[4] 14:17 14:18[4] 14:19 14:20 14:22[4] 14:24[2] 14:25[2] 14:26[2] 14:29[2] 14:30 14:31 14:33[2]

14:34 14:35 14:36[2] 14:38 14:39[2] 14:40[3] 14:41 14:43[2] 14:44 14:45[3] 15:1 15:2 15:3 15:5 15:7 15:9 15:10 15:14[2] 15:15 15:16[2] 15:17 15:18 15:22[2] 15:23 15:24[2] 15:25[4] 15:26[2] 15:27 15:28[2] 15:29 15:30 15:31 15:32 15:33[3] 15:34 15:35 15:36[3] 15:37 15:38[2] 15:39[5] 15:40[2] 16:1[3] 16:2[2] 16:3[4] 16:4 16:5[4] 16:6 16:7[3] 16:8 16:9 16:10[3] 16:11[2] 16:12[2] 16:13 16:14[2] 16:15[2] 16:16[4] 16:17[5] 16:18[5] 16:19[2] 16:20[2] 16:22[3] 16:23 16:24 16:25[4] 16:26[2] 16:27[7] 16:28 16:30[3] 16:31 16:32[5] 16:33[3] 16:34 16:35[3] 16:36 16:37 16:38 16:39[2] 16:40 16:41 16:42[4] 16:43[2] 16:44 16:45 16:46[5] 16:47[5] 16:48[3]

16:49 16:50[2] 17:1 17:2 17:3 17:4 17:5[2] 17:6[3] 17:7 17:8[5] 17:9[3] 17:10[2] 17:11 17:12 18:1[5] 18:2[3] 18:3[3] 18:4[3] 18:5[2] 18:6 18:7[4] 18:8[2] 18:9[3] 18:11[3] 18:12[2] 18:13 18:15 18:16 18:17 18:18[2] 18:19[3] 18:20[2] 18:21 18:22 18:23 18:25 18:26 18:27[2] 18:28 18:30 18:31[2] 18:32 19:1[2] 19:2 19:3[2] 19:4[2] 19:5[3] 19:6[4] 19:7[3] 19:8[3] 19:9[3] 19:10[4] 19:12 19:13 19:14 19:15 19:16 19:17[2] 19:18[6] 19:19[6] 19:20 19:21[2] 19:22[2] 20:1[3] 20:2[3] 20:3[2] 20:4[2] 20:5 20:6[4] 20:7 20:8[6] 20:9 20:10[3] 20:11[5] 20:12[2] 20:13 20:14 20:15[3] 20:16[4] 20:18 20:19[3] 20:20[3] 20:22[2] 20:23[2] 20:25[2] 20:26[4] 20:27[2]

20:28[5] 20:29 21:1[2] 21:2[2] 21:3[5] 21:4[2] 21:5[3] 21:6[3] 21:7[3] 21:8[3] 21:9[3] 21:10[2] 21:11[2] 21:12 21:13[2] 21:14 21:15[2] 21:16[2] 21:18 21:19[2] 21:20 21:21 21:23[4] 21:24[2] 21:25[3] 21:26 21:27 21:28 21:29 21:30 21:32[3] 21:33[4] 21:34[4] 21:35[3] 22:1[2] 22:2 22:3[2] 22:4[2] 22:5 22:6[2] 22:7[4] 22:8[3] 22:9[2] 22:10 22:11 22:12 22:13[2] 22:14[3] 22:15[2] 22:16[2] 22:17 22:18[3] 22:20[3] 22:21[3] 22:22[3] 22:23[5] 22:24 22:25[3] 22:26[2] 22:27[3] 22:28[2] 22:29 22:30[2] 22:31[4] 22:32 22:33[3] 22:34 22:35 22:36 22:37 22:38 22:39 22:40[4] 22:41[2] 23:1[3] 23:2[4] 23:3[4] 23:4[4] 23:5[3] 23:6[3] 23:7[3] 23:9[2] 23:10[2] 23:11[2] 23:12[2] 23:13[3] 23:14[4]

DE

JOS

18:20 18:21^2 18:22^3 18:23^3 18:24^3 18:25^2 18:26^3 18:27^3 18:28^3 19:1^2 19:2^3 19:3^3 19:4^3 19:5^3 19:6^3 19:7^3 19:8 19:10^2 19:11^4 19:12^3 19:13^2 19:14^2 19:15^5 19:17 19:18^3 19:19^3 19:20^3 19:21^4 19:22^4 19:23 19:24 19:25^4 19:26^5 19:27^5 19:28^4 19:29^4 19:30^3 19:33^4 19:34^5 19:35^3 19:36^3 19:37^3 19:38^4 19:39 19:40 19:41^3 19:42^3 19:43^3 19:44^3 19:45^3 19:46^2 19:47^6 19:50^2 19:51^2 20:3^2 20:4^3 20:5^2 20:6^4 20:7^3 20:8^3 20:9^2 21:1^2 21:2 21:3^2 21:4^4 21:5^3 21:6^4 21:7^2 21:8 21:9^2 21:11 21:12 21:13 21:14^2 21:15^2 21:16^3 21:17 21:18 21:20 21:21 21:22^2 21:23 21:25^2 21:27^2 21:28 21:30 21:31

21:32^3 21:34^2 21:36^2 21:37 21:38^2 21:41 21:43^3 21:44^2 22:1^2 22:2^2 22:4^3 22:5^6 22:6^2 22:7 22:8^6 22:9^4 22:10^3 22:11^3 22:12 22:13^3 22:14^2 22:15^4 22:18 22:19 22:20^2 22:21^3 22:22 22:24 22:25^2 22:27^4 22:28 22:29 22:30^5 22:31^3 22:32^4 22:33^4 22:34^2 23:1^2 23:2^7 23:3 23:5^3 23:6 23:9 23:12^4 23:13^3 23:14^4 23:16^4 24:1^6 24:2^3 24:3^4 24:4^4 24:5^3 24:6^4 24:7^6 24:8^4 24:9^3 24:11^9 24:12 24:13^4 24:14^5 24:15^2 24:16^2 24:17^4 24:18 24:19 24:20^3 24:21 24:22^2 24:23 24:24^2 24:25^2 24:26^3 24:27 24:29^2 24:30 24:31^3 24:32^2 24:33^2

JG

1:2 1:3^2 1:4^4 1:5^4 1:6^4 1:7^5 1:8^3 1:9^3 1:10^4 1:11^2 1:12^2 1:13^2 1:14^3 1:15^3 1:16^3 1:17^4 1:18^2 1:19^2 1:20^2 1:21 1:22^2 1:23 1:24^3 1:25^2 1:26^3 1:27^5 1:28^2 1:30 1:33 1:34 1:35 1:36^2 2:1^4 2:2 2:3 2:4^2 2:5^2 2:6 2:7^2 2:8^2 2:9 2:10^2 2:11^2 2:12^4 2:13^3 2:14^3 2:15^2 2:17^2 2:18^3 2:19^3 2:20^3 3:3^3 3:4 3:5^5 3:6^3 3:7^4 3:8^2 3:9 3:10^5 3:11^2 3:12^2 3:13^5 3:15 3:16 3:17^2 3:18 3:19^2 3:20^4 3:21^3 3:22^3 3:23^2 3:24 3:25^4 3:26^3 3:27^3 3:28^4 3:29^3 3:30 3:31^2 4:1 4:2 4:3^2 4:4 4:5^3 4:6^6 4:7^3 4:8 4:9^3 4:10^4 4:11 4:12 4:13^2

4:14^2 4:15^4 4:16^3 4:17 4:18^3 4:19^4 4:20^3 4:21^5 4:22^5 4:24^2 5:1 5:4 5:6 5:10 5:12 5:14 5:15^2 5:17^2 5:18 5:19 5:25 5:26^3 5:28 5:31 6:1^2 6:2^4 6:3^3 6:4^3 6:5^4 6:6^2 6:7 6:8 6:9^4 6:10 6:11^3 6:12^2 6:13^3 6:14^3 6:15^2 6:16^2 6:17 6:18^3 6:19^6 6:20^5 6:21^5 6:22 6:23 6:24 6:25^3 6:26^3 6:27^3 6:28^3 6:29^3 6:30 6:31 6:33^4 6:34^2 6:35^5 6:36 6:37^2 6:38^3 6:39^3 6:40^2 7:1^2 7:2 7:3^5 7:4^4 7:5 7:6 7:7^3 7:8^4 7:9 7:11^2 7:12^4 7:13^6 7:14^3 7:15^4 7:16^3 7:17^3 7:18^3 7:19^4 7:20^6 7:21^4 7:22^4 7:23^4 7:24^5 7:25^7

8:1^2 8:2 8:3^2 8:4^3 8:5^3 8:6^2 8:7^3 8:8^3 8:9 8:10^3 8:11^3 8:12^5 8:13 8:14^5 8:15^4 8:16^4 8:17^2 8:18^2 8:19 8:20^2 8:21^5 8:22^2 8:23 8:24 8:25^3 8:26^5 8:27^4 8:28 8:29^2 8:30^2 8:31 8:32^2 8:33^3 8:34 9:1^3 9:2^2 9:3^2 9:4^3 9:5^3 9:6^4 9:7^5 9:8 9:9^2 9:10^2 9:11^2 9:12 9:13^3 9:14 9:15^4 9:16^4 9:17^2 9:18^4 9:19^3 9:20^5 9:21^4 9:23^2 9:24^3 9:25^3 9:26^3 9:27^8 9:28^3 9:29^3 9:30 9:31^3 9:32^2 9:33^4 9:34^3 9:35^4 9:36^2 9:37^3 9:38 9:39^2 9:40^4 9:41^3 9:42^2 9:43^7 9:44^5 9:45^5 9:46 9:47 9:48^8 9:49^5 9:50^2 9:51^5 9:52^3 9:53^2 9:54^4

9:55 9:57^2 10:1^2 10:2^4 10:3^3 10:4^2 10:5 10:6^{10} 10:7^3 10:8^2 10:9^2 10:10^2 10:11^3 10:12^4 10:13 10:14 10:15 10:16^3 10:17^3 10:18^2 11:1^2 11:2^4 11:3^3 11:4 11:5 11:6^2 11:7^3 11:8^3 11:9^2 11:10 11:11^3 11:12 11:13^2 11:14 11:15 11:16^2 11:17^2 11:18^4 11:19^2 11:20^2 11:21^3 11:22^2 11:23 11:25 11:26^4 11:27 11:29^4 11:30^2 11:31 11:32 11:33^2 11:34^4 11:35^4 11:37^4 11:38^4 11:39^4 12:1^4 12:2^3 12:3^3 12:4^3 12:5^2 12:6^4 12:7^2 12:8 12:9^3 12:10 12:11^2 12:12^2 12:13 12:14^4 12:15^2 13:1^2 13:2^3 13:3^4 13:4^2 13:5^3 13:6^2 13:7^2 13:8^2 13:9^2 13:10^4 13:11^5 13:12^2 13:13 13:15 13:16^2 13:17

13:18 13:19^4 13:20^2 13:21 13:22 13:23 13:24^4 13:25^2 14:1^2 14:2^4 14:3^2 14:4 14:5^4 14:6^3 14:7^3 14:8^4 14:9^6 14:10 14:11 14:12^3 14:13^2 14:14^3 14:15^2 14:16^6 14:17^3 14:18^3 14:19^7 15:1 15:2 15:3 15:4^5 15:5^4 15:6^5 15:7^2 15:8^4 15:9^2 15:10^2 15:11^2 15:12^2 15:13^4 15:14^4 15:15^4 15:16 15:17^2 15:18^5 15:19^3 15:20 16:1^2 16:2^4 16:3^8 16:4 16:5^5 16:6^2 16:7^2 16:8 16:9^2 16:10^2 16:11^2 16:12^4 16:13^3 16:14^5 16:15^2 16:16^2 16:17^3 16:18^3 16:19^5 16:20^5 16:21^4 16:23 16:24^2 16:25^4 16:26 16:27^4 16:28^3 16:29^3 16:30^4 16:31^6 17:1 17:2^3 17:3^2 17:4^4 17:5^4 17:7^2 17:8^2 17:9^3 17:10^6 17:11^2

17:12^3 18:1 18:2^4 18:3^4 18:4^4 18:5 18:6 18:7^6 18:8^3 18:9^4 18:10 18:11^2 18:12^2 18:13^2 18:14^4 18:15^3 18:16 18:17^7 18:18^4 18:19^5 18:20^5 18:21^4 18:22^2 18:23^3 18:24^5 18:25^2 18:26^3 18:27^6 18:28^5 18:29 18:30^2 18:31 19:1 19:2^3 19:3^6 19:4^4 19:5^3 19:6^5 19:7 19:8^4 19:9^4 19:10^3 19:11^4 19:12 19:13^2 19:14^3 19:15^3 19:16^2 19:17^3 19:18^3 19:19^5 19:20 19:21^4 19:22^2 19:23^2 19:24^3 19:25^4 19:26 19:27^5 19:28^4 19:29^4 19:30^2 20:1 20:2 20:4^2 20:5^4 20:6^4 20:7 20:8 20:10^3 20:12 20:13 20:15^2 20:16 20:17 20:18^5 20:19^2 20:20^2 20:21^3 20:22^2 20:23^4 20:24 20:25^2 20:26^7 20:27 20:28^2 20:29

20:30^2 20:31^5 20:32^2 20:33^3 20:34^2 20:35^4 20:37^4 20:38 20:39^2 20:40 20:41 20:42 20:43^2 20:44 20:45^5 20:46 20:47^2 20:48^3 21:2^4 21:3 21:4^4 21:5 21:6^2 21:8^2 21:9 21:10^4 21:11^2 21:12^2 21:13^2 21:14^3 21:15 21:17 21:19 21:20 21:21^4 21:22 21:23^6 21:24^3

RU

1:1^3 1:2^6 1:3^3 1:4^3 1:5^4 1:7^2 1:8^2 1:9^2 1:10 1:11 1:12 1:14^3 1:15^2 1:16^3 1:17^3 1:19^2 1:20 1:21^2 1:22^2 2:1^2 2:2^3 2:3^4 2:4^3 2:6^2 2:7^3 2:9^3 2:10^2 2:11^6 2:12 2:13 2:14^8 2:15^2 2:16^3 2:17^2 2:18^5 2:19^4 2:20^3 2:21 2:22 2:23^2 3:2 3:3^4 3:4^5 3:5 3:6^2 3:7^6 3:8^3 3:9^2 3:10 3:11 3:12 3:13 3:14^3 3:15^4 3:16^2 3:17 4:1^4 4:2^3 4:3 4:4^4 4:6 4:7^3 4:9^4 4:10 4:11^5 4:12 4:13^3 4:14 4:15^2 4:16^3 4:17^2 4:19^2 4:20^2 4:21^2 4:22^2

1 SA

1:1 1:2^3 1:3^4 1:4^3 1:6 1:7^2 1:8^2 1:9 1:10^3 1:11^5 1:12 1:14 1:15^2 1:16 1:17^2 1:18^3 1:19^6 1:20 1:21^3 1:22^2 1:23^2 1:24^5 1:25^2 1:26 1:27 1:28 2:1^2 2:3 2:4 2:5^2 2:6^2 2:7^2 2:8^3 2:9 2:10^2 2:11^2 2:13 2:14 2:15 2:16^3 2:19 2:20^3 2:21^4 2:22^2 2:23 2:26^3 2:27^2 2:28^2 2:29^2 2:30^3 2:31 2:32^2 2:33^3

2:34^2 2:35^4 2:36^4 3:1 3:2^2 3:3^2 3:4 3:5^5 3:6^5 3:8^5 3:9^2 3:10^3 3:11 3:13 3:14 3:15^3 3:16^2 3:17^2 3:18^3 3:19^3 3:20 3:21 4:1^3 4:2^3 4:3 4:4^2 4:5 4:6^2 4:7^2 4:9^2 4:10^4 4:11^3 4:12^3 4:13^3 4:14^3 4:15^2 4:16^3 4:17^6 4:18^5 4:19^5 4:20 4:21^3 4:22 5:1^2 5:2 5:3^3 5:4^2 5:6^3 5:7^2 5:8^4 5:10^2 5:11^4 5:12^2 6:1 6:2^2 6:3^2 6:4^2 6:5^4 6:6^2 6:7^3 6:8^4 6:9 6:10^4 6:11^3 6:12^4 6:13^4 6:14^4 6:15^5 6:16 6:17 6:18^2 6:19^4 6:20^2 6:21^2 7:1^4 7:2^2 7:3^5 7:4^2 7:5^2 7:6^6 7:7^2 7:8 7:9^4 7:10^3 7:11^3 7:12^3 7:13^2

7:14^4 7:15 7:16^4 7:17^3 8:1 8:2 8:3^3 8:4 8:5^2 8:6 8:7 8:8 8:9 8:10 8:11^4 8:12^6 8:13^3 8:14^4 8:15^4 8:16^5 8:17 8:18^2 8:19 8:20^3 8:21^2 8:22^3 9:2^4 9:3^3 9:4^4 9:5^3 9:6^2 9:7 9:8^2 9:9 9:11^2 9:12^2 9:13 9:14^2 9:16 9:17 9:18 9:19^4 9:20^3 9:21^3 9:22^4 9:23 9:24^5 9:25 9:26^5 9:27^2 10:1^3 10:2^3 10:3^4 10:4^2 10:5^5 10:6^3 10:7 10:8^4 10:9^2 10:10^3 10:11 10:12^2 10:13 10:14^4 10:15 10:16 10:17 10:18^4 10:19^4 10:20 10:21^2 10:22 10:23^4 10:24^3 10:25^2 10:26^2 10:27^2 11:1^3 11:2^2 11:3^2 11:4^3 11:5^3 11:6^2 11:7^6 11:8^2 11:9^4

11:10 11:11^4 11:12 11:13 11:14^2 11:15^5 12:1^2 12:2^5 12:3^2 12:4 12:5^3 12:6^3 12:7^3 12:8^3 12:9^4 12:10^5 12:11^6 12:12 12:13^2 12:14^4 12:16 12:17^3 12:18^4 12:19 12:20 12:21 12:23 12:24 12:25 13:1 13:2^3 13:3^3 13:4^3 13:5^5 13:6^4 13:7^3 13:8^2 13:9^3 13:10^2 13:11^4 13:12^2 13:13 13:14 13:15^3 13:16^3 13:17 13:18^2 13:20^3 13:21^4 13:22^2 13:23 14:1 14:2^2 14:3^2 14:4^4 14:5 14:6^2 14:7 14:8 14:9 14:10 14:11^2 14:12^5 14:13^5 14:14^2 14:15^4 14:16^3 14:17^3 14:18 14:19^3 14:20^5 14:21 14:23 14:24 14:25^2 14:26 14:27^3 14:28^2 14:31^2 14:32^6 14:33 14:34^8 14:35 14:36^4 14:37 14:38^3 14:40^3

14:41^2 14:42^3 14:43^3 14:44^2 14:45 14:46 14:47^6 14:48^3 14:49^4 14:50^2 14:51^2 14:52^2 15:3^7 15:4^3 15:5^2 15:6 15:7 15:8^2 15:9^3 15:11^3 15:12^5 15:13^2 15:14^2 15:15^3 15:16^2 15:17^2 15:18^4 15:19 15:20^4 15:21 15:22^3 15:23^2 15:24^3 15:25 15:26^2 15:27^2 15:28^2 15:29 15:30^2 15:31 15:32^2 15:33^2 15:34 15:35^2 16:1^2 16:2^3 16:3^3 16:4^4 16:5^5 16:6^2 16:8^2 16:9 16:10 16:11^5 16:12^5 16:13^3 16:14 16:15 16:16^2 16:17^2 16:18^6 16:19 16:20^4 16:21^4 16:22 16:23^4 17:1^3 17:2^4 17:3^3 17:4^2 17:5^3 17:6^2 17:7^3 17:8^5 17:9^3 17:10 17:11^2 17:12^2 17:13^5 17:14^2 17:15 17:16^3 17:17^3 17:18^3 17:19^2 17:20^6 17:21

17:22^4 17:23^3 17:24^2 17:25^4 17:26^2 17:27 17:28^5 17:29 17:30^3 17:31^2 17:32^2 17:33^2 17:34^4 17:35^6 17:36^2 17:37^3 17:38^2 17:39^4 17:40^5 17:41^3 17:42^4 17:43^2 17:44^3 17:45^2 17:46^4 17:47^3 17:48^4 17:49^5 17:50^3 17:51^6 17:52^7 17:53^2 17:54^2 17:55^2 17:56 17:57^2 17:58^2 18:1^2 18:2^2 18:3 18:4^5 18:5^5 18:6^3 18:7^3 18:8^5 18:9^2 18:10^4 18:11^2 18:12^2 18:13^3 18:14^2 18:16^2 18:17^2 18:18^2 18:20^3 18:21^2 18:22^3 18:23^3 18:24 18:25 18:26^2 18:27^6 18:28^3 18:29^2 18:30 19:1^2 19:2^3 19:3^4 19:4^3 19:5^3 19:6^2 19:7^4 19:8^5 19:9^2 19:10^4 19:11^2 19:12^2 19:13^4 19:14 19:15 19:16 19:17^3 19:18^6 19:19 19:20^4 19:21^4 19:22^5

19:23^4 19:24^4 20:1^4 20:2^2 20:3^5 20:5^2 20:9 20:11^3 20:12^4 20:13^3 20:14 20:17 20:18 20:19^3 20:20 20:21^2 20:23^3 20:24 20:25^4 20:27^2 20:28 20:29^4 20:30^2 20:31 20:32^2 20:33 20:34 20:35^2 20:36^2 20:37^2 20:38^3 20:39 20:40^2 20:41^5 20:42^7 21:1^3 21:2^5 21:4^2 21:5^4 21:7 21:8^2 21:9^2 21:10^3 21:11^2 21:12^2 21:13^4 22:1^3 22:2^5 22:3^4 22:4^2 22:5^3 22:6^2 22:7^3 22:8^2 22:9 22:10^3 22:11^2 22:12^2 22:13^4 22:14^4 22:16^2 22:17^4 22:18^6 22:19^6 22:20^2 22:21 22:22 23:1 23:2^4 23:3 23:4^2 23:5^4 23:6 23:7^3 23:8^2 23:9^2 23:11 23:12^2 23:13^5 23:14^3 23:15^2 23:16^3 23:17^4 23:18^3 23:20 23:21 23:22^3

23:23^4 23:24^3 23:25^4 23:26^6 23:27 23:28 23:29^2 24:1 24:2^2 24:3^4 24:4^2 24:5 24:6 24:7^2 24:8^4 24:9 24:10^2 24:11^3 24:12^2 24:15^5 24:16^3 24:17 24:18 24:20^2 24:21 24:22^3 25:1^6 25:2^5 25:3^5 25:4 25:5^4 25:6^3 25:7 25:8^2 25:9^2 25:10^3 25:11^3 25:12^3 25:13^5 25:14 25:15 25:16 25:17^2 25:18^7 25:19 25:20^4 25:21 25:22 25:23^4 25:24^4 25:25 25:26^3 25:27 25:28 25:29^2 25:30^2 25:32 25:33^3 25:34 25:35^2 25:36^3 25:37^2 25:38 25:39^4 25:40 25:41^3 25:42^5 25:43 26:1 26:2 26:3^2 26:4 26:5^6 26:6^3 26:7^4 26:8 26:9^2 26:10 26:11^2 26:12^3 26:13 26:14^3 26:15^2 26:16^2 26:17^3 26:18 26:21

26:22^4 26:23 26:24^2 26:25^2 27:1^2 27:2^2 27:3^3 27:4^2 27:5 27:7^2 27:8^5 27:9^9 27:10^4 27:11^2 27:12 28:1^3 28:2^2 28:3^4 28:4^5 28:5^2 28:6 28:7^2 28:8^7 28:9^2 28:10 28:11 28:12^2 28:13^2 28:14^6 28:15^4 28:16 28:17^2 28:19^2 28:20^2 28:21^5 28:22^2 28:23^3 28:24^6 28:25^4 29:1 29:2^3 29:3^2 29:4^3 29:5 29:6^3 29:7 29:8^2 29:9^2 29:10^2 29:11^2 30:1^5 30:2^2 30:3^5 30:4^2 30:5^2 30:6^2 30:7^2 30:8^3 30:9^2 30:10 30:11^5 30:12^4 30:13^4 30:14^3 30:15^3 30:16^4 30:17^3 30:18^2 30:19 30:20^3 30:21^4 30:22^4 30:23 30:25^2 30:26 30:27^2 30:28^3 30:29^3 30:30^3 30:31^3 31:1^2 31:2^5 31:3^3 31:4^4 31:5^2 31:6^3 31:7^7

31:8[2]
31:9[4]
31:10[2]
31:11
31:12[5]
31:13[3]

2 SA

1:1
1:2[3]
1:3[2]
1:4[6]
1:5[2]
1:6[3]
1:7[3]
1:8[2]
1:9
1:10[4]
1:11[2]
1:12[6]
1:13[2]
1:14
1:15[4]
1:16
1:17[2]
1:19[2]
1:22
1:23[3]
1:27
2:1[4]
2:2[2]
2:3[2]
2:4[3]
2:5[3]
2:6[2]
2:7[2]
2:8
2:9[6]
2:10
2:11[2]
2:12[2]
2:13[5]
2:14[3]
2:15[2]
2:16[2]
2:17[3]
2:18[4]
2:19[2]
2:20[2]
2:21[3]
2:22
2:23[4]
2:24[2]
2:25[3]
2:26
2:27
2:28[2]
2:29[5]
2:30[3]
2:31[2]
2:32[5]
3:1[4]
3:2[2]
3:3[2]
3:4
3:5
3:6[2]
3:7[2]
3:8[3]
3:9
3:10[2]
3:11
3:12[2]
3:13
3:14
3:15[2]
3:16[2]
3:17
3:18
3:19[3]
3:20[3]
3:21[6]
3:22[4]
3:23[3]
3:24[2]
3:25[3]
3:26
3:27[2]
3:28[2]
3:29[2]
3:30
3:31[5]
3:32[4]
3:33[2]
3:34
3:35[2]
3:36[2]
3:37
3:38[2]
3:39[2]
4:1[2]
4:2[2]
4:3[2]
4:4[7]
4:5[3]
4:6[4]
4:7[5]
4:8[4]
4:9[3]
4:10
4:11
4:12[6]
5:1[2]
5:2[3]
5:3[2]
5:4
5:5[4]
5:6[3]
5:8[6]
5:9[3]
5:10[3]
5:11[5]
5:12[2]
5:13[4]
5:14[4]
5:15[3]
5:16[3]
5:17[2]
5:18
5:19[2]
5:20[3]
5:21[3]
5:22[2]
5:23[2]
5:24
5:25
6:2[2]
6:3[4]
6:4[2]
6:5[6]
6:6[2]
6:7[3]
6:8[2]
6:9[2]
6:11[3]
6:12[3]
6:13[2]
6:14[2]
6:15[2]
6:16[4]
6:17[4]
6:18[2]
6:19[3]
6:20[2]
6:21[2]
6:22[3]
7:1[2]
7:3
7:4
7:5
7:6
7:9[3]
7:10[2]
7:11[2]
7:12[3]
7:13
7:14[4]
7:16[2]
7:17
7:18[3]
7:19[2]
7:20
7:21
7:23[5]
7:24
7:25
7:26[2]
7:28[3]
7:29
8:1[3]
8:2[5]
8:4[4]
8:5[2]
8:6[3]
8:7[2]
8:8[2]
8:9
8:10[5]
8:11
8:12[5]
8:13
8:14[3]
8:15[3]
8:16[2]
8:17[3]
8:18[3]
9:1
9:2[3]
9:3[2]
9:4[2]
9:5
9:6[3]
9:7[3]
9:8[2]
9:9[2]
9:10[4]
9:12[2]
9:13
10:1[2]
10:2
10:3[3]
10:4[3]
10:5[2]
10:6[5]
10:7[2]
10:8[6]
10:9[2]
10:10
10:11[2]
10:12[3]
10:13[3]
10:14[3]
10:15
10:16[4]
10:17[5]
10:18[4]
10:19[2]
11:1[5]
11:2[4]
11:3[3]
11:4[5]
11:5[4]
11:6[2]
11:7[3]
11:8[4]
11:9
11:10
11:11[3]
11:12[3]
11:13[4]
11:14[2]
11:15[3]
11:16
11:17[4]
11:18
11:19
11:20
11:22[2]
11:23[3]
11:24[3]
11:25[2]
11:26
11:27[2]
12:1[2]
12:2
12:3[3]
12:4[4]
12:5[2]
12:6[2]
12:7[2]
12:8[6]
12:9[2]
12:10
12:11[3]
12:12
12:13
12:15
12:16[3]
12:17[2]
12:18[3]
12:19
12:20[7]
12:21[2]
12:22[2]
12:24[6]
12:25[2]
12:26[2]
12:27[3]
12:28[3]
12:29[4]
12:30[3]
12:31[7]
13:1[2]
13:2[2]
13:3
13:4[2]
13:5[5]
13:6[3]
13:7
13:8[5]
13:9[4]
13:10[4]
13:11[2]
13:12
13:13[2]
13:14
13:15
13:16
13:17[2]
13:18[2]
13:19[4]
13:20
13:22
13:23[2]
13:24[3]
13:25[2]
13:26
13:27
13:28[2]
13:29[3]
13:30[2]
13:31[3]
13:32[2]
13:34[3]
13:35
13:36[5]
13:37[2]
13:38[2]
13:39
14:2[5]
14:3[2]
14:4[3]
14:5[2]
14:6[4]
14:7[5]
14:8[2]
14:9[4]
14:10[2]
14:11
14:12
14:13
14:14
14:15
14:16
14:17
14:18[2]
14:19[4]
14:20
14:21
14:22[4]
14:23[2]
14:24[3]
14:26
14:27[2]
14:28
14:29
14:30[3]
14:31[2]
14:32[2]
14:33[4]
15:1[3]
15:2[5]
15:3[2]
15:4
15:5[3]
15:6
15:7[2]
15:9[2]
15:11[3]
15:12[2]
15:13
15:14[4]
15:15
15:16[3]
15:17[3]
15:18[4]
15:19[2]
15:20[3]
15:21[3]
15:22[5]
15:23[3]
15:24[4]
15:25[3]
15:27[2]
15:29
15:30[6]
15:31[2]
15:32[2]
15:34
15:35[3]
15:36[2]
15:37
16:1[5]
16:2[5]
16:3[3]
16:4
16:5[2]
16:6[5]
16:7[2]
16:8[2]
16:9
16:10
16:11[3]
16:12
16:13[5]
16:14[3]
16:15[3]
16:16
16:17
16:18[4]
16:19
16:21[2]
16:22
16:23[2]
17:1[2]
17:2[5]
17:3
17:4[2]
17:5
17:6
17:7
17:8[4]
17:9
17:10[2]
17:11
17:12[3]
17:13
17:14[2]
17:15[5]
17:16[2]
17:17[5]
17:18[2]
17:19[4]
17:20[5]
17:21[5]
17:22[2]
17:23[7]
17:24[2]
17:25
17:26
17:27[3]
17:28[9]
17:29[7]
18:1[3]
18:2[4]
18:4[4]
18:5[4]
18:6
18:7
18:9[7]
18:10[3]
18:11[5]
18:12[3]
18:13
18:14[2]
18:15[3]
18:16[2]
18:17[4]
18:18[3]
18:19
18:20
18:21[2]
18:22
18:23[2]
18:24[5]
18:25[5]
18:26[4]
18:27[3]
18:28[4]
18:29[3]
18:30[4]
18:31[2]
18:32[3]
18:33[4]
19:1[2]
19:2
19:3
19:4
19:5[5]
19:6[2]
19:7[2]
19:8[3]
19:9[3]
19:10
19:11[2]
19:12
19:13[3]
19:14
19:15
19:16[2]
19:17[5]
19:18[3]
19:19
19:21
19:23
19:24[2]
19:25
19:26[2]
19:27
19:29[2]
19:30
19:31[2]
19:32
19:33[2]
19:34
19:35[3]
19:36
19:37[3]
19:38[3]
19:39[4]
19:40[3]
19:41[5]
19:42
19:43[4]
20:1[3]
20:2
20:3[4]
20:4
20:6[3]
20:7[5]
20:8[3]
20:9[2]
20:10[4]
20:11[3]
20:12[3]
20:14[5]
20:15[5]
20:17[3]
20:18
20:19[2]
20:20[2]
20:21[2]
20:22[5]
20:23[2]
20:24[2]
20:25[3]
20:26
21:1[3]
21:2[5]
21:3
21:4[2]
21:5[2]
21:6[2]
21:7
21:8[2]
21:9[4]
21:10[3]
21:11
21:12[3]
21:13[3]
21:14[4]
21:15[4]
21:16
21:17[2]
21:18
21:19
21:20[4]
21:21
21:22[2]
22:1[2]
22:2[3]
22:3[2]
22:7[3]
22:8[2]
22:9
22:10[2]
22:11[3]
22:12[2]
22:14
22:15[3]
22:16
22:18
22:22
22:23
22:24
22:26
22:27
22:28
22:29
22:32
22:33[2]
22:34
22:36
22:38[2]
22:39[2]
22:43
22:46
22:47[2]
22:48
22:49
22:50
22:51[2]
23:1[2]
23:2
23:4
23:5[2]
23:7[2]
23:9[2]
23:10[4]
23:11[3]
23:12[3]
23:13[3]
23:14[2]
23:15[2]
23:16[4]
23:17
23:18[4]
23:20[2]
23:21[4]
23:22
23:23
23:39
24:1[3]
24:2
24:3[2]
24:4[3]
24:5[3]
24:6[3]
24:7[4]
24:8
24:9[3]
24:10[3]
24:12
24:13[3]
24:14[2]
24:15
24:16[3]
24:17[4]
24:18[2]
24:19
24:20[5]
24:21[2]
24:22[4]
24:23
24:24[2]
24:25[4]

1 KI

1:1[2]
1:2[3]
1:3[5]
1:4[3]
1:5[3]
1:6[3]
1:7[3]
1:8[5]
1:9[5]
1:10[3]
1:11[2]
1:12
1:13[3]
1:14[3]
1:15[3]
1:16[3]
1:17[2]
1:18[2]
1:19[6]
1:20
1:21
1:22
1:23
1:24
1:25[9]
1:26[3]
1:27
1:28[3]
1:29[2]
1:30
1:31[2]
1:32[4]
1:33[2]
1:34[4]
1:35[3]
1:36[2]
1:37
1:38[6]
1:39[4]
1:40[3]
1:41[3]
1:42[3]
1:43[2]
1:44[6]
1:45[3]
1:46
1:47[3]
1:48[3]
1:49[3]
1:50[4]
1:51
1:52
1:53[4]
2:1
2:2
2:3[5]
2:4
2:5[5]
2:6
2:7
2:8[2]
2:9
2:10
2:11[3]
2:12
2:13[3]
2:14
2:15[3]
2:16[2]
2:17
2:18
2:19[5]
2:20
2:21
2:22[5]
2:23
2:24[2]
2:25[2]
2:26[2]
2:28[2]
2:29[2]
2:30[5]
2:31[4]
2:32[4]
2:33[4]
2:34[3]
2:35[2]
2:36[5]
2:37
2:38[2]
2:39
2:40[5]
2:41[2]
2:42[6]
2:43
2:45[2]
2:46[2]
3:1[5]
3:3[2]
3:4
3:5
3:6[4]
3:7[2]
3:8
3:9
3:10
3:11[2]
3:12
3:13[2]
3:14[2]
3:15[7]
3:16
3:17[3]
3:18[2]
3:19
3:20[4]
3:21
3:22[4]
3:23[3]
3:24[2]
3:25[3]
3:26[2]
3:27[2]
3:28[3]
4:2
4:3
4:4[3]
4:5[3]
4:6[2]
4:7[2]
4:8
4:9[3]
4:10
4:12[2]
4:16
4:19[2]
4:20[3]
4:21[3]
4:22[2]
4:23[5]
4:24
4:25[3]
4:26[2]
4:27[2]
4:28
4:29[3]
4:30[2]
4:31[4]
4:32[3]
4:33[4]
4:34
5:1
5:2
5:5
5:6
5:7[2]
5:8[3]
5:9[4]
5:10
5:11[2]
5:12[4]
5:13
5:14[3]
5:15[3]
5:16
5:17[3]
5:18[4]
6:1[2]
6:2[3]
6:3[2]
6:4
6:5[3]
6:6[2]
6:7
6:8[2]
6:9[3]
6:10[2]
6:11
6:12[2]
6:13[2]
6:14
6:15[4]
6:16[2]
6:17
6:18[2]
6:19
6:20[5]
6:21[2]
6:22
6:23
6:24[2]
6:25[2]
6:26
6:27[4]
6:28
6:29[4]
6:30[2]
6:31[2]
6:32[6]
6:34[2]
6:35[4]
6:36[2]
6:38[2]
7:1
7:2[2]
7:3
7:4[2]
7:5[3]
7:6[5]
7:7
7:8
7:9[2]
7:10[2]
7:11[2]
7:12[3]
7:13[2]
7:14[6]
7:15
7:16[2]
7:17[3]
7:18[3]
7:19
7:20[2]
7:21[5]
7:22
7:23[3]
7:24
7:25[5]
7:26[2]
7:27[3]
7:28[2]
7:29[5]
7:30[3]
7:31[4]
7:32[4]
7:33[4]
7:34[2]
7:35[3]
7:36[3]
7:37
7:38[2]
7:39[3]
7:40[3]
7:41[2]
7:42
7:43[2]
7:44[2]
7:45[4]
7:46
7:47
7:48[2]
7:49[4]
7:50[7]
7:51[3]
8:1
8:2
8:3[2]
8:4[4]
8:5[3]
8:6
8:7[2]
8:8[3]
8:9
8:14[3]
8:15[2]
8:17
8:18
8:20[4]
8:21
8:22[2]
8:23
8:24
8:26
8:27
8:28[2]
8:29
8:30[4]
8:31[2]
8:32[3]
8:33[4]
8:34[2]
8:35[3]
8:36[3]
8:38[2]
8:39[3]
8:42[3]
8:43[2]
8:44[2]
8:45[2]
8:46[2]
8:47[3]
8:48[4]
8:49[2]
8:50[3]
8:51
8:52
8:54
8:55
8:58[3]
8:59[3]
8:60
8:61
8:62[2]
8:63[5]
8:64[4]
8:65[3]
8:66[4]
9:1[3]
9:3[4]
9:4[4]
9:6[4]
9:7[3]
9:8[4]
9:9[4]
9:10[2]
9:11[2]
9:12[2]
9:13[2]
9:14
9:15[7]
9:16[4]
9:17[2]
9:18[2]
9:19[6]
9:20[2]
9:22[5]
9:23
9:25[3]
9:26
9:27
9:28[4]
10:1
10:2[4]
10:3
10:4[2]
10:5[6]
10:6[2]
10:7[3]
10:8
10:9
10:10[4]
10:11[2]
10:12[3]
10:13[3]
10:14
10:15[3]
10:16
10:17[2]
10:18
10:19[3]
10:20[2]
10:21[2]
10:22[3]
10:23
10:24
10:25[6]
10:26[6]
10:27
10:28[2]
10:29[6]
11:1
11:3[3]
11:4
11:5
11:6[2]
11:7
11:8[2]
11:9
11:10
11:11[3]
11:13
11:14
11:15
11:17
11:18[6]
11:19
11:20[2]
11:21[2]
11:22
11:23
11:24[5]
11:25[3]
11:26
11:27[2]
11:28[2]
11:29[3]
11:30[2]
11:31[2]
11:32
11:33[5]
11:34
11:35
11:36
11:37[3]
11:38[6]
11:39
11:40[3]
11:41[3]
11:42
11:43[3]
12:1
12:2[2]
12:3[4]
12:4[2]
12:5[2]
12:6[2]
12:7[4]
12:8[2]
12:9
12:10
12:11
12:12
12:13[2]
12:14[2]
12:18
12:20[3]
12:21[2]
12:23[3]
12:24
12:25[3]
12:26
12:27[2]
12:28[2]
12:29[2]
12:30
12:31[2]
12:32[3]
12:33[3]
13:1[2]
13:2[4]
13:3[2]
13:4[2]
13:5
13:6[6]
13:7[3]
13:8
13:10
13:11[2]
13:12
13:13[2]
13:14[4]
13:15
13:16
13:18[2]
13:19[2]
13:20
13:21[2]
13:22[3]
13:23[2]
13:24[4]
13:25[5]
13:26[2]
13:27[2]
13:28[4]
13:29[5]
13:30[2]
13:31
13:32
13:33
13:34[2]
14:2[3]
14:3[4]
14:4[4]
14:5[2]
14:6
14:7
14:8[4]
14:9[3]
14:10[4]
14:11
14:12
14:13[2]
14:15[2]
14:16[2]
14:17[4]
14:18[2]
14:19[2]
14:20[4]
14:21[4]
14:22[2]
14:23[3]
14:24[2]
14:25
14:26[3]
14:27[2]
14:28[2]
14:29
14:30[2]
14:31[4]
15:2
15:3[2]
15:4
15:5
15:6[2]
15:7[3]
15:8[3]
15:9
15:10[3]
15:11
15:12[2]
15:13[3]
15:15[4]
15:16[2]
15:17[2]
15:18[4]
15:19[5]
15:20[5]
15:21[2]
15:22[4]
15:23[3]
15:24[3]
15:25[2]
15:26[3]
15:27[3]
15:28
15:29
15:30
15:31
15:32[2]
15:33
15:34[3]
16:2[3]
16:3[2]
16:4
16:5
16:6[2]
16:7[3]
16:8
16:9
16:10[5]
16:11
16:13[2]
16:14
16:15[2]
16:16[2]
16:17[3]
16:18[3]
16:19
16:20
16:21
16:22
16:23
16:24[3]
16:25
16:26
16:27
16:28[2]
16:29[4]
16:30
16:31[4]
16:32
16:33[2]
16:34
17:1
17:2
17:3[2]
17:4[2]
17:5[2]
17:6[5]
17:7
17:8
17:9
17:10[4]
17:11[2]
17:12[6]
17:13[5]
17:15[5]
17:16
17:17[2]
17:18[2]
17:19[4]
17:20[2]
17:21[3]
17:22[3]
17:23[4]
17:24[2]
18:1[2]
18:2[2]
18:3
18:4[3]
18:5[3]
18:6
18:7[4]
18:8
18:9
18:10[2]
18:11
18:12[4]
18:13[2]
18:14[2]
18:15
18:16[2]
18:17
18:18[3]
18:19[4]
18:20
18:21[3]
18:22
18:23[7]
18:24[5]
18:25[3]
18:26[4]
18:27[3]
18:28[3]
18:29[2]
18:30[3]
18:31
18:32[2]
18:33[6]
18:34[4]
18:35[2]
18:36[5]
18:37
18:38[5]
18:39[2]
18:40[4]
18:41[2]
18:42[4]
18:43[5]
18:44[3]
18:45[5]
18:46[3]
19:1[2]
19:2
19:3[4]
19:4[4]
19:5[4]
19:6[6]
19:7[4]
19:8[5]
19:9[4]
19:10[4]
19:11[7]
19:12[2]
19:13[5]
19:14[4]
19:15[2]
19:16[2]
19:17[2]
19:18
19:19[3]
19:20[6]
19:21[8]
20:1[8]
20:2[2]
20:3[2]
20:4[3]
20:5[5]
20:6[4]
20:7[6]
20:8[2]
20:9[2]
20:10[3]
20:11[2]
20:12[3]
20:13[2]
20:14[3]
20:15[3]
20:16[3]
20:17[3]
20:18
20:19
20:20[4]
20:21[4]
20:22[4]
20:23[2]
20:24[2]
20:25[6]
20:26[2]
20:27[4]
20:28[4]
20:29[3]
20:30[4]
20:31[3]
20:32[4]
20:33[3]
20:34[3]
20:35[2]
20:36[2]
20:37[2]
20:38[2]
20:39[5]
20:40[3]
20:41[3]
20:42[2]
20:43[3]
21:1
21:2[2]
21:3
21:4[5]
21:5
21:6[3]
21:7[3]
21:8[3]
21:9[2]
21:10[4]
21:11[3]
21:12
21:13[5]
21:14
21:15[2]
21:16
21:17
21:19[3]
21:20[2]
21:21[4]
21:22[3]
21:23
21:24
21:26
21:27[5]
21:28
22:1[2]
22:2
22:3[3]
22:4[2]
22:5
22:6[2]
22:7
22:8[2]
22:9
22:10[3]
22:11[2]
22:12[2]
22:13[2]
22:14
22:15[3]
22:16
22:17[2]
22:18
22:19[3]
22:20[4]
22:21[3]
22:22[6]
22:23
22:24[2]
22:25
22:26[3]
22:27[3]
22:28[2]
22:29
22:30[4]
22:31
22:32[3]
22:33
22:34[3]
22:35[4]
22:36
22:37[2]
22:38[3]
22:39[3]
22:40
22:41
22:42[4]
22:43[2]
22:44
22:45[2]
22:46
22:50[3]
22:51
22:52[4]
22:53[2]

2 KI

1:2[4]
1:3
1:4
1:5
1:6[3]
1:7[2]
1:8[3]
1:9[3]
1:10[7]
1:11[2]
1:12[7]
1:13[7]
1:14
1:15[3]
1:16
1:17
2:1
2:2[3]
2:3[3]
2:4[3]
2:5[3]
2:6[4]
2:7[3]
2:8[5]
2:9[2]
2:10
2:11[5]
2:12[6]
2:13[2]
2:14[6]
2:15[3]
2:16[4]
2:17[2]
2:18
2:19[2]
2:20[3]
2:21[3]
2:23[4]
2:24[6]
2:25[2]
3:1
3:2[2]
3:4[3]
3:6[2]
3:7[4]
3:8[2]
3:9[5]
3:10
3:11[2]
3:12[3]
3:13[3]
3:14
3:15
3:16
3:17[2]
3:18
3:19[5]
3:20[2]
3:21[3]
3:22[3]
3:23[2]
3:24[2]
3:25[6]
3:26
3:27[4]
4:1[2]
4:2[2]
4:4[4]
4:5[3]
4:6[3]
4:7[5]
4:8[3]
4:9
4:10[5]
4:11[3]
4:12[2]
4:13[2]
4:14[3]
4:15[2]
4:16[2]
4:17[2]
4:18
4:19[2]
4:20[3]
4:21[4]
4:22[4]
4:23[2]
4:24[2]
4:25[2]
4:26[2]
4:27[4]
4:29[4]
4:30[4]
4:31[3]
4:32[2]
4:33
4:34
4:35[6]
4:36[3]
4:37[4]
4:38[5]
4:39[5]
4:40[3]
4:41[3]
4:42[4]
4:43[2]
4:44[2]
5:1
5:2[3]
5:3
5:4[3]
5:5[6]
5:6
5:7[4]
5:8[2]
5:9[2]
5:10[4]
5:11[6]
5:12[3]
5:13[3]
5:14[3]
5:15[5]
5:16
5:17
5:18[2]
5:19
5:20
5:21[2]
5:22[2]
5:23[5]
5:24[4]
5:25[3]
5:26[8]
5:27
6:1
6:2[2]
6:3[3]
6:4
6:5[2]
6:6[5]
6:7[2]
6:8[2]
6:9
6:10[3]
6:11[2]
6:12
6:13[4]
6:14[4]
6:15[4]
6:16
6:17[6]
6:18[3]
6:19[2]
6:20[4]
6:21
6:22[5]
6:23[4]
6:24[3]
6:25[3]
6:26
6:27
6:28[3]
6:29[3]
6:30[4]
6:31
6:32[2]
6:33[2]

AND—*continued*

7:1 7:2^2 7:3^2 7:4^4 7:5^2 7:6^3 7:7^5 7:8^{13} 7:9^2 7:10^5 7:11^2 7:12^3 7:13^4 7:14^2 7:15^5 7:16^3 7:17^3 7:18^2 7:19^3 7:20^2 8:1^4 8:2^4 8:3^3 8:4 8:5^4 8:6^2 8:7^3 8:8^3 8:9^4 8:10 8:11^2 8:12^5 8:13^2 8:14^2 8:15^4 8:16 8:17^2 8:18^2 8:19 8:20 8:21^5 8:23^2 8:24^3 8:26^3 8:27^2 8:28^2 8:29^2 9:1^4 9:2^4 9:3^4 9:5^4 9:6^4 9:7^2 9:8^3 9:9^2 9:10^4 9:11^3 9:12^3 9:13^3 9:14 9:15 9:16^2 9:17^6 9:18^3 9:19^2 9:20^3 9:21^6 9:22^3 9:23^2 9:25^2 9:26^3 9:27^5 9:28^2 9:29 9:30^4 9:31 9:32^3 9:33^4 9:34^4 9:35^3 9:36^2 9:37 10:1^4 10:2^3 10:3^3 10:4 10:5^4

10:6^2 10:7^4 10:8^3 10:9^4 10:11^3 10:12^4 10:13^4 10:14^4 10:15^6 10:16^2 10:17 10:18^2 10:19 10:20^2 10:21^4 10:22^2 10:23^4 10:24^3 10:25^7 10:26^2 10:27^3 10:29 10:30^2 10:32 10:33^3 10:34^2 10:35^3 10:36^2 11:1^2 11:2^2 11:3^2 11:4^7 11:5 11:6^2 11:7 11:8^4 11:9^3 11:10^2 11:11^2 11:12^7 11:13^2 11:14^7 11:15^2 11:16^2 11:17^4 11:18^5 11:19^7 11:20^3 12:1^2 12:2 12:3 12:4^2 12:5 12:6 12:7^2 12:8 12:9^3 12:10^4 12:11^3 12:12^5 12:14 12:16 12:17^3 12:18^8 12:19 12:20^3 12:21^4 13:1^2 13:2^2 13:3^2 13:4^2 13:5^2 13:6 13:7^3 13:8^2 13:9^3 13:10^2 13:11 13:12^3 13:13^3 13:14^4 13:15^4 13:16^3 13:17^5 13:18^5 13:19^2 13:20^3

13:21^5 13:23^5 13:24 13:25^2 14:2^4 14:3 14:4 14:5 14:7^2 14:9^3 14:10^3 14:11^2 14:12^2 14:13^3 14:14^6 14:15^2 14:16^3 14:17 14:18 14:19^2 14:20^2 14:21^2 14:22 14:23^2 14:24 14:27 14:28^4 14:29^2 15:1 15:2^3 15:3 15:4 15:5^3 15:6^2 15:7^2 15:8 15:9 15:10^4 15:11 15:12 15:13^2 15:14^4 15:15^2 15:16^3 15:17^2 15:18 15:19^2 15:20^2 15:21^2 15:22^2 15:23 15:24 15:25^5 15:26^2 15:27^2 15:28 15:29^8 15:30^4 15:31^2 15:33^3 15:34 15:35 15:36 15:37 15:38^3 16:2^2 16:3 16:4^4 16:5^2 16:6^3 16:7^3 16:8^4 16:9^4 16:10^4 16:11 16:12^2 16:13^4 16:14^3 16:15^9 16:17^4 16:18^2 16:20^3 17:2 17:3^2 17:4^3 17:5^2 17:7

17:8^2 17:9^2 17:10^3 17:11^2 17:13^5 17:15^6 17:16^5 17:17^5 17:18 17:20^3 17:21^3 17:24^8 17:25 17:26^2 17:27^3 17:28^2 17:29 17:30^3 17:31^4 17:32 17:33 17:34 17:35 17:36^2 17:37^5 17:38 17:39 17:41^2 18:2^3 18:3 18:4^4 18:6 18:7^4 18:8 18:9^2 18:10 18:11^4 18:12^2 18:13 18:14^3 18:15^2 18:16^2 18:17^7 18:18^3 18:19 18:20 18:21 18:22^3 18:23 18:24 18:25 18:26^3 18:27^2 18:28^2 18:30 18:31^4 18:32^6 18:34^2 18:37^3 19:1^3 19:2^2 19:3^4 19:4 19:6 19:7^3 19:8 19:11 19:12^3 19:13^3 19:14^4 19:15^3 19:16^3 19:17 19:18^2 19:21 19:22^3 19:23^5 19:24^2 19:25 19:26^3 19:27^3 19:28^3 19:29^6 19:30^2 19:31 19:33 19:34

19:35^4 19:36^3 19:37^4 20:1^3 20:2 20:3^3 20:4 20:5 20:6^5 20:7^4 20:8^2 20:9 20:10 20:11^2 20:12 20:13^7 20:14^3 20:15^2 20:16 20:17 20:18^2 20:19^2 20:20^5 20:21^2 21:1^3 21:2 21:3^4 21:4 21:5 21:6^5 21:7^3 21:8 21:9 21:10 21:11^2 21:12 21:13^4 21:14^4 21:15 21:17^2 21:18^3 21:19^3 21:20 21:21^3 21:22^2 21:23^2 21:24^2 21:26^2 22:1^3 22:2^2 22:3 22:5^2 22:6^4 22:8^3 22:9^4 22:10^2 22:11 22:12^5 22:13^2 22:14^5 22:15 22:16 22:17^2 22:19^5 23:20^3 23:1^3 23:2^8 23:3^7 23:4^7 23:5^5 23:6^4 23:7 23:8^3 23:10 23:11^2 23:12^4 23:13^3 23:14^3 23:15^5 23:16^5 23:17^2 23:18 23:19^2 23:20^3 23:21 23:24^5 23:25^3

23:27^3 23:28 23:29^2 23:30^6 23:31^3 23:32 23:33^3 23:34^5 23:35^3 23:36^3 23:37 24:1^2 24:2^5 24:4 24:5 24:6 24:7 24:8^2 24:9 24:10 24:11^2 24:12^6 24:13^3 24:14^5 24:15^5 24:16^4 24:17^2 24:18^3 24:19 24:20 25:1^4 25:2 25:3^2 25:4^3 25:5^3 25:6^2 25:7^4 25:8 25:9^4 25:10 25:11 25:12 25:13^4 25:14^5 25:15^4 25:16 25:17^5 25:18^3 25:19^4 25:20^2 25:21^2 25:22 25:23^6 25:24^5 25:26^4 25:27^3 25:28^2 25:29^2 25:30

1 CH

1:4 1:5^6 1:6^3 1:7^3 1:8^2 1:9^7 1:10 1:11^4 1:12^3 1:13^2 1:14^2 1:15^3 1:16^3 1:17^8 1:18^2 1:19^2 1:20^4 1:21^2 1:22^3 1:23^3 1:28 1:29^2 1:30^2 1:31

1:32^7 1:33^5 1:34^2 1:35^3 1:36^4 1:37 1:38^7 1:39^3 1:40^5 1:41^4 1:42^3 1:43^2 1:44 1:45 1:46^2 1:47 1:48 1:49 1:50^3 1:51 2:1^2 2:2^2 2:3^4 2:4^2 2:5 2:6^5 2:7 2:8 2:9^2 2:10^2 2:11^2 2:12^2 2:13^3 2:16^4 2:17^2 2:18^4 2:19 2:20^2 2:21^2 2:22^2 2:23^3 2:24 2:25^5 2:27^3 2:28^4 2:29^3 2:30^2 2:31^3 2:32^3 2:34 2:35^2 2:36^2 2:37^2 2:38^2 2:39^2 2:40^2 2:41^2 2:42 2:43^4 2:44^2 2:45^2 2:46^4 2:47^4 2:48 2:49^2 2:52^2 2:53^5 2:54^2 2:55^2 3:4^4 3:5^4 3:6^2 3:7^3 3:8^3 3:9 3:10 3:15 3:16 3:17 3:18^3 3:19^5 3:20^4 3:21^2 3:22^4 3:23^3 3:24^7 4:1^3

4:2^3 4:3^4 4:4^2 4:5^2 4:6^4 4:7^3 4:8^3 4:9^2 4:10^5 4:11 4:12^3 4:13^3 4:14^2 4:15^3 4:16^3 4:17^7 4:18^4 4:19^2 4:20^5 4:21^2 4:22^6 4:23^2 4:24^2 4:26 4:27^2 4:28^3 4:29^3 4:30^3 4:31^4 4:32^4 4:33^2 4:34^3 4:35^2 4:36^7 4:37 4:38 4:39 4:40^5 4:41^5 4:42^4 4:43^2 5:1 5:2 5:3^2 5:7^2 5:8^2 5:9 5:10^2 5:11 5:12^3 5:13^7 5:16^3 5:17 5:18^7 5:19^3 5:20^4 5:21^5 5:22 5:23^3 5:24^8 5:25^2 5:26^9 6:1 6:2^3 6:3^5 6:5^2 6:6^2 6:7 6:8^2 6:9^2 6:10 6:11^2 6:12^2 6:13^2 6:14^2 6:15^2 6:16 6:17^2 6:18^4 6:19^2 6:23^2 6:24 6:25^2 6:26 6:28^2 6:31 6:32^2

6:33 6:44 6:49^4 6:50 6:55^2 6:56 6:57^4 6:58 6:59^2 6:60^3 6:61 6:62^4 6:63^2 6:64 6:65^3 6:66 6:67 6:68^2 6:69^2 6:70^2 6:71 6:72 6:73^2 6:74^2 6:75^2 6:76^3 6:78^2 6:79 6:80^2 6:81^2 7:1^2 7:2^8 7:3^4 7:4^3 7:5^2 7:6^2 7:7^9 7:8^9 7:9^2 7:10^7 7:11^2 7:12^2 7:13^3 7:15^4 7:16^5 7:17 7:18^3 7:19^4 7:20^5 7:21^4 7:22^2 7:23^3 7:24^3 7:25^3 7:28^7 7:29^5 7:30^4 7:31^2 7:32^4 7:33^3 7:34^3 7:35^4 7:36^4 7:37^5 7:38^3 7:39^3 7:40^4 8:1 8:2 8:3^3 8:4^3 8:5^3 8:6^2 8:7^5 8:8^2 8:9^4 8:10^3 8:11^2 8:12^3 8:13 8:14 8:15^3 8:16^3 8:17^4 8:18^2 8:19^3 8:20^3

8:21^3 8:22^3 8:23^3 8:24^3 8:25^2 8:26^3 8:27^3 8:29 8:30^5 8:31^3 8:32^2 8:33^6 8:34^2 8:35^4 8:36^5 8:37 8:38^5 8:39^2 8:40^4 9:1^2 9:2 9:3^4 9:5^2 9:6^3 9:7 9:8^3 9:9^3 9:10^3 9:11 9:12^2 9:13^3 9:14 9:15^3 9:16^2 9:17^5 9:19^3 9:20^2 9:21 9:22^2 9:23 9:24 9:25 9:26^2 9:27^2 9:28^2 9:29^5 9:30 9:31 9:32 9:33^2 9:35 9:36^5 9:37^4 9:38^2 9:39^6 9:40^2 9:41^4 9:42^5 9:43^2 9:44^5 10:1^2 10:2^5 10:3^3 10:4^3 10:5^2 10:6^2 10:7^6 10:8^2 10:9^4 10:10^2 10:11 10:12^5 10:13 10:14^2 11:1 11:2^4 11:3^2 11:4^2 11:5 11:6^3 11:7 11:8^2 11:9 11:10 11:11 11:12 11:13^2

11:14^4 11:15 11:16^2 11:17^2 11:18^4 11:19 11:20^2 11:22^2 11:23^5 11:24 11:25 11:42 11:43 11:44 11:45 11:46^3 11:47^2 12:1 12:2^3 12:3^4 12:4^6 12:5^4 12:6^4 12:7^2 12:8^4 12:14 12:15^2 12:16^2 12:17^4 12:18^4 12:19 12:20^6 12:21^2 12:22^2 12:24^2 12:25 12:26 12:27^3 12:28^3 12:29 12:30^2 12:31^2 12:32^2 12:34^4 12:35^3 12:36 12:37^4 12:38 12:39^2 12:40^{11} 13:1^3 13:2^5 13:3 13:4 13:6^2 13:7^3 13:8^8 13:9 13:10^3 13:11 13:12 13:14^3 14:1^2 14:2 14:3^3 14:4^2 14:5^3 14:6^2 14:7^3 14:8^3 14:9^2 14:10^3 14:11 14:12^2 14:14^2 14:15 14:16 14:17^2 15:1^3 15:2 15:3 15:4^2 15:5^2 15:6^2 15:7^2 15:8 15:9

15:10^2 15:11^6 15:12^2 15:14 15:15 15:16^3 15:17^2 15:18^{12} 15:19 15:20^8 15:21^6 15:22 15:23^2 15:24^9 15:25^2 15:26^2 15:27^4 15:28^4 15:29^3 16:1^2 16:2^2 16:3^4 16:4^4 16:5^9 16:6 16:7 16:11 16:12 16:16 16:17^2 16:19 16:20^2 16:22 16:25 16:27^2 16:28 16:29^2 16:31^2 16:32^2 16:35^4 16:36^3 16:37 16:38^3 16:39^2 16:40^2 16:41^3 16:42^5 16:43^2 17:3 17:4 17:5 17:8^3 17:9^3 17:10 17:11^2 17:13^2 17:14^2 17:15 17:16^4 17:17^2 17:19 17:21^2 17:22 17:23^2 17:24 17:26^2 17:27 18:1^3 18:2^3 18:3 18:4^3 18:5^2 18:6^2 18:7^2 18:8^3 18:10^5 18:11^5 18:13^2 18:14^2 18:15^2 18:16^3 18:17^3 19:1 19:2^2 19:3^2 19:4^3 19:5^4

19:6^5 19:7^6 19:8^2 19:9^3 19:10^2 19:11^2 19:12 19:13^3 19:14^2 19:15^2 19:16^3 19:17^5 19:18^3 19:19^2 20:1^6 20:2^5 20:3^6 20:4^2 20:5^2 20:6^5 20:8^2 21:1^2 21:2^3 21:3 21:4^2 21:5^5 21:6 21:7 21:8 21:9 21:10 21:11 21:12 21:13 21:14 21:15^5 21:16^4 21:17^3 21:18 21:19 21:20^3 21:21^4 21:23^4 21:24 21:26^5 21:27^2 21:29 22:1 22:2^2 22:3^2 22:4^2 22:5^2 22:6 22:7 22:8 22:9^3 22:10^3 22:11^2 22:12^2 22:13^2 22:14^5 22:15^3 22:16^4 22:18^2 22:19^3 23:1 23:2^2 23:3^3 23:4^3 23:5 23:6^2 23:7 23:8^2 23:9^2 23:10^3 23:11^3 23:12 23:13^4 23:15 23:17^2 23:19 23:20 23:21^2 23:22^3 23:23^2 23:24 23:26

23:27 23:28^3 23:29^6 23:30^3 23:31^2 23:32^3 24:1^2 24:2^3 24:3^2 24:4^3 24:5^2 24:6^7 24:17^2 24:18^2 24:20 24:23 24:26 24:27^3 24:30^2 24:31^4 25:1^5 25:2^3 25:3^4 25:4^3 25:5^2 25:6^2 25:7 25:8 25:9 25:10 25:11 25:12 25:13 25:14 25:15 25:16 25:17 25:18 25:19 25:20 25:21 25:22 25:23 25:24 25:25 25:26 25:27 25:28^2 25:29^2 25:30^2 25:31^2 26:2 26:4^2 26:7^3 26:8^3 26:9^2 26:11 26:13 26:14^2 26:15 26:16 26:17^2 26:18 26:19 26:20^2 26:22 26:23^2 26:24 26:25^5 26:26^4 26:28^6 26:29^2 26:30^4 26:31 26:32^4 27:1^5 27:2^2 27:4^3 27:5^2 27:6^2 27:7^3 27:8^2 27:9^2 27:10^2 27:11^2 27:12^2 27:13^2

27:14^2 27:15^2 27:23 27:25^4 27:26^5 27:27 27:28^3 27:29^2 27:30 27:31 27:32^2 27:33^2 27:34^3 28:1^9 28:2^4 28:3 28:4^2 28:5 28:6^3 28:7 28:8^3 28:9^4 28:10 28:11^5 28:12^3 28:13^3 28:15^4 28:16^2 28:17^4 28:18^3 28:20^3 28:21^4 29:1^2 29:2^7 29:3^2 29:4 29:5^3 29:6^3 29:7^5 29:8 29:9 29:10^2 29:11^6 29:12^6 29:13 29:14^2 29:15^2 29:16 29:17^2 29:18^2 29:19^4 29:20^5 29:21^4 29:22^5 29:23 29:24^3 29:25^2 29:27^3 29:28^3 29:29^3 29:30^4

2 CH

1:1^3 1:2^3 1:3 1:5^2 1:6^2 1:7 1:8^2 1:10^2 1:11^3 1:12^4 1:13 1:14^6 1:15^3 1:16^2 1:17^6 2:1^2 2:2^5 2:3^2 2:4^6 2:5 2:6 2:7^8

2:8^2 2:10^4 2:12^3 2:13 2:14^7 2:15^2 2:16^3 2:17^5 2:18^5 3:2 3:3 3:4^4 3:5^3 3:6^2 3:7^3 3:8^3 3:9^2 3:10^2 3:11^2 3:12^2 3:13^2 3:14^5 3:15^2 3:16^4 3:17^4 4:1^2 4:2^2 4:3 4:4^5 4:5^4 4:6^2 4:7^3 4:8^3 4:9^3 4:10 4:11^4 4:12^3 4:13 4:14 4:15 4:16^3 4:17 4:19^2 4:21^4 4:22^6 5:1^4 5:2 5:4^2 5:5^4 5:6^2 5:7 5:8^2 5:9^2 5:11^2 5:12^5 5:13^6 6:2 6:3^3 6:4 6:6 6:10^2 6:11 6:12^2 6:13^6 6:14^2 6:15^2 6:18 6:19^2 6:20 6:21^2 6:22^2 6:23^3 6:24^5 6:25^3 6:26^3 6:27^3 6:29^2 6:30^2 6:32^3 6:33^3 6:34^2 6:35^2 6:36^3 6:37^3 6:38^4 6:39^3 6:40

6:41^2 7:1^3 7:2^3 7:3^4 7:4 7:5^5 7:6^3 7:7^3 7:8 7:9^2 7:10^5 7:11^3 7:12^3 7:14^5 7:15 7:16^3 7:17^4 7:19^5 7:20^3 7:21^2 7:22^4 8:1^2 8:2 8:3^2 8:4^2 8:5^2 8:6^7 8:7^4 8:9^3 8:10^2 8:11 8:13^4 8:14^3 8:15^2 8:16 8:17 8:18^6 9:1^5 9:2^2 9:3^2 9:4^6 9:5^2 9:6^2 9:7^2 9:8 9:9^4 9:10^3 9:11^5 9:12^2 9:13^2 9:14^4 9:15 9:16^2 9:17 9:18^3 9:19^2 9:20^2 9:21^3 9:22^2 9:23 9:24^5 9:25^4 9:26^2 9:27^2 9:28^2 9:29^3 9:30 9:31^3 10:1 10:2 10:3^4 10:4^2 10:5^2 10:6 10:7^3 10:8 10:9 10:10 10:12 10:13^2 10:14 10:16^3 10:18 10:19 11:1^3 11:3^2 11:4^2

11:5^2 11:6^2 11:7^3 11:8^3 11:9^3 11:10^4 11:11^5 11:12^4 11:13^2 11:14^4 11:15^3 11:16 11:17^2 11:18^2 11:19^2 11:20^4 11:21^6 11:22 11:23^5 12:1^3 12:2 12:3^3 12:4^2 12:5^3 12:6^2 12:7^2 12:8 12:9^2 12:10 12:11^3 12:12^2 12:13^4 12:14 12:15^4 12:16^3 13:2^2 13:3 13:4^3 13:5 13:6 13:7^4 13:8^3 13:9^3 13:10^3 13:11^4 13:12^2 13:13 13:14^4 13:15^3 13:16^2 13:17^2 13:18 13:19^4 13:20^2 13:21^4 13:22^3 14:1^2 14:2^2 14:3^2 14:4^3 14:5^2 14:6^2 14:7^5 14:8^5 14:9^3 14:10 14:11^3 14:12^2 14:13^5 14:14^2 14:15^3 15:1 15:2^5 15:3^2 15:4 15:5 15:6^2 15:7 15:8^6 15:9^5 15:11^2 15:12^2 15:14^4 15:15^4 15:16^4 15:18^4 15:19^2

16:1[2] 16:2[3] 16:3[3] 16:4[6] 16:5[2] 16:6[4] 16:7[2] 16:8[2] 16:9 16:10[2] 16:11[3] 16:12[2] 16:13[3] 16:14[4] 17:1[2] 17:2[3] 17:3[2] 17:4[2] 17:5[3] 17:6[2] 17:7[4] 17:8[11] 17:9[4] 17:10 17:11[5] 17:12[3] 17:13[2] 17:14[2] 17:15[3] 17:16[2] 17:17[3] 17:18[3] 18:1[2] 18:2[5] 18:3[4] 18:4 18:5[2] 18:7[2] 18:8[2] 18:9[4] 18:10[2] 18:11[2] 18:12[2] 18:13 18:14[4] 18:15 18:16 18:17 18:18[2] 18:19[4] 18:20[3] 18:21[5] 18:22 18:23[2] 18:24 18:25[2] 18:26[3] 18:27[2] 18:28 18:29[3] 18:31[3] 18:33[2] 18:34[2] 19:1 19:2[3] 19:3 19:4[3] 19:5 19:6 19:7 19:8[3] 19:9[2] 19:10[7] 19:11[3] 20:1[2] 20:2 20:3[3] 20:4 20:5[2] 20:6[4] 20:7 20:8[2] 20:9[3] 20:10[4] 20:13[2] 20:15[3] 20:16

20:17[2] 20:18[3] 20:19[2] 20:20[5] 20:21[3] 20:22[4] 20:23[3] 20:24[3] 20:25[4] 20:26 20:27[2] 20:28[3] 20:29 20:31[5] 20:32[2] 20:34 20:35 20:36[2] 20:37 21:1[2] 21:2[6] 21:3[3] 21:4[2] 21:5[2] 21:6[2] 21:7[2] 21:8 21:9[4] 21:11[2] 21:12 21:13[3] 21:14[3] 21:15 21:16 21:17[5] 21:18 21:19[2] 21:20[3] 22:1 22:2[2] 22:5[2] 22:6[2] 22:7 22:8[3] 22:9[4] 22:10 22:11[3] 22:12[2] 23:1[6] 23:2[4] 23:3[2] 23:4 23:5[3] 23:6 23:7[3] 23:8[2] 23:9[2] 23:10[2] 23:11[6] 23:12 23:13[8] 23:14[2] 23:15 23:16[3] 23:17[4] 23:18 23:19 23:20[6] 23:21[2] 24:1 24:2 24:3[3] 24:4 24:5[5] 24:6[4] 24:7 24:8[2] 24:9[2] 24:10[4] 24:11[6] 24:12[6] 24:13[3] 24:14[7] 24:15[2] 24:16[2] 24:17 24:18[5]

24:19 24:20[2] 24:21[2] 24:22[2] 24:23[5] 24:24 24:25[4] 24:26[2] 24:27[3] 25:1[4] 25:2 25:5[7] 25:8 25:9[2] 25:10 25:11[4] 25:12[8] 25:13[2] 25:14[3] 25:15 25:16[3] 25:17 25:18[3] 25:19[2] 25:21[2] 25:22[2] 25:23[3] 25:24[5] 25:25 25:26[2] 25:27[2] 25:28 26:1 26:2 26:3[2] 26:4 26:5[2] 26:6[7] 26:7[3] 26:8[2] 26:9[3] 26:10[11] 26:11 26:12 26:13[3] 26:14[6] 26:15[4] 26:16 26:17[2] 26:18[2] 26:19[2] 26:20[4] 26:21[3] 26:22 26:23[2] 27:1[2] 27:2[2] 27:3 27:4[2] 27:5[5] 27:7[3] 27:8[2] 27:9[3] 28:1 28:2 28:3 28:4[3] 28:5[4] 28:6 28:7[3] 28:8[4] 28:9[3] 28:10[3] 28:11 28:12[3] 28:13[3] 28:14[2] 28:15[10] 28:17[2] 28:18[8] 28:19 28:20[2] 28:21[3] 28:22 28:23[2] 28:24[4] 28:25[2]

28:26[3] 28:27[3] 29:1[4] 29:2 29:3 29:4[3] 29:5[3] 29:6[4] 29:7[2] 29:8[3] 29:9[3] 29:11[2] 29:12[4] 29:13[4] 29:14[4] 29:15[3] 29:16[3] 29:17[2] 29:18[3] 29:19[2] 29:20[2] 29:21[7] 29:22[3] 29:23[3] 29:24[3] 29:25[4] 29:26[2] 29:27[3] 29:28[4] 29:29[3] 29:30[5] 29:31[6] 29:32[3] 29:33[2] 29:34 29:35[2] 29:36[2] 30:1[4] 30:2[2] 30:4[2] 30:6[5] 30:7[2] 30:8 30:9[3] 30:10[2] 30:11[3] 30:12 30:13 30:14[4] 30:15[4] 30:16 30:18[2] 30:20[2] 30:21[3] 30:22[3] 30:23[2] 30:24[4] 30:25[5] 30:27[3] 31:1[6] 31:2[6] 31:3[4] 31:4 31:5[5] 31:6[5] 31:7 31:8[4] 31:9 31:10[4] 31:11 31:12[4] 31:13[12] 31:14[2] 31:15[5] 31:16 31:17[2] 31:18[3] 31:19 31:20[4] 31:21[4] 32:1[4] 32:2[2] 32:3[2] 32:4[2] 32:5[6] 32:6[3] 32:7

32:8[2] 32:9[2] 32:11 32:12[4] 32:13 32:16[2] 32:17 32:18 32:19 32:20[3] 32:21[4] 32:22[3] 32:23[2] 32:24[3] 32:25[2] 32:26 32:27[8] 32:28[4] 32:29[2] 32:30[2] 32:32[3] 32:33[5] 33:1[2] 33:3[4] 33:5 33:6[5] 33:7[3] 33:8[2] 33:9[2] 33:10[2] 33:11[2] 33:12[2] 33:13[4] 33:14[3] 33:15[5] 33:16[4] 33:18[2] 33:19[6] 33:20[2] 33:21[2] 33:22 33:23[2] 33:24[2] 33:25 34:1[2] 34:2[3] 34:3[5] 34:4[7] 34:5[3] 34:6[3] 34:7[4] 34:8[3] 34:9[6] 34:10[3] 34:11[3] 34:12[6] 34:13[4] 34:14 34:15[3] 34:16[2] 34:17[3] 34:18 34:19 34:20[5] 34:21[2] 34:22[3] 34:23 34:24 34:25[2] 34:26 34:27[5] 34:28[2] 34:29[2] 34:30[8] 34:31[6] 34:32[3] 34:33[3] 35:1 35:2[2] 35:3[2] 35:4[2] 35:5[2] 35:6[2] 35:7[3] 35:8[6] 35:9[6] 35:10[2]

35:11[3] 35:12[2] 35:13[4] 35:14[4] 35:15[5] 35:16 35:17[2] 35:18[6] 35:20 35:22 35:23[2] 35:24[6] 35:25[5] 35:26 35:27[3] 36:1 36:2[2] 36:3[3] 36:4[5] 36:5[3] 36:6 36:7 36:8[4] 36:9[3] 36:10[4] 36:11[2] 36:12[2] 36:13[2] 36:14[2] 36:15[3] 36:16[2] 36:17 36:18[5] 36:19[4] 36:20[2] 36:21 36:22 36:23[3]

EZR

1:1 1:2 1:3[2] 1:4[4] 1:5[3] 1:6[3] 1:7 1:8 1:9[2] 1:10[2] 1:11[2] 2:1[2] 2:3 2:4 2:5 2:6[2] 2:7 2:8 2:9 2:10 2:11 2:12 2:13 2:14 2:15 2:16 2:17 2:18 2:19 2:20 2:21 2:22 2:23 2:24 2:25[3] 2:26[2] 2:27 2:28[2] 2:29 2:30 2:31 2:32 2:33[2] 2:34 2:35[2]

2:36 2:37 2:38 2:39 2:40[2] 2:41 2:42 2:58[2] 2:59[3] 2:60 2:61[2] 2:63[2] 2:64[2] 2:65[4] 2:66[2] 2:67[2] 2:68 2:69[3] 2:70[6] 3:1[2] 3:2[4] 3:3[3] 3:4 3:5[3] 3:7[5] 3:8[5] 3:9[3] 3:10[2] 3:11[3] 3:12[3] 3:13 4:1 4:2[3] 4:3[2] 4:4 4:5 4:6[2] 4:7[4] 4:8 4:9[3] 4:10[5] 4:11 4:12[3] 4:13[3] 4:14[2] 4:15[4] 4:16 4:17[4] 4:19[5] 4:20[2] 4:21 4:23[4] 5:1[2] 5:2[3] 5:3[4] 5:5 5:6[2] 5:8[3] 5:9[2] 5:11[4] 5:12 5:14[4] 5:15[2] 5:16[3] 5:17 6:1 6:2[2] 6:3[2] 6:4[2] 6:5[5] 6:6 6:7 6:9[4] 6:10[2] 6:11[2] 6:12[2] 6:13 6:14[6] 6:15 6:16[2] 6:17[2] 6:18[2] 6:19 6:20[4] 6:21[2] 6:22[2] 7:6[2]

7:7[6] 7:8 7:9 7:10[3] 7:11 7:12 7:13[2] 7:14[2] 7:15[2] 7:16[3] 7:17[2] 7:18[3] 7:20 7:21 7:22[4] 7:23 7:24 7:25[3] 7:26[2] 7:28[5] 8:1 8:3[2] 8:4 8:5 8:6 8:7[2] 8:8[2] 8:9[2] 8:10[3] 8:11[3] 8:12[3] 8:13[3] 8:14[2] 8:15[5] 8:16[7] 8:17[3] 8:18[3] 8:19[3] 8:20[2] 8:21[2] 8:22[2] 8:23[2] 8:24 8:25[6] 8:26[3] 8:27 8:28[3] 8:29[3] 8:30[3] 8:31[3] 8:32[2] 8:33[5] 8:34[2] 8:35[2] 8:36[4] 9:1[3] 9:2[2] 9:3[5] 9:4 9:5[4] 9:6[3] 9:7[4] 9:8[3] 9:9[3] 9:10 9:12[2] 9:13[3] 9:14 10:1[4] 10:2[3] 10:3[3] 10:4 10:5[3] 10:6[2] 10:7[2] 10:8[3] 10:9[3] 10:10[3] 10:11[3] 10:12 10:13[2] 10:14[3] 10:15[3] 10:16[4] 10:17 10:18[5] 10:19[2]

10:20[2] 10:21[5] 10:22[2] 10:23[3] 10:24[3] 10:25[6] 10:26[5] 10:27[4] 10:28 10:29[4] 10:30[4] 10:31 10:32 10:33 10:34[2] 10:37 10:38[2] 10:39[3] 10:41 10:42 10:43 10:44

NE

1:1 1:2[2] 1:3[3] 1:4[5] 1:5[4] 1:6[4] 1:7 1:9[2] 1:10[2] 1:11[3] 2:1[3] 2:3[2] 2:5[2] 2:6[2] 2:8[4] 2:9[2] 2:10 2:11 2:12[2] 2:13[4] 2:14 2:15[4] 2:16 2:17[2] 2:18[2] 2:19[4] 2:20[2] 3:1[2] 3:2[2] 3:3[2] 3:4[3] 3:5 3:6[4] 3:7[3] 3:8 3:9 3:10[2] 3:11[2] 3:12[2] 3:13[4] 3:14[2] 3:15[5] 3:16[2] 3:19 3:22 3:23 3:25 3:26 3:30 3:31[2] 3:32[2] 4:1[2] 4:2[3] 4:3 4:4[2] 4:5[2] 4:6 4:7[5] 4:8[3] 4:9[2] 4:10[2]

4:11[3] 4:12 4:13[2] 4:14[9] 4:15[2] 4:16[2] 4:17[2] 4:18[2] 4:19[5] 4:21 4:22 5:1[2] 5:2[2] 5:3 5:4[2] 5:5[4] 5:6[2] 5:7[4] 5:8[3] 5:10[3] 5:11[3] 5:12[2] 5:13[6] 5:14[2] 5:15[2] 5:16 5:17[2] 5:18[2] 6:1[4] 6:2 6:3[2] 6:4 6:6[2] 6:7[3] 6:10[2] 6:11[2] 6:12[2] 6:13[3] 6:14[3] 6:15[2] 6:16[2] 6:17 6:18 6:19[2] 7:1[4] 7:2[2] 7:3[5] 7:4[2] 7:5[5] 7:6[2] 7:8 7:9 7:10 7:11[3] 7:12 7:13 7:14 7:15 7:16 7:17 7:18 7:19 7:20 7:21 7:22 7:23 7:24 7:25 7:26[2] 7:27 7:28 7:29[2] 7:30[2] 7:31[2] 7:32[2] 7:33 7:34 7:35 7:36 7:37[2] 7:38 7:39 7:40 7:41 7:42 7:43[2] 7:44

7:45 7:60[2] 7:61[2] 7:62 7:63[2] 7:65[2] 7:66[2] 7:67[5] 7:68[2] 7:69[2] 7:70[2] 7:71[3] 7:72[4] 7:73[7] 8:1[2] 8:2[3] 8:3[4] 8:4[13] 8:5[2] 8:6[4] 8:7[4] 8:8[2] 8:9[3] 8:10[2] 8:12[4] 8:13[2] 8:14 8:15[6] 8:16[6] 8:17[3] 8:18[2] 9:1[3] 9:2[4] 9:3[4] 9:4[3] 9:5[6] 9:6[4] 9:7[2] 9:8[6] 9:9[2] 9:10[4] 9:11[2] 9:12 9:13[4] 9:14[3] 9:15[3] 9:16[3] 9:17[5] 9:18[2] 9:19 9:20[2] 9:21 9:22[4] 9:23 9:24[4] 9:25[8] 9:26[4] 9:27[2] 9:28[2] 9:29[5] 9:30 9:31 9:32[6] 9:34 9:35[3] 9:36[2] 9:37[3] 9:38[4] 10:1 10:9 10:10 10:26 10:28[4] 10:29[6] 10:30 10:31[3] 10:33[5] 10:34[2] 10:35[2] 10:36[3] 10:37[5] 10:38[2] 10:39[6] 11:1[2] 11:2 11:3[3] 11:4[2]

11:5 11:6 11:7 11:8[2] 11:9[2] 11:12[3] 11:13[3] 11:14[3] 11:16[2] 11:17[3] 11:18 11:19[2] 11:20[2] 11:21[2] 11:24 11:25[6] 11:26[3] 11:27[3] 11:28[3] 11:29[3] 11:30[4] 11:31[3] 11:32 11:35 11:36[2] 12:1[2] 12:6 12:7 12:8[2] 12:9 12:10[2] 12:11[2] 12:12 12:19 12:22[2] 12:24[3] 12:25 12:26[2] 12:27[3] 12:28[2] 12:29[2] 12:30[5] 12:31 12:32[2] 12:33[2] 12:34[3] 12:35 12:36[4] 12:37 12:38[3] 12:39[6] 12:40[2] 12:41[2] 12:42[9] 12:43[2] 12:44[4] 12:45[4] 12:46[3] 12:47[5] 13:1[2] 13:2 13:4 13:5[7] 13:6[2] 13:7[2] 13:8 13:9[3] 13:10[2] 13:11[3] 13:12[2] 13:13[5] 13:14[2] 13:15[5] 13:16[3] 13:17[2] 13:18[2] 13:19[3] 13:20 13:21 13:22[4] 13:23 13:24[2] 13:25[5] 13:26 13:28 13:29[2]

13:30[2] 13:31[3]

ES

1:1[2] 1:3[3] 1:4[2] 1:5[2] 1:6[7] 1:7[2] 1:8 1:10[2] 1:11 1:12 1:13 1:14[4] 1:16[3] 1:18[2] 1:19[3] 1:20[2] 1:21[3] 1:22[2] 2:1[2] 2:3[2] 2:4[3] 2:7[4] 2:8[2] 2:9[6] 2:11[2] 2:12[2] 2:14[2] 2:15 2:17[4] 2:18[3] 2:19 2:21[2] 2:22[2] 2:23[2] 3:1[2] 3:2[2] 3:4 3:5 3:6 3:7 3:8[3] 3:9 3:10[2] 3:11 3:12[5] 3:13[5] 3:15[3] 4:1[4] 4:2 4:3[7] 4:4[4] 4:5[2] 4:7[2] 4:8[2] 4:9[2] 4:10 4:11 4:12 4:14[3] 4:16[5] 4:17 5:1[2] 5:2[3] 5:3 5:4[2] 5:5 5:6[3] 5:7[2] 5:8[4] 5:9 5:10 5:11[5] 5:12 5:14[4] 6:1[2] 6:2[2] 6:3[2] 6:4 6:5[2]

6:6 6:7 6:8[2] 6:9[4] 6:10[3] 6:11[4] 6:12[2] 6:13[3] 6:14[2] 7:1 7:2[4] 7:3[3] 7:4[3] 7:5[2] 7:6[3] 7:7[2] 7:8 7:9 8:1 8:2[3] 8:3[4] 8:4 8:5[4] 8:7[2] 8:8[2] 8:9[9] 8:10[5] 8:11[5] 8:13 8:14[3] 8:15[7] 8:16[3] 8:17[6] 9:1 9:2 9:3[4] 9:4[2] 9:5[2] 9:6[2] 9:7[3] 9:8[3] 9:9[4] 9:12[5] 9:13 9:14[3] 9:15 9:16[4] 9:17[3] 9:18[4] 9:19[3] 9:20[3] 9:21 9:22[5] 9:23[2] 9:24[2] 9:25[2] 9:26[2] 9:27[4] 9:28[4] 9:29 9:30[3] 9:31[4] 9:32[2] 10:1[2] 10:2[4] 10:3[3]

JOB

1:1[4] 1:2[2] 1:3[4] 1:4[5] 1:5[5] 1:6 1:7[5] 1:8[3] 1:9 1:10[3] 1:11[2] 1:12 1:13[3] 1:14[3] 1:15[3] 1:16[5] 1:17[5]

1:18[3] 1:19[5] 1:20[4] 1:21[3] 2:1 2:2[6] 2:3[4] 2:4[2] 2:5[3] 2:6 2:7 2:8[2] 2:9 2:10 2:11[3] 2:12[5] 2:13[2] 3:1 3:2[2] 3:3 3:5 3:13 3:14 3:17 3:19[2] 3:20 3:21 3:22 3:23 3:24 3:25 4:1 4:3 4:4 4:5[2] 4:6 4:8 4:9 4:10[2] 4:11 4:12 4:14 4:16 4:18 5:1 5:2 5:4 5:5[2] 5:8[2] 5:9 5:10 5:13 5:14 5:15 5:16 5:18[2] 5:20 5:22 5:23 5:24[3] 5:25 5:27[3] 6:1 6:2 6:8 6:9 6:11 6:13 6:15 6:16 6:18 6:20 6:21 6:24[2] 6:26 6:27 7:2 7:3 7:4[3] 7:5[2] 7:6 7:8 7:9 7:14 7:15 7:17 7:18[2]

7:21[3] 8:1 8:2 8:4 8:5 8:6[2] 8:8 8:9 8:10 8:12 8:13 8:14 8:16 8:17 8:19 8:21 8:22 9:1 9:4[2] 9:5[2] 9:6 9:7[2] 9:8 9:9[2] 9:10 9:11 9:14 9:16 9:17 9:19 9:22 9:24 9:27 9:30 9:31 9:32 9:34 9:35 10:3 10:6 10:7 10:8 10:9 10:10 10:11[3] 10:12[2] 10:13 10:14 10:15 10:16 10:17[2] 10:18 10:20 10:21 10:22[2] 11:1 11:2 11:3 11:4 11:5 11:6 11:9 11:10 11:13 11:14 11:15 11:16 11:17 11:18[2] 11:19 11:20[2] 12:1[2] 12:2 12:4 12:6 12:7[3] 12:8[2] 12:10 12:11 12:12 12:13[2] 12:14[2] 12:15[2] 12:16[2] 12:17 12:18 12:19

12:20 12:21 12:22 12:23[2] 12:24 12:25[2] 13:1 13:3 13:5 13:6 13:7 13:11 13:13 13:14 13:17 13:21 13:22[2] 13:23[2] 13:24 13:25[2] 13:26 13:27 13:28 14:1 14:2[2] 14:3[2] 14:7 14:8 14:9 14:10[2] 14:11[2] 14:12 14:13 14:15 14:17 14:18[2] 14:19 14:20[2] 14:21[2] 14:22 15:1 15:2 15:4 15:5 15:6 15:8 15:9 15:10 15:12 15:13 15:14 15:16 15:17 15:18 15:19 15:20 15:22 15:24 15:25 15:27 15:28[2] 15:30 15:32 15:33 15:34 15:35[2] 16:1 16:4 16:5 16:6 16:8[2] 16:11 16:12[2] 16:13 16:15 16:16 16:18 16:19 17:2 17:6 17:7 17:8 17:9[2] 17:10 17:14 17:15 18:1

18:2 18:3 18:4 18:5 18:6 18:7 18:8 18:9 18:10 18:11 18:12 18:14 18:16 18:17 18:18 18:21 19:1 19:2 19:4 19:5 19:6 19:8 19:9 19:10[2] 19:11 19:12[2] 19:13 19:14 19:15 19:16 19:18 19:19 19:20[2] 19:22 19:24 19:25 19:26 19:27[2] 20:1 20:2 20:3 20:5 20:6 20:8 20:10 20:13 20:15 20:17 20:18[2] 20:19 20:23 20:24 20:25 20:27 20:28 20:29 21:1 21:2 21:3 21:4 21:5[2] 21:6 21:8 21:10[2] 21:11 21:12[2] 21:13 21:15 21:17 21:18 21:19 21:20 21:23 21:24 21:25[2] 21:26 21:27 21:28 21:29 21:31 21:32 21:33 22:1 22:5 22:6 22:7 22:8

22:9 22:10 22:11 22:12 22:13 22:14 22:17 22:19^2 22:21 22:22 22:24 22:25 22:26 22:27^2 22:28^2 22:29 22:30 23:1 23:4 23:5 23:8 23:11 23:13^2 23:14 23:16 24:2 24:5 24:6 24:8 24:9 24:10 24:11^2 24:12 24:14^2 24:15 24:19 24:20 24:21 24:22 24:24^2 24:25^2 25:1 25:2 25:3 25:5 25:6 26:1 26:3 26:4 26:5 26:6 26:7 26:8 26:9 26:10 26:11 26:12 27:1 27:2 27:3 27:6 27:7 27:13 27:14 27:15 27:16 27:17 27:18 27:19 27:21^2 27:22 27:23 28:1 28:2 28:3^2 28:5 28:6 28:7 28:10 28:11 28:12 28:14 28:17^2 28:20 28:21 28:22 28:23

28:24 28:25 28:26 28:27^2 28:28^2 29:1 29:3 29:6 29:8^3 29:9 29:10 29:11 29:12^2 29:13 29:14^2 29:15 29:16 29:17^2 29:18 29:19 29:20 29:21^2 29:22 29:23^2 29:24 29:25^2 30:3^2 30:4 30:6 30:9 30:10 30:11 30:12 30:15 30:16 30:17 30:19^2 30:20^2 30:22 30:23 30:26 30:27 30:28 30:29 30:30 30:31 31:2 31:3 31:4 31:7^2 31:8 31:10 31:12 31:14 31:15 31:17 31:18 31:20 31:22 31:23 31:25 31:27 31:34 31:35 31:36 31:40 32:3 32:6^4 32:7 32:8 32:12 32:16 32:20 33:1 33:3 33:4 33:8 33:16 33:17 33:18 33:19 33:20 33:21 33:22 33:24 33:26^2 33:27^3

33:28 33:31 33:33 34:1 34:2 34:5 34:8 34:10 34:11 34:14 34:15 34:17 34:18 34:20^3 34:24 34:25 34:27 34:28 34:29 34:33 34:34 34:35 34:37 35:1 35:3 35:4 35:5^2 35:8 35:11 36:1 36:2 36:3 36:5^2 36:7 36:8^2 36:9 36:10 36:11^2 36:12 36:14 36:15 36:16 36:17 36:26 36:28 36:30 36:32 37:1 37:2 37:3 37:4 37:6 37:8 37:9 37:10 37:12 37:14 37:15 37:18 37:21^2 37:23^2 38:1 38:3 38:7 38:9 38:10^3 38:11^2 38:12 38:14 38:15^2 38:19 38:20 38:23 38:27^2 38:29 38:30 38:35 38:38 38:40 39:4 39:6 39:8 39:12 39:13 39:14 39:15 39:18

39:21 39:22 39:23 39:24 39:25^2 39:26 39:27 39:28^2 39:29 39:30 40:1 40:3 40:6 40:7 40:10^3 40:11^2 40:12^2 40:13 40:16 40:21 40:23 41:18 41:19 41:21 41:22 41:27 42:1 42:2 42:4^2 42:6^2 42:7^2 42:8^4 42:9^3 42:10 42:11^6 42:12^3 42:13 42:14^3 42:15^2 42:16^3 42:17

PS

1:2^2 1:3^2 2:1 2:2^2 2:3 2:5 2:8^2 2:11 2:12 3:3 3:4 3:5 4:1 4:2 4:4^2 4:5 4:7 4:8 5:2 5:3 5:6 5:7 6:10^2 7:1 7:5^2 7:6 7:8 7:9 7:11 7:12 7:14^2 7:15^2 7:16 7:17 8:2^2 8:3 8:4 8:5^2 8:7^2 8:8^2

9:2 9:3 9:4 9:5 9:6 9:8 9:10 9:17 10:3 10:7^3 10:10 10:14 10:15 10:16 10:18 11:5 11:6^2 12:2 12:3 13:3 13:4 14:2 14:4 14:7 15:2^2 15:4 16:3 16:5 16:9 17:3 17:6 17:12 17:14^2 18 *tit.*^{2} 18:2^4 18:4 18:6^2 18:7^2 18:8 18:9^2 18:10^2 18:11 18:12 18:13^2 18:14^3 18:15 18:17 18:21 18:22 18:23 18:26 18:29 18:32 18:33 18:35^2 18:37 18:43 18:45 18:46^2 18:47 18:49 18:50^2 19:1 19:2 19:4 19:5 19:6^2 19:9 19:10 19:11 19:13 19:14^2 20:2 20:3 20:4 20:5 20:7 20:8^2 21:1 21:2 21:4^2 21:5 21:7 21:9 21:10 21:13 22:1

22:2^2 22:4 22:5^2 22:6^2 22:13 22:14 22:15^2 22:16 22:17 22:18 22:23 22:26 22:27^2 22:28 22:29^2 22:31 23:4 23:6^2 24:1^2 24:2 24:4 24:5 24:7^2 24:8 24:9 25:5 25:6 25:8 25:9 25:10^2 25:13 25:14 25:16^2 25:18^2 25:19 25:20 25:21 26:2^2 26:3 26:5 26:7 26:8 26:10 26:11 27:1 27:2^2 27:4 27:6 27:7 27:10 27:11 27:12 27:14 28:3 28:4 28:5 28:7^3 28:8 28:9^2 29:1 29:6 29:9^2 30 *title* 30:1 30:2 30:4 30:6 30:7 30:8 30:10 30:11 30:12 31:3^2 31:7 31:8 31:9 31:10^2 31:11 31:15 31:17 31:18 31:23 31:24 32:2 32:4 32:5^2 32:8

32:9 32:11^2 33:2 33:4 33:5 33:6 33:9^2 33:12 33:19 33:20 34 *title* 34:2 34:3 34:4^2 34:5^2 34:6^2 34:7 34:8 34:10 34:12 34:13 34:14^2 34:15 34:17^2 34:18 34:21 34:22 35:2^2 35:3 35:4^2 35:5 35:6^2 35:8 35:9 35:10 35:13 35:15^3 35:21 35:23^2 35:24 35:26^2 35:27 35:28^2 36:3^2 36:5 36:6 36:8 36:10 36:11 36:12 37:2 37:3^2 37:4 37:5 37:6^2 37:7 37:8 37:10^2 37:11 37:12 37:14^3 37:15 37:18 37:19 37:20 37:21^2 37:22 37:23 37:25 37:26^2 37:27^2 37:28 37:29 37:30 37:32 37:34^2 37:35 37:36 37:37 37:40^3 38:2 38:5 38:7 38:8 38:9 38:11^2 38:12^2

38:13 38:14 38:17 38:19^2 39:2 39:4 39:5 39:6 39:7 39:12^2 39:13 40:1 40:2^2 40:3^3 40:4 40:5^2 40:6^2 40:10^2 40:11 40:14^2 40:16 40:17^2 41:2^3 41:5 41:6 41:8 41:10 41:12^2 41:13^2 42:2 42:3 42:4 42:5 42:6 42:7 42:8^2 42:11^2 43:1^2 43:3^2 43:5^2 44:2^2 44:3^2 44:7 44:8 44:9^2 44:10 44:11 44:12 44:13 44:15 44:16^2 44:19 44:24^2 44:26 45:3 45:4^4 45:6 45:7 45:8^2 45:10^3 45:11 45:12 45:15 45:17 46:1 46:2 46:3 46:5 46:9 46:10 47:3 48 *title* 48:1 48:5^2 48:6 48:12 48:14 49:2^2 49:3 49:6 49:8 49:9 49:10^2 49:11 49:14^2 49:18 49:20

50:1 50:3^2 50:4 50:6 50:7^2 50:10 50:11 50:12 50:14 50:15^2 50:17 50:18 50:19 50:20 50:21^2 50:22 50:23 51:2 51:3 51:4^2 51:5 51:6 51:7^2 51:8 51:9 51:10 51:11 51:12 51:13 51:14 51:15 51:17^2 51:19 52 *tit.*^{2} 52:3 52:5^2 52:6^2 52:7 52:8 52:9 53:1 53:6 54 *title* 54:1 54:3 54:7 55:1 55:2^2 55:3 55:4 55:5^2 55:6^2 55:7 55:8 55:9^2 55:10^2 55:11 55:13 55:14 55:15^2 55:16 55:17^4 55:19 55:22 55:23 57:3^2 57:4^3 57:7 57:8 57:10 58:9 59 *title* 59:2 59:4^2 59:6 59:11 59:12^3 59:13 59:14^3 59:15^2 59:16 59:17 60 *tit.*^{2} 60:5 60:6 60:7 60:10

61:3 61:6 61:7 62:2 62:3 62:6 62:7^2 62:9 62:10 63:1 63:2 63:5^2 63:6 64:3 64:4 64:6 64:9^2 64:10^2 65 *title* 65:1 65:4 65:5 65:7 65:8 65:9 65:11 65:12 66:4 66:5 66:8 66:9 66:12 66:14 66:16^2 66:17 67:1^2 67:4^2 67:6 67:7 68:4 68:5 68:12 68:13 68:20 68:21 68:23 68:27^2 68:33 68:34 68:35 69:5 69:8 69:9 69:10 69:11 69:12 69:14^2 69:15 69:17 69:18 69:19^2 69:20^3 69:21 69:22 69:23 69:24 69:25 69:26 69:27 69:28 69:29 69:30 69:31 69:32^2 69:33 69:34^2 69:35^2 69:36 70:2^2 70:4^2 70:5^2 71:2^2 71:3 71:4 71:8 71:10 71:11

71:13^2 71:14^2 71:15 71:17 71:18^2 71:20^2 71:21 71:23 72:1 72:2 72:3 72:4 72:5 72:7 72:8 72:9 72:10^2 72:12 72:13^2 72:14^2 72:15^3 72:16 72:17 72:19^3 73:8 73:9 73:10 73:11^2 73:13 73:14 73:21 73:22 73:24 73:25 73:26^2 74:6 74:14 74:15 74:16 74:17 74:18 74:21 75:3 75:4 75:7 75:8^3 76:2 76:3^2 76:4 76:5 76:6 76:7 76:8 76:11 77:1 77:2 77:3^2 77:6 77:7 77:10 77:12 77:15 77:18 77:19^2 77:20 78:3^2 78:4^2 78:5 78:6 78:7 78:8^3 78:9 78:10 78:11^2 78:13^2 78:14 78:15 78:16 78:17 78:18 78:20 78:21^2 78:22 78:23 78:24^2 78:26 78:27

78:28 78:29 78:31^2 78:32 78:33 78:34^2 78:35^2 78:36 78:38^2 78:39 78:40 78:41^2 78:43 78:44^2 78:45 78:46 78:47 78:48 78:49^2 78:51 78:52 78:53 78:54 78:55^2 78:56^2 78:57 78:58 78:59 78:61^2 78:62 78:63 78:64 78:65 78:66 78:67 78:69 78:70 78:71 78:72 79:3 79:6 79:7 79:9^2 79:12 79:13 80:2^4 80:3^2 80:5 80:6 80:7^2 80:8 80:9^2 80:10 80:11 80:13 80:14^2 80:15^2 80:18 80:19 81:2 81:4 81:7 81:8 81:10 81:11 81:12 81:13 81:14 81:16 82:2 82:3^2 82:4 82:6 82:7 83:1 83:2 83:3 83:4 83:6^2 83:7^2 83:11^2 83:14 83:15 83:17^2 84:2 84:3^2 84:9

84:11^2 85:4 85:7 85:8 85:10^2 85:11 85:12 85:13 86:1 86:5^2 86:6 86:9^2 86:10 86:12 86:13 86:14^2 86:15^3 86:16^2 86:17^2 87:4^2 87:5^3 88:1 88:3 88:5 88:7 88:8 88:10 88:12 88:13 88:15 88:18^2 89:4 89:5 89:7 89:11 89:12^2 89:13 89:14^2 89:16 89:17 89:18 89:19 89:23^2 89:24^2 89:25 89:26 89:28 89:29 89:30 89:31 89:32 89:36 89:37 89:38 89:43 89:44 89:48 89:52 90:2 90:3 90:4 90:6^2 90:7 90:10^4 90:13 90:14 90:15 90:16 90:17^2 91:2 91:3 91:4^2 91:7 91:8 91:13^2 91:15^2 91:16 92:1 92:2 92:3 92:5 92:7 92:11 92:14 92:15 94:4^2 94:5

94:6^2 94:8 94:12 94:15 94:21 94:22 94:23^2 95:2 95:3 95:5 95:6 95:7^2 95:8^2 95:9 95:10^2 96:4 96:6^2 96:7 96:8 96:11^2 96:12 96:13 97:2^2 97:3 97:4 97:6 97:8^2 97:11 97:12 98:1 98:3 98:4^2 98:5 98:6 98:7^2 98:9 99:2 99:3 99:4 99:5 99:6^3 99:7 99:9 100:3^2 100:4^2 100:5 101:1 101:2^2 101:5 102:*title* 102:1 102:3 102:4 102:7 102:8 102:9 102:10^2 102:11 102:12 102:13 102:14 102:15 102:17 102:18 102:21 102:22 102:25 102:26 102:27 102:28 103:1 103:2 103:4 103:6 103:8^2 103:16^2 103:17 103:18 103:19 104:1 104:14 104:15^3 104:18 104:20 104:21 104:22 104:23

104:25^4 104:29 104:30 104:32^2 104:35 105:4 105:5 105:9 105:10^2 105:13 105:15 105:20^2 105:21 105:22 105:23 105:24^2 105:26 105:27 105:28^2 105:29 105:31^2 105:32 105:33^2 105:34^3 105:35^2 105:37 105:39 105:40^2 105:41 105:42 105:43^2 105:44^2 105:45 106:3 106:9 106:10^2 106:11 106:14 106:15 106:16 106:17^2 106:18 106:19 106:22 106:25 106:27 106:28 106:29 106:30^2 106:31 106:35 106:36 106:37 106:38^3 106:39 106:41^2 106:42 106:43 106:45^2 106:47^2 106:48 107:3^3 107:5 107:6 107:7 107:8 107:9 107:10^2 107:11 107:12 107:13 107:14^2 107:15 107:16 107:17 107:18 107:19 107:20^2 107:21 107:22^2 107:24 107:25 107:27^3 107:28 107:31 107:32 107:33

107:35 107:36 107:37^2 107:38 107:39^2 107:40 107:41 107:42^2 107:43 108:1 108:2 108:3 108:4 108:5 108:6 108:7 108:11 109:2 109:3 109:5^2 109:6 109:7 109:8 109:9 109:10 109:11 109:13 109:14 109:16 109:18 109:19 109:20 109:22^2 109:23 109:24 109:29 110:4 111:1 111:3^2 111:4 111:7 111:8^3 111:9 112:3^2 112:4^2 112:5 112:10^2 113:2 113:4 113:6 113:7 113:9 114:2 114:3 114:4 114:6 115:1 115:4 115:9 115:10 115:11 115:13 115:14^2 115:15 115:18 116:1 116:3^2 116:5 116:6 116:8 116:13 116:16 116:17 117:2 118:5 118:14^2 118:15 118:17 118:19 118:21 118:24 118:28 119:2 119:15 119:17 119:22 119:23

119:24 119:26 119:29 119:33 119:34 119:36 119:37 119:43 119:44 119:45 119:46 119:47 119:48 119:52 119:55 119:59 119:60 119:63 119:66 119:68 119:72 119:73 119:75 119:79 119:90 119:105 119:106 119:108 119:114 119:116 119:117^2 119:120 119:121 119:123 119:124 119:128 119:131 119:132 119:133 119:135 119:137 119:138 119:141 119:142 119:143 119:144 119:146 119:147 119:151 119:153 119:154 119:157 119:158 119:160 119:163 119:165 119:166 119:167 119:168 119:174 119:175^2 120:1 120:2 121:8^2 122:7 122:8 123:2 123:4 124:7 124:8 125:4 126:2 126:6 127:3 128:2 128:5 128:6 129:5 130:5 130:7 130:8 131:2 131:3 132:1 132:2 132:8 132:9

132:12 132:16 133:1 133:3 134:2 134:3 135:4 135:5 135:6^2 135:9^2 135:10 135:11^2 135:12 135:13 135:14 135:15 136:9 136:11 136:12 136:14 136:15 136:18 136:20 136:21 136:24 137:3 137:9 138:2 138:3 138:7 139:1 139:2 139:3^2 139:5^2 139:9 139:10 139:12 139:14^2 139:15 139:16 139:20 139:21 139:23^2 139:24^2 140:5 140:12 141:2 141:4 141:5 141:7 141:9 142:4 142:5 143:1 143:2 143:12^2 144:1 144:2^3 144:5^2 144:6^2 144:7 144:8 144:9 144:11^2 144:13 145:1^2 145:2^2 145:3^2 145:4 145:5 145:6^2 145:7 145:8^2 145:9 145:10 145:11 145:12 145:13 145:14 145:15 145:16 145:17 145:19 145:21^2 146:6^2 146:9 147:1

147:3 147:5 147:9 147:14 147:18[2] 147:19 147:20 148:3 148:4 148:5 148:6 148:7 148:8[2] 148:9[2] 148:10[2] 148:11[2] 148:12[2] 148:13 149:1 149:3 149:6 149:7 149:8 150:3 150:4[2]

PR

1:2 1:3 1:4 1:5[2] 1:6[2] 1:7 1:8 1:9 1:12 1:16 1:18 1:22[2] 1:24[2] 1:25 1:27[2] 1:29 1:31 1:32 1:33 2:1 2:2 2:3 2:4 2:5 2:6 2:8 2:9[2] 2:10 2:14 2:15 2:17 2:18 2:20 2:21 2:22 3:2[2] 3:3 3:4[2] 3:5 3:6 3:7 3:8 3:9 3:10 3:13 3:14 3:15 3:16[2] 3:17 3:18 3:20 3:21 3:22 3:23 3:24 3:26 3:28[2] 3:31

4:1 4:3 4:4[2] 4:6[2] 4:7 4:8 4:10[2] 4:12 4:14 4:15 4:16 4:17 4:18 4:22 4:24 4:25 4:26 5:1 5:2 5:3 5:7 5:8 5:9 5:10 5:11[2] 5:12[2] 5:13 5:14 5:15 5:16 5:17 5:18 5:19[2] 5:20[2] 5:21 5:22 5:23 6:3[2] 6:5 6:6 6:8 6:11 6:17 6:19 6:20 6:21 6:22 6:23[2] 6:26 6:27 6:28 6:33[2] 7:1 7:2[2] 7:4 7:7 7:8 7:9 7:10[2] 7:11 7:12 7:13[2] 7:15 7:17 7:20 7:23 7:24 8:1 8:4 8:5 8:6 8:7 8:9 8:10[2] 8:11 8:12 8:13[3] 8:14 8:15 8:16 8:17 8:18[2] 8:19 8:21 8:30 8:31 8:33[2]

8:35 9:5 9:6[2] 9:7 9:8 9:9[2] 9:10 9:11 9:13 9:16 9:17 9:18 10:18 10:22 10:26 11:7 11:8 11:10 11:15 11:16 11:24[2] 11:25 11:29 11:30 11:31 12:7 12:9[2] 12:14 12:28 13:4 13:5 13:18 13:22 14:6 14:10 14:13 14:14 14:16[2] 14:17 14:19 14:22 14:26 15:3 15:10 15:11 15:16 15:17 15:23 15:30 15:33 16:1 16:3 16:6[2] 16:11 16:13 16:15 16:16 16:18 16:20 16:21 16:23 16:24 16:27 16:28 16:29 16:32 17:1 17:2 17:3 17:4 17:5 17:6 17:15 17:17 17:18 17:19 17:20 17:21 17:25 17:27 17:28 18:1 18:3 18:4 18:6 18:7 18:8

18:10 18:11 18:12 18:13 18:15 18:16 18:17 18:18 18:19 18:20 18:21[2] 18:22 18:24 19:1 19:2 19:3 19:5 19:6 19:9 19:11 19:13 19:14[2] 19:15 19:17 19:18 19:20 19:22 19:23 19:24 19:25[3] 19:26[2] 19:28 19:29 20:1 20:4 20:10 20:11 20:12 20:13 20:15 20:16 20:18 20:22 20:23 20:25 20:26 20:28 20:29 21:3 21:4[2] 21:6 21:8 21:11 21:14 21:17 21:18 21:19 21:20 21:21[2] 21:22 21:23 21:24 21:26 22:1[2] 22:2 22:3[2] 22:4[3] 22:5 22:6 22:7 22:8 22:10[2] 22:12 22:16 22:17[2] 22:20 22:23 22:24 22:25 23:2 23:7 23:8 23:10 23:12 23:14 23:18 23:19[2]

23:21[2] 23:22 23:23[3] 23:24 23:25[2] 23:26 23:27 23:28 23:32 23:33 23:35[2] 24:2 24:3 24:4[2] 24:6 24:9 24:11 24:12[2] 24:13 24:14 24:16 24:17 24:18[2] 24:21[2] 24:22 24:25 24:27[2] 24:28 24:30 24:31[3] 24:32[2] 24:34 25:3[2] 25:4 25:5 25:6 25:9 25:10 25:12 25:14 25:15 25:16 25:17 25:18[2] 25:19 25:20 25:21 25:22 25:24 25:26 25:28 26:1 26:3 26:6 26:10 26:17 26:18 26:19 26:21 26:22 26:23 26:24 26:27 26:28 27:2[2] 27:3 27:4 27:9 27:10 27:11 27:12[2] 27:13 27:15 27:16 27:20 27:21 27:23 27:24 27:25[2] 27:26 27:27[2] 28:2 28:8 28:13 28:15 28:22 28:24

29:1 29:6 29:13 29:15 29:17 29:22 29:24 29:27 30:1 30:2 30:4 30:6 30:8 30:9[4] 30:10 30:11 30:12 30:13 30:14[2] 30:16[2] 30:17[2] 30:19 30:20[2] 30:21 30:22 30:23 30:28 30:30 30:31 30:33 31:2[2] 31:5[2] 31:6 31:7[2] 31:9[2] 31:12 31:13[2] 31:15[2] 31:16 31:17 31:19 31:22 31:24[2] 31:25[2] 31:26 31:27 31:28[2] 31:30 31:31

EC

1:4 1:5[2] 1:6[2] 1:9[2] 1:13[2] 1:14[2] 1:15 1:16[2] 1:17[3] 1:18 2:1 2:2 2:3 2:5[2] 2:7[3] 2:8[6] 2:9 2:10[2] 2:11[4] 2:12[3] 2:14 2:15 2:16 2:17 2:19[2] 2:21[3] 2:22 2:23 2:24[2] 2:26[4] 3:1 3:2[2]

3:3[2] 3:4[2] 3:5[2] 3:6[2] 3:7[2] 3:8[2] 3:12 3:13[3] 3:14 3:15[2] 3:16[2] 3:17[2] 3:18 3:20 3:21 4:1[4] 4:4[2] 4:5 4:6 4:7 4:8[2] 4:12[2] 4:13[2] 4:16 5:1 5:2[2] 5:3 5:5 5:6 5:7 5:8[3] 5:11 5:14[2] 5:15 5:16[2] 5:17[2] 5:18[3] 5:19[4] 6:1 6:2[2] 6:3[3] 6:4[2] 6:7 6:9 7:1 7:2 7:7 7:8 7:11 7:12 7:15 7:20 7:24 7:25[5] 7:26[3] 8:1[2] 8:2 8:4 8:5[2] 8:6 8:8 8:9 8:10[3] 8:12 8:15[2] 8:16 9:1[2] 9:2[5] 9:3[2] 9:6[2] 9:7 9:8 9:9 9:11[2] 9:12 9:13 9:14[4] 9:15 9:16 10:1 10:3 10:6 10:7 10:8 10:9 10:10 10:11

10:13 10:14 10:16 10:17[2] 10:18 10:19 10:20[2] 11:2 11:3 11:4 11:6 11:7 11:8 11:9[3] 11:10[2] 12:3[3] 12:4[3] 12:5[5] 12:7 12:9[3] 12:10 12:11 12:12[2] 12:13

CA

1:4 1:8 1:17 2:1 2:3 2:4 2:6 2:7 2:10[2] 2:11 2:12 2:13[2] 2:14 2:16 2:17[2] 3:2[2] 3:4[2] 3:5 3:11[2] 4:2 4:3 4:6[2] 4:8 4:10 4:11[2] 4:14[3] 4:15 4:16[2] 5:2 5:4 5:5[2] 5:6 5:10 5:11 5:12 5:16 6:2 6:3 6:6 6:8[2] 6:9[3] 6:10 6:11[2] 7:5 7:6 7:7 7:8 7:9 7:10 7:12 7:13[2] 8:2 8:3 8:8 8:9 8:10 8:12 8:14

ISA

1:1[2] 1:2[2] 1:3 1:5[2] 1:6[2] 1:7 1:8 1:9 1:11[2] 1:13 1:14 1:15 1:18 1:19 1:20 1:23[2] 1:24 1:25[3] 1:26[2] 1:27 1:28[3] 1:29 1:30 1:31[4] 2:1 2:2[3] 2:3[6] 2:4[4] 2:5 2:6[2] 2:7 2:9[2] 2:10[2] 2:11[2] 2:12[3] 2:13[3] 2:14[2] 2:15[2] 2:16[2] 2:17[3] 2:18 2:19[3] 2:20[2] 2:21[2] 3:1[3] 3:2[4] 3:3[4] 3:4[2] 3:5[3] 3:6 3:8[2] 3:9 3:12[2] 3:13 3:14 3:15 3:16[4] 3:17 3:18[2] 3:19[2] 3:20[4] 3:21 3:22[3] 3:23[3] 3:24[5] 3:25 3:26[3] 4:1[2] 4:2[3] 4:3[2] 4:4[2] 4:5[4] 4:6[4] 5:2[7] 5:3[3] 5:5[4] 5:6[2] 5:7[2] 5:9 5:10 5:12[4] 5:13[2] 5:14[5] 5:15[3] 5:16

5:17 5:18 5:19[3] 5:20[3] 5:21 5:22 5:23 5:24[3] 5:25[4] 5:26[3] 5:28[2] 5:29[3] 5:30[4] 6:1[2] 6:2[2] 6:3[2] 6:4[2] 6:5 6:7[4] 6:8 6:9[3] 6:10[6] 6:11[3] 6:12[2] 6:13[3] 7:1[2] 7:2[3] 7:3 7:4[3] 7:5 7:6[3] 7:8[3] 7:9[2] 7:13 7:14[2] 7:15[2] 7:16 7:17[2] 7:18[2] 7:19[5] 7:20[2] 7:21[2] 7:22[2] 7:23[2] 7:24[2] 7:25[3] 8:1 8:2[2] 8:3[3] 8:4[2] 8:6[2] 8:7[4] 8:8[3] 8:9[4] 8:10[2] 8:11 8:13[2] 8:14[3] 8:15[5] 8:17[2] 8:18[2] 8:19[3] 8:20 8:21[6] 8:22[4] 9:1[2] 9:3[2] 9:4 9:5[2] 9:6[2] 9:7[4] 9:8 9:9[3] 9:11 9:12[2] 9:14[2] 9:15[2] 9:16 9:17[3] 9:18[3] 9:19 9:20[4] 9:21[2] 10:1 10:2[2] 10:3[3] 10:4

10:5 10:6[3] 10:7 10:10[2] 10:11[2] 10:12[2] 10:13[4] 10:14[3] 10:16 10:17[5] 10:18[4] 10:19 10:20[2] 10:24 10:25[2] 10:26[2] 10:27[3] 10:33[2] 10:34[2] 11:1[2] 11:2[4] 11:3[2] 11:4[3] 11:5[2] 11:6[5] 11:7[3] 11:8[2] 11:10[2] 11:11[8] 11:12[3] 11:13[2] 11:14[2] 11:15[4] 11:16 12:1[2] 12:2[2] 12:4 12:6 13:5 13:7 13:8[2] 13:9[2] 13:10[2] 13:11[4] 13:13[2] 13:14[3] 13:15 13:16 13:17 13:18 13:19[2] 13:21[3] 13:22[4] 14:1[4] 14:2[6] 14:3[3] 14:4 14:5 14:6 14:7 14:8 14:10 14:11[2] 14:16 14:17 14:19 14:20 14:22[4] 14:23[2] 14:24 14:25[2] 14:26 14:27[3] 14:29 14:30[4] 14:31 14:32 15:1[2] 15:2[3] 15:3 15:4[2] 15:7 15:8 15:9 16:5[4] 16:6[2] 16:8

16:9[2] 16:10[3] 16:11 16:12 16:14[3] 17:1 17:2 17:3[2] 17:4[2] 17:5[3] 17:7 17:8 17:9[2] 17:10[2] 17:11[2] 17:12 17:13[3] 17:14[3] 18:2[2] 18:3[2] 18:4[2] 18:5[3] 18:6[3] 18:7[3] 19:1[3] 19:2[4] 19:3[6] 19:4[2] 19:5[3] 19:6[4] 19:7[2] 19:8[2] 19:9 19:10[2] 19:12[2] 19:14 19:16[2] 19:17 19:18 19:19 19:20[5] 19:21[5] 19:22[5] 19:23[3] 19:24 19:25[2] 20:1[2] 20:2[4] 20:3[4] 20:4[3] 20:5[3] 20:6[2] 21:2 21:5 21:7[3] 21:8[2] 21:9[4] 21:10 21:12 21:15[2] 21:16 21:17 22:5[3] 22:6[3] 22:7[2] 22:8[2] 22:9 22:10[2] 22:12[4] 22:13[5] 22:14 22:15 22:16[2] 22:17 22:18[2] 22:19[2] 22:20 22:21[5] 22:22[4] 22:23[2] 22:24[2] 22:25[3] 23:3[2] 23:9 23:12 23:13 23:15

23:17[3] 23:18[3] 24:1[3] 24:2 24:3 24:4[2] 24:6[2] 24:12 24:13 24:17[2] 24:18[3] 24:20[5] 24:21[2] 24:22[3] 24:23[3] 25:1 25:6 25:7[2] 25:8[2] 25:9[3] 25:10 25:11[2] 25:12[2] 26:1 26:6 26:8 26:10 26:11 26:14[2] 26:17 26:19[2] 26:20 26:21 27:1[3] 27:3 27:4 27:5 27:6[2] 27:9[2] 27:10[4] 27:11[2] 27:12[2] 27:13[4] 28:2 28:4[2] 28:5 28:6[2] 28:7[2] 28:8 28:9[2] 28:10 28:11 28:12 28:13[5] 28:15[2] 28:17[3] 28:18[2] 28:19[2] 28:20 28:21 28:23[2] 28:24 28:25[4] 28:26 28:27 28:29 29:2[3] 29:3[3] 29:4[5] 29:5 29:6[4] 29:7[3] 29:8[5] 29:9[2] 29:10[2] 29:11[2] 29:12[2] 29:13[2] 29:14[2] 29:15[3] 29:17[2] 29:18[3] 29:19 29:20[2] 29:21[2] 29:23[2] 29:24

30:1 30:2[2] 30:3 30:4 30:5 30:6[4] 30:7 30:8[2] 30:10 30:12[3] 30:14 30:15[3] 30:16 30:17 30:18[2] 30:20[2] 30:21[2] 30:22 30:23[3] 30:24[2] 30:25[3] 30:26[2] 30:27[2] 30:28[2] 30:29 30:30[5] 30:32[3] 30:33[2] 31:1[3] 31:2[3] 31:3[5] 31:4[2] 31:5 31:7 31:8[2] 31:9[3] 32:1 32:2[2] 32:3[2] 32:4 32:6[3] 32:8 32:10 32:11[2] 32:13 32:15[2] 32:16 32:17[3] 32:18[3] 32:19 32:20 33:1[4] 33:4[2] 33:5 33:6[3] 33:9[4] 33:12 33:13 33:15[2] 33:21 33:24 34:1[3] 34:2 34:3[2] 34:4[4] 34:5 34:6[3] 34:7[4] 34:8 34:9[3] 34:10 34:11[4] 34:12 34:13[4] 34:14[2] 34:15[3] 34:16[2] 34:17[2] 35:1[3] 35:2[4] 35:3 35:4 35:5 35:6[2] 35:7[3] 35:8[3] 35:10[6]

36:1 36:2[2] 36:3[2] 36:4 36:5 36:6 36:7[3] 36:8 36:9[2] 36:10[2] 36:11[3] 36:12[2] 36:13[2] 36:16[4] 36:17[3] 36:19[2] 36:21 36:22[2] 37:1[3] 37:2[3] 37:3[4] 37:4 37:6 37:7[3] 37:8 37:9[2] 37:11 37:12[3] 37:13[3] 37:14[4] 37:15 37:16 37:17[3] 37:18 37:19[2] 37:22 37:23[3] 37:24[5] 37:25[2] 37:26 37:27[3] 37:28[3] 37:29[3] 37:30[6] 37:31[2] 37:32 37:34 37:35 37:36[4] 37:37[3] 37:38[4] 38:1[3] 38:2 38:3[4] 38:5 38:6[3] 38:7 38:9 38:12 38:15 38:16[2] 38:21[2] 39:1[2] 39:2[7] 39:3[3] 39:4 39:6 39:7[2] 39:8 40:2 40:4[4] 40:5[2] 40:6[2] 40:10[2] 40:11[2] 40:12[4] 40:14[4] 40:15 40:16 40:17[2] 40:19[2] 40:22[2] 40:24[3] 40:26 40:27[2] 40:29 40:30[2]

40:31[3] 41:1 41:2[2] 41:3 41:4[2] 41:5[2] 41:6 41:7[2] 41:9[3] 41:11[2] 41:12[2] 41:14[2] 41:15[2] 41:16[4] 41:17[3] 41:18[2] 41:19[4] 41:20[4] 41:22[2] 41:23 41:24 41:25[3] 41:26 41:27 41:28[2] 41:29 42:3 42:4 42:5[3] 42:6[3] 42:7 42:8 42:9 42:10[3] 42:11 42:12 42:14[2] 42:15[4] 42:16[3] 42:18 42:19 42:21 42:22[4] 42:23 42:24 42:25[2] 43:1 43:2 43:3 43:4[2] 43:5 43:6[2] 43:8 43:9[3] 43:10[3] 43:11 43:12[2] 43:13[2] 43:14[2] 43:16 43:17[2] 43:19 43:20 43:25 43:27 43:28[2] 44:1 44:2[2] 44:3[2] 44:4 44:5[3] 44:6[3] 44:7[5] 44:8 44:9[2] 44:11[2] 44:12[4] 44:13[2] 44:14[3] 44:15[4] 44:16[2] 44:17[4] 44:18 44:19[3] 44:21 44:22 44:23[2]

44:24 44:25[2] 44:26[2] 44:27 44:28[2] 45:1[2] 45:2[2] 45:3[2] 45:4 45:5 45:6[2] 45:7[2] 45:8[3] 45:11[2] 45:12[2] 45:13[2] 45:14[5] 45:16 45:18[2] 45:20[2] 45:21[3] 45:22[2] 45:23 45:24[2] 45:25 46:1 46:3 46:4[4] 46:5[2] 46:6[3] 46:7[2] 46:8 46:9[2] 46:10[2] 46:13[3] 47:1[2] 47:2 47:3 47:5 47:6 47:7 47:8 47:9[2] 47:10[3] 47:11[3] 47:12 47:13 48:1[2] 48:2 48:3[3] 48:4[2] 48:5[2] 48:6[2] 48:7 48:8 48:9 48:11 48:12 48:13 48:14[2] 48:15 48:16[2] 48:18 48:19 48:21[2] 49:1 49:2[2] 49:3 49:4[2] 49:5[2] 49:6[2] 49:7[4] 49:8[3] 49:9 49:11[2] 49:12[3] 49:13[3] 49:14 49:17 49:18[3] 49:19[3] 49:21[4] 49:22[3] 49:23[4] 49:25[2] 49:26[4] 50:1

50:2 50:3 50:5 50:6[2] 50:10[2] 50:11 51:1 51:2[3] 51:3[4] 51:4[2] 51:5[2] 51:6[4] 51:8[2] 51:9 51:11[5] 51:12 51:13[4] 51:14 51:16[4] 51:17 51:19[3] 51:21 51:22 51:23[2] 52:1 52:2 52:3 52:4 52:5 52:10 52:12 52:13[2] 52:14 52:15 53:1 53:2[2] 53:3[4] 53:4[2] 53:5 53:6 53:7[2] 53:8[2] 53:9[2] 53:10 53:11 53:12[4] 54:1 54:2[2] 54:3[3] 54:4 54:5 54:6[2] 54:10 54:11[2] 54:12[2] 54:13[2] 54:14 54:16[2] 54:17[2] 55:1[4] 55:2[3] 55:3[3] 55:4 55:5[2] 55:7[4] 55:9 55:10[5] 55:11 55:12[3] 55:13[2] 56:1[2] 56:2[2] 56:4[2] 56:5[3] 56:6[2] 56:7[2] 56:11 56:12[3] 57:1[2] 57:3 57:4 57:7 57:8[3] 57:9[4] 57:11[3] 57:12 57:13

57:14
57:15^{4}
57:16
57:17^{3}
57:18^{3}
57:19^{2}
57:20
58:1^{2}
58:2^{2}
58:3^{3}
58:4^{2}
58:5^{3}
58:6^{2}
58:7^{2}
58:8^{2}
58:9^{3}
58:10^{3}
58:11^{5}
58:12^{2}
58:13^{2}
58:14^{2}
59:2^{2}
59:3
59:4^{2}
59:5^{2}
59:6
59:7^{2}
59:8
59:10
59:11
59:12^{2}
59:13^{4}
59:14^{3}
59:15^{3}
59:16^{3}
59:17^{3}
59:19
59:20^{2}
59:21^{2}
60:1
60:2^{2}
60:3^{2}
60:4^{2}
60:5^{3}
60:6^{3}
60:7
60:8
60:9^{3}
60:10^{2}
60:11
60:12
60:13^{2}
60:14^{2}
60:15
60:16^{3}
60:17^{4}
60:18
60:19
60:20
60:22
61:1
61:2
61:4^{2}
61:5^{4}
61:6
61:7
61:8^{2}
61:9^{2}
61:10
61:11^{2}
62:1^{2}
62:2^{3}
62:3
62:4^{2}
62:5
62:7^{2}
62:8^{2}
62:9^{2}
62:11
62:12^{2}
63:2
63:3^{4}
63:4
63:5^{4}
63:6^{3}
63:7^{3}
63:9^{4}
63:10^{2}
63:11
63:15^{4}
63:16
63:17
64:5^{2}
64:6^{3}
64:7^{2}
64:8^{2}
64:11^{2}
64:12
65:3
65:4^{2}
65:7^{2}
65:8
65:9^{4}
65:10^{2}
65:11
65:12^{2}
65:14
65:15^{2}
65:16^{2}
65:17^{2}
65:18^{2}
65:19^{3}
65:21^{4}
65:22^{3}
65:23
65:24^{2}
65:25^{3}
66:1^{2}
66:2^{3}
66:3
66:4^{2}
66:5
66:9^{2}
66:10
66:11^{2}
66:12^{2}
66:13
66:14^{4}
66:15^{2}
66:16^{2}
66:17^{3}
66:18^{4}
66:19^{5}
66:20^{5}
66:21^{2}
66:22^{2}
66:23^{2}
66:24^{3}

JER

1:5^{2}
1:7
1:9^{2}
1:10^{5}
1:11
1:13^{3}
1:15^{4}
1:16^{3}
1:17^{2}
1:18^{3}
1:19
2:2
2:3
2:4
2:5^{2}
2:6^{3}
2:7^{3}
2:8^{3}
2:9
2:10^{4}
2:12
2:13
2:15^{2}
2:16
2:18
2:19^{4}
2:20^{8}
2:22
2:25^{2}
2:26^{2}
2:27^{3}
2:37^{2}
3:1^{2}
3:2^{3}
3:3^{2}
3:5
3:6^{2}
3:7^{2}
3:8^{3}
3:9^{3}
3:10
3:11
3:12^{4}
3:13^{2}
3:14^{3}
3:15^{2}
3:16^{2}
3:17
3:18
3:19^{3}
3:21^{2}
3:22
3:23
3:24^{2}
3:25^{3}
4:1
4:2^{4}
4:3^{2}
4:4^{3}
4:5^{4}
4:6
4:7^{2}
4:8
4:9^{4}
4:10
4:11
4:13
4:15
4:16
4:18
4:20
4:21
4:22
4:23^{4}
4:24^{2}
4:25^{2}
4:26^{3}
4:28^{2}
4:29^{3}
4:30
4:31
5:1^{5}
5:2
5:5^{3}
5:6^{2}
5:7^{2}
5:9
5:10
5:11
5:12
5:13^{2}
5:14^{2}
5:17^{5}
5:19^{2}
5:20
5:21^{3}
5:22
5:23^{2}
5:24
5:25
5:27
5:28
5:30
5:31^{3}
6:1^{3}
6:2
6:4
6:5^{2}
6:6
6:7^{2}
6:10^{2}
6:11
6:12^{2}
6:13
6:16^{4}
6:18
6:20
6:21^{3}
6:22
6:23^{3}
6:24
6:25
6:26
6:27^{2}
6:28
7:2^{2}
7:5^{2}
7:6^{2}
7:7
7:9^{4}
7:10^{3}
7:12
7:13^{4}
7:14^{2}
7:15
7:17
7:18^{3}
7:20^{5}
7:21
7:23^{3}
7:24^{3}
7:25
7:28
7:29^{3}
7:31^{2}
7:33^{3}
7:34^{3}
8:1^{4}
8:2^{7}
8:3
8:4^{2}
8:6
8:7^{3}
8:8
8:9^{2}
8:10
8:13^{2}
8:14^{3}
8:15^{2}
8:16^{3}
8:17
8:19
8:20
9:1^{2}
9:2
9:3^{2}
9:4^{2}
9:5^{3}
9:7
9:10^{3}
9:11^{3}
9:12^{2}
9:13^{2}
9:14
9:15
9:16
9:17^{2}
9:18^{3}
9:20^{3}
9:21^{2}
9:22
9:24^{2}
9:26^{6}
10:2
10:4^{2}
10:6
10:7
10:8
10:9^{3}
10:10^{2}
10:11^{2}
10:12
10:13^{2}
10:14
10:15
10:16
10:18
10:19
10:20^{3}
10:21^{2}
10:22^{2}
10:25^{4}
11:2^{2}
11:3
11:4^{2}
11:5^{2}
11:6^{2}
11:7
11:9^{2}
11:10^{2}
11:11
11:12^{2}
11:13
11:15
11:16^{2}
11:17
11:18^{2}
11:19^{2}
11:20
11:22
11:23
12:2
12:3^{2}
12:4^{2}
12:5^{2}
12:6
12:9
12:11
12:13
12:14
12:15^{4}
12:16
12:17
13:1^{3}
13:2
13:3
13:4^{2}
13:5
13:6^{2}
13:7^{3}
13:9
13:10^{2}
13:11^{4}
13:12
13:13^{3}
13:14^{2}
13:15
13:16^{3}
13:17^{2}
13:18
13:19
13:20
13:21
13:22^{2}
13:25
13:27^{2}
14:2^{2}
14:3^{4}
14:5
14:6
14:8
14:9
14:10
14:12^{4}
14:14^{3}
14:15^{3}
14:16^{3}
14:17^{2}
14:18^{2}
14:19^{4}
14:20
15:1^{2}
15:2^{4}
15:3^{5}
15:4
15:6
15:7
15:8
15:9^{2}
15:10
15:11
15:12
15:13^{2}
15:14
15:15^{2}
15:16^{3}
15:18^{2}
15:19^{2}
15:20^{3}
15:21^{2}
16:3^{3}
16:4^{4}
16:5
16:6
16:8
16:9^{3}
16:10^{2}
16:11^{5}
16:12
16:13^{2}
16:15^{2}
16:16^{5}
16:18^{3}
16:19^{4}
16:20
16:21^{2}
17:1^{2}
17:2
17:3^{2}
17:4^{2}
17:5^{2}
17:6^{2}
17:7
17:8^{3}
17:9
17:10
17:11^{3}
17:13
17:14^{2}
17:18
17:19^{3}
17:20^{3}
17:21
17:24
17:25^{5}
17:26^{10}
17:27^{3}
18:2^{2}
18:3
18:4
18:7^{3}
18:9^{3}
18:11^{4}
18:12^{2}
18:15
18:16^{2}
18:17
18:18^{3}
18:19
18:20
18:21^{4}
18:22
19:1^{3}
19:2^{2}
19:3^{2}
19:4^{3}
19:7^{6}
19:8^{3}
19:9^{5}
19:11^{3}
19:12^{2}
19:13^{3}
19:14^{2}
19:15
20:2
20:3
20:4^{6}
20:5^{5}
20:6^{6}
20:7^{2}
20:8^{2}
20:9^{2}
20:10^{3}
20:11
20:12^{2}
20:16^{4}
20:17
20:18
21:1
21:4^{2}
21:5^{4}
21:6^{2}
21:7^{8}
21:8^{2}
21:9^{4}
21:10^{2}
21:11
21:12^{2}
21:13
21:14^{2}
22:1
22:2^{3}
22:3^{3}
22:4^{2}
22:6^{2}
22:7^{3}
22:8^{2}
22:9^{2}
22:12
22:13^{2}
22:14^{2}
22:15^{4}
22:16
22:17^{4}
22:19
22:20^{3}
22:22^{2}
22:25^{3}
22:26^{3}
22:28^{2}
22:30
23:1
23:2^{2}
23:3^{4}
23:4^{2}
23:5^{4}
23:6^{2}
23:8^{3}
23:9^{2}
23:10^{2}
23:11
23:12
23:13
23:14^{2}
23:15
23:16
23:17
23:18^{3}
23:20
23:22^{2}
23:23
23:24
23:28
23:29
23:31
23:32^{3}
23:33
23:34^{4}
23:35^{2}
23:36
23:37
23:38
23:39^{4}
23:40^{2}
24:1^{4}
24:2
24:3^{2}
24:6^{5}
24:7^{3}
24:8^{4}
24:9^{3}
24:10^{3}
25:2
25:3^{3}
25:4^{2}
25:5^{4}
25:6^{4}
25:9^{9}
25:10^{3}
25:11^{3}
25:12^{4}
25:13
25:14^{3}
25:15
25:16^{3}
25:17
25:18^{4}
25:19^{3}
25:20^{7}
25:21^{2}
25:22^{3}
25:23^{3}
25:24^{2}
25:25^{3}
25:26^{4}
25:27^{4}
25:28
25:29
25:30^{2}
25:32
25:33
25:34^{4}
25:35
25:36
25:37
25:38
26:2
26:3
26:4
26:5
26:6
26:7^{2}
26:8^{2}
26:9^{2}
26:10
26:11^{2}
26:12^{2}
26:13^{3}
26:14
26:15
26:16^{2}
26:17
26:18^{3}
26:19^{3}
26:20^{2}
26:21^{4}
26:22^{2}
26:23^{3}
27:2^{2}
27:3^{5}
27:4
27:5^{3}
27:6^{2}
27:7^{5}
27:8^{5}
27:10^{2}
27:11^{3}
27:12^{3}
27:13^{2}
27:15^{2}
27:16
27:17
27:18^{3}
27:19^{3}
27:20^{2}
27:21^{2}
27:22^{2}
28:1^{3}
28:3
28:4
28:5
28:6
28:7
28:8^{4}
28:10
28:11^{2}
28:13
28:14^{2}
29:1^{3}
29:2^{5}
29:3
29:5^{3}
29:6^{6}
29:7^{2}
29:8
29:10
29:11
29:12^{3}
29:13^{2}
29:14^{5}
29:16^{2}
29:17^{2}
29:18^{6}
29:19
29:21^{2}
29:22^{2}
29:23^{3}
29:25^{3}
29:26^{2}
29:28^{3}
29:29
29:31^{2}
29:32
30:3^{3}
30:4^{2}
30:5
30:6^{2}
30:8^{2}
30:9
30:10^{5}
30:11
30:12
30:16^{3}
30:17
30:18^{3}
30:19^{5}
30:20^{2}
30:21^{4}
30:22^{2}
30:24
31:1
31:4^{2}
31:5
31:6
31:7^{2}
31:8^{3}
31:9^{2}
31:10^{3}
31:11
31:12^{8}
31:13^{3}
31:14^{2}
31:15
31:16^{2}
31:17
31:18^{2}
31:19
31:23^{2}
31:24^{3}
31:25
31:26^{2}
31:27^{2}
31:28^{6}
31:29
31:31
31:33^{3}
31:34^{3}
31:35^{2}
31:37
31:39^{2}
31:40^{3}
32:2
32:3^{2}
32:4^{3}
32:5^{2}
32:6
32:8^{2}
32:9^{2}
32:10^{4}
32:11^{2}
32:12^{2}
32:13
32:14^{2}
32:15^{2}
32:17^{3}
32:18
32:19^{2}
32:20^{4}
32:21^{5}
32:22^{2}
32:23^{2}
32:24^{5}
32:25^{2}
32:28^{2}
32:29^{4}
32:30
32:31
32:32^{4}
32:33^{3}
32:35^{2}
32:36^{3}
32:37^{4}
32:38^{2}
32:39^{3}
32:40
32:41^{2}
32:43
32:44^{8}
33:3^{3}
33:4^{2}
33:5^{2}
33:6^{4}
33:7^{3}
33:8^{3}
33:9^{5}
33:10^{4}
33:11^{3}
33:12^{2}
33:13^{4}
33:14
33:15^{3}
33:16^{2}
33:18^{2}
33:19
33:20^{3}
33:21
33:22
33:25^{3}
33:26^{3}
34:1^{4}
34:2^{3}
34:3^{5}
34:5^{2}
34:7^{2}
34:9
34:10^{3}
34:11^{4}
34:14
34:15^{3}
34:16^{5}
34:17^{3}
34:18^{2}
34:19^{3}
34:20^{3}
34:21^{4}
34:22^{5}
35:2^{3}
35:3^{3}
35:4
35:5^{3}
35:10^{2}
35:11^{2}
35:13^{2}
35:14
35:15^{5}
35:17^{2}
35:18^{3}
36:1
36:2^{3}
36:3
36:4
36:5
36:6^{2}
36:7^{2}
36:8
36:9^{2}
36:12^{6}
36:14^{2}
36:15^{2}
36:16^{2}
36:17
36:18
36:19^{2}
36:20^{2}
36:21^{3}
36:23^{2}
36:25^{2}
36:26^{3}
36:27
36:28
36:29^{4}
36:30^{2}
36:31^{6}
36:32^{2}
37:1
37:3^{2}
37:4
37:5
37:8^{4}
37:10^{2}
37:11
37:13^{2}
37:14
37:15^{2}
37:16^{2}
37:17^{4}
37:21
38:1^{3}
38:2^{2}
38:4
38:6^{3}
38:8
38:9
38:10
38:11^{4}
38:12^{3}
38:13^{2}
38:14^{2}
38:15
38:17^{3}
38:18^{2}
38:19^{2}
38:20
38:22^{4}
38:23^{3}
38:24
38:25^{3}
38:27^{2}
38:28
39:1^{2}
39:2
39:3^{2}
39:4^{4}
39:5^{2}
39:7
39:8^{3}
39:9
39:10^{2}
39:12^{2}
39:13^{3}
39:14^{2}
39:16^{3}
39:17
39:18
40:1
40:2^{2}
40:3^{2}
40:4^{3}
40:5^{3}
40:6
40:7^{5}
40:8^{6}
40:9^{4}
40:10^{4}
40:11^{4}
40:12^{3}
40:13
40:14
40:15^{3}
41:1^{2}
41:2^{3}
41:3^{2}
41:4^{2}
41:5^{4}
41:6^{2}
41:7^{3}
41:8^{4}
41:9
41:10^{3}
41:11
41:12^{2}
41:13
41:14^{2}
41:15
41:16^{4}
41:17^{2}
42:1^{3}
42:2^{2}
42:3
42:4
42:5
42:6
42:8^{2}
42:9
42:10^{3}
42:11
42:12^{2}
42:14
42:15^{2}
42:16^{2}
42:17
42:18^{6}
42:20^{2}
42:21
42:22^{2}
43:1
43:2^{2}
43:3
43:4^{2}
43:5
43:6^{6}
43:9
43:10^{4}
43:11^{4}
43:12^{5}
43:13
44:1^{3}
44:2^{3}
44:3
44:4
44:6^{5}
44:7^{2}
44:8^{2}
44:9^{5}
44:10
44:11
44:12^{9}
44:13
44:15
44:17^{6}
44:18^{3}
44:19^{3}
44:20^{2}
44:21^{5}
44:22^{3}
44:23^{2}
44:24
44:25^{4}
44:27^{3}
44:28
44:29
44:30^{2}
45:3
45:4
45:5
46:3^{2}
46:4^{3}
46:5^{4}
46:6
46:8^{4}
46:9^{5}
46:10^{3}
46:11
46:12^{2}
46:13
46:14^{4}
46:16^{3}
46:18
46:19
46:21^{2}
46:22
46:23
46:25^{4}
46:26^{4}
46:27^{5}
47:2^{5}
47:3
47:4^{2}
47:6
47:7
48:1^{2}
48:2
48:3
48:6
48:7^{3}
48:8^{3}
48:9
48:10
48:11^{3}
48:12^{2}
48:13
48:14
48:15^{2}
48:16
48:17^{2}
48:18^{2}
48:19^{3}
48:20
48:21^{3}
48:22^{3}
48:23^{3}
48:24^{3}
48:25
48:26
48:28^{2}
48:29^{3}
48:31
48:32
48:33^{4}
48:34
48:35
48:36
48:37^{2}
48:38
48:39
48:40
48:41^{2}
48:42
48:43^{2}
48:44
48:45^{3}
48:46
49:1
49:2^{2}
49:3^{4}
49:5^{2}
49:6
49:10^{4}
49:11
49:12
49:13^{2}
49:14^{3}
49:15
49:16
49:17
49:18^{2}
49:19^{3}
49:20
49:22^{3}
49:23
49:24^{3}
49:26
49:27^{2}
49:28^{2}
49:29^{4}
49:30
49:32^{3}
49:33^{2}
49:36^{3}
49:37^{3}
49:38^{3}
50:1
50:2^{3}
50:3^{2}
50:4^{4}
50:5
50:7
50:8^{2}
50:9^{2}
50:10
50:12
50:13
50:16^{2}
50:17
50:18
50:19^{5}
50:20^{4}
50:21^{3}
50:22
50:23
50:24^{3}
50:25
50:26
50:28
50:30
50:32^{5}
50:33^{2}
50:34
50:35^{3}
50:36^{2}
50:37^{4}
50:38^{2}
50:39^{2}
50:40^{2}
50:41^{2}
50:42^{3}
50:43^{2}
50:44^{2}
50:45
50:46
51:1
51:2^{2}
51:3^{2}
51:4
51:6
51:8
51:9^{2}
51:10
51:12
51:13
51:14
51:15
51:16^{2}
51:17
51:19
51:20^{2}
51:21^{4}
51:22^{5}
51:23^{5}
51:24^{2}
51:25^{3}
51:26
51:27
51:28
51:29^{2}
51:31
51:32^{3}
51:33
51:35^{2}
51:36^{3}
51:37^{2}
51:39^{3}
51:41
51:43
51:44^{3}
51:45
51:46^{4}
51:47^{2}
51:48^{2}
51:50
51:52
51:53
51:54
51:55
51:56
51:57^{6}
51:58^{4}
51:59
51:61^{3}
51:63^{2}
51:64^{3}
52:1^{3}
52:2
52:3
52:4^{4}
52:6
52:7^{3}
52:8^{2}
52:9^{5}
52:10^{5}
52:11^{3}
52:13^{4}
52:14
52:15^{3}
52:16
52:17^{3}
52:18^{5}
52:19^{8}
52:20
52:21^{3}
52:22^{4}
52:23^{3}
52:24^{3}
52:25^{3}
52:26
52:27^{2}
52:28^{2}
52:29
52:30^{3}
52:31^{4}
52:32^{2}
52:33^{2}
52:34

LA

1:1
1:2
1:3
1:4
1:6^{2}
1:7^{3}
1:8
1:11
1:12
1:13^{3}
1:14
1:17
1:18^{2}
1:19
1:20
1:21
1:22^{2}
1:25
2:1^{2}
2:2^{2}
2:3
2:4
2:5^{2}
2:6^{4}
2:8
2:9^{2}
2:10
2:11
2:12
2:14^{3}
2:15
2:16
2:17^{2}
2:18
2:20^{3}
2:21^{3}
2:22
3:2
3:4
3:5
3:8
3:10
3:11
3:12
3:14
3:17
3:18^{2}
3:19^{2}
3:20
3:26
3:28
3:37
3:38
3:40^{2}
3:42
3:43
3:47^{2}
3:49
3:50
3:53
3:60
3:61
3:62
3:63
3:66
4:4
4:6
4:11^{2}
4:12^{2}
4:13
4:15
4:21
5:1
5:3
5:5
5:6
5:7^{2}
5:11
5:13
5:20
5:21

EZE

1:1
1:3
1:4^{5}
1:5
1:6^{2}
1:7^{3}
1:8^{3}
1:10^{2}
1:11^{2}
1:12^{2}
1:13^{3}
1:14^{2}
1:16^{4}
1:17
1:18
1:19^{2}
1:21^{2}
1:22
1:23^{2}
1:24
1:25
1:26^{2}
1:27^{3}
1:28^{2}
2:1^{2}
2:2^{2}
2:3^{2}
2:4^{2}
2:5
2:6^{3}
2:7
2:8
2:9^{2}
2:10^{6}
3:1
3:2
3:3^{3}
3:4^{2}
3:5
3:6
3:7
3:8
3:10
3:11^{3}
3:12
3:13^{2}
3:14^{2}
3:15^{2}
3:16
3:17
3:18
3:19
3:20^{3}
3:21
3:22^{3}
3:23^{3}
3:24^{3}
3:25^{2}
3:26^{2}
3:27^{2}
4:1^{2}
4:2^{4}
4:3^{5}
4:4
4:5
4:6^{2}
4:7
4:8^{2}
4:9^{8}
4:10
4:12^{2}
4:13
4:15
4:16^{4}
4:17^{3}
5:1^{4}
5:2^{4}
5:3
5:4^{2}
5:5
5:6^{3}
5:7^{2}
5:8
5:9^{2}
5:10^{3}
5:11
5:12^{4}
5:13^{3}
5:14
5:15^{4}
5:16^{3}
5:17^{5}
6:1
6:2
6:3^{4}
6:4^{3}
6:5^{2}
6:6^{6}
6:7^{2}
6:9^{3}
6:10^{2}
6:11^{3}
6:12^{8}
6:13^{2}
6:14^{2}
7:3^{3}
7:4^{3}
7:7
7:8^{3}
7:9^{3}
7:15^{4}
7:16
7:17
7:18^{3}
7:19^{2}
7:20
7:21^{3}
7:22^{2}
7:23
7:24^{2}
7:25^{2}
7:26^{2}
7:27^{4}
8:1^{2}
8:2^{2}
8:3^{5}
8:4
8:5
8:6
8:7^{2}
8:8
8:9^{2}
8:10^{4}
8:11^{3}
8:13
8:14
8:15
8:16^{6}
8:17^{2}
8:18
9:2^{5}
9:3^{2}
9:4^{3}
9:5^{2}
9:6^{4}
9:7^{4}
9:8^{4}
9:9^{4}
9:10
9:11
10:1
10:2^{5}
10:3
10:4^{3}
10:5
10:6^{2}
10:7^{4}
10:8
10:9^{3}
10:10
10:12^{5}
10:14^{4}
10:15
10:16^{2}
10:17
10:18
10:19^{4}
10:20
10:21^{2}
10:22^{2}
11:1^{4}
11:2
11:3
11:5^{2}
11:6
11:7
11:8
11:9^{3}
11:10
11:12
11:13^{3}
11:15
11:16
11:17^{2}
11:18^{3}
11:19^{4}
11:20^{4}
11:21
11:22^{2}
11:23^{2}
11:24
12:2^{2}
12:3^{2}
12:4
12:5
12:6
12:7^{3}
12:8
12:10
12:11
12:12^{2}
12:13^{2}
12:14^{3}
12:15^{2}
12:16^{2}
12:18^{2}
12:19^{3}
12:20^{3}
12:21
12:22
12:23^{2}
12:25^{2}
12:27
13:1
13:2
13:3
13:6^{3}
13:7
13:8
13:9^{3}
13:10^{3}
13:11^{2}
13:13^{2}
13:14^{4}
13:15^{2}
13:16^{2}
13:17
13:18^{3}
13:19^{4}
13:20^{2}
13:21^{3}
13:22
13:23
14:1
14:2
14:3
14:4^{3}
14:6^{2}
14:7^{3}
14:8^{5}
14:9^{3}
14:10
14:11^{3}
14:13^{4}
14:14
14:15
14:17^{2}
14:19^{2}
14:20
14:21^{4}
14:22^{4}
14:23^{3}
15:1
15:4
15:5
15:7^{3}
15:8
16:3^{3}
16:4

16:6[2] 16:7[5] 16:8[5] 16:9 16:10[3] 16:11[2] 16:12[3] 16:13[8] 16:14 16:15[2] 16:16[3] 16:17[3] 16:18[4] 16:19[3] 16:20[2] 16:21 16:22[4] 16:23 16:24 16:25[3] 16:26 16:27 16:28 16:29 16:31[2] 16:33 16:34[3] 16:36[3] 16:37[2] 16:38[4] 16:39[6] 16:40[2] 16:41[4] 16:42[3] 16:43 16:45[4] 16:46[4] 16:48 16:49[3] 16:50[2] 16:51 16:52 16:53[3] 16:54 16:55[5] 16:57 16:58 16:60 16:61[3] 16:62[2] 16:63[2] 17:1 17:2 17:3[2] 17:4 17:5[2] 17:6[5] 17:7[3] 17:8 17:9 17:12[3] 17:13[3] 17:15[2] 17:16 17:17[2] 17:18 17:19 17:20[4] 17:21[3] 17:22[3] 17:23[4] 17:24[3] 18:2 18:5[2] 18:6 18:7[2] 18:8 18:9 18:10 18:11[2] 18:12[2] 18:13 18:14[2] 18:16 18:18 18:19[3] 18:20

18:21[3] 18:23[2] 18:24[3] 18:26[2] 18:27 18:28 18:30 18:31[2] 18:32 19:2 19:3[2] 19:4 19:5[2] 19:6[4] 19:7[4] 19:8 19:9[2] 19:10 19:11[3] 19:12[2] 19:13[2] 19:14[2] 20:1[2] 20:3 20:5[3] 20:6 20:7 20:8 20:10 20:11[2] 20:12 20:13[2] 20:15 20:16 20:19[2] 20:20[3] 20:22 20:23 20:24[2] 20:25 20:26 20:27 20:28[4] 20:29 20:30 20:31 20:32[2] 20:33[2] 20:34[4] 20:35[2] 20:37[2] 20:38[4] 20:39[2] 20:40[2] 20:41[2] 20:42 20:43[3] 20:44 20:46 20:47[4] 20:48 21:1 21:2[2] 21:3[4] 21:4 21:6 21:7[6] 21:9[2] 21:11[2] 21:12 21:13 21:14[2] 21:15 21:17 21:19 21:20 21:22 21:23 21:25 21:26[2] 21:27[2] 21:28[3] 21:31[3] 22:3 22:4[4] 22:5[2] 22:7[2]

22:8 22:9 22:11[3] 22:12[3] 22:13 22:14 22:15[3] 22:16[2] 22:17 22:18[3] 22:20[7] 22:21[2] 22:22 22:23 22:25 22:26[5] 22:27 22:28[2] 22:29[3] 22:30[2] 23:3[2] 23:4[6] 23:5[2] 23:6 23:7 23:8[2] 23:10[3] 23:11[2] 23:12 23:14 23:16[2] 23:17[4] 23:18 23:20 23:23[6] 23:24[7] 23:25[6] 23:26 23:27 23:29[6] 23:30 23:32[2] 23:33[2] 23:34[3] 23:35[2] 23:36 23:37[3] 23:38 23:39 23:40[3] 23:41[3] 23:42[3] 23:43 23:44 23:45[3] 23:46[2] 23:47[4] 23:49[3] 24:3[3] 24:4 24:5[3] 24:6 24:10[2] 24:11[2] 24:12 24:13 24:14[2] 24:17[3] 24:18[2] 24:19 24:21[3] 24:22 24:23[3] 24:24 24:25[2] 24:27[4] 25:2 25:3[3] 25:4[3] 25:5[3] 25:6[2] 25:7[4] 25:8 25:9 25:10 25:11[2] 25:12[2]

25:13[4] 25:14[4] 25:15 25:16[2] 25:17[2] 26:1 26:3 26:4[3] 26:5 26:6[2] 26:7[4] 26:8[3] 26:9[2] 26:10[2] 26:11 26:12[7] 26:13[2] 26:14 26:16[3] 26:17[3] 26:19 26:20[2] 26:21 27:3 27:7 27:8 27:9 27:10[6] 27:11 27:12 27:13[2] 27:14[2] 27:15 27:16[4] 27:17[5] 27:18 27:19[3] 27:21[3] 27:22[3] 27:23[3] 27:24[3] 27:25[2] 27:27[5] 27:29[2] 27:30[3] 27:31[4] 27:32[2] 27:33 27:34 27:35 27:36 28:2[2] 28:4[3] 28:5[2] 28:7[2] 28:8 28:9 28:12[2] 28:13[5] 28:14[2] 28:16[2] 28:18 28:19 28:21 28:22[4] 28:23[3] 28:24[2] 28:25 28:26[4] 29:2[2] 29:3[2] 29:4[3] 29:5[3] 29:6 29:7[3] 29:8[2] 29:9[4] 29:10[3] 29:12[4] 29:14[3] 29:16 29:17[2] 29:18 29:19[4] 29:21[2] 30:2 30:4[4]

30:5[5] 30:6 30:7[2] 30:8 30:9 30:11[3] 30:12[4] 30:13[3] 30:14[3] 30:15[2] 30:16[3] 30:17[2] 30:18[2] 30:19 30:20 30:21 30:22[3] 30:23[2] 30:24[3] 30:25[3] 30:26[3] 31:1 31:2 31:3[2] 31:4 31:5[2] 31:6[2] 31:8 31:10[2] 31:12[6] 31:13 31:15[4] 31:16[2] 31:17 31:18[2] 32:1 32:2[5] 32:3 32:4[2] 32:5[2] 32:6 32:7[2] 32:8 32:10[2] 32:12[2] 32:14 32:15 32:16 32:18[2] 32:19 32:20 32:22 32:23 32:24 32:26 32:27[2] 32:28 32:29[2] 32:30[3] 32:31[2] 32:32[2] 33:2[2] 33:3 33:4[2] 33:5 33:6[3] 33:7 33:10[2] 33:11 33:13 33:14[2] 33:16 33:18 33:19[2] 33:21 33:22[3] 33:24 33:25[3] 33:26[2] 33:27[3] 33:28[2] 33:30[3] 33:31[3] 33:32[2] 33:33 34:1 34:2

34:3 34:4 34:5[2] 34:6[2] 34:8[2] 34:10[2] 34:11 34:12[2] 34:13[5] 34:14[2] 34:15 34:16[4] 34:17[3] 34:18 34:19[2] 34:20 34:21[2] 34:22[3] 34:23[3] 34:24[2] 34:25[4] 34:26[3] 34:27[5] 34:28[2] 34:29[2] 34:30 34:31 35:2 35:3[3] 35:4[2] 35:5 35:6 35:7[2] 35:8[3] 35:9[2] 35:10[2] 35:11[2] 35:12[2] 35:13 35:15[2] 36:1 36:3[4] 36:4[4] 36:5 36:6[4] 36:8 36:9[3] 36:10[3] 36:11[7] 36:12[3] 36:13 36:17 36:18 36:19[3] 36:20[2] 36:23[2] 36:24[2] 36:25[2] 36:26[3] 36:27[4] 36:28[3] 36:29[3] 36:30[2] 36:31[3] 36:32 36:33 36:34 36:35[5] 36:36[2] 36:38 37:1[2] 37:2[3] 37:3[2] 37:4 37:5 37:6[6] 37:7[3] 37:8[3] 37:9[2] 37:10[3] 37:11 37:12[3] 37:13[2] 37:14[4] 37:16[4] 37:17[2] 37:18

37:19[4] 37:20 37:21[3] 37:22[3] 37:23[2] 37:24[4] 37:25[5] 37:26[3] 37:27 37:28 38:1 38:2[2] 38:3[2] 38:4[6] 38:5[2] 38:6[3] 38:7[3] 38:8[2] 38:9[3] 38:10 38:11[2] 38:12[3] 38:13[4] 38:14 38:15[3] 38:16[2] 38:19 38:20[7] 38:21 38:22[7] 38:23[3] 39:1[2] 39:2[4] 39:3[2] 39:4[3] 39:6[3] 39:7[2] 39:8 39:9[8] 39:10[2] 39:11[5] 39:12 39:13 39:14 39:15 39:16 39:17[4] 39:18[2] 39:19[2] 39:20[2] 39:21[3] 39:22 39:23[2] 39:24[2] 39:25[2] 39:26[2] 39:27[2] 39:28 40:1[2] 40:2 40:3[4] 40:4[3] 40:5[4] 40:6[3] 40:7[4] 40:9[2] 40:10[4] 40:11[2] 40:12[3] 40:13 40:15 40:16[5] 40:17[2] 40:18 40:19 40:20[2] 40:21[6] 40:22[5] 40:23[3] 40:24[3] 40:25[4] 40:26[4] 40:27[2] 40:28[2] 40:29[7] 40:30[3] 40:31[3]

40:32[2] 40:33[6] 40:34[4] 40:35[2] 40:36[4] 40:37[4] 40:38[2] 40:39[4] 40:40[2] 40:41 40:42[6] 40:43[2] 40:44[2] 40:45 40:46 40:47[2] 40:48[5] 40:49[4] 41:1[2] 41:2[5] 41:3[3] 41:4[2] 41:5 41:6[3] 41:7[3] 41:9 41:10 41:11[3] 41:12[2] 41:13[2] 41:14 41:15[4] 41:16[4] 41:17[3] 41:18[4] 41:19 41:20[2] 41:21 41:22[5] 41:23[2] 41:24[2] 41:25[2] 41:26[5] 42:1[2] 42:2 42:3 42:4[2] 42:5 42:6 42:7 42:8 42:9 42:10 42:11[4] 42:12 42:13[4] 42:14[2] 42:15 42:19 42:20[2] 43:2[3] 43:3[3] 43:4 43:5[2] 43:6[2] 43:7[3] 43:8[3] 43:9[2] 43:10 43:11[11] 43:13[5] 43:14[4] 43:15[2] 43:16 43:17[5] 43:18[2] 43:19 43:20[5] 43:21 43:22[2] 43:23 43:24[3] 43:25 43:26[2] 43:27[4] 44:1 44:2

44:3 44:4[3] 44:5[5] 44:6 44:7[3] 44:8 44:10 44:11[3] 44:12[2] 44:13[2] 44:14 44:15[2] 44:16[2] 44:17[3] 44:18 44:19[4] 44:23[4] 44:24[5] 44:25 44:26 44:27 44:28[2] 44:29[3] 44:30[2] 45:1[2] 45:2 45:3[5] 45:4[2] 45:5[3] 45:6[3] 45:7[6] 45:8[2] 45:9[3] 45:10[2] 45:11[2] 45:12[2] 45:13 45:15[3] 45:17[8] 45:18 45:19[4] 45:20[2] 45:22[2] 45:23[3] 45:24[3] 45:25[2] 46:1 46:2[5] 46:3 46:4[2] 46:5[3] 46:6[3] 46:7[4] 46:8[2] 46:9 46:10[2] 46:11[5] 46:12[3] 46:14[2] 46:15[2] 46:19 46:20 46:21[2] 46:22 46:23[2] 47:1[2] 47:2[2] 47:3[2] 47:4[2] 47:5 47:6[2] 47:7 47:8[2] 47:9[3] 47:10 47:11 47:12[4] 47:14[2] 47:15 47:16 47:17[4] 47:18[5] 47:19[2] 47:22[3] 47:23 48:1 48:2

48:3 48:4 48:5 48:6 48:7 48:8[4] 48:9[3] 48:10[7] 48:12 48:13[5] 48:14 48:15[4] 48:16[8] 48:17[8] 48:18[4] 48:19 48:20[2] 48:21[8] 48:22[2] 48:24 48:25 48:26 48:27 48:28[2] 48:29 48:30[2] 48:31 48:32[4] 48:33[3] 48:34 48:35

DA

1:1 1:2[2] 1:3[3] 1:4[6] 1:5[2] 1:6 1:7[3] 1:9 1:10[2] 1:11 1:12[2] 1:13[2] 1:14 1:15[2] 1:16[2] 1:17[4] 1:19[3] 1:20[3] 1:21 2:1[2] 2:2[4] 2:3[2] 2:4 2:5[2] 2:6[4] 2:7[2] 2:8 2:9[2] 2:10 2:11[2] 2:12[2] 2:13[3] 2:14 2:15 2:16[2] 2:17[2] 2:18 2:20[3] 2:21[4] 2:22[2] 2:23[3] 2:24[2] 2:25 2:26[2] 2:27 2:28[2] 2:29 2:30 2:31[2] 2:32[2] 2:33 2:34[2]

2:35[5] 2:36 2:37[2] 2:38[3] 2:39[2] 2:40[4] 2:41[3] 2:42[3] 2:43 2:44[4] 2:45[4] 2:46[3] 2:47[3] 2:48[3] 2:49[2] 3:1 3:2[2] 3:3[3] 3:4 3:5[2] 3:6[2] 3:7[3] 3:8 3:9 3:10[3] 3:11[2] 3:12 3:13[2] 3:14[2] 3:15[4] 3:16[2] 3:17 3:19[3] 3:20[3] 3:21[3] 3:22[2] 3:23[2] 3:24[4] 3:25[3] 3:26[5] 3:27[3] 3:28[5] 3:29[3] 3:30 4:1 4:2 4:3[2] 4:4 4:5[2] 4:7[2] 4:8[2] 4:9[2] 4:10[2] 4:11[3] 4:12[4] 4:13[2] 4:14[4] 4:15[3] 4:16[2] 4:17[3] 4:19[4] 4:20[2] 4:21[3] 4:22[3] 4:23[7] 4:24 4:25[5] 4:26 4:27[2] 4:30[2] 4:32[4] 4:33[4] 4:34[6] 4:35[4] 4:36[6] 4:37[4] 5:1 5:2[3] 5:3[3] 5:4[3] 5:5[2] 5:6[2] 5:7[6] 5:9[2] 5:10[3] 5:11[4] 5:12[5]

5:13[2] 5:14[3] 5:15[2] 5:16[5] 5:17[3] 5:18[3] 5:19[6] 5:20[2] 5:21[5] 5:22 5:23[9] 5:24 5:25 5:26 5:27 5:28[2] 5:29[3] 5:31[2] 6:1 6:2[2] 6:3[2] 6:4 6:6[2] 6:7[3] 6:8[2] 6:9 6:10[3] 6:11[2] 6:12[3] 6:13 6:14[2] 6:15[2] 6:16[3] 6:17[4] 6:18[2] 6:19 6:20[3] 6:22[2] 6:23[2] 6:24[6] 6:25 6:26[4] 6:27[4] 6:28 7:1[2] 7:2[2] 7:3 7:4[4] 7:5[4] 7:6[2] 7:7[8] 7:8[3] 7:9[3] 7:10[3] 7:11[2] 7:12 7:13[3] 7:14[5] 7:15 7:16[2] 7:18[2] 7:19[2] 7:20[4] 7:21[2] 7:22[2] 7:23[3] 7:24[4] 7:25[7] 7:26[2] 7:27[5] 7:28 8:2[4] 8:3[4] 8:4[3] 8:5[3] 8:6[2] 8:7[7] 8:8[2] 8:9[3] 8:10[4] 8:11[2] 8:12[4] 8:13[3] 8:14[2] 8:15[2] 8:16[2] 8:17[2]

8:18 8:19 8:20 8:21[2] 8:23[2] 8:24[6] 8:25[3] 8:26[2] 8:27[4] 9:3[4] 9:4[6] 9:5[4] 9:6[2] 9:7[3] 9:8 9:9 9:11 9:12[2] 9:13 9:14 9:15[2] 9:16[3] 9:17[2] 9:18[3] 9:19[2] 9:20[5] 9:22[4] 9:23[2] 9:24[7] 9:25[5] 9:26[6] 9:27[5] 10:1[3] 10:4[2] 10:5[2] 10:6[5] 10:7 10:8[3] 10:9[2] 10:10[2] 10:11[3] 10:12[2] 10:13[2] 10:15[2] 10:16[4] 10:18[2] 10:19[3] 10:20[2] 10:21 11:1 11:2[3] 11:3[2] 11:4[3] 11:5[4] 11:6[4] 11:7[3] 11:8[4] 11:9 11:10[5] 11:11[4] 11:12[2] 11:13[3] 11:14 11:15[3] 11:16[2] 11:17[2] 11:18 11:19[2] 11:21[2] 11:22[2] 11:23[2] 11:24[2] 11:25[4] 11:26[2] 11:27[2] 11:28[3] 11:29 11:30[3] 11:31[4] 11:32[3] 11:33[3] 11:35[3] 11:36[5] 11:38[4] 11:39[3] 11:40[7] 11:41[3]

11:42 11:43[4] 11:44[2] 11:45[2] 12:1[3] 12:2[3] 12:3[3] 12:4[3] 12:5[2] 12:6 12:7[5] 12:8 12:9[2] 12:10[3] 12:11[3] 12:12[3] 12:13

HO

1:1[2] 1:2[2] 1:3[2] 1:4[3] 1:5 1:6[3] 1:7[2] 1:8 1:9 1:10 1:11[3] 2:1 2:2 2:3[4] 2:4 2:5[3] 2:6 2:7[3] 2:8[4] 2:9[4] 2:10[2] 2:11[2] 2:12[4] 2:13[5] 2:14[2] 2:15[4] 2:16[2] 2:17 2:18[7] 2:19[4] 2:20 2:21[2] 2:22[4] 2:23[4] 3:1 3:2[2] 3:3[2] 3:4[5] 3:5[4] 4:2[5] 4:3[2] 4:5 4:8 4:9[3] 4:10[2] 4:11[2] 4:12[2] 4:13[4] 4:14 4:15 4:19 5:1[3] 5:2 5:3[2] 5:4 5:5[2] 5:6 5:8 5:11 5:12 5:13[2] 5:14[3] 5:15[2] 6:1[3] 6:2

6:3[2] 6:4 6:5 6:6[2] 6:8 6:9 7:1[3] 7:2 7:3 7:7 7:9[2] 7:10[2] 7:14[3] 7:15 8:1 8:4[2] 8:7 8:10 8:13[2] 8:14[3] 9:2[2] 9:3 9:5 9:7 9:8 9:10[2] 9:11[2] 9:14 9:17 10:5 10:6 10:8[3] 10:10 10:11[3] 10:12 10:14 11:1 11:2 11:4[2] 11:6[3] 11:7 11:9[2] 11:11[2] 11:12[3] 12:1[4] 12:2 12:3 12:4[3] 12:6[2] 12:8 12:9 12:10[2] 12:12[3] 12:13[2] 12:14 13:2[4] 13:3[2] 13:4 13:6 13:8[2] 13:10[2] 13:11 13:15[2] 13:16 14:2[2] 14:5 14:6[2] 14:7 14:8 14:9[3]

JOE

1:2 1:3[2] 1:4[2] 1:5[2] 1:6[2] 1:7[2] 1:9 1:11 1:12[2] 1:13[2] 1:14[2] 1:15

1:16 1:19 1:20 2:1 2:2[3] 2:3[3] 2:4 2:7[2] 2:8 2:9 2:10[2] 2:11[3] 2:12[3] 2:13[6] 2:14[3] 2:16[2] 2:17[3] 2:18 2:19[5] 2:20[5] 2:21 2:22 2:23[3] 2:24[3] 2:25[3] 2:26[4] 2:27[4] 2:28[3] 2:29[2] 2:30[4] 2:31[2] 2:32[3] 3:1[2] 3:2[4] 3:3[3] 3:4[5] 3:5[2] 3:6 3:7 3:8[3] 3:10 3:11[2] 3:12 3:15[2] 3:16[4] 3:17 3:18[5] 3:19 3:20

AM

1:1 1:2[4] 1:3 1:5[3] 1:6 1:8[4] 1:9[2] 1:11[4] 1:13 1:14 1:15[2] 2:1 2:2[3] 2:3[2] 2:4[3] 2:5 2:6[2] 2:7[3] 2:8[2] 2:9[2] 2:10 2:11[2] 2:12 2:14 2:15 2:16 3:5 3:6[2] 3:9[4] 3:10 3:11[2]

3:12 3:13 3:14[2] 3:15[3] 4:1 4:2 4:3[2] 4:4[3] 4:5[3] 4:6[2] 4:7[4] 4:9[4] 4:10[2] 4:11[2] 4:12 4:13[3] 5:3 5:4 5:5[2] 5:6[3] 5:7 5:8[4] 5:10 5:11 5:12[2] 5:14[2] 5:15[2] 5:16[3] 5:17 5:18 5:19[3] 5:20[2] 5:21 5:22 5:24 5:26 6:1 6:2[2] 6:3 6:4[3] 6:5 6:6 6:7 6:8 6:9 6:10[4] 6:11[2] 6:12 6:14 7:1[2] 7:2 7:4[3] 7:7 7:8[2] 7:9[3] 7:11 7:12[2] 7:13 7:14[2] 7:15[2] 7:16 7:17[5] 8:1 8:2[2] 8:3 8:5[3] 8:6[2] 8:8[4] 8:9[2] 8:10[6] 8:12[4] 8:13 8:14[3] 9:1[4] 9:3[4] 9:4[4] 9:5[5] 9:6[2] 9:7[2] 9:8 9:9 9:11[3] 9:12 9:13[3] 9:14[6] 9:15[2]

OB

1[2] 4 7 8 9 10 11[2] 16[2] 17[2] 18[6] 19[5] 20[2] 21[2]

JON

1:2 1:3[3] 1:4 1:5[4] 1:6 1:7[2] 1:8[2] 1:9[3] 1:10 1:11 1:12[2] 1:13 1:14[2] 1:15[2] 1:16[2] 1:17[2] 2:2[3] 2:3[2] 2:7 2:10[2] 3:1 3:2 3:3 3:4[4] 3:5[2] 3:6[4] 3:7[3] 3:8[3] 3:9[2] 3:10[3] 4:1 4:2[5] 4:5[3] 4:6[2] 4:7 4:8[4] 4:9[2] 4:10 4:11[3]

MIC

1:1[2] 1:2[2] 1:3[2] 1:4[3] 1:5[2] 1:6[3] 1:7[4] 1:8[3] 1:16 2:1 2:2[6] 2:4[2] 2:10 2:11[2] 2:13[4] 3:1[2] 3:2[2] 3:3[4] 3:5[2] 3:6[3] 3:7 3:8[3] 3:9[2] 3:10

3:11^{3} 3:12^{2} 4:1^{2} 4:2^{7} 4:3^{4} 4:4^{2} 4:5^{2} 4:6^{2} 4:7^{3} 4:8 4:10^{3} 4:11 4:13^{5} 5:4^{3} 5:5^{3} 5:6^{3} 5:7 5:8^{3} 5:9 5:10^{2} 5:11^{2} 5:12^{2} 5:13^{2} 5:14 5:15^{2} 6:1 6:2^{2} 6:3 6:4^{3} 6:5 6:6 6:8^{2} 6:9^{2} 6:10 6:11 6:12^{2} 6:14^{3} 6:15 6:16^{3} 7:2 7:3^{2} 7:4 7:9^{2} 7:10 7:12^{4} 7:14 7:16 7:17 7:18 7:19 7:20

NA

1:2^{3} 1:3^{4} 1:4^{4} 1:5^{3} 1:6^{2} 1:7 1:8 1:10 1:12 1:13 1:14^{2} 2:2 2:3 2:5 2:6 2:7^{2} 2:9 2:10^{6} 2:11^{3} 2:12^{3} 2:13^{4} 3:1 3:2^{3} 3:3^{4} 3:4 3:5^{3} 3:6^{3} 3:7^{2} 3:8 3:9^{3} 3:10^{2} 3:14 3:16 3:17^{2} 3:18

HAB

1:2^{2} 1:3^{4} 1:4 1:5^{2} 1:6 1:7^{2} 1:8^{3} 1:9 1:10^{3} 1:11^{2} 1:12 1:13^{2} 1:14 1:15^{2} 1:16^{2} 1:17 2:1^{3} 2:2^{3} 2:3 2:5^{3} 2:6^{3} 2:7^{2} 2:8^{2} 2:10 2:11 2:12 2:13 2:15 2:16^{2} 2:17^{3} 2:18 2:19^{2} 3:2 3:3^{2} 3:4^{2} 3:5 3:6^{3} 3:7 3:8 3:10^{2} 3:11^{2} 3:16 3:17^{2} 3:19^{2}

ZEP

1:3^{4} 1:4^{3} 1:5^{4} 1:6^{2} 1:8^{3} 1:9 1:10^{3} 1:12^{2} 1:13^{2} 1:14 1:15^{4} 1:16^{2} 1:17^{3} 2:4^{2} 2:6^{3} 2:7^{2} 2:8^{2} 2:9^{4} 2:10 2:11 2:13^{4} 2:14^{2} 2:15^{2} 3:1 3:4 3:7 3:11 3:12^{2} 3:13^{2} 3:14 3:16 3:19^{4} 3:20

HAG

1:1 1:4 1:6^{2} 1:8^{4} 1:9^{3} 1:10 1:11^{3} 1:12^{3} 1:14^{5} 1:15 2:1 2:2^{2} 2:3 2:4^{3} 2:6^{4} 2:7^{2} 2:8 2:9 2:10 2:12^{3} 2:13^{2} 2:14^{4} 2:15^{2} 2:17^{2} 2:18^{2} 2:19^{3} 2:20^{2} 2:21 2:22^{6} 2:23

ZEC

1:3 1:4 1:5 1:6^{4} 1:7 1:8^{4} 1:9 1:10^{3} 1:11^{5} 1:12^{3} 1:13^{2} 1:14 1:15^{2} 1:16 1:17^{2} 1:18^{2} 1:19^{3} 1:20 1:21 2:1^{2} 2:2^{2} 2:3^{2} 2:4^{2} 2:5 2:6 2:9^{2} 2:10^{3} 2:11^{4} 2:12^{2} 3:1^{2} 3:2 3:3 3:4^{4} 3:5^{3} 3:6 3:7^{3} 3:8 3:9 3:10 4:1^{2} 4:2^{5} 4:3^{2} 4:4 4:5^{2} 4:6 4:7 4:9 4:10^{2} 4:11^{2} 4:12^{2} 4:13^{3} 5:1^{3} 5:2^{3} 5:3 5:4^{5} 5:5^{2} 5:6^{2} 5:7^{2} 5:8^{3} 5:9^{5} 5:11^{3} 6:1^{5} 6:2 6:3^{3} 6:4 6:5^{2} 6:6^{2} 6:7^{6} 6:8 6:9 6:10^{3} 6:11^{3} 6:12^{3} 6:13^{5} 6:14^{4} 6:15^{4} 7:1 7:2^{2} 7:3^{2} 7:5^{3} 7:6^{3} 7:7^{3} 7:8 7:9^{2} 7:10^{2} 7:11^{2} 7:12 7:13^{2} 8:2 8:3^{3} 8:4^{2} 8:5^{2} 8:7 8:8^{5} 8:12^{3} 8:13^{3} 8:14 8:15 8:16 8:17^{2} 8:18 8:19^{6} 8:20 8:21^{2} 8:22^{2} 9:1 9:2^{2} 9:3^{3} 9:4^{2} 9:5^{5} 9:6^{2} 9:7^{4} 9:8^{3} 9:9^{3} 9:10^{5} 9:13^{2} 9:14^{4} 9:15^{6} 9:16 9:17^{2} 10:1 10:2^{2} 10:3^{2} 10:5^{3} 10:6^{5} 10:7^{3} 10:8^{2} 10:9^{4} 10:10^{4} 10:11^{5} 10:12^{3} 11:5^{3} 11:6^{3} 11:7^{4} 11:8^{2} 11:9^{2} 11:10^{2} 11:11^{2} 11:12^{2} 11:13^{3} 11:14 11:15 11:16 11:17^{2} 12:1^{2} 12:2 12:3 12:4^{3} 12:5 12:6^{4} 12:7 12:8^{2} 12:9 12:10^{6} 12:12^{3} 12:13^{2} 12:14 13:1^{2} 13:2^{4} 13:3^{4} 13:4 13:6 13:7^{3} 13:8^{2} 13:9^{5} 14:1 14:2^{5} 14:3 14:4^{6} 14:5^{3} 14:6 14:8^{3} 14:9^{2} 14:10^{3} 14:11^{2} 14:12^{3} 14:13^{3} 14:14^{4} 14:15^{3} 14:16^{2} 14:17 14:18^{2} 14:19 14:20 14:21^{5}

MAL

1:3^{3} 1:4^{3} 1:5^{2} 1:6^{3} 1:7 1:8^{3} 1:9 1:11^{2} 1:12 1:13^{4} 1:14^{3} 2:1 2:2^{2} 2:3^{2} 2:4 2:5^{3} 2:6^{3} 2:7 2:9 2:11^{3} 2:12^{2} 2:13^{2} 2:14^{2} 2:15^{3} 2:17 3:1^{2} 3:2^{2} 3:3^{5} 3:4^{2} 3:5^{8} 3:7^{2} 3:8 3:9 3:10^{2} 3:11^{2} 3:12 3:14^{2} 3:15 3:16^{4} 3:17^{2} 3:18^{3} 4:1^{3} 4:2^{2} 4:3 4:4 4:5 4:6^{3}

MT

1:2^{3} 1:3^{4} 1:4^{3} 1:5^{3} 1:6^{2} 1:7^{3} 1:8^{3} 1:9^{3} 1:10^{3} 1:11^{2} 1:12^{2} 1:13^{3} 1:14^{3} 1:15^{3} 1:16 1:17^{2} 1:19 1:21^{2} 1:23^{2} 1:24 1:25^{2} 2:2 2:3 2:4^{2} 2:5 2:6 2:8^{5} 2:9^{2} 2:11^{6} 2:12 2:13^{5} 2:14^{2} 2:15 2:16^{4} 2:18^{3} 2:20^{3} 2:21^{4} 2:23^{2} 3:2 3:4^{4} 3:5^{2} 3:6 3:7 3:9 3:10^{2} 3:11 3:12^{2} 3:14 3:15 3:16^{4} 3:17 4:2^{2} 4:3 4:4 4:5 4:6^{2} 4:8^{2} 4:9^{2} 4:10 4:11^{2} 4:13^{3} 4:15 4:16^{2} 4:17 4:18^{2} 4:19^{2} 4:20^{2} 4:21^{3} 4:22^{3} 4:23^{4} 4:24^{7} 4:25^{5} 5:1^{2} 5:2^{2} 5:6 5:11^{2} 5:12 5:13 5:15^{2} 5:16 5:18 5:19^{2} 5:20 5:21 5:22 5:23 5:24^{3} 5:25^{2} 5:29^{3} 5:30^{3} 5:32 5:38 5:40^{2} 5:41 5:42 5:43 5:44^{2} 5:45^{3} 5:47 6:2 6:4 6:5 6:6^{2} 6:8 6:12 6:13^{3} 6:17 6:18 6:19^{3} 6:20 6:24^{3} 6:25 6:28 6:29 6:30 6:33^{2} 7:2 7:3 7:4 7:5 7:6^{2} 7:7^{3} 7:8^{2} 7:12 7:13^{2} 7:14^{2} 7:19 7:22^{2} 7:23 7:24 7:25^{5} 7:26^{2} 7:27^{6} 7:28 7:29 8:2^{2} 8:3^{3} 8:4^{2} 8:5 8:6 8:7^{2} 8:8^{2} 8:9^{6} 8:10 8:11^{5} 8:12 8:13^{3} 8:14^{2} 8:15^{4} 8:16^{2} 8:17 8:19^{2} 8:20^{2} 8:21^{2} 8:22 8:23 8:24 8:25^{2} 8:26^{4} 8:27 8:28 8:29 8:30 8:32^{4} 8:33^{4} 8:34^{2} 9:1^{3} 9:2^{2} 9:3 9:4 9:5 9:6 9:7 9:8 9:9^{4} 9:10^{4} 9:11^{2} 9:13^{2} 9:14 9:15^{2} 9:16 9:17^{3} 9:18^{3} 9:19^{3} 9:20^{2} 9:22^{2} 9:23^{3} 9:24 9:25^{2} 9:26 9:27^{2} 9:28^{2} 9:30^{2} 9:33^{2} 9:35^{5} 9:36 10:1^{3} 10:2^{2} 10:3^{3} 10:4 10:5^{2} 10:7 10:11^{2} 10:12 10:13 10:14 10:15 10:16 10:17 10:18^{3} 10:21^{4} 10:25 10:26 10:27 10:28^{2} 10:29 10:35^{2} 10:36 10:37 10:38^{2} 10:39 10:40 10:41 10:42 11:1^{2} 11:3 11:4^{3} 11:5^{3} 11:6 11:7 11:9 11:12^{2} 11:13 11:14 11:16 11:17^{3} 11:18 11:19^{4} 11:21^{2} 11:22 11:23 11:25^{4} 11:27^{2} 11:28^{2} 11:29^{3} 11:30 12:1^{3} 12:3 12:4 12:5 12:6 12:7 12:9 12:10^{2} 12:11^{3} 12:13^{2} 12:14 12:15^{2} 12:16 12:18 12:20 12:21 12:22^{4} 12:23^{2} 12:25^{3} 12:26 12:27 12:29^{2} 12:30 12:31 12:32 12:33^{2} 12:35 12:37 12:38 12:39^{3} 12:40^{2} 12:41^{2} 12:42^{2} 12:43 12:44^{2} 12:45^{4} 12:46 12:47 12:48^{2} 12:49^{3} 12:50^{2} 13:1 13:2^{3} 13:3 13:4^{3} 13:5 13:6^{2} 13:7^{3} 13:8 13:10^{2} 13:11 13:12 13:13 13:14^{4} 13:15^{6} 13:16 13:17^{4} 13:19^{2} 13:20 13:21 13:22^{3} 13:23^{2} 13:25^{2} 13:26 13:27 13:28 13:30^{2} 13:31 13:32^{2} 13:33 13:34 13:36^{2} 13:37 13:39 13:40 13:41 13:42^{2} 13:44^{3} 13:46^{2} 13:47 13:48^{2} 13:49 13:50^{2} 13:52 13:53 13:54^{3} 13:55^{4} 13:56 13:57^{2} 13:58 14:2^{2} 14:3^{2} 14:5 14:6 14:8 14:9^{2} 14:10^{2} 14:11^{3} 14:12^{5} 14:13 14:14^{4} 14:15^{3} 14:17^{2} 14:19^{7} 14:20^{3} 14:21^{2} 14:22^{2} 14:23^{2} 14:25 14:26^{2} 14:28^{2} 14:29^{2} 14:30 14:31^{3} 14:32 14:33 14:34 14:35^{2} 14:36^{2} 15:1 15:3 15:4^{2} 15:6 15:8 15:10^{3} 15:12 15:13 15:14 15:15 15:16 15:17 15:18 15:21^{2} 15:22^{2} 15:23^{2} 15:24 15:25 15:26^{2} 15:27 15:28^{2} 15:29^{4} 15:30^{4} 15:31^{2} 15:32^{3} 15:33 15:34^{3} 15:35 15:36^{6} 15:37^{3} 15:38^{2} 15:39^{3} 16:1 16:2 16:3^{2} 16:4^{4} 16:5 16:6^{2} 16:7 16:9 16:10 16:11 16:12 16:14^{2} 16:16^{2} 16:17^{3} 16:18^{3} 16:19^{3} 16:21^{5} 16:22 16:23 16:24^{2} 16:25 16:26 16:27 17:1^{3} 17:2^{3} 17:3^{2} 17:4^{3} 17:5 17:6^{2} 17:7^{4} 17:8 17:9 17:10 17:11^{3} 17:12 17:14^{2} 17:15^{2} 17:16^{2} 17:17^{2} 17:18^{3} 17:19 17:20^{3} 17:21 17:22 17:23 17:24^{2} 17:25 17:27^{5} 18:2^{2} 18:3^{2} 18:5 18:6 18:8 18:9^{2} 18:12^{4} 18:13^{2} 18:15^{2} 18:17^{2} 18:18 18:21^{2} 18:24 18:25^{4} 18:26^{2} 18:27^{2} 18:28^{3} 18:29^{3} 18:30^{2} 18:31^{2} 18:34^{2} 19:1^{2} 19:2^{2} 19:3 19:4^{3} 19:5^{4} 19:7 19:9^{3} 19:12^{2} 19:13^{2} 19:14 19:15^{2} 19:16^{2} 19:17 19:19^{2} 19:21^{5} 19:24 19:26 19:27^{2} 19:28 19:29^{2} 19:30^{2} 20:2 20:3^{2} 20:4^{3} 20:5^{2} 20:6^{3} 20:7 20:8 20:9 20:10 20:11 20:12^{2} 20:13 20:14 20:16 20:17^{2} 20:18^{3} 20:19^{4} 20:20 20:21^{2} 20:22^{2} 20:23^{3} 20:24 20:25^{2} 20:27 20:28 20:29 20:30 20:31 20:32^{3} 20:34^{3} 21:1^{2} 21:2^{3} 21:3^{2} 21:5^{2} 21:6^{2} 21:7^{4} 21:8^{2} 21:9^{2} 21:10 21:11 21:12^{5} 21:13 21:14^{3} 21:15^{4} 21:16^{2} 21:17^{3} 21:19^{4} 21:20 21:21^{3} 21:22 21:23^{4} 21:24^{2} 21:25 21:27^{3} 21:28^{2} 21:29^{2} 21:30^{5} 21:31 21:32^{3} 21:33^{3} 21:34 21:35^{4} 21:36 21:38 21:39^{3} 21:41 21:42 21:43 21:44 21:45^{2} 22:1^{3} 22:3^{2} 22:4^{3} 22:5 22:6^{3} 22:7^{3} 22:9 22:10^{3} 22:11 22:12^{2} 22:13^{4} 22:15 22:16^{2} 22:18 22:19 22:20^{2} 22:21 22:22^{2} 22:23 22:24 22:25^{2} 22:26 22:27 22:29 22:32^{2} 22:33 22:35 22:37^{2} 22:38 22:39 22:40 22:46 23:1 23:2 23:3^{2} 23:4^{2} 23:5 23:6^{2} 23:7^{2} 23:8 23:9 23:12^{2} 23:13 23:14^{2} 23:15^{3} 23:17 23:18 23:19 23:20 23:21^{2} 23:22^{2} 23:23^{6} 23:24 23:25^{3} 23:26 23:27^{2} 23:28 23:29^{2} 23:30 23:34^{6} 23:35 23:37^{2} 24:1^{3} 24:2 24:3^{3} 24:4^{2} 24:5 24:6^{2} 24:7^{4} 24:9^{2} 24:10^{3} 24:11^{2} 24:12 24:14^{2} 24:19^{2} 24:22 24:24^{3} 24:27 24:29^{3} 24:30^{4} 24:31^{2} 24:32 24:35 24:36 24:38^{2} 24:39^{2} 24:40 24:41 24:43 24:45 24:48 24:49^{3} 24:50 24:51^{3} 25:1 25:2^{2} 25:3 25:5 25:6 25:7 25:8 25:9^{2} 25:10^{3} 25:12 25:14 25:15^{3} 25:16^{2} 25:17 25:18^{2} 25:19 25:20^{2} 25:21 25:22 25:23 25:24^{2} 25:25^{3} 25:26^{3} 25:27 25:28 25:29 25:30^{2} 25:31 25:32^{2} 25:33 25:35^{2} 25:36^{3} 25:37^{2} 25:38^{2} 25:39 25:40^{2} 25:41 25:42^{2} 25:43^{4} 25:44 25:46 26:1 26:2 26:3^{2} 26:4^{2} 26:7 26:9 26:15^{3} 26:16 26:18^{2} 26:19^{2} 26:21 26:22^{2} 26:23^{3} 26:25 26:26^{5} 26:27^{3} 26:30 26:31 26:33 26:36^{2} 26:37^{4} 26:38 26:39^{3} 26:40^{3} 26:41 26:42 26:43^{2} 26:44^{3} 26:45^{3} 26:47^{4} 26:49^{2} 26:50^{3} 26:51^{4} 26:53 26:55^{2} 26:56 26:57^{2} 26:58^{2} 26:59^{2} 26:61^{2} 26:62^{2} 26:63^{2} 26:64 26:66 26:67^{2} 26:69 26:71^{2} 26:72 26:73^{2} 26:74^{2} 26:75^{3} 27:1 27:2^{2} 27:3^{2} 27:4 27:5^{4} 27:6^{2} 27:7^{2} 27:9 27:10 27:11^{3} 27:12^{2} 27:14 27:16 27:20^{2} 27:21 27:23 27:24 27:25^{2} 27:26 27:27 27:28^{2} 27:29^{3} 27:30^{3} 27:31^{3} 27:32 27:33 27:34 27:35^{3} 27:36 27:37 27:38 27:39 27:40^{2} 27:41 27:42 27:46 27:48^{5} 27:51^{3} 27:52^{2} 27:53^{3} 27:54^{2} 27:55 27:56^{3} 27:58 27:59 27:60^{3} 27:61^{2} 27:62 27:64^{2} 27:66^{2} 28:1 28:2^{4} 28:3 28:4^{2} 28:5^{2} 28:7^{3} 28:8^{3} 28:9^{4} 28:10 28:11 28:12^{2} 28:13 28:14^{2} 28:15^{2} 28:17 28:18^{3} 28:19^{3} 28:20

MK

1:4 1:5^{3} 1:6^{4} 1:7^{2} 1:9^{2} 1:10 1:11 1:12 1:13^{3} 1:15^{3} 1:16 1:17^{2} 1:18^{2} 1:19^{2} 1:20^{3} 1:21^{3} 1:22^{2} 1:23^{2} 1:25^{2} 1:26^{2} 1:27^{2} 1:28 1:29^{3} 1:30 1:31^{5} 1:32^{2} 1:33 1:34^{3} 1:35^{3} 1:36^{2} 1:37 1:38 1:39^{2} 1:40^{3} 1:41^{3} 1:42^{2} 1:43^{2} 1:44^{2} 1:45^{3} 2:1^{2} 2:2^{2} 2:3 2:4^{2} 2:6 2:8 2:9^{2} 2:11^{2} 2:12^{3} 2:13^{3} 2:14^{4} 2:15^{4} 2:16^{5} 2:18^{5} 2:19 2:20 2:21 2:22^{3} 2:23^{2} 2:24 2:25^{3} 2:26^{2} 2:27^{2} 3:1^{2} 3:2 3:3 3:4 3:5^{3} 3:6^{2} 3:7^{2} 3:8^{5} 3:9 3:11^{2} 3:12 3:13^{3} 3:14^{2} 3:15^{2} 3:16 3:17^{3} 3:18^{8} 3:19^{2} 3:20 3:21 3:22^{2} 3:23^{2} 3:25 3:26^{2} 3:27^{2} 3:28 3:31^{2} 3:32^{3} 3:33 3:34^{3} 3:35^{2} 4:1^{3} 4:2^{2} 4:4^{3} 4:5^{2} 4:6 4:7^{4} 4:8^{6} 4:9 4:10 4:11 4:12^{4} 4:13 4:15^{2} 4:16 4:17^{2} 4:18 4:19^{4} 4:20^{4} 4:21^{2} 4:24^{2} 4:25 4:26 4:27^{5} 4:30 4:32^{2} 4:33 4:34 4:35 4:36^{2} 4:37^{2} 4:38^{3} 4:39^{5} 4:40 4:41^{3} 5:1 5:2 5:3 5:4^{3} 5:5^{4} 5:6 5:7^{2} 5:9^{2} 5:10 5:12 5:13^{5} 5:14^{4} 5:15^{6} 5:16^{2} 5:17 5:18 5:19^{2} 5:20^{3} 5:21^{2} 5:22^{2} 5:23^{3} 5:24^{2} 5:25 5:26^{3} 5:27 5:29^{2} 5:30^{2} 5:31^{2} 5:32 5:33^{3} 5:34^{2} 5:37^{3} 5:38^{4} 5:39^{2} 5:40^{4} 5:41^{2} 5:42^{3} 5:43^{2} 6:1^{3} 6:2^{3} 6:3^{5} 6:4^{2} 6:5^{2} 6:6^{2} 6:7^{4} 6:8 6:9 6:10 6:11^{2} 6:12^{2} 6:13^{3} 6:14^{3} 6:15 6:17^{2} 6:19 6:20^{4} 6:21^{2} 6:22^{5} 6:23 6:24^{3} 6:25^{3} 6:26^{2} 6:27^{4} 6:28^{3} 6:29^{3} 6:30^{3} 6:31^{4} 6:32 6:33^{5} 6:34^{3} 6:35^{3} 6:36^{2} 6:37^{4} 6:38^{3} 6:39 6:40^{2} 6:41^{6} 6:42^{2} 6:43^{2} 6:44 6:45^{2} 6:46 6:47^{2} 6:48^{3} 6:49 6:50^{3} 6:51^{4} 6:53^{2} 6:54 6:55^{2} 6:56^{3} 7:1 7:2 7:3 7:4^{4} 7:5 7:6 7:8^{2} 7:12 7:13 7:14^{2} 7:17 7:18 7:19 7:20 7:23 7:24^{5} 7:25^{2} 7:26 7:27 7:28^{2} 7:29 7:30^{2} 7:31^{2} 7:32^{3} 7:33^{4} 7:34^{2} 7:35^{3} 7:36 7:37^{2} 8:1^{2} 8:2 8:3 8:4 8:5^{2} 8:6^{6} 8:7^{3} 8:8^{2} 8:9^{2} 8:10^{2} 8:11^{2} 8:12^{2} 8:13^{3} 8:15^{2} 8:16 8:17 8:18 8:20^{2} 8:21 8:22^{3} 8:23^{4} 8:24^{2} 8:25^{3} 8:26 8:27^{3} 8:28^{2} 8:29^{3} 8:30 8:31^{6} 8:32^{3} 8:33 8:34^{3} 8:35 8:36 8:38^{2} 9:1 9:2^{5} 9:3 9:4^{2} 9:5^{5} 9:7^{2} 9:8 9:9 9:10 9:11 9:12^{5} 9:13 9:14^{2} 9:15^{2} 9:16 9:17^{2} 9:18^{6} 9:19

9:20^{4} 9:21^{2} 9:22^{3} 9:24^{2} 9:25^{2} 9:26^{4} 9:27^{2} 9:28 9:29^{2} 9:30^{3} 9:31^{3} 9:32 9:33^{2} 9:35^{4} 9:36^{3} 9:37 9:38^{3} 9:42^{2} 9:43 9:44 9:45 9:46 9:47 9:48 9:49 9:50 10:1^{4} 10:2^{2} 10:3^{3} 10:4^{2} 10:5^{2} 10:6 10:7^{2} 10:8 10:10 10:11^{2} 10:12^{2} 10:13^{2} 10:14^{2} 10:16^{2} 10:17^{3} 10:18 10:19 10:20^{2} 10:21^{5} 10:22^{2} 10:23^{2} 10:24^{2} 10:26 10:27 10:28 10:29^{3} 10:30^{6} 10:31 10:32^{6} 10:33^{4} 10:34^{5} 10:35^{2} 10:36 10:37 10:38 10:39^{3} 10:40 10:41^{2} 10:42^{3} 10:44 10:45 10:46^{3} 10:47^{2} 10:48 10:49^{3} 10:50^{2} 10:51^{2} 10:52^{3} 11:1^{2} 11:2^{3} 11:3^{2} 11:4^{3} 11:5 11:6^{2} 11:7^{3} 11:8^{3} 11:9^{2} 11:11^{4} 11:12 11:13^{2} 11:14^{3}

11:15^{6} 11:16 11:17 11:18^{3} 11:19 11:20 11:21 11:22 11:23^{2} 11:24 11:25 11:27^{4} 11:28^{2} 11:29^{4} 11:31 11:33^{3} 12:1^{6} 12:2 12:3^{2} 12:4^{4} 12:5^{4} 12:7 12:8^{3} 12:9^{2} 12:10 12:11 12:12^{3} 12:13^{2} 12:14^{2} 12:16^{4} 12:17^{3} 12:18 12:19^{3} 12:20^{2} 12:21^{3} 12:22^{2} 12:24 12:26^{3} 12:28^{3} 12:29 12:30^{4} 12:31 12:32^{2} 12:33^{6} 12:34^{2} 12:35^{2} 12:37^{2} 12:38^{2} 12:39^{2} 12:40 12:41^{3} 12:42^{2} 12:43^{2} 13:1^{2} 13:2 13:3^{4} 13:4 13:5 13:6 13:7^{2} 13:8^{4} 13:9^{3} 13:10 13:11 13:12^{3} 13:13 13:15 13:16 13:17 13:18 13:20 13:21 13:22^{3} 13:24 13:25^{2} 13:26^{2} 13:27^{2} 13:28 13:31 13:32 13:33 13:34^{3} 13:37 14:1^{4} 14:3^{3} 14:4^{2} 14:5^{2}

14:6 14:7 14:10 14:11^{3} 14:12^{2} 14:13^{3} 14:14 14:15^{2} 14:16^{4} 14:17 14:18^{2} 14:19^{3} 14:20^{2} 14:22^{5} 14:23^{3} 14:24 14:26 14:27^{2} 14:30 14:32^{2} 14:33^{5} 14:34^{2} 14:35^{3} 14:36 14:37^{3} 14:38 14:39^{3} 14:40 14:41^{3} 14:43^{5} 14:44^{2} 14:45^{3} 14:46^{2} 14:47^{3} 14:48^{3} 14:49 14:50^{2} 14:51^{2} 14:52^{2} 14:53^{4} 14:54^{3} 14:55^{3} 14:57^{2} 14:58 14:60^{2} 14:61^{2} 14:62^{3} 14:63 14:64 14:65^{5} 14:66 14:67^{3} 14:68^{2} 14:69^{2} 14:70^{3} 14:71 14:72^{3} 15:1^{6} 15:2^{2} 15:3 15:4 15:7 15:8 15:12^{2} 15:13 15:14 15:15^{2} 15:16^{2} 15:17^{3} 15:18 15:19^{3} 15:20^{3} 15:21^{2} 15:22 15:23 15:24 15:25^{2} 15:26 15:27^{2} 15:28^{2} 15:29^{3} 15:30 15:32^{2} 15:33 15:34 15:35 15:36^{4}

15:37^{2} 15:38 15:39^{2} 15:40^{3} 15:41^{2} 15:42 15:43^{2} 15:44^{2} 15:45 15:46^{5} 15:47^{2} 16:1^{4} 16:2 16:3 16:4 16:5^{2} 16:6 16:7 16:8^{3} 16:10^{3} 16:11^{2} 16:12 16:13^{2} 16:14^{2} 16:15^{2} 16:16 16:17 16:18^{2} 16:19 16:20^{3}

LU

1:2 1:5^{2} 1:6^{2} 1:7^{2} 1:8 1:10 1:11 1:12^{2} 1:13^{2} 1:14^{3} 1:15^{2} 1:16 1:17^{3} 1:18^{2} 1:19^{3} 1:20^{2} 1:21^{2} 1:22^{3} 1:23 1:24^{2} 1:26 1:27 1:28^{2} 1:29^{2} 1:30 1:31^{3} 1:32^{2} 1:33^{2} 1:35^{3} 1:36^{2} 1:38^{2} 1:39^{2} 1:40^{2} 1:41^{2} 1:42^{3} 1:43 1:45 1:46 1:47 1:49 1:50 1:52 1:53 1:55 1:56^{2} 1:57 1:58^{3} 1:59^{2} 1:60^{2} 1:61 1:62 1:63^{2} 1:64^{4}

1:65^{2} 1:66^{2} 1:67^{2} 1:68 1:69 1:71 1:72 1:75 1:76 1:79 1:80^{3} 2:1 2:2 2:3 2:4^{2} 2:6 2:7^{3} 2:8 2:9^{3} 2:10 2:12 2:13^{2} 2:14 2:15^{2} 2:16^{4} 2:17 2:18 2:19 2:20^{3} 2:21 2:22 2:24 2:25^{4} 2:26 2:27^{2} 2:28^{2} 2:32 2:33^{2} 2:34^{4} 2:36^{2} 2:37^{4} 2:38^{2} 2:39 2:40^{3} 2:42 2:43^{3} 2:44^{2} 2:45 2:46^{2} 2:47^{2} 2:48^{3} 2:49 2:50 2:51^{3} 2:52^{4} 3:1^{4} 3:2 3:3 3:5^{4} 3:6 3:8 3:9^{2} 3:10 3:11^{2} 3:12 3:13 3:14^{4} 3:15^{2} 3:16 3:17^{2} 3:18 3:19 3:21 3:22^{2} 3:23 4:1^{2} 4:2^{2} 4:3 4:4 4:5 4:6^{3} 4:8^{3} 4:9^{3} 4:11 4:12 4:13 4:14^{2}

4:15 4:16^{3} 4:17^{2} 4:18 4:20^{4} 4:21 4:22^{3} 4:23 4:24 4:25 4:27^{2} 4:28 4:29^{3} 4:31^{2} 4:33^{2} 4:35^{4} 4:36^{4} 4:37 4:38^{4} 4:39^{5} 4:40^{2} 4:41^{3} 4:42^{5} 4:43 4:44 5:1 5:2^{2} 5:3^{4} 5:4 5:5^{2} 5:6^{2} 5:7^{4} 5:9 5:10^{3} 5:11^{2} 5:12^{2} 5:13^{3} 5:14^{3} 5:15 5:16^{2} 5:17^{5} 5:18^{3} 5:19^{2} 5:20 5:21^{2} 5:23 5:24^{2} 5:25^{3} 5:26^{3} 5:27^{3} 5:28^{2} 5:29^{3} 5:30^{3} 5:31 5:33^{4} 5:34 5:35 5:36^{2} 5:37^{3} 5:38 6:1^{3} 6:2 6:3^{2} 6:4^{3} 6:5 6:6^{3} 6:7^{2} 6:8^{4} 6:10^{3} 6:11^{2} 6:12^{2} 6:13^{2} 6:14^{3} 6:15^{2} 6:16^{2} 6:17^{8} 6:18^{2} 6:19^{2} 6:20^{2} 6:22^{3} 6:23 6:25 6:28 6:29^{2} 6:30 6:31 6:33

6:34 6:35^{5} 6:37^{3} 6:38^{3} 6:39 6:41 6:42 6:45 6:46^{2} 6:47^{2} 6:48^{4} 6:49^{3} 7:2^{2} 7:3^{2} 7:4 7:5 7:6 7:7 7:8^{6} 7:9^{2} 7:10 7:11^{3} 7:12^{2} 7:13^{2} 7:14^{4} 7:15^{3} 7:16^{3} 7:17^{2} 7:18 7:19 7:21^{4} 7:23 7:24 7:25 7:26 7:29^{2} 7:30 7:31^{2} 7:32^{4} 7:33 7:34^{4} 7:36^{3} 7:37 7:38^{5} 7:39 7:40^{2} 7:41 7:42 7:43 7:44^{3} 7:48 7:49 7:50 8:1^{4} 8:2^{2} 8:3^{3} 8:4^{2} 8:5^{3} 8:6^{2} 8:7^{3} 8:8^{4} 8:9 8:10^{2} 8:12 8:13^{2} 8:14^{5} 8:15^{2} 8:17 8:18 8:19^{2} 8:20^{2} 8:21^{4} 8:22^{2} 8:23^{3} 8:24^{6} 8:25^{4} 8:26 8:27^{2} 8:28^{2} 8:29^{4} 8:30^{2} 8:31 8:32^{3} 8:33^{3} 8:34^{3} 8:35^{4}

8:37^{2} 8:39^{3} 8:40 8:41^{4} 8:42 8:43 8:44^{2} 8:45^{4} 8:46 8:47^{3} 8:48 8:50 8:51^{5} 8:52^{2} 8:53 8:54^{3} 8:55^{3} 8:56 9:1^{3} 9:2^{2} 9:3 9:4^{2} 9:5 9:6^{3} 9:7 9:8^{2} 9:9^{2} 9:10^{3} 9:11^{4} 9:12^{5} 9:13^{3} 9:14 9:15^{2} 9:16^{4} 9:17^{3} 9:18^{2} 9:19 9:21^{2} 9:22^{5} 9:23^{3} 9:25 9:26^{3} 9:28^{4} 9:29^{3} 9:30^{2} 9:31 9:32^{3} 9:33^{4} 9:34^{2} 9:35 9:36^{3} 9:37 9:38 9:39^{4} 9:40^{2} 9:41^{3} 9:42^{5} 9:43 9:45^{2} 9:46 9:47^{2} 9:48^{2} 9:49^{3} 9:50 9:51 9:52^{3} 9:53 9:54^{3} 9:55^{2} 9:56 9:57 9:58^{2} 9:59^{2} 9:60 9:61 9:62^{2} 10:1^{3} 10:4 10:5 10:6 10:7^{2} 10:8^{2} 10:9^{2} 10:10^{2} 10:13^{2} 10:14 10:15

10:16^{2} 10:17 10:18 10:19^{3} 10:21^{4} 10:22^{3} 10:23^{2} 10:24^{4} 10:25^{2} 10:27^{5} 10:28^{2} 10:29 10:30^{4} 10:31^{2} 10:32^{3} 10:33 10:34^{6} 10:35^{4} 10:37^{2} 10:38 10:39^{2} 10:40^{2} 10:41^{3} 10:42 11:1 11:2 11:4^{2} 11:5^{3} 11:6 11:7^{4} 11:8^{2} 11:9^{4} 11:10^{2} 11:14^{4} 11:16 11:17 11:19 11:22^{2} 11:24 11:25^{2} 11:26^{4} 11:27^{3} 11:28 11:29^{2} 11:31^{2} 11:32^{2} 11:37^{3} 11:38 11:39^{3} 11:41 11:42^{5} 11:43 11:44^{2} 11:45 11:46^{2} 11:47 11:48 11:49^{3} 11:51 11:52 11:53^{3} 11:54 12:3 12:4^{2} 12:6 12:10 12:11^{3} 12:13 12:14 12:15^{2} 12:16 12:17 12:18^{4} 12:19^{2} 12:21 12:22 12:23 12:24 12:25 12:27 12:28 12:29 12:30 12:31 12:33 12:35 12:36^{2}

12:37^{3} 12:38^{2} 12:39^{2} 12:42^{2} 12:45^{6} 12:46^{3} 12:47^{2} 12:48^{2} 12:49 12:50 12:52 12:53^{3} 12:54^{2} 12:55^{2} 12:56 12:57 12:58^{2} 13:2 13:4 13:6^{3} 13:7 13:8^{2} 13:9^{2} 13:10 13:11^{3} 13:12^{2} 13:13^{3} 13:14^{4} 13:15^{2} 13:16 13:17^{2} 13:18 13:19^{4} 13:20 13:21 13:22^{3} 13:23 13:24 13:25^{5} 13:26^{2} 13:28^{5} 13:29^{5} 13:30^{2} 13:31 13:32^{5} 13:33^{2} 13:34^{2} 13:35 14:1 14:2 14:3^{2} 14:4^{4} 14:5^{2} 14:6 14:7 14:9^{4} 14:10 14:11 14:12 14:14 14:15 14:16 14:17 14:18^{3} 14:19^{2} 14:20^{2} 14:21^{6} 14:22^{2} 14:23^{3} 14:25^{3} 14:26^{7} 14:27^{2} 14:28 14:29 14:30 14:31 14:32 15:1 15:2^{3} 15:3 15:4^{2} 15:5 15:6^{2} 15:7 15:8^{2} 15:9^{2} 15:11

15:12^{2} 15:13^{3} 15:14^{2} 15:15^{3} 15:16^{2} 15:17^{3} 15:18^{3} 15:19 15:20^{6} 15:21^{3} 15:22^{3} 15:23^{4} 15:24^{3} 15:25^{2} 15:26^{2} 15:27^{3} 15:28^{3} 15:29^{2} 15:31^{2} 15:32^{4} 16:1^{2} 16:2^{2} 16:5 16:6^{4} 16:7^{4} 16:8 16:9 16:10 16:12 16:13^{3} 16:14^{2} 16:15 16:16^{2} 16:17^{2} 16:18^{2} 16:19^{2} 16:20 16:21^{2} 16:22^{3} 16:23^{3} 16:24^{4} 16:25^{2} 16:26^{2} 16:29 16:30 16:31^{2} 17:2 17:3 17:4^{2} 17:5 17:6^{3} 17:7^{2} 17:8^{6} 17:11^{2} 17:12 17:13^{2} 17:14^{2} 17:15^{2} 17:16^{2} 17:17 17:19 17:20^{2} 17:22^{2} 17:23 17:25 17:26 17:27^{2} 17:29^{2} 17:31^{2} 17:33 17:34 17:35 17:36 17:37^{3} 18:1^{2} 18:3^{2} 18:4 18:6 18:7^{2} 18:9^{2} 18:10 18:11 18:13 18:14 18:15 18:16^{2} 18:18

18:19 18:20 18:21 18:22^{3} 18:23 18:24 18:26 18:27 18:28 18:29 18:30 18:31^{2} 18:32^{3} 18:33^{3} 18:34^{2} 18:35 18:36 18:37 18:38 18:39 18:40^{3} 18:41 18:42 18:43^{3} 19:1^{2} 19:2^{2} 19:3^{2} 19:4^{2} 19:5^{4} 19:6^{3} 19:7 19:8^{3} 19:9 19:10 19:11^{3} 19:12 19:13^{3} 19:14 19:15 19:17 19:18 19:19 19:20 19:21 19:22^{2} 19:24^{2} 19:25 19:26 19:27 19:28 19:29^{2} 19:30 19:31 19:32^{2} 19:33 19:34 19:35^{3} 19:36 19:37^{2} 19:38 19:39 19:40^{2} 19:41^{2} 19:43^{2} 19:44^{3} 19:45^{3} 19:47^{3} 19:48 20:1^{3} 20:2 20:3^{3} 20:5 20:6 20:7 20:8 20:9^{2} 20:10^{2} 20:11^{4} 20:12^{3} 20:15 20:16^{3} 20:17^{2} 20:19^{3} 20:20^{3} 20:21^{2} 20:23 20:24^{2}

20:25^{2} 20:26^{3} 20:27 20:28^{2} 20:29^{2} 20:30^{2} 20:31^{4} 20:34^{2} 20:35 20:36 20:37^{3} 20:40 20:41 20:42 20:46^{3} 20:47 21:1^{2} 21:2 21:3 21:5^{2} 21:7^{2} 21:8^{2} 21:9^{2} 21:10 21:11^{5} 21:12^{3} 21:13 21:15 21:16^{5} 21:17 21:20 21:21^{2} 21:23^{2} 21:24^{3} 21:25^{5} 21:26 21:27^{2} 21:28^{2} 21:29^{2} 21:30 21:33 21:34^{4} 21:36^{2} 21:37^{3} 21:38 22:1^{2} 22:4^{3} 22:5^{2} 22:6^{2} 22:8^{3} 22:9 22:10 22:11 22:12 22:13^{3} 22:14^{2} 22:15 22:17^{4} 22:19^{4} 22:22 22:23 22:24 22:25^{2} 22:26 22:29 22:30^{2} 22:31 22:32 22:33^{2} 22:34 22:35^{4} 22:36^{3} 22:37 22:38^{2} 22:39^{3} 22:40 22:41^{3} 22:43 22:44^{2} 22:45^{2} 22:46^{2} 22:47^{3} 22:50^{2} 22:51^{4} 22:52^{3} 22:53 22:54^{3}

22:55^{2} 22:56^{2} 22:57 22:58^{3} 22:59 22:60^{2} 22:61^{3} 22:62^{2} 22:63^{2} 22:64^{2} 22:65 22:66^{4} 22:67 22:68 22:70 22:71 23:1^{2} 23:2^{2} 23:3^{3} 23:4 23:5 23:7 23:8^{2} 23:10^{3} 23:11^{4} 23:12^{2} 23:13^{3} 23:14 23:15 23:16 23:18^{2} 23:19 23:22^{2} 23:23^{3} 23:24 23:25^{2} 23:26^{2} 23:27^{3} 23:28 23:29^{2} 23:30 23:32 23:33^{3} 23:34^{2} 23:35^{2} 23:36^{2} 23:37 23:38^{3} 23:39^{2} 23:41 23:42 23:43 23:44^{2} 23:45^{2} 23:46^{2} 23:48^{2} 23:49^{2} 23:50^{3} 23:51 23:52 23:53^{3} 23:54^{2} 23:55^{3} 23:56^{4} 24:1 24:2 24:3^{2} 24:4 24:5^{2} 24:7^{2} 24:8 24:9^{3} 24:10^{3} 24:11^{2} 24:12^{3} 24:13 24:14 24:15^{3} 24:17^{2} 24:18^{2} 24:19^{4} 24:20^{3} 24:21 24:22 24:23 24:24^{2} 24:25

24:26 24:27^{2} 24:28^{2} 24:29^{2} 24:30^{4} 24:31^{3} 24:32^{2} 24:33^{4} 24:34 24:35^{2} 24:36^{2} 24:37^{2} 24:38^{2} 24:39^{3} 24:40^{2} 24:41^{2} 24:42^{2} 24:43^{2} 24:44^{3} 24:46^{3} 24:47^{2} 24:48 24:49 24:50^{3} 24:51^{2} 24:52^{2} 24:53^{2}

JOH

1:1^{2} 1:3 1:4 1:5^{2} 1:10^{2} 1:11 1:14^{4} 1:15 1:16^{2} 1:17 1:19^{2} 1:20^{2} 1:21^{3} 1:24 1:25^{2} 1:29 1:31 1:32^{2} 1:33^{2} 1:34^{2} 1:35 1:36 1:37^{2} 1:38^{2} 1:39^{3} 1:40 1:41 1:42^{2} 1:43^{2} 1:44 1:45^{2} 1:46^{2} 1:47 1:48 1:49 1:50 1:51^{3} 2:1^{2} 2:2^{2} 2:3 2:6 2:7 2:8^{3} 2:9 2:10^{2} 2:11^{2} 2:12^{4} 2:13^{2} 2:14^{4} 2:15^{5} 2:16 2:17 2:18 2:19^{2} 2:20^{2} 2:22^{2}

2:25 3:2 3:3 3:4 3:5 3:6 3:8^{2} 3:9 3:10^{2} 3:11^{2} 3:12 3:13 3:14 3:19^{2} 3:22^{3} 3:23^{3} 3:25 3:26^{3} 3:27 3:29 3:31 3:32^{3} 3:35 3:36 4:1 4:3 4:4 4:6 4:10^{3} 4:11 4:12^{3} 4:13 4:16 4:17 4:18 4:20 4:23^{2} 4:24^{2} 4:27^{2} 4:28^{2} 4:30 4:34 4:35^{2} 4:36^{3} 4:37^{2} 4:38 4:39 4:40 4:41 4:42^{2} 4:43 4:46 4:47^{2} 4:48 4:50^{2} 4:51^{2} 4:52 4:53^{2} 5:1 5:4 5:5^{2} 5:6 5:8 5:9^{4} 5:11 5:12 5:13 5:14 5:15 5:16^{2} 5:17 5:19 5:20^{2} 5:21 5:24^{2} 5:25^{2} 5:27 5:29^{2} 5:30 5:32 5:33 5:35^{2} 5:37 5:38 5:39 5:40 5:43

5:44 6:2 6:3^{2} 6:4 6:5 6:6 6:9 6:10 6:11^{4} 6:13^{2} 6:15 6:16 6:17^{4} 6:18 6:19^{3} 6:21 6:22 6:24 6:25 6:26^{2} 6:29 6:30 6:33 6:35^{2} 6:36 6:37 6:39 6:40^{3} 6:42^{2} 6:43 6:44 6:45^{2} 6:49 6:50 6:51 6:53 6:54^{2} 6:55 6:56^{2} 6:57 6:58 6:62 6:63 6:64 6:65 6:66 6:69^{2} 6:70 7:3 7:4 7:11 7:12 7:14 7:15 7:16 7:18 7:19 7:20 7:21^{2} 7:22 7:26 7:28^{2} 7:29 7:31^{2} 7:32^{2} 7:33 7:34^{2} 7:35 7:36^{2} 7:37^{2} 7:42 7:44 7:45^{2} 7:51 7:52^{2} 7:53 8:2^{4} 8:3^{3} 8:6 8:7 8:8^{2} 8:9^{3} 8:10 8:11^{2} 8:14^{3} 8:16^{2} 8:18

8:20 8:21^{2} 8:23 8:25 8:26^{2} 8:28 8:29 8:32^{2} 8:33 8:35 8:38 8:39 8:42 8:44^{3} 8:45 8:46 8:48^{2} 8:49 8:50^{2} 8:52^{2} 8:53 8:55^{2} 8:56^{2} 8:57 8:59^{2} 9:1 9:2 9:6^{2} 9:7^{3} 9:8^{2} 9:11^{7} 9:14^{2} 9:15^{2} 9:16 9:18 9:19 9:20^{2} 9:24 9:25 9:27 9:28 9:30^{2} 9:31 9:34^{3} 9:35 9:36 9:37^{2} 9:38^{2} 9:39^{2} 9:40^{2} 10:1 10:3^{3} 10:4^{2} 10:5 10:8 10:9^{2} 10:10^{3} 10:12^{5} 10:13 10:14^{2} 10:15 10:16^{4} 10:18 10:20^{2} 10:22^{2} 10:23 10:24 10:25 10:27^{2} 10:28^{2} 10:29 10:30 10:33 10:35 10:36 10:38^{2} 10:40^{2} 10:41^{2} 10:42 11:1 11:2 11:5^{2} 11:8 11:11 11:15 11:19^{2} 11:20

11:25 11:26^{2} 11:28^{3} 11:29 11:31^{2} 11:32 11:33^{2} 11:34^{2} 11:37 11:38 11:41^{2} 11:42 11:43 11:44^{4} 11:45 11:46 11:47^{2} 11:48^{3} 11:49 11:50 11:51 11:52 11:54 11:55^{2} 11:56 11:57 12:1 12:3^{3} 12:5 12:6^{2} 12:9 12:11 12:13^{2} 12:14 12:16 12:17 12:20 12:21 12:22^{3} 12:23 12:24 12:25 12:26 12:27 12:28 12:29 12:30 12:32 12:34 12:36^{2} 12:38 12:40^{3} 12:41 12:44 12:45 12:47^{2} 12:48 12:49 12:50 13:2 13:3^{2} 13:4^{3} 13:5^{2} 13:6 13:7 13:9 13:10 13:12^{2} 13:13^{2} 13:14 13:20 13:21^{2} 13:26 13:27 13:30 13:31 13:32 13:33 14:3^{3} 14:4^{2} 14:5 14:6 14:7^{2} 14:8 14:9^{2} 14:10 14:11

14:12 14:13 14:16^{2} 14:17 14:19 14:20^{2} 14:21^{4} 14:22 14:23^{4} 14:24 14:26 14:28 14:29 14:30 14:31 15:1 15:2 15:4 15:5 15:6^{4} 15:7^{2} 15:10 15:11 15:16^{3} 15:22 15:24^{2} 15:27 16:3 16:4 16:5 16:8^{3} 16:10 16:13 16:14 16:15 16:16^{3} 16:17^{4} 16:19^{4} 16:20^{2} 16:22^{3} 16:23 16:24 16:26 16:27 16:28^{2} 16:29 16:30 16:32^{2} 17:1^{2} 17:3^{2} 17:5 17:6^{2} 17:8^{3} 17:10^{3} 17:11^{2} 17:12 17:13^{2} 17:14 17:19 17:21 17:22 17:23^{3} 17:25 17:26^{3} 18:1 18:2 18:3^{2} 18:4 18:5 18:6 18:7 18:10^{2} 18:13^{3} 18:13 18:15^{3} 18:16^{2} 18:18^{5} 18:19 18:20^{2} 18:22 18:25^{3} 18:27 18:28^{2} 18:29 18:30 18:31 18:33^{2}

18:35 18:37 18:38^{2} 19:1 19:2^{3} 19:3^{2} 19:4 19:5^{2} 19:6^{2} 19:7 19:9^{2} 19:10 19:12 19:13 19:14^{3} 19:16^{2} 19:17 19:18^{2} 19:19^{3} 19:20^{3} 19:23^{2} 19:24 19:25^{2} 19:26 19:27 19:29^{3} 19:30^{2} 19:31 19:32^{2} 19:33 19:34^{2} 19:35^{3} 19:37 19:38^{3} 19:39^{3} 19:40 19:41 20:1 20:2^{4} 20:3^{2} 20:4^{2} 20:5^{2} 20:6^{2} 20:7 20:8^{2} 20:11^{2} 20:12^{2} 20:13^{2} 20:14^{3} 20:15 20:16 20:17^{4} 20:18^{2} 20:19^{2} 20:20^{2} 20:22^{2} 20:23 20:25^{2} 20:26^{4} 20:27^{4} 20:28^{3} 20:29 20:30 20:31 21:1 21:2^{4} 21:3^{2} 21:6^{3} 21:7 21:8 21:9^{2} 21:11^{4} 21:12^{2} 21:13^{3} 21:17 21:18^{3} 21:19 21:20 21:21 21:24^{2} 21:25

AC

1:1 1:3

1:4 1:7 1:8^{4} 1:9^{2} 1:10 1:13^{8} 1:14^{3} 1:15^{3} 1:16 1:17 1:18^{2} 1:19 1:20^{2} 1:21 1:23^{2} 1:24^{2} 1:25 1:26^{3} 2:1 2:2^{2} 2:3^{2} 2:4^{2} 2:5 2:6 2:7^{2} 2:8 2:9^{6} 2:10^{4} 2:11 2:12^{2} 2:14^{3} 2:17^{5} 2:18^{3} 2:19^{4} 2:20^{2} 2:21 2:22^{2} 2:23^{3} 2:26 2:29^{3} 2:30 2:33^{2} 2:36 2:37^{3} 2:38^{2} 2:39^{2} 2:40^{2} 2:41 2:42^{4} 2:43^{3} 2:44^{2} 2:45^{3} 2:46^{3} 2:47^{2} 3:1 3:2 3:3 3:4 3:5 3:6^{2} 3:7^{4} 3:8^{5} 3:9^{2} 3:10^{3} 3:11^{2} 3:12 3:13^{3} 3:14^{2} 3:15 3:16^{2} 3:17 3:19 3:20 3:23 3:24^{2} 3:25^{2} 4:1^{3} 4:2 4:3^{2} 4:4 4:5^{3} 4:6^{5} 4:7 4:8 4:10 4:13^{4} 4:14

4:16 4:18^{2} 4:19^{2} 4:20 4:23^{3} 4:24^{5} 4:25 4:26^{2} 4:27^{2} 4:28 4:29^{2} 4:30^{2} 4:31^{3} 4:32^{2} 4:33^{2} 4:34 4:35^{2} 4:36^{2} 4:37^{2} 5:2^{3} 5:3 5:4 5:5^{3} 5:6^{3} 5:7 5:8^{2} 5:9 5:10^{4} 5:11^{2} 5:12^{3} 5:13 5:14^{2} 5:15^{2} 5:16^{2} 5:17^{2} 5:18^{2} 5:19^{2} 5:20 5:21^{6} 5:22^{2} 5:23 5:24^{2} 5:25^{2} 5:26 5:27^{2} 5:28^{2} 5:29^{2} 5:30 5:31^{2} 5:32^{2} 5:33 5:34 5:35 5:36^{2} 5:37^{2} 5:38^{2} 5:40^{4} 5:41 5:42^{3} 6:1 6:2^{2} 6:3 6:4 6:5^{9} 6:6 6:7^{3} 6:8^{3} 6:9^{4} 6:10^{2} 6:11 6:12^{6} 6:13^{2} 6:14 6:15 7:2^{2} 7:3^{3} 7:4^{2} 7:5^{2} 7:6^{3} 7:7^{3} 7:8^{5} 7:9 7:10^{5} 7:11^{3} 7:13^{2} 7:14^{3} 7:15^{2}

7:16^{2} 7:17 7:19 7:20^{2} 7:21^{2} 7:22^{3} 7:23 7:24^{3} 7:26^{2} 7:27 7:29 7:30 7:31 7:32^{3} 7:34^{3} 7:35^{2} 7:36^{3} 7:38 7:39 7:41^{3} 7:42^{2} 7:43^{2} 7:46 7:49 7:51^{2} 7:52^{2} 7:53 7:54 7:55^{2} 7:56^{2} 7:57^{2} 7:58^{3} 7:59^{2} 7:60^{3} 8:1^{4} 8:2^{2} 8:3^{2} 8:5 8:6^{2} 8:7^{2} 8:8 8:9 8:11 8:12^{2} 8:13^{3} 8:14 8:17 8:18 8:22 8:23 8:24 8:25^{3} 8:26^{2} 8:27^{4} 8:28 8:29 8:30^{3} 8:31^{3} 8:32 8:33 8:34^{2} 8:35^{2} 8:36^{2} 8:37^{3} 8:38^{4} 8:39^{2} 8:40 9:1 9:2 9:3^{2} 9:4^{2} 9:5^{2} 9:6^{5} 9:7 9:8^{3} 9:9^{2} 9:10^{3} 9:11^{3} 9:12^{2} 9:14 9:15^{2} 9:17^{4} 9:18^{4} 9:19 9:20 9:21^{2} 9:22

9:23 9:24^{2} 9:25 9:26^{2} 9:27^{4} 9:28^{2} 9:29^{2} 9:30 9:31^{5} 9:32 9:33^{2} 9:34^{3} 9:35^{3} 9:36 9:37^{2} 9:38^{2} 9:39^{4} 9:40^{5} 9:41^{4} 9:42^{2} 9:43 10:2^{2} 10:3 10:4^{4} 10:5^{2} 10:7^{2} 10:8 10:9 10:10^{2} 10:11^{3} 10:12^{3} 10:13^{2} 10:15 10:16 10:17 10:18^{2} 10:20^{2} 10:21 10:22^{4} 10:23^{3} 10:24^{4} 10:25^{3} 10:27^{2} 10:28 10:30^{3} 10:31^{2} 10:32 10:33 10:34 10:35 10:37 10:38^{2} 10:39^{3} 10:40 10:41 10:42^{3} 10:45 10:46 10:48 11:1^{2} 11:2 11:3 11:4 11:5^{2} 11:6^{4} 11:7^{2} 11:10^{2} 11:11 11:12^{2} 11:13^{3} 11:14 11:15 11:18 11:19^{2} 11:20^{2} 11:21^{3} 11:22 11:23^{2} 11:24^{3} 11:26^{4} 11:27 11:28^{2} 11:30^{2} 12:2 12:3 12:4^{2} 12:6^{2}

12:7^{5} 12:8^{5} 12:9^{3} 12:10^{4} 12:11^{3} 12:12 12:13 12:14^{2} 12:15 12:16^{2} 12:17^{4} 12:19^{5} 12:20^{3} 12:21^{2} 12:22^{2} 12:23^{3} 12:24 12:25^{3} 13:1^{5} 13:2^{2} 13:3^{3} 13:4 13:5^{2} 13:6 13:7^{2} 13:10^{2} 13:11^{5} 13:13^{2} 13:14^{2} 13:15^{3} 13:16^{2} 13:17^{2} 13:18 13:19 13:20^{2} 13:21^{2} 13:22^{2} 13:25 13:26^{2} 13:27 13:28 13:29^{2} 13:31 13:32 13:34 13:36^{2} 13:38 13:39 13:41^{2} 13:42 13:43^{2} 13:44 13:45^{2} 13:46^{3} 13:48^{3} 13:49 13:50^{5} 13:51 13:52^{2} 14:1^{3} 14:2 14:3^{2} 14:4^{2} 14:5^{3} 14:6^{3} 14:7 14:8 14:9 14:10^{2} 14:11 14:12^{2} 14:13^{2} 14:14^{2} 14:15^{5} 14:17^{3} 14:18 14:19^{3} 14:20^{2} 14:21^{4} 14:22^{2} 14:23^{2} 14:24 14:25 14:26 14:27^{3} 14:28 15:1^{2}

15:2^{5} 15:3^{3} 15:4^{4} 15:5 15:6^{2} 15:7^{4} 15:8 15:9^{2} 15:12^{3} 15:13^{2} 15:15 15:16^{3} 15:17 15:20^{3} 15:22^{3} 15:23^{5} 15:24 15:25 15:27 15:28 15:29^{3} 15:30 15:32^{3} 15:33 15:35^{2} 15:36^{3} 15:37 15:38 15:39^{3} 15:40^{2} 15:41^{2} 16:1^{3} 16:2 16:3^{2} 16:4^{2} 16:5^{2} 16:6^{2} 16:8 16:9^{3} 16:10 16:11 16:12^{3} 16:13^{3} 16:14 16:15^{4} 16:16 16:17^{2} 16:18^{3} 16:19^{3} 16:20 16:21 16:22^{3} 16:23 16:24 16:25^{4} 16:26^{3} 16:27^{3} 16:29^{3} 16:30^{2} 16:31^{3} 16:32^{2} 16:33^{4} 16:34^{2} 16:35 16:36^{2} 16:37^{3} 16:38^{2} 16:39^{4} 16:40^{4} 17:1 17:2^{2} 17:3^{3} 17:4^{5} 17:5^{4} 17:6^{2} 17:7 17:8^{2} 17:9^{2} 17:10^{2} 17:11 17:12 17:13 17:14^{2} 17:15^{3} 17:17^{2} 17:18^{3} 17:19^{2}

17:21 17:22 17:23 17:24^{2} 17:25^{2} 17:26^{3} 17:27 17:28^{2} 17:29 17:30 17:32^{2} 17:34^{3} 18:1 18:2^{2} 18:3^{2} 18:4^{3} 18:5^{3} 18:6^{3} 18:7^{2} 18:8^{3} 18:9 18:10 18:11^{2} 18:12^{2} 18:14 18:15^{2} 18:16 18:17^{2} 18:18^{5} 18:19^{3} 18:21 18:22^{3} 18:23^{3} 18:24^{2} 18:25^{2} 18:26^{3} 18:27 18:28 19:1^{2} 19:3^{2} 19:6^{3} 19:7 19:8^{3} 19:9^{2} 19:10^{2} 19:11 19:12^{2} 19:14^{2} 19:15^{3} 19:16^{4} 19:17^{4} 19:18^{3} 19:19^{3} 19:20 19:21 19:22 19:23 19:25 19:26^{2} 19:27^{2} 19:28^{2} 19:29^{3} 19:30 19:31 19:32^{2} 19:33^{3} 19:35^{2} 19:36 19:38^{2} 19:41 20:1^{3} 20:2^{2} 20:3^{2} 20:4^{7} 20:6^{2} 20:7^{2} 20:8 20:9^{4} 20:10^{3} 20:11^{3} 20:12^{2} 20:13^{2} 20:14^{2} 20:15^{5} 20:17^{2} 20:18 20:19^{2}

20:20^{3} 20:21^{2} 20:22 20:23 20:24 20:25 20:28 20:31^{2} 20:32^{3} 20:34 20:35 20:36^{2} 20:37^{3} 20:38 21:1^{4} 21:2^{2} 21:3^{2} 21:4 21:5^{6} 21:6^{2} 21:7^{3} 21:8^{4} 21:9 21:10 21:11^{5} 21:12^{2} 21:13 21:14 21:15^{2} 21:16 21:17 21:18^{2} 21:19 21:20^{3} 21:21 21:24^{4} 21:25^{4} 21:26 21:27^{2} 21:28^{4} 21:30^{5} 21:31 21:32^{4} 21:33^{4} 21:34^{2} 21:35 21:37 21:38 21:39 21:40^{3} 22:1 22:2^{2} 22:3^{2} 22:4^{3} 22:5^{2} 22:6^{2} 22:7^{2} 22:8^{2} 22:9^{2} 22:10^{4} 22:11 22:12 22:13^{3} 22:14^{3} 22:15 22:16^{3} 22:17 22:18^{2} 22:19^{2} 22:20^{3} 22:21 22:22^{3} 22:23^{3} 22:24 22:25^{2} 22:26 22:27 22:28^{2} 22:29^{2} 22:30^{4} 23:1^{2} 23:2 23:3 23:4 23:6^{3} 23:7^{3} 23:9^{3}

23:10^{3} 23:11^{2} 23:12^{2} 23:13 23:14^{3} 23:15 23:16^{3} 23:17 23:18^{3} 23:19^{2} 23:20 23:21 23:22 23:23^{4} 23:24^{2} 23:25 23:27^{2} 23:28 23:30^{2} 23:31 23:32 23:33 23:34^{2} 23:35 24:1^{2} 24:2^{2} 24:3 24:5^{2} 24:6 24:7 24:9 24:12 24:14 24:15^{2} 24:16^{2} 24:17 24:19 24:22^{2} 24:23^{3} 24:24^{2} 24:25^{3} 24:26 24:27 25:2^{2} 25:3 25:4 25:5 25:6^{2} 25:7^{3} 25:9^{2} 25:13^{2} 25:14 25:15 25:16 25:17 25:19 25:20^{2} 25:23^{4} 25:24^{3} 25:25 25:26 25:27 26:1 26:3 26:6^{2} 26:7 26:10^{2} 26:11^{3} 26:12 26:13 26:14^{2} 26:15^{2} 26:16^{3} 26:17 26:18^{3} 26:20^{5} 26:21 26:22^{2} 26:23^{3} 26:24 26:25 26:29^{2} 26:30^{4} 26:31 27:1^{2} 27:2

27:3^{3} 27:4 27:5^{2} 27:6^{2} 27:7^{2} 27:8 27:9 27:10^{3} 27:11 27:12^{2} 27:13 27:15^{2} 27:16 27:17^{2} 27:18 27:19 27:20^{2} 27:21^{4} 27:22 27:23 27:24 27:27 27:28^{4} 27:29 27:30 27:31 27:32 27:33^{2} 27:35^{3} 27:36 27:37^{2} 27:38^{2} 27:39 27:40^{4} 27:41^{3} 27:42^{2} 27:43^{2} 27:44^{3} 28:1 28:2^{3} 28:3^{3} 28:4 28:5^{2} 28:6^{2} 28:7 28:8^{5} 28:9 28:10 28:11^{2} 28:12 28:13^{4} 28:14^{2} 28:15^{3} 28:16 28:17^{3} 28:20 28:21 28:23^{3} 28:24^{2} 28:25 28:26^{4} 28:27^{6} 28:28 28:29^{2} 28:30^{2} 28:31

RO

1:4 1:5 1:7^{2} 1:12 1:14^{2} 1:16 1:18 1:20 1:21 1:23^{4} 1:25^{2} 1:27^{2} 1:28 2:3^{2} 2:4^{2} 2:5^{2}

2:7^{2} 2:8^{2} 2:9^{2} 2:10^{2} 2:12 2:15 2:17^{2} 2:18^{2} 2:19 2:20^{2} 2:27^{2} 2:29^{2} 3:4 3:8^{2} 3:9 3:14 3:16 3:17 3:19 3:21 3:22 3:23 3:26 3:30 4:3 4:7 4:11 4:12 4:14 4:17 4:19 4:21 4:22 4:25 5:2 5:3 5:4^{2} 5:5 5:11 5:12^{2} 5:15 5:16 5:17 6:13 6:19 6:22^{2} 7:6 7:9 7:10 7:11 7:12^{3} 7:23 8:2 8:3 8:6 8:10 8:17^{2} 8:22 8:23 8:27 8:28 8:30^{2} 9:2 9:4^{5} 9:5 9:9 9:10 9:15 9:17 9:18 9:21 9:22 9:23 9:25 9:26 9:28 9:29^{2} 9:33^{2} 10:1 10:3 10:8 10:9 10:10 10:12 10:14^{2} 10:15^{2}

10:17 10:18 10:19 10:20 10:21 11:3^{3} 11:6 11:7 11:8 11:9^{4} 11:10 11:12 11:14 11:16 11:17^{4} 11:20 11:22 11:23 11:24 11:26^{2} 11:29 11:33^{2} 11:35 11:36^{2} 12:2^{3} 12:4 12:5 12:14 12:15 13:2 13:3 13:9 13:11 13:12 13:13^{3} 13:14 14:3 14:6^{3} 14:7 14:8 14:9^{3} 14:11 14:14 14:17^{3} 14:18 14:19 14:23 15:1 15:4 15:5 15:6 15:9^{2} 15:10 15:11^{2} 15:12^{2} 15:13 15:14 15:18 15:19^{2} 15:21 15:23 15:24 15:26 15:27 15:28 15:29 15:30 15:31 15:32 16:2^{2} 16:3 16:7^{2} 16:9 16:12 16:13^{2} 16:14 16:15^{4} 16:17^{2} 16:18^{2} 16:19 16:20 16:21^{3} 16:23^{2} 16:25 16:26 16:*sub.*

1 CO

1:1 1:2 1:3^{2} 1:5 1:10^{2} 1:12^{3} 1:14 1:16 1:19 1:22 1:23 1:24^{2} 1:25 1:27 1:28^{3} 1:30^{3} 2:1 2:2 2:3^{3} 2:4^{3} 3:1 3:2 3:3^{3} 3:4 3:5 3:8^{2} 3:10 3:13 3:16 3:20 3:23^{2} 4:1 4:5^{2} 4:6^{2} 4:7 4:8 4:9^{2} 4:11^{4} 4:12 4:13 4:17 4:19 4:21 5:1 5:2^{2} 5:4 5:8^{2} 6:1 6:2 6:6 6:8^{2} 6:11^{2} 6:13^{3} 6:14^{2} 6:15 6:19 6:20 7:2 7:3 7:4 7:5^{2} 7:6 7:7 7:8 7:10 7:11^{2} 7:12 7:13^{2} 7:14 7:17 7:19 7:28^{2} 7:30^{3} 7:31 7:34^{2} 7:35^{2} 7:36 7:37 7:40 8:2 8:4 8:5 8:6^{3} 8:7 8:11

8:12 9:4 9:5^{2} 9:6 9:7^{2} 9:10 9:13 9:20 9:23 9:25 9:27 10:1 10:2^{2} 10:3 10:4^{2} 10:7^{2} 10:8^{2} 10:9 10:10 10:11 10:17 10:20^{2} 10:21^{2} 10:26 10:27 10:28 11:2 11:3^{2} 11:7 11:18 11:21^{2} 11:22^{2} 11:24^{2} 11:26 11:27^{2} 11:28^{2} 11:29^{2} 11:30^{2} 11:34^{2} 12:3 12:5 12:6 12:11 12:12^{2} 12:13 12:16 12:19 12:21 12:23^{2} 12:26 12:27 12:28 12:31 13:1^{2} 13:2^{5} 13:3^{3} 13:4 13:9 13:13 14:1 14:3^{2} 14:7 14:10 14:11 14:15^{2} 14:21^{2} 14:23^{2} 14:24 14:25^{3} 14:27^{2} 14:28^{2} 14:29 14:31 14:32 14:35 14:39 14:40 15:1 15:4^{2} 15:5 15:8 15:10 15:11 15:14^{2} 15:15 15:17 15:20

15:24^{2} 15:28 15:30 15:32 15:34 15:35 15:37 15:38 15:39 15:40^{2} 15:41^{2} 15:44 15:45 15:46 15:48 15:49 15:50 15:52^{2} 15:53 15:54 15:56 16:3 16:4 16:6^{2} 16:9^{2} 16:15 16:16^{2} 16:17^{2} 16:18 16:19 16:*sub*^{3}

2 CO

1:1 1:2^{2} 1:3 1:6^{3} 1:7 1:10 1:12^{2} 1:13 1:15 1:16^{3} 1:17 1:18 1:19^{3} 1:20 1:21 1:22 2:3 2:4 2:7 2:12 2:14 2:15 2:16^{2} 3:2 3:4 3:7 3:13 3:17 4:5 4:7 4:13^{2} 4:14 4:17 5:8^{2} 5:11 5:12 5:15^{2} 5:18^{2} 5:19 6:2 6:7 6:8^{3} 6:9^{3} 6:10 6:14 6:15 6:16^{4} 6:17^{3} 6:18^{3} 7:1 7:3 7:7

7:13 7:15^{2} 8:2 8:3 8:4 8:5^{2} 8:7^{4} 8:8 8:10 8:12 8:13 8:15 8:18 8:19^{2} 8:22 8:23^{2} 8:24^{2} 9:2 9:4 9:5^{2} 9:6 9:8 9:10^{2} 9:13^{2} 9:14 10:1 10:5^{2} 10:6 10:8 10:10^{2} 10:12 10:16 11:1 11:9^{4} 11:14 11:25 11:27^{3} 11:29^{2} 11:31 11:33 12:1 12:3 12:4 12:7 12:9 12:12^{2} 12:14 12:15^{2} 12:18 12:20 12:21^{5} 13:2^{3} 13:9^{2} 13:10 13:11^{2} 13:14 13:*sub.*

GA

1:1 1:2 1:3^{2} 1:4 1:5 1:7 1:13 1:14 1:15 1:16 1:17 1:18 1:21 1:22 1:24 2:1 2:2 2:4 2:9^{4} 2:12 2:13 2:14 2:15 2:16 2:20^{2} 3:5 3:6 3:8 3:12 3:16^{3} 3:17^{2} 3:19 3:29^{2} 4:2 4:6 4:7 4:9 4:10^{3} 4:14 4:15 4:18 4:20 4:25^{2} 4:27 4:30 5:1 5:11 5:15 5:16 5:17^{2} 5:21 5:24^{2} 6:2 6:4^{2} 6:9 6:14 6:16^{3}

EPH

1:1 1:2^{2} 1:3 1:4 1:8 1:10 1:15 1:17 1:18 1:19 1:20 1:21^{4} 1:22^{2} 2:1^{2} 2:3^{2} 2:6^{2} 2:8 2:12^{2} 2:14 2:16 2:17^{3} 2:19^{2} 2:20^{2} 3:5 3:6^{2} 3:9 3:10 3:12 3:15 3:17 3:18^{3} 3:19 4:2 4:4 4:6^{3} 4:8 4:11^{5} 4:13 4:14^{3} 4:16 4:17 4:21 4:23 4:24^{2} 4:26 4:30 4:31^{4} 4:32 5:2^{3} 5:3 5:5 5:9^{2} 5:11 5:14^{2} 5:18 5:19^{3} 5:20 5:23 5:25 5:26 5:27 5:29 5:30 5:31^{3} 5:32 5:33 6:2 6:3 6:4^{2} 6:5 6:7 6:9 6:10 6:12 6:13 6:14 6:15 6:17^{2} 6:18^{3} 6:19 6:21^{2} 6:22 6:23^{2}

PHP

1:1^{2} 1:2^{2} 1:7^{2} 1:9^{3} 1:10 1:11 1:13 1:14 1:15^{2} 1:18^{2} 1:19 1:20 1:21 1:23 1:25^{3} 1:27 1:28^{2} 1:30 2:1 2:7^{2} 2:8^{2} 2:9 2:10^{2} 2:11 2:12 2:13 2:14 2:15^{2} 2:17^{3} 2:18 2:25^{3} 2:26 2:27 2:28 2:29 3:3^{2} 3:8^{2} 3:9 3:10 3:13 3:15 3:17 3:18 3:19 4:1^{2} 4:2 4:3 4:4 4:6 4:7^{2} 4:8 4:9^{4} 4:12^{4} 4:15 4:16 4:18 4:20

COL

1:1 1:2^{3} 1:3 1:4 1:6^{2} 1:9^{2} 1:10 1:11 1:13 1:16^{3} 1:17^{2} 1:18 1:20 1:21^{2} 1:22^{2} 1:23^{3} 1:24 1:26 1:28 2:1^{2} 2:2^{2} 2:3 2:4 2:5^{2} 2:7^{2} 2:8^{2} 2:10 2:13^{2} 2:14 2:15^{2} 2:18 2:19^{3} 2:22 2:23^{2} 3:3 3:5 3:10 3:11 3:12 3:13 3:14 3:15^{2} 3:16^{3} 3:17^{2} 3:19 3:23^{2} 3:25 4:1 4:2 4:7 4:8 4:9 4:10 4:11 4:12 4:13^{2} 4:14 4:15^{2} 4:16^{2} 4:17 4:*sub.*

I TH

1:1^{5} 1:3^{3} 1:5^{2} 1:6^{2} 1:7 1:8 1:9^{2} 2:2 2:9^{2} 2:10^{3} 2:11^{2} 2:12 2:15^{4} 2:18 2:20 3:2^{4} 3:4 3:5 3:6^{3} 3:7 3:10^{2} 3:11^{2} 3:12^{3} 4:1^{3} 4:4 4:6^{2} 4:10^{2} 4:11^{3} 4:12 4:14 4:15 4:16^{2} 4:17^{2} 5:1 5:3^{2} 5:5 5:6 5:7 5:8^{2} 5:11 5:12^{3} 5:13^{2} 5:15 5:23^{4}

2 TH

1:1^{3} 1:2^{2} 1:3 1:4^{2} 1:7 1:8 1:9 1:10 1:11^{2} 1:12^{2} 2:1 2:3 2:4 2:6 2:8^{2} 2:9^{2} 2:10 2:11 2:13 2:15 2:16^{3} 2:17^{2} 3:1 3:2^{2} 3:3 3:4^{2} 3:5^{2} 3:6 3:8^{2} 3:12^{2} 3:14^{2}

1 TI

1:1 1:2 1:4 1:5 1:9^{4} 1:10 1:12 1:13^{2} 1:14^{2} 1:15 1:17^{2} 1:19 1:20 2:1 2:2 2:3 2:4 2:5^{3} 2:7^{3} 2:8 2:9 2:14 2:15^{2} 3:7 3:10 3:12 3:13 3:15 3:16 4:1 4:3^{2} 4:4 4:5 4:6 4:7^{2} 4:8 4:9 4:10 4:11 4:16^{2} 5:1 5:4^{2} 5:5^{4} 5:7 5:8^{2} 5:13^{3} 5:16 5:17 5:18 5:21 5:23 5:24 5:25 6:1 6:2^{3} 6:3^{2} 6:4 6:5 6:7 6:8^{2} 6:9^{4} 6:10 6:11 6:12 6:13 6:15 6:16 6:20^{2}

2 TI

1:2 1:3 1:5^{2} 1:7^{2} 1:9^{2} 1:10^{2} 1:11^{2} 1:12 1:13 1:15 1:16 1:17 1:18 2:2 2:5 2:7 2:16 2:17^{2} 2:18 2:20^{4} 2:21^{2} 2:23 2:24 2:26 3:6 3:7 3:8 3:12 3:13^{3} 3:14 3:15 3:16 4:1^{2} 4:2 4:4^{2} 4:6 4:8 4:10 4:11 4:12 4:13 4:17^{3} 4:18^{3} 4:19^{2} 4:21^{4}

TIT

1:1^{2} 1:4^{2} 1:5 1:9 1:10^{2} 1:14 1:15^{2} 1:16^{2} 2:9 2:12^{2} 2:13^{2} 2:14 2:15^{2} 3:1 3:3^{2} 3:4 3:5 3:8^{2} 3:9^{4} 3:10 3:11 3:13 3:14

PHM

1 2^{3} 3^{2} 5^{2} 7 9 11 16

HEB

1:1 1:3^{2} 1:5^{2} 1:6^{2} 1:7^{2} 1:8 1:9 1:10^{2} 1:11 1:12^{3} 2:2^{2} 2:3 2:4^{3} 2:7^{2} 2:9 2:10 2:11 2:13^{3} 2:14 2:15 2:17 3:1 3:5 3:6 3:9 3:10^{2} 3:18 4:4 4:5 4:6 4:12^{7} 4:13 4:16 5:1 5:2 5:3 5:4 5:7^{3} 5:9 5:11 5:12^{2} 5:14 6:1 6:2^{3} 6:3 6:4^{2} 6:5^{2} 6:6 6:7 6:8^{2} 6:9 6:10^{2} 6:11 6:12 6:14 6:15 6:16 6:19^{2} 7:1 7:2 7:5 7:6 7:7 7:8 7:9 7:11 7:15 7:18 7:20 7:21 7:23 7:26 7:27 8:2^{2} 8:3 8:5 8:8 8:9 8:10^{3} 8:11^{2} 8:12^{2} 8:13 9:1 9:2^{2} 9:3 9:4^{3} 9:5 9:7 9:9 9:10^{3} 9:11 9:12 9:13^{2} 9:15 9:19^{5} 9:21 9:22^{2} 9:27 9:28 10:1 10:4 10:5 10:6 10:8^{3} 10:11^{2} 10:16 10:17^{2} 10:20 10:21 10:22 10:24^{2} 10:25 10:27 10:29^{2} 10:30 10:33^{2} 10:34^{2} 10:37^{2} 11:4 11:5 11:6 11:7 11:8 11:9 11:10 11:11 11:12^{2} 11:13^{4} 11:15 11:17 11:20 11:21 11:22 11:23 11:28 11:32^{6} 11:35 11:36^{3} 11:37 11:38^{3} 11:39 12:1^{2} 12:2^{2} 12:3 12:5 12:6 12:8 12:9^{2} 12:12 12:13 12:14 12:15 12:18^{3} 12:19^{2} 12:20 12:21^{2} 12:22^{2} 12:23^{3} 12:24^{2} 12:27 12:28 13:3 13:4^{2} 13:5 13:6 13:8^{2} 13:9 13:16 13:17^{2} 13:21 13:22 13:24

JAS

1:1 1:4 1:5^{2} 1:6 1:11^{2} 1:14 1:15 1:17^{2} 1:21^{2} 1:22 1:23 1:24^{2} 1:25 1:26 1:27^{4} 2:2 2:3^{3} 2:4 2:5 2:6 2:9 2:10 2:12 2:13 2:14 2:15 2:16^{2} 2:18^{2} 2:19 2:22 2:23^{3} 2:24 2:25 3:2 3:3 3:4 3:5 3:6^{3} 3:7^{4} 3:9 3:10 3:11 3:12 3:13 3:14^{2} 3:16^{2} 3:17^{3} 3:18 4:1 4:2^{4} 4:3 4:4 4:7 4:8^{2} 4:9^{3} 4:10 4:11^{2} 4:12 4:13^{4} 4:14 4:15 4:17 5:1 5:2 5:3^{3} 5:4 5:5 5:6^{2} 5:7^{2} 5:10 5:11^{2} 5:12 5:14 5:15^{3} 5:16 5:17^{3} 5:18^{3} 5:19 5:20

1 PE

1:1 1:2^{2} 1:3 1:4^{2} 1:7^{2} 1:8 1:10 1:11 1:13 1:17 1:18 1:19 1:21^{2} 1:23 1:24^{2} 1:25 2:1^{4} 2:4 2:6 2:8^{2} 2:11 2:14 2:16 2:18 2:20 2:25 3:3 3:4 3:6 3:7 3:10^{2} 3:11^{2} 3:12 3:13 3:14^{2} 3:15^{2} 3:19 3:22^{3} 4:3 4:5 4:7 4:8 4:11^{2} 4:14 4:17 4:18^{2} 5:1^{2} 5:4 5:5^{2} 5:11^{2} 5:12 5:13

2 PE

1:1^{2} 1:2^{2} 1:3^{2} 1:4 1:5^{2} 1:6^{3} 1:7^{2} 1:8 1:9^{2} 1:10 1:11 1:12 1:16 1:17 1:18 1:19 2:1 2:2 2:3^{2} 2:4 2:5 2:6^{2} 2:7 2:8 2:9 2:10 2:11 2:12^{2} 2:13^{2} 2:14 2:15 2:20^{2} 2:22 3:2^{2} 3:4 3:5^{2} 3:7^{2} 3:8 3:10^{2} 3:11 3:12^{2} 3:13 3:14 3:15 3:16 3:18^{3}

1 JO

1:1 1:2^{4} 1:3^{3} 1:4 1:5^{2} 1:6^{2} 1:7 1:8 1:9^{2} 1:10 2:1 2:2^{2} 2:3 2:4 2:8^{2} 2:9 2:10 2:11^{2} 2:14^{2} 2:16^{2} 2:17^{2} 2:18 2:20 2:21 2:22 2:24 2:25 2:27^{4} 2:28^{2} 3:2 3:3 3:5^{2} 3:9 3:10 3:12^{3} 3:15 3:16 3:17^{2} 3:18 3:19^{2} 3:20 3:22^{2} 3:23^{2} 3:24^{3} 4:3^{3} 4:4 4:5 4:6 4:7^{2} 4:10 4:12 4:13 4:14^{2} 4:15 4:16^{4} 4:20 4:21 5:1 5:2 5:3 5:4 5:6^{3} 5:7^{2} 5:8^{4} 5:11^{2} 5:12 5:13 5:14 5:15 5:16 5:17 5:18 5:19 5:20^{4}

2 JO

1^{2} 2 3^{3} 5 6 7 9^{2} 10 12^{2}

3 JO

2 3 5 10^{3} 12^{3} 13 14

JUDE

1^{3} 2^{2} 3 4^{2} 6 7^{3} 8 11^{2} 14 15^{2} 16 22 23 24 25^{3}

RE

1:1^{2} 1:2^{2} 1:3^{2} 1:4^{4} 1:5^{4} 1:6^{5} 1:7^{2} 1:8^{4} 1:9^{4} 1:10 1:11^{10} 1:12^{2} 1:13^{2} 1:14^{2} 1:15^{2} 1:16^{3} 1:17^{3} 1:18^{4} 1:19^{2} 1:20^{2} 2:2^{6} 2:3^{4} 2:5^{3} 2:8^{3} 2:9^{4} 2:10^{2} 2:12 2:13^{3} 2:14 2:16 2:17^{2} 2:18^{2} 2:19^{6} 2:20^{2} 2:21^{2} 2:22 2:23^{4} 2:24^{2} 2:26^{2} 2:27 2:28 3:1^{3} 3:2 3:3^{4} 3:4 3:5^{2} 3:7^{4} 3:8^{3} 3:9^{3} 3:12^{4} 3:14^{2} 3:16 3:17^{7} 3:18^{3} 3:19^{2} 3:20^{4} 3:21 4:1^{3} 4:2^{3} 4:3^{3} 4:4^{5} 4:5^{4} 4:6^{4} 4:7^{4} 4:8^{6} 4:9^{4} 4:10^{4} 4:11^{4} 5:1^{2} 5:2^{2} 5:3 5:4^{2} 5:5^{2} 5:6^{5} 5:7^{2} 5:8^{4} 5:9^{6} 5:10^{3} 5:11^{6} 5:12^{6} 5:13^{10} 5:14^{5} 6:1^{3} 6:2^{6} 6:3^{2} 6:4^{4} 6:5^{5} 6:6^{4} 6:7^{2} 6:8^{8} 6:9^{2} 6:10^{3} 6:11^{3} 6:12^{4} 6:13 6:14^{3} 6:15^{8} 6:16^{4} 6:17 7:1 7:2^{3} 7:4^{4} 7:9^{6} 7:10^{2} 7:11^{5} 7:12^{7} 7:13^{2} 7:14^{4} 7:15^{3} 7:17^{2} 8:1 8:2^{2} 8:3^{3} 8:4 8:5^{7} 8:6 8:7^{5} 8:8^{3} 8:9^{3} 8:10^{4} 8:11^{3} 8:12^{6} 8:13^{2} 9:1^{3} 9:2^{4} 9:3^{2} 9:4 9:5^{2} 9:6^{4} 9:7^{3} 9:8 9:9^{2} 9:10^{3} 9:11 9:12 9:13^{2} 9:15^{4} 9:16^{2} 9:17^{8} 9:18^{2} 9:19^{3} 9:20^{6} 10:1^{4} 10:2^{3} 10:3^{2} 10:4^{3} 10:5^{2} 10:6^{7} 10:8^{4} 10:9^{5} 10:10^{4} 10:11^{4} 11:1^{5} 11:2^{3} 11:3^{3} 11:4 11:5^{3} 11:6^{2} 11:7^{3} 11:8^{2} 11:9^{6} 11:10^{3} 11:11^{4} 11:12^{3} 11:13^{5} 11:14 11:15^{5} 11:16^{3} 11:17^{3} 11:18^{8} 11:19^{7} 12:1^{3} 12:2^{2} 12:3^{4} 12:4^{3} 12:5^{3} 12:6^{2} 12:7^{4} 12:8 12:9^{3} 12:10^{5} 12:11^{3} 12:12^{2} 12:13 12:14^{3} 12:15 12:16^{3} 12:17^{3} 13:1^{5} 13:2^{6} 13:3^{3} 13:4^{2} 13:5^{4} 13:6^{3} 13:7^{5} 13:8 13:10 13:11^{3} 13:12^{3} 13:13 13:14^{2} 13:15^{2} 13:16^{4} 13:17 13:18^{2} 14:1^{4} 14:2^{3} 14:3^{6} 14:4 14:5 14:6^{5} 14:7^{5} 14:8 14:9^{3} 14:10^{3} 14:11^{5} 14:12 14:13^{2} 14:14^{4} 14:15^{2} 14:16^{2} 14:17 14:18^{3} 14:19^{3} 14:20^{3} 15:1^{2} 15:2^{5} 15:3^{4} 15:4^{2} 15:5^{2} 15:6^{3} 15:7^{2} 15:8^{3} 16:1^{2} 16:2^{5} 16:3^{3} 16:4^{3} 16:5^{3} 16:6^{2} 16:7^{2} 16:8^{2} 16:9^{3} 16:10^{3} 16:11^{3} 16:12^{2} 16:13^{3} 16:14 16:15^{2} 16:16 16:17^{2} 16:18^{5} 16:19^{3} 16:20^{2} 16:21^{2} 17:1^{2} 17:2 17:3^{2} 17:4^{6} 17:5^{2} 17:6^{3} 17:7^{3} 17:8^{6} 17:9 17:10^{4} 17:11^{4} 17:12 17:13^{2} 17:14^{5} 17:15^{4} 17:16^{5} 17:17^{2} 17:18 18:1^{2} 18:2^{5} 18:3^{2} 18:4^{2} 18:5 18:6 18:7^{4} 18:8^{3} 18:9^{3} 18:11^{2} 18:12^{13} 18:13^{14} 18:14^{3} 18:15 18:16^{6} 18:17^{4} 18:18 18:19^{3} 18:20^{2} 18:21^{3} 18:22^{5} 18:23^{3} 18:24^{3} 19:1^{4} 19:2^{2} 19:3^{3} 19:4^{4} 19:5^{3} 19:6^{3} 19:7^{3} 19:8^{2} 19:9^{2} 19:10^{3} 19:11^{6} 19:12^{2} 19:13^{2} 19:14^{2} 19:15^{4} 19:16^{3} 19:17^{3} 19:18^{7} 19:19^{4} 19:20^{3} 19:21^{2} 20:1^{2} 20:2^{3} 20:3^{4} 20:4^{8} 20:6^{3} 20:7 20:8^{2} 20:9^{5} 20:10^{6} 20:11^{4} 20:12^{5} 20:13^{4} 20:14^{2} 20:15 21:1^{4} 21:2 21:3^{5} 21:4^{2} 21:5^{3} 21:6^{3} 21:7^{2} 21:8^{8} 21:9^{2} 21:10^{3} 21:11 21:12^{5} 21:13 21:14^{2} 21:15^{2} 21:16^{5} 21:17^{3} 21:18^{2} 21:19 21:21^{2} 21:22^{2} 21:23^{2} 21:24^{3} 21:25 21:26 21:27 22:1 22:2^{2} 22:3^{3} 22:4^{2} 22:5^{4} 22:6^{3} 22:8^{4} 22:9^{2} 22:10 22:11^{3} 22:12^{2} 22:13^{3} 22:14 22:15^{6} 22:16^{3} 22:17^{5} 22:19^{3}

ARE

1526

GE

2:4 6:9 7:2 7:8 9:2 9:19 10:1 10:20 10:31 10:32 11:10 11:27 18:15 18:24 19:5 19:15 19:21 20:7 20:16 25:6 25:12 25:13 25:16 25:17 25:19 25:23 27:22 27:41 27:46 29:4 31:12 31:15 31:43^{3} 31:49 32:17 33:5 33:8 33:13^{2} 33:15 34:21 34:22 35:2 35:26 36:1 36:5 36:9 36:10 36:13 36:16 36:17^{3} 36:18 36:19^{2} 36:20

36:21
36:24
36:26
36:27
36:28
36:29
26:30
36:31
36:40
37:2
37:17
38:25^{2}
40:12
40:18
41:26
41:27
42:9^{2}
42:10
42:11^{3}
42:12
42:13
42:14
42:16
42:21
42:31^{2}
42:33
42:34^{2}
42:36
43:18
44:16
45:6
45:11
45:16
46:8
46:18
46:22
46:25
46:31
46:32
47:1^{2}
47:3
47:4
47:5
47:9
48:5
48:8
48:9
49:5^{2}
49:28
50:3

EX

1:1
1:9
1:19^{3}
2:18
3:7
4:18
4:19
5:5
5:16
5:17^{2}
6:15
6:16
6:19
6:24
6:25
6:26
6:27^{2}
7:17
8:21
9:27
10:8
10:11
12:13
14:3
15:4
16:7
16:8^{2}
16:16
19:6
21:1
24:14
25:22
25:26
28:3
28:4
28:24
29:33
30:13
30:14
31:6
32:2
32:22
33:5
33:16
35:1
39:6
40:4

LE

4:12^{2}
4:13
5:17
10:14
11:2^{2}
11:8
11:9
11:13^{2}
11:26
11:27
11:28
11:31
11:32
11:35
11:42
12:6
14:37
16:4
18:17
18:24
23:2
23:4
23:17
23:37
23:42
25:7
25:23
25:33
25:42
25:44
25:45
25:55^{2}
26:25
26:36
26:39
26:46
27:34

NU

1:3
1:5
1:17
1:44
2:32
3:1
3:2
3:3
3:9
3:13
3:18
3:20
3:21
3:27
3:33
3:46^{2}
4:15
4:20
4:41
6:13
8:16
8:17
9:7^{2}
10:4
10:29
10:31
11:21
13:16
13:28
13:30
13:31
13:32
14:9
14:35
14:43^{2}
15:13
15:15
15:16
16:3
16:5
16:11
16:37
18:6
18:17
18:18
20:16
22:4
22:6
22:9
22:12
24:3
24:5
24:6
24:15
26:2
26:7
26:14
26:18
26:22
26:25
26:27
26:30
26:34
26:35
26:36
26:37^{2}
26:41
26:42^{2}
26:47
26:50
26:57
26:58
26:63
27:1
30:14
30:16
31:12
31:49
32:14
32:51
33:1
33:2
34:17
34:19
34:29
35:33
36:3
36:4
36:13

DE

1:2
1:10
1:11
1:20
1:28
2:4
2:25
3:18
4:4
4:20
4:30
4:32
4:45
5:3
6:1
6:14
7:6
7:17
7:20
8:9
9:12
9:29
11:12
11:30
12:1
12:9
13:7
13:13
14:1
14:2
14:4
14:7
14:9
14:12
14:29
16:11
16:14
17:14
18:12
20:2
20:15^{2}
21:2
21:6
22:5
22:17
23:8
23:18
24:14
25:16
27:12
28:58
29:1
29:5
29:20
29:21
29:29
30:1
30:10
31:17
31:18
31:21
32:4
32:5
32:20
32:21
32:28
32:32^{2}
32:37
33:3
33:17^{3}
33:27

JOS

1:3
3:8
4:9
6:17^{2}
6:19
7:3
7:29
8:5
9:8^{2}
9:9
9:11
9:13
9:22
9:23
9:25
10:6
10:17
12:1
12:7
13:14
13:17
13:30
13:32
14:1
14:32
16:3
17:3
17:9
17:16^{2}
18:3
19:14
19:29
19:35
19:51
21:9
22:10
22:17
23:14
23:15
24:22^{2}
24:23

JG

3:1
5:11
6:2
7:2^{2}
7:3
7:18
8:6
8:15^{2}
9:2
9:18
10:4^{2}
11:7
12:3
12:4
15:10^{2}
15:11
15:12
18:9
18:24
19:18
20:7
20:13
20:32
20:39
21:16

RU

1:11
4:9
4:10
4:11
4:18

1 SA

2:3
2:4
2:8
4:8
4:17
6:17
9:20
10:2
10:7
12:2
12:22
16:11
16:16
17:8
19:22
20:21
20:22
21:5
26:16
29:10

2 SA

1:4^{3}
1:19
1:25
1:27
3:28
5:1
5:8
7:9
11:11
13:33
14:14
14:20
15:3
15:13
15:15
16:4
16:21
17:2
17:10
17:12
17:16
19:11
19:12^{3}
19:19
22:28
22:39
24:14

1 KI

1:20
1:45
4:8
4:13
8:8
8:13
10:8^{2}
10:27
11:41
13:3
13:32
14:19
14:29
15:7
15:23
15:31
16:5
16:14
16:20
16:27
18:22
18:25
20:3
20:17
20:23
20:31
22:39
22:45

2 KI

1:5
1:18
3:23
5:12
6:9
6:16
7:12
7:13^{5}
8:23
9:22
10:2^{2}
10:5
10:13^{2}
10:34
12:19
13:8
13:12
14:15
14:18
14:28
15:6
15:11
15:15
15:21
15:26
15:31
15:36
16:19
18:20
18:26
18:34^{2}
18:35
19:3
19:4
20:14
20:15
20:20
21:17
21:25
23:28
24:5

1 CH

1:29
1:31
1:33
1:54
2:1
2:18
2:55
4:2
4:4
4:12
4:18
4:22
5:14
6:19
6:31
6:33
6:50
6:54
6:65
7:8
7:33
8:6^{2}
8:38
8:40
9:33
9:44
11:1
11:10
12:1
12:15
12:18
12:23
13:2^{2}
14:4
15:12
16:14
16:26
16:27^{2}
17:8
19:3
21:3
21:13
22:15
24:1
26:19
29:15^{2}
29:17
29:29

2 CH

1:15
2:7
3:3
6:37
7:14
8:11
9:7^{2}
9:27
9:29
11:10
12:15
13:7
13:8
13:9
13:10
13:22
16:11
17:14
19:3
20:12
20:34
23:6
24:26
24:27
25:26
26:18
27:7
28:10
28:26
29:9
29:19
30:6
32:32
33:18
33:19
34:21
34:24
34:31
35:25
35:27
36:8

EZR

2:1
4:10
4:12
5:4
5:11
6:6
6:9
7:13
7:19
7:21
7:25
8:1
8:13
8:28^{3}
9:6
9:15
10:3
10:13^{2}

NE

1:3^{3}
1:10
2:3
2:17^{2}
4:2
4:4
4:10
4:19
5:2
5:5
5:17
6:8
7:6
9:6
9:36^{2}
9:37
10:39
11:3
11:7
12:1

ES

1:16
3:8
4:16
7:4
8:5
8:9
9:13
10:2

JOB

1:19
3:8
3:19
3:22
3:24
4:9
4:10
4:11
4:19
4:20
5:4^{2}
6:3
6:4
6:7
6:16
6:17
6:18
6:21^{2}
6:25
6:26
7:1
7:3
7:6^{2}
7:8
7:16
8:9^{2}
8:13
8:17
9:25
9:26
10:5^{2}
10:17
10:20
11:16
12:2
12:6
12:16
13:4^{2}
13:12
13:23
14:5^{2}
14:21
15:10
15:11
15:15
15:28
16:2
16:22
17:1^{2}
17:2
17:7
17:11^{2}
18:3
18:21
19:3
19:13
19:19
19:22
20:11
20:25
21:7
21:9
21:18
21:22
21:24^{2}
21:28
21:33
22:10
22:12
22:14
22:19
22:29
23:14
24:1
24:8
24:13
24:17
24:23
24:24^{3}
25:2
25:5
26:5
26:11
26:14
27:12
28:4^{2}
28:6
30:1
30:15
30:17
30:30
31:40
32:6
32:9
34:18
34:19
34:21
34:25
35:5
36:7^{2}
36:20
37:17
37:24
38:6
38:30
38:35
39:4
39:30
40:17
40:18^{2}
41:14
41:15
41:17
41:18
41:23^{2}
41:25
41:28
41:29
41:30

PS

1:4^{2}
2:12
3:1^{2}
6:2
9:3
9:6
9:15
10:5^{2}
10:8
10:16
12:4
12:6
12:8
14:1
14:3^{2}
16:3
16:6
16:11
17:2
17:10
17:14^{2}
18:38
19:8
19:9
19:10
20:8^{2}
21:11
22:14
25:10
25:15
25:17
25:19
27:12
31:10
31:15
32:11
33:4
34:15^{2}
34:18
34:19
35:19
35:20
36:3
36:6
36:12^{2}
37:23
37:28
37:34
38:4^{2}
38:5
38:7
38:14
38:19^{3}
38:20
39:6
40:5^{3}
40:12
42:7
44:13
44:22^{2}
45:5
47:9
49:14
50:11
51:17
53:1
53:3
54:3
55:4
55:5
55:10
56:5
56:8
56:12
57:4^{2}
57:6
58:3
58:4
59:3
59:7
62:9^{3}
65:5
65:8
65:13^{2}
68:6
68:17
69:1
69:4^{2}
69:5
69:9
69:19
71:13
71:24^{2}
72:20
73:1
73:4
73:5^{2}
73:8
73:10
73:12
73:19^{2}
73:27
74:20
75:3
76:5
76:6
77:19
79:1
79:4^{2}
79:8
79:11
82:5
82:6^{2}
83:5
84:1
84:4
84:5
85:10
86:8
86:14
87:3
87:7
88:5
89:7
89:11
89:14
89:49
90:4
90:5^{2}
90:7^{2}
90:9
90:10
92:5^{2}
93:5
94:11
95:4
95:7
96:5
96:6^{2}
97:2^{2}
100:3
102:3^{2}
102:8^{2}
102:11
102:20
102:22
102:24
102:25
103:6
103:14
103:15
104:16
104:17
104:18
104:24
104:25
104:28
104:29
104:30
105:7
106:3
107:17
107:27
107:29
107:30
107:38
107:39
109:2
109:4
109:24
111:2
111:7^{2}
111:8
113:6
115:4
115:8
115:15
115:16
116:10
118:12
119:1
119:2
119:21
119:24
119:39
119:75^{2}
119:84
119:85
119:86
119:91
119:98
119:99
119:103
119:111
119:129
119:137
119:138
119:143
119:150
119:151
119:156
119:157
119:168
119:172
120:7
122:5
123:3
123:4
124:7
125:2
125:4
126:3
127:3
127:4^{2}
135:15
139:12
140:2
141:6
141:7
141:8
142:6
144:4
145:9
146:8

PR

1:19
2:15
3:15
3:17^{2}
3:20
4:22
4:23
5:6
5:11
5:21
6:16
6:23
8:8
8:9
8:11
8:18
8:32
9:17
9:18^{2}
10:6
11:20^{4}
12:5^{2}
12:6
12:7^{2}
12:10
12:22^{2}
13:8
14:4
14:12
14:18
15:3
15:11
15:15
15:22^{2}
15:26^{2}
16:2
16:11^{2}
16:13
16:24
16:25
17:6^{2}
17:15
17:24
18:4
18:7
18:8
18:19
18:21
19:7
19:13
19:14
19:21
19:29
20:7
20:10
20:15
20:23
20:24
22:3
22:4
22:5
22:26
23:3
24:11^{2}
24:21
25:1
26:7
26:21
26:22
26:23
26:25
26:28
27:6^{2}
27:12
27:15
27:20^{2}
27:24
27:25
27:26^{2}
28:1
28:2
29:2
29:12
29:16
30:12
30:13^{2}
30:14
30:15^{2}
30:18
30:24^{2}
30:25
30:26
30:29
31:8
31:21
31:25

EC

1:8
1:11
1:13
1:14
2:14
2:23
3:18
3:20
4:1
4:2^{2}
4:9
5:7
5:11
7:19
7:21
8:8
8:13
9:1
9:3
9:12^{3}
9:16
9:17
10:12
11:10
12:3
12:11^{2}

CA

1:10
1:17
3:7
4:2^{2}
4:3^{2}
4:5^{2}
4:11
4:13
5:11
5:12
5:13
5:14
5:15
6:6
6:7
6:8
7:1^{2}
7:3^{2}
7:9
7:13

ISA

1:4^{2}
1:7
1:14
1:15
1:23
2:6
2:13
2:14
3:8
3:12
3:16
4:2
5:12
5:13^{2}
5:21
5:22
5:28
7:2
8:18
9:10^{2}
9:16
10:8
10:14
10:20
10:29
14:19
16:4
16:7
16:8^{3}
17:2
19:11
19:12^{2}
19:13^{2}
21:3
22:2
22:3^{4}
22:9
23:8
24:6
24:17
24:18
24:21
24:22
25:1
26:9
26:14^{2}
27:7
27:9
27:11
28:1^{2}
28:7^{3}
28:8
28:9
28:15
28:27^{2}
29:9
29:15
29:20
30:18
30:27
31:1^{2}
31:3
32:7
32:9
32:11
33:13^{2}
33:14
33:23
35:4
36:5
36:11
36:19^{2}
36:20
37:3
39:3
40:11
40:15^{2}
40:17^{2}
40:22
41:23^{2}
41:24
41:29^{3}
42:9
42:17
42:22^{3}
43:10
43:12
43:17^{2}
44:7
44:8
44:9^{2}
44:11
45:16
45:19
45:20
45:24
46:1
46:2
46:3^{2}
46:10
46:12
48:1^{2}
48:7
49:9
51:1^{2}
51:19
51:20
52:7
53:5
54:1
55:8^{2}
55:9^{2}
56:8
56:10^{3}
56:11^{2}
57:1
57:4
57:6
57:20
58:7
59:3
59:6
59:7^{2}
59:10
59:12^{2}
60:8
61:1^{2}
61:9
61:11
63:8
63:19
64:6^{2}
64:8^{2}
64:9
64:10
64:11
65:5
65:11
65:16^{2}
65:22
65:23
65:24

JER

2:5
2:11
2:15
2:28^{2}
2:31
4:13^{2}
4:17
4:20
4:22^{2}
5:3
5:4^{2}
5:6^{2}
5:7
5:10
5:16
5:23
5:26
5:27^{2}
5:28
6:4
6:20
6:23
6:28^{3}
6:29^{2}
7:4
7:10
8:8
8:9^{2}
8:16
8:20
9:3
9:10^{3}
9:19^{2}
9:25
9:26^{3}
10:2
10:3
10:5
10:8
10:9
10:15
10:20
12:1
12:4
12:12
13:22
13:23
14:2
14:7
14:9
14:18
14:22
15:2^{4}
15:8
16:3
16:17^{2}
16:20
18:6
21:4
21:7
22:6
22:17
22:20
22:28^{2}
23:10
23:11
23:14
23:26
24:2
24:3
24:5
24:8
25:12
25:22
25:23
25:26
25:31
25:34
25:37
27:5
27:18
29:1
29:4
29:16
29:17
29:22
29:25
30:4
30:6
31:20
31:29
32:19
32:24
32:35
33:4
34:21
35:14
37:19
38:19
38:22^{3}
40:15
41:12
42:2
42:11
43:11^{3}
44:2
44:6
44:10
44:14
44:24
44:27
44:28
46:5^{2}
46:7
46:8
46:12
46:15
46:21^{3}
46:23^{2}
48:14
48:15
48:17
48:32
48:36
48:41
48:46
49:23
49:32
50:2^{2}
50:11
50:15^{2}
50:37
50:38
50:43
51:4
51:7
51:18
51:30
51:32^{2}
51:43
51:51^{2}
51:56
51:60
51:64

LA

1:2^{2}
1:4^{2}
1:5^{2}
1:6^{2}
1:14
1:16
1:18
1:20
1:21
1:22
2:9^{2}
2:11
2:21
3:22
3:23
4:1
4:2
4:5
4:8
4:9
4:18
4:19
5:3^{2}
5:5
5:7
5:12
5:17

EZE

2:4
2:5
2:7
3:7
3:26
3:27
5:2
5:5
5:6
5:7^{2}
5:12^{4}
5:14
5:15
7:9
11:2
11:7
11:12
11:15
12:2
12:10
12:14
12:20
12:22
12:23
12:27
13:4
14:5
16:7
16:27
16:38
16:52
16:57
18:2
18:4
18:25
18:29^{2}
20:3
20:30
20:34
21:14
21:24^{2}
21:29
22:9
22:18^{2}
22:19
22:27
23:45
24:19
25:9
26:6
26:18
26:19
27:4
27:27
28:8
28:24
28:25
29:12^{2}
30:7^{2}

31:12^{3} 31:14 32:20 32:21 32:22 32:23 32:24 32:25 32:26 32:27^{2} 32:28 32:29 32:30^{2} 32:32 33:24 33:27 33:30 34:3 34:12 34:30 34:31 35:8 35:12^{2} 36:2 36:3^{2} 36:4^{2} 36:7 36:8 36:20^{2} 36:35^{2} 37:11^{3} 38:7 38:11 38:12^{2} 38:20 38:22 40:46 42:13 42:14^{2} 43:13 43:18 43:27 44:10 45:14 46:24 48:1^{2} 48:11 48:15 48:29 48:30

DA

1:10 2:20 2:28 3:12 3:16 4:3^{2} 4:18 4:35 4:37 5:23 7:17^{2} 7:24 8:20 8:23 9:7^{2} 9:16^{2} 9:19 9:24 9:26 10:16 12:9

HO

1:9 1:10^{2} 2:12 4:4 4:6 4:14 5:2 6:5 7:2 7:4 7:7^{2} 7:9 7:16 8:9 9:6 9:7^{2} 9:15 11:7 11:8 12:7 12:11^{2} 14:3 14:9

JOE

1:6 1:7 1:12 1:17^{2} 1:18^{2} 1:20

AM

4:1 5:16 6:1^{2} 6:6 9:7 9:8 9:12

OB

6^{2}

JON

4:11

MIC

1:4 1:5^{2} 1:16 2:7 2:13 4:11 6:10 6:12 7:6 7:11

NA

1:3 1:6 1:10 2:3 3:13 3:17^{2}

HAB

1:3^{2} 1:6 1:7 1:8^{2} 1:15 3:6

ZEP

1:6 1:8 1:11^{2} 1:12 3:3^{2} 3:4 3:6^{2} 3:18^{2}

HAG

1:6

ZEC

1:5 1:9 1:10 1:15 1:19 1:21^{2} 3:8 4:2 4:4 4:10 4:11 4:14 6:4 6:5 6:6 6:10 6:15 8:16 8:17 11:2 13:6

MAL

1:4 2:8 3:6 3:7 3:15^{2}

MT

1:17^{3} 2:2 2:18 2:20 5:3 5:4 5:5 5:6 5:7 5:8 5:9 5:10^{2} 5:11 5:13 5:14 5:15^{2} 5:26 7:15 8:26 9:12 9:17 9:37 10:2 10:28 10:29 10:30 10:31 11:5^{2} 11:8 11:11 11:27 11:28 12:5 12:48 13:15 13:16 13:38^{2} 13:39 13:40 13:56 18:20 19:12^{2} 19:26 19:30 20:22^{2} 20:25 22:4^{3} 22:14^{2} 22:21^{2} 22:30^{2} 23:8 23:13 23:25 23:27^{2} 23:28 23:31 23:37 24:8 24:19 25:8 26:55

MK

2:17^{2} 4:11^{2} 4:15 4:16^{2} 4:17 4:18^{2} 4:20^{2} 4:40 5:9 6:2 6:3 7:15 7:18 9:23 10:8 10:27 10:31 10:42 12:17^{2} 12:25^{3} 13:1 13:8 13:17 13:25 13:32 14:36 14:48

LU

1:1 4:18 5:20 5:31^{2} 5:38 6:21^{2} 6:22 6:24 6:25 7:22^{2} 7:25^{2} 7:28 7:31 7:32 7:47^{2} 7:48 8:12 8:13 8:14^{2} 8:15 8:21 9:12 9:55 9:61 10:2 10:8 10:9 10:17 10:20^{2} 10:22 10:23 11:7 11:21 11:28 11:41 11:44^{2} 12:6 12:7^{2} 12:24 12:37 12:38 13:14 13:23 13:25 13:27 13:30^{2} 13:34 14:17 16:8 16:15 17:10^{2} 17:17 17:18 18:11 18:27^{2} 18:31 18:42 20:34 20:35 20:36^{2} 21:21^{3} 21:22 21:23 21:26 22:10 22:25 22:28 22:38 23:29^{2} 24:17^{2} 24:18 24:38 24:44 24:48

JOH

3:21 4:35^{2} 4:38 5:28 5:39 6:9 6:49 6:58 6:63^{2} 6:64 6:69 7:7 7:23 7:47 7:49 8:10 8:23^{2} 8:31 8:37 8:44 8:47 8:53 9:28 9:40 10:8 10:12 10:16 10:21 10:26 10:30 10:34 11:9 13:10 13:11 13:17 13:35 14:2 15:3 15:5 15:6 15:14 15:19 16:15 16:30 17:7 17:9 17:10^{2} 17:11^{2} 17:14 17:16 17:22 20:23^{2} 20:29 20:30 20:31 21:25

AC

2:7 2:13 2:15 2:32 2:39 3:15 3:25 5:9 5:25 5:32 7:1 7:26 10:4 10:21 10:31 10:33^{2} 10:39 13:27 13:31 13:39 14:11 14:15^{2} 15:18 15:19 15:23 16:17 16:21 16:28 17:6 17:22 17:28 17:29 19:15 19:26 19:37 19:38^{2} 19:40 20:32 21:20^{2} 21:21^{2} 21:24 22:3 22:10 23:15 23:21 23:35 24:2 24:11 24:14 25:5 25:24 26:3 26:18 26:26 28:27

RO

1:6 1:15 1:20^{3} 1:28 1:32 2:2 2:8 2:13 2:14 2:18 2:19 3:9^{2} 3:12^{2} 3:15 3:16 3:19 3:25 4:7^{3} 4:12 4:14 6:2 6:4 6:13 6:14 6:15 6:16 6:21 7:4 7:6 8:1 8:5^{2} 8:8 8:9 8:12 8:14^{2} 8:16 8:18 8:24 8:28 8:36^{2} 8:37 9:4 9:5 9:6^{2} 9:7^{2} 9:8^{3} 9:26 10:15 10:19 11:14 11:16 11:28^{2} 11:29 11:33 11:36 12:5 13:1 13:3 13:6 14:8 14:20 15:1 15:14 15:26 15:27 16:7 16:10 16:11 16:14 16:15 16:18

1 CO

1:2 1:5 1:11^{2} 1:18 1:24 1:26 1:27 1:28^{2} 1:30 2:6 2:12 2:14^{2} 3:2 3:3^{2} 3:4 3:8 3:9^{3} 3:16 3:17 3:20 3:21 3:22 3:23 4:8^{2} 4:9 4:10^{6} 4:11^{2} 4:13^{2} 4:18 4:19 5:2 5:4 5:7 5:12^{2} 5:13 6:2 6:4 6:11^{3} 6:12^{3} 6:15 6:19 6:20^{2} 7:14 7:23 7:33 8:4 8:5 8:6^{2} 8:8^{2} 8:9 8:10 9:1 9:2 9:12 9:13 9:20^{2} 9:21^{2} 10:11^{2} 10:13 10:17^{2} 10:18 10:22 10:23^{3} 11:19 11:32^{2} 12:4 12:5 12:6 12:12 12:13 12:20 12:22 12:27 12:29^{4} 14:10 14:12 14:22 14:23^{2} 14:32 14:34 14:37 15:2 15:6 15:15 15:17 15:18^{2} 15:19 15:23 15:27 15:29^{2} 15:35 15:40 15:48^{4} 16:9 16:18

2 CO

1:1 1:4^{2} 1:7 1:14^{2} 1:20 1:24 2:11 2:15^{2} 2:16 2:17 3:2 3:3 3:5 3:18 4:3 4:8^{2} 4:11 4:15 4:18^{6} 5:4 5:6^{3} 5:8 5:11^{2} 5:17^{2} 5:18 5:20 6:12 6:16 7:3 7:6 8:23 10:4 10:7 10:10 10:11^{3} 10:12 10:14 11:13 11:19 11:22^{3} 11:23 11:28 13:4 13:6 13:9^{3}

GA

1:2 1:6 2:15 2:17 3:3^{2} 3:7^{2} 3:9 3:10^{3} 3:25 3:26 3:28 3:29 4:6 4:8 4:9 4:12 4:24^{2} 4:28 4:31 5:4^{2} 5:17 5:18 5:19^{2} 5:24 6:1 6:10 6:13

EPH

1:1 1:10^{2} 2:5 2:8 2:10 2:11 2:13 2:19 2:20 2:22 4:1 4:4 4:25 4:30 5:4 5:8 5:12 5:13 5:16 5:30 6:5

PHP

1:1 1:7 1:10 1:11 1:13 1:14 2:21 3:3 3:13^{2} 3:18 4:3 4:8^{6} 4:21 4:22

COL

2:3 2:10 2:11 2:12 2:17 2:20 2:22 3:1 3:3 3:5 3:15 4:5 4:9 4:11^{2} 4:13 4:15

1 TH

2:10 2:14 2:15 2:19 2:20 3:3 4:9 4:10 4:12 4:13 4:15^{2} 4:17 5:4 5:5^{2} 5:7 5:8 5:12 5:14

2 TH

1:3 1:7 2:13 3:11^{2} 3:12 5:15

1 TI

2:2 3:7 5:3 5:16 5:24 5:25^{2} 6:1 6:2 6:17

2 TI

1:15^{2} 2:19 2:20 2:26 3:3 3:6 3:15

TIT

1:5 1:10 1:12 1:15^{2} 3:8 3:9 3:15

PHM

7

HEB

1:10 1:14 2:10^{2} 2:11^{2} 2:14 2:18 3:6 3:14 4:13 4:15 5:2 5:11 5:12 5:14 6:9 7:5 7:13 8:4 9:15 9:17 9:22 9:24 10:8 10:10 10:14 10:39 11:3 12:1 12:8^{2} 12:11 12:18 12:22 12:23 12:27^{2} 13:3 13:11

JAS

1:1 2:4^{2} 2:7 2:9 2:16 3:4^{2} 3:9 5:2^{2} 5:4 5:17

1 PE

1:5 1:6 1:12 2:5 2:9 2:10 2:14 2:25 3:6^{2} 3:9 3:12^{2} 3:14 4:6 4:13 4:14 5:1 5:9^{2} 5:14

2 PE

1:4 2:10^{2} 2:11 2:13 2:15 2:17^{2} 2:19 2:20 3:5 3:7^{2} 3:10 3:16^{2}

1 JO

2:5 2:12 2:14 2:15 2:18 3:2 3:10 3:19 3:22 4:1^{2} 4:4 4:5 4:6 4:17 5:3 5:7^{2} 5:8 5:19 5:20

2 JO

7

JUDE

1 4 7 12^{2} 15 16

RE

1:3 1:4^{2} 1:11 1:19 1:20^{2} 2:2^{3} 2:9^{3} 2:18 3:2 3:4 3:9^{2} 4:5 4:11 5:6 5:8 5:13^{2} 7:13^{2} 7:14 7:15 8:13 9:14 10:6^{3} 11:4 11:15 13:8 14:4^{2} 14:5 14:12 14:13 14:18 15:3^{2} 15:4 16:6 16:7 16:14 17:9 17:10^{2} 17:12 17:14^{2} 17:15 18:3 18:14^{2} 19:2 19:9^{3} 20:7 20:8 20:10 21:4 21:5 21:12 21:16 21:22 21:24 21:27 22:6 22:14 22:15 22:18 22:19

AS

5613

GE

3:5 3:22 4:20 4:21 7:9 7:16 8:21 9:3 10:9 10:19^{2} 11:2 12:4 13:10 13:16 16:6 17:4 17:15 17:20 17:23 18:5 18:25 18:33^{2} 19:8 19:14 19:28 21:1^{2} 21:4 21:16 22:14 22:17^{2} 23:9^{2} 24:22 24:51 25:18 26:4 26:29^{2} 27:4 27:9 27:12 27:14 27:19 27:23 27:27 27:30 27:42 27:46 28:6 28:14 31:2 31:5 31:26 32:12 32:25 32:28 32:31 33:10 33:14 34:12 34:15 34:22 34:31 35:18 36:24 38:11 38:29 39:10 39:18 40:10 40:22 41:13 41:19 41:21 41:38 41:39^{2} 41:49 41:54 42:27 42:35 43:6 43:17 43:34 44:1 44:3 44:15 44:17 44:18 47:11 47:21 47:30 48:5 48:7 49:4 49:9 49:16 49:27 50:6 50:12 50:20^{2}

EX

1:17 1:19 2:14 4:6 4:7 5:7 5:13 5:14 5:20 7:6 7:10 7:13 7:20 7:22 8:15 8:19 8:27 9:12 9:17 9:18 9:24 9:29^{2} 9:30 9:35 10:10 10:14 11:6 12:25 12:28 12:31 12:32 12:36 12:48 12:50 13:11 14:28 15:5 15:7 15:8 15:10 15:16^{2} 16:5^{2} 16:10 16:14^{2} 16:22 16:24 16:34 17:10 18:21 19:18 21:7 21:22^{2} 22:25 23:15 24:10^{2} 27:8 28:32 30:37 32:1 32:13 32:17 32:19^{2} 32:23 33:9 33:11 34:4 34:10 34:18 35:22^{2} 38:21 39:1 39:5 39:6 39:7 39:21 39:23 39:26 39:29 39:31 39:43 40:15 40:19 40:21 40:23 40:25 40:27 40:29 40:32

LE

2:12 4:10 4:20 4:21 4:25^{2} 4:31 4:35 5:13^{2} 6:17^{2} 7:7 7:10^{2} 7:19 7:21 8:4 8:9 8:13 8:17 8:21 8:29 8:31 8:34 9:7 9:10 9:15 9:21 10:5 10:15 10:18 11:94 12:5 13:43 14:6 14:13 14:22 14:30 14:31 14:35 15:25 15:26^{2} 16:15 16:34 18:19^{2} 18:22 18:28 19:16 19:18 19:23^{2} 19:34^{2} 20:6 20:13 20:25 22:13 24:16^{2} 24:19 24:20 24:22^{2} 24:23 25:31 25:39 25:40^{2} 25:42 25:46 25:53 26:19^{2} 26:34^{2} 26:35^{2} 26:36 26:37 27:12 27:14 27:21 27:23

NU

1:19 2:17 2:33 3:16 3:42 3:51 4:15 4:29 4:49 5:4 8:3 8:16 8:19 8:21 8:22 9:15 9:18^{2} 10:31 11:7^{2} 11:8 11:12 11:31^{3} 12:10 12:12 13:21 13:33 14:15 14:17 14:19 14:21^{2} 14:28^{3} 14:32 15:14 15:15 15:20 15:36 16:31 16:40^{3} 16:45 16:47 17:11 18:6 18:7 18:18^{2} 18:24 18:27^{2} 18:30^{2} 20:9 20:27 21:34 22:4 22:8 23:2 23:22 23:24^{2} 23:30 24:1 24:6^{4} 24:8 24:9^{2} 26:4 27:11 27:13 27:17 27:22 27:23 28:8^{2} 31:7 31:31 31:41 31:47 32:25 32:27 32:31 33:56 34:6 36:10

DE

1:10 1:11^{2} 1:17^{2} 1:19 1:21 1:31 1:40 1:44 2:1 2:5 2:10 2:11 2:12 2:14 2:21 2:22 2:29 2:30 3:2 3:6 3:20^{2} 4:5 4:7 4:8 4:20 4:32 4:33 4:38 5:12

5:14[2]
5:16
5:26
5:31
5:32
6:3
6:8
6:16
6:19
6:24
6:25
8:5
8:18
8:20
9:3[3]
9:18
9:21[2]
9:25
10:5
10:9
10:15
10:22
11:4
11:10[2]
11:18
11:21
11:25
12:9
12:12
12:15[2]
12:16
12:19[2]
12:20
12:21
12:22
12:24
13:6
13:11
13:17
14:7
15:6
15:21
15:22[2]
15:23
16:9
16:10
16:17
17:14
17:16
18:2
18:7
18:14
19:5
19:19
20:6
20:8[2]
20:17
22:11
22:26
23:23
24:8
26:15
26:18
26:19
27:3
28:9
28:29
28:49[2]
28:62
28:63
29:13[2]
29:28
30:9
31:3
31:4
31:13[2]
31:21
32:2[4]
32:10
32:11
32:31
32:50
33:20
33:25
34:9

JOS

1:3
1:5
1:15
1:17[2]
2:7[2]
2:11[2]
3:7
3:13[2]
3:15
4:8[2]
4:12
4:14
4:18
4:23
5:5
5:14
6:22
7:5
8:2
8:5
8:6
8:15
8:19[2]
8:29[2]
8:31[2]
8:33[3]
9:4
9:21
9:25
10:1
10:2
10:11
10:28
10:30
10:39[2]
10:40
11:4
11:9
11:12
11:13
11:15
11:20
13:6
13:8
13:14
13:33
14:2
14:5
14:7
14:10
14:11
14:12
15:18
15:63
17:14
21:8
22:4
23:5
23:8
23:9
23:10
23:15
24:15

JG

1:7
1:20
2:3
2:15[2]
2:22
3:1[2]
3:2
4:22
5:31
6:5
6:16
6:27
6:36
6:37
7:5
7:12
7:17
8:8
8:18
8:19
8:21
8:33[2]
9:33[3]
9:36
9:48
11:36
13:9
13:23[2]
14:6
14:20
15:10
15:11
15:14
16:7
16:9
16:11
16:20
17:8
17:11
19:22
20:1
20:8
20:11
20:30
20:31
20:32
20:39
20:48[2]

RU

1:8
3:10
3:13

1 SA

1:7
1:12
1:26
1:28[2]
2:2
2:16[2]
3:10
4:9
5:10
6:6
6:12
7:10
9:11
9:13[2]
9:20
9:27
10:7
12:15
12:23
13:5
13:7
13:10[2]
14:14
14:39
14:45
15:22[2]
15:23[2]
15:27
15:33
16:7
17:20[2]
17:23
17:36
17:55
17:57
18:1
18:3
18:6
18:10
19:6
19:7
19:9
19:20
20:3[2]
20:13
20:17
20:20
20:21
20:23
20:25
20:31[2]
20:36
20:41[2]
20:42
22:8
22:13
22:14
23:11
24:4
24:13
24:18
25:15[2]
25:20
25:25
25:26[3]
25:29
25:34
25:37
26:10
26:16
26:20
26:24
27:8
28:10
28:17
29:6
29:8
29:9
29:10[2]
30:24

2 SA

1:6
1:21
2:18[2]
2:23
2:27
3:9
3:33
3:34
3:36
4:4
4:6
4:9
5:20
5:25
6:16
6:18
6:19
6:20
7:10
7:11
7:15
7:25
8:3
9:8
9:11
10:2
11:11
11:25
12:3
12:5
13:13[2]
13:29
13:35
13:36
14:2
14:11
14:13
14:14
14:17
14:19
14:25
15:10
15:21
15:26
15:30
15:34
16:2
16:5
16:13[2]
16:19
16:23
17:3
17:8
17:10
17:11
17:12[2]
18:33
19:3
19:14
19:18
19:27
19:30
20:8
22:23
22:31
22:43[3]
22:45[2]
23:4[2]
23:6
24:19
24:23

1 KI

1:29
1:30
1:37
1:41
2:3
2:24[2]
2:31
2:38
3:6[2]
3:14
4:20
4:29
5:5
5:12
8:20
8:24
8:25
8:43
8:53
8:57
8:59
8:61
9:2
9:4
9:5
9:10
10:27[2]
11:4
11:6
11:11
11:33
11:38[2]
12:12
12:17
13:6
13:18
13:20
13:21
14:6
14:7
14:8
14:10
14:15
15:3
15:11
16:2
16:9
16:11[2]
16:31
17:1
17:11
17:12
17:13
18:7
18:10
18:12[2]
18:15
18:32[2]
19:2
19:5
20:11
20:12
20:34
20:36[4]
20:39
20:40
21:11[2]
21:26
22:4[3]
22:14
22:17

2 KI

1:16
2:2[2]
2:4[2]
2:6[2]
2:11
2:19
2:23
3:7[3]
3:14
3:22[2]
4:8[2]
4:30[2]
4:40
5:16
5:20
5:27[2]
6:5
6:26
7:7
7:10
7:13[2]
7:17
7:18
8:5
8:18
8:19
8:27
9:17
9:22
9:31
9:37
10:2[2]
10:12
10:15
10:25[2]
11:8[2]
11:14
12:9
13:5
13:21
13:23
14:3
14:4
14:5[2]
15:9
17:2
17:4
17:11
17:23
17:41
19:13
19:26[4]
19:29
19:37
21:3
21:13
21:20
22:18
23:16
23:21
23:27
24:13
25:15
25:22

1 CH

5:1
6:26
12:8[2]
12:20
12:33
12:36
14:16
15:15
15:29
16:37
17:1
17:9
17:13
17:23
18:3
21:3
21:15
21:17
21:21
22:7
22:11
23:24
24:19
25:8[3]
26:13[2]
26:21
28:2
28:7
29:11
29:15[2]
29:17
29:23
29:25

2 CH

1:12
1:15[3]
2:3
2:16[2]
3:16
4:6
5:13[2]
6:8
6:10
6:15
6:16
6:31
6:33
7:17[2]
7:18
8:7
8:14
9:9
9:27[2]
10:12
10:17
11:16
13:10
13:15
16:3
18:3[2]
18:13
18:16
20:9
20:20
20:21
20:33
21:6
21:7
23:3
23:13
23:18[2]
24:12[2]
25:4
25:16
26:5[2]
29:8
29:31[2]
30:5
30:7
30:8
31:3
31:5[2]
31:15[2]
32:17
32:19
33:22
33:23
34:26
35:12
35:18
36:21[2]

EZR

2:62
3:1
3:2
3:4[2]
3:5
4:2
4:3
6:18
6:21
7:14
7:25
7:27
7:28
8:27
8:31
9:7
9:13
9:15
10:3
10:12

NE

1:1
2:16
2:18
5:5[2]
5:12
6:8
6:11[2]
7:64
8:1
8:15
9:10
9:11
9:23
9:24
10:34
10:36
13:15

ES

2:9
2:20[2]
3:11
4:14
5:5
5:8
5:13
6:10
7:8
8:8
9:2
9:22
9:23[2]
9:27[2]
9:31[2]

JOB

2:10
3:6
3:16[2]
4:8
5:7
5:14
5:25
5:26
6:7
6:15[2]
6:26
7:2[2]
7:9
7:20
9:26[2]
9:32
10:4
10:5[2]
10:9
10:10
10:16
10:19
10:22[2]
11:8[2]
11:16
11:17
11:20
12:3[3]
12:4
12:5
13:9
13:28[2]
14:2
14:6
14:11
15:24
15:33[2]
16:4
16:21
17:6
17:7
17:10
17:15
18:3
18:20
19:11
19:22
20:8[2]
21:4
21:18[2]
21:33
22:2
22:8
22:24[2]
23:10
24:5
24:14
24:17
24:18
24:20
24:24[2]
26:3
27:2
27:6
27:7[2]
27:16[2]
27:18[2]
27:20
27:21
28:5[2]
29:2[2]
29:4
29:14
29:18
29:23[2]
29:25[2]
30:5
30:14
30:15[2]
30:18
31:18
31:33
31:36
31:37
32:19
34:3
34:26
35:8
37:18
38:8
38:14[2]
38:19
38:30
39:16
39:20
40:15
40:18
41:5
41:15
41:20
41:24[4]
41:27[2]
41:29
42:7
42:9
42:10[2]
42:15

PS

5:7
5:12
10:5
10:9
11:1
12:6
14:4
17:8
17:12[2]
17:15
18:30
18:42[2]
18:44[2]
19:5[2]
21:9
22:13
25:10
26:11
27:12
31:12
32:9[2]
33:7
33:22
34:18
35:5
35:13
35:14[2]
37:2
37:6[2]
37:14
37:20
37:22
38:4
38:10
38:13[2]
38:14
39:5[2]
39:12
40:4
40:16
41:12
42:1
42:10
44:22
48:6
48:8
50:21
53:4
55:16
55:20
58:3[2]
58:7[2]
58:8
58:9
61:6
62:3[2]
62:2
62:5
65:3
66:10
68:2[2]
68:13
68:14
68:15[2]
68:17
68:21
69:13
70:4
71:7
72:5[2]
72:6
72:7
72:17[2]
73:1
73:2
73:5
73:6[2]
73:19
73:20
73:22
74:5
77:13
78:8
78:13
78:15
78:27[2]
78:65
83:9[3]
83:10
83:11[2]
83:13
83:14[2]
87:7[2]
88:4
89:10
89:11
89:29
89:36
89:37[2]
90:4[2]
90:5[2]
90:9
92:7
95:8
102:3
102:7
102:26
103:11
103:12[2]
103:13
103:15[3]
103:18
104:2
104:6
104:17
104:33[2]
106:9
107:10
109:17[2]
109:18[2]
109:19
109:23
109:29
116:2[2]
118:12
119:14[2]
119:70[2]
119:111
119:132
119:162
122:3
123:2[2]
124:6
124:7
125:1
125:2
125:5[2]
126:4
127:4
128:3
129:6
131:2[2]
133:1
133:3[2]
137:8
139:12
139:16
140:9
141:2[2]
141:7
143:3
143:6
144:4
144:12[2]
147:20

PR

1:12[2]
1:27[2]
2:14[4]
3:12
4:18
4:19
5:3
5:4
5:19
6:5[2]
6:11[2]
7:2
7:22
7:23
8:26
8:30
9:4
9:16
10:20
10:23
10:25
10:26
11:19
11:20
11:22
11:28
12:4
15:19
16:14
16:15
16:24
16:27
17:8
17:14
18:4[2]
18:8
18:11
19:12[2]
19:24
20:2
20:19
21:1
21:8
21:29
23:5
23:7
23:28
23:34[2]
24:29
24:34[2]
25:12
25:13
25:16
25:20[2]
25:25
25:26
26:1[2]
26:2
26:8
26:9
26:11
26:14
26:18
26:21
26:22
27:8
27:19
27:21
28:1
28:4
28:15
30:14
31:8

EC

2:8
2:13
2:15
2:16
3:19
4:1
5:15[2]
5:16
6:12
7:6
7:26
8:1
8:13
9:2[2]
9:12[2]
10:5
10:7
11:5
12:7
12:11[2]

CA

1:3
1:5
1:7
1:14
2:2
2:3
4:1
4:11
5:11[2]
5:12
5:13
5:14[2]
5:15[3]
6:4[3]
6:5
6:6
6:7
6:10[4]
6:13
7:4[2]
7:8
8:1
8:6[4]
8:10

ISA

1:7
1:8[3]
1:9
1:18[4]
1:26[2]
1:30[2]
1:31[2]
3:9
3:12
3:16
5:18
5:24[3]
6:13
7:2
8:6
9:1
9:3
9:4
9:18
9:19
10:9[3]
10:10
10:11
10:14[2]
10:15[3]
10:18
10:20
10:22
10:26
10:32
11:9
11:16
13:4
13:6
13:8[2]
13:14[2]
13:17
13:19
14:10
14:17
14:19[2]
14:24[2]
16:2
16:3
16:14
17:3
17:5[2]
17:6
17:9
17:13
19:14
20:3
21:1
21:3
22:16
22:23
23:5
23:10
23:15
24:2[6]
24:13[2]
24:22
25:4
25:5
25:10
25:11
26:17
26:18
26:19
26:20
27:7
27:9
28:2
28:4
28:21[2]
29:2[2]
29:4
29:5
29:7
29:8[2]
29:11
29:13
29:16
29:17
30:13
30:14
30:17[2]
30:22
30:26[2]
30:27
30:28
30:29[2]
31:4
31:5
32:2[3]
33:4
33:11
33:12[2]
34:4[3]
35:1
35:6
37:12
37:27[4]
37:30
37:38
38:12
38:13
38:14
38:19
40:6
40:15[3]
40:17
40:22[3]
40:23
40:24
40:31
41:2[2]
41:11
41:12[2]
41:15
41:25[2]
42:13
42:19[3]
43:17
44:4[2]
44:7
44:22[2]
47:3
47:4
47:8
47:14
48:18[2]
48:19
49:18[3]
49:26
50:4
50:9
51:9
51:12
51:13
51:20
51:23[2]
52:14
53:2[2]
53:3
53:7[2]
54:6
54:9[2]
55:9
55:10
56:12
58:2
58:4
58:5
58:8
58:10
59:10[3]
59:12
59:17[2]
59:21
60:8[2]
61:10[2]
61:11[2]
62:1[2]
62:5[2]
63:13
63:14
64:2
64:6[3]
65:8
65:22
66:3[4]
66:8[2]
66:13
66:20
66:22

JER

2:26
2:36
3:2
3:5
3:20
4:13[2]
4:17
4:31[2]
5:8
5:9
5:16
5:19
5:26
5:27
5:29
6:7
6:9[2]
6:23
6:24
6:26
7:14
7:15
8:6
9:8
9:9
9:22[2]
10:5
10:6
10:7
11:5
12:8
12:9
12:16
13:5
13:10
13:11
13:21[2]
13:24
14:8[2]
14:9[2]
15:2[4]
15:18[2]
15:19
16:4
17:8
17:11
17:16
17:22
18:4
18:6[2]
18:17
19:11
19:12
19:13
20:9
20:11
21:7
22:23
22:24
23:12
23:14[2]
23:27
23:29
23:34
24:8
25:18
25:30
25:38
26:11
26:14[2]
26:18
27:13
30:6
30:20
31:5
31:10
31:12
31:18
31:23
31:28
32:20
32:31
32:42
33:7
33:11
33:22
38:16
39:12
40:3
40:10
41:6[2]
42:2
42:18
43:11[3]
43:12
44:6
44:13
44:14
44:16
44:17
44:22
44:23
44:30
46:7[2]
46:18[3]
46:22
46:26
48:8
48:13
48:34
48:40
48:41
49:16[2]
49:18
49:22[2]
49:24
50:8
50:9
50:11[2]
50:15
50:18
50:26
50:37
50:40
50:43
51:14
51:27
51:30
51:38
51:49

LA

1:1
1:15
1:17
1:20
1:22
2:4
2:5
2:6
2:7
2:12
2:22
3:6
3:10[2]
3:12
3:45
4:2
4:6
4:14
4:17[2]
5:3
5:21

EZE

1:1
1:4
1:10
1:13
1:14
1:15
1:16
1:18
1:22
1:24[2]
1:26[2]
1:27[3]
1:28
3:3
3:9
3:23
4:12
5:11
7:17
7:20
8:1
8:2[3]
9:10
9:11
10:1[2]
10:5
10:9
10:10[2]
10:11[2]
10:13
11:16
11:21
12:4[2]
12:7[2]
12:11
12:23
14:10
14:16
14:18
14:20
15:6
16:4
16:7
16:31
16:32
16:38
16:44
16:47
16:48[2]
16:50
16:57
16:59
17:5
17:16
17:19
18:3
18:4
18:18
20:3
20:31
20:32[2]
20:33
20:36
20:39
21:7
21:10
21:23
22:20
22:22
23:16[2]
23:18
23:20
23:44
24:18
24:22
26:3
26:10
28:2
28:6
28:16
30:9
30:18
32:2
33:11
33:12
33:17
33:27
33:31[2]
33:32
34:8
34:12
34:17
34:19
35:6
35:11
35:15
36:17
36:38[2]
37:7[2]
37:10
38:16
40:2
40:40
41:21
41:25
42:6
42:9
42:11[4]
42:12
43:22
46:5
46:7
46:11
46:12
47:10
47:14[2]
47:15
47:22
48:1
48:8
48:11
48:23

DA

1:4
1:13
1:17
2:29
2:30
2:40[3]
2:41
2:42
2:43
2:45
4:18
4:25
4:32
4:33
4:35
5:12
6:4
6:10
6:22
7:4
7:9[2]
7:12
7:28
8:5
8:15
8:18
9:7
9:12

9:13, 9:15, 10:4, 10:6[2], 10:17, 11:29[2], 11:32, 12:1, 12:3[2]

HO
1:10, 2:3[2], 2:15[2], 4:4, 4:7, 4:16[2], 5:12[2], 5:14[2], 6:3[2], 6:4[2], 6:5, 6:9, 7:4, 7:6, 7:7, 7:12[2], 8:1, 8:8, 8:12, 9:1, 9:4, 9:9, 9:10[2], 9:11, 9:13, 10:4, 10:7[2], 10:11, 10:14, 11:2, 11:4, 11:8[2], 11:11[2], 12:9, 12:11, 13:3[4], 13:7[2], 13:8, 14:5[3], 14:6[2], 14:7[3]

JOE
1:15, 2:2, 2:3, 2:4[2], 2:5, 2:32

AM
2:9, 2:13, 3:12, 4:11[2], 5:11, 5:14, 5:16, 5:19, 5:24[2], 7:15, 8:8[2], 8:10[2], 9:5, 9:7, 9:9, 9:11

OB
4, 11, 15, 16[2]

JON
1:14

MIC
1:4[2], 1:6[2], 1:8, 1:16, 2:8[2], 2:12[2], 3:3[2], 3:4, 3:12[2], 4:9, 4:12, 5:7[2], 5:8[2], 5:15, 7:1[2], 7:4, 7:10, 7:14

NA
1:10[3], 2:2, 2:7, 3:6, 3:15[2], 3:17[2]

HAB
1:8, 1:9[2], 1:14[2], 2:5[2], 2:14, 3:4, 3:14[2]

ZEP
1:8, 1:17[2], 2:2, 2:9

HAG
1:12, 2:3, 2:19, 2:23

ZEC
1:4, 1:6, 2:4, 2:6, 4:1, 5:3[2], 7:3, 7:12, 7:13, 8:11, 8:13, 8:14, 9:1, 9:3[2], 9:7[2], 9:11, 9:13, 9:14, 9:15[2], 9:16[3], 10:2, 10:3, 10:5, 10:6, 10:7, 10:8, 12:8[3], 12:10[2], 12:11, 13:9[2], 14:3, 14:5, 14:10, 14:15

MAL
2:9, 3:3[2], 3:4[2], 3:17, 4:1, 4:2

MT
1:18, 1:24, 5:48, 6:2, 6:5, 6:7, 6:10, 6:12, 6:16, 7:29[2], 8:13, 9:9, 9:10, 9:15[2], 9:32, 9:36, 10:7, 10:16[3], 10:25[2], 11:7, 12:13, 12:40, 13:40, 13:43, 14:5, 14:36[2], 15:28, 15:33, 17:2[2], 17:9, 17:20, 18:3, 18:4, 18:17, 18:19, 18:25, 18:33, 19:19, 20:14, 20:28, 20:29, 21:6, 21:18, 21:23, 21:26, 22:9[2], 22:10[2], 22:30, 22:31, 22:39, 23:37, 24:3, 24:21, 24:27, 24:37, 24:38, 24:44, 25:14, 25:32, 25:40, 25:45, 26:7, 26:19, 26:21, 26:24, 26:26, 26:39[2], 26:55, 27:10, 27:32, 27:65[2], 28:1, 28:3, 28:4, 28:6, 28:9, 28:15

MK
1:2, 1:16, 1:22[2], 1:42[2], 2:2, 2:14, 2:15, 2:19[2], 2:23, 3:5, 3:10[2], 3:20, 4:4, 4:18, 4:20, 4:26, 4:33, 4:36, 5:36, 6:15, 6:31, 6:34, 6:56[2], 7:4, 7:6, 7:8, 8:24, 9:3[2], 9:9, 9:13, 9:26, 10:1, 10:15, 10:32, 10:46, 11:2[2], 11:6, 11:20, 11:27, 12:25, 12:26, 12:31, 12:33, 13:1, 13:3, 13:19, 13:34, 14:3, 14:16, 14:18, 14:21, 14:22, 14:45[2], 14:48, 14:66, 15:8, 16:7, 16:10, 16:12, 16:14

LU
1:1, 1:2, 1:23[2], 1:44[2], 1:55, 1:70, 2:15, 2:20, 2:23, 2:43, 3:4, 3:15, 3:23, 4:16, 5:1, 5:14, 5:17, 6:3, 6:10, 6:22, 6:31, 6:34, 6:36, 6:40, 8:5, 8:6[2], 8:23, 8:42, 9:18, 9:29, 9:33, 9:34, 9:42, 9:53, 9:54, 9:57, 10:3, 10:7, 10:8, 10:18, 10:27, 10:33, 10:38, 11:1[2], 11:2, 11:8[2], 11:27, 11:30, 11:36, 11:37, 11:41, 11:44, 11:53, 12:58, 13:34, 14:1, 14:22, 15:19, 15:25, 15:30[2], 17:6, 17:11, 17:12, 17:14, 17:24, 17:26, 17:28, 18:11[2], 18:13, 18:17, 18:35, 19:9, 19:11, 19:32, 19:33, 19:36, 20:1, 21:5, 21:6, 21:35, 22:13, 22:26[2], 22:27, 22:29, 22:31, 22:39, 22:44, 22:52, 22:56, 22:66[2], 23:7[2], 23:14, 23:24, 23:26, 24:4, 24:5, 24:11, 24:17, 24:24, 24:28, 24:36, 24:39, 24:50[2]

JOH
1:12[2], 1:14, 1:23, 1:36, 3:14, 4:51, 5:21, 5:23, 5:26, 5:30, 6:11[2], 6:31, 6:57, 6:58, 6:59, 7:10, 7:28, 7:38, 8:6, 8:20, 8:28, 8:30, 9:1, 9:5[2], 9:29, 10:15, 10:26, 11:20[2], 11:29[2], 11:56, 12:14, 12:50, 13:15, 13:33, 13:34, 14:27, 14:31, 15:4, 15:6, 15:9, 15:10, 15:12, 16:21[2], 17:2[3], 17:11, 17:14, 17:16, 17:18, 17:21, 17:22, 17:23, 18:6[2], 19:40, 20:9, 20:11, 20:21, 21:8, 21:9[2]

AC
1:10, 1:11, 1:19, 2:2, 2:3, 2:4, 2:15, 2:22, 2:39[2], 2:45, 2:47, 3:6, 3:11, 3:12, 3:17, 3:24[2], 4:1, 4:6[2], 4:34[2], 4:35, 5:11[2], 5:35, 5:36[2], 5:37[2], 6:15, 7:5[2], 7:26, 7:28, 7:31, 7:40, 7:42, 7:44, 7:48, 7:51, 8:3, 8:16, 8:32, 8:36, 9:3, 9:17, 9:18, 9:32, 9:38, 10:9, 10:11, 10:25, 10:27, 10:29[2], 10:45, 10:47[2], 11:15[2], 11:17[2], 11:19[2], 11:22[2], 12:13, 12:18[2], 13:1, 13:2, 13:17, 13:25, 13:33, 13:34, 13:48[2], 14:20, 15:8, 15:11, 15:15, 15:24, 16:4, 16:16, 17:2, 17:14, 17:23, 17:25, 17:28, 17:29, 19:2, 20:3, 20:9, 21:10, 21:25, 21:31, 21:37, 22:3, 22:5, 22:6, 22:23, 22:25, 23:11, 23:15, 23:20, 23:31, 24:10, 24:25, 25:10, 25:18, 26:12, 26:24, 26:29, 27:25, 27:27, 27:30[2], 28:10, 28:15[2], 28:22

RO
1:13, 1:15, 1:17, 1:21, 1:28, 2:12[4], 2:24, 3:4, 3:5, 3:7, 3:8[2], 3:10, 4:1, 4:6, 4:17[2], 5:12, 5:15, 5:16, 5:18, 5:19, 5:21, 6:3, 6:4, 6:13[3], 6:19, 7:1[2], 7:2, 8:14[2], 8:26, 8:36[2], 9:5, 9:6, 9:13, 9:25, 9:27, 9:29[2], 9:32, 9:33, 10:15, 11:8, 11:13, 11:26, 11:28[2], 11:30, 12:3, 12:4, 12:18[2], 13:9, 13:13, 14:11, 15:3, 15:7, 15:9, 15:15, 15:21, 16:2

1 CO
1:6, 1:31, 2:9, 3:1[3], 3:3, 3:5, 3:10, 3:15, 4:1, 4:7, 4:8, 4:9, 4:13, 4:14, 4:17, 4:18, 5:1[2], 5:3[2], 5:7, 7:7, 7:8, 7:17[2], 7:25, 7:29, 7:30[3], 7:31, 7:39[2], 8:1, 8:2, 8:4, 8:5, 8:7, 9:5[3], 9:8, 9:20[2], 9:21, 9:22, 9:26[2], 10:6, 10:7[2], 10:8, 10:9, 10:10, 10:13, 10:15, 10:33, 11:1, 11:2, 11:5, 11:7, 11:12, 11:25[2], 11:26[2], 12:2, 12:11, 12:12, 12:18, 13:1, 13:11[3], 13:12, 14:12, 14:33, 14:34, 15:8, 15:22, 15:38, 15:48[2], 15:49, 15:58, 16:1, 16:2, 16:10, 16:12

2 CO
1:5, 1:7, 1:14[2], 1:18, 1:23, 2:17[3], 3:1, 3:3, 3:5, 3:13, 3:18[2], 4:1, 4:13, 5:20, 6:1, 6:4, 6:8, 6:9[3], 6:10[3], 6:13, 6:16, 7:14, 8:5, 8:6, 8:7, 8:11, 8:15, 9:1, 9:3, 9:5[2], 9:7, 9:9, 10:2, 10:7, 10:9, 10:11, 10:14[3], 11:2, 11:3, 11:10, 11:12, 11:15, 11:16, 11:17, 11:21[2]

2 CO
11:23, 12:20, 13:2, 13:7

GA
1:9, 2:7, 2:14[2], 3:6, 3:10[2], 3:16[2], 3:27[2], 4:1[2], 4:12[2], 4:14[2], 4:28, 4:29, 5:14, 5:21, 6:10, 6:12[2], 6:16[2]

EPH
1:4, 2:3, 3:3, 3:5, 4:4, 4:17, 4:21, 4:32, 5:1, 5:2, 5:3, 5:8, 5:15, 5:22, 5:23, 5:24, 5:25, 5:28, 5:29, 5:33, 6:5[2], 6:6, 6:7, 6:20

PHP
1:7, 1:20, 1:27, 2:8, 2:12[2], 2:15, 2:22, 2:23, 3:5, 3:12, 3:15, 3:17, 4:15

COL
1:6[2], 1:7, 2:1, 2:6, 2:7, 2:20, 3:12, 3:13, 3:18, 3:22, 3:23, 4:4

1 TH
1:5, 2:2, 2:4[2], 2:5, 2:6, 2:7, 2:11[2], 2:13, 2:14, 3:4, 3:6, 3:12, 4:1, 4:5, 4:6, 4:9, 4:11, 4:13, 5:2, 5:3, 5:4, 5:6, 5:11

2 TH
1:3, 2:2, 2:4, 3:1, 3:15[2]

1 TI
1:3, 5:1[2], 5:2, 6:1

2 TI
2:3, 2:9, 2:17, 3:8, 3:9

TIT
1:5, 1:7, 1:9, 2:3

PHM
9, 14, 16, 17

HEB
1:4, 1:11, 1:12, 2:14, 3:2, 3:3, 3:5, 3:6, 3:7, 3:8, 3:15, 4:2[2], 4:3[2], 4:7, 4:10, 4:15, 5:3, 5:4, 5:6, 5:12, 6:19, 7:9, 7:20, 7:27, 8:5, 9:8, 9:9, 9:25, 9:27, 10:25[2], 11:7, 11:9, 11:12[4], 11:27, 11:29, 12:5, 12:7, 12:16, 12:20, 12:27, 13:3[2], 13:5, 13:17

JAS
1:10, 2:8, 2:9, 2:12, 2:26, 5:3, 5:5, 5:17

1 PE
1:14, 1:15, 1:18[2], 1:19, 1:24[2], 2:2, 2:4, 2:5, 2:11, 2:12, 2:13, 2:14, 2:16[2], 2:25, 3:6[3], 3:7[2], 3:8, 3:16, 4:1, 4:10[2], 4:11[2], 4:12, 4:13, 4:15[4], 4:16, 4:19, 5:3, 5:8, 5:12

2 PE
1:3, 1:13, 1:14, 1:19, 1:21, 2:1, 2:12, 2:13, 3:4, 3:8[2], 3:9, 3:10, 3:15, 3:16[2]

1 JO
1:7, 2:6, 2:18, 2:27[2], 3:2, 3:3, 3:7, 3:12, 3:23, 4:17

2 JO
4, 5, 6

3 JO
2, 3

JUDE
7, 10

RE
1:10, 1:14[3], 1:15[2], 1:16, 1:17, 2:24[3], 2:27[2], 3:3, 3:19[2], 3:21, 4:1, 4:7, 5:6, 5:13, 6:1, 6:11, 6:12[2], 6:13, 6:14, 8:8, 8:10, 8:12, 9:2, 9:3, 9:5, 9:7[2], 9:8[2], 9:9[2], 9:17, 10:1[2], 10:3, 10:7, 10:9, 10:10[3], 11:6[2], 12:4[4], 12:15, 13:2[2], 13:3, 13:11, 13:15[2], 14:2[2], 14:3, 15:2, 16:3, 16:15, 16:18, 17:12[2], 18:6, 18:17[2], 19:6[3], 19:12, 20:8, 21:2, 21:11, 21:16[2], 21:21, 22:1, 22:12

BE

1961, *1510*

GE
1:3, 1:6, 1:9[2], 1:14[2], 1:15, 1:22, 1:28, 1:29, 2:18, 2:23, 2:24, 3:5[2], 3:6, 3:12, 3:16, 4:7[2], 4:12, 4:14[2], 4:15, 4:24, 6:3, 6:15, 6:19, 6:21, 8:17, 9:1[2], 9:2, 9:3, 9:6, 9:7, 9:11[2], 9:13, 9:14, 9:15, 9:16, 9:20, 9:25[2], 9:26[2], 9:27, 10:8, 11:4, 11:6, 12:2, 12:3, 12:13, 13:8[2], 13:16, 14:19, 14:20, 15:4[2], 15:5[2], 15:13, 15:15, 16:2, 16:3, 16:5, 16:10, 16:12, 17:1, 17:4, 17:5[2], 17:7, 17:8, 17:10, 17:11, 17:12, 17:13[2], 17:14, 17:15, 17:16, 17:17, 18:4, 18:11, 18:18, 18:24, 18:25[2], 18:29, 18:30[2], 18:31, 18:32[2], 19:9, 19:15, 19:17, 19:22, 20:9, 21:10, 21:12[2], 21:30, 22:14, 22:17, 23:8, 24:5, 24:8[2], 24:14, 24:27, 24:41[2], 24:44, 24:51, 24:60, 25:22, 25:23[2], 26:3, 26:4, 26:11, 26:22, 26:28, 27:13, 27:21, 27:29[2], 27:33, 27:39, 27:45, 28:3, 28:9, 28:14[2], 28:20, 28:21, 28:22, 29:4, 29:7, 29:8, 29:15, 29:26, 29:29, 29:34, 30:32, 30:33, 30:34, 31:3, 31:8[2], 31:30, 31:44, 31:52[2], 32:12, 32:18, 32:28, 33:14, 34:7, 34:10, 34:15[3], 34:17[2], 34:22[2], 34:23, 34:30, 35:2, 35:10[2], 35:11[2], 36:43, 37:14, 37:27, 37:32, 37:35, 38:9, 38:11, 38:15, 38:23, 38:24, 38:29, 39:10, 40:14, 40:27, 40:36[2], 41:21, 41:30, 41:31[2], 41:40[3], 41:52, 42:15, 42:16[3], 42:19[2], 42:20, 42:32, 42:33, 43:3, 43:5, 43:9, 43:11, 43:14, 43:23, 43:29, 44:9[2], 44:10[3], 44:17, 44:26[2], 44:30, 44:34, 45:5, 45:6, 45:10, 46:15, 47:19[2], 47:24, 47:25, 48:5, 48:6[2], 48:16, 48:19[2], 48:21, 49:6, 49:7, 49:8, 49:10, 49:12, 49:13[2], 49:17, 49:20, 49:26, 49:29, 50:18

EX
1:16[2], 2:4, 3:12[2], 4:12, 4:14, 4:15, 4:16[4], 4:18, 5:8, 5:9, 5:11, 5:18, 5:21, 6:7, 6:14[2], 7:1, 7:17, 7:19, 8:20, 8:21, 8:22, 8:23, 9:3, 9:9, 9:15, 9:16, 9:19[2], 9:22, 9:28, 9:29, 10:5, 10:7, 10:10, 10:14, 10:21[2], 10:24, 10:26, 11:6[2], 11:9, 12:2[2], 12:15, 12:16[2], 12:19, 12:25, 12:32, 12:42[2], 12:46, 12:48, 13:3, 13:7[3], 14:4, 15:9, 15:15, 16:12, 16:23, 16:32, 16:33, 16:34, 19:12, 19:13, 20:26, 21:8, 21:12, 21:15, 21:16[2], 21:17, 21:19, 21:20, 21:21, 21:22, 21:28[2], 21:29[2], 21:30, 21:31, 21:32, 22:2[3], 22:3[3], 22:4[2], 22:5, 22:6, 22:7[2], 22:8[2], 22:9[2], 22:10, 22:11, 22:12, 22:13, 22:14, 22:15[2], 22:16, 22:19, 22:20, 22:24, 22:25, 22:30, 22:31, 23:1, 23:12[2], 23:13[2], 23:22, 23:26, 23:30, 23:33, 24:7, 24:12, 25:7, 25:10, 25:12, 25:14, 25:15[2]

25:17
25:20
25:23
25:27
25:28
25:31[2]
25:34
25:35
25:36[2]
25:38
26:2
26:3[2]
26:6
26:7
26:8[2]
26:11
26:16[2]
26:17
26:20
26:24[4]
26:25
26:31
26:32
26:37
27:1[2]
27:2
27:5
27:7[2]
27:9
27:10[2]
27:11
27:12
27:13
27:14
27:15
27:16[2]
27:17[2]
27:18
27:19
27:21
28:7
28:8
28:11
28:16[3]
28:17[2]
28:18
28:20
28:21[2]
28:28[2]
28:30
28:32[2]
28:35[2]
28:37[2]
28:38[3]
28:43[2]
29:9
29:10
29:21
29:26
29:28[2]
29:29[3]
29:34
29:37[2]
29:42
29:43
29:45
30:2[4]
30:4
30:12
30:13
30:16
30:21
30:25
30:29[2]
30:31
30:32[2]
30:33
30:34
30:36
30:37
30:38
31:14[2]
31:15[2]
32:5
32:8
33:16[2]
33:19[2]
33:23
34:2
34:3
34:12
34:25
35:2[3]
35:9
35:27
35:29
36:6
36:18
36:34
37:3
37:27
38:5
38:26
39:7
39:21[2]
39:37
40:4
40:9
40:10
40:15

LE

1:3
1:4
1:9
1:10
1:14
1:15
2:1
2:2
2:3
2:4
2:5[2]
2:7[2]
2:10
2:11
2:12
2:13
3:1[2]
3:6
3:12
3:17
4:2
4:12
4:13[2]
4:15
4:20
4:22
4:26
4:27[2]
4:31
4:35
5:2[3]
5:3[4]
5:4[3]
5:5[2]
5:7
5:9
5:10
5:11
5:13[2]
5:16
5:17
5:18
6:4
6:7
6:9
6:12[2]
6:13
6:16
6:17
6:18[2]
6:21
6:22
6:23[2]
6:25
6:26
6:27
6:28[3]
6:30[2]
7:6
7:9
7:14
7:15
7:16[2]
7:17
7:18[4]
7:19[3]
7:20
7:21
7:24
7:25
7:26
7:27[2]
7:30
7:31
7:36
8:5
8:33
10:3[2]
10:9
10:14
10:15
11:7
11:10
11:11
11:12
11:13
11:20
11:23
11:24[2]
11:25
11:26
11:27
11:28
11:29
11:31[2]
11:32[6]
11:33
11:34[4]
11:35[4]
11:36[2]
11:37[2]
11:38[2]
11:39
11:40[2]
11:41[2]
11:43
11:44
11:45[2]
11:47[2]
12:2[2]
12:3
12:4
12:5
12:7
12:8[2]
13:2[2]
13:3
13:4[3]
13:5
13:6[2]
13:7
13:9
13:10[2]
13:14
13:15
13:16
13:17
13:19[2]
13:20[2]
13:21[3]
13:24
13:25[2]
13:26[3]
13:27
13:28
13:30[2]
13:31
13:32[2]
13:33
13:34[3]
13:36
13:37
13:39
13:42
13:43
13:45
13:46[3]
13:47
13:48
13:49[2]
13:51
13:52
13:53
13:55[2]
13:56
13:58[4]
14:2[2]
14:3
14:4
14:5
14:7
14:8[2]
14:9[2]
14:11
14:14
14:17
14:18
14:19
14:20
14:21[2]
14:22
14:25
14:28
14:29
14:31
14:34
14:36
14:37
14:39
14:41
14:44
14:46
14:54
15:3[2]
15:4
15:5
15:6
15:7
15:8
15:9
15:10[2]
15:11
15:12[2]
15:13
15:16
15:17[2]
15:18
15:19[3]
15:20[2]
15:21
15:22
15:23[2]
15:24[3]
15:25[2]
15:26[2]
15:27[2]
15:28[2]
16:4[2]
16:10[2]
16:17
16:29[2]
16:30
16:31
16:34
17:3
17:4[2]
17:7
17:8
17:9
17:10
17:13[2]
17:14
17:15[3]
18:9
18:29
19:3
19:6[2]
19:7[2]
19:8
19:20[2]
19:22
19:23[2]
19:24
19:29
19:31
19:34
20:2[2]
20:7
20:9[2]
20:10
20:11[2]
20:12[2]
20:13[2]
20:14[2]
20:15
20:16[2]
20:17
20:18
20:21
20:26[2]
20:27[2]
21:1
21:3
21:6[2]
21:8
21:9
21:17
21:18
21:20
22:3[2]
22:4
22:5
22:6
22:7
22:12
22:13
22:18
22:20
22:21[3]
22:23
22:25[2]
22:27[2]
22:28
22:30
22:32
22:33
23:2
23:3
23:10
23:11
23:13[2]
23:14
23:15
23:17[2]
23:18
23:20
23:21[2]
23:27[2]
23:29[3]
23:30
23:31
23:32
23:34
23:35
23:36
23:37
23:39[2]
23:41
24:3
24:5
24:7
24:9
24:12
24:16[2]
24:17
24:19
24:20
24:21
25:4
25:6
25:7
25:8
25:10
25:11
25:12
25:23
25:25
25:26
25:28
25:30[2]
25:31[2]
25:34
25:35[2]
25:38
25:39[2]
25:40
25:42
25:44
25:45
25:46
25:48
25:49
25:50[2]
25:51
25:53
25:54
26:12[2]
26:13
26:17
26:20
26:22
26:23
26:25
26:26
26:32
26:33
26:34
26:41
26:43
26:44
26:45
27:2
27:3[2]
27:4[2]
27:5[2]
27:6[3]
27:7[3]
27:8
27:9[2]
27:10
27:11
27:12[2]
27:14[2]
27:15
27:16[2]
27:18
27:19
27:20
27:21[2]
27:25[2]
27:26[2]
27:27[3]
27:28
27:29[3]
27:32
27:33[3]

NU

1:4
1:51[2]
1:53
2:3
2:5[2]
2:7
2:10[2]
2:12[2]
2:14
2:18[2]
2:20[2]
2:22
2:25[2]
2:27[2]
2:29
3:10
3:12
3:13
3:24
3:25
3:30
3:31
3:32
3:36
3:38[2]
3:45
3:46
3:48
4:4
4:7
4:27
4:28
4:45
5:6
5:8[2]
5:9
5:10[2]
5:13[5]
5:14[4]
5:19
5:20
5:27[2]
5:28[3]
5:30
5:31
6:5[2]
6:12
6:13
6:25
7:5
8:14
8:19
9:10[2]
9:13
10:7
10:8
10:9[2]
10:10
10:31
10:32[2]
10:35
11:16
11:20
11:22[2]
12:6
12:12
12:14[3]
13:18
13:19[2]
13:20[3]
13:28
13:31
14:3
14:11
14:17
14:21
14:31
14:33
14:35
14:40
14:42
14:43
15:2
15:11
15:14
15:15[2]
15:16
15:19
15:24[2]
15:25
15:26
15:28
15:30[2]
15:31[2]
15:34
15:35
15:39
15:40
15:41
16:7[2]
16:16
16:22
16:26
16:29
16:38
16:40[2]
17:3
17:10
17:13
18:2
18:4
18:5
18:7
18:9[2]
18:10
18:13
18:14
18:15[2]
18:16
18:17
18:18
18:23
18:27
18:30
19:7
19:8
19:9
19:10[2]
19:11
19:12[2]
19:13[2]
19:14
19:16
19:17
19:19
19:20[2]
19:21[2]
19:22[2]
20:24
20:26
21:22
22:11
23:9
23:10
23:23
24:7[3]
24:18[2]
24:20
24:22
25:4
26:53
26:54
26:55
26:56
27:4
27:11
27:13
27:17
27:20
28:7[2]
28:14
28:15
28:17
28:18
28:19
28:20
28:24
28:26
28:31
29:3
29:8
29:9
29:13
29:14
29:18
29:21
29:24
29:27
29:30
29:33
29:37
31:2
31:23[2]
31:24
32:5
32:22[3]
32:23
32:26
32:29
32:32
32:54
32:55
34:3[2]
34:4
34:5
34:6
34:7
34:8
34:9[2]
34:12[2]
35:3
35:5[2]
35:6
35:7
35:8
35:10
35:11
35:12
35:14
35:15
35:16
35:17
35:18
35:21
35:27
35:29
35:30
35:31
35:33
36:3[4]
36:4[3]
36:8

DE

1:1
1:17
1:21
1:29
1:39
1:42
2:4
2:25
4:19
4:20
4:26
4:27
4:30
5:16
5:29
5:33
6:2
6:3
6:6
6:8
6:10
6:11
6:15
6:18
6:25
7:4
7:6
7:10
7:14[2]
7:16
7:18
7:20
7:21
7:23
7:24
7:25
7:26
8:14
8:19
8:20
10:5
10:16
11:8
11:15
11:16
11:17[2]
11:18
11:21
11:24[2]
11:25
12:11
12:21
12:23
12:27
12:30[2]
13:5
13:9
13:14
13:16[2]
14:2
14:19
14:24[2]
14:29
15:4
15:7
15:9[3]
15:10
15:12
15:16
15:17
15:21[2]
16:4
16:8
17:2
17:4[2]
17:6[2]
17:7
17:9
17:18
17:19
17:20
18:3[2]
18:10
18:13
18:22
19:2
19:9
19:10[2]
19:15
19:17
19:18
20:1
20:3
20:11[3]
20:20[2]
21:1[2]
21:3
21:6
21:8[2]
21:13[2]
21:14
21:15
21:16
21:22[2]
21:23
22:2[2]
22:6[2]
22:7
22:9
22:19
22:20[2]
22:22
22:23
23:10
23:11
23:13
23:14
23:17
23:21
23:22
24:2
24:3
24:4
24:5[2]
24:7
24:12
24:13
24:14
24:15
24:16[3]
24:19
24:20
24:21
25:1
25:2[4]
25:6[2]
25:9
25:10
25:15
25:19
26:1
26:3
26:12
26:17
26:18
26:19
27:2
27:4[2]
27:15
27:16
27:17
27:18
27:19
27:20
27:21
27:22
27:23
27:24
27:25
27:26
28:3[2]
28:4
28:5
28:6[2]
28:7
28:10
28:13[2]
28:16
28:17
28:18
28:19[2]
28:20
28:23[2]
28:24
28:25[2]
28:26
28:27
28:29
28:31[4]
28:32[2]
28:33
28:34
28:35
28:44[2]
28:45
28:46
28:51
28:54
28:56
28:61
28:62
28:63
28:68
29:13
29:18[2]
30:4
30:17
31:6[2]
31:7
31:8[2]
31:16
31:17[2]
31:19
31:21
31:23[2]
31:26
32:20
32:24
32:38
32:43
32:50
33:6
33:7[2]
33:8
33:13
33:20
33:24[2]
33:25[2]
33:28
33:29

JOS

1:4
1:5[2]
1:6
1:7
1:9[3]
1:17
1:18[3]
2:3
2:14
2:16
2:17
2:19[6]
2:20
2:21
3:4
3:7
3:13
4:6
4:7
6:17
6:26
7:12
7:14[2]
7:15[2]
8:1
8:4
8:8
9:6
9:13
9:20
9:21
9:23
10:25
11:6
13:1
14:9
14:12[3]
15:4
17:15[2]
17:18[3]
20:3
20:6
21:13
21:21
21:27
21:32
21:38
22:18[2]
22:19
22:22
22:27
22:28
22:34
23:4
23:6
23:13
23:16
24:27[2]

JG

2:3[2]
2:6
4:9
4:20
5:24[2]
5:31
6:13[2]
6:16
6:23
6:31[2]
6:37[2]
6:39[3]
7:4
7:11
7:17
8:5
9:9
9:11
9:13
9:24
9:31
9:33
10:18
11:6
11:8
11:9
11:10
11:26
11:27
11:31[2]
11:37
13:5
13:7
13:8
14:11
15:3
15:7
16:6
16:7[2]
16:9
16:10
16:11[2]
16:12
16:13
16:14
16:17[2]
16:20
16:28
17:2
17:10
18:5
18:9
18:19[3]
18:25
19:6[2]
19:9
19:20
19:28
20:9
21:3
21:5
21:17[3]
21:18
21:22[3]

RU

1:11
1:16
1:17
2:4
2:9
2:12
2:13
2:19
2:20
3:1
3:4
3:10
3:13
3:14
3:18
4:10[2]
4:11
4:12
4:14[2]
4:15

1 SA

1:14
1:22
1:28
2:9
2:10
2:28
2:30[2]
2:31
2:32
2:33
2:34
3:9
3:14
3:20
4:9[2]
4:19
5:8
6:3[2]
6:4
8:11[2]
8:13[3]
8:17
8:20
9:13[2]
9:16
10:1
10:6
10:7
10:21
11:3
11:7
11:9
11:13
12:15
12:25
13:14
14:6
14:10
14:21
14:24[2]
14:28
14:39
14:40[2]
15:1
15:11
15:13
15:18
15:33
16:16
17:9[3]
17:25
17:26
17:27
17:36
17:37
18:17[3]
18:18
18:21[3]
18:22
18:23
18:25
18:26
18:27
19:6
19:11
19:22
20:3
20:7[2]
20:8
20:9
20:12
20:13
20:18[2]
20:23
20:29
20:31
20:32
20:42
22:3
22:15
22:23
23:3
23:17[2]
23:20
23:21
23:23
24:12
24:13
24:15
24:20[2]
25:6[3]
25:10
25:11
25:24
25:26
25:27
25:29
25:31
25:32
25:33[2]
25:39
25:41
26:9
26:19[2]
26:24
26:25
27:11
27:12
28:13
28:19
29:4[2]
29:10
30:24

2 SA

1:5
1:16
2:5
2:7[2]
2:26
3:12
3:35
3:39
5:2
5:14
5:24
6:22[2]
7:8
7:11
7:12
7:14[2]
7:16[2]
7:24
7:26[2]
7:28
7:29
10:5
10:11[2]
10:12
11:15
11:20
11:24
12:9
12:10
12:22
12:28
13:12
13:13
13:15
13:25
13:28
14:2[2]
14:9
14:14[2]
14:15
14:17[2]
14:25
14:32
15:20
15:21[2]
15:33
15:34[2]
15:35
16:2[2]
16:12
16:18
16:19
16:21
17:3
17:8[2]
17:9
17:10
17:11
17:12[2]
17:13[2]
17:16
17:17
17:20
18:25
18:28
18:32
19:7
19:13
19:21
19:22[2]
19:35
19:37
19:42
19:43
20:1
20:4
20:20
20:21
21:5
21:6
22:4[2]
22:44
22:45
22:46
22:47[2]
23:1
23:3
23:4
23:5
23:6[2]
23:7[2]
23:8
23:17
24:3
24:13
24:17
24:21
24:22

1 KI

1:2
1:5
1:21
1:35[2]
1:37
1:48
1:52
2:2
2:7
2:19
2:21
2:24
2:33
2:37
2:39
2:45
3:13
3:26
5:6
5:7
5:9
6:6
8:5
8:15
8:16
8:26
8:29[2]
8:31
8:33
8:37[3]
8:38
8:46
8:51
8:52[2]
8:56
8:57
8:59
8:61
9:3
9:7
9:8
10:9
10:27[2]
11:37
11:38[2]
12:7[2]
12:10
13:2[2]
13:3[2]
13:6
14:2[3]
14:5[2]
14:6
14:10
17:1
17:4
18:21
18:24
18:27
18:31
18:36
19:15
19:16[2]
20:6
20:18[2]
20:23
20:25
20:39[2]
20:40
21:7
22:3
22:13
22:22

2 KI

1:10
1:12
1:13
1:14
1:15
2:9[2]
2:10[2]
2:16
2:21
3:17
4:1
4:10
4:13[2]
4:14
4:23
5:10
5:12
5:13
5:17
5:22
5:23
6:3
6:6[2]
6:8
7:1
7:2
7:12
7:18
7:19
8:13
8:29
9:10
9:15[2]
9:37
10:6
10:9
10:15
10:19[2]
10:23
10:24
11:5
11:6[2]
11:8[2]
11:15
11:17
12:5
12:15
14:6[3]
15:19
16:15
18:23
18:29
18:30
19:4
19:6
19:10
19:11
19:25
19:26
19:29
20:8
20:17[2]
20:18
20:19
22:17[2]
22:20
23:27
25:12
25:24[2]

1 CH

1:10
4:10
5:2
6:17
9:22
11:2
11:6
12:17[3]
12:18[2]
13:2
14:15
15:16
16:15
16:25[2]
16:30[2]
16:31
16:36
16:38
17:7
17:9
17:10
17:11[3]
17:13[2]
17:14
17:21
17:23
17:24[3]
17:27[2]
19:5
19:12[2]
19:13
21:3[2]
21:12
21:17[3]
21:22
22:5[2]
22:9[3]
22:10[2]
22:11
22:13[2]
22:16[2]
22:19
28:4[2]
28:6[2]
28:7
28:9
28:10
28:20[3]
28:21[3]
29:2[2]
29:5
29:10
29:14
29:22[2]

2 CH

1:9
2:8
2:9
2:12
2:14
2:18[2]
4:18
5:6
5:13
6:4
6:5[2]
6:6
6:17
6:20
6:22
6:24
6:28[4]
6:29
6:36
6:40[2]
6:41
7:13
7:15
7:16[2]
7:18
7:20
7:21
7:22
9:8[2]
10:3
10:4[2]
10:7[2]
10:10
11:22
12:7
12:8
13:8
13:9
15:2[2]
15:7[3]
15:13
18:3

18:10 18:12 18:14 18:21 19:7 19:11[2] 20:2 20:15 20:17[2] 20:20 22:6 23:4 23:5[2] 23:7[2] 23:14 23:15 23:16 25:8 25:14 25:16 26:15 26:18 29:11 29:24 30:7 30:8 30:19 31:4 32:7[3] 32:14 33:4 34:25[2] 34:28 35:3 36:22 36:23

EZR

1:1 1:3 4:12 4:13[2] 4:15 4:16 4:21[2] 5:8 5:15 5:17[2] 6:3[2] 6:4 6:5 6:6 6:8[2] 6:9 6:11[3] 6:12 7:20 7:21 7:23[2] 7:24 7:26[2] 7:27 9:12 9:14[2] 10:3 10:4[2] 10:8 10:14

NE

1:6 1:11 2:3 2:6 2:7 2:17 4:5 4:7 4:12 4:14 4:22 5:5 5:8 5:13 5:14 6:6 6:7 6:9[2] 6:13 7:3[3] 7:5 8:10 8:11 9:5 10:38 11:23 13:5 13:19[4]

ES

1:17[2] 1:19[2] 1:20 1:22 2:2 2:3 2:4 2:9 3:9[2] 3:14[2] 4:14 5:3 5:6[2] 5:14[3] 6:6 6:8 6:9[2] 6:11 6:13 7:2[2] 7:3 7:4[2] 8:5[2] 8:13[2] 9:1 9:12[2] 9:13[2] 9:14 9:25 9:28

JOB

1:5 1:21 3:4 3:6 3:7 3:9 3:17 4:2 4:17[2] 5:1 5:11[2] 5:21[2] 5:22 5:23[2] 5:24 5:25 6:3 6:6 6:14 6:28 6:29 7:4 7:21 8:2 8:14[2] 8:22 9:2 9:29 10:15[2] 11:2[2] 11:12[2] 11:14 11:15 11:17[2] 11:18 11:20 12:14[2] 13:5 13:16 13:18 14:7 15:14[2] 15:29 15:31 15:32[2] 15:34 17:8 17:9 18:2 18:4[2] 18:5 18:6[2] 18:7 18:12[2] 18:14 18:15 18:16[2] 18:18 18:20 19:4 19:27 19:29 20:8[2] 20:12 20:18 20:21 20:22 20:26 21:2 21:4 21:5 21:30 21:32 21:33 22:2[2] 22:21 22:23 22:25 22:28 23:7 24:20[2] 24:23[2] 24:25 25:4[2] 27:7 27:14[2] 27:15 27:19 28:12 28:15[2] 28:16 28:17 28:18 28:19 31:6 31:8 31:11 31:22 31:28 31:31 32:20 33:3 33:7 33:21 33:23 33:25 33:26 33:30 34:10 34:20[2] 34:29 34:30 34:31 34:33 34:36 35:2 35:3[2] 35:6 35:7 36:4 36:8[2] 36:16[2] 36:26 37:6 37:20[2] 38:11 38:13 38:15 39:9 40:8 41:9 41:17 41:23 41:32 42:2

PS

1:3 2:10[2] 2:12 3:2 3:6 4:3 4:4 4:6 5:11 6:10[2] 7:3 9:2 9:9 9:17 9:18 9:19 9:20 10:2 10:6[2] 11:3 11:6 13:2 14:7 15:5 16:4 16:8 17:15 18:3[2] 18:45 18:46[2] 19:10 19:13[2] 19:14 21:7 21:13 22:3 22:11 22:19 22:25 22:26 22:29 22:30 22:31 24:7 25:2 25:3[2] 25:20 26:11 27:1 27:2 27:6 27:14 28:1[2] 28:6 30:6 30:10 30:12 31:1 31:2 31:7 31:17[3] 31:18 31:21 31:24 32:6 32:9[2] 32:10 32:11 33:22 34:1 34:2 34:18 34:21 34:22 35:4[2] 35:5 35:6 35:9 35:22 35:26[2] 35:27[2] 36:2[2] 36:3 36:8 36:12 37:1 37:2 37:3 37:9 37:10[2] 37:14 37:15 37:17 37:18 37:19[2] 37:20 37:22[3] 37:24 37:28 37:36 37:38[2] 38:18 38:21 39:13 40:5[2] 40:13 40:14[2] 40:15 40:16[2] 41:2 41:4 41:10 41:13 42:8 45:12 45:14[2] 45:15 45:16 45:17 46:2[2] 46:3 46:5 46:10[3] 48:1 48:11 48:14 49:3 49:16 50:3 50:22 51:4[2] 51:7[2] 51:13 51:19 53:6 55:6 55:20 55:22 56:1 56:2 56:11 57:1[3] 57:5[2] 57:11[2] 58:3 58:7 59:5 59:12 59:13 59:15 60:4 60:5 62:2 62:3[2] 62:6 62:9 63:5 63:10 63:11[2] 64:7 64:10 65:1 65:4 66:8 66:9 66:20 67:1 67:2 67:4 68:1 68:3 68:13 68:19 68:23 68:35 69:6[2] 69:14 69:23 69:25 69:28[2] 69:32 70:2[2] 70:3 70:4[2] 71:1 71:3 71:6 71:8 71:12 71:13[2] 72:14 72:15[3] 72:16 72:17[2] 72:18 72:19[2] 74:14 75:10 76:7 76:8 76:11[2] 77:2 77:7 77:9 78:6 78:8 79:2 79:5 79:10 80:3 80:4 80:7 80:17 80:19 81:9 83:1 83:4 83:17[2] 84:4 84:10 85:6 86:3 86:17 87:5 87:7 88:11 88:12 89:2 89:6[2] 89:7[2] 89:16 89:17 89:21 89:24[2] 89:37 89:52 90:10 90:14 90:17 91:4 91:5 91:15 92:7 92:9 92:10 92:13 92:14 93:1 94:8 94:13 96:4[2] 96:10[2] 96:11 96:12 97:1 97:7 98:8 99:1 100:4 101:6 102:18[2] 102:26 102:28 104:5 104:12 104:34[2] 104:35[2] 106:8 106:46 106:48 107:30 108:5 108:6 109:7[2] 109:8 109:9 109:10 109:12[2] 109:13[2] 109:14[2] 109:15 109:17 109:19 109:20 109:28 109:29 110:3 111:4 111:5 112:2[2] 112:3 112:6[2] 112:7 112:8 112:9 112:10 113:2 113:3 113:9 118:26 119:6 119:46 119:58 119:74 119:76 119:78 119:80[2] 119:116 119:117 119:122 119:128 119:132 120:3[2] 121:3 122:7 122:8 124:6 125:1[2] 125:4 125:5 127:5 128:1[2] 128:3 128:4 129:5 129:6 129:8 130:2 130:4 132:9 135:21 137:8[2] 138:6 139:11 140:10 140:11 141:2 141:5[3] 143:2 143:7 144:1 144:12[2] 144:13 144:14[3] 145:3 145:14 148:4 149:2 149:5 149:6

PR

1:9 1:31 1:33 2:22[2] 3:7 3:8 3:10 3:11 3:15 3:22 3:24[2] 3:25 3:26 3:35 4:10 4:12 4:26 5:10[2] 5:16 5:17 5:18 5:19 5:20 5:22 6:1 6:6 6:15 6:18 6:27 6:28 6:29 6:31 6:33 8:5 8:6 8:11[2] 8:33 9:9 9:11[2] 9:12[2] 10:9 10:24 10:27 10:28 10:29 10:30 10:31 11:6 11:9 11:18 11:21[2] 11:25[2] 11:26 11:29 11:31 12:3[2] 12:8[2] 12:11 12:14[2] 12:19 12:21 12:24 13:4 13:9 13:11 13:13[2] 13:18[2] 13:20[2] 13:21 14:11 14:14[2] 14:22 16:3 16:5 16:7 16:16 16:19 16:21 16:31 17:5 17:11 17:14 18:19 18:20[2] 19:2 19:5 19:9 19:20 19:23 20:3 20:11[2] 20:13 20:17 20:20 20:21[2] 21:13 21:15 21:17[2] 21:18 21:20 22:1 22:5 22:9 22:11 22:13 22:18 22:19 22:26 23:2 23:3 23:4 23:15 23:17 23:18 23:19 23:20 23:25 23:34 24:1 24:4 24:8 24:11 24:14[3] 24:17 24:19 24:20[2] 24:25 24:28 25:5 25:7[2] 25:16 25:17 25:21[2] 26:4 26:5 26:26 27:11 27:14 27:18 27:23 28:2 28:6 28:9 28:18 28:20 28:22 28:25 28:26 29:1 29:14 29:19 29:25 30:6 30:9[2] 30:10 30:18 30:24 30:29 31:6 31:30

EC

1:9[2] 1:10 1:11 1:13 1:15[2] 2:16 2:18 2:19 3:2 3:10[2] 3:14[2] 3:15 3:22 4:11 4:13 5:1 5:2[3] 5:6 5:8 5:10 6:3[2] 6:4 6:11 6:12 7:9[2] 7:14 7:16 7:17[2] 7:23 7:26 8:1 8:3 8:7[2] 8:12[2] 8:13 8:14 8:15 8:17 9:8 10:9[2] 10:10 10:14[2] 11:2 11:3[2] 11:6 11:8 12:2 12:3 12:4[2] 12:5[3] 12:6[3] 12:12 12:14[2]

CA

1:4 1:7 2:17 7:8 8:1 8:3 8:7 8:8 8:9[2] 8:14

ISA

1:5 1:18[4] 1:19 1:20 1:26 1:27 1:28[2] 1:29[2] 1:30 1:31 2:2[2] 2:6 2:11[3] 2:12[2] 2:17[3] 2:22 3:4 3:5 3:6 3:7 3:10 3:11[2] 3:24 4:1 4:2[2] 4:3 4:5 4:6 5:5[2] 5:6 5:8[2] 5:9 5:15[3] 5:16[2] 5:24 5:27[3] 5:28 5:29 6:10 6:11[2] 6:12 6:13[3] 7:4 7:8[2] 7:9 7:16 7:23[2] 7:25[2] 8:4 8:9[3] 8:12 8:13[2] 8:14 8:15[3] 8:20 8:21 8:22 9:1 9:5 9:6[2] 9:7 9:19 9:20 9:21 10:2 10:17 10:18 10:19 10:22 10:24 10:27[2] 10:30 10:33[2] 11:5 11:9 11:10[2] 11:11 11:13 11:16[2] 12:2 13:6 13:7 13:8[3] 13:10 13:14 13:15 13:16[2] 13:19 13:20[2] 13:21 13:22 14:1 14:14 14:15 14:20[2] 14:29 14:30 15:2 15:4[2] 15:6 15:9 16:2[2] 16:4 16:5 16:6 16:10[2] 16:14 17:1 17:2 17:3 17:4 17:5[2] 17:6 17:9[2] 17:11 17:13 18:6 18:7 19:1 19:5 19:6 19:7[2] 19:9 19:10 19:15 19:16[2] 19:17[2] 19:18 19:19 19:20 19:21 19:22 19:23 19:24 19:25 20:5 20:6 21:17 22:14 22:18 22:21 22:23 22:25[3] 23:2 23:4 23:5 23:15 23:16 23:18 24:2 24:3 24:9 24:13[2] 24:16 24:18 24:20[3] 24:22[3] 24:23 25:2[2] 25:5 25:9[2] 25:10 26:6 26:10 26:20 27:9 27:10 27:11 27:12 27:13 28:3 28:4 28:5 28:10 28:13 28:18[2] 28:19 28:21 28:22[2] 28:28 29:2[2] 29:4[3] 29:5[2] 29:6 29:7 29:8[2] 29:14 29:16 29:17[2] 29:22 30:3 30:5 30:8 30:13 30:14 30:15[2] 30:16 30:17 30:18[2] 30:19 30:20 30:23 30:25 30:26[2] 30:28 30:30 30:31 30:32 31:4 31:8 31:9 32:2 32:3 32:4 32:5[3] 32:11 32:14[3] 32:15[3] 32:17 32:19 33:1 33:2[2] 33:4 33:6 33:10 33:12[2] 33:16[3] 33:20[3] 33:21 33:24 34:3[2] 34:4[2] 34:5 34:7 34:9 34:10 34:12[2] 34:13 34:15 35:1 35:2 35:4 35:5[2] 35:7 35:8[3] 35:9[2] 36:8 36:14 36:15 37:4 37:6 37:10 37:11 37:26 37:27 37:30 38:7 39:6[2] 39:7 39:8 40:4[3] 40:5 40:9 40:20 40:24[2] 40:25 40:30 40:31 41:6 41:7 41:10 41:11[2] 41:12 41:22 41:23 42:2 42:4 42:17[2] 43:2[2] 43:9[3] 43:10 43:26 44:8 44:9 44:11[3] 44:15 44:21 44:26[2] 44:27 44:28[2] 45:1 45:14 45:16 45:17[2] 45:18 45:22 45:24 45:25 46:5 46:13 47:1 47:3[2] 47:5 47:7 47:11 47:12[2] 47:14[2] 47:15 48:11 48:14 49:3 49:5[4] 49:6[2] 49:9 49:11 49:13 49:19[2] 49:22 49:23[3] 49:24 49:25[2] 49:26 50:7[2] 51:3 51:6[2] 51:7 51:8 51:11 51:12[2] 51:14 51:19 52:3 52:11 52:12 52:13[2] 53:11 54:3 54:4[3] 54:5 54:9 54:10[2] 54:13[2] 54:14[2] 55:6[2] 55:12[2] 55:13 56:1 56:5 56:7[2] 57:16 58:4 58:8 58:10 58:11 58:12[2] 60:2 60:4 60:5[2] 60:7 60:11[3] 60:12 60:18 60:19[2] 60:20[2] 60:21[2] 61:3[2] 61:5 61:6 61:7 61:9 61:10 62:2 62:3 62:4[4] 62:8 62:10 62:12 62:16 63:3 64:5 64:9 65:10 65:13[3] 65:17 65:18 65:19 65:20[2] 65:25 66:5 66:8[2] 66:10 66:12[2] 66:13 66:14 66:16 66:17 66:24[2]

JER

1:8 1:17 2:10 2:12[3] 2:36 3:1 3:3 3:16[2] 3:17 4:7 4:9 4:11 4:13 4:14 4:27 4:28 4:29 5:1 5:6 5:9 5:13 5:29 6:6 6:8 6:11 6:12 6:15 6:22 7:20[2] 7:23[3] 7:32[2] 7:33 7:34 8:2[3] 8:3 8:12 8:13 8:14 8:17 9:2 9:9 10:2 10:5[2] 10:10 10:21 11:3 11:4 11:5 11:11 11:19 11:23 12:13 12:16 13:10 13:11 13:12[2] 13:15 13:19[3] 13:21 13:27[2] 14:8 14:9 14:15[2] 14:16 15:1 15:4 15:11 15:18[2] 15:19 16:4[5] 16:6 16:14 17:5 17:6 17:8[3] 17:11 17:13[2] 17:14[2] 17:17 17:18[4] 17:27 18:14 18:16 18:20 18:21[4] 18:22 18:23 19:6 19:7 19:8 19:11[2] 19:13 20:6 20:10 20:11[2] 20:14[2] 20:15 20:16 20:17 20:18 21:2 21:9 21:10 22:19 22:22 22:23 23:1 23:3 23:4[2] 23:6[2] 23:12[2] 23:26 23:36 23:40 24:2 24:3 24:7[2] 24:8 24:9[2] 25:10 25:11 25:16[2] 25:27 25:28 25:29[2] 25:32 25:33[3] 25:36 26:3 26:9[2] 26:18 27:16 27:17 27:18[2] 27:22[2] 28:9 29:4 29:6 29:7 29:8[2] 29:10 29:14[2] 29:17 29:18[2] 29:22 29:26 30:7 30:10[3] 30:13 30:16[2] 30:18 30:19[2] 30:20[2] 30:21 30:22[2] 31:1 31:4[2] 31:6 31:12 31:14 31:15 31:16 31:18 31:30 31:33[3] 31:37 31:38 31:40[2] 32:4 32:5 32:15 32:36 32:38[2] 32:43 33:9 33:10[2] 33:12 33:16[2] 33:20 33:21 33:22 33:24 33:25 33:26 34:3 34:16 34:17 34:20 35:7 36:3 36:7 36:19 36:30 37:17 37:20 38:3 38:4 38:17 38:18 38:20 38:22 38:23[2] 39:16 39:17 39:18 40:9 40:15 42:2 42:5 42:6[3] 42:11[2] 42:17 42:18[2] 44:8[2] 44:12[3] 44:26 44:27[2] 44:29 46:10 46:11 46:19 46:23 46:24[2] 46:26 46:27[2] 47:2 47:6[3] 47:7 48:2[2] 48:3 48:4 48:6 48:7 48:8 48:9 48:10[2] 48:13 48:26 48:28 48:30 48:33 48:34 48:37[2] 48:38 48:39 48:41 48:42 48:43 48:44 48:46 49:2[4] 49:5[2] 49:10 49:13 49:17[2] 49:22 49:23 49:26 49:32 49:33 49:36 49:37 50:5 50:8 50:9[2] 50:10[2] 50:12[3] 50:13[3] 50:19 50:20[3] 50:26 50:30 50:33 50:36 50:37 50:38 50:39[2] 50:41 51:2 51:6 51:8[2] 51:26 51:29 51:35 51:46 51:47 51:58[3] 51:62 51:63 51:64

LA

1:12 1:17 1:21 2:6 2:20 3:6 3:29[2]

4:9^2 4:21^2 5:6 5:21

EZE

2:6^6 2:8 3:9^2 3:12 3:20 3:23 3:26^2 4:3^2 4:7 4:10 4:17 5:12 5:13^2 5:15 5:16 6:4^2 6:6^6 6:8 6:9 6:13 7:4 7:11 7:16 7:17^2 7:18 7:19^2 7:24 7:25 7:26 7:27^2 9:4 11:3 11:11^2 11:16 11:20^2 12:3^2 12:11 12:13 12:19 12:20^2 12:24 12:25 12:28^2 13:9^3 13:11 13:12 13:13 13:14^2 13:20 13:21^2 14:3 14:9 14:10 14:11^3 14:15 14:16^2 14:18 14:22^3 15:3 15:5 16:16 16:20 16:25 16:28 16:42^2 16:52 16:54 16:61 16:63 17:8 17:14 17:15 17:20 17:21 17:23 18:5 18:13 18:20^2 18:22 18:24 18:30 19:9 19:14^2 20:3 20:9 20:12 20:14 20:20 20:22 20:31 20:32^2 20:41 20:47^2 20:48 21:7^4 21:11^2 21:12^3 21:13 21:14 21:15 21:23^2 21:24^2 21:26 21:27 21:32^3 22:5^2 22:14 22:21 22:22 22:25 22:29 22:32 22:33 22:46 22:48 24:8 24:10 24:11^3 24:12 24:13 24:23 24:25 24:27^3 25:10 26:1 26:5 26:6 26:13 26:14^2 26:16 26:17 26:18 26:20 26:21^3 27:7 27:30 27:34 27:35^2 27:36^2 28:9 28:19^3 28:22^2 28:23 28:24 28:25 29:5 29:7 29:9 29:11 29:12 29:14 29:15 29:16 29:19 30:3 30:4^2 30:7^2 30:8 30:11 30:13 30:16 30:18 30:21^2 31:13 31:16 31:17 31:18^2 32:6 32:10 32:12 32:15 32:19 32:25 32:27 32:28 32:30^2 32:31 32:32 33:4 33:5 33:6 33:10 33:12 33:13 33:27^2 33:28 34:2 34:10 34:14 34:16 34:22 34:23 34:24 34:26 34:27 34:28 34:29 35:4 35:10 35:15 36:3 36:9 36:10^2 36:12 36:23 36:25 36:28^2 36:32^2 36:33 36:34 36:37 36:38 37:19 37:20 37:21 37:22^3 37:23^2 37:24 37:25 37:26 37:27^3 37:28 38:7^2 38:8 38:9 38:16^2 38:19 38:20 38:21 38:23 39:4 39:12 39:13^2 39:16 39:19^2 39:20 39:25 39:28 42:13 43:10 43:11 43:12 43:13^3 43:14^2 43:15^2 43:16 43:17^3 43:19 43:27 44:2^3 44:7 44:11 44:14 44:17 44:28 44:29 44:30 44:31 45:1^3 45:2 45:3 45:4^2 45:6 45:7^2 45:8 45:11^2 45:12^2 45:17 45:21 46:1^3 46:2 46:4 46:5^2 46:6^2 46:11 46:16^2 46:17^2 46:18 47:5 47:8 47:9^2 47:10^2 47:11^2 47:12^2 47:13 47:15 47:17 47:20 47:22 48:8^2 48:9 48:10^2 48:11 48:12 48:13 48:15^2 48:16 48:17 48:18^3 48:20 48:21^3 48:22 48:28 48:31 48:35

DA

1:13 2:5^2 2:9 2:13^2 2:20 2:28 2:40 2:41^2 2:42 2:44^2 3:6 3:11 3:15^2 3:17 3:18 3:19 3:28 3:29^2 4:1 4:15^2 4:16^2 4:19 4:23^2 4:25 4:26 4:27^2 4:32 5:7^2 5:10 5:12 5:16^2 5:17 5:29 6:1 6:7 6:8 6:12 6:15 6:17 6:25 6:26^2 7:14 7:23^2 7:24 7:25 7:27 8:13^2 8:14 8:17 8:19^2 8:24 8:25 8:26 9:16 9:25^2 9:26^2 9:27 10:19^2 11:2 11:4^3 11:5^3 11:6 11:10^2 11:11^2 11:12^2 11:15 11:16 11:17 11:19 11:20 11:22^2 11:25 11:27^2 11:28 11:29 11:30 11:32 11:34 11:36^2 11:41 11:43 12:1^3 12:3 12:4 12:6 12:7^2 12:8 12:10 12:11^2 12:13

HO

1:9 1:10^3 1:11^2 2:4 2:16 2:17 3:3^2 4:3 4:6 4:9 4:19 5:9^2 5:12 5:14 7:4^2 7:16 8:4 8:5 8:6 8:7 8:8 8:11 9:4^3 9:6 9:12 9:17 10:2 10:6^2 10:8 10:10 10:14 10:15 11:5 13:3 13:7 13:10 13:14^2 13:15^2 13:16^2 14:5 14:6 14:7

JOE

1:11 2:2 2:6 2:8 2:10 2:18 2:19 2:21 2:22 2:23 2:24 2:26^2 2:27 2:31 2:32^2 3:12 3:15 3:16 3:17 3:19^2

AM

3:4 3:6^3 3:11^2 3:12 3:14 5:6 5:14 5:15^2 5:16 5:17 5:20 6:2 6:7 7:3 7:6 7:9^2 7:11 7:17^2 8:3^2 8:5 8:7 8:8 9:1 9:2 9:5 9:15

OB

9 10 15 16 17^2 18^2 21

JON

1:4 1:6 1:11 1:12 3:4 3:7 3:8 4:4 4:6 4:9^2

MIC

1:2 1:4^2 1:7^2 1:14 2:4 2:11 3:6^3 3:7 3:12 4:1^2 4:10^2 4:11 5:2 5:4 5:5 5:7 5:8 5:9^2 6:7 6:14^2 7:4 7:8 7:10 7:11^2 7:13 7:16^2 7:17

NA

1:10^2 1:12^2 1:14 2:3^2 2:5 2:6^2 2:7^2 2:13 3:11^2 3:12^2 3:13

HAB

1:5 1:10 2:5 2:7 2:9 2:14 2:16^3 3:17^3

ZEP

1:10 1:17 1:18^2 2:3^2 2:4^2 2:5 2:6 2:7 2:9 2:11 2:12 2:14 3:7 3:8 3:11^2 3:13 3:14 3:16^2

HAG

1:2 1:8 2:4^2 2:9 2:12 2:13^2

ZEC

1:4 1:9 1:16^2 1:17 1:19 2:4 2:5^2 2:9 2:11^2 2:13 3:9 4:5 4:12 4:13 5:3^2 5:11 6:13^2 6:14 8:3 8:5 8:6^2 8:8^2 8:9^2 8:11 8:12 8:13^2 8:19 9:1^2 9:2 9:4 9:5^3 9:7^2 9:10^2 9:14 9:15 9:16 10:5^2 10:6 10:7^2 10:10 10:11 11:5 11:9^2 11:16 11:17^3 12:2 12:3^2 12:5 12:6 12:8^2 12:10 12:11 13:1 13:2 13:4 13:7 13:8^2 14:1 14:2^2 14:4 14:6 14:7^3 14:8^2 14:9^2 14:10^2 14:11^2 14:12 14:13 14:14 14:15^2 14:17^2 14:18 14:19 14:20^2 14:21^2

MAL

1:5 1:6^2 1:8 1:9 1:11^3 1:14 2:4 3:4 3:5 3:10^2 3:12 3:17 4:1 4:3

MT

1:22 1:23 2:4 2:13 2:15 2:18 2:23^2 3:15 4:1 4:3^2 4:6 4:14 5:4 5:6 5:9 5:12 5:13^3 5:14 5:18 5:19^2 5:21 5:22^3 5:24 5:25 5:29 5:30 5:37 5:45 5:48 6:1 6:4 6:5^2 6:7 6:8 6:9 6:10 6:16 6:21 6:22^2 6:23^3 6:31 6:33 7:1 7:2^2 7:7^2 7:8 7:13 7:14 7:26 8:3 8:8 8:12^2 8:13 8:17 9:2^2 9:5 9:12 9:15 9:21 9:22 9:29 10:13^2 10:14 10:16 10:18 10:19 10:21 10:22^2 10:23 10:25 10:26^2 10:36 11:6 11:22 11:23 11:24 12:11 12:17 12:27 12:31^2 12:32^2 12:37^2 12:39 12:40 12:45 13:12^2 13:15 13:35 13:40 13:42 13:49 13:50 14:9 14:27^2 14:28 15:5 15:6 15:13 15:14 15:28 15:31 16:2 16:3 16:4 16:19^2 16:21^2 16:22^2 16:23^2 16:28 17:4 17:7 17:9 17:17 17:20 17:22 17:23 18:3 18:7 18:8 18:9 18:12 18:13 18:16 18:17 18:18^2 18:19 18:25^2 19:5 19:9 19:10 19:12 19:21 19:25 19:30^2 20:16^2 20:18 20:22 20:23^2 20:26^3 20:27^2 20:28 20:33 21:4 21:13 21:21^3 21:43 21:44 22:13 22:28 23:4 23:5 23:7 23:8 23:10 23:11 23:12^2 23:26 23:31 24:2^2 24:3^2 24:6 24:7 24:9^2 24:10 24:13 24:14 24:16 24:20 24:21^2 24:22^3 24:27 24:28 24:29^2 24:34 24:37 24:39 24:40^2 24:41^2 24:43 24:44 24:51 25:1 25:9 25:29^2 25:30 25:32 26:2 26:5 26:13^2 26:31^2 26:33^2 26:37 26:39 26:42 26:46 26:54^2 26:56 26:63^2 27:22 27:23 27:25 27:26 27:35 27:40 27:42 27:49 27:58 27:64^2 28:10

MK

1:41 2:5 2:9 2:20 2:22^2 3:14 3:24 3:25 3:26 3:28 4:12^2 4:21^2 4:22 4:24^2 4:25^2 4:31 4:39 5:18 5:23 5:28 5:34 5:36 5:43 6:9 6:11 6:27 6:50 7:4 7:11^2 7:24 7:27 7:34 8:12 8:31^2 8:33^2 8:38^2 9:1 9:5 9:12 9:19 9:34 9:35^2 9:43 9:45^2 9:47 9:49 10:8 10:12 10:26 10:31 10:33 10:38 10:39 10:40 10:41 10:43^3 10:44^2 10:45 10:49^2 11:2 11:10 11:17 11:22^2 12:7 12:23 13:2^2 13:4^3 13:7^3 13:8^2 13:9^2 13:10 13:11 13:12 13:13^2 13:14 13:18 13:19^2 13:20 13:24 13:25 13:30 14:2 14:9^2 14:19 14:27^2 14:29 14:33^2 14:49 14:64 15:15 16:6 16:16^2

LU

1:15^2 1:20^3 1:29 1:32^2 1:33 1:34 1:35^2 1:37 1:38 1:45 1:57 1:60 1:66 1:68 1:71 1:76 2:1 2:3 2:5 2:6 2:10 2:12 2:23 2:34 2:35 2:49 3:5^4 3:7 3:12 3:14 3:23 4:7 4:9 5:13 5:15 5:23 5:35 5:37 5:38 6:17 6:20 6:21 6:35^2 6:36 6:37^3 6:38^2 6:40 7:23 8:9 8:12 8:17^2 8:18^2 8:38 8:43 8:48 8:50 9:22^3 9:25 9:26^2 9:27 9:33 9:41 9:44 9:46 9:48 9:51 10:5 10:6 10:11 10:12 10:14 10:15 10:42 11:2^2 11:9^2 11:10 11:18 11:19 11:29 11:30 11:35 11:36^2 11:46 11:50 11:51 12:2^2 12:3^2 12:4 12:9 12:10^2 12:19 12:20^2 12:26 12:29 12:31 12:34 12:35 12:39 12:40 12:45 12:47 12:48^2 12:49 12:50^2 12:52 12:53 12:55 12:58 13:14 13:16 13:23 13:24 13:28 13:30^2 13:32 13:33 14:8 14:11^2 14:12 14:14^2 14:23 14:26 14:27 14:31 14:33^2 14:34 15:7 15:14 15:19 15:21 15:23 15:24 15:32 16:2 16:21 16:31 17:6^2 17:24 17:25 17:26 17:30 17:31 17:34^3 17:35^2 17:36^2 17:37 18:13 18:14^2 18:26 18:31 18:32^2 18:40 19:7 19:15 19:19 19:26^2 19:38 20:6 20:13 20:14 20:18 20:25^2 20:35 21:6^2 21:7^2 21:8 21:9 21:11^2 21:15 21:16^2 21:17 21:22^2 21:23 21:24^3 21:25 21:26 21:32 21:34 21:36 22:7 22:16 22:24 22:26^2 22:37 22:42^2 22:52 23:23 23:24 23:31 23:32 23:35 23:37 23:39 23:43 24:7^2 24:20 24:36 24:44 24:47 24:49

JOH

1:25 1:31 1:42 3:2 3:3 3:4^2 3:5 3:7 3:9 3:14 3:17 3:20 3:21 3:27 4:14 5:6 5:34 6:12 6:20 6:45 7:4 7:17 7:23 8:5 8:33^2 8:36 8:41 8:55 9:3 9:22 9:25 9:27 9:31 9:39 10:9 10:16 10:24 10:35 11:4 12:23 12:26 12:31 12:32 12:34 12:36 12:38 12:40 12:42 13:18 13:24 13:32 14:1 14:3 14:13 14:17 14:21 14:27^2 15:7 15:8 15:11 15:25 16:1 16:20^2 16:24 16:32 16:33 17:11 17:12 17:19 17:21^2 17:22 17:23 17:24 17:26 18:9 18:28 18:32 18:36 19:16 19:24^2 19:28 19:31^2 19:36^2 20:15 20:19 20:21 20:26 20:27 21:18 21:25^2

AC

1:5 1:8 1:20 1:22^2 2:14 2:20 2:21 2:24 2:25 2:38 2:47 3:14 3:19^2 3:23 3:25 4:9 4:10 4:12 4:19 4:28 4:30 5:31 5:36 5:38 5:39^2 7:7 7:35 8:20 8:22 8:36 9:6 9:17 10:42 10:47 10:48 11:14 11:16 11:28 12:19 13:11 13:22 13:28 13:38 13:39 13:42 13:47^2 14:3 14:9 15:1^2 15:11 15:24 16:13 16:15 16:30 16:31 17:18 17:27 18:6 18:9 18:15^2 19:2 19:26 19:27^3 19:36^2 19:39 19:40 20:16 21:13 21:14^2 21:24 21:26 21:33 21:34 21:37 22:5 22:10 22:15 22:16 22:24^2 23:3 23:11 23:29 23:35 24:4 24:15 24:21 25:4 25:5 25:6 25:9 25:10 25:11^2 25:17 25:19 25:20 25:21^2 26:3 26:8 26:23 26:28 27:10 27:20 27:22^2 27:24 27:25^2 27:26 27:31 28:27 28:28

RO

1:1 1:4 1:7^2 1:11 1:12 1:19 1:22 2:12 2:13 2:25 2:26 3:4^2 3:8 3:19 3:20 3:25 3:26 4:11^3 4:13 4:14 4:16^2 4:17 4:18 4:24 5:9 5:10 5:15 5:19 6:5 6:6 6:8 6:11 6:17 7:2 7:3^4 7:4 7:10 8:4 8:6^2 8:7 8:9 8:10 8:17^2 8:18^2 8:21 8:26 8:29^2 8:31^2 8:39 9:7 9:17 9:26 9:27^2 9:33 10:1 10:9 10:11 10:13 10:15 11:6 11:9 11:10 11:13 11:15^2 11:16^2 11:17 11:19 11:20 11:22 11:23 11:24^2 11:25^3 11:26 11:35 11:36 12:2^2 12:9 12:10 12:16^2 12:18 12:21 13:1^2 13:3 13:4 13:5 13:9 14:4 14:5 14:9 14:14 14:15 14:16 15:5 15:12 15:16^2 15:24^2 15:31^2 15:32 15:33 16:11 16:20 16:24 16:27

1 CO

1:1 1:2 1:3 1:8 1:10^2 1:17 3:13^2 3:15^2 3:18^2 4:2 4:3 4:6 4:16 4:17 5:2 5:5 5:7 5:11 6:2 6:5 6:7 6:9 6:12 6:16

BE—*continued* 1665

7:5 7:11 7:12 7:13 7:18 7:21 7:23 7:25 7:26 7:27 7:29 7:34 7:39[2] 8:5[2] 8:10 9:2 9:10 9:12 9:15 9:19 9:23 9:27 10:1 10:7 10:13[2] 10:21 10:27 10:30 10:33 11:1 11:5 11:6 11:16 11:18 11:19[2] 11:27 11:31 11:32 12:13[2] 12:22 12:23 12:25 12:26 13:3 13:8[3] 13:10 14:7 14:9[2] 14:10 14:11[2] 14:20[3] 14:23 14:26 14:27 14:28 14:30 14:31 14:34 14:37 14:38[2] 14:40 15:9 15:12 15:13 15:14 15:15 15:17 15:22 15:26 15:28[3] 15:33 15:37 15:51 15:52[2] 15:54 15:57 15:58 16:2 16:4 16:6 16:10 16:13 16:14 16:22 16:23 16:24

2 CO

1:2 1:3 1:4 1:6[2] 1:7 1:11 1:16 1:17 2:4 2:7 2:9 2:14 3:3 3:7 3:8 3:9 3:16 4:3 4:7 4:10 4:11 5:2 5:3[2] 5:4[2] 5:8[2] 5:9 5:10 5:13[2] 5:17 5:20 5:21 6:3 6:13 6:14 6:16[2] 6:17 6:18[2] 7:10 7:11 8:9 8:10 8:11 8:12 8:13 8:14[2] 8:16 8:23 9:3[2] 9:4 9:5 9:15 10:2[2] 10:8 10:11 10:15 11:3 11:6 11:7 11:12 11:15[2] 12:6 12:7[2] 12:11 12:13 12:14 12:15[2] 12:16[2] 12:20[2] 13:1 13:5[2] 13:7 13:11[4] 13:14

GA

1:3 1:5 1:7 1:8 1:9 1:10 2:3 2:6[2] 2:9 2:11 2:16[2] 2:17 3:4 3:8 3:9 3:15[2] 3:18 3:22 3:23 3:24 3:29 4:1 4:9 4:12 4:18 4:19 4:20 4:21 4:30 5:1 5:2 5:10[2] 5:15 5:18 5:26 6:1[2] 6:3 6:7 6:9 6:12 6:16 6:18

EPH

1:2 1:3 1:4 1:12 1:23 3:6 3:10 3:16 3:18 3:19 3:21 4:14 4:21 4:23 4:26 4:31 4:32 5:1 5:3 5:7 5:17 5:18[2] 5:24 5:27 5:31[2] 6:3 6:5 6:8 6:10 6:11 6:13 6:16 6:19 6:23 6:24

PHP

1:2 1:10 1:20[3] 1:23 1:26 1:27 1:30 2:1 2:2 2:3 2:5 2:6 2:15 2:17 2:19 2:28 3:9 3:15[3] 3:17 3:21 4:2 4:5 4:6[2] 4:8[2] 4:9 4:11 4:12[3] 4:20 4:23

COL

1:2 1:9 1:12 1:16 1:20 1:23 2:2 2:5 2:20 3:1 3:15 3:19 3:21 4:6 4:16 4:18

1 TH

1:1 2:4 2:9 2:16 3:1 3:3 3:5 4:11 4:13 4:17 5:6 5:7 5:8 5:13 5:14 5:23 5:27 5:28

2 TH

1:5 1:7 1:9 1:10[2] 1:12 2:2[2] 2:3 2:6 2:7 2:8 2:10 2:12 2:14 2:15 3:1 3:2 3:8 3:13 3:14 3:16 3:18

1 TI

1:7 1:10 1:17 2:1 2:4 2:6 2:12 2:15 3:2 3:8 3:10 3:11 3:12 4:3 4:4[2] 4:6 4:12 5:7 5:9 5:13 5:16 5:17 5:22 5:25 6:1 6:8 6:9 6:16 6:17 6:18 6:21

2 TI

1:4 1:8 1:15 2:1 2:2 2:4 2:6 2:11 2:15 2:21 2:24 3:2 3:9 3:17 4:2 4:4 4:6 4:15 4:16 4:17 4:18 4:22

TIT

1:6 1:7 1:9 1:11 1:13 2:2 2:3 2:4 2:5[2] 2:6 2:8[2] 2:9 3:1 3:2 3:7 3:8 3:12 3:13 3:14 3:15

PHM

8 14 22

HEB

1:5[2] 1:12 1:14 1:25 2:3 2:17[2] 3:5 3:12 3:13 4:15 5:5 5:11 5:12[2] 6:8 6:12 7:11 8:4 8:10[2] 8:12 9:6 9:23 10:2 10:13 10:29 11:16 11:18 11:24 11:40 12:3 12:8 12:9 12:10 12:11 12:13[2] 12:15 12:16 12:18 12:19 12:20 12:27 12:28 13:2 13:5 13:9[2] 13:19 13:21 13:25

JAS

1:4 1:5 1:13 1:18 1:19 1:22 1:23 1:25 1:26 2:12 2:15 2:16 3:1 3:4 3:10 3:17 4:4 4:9[2] 4:14 5:3 5:7 5:8 5:9 5:12 5:15 5:16

1 PE

1:2 1:3 1:5 1:6 1:7[2] 1:13[2] 1:15 1:16 1:21 2:3 2:6 2:7 2:13 2:18 2:20 3:1[2] 3:3 3:4 3:7 3:8[2] 3:13 3:14 3:15 3:16 3:17 4:6 4:7 4:11[2] 4:13[2] 4:14 4:16 4:17 4:18 5:1 5:5 5:8 5:11 5:14

2 PE

1:2 1:4 1:8[2] 1:11 1:12[2] 1:15 2:1 2:2 2:4 2:9 2:12 3:2 3:8 3:11[2] 3:12 3:14[2] 3:16 3:18

1 JO

1:4 2:19 2:28 3:1 3:2[2] 4:10 4:14

2 JO

2 3 12

3 JO

2 8 14

JUDE

2 18 19 25

RE

1:4 1:6 1:19 2:10[2] 2:11 2:19 2:27 3:2 3:5 3:18[2] 3:19 4:1 5:13 6:11[2] 6:17 7:12 9:5 10:6 10:7 10:9 11:5 11:9 11:18 12:2 12:4 12:15 13:15 14:10 16:5 16:12 17:17 18:4 18:9 18:21[2] 18:22[4] 18:23 19:7 19:8 20:3[2] 20:6 20:7 20:10 21:3[3] 21:4[2] 21:7[2] 21:25[2] 22:3[2] 22:4 22:5 22:6 22:11[4] 22:12 22:21

BUT

235

GE

2:6 2:17 2:20 3:3 4:2 4:5 6:8 6:18 8:9 9:4 11:30 12:12 13:13 15:4 15:10 15:16 16:6 17:5 17:15 17:21 18:15 18:22 18:27 18:32 19:2 19:4 19:10 19:14 19:26 20:3[2] 20:4 20:12 21:23 21:26 22:7 23:6 23:13 24:4 24:33 24:38 25:6 25:28 26:29 27:22 27:38 28:17 28:19 29:17 29:20 29:31 30:42 31:5 31:7 31:29 31:36 31:34 31:35 31:47 32:28 34:12 34:15 34:17 35:8 35:10 35:16 35:18 37:11 37:22 37:35 38:20 39:8 39:9 39:21 40:14 40:22 40:23 41:8 41:21 41:24 41:54 42:4 42:7 42:8 42:10 42:12 42:20 42:34 43:5 43:34 44:17 45:8 45:22 46:12 47:18 47:30 48:7 48:19 48:21 49:19 49:24 50:20[2]

EX

1:12 1:16 1:17[2] 2:15 2:17 3:22 4:1 4:10 4:21 5:16 5:17 6:3 6:9 7:4 7:12 8:15 8:18 8:29 9:6 9:30 9:32 10:8 10:20 10:23 10:27 11:7 12:9 12:44 13:15 13:18 14:9 14:16 14:20 14:29 15:19 16:8 16:20 16:26 17:12 18:22 18:26 19:13 19:24 20:10 20:19 21:13 21:14 21:18 21:28 21:29[2] 22:15 23:11 23:22 23:24 24:2 29:14 29:33 31:15 31:18 33:11 33:23 34:13 34:20 34:21 34:34 35:2 36:38 40:37

LE

1:9 1:13 1:17 2:12 5:8 5:11 6:28 7:16 7:17 7:20 7:24 7:31 8:17 10:6 11:4 11:5 11:6 11:11 11:23 11:36 11:38 12:5 13:6 13:7 13:14 13:21[2] 13:23 13:26[2] 13:28 13:33 13:35 13:37 14:9 14:53 15:28 16:10 17:16 19:14 19:15 19:18 19:24 19:34 20:24 21:2 21:4 21:14 22:11 22:13[2] 22:20 22:23 22:32 23:3 23:8 23:25 25:4 25:17 25:28 25:31 25:34 25:36 25:40 25:43 25:46 25:52 26:14 26:15 26:23 26:27 26:45 27:8 27:13 27:18 27:21 27:29

NU

1:47 1:50 1:53 2:33 3:38 4:15 4:19 4:20 5:8 5:20 5:28 6:12 7:9 8:26 9:13 9:22 10:4 10:7[2] 10:30 11:6 11:20 11:26[2] 12:14 13:31 14:10 14:21 14:24 14:31 14:32 14:38 14:41 14:44 15:30 16:9 16:30 16:41 18:2 18:17 18:23 18:24 19:12 19:20 21:22 21:23 22:20 22:24 22:35 23:13 23:26 24:1 24:4 24:11 24:13 24:16 24:17[2] 24:20 26:33 26:64 27:3 28:19 28:27 29:8 29:36 30:5 30:8 30:9 30:12 30:14 30:15 31:18 32:17 32:23 32:27 32:30 33:55 35:8 35:20 35:22 35:26 35:28 35:30 35:31 35:33 36:9

DE

1:11 1:12 1:17 1:21 1:26 1:28 1:30 1:38 1:40 1:43 1:45 3:7 3:19 3:26 4:4 4:9 4:12 4:20 4:22[2] 4:26 4:29 5:3 5:14 5:31 7:5 7:8 7:15 7:18 7:23 7:26 8:3 8:18 9:4 9:5 9:19 10:12 11:7 11:11 11:28 12:5 12:10 12:14 12:18 13:9 14:7 14:12 14:20 15:3 15:6[2] 15:8 16:6 17:6 17:16 18:14 18:20 18:22 19:11 19:13 19:21 20:12 20:14 20:16 20:17 21:14 21:17 21:23 22:7 22:20 22:25 22:26 22:28 22:29 23:5 23:11 23:20 23:22 23:24 23:25 24:5 24:18 25:15 26:14 27:15 28:38 28:39 28:40 28:41 28:65 29:15 29:20 29:29 30:14 30:17[2] 32:15 32:52 34:4 34:6

JOS

1:8 1:14 2:4 2:6 2:22 5:5 5:12 5:14 6:13 6:19 6:22 7:1 7:3[2] 7:12 8:4 8:9 8:14 9:12 9:19 9:21 10:16 10:19 10:30 10:37 10:40 11:13 11:14 11:20 13:13 13:33 14:3 14:8 15:63 16:10 17:3[2] 17:8 17:12 17:13 17:14 17:18 18:7 21:12 22:3 22:5 22:7 22:18 22:19 22:27 22:28 23:8 23:9 23:13 24:4 24:10 24:12 24:15 24:21

JG

1:6 1:19 1:21 1:25 1:27 1:29 1:30 1:32 1:33 1:35 2:2 2:3 2:17[2] 3:15 3:16 3:19 4:8 4:16 5:31 6:10 6:13 6:34 6:39[2] 7:6 7:10 7:19 8:20 9:9 9:11 9:20 9:51 11:16 11:17[2] 11:18 11:20[2] 11:27 13:3 13:6 13:7 13:9 13:21 13:23 14:4 14:6 14:9 14:13 14:16 14:20 15:1[2] 15:13[2] 15:19 16:21 17:6 19:10[2] 19:16 19:18 19:24 19:25 19:28 20:9 20:13 20:14 20:32 20:34 20:40 20:42 20:47

RU

1:14 1:17 2:8 3:3 3:13 4:4

1 SA

1:2 1:5[2] 1:11 1:13 1:15 1:22 2:15 2:16 2:18 2:25 2:30 4:20 5:6 6:3 6:9 7:10 8:3 8:6 8:7 8:19 9:4[2] 9:7 9:27 10:12 10:16 10:19 10:27[2] 12:10 12:12 12:15[2] 12:20 12:23 12:25 13:8 13:14 13:16 13:20 13:22 14:1 14:10 14:26 14:27 14:37 14:39 14:41 14:43 15:3 15:9[2] 15:19 15:21 16:7[2] 16:14 17:9 17:15 17:33 17:42 17:45 17:50 17:54 18:8[2] 18:16 18:17 18:19 18:25[2] 19:2 19:10 20:2 20:3[2] 20:5 20:7 20:13 20:15 20:22 20:39 21:4 21:6 22:17 22:23 23:14 23:24 23:27 24:7 24:10 24:12 24:13 24:22 25:3 25:14 25:15 25:19 25:25 25:29 25:31 25:37 25:44 26:3 26:7 26:11 26:19 26:23 28:23[2] 29:2 29:8 30:2 30:6 30:10 30:24 31:4

2 SA

2:8 2:10 2:30 2:31 3:1 3:13 3:22 3:26 4:12 5:17 5:23 6:10 7:2 7:6 7:15 7:19 8:4 9:10 10:11 11:1 11:9 11:13 11:27 12:3 12:4 12:12 12:17 12:19 12:21 12:23 13:3 13:14 13:16 13:20 13:21 13:25 13:27 13:34 13:37 14:2 14:6 14:25 14:29 15:3 15:10 15:20 15:26 15:34 16:18 17:16 17:18 18:3[2] 18:20 18:22 18:23 18:29 19:4 19:21 19:27 19:28 19:37 20:2 20:3 20:5 20:10 20:21 21:2 21:7 21:8 21:17 22:19 22:28 22:42[2] 23:6 23:7 23:12 23:16 23:21 23:23 24:3 24:17 24:24

1 KI

1:1 1:4 1:8 1:10 1:19 1:26 1:52 2:7 2:8 2:9 2:26 2:30 2:33 3:7 3:11 3:21 3:22[2] 3:23 3:26[2] 5:4 7:1 7:31 8:16

8:19 8:27 8:41 9:6[2] 9:22 9:24 11:1 11:10 11:12 11:13 11:22 11:32 11:34 11:35 11:39 12:8 12:10 12:11 12:14 12:17 12:20 12:22 13:13 13:18 13:22 14:4 14:9 14:14 15:14 16:22 16:25 17:1 17:12 17:13 18:12 18:18 18:21 18:22 18:25 18:26 19:4 19:11[2] 19:12 20:9 20:16 20:23 20:27 20:28 20:30 21:5 21:15 21:25 21:29 22:8[2] 22:16 22:18 22:24 22:30 22:31 22:48 22:49

2 KI

1:3 1:4 1:6 1:16 2:10 2:17 2:19 3:2 3:5 3:11 3:15 3:18 3:24 3:26 4:27 4:31 4:41 5:1 5:11 5:15 5:16[2] 5:17 5:20[2] 5:25 6:5 6:12 6:19 6:32[2] 7:2 7:4 7:10 7:19 8:13 9:15 9:18 9:27 9:35 10:4 10:9 10:18 10:19 10:23 10:31 11:2 11:15 12:3 12:6 12:7 12:9 12:14 13:6 13:7 13:11 13:19 13:22 14:6[2] 14:11 14:19 14:27 15:25 16:3 16:5 17:2 17:14 17:18 17:19 17:36 17:39 17:40 18:6 18:12 18:20[2] 18:22 18:27 18:36 19:18 19:27 20:10 21:9 22:18 23:9 23:23 23:35 25:12 23:25

1 CH

2:30 2:34 4:27 5:1 5:2 6:49 6:56 7:14 10:4 11:18[2] 11:25 12:17 12:19 13:13 15:2 16:5 16:19 16:26 17:1 17:5 17:14 18:4 19:3 19:12 19:18 20:1 20:7 21:3 21:6 21:8 21:13 21:17 21:24 21:30 22:8 23:11 23:17 23:22 24:2 27:23 27:24 28:3 28:9 29:1 29:14

2 CH

1:4 1:11 2:6 4:6 5:9 6:2 6:6 6:8 6:9 6:18 6:32 7:19 8:8 8:9[2] 10:8 10:10 10:11 10:14[2] 10:17 10:18 11:2 12:7 13:10 13:11 13:13 13:21 15:2 15:4 15:5 15:17 16:12 17:4 18:6 18:7[2] 18:15 18:17 18:29 18:31 19:6 20:10 20:12 20:15 21:3 21:13 21:20 22:10 22:11 23:6[2] 23:7 24:15 24:19 24:22 24:25 25:2 25:4[3] 25:7 25:8 25:9 25:13 25:20 25:27 26:16 26:18 28:1 28:9 28:10 28:20 28:21 28:23 28:27 29:34 30:8 30:10 30:18 32:8 32:9 32:25 33:2 33:10 33:22 33:23 33:25 35:13 35:21[2] 35:22 36:13 36:16

EZR

2:59 2:62 3:6 3:12 4:3[2] 5:5 5:12 5:13 8:22 9:9 10:13

NE

1:9 2:2 2:14 2:19 2:20 3:3 3:4 3:5 3:15 4:1 4:7 5:15[2] 6:2 6:8 6:12 7:4 7:61 7:64 9:16 9:17[2] 9:28 9:29 9:33 11:3 11:21 13:2 13:6 13:24

ES

1:12 1:16 1:17 2:15 3:2 3:15 4:4 4:11 4:14 5:9 5:12 6:12 6:13 7:4 9:10 9:15 9:16[2] 9:18 9:25

JOB

1:11 2:5 2:6 2:10 3:9 3:21 4:2 4:5 4:16 5:3 5:15 6:1 6:14 6:25 7:21 8:9 8:15[2] 9:2 9:11 9:15 9:18 9:35 11:5 11:20 12:2 12:3 12:7 13:4 13:15 14:10 14:12[2] 14:13 14:21 14:22 16:5 16:7 16:12 16:20 17:10 19:7[2] 19:28 20:5 20:13 21:1 22:8 22:18 22:20 23:6 23:8[2] 23:9 23:10 23:13 24:24 26:1 27:14[2] 27:17 27:19 28:12 30:1 31:32 32:8 32:16 35:10 35:12 35:15 36:6 36:7 36:12 36:13 36:17 37:21 38:11 40:5[2] 42:5

PS

1:2 1:4 1:6 2:12 3:3 5:7 5:11 6:3 7:9 9:7 9:20 11:5 13:5 15:4 16:3 18:18 18:27 18:41[2] 20:7 20:8 22:2 22:6 22:9 22:19 22:24 26:11 28:3 30:5 31:6 31:11 31:14 32:11 34:10 34:19 35:13 35:15 35:20 37:9 37:11 37:17 37:20 37:21 37:28 37:36 37:38 37:39 38:13 38:19 40:17 41:10 44:3 44:7 44:9 49:15 50:16 50:21 52:7 52:8 55:13 55:21 55:23[2] 59:8 59:16 62:4 63:9 63:11[2] 64:7 66:19 68:3 68:6 68:21 69:13 69:20[2] 69:29 70:5 71:7 71:14 73:2 73:4 73:25 73:26 73:28 74:6 75:7 75:8 75:9 75:10 77:10 78:7 78:30 78:38 78:50 78:52 78:53 78:57 78:68 81:7 81:11 81:15 85:8 86:15 88:13 89:24 89:38 90:4 91:7 92:8 92:10 94:15 94:22 96:5 102:12 102:26 102:27 103:17 105:12 106:7 106:14 106:15 106:25 106:35 106:43 109:4 109:16 109:21 109:28[2] 115:1 115:3 115:5[2] 115:6[2] 115:7[2] 115:16 115:18 118:10 118:11 118:13 118:17 118:18 119:23 119:61 119:67 119:69 119:70 119:78 119:81 119:87 119:95 119:96 119:113 119:161 119:163 120:7 125:1 125:5 127:1 127:5 130:4 132:18 135:16[2] 135:17 136:15 138:6 139:4 139:12 141:8 142:4 145:20 146:9

PR

1:7 1:25 1:28[2] 1:33 2:22 3:1 3:32 3:33 3:34 3:35 4:18 5:4 6:31 6:32 8:36 9:12 9:18 10:1 10:2 10:3 10:4 10:5 10:6 10:7 10:8 10:9 10:10 10:11 10:12 10:13 10:14 10:17 10:19 10:21 10:23 10:24 10:25 10:27 10:28 10:29 10:30 10:31 10:32 11:1 11:2 11:3 11:4 11:5 11:6 11:9 11:11 11:12 11:13 11:14 11:17 11:18 11:20 11:21 11:23 11:24 11:26 11:27 11:28 12:1 12:2 12:3 12:4 12:5 12:6 12:7 12:8 12:10 12:11 12:12 12:13 12:15 12:16 12:17 12:18 12:19[2] 12:20 12:21 12:22 12:23 12:24 12:25 12:26 12:27 13:1 13:2 13:3 13:4 13:5 13:6 13:8 13:9 13:10 13:11 13:12 13:13 13:15 13:16 13:17 13:18 13:19 13:20 13:21 13:23 13:24 13:25 14:1 14:2 14:3 14:4 14:5 14:6 14:8 14:9 14:11 14:12 14:15 14:16 14:18 14:20 14:21 14:22 14:23 14:24 14:25 14:28 14:29 14:30 14:31 14:32 14:33 14:34 14:35 15:1 15:2 15:4 15:5 15:6 15:7 15:8 15:9 15:13 15:14 15:15 15:18 15:19 15:20 15:21 15:22 15:25 15:26 15:27 15:28 15:29 15:32 16:2 16:9 16:14 16:22 16:25 16:33 17:3 17:9 17:22 17:24 18:2 18:14 18:17 18:23 19:4 19:12 19:16 20:3 20:5 20:6 20:14 20:15 20:17 20:21 20:22 21:2 21:5 21:8 21:12 21:13 21:15 21:20 21:26 21:28 21:29 21:31 22:3 22:15 23:7 23:17 24:16 24:25 25:2 27:3 27:4 27:6 27:7 27:12 28:1 28:2 28:4 28:5 28:7 28:10 28:11 28:12 28:13 28:14 28:16 28:18 28:19 28:20 28:25 28:26 28:27 28:28 29:2 29:3 29:4 29:6 29:7 29:8 29:10 29:11 29:15 29:16 29:18 29:23 29:25 29:26 30:24 30:26 31:29 31:30

EC

1:4 2:14 2:26 3:12 4:1 4:10 4:11 5:7 5:12 5:14 6:2 7:4 7:12 7:14 7:23 7:26 7:28[2] 7:29 8:13 9:5 9:11 9:18 10:2 10:10 10:12 10:19 11:8 11:9

CA

1:5 1:6 3:1 3:2 3:4[2] 5:2 6:6[3] 6:9

ISA

1:3 1:6 1:20 1:21 5:6 5:7[2] 5:12 5:16 5:25 6:9[2] 6:13 7:1 7:12 7:13 7:25 8:14 9:5 9:10[2] 9:12 9:17 9:21 10:4 10:7 10:20 11:4 11:14 13:21 14:19 16:6 16:12 16:14 17:11 17:13 22:11 24:16 26:11 26:13 28:7 28:13 28:27 29:8[2] 29:9[2] 29:13 29:23 30:1[2] 30:5[2] 30:16 30:20 31:1 31:2 31:8 32:8 33:21 34:11 34:12 35:8 35:9 36:5[2] 36:7 36:12 36:21 37:19 37:28 38:17 40:8 40:31 41:8 42:19 42:20[2] 42:22 43:1 43:22[2] 43:24 45:17 46:2 47:9 48:1 48:10 49:14 49:25 51:6 51:8 51:15 51:21 51:23 53:5 54:7 54:8 54:10 54:15 55:10 55:11 57:3 57:13[2] 57:20 59:2 59:9[2] 59:11[2] 60:2 60:10 60:18 60:19 61:6 62:4 62:9 63:10 63:18 64:6 64:8 65:6 65:11 65:12 65:13[3] 65:14 65:18 65:20 66:2 66:4 66:5

JER

1:7 1:19 2:7 2:11 2:25 2:27 2:28 2:34 3:1 3:7 3:8 3:10 3:19 3:22 5:3[2] 5:5 5:10 5:23 6:16 6:17 6:19 7:12 7:13[2] 7:23 7:24[2] 7:26 7:27[2] 7:28 7:32 8:6 8:7 8:15 9:3 9:8 9:14 9:24 10:5 10:8 10:10 10:19 10:24 11:8[2] 11:12 11:19 11:20 12:3 12:13[2] 12:17 13:11 13:14 13:17 14:12 14:13 15:19 15:20 16:4 16:15 17:6 17:8 17:18[2] 17:22 17:23[2] 17:24 17:27 18:12 18:23 19:6 20:3 20:9 20:11 20:12 21:9 21:14 22:5 22:10 22:12 22:17[2] 22:21 22:27 23:8 23:22 23:38 25:3 25:4 26:5 26:15 26:21 26:37 26:38 26:42 26:46 27:11 27:18 28:13 28:15 29:19 30:7 30:9 30:11 31:30 31:33 32:4 32:23 32:34 32:40 33:5 34:3 34:5 34:11 34:14 34:16 35:6 35:7 35:10 35:11 35:14[2] 35:15 35:16 35:17[3] 36:20 36:25 36:26[2] 36:31 36:37[2] 37:14 38:2 38:4 38:18 38:20 38:21 38:23 38:25 39:5 39:10 39:12 39:17 39:18 40:4 40:10 40:14 40:16 41:8 41:11 41:15 42:13 42:14 42:21 43:1 43:3 43:5 44:5 44:14 44:17 44:18 45:5 46:20 46:27 46:28[2] 48:30 48:45 49:10 49:12 49:19 49:39 50:13 50:44 51:9 51:26 51:62 52:8 52:16

LA

1:19 2:14 3:2 3:32 5:22

EZE

2:8 3:5 3:7 3:14 3:18 3:19 3:20 3:25 3:27 7:4 7:14 7:16 7:20 7:26 8:6 9:6 9:10 10:11 11:7 11:11 11:12 11:21 12:16 12:23 12:28 14:11 14:14 14:16 14:18 14:20 16:5 16:15 16:32 16:33 16:43 16:47 16:51 16:61 17:14 17:15 18:5 18:7 18:11 18:16 18:21 18:24 19:12 20:8 20:9 20:13 20:14 20:16 20:18 20:24 20:39 21:23 22:30 24:23 28:9 29:4 29:16 30:24 30:25 32:27 33:5 33:6[2] 33:8 33:9 33:11 33:13 33:17 33:19 33:24 33:31[2] 33:32 34:3 34:4 34:8 34:16 34:18[2] 34:28 36:8 36:21 36:22 37:8 37:23 38:8 38:28 39:2 41:6 42:6 42:14 44:8 44:13 44:14 44:15 44:22 44:25 46:1 46:2 46:9[2] 46:17[2] 46:18 47:11

DA

1:4 1:8 2:6 2:9[2] 2:28 2:30[2] 2:41 2:43 2:44 2:49 3:15 3:18 4:7 4:8 4:18 5:8 5:15 5:20 5:23 6:4 6:13 7:18 7:26 7:28 8:3 8:4 8:7 8:17 8:18 8:22 8:24 8:25 8:27 9:7 9:18 9:26 10:1 10:7 10:13[2] 10:21[2] 11:6[2] 11:7 11:10 11:11 11:12 11:14 11:16 11:17 11:18 11:19 11:20 11:21 11:25 11:27 11:29 11:32 11:34 11:38 11:41 11:43 11:44 12:4 12:8 12:10[2] 12:13

HO

1:6 1:7 2:7[2] 5:6 6:7 7:16 8:4 8:6 8:12 8:13 8:14 9:3 9:8 9:10 9:13 10:11 11:3 11:5 11:12 13:1 13:4 13:9 14:9

JOE

2:20 3:16 3:20

AM

1:4 1:7 1:10 1:12 1:14 2:2 2:5 2:12 3:7 3:8 4:8 5:5 5:11[2] 5:24 5:26 6:6 6:14 7:13 7:14 8:11

OB

12 17

JON

1:3 1:4 1:5 1:13 2:9 3:8 4:1 4:7

MIC

1:12 3:4 3:8 4:1 4:4 4:12 5:2 6:8 6:14[2] 6:15[3]

NA

1:7 2:8[2] 3:17

HAB

2:1 2:4 2:5 2:20

ZEP

1:13[2] 1:18 3:5 3:7

HAG

1:6[3] 2:16

ZEC

1:4 1:6 1:15 1:21 4:6 7:11 7:14 8:11 8:13 9:7 11:6 11:16 13:5 13:8 14:7[2] 14:11

MAL

1:4[2] 1:12 1:14 2:8 2:9 3:2 3:7 3:8 4:2

MT

1:20 2:19 2:22 3:7 3:11 3:12 3:14 4:4[2] 5:13[2] 5:15 5:17 5:19 5:22[2] 5:28 5:32 5:33 5:34 5:37 5:39[2] 5:44 6:3 6:6 6:7 6:13 6:15 6:17 6:18 6:20 6:23 6:33 7:3 7:15 7:17 7:21 8:4 8:8 8:12 8:20 8:22 8:24 8:27

9:6
9:8
9:12[2]
9:13[2]
9:14
9:15
9:17
9:18
9:21
9:22
9:24
9:25
9:31
9:34
9:36
9:37
10:6
10:13
10:17
10:19
10:20
10:22
10:23
10:28[2]
10:30
10:33
10:34
11:8
11:9
11:16
11:19
11:22
11:24
11:27
12:2
12:3
12:4
12:6
12:7
12:15
12:24[2]
12:28
12:31
12:32
12:36
12:39[2]
12:48
13:8
13:11
13:12
13:16
13:20
13:21
13:23
13:25
13:26
13:29
13:30
13:32
13:38
13:48
13:57
14:6
14:16
14:17
14:24
14:27
14:30
15:3
15:5
15:8
15:9
15:11
15:13
15:18
15:20
15:23
15:24[2]
15:26
16:3
16:4
16:12
16:15
16:17
16:23[2]
17:12[2]
17:21
18:6
18:7
18:16
18:17
18:22
18:25
18:28
18:30
19:6
19:8
19:11
19:14
19:17[2]
19:22
19:26[2]
19:30
20:10
20:12
20:13
20:16
20:20
20:22
20:23[2]
20:25
20:26[2]
20:28
20:31
21:13
21:19
21:21
21:26
21:28
21:29
21:32
21:37
21:38
21:44
21:46
22:5
22:7
22:8
22:14
22:18
22:30
22:31
22:32
22:34
23:3
23:4
23:5
23:8
23:11
23:13
23:16
23:18
23:25
23:27
23:28
24:6
24:13
24:20
24:22
24:35
24:36[2]
24:37
24:43
24:48
25:4
25:9[2]
25:12
25:18
25:29
25:33
25:46
26:5
26:8
26:11
26:24
26:29
26:32
26:39
26:41
26:54
26:56
26:58
26:60
26:63
26:70
27:20
27:23
27:24
28:17

MK

1:8
1:30
1:44
1:45[2]
2:6
2:7
2:10
2:17[2]
2:18
2:20
2:22
2:26
3:4
3:7
3:26
3:29[2]
4:6
4:11
4:15
4:17
4:22
4:29
4:32
4:34
5:6
5:19
5:26
5:28
5:33
5:39
5:40
6:4[2]
6:9
6:16
6:19
6:49
6:56
7:5
7:6
7:11
7:15
7:19
7:24
7:27
7:36
8:27
8:29
8:33[2]
8:35
9:13
9:22
9:27
9:29
9:32
9:34
9:37
9:39
9:50
10:6
10:8
10:14
10:18
10:24
10:27
10:30
10:31
10:38
10:40[2]
10:42
10:43[2]
10:45
10:48
11:13
11:17
11:23
11:26
11:32
12:7
12:12
12:14
12:15
12:25
12:27
12:32
12:44
13:7
13:9
13:11[3]
13:13
13:14
13:17
13:20
13:23
13:24
13:31
13:32[2]
14:2
14:7
14:21
14:28
14:29
14:31
14:36
14:38
14:49
14:56
14:59
14:61
14:68
14:71
15:3
15:5
15:9
15:11
15:23
16:7
16:16

LU

1:13
1:60
2:19
2:37
2:44
2:51
3:16
3:17
3:19
4:4
4:25
4:26
4:30
5:2
5:14
5:15
5:21
5:22
5:24
5:30
5:31
5:32
5:33
5:35
5:38
6:4
6:8
6:24
6:27
6:35
6:40
6:41
6:49
7:7
7:25
7:26
7:28
7:30
7:35
7:44
7:45
7:46
7:47
8:10
8:15
8:16
8:23
8:27
8:35
8:38
8:42
8:50
8:52
8:56
9:9
9:13[2]
9:19
9:20
9:24
9:27
9:32
9:43
9:45
9:55
9:56
9:58
9:59
9:60
9:61
10:2
10:10
10:12
10:14
10:20
10:22[2]
10:29
10:33
10:40
10:42
11:4
11:15
11:17
11:20
11:22
11:28
11:29
11:33
11:34
11:39
11:41
11:42
12:5
12:7
12:9
12:10
12:20
12:31
12:45
12:48
12:50
12:51
12:56
13:3
13:5
13:27
14:10
14:13
14:34
14:35
15:20
15:22
15:30
16:15
16:25[2]
16:30
17:1[2]
17:7
17:17
17:25
17:29
18:4
18:13
18:15
18:16
18:39
19:14
19:27
19:42
19:46
19:47
20:6
20:10
20:14
20:18
20:21
20:23
20:35
20:38
21:4
21:7
21:9[2]
21:12
21:18
21:23
21:33
22:21
22:22
22:26[2]
22:27
22:32
22:36
22:42
22:48
22:53
22:56
23:9
23:21
23:25
23:28[2]
23:40
23:41
24:6
24:16
24:21
24:24
24:29
24:37
24:49

JOH

1:8
1:12
1:13
1:17
1:20
1:26
1:31
1:33
2:9
2:10
2:21
2:24
3:8
3:13
3:15
3:16
3:17
3:18
3:21
3:28
3:29
3:30
3:36
4:2
4:14[2]
4:23
4:32
5:7
5:17
5:18
5:19
5:22
5:24
5:30
5:34[2]
5:36
5:42
5:47
6:9
6:20
6:22
6:26
6:27
6:32
6:36
6:38
6:39
6:64
7:6
7:7
7:10[2]
7:12
7:16
7:18
7:22
7:24
7:26
7:27
7:28
7:29
7:30
7:39
7:41
7:44
7:49
8:5
8:6
8:10
8:12
8:14
8:16
8:26
8:28
8:35
8:37
8:40
8:42
8:49
8:55[2]
8:59
9:3
9:9
9:18
9:21
9:28
9:31
9:41
10:1
10:2
10:5
10:6
10:8
10:10
10:12
10:18
10:26
10:33
10:38
10:39
10:41
11:4
11:10
11:11
11:13
11:20
11:22
11:30
11:42
11:46
11:51
11:52
11:54
12:2
12:6
12:8
12:9
12:10
12:16
12:24
12:27
12:30
12:37
12:42
12:44
12:47
12:49
13:7
13:9
13:10[2]
13:18
13:36
14:6
14:10
14:17
14:19
14:24
14:26
14:31
15:15
15:16
15:19[2]
15:21
15:22
15:24
15:25
15:26
16:4
16:5
16:6
16:7
16:12
16:13
16:20[2]
16:21
16:22
16:25[2]
16:33
17:9
17:11
17:12
17:15
17:20
17:25
18:16
18:23
18:28
18:36
18:39
18:40
19:9
19:12
19:13
19:15[2]
19:21
19:24
19:33
19:34
19:38
20:7
20:11
20:17
20:24
20:25
20:27
20:31
21:4[2]
21:8
21:18
21:23

AC

1:4
1:5
1:8
2:14
2:15
2:16
2:34
3:6
3:14
3:18
4:15
4:17
4:19
4:20
4:32
5:1
5:3
5:4
5:13
5:19
5:21
5:22
5:23
5:39
6:4
7:9
7:12
7:17
7:25
7:27
7:39
7:47
7:55
8:9
8:12
8:20
8:40
9:7
9:8
9:15
9:21
9:22
9:24
9:26
9:27
9:29
9:40
10:10
10:14
10:26
10:28
10:35
10:41
11:4
11:8
11:9
11:16
11:19
12:5
12:9
12:14
12:15
12:16
12:17
12:20
12:24
13:8
13:14
13:25
13:30
13:37
13:45
13:46
13:50
13:51
14:2
14:4
15:5
15:11
15:20
15:38
16:1
16:7
16:18
16:28
16:37[2]
17:5
17:13
17:14
17:21
17:30
18:9
18:15
18:19
18:21[2]
19:9[2]
19:15
19:22
19:26
19:27
19:34
19:39
20:20
20:24
21:13
21:24
21:39
22:9
22:28
23:6
23:8
23:9
23:21
23:29
24:7
24:11
24:14
24:27
25:4
25:9
25:11
25:19
25:21
25:25
26:16
26:20
26:25[2]
26:29
27:10
27:14
27:21
27:22
27:27
27:39
27:41
27:43
28:6
28:16
28:19
28:22

RO

1:13
1:21
1:32
2:2
2:5
2:8[2]
2:10
2:13
2:25
2:29[2]
3:4
3:5
3:21
3:27
4:2
4:4
4:5[2]
4:10
4:12
4:13
4:16
4:20
4:24
5:3
5:8
5:11
5:13
5:15
5:16
5:20
6:10
6:11
6:13
6:14
6:15
6:17[2]
6:22
6:23
7:2
7:3
7:6
7:7
7:8
7:9
7:13
7:14
7:15
7:17
7:18
7:19
7:20
7:23
7:25
8:1
8:4
8:5
8:6
8:9[2]
8:10
8:11
8:13
8:15
8:20
8:23
8:24
8:25
8:26
8:32
9:7
9:8
9:10
9:11
9:13
9:16
9:20
9:24
9:31
9:32
10:2
10:6
10:8
10:16
10:18
10:19
10:20
10:21
11:4
11:6
11:7
11:11
11:15
11:18[2]
11:20
11:22
11:28
12:2
12:3
12:16
12:19
12:21
13:1
13:3
13:4
13:5
13:8
13:14
14:1
14:10
14:13
14:14
14:15
14:17
14:20
15:3
15:21
15:23
15:25
16:4
16:18
16:19
16:26

1 CO

1:10
1:17
1:18
1:23
1:24
1:27
1:30
2:4
2:5
2:7
2:9
2:10
2:12
2:13
2:14
2:15
2:16
3:1
3:6
3:7
3:10
3:15
4:3
4:4
4:10[3]
4:14
4:19[2]
4:20
5:3
5:8
5:11
5:13
6:6
6:11
6:12[2]
6:13[2]
6:17
6:18
7:4[2]
7:6
7:7
7:9
7:10
7:11
7:14
7:15[2]
7:17
7:19
7:21
7:28[2]
7:29
7:32
7:33
7:34
7:35
7:36
7:37
7:38
7:39
7:40
8:1
8:3
8:4
8:6[2]
8:8
8:9
8:12
9:12
9:15
9:17
9:21
9:24
9:25
9:27
10:5
10:13[2]
10:20
10:23[2]
10:24
10:28
10:29
10:33
11:3
11:5
11:6
11:7
11:8
11:9
11:12
11:15
11:16
11:17
11:28
11:32
12:3
12:4
12:5
12:6
12:7
12:11
12:14
12:18
12:20[2]
12:24
12:25
12:31
13:6
13:8
13:10
13:11
13:12[2]
13:13
14:1
14:2
14:3
14:4
14:5
14:14
14:17
14:20
14:22[3]
14:24
14:28
14:33
14:34
14:38
15:6
15:10[3]
15:13
15:20
15:23
15:27
15:35
15:37
15:38
15:39
15:40
15:46
15:51
15:57
16:7
16:8
16:11
16:12[2]

2 CO

1:9[2]
1:12
1:18
1:19
1:24
2:1
2:4
2:5[2]
2:13
2:17[2]
3:3[2]
3:5
3:6[2]
3:7
3:14
3:15
3:18
4:2[2]
4:3
4:5
4:7
4:8
4:9[2]
4:12
4:16
4:17
4:18[2]
5:4
5:11
5:12
5:15
6:4
6:12
7:5
7:7
7:8
7:9
7:10
7:12
7:14
8:5
8:8
8:10
8:14
8:16
8:17
8:19
8:21
8:22
9:6
9:12
10:1
10:2
10:4
10:10
10:12
10:13[2]
10:15
10:17
10:18
11:3
11:6[2]
11:12
11:17
12:5
12:6
12:14[2]
12:16
12:19
13:3
13:4
13:6
13:7
13:8

GA

1:1
1:7
1:8
1:11
1:12
1:15
1:17
1:19
1:23
2:2
2:3
2:6
2:7
2:11
2:12
2:14
2:16
2:17
2:20
3:11
3:12
3:15
3:16
3:18
3:20
3:22
3:23
3:25
4:2
4:4
4:7
4:9
4:14
4:17
4:18
4:23[2]
4:26
4:29
4:31
5:6
5:10
5:13
5:15
5:18
5:22
6:4
6:8
6:13
6:14
6:15

EPH

1:21
2:4
2:13
2:19
4:7
4:9
4:15
4:20
4:28
4:29
5:3
5:4
5:8
5:11
5:13
5:15
5:17
5:18
5:27
5:29
5:32
6:4
6:6
6:12
6:21

PHP

1:12
1:17
1:20
1:22
1:28
1:29
2:3
2:4
2:7
2:12
2:19
2:22
2:24
2:25
2:27[2]
3:1
3:7
3:8[2]
3:9
3:12
3:13
4:6
4:10[2]
4:15
4:17
4:18
4:19

COL

1:26
2:17
3:8
3:11
3:22
3:25

1 TH

1:5
1:8
2:2
2:4[2]
2:7
2:8
2:13
2:17
2:18
3:6
4:7
4:8
4:9
4:10
4:13
5:1
5:4
5:6
5:8
5:9
5:15

2 TH

2:12
2:13
3:3
3:8
3:9
3:11
3:13
3:15

1 TI

1:8
1:9
1:13
2:10
2:12[2]
2:14
3:3
3:15
4:7
4:8
4:12
5:1
5:4
5:6
5:8
5:11
5:13
5:19
5:23
6:2
6:4
6:6
6:9
6:11
6:17

2 TI

1:7
1:8
1:9
1:10
1:17
2:9
2:14
2:16
2:20[2]
2:22
2:23
2:24
3:5
3:9
3:10
3:11
3:13
3:14
4:3
4:5
4:8
4:13
4:16
4:20

TIT

1:3
1:8
1:15[2]
1:16
2:1
2:10
3:2
3:4
3:5
3:9

PHM

11
14[2]
16[2]
22

HEB

1:8
1:11
1:12
1:13
2:6
2:8
2:9
2:16
3:4
3:6
3:13
3:17
3:18
4:2
4:13
4:15
5:4
5:5
5:14
6:8
6:9
6:12
7:3
7:6
7:8
7:16
7:19
7:21
7:24
7:28
8:6
9:7
9:11
9:12
9:23
9:24
9:26
9:27
10:3
10:5
10:25
10:27
10:32
10:38
10:39[2]
11:6
11:13
11:16
12:8
12:10
12:11
12:13
12:22
12:26[2]
13:4
13:14
13:15
13:19

JAS

1:4
1:6
1:10
1:11
1:14
1:22
1:25[2]
1:26
2:6
2:9
2:20
3:8
3:14
3:15
3:17
4:6[2]
4:11[2]
4:16
5:12[2]

1 PE

1:12
1:15
1:19
1:20
1:23
1:25
2:4
2:7
2:9
2:10[2]
2:16
2:18
2:20
2:23
2:25
3:4
3:9
3:12
3:14
3:15
3:18
3:21
4:2
4:4
4:6
4:7
4:13
4:14
4:15
4:16
5:2[2]
5:3
5:10

2 PE

1:9
1:16
1:21
2:1
2:4
2:5
2:10
2:12
2:16
2:22
3:7
3:8
3:9[2]
3:10
3:18

1 JO

1:7
2:2
2:5
2:7
2:11
2:16
2:17
2:19[2]
2:20
2:21
2:22
2:23
2:27[2]
3:2
3:17
3:18
4:1
4:10
4:18
5:5
5:6
5:18

2 JO

1
5
8
12

3 JO

11[2]
9
13
14

JUDE

6
9
10[2]
17
20

RE

2:6
2:9[2]
2:14
2:24
2:25
3:5
3:9
9:4
9:5
9:11
10:7
10:9
11:2
12:12
14:3
19:12
20:5
20:6
21:8
21:27
22:3

BY

GE
7:3, 7:22, 9:6, 9:11, 10:5, 10:32, 14:6, 14:15, 16:2, 16:7, 18:2, 18:8, 19:36, 20:3, 21:23, 21:28, 21:29, 22:13, 22:16, 23:20, 24:3, 24:11, 24:13, 24:30, 24:43, 25:11, 25:13, 25:16, 26:18, 27:40, 29:2, 30:3, 30:27, 30:40, 31:24, 31:31, 31:39, 31:40, 31:53, 32:16, 33:8, 35:4, 36:37, 36:40, 37:28, 38:14, 38:16, 38:18, 38:19, 38:20, 38:21, 38:24, 38:25, 39:10^{2}, 39:12, 39:16, 41:1, 41:3, 41:31, 41:32, 41:47, 42:15, 42:16, 42:23, 42:38, 43:32^{3}, 45:1, 45:7, 45:23, 45:24, 47:13, 48:7, 49:17, 49:22, 49:24, 49:25^{2}

EX
2:3, 2:5, 2:15, 2:23^{2}, 3:7, 3:19, 4:4, 4:13, 4:24, 6:3^{2}, 7:4, 7:15, 8:24, 9:35, 12:14, 12:26, 12:31, 12:51, 13:3, 13:14, 13:16, 13:21^{3}, 13:22, 14:2, 14:9, 14:20, 14:21, 15:16, 15:27, 16:3^{2}, 18:8, 18:13, 18:14, 18:19, 20:26, 21:3^{2}, 21:4, 22:25, 22:26, 23:30, 25:14, 26:9^{2}, 28:28, 29:11, 29:18, 29:25, 29:28, 29:32, 29:38, 29:41, 29:43, 30:4, 30:6, 30:20, 31:2, 32:13, 32:27, 33:6, 33:12, 33:17, 33:21, 33:22^{2}, 34:6, 34:7, 35:29, 35:30, 36:16^{2}, 37:3, 37:5, 37:27, 38:21, 39:4, 39:21, 40:29, 40:38^{2}

LE
1:5, 1:9, 1:13, 1:16, 1:17, 2:2, 2:3, 2:9, 2:10, 2:11, 2:14, 2:16, 3:3, 3:4, 3:5, 3:9^{2}, 3:10, 3:11, 3:14, 3:15, 3:16, 4:9, 4:35, 5:12, 5:15, 5:17, 6:2, 6:17, 6:18, 7:4, 7:5, 7:25, 7:30, 7:34, 7:35, 7:36, 8:21, 8:28, 8:36, 10:11, 10:12, 10:13, 10:15^{2}, 16:21, 16:31, 19:12, 19:31, 20:25^{3}, 21:6, 21:9, 21:21, 22:4, 22:22, 22:27, 23:8, 23:13, 23:18, 23:25, 23:27, 23:36^{2}, 23:37, 24:7, 24:8, 24:9^{2}, 25:39, 25:47^{3}, 26:7, 26:8, 26:23^{2}, 26:26, 26:46, 27:2

NU
1:2^{2}, 1:3, 1:17, 1:18^{2}, 1:20^{3}, 1:22^{3}, 1:24^{2}, 1:26^{2}, 1:28^{2}, 1:30^{2}, 1:32^{2}, 1:34^{2}, 1:36^{2}, 1:38^{2}, 1:40, 1:42, 1:45, 1:52^{2}, 2:2, 2:12, 2:17, 2:20, 2:25, 2:27, 2:32, 2:34, 3:15, 3:17, 3:18, 3:19, 3:20, 3:26^{2}, 3:43, 3:47, 3:49, 4:2, 4:22, 4:26^{2}, 4:29, 4:32, 4:36, 4:37, 4:38, 4:40, 4:42, 4:45, 4:49, 5:2, 5:19, 6:9, 6:11, 7:84, 9:6, 9:7, 9:10, 9:16^{2}, 9:21^{2}, 9:23, 10:13, 10:34, 11:31, 12:2, 13:3, 13:22, 13:29^{2}, 14:3, 14:14^{2}, 14:18, 14:25, 14:36, 14:37, 14:43, 15:3, 15:10, 15:13, 15:14, 15:23, 15:24, 15:25, 15:28, 16:40, 18:8^{2}, 18:11, 18:19, 18:32, 20:17, 20:18, 20:19, 20:23, 21:1, 21:4, 21:18, 21:22, 21:27, 21:33, 22:1, 22:5, 23:3, 23:6, 23:15, 23:17, 24:6, 26:3, 26:55, 26:63^{2}, 27:2, 27:23, 28:2, 28:3^{2}, 28:6, 28:8, 28:13, 28:19, 28:24, 29:6, 29:13, 29:36, 30:3, 30:10, 31:12, 31:17, 31:18, 31:35, 33:2, 33:10, 33:48, 33:49, 33:50, 33:54, 34:3, 34:13, 34:18, 35:1, 35:20, 35:30, 35:33, 36:2^{2}, 36:13^{2}

DE
1:2, 1:7, 1:19, 1:22, 1:33^{3}, 1:40, 2:1, 2:8^{2}, 2:27, 2:30, 2:36^{2}, 3:12, 4:34^{7}, 4:48, 5:5, 5:15, 5:31, 6:7, 6:13, 7:22, 8:3^{2}, 9:29^{2}, 10:20, 11:19, 11:30, 12:30, 14:22, 15:20, 16:1, 18:1, 20:19, 21:5, 21:17, 22:4, 23:10^{2}, 24:9, 25:2, 25:11, 25:17, 25:18, 27:16, 28:10, 28:68, 29:16, 33:12, 33:14^{2}, 33:29

JOS
2:12, 2:15, 2:18, 3:4^{2}, 4:6, 5:1, 5:4, 5:7, 5:13, 7:14^{2}, 7:16, 7:17, 7:18, 8:3, 8:15, 9:13, 9:18, 9:19, 10:18, 11:7, 11:23, 13:6, 13:14, 13:16, 13:22, 13:29, 13:31, 13:32, 14:2^{2}, 15:1, 15:6, 15:8, 16:1, 16:6, 16:8, 17:2^{2}, 18:9, 18:20, 19:49, 19:51, 20:2, 20:8, 20:9, 21:2, 21:4, 21:5, 21:6, 21:7, 21:8^{2}, 21:9, 21:40^{2}, 22:9, 22:10, 23:4, 23:7, 24:26

JG
2:18, 3:1, 3:4^{2}, 3:15, 3:19^{2}, 4:11, 5:10, 5:19, 5:22, 6:11, 6:25, 6:27^{2}, 6:28, 6:30, 6:36, 6:37, 7:1, 7:5, 7:7, 7:12, 8:11, 9:6, 9:9, 9:25, 9:32, 9:34, 9:37^{2}, 11:18, 11:26, 16:5, 16:26, 17:10, 18:3, 18:16, 18:28, 19:11, 19:14, 20:5, 20:9, 21:7, 21:11, 21:12

RU
2:8, 2:21, 2:23, 4:1

1 SA
1:7, 1:9, 1:25, 2:3, 2:9, 2:16, 2:23, 2:28, 3:21, 4:13, 4:18, 4:20, 5:2, 5:8, 5:9, 9:23, 10:2, 10:19^{2}, 10:21, 11:7, 11:9, 14:4, 14:6^{2}, 14:36, 16:9, 16:20, 17:2, 17:23, 17:26, 17:35, 17:43, 17:52, 18:25, 18:30, 20:7, 20:9, 20:19, 20:25^{2}, 23:7, 24:3, 24:21, 25:13, 25:16, 25:20, 25:22, 25:34, 26:3, 26:7, 26:24^{2}, 27:1, 28:6^{3}, 28:8^{2}, 28:10, 28:15^{2}, 28:17, 29:1, 29:2^{2}, 30:15, 30:24

2 SA
1:16, 1:12, 2:13, 2:15, 2:16, 2:24, 3:5, 3:18, 6:2, 6:7, 10:2, 10:8, 11:14, 12:14, 12:25, 13:31, 13:32, 13:34, 15:30, 15:36, 16:2, 16:13, 17:11, 17:17, 17:22, 18:4^{3}, 18:23, 19:3, 19:7, 19:37, 20:9, 20:11, 20:12, 20:21, 21:10^{2}, 21:22^{2}, 22:9, 22:30^{2}, 22:35, 23:2, 23:4, 23:15, 23:16, 24:16

1 KI
1:9^{2}, 1:17, 1:27, 1:30, 2:8, 2:23, 2:25, 2:42, 3:5, 4:12, 4:20, 5:9, 5:11, 5:14, 5:21, 5:22, 7:20, 8:38^{2}, 8:43, 8:53, 8:56, 9:8, 10:5, 10:25, 10:29, 12:15, 13:1^{2}, 13:2, 13:5, 13:9^{2}, 13:10, 13:17^{2}, 13:18, 13:24^{3}, 13:25^{2}, 13:28, 13:32, 14:4, 14:18, 15:13, 15:29, 15:30, 16:7, 16:12, 16:13^{2}, 16:34, 17:3, 17:5, 17:16, 17:20, 17:24, 18:4, 18:6^{2}, 18:13, 18:24, 19:2, 19:11, 19:19, 20:14^{2}, 20:38, 20:39^{2}, 21:1, 21:23, 22:8, 22:19, 22:28

2 KI
2:1, 2:7, 2:11, 2:13, 2:23, 3:11, 3:20, 4:8, 4:9, 4:27, 5:1, 6:14, 6:26, 6:30, 8:8, 8:21, 9:27^{2}, 9:36, 10:6, 10:10, 10:33, 11:11, 11:14^{2}, 11:16^{2}, 11:19, 13:7, 13:25, 14:7, 14:9, 14:25, 14:27, 16:15, 17:4, 17:6, 17:13^{3}, 17:23, 18:11, 18:17, 18:31, 19:7, 19:11, 19:23, 19:28^{2}, 19:33^{2}, 20:11, 21:10, 23:3, 23:11, 24:2, 25:4^{3}

1 CH
1:48, 3:3, 4:38, 4:41, 5:7, 5:10, 5:17, 6:15, 6:61, 6:63, 6:65^{2}, 6:78, 7:4, 7:5, 7:7, 7:9, 7:11, 7:29, 8:28, 9:1, 9:22, 9:23, 9:28, 11:3, 11:11, 11:14, 11:18, 12:22, 12:31, 14:11, 15:16, 16:41, 17:21, 18:3, 19:4, 19:9, 20:8^{2}, 21:15, 21:25, 21:26, 23:3^{2}, 23:24^{2}, 23:27, 23:31, 24:5, 24:27, 26:16, 26:25, 27:1, 28:1, 28:12, 28:14^{2}, 28:15^{2}, 28:16, 28:17^{2}, 28:18, 28:19, 29:5, 29:8

2 CH
1:17, 2:16, 3:3, 5:11, 5:14, 6:23^{4}, 6:33, 6:34, 7:6, 7:12, 7:14, 7:20, 7:21, 8:14, 8:18, 9:4, 9:18, 9:24, 10:15, 12:7, 13:5, 16:14, 18:7, 18:27, 19:5, 20:15, 20:16, 21:9, 21:15^{3}, 21:19, 22:7, 23:10^{2}, 23:13, 23:18^{2}, 24:11^{2}, 24:13, 25:18, 26:11^{2}, 26:15, 28:15, 29:9, 29:15, 29:25, 29:27, 30:12, 30:21, 31:6, 31:15, 31:17^{2}, 31:19^{2}, 32:11^{2}, 33:8, 34:14, 35:4, 35:6, 35:20, 36:13, 36:15, 36:21, 36:22

EZR
1:1, 1:8, 2:62, 3:4, 3:11, 4:16, 4:23, 5:5, 6:9, 7:23, 8:3, 8:18, 8:20, 8:31, 8:33, 8:34^{2}, 9:11, 10:16, 10:17, 10:44

NE
1:10^{2}, 2:6, 2:13^{2}, 2:15^{2}, 3:15, 3:23, 3:25, 4:3, 4:12, 4:18^{2}, 7:3, 7:5, 7:64, 8:14, 8:18, 9:12^{2}, 9:14, 9:19^{2}, 9:30, 10:29, 10:34, 10:35, 12:37, 13:18, 13:25, 13:26

ES
1:12, 1:15, 2:14, 3:13, 3:15, 7:7, 8:5, 8:10, 8:14^{2}, 9:25

JOB
4:9^{2}, 6:16, 9:11, 11:7, 15:30, 16:12, 17:7, 18:8, 18:9, 20:29, 21:29, 22:30, 26:12, 26:13, 27:11, 28:8, 28:9, 28:25, 29:3, 29:19, 30:4, 30:18, 31:9, 31:11, 31:23, 31:28, 31:30, 31:33, 33:18, 35:9^{2}, 36:12, 36:22, 36:31, 36:32, 37:10, 37:11, 37:12, 37:17, 37:19, 38:2, 38:24, 39:9, 39:26, 41:18, 41:25, 42:5

PS
1:3, 5:10, 9:16, 10:10, 17:4, 17:7, 18:8, 18:29^{2}, 18:34, 19:11, 30:7, 33:6^{2}, 30:16^{2}, 30:17, 37:23, 38:8, 39:10, 41:11, 44:3, 44:12, 44:16, 48:4, 49:7, 50:5, 54:1^{2}, 56:7, 59:11, 63:10, 65:5, 65:6, 66:7, 66:12, 68:4, 71:6, 72:3, 73:23, 74:7, 74:13, 77:20, 78:17, 78:18, 78:26, 78:49, 78:55, 78:64, 78:65, 78:72, 79:10, 80:12, 88:9, 89:35, 89:39, 89:41, 90:7^{2}, 90:10, 91:5^{2}, 94:20, 102:5, 104:8^{2}, 106:22, 107:7, 119:9, 121:6^{2}, 128:3, 129:8, 134:1, 136:5, 137:1, 140:5, 147:4

PR
3:19^{2}, 3:20, 3:28, 3:29, 4:15, 6:26, 7:26, 8:2, 8:15, 8:16, 8:30, 9:11, 11:5, 11:11^{2}, 12:3, 12:13, 12:14, 13:2, 13:10, 13:11^{2}, 14:4, 15:13, 15:23, 16:6, 16:12, 20:4, 20:11, 20:18, 20:28, 21:6, 22:4, 24:3, 24:4, 24:6, 24:30^{2}, 25:15, 26:2, 26:6, 26:17^{2}, 26:26, 26:28, 27:9, 28:2, 28:8, 29:19, 30:27, 31:18

EC
1:13, 5:3, 5:9, 5:14, 7:3, 7:11, 7:23, 7:26, 7:27, 9:1, 9:15, 10:3, 10:18, 12:11, 12:12

CA
1:7, 1:8, 2:7, 3:1, 3:5, 5:4, 5:12, 7:4

ISA
1:7, 3:5^{2}, 3:25, 4:1, 4:4^{2}, 4:5^{2}, 7:20^{2}, 9:1, 10:13^{2}, 10:34, 13:15, 15:5, 18:2, 19:7^{3}, 20:2, 22:3, 22:5, 22:14, 23:3, 26:13, 27:7, 27:9, 27:12, 29:13, 32:8, 34:17, 36:2, 36:16, 37:7, 37:11, 37:24^{2}, 37:29^{2}, 37:34^{2}, 38:8, 38:16, 40:26^{3}, 41:3, 42:16, 43:1, 43:7, 44:4, 44:5^{2}, 44:24, 45:3, 45:4, 45:23, 46:3, 48:1^{2}, 48:17, 49:10, 49:19, 50:4, 51:18, 51:19, 52:12, 53:11, 54:15, 60:19, 62:2, 62:8^{2}, 63:12, 63:19, 64:4, 65:1, 65:5, 65:15, 65:16, 66:16^{2}

JER
2:8, 2:17, 2:34, 4:26, 5:7^{2}, 5:22, 5:31, 6:5, 6:25, 7:10, 7:11, 7:14, 7:30, 8:2, 8:5, 10:12^{3}, 10:14, 11:21, 11:22^{2}, 12:16^{2}, 13:5, 13:24, 14:9, 14:12^{3}, 14:15, 15:16, 16:4^{2}, 17:2, 17:8^{2}, 17:11, 17:19, 17:20, 17:21, 18:21^{2}, 19:2, 19:7, 20:2, 20:4, 21:9^{3}, 22:2, 22:4, 22:5, 22:8, 22:13^{2}, 23:27, 23:32^{2}, 25:29, 27:3, 27:5^{2}, 27:8, 27:13^{3}, 29:3, 29:19, 29:22, 31:9, 31:32, 31:35^{2}, 32:17, 32:34, 32:36^{3}, 33:4^{2}, 34:4, 34:15, 37:2, 38:2^{3}, 38:11, 38:23, 39:4^{3}, 39:18, 41:12, 41:17, 42:17^{3}, 42:22^{3}, 44:12^{4}, 44:13^{3}, 44:15, 44:18^{2}, 44:26, 44:27^{2}, 46:2, 46:6, 46:10, 46:18, 48:19, 49:3, 49:9, 49:13, 49:17, 50:1, 50:13, 51:14, 51:15^{3}, 51:17^{2}, 52:7^{5}

LA
1:12, 2:15, 2:21, 3:1, 5:12

EZE
1:1, 1:3, 1:15, 1:19, 3:15, 4:10, 4:11, 4:16^{2}, 5:12, 5:14, 6:11^{3}, 6:12^{2}, 8:3, 9:2, 9:3, 9:11, 10:9^{3}, 10:15, 10:16, 10:20, 10:22, 11:10, 11:24, 12:3, 12:4, 12:7, 13:19, 13:22, 14:3, 14:7, 14:13, 14:14, 14:20, 16:6, 16:8, 16:15, 16:25, 16:36, 16:56, 16:61, 17:5, 17:7, 17:8, 17:9, 17:14, 17:17, 17:18, 17:21, 18:7, 18:12, 18:16, 18:18, 19:7, 19:10^{2}, 20:3, 20:31^{2}, 21:12, 22:7^{2}, 22:12, 23:21, 23:25^{2}, 24:6, 24:21, 25:12, 25:13, 25:14, 25:15, 26:6, 26:10, 26:11, 27:12, 27:16, 27:34, 28:5^{2}, 28:10, 28:16, 28:17, 28:18^{2}, 28:23, 29:7, 30:5, 30:6, 30:10, 30:12, 30:17, 31:7, 31:9, 31:12, 31:14, 31:18, 32:12, 32:20, 32:21, 32:22, 32:23, 32:24, 32:25, 32:26, 32:29^{2}, 32:30, 32:31, 34:13, 34:27, 34:30, 35:5, 36:17^{2}, 36:34, 36:37, 37:2, 37:18, 38:17, 39:15, 39:23, 40:2, 40:5, 40:7, 40:18, 40:22, 40:28, 40:38, 40:41, 40:49^{2}, 41:7, 41:17^{2}, 42:20, 43:3, 43:4, 43:6, 43:7^{2}, 43:8^{3}, 43:13, 44:2^{2}, 44:3^{2}, 45:1, 46:2^{2}, 46:8^{2}, 46:9^{5}, 46:14, 46:16, 46:18, 46:21, 47:2, 47:12, 47:16, 47:18, 47:22, 48:2, 48:3, 48:4, 48:5, 48:6, 48:7, 48:8, 48:12, 48:17, 48:20, 48:24, 48:25, 48:26, 48:28, 48:29

DA
4:17^{2}, 4:27^{2}, 4:30, 5:10, 7:2, 7:8, 7:16, 8:2, 8:11, 8:12, 8:24, 8:25, 9:2, 9:3, 9:5, 9:10, 9:11, 9:12, 9:18, 9:19, 10:4, 10:16, 11:2, 11:12, 11:16, 11:18, 11:21, 11:32, 11:33^{4}, 12:7

HO
1:2, 1:7^{6}, 2:17, 4:2, 6:5^{2}, 6:9, 7:16, 8:4, 8:9, 11:3, 12:3^{2}, 12:10, 12:13^{2}, 13:7, 13:16, 14:1

AM
2:8 4:2 5:3[2] 6:8 6:10 6:13 7:2 7:4 7:5 7:7 7:8 7:11 7:17[2] 8:2 8:5 8:8 8:14 9:5 9:10 9:12

OB
5 9

JON
2:4 3:7

MIC
2:2 2:5 2:8 2:12 2:13 3:8 7:18

NA
1:6

HAB
1:16 2:4 2:5 2:10 2:12 3:10 3:13

ZEP
1:5[2] 1:18 2:12 2:15

HAG
1:1 1:3 2:1 2:10 2:13 2:22 3:6

ZEC
1:8 3:5 3:7 4:3 4:6[3] 4:14 5:4 7:7 7:12 8:9 9:8 9:11

MAL
1:1 1:9 2:10

MT
1:22 2:5 2:14 2:15 2:17 2:23 3:3 4:4[2] 4:14 4:15 4:18 5:21 5:26 5:27 5:33 5:34 5:35[2] 5:36 6:27 7:16 7:20 8:17 8:28 9:25 11:12 12:17 12:24 12:27[2] 12:28 12:33 12:37[2] 13:1 13:4 13:14 13:19 13:21[2] 13:35 14:13 15:3 15:5[2] 17:21 18:7 18:28 20:30 21:4 21:23 21:24 21:27 22:1 22:31 23:16[2] 23:18[2] 23:20[3] 23:21[3] 23:22[3] 24:15 26:4 26:24 26:73 27:9 27:32 27:35 27:39 27:64 28:9 28:13

MK
1:16 1:31 2:13 2:14 3:22 4:1[2] 4:2 4:4 4:15 5:4 5:7 5:21 5:22 5:41 6:2 6:7 6:25 6:32 6:39 6:40[2] 6:48 7:11[2] 7:26 8:3 8:23 8:27 9:2 9:27 9:29[2] 9:33 9:34 10:1 10:46 11:4 11:20 11:28 11:29 11:33 12:1 12:36 13:14 14:1 14:19 14:21 14:47 14:69 14:70 15:21 15:29 15:35

LU
1:61 1:70 1:77 2:8 2:18 2:26 2:27 3:19 4:1 4:3[2] 4:4[2] 5:1 5:2 5:15 5:17 5:19 6:44 7:7 8:4 8:5 8:12 8:20 8:36 8:54 9:7 9:14 9:47 10:4 10:19 10:31[2] 10:32 11:3 11:9[2] 13:17 16:22 17:6 17:7 18:5 18:31 18:35 18:36 18:37 19:8 19:15 19:24 20:2 20:8 21:9 21:16 21:24 22:22 22:56 23:8 24:4 24:12 24:32

JOH
1:3 1:10 1:17[2] 1:42 3:2 3:34 5:2 6:15 6:18 6:57[2] 7:50 8:9[2] 8:59 9:1 9:7 9:21 10:1 10:2 10:3 10:9 11:39 11:42 12:11 12:29 13:35 14:6 16:30 19:7 19:25 19:39 20:7 21:19

AC
1:3 1:10 1:16 1:25 2:16 2:22[2] 2:23[2] 2:33 2:43 3:7 3:12 3:16 3:18 3:21 4:7[2] 4:9 4:10[2] 4:16 4:25 4:30[2] 4:36 5:10 5:12 5:15 5:19 6:10 7:25 7:35 7:42 7:53 9:8 9:13 9:25[2] 9:36 9:39 10:6 10:22 10:32 10:36 11:4 11:5 11:28 11:30 12:9 12:20 13:4 13:8 13:11 13:19 13:21 13:36 13:39[2] 13:45 14:3 15:3 15:7 15:9 15:12 15:23 15:27 15:40 16:2 16:8 16:13 16:16 17:10 17:23 17:29 17:31 18:3 18:9 18:21 18:28 19:10 19:11 19:13 19:25 20:16 20:19 20:31 21:19 22:10 22:11 22:24 22:25 23:2 23:4 23:10 23:11 23:19 23:31 24:2[2] 24:8 24:14 24:21 26:18 27:2 27:11 27:12 27:13 27:16 27:23 28:16 28:25

RO
1:2 1:4 1:5 1:10[2] 1:12 1:17 1:20 2:7 2:12 2:14 2:16 2:27[2] 3:20[2] 3:21 3:22 3:24 3:27[2] 3:28 3:30 4:2 4:16 5:1 5:2[2] 5:5 5:9 5:10[2] 5:11 5:12[2] 5:15[2] 5:16[2] 5:17[3] 5:18[2] 5:19[2] 5:21 6:4[2] 7:2 7:4 7:5 7:7 7:8 7:11 7:13[2] 8:11 8:14 8:20 8:24 9:10[2] 9:32[2] 10:5 10:17[2] 10:19[2] 11:6 11:14 11:20 11:24 12:1 12:2 14:14 15:16 15:18[2] 15:19 15:24 15:28 15:32 16:18 16:25 16:*sub.*

1 CO
1:4 1:5 1:9 1:10 1:11 1:21[2] 2:10 3:5 3:13 3:15 4:4 6:2 6:11 6:14 7:6 7:14[2] 7:39 8:6[2] 8:9 9:22 9:27 10:30 11:12 12:3[2] 12:8[2] 12:9[2] 12:13 14:6[4] 14:9 14:19 14:27[3] 14:30 14:31 15:2 15:10 15:21[2] 15:31 16:2 16:3 16:7 16:*sub.*

2 CO
1:1 1:4 1:5 1:11[3] 1:12 1:16 1:19[2] 1:20 1:24 2:2 2:14 3:3 3:10 3:18 4:2 4:14 4:16 5:7[2] 5:18 5:20 6:6[6] 6:7[3] 6:8[2] 7:6 7:7[2] 7:9 7:13 8:5 8:8[2] 8:14 8:19 8:20 9:12 9:13 9:14 10:1 10:9 10:11 10:12 10:15 11:3 11:26[2] 11:33 12:17 13:4[2] 13:*sub.*

GA
1:1[2] 1:15 1:22 2:2[2] 2:15 2:16[5] 2:17 2:20 2:21 3:2[2] 3:3 3:5[2] 3:11[2] 3:18 3:19 3:21 3:22 3:24 3:26 4:8 4:22 4:23 5:4 5:5 5:6 5:13 6:14

EPH
1:1 1:5 2:3 2:5 2:8 2:11[2] 2:13 2:16 2:18 3:3 3:5 3:6 3:7 3:9 3:10 3:12 3:16 3:17 3:21 4:14 4:16 4:21 5:13 5:26 5:*sub.*

PHP
1:11 1:14 1:20 1:26 1:28 3:9 3:11 3:16 4:6 4:19 4:*sub.*

COL
1:1 1:16 1:17 1:20 1:21 2:11 2:18 2:19 3:17 4:18 4:*sub.*

1 TH
3:3 3:5 3:7 4:1 4:2 4:15 5:9 5:27

2 TH
2:1[2] 2:2[3] 2:3 3:12 3:14 3:16

1 TI
1:1 1:18 4:5 4:14 5:21

2 TI
1:1 1:6 1:10 1:14 2:26 3:16 4:17

TIT
1:9 3:5[2] 3:7

PHM
6 7 *sub.*

HEB
1:1 1:2[2] 1:3[2] 1:4 2:2 2:3[2] 2:9 2:10 3:4 3:16 5:3 5:8 5:14 6:7 6:13[2] 6:16 6:17 6:18 7:2 7:11 7:19 7:21 7:22 7:23 7:25 8:6 8:9 9:11 9:12[2] 9:15 9:22 9:26 10:1 10:8 10:10 10:14 10:19 10:20 10:33 10:38 11:2 11:3 11:4[3] 11:5 11:7[3] 11:8 11:9 11:12 11:17 11:20 11:21 11:22 11:23 11:24 11:27 11:29[2] 11:30 11:31 13:11 13:15 13:*sub.*

JAS
2:7 2:12 2:18 2:21 2:22 2:24[2] 2:25 5:4 5:12[3] 5:17

1 PE
1:3 1:5 1:12 1:18 1:21 1:23 1:25 2:5 2:12 2:14 2:24 3:1 3:18 3:19 3:20 3:21 5:2 5:12

2 PE
1:4 1:13 1:21[2] 2:2 3:1 3:2 3:5 3:7

1 JO
3:24 5:2 5:6[3]

3 JO
14

JUDE
1 12 23

RE
1:1 5:9 8:13 9:2 9:18[4] 9:20 10:6 12:11[2] 13:14[2] 14:20 17:12 18:15 18:17 18:19 18:23 21:25

FOR

3588, *1063*

GE
1:14[3] 1:15 1:29 1:30 2:5 2:5 2:9 2:17 2:18 2:20 3:5 3:6 3:17 3:19 3:22 3:23 3:25 5:24 6:3 6:7 6:12 6:13 6:21 7:1 7:4 8:9[2] 8:21[2] 9:3 9:6 9:12 9:13 9:25 11:3 12:10 12:13 12:16 13:6 13:8 13:15[2] 13:17 14:13 15:6 15:16 16:10 16:13 17:4 17:5 17:7 17:8 17:13 17:15 17:19 17:20 18:5 18:14 18:15 18:19 18:24 18:26 18:28 18:29 18:31 18:32 19:8 19:13 19:14 19:17 19:21 19:22 19:30 20:3 20:6 20:7 20:11 20:18 21:2 21:7 21:10 21:12 21:16 21:17 21:18 21:30 22:2 22:3 22:7 22:12 22:13 22:16 23:2 23:8 23:9 23:13 23:18 23:20 24:10 24:19 24:20 24:22 24:23 24:31 24:32 24:40 24:44[2] 24:62 24:65 25:21 25:30 26:3 26:7[2] 26:9 26:14 26:15 26:16 26:18 26:21 26:22[2] 26:24[2] 27:5 27:9 27:36[2] 27:37 27:41 28:11 28:15 28:18 28:22 29:2 29:9 29:15 29:18 29:20[2] 29:21 29:24 29:25 29:27 29:32 30:13 30:15 30:16 30:26[2] 30:27[2] 30:30[2] 30:31 30:33[2] 31:12 31:14 31:15 31:16 31:18 31:31 31:32 31:35 31:41 31:44 31:45 31:49 31:52 32:10 32:11 32:12 32:13 32:20 32:26 32:28 32:30 33:10 33:17 33:19 34:8 34:14 34:18 34:21[3] 34:22 36:7 37:7 37:8[2] 37:17 37:27 37:28 37:34 37:35[2] 38:6 38:11 38:14 38:16 39:5 40:15 40:17 41:8 41:19 41:31 41:32 41:36 41:49 41:51 41:52 41:55 41:57 42:2 42:4 42:5 42:18 42:19 42:23 42:25 42:27 42:30 42:33 42:38 43:5 43:9[2] 43:10 43:16 43:18 43:25 43:30 43:32[4] 44:4 44:14 44:17 44:18 44:22 44:26 44:32[3] 44:34 45:3 45:5 45:6 45:11 45:19[2] 45:20 45:21 45:23 45:26 46:3 46:32 46:34 47:4[3] 47:13 47:14 47:15[2] 47:16 47:17[6] 47:19 47:20[2] 47:21 47:22 47:23[2] 47:24[5] 48:4 48:7 48:10 48:14 48:18 49:6 49:7[2] 49:13 49:18 49:30 50:3[3] 50:5 50:10 50:13[2] 50:17 50:19 50:20

EX
1:5 1:11 1:18 1:19 2:3 2:7 2:9 2:19 2:22 3:5 3:6 3:7 3:15 4:1 4:19 5:7 5:8 5:18 5:23 6:1 6:7 6:8 6:9[2] 7:9 7:12 7:24[2] 8:8 8:9[3] 8:17 8:25[2] 8:26 8:28 9:2 9:11 9:14 9:15 9:16[2] 9:19 9:27 9:28 9:30 9:31 9:32 10:1 10:5 10:9 10:10 10:11 10:12 10:15 10:16 10:23 10:26 10:28 12:3 12:4[2] 12:12 12:13 12:14[2] 12:15 12:17[2] 12:19 12:21 12:23 12:24[2] 12:30 12:31 12:33 12:39[2] 12:42 12:44 12:48 13:3 13:9[3] 13:16[3] 13:17 13:19 14:3 14:12[2] 14:13[2] 14:14 14:25[2] 15:1 15:17 15:18 15:19 15:21 15:23 15:25 15:26 16:3 16:4 16:7 16:8 16:9 16:15 16:16[2] 16:22 16:23 16:25 16:27 16:29 16:32 16:33 17:1 17:3 17:14[2] 17:16 18:1[2] 18:3 18:4 18:8 18:9 18:11 18:12 18:18[2] 18:19 18:22 19:2 19:5 19:7 19:9 19:11 19:23 20:5 20:7 20:11 20:20 20:25 21:2 21:6 21:19 21:21 21:23 21:24[4] 21:25[3] 21:26 21:27 21:30 21:36 22:1[2] 22:2 22:3[3] 22:9[6] 22:13 22:15 22:21 22:27[3] 23:7 23:8 23:9 23:15 23:21[2] 23:23 23:31 23:33 24:14 25:6[3] 25:12 25:26 25:27 26:14 26:15 26:17 26:18 26:19[2] 26:20 26:22 26:23 26:24[2] 26:26 26:27[3] 26:29[2] 26:36 26:37[2] 27:4 27:6 27:9[3] 27:11 27:12 27:16 27:20 27:21 28:2[3] 28:4 28:12[2] 28:29 28:40[5] 28:43 29:9 29:22 29:24 29:25[2] 29:26 29:27[2] 29:28[2] 29:36[3] 29:37 29:40 29:41 30:4[2] 30:12 30:15 30:16[2] 30:19 30:21 30:37[2] 31:10 31:11 31:13 31:14[2] 31:16 31:17[2] 32:1[2] 32:7 32:12 32:13 32:18[2] 32:23[3] 32:25 32:29 32:30 33:3[2] 33:5 33:16 33:17 33:20 34:7 34:9[2] 34:10 34:12 34:14[2] 34:18 34:24 34:27 35:8[3] 35:9[2] 35:14[2] 35:15 35:17 35:19 35:21[2] 35:24 35:27[2] 35:28[3] 35:29 36:1 36:3 36:5 36:6 36:7[2] 36:14 36:19 36:20 36:22 36:23[2] 36:24[2] 36:25 36:27 36:28 36:31 36:32[3] 36:34 36:36 36:37 37:3 37:12 37:13 37:14 37:27[2] 38:4 38:5[2] 38:11 38:12 38:13 38:15 38:17 38:18 38:21 38:24 38:26[3] 38:27 38:28 38:30 39:1 39:4 39:7 39:27 39:37 39:38 39:40[2] 39:41 40:5 40:15 40:38

LE
1:4[2] 1:10 1:14 2:11 2:12[2] 2:14 3:6 3:7 3:16 3:17 4:3[2] 4:14 4:20[2] 4:21 4:26 4:28 4:31[2] 4:32 4:33 4:35 5:6[3] 5:7[3]

5:8
5:10[3]
5:11[3]
5:13
5:15[2]
5:16[2]
5:18[2]
6:6
6:7[2]
6:15
6:17
6:18
6:20
6:21
6:22
6:23[2]
6:26
7:5
7:7
7:12
7:13
7:14
7:15
7:19
7:25
7:30
7:32
7:33
7:34[2]
7:36
8:2
8:14[2]
8:21
8:27
8:28
8:29[2]
8:33
8:34
8:35
9:2[2]
9:3[2]
9:4[2]
9:7[3]
9:8
9:15[2]
9:18[2]
9:21
10:7
10:9
10:12
10:13
10:14
10:15[2]
10:17
11:24
11:35[2]
11:42
11:44[2]
11:45[2]
12:2
12:6[4]
12:7[2]
12:8[3]
13:7
13:11
13:15
13:28
13:36
13:52
14:4
14:6
14:10
14:12[2]
14:13
14:18
14:19
14:20
14:21[3]
14:23
14:24
14:29
14:31[3]
14:34
14:53
14:54
14:55
14:56[3]
15:13
15:15[4]
15:30[4]
16:2
16:3[2]
16:5[2]
16:6[3]
16:8[2]
16:9
16:10
16:11[4]
16:15
16:16[2]
16:17[3]
16:18
16:24[2]
16:26
16:27[2]
16:29
16:30[2]
16:31
16:33[5]
16:34[2]
17:5
17:6
17:7
17:11[4]
17:14[3]
18:10
18:13
18:17
18:19
18:24
18:27
18:29
19:2
19:10
19:21
19:22[2]
19:23
19:28
19:34
20:7
20:9
20:19
20:23
20:26
21:1
21:2[6]
21:3[2]
21:6
21:7
21:8[2]
21:11[2]
21:12
21:15
21:18
21:23
22:9
22:16
22:18[3]
22:20[2]
22:23[2]
22:25
22:27
23:11
23:12
23:13
23:14
23:18
23:19[2]
23:20[2]
23:21
23:28[2]
23:29
23:31
23:34
23:41
24:2
24:3
24:7
24:9
24:18
24:20[3]
24:22[2]
25:4
25:5
25:6[6]
25:7[2]
25:12
25:16
25:17
25:21
25:23[3]
25:24
25:30
25:33
25:34
25:37
25:46[3]
25:51
25:55
26:1
26:9
26:16
26:18[2]
26:20
26:24
26:27
26:28
26:44[2]
26:45
27:2
27:5
27:6
27:7
27:10[3]
27:34

NU

1:44
1:48
3:13
3:25
3:26[2]
3:38
3:41
3:46
4:16
4:24
4:25
4:26[2]
4:29
4:35
4:39
4:43
5:8
5:15[2]
6:7[4]
6:11[4]
6:12
6:14[3]
6:17
6:20[2]
6:21
7:3[2]
7:10
7:11
7:13
7:15
7:16
7:17
7:19[2]
7:21
7:22
7:23
7:25
7:27
7:28
7:29
7:31
7:33
7:34
7:35
7:37
7:39
7:40
7:41
7:43
7:45
7:46
7:47
7:49
7:51
7:52
7:53
7:55
7:57
7:58
7:59
7:61
7:63
7:64
7:65
7:67
7:69
7:70
7:71
7:73
7:75
7:76
7:77
7:79
7:81
7:82
7:83
7:87[2]
7:88
8:8
8:11
8:12[3]
8:13
8:15
8:16
8:17[2]
8:18
8:19
8:21
9:14[2]
10:2[2]
10:6
10:8[2]
10:10
10:29
10:33
11:13
11:14
11:18[2]
11:22
11:29
11:31
12:1
13:30
13:31
14:3
14:9[2]
14:11
14:13
14:14
14:32
14:34
14:40
14:42
14:43
15:5[2]
15:6[2]
15:7[2]
15:8[2]
15:10[2]
15:11[3]
15:15[3]
15:16[2]
15:20
15:24[3]
15:25[3]
15:27
15:28[2]
15:29[3]
15:39
16:11
16:28
16:34
16:37
16:38[2]
16:39
16:46[2]
16:47
17:3[2]
17:6
17:8
17:10
18:4
18:6
18:7
18:8
18:9[2]
18:11
18:16
18:17[2]
18:19[2]
18:21[2]
18:23
18:26[2]
18:31[2]
19:9[3]
19:10[2]
19:17[2]
20:2
20:19
20:24
20:29
21:5
21:7[2]
21:13
21:24
21:26
21:28
21:34
22:6[3]
22:12
22:13
22:17
22:22
22:29
22:34
23:9
24:1
24:18
24:20
24:24
25:11
25:13[2]
25:18[2]
26:53
26:62
26:65
27:14
27:21
28:2[2]
28:3
28:5
28:6
28:7[2]
28:9
28:12[4]
28:13[2]
28:15
28:19
28:20[2]
28:21
28:22[2]
28:23
28:27
28:30
29:2
29:3[2]
29:4
29:5[2]
29:6
29:8
29:10
29:11
29:16
29:18[3]
29:19
29:21[3]
29:22
29:24[3]
29:25
29:27[3]
29:28
29:30[3]
29:31
29:33[3]
29:34
29:37[3]
29:38
29:39[4]
31:18
31:29
31:50[2]
31:53[2]
31:54[2]
32:1
32:4
32:5
32:9
32:12
32:15
32:16[2]
32:19
32:24[2]
32:27
32:29
32:36
33:4
33:14
33:53
33:54
34:2
34:6[2]
34:7
34:14
34:23
35:2
35:3[3]
35:6[2]
35:11
35:12
35:13
35:15[3]
35:21
35:29
35:31
35:32
35:33
35:34
36:2
36:7
36:11

DE

1:10
1:14
1:17[2]
1:30[2]
1:37
1:38
1:40
1:42
2:5[2]
2:6[2]
2:7
2:9[3]
2:15
2:19[2]
2:28[2]
2:30
2:35
2:36
3:2
3:7
3:11
3:18
3:19
3:22[2]
3:24
3:26
3:27
3:28
4:1
4:3
4:6
4:7[2]
4:15
4:21[2]
4:24
4:31
4:32
4:34
4:38
4:40
5:5
5:9
5:11
5:23
5:25
5:26
5:29
5:31
6:8
6:15
6:24
7:4
7:6
7:7
7:16
7:21
7:25
7:26
8:7
8:10
8:18
9:4[2]
9:5[3]
9:6[2]
9:12
9:19
9:20
10:13
10:17
10:19
10:21
10:22
11:2
11:10
11:12
11:15
11:18
11:22
11:25
11:31
12:9
12:23
12:28
12:31[2]
13:3
13:16[2]
14:1
14:2
14:7
14:21
14:24
14:26[6]
14:27
15:4[2]
15:6
15:8
15:10
15:11
15:17
15:18
16:1
16:3
16:19
17:1
17:8
18:5[2]
18:12
18:14[2]
19:5
19:9
19:10
19:11
19:15[2]
19:21[5]
20:1
20:4[2]
20:7
20:16
20:19[2]
20:20
21:5
21:14
21:17[2]
21:23[2]
22:5
22:8
22:20
22:26
22:27
23:3
23:6
23:7
23:14
23:18[2]
23:21
24:4[2]
24:6
24:15
24:16[3]
24:19[3]
24:20[3]
24:21[3]
25:11
25:16
25:19
26:1
26:3
26:14[2]
28:20
28:32
28:34
28:38
28:39
28:40
28:41
28:46[3]
28:47
28:56
28:57[2]
28:62
28:67[2]
28:68
29:8
29:13
29:16
29:26
29:29
30:9[2]
30:11
30:12
30:13
30:20
31:6
31:7
31:18
31:19[2]
31:20
31:21[2]
31:23
31:26
31:27
31:29
32:4
32:9
32:20
32:22
32:28
32:31
32:32
32:35
32:36[2]
32:40[2]
32:43
32:47[2]
32:49
33:2
33:7
33:9
33:13[3]
33:14[2]
33:15[2]
33:16[2]
33:19
33:21
34:8[2]
34:9

JOS

1:6[2]
1:8
1:9
1:11
2:3
2:5
2:10[2]
2:11
2:14
2:15
2:24
3:4
3:5
3:15
4:7[2]
4:10
4:13
4:23
4:24
5:6
5:7
5:13[2]
5:15
6:16
7:1
7:3
7:5
7:9
7:11
7:13
8:2[2]
8:6[2]
8:7
8:18
8:26
8:27
8:28
9:9
9:11
9:12
9:22
9:23
9:27[2]
10:4
10:6
10:8
10:14[2]
10:18
10:19
10:24
10:25
10:42
11:6
11:10
11:13
11:14
11:20
11:23
12:6
12:7
13:6
13:7
13:12
13:32
14:1
14:2[2]
14:3
14:4[3]
14:9
14:11
14:12
14:13
15:19
15:63
16:9
17:1[3]
17:2[7]
17:15[2]
17:16
17:18[2]
18:4
18:6
18:7
18:8
18:10
19:1
19:9[2]
19:10
19:17
19:24
19:32
19:40
19:47
19:49
19:51
20:2
20:6
20:9[2]
21:2
21:4
21:10
21:12
21:13
21:21[2]
21:26
21:27
21:32
21:38
21:40
22:17
22:24
22:25
22:26[2]
22:28[2]
22:29[3]
22:34
23:2[5]
23:3[2]
23:4
23:9[2]
23:10[2]
23:13
24:1[4]
24:13
24:15
24:17
24:18
24:19
24:27
24:31
24:32

JG

1:1
1:15
1:32
1:34
2:7
2:10
2:15
2:18
2:28
4:3
4:5
4:9[2]
4:14
4:17
4:19
4:21
5:2
5:15
5:16
5:30
6:4
6:5[3]
6:22
6:31[3]
6:38
6:40
7:2
7:4
7:9
7:12[2]
7:14
7:15
8:5
8:10
8:11
8:20
8:21
8:22
8:24
8:30
9:2
9:3
9:5
9:17[2]
9:21
9:25
9:28
10:16
11:2
11:18
11:35
11:36
11:37
11:38
12:6
12:9
13:5[2]
13:7
13:15
13:16
13:20
14:2
14:3[2]
14:4
14:10
15:18
16:2
16:17
16:18[2]
16:19
16:23[2]
16:24
16:25[2]
16:28
17:3
18:1
18:9
18:10
18:19
18:26
19:6
19:15
19:19[4]
20:6
20:10
20:27
20:28
20:36
20:39
20:41
21:5
21:6
21:7[2]
21:9
21:15
21:16[2]
21:17
21:18
21:22[2]

RU

1:6
1:12
1:13[4]
1:16
1:20
2:13[2]
2:16
3:1
3:9
3:10
3:11
3:17
3:18
4:4
4:6[2]
4:7
4:8
4:15

1 SA

1:5
1:6
1:16[2]
1:22[2]
1:27
2:2
2:3
2:5
2:8
2:9
2:14
2:15[2]
2:17
2:20
2:23
2:24
2:25
2:30[2]
2:32
2:35
2:36
3:5
3:6
3:8
3:9
3:10
3:13[3]
3:14
3:21
4:7[2]
4:10
4:13[2]
4:18
4:19
4:20
4:22
5:7
5:11
6:2
6:4
6:8
6:17[6]
7:2
7:5
7:8
7:9[2]
7:17
8:7
8:11[2]
9:5[2]
9:7
9:9
9:12[2]
9:13[2]
9:14
9:16
9:19
9:20[2]
9:24[2]
10:2[2]
10:7
11:2
11:13
12:19[2]
12:21[2]
12:22[2]
12:23[2]
12:24[2]
13:6
13:7
13:13[2]
13:19
13:21[4]
14:6[2]
14:10
14:12
14:18
14:24
14:26
14:31
14:39
14:44
14:45
15:2
15:6
15:11
15:15
15:23
15:24
15:26
15:29
15:35
16:1[2]
16:7[2]
16:11
16:12
16:22
17:8
17:12
17:17
17:20
17:21
17:26
17:28
17:31
17:33
17:39[2]
17:42
17:47
18:11
18:17[2]
19:5[2]
19:13
19:16
20:4
20:6[2]
20:8[2]
20:9
20:15
20:17
20:21
20:22
20:23
20:26
20:29
20:31[2]
20:34[2]
20:42
21:6
21:8
21:9
21:10
22:3
22:8
22:10
22:13
22:15[2]
22:23
23:4
23:7
23:10
23:17
23:21
23:22
23:26[2]
23:27
24:10
24:11
24:17
24:19
25:8
25:11
25:17[2]
25:21
25:25
25:28
25:34
25:36
25:39
26:9
26:12
26:15
26:18
26:19
26:20
26:21
26:23
27:1
27:4
27:5
27:8
27:12
28:1
28:2
28:9
28:10
28:12
28:13
28:15
28:17
28:20
29:4
29:6
30:6[3]
30:8
30:10
30:12
30:24
30:25
30:26
31:4

2 SA

1:9
1:12[4]
1:16
1:21
1:26
2:7
2:26
3:6
3:8
3:14
3:17
3:18
3:22
3:27
3:28
3:37
3:39
4:2
4:7
4:10
5:12
5:19
5:24
6:6
6:7
6:17
7:3
7:5
7:10
7:13[2]
7:16[2]
7:19
7:20
7:21
7:22
7:23[3]
7:24[2]
7:25
7:26
7:27
7:29[3]
8:4
8:10
9:1
9:7[2]
9:10
9:11
9:13
10:2
10:11[2]
10:12[2]
11:4
11:22
11:25
11:26
12:4[2]
12:12
12:16
12:18
12:21
12:22
13:2[3]
13:12
13:13[2]
13:18
13:22
13:32[2]
13:33
13:37
13:39
14:2
14:7
14:13
14:14
14:16
14:17
14:19
14:25
14:26
14:29
14:32
14:33
15:2
15:6
15:8
15:12[2]
15:14
15:19
15:34
16:2[2]
16:3
16:11
16:12
17:8
17:10
17:11
17:14
17:17
17:21
17:29[2]
18:3[3]
18:5
18:8
18:12
18:13
18:16
18:18[2]
18:31
19:1
19:2[2]
19:6[2]
19:7
19:8
19:9
19:20
19:21
19:22
19:26
19:28
19:32
19:38
19:42
20:11
21:1[2]
21:3
21:4
21:8
21:10
21:14
22:18[2]
22:22
22:23[3]
22:29
22:30
22:31
22:32
22:51[2]
23:5
24:2
24:10
24:14
24:22
24:24
24:25

1 KI

1:2
1:3
1:31
1:35
1:42
1:51
2:7
2:9
2:15
2:17
2:18
2:19[2]
2:20
2:22[6]
2:26
2:28
2:33[2]
2:36
2:37[2]
2:42[2]
2:45
3:4
3:8
3:9
3:11[2]
3:26
3:27
4:7
4:21
4:22
4:24
4:26
4:27[2]
4:28
5:1[2]
5:3
5:6[2]
5:8
5:9
5:11
6:2
6:4
6:6
6:16[3]
6:31
6:33
7:7
7:8
7:12[2]
7:15
7:17[3]
7:18
7:36
7:40
7:42
7:45
7:50[2]
7:51
8:5
8:7
8:11
8:13
8:17
8:20
8:21
8:36
8:39
8:42
8:43
8:44
8:46
8:48
8:51
8:52
8:53
8:64
8:66[3]
9:3
9:5
9:7
9:15
9:16[2]
9:19[2]
9:22
9:24
10:9
10:12[3]
10:23[2]
10:26
10:27
10:29[4]
11:2
11:4
11:5
11:7
11:8
11:12
11:13[2]
11:15
11:16
11:31
11:32[2]
11:34
11:38
11:39[2]
12:1
12:2
12:5
12:7
12:15
12:17
12:24
12:28
12:30
13:6
13:9
13:12
13:17
13:23[2]
13:32
14:4
14:5[3]
14:6
14:9
14:11
14:13[2]
14:15
14:18
14:23
15:4
15:27
16:7
16:13
16:19
16:24
16:26
16:31
16:32
17:5
17:12
17:13[2]
17:14
18:4
18:23
18:25[2]
18:26
18:27
18:41
19:3
19:4[2]
19:7
19:10[2]
19:14
19:20
20:7[5]
20:9
20:10[2]
20:18[2]
20:22
20:25[2]
20:34
20:38
20:39
20:42[2]
21:2[2]
21:4
21:6[2]
21:15[2]
21:22
22:6
22:8
22:12
22:15
22:34
22:43
22:48[2]
22:53

2 KI

2:2
2:4
2:6
2:9
2:18
3:2
3:9[2]
3:13
3:17
3:26[2]
4:2
4:10
4:13[3]
4:14
4:24
4:27
4:38
4:39
4:40
4:41
4:43
5:3
5:17
5:27
6:1
6:5
6:9
6:11[2]
6:16
6:23
6:25[2]
6:33
7:1[2]
7:6
7:7
7:16[2]
7:18[2]
7:20
8:1[2]
8:3[2]
8:5[2]
8:18
8:19
8:27
9:8
9:16
9:20
9:25
9:34
10:3
10:10
10:16
10:19
10:20
10:22
10:24
10:31
11:15
12:7[2]
12:12[2]
12:13
12:15
12:20
13:4
13:7[2]
14:6[3]
14:10
14:26[3]
14:28
15:14
16:8
16:9
16:15
16:18[2]
17:4
17:7
17:12
17:21
17:22
17:32
17:37[2]
18:4
18:6
18:20
18:24[2]
18:26
18:29
18:31
18:36
19:3
19:4

19:8
19:18
19:31
19:34^{8}
20:1
20:6^{2}
20:10
20:12
21:3^{2}
21:5
21:7
22:13^{4}
23:4^{3}
23:7
23:13^{3}
24:3
24:4^{2}
24:7
24:16
24:20
25:3
25:16
25:22
25:26
25:30

1 CH

4:14
4:23
4:39
4:40
4:41
4:42
5:1
5:2
5:20
5:22
6:26
6:49^{2}
6:54
6:70
7:4^{2}
7:11
9:1
9:13
9:26
9:33
10:4
10:13^{2}
11:9
11:19
11:20
11:21
12:8
12:18
12:19
12:21
12:22
12:25
12:29
12:37
12:39^{2}
12:40
13:3
13:4
13:9
14:2
14:10
14:15
15:1^{2}
15:2^{2}
15:3
15:11^{3}
15:12
15:13^{2}
15:22
15:23
15:24
16:1
16:17^{2}
16:21
16:25
16:26
16:34^{3}
16:36
16:41
16:42
17:2
17:5
17:9
17:12
17:14^{2}
17:17^{2}
17:18^{3}
17:19
17:22^{2}
17:23
17:24
17:25
17:27^{3}
18:10
19:3
19:5
19:12^{2}
19:13^{2}
21:6
21:8
21:13
21:17
21:22
21:23^{3}
21:24^{3}
21:25
21:29
21:30
22:1
22:3^{3}
22:4
22:5^{2}
22:6^{2}
22:7
22:9
22:10^{2}
22:14^{2}
22:15
22:18
23:13^{2}
23:24
23:25^{2}
23:26
23:27
23:28
23:29^{7}
24:5
24:6^{2}
25:6^{2}
25:9
26:5
26:6
26:8^{2}
26:10
26:13
26:14
26:29^{2}
26:31
26:32
27:2
27:3
27:5
27:7
27:8
27:9
27:10
27:11
27:12
27:13
27:14
27:15
27:24
27:26
27:27
28:2^{4}
28:3
28:4^{2}
28:5
28:6
28:7
28:8^{4}
28:9^{2}
28:10^{2}
28:13^{3}
28:14^{4}
28:15^{7}
28:16^{3}
28:17^{4}
28:18^{2}
28:20^{2}
28:21^{3}
29:1^{3}
29:2^{6}
29:3
29:5^{3}
29:7
29:9
29:10
29:11
29:14
29:15
29:16
29:17
29:18
29:19
29:21

2 CH

1:3
1:4^{3}
1:9
1:10
1:11
1:15
1:17^{4}
2:1^{2}
2:4^{3}
2:5
2:8
2:9
2:12^{2}
3:3
3:6
4:6^{2}
4:9
4:11^{2}
4:16
4:18
4:19
4:22
5:1
5:6
5:8
5:11
5:13^{3}
5:14
6:2^{3}
6:7
6:8
6:9
6:10^{2}
6:13
6:27
6:30
6:32
6:33
6:34
6:36
6:38
7:3^{3}
7:6
7:7
7:9
7:10
7:12
7:16^{2}
7:17
7:20
8:7
8:9
8:11^{2}
8:14
9:6
9:8^{2}
9:11
9:21
9:25
10:1
10:7
10:10
10:11
10:15
10:17
11:4
11:5
11:14^{2}
11:15^{3}
11:17
11:21
11:22
12:13
13:5
13:8
13:10
13:11
13:12^{2}
14:3
14:6
14:11
14:13
14:14^{2}
15:3
15:6
15:7
15:9
15:15
16:9
16:10
16:14^{2}
17:18
18:2^{2}
18:5
18:7
18:8
18:11
18:32
18:33
19:6^{3}
19:7
19:8^{2}
19:11
20:7
20:8
20:9
20:12
20:15
20:17
20:21^{2}
20:23
20:25
20:26
20:27
20:30
20:33
21:6
21:7
21:19
22:1
22:3
22:4
22:7
22:9
22:11
23:6
23:8
23:14
24:3
24:6^{2}
24:7
24:14
24:18
24:24
24:25^{2}
25:4^{3}
25:6
25:7
25:8^{2}
25:9
25:20
26:8
26:10^{2}
26:14
26:15
26:16
26:18^{2}
26:21
26:23
28:2^{2}
28:6
28:10
28:11
28:13^{2}
28:17
28:19^{2}
28:21
28:23
29:6
29:9^{2}
29:11
29:21^{4}
29:23
29:24^{3}
29:25
29:32
29:34
29:35
29:36
30:2
30:3
30:5
30:8
30:9^{2}
30:14
30:17^{2}
30:18^{2}
30:24
30:26
31:2^{2}
31:3^{5}
31:10
31:16
31:18
32:1
32:7^{3}
32:15
32:20
32:25
32:26
32:27^{6}
32:28^{3}
32:29
33:3^{2}
33:4
33:5
33:7
33:8
33:22
34:3
34:11
34:21^{3}
34:26
35:7^{2}
35:8
35:9
35:14^{4}
35:15^{2}
35:21
35:23
35:24
35:25
36:17
36:21

EZR

1:4
2:68
3:3
3:11^{2}
3:12
3:13
4:2
4:14
4:15
6:8
6:9
6:10
6:11
6:17^{2}
6:18
6:20^{4}
6:22
7:9
7:10
7:16
7:19
7:20
7:23^{2}
8:16^{11}
8:17
8:20
8:21^{3}
8:22^{2}
8:23
8:35^{2}
9:2^{3}
9:6
9:7
9:8
9:9
9:10
9:12^{3}
9:13^{2}
9:15^{2}
10:1
10:4
10:6
10:9
10:13
10:14
10:19

NE

1:5
1:6
1:11
2:3
2:4
2:6
2:8^{3}
2:14
2:18
4:4^{2}
4:5
4:6
4:14
4:18
4:20
4:23
5:2^{2}
5:4
5:5
5:18^{3}
5:19^{2}
6:6
6:9
6:10
6:12
6:13
6:16
6:18
7:2
8:4
8:5
8:9
8:10^{3}
8:11
8:17
9:5
9:8
9:10
9:15^{3}
9:20
9:31^{2}
9:33
9:35
9:36
10:30
10:31^{2}
10:33^{8}
10:34
10:39
11:23^{3}
11:25
12:29
12:43
12:44^{8}
12:46
13:1
13:5
13:6
13:7
13:10
13:13
13:14^{2}
13:25
13:31^{3}

ES

1:8
1:9
1:11
1:13
1:17
1:20
1:22
2:2
2:3
2:7^{2}
2:9
2:10
2:12^{2}
2:15
2:20
3:2
3:4
3:6
3:8
3:13
3:14
4:2
4:5
4:7
4:8
4:14^{2}
4:16
5:4
5:8
5:9
5:10
6:3^{2}
6:4
6:7
7:4^{2}
7:7^{2}
7:9^{2}
7:10
8:1
8:6
8:8^{2}
8:11^{2}
8:13
8:17
9:2
9:4^{2}
9:15
9:16
9:26
9:31^{2}
10:3

JOB

1:4
1:5
1:9
2:4^{2}
2:11
2:13
3:6
3:9
3:13
3:14
3:21^{3}
3:24
3:25
4:11
4:20
5:2
5:18
5:23
5:27
6:3
6:4
6:8
6:10
6:19
6:21
6:22
6:27
6:28
7:2
7:16
7:21
8:4
8:6
8:9
9:17
9:32
10:16
11:4
11:11
11:12
11:15
13:7^{2}
13:8
13:16
13:19
13:24
13:26
14:7
14:16
14:20
15:5
15:22
15:23
15:25
15:31
15:34
16:12
16:17
16:21^{2}
17:1
17:4
17:10^{2}
17:15
18:4
18:8
18:10^{2}
19:15
19:17
19:21
19:24
19:25
19:27
19:29
20:2
20:5
20:7
20:18
20:21
21:4
21:14
21:19
21:21
21:28
22:4
22:6^{2}
22:8
22:17
22:26
23:7
23:14^{2}
23:16
24:3
24:5^{3}
24:8
24:15
24:16
24:17
24:24
27:8
27:14
27:22
28:1^{2}
28:5
28:15^{2}
28:17
28:18
28:24
28:25
28:26^{2}
29:13
29:23^{3}
30:3
30:4
30:23^{2}
30:25^{2}
30:26^{2}
31:2
31:11
31:12
31:18
31:19
31:23
31:28
32:11
32:16
32:18
32:22
33:10
33:13
33:14
33:26
33:32
34:3
34:5
34:9
34:11
34:19
34:21
34:23
34:36
34:37
35:3
36:4
36:7
36:21
36:27
36:31
37:6
37:13^{2}
37:19
38:3
38:7
38:9
38:10
38:19
38:25^{2}
38:39
38:41^{2}
41:4^{2}
41:5
42:3
42:7
42:8^{3}
42:10
42:12

PS

1:6
2:8^{2}
3:2
3:3
3:5
3:7
4:3
4:8
5:2
5:4
5:7
5:9
5:10
5:11
5:12
6:2^{2}
6:4
6:5
6:8
7:6
7:7
7:9
7:13
8:5
9:4
9:5
9:7^{2}
9:9
9:10
9:12
9:18^{2}
10:3
10:5
10:6
10:14
10:16
11:2
11:7
12:1^{2}
12:5^{2}
12:7
13:1
14:5
16:1
16:10
16:11
17:6
17:15
18:17^{2}
18:21
18:22
18:23
18:27
18:28
18:29
18:30
18:31
18:39
18:50
19:4
19:9
21:3
21:4
21:6^{2}
21:7
21:11
22:11^{2}
22:16
22:21
22:24
22:26
22:28
22:30
23:3
23:4
23:6
24:2
25:5
25:6
25:7
25:11^{2}
25:15
25:16
25:19
25:20
25:21
26:1
26:3
26:11
27:5
27:12
28:9
29:10
30:1
30:5^{2}
30:11
30:12
31:2
31:3^{2}
31:4^{2}
31:7
31:9
31:10
31:13
31:16
31:17
31:19^{2}
31:21
31:22
31:23
32:4
32:6
32:11
33:1^{2}
33:4
33:9
33:11
33:12
33:17
33:20
33:21
34:9
35:2
35:7^{3}
35:10
35:12
35:13
35:14
35:20
35:27
36:2
36:9
37:2
37:7
37:9
37:10
37:13
37:17
37:18
37:22
37:24
37:27
37:28^{2}
37:29
37:37
38:2
38:4^{2}
38:7
38:10
38:12
38:15
38:16
38:17
38:18^{2}
38:20
39:7
39:11
39:12
40:1
40:12
40:15
41:4
41:12^{2}
42:2^{2}
42:4
42:5^{2}
42:11
43:2
43:5
44:*title*
44:3
44:4
44:6
44:8
44:10
44:11
44:12
44:16
44:21
44:22^{2}
44:23
44:25
44:26^{2}
45:*title*
45:2
45:6
45:11
45:17
46:*title*
47:*title*
47:2
47:4
47:7
47:9
48:*title*
48:2
48:3
48:4
48:8
48:14^{2}
49:*title*
49:7
49:8^{2}
49:9
49:10
49:11
49:15
49:17
50:6
50:8
50:10
50:12
51:3
51:16
52:5
52:8
52:9^{2}
53:5
54:3
54:6
54:7
55:3
55:6
55:9
55:12
55:15
55:16
55:18
56:1
56:2
56:5
56:6
56:9^{2}
56:13
57:1
57:2
57:6
57:10
58:11
59:3^{4}
59:7
59:9
59:12^{2}
59:15
59:16
59:17
60:2
60:11
60:12
61:3^{2}
61:4
61:5
61:7
61:8
62:*title*
62:5
62:8
62:12
63:1^{2}
63:10
64:9
65:1
65:3
65:9
65:13
66:7
66:10
66:16
67:4^{2}
68:10
68:16
68:18^{2}
68:28
69:1
69:3
69:6^{2}
69:7
69:9
69:13
69:16
69:17
69:20^{2}
69:21
69:22
69:26
69:33
69:35
70:3
71:3
71:5
71:10^{2}
71:11
71:12
71:15
71:24^{2}
72:12
72:15
72:17
72:19
73:2
73:3
73:4
73:14
73:16
73:26
73:27
73:28
74:1
74:4
74:10
74:12
74:19
74:20
75:1
75:6
75:8
75:9
77:7
77:8^{2}
78:5
78:18
78:20
78:29
78:32^{2}
78:37
78:39
78:58
78:69
79:5
79:7
79:8
79:9^{2}
79:13
80:15
80:17
81:4^{2}
81:5
81:15
82:8
83:2
83:5
83:10
83:17
84:*title*
84:2^{2}
84:3
84:10
84:11
85:*title*
85:5
85:8
86:1
86:2
86:3
86:4
86:5
86:7
86:10
86:12
86:13
86:17
87:*title*
88:*title*
88:3
89:1
89:2^{2}
89:4
89:6
89:11
89:17
89:18
89:28^{2}
89:29
89:36
89:37
89:46
89:52
90:4
90:7
90:9
90:10
91:5^{2}
91:6^{2}
91:11
92:*title*
92:4
92:7
92:8
92:9^{2}
93:5
94:13
94:14
94:16^{2}
95:3
95:7
96:4
96:5
96:13^{2}
97:9
97:11^{2}
98:1
98:9
99:3
99:5
99:9
100:5
102:3
102:9
102:10
102:12
102:13
102:14
102:18
102:19
103:6
103:9
103:11
103:14
103:15
103:16
104:5
104:8
104:14^{2}
104:17
104:18^{2}
104:19
104:31
105:8
105:10^{2}
105:14
105:16
105:17
105:32
105:38
105:39
105:42
106:1^{3}
106:8
106:13
106:31^{2}
106:32
106:43
106:45
107:1^{3}
107:8^{2}
107:9
107:15^{2}
107:16
107:21^{2}
107:25
107:31^{2}
107:34
107:36
108:4
108:13
109:2
109:4
109:5^{2}
109:19
109:21^{2}
109:22
109:31
110:4
111:3
111:8
111:9
111:10
112:3
112:6
112:9
113:2
115:1^{2}
115:18
116:7
116:8
116:12
117:2^{2}
118:1^{2}
118:2
118:3
118:4
118:12
118:21
118:29^{3}
119:20
119:22
119:28
119:35
119:39
119:42
119:43
119:44
119:45
119:50
119:66
119:71
119:76
119:77
119:78
119:81
119:82
119:83
119:85
119:89
119:91
119:93
119:94
119:95
119:98
119:99
119:102
119:110
119:111^{2}
119:115
119:118
119:120
119:122^{2}
119:123^{2}
119:126^{2}
119:131^{2}
119:152
119:153
119:155
119:160
119:166
119:168
119:172
119:173
119:174
119:176
120:7^{2}
121:8
122:5
122:6
122:8
123:3
125:1
125:2
125:3
125:5
126:2
126:3
127:2^{2}
128:2
130:5
130:6^{3}
130:7
131:1
131:3
132:5^{2}
132:9
132:10
132:12
132:13^{2}
132:14^{2}
132:16
132:17
133:1
133:3^{2}
135:3^{3}
135:4^{2}
135:5
135:7
135:12
135:13
135:14
136:1^{3}
136:2^{3}
136:3^{2}
136:4^{2}
136:5^{2}
136:6^{2}
136:7^{2}
136:8^{2}
136:9^{2}
136:10^{2}
136:11^{2}
136:12^{2}
136:13^{2}
136:14^{2}
136:15^{2}
136:16^{2}
136:17^{2}
136:18^{2}
136:19^{2}
136:20^{2}
136:21^{3}
136:22^{2}
136:23^{2}
136:24^{2}
136:25^{2}
136:26^{2}
137:3
138:2^{3}
138:5
138:8
139:4
139:6
139:13
139:14
139:20
140:2
140:5^{2}
140:9
141:5
141:6
141:9
142:3
142:4
142:6^{2}
142:7
143:2
143:3
143:8^{2}
143:10
143:11^{2}
143:12
145:1
145:2
145:21
146:5
146:6
146:7
146:10
147:1^{2}
147:8
147:13
147:20
148:5
148:6
148:13
149:4
150:2

PR

1:9
1:11^{2}
1:16
1:18^{2}
1:29
1:32
2:3
2:4^{2}
2:6
2:7
2:18
2:21
3:2
3:12
3:14
3:26
3:32
4:2
4:3
4:13
4:16
4:17
4:22
4:23
5:3
5:21
6:1
6:23
6:26^{2}
6:34
7:6
7:19
7:23
7:26
8:6
8:7
8:11
8:32
8:35
9:4
9:11
9:12
9:14
9:16
10:13
10:21
11:15^{2}
12:6
12:19^{2}
13:22
13:23
16:4^{2}
16:12
16:25
16:26
17:3^{2}
17:13
17:17
17:26
18:6
18:16
19:10^{2}
19:18
19:19
19:29^{2}
20:3
20:16^{2}
21:8
21:12
21:18^{2}
21:25
21:29
22:9
22:11
22:18
22:23
22:26
23:3
23:5
23:7
23:9
23:11
23:13
23:18
23:21
23:27
23:28
24:2
24:6
24:7
24:16
24:20
24:22
24:27
25:3^{2}
25:4
25:7
25:13
25:16
25:22
25:27
26:1
26:3^{3}
26:25
27:1
27:10
27:13^{2}
27:21^{2}
27:24^{2}
27:26
27:27^{4}
28:2
28:8
28:21^{2}
29:5
29:14
29:19
30:8
30:18
30:21^{2}
30:22
30:23
30:30
31:4^{3}
31:8
31:10
31:21^{2}

EC

1:4
1:18
2:3
2:10
2:12
2:16^{2}
2:17
2:21^{2}
2:22
2:23
2:24
2:25
2:26
3:12
3:14
3:17^{3}
3:19^{2}
3:22^{2}
4:4
4:8
4:9
4:10^{2}
4:14
5:1
5:2
5:3
5:4
5:7
5:8
5:9
5:13
5:16
5:18^{2}
5:20
6:2
6:4
6:7
6:8
6:12^{3}
7:2
7:3

7:5 7:6 7:9 7:10 7:12 7:13 7:18 7:20 7:22 8:3 8:7^{2} 8:15 8:16 9:1 9:4^{2} 9:5^{2} 9:6 9:7 9:9 9:10 9:12 10:1 10:4 10:17^{2} 10:19 10:20 11:1 11:2 11:6 11:7 11:8 11:9 11:10 12:13 12:14

CA

1:2 1:7 2:5 2:11 2:14 2:15 3:10 4:4 5:2 5:4 6:5 7:6 7:9 7:13 8:6 8:7 8:8^{2} 8:11

ISA

1:2 1:17 1:20 1:29^{2} 1:30 2:3 2:10^{2} 2:12 2:19^{2} 2:20 2:21 2:22 3:1 3:7 3:8 3:9 3:10 3:11 3:12 3:14 4:2 4:5 4:6^{3} 5:7 5:20^{4} 5:23 5:25

6:5^{2} 6:8 7:4^{2} 7:6 7:8 7:13 7:16 7:18^{2} 7:22^{2} 7:23 7:25^{2} 8:2 8:10 8:11 8:14^{5} 8:17 8:18^{2} 8:19 9:4 9:5 9:6 9:7 9:12 9:13 9:16 9:17^{2} 9:18 9:21 10:3 10:4 10:8 10:13^{2} 10:17^{2} 10:22 10:23 10:25 10:26 11:4 11:9 11:10 11:12 11:16 12:2 12:5 12:6 13:3 13:6 13:10 13:11^{2} 13:17 14:1 14:2 14:9^{2} 14:13 14:21^{2} 14:22 14:23 14:27 14:29 14:31 15:5^{3} 15:6^{2} 15:8 15:9^{2} 16:2 16:4 16:7^{2} 16:8 16:9^{3} 16:11^{2} 17:2 18:4 18:5 19:10 19:15 19:20^{3} 20:3 20:6 21:6 21:15 21:16 21:17 22:5 22:11 22:13 22:16 22:23

22:25 23:1 23:4 23:13 23:14 23:18^{3} 24:3 24:11 24:14 24:18 25:1 25:2 25:4 25:8 25:9^{2} 25:10^{2} 26:1 26:4^{2} 26:5 26:8 26:9 26:11 26:12^{2} 26:19 26:20 26:21^{2} 27:11 28:5^{2} 28:6^{2} 28:8 28:10 28:11 28:15 28:16 28:18 28:19^{3} 28:20 28:21 28:22 28:26 28:27 29:10 29:11 29:14 29:16 29:20^{2} 29:21^{3} 30:4 30:7 30:8^{2} 30:15 30:16 30:18 30:19 30:31 30:33^{2} 31:1 31:4^{4} 31:7^{2} 31:9 32:6 32:10 32:12^{3} 32:14^{2} 32:15 32:17 33:2 33:5 33:22 34:2 34:5 34:6 34:8^{2} 34:10^{2} 34:13 34:14 34:16 34:17^{2} 35:1 35:6 35:8 36:5 36:9^{2} 36:11 36:14 36:16 36:21

37:3 37:4 37:8 37:19 37:32 37:35^{2} 38:1 38:14 38:17^{2} 38:18^{2} 38:21^{2} 39:1 39:8 40:2^{2} 40:3 40:5 40:8 40:10 40:16 40:26 41:7 41:10^{2} 41:13 41:17 41:22 41:28 42:4 42:6^{2} 42:21 42:22^{2} 42:23 42:24^{2} 43:1 43:3^{3} 43:4^{2} 43:5 43:7^{2} 43:14 43:21 43:25 44:3 44:7 44:10 44:14 44:15^{2} 44:17 44:18 44:21 44:22 44:23^{2} 45:4 45:13 45:18 45:22 46:9 46:13 47:1 47:4 47:5 47:7 47:9^{2} 47:10 48:2 48:8 48:9^{3} 48:11^{3} 48:21 49:4 49:6 49:8 49:10 49:13 49:19 49:20 49:23^{2} 49:25 50:1^{2} 50:2 50:7 51:2 51:3 51:4^{2} 51:6^{2} 51:8^{2} 51:10 51:19 52:1

52:3^{2} 52:4 52:5 52:8 52:9 52:12^{2} 52:15 53:2 53:5^{2} 53:8^{2} 53:10 53:11 53:12 54:1 54:3 54:4^{3} 54:5 54:6 54:7 54:8 54:9^{2} 54:10 54:14^{2} 54:15 54:16 55:2^{2} 55:4 55:5^{2} 55:7 55:8 55:9 55:10 55:12 55:13^{2} 56:1 56:4 56:7^{2} 56:11 57:8 57:12 57:15 57:16^{3} 57:17 58:4 58:5 58:14 59:3 59:4^{2} 59:9^{2} 59:10 59:11^{2} 59:12^{3} 59:14 59:17^{2} 59:21^{2} 60:1 60:2 60:9 60:10 60:12 60:17^{4} 60:19 60:20 60:21 61:3^{3} 61:7^{2} 61:8^{2} 61:10 61:11 62:1^{2} 62:4 62:5 62:8^{2} 62:10 63:3 63:4 63:8 63:17 64:3 64:4^{3} 64:5 64:7 64:9 64:12 65:1 65:5 65:8^{2}

65:10^{2} 65:11 65:14^{3} 65:15^{2} 65:17 65:18^{2} 65:20 65:22 65:23^{2} 66:2 66:5 66:8 66:10^{2} 66:12 66:15 66:16 66:18 66:20 66:21^{2} 66:22 66:24

JER

1:6 1:7 1:8 1:12 1:15 1:18 1:19 2:10 2:11 2:13 2:20 2:22 2:25 2:27 2:28 2:37 3:2 3:5 3:8 3:10 3:12^{2} 3:14 3:18 3:21 3:22 3:23 3:24 3:25 4:3 4:6 4:8^{2} 4:13 4:15 4:20 4:22 4:27 4:28 4:29 4:31^{2} 5:4 5:5 5:7 5:9 5:10 5:11 5:22 5:26 5:29 6:1 6:4^{2} 6:6 6:11 6:12 6:13 6:16^{2} 6:22 6:25 6:26^{2} 6:27 6:29 7:5 7:7

7:12 7:16^{3} 7:22 7:29 7:30 7:32 7:33^{2} 7:34 8:2 8:10 8:11 8:14 8:15^{2} 8:16 8:17 8:21 9:1 9:2 9:3^{2} 9:4 9:7^{2} 9:9 9:10^{2} 9:12 9:17^{2} 9:18 9:19 9:21 9:24 9:26 10:2 10:3^{2} 10:5 10:7 10:14 10:16 10:18 10:19 10:21 10:25 11:7 11:13 11:14^{4} 11:17^{2} 11:20 11:23 12:3^{2} 12:4 12:6 12:12 13:7 13:10 13:11^{5} 13:15 13:16 13:17 13:18 13:21 13:22 14:4 14:7^{2} 14:8 14:11^{2} 14:16 14:17 14:19^{3} 14:20 14:21 14:22 15:2^{4} 15:4 15:5 15:13 15:14 15:15 15:16 15:17 15:20 16:3 16:4^{2} 16:5^{2} 16:6^{2} 16:7^{4} 16:9 16:12 16:16^{2} 16:17

17:3 17:4^{2} 17:6 17:8 17:14 17:16 17:25 18:18 18:20^{4} 18:22^{2} 19:5 19:7^{2} 20:4 20:8 20:10^{2} 20:11 20:12 20:13 21:2^{2} 21:9 21:10 22:4 22:6 22:10^{3} 22:11 22:13 22:17^{4} 22:18^{2} 22:20 22:22 22:30 23:10^{2} 23:11 23:12 23:15 23:18 23:27 23:34 23:36^{2} 24:5 24:6^{2} 24:7 24:9 25:5 25:12 25:14 25:15 25:29^{3} 25:31 25:34 25:36 25:38 26:11 26:14 26:15^{2} 26:16 27:10 27:14 27:15 27:16 27:19 28:4 28:13 28:14 29:6 29:7^{2} 29:8 29:9 29:10 29:11 29:13 29:26 29:28 29:32 30:3 30:5 30:7 30:8 30:10 30:11 30:12 30:14^{2} 30:15^{2} 30:16 30:17 30:21 31:6

31:7^{2} 31:9 31:11 31:12^{4} 31:13 31:15^{2} 31:16 31:18 31:20^{2} 31:22 31:25 31:30 31:34^{2} 31:35^{2} 31:36 31:37 31:40 32:2 32:3 32:7 32:8^{2} 32:15 32:17 32:19 32:25^{2} 32:27 32:30^{2} 32:31 32:39^{2} 32:42 32:44^{2} 33:4 33:5 33:9^{2} 33:11^{4} 33:17 33:26 34:5^{2} 34:7 34:11^{2} 34:16^{2} 34:17 34:20 35:6^{2} 35:9 35:11^{2} 35:14 35:19 36:7 36:31 37:2 37:3 37:4 37:9 37:10 37:11 37:15 37:17 38:2^{2} 38:4^{2} 38:5 38:9^{2} 38:27 39:16^{2} 39:18^{2} 40:4 40:10 40:16 41:8 41:9 41:18 42:2^{3} 42:5 42:10 42:11 42:18 42:20^{2} 42:21 43:1 43:3 43:7 43:11^{3} 44:11 44:13 44:14 44:16 44:17

44:27^{2} 44:29 45:3^{4} 45:5^{3} 46:5 46:10^{2} 46:11 46:12 46:14 46:19 46:21 46:22 46:27 46:28^{2} 47:3 48:1 48:5^{2} 48:7 48:9 48:14 48:18 48:20 48:26 48:27^{3} 48:31^{3} 48:32 48:34 48:36^{2} 48:37 48:38 48:40 48:44 48:46 49:3^{2} 49:8 49:12 49:13 49:15 49:19 49:23 49:30 49:33 49:37 50:3 50:9 50:14 50:15 50:16 50:20^{2} 50:24 50:25 50:27 50:29 50:31 50:38 50:39 50:44 51:2 51:5 51:6 51:8^{2} 51:9 51:11 51:12 51:17 51:19 51:20 51:26^{3} 51:29 51:33 51:36 51:37 51:46 51:48^{2} 51:51 51:56 51:62 52:3 52:6 52:16^{2} 52:34

LA

1:5^{2} 1:9 1:10 1:11^{2} 1:13 1:16 1:18 1:19 1:20^{2} 1:22^{2} 2:11 2:13^{2} 2:14^{2} 2:16 2:19^{2} 3:12 3:25 3:26 3:27 3:31 3:33 3:39 3:48 4:4 4:6 4:9^{2} 4:13 4:17^{3} 4:18 4:19 5:4 5:17^{2} 5:19 5:20

EZE

1:10 1:13 1:18 1:20 1:21 2:1 2:2 2:7 3:3 3:5 3:7^{2} 3:26 3:27 4:3 4:5 4:6 4:14 4:15 4:17 5:4 5:6 5:16 6:9 6:11^{2} 7:6 7:8 7:11 7:12 7:13^{2} 7:14 7:16 7:20 7:21^{2} 7:22 7:23 8:12 8:14 8:17 9:4 9:9 9:10 10:10 10:13 10:17 11:5 11:12 11:21 12:2 12:3 12:4 12:6^{2}

12:7 12:24 12:25^{2} 12:27 13:5 13:16 13:19^{2} 13:23 14:7 14:21 15:4^{2} 15:5^{2} 15:6 16:4 16:14^{2} 16:19 16:21 16:33 16:52 16:56 16:59 16:61 16:63 17:17 17:20 18:17 18:18 18:24 18:26 18:31 18:32 19:1 19:11 19:14 20:6 20:9 20:14 20:16 20:22 20:28^{2} 20:31 20:39 20:40 20:42 20:43 20:44 21:7 21:12 21:15 21:21 21:22 21:28 21:32^{2} 22:10 22:30^{2} 23:8 23:10 23:14 23:20 23:21 23:28 23:34 23:37 23:39 23:40^{2} 23:46 24:7 24:9 24:17 24:23 25:4 25:5^{2} 25:6 25:7 25:15 26:5^{5} 26:7 26:17 26:19 26:21 27:2 27:3 27:5 27:15 27:18 27:20 27:31^{2}

27:32 28:10 28:23 29:3 29:5 29:15 29:18^{2} 29:19 29:20^{2} 30:3 30:9 30:18 31:7 31:11 31:14^{2} 31:15^{3} 32:2 32:10^{2} 32:11 32:16^{3} 32:18 32:32 33:2 33:11 33:12^{2} 33:13^{2} 33:17 33:24 33:28 33:31 33:32 34:8 34:10^{2} 34:11 34:17 34:19 34:29 36:5 36:8 36:9^{2} 36:18^{2} 36:21 36:22^{2} 36:24 36:29 36:31^{2} 36:32^{2} 36:37^{2} 37:10 37:16^{4} 37:25^{2} 37:26 37:28 38:7 38:19 38:21 39:5 39:10 39:17 39:19 39:23 39:25 39:29 40:4 40:17 40:42 40:45 40:46 41:6 41:7 41:9 41:24^{2} 42:3^{2} 42:5 42:6 42:8 42:13 42:14^{2} 43:7 43:9 43:19 43:22 43:24 43:25 44:3 44:8 44:11

44:14^{2} 44:22 44:25^{6} 44:28 45:1 45:2^{2} 45:4^{3} 45:5^{3} 45:6 45:7 45:14 45:15^{4} 45:16 45:17 45:20^{2} 45:22^{3} 45:23 45:24^{3} 46:5^{2} 46:7^{3} 46:14 46:15 46:17 47:1 47:5 47:9 47:12^{3} 47:14 47:22 48:1^{2} 48:2 48:3 48:4 48:5 48:6 48:7 48:10^{2} 48:11 48:14 48:15^{3} 48:18 48:21^{2} 48:22 48:23 48:29

DA

1:7 1:10 1:17 2:2 2:4 2:9^{2} 2:12 2:20^{2} 2:23 2:29 2:30^{3} 2:35 2:37 2:44 3:9 4:12 4:18 4:19 4:21 4:22 4:30^{2} 4:34 4:36 5:10 5:19 6:6 6:7 6:21 6:23 6:26^{2} 7:12 7:18^{2} 7:28 8:8 8:15 8:17 8:19 8:22

8:26^{2} 9:12 9:14^{2} 9:16^{2} 9:17 9:18^{3} 9:19^{2} 9:20 9:23 9:24 9:26 9:27^{2} 10:7 10:8 10:11 10:12^{2} 10:14^{2} 10:17^{3} 10:19 11:4^{2} 11:6 11:13 11:17 11:18 11:23 11:24 11:25 11:27 11:30 11:35 11:36 11:37 11:39 12:1 12:3 12:7^{2} 12:9 12:13

HO

1:2 1:4 1:6 1:9 1:11 2:2 2:4 2:5^{2} 2:7 2:8^{2} 2:15 2:17 2:18 2:19 3:2^{2} 3:3^{3} 3:4 4:1 4:4 4:6 4:9 4:10 4:12 4:14 4:16 5:1 5:3 5:4 5:7 5:14 6:1 6:4 6:6 6:9^{2} 6:11 7:1 7:6 7:10 7:13 7:14 7:16 8:6 8:7 8:9 8:10

8:12 8:13 9:1^{2} 9:4^{2} 9:6^{2} 9:7 9:11 9:15^{2} 10:3 10:5^{2} 10:6 10:7 10:12 11:9 12:12^{2} 13:4 13:13 13:16 14:1 14:3 14:4 14:9

JOE

1:5 1:6 1:8 1:10 1:11^{2} 1:13 1:15^{2} 1:17 1:19 1:20 2:1^{2} 2:11^{3} 2:13 2:18 2:21 2:22^{2} 2:23^{2} 2:32 3:1 3:2^{2} 3:3^{3} 3:8 3:12 3:13^{3} 3:14 3:19 3:20 3:21^{2}

AM

1:3^{2} 1:6^{2} 1:9^{2} 1:11^{3} 1:13^{2} 2:1^{2} 2:4^{2} 2:6^{4} 2:11^{2} 3:2 3:5 3:10 4:5 4:13 5:3 5:4 5:5 5:8 5:12 5:13 5:17 5:18 5:23 6:6 6:10 6:11 6:12 7:2 7:3 7:5

7:6 7:11 7:13 8:6^{2} 8:8 8:11 8:13 9:4^{2} 9:6 9:9

OB

10^{2} 15 16 18^{2}

JON

1:2 1:7 1:8 1:10 1:11 1:12^{2} 1:13 1:14^{2} 2:3 2:6 3:6 4:2 4:3^{2} 4:8 4:9 4:10

MIC

1:3 1:5^{2} 1:7 1:9^{2} 1:12^{2} 1:13 1:16^{2} 2:4 2:9 2:10 3:1 3:3 3:7 3:11^{3} 3:12 4:2 4:4 4:5^{2} 4:7 4:9 4:10 4:12 4:13 5:4 5:7^{2} 6:2 6:4 6:7^{2} 6:12 6:16 7:1 7:2 7:3 7:6 7:7 7:9 7:13 7:18

NA

1:2 1:10 1:13 1:14 1:15 2:2^{2} 2:9 2:12^{2} 3:7 3:10 3:14 3:19

HAB

1:3 1:4 1:5 1:6 1:9 1:10 1:12^{2} 2:3^{3} 2:7 2:8 2:11 2:13 2:14 2:16 2:17^{2} 3:13^{2}

ZEP

1:6 1:7^{2} 1:11 1:18 2:4 2:6^{2} 2:7^{2} 2:10 2:11 2:14 2:15 3:8^{2} 3:9 3:11^{2} 3:13 3:18 3:20

HAG

1:4 1:9 1:11 2:4 2:6 2:16 2:23

ZEC

1:5 1:14^{2} 1:15 2:4 2:5 2:6 2:8^{2} 2:9 2:10 2:13 3:8^{2} 3:9 4:10^{2} 5:3 5:9 6:14 7:6^{2} 7:14 8:2^{2} 8:4 8:10^{4} 8:12 8:14 8:17 8:23 9:5 9:7

9:8
9:11
9:13
9:16
9:17
10:2
10:3
10:6[2]
10:8[2]
10:10
11:2[2]
11:3[2]
11:5
11:6
11:12
11:16
12:1
12:3
12:10[4]
13:1[2]
13:3
13:5
14:2
14:5

MAL

1:3
1:4
1:8
1:10[2]
1:11[2]
1:14
2:1
2:5
2:7[2]
2:11
2:16[2]
3:2
3:6
3:9
3:11
3:12
3:16
4:1
4:3
4:4

MT

1:20
1:21
2:2
2:5
2:6
2:8
2:13
2:18
2:20
3:2
3:3
3:8
3:9
3:15
4:6
4:10
4:17
4:18
5:3
5:4
5:5
5:6
5:7
5:8
5:9
5:10[2]
5:11
5:12[2]
5:13
5:18
5:20
5:29[2]
5:30[2]
5:32
5:34
5:35[2]
5:37
5:38[2]
5:41
5:45
5:46
6:5
6:7[2]
6:8
6:13[2]
6:14
6:16
6:19
6:20
6:21
6:24
6:25[2]
6:26
6:28
6:32[2]
6:34[3]
7:2
7:8
7:12
7:13
7:29
8:4
8:9
9:5
9:13
9:16
9:21
9:24
10:10[2]
10:15[2]
10:17
10:18[2]
10:19
10:20
10:22
10:23
10:25
10:26
10:29
10:35
10:39
11:3
11:8
11:9
11:10
11:13
11:14
11:18
11:21
11:22[2]
11:23
11:24[2]
11:26
11:29
11:30
12:4[3]
12:8
12:33
12:34
12:37
12:40
12:42
12:50
13:12
13:15
13:16[2]
13:17
13:21[2]
13:44
14:3[2]
14:4[2]
14:9
14:24
14:26
15:2
15:4
15:9
15:19
15:23
16:2
16:3
16:17
16:23
16:25[2]
16:26[2]
16:27
17:4[4]
17:15[2]
17:20
17:27
18:6
18:7
18:8
18:9
18:10
18:11
18:19
18:20
19:3[2]
19:5
19:9
19:12[2]
19:14
19:22
19:24[2]
19:29
20:1
20:2
20:13
20:15
20:16
20:23
20:28
21:19
21:26
21:32
21:46
22:2
22:14
22:16[2]
22:28
22:30
23:3
23:4
23:5
23:8
23:9
23:10
23:13[2]
23:14[2]
23:15
23:17
23:19
23:23
23:25
23:27
23:39
24:1
24:5
24:6
24:7
24:9
24:14
24:21
24:22
24:24
24:27
24:28
24:38
24:42
24:44
24:50
25:8
25:9[2]
25:13
25:14
25:29
25:34
25:41
25:42
26:9[2]
26:10
26:11
26:12[2]
26:13
26:15
26:17
26:24
26:28[3]
26:31
26:52
26:55
26:73
27:6
27:10
27:18[2]
27:19
27:43
27:47
28:2
28:4
28:5
28:6

MK

1:4
1:16
1:22
1:27
1:37
1:38
1:44[2]
2:4
2:15
2:26
2:27[2]
3:5
3:10[2]
3:21
3:32
3:35
4:17[2]
4:22
4:25
4:28
5:8
5:9
5:19
5:20
5:28
5:42
6:8
6:11[3]
6:14
6:17[3]
6:18[2]
6:20
6:26[2]
6:31
6:36
6:48
6:50
6:52[2]
7:3
7:7
7:8
7:10
7:12
7:21
7:25
7:27
7:29
8:3
8:33
8:35[2]
8:36
8:37
9:5[4]
9:6[2]
9:31
9:34
9:39
9:40
9:41
9:42
9:43
9:45
9:47
9:49
10:2
10:5
10:7
10:14
10:22
10:24
10:25[2]
10:27
10:29
10:35
10:36
10:40
10:45[2]
11:13
11:14
11:18
11:23
11:32
12:1
12:12
12:14[2]
12:23
12:25
12:32
12:36
12:40
12:44
13:6
13:7
13:8
13:9[3]
13:11
13:13
13:16
13:19
13:20
13:22
13:33
13:34
13:35
14:5[2]
14:7
14:9
14:15
14:21
14:24
14:27
14:40
14:55
14:56
14:70
15:10[2]
15:43
16:4
16:8[2]

LU

1:13
1:15
1:17
1:18
1:21
1:22
1:30
1:33
1:37
1:44[2]
1:45
1:48[2]
1:49
1:55
1:63
1:68
1:69
1:76
2:7
2:10
2:11
2:20
2:21
2:25
2:27
2:30
2:34[2]
2:38
3:3
3:8
3:19[2]
4:6
4:8
4:10
4:13
4:16
4:32
4:36
4:38
4:41
4:43
5:4
5:8
5:9
5:14[2]
5:39
6:4
6:19
6:20
6:21[2]
6:22
6:23[3]
6:24
6:25[2]
6:26
6:28
6:32[2]
6:33
6:34
6:35[2]
6:38
6:43
6:44[2]
6:45
6:48
7:4
7:5
7:6
7:8
7:19
7:20
7:24
7:25
7:26
7:28
7:33
7:39
7:44
7:47
8:13
8:17
8:18
8:19
8:25
8:29[2]
8:37
8:40[2]
8:42
8:46
8:47
9:3
9:5
9:12
9:13
9:14
9:24[2]
9:25
9:26
9:33[4]
9:38
9:44
9:48
9:51[2]
9:52
9:56
9:62
10:7
10:12[2]
10:13
10:14[2]
10:21
10:24
11:4
11:6
11:10
11:11
11:30
11:31
11:32
11:42
11:43
11:44
11:46
11:47
11:48
11:52
11:54
12:2
12:6
12:12
12:15
12:19
12:21
12:22[2]
12:24
12:26
12:30
12:32
12:34
12:36
12:40
12:46
12:48
12:52
13:17
13:24
13:31
13:33
14:11
14:14[2]
14:17
14:24
14:28
14:35[2]
15:1
15:6
15:9
15:24
15:30
15:32
16:2
16:3
16:8
16:13
16:15
16:17
16:24
16:28
17:2
17:21
17:24
18:4
18:14
18:16
18:23
18:25[3]
18:29
18:32
19:3
19:4
19:5
19:10
19:12
19:21
19:26
19:37
19:43
19:48
20:6
20:9
20:19
20:22
20:33
20:36
20:38[2]
20:48
21:4
21:6
21:8
21:9
21:12
21:13
21:15
21:17
21:22
21:23
21:26[3]
21:28
21:35
21:38
22:2
22:16
22:18
22:19
22:20
22:27
22:32
22:37[2]
22:45
22:59
22:71
23:8
23:12
23:15
23:17
23:19[2]
23:25
23:28[3]
23:29
23:31
23:34
23:41
23:51
24:29
24:39
24:41

JOH

1:7
1:15
1:16
1:17
1:30
1:39
2:25
3:2
3:16
3:17
3:20
3:24
3:34[3]
4:8
4:9
4:18
4:22
4:23
4:35
4:39
4:42
4:44
4:45
4:47
5:3
5:4
5:10
5:13
5:19
5:20
5:21
5:22
5:26
5:28
5:35
5:36
5:38
5:39
5:46[2]
6:6
6:7
6:24
6:27[3]
6:33
6:38
6:51[2]
6:55
6:58
6:64
6:71
7:1
7:4
7:5
7:8
7:12
7:13
7:29
7:39
7:52
8:14
8:16
8:20
8:24
8:29
8:35
8:42
8:44
9:21
9:22
9:29
9:39
10:4
10:5
10:10
10:11
10:13
10:15
10:19
10:32
10:33[2]
11:4
11:15
11:28
11:39
11:47
11:50[2]
11:51
11:52
11:53
11:56
12:5
12:6
12:8
12:9
12:18[2]
12:27
12:30
12:34
12:35
12:43
12:47
12:49
13:11
13:13
13:15
13:28
13:29
13:37
13:38
14:2
14:3
14:11
14:16
14:17
14:28
14:30
15:5
15:13
15:15[2]
15:21
15:22
16:7[2]
16:13
16:14
16:21
16:26
16:27
17:8
17:9[4]
17:19
17:20[2]
17:24
18:2
18:13
18:14
18:18
18:31
18:37
19:6
19:20
19:24[2]
19:31
19:36
19:38
19:42
20:9
20:17
20:19
21:6
21:7
21:8
21:11

AC

1:4
1:5
1:7
1:17
1:20
2:15
2:25[2]
2:34
2:38
2:39
3:10
3:22
4:3
4:12
4:16
4:20
4:21[2]
4:22
4:27
4:28
4:34
5:8[2]
5:26
5:31
5:36
5:38
5:41
6:14
7:5
7:16
7:21
7:25
7:33
7:40[2]
7:46
8:3
8:7
8:15
8:16
8:21
8:23
8:24
8:27
8:33
9:5
9:11[2]
9:15
9:16[2]
9:21
10:4
10:5
10:14
10:17
10:20
10:22
10:24
10:28
10:29[2]
10:38
10:46
11:8
11:13
11:24
11:25
12:5
12:14
12:19
13:2
13:7
13:8
13:11
13:15
13:27
13:36
13:41
13:47[2]
14:26
15:6
15:14
15:21
15:26
15:28
15:31
16:3
16:4
16:10
16:21
16:28
16:29
17:15
17:16
17:20
17:21
17:23
17:26
17:28[2]
18:3
18:10[2]
18:15
18:17
18:18
18:28
19:8
19:22
19:24[2]
19:32
19:37
19:40[2]
20:1
20:3
20:5
20:10
20:13
20:16[3]
20:27
20:29
20:38
21:3
21:13[2]
21:22
21:26
21:29
21:34
21:35
21:36
22:5
22:10
22:11
22:15
22:18
22:21
22:22
22:25
22:26
23:3
23:5
23:8
23:11
23:17
23:21[3]
23:30
24:5
24:10
24:11
24:21
24:24
24:25[2]
24:26
25:3
25:8
25:11
25:16
25:27
26:1[2]
26:2
26:6
26:7
26:14
26:16[2]
26:20
26:21
26:24
26:26[3]
27:22
27:23
27:25
27:29
27:34[3]
28:2
28:20[3]
28:22
28:27

RO

1:5[2]
1:8
1:9
1:11
1:16[2]
1:17
1:18
1:19
1:20
1:25
1:26[2]
2:1[2]
2:7
2:11
2:12
2:13
2:14
2:24
2:25
2:26
2:28
3:3
3:6
3:7
3:9
3:20
3:22
3:23
3:25
4:2
4:3[2]
4:5
4:9[2]
4:13
4:14
4:15
4:22
4:23
4:24
4:25[2]
5:6[2]
5:7[3]
5:8
5:10
5:12
5:13
5:15
5:16
5:17
5:19
6:5
6:7
6:10
6:14[2]
6:19
6:20
6:21
6:23
7:1
7:2
7:5
7:7
7:8
7:9
7:11
7:14
7:15[2]
7:18[2]
7:19
7:22
8:2
8:3[2]
8:5
8:6
8:7
8:13
8:14
8:15
8:18
8:19[2]
8:20
8:22
8:23
8:24[3]
8:25[2]
8:26[3]
8:27
8:28
8:29
8:31
8:32
8:34
8:36[2]
8:38
9:3[2]
9:5
9:6
9:8
9:9
9:11
9:15
9:17[2]
9:19
9:28
9:32
10:1
10:2
10:3
10:4[2]
10:5
10:10
10:11
10:12[2]
10:13
10:16
11:1
11:7
11:11
11:13
11:15
11:16
11:21
11:23
11:24
11:25
11:27
11:28[2]
11:29
11:30
11:32
11:34
11:36[2]
12:3
12:4
12:17
12:19
12:20
13:1
13:3
13:4[4]
13:5[2]
13:6[3]
13:8
13:9
13:11
13:14
14:2
14:3
14:4
14:6
14:7
14:8
14:9
14:10
14:11
14:15
14:17
14:18
14:19
14:20[2]
14:23
15:2
15:3
15:4[2]
15:8
15:9[2]
15:18
15:22
15:24
15:26[2]
15:27
15:30[3]
15:31
16:2
16:4
16:18
16:19
16:26
16:27

1 CO

1:4
1:7
1:11
1:13
1:17
1:18
1:19
1:21
1:22
1:26
2:2
2:8
2:9
2:10
2:11
2:14
2:16
3:2
3:3[2]
3:4
3:9
3:11
3:13
3:17
3:19[2]
3:21
4:4
4:6[2]
4:7
4:9[2]
4:10
4:15[2]
4:17
4:20
5:3
5:5
5:7[2]
5:10
5:12
6:12
6:13[5]
6:16
6:20
7:1
7:5
7:7
7:8
7:9
7:14
7:16
7:21
7:22
7:26[2]
7:31
7:32
7:33
7:34[2]
7:35[2]
8:5
8:7
8:8
8:9
8:10
9:2
9:9[2]
9:10[2]
9:15[2]
9:16[2]
9:17
9:19
9:23
9:25
10:4
10:5
10:11[2]
10:17[2]
10:23[2]
10:25
10:26
10:27
10:28
10:29
10:30[3]
11:5
11:6
11:7
11:8
11:9[2]
11:10
11:12
11:15[2]
11:17[2]
11:18
11:19
11:21
11:23
11:24
11:26
11:29
11:30
11:31
11:33
12:8
12:12
12:13
12:14
12:24
12:25
13:9
13:12
14:2[2]
14:5
14:8
14:9
14:14
14:17
14:21
14:22[3]
14:31
14:33
14:34
14:35[2]
15:3[2]
15:9
15:16
15:21
15:22
15:25
15:27
15:29[2]
15:32
15:34
15:41
15:52
15:53
16:1
16:5
16:7
16:9
16:10
16:11[2]
16:17
16:18

2 CO

1:5
1:6[2]
1:8
1:11[2]
1:12
1:13
1:19
1:20
1:23
1:24[2]
2:2
2:4
2:9
2:10[2]
2:11
2:15
2:16
2:17
3:6
3:7
3:9
3:10
3:11
3:14
4:5[2]
4:6
4:11[2]
4:15[2]
4:16
4:17[3]
4:18
5:1
5:2
5:4[2]
5:5
5:7
5:10
5:12
5:13[2]
5:14[2]
5:15[2]
5:20
5:21[2]
6:2
6:13
6:14
6:16
7:3
7:5
7:8[3]
7:9
7:10
7:11
7:12[3]
7:13
7:14
8:3
8:9[2]
8:10[2]
8:12
8:13
8:14[2]
8:16
8:17
8:21
9:1[2]
9:2[2]
9:7
9:9
9:10
9:12
9:13[2]
9:14[2]
9:15
10:3
10:4
10:8[3]
10:10
10:12
10:14[2]
10:18
11:2[2]
11:4
11:5
11:9
11:13
11:14
11:19
11:20
11:31
12:1
12:4
12:6[2]
12:8
12:9[2]
12:10[2]
12:11[2]
12:13
12:14[4]
12:15
12:19
12:20
13:4[2]
13:8[2]
13:9

GA

1:4
1:5
1:10[2]
1:12
1:13
2:5
2:6
2:8
2:12
2:16
2:18
2:19
2:20
2:21
3:6
3:10[2]
3:11
3:13[2]
3:18
3:21
3:26
3:27
3:28
4:12
4:15
4:20
4:22
4:24
4:25
4:27[2]
4:30
5:3
5:5[2]
5:6
5:13[2]
5:14
5:17
6:3
6:5
6:7
6:8
6:9
6:12
6:13
6:15
6:17

EPH

1:16
2:4
2:8
2:10
2:14
2:15
2:18
2:22
3:1[2]
3:13
3:14
4:12[3]
4:25
4:32
5:2[2]
5:5
5:6
5:8
5:9
5:12
5:13
5:20
5:23
5:25
5:29
5:30
5:31
6:1
6:12
6:18
6:19
6:20
6:22

PHP

1:4
1:5
1:7
1:8
1:17
1:19
1:21
1:23
1:24
1:25
1:26
1:27
1:29[2]
2:13
2:18
2:20[2]
2:21
2:26
2:27
2:30
3:1
3:3
3:7
3:8[2]
3:12
3:14
3:17
3:18
3:20[2]
4:1
4:6
4:11
4:16
4:20

COL

1:3
1:5[2]
1:7
1:9[2]
1:16
1:19
1:24[2]
1:25
2:1[4]
2:5
2:9
3:3
3:6
3:20
3:24
3:25
4:3[2]
4:8
4:12
4:13[2]

1 TH

1:2
1:5[2]
1:8
1:9
1:10
2:1
2:3
2:5

2:9^{2} 2:13 2:14^{2} 2:16 2:17 2:19 2:20 3:3 3:4 3:5 3:8 3:9^{4} 4:2 4:3 4:7 4:9 4:14 4:15 4:16 5:2 5:3 5:7 5:8 5:9 5:10 5:13 5:15 5:18 5:25

2 TH

1:3 1:4 1:5 1:11 2:3 2:7 2:11 2:13 3:1 3:2 3:5 3:7^{2} 3:8 3:10 3:11

1 TI

1:9^{7} 1:10^{5} 1:12 1:16^{2} 1:17 2:1 2:2^{2} 2:3 2:5 2:6 2:13 3:5 3:13 4:4 4:5 4:8 4:10 5:4 5:8^{2} 5:10 5:11 5:15 5:18 5:23 6:7 6:10 6:19

2 TI

1:7 1:12^{2} 1:16 2:5 2:10 2:11 2:16 2:21 3:2 3:6 3:9 3:16^{4} 4:3 4:6 4:8 4:10 4:11^{2} 4:15 4:18

TIT

1:5 1:7 1:10 1:11 2:11 2:13 2:14 3:3 3:9 3:12 3:14

PHP

1:7 1:9 1:10 1:15^{3} 1:22

HEB

1:5 1:8 1:14 2:2 2:5 2:8 2:9^{2} 2:10^{2} 2:11 2:16 2:17 2:18 3:3 3:4 3:5 3:14 3:16 4:2 4:3 4:4 4:8 4:10 4:12 4:15 5:1^{3} 5:2 5:3^{3} 5:6 5:12^{2} 5:13^{2} 6:4^{2} 6:7^{2} 6:10 6:13 6:16^{2} 6:18^{2} 6:20^{2} 7:1^{2} 7:10 7:11 7:12 7:13 7:14 7:15 7:17^{2} 7:18^{2} 7:19 7:21^{2} 7:25 7:26 7:27^{3} 7:28^{2} 8:3 8:4 8:5 8:7^{2} 8:8 8:10 8:11 8:12 9:2 9:7^{2} 9:9 9:12 9:13 9:15^{2} 9:16^{2} 9:17 9:19 9:24^{2} 9:26 9:28 10:1 10:2 10:4 10:6 10:8 10:10 10:12^{2} 10:14^{2} 10:15 10:18 10:20 10:23 10:26^{2} 10:27 10:30 10:34 10:36 10:37 11:1 11:2 11:5 11:6 11:8 11:10^{2} 11:14 11:16^{2} 11:25 11:26 11:27 11:32 11:40 12:2 12:3 12:6 12:7 12:10^{3} 12:11 12:13 12:16 12:17^{2} 12:18 12:20 12:25 12:29 13:2 13:5 13:8 13:9 13:11^{2} 13:14 13:16 13:17^{4} 13:18^{2} 13:21 13:22

JAS

1:6 1:7 1:11 1:12 1:13 1:20 1:23 1:24 2:2 2:10 2:11 2:13 2:23 2:26 3:2 3:7 3:16 4:14^{2} 4:15 5:1 5:3 5:7^{2} 5:8 5:10 5:14 5:16

1 PE

1:4 1:6 1:13 1:16 1:20 1:23 1:24 1:25 2:13 2:14^{2} 2:15 2:16 2:19^{2} 2:20^{3} 2:21^{2} 2:25 3:5 3:9^{2} 3:10 3:12 3:14 3:17^{3} 3:18^{3} 4:1^{2} 4:6^{2} 4:8 4:11 4:14^{2} 4:17 5:2 5:5 5:7^{2} 5:11

2 PE

1:8 1:10 1:11 1:16 1:17 1:21 2:4 2:8 2:16 2:17 2:18 2:19 2:20 2:21^{2} 3:4 3:5 3:12 3:13 3:14 3:18

1 JO

1:2 2:2^{3} 2:12 2:16 2:17 2:19 3:2 3:4 3:8^{2} 3:9 3:11 3:16^{2} 3:20 4:7 4:8 4:10 4:20 5:3 5:4 5:7 5:9 5:16^{2}

2 JO

2^{2} 7 11

3 JO

3 7

JUDE

3^{2} 4 7 11^{2} 13 21

RE

1:3 1:6 1:9^{2} 1:18 2:3 3:2 3:4 3:8 4:9 4:10 4:11^{2} 5:9 5:13 5:14 6:6^{2} 6:9^{2} 6:11 6:17 7:12 7:17 8:12 9:15^{2} 9:19^{2} 10:6 11:2 11:15 12:4 12:10 12:12 12:14 13:18 14:4 14:5 14:7 14:11 14:15^{3} 14:18 15:1 15:4^{3} 15:7 16:6^{2} 16:10 16:14 16:21 17:14 17:17 18:3 18:5 18:7 18:8 18:9 18:10^{2} 18:11 18:15 18:17 18:19 18:20 18:23^{2} 19:2^{2} 19:3 19:6 19:7 19:8 19:10 20:4^{2} 20:10 20:11 21:1 21:2 21:4 21:5 21:22 21:23 21:25 22:2 22:5^{2} 22:9 22:10 22:15 22:18

FROM

575

GE

1:4 1:6 1:7 1:14 1:18 2:2 2:3 2:6 2:10 2:22 3:8 3:23 4:1 4:10 4:11^{2} 4:14 4:16 6:7 6:17 7:4 7:23 8:2 8:3 8:7 8:8^{2} 8:11 8:13 8:21 9:10 9:24 10:19 10:30 11:2 11:6 11:8 11:9 11:31 12:1 12:8 13:3 13:9 13:11 13:14^{2} 13:17 14:23 15:18 16:2 16:6 16:8 17:14 17:22 18:2 18:3 18:16^{2} 18:22 18:25^{2} 19:4 19:24 19:26 20:1 20:6 20:13 22:12 23:3 23:6 24:5 24:7^{2} 24:8 24:41^{2} 24:46 24:50 24:62 25:6 25:18 25:23 25:29 26:16 26:22 26:23 26:26 26:27 26:31 27:9 27:30^{2} 27:39 27:40 27:45^{2} 28:2 28:6 28:10 29:3 29:8 29:10 30:2 30:32 31:13 31:16 31:27 31:31 31:40 31:49 32:11^{2} 33:18 35:1 35:7 35:13 35:16 36:6 37:25 38:14 38:17 38:19 38:20 39:5 39:9 40:19^{2} 41:42 41:46 42:2 42:7 42:24^{2} 43:34 44:28 44:29 45:1 46:5 46:34 47:10 47:18 47:21 48:7 48:12 48:16 48:17 49:9 49:10^{2} 49:24 49:26 49:32 50:25

EX

2:15 3:5 4:3 5:4 5:5 5:19 5:20 6:6 6:7 6:26 6:27 7:5 8:8^{2} 8:9 8:11^{4} 8:12 8:29^{4} 8:30 8:31^{3} 9:15 9:33 10:5 10:6 10:11 10:17 10:18 10:23 10:28 11:5 11:8 12:5^{2} 12:15^{2} 12:19 12:29 12:31 12:37 12:41 12:42 13:3^{2} 13:10 13:14^{2} 13:20 13:22 14:5 14:19 14:25 15:22 16:1 16:4 16:6 16:32 17:1 17:14 17:16 18:4 18:10 18:13 18:14 19:2 19:14 20:22 21:14 21:22 22:12 23:7 23:15 23:25 23:28 23:29 23:30 23:31^{2} 25:15 25:22^{2} 26:4 26:28 27:21 28:1 28:28 28:42 29:28^{2} 30:14 30:33 30:38 31:14 32:12^{2} 32:15 32:27 33:5 33:7 33:16 34:18 34:29^{2} 35:5 35:20 36:4 36:6 36:11 36:22 36:33 38:26 39:21 40:36

LE

2:9 2:13 4:8 4:10 4:13 4:19 4:31 4:35 5:2 5:3 5:4 5:6 5:8 7:20 7:21 7:25 7:27 7:34^{2} 8:28 9:22 9:24 10:2 10:4 10:7 12:7 13:12 13:41 13:58 14:7 14:19 15:3 15:16 15:31 15:32 16:12 16:19 16:30 17:4 17:9 17:10 18:29 19:8 20:3 20:4 20:5 20:6 20:18 20:24 20:25 20:26 21:7 22:2 22:3 22:4 22:25 22:27 23:15^{2} 23:29 23:30 23:32 24:3 24:8 25:41 25:50 26:36 27:3 27:5 27:6 27:7 27:17 27:18

NU

1:3 1:18 1:20 1:22 1:24 1:26 1:28 1:30 1:32 1:34 1:36 1:38 1:40 1:42 1:45 3:12 3:15 3:22 3:28 3:34 3:39 3:40 3:43 4:2 4:3 4:13 4:18 4:23 4:30 4:35 4:39 4:43 4:47 5:13 5:19 5:31 6:3 6:4 7:89 8:6 8:14 8:16 8:19 8:24 8:25 9:13 9:17 9:21 10:9 10:11 10:33 11:31^{2} 11:35 12:10 12:14 12:15 12:16 13:3 13:21 13:23 13:24 13:25 14:9 14:13 14:19 14:29 14:43 15:23 15:30 16:9 16:15 16:21 16:24 16:26 16:27 16:33 16:35 16:45 16:46^{2} 17:5 17:9 17:10 18:6 18:9 18:16 18:26 18:30 18:32 19:13 19:20 20:6 20:9 20:14 20:21 20:22 20:28 21:4 21:7 21:11 21:12 21:13 21:16 21:18 21:19^{2} 21:20 21:24 21:28 22:5 22:16 22:33^{2} 23:7 23:9^{2} 23:13^{2} 23:27 24:11 24:24 25:4 25:7 25:8 25:11 26:2 26:4 26:62 27:4 30:14 31:14 31:42 32:7 32:8 32:11 32:15 32:21 33:3 33:5 33:6 33:7 33:8 33:9 33:10 33:11 33:13 33:14 33:15 33:16 33:17 33:18 33:19 33:20 33:21 33:22 33:23 33:24 33:25 33:26 33:27 33:28 33:29 33:30 33:32 33:33 33:34 33:35 33:36 33:37 33:41 33:42 33:43 33:44 33:45 33:46 33:47 33:48 33:49 33:52 33:55 34:3 34:4^{2} 34:5 34:7 34:8 34:10 34:11 35:4 35:5 35:8^{2} 35:12 36:3^{2} 36:4 36:7 36:9

DE

1:2 1:19 2:8^{3} 2:12 2:14^{2} 2:15 2:16 2:22 2:36^{2} 3:4 3:8 3:12 3:16 3:17 4:2 4:3 4:9 4:26 4:29 4:32 4:34 4:38 4:48 5:6 6:12 6:15 6:19 6:23 7:4 7:8 7:15 7:20 7:24 8:14 9:4^{2} 9:5 9:7 9:12 9:14 9:15 9:23 9:24 10:5 10:6 10:7^{2} 11:10 11:12 11:17 11:23 11:24^{2} 12:10 12:21 12:29 12:30 12:32 13:5^{2} 13:7^{2} 13:10^{2} 13:13 13:17 13:24 15:7 15:12 15:13 15:16 15:18 16:9 17:7 17:11 17:12 17:15 17:20 18:3^{2} 18:6 18:12 18:15 18:18 19:2 19:13 19:19 20:15 21:9 21:13 21:21 22:1 22:4 22:8 22:21 22:22 22:24 23:9 23:13 23:14 23:15 24:7 25:9 25:19^{2} 26:15^{2} 28:14 28:21 28:24 28:31 28:35 28:49^{2} 28:57 28:63 28:64 29:11 29:18 29:20 29:22 30:3 30:4^{2} 30:11 31:3 31:17 31:29 32:20 32:26 32:42 33:2^{4} 33:7 33:16 33:22 33:27 34:1

JOS

1:4 1:7 2:13 2:23 3:1 3:3 3:9 3:13^{2} 3:14 3:16^{2} 4:23^{2} 5:1 5:9 5:15 6:18 7:2 7:5 7:9 7:12 7:13 7:19 7:26 8:4 8:6 8:7 8:16 8:29 9:6 9:8 9:9 9:22 9:23 9:24 10:6 10:7 10:9 10:11^{2} 10:29 10:31 10:34 10:36 10:41 11:17 11:21^{6} 11:23 12:1 12:2^{3} 12:3^{2} 12:7 13:3 13:4 13:5 13:6^{2} 13:9 13:16 13:26^{2} 13:30 14:7 14:15 15:2^{2} 15:4 15:5 15:7 15:9 15:10 15:46 16:1^{2} 16:2 16:7 16:8 17:7 18:4 18:12 18:13 18:14 18:15 18:17 19:12 19:13 19:29 19:33^{2} 19:34 20:3 20:6 22:9 22:16 22:17 22:18 22:23 22:25 22:29 22:32^{2} 23:1 23:4 23:5^{2} 23:9 23:13^{2} 23:15 23:16 24:3 24:8 24:12 24:17 24:18

JG

1:11 1:14 1:36^{2} 2:1 2:3 2:19^{2} 2:21 3:3 3:19^{2} 3:20 3:21 3:27 4:11 4:13 4:14 5:5^{2} 5:11 5:20 6:8 6:9 6:11 6:13 6:14 7:3 8:13 8:22 9:20^{3} 9:35 9:36 9:48 10:11^{4} 10:16 11:3 11:13 11:16 11:22^{2} 11:23 11:24 11:29 11:31 11:33 12:9 13:5 13:7 13:20 15:13 15:14 16:12 16:17^{2} 16:19 16:20 17:2 17:3 17:8 18:2^{3} 18:7 18:11 18:22 18:28 19:2 19:16 19:18^{2} 19:30 20:1 20:13 20:31 20:32 21:6 21:8 21:19 21:24

RU

1:6 1:13 1:16 2:4 2:7 2:8 4:10^{2}

1 SA

1:14 2:8 2:19 2:30 2:33 3:17^{2} 3:18 3:20 4:4 4:18 4:21 4:22 5:1 6:3 6:5 6:7 6:20 7:3 7:14^{2} 7:16 9:2 9:25 10:2 10:3 10:5 10:9 10:23 12:2 12:20 13:5 13:8 13:11 13:15 14:17 14:21 14:31 14:46 15:2 15:6^{2} 15:7 15:11 15:15 15:23 15:26 15:28 16:1 16:13 16:14^{2} 16:15 16:16 16:22^{2} 17:15 17:24 17:26 17:30 17:33 17:46 17:53 17:57 18:6 18:9 18:10 18:12 18:13 19:8 19:9 20:1 20:2 20:9 20:15^{2} 20:34 21:4 21:5 21:6 21:15 23:13 23:28 23:29 24:1 24:13 25:10 25:26^{2} 25:33^{2} 25:34 25:39^{2} 26:12^{2} 26:19 28:15 28:16 28:23 30:17 30:25 31:1 31:12

2 SA

1:1 1:2 1:3 1:4 1:22^{2} 2:12 2:19 2:21 2:22 2:26 2:27 2:30 3:10^{2} 3:15^{2} 3:22 3:26^{2} 3:28 4:11 5:9 5:13 5:25 6:2^{2} 6:12 7:1 7:8^{2} 7:11 7:15^{2} 7:23 8:4 8:13 9:5 10:14 11:2^{2} 11:4 11:8 11:10 11:15 11:20 11:21 11:24 12:10 12:17 12:20 12:30 13:4 13:9^{2} 13:13 13:17 13:32 14:14 14:18 14:19 14:25 14:32 15:12^{2} 15:14 15:18 15:28 17:11 18:13 18:16 19:7 19:24 19:31 20:2^{2} 20:20 20:21 20:22 21:5 21:10 21:12^{2} 22:3 22:4

22:14
22:17
22:18[2]
22:22
22:23
22:24
22:44
22:49[2]
23:11
23:17
24:2
24:4
24:15
24:21
24:25

1 KI

1:45
1:53
2:13
2:27
2:31[2]
2:33
2:40
2:41
3:20
4:12
4:21
4:24
4:25
4:33
4:34
5:9
6:24
7:7
7:9
7:23
8:35
8:51
8:53
8:54[2]
8:64
9:6
9:12
9:28
10:3
10:11[2]
11:9
11:11
11:23
12:2
12:15
12:24
12:25
13:4
13:5
13:12
13:14
13:21
13:26
13:33
13:34
14:7
14:8
14:10
15:5
15:13
15:19
16:17
18:12[2]
19:17
19:21
20:33
20:34
20:36[2]
20:41
21:21
22:24
22:33
22:43

2 KI

1:4
1:6
1:10[2]
1:12[2]
1:14
2:1
2:3
2:5
2:9
2:10
2:13
2:14
2:21
2:23
2:25[2]
3:26
4:5
4:27
4:42
5:19
5:21
5:22
5:24
5:26
5:27
6:32
8:14
8:20
8:22
9:2
9:8
10:21
10:29[2]
10:31
10:33[2]
11:2[2]
11:11
11:19
12:18
13:5
13:6
13:11
13:17
13:23
14:13
14:24
14:25
14:27
15:9
15:14
15:16
15:18
15:24
15:28
16:3
16:6
16:11[2]
16:12
16:14[2]
16:17[2]
16:18
17:7
17:8
17:9
17:13
17:21
17:22
17:24[5]
17:27
17:28
17:33
18:6
18:8
18:14
18:16[2]
18:17
19:8
20:14[3]
20:18
21:16
23:6
23:8
23:12
23:17
23:22
23:26
23:30
24:7
24:15
24:20
25:5

1 CH

2:23
4:10
5:9
5:23
9:25
10:1
11:8
11:13
13:5[2]
14:14
14:16
16:20[2]
16:23
16:35
17:5[2]
17:7[2]
17:8
17:13[2]
17:21
18:4
18:8[2]
18:11[6]
19:7
20:2
21:2
21:22
21:26
22:9
23:3
23:24
23:27
27:23

2 CH

1:4
1:13[2]
4:2
5:9
6:21[2]
6:23
6:25
6:26
6:27
6:30
6:32
6:33[2]
6:35
6:39[2]
7:1
7:8
7:14[2]
8:15
9:2
9:10
9:26
10:2
11:4
11:14
12:12
13:19
15:8
15:16
16:3
16:9
18:23
18:31
18:32
19:2
19:4
20:2
20:10
20:32
21:8
21:10[2]
21:12
22:11[2]
23:10
23:20
24:5
24:23
24:25
25:5
25:12
25:13
25:14
25:23
25:27
26:18
26:19
26:20
26:21
28:8
28:12
29:6
29:10
30:5
30:6
30:8
30:9
30:10
31:16
31:17
32:22[2]
32:23
33:8
34:3
34:33
35:11
35:15
35:18
35:21
35:22[2]
36:12
36:13
36:20

EZR

1:11
2:59
2:62
3:6
3:7
3:8
3:13
4:12
4:14
4:21
6:6
6:11
6:21
7:6
7:9
8:1
8:31[2]
9:1
9:5
9:8
9:11
10:6
10:8
10:11[2]
10:14

NE

1:9
3:15
3:20
3:21
3:24
3:25
3:28
4:5
4:12
4:16
4:19
4:21
5:13[2]
5:14[2]
5:17
6:9
7:61
7:64
8:3
8:18
9:2
9:13
9:15
9:19
9:20
9:27
9:28
9:35
10:28
11:30
11:31
12:28
12:29
12:38
12:39
13:3
13:21
13:28
13:30

ES

1:1
1:7
1:19
2:6
3:7[2]
3:8
3:10
4:4
4:14
7:7
8:2
8:9
8:15
9:16
9:22[3]
9:28[2]

JOB

1:7[2]
1:12
1:16
1:19
2:2[3]
2:7[2]
2:11
3:4
3:10
3:11
3:17
3:19
4:2
4:13
4:20
5:4
5:15[3]
5:20[2]
5:21
6:13
6:14
6:23[2]
7:19
8:18
9:34
10:14
10:19
13:20
13:21
14:6
14:11
15:18
17:4
18:17
18:18
19:9
19:13[2]
20:24
20:29
21:9
21:14
21:16
22:6
22:7
22:17
22:18
22:22
22:23
23:7
23:12
23:17
24:1
24:9
24:10
24:12
26:4
26:5
27:5
28:4[2]
28:11
28:21[2]
28:28
30:5
30:10
31:2[2]
31:16
31:18[2]
31:22[2]
31:23
33:17[2]
33:18[2]
33:24
33:28
33:30
34:10[2]
34:27
35:3
36:3
36:7
36:10
38:15
39:22
39:29
42:2

PS

2:3
2:12
3:*title*
6:8
7:1
9:13
12:1
12:5
12:7
13:1
14:2
17:2
17:4
17:7
17:9[2]
17:13
17:14[2]
18:*title*
18:3
18:16
18:17[2]
18:21
18:22
18:43
18:48[2]
19:6[2]
19:12
19:13[2]
20:2
20:6
21:10[2]
22:1[2]
22:10[2]
22:11
22:19
22:20[2]
22:21[2]
22:24
24:5[2]
27:9
30:3
31:11
31:15[2]
31:20[2]
31:22
32:7
33:13
33:14
33:19
34:4
34:13[2]
34:14
34:16
35:10[2]
35:17[2]
35:22
37:8
37:27
37:40
38:9
38:10
38:11
38:21
39:2
39:8
39:10
40:10
40:11
41:13
42:6[2]
43:1
44:7
44:10
44:18
49:14
49:15
50:1
50:4
51:2[2]
51:9
51:11[2]
51:14
53:2
55:1
55:8
55:11
55:12
55:18
56:13[2]
57:3[2]
58:3
59:*title*
59:1[2]
59:2[2]
60:11
61:2
61:3
62:1
62:4
62:5
64:1
64:2[2]
66:20
68:20
68:22[2]
68:26
69:5
69:14
69:17
71:5
71:6
71:12
71:17
71:20
72:8[2]
72:14
73:27[2]
75:6[3]
76:8
78:4
78:23
78:30
78:42
78:50
78:70
78:71
80:14
80:18
81:6[2]
83:4
84:7
84:11
85:3
85:11
86:13
88:5
88:8
88:14
88:15
88:18
89:33
89:48
90:2
91:3[2]
93:2
94:13
96:2
101:4
101:8
102:2
102:19[2]
103:4
103:12[2]
103:17
104:13
104:21
105:13[2]
106:10[2]
106:47
106:48
107:2
107:3[4]
107:20
107:41
108:12
109:15
109:17
109:20
109:31
110:3
113:2
113:3
114:1
115:18
116:8[3]
119:10
119:19
119:21
119:22
119:29
119:37
119:51
119:101
119:102
119:110
119:115
119:118
119:134
119:150
119:155
119:157
119:160
120:2[2]
121:1
121:2
121:7
121:8
125:2
129:1
129:2
130:8
131:3
132:11
135:7
136:11
136:24
139:7[2]
139:12
139:15
139:19
140:1[2]
140:4[2]
140:9
142:6
143:7
143:9
144:7[2]
144:10
144:11
148:1
148:7

PR

1:15
1:33
2:12
2:16[2]
2:22
3:7
3:21
3:26
3:27
4:5
4:15
4:21
4:24[2]
4:27
5:7
5:8
6:5[2]
6:24[2]
7:5[2]
8:23[2]
10:2
11:4
13:14
13:19
14:7
14:14
14:16
14:27
15:24
15:29
16:1
16:6
16:17
17:13
19:4
19:7
19:14
19:27
20:3
20:9
21:23
22:5
22:6
22:15
22:27
23:4
23:13
23:14
24:18
25:4
25:5
25:17
25:25
27:22
28:9
29:21
29:26
30:8
30:12
30:14[2]
31:14

EC

1:7
2:10[2]
2:24
3:5
3:11
3:14
7:18
7:23
7:26
8:10
10:5
11:10[2]
12:11

CA

3:4
4:1
4:2
4:8[6]
4:15
5:7
6:5[2]
6:6
8:5

ISA

1:6
1:15
1:16
2:3
2:6
2:22
3:1
4:4
4:6[3]
5:23
5:26[2]
6:6
7:17[2]
8:17[2]
8:18
9:7
9:14
10:2[2]
10:3
10:27[2]
11:11[8]
11:12
11:16
13:5[2]
13:6
13:20
14:3[3]
14:9[2]
14:12
14:22
14:25[2]
14:31
15:1
15:4
16:1
17:1
17:3[2]
18:2
18:7[2]
19:5
20:2[2]
20:6
21:1[2]
21:15[4]
22:3
22:4
22:14
22:19[2]
22:24
23:1
24:14
24:16
24:18[2]
25:4[2]
25:8[2]
27:12
28:9[2]
28:19
28:22
28:29
29:13
29:15
30:6
30:11
30:14
30:27
31:6
31:8
32:2[2]
32:15
33:15[3]
34:4[2]
34:10
34:17
36:2
37:8
37:14
37:20
38:7
38:12[2]
38:13
38:17
39:3[2]
39:7
40:21[2]
40:27[2]
41:2
41:4
41:9[2]
41:25[2]
41:26
42:7
42:10
42:11
43:5[2]
43:6[2]
44:2
44:8
44:24
45:6[2]
45:8
45:21[2]
46:3[2]
46:7
46:10[2]
46:11[2]
46:12
47:11
47:12
47:13
47:14
47:15
48:3
48:5
48:6
48:7
48:8[2]
48:16[2]
48:19
48:20
49:1[3]
49:5
49:12[4]
49:24
50:6
51:4
51:8
52:2[2]
52:11
53:3
53:8[2]
54:8
54:10
54:14[2]
55:10
56:2[2]
56:3
56:6
56:11
57:1
58:7
58:9
58:13[2]
59:2
59:9
59:11
59:13[2]
59:15
59:19[2]
59:20
59:21
60:4
60:6
60:9
63:1[2]
63:15[2]
63:16
63:17[2]
64:7
65:16
66:6[2]
66:23[2]

JER

2:5
2:25[2]
2:35
2:37
3:1
3:4
3:19
3:20
3:23[2]
3:24
3:25
4:6
4:7[2]
4:8
4:12
4:14
4:15[2]
4:16
4:28
5:15
5:25
6:8
6:13[2]
6:20[2]
6:22[2]
7:1
7:28
7:34[2]
8:10[2]
8:13
8:16
9:2
9:3
9:21[2]
10:9[2]
10:11[2]
10:13
11:1
11:4
11:15
11:19
12:2
12:12
12:14
13:6
13:7
13:20
13:25
15:7
15:19
16:5
16:15[2]
16:16[2]
16:17[2]
16:19
17:4
17:5
17:8
17:12
17:13
17:16
17:26[6]
18:1
18:8
18:11
18:14[2]
18:15
18:18[3]
18:20
18:22
18:23
19:14
20:2
20:7[3]
20:13
20:17
21:1
22:20
22:21
23:8
23:14
23:15
23:22[2]
23:30
24:1
24:10
25:3
25:5[2]
25:10
25:30[2]
25:32[2]
25:33
26:1
26:3
26:10
27:1
27:10
27:16
27:20
28:3
28:6
28:10
28:11
28:12
28:16
29:1[2]
29:2
29:4
29:14[2]
29:20
30:1
30:8
30:10[2]
30:21
31:8[2]
31:11
31:13
31:16[3]
31:34
31:36[2]
31:38
32:1
32:30
32:31[2]
32:40[2]
33:5
33:8
34:1
34:8
34:12
34:14
34:21
35:1
35:15
36:1
36:2[2]
36:3
36:4
36:6
36:7
36:9
36:29
36:32
37:5
37:9
37:11
37:17
38:10
38:14
38:25
40:1[2]
40:4
41:5[3]
41:6
41:14
41:15
41:16[3]
42:1
42:4
42:8
42:11
42:17
43:5
43:12
44:7
44:5
44:12
46:16
46:27[2]
47:4
48:2
48:3
48:10
48:11[2]
48:18
48:33[3]
48:34
48:42
48:44
48:45
49:5
49:7
49:14
49:16
49:19[2]
49:32
49:36
49:38
50:6
50:9[2]
50:16
50:26
50:39
50:41[2]
50:44[2]
51:16
51:25
51:45
51:48
51:53
51:54[2]
51:64
52:3
52:8
52:29

LA

1:6
1:13
1:14
1:16
2:1
2:3
2:8
2:9
3:17
3:18
3:50
3:66
5:14[2]
5:16
5:19

EZE

1:19
1:21
1:25
1:27[2]
3:12
3:17
3:18
3:19[2]
3:20
4:8
4:10
4:11
4:14
6:9
7:20
7:22
7:26[2]
8:2[2]
8:6
9:2
9:3
10:2
10:4
10:6[2]
10:7
10:16[2]
10:18
10:19
11:15
11:17
11:18
11:23
11:24
12:3
12:16[3]
12:19
13:20
13:22
14:5
14:6[2]
14:7
14:8
14:9
14:11
14:13
14:17
14:19
14:21
15:7
16:9
16:34
16:41
16:42
17:22
18:8
18:17
18:21
18:23
18:26
18:27
18:28
18:30
18:31
19:8
20:17
20:34
20:38
20:41
20:47
21:3
21:4[2]
22:5
22:26
23:8
23:17
23:18[2]
23:22
23:27[2]
23:28
23:40
23:42
24:13
24:16
24:25
25:7
25:9[2]
25:13[2]
26:4
26:7
26:16
27:5
27:7[2]
27:29
28:3
28:15
28:16
28:18
28:25
29:10
29:13
30:6
30:9
31:12
32:13
33:6
33:7
33:8
33:9[2]
33:11[2]
33:12
33:14
33:18
33:19
33:30
34:10[2]
34:13[2]
35:7
36:24
36:25[2]
36:29
36:33
37:9
37:21
38:8
38:15
39:2
39:22
39:23
39:24
39:27
39:29
40:13
40:15
40:19
40:23
40:27
41:7
41:16
41:20
42:6
42:9[2]
43:2
43:9
43:14[2]
43:15
44:10[2]
44:15
45:7[3]
45:9
46:18
47:1[3]
47:10
47:15
47:17
47:18[5]
47:19
47:20
48:1
48:2
48:3
48:4
48:5
48:6
48:7
48:8[2]
48:22[2]
48:23
48:24
48:25
48:26
48:27
48:28
48:35

DA

2:1
2:5
2:8
2:15
3:17
4:3
4:13
4:14[2]
4:16
4:23
4:25
4:31[2]
4:32
4:33
4:34
5:20[2]
5:21
5:24
6:18
6:20
6:27
7:3[2]
7:4
7:7
7:10
7:19
7:23
7:24
8:5
9:5[2]
9:12
9:16
9:25
10:12
11:22
12:11

HO

1:2
2:2
2:15
4:12
5:3
5:6
7:4
7:13
8:6
9:1
9:11[3]
9:12
10:5
10:9
11:2
11:7
11:10
12:9
13:4
13:14[3]
13:15
14:4
14:8

JOE

1:5
1:9
1:12
1:13
1:15
1:16
2:20
3:6
3:16
3:20

AM

1:2[2]
1:5[2]
1:8[2]
2:3
2:9[2]
2:10
2:14
3:1
3:5
3:11
4:7
5:11
5:12
5:19
5:23
6:2
6:14
8:12[2]
9:3
9:7[2]
9:8

OB

1

JON

1:3[2]
1:10
1:15
2:6
3:5
3:6[2]
3:8[2]
3:9
3:10
4:3
4:6

MIC

1:2
1:12
1:16
2:4
2:8[2]
2:9[2]
3:2[2]
3:3
3:4
4:2
4:7
4:10
5:2[2]
5:6
5:7
6:5
7:5
7:12[5]
7:20

NA

1:13
2:13
3:7
3:8

HAB

1:8
1:12
2:9
3:3[2]
3:17

ZEP

1:2
1:3
1:4
1:6
1:10[3]
1:11
3:10

HAG

1:10[2]
2:15[2]
2:18[3]
2:19

ZEC

1:4[2]
1:6
3:4[2]
6:1
6:5
6:10
6:12
8:7[2]
9:5
9:7
9:10[4]
13:5
14:2
14:5
14:8
14:10[3]
14:13
14:16

FROM—*continued*

MAL 1:5 1:11 2:6 3:5 3:7^{2}

MT 1:17^{3} 1:21 1:24 2:1 2:16 3:7 3:13 3:17 4:17 4:21 4:25^{5} 5:18 5:29 5:30 5:42 6:13 7:23 8:1 8:11 8:30 9:9 9:15 9:16 9:22 11:12 11:25 12:15 12:38 12:42 12:44 13:12 13:27 13:35 13:49 14:2 15:8 15:18 15:27 15:28 15:29 16:1 16:21 16:22 17:9^{2} 17:18 18:8 18:9 18:35 19:1 19:8 19:12 19:20 20:8 20:29 21:8 21:25^{2} 21:43 22:46 23:35 24:1 24:29 24:31 25:28 25:29 25:32^{2} 25:34 25:41 26:16 26:39 26:42 26:47 27:31 27:40 27:42 27:45 27:51 27:55 27:64 28:2^{2} 28:7 28:8

MK 1:9 1:11 1:42 1:45 2:20 2:21 3:7^{2} 3:8^{3} 3:22 4:25 5:35 6:1 6:2 6:10 6:14 6:16 7:1 7:4 7:6 7:15 7:17 7:18 7:21 7:23 7:24 7:31 7:33 8:3 8:4 8:11 9:9^{2} 9:10 10:1 10:6 10:20 11:12 11:20 11:30 11:31 12:2 12:25 12:34 13:19 13:27^{2} 14:35 14:36 14:43 14:52 15:20 15:30 15:32 15:38 16:3 16:8 16:12

LU 1:2 1:3 1:15 1:26 1:38 1:45 1:48 1:50 1:52 1:71^{2} 1:78 2:1 2:4 2:15 2:36 2:37 3:7 3:22 4:1 4:9 4:13 4:42 5:3 5:8 5:10 5:13 5:35 6:17 6:22 7:6 7:18 7:37 8:49 9:5 9:7 9:33 9:37 9:39 9:45 9:54 10:7 10:18 10:21 10:30 10:42 11:4 11:7 11:16 11:22 11:31 11:50 11:51 12:36 12:52 12:58 13:12 13:15 13:16 13:27 13:29^{4} 16:3 16:18 16:21 16:26^{2} 16:30 16:31 17:7 17:29 18:21 18:34 19:8 19:24 19:26^{2} 19:39 19:42 20:4 20:5 20:35 21:11 22:41 22:42 22:43 22:45 23:5 23:49 23:55 24:2 24:9 24:13 24:46 24:49 24:51

JOH 1:6 1:19 1:31 2:22 3:2 3:13 3:27 3:31^{2} 4:11 5:24 5:34 5:41 5:44 6:23 6:31 6:32^{2} 6:33 6:38 6:41 6:42 6:50 6:51 6:58 6:64 6:66 7:29 8:23^{2} 8:25 8:42 8:44 9:29 9:30 10:5 10:18 10:32 11:41 11:53 12:1 12:9 12:17 12:27 12:28 12:32 12:36 13:3 13:4 14:7 15:26^{2} 15:27 16:22 16:27 16:28 16:30 17:8 17:15 18:3 18:28 18:36 19:11 19:12 19:23 19:27 20:1 20:9 21:8 21:14

AC 1:4 1:11 1:12^{2} 1:22^{2} 1:25 2:2 2:40 2:46 3:2 3:15 3:19 3:23 3:24 3:26 4:2 4:10 5:38 5:41 7:3 7:4 7:33 7:39 8:10 8:26 8:33 9:3 9:8 9:14 9:18 10:17 10:21 10:22 10:23 10:37 10:41 11:4 11:5 11:9 11:11 11:27 12:7 12:10 12:11 12:19 12:25 13:4 13:8 13:13^{2} 13:14 13:29 13:30 13:31 13:34 13:39^{2} 13:46 14:8 14:15 14:17 14:19 14:26 15:1 15:18 15:19 15:20^{4} 15:24 15:29^{5} 15:33 15:38^{2} 15:39 16:11 16:12 17:3 17:27 17:31 17:33 18:1 18:2^{2} 18:5 18:6 18:16 18:21 19:9 19:12^{2} 19:35 20:6 20:9 20:17 20:18 20:20 20:26 21:1^{2} 21:7 21:10 21:25^{4} 22:5 22:6 22:22 22:29 22:30 23:10 23:21 24:18 25:1 25:7 26:4 26:5 26:10 26:12 26:13 26:17^{2} 26:18^{2} 26:23 26:26 27:4 27:21 27:34 27:43 28:13 28:15 28:17 28:23

RO 1:4 1:7 1:17 1:18 1:20 4:24 5:9 5:14 6:4 6:7 6:9 6:13 6:17^{2} 6:18 6:20 6:22 7:2 7:3 7:4 7:6 7:24 8:2 8:11^{2} 8:21 8:35 8:39 9:3 10:6 10:7 10:9 11:15 11:26 15:19 15:22 15:31 16:*sub.*

1 CO 1:3^{2} 4:7 5:2 5:13 7:11 7:27 9:19 10:14 14:36 15:12 15:20 15:41 15:47 16:*sub.*

2 CO 1:2^{2} 1:10 2:3 2:13 3:1 3:18 5:2 5:5 5:6 6:17 7:1 11:3 11:9^{2} 11:12 12:8 13:*sub.*

GA 1:1 1:3^{2} 1:4 1:6 1:8 1:15 2:12 3:13 4:1 4:24 5:4 6:17 6:*sub.*

EPH 1:2^{2} 1:20 2:12^{2} 3:9 4:16 4:31 4:18 5:14 6:23 6:*sub.*

PHP 1:2^{2} 1:5 3:20 4:15 4:18 4:*sub.*

COL 1:2 1:13 1:16 1:18 1:23 1:26^{2} 2:12 2:19 2:20 4:16 4:*sub.*

1 TH 1:1 1:8 1:9 1:10^{3} 2:17 3:6 4:3 4:16 5:22 5:*sub.*

2 TH 1:2 1:7 1:9^{2} 2:1 2:13 3:2 3:3 3:6 3:*sub.*

1 TI 1:2 1:6 4:1 4:3 5:13 6:5 6:10 6:*sub.*

2 TI 1:2 1:3 1:15 2:8 2:19 2:21 3:5 3:15 4:4 4:18 4:*sub.*

TIT 1:4 1:14 2:14 3:*sub.*

PHM 3 *sub.*

HEB 3:12 4:3 4:4 4:10^{2} 5:1 5:7 6:1 6:7 7:6 7:26 8:11 9:14 10:13 10:22 11:15 11:19^{2} 12:25^{2} 13:20 13:*sub.*

JAS 1:17^{2} 1:27 3:15 3:17 4:1 4:7 5:19 5:20^{2}

1 PE 1:3 1:12 1:18^{2} 1:21 2:11 3:10 4:1

2 PE 1:9 1:17^{2} 1:18 2:8 2:14 2:18 2:21 3:4 3:17

1 JO 1:1 1:7 1:9 2:7^{2} 2:13 2:14 2:19 2:20 2:24^{2} 3:8 3:11 3:14 3:17 4:21 5:21

2 JO 3^{2} 4 5 6

JUDE 14 24

RE 1:4^{2} 1:5^{2} 2:5 3:10 3:12 6:4 6:16^{2} 7:2 7:17 8:10 9:1 9:6 9:13 10:1 10:4 10:8 11:11 11:12 12:14 13:8 13:13 14:2 14:3 14:4 14:13^{2} 14:18 15:8^{2} 16:17 17:8 18:1 18:4 18:14^{2} 20:1 20:9 20:11 21:2 21:4 21:10 22:19^{2}

HE

1931, *846*

GE 1:5 1:10 1:16 1:27^{2} 1:31 2:2^{2} 2:3 2:8^{2} 2:19 2:21^{2} 2:22 3:1 3:6 3:10 3:11 3:16 3:17 3:22 3:23 3:24 4:4 4:5 4:9 4:10 4:17 4:20 4:21 4:26 5:1 5:2 5:4^{2} 5:7 5:8 5:10 5:11 5:13 5:14 5:16 5:17 5:18 5:19 5:20 5:22 5:24 5:26 5:27 5:29 5:30 5:31 6:3 6:6 6:22 8:6 8:7 8:8 8:9 8:10 8:12 9:6 9:19 9:21 9:25 9:26 9:27 9:29 10:8 10:9 11:11 11:13 11:15 11:17 11:19 11:23 11:25 12:4 12:7 12:8^{2} 12:11^{2} 12:16 12:20 12:26 13:1^{2} 13:3 13:4 14:13 14:14 14:15 14:16 14:18 14:19 14:20 15:4 15:5^{2} 15:6 15:7 15:8 15:9 15:10^{2} 15:13 16:3 16:8 16:12^{3} 17:12 17:13 17:14 17:20 17:22 17:24 17:25 18:1 18:2^{2} 18:7 18:8^{2} 18:9 18:10 18:15 18:19^{2} 18:28 18:29^{2} 18:30^{2} 18:31^{2} 18:32^{2} 18:33 19:1 19:2 19:3^{2} 19:9 19:14 19:16 19:17 19:21 19:25 19:27 19:28 19:29 19:30^{2} 19:33 19:35 20:4 20:5^{2} 20:7 20:13 20:16^{2} 21:1 21:13 21:17 21:20 21:21 21:30 21:31 22:1 22:2 22:6 22:7^{2} 22:11 22:12 23:8 23:9^{3} 23:13 23:16 24:2 24:7 24:10 24:11 24:12 24:15 24:27 24:30^{4} 24:31 24:32 24:33^{2} 24:34 24:35 24:36 24:40 24:52 24:53 24:54^{2} 24:56 24:62 24:63 24:66 24:67 25:5 25:6 25:7 25:17 25:18 25:20 25:28 25:29 25:33 25:34 26:7^{3} 26:8 26:11 26:13 26:14 26:18 26:20 26:21 26:22^{3} 26:23 26:25 26:30 26:33 26:34 27:1^{3} 27:2 27:9 27:10 27:14 27:18 27:20 27:22 27:23^{2} 27:24 27:25^{5} 27:27 27:29 27:31 27:32 27:33^{2} 27:34 27:35 27:36^{6} 27:45 28:5 28:6 28:9 28:11^{2} 28:12 28:16 28:17 28:18 28:19 29:1 29:5 29:6 29:7 29:9 29:12 29:13^{2} 29:14 29:20 29:23^{2} 29:25 29:28 29:30 29:31 29:33 30:2 30:15 30:16 30:28 30:29 30:31 30:35^{2} 30:36 30:38 30:40 30:42 31:1^{2} 31:8^{2} 31:12 31:15 31:18^{3} 31:20 31:21 31:23 31:33^{2} 31:35 31:49 32:2^{2} 32:4 32:6 32:7 32:11 32:13 32:14 32:16 32:17 32:18 32:19 32:20^{2} 32:22 32:23^{2} 32:25^{4} 32:26^{2} 32:27^{2} 32:28 32:29^{2} 32:31^{2} 32:32 33:1 33:2 33:3^{2} 33:5^{2} 33:8^{2} 33:11^{2} 33:12 33:13 33:15 33:18 33:19^{2} 33:20 34:2 34:3 34:5 34:7 34:13 34:19^{2} 34:31 35:6 35:7^{2} 35:9 35:10 35:13 35:14^{3} 36:6 36:24 36:43 37:3^{2} 37:5 37:6 37:9 37:10 37:13 37:14^{3} 37:15 37:16 37:18 37:21 37:22 37:27 37:29 37:30 37:33 37:35^{2} 38:2 38:3 38:5 38:9^{3} 38:10^{2} 38:11^{2} 38:12 38:15 38:16^{2} 38:17 38:18^{2} 38:20 38:21 38:22 38:26 38:29 39:2^{2} 39:3 39:4^{4} 39:5^{3} 39:6^{5} 39:8^{3} 39:9 39:10 39:12 39:13 39:14^{2} 39:15^{2} 39:18 39:20 39:22 39:23 40:3 40:4 40:7 40:16 40:20^{2} 40:21^{2} 40:22 41:1 41:5 41:8 41:11 41:12^{2} 41:13^{3} 41:14 41:25 41:28 41:43^{3} 41:45 41:46 41:48^{2} 41:49 41:51 41:52 41:55 42:2 42:4 42:6 42:7^{2} 42:9 42:12 42:17 42:21 42:23 42:24 42:25 42:27 42:28 42:38^{2} 43:7 43:14 43:16 43:18 43:23^{2} 43:24 43:27^{2} 43:28 43:29^{2} 43:30^{2} 43:31 43:34 44:1 44:2 44:5 44:6^{2} 44:10^{2} 44:12 44:14 44:16 44:17^{2} 44:20 44:22 44:28 44:31^{2} 45:1 45:2 45:4 45:8 45:14 45:15 45:22^{2} 45:23 45:24^{2} 45:26^{2} 45:27^{2} 46:1 46:2 46:3 46:7 46:28 46:29 47:2 47:17 47:21 47:22 47:29 47:30 47:31^{2} 48:1 48:9 48:10^{3} 48:12 48:15 48:17 48:19^{3} 48:20^{2} 49:4 49:8 49:9^{2} 49:11 49:13 49:15 49:19 49:20 49:21 49:27^{2} 49:28 49:29 49:33 50:6 50:10 50:12 50:14^{2} 50:16 50:21 50:22 50:24 50:26

EX 1:9 1:16 1:21 2:2 2:10 2:11^{2} 2:12^{3} 2:13^{2} 2:14 2:15^{2} 2:18 2:20^{3} 2:21 2:22 3:1 3:2 3:4^{2} 3:5 3:6^{2} 3:12 3:14 3:20 4:2 4:3^{2} 4:4 4:6^{2} 4:7^{2} 4:13 4:14^{5} 4:16^{3} 4:20 4:21 4:23 4:26 4:27 4:28 4:31 5:3 5:17 5:23 6:1 6:11 7:2 7:13^{2} 7:14 7:15^{2} 7:20 7:22 7:23 8:8 8:10^{2} 8:12 8:15 8:19 8:20 8:27 8:31 8:32 9:7 9:12 9:20 9:21 9:34^{2} 9:35 10:6 10:8 10:10 10:16 10:17 10:18 10:20 10:27 11:1^{3} 11:8 11:10 12:19 12:23 12:25 12:27 12:30 12:31 12:44 12:48 13:5 13:11 13:19 13:22 14:4 14:6 14:7 14:8 14:13 15:1^{2} 15:2^{2} 15:4 15:21^{2} 15:25^{4} 16:7 16:9 16:18^{2} 16:23 16:29 17:7 17:11 17:12 17:16 18:2 18:3 18:4 18:5 18:6 18:9 18:11 18:14 18:24 18:27 19:13 19:15 19:24 21:2^{2} 21:3^{3} 21:4 21:6^{2} 21:8^{3} 21:9^{2} 21:10^{2} 21:11 21:12^{2} 21:13 21:14 21:16^{3} 21:17 21:18 21:19^{3} 21:20^{2} 21:21^{3} 21:22^{2} 21:26 21:27^{2} 21:29^{2} 21:30 21:31 21:32 21:35 21:36 22:1 22:2 22:3^{3} 22:4 22:5 22:6 22:8 22:9 22:11^{2} 22:12 22:13 22:14 22:15 22:16 22:17 22:20^{2} 22:27^{2} 23:21 23:25 24:1 24:5 24:6 24:7 24:11 24:14 24:16 25:39 28:1 28:3 28:4 28:29 28:30 28:35^{3} 29:21 29:30 30:7^{2} 30:8 30:10 31:15 31:17 31:18^{2} 32:4^{2} 32:5 32:12 32:14 32:17 32:18 32:19^{3} 32:20 32:27 32:29 33:8 33:11 33:14 33:15 33:18 33:19 33:20 34:4 34:9 34:10 34:28^{3} 34:29^{2} 34:32 34:33

34:34^{4} 34:35 35:31 35:34^{3} 35:35 36:8 36:10^{2} 36:11^{2} 36:12^{2} 36:13 36:14^{2} 36:16 36:17^{2} 36:18 36:19 36:20 36:22 36:23 36:24 36:25 36:27 36:28 36:29 36:31 36:33 36:34 36:35^{2} 36:36^{2} 36:37 36:38 37:2 37:3 37:4 37:5 37:6 37:7^{2} 37:8 37:10 37:11 37:12 37:13 37:15 37:16 37:17^{2} 37:23 37:24 37:25 37:26^{2} 37:27 37:28 37:29 38:1 38:2^{2} 38:3^{2} 38:4 38:5 38:6 38:7^{2} 38:8 38:9 38:28 38:30 39:2 39:7 39:8 39:22 40:13 40:16 40:19 40:20 40:21 40:22 40:23 40:24 40:25 40:26 40:27 40:28 40:29 40:30 40:33

LE

1:3 1:4

1:5 1:6 1:9 1:10 1:11 1:12 1:13 1:14 1:16 1:17 2:1 2:2^{2} 2:8 3:1^{2} 3:2 3:3 3:4 3:6 3:7^{2} 3:8 3:9^{2} 3:10 3:12 3:13 3:14 3:15 4:3 4:4 4:8 4:9 4:12^{2} 4:18 4:19 4:20^{3} 4:21^{2} 4:23^{2} 4:24 4:26 4:27 4:28^{3} 4:29 4:31 4:32^{2} 4:33 4:35^{2} 5:1^{3} 5:2 5:3^{3} 5:4^{2} 5:5^{3} 5:6 5:7^{3} 5:8 5:9 5:10^{2} 5:11^{4} 5:12 5:13 5:15 5:16^{2} 5:17^{2} 5:18^{2} 5:19 6:4^{5} 6:5^{2} 6:6 6:7 6:10^{2} 6:11 6:12 6:15 6:20 7:2 7:3 7:4 7:8 7:11 7:12^{2} 7:13 7:14 7:15 7:16 7:29 7:30 7:33 7:35 7:36

7:38 8:7^{2} 8:8^{2} 8:9^{2} 8:11 8:12 8:14 8:15 8:16 8:17 8:18 8:19 8:20 8:21 8:22 8:23 8:24 8:25 8:26 8:27 8:33 8:34 9:2 9:9 9:10 9:11 9:12^{2} 9:13 9:14 9:15 9:16 9:17 9:18^{2} 9:20 10:1 10:16 10:20 11:4^{2} 11:5^{2} 11:6^{2} 11:7^{3} 11:28 11:39 11:40^{2} 13:2 13:6 13:7^{2} 13:9 13:11 13:13^{2} 13:14 13:16 13:17 13:33^{2} 13:34 13:36 13:37 13:39 13:40^{2} 13:41^{3} 13:44^{2} 13:45 13:46^{3} 13:51 13:52 13:54 13:56 14:2 14:6 14:7 14:8^{3} 14:9^{5} 14:10^{2} 14:12 14:13^{2} 14:18 14:19 14:20 14:21^{2} 14:22 14:23 14:25 14:29 14:30^{2} 14:31 14:35 14:37

14:41 14:42 14:43^{2} 14:45^{2} 14:46 14:47^{2} 14:49 14:50 14:51 14:52 14:53 15:2 15:4^{2} 15:6^{2} 15:7 15:8^{2} 15:9 15:10 15:11^{2} 15:12 15:13^{2} 15:14 15:16 15:23 15:24^{2} 16:2^{2} 16:4^{4} 16:5 16:7 16:12 16:13^{2} 16:14^{2} 16:15^{2} 16:16^{2} 16:17^{2} 16:18 16:19 16:20^{2} 16:22 16:23^{2} 16:24 16:25 16:26 16:28^{2} 16:32^{2} 16:33^{3} 16:34 17:4 17:13 17:15^{2} 17:16^{2} 18:5 19:8 19:21 19:22^{2} 20:2^{2} 20:3 20:4 20:9 20:10 20:13 20:14 20:15 20:17^{2} 20:18 20:19 20:20 20:21 21:3 21:4 21:7 21:8^{2} 21:10 21:11 21:13 21:14^{2} 21:15 21:17 21:18^{3} 21:21^{2} 21:22 21:23^{3} 22:3 22:4^{2} 22:5^{3} 22:6 22:7

22:8 22:11^{2} 22:14 22:18 23:11 23:12 23:29 24:4 24:8 24:9 24:16^{4} 24:17 24:18 24:19 24:20 24:21^{4} 25:15 25:16 25:25 25:27^{2} 25:28^{2} 25:29^{2} 25:35^{2} 25:40 25:41^{3} 25:48^{2} 25:49^{2} 25:50^{2} 25:51^{2} 25:52^{2} 25:53 25:54^{3} 27:8^{2} 27:10^{2} 27:11 27:13^{2} 27:15^{2} 27:17 27:18 27:19^{2} 27:20^{2} 27:22 27:23 27:27 27:28 27:31 27:33^{3}

NU

1:19 3:3 3:16 3:50 5:7^{2} 5:14^{2} 5:15^{2} 5:23 5:24 5:27 5:30 6:3^{2} 6:4 6:5^{2} 6:6^{2} 6:7 6:8 6:9^{3} 6:10 6:11 6:12 6:13 6:14^{2} 6:17 6:21^{2} 7:7 7:8 7:9 7:12 7:17 7:19 7:23 7:29 7:35 7:41 7:47

7:53 7:59 7:65 7:71 7:77 7:83 7:89^{2} 8:3 8:4 9:10 9:13 9:14 10:30 10:31 10:36 11:3 11:30 11:32 11:34 12:1^{2} 12:2 12:6 12:8 12:9 12:12 14:8 14:16^{2} 14:24^{2} 15:4 15:9 15:14 15:27 15:28 15:30 15:31 15:36 16:4 16:5^{3} 16:7 16:10 16:26 16:31 16:37 16:40 16:47 16:48 17:11 19:3 19:5 19:7^{2} 19:8 19:10 19:11 19:12^{4} 19:13 19:19 19:20^{2} 19:21^{2} 20:9 20:10 20:11 20:13 20:16 20:20 20:24 21:1 21:3 21:7 21:8 21:9^{2} 21:14 21:23 21:29 21:33 22:5 22:6^{2} 22:8 22:22^{2} 22:25 22:27 22:30 22:31^{2} 22:36 22:41 23:3^{2} 23:4 23:6^{3}

23:7 23:12 23:14 23:15 23:17^{2} 23:18 23:19^{6} 23:20 23:21^{2} 23:22 23:24^{2} 24:1^{2} 24:2 24:3 24:4 24:7 24:8^{2} 24:9^{4} 24:10 24:15 24:16 24:19 24:20^{3} 24:21 24:23 24:24 26:7 26:8 26:11 26:13^{2} 26:15 27:3 27:4 27:9 27:10 27:11 27:21^{2} 27:22 27:23 30:2^{2} 30:5 30:7 30:8^{2} 30:12 30:14^{4} 30:15^{3} 32:10 32:13 32:15 32:21 32:40 33:39 35:6 35:8 35:12 35:16^{3} 35:17^{4} 35:18^{4} 35:19^{2} 35:20^{2} 35:21^{4} 35:22 35:23 35:25^{2} 35:26 35:27 35:28 35:31 35:32

DE

1:4 1:11 1:27 1:30^{2} 1:36^{3} 1:38^{2} 2:7 2:22^{2} 2:30 2:32 3:1 3:22 3:28^{2} 4:13^{3}

4:23 4:31^{2} 4:35 4:36^{3} 4:37^{2} 4:39 4:42 5:22^{2} 5:24 6:10 6:17 6:23^{3} 6:24 6:25 7:8^{2} 7:9 7:10^{2} 7:12 7:13^{3} 7:24 8:3^{2} 8:10 8:16^{2} 8:18^{3} 9:3^{3} 9:5 9:25 9:28^{3} 10:4 10:6 10:15 10:18 10:21^{2} 11:3 11:4^{2} 11:5 11:6 11:7 11:17 11:25 12:10 12:12 12:15 12:20 12:31 13:2 13:5 13:10^{2} 13:17 14:21 14:23 14:27 14:29 15:2 15:6 15:8 15:9 15:16^{3} 15:17 15:18 16:16 16:17^{2} 17:6^{2} 17:16^{2} 17:17^{2} 17:18^{2} 17:19^{2} 17:20^{3} 18:2 18:6 18:7 18:18 18:19 19:4^{2} 19:5^{2} 19:6^{3} 19:8^{2} 19:11 19:12 19:15 19:19 20:4 20:5 20:6^{2} 20:7 21:16^{3} 21:17^{3}

21:20^{2} 21:21 21:22 21:23 22:3 22:16 22:17 22:19^{2} 22:24 22:27 22:29^{2} 23:1 23:2 23:6 23:7 23:10^{2} 23:11^{2} 23:14 23:16^{2} 24:1 24:5^{4} 24:13 24:14 24:15^{2} 25:3^{2} 25:4 25:7 25:8 25:18^{2} 26:5 26:9 26:18 26:19^{2} 27:16 27:17 27:18 27:19 27:20^{2} 27:21 27:22 27:23 27:24 27:25 27:26 28:8 28:9 28:21 28:44^{2} 28:45 28:48^{2} 28:51^{2} 28:52^{2} 28:54 28:55^{3} 28:60 29:1 29:13^{4} 29:19^{2} 29:25^{2} 29:26 30:4 30:5 30:9 30:20 31:2 31:3^{3} 31:4^{2} 31:6^{2} 31:8^{3} 31:11 31:23 32:4^{2} 32:6^{2} 32:7 32:8^{2} 32:10^{4} 32:13^{3} 32:15 32:19 32:20 32:36 32:37 32:39 32:43 32:44 32:46 33:2^{3}

33:3 33:5 33:7 33:8 33:9 33:12^{2} 33:13 33:17 33:18 33:20^{3} 33:21^{4} 33:22^{2} 33:23 33:24 33:27 34:6 34:7

JOS

1:15 1:17 1:18^{2} 2:11 3:1 3:10 4:4 4:21 4:23 5:6^{2} 5:7 5:13 5:14 6:7 6:26^{2} 7:6 7:15^{5} 7:17^{3} 7:18 7:24 8:4 8:10 8:12 8:14^{2} 8:18 8:19 8:26^{2} 8:27 8:29 8:32^{2} 8:33 8:34 9:9 9:10 9:22 9:26 9:27 10:1^{2} 10:7 10:12 10:28^{4} 10:30^{3} 10:32 10:33 10:35^{2} 10:37^{2} 10:39^{5} 10:40 11:1 11:9 11:11 11:12 11:15 11:17 11:20^{2} 13:14^{2} 13:33 14:3 14:10 14:14 15:13 15:15 15:16 15:17 15:19 17:1^{3}

17:4 19:50^{2} 20:4^{2} 20:5 20:6^{3} 20:9 21:43 21:44 22:4 22:7 22:8 22:18 22:22^{2} 23:3 23:5 23:10^{2} 23:15 23:16^{2} 24:7 24:10 24:17 24:18 24:19^{3} 24:20^{2} 24:23 24:27 24:31

JG

1:3 1:5 1:6^{2} 1:7 1:11 1:12 1:13 1:19 1:20 1:25 1:33 2:7 2:10 2:14^{2} 2:20 2:21 2:23 3:4 3:8 3:10 3:13 3:16 3:17 3:18^{2} 3:19 3:20^{3} 3:22 3:24^{2} 3:25 3:27^{3} 3:28 3:31 4:3^{2} 4:10 4:18 4:19 4:20 4:21^{2} 4:22 5:13 5:15 5:25 5:27^{7} 5:31 6:15 6:17 6:18 6:19^{2} 6:20 6:22 6:27^{3} 6:30^{3} 6:31^{2} 6:32^{2} 6:34 6:35^{2}

6:38 7:5 7:8 7:11 7:15 7:16^{2} 7:17 8:2 8:3 8:4 8:5 8:8 8:9 8:12 8:14 8:15 8:16^{2} 8:17 8:18 8:19 8:20^{3} 8:26 8:30 8:31 8:35 9:3 9:5 9:7 9:18 9:28 9:29 9:31 9:33 9:36 9:40 9:43^{2} 9:45 9:48 9:54^{2} 9:56 10:1 10:2 10:4 10:7 10:18^{2} 11:1 11:17 11:25^{2} 11:28 11:29^{2} 11:33 11:34 11:35^{2} 11:38^{2} 11:39 12:5 12:6^{2} 12:9^{3} 12:11 12:14^{2} 13:5 13:6^{2} 13:7 13:11 13:16 13:21 13:23^{3} 14:2 14:4 14:6^{5} 14:7 14:8^{2} 14:9^{4} 14:14 14:15 14:16 14:17 14:18 14:19^{2} 14:20 15:1 15:5^{2} 15:6 15:8^{2} 15:10 15:11 15:14

15:15 15:17^{2} 15:18 15:19^{3} 15:20 16:4 16:9 16:11 16:12 16:13 16:14 16:17 16:18^{2} 16:20^{2} 16:21 16:22 16:25^{2} 16:30^{3} 16:31 17:2 17:3 17:4 17:7 17:8^{3} 17:9 18:4 18:20 18:24 18:26 18:27 18:30 18:31 19:3 19:4 19:5 19:7 19:8 19:9 19:10 19:13 19:15^{2} 19:16 19:17^{2} 19:18 19:21 19:28 19:29^{2} 21:5 21:18

RU

1:1 2:14 2:19 2:20 2:21 3:2 3:3 3:4^{3} 3:7 3:9 3:10 3:13^{2} 3:14 3:15^{2} 3:17^{2} 3:18 4:1^{2} 4:2 4:3 4:4 4:8 4:13 4:15 4:17

1 SA

1:2 1:4 1:5^{2} 1:7 1:22 1:28^{3} 2:6

2:7 2:8^{2} 2:9 2:10^{2} 2:14 2:15 2:16 2:23 2:35 3:2 3:4 3:5^{3} 3:6 3:8 3:9 3:13^{2} 3:16 3:17^{2} 3:18 4:13 4:14 4:15 4:16^{2} 4:18^{5} 5:6 5:9 6:5 6:6 6:9 6:19^{2} 6:20 7:3 7:8 7:16 7:17^{2} 8:1 8:11^{2} 8:12 8:13 8:14 8:15 8:16 8:17 8:21 9:2^{3} 9:4^{2} 9:6^{4} 9:12^{3} 9:13^{3} 9:16 9:26 9:27 10:9 10:10 10:11 10:13^{2} 10:14 10:16^{2} 10:21^{2} 10:22 10:23^{2} 10:27 11:6 11:7 11:8 11:12 12:5^{2} 12:7 12:9 12:17 12:24 13:1 13:2 13:7 13:8 13:9 13:10^{2} 13:13 14:1 14:27 14:33 14:35 14:37 14:39 14:40 14:45^{2} 14:47^{2}

14:48 14:52 15:2^{2} 15:8 15:11^{2} 15:12 15:16 15:23 15:27 15:29^{2} 15:30 15:35 16:2 16:5^{2} 16:6 16:8 16:9 16:11^{3} 16:12^{3} 16:16 16:21^{2} 16:22 17:5^{2} 17:6 17:8 17:9 17:12 17:20 17:23 17:25 17:26 17:28^{2} 17:30 17:31 17:33 17:35 17:36 17:37 17:38^{2} 17:39^{2} 17:40^{3} 17:42^{2} 17:47 17:49 17:54 17:55 18:1 18:3 18:5 18:8^{2} 18:10 18:11 18:13 18:15^{2} 18:16 18:27^{2} 19:4 19:5 19:6 19:7 19:9 19:10^{2} 19:12 19:14 19:17^{2} 19:18 19:21 19:22^{2} 19:23^{3} 19:24 20:1 20:2^{2} 20:3^{2} 20:6 20:7^{2} 20:13 20:17^{3} 20:26^{3} 20:29^{3} 20:30 20:31 20:32^{2} 20:34 20:36^{2} 20:42 21:13 22:2

22:3 22:4 22:10 22:12 22:13 22:17 22:18 22:19 22:22 22:23 23:6 23:7 23:9 23:11 23:13 23:17 23:22 23:23^{2} 23:25^{2} 24:3 24:5 24:6^{2} 24:10 24:17 24:19 25:2^{2} 25:3 25:14 25:17 25:21 25:25 25:29 25:30 25:36^{2} 25:37 25:38 25:39 26:3 26:10 26:18 27:2 27:3 27:4 27:11 27:12^{2} 28:5 28:8^{2} 28:9 28:11 28:14^{4} 28:17 28:20 28:21 28:23^{3} 29:3 29:4^{3} 29:9 30:8 30:9 30:10 30:11 30:12^{2} 30:13 30:15 30:16 30:21 30:25 30:26 31:3 31:4 31:5

2 SA

1:2^{2} 1:3 1:4 1:7^{2} 1:8 1:9 1:10^{2} 1:13 1:15^{2} 1:18 1:21 2:1

2:10 2:19 2:20 2:23^{2} 2:30 3:11^{2} 3:13 3:16 3:21 3:22^{2} 3:23^{2} 3:24 3:25 3:26 3:27 3:28 3:30 4:4^{2} 4:7 5:2 5:4^{2} 5:5^{2} 5:8 5:12 5:13 5:20 5:23 6:7 6:8 6:13 6:18 6:19 7:11 7:13 7:14^{2} 7:18 8:2^{2} 8:3 8:6 8:10 8:11^{2} 8:13 8:14^{3} 9:2^{2} 9:4^{2} 9:6^{2} 9:8 9:11 9:13 10:3 10:5 10:7 10:9 10:10^{2} 10:11 10:17 11:2 11:4 11:13^{3} 11:15^{2} 11:16^{2} 11:20 11:21 12:1 12:3 12:4 12:5 12:6^{3} 12:11 12:17^{2} 12:18^{2} 12:19 12:20^{3} 12:22 12:23^{2} 12:24 12:25 12:30 12:31^{2} 13:2 13:4 13:8 13:9 13:11 13:13 13:14 13:15^{2}

13:16 13:17 13:20 13:21 13:22 13:25^{2} 13:26 13:27 13:32 13:36 13:39^{2} 14:7 14:10 14:11 14:12 14:14 14:15 14:19^{2} 14:26^{4} 14:29^{3} 14:30^{2} 14:33^{2} 15:2 15:5 15:9 15:12 15:14 15:25 15:26 15:30^{2} 15:32 16:3^{2} 16:5^{2} 16:13 16:21 16:23 17:2 17:5 17:9 17:10 17:12 17:13 17:23 17:24 18:9 18:14^{2} 18:18^{2} 18:23^{2} 18:25^{2} 18:26 18:27 18:28 18:30 18:33^{2} 19:9^{2} 19:14 19:18^{2} 19:21 19:24 19:25 19:26 19:27 19:32^{3} 19:39 19:42 20:1 20:3 20:5^{2} 20:6 20:8^{2} 20:10^{2} 20:11^{2} 20:12^{2} 20:13 20:14 20:17^{4} 20:22 21:1 21:4 21:9 21:13 21:16 21:20 21:21 22:2 22:3 22:7

22:8 22:10 22:11[2] 22:12 22:15 22:17[3] 22:18 22:20[3] 22:21 22:31 22:33 22:34 22:35 22:42 22:51 23:3 23:4 23:5[2] 23:8[2] 23:10 23:12 23:16 23:17[2] 23:18 23:19[3] 23:20[2] 23:21[2] 23:23[2] 24:1 24:10 24:17

1 KI

1:1 1:5 1:6 1:7 1:10 1:13 1:17 1:19[2] 1:23[3] 1:24 1:25 1:26 1:30 1:35[2] 1:37 1:41 1:42 1:51[2] 1:52 1:53 2:1 2:4[2] 2:5[2] 2:8 2:11[2] 2:13 2:14 2:15 2:17[3] 2:22 2:24 2:25[2] 2:27[2] 2:28 2:29 2:30[2] 2:31 2:32 2:34 2:46 3:1 3:3 3:6 3:15 4:2 4:15 4:24[2] 4:31 4:32 4:33[2] 5:1 5:5

5:7 5:12 5:14 6:4 6:5[2] 6:6 6:9 6:10 6:15[2] 6:16[2] 6:19 6:20 6:21[2] 6:22[3] 6:23 6:27 6:28 6:29 6:30 6:31 6:32 6:33 6:35 6:36 6:38 7:1 7:2 7:6 7:7[2] 7:8[2] 7:14[3] 7:15 7:16 7:18[2] 7:21[3] 7:23 7:27 7:37 7:38 7:39[3] 7:40 7:51 8:12 8:15 8:19 8:20 8:21[2] 8:23 8:42 8:54 8:55 8:56[2] 8:57 8:58 8:59 8:63 8:64 8:66 9:1 9:2 9:13[2] 9:24 9:25[3] 10:3 10:4 10:5 10:9 10:15 10:17 10:26[2] 10:27 11:2 11:8 11:10[2] 11:14 11:15 11:16 11:17 11:19 11:22 11:24 11:25[2] 11:26 11:27 11:28[2] 11:29 11:31

11:32 11:34 11:41 12:2 12:4 12:5 12:6 12:8 12:9 12:15 12:18 12:21 12:29[2] 12:31 12:32[5] 12:33[4] 13:2[2] 13:3 13:4[3] 13:10[2] 13:11 13:12 13:13[2] 13:14[2] 13:15 13:16 13:18[3] 13:19 13:21 13:23[4] 13:24 13:26[2] 13:27 13:28 13:30 13:31[2] 13:32 13:33[2] 14:3 14:5 14:6 14:13 14:15[2] 14:16 14:18 14:19[2] 14:20 14:21[2] 14:26[3] 14:29 15:2 15:3[2] 15:5 15:7 15:10 15:12 15:13 15:15 15:17 15:19 15:20 15:21 15:23[3] 15:26[2] 15:29[5] 15:30[3] 15:31 15:34[2] 16:5 16:7[2] 16:9 16:11[4] 16:12 16:14 16:18 16:19[2] 16:20 16:23 16:24[2] 16:26[2] 16:27[2] 16:31 16:32 16:34[2] 17:5[2] 17:6 17:10[3]

17:11 17:15 17:16 17:19[3] 17:20 17:21 17:22 18:7 18:8 18:9 18:10[2] 18:12[2] 18:14 18:17 18:18 18:27[5] 18:30 18:32[2] 18:33 18:34[2] 18:35 18:39[2] 18:42 18:43[2] 18:44[2] 18:46 19:1 19:3[2] 19:4[3] 19:5 19:6[2] 19:8 19:9[2] 19:10 19:11 19:13 19:14 19:19[2] 19:20[2] 19:21[2] 20:1 20:2 20:7 20:9 20:11 20:12[3] 20:14[3] 20:15[2] 20:16 20:18 20:25 20:28 20:31 20:32[3] 20:33[2] 20:34 20:36[2] 20:37[2] 20:39[3] 20:40 20:41[2] 20:42 21:4[2] 21:6[2] 21:10 21:13 21:15 21:18[2] 21:20 21:26 21:27 21:29 22:4 22:8 22:11 22:15[2] 22:17 22:18 22:19 22:20 22:22[2] 22:28 22:34 22:38 22:39[3] 22:42[2] 22:43[2]

22:45[2] 22:46 22:52 22:53

2 KI

1:2 1:5 1:7[2] 1:8[2] 1:9[3] 1:11[2] 1:13 1:15 1:16 1:17[2] 1:18 2:3 2:4 2:5 2:6 2:10 2:12[3] 2:13 2:14[2] 2:16 2:17[2] 2:18[2] 2:20 2:21 2:22 2:23[2] 2:24 2:25[2] 3:2[2] 3:3[2] 3:7[2] 3:8[2] 3:16 3:18 3:26 3:27 4:3 4:6 4:7 4:8[2] 4:10[2] 4:11[2] 4:12[2] 4:13 4:14 4:15[2] 4:16 4:18 4:19[2] 4:20[2] 4:23 4:25 4:29 4:30 4:31 4:33 4:34[2] 4:35 4:36[3] 4:38 4:41[3] 4:42 4:43 4:44 5:1[2] 5:3 5:5 5:6 5:7[2] 5:8[2] 5:11 5:12 5:13 5:14[2] 5:15[3] 5:16[3] 5:18 5:19[2]

5:20 5:21 5:22 5:23 5:24[3] 5:25[2] 5:26 5:27 6:2 6:3 6:4 6:5 6:6[2] 6:7[2] 6:11 6:13[3] 6:14 6:16 6:17[2] 6:18 6:19 6:21 6:22 6:23[2] 6:27 6:30[3] 6:31 6:32 6:33[2] 7:2 7:11 7:17[2] 7:19 7:20 8:1 8:5[3] 8:10 8:11[2] 8:12 8:13 8:14[3] 8:15[2] 8:17[3] 8:18[2] 8:19 8:21 8:23 8:26[2] 8:27[2] 8:28 8:29[2] 9:5[3] 9:6[2] 9:10 9:11 9:12[2] 9:14 9:15 9:17[2] 9:18 9:19 9:20[2] 9:22[2] 9:24 9:27[2] 9:32 9:33[2] 9:34[2] 9:36[2] 10:5[2] 10:6 10:8 10:9 10:10 10:11 10:12[2] 10:14[2] 10:15[5] 10:16 10:17[4] 10:19[2] 10:22[2] 10:24 10:25 10:31 10:34

11:2 11:3 11:5 11:8[3] 11:12 11:19[2] 11:21 12:1 12:18 12:19 12:21 13:2[2] 13:3 13:4 13:7 13:8 13:11[3] 13:12[2] 13:14 13:15 13:16[2] 13:17[4] 13:18[4] 13:21 13:23 13:25 14:2[2] 14:3[2] 14:5 14:6 14:7 14:11 14:14 14:15[2] 14:19 14:20 14:22 14:24[2] 14:25[2] 14:27[2] 14:28[3] 15:2[3] 15:3 15:5 15:6 15:9[2] 15:12 15:13 15:15 15:16[2] 15:18[2] 15:21 15:24[2] 15:25 15:26 15:28[2] 15:31 15:33[3] 15:34[2] 15:35 15:36 16:2 16:3 16:4 16:13 16:14 16:18 16:19 17:2 17:4[2] 17:15[2] 17:20 17:21 17:22 17:23 17:26 17:34 17:37 17:39 18:2[3] 18:3 18:4[2] 18:5 18:6 18:7[3] 18:8

18:22 18:27 18:29 18:32 19:1 19:2 19:7 19:8[2] 19:9[3] 19:32 19:33[2] 19:37 20:7 20:9 20:11 20:12 20:15 20:19 20:20 21:1 21:2 21:3[2] 21:4 21:5 21:6[2] 21:7[2] 21:16[2] 21:17[2] 21:19[2] 21:20 21:21 21:22 21:25 21:26 22:1[2] 22:2 22:4 22:8 22:11 23:2 23:4 23:5 23:6 23:7 23:8 23:10 23:11 23:14 23:15 23:16 23:17 23:18 23:19 23:20 23:24 23:28 23:29[2] 23:31[2] 23:32 23:33 23:34 23:35[2] 23:36[2] 23:37 24:1 24:2 24:3 24:4[2] 24:5 24:8[2] 24:9 24:12 24:13 24:14 24:15[2] 24:18[2] 24:19 24:20 25:1 25:9[2] 25:19 25:22 25:25 25:27 25:28 25:29

1 CH

1:10 2:3 2:21[2] 2:23 3:4[2] 4:10 5:1[2] 5:6 5:9 5:20 5:26 6:10 7:23[2] 8:7 8:8 8:9 8:11 10:3 10:4 10:5 10:13[2] 10:14 11:2 11:8 11:11 11:13 11:19 11:20[2] 11:21[3] 11:22[2] 11:23[2] 11:25 12:1 12:18 12:19[2] 12:20 13:10[3] 13:14 14:4 15:3 15:22[2] 16:2 16:3 16:4 16:12 16:14 16:15 16:16 16:21[2] 16:25 16:33 16:34 16:37 16:40 17:12 17:13 18:2 18:3 18:6 18:10[2] 18:11 18:13[2] 19:3 19:5 19:8 19:10 19:11 19:12 19:17 20:2 20:3 20:6 20:7 21:3 21:6 21:7 21:15[2] 21:19 21:26 21:27 21:28 21:30 22:2 22:6 22:10[2]

22:11 22:18[2] 23:1 23:2 23:13[2] 25:10 25:11 25:12 25:13 25:14 25:15 25:16 25:17 25:18 25:19 25:20 25:21 25:22 25:23 25:24 25:25 25:26 25:27 25:28 25:29 25:30 25:31 26:10 27:23 27:24 28:4[2] 28:5 28:6[2] 28:7 28:9[2] 28:12 28:14 28:16 28:17 28:20 29:27[3] 29:28

2 CH

1:4 1:5 1:14[2] 1:15 2:11[2] 2:18 3:2 3:4 3:5[2] 3:6 3:7 3:8[2] 3:9 3:10 3:14 3:15 3:16 3:17 4:1 4:2 4:6 4:7 4:8[2] 4:9 4:10 4:11 4:14[2] 4:21 5:1 5:13 6:1 6:4[2] 6:9 6:10 6:11 6:12 6:13 7:3 7:7 7:10

7:11 7:21 7:22 8:4[2] 8:5 8:11[2] 8:12 8:14 9:2 9:3 9:4 9:8 9:15 9:25 9:26 9:27 9:31 10:2 10:4 10:5 10:6 10:8 10:9 10:15 10:18 11:1[2] 11:6 11:11 11:12 11:15[2] 11:20 11:21 11:22 11:23[3] 12:1 12:4 12:9[2] 12:12[2] 12:13[2] 12:14[2] 13:2 13:20 14:3 14:5 14:6[2] 14:7[2] 15:2[3] 15:4 15:8[2] 15:9 15:15 15:16 15:18[2] 16:1 16:3 16:5 16:6 16:8 16:10 16:12 16:14 17:2 17:3 17:5 17:6 17:7 17:8 17:11 17:12 17:13 18:2[2] 18:3 18:7 18:14[2] 18:16 18:17 18:18 18:19 18:21 18:27 18:33 18:34 19:4 19:5 19:9 20:15

20:21[2] 20:31[3] 20:32 20:36 21:2 21:3[2] 21:4 21:5[2] 21:6[2] 21:7[2] 21:9 21:10 21:11 21:19 21:20[3] 22:2[2] 22:3 22:4 22:5 22:6[3] 22:7[2] 22:8 22:9[3] 22:12 23:3 23:7[3] 23:10 23:19 23:20 24:1[2] 24:3 24:5 24:15[3] 24:16 24:19 24:20 24:22[2] 24:25 25:1[2] 25:2 25:3 25:4 25:5 25:6 25:14 25:15 25:16 25:20 25:21 25:24 25:27 26:2 26:3[2] 26:4 26:5[2] 26:6 26:8 26:10[2] 26:15[3] 26:16[2] 26:19 26:20 26:21 26:23 27:1[2] 27:2[2] 27:3[2] 27:4[2] 27:5 27:6 27:8[2] 28:1[3] 28:2 28:3 28:4 28:5 28:9[2] 28:19 28:21 28:22 28:23[2] 28:24 28:25 29:1[2] 29:2 29:3

29:4 29:8 29:21[2] 29:23 29:25 30:6 30:8 30:19 31:3 31:4 31:21[2] 32:2 32:3 32:5 32:6 32:9 32:17 32:21[2] 32:23 32:24[2] 32:26 32:27 32:29 32:31 33:1[2] 33:3[2] 33:4 33:5 33:6[3] 33:7[2] 33:12[2] 33:13[2] 33:14 33:15[2] 33:16 33:19[2] 33:21 33:22 34:1[2] 34:2 34:3[3] 34:4[2] 34:5 34:6 34:7[2] 34:8[2] 34:19 34:30 34:32 35:2 35:21[2] 35:22 35:24[2] 36:2[2] 36:5[3] 36:8 36:9[3] 36:11 36:12 36:13[2] 36:14 36:15 36:17[2] 36:18 36:20 36:22 36:23

EZR

1:1 1:2 1:3 1:4 3:11 3:12 3:14 6:17 7:6 7:8 7:9[2] 8:23 8:31 8:35 10:1 10:6[3]

NE

1:2 2:8 2:18 2:20 3:12 3:14 3:15 4:1 4:2 4:3[2] 4:18 5:13 6:10 6:12 6:13 6:18 7:2 8:3 8:5[2] 8:10 8:18 9:29 12:8 13:2 13:5

ES

1:3 1:4 1:10 1:20 1:22 2:1 2:4 2:7 2:9[2] 2:17 2:18 3:4[3] 3:6 4:4 4:5 4:8 4:11 5:5 5:9[2] 5:10[2] 5:11 5:14 6:1 6:4 7:5[2] 7:7 7:8 7:10 8:1 8:2 8:3 8:5 8:7 8:10 9:25[3] 9:30

JOB

1:10 1:11[2] 1:12 1:16 1:17 1:18 2:3 2:4 2:5 2:6 2:8[2] 2:10 4:18[2] 5:12 5:13 5:15 5:18[2] 5:19

5:20 6:5 6:9 6:14 7:9 7:10 8:4 8:6 8:15[2] 8:16 8:18 8:20 8:21 9:3[2] 9:4 9:11[2] 9:12 9:16[2] 9:17 9:18 9:19 9:22 9:23 9:24[2] 9:32 11:6 11:10 12:4 12:5 12:13 12:14[2] 12:15[2] 12:17 12:18 12:19 12:20 12:21 12:22 12:23[2] 12:24 12:25 13:9 13:10 13:15 13:16 13:19 13:28 14:2[2] 14:5 14:6[2] 14:10 14:14 14:20 14:21[2] 15:3[2] 15:14[3] 15:15 15:23[2] 15:25 15:26 15:27 15:28 15:29[2] 15:30[2] 15:33 16:7 16:9[2] 16:12[2] 16:13[2] 16:14[2] 17:3 17:5 17:6 17:9 18:4 18:8[2] 18:17 18:18 18:19 19:8[2] 19:9 19:10[2] 19:11[2] 19:13 19:16 19:25 20:7[2]

20:8[2] 20:12 20:13 20:15[2] 20:16 20:17 20:18[3] 20:19[3] 20:20[3] 20:22 20:23[2] 20:24 21:19[2] 21:20 21:21 21:22 21:31 21:32 22:2 22:4[2] 22:8 22:13 22:14[2] 22:28 22:27 22:29 22:30 23:5[2] 23:6[2] 23:8 23:9[2] 23:10[2] 23:13[3] 23:14 23:17 24:18[2] 24:20 24:21 24:22[2] 24:23 25:2 25:4 26:7 26:8 26:9 26:10 26:12[2] 26:13 27:7 27:9 27:10[2] 27:16 27:17 27:18 27:19[3] 27:21 27:22 28:3 28:9[2] 28:10 28:11[2] 28:23 28:24 28:25 28:26 28:27[2] 28:28 30:11 30:19 30:24 31:4 31:14 31:15 31:18 31:20 32:1 32:2 32:4 32:14 33:10[2] 33:11[2] 33:13 33:16 33:17 33:18 33:19 33:24

33:25 33:26[3] 33:27 33:28 34:9[2] 34:10[2] 34:11 34:14[2] 34:17 34:21 34:23[2] 34:24 34:25[2] 34:26 34:28 34:29[2] 34:33 34:37[2] 35:7 35:15[2] 35:16 36:4 36:5 36:6 36:7[2] 36:9 36:10 36:13 36:15 36:16 36:18 36:19 36:22 36:27 36:30 36:31[2] 36:32 37:3 37:4[2] 37:5 37:6 37:7 37:11[2] 37:12 37:13 37:17 37:20 37:23[2] 37:24 39:7[2] 39:8 39:10 39:12 39:17 39:21[2] 39:22[2] 39:24[2] 39:25[2] 40:2[2] 40:15 40:17 40:19[2] 40:21 40:23[3] 40:24 41:3[2] 41:4 41:25 41:26 41:29 41:30 41:31[2] 41:32 41:34[2] 42:3 42:10[2] 42:12 42:13 42:14

PS

1:2 1:3[2] 2:4 2:5

2:12 3:*title* 3:4 7:*title* 7:2 7:12[3] 7:13[2] 7:14 7:15[2] 9:7 9:8[2] 9:12[3] 9:16 10:5 10:6 10:8[2] 10:9[4] 10:10 10:11[3] 10:13 11:6 13:6 15:2 15:3 15:4[2] 15:5[2] 16:8 18:*title* 18:6 18:7 18:10[2] 18:11 18:14[2] 18:16[3] 18:17 18:19[3] 18:20 18:30 18:33 18:34 18:41 18:48 18:50 19:4 20:6 21:1 21:4 21:7 22:8[3] 22:9 22:24[4] 22:28 22:31 23:2[2] 23:3[2] 24:2 24:4 24:5 24:10 25:8 25:9[2] 25:12[3] 25:14 25:15 27:5[3] 27:14 28:5 28:6 28:8 29:6 31:21 31:24 32:1 32:10 33:5 33:7[2] 33:9[2] 33:10 33:12 33:13 33:14 33:15[2] 33:17 33:20 34:*title*[2] 34:4 34:12[2]

34:20
35:8
35:14
36:2
36:3
36:4[3]
37:4
37:5
37:6
37:13
37:23
37:24[2]
37:26
37:33
37:34
37:36[3]
37:39
37:40
39:6
40:1
40:2
40:3
41:1
41:2
41:5
41:6[4]
41:8[2]
44:21
45:11
46:6
46:8
46:9[3]
47:2
47:3
47:4[2]
47:9
48:14
49:9
49:10
49:12
49:15
49:17
49:18[2]
49:19
50:4[2]
50:9
51:*title*
52:5
54:5
54:7
55:12
55:17
55:18
55:19
55:20[2]
55:22[2]
56:1
57:*title*
57:3
58:7
58:9
58:10[2]
58:11
60:*title*
60:12
61:7
62:2[2]
62:6[2]
63:*title*
65:4
66:5
66:6
66:7
66:16
66:17
66:19
68:6
68:20
68:33
68:35
71:6
72:2
72:4[2]
72:6
72:8
72:12[2]
72:13
72:14
74:5
75:7
75:8
76:3
76:12[2]
77:1
77:7
77:9
78:4
78:5[2]
78:11
78:12
78:13[2]
78:14
78:15
78:16
78:20[3]
78:23
78:25
78:26[2]
78:27
78:28
78:29
78:33
78:34
78:38[2]
78:39
78:42
78:43
78:45
78:46
78:47
78:48
78:49
78:50[3]
78:53
78:54
78:55
78:59
78:60[2]
78:62
78:66[2]
78:67
78:68
78:69[2]
78:70
78:71
78:72
81:5[2]
81:16
82:1
84:11
85:8
87:6
89:26
89:41
89:48[2]
91:1
91:2
91:3
91:4
91:11
91:14[2]
91:15
92:12
92:15
93:1[2]
94:9[4]
94:10[4]
94:14
94:23
95:5
95:7
96:4
96:10
96:13[3]
97:10[2]
98:1
98:2
98:3
98:9[2]
99:1
99:2
99:5
99:6
99:7[2]
100:3[2]
101:6[2]
101:7[2]
102:*title*
102:16
102:17
102:19
102:23[2]
103:7
103:9[2]
103:10
103:12
103:14[2]
103:15
104:10
104:13
104:14[2]
104:16
104:19
104:32[2]
105:5
105:7
105:8[2]
105:9
105:14[2]
105:16[2]
105:17
105:18
105:21
105:24
105:25
105:26[2]
105:28
105:29
105:31
105:32
105:33
105:34
105:36
105:37
105:39
105:40
105:41
105:42
105:43
106:1
106:3
106:8[2]
106:9[2]
106:10
106:15
106:23[3]
106:26
106:33
106:40
106:41
106:43
106:44[2]
106:45
106:46
107:1
107:2
107:6
107:7
107:9
107:12
107:13
107:14
107:16
107:19
107:20
107:25
107:28
107:29
107:30
107:33
107:35
107:36
107:38
107:40
107:41
108:13
109:7
109:11
109:15
109:16[2]
109:17[2]
109:18
109:19
109:31
110:6[3]
110:7[2]
111:4
111:5[2]
111:6[2]
111:9[2]
112:4
112:5
112:6
112:7
112:8[2]
112:9[2]
112:10
113:7
113:8
113:9
115:3[2]
115:9
115:10
115:11
115:12[3]
115:13
115:16
116:1
116:2
116:6
118:1
118:18
118:26
118:29
120:1
121:3[2]
121:4
121:7
123:2
126:6
127:2
129:4
129:7
130:8
132:2
132:11
132:13
135:6
135:7[3]
135:14
136:1
137:8
137:9
138:6[2]
142:*title*
143:3[2]
144:2
144:10
145:19[2]
145:20
146:4
146:5
146:9
147:2
147:3
147:4[2]
147:6
147:9
147:10[2]
147:13[2]
147:14
147:15
147:16[2]
147:17
147:18[2]
147:19
147:20
148:5
148:6[2]
148:14
149:4

PR

2:7[2]
2:8
3:6
3:12[2]
3:19
3:29
3:30
3:33
3:34[2]
4:4
5:21
5:22
5:23[2]
6:13[3]
6:14[2]
6:15
6:19
6:29
6:30[2]
6:31[3]
6:32
6:33
6:34
6:35[2]
7:8
7:19
7:20
7:22
8:26
8:27[2]
8:28[2]
8:29[2]
8:36
9:7[2]
9:8[2]
9:9[2]
9:18
10:3
10:4
10:5[2]
10:9
10:10
10:17[2]
10:18[2]
10:19
10:22
11:12
11:13
11:15[2]
11:17
11:19
11:25
11:26
11:27[2]
11:28
11:29
11:30
12:1
12:2
12:8
12:9[2]
12:11[2]
12:15
12:17
12:27
13:3[2]
13:11
13:13
13:18
13:20
13:24[2]
14:2[2]
14:17
14:21[3]
14:29[2]
14:31[2]
15:5
15:9
15:10
15:12
15:15
15:18
15:24
15:25
15:27[2]
15:29
15:32[2]
16:5
16:7
16:17
16:20[2]
16:26
16:30[2]
16:32[3]
17:5
17:9[2]
17:15[2]
17:16
17:19[2]
17:20[2]
17:21
17:27
17:28[2]
18:9
18:13[2]
18:17
18:20
19:1
19:2
19:5
19:7
19:8[2]
19:9
19:16[2]
19:17[3]
19:23[2]
19:25
19:26
20:4
20:14[2]
20:19
20:22
21:1[2]
21:11
21:13
21:17[2]
21:21
21:26
21:27
21:29
22:5
22:6[3]
22:8
22:9[2]
22:11
22:12
22:14
22:16[2]
22:22
22:27
22:29[2]
23:7[3]
23:9
23:11
23:13
23:24
23:34[2]
24:7
24:8
24:12[4]
24:17
24:18
24:24
24:29
25:10
25:13
25:17
25:20[2]
25:21
25:28
26:5
26:6
26:8[2]
26:17
26:24
26:25
26:27
27:14
27:18
28:6[2]
28:7
28:8[2]
28:9
28:10
28:13
28:14
28:16
28:18
28:19[2]
28:20
28:22
28:23[2]
28:25[2]
28:26[2]
28:27[2]
29:1
29:3
29:4
29:9
29:17[2]
29:18[2]
29:19[2]
29:21
29:24
29:27
30:5
30:6
30:10
30:22[2]
30:31
31:11
31:23
31:28

EC

1:3
1:5
1:18
2:19[2]
2:21
2:22
2:24[2]
2:26[2]
3:9[3]
3:11[2]
4:3
4:8[2]
4:10[2]
4:14[2]
5:4
5:8
5:10[2]
5:12
5:14
5:15[4]
5:16[3]
5:17[2]
5:18
5:20
6:2[2]
6:3[2]
6:4
6:5
6:6[2]
6:10[2]
6:12
7:13
7:18
8:3
8:7
8:8
8:13[2]
8:17[2]
9:2[2]
9:9
9:15
10:3[3]
10:8
10:9
10:10[2]
10:15
11:4[2]
12:4
12:9[2]

CA

1:13
2:3
2:8
2:9[2]
2:16
3:10
5:6[2]
5:16
6:3
8:11

ISA

1:1
1:11
2:3
2:4
2:12
2:18
2:19
2:21
2:22
3:7
4:3[2]
5:2[2]
5:7
5:14
5:25
5:26
6:2[3]
6:6
6:7
6:9
6:11
7:13
7:15[2]
7:22
8:7
8:8[3]
8:14
9:1
9:15[2]
9:20[2]
10:7
10:8
10:13
10:16
10:24
10:26
10:28[3]
10:32[2]
10:34
11:3
11:4[3]
11:12
11:15
11:16
12:2
12:5
13:9
14:6[2]
14:30
15:8
16:5
16:6
16:12[2]
17:5
17:8
17:14
18:3[2]
18:5
19:16
19:17
19:20[2]
19:22[2]
20:2
21:4
21:6
21:7[2]
21:8
21:9[2]
21:11
22:8
22:16
22:19
22:21
22:22[2]
22:23
23:11[2]
23:12
23:13
24:18[2]
25:7
25:8[2]
25:9
25:11[3]
25:12
26:3
26:5
26:10[2]
27:1
27:5[2]
27:6
27:7[3]
27:8
27:9
27:10
27:11[2]
28:4[2]
28:9[2]
28:11
28:12
28:16
28:20
28:21[2]
28:24
28:25[2]
28:28
29:8[5]
29:10
29:11
29:12
29:16[2]
29:23
30:14[2]
30:18[3]
30:19[3]
30:23
30:32
30:33
31:2
31:3[2]
31:4
31:5[2]
31:8
31:9
32:6
32:7
32:8
33:4
33:5[2]
33:8[3]
33:15[2]
33:16
33:18
33:22
34:2[2]
34:11
34:17
35:4
36:2
36:7
36:12
36:14
37:1
37:2
37:7
37:8[2]
37:9[4]
37:33
37:34[2]
37:38
38:7
38:9
38:12
38:13
38:15
38:19
38:21
39:1[2]
39:4
39:8
40:5
40:6
40:11[2]
40:14
40:15
40:20[3]
40:22
40:23
40:24
40:26[2]
40:29[2]
41:2
41:3[2]
41:4
41:7[2]
41:24
41:25[3]
41:26
42:1
42:2
42:3[3]
42:4[2]
42:5[3]
42:13[3]
42:19
42:20
42:21
42:24
42:25[3]
43:1
43:10
43:13
43:25
44:12[2]
44:13[3]
44:14[3]
44:15[4]
44:16[4]
44:17[2]
44:18
44:20[2]
44:24
44:28
45:9
45:13[2]
45:18[3]
46:4
46:6
46:7[3]
48:12
48:14
48:15
48:21[3]
49:1
49:2[3]
49:6
49:7
49:10[2]
50:4[2]
50:8
50:9
51:3[2]
51:12
51:13
51:14[2]
52:6
52:9
52:13
52:15
53:2[2]
53:3[2]
53:4
53:5[2]
53:7[4]
53:8[3]
53:9[2]
53:10[3]
53:11[2]
53:12[4]
54:5
55:1
55:5
55:6[2]
55:7[2]
57:2
57:13
57:17
58:9
59:2
59:5
59:15
59:16
59:17[2]
59:18[2]
60:9
61:1
61:3
61:10[2]
62:7[2]
63:7
63:8[2]
63:9[3]
63:10[2]
63:11[3]
64:4
65:16[2]
66:3[8]
66:5

JER

2:14[2]
2:17
2:26
3:1
3:5[2]
4:7
4:13
5:12
5:24
5:26
8:4
8:8
9:8
9:12[2]
9:24
10:10
10:12[2]
10:13[3]
10:16
11:16
12:4
13:16[2]
13:21
14:10
14:22
15:4
16:15
17:6
17:8
17:11
18:3
18:4[2]
19:4
20:4
20:10
20:13
20:17
21:2
21:7[2]
21:9[3]
21:10
22:4
22:10
22:11
22:12
22:16
22:19
22:28[2]
23:6
23:17
23:20[2]
23:28
23:31
25:30[2]
25:31[2]
25:38
26:11
26:13
26:16
26:19[2]
26:21
27:20
29:21
29:28
29:31
29:32[3]
30:7
30:21
30:24[2]
31:10
31:11
31:20
32:3
32:5[2]
32:28
33:1
33:15
33:21
33:24
34:2
34:3
34:14
34:16
35:8
35:14
35:16
35:18
36:4
36:12
36:13
36:18
36:21
36:23
36:25[2]
36:30
37:2[2]
37:13[2]
37:14
37:17
38:2[3]
38:4
38:5[2]
38:9[2]
38:10
38:26
38:27
38:28
39:4
39:5
39:7
39:12
39:14[2]
39:15
40:1
40:3
40:5[2]
40:11
40:15
41:4
41:6[3]
41:7
41:9
41:16[3]
42:8
42:12
42:21
43:10
43:11[2]
43:12[3]
43:13[2]
45:1
46:8
46:10
46:16
46:17
46:18
47:7
48:10
48:11[2]
48:18
48:26
48:27
48:29
48:36
48:40
48:42
48:44[2]
49:1
49:10[2]
49:12
49:19
49:20[3]
49:22
50:8
50:19
50:34[2]
50:44
50:45[3]
51:6
51:12
51:15[2]
51:16[3]
51:19
51:34[5]
51:40
51:44
51:59
52:1
52:2
52:3
52:4
52:9
52:10
52:11
52:13
52:25
52:29
52:33

LA

1:13[4]
1:14
1:15
2:2[3]
2:4[3]
2:5[3]
2:6[2]
2:7[2]
2:8[3]
2:9
2:17[6]
3:2
3:3[2]
3:4[2]
3:5
3:6
3:7[2]
3:8
3:9[2]
3:10
3:11[2]
3:12
3:13
3:15[2]
3:16[2]
3:27
3:28
3:29
3:30
3:32[2]
3:33
3:37
4:11
4:16
4:22[3]

EZE

2:1
2:2
2:3
2:10
3:1
3:2
3:3
3:4
3:10
3:19[2]
3:20[3]
3:21[3]
3:22
3:27[2]
4:15
4:16
6:12[3]
7:15[2]
7:20
8:3
8:5
8:6
8:7
8:8
8:9
8:12
8:13
8:14
8:15
8:16
8:17
9:1
9:3[2]
9:5
9:7
9:9
11:2
12:12[2]
12:13[3]
12:27[2]
13:22
14:9
17:4[2]
17:5[7]
17:7
17:9
17:13
17:15[4]
17:16[3]
17:18[3]
17:19[2]
17:20[2]
18:8
18:9[2]
18:10
18:13[4]
18:14[2]
18:17[2]
18:18[2]
18:19
18:21[3]
18:22[3]
18:23
18:24[5]
18:26[2]
18:27[2]
18:28[4]
19:4
19:6[2]
19:7[2]
19:8
20:11
20:13
20:21
20:49
21:11
21:21[3]
21:23
21:27
24:24
24:26
26:8[2]
26:9[2]
26:10
26:11[2]
29:9
29:18[2]
29:19
29:20
30:11
30:24
30:25
31:5
31:10
31:11
31:15
32:25
32:32
33:3[2]
33:5[2]
33:6
33:9[2]
33:12[3]
33:13[4]
33:14
33:15[3]
33:16[3]
33:18
33:19
33:22[2]
33:24
34:12
34:17
34:23[2]
37:3
37:4
37:9
37:10
37:11
38:17
39:15
40:2
40:3[2]
40:5
40:6
40:8
40:9
40:11
40:13
40:14
40:17
40:19
40:20
40:23
40:24[2]
40:27
40:28[2]
40:32[2]
40:35
40:45
40:47
40:48
40:49
41:1
41:2
41:3
41:4[2]
41:5
41:13
41:15
41:22
42:1[2]
42:13
42:15[2]
42:16
42:17
42:18
42:19
42:20
43:1
43:7
43:18
43:21
44:1
44:3[2]
44:4
44:26
44:27[2]
44:30
45:17
45:23
45:24
45:25
46:2[2]
46:5
46:7
46:8[2]
46:9[4]
46:11
46:12[3]
46:17
46:18
46:19
46:20
46:21
46:24
47:1
47:2
47:3[2]
47:4[2]
47:5
47:6[2]
47:8

DA

1:2[2]
1:3
1:5
1:7
1:8[4]
1:10
1:14
1:18
1:20
2:15
2:16[2]
2:21[3]
2:22[2]
2:24
2:29
2:38
2:49
3:1
3:11
3:17
3:19
3:20
3:25
4:14
4:17
4:25
4:29
4:32
4:33
4:35
4:37
5:2
5:12
5:19[9]
5:20
5:21[4]
5:29
6:4
6:7
6:10[3]
6:14[2]
6:16
6:20[2]
6:23
6:26
6:27[2]
7:1
7:16
7:23
7:24[2]
7:25
8:4
8:5
8:6
8:7[2]
8:8[2]
8:11
8:14
8:17[3]
8:18[2]
8:19
8:24
8:25[4]
9:2
9:10
9:12[2]
9:14
9:22
9:27[3]
10:1
10:11[2]
10:12
10:15
10:18
10:19
10:20
11:2
11:4[2]
11:5
11:6[3]
11:8
11:10
11:11
11:12[3]
11:16[2]
11:17[3]
11:18[2]
11:19[2]
11:20
11:21
11:23[2]
11:24[4]
11:25[2]
11:28[2]
11:29
11:30[3]
11:32
11:36
11:37[2]
11:38[2]
11:39[3]
11:40
11:41
11:42
11:43
11:44
11:45[2]
12:7[2]
12:9
12:12

HO

1:3
5:6
5:11
5:13
6:1[4]
6:2[2]
6:3
6:11
7:4
7:5
7:8
7:9[2]
8:1
8:13
9:9[2]
10:1[2]
10:2[2]
10:12
11:5
11:10[2]
12:1
12:2
12:3[2]
12:4[4]
12:7[2]
12:12
12:13
13:1[3]
13:13[2]
13:15[2]
14:5
14:9[2]

JOE

1:6
1:7[2]
2:11
2:13
2:14
2:20
2:23[2]

AM

1:1
1:2
1:11[2]
1:15
2:1
2:9
2:15[3]
2:16
3:4[2]
3:7
3:11
4:2
4:13
5:6
6:10[3]
6:11
7:1
7:2
7:5
7:7
8:2
9:1[3]
9:3
9:5
9:6[2]

OB

12

JON

1:3[2]
1:5
1:9
1:10[2]
1:12
2:2
3:4
3:6[2]
3:7
3:10[3]
4:1
4:2
4:5
4:8
4:9

MIC

1:1
1:9
1:11
1:15
2:4[3]
2:11
3:4[2]
3:5
4:2
4:3
4:12
5:1
5:2
5:3
5:4[2]
5:5
5:6[3]
5:8
6:2
6:8
7:3
7:9[2]
7:12
7:18[2]
7:19[3]

NA

1:2
1:4
1:7
1:8
1:9
1:12
1:15
2:1
2:5

HAB

1:11
1:13
2:1
2:2
2:5[2]
2:9[2]
3:4
3:6[2]

3:16^2 3:19^2

ZEP

1:7 1:12 1:18 2:11 2:13 2:14 3:5^3 3:15 3:17^4

HAG

1:6

ZEC

1:6 1:8 1:19 1:21 2:2 2:8^2 2:13 3:1 3:4^2 4:6 4:7 4:9 4:13 4:14 5:2 5:3 5:6^2 5:8^3 5:11 6:7 6:8 6:12^2 6:13^3 7:13 9:4 9:7^3 9:9 9:10 10:11 11:16 12:8 13:3 13:4 13:5 13:6 14:3

MAL

1:8 1:9^2 2:5 2:6 2:7 2:11 2:13 2:15^3 2:16 2:17 3:1^2 3:2^2 3:3^2 3:11 4:6

MT

1:20 1:21 1:25 2:2 2:3 2:4^2 2:7 2:8 2:14^2 2:16^3 2:21 2:22^3 2:23^2 3:3 3:7^2 3:11^2 3:12^2 3:15 3:16^2 4:2^2 4:3 4:4 4:6 4:12 4:13 4:19 4:21^2 4:24 5:1^2 5:2 5:19 5:45 6:24^2 6:30 7:8 7:9 7:10^2 7:21 7:29 8:1 8:9^3 8:10 8:14 8:15 8:16 8:18 8:23 8:24 8:26^2 8:28 8:32 8:34 9:1 9:6 9:7 9:9^3 9:12 9:18 9:22 9:24 9:25 9:28 9:29 9:34 9:36^2 9:37 9:38 10:1^2 10:22 10:25 10:37^2 10:38 10:39^2 10:40^2 10:41^2 10:42 11:1 11:2 11:3 11:6 11:10 11:11^2 11:15 11:18 11:20 11:27 12:3^2 12:4 12:9^2 12:11^2 12:13^2 12:15^2 12:18 12:19

12:20^3 12:22 12:26 12:29^2 12:30^2 12:39 12:43 12:44^3 12:45 12:46 12:48 12:49 13:2 13:3 13:4 13:11 13:12^2 13:19 13:20^2 13:21^2 13:22^3 13:23^2 13:24 13:28 13:29 13:31 13:33 13:34 13:37^2 13:44^2 13:46^2 13:52 13:53 13:54^2 13:58 14:2 14:5^2 14:7 14:9 14:10 14:13 14:14 14:18 14:19^2 14:22 14:23^3 14:29^2 14:30^3 15:3 15:4 15:6 15:10 15:13 15:23 15:24 15:26 15:30 15:35 15:36 15:39 16:1 16:2 16:4 16:8 16:12 16:13 16:15 16:20^2 16:21 16:23 16:26 16:27 17:5 17:13 17:15^2 17:18 17:23 17:25^2 18:6 18:12 18:13^2 18:15 18:16 18:17^2 18:24 18:25^2 18:28

18:30^2 18:32 18:34 19:1 19:2 19:4^2 19:8 19:11 19:12 19:13 19:15 19:17 19:18 19:22^2 20:2^2 20:3 20:5 20:6 20:7 20:13 20:19 20:21 20:23 21:3 21:9 21:10 21:14 21:15 21:17^2 21:18^2 21:19^2 21:23^2 21:25 21:27 21:28 21:29^2 21:30^2 21:31 21:34 21:36 21:37 21:40 21:41 21:45 22:4 22:7^2 22:8 22:11 22:12 22:20 22:21 22:25 22:34 22:42 22:43 22:45 23:11 23:12 23:15 23:16 23:18 23:22 23:39 24:3 24:13 24:26^2 24:31 24:43 24:46 24:47 24:50^2 25:12 25:15 25:16 25:17^2 25:18 25:20 25:22 25:24 25:29^2 25:31 25:32 25:33 25:41 25:45 26:1 26:7

26:10 26:16 26:18 26:20 26:21 26:23^2 26:24 26:25 26:27 26:37 26:38 26:39 26:40 26:42 26:43 26:44 26:45 26:46 26:47 26:48^2 26:49 26:53 26:65 26:66 26:68 26:70 26:71 26:72 26:74 26:75 27:3^2 27:5 27:12^2 27:14 27:18 27:19 27:23 27:24^2 27:26^3 27:34^2 27:42^3 27:43^3 27:50 27:58 27:59 27:60^2 27:63 27:64 28:6^3 28:7^2

MK

1:6 1:8 1:10 1:13 1:16^2 1:19^2 1:20 1:21 1:22 1:23 1:26 1:27 1:31 1:34 1:35 1:38 1:39 1:42^2 1:43 1:45 2:1^2 2:2 2:4 2:5 2:8 2:10 2:12 2:13^2 2:14^3 2:16 2:17 2:23 2:25^3

2:26 2:27 3:1 3:2 3:3 3:4 3:5^3 3:8 3:9 3:10 3:12 3:13^2 3:14^2 3:16 3:17 3:21 3:22^2 3:23 3:26 3:27^2 3:29 3:30 3:33 3:34 4:1^2 4:2 4:4 4:9^2 4:10 4:11 4:13 4:21 4:24 4:25^3 4:26 4:27 4:29 4:30 4:33 4:34^2 4:35 4:36 4:38^2 4:39 4:40 5:2 5:4 5:5 5:6^2 5:8 5:9^2 5:10^2 5:18^3 5:21 5:22^2 5:32 5:34 5:35 5:36 5:37 5:38 5:39^2 5:40^2 5:41 5:43 6:1 6:2 6:5 6:6^2 6:7 6:10 6:14 6:16^2 6:17 6:20^2 6:23 6:26 6:27 6:31 6:34^2 6:37 6:38 6:39 6:41^3 6:45^2 6:46^2 6:47

6:48^2 6:50 6:51 6:55 6:56 7:6 7:9 7:11 7:14^2 7:17 7:18 7:20 7:24^2 7:26 7:29 7:31 7:33^2 7:34 7:35 7:36^2 7:37^2 8:5 8:6^2 8:7 8:9 8:10 8:12 8:13 8:15 8:17 8:21 8:22 8:23^4 8:24 8:25^2 8:26 8:27 8:29 8:30 8:31 8:32 8:33^2 8:34^2 8:36 8:38 9:1 9:2 9:6 9:9 9:12^2 9:14^2 9:16 9:18^3 9:19 9:20^2 9:21 9:25 9:26^2 9:27 9:28 9:29 9:30 9:31^3 9:33^2 9:35 9:36^3 9:38^2 9:40 9:41 9:42 10:1^3 10:3 10:5 10:11 10:13 10:14 10:15 10:16 10:17 10:20 10:22^2 10:30 10:32 10:34 10:36 10:46 10:47^2

10:48^2 10:49 10:50 10:52 11:1 11:3 11:7 11:9 11:11^2 11:12 11:13^4 11:17 11:19 11:21 11:23^3 11:27 11:31 11:32 12:1 12:2^2 12:4 12:5 12:6 12:9 12:12 12:15 12:16 12:21 12:27 12:28 12:32 12:34^2 12:35 12:37 12:38 12:43 13:1 13:3 13:13 13:20^2 13:21 13:27 13:36 14:3 14:11^2 14:13 14:14 14:15 14:16 14:17 14:20 14:21 14:23^3 14:24 14:31 14:32 14:33 14:35 14:36 14:37 14:39 14:40^2 14:41 14:42 14:43 14:44^2 14:45^2 14:52 14:54 14:61 14:68^2 14:70 14:71 14:72^2 15:2 15:3 15:6 15:8 15:10 15:11 15:14 15:15 15:23 15:28 15:31^2 15:35 15:39^2

15:41 15:44^3 15:45^2 15:46 15:47 16:6^3 16:7^2 16:9^2 16:11 16:12 16:14^2 16:15 16:16^2 16:19

LU

1:8 1:9 1:12 1:15^2 1:16 1:17 1:21 1:22^4 1:23 1:25 1:32 1:33 1:48 1:49 1:51^2 1:52 1:53^2 1:54 1:55 1:60 1:62 1:63 1:64 1:68 1:70 1:73 1:74 2:4 2:21 2:26^2 2:27 2:28 2:42 2:49 2:50 2:51 3:3 3:7 3:11^3 3:13 3:14 3:15 3:16 3:17^2 3:18 3:20 4:2^2 4:9 4:10 4:13 4:15 4:16^3 4:17^2 4:18^2 4:20^2 4:21 4:23 4:24 4:30 4:35 4:36 4:38 4:39 4:40 4:41^2 4:42^2 4:43 5:1 5:3^3

5:4^2 5:8 5:9 5:12 5:13 5:14 5:16 5:17 5:20^2 5:22 5:24 5:25^2 5:27^2 5:28 5:34 5:36 5:39 6:1 6:4 6:5 6:6 6:7 6:8^2 6:10^2 6:12 6:13^3 6:14 6:17 6:20 6:35 6:39 6:47 6:48 6:49 7:1^2 7:3^3 7:4^2 7:5^2 7:6 7:8^3 7:9 7:11 7:12 7:13 7:14^2 7:15^2 7:19 7:20 7:21^2 7:23 7:24 7:27 7:28^2 7:33 7:36^2 7:39^2 7:40 7:42 7:43^3 7:44 7:48 7:50 8:1 8:4 8:5 8:8^3 8:10 8:16 8:18 8:21 8:22^2 8:23 8:24 8:25^2 8:27 8:28^2 8:29^3 8:30 8:31 8:32^2 8:36 8:37 8:38 8:39 8:41^2 8:42^2 8:44

8:48 8:49 8:50 8:51^2 8:52 8:54 8:55 8:56 9:1 9:2 9:3 9:7 9:9 9:10 9:11 9:13 9:14 9:16^2 9:18^2 9:20 9:21 9:23 9:25 9:26 9:28 9:29 9:31 9:33 9:34 9:38 9:39^2 9:42 9:43 9:48 9:49 9:50 9:51^2 9:53 9:55 9:59^2 10:1 10:2^2 10:16^3 10:18 10:22 10:23 10:26 10:27 10:28 10:29 10:31^2 10:32 10:33^4 10:35^2 10:37^2 10:38 11:1^2 11:2 11:5 11:7 11:8^4 11:10 11:11^3 11:12^2 11:14 11:15 11:17 11:22^3 11:23^2 11:24^2 11:25^2 11:26 11:27 11:28 11:29 11:33 11:37^2 11:38^2 11:40 11:46 11:53 12:1 12:5 12:9 12:13 12:14 12:15^2

12:16 12:17 12:18 12:21 12:22 12:28 12:36^2 12:37^2 12:38 12:39 12:43 12:44^2 12:46^2 12:48 12:54 12:58 13:6^2 13:7 13:8 13:10 13:12 13:13 13:17 13:18 13:20 13:22 13:23 13:25 13:27 13:32 13:35 14:1 14:4 14:7^2 14:9 14:10^2 14:11 14:12 14:15^2 14:16 14:25 14:26 14:28 14:29 14:31 14:32 14:33^3 14:35 15:3 15:4^2 15:5^2 15:6^2 15:11 15:12 15:14^2 15:15^2 15:16 15:17^2 15:20^3 15:24 15:25^2 15:26 15:27^2 15:28 15:29 15:31 16:1^2 16:2 16:5 16:6^2 16:7^3 16:8 16:10^2 16:13^2 16:15 16:23 16:24^2 16:25 16:27 16:28 16:30 16:31 17:1 17:2^2 17:3 17:4 17:7

17:9^2 17:11^2 17:12 17:14^2 17:15^2 17:16 17:19 17:20^2 17:22 17:25 17:31^2 17:37 18:1 18:4^2 18:7 18:8^2 18:9 18:14 18:15 18:21 18:22 18:23^3 18:24^2 18:27 18:29 18:31 18:32 18:33 18:35 18:36 18:38 18:39^2 18:40^2 18:41 18:43 19:1 19:3^3 19:4^2 19:5 19:6 19:7 19:9 19:11^2 19:12 19:13 19:15^4 19:17 19:19 19:22 19:24 19:25 19:26 19:28^2 19:29^2 19:32 19:36 19:37 19:40 19:41^2 19:45 19:47 20:1 20:2 20:3 20:5 20:9 20:10 20:11 20:12 20:16 20:17 20:19 20:23 20:25 20:28 20:30 20:37 20:38 20:41 20:44 21:1 21:2 21:3 21:5 21:8 21:10 21:29

21:37^2 22:4^2 22:6 22:8 22:10^2 22:12 22:13 22:14 22:15 22:17 22:19 22:22 22:25 22:26^3 22:27^4 22:31 22:33 22:34 22:35 22:36^3 22:37 22:38 22:39^2 22:40^2 22:41 22:44 22:45^2 22:47^2 22:51 22:56 22:57 22:59 22:60 22:61 22:67 22:70 23:2 23:3 23:5 23:6 23:7^3 23:8^4 23:9^2 23:13 23:17 23:22^2 23:23 23:25^2 23:26 23:35^2 23:42 23:46^2 23:47 23:50 23:51 23:53 24:6^3 24:12 24:17 24:19 24:21 24:23 24:25 24:27 24:28^2 24:29 24:30^2 24:31 24:32^2 24:35 24:38 24:40^2 24:41 24:43 24:44 24:45 24:50^2 24:51^2

JOH

1:8 1:10 1:11 1:12 1:15^3

1:18 1:20 1:21^2 1:23 1:27 1:30^2 1:31 1:33^2 1:36^2 1:39^2 1:41 1:42^2 1:51 2:5 2:8 2:12 2:15^2 2:21 2:22^2 2:23^2 2:24 2:25 3:3 3:4^2 3:5 3:13 3:16 3:18^3 3:21 3:22 3:26 3:29 3:30 3:31^3 3:32^2 3:33 3:34 3:36^2 4:4 4:5 4:10 4:18 4:25^2 4:26 4:27 4:32 4:36^3 4:39 4:40^2 4:43 4:45^2 4:46 4:47^4 4:50 4:51 4:52^2 4:54 5:4 5:6^2 5:11^2 5:13 5:16 5:18 5:19^2 5:20 5:21 5:23 5:24 5:26 5:27 5:32 5:33 5:35 5:38 5:46 6:2 6:3 6:5 6:6^3 6:11^2 6:12 6:15 6:20 6:29 6:31 6:33 6:35^2

6:39 6:41 6:42 6:46 6:47 6:51 6:56 6:57^2 6:58 6:59^2 6:61 6:62 6:65 6:71^2 7:1 7:4 7:9^2 7:10 7:11 7:12^2 7:17 7:18^2 7:25 7:26 7:27^2 7:28^2 7:29 7:31 7:35^2 7:36 7:38 7:39 7:50 7:51 8:2^2 8:6 8:7^2 8:8 8:10 8:12 8:20 8:22^2 8:23 8:24 8:26 8:27 8:28 8:29 8:30 8:42 8:44^4 8:47 8:51 8:52 8:54 8:56 9:1 9:2 9:6^3 9:7 9:8^2 9:9^4 9:11 9:12^2 9:15^3 9:16 9:17^3 9:18 9:19 9:20 9:21^3 9:22^2 9:23 9:25^2 9:26^2 9:27 9:29 9:30^2 9:31 9:33 9:31 9:33 9:35^2 9:36^2 9:37 9:38^2 10:1

10:2 10:3 10:4^2 10:6 10:9 10:12 10:13 10:20 10:35 10:39 10:40 11:3 11:4 11:6^4 11:7 11:8 11:9^2 11:10 11:11^2 11:12^2 11:13 11:17^2 11:24 11:25^3 11:33 11:36 11:39^2 11:43^2 11:44 11:51^2 11:52 11:56 11:57^2 12:1 12:6^3 12:9^2 12:14 12:17 12:18 12:25^2 12:33^2 12:35^2 12:37 12:38 12:40 12:41 12:44 12:45 12:48 12:49 13:1^2 13:3 13:4 13:5^2 13:6 13:10 13:11^2 13:12^2 13:16^2 13:18 13:19 13:20^2 13:21 13:22 13:24^2 13:25 13:26^3 13:28 13:29 13:30 13:31 14:9 14:10 14:12^3 14:16^2 14:17 14:21^3 14:23 14:24 14:26 15:2^2 15:5 15:6 15:23 15:26 16:2 16:8^2

16:13^6 16:14^2 16:15 16:17 16:18^2 16:23 17:2 18:1^2 18:5 18:6^2 18:7 18:8 18:9 18:13 18:14 18:17 18:22 18:25 18:30 18:32^2 18:38^2 19:7^2 19:8 19:11 19:13 19:14 19:16 19:17 19:21 19:26^2 19:27 19:30^2 19:33 19:35^3 19:38^2 19:41 20:5^2 20:8 20:9 20:18 20:20^2 20:22^2 20:25 20:27 21:1 21:6 21:7^2 21:14 21:15^2 21:16^3 21:17^3 21:19^4 21:20 21:22 21:23^2

AC

1:2^3 1:3 1:4 1:7 1:9^2 1:10 1:17 1:18 1:22 1:25^2 1:26 2:24 2:25 2:29 2:30 2:31 2:33 2:34 2:40 3:5 3:7 3:8 3:10 3:12 3:13 3:18 3:20 3:22

4:9 4:32 4:35 5:37 6:10 7:2^{3} 7:4^{2} 7:5^{4} 7:8 7:10 7:12 7:15 7:21 7:23 7:24 7:25 7:26 7:27 7:29 7:31^{2} 7:36^{2} 7:38 7:44^{3} 7:55 7:60^{3} 8:3 8:6 8:11 8:13^{2} 8:16 8:18 8:19 8:27 8:31^{3} 8:32^{3} 8:37 8:38^{2} 8:39 8:40^{2} 9:2^{2} 9:3^{2} 9:4 9:5 9:6 9:8 9:9 9:10 9:11 9:12 9:13 9:14 9:15 9:16 9:18 9:19^{2} 9:20^{2} 9:21^{2} 9:26^{2} 9:27^{3} 9:28 9:29 9:32 9:33 9:34 9:38 9:39 9:41^{2} 9:43 10:3 10:4^{3} 10:6^{2} 10:7 10:8^{2} 10:10^{2} 10:17^{2} 10:21 10:23 10:27^{2} 10:28 10:32^{2} 10:35 10:36 10:39 10:41 10:42^{2} 10:48 11:13^{2} 11:16 11:17 11:22 11:23 11:24 11:26^{2} 12:2 12:3^{2} 12:4^{2} 12:7 12:8^{2} 12:9^{2} 12:11 12:12^{2} 12:17^{3} 12:19^{2} 12:23^{2} 13:11 13:12 13:17 13:18 13:19^{2} 13:20 13:22^{3} 13:25^{2} 13:28 13:31 13:33 13:34^{2} 13:35 13:36 13:37 14:9 14:10 14:12 14:17^{2} 14:19 14:20^{2} 14:27 15:8 15:41 16:1 16:10 16:18 16:27 16:29 16:33^{2} 16:34^{2} 17:16 17:17 17:18^{2} 17:24 17:25^{2} 17:27 17:31^{4} 18:3^{2} 18:4 18:6 18:7 18:11 18:16 18:18 18:19^{2} 18:20 18:21 18:22^{2} 18:23^{2} 18:25 18:26 18:27^{2} 18:28 19:2 19:3 19:8 19:9 19:21 19:22^{2} 19:25 19:31 19:34 19:35 19:41^{2} 20:2^{2} 20:3^{2} 20:9 20:11^{2} 20:13 20:14 20:16^{2} 20:17 20:18 20:28 20:35 20:36^{2} 20:38 21:4 21:11^{2} 21:14 21:19^{2} 21:33^{2} 21:34 21:35^{2} 21:37 21:40^{2} 22:2^{2} 22:8 22:14 22:21 22:22 22:24^{2} 22:26 22:27 22:39^{3} 22:30^{3} 23:5 23:6 23:7 23:15^{2} 23:16 23:17 23:18 23:20 23:23 23:25 23:27 23:34^{4} 23:35^{2} 24:2 24:22 24:23^{2} 24:24 24:25 24:26^{3} 25:1 25:3 25:4 25:6^{2} 25:7 25:8 25:12 25:16 25:20 25:22 25:24 25:25^{2} 26:15 26:23 26:24 26:25 26:30 26:32 27:6 27:35^{4} 28:4 28:5 28:6^{2} 28:15 28:17 28:23 28:29

RO

1:2 2:28 2:29 3:26 3:29^{2} 4:2 4:10 4:11^{3} 4:12 4:13 4:17 4:18 4:19^{2} 4:20 4:21^{2} 6:7 6:10^{4} 7:1 7:2 8:9 8:11 8:24 8:27^{2} 8:29^{3} 8:30^{6} 8:32^{2} 8:34 9:15 9:18^{4} 9:19 9:23^{2} 9:24 9:25 9:28 10:21 11:2^{2} 11:7 11:21 11:32 12:3 12:7 12:8^{4} 12:20 13:4^{3} 13:8 14:2 14:4^{2} 14:6^{7} 14:9 14:18 14:22^{2} 14:23^{3} 15:10 15:12 15:21

1 CO

1:31 2:14 2:15^{2} 2:16 3:7^{2} 3:8^{2} 3:10 3:14^{2} 3:15^{2} 3:18 3:19 4:4 5:2 6:16^{2} 6:17 6:18 7:13 7:20 7:22^{2} 7:24 7:32^{2} 7:33^{2} 7:36^{3} 7:37^{2} 7:38^{2} 8:2^{3} 9:10^{3} 10:12^{2} 10:22 11:7 11:23 11:24^{2} 11:25^{2} 11:26 11:29 12:11 14:2^{2} 14:3 14:4^{2} 14:5^{3} 14:11 14:13 14:16^{2} 14:24^{2} 14:25 15:4^{2} 15:5 15:6 15:7 15:8 15:12 15:15^{2} 15:24^{2} 15:25^{2} 15:27^{3} 16:10^{2} 16:11 16:12^{2}

2 CO

1:10 1:21 2:2 2:5 4:14 5:5 5:10 5:15 5:17 5:21 6:2 6:15 7:7^{2} 7:15 8:6^{2} 8:9^{2} 8:12 8:15^{2} 8:17^{2} 8:23 9:6^{2} 9:7 9:9^{2} 9:10 10:7^{2} 10:17 10:18 11:4 12:4 12:6^{2} 12:9 13:4^{2}

GA

1:4 1:23^{2} 2:8 2:11 2:12^{2} 3:5^{2} 3:16 4:1^{2} 4:23^{2} 4:29 5:3 5:10^{2} 6:3^{2} 6:4 6:7 6:8^{2}

EPH

1:4 1:6 1:8 1:9 1:10 1:20^{2} 2:1 2:4 2:7 2:14 2:16 3:3 3:11 3:16 4:8^{3} 4:9^{2} 4:10^{2} 4:11 4:28 5:14 5:23 5:26 5:27 5:28 6:8^{2} 6:22

PHP

1:6 2:8 2:22 2:25 2:26^{2} 2:27 2:30 3:4^{2} 3:21

COL

1:17 1:18^{2} 1:21 2:13 2:15 2:18 3:25^{2} 4:8 4:10 4:13

1 TH

1:10 3:13 4:8 5:24

2 TH

1:10 2:4^{2} 2:6 2:7^{2} 2:14 3:6 3:10 3:14

1 TI

1:12 3:1 3:5 3:6 3:7 5:8 6:4 6:15

2 TI

1:12 1:16 1:17^{2} 1:18^{2} 2:4 2:5 2:12 2:13^{2} 2:21 4:11 4:15

TIT

1:9^{2} 2:8 2:14 3:5 3:6 3:11

PHM

13 15 18

HEB

1:2^{2} 1:3 1:4 1:5^{2} 1:6^{2} 1:7 1:8 1:13 2:5 2:8^{2} 2:9 2:11^{2} 2:14^{2} 2:16^{2} 2:17 2:18^{2} 3:3 3:4 3:17 3:18 4:3 4:4 4:7 4:8 4:10^{2} 5:1 5:2 5:3 5:4 5:5 5:6 5:7^{2} 5:8^{3} 5:9 5:13 6:13^{2} 6:15^{2} 7:6 7:8^{2} 7:10 7:13 7:17 7:20 7:24 7:25^{2} 7:27^{2} 8:4^{2} 8:5^{2} 8:6^{2} 8:8 8:13^{2} 9:7 9:12 9:15 9:19 9:21 9:25 9:26^{2} 9:28 10:5^{2} 10:8 10:9^{3} 10:12 10:14 10:15 10:20 10:23 10:28 10:29^{2} 10:37 11:4^{3} 11:5^{3} 11:6^{3} 11:7 11:8^{4} 11:9 11:10 11:16 11:17^{2} 11:19 11:21 11:22 11:23^{2} 11:24 11:26 11:27^{2} 11:28^{2} 12:6^{2} 12:7 12:10 12:17^{4} 12:26 13:5 13:12 13:23

JAS

1:6 1:7 1:9 1:10^{2} 1:12^{2} 1:13^{2} 1:14 1:18 1:23 1:24^{2} 1:25 2:5 2:10 2:11 2:13 2:14 2:21 2:23 4:6^{2} 4:7 4:8 4:10 4:11 5:6 5:7 5:15 5:17 5:18 5:20

1 PE

1:15 2:6 2:7 2:23^{3} 3:10 3:13 3:18 3:19 4:1 4:2 4:14^{2} 5:6 5:7 5:8

2 PE

1:9^{2} 1:17 2:19

1 JO

1:7 1:9 2:2 2:4 2:6^{3} 2:9^{2} 2:10 2:11^{2} 2:17 2:22^{2} 2:23 2:25 2:28 2:29 3:2^{2} 3:3 3:5 3:7^{2} 3:8^{2} 3:9^{2} 3:10 3:12 3:14 3:16 3:23 3:24^{4} 4:4^{2} 4:6^{2} 4:8 4:10 4:13^{2} 4:15 4:16 4:17 4:18 4:19 4:20^{5} 4:21 5:5^{2} 5:6 5:9 5:10^{3} 5:12^{2} 5:14 5:15 5:16^{3} 5:18

2 JO

9^{2} 11

3 JO

10^{2} 11^{2}

JUDE

6 9

RE

1:1 1:2 1:3 1:7 1:16 1:17 1:18 2:1 2:7 2:11^{2} 2:12 2:17^{2} 2:23 2:26 2:27 2:29 3:1 3:5 3:6 3:7^{4} 3:12 3:13 3:20 3:22 4:3 5:7 5:8 6:2^{2} 6:3 6:5^{2} 6:7 6:9 6:12 7:2 7:14 7:15 8:1 8:3 9:2 9:5 10:2^{2} 10:3 10:7^{2} 10:9 10:11 11:5 11:15 12:9 12:12^{2} 12:13^{2} 12:15 13:6 13:10^{2} 13:11^{2} 13:12 13:13^{2} 13:14 13:15 13:16 13:17 14:4 14:10 14:16 14:17 16:15^{2} 16:16 17:3 17:10^{2} 17:11 17:14 17:15 18:2 18:22 19:2 19:9^{2} 19:10 19:11^{2} 19:12^{2} 19:13 19:15^{3} 19:16 19:17 19:20 20:2 20:3^{2} 20:6 21:3 21:5^{2} 21:6 21:7^{2} 21:10 21:15 21:16 21:17 22:1 22:6 22:7 22:9 22:10 22:11^{4} 22:20

HER

846

GE

2:22 3:6^{2} 3:15 4:11 4:12 8:9^{2} 8:11 8:15 12:16 12:19^{2} 16:2 16:3^{3} 16:4 16:5 16:6^{3} 16:7^{2} 16:9 16:10 16:11 16:13 17:15 17:16^{2} 19:33 20:4 20:6 20:7 20:13 21:10 21:12 21:14^{2} 21:16^{2} 21:17 21:19 23:2 24:15 24:16^{2} 24:17 24:18 24:20 24:21 24:22 24:28 24:43 24:45^{2} 24:46 24:47^{2} 24:51 24:53 24:55 24:57 24:58 24:59 24:60 24:61 24:64 24:67^{2} 25:1 25:22 25:23^{3} 26:9 27:6 27:15^{3} 27:17 27:42^{2} 29:9 29:12^{2} 29:19 29:20 29:21 29:23 29:27 29:28 29:29 29:31 30:1 30:3^{2} 30:4^{2} 30:9^{2} 30:15 30:16 30:21 30:22^{2} 31:19 31:35 33:2 33:7 34:2^{4} 34:8 34:11^{2} 35:17 35:18 35:20 38:2^{2} 38:8 38:11 38:14^{3} 38:15^{3} 38:16 38:18^{2} 38:19^{3} 38:20 38:22 38:23^{3} 38:24^{2} 38:25 38:26^{2} 38:27^{2} 39:7 39:10^{3} 39:12 39:13 39:14 39:16 40:10 48:7

EX

2:5^{2} 2:8 2:9 2:10 3:22^{3} 4:25 11:2 15:20^{2} 18:2 18:3 18:6^{2} 21:4^{2} 21:8^{5} 21:9^{2} 21:10^{3} 21:11 21:22^{2} 22:16^{2} 22:17^{2}

LE

11:19 12:2 12:4^{2} 12:5^{2} 12:6 12:7^{3} 12:8 15:19^{3} 15:20 15:21 15:23 15:24^{2} 15:25^{5} 15:26^{4} 15:28 15:29 15:30^{2} 15:33^{3} 18:7 18:11 18:15 18:17^{5} 18:18^{4} 18:19^{2} 18:20 18:25 19:20 19:29 20:14 20:17 20:18^{4} 21:3 21:7 21:9 21:13 22:13^{3} 22:28 25:19 25:22 26:4 26:10 26:20 26:34^{2} 26:43

NU

5:13^{3} 5:15^{2} 5:16^{2} 5:18 5:19 5:24 5:27^{6} 5:29 5:30 5:31 12:12 12:13 12:14^{4} 16:30 16:32 19:3^{3} 19:4^{2} 19:5^{4} 19:8 22:23 22:25 22:33 25:8 26:59 30:3 30:4^{8} 30:5^{8} 30:6^{2} 30:7^{5} 30:8^{6} 30:9^{2} 30:10^{2} 30:11^{5} 30:12^{6} 30:13^{2} 30:14^{6} 30:15 30:16^{2} 36:8

DE

11:6 11:17 14:18 20:7^{2} 21:11^{2} 21:12^{3} 21:13^{6} 21:14^{5} 22:13^{3} 22:14^{4} 22:15 22:16 22:17 22:19 22:21^{4} 22:23^{2} 22:25^{3} 22:27^{2} 22:28^{2} 22:29^{3} 24:1^{5} 24:3^{5} 24:4^{3} 25:5^{4} 25:8 25:11^{2} 25:12^{2} 28:30 28:56^{6} 28:57^{3} 32:11^{4} 32:22

JOS

2:14 2:15 2:17 6:17 6:22 6:23^{4} 6:25 8:2^{2} 10:1^{2} 10:39 13:17 15:18^{3} 15:19 15:45^{2} 15:47^{4} 17:11^{6} 17:16 21:13^{2} 21:14^{2} 21:15^{2} 21:16^{3} 21:17^{2} 21:18^{2} 21:21^{2} 21:22^{2} 21:23^{2} 21:24^{2} 21:25^{2} 21:27^{2} 21:28^{2} 21:29^{2} 21:30^{2} 21:31^{2} 21:32^{3} 21:34^{2} 21:35^{2} 21:36^{2} 21:37^{2} 21:38^{2} 21:39^{2}

JG

1:14^{3} 1:15 1:27^{5} 4:5 4:8 4:18 4:19 4:20 4:21 4:22 5:26^{2} 5:27^{2} 5:29^{2} 11:26^{2} 11:34 11:35 11:37 11:38^{3} 11:39^{2} 13:3 13:6 13:9^{2} 13:10 13:13 13:14^{3} 14:3^{2} 14:8 14:16 14:17^{2} 15:1 15:2^{6} 15:6^{3} 16:1 16:5^{2} 16:7 16:8 16:9 16:11 16:13 16:16 16:17^{2} 16:18^{2} 16:19 19:2 19:3^{5} 19:25^{4} 19:26 19:27^{2} 19:28^{2} 19:29^{3} 20:6^{2}

RU

1:3 1:5^{2} 1:6 1:7^{2} 1:8^{2} 1:9 1:10 1:14^{2} 1:15^{2} 1:18^{2} 1:22^{2} 2:1 2:2 2:3 2:10 2:11 2:14^{2} 2:15^{2} 2:16^{2} 2:18^{2} 2:19^{3} 2:20^{2} 2:22 2:23 3:1^{2} 3:5 3:6^{2} 3:7 3:15 3:16^{3} 4:13^{2} 4:16 4:17

1 SA

1:4^{2} 1:5 1:6^{4} 1:7 1:8^{2} 1:12 1:13^{3} 1:14 1:18^{2} 1:19 1:22 1:23^{3} 1:24 2:19 4:19^{4} 4:20^{3} 4:21^{2} 18:17 18:21 25:19^{2} 25:20 25:23 25:35^{2} 25:39 25:40 25:41 25:42 28:7^{2} 28:10 28:13 28:14

2 SA

3:15^{2} 3:16^{3} 6:16 6:23 11:4^{4} 11:26^{2} 11:27 12:24^{2} 13:1 13:2 13:5 13:6 13:8 13:10 13:11^{2} 13:14^{3} 13:15^{4} 13:16 13:17 13:18^{3} 13:19^{5} 13:20^{3} 13:22 14:2 14:3 14:4 14:5 16:8 20:17 20:22 21:10

1 KI

1:2^{3} 1:3 1:4 1:19^{2} 1:20 2:1 2:17 3:20 3:26^{3} 3:27 9:24^{2} 10:2 10:3^{3} 10:5 10:13^{4} 14:5^{2} 14:6 15:13^{2} 17:10 17:11 17:13 17:15 17:19^{2} 17:20 21:6

2 KI

4:2 4:5^{3} 4:6^{2} 4:9 4:12 4:13 4:14^{2} 4:15^{2} 4:17 4:20 4:22 4:24 4:25 4:26^{2} 4:27^{4} 4:30 4:36 4:37 5:3 6:28 6:29^{2} 8:2 8:3^{2} 8:5^{3} 8:6 8:10 9:22 9:30^{2} 9:33^{4} 9:34 9:35^{3} 11:1 11:3 11:14 11:15^{3} 11:16 19:21 22:14

1 CH

2:18 5:16 6:57^{2} 6:58^{2} 6:59^{2} 6:60^{3} 6:67^{2} 6:68^{2} 6:69^{2} 6:70^{2} 6:71^{2} 6:72^{2} 6:73^{2} 6:74^{2} 6:75^{2} 6:76^{3} 6:77^{2} 6:78^{2} 6:79^{2} 6:80^{2} 6:81^{2} 7:29^{4} 15:29 18:1

2 CH

8:11 9:1 9:2^{3} 9:4 9:12^{3} 10:20 15:16^{2} 22:10 23:13 23:14^{3} 23:15^{2} 34:22 36:21

ES

1:11 1:19 2:1 2:7 2:9^{6} 2:10^{3} 2:11 2:13^{2} 2:14 2:15^{2} 2:17^{2} 2:20^{3} 4:4^{2} 4:5 4:8^{3} 5:1 5:3 5:12 8:1

JOB

5:16 9:6 21:10 31:10 31:18 39:14 39:16^{2} 39:17^{2} 39:26 39:27

HIM

846

17:15 17:18 17:19 18:4 18:5^{2} 18:18 18:19 18:20 18:22 19:6^{3} 19:11^{3} 19:12^{2} 19:13 19:16 19:19 20:5 20:6 20:7 20:8 21:1 21:2 21:5 21:15 21:17 21:18 21:19^{2} 21:21 21:22 21:23 22:2^{2} 22:4 22:18 22:19 22:26 23:10 23:16^{2} 24:1 24:7^{2} 24:13 24:15 25:2 25:3^{2} 25:5 25:8^{2} 25:9 25:10 25:11^{3} 26:3 28:44 28:55 29:15^{2} 29:20^{2} 29:21 30:20 31:7 31:14 31:29 32:10^{4} 32:12^{2} 32:13^{2} 32:15 32:16^{2} 33:7^{3} 33:9 33:11^{2} 33:12^{2} 33:16^{2} 33:24^{2} 34:1 34:4 34:6 34:9^{2} 34:11

JOS

1:18 2:19 2:23 4:14 5:3 5:13^{3} 5:14 6:5 6:7 6:20 7:3 7:19 7:24 7:25 7:26 8:11 8:14 8:23 9:6 9:9^{2} 10:7 10:15 10:23 10:24 10:29 10:31 10:33^{2} 10:34 10:36 10:38 10:43 11:7 11:9 13:1 14:6 14:7 14:13 15:16 15:17 15:18^{2} 19:50 20:4^{2} 20:5^{2} 22:5^{2} 22:14 22:27 22:30 23:3^{2} 23:14 24:22 24:30 24:33^{2}

JG

1:7 1:12 1:13 1:14^{2} 1:15 1:24 1:25 2:9 3:10 3:13 3:15 3:16 3:19^{2} 3:20 3:23 3:27 3:28 3:31 4:6 4:7 4:13 4:14 4:18^{2} 4:19^{2} 4:21 4:22^{2} 5:13 5:25 5:28^{2} 5:31 6:12^{2} 6:13 6:14 6:15 6:16 6:17 6:19 6:20 6:23 6:25 6:27 6:31^{5} 6:32^{2} 6:34 6:35 7:1 7:3 7:5 7:8 7:9 7:19 8:1^{2} 8:3 8:4 8:8^{2} 8:14^{2} 8:31 9:3 9:4^{2} 9:5^{2} 9:16 9:19 9:24 9:25 9:26 9:28^{2} 9:33 9:34 9:35 9:36 9:38^{2} 9:40^{2} 9:44 9:48^{3} 9:54^{3} 10:3 10:6 11:2^{2} 11:3 11:11 11:15 11:19 11:28 11:34 11:36 12:5 12:6^{3} 12:8 12:11 12:13 13:6 13:10 13:11 13:12 13:18 13:23 13:24 13:25 14:3 14:5 14:6^{2} 14:11^{2} 14:13 14:16 14:17^{2} 14:18 14:19 15:1 15:10 15:12 15:13^{3} 15:14^{2} 16:2^{3} 16:5^{4} 16:8 16:9 16:12^{2} 16:14 16:15 16:16^{2} 16:19^{4} 16:20 16:21^{3} 16:24 16:25 16:26 16:31^{3} 17:9^{2} 17:10 17:11 18:3 18:5 18:15 18:16 18:25 18:26 19:1 19:2^{2} 19:3^{4} 19:4^{2} 19:7 19:9 19:10^{2} 19:12 19:15 19:18 19:21 19:22 19:25 19:28 20:23 21:5

RU

2:2 2:4 2:10 3:13 4:1 4:15

1 SA

1:11 1:17 1:20 1:22 1:23^{2} 1:24^{3} 1:27 1:28 2:3 2:16^{2} 2:19^{2} 2:25^{2} 2:27 2:28 2:35 2:36 3:7 3:13 3:18^{4} 3:19 5:3 5:4 6:3 6:4 6:8 7:3 7:9 8:5 8:10 8:12 9:5 9:6 9:13^{2} 9:16 9:17 10:1 10:9 10:10^{2} 10:11 10:14 10:16 10:19 10:21 10:23 10:24^{2} 10:26 10:27^{2} 11:3 11:5 12:14 12:24 13:2 13:7 13:8 13:10^{2} 13:14^{2} 13:15^{2} 14:2 14:7 14:13^{2} 14:17 14:20 14:34 14:37 14:39 14:43 14:52^{2} 15:2 15:12 15:13 15:16 15:28 15:32 16:1 16:3 16:6 16:7 16:8 16:11 16:12^{2} 16:13 16:14 16:15 16:17 16:18 16:21^{2} 16:23 17:7 17:8 17:9^{2} 17:13 17:20 17:24 17:25^{3} 17:26 17:27^{2} 17:30^{2} 17:31 17:32 17:33 17:35^{5} 17:38 17:39 17:40 17:41 17:42 17:50 17:51 17:57^{2} 17:58 18:1 18:2^{2} 18:3 18:4 18:5^{2} 18:8 18:12 18:13^{3} 18:14 18:15 18:17^{2} 18:20 18:21^{3} 18:24 18:27 18:28 19:4 19:7 19:8 19:11^{3} 19:15^{2} 19:18^{2} 19:23 20:2 20:7 20:17^{2} 20:24 20:26 20:30 20:31 20:32 20:33^{2} 20:34 20:35 20:36 20:40 21:1 21:5 21:6 21:11^{2} 21:14 22:1 22:2^{2} 22:4 22:6^{2} 22:7 22:10^{3} 22:13^{3} 22:15 22:17 23:3 23:4 23:7 23:9 23:14^{2} 23:17 23:20 23:22 23:23 23:25 24:1 24:4^{2} 24:5 24:6 24:8 24:19 25:1^{2} 25:5 25:6 25:12 25:17 25:21 25:22 25:25 25:35 25:36^{2} 25:37^{2} 25:39 25:40 26:2 26:3 26:5 26:7 26:8^{2} 26:9 26:10 26:19 26:24 27:2 27:4 27:6 27:12 28:3^{2} 28:6 28:7 28:8^{2} 28:9 28:17 28:20 28:21 28:23 29:3 29:4^{4} 29:6 30:4 30:6 30:8 30:9 30:11^{2} 30:12^{2} 30:13 30:15 30:16 30:21 31:3 31:5

2 SA

1:3^{2} 1:4 1:5 1:6^{2} 1:7 1:8 1:10^{2} 1:11 1:13 1:14 1:15^{2} 1:16 2:1 2:3 2:5 2:8 2:9 2:20 2:21^{2} 2:23^{2} 2:32 3:9 3:11 3:16 3:20^{2} 3:22 3:23^{2} 3:24 3:26 3:27^{3} 3:31 3:34 4:4 4:6 4:7^{3} 4:10^{3} 5:10 5:12 5:13 5:14 5:25 6:2 6:7 6:10 6:12 6:16 7:1 7:14 7:15 7:23 8:4 8:10^{3} 9:1 9:2^{2} 9:3 9:4 9:5 9:7 9:10 10:1 10:2 10:9 10:12 10:13^{2} 10:17 11:1 11:4 11:7 11:8 11:13^{3} 11:15 11:21 11:22 11:25 11:27 12:1^{2} 12:3 12:4 12:9 12:17^{2} 12:18^{3} 12:20 12:21 12:23^{2} 12:24 13:2 13:4^{2} 13:5^{2} 13:6 13:7 13:9^{2} 13:11 13:12 13:16 13:17 13:25^{2} 13:26 13:27^{2} 13:28 13:29 13:34 14:3 14:6 14:7^{2} 14:10 14:14 14:24^{2} 14:25 14:26 14:29^{2} 14:31 14:32 14:33 15:1^{2} 15:2 15:3 15:4 15:5^{4} 15:9 15:14 15:16 15:17 15:18^{2} 15:22 15:24 15:26^{2} 15:30 15:32 16:1 16:10^{2} 16:11^{3} 16:13^{2} 16:14 16:15 16:18 17:2^{3} 17:6 17:10 17:12 17:16 17:22 17:23 17:24 17:29 18:1 18:9 18:11^{3} 18:15 18:17^{2} 18:19 18:20 18:23 18:30 19:17^{2} 19:23 19:25 19:29 19:30 19:31 19:37^{2} 19:38 19:39 19:40 19:41 20:5 20:6^{2} 20:7 20:8 20:9 20:10^{2} 20:11^{2} 20:12^{2} 20:14 20:15 20:17 20:21 21:4 21:15 21:17^{3} 21:21 22:1 22:3 22:13 22:24 22:31 23:9 23:10 23:11 23:21^{2} 23:23 24:2 24:10 24:13^{3} 24:16 24:18 24:20 24:22

1 KI

1:1 1:2^{2} 1:4 1:5^{2} 1:6^{2} 1:7 1:13 1:17 1:20 1:25 1:27 1:33 1:34 1:35^{2} 1:38 1:40 1:41 1:42 1:44^{2} 1:45 1:52^{2} 1:53^{2} 2:8 2:9^{2} 2:16 2:19 2:22^{2} 2:25 2:29 2:30 2:31 2:34^{2} 2:36 2:42 2:46 3:6^{2} 3:11 3:16 3:28 4:10 4:12 4:13^{2} 4:24 5:1 5:3 5:12 8:5^{2} 8:24 8:25 8:31^{2} 8:32 8:57 8:58 8:62 8:65 9:2 9:3 9:12 10:1 10:2 11:9 11:10 11:17 11:18^{3} 11:19 11:20 11:22 11:23 11:24 11:28 11:29 11:30 11:34 12:1 12:3 12:7 12:8^{2} 12:10^{2} 12:13 12:18^{2} 12:20^{2} 13:4^{3} 13:6 13:11 13:13 13:14^{2} 13:18^{3} 13:19 13:20 13:23 13:24^{2} 13:26^{5} 13:29 13:30 13:31 13:33 14:3 14:10^{2} 14:11^{2} 14:13^{3} 14:14 14:18^{2} 14:22 15:3 15:4^{2} 15:5 15:8 15:27^{2} 15:28 15:29 16:4^{2} 16:7^{2} 16:9 16:10^{2} 16:11 16:17 16:18 16:21 16:25 16:30 16:31^{2} 16:33 17:2 17:6 17:8 17:17 17:19^{3} 17:21 17:22 17:23^{2} 18:7^{2} 18:8 18:15 18:16 18:17 18:21^{3} 18:24 18:30 18:33 19:5^{2} 19:6 19:7 19:9^{2} 19:13 19:15 19:17^{2} 19:18 19:19^{3} 19:20 19:21^{2} 20:1 20:2 20:7 20:8^{2} 20:9 20:10 20:11^{2} 20:16 20:17 20:22 20:23 20:31 20:33^{4} 20:34^{3} 20:35 20:36^{4} 20:37^{2} 20:40 20:41 20:42 21:4^{2} 21:5^{2} 21:6 21:7 21:10^{4} 21:13^{4} 21:19^{2} 21:21^{2} 21:24^{2} 22:7 22:8 22:11 22:13 22:15^{2} 22:16 22:19 22:21 22:22^{2} 22:26 22:27 22:32 22:33 22:53

2 KI

1:5 1:6^{2} 1:8 1:9^{3} 1:10 1:11^{2} 1:12 1:13^{2} 1:15^{3} 1:16 2:2 2:3 2:4 2:5 2:6 2:12 2:13 2:14 2:15^{3} 2:16 2:17^{2} 2:18 2:20 2:23^{2} 3:11 3:12^{2} 3:13 3:15 3:26^{2} 3:27^{2} 4:1 4:5 4:8 4:10 4:12 4:13 4:19 4:20^{2} 4:21^{2} 4:23 4:27 4:29^{2} 4:31^{2} 4:35 4:36 4:38 5:1 5:3 5:5 5:6 5:8 5:10 5:13 5:15 5:16 5:19^{2} 5:20^{2} 5:21^{3} 5:23^{2} 5:25 5:26 6:6 6:10^{2} 6:13^{2} 6:15 6:18 6:26 6:28 6:29^{2} 6:31 6:32^{5} 6:33 7:17^{2} 7:20^{2} 8:6 8:7 8:8 8:9^{3} 8:10^{2} 8:14 8:19^{2} 8:21^{2} 8:29 9:1 9:2^{2} 9:6 9:8^{2} 9:11 9:13 9:15 9:17 9:18 9:21 9:25^{2} 9:26 9:27^{2} 9:28^{2} 9:32 9:36 10:3 10:4 10:7 10:8 10:9 10:11 10:15^{6} 10:16 10:17 10:18 10:22 10:24^{2} 10:35 11:2^{3} 11:4 11:8 11:12^{4} 11:15 12:2 12:21^{2} 13:4 13:9 13:14 13:15^{2} 13:19 13:20 13:25 14:19^{3} 14:20 14:21 15:7 15:10^{3} 15:14 15:16 15:19 15:25^{4} 15:30^{2} 16:5 16:9 17:2 17:3^{2} 17:4^{2} 17:17 17:27 17:36^{3} 18:5^{3} 18:6 18:7^{2} 18:15 18:21 18:36^{2} 18:37 19:3 19:7^{2} 19:16 19:21 19:37 20:1^{2} 20:2 20:4 20:14 21:6 21:11 21:23 22:18 23:1 23:2 23:17 23:13 23:25^{4} 23:26 23:29^{3} 23:30^{5} 23:33 24:1 24:2 24:12 25:5^{2} 25:6^{2} 25:7^{2} 25:25^{2} 25:28^{2} 25:29 25:30

1 CH

2:3^{2} 2:4 2:9 2:19^{2} 2:21 2:24 2:29 2:35 3:1 3:4 3:5 4:6 4:9 4:10 5:2 5:20 7:22 9:20 10:3 10:9 10:14 11:9 11:10^{2} 11:11 11:12 11:23^{2} 11:25 11:42 12:19 12:20 12:22 12:23 12:27 13:10 14:1 14:2 14:10 14:14 14:16 14:17 15:1 15:2 15:13 15:27 15:29 16:5 16:9^{2} 16:29 16:30 17:13^{2} 17:14 17:25 18:4 18:10^{3} 19:2^{2} 19:10 19:14^{2} 19:17 20:7 21:11 21:12 21:15 21:20 21:26 21:28 22:6 22:9 23:13 24:19 25:5 26:10 27:7 28:6 28:9^{3} 29:22 29:23 29:25^{2} 29:30

2 CH

1:1^{2} 1:3 1:7 2:3^{2} 2:4^{2} 2:6^{4} 2:14 2:15 5:6 6:15 6:16 6:22^{2} 6:23 7:8 7:12 8:18 9:1 10:1 10:3 10:7 10:8^{3} 10:10^{2} 10:18^{2} 11:13 11:15 11:18 11:19 11:20 11:22 12:1 12:3 12:12^{2} 13:3 13:5 13:7 13:10 13:11 13:19 13:20 14:1 14:5 14:6 14:7 14:10 14:13 15:2^{4} 15:4 15:5^{2} 15:9^{2} 15:15 16:7 16:9 16:10^{2} 16:14^{3} 17:11 17:14 17:15^{2} 17:16^{2} 17:17 17:18^{2} 18:2^{4} 18:3 18:6 18:7 18:10 18:12 18:14 18:15 18:20^{2} 18:21 18:25 18:26 18:30 18:31^{3} 18:32 19:2 20:30 20:36 21:7 21:9^{2} 21:12 21:17 21:18 21:19 21:20 22:6 22:9^{4} 22:11^{4} 23:1 23:11^{4} 23:14 23:16 24:3 24:6 24:16 24:21^{2} 24:22 24:23 24:25^{6} 24:26 24:27 25:3 25:7 25:10 25:13 25:15^{2} 25:16^{2} 25:23 25:27^{3} 25:28 26:1 26:5 26:7 26:17^{2} 26:18 26:20^{3} 26:23 27:5^{2} 27:9 28:5^{3} 28:16 28:20^{3} 28:21 28:23^{2} 28:24 28:27^{2} 29:6 29:11^{3} 29:29 30:9 31:10 31:15 32:3 32:6 32:7^{2} 32:8 32:9 32:15 32:17 32:21 32:24^{2} 32:25^{2} 32:29^{2} 32:31^{3} 32:33^{2} 33:6 33:11^{2} 33:13^{3} 33:18 33:19 33:20 33:24^{2} 34:26 35:20 35:21 35:22^{2} 35:24^{3} 36:1 36:3 36:4 36:6^{3} 36:8 36:10 36:13 36:17 36:20 36:23^{3}

EZR

1:2 1:3^{2} 1:4 4:2 4:6 4:11 5:7 5:15 6:11 7:6^{2} 7:9 7:26 8:3 8:4 8:5 8:6 8:7 8:8 8:9 8:10 8:11 8:12 8:19 8:21 8:22^{2} 8:33 10:1

NE

1:5 1:11 2:1 2:6^{2} 3:2 3:8^{2} 3:10 3:12 3:16 3:17^{2} 3:18 3:19 3:20 3:21 3:22 3:23^{2} 3:24 3:25 3:29 3:30^{2} 3:31 4:3 6:8 6:12^{2} 6:18 6:19 8:4 9:7^{2} 9:8 11:8 13:5 13:7 13:26^{3} 13:28

ES

1:3 1:12 1:14 1:17 1:19 2:2 2:9^{2} 2:20 3:1^{2} 3:2^{2} 3:4 3:5 3:6 4:4 4:5 4:7^{2} 4:8^{3} 4:10 4:11 4:17 5:4 5:9 5:11^{2} 5:14 6:3^{2} 6:4 6:5^{2} 6:6 6:9^{2} 6:11^{2} 6:13^{4} 6:14 7:7 7:9 8:3 8:7 10:2

JOB

1:2 1:8 1:10 2:3^{3} 2:8 2:9 2:11^{3} 2:12 2:13^{2} 3:20 4:4 6:10 6:14 7:8 7:10 7:17^{2} 7:18^{2} 8:4 8:18^{2} 9:3^{2} 9:4 9:11^{2} 9:12^{2} 9:13 9:14^{2} 9:32 9:34 9:35 11:10 11:13 12:4 12:5 12:13 12:16 13:7 13:9 13:15^{2} 13:16 14:6 14:20^{2} 14:22^{2} 15:21 15:24^{2} 15:26 15:31 18:6 18:7 18:9^{2} 18:10^{2} 18:11^{2} 18:14 18:20 18:21 19:11 19:16 19:28 20:7 20:9^{3} 20:11 20:14 20:16 20:22 20:23^{2} 20:24 20:25 20:26^{2} 20:27 20:29 21:15^{2} 21:19 21:21 21:31 21:33^{3} 22:3 22:14 22:27 23:3 23:4 23:7 23:8 23:9^{2} 23:13 23:14 23:15 24:1 24:10 24:20^{2} 24:23 25:2 26:2 26:3

4:8[2] 4:9[3] 4:12 4:13 4:14 4:17 4:20 4:22 4:29[3] 4:35[5] 4:37 4:38 4:40 4:42[3] 5:3 5:5 5:9 5:11 5:12 5:13[2] 5:14 5:15[2] 5:18[3] 5:19[2] 5:20 5:27 5:28 5:29 5:33 6:3 6:4 6:7[2] 6:13 6:17 6:19[2] 6:29[2] 6:30 7:2 7:3[2] 7:4 7:6[2] 7:9[3] 7:11 7:14 7:15 7:17 7:18 7:19 7:20 7:29 7:30 7:36[2] 7:38 7:39[2] 7:40 7:42 7:43 7:49 8:1 8:3 8:4 8:8 8:9 8:18[2] 8:19[2] 8:20 8:24[2] 8:25 8:27 8:28 8:29 8:30[2] 8:31

8:32 8:37 8:38[3] 8:39 8:40[2] 8:41 8:42 8:44 8:45 8:47[3] 8:49 8:50 8:53 9:7 9:9 9:10 9:11 9:12 9:18 9:23 9:26 9:30 9:32[2] 9:33 9:35 9:37 9:39[4] 9:40 9:42[3] 9:45 9:47[2] 9:48 9:49 9:50[2] 9:52 9:53 9:57 9:58 9:60 9:62 10:16 10:22 10:23 10:25 10:26 10:28 10:30[3] 10:31 10:32 10:33[2] 10:34[4] 10:35[2] 10:36 10:37[2] 10:38 10:40 11:1 11:5[2] 11:6 11:8[2] 11:10 11:11[2] 11:12 11:13 11:16[2] 11:22[3] 11:26 11:27 11:37[2] 11:39 11:45 11:53[2] 11:54[2]

12:5[2] 12:8 12:10[2] 12:13 12:14 12:20 12:36 12:41 12:44 12:46[3] 12:48[2] 12:58 13:1 13:8 13:12 13:15[2] 13:17 13:23 13:31 14:1 14:2 14:4[3] 14:5 14:6 14:8 14:9 14:12[2] 14:15[2] 14:16 14:18 14:25 14:29 14:31[2] 14:35 15:1[2] 15:15 15:16 15:18 15:20[2] 15:21 15:22 15:27[2] 15:28 15:30 15:31 16:1 16:2[2] 16:5 16:6 16:7 16:14 16:27 16:29 16:31 17:1 17:2 17:3[2] 17:4 17:7 17:8 17:9 17:12 17:16 17:19 17:31[2] 17:37 18:3 18:7 18:15 18:16 18:18 18:19 18:22

18:31 18:33[2] 18:37 18:39 18:40[3] 18:42 18:43 19:4 19:5[2] 19:6 19:8 19:9 19:14[2] 19:15 19:17 19:19 19:22 19:24[2] 19:25 19:26[2] 19:30[2] 19:31[3] 19:34 19:35 19:39 19:47 19:48 20:1 20:2 20:5 20:10[3] 20:11[3] 20:12[2] 20:13[2] 20:14[2] 20:15[2] 20:18 20:19 20:20[2] 20:21 20:27[2] 20:38 20:40 20:44 21:7 21:38[2] 22:2 22:4 22:5 22:6 22:9 22:10 22:14 22:21 22:26 22:33 22:36[2] 22:39 22:43[2] 22:47 22:48 22:49[2] 22:51 22:52 22:54[3] 22:56[3] 22:57[2] 22:58 22:59 22:61 22:63[2] 22:64[3] 22:65

22:66 23:1 23:2 23:3[2] 23:7 23:8[3] 23:9[2] 23:10 23:11[4] 23:14[2] 23:15[2] 23:16[2] 23:21[2] 23:22[3] 23:25 23:26[2] 23:27[2] 23:32 23:33 23:35[2] 23:36[3] 23:38 23:39 23:40 23:43 23:49 23:55 24:16 24:18 24:19 24:20[2] 24:24 24:29 24:31 24:42 24:52

JOH

1:3[2] 1:4 1:7 1:10[2] 1:11 1:12 1:15 1:18 1:19 1:21 1:22 1:25[2] 1:29 1:31 1:32 1:33[2] 1:37 1:38 1:39 1:40 1:41 1:42[2] 1:43 1:45[2] 1:46[2] 1:47[2] 1:48[2] 1:49 1:50 1:51 2:3 2:10 2:11 2:18

3:2[2] 3:3 3:4 3:9 3:10 3:15 3:16 3:17 3:18 3:26[2] 3:27 3:28 3:29 3:34 3:36 4:9 4:11 4:14[3] 4:15 4:19 4:23 4:24[2] 4:25 4:30 4:31 4:33 4:34 4:39 4:40[2] 4:42 4:45 4:47[2] 4:48 4:49 4:50[2] 4:51[2] 4:52[2] 4:53 5:6[2] 5:7 5:8 5:10 5:12 5:14[2] 5:15 5:16 5:18 5:20[2] 5:23 5:24 5:27 5:38 5:43 6:2 6:5 6:6 6:7 6:8 6:15[2] 6:21 6:25[2] 6:27 6:28 6:29 6:30 6:34 6:37 6:38 6:40[3] 6:41 6:44[2] 6:54 6:56

6:64 6:65 6:66 6:68 6:71 7:1 7:3 7:5 7:11 7:12 7:13 7:18[2] 7:26 7:29[2] 7:30[2] 7:31 7:32[2] 7:33 7:35 7:37 7:39 7:43 7:44[2] 7:45 7:48 7:51 7:52 8:2 8:3 8:4 8:6[2] 8:7[2] 8:13 8:19 8:20 8:25 8:26 8:29 8:30 8:31 8:33 8:39 8:41 8:44 8:48 8:52 8:55[4] 8:57 8:59 9:2 9:3 9:4 9:7 9:8 9:9 9:10 9:12 9:13 9:15 9:17 9:18[2] 9:21 9:23 9:24 9:26 9:28 9:31 9:34[2] 9:35[3] 9:36 9:37[2] 9:38 9:40[2]

10:3 10:4 10:5 10:20 10:21 10:24[2] 10:31 10:33 10:36 10:38 10:39 10:41 10:42 11:3 11:8 11:10 11:11 11:15 11:16 11:20 11:24 11:27 11:29 11:30 11:32[2] 11:34[2] 11:36 11:39[2] 11:44[2] 11:45 11:48[2] 11:53 11:57 12:2[2] 12:4 12:11 12:13 12:16[2] 12:17[2] 12:18 12:19 12:21 12:26[2] 12:29 12:34 12:37 12:41 12:42[2] 12:44 12:45 12:47 12:48[2] 13:2 13:6 13:7 13:8[2] 13:9 13:10 13:11 13:16 13:20 13:24 13:25 13:27[2] 13:28 13:29 13:31 13:32[3] 13:36[2] 13:37 13:38 14:5 14:6

14:7[2] 14:8 14:9 14:17[3] 14:21[2] 14:22 14:23[4] 15:5 15:21 16:5 16:7 16:19 16:29 17:2[2] 18:2 18:4 18:5[2] 18:12 18:13 18:20 18:23 18:24 18:25 18:26 18:30[2] 18:31[3] 18:33 18:34 18:37 18:38 19:1 19:2 19:3 19:4[2] 19:6[6] 19:7 19:9 19:10 19:12 19:15[3] 19:16[2] 19:18[2] 19:32 19:36 19:37 19:38 20:2 20:6 20:13 20:15[5] 20:16 20:25 20:28 20:29 21:3 21:5 21:7 21:12 21:15[2] 21:16[3] 21:17[4] 21:19 21:21 21:22 21:23

AC

1:6 1:9 1:11 2:22 2:23

2:25 2:30 3:4 3:7[2] 3:9 3:10 3:13[2] 3:16[2] 3:22 3:26 4:10 5:6[3] 5:17 5:21 5:31 5:32 5:36 5:37[2] 5:40 6:11 6:12[3] 6:14 6:15 7:3 7:4 7:5[3] 7:8[2] 7:9 7:10[3] 7:14 7:21[2] 7:24[2] 7:27 7:30 7:31 7:33 7:35 7:37 7:38 7:39 7:40 7:47 7:54 7:55 7:58[2] 8:2 8:11 8:30[2] 8:31 8:35 8:38 8:39 9:2 9:3 9:4 9:6 9:7 9:8[2] 9:10 9:11 9:12 9:15 9:16 9:17 9:21 9:23 9:24 9:25[2] 9:26 9:27[3] 9:29 9:30[2] 9:34

9:35 9:38[2] 9:39[2] 9:40 10:3[2] 10:4[2] 10:7 10:11 10:13 10:15 10:19 10:21 10:23 10:25[2] 10:26 10:27 10:35[2] 10:38 10:40[2] 10:41 10:43[2] 10:48 11:2 11:13 11:26[2] 12:4[5] 12:5 12:6 12:7[2] 12:8[2] 12:9 12:10 12:16 12:17 12:19[2] 12:20 12:23 13:9 13:11[2] 13:22 13:27[2] 13:28 13:29[3] 13:30 13:31 13:34 13:39 14:9 14:19 14:20 15:21 15:38 16:3[3] 16:9 16:32 17:15[2] 17:16 17:17 17:18 17:19[2] 17:23 17:27[2] 17:28[2] 17:31 17:34 18:12 18:17 18:18 18:20 18:26[2] 18:27 19:2 19:4[2]

19:22 19:30 19:31[2] 19:33 19:38 20:1 20:3 20:4 20:10[3] 20:14 20:16 20:18 20:37 20:38 21:8 21:11 21:12 21:20 21:27[2] 21:29 21:30 21:31 21:33[2] 21:34 21:36 21:40 22:9 22:13 22:18 22:20 22:22 22:24[2] 22:25 22:27 22:29[3] 22:30[2] 23:2[2] 23:3 23:9 23:10[2] 23:11 23:15[3] 23:17[2] 23:18[3] 23:19[3] 23:20 23:21[2] 23:22 23:23 23:24 23:27 23:28[2] 23:30 23:31 23:32 23:33 23:35 24:2 24:7 24:8 24:10 24:23[2] 24:24 24:26[4] 25:2[2] 25:3[3] 25:5 25:15 25:16 25:19 25:20 25:21[2] 25:22

25:25 25:26 25:27 26:26 27:3 28:6 28:8[2] 28:16 28:21 28:23[2] 28:30 28:31

RO

1:20 1:21 3:26 4:3 4:4 4:5[2] 4:17 4:22 4:23 4:24 5:9 5:14 6:4 6:6 6:8 6:9 7:4 8:11 8:17 8:20 8:32[2] 8:37 9:11 9:16[2] 9:20 9:33 10:9 10:11 10:12 10:14[2] 11:4 11:35[2] 11:36[3] 12:8 12:20[2] 13:4 14:1 14:3[5] 14:4 14:14[2] 14:15 15:11 15:12 16:25

1 CO

1:5 1:30 1:31 2:2 2:9 2:11 2:14 2:16 3:17 3:18 5:3

7:12[2] 7:13 7:15 7:17 7:18[2] 7:36 8:3 8:6[2] 8:10 10:12 11:14 11:28 11:34 12:18 14:2 14:11 14:13 14:28[2] 14:37 14:38 15:27[2] 15:28[3] 15:38 16:2[2] 16:11[3] 16:12 16:22

2 CO

1:19 1:20[2] 2:7[2] 2:8 5:9 5:15 5:16 5:21[2] 6:1 7:14 7:15 8:18 9:7 10:7 10:19 11:4 12:18 13:4[2]

GA

1:1 1:6 1:8 1:9 1:16 1:18 2:11 2:13 3:6 4:29 5:8 6:6[2]

EPH

1:4[2] 1:10 1:11 1:17 1:20[2] 1:22 1:23 2:18 3:12 3:20 3:21 4:15 4:21[2] 4:28[3] 6:9

PHP

1:29 2:7 2:9[2] 2:22 2:23 2:27[2] 2:28[2] 2:29 3:9 3:10

COL

1:16[3] 1:17 1:19 1:20[2] 2:6 2:7 2:9 2:10 2:12[3] 2:13 3:4 3:10[2] 3:17 4:10 4:13

1 TH

4:14 5:10

2 TH

1:12 2:1 2:9 3:14 3:15[2]

1 TI

1:16 5:1

2 TI

1:12 1:18 2:4[2] 2:11[2] 2:12[2] 2:26 4:11 4:14

TIT

1:16

PHM

12 15 17

HEB

1:5 1:6 2:3 2:6[2] 2:7[3] 2:8[3] 2:10 2:13 2:14 2:16[2] 2:17 3:3[2] 4:13 5:5 5:7[2] 5:9 6:6 7:1 7:6 7:10 7:21[2] 7:25 9:9 9:28 10:30 10:38 11:5 11:6[2] 11:9 11:11 11:12 11:19[2] 11:27 12:2 12:3 12:5 12:25[3] 13:13 13:15

JAS

1:5[2] 1:6 1:12 2:3[2] 2:5 2:14 2:23 3:13 4:17[2] 5:13[2] 5:14[3] 5:15[2] 5:19 5:20

1 PE

1:8 1:21[3] 2:6 2:9 2:14 2:23 3:6 3:10 3:11[2] 3:22 4:5 4:11[2] 4:16[2] 4:19 5:7 5:11

2 PE

1:3 1:17 1:18 3:14 3:15 3:18

1 JO

1:5[2] 1:6 1:10 2:3 2:4[2] 2:5[2] 2:6 2:8 2:10 2:13 2:14 2:15 2:27[2] 2:28[2] 2:29 3:1 3:2[2] 3:3 3:5 3:6[3] 3:9 3:12 3:15 3:17[2] 3:19 3:22 3:24[2] 4:9 4:13 4:15 4:16 4:19 4:21 5:1[3] 5:10 5:14 5:15 5:16 5:18 5:20[2]

2 JO

10[2] 11

JUDE

9 15 24

RE

1:1 1:4 1:5 1:6 1:7[3] 1:17 2:7[2] 2:11 2:17[8] 2:26 2:28 2:29 3:6 3:12[6] 3:13 3:20[2] 3:21 3:22 4:8 4:9 4:10[2] 5:1 5:7 5:13 5:14 6:2[2] 6:4[2] 6:5 6:8[2] 6:16 7:14 7:15 8:3 9:1 10:6 10:9 12:9 12:11 13:2 13:4 13:5[2] 13:7[2] 13:8 13:9 13:12 13:18 14:1 14:7[2] 14:15 14:18 16:8 16:9 17:14 19:5 19:7 19:10 19:11 19:14 19:19 19:20[2] 19:21 20:2 20:3[3] 20:6 20:11 21:7 22:3 22:11[4] 22:17[3] 22:18

HIS

848

GE

1:11 1:12[2] 1:21 1:24[2] 1:25[2] 1:27 2:2[2] 2:3 2:7 2:21 2:24[2] 2:25 3:8 3:15 3:20 3:21 3:22 4:1 4:2 4:4[2] 4:5[2] 4:7 4:8[2] 4:17[2] 4:20 4:23 4:25[2] 4:26 5:3 5:29 6:3 6:5 6:6 6:9 6:12 6:20 7:2[2] 7:7 7:13 7:14[2] 8:9 8:18 8:21[2] 9:1 9:6 9:8 9:21 9:22 9:24 9:25 9:26 9:27 10:5 10:10 10:15 10:25 11:28 11:31[2] 12:5 12:8 12:11 12:12 12:17 12:20[2] 13:1 13:3[2] 13:10 13:12 13:18 14:12 14:14[2] 14:15 14:16 14:17 16:3 16:11 16:12[2] 16:15 17:3 17:14 17:17 17:19[2] 17:23[2] 17:24 17:25[2] 17:26 17:27 18:2 18:19 18:33[2] 19:1 19:3 19:14[2] 19:16[2] 19:26 19:30[2] 19:37 19:38 20:2 20:7 20:8 20:14 20:17 21:2 21:3 21:4 21:5 21:7 21:11 21:21 21:22 21:32 22:3[2] 22:4 22:5 22:6[2] 22:7 22:9 22:10 22:13[3] 22:17 22:19 22:21 22:24 23:3 23:6 23:9 23:10 23:18 23:19 24:2 24:7 24:9 24:10[2] 24:11 24:20 24:21 24:26 24:27 24:29 24:30[2] 24:32[2] 24:40 24:48 24:59 24:61 24:63 24:67[3] 25:6 25:8 25:9 25:10 25:11 25:17 25:18 25:21[2] 25:25 25:26[2] 25:28 25:30

25:33 25:34 26:7 26:8 26:11^{2} 26:15 26:17 26:18^{2} 26:25 26:26 27:1^{2} 27:5 27:10 27:11 27:13 27:14^{2} 27:16 27:18 27:19 27:20 27:22 27:23 27:26 27:27 27:30 27:31^{2} 27:32 27:34^{2} 27:37 27:38^{2} 27:39 27:40 27:41^{2} 28:7 28:8 28:9 28:11 28:16 28:18 29:1 29:3 29:6 29:10^{3} 29:11 29:13^{2} 29:23 29:24 29:28 29:29 29:32 29:33 29:34 29:35 30:6 30:8 30:11 30:13 30:14 30:18 30:20 30:24 30:35 30:40 31:4 31:17 31:18^{3} 31:19 31:21 31:23 31:25^{2} 31:46 31:53 31:54 31:55^{3} 32:1 32:3 32:13^{2} 32:16^{2} 32:20 32:22^{3} 32:25 32:31 33:1 33:3 33:4 33:5 33:14

33:16 33:17 33:18 33:19 34:3 34:4 34:5^{4} 34:13 34:19 34:20 34:24^{3} 34:25 34:26 35:2 35:7 35:10 35:18^{2} 35:21 35:22 35:27 35:29 36:2 36:6^{8} 36:24 36:32 36:33 36:34 36:35^{2} 36:36 36:37 36:38 36:39^{3} 37:1 37:2^{3} 37:3^{2} 37:4^{2} 37:5 37:8^{3} 37:9 37:10^{3} 37:11^{2} 37:12 37:17 37:20 37:22 37:23^{3} 37:26^{2} 37:27 37:29 37:30 37:34^{3} 37:35^{3} 38:1 38:3 38:4 38:5 38:6 38:9^{3} 38:11^{2} 38:12^{2} 38:13 38:16 38:20^{2} 38:28^{2} 38:29^{3} 38:30^{3} 39:2 39:3^{2} 39:4^{3} 39:5 39:7 39:8 39:9 39:11 39:12^{2} 39:13 39:15 39:16^{2} 39:18 39:19^{3} 39:23 40:1 40:2 40:5^{2} 40:7 40:9 40:13^{2}

40:20^{2} 40:21 41:8^{2} 41:10 41:11 41:12 41:14 41:37 41:38 41:42^{3} 41:44 42:1 42:4 42:7 42:8 42:21 42:22 42:25 42:27^{4} 42:28 42:35 42:37 42:38 43:8 43:16 43:21 43:29^{3} 43:30^{3} 43:31 43:33^{2} 44:1^{2} 44:2 44:4 44:11^{2} 44:13 44:14 44:19 44:20^{4} 44:22^{3} 44:30 44:33 45:1 45:3^{3} 45:4 45:8 45:14^{2} 45:15^{2} 45:16 45:23^{2} 45:24 46:1^{2} 46:4 46:6 46:7^{5} 46:8 46:15^{3} 46:18 46:25 46:26 46:28 46:29^{4} 46:31^{2} 47:2 47:3 47:7 47:11^{2} 47:12^{3} 47:20 47:29 48:1 48:9 48:12^{2} 48:13^{2} 48:14^{3} 48:17^{3} 48:18^{2} 48:19^{3} 49:1 49:10 49:11^{4} 49:12^{2} 49:13 49:15 49:16 49:17 49:20 49:24^{2}

49:26 49:28 49:31^{2} 49:33^{3} 50:1 50:2^{2} 50:4 50:7^{2} 50:8^{2} 50:10 50:12 50:13 50:14^{3} 50:18^{2} 50:22 50:24

EX

1:1 1:6 1:9 1:22 2:4 2:7 2:10 2:11^{2} 2:20 2:21 2:22 2:24 3:1 3:6 3:13 4:4^{2} 4:6^{3} 4:7^{4} 4:14 4:15^{2} 4:18 4:20^{3} 4:21 4:25 5:2 5:21 6:1 6:11 6:20 7:2 7:10^{2} 7:12 7:20 7:23^{2} 8:6 8:15 8:17^{2} 8:24 8:29^{2} 8:31^{2} 8:32 9:20^{2} 9:21^{2} 9:23 9:33 9:34^{2} 10:1^{2} 10:13 10:22 10:23 11:2 11:5 11:7 11:10 12:4^{3} 12:9^{2} 12:22 12:29 12:30 12:48 13:10 13:13 14:4 14:5 14:6^{2} 14:9^{2} 14:17^{3}

14:18^{2} 14:21 14:23^{2} 14:27^{2} 14:31 15:1 15:3 15:4^{2} 15:19^{2} 15:21 15:26^{2} 16:16^{2} 16:18 16:21 16:29^{2} 17:11^{2} 17:12^{2} 17:13 18:1 18:5^{2} 18:7 18:8 18:15 18:16 18:24 18:27^{3} 20:7 20:17^{4} 20:20 21:3 21:4 21:6^{3} 21:7 21:9 21:13 21:14 21:15^{2} 21:16 21:17^{2} 21:18^{2} 21:19^{2} 21:20^{3} 21:21 21:26^{3} 21:27^{3} 21:28 21:29^{3} 21:30 21:34 21:36^{2} 22:3 22:4 22:5^{3} 22:7 22:8^{2} 22:9^{2} 22:10 22:11^{2} 22:14 22:15 22:16 22:27^{2} 22:30 23:3 23:4 23:5 23:6 23:19 23:21 23:22 24:10^{2} 24:11 24:13 25:2 25:31^{5} 26:19^{2} 27:2 27:3^{6} 27:11 27:21 28:1 28:4 28:12 28:21 28:29 28:30 28:35

28:38 28:41 28:43^{2} 29:4 29:6 29:7 29:8 29:9^{2} 29:10 29:14^{2} 29:15 29:16 29:17^{3} 29:19 29:20^{2} 29:21^{6} 29:24 29:27 29:28 29:29 29:30 29:31 29:32 29:35 29:44 30:12 30:18 30:19 30:21 30:27^{2} 30:28^{2} 30:30 30:33 30:38 31:8^{2} 31:9^{2} 31:10 31:14 32:11 32:14 32:15 32:19 32:27^{5} 32:29^{2} 33:4 33:8 33:10 33:11^{2} 34:4 34:8 34:15 34:20 34:26 34:29 34:30 34:33 34:35 35:11^{7} 35:13^{2} 35:14^{2} 35:15 35:16^{4} 35:17 35:19 35:21^{2} 35:34 36:4 36:24^{2} 37:16^{4} 37:17^{5} 37:20^{2} 37:32^{3} 39:5 39:14 39:21 39:27 39:33^{6} 39:39^{4} 39:40^{4} 39:41 40:10 40:11 40:12 40:14 40:18^{2} 40:31

LE

1:3^{2} 1:4 1:9^{2} 1:10 1:11 1:12^{3} 1:14^{2} 1:15 1:16^{2} 2:1 2:2 2:3 2:10 3:1 3:2^{2} 3:6 3:7 3:8^{2} 3:12 3:13 3:14 4:3 4:4 4:6 4:11^{5} 4:17 4:19 4:22 4:23^{3} 4:24 4:25^{2} 4:26^{2} 4:28^{4} 4:29 4:30 4:33 4:34 4:35 5:1 5:4 5:6^{3} 5:7 5:8^{2} 5:10 5:11 5:12 5:13 5:15 5:17 5:18 6:2^{2} 6:5 6:6 6:9 6:10^{3} 6:11 6:15 6:16 6:20 6:22^{2} 6:25 7:13^{2} 7:15 7:16^{2} 7:18^{2} 7:20^{2} 7:21 7:25 7:27 7:29^{3} 7:30 7:31 7:33 7:34 7:35 8:2 8:6 8:9^{2} 8:11^{2} 8:14 8:15 8:17^{3} 8:18 8:22 8:23^{2}

8:27 8:30^{6} 8:31^{2} 8:36 9:1 9:9 9:22 10:1 10:3 10:6 10:12 11:14 11:15 11:16 11:22^{4} 11:25 11:27 11:28 11:29 11:40^{2} 12:3 13:2^{3} 13:3 13:4 13:5 13:6 13:7 13:11 13:12^{2} 13:13 13:23 13:28 13:34 13:35 13:37 13:40 13:41^{3} 13:42^{2} 13:43^{2} 13:44^{2} 13:45^{3} 13:46 13:55 14:2 14:8^{3} 14:9^{7} 14:14^{2} 14:15 14:16^{3} 14:17^{3} 14:19 14:23 14:25^{2} 14:26 14:27^{2} 14:28^{3} 14:32 14:47^{2} 15:2^{2} 15:3^{7} 15:5^{2} 15:6 15:7 15:8 15:10 15:11^{2} 15:13^{4} 15:15 15:16 15:21 15:22 15:27 16:4^{2} 16:6^{2} 16:11 16:12 16:14^{2} 16:15 16:17 16:19 16:21 16:24^{3} 16:26^{2} 16:28^{2} 16:32 17:2 17:4

17:9 17:10 17:14 17:15 17:16^{2} 19:3^{2} 19:8^{2} 19:21 19:22 20:2 20:3^{2} 20:4 20:5 20:6 20:9^{5} 20:10 20:11 20:12 20:17^{6} 20:19 20:20^{2} 20:21^{2} 21:1 21:2^{6} 21:3^{2} 21:4 21:7 21:10^{3} 21:11^{2} 21:12^{2} 21:14 21:15^{2} 21:17 21:20^{2} 21:21 21:22 21:24 22:2 22:3 22:6 22:7 22:11^{3} 22:18^{3} 22:21 22:23 23:29 23:30 23:37 24:9 24:11 24:14 24:15^{2} 24:19 25:10 25:13 25:25^{3} 25:27 25:28 25:30 25:33 25:41^{3} 25:48 25:49^{3} 25:50 25:51 25:52^{2} 25:54 27:8 27:14 27:15^{2} 27:16 27:17 27:18 27:22 27:28 27:31

NU

1:4 1:44 1:52^{2} 2:2 2:4 2:6 2:8

2:11 2:13 2:15 2:17 2:19 2:21 2:23 2:26 2:28 2:30 3:7 3:9 3:10 3:38 3:48 3:51 4:5 4:9^{3} 4:19^{3} 4:25 4:27 4:49 5:7 5:9 5:10^{2} 5:14^{2} 5:15 5:18 5:30 6:4 6:5^{3} 6:7^{6} 6:8 6:9^{3} 6:11 6:12^{2} 6:13 6:14 6:16^{2} 6:17^{2} 6:18^{2} 6:19 6:21^{4} 6:23 6:25 6:26 7:5 7:11 7:12 7:13 7:19 7:25 7:31 7:37 7:43 7:49 7:55 7:61 7:67 7:73 7:79 8:8 8:13 8:19 8:22 9:2 9:3 9:7 9:13^{3} 10:14 10:18 10:22 10:25 11:1 11:10 11:28 11:29 12:12 14:24 15:4 15:24^{2} 15:30 15:31^{2} 16:4 16:5^{2} 16:6 16:17^{3}

16:18 16:40 17:2 17:9 19:3 19:4 19:5 19:7^{2} 19:8^{2} 19:10 19:13 19:19 19:21 20:8 20:11^{2} 20:21 20:24 20:25 20:26^{3} 20:28^{2} 21:23^{2} 21:24 21:26^{2} 21:29^{2} 21:33 21:34^{2} 21:35^{3} 22:5 22:18 22:21 22:22^{2} 22:23^{2} 22:31^{4} 23:6 23:7 23:10 23:16 23:17 23:18 23:21 24:1 24:2^{2} 24:3 24:4 24:7^{4} 24:8^{2} 24:10 24:13 24:15 24:16 24:18 24:20^{2} 24:21 24:23 24:25^{2} 25:5 25:6 25:7 25:13^{2} 26:54 27:1 27:3 27:4 27:8^{2} 27:9^{2} 27:10^{2} 27:11^{4} 27:21^{2} 27:23 28:10 28:15 28:24 28:31 29:6 29:16^{2} 29:22^{2} 29:25^{2} 29:28^{2} 29:31^{2} 29:34^{2} 29:38^{2} 30:2^{3} 30:4 30:7 30:11 30:14^{2} 30:16^{2}

31:6 32:18 32:21 32:42 33:54 35:8^{2} 35:21 35:23^{2} 35:25 35:26 35:27 35:28^{2} 35:32 36:2 36:7 36:8 36:9

DE

1:16 1:31 1:36 1:41 2:12 2:24 2:30^{2} 2:31^{2} 2:32 2:33^{2} 2:34 3:1 3:2^{2} 3:3 3:4 3:11 3:14 4:13 4:20 4:30 4:36^{3} 4:37^{2} 4:40^{2} 4:42 4:47 5:11 5:21^{5} 5:24^{3} 6:2^{2} 6:13 6:17^{2} 7:3^{2} 7:7 7:9 7:10 7:22 8:2 8:5 8:6 8:11^{3} 8:18 9:23 10:6^{2} 10:8 10:9^{2} 10:12 10:13 10:20 11:1^{4} 11:2^{3} 11:3^{3} 11:14 11:22 12:5^{2} 12:8 12:11 12:21 13:4^{2} 13:17 13:18 14:13 14:14 14:15 14:21 14:23 14:24

15:2^{2} 15:8 15:17 16:2 16:6 16:11 17:2 17:17 17:18 17:19^{2} 17:20^{5} 18:1 18:5 18:6 18:7^{2} 18:8 18:10^{2} 18:18 19:4 19:5^{3} 19:6^{3} 19:9 19:11 19:12 19:18 19:19 20:5 20:6 20:7 20:8^{3} 21:16 21:17^{2} 21:18^{2} 21:19^{4} 21:20 21:21 21:23 22:1 22:3^{2} 22:4 22:19^{2} 22:24 22:26 22:29^{2} 22:30^{2} 23:1 23:2 23:7 23:15^{2} 24:1^{2} 24:2 24:3^{2} 24:4 24:5 24:7 24:10^{2} 24:12 24:13 24:15^{3} 24:16 25:2^{2} 25:6^{2} 25:7^{3} 25:8 25:9^{5} 25:10^{2} 26:2 26:17^{5} 26:18^{2} 27:10^{2} 27:16^{2} 27:17 27:20^{2} 27:22^{3} 27:23 27:24 28:1 28:9 28:12^{2} 28:15^{2} 28:40 28:45^{2} 28:54^{4} 28:55 29:2 29:12 29:19

29:20^{2} 29:23^{2} 30:2 30:8 30:10^{2} 30:16^{4} 30:20 32:4^{2} 32:5 32:9^{2} 32:10 32:15 32:19^{2} 32:36^{2} 32:43^{5} 32:50 33:1 33:2 33:3 33:6 33:7^{3} 33:9^{4} 33:11^{2} 33:12 33:13 33:16 33:17^{3} 33:21 33:24^{2} 33:26 33:28 34:6 34:7^{2} 34:9 34:11^{2}

JOS

2:19^{3} 3:15 4:5 4:14 4:18 5:13^{3} 5:14^{2} 6:26^{2} 6:27 7:6^{2} 7:18 7:22 7:24^{6} 7:26 8:1^{3} 8:14 8:18 8:19 8:26 8:29 9:24 10:21 10:33 11:15 13:27 15:17 17:3 17:6 17:10 20:4 20:5^{2} 20:6^{2} 21:12 22:5^{2} 22:20 22:29 23:3 23:4 23:10 24:24 24:28 24:30 24:33

JG

1:2 1:3

1:6^{2} 1:13 1:17 2:6 2:9 3:10^{2} 3:16^{2} 3:20 3:21^{3} 3:22 3:24^{3} 4:7^{2} 4:10 4:11 4:13 4:15^{4} 4:17 4:21 4:22 5:11 5:17 5:26^{2} 5:31 6:11 6:13 6:21^{2} 6:27^{2} 6:31 6:32 7:5^{2} 7:7 7:8 7:11 7:13 7:14^{2} 7:21 7:22 8:20^{2} 8:21 8:24 8:25 8:27^{2} 8:29 8:30 8:31 8:32 9:1^{2} 9:3 9:5^{2} 9:7 9:16^{2} 9:17 9:18^{2} 9:19 9:21 9:24 9:26 9:28 9:30 9:31 9:41 9:48^{2} 9:49 9:53 9:54^{2} 9:55 9:56^{2} 10:16 11:2 11:3 11:11 11:20^{2} 11:21 11:23 11:32 11:34^{3} 11:35 11:39 12:9 13:2 13:5 13:6^{2} 13:7 13:11 13:19 13:20 13:21

13:22 13:23 13:24 14:2^{2} 14:3^{3} 14:4^{2} 14:5^{2} 14:6^{3} 14:9^{2} 14:10 14:19^{2} 14:20^{2} 15:1 15:6^{2} 15:14^{3} 15:15 15:17 15:19 16:3 16:5 16:9 16:12 16:14 16:16 16:17 16:18^{2} 16:19^{2} 16:20 16:21 16:22 16:29^{2} 16:30^{3} 16:31^{3} 17:2^{2} 17:3^{2} 17:4^{2} 17:5^{2} 17:6 17:11 17:12 18:4 18:26 18:30 19:2 19:3 19:4 19:5 19:7 19:9^{3} 19:10 19:11 19:12 19:13 19:15^{2} 19:16 19:17 19:21 19:24 19:25 19:27^{2} 19:28 19:29^{2} 20:8^{2} 21:1 21:21 21:22 21:24^{3} 21:25

RU

1:1^{2} 1:2^{2} 1:6 2:1 2:5 2:15 2:20 2:22 3:4 3:7^{2} 3:8 3:14 4:5 4:7^{2} 4:8

4:10^{3} 4:13 4:14 4:17

1 SA

1:1 1:3 1:4 1:11^{2} 1:19 1:20 1:21^{2} 1:23 2:9 2:10^{2} 2:11 2:13 2:19 2:20 2:22 3:2^{2} 3:9 3:12 3:13^{2} 3:19 4:10 4:12^{2} 4:13 4:15 4:18 4:19 5:3^{2} 5:4^{2} 5:7 5:11 6:2 6:3 6:5 6:9^{2} 7:1 7:15 7:17^{2} 8:1 8:2^{2} 8:3^{2} 8:11^{3} 8:12^{4} 8:14 8:15 8:16 8:17 8:22 9:2 9:3 9:5 9:7 9:10 9:15 9:22 10:1^{2} 10:9 10:14 10:16 10:23 10:25 10:27 11:6 11:7 12:3 12:5 12:14 12:22^{3} 13:2 13:14^{2} 13:16 13:20^{4} 13:22 14:1^{2} 14:6 14:7 14:12^{2} 14:13^{4} 14:14 14:17

14:20 14:26^{2} 14:27^{5} 14:34^{3} 14:45 14:47 14:49 14:50 15:1 15:27 15:34 15:35 16:1 16:4 16:5 16:7^{2} 16:10 16:13 16:16 16:17 16:20 16:21 16:23 17:5 17:6^{2} 17:7^{2} 17:13 17:15 17:17 17:22^{2} 17:25^{2} 17:28 17:33 17:34 17:35^{2} 17:38^{2} 17:39^{2} 17:40^{4} 17:43 17:49^{5} 17:51^{2} 17:54^{2} 17:57 18:1 18:2 18:3 18:4^{4} 18:7^{2} 18:10 18:11 18:13 18:14 18:22^{2} 18:26 18:27^{2} 18:30 19:1^{2} 19:4^{3} 19:5^{2} 19:7 19:9^{4} 19:13 19:16 19:24 20:6 20:17 20:25 20:27 20:32 20:33 20:34 20:36 20:38 20:40^{2} 20:41 21:7 21:11^{2} 21:12 21:13^{3} 21:14 22:1^{2} 22:6^{3} 22:7 22:11 22:15 23:5 23:6

23:8
23:11
23:13
23:14
23:15
23:16
23:18
23:22[2]
23:24
23:25
23:26[3]
24:2
24:3[2]
24:6
24:7[2]
24:8
24:16
24:19
24:22
25:1
25:2
25:3[2]
25:4
25:10
25:13[4]
25:17
25:20
25:24
25:25[2]
25:36
25:37[2]
25:39[2]
25:42
25:43
25:44
26:5
26:7[2]
26:9
26:10
26:11
26:16
26:18
26:19
26:23[2]
26:25[2]
27:1[2]
27:3[3]
27:8
27:11
27:12
28:3
28:5
28:7[2]
28:14
28:18
28:23
28:25
29:2
29:4[2]
29:5[2]
29:11
30:1
30:3
30:6[3]
30:12
30:18
30:22[2]
30:24[2]
30:26
30:31
31:2
31:4[2]
31:5[2]
31:6[3]
31:7
31:8
31:9[2]
31:10
31:12

2 SA

1:2[2]
1:4
1:5
1:6
1:10[2]
1:11
1:12
1:17
2:2
2:3[2]
2:16[3]
2:21
2:27
2:29
2:32[2]
3:2
3:3
3:8[2]
3:12
3:27
3:29
3:30
3:32
3:38
3:39
4:1
4:4[3]
4:6
4:7[3]
4:8
4:9
4:10
4:11[3]
4:12
5:6
5:12[2]
5:21
6:6
6:7
6:11
6:14
6:17
6:19
6:20[2]
6:21
7:1[2]
7:12
7:13
7:14
7:25
7:27
8:3
8:10
8:15
9:3
9:6
9:9
9:11
9:13
10:1[2]
10:2[3]
10:3
10:10
11:1
11:2
11:9[2]
11:10
11:13[3]
11:27[2]
12:4[2]
12:9[2]
12:15
12:17
12:19[2]
12:20[2]
12:21
12:24[2]
12:25
12:30
13:2
13:8
13:17
13:18
13:22
13:24
13:28
13:29
13:31[2]
13:32
13:33
13:34
13:36
13:37
14:7[2]
14:9
14:13
14:14
14:15
14:16
14:22[2]
14:24[2]
14:25[3]
14:26[2]
14:30
14:31
14:33
15:5
15:12
15:14
15:16
15:18
15:22
15:25
15:30[2]
15:32[2]
16:6[2]
16:9
16:11
16:12
16:13
16:18
16:19
16:22
17:6
17:8
17:18
17:23[6]
18:9
18:14
18:17
18:18[2]
18:19
18:24
18:25
18:28
19:2
19:4
19:8
19:11[2]
19:17[2]
19:19
19:24[3]
19:30
19:39
19:41
20:1
20:3[2]
20:8
20:10[2]
20:21[2]
20:22
21:1
21:2
21:4
21:6
21:12
21:13
21:14[2]
21:15
21:22
22:1
22:7[2]
22:9[2]
22:10
22:14
22:23[2]
22:25
22:31
22:51[3]
23:2
23:8
23:10[2]
23:18
23:21[2]
23:23
24:14
24:16
24:20[2]
24:21

1 KI

1:2
1:6[2]
1:9
1:10
1:21
1:23
1:37
1:47
1:49
1:51
2:1
2:3[5]
2:4
2:5[4]
2:6
2:9
2:10
2:12[2]
2:15
2:19[2]
2:22
2:23
2:32
2:33[4]
2:34
2:35
2:40[2]
3:1
3:5
3:6
3:15
4:7
4:21
4:25[2]
4:26
4:27
4:28
4:31
4:32
4:34
5:1[2]
5:3[2]
5:10
5:11
7:1[2]
7:8
7:14[2]
7:23
7:31
8:6
8:14
8:15[2]
8:20
8:22
8:28
8:31
8:32[3]
8:38[2]
8:39
8:54[2]
8:56[3]
8:58[4]
8:59[2]
8:61[2]
8:66[2]
9:11
9:15
9:16
9:19[3]
9:22[5]
9:27
10:5[5]
10:13
10:24[2]
10:25
11:3[2]
11:4[5]
11:6
11:8
11:9
11:17
11:19
11:20
11:21
11:23
11:26
11:27[2]
11:33
11:34[2]
11:35
11:36
11:41
11:43[4]
12:4
12:6
12:15
12:18
12:24
12:26
12:33
13:4[2]
13:11
13:12
13:13
13:19
13:24
13:27
13:28
13:30[2]
13:31[2]
13:33
14:2
14:4[2]
14:8
14:18
14:20[3]
14:21[2]
14:31[5]
15:2
15:3[4]
15:4[2]
15:5
15:6
15:8[3]
15:10
15:11
15:12
15:13
15:14
15:15
15:18
15:23[3]
15:24[5]
15:26[2]
15:28
15:29
15:30
15:34
16:3
16:4
16:5
16:6[3]
16:7[2]
16:9[3]
16:10
16:11[3]
16:13
16:19[2]
16:20
16:26
16:27
16:28[3]
16:34[3]
17:17
17:19
17:23
18:3
18:7
18:42[2]
18:43
18:46
19:3[2]
19:6
19:13[2]
19:19
20:1
20:11
20:12
20:20
20:24
20:31
20:35
20:38
20:39
20:41
20:42[2]
20:43
21:4[3]
21:5
21:7
21:8[2]
21:11[2]
21:25
21:27[2]
21:29[3]
22:3
22:10
22:17
22:19[3]
22:22
22:31[2]
22:34
22:35
22:36[2]
22:38[2]
22:40[3]
22:42
22:43
22:45
22:46
22:50[5]
22:52[2]
22:53

2 KI

1:2
1:8
1:9
1:10
1:11
1:12
1:13[2]
1:16
1:17
2:8
2:12
3:2[3]
3:25
3:27[2]
4:12
4:18
4:19[2]
4:20
4:25
4:32
4:34[6]
4:35
4:37
4:38
4:39
4:43
5:1
5:3
5:4
5:6
5:7[2]
5:8
5:9[2]
5:11[2]
5:13
5:14
5:15
5:20
5:23
5:25
5:26
5:27
6:7
6:8
6:11
6:12
6:15
6:17
6:24
6:30[2]
6:32[2]
7:12
7:13
8:11
8:14
8:15[2]
8:18
8:19[2]
8:20
8:24[4]
8:26
9:2
9:3
9:6
9:11[2]
9:13
9:21[2]
9:23
9:24[4]
9:25[2]
9:26
9:28[3]
9:31
9:32
9:36
10:3
10:10
10:11[3]
10:15
10:16
10:19[2]
10:24
10:31
10:34
10:35[3]
11:2
11:8[2]
11:9
11:11[2]
11:18[2]
12:1
12:2
12:5
12:17
12:18[2]
12:20
12:21[4]
13:8
13:9[3]
13:12
13:13[2]
13:14[2]
13:16[2]
13:21
13:23[2]
13:24[2]
13:25
14:2
14:3[2]
14:5[3]
14:6
14:15
14:16[3]
14:20
14:21
14:22
14:25
14:28
14:29[3]
15:2
15:3
15:5
15:7[4]
15:9
15:10
15:14
15:15
15:18
15:19[2]
15:22[3]
15:25[2]
15:30
15:33
15:34
15:38[5]
16:2[2]
16:3
16:13[4]
16:15
16:20[4]
17:3
17:15[3]
17:18
17:20
17:23[2]
18:2
18:3
18:6
18:12
18:21
18:29
18:31[3]
18:33
19:1
19:4
19:7[2]
19:19
19:23[2]
19:37[4]
20:2
20:13[5]
20:20
20:21[3]
21:1
21:3
21:6
21:7
21:10
21:11
21:12
21:16
21:17
21:18[4]
21:19
21:20
21:21[2]
21:22
21:23
21:24[2]
21:26[3]
22:1
22:2
22:11
23:3[3]
23:10[2]
23:18[2]
23:25[3]
23:26[2]
23:29
23:30[3]
23:31
23:32
23:34[2]
23:35
23:36
23:37
24:1[2]
24:2
24:3
24:6[3]
24:7
24:8
24:9
24:11
24:12[5]
24:15
24:17[3]
24:18
24:20
25:1[2]
25:5
25:7
25:28
25:29[2]
25:30[2]

1 CH

1:13
1:19[2]
1:43
1:44
1:45
1:46[2]
1:47
1:48
1:49
1:50[3]
2:4
2:13
2:18
2:35[2]
2:42
3:3
3:10[3]
3:11[3]
3:12[3]
3:13[3]
3:14[2]
3:16[2]
3:17
4:9[3]
4:18
4:19
4:23
4:25[3]
4:26[3]
4:27
5:1[2]
5:2
5:4[3]
5:5[3]
5:6
5:7
6:20[3]
6:21[4]
6:22[3]
6:23[3]
6:24[4]
6:26[2]
6:27[3]
6:29[3]
6:30[3]
6:39[2]
6:49
6:50[3]
6:51[3]
6:52[3]
6:53[2]
7:14
7:16[3]
7:18
7:20[4]
7:21[2]
7:22
7:23[3]
7:24
7:25[3]
7:26[3]
7:27[2]
7:35
8:1
8:8
8:9
8:10
8:30
8:37[3]
8:39[2]
9:5
9:19[2]
9:36
9:43[3]
10:2
10:4[2]
10:5
10:6[2]
10:7
10:8
10:9[2]
10:10[2]
10:12
10:13
11:10
11:11
11:20
11:23
11:25
11:45
12:15
12:19
12:28
13:9
13:10
13:14
14:2[2]
14:4
15:3
15:5
15:6
15:7
15:8
15:9
15:10
15:17
16:7
16:8[2]
16:9
16:10
16:11[2]
16:12[3]
16:13[2]
16:14
16:15
16:16
16:23
16:24[2]
16:27[2]
16:29
16:34
16:37
16:39
16:41
16:43[2]
17:1
17:11
17:12
17:13
17:14
17:21
17:23
17:25
18:3
18:10[2]
18:14
19:1[2]
19:2[2]
19:3
19:7
19:11
19:13
19:15
19:19
20:2
20:8
21:3
21:13
21:16[2]
21:20
21:21
21:23
21:27
22:5
22:6
22:9[3]
22:10[2]
22:17
22:18
23:1
23:13[2]
23:14
23:25
25:9
25:10[2]
25:11[2]
25:12[2]
25:13[2]
25:14[2]
25:15[2]
25:16[2]
25:17[2]
25:18[2]
25:19[2]
25:20[2]
25:21[2]
25:22[2]
25:23[2]
25:24[2]
25:25[2]
25:26[2]
25:27[2]
25:28[2]
25:29[2]
25:30[2]
25:31[2]
26:6
26:10
26:14
26:15
26:22
26:25[5]
26:26
26:28
26:29
26:30
26:31
26:32
27:2
27:4[2]
27:5
27:6[2]
27:7[2]
27:8
27:9
27:10
27:11
27:12
27:13
27:14
27:15
28:1
28:2
28:6
28:7
28:11
28:19
28:20
29:5
29:23
29:28[2]
29:30[2]

2 CH

1:1[2]
1:8
2:1
2:11
2:12
2:14
2:15
2:17
3:1
3:2
4:16
5:1
5:7
5:13
6:3
6:4[2]
6:10
6:12
6:13[2]
6:19
6:22
6:23[3]
6:29[3]
6:30
7:3
7:6
7:10
7:11
8:1
8:6
8:9[3]
8:14
8:18
9:4[5]
9:8
9:23[2]
9:24
9:31[4]
10:4
10:6
10:15
10:18
11:4
11:12
11:14
11:21[2]
11:22
11:23
12:8
12:13[2]
12:14
12:16[3]
13:2
13:5
13:6
13:12
13:17
13:22[2]
14:1[4]
14:2
14:11
14:13
15:9
15:17
15:18
16:4
16:5
16:12[4]
16:13[2]
16:14
17:1[2]
17:2
17:3
17:4[2]
17:5
17:6
17:7[2]
18:7
18:9
18:16
18:18[3]
18:21
18:33
18:34
19:1
20:18[2]
20:20
20:21
20:25
20:30
20:31
20:32
21:1[4]
21:4[2]
21:7
21:8
21:9[2]
21:10[2]
21:17[3]
21:18
21:19[4]
22:1[2]
22:2
22:3[2]
22:4[3]
22:9
22:11
23:7[2]
23:8
23:10[2]
23:11
23:13
23:17[2]
24:1
24:11
24:13
24:16
24:22[2]
24:25[2]
24:27[3]
25:1
25:3[2]
25:4
25:11
25:14
25:22
25:28
26:1
26:2
26:3
26:4
26:8
26:15
26:16[3]
26:19[2]
26:20
26:21[2]
26:23[4]
27:1
27:2
27:6[2]
27:7[2]
27:9[3]
28:1
28:3
28:5
28:22
28:25
28:26[2]
28:27[3]
29:1
29:2
29:3
29:10
29:19[2]
29:25
30:2
30:6
30:8[2]
30:9
30:19[2]
30:27
31:1
31:2
31:3
31:8
31:10
31:12
31:13
31:16
31:20
31:21[2]
32:3[2]
32:9[2]
32:12[2]
32:14
32:15
32:16[2]
32:17
32:21[3]
32:25
32:26
32:30
32:31
32:32
32:33[4]
33:3
33:6
33:7
33:10
33:12[2]
33:13[2]
33:18[2]
33:19[3]
33:20[4]
33:22[2]
33:23
33:24[2]
33:25[2]
34:2
34:3[2]
34:4
34:8[2]
34:19
34:27
34:31[6]
34:33
35:3
35:4
35:8
35:9
35:22
35:23
35:24[2]
35:26
35:27
36:1
36:4[3]
36:5
36:7
36:8[3]
36:10
36:12
36:13[2]
36:15[3]
36:16[3]
36:17
36:18
36:20
36:22
36:23[2]

EZR

1:1
1:3[2]
1:4
1:7
2:1
2:68
3:2[2]
3:3
3:9[3]
3:11
4:6
5:6
5:15
5:17
6:5
6:7
6:10
6:11[2]
6:12
7:6[2]
7:9
7:10
7:11
7:13
7:14
7:15
7:23
7:28
8:17
8:18[2]
8:19
8:22[2]
8:25[2]
9:8
10:8
10:11
10:18

NE

1:5
2:1
2:20
3:1
3:10
3:12
3:17
3:23
3:28
3:29
3:30
4:2
4:15
4:17
4:18[2]
4:22
5:7
5:13[2]
6:5[2]
6:11
6:18
6:19
7:3[2]
7:6
8:4[2]
8:16
9:8[2]
9:10[2]
10:29[2]
11:3
11:13
11:17
11:20
12:8
12:36
12:45
12:47
13:10
13:26
13:30

ES

1:2
1:3[3]
1:4[2]
1:8
1:12[2]
1:20
1:22
2:3
2:7[2]
2:8
2:15
2:16[2]
2:17
2:18[2]
3:1
3:10[2]
4:1
4:3
4:4
4:11
4:17
5:1
5:2[2]
5:10[2]
5:11[2]
5:14[2]
6:6
6:8
6:12[2]
6:13[3]
7:5
7:7[2]
8:2
8:3[2]
8:5[2]
8:7
8:17
9:1
9:4
9:25[3]
10:2[2]
10:3[3]

JOB

1:3
1:4[2]
1:10[3]
1:13[2]
1:20[2]
2:3
2:4
2:5[2]
2:6
2:7[2]
2:9
2:10
2:11
2:12
2:13
3:1[2]
3:19
4:9
4:17
4:18[2]
5:3
5:4
5:18
5:26
6:5
6:9
6:14
7:1
7:2
7:10[2]
8:12
8:15
8:16[2]
8:17
8:18
8:19
9:5
9:13
9:33
9:34[2]
11:5
11:11[3]
12:4
12:5
12:11
12:16
13:8
13:11[2]
14:5[3]
14:6
14:18
14:20
14:21
14:22[2]
15:2
15:15[2]
15:20
15:21
15:23
15:25
15:26[2]
15:27[3]
15:29
15:30[2]
15:31
15:32[2]
15:33[2]
16:9[3]
16:12
16:13
16:21
17:5[2]
17:9
18:4[2]
18:5
18:6[2]
18:7[2]
18:8
18:11
18:12[2]
18:13[2]
18:14[2]
18:15[3]
18:16[2]
18:17
18:19[2]
18:20
19:6
19:11[2]
19:12
20:6[2]
20:7
20:9
20:10[2]
20:11[2]
20:12[2]
20:13
20:14[2]
20:15
20:18
20:20
20:21[2]
20:22
20:23[2]
20:25
20:26
20:27
20:28[3]
21:17
21:19[2]
21:20[2]
21:21[2]
21:23
21:24[2]
21:25
21:31[2]
22:22[2]
23:3
23:6
23:11[2]
23:12[2]
23:13
23:15
24:1
24:6
24:15
24:22
24:23
25:2
25:3[2]
25:5
26:8
26:9[2]
26:11
26:12[2]
26:13[2]
26:14[2]
27:1
27:8
27:9
27:14[2]
27:15
27:18
27:19
27:21
27:22
27:23
28:9
28:10
29:1
29:3[2]
29:17
30:24[2]
31:20
31:23
31:30
31:31
32:1
32:2
32:3[2]
32:5
32:12
32:14
33:10
33:13
33:17
33:18[2]
33:19[2]
33:20[2]
33:21[2]
33:22[2]
33:23
33:25[2]
33:26[2]
33:28[2]
33:30
34:11
34:14[3]
34:19
34:21[2]
34:27
34:29
34:35
34:36
34:37[3]
35:15
35:16
36:7
36:15
36:18
36:23
36:24
36:26
36:29
36:30
37:1
37:2[2]
37:3
37:4[2]
37:5
37:6
37:7
37:11
37:12
37:13
37:15
38:12
38:32[2]
38:41[2]
39:6
39:8
39:10
39:11
39:18
39:19
39:20
39:21
40:16[4]
40:17[2]
40:18[2]
40:19
40:23
40:24[2]
41:1
41:2[2]
41:7[2]
41:12[3]
41:13[2]
41:14[2]
41:15[2]
41:18[2]
41:19[2]
41:20
41:21[2]
41:22
41:23
41:24
41:33
42:10
42:11[4]
42:12
42:16[2]

PS

1:2[2]
1:3[3]
2:2
2:5[2]
2:12
3:*title*
3:4
7:12[2]
7:13
7:16[4]
7:17
8:6
9:7
9:11
9:16
10:2
10:3
10:4[2]
10:5[3]
10:6
10:7[2]
10:8
10:9[2]
10:10
10:11[2]
10:13
10:15
10:16
11:4[3]
11:5
11:7
12:2
14:1
14:6
14:7
15:2
15:3[3]
15:4

15:5
17:12
18:*title*
18:6^{2}
18:8^{2}
18:9^{2}
18:11^{2}
18:12
18:13
18:14
18:22^{2}
18:24
18:30
18:50^{3}
19:1
19:5
19:6^{2}
19:12
20:6^{3}
21:2^{2}
21:3
21:5
21:9
22:24
22:29
22:31
23:3
24:3
24:4
24:5
25:9
25:10^{2}
25:13^{2}
25:14
25:22
27:4
27:5^{2}
27:6
28:5
28:8
29:2
29:9^{2}
29:11^{2}
30:4^{2}
30:5^{2}
31:21
31:23
33:4
33:6
33:11
33:12
33:14
33:17
33:18
33:21
34:1
34:3
34:6
34:9
34:15
34:20
34:22
35:8
35:9
35:14
35:27
36:1
36:2^{2}
36:3
36:4
37:7
37:10
37:12
37:13
37:23
37:24
37:25
37:26
37:28
37:30
37:31^{3}
37:33
37:34
38:13
39:5
39:11
40:4
41:2
41:3^{2}
41:5
41:6
41:9
42:5
42:8^{2}
46:6
47:8
48:1
49:7
49:16
49:17
49:18
49:19
50:4
50:6
50:23
52:7^{3}
53:1
53:6
54:7
55:20^{2}
55:21^{3}
56:4
56:10^{2}
57:3^{2}
58:7^{2}
58:9
58:10
59:9
60:6
61:6
62:4
62:12
64:9
65:6
66:2^{2}
66:5
66:7^{2}
66:8
66:20
67:1
68:1
68:4^{2}
68:5
68:21^{2}
68:33
68:34^{2}
68:35
69:33
69:36^{2}
72:7
72:9
72:14
72:15^{2}
72:17^{2}
72:19^{2}
73:10
76:1
76:2^{2}
77:8^{2}
77:9
78:4^{2}
78:7
78:10
78:11^{2}
78:20
78:22
78:26
78:32
78:37
78:38^{2}
78:42
78:43^{2}
78:49
78:50
78:52
78:54^{2}
78:56
78:61^{2}
78:62^{2}
78:66
78:69
78:70
78:71^{2}
78:72^{2}
79:7
81:6^{2}
85:8^{2}
85:9
85:13
87:1
89:23^{2}
89:24
89:25^{2}
89:29^{2}
89:30
89:36^{2}
89:39
89:40^{2}
89:41
89:42^{2}
89:43
89:44^{2}
89:45
89:48
91:4^{3}
91:11
91:14
94:14^{2}
95:2
95:4^{2}
95:5^{2}
95:7^{3}
96:2^{2}
96:3^{2}
96:6
96:8^{2}
96:13
97:2
97:3
97:4
97:6^{2}
97:10
97:12
98:1^{2}
98:2^{2}
98:3^{2}
99:5
99:6^{2}
99:7
99:9
100:2
100:3^{2}
100:4^{3}
100:5^{2}
101:5
102:*title*
102:16
102:19
102:21
103:1
103:2
103:7^{2}
103:9
103:11
103:13
103:15
103:17
103:18^{2}
103:19^{2}
103:20^{3}
103:21^{3}
103:22^{2}
104:3^{2}
104:4^{2}
104:13
104:15
104:19
104:23^{2}
104:31
105:1^{2}
105:2
105:3
105:4^{2}
105:5^{3}
105:6^{2}
105:7
105:8
105:9
105:19
105:21^{2}
105:22^{3}
105:24
105:25^{2}
105:26
105:27
105:28
105:42^{2}
105:43^{2}
105:45^{2}
106:1
106:2
106:8^{2}
106:12^{2}
106:13^{2}
106:23^{2}
106:24
106:26
106:33^{2}
106:40^{2}
106:45^{2}
107:1
107:8^{2}
107:15^{2}
107:20
107:21^{2}
107:22
107:24
107:31^{2}
108:7
109:6
109:7
109:8^{2}
109:9^{2}
109:10
109:11
109:12
109:13
109:14^{2}
109:18^{3}
109:31
110:5
111:3^{2}
111:4
111:5
111:6^{2}
111:7^{2}
111:9^{3}
111:10^{2}
112:1
112:2
112:3^{2}
112:5
112:7
112:8^{3}
112:9^{2}
112:10
113:4
113:8
114:2^{2}
116:2
116:12
116:14
116:15
116:18
118:1
118:2
118:3
118:4
118:29
119:2
119:3
119:9
125:2
126:6
127:2
127:3
127:5
128:1
129:7^{2}
130:5
130:8
131:2
132:1
132:7^{2}
132:13
132:18^{2}
133:2
135:3
135:4
135:7
135:9
135:12
135:14^{2}
136:1
136:2
136:3
136:4
136:5
136:6
136:7
136:8
136:9
136:10
136:11
136:12
136:13
136:14
136:15^{2}
136:16^{2}
136:17
136:18
136:19
136:20
136:21
136:22^{2}
136:23
136:24
136:25
136:26
140:8
144:4
144:10
145:3
145:9^{2}
145:12^{2}
145:17^{2}
145:21
146:4^{3}
146:5^{2}
147:5
147:9
147:11
147:15^{2}
147:17^{2}
147:18^{2}
147:19^{3}
147:20
148:2^{2}
148:8
148:13^{2}
148:14^{2}
149:1
149:3
149:4
149:9
150:1^{2}
150:2^{2}

PR

2:6
2:8
3:11
3:20
3:31
3:32
5:21
5:22^{2}
5:23
6:13^{3}
6:14
6:15
6:27^{2}
6:28
6:29
6:30
6:31
6:32
6:33
7:23^{2}
8:22^{2}
8:29^{2}
8:30
8:31
8:36
10:1
10:9
10:15
10:19
11:1
11:5^{2}
11:7
11:8
11:9^{2}
11:12^{2}
11:17^{2}
11:19
11:20
11:28
11:29
12:4
12:8
12:10
12:11
12:13
12:14
12:15
12:25
12:26
13:1
13:2
13:3^{3}
13:8
13:16
13:22
13:24^{2}
13:25
14:2^{2}
14:8
14:10^{2}
14:14
14:15
14:20
14:21
14:26
14:31
14:32^{2}
14:35
15:5
15:8
15:20
15:23
15:27
15:32
16:2
16:7
16:9^{2}
16:10
16:11
16:15^{2}
16:17^{2}
16:23^{2}
16:26
16:27
16:29
16:30
16:32
17:5
17:12
17:13
17:18
17:19
17:21
17:25
17:27
17:28^{2}
18:2
18:6
18:7^{3}
18:9
18:11^{2}
18:14
18:17^{2}
18:20^{2}
19:1^{2}
19:2
19:3^{2}
19:4
19:7
19:8
19:11^{2}
19:12
19:13
19:16^{2}
19:18
19:22
19:24^{3}
19:26^{2}
20:2
20:6
20:7^{2}
20:8
20:11^{2}
20:14
20:16
20:17
20:19
20:20^{3}
20:24
20:28
21:2
21:8
21:10^{2}
21:13
21:23^{3}
21:24
21:25
21:29^{2}
22:5
22:8
22:9
22:11^{2}
22:16
22:25
22:29
23:3
23:6
23:7^{2}
23:14
23:31
24:7
24:12
24:15
24:18
24:26
24:29
25:5
25:13
25:18
25:22
25:28
26:4
26:5^{2}
26:11^{2}
26:12
26:14^{2}
26:15^{3}
26:16
26:19
26:24
26:25
26:26
27:8
27:13
27:14
27:16
27:17
27:18
27:21
27:22
28:6^{2}
28:7
28:8
28:9^{2}
28:10
28:11
28:13
28:14
28:16
28:18
28:19
28:24^{2}
28:25
28:26
28:27
29:1
29:3^{2}
29:5^{2}
29:10
29:11
29:12
29:14
29:15
29:20
29:21^{2}
29:24
29:25
30:4^{3}
30:6
30:10
30:17^{2}
31:1
31:7^{2}

EC

1:3
1:5
1:6
2:14
2:21
2:22^{2}
2:23^{3}
2:24^{2}
2:26
3:11
3:12
3:13
3:22^{2}
4:4
4:5^{2}
4:8^{2}
4:10
4:14
4:15
5:14
5:15^{3}
5:17^{2}
5:18^{3}
5:19^{2}
5:20^{2}
6:2
6:3^{2}
6:4
6:7
6:12
7:2
7:15^{3}
8:1^{2}
8:3
8:9
8:12
8:13
8:15^{2}
8:16
9:12
9:15
9:16
10:2^{2}
10:3
10:13^{2}
12:5
12:13

CA

1:2
1:4
1:12
2:3^{2}
2:4
2:6^{2}
2:16
3:8^{2}
3:11^{3}
4:16^{2}
5:4
5:11^{2}
5:12
5:13^{2}
5:14^{2}
5:15^{2}
5:16
6:2
7:10
8:3^{2}
8:7
8:10

ISA

1:3^{2}
2:3^{2}
2:10
2:19
2:20^{2}
2:21
2:22
3:5
3:6^{2}
3:8
3:11
3:14
5:1
5:7
5:12
5:19
5:25^{4}
6:1
6:2^{2}
6:3
6:6
7:2^{2}
7:14
8:3
8:7^{5}
8:8
8:17
9:4^{3}
9:6^{2}
9:7^{2}
9:11
9:12^{2}
9:17^{2}
9:19
9:20
9:21^{2}
10:4^{2}
10:7^{2}
10:12^{2}
10:16^{2}
10:17^{3}
10:18^{2}
10:19
10:24
10:26
10:27^{2}
10:28
10:32
11:1
11:3^{2}
11:4^{2}
11:5^{2}
11:8
11:10
11:11^{2}
11:15^{2}
11:16
12:4^{3}
13:6
13:10
13:13
13:14^{2}
14:17
14:18
14:21
14:25^{2}
14:27
14:29
14:31
14:32
15:4
15:5
16:6^{4}
16:12
17:4
17:5
17:7^{2}
17:8^{2}
17:9
19:1
19:2^{2}
19:14
22:21
22:22
22:23
22:24
23:11
24:2
24:23
25:4
25:8
25:9
25:11^{2}
26:21
27:1
27:8
27:9
28:4
28:5
28:21^{4}
28:25
28:28^{2}
29:8^{2}
29:22
29:23
30:4^{2}
30:26
30:27^{3}
30:28
30:30^{3}
31:2
31:3
31:4
31:7^{2}
31:8
31:9^{3}
32:6
33:6
33:15^{3}
33:16^{2}
33:17
34:2
34:14
34:16
34:17
36:6
36:16^{3}
36:18
37:1
37:4
37:7^{2}
37:20
37:24^{2}
37:38^{4}
38:2
38:9
39:2^{5}
40:10^{3}
40:11^{3}
40:12
40:13
40:26
40:28
41:2^{3}
41:3
41:6^{2}
42:2
42:4
42:10
42:12
42:13
42:21
42:24^{2}
42:25
44:5
44:6
44:11
44:12^{2}
44:13
44:17
44:19
44:20
44:26^{2}
45:1
45:9
45:10
45:11
45:13
46:3
47:4
47:15
48:2
48:14^{2}
48:15
48:16
48:19
48:20
49:2^{2}
49:5
49:7
49:13^{2}
50:10^{2}
51:14
51:15
51:17
51:22
52:9
52:10
52:14^{2}
53:5
53:6
53:7^{2}
53:8
53:9^{3}
53:10^{4}
53:11^{2}
53:12
54:5
54:16
55:7^{2}
56:2
56:3
56:6
56:10
56:11
57:2
57:13
57:17^{2}
57:18^{2}
58:5^{2}
59:1
59:2
59:16^{2}
59:17
59:18^{2}
59:19
60:2
60:22
62:8^{2}
62:11^{2}
63:1^{2}
63:7
63:9^{3}
63:10
63:11^{3}
63:12
65:15
65:20
66:5
66:6
66:13
66:14^{3}
66:15^{3}
66:16

JER

1:2
1:9
1:15
2:3
2:15^{2}
2:35
3:1
3:5
4:7^{3}
4:13^{2}
4:26
5:8
5:24
6:3
6:21
7:5
7:29
8:1
8:6^{2}
8:16^{2}
9:4
9:5
9:8^{3}
9:20
9:23^{3}
10:10^{2}
10:12^{3}
10:13^{2}
10:14^{2}
10:16^{2}
10:23
10:25
11:19
12:15^{2}
13:23^{2}
16:12
17:5
17:10^{2}
17:11^{2}
18:11
18:12
18:16
18:18
19:3
19:9
20:9^{2}
21:2
21:7
21:9
22:4^{2}
22:6
22:7
22:8
22:10
22:11
22:13^{4}
22:18
22:28
22:30^{2}
23:6
23:9
23:14
23:18^{2}
23:20
23:27
23:30
23:34
23:35^{2}
23:36
24:8
25:4
25:5
25:19^{3}
25:30^{3}
25:38^{2}
26:3
26:21^{2}
26:23
27:7^{3}
27:8
27:12
28:11
29:32
30:6^{2}
30:8
30:18
30:21
30:24
31:10
31:30^{2}
31:34^{2}
31:35
32:4^{2}
32:18
32:19^{2}
33:2
33:11
33:21
33:26
34:1^{2}
34:3^{2}
34:9^{3}
34:10^{2}
34:14
34:15
34:16^{2}
34:17^{2}
34:21
35:3^{2}
35:14
35:15
35:18
36:3
36:7
36:14
36:17
36:18
36:24
36:30
36:31^{2}
37:2
37:10
37:17
38:2
39:1
39:6
40:3
42:11
43:10^{2}
43:12
44:21
44:23^{3}
44:30^{4}
46:8
46:10
46:26
47:3^{3}
48:7
48:10
48:11^{3}
48:12
48:15
48:16
48:17
48:25
48:26
48:29
48:30^{2}
48:35
48:40
49:1^{2}
49:2
49:3^{2}
49:10^{4}
49:20
49:22
50:16^{2}
50:17
50:18
50:19^{2}
50:25^{2}
50:28
50:32
50:34
50:43
50:45
51:3^{2}
51:5
51:6
51:9
51:11^{2}
51:15^{3}
51:16^{2}
51:17^{2}
51:19^{2}
51:21^{2}
51:23^{2}
51:28
51:31
51:34
51:44
51:45
51:59
52:1
52:3
52:4^{2}
52:8
52:10
52:11
52:27
52:31
52:32
52:33^{2}
52:34^{3}

LA

1:10
1:12
1:14
1:17
1:18
2:1^{3}
2:2
2:3^{2}
2:4^{3}
2:5
2:6^{3}
2:7^{2}
2:8
2:17
3:1
3:3
3:12
3:13
3:22
3:27
3:29
3:30
3:32
3:34
3:36
3:39
4:4
4:11
4:20

EZE

1:15
1:27^{2}
3:12
3:18^{4}
3:19^{3}
3:20^{4}
7:13
7:16
7:20
8:2^{2}
8:11^{2}
8:12
9:1^{2}
9:2^{2}
9:3
9:11
10:7
12:12^{3}
12:14
13:22
14:4^{5}
14:7^{4}
16:15
17:4
17:14
17:15
17:17
17:18
17:19
17:20
17:21^{2}
17:22
18:6
18:7^{2}
18:8
18:11
18:12
18:13
18:14
18:15^{2}
18:16
18:17^{2}
18:18^{4}
18:21
18:22
18:23
18:24^{4}
18:26^{2}
18:27^{2}
18:28
18:30
19:7
19:9
20:7
20:39
21:3
21:4
21:5
21:21
21:22
21:30
22:11^{4}
25:9^{2}
26:3
26:9
26:10
26:11
29:3
29:18^{2}
29:19
29:20
30:11
30:22
30:24
31:2
31:3
31:4
31:5^{3}
31:6^{3}
31:7^{3}
31:8^{3}
31:9
31:10^{3}
31:11^{3}
31:13^{2}
31:16^{2}
31:18
32:10
32:22^{2}
32:31
32:32
33:4^{2}
33:5^{2}
33:6^{2}
33:8^{3}
33:9^{3}
33:11
33:12^{3}
33:13^{3}
33:14
33:16
33:18
33:19
33:20
33:26
33:30
34:12^{2}
34:26
35:8
36:20
37:7
37:16^{2}
37:19
38:6
38:21
38:22
39:11
40:3
43:2^{2}
43:17
44:27
45:8
46:2^{2}
46:7
46:12^{3}
46:16^{2}
46:17^{5}
46:18^{3}
47:3
47:12
47:23
48:1

DA

1:2^{3}
1:3
1:8
1:20
2:1^{2}
2:2
2:7
2:13
2:17^{2}
2:18
2:20
2:32^{4}
2:33^{2}
2:34
2:46
3:13
3:19
3:20
3:24
3:28^{2}
4:3^{4}
4:14^{4}
4:15^{2}
4:16
4:19
4:23
4:33^{3}
4:34
4:35^{2}
4:37
5:1
5:2^{4}
5:3^{3}
5:6^{3}
5:7
5:9^{2}
5:10
5:20^{4}
5:21^{3}
5:22
5:23
5:29
6:5
6:10^{5}
6:11
6:13
6:14
6:17^{2}
6:18^{2}
6:22
6:23
6:26^{2}
7:1^{2}
7:9^{3}
7:11
7:14^{2}
7:19^{2}
7:20^{2}
7:25
7:26
8:4^{2}
8:5
8:6
8:7^{2}
8:11
8:21
8:22
8:24^{2}
8:25^{3}
9:2
9:4
9:10^{2}
9:12
9:14^{2}
9:17
10:6^{6}
10:9^{2}
11:2^{2}
11:3
11:4^{4}
11:5^{2}
11:6
11:7
11:9^{2}
11:10^{2}
11:11
11:12
11:15
11:16^{2}
11:17^{3}
11:18^{3}
11:19^{2}
11:20
11:21
11:24^{3}
11:25^{2}
11:26^{2}
11:28^{3}
11:31
11:36
11:37
11:39^{2}
11:41
11:42
11:43
11:45^{2}
12:7^{2}

HO

1:4
1:9
3:5
5:5
5:13^{2}
6:2
6:3
7:5
7:9
7:10
8:14^{2}
9:8^{2}
9:13
10:1^{2}
10:6
10:11
11:5
11:6^{2}
12:2^{2}
12:3^{2}
12:5
12:7
12:14^{3}
13:12
13:15^{3}
14:5
14:6^{3}
14:7

JOE

2:7
2:8
2:11^{4}
2:16
2:18^{2}
2:19
2:20^{4}
3:16^{2}

AM

1:2
1:11^{3}
1:15
2:4
2:7^{2}
2:9^{2}
2:14
3:4
3:7^{2}
4:2
4:13^{2}
5:8
5:19
6:8
7:7
7:10
7:17
9:6^{3}
9:11

OB

3
6
11^{2}
14^{2}

JON

1:5
1:7
2:1
3:6^{2}
3:7
3:8
3:9
4:6^{2}

MIC

1:2
1:3
1:11
2:2^{2}
2:7
3:4
3:8^{2}
4:2^{2}
4:4^{2}
4:5
4:12
5:3
5:4
6:2
7:2
7:3
7:6
7:9
7:18^{2}

NA

1:2^{2}
1:3^{2}
1:5
1:6^{3}
1:8
1:14
2:3^{2}
2:5
2:12^{4}

HAB

1:11^{3}
2:4^{2}
2:5
2:6
2:9^{2}
2:15
2:18
2:20
3:3^{2}
3:4^{3}
3:5
3:6
3:10^{2}
3:14^{2}
3:16

ZEP

1:7
1:18
2:3
2:11
2:13
2:15
3:5
3:17

HAG

1:9
2:12^{2}
2:22

ZEC
1:21 2:1 2:8 2:12 2:13 3:1 3:5[2] 3:10 4:1 4:2 5:4 6:12 6:13[2] 7:9 7:10 7:12 8:4[2] 8:10 8:16 8:17 9:7[4] 9:10 9:14 9:16[2] 9:17[2] 10:3[2] 10:12 11:6[2] 11:17[4] 12:4 12:10[2] 13:3[4] 13:4 14:4 14:9 14:13[3]

MAL
1:3[2] 1:6[2] 1:12 1:14 2:6[2] 2:7 2:10 2:15 2:16 3:1 3:2 3:5[2] 3:14 3:16 3:17 4:2

MT
1:2 1:11 1:18 1:21 1:23 1:24 1:25 2:2 2:11 2:13 2:14 2:20 2:22 3:3 3:4[3] 3:7 3:12[3] 4:6 4:18 4:21 4:24 5:1 5:2 5:13 5:22[2] 5:28 5:31 5:32 5:35 5:45 6:27 6:29 6:33 7:9 7:24 7:26 7:28 8:3[2] 8:13 8:14 8:16 8:20 8:21 8:23 8:25 9:1 9:7 9:10 9:11 9:19 9:20 9:21 9:31 9:37 9:38 10:1 10:2[2] 10:10 10:24[2] 10:25[3] 10:35 10:36 10:38 10:39[2] 10:42 11:1 11:2 11:20 12:1 12:10 12:19 12:21 12:26 12:29[2] 12:33[3] 12:46[2] 12:49[2] 13:19 13:24 13:25[2] 13:31 13:36 13:41[2] 13:52 13:54 13:55[2] 13:56 13:57[2] 14:2 14:3 14:11 14:12 14:15 14:19 14:22 14:31 14:36 15:5[2] 15:6[2] 15:12 15:23 15:32 15:33 15:36 16:5 16:13 16:20 16:21 16:24[2] 16:25[2] 16:26[2] 16:27[3] 16:28 17:1 17:2[2] 17:10 17:27 18:6 18:15 18:23 18:25[2] 18:28 18:29[2] 18:31 18:32 18:34 18:35 19:3 19:5 19:9 19:10[2] 19:13 19:15 19:23 19:25 19:28 20:1 20:2 20:8 20:28 21:34 21:35 21:37 21:38 21:41 21:45 22:2 22:3 22:5[2] 22:6 22:7 22:8 22:15 22:24[3] 22:25[2] 22:33 22:45 23:1 24:1 24:17 24:18 24:31[2] 24:32 24:43 24:45[2] 24:46 24:47 24:48[2] 24:49 24:51 25:14[2] 25:15[2] 25:18 25:21 25:23 25:26 25:31[2] 25:32 25:33 25:34 25:41 26:1 26:7 26:8 26:23 26:39 26:45 26:51[3] 26:52 26:52 26:63 26:65[2] 26:67 27:19 27:24 27:25 27:29[2] 27:31 27:32 27:35 27:37[2] 27:44 27:53 27:60 27:64 28:3[2] 28:7 28:8 28:9 28:13

MK
1:3 1:6 1:16 1:19 1:22 1:28 1:41 2:8 2:15[2] 2:16 2:23 3:5 3:7 3:9 3:21 3:27[2] 3:31[2] 4:2 4:34 5:3 5:15 5:22 5:27 5:28 5:31 6:1[2] 6:2 6:3 6:4[3] 6:5 6:14 6:17 6:21[2] 6:26 6:27 6:28 6:29[2] 6:35 6:41 6:45 6:56 7:2 7:11 7:12[2] 7:17 7:19 7:25 7:32[2] 7:33[3] 7:35[2] 8:1 8:4 8:6 8:10 8:12 8:23[2] 8:25[2] 8:26 8:27[2] 8:33 8:34[2] 8:35[2] 8:36 8:37 8:38 9:3 9:14 9:18 9:21 9:28 9:31 9:36 9:41 9:42 9:50 10:2 10:7[2] 10:10 10:11 10:13 10:16[2] 10:23 10:24 10:45 10:48 10:50 10:52 11:1 11:18 11:23 12:6 12:13 12:19[4] 12:33 12:37 12:38 12:43 13:1 13:15 13:16 13:27[2] 13:34[3] 14:3 14:12 14:13 14:16 14:32 14:47 14:51 14:61 14:63 14:65 15:17 15:20 15:21 15:24 15:26 15:27[2] 16:7

LU
1:5 1:8 1:9 1:13 1:14 1:15 1:23 1:24 1:29 1:31 1:32 1:33 1:48 1:49 1:50 1:51 1:54[2] 1:55 1:59 1:60 1:62 1:63 1:64[2] 1:67 1:68 1:69 1:70 1:72 1:76 1:77 1:80 2:3 2:5 2:21 2:28 2:33 2:34 2:41 2:43 2:47 2:48 2:51 3:1 3:4 3:17[3] 3:18 3:19 4:10 4:16 4:22 4:24 4:30 4:32[2] 4:40 5:12 5:13 5:19 5:25 5:29 5:30 6:1 6:10 6:13 6:14 6:17 6:20[2] 6:40[2] 6:44 6:45[3] 7:1 7:3 7:11 7:12 7:15 7:16 7:19 7:38[3] 8:5 8:9 8:19[2] 8:22 8:35 8:39 8:41 8:44 9:1 9:14 9:18 9:23 9:24[3] 9:26[2] 9:29[2] 9:31 9:32 9:42 9:43 9:51 9:52 9:53 9:54 9:58 9:62 10:1 10:2 10:7 10:23 10:30 10:34[2] 10:39 11:1[2] 11:6 11:8[2] 11:18 11:21[2] 11:22[2] 11:54 12:1 12:22 12:25 12:27 12:39 12:42[2] 12:43 12:45[2] 12:46 12:47[2] 13:6 13:7 13:13 13:15[2] 13:17 13:19 14:17 14:21[2] 14:26[2] 14:27 14:34 15:5 15:6 15:12[2] 15:13[2] 15:15 15:16 15:20[3] 15:22[3] 15:25 15:28 15:29 16:1[2] 16:5 16:18 16:20 16:21 16:23[2] 16:24 17:2 17:16[2] 17:24 17:31 17:33[2] 18:7 18:13[2] 18:14 18:15 18:39 18:43 19:13 19:14 19:29 20:20 20:26[2] 20:28[3] 20:44 20:45 22:4 22:36[2] 22:39 22:44 22:45 22:50 22:51 22:71 23:11 23:34 23:49 23:55 24:8 24:23 24:26 24:40[2] 24:47 24:50

JOH
1:11[2] 1:12 1:14 1:16 1:35 1:41 2:2 2:5 2:11[2] 2:12[3] 2:17 2:21 2:22 2:23 3:4 3:16 3:17 3:20 3:21 3:22 3:32 3:33[2] 3:35 4:2 4:3 4:5 4:6 4:8 4:12[2] 4:27 4:31 4:34 4:41 4:44 4:47 4:50 4:51 4:53 5:9 5:18 5:28 5:35 5:37[2] 5:38 5:43 5:47 6:2 6:3 6:5 6:8 6:12 6:16 6:22[3] 6:24 6:52 6:53 6:60 6:61 6:66 7:3 7:5 7:10 7:16 7:17 7:18[2] 7:30 7:38 7:53 8:6 8:20 8:44 8:55 9:1 9:2[2] 9:3 9:7 9:14 9:15 9:18[2] 9:20 9:21 9:22 9:23 9:27 9:28 9:31 10:3[2] 10:4[2] 10:11 11:2 11:3 11:7 11:12 11:13 11:16 11:32 11:41 11:44 11:54 12:3 12:4 12:16 12:17 12:25[2] 12:41 12:50 13:1[2] 13:3 13:4 13:10 13:12 13:16 13:18 13:23 15:10 15:13[2] 15:15 15:19 15:20 16:17 16:29 16:32 17:1 18:1[2] 18:2 18:10 18:19[2] 18:22 18:25 18:26 19:2 19:17 19:23[2] 19:25[2] 19:26[2] 19:27 19:29 19:30 19:33 19:34 19:35 20:7 20:20[2] 20:25[2] 20:26 20:30 20:31 21:2 21:7 21:14 21:20 21:24

AC
1:3 1:7 1:14 1:18 1:20[2] 1:22 1:25 2:6 2:14 2:29 2:30[2] 2:31[2] 2:41 3:2 3:4 3:7 3:13 3:16[2] 3:18 3:21 3:26[2] 4:26 4:32 5:1 5:2 5:7 5:10 5:31 5:32 5:41 6:15 7:4 7:5[2] 7:6 7:10[2] 7:13 7:14[2] 7:20 7:23[2] 7:25[2] 7:27 8:1 8:2 8:28 8:32[2] 8:33[4] 8:35 8:39 9:8 9:12[2] 9:17[2] 9:18 9:33 9:41 10:2 10:7 10:22 10:24 10:25 10:34 10:43 11:13 11:29 12:1 12:7[2] 12:10 12:11 12:15 12:21 13:8 13:9 13:13 13:16 13:23 13:24 13:25[2] 13:31 13:36[2] 14:3 14:8[2] 14:14 14:18 16:1 16:3 16:27[2] 16:32 16:33 16:34[2] 17:2 17:16 17:28 18:2 18:6 18:8 18:14 18:18[2] 19:6 19:12 19:31 19:33 20:7 20:10 20:28 20:32 20:38 21:11 21:19 22:14[2] 22:15 22:20 22:30 23:29 23:30 24:8 24:23 24:24 27:3 28:3 28:4 28:8 28:23 28:30

RO
1:2 1:3 1:5 1:9 1:20 2:4 2:6 2:18 2:26 3:7 3:20 3:24 3:25[2] 3:26 4:5 4:13 4:19 4:23 5:8 5:9 5:10[2] 6:3 6:5[2] 6:16 8:3 8:9 8:11 8:28 8:29 8:32 9:19 9:22[2] 9:23 11:1 11:2 11:22 11:33[2] 11:34 12:20 13:10 14:4 14:5 14:13 15:2[2] 15:9 15:10 16:13 16:15

1 CO
1:9 1:29 2:10 3:8[2] 5:1 6:5 6:14 6:18 7:2 7:4 7:7 7:11 7:33 7:36 7:37[4] 9:7 9:10 10:24 10:28 11:4[2] 11:7 11:21 14:25[2] 14:30 15:10 15:23[2] 15:25 15:27 15:38 16:12

2 CO
2:11 2:14 3:7 3:13 5:10 7:7 7:12[2] 7:13 7:15 8:9 8:17 9:7 9:9 9:15 10:10[3] 11:3 11:15 11:33

GA
1:15 1:16 3:16 4:4 4:6 5:10 6:4 6:5 6:8

EPH
1:5 1:6 1:7[2] 1:9[2] 1:11 1:12 1:14 1:18[2] 1:19[2] 1:20 1:22 1:23 2:4 2:7[2] 2:10 2:15 3:5 3:6 3:7 3:16[2] 4:25 4:28 5:28 5:29 5:30[3] 5:31[2] 5:33 6:10

PHP
1:29 2:4 2:13 2:30 3:10[3] 3:21 4:19

COL
1:9 1:11 1:13 1:14 1:20 1:22[2] 1:24 1:26 1:29 2:14 2:18 3:9 4:15

1 TH
1:10 2:11 2:12 2:19 3:13 4:4 4:6 4:8

2 TH
1:7 1:9 1:10 1:11 2:6 2:8[2] 3:4[2] 3:5

1 TI
5:8[2] 5:18 6:1 6:15

2 TI
1:8 1:9 2:19 2:26 4:1[2] 4:8 4:14 4:18

TIT
1:3 3:5 3:7

HEB
1:2 1:3[3] 1:7[2] 2:4 2:8 3:2 3:5 3:6 3:7 3:15 3:18 4:1 4:4 4:7 4:10[3] 4:13 5:7 6:10 6:17 7:10 7:27 8:11[2] 9:12 10:13[2] 10:20 10:30 11:4 11:5 11:7 11:17 11:21 11:22 11:23 12:10 12:16 13:12 13:13 13:15 13:21[2]

JAS
1:8 1:11 1:14 1:18[2] 1:23 1:24 1:25 1:26[2] 2:21 2:22 3:13 4:11[2] 5:20

1 PE
1:3 2:9 2:21 2:22 2:24[2] 3:10[2] 3:12 4:2 4:13 5:10

2 PE
1:3 1:9 1:16 2:8 2:16 2:22 3:4 3:9 3:13 3:16

1 JO
1:3 1:7 1:10 2:3 2:4 2:5 2:9 2:10 2:11[2] 2:12 2:28 3:9 3:10 3:12[3] 3:14 3:15 3:16 3:17[2] 3:22[2] 3:23[2] 3:24 4:9 4:10 4:12 4:13 4:20[2] 4:21 5:2 5:3[2] 5:9 5:10 5:11 5:14 5:16 5:20

2 JO
6 11

3 JO
7 10

JUDE
14 24

RE
1:1[3] 1:4 1:5 1:6 1:14[3] 1:15[2] 1:16[4] 1:17[2] 2:1 2:5 2:18[2] 3:5[3] 3:21 6:5 6:8 6:17 7:15 9:11 10:1[3] 10:2[3] 10:5 10:7 11:15 11:19[2] 12:3 12:4 12:5 12:7[2] 12:9 12:10 12:15 12:16 13:1[2] 13:2[4] 13:3[2] 13:6[8] 13:17 13:18 14:1 14:7 14:9[4] 14:10 14:11[2] 14:14[2] 14:16 14:19 15:2[3] 15:8 16:2[2] 16:3 16:4 16:8 16:10[2] 16:12 16:15[2] 16:17 16:19 17:17 18:1 19:2[2] 19:5 19:7 19:10 19:12[2] 19:13 19:15 19:16[2] 19:19 19:20 19:21 20:1 20:4[2] 20:7 21:3 21:7 22:3 22:4[2] 22:6[2] 22:12 22:14 22:19

I

589, *1473*

GE
1:25 1:30 2:18 3:10[2] 3:11 3:12 3:13 3:15 3:16 3:17 4:1 4:9 4:13 4:14 4:23 6:7[2] 6:13 6:17 6:18 7:1 7:4[2] 8:21[2] 9:3 9:5 9:9 9:11 9:12 9:13 9:14 9:15 9:16 9:17 12:1 12:2 12:3 12:7 12:11 12:13 12:19 13:8 13:9[2] 13:15 13:16 13:17 13:22 13:23[3] 15:1 15:2 15:7 15:8 15:14 15:18 16:2 16:5[2] 16:8 16:10 16:13 17:1 17:2 17:5 17:6 17:7 17:8[2] 17:16[2] 17:19 17:20[2] 17:21 18:3 18:4 18:5 18:10 18:12 18:13 18:14 18:15 18:17 18:19 18:21[2] 18:26[2] 18:27 18:28 18:29 18:30[2] 18:31[2] 18:32 19:2 19:7 19:8[2] 19:19 19:21 19:22 19:34 20:5 20:6[3] 20:9 20:11 20:13 20:16 21:7 21:13 21:18 21:23 21:24 21:26[2] 21:30 22:1 22:2 22:5 22:7 22:11 22:12 22:16 22:17 23:4[2] 23:8 23:11[2] 23:13[2] 24:2 24:3[2] 24:5 24:7 24:12 24:13 24:14[4] 24:17 24:19 24:23 24:24 24:27 24:31 24:33 24:34 24:37 24:39 24:40 24:42[2] 24:43[2] 24:44 24:45[2] 24:46[2] 24:47[2] 24:48 24:49 24:56 24:58 25:22 25:30[2] 25:32 26:2 26:3[3] 26:4 26:9 26:24[2] 27:1 27:2 27:3 27:4[2] 27:6 27:7 27:8

27:9 27:11 27:12 27:18 27:19^{2} 27:21 27:24 27:25 27:32 27:33 27:37^{3} 27:41 27:45^{2} 27:46 28:13^{2} 28:15^{2} 28:16 28:20 28:21 28:22^{2} 29:18 29:19^{2} 29:21 29:25 29:33 29:34 29:35 30:1 30:2 30:3 30:8 30:13 30:14 30:16 30:18 30:20 30:25 30:26^{2} 30:27^{2} 30:28 30:29 30:30^{2} 30:31^{2} 30:32 30:34 31:3 31:5 31:6 31:10 31:11 31:12 31:13 31:31 31:35 31:38^{2} 31:39^{2} 31:40 31:41 31:43 31:44 31:51 31:52 32:4 32:5^{3} 32:9 32:10^{3} 32:11^{2} 32:12 32:20^{2} 32:26 32:29 32:30 33:8 33:9 33:10^{4} 33:11^{2} 33:12 33:14^{3} 34:8 34:11 34:12 34:30^{3} 35:3^{2} 35:11 35:12^{3} 37:6^{2} 37:9 37:10 37:13^{2} 37:14 37:16^{2} 37:17 37:30^{2} 37:35 38:16 38:17 38:18 38:22 38:23 38:25^{2} 38:26^{2} 39:9^{2} 39:14 39:15 39:18 40:8 40:11^{2} 40:14 40:15^{2} 40:16^{2} 41:9 41:11 41:15^{2} 41:17 41:19 41:21 41:22 41:24 41:28 41:40 41:41 41:44 42:2 42:14 42:18 42:22 42:33 42:34^{2} 42:37^{2} 43:9^{2} 43:14^{2} 43:23 44:15 44:17 44:18 44:21 44:28^{2} 44:30 44:32^{2} 44:33 44:34^{2} 45:3 45:4^{2} 45:11 45:18 45:28^{2} 46:2 46:3^{2} 46:4^{2} 46:30 46:31 47:16 47:23 47:29^{3} 47:30^{2} 48:4^{2} 48:5 48:7^{2} 48:9 48:11 48:19^{2} 48:21 48:22^{2} 49:1 49:7 49:29 49:31 50:4^{2} 50:5^{4} 50:17 50:19 50:21 50:24

EX

2:7 2:9 2:10 2:22 3:3 3:4 3:6 3:7^{2} 3:8 3:9 3:10 3:11^{3} 3:12^{2} 3:13^{2} 3:14^{3} 3:16 3:17^{2} 3:19 3:20^{2} 3:21 4:10^{2} 4:11 4:12 4:13 4:14 4:15 4:18 4:21^{2} 4:23^{2} 5:2^{3} 5:10 5:23 6:1 6:2 6:3^{2} 6:4 6:5^{2} 6:6^{4} 6:7^{3} 6:8^{4} 6:29^{2} 6:30 7:1 7:2 7:3 7:4 7:5^{2} 7:17^{2} 8:2 8:8 8:9 8:21 8:22^{2} 8:23 8:28 8:29^{2} 9:14 9:15^{2} 9:16 9:18 9:27 9:28 9:29^{2} 9:30 10:1^{2} 10:2^{3} 10:4 10:10 10:16 10:17 10:29 11:1 11:4 11:8 12:8 12:12^{3} 12:13^{3} 12:15^{2} 12:17 14:4^{3} 14:17^{3} 14:18^{2} 15:1 15:2^{2} 15:9^{4} 15:26^{3} 16:4^{2} 16:12^{2} 16:32^{2} 17:4 17:6 17:9 17:14 18:3 18:6 18:11 18:16^{2} 18:19 19:4^{2} 19:9^{2} 20:2 20:5 20:22 20:24^{3} 21:5^{2} 21:13 22:23 22:24 22:27^{2} 23:7 23:13 23:15 23:20^{2} 23:22^{2} 23:23 23:25 23:26 23:27^{2} 23:28 23:29 23:30 23:31^{2} 24:12^{2} 25:8 25:9 25:16 25:21 25:22^{3} 28:3 29:35 29:42 29:43 29:44^{2} 29:45 29:46^{3} 30:6 30:36 31:2 31:3 31:6^{4} 31:11 31:13 32:8 32:9 32:10^{2} 32:13^{3} 32:18 32:24^{2} 32:30^{2} 32:32 32:33 32:34^{3} 33:1^{2} 33:2^{2} 33:3^{2} 33:5^{2} 33:12 33:13^{4} 33:14 33:16^{2} 33:17^{2} 33:18 33:19^{4} 33:22^{2} 33:23 34:1 34:9^{2} 34:10^{3} 34:11^{2} 34:18 34:24 34:27

LE

6:17 7:34 8:31 8:35 10:3^{2} 10:13 10:18 10:19 11:44^{2} 11:45^{2} 14:34^{2} 16:2 17:10 17:11 17:12 17:14 18:2 18:3 18:4 18:5 18:6 18:21 18:24 18:25 18:30 19:3 19:4 19:10 19:12 19:14 19:16 19:18 19:25 19:28 19:30 19:31 19:32 19:34 19:36 19:37 20:2 20:3 20:5 20:6 20:7 20:8 20:22 20:23^{2} 20:24^{3} 20:25 20:26 21:8 21:12 21:15 21:23 22:2 22:3 22:8 22:9 22:16 22:30 22:31 22:32^{2} 22:33 23:10 23:22 23:30 23:43^{3} 25:2 25:17 25:21 25:38 25:42 25:55^{2} 26:1 26:2 26:4 26:6^{2} 26:9 26:11 26:12 26:13^{2} 26:16^{2} 26:17 26:18 26:19^{2} 26:21 26:22 26:24 26:25^{2} 26:26 26:28^{3} 26:30 26:31^{2} 26:32 26:33 26:36 26:41 27:42^{3} 27:44^{3} 27:45^{4}

NU

3:12 3:13^{3} 3:41 3:45 5:3 6:27 8:16 8:17^{2} 8:18 8:19 9:8 10:10 10:29 10:30^{2} 10:31 11:11 11:12^{2} 11:13 11:14 11:15^{2} 11:17^{2} 11:21^{2} 12:6 12:8 12:11 12:13 13:2 14:11 14:12 14:17 14:19 14:20 14:21 14:22 14:23 14:24 14:27^{2} 14:28^{2} 14:30 14:31 14:35^{2} 15:2 15:18 15:41^{2} 16:8 16:15^{2} 16:21 16:26 16:28 16:45 17:4 17:5^{2} 18:6^{2} 18:7 18:8^{2} 18:11 18:12 18:19 18:20 18:21 18:24^{2} 18:26 20:12 20:17 20:18 20:19^{3} 20:24 21:2 21:16 21:34 22:6^{4} 22:8 22:11 22:16 22:17^{3} 22:18 22:19^{2} 22:20 22:28 22:29^{2} 22:30^{3} 22:32 22:33 22:34^{3} 22:35 22:37^{2} 22:38^{3} 23:3^{2} 23:4^{2} 23:8^{2} 23:9^{2} 23:11 23:12 23:13 23:15 23:20^{2} 23:26^{2} 23:27^{2} 24:10 24:11 24:12 24:13^{2} 24:14^{2} 24:17^{2} 25:11 25:12 27:12 32:8 32:11 33:53 33:56^{2} 35:34^{2}

DE

1:8 1:9^{2} 1:12 1:13 1:15 1:16 1:17 1:18 1:20 1:23 1:29 1:35 1:36 1:39 1:42 1:43 2:5^{2} 2:9^{2} 2:13 2:19^{2} 2:24 2:25 2:26 2:27^{2} 2:28^{3} 2:29 2:31 3:2 3:12 3:13 3:15 3:16 3:18 3:19^{2} 3:20 3:21 3:23 3:25 4:1 4:2^{2} 4:5 4:8 4:10 4:21^{2} 4:22^{2} 4:26 4:40 5:1 5:5 5:6 5:9 5:28 5:31^{2} 6:2 6:6 7:11 7:17^{2} 8:1 8:11 8:19 9:9^{3} 9:12 9:13 9:14^{2} 9:15 9:16 9:17 9:18^{2} 9:19 9:20 9:21^{2} 9:23 9:24 9:25^{2} 9:26 10:2 10:3 10:5^{2} 10:10 10:11 10:13 11:2 11:8 11:13 11:14 11:15 11:22 11:26 11:27 11:28 11:32 12:11 12:14 12:20 12:21 12:28 12:30 12:32 13:18 15:5 15:11 15:15 15:16 18:16 18:18^{2} 18:19 18:20 19:7 19:9 22:14^{3} 22:16 22:17 24:8 24:18 24:22 26:3^{2} 26:8 26:10 26:13^{3} 26:14^{3} 27:1 27:4 27:10 28:1 28:13 28:14 28:15 28:68 29:5 29:6 29:14 29:19^{2} 30:1 30:2 30:8 30:11 30:15 30:16 30:18 30:19^{2} 31:2^{2} 31:5 31:14 31:16 31:17^{2} 31:18 31:20^{2} 31:21^{3} 31:23^{2} 31:27^{2} 31:28 31:29^{2} 32:1 32:3 32:20^{2} 32:21^{2} 32:23^{2} 32:24 32:26^{3} 32:27 32:39^{6} 32:40^{2} 32:41^{2} 32:42 32:46 32:49 32:52 33:9 34:4^{3}

JOS

1:2 1:3^{2} 1:5^{3} 1:6 1:9 2:4 2:5 2:9 2:12^{2} 3:7^{3} 5:9 5:14 6:2 6:10 7:8 7:11 7:12 7:19 7:20^{2} 7:21^{2} 8:1 8:5 8:8 8:18 10:8 11:6 13:6^{2} 14:7^{2} 14:8 14:10 14:11^{2} 14:12 15:16 17:14 18:4 18:6 18:8 20:2 22:2 23:2 23:4^{2} 23:14 24:3 24:4^{2} 24:5^{4} 24:6 24:7 24:8^{3} 24:10^{2} 24:11 24:12 24:13

JG

1:1 1:2 1:7 1:12 2:1^{4} 2:3^{2} 2:20 2:21 2:22 3:19 3:20 4:7^{2} 4:8^{2} 4:9 4:19^{2} 4:22 5:3^{3} 5:7^{2} 6:8 6:9 6:10^{2} 6:14 6:15^{2} 6:16 6:17 6:18^{3} 6:22 6:37^{2} 6:38^{2} 7:4^{3} 7:7 7:9 7:13 7:17^{2} 7:18^{2} 8:2 8:3 8:5^{2} 8:7 8:9^{2} 8:19 8:23 8:24 9:2^{2} 9:9 9:11 9:13 9:29 9:38 9:48 10:11 10:12 10:13 11:9 11:17 11:27 11:31^{2} 11:35^{2} 11:37^{2} 12:2^{2} 12:3^{2} 13:4 13:6 13:11 13:13 13:14 13:15 13:16 14:2 14:12^{2} 14:16^{2} 15:1 15:2^{3} 15:3^{2} 15:7^{2} 15:11 15:16 15:18 16:6 16:7 16:10 16:11 16:15 16:17^{3} 16:20 16:26^{2} 16:28^{3} 17:2 17:3^{2} 17:9^{3} 17:10 17:13^{2} 18:4 18:24^{2} 19:6 19:8 19:9 19:11 19:18^{3} 19:23 19:24 20:4^{2} 20:6 20:23 20:28^{3}

RU

1:12^{4} 1:16^{2} 1:17^{2} 1:21 2:2 2:7 2:9 2:10^{2} 2:13 2:19 3:1 3:5 3:9 3:11 3:12^{2} 3:13 4:4^{4} 4:6^{3} 4:9 4:10

1 SA

1:8 1:11 1:15^{2} 1:16 1:20 1:22^{2} 1:26 1:27^{2} 1:28 2:1 2:16 2:23 2:24 2:27 2:28^{2} 2:29 2:30^{2} 2:31 2:33 2:35^{2} 2:36^{2} 3:4 3:5^{2} 3:6 3:8 3:11 3:12^{4} 3:13^{2} 3:14 3:16 3:17 4:16^{2} 7:5 7:7 7:8 9:8^{2} 9:16^{2} 9:17 9:18 9:19^{2} 9:21 9:23^{2} 9:24^{2} 9:26 9:27 10:2 10:8^{2} 10:15 10:18 11:2^{2} 12:1 12:2^{2} 12:3^{7} 12:7 12:17 12:23^{2} 13:11 13:12^{3} 14:7 14:24 14:29^{2} 14:37 14:40 14:43^{2} 15:2 15:6 15:11 15:13 15:14 15:16 15:20 15:24^{3} 15:25^{2} 15:26 15:30^{3} 16:1^{3} 16:2^{2} 16:3^{2} 16:5 16:7 16:18 16:22 17:8 17:9 17:10 17:28 17:29 17:35^{2} 17:39^{2} 17:43 17:44 17:45 17:46^{2} 17:55 17:58 18:11 18:17 18:18^{2} 18:21 18:23 19:2 19:3^{4} 19:15 19:17 20:1 20:3 20:4 20:5^{2} 20:9^{2} 20:12^{2} 20:13 20:14^{2} 20:20^{2} 20:21^{2} 20:22 20:23 20:29^{3} 20:30 20:36 21:2^{3} 21:5 21:8 21:15 22:3^{2} 22:9 22:12 22:15 22:22^{2} 23:2 23:4 23:11 23:17 23:22 23:23^{2} 24:4 24:6 24:10^{2} 24:11^{2} 24:17^{2} 24:20 25:7 25:8 25:11^{3} 25:19 25:21 25:22 25:24 25:25^{2} 25:28 25:35 26:6 26:8^{2} 26:11^{2} 26:18 26:19 26:21^{3} 26:23 27:1^{3} 27:5^{2} 28:2 28:7 28:8^{2} 28:11 28:13 28:15^{3} 28:21 28:22 28:23 29:3 29:6 29:8^{3} 29:9 30:7 30:8^{2} 30:13^{2} 30:15

2 SA

1:3 1:4 1:6 1:7^{2} 1:8^{2} 1:9 1:10^{3} 1:13 1:16 1:26 2:1^{2} 2:6 2:20 2:22^{2} 3:8 3:9 3:13^{2} 3:14 3:18 3:21 3:28 3:35 3:39 4:10^{2} 4:11 5:19^{2} 6:21 6:22^{2} 7:2 7:6^{2} 7:7^{3} 7:8 7:9 7:10 7:11 7:12^{2} 7:13 7:14^{2} 7:15 7:18 7:27 9:1 9:3 9:7 9:8 9:9 10:2 10:11 11:5 11:11^{2} 12:7 12:8^{2} 12:11^{2} 12:12 12:13 12:22 12:23^{3} 12:27 12:28 13:4 13:5^{2} 13:6^{2} 13:10 13:12^{3} 13:24 13:26 13:28^{2} 14:2 14:5 14:8 14:11 14:12 14:15^{2} 14:18^{2} 14:21 14:22 14:32^{3} 15:4^{2} 15:7^{2} 15:8^{2} 15:20^{3} 15:25 15:26 15:28 15:31 15:34^{3} 16:4^{2} 16:9 16:10 16:18^{2} 16:19^{4} 17:1 17:2^{2} 17:3 17:11 17:15 18:2 18:4 18:10 18:11 18:12^{2} 18:13 18:14 18:18 18:22 18:29^{2} 18:33 19:6 19:7 19:20^{2} 19:22^{3} 19:26^{2} 19:28 19:29 19:33 19:34^{2} 19:35^{5} 19:37^{2} 19:38^{2} 20:16^{2} 20:17^{2} 20:19 20:20 20:21 21:3^{2} 21:4 21:6 22:3 22:4^{2} 22:7 22:22 22:23 22:24 22:30^{2} 22:38^{2} 22:39 22:41 22:43^{2} 22:44 22:50^{2} 23:17 24:2 24:10^{4} 24:12^{2} 24:13 24:14 24:17 24:24^{2}

1 KI

1:5 1:12 1:14 1:21 1:30 1:35 2:2 2:7 2:8^{3} 2:14 2:15 2:16 2:17 2:18 2:20^{3} 2:26 2:30 2:42^{2} 2:43 3:5 3:7^{2} 3:9 3:12 3:13 3:14 3:17 3:18 3:21^{3} 5:5^{2} 5:6 5:8 5:9 6:12^{2} 6:13 8:12 8:16^{3} 8:20 8:21 8:26 8:27 8:43 8:44 8:48 8:59 9:3^{2} 9:4 9:5 9:6 9:7^{4} 10:6 10:7^{3} 11:11^{2} 11:12^{2} 11:13^{2} 11:21 11:31 11:32 11:34^{3} 11:35 11:36^{2} 11:37 11:38^{3} 11:39 12:6 12:11^{2} 12:14 13:7 13:8^{2} 13:14 13:16^{2} 13:18 13:31 14:2^{2} 14:6 14:7 14:10 15:19 16:2 16:3 17:1 17:4 17:9 17:10^{2} 17:12^{3} 17:18 17:20 17:21 17:24 18:1 18:8 18:9 18:12^{4} 18:13^{2} 18:15^{2} 18:18 18:22^{2} 18:23 18:24 18:36^{2} 19:2 19:4 19:10^{3} 19:14^{3} 19:18 19:20^{3} 20:4^{2} 20:5 20:6 20:7^{2} 20:9^{2} 20:13^{2} 20:28^{2} 20:31 20:32 20:34^{2} 20:35 20:37 20:42 21:2^{3} 21:3 21:4 21:6^{3} 21:7 21:20 21:21 21:29^{2} 22:4 22:5 22:6^{2} 22:8 22:13 22:14 22:16 22:17 22:18 22:19 22:21 22:22^{2} 22:27 22:30 22:34

2 KI

1:2 1:10 1:12 1:13 2:2^{2} 2:3 2:4^{2} 2:5 2:6^{2} 2:9^{3} 2:10 2:18 2:19 2:21 3:7^{2} 3:13 3:14^{3} 4:2 4:9 4:10 4:13 4:22^{2} 4:24 4:26 4:28^{2} 4:30 4:43 5:5 5:6 5:7^{2} 5:11 5:12 5:15^{2} 5:16^{2} 5:17 5:18^{2} 5:20 5:22 6:3^{2} 6:13 6:17 6:18 6:19 6:21^{2} 6:27 6:29 6:33 7:12 7:13^{2} 8:4 8:8 8:9 8:12 9:3 9:5 9:6 9:7 9:8 9:9 9:12 9:17 9:25 9:26^{2} 10:9 10:19 10:24 16:7 17:13^{2} 17:38 18:14^{2} 18:20 18:23^{2} 18:25 18:26 18:32 19:7^{2} 19:19 19:20 19:23^{2} 19:24^{2} 19:25^{3} 19:27 19:28^{2} 19:34 20:3^{2} 20:5^{3} 20:6^{3} 20:8 20:15 21:4 21:7^{2} 21:8^{3} 21:13^{2} 21:14 22:8 22:16 22:19^{2} 22:20^{2} 23:17 23:27^{4}

1 CH

4:9 5:3 11:19^{2} 13:12 14:10^{2} 15:12 16:18 17:1 17:5^{2} 17:6^{3} 17:7 17:8 17:9 17:10^{3} 17:11^{2} 17:12 17:13^{3} 17:14 17:16 19:2 19:12 21:2 21:8^{4} 21:10^{2} 21:12 21:13 21:17^{3} 21:22 21:23^{2} 21:24^{2} 22:5 22:9^{2} 22:10^{2} 22:14^{2} 23:5 28:2 28:6^{2} 28:7 29:2 29:3^{4} 29:14 29:17^{3} 29:19

2 CH

1:7 1:10 1:11 1:12 2:4 2:5 2:6^{2}

2:8
2:9
2:10
2:13
6:2
6:5^3
6:6
6:10
6:11
6:18
6:33
6:34
6:38
6:40
7:12
7:13^3
7:14
7:16
7:17
7:18^2
7:19
7:20^4
9:5
9:6^3
10:11
10:14^2
12:5
12:7^2
16:3
18:3
18:4
18:5
18:7
18:12
18:13
18:14
18:15
18:16
18:17
18:18
18:20
18:21
18:26
18:29
18:33
20:11
25:9
25:16
28:23
32:13
33:7^2
33:8^3
34:15
34:24
34:27
34:28^2
35:21^3
35:23

EZR

4:19
6:8
6:11
6:12
7:13
7:21^2
7:28^2
8:15^2
8:16
8:17^2
8:21
8:22
8:24
8:26
8:28
9:3^2
9:4
9:5^2
9:6

NE

1:1
1:2
1:4^2
1:5
1:6^2
1:8^2
1:9^2
1:11^3
2:1^2
2:2
2:4
2:5^2
2:6
2:7^2
2:8
2:9
2:11
2:12^4
2:13
2:14
2:15
2:16^3
2:17
2:18
2:20
4:13^2
4:14
4:19
4:22
4:23
5:6^2
5:7^3
5:8
5:9
5:10^2
5:11
5:12
5:13
5:14^2
5:15
5:16
5:18
5:19
6:1^2
6:3^4
6:4
6:8
6:10
6:11^4
6:12
6:13
7:1
7:2
7:3
7:5
7:7
9:8
12:31
12:38
12:40
13:6^3
13:7
13:8
13:9^2
13:10
13:11^2
13:13
13:14
13:15^2
13:17
13:19^2
13:21^2
13:22
13:23
13:25
13:28
13:30

ES

3:9
4:11
4:16^4
5:4
5:8^3
5:12
5:13
7:3
7:4^2
8:5^2
8:6^2
8:7

JOB

1:15
1:16
1:17
1:19
1:21^2
3:3
3:11^3
3:12
3:13^3
3:16
3:24
3:25^2
3:26^3
4:7
4:8
4:16^2
5:3^2
5:8^2
6:8^2
6:10^3
6:11^2
6:22
6:24^2
6:28
6:29
7:3
7:4^4
7:8
7:11^3
7:12
7:13
7:16^2
7:19
7:20^3
7:21^2
8:8
8:18
9:1
9:11^2
9:14
9:15^3
9:16^2
9:19
9:20^3
9:21^3
9:22
9:27^3
9:28^2
9:29^2
9:30
9:32^2
9:35
10:1^2
10:2
10:7
10:9
10:13
10:14
10:15^4
10:18
10:19^3
10:20
10:21^2
11:4
12:3^2
12:4
13:2^2
13:3^2
13:13
13:14
13:15^2
13:18^3
13:19^2
13:20
13:22
14:14
14:15
15:6
15:17^3
16:1
16:4^2
16:5
16:6^3
16:12
16:15
16:22^2
17:6
17:10
17:13^2
17:14
19:4
19:7^3
19:8
19:10
19:15
19:16^2
19:17
19:18
19:19
19:20
19:25
19:26
19:27
20:2
20:3
21:3^2
21:6^2
21:27
22:22
23:3^3
23:4
23:5
23:7
23:8^2
23:9^2
23:10^2
23:11
23:12^3
23:15^4
23:17
27:5^3
27:6^2
27:11^2
29:1
29:3
29:4
29:6
29:7^2
29:12
29:13
29:14
29:15^2
29:16^3
29:17
29:18^3
29:24
29:25
30:1^2
30:9^2
30:19
30:20^2
30:23
30:25
30:26^2
30:28^3
30:29
31:1^2
31:5
31:9
31:13
31:14
31:16
31:18
31:19
31:21^2
31:23
31:24
31:25
31:26
31:28
31:29
31:30
31:32
31:33
31:34^2
31:36
31:37^2
31:39
32:6^2
32:7
32:10^2
32:11^2
32:12
32:14
32:16
32:17^3
32:18
32:20^3
32:21
32:22
33:2
33:2
33:6^2
33:8
33:9^2
33:12
33:24
33:27
33:31
33:32
33:33
34:5
34:6
34:31^2
34:32^3
34:33
35:3^2
35:4
36:2^2
36:3
37:20
38:3
38:4
38:9
38:23
39:6
40:4^3
40:5^3
40:7
40:14
40:15
41:11
41:12
42:2
42:3^3
42:4^3
42:5
42:6
42:8^2

PS

2:6
2:7^2
2:8
3:4
3:5^2
3:6
4:1^2
4:3
4:8
5:2
5:3
5:7^2
6:2
6:6^3
7:1
7:3
7:4^2
7:17
8:3
9:1^2
9:2^2
9:13
9:14^2
10:6^2
11:1
12:5^2
13:2
13:3
13:4^2
13:5
13:6
16:1
16:4
16:6
16:7
16:8^2
17:3
17:4
17:6
17:15^3
18:1
18:2
18:3^2
18:6
18:21
18:22
18:23^2
18:29^2
18:37^2
18:38
18:40
18:42^2
18:43
18:49
19:13^2
20:6
22:2
22:6
22:9
22:10
22:14
22:17
22:22^2
22:25
23:1
23:4^2
23:6
25:1
25:2
25:5
25:16
25:20
25:21
26:1^3
26:3
26:4^2
26:5
26:6^2
26:7
26:8
26:11
26:12
27:1^2
27:3
27:4^3
27:6^3
27:7
27:8
27:13^2
27:14
28:1^2
28:2^2
28:7^2
30:1
30:2
30:3
30:6^2
30:7
30:8^2
30:9
30:12
31:1
31:5
31:6^2
31:7
31:9
31:11
31:12^2
31:13
31:14^2
31:17
31:22^3
32:3
32:5^4
32:8^2
34:1
34:4
34:11
35:3
35:11
35:13
35:14^2
35:15
35:18^2
37:25^2
37:35
37:36
38:6^3
38:8^2
38:13^2
38:14
38:15
38:16
38:17
38:18^2
38:20
39:1^4
39:2^2
39:3^2
39:4^2
39:7
39:9^2
39:10
39:12
39:13^2
40:1
40:5
40:7^2
40:8
40:9^2
40:10^3
40:12
40:17
41:4^2
41:9
41:10
41:11
42:2
42:4^4
42:5
42:6
42:9^2
42:11
43:2
43:4^2
43:5
44:6
45:1^2
45:17
46:10^3
49:4^2
49:5
50:7^3
50:8
50:9
50:11
50:12^2
50:13
50:15
50:21^3
50:22
50:23
51:3
51:4
51:5
51:7^2
51:13
51:16
52:8^2
52:9^2
54:6^2
55:2
55:6^3
55:7
55:8
55:9
55:12^2
55:16
55:17
55:23
56:3^2
56:4^3
56:9^2
56:10^2
56:11^2
56:12
56:13
57:1
57:2
57:4
57:7
57:8
57:9^2
59:8
59:16^2
59:17
60:6^2
60:8
61:2^2
61:4^2
61:8^2
62:2
62:6
62:11
63:1
63:2
63:4^3
63:6
63:7
66:13^2
66:14
66:15^2
66:16
66:17
66:18
68:22^2
69:2^2
69:3^2
69:4^2
69:7
69:8
69:10
69:11^2
69:12
69:17
69:20^3
69:29
69:30
70:5
71:1
71:3
71:6
71:7
71:14
71:15
71:16^2
71:17
71:18^2
71:22^2
71:23
73:3^2
73:13
73:14
73:15^3
73:16
73:17^2
73:21
73:22^2
73:23
73:25^2
73:28^2
75:2^2
75:3
75:4
75:9^2
75:10
77:1
77:2
77:3^2
77:4^2
77:5
77:6^2
77:10^2
77:11^2
77:12
78:2^2
81:5^2
81:6
81:7^3
81:8
81:10^2
81:12
81:14
81:16
82:6
84:10
85:8
86:1
86:2
86:3
86:4
86:7
86:11
86:12^2
87:4
88:1
88:4^2
88:8^2
88:9^2
88:13
88:15^3
89:1^2
89:2
89:3^2
89:4
89:19^2
89:20^2
89:23
89:25
89:27
89:28
89:29
89:32
89:33
89:34
89:35^2
89:50
91:2^2
91:14^2
91:15^3
91:16
92:4
92:10
94:18
95:10
95:11
101:1^2
101:2^2
101:3^2
101:4
101:5^2
101:8^2
102:2^2
102:4
102:6^2
102:7
102:9
102:11
102:24
104:33^4
104:34
105:11
106:5^3
108:1
108:2
108:3^2
108:7^2
108:9^2
109:4
109:22
109:23^2
109:25
109:30^2
110:1
110:2
110:3^2
110:5
110:7
111:1
116:1
116:2^2
116:3
116:4^2
116:6
116:9
116:10^3
116:11
116:12
116:13
116:14
116:16^2
116:17
116:18
118:5
118:6
118:7
118:10
118:11
118:12
118:13
118:17
118:19^2
118:21
118:25^2
118:28^2
119:6^2
119:7^2
119:8
119:10
119:11^2
119:13
119:14
119:15
119:16^2
119:17
119:18
119:19
119:22
119:26
119:27
119:30^2
119:31
119:32
119:33
119:34^2
119:35
119:39
119:40
119:42^2
119:43
119:44
119:45^2
119:46
119:47^2
119:48^3
119:51
119:52
119:55
119:56^2
119:57^2
119:58
119:59
119:60
119:61
119:62
119:63
119:66
119:67^3
119:69
119:70
119:71^2
119:73
119:74
119:75
119:76
119:77
119:78
119:80
119:81
119:83^2
119:87
119:88
119:92
119:93
119:94^2
119:95
119:96
119:97
119:99
119:100^2
119:101^2
119:102
119:104^2
119:106^3
119:107
119:108
119:109
119:110
119:111
119:112
119:113^2
119:114
119:115
119:116
119:117^2
119:119
119:120
119:121
119:125^2
119:127
119:128^2
119:131^2
119:134
119:141^2
119:144
119:145^2
119:146^2
119:147^2
119:148
119:152
119:153
119:157
119:158
119:159
119:162
119:163^2
119:164
119:166
119:167
119:168
119:173
119:174
119:176^2
120:1
120:5^2
120:7^2
121:1
122:1
122:8
122:9
123:1
130:1
130:5^2
130:6
131:1
131:2
132:3
132:4
132:5
132:11
132:12
132:14^2
132:15^2
132:16
132:17^2
132:18
135:5
137:5
137:6^2
138:1^2
138:2
138:3
138:7
139:6
139:7^2
139:8
139:9
139:11
139:14^2
139:15
139:18^3
139:21^2
139:22^2
140:6
140:12
141:1^2
141:10
142:1^2
142:2^2
142:3
142:4
142:5^2
142:6^2
142:7
143:5^3
143:6
143:7
143:8^3
143:9
143:12
144:2
144:9^2
145:1^2
145:2^2
145:5
145:6
146:2^4

PR

1:23^2
1:24^2
1:26^2
1:28
3:28
4:2
4:3
4:11^2
5:12
5:14
7:6
7:7
7:14^2
7:15^2
7:16
7:17
8:4
8:6
8:12
8:13
8:14^2
8:17
8:20
8:21^2
8:23
8:24
8:25
8:27
8:30^2
9:5
20:9^2
20:22
22:13
22:19
22:20
22:21
23:35^4
24:29^2
24:30
24:32
26:19
27:11
30:2
30:3
30:7^2
30:9^2
30:18
30:20

EC

1:12
1:13
1:14
1:16^2
1:17^2
2:1^2
2:2
2:3^2
2:4^3
2:5^2
2:6
2:7^2
2:8^2
2:9
2:10^2
2:11^2
2:12
2:13
2:14
2:15^3
2:17
2:18^3
2:19^2
2:20^2
2:24
2:25
3:10
3:12
3:14
3:16
3:17
3:18
3:22
4:1
4:2
4:4
4:7^2
4:8
4:15
5:13
5:18
6:1
6:3
7:15
7:23^3
7:25
7:26
7:27
7:28^3
7:29
8:2
8:9
8:10
8:12
8:14
8:15
8:16
8:17
9:1
9:11
9:13
9:16
10:5
10:7
12:1

CA

1:5
1:6^2
1:7
1:9
2:1
2:3
2:5
2:7
2:16
3:1^3
3:2^4
3:3
3:4^4
3:5
4:6
5:1^4
5:2
5:3^4
5:5
5:6^4
5:8^2
6:3
6:11
6:12
7:8^3
7:10
7:12
7:13
8:1^3
8:2^2
8:4
8:5
8:10^2

ISA

1:2
1:11^2
1:13
1:14
1:15^2
1:24
1:25
1:26
3:4
3:7
5:1
5:2
5:3
5:4^2
5:5^3
5:6^2
6:1
6:5^4
6:8^4
6:11
8:2
8:3
8:17^2
8:18
10:6^2
10:11^2
10:12
10:13^4
10:14
12:1
12:2
13:3^2
13:11^2
13:12
13:13
13:17
14:13^2
14:14^2
14:22
14:23^2
14:24^2
14:25
14:30
15:9
16:9^2
16:10
18:4^2
19:2
19:3
19:4
19:11
21:2
21:3^2
21:8^2
21:10^2
22:4^2
22:19
22:20
22:21^2
22:22
22:23
23:4^2
24:16
25:1^2
26:9^2
27:3^3
27:4^2
28:16
28:17
28:22
29:2
29:3^2
29:11^2
29:12^2
29:14
30:7
33:10^3
33:13
33:24
36:5^2
36:8^2
36:10
36:11
36:17
37:7^2
37:24^3
37:25^2
37:26^3
37:28
37:29^2
37:35
38:3^2
38:5^3
38:6^2
38:8
38:10^3
38:11^3
38:12
38:13
38:14^3
38:15^2
38:17
38:19
38:22
39:4
40:6
40:25
41:4^2
41:8
41:9^2
41:10^5
41:13^2
41:14
41:15
41:17^2
41:18^2
41:19^2
41:25
41:27
41:28^2
42:1^2
42:6
42:8^2
42:9^2
42:14^4
42:15^3
42:16^4
42:19
43:1^2
43:2
43:3^2
43:4^2
43:5^2
43:6
43:7^3
43:10^2
43:11^2
43:12^3
43:13^2
43:14
43:15
43:19^2
43:20
43:21
43:23
43:25
43:28
44:1
44:2
44:3^2
44:5
44:6^2
44:7^2
44:8^2
44:16^2
44:19^5
44:21
44:22^2
44:24
44:26
44:27
45:1^2
45:2^2
45:3^2
45:4^2
45:5^2
45:6
45:7^3
45:8
45:12^3
45:13^2
45:18
45:19^4
45:21
45:22
45:23
45:24
46:4^5
46:9^2
46:10
46:11^4
46:13^2
47:3^2
47:6^2
47:7
47:8^3
47:10
48:3^2
48:4
48:5^2
48:6
48:7
48:8
48:9^3
48:10^2
48:11^2
48:12^3
48:13
48:15^4
48:16^2
48:17
49:3
49:4^3
49:5
49:6
49:8^3
49:11
49:15
49:16
49:18
49:20
49:21^2
49:22
49:23
49:25^2
49:26^2
50:1^2
50:2^5
50:3^2
50:4
50:5
50:6^2
50:7^4
51:2
51:4
51:12^2
51:15
51:16^3
51:19
51:22
51:23
52:5
52:6^2
53:12
54:7^2
54:8^2
54:9^3
54:11
54:12
54:16^2
55:3
55:4
55:11^2
56:3
56:5^2
56:7
56:8
56:12
57:6
57:11
57:12
57:15
57:16^3
57:17^2
57:18^2
57:19^2
58:5
58:6
58:9
58:14
59:21
60:7
60:10^2
60:13
60:15
60:16
60:17^3
60:21
60:22
61:8^4
61:10
62:1^2
62:6
62:8
63:1
63:3^3
63:5^2
63:6^2
63:7
65:1^3
65:2^2
65:5
65:6
65:7
65:8^2
65:9
65:12^4
65:17
65:18^2
65:19
65:24^2
66:2
66:4^4
66:9^2
66:12
66:13
66:18^2
66:19^2
66:21
66:22

JER

1:5^4
1:6^3
1:7^3
1:8
1:9
1:10
1:11^2
1:12
1:13^2
1:15
1:16
1:17^2
1:18
1:19
2:2
2:7
2:9^2
2:20^2
2:21
2:23^2
2:25^2
2:30
2:31
2:34
2:35^3
3:7
3:8^2
3:12
3:14^3
3:15
3:18
3:19^3
3:22
4:6
4:10
4:12
4:19^2
4:21
4:23
4:24
4:25
4:26
4:27
4:28^3
4:31
5:1
5:4
5:5
5:7^2
5:9
5:14
5:15
5:29
6:2
6:8
6:10
6:11^3
6:12
6:15
6:17
6:19
6:21
6:27
7:3
7:7^2
7:11
7:12^2
7:13^2
7:14^3
7:15^2
7:16
7:22^2
7:23^3
7:25
7:31
7:34
8:6^2
8:10
8:13
8:17
8:18
8:21^2
9:1
9:2^2
9:7^2
9:9
9:10
9:11
9:13
9:15
9:16^3
9:24^2
9:25
10:18
10:19^2
10:23
11:4^4
11:5^3
11:7^2
11:8^2
11:10
11:11^2
11:14
11:18
11:19^2
11:20
11:22
11:23
12:1
12:7^3
12:8
12:14^2
12:15^2
12:17
13:2
13:5
13:6
13:7^2
13:9
13:11
13:13
13:14^2
13:24
13:26
13:27
14:12^3
14:13^2
14:14^2
14:15

14:16 14:18^{2} 15:3 15:4 15:6^{2} 15:7^{3} 15:8^{2} 15:9 15:10 15:11 15:13 15:14 15:15 15:16^{2} 15:17 15:19 15:20^{2} 15:21^{2} 16:5 16:9 16:13^{2} 16:15^{2} 16:16^{2} 16:18 16:21^{2} 17:3 17:4^{2} 17:10^{2} 17:14^{2} 17:16^{2} 17:22 17:27 18:2 18:3 18:6 18:7 18:8^{3} 18:9 18:10^{3} 18:11 18:17^{2} 18:20 19:2 19:3 19:5 19:7^{3} 19:8 19:9 19:11 19:12 19:15^{2} 20:4^{2} 20:5^{2} 20:7^{3} 20:8^{3} 20:9^{4} 20:10 20:12 20:14 20:18 21:2 21:4^{2} 21:5 21:6 21:7 21:8 21:10 21:13 21:14^{2} 22:5 22:6 22:7 22:14 22:21^{2} 22:24^{2} 22:25 22:26 23:2 23:3^{2} 23:4 23:5 23:6 23:8 23:9 23:11 23:12 23:13

23:14 23:15 23:21^{2} 23:23 23:24^{2} 23:25^{3} 23:30 23:31 23:32^{2} 23:33 23:34 23:38 23:39^{4} 23:40 24:3 24:5^{2} 24:6^{4} 24:7^{3} 24:8 24:9^{2} 24:10^{2} 25:3 25:6 25:9 25:10 25:12 25:13^{2} 25:14 25:15 25:16 25:17 25:27 25:29^{2} 26:2 26:3^{2} 26:4 26:5 26:6 26:14 27:5 27:6^{2} 27:8^{2} 27:10 27:11 27:12 27:15^{2} 27:16 27:22^{2} 28:2 28:3 28:4^{2} 28:7 28:11 28:14^{2} 28:16 29:4 29:7 29:8 29:10 29:11^{2} 29:12 29:14^{6} 29:17 29:18^{2} 29:19 29:20 29:21 29:23^{2} 29:31 29:32^{2} 30:2 30:3^{3} 30:6 30:8 30:9 30:10 30:11^{5} 30:14 30:15 30:16 30:17^{2} 30:18 30:19^{2} 30:20 30:21 30:22 31:1

31:2 31:3^{2} 31:4 31:8 31:9^{3} 31:13 31:14 31:18^{3} 31:19^{6} 31:20^{3} 31:25^{2} 31:26 31:27 31:28^{2} 31:31 31:32^{3} 31:33^{2} 31:34^{2} 31:37 32:3 32:5 32:8^{2} 32:9 32:10 32:11 32:12 32:13 32:16^{2} 32:27 32:28 32:31 32:33 32:35 32:37^{3} 32:38 32:39 32:40^{3} 32:41^{2} 32:42^{3} 32:44 33:3 33:5^{2} 33:6^{2} 33:7 33:8^{2} 33:11 33:14^{2} 33:15 33:22 33:25 33:26^{3} 34:2 34:5 34:13^{2} 34:17^{2} 34:18 34:20 34:21 34:22^{2} 35:3 35:4 35:5^{2} 35:14 35:15^{2} 35:17^{4} 36:2^{2} 36:3^{2} 36:5^{2} 36:18 36:31^{3} 37:14 37:18 37:20^{3} 38:14 38:15^{2} 38:16^{2} 38:19 38:20^{2} 38:25 38:26 39:16 39:17 39:18 40:4^{2} 40:10 40:15^{2}

42:4^{4} 42:10^{4} 42:11 42:12 42:17 42:19 42:21 43:10^{2} 43:12 44:2 44:4^{2} 44:10 44:11 44:12 44:13^{2} 44:26 44:27 44:29 44:30^{2} 45:3^{2} 45:4^{4} 45:5^{2} 46:5 46:8^{2} 46:18 46:25 46:26 46:27 46:28^{5} 48:12 48:30 48:31^{2} 48:32 48:33 48:35 48:38 48:44 48:47 49:2 49:5 49:6 49:8^{2} 49:10^{2} 49:11 49:13 49:14 49:15 49:16 49:19^{2} 49:27 49:32^{2} 49:35 49:36 49:37^{4} 49:38 49:39 50:9 50:18^{2} 50:19 50:20^{2} 50:21 50:24 50:31^{2} 50:32 50:44^{2} 51:1 51:14 51:20^{2} 51:21^{2} 51:22^{3} 51:23^{3} 51:24 51:25^{2} 51:36^{2} 51:39^{2} 51:40 51:44^{2} 51:47 51:52 51:57 51:64

LA

1:11 1:14 1:16 1:18^{2} 1:19 1:20^{2} 1:21 2:13^{4} 2:22 3:1 3:7 3:8 3:14 3:17 3:18 3:21^{2} 3:24 3:54^{2} 3:55 3:57 3:63

EZE

1:1^{2} 1:4 1:15 1:24 1:27^{2} 1:28^{3} 2:1 2:2 2:3 2:4 2:8^{2} 2:9 3:2 3:3^{2} 3:6 3:8 3:9 3:10 3:12 3:13 3:14 3:15^{2} 3:17 3:18^{2} 3:20^{2} 3:22 3:23^{3} 3:26 3:27^{2} 4:5 4:6 4:8 4:13 4:14^{2} 4:15 4:16 5:2 5:5 5:8^{2} 5:9^{3} 5:10^{2} 5:11^{3} 5:12^{2} 5:13^{4} 5:14 5:15^{2} 5:16^{3} 5:17^{3} 6:3^{3} 6:4 6:5^{2} 6:7 6:8 6:9 6:10^{3} 6:12 6:13 6:14^{2} 7:3 7:4^{3} 7:8^{2} 7:9^{3} 7:20 7:21

7:22 7:24^{2} 7:27^{3} 8:1 8:2 8:4 8:5 8:6 8:7 8:8 8:10 8:18^{3} 9:8^{2} 9:10^{2} 9:11 10:1 10:9 10:15 10:20^{2} 10:22 11:1 11:5 11:7 11:8 11:9 11:10^{2} 11:11 11:12 11:13^{2} 11:16^{3} 11:17^{2} 11:19^{3} 11:20 11:21 11:24 11:25 12:6 12:7^{6} 12:11^{2} 12:13^{2} 12:14^{2} 12:16^{2} 12:20 12:23 12:25^{4} 12:28 13:7 13:8 13:9 13:13 13:14^{2} 13:15 13:20^{2} 13:21^{2} 13:22 13:23^{2} 14:3 14:4 14:5 14:7 14:8^{3} 14:9^{2} 14:11 14:13 14:15 14:16 14:17^{2} 14:18 14:19 14:20 14:21 14:22^{2} 14:23^{2} 15:6^{2} 15:7^{3} 15:8 16:3 16:6^{3} 16:7 16:8^{3} 16:9^{3} 16:10^{3} 16:11^{2} 16:12 16:14 16:17 16:19^{2}

16:27 16:37^{2} 16:38^{2} 16:39 16:41 16:42^{2} 16:43 16:48 16:50^{2} 16:53^{2} 16:59 16:60^{2} 16:61 16:62^{2} 16:63 17:16 17:19^{2} 17:20^{2} 17:21 17:22^{2} 17:23 17:24^{2} 18:3 18:23 18:30 18:32 20:3^{2} 20:5^{3} 20:6^{2} 20:7^{2} 20:8^{2} 20:9^{2} 20:10 20:11 20:12^{2} 20:13^{2} 20:14^{2} 20:15^{3} 20:17 20:18 20:19 20:20 20:21^{2} 20:22^{2} 20:23^{2} 20:25 20:26^{3} 20:28^{2} 20:29 20:31^{3} 20:33^{2} 20:34 20:35^{2} 20:36^{2} 20:37^{2} 20:38^{3} 20:40^{2} 20:41^{3} 20:42^{3} 20:44^{2} 20:47 20:48 20:49 21:3 21:4 21:5 21:15 21:17^{3} 21:24 21:27^{2} 21:30^{2} 21:31^{2} 21:32 22:4 22:13 22:14^{2} 22:15 22:16^{2} 22:19 22:20^{2} 22:21 22:22 22:26 22:30^{3} 22:31^{3} 23:9 23:13

23:22^{2} 23:24 23:25 23:27 23:28 23:30 23:31 23:34 23:43 23:46 23:48 23:49 24:8 24:9 24:13^{2} 24:14^{5} 24:16 24:18^{3} 24:20 24:21 24:22 24:24 24:25 24:27 25:4 25:5^{2} 25:7^{5} 25:9 25:11^{2} 25:13^{2} 25:14 25:16^{2} 25:17^{3} 26:2 26:3 26:4 26:5 26:6 26:7 26:13 26:14^{2} 26:19^{2} 26:20^{2} 26:21 27:3 28:2^{2} 28:7 28:9 28:10 28:14 28:16^{2} 28:17^{2} 28:18^{2} 28:22^{4} 28:23^{2} 28:24 28:25^{2} 28:26^{2} 29:3^{2} 29:4^{3} 29:5 29:6 29:8 29:9^{2} 29:10^{2} 29:12^{2} 29:13 29:14 29:15 29:16 29:19 29:20 29:21^{3} 30:8^{2} 30:10 30:12^{3} 30:13^{3} 30:14 30:15^{2} 30:16 30:18 30:19^{2} 30:21 30:22^{2} 30:23 30:24 30:25^{3}

30:26^{2} 31:9 31:11^{2} 31:15^{4} 31:16^{2} 32:3 32:4^{3} 32:5 32:6 32:7^{3} 32:8 32:9^{2} 32:10^{2} 32:12 32:13 32:14 32:15^{3} 32:32 33:2 33:6 33:7 33:8^{2} 33:11^{2} 33:13 33:14 33:20 33:22 33:27^{2} 33:28 33:29^{2} 33:30 34:8 34:10^{3} 34:11^{2} 34:12 34:13 34:14 34:15^{2} 34:16^{3} 34:17 34:20^{2} 34:22^{2} 34:23 34:24^{2} 34:25 34:26^{2} 34:27^{2} 34:29 34:30 34:31 35:3^{3} 35:4^{2} 35:6^{2} 35:7 35:8 35:9^{2} 35:11^{4} 35:12^{2} 35:13 35:14 35:15^{2} 36:5 36:6 36:7 36:9^{2} 36:10 36:11^{3} 36:12 36:15 36:18 36:19^{2} 36:21 36:22 36:23^{3} 36:24 36:25^{2} 36:26^{4} 36:27 36:28^{2} 36:29^{2} 36:30 36:32 36:33^{2} 36:36^{3} 36:37^{2} 36:38

37:3 37:5 37:6^{2} 37:7^{3} 37:8 37:10 37:12 37:13^{2} 37:14^{2} 37:19 37:21 37:22 37:23^{2} 37:25 37:26^{2} 37:27 37:28 38:3 38:4^{2} 38:11^{2} 38:16^{2} 38:17^{2} 38:19 38:21 38:22^{2} 38:23^{3} 39:1 39:2 39:3 39:4 39:5 39:6^{2} 39:7^{3} 39:8 39:11 39:13 39:17 39:19 39:21^{3} 39:22 39:23 39:24 39:25 39:27 39:28^{2} 39:29^{2} 40:4^{2} 41:8 43:3^{5} 43:6 43:7 43:8 43:9 43:27 44:4 44:5 44:12 44:14 44:28^{2} 47:5 47:5 47:7 47:14

DA

1:10 1:12 2:3 2:8 2:9 2:23 2:24 2:25 2:26 2:30 3:14 3:15 3:25 3:29 4:2 4:4 4:5 4:6 4:7 4:8 4:9^{2} 4:10 4:13 4:30 4:34^{3} 4:36 4:37 5:11 5:14 5:16 5:17 6:22 6:26 7:2 7:4 7:6 7:7 7:8 7:9 7:11^{2} 7:13 7:15 7:16 7:19 7:21 7:28 8:2^{5} 8:3 8:4 8:5 8:6 8:7 8:13 8:15^{2} 8:16 8:17^{2} 8:18 8:19 8:27^{3} 9:2 9:3 9:4 9:16 9:20 9:21^{2} 9:22 9:23 10:2^{2} 10:4 10:5 10:7 10:8^{2} 10:9^{3} 10:11^{3} 10:12 10:13 10:14 10:15^{2} 10:16^{2} 10:19 10:20^{3} 10:21 11:1^{2} 11:2 12:5 12:7 12:8^{3}

HO

1:4 1:5 1:6^{2} 1:7 1:9 2:2 2:3 2:4 2:5 2:6 2:7 2:8 2:9 2:10 2:11 2:12^{2} 2:13 2:14 2:15 2:17 2:18^{2} 2:19^{2} 2:20 2:21^{2} 2:23^{3} 3:2 3:3^{2} 4:5 4:6^{2} 4:7 4:9 4:14 5:2 5:3 5:9 5:10 5:11 5:12 5:14^{4} 5:15 6:4^{2} 6:5^{2} 6:6 6:10 6:11 7:1 7:2 7:12^{3} 7:13 7:15 8:4 8:10 8:12 8:14 9:10^{2} 9:12^{2} 9:13 9:15^{3} 9:16 10:10 10:11^{2} 11:1 11:3^{2} 11:4^{3} 11:8^{4} 11:9^{4} 11:11 12:8^{2} 12:9 12:10^{2} 12:11 13:5 13:7^{2} 13:8^{2} 13:10 13:11 13:14^{4} 14:4^{2} 14:5 14:8^{3}

JOE

1:19 2:19 2:20 2:25^{2} 2:27^{2} 2:28 2:29 2:30 3:1 3:2 3:4 3:7 3:8 3:10 3:12 3:17 3:21^{2}

AM

1:3 1:4 1:5 1:6 1:7 1:8^{2} 1:9 1:10 1:11 1:12 1:13 1:14 2:1 2:2 2:3 2:4 2:5 2:6 2:9^{2} 2:10 2:11 2:13 3:1 3:2^{2} 3:14^{2} 3:15 4:6 4:7^{2} 4:9 4:10^{3} 4:11 4:12^{2} 5:1 5:17 5:21^{3} 5:22^{2} 5:23 5:27 6:8^{2} 6:14 7:2^{2} 7:5^{2} 7:8^{3} 7:9 7:14^{3} 7:15 8:2 8:7 8:9^{2} 8:10^{3} 8:11 9:1^{2} 9:2 9:3^{2} 9:4^{2} 9:7 9:8^{2} 9:9^{2} 9:11^{3} 9:14 9:15^{2}

OB

2 4 8

JON

1:9^{2} 1:12 2:2^{2} 2:4^{3} 2:6 2:7 2:9^{3} 3:2 4:2^{4} 4:3 4:9 4:11

MIC

1:6^{3} 1:7 1:8^{3} 1:15 2:3 2:11 2:12^{3} 3:1^{2} 3:8 3:9 4:6^{3} 4:7 4:13^{3} 5:10^{2} 5:11 5:12 5:13 5:14^{2} 5:15 6:3^{2} 6:4^{2} 6:6^{2} 6:7 6:11 6:13 6:14 6:16 7:1 7:7^{2} 7:8^{3} 7:9^{3} 7:15

NA

1:12^{2} 1:13 1:14^{2} 2:13^{3} 3:5^{3} 3:6 3:7

HAB

1:2 1:5 1:6 2:1^{3} 3:2 3:7 3:16^{3} 3:18^{2}

ZEP

1:2 1:3^{3} 1:4^{2} 1:8 1:9 1:10 1:12 1:17 2:5 2:8 2:9 2:15 3:6^{2} 3:7^{2} 3:8^{2} 3:9 3:11 3:12 3:18 3:19^{3} 3:20^{4}

HAG

1:8^{2} 1:9 1:11 1:13 2:4 2:5 2:6 2:7^{2} 2:9 2:15 2:17 2:19 2:21 2:22^{3} 2:23^{2}

ZEC

1:3 1:6 1:8 1:9^{2} 1:14 1:15^{2} 1:16 1:18 1:19 1:21 2:1 2:2 2:5 2:6 2:9 2:10^{2} 2:11 3:4^{2} 3:5 3:7 3:8 3:9^{3} 4:2^{2} 4:4 4:5 4:11 4:12 4:13 5:1 5:2^{2} 5:4 5:6 5:9 5:10 6:1 6:4 7:3^{2} 7:13 7:14 8:2^{2} 8:3 8:7 8:8^{2} 8:10 8:11 8:12 8:13 8:14^{2} 8:15 8:17 8:21 9:6 9:7 9:8^{2} 9:10 9:11 9:12^{2} 9:13 10:3 10:6^{6} 10:8^{2} 10:9 10:10^{2} 10:12 11:5 11:6^{3} 11:7^{5} 11:8 11:9^{2} 11:10^{3} 11:12 11:13^{2} 11:14^{2} 11:16 12:2 12:3 12:4^{2} 12:6 12:9 12:10 13:2^{2} 13:5^{2} 13:6 13:7 13:9^{3} 14:2

MAL

1:2^{2} 1:3 1:4 1:6^{2} 1:9 1:10^{2} 1:13 1:14 2:2^{3} 2:3 2:4 2:5 2:9 3:1 3:5^{2} 3:6^{2} 3:7 3:10 3:11 3:17^{2} 4:3 4:4 4:5 4:6

MT

2:8 2:13 2:15 3:9 3:11^{3} 3:14 3:17 4:9 4:19 5:17^{2} 5:18 5:20 5:22 5:26 5:28 5:32 5:34 5:39 5:44 6:2 6:5 6:16 6:25 6:29 7:23^{2} 7:24 8:3 8:7 8:8 8:9^{2} 8:10^{2} 8:11 8:19 9:13^{2} 9:21^{2} 9:28 10:15 10:16 10:23 10:27 10:32 10:33

10:34^{2} 10:35 10:42 11:9 11:10 11:11 11:16 11:22 11:24 11:25 11:28 11:29 12:6 12:7 12:18^{2} 12:27 12:28 12:31 12:36 12:44^{2} 13:13 13:15 13:17 13:30 13:35^{2} 14:27 15:24 15:32^{2} 16:11 16:13 16:15 16:18^{2} 16:19 16:28 17:5 17:12 17:16 17:17^{2} 17:20 18:3 18:10 18:13 18:18 18:19 18:20 18:21 18:22 18:26 18:29 18:32 18:33 19:9 19:16^{2} 19:20^{2} 19:23 19:24 19:28 20:4 20:13 20:14 20:15^{2} 20:22^{2} 20:23 20:32 21:21 21:24^{3} 21:27^{2} 21:29 21:30 21:31 21:43 22:4 22:32 22:44 23:34 23:36 23:37 23:39 24:2 24:5 24:25 24:34 24:47 25:12^{2} 25:20 25:22 25:23

25:24 25:25 25:26^{2} 25:27 25:35^{3} 25:36^{2} 25:40 25:42^{2} 25:43 25:45 26:13 26:15 26:18 26:21 26:22 26:25 26:29^{3} 26:31 26:32^{2} 26:33 26:34 26:35^{2} 26:36 26:39 26:42 26:48 26:53 26:55 26:61 26:63 26:64 26:70 26:72 26:74 27:4^{2} 27:17 27:19 27:21 27:22 27:24 27:43 27:63 28:5 28:7 28:20^{2}

MK

1:7^{2} 1:8 1:11 1:17 1:24 1:38^{2} 1:41 2:11 2:17 3:28 5:7^{2} 5:23 5:28^{2} 5:41 6:11 6:16 6:22 6:23 6:24 6:25 6:50 8:2 8:3 8:12 8:19 8:24 8:27 8:29 9:1 9:13 9:17 9:18 9:19^{2} 9:24 9:25 9:41 10:15 10:17^{2}

10:20 10:29 10:36 10:38^{2} 10:39^{2} 10:51^{2} 11:23 11:24 11:29^{3} 11:33^{2} 12:15 12:26 12:36 12:43 13:6 13:23 13:30 13:37^{2} 14:9 14:14 14:18 14:19^{2} 14:25^{3} 14:27 14:28^{2} 14:29 14:30 14:31^{2} 14:32 14:36 14:44 14:49 14:58^{2} 14:62 14:68^{2} 14:71 15:9 15:12

LU

1:18^{2} 1:19 1:34 2:10 2:48 2:49 3:8 3:16^{3} 3:22 4:6^{3} 4:24 4:25 4:34 4:43^{2} 5:5 5:8 5:13 5:24 5:32 6:9 6:27 6:46 6:47 7:6 7:7 7:8^{2} 7:9^{2} 7:14 7:26 7:27 7:28 7:31 7:40 7:43 7:44 7:45 7:47 8:28^{2} 8:46 9:9 9:18 9:20 9:27 9:38 9:40 9:41 9:57 9:61 10:3 10:12 10:18 10:19 10:21 10:24 10:25 10:35^{2} 11:6 11:7 11:8 11:9 11:18 11:19 11:20 11:24^{2} 11:49 11:51 12:4 12:5^{2} 12:8 12:17^{2} 12:18^{3} 12:19 12:22 12:37 12:44 12:49^{2} 12:50^{2} 12:51^{2} 12:59 13:3 13:5 13:8 13:18 13:20 13:24 13:25 13:27^{2} 13:32^{3} 13:33 13:34 13:35 14:18^{3} 14:19^{3} 14:20^{2} 14:24 15:6 15:7 15:9^{2} 15:10 15:17 15:18^{2} 15:21 15:29^{3} 15:31 16:2 16:3^{3} 16:4^{2} 16:9 16:24 16:27 16:28 17:4 17:8^{2} 17:9 17:34 18:4 18:5 18:8 18:11^{2} 18:12^{3} 18:14 18:17 18:18 18:21 18:29 18:41^{2} 19:5 19:8^{3} 19:13 19:20 19:21 19:22^{4} 19:23 19:26 19:27 19:40 20:3 20:8^{2} 20:13^{2} 20:43 21:3 21:8 21:15 21:32 22:11 22:15^{2} 22:16^{2} 22:18^{2} 22:29 22:32 22:33 22:34 22:35 22:37 22:53 22:57 22:58 22:60 22:67 22:68 22:70 23:4 23:14 23:15 23:16 23:22^{2} 23:43 23:46 24:39 24:44^{2} 24:49

JOH

1:15 1:20 1:21 1:23 1:26 1:27 1:30 1:31^{2} 1:32 1:33 1:34 1:48 1:50^{2} 1:51 2:4 2:19 3:3 3:5 3:7 3:11 3:12^{2} 3:28^{3} 3:30 4:14^{2} 4:15 4:17^{2} 4:19 4:25 4:26 4:29 4:32 4:35 4:38 4:39 5:7^{2} 5:17 5:19 5:24 5:25 5:30^{4} 5:31 5:32 5:34^{2} 5:36^{2} 5:41 5:42 5:43 5:45 6:20 6:26 6:32 6:35 6:36 6:37 6:38 6:39 6:40 6:41 6:42 6:44 6:47 6:48 6:51^{3} 6:53 6:54 6:56 6:57 6:63 6:65 6:70 7:7 7:8 7:17 7:21 7:23 7:28^{2} 7:29^{2} 7:33^{2} 7:34 7:36 8:11 8:12 8:14^{6} 8:15 8:16^{3} 8:18 8:21^{2} 8:22 8:23^{2} 8:24^{2} 8:25 8:26^{3} 8:28^{3} 8:29 8:34 8:37 8:38^{2} 8:40 8:42^{2} 8:45 8:46 8:49^{2} 8:50 8:51 8:54 8:55^{5} 8:58^{2} 9:4 9:5^{2} 9:7 9:9 9:11^{2} 9:12 9:15 9:25^{4} 9:27 9:36 9:38 9:39 10:1 10:7^{2} 10:9 10:10 10:11 10:14 10:15^{2} 10:16^{2} 10:17^{2} 10:18^{4} 10:25^{2} 10:26 10:27 10:28 10:30 10:32 10:34 10:36^{2} 10:37 10:38^{2} 11:11^{2} 11:15^{2} 11:22 11:24 11:25 11:27 11:40 11:41 11:42^{2} 12:24 12:26 12:27^{2} 12:28 12:32^{2} 12:40 12:46 12:47^{2} 12:48 12:49^{3} 12:50^{3} 13:7 13:8 13:12 13:13 13:14 13:15^{2} 13:16 13:18^{2} 13:19^{2} 13:20^{2} 13:21 13:26 13:33^{4} 13:34^{2} 13:36 13:37 13:38 14:2^{2} 14:3^{3} 14:4 14:5 14:9 14:10^{3} 14:11 14:12^{3} 14:13 14:14 14:16 14:18^{2} 14:19 14:20^{2} 14:21 14:25 14:26 14:27^{3} 14:28^{5} 14:29 14:30 14:31^{2} 15:1 15:3 15:4 15:5^{2} 15:9 15:10 15:11 15:12 15:14 15:15^{4} 15:16 15:17 15:19 15:20 15:22 15:24 15:26 16:1 16:4^{4} 16:5 16:6 16:7^{5} 16:10 16:12 16:15 16:16 16:17 16:19 16:20 16:22 16:23 16:25^{2} 16:26^{2} 16:27 16:28^{2} 16:32 16:33^{2} 17:4^{2} 17:5 17:6 17:8^{2} 17:9^{2} 17:10 17:11^{2} 17:12^{3} 17:13^{2} 17:14^{2} 17:15 17:16 17:18 17:19 17:20 17:21 17:22 17:23 17:24^{2} 17:25 17:26 18:5 18:6 18:8^{2} 18:9 18:11 18:17 18:20^{3} 18:21^{2} 18:23 18:25 18:26 18:35 18:36 18:37^{4} 18:38 18:39^{2} 19:4^{2} 19:6 19:10 19:15 19:21 19:22^{2} 19:28 20:13 20:15 20:17^{2} 20:21 20:25^{2} 21:3 21:16 21:17 21:18 21:22^{2} 21:23^{2} 21:25

AC

1:1 2:17 2:18 2:19 2:25^{2} 2:35 3:6^{3} 3:17 5:38 7:3 7:7 7:32 7:34^{4} 7:43 7:56 8:19 8:23 8:31 8:34 8:37 9:5 9:10 9:13 9:16 10:14 10:20 10:21 10:26 10:28 10:29^{3} 10:30^{2} 10:33 10:34 10:37 11:5^{2} 11:6^{2} 11:7 11:8 11:11 11:15 11:16 11:17^{2} 12:11 13:2 13:22 13:25^{3} 13:33 13:34 13:41 13:46 13:47 15:16^{3} 16:18 16:30 17:3 17:22 17:23^{3} 18:6^{2} 18:10^{2} 18:14 18:15 18:21^{2} 19:15^{2} 19:21^{2} 20:18^{2} 20:20 20:22 20:24^{3} 20:25^{2} 20:26^{2} 20:27 20:29 20:31 20:32 20:33 20:35 21:13 21:37 21:39^{2} 22:1 22:3 22:4 22:5 22:6 22:7 22:8^{2} 22:10^{2} 22:11^{2} 22:13 22:17^{3} 22:19^{2} 22:20 22:21 22:28^{2} 23:1 23:5 23:6^{2} 23:27 23:28^{2} 23:29 23:30 23:35 24:4^{2} 24:10^{2} 24:11 24:14^{2} 24:16 24:17 24:20 24:21^{2} 24:22 24:25^{2} 25:8 25:10^{3} 25:11^{3} 25:15 25:16 25:17 25:18 25:20^{2} 25:21^{2} 25:22 25:25^{2} 25:26^{3} 26:2^{3} 26:3^{2} 26:5 26:6 26:7 26:9^{2} 26:10^{3} 26:11^{2} 26:12 26:13 26:14 26:15^{2} 26:16^{2} 26:17 26:19 26:22 26:25 26:26^{2} 26:27 26:29^{2} 27:10 27:22 27:23^{2} 27:25 27:34 28:17^{2} 28:19^{2} 28:20^{2} 28:27

RO

1:8 1:9^{2} 1:10 1:11^{2} 1:12 1:13^{3} 1:14 1:15 1:16 3:5 3:7 3:26 4:17 6:19 7:1 7:7^{2} 7:9^{2} 7:10 7:14 7:15^{6} 7:16^{3} 7:17 7:18^{2} 7:19^{4} 7:20^{3} 7:21^{2} 7:22 7:23 7:24 7:25^{2} 8:18 8:38 9:1^{2} 9:2 9:3 9:9 9:13^{2} 9:15^{4} 9:17^{2} 9:25 9:33 10:18 10:19^{3} 10:20^{2} 10:21 11:1^{2} 11:3 11:4 11:11 11:13^{3} 11:14 11:19 11:25 11:27 12:1 12:3 12:19 14:11 14:14 15:8 15:9 15:14 15:15 15:16 15:17^{2} 15:18 15:19 15:20^{2} 15:22 15:24^{4} 15:25 15:28^{2} 15:29^{3} 15:30 15:31^{2} 15:32 16:1 16:4 16:17 16:19^{2} 16:22

1 CO

1:4 1:10 1:12^{5} 1:14^{2} 1:15 1:16^{3} 1:19 2:1^{2} 2:2 2:3 3:1 3:2 3:4^{2} 3:6 3:10 4:3^{2} 4:4^{2} 4:6 4:8 4:9 4:14^{2} 4:15 4:16 4:17^{2} 4:18 4:19 4:21 5:3^{2} 5:9 5:11 5:12 6:5 6:12 6:15 7:6 7:7^{2} 7:8^{2} 7:10^{2} 7:12 7:17 7:25^{2} 7:26^{2} 7:28 7:29 7:32 7:35^{2} 7:40^{2} 8:13^{2} 9:1^{3} 9:2^{2} 9:6 9:8 9:15^{2} 9:16^{3} 9:17 9:18^{3} 9:19^{3} 9:20^{3} 9:21 9:22^{4} 9:23^{2} 9:26^{2} 9:27^{3} 10:1 10:15^{2} 10:19 10:20^{2} 10:29 10:30^{3} 10:33 11:1 11:2^{2} 11:3 11:17^{2} 11:18^{2} 11:22^{3} 11:23^{2} 11:34^{2} 12:1 12:3 12:15^{2} 12:16^{2} 12:21^{2} 12:31 13:1^{2} 13:2^{4} 13:3^{2} 13:11^{6} 13:12^{3} 14:5 14:6^{3} 14:11^{2} 14:14 14:15^{4} 14:18^{2} 14:19^{2} 14:21 14:37 15:1^{2} 15:2 15:3^{2} 15:9^{2} 15:10^{4} 15:11 15:31^{3} 15:32 15:34 15:50 15:51 16:1 16:2 16:3^{2} 16:4 16:5^{3} 16:6^{2} 16:7^{2} 16:8 16:10 16:11 16:12 16:15 16:17

2 CO

1:13 1:15 1:17^{4} 1:23^{2} 2:1^{2} 2:2 2:3^{4} 2:4^{2} 2:5 2:8 2:9^{2} 2:10^{4} 2:12 2:13^{3} 4:13^{2} 5:8 5:11 6:2^{2} 6:13 6:16^{2} 6:17 7:3^{2} 7:4^{2} 7:7 7:8^{4} 7:9 7:12^{2} 7:14^{3} 7:16^{2} 8:3 8:8 8:10 8:13 8:22 9:2^{2} 9:3^{2} 9:5 9:6 10:1 10:2^{4} 10:8^{2} 10:9^{2} 11:2^{3} 11:3 11:5^{2} 11:6 11:7^{2} 11:8 11:9^{4} 11:11 11:12^{3} 11:16^{2} 11:17^{2} 11:18 11:21^{3} 11:22^{3} 11:23^{2} 11:24 11:25^{4} 11:29^{2} 11:30^{2} 11:31 11:33 12:1 12:2^{3} 12:3^{2} 12:5^{2} 12:6^{4} 12:7^{2} 12:8 12:9 12:10^{3} 12:11^{4} 12:13 12:14^{3} 12:15^{3} 12:16^{2} 12:17^{2} 12:18^{2} 12:20^{5} 12:21^{2} 13:1 13:2^{5} 13:6 13:7 13:10^{2}

GA

1:6 1:9 1:10^{4} 1:11 1:12^{2} 1:13 1:16^{2} 1:17^{2} 1:18 1:19 1:20^{2} 1:21 2:1 2:2^{3} 2:10 2:11 2:14^{2} 2:18^{3} 2:19^{2} 2:20^{5} 2:21 3:2 3:15 3:17 4:1 4:11 4:12^{3} 4:13 4:15 4:16^{2} 4:18 4:19 4:20^{2} 5:2 5:3 5:13 5:11^{3} 5:12 5:16 5:21^{2} 6:11 6:14^{2} 6:17

EPH

1:15^{2} 3:1 3:3 3:7 3:8 3:13 3:14 4:1 4:17 5:32 6:19 6:20^{3} 6:21 6:22

PHP

1:3 1:7 1:8 1:9 1:12 1:17 1:18 1:19 1:20 1:21 1:22^{2} 1:23 1:25^{2} 1:27^{2} 2:16^{2} 2:17^{2} 2:19^{3} 2:20 2:23^{2} 2:24^{2} 2:25 2:27 2:28^{2} 3:4^{2} 3:7 3:8^{3} 3:10 3:11 3:12^{4} 3:13^{2} 3:14 3:18 4:2 4:3 4:4 4:10 4:11^{3} 4:12^{3} 4:13 4:15 4:17^{2} 4:18^{2}

COL

1:2 1:20 1:23 1:25 1:29 2:1^{2} 2:4 2:5^{2} 4:3 4:4^{2} 4:8 4:13

1 TH

2:18 3:5^{2} 4:9 4:13 5:1 5:23 5:27

2 TH

2:5^{2} 3:17

1 TI

1:3^{2} 1:12 1:13 1:15 1:16 1:18 1:20 2:1 2:7^{2} 2:8 2:12 3:14 3:15 4:13 5:14 5:21 6:13

2 TI

1:3 1:4 1:5 1:11 1:12^{5} 2:7 2:9 2:10 3:11 4:1 4:6 4:7^{3} 4:12 4:13 4:16 4:17 4:20

TIT

1:5^{2} 3:8 3:12^{2}

PHM

4 8 9 10^{2} 12 13 14 19^{3} 21^{2} 22^{2}

HEB

1:5^{2} 1:13 2:12^{2} 2:13^{2} 3:10 3:11 4:3 5:5, 6:14^{2} 7:9 8:8 8:9^{3} 8:10^{3} 8:12^{2} 10:7^{2} 10:9 10:16^{3} 10:17 10:30 11:32 12:21 12:26 13:5 13:6 13:19^{2} 13:22^{2} 13:23

JAS

1:13 2:18^{2}

1 PE

1:16 2:6 2:11 5:1 5:12^{2}

2 PE

1:12 1:13^{2} 1:14 1:15 1:17 3:1^{2}

1 JO

2:1 2:4 2:7 2:8 2:12 2:13^{3} 2:14^{2} 2:21 2:26 4:20 5:13 5:16

2 JO

1^{2} 4^{2} 5^{2} 12^{2}

3 JO

1 2 3 4 9 10^{2} 13^{2} 14^{2}

JUDE

3 5

RE

1:8 1:9 1:10 1:11 1:12^{2} 1:17^{3} 1:18^{2} 2:2 2:4 2:5 2:6 2:7 2:9^{2} 2:10 2:13 2:14 2:15 2:16 2:17 2:19 2:20 2:21 2:22 2:23^{3} 2:24^{2}1 2:25 2:26 2:27 2:28 3:1 3:2 3:3^{2} 3:5^{2} 3:8^{2} 3:9^{3} 3:10 3:11 3:12^{3} 3:15^{2} 3:16 3:17 3:18 3:19^{2} 3:20^{2} 3:21^{2} 4:1^{3} 4:2 4:4 5:1 5:2 5:4 5:6 5:11^{2} 5:13 6:1^{2} 6:2 6:3 6:5^{2} 6:6 6:7 6:8 6:9 6:12 7:1 7:2 7:4 7:9 7:14 8:2 8:13 9:1 9:13 9:16 9:17 10:1 10:4^{2} 10:5 10:8 10:9 10:10^{2} 11:3 12:10 13:1 13:2 13:3 13:11 14:1 14:2^{2} 14:6 14:13 14:14 15:1 15:2 15:5 16:1 16:5 16:7 16:13 16:15 17:1 17:3 17:6^{3} 17:7 18:1 18:4 18:7 19:1 19:6 19:10^{2} 19:11 19:17 19:19 20:1 20:4 20:11 20:12 21:1 21:2 21:3 21:5 21:6^{2} 21:7 21:9 21:22 22:7 22:8^{3} 22:9 22:12 22:13 22:16^{2} 22:18 22:20

IN

1722

GE

1:1 1:6 1:11 1:12 1:14 1:15 1:17 1:20 1:22^{2} 1:26 1:27^{2} 1:29 2:3 2:4 2:5 2:8 2:9 2:17 3:3 3:5 3:8 3:10 3:16 3:19 4:3 4:8 4:12 4:14 4:16 4:20 4:21 5:1 5:2 5:3 6:4^{2} 6:5 6:8 6:9 6:14 6:16^{2} 6:17 7:1 7:7 7:9 7:11 7:12 7:15 7:16^{2} 7:22^{2} 7:23 8:1 8:4 8:5 8:9 8:11 8:13 8:14 8:17 8:21 9:6 9:7 9:13 9:14 9:16 9:27 10:5^{2} 10:8 10:10 10:20 10:25 10:32 11:2 11:28 11:31 11:32 12:3 12:5 12:6 12:10^{2} 13:2 13:7 13:12 13:17 13:18 14:1 14:3 14:4 14:5^{3}

14:6 14:7 14:8 14:12 14:13 14:14 15:1 15:3 15:6 15:10 15:13 15:15 15:16 15:18 16:2 16:3^{2} 16:4 16:5 16:6 16:7 16:12 17:7 17:9 17:12 17:13^{2} 17:17 17:21 17:23^{2} 17:24 17:25 17:26 17:27 18:1^{2} 18:3 18:9 18:10 18:11 18:18 18:26 19:1 19:2^{2} 19:3 19:5 19:8 19:12^{2} 19:14^{2} 19:15 19:17 19:19 19:27 19:29 19:30^{2} 19:31 19:33 19:34 20:1 20:3 20:5 20:6^{2} 20:8^{2} 20:11 21:2 21:7 21:11 21:12^{3} 21:14^{2} 21:15 21:18 21:20 21:21 21:22 21:33 21:34 22:3 22:6 22:9 22:13^{2} 22:14 22:17 22:18 23:2 23:6 23:9 23:10^{2} 23:11 23:13 23:16
23:17 23:18^{2} 23:19^{2} 24:1^{2} 24:10 24:23 24:25 24:27 24:31 24:37 24:45 24:48 24:54 24:62 24:63 24:65 25:8 25:9 25:18 25:23 25:24 25:27 26:1 26:2 26:3 26:4 26:6 26:12 26:15 26:17 26:18 26:19 26:22 26:29 26:31^{2} 27:15 27:30 27:41 27:45 28:11 28:14 28:15 28:16 28:18 28:20 28:21 29:2 29:3 29:21 29:23^{2} 29:25 29:26 29:30 30:2 30:3 30:4 30:14^{2} 30:16^{2} 30:27 30:33 30:35 30:37^{2} 30:38 30:40 30:41 30:42 31:10 31:11 31:14 31:18^{2} 31:20 31:23 31:24 31:25^{2} 31:28 31:29 31:34 31:40 31:41 31:54 31:55 32:5 32:21 32:32 33:8 33:10 33:15
33:18 34:5 34:7^{2} 34:11 34:15 34:19 34:21 34:28^{2} 34:29 34:30 35:3^{2} 35:4^{2} 35:6 35:13 35:14 35:17 35:18 35:19 35:22 35:26 36:5 36:6 36:8 36:9 36:16 36:17 36:21 36:24 36:30 36:31 36:32 36:33 36:34 36:35^{2} 36:36 36:37 36:38 36:39 36:43 37:1^{2} 37:7 37:12 37:13 37:15 37:17 37:22 37:24 37:29 37:31 37:33 38:1 38:2 38:7 38:8 38:9 38:11^{2} 38:12 38:13 38:14 38:16^{3} 38:18^{2} 38:21 38:22 38:24 38:25 38:27^{2} 39:2 39:3 39:4 39:5^{3} 39:6 39:8 39:9 39:12 39:13 39:14^{2} 39:17 39:20 39:21 39:22 40:3^{2} 40:4 40:5^{2} 40:6^{2} 40:7 40:9 40:10
40:11 40:16 40:17 41:2 41:8 41:10^{2} 41:11 41:14 41:16 41:17 41:18 41:19 41:22^{2} 41:30 41:31 41:34 41:35 41:36 41:37^{2} 41:38 41:40 41:42 41:43 41:44 41:47 41:48^{3} 41:52 41:53 41:54^{2} 41:56 41:57 42:1 42:2 42:3 42:5 42:13 42:16^{2} 42:19 42:21 42:27^{2} 42:28 42:32 42:34 42:35 42:38 43:1 43:11^{2} 43:12^{3} 43:15 43:18^{2} 43:21^{3} 43:22^{2} 43:23 43:26 43:28 44:1 44:2 44:5^{2} 44:8 44:12 44:17^{2} 44:18 44:28 44:30 45:6^{2} 45:7 45:10 45:13 45:16 46:2 46:5 46:6 46:12 46:15 46:20 46:27 46:31 46:34 47:1 47:4^{3} 47:6^{2} 47:7 47:9 47:11^{3} 47:13 47:14^{2} 47:15^{3}
47:17 47:18 47:24 47:25 47:27^{2} 47:28 47:29^{2} 47:30 48:3 48:5 48:6 48:7^{3} 48:9 48:13^{2} 48:16 48:20 49:1 49:5 49:6^{2} 49:7^{2} 49:8 49:11^{2} 49:17 49:24 49:27 49:29^{2} 49:30^{3} 50:4^{2} 50:5^{2} 50:8 50:11 50:13 50:19 50:22 50:26^{2}

EX

1:5 1:14^{4} 1:19 2:3 2:11 2:12 2:15 2:22 2:23 3:1 3:2 3:7 3:16 3:20 3:21 3:22 4:2 4:4 4:14 4:15 4:17 4:18^{3} 4:19 4:20 4:21 4:24 4:27 4:30 5:1^{2} 5:14 5:16 5:19 5:20 5:21^{3} 5:23 6:5 6:8 6:11 6:28 7:3 7:10 7:11 7:15^{2} 7:16 7:17^{3} 7:18 7:19^{2} 7:20^{4}
7:21 8:9 8:11 8:17^{2} 8:20 8:22^{3} 8:25 8:28 8:29 9:1 9:3 9:5 9:8 9:9 9:13 9:14 9:16^{2} 9:18 9:19^{2} 9:21 9:22 9:24 9:25 9:26 9:31 10:1 10:2^{2} 10:3 10:14 10:15 10:16 10:19 10:22 10:23 10:28 11:2 11:3^{4} 11:5 11:8 11:9 12:1 12:3 12:6 12:8 12:11^{2} 12:12 12:16^{3} 12:17^{2} 12:18 12:19^{2} 12:20 12:22^{3} 12:23 12:27 12:29^{2} 12:30^{2} 12:33 12:34 12:36 12:40 12:42 12:46 12:48 13:3 13:4 13:5 13:6 13:7 13:8 13:9 13:10 13:14 13:15 13:20^{2} 13:21^{2} 14:3^{2} 14:11^{2} 14:12^{2} 14:23 14:24 14:27 14:29 15:4 15:6^{2} 15:7 15:8 15:10
15:11^{2} 15:13^{2} 15:17^{5} 15:19^{2} 15:20 15:22 15:26 16:2 16:3 16:4 16:5 16:7 16:8^{2} 16:10 16:12 16:13 16:16 16:25 16:26 16:29 16:32 17:1 17:5 17:6^{2} 17:8 17:9 17:14^{2} 18:1 18:2 18:3 18:5 18:6 18:7 18:8 18:11 18:12^{2} 18:14 18:15 18:17 18:23 18:24 18:27 19:1 19:2 19:9 19:11 19:16^{2} 19:18 20:4^{2} 20:7^{2} 20:10 20:11 20:24 21:2 21:3 21:13 21:16 21:29^{2} 21:36^{2} 22:4 22:5^{2} 22:6 22:13 22:21 22:23 22:31 23:2 23:3 23:6 23:9 23:10 23:11 23:13 23:14 23:15^{2} 23:16^{3} 23:17 23:19 23:20 23:21 23:23 23:26 23:29 23:33 24:4 24:6 24:7
24:10 24:17 24:18 25:7^{2} 25:12^{3} 25:15 25:18 25:21 25:22 25:26 25:33^{3} 25:34 25:40 26:4^{3} 26:5^{3} 26:10^{2} 26:13 26:17^{2} 26:23 26:28 26:30 26:33 26:34 27:4 27:8 27:11 27:19 27:21 28:1 28:3 28:4 28:11^{2} 28:17 28:20^{2} 28:24 28:25 28:26^{2} 28:29^{2} 28:30^{2} 28:32^{2} 28:35 28:38 28:41 28:43^{2} 29:1 29:3 29:17 29:24^{2} 29:29 29:30^{2} 29:31 29:32 29:39 29:44 30:10^{2} 30:30 30:36 31:3^{4} 31:4^{3} 31:5^{3} 31:6 31:10 31:15^{2} 31:17 32:2 32:3 32:12 32:15 32:17 32:20 32:26 32:27 32:34 33:3^{2} 33:5 33:10 33:12 33:13^{2} 33:16 33:17 33:22 34:1 34:2^{3} 34:4^{2} 34:5 34:6 34:9
34:10^{2} 34:12 34:18^{2} 34:21^{2} 34:23 34:24 34:26 34:29 34:32^{2} 34:34 34:35 35:15 35:19^{5} 35:26 35:31^{4} 35:32^{3} 35:34 35:35^{4} 36:1 36:2 36:11^{3} 36:12^{3} 36:17 36:28 36:29 37:13 37:19^{2} 37:20 38:18 38:23^{3} 38:24 39:1 39:3^{4} 39:6 39:10 39:13^{2} 39:16 39:17 39:18 39:23 39:26 39:37 39:41^{2} 40:4^{4} 40:13 40:15 40:17^{2} 40:18 40:22 40:23 40:24 40:26 40:36 40:38

LE

1:7 1:8 1:9 1:12 2:4 2:5 2:6 2:7 2:11 4:6 4:7 4:17 4:18 4:29 4:33 5:4 5:5^{2} 5:13 5:15 5:16 5:24 6:2^{3} 6:3 6:5^{2} 6:7 6:9 6:12^{2} 6:16^{2} 6:18
6:20^{2} 6:21^{2} 6:22 6:25 6:26^{2} 6:27 6:28^{2} 6:30^{2} 7:2 7:6 7:9^{3} 7:24^{2} 7:26 7:35^{2} 7:36 7:38^{3} 8:8 8:21 8:31 8:33 9:9 10:3 10:5 10:13 10:14 10:17 10:18^{2} 10:19 11:9^{4} 11:10^{4} 11:11 11:12 11:13 11:33 11:34 11:46 12:3 12:4 12:5^{2} 13:2^{2} 13:3^{3} 13:4^{2} 13:5^{2} 13:6 13:7 13:8 13:9 13:10^{2} 13:11 13:12 13:14 13:18^{2} 13:19 13:20 13:22 13:23 13:24 13:25^{2} 13:26 13:27 13:28^{2} 13:30^{2} 13:31^{2} 13:32^{3} 13:34^{3} 13:35 13:36 13:37 13:38 13:39^{2} 13:42^{2} 13:43^{3} 13:44 13:45 13:46 13:47 13:48^{3} 13:49^{5} 13:51^{5} 13:52^{3} 13:53^{4} 13:55 13:57^{4} 13:59^{2} 14:2 14:3 14:5
14:6 14:8 14:9 14:13^{2} 14:16^{2} 14:17 14:18 14:27 14:28 14:29 14:32 14:34 14:35 14:36^{2} 14:37^{2} 14:39 14:40 14:42 14:43 14:44^{2} 14:47^{2} 14:48^{2} 14:50 14:51^{2} 15:3 15:5 15:6 15:7 15:8 15:10 15:11^{2} 15:12 15:13 15:16 15:18 15:19 15:20 15:21 15:22 15:27 15:31 16:2 16:4 16:16^{2} 16:17^{3} 16:21 16:22 16:24 16:26 16:27^{3} 16:28 16:29 16:32 17:3 17:5 17:11 17:15 18:3 18:5 18:15 18:18 18:24^{2} 19:6 19:15^{2} 19:17^{2} 19:24 19:25 19:28 19:33 19:34 19:35^{4} 20:2 20:12 20:17 20:23 21:5 21:11 21:13 21:17 21:20 21:23 22:2 22:11 22:13 22:18 22:21 22:23
22:24 22:25^{2} 22:28 23:3 23:4 23:5 23:7 23:8 23:14 23:21 23:24^{2} 23:28 23:29 23:30 23:31 23:32 23:39^{2} 23:41^{3} 23:42^{2} 23:43 24:3^{2} 24:5 24:6 24:8 24:9 24:10 24:12 24:16 24:19 24:20 25:1 25:3 25:4 25:7 25:9 25:11^{2} 25:13 25:18^{2} 25:19 25:20 25:21 25:22 25:24 25:28^{2} 25:29 25:30^{2} 25:31 25:33 25:35 25:45 25:53 25:54^{2} 26:1 26:3 26:4 26:5 26:6 26:16 26:20 26:22 26:26 26:28 26:34 26:35 26:36 26:39^{3} 26:44 26:45 26:46 27:21 27:23 27:24 27:34

NU

1:1^{3} 1:3 1:16 1:19 1:45 2:9 2:16^{2} 2:17^{2} 2:24 2:31
3:1^{2} 3:3 3:4^{3} 3:13^{2} 3:14 3:25 3:28 4:3 4:4 4:6 4:8 4:12^{2} 4:15 4:16^{2} 4:19 4:20 4:23^{2} 4:27^{3} 4:28 4:31 4:33 4:35 4:37 4:39 4:41 4:43 4:47 5:3 5:17^{2} 5:18^{2} 5:23 6:5 6:9 6:18 7:10 7:84 8:15 8:17 8:19 8:22^{2} 8:24 8:26 9:1^{2} 9:3^{2} 9:5 9:7 9:10 9:13^{2} 9:14 9:17 9:18 9:20 9:21 9:22 9:23 10:9 10:10^{3} 10:11 10:12 10:14 10:29 10:33 11:1 11:5 11:8^{3} 11:9 11:10 11:11 11:12 11:15 11:18^{2} 11:25 11:26^{2} 11:27 11:31 12:5^{2} 12:6^{2} 12:7 12:8 12:14^{2} 12:15 12:16 12:19^{4} 12:22 12:28 12:29^{2} 12:32
12:33^{2} 14:2^{2} 14:8 14:10 14:13 14:14^{2} 14:16 14:22^{2} 14:25 14:28 14:29 14:31 14:32 14:33^{2} 14:34 14:35 14:40 14:45 15:3^{3} 15:8 15:13 15:14 15:15 15:21 15:26 15:30 15:32 15:34 15:38 16:2 16:7 16:13 16:17 16:18^{2} 16:21 16:26 16:27 16:45 16:49 17:4 17:7 18:10 18:11 18:13^{2} 18:14 18:15 18:20 18:21 18:31^{2} 19:5 19:7 19:8^{2} 19:9 19:14^{2} 19:16^{2} 19:17 19:18 19:19 20:1^{2} 20:5 20:12 20:13 20:15 20:16^{2} 20:23 20:27 20:28 21:1 21:5 21:10 21:11 21:12 21:13 21:14^{2} 21:20^{2} 21:25^{3} 21:27 21:31 22:1 22:7 22:13 22:21 22:22 22:23^{2} 22:24 22:26 22:29
22:31^{2} 22:34 22:36^{2} 22:38 23:5 23:12 23:16 23:21^{2} 24:2 24:7 24:14 24:21 25:1 25:6^{2} 25:7 25:9 25:11 25:15 25:18^{3} 26:2 26:3 26:9 26:19 26:59 26:63 26:64 26:65 27:3^{4} 27:14^{4} 27:17^{2} 27:18 27:19 27:21 28:2 28:4 28:6 28:7 28:11 28:16 28:17 28:18 28:23 28:26 29:1 29:39 30:3^{2} 30:5 30:7 30:10 30:14 30:16^{2} 31:6 31:10 31:16 31:35 31:36 32:5 32:13^{2} 32:14 32:15 32:17 32:26 32:30 32:33 32:39 33:3^{2} 33:5 33:6^{2} 33:8^{2} 33:9 33:11 33:12 33:13 33:15 33:18 33:20 33:22 33:23 33:24 33:25 33:28 33:29 33:31 33:33 33:36 33:37 33:38^{2}
33:39 33:40^{2} 33:41 33:42 33:43 33:44^{2} 33:45 33:46 33:47 33:48 33:49 33:50 33:54 33:55^{3} 34:29 35:1 35:2 35:3 35:5 35:12 35:14 35:21 35:25 35:28 35:29 35:32 36:8 36:12 36:13

DE

1:1^{2} 1:3^{3} 1:4^{2} 1:5 1:6^{2} 1:7^{4} 1:8 1:17 1:25 1:27 1:30 1:31^{2} 1:32 1:33^{4} 1:37 1:38 1:39^{2} 1:44^{2} 1:46 2:4 2:7 2:8 2:9 2:10 2:12^{2} 2:14 2:20 2:21 2:22^{2} 2:23^{2} 2:24 2:25 2:29^{2} 2:37 3:4 3:10 3:11 3:19 3:24^{2} 3:29 4:1 4:5 4:6 4:7 4:10 4:14 4:15 4:17 4:18 4:19 4:21 4:22 4:25^{2} 4:27
4:30^{2} 4:34 4:37 4:38 4:39^{2} 4:42 4:43^{4} 4:46^{2} 5:1 5:2 5:4 5:8^{3} 5:11^{2} 5:14 5:15 5:16 5:22^{2} 5:29 5:31 5:33^{2} 6:1 6:3 6:6 6:7 6:16 6:18^{2} 6:20 6:21 6:23 7:7 7:13 7:17 8:1 8:2^{2} 8:5 8:6 8:9 8:11 8:16 8:17 9:1 9:4^{2} 9:7 9:8 9:9 9:10^{2} 9:15 9:18^{2} 9:28 10:2^{2} 10:3 10:4^{2} 10:5 10:6^{2} 10:8 10:10 10:11 10:12 10:15 10:18 10:19 11:3 11:5 11:6^{2} 11:8 11:9 11:10 11:14^{2} 11:15 11:18^{2} 11:19 11:21 11:22 11:29 11:30^{2} 11:31 12:1 12:7 12:8 12:10^{2} 12:13 12:14^{2} 12:15 12:18^{2} 12:21 12:25 12:28
12:29 12:31 13:5 13:12 13:18 14:9 14:21^{2} 14:23 14:25 14:29 15:4 15:7 15:8 15:9 15:10^{2} 15:11 15:12 15:15 15:18^{2} 15:20 16:1 16:2 16:3 16:4 16:6 16:7^{2} 16:11 16:12 16:13 16:14 16:15^{3} 16:16^{5} 16:18 17:2 17:4 17:8 17:9 17:15 17:18 17:20^{2} 18:5 18:7 18:16^{2} 18:18 18:19 18:20^{2} 18:21 18:22 19:1^{2} 19:2 19:4 19:6 19:9 19:10 19:11 19:14^{2} 19:15 19:17 20:5 20:6 20:7 20:14 20:19^{2} 21:1^{2} 21:3 21:4 21:5 21:6 21:9 21:13^{2} 21:14 21:23 22:1 22:3 22:6^{2} 22:7 22:13 22:15 22:19 22:21^{2} 22:23 22:24 22:25 22:26 22:27 23:1 23:4

16:3
16:4
16:8[2]
16:18
16:19
16:20[2]
17:1[2]
17:2
17:4[2]
17:6[4]
17:8
17:9
17:10
17:11
17:14
17:17
17:19
17:22
17:24[2]
17:26
17:28
17:29[2]
17:31
17:32
18:1
18:2
18:3
18:4
18:5
18:9
18:10
18:11[3]
18:13
18:15
18:17
18:22[2]
18:26[3]
18:28
18:30
19:7
19:10
19:12
19:27
19:28[2]
19:29[2]
19:35[2]
19:37[2]
20:1[2]
20:3[2]
20:11
20:13[3]
20:15[2]
20:17[2]
20:18
20:19
20:20
20:21
21:1
21:2
21:4[2]
21:5
21:6
21:7[3]
21:12
21:15
21:16[2]
21:17
21:18[3]
21:19
21:20
21:21[2]
21:22
21:23
21:24
21:25
21:26[3]
22:1
22:2[2]
22:3
22:5
22:8
22:9
22:14[2]
22:20
23:2[2]
23:3
23:4
23:5[3]
23:8[2]
23:9
23:10
23:11[2]
23:12
23:14
23:16
23:19[2]
23:21
23:22
23:23[2]
23:24[4]
23:28
23:29
23:30[3]
23:31
23:32
23:33[3]
23:34
23:36
23:37
24:1
24:5
24:6
24:8
24:9
24:12
24:13[2]
24:17
24:18
24:19
24:20
25:1[3]
25:3
25:5
25:8
25:11
25:13[3]
25:15[2]
25:19[3]
25:21
25:22
25:24
25:27[3]
25:28

1 CH

1:19
1:43
1:44
1:45
1:46[2]
1:47
1:48
1:49
1:50
2:3
2:4
2:6
2:7
2:21
2:22
2:24
3:1
3:4[2]
3:5
4:22
4:38
4:41[2]
5:8
5:9[2]
5:10[2]
5:11
5:12
5:16[4]
5:17[2]
5:18
5:20[2]
5:22
5:23
6:10[2]
6:31
6:32
6:54
6:55
6:62
6:67
6:71
6:76
6:78
6:80
7:2[2]
7:5
7:21
7:23
7:29
8:8
8:28
8:32
9:1
9:2[2]
9:3
9:9
9:16
9:18[2]
9:20
9:22[3]
9:24
9:25
9:26
9:28
9:31
9:33[2]
9:35
10:1
10:7[2]
10:8
10:10[2]
10:12
11:2[2]
11:3
11:7
11:10
11:14
11:15
11:16
11:19
11:22[2]
11:23
12:2
12:15
12:17
12:21
12:33
12:35
12:36
12:40
13:2[2]
13:3
13:4
13:7
13:14
14:4
14:9
14:11
14:13
14:15
15:1
15:29
16:1
16:2
16:10
16:14
16:19
16:27[2]
16:29
16:35
16:39
16:40
17:1[2]
17:2
17:4
17:5
17:8
17:9
17:14[2]
17:17
17:19
17:21
17:25
18:6
18:12
18:13
19:1
19:4
19:9[2]
19:10
19:11
19:13
19:17[2]
19:18
20:2
20:3
21:12
21:13
21:16[2]
21:18
21:19
21:23
21:28
21:29[2]
22:2
22:3[2]
22:4
22:7
22:8
22:9
22:14[2]
22:15
23:11
23:13
23:25
23:28[3]
23:29
23:31[2]
23:32
24:3
24:19
24:31
25:5
25:6
25:7
26:12
26:27
26:30[2]
26:31
27:1[2]
27:2
27:4
27:5
27:6
27:7
27:8
27:9
27:10
27:11
27:12
27:13
27:14
27:15
27:21
27:24
27:25[4]
27:28
27:29[2]
28:2
28:8[2]
28:13
28:19
29:2
29:11[2]
29:12[2]
29:17[2]
29:18
29:21
29:25[2]
29:27[2]
29:28[2]
29:29[3]

2 CH

1:1
1:2
1:3
1:7
1:8
1:9
1:10
1:11
1:14
1:15
2:2
2:7[7]
2:8
2:9
2:11
2:14[10]
2:16
2:17
2:18
3:1[3]
3:2[2]
3:4
3:10
3:16
4:2
4:3
4:6[3]
4:7
4:8
4:17[2]
4:18
5:1
5:3[2]
5:5
5:7
5:10
5:12
5:13
6:1
6:5
6:7
6:8[3]
6:10
6:11
6:12
6:13
6:14[2]
6:16[2]
6:18
6:22
6:24
6:28[2]
6:29
6:31[2]
6:32
6:37[2]
6:38
6:40
6:41
7:8
7:9
7:10
7:11[2]
7:15
7:18
8:4[2]
8:6[2]
8:8
8:11
8:13[4]
8:17
9:1[2]
9:4
9:5
9:8
9:11
9:13
9:16
9:19
9:20
9:22
9:23
9:25
9:27[3]
9:29[3]
9:30
9:31[2]
10:2
10:16[2]
10:17
11:3
11:5[2]
11:10[2]
11:11
11:12
11:13
11:17
11:23
12:2
12:5
12:12
12:13[2]
12:15
12:16[2]
13:1
13:2
13:3[2]
13:4
13:8
13:11
13:20
13:22
14:1[3]
14:2
14:6[2]
14:10[2]
14:11
14:14
14:15
15:3
15:5[2]
15:9
15:10[2]
15:16
16:1[2]
16:9
16:10[2]
16:11
16:12[3]
16:13
16:14[3]
17:1
17:2[3]
17:3
17:4
17:5[2]
17:6
17:7[2]
17:9
17:12
17:13[3]
17:19
18:1
18:2
18:3
18:9[3]
18:15
18:16
18:21
18:22
18:26[2]
18:27
18:34
19:1
19:3[2]
19:5
19:6
19:8
19:9
19:10
19:11
20:2
20:5[2]
20:6[2]
20:9[3]
20:14
20:17
20:20[2]
20:24
20:25[2]
20:26
20:27
20:31
20:32[2]
20:34[2]
20:36
21:1[2]
21:3
21:5
21:6[2]
21:8
21:9
21:11
21:12[2]
21:13
21:17
21:18
21:19
21:20[3]
22:1
22:2
22:3
22:4
22:6
22:9
22:11
22:12
23:1
23:2
23:3
23:5
23:6
23:7[2]
23:8
23:9
23:10
23:13
23:14
23:17
23:18[2]
23:19[2]
24:1
24:2
24:6
24:9[2]
24:10
24:11
24:13
24:14
24:16[2]
24:21
24:25[3]
24:27[2]
25:1
25:2
25:4[2]
25:10
25:12
25:17
25:18[3]
25:21
25:24
25:26
25:27
25:28
26:1
26:3
26:4
26:5[2]
26:7
26:8
26:9
26:10[5]
26:15
26:17
26:19[3]
26:20
26:21
26:23[2]
27:1
27:2
27:4[2]
27:7
27:8
27:9[2]
28:1[2]
28:2
28:3[2]
28:4
28:6[2]
28:9
28:13
28:22
28:24[2]
28:25
28:26
28:27[3]
29:1
29:2
29:3[2]
29:4
29:6
29:7
29:9
29:10
29:17[2]
29:18
29:19[2]
29:25
29:31
29:34
29:35[2]
30:2[2]
30:5
30:12
30:13
30:14
30:15
30:16
30:17
30:25
30:26[2]
31:1[2]
31:2
31:3
31:4[2]
31:5[2]
31:6[2]
31:7[2]
31:11
31:12
31:15[2]
31:16
31:17
31:18[2]
31:19[2]
31:21[4]
32:5[2]
32:6
32:10[2]
32:18
32:21
32:23
32:24
32:26
32:29
32:30
32:31[3]
32:32[2]
32:33[2]
33:1
33:2
33:4[2]
33:5
33:6[2]
33:7[3]
33:12
33:14[3]
33:15
33:17
33:18[2]
33:20[2]
33:21
33:22
33:24
33:25
34:1
34:2[2]
34:3[2]
34:4[2]
34:6
34:8
34:10[2]
34:13
34:15
34:17
34:21[3]
34:22[2]
34:24
34:28
34:30[2]
34:31[2]
34:32
34:33
35:1
35:2
35:3
35:5
35:10[2]
35:12
35:13[3]
35:14
35:15
35:18
35:19
35:22
35:24[2]
35:25[3]
35:26
35:27
36:1[2]
36:2
36:3
36:5[2]
36:6
36:7
36:8[3]
36:9[2]
36:11
36:12
36:14
36:17
36:22[2]
36:23[2]

EZR

1:1[2]
1:2
1:3[2]
1:4[2]
1:5
1:7
2:42
2:68
2:70[2]
3:1
3:2
3:8[2]
3:6
3:10
3:11
4:4
4:6[2]
4:7[3]
4:8
4:10
4:15[2]
4:17
4:23
5:1[2]
5:8[2]
5:13
5:14
5:15[2]
5:16[2]
5:17
6:1[2]
6:2[2]
6:3
6:5
6:7
6:15
6:18[3]
6:22
7:1
7:6
7:7
7:8[2]
7:10
7:13
7:14
7:15
7:16[2]
7:17
7:25
7:27[2]
8:1
8:15
8:22
8:29
8:31
8:33
9:2
9:7
9:8[2]
9:9[4]
9:14
9:15
10:2
10:9
10:13
10:14
10:16

NE

1:1[3]
1:3[2]
1:11
2:1[3]
2:5
2:12[2]
2:15
2:17
2:20
3:17
3:26
4:2
4:4
4:11
4:13
4:16
4:17
4:20
4:21
4:22
5:5
5:9
5:14
5:16
5:18
6:2[2]
6:5[2]
6:7
6:10[2]
6:11
6:14
6:15[2]
6:16
6:17
6:18[2]
6:19
7:3
7:73[2]
8:5
8:7
8:8[2]
8:14[3]
8:15[2]
8:16[4]
8:18
9:1
9:3[2]
9:9
9:12[3]
9:15
9:17
9:19[3]
9:21
9:23
9:24
9:25[2]
9:27
9:28
9:29
9:30
9:33
9:35[3]
9:36
9:37
10:29
10:34
10:36[2]
10:37
11:1[2]
11:3[4]
11:17
11:18
11:20[2]
11:21
11:24
11:25[3]
11:27
11:28
11:30[2]
11:31
11:36[2]
12:7
12:9
12:12
12:22
12:23
12:26[2]
12:39
12:40
12:46
12:47[2]
13:1[2]
13:6[2]
13:7[2]
13:11
13:15[5]
13:16
13:19
13:23
13:24[2]
13:27
13:28
13:30

ES

1:1
1:2[2]
1:3
1:5[2]
1:7[2]
1:9
1:10
1:12
1:14
1:16
1:17[2]
1:22
2:3
2:5
2:12
2:14[3]
2:15[2]
2:16[2]
2:17
2:19
2:21[2]
2:22
2:23
3:2
3:3
3:7[2]
3:8
3:12
3:13
3:14
3:15
4:3[2]
4:8
4:11
4:13
4:16[2]
5:1[2]
5:2[3]
5:8
5:9
5:12
5:14
6:4
6:5[2]
6:6[2]
7:3
7:5
7:7
7:8
7:9
8:5[3]
8:8[2]
8:9
8:10
8:11
8:12
8:13
8:15
8:17[2]
9:1[3]
9:2
9:4
9:6
9:11
9:12[2]
9:13
9:15
9:16
9:19
9:20
9:31
9:32
10:2

JOB

1:1
1:4
1:5[2]
1:7[2]
1:8
1:10
1:12
1:13
1:18
1:22
2:2[2]
2:3
2:6
2:10
3:3
3:20[2]
3:23
3:26
4:13
4:18
4:19[3]
4:21
5:4
5:13
5:14[3]
5:19[2]
5:20[2]
5:23
5:24
5:26[3]
6:2
6:4
6:6
6:10
6:13
6:29
6:30
7:11[2]
7:21[2]
8:12
8:16
9:4[2]
9:5
9:29
9:31
9:32
10:1
10:3
10:13
11:4
11:14[2]
11:18
12:5
12:9
12:10
12:12
12:24
12:25
13:14[2]
13:15
13:27
14:8[2]
14:13
14:17
15:9
15:15[2]
15:21[2]
15:28[2]
15:31
16:4
16:8
16:9
16:15
16:17
16:19
17:2
17:3
17:13
17:16
18:3
18:4
18:6
18:10[2]
18:15
18:17
18:19
19:2
19:8
19:15[2]
19:23
19:24
19:26
19:28
20:11
20:12
20:14
20:20
20:22[2]
20:26[2]
20:28
21:7
21:8
21:13[2]
21:16
21:17
21:21[2]
21:23
21:25
21:26
21:32
21:34[2]
22:8
22:12
22:14
22:22
22:26
23:6
23:13
24:5
24:6
24:7
24:13
24:14
24:16[2]
24:17
24:18
24:23
25:2
25:5
26:8
27:3[2]
27:10
27:15
27:20
28:13
28:14
29:2[2]
29:4
29:7
29:18
29:20[2]
29:25
30:1
30:2
30:3
30:6[3]
30:10
30:14[2]
30:17[2]
30:24
30:25
30:28
31:6
31:15[2]
31:21
31:26
31:32
31:33
32:1
32:5
32:8
32:22
33:2
33:5
33:6
33:8
33:9
33:11
33:12
33:15[3]
34:8
34:20
34:24[2]
34:25
34:26
35:10
35:14
35:15[2]
35:16
36:4
36:5
36:8[2]
36:11[2]
36:13
36:14
36:15[2]
36:20
36:31
37:8
37:12
37:16
37:20
37:23[3]
38:16
38:32
38:33
38:36
38:37
38:40[3]
39:4
39:10
39:14[2]
39:16
39:21[2]
40:12
40:13[2]
40:16[2]
40:21
41:9
41:22
41:23
42:6
42:11
42:15

PS

1:1[3]
1:2[2]
1:3
1:5[2]
2:4[2]
2:5[2]
2:9
2:12
3:2
4:1
4:4
4:5
4:7[2]
4:8[2]
5:3[2]
5:4
5:5
5:7[2]
5:8
5:9
5:10
5:11[2]
6:1[2]
6:5[2]
7:1
7:2
7:3
7:5
7:6
7:8
7:10
8:1
8:9
9:2
9:4
9:8[2]
9:9
9:10
9:11
9:14[2]
9:15[2]
9:16
9:19
9:20
10:1
10:2[2]
10:4
10:6[2]
10:8[2]
10:9[3]
10:13
11:1
11:2
11:4[2]
12:5
12:6
13:2[2]
13:5[2]
14:1
14:5[2]
15:1[2]
15:2
15:4
16:1
16:3[2]
16:6
16:7
16:9
16:10
16:11
17:3
17:5[2]
17:7
17:10
17:11
17:12
17:14
17:15
18:*title*
18:2
18:6
18:13
18:18
18:19
18:24
18:30
18:42
19:4
19:11
19:14
20:1
20:5[2]
20:7[2]
21:1[2]
21:5
21:7
21:9[2]
21:13
22:2[2]
22:4
22:5
22:8
22:14
22:22
22:25
23:2
23:3
23:5
23:6
24:3
24:7
24:8
24:9
25:2
25:5
25:8
25:9
25:12
25:20
26:1[2]
26:3
26:4
26:6
26:10
26:11
26:12[2]
27:3
27:4[2]
27:5[3]
27:6
27:9
27:11
27:13
28:3
28:7
29:2
29:9
30:5[2]
30:6
30:9
31:1[2]
31:6
31:7[2]
31:8
31:9
31:14
31:15
31:17
31:19
31:20[2]
31:21
31:22
31:24
32:2
32:6[2]
32:8
32:9
32:10
32:11[2]
33:1
33:4
33:7
33:8
33:18
33:19
33:21[2]
33:22
34:1
34:2
34:8
34:22
35:7
35:9[2]
35:15
35:16
35:18
35:20
35:25
35:27
36:2
36:4
36:5
36:9
36:10
37:3[2]
37:4
37:5
37:7[2]
37:8
37:11
37:19[2]
37:23
37:31
37:33
37:35
37:39
37:40
38:1[2]
38:2
38:3[2]
38:7
38:14
38:15
39:6[2]
39:7
40:3[2]
40:5
40:7
40:9
40:16
41:1
41:3
41:8
41:12
42:4
42:5[2]
42:8[2]
42:10
42:11
43:5
44:1[2]
44:3
44:6
44:8
44:17
44:19
45:4
45:5
45:9
45:14
45:16
45:17
46:1
46:5
46:8
46:9[2]
46:10
48:1[2]
48:3
48:6
48:8[2]
48:9
49:5
49:6[2]
49:12
49:14[3]
49:20
50:15
50:16
50:21
50:22
51:*title*
51:4
51:5[2]
51:6[2]
51:10
51:16
51:18
52:1
52:7[2]
52:8[2]
53:1
53:5
54:5
55:2
55:3
55:7
55:9
55:10
55:11
55:14
55:15
55:18
55:21
55:23
56:*title*
56:3
56:4[2]
56:7
56:8
56:10[2]
56:11
56:13
57:*title*
57:1[2]
58:2[2]
58:6
58:7
58:9
58:10
58:11
59:3
59:7
59:8
59:12
59:13[2]
59:16[2]
60:*title*
60:6
61:4[2]
62:4
62:7[2]
62:8
62:9
62:10[2]
63:*title*
63:1
63:2
63:4
63:6
63:7
63:11
64:1
64:4
64:5
64:10[3]
65:1
65:4
65:5
65:8
66:3
66:5
66:6
66:9
66:14
66:18
68:5
68:6[2]
68:14[2]
68:16[2]
68:17[2]
68:21
68:23[2]
68:24
68:26
68:30
68:34
69:1
69:2
69:12
69:13[3]
69:17
69:21
69:25
69:35
70:4
71:1
71:2
71:9
71:16
72:4
72:7
72:9
72:14
72:16
72:17
73:4
73:5
73:11
73:12[2]
73:13[2]
73:19

73:21
73:25
73:28
74:3
74:4
74:8[2]
74:12
74:13
74:14
75:8
76:1[2]
76:2[2]
76:7
77:2[2]
77:6
77:9
77:13
77:18
77:19[2]
78:2
78:5[2]
78:7
78:9
78:10
78:12[3]
78:14
78:15
78:17
78:18
78:19
78:22[2]
78:26[2]
78:28
78:30
78:33[2]
78:37
78:40[2]
78:43[2]
78:51[2]
78:52
78:55
78:66
79:10
80:5
81:3[2]
81:5
81:7[2]
81:9
81:12
81:13
82:1
82:5
83:4
83:12
84:4
84:5[2]
84:7
84:10[3]
84:12
85:6
85:9
85:13
86:2
86:5
86:7
86:11
86:15
87:1
87:5
87:7
88:5
88:6[3]
88:11[2]
88:12[2]
88:13
89:2
89:5
89:6
89:7[2]
89:10
89:12
89:15
89:16[2]
89:17
89:19
89:24
89:25[2]
89:30
89:37
89:43
89:47
89:49
89:50
90:1
90:4[2]
90:5
90:6[2]
90:8
90:9
91:1
91:2
91:6
91:11
91:12
91:15
92:2
92:4
92:12
92:13[2]
92:14
92:15
94:5
94:15
94:17
94:19
94:23
95:4
95:8[3]
95:10
95:11
96:6
96:9
97:11
97:12
98:2
99:2
99:4
99:7
101:2
101:6
101:7
102:2[3]
102:14
102:16
102:21[2]
102:23
102:24
103:8
103:19
103:22
104:3
104:22
104:24
104:27
104:31
104:34
105:7
105:12[2]
105:18
105:23
105:27
105:30[2]
105:31
105:32
105:35
105:36
105:39
105:41
106:5
106:7
106:14[2]
106:16
106:18
106:19
106:21
106:22
106:23
106:25
106:26
106:27
106:29
106:47
107:4[2]
107:5
107:6
107:10[3]
107:13
107:14
107:16
107:19
107:23[2]
107:24
107:26
107:28
107:32[2]
107:40
108:7
109:13
109:17
111:1[2]
111:8
112:1
112:3
112:4
112:6
112:7
113:6[2]
115:3
115:8
115:9
115:10
115:11
116:9
116:11
116:14
116:15
116:18
116:19[2]
118:5[2]
118:8[2]
118:9[2]
118:10
118:11
118:12
118:15
118:23
118:24
118:26
119:1[2]
119:3
119:11
119:14[2]
119:15
119:16
119:19
119:23
119:35
119:37
119:40
119:42
119:43
119:47
119:48
119:50
119:51
119:54
119:55
119:70
119:74
119:78
119:80
119:81
119:83
119:89
119:92
119:109
119:114
119:133
119:147
119:148
119:161
120:1
120:5[2]
121:8
123:1
124:8
125:1
125:4
126:4
126:5[2]
127:1[2]
127:4
127:5
128:1
129:8
130:5
130:7
131:1[2]
131:3
132:6
132:11
133:1
134:1
134:2
135:2[2]
135:6[3]
135:17
135:18
136:10
136:15
136:23
137:2
137:4
137:7
138:3[2]
138:5
138:7
139:4
139:8
139:9
139:15[2]
139:16[2]
139:18
139:20
139:24[2]
140:2
140:7
140:11
140:13
141:5
141:6
141:8
142:*title*
142:3
142:5
143:1[2]
143:2
143:3
143:8[2]
144:2
144:12
144:13
144:14[2]
144:15
145:15
145:17[2]
145:18
146:3[3]
146:4
146:5
147:3
147:10[2]
147:11[3]
147:14
148:1
149:1
149:2[2]
149:3
149:4
149:5
149:6[2]
150:1[2]

PR

1:14
1:15
1:17[2]
1:20
1:21[3]
1:22
2:13
2:14
2:15
2:20
2:21[2]
3:4
3:5
3:6
3:7
3:12
3:16[2]
3:23
3:27
3:33
4:3
4:11[2]
4:14
4:21
5:10
5:14[2]
5:16
5:23
6:8[2]
6:14
6:18
6:25
6:27
6:29
6:34
7:9[3]
7:11
7:12[2]
7:25
8:2[2]
8:3
8:8[2]
8:20[2]
8:22
8:31
9:4
9:6
9:9
9:14
9:16
9:17
9:18
10:5[2]
10:8
10:13
10:17
10:19
11:4
11:6
11:8
11:14
11:20
11:21
11:22
11:28
11:31
12:4
12:6
12:15
12:20
12:25
12:27
12:28[2]
13:6
13:23
14:2[2]
14:3
14:7
14:13
14:14
14:23
14:26
14:28[2]
14:32[2]
14:33[2]
15:3
15:4
15:6[2]
15:22
15:23
16:1
16:2
16:5[2]
16:10[2]
16:15
16:20
16:21
16:27
16:31
17:8
17:12
17:16
17:18
17:24
18:2
18:5
18:9
18:11
18:17
18:21
19:1[2]
19:20
19:21
19:24
20:4
20:5
20:7
20:8
20:20
21:1
21:2
21:9[2]
21:10
21:14[2]
21:16
21:19
21:20
21:24
22:5[2]
22:6
22:13
22:15
22:18
22:19
22:20
22:22
22:29
23:7
23:9
23:17
23:19
23:28
23:32
23:34
24:6
24:7
24:10
24:23
24:27
25:5
25:6[2]
25:7
25:8
25:11
25:13
25:19[2]
25:20
25:24[2]
26:1[2]
26:5
26:7
26:8
26:9
26:12
26:13[2]
26:15
26:16
26:19
26:25
27:10
27:14
27:15
27:19
27:22
28:6[2]
28:10[2]
28:11
28:18
28:25
28:26
29:2
29:6
29:11
29:20
29:22
29:23
29:25
29:27
30:4[2]
30:5
30:9
30:12
30:19[2]
30:25
30:26
30:28
30:29
30:32
31:8
31:11
31:23
31:25
31:26
31:31

EC

1:1
1:12
1:16
1:18
2:1
2:3
2:5
2:7[2]
2:9
2:10
2:14[2]
2:15[2]
2:16
2:21[3]
2:23
2:24
2:26
3:9
3:10
3:11[2]
3:12[2]
3:17
3:18
3:22
4:14
4:15
4:16
5:2
5:4
5:7
5:8
5:14
5:15
5:16
5:17
5:19
5:20
6:4[2]
6:12
7:4[2]
7:8[2]
7:9[2]
7:14[2]
7:15[3]
7:19
8:2
8:3
8:8[2]
8:10
8:11
9:1[2]
9:3
9:6
9:9[2]
9:10
9:12[3]
9:15
9:17
10:1
10:6[2]
10:16
10:17
10:20[2]
11:3
11:5
11:6[2]
11:8
11:9[4]
12:1[2]
12:3
12:4
12:5
12:9

CA

1:4
1:9
1:14
2:12
2:14[2]
3:2[2]
3:8[2]
3:11[2]
4:7
5:4
6:2
6:13
7:4
7:5
7:11
8:8
9:10
9:13

ISA

1:1
1:6
1:7
1:8[2]
1:11
1:21
2:2[2]
2:3
2:5
2:6
2:10
2:11
2:17
2:20
2:22
3:7
3:14
3:18
3:25
4:1
4:2
4:3[3]
4:6
5:1
5:2
5:4
5:8
5:9
5:11
5:12
5:16[2]
5:21[2]
5:25
5:30[2]
6:1
6:5
6:6
6:12
6:13[2]
7:1
7:3
7:6
7:11[2]
7:13[3]
7:19[2]
7:20
7:21
7:22
7:23
8:1
8:6
8:9[3]
8:11
8:18[2]
8:20
9:1[2]
9:2[2]
9:3
9:4
9:5
9:9
9:14
9:17
9:18
10:3[2]
10:5
10:7
10:17
10:20[2]
10:23
10:24
10:25
10:27
11:3
11:9
11:10
11:11
11:15
11:16
12:1
12:4
12:5
12:6
13:3
13:4
13:8
13:10
13:13[2]
13:17
13:20
13:22[2]
14:1
14:2
14:3
14:6
14:13[2]
14:18[2]
14:20
14:25
14:28
14:30
14:31
14:32
15:1[2]
15:4[2]
15:5
16:3
16:5[3]
16:10[2]
17:4
17:5
17:6[3]
17:9
17:11[3]
18:2
18:4[2]
18:5
18:7
19:1
19:3
19:9
19:10
19:14[2]
19:16
19:17
19:18[2]
19:19[2]
19:20[2]
19:21
19:23
19:24[2]
20:1
20:6
21:1
21:5
21:8[2]
21:13[2]
22:2
22:3
22:5
22:7
22:8
22:12
22:14
22:16
22:20
22:23
22:25[2]
23:1
23:13
23:15
24:11
24:12
24:13
24:15[2]
24:18
24:21
24:22[2]
24:23[2]
25:4
25:5
25:6
25:7
25:8
25:9[2]
25:10
25:11
26:1[2]
26:2
26:3[2]
26:4[2]
26:8
26:9[2]
26:10[2]
26:12
26:16
26:17[3]
26:18[2]
26:19
27:1[2]
27:2
27:4[2]
27:8[2]
27:9
27:12
27:13[4]
28:4
28:5
28:6
28:7[2]
28:14
28:16
28:20
28:21[2]
28:25[2]
28:29[2]
29:15
29:18
29:19[2]
29:21
29:23
29:24
30:2[2]
30:3
30:7
30:8[2]
30:12
30:13
30:14[2]
30:15[3]
30:19
30:21
30:23[2]
30:25
30:26
30:28
30:29
30:32[2]
31:1[2]
31:7
31:9[2]
32:1[2]
32:2[2]
32:13
32:16[2]
32:18[3]
32:19
33:2
33:12
33:14
33:17
34:5
34:6[2]
34:11
34:13[2]
35:6[2]
35:7
36:1
36:2
36:6[2]
36:7
36:11[3]
36:13
36:15
37:7
37:10
37:12
37:28
37:29[2]
37:30
37:36[2]
37:38[2]
38:1[2]
38:3[2]
38:8
38:10
38:11
38:15
38:16
38:17
38:20
39:2[3]
39:4[2]
39:6[2]
39:7
39:8
40:3[2]
40:11
40:12[4]
40:14
40:22
40:24
40:26
41:16[2]
41:18[2]
41:19[2]
42:1
42:2
42:4
42:6
42:7
42:12
42:16
42:17
42:22[2]
42:24
43:4
43:14
43:16[2]
43:19[2]
43:20[2]
43:26
44:7
44:12
44:13
44:16
44:19
44:20
44:23
45:2[2]
45:13
45:14[2]
45:17
45:18
45:19[3]
45:23
45:24
45:25
46:6
46:7
46:13
47:1
47:8
47:9[3]
47:10[2]
47:13
48:1
48:10
48:16
49:2[2]
49:3
49:4[2]
49:5
49:8[2]
49:9[3]
49:20
49:21
49:22
50:4
50:10[2]
50:11[3]
51:6
51:7
51:9[2]
51:14
51:16[2]
51:20
52:6
52:10
53:9[2]
53:10
54:6
54:8
54:14
54:16
54:17
55:2
55:11
56:5
56:7
56:9
57:2[2]
57:5
57:6
57:10
57:13
57:15
57:17
58:2
58:3
58:10
58:11
58:12
58:14
59:4
59:6
59:7
59:8
59:9
59:10[2]
59:13
59:14
59:19
59:20
59:21
60:10[2]
60:18
60:22
61:3
61:6
61:7[2]
61:8
61:10[2]
61:11
62:2[2]
62:4
62:7
62:9
63:1[3]
63:2[2]
63:3[2]
63:4
63:6[2]
63:9[3]
63:13
64:5[2]
65:2
65:3
65:4[2]
65:5
65:8[2]
65:10
65:16[3]
65:18
65:19[3]
65:23
65:25
66:3
66:4
66:8
66:13
66:17[2]
66:20[3]

JER

1:1[2]
1:2[2]
1:3[2]
1:5
1:9
2:2[3]
2:5
2:17
2:18[2]
2:19
2:23
2:24[2]
2:27
2:28
2:30
2:34
2:37
3:2[2]
3:6
3:16[2]
3:18
3:23[2]
3:25
4:2[5]
4:5[3]
4:11
4:19
4:20
4:30
4:31
5:1
5:6
5:7
5:8
5:13
5:14
5:18
5:19[2]
5:20[2]
5:24[2]
5:30
5:31
6:1[2]
6:3
6:6
6:7
6:10
6:11
6:16
6:23
6:24
6:26
6:29
7:2[2]
7:3
7:4
7:6
7:7[2]
7:8
7:10
7:11
7:12
7:17[2]
7:22
7:23
7:24[2]
7:30[2]
7:31[2]
7:32
8:3
8:7
8:8[2]
8:9
8:12
8:16
8:18
8:19[3]
8:22
9:2
9:4
9:6
9:8
9:23[3]
9:24[3]
9:26[3]
10:5
10:6
10:7
10:13
10:14[2]
10:15
10:23[2]
10:24
11:4
11:6[2]
11:7
11:8
11:12
11:14
11:15
11:17
11:21
12:2
12:5[2]
12:8
12:16
13:1
13:4
13:10
13:17
13:21
13:22
13:25
13:27
14:4
14:5
14:6
14:8[2]
14:9
14:13
14:14
14:15[2]
14:16
15:4
15:7
15:11[2]
15:13
15:14
15:15
15:17[2]
16:2
16:3[2]
16:6
16:7
16:9[2]
16:19
17:3
17:4[2]
17:5
17:6[3]
17:7
17:8
17:11
17:13
17:17
17:19[3]
17:20
17:21
17:24
17:25
17:29[2]
18:4
18:6[2]
18:10
18:15[3]
18:17
18:21
18:23
19:4
19:7
19:9
19:10
19:11
19:14
20:1
20:2[2]
20:6
20:7
20:9[3]
20:16
21:4
21:5[3]
21:7
21:9
21:12
21:14
22:2
22:3
22:4[2]
22:12
22:15
22:20
22:21
22:23[2]
22:30[2]
23:5
23:8
23:11
23:12
23:13[2]
23:14[2]
23:18
23:19
23:20
23:22
23:24
23:25
23:26
23:29
24:8[2]
24:9
25:1
25:5
25:13
25:23
25:24
25:34
26:1
26:2[2]
26:4
26:7
26:9[2]
26:10
26:14
26:15
26:16
26:18
26:20
27:1
27:11
27:15
27:18[2]
27:19
27:21[2]
28:1[5]
28:5[3]
28:7[2]
28:11
28:15
28:17
29:5
29:7
29:8
29:9
29:10
29:15
29:16
29:21
29:22[2]
29:23[2]
29:25
29:26[4]
29:28[2]
29:29
29:31
30:2
30:6
30:8
30:10
30:11
30:24
31:2
31:4
31:9
31:10
31:12
31:13
31:15
31:17
31:22
31:23[2]
31:24[2]
31:29
31:32
31:33[2]
32:1
32:2[2]
32:7
32:8[3]
32:9
32:10
32:12[3]
32:14
32:15
32:19[2]
32:20[2]
32:23[2]
32:34
32:35
32:37[3]
32:40
32:41
32:43
32:44[6]
33:1
33:5[2]
33:10[3]
33:12[2]
33:13[6]
33:15[3]
33:16
33:20
34:5
34:6
34:13
34:15[3]
34:17
34:18
35:1
35:7[2]
35:8
35:9
35:10
35:15
36:1
36:6[4]
36:8[2]
36:9[3]
36:10[5]
36:13
36:14[3]
36:15[2]
36:18
36:20[3]
36:21[2]
36:22[2]
36:23
36:28[2]
36:30[2]
36:32
37:1
37:4
37:10
37:12
37:13
37:15[2]
37:17
37:18
37:21[2]
38:2
38:4[2]
38:5
38:6[3]
38:7[3]
38:9[3]
38:13
38:14
38:22[2]
38:28
39:1[2]
39:2[2]
39:3[2]
39:5[2]
39:6
39:9
39:10
39:15
39:16
39:17
39:18
40:1
40:6
40:7[2]
40:9
40:10[2]
40:11[3]
40:13
40:15[3]
41:1[2]
41:6
41:8
41:10[2]
41:12
41:17
41:18
42:10
42:13
42:16
42:20
42:22
43:4
43:5
43:8
43:9[5]
43:12[2]
43:13
44:1[2]
44:3
44:6[2]
44:8[2]
44:9[2]
44:10[2]
44:12
44:13
44:15[2]
44:16
44:17[2]
44:21[2]
44:23[3]
44:24
44:26[3]
44:27
44:29
45:1[2]
45:3
45:5
46:2[2]
46:10
46:11
46:14[4]
46:19
46:21
46:25
46:26
46:27
46:28
48:2
48:5[2]
48:6
48:7[2]
48:11
48:18
48:20
48:26[2]
48:28[3]
48:35[2]
48:38
48:41[2]
48:44
48:47
49:1
49:2
49:4[2]
49:7
49:11
49:16
49:18[2]
49:21
49:22
49:24
49:26[2]
49:27
49:32
49:33
49:34
49:38
49:39
50:2[2]
50:4[2]
50:5
50:9[2]
50:14
50:16
50:20[2]
50:22
50:25
50:28
50:30[2]
50:32
50:37
50:39
50:42
50:43
51:1
51:2
51:3
51:4[2]
51:6
51:7
51:10
51:13
51:16
51:17
51:18
51:20
51:21[2]
51:22[3]
51:23[3]
51:24[2]
51:27
51:30
51:39
51:44
51:46[3]
51:47
51:58[2]
51:59
51:60
51:62
52:1
52:2
52:3
52:4[3]
52:6[3]
52:8
52:9
52:10
52:11[2]
52:12[2]
52:15
52:17[2]
52:19[2]
52:20
52:25[2]
52:27[2]
52:28
52:29
52:31[4]
52:32

LA

1:2
1:4

1:7 1:9 1:12 1:15^2 1:19 1:20 2:1^2 2:2 2:3 2:4 2:5 2:6^2 2:7^2 2:11 2:12 2:17 2:19^3 2:20 2:21^2 2:22^2 3:6 3:10^2 3:11 3:20^2 3:24 3:27 3:29 3:36 3:41 3:45 3:53 3:57 3:66 4:1 4:3 4:5^2 4:6 4:7 4:8 4:10 4:11 4:13 4:14 4:17 4:18 4:19 4:20 4:21 5:11^2

EZE

1:1^3 1:2 1:3 1:16 1:20 1:21 1:28^2 3:3 3:10 3:14^2 3:18 3:19 3:20 4:9 4:12 4:14 4:16 5:2^2 5:3^2 5:4 5:5 5:6 5:7 5:8^2 5:9 5:10^2 5:12 5:13^2 5:14 5:15^4 6:6 6:7 6:9 6:10

6:13 6:14 7:4 7:7 7:9 7:13 7:15^2 7:19^2 7:20 8:1^4 8:3 8:4 8:5 8:7 8:8^2 8:9 8:10 8:11^2 8:12^2 8:18^2 9:1^2 9:2^2 9:4 9:5 9:7 9:8 10:1 10:2^3 10:3 10:6 10:8 10:10 10:13 10:17 10:19 11:2 11:6 11:7 11:10 11:11^2 11:12 11:16 11:20 11:24 12:2 12:3^2 12:4^2 12:5 12:6^2 12:7^3 12:8 12:10 12:11 12:12 12:13 12:15 12:22 12:23 12:25 13:4 13:5^2 13:9^2 13:13^3 13:14 13:21 14:3 14:4 14:5 14:7^2 14:14 14:16 14:18 14:19 14:20 14:23 16:4^2 16:5^2 16:6^3 16:12 16:15 16:22^2 16:24 16:29 16:31^4 16:34^3 16:38 16:41

16:43 16:47 16:49^2 16:51 16:52 16:53 16:54^2 16:56 16:59 16:60 17:5 17:8 17:9 17:10 17:15 17:16^2 17:17 17:20 17:23^2 18:3 18:9 18:17 18:18 18:22 18:24^3 18:26 18:32 19:4 19:8 19:9^2 19:10 19:11 19:12 19:13^2 20:1^2 20:5^2 20:6 20:8 20:9^2 20:11 20:13^4 20:14 20:15 20:16 20:17 20:18^2 20:19 20:21^3 20:22^2 20:23 20:26^2 20:27^2 20:36 20:40^3 20:41 20:43 20:47^2 21:20 21:21 21:22 21:23 21:24^2 21:30^2 21:31 21:32 22:3 22:4^2 22:6 22:7^3 22:9^3 22:10^2 22:11^2 22:12 22:13 22:14 22:15 22:16 22:18 22:20^2 22:21^2 22:22^2 22:24 22:25^2 22:27 22:30 23:3^2 23:8

23:11^3 23:15 23:19^2 23:21 23:31 23:32 23:37 23:38 23:39 23:43 23:44^3 23:45 24:1^3 24:7 24:11 24:12 24:13 24:18^2 24:25 24:26 24:27 25:4^2 25:6 25:10 25:14 26:1^2 26:5 26:6 26:8 26:12 26:15 26:17 26:18^2 26:20^3 27:4 27:8 27:9^2 27:10^2 27:11 27:12 27:13 27:14 27:16 27:17 27:18^2 27:19^2 27:20 27:21^3 27:22 27:24^3 27:25^2 27:26 27:27^4 27:30 27:32 27:34^2 27:35 28:2^2 28:8 28:9 28:12 28:13^3 28:14 28:15^2 28:18 28:22^3 28:23 28:25^3 29:1^3 29:3 29:4 29:12 29:17^3 29:21^2 30:4^2 30:5 30:6 30:7^2 30:8 30:9^3 30:13 30:14^2 30:16 30:18 30:19 30:20^3 30:24

31:1^3 31:2 31:3 31:6 31:7^2 31:8^3 31:9 31:10^2 31:12 31:14^2 31:15 31:16 31:17 31:18^3 32:1^3 32:2 32:3 32:10 32:17^2 32:19 32:20 32:23^2 32:24 32:25^3 32:26 32:27 32:28 32:32^2 33:6 33:8 33:9 33:10 33:11 33:12^3 33:15 33:21^3 33:22^2 33:27^4 33:30 34:12^2 34:13 34:14^3 34:25^2 34:26 34:27 34:29 35:5^2 35:8^3 36:2 36:3 36:5 36:6^2 36:15 36:17 36:23^2 36:27 36:28 36:31 36:33^2 36:34 36:38 37:1^2 37:2 37:6 37:8 37:14^2 37:17 37:19^2 37:20 37:22 37:24 37:25 37:26 37:28 38:8 38:12 38:14 38:16^2 38:17^2 38:18 38:23 39:6 39:7^2 39:9 39:11^2 39:15 39:26

39:27^2 40:1^4 40:2 40:3^2 40:5 40:25^2 40:27 40:29^2 40:33 40:39 40:44 41:6^2 42:3 42:6 42:8 42:10 42:12 43:7^2 43:8^2 43:9 43:11^2 43:16 43:17 43:18 43:21 44:2^2 44:3 44:5 44:7^4 44:8 44:9^2 44:11 44:13 44:17^2 44:19 44:24^3 44:27^2 44:28 44:29 44:30 45:1 45:2^2 45:3 45:8^2 45:16 45:17^4 45:18^2 45:21^2 45:25^3 46:1 46:3^2 46:4 46:6 46:8 46:9^3 46:10^2 46:11^2 46:21 46:22 46:23 47:3 47:5 47:19 47:22 47:23 48:8^3 48:9^2 48:10^5 48:13^2 48:15^2 48:18 48:21 48:22 48:28

DA

1:1 1:4^5 1:8 1:14 1:15 1:17^2 1:18^2 1:20^2 2:1

2:4 2:5 2:16 2:19 2:22 2:24^2 2:25^2 2:27 2:28^2 2:40 2:41 2:44^2 2:45 2:49 3:1^2 3:13 3:16 3:20 3:21 3:24 3:25 3:28 3:29 3:30 4:1 4:4^2 4:6 4:7 4:8^2 4:9 4:10^2 4:12^2 4:13 4:15^3 4:17 4:18^2 4:21 4:23^2 4:25 4:29 4:31 4:32 4:35 4:36 4:37 5:2 5:3 5:5 5:7^2 5:8 5:9 5:11^4 5:12 5:13 5:14^2 5:15 5:16 5:20 5:21 5:23^2 5:27 5:29 5:30 6:3 6:4 6:10 6:19^2 6:22 6:23 6:24 6:25 6:26 6:27^2 6:28^2 7:1 7:2 7:5 7:7^2 7:8 7:13 7:15^2 7:19 7:21 7:23 7:28^2 8:1 8:2^4

8:6 8:7 8:18 8:22 8:23 8:25^2 9:1 9:2^2 9:6 9:10 9:11 9:13 9:14 9:21^2 9:24 9:25 9:27 10:1 10:2 10:3 10:4 10:5 10:6 10:8^2 10:9 10:14 10:17^2 10:21^2 11:1 11:2 11:6^2 11:7 11:14 11:16 11:20^4 11:21^2 11:38 11:39 11:45 12:1 12:2 12:6 12:7 12:13

HO

1:1^2 1:5 1:10 2:3 2:9^2 2:10 2:15^2 2:18 2:19^4 2:20 2:21 2:23 3:5 4:1 4:5^2 4:16 4:19 5:4 5:5 5:8^2 5:9 5:11 5:15 6:2^2 6:9 6:10 7:1 7:2 7:5 7:6^2 7:16 8:6 9:2 9:3^2 9:5^2 9:6 9:8^2 9:9 9:10^2

9:13 9:15 10:4^2 10:9 10:10^2 10:12^2 10:13^2 10:14^2 10:15 11:9 11:11 12:3 12:4 12:7 12:8^2 12:9^2 12:10^3 13:1^2 13:5 13:9 13:10 13:11^2 13:13 13:16 14:3 14:9

JOE

1:2^2 1:13 2:1^2 2:5 2:8 2:9^2 2:15 2:23^2 2:26 2:27 2:29 2:30^2 2:32^2 3:1^2 3:13 3:14^2 3:17 3:18 3:19 3:21

AM

1:1^2 1:14^3 2:7 2:8 2:16 3:4 3:5 3:6^2 3:9^5 3:10 3:12^4 3:13 3:14 4:1 4:6^2 5:6^2 5:7 5:10 5:11 5:12 5:13 5:15 5:16^2 5:17 5:20 5:21 5:25 6:1^2 6:6 6:9 6:13 6:14 7:1 7:7

7:8 7:10 7:17^2 8:3^2 8:9^2 8:11 8:13 9:1 9:3^2 9:6^2 9:9 9:11^2

OB

1 3^2 7 8 11^2 12^3 13^3 14^2 18 20

JON

1:4 1:5 1:17 2:3 2:7 3:6 3:8 4:2 4:5 4:8 4:10^2

MIC

1:1 1:10^2 1:11 1:13 2:1 2:4 2:5 2:11 2:12 3:2 3:4 4:1^2 4:2 4:5^2 4:6 4:7 4:9^2 4:10^3 4:13 5:1 5:2 5:4^2 5:5 5:6 5:7 5:8^2 5:10 5:15 6:10 6:12 6:13^2 6:14 6:16 7:2 7:5^3 7:6^2 7:8 7:11^2 7:12 7:14^4 7:18

NA

1:3^3 1:6 1:7^2 1:13 2:1 2:3^2 2:4^2 2:5 2:10 2:12 2:13 3:10^2 3:13 3:17^2 3:18

HAB

1:5 1:15^2 2:4 2:13 2:19 2:20 3:2^3 3:7 3:11 3:12^2 3:16^2 3:17^2 3:18^2

ZEP

1:1 1:9 1:10 1:11 1:18^2 2:3 2:7^2 2:14^4 2:15^2 3:2 3:5 3:11^2 3:12 3:13 3:15 3:16 3:17^2 3:19 3:20

HAG

1:1^3 1:4 1:6 1:8 1:13 1:14 1:15^2 2:1^2 2:3^3 2:9 2:10^2 2:12 2:15 2:17 2:19 2:20 2:22 2:23

ZEC

1:1^2 1:7 1:8 1:16 2:1 2:5 2:10

2:11^2 2:12 3:7 3:9 3:10 4:10 5:4 5:7 5:9 5:11 6:2^2 6:3^2 6:8 6:14 6:15 7:1^3 7:3^2 7:5 7:7 7:10 7:12 8:3 8:4^2 8:5 8:6^3 8:8^3 8:9^2 8:10 8:11 8:15 8:16 8:17 8:22 8:23 9:1 9:4 9:6 9:7 9:16 10:1^2 10:2 10:3 10:5^2 10:9 10:11 10:12^2 11:8 11:11 11:13 11:16^2 12:2 12:3^2 12:4 12:5^2 12:6^4 12:8 12:9 12:10^2 12:11^3 13:1 13:2 13:3 13:4 13:6^2 13:8 14:1 14:3 14:4^2 14:5 14:6 14:8^3 14:9 14:10 14:11 14:12^2 14:13 14:14 14:15 14:20^2 14:21^4

MAL

1:7 1:10 1:11

1:12 1:14 2:6^3 2:9 2:11^2 2:17^2 3:1 3:3 3:4^2 3:5 3:8 3:10 3:11 3:17 4:2 4:3 4:4

MT

1:20^2 2:1^2 2:2 2:5 2:6 2:9 2:12 2:13 2:16^2 2:18 2:19^2 2:22^3 2:23 3:1^2 3:3 3:6 3:12 3:17 4:6 4:13^2 4:16^2 4:21 4:23 5:3 5:8 5:11 5:15 5:16 5:18 5:19^2 5:20 5:21 5:22^3 5:25 5:28 5:45 5:48 6:1 6:2^2 6:4^2 6:5^2 6:6^2 6:9 6:10^2 6:18^2 6:20 6:23 6:29 7:3^2 7:4 7:11 7:13^2 7:15 7:21 7:22^4 8:10 8:11 8:13 8:24 8:32 9:4 9:10 9:16 9:25 9:31 9:33

9:35 10:9 10:11 10:15 10:16 10:17 10:19 10:20 10:23 10:27^3 10:28 10:32 10:33 10:35^2 10:41^2 10:42^2 11:1 11:2 11:6 11:8^2 11:11 11:16 11:21^3 11:23^2 11:24 11:26 11:29 12:5^2 12:6 12:18 12:19 12:21 12:32^2 12:36 12:40^2 12:41 12:42 12:50 13:3 13:10 13:13 13:14 13:19 13:21 13:24 13:27 13:30^3 13:31 13:32 13:33 13:34 13:35 13:40^2 13:43 13:44 13:54 13:57^3 14:2 14:3 14:8 14:10 14:11 14:24 14:25 14:33 15:9 15:17 15:32 15:33 16:3 16:17 16:19^2 16:26 16:27 16:28 17:5 17:22 18:1 18:2 18:4 18:5 18:6^2 18:10^2 18:14 18:16 18:18^2 18:19

18:20^2 19:21 19:28^2 20:1 20:3 20:17 20:21 21:8^2 21:9^2 21:12 21:14 21:15 21:18 21:19 21:22 21:24 21:28 21:32 21:33 21:41 21:42^2 22:11 22:12 22:15 22:16 22:28 22:30^3 22:36 22:43 23:2 23:6 23:7 23:9 23:13^2 23:30^2 23:34 23:39 24:5 24:7 24:14 24:15 24:16 24:18 24:19 24:20 24:26^2 24:30^2 24:38^2 24:40 24:43 24:44 24:45 24:48 24:50^2 25:4 25:10 25:18 25:25 25:31 25:35 25:36 25:38 25:39 25:43^2 25:44 26:6^2 26:12 26:13 26:23 26:29 26:55^2 26:58 26:61 26:64 26:67 26:69 27:4 27:5 27:7 27:19 27:29 27:40 27:43 27:44 27:51 27:59 27:60^2

28:1 28:18^2 28:19

MK

1:2 1:3 1:4 1:5 1:9^2 1:11 1:13 1:14 1:19 1:20 1:23 1:35 1:39 1:45 2:1 2:6 2:8^2 2:15 2:20 2:26 3:23 3:29 4:2 4:11 4:15 4:17 4:19 4:28 4:29 4:31^2 4:36 4:38 5:4 5:5^2 5:13 5:14^2 5:15 5:20 5:27 5:29 5:30^2 5:33 5:34 5:39 5:40 6:2 6:4^2 6:8 6:10 6:11 6:14 6:17 6:22 6:25^2 6:27 6:28 6:29 6:40 6:47 6:48 6:51 6:55 6:56 7:7 7:32 8:1 8:4 8:12 8:14 8:26 8:37 8:38^2 9:33 9:36^2 9:37 9:38 9:39 9:41 9:42 9:50

10:10 10:16 10:21 10:24 10:30^2 10:32 10:37 10:52 11:4 11:8^2 11:9 11:10^2 11:15 11:20 11:22 11:23 11:25 11:26 11:27 12:4 12:11 12:13 12:14 12:23 12:25^2 12:26^2 12:35 12:38^3 12:39 12:41 12:42 12:43 12:44^2 13:6 13:8 13:9 13:11 13:14 13:16 13:17 13:18 13:19 13:24 13:25 13:26 13:29 13:32 13:35 14:3^2 14:14 14:17 14:20 14:25 14:30 14:31 14:49 14:60 14:62 14:66 15:1 15:7 15:29 15:38 15:41 15:43 15:46^2 16:2 16:7 16:12 16:17

LU

1:1^2 1:3 1:5 1:6 1:7 1:8 1:15 1:17 1:18 1:19 1:20 1:21 1:22

1:25 1:26 1:28 1:29 1:31 1:36 1:39 1:41 1:44^2 1:47 1:51 1:54 1:66 1:69 1:75 1:79^2 1:80^2 2:1 2:7^3 2:8^2 2:11 2:12^2 2:14 2:16 2:19 2:21 2:23 2:24 2:25 2:27 2:28 2:29 2:34 2:38^2 2:40 2:43 2:44 2:46^2 2:51 2:52 3:1 3:2 3:4^2 3:15^2 3:17 3:18 3:20 3:22^2 4:2 4:5 4:11 4:14 4:15 4:20 4:21 4:23^2 4:24 4:25^2 4:27^2 4:28 4:33 4:35 4:44 5:7 5:12 5:18^2 5:19 5:22 5:29 5:35 6:1 6:8 6:12^2 6:17 6:23^3 6:41^2 6:42^3 7:1 7:7 7:9 7:21 7:23 7:25^2 7:28 7:32 7:37^2 7:45

1:12 1:13[2] 1:15 1:17 1:18 1:19[2] 1:21 2:1 2:5 2:8 2:10 2:11 2:12
2:13 2:18 2:19 2:22 3:1 3:3 3:5 3:7 3:10[2] 3:11 3:14 3:16[3] 3:18[2]

1 JO
1:5 1:6 1:7[2] 1:8 1:10 2:4 2:5[2] 2:6 2:8[2] 2:9[2] 2:10[2] 2:11[2]
2:14 2:15[2] 2:16 2:24[2] 2:27[2] 2:28 3:3 3:5 3:6 3:9 3:10 3:14 3:15 3:17
3:18[4] 3:22 3:24[3] 4:2 4:3[2] 4:4[2] 4:9 4:12[2] 4:13[2] 4:15[2] 4:16[3] 4:17[2] 4:18[2] 5:7
5:8[2] 5:10 5:11 5:14 5:19 5:20[2]

2 JO
1 2 3 4 6
7 9[2]

3 JO
1 2 3[2] 4

JUDE
1 4
5 6 7 10 11[2] 12 16 18 20 21

RE
1:4
1:5 1:9[3] 1:10 1:11[2] 1:13 1:16[2] 1:20 2:1[2] 2:7 2:8 2:12 2:13 2:17 2:18
2:24 3:1 3:4[2] 3:5 3:7 3:12 3:18 3:20 3:21[2] 4:1 4:2[2] 4:3 4:4 4:6
5:1 5:3[2] 5:6[2] 5:13[3] 6:5 6:6 6:15[2] 7:3 7:9 7:13 7:14 7:15 7:17 8:1
8:9 9:4 9:6 9:10 9:11[2] 9:14 9:17 9:19[2] 10:2 10:7 10:8 10:9 10:10 11:3
11:5 11:6 11:8 11:9 11:12 11:13 11:15 11:19[2] 12:1 12:2 12:3 12:7 12:8
12:10 12:12 13:6[2] 13:8 13:13 13:14 13:16[2] 14:1 14:5 14:6 14:9[2] 14:10[2] 14:13
14:14 14:15 14:16 14:17 14:18 14:19 15:1[2] 15:5 15:6 16:3 16:16 16:19 17:3
17:4[2] 17:8 17:17 18:6 18:7 18:8 18:10 18:16 18:17 18:19[2] 18:22[3] 18:23[2] 18:24
19:1 19:8 19:11 19:13 19:14[2] 19:17[2] 20:1 20:4 20:6 20:8 20:12 20:13[2] 20:15
21:8 21:10 21:14 21:23 21:24 21:27[2] 22:2 22:3 22:4 22:14 22:16 22:18 22:19

IS

1961, *2076*

GE
1:11 1:29[2] 1:30 2:9 2:11[3] 2:12[2] 2:13[2] 2:14[3] 2:18 2:23 3:3 3:13 3:17 3:22 4:6 4:9 4:13 5:1 6:3 6:13 6:14 6:17[2] 6:21 7:15 8:17 8:21 9:4 9:10 9:12[2] 9:15 9:16 9:17[2] 9:18 10:9 10:12 10:6 11:9 12:12 12:18 12:19 13:9 13:18 14:2 14:3 14:6 14:7 14:8 14:15 14:17 14:23 15:2 15:3 15:13 15:16 16:6 16:14 17:4 17:10 17:12[3] 17:13 17:14 17:17 18:9 18:14 18:20 18:21
19:8 19:13 19:19 19:20 19:31 19:37 19:38 20:2 20:3 20:5[2] 20:7 20:11 20:12 20:13[2] 20:15 20:16 21:13 21:17 21:22 22:7 22:14 22:17 23:2 23:9[2] 23:11 23:15 23:19 23:20 24:23 24:35 24:51 24:65[2] 25:9 25:18 26:7 26:9 26:10 26:20 27:11 27:20 27:22 27:27 27:33 27:36 28:16 28:17[2] 29:6 29:7 29:19 29:25 30:15 30:30 30:33 31:5 31:14 31:16 31:29 31:32 31:35 31:36 31:43 31:48 31:50[2] 32:2 32:8 32:18[2] 32:20 32:27
32:29 32:30 32:32 33:11 33:17 33:18 34:14 34:21 35:6[2] 35:10 35:19 35:20 35:27 36:1 36:8 36:19 36:43 37:10 37:22 37:26 37:27 37:30 37:33[2] 38:14 38:18 38:21 38:24 39:8 39:9 40:8 40:12 40:18 41:15 41:16 41:25[2] 41:26 41:28[2] 41:32[2] 41:38[2] 41:39 42:2 42:13[2] 42:14 42:21 42:22 42:28[3] 42:30 42:32[2] 42:36[2] 42:38[2] 43:7 43:27[2] 43:28[2] 43:29 43:32 44:5 44:10 44:15 44:16 44:17 44:20[2] 44:28 44:30 44:31 45:12 45:20 45:26[2] 45:28[2]
46:33 46:34 47:3 47:4 47:6 47:18[2] 47:23 48:1 48:7 48:18 49:9 49:14 49:21 49:22 49:24 49:28 49:29 49:30 49:32 50:10 50:11[2] 50:20

EX
1:22 2:6 2:14 2:18 2:20[2] 3:3 3:5 3:9 3:13 3:15[2] 3:16 4:2 4:14 4:22 5:2 5:16[2] 5:22 7:14 7:17 7:18 8:10 8:19 8:26 9:3[2] 9:4 9:14 9:27 9:28 9:29 10:5 10:7 10:10 11:5 12:11 12:19 12:22[2] 12:27 12:42[2] 12:43 12:44 12:48 12:49 13:2
13:8 13:14 14:12 15:2[3] 15:3[2] 15:6 15:11[2] 15:26 16:12 16:15 16:16 16:23[2] 16:25 16:26 16:32 16:36 17:3 17:7 18:11 18:14 18:17 18:18[2] 19:5 20:4[3] 20:10[2] 20:11 20:17 20:20 21:21 21:30 22:16 22:25 22:27[2] 22:31 23:16 23:21 25:3 26:5 26:10 27:21 28:8 28:26 29:1 29:13[2] 29:14 29:18 29:21 29:22[2] 29:23 29:25 29:27[4] 29:28 29:30 29:32 29:34 29:38 30:6[2] 30:10 30:13 30:32 31:7 31:13 31:14 31:15 31:17 32:1 32:5 32:9
32:17 32:18[2] 32:23 32:26 33:13 33:16 33:21 34:9 34:10 34:14[2] 34:19[2] 35:4 35:5 36:25 38:21 38:26 40:9

LE
1:5 1:8[2] 1:12[2] 1:13 1:17[2] 2:3 2:6 2:8[2] 2:9 2:10[2] 2:15 2:16 3:3 3:4[2] 3:5[3] 3:9 3:10[2] 3:11 3:14 3:15[2] 3:16[2] 4:3 4:5 4:7[2] 4:8 4:9[2] 4:14 4:16 4:18[3] 4:21 4:22 4:24 4:31 4:35 5:1 5:8 5:9 5:11 5:12 5:17 5:19 6:4 6:9[2] 6:14 6:15 6:17[2] 6:20[2] 6:21
6:22[2] 6:25[3] 6:27 6:28 6:29 6:30 7:1[2] 7:4[3] 7:5 7:6 7:7[3] 7:9[2] 7:11 7:15 7:24 7:35 7:37 8:5 8:28 8:31 9:6 10:3 10:7 10:12 10:13 10:17 11:3 11:4 11:5 11:6 11:7 11:10 11:26 11:32 11:33 11:36 11:37 11:46 12:7 13:3[2] 13:6 13:8 13:9 13:11[2] 13:13 13:15[2] 13:17 13:18 13:20 13:22 13:23 13:24 13:25[2] 13:27 13:28[2] 13:30 13:31 13:36 13:37[3] 13:39[2] 13:40[3] 13:41[2] 13:42 13:44[3] 13:45 13:46 13:47 13:49
13:51[3] 13:52[2] 13:54 13:55[3] 13:57[2] 13:59 14:4 14:7 14:8 14:11 14:13[3] 14:14 14:16 14:17[2] 14:18[2] 14:19 14:22 14:25 14:27 14:28[2] 14:29[2] 14:31[2] 14:32[3] 14:35 14:36 14:40 14:43 14:44[2] 14:46 14:48 14:54 14:57[3] 15:2 15:3 15:4 15:8 15:13 15:17 15:31 15:32[2] 15:33[2] 16:2 16:6 16:11[2] 16:13 16:15 16:18 17:2 17:11[2] 17:14[3] 18:6 18:7 18:8 18:10 18:11 18:12 18:13 18:14 18:15 18:16 18:17 18:19 18:22 18:23 18:25 18:27 19:7 19:13
19:20 20:14 20:17 20:21 20:27 21:2[2] 21:3 21:7[2] 21:10[2] 21:12 21:19 22:4[2] 22:7[2] 22:8 22:11 22:13 22:24 22:25 22:27 23:3[2] 23:5 23:6 23:8 23:28 23:36 24:9 24:16 25:5 25:12 25:23 25:28 25:29 25:30 25:34 25:48 25:49 27:22 27:26 27:28 27:30[2]

NU
1:51 3:26 3:47 3:48 4:15 4:16 4:24 4:25 4:26[2] 4:28 4:31 4:33 5:2 5:15 5:17 5:18 5:29[2] 6:4 6:7 6:8 6:13 6:18 6:19 6:20 6:21
8:24 9:13[2] 10:7 11:6[2] 11:14 11:17 11:20 11:23 12:7[2] 12:12 13:18 13:19 13:20 13:27 13:32 14:7 14:9[2] 14:18 14:42 15:25 15:29 16:3 16:5 16:11 16:13 16:40 16:46 18:11[2] 18:13[2] 18:16 18:19 18:31 19:2[2] 19:9[2] 19:13[2] 19:14[2] 19:15 19:16 19:20 20:5[2] 20:13 21:5[2] 21:8 21:11 21:13[2] 21:14 21:16 21:20 21:28 21:30 22:5[2] 22:6[2] 22:11 22:32 22:36[2] 23:19 23:21[2] 23:23[2] 24:9[2] 24:21 26:9 27:11 27:14 27:18 28:3 28:6 28:10 28:14
28:16 28:17 28:23 29:1 30:1 30:9 30:20 30:21 32:4 32:19 33:6 33:7 33:36 34:2 34:13 35:16 35:17 35:18 35:21 35:31 35:32 35:33 36:6

DE
1:14 1:16 1:17[2] 1:25 1:28 1:36[2] 3:11 3:12 3:16 3:18 3:24 3:25 4:6[2] 4:7[2] 4:8 4:17 4:18 4:24 4:31 4:32 4:35[2] 4:38 4:39[2] 4:44 4:48[2] 5:8[3] 5:14[2] 5:21 5:26 6:4 6:15 6:18 6:24 7:9 7:21 7:25[2] 7:26 8:13[2] 8:18[2] 9:3 9:13 10:9
10:14[2] 10:15 10:17 10:21[2] 11:10[2] 11:11 12:8 12:12 12:18 12:22 12:23 12:25 12:28 13:6 13:11 13:14 13:15 13:18 14:8 14:10 14:19 14:21 14:27 15:2[2] 15:3 15:9 15:16 16:11 16:17 16:20 17:1[2] 17:4 17:6 17:15 17:18 18:2 18:22 19:4 19:6[2] 19:16 19:17 20:1 20:4 20:5 20:6 20:7 20:8[2] 20:11 20:14 20:19 21:2 21:3 21:4 21:6 21:9 21:16 21:17[2] 21:20[2] 21:23[2] 22:23 22:26[2] 22:23[2] 23:1 23:7 23:10 23:11 23:15 23:19
23:23 24:2 24:4[2] 24:14 24:15 25:6 26:11 26:12 28:23[2] 28:43 28:54 28:61 29:5 29:11 29:15 29:23[2] 29:28 30:11[2] 30:12 30:13 30:14 30:20 31:6 31:8 31:11 31:12 31:17 32:4[3] 32:5 32:6 32:9[2] 32:20 32:21 32:22 32:27 32:28 32:31 32:32 32:33 32:34 32:35 32:36[2] 32:39[2] 32:47[2] 32:49[2] 33:1 33:7 33:17 33:22 33:26 33:27 33:29[2] 34:1 34:4

JOS
1:2 1:8 1:9 2:9 2:11 3:10 3:16 4:24 5:4 5:9 5:15
6:7 7:2 7:13 7:15 8:18 8:31 8:34 9:12[2] 10:13 11:4 12:2[2] 12:9 13:2 13:3[2] 13:4 13:9[2] 13:16[2] 13:25 13:28 14:11 15:7[2] 15:8[2] 15:9 15:10 15:12 15:13 15:20 15:25 15:49 15:54 15:60 16:8 17:10 17:16 17:18 18:7 18:13 18:14 18:16 18:17 18:28[2] 19:8 19:11 19:16 19:23 19:31 19:39 19:48 20:7 21:11 22:9 22:16 22:17 22:28 22:29 22:31 22:34 23:3 23:6 23:10 24:17 24:18 24:19[2] 24:30

JG
1:26
4:11 4:14[2] 4:20 5:9 5:28 6:12 6:13 6:15 6:24 6:25 6:31 7:1 7:3 7:14 8:2 8:21[2] 9:2 9:3 9:18 9:28[3] 9:32 9:33[2] 9:38[3] 10:8 10:18 13:17 13:18 14:3 14:15 14:18[2] 15:2 15:11 15:19 16:2[2] 16:3 16:9 16:15 17:2 18:6 18:9 18:10[2] 18:12 18:14 18:19 18:24 19:10 19:12 19:18 19:19[4] 19:23 19:24 20:5 20:12[2] 21:3 21:5 21:6 21:8 21:11 21:12 21:19[2]

RU
1:13 1:15 1:19 2:5 2:6
2:19 2:20 2:22 3:2 3:12[2] 4:3 4:4 4:11 4:15 4:17[2]

1 SA
1:8 2:1[2] 2:2[3] 2:3 2:5 2:20 2:24 2:35 2:36 3:17 3:18 4:7 4:16 4:17[2] 4:21 4:22[2] 5:7 6:3 6:9 6:20 9:6[2] 9:7[2] 9:9 9:11 9:12[3] 9:16 9:18 9:19 9:20[2] 9:24 10:1 10:5 10:7 10:11[3] 10:12[2] 10:24 11:12 12:5[3] 12:6 12:17[2] 13:5 14:1 14:2 14:6 14:7 14:17 15:7 15:11 15:22 15:23 15:28[2] 15:29 15:32 16:6 16:12
16:16[2] 16:18[2] 16:19 17:25[2] 17:26 17:29 17:46 17:47 18:18 19:14 19:17 19:19 19:22 19:24 20:1[2] 20:2 20:3 20:5 20:6 20:7[2] 20:18 20:21 20:26[2] 20:37 21:3[2] 21:4[2] 21:5 21:8 21:9[3] 21:11 21:14 22:8[3] 22:14[3] 22:17 23:7 23:19 23:22[2] 24:1 24:6 24:10 24:11 24:14 24:16 25:10[2] 25:17[2] 25:25[4] 25:29 26:1 26:3 26:4 26:5 26:11 26:15 26:16[2] 26:17[2] 26:18 26:20 27:1 28:7 28:14[2] 28:15 28:16[2] 29:1 29:3 29:5 29:6 30:20 30:24

2 SA
1:9[2] 1:18 1:19 1:21 2:7 2:16 3:12 3:13 3:23 3:24[2] 3:29 3:38 4:10 5:7 6:2 7:3[2] 7:18 7:19 7:22 7:23 7:26 10:1[2] 10:2 10:3[2] 10:4[2] 10:8 11:3 11:21 11:24 12:14 12:18 12:19 12:21 12:23 13:16[2] 13:20 13:23 13:28 13:30 13:32 13:33 13:35 14:5 14:7[2] 14:13 14:15 14:17 14:19 14:20 14:30 15:2 15:3 15:31 16:3 16:17 17:2 17:3 17:7 17:8 17:9 17:10[2] 17:11 17:14 17:20 17:29 18:3

18:13 18:18 18:20 18:25 18:27[2] 18:28 18:29 18:32[2] 19:9 19:10 19:11 19:26 19:27[2] 19:30 19:42 20:11 20:21 21:1 22:2 22:3 22:4 22:31[3] 22:32 22:33 22:35 22:48 22:51 23:5 23:15 23:17 24:16 24:21

1 KI

1:9 1:25 1:26 1:41 1:45 2:3 2:15[2] 2:22 2:29 2:35 2:38 2:42 2:43 2:44 3:6 3:8 3:9 3:22 3:27 4:12 4:13 4:20 4:29 4:33 5:4 5:6 6:1 6:17 6:38 8:1 8:2 8:21 8:23 8:24 8:35 8:41 8:46 8:60[2] 9:14 9:26 11:7 11:11 11:33 11:38 12:24 12:28 12:32 13:3 13:26 13:31 14:2 14:5 14:10 14:13 14:15 15:19 17:3 17:5 17:24 18:8 18:10[2] 18:11 18:14 18:24 18:27[4] 18:39[2] 18:41 18:43 19:4 19:7 20:3 20:6 20:28[2] 20:32[2] 21:2 21:5 21:14[2] 21:15 21:18[3] 21:21 22:3 22:7 22:8 22:13 22:16 22:32

2 KI

1:3[2] 1:6[2] 1:8 1:16[2] 2:14 2:19[2] 3:11[2] 3:12 3:18 4:1[2] 4:4 4:6 4:9 4:13 4:14[2] 4:23 4:25 4:26[4] 4:27 4:31 4:40 5:3 5:4 5:6 5:8 5:15 5:21 5:22 5:26 6:1 6:11 6:12 6:13[2] 6:19[2] 6:32 6:33 7:4 7:9 8:5[2] 8:7 8:13 9:8 9:11 9:12 9:13 9:17 9:18 9:19 9:20 9:22 9:23 9:27 9:32 9:34 9:36 9:37 10:5 10:15[3] 10:30 10:33 11:5 12:4[2] 14:6 18:10 18:17 18:19 18:21 18:22 19:3[2] 19:9 19:13 19:21 19:28 19:30 20:3 20:10 20:15 20:17 20:19[2] 22:4 22:5 22:13[4] 23:10 23:17[2] 23:21 25:4 25:8

1 CH

1:27 5:1 6:10 7:31 11:4 11:5 11:11 11:17 12:17 13:6[2] 13:11 14:15 16:14 16:25[2] 16:32 16:34 16:40 17:2[2] 17:16 17:20[2] 17:21 17:24 19:13 21:15 21:17[2] 21:23 21:24 22:1[2] 22:5[2] 22:14 22:16 22:18[2] 22:19 23:29[2] 27:6 29:1[3] 29:5 29:11[3] 29:12[2] 29:14 29:15 29:16

2 CH

1:10 1:12 2:4 2:5[2] 2:6 5:2 5:9 5:13 6:11 6:14 6:15 6:26[2] 6:32[2] 6:33 6:36 6:40 7:3 7:15 7:21 11:4 12:6 13:4 13:6 13:10 13:12 14:7 14:11 15:2 16:3 16:7 16:9 18:6 18:7[2] 18:31 19:2 19:6 19:7 19:11 20:2 20:6[2] 20:9 20:15 22:9 23:4 23:18 25:4 25:7 25:9 26:23 28:11 28:13[2] 28:22 29:10 30:9 31:3 31:10 32:7 32:8[2] 34:21[4] 35:12 35:21 36:23[2]

EZR

1:2 1:3[4] 1:4 1:5 1:9 2:68 3:2 3:4 3:11 4:11 4:15 4:19 4:24 5:2 5:8[2] 5:15 5:16[2] 5:17 6:2 6:5[2] 6:12 6:18[2] 7:11 7:14 7:15 7:16 7:17 7:23 7:25 7:27 8:1 8:22[2] 9:6 9:7 9:11 9:13 9:15 10:2 10:13[2] 10:23

NE

1:3 2:2[2] 2:19 4:10[2] 4:14 4:19 5:5[2] 5:9 5:14 6:6 6:7 6:11 8:9[2] 8:10[3] 8:11 8:15 9:5 9:6 9:10 9:18 9:33 10:34 10:36 13:11 13:17

ES

1:1 1:19 1:20 2:7 2:16[2] 3:7[3] 3:8[2] 3:11 3:13 4:11[2] 4:16 5:3 5:6[2] 5:7 6:3 6:4 6:8 7:2[2] 7:5[2] 7:6 8:8 8:9 8:12 9:1 9:12[2] 9:24

JOB

1:8 1:10 1:12 1:16 2:3 2:6 3:3 3:19 3:20[2] 3:23[2] 3:25[2] 4:5 4:6 4:19 4:21 5:4 5:7 5:13 5:17 5:27 6:6[2] 6:11[2] 6:12[2] 6:13[2] 6:14 6:16 6:17 6:26 6:28 6:29 6:30 7:1 7:5[2] 7:7 7:9 7:17 8:12 8:16 8:19 9:1 9:4 9:19 9:22 9:24[2] 9:32 9:33 9:35 10:1 10:3 10:7 10:13 10:22 11:4 11:6 11:8 11:9 11:18 12:4 12:5[3] 12:10 12:12 12:13 12:16 12:24 13:9 13:19 13:28 14:1[2] 14:2 14:7 14:10 14:17 14:18 15:9 15:11 15:14[2] 15:16 15:20 15:21 15:22 15:23[2] 15:31 16:6 16:8 16:16[2] 16:17 16:19[2] 17:1 17:3 17:7 17:12 17:13 17:15 17:16 18:8 18:10 18:15 18:21 19:7 19:17 19:28 19:29 20:5 20:7 20:14[2] 20:23[2] 20:25 20:26 20:29 21:4 21:8 21:9 21:15 21:16[2] 21:17 21:21 21:28 21:30 22:2 22:3[2] 22:5 22:12 22:18 22:20 22:29 22:30 23:2[2] 23:8 23:13 23:14 24:14 24:17 24:18[2] 24:22 25:3 25:4 25:6[2] 26:2 26:3 26:6 26:8 26:14 27:3[2] 27:8 27:11 27:13 27:14 27:19 28:1 28:2[2] 28:5 28:7 28:11 28:12 28:13 28:14[2] 28:18 28:20 28:21 28:28[2] 30:16 30:18 30:30 30:31 31:2 31:3 31:11[2] 31:12 31:28 31:35 32:8 32:19[2] 33:9 33:12 33:19 33:21 33:24 34:4 34:6 34:7 34:17 34:18 34:22 34:31 34:36 35:2 35:10 35:14 35:15 36:4[2] 36:5[2] 36:14 36:16 36:18 36:26 37:1 37:4 37:10[2] 37:12 37:16 37:18 37:20 37:22 37:23 38:2 38:14 38:15 38:19[2] 38:21 38:24 38:26[2] 38:30 39:8 39:11 39:16[2] 39:20 39:22 39:24 39:30 40:11 40:12 40:16[2] 40:19 41:9 41:10[2] 41:11[2] 41:16 41:22 41:24 41:33[2] 41:34 42:3 42:7[2] 42:8

PS

1:1 1:2 2:12 3:2 3:8 4:3 5:9[3] 6:3 6:5 6:7 7:2 7:4 7:8 7:10 7:11 7:15 8:1 8:4 8:9 9:6 9:15 9:16[2] 10:4 10:7[2] 10:11 10:16 11:4[2] 12:4 14:1[2] 14:3 14:5 14:6 15:4 16:3 16:5 16:8 16:9 16:11 17:12 17:13 18:2 18:3 18:30[3] 18:31[2] 18:32 18:34 18:47 19:3[3] 19:4 19:5 19:6[2] 19:7[2] 19:8 19:9 19:11[2] 21:5 22:11[2] 22:14[2] 22:15 22:28[2] 23:1 24:1 24:6 24:8 24:10[2] 25:8 25:11 25:12 25:14 26:3 26:10[2] 27:1[2] 28:3 28:7 28:8[2] 29:3[2] 29:4[2] 30:5 30:9 31:9 31:10 31:19 32:1[3] 32:2[2] 32:4 32:6 33:1 33:4 33:5 33:12[2] 33:16[2] 33:17 33:18 33:20 34:8[2] 34:9 34:12 34:16 34:18 34:20 35:10[2] 36:1 36:4 36:5 36:6 36:7 36:9 37:13 37:16 37:26[2] 37:31 37:33 37:37 37:39[2] 38:3[2] 38:7 38:9[2] 38:10 38:17 38:20 39:1 39:4 39:5[2] 39:7 39:11 40:4 40:7 40:8 41:1 42:3 42:6 42:10 42:11 43:5 44:15 44:17 44:18 44:25 45:1[2] 45:2 45:6[2] 45:11 45:13[2] 46:1 46:4 46:5 46:7[2] 46:11[2] 47:2[2] 47:5 47:7 47:9 48:1 48:2 48:3 48:10[2] 48:14 49:8 49:11 49:12 49:13 49:16[2] 49:20[2] 50:6 50:10 50:12 51:3 52:*title* 52:7 52:9 53:1[2] 53:3[2] 54:4[2] 54:6 55:4 55:11 55:15 56:9 57:4 57:6 57:7[2] 57:10 58:4 58:11[2] 59:8 59:17 60:7[4] 60:8 60:11 60:12 61:2[2] 62:2[2] 62:5 62:6[2] 62:7[2] 62:8 63:1 63:3 64:6 65:4 65:9 66:5 66:10 68:2 68:5 68:15 68:16 68:17 68:20[2] 68:27 68:34[2] 68:35 69:2 69:3 69:13 69:16 71:11 71:18 71:19[2] 73:1 73:4 73:11 73:25 73:26 73:28 74:9[2] 74:12 74:16[2] 75:1 75:7 75:8[3] 76:1[2] 76:2 76:12 77:8 77:10 77:13[2] 77:19 79:10[2] 80:16[2] 83:8 83:18 84:5[2] 84:10 84:11 84:12 85:9 85:12 86:8 86:13 87:1 88:3 89:7 89:8 89:10 89:11 89:13[2] 89:15 89:18[2] 89:19 89:34 89:41 89:47 89:48 90:4 90:6 90:9 90:10[2] 90:11 91:2 91:9 92:1 92:7 92:15[3] 93:1[3] 93:2 93:4 94:12 94:22[2] 95:3 95:4 95:5 95:7 95:10 96:4[2] 96:12 97:11 99:2[2] 99:3 99:5 99:9 100:3[2] 100:5[2] 102:*title* 102:4 102:13 103:1 103:5 103:8 103:11[2] 103:12 103:16 103:17 103:20 104:13 104:20 104:24 104:25 104:26 105:7 106:1 107:1 107:40 107:43 108:1 108:4 108:8[4] 108:9 108:12 108:13 109:19 109:21 109:22 109:27 111:3 111:4 111:9 111:10 112:1 112:4 112:7 112:8 113:3 113:4 113:5 115:2 115:3 115:8 115:9 115:10 115:11 116:5[2] 116:15 117:2 118:1 118:6 118:8 118:9 118:14[2] 118:15 118:16 118:22 118:23[2] 118:24 118:27 118:29 119:38 119:50 119:64 119:70 119:71 119:72 119:77 119:89 119:90 119:96 119:97 119:105 119:109 119:118 119:126 119:140 119:142[2] 119:144 119:155 119:160 119:174 120:5 121:5[2] 122:3[2] 123:4 124:7[2] 124:8 125:2 127:2 127:3 127:5 128:1 129:4 130:4 130:7[2] 131:1 131:2[2] 132:14 133:1 133:2 135:3[2] 135:5[2] 135:17 135:18 136:1 138:5 139:4 139:6 139:17 140:3 143:4[2] 143:10 144:3 144:4 144:8 144:10 144:11 144:15[4] 145:3[2] 145:8 145:9 145:13 145:17 145:18 146:3 146:5[2] 146:6 147:1[3] 147:5[2] 148:13[2]

PR

1:7 1:17 1:19 2:7 2:10 3:13 3:14 3:15 3:16 3:18[2] 3:19 3:27[2] 3:32[2] 3:33 4:7 4:13 4:16 4:18 4:19 5:3 5:4 6:14 6:23[2] 6:26 6:30 6:34 7:11 7:12 7:19 7:23 7:27 8:4 8:7 8:8 8:11 8:13 8:14 8:19 8:34 9:4 9:10[2] 9:13[2] 9:16 9:17 10:1 10:5[2] 10:7 10:11 10:13[3] 10:14 10:15[2] 10:17 10:18 10:19 10:20[2] 10:23 10:25[2] 10:26 10:29 10:32 11:1[2] 11:2 11:8 11:10 11:11[2] 11:12 11:13 11:14[2] 11:15[2] 11:17 11:22[2] 11:23[2] 11:24[3] 11:30[2] 12:1 12:4[2] 12:8 12:9[2] 12:11 12:13 12:15[2] 12:16 12:18[2] 12:19 12:20[2] 12:26 12:27 12:28[2] 13:5 13:6 13:7[2] 13:10 13:12 13:14 13:15 13:17 13:19[2] 13:22 13:23[3] 14:2 14:3 14:4[2] 14:6 14:8[2] 14:9 14:12 14:13[2] 14:16 14:17[2] 14:20 14:21 14:23 14:24[2] 14:26 14:27 14:28[2] 14:29[3] 14:30 14:32 14:33[2] 14:34 14:35[2] 15:4[2] 15:5 15:6[2] 15:8[2] 15:9 15:10 15:13 15:15 15:16 15:17[2] 15:18 15:19[2] 15:21[2] 15:23 15:24 15:27 15:29 15:33[2] 16:1 16:5[2] 16:6 16:8 16:10 16:12 16:14 16:15[2] 16:16 16:17 16:19 16:20 16:22 16:25 16:27 16:29 16:31 16:32[2] 16:33[2] 17:1 17:3 17:5 17:8 17:14 17:16 17:17 17:24 17:25 17:26 17:27 17:28[2] 18:5 18:7 18:9[3] 18:10[2] 18:11 18:12[2] 18:13 18:17 18:19 18:24 19:1[3] 19:2 19:4 19:6 19:10 19:11 19:12[2] 19:13 19:14 19:18 19:22[2] 19:26 20:1[4] 20:2 20:3 20:5 20:11 20:14[3] 20:15 20:16 20:17 20:18 20:23 20:25[2] 20:27 20:28 20:29[2] 21:1 21:2 21:3 21:4 21:5 21:6 21:8[2] 21:9 21:11[3] 21:15 21:19 21:20 21:24 21:27 21:30 21:31[2] 22:1 22:2 22:6 22:7 22:13 22:14[2] 22:15 22:18 22:22 23:1 23:5 23:7[2] 23:11 23:18 23:22 23:27[2] 23:31 24:3[2] 24:5 24:6 24:7 24:9[2] 24:10 24:13[2] 24:23 25:2[2] 25:3 25:7 25:11 25:12 25:13 25:14 25:15 25:16 25:18 25:19 25:20 25:24 25:25 25:26 25:27[2] 25:28[2] 26:1 26:7 26:8 26:9 26:12 26:13[2] 26:16 26:17 26:19 26:20[2] 26:21 26:26 27:3[2] 27:4[3] 27:5 27:7 27:8 27:10[2] 27:13 27:21 28:3 28:6[2] 28:7[2] 28:11 28:12[2] 28:14 28:15 28:16 28:18 28:21 28:24[2] 28:25 28:26 29:6 29:9 29:18[2] 29:20[2] 29:24 29:27[3] 30:4[2] 30:5[2] 30:9 30:11 30:12[2] 30:13 30:14 30:15 30:16[2] 30:20 30:21 30:22 30:23[2] 30:28 30:30 30:31 31:4[2] 31:6 31:10 31:14 31:15 31:18 31:21 31:22 31:23 31:26 31:30[2]

EC

1:2 1:7 1:8 1:9[4] 1:10 1:11 1:14 1:15[2] 1:17 1:18 2:1 2:2 2:15 2:16[2] 2:17[3] 2:19 2:21[3] 2:23 2:24 2:26[3] 3:1 3:2 3:12 3:13 3:15[3] 3:17 3:19 3:22[2] 4:3[2] 4:4[2] 4:6 4:8[6] 4:10 4:12 4:13 4:14 4:16[2] 5:2 5:3 5:5 5:8 5:9[2] 5:10 5:11 5:12 5:13 5:14 5:16 5:18[2] 5:19 6:1[2] 6:2[2] 6:3 6:7[2] 6:9[2] 6:10[4] 6:11 6:12 7:1 7:2[2] 7:3[2] 7:4[2] 7:5 7:6[2] 7:8[2] 7:10 7:11[2] 7:12[3] 7:15[2] 7:18 7:20 7:24 7:26 8:1 8:4[2] 8:6[2] 8:9[2] 8:10 8:11[2] 8:14[3] 8:16[2] 8:17 9:1 9:2[3] 9:3[4] 9:4[3] 9:5 9:6[2] 9:9 9:10 9:11 9:16[2] 9:18 10:1 10:2 10:3[2] 10:5 10:6 10:10 10:11 10:13[2] 10:14 10:16 10:17 10:19 11:5[2] 11:7[2] 11:8 12:4 12:5 12:8 12:12[2] 12:13

CA

1:1 1:2 1:3 1:13 1:14 1:16 2:2 2:3 2:6 2:9 2:11[2] 2:12[2] 2:14[2] 2:16 3:6 3:7

4:1
4:2
4:3
4:4
4:7
4:10[2]
4:11
4:12
5:2[2]
5:9[2]
5:10
5:11
5:14
5:15
5:16[4]
6:1[2]
6:2
6:3
6:5
6:6
6:9[2]
6:10
7:2[2]
7:4[2]
7:5[2]
7:7
7:10
8:5
8:6[2]
8:12[2]

ISA

1:5
1:6
1:7[2]
1:8
1:11
1:13[2]
1:21
1:22
2:7[4]
2:8
2:12[2]
2:22[2]
3:7
3:8[2]
3:14
4:3[2]
5:7
5:16
5:25[3]
5:30
6:3[2]
6:5
6:7
7:2
7:8[2]
7:9[2]
7:13
7:18[2]
7:20
7:22
8:10
8:20[2]
9:5
9:6[2]
9:12[2]
9:15
9:17[3]
9:19
9:21[2]
10:4[2]
10:5
10:7
10:9[3]
10:28[2]
10:29[2]
10:32
12:1
12:2[3]
12:4
12:5
12:6
13:6
13:15[2]
13:22
14:6
14:7[2]
14:8
14:9
14:11[2]
14:16
14:26[4]
14:27
14:29
15:1[2]
15:2
15:6[2]
15:8
16:4
16:6
16:9
16:10
16:12[2]
16:13
17:1
17:14[2]
18:1
18:5[2]
19:11
20:6
21:2
21:9[2]
22:5
22:15
22:25
23:1[3]
23:3[2]
23:7[2]
23:10
23:14
24:5
24:10[2]
24:11[3]
24:12[2]
24:13
24:19[3]
25:4
25:7
25:9[2]
25:10
26:3
26:4
26:7
26:8
26:11
26:17
26:19
27:1
27:4
27:7
27:9
27:11
28:1
28:4[2]
28:8
28:12[2]
28:14
28:20
28:27
28:28
28:29
29:8[2]
29:11[4]
29:12[2]
29:13
29:17
29:20[2]
30:7
30:9
30:14
30:18
30:21
30:27
30:29
30:33[3]
31:2
31:3
31:4
31:9
33:5
33:6
33:9[2]
33:17
33:18[3]
33:22[3]
33:23
34:1[2]
34:9[2]
34:8
36:4
36:6
36:7
37:3[2]
37:4
37:9
37:13
37:21
37:29
37:31
38:3
38:8
38:12[2]
38:16
38:22
39:4[2]
39:6
39:8
40:2[2]
40:6[2]
40:7
40:10
40:16
40:20
40:22
40:26
40:27[2]
40:28[2]
41:7
41:17
41:24
41:26[4]
42:8
42:10
42:19[3]
42:21
42:22
43:7
43:9
43:11
43:13
43:14
44:3
44:6
44:8[2]
44:10
44:12[2]
44:16
44:19
44:20
44:28
45:5[2]
45:6[2]
45:14[3]
45:18
45:21[2]
45:22
45:23
46:9[2]
47:1
47:4
48:2
48:4
48:22
49:4
49:6
49:7
49:20
50:1[3]
50:2[2]
50:4
50:8[2]
50:9
50:10
51:5[2]
51:7
51:13
51:15
51:18[2]
52:5[2]
52:6
53:1
53:2
53:3
53:7[2]
54:5[2]
54:9
54:17[3]
55:2[2]
55:6
56:1
56:2
57:1
57:6
57:10
57:15[2]
57:19[2]
57:21
58:5[2]
58:6
58:7
59:1
59:5
59:6
59:8
59:9
59:11[2]
59:14[2]
59:21[2]
60:1[2]
61:1
62:11
63:1[2]
63:4[2]
63:11[2]
63:15
63:16
64:5
64:7
64:10
64:11
65:4
65:6
65:8[2]
66:1[4]
66:2
66:3

JER

1:13
2:6
2:8
2:14[3]
2:19[2]
2:22
2:25
2:26[3]
2:34
3:6
3:23[2]
4:7[3]
4:8
4:18[2]
4:20[2]
4:22
4:31[2]
5:12
5:13
5:15[2]
5:16
5:19
5:27
5:30
6:6[2]
6:7[2]
6:10[2]
6:11
6:13
6:14
6:16
6:18
6:25
6:29
7:10
7:11[2]
7:14
7:28[3]
7:30
7:31
8:5
8:8[2]
8:9
8:10
8:11
8:16
8:18
8:19
8:20[2]
8:22[3]
9:6
9:8
9:12[3]
9:19
9:21[2]
10:5
10:6[2]
10:7
10:8
10:9[2]
10:10[2]
10:13
10:14[4]
10:16[4]
10:19[3]
10:20[2]
10:22
10:23[2]
11:5
11:9
11:15
11:19
12:8
12:9
12:11
13:4
13:10
13:17
13:20
13:25
14:2
14:4
14:17[2]
14:19[2]
15:9
15:10
15:14
15:18
16:10[2]
16:17
16:19
16:21
17:1[2]
17:7[2]
17:9
17:12
17:15
18:6
18:12
19:2
20:11
20:15
21:12
22:14
22:28[3]
23:6
23:9
23:10[3]
23:15
23:19
23:28
23:29
23:33
25:3
25:13
25:18
25:29
25:38
26:11
26:16
28:6
29:26
29:28
30:7[3]
30:12[2]
30:13
30:15
30:17
30:21
31:9
31:17
31:20[2]
31:35
32:7[2]
32:8[4]
32:14
32:17
32:18
32:24[2]
32:25
32:27
32:34
32:43[2]
33:2
33:5
33:11
33:12
33:16
34:8
34:15
36:7
37:7
37:14
37:17[2]
38:5
38:9[3]
38:14
38:21
40:3
40:4
41:17
43:9
43:13
44:22
44:23
45:3
46:7
46:10
46:17
46:18[2]
46:20
47:2
47:5[2]
48:1[3]
48:4
48:11
48:15[2]
48:16
48:17
48:19
48:20[3]
48:21
48:25[2]
48:29
48:32
48:33
48:38
48:39
48:41
48:47
49:3
49:7[3]
49:10[2]
49:14
49:19[3]
49:21
49:23[2]
49:24
49:25
49:29
50:2[3]
50:15
50:17
50:22
50:23[2]
50:25
50:27
50:31
50:34[2]
50:35
50:36[2]
50:37[2]
50:38[2]
50:44[3]
50:46[2]
51:6
51:8
51:9[2]
51:11[2]
51:13
51:16
51:17[4]
51:19[4]
51:31
51:33[2]
51:41[3]
51:42[2]
51:48
51:55
51:56[2]
51:57
52:28

LA

1:1
1:3
1:4
1:6
1:8
1:9
1:12[2]
1:14
1:16
1:17[2]
1:18
1:20[2]
1:21
1:22
2:9
2:11
2:12
2:13
2:15
2:16
2:3
2:18
2:20
2:22
2:23
2:24
2:25
2:26
2:27
2:30
2:37
2:47
4:1[2]
4:3
4:6
4:8[3]
4:15
4:18[2]
4:22
5:1
5:2
5:4
5:8
5:15[2]
5:16
5:17
5:18

EZE

1:28
3:21
4:14
5:5
6:12[3]
7:2
7:3
7:5
7:6[3]
7:10[2]
7:11
7:12[2]
7:13[2]
7:14
7:15[3]
7:19
7:23[2]
8:17
9:6
9:9[2]
10:15
10:20
11:3[2]
11:7
11:15
11:23
12:12
12:19
12:22
12:23
12:27
13:12[2]
13:15
13:16
15:2[2]
15:4[3]
15:5
16:7
16:20
16:30
16:34[2]
16:44[2]
16:46[2]
17:12
18:4
18:5
18:9
18:10
18:18
18:19
18:21
18:25[2]
18:27
18:29
19:2
19:10
19:13
19:14[2]
20:6
20:15
20:29[2]
21:9
21:10[2]
21:11[2]
21:13
21:14
21:15[2]
21:16
21:25
21:26[2]
21:27
21:28[2]
21:29
22:18
22:22
22:24
22:25
23:4
23:20[2]
23:22
23:28
23:37
23:45
24:6[2]
24:7
24:13
24:24
24:27
25:8
26:2[3]
26:10
26:15
28:5
29:3
29:9
30:3[2]
30:5
30:12
31:10
31:18
32:16
32:20
32:22
32:23
32:24
32:25
32:26
32:29
33:6
33:14
33:16
33:17[2]
33:19
33:20
33:21
33:24
33:27
33:30
34:5
34:12
36:35
37:11
37:19
38:8[3]
39:4
39:8[3]
40:45[2]
40:46[2]
41:4
41:22[2]
42:13
42:15
43:4
43:12[2]
43:13
44:3
44:9
44:22
44:26
44:31
45:13
45:14
45:20
46:11
46:20
47:16[2]
47:17
47:18
47:19
47:20
48:12
48:14
48:22
48:29
48:35

DA

2:5
2:8
2:9
2:10[2]
2:11[3]
2:15
2:22
2:28
2:30
2:36
2:43
2:45
2:47[2]
3:4
3:14
3:15
3:17
3:25
3:29
4:3[2]
4:8
4:9
4:17
4:18
4:22[2]
4:24[3]
4:30
4:31[2]
4:34[2]
4:37
5:11[2]
5:14[2]
5:23
5:25
5:26
5:28
6:12
6:13
6:15
6:20
6:26
7:14
7:27
7:28
8:2
8:21[3]
8:26
9:11[2]
9:13[2]
9:14
9:17
9:18
10:4
10:14
10:17
10:21[2]
11:35
11:36
12:12

HO

2:2
4:1
4:13
4:17
4:18
5:1
5:3[2]
5:4
6:3
6:4
6:8[2]
6:10[2]
7:7
7:8
7:11
8:3
8:5
8:6
8:8[2]
9:7[2]
9:8
9:13
9:15
9:16[2]
10:1
10:2
10:5
10:7
10:10
10:11[2]
10:12
11:8
11:12
12:1
12:5
12:7
13:3
13:4
13:8
13:9
13:10
13:12[2]
13:13
14:4
14:8
14:9

JOE

1:5
1:6
1:9
1:10[3]
1:11
1:12[2]
1:13
1:15
1:16
1:17[2]
2:1
2:3
2:4
2:11[3]
2:13
2:17
3:13[3]
3:14

AM

2:11
2:13[2]
2:15
2:16
3:5
4:3
4:13[2]
5:2[3]
5:8
5:11
5:12
5:13
5:18[2]
5:27
6:8
6:10[2]
7:2
7:5
7:10
7:13[2]
8:2
9:5
9:6[2]
9:9
9:11

OB

1
3
7
15
20

JON

1:2
1:7
1:8[3]
1:12
2:9
3:8
4:3
4:8

MIC

1:2
1:5[3]
1:9[3]
1:13
2:1[2]
2:3
2:7
2:8
2:10[2]
2:13
3:1
3:8
3:11
4:6
4:9[2]
5:2
6:8
6:10
6:12
7:1[2]
7:2[2]
7:4[2]
7:10[2]
7:18

NA

1:2[2]
1:3
1:5
1:6
1:7
1:11
1:15
2:1
2:3
2:8
2:9
2:10[2]
2:11
3:1
3:3[2]
3:7
3:17
3:18
3:19[2]

HAB

1:4
1:13
1:16
2:3
2:4[2]
2:5[2]
2:6
2:13
2:19
2:20
3:19

ZEP

1:7
1:8
1:14[2]
1:15
2:5
2:15[3]
3:1
3:5
3:6[2]
3:8
3:15
3:17

HAG

1:2
1:4
1:6
1:9
1:10[2]
2:3[2]
2:6
2:8[2]
2:13
2:14[4]
2:19

ZEC

1:7
1:11
2:2[2]
2:13
3:2
4:1
4:6
5:2
5:3
5:5
5:6[3]
5:7
5:8
6:12
7:13
8:23[2]
9:9
9:11
9:17[2]
10:5
10:7
11:2[2]
11:3[3]
11:9
11:16
12:8
12:10
13:7
13:8
13:9[4]
14:4
14:16

MAL

1:6[2]
1:7
1:8[2]
1:10
1:12[2]
1:13
1:14
2:1
2:7
2:11
2:14
2:17[2]
3:2
3:14[2]

MT

1:16
1:20[2]
1:23
2:2[2]
2:5
3:2
3:3
3:9
3:10[2]
3:11
3:12
3:17
4:4
4:6
4:7
4:10
4:13
4:16
4:17
5:3
5:10
5:12
5:13
5:14
5:16
5:22
5:29
5:30
5:32
5:34
5:35[2]
5:37
5:45
5:48[2]
6:1
6:6
6:10
6:13
6:18
6:21
6:22
6:23[2]
6:25
6:30[2]
6:34
7:3[2]
7:4
7:6
7:9
7:11
7:12
7:13
7:14[2]
7:19
7:21
8:27
9:5
9:15
9:16[2]
9:18
9:24
9:37
10:2
10:7
10:10
10:11
10:20
10:24
10:25
10:26
10:28
10:32
10:35
10:37[2]
10:38
11:6
11:10[2]
11:11[2]
11:14
11:16
11:19
11:30[2]
12:2
12:6
12:8
12:10
12:12[2]
12:18
12:23
12:25
12:26
12:38
12:30[2]
12:33
12:41
12:42
12:43
12:44
12:45
12:48
12:50[2]
13:11[2]
13:14
13:15
13:19
13:20
13:21
13:22
13:23
13:24
13:31
13:32[3]
13:33
13:37
13:38
13:39[2]
13:44
13:45
13:47
13:52[3]
13:55[2]
13:57
14:2[2]
14:4
14:15[2]
14:26
14:27
15:5
15:8
15:17
15:22
15:26
15:28
16:2[2]
16:3
16:7
16:11
16:17
16:26
17:4
17:5
17:12
17:15
18:1
18:4
18:8
18:9
18:10
18:11
18:12
18:14[2]
18:19
18:23
19:3
19:9
19:10
19:11
19:12
19:14
19:17[2]
19:24
19:26
20:1[2]
20:4
20:7
20:14
20:15[2]
20:23[2]
21:9
21:10
21:11
21:13
21:20
21:21
21:38
21:42[3]
22:2
22:8
22:17
22:20
22:23
22:32
22:36
22:38
22:39
22:42
22:45
23:8
23:9[2]
23:10
23:11
23:16[2]
23:17
23:18[2]
23:19
23:26
23:38
23:39
24:6
24:17
24:18
24:23
24:26[2]
24:28
24:32[2]
24:33
24:45
24:46
24:50
25:14
25:25
26:2[2]
26:8
26:18
26:22
26:24[2]
26:25
26:26
26:28[2]
26:31
26:38
26:41[2]
26:45[2]
26:46
26:48
26:62
26:66
26:68
27:4
27:6[2]
27:17
27:22
27:33
27:37
27:46
27:64
28:6[2]
28:7
28:15
28:18

MK

1:2
1:15[2]
1:27[2]
2:9
2:16
2:19
2:21
2:22
2:24
2:26
2:28
3:4
3:17
3:21
3:29
3:33
3:35
4:11
4:15
4:21
4:22
4:26
4:29[2]
4:31[3]
4:32
4:40
4:41
5:9[2]
5:35
5:39
5:41
6:2[2]
6:3
6:4
6:15[2]
6:16[2]
6:18
6:35[2]
6:50
7:2
7:6[2]
7:11[2]
7:15
7:27
7:29
7:34
8:16
8:21
9:5
9:7
9:12
9:13[2]
9:21
9:26
9:31[2]
9:39
9:40[2]
9:42
9:43
9:44
9:45
9:46
9:47
9:48
9:50
10:2
10:14
10:18[2]
10:24
10:25
10:27
10:29
10:40[2]
11:9
11:17
11:21
11:25
11:26
12:7
12:10
12:11
12:14
12:16
12:18
12:27
12:28
12:29[2]
12:30
12:31[2]
12:32[2]
12:33
12:35
12:37
13:11
13:15
13:16
13:21[2]
13:28[2]
13:29
13:33
13:34
14:8
14:14
14:19[2]
14:20
14:21[2]
14:22
14:24[2]
14:27
14:34
14:38[2]
14:41[3]
14:42
14:44
14:58
14:60
14:69
15:22
15:34
15:42
16:6[2]
16:16

LU

1:13
1:28
1:36
1:42
1:43
1:45
1:49[2]
1:50
1:61[2]
1:63
2:4
2:11[2]
2:15
2:23
2:24
2:34
2:49
3:4
3:8
3:9[2]
3:13
3:17
4:4
4:6
4:8
4:10
4:12
4:18
4:21
4:22
4:24
4:36
5:21
5:23
5:34
5:39
6:2
6:4
6:5
6:9
6:20
6:23
6:35
6:36
6:40[2]
6:41[2]
6:42[3]
6:44
6:45[2]
6:47
6:48
6:49
7:16
7:22
7:23
7:27
7:28[3]
7:34
7:35
7:39[2]
7:47
7:49
8:10
8:11[2]
8:17
8:25[2]
8:26
8:30
8:46
8:49
8:52
9:9
9:19
9:25
9:33
9:35
9:38
9:48
9:50[2]
9:56
9:62
10:2
10:7
10:9
10:11
10:22[2]
10:26
10:29
10:42
11:4
11:6
11:7
11:8
11:11
11:17
11:20
11:23[2]
11:24
11:26
11:27
11:29
11:31
11:32
11:34[5]
11:35
11:39
11:40[2]

12:1 12:2 12:6 12:21[2] 12:23[2] 12:26 12:27 12:28[2] 12:32 12:34 12:42 12:43 12:46 12:48 12:54 12:56 12:57 13:18 13:19 13:21 13:25 13:35[2] 14:3 14:15 14:22[2] 14:29 14:32 14:34 14:35 15:4 15:10 15:24[2] 15:27 15:31 15:32[2] 16:2 16:10[5] 16:12[2] 16:15[2] 16:16 16:17 16:18 16:25 16:26 17:1 17:7 17:21 17:30 17:31 17:37 18:16 18:19[2] 18:25 18:29 19:7 19:9[2] 19:10 19:20 19:46[2] 20:2 20:14 20:17[3] 20:22 20:27 20:33 20:38 20:41 20:44 21:9 21:20 21:30 21:31 21:37 22:1 22:11 22:19[2] 22:20[2] 22:21 22:22 22:26[2] 22:27[2] 22:37 22:38 22:53 22:59 22:64 23:2 23:15 23:33 23:38 24:6[2] 24:21 24:29[2] 24:34 24:39 24:46

JOH

1:15 1:18 1:19 1:27 1:30[2] 1:33 1:34 1:38 1:41 1:42 1:47 2:4 2:10 3:4 3:6[4] 3:8[2] 3:13 3:18[3] 3:19[2] 3:29[2] 3:31[4] 3:33 4:5 4:9 4:10 4:11 4:18 4:20 4:22 4:23 4:24 4:25[2] 4:29 4:34 4:37 4:42 4:54 5:2[2] 5:7 5:10[2] 5:12 5:24 5:25[2] 5:27 5:28 5:30 5:31 5:32[2] 5:45 6:1 6:7 6:9 6:14 6:20 6:29 6:31 6:33 6:39 6:40 6:42[2] 6:45 6:46 6:50 6:51 6:55[2] 6:58 6:60 6:70 7:4 7:6[2] 7:8 7:11 7:12 7:16 7:18[2] 7:22 7:25 7:26 7:27[2] 7:28 7:36 7:40 7:41 8:7 8:13 8:14 8:16 8:17[2] 8:19 8:26 8:29 8:34 8:39 8:44[2] 8:47 8:50 8:52 8:53 8:54[3] 9:4 9:7 9:8 9:9[2] 9:11 9:12 9:16[2] 9:17 9:19 9:20 9:21 9:23 9:24 9:29 9:30[2] 9:36 9:37 10:1 10:2 10:12 10:13 10:20 10:29[2] 10:34 10:38 11:3 11:4 11:10 11:14 11:16 11:28 11:50 12:13 12:14 12:19 12:23 12:27 12:31 12:34 12:35 12:50 13:10[2] 13:16[2] 13:19 13:25 13:26 13:31[2] 14:21 14:22 14:24 14:26 14:28 14:29 15:1 15:6[2] 15:8 15:12 15:20 15:25 15:26 16:7 16:8 16:11 16:13 16:17 16:18 16:21[4] 16:32 17:1 17:3 17:12 17:17 18:31 18:36[2] 18:37 18:38 19:13 19:17 19:30 19:35 19:40 20:16 20:31 21:7 21:14 21:20 21:22 21:23 21:24[2]

AC

1:7 1:8 1:11 1:12 1:19[2] 1:20 2:15 2:16 2:25 2:29[2] 2:34 2:39 3:2 3:11 3:16 4:9 4:11[2] 4:12[2] 4:16 4:24 4:36 5:9 5:17 5:32 6:2 6:9 7:33 7:34 7:37 7:38 7:40 7:42 7:49[3] 8:10 8:21 8:26 8:33 8:36 8:37 9:5 9:11 9:15 9:20 9:21 9:22 9:36 10:4 10:5 10:6 10:14 10:21 10:28[2] 10:30 10:32[2] 10:34 10:35 10:36 11:13 12:15 12:22 13:8 13:9 13:11 13:26 13:33 13:38 13:40 15:15 15:16 15:17 15:19 16:12 17:3 17:7 17:19 17:24 17:25 17:29 19:4 19:27 19:28 19:34 19:35[2] 19:38 20:10 20:32 20:35 21:22 21:28 22:22 22:25 22:26 23:5 23:8 23:19 25:14 25:16[2] 26:14 26:18 27:8 27:12 27:16 27:33 27:34 28:4 28:22 28:27 28:28

RO

1:8 1:9 1:12 1:15 1:16 1:17[2] 1:18 1:19 1:25 1:26 1:27 2:2 2:11 2:24[2] 2:25 2:27 2:28[4] 2:29[4] 3:1 3:4 3:5 3:8 3:10[2] 3:11[2] 3:12 3:13[2] 3:14 3:18 3:20 3:21 3:22[2] 3:24 3:27[2] 3:28 3:29[2] 3:30 4:4 4:5 4:8 4:14 4:15[2] 4:16[4] 4:17 5:5[2] 5:13[2] 5:14 5:15 5:16[2] 6:6 6:7[2] 6:21 6:23[2] 7:2[2] 7:3[2] 7:4 7:7 7:12 7:13 7:14 7:16 7:17 7:18[3] 7:20 7:21 7:23 8:1 8:6[2] 8:7[2] 8:9 8:10[2] 8:24[2] 8:27 8:33 8:34[4] 8:36 8:39 9:5 9:8 9:9 9:13 9:14 9:16 9:30 9:33 10:1 10:2 10:4 10:5 10:6[2] 10:7 10:8[2] 10:10 10:12[2] 10:15 10:20 11:5 11:6[4] 11:8 11:11 11:16 11:24 11:25 11:26 11:27 12:1 12:2 12:3 12:6 12:9[2] 12:19[2] 13:1 13:3 13:4[3] 13:7 13:9 13:10 13:11[2] 13:12[2] 14:1 14:2 14:4 14:11 14:14[2] 14:17 14:18 14:20 14:21[3] 14:22 14:23[3] 15:3 15:9 15:15 15:21 15:27 16:1[2] 16:5[2] 16:19[2] 16:25 16:26

1 CO

1:2 1:4 1:9 1:13 1:18[2] 1:19 1:20[3] 1:25[2] 1:30 1:31 2:9 2:11 2:12 2:15[2] 3:3 3:5[2] 3:7 3:10 3:11[2] 3:13 3:17 3:19[2] 3:23 4:2 4:3 4:4 4:6 4:17 4:20 5:1[3] 5:6 5:7 5:11 6:5 6:7 6:13 6:16[2] 6:17 6:18 6:19[2] 7:1 7:8 7:9 7:14[2] 7:15 7:18[2] 7:19[2] 7:22[4] 7:24 7:26[2] 7:29 7:32 7:33 7:34[2] 7:35 7:39[2] 7:40 8:3 8:4[2] 8:6 8:7[2] 8:10 9:3 9:9 9:10 9:11 9:16 9:17 9:18 9:25 10:7 10:13[2] 10:16[2] 10:19[3] 10:25 10:26 10:27 10:28[2] 10:29 11:3[3] 11:5 11:7[2] 11:8 11:11 11:12[2] 11:13 11:14 11:15[2] 11:20 11:21[2] 11:24[2] 11:25 12:3 12:6 12:7 12:8 12:12[2] 12:14 12:15 12:16 13:4[2] 13:5 13:10[3] 13:13 14:5 14:7 14:9 14:10 14:14 14:15 14:17 14:21 14:24[2] 14:25 14:26 14:33 14:34 14:35 15:12 15:13 15:14[2] 15:16 15:17 15:20 15:26 15:27[2] 15:36 15:39[2] 15:40[2] 15:41 15:42[3] 15:43[4] 15:44[4] 15:45 15:46[3] 15:47[2] 15:48[2] 15:54[2] 15:55[2] 15:56[2] 15:58 16:9 16:15 16:19

2 CO

1:1 1:6[3] 1:7 1:12 1:18 1:21 2:2 2:3 2:6 2:16 3:5 3:11[2] 3:13 3:14 3:15[2] 3:17[3] 4:3 4:4 4:13 4:16 4:17 5:2 5:5 5:13[2] 5:17 6:2[2] 6:11[2] 7:4[2] 7:14 7:15 8:10 8:12 8:15 8:18 8:19 8:20 8:23 9:1 9:8 9:9 9:12 10:6 10:7[2] 10:10 10:15[2] 10:18 11:3 11:10 11:14 11:15 11:21 11:29[2] 11:31 12:1 12:4 12:9[2] 12:13 13:1 13:3[2] 13:5 13:7

GA

1:7 1:11 2:16 2:17 2:21 3:10[2] 3:11[2] 3:12 3:13[2] 3:16 3:18 3:20[2] 3:21 3:25 3:28[2] 4:1 4:2 4:15 4:18 4:22 4:24 4:25[3] 4:26[3] 4:27 4:29 5:3[2] 5:4 5:11 5:14 5:22 5:23 6:3 6:6 6:7 6:14

EPH

1:14 1:18 1:19 1:21[2] 1:23 2:4 2:8 2:11 2:14 3:2 3:5 3:8 3:9 3:13 3:15 3:18 3:20 4:4 4:6 4:7 4:9 4:10 4:15 4:18 4:21 4:22 4:24 4:28 4:29 5:5 5:9 5:10 5:12 5:13 5:17 5:18 5:23[3] 5:24 6:1 6:2 6:9[2] 6:17

PHP

1:7 1:8 1:18 1:21[2] 1:22 1:23 1:24 1:28 1:29 2:9 2:11 2:13 3:1[2] 3:6 3:9[3] 3:19[3] 3:20 3:21 4:5

COL

1:5 1:6[2] 1:7 1:15 1:17 1:18[2] 1:23 1:24[2] 1:25 1:26 1:27[2] 2:10 2:17 3:3 3:4 3:5 3:10 3:11[2] 3:14 3:18 3:20 3:25 4:1 4:7 4:9 4:11 4:12 4:15 4:16

1 TH

1:1 1:8 2:5 2:13 2:16 2:19 3:10 4:3 4:6 5:15 5:18 5:21 5:24

2 TH

1:3 1:5 1:6 2:2 2:4[3] 2:9 3:1 3:3 3:17

1 TI

1:1 1:4 1:5 1:8 1:9 1:10 1:14 1:15 1:20 2:3 2:5 3:1 3:13 3:15 3:16 4:4 4:5 4:8[3] 4:9 4:10 4:14 5:4 5:5 5:6 5:8 5:18 6:3 6:4 6:5 6:6 6:7 6:10 6:15 6:20 6:*sub.*

2 TI

1:1 1:5 1:6 1:10 1:12 1:13 2:1 2:5 2:9 2:10 2:11 2:17 2:18 3:15 3:16[2] 4:6 4:8 4:10 4:11[2]

TIT

1:1 1:3 1:13 1:15[2] 2:8 3:8 3:10 3:11[2]

PHM

6 8 12

HEB

1:8[2] 2:6 2:8 2:11 2:14 2:18 3:4[2] 3:13 3:15 4:7 4:10 4:12[2] 4:13[2] 4:14 5:1 5:2 5:4 5:13[2] 6:4 6:7 6:8[3] 6:10 6:16 6:20 7:2 7:5 7:6 7:7 7:8 7:12 7:14 7:15 7:16 7:18 7:25 7:26 7:28 8:1[2] 8:3[2] 8:6 8:10 8:13 9:2 9:3 9:11 9:15 9:16 9:17[2] 9:20 9:22 9:23 9:24 9:27 10:3 10:4 10:7 10:15 10:16 10:18[2] 10:20 10:23 10:25 10:31 11:1 11:6[3] 11:7 11:10 11:12 11:16[2] 11:18 11:27 12:1 12:2 12:7 12:13 12:29 13:4 13:6 13:9 13:11 13:15 13:16 13:17 13:21 13:23

JAS

1:6 1:8 1:9 1:10 1:11 1:12[2] 1:13 1:14[2] 1:15 1:17[2] 1:21 1:23 1:26 1:27 2:10 2:17 2:19 2:20 2:24 2:26[2] 3:2 3:5 3:6[3] 3:7 3:8 3:13 3:15 3:16[2] 3:17[2] 3:18 4:4[2] 4:12[2] 4:14[2] 4:16 4:17 5:3 5:4 5:11 5:13[2] 5:14

1 PE

1:13 1:15 1:16 1:24 1:25[2] 2:3 2:6 2:7[2] 2:15 2:19 2:20[2] 2:22 3:4[2] 3:12 3:13[2] 3:15 3:17 3:20 3:22[2] 4:5 4:7 4:12 4:14[2] 4:17 5:2 5:12 5:13

2 PE

1:4 1:9 1:17 1:20 2:17 2:19[2] 2:20 2:22[2] 3:4 3:8 3:9[2] 3:15

1 JO

1:3 1:5[3] 1:7 1:8 1:9 1:10 2:2 2:4[2] 2:5 2:7 2:8[2] 2:9[2] 2:10 2:11 2:13 2:14 2:15 2:16[3] 2:18[2] 2:21 2:22[3] 2:25 2:27[2] 2:29[2] 3:2 3:3 3:4 3:5 3:7[2] 3:8 3:9[2] 3:10 3:11 3:15 3:20 3:23 4:2[2] 4:3[4] 4:4[3] 4:6 4:7[2] 4:8 4:10 4:12 4:15 4:16 4:17[2] 4:18[2] 4:20 5:1[3] 5:3 5:4[2] 5:5[2] 5:6[3] 5:9[2] 5:11[2] 5:14 5:16[2] 5:17[2] 5:18[2] 5:20[4]

2 JO

6[2] 7 11

3 JO

3 11[3] 12

JUDE

13 24

RE

1:3[2] 1:4[2] 1:5 1:8[2] 1:9 2:7 2:8 2:13 3:7[2] 3:12 4:8[2] 5:2 5:12 5:13 6:13 6:14 6:17 7:17 8:11 9:11[2] 9:12 9:13 9:19 10:8 11:2[2] 11:8 11:14 11:18 12:10[2] 12:12 12:14 13:4[2] 13:10 13:18[3] 14:7 14:8[2] 14:10 14:12 14:15[2] 14:17 15:1 16:15 16:17 17:8[3] 17:9 17:10[2] 17:11[3] 17:14 17:18 18:2[3] 18:8 18:10 18:17 18:18 18:19 19:7 19:8 19:10 19:13 20:2 20:5 20:6 20:8 20:12 20:14 21:3 21:6[2] 21:8 21:16 21:17 21:23 22:7 22:10 22:11[4] 22:12 22:17

IT

846

GE

1:4 1:6 1:7 1:9 1:10 1:11 1:12 1:15 1:18 1:21 1:24 1:25 1:28 1:29 1:30 1:31 2:3[2] 2:5[3] 2:10 2:11 2:13 2:14 2:15 2:17 2:18 3:3 3:6 3:15 3:17[2] 3:18 3:19 4:3 4:8 4:12 4:14 6:1 6:6[2] 6:7 6:12 6:14 6:15[2] 6:16[2] 6:21 7:4 7:10 7:17 8:6 8:13 9:5 9:13 9:14 9:16 9:23 10:9 11:2 11:9 12:11 12:12 12:13 12:14 13:10 13:15 13:17 14:1 15:6 15:7 15:8 15:17 16:2 16:6 16:10 16:14 17:11 18:6 18:7 18:8 18:10 18:11 18:21 18:28 18:29 18:30 18:31 18:32 19:13 19:17 19:20[2] 19:29 19:34 20:13 20:15 21:12 21:14 21:16 21:22 21:26 22:1 22:6 22:14 22:20 23:8 23:9 23:11[2] 23:13[2] 24:14 24:15 24:22 24:30 24:43 24:52 24:65 25:11 25:22 26:8 26:21 26:22 26:32 26:33 27:1 27:4 27:5 27:10 27:20[2] 27:25[2]

27:30 27:31 27:33 27:40 28:12[2] 28:13[2] 28:16 28:18 29:2 29:7 29:10 29:13 29:19 29:23 29:25 29:26 30:15 30:25 30:28 30:30 30:33 30:34 30:35 30:41 31:2 31:5 31:10 31:22 31:29 31:32 31:35 31:37 31:39 31:44 31:45 31:47[2] 31:48 32:8 32:18 32:29 33:11 33:15 33:20 34:7 34:21 34:25 35:8 35:12 35:17 35:18 35:22[2] 37:5 37:9 37:10 37:14 37:21 37:23 37:24 37:25 37:26 37:32[2] 37:33[2] 38:1 38:9[2] 38:13 38:17 38:18 38:23 38:24[2] 38:27 38:28 38:29 39:5 39:7 39:10 39:11 39:13 39:15 39:18 39:19 39:22 39:23 40:1 40:8 40:10[2] 40:12 40:14

40:20 41:1 41:7 41:8 41:13[2] 41:15[2] 41:16 41:21 41:24 41:31 41:32[2] 41:42 41:49 42:6 42:14 42:27 42:28 42:35 42:2 42:11 42:12[2] 42:21[2] 44:5 44:9 44:10[2] 44:24 44:31 45:8 45:12 45:16 45:28 46:33 47:18 47:24 47:26 48:1 48:14 48:17[2] 48:19[2] 49:4 49:7[2] 49:15 49:28 50:9 50:11 50:20[2]

EX

1:10 1:16[2] 1:21 2:3[2] 2:5 2:6 2:9[2] 2:11 2:18 2:20 2:23 3:21 4:3[4] 4:4[3] 4:6 4:7[2] 4:8 4:9[2] 4:24 4:25 5:11 5:19 5:22 6:8[2] 6:28 7:9[2] 7:10 8:10 8:16 8:17 8:26 9:8 9:9 9:10[2] 9:18 9:24[2] 9:28

10:10 10:13 11:6[2] 12:2 12:4 12:5 12:6[2] 12:7[2] 12:8 12:9 12:10[2] 12:11[3] 12:14[2] 12:22 12:25 12:26 12:27 12:29 12:34 12:39 12:41[2] 12:42 12:46 12:47 12:48 12:51 13:2 13:5 13:9 13:11[2] 13:13 13:14 13:15 13:16 13:17 14:2 14:5 14:12 14:16 14:20[3] 14:24 14:27 15:23 16:5[2] 16:10 16:13 16:15[3] 16:16 16:18 16:19 16:20[2] 16:21[2] 16:22 16:24[2] 16:25 16:26[2] 16:27 16:31[2] 16:32 16:33 16:34 17:6 17:11 17:12 17:14 17:15 18:13 18:18 18:22 19:12 19:13[3] 19:16 19:18 19:23 20:8 20:10 20:11 20:18 20:25[3] 21:26 21:29 21:31 21:33 21:34 21:35 21:36 22:1[2]

22:4 22:7 22:9 22:10[2] 22:11[2] 22:12 22:13[2] 22:14[3] 22:15[4] 22:26 22:27[2] 22:30[2] 22:31 23:4 23:11 23:13 23:15 23:23 24:6 24:8 24:10[2] 24:16 25:2 25:9 25:11[3] 25:12[3] 25:15 25:24 25:25 25:26 25:32 25:36 25:37 25:39 26:6 26:11 26:13[2] 26:24[2] 26:31 26:32 27:2[2] 27:4 27:5 27:7 27:8[3] 27:21[2] 28:7[2] 28:8 28:15[2] 28:16 28:17 28:25 28:28 28:32[5] 28:33 28:35 28:36 28:37[3] 28:38[2] 28:43 29:7 29:12 29:14 29:16 29:18[2] 29:20 29:21 29:22 29:25 29:26[2] 29:28[3] 29:34[2] 29:36[3] 29:37[2] 30:1 30:2 30:3[2] 30:4[5] 30:6 30:7 30:8 30:10[3] 30:16[2] 30:18 30:21 30:25[2] 30:32[5]

30:33[2] 30:35 30:36[3] 30:37 31:13 31:14[2] 31:17 32:4[2] 32:5[2] 32:8 32:9 32:13 32:18[2] 32:19 32:20[4] 32:24[3] 32:30 33:1 33:7[3] 33:8 33:9 33:16[2] 33:22 34:9 34:10 34:12 34:29 35:5 35:24 36:2 36:3 36:6 36:7 36:13 36:18 36:35 36:38 37:1[3] 37:2[2] 37:3[4] 37:11 37:13 37:21 37:22 37:24 37:25[4] 37:26[4] 37:27[3] 38:1 38:2[2] 38:4 38:7 38:8 38:21 38:30 39:3[2] 39:4[3] 39:5 39:9 39:10 39:18 39:19 39:20 39:21 39:23 39:30 39:31[2] 39:43[2] 40:4 40:9[2] 40:10 40:11 40:17 40:19 40:23 40:29 40:37 40:38

LE

1:3 1:4 1:6 1:10 1:11

1:12 1:13[3] 1:15[2] 1:16 1:17[4] 2:1 2:2[2] 2:3 2:4 2:5 2:6[2] 2:7 2:8[2] 2:9[2] 2:10 2:15[2] 2:16[2] 3:1[3] 3:2 3:4 3:5[2] 3:6 3:7 3:8 3:9 3:10 3:11[2] 3:12 3:13[2] 3:15 3:16 3:17 4:5 4:8 4:9 4:10 4:14 4:17 4:19 4:20 4:21 4:24[2] 4:25 4:26 4:30 4:31[2] 4:32 4:33 4:34 4:35 5:1[2] 5:2[2] 5:3[3] 5:4[3] 5:5 5:8 5:9 5:10 5:11[2] 5:12[4] 5:13 5:16[2] 5:17 5:18[2] 5:19 6:3 6:4 6:5[3] 6:7 6:9[2] 6:12[4] 6:13 6:14 6:15[3] 6:16[2] 6:17 6:18[2] 6:20 6:21[3] 6:22[3] 6:23 6:25 6:26[3] 6:27 6:28[3] 6:29 6:30

7:1 7:3 7:4 7:5 7:6[2] 7:7 7:9 7:12 7:14[2] 7:15[2] 7:16[2] 7:18[5] 7:19 7:24 7:25 7:26 7:27 7:30 8:7 8:15[4] 8:16 8:19 8:21 8:23[3] 8:28 8:29[2] 8:30 8:31[2] 9:1 9:9 9:15[2] 9:16 9:17 10:3 10:9 10:12[2] 10:13[2] 10:15[2] 10:16 10:17[2] 10:18[2] 10:19 11:32[6] 11:33[2] 11:35 11:37 11:38 11:40[2] 11:41 12:7 13:2 13:3 13:6 13:8 13:10 13:11 13:13 13:15 13:19 13:20[3] 13:21[2] 13:22[2] 13:23 13:25[4] 13:26[2] 13:27[2] 13:28[3] 13:30[3] 13:31[2] 13:32 13:39 13:42 13:43 13:47 13:48 13:49 13:50 13:51 13:52[2] 13:54 13:55[5] 13:56 13:57[2] 13:58[2] 13:59[2] 14:6 14:9

14:13 14:14 14:15 14:25 14:35[2] 14:36 14:43 14:44[2] 14:45 14:46 14:48 14:53 14:57[2] 15:3 15:23[2] 15:25 16:12 16:14 16:15 16:18[2] 16:19[3] 16:29 16:31 17:3 17:4 17:9[2] 17:11[2] 17:13 17:14[3] 17:15 18:8 18:16 18:17 18:22 18:23 18:25 18:28[2] 19:5 19:6[3] 19:7[3] 19:8 19:23[2] 19:25 20:14 20:17 20:21 20:24[2] 21:24 22:7 22:9[2] 22:11 22:14[2] 22:20 22:21 22:23 22:27[2] 22:28[2] 22:29 22:30[2] 23:3 23:11 23:14 23:21[2] 23:27 23:28 23:29 23:30 23:31 23:32 23:36 23:41[3] 24:3[2] 24:7 24:8 24:9[3] 24:18 24:19 24:20 24:21 25:5 25:10 25:11[2] 25:12[2] 25:16 25:21 25:25 25:26[2]

25:27 25:28[3] 25:29[3] 25:30[3] 25:34 25:50 26:1 26:16 26:32 26:34 26:35[4] 26:37 27:4 27:5 27:6 27:7[2] 27:9 27:10[3] 27:11 27:12[4] 27:13 27:14[4] 27:15[3] 27:17 27:18 27:19[3] 27:20 27:21 27:24 27:26[3] 27:27[5] 27:30 27:33[5]

NU

1:50[2] 1:51[2] 3:26 4:5 4:6 4:9 4:10[2] 4:11 4:14[4] 4:15 4:25 5:7[2] 5:10 5:13 5:15[2] 5:17 5:25 5:26 5:27 6:9 6:18 7:1[3] 7:5 7:10 7:84 7:88 8:24 9:3[3] 9:11[2] 9:12[3] 9:15 9:16 9:20 9:21[2] 9:22[2] 10:11 10:29 10:32[2] 10:35 10:36 11:1[2] 11:8[6] 11:9 11:14 11:17[2] 11:18 11:20[2] 11:25[2] 11:31[3] 11:33

12:2 13:18 13:19 13:20 13:23 13:27[2] 13:30[2] 13:32[2] 14:3 14:7 14:8 14:11 14:13 14:14 14:23 14:24 14:35 14:41 15:11 15:19 15:20 15:24 15:25[2] 15:26 15:28 15:34 15:39[2] 16:4 16:7 16:9 16:13 16:31 16:42[2] 17:5 17:8 18:10[3] 18:11 18:13 18:15 18:19 18:23 18:26 18:27 18:29 18:30[2] 18:31[2] 18:32[3] 19:6 19:9[2] 19:10 19:12 19:15 19:18[2] 19:21 19:22 20:5 20:8 20:19 21:8[3] 21:9[2] 21:14 21:17 21:18 21:28 21:34 21:41 23:19[2] 23:20 23:22 23:23 23:27 24:1 24:8 25:7 25:13 26:1 27:11[2] 27:13 28:6 28:24 29:1 29:11 30:7[2] 30:8 30:11 30:13[2] 31:23[3]

31:29[2] 31:54 32:39[2] 32:42 33:53 33:55 33:56 34:5 34:12 35:23 35:25 35:33[2] 36:3 36:9

DE

1:3 1:17[2] 1:21 1:24 1:25[2] 1:36 1:39[2] 2:16 2:19 2:24 3:9 3:11[2] 3:26 3:27 4:2 4:5 4:14 4:26[2] 4:32 4:35 4:38 4:39 4:40 5:12 5:14 5:16 5:23 5:27[2] 5:29 5:31 5:33 6:1 6:3[2] 6:10 6:18 6:24 6:25 7:1 7:12 7:25[2] 7:26[4] 8:9 8:18[2] 8:19 9:6 9:11 9:13 9:21[4] 10:15 10:8 11:10 11:11 11:12 11:13 11:29[2] 11:31 12:1 12:16 12:24[2] 12:25 12:28 12:32[2] 13:14 13:15 13:16[3] 14:8[2] 14:10 14:21[3] 14:24

14:25 14:28 15:2[3] 15:3 15:4 15:9 15:16 15:17 15:18 15:20 15:21[2] 15:22[2] 15:23 16:3 16:7 17:4[3] 17:14 17:18 17:19 18:3 18:19 18:22 19:2 19:13 19:14 20:2 20:5[2] 20:6[2] 20:9 20:10[2] 20:11[3] 20:12[2] 20:13 20:19[2] 20:20 21:1[2] 21:3 21:7 21:14 21:16 22:2[4] 22:7 23:11 23:13 23:16 23:20 23:21[3] 23:22 24:1[2] 24:3 24:13 24:15[3] 24:19 24:20 24:21[2] 25:2 25:6 25:8 25:9 25:19[3] 26:1[2] 26:2 26:4 26:10 26:12 27:2 27:4 27:15 28:1 28:15 28:21 28:24 28:38 28:63[2] 28:67[2] 28:68 29:8 29:19 29:22 29:23 29:27 29:28 30:1 30:5 30:11[2] 30:12[4] 30:13[4]

30:14 30:16 30:18 31:6 31:7 31:8 31:9 31:13 31:19[2] 31:21[2] 31:22 31:24 31:26[2] 32:19 32:27 32:47[3] 34:4[2]

JOS

1:1 1:7 1:11 1:15 2:2 2:5[2] 2:14 2:19 2:21 3:2 3:3[2] 3:4[2] 3:13 3:34 4:1 4:7 4:11 4:18 4:24 5:1 5:8 5:13 6:5 6:8 6:11 6:15 6:16 6:17 6:18 6:20 6:26 7:9 7:11 7:14 7:15 7:19 7:21 7:22[2] 8:2 8:5 8:7 8:8 8:14[2] 8:18 8:19 8:24[2] 8:25 8:28 8:29 8:31 9:1 9:12[2] 9:16 9:24 9:25 10:1[2] 10:2 10:4 10:5 10:11 10:14[2] 10:17 10:18 10:20 10:24 10:27

10:28 10:30[3] 10:31[2] 10:32[2] 10:34[2] 10:35[2] 10:36 10:37[3] 10:38 10:39 11:1 11:20 11:23 12:6 13:6 14:7 15:3 15:4 15:16 15:17 15:18 16:6 16:7 17:9 17:10[2] 17:13 17:18[3] 18:4 18:5 18:8 18:9 18:20 19:14 19:47[3] 21:11 21:12 21:18 21:22 21:23 21:24 21:27 21:28[2] 21:30 21:34 21:43 23:1 23:10 23:15 24:4 24:15 24:17 24:26 24:27[2] 24:29 24:32

JG

1:1 1:8[2] 1:12 1:13 1:14 1:17 1:28 2:4 2:18 2:19 2:22 3:16 3:21 3:27 4:20 4:21 6:3 6:5 6:7 6:11 6:18 6:19[2] 6:24[2] 6:25[2] 6:27[3] 6:28 6:30 6:31

6:37 6:38 6:39 6:40 7:4 7:9[2] 7:13[3] 7:15 7:17 8:27[2] 8:33 9:7 9:25 9:33 9:42 9:45 9:47 9:48[2] 9:50 9:51 9:52[2] 11:4 11:5 11:23 11:31[2] 11:35 11:39[2] 12:5 12:6 13:16 13:18 13:19 13:20[2] 14:4 14:11 14:12[2] 14:13[2] 14:15[2] 14:16[3] 14:17 15:1 15:15 15:17 16:2[2] 16:4 16:9 16:14 16:16 16:25 16:29 17:2 17:3 18:2 18:9 18:10 18:12 18:19 18:28[2] 19:1 19:5 19:11 19:26 19:30[3] 20:9 20:28 21:4 21:22

RU

1:1 1:13 1:19 2:6 2:11 2:17 2:18 2:22 3:1 3:4 3:8 3:12 3:13 3:14 3:15[3] 4:4[6] 4:5 4:6[2] 4:7 4:8 4:16[2] 4:17

1 SA

1:12 1:20 2:14 2:16[2] 2:19 2:24 2:30 2:36 3:2 3:9 3:11 3:17 3:18 4:3[2] 4:13 4:18 4:20 5:1 5:2[2] 5:7 5:9[2] 5:10 5:11[2] 6:2 6:3[2] 6:8[3] 6:9[3] 6:13 6:15 6:16 6:21 7:1 7:2[2] 7:6 7:7 7:9 7:12[2] 8:1 9:20 9:23 9:24[4] 9:26 10:1[2] 10:5 10:7 10:9 10:11 10:12 10:25[2] 11:2 11:7 11:9 11:11[2] 12:3 12:6 12:15 12:17 12:22 13:3 13:10 13:22 14:1 14:6 14:14 14:15 14:19 14:27 14:39 15:11[2] 15:12 15:27 15:28 16:2 16:6 16:16 16:18[2] 16:23

17:25 17:27 17:35 17:39 17:48 17:49 17:51 17:54 18:1 18:4 18:6 18:10 18:11 18:19 18:23 18:26 18:30 19:5 19:13[2] 19:19 19:21 20:2[2] 20:4 20:7 20:9[2] 20:12 20:13[2] 20:16 20:27 20:33 20:35 21:5[3] 21:6 21:9[3] 22:1 22:15 22:17 22:22 23:6 23:7 23:13 23:22 23:23 24:1[2] 24:4 24:5 24:11 24:16 25:11 25:20 25:27 25:30 25:37 25:38 26:12[2] 26:17 26:22 27:4 28:1 28:14 28:17 28:24[2] 28:25 29:4 30:1[2] 30:3 30:25[2] 31:4 31:8 31:9

2 SA

1:1 1:2[2] 1:18 1:20[2] 2:1 2:23 2:26[2] 3:18 3:24 3:26 3:28 3:29 3:35

3:36[2] 3:37 4:4 4:12 5:9 5:24 6:3 6:4 6:6[2] 6:10 6:12 6:13 6:17[2] 6:21 7:1 7:4 7:15 7:25 7:29[3] 8:1 10:3[2] 10:5 10:7 10:17 11:1 11:2 11:14 11:16 11:25 12:3[2] 12:4 12:12 12:15 12:18 12:21 12:28 12:29[2] 12:30 13:1 13:2 13:5[2] 13:8 13:23 13:30 13:35 13:36 14:15[2] 14:26[3] 14:30 14:32 15:1 15:2 15:5 15:7 15:25 15:32 15:35[2] 16:11 16:12 16:16 17:9[3] 17:13 17:21 17:27 18:3 18:10 18:18 18:29 19:1 19:6 19:19 19:25 19:36 20:8[2] 20:15 20:20[2] 20:22 21:1 21:10 21:11 21:18 22:9 22:48 23:5 23:12 23:16[3] 23:17[2]

24:3
24:12
24:16^{2}
24:24

1 KI

1:11
1:18
1:21
1:27
1:41
1:48
1:51
2:3
2:15
2:29
2:37
2:39
2:41
3:6
3:15
3:18
3:19
3:20
3:21^{3}
3:26^{3}
3:27
5:7
6:1
6:7
6:9
6:14
6:16
6:17
6:20
6:21
6:38
7:3
7:7
7:23^{2}
7:24^{3}
7:25
7:26^{2}
7:27
7:31^{2}
8:10
8:15
8:17
8:18
8:24^{2}
8:54
9:1
9:8
9:10
9:16^{2}
9:28
10:6
10:7
10:18
10:21
11:4
11:11
11:12^{2}
11:15
11:29
11:30
11:35
11:38
12:2^{2}
12:10
12:20
12:28
13:3
13:4^{2}
13:6
13:9
13:17
13:20
13:23
13:24
13:25
13:26
13:29^{2}
13:31
13:34^{2}
14:5
14:6
14:8
14:10
14:11
14:25
14:28
15:13
15:21
15:29
16:11
16:18
16:31^{2}
17:4
17:7
17:11
17:12^{2}
17:13
17:17
18:1
18:4
18:6
18:12
18:13
18:17
18:23^{3}
18:24
18:25
18:26
18:27
18:29
18:33
18:34^{4}
18:36^{2}
18:39
18:44
18:45
19:4
19:10
19:13^{2}
19:14
19:17
20:1
20:6^{3}
20:11
20:12
20:13
20:26
20:29
20:33
20:40
21:1
21:2^{6}
21:3
21:6^{2}
21:11
21:15
21:16^{2}
21:18
21:27
22:2
22:3
22:6
22:12
22:15
22:32^{2}
22:33^{2}
22:43

2 KI

1:3
1:6
1:8
1:16
2:1
2:3
2:5
2:8
2:9
2:10^{2}
2:11
2:12
2:20
3:5
3:14
3:15
3:20
3:25^{3}
4:6
4:8^{2}
4:10
4:11
4:18
4:23^{2}
4:25
4:26^{4}
4:27
4:40
4:41
4:44
5:7
5:8
5:13
5:16
5:26
6:5
6:6^{2}
6:7^{2}
6:13
6:20
6:24
6:25
6:30
7:2
7:7
7:8^{2}
7:11
7:13
7:18
7:19
7:20
8:1
8:3
8:5
8:7
8:15^{3}
9:3
9:12
9:13
9:15^{3}
9:17
9:18
9:19
9:22^{2}
9:30
10:7
10:9
10:15^{2}
10:19
10:20
10:25
10:27
11:6
11:18
12:5
12:6
12:7
12:9^{2}
12:10
12:11
12:12
12:16
12:17
12:18
13:16
13:17
13:19
13:21
14:5
14:17
14:22
14:26
15:12
15:16
16:8
16:9^{2}
16:10
16:11
16:14
16:15
16:17^{2}
17:5
17:7
17:25
18:1
18:4^{2}
18:9^{2}
18:10
18:16
18:21^{2}
18:25^{2}
18:26
19:1^{2}
19:4
19:14^{2}
19:25^{3}
19:26
19:32^{2}
19:34
19:35
19:37
20:4
20:7
20:10
20:11
20:19
21:12
21:13^{2}
22:3
22:5^{2}
22:8
22:9
22:10
22:11
23:6^{2}
23:15
23:16
23:17
23:21
23:35
24:2
24:11
24:20
25:1^{3}
25:17
25:24
25:25
25:27

1 CH

4:10
6:10
6:55
7:23
9:32
10:4
10:8
10:13
11:7
11:14
11:18^{4}
11:19^{3}
12:15
12:17
12:22
13:2^{2}
13:3
13:6
13:13
14:8
14:15
15:1
15:3
15:12
15:13
15:26
15:29
16:1^{2}
16:19
16:30
17:3
17:11
17:13
17:24
17:27^{3}
18:1
19:1
19:8
19:17
20:1^{2}
20:2^{3}
20:3
20:4
20:8
21:2
21:10
21:15^{2}
21:17^{2}
21:22
21:23^{2}
21:24
21:30
22:5
22:7
22:14
23:26
26:28
27:24
28:8
28:10
28:20
29:12

2 CH

1:4^{2}
1:5
1:6
2:4
2:16^{2}
3:4^{2}
3:8
4:3^{3}
4:4
4:5^{3}
4:15
5:9
5:11
5:13
6:7
6:8^{2}
6:11
6:13^{2}
6:15^{2}
7:20
7:21
7:22
8:1
8:3
8:16
9:5
9:6
9:17
9:20
10:2^{2}
10:10
12:1
12:2
13:15
14:11
15:16^{2}
16:5^{2}
18:5
18:11
18:31^{2}
18:32^{2}
19:7
20:1
20:7
20:25
20:32
20:34
21:17
21:19
22:8
23:17
23:18^{2}
24:4
24:5
24:8
24:11^{3}
24:12
24:13
24:14
24:22^{2}
24:23
25:3
25:4
25:8
25:14
25:16
25:20
26:2
26:18^{2}
28:21
29:10
29:16^{3}
29:22
30:3
30:5^{2}
30:18
31:3
31:21
32:5
32:12
32:30
33:14
34:4
34:10^{2}
34:11
34:12
34:16
34:17
34:18
34:19
34:32
35:3
35:12
36:22

EZR

1:1
2:68
3:2
3:4
4:12
4:13
4:14
4:19
4:24
5:8
5:16
5:17^{2}
6:9
6:12
6:14
6:18
7:10
7:20
7:21
7:23
7:24
7:26
9:7
9:11^{2}
9:12
9:15
10:3
10:4
10:9
10:13

NE

1:1
1:4
2:1^{2}
2:5^{2}
2:6
2:7
2:10^{2}
2:16
2:19
3:1^{3}
3:13
3:14
3:15^{2}
4:1
4:7
4:8
4:12
4:15^{2}
4:16
5:5
5:9
6:1
6:3
6:6^{2}
6:7
6:9
6:16
7:1
7:64
8:5
8:15
9:8
9:10
9:23
9:36
9:37
9:37
9:38^{2}
10:31
10:34^{2}
10:36
11:23
13:3
13:8
13:19

ES

1:1
1:17
1:19^{3}
1:20
1:22
2:8
2:10
2:22
2:23^{2}
3:4
3:8
3:9^{3}
3:10
3:11
3:12
4:4^{2}
4:5^{2}
4:8^{2}
5:1
5:2
5:3
5:4
5:6^{2}
5:8
6:2
6:9
6:11
7:2^{2}
7:3
8:2
8:5^{2}
8:8^{2}
8:9
8:10
9:1
9:12^{2}
9:13^{2}
9:14
9:17
9:18
9:27
9:32

JOB

1:5^{2}
1:7
1:19
2:2
3:3
3:4^{2}
3:5^{3}
3:6^{3}
3:8
3:9^{2}
3:10^{2}
3:21^{2}
4:5^{2}
4:16
4:20
5:5
5:21
5:27^{4}
6:3
6:9
6:17
6:28
6:29^{2}
7:16
8:12^{2}
8:15^{3}
8:18
9:1
9:7
9:20
9:22
9:35
10:16
11:8
11:11
11:14
11:16
12:8
12:14
13:1
13:5
13:9
14:7^{2}
14:9
14:21^{2}
15:18
15:23
15:32
17:15
18:2
18:13
18:14
18:15^{2}
19:4
20:12
20:13^{3}
20:14
20:18
20:23
20:25
20:26
21:4
21:19
22:3^{2}
22:8
22:19
22:28
22:30
24:23
24:25
25:5
26:3
26:9
27:6
27:12
27:14
27:17^{2}
28:1
28:5^{3}
28:6^{2}
28:8^{2}
28:13
28:14^{2}
28:15
28:16
28:17^{2}
28:19^{2}
28:21
28:27^{4}
29:11^{2}
29:14
29:24
30:18
30:22
31:11
31:12
31:26
31:36^{2}
32:19
33:14
33:21
33:27
34:9
34:10
34:18
34:29
34:31
34:33^{2}
35:3
35:13
35:15^{2}
36:25^{2}
36:30
36:32
36:33
37:3
37:4
37:12
37:13
37:20
38:5
38:8^{2}
38:9
38:10
38:13^{2}
38:14
38:18
38:20
38:21
38:26
38:29
39:12
39:24
40:2
40:24
42:7

PS

6:7
7:2
7:5
7:12
7:15
10:11
10:13
10:14^{2}
17:12
18:8
18:32
18:47
19:6
21:4
22:14
22:30
24:2^{2}
25:11
30:9
33:9^{2}
34:14
35:9
35:15
35:21
35:25
37:5
37:10
37:34
38:10
39:4
39:9
40:3
40:7
40:14
41:6
48:5
48:8
48:13
49:8
50:1
51:16
52:9^{2}
54:6
55:10^{2}
55:12^{3}
55:13
60:2^{2}
60:4
60:12
63:9
65:9^{3}
65:10
68:9
68:11
68:14^{2}
68:16
69:18
69:22
69:35
69:36
73:16
73:28
74:11
75:3
75:8
78:28
80:8
80:9^{3}
80:10
80:13^{2}
80:16^{2}
81:10
84:6
86:17
87:5
89:37
89:39
90:4
90:6^{2}
90:10
90:13
90:17
91:7
92:1
92:7
93:1
94:7
94:15
96:5
96:10
96:10
99:3
100:3
101:3
103:16^{3}
104:5
104:6
104:20
104:32
105:12
105:28
106:9
106:32
107:42
108:13
109:17^{2}
109:18
109:19
109:23
109:27
112:10
114:3
118:8
118:9
118:23
118:24
119:20
119:33
119:34
119:71
119:90
119:97
119:106
119:126
119:130
119:140
119:175
124:1
124:2
127:1
127:2
128:2
129:6
132:6^{2}
132:11
132:13
133:1
133:2
135:3
136:14
137:7^{2}
139:4
139:6^{2}
141:5^{2}
144:10
147:1^{2}

PR

1:21
1:22
3:8
3:14
3:25
3:27^{3}
3:28
4:5
4:15^{3}
4:23
6:22^{3}
6:32
7:23
8:11
8:33
9:12
10:22^{2}
10:23
10:24
11:10
11:11
11:15
11:19
11:24
11:26
11:27
12:25
13:12
13:19
14:1
14:6
15:23
16:12
16:14
16:16
16:19
16:22
16:26
16:31
17:8^{3}
17:14
17:16
17:21
18:4
18:10
18:13^{2}
18:21
19:2
19:11
19:19
19:23
19:24
20:3
20:5
20:11
20:14^{2}
20:25
21:1
21:9
21:15
21:19
21:20
21:27
22:6
22:15
22:18
23:23
23:31
23:32
23:35^{2}
24:3
24:12^{3}
24:13
24:14
24:18^{2}
24:23
24:27
24:31
24:32^{2}
25:2
25:7^{2}
25:10
25:16
25:24
25:27
26:15^{2}
26:27
26:28
27:14
28:8
28:24
29:4
29:7
29:14
29:24
30:15
30:16
30:17^{2}
30:21
31:4^{2}
31:15
31:16
31:24

EC

1:6
1:8
1:9
1:10^{2}
2:2^{2}
2:15^{2}
2:18
2:21
2:24
3:10
3:13
3:14^{4}
4:8
5:4
5:5
5:6
5:18^{2}
6:1
6:2^{2}
6:10^{2}
7:2^{2}
7:5
7:11
7:12
7:18
7:23
7:24
8:7
8:8
8:12
8:13
8:14^{2}
8:17^{4}
9:10
9:12
9:13
9:14^{4}
9:15
10:8
11:1
11:3
11:7
12:7^{3}
12:14^{2}

CA

3:4
3:7
3:10
5:2
5:3
6:13
8:7^{2}
8:13

ISA

1:6
1:7^{2}
1:13
1:20
1:21^{2}
1:31
2:2^{2}
3:9
3:10
3:11
3:24
4:3
5:2^{5}
5:4^{3}
5:5^{2}
5:6^{3}
5:14
5:18
5:19^{2}
5:29^{2}
6:2
6:7
6:13^{2}
7:1^{3}
7:2
7:6^{2}
7:7^{2}
7:8
7:11
7:13
7:18
7:20
7:21
7:22
7:23^{2}
7:25
8:1
8:10^{2}
8:20
8:21
9:7^{2}
9:8
9:18
10:7
10:12
10:13
10:15^{3}
10:17
10:20
10:26
10:27
10:30
11:10
11:11
11:15
11:16
13:6
13:9
13:14
13:17
13:20^{2}
14:2
14:9^{2}
14:23^{2}
14:24^{2}
14:27^{2}
14:32
15:5
16:2
16:5
16:12^{2}
17:1
17:4
17:5^{2}
17:6
17:10
19:1
19:16
19:17
19:20
19:21
20:1
21:1
21:3^{2}
21:17
22:5
22:7
22:11
22:14
22:20
22:25^{2}
23:1^{2}
23:9
23:13^{2}
23:15
23:17
23:18
24:1^{2}
24:2^{2}
24:9
24:13
24:18
24:20
24:21
25:2
25:8
25:9
26:5^{3}
26:6
26:15
26:18
26:20
27:3^{3}
27:8^{2}
27:11
27:12
27:13
28:4^{3}
28:15
28:18
28:19^{4}
28:20^{2}
28:28^{3}
29:2
29:5
29:8
29:11
29:16^{2}
29:17
30:8^{3}
30:14^{2}
30:19
30:21
30:22
30:23
30:32^{2}
30:33^{3}
31:5^{2}
32:19
34:1
34:5
34:6
34:8
34:10^{3}
34:11^{3}
34:13
34:16^{2}
34:17^{2}
35:2^{2}
35:8^{3}
35:9
36:1
36:6^{2}
36:7
36:10^{2}
36:11
37:1^{2}
37:4
37:9
37:14^{2}
37:26^{3}
37:27
37:33^{2}
37:35
37:38
38:8
38:15
38:17
38:21
40:5^{2}
40:7
40:9
40:19
40:21
40:22
41:4
41:5
41:7^{3}
41:20
41:23
42:5^{2}
42:21
42:25^{3}
43:9
43:13
43:19^{2}
44:7^{2}
44:8
44:12^{2}
44:13^{5}
44:14
44:15^{4}
44:17^{3}
44:19^{3}
44:23
45:8
45:9
45:12
45:18^{4}
45:21
46:6
46:8
46:11^{4}
46:13
47:7
47:10
47:11^{2}
47:14
48:5^{3}
48:6
48:11
48:16
48:20
49:6
50:1
50:2
51:9
51:10
51:22
51:23
52:6
53:3
53:10
54:14
55:10^{2}
55:11^{4}
55:13
56:2^{2}
56:6
57:1
57:8
57:11
57:20
58:5^{2}
58:7
58:14
59:1^{2}
59:11
59:15^{2}
59:16
60:22
61:11
62:9^{4}
63:5
63:18
65:6
65:8^{2}
65:9
65:24
66:18
66:23

JER

1:3
1:12
2:19
2:34
3:5
3:7
3:9
3:16^{4}
3:17
4:4
4:9
4:11
4:18^{2}
4:23
4:28^{3}
5:1
5:12
5:13
5:14
5:15^{2}
5:19
5:20
5:22^{3}
5:31
6:10
6:11
6:19
7:11
7:12
7:20
7:23
7:29
7:30
7:31
7:32
8:8
8:16
9:8
9:12
10:4^{3}
10:5
10:7
10:18
10:19
10:23
11:5^{2}
11:16^{2}
11:18^{2}
12:8^{2}
12:11^{3}
12:15
12:16
13:1^{2}
13:2
13:4
13:5
13:6
13:7^{2}
13:16^{2}
13:17
13:19^{2}
13:27
14:5
14:7
15:2
15:8
15:9
15:11
16:10
16:14
17:1
17:9
17:15
17:21
17:24
17:27^{2}
18:4^{2}
18:7
18:9
18:10^{2}
19:4
19:5^{2}
19:15
20:3
20:4
20:10
21:10^{2}
21:12
21:14^{2}
22:14
22:15
22:16
22:17
23:18
23:19
23:20
25:12^{2}
25:13
25:15
25:18
25:28
26:8
26:21
27:5^{2}
27:8
27:11
28:1
28:10
29:7
30:3
30:7^{3}
30:8
30:23
30:24^{3}
31:10
31:28
31:33
31:39
31:40
32:3
32:7
32:8
32:10
32:23
32:24^{3}
32:28
32:29
32:31^{2}
32:34
32:35
32:36
32:43^{2}
33:2^{2}
33:5
33:6
33:9^{2}
34:2
34:22^{3}
35:11
36:1
36:3
36:7
36:9
36:15^{2}
36:16
36:21^{2}
36:23^{3}
36:28
36:32
37:8^{2}
37:11
37:14
38:3
38:15
38:18
38:20
38:25
39:1
39:4
40:3
40:4^{3}
40:5
40:9
40:15
41:1
41:4^{2}
41:6
41:7
41:9^{2}
41:13
42:4^{2}
42:6^{3}
42:7
42:16
42:17
42:20
42:21
43:1
44:21
46:10
46:20
46:23
46:26
47:6
47:7^{3}
48:1
48:2^{2}
48:9
48:20^{2}
48:30^{2}
48:39
48:44
49:2
49:12
49:17
49:18
49:23
49:27
49:33
49:39
50:13^{2}
50:15
50:21
50:29
50:32
50:38
50:39^{2}
51:11^{2}
51:33
51:62^{3}
51:63^{3}
52:3
52:4^{3}
52:21^{2}
52:22
52:31

LA

1:12
1:13
1:21
2:6
2:16
3:22
3:26
3:27
3:28
3:37^{2}
4:4
4:8^{2}
4:11
4:15
5:18

EZE

1:1
1:4
1:13
1:16
1:26
1:27^{3}
1:28
2:10^{2}
3:3^{2}
3:16
4:1^{2}
4:2^{5}
4:3^{4}
4:4^{2}
4:7
4:10

4:12^{2}
5:1
5:2
5:5
5:13
5:15^{2}
5:17
7:6^{2}
7:7^{3}
7:10
7:19
7:20^{2}
7:21^{2}
7:22^{2}
8:1
8:17
9:8
10:1
10:6
10:7^{2}
10:11
10:13
11:3
11:7^{2}
11:13
11:15
12:3
12:6^{2}
12:7^{2}
12:11
12:13
12:25^{2}
13:7
13:10
13:11^{3}
13:12^{2}
13:13^{2}
13:14^{2}
13:15^{2}
14:13^{3}
14:14
14:15^{2}
14:16
14:17
14:18
14:19^{2}
14:20
14:21
14:22
14:23
15:3
15:4^{4}
15:5^{5}
16:5
16:14
16:15
16:16
16:19^{2}
16:23
17:4^{2}
17:5^{3}
17:6^{2}
17:7
17:8^{4}
17:9^{4}
17:10^{5}
17:14^{2}
17:19
17:21
17:22^{2}
17:23^{3}
17:24
18:4
18:20
19:3^{3}
20:1
20:9
20:14
20:22
20:28
20:42
20:47
20:48^{2}
21:5
21:7^{3}
21:10^{4}
21:11^{4}
21:12^{2}
21:13^{2}
21:14
21:15^{2}
21:17
21:19
21:23
21:27^{4}
21:28
21:30
21:32
23:3
23:14^{2}
23:20^{2}
23:30
23:32
23:34^{3}
23:39
23:41
24:3^{2}
24:4^{2}
24:5^{3}
24:6^{3}
24:7^{3}
24:8^{2}
24:10
24:11^{5}
24:14^{3}
24:25
24:26
25:3^{2}
25:13^{2}
25:15
26:1
26:5^{3}
26:14
26:17
27:27
27:32
28:2
28:3
28:10
28:18
28:21
29:3
29:9
29:11^{3}
29:15^{2}
29:16
29:17
29:18
29:19
29:20
30:3
30:6
30:9
30:12
30:20
30:21^{3}
30:25
31:1
32:1
32:15
32:17
33:9
33:13
33:21
33:33
34:18
34:24
35:2
35:3
35:7
35:10
35:15^{2}
36:5
36:10
36:17
36:18
36:29
36:32
36:34
36:36
36:37
37:14^{2}
37:16
37:26
38:8
38:10
38:14
38:16
38:18
38:19^{4}
39:5
39:8^{2}
39:11^{2}
39:13
39:14
39:15^{2}
40:22
40:25
40:26^{2}
40:29^{2}
40:31
40:33
40:34
40:35
40:36
40:37
40:49
41:15
41:18
41:19
42:15
42:20^{2}
43:8
43:11
43:17
43:18
43:20^{3}
43:21
43:22
43:23
43:26
43:27
44:1
44:2^{4}
44:3^{2}
44:6
44:7
44:17
44:24
44:28
44:31
45:3
45:4
45:6
45:9
45:17
45:19
46:1^{2}
46:6
46:9
46:13
46:14
46:16
46:17^{2}
46:23
47:5
47:9
47:10^{2}
47:12
47:14^{2}
47:22^{2}
47:23
48:8
48:11
48:14^{2}
48:18
48:19
48:21
48:35

DA

1:1
2:7
2:11^{2}
2:40
2:41
2:44^{2}
2:45
2:47
3:1
3:4
3:14
3:17
3:18
3:19
4:2
4:12^{3}
4:14
4:15
4:17^{2}
4:21
4:22
4:23^{2}
4:25
4:27
4:31
4:32
5:21
5:26
6:1
6:5
6:8
6:17
7:4^{2}
7:5^{5}
7:6^{2}
7:7^{6}
7:23^{2}
7:26
8:2
8:8
8:10^{2}
8:12^{2}
8:15
8:22
8:26
8:27
9:13
9:14
9:27
11:12
11:18
11:27
11:39
11:35
12:6
12:7

HO

1:5
1:10^{3}
2:7
2:16
2:21
6:4
7:4
7:6
7:9
8:4
8:5
8:6^{3}
8:7^{3}
8:13
8:14
9:7
10:5^{4}
10:6
10:10
10:12
13:2

JOE

1:3
1:5
1:7^{2}
1:15
2:1
2:2
2:11
2:29
2:32
3:8
3:18

AM

1:14
2:2
2:5
2:11
3:6
4:7^{3}
5:6^{2}
5:13
5:15
5:18
5:20
6:9
7:1
7:2
7:3
7:4
7:13^{2}
8:8^{2}
8:9
8:10
8:12
9:4
9:5^{2}
9:6
9:8
9:11

OB

15
18

JON

1:2
1:3
1:5
1:13
1:14
2:10
3:2
3:7
3:10
4:1
4:3
4:5
4:6^{2}
4:7^{2}
4:8^{2}
4:10

MIC

1:5
1:7
1:9
1:10
2:1^{2}
2:4
2:10^{2}
2:13
3:1
3:6
4:1^{3}
4:4
4:8
5:10
6:9
7:3
7:10

NA

1:4
3:1
3:7
3:8
3:9
3:15

HAB

1:10
2:2^{2}
2:3^{5}
2:11
2:13
2:18
2:19^{3}

ZEP

1:8
1:12
1:14
2:3
2:14
3:16
3:18

HAG

1:4
1:6
1:8
1:9^{3}
2:3^{3}
2:6
2:12
2:13^{2}
2:18

ZEC

1:16
1:21
4:2
4:3
4:7
4:9
5:3^{2}
5:4^{4}
5:6
5:8
5:11^{2}
7:1
7:13
8:6^{2}
8:13
8:20
8:23
9:2
9:5^{2}
10:7
11:9^{2}
11:10
11:11^{2}
11:13
12:3^{2}
12:9
13:2
13:3
13:4
13:9
14:4
14:6
14:7^{3}
14:8^{2}
14:10
14:11
14:13
14:16
14:17

MAL

1:7^{3}
1:12
1:13^{2}
2:2^{2}
2:3
2:13
3:10
3:14^{2}
3:16
4:1

MT

1:22
2:5
2:9
2:15
2:23
3:15^{2}
4:4
4:6
4:7
4:10
4:14
5:13^{2}
5:15^{2}
5:21
5:27
5:29^{3}
5:30^{3}
5:31
5:33
5:34
5:35^{2}
5:38
5:43
6:10
7:2
7:7^{2}
7:8
7:14
7:25^{2}
7:27^{2}
7:28
8:9
8:10
8:13
8:17
9:8
9:10
9:11
9:16
9:29
9:30
9:33
10:11
10:12
10:13^{2}
10:15
10:19
10:20
10:25
10:39^{2}
11:1
11:10
11:12
11:14
11:16
11:22
11:23
11:24
11:26
12:2
12:10
12:11^{3}
12:12
12:13^{2}
12:15
12:17
12:24
12:32^{2}
12:39
12:41
12:42
12:44
12:45
13:11^{2}
13:19
13:21
13:23
13:27
13:32
13:35
13:40
13:46
13:48
13:49
13:58
14:4
14:9
14:11
14:12
14:13
14:15
14:26
14:27
14:28
15:5
15:26^{2}
15:28
16:2^{2}
16:3
16:4
16:7
16:11
16:17
16:18
16:22
16:25^{2}
17:4
17:6
17:26
18:6
18:7
18:8
18:9^{3}
18:13
18:14
18:17
18:19
19:1
19:3
19:8
19:9
19:10
19:11
19:12^{2}
19:24
19:25
20:11
20:15
20:23^{2}
20:24
20:26
21:4
21:15
21:13^{2}
21:19^{2}
21:20
21:21
21:25
21:32
21:33^{2}
21:34
21:42
21:44^{2}
22:5
22:17
22:39
23:16
23:18^{2}
23:20
23:21
24:23
24:24
24:26
24:33
25:28
25:40^{2}
25:45^{2}
26:1
26:7
26:8
26:10
26:12
26:22
26:24^{2}
26:25
26:26^{3}
26:27^{2}
26:29
26:31
26:39
26:42
26:54
26:61
26:62
27:6^{2}
27:24
27:29
27:35
27:40
27:48^{2}
27:59
27:60
27:65
28:1
28:2

MK

1:2
1:9
2:1
2:4
2:9
2:12
2:15
2:16
2:17
2:21
2:23
3:4
3:5
3:21
4:4^{2}
4:5^{3}
4:6^{3}
4:7^{2}
4:11
4:16
4:19
4:20
4:22
4:24
4:30
4:31^{2}
4:32
4:33
4:37
4:40
5:14^{2}
5:16^{2}
5:43
6:11
6:15^{2}
6:16
6:18
6:22
6:23^{2}
6:28^{2}
6:29
6:49
6:50
6:56
7:6
7:11
7:18
7:19
7:24
7:27^{2}
7:36
8:16
8:17
8:21
8:26
8:35^{2}
8:36
9:5
9:12
9:13
9:21
9:22
9:30
9:33
9:42
9:43^{2}
9:45^{2}
9:47^{2}
9:50
10:2
10:14
10:24
10:25
10:27
10:40^{2}
10:41
10:43
10:47
11:2
11:13
11:14
11:17^{2}
11:18
11:30
12:1^{2}
12:11
12:14
12:15
12:16
13:11
13:14
13:22
13:29
14:3
14:5
14:11
14:19^{2}
14:20
14:21^{2}
14:22
14:23^{2}
14:25
14:27
14:35
14:41
14:60
14:70
15:2
15:17
15:23
15:25
15:29
15:35
15:36
15:42
15:45
16:4
16:13
16:18

LU

1:3
1:8
1:23
1:38
1:41
1:59
2:1
2:6
2:15
2:17
2:18
2:20
2:23
2:26
2:43
2:46
2:49
3:4
3:21
4:3
4:4
4:6
4:8
4:10
4:12
4:17
4:20
4:39
4:42
5:1
5:8
5:12
5:17
6:1
6:4
6:6
6:9^{2}
6:12
6:13
6:38^{2}
6:48^{2}
6:49
7:8
7:11
7:27^{2}
7:39
8:1
8:5^{2}
8:6^{3}
8:7^{2}
8:10
8:15
8:16^{2}
8:20
8:22
8:29
8:34
8:36
8:40
8:50
9:7
9:11
9:18
9:24
9:28
9:33^{2}
9:36
9:37
9:39
9:45^{2}
9:51
9:57
10:6
10:12
10:14
10:21
10:38
11:1
11:9^{2}
11:10
11:14^{2}
11:25
11:27
11:28
11:29
11:32
11:33
11:38
11:51
12:10^{2}
12:32
12:49
12:50
12:54
12:55
12:56
13:7^{2}
13:8^{3}
13:9^{2}
13:18
13:19^{3}
13:21
13:33
14:1
14:3
14:18
14:22
14:28
14:29^{2}
14:34
14:35^{2}
15:4
15:5^{2}
15:8
15:9
15:22
15:23
15:32
16:2
16:16
16:17
16:22
17:1
17:2
17:6
17:11
17:14
17:22
17:26^{2}
17:28
17:29
17:30
17:31
17:33^{2}
18:15
18:25
18:26
18:35
18:36
18:43
19:7
19:15
19:24
19:29
19:41
19:46^{2}
20:1
20:4
20:7
20:9
20:13
20:16
20:18^{2}
20:22
20:24
21:5
21:13
21:14
21:21
21:35
22:16
22:17
22:19
22:22
22:23
22:36
22:38
22:44
22:64
22:66
23:3
23:24
23:26
23:44
23:53^{3}
24:4
24:10
24:15
24:21
24:24
24:29
24:30^{2}
24:39
24:43
24:46^{2}
24:51

JOH

1:5
1:27^{2}
1:32
1:39
2:5
2:8
2:9
2:17
2:19
2:20
3:8^{3}
3:27
4:6
4:9
4:10
4:53
5:10^{2}
5:13
5:15
6:17
6:20
6:31
6:39
6:42
6:45
6:60
6:61
6:63
6:65
6:71
7:7^{2}
7:10
7:17
7:22
7:51
8:9
8:17
8:44
8:54
8:56
9:4
9:14
9:27
9:32
9:37
10:10
10:17
10:18^{4}
10:22^{2}
10:34
11:2
11:22
11:38^{2}
11:42
11:50
11:57
12:13
12:14
12:24^{3}
12:25
12:28^{2}
12:29^{2}
13:19^{2}
13:24
13:25
13:26^{3}
13:30
14:2
14:8
14:14
14:17
14:21
14:22
14:27
14:29^{2}
15:2^{2}
15:4
15:7
15:16
15:18^{2}
16:7
16:14
16:15
16:23
16:26
18:10
18:11
18:14
18:18
18:25
18:28
18:31
18:34
19:2
19:11
19:14
19:19
19:20
19:24^{3}
19:29^{2}
19:30
19:31
19:35
19:40
20:1
20:14
20:27
21:4
21:6
21:7^{2}
21:8
21:12

AC

1:7
1:19
1:20
2:2
2:3
2:15
2:17
2:21
2:24^{2}
3:10
3:12
3:17
3:23
4:3
4:5
4:10
4:14
4:16
4:17
4:19
4:37^{2}
5:2^{2}
5:4^{4}
5:7
5:9
5:38
5:39^{2}
6:12
6:15
7:5^{2}
7:23
7:31^{2}
7:42
7:44
7:53
9:5
9:6
9:18
9:32
9:37
9:42
9:43
10:4
10:11
10:28
10:42
11:4
11:5^{2}
11:26
11:30
12:3
12:9
12:15^{2}
12:18
12:22
13:17
13:33
13:38
13:41
13:46
14:1
14:6
15:5
15:15
15:16
15:22
15:25
15:28
15:34
16:16
16:35
17:14
18:14
18:15^{2}
19:1
19:19
19:39
20:16
20:35
21:1
21:3
21:20
21:22
21:35
22:6
22:10
22:17
22:22
22:25
23:5
23:12
23:30
23:31
24:3
24:21
25:16
25:27
26:8
26:14
27:1
27:8
27:14
27:25^{2}
27:28^{2}
27:35
27:39^{2}
27:44
28:8
28:17
28:19
28:22
28:28^{2}

RO

1:16
1:17
1:19
2:24
2:27
3:4
3:10
3:19
3:27
3:30
4:3
4:10
4:16^{2}
4:17
4:22
4:23^{2}
4:24
5:16
6:12
7:11
7:13
7:16
7:17^{2}
7:20^{2}
8:3
8:7
8:25
8:33
8:34
8:36
9:12
9:13
9:16
9:20
9:26^{2}
9:28
9:32^{2}
9:33
10:8
10:15
11:6^{3}
11:7
11:8
11:26
11:35
12:8
12:18
12:19
13:9
13:11
14:6^{2}
14:11
14:14
14:20
14:21
14:22
15:3
15:9
15:21
15:26
15:27

1 CO

1:11
1:18
1:19
1:21
1:31
2:8
2:9
3:2
3:13^{3}
3:19
4:2
4:3
4:7^{2}
4:9
4:12
5:1
6:5
6:13
7:1
7:5
7:8
7:9
7:21^{2}
7:26
7:29
7:31
8:7
9:9
9:10
9:11
9:15
9:25
9:27
10:7
10:13
10:16^{2}
10:28
11:6
11:13
11:14
11:15
11:18
11:24
11:25
12:6
12:15
12:16
12:18
12:26^{2}
13:3
13:8
14:7
14:9
14:10
14:15
14:21
14:26
14:27
14:34
14:35
14:36
15:11
15:27
15:32
15:36
15:37
15:38^{2}
15:42^{2}
15:43^{4}
15:44^{2}
15:45
16:4
16:6
16:15

2 CO

1:6^{2}
2:10^{2}
3:16
4:3
4:13
5:10
5:13^{2}
7:8
7:11
7:12
8:11
8:12
8:15
9:1
9:5
9:9
11:15
11:17^{2}
12:1
12:4
12:8
12:13
12:16

GA

1:12^{2}
1:13
1:15
2:6
3:4
3:5
3:6
3:10
3:11
3:13
3:15^{2}
3:17
3:18^{2}
3:19^{2}
4:15
4:18
4:22
4:27
4:29

EPH

2:8
3:5
4:9
4:29
5:3
5:12
5:25
5:26
5:27^{2}
5:29
5:32
6:3

PHP

1:6
1:7
1:20
1:27
1:29
2:6
2:13
2:23
2:25
3:1
3:21
4:*sub.*

COL

1:6^{3}
1:9
1:19
2:14
2:15
3:18
3:23
4:4
4:16
4:17

1 TH

2:1
2:13^{2}
3:1
3:4
4:10
5:24

2 TH

1:3
1:6
3:1

1 TI

1:8
1:13
4:4
4:5
5:16
6:7

2 TI

2:11
4:16

TIT

3:*sub.*

PHM

14
19^{2}

HEB

2:10
2:17
3:13
3:15
3:17
4:1
4:2
4:6^{2}
4:7
6:4
6:7^{2}
6:17
6:18
7:8
7:11
7:14
7:15
8:3
9:5
9:17
9:23
9:27
10:4
10:7
10:31
11:2

11:4
11:6
11:18
12:11
12:13
12:17
12:20
13:9
13:17

JAS

1:2
1:5
1:11^2
1:15^2
2:14
2:16
2:17
2:23
3:6^2
3:8
4:3
4:14
4:17^2
5:3
5:7
5:17^2

1 PE

1:7
1:11
1:12
1:16
2:6
2:13
2:20^4
3:3
3:4
3:11
3:17
4:4
4:11
4:12
4:17

2 PE

1:13
2:13
2:21^2
2:22

1 JO

1:2
2:18^2
2:21
2:27
3:1
3:2
4:3^2
5:6
5:16

2 JO

6

JUDE

3

RE

1:9
1:11
2:17
3:8
4:1
5:6
6:1
6:11
6:14
7:2
8:3
8:5^2
8:8
8:10^2
8:12
9:4
9:5
9:6
9:7
9:9
10:1
10:9^4
10:10^3
11:2^2
11:6
12:4
13:3
13:7
13:18
14:3
14:19
15:2
16:3
16:17
18:21
19:6
19:10
19:15
20:11
20:13
21:6
21:16
21:18
21:21
21:22
21:23^2
21:24^2
21:25
21:26
21:27
22:2
22:3
22:9

ME

1691 or *3165*

GE

3:12
3:13
4:10
4:14^2
4:25
6:7
6:13
7:1
9:12
9:13
9:15
9:17
12:12
12:13
12:18^2
12:19
13:8
13:9
14:21
14:24
15:2
15:3
15:9
16:2
16:5
16:13^2
17:1
17:2
17:4
17:7
17:10
17:11
18:21
18:27
18:31
19:8
19:19^2
19:20
20:5
20:6
20:9^2
20:11
20:13^3
21:6
21:16
21:23^2
21:26
21:30
22:12
23:4
23:8
23:9^2
23:11
23:13^2
23:15^2
24:5
24:7^2
24:12
24:17
24:23
24:27
24:30
24:37
24:39
24:40
24:43
24:44
24:45
24:48^2
24:49^2
24:54
24:56^2
25:30
25:31
25:32
25:33
26:7
26:27
27:3
27:4
27:7
27:9
27:12^2
27:13^2
27:19^2
27:20
27:25
27:26
27:31
27:33
27:34
27:36^2
27:38
27:46
28:20^2
28:22
29:15
29:19
29:21
29:25^2
29:27
29:32
29:33
29:34
30:1
30:6^2
30:13
30:14
30:16
30:18
30:20^2
30:24
30:25
30:26^2
30:27
30:28
30:29
30:31^2
30:33^2
31:5^2
31:7^2
31:9
31:11
31:13
31:26
31:27
31:28
31:29
31:31
31:32
31:35
31:36
31:40
31:42^2
31:44
31:48
31:49
31:50
31:51
31:52
32:9
32:11^2
32:16
32:20^2
32:26^2
32:29
33:10
33:11
33:13
33:14
33:15^3
34:4
34:11^2
34:12^3
34:30^4
35:3^2
37:9
37:14
37:16
38:16^2
38:17
39:7
39:8
39:9
39:12
39:14^2
39:15
39:17^2
39:18
39:19
40:8
40:9
40:14^4
40:15
41:10^2
41:13
41:16
41:24
41:51
41:52
42:20
42:33
42:34
42:36^2
43:6
43:8
43:9
43:16
43:29
44:21
44:27
44:28
44:29
44:34
45:1
45:4
45:5^2
45:7
45:8^2
45:9^2
45:10
45:18
46:30
46:31
47:29^2
47:30^2
47:31
48:3^2
48:4
48:7^2
48:9^2
48:15
48:16
48:29
50:5^4
50:20

EX

2:9
2:14
3:9
3:13^2
3:14
3:15
3:16
4:1
4:18
4:23
4:25
5:1
5:22
6:7
6:12^2
6:30
7:16^2
8:1
8:9
8:20
8:28
9:1
9:13
9:14
10:3^2
10:17
10:28
11:8
12:32
13:2
13:8
14:15
14:17
14:18
17:2
17:4
18:4
18:15
18:16
19:5
19:6
20:5
20:6
20:23
20:24
20:25
22:23
22:27
22:29
22:30
22:31
23:14
23:15
23:33
24:12
25:2
25:8
25:30
28:1
28:3
28:4
28:41
29:1
29:44
30:30
30:31
31:13
31:17
32:2
32:10
32:23
32:24
32:26
32:32
32:33
33:12^3
33:13
33:15
33:18
33:20
33:21
34:2
34:20
40:13
40:15

LE

10:3
10:19
14:35
20:26
22:2
25:23
26:14
26:18
26:21^2
26:23^2
26:27^2
26:40^2

NU

3:13
3:41
8:16^2
11:11
11:12
11:13
11:14
11:15^3
11:16
14:11^2
14:22
14:23
14:24
14:27^2
14:29
14:35
16:28
16:29
17:5
17:10
18:9
20:12^2
20:18
21:22
22:5
22:6
22:8
22:10
22:11
22:13
22:16
22:17^2
22:18
22:19
22:28
22:29
22:32
22:33^3
22:34^2
22:37
23:1^2
23:3^2
23:7^2
23:10
23:11
23:13^2
23:18
23:27
23:29^2
24:12
24:13
27:14
28:2^2
32:11

DE

1:14
1:17
1:21
1:23
1:37
1:41
1:42
2:1
2:2
2:9
2:17
2:27
2:28^2
2:29
2:31
3:2
3:25
3:26^4
4:5
4:10^3
4:14
4:21
5:7
5:9
5:10
5:22
5:23
5:28^2
5:29
5:31
7:4
8:17
9:4
9:10
9:11
9:12
9:13
9:14
9:19
10:1^2
10:4
10:5
10:10
10:11
17:14^2
18:15
18:16^2
18:17
26:10
26:13
26:14
28:20
31:2
31:16
31:19
31:20
31:28
32:21^2
32:34
32:35
32:39
32:41
32:51^2

JOS

2:4
2:12^2
7:19^2
8:5
10:4^2
10:22
14:6
14:7
14:8
14:10
14:11
14:12^2
15:19^3
17:14^2
18:4
18:6
18:8
24:15

JG

1:3
1:7
1:15^3
3:28
4:8^2
4:18
4:19
5:13
6:17^2
6:39^2
7:2^3
7:17
7:18
8:5
8:15
8:24
9:7
9:9
9:15
9:48
9:54^2
10:12
10:13
11:7^3
11:9^2
11:12^2
11:17
11:27^2
11:31
11:35^2
11:36
11:37^2
12:2
12:3^3
12:5
13:6^2
13:7
13:10^2
13:16
14:2
14:3^2
14:12
14:13^2
14:16^3
15:11
15:12^2
16:6
16:7
16:10^3
16:11
16:13^3
16:15^3
16:17
16:18
16:26
16:28^2
16:30
17:2
17:10^2
17:13
18:4^2
18:24
19:18
19:19
19:20
20:5^3

RU

1:8
1:11
1:13^2
1:16
1:17^2
1:20^3
1:21^4
2:2
2:7
2:10
2:11
2:13^2
2:21
3:5
3:17^2
4:4

1 SA

1:11
1:27
2:16
2:28
2:29
2:30^4
2:35
2:36
3:5
3:6
3:8
3:17^2
8:7
8:8
9:16
9:18
9:19^2
9:21
10:2
10:8
10:15
12:1
12:3
12:12
12:23
13:9
13:11
13:12
14:12
14:33
14:34
14:42
14:43
15:1
15:11^2
15:16
15:20
15:25
15:30^2
15:32
16:1
16:2
16:3
16:5
16:17^2
16:19
16:22
17:8
17:9^2
17:10
17:35
17:37^2
17:43
17:44
17:45
18:8
18:17
19:15
19:17^3
20:2^2
20:3
20:5
20:6^2
20:8^3
20:10
20:14
20:23
20:28
20:29^3
20:31
20:42
21:2^2
21:3
21:8
21:9
21:14
22:3
22:8^5
22:13^2
22:15
22:17
22:23^2
23:11
23:12
23:21
23:22
23:23
24:10
24:12^2
24:15^2
24:17
24:18^3
24:19
24:21^2
25:19
25:21
25:24^2
25:32
25:33
25:34^2
26:6
26:7
26:19^2
26:24
27:1^3
27:5
28:1
28:7
28:8^2
28:9
28:11
28:12
28:15^6
28:16
28:17
28:19
28:21
28:22
29:3^2
29:6^2
30:7
30:13
30:15^4
31:4^3

2 SA

1:4
1:7^2
1:8
1:9^5
1:26^2
2:7
2:22
3:8
3:12
3:14^2
3:35
3:39
4:10
5:20
6:9
6:21^2
7:5^2
7:7
7:18
10:2
10:11^2
11:6
12:10
12:22
12:23
13:4
13:5
13:6
13:9
13:11
13:12
13:13
13:16^2
13:17
14:9
14:10
14:15
14:17
14:18
14:32^4
15:4
15:7
15:8
15:25^2
15:26
15:28
15:33^2
15:34
15:36
16:3
16:9
16:12
17:1
18:13
18:19
18:22
18:23
18:29
19:13^2
19:19
19:22
19:25
19:26
19:33^2
19:36
19:38^2
20:4
20:20
22:3
22:5^2
22:6^2
22:17^2
22:18^3
22:19
22:20^3
22:21^2
22:23
22:25
22:34
22:36^2
22:37
22:40^3
22:41
22:44^3
22:45^2
22:48
22:49^4
23:2
23:3
23:5
23:15
23:17
24:13
24:14
24:17
24:24

1 KI

1:12
1:13
1:17
1:24
1:26^2
1:30
1:51
2:4^2
2:5
2:7
2:8^2
2:15
2:16
2:17
2:20
2:23
2:24^3
2:28
2:30
2:31
2:32
2:42
3:20
3:24
5:4
5:6
5:8
5:9
8:25^2
9:3
9:4
9:6
9:13
10:7
11:21
11:22^2
11:33
11:36^2
12:5
12:9
12:12
12:24
12:27
13:6^2
13:7
13:8
13:9
13:13
13:15
13:17
13:18
13:27
13:31
14:2
14:8
14:9^2
15:19^2
16:2
17:10
17:11
17:12
17:13^2
17:18
17:19
18:9
18:12
18:14
18:19
18:30
18:37^2
19:2
19:18
19:20
20:5
20:7
20:10^2
20:32
20:35
20:36
20:37
20:39
21:2
21:3
21:6
21:20
21:22
21:29^2
22:4
22:8
22:14
22:16
22:18
22:24
22:28
22:34

2 KI

2:2
2:4
2:6
2:9
2:10
2:20
3:7^2
3:15
4:2
4:6
4:22
4:24
4:27^2
4:28
5:7^2
5:8
5:11
5:22^2
6:11
6:19
6:28
6:31
8:4
8:10
8:13
8:14
9:12
9:18
9:19
10:6
10:15
10:16
10:19
16:7^2
16:15
18:14^2
18:20
18:22
18:25
18:27^2
18:31^2
19:6
19:20
19:27
19:28
20:8
21:15
22:10
22:13
22:15
22:17^2
22:19

1 CH

4:10^2
10:4^2
11:17
11:19
12:17^3
13:12
17:4
17:6
17:12
17:16
17:17
19:2
19:12^2
21:2
21:12
21:13^2
21:17
21:22^2
22:7
22:8
28:2^2
28:3
28:4^3
28:5
28:6
28:19^2
29:17

2 CH

1:8
1:9
1:10
2:3
2:7^2
2:8
2:9
6:16
7:17
9:6
10:5
10:6
10:9
10:12
11:4
12:5
13:4
15:2
16:3^2
18:3
18:7
18:15
18:17
18:23
18:27
18:33
20:20
28:11
28:23
29:5
34:18
34:21
34:23
34:25^2
34:27
35:21^2
35:23
36:23^2

EZR

1:2^2
4:18
4:21
7:28^3
8:1
9:1
9:4

NE

1:3
1:9
2:2
2:4
2:5
2:6^2
2:7^2
2:8^3
2:9
2:12^2
2:14
2:18^2
4:18
4:23
5:15
5:18^2
5:19
6:2^2
6:4
6:5
6:12
6:13
6:14
6:19^2
12:40
13:8
13:14
13:22
13:28
13:31

ES

4:16
5:13
7:3
7:8

JOB

2:3
3:12
3:25^2
4:12
4:14
6:4
6:8
6:9^2
6:13^2
6:22^2
6:23^2
6:24^2
6:28
7:3
7:8
7:12
7:13
7:14^2
7:16
7:19^2
7:20
7:21
9:11
9:16
9:17
9:18^2
9:19
9:20^2
9:28
9:31^2
9:34^2
9:35
10:2^3
10:8^3
10:9^2
10:10^2
10:11^2
10:12
10:14^2
10:15
10:16^2
10:17^3
10:18^2
10:20
13:13^2
13:15
13:19
13:20
13:21^2
13:22^2
13:23
13:24
13:26^2
14:3
14:13^4
15:17
16:7
16:8^3
16:9^4
16:10^3
16:11^2
16:12^4
16:13
16:14^2
16:20
17:1
17:2
17:3^2
17:6
19:2
19:3^2
19:5^2
19:6^2
19:9
19:10
19:11^2
19:12
19:13^2
19:14
19:15
19:16
19:18^2
19:19^2
19:21^3
19:22
19:27
19:28
20:2
20:3
21:3
21:4
21:5
21:16
21:27
21:34
22:18
23:5^2
23:6^2
23:10
23:14
23:16
24:15
24:25
27:3
27:5
27:6
27:7
28:14^2
29:2
29:5^2
29:6
29:8
29:11^4
29:13
29:14
29:20
29:21
29:23
30:1
30:2
30:10^2
30:11^2
30:12
30:14^2
30:15
30:16^2
30:17
30:18
30:19
30:20^2
30:21^2
30:22^2
30:23
30:26
30:27
30:30
31:6
31:8
31:13
31:15
31:18
31:20
31:23
31:29
31:34
31:35
31:36
31:38
32:10
32:14
32:18^2
32:21^2
32:22
33:4^2
33:5^2
33:9
33:10^2
33:27
33:31
33:32
33:33
34:2
34:10
34:32
34:34^2
36:2
38:3
40:7
40:8
41:10
41:11
42:3
42:4
42:7
42:8

PS

2:7
2:8
3:1^2
3:3
3:4
3:5^2
3:6
3:7
4:1^3
4:8^2
5:7
5:8
6:1^2
6:2^2
6:4
6:8
7:1^3
7:4
7:6
7:8^2
9:13^3
13:1^2
13:2
13:3
13:4
13:6
16:1
16:6
16:7^2
16:8
16:11
17:3^2
17:4
17:6^2
17:8^2
17:9^2
17:15
18:4^2
18:5^2
18:16^2
18:17^3
18:18
18:19^3
18:20^2
18:22^2
18:24
18:32
18:33
18:35^3
18:36
18:39^2
18:40^2
18:43^3
18:44^3
18:47^2
18:48^4
19:12
19:13
22:1^2
22:7^2
22:9^2
22:11
22:12^2
22:13
22:15
22:16^2
22:17
22:19^2
22:21^2
23:2^2
23:3
23:4^2
23:5
23:6
25:2
25:4^2
25:5^2
25:7
25:16^2
25:17
25:19
25:20^3
25:21
26:1
26:2^3
26:11^3
27:2
27:3^2
27:5^3
27:6
27:7^2
27:9^3
27:10^2
27:11^2
27:12^2
28:1^2
28:3
30:1^2
30:2
30:3
30:10
30:11^2

31:1^{2} 31:2^{3} 31:3^{2} 31:4^{2} 31:5 31:8 31:9 31:13^{2} 31:13 31:15^{2} 31:16 31:17 31:21 32:4 32:7^{2} 34:3 34:4^{2} 34:11 35:1^{2} 35:3 35:7 35:12 35:13 35:15^{2} 35:16 35:19^{2} 35:21 35:22 35:24^{2} 35:26 36:11^{2} 38:1^{2} 38:2^{2} 38:4 38:10^{2} 38:12 38:16^{3} 38:17 38:19 38:21^{2} 38:22 39:1 39:3 39:4 39:8^{2} 39:10 39:13 40:1 40:2 40:7 40:11^{2} 40:12^{3} 40:13^{2} 40:14 40:15 40:17 41:4 41:5 41:6 41:7^{3} 41:9 41:10^{2} 41:11^{2} 41:12^{3} 42:3 42:4 42:5 42:6 42:7 42:8 42:9 42:10^{2} 42:11 43:1^{2} 43:2 43:3^{2} 43:5 44:6 44:15^{2} 49:5 49:15 50:5^{2} 50:8 50:15^{2} 50:23 51:1 51:2^{2}

51:3 51:6 51:7^{2} 51:8 51:10^{2} 51:11^{2} 51:12 51:14 54:1^{2} 54:3 54:7 55:2^{2} 55:3^{2} 55:4^{2} 55:5^{2} 55:12^{3} 55:16^{2} 55:18^{2} 56:1^{3} 56:2^{2} 56:4 56:5 56:9 56:11 56:12 57:1^{2} 57:2 57:3^{2} 57:5 59:1^{3} 59:2 59:3 59:4 59:10^{2} 60:5 60:8 60:9^{2} 61:2 61:3 61:5 63:8 64:2 65:3 65:18 65:19 65:20 69:1 69:2 69:4^{2} 69:9^{2} 69:12 69:13^{2} 69:14^{4} 69:15^{3} 69:16^{2} 69:17 69:18 69:21^{2} 69:29 70:1^{2} 70:5 71:1 71:2^{4} 71:3 71:4 71:6 71:9^{2} 71:10 71:12 71:17 71:18 71:20^{3} 71:21 73:2 73:16 73:23 73:24^{2} 73:28 77:1 81:8 81:11 81:13 86:1 86:3 86:7 86:11 86:13

86:14 86:16^{2} 86:17^{4} 87:4 88:6 88:7^{2} 88:8^{2} 88:14 88:16^{2} 88:17^{2} 88:18 89:26 89:36 91:14 91:15 92:4 92:11 94:16^{2} 94:18 94:19 95:9^{2} 101:2 101:3 101:4 101:6^{2} 102:2^{3} 102:8^{3} 102:10^{2} 102:24 103:1 106:4^{2} 108:6 108:10^{2} 109:2^{2} 109:3^{2} 109:5 109:21^{2} 109:22 109:25 109:26^{2} 116:2 116:3^{2} 116:6 116:12 118:5^{2} 118:6 118:7^{2} 118:10 118:11^{2} 118:12 118:13^{2} 118:18^{2} 118:19 118:21 119:8 119:10^{2} 119:12 119:19 119:22 119:23 119:25 119:26^{2} 119:27 119:28 119:29^{2} 119:30 119:31 119:33 119:34 119:35 119:36 119:37 119:40 119:41 119:42 119:49 119:50 119:51 119:53 119:58 119:61 119:64 119:66 119:68 119:69 119:71 119:72

119:73^{3} 119:74 119:75 119:77 119:78 119:79 119:82 119:84 119:85 119:86^{2} 119:87 119:88 119:93 119:94 119:95^{2} 119:98^{2} 119:102 119:107 119:108 119:110 119:115 119:116^{2} 119:117 119:121 119:122 119:124 119:125 119:132^{2} 119:133 119:134 119:135 119:139 119:143 119:144 119:145 119:146 119:149 119:153 119:154^{2} 119:156 119:159 119:161 119:169 119:170 119:171 119:173 119:175 120:1 120:5 122:1 129:1 129:2^{2} 131:1 138:3^{2} 138:7^{2} 138:8 139:1^{2} 139:5^{2} 139:6 139:10^{2} 139:11^{2} 139:13 139:17 139:19 139:23^{2} 139:24 140:1^{2} 140:4^{2} 140:5^{2} 140:9 141:1 141:4 141:5^{2} 141:9 142:3^{2} 142:4^{2} 142:6 142:7 143:1 143:3 143:4^{2} 143:7^{2} 143:8^{2} 143:9^{2} 143:10^{2} 143:11 144:2 144:7^{2} 144:11^{2}

PR

1:28^{3} 1:33 4:4^{2} 5:7 5:13 7:14 7:24 8:15 8:16 8:17^{3} 8:18 8:21 8:22 8:32 8:34 8:35 8:36^{2} 9:11 22:26 22:35^{2} 24:29 27:11 30:7 30:8^{4} 30:18

EC

1:16 2:4^{3} 2:5 2:6 2:7^{2} 2:8^{2} 2:9^{2} 2:15 2:17 2:18 7:23 9:13

CA

1:2 1:4^{2} 1:6^{4} 1:7 1:13 1:14 2:4^{2} 2:5^{2} 2:6 2:10 2:14^{2} 3:3 3:4 4:6 4:8^{2} 5:2 5:6 5:7^{4} 6:5 6:12 7:10 8:2 8:3 8:6 8:12 8:13

ISA

1:2 1:11 1:12 1:13 1:14 1:24^{2} 3:7 5:3 6:5 6:6 6:8 8:1 8:2 8:3 8:5 8:11^{2} 8:18 10:4 12:1 21:2 21:3 21:4^{2} 21:6 21:11 21:16 22:4^{2} 24:16 26:9 27:4^{2} 27:5^{2} 29:2 29:13^{3} 29:16 30:1 31:4 36:5 36:7 36:10 36:12^{2} 36:16^{2} 37:6 37:21 37:28 37:29 38:12^{3} 38:13 38:14 38:15 38:16^{2} 38:20 39:3 40:25 41:1 43:10^{3} 43:11 43:20 43:22^{2} 43:23^{2} 43:24^{4} 43:26 43:27 44:6 44:7 44:8 44:17 44:21 44:22 45:4 45:5^{2} 45:6 45:11^{2} 45:19 45:21^{2} 45:22 45:23 46:3^{2} 46:5^{3} 46:9 46:12 47:8 47:10^{2} 48:12 48:16^{2} 48:19 49:1^{2} 49:2^{3} 49:3 49:5 49:14^{2} 49:16 49:20^{2} 49:21 49:23 50:4 50:7 50:8^{3} 50:9^{2} 51:1 51:4^{3} 51:5 51:7 54:9 54:15 54:17 55:3 55:11 56:3 56:4 56:11 57:8 57:11^{2} 57:13 57:16 57:17 58:2^{2} 59:21 60:9 61:1^{3} 61:10^{2} 63:3 63:5^{2} 63:15 65:1^{4} 65:3 65:5 65:6 65:7 65:10 66:1 66:22 66:23 66:24

JER

1:4 1:7 1:9 1:11 1:12 1:13 1:14 1:16 2:1 2:2 2:5^{2} 2:8^{2} 2:13 2:21 2:22 2:27^{2} 2:29^{2} 2:32 2:35 3:1 3:4 3:6 3:7 3:10 3:11 3:19^{2} 3:20 4:1 4:12 4:17 4:19 4:22 4:31 5:5 5:7 5:11 5:19 5:22 6:7 6:20^{2} 7:10 7:16 7:18 7:19 7:26 8:18 8:19 8:21 9:3 9:6 9:24 10:19 10:20 10:24^{2} 11:6 11:9 11:11 11:14 11:17 11:18^{2} 11:19 11:20 12:1 12:3^{2} 12:8^{2} 12:9 12:11 13:1 13:3 13:5 13:6 13:8 13:11^{2} 13:22 13:25^{2} 14:11 14:14 15:1^{2} 15:6 15:8 15:10^{4} 15:15^{4} 15:16 15:17 15:18 15:19 16:1 16:11^{2} 16:12 17:13 17:14^{2} 17:15 17:16 17:17 17:18^{3} 17:19 17:24 17:27 18:5 18:15 18:19^{2} 18:22 18:23^{2} 19:4 20:7^{2} 20:8 20:11 20:12 20:14 20:17^{2} 22:6 22:14 22:16 23:9 23:14 23:17 24:1 24:3 24:4 24:7^{2} 25:3 25:6 25:7^{2} 25:15 25:17 26:3 26:4 26:12 26:14^{2} 26:15^{2} 27:2 27:5 28:1 28:8 29:12^{2} 29:13^{2} 30:20 30:21^{2} 31:3 31:18^{2} 31:26 31:34 31:36^{2} 32:6 32:8^{2} 32:25 32:27 32:29 32:30^{2} 32:31 32:32 32:33 32:39 32:40 33:3 33:8^{2} 33:9 33:18 33:22 34:14 34:15 34:17 34:18 35:14 35:15 35:16 35:19 36:18 37:7^{2} 37:18 37:20 38:14 38:15^{2} 38:19^{2} 38:21 38:26 39:18 40:4^{2} 40:10 40:15 42:9 42:10 42:20 42:21 44:3 44:8 49:4 49:11 49:19^{3} 50:44^{3} 51:1 51:34^{5} 51:35 51:53

LA

1:12^{2} 1:13^{2} 1:14 1:15^{2} 1:16 1:19 1:20 1:21^{2} 1:22 3:2^{2} 3:3^{2} 3:5^{2} 3:6 3:7 3:10 3:11^{2} 3:12 3:15^{2} 3:16 3:20 3:52 3:53 3:60 3:61 3:62^{2}

EZE

2:1 2:2^{4} 2:3^{3} 2:9 2:10 3:1 3:2 3:3 3:4 3:7 3:10 3:12^{2} 3:14^{3} 3:16 3:17 3:22^{2} 3:24^{4} 4:15 4:16 6:1 6:9^{2} 7:1 8:1^{2} 8:3^{3} 8:5 8:6 8:7 8:8 8:9 8:12 8:13 8:14 8:15 8:16 8:17^{2} 9:9 9:10 9:11 11:1^{2} 11:2 11:5^{2} 11:14 11:24^{3} 11:25 12:1 12:8 12:17 12:21 12:26 13:1 13:19 14:1^{2} 14:2 14:5 14:7^{2} 14:11 14:12 14:13 15:1 16:1 16:20 16:26 16:43 16:50 17:1 17:11 17:20 18:1 20:1 20:2 20:3 20:8^{2} 20:12 20:13 20:20 20:21 20:27^{2} 20:38 20:39 20:40 20:45 20:49 21:1 21:8 21:18 22:1 22:12 22:17 22:18 22:23 22:30 23:1 23:35^{2} 23:36 23:37 23:38 24:1 24:15 24:19 24:20 25:1 26:1 26:2 27:1 28:1 28:11 28:20 29:1 29:17 29:20 30:1 30:9 30:20 31:1 32:1 32:17 33:1 33:7 33:21 33:22^{2} 33:23 34:1 35:1 35:13^{2} 36:16 36:17 37:1^{3} 37:2 37:3 37:4 37:9 37:10 37:11 37:15 38:1 38:16 39:23 39:26 40:1^{2} 40:2^{2} 40:3 40:4 40:17 40:24 40:28 40:32 40:35 40:45 40:48 40:49 41:1 41:4 41:22 42:1^{2} 42:13 42:15 43:1 43:5^{2} 43:6^{2} 43:7 43:8 43:9 43:18 43:19^{2} 44:1 44:2 44:4 44:5 44:10^{2} 44:13^{2} 44:15^{5} 44:16 46:19 46:20 46:21^{2} 46:24 47:1 47:2^{2} 47:3 47:4^{2} 47:6^{3} 47:8

DA

1:10 2:5^{2} 2:6^{2} 2:8 2:9^{4} 2:23^{2} 2:24 2:26 2:30^{2} 4:1 4:5^{2} 4:6^{2} 4:7 4:8 4:9 4:18 4:34 4:36^{4} 5:7 5:15^{2} 5:16 6:22^{2} 7:15 7:18^{2} 7:28^{3} 8:1^{3} 8:14 8:15 8:17 8:18^{3} 9:21 9:22^{2} 10:7 10:8^{2} 10:10^{2} 10:11^{2} 10:12 10:13^{2} 10:15 10:16^{2} 10:17^{3} 10:18^{2} 10:19^{2} 10:21

HO

2:5 2:7 2:12 2:13 2:16^{2} 2:19^{2} 2:20 2:23 3:1 3:2 3:3 4:6 4:7 5:3 5:15 6:7 7:7 7:13^{3} 7:14^{2} 7:15 8:2 8:4 11:7 11:8 11:12 12:8^{2} 13:4^{2} 13:6 13:9 13:10 14:8

JOE

2:12 3:4^{3}

AM

4:6 4:8 4:9 4:10 4:11 5:4 5:22 5:23 5:25 7:1 7:4 7:7 7:8 7:15^{2} 8:1 8:2 9:7

OB

4

JON

1:2 1:12^{2} 2:2 2:3^{3} 2:5^{2} 2:6 2:7 4:3 4:8

MIC

2:4 5:2 6:1 7:1 7:7 7:8^{2} 7:9^{2} 7:10

HAB

1:3^{3} 2:1^{2} 2:2 3:14 3:19

ZEP

2:15 3:7 3:8 3:11

HAG

2:14 2:17

ZEC

1:3 1:4 1:9^{2} 1:13 1:14^{2} 1:19^{2} 1:20 2:2 2:3 2:8 2:9 2:11 3:1 4:1^{2} 4:2 4:4 4:5^{2} 4:6 4:8 4:9 4:13 5:2 5:3 5:5^{2} 5:10 5:11 6:4 6:5 6:8^{2} 6:9 6:15 7:4 7:5^{2} 8:1 8:14 8:18 9:13 10:9 11:7 11:8 11:11 11:12 11:13 11:15 12:10 13:5

MAL

2:5 2:6 3:1 3:5 3:7 3:8 3:9 3:10 3:13

MT

2:8 3:11 3:14 4:9 4:19 7:4 7:21 7:22 7:23 8:2 8:9 8:21 8:22 9:9 10:32 10:33 10:37^{4} 10:38^{2} 10:40^{3} 11:6 11:27 11:28 11:29 12:30^{3} 14:8 14:18 14:28 14:30 15:5 15:8^{3} 15:9 15:22 15:25 15:32 16:23^{2} 16:24^{2} 17:17 17:27 18:5 18:6 18:21 18:26 18:28 18:29 18:32 19:14 19:17 19:21 19:28 20:13 20:15 21:2 21:24 22:18 22:19 23:39 25:20 25:22 25:35^{2} 25:36^{3} 25:40 25:41 25:42^{2} 25:43^{3} 25:45 26:10 26:11 26:15 26:21 26:23^{2} 26:31 26:34 26:38 26:39 26:40 26:42 26:46 26:53 26:55^{2} 26:75 27:10 27:46 28:10 28:18

MK

1:7 1:17 1:40 2:14 5:7 5:31 6:22 6:23 6:25 7:6^{2} 7:7 7:11 7:14 8:2 8:33 8:34^{2} 8:38 9:19 9:37^{4} 9:39 9:42 10:14 10:18 10:21 10:47 10:48 11:29 11:30 12:15^{2} 14:6 14:7 14:18^{2} 14:20 14:27 14:30 14:36 14:42 14:48 14:49 14:72 15:34

LU

1:3 1:25^{2} 1:38 1:43^{2} 1:48 1:49 2:49 4:6 4:7 4:8 4:18^{3} 4:23 5:6 5:12 5:27 6:42 6:46 6:47 7:8 7:23 7:42 7:44 7:45 8:28 8:45^{2} 8:46^{2} 9:23^{2} 9:26 9:48^{3} 9:59^{2} 9:61 10:16^{4} 10:22 10:40^{2} 11:5 11:6 11:7^{2} 11:23^{3} 12:8 12:9 12:13 12:14 13:27 13:35 14:18 14:19 14:26 14:27 15:6 15:9 15:12^{2} 15:19 15:29 15:31 16:3 16:4 16:24 17:8 18:3 18:5^{2} 18:13 18:16 18:19 18:22 18:38 18:39 19:27 20:3 20:23 20:24 22:19 22:21^{2} 22:28 22:29 22:34 22:37^{2} 22:42 22:53 22:61 22:68^{2} 23:14 23:28 23:42 23:43 24:39^{2} 24:44

JOH

1:15^{3} 1:27^{2} 1:30^{3} 1:33^{2} 1:43 1:48 2:17 3:28 4:7 4:9 4:10 4:15 4:21 4:29 4:34 4:39 5:7^{2} 5:11^{2} 5:24 5:30 5:32^{2} 5:36^{3} 5:37^{2} 5:39 5:40 5:43 5:46^{2} 6:26 6:35^{2} 6:36 6:37^{3} 6:38 6:39^{2} 6:40 6:44^{2} 6:45 6:47 6:56 6:57^{2} 6:65 7:7 7:16 7:19 7:23 7:28^{2} 7:29 7:33 7:34^{2} 7:36^{2} 7:37 7:38 8:12 8:16 8:18^{2} 8:19^{2} 8:21 8:26 8:28 8:29^{3} 8:37 8:40 8:42^{2} 8:45 8:46^{2} 8:49 8:54 9:4 9:11 10:8 10:9 10:15 10:17 10:18 10:25 10:27 10:29 10:32 10:37 10:38^{2} 11:25 11:26 11:41 11:42^{2} 12:8 12:26^{3} 12:27 12:30 12:32 12:44^{3} 12:45^{2} 12:46 12:47 12:48 12:49^{2} 12:50 13:8 13:13 13:18^{2} 13:20^{3} 13:21 13:33 13:36^{2} 13:38 14:1 14:6 14:7 14:9^{2} 14:10^{2} 14:11^{3} 14:12 14:15 14:19^{2} 14:20 14:21^{2} 14:23^{2} 14:24^{2} 14:28 14:30 14:31 15:2 15:4^{2} 15:5^{2} 15:6 15:7 15:9 15:16 15:18 15:20 15:21 15:23 15:24 15:25 15:26 15:27 16:3 16:5^{2} 16:9 16:10 16:14 16:16^{2} 16:17^{2} 16:19^{2} 16:23 16:27 16:32^{2} 16:33 17:4 17:5 17:6^{2}

17:7
17:8[2]
17:9
17:11
17:12
17:18
17:20
17:21[2]
17:22
17:23[3]
17:24[4]
17:25
17:26
18:8
18:9
18:11
18:21[2]
18:23
18:34
18:35
19:10
19:11[2]
20:15
20:17
20:21
20:29
21:15
21:16
21:17[2]
21:19
21:22

AC

1:4
1:8
2:28[2]
2:29
3:22
5:8
7:7
7:28
7:37
7:42
7:49
8:19
8:24[2]
8:31
8:36
9:4
9:6
9:15
9:17
10:28
10:29
10:30
11:5
11:7
11:9
11:11
11:12[2]
12:8
12:11
13:2
13:25
15:13
16:15
20:19
20:22
20:23
20:24
20:34
21:39
22:5
22:6
22:7[2]
22:8
22:9[2]
22:10
22:11
22:13[2]
22:18[2]
22:21
22:27
23:3[2]
23:11
23:18[2]
23:19
23:22
23:30
24:12
24:13
24:18
24:19
24:20
25:5
25:9
25:11[2]
25:15
25:24
25:27
26:3
26:5
26:13[2]
26:14[2]
26:18
26:21[2]
26:28
26:29
27:21
27:23
27:25
28:18[2]

RO

1:12
1:15
7:8
7:11[2]
7:13[2]
7:17
7:18[2]
7:20
7:21
7:23
7:24
8:2
9:1
9:19
9:20
10:20[2]
14:11
15:3
15:15
15:18
15:30[2]
16:7

1 CO

1:11
1:17
3:10
4:3
4:4
4:16
6:12[2]
7:1
9:3
9:15[2]
9:16[2]
9:17
10:23[2]
11:1
11:2
11:24
11:25
13:3
14:11
14:21
15:8
15:12[2]
15:32
16:4
16:6
16:9
16:11
16:21

2 CO

1:17
1:19
2:2[2]
2:5
2:12
7:7
9:1
9:4
11:2
11:9
11:10[2]
11:16[2]
11:28
11:32
12:1
12:6[3]
12:7[2]
12:8
12:9[2]
12:11
12:18
12:21
13:3
13:10

GA

1:2
1:11
1:15[2]
1:16
1:17
1:24
2:1
2:3
2:6[2]
2:7
2:8
2:9[2]
2:20[3]
4:12
4:14
4:15
4:21
6:14
6:17

EPH

3:2
3:3
3:7
3:8
6:19[2]

PHP

1:7
1:12
1:26
1:30[2]
2:18
2:22
2:23
2:27
2:30
3:1
3:7
3:17
4:9
4:10
4:13
4:15
4:21

COL

1:25
1:29
4:11
4:18

1 TI

1:12[2]
1:16

2 TI

1:8
1:13
1:15
1:16
1:17[2]
1:18
2:2
3:11[2]
4:8[2]
4:9
4:10
4:11[2]
4:14
4:16[2]
4:17[2]
4:18[2]

TIT

1:3
3:12
3:15

PHM

11
13[2]
16
17
19
20
22

HEB

1:5
2:13
3:9[2]
8:10
8:11
10:5
10:7
10:30
10:34
11:32
13:6

JAS

2:18

2 PE

1:14

JUDE

3

RE

1:10
1:12
1:17[2]
3:4
3:18
3:20
3:21
4:1
5:5
7:13
7:14
10:4
10:8
10:9[2]
10:11
11:1
14:13
17:1[2]
17:3
17:7
17:15
19:9[2]
19:10
21:5
21:6
21:9[2]
21:10[2]
21:15
22:1
22:6
22:8
22:9
22:10
22:12

MY

1700 or *345c*

GE

2:23
4:9
4:13
4:23[3]
6:2
6:18
9:11
9:13
9:15
12:13[2]
12:19
13:8
15:2
15:3
16:2
16:5[2]
16:8
17:2
17:4
17:7
17:9
17:10
17:13
17:14
17:19
17:21
18:3
18:12
19:2
19:8
19:18
19:19
19:20
19:34
20:2
20:5[3]
20:9
20:11
20:12[2]
20:13[2]
20:15
21:10
21:23
21:30
22:7
22:8
22:18
23:4
23:6
23:8
23:11[2]
23:13
23:15
24:2
24:3
24:4
24:6
24:7[3]
24:8
24:12[2]
24:14
24:27[3]
24:35
24:36
24:37[2]
24:38[2]
24:39
24:40
24:41[2]
24:42
24:44
24:48[3]
24:49
24:54
24:56
24:65
26:5[2]
26:7
26:9
26:24
27:1
27:2
27:4
27:7
27:8
27:11
27:12
27:13
27:18[2]
27:19
27:20
27:21
27:24
27:25
27:26
27:27
27:31
27:34
27:36
27:37
27:38[2]
27:41
27:43
27:46[2]
28:21
29:4
29:14
29:15
29:21
29:32[2]
29:34
30:3[2]
30:6
30:8
30:15[2]
30:16
30:18[2]
30:20
30:23
30:25
30:26[2]
30:30
30:32
30:33[2]
31:5
31:6
31:7
31:26
31:28
31:29
31:30
31:35
31:36
31:37[2]
31:39
31:40
31:41
31:42[2]
31:43[4]
31:50[2]
32:4
32:5
32:9[2]
32:10
32:11
32:17
32:18
32:29
32:30
33:8
33:9
33:10[2]
33:11
33:13
33:14[2]
33:15
34:8
34:30
35:3
37:7[2]
37:16
37:33
37:35
38:11
38:26
39:8[2]
39:15
39:18
40:9
40:11
40:16[2]
40:17
41:9
41:17
41:22
41:40[2]
41:51[2]
41:52
42:10
42:28[2]
42:36
42:37[2]
42:38[2]
43:3
43:5
43:9
43:14
43:29
44:2
44:5
44:7
44:9
44:10
44:16[2]
44:17
44:18[2]
44:19
44:20
44:22
44:23
44:24[2]
44:27[2]
44:29
44:30
44:32[2]
44:33
44:34[2]
45:3
45:9
45:12[2]
45:13[3]
45:28
46:31[2]
47:1[2]
47:6
47:9[3]
47:18[3]
47:25
47:29
47:30
48:9
48:11
48:15[2]
48:16[2]
48:18
48:19
48:22[2]
49:3[3]
49:4
49:6
49:9
49:26
49:29[2]
50:5[3]
50:25

EX

3:7
3:10
3:15[2]
3:20[2]
4:1
4:10
4:13
4:18
4:22[2]
4:23
5:1
6:3
6:4
6:5
7:3[2]
7:4
7:16
8:1
8:8
8:20
8:21
8:22
8:23
9:1
9:13
9:14
9:15
9:16[2]
9:17
9:27
9:29
10:1
10:2
10:3
10:4
10:17
10:28[2]
11:9
12:31
13:15
13:19
15:2[4]
15:9[3]
16:4
16:28[2]
18:4
18:19
19:5[2]
20:6
20:24
21:5[3]
22:24
22:25
23:18[2]
23:21
23:27
25:2
29:43
31:13
32:10
32:22
32:33
33:12
33:14
33:17
33:19
33:20
33:22[2]
33:23[2]
34:9
34:25

LE

6:17
15:31
17:10
18:4
18:5[2]
18:26[2]
19:3
19:12
19:19
19:30[2]
19:37[2]
20:3[3]
20:5
20:6
20:8
20:22[2]
21:23
22:2
22:3
22:31
22:32
23:2
25:18[2]
25:21
25:42
25:55
26:2[2]
26:3[2]
26:9
26:11[2]
26:12
26:15[4]
26:17
26:25
26:30
26:42[3]
26:43[2]
26:44

NU

6:27
10:30
11:15
11:23
11:28
11:29
12:6
12:7
12:8
12:11
12:17
14:22[3]
14:24
14:34
15:40
20:19[2]
20:24
21:2
22:18
22:38
23:10
23:12
24:14
25:11[3]
25:12
27:14
28:2[3]
32:25
32:27
36:2[2]

DE

2:28
4:5
4:10
5:10
5:29
8:17
9:4
9:15
9:17
11:13
11:18
18:16
18:18
18:19[2]
18:20
22:16
22:17
25:7[2]
26:5
26:14[2]
31:16
31:17[2]
31:18
31:20
31:27
31:29
32:1
32:2[2]
32:20
32:34
32:39
32:40
32:41
32:42

JOS

1:2
1:7
2:12
2:13[4]
5:14
7:11
7:19
7:21
9:23
14:8[2]
14:9
14:11[2]
15:16
22:2
24:15

JG

1:3
1:7
1:12
2:1
2:2
2:20[2]
4:18
5:9
5:21
6:10
6:13
6:15[3]
6:18
8:19[2]
8:23
9:9
9:11[2]
9:13
9:15
9:17
9:18
9:29
11:7
11:12
11:13
11:19
11:31
11:35[2]
11:36
11:37[2]
12:2
12:3[3]
13:8
13:18
14:3
14:16[3]
14:18[2]
15:1
16:13
16:17[2]
16:28
17:2
17:3[2]
17:13
18:24
19:23
19:24
20:4
20:5
20:6
20:23
20:28

RU

1:11[2]
1:12
1:13
1:16[2]
2:2
2:8[2]
2:13
2:21[2]
2:22
3:1
3:10
3:11[2]
3:16
3:18
4:4
4:6
4:10

1 SA

1:15[2]
1:16
1:26[2]
1:27
2:1[2]
2:24
2:28
2:29[3]
2:32
2:35
3:6
3:16
4:16
9:5
9:16[3]
9:17
9:21
10:2
12:2[2]
12:5
14:29
14:39
14:40
14:42
15:11
15:25
15:30
16:22
18:17
18:18[2]
18:21
19:2
19:3[2]
20:1[2]
20:2[2]
20:9
20:12
20:13[2]
20:15
20:29[2]
20:42
21:2
21:8[2]
21:15[2]
22:3[2]
22:8[3]
22:12
22:15
22:23
23:10
23:12
23:17[2]
24:6
24:8
24:10
24:11[3]
24:15
24:16
24:21[3]
25:5
25:11[4]
25:24
25:25[2]
25:26[2]
25:27[2]
25:28[2]
25:29
25:30
25:31[3]
25:39
25:41
26:17[3]
26:18
26:19
26:20
26:21[2]
26:23
26:24
26:25
27:12
28:9
28:21[2]
29:6
29:8
29:9
30:13
30:15
30:23

2 SA

1:9
1:10
1:26
2:22
3:7
3:12
3:13[2]
3:14
3:18[2]
3:21
3:28
4:8
4:9
5:2
7:5
7:7
7:8[2]
7:10
7:11
7:13
7:14
7:15
7:18
9:7
9:10
9:11[2]
11:11[3]
12:28
13:4
13:5[2]
13:6[2]
13:11
13:12
13:13
13:20
13:25
13:26
13:32
13:33
14:7[2]
14:9[2]
14:11
14:12
14:15
14:16
14:17[2]
14:18
14:19[2]
14:20
14:22
14:24
14:31
15:7
15:15
15:21[2]
16:3
16:4
16:9
16:11[3]
18:5
18:18
18:22
18:28
18:31
18:32
18:33[5]
19:4
19:12[3]
19:13[2]
19:19[2]
19:20
19:26[2]
19:27[2]
19:28[2]
19:30
19:35
19:37[3]
20:9
22:2[3]
22:3[6]
22:7[4]
22:18
22:19[2]
22:21[2]
22:22
22:25[2]
22:29[2]
22:30
22:33[2]
22:34[2]
22:35
22:37
22:39
22:44
22:47[2]
23:2
23:5[2]
24:3[2]
24:17
24:21
24:22
24:24

1 KI

1:2[3]
1:13[2]
1:17[2]
1:18
1:20[2]
1:21[2]
1:24[2]
1:27[2]
1:29
1:30[2]
1:31
1:33
1:35
1:36
1:37[2]
1:48
2:15
2:20
2:24
2:26[2]
2:31
2:32
2:38
2:44
3:6
3:7
3:14[3]
3:17
3:20[2]
3:21
3:22[2]
3:23[2]
3:26
5:3
5:4
5:5[3]
5:6
5:9[3]
5:12[4]
5:13
8:15
8:16[3]
8:17
8:18[2]
8:19
8:20
8:24
8:25[2]
8:26
8:28
8:29
8:59
9:3
9:4[2]
9:7[2]
9:13
11:11[2]
11:13
11:32
11:33[3]
11:34[3]
11:36[2]
11:38[5]
12:10[2]
12:11[2]
12:14[2]
13:6
13:30
13:31
14:7
14:8[2]
15:19
16:2[2]
17:1
17:12
17:18[2]
17:20
17:21
18:7
18:10
18:12
18:13
19:4[2]
19:10
19:14
19:20[2]
20:4
20:6
20:7[4]
20:9
20:32
20:34[2]
21:2
21:3
21:4
21:6
22:4[2]
22:49

2 KI

1:13
1:14
2:12[2]
2:19
3:7[2]
4:1[2]
4:16
4:19[2]
4:28
4:29[2]
5:3
5:6
5:13
5:18[2]
5:20
5:22
6:8
6:12
6:15
6:21
6:26
6:28
6:29
8:5
8:9
8:12
9:7
9:32
10:6
10:9
10:15
10:16
13:14[2]
14:9
17:13[3]
18:23
18:24
18:27
19:12
19:23
19:24
19:28[2]
19:34
20:5
20:6
20:15
20:19
21:4
21:7
21:8
21:15
22:17
23:27[2]

1 CH

4:10
11:2[2]
11:19
16:22
17:4
17:6
17:7[2]
17:9
17:10
17:13[2]
17:14
17:25
21:3[3]
21:17[2]
21:23
22:5
22:7[3]
22:8[2]
22:10[2]
22:11
22:14
28:2[2]
28:3
28:4[3]
28:5[2]
28:6[3]
28:7[2]
28:9
28:20
29:1
29:2[2]
29:3[3]
29:14
29:17
29:19

2 CH

1:8
1:9
1:11
2:3
2:4
2:7
2:8
2:13
2:14
2:15
6:4
6:5[3]
6:6[2]
6:7
6:8[2]
6:9
6:10
6:15
6:16[3]
6:19
6:40
7:13
7:14[3]
7:16
7:17[2]
7:19[2]
7:20[3]
8:11
10:10[2]
10:11[2]
10:14[2]
12:7
12:8
16:3
18:3
18:13
25:16
25:18
29:11
32:13
32:14
32:15
33:4
33:7
34:25

EZR

7:13
7:28
9:3[4]
9:5[6]
9:6[3]
10:3

NE

1:2
1:6
1:9
2:3[2]
2:5
2:8
2:12[2]
2:18
4:16
4:23[2]
5:10[2]
5:14
5:16
5:17
5:19
6:9
6:14
6:19
7:2
7:5
13:14[3]
13:19
13:22
13:29
13:31

ES

4:16
5:7[2]
5:8[2]
7:3[4]
7:4[2]
8:6[2]

JOB

1:5
1:8
1:21
2:3
3:10
3:24
4:14
4:15[2]
5:8
6:2[2]
6:3
6:4
6:7[2]
6:8
6:11[2]
6:12[2]
6:13
6:15
6:21
6:24
6:29
6:30[2]
7:5[2]
7:6
7:7
7:11[3]
7:13[3]
7:15[2]
7:16
7:19
7:21
9:14
9:15
9:16
9:17
9:18
9:21[2]
9:25
9:27[2]
9:28
9:30
10:1[4]
10:6
10:12
10:15
10:20
11:4
13:6[2]
13:14[3]
13:16
13:17[2]
13:18
13:19
13:23[2]
13:26
13:27[3]
14:14[2]
14:16[2]
14:17
16:4
16:5[2]
16:6
16:7
16:8[2]
16:12
16:13[2]
16:15[3]
16:16[2]
16:17
16:18[2]
16:19[2]
16:20
17:1[2]
17:7
17:11[3]
17:13
17:14[3]
17:14[2]
19:2
19:5
19:8[2]
19:9[2]
19:12
19:13
19:14[2]
19:15
19:16[2]
19:17[2]
19:19
19:20[4]
19:21
19:22
19:23
19:25
19:26[2]
19:27
20:2
20:3[2]
21:2
21:4[2]
21:6
23:2[3]
23:4[2]
23:7
23:11
23:12
23:16
23:17
24:25
27:2[2]
27:3[2]
27:4[2]
27:6[2]

29:3 29:4[2] 29:5 29:6 29:7 29:14 29:18[2] 29:19[2] 29:20[3] 29:21 29:22[2] 29:24 30:1 30:10 30:11 30:12[2] 30:13[2] 30:15[2] 30:16 30:17[2] 30:18[3] 30:22 30:25 30:27 30:30[2] 30:31[2] 31:4[2] 31:5 31:7 31:8 31:9 31:10 31:13[2] 31:17 31:18[2] 31:20 31:21[2] 31:22 31:24[2] 31:25 31:27[3] 31:30 31:31 31:32 31:33[2] 31:35 31:36 31:37 31:38 32:17 32:19 32:20 32:22 33:1[2] 33:2[3] 33:3[2] 33:7[2] 33:11[2] 34:2 34:5 34:6[2] 34:16 34:36 35:2 35:3 35:10 36:3[2] 36:4 37:1 38:10 40:4 40:8 40:7[2] 42:8[3]

PS

2:6[2] 2:7 3:2 3:3 3:4 3:7 4:1[2] 4:2 4:7 5:1[2] 5:2[3] 5:3[2] 5:8 6:2 6:3 6:4 6:6[4] 6:8 6:9[2] 7:1[3] 7:2 7:3[2] 7:5[2] 7:8 7:10 9:1 9:4[2] 9:13 11:1[2] 13:2[2] 13:3 13:5 14:4 16:1 16:2[3] 16:3 16:4 16:5[2] 16:7 16:8 16:9[3] 16:10 17:1[2] 17:2 17:3 17:5[2] 17:6 17:9 17:13 18:1 18:2[8] 18:6[4] 18:17 18:18[2] 18:20[2] 18:21 18:24[2] 18:28[3] 18:29 18:32 18:33[2] 18:34 18:36[2] 18:38 18:46[2] 19:14[4] 22:1[3] 22:2 22:9 22:10[2] 22:14[3] 22:15[2] 22:16[2] 22:17 22:18[2] 22:19 22:20[2] 22:22 22:25[2] 23:1 23:3 23:5[2] 23:6 25:1 25:2 25:5 25:7[2] 25:15 25:17[2] 25:18[2] 25:20 26:2[2] 26:9[2] 26:11 27:1[3] 27:2[2] 27:3 27:4 27:7 27:8[2] 27:9[2] 27:10[2] 28:1 28:2[2] 28:6 28:7[5] 30:1 30:2 30:3 30:6 30:7 30:9 30:10 30:11[2] 30:12[2] 31:1 31:2 31:3[2] 31:4 31:5 31:7[2] 31:8 31:9[2] 31:10[4] 31:11 31:13 31:14 31:15 31:22[2] 32:3[2] 32:4 32:5[2] 32:7 34:1 34:2 34:4 35:1 35:3 35:4[2] 35:7 35:9 35:10 35:11 35:12 35:13[3] 35:14 35:17[2] 35:23[4] 35:24 35:27 35:28 36:1 38:3[3] 38:5[2] 38:7[2] 38:8 38:9[2] 38:10[2] 38:11[4] 38:12[2] 38:15 38:16 38:17 38:18 38:21 38:22 39:1[3] 39:2[2] 39:3[2] 39:4 39:5 39:7 39:8 39:9 39:12[4] 40:1 40:2[2] 40:3 40:5 40:8[2] 40:9 40:10 40:12 40:14 40:17[3] 41:4 41:7 41:9 42:1 42:2 42:3[2] 42:4 42:5 42:6[2] 42:8[2] 42:9 42:10 42:11[3] 43:1 43:2 43:4[2] 43:5[2] 44:4 44:6[2] 44:15[2] 45:1[2] 49:3[2] 49:4 49:5 49:15 50:5 50:7 50:16[2] 50:17 51:1 51:2 51:3[2] 51:5 51:9 51:14[2] 51:15[2] 53:4 54:2[2] 54:3 54:4 55:1[2] 55:2 55:4 55:8 55:13 55:17 55:18 56:4 56:5 56:6[2] 56:8[2] 56:11 56:13[2] 57:1[2] 57:4 57:6[2] 57:7[2] 57:8 59:1 59:3[3] 59:4 59:9 59:10[2] 59:11 59:16[2] 59:17[3] 60:7 60:8[2] 61:1[2] 61:2 61:5 61:8 62:1[2] 62:2[3] 62:5[2] 62:6[3] 62:7[4] 63:1[3] 63:3 63:4 63:5[2] 63:6 63:7 63:8 63:9 64:1[3] 66:13 66:14[2] 66:16 66:17[2] 66:18 66:19 66:20 68:22 68:24[2] 69:1 69:3[3] 69:5[2] 69:6[2] 69:7 69:8 69:10[2] 69:11 69:13 69:18 69:19[3] 69:20 69:21[2] 70:2[2] 70:5[2] 71:1 71:3[3] 71:4 71:5[3] 71:6[2] 71:7 71:8 71:9 71:10 71:12[2] 71:13[2] 71:15 71:17 71:21 71:22 71:23[2] 71:24[2] 73:2[2] 73:13[2] 73:21[2] 73:23 73:26[4] 73:28 74:12 77:1[2] 77:2[2] 77:3 77:6[2] 77:10 78:1[3] 78:2 81:8 81:11[2] 81:13[2] 81:14 83:13 84:2[3] 84:3[2] 84:8 84:10 86:2[2] 86:4 86:6[2] 86:7 86:11 86:12[2] 86:13 86:14 87:7 88:1 88:2[2] 88:3[2] 88:9 88:13 88:14 88:15 89:1 89:3[2] 89:20[2] 89:21 89:24[3] 89:26[3] 89:27 89:28[2] 89:30[2] 89:31[2] 89:33[2] 89:34[2] 89:35 89:47 89:50 91:2[3] 91:9 91:14 91:16 92:10 92:11[2] 92:15 94:17[2] 94:18 94:19[2] 94:22[3] 95:9 95:10 95:11[2] 101:2 101:7[2] 102:1[2] 102:3[2] 102:4[2] 102:5[3] 102:9 102:11 102:23[2] 102:24[2] 103:1 103:2 103:22 104:1[2] 104:33[2] 104:34 104:35 105:15 108:1[2] 108:8 108:9[2] 109:1 109:4[2] 109:5 109:20 109:22 109:24[2] 109:26 109:30 110:1[2] 111:1 116:1[2] 116:4 116:7 116:8[2] 116:11 116:14 116:16 116:18 118:6 118:7[2] 118:14[2] 118:21 118:28[2] 119:5 119:13 119:20 119:24[2] 119:25 119:26 119:28 119:32 119:34 119:39 119:43 119:48 119:50[2] 119:54[2] 119:57 119:58 119:59[2] 119:69 119:76 119:77 119:80 119:81 119:92 119:97 119:99[2] 119:101 119:103[2] 119:105[2] 119:108 119:109[2] 119:111 119:114[2] 119:115 119:116 119:120 119:129 119:131 119:133 119:139 119:143 119:145 119:149 119:154 119:157 119:161 119:167 119:168 119:169 119:170 119:171 119:172 119:174 119:175 120:1 120:2 120:6 121:1 121:2 122:8 129:1 129:2 129:3 130:2[2] 130:5 130:6 131:1 131:2 131:3[2] 132:12[2] 132:14 137:5 137:6 138:1 138:3 139:2[2] 139:3[3] 139:4 139:8 139:13[2] 139:14 139:15 139:16[2] 139:23[2] 140:4 140:6[2] 140:7[2] 141:1 141:2[2] 141:3[2] 141:4 141:5[2] 141:6 141:8[2] 142:1[3] 142:2[2] 142:3[2] 142:4[2] 142:5[2] 142:6[2] 142:7 143:1[2] 143:3[2] 143:4[2] 143:6[2] 143:7 143:8 143:10 143:11 143:12 144:1[3] 144:2[6] 145:1 145:21 146:1 146:2

PR

1:8 1:10 1:15 1:23[3] 1:24 1:25[2] 1:30[2] 2:1[3] 3:1[3] 3:11 3:21 4:2 4:3[2] 4:4[2] 4:5 4:10[2] 4:20[3] 5:1[3] 5:7 5:12 5:13 5:20 6:1 6:3 6:20 7:1[3] 7:2[2] 7:4 7:6[2] 7:14 7:16 7:17 7:24 8:4 8:6 8:7[2] 8:8 8:10 8:19[2] 8:31 8:32 8:34[2] 9:5 19:27 20:9[2] 22:17 23:15[2] 23:16 23:19 23:26[2] 24:13 24:21 27:11[2] 30:9 31:2[3]

EC

1:13 1:16 1:17 2:7 2:9 2:10[6] 2:11 2:15[2] 2:18 2:19 2:20 4:8 7:15 7:28 8:9 9:1 12:12

CA

1:6 1:7 1:9 1:12 1:13[2] 1:14 1:15 1:16 2:2 2:3[2] 2:6 2:7 2:8 2:9 2:10[3] 2:13[2] 2:14 2:16 2:17 3:1[2] 3:2 3:3 3:4[2] 3:5 4:1 4:7 4:8 4:9[4] 4:10[2] 4:11 4:12[2] 4:16[2] 5:1[9] 5:2[8] 5:3[2] 5:4[2] 5:5[3] 5:6[3] 5:7 5:8 5:10 5:16[2] 6:2 6:3[2] 6:4 6:9[2] 6:12 7:9 7:10 7:11 7:12 7:13 8:1[2] 8:2[2] 8:3 8:4 8:10 8:12 8:14

ISA

1:3 1:12 1:14 1:25 3:7 3:12[2] 3:15 5:1[3] 5:3[2] 5:4 5:5 5:13 6:7 7:13 8:4[2] 8:16 10:2 10:6 10:8 10:10 10:13[2] 10:14 10:24 11:9 12:2[4] 13:3[3] 14:13 14:25[2] 15:5 16:9 16:11 18:4[2] 19:25[2] 20:3 21:3 21:4[2] 21:8[2] 21:10[2] 22:4 22:20 24:16[2] 25:1 26:9[2] 26:19 26:20 27:5 28:23[2] 29:23 30:1 30:2 32:9[2] 32:13 32:18 33:13 34:5[2] 34:16 36:8 36:9 36:12 36:19 36:20[2] 37:12 37:24 37:29[2] 37:35 38:10[2] 38:12 38:13 38:15[2] 38:16 38:17[2] 38:20 39:4 39:8 40:1 40:27[3] 41:8[2] 41:9 41:10 41:25 42:1[3] 42:8[3] 42:14 42:19[2] 43:4 43:6[2] 43:7[2] 43:10[2] 43:12 43:13 43:20[2] 43:21 44:1 44:2 44:3[2] 44:8 44:17 44:20 44:21[2] 44:28[2] 45:4 45:11[2] 45:12 45:13[2] 45:23 46:10[2] 46:11 46:13[3] 47:6 48:3 48:5[2] 48:9[2] 48:11[2] 48:12 48:13 48:18 49:1[2] 49:2 49:3 49:4[4] 49:5[2] 49:6[2] 49:11[2] 49:14 49:16 49:21 49:22 50:1 50:2[2] 50:6[3] 50:7 51:4[3] 51:5[2] 51:6[2] 51:7 51:8[2] 51:16[2] 51:22 52:4 52:5[2] 52:6[2] 52:13 53:8 53:11 54:8 54:10[2] 55:8[2] 55:9[2] 55:11[2] 56:1[2] 56:4[2] 56:5 56:6 56:7[2] 57:11 57:13 57:14 57:21 58:1 58:2 58:13 59:21[3] 60:7 60:10[2] 60:13[2] 60:21[2] 61:10[2] 62:1 62:9 63:3[3] 63:4 63:5 63:6 63:8 65:1 65:2 65:3 65:5 65:8 65:9[2] 65:10 65:11 65:13[3] 65:14 65:15 65:19 65:22 65:25 66:1[3] 66:2 66:5 66:18 66:19[3] 66:20

JER

1:9[2] 1:12 1:16 2:7 2:11 2:13 2:19 2:27 2:31 2:32 3:4[2] 3:13 3:19 4:1 4:4 4:11 4:19[6] 4:20[2] 4:22 4:31 5:9 5:14 5:22 5:26 5:29 5:31 6:8 6:12 6:14 6:19[2] 6:26 6:27 7:10 7:11 7:12[3] 7:14 7:15 7:20 7:23[2] 7:25 7:30[2] 7:31 8:7 8:11 8:18 8:19 8:20 8:21 9:1[2] 9:2 9:7 9:9 9:13[2] 10:19[2] 10:20[5] 11:4[2] 11:7[2] 11:15 11:20 12:7 12:10[3] 12:14 12:16[4] 13:2 13:10 13:17 14:14 14:15 14:17 15:1[2] 15:6 15:7 15:10 15:15 15:18[2] 15:19 16:5 16:11 16:17[2] 16:18 16:19[3] 16:21[2] 17:3 17:14 17:16 17:17 18:2 18:10[2] 18:15 18:20 18:22 19:5 19:15 20:9 20:10[2] 20:11 20:12 20:14 20:15 20:17[2] 20:18 21:10 21:12 22:18 22:21 22:24 23:1 23:2[2] 23:3 23:9 23:11 23:13 23:22[3] 23:25 23:27[3] 23:28[2] 23:29 23:30 23:32 23:39 24:7 25:8 25:9 25:13 25:15 25:29 26:4 26:5 27:5[2] 27:6 27:15 29:9 29:10 29:19[2] 29:21 29:23 29:32 30:3 30:10 30:22 31:1 31:9 31:14[2] 31:18 31:19[2] 31:20[2] 31:26 31:32 31:33[2] 32:7 32:8 32:9 32:31[2] 32:34 32:35 32:37 32:38 32:40 32:41[2] 33:5[2] 33:20[2] 33:21[3] 33:22 33:24 33:25 33:26 34:15[2] 34:16 34:18 35:13 36:6 37:20[2] 38:9 38:26 39:16 42:18[2] 43:10 44:4 44:6 44:10[2] 44:11 44:26[2] 44:29 45:3[2] 46:10 46:27 46:28 49:25 49:37 49:38 50:6 51:20 51:34 51:35[2] 51:45

LA

1:9 1:12 1:13[2] 1:14[3] 1:15[2] 1:16[2] 1:18[3] 1:19[2] 1:20 1:21 1:22[3] 2:11[3] 2:21[2] 2:22 3:4[3] 3:7 3:9[2] 3:11 3:13 3:14 3:16 3:17 3:18[2] 3:19 3:20 3:21 3:24[2] 3:48 3:51 3:53 3:56[3] 3:58[2] 3:59[2] 4:3 4:6 4:10

EZE

1:28 2:2 2:7 3:2 3:3 3:4 3:10 3:14 3:17 3:23 3:24 4:14[3] 5:6[3] 5:7[2] 5:11 5:12 5:13[3] 5:14 7:8 7:14 7:22 8:6 9:6 9:8 10:2 10:13 10:19 11:12[2] 11:13 11:20[2] 12:7[2] 12:13[2] 12:28[2] 13:9 13:10 13:13[2] 13:15 13:18 13:19[2] 13:21 13:23 14:8[2] 14:9[2] 14:11 14:19 14:21 15:7[2] 16:8 16:14 16:17[2] 16:19 16:21 16:27 16:42[2] 16:60 16:62 17:9[2] 17:19 17:20[2] 18:17[2] 18:19 18:21 18:25 18:29 20:8[2] 20:9 20:11[2] 20:12 20:13[4] 20:14 20:15 20:16[3] 20:19[2] 20:20 20:21[5] 20:22 20:24[3] 20:39 20:44 21:3 21:4 21:5 21:10 21:12[2] 21:17 21:31 22:8 22:20 22:22 22:26[2] 22:31 23:18[2] 23:25 23:38[2] 23:39 24:13 24:18 24:21 25:3 25:14[4] 25:17 28:25 29:3 30:15 30:24 30:25 32:3 32:10 32:32 33:7 33:22[2] 33:31 34:6[2] 34:8[5] 34:10[3] 34:11 34:12 34:15 34:17 34:19 34:22 34:23 34:24 34:26 34:30 34:31[2] 36:5[2] 36:6[2] 36:8 36:12 36:18 36:20 36:23 36:27[3] 36:28 37:12 37:13 37:14 37:23 37:24[3] 37:25[2] 37:26 37:27[2] 37:28 38:16[2] 38:14 38:17 38:18[2] 38:19[2] 38:20 38:21 39:7[3] 39:17 39:19 39:20 39:21[3] 39:23 39:24 39:25 39:29[2] 43:3 43:7[3] 43:8[3] 44:4 44:7[5] 44:8[2] 44:9 44:11 44:13 44:15 44:16[3] 44:23 44:24[4] 45:8[2] 45:9 46:18 48:11

DA

1:10[2] 2:3 2:23 3:14 3:15 4:4 4:5[2] 4:8 4:9 4:10 4:13[2] 4:18 4:19 4:24 4:27 4:30[2] 4:36[5] 5:13 6:22 6:26 7:2 7:15[2] 7:28[3] 8:17 8:18 9:3 9:4[2] 9:18 9:19 9:20[5] 10:3 10:8 10:9[2] 10:10[2] 10:15 10:16[4] 10:17[2] 10:19 12:8

HO

1:9 1:10 2:2 2:5[6] 2:7 2:9[4] 2:12[2] 2:23[3] 4:6 4:8 4:12 5:10 5:15[2] 6:5 6:11 7:2 7:12 8:1[2] 8:2 8:12 9:8 9:17 10:10 11:1 11:7 11:8 12:8 13:11

JOE

1:6 1:7[2] 1:13 2:1 2:25 2:26 2:27 2:28 2:29 3:2[2] 3:3 3:5[3] 3:17

AM

2:7 7:8 7:15 8:2 9:3 9:10 9:12 9:14

OB

13 16

JON

1:12 2:2 2:5 2:6[2] 2:7[2] 4:2[2] 4:3

MIC

1:9 2:4 2:7 2:8 2:9[2] 3:3 3:5 6:1 6:5 6:7[4] 6:16 7:1 7:7[2] 7:9

HAB

1:12 2:1 3:16[3] 3:18 3:19[3]

ZEP

2:8 2:9[2] 2:12 3:8[3] 3:10[2] 3:11

HAG

2:5 2:23

ZEC

1:6[3] 1:9 1:16 1:17 2:11 3:7[4] 3:8 4:4 4:5 4:6 4:13 5:4 6:4 6:8 8:7 8:8 11:4 11:8 11:10[2] 11:12[2] 12:5 13:5 13:6 13:7[2] 13:9[3] 14:5

MAL
1:6[2] 1:11[3] 1:14 2:2 2:4 2:5[2] 2:9 3:1 3:17 4:2 4:4

MT
2:6 2:15 3:17 5:11 7:21 8:6 8:8 8:9[2] 8:21 9:18 10:18 10:22 10:32 10:33 10:39 11:10 11:27 11:29 11:30[2] 12:18[4] 12:44 12:48[2] 12:49[2] 12:50[2] 13:30 13:35 15:13 15:22 16:17 16:18 16:25 17:5 17:15 18:5 18:10 18:19 18:20 18:21 18:35 19:20 19:29 20:21 20:23[4] 21:13 21:28 21:37 22:4[3] 22:44 24:5 24:9 24:35 24:37 24:48 25:27[2] 25:34 25:40 26:12[2] 26:18[2] 26:26 26:28 26:29 26:38 26:39 26:42 26:53 27:35[2] 27:46[2] 28:10

MK
1:2 1:11 3:33[2] 3:34[2] 3:35[2] 5:9 5:23 5:31 6:23 8:34 8:38 9:7 9:17 9:37 9:39 9:41 10:20 10:29 10:40[2] 10:51 11:17 12:6 12:36[2] 13:6 13:9 13:13 13:31 14:8 14:14 14:22 14:24 14:34 15:34[2] 16:17

LU
1:18 1:20 1:25 1:43 1:44 1:46 1:47[2] 2:49 3:22 6:47 7:6 7:7 7:8 7:27 7:44[2] 7:45 7:46[2] 8:21[2] 9:24 9:26 9:35 9:38 9:48 9:59 9:61 10:22 10:29 10:40 11:7 11:24 12:4 12:13 12:17 12:18[3] 12:19 12:45 14:23 14:24 14:26 14:27 14:33 15:6 15:17 15:18 15:24 15:29 16:3 16:5 16:21 16:24 16:27 18:41 19:8 19:23[2] 19:46 20:13 20:42[2] 21:8 21:12 21:17 21:33 22:11 22:19 22:20 22:28 22:29 22:30[2] 22:42 23:46

JOH
2:16 3:29 4:34 4:49 5:17 5:24 5:30 5:31 5:43 5:47 6:32 6:51 6:54[2] 6:55[2] 6:56[2] 6:65 7:6 7:8 8:14 8:16 8:19[2] 8:21 8:28 8:31[2] 8:37 8:38 8:43[2] 8:49 8:51 8:52 8:54[2] 8:56 10:14 10:15 10:16 10:17[2] 10:18 10:25 10:26 10:27[2] 10:28 10:29[2] 10:30 10:32 10:37 11:21 11:32 12:7 12:26[2] 12:27 12:48 13:6 13:8 13:9[3] 13:35 13:37 13:38 14:2 14:7 14:12 14:13 14:14 14:15 14:20 14:21[2] 14:23 14:24 14:26 14:27 14:28 15:1 15:7 15:8[2] 15:9 15:10[3] 15:11 15:12 15:14 15:15 15:16 15:20 15:21 15:23 15:24 16:5 16:10 16:23 16:24 16:26 17:13 17:24 18:11 18:36[4] 18:37 19:24[2] 20:13 20:17[4] 20:21 20:25[2] 20:27[2] 20:28[2] 21:15 21:16 21:17

AC
2:14 2:17 2:18[3] 2:25[2] 2:26[3] 2:27 2:34[2] 7:34 7:49[3] 7:50 7:59 9:15 9:16 10:30 11:8 13:22 13:33 15:7 15:17 15:19 16:15 20:24[2] 20:25 20:29 20:34 22:1 22:6 24:14 24:17 25:26 26:4[2] 26:10 28:19

RO
1:8 1:9[3] 2:16 3:7 7:4 7:18 7:23[3] 9:1 9:2 9:3[2] 9:17[2] 9:25[2] 9:26 10:1 10:21 11;3 11:14 11:27 12:3 15:14 15:24[3] 15:31 16:3 16:4 16:5 16:7[2] 16:8 16:9 16:11 16:21[2] 16:25

1 CO
1:4 1:11 2:4[2] 4:14 4:17[2] 5:4 7:25 7:40 8:13[2] 9:1 9:15 9:17 9:18[2] 9:27 10:14 10:29 11:24 11:25 11:33 13:3[2] 14:14[2] 14:18 14:19[2] 14:58 16:6 16:18 16:24

2 CO
1:16 1:23 2:3 2:13[2] 6:13 6:16 6:18 7:4[2] 8:10 8:23 11:1 12:9[3] 12:21

GA
1:13 1:14[2] 1:15 4:14[2] 4:19 4:20 6:17

EPH
1:16 3:4 3:13 3:14 16:10 16:19 16:21

PHP
1:3 1:7[3] 1:8 1:13 1:14 1:16 1:19 1:20[3] 1:21 1:22 1:26 2:2 2:12[3] 2:25[2] 3:1 3:8 4:1[3] 4:3[2] 4:14 4:16 4:19

COL
1:24[2] 2:1 4:7 4:10 4:11 4:18

1 TI
1:2 1:11

2 TI
1:2 1:3[2] 1:6 1:16 2:1 2:8 3:10 4:6 4:7 4:16

PHM
4[2] 10[2] 20 23 24

HEB
1:5 1:13 2:12 2:13 3:9 3:10 3:11[2] 4:3[2] 4:5 5:5 8:9 8:10 10:16 10:34 10:38 12:5 13:6

JAS
1:2 1:16 1:19 2:1 2:3 2:5 2:14 2:18[2] 3:1 3:10 3:12 5:10 5:12

1 PE
5:13

2 PE
1:14 1:15 1:17

1 JO
2:1 3:13 3:18

3 JO
4

RE
1:20 2:3 2:13[3] 2:16 2:20 2:26 2:27 3:5 3:8[2] 3:10 3:12[5] 3:16 3:20 3:21[2] 10:10[2] 11:3 18:4 21:7 22:12

NOT

3808, *3756*

GE
2:5[2] 2:16 2:18 2:20 2:25 3:1 3:3 3:4 3:11 3:17 4:5 4:7[2] 4:9 4:12 5:24 6:3 7:2 7:8 8:12 8:21 8:22 9:4 9:23 11:7 12:18 13:6[2] 13:9 14:23[2] 15:1 15:4 15:10 15:13 15:16 16:10 17:12 17:14 17:15 18:3 18:15 18:21 18:24 18:25 18:28 18:29 18:30[2] 18:31 18:32[2] 19:7 19:8 19:17 19:18 19:20 19:21 19:31 19:33 19:35 20:4 20:5 20:6 20:7 20:9 20:11 20:12 21:10 21:12 21:16 21:17 21:23 21:26 22:12[2] 22:16 24:3 24:5 24:6 24:8[2] 24:21 24:27 24:33 24:37 24:39 24:41 24:49 24:56 26:2 26:22 26:24 26:29 27:1 27:2 27:12 27:21 27:23 27:36[2] 28:1 28:6 28:8 28:15 28:16 29:25 29:26 30:31 30:33 30:40 30:42 31:2 31:5 31:7 31:15 31:20 31:24 31:27 31:28 31:29 31:32[2] 31:33 31:34 31:35[2] 31:38[2] 31:39 31:52[2] 32:10 32:25 32:26 32:32 34:7 34:17 34:19 34:23 35:5 35:10 35:17 36:7 37:4 37:13 37:21 37:27 37:29 37:30 38:9 38:14 38:16 38:20 38:23 38:26 39:6 39:8 39:10 39:23 40:8 40:23 41:16 41:21 41:31 41:36 42:2 42:4 42:8 42:13 42:15 42:20 42:21 42:22[3] 42:23 42:32 42:36[2] 42:37 42:38 43:3 43:5[3] 43:8 43:9 43:23 43:32 44:4 44:5 44:15 44:18 44:26 44:28 44:30 44:31 44:32 44:34 45:1 45:3 45:5 45:8 45:9 45:20 45:24 45:26 46:3 47:9 47:18[2] 47:19[2] 47:22[2] 47:26 47:29 48:10 48:11 48:18 49:4 49:6 49:10 50:19 50:21

EX
1:8 1:17 1:19 2:3 3:2 3:3 3:5 3:19[2] 3:21 4:1[2] 4:8 4:9 4:10 4:11 4:14 4:21 5:2 5:8 5:9 5:10 5:11 5:14 5:19 6:3 6:9 6:12 7:4 7:13 7:16 7:24 8:15 8:18 8:19 8:21 8:26[2] 8:28 8:29[2] 8:31 9:6 9:7[2] 9:11 9:12 9:17 9:18 9:19 9:21 9:30 9:32[2] 9:33 10:7 10:11 10:15 10:19 10:20 10:23 10:26[2] 10:27 11:7 11:9 11:10 12:9 12:13 12:23 12:30[2] 12:39[2] 12:45 12:46 13:13 13:17 13:22 14:12 14:13 14:20 14:28 15:23 16:8 16:15 16:20 16:24 16:25 17:7 17:17 17:18 19:12 19:13[2] 19:15 19:24 20:4 20:5 20:7[2] 20:10 20:13 20:14 20:15 20:16 20:17[2] 20:19 20:20[2] 20:23 20:25 20:26 21:5 21:7 21:8 21:10 21:11 21:13 21:18 21:21 21:28 21:29 21:33 21:36 22:8 22:11[2] 22:13 22:14 22:15 22:16 22:18 22:22 22:25 22:28 22:29 23:1[2] 23:2 23:6 23:7[2] 23:9 23:18 23:19 23:21[2] 23:24 23:29 23:33 24:2 24:11 25:15 28:28 28:32 28:35 28:43 29:33 29:34 30:15[2] 30:20 30:21 30:32 30:37 32:1 32:18 32:22 32:23 32:32 33:3 33:11 33:12 33:15[2] 33:16 33:20 33:23 34:10 34:20 34:25 34:26 34:29 39:21 39:23 40:35 40:37[2]

LE
1:17 2:12 4:1 4:13 4:22 4:27 5:1 5:7 5:8 5:11 5:17 5:18 6:12 6:17 6:23 7:15 7:18 7:19 8:33 8:35 10:1 10:6 10:7 10:9 10:17 10:18 11:4[2] 11:5 11:6 11:7 11:8[2] 11:10 11:11 11:13 11:26 11:41 11:42 11:43 11:47 12:8 13:4[2] 13:5 13:6 13:11 13:21 13:23 13:28 13:31 13:32[2] 13:33 13:34 13:36 13:53 13:55[2] 14:32 14:36 14:48 15:11 15:31 16:2[2] 16:13 16:22 17:4 17:9 17:16 18:3[2] 18:7[2] 18:8 18:9 18:10 18:11 18:12 18:13 18:14[2] 18:15[2] 18:16 18:17 18:19 18:20 18:21 18:22 18:24 18:26 18:28 18:30[2] 19:4 19:7 19:9 19:10 19:11 19:12 19:13[2] 19:14 19:15 19:16 19:17[2] 19:18 19:19[2] 19:20[3] 19:23 19:26 19:27 19:28 19:29 19:31 19:33 20:4 20:19 20:22 20:23 20:25 21:4 21:5 21:6 21:7 21:10 21:14 21:17 21:18 21:21 21:23[2] 22:2 22:4 22:6 22:8 22:10 22:12 22:15 22:20[2] 22:22 22:23 22:24 22:25 22:28 23:22 23:29 25:5 25:11 25:14 25:17 25:20 25:23 25:28 25:30[2] 25:34 25:37 25:39 25:42 25:43 25:46 25:53 25:54 26:11 26:13 26:14[2] 26:15 26:18 26:20 26:21 26:23 26:26 26:27 26:31 26:35 26:44 27:10 27:11 27:20[2] 27:22 27:27 27:33[2]

NU
1:47 1:49 2:33 4:15 4:18 4:19 4:20 5:3 5:14 5:19 5:28 6:7 9:6 9:7 9:13[2] 9:19 9:22 10:7 10:30 10:31 11:11 11:14 11:15 11:17 11:19 11:23 11:25 11:26 12:2 12:7 12:8[2] 12:11 12:12 12:14 12:15 12:20 13:31 14:3 14:9[2] 14:16 14:22 14:23 14:30 14:41 14:42[3] 14:43 14:44 15:22 15:34 15:39 16:12 16:14[2] 16:15[2] 16:28 16:29 16:40[2] 17:10 18:3 18:4 18:17 19:12[2] 19:13[2] 19:20[2] 20:12[2] 20:17[2] 20:18 20:20 20:24 21:22[2] 21:23 21:34 22:12[2] 22:30 22:34 22:37[2] 23:8[2] 23:9 23:12 23:13 23:19[3] 23:21 23:24 23:26 24:1 24:12 24:17[2] 25:11 26:11 26:62 26:64 26:65 27:3 27:17 29:7 30:2 30:5 30:11 30:12 31:18 31:23 31:35 31:49 32:5 32:9 32:11 32:18 32:19 32:23 32:30 33:55 35:12 35:23[2] 35:27 35:30 35:33 35:34 36:7

DE
1:9 1:17[2] 1:21 1:26 1:29 1:32 1:35 1:37 1:42[2] 1:43 1:45 2:5[3] 2:9[2] 2:19[2] 2:30 2:36 2:37 3:2 3:4[2] 3:11 3:22 3:26 3:27 4:2 4:21[2] 4:22 4:26 4:31 4:42 5:3 5:5 5:8 5:9 5:11[2] 5:14 5:17 5:32 6:10 6:11[3] 6:14 6:16 7:3 7:7 7:10 7:14 7:18 7:21 7:22 7:25 8:3[2] 8:4 8:9 8:11[2] 8:16 8:20 9:4 9:5 9:6 9:7 9:23 9:26 9:27 9:28 10:10 10:17 11:2[3] 11:10 11:16 11:17 11:28[2] 11:30 12:4 12:8 12:9 12:13 12:16 12:17 12:19 12:23[2] 12:24 12:25 12:30[2] 12:31 12:32 13:2 13:3 13:6 13:8 13:13 13:16 14:1 14:3 14:7[2] 14:8[2] 14:10[2] 14:12 14:19 14:21[2] 14:24 14:27 15:2 15:6[2] 15:7 15:9 15:10 15:13 15:16 15:18 15:21 15:23 16:5 16:16 16:19[2] 16:21 17:1 17:3 17:7 17:11 17:12 17:15[2] 17:16 17:17 17:20[2] 18:9 18:10 18:14 18:16[2] 18:19 18:20 18:21 18:22[3] 19:4 19:6[2] 19:10 19:13 19:14 19:15 19:21 20:1 20:3[3] 20:5 20:6 20:7 20:15 20:18 20:19[2] 20:20 21:1 21:3[2] 21:7 21:8 21:14[2] 21:16 21:18[2] 21:20 21:23[2] 22:1 22:2[2] 22:3 22:4 22:5 22:6 22:8 22:9 22:10 22:11 22:14 22:17 22:19 22:20 22:24 22:28 22:29 22:30 23:1 23:2[2] 23:3[2] 23:4 23:5 23:6 23:7[2] 23:10[2] 23:15 23:16 23:18 23:19 23:20 23:21 23:24 23:25 24:4[2] 24:5 24:10 24:12 24:14 24:16 24:17 24:19 24:20 24:21 25:3 25:4 25:5 25:6 25:7[2] 25:8 25:9 25:12 25:13 25:14 25:18 25:19 26:13 26:14 27:5 27:26 28:12 28:13[2] 28:14 28:15 28:27 28:29

28:30[2] 28:31[2] 28:33 28:40 28:41 28:44 28:45 28:47 28:49 28:50 28:51 28:55 28:56 28:58 28:61 28:62 29:4 29:5[2] 29:6 29:15 29:20 29:23 29:26[2] 30:11 30:12 30:17 30:18 31:2 31:6[2] 31:8[2] 31:13 31:17[2] 31:21 32:5 32:6[2] 32:17[3] 32:21[2] 32:27[2] 32:31 32:34 32:47 32:51 32:52 33:6[2] 33:9 33:11 34:4 34:7 34:10

JOS

1:5[2] 1:7 1:8 1:9[2] 1:18 2:4 2:5 2:14 2:22 3:4[2] 5:5 5:6[2] 5:7 6:10 7:3[2] 7:12 7:13 7:19 8:1 8:4 8:14 8:17[2] 8:26 8:35[2] 9:14 9:18 9:19 9:26 10:6 10:8[2] 10:13[2] 10:19[2] 10:25 11:6 11:11 11:19 13:13 13:33 15:63 16:10 17:12 17:13 17:16 17:17 18:2 20:5[2] 20:9 21:44 21:45 22:3 22:17 22:19 22:20[2] 22:22 22:24 22:26 22:27 22:28 22:31 22:33 23:6 23:7 23:14[2] 24:10 24:12 24:13[3] 24:19

JG

1:19 1:21 1:28 1:32 1:34 2:2 2:3 2:10 2:14 2:17[2] 2:19 2:20 2:21 2:22 3:1 3:22 3:25 3:28 3:29 4:6 4:8[2] 4:9 4:14 4:16 4:18 5:23 5:30[2] 6:10[2] 6:13 6:14 6:18 6:23[2] 6:27 6:39 7:4[2] 8:1 8:2 8:19 8:20 8:23 8:34 9:15 9:20 9:28 9:38 9:41 9:54 10:6 10:11 11:2 11:7 11:10 11:15 11:17[2] 11:18 11:20 11:24 11:26 11:27 11:28 12:1 12:2 12:3 12:6 13:2 13:3 13:4[2] 13:6 13:9 13:14 13:16[2] 13:23 14:4 14:6 14:9 14:14 14:15 14:16[3] 14:18[2] 15:1 15:2 15:11 15:12 15:13 16:8 16:9 16:15[2] 16:17 16:20 18:1 18:9 18:25 19:10 19:12[2] 19:20 19:23[2] 19:24 19:25 20:8 20:13 20:16 20:34 21:1 21:5[2] 21:7 21:8 21:14 21:17 21:18 21:22[2]

RU

1:16 1:20 2:8[2] 2:9[2] 2:11 2:13 2:15 2:16 2:20 2:22 3:1 3:2 3:3 3:10 3:11 3:13 3:14 3:17 3:18 4:4 4:10 4:14

1 SA

1:7 1:8[2] 1:11 1:13 1:16 1:22[2] 2:3 2:12 2:15 2:16[2] 2:25 2:31 2:32 2:33 3:2 3:5 3:6 3:7 3:13 3:14 3:17 4:7 4:9 4:15 4:20[2] 5:7 5:11 5:12 6:3[2] 6:6 6:9[2] 6:10 7:8 8:3 8:5 8:7[2] 8:18 9:2 9:4[3] 9:7 9:13 9:20[2] 9:21 10:1 10:16 10:21 11:7 11:11 11:13 12:4 12:5 12:14 12:15 12:17 12:19 12:20[2] 12:21 12:22 13:8 13:11 13:12 13:13 13:14[2] 14:1 14:3 14:9 14:17 14:27 14:31 14:34 14:36 14:37 14:39 14:45[2] 15:3 15:9 15:11 15:17 15:19 15:26 15:29[2] 16:7[2] 16:10 16:11 17:8 17:29 17:33 17:39[2] 17:47 18:17 18:25 18:26 19:4[2] 19:6 19:11 20:2[2] 20:3 20:5 20:9 20:12 20:14[2] 20:15[2] 20:26[3] 20:27 20:29 20:30 20:31 20:37 20:38 20:39 21:8 21:11[2] 22:5 22:15 22:17[2] 22:23 23:14 23:17[2] 23:19 24:7 24:10 24:11[2] 24:12 24:13 24:18 24:21[2] 25:7 25:11 25:15 25:19 25:25[2] 25:28 25:34 26:1 26:8 26:9 26:14 26:15[2] 26:16[2] 26:20 26:23 28:6 28:13 28:18 28:23 29:3 29:4[2] 29:5 29:6[2] 29:7 29:8 29:9 30:2[2] 30:10 30:17 30:21 30:22[2] 30:23 31:4

2 SA

1:10 1:14 1:20[2] 1:21 1:22[2] 1:23 2:19 2:21 2:26 3:8 3:11 3:13 3:22 3:26 3:29 3:34 3:37 3:38 4:11 5:6 5:8 5:23 6:10 7:6 7:7 7:15 9:3 9:7 10:3 11:3 11:9 11:10[3] 11:11 11:13 11:20 11:21 11:25 12:13 12:17 12:18 12:23 13:4 13:12[2] 13:13 13:14 13:16 13:20 13:25[2] 13:26 13:28[2] 13:30 13:32 13:33 14:2 14:7 14:10 14:11[2] 14:13 14:14 14:18 14:19 14:24[2] 14:28 14:29[2] 15:11 15:14 15:27 15:35 16:17 16:19 17:6 17:7 17:8 17:12 17:13 17:16 17:17 17:19 17:20 17:22 17:23 18:3[2] 18:11 18:12 18:14 18:20 18:29 19:7[2] 19:10 19:13[2] 19:19 19:21 19:22 19:23 19:25 19:43 20:3 20:10 20:21 21:2 21:17 22:22 22:23 22:37 22:38 22:39 22:42 22:44 23:5[2] 23:16 23:17[2] 23:19[2] 23:23 24:14

1 KI

1:4 1:6 1:8 1:10 1:11 1:18 1:19 1:26 1:27 1:51 1:52 2:4 2:6 2:8 2:9 2:16 2:17 2:20[2] 2:23 2:26 2:28 2:32 2:36 2:42 2:43 3:7 3:11 3:13[2] 3:21 5:3 5:6 6:6 6:13 7:31 8:5 8:8 8:11 8:19 8:25 8:41 8:46 8:56 8:57 9:5 9:6 9:12 9:20 9:21 10:3[2] 10:7[2] 10:20 11:2 11:4 11:6 11:10[2] 11:11 11:12 11:13 11:33 11:34 11:39 11:41 12:15 12:16 12:24 12:31 13:4 13:8 13:10 13:16 13:21 13:22 13:28 13:33 14:2 14:4 14:8 14:29 15:3 15:5 15:7 15:14 15:17 15:23 15:29 15:31 16:11 16:14 16:15 16:20 16:27 17:1 17:12 17:13 17:14 17:16 18:5 18:10[3] 18:12 18:13 18:18 18:21 18:40 18:44 19:2 19:4 19:11[2] 19:12 19:18[2] 20:7 20:8 20:9 20:11 20:28 20:36 21:4 21:6 21:15 21:29 22:3 22:7 22:8[2] 22:17 22:18 22:28 22:33 22:39 22:43[2] 22:45 22:48 22:49

2 KI

1:3[2] 1:4 1:6[3] 1:15 1:16[2] 1:18 2:2 2:4 2:6 2:10[2] 2:16 2:17 2:18[2] 2:21 3:2 3:3 3:11 3:14[2] 3:17 3:26 4:2 4:3 4:6 4:16 4:24 4:27 4:28[2] 4:29[2] 4:30 4:31 4:39 4:40 5:12[2] 5:13 5:17 5:20 5:26 6:9 6:10 6:11 6:16 6:19 6:22 6:27 6:32 7:2 7:9 7:19 8:19 8:23 9:3 9:18 9:20 9:37 10:4 10:5 10:19 10:21[2] 10:29 10:31 10:34 11:2 11:6 11:15 12:3 12:6 12:7 12:13 12:15 12:16 12:19 13:2 13:6 13:8 13:11 13:12 13:23 14:3 14:4 14:6[2] 14:11 14:15 14:18 14:24 14:26 14:27 14:28 15:4 15:6 15:9 15:16 15:18 15:20 15:21 15:24 15:28 15:35 15:36 16:2 16:5 16:19 17:2 17:9 17:12 17:14[2] 17:15 17:19[2] 17:22 17:25 17:26[2] 17:34 17:35 17:37 17:38 17:40 18:6 18:7 18:12[2] 18:22 18:26 18:27 18:29[2] 18:30 18:31 18:32[2] 18:36[2] 19:3 19:6 19:10[2] 19:25 19:32 19:33 20:1 20:13 20:15 20:19 20:20 21:9 21:17 21:22 21:25 22:2 22:13 22:17 22:20 23:9 23:22 23:26 23:28 23:33 24:4 24:5 24:7 25:24

1 CH

4:10 4:27 5:1 10:4 10:13 10:14 11:5 11:18 11:19 11:21 11:25 12:19 12:33 13:3 13:13 14:14 15:13[2] 16:22 16:30 17:4 17:5 17:6 17:13 19:3 21:3 21:6 21:13 21:17[2] 21:24 21:30 22:8 22:13 22:18[2] 23:11 26:10 27:23 27:24 28:3 28:30[2] 29:1 29:25

2 CH

1:11 4:18 5:6 5:9 5:11 5:14 6:9 6:16 6:32 6:36 6:42 7:2 7:7 7:18 8:7 8:8 8:11 8:15 9:2 9:6[2] 9:19 9:20 9:29 10:15 10:16 11:4 12:7[2] 12:12 12:14 12:15 13:5 13:7 13:9 13:10 13:12[2] 14:11 14:13 15:7 15:13 15:17 16:7 16:8 16:12 17:3 17:4 18:6 18:7 18:17[2] 18:27 18:30 18:32 19:6 19:10[2] 20:6[3] 20:7 20:10[2] 20:12 20:15[2] 20:17[2] 20:32 20:33[2] 20:37 21:7 21:12 21:20 22:11 23:8 23:14 24:5 24:6 24:19 24:22 24:25 25:2 25:4[2] 25:7[2] 25:13 25:15 25:16 25:20 25:26 26:18 27:2 28:1 28:10 28:13 28:20 28:21 28:27 29:7 29:11 29:34 30:3[2] 30:5 30:7 30:8 30:9 30:17[2] 30:18 30:19 30:26 32:7 32:11 32:12 32:13 32:15 32:17[2] 32:25 32:26 33:10 33:23 34:21 34:25 34:33 35:3 35:15 35:21[2] 35:22[2] 36:12

EZR

2:59 2:62 2:63 3:6 3:13 4:13 4:14 4:21 4:22 5:5 5:16 6:8 7:24 7:25 7:26 9:1 9:9 9:12 9:14 10:8 10:13

NE

1:7 2:1 2:2 2:3 2:16 3:5 4:5[2] 4:10 4:11 4:14 5:9[2] 5:13 5:14 5:15 5:18 6:1 6:9 6:11 6:12 7:3 7:4 7:61 7:64 7:65 8:9 8:17 9:16 9:17 9:19[2] 9:20 9:21[2] 9:29[2] 9:30 9:31 9:32 9:35 10:30 10:31 10:39 13:1 13:2 13:6 13:10 13:14 13:18[2] 13:19 13:24 13:25 13:26

ES

1:15 1:16 1:17 1:19 2:10[2] 2:20 3:2 3:4 3:5 3:8 4:4 4:11[2] 4:13 4:16 5:9 6:1 6:13 7:4 9:10 9:15 9:16 9:27 9:28 10:2

JOB

1:10 1:12 1:22 2:10[2] 2:12 3:4 3:6[2] 3:10 3:11[2] 3:16 3:18 3:21 3:26 4:6 4:16 4:21 5:6 5:17 5:24 6:10[2] 6:13 6:29 7:1[2] 7:8 7:11 7:16 7:19 7:21[2] 8:10 8:12 8:15[2] 8:18 8:20 9:5 9:7 9:11[2] 9:13 9:15 9:16 9:18 9:21 9:24 9:28 9:32 9:34 9:35[2] 10:2 10:7 10:10 10:14 10:15 10:19 10:20 10:21 11:2 11:11 11:14 11:15 11:20 12:3[2] 12:9 12:11 13:2 13:11 13:16 13:20[2] 13:21 14:2 14:4 14:6 14:7 14:12[2] 14:21[2] 15:6 15:9[2] 15:15 15:18 15:22 15:29 15:30 15:31 15:32 16:6 16:13 16:17 16:18 16:22 17:2[2] 17:4 18:5 18:21 19:3 19:7 19:22 19:27 20:4 20:8 20:13 20:17 20:18[2] 20:19 20:20[2] 20:26 21:4 21:10[2] 21:14 21:16 21:29[2] 22:5 22:7 22:11 22:12 22:14 22:20 23:8 23:11 23:17 24:1[2] 24:12 24:13 24:16 24:18 24:21[2] 24:25 25:3 25:5[2] 26:8 27:4 27:5 27:6[2] 27:11 27:14 27:15 27:19[2] 27:22 28:7 28:8 28:13 28:14[2] 28:17 28:19 29:16 29:22 29:24[2] 30:10 30:20[2] 30:24 30:25[2] 30:27 31:3 31:4 31:15[2] 31:17 31:20[2] 31:23 31:31[2] 31:32 31:34 32:6 32:9 32:13 32:14 32:16 32:21 32:22 33:7 33:12 33:13 33:14 33:21 33:27 33:33 34:12 34:19 34:23 34:27 34:30 34:31 34:32 34:33 35:13 35:14 35:15[2] 36:4 36:5 36:6 36:7 36:12 36:13 36:19 36:20 36:21 36:26 36:32 37:4 37:21 37:23 37:24 39:4 39:16 39:22 40:5 40:23 41:9 41:12 41:33 42:3[2] 42:7 42:8

PS

1:1 1:3 1:4 1:5 3:6 4:4 5:4 5:5 6:1 7:12 9:10 9:12 9:18[2] 9:19 10:4[2] 10:6 10:12 10:13 14:3 14:4 15:3 15:4 15:5 16:2 16:4 16:8 16:10 17:1 17:3 17:5 18:21 18:22 18:36 18:38 18:41 18:43 19:3 19:13 21:2 21:7 21:11 22:2[2] 22:5 22:11 22:19 22:24 23:1 24:4 25:2[2] 25:7 25:20 26:1 26:4 26:5 26:9 27:3 27:9[3] 27:12 28:1 28:3 28:5[2] 30:1 30:3 30:12 31:8 31:17 32:2 32:5 32:6 32:9 33:16 34:5 34:10 34:20 35:11 35:15[2] 35:19 35:20 35:22[2] 35:24 35:25[2] 36:4[2] 36:11[2] 36:12 37:1 37:7 37:8 37:10[2] 37:19 37:21 37:24 37:25 37:28 37:33 37:36[2] 38:1 38:9 38:13[2] 38:14 38:21[2] 39:1 39:6 39:8 39:9 39:12 40:4 40:6[2] 40:9 40:10[2] 40:11 40:12 41:2 41:11 44:3 44:6 44:9 44:12 44:17 44:18 44:21 44:23 46:2 46:5 49:9 49:12 49:16 49:17 49:20 50:3 50:8 50:12 51:11[2] 51:16[2] 51:17 52:7 53:3 53:4 54:*title* 54:3 55:1 55:11 55:12 55:19 55:23 56:4 56:8 56:11 56:13 58:5 58:8 59:3 59:5 59:11 59:13 59:15 60:10[2] 62:2 62:6 62:10[3] 64:4 66:7 66:9 66:18 66:20 69:4 69:5 69:6[2] 69:14 69:15[2] 69:17 69:23 69:27 69:28 69:33 71:9[2] 71:12 71:15 71:18 73:5 74:9 74:19[2] 74:21 74:23 75:4[2] 75:5[2] 77:2 77:19 78:4 78:7 78:8[3] 78:10 78:22[2] 78:30 78:32 78:37 78:38 78:39 78:42 78:44 78:50 78:53 78:56 78:63 78:67 79:6[2] 79:8 80:18 81:5 81:11 82:5 83:1[3] 85:6 85:8 86:14 89:22 89:30 89:31 89:33 89:34 89:35 89:43 89:48 91:5 91:7 92:6 94:7 94:9[2] 94:10[2] 94:14 95:8 95:10 95:11 96:10 100:3 101:3 101:4 101:5 101:7[2] 102:2 102:17 102:24

103:2
103:9
103:10
104:5
104:9^{2}
105:15
105:28
105:37
106:7^{2}
106:11
106:13
106:23
106:24
106:25
106:34
107:38
108:11^{2}
109:1
109:14
109:16
109:17
110:4
112:6
112:7
112:8
115:1^{2}
115:5^{2}
115:6^{2}
115:7^{2}
115:17
118:6
118:17
118:18
119:6
119:8
119:10
119:11
119:16
119:19
119:31
119:36
119:43
119:46
119:51
119:60
119:61
119:80
119:83
119:85
119:87
119:102
119:109
119:110
119:116
119:121
119:122
119:133
119:136
119:141
119:153
119:155
119:157
119:158
119:176
121:3^{2}
121:6
124:1
124:2
124:6
125:3
127:5
129:2
129:7
131:1
132:3
132:4
132:10
132:11
135:16^{2}
135:17
137:6^{2}
138:8
139:4
139:12
139:15
139:21^{2}
140:8^{2}
140:10
140:11
141:4^{2}
141:5
141:8
143:2
143:7
146:3
147:10^{2}
147:20^{2}
148:6

PR

1:8
1:10
1:15
1:28^{2}
1:29
3:1
3:3
3:5
3:7
3:11
3:15
3:21
3:23
3:24
3:25
3:27
3:28
3:29
3:30
3:31
4:2
4:5
4:6
4:12^{2}
4:13
4:14^{2}
4:15
4:16
4:19
4:21
4:27
5:6
5:7
5:8
5:13
5:17
6:4
6:20
6:25
6:27
6:28
6:29
6:30
6:33
6:34
6:35
7:11
7:19
7:23
7:25^{2}
8:1
8:10
8:11
8:26
8:29
8:33
9:8
9:18
10:8
10:19
10:30
11:4
11:21
12:3^{2}
12:7
12:27
13:1
13:8
14:5
14:6
14:7
14:10
14:22
15:7
15:12
16:5
16:10
16:25
17:5
17:7
17:13
17:26
18:5
19:2
19:5^{2}
19:9
19:10
19:18
19:23
19:24
20:1
20:4
20:13
20:19
20:21
20:22
20:23
21:13
21:17
21:26
22:6
22:20
22:22
22:24
22:26
22:28
22:29
23:3
23:4
23:5
23:6
23:7
23:9
23:10^{2}
23:13^{2}
23:17
23:18
23:20
23:22
23:23
23:31
23:35^{2}
24:1
24:7
24:12^{4}
24:14
24:15^{2}
24:17^{2}
24:19
24:21
24:23
24:28^{2}
24:29
25:6^{2}
25:8^{2}
25:9
25:10
25:27^{2}
26:1
26:2
26:4
26:7
26:17
26:19
26:25
27:1^{2}
27:2^{2}
27:10
27:22
27:24
28:5
28:13
28:20
28:21
28:22
28:27
29:7
29:19^{2}
29:24
30:2
30:6
30:7
30:10
30:11
30:12
30:15
30:16^{2}
30:18
30:25
30:30
31:3
31:4^{2}
31:12
31:18
31:21
31:27

EC

1:7
1:8
2:10^{2}
2:21
2:23
4:3
4:8
4:10
4:12
4:16
5:1
5:2^{2}
5:4
5:5^{2}
5:6
5:8
5:10
5:12
5:20
6:2
6:3
6:5
6:6
6:7
7:9
7:10^{2}
7:16
7:17
7:18
7:20^{2}
7:28^{2}
8:3^{2}
8:7
8:11
8:13^{2}
8:17^{2}
9:2
9:5
9:11
9:12
9:16
10:4
10:10
10:15
10:17
10:20^{3}
11:2
11:4^{2}
11:5^{2}
11:6^{2}
12:1
12:2

CA

1:6^{2}
1:8
2:7
3:1
3:2
3:4
3:5
5:6
6:6
7:2
8:1
8:4

ISA

1:3^{2}
1:6
1:11
1:15
1:23
2:4
2:9
3:7
3:9
5:4
5:6
5:12
5:25
6:9^{2}
7:1
7:4
7:7
7:8
7:9^{2}
7:12
7:17
7:25
8:10
8:11
8:12
8:19
8:20
9:1
9:3
9:12
9:13
9:17
9:20
9:21
10:4
10:7^{2}
10:8
10:9^{3}
10:11
10:24
11:3
11:9
11:13^{2}
12:2
13:17^{2}
13:18
13:22
14:17
14:20
14:21
14:29
16:3
16:6
16:12
17:8
17:10
17:14
22:2
22:4
22:11
22:14
23:4
23:13
23:18
24:9
24:20
26:10^{2}
26:11
26:14^{2}
26:18
27:4
27:9
27:11
28:12
28:15
28:16
28:18
28:22
28:25
28:27
28:28
29:9^{2}
29:12^{2}
29:16
29:17
29:22
30:1^{2}
30:2
30:5
30:6
30:9
30:10^{2}
30:14^{2}
30:15
30:20
31:1
31:2
31:3^{2}
31:4
31:8^{2}
32:3
32:10
33:1^{2}
33:19^{2}
33:20^{2}
33:23^{2}
33:24
34:10
35:4
35:8^{2}
35:9
36:7
36:11
36:12
36:14^{2}
36:15
36:16
36:21^{2}
37:3
37:6
37:10^{2}
37:26
37:33
37:34
38:1
38:11
39:2
39:4
40:9
40:16
40:20^{2}
40:21^{4}
40:24^{3}
40:26
40:28^{3}
40:31^{2}
41:3
41:7
41:9
41:10^{2}
41:12
41:13
41:14
41:17
42:2
42:3^{2}
42:4
42:8
42:16^{3}
42:20^{2}
42:24^{2}
42:25^{2}
43:1
43:2^{2}
43:5
43:6
43:17
43:18
43:19
43:22
43:23^{2}
43:25
44:2
44:8^{3}
44:9^{2}
44:18
44:20
44:21
45:1
45:4
45:5
45:13
45:17
45:18
45:19^{2}
45:21
45:23
46:2
46:7^{2}
46:10
46:13^{2}
47:3
47:7
47:8
47:11^{3}
47:14^{2}
48:1
48:6^{2}
48:7^{2}
48:8^{3}
48:9
48:10
48:11
48:16
48:19
48:21
49:5
49:10
49:15^{2}
49:23
50:5
50:6
50:7^{2}
51:6
51:7
51:9
51:10
51:14
51:21
52:12
52:15^{2}
53:3
53:7^{2}
54:1^{2}
54:2
54:4^{4}
54:9
54:10
54:11
54:14^{2}
54:15
55:2^{2}
55:5^{2}
55:8
55:10
55:11
55:13
56:5
57:4
57:10^{2}
57:11^{3}
57:12
57:16
58:1
58:2
58:3
58:4
58:6
58:7^{2}
58:11
58:13
59:1
59:2
59:6
59:8^{2}
59:21
60:11
60:12
62:1^{2}
62:6
62:8
62:12
63:8
63:13
63:16
63:19
64:3
64:4
64:9
65:1^{3}
65:2
65:5
65:6
65:8^{2}
65:12^{3}
65:17
65:20
65:22^{2}
65:23
65:25
66:4^{2}
66:9
66:19
66:24

JER

1:7
1:8
1:17
1:19
2:2
2:8^{3}
2:11
2:17
2:19
2:20
2:23^{2}
2:24
2:27
2:34
2:35
2:37
3:1
3:2
3:4
3:5
3:8
3:10
3:12^{2}
3:13
3:19
3:25
4:1
4:3
4:6
4:8
4:11
4:22
4:27
4:28
4:29
5:3^{2}
5:4
5:9^{2}
5:10^{2}
5:12
5:13
5:15
5:18
5:19
5:21^{2}
5:22^{4}
5:28^{2}
5:29^{2}
6:8
6:15
6:16
6:17
6:19
6:20
6:25
6:29
7:4
7:6^{2}
7:9
7:13^{2}
7:16^{2}
7:17
7:19
7:20
7:22
7:24^{2}
7:26
7:27^{2}
7:28
7:31
8:2
8:4^{2}
8:6
8:7
8:12
8:17
8:19^{2}
8:20
8:22
9:3^{2}
9:4
9:5
9:9^{2}
9:13
9:23^{2}
10:2^{2}
10:4
10:5^{2}
10:7
10:10
10:11
10:16
10:20
10:21^{2}
10:23^{2}
10:24
10:25^{2}
11:3
11:8^{2}
11:11^{2}
11:12
11:14^{2}
11:19
11:21^{2}
12:4
12:6
12:13
12:17
13:1
13:11
13:12
13:14
13:15
13:17
13:21
13:27
14:9
14:10^{2}
14:11
14:12^{2}
14:13
14:15^{2}
14:17
14:18
14:21^{3}
14:22
15:1
15:7
15:14
15:15
15:17
15:19
15:20
16:2
16:4
16:5
16:6
16:8
16:11
16:12
16:13^{2}
16:17
17:4
17:6^{2}
17:8^{2}
17:11^{2}
17:16
17:17
17:18^{2}
17:23^{2}
17:27^{3}
18:10
18:15
18:17
18:18^{2}
18:23
19:5
19:15
20:3
20:9^{2}
20:11^{2}
20:14
20:16
20:17
21:7
21:10
22:5
22:6
22:10
22:11
22:13
22:15
22:16
22:17
22:18^{2}
22:21^{2}
22:26
22:27
22:28
22:30
23:2
23:10
23:16^{2}
23:20
23:21^{2}
23:23
23:24^{2}
23:29
23:32^{2}
23:38
23:40
24:2
24:6^{2}
25:3
25:4
25:6^{2}
25:7
25:8
25:29
25:33
26:2
26:4
26:5
26:16
26:19
26:24
27:8^{2}
27:9^{2}
27:13
27:14^{2}
27:15
27:16
27:17
27:18
27:20
28:15
29:6
29:8
29:9
29:11
29:16
29:19^{2}
29:23
29:27
29:31
29:32
30:5
30:10
30:11^{2}
30:14
30:19^{2}
30:24
31:9
31:12
31:15
31:32
31:40
32:4
32:5
32:23
32:33^{2}
32:35
32:40^{2}
33:3
33:20
33:21
33:24
33:25^{2}
33:26
34:3
34:4
34:14
34:17
34:18
35:13
35:14^{2}
35:15^{2}
35:16
35:17^{2}
35:19
36:24
36:25^{2}
36:31
37:4
37:9^{2}
37:14^{2}
37:19
37:20
38:4
38:5
38:15^{2}
38:16
38:17
38:18^{2}
38:20
38:23
38:24
38:25^{2}
38:26
38:27
39:16
39:17
39:18
40:3
40:5
40:7
40:9
40:14
40:16
41:8^{2}
42:5
42:10^{2}
42:11^{2}
42:13
42:19
42:21
43:2^{2}
43:4
43:7
44:3
44:4
44:5
44:10
44:16
44:21^{2}
44:23
44:27
45:5
46:5
46:6
46:11
46:15
46:21
46:27^{2}
46:28^{3}
47:3
48:11^{2}
48:27
48:30^{2}
49:9
49:10^{2}
49:12^{2}
49:25
49:36
50:2
50:5
50:7
50:13
50:20
50:24
50:42
51:3
51:5
51:6
51:9
51:19
51:26
51:39
51:44
51:50
51:57
51:63

LA

1:9
1:10
1:14
2:1
2:2
2:8
2:14
2:17
2:18
2:21
3:2
3:22^{2}
3:31
3:33
3:36
3:37
3:38
3:42
3:43
3:44
3:49
3:56
3:57
4:8
4:12
4:14
4:15
4:16^{2}
4:17
5:7
5:12

EZE

1:9
1:12
1:17
2:6^{2}
2:8
3:5
3:6^{2}
3:7^{2}
3:9
3:18
3:19
3:20^{2}
3:21^{2}
3:25
3:26
4:8
4:14^{2}
5:6
5:7
5:9^{2}
6:10
7:4
7:7
7:9
7:12
7:13^{2}
7:19^{2}
8:12
8:18^{2}
9:5
9:6
9:9
9:10
10:11^{2}
10:16
11:3
11:11
11:12
12:2^{2}
12:6
12:9
12:12
12:13
13:5
13:6
13:7^{3}
13:9
13:12
13:19^{2}
13:22^{2}
14:23
16:4^{2}
16:16
16:22
16:28
16:29
16:31
16:43^{2}
16:47
16:48
16:56
16:61
17:9
17:10
17:12
17:14
17:18
18:3
18:6
18:7
18:8
18:11
18:12
18:13
18:14
18:15^{2}
18:16
18:17^{2}
18:18
18:19
18:20
18:21
18:22
18:23
18:24
18:25^{3}
18:28
18:29^{3}
18:30
20:3
20:7
20:8^{2}
20:9
20:13
20:14
20:15
20:16
20:18
20:21
20:22
20:24
20:25^{2}
20:31
20:32
20:38
20:39
20:44
20:47
20:48
20:49
21:5
21:26
22:24
22:28
22:30
23:27
23:48
24:6
24:7
24:8
24:12
24:13^{2}
24:14
24:17^{2}
24:19
24:22
24:23
24:25
25:10
26:15
26:19
26:20
28:2
29:5
30:21
31:8^{3}
32:7
32:9
32:27
33:4
33:5
33:6^{2}
33:8
33:9
33:12^{2}
33:13
33:15
33:17^{2}
33:20
33:31
33:32
34:2
34:3
34:4
34:8
34:10
35:6
35:9
36:22
36:31
36:32
37:18
38:14
39:7
41:6
42:6
42:14
44:2
44:8
44:13
44:18
44:19
44:31
46:2
46:9
46:18^{2}
46:20
47:5^{2}
47:11
47:12
48:11
48:14

DA

1:8^{2}
2:5
2:9
2:10
2:11
2:18
2:24
2:30
2:43^{2}
2:44
3:6
3:11
3:12^{2}
3:14
3:15
3:16
3:18^{2}
3:24
3:28
4:7
4:18
4:19
4:30
5:8
5:10
5:15
5:22
5:23^{2}
6:5
6:8^{2}
6:12^{2}
6:13
6:17
6:22
6:26
7:14^{2}
8:5
8:22
8:24
9:11
9:12
9:13
9:14
9:18
9:19
9:26
10:7
10:12
10:19
11:4
11:6
11:12
11:15
11:17
11:19
11:21
11:24
11:25
11:27
11:29
11:38
11:42
12:8

HO

1:7
1:9^{2}
1:10
2:2
2:4
2:6
2:7^{2}
2:8
2:23^{2}
3:3^{2}
4:10^{2}
4:14^{2}
4:15^{2}
5:3
5:4^{2}
5:6
5:13
6:6
7:2
7:8
7:9^{2}
7:10
7:14
7:16
8:4^{2}
8:6
8:13
9:1
9:2
9:3
9:4^{2}
9:12
9:17
10:3
10:9
11:3
11:5
11:9^{4}
13:13
14:3^{2}

JOE

1:16
2:2
2:7
2:8
2:13
2:17
2:21
2:22
3:21

AM

1:3
1:6
1:9^{2}
1:11
1:13
2:1
2:4^{2}
2:6
2:11
2:12
2:14
2:15
3:6^{2}
3:8
3:10
4:6
4:7^{2}
4:8^{2}
4:9
4:10
4:11
5:5^{2}
5:11^{2}
5:14
5:18
5:20^{2}
5:21
5:22
5:23
6:6
6:10
6:13
7:3
7:6
7:8
7:10
7:13
7:16^{2}
8:2
8:8
8:11
8:12
9:1^{2}
9:4
9:7^{2}
9:8
9:9
9:10

OB

5^{2}
8
12
13^{2}
16
18

JON

1:6
1:13
1:14^{2}
3:7
3:9
3:10
4:2
4:10
4:11

MIC

1:5^{2}
1:10^{2}
1:11
2:3
2:6^{2}
2:7
2:10
3:1
3:4
3:5
3:6^{2}
3:11
4:3
4:12
5:7
5:15
6:14^{2}
6:15^{3}
7:5^{2}
7:8
7:18

NA

1:3
1:9
3:1
3:17
3:19

HAB

1:2^{2}
1:5
1:6
1:12^{2}
1:13
1:17
2:3^{2}
2:4
2:6^{2}
2:7
2:13
3:17

ZEP

1:6
1:12
1:13^{2}
2:1
3:2^{4}
3:3
3:5^{2}
3:7
3:11
3:13
3:15
3:16^{2}

HAG

1:2
1:6^{2}
2:3
2:5
2:17
2:19

ZEC

1:4^{2}
1:6
1:12
3:2
4:5
4:6
4:13
7:6
7:7
7:10
7:11
7:13^{2}
7:14
8:11
8:13
8:14
8:15
9:5
10:6
10:10
11:5^{2}
11:6
11:9
11:12
11:16
12:7
13:3
14:2
14:6
14:7
14:17
14:18^{3}
14:19

MAL

1:2
1:8^{2}
2:2^{3}
2:6
2:9
2:10^{2}
2:13
2:15
2:16
3:5
3:6^{2}
3:7
3:10^{2}
3:11
3:18

MT

1:19
1:20
1:25
2:6
2:12
2:18^{2}
3:9
3:10
3:11
4:4
4:7
5:17^{2}
5:21
5:27
5:29
5:30
5:33
5:34
5:36
5:39
5:42
5:46
5:47
6:1
6:2
6:3
6:5
6:7
6:8
6:13
6:15
6:16
6:18
6:19
6:20
6:25
6:26^{2}
6:28
6:29
6:30
7:1^{2}
7:3
7:6
7:19
7:21

7:22 7:25 7:26 7:29 8:8 8:10^2 8:20 9:12 9:13^2 9:14 9:24 10:5^2 10:13 10:14 10:20 10:23 10:24 10:26^2 10:28^2 10:29^2 10:31 10:34^2 10:37^2 10:38^2 11:6 11:11 11:17^2 11:20 12:2 12:3 12:4 12:5 12:7^2 12:11 12:16 12:19 12:20^2 12:23 12:24 12:25 12:30^2 12:31 12:32 13:5 13:11 13:12 13:13^2 13:14^2 13:17^2 13:19 13:21 13:27 13:34 13:55^2 13:56 13:57 13:58 14:4 14:16 14:27 15:2 15:6 15:11 15:13 15:17 15:20 15:23 15:24 15:26 15:32 16:3 16:9 16:11^2 16:12 16:17 16:18 16:22 16:23 16:28 17:7 17:12 17:16 17:19 17:21 17:24 18:3 18:10 18:12 18:13 18:14 18:16 18:22 18:25 18:30 18:33 18:35 19:4 19:6 19:8 19:10 19:14 19:18^3 20:13 20:15 20:22 20:23 20:26 20:28 21:21^2 21:25 21:29 21:30 21:32^2 22:3 22:8 22:11 22:12 22:16 22:17 22:29 22:31 22:32 23:3^2 23:4 23:8 23:23 23:30 23:37 23:39 24:2^3 24:6^2 24:17 24:20 24:21 24:23 24:26^2 24:29 24:34 24:35 24:36 24:39 24:42 24:43 24:44 24:50^2 25:9^2 25:12 25:24^2 25:26^2 25:29 25:43^3 25:44 25:45^2 26:5 26:11 26:24 26:29 26:35 26:39 26:40 26:41 26:42 26:70 26:72 26:74 27:6 27:13 27:34 28:5 28:6 28:10

MK

1:7 1:22 1:35 2:2 2:4 2:17 2:18 2:24 2:26 2:27 3:12 3:20 4:5 4:12^2 4:13 4:21 4:22 4:25 4:27 4:34 4:38 5:3 5:7 5:10 5:19 5:36 5:39 6:3^2 6:4 6:9 6:11 6:18 6:19 6:26 6:34 6:50 6:52 7:3 7:4 7:5 7:18 7:19 7:24 7:27 8:17 8:18^2 8:21 8:33 9:1 9:6 9:18 9:28 9:30 9:32 9:37 9:38^2 9:39 9:40 9:41 9:44^2 9:46^2 9:48^2 10:9 10:14 10:15^2 10:19^4 10:27 10:38 10:40 10:43 10:45 11:13 11:16 11:17 11:23 11:26 11:31 12:10 12:14^2 12:15 12:24^2 12:26 12:27 12:34 13:2^2 13:7^2 13:11 13:14 13:15 13:16 13:18 13:19 13:21 13:24 13:30 13:31 13:32 13:33 13:35 14:2 14:7 14:29 14:31 14:36 14:37 14:49 14:56 14:68 14:71 15:23 16:6^2 16:11 16:14 16:16 16:18

LU

1:13 1:20^2 1:22 1:30 1:34 1:60 2:10 2:26 2:37 2:43 2:45 2:49 2:50 3:8 3:9 3:15 3:16 4:4 4:12 4:22 4:35 4:41 4:42 5:10 5:19 5:31 5:32 5:36 6:2 6:3 6:4 6:29 6:30 6:37^4 6:39 6:40 6:41 6:42 6:43 6:44 6:46 6:48 6:49 7:6^3 7:9^2 7:13 7:23 7:28 7:30 7:32^2 7:45 7:46 8:10^2 8:17^2 8:18 8:19 8:28 8:31 8:47 8:49 8:50 8:52^2 9:5 9:27 9:33 9:40 9:45^2 9:49 9:50^2 9:53 9:55 9:56 9:58 10:6 10:7 10:10 10:20 10:24^2 10:40 10:42 11:4 11:7 11:8 11:23^2 11:35 11:38 11:40 11:42 11:44^2 11:46 11:52 12:2^2 12:4 12:6^2 12:7 12:10 12:15 12:21 12:26 12:27^3 12:29 12:32 12:33^2 12:39 12:40 12:46^2 12:47 12:48 12:56 12:57 12:59 13:9 13:14 13:15 13:16 13:24 13:25 13:27 13:34 13:35 14:5 14:6 14:8 14:12 14:26 14:27 14:28 14:29 14:30 14:31 14:33 15:4 15:8 15:13 15:28 16:11 16:12 16:31 17:8 17:9 17:17 17:18 17:20 17:22 17:23 17:31^2 18:1 18:2 18:4^2 18:7 18:11 18:13 18:16 18:17 18:20^4 18:30 19:3 19:14 19:21^2 19:22^2 19:23 19:26 19:27 19:44^2 19:48 20:5 20:7 20:26 20:38 20:40 21:6^2 21:8^2 21:9^2 21:14 21:15 21:18 21:21 21:32 21:33 22:16 22:18 22:26 22:27 22:32 22:34 22:40 22:42 22:57 22:58 22:60 22:67 22:68 23:28 23:34 23:40 23:51 24:3 24:6 24:11 24:16 24:18 24:23 24:24 24:26 24:32 24:39 24:41

JOH

1:3 1:5 1:8 1:10 1:11 1:13 1:20^2 1:21 1:25 1:26 1:27 1:31 1:33 2:4 2:9 2:12 2:16 2:24 2:25 3:7 3:8 3:10 3:11 3:12 3:15 3:16 3:17 3:18^3 3:24 3:28 3:34 3:36^2 4:2 4:15 4:18 4:22 4:29 4:32 4:35 4:42 4:48 5:10 5:13 5:18 5:23^2 5:24 5:28 5:30 5:31 5:34 5:38^2 5:40 5:41 5:42 5:43 5:44 5:45 5:47 6:7 6:17 6:20 6:22 6:24 6:26 6:27 6:32 6:36 6:38 6:42 6:43 6:46 6:50 6:58 6:64^2 6:70 7:1 7:6 7:8^2 7:10 7:16 7:19 7:22 7:23 7:24 7:25 7:28^2 7:30 7:34 7:35 7:36 7:39^2 7:42 7:45 7:49 8:6 8:12 8:13 8:16 8:20 8:23 8:24 8:27 8:29 8:35 8:40 8:41 8:43 8:44 8:45 8:46 8:47^2 8:48 8:49 8:50 8:55^2 8:57 9:8 9:12 9:16^2 9:18 9:21^2 9:25 9:27 9:29 9:30 9:31 9:32 9:33 9:39 10:1 10:5^2 10:6 10:8 10:10 10:12^2 10:13 10:16 10:21 10:25 10:26^2 10:33 10:34 10:37^2 10:38 11:4 11:9^2 11:15 11:21 11:30 11:32 11:37^2 11:40 11:50 11:51 11:52 11:56 12:5 12:6 12:8 12:9 12:15 12:16 12:30 12:35 12:37 12:39 12:40 12:42 12:44 12:46 12:47^3 12:48 12:49 13:7 13:8 13:9 13:10^2 13:11 13:16 13:18 13:36 13:38 14:1 14:2 14:5 14:9 14:10^2 14:17 14:18 14:22^2 14:24^3 14:27^2 14:30 15:2 15:6 15:15^2 15:16 15:19 15:20 15:21 15:22^2 15:24^2 16:1 16:3 16:4 16:7^2 16:9 16:13 16:16 16:17 16:19 16:26 16:30 16:32 17:9 17:14^2 17:15 17:16^2 17:25 18:1 18:17^2 18:25^2 18:26 18:28 18:30^2 18:31 18:36^3 18:40 19:10^2 19:12 19:21 19:24 19:31 19:33 19:36 20:2 20:5 20:7 20:9 20:13 20:14 20:17^2 20:24 20:25 20:27 20:29 20:30 21:4 21:6 21:8 21:11 21:18 21:23^3 21:25

AC

1:4 1:5 1:7 2:7 2:15 2:24 2:25 2:27 2:31 2:34 3:23 4:18 5:4^3 5:7 5:22 5:28^2 5:40 5:42 6:2 6:10 6:13 7:5 7:18 7:19 7:25 7:32 7:39 7:40 7:48 7:50 7:52 7:53 7:60 8:21 8:32 9:21 9:26 9:38 10:14 10:15 10:28 10:41 10:47 11:8 11:9 12:9 12:14 12:19 12:22 12:23 13:10 13:11 13:25^2 13:27 13:35 13:39 14:17 14:18 15:19 15:38^2 16:7 16:21 17:4 17:5 17:6 17:12 17:24 17:27 17:29 18:9^2 18:20 19:2 19:9 19:26 19:27 19:30 19:31 19:32 19:35 20:10 20:12 20:16 20:22 20:27 20:29 20:31 21:4 21:12 21:13 21:14 21:21 21:34 21:38 22:9 22:11 22:18 22:22 23:5^2 23:9 23:21 24:4 25:7 25:11 25:16 25:24 25:27 26:19 26:25 26:26 26:29 26:32 27:7 27:10 27:12 27:14 27:15 27:21 27:24 27:34 27:39 28:4 28:19 28:24 28:25 28:26^2

RO

1:13 1:16 1:21 1:28^2 1:32 2:4 2:8 2:13 2:14^2 2:21^2 2:22 2:26 2:27 2:28 2:29^2 3:3 3:8 3:10 3:12 3:17 3:29 4:2 4:4 4:5 4:8 4:10 4:11 4:12 4:13 4:16 4:17 4:19^2 4:20 4:23 5:3 5:5 5:11 5:13 5:14 5:15 5:16 6:3 6:6 6:12 6:14^2 6:15 6:16 7:1 7:6 7:7^3 7:15^2 7:16 7:18 7:19^2 7:20 8:1 8:3 8:4 8:7 8:9^2 8:12 8:15 8:18 8:20 8:23 8:24 8:25 8:26 8:32^2 9:1 9:6^2 9:8 9:10 9:11^2 9:16 9:21 9:24 9:25^2 9:26 9:30 9:31 9:32 9:33 10:2 10:3 10:6 10:11 10:14^2 10:16 10:18 10:19 10:20^2 11:2^2 11:4 11:7 11:8^2 11:10 11:18^2 11:20 11:21^2 11:23 11:25 11:30 11:31 12:2 12:3 12:4 12:11 12:14 12:16^2 12:19 12:21 13:3^2 13:4 13:5 13:9^5 13:13^3 13:14 14:1 14:3^4 14:6^4 14:13 14:15^2 14:16 14:17 14:20 14:22 14:23^2 15:1 15:3 15:18^2 15:20 15:21^2 15:31 16:4 16:18

1 CO

1:16 1:17^2 1:20 1:21 1:26^3 1:27 1:28 2:1 2:2 2:4 2:5 2:6 2:8 2:9 2:12 2:13 2:14 3:1 3:2^2 3:4 3:16 4:3 4:4 4:6 4:7^2 4:14 4:15 4:18 4:19 4:20 5:1 5:2 5:6^2 5:8 5:9 5:10 5:11^2 5:12 6:1 6:2 6:3 6:5^2 6:7^2 6:9^3 6:12^2 6:13 6:15 6:16 6:19^2 7:1 7:4^2 7:5^2 7:6 7:10^2 7:11 7:12^3 7:13^2 7:15 7:18^2 7:21 7:23 7:27^2 7:28^2 7:30^3 7:31 7:35 7:36 7:38 8:7 8:8^2 8:10 9:1^4 9:2 9:4 9:5 9:6 9:7^2 9:8 9:9 9:12^2 9:13 9:16 9:18 9:21 9:24 9:26^2 10:1 10:5 10:6 10:13 10:16^2 10:18 10:20^2 10:23 10:27 10:28 10:29 10:33 11:6 11:7 11:8 11:14 11:17^2 11:20 11:22^3 11:29 11:31 11:32 11:34 12:1 12:14 12:15^3 12:16^3 13:1 13:2 13:3 13:4^3 13:5^3 13:6 14:2 14:11 14:16 14:17 14:20 14:21 14:22^4 14:23 14:24 14:33 14:34 14:39 15:9 15:10^2 15:13 15:14 15:15^2 15:16^2 15:17 15:29 15:32 15:33 15:34^2 15:36 15:37 15:39 15:46 15:51 15:58 16:7 16:12 16:22

2 CO

1:8 1:9 1:12 1:18 1:19 1:23 1:24 2:1 2:4 2:5^2 2:11 2:13 2:17 3:3^2 3:5 3:6 3:7 3:8 3:13^2 4:1 4:2 4:4 4:5 4:7 4:8^2 4:9^2 4:16 4:18^2 5:1 5:3 5:4 5:7 5:12^2 5:15 5:19 6:1 6:3 6:9 6:12 6:14 6:17 7:3 7:7 7:8 7:9 7:10 7:12 7:14 8:5 8:8 8:10 8:12^2 8:13 8:19 8:21 9:4 9:5 9:7 9:12 10:2 10:3 10:4 10:8^2 10:9 10:12^2 10:13 10:14^2 10:15 10:16 10:18 11:4^3 11:5 11:6 11:11 11:17 11:29^2 11:31 12:1 12:4 12:5 12:6 12:13 12:14^2 12:16 12:18^2 12:20^2 12:21 13:2 13:3 13:5 13:6 13:7 13:10

GA

1:1 1:7 1:10 1:11 1:16 1:20 2:5 2:14 2:15 2:16^2 2:20 2:21 3:1 3:10 3:12 3:16 3:20 4:8 4:12 4:14 4:17 4:18 4:21 4:27^2 4:30 4:31 5:1 5:7 5:8 5:13 5:15 5:16 5:18 5:21 5:26 6:4 6:7^2 6:9^2

EPH

1:16 1:21 2:8 2:9 3:5 3:13 4:17 4:20 4:26^2 4:30 5:3 5:4 5:7 5:15 5:17 5:18 5:27 6:4 6:6 6:7 6:12

PHP

1:16 1:21 1:29 2:4 2:6 2:12 2:16 2:21 2:27 2:30 3:1 3:9 3:12 3:13 4:11 4:17

COL

1:9 1:23 2:1 2:8 2:18 2:19 2:21^3 2:23 3:2 3:9 3:19 3:21 3:22 3:23

1 TH

1:5 1:8 2:1 2:3 2:4 2:8 2:9 2:13 2:15 2:17 2:19 4:5^2 4:7 4:8 4:9 4:13^2 4:15 5:3 5:4 5:5 5:6 5:9 5:19 5:20

2 TH

1:8 1:2 1:3 1:5 2:10 2:12 3:2 3:6 3:7 3:8 3:9 3:10 3:11 3:13 3:14 3:15

1 TI

1:9 1:20 2:7 2:9 2:12 2:14 3:3^4 3:5 3:6 3:8^3 3:11 4:14 5:1 5:8 5:9 5:13^2 5:16 5:18 5:19 6:1 6:2 6:3 6:17

2 TI

1:7 1:8 1:9 1:12 1:16 2:5 2:9 2:13 2:14 2:15 2:20 2:24 4:3 4:8 4:16

TIT

1:6 1:7^4 1:11 1:14 2:3^2 2:5 2:9 2:10 3:5 3:14

PHM

14 16 19

HEB

1:12 1:14 2:5 2:8^2 2:11 2:16 3:8 3:10 3:11 3:15 3:16 3:17 3:18^2 3:19 4:2^2 4:6 4:7 4:8 4:13 4:15 5:5 5:12 6:1 6:10 6:12 7:6 7:11 7:16 7:20 7:21 7:23 7:27 8:2 8:4 8:9^3 8:11 9:7 9:8 9:9 9:11^2 9:24 10:1 10:2 10:4 10:5 10:8 10:25 10:35 10:37 10:39 11:1 11:3 11:5^2 11:7 11:8 11:13 11:16 11:23 11:27 11:31^2 11:35 11:38 11:39 11:40 12:4 12:5 12:7

12:8 12:9 12:18 12:19 12:20 12:25[3] 12:26 13:2 13:6 13:9[3] 13:16 13:17

JAS
1:5 1:7 1:16 1:20 1:22 1:23 1:25 1:26 2:1 2:4 2:5 2:6 2:7 2:11[2] 2:14 2:16 2:17 2:21 2:24 2:25 3:1 3:2 3:10 3:14[2] 3:15 4:1 4:2[3] 4:3 4:4 4:11[2] 4:14 4:17 5:6 5:9 5:12 5:17[2]

1 PE
1:4 1:8[2] 1:12 1:14 1:18 1:23 2:6 2:10[2] 2:16 2:18 2:23[2] 3:1 3:3 3:4 3:6 3:7 3:9 3:14 3:21 4:4 4:12 4:16 4:17 5:2[2] 5:4

2 PE
1:12 1:16 1:21 2:3[2] 2:4 2:5 2:10 2:11 2:12 2:21 3:8 3:9[2]

1 JO
1:6 1:8 1:10[2] 2:1 2:2 2:4[2] 2:11 2:15[2] 2:16 2:19[2] 2:21[2] 2:23 2:27 2:28 3:1[2] 3:2 3:6[2] 3:9 3:10[3] 3:12 3:13 3:14 3:18 3:21 4:1 4:3[2] 4:6[2] 4:8[2] 4:10 4:18 4:20[2] 5:3 5:6 5:10[2] 5:12[2] 5:16[3] 5:17 5:18[2]

2 JO
1 5 7 8 9[2] 10[2] 12

3 JO
9 10 11[2] 13

JUDE
5 6 9 10 19

RE
1:17 2:2[2] 2:3 2:9 2:11 2:13 2:21 2:24[2] 3:2 3:3[2] 3:4 3:5 3:8 3:9 3:17 3:18 4:8 5:5 6:6 6:10 7:1 7:3 8:12 9:4[2] 9:5 9:6 9:20[3] 10:4 11:2 11:6 11:9 12:8 12:11 13:8 13:15 14:4 15:4 16:9 16:11 16:18 16:20 17:8[3] 17:10 17:11 18:4[2] 19:10 20:4 20:5 20:15 21:25 22:9 22:10

O

5599

GE
17:18 27:34 27:38 32:9 43:20 49:6 49:18

EX
4:10 4:13 15:6[2] 15:11 15:16 15:17[2] 32:4 32:8 34:9

NU
10:36 12:13 16:22 21:17 21:29 24:5[2]

DE
3:24 4:1 5:1 5:29 6:3 6:4 9:1 9:26 20:3 21:8 26:10 27:9 32:1[2] 32:6 32:29 32:43 33:23 33:29[2]

JOS
7:7 7:8 7:13

JG
3:19 5:3[2] 5:21 5:31 6:22 13:8 16:28[2] 21:3

1 SA
1:11 4:9 17:55 20:12 23:10 23:11 23:20 26:17

2 SA
1:25 7:18 7:19[2] 7:22 7:25 7:27 7:28 7:29 14:4 14:9 14:22 15:31 15:34 16:4 18:33[2] 19:4 19:26 20:1 22:29 22:50 23:17 24:10

1 KI
1:13 1:20 1:24 3:7 3:17 3:26 8:28 8:53 12:16 12:28 13:2 17:18 17:20 17:21 18:26 18:37 19:4 20:4 21:20 22:28

2 KI
1:11 1:13 4:40 6:12 6:26 8:5 9:5[2] 9:23 13:14 19:15 19:19 20:3

1 CH
16:13 16:34 16:35 17:16 17:17[2] 17:19 17:20 17:25 17:27 21:17 29:11[2] 29:16 29:18

2 CH
1:9 6:14 6:16 6:17 6:19 6:41[2] 6:42 10:16 13:12 14:11[2] 20:6 20:12 20:17 20:20 25:7

EZR
9:6 9:10 9:15

NE
1:5 1:11 4:4 6:9 13:14 13:22 13:29 13:31

ES
7:3

JOB
7:7 7:20 13:5 14:13 16:18 16:21 19:21 33:31 34:2 37:14

PS
2:10 3:3 3:7[2] 4:1 4:2 5:1 5:3 5:8 5:10 6:1 6:2[2] 6:3 6:4 7:1 7:3 7:6 7:8 8:1 8:9 9:1 9:2 9:6 9:13 9:19 10:1 10:12[2] 12:7 13:1 13:3 16:1 16:2 17:1 17:6 17:7 17:13 17:14 18:1 18:15 18:49 19:14 21:1 22:2 22:3 22:19[2] 24:6 24:7 24:9 25:1 25:2 25:4 25:6 25:7 25:11 25:17 25:22 25:25 26:1 26:2 26:6 27:7 27:9 27:11 28:1 29:1 30:1 30:2 30:3 30:4 30:8 30:10 30:12 31:1 31:5 31:9 31:14 31:17 31:23 33:1 33:22 34:3 34:8 34:9 35:1 35:22[2] 35:24 36:6 36:7 36:10 38:1 38:15[2] 38:21[2] 38:22 39:12 39:13 40:5 40:8 40:9 40:11 40:13[2] 40:17 41:10 42:1 42:5 42:6 42:11 43:1[2] 43:3 43:4 43:5 44:1 44:4 44:23 45:3 45:6 45:10 47:1 48:9 48:10 50:7[2] 51:1 51:10 51:14 51:15 51:17 52:1 52:4 54:1 54:2 54:6 55:1 55:9 55:23 56:1 56:2 56:7 56:12 57:1 57:5 57:7 57:9 57:11 58:1[2] 58:6[2] 59:1 59:3 59:5 59:8 59:11 59:17 60:1[2] 60:10[2] 61:1 61:5 61:7 62:12 63:1 64:1 65:1 65:2 65:5 66:8 66:10 67:3 67:4 67:5 68:7 68:9 68:10 68:24 68:28 68:32 68:35 69:1 69:5 69:6[2] 69:13[2] 69:16 69:29 70:1[2] 70:5[2] 71:1 71:4 71:5 71:12[2] 71:17 71:18 71:19[2] 71:22[2] 72:1 73:20 74:1 74:10 74:18 74:19 74:21 74:22 75:1 76:6 77:13 77:16 78:1 79:8 79:9 79:12 80:1 80:3 80:4 80:7 80:14 80:19 81:8[2] 82:8 83:1[2] 83:13 83:16 84:1 84:3 84:8[2] 84:9 84:12 85:4 85:7 86:1 86:2 86:3 86:4 86:6 86:8 86:9 86:11 86:12 86:14 86:15 86:16 87:3 88:1 88:13 89:5 89:8 89:15 89:51 90:13 90:14 92:1 92:5 92:9 93:3 93:5 94:1[2] 94:5 94:12 94:18 95:1 95:6 96:1 96:7 96:9 97:8 98:1 99:8 101:1 101:2 102:1 102:12 102:24 103:1 103:2 103:22 104:1[2] 104:24 104:35 105:1 105:6 106:1 106:4[2] 106:47 107:1 108:1 108:3 108:5 107:11[2] 109:1 109:21 109:26[2] 113:1 114:5 115:1 115:9 115:10 116:4 116:7 116:16 116:19 117:1 118:1 118:25[2] 118:29 119:5 119:8 119:10 119:12 119:31 119:33 119:41 119:52 119:55 119:57 119:64 119:64 119:75 119:89 119:97 119:107 119:108 119:137 119:145 119:149 119:151 119:156 119:159 119:169 119:174 120:2 122:2 123:1 123:3 125:4 126:4 130:1 130:3 132:8 135:1 135:9 135:13[2] 135:19[2] 135:20 136:1 136:2 136:3 136:26 137:7 137:8 139:4 139:19 139:21 139:23 140:4 140:6 140:7 140:8 141:3 141:7 141:8 142:5 143:7 143:9 143:11 144:5 144:9 145:1 145:10 146:1 147:12[2]

PR
4:10 5:7 6:9 7:24 8:4 8:5 8:32 30:13 31:4

EC
10:16 10:17 11:9

CA
1:5 1:7 1:8 1:9 2:7 2:14 3:5 3:11 4:11 4:16 5:1 5:8 5:9 5:16 6:1 6:4 6:13 7:1 7:6 7:13 8:1 8:4 8:12

ISA
1:5[2] 2:5 5:3 8:8 8:9 10:5 10:24 10:30[2] 12:12 14:12 14:31[2] 16:9 21:2[2] 21:10 21:13 23:4 23:10 23:12 24:17 26:8 26:13 26:15 27:12 33:2 37:16 37:17[2] 37:20 38:3 38:14 38:16 40:9[2] 40:27[2] 41:1 43:1[2] 43:22 44:1 44:2 44:21[2] 44:23[2] 45:15 46:3 46:8 47:1[2] 47:5 48:1 48:12 48:18 49:1 49:3 49:13[3] 51:4 51:9 51:17 52:1[2] 52:2[2] 54:1 54:11 62:6 63:16 63:17 64:4 64:8 64:9

JER
2:4 2:12 2:28 2:31 3:20 4:1 4:14 4:19 5:3 5:15 5:21 6:8 6:18 6:19 6:23 6:26 7:29 9:20 10:1 10:6 10:7 10:17 10:23 10:24 11:5 11:13 11:20 12:1 12:3 13:27 14:7 14:8 14:9 14:20 14:22 15:5 15:15 15:16 16:19 17:3 17:12 17:13 17:14 18:6[2] 18:19 19:3 20:7 20:12 21:12 21:13 22:2 22:23 22:29 30:10[2] 31:4 31:7 31:10 31:21 31:22 31:23 32:25 34:4 37:20 42:19 45:2 46:11 46:19 46:27[2] 46:28 47:6 48:2 48:19 48:28 48:32 48:43 48:46 49:3 49:4 49:8 49:16 49:30 50:11 50:24 50:31 50:42 51:13 51:25 51:62

LA
1:9 1:11 1:20 2:13[2] 2:18 2:20 3:55 3:58 3:59 3:61 3:64 4:21 4:22 5:1 5:19 5:21

EZE
3:25 7:7 8:15 8:17 10:13 11:4 11:5 12:25 13:4 13:11 16:35 18:25 18:29 18:30 18:31 20:31 20:39 20:44 23:22 26:3 27:3[2] 27:8 28:16 28:22 33:7 33:8 33:10 33:11 33:20 34:9 34:17 35:3 35:15 36:8 36:22 36:32 37:3 37:4 37:9 37:12 37:13 38:3 38:16 39:1 44:6 45:9

DA
2:4 2:23 2:29 2:31 2:37 3:4 3:9 3:10 3:12 3:14 3:16 3:17 3:18 3:24 4:9 4:18 4:22 4:24 4:27 4:31 5:10 5:18 5:22 6:7 6:8 6:12 6:13 6:15 6:20 6:21 6:22 8:17 9:4 9:7 9:8 9:15 9:16 9:17 9:18 9:19[4] 9:22 10:11 10:16 10:19 12:4 12:8

HO
5:1[2] 5:3 5:8 6:4[2] 5:11 8:5 9:1 9:14 10:9 13:9 13:14[2] 14:1

JOE
1:11[2] 1:19 2:17 2:21 3:4 3:11

AM
2:11 3:1 4:5 4:12[2] 5:1 5:25 6:14 7:2 7:5 7:12 8:4 8:14 9:7

OB
9

JON
1:6 1:14[2] 2:6 4:2 4:3

MIC
1:2 1:13 1:15 2:7 2:12 3:1 4:8 4:10 4:13 5:1 6:2 6:3 6:5 6:8 7:8

NA
1:15 3:18

HAB
1:2 1:12[2] 3:2[2]

ZEP
2:1 2:5 3:14[3]

HAG
1:4 2:4[2] 2:23

ZEC
1:9 1:12 2:7 2:10 2:13 3:2 3:8 4:7 8:13 9:9[2] 9:13[2] 11:1 11:2 11:7 13:7

MAL
1:6 2:1

MT
3:7 6:30 8:26 11:25 12:34 14:31 15:22 15:28 16:3 16:8 17:17 18:32 20:30 20:31 23:37 26:39 26:42

MK
9:19 12:29

LU
3:7 5:8 9:41 10:21 12:28 13:34 24:25

JOH
17:5 17:25

AC
1:1 7:42 13:10 18:14 25:26 26:13 26:19

RO
2:1 2:3 7:24 9:20 11:33

1 CO
7:16[2] 15:55[2]

2 CO
6:11

GA
3:1

1 TI
6:11 6:20

HEB
1:8 10:7 10:9

JAS
2:20

RE
4:11 6:10 11:17 15:4 16:5

OF

GE
1:2[3] 1:6 1:10 1:14 1:15 1:17 1:20 1:24 1:25 1:26[2] 1:27 1:28[2] 1:29[2] 1:30[2] 2:1 2:4[2] 2:5[2] 2:6 2:7[3] 2:9[5] 2:10 2:11[2] 2:12 2:13[2] 2:14[2] 2:17[4] 2:19[3] 2:20[2] 2:21 2:23[2] 3:1[3] 3:2[3] 3:3[4] 3:6 3:7 3:8[4] 3:11 3:12 3:14[2] 3:17[6] 3:18 3:19[2] 3:20 3:21 3:22[3] 3:23 3:24[4] 4:2[2] 4:3[3] 4:4[3] 4:10 4:14 4:16[3]

4:17[2] 4:19[2] 4:20[2] 4:21 4:22[2] 4:23 4:25 4:26 5:1[3] 5:4 5:8 5:11 5:14 5:17 5:20 5:23 5:27 5:29[2] 5:31 6:1 6:2[2] 6:4[4] 6:5[3] 6:7[3] 6:8 6:9 6:14[2] 6:15[4] 6:16 6:17[2] 6:19[3] 6:20[5] 6:21 7:2[2] 7:3[3] 7:4 7:6 7:7[2] 7:8[4] 7:10 7:11[4] 7:13[2] 7:14 7:15[2] 7:16 7:18 7:21[4] 7:22[2] 7:23[3] 8:2[2] 8:3 8:4[2] 8:5[2] 8:6[2] 8:8 8:9[2] 8:10 8:13[3] 8:14 8:16 8:17[4] 8:19 8:20[2] 8:21 9:2[5] 9:5[5] 9:6 9:10[6] 9:11 9:12 9:13 9:15 9:16 9:17 9:18[3] 9:19[2] 9:21 9:22[2] 9:23 9:25 9:26 9:27 9:29 10:1[2] 10:2 10:3 10:4

10:5 10:6 10:7[2] 10:10[2] 10:11 10:14 10:18 10:19 10:20 10:21[3] 10:22 10:23 10:30 10:31 10:32 11:1[2] 11:2 11:4 11:5 11:8 11:9[3] 11:10 11:27 11:28[2] 11:29[5] 11:31[3] 11:32 12:1 12:2 12:3 12:4 12:5[2] 12:6[2] 12:8[2] 12:13 12:15 12:17[2] 13:1 13:4[2] 13:7[2] 13:10[3] 13:11 13:12[2] 13:13 13:16[2] 13:17[2] 13:18 14:1[5] 14:2[5] 14:3 14:7 14:8[6] 14:9[4] 14:10[3] 14:11 14:13[3] 14:15 14:17[4] 14:18[2] 14:19[2] 14:20 14:21 14:22[2] 14:24 15:1 15:2[2] 15:4[2] 15:7[2] 15:9[3] 15:12 15:13 15:16 15:18 16:2 16:3 16:7[2] 16:8 16:9 16:10 16:11 16:12[2] 16:13 17:4 17:5 17:6[2] 17:8 17:11

17:12[2] 17:14 17:16[4] 17:23[2] 17:24 17:25 17:27[2] 18:1[2] 18:5 18:6 18:10 18:11 18:13 18:14 18:18 18:19[2] 18:20 18:21 18:25 18:28[2] 19:1 19:4[2] 19:8 19:11 19:12 19:13[2] 19:14 19:15 19:16[2] 19:22 19:24 19:25 19:26 19:28[3] 19:29[3] 19:30 19:31 19:32 19:34 19:36 19:37 19:38[2] 20:2[2] 20:5[2] 20:6 20:11 20:12[2] 20:13 20:16[2] 20:18[3] 21:2 21:3 21:9 21:10 21:11 21:12[2] 21:13[2] 21:14[2] 21:15 21:16 21:17[4] 21:19 21:21[3] 21:22 21:25[2] 21:26 21:27 21:28 21:30 21:31 21:32[2] 21:33 22:2[3] 22:3 22:6[2] 22:8 22:9 22:11[2] 22:13 22:14[2] 22:15[2] 22:17[2] 22:18 22:21 23:1[2] 23:2 23:3

23:4[2] 23:5 23:6[2] 23:7[2] 23:8[2] 23:9[3] 23:10[5] 23:11[2] 23:12 23:13[3] 23:15 23:16[3] 23:17 23:18[3] 23:19[3] 23:20[2] 24:2 24:3[4] 24:7[2] 24:9 24:10[4] 24:11[2] 24:12 24:13[3] 24:15[2] 24:17 24:22[3] 24:24[2] 24:27[3] 24:28 24:30 24:31 24:37[2] 24:40[2] 24:42 24:43[2] 24:47 24:48 24:53[2] 24:60[3] 24:62 25:3 25:4[2] 25:6 25:7[2] 25:8 25:9[3] 25:10[2] 25:11 25:12 25:13[3] 25:16 25:17[2] 25:18 25:19 25:20[2] 25:21 25:22 25:23 25:27 25:28 25:34 26:1[2] 26:2 26:4[2] 26:7[3] 26:8 26:9 26:10 26:14[3] 26:15 26:17 26:18[3] 26:19 26:20[2] 26:21 26:22 26:24 26:25 26:26[2] 26:29 26:33 26:34[2] 26:35 27:2 27:9 27:15

27:16[3] 27:17 27:19 27:22 27:25 27:27[3] 27:28[4] 27:30[2] 27:31 27:33 27:34 27:39[3] 27:41[2] 27:42 27:45 27:46[7] 28:1[2] 28:2[3] 28:3 28:4 28:5[2] 28:6[2] 28:8 28:9[2] 28:11[2] 28:12[2] 28:13[2] 28:14[2] 28:15 28:16 28:17[2] 28:18 28:19[2] 28:22 29:1[2] 29:2[2] 29:4 29:5 29:10[3] 29:13 29:14 29:16[2] 29:22 30:2 30:14[2] 30:16 30:32 30:35 30:36 30:37[2] 30:40[2] 30:41 31:1[2] 31:2 31:3 31:5 31:9 31:11 31:13 31:15 31:18[2] 31:25 31:29[2] 31:33 31:35 31:37 31:38 31:39[3] 31:42[4] 31:48 31:53[4] 32:1 32:2 32:3[2] 32:9[2] 32:10[3] 32:11[2] 32:12 32:13 32:16 32:20 32:24 32:25[3] 32:30 32:32[3] 33:8 33:10

33:15[2] 33:17 33:18[2] 33:19[4] 34:1[2] 34:2[2] 34:3 34:6 34:7[2] 34:8 34:13 34:15 34:19 34:20[2] 34:23 34:24[4] 34:25[2] 34:26[2] 34:27 34:30 35:1 35:3 35:5[2] 35:6 35:7 35:8 35:9 35:11[3] 35:14 35:15 35:20 35:21 35:22 35:23 35:24 35:25 35:26[2] 35:27 35:28 35:29 36:1 36:2[5] 36:3 36:5[2] 36:6[3] 36:7 36:9[2] 36:10[5] 36:11 36:12 36:13[2] 36:14[3] 36:15[4] 36:16[3] 36:17[4] 36:18[3] 36:19 36:20 36:21[3] 36:22 36:23 36:24[2] 36:25[2] 36:26 36:27 36:28 36:29 36:30[2] 36:31[2] 36:32[2] 36:33[2] 36:34[2] 36:35[3] 36:36 36:37 36:38 36:39[4] 36:40[2] 36:43[3] 37:1 37:2[2] 37:3[2] 37:14[2] 37:20 37:21 37:22 37:23[2]

37:25 37:28[2] 37:31 37:32 37:36[2] 38:2 38:7 38:12[2] 38:19 38:20 38:21 38:22 38:27 39:1[4] 39:2 39:5 39:11[2] 39:14 39:19 39:21[2] 39:22[2] 39:23 40:1[3] 40:2[3] 40:3[2] 40:4 40:5[4] 40:7 40:8 40:12 40:14[2] 40:15[2] 40:17[3] 40:20[2] 41:1 41:2 41:3[2] 41:5 41:8 41:10 41:11 41:12 41:14 41:15 41:16 41:17 41:18 41:19 41:25 41:27 41:29[2] 41:30[2] 41:31 41:33 41:34[2] 41:35[2] 41:36[2] 41:37[2] 41:38 41:41 41:42 41:43 41:44 41:45[3] 41:46[3] 41:48[3] 41:49 41:50[3] 41:51 41:52[2] 41:53[2] 41:54[2] 41:55 41:56[2] 42:5[2] 42:6 42:7 42:9[2] 42:12 42:13[2] 42:15 42:16[2] 42:19[3] 42:21 42:27 42:29 42:30[2]

42:32[2] 42:33[3] 42:35[2] 42:36 43:2 43:7[3] 43:9 43:11 43:12 43:14 43:16 43:18 43:19[2] 43:21 43:23 43:27[2] 43:29 43:34 44:1 44:2 44:4 44:8[3] 44:9 44:16 44:20 44:24 44:31 44:33 45:2 45:8[2] 45:9 45:10 45:11 45:12 45:13[2] 45:17 45:18[2] 45:19[2] 45:20 45:21[2] 45:22[4] 45:23 45:25 45:26 45:27[2] 46:1 46:2 46:3 46:6 46:8 46:9 46:10[2] 46:11 46:12[3] 46:13 46:14 46:15[2] 46:16 46:17[2] 46:18 46:19 46:20[3] 46:21 46:22 46:23 46:24 46:25 46:26 46:27[3] 46:28 46:31 46:34 47:1 47:2 47:4[2] 47:6[4] 47:9[8] 47:11[3] 47:13 47:14 47:15[2] 47:17 47:18[2] 47:20 47:21[2] 47:22[2] 47:24[2]

47:25 47:26[2] 47:27[2] 47:28[2] 47:30 48:3 48:4 48:5 48:6 48:7[2] 48:10 48:16[2] 48:17 48:19 48:21 48:22[2] 49:2 49:3[3] 49:5 49:8 49:10 49:11 49:13[2] 49:16[2] 49:20 49:24[4] 49:25[5] 49:26[6] 49:28 49:29 49:30[4] 49:32[3] 50:3 50:4[3] 50:5 50:7[4] 50:8[2] 50:10 50:11[2] 50:13[5] 50:17[4] 50:19 50:23[3] 50:24 50:25[2]

EX

1:1[2] 1:5[2] 1:7 1:9[2] 1:10 1:12[2] 1:13 1:14 1:15[4] 1:16 1:17 1:18 2:1[3] 2:3 2:5 2:6 2:7 2:10 2:11 2:13 2:15[2] 2:16 2:19[2] 2:23[5] 2:25 3:1[4] 3:2[4] 3:4[2] 3:6[4] 3:7[2] 3:8[4] 3:9[2] 3:10[2] 3:11[2] 3:12 3:13 3:14 3:15[5]

3:16[5] 3:17[3] 3:18[3] 3:19 3:21 3:22[4] 4:5[4] 4:7 4:8[2] 4:9[3] 4:10[2] 4:13 4:14 4:16[2] 4:20[2] 4:25 4:26 4:27 4:28 4:29 4:30 5:1 5:3 5:4 5:5 5:6 5:8 5:10 5:11 5:12[2] 5:14[2] 5:15[2] 5:18 5:19[3] 5:21[2] 6:1 6:3 6:4[2] 6:5[2] 6:6[3] 6:7 6:9[2] 6:11[3] 6:12[2] 6:13[5] 6:14[4] 6:15[3] 6:16[4] 6:17 6:18[2] 6:19[2] 6:20[2] 6:21 6:22 6:23[2] 6:24[2] 6:25[4] 6:26[2] 6:27[2] 6:28 6:29 6:30 7:2[2] 7:3 7:4[3] 7:5 7:11 7:16 7:18[2] 7:19[5] 7:20[2] 7:21[3] 7:24[2] 8:3 8:5 8:6[2] 8:7 8:12 8:13[4] 8:16[2] 8:17[3] 8:19 8:21[4] 8:22[3] 8:24[5] 8:26[2] 8:29

8:31[2] 9:1 9:3 9:4[4] 9:6[4] 9:7[3] 9:8[3] 9:9[2] 9:10 9:11 9:12 9:13 9:20[2] 9:21 9:22[3] 9:23 9:24 9:25[3] 9:26[2] 9:29 9:33 9:35[2] 10:1 10:2 10:3 10:5[3] 10:6[2] 10:12[3] 10:13 10:14[2] 10:15[5] 10:19 10:20 10:21 10:22 10:23 11:2[5] 11:3[4] 11:4 11:5[4] 11:6 11:7[2] 11:9 11:10[2] 12:1 12:2[2] 12:3[3] 12:4 12:5 12:6[3] 12:7[2] 12:9 12:10[2] 12:12[3] 12:13 12:15 12:16 12:17[3] 12:18[2] 12:19 12:21 12:22[3] 12:27[3] 12:28 12:29[4] 12:31 12:33 12:35[5] 12:36 12:37 12:39[3] 12:40[2] 12:41[3] 12:42[4] 12:43 12:46[2] 12:47 12:50 12:51[3] 13:2[3] 13:3[3] 13:5 13:8[2] 13:9 13:11 13:12 13:13[2]

13:14[2] 13:15[4] 13:16[2] 13:17[2] 13:18[5] 13:19[2] 13:20 13:21[2] 13:22[2] 14:2 14:3[2] 14:5[3] 14:7[2] 14:8[4] 14:9 14:10[2] 14:11 14:13 14:15 14:16[2] 14:17 14:19[3] 14:20[2] 14:22[2] 14:23 14:24[4] 14:25 14:27 14:28[2] 14:29[2] 14:30[2] 15:1 15:3 15:7 15:8[2] 15:14 15:15[3] 15:16 15:17 15:19[4] 15:20 15:22 15:23[3] 15:26[2] 15:27 16:1[6] 16:2[2] 16:3[3] 16:6[2] 16:7 16:9[2] 16:10[3] 16:12[2] 16:14 16:15 16:16[2] 16:17 16:19 16:20[2] 16:22 16:23 16:27 16:29[2] 16:31[2] 16:32[2] 16:33 16:35[3] 16:36 17:1[4] 17:3 17:5[2] 17:6[3] 17:7[4] 17:9[2] 17:10 17:12 17:13 17:14[2] 17:15 18:1[3] 18:3[2] 18:4[3] 18:5 18:7 18:9[2] 18:10[5] 18:12

18:15 18:16 18:21[6] 18:24 18:25[5] 19:1[4] 19:2 19:3[3] 19:6[2] 19:7 19:8 19:9 19:11 19:12 19:16 19:17[2] 19:18 19:19 19:20[2] 19:21 20:2[4] 20:4 20:5[2] 20:6 20:7 20:10 20:18 20:22 20:23[2] 20:24 20:25[2] 21:9 21:10 21:19 21:26[2] 21:28 21:30[2] 21:32 21:34[2] 21:35 22:5[4] 22:6 22:7 22:8 22:9[2] 22:11[2] 22:14 22:17 22:21 22:25 22:28 22:29[3] 22:31 23:5 23:8 23:9[2] 23:11[2] 23:12 23:13[3] 23:15[2] 23:16[5] 23:18[2] 23:19[3] 23:21 23:25 23:26 23:29 23:31[2] 24:1[2] 24:3 24:4[2] 24:5[3] 24:6[2] 24:7[2] 24:8 24:9 24:10[3] 24:11[2] 24:12 24:18 24:16[3] 24:17[5] 24:18 25:2[2] 25:3 25:9[2] 25:10

25:11 25:12[3] 25:13 25:14 25:15 25:17 25:18[3] 25:19 25:20 25:22[2] 25:23 25:24 25:25 25:26 25:27 25:28 25:29 25:31[3] 25:32[6] 25:33 25:35[4] 25:36[3] 25:38 25:39[2] 26:1[2] 26:2[3] 26:4[4] 26:5 26:6 26:7 26:8[3] 26:9 26:10[2] 26:11 26:12[3] 26:13[4] 26:14[2] 26:15 26:16[2] 26:17 26:19 26:20 26:21 26:22 26:23 26:24 26:25 26:26[3] 26:27[4] 26:28 26:29 26:31[2] 26:32[2] 26:33 26:34 26:35 26:36[2] 26:37[3] 27:1 27:2[2] 27:3 27:4[2] 27:5[2] 27:6 27:7 27:9[3] 27:10[3] 27:11[4] 27:12[2] 27:13 27:14[2] 27:16[3] 27:17[2] 27:18[3] 27:19[3] 27:20 27:21[3] 28:1 28:3 28:6[4] 28:8[4] 28:9[2] 28:10[2] 28:11[5] 28:12[3] 28:13 28:14[2]

28:15[7] 28:17[2] 28:21[3] 28:22[2] 28:23[2] 28:24[2] 28:25[2] 28:26[3] 28:27[3] 28:28[3] 28:29[3] 28:30[3] 28:31[2] 28:32[4] 28:33[5] 28:34 28:36[2] 28:37 28:38[2] 28:39[3] 28:43 29:2 29:4 29:5[2] 29:10[2] 29:11[2] 29:12[4] 29:14 29:15 29:17 29:19 29:20[7] 29:21[3] 29:22[2] 29:23[4] 29:24 29:25 29:26[2] 29:27[6] 29:28[4] 29:29 29:30 29:31 29:32[3] 29:34[3] 29:38 29:40[5] 29:41 29:42[2] 29:43 29:44 29:45 29:46[2] 30:1 30:2 30:3 30:4[2] 30:5 30:6 30:10[3] 30:12[2] 30:13[2] 30:16[5] 30:18[3] 30:20 30:23[3] 30:24[3] 30:25[2] 30:26[2] 30:27 30:28 30:31 30:32 30:33 30:34 30:35 30:36[3] 31:2[4] 31:3[2] 31:5[3] 31:6[4] 31:7[3] 31:8 31:9 31:10[2] 31:13 31:15

31:16 31:17 31:18[4] 32:1[4] 32:2[3] 32:4[2] 32:7[2] 32:8[3] 32:10 32:11[2] 32:12[2] 32:13[2] 32:14 32:15 32:16[2] 32:17[2] 32:18[3] 32:19 32:20[2] 32:22 32:23[3] 32:26[2] 32:27 32:28[3] 32:31 32:32 32:33 32:34 33:1[2] 33:3 33:5[2] 33:6[2] 33:7[2] 33:9 33:11[2] 33:16 33:19 33:22 34:1 34:2 34:4[2] 34:5 34:7 34:10 34:12 34:15[2] 34:16 34:18[2] 34:20[2] 34:22[4] 34:23 34:25[3] 34:26[3] 34:27 34:28 34:29 34:30[2] 34:31 34:32 34:34 34:35[3] 35:1[2] 35:2 35:4[2] 35:5[2] 35:12 35:15 35:16 35:17[2] 35:18[2] 35:19[2] 35:20[3] 35:21[2] 35:22[2] 35:23 35:24[2] 35:25[4] 35:29[3] 35:30[5] 35:31[2] 35:33[3] 35:34[3] 35:35[8] 36:1[4] 36:3[4] 36:4 36:5

36:6 36:8[2] 36:9[3] 36:11[4] 36:12[2] 36:13 36:14 36:15[3] 36:17[2] 36:18 36:19[2] 36:20 36:21[2] 36:22 36:24 36:25 36:26 36:27 36:28 36:29 36:30 36:31[3] 36:32[3] 36:34 36:35[2] 36:36[3] 36:37[2] 36:38[2] 37:1[4] 37:2 37:3[4] 37:4 37:5 37:6 37:7[3] 37:8 37:9 37:10 37:11 37:12[2] 37:13 37:16 37:17[3] 37:18[5] 37:19[2] 37:21[4] 37:22[3] 37:23 37:24[2] 37:25[5] 37:26[3] 37:27[2] 37:28 37:29 38:1[2] 38:2 38:3[2] 38:4[2] 38:5 38:6 38:7 38:8[7] 38:9[2] 38:10[2] 38:11[3] 38:12[3] 38:14[2] 38:15[2] 38:16[2] 38:17[6] 38:18[3] 38:19[4] 38:20[3] 38:21[6] 38:22[4] 38:23[3] 38:24[3] 38:25[3] 38:26 38:27[5] 38:28 38:29 38:30[3] 38:31[4] 39:1[2] 39:2 39:5[3]

39:6[3] 39:7[2] 39:8[3] 39:10 39:13 39:14[3] 39:15[2] 39:16[2] 39:17[2] 39:18[2] 39:19[4] 39:20[3] 39:21[3] 39:22[3] 39:23[2] 39:24[2] 39:25[2] 39:26 39:27[2] 39:28[3] 39:29[2] 39:30[3] 39:31 39:32[4] 39:34[3] 39:35 39:39 39:40[4] 39:41 39:42 40:2[3] 40:3 40:5[3] 40:6[4] 40:8 40:10 40:12[2] 40:17 40:19 40:21[2] 40:22[2] 40:24[2] 40:26 40:28 40:29[4] 40:30 40:32 40:33 40:34[2] 40:35[2] 40:36 40:38[2]

LE

1:1[2] 1:2[5] 1:3[4] 1:4 1:5[2] 1:7 1:9 1:10[3] 1:11 1:13 1:14[3] 1:15 1:16 1:17 2:1 2:2[4] 2:3[3] 2:4[2] 2:5 2:7 2:8 2:9 2:10[2] 2:11 2:12 2:13[3] 2:14[4] 2:16[4] 3:1[2] 3:2[3] 3:3[2]

3:5 3:6^{2} 3:8^{2} 3:9^{2} 3:11 3:13^{3} 3:16 4:2^{4} 4:3 4:4^{2} 4:5^{2} 4:6^{2} 4:7^{9} 4:8 4:10^{3} 4:11 4:13^{4} 4:14 4:15^{2} 4:16^{2} 4:17 4:18^{7} 4:22^{2} 4:23 4:24 4:25^{6} 4:26^{2} 4:27^{3} 4:28 4:29^{2} 4:30^{4} 4:31 4:33 4:34^{5} 4:35^{2} 5:1^{2} 5:2^{3} 5:3^{2} 5:4^{2} 5:5 5:9^{5} 5:11^{2} 5:12 5:13 5:15^{4} 5:16 5:17^{2} 5:18 6:3 6:5 6:6 6:7 6:9^{3} 6:12 6:14^{2} 6:15^{5} 6:16^{2} 6:17 6:18^{2} 6:20^{5} 6:21^{2} 6:22 6:25 6:26^{2} 6:27 6:30 7:1 7:3 7:8 7:10 7:11^{2} 7:12^{2} 7:13^{2} 7:14^{3} 7:15^{3} 7:16^{2} 7:17^{2} 7:18^{4} 7:20^{3} 7:21^{4} 7:23^{5} 7:24^{4} 7:25^{2} 7:26^{4} 7:27 7:29^{4} 7:30

7:32^{2} 7:33^{2} 7:34^{4} 7:35^{6} 7:36^{2} 7:37^{7} 7:38^{2} 8:2 8:3^{2} 8:4^{2} 8:7 8:12 8:14 8:15^{2} 8:18 8:22^{2} 8:23^{5} 8:24^{4} 8:26^{3} 8:29^{2} 8:30^{2} 8:31^{3} 8:32^{2} 8:33^{4} 8:35^{3} 8:36 9:1 9:3^{3} 9:5 9:6 9:7 9:8 9:9^{3} 9:10 9:17 9:18 9:19^{2} 9:22 9:23^{2} 10:1^{2} 10:4^{3} 10:5 10:6 10:7^{3} 10:9 10:11^{2} 10:12^{2} 10:13^{2} 10:14^{4} 10:15 10:16^{2} 10:17 10:18 11:2 11:4^{2} 11:8 11:9 11:10^{2} 11:11 11:21 11:22 11:25 11:26 11:27 11:28 11:32^{2} 11:33 11:34 11:35 11:36 11:37 11:38 11:39 11:40^{3} 11:44 11:45^{2} 11:46^{4} 12:2^{2} 12:3 12:4^{2} 12:5 12:6^{4} 13:2^{4} 13:3^{3} 13:4 13:7^{2} 13:9

13:11 13:12 13:19 13:20^{2} 13:25^{2} 13:27 13:28^{2} 13:31^{2} 13:38 13:39 13:41 13:43^{2} 13:47 13:48^{2} 13:49^{2} 13:51 13:52 13:53 13:56^{5} 13:57 13:58 13:59^{4} 14:2^{2} 14:3^{2} 14:5 14:6 14:8 14:10^{2} 14:11^{2} 14:14^{6} 14:15^{3} 14:16 14:17^{7} 14:18^{2} 14:21^{2} 14:23^{2} 14:24^{2} 14:25^{7} 14:26^{2} 14:27 14:28^{7} 14:29^{2} 14:30^{2} 14:32^{2} 14:34^{4} 14:37 14:38^{2} 14:39 14:42 14:45^{3} 14:50 14:51 14:52 14:53 14:54^{2} 14:55^{2} 14:57 15:2^{3} 15:7 15:10 15:12^{2} 15:13 15:14^{2} 15:16 15:17 15:18 15:25^{7} 15:26^{3} 15:28 15:29^{2} 15:30 15:31 15:32^{2} 15:33^{6} 16:1^{2} 16:5^{4} 16:6 16:7^{2} 16:11^{2} 16:12^{3} 16:13 16:14^{3} 16:15^{2} 16:16^{6} 16:17^{2} 16:18^{5} 16:19^{3}

16:20^{2} 16:21^{5} 16:23 16:24 16:25 16:29^{2} 16:31 16:33^{2} 16:34 17:2 17:3^{3} 17:4^{3} 17:5^{3} 17:6^{3} 17:8^{3} 17:9^{2} 17:10^{4} 17:11 17:12^{2} 17:13^{3} 17:14^{6} 17:15^{2} 18:2 18:3^{4} 18:6^{2} 18:7^{2} 18:8 18:9^{3} 18:10^{2} 18:11^{2} 18:12 18:13 18:14 18:15 18:16 18:17 18:21^{2} 18:24 18:26^{2} 18:27 18:29 18:30 19:2^{2} 19:5 19:8 19:9^{3} 19:10 19:12 19:13 19:15^{2} 19:16 19:18 19:19 19:21^{2} 19:22 19:23^{2} 19:25 19:27^{2} 19:29 19:32 19:34 19:36^{2} 20:2^{6} 20:3 20:4^{2} 20:11 20:12 20:13 20:17 20:18^{2} 20:19^{2} 20:23 20:25 21:1 21:5 21:6^{3} 21:8 21:9 21:12^{4} 21:14 21:17^{2} 21:21^{4} 21:22^{3} 21:24 22:2^{2} 22:3^{2} 22:4^{3}

22:5 22:6 22:7 22:8 22:10^{3} 22:11^{2} 22:12^{2} 22:13 22:14 22:15^{2} 22:16 22:18^{4} 22:19^{3} 22:21 22:22 22:25^{3} 22:29 22:30 22:32 22:33^{2} 23:2^{2} 23:3^{2} 23:4 23:5 23:6^{2} 23:10^{3} 23:12 23:13^{3} 23:15 23:17^{3} 23:18^{2} 23:19^{3} 23:20 23:22^{4} 23:24^{4} 23:27^{2} 23:28 23:31 23:32^{2} 23:34^{3} 23:37 23:38 23:39^{2} 23:40^{4} 23:43^{3} 23:44^{2} 24:2 24:3^{2} 24:8 24:9^{2} 24:10^{4} 24:11^{4} 24:12 24:15 24:16^{2} 24:22^{2} 24:23^{3} 25:2 25:4 25:5^{4} 25:6 25:8^{3} 25:9^{3} 25:11^{2} 25:12 25:13 25:14 25:15^{4} 25:16^{5} 25:22^{2} 25:24 25:25^{2} 25:27 25:28^{2} 25:30 25:31^{2} 25:32^{3} 25:33^{6} 25:34^{2} 25:36 25:38^{3} 25:40 25:41 25:42^{2} 25:44^{2} 25:45^{4} 25:46

25:47 25:48 25:49^{2} 25:50^{4} 25:51^{2} 25:52^{2} 25:54 25:55^{3} 26:1 26:4 26:6 26:8^{2} 26:10 26:13^{3} 26:16 26:19 26:20 26:22 26:25^{2} 26:26 26:29^{2} 26:30 26:31 26:36^{3} 26:38 26:39^{2} 26:40 26:41^{3} 26:43^{3} 26:44 26:45^{4} 26:46^{2} 27:2 27:3^{3} 27:5 27:6^{3} 27:9 27:11 27:15^{2} 27:6^{3} 27:16^{4} 27:17 27:18 27:19^{2} 27:22^{2} 27:23^{2} 27:24^{3} 27:25 27:26 27:27^{2} 27:28^{4} 27:29 27:30^{5} 27:31 27:32^{3} 27:34

NU

1:1^{5} 1:2^{5} 1:4^{3} 1:5^{4} 1:6^{2} 1:7^{2} 1:8^{2} 1:9^{2} 1:10^{6} 1:11^{2} 1:12^{2} 1:13^{2} 1:14^{2} 1:15^{2} 1:16^{4} 1:18^{3} 1:19 1:20^{3} 1:21^{3} 1:22^{5} 1:23^{3} 1:24^{4} 1:25^{3} 1:26^{4} 1:27^{3} 1:28^{4} 1:29^{3}

1:30^{4} 1:31^{3} 1:32^{6} 1:33^{3} 1:34^{4} 1:35^{3} 1:36^{4} 1:37^{3} 1:38^{4} 1:39^{3} 1:40^{4} 1:41^{3} 1:42^{4} 1:43^{3} 1:44^{2} 1:45^{3} 1:47 1:49^{3} 1:50 1:52 1:53^{5} 1:54 2:2^{4} 2:3^{7} 2:4 2:5^{4} 2:7^{4} 2:9 2:10^{5} 2:12^{4} 2:13 2:14^{4} 2:15 2:16 2:17^{3} 2:18^{5} 2:19 2:20^{4} 2:21 2:22^{4} 2:23 2:24^{2} 2:25^{5} 2:26 2:27^{4} 2:28 2:29^{4} 2:30 2:31 2:32^{4} 2:33 2:34^{2} 3:1 3:2^{2} 3:3 3:4^{2} 3:6 3:7^{3} 3:8^{5} 3:9^{2} 3:12^{3} 3:13 3:14 3:15^{2} 3:16 3:17 3:18^{2} 3:19 3:20^{3} 3:21^{4} 3:22^{3} 3:23 3:24^{4} 3:25^{5} 3:26^{3} 3:27^{6} 3:28^{2} 3:29^{3} 3:30^{5} 3:31 3:32^{4} 3:33^{4} 3:34^{2} 3:35^{6} 3:36^{3} 3:37 3:38^{4}

3:39^{2} 3:40^{4} 3:41^{6} 3:42 3:43^{3} 3:45^{4} 3:46^{4} 3:47 3:48 3:49 3:50^{4} 3:51^{2} 4:2^{4} 4:3 4:4^{3} 4:5 4:6^{2} 4:7^{2} 4:8^{2} 4:9^{2} 4:10 4:11^{2} 4:12^{3} 4:14^{3} 4:15^{6} 4:16^{4} 4:18^{2} 4:22^{3} 4:23 4:24^{2} 4:25^{5} 4:26^{4} 4:27^{3} 4:28^{6} 4:29^{2} 4:30^{2} 4:31^{3} 4:32^{3} 4:33^{6} 4:34^{3} 4:35 4:36 4:37^{5} 4:38^{3} 4:39 4:40^{2} 4:41^{6} 4:42^{4} 4:43 4:44 4:45^{5} 4:46^{3} 4:47^{3} 4:48 4:49^{3} 5:2^{2} 5:4^{2} 5:6 5:8 5:9^{3} 5:12 5:13 5:14^{4} 5:15^{4} 5:17^{2} 5:18 5:19 5:20 5:21 5:25 5:26 5:29^{2} 5:30 6:2^{2} 6:3^{3} 6:4^{2} 6:5^{4} 6:7 6:8 6:9^{2} 6:10^{2} 6:12^{2} 6:13^{4} 6:14^{2} 6:15^{3} 6:17^{2} 6:18^{6}

6:19^{4} 6:21^{3} 6:23 6:27 7:2^{4} 7:3 7:5^{3} 7:7 7:8^{3} 7:9^{2} 7:10 7:11 7:12^{3} 7:13^{4} 7:14^{3} 7:15 7:16 7:17^{4} 7:18^{2} 7:19^{4} 7:20^{2} 7:21 7:22 7:23^{4} 7:24^{3} 7:25^{4} 7:26^{2} 7:27 7:28 7:29^{4} 7:30^{3} 7:31^{5} 7:32^{2} 7:33 7:34 7:35^{4} 7:36^{3} 7:36^{3} 7:37^{4} 7:38^{2} 7:39 7:40 7:41^{4} 7:42^{3} 7:43^{5} 7:44^{2} 7:45 7:46 7:47^{4} 7:48^{3} 7:49^{4} 7:50^{2} 7:51 7:52 7:53^{4} 7:54^{3} 7:55^{6} 7:56^{2} 7:57 7:58 7:59^{4} 7:60^{3} 7:61^{4} 7:62^{2} 7:63 7:64 7:65^{4} 7:66^{3} 7:67^{4} 7:68^{2} 7:69 7:70 7:71^{4} 7:72^{3} 7:73^{4} 7:74^{2} 7:75 7:76 7:77^{4} 7:78^{3} 7:79^{4} 7:80^{2} 7:81 7:82 7:83^{4} 7:84^{4} 7:85^{2}

7:86^{3} 7:87^{2} 7:88^{3} 7:89^{3} 8:4^{2} 8:6 8:7 8:9^{3} 8:10 8:11^{3} 8:12 8:14 8:15^{2} 8:16^{5} 8:17^{3} 8:18^{2} 8:19^{7} 8:20^{3} 8:22 8:24^{2} 8:25 8:26 9:1^{4} 9:2 9:3^{2} 9:4 9:5^{3} 9:6 9:7^{3} 9:10^{4} 9:11 9:12^{3} 9:13 9:14 9:15^{2} 9:16 9:17^{2} 9:18^{3} 9:19^{2} 9:20^{2} 9:22 9:23^{5} 10:2^{4} 10:3^{2} 10:4^{2} 10:8 10:10^{3} 10:11^{2} 10:12^{4} 10:13^{2} 10:14^{4} 10:15^{4} 10:16^{4} 10:17^{2} 10:18^{2} 10:19^{4} 10:20^{4} 10:22^{4} 10:23^{4} 10:24^{4} 10:25^{5} 10:26^{4} 10:27^{4} 10:28^{2} 10:29^{2} 10:31 10:33^{2} 10:34^{2} 10:36 11:1^{2} 11:3^{2} 11:4 11:7 11:8^{3} 11:10^{2} 11:11 11:15 11:16^{4} 11:17^{2} 11:18 11:20 11:22 11:24^{3} 11:25 11:26^{4} 11:28^{3} 11:30

11:31 11:33 11:34 12:1 12:3 12:4 12:5^{2} 12:8 12:12^{2} 12:16 13:2^{4} 13:3^{4} 13:4^{3} 13:5^{2} 13:6^{3} 13:7^{3} 13:8^{3} 13:9^{3} 13:10^{3} 13:11^{5} 13:12^{3} 13:13^{3} 13:14^{3} 13:15^{3} 13:16^{2} 13:17 13:20^{4} 13:21 13:22 13:23^{4} 13:24^{3} 13:25 13:26^{4} 13:27 13:28 13:29^{2} 13:32^{3} 13:33^{2} 14:2^{2} 14:5^{3} 14:6^{3} 14:7^{2} 14:9 14:10^{3} 14:12 14:14^{3} 14:15 14:17 14:18^{2} 14:19^{2} 14:21 14:23 14:25 14:27^{2} 14:29 14:30^{2} 14:34^{2} 14:38^{3} 14:39 14:40 14:41 14:44^{3} 15:2^{2} 15:3^{2} 15:4^{3} 15:5^{2} 15:6^{3} 15:7^{2} 15:9^{3} 15:10^{2} 15:13^{2} 15:14 15:15 15:18 15:19^{2} 15:20^{3} 15:21^{2} 15:23 15:24^{2} 15:25^{2} 15:26^{2} 15:27 15:29 15:31 15:32 15:38^{4} 15:39

15:41^{2} 16:1^{6} 16:2^{4} 16:3 16:7 16:8^{2} 16:9^{4} 16:10 16:12 16:13 16:14^{2} 16:15 16:17 16:18^{2} 16:19^{3} 16:22^{2} 16:24 16:25 16:26^{2} 16:27^{2} 16:28 16:29^{2} 16:31 16:34 16:37^{2} 16:38^{2} 16:39 16:40^{4} 16:41^{3} 16:42^{2} 16:43 16:47 16:49 16:50^{2} 17:2^{6} 17:3^{3} 17:4 17:5^{2} 17:6^{3} 17:7 17:8^{3} 17:9 17:12 17:13 18:1^{2} 18:2^{4} 18:3^{2} 18:4^{3} 18:5^{3} 18:6^{3} 18:7^{2} 18:8^{5} 18:9^{5} 18:11^{4} 18:12^{4} 18:13 18:15^{3} 18:16^{2} 18:17^{3} 18:18 18:19^{3} 18:20 18:21^{3} 18:22^{2} 18:23^{3} 18:24^{3} 18:26^{4} 18:27^{2} 18:28^{3} 18:29^{4} 18:30^{2} 18:31 18:32^{4} 19:2^{2} 19:4^{3} 19:6^{2} 19:9^{4} 19:10^{2} 19:11 19:13^{3} 19:16 19:17^{3} 19:20^{2} 19:21^{2} 20:1^{2} 20:4 20:5^{5}

20:6^{4} 20:8 20:10 20:12^{2} 20:13^{2} 20:14 20:16^{2} 20:17^{2} 20:19^{2} 20:22 20:23^{2} 20:24^{2} 20:26 20:27 20:28^{2} 20:29 21:1^{2} 21:3^{2} 21:4^{4} 21:5 21:6 21:9^{2} 21:10 21:12 21:13^{4} 21:14^{3} 21:15^{3} 21:18^{2} 21:20^{2} 21:21 21:22^{2} 21:24^{4} 21:25 21:26^{4} 21:27 21:28^{5} 21:29^{2} 21:31 21:33^{2} 21:34 22:1^{2} 22:2 22:3^{3} 22:4^{4} 22:5^{5} 22:6 22:7^{4} 22:8 22:10^{3} 22:11^{2} 22:13 22:14 22:16 22:18^{2} 22:21 22:22 22:23^{2} 22:24^{2} 22:25 22:26 22:27 22:28 22:31^{2} 22:32 22:34 22:35^{2} 22:36^{2} 22:41^{2} 23:6 23:7^{3} 23:9 23:10^{4} 23:13 23:14^{2} 23:17 23:18 23:19 23:21 23:22^{2} 23:23^{2} 23:24^{2} 23:28 24:2 24:3 24:4^{2} 24:6 24:7

24:8^{2} 24:13^{3} 24:15 24:16^{3} 24:17^{4} 24:19^{2} 24:20 24:24 25:1 25:2 25:3 25:4^{2} 25:5 25:6^{8} 25:7^{2} 25:8^{4} 25:11^{4} 25:12 25:13^{2} 25:14^{3} 25:15^{3} 25:18^{5} 26:1 26:2^{3} 26:3 26:4^{4} 26:5^{6} 26:6^{4} 26:7^{2} 26:8 26:9^{2} 26:11 26:12^{7} 26:13^{4} 26:14 26:15^{7} 26:16^{4} 26:17^{4} 26:18^{3} 26:19^{2} 26:20^{7} 26:21^{5} 26:22^{2} 26:23^{6} 26:24^{4} 26:25^{2} 26:26^{8} 26:27^{2} 26:28 26:29^{6} 26:30^{5} 26:31^{4} 26:32^{4} 26:35^{7} 26:36^{3} 26:37^{4} 26:38^{7} 26:39^{4} 26:40^{5} 26:41^{2} 26:42^{4} 26:43^{2} 26:44^{8} 26:45^{6} 26:46^{2} 26:47^{3} 26:48^{6} 26:49^{4} 26:50^{2} 26:51^{2} 26:53 26:54 26:55^{2} 26:57^{7} 26:58^{6} 26:59^{2} 26:62^{3} 26:63^{2} 26:65^{3} 27:1^{9} 27:2^{2} 27:3^{2} 27:4^{2} 27:7^{3} 27:8 27:11^{3} 27:12

27:14^{4} 27:16^{2} 27:17 27:18 27:20^{3} 27:21^{2} 27:23 28:2 28:3 28:5 28:7 28:8^{2} 28:9^{2} 28:10 28:11^{2} 28:12^{2} 28:13^{2} 28:14^{5} 28:15 28:16^{2} 28:17 28:18 28:19 28:20 28:24^{2} 28:26 28:27 28:28 28:30 29:1^{2} 29:2 29:3 29:5 29:6 29:7 29:8 29:9 29:11^{3} 29:12 29:13^{2} 29:14^{3} 29:15 29:16 29:17 29:19 29:20 29:23 29:25 29:26 29:29 29:32 29:36^{2} 29:40 30:1^{2} 30:2 30:5^{2} 30:6 30:8 30:9^{2} 30:12^{2} 31:2^{2} 31:3^{2} 31:4^{2} 31:5^{3} 31:6^{2} 31:8^{4} 31:9^{3} 31:11^{2} 31:12^{3} 31:13 31:14^{2} 31:16^{4} 31:20^{3} 31:21^{2} 31:23 31:26^{4} 31:28^{7} 31:29^{2} 31:30^{11} 31:32^{2} 31:35 31:36 31:37 31:38 31:39 31:40 31:42^{2}

31:47^{7} 31:48^{2} 31:49^{3} 31:50^{2} 31:51 31:52^{5} 31:53 31:54^{5} 32:1^{5} 32:2^{3} 32:4 32:6^{2} 32:7^{2} 32:9^{3} 32:11^{2} 32:12^{2} 32:13 32:14 32:17^{3} 32:18 32:21 32:24 32:25^{2} 32:25 32:28^{4} 32:29^{3} 32:30 32:31^{2} 32:32^{2} 32:33^{2} 32:34 32:37 32:39^{2} 32:40 32:41 33:1^{5} 33:2 33:3^{3} 33:5 33:6 33:8^{2} 33:9 33:11 33:12^{2} 33:15 33:16 33:36 33:38^{5} 33:40^{4} 33:44 33:47 33:48^{2} 33:49 33:50 33:51^{2} 33:52 33:53 33:54 33:55^{2} 34:2^{3} 34:3^{3} 34:4 34:5^{2} 34:8^{2} 34:9 34:11^{3} 34:12 34:13 34:14^{7} 34:17^{2} 34:18 34:19^{4} 34:20^{4} 34:21^{3} 34:22^{4} 34:23^{5} 34:24^{4} 34:25^{4} 34:26^{4} 34:27^{4} 34:28^{4} 34:29^{2} 35:1 35:2^{3} 35:3 35:4^{2} 35:5

35:8^{4} 35:10^{2} 35:11 35:13 35:14^{2} 35:15 35:16 35:18 35:19 35:20^{2} 35:21 35:22 35:24 35:25^{5} 35:26^{2} 35:27^{5} 35:28^{4} 35:29 35:30 35:31^{2} 35:32^{2} 35:33^{2} 35:33^{2} 35:34 36:1^{10} 36:2^{2} 36:3^{7} 36:4^{5} 36:5^{4} 36:6^{3} 36:7^{6} 36:8^{7} 36:9^{3} 36:10 36:11 36:12^{5} 36:13^{3}

DE

1:2 1:3^{2} 1:4^{2} 1:5 1:7^{2} 1:10 1:11 1:15 1:17^{2} 1:19^{2} 1:20 1:21 1:22 1:23^{2} 1:24 1:25^{2} 1:26 1:27^{3} 1:28 1:29 1:34 1:35^{2} 1:36 1:38 1:40 1:41 1:43 2:1 2:4^{3} 2:5 2:6^{2} 2:7 2:8^{4} 2:9^{2} 2:12^{2} 2:14^{2} 2:15 2:16 2:18 2:19^{5} 2:20 2:22 2:24 2:25^{4} 2:26^{4} 2:29

2:30 2:34 2:35 2:36^{2} 2:37^{3} 3:1 3:2 3:3 3:4^{2} 3:6^{2} 3:7 3:8^{4} 3:10^{3} 3:11^{8} 3:13^{5} 3:14^{3} 3:16^{2} 3:17 3:18 3:26 3:27 4:1 4:2 4:3 4:4 4:6 4:9 4:11 4:12^{3} 4:13 4:15^{3} 4:16^{2} 4:17^{2} 4:18^{2} 4:19 4:20^{3} 4:23^{2} 4:25^{2} 4:28 4:31 4:32^{2} 4:33^{3} 4:34 4:36^{3} 4:37 4:42 4:43^{3} 4:44 4:45^{2} 4:46^{4} 4:47^{3} 4:48 4:49^{2} 5:3 5:4^{2} 5:5^{2} 5:6^{3} 5:8 5:9^{2} 5:10 5:11 5:14^{2} 5:15 5:22^{5} 5:23^{3} 5:24^{2} 5:25 5:26^{4} 5:28^{3} 6:2 6:3 6:7 6:9 6:11 6:12^{3} 6:14^{2} 6:15^{2} 6:17 6:18 6:21 7:4 7:6 7:7 7:8^{4} 7:18^{4} 7:15^{2} 7:18

7:19 7:22 7:25 8:8^{2} 8:6 8:7^{4} 8:8^{2} 8:9 8:14^{3} 8:15^{2} 8:20 9:2^{3} 9:4 9:5^{2} 9:7^{2} 9:9^{2} 9:10^{5} 9:11^{3} 9:12^{2} 9:14 9:15 9:16 9:17 9:18^{2} 9:19 9:21 9:23 9:26 9:27 10:1^{2} 10:8^{2} 10:4^{3} 10:6^{3} 10:7^{2} 10:8^{3} 10:12 10:13 10:14 10:16 10:17^{2} 10:18 10:19 10:22 11:2 11:3^{2} 11:4^{2} 11:6^{3} 11:7 11:10^{2} 11:11^{3} 11:12^{3} 11:14 11:19 11:20 11:21^{2} 11:24 11:25^{2} 11:27 11:28^{2} 11:30^{2} 12:1 12:3^{3} 12:5 12:6^{3} 12:11 12:14 12:15^{3} 12:17^{7} 12:21^{2} 12:22 12:25 12:27^{3} 12:28 13:1 13:3^{2} 13:5^{7} 13:6^{2} 13:7^{4} 13:9 13:10^{3} 13:12 13:13^{2} 13:15^{3} 13:16^{2} 13:17^{2} 13:18^{2} 14:1

14:7^{2} 14:8 14:9 14:11 14:12 14:20 14:21^{2} 14:22 14:23^{5} 14:28^{2} 14:29 15:1 15:2^{3} 15:3 15:5 15:7^{3} 15:9 15:11 15:14^{4} 15:15 15:19^{4} 16:1^{3} 16:2 16:3^{6} 16:4 16:5 16:6^{2} 16:10^{3} 16:13 16:15 16:16^{3} 16:17 16:19^{2} 16:21^{2} 17:2^{2} 17:3^{2} 17:4 17:6^{3} 17:7^{2} 17:8 17:9 17:10 17:18^{3} 17:19^{2} 17:20 18:1^{2} 18:4^{5} 18:5^{2} 18:6^{3} 18:7 18:8^{2} 18:9 18:12 18:14 18:15^{2} 18:16^{3} 18:19 18:20 18:22^{2} 19:2 19:3 19:4 19:5 19:6^{2} 19:11 19:12^{3} 19:13 19:14 19:15^{2} 20:1^{3} 20:3 20:6^{2} 20:9^{2} 20:11 20:13 20:14 20:15^{2} 20:16^{2} 20:19^{2} 21:3 21:4 21:5^{2} 21:6 21:8 21:9^{2} 21:13 21:16^{2}

21:17^{4} 21:18^{2} 21:19^{2} 21:20 21:21 21:22 21:23 22:3 22:9^{2} 22:11^{2} 22:12 22:14 22:15^{3} 22:17^{3} 22:18 22:19^{3} 22:20 22:21^{2} 22:22 22:24 22:26 22:29 23:1 23:2^{2} 23:3^{2} 23:4^{4} 23:8^{2} 23:10^{2} 23:14 23:16 23:17^{4} 23:18^{3} 23:19^{3} 23:21 23:23 23:25 24:1 24:2 24:3^{2} 24:7^{3} 24:8 24:9 24:14^{2} 24:17^{2} 24:19 24:21 24:22 25:5^{3} 25:6^{2} 25:7 25:8 25:9 25:10 25:11^{3} 25:17 25:18 25:19 26:1 26:2^{4} 26:4^{2} 26:7 26:8 26:10 26:12^{3} 26:13 26:14 27:1 27:3^{2} 27:5 27:6^{2} 27:8 27:9 27:10 27:14 27:15^{2} 27:18 27:19 27:21 27:22^{2} 27:26 28:1^{2} 28:2 28:4^{5} 28:9 28:10^{3} 28:11^{3} 28:12

28:13 28:14 28:15 28:18^{4} 28:20 28:24 28:25 28:26 28:27 28:28 28:33 28:34 28:35^{2} 28:39 28:42 28:45 28:47^{2} 28:48^{2} 28:49 28:50^{2} 28:51^{4} 28:53^{3} 28:54^{2} 28:55^{3} 28:56^{2} 28:57 28:58 28:59^{3} 28:60^{2} 28:61 28:62^{2} 28:64 28:65^{3} 28:66 28:67^{2} 29:1^{3} 29:2 29:7^{2} 29:8 29:9 29:10^{3} 29:11^{2} 29:16 29:18 29:19^{2} 29:20 29:21^{4} 29:22^{2} 29:23 29:24 29:25^{4} 29:27 29:28 29:29 30:4^{2} 30:6 30:8 30:9^{4} 30:10^{2} 30:20 31:4^{2} 31:6^{2} 31:7^{2} 31:9^{4} 31:10^{2} 31:12 31:14^{2} 31:15^{3} 31:16^{2} 31:19^{2} 31:21^{2} 31:22 31:23^{3} 31:24^{2} 31:25^{2} 31:26^{4} 31:28 31:29^{2} 31:30^{3} 32:1 32:3 32:4 32:5 32:7^{2} 32:8^{4} 32:9 32:10

32:13^{4} 32:14^{8} 32:15 32:18 32:19^{3} 32:22 32:24^{3} 32:25 32:26 32:27 32:28 32:32^{5} 32:33^{2} 32:35 32:38^{2} 32:39 32:42^{3} 32:43 32:44^{3} 32:45 32:46 32:49^{3} 32:51^{5} 32:52 33:1^{2} 33:2 33:3 33:4^{2} 33:5^{2} 33:7^{2} 33:8^{2} 33:11^{3} 33:12^{2} 33:13^{3} 33:15^{2} 33:16^{5} 33:17^{5} 33:18 33:19^{4} 33:20^{2} 33:21^{3} 33:22 33:23^{2} 33:24 33:26 33:28^{2} 33:29 34:1^{4} 34:2^{2} 34:3^{3} 34:5^{3} 34:6^{2} 34:8^{3} 34:9^{4} 34:11 34:12

JOS

1:1^{3} 1:2 1:3 1:4^{2} 1:5 1:6 1:8^{2} 1:9 1:10 1:12 1:13 1:14 1:15 1:18 2:1^{2} 2:2^{3} 2:3 2:5^{2} 2:6^{2} 2:9^{2} 2:10^{3} 2:11 2:17 2:18 2:19^{2} 2:20 2:23

2:24^{2} 3:1 3:3^{2} 3:6^{2} 3:7 3:8^{3} 3:9^{2} 3:11^{3} 3:12^{3} 3:13^{6} 3:14 3:15^{3} 3:16 3:17^{3} 4:2^{2} 4:3^{3} 4:4^{3} 4:5^{6} 4:7^{5} 4:8^{6} 4:9^{3} 4:10 4:11^{2} 4:12^{4} 4:13 4:14^{2} 4:16^{2} 4:17 4:18^{6} 4:19^{3} 4:20 4:21 4:23 4:24^{2} 5:1^{7} 5:2 5:3^{2} 5:4^{3} 5:5 5:6^{4} 5:9^{2} 5:10^{3} 5:11^{2} 5:12^{6} 5:14^{2} 5:15 6:1^{2} 6:2 6:3 6:4 6:5^{2} 6:6^{3} 6:7 6:8^{3} 6:10 6:11 6:12 6:13^{3} 6:15 6:18^{2} 6:19^{2} 6:20 6:21 6:23 6:24^{4} 6:26 7:1^{9} 7:2 7:4^{2} 7:5^{3} 7:6^{2} 7:7 7:9^{2} 7:11 7:12 7:13^{2} 7:15 7:16 7:17^{3} 7:18^{5} 7:19 7:20 7:21^{4} 7:23^{3} 7:24^{3} 7:26^{4} 8:1^{2}

8:3^{2} 8:8 8:9 8:10 8:11^{2} 8:12 8:13^{3} 8:14^{2} 8:15 8:19 8:20^{2} 8:21^{2} 8:22^{3} 8:23 8:24^{4} 8:25^{2} 8:26 8:27^{2} 8:29^{4} 8:30 8:31^{5} 8:32^{4} 8:33^{6} 8:34^{2} 8:35^{2} 9:1 9:3 9:5 9:6 9:7 9:9^{3} 9:10^{3} 9:11 9:12 9:13^{2} 9:14^{2} 9:15 9:16 9:17 9:18^{3} 9:19 9:20 9:21^{2} 9:23^{4} 9:24^{3} 9:26^{3} 9:27^{3} 10:1^{2} 10:2 10:3^{5} 10:4 10:5^{6} 10:6^{2} 10:7^{2} 10:8 10:11 10:12^{3} 10:13^{2} 10:14 10:18 10:19 10:20^{3} 10:21^{2} 10:22^{2} 10:23^{6} 10:24^{5} 10:25 10:27^{2} 10:28^{3} 10:30^{3} 10:32^{2} 10:33 10:35 10:37 10:39 10:40^{5} 10:41 10:42 11:1^{4} 11:2^{4} 11:3 11:5 11:6 11:7^{2} 11:8^{2} 11:10 11:11

11:12^{4} 11:13 11:14^{3} 11:15 11:16^{3} 11:17 11:19^{2} 11:20 11:21^{2} 11:22^{3} 12:1^{3} 12:2^{5} 12:3^{2} 12:4^{4} 12:5^{3} 12:6^{4} 12:7^{4} 12:9^{2} 12:10^{2} 12:11^{2} 12:12^{2} 12:13^{2} 12:14^{2} 12:15^{2} 12:16^{2} 12:17^{2} 12:18^{2} 12:19^{2} 12:20^{2} 12:21^{2} 12:22^{2} 12:23^{4} 12:24 13:2 13:3^{2} 13:4^{2} 13:5 13:6^{2} 13:7 13:8 13:9^{3} 13:10^{4} 13:11 13:12^{3} 13:13 13:14^{3} 13:15^{2} 13:16^{2} 13:19 13:21^{5} 13:22^{2} 13:23^{4} 13:24 13:25^{3} 13:26 13:27^{5} 13:28^{2} 13:29^{4} 13:30^{3} 13:31^{6} 13:32 13:33^{2} 14:1^{7} 14:2 14:3 14:4 14:5 14:6^{3} 14:7 14:8 14:10 14:13 14:14^{3} 15:1^{6} 15:2 15:4 15:5^{3} 15:6^{3} 15:7^{3} 15:8^{7} 15:9^{4} 15:10 15:11^{2} 15:12^{2} 15:13^{5} 15:14^{2} 15:15^{2}

15:17^{2} 15:18 15:19 15:20^{3} 15:21^{4} 15:47 15:62 15:63^{3} 16:1^{3} 16:2 16:3^{2} 16:4 16:8^{3} 16:9^{3} 17:1^{5} 17:2^{10} 17:3^{5} 17:4^{3} 17:5 17:6^{3} 17:7^{2} 17:8^{3} 17:9^{6} 17:11^{4} 17:12^{2} 17:13 17:14 17:15^{2} 17:16^{6} 17:17 17:18 18:1^{3} 18:3^{2} 18:4 18:5 18:7^{3} 18:10 18:11^{6} 18:12^{2} 18:13^{2} 18:14^{3} 18:15^{2} 18:16^{6} 18:17^{3} 18:19^{4} 18:20^{3} 18:21^{4} 18:28^{2} 19:1^{4} 19:8^{4} 19:9^{9} 19:10^{2} 19:12 19:14 19:16^{2} 19:17 19:22 19:23^{3} 19:24^{2} 19:27^{2} 19:31^{3} 19:32^{2} 19:39^{3} 19:40^{2} 19:41 19:47^{5} 19:48^{3} 19:49^{3} 19:50 19:51^{8} 20:2^{3} 20:3 20:4^{5} 20:5 20:6 20:7 20:8^{6} 20:9^{3} 21:1^{7} 21:2^{2} 21:3^{3} 21:4^{8} 21:5^{9} 21:6^{10} 21:7^{7} 21:8^{2}

21:9^{6} 21:10^{5} 21:11^{3} 21:12^{2} 21:13^{2} 21:16 21:17^{2} 21:19^{2} 21:20^{7} 21:21 21:23^{2} 21:25^{2} 21:26^{2} 21:27^{6} 21:28^{2} 21:30^{2} 21:32^{3} 21:33 21:34^{5} 21:36^{2} 21:38^{3} 21:40^{3} 21:41^{3} 21:44 21:45^{2} 22:1 22:2 22:3^{2} 22:4^{2} 22:5 22:7^{2} 22:8 22:9^{10} 22:10^{5} 22:11^{8} 22:12^{4} 22:13^{6} 22:14^{5} 22:15^{4} 22:16^{2} 22:17^{2} 22:18 22:19^{4} 22:20^{2} 22:21^{5} 22:22^{2} 22:24^{2} 22:25^{2} 22:27 22:28^{2} 22:29 22:30^{6} 22:31^{7} 22:32^{7} 22:33^{3} 22:34^{2} 23:3 23:5 23:6^{2} 23:7^{2} 23:10 23:12 23:13 23:14^{2} 23:16^{2} 24:1^{2} 24:2^{4} 24:3^{2} 24:6 24:8 24:9^{3} 24:10 24:11 24:12 24:13 24:14 24:15^{2} 24:17^{3} 24:23 24:26^{3} 24:27 24:29^{2} 24:30^{3} 24:31^{3} 24:32^{10} 24:33

JG

1:1^{2} 1:4 1:8^{2} 1:9 1:10 1:11^{2} 1:13 1:14 1:15 1:16^{6} 1:17 1:19^{3} 1:20 1:21^{2} 1:22 1:23^{2} 1:24 1:25 1:26 1:27^{4} 1:30^{2} 1:31^{7} 1:32 1:33^{5} 1:34 1:35^{2} 1:36 2:1^{2} 2:2 2:4^{2} 2:5 2:6 2:7^{3} 2:8^{2} 2:9^{3} 2:11^{2} 2:12^{5} 2:14^{3} 2:15 2:16^{2} 2:17^{2} 2:18^{5} 2:20 2:21 2:22 2:23 3:1^{2} 3:2^{2} 3:3^{2} 3:4^{2} 3:5 3:7^{2} 3:8^{4} 3:9^{3} 3:10^{2} 3:11 3:12^{4} 3:13^{2} 3:14^{2} 3:15^{4} 3:16 3:17 3:20 3:22 3:23 3:24 3:25 3:27^{2} 3:28 3:29^{2} 3:30 3:31^{2} 4:1^{2} 4:2^{4} 4:3^{3} 4:4 4:5^{2} 4:6^{7} 4:7 4:9 4:11^{4} 4:12 4:13^{3} 4:15 4:16^{3}

4:17^{4} 4:19 4:20^{2} 4:21 4:23^{2} 4:24^{4} 5:1 5:2 5:3 5:4^{3} 5:5 5:6^{3} 5:7 5:9 5:11^{5} 5:12 5:14^{5} 5:15^{3} 5:16^{3} 5:18 5:19^{3} 5:21 5:22^{2} 5:23^{3} 5:24 5:28^{2} 5:30^{6} 6:1^{3} 6:2^{3} 6:3 6:4 6:6^{2} 6:7^{3} 6:8^{4} 6:9^{4} 6:10 6:11 6:12^{2} 6:13^{2} 6:14 6:19^{2} 6:20 6:21^{5} 6:22^{2} 6:24 6:25^{2} 6:26^{2} 6:27^{2} 6:28^{2} 6:29 6:30^{2} 6:33^{2} 6:34 6:37 6:38^{2} 7:1^{4} 7:3^{2} 7:4^{2} 7:5 7:6^{2} 7:8^{2} 7:11 7:12 7:13^{2} 7:14^{3} 7:15^{3} 7:17 7:18^{3} 7:19^{2} 7:20^{2} 7:22 7:23^{4} 7:24 7:25^{3} 8:1 8:2^{4} 8:3^{2} 8:5^{3} 8:6^{2} 8:7 8:8^{2} 8:9 8:10^{3} 8:11^{2} 8:12 8:13 8:14^{4}

8:15^{2} 8:16^{3} 8:17^{2} 8:18^{2} 8:19 8:22^{2} 8:24^{2} 8:25 8:26^{3} 8:28^{2} 8:29 8:30 8:32^{3} 8:33 8:34^{3} 8:35 9:1^{3} 9:2^{3} 9:3^{3} 9:4^{3} 9:5^{2} 9:6^{3} 9:7^{2} 9:15^{2} 9:16 9:17^{2} 9:18^{2} 9:20^{4} 9:21 9:23^{2} 9:24^{3} 9:25^{2} 9:26^{2} 9:27 9:28^{4} 9:30^{3} 9:31 9:35^{3} 9:36^{2} 9:37^{2} 9:39 9:40 9:43 9:44^{2} 9:46^{4} 9:47^{2} 9:49^{2} 9:51^{2} 9:52 9:53 9:54 9:55 9:56 9:57^{4} 10:1^{3} 10:4 10:6^{8} 10:7^{4} 10:8^{3} 10:9^{2} 10:10 10:11^{2} 10:12 10:14 10:15 10:16 10:17^{2} 10:18^{3} 11:1^{2} 11:2 11:3 11:4^{2} 11:5^{4} 11:6 11:7^{2} 11:8^{3} 11:9^{2} 11:10 11:11 11:12^{2} 11:13^{4} 11:14^{2} 11:15^{3} 11:17^{3} 11:18^{7} 11:19^{2} 11:21^{4}

11:22 11:23 11:25^{2} 11:26 11:27^{2} 11:28^{3} 11:29^{4} 11:30 11:31^{2} 11:32 11:33^{3} 11:35 11:36^{4} 11:39 11:40^{2} 12:1^{2} 12:2^{2} 12:3 12:4^{3} 12:5^{2} 12:6^{2} 12:7^{2} 12:8 12:12 12:13 12:15^{3} 13:1^{3} 13:2^{3} 13:3 13:5^{2} 13:6^{3} 13:7 13:8 13:9^{2} 13:13^{2} 13:14^{2} 13:15 13:16^{3} 13:17 13:18 13:20^{2} 13:21^{2} 13:25^{2} 14:1^{2} 14:2^{2} 14:3^{2} 14:4 14:5 14:6 14:8^{3} 14:9^{2} 14:12^{2} 14:13 14:14^{2} 14:16 14:17 14:18 14:19^{3} 15:1 15:2 15:5 15:6 15:7 15:8 15:10 15:11^{2} 15:12 15:14 15:15 15:16^{2} 15:17^{2} 15:18^{2} 15:20 16:2 16:3^{3} 16:4 16:5^{3} 16:8 16:9 16:13 16:14^{2} 16:18^{2} 16:19 16:20 16:21 16:22 16:23

16:24^{2} 16:25 16:27^{2} 16:28 16:29^{3} 16:31^{2} 17:1 17:2^{3} 17:3 17:4^{2} 17:5^{2} 17:7^{3} 17:8^{2} 17:9 17:10^{2} 17:11 17:12 18:1^{2} 18:2^{4} 18:3^{2} 18:5 18:7 18:10 18:11^{5} 18:13 18:14 18:15^{2} 18:16^{4} 18:17^{2} 18:19 18:20 18:22^{2} 18:23 18:25^{2} 18:26 18:27 18:29^{3} 18:30^{6} 18:31 19:1^{2} 19:3^{2} 19:5 19:6 19:8 19:11 19:12^{3} 19:13 19:15 19:16^{3} 19:17 19:18^{2} 19:19 19:22^{3} 19:23 19:26^{2} 19:27^{2} 19:29 19:30^{4} 20:1^{2} 20:2^{5} 20:3^{3} 20:4 20:5 20:6^{2} 20:7 20:8^{2} 20:10^{5} 20:11 20:12^{2} 20:13^{4} 20:14^{3} 20:15^{3} 20:17^{2} 20:18^{5} 20:19 20:20^{2} 20:21^{3} 20:22 20:23^{3} 20:24^{2} 20:25^{3} 20:26^{2} 20:27^{4} 20:28^{3} 20:30^{2} 20:31^{5} 20:32^{2}

20:33^{6} 20:34 20:35^{2} 20:36^{2} 20:37 20:38^{2} 20:39^{3} 20:40^{3} 20:41^{2} 20:42^{4} 20:44^{2} 20:45^{3} 20:46^{2} 20:48^{4} 21:1^{2} 21:2 21:3 21:5^{2} 21:6 21:7 21:8^{2} 21:9^{2} 21:10^{3} 21:12^{2} 21:13 21:14^{2} 21:15 21:16^{2} 21:17^{2} 21:18^{2} 21:19^{4} 21:20 21:21^{5} 21:23^{2} 21:24

RU

1:1^{2} 1:2^{5} 1:4^{4} 1:5^{2} 1:6^{2} 1:7^{2} 1:9^{2} 1:13 1:22^{3} 2:1^{4} 2:2 2:3^{3} 2:6^{2} 2:9 2:10 2:11 2:12^{2} 2:13 2:14 2:16^{2} 2:17 2:19 2:20^{3} 2:23^{3} 3:2 3:7^{2} 3:10 3:11 3:13^{3} 3:15 3:17 4:1 4:2^{2} 4:3^{3} 4:4 4:5^{5} 4:9^{2} 4:10^{4} 4:11^{2} 4:12^{3} 4:15^{2} 4:17^{2} 4:18

1 SA

1:1^{6} 1:2^{2}

1:3^{4} 1:7 1:9^{2} 1:10 1:11^{2} 1:15 1:16^{3} 1:17^{2} 1:20 1:24^{3} 1:27 2:3^{2} 2:4 2:8^{3} 2:9 2:10^{4} 2:12^{2} 2:13 2:15 2:17 2:20 2:22^{2} 2:23 2:25 2:27^{2} 2:28^{5} 2:29^{2} 2:30^{2} 2:31 2:33^{9} 2:34 2:36^{4} 3:1 3:3^{3} 3:7 3:11 3:14^{2} 3:15^{2} 3:17 3:19 3:20 3:21 4:1 4:2 4:3^{6} 4:4^{6} 4:5^{2} 4:6^{4} 4:8^{2} 4:10 4:11^{2} 4:12^{2} 4:13 4:14^{2} 4:16^{2} 4:17 4:18^{3} 4:19 4:20 4:21^{2} 4:22 5:1 5:2^{2} 5:3^{2} 5:4^{4} 5:5^{2} 5:6^{2} 5:7^{3} 5:8^{7} 5:9^{2} 5:10^{4} 5:11^{4} 5:12 6:1^{2} 6:2 6:3 6:4^{2} 6:5^{3} 6:8^{2} 6:9 6:11^{3} 6:12^{3} 6:13 6:14^{2} 6:15^{3} 6:16 6:18^{7}

6:19^{4} 6:20 6:21^{2} 7:1^{4} 7:2 7:3^{3} 7:4 7:6 7:7^{4} 7:8^{3} 7:11^{2} 7:12 7:13^{9} 7:14^{2} 7:15 8:2^{2} 8:4 8:7 8:8 8:9 8:10^{2} 8:11 8:12^{2} 8:14 8:15^{2} 8:17 8:18 8:19 8:21^{2} 8:22 9:1^{6} 9:2^{2} 9:3^{2} 9:4^{3} 9:5 9:6 9:7 9:8^{3} 9:9 9:10 9:12 9:16^{4} 9:17 9:20 9:21^{6} 9:23 9:25 9:26^{3} 9:27^{2} 10:1 10:2^{2} 10:3^{3} 10:4^{2} 10:5^{3} 10:6 10:8 10:10^{2} 10:11 10:12 10:13 10:16^{2} 10:18^{8} 10:19 10:20^{2} 10:21^{3} 10:22 10:23 10:25 10:26 10:27 11:1 11:3^{2} 11:4^{2} 11:5^{3} 11:6 11:7^{4} 11:8^{2} 11:9^{2} 11:10 11:11^{3} 11:15^{2} 12:3 12:4 12:6^{2} 12:7^{2} 12:8 12:9^{6}

12:10^2 12:11^2 12:12^2 12:14 12:15^3 12:17 13:2^3 13:3^2 13:4 13:7^2 13:10 13:13 13:15 13:16 13:17^3 13:18^2 13:19 13:22^3 13:23^2 14:1 14:2 14:3^3 14:4^2 14:5 14:6 14:11^3 14:12^2 14:14^2 14:16^2 14:18^3 14:19 14:22 14:24^2 14:25 14:27 14:28 14:29 14:30^2 14:36 14:37^2 14:38 14:41 14:43 14:45 14:47^2 14:48^2 14:49^4 14:50^5 14:51^3 14:52 15:1^2 15:2 15:4 15:5 15:6^2 15:8^2 15:9^3 15:10 15:13^2 15:14^2 15:15^2 15:17^2 15:19^2 15:20^2 15:21^2 15:22^2 15:23^2 15:24 15:26 15:27 15:28^2 15:29 15:30 15:32^2 15:34 15:35 16:4 16:7 16:10 16:12 16:13^3 16:14 16:18^3 16:20 17:2^2 17:4^3 17:5^4

17:6^2 17:7^2 17:8 17:10 17:11 17:12^3 17:13^2 17:17 17:18 17:19^2 17:22^2 17:23^3 17:24 17:25 17:26 17:28 17:32 17:33 17:34 17:35 17:36^2 17:37^6 17:38^2 17:40 17:42 17:44^2 17:45^4 17:46^2 17:50 17:51 17:51 17:52^4 17:53 17:54 17:55 17:57^2 17:58 18:1^3 18:4 18:5^3 18:6^4 18:10 18:11 18:12 18:15 18:17 18:21^2 18:23 18:24 18:25^3 18:27 18:29 18:30^2 19:3 19:4 19:6 19:10 19:13 19:16 19:20^3 19:23 20:6 20:8 20:11 20:12 20:14 20:15^2 20:16^2 20:21 20:23 20:27^2 20:28 20:30^3 20:31 20:33 20:34 20:37 20:41 20:42^2 21:1 21:2 21:3 21:5^2 21:7^3 21:9^2 21:10^2 21:11^3

21:12^2 21:13 21:15 22:3^2 22:4 22:6^2 22:7^4 22:8^3 22:9^3 22:10^2 22:11^2 22:12 22:13^2 22:15^3 22:17^3 22:19^3 22:20^3 22:22^2 23:2 23:3 23:4 23:5 23:6 23:10 23:11^2 23:12^2 23:13 23:14 23:15 23:17 23:19^4 23:20 23:21 23:23^2 23:24^2 23:25^2 23:26^3 24:1 24:2^2 24:3 24:4^3 24:6 24:7 24:8 24:11^2 24:12 24:13 24:14 24:15 24:16 24:20 24:21 25:1 25:3^6 25:9 25:10 25:14^2 25:17 25:18^4 25:20 25:21 25:22 25:24 25:25^2 25:28^2 25:29^5 25:31 25:32 25:34 25:35 25:36 25:37 25:39^3 25:40 25:41^2 25:42^2 25:43^2 25:44^2 26:1 26:2^3 26:3 26:5^2 26:6 26:11 26:12 26:13 26:14

26:15 26:16 26:19^3 26:20^2 26:22 26:24^2 27:1^5 27:2^2 27:6 27:7 27:8^3 27:10^3 27:11 28:2 28:3 28:5 28:6 28:7 28:9 28:13 28:14 28:16 28:17 28:18 28:19^3 28:20^2 28:22^2 29:1 29:3^4 29:4^3 29:5 29:6 29:7 29:8 29:9^2 29:11 30:5 30:6^2 30:12^3 30:13 30:14^2 30:15 30:16^5 30:17^2 30:22^3 30:26^5 30:29^2 31:1 31:3 31:7^3 31:9^2 31:10 31:11^2 31:12^3

2 SA

1:1^2 1:2 1:3^2 1:4 1:12^2 1:13 1:15 1:18^3 1:19 1:20^3 1:21^4 1:22^4 1:24^2 1:25 1:26 1:27 2:1^3 2:3 2:4^3 2:5^2 2:7 2:8^3 2:10 2:11 2:12^3 2:13^5 2:15^4 2:17^2 2:18^2

2:21^2 2:23 2:24^3 2:25^2 2:30 2:31^3 2:32^2 3:1^3 3:2 3:3^5 3:4^2 3:6^3 3:7 3:8^2 3:9 3:10^2 3:13 3:14 3:15 3:17 3:18^6 3:19^3 3:22 3:23 3:25 3:26 3:27 3:28^2 3:29^2 3:32 3:36 3:37^2 3:39^2 4:2^6 4:4^3 4:5^3 4:6 4:8^5 4:9^2 4:10 4:11 4:12^2 5:1 5:3 5:6 5:7^2 5:8 5:9 5:10 5:11 5:13 5:14 5:17 5:18 5:19 5:20^2 5:22 5:23 5:24^3 6:1 6:2^4 6:3^4 6:4^3 6:5^3 6:6^2 6:7^2 6:8 6:9^2 6:10^3 6:11^2 6:12^6 6:13 6:15^3 6:16^2 6:17^2 6:18^3 6:19^4 6:20^5 6:21 6:22^3 6:23^2 7:2^2 7:4 7:6^2 7:7^4 7:8 7:9^2

7:10^2 7:12 7:13 7:14^3 7:19^2 7:26^2 7:27^2 7:29^2 8:1^2 8:3^2 8:4 8:5^3 8:6 8:7^2 8:8 8:9^2 8:10^3 8:11 8:12^{10} 8:13^2 8:14 8:16^2 8:17^2 8:18 9:1^2 9:2^2 9:3^3 9:4^2 9:5^3 9:6^2 9:7 9:11 9:12 10:1^2 10:2^4 10:3^2 10:4 10:6^6 10:7^2 10:8^4 10:9^3 10:10^3 10:11 10:12^2 10:14^2 10:16^2 10:18^3 10:19 11:1 11:2 11:3 11:7 11:8^2 11:9^2 11:11 11:13 11:14 11:15 11:17^4 11:19^2 11:21^2 11:23 11:24 11:26 12:3^2 12:4^2 12:7^3 12:8^2 12:9^3 12:10 12:11^2 12:14 12:17 12:18 12:20 12:25^2 12:26 12:27 12:28 12:30^2 12:31^4 13:1 13:3 13:6 13:10 13:11 13:13

13:18 13:19 13:21 13:29 13:30 13:32^2 13:34 13:36 13:37 13:39 14:1 14:4 14:9 14:11^2 14:13 14:15 14:16^4 14:17^2 14:19^2 14:20^3 14:22 14:25 14:26 14:27 15:2^5 15:3 15:6^2 15:10^2 15:11 15:13^2 15:14 15:23 15:24^4 15:25^2 15:27 15:28 15:29 15:31 15:32 15:34 15:35 16:1^7 16:3^2 16:5^4 16:6 16:7 16:8^3 16:10 16:11 16:15 16:18 16:19 16:21^2 16:22^2 16:23^3 17:4 17:8^2 17:9 17:10 17:12 17:14^5 17:15 17:16 17:18 17:20 17:21 17:22 17:23 17:24 17:25^3 17:26 17:27^7 17:29 18:1 18:2^5 18:3^3 18:6 18:7^3 18:8 18:9^3 18:11 18:12 18:14 18:17 18:19^2 18:22 18:23

18:27^3 18:31 18:32 19:5^5 19:9^6 19:10 19:11^2 19:13^4 19:14^3 19:16^3 19:17^3 19:18 19:19 19:20^2 19:21 19:22 19:24 19:27 19:28 19:29 19:32 19:35 19:37^2 19:38 19:40 19:41^2 19:42^4 19:43^5 20:1^3 20:2^3 20:3 20:4 20:5 20:6 20:7^2 20:10 20:11 20:12^2 20:13^2 20:14 20:15 20:16 20:17 20:19^2 20:21^2 20:22^2 20:23^2 20:24 21:1^2 21:2^6 21:3 21:4^2 21:5^2 21:6^2 21:7^4 21:8^5 21:9^3 21:10^5 21:11^2 21:12^4 21:13^3 21:14^3 21:16^4 21:17^3 21:18^2 21:19^3 21:20 21:21^2 21:22^2 22:1^5 22:3^2 22:5^2 22:6^2 22:7 22:8 22:9^2 22:11 22:12 22:13 22:16^5 22:17 22:19 22:21 22:22 22:31 22:35 22:36

22:41 22:43^2 22:44^2 22:46 22:47^2 22:51 23:1^5 23:2 23:3^3 23:4^2 23:6^2 23:7 23:8 23:9^3 23:11^2 23:12 23:13^4 23:14 23:15^3 23:16^3 23:17^2 23:18^2 23:20^6 23:21 23:22 23:24 23:29^5 23:30^2 23:32^2 23:33 23:34^3 23:36^2 23:37 24:1 24:2^3 24:3 24:4^4 24:5^3 24:6 24:7^4 24:8 24:9^3 24:10 24:11 24:12 24:13 24:14^2 24:15 24:16^3 24:18 24:19 24:21 24:22 24:24^3

1 KI

1:3 1:5 1:7 1:8 1:9^2 1:11^2 1:12 1:19^2 1:20^2 1:25 1:26 1:27 1:29 1:30 1:32 1:33 1:36^2 1:37 1:38 1:39^2 1:40 1:41^3 1:42 1:44 1:46 1:47 1:48 1:50^2 1:51

1:52 2:1 2:2 2:3^2 2:4 2:5^7 2:7^3 2:8^2 2:10 2:12 2:13^2 2:16 2:20 2:22 2:24 2:25^2 2:26^2 2:27^2 2:28^2 2:29^2 2:30 2:31 2:32^6 2:33^2 2:34 2:35^2 2:39^5 2:43 2:45 2:46 3:1^5 3:3 3:6 3:7 3:8 3:11 3:15 3:17 3:28 4:2 4:3^2 4:4 4:5 4:6 4:8 4:9 4:10 4:11^2 4:12 4:13^4 4:14 4:15 4:16 4:17 4:18 4:19^6 4:21^3 4:22^2 4:23 4:25 4:26 4:29 4:30^3 4:31 4:33^6 4:34^4 5:1^3 5:3^2 5:5 5:6 5:7 5:8^2 5:11 5:13 5:16 5:17 6:1^4 6:3^2 6:4 6:5^4 6:6^2 6:7^2 6:8^2 6:9 6:10 6:11 6:13

6:15^6 6:16^2 6:18 6:19^2 6:20 6:21 6:23 6:24^4 6:25 6:26^2 6:27^4 6:29^2 6:30 6:31^3 6:32^2 6:33^3 6:34^3 6:36^2 6:37^2 6:38 7:2^3 7:7^2 7:8 7:9^2 7:10^3 7:11 7:12^5 7:13 7:14^3 7:15^4 7:16^4 7:17^3 7:19^2 7:21 7:22^2 7:23 7:24 7:26^2 7:27^3 7:28 7:29 7:30^2 7:31^3 7:32^2 7:33^2 7:34^2 7:35^4 7:36^2 7:37 7:38^2 7:39^3 7:40^2 7:41^4 7:42^2 7:43^2 7:46 7:47 7:48^3 7:49^2 7:50^5 7:51^3 8:1^9 8:2 8:3 8:4^2 8:5 8:6^4 8:7 8:8 8:9^4 8:10^2 8:11^3 8:14^2 8:15 8:16^3 8:17^3 8:18 8:19 8:20^4 8:21^3 8:22^3 8:23 8:25^2 8:26 8:27 8:28 8:29

8:30^2 8:34 8:36^2 8:37 8:38 8:39^2 8:41 8:42^3 8:43 8:46 8:47 8:51^3 8:52^2 8:53^3 8:54^2 8:55 8:56^2 8:59^2 8:60 8:63^3 8:64^4 8:65 8:66 9:1^2 9:4 9:5^2 9:7^2 9:9^2 9:10^2 9:11^2 9:13 9:14^3 9:15 9:19^2 9:20^3 9:21^2 9:22^4 9:23 9:24^2 9:26^3 9:27^2 10:1^4 10:2 10:4 10:5^4 10:6^2 10:9 10:10^4 10:11^2 10:12^2 10:13^2 10:14^2 10:15^7 10:16^2 10:17^4 10:18 10:19^2 10:21^8 10:22^3 10:23 10:25^2 10:28 10:29^4 11:1 11:2^2 11:4 11:5^2 11:6 11:7^3 11:9 11:11 11:12^2 11:14 11:15 11:17 11:18^3 11:19^3 11:20^2 11:21 11:23^2 11:24 11:25 11:26^2 11:27^2 11:28^3 11:29

11:31^3 11:32^2 11:33^4 11:34^2 11:35 11:39 11:40^2 11:41^4 11:43 12:2^3 12:3 12:4 12:8 12:14 12:15 12:16 12:17^2 12:19 12:20^2 12:21^4 12:22^2 12:23^4 12:24^3 12:26 12:27^4 12:28^3 12:31^4 12:32^2 12:33^3 13:1^3 13:2^3 13:4^2 13:5^2 13:6^3 13:7 13:8 13:9 13:11 13:12 13:14^2 13:17 13:18 13:20 13:21^2 13:22^2 13:26^3 13:29^2 13:31 13:32^3 13:33^5 13:34^2 14:1 14:2 14:3^2 14:4^2 14:5^2 14:6^2 14:7 14:8 14:10^3 14:11^2 14:13^3 14:14 14:15 14:16^2 14:17 14:18^2 14:19^5 14:21^3 14:22 14:24^2 14:25^2 14:26^4 14:27^3 14:28 14:29^5 14:31 15:1^2 15:2 15:3^2 15:5^3 15:6 15:7^5 15:8 15:9^2 15:10 15:11

15:12 15:15 15:16 15:17^2 15:18^7 15:19^2 15:20^3 15:21 15:22^2 15:23^6 15:24 15:25^3 15:26^2 15:27^3 15:28^2 15:29^2 15:30^3 15:31^5 15:32 15:33^3 15:34^2 16:1^2 16:2^2 16:3^4 16:4^3 16:5^5 16:7^6 16:8^3 16:9^3 16:10^2 16:11^3 16:12^2 16:13^3 16:14^5 16:15^2 16:16 16:18 16:19^2 16:20^5 16:21^3 16:22 16:23^2 16:24^5 16:25 16:26^3 16:27^5 16:29^4 16:30^2 16:31^4 16:32 16:33^2 16:34^2 17:1^3 17:2 17:4 17:5 17:6 17:8 17:10^2 17:11 17:12 17:14^3 17:15 17:16^3 17:17^2 17:18 17:19 17:22^2 17:23 17:24^2 18:1 18:3 18:4 18:5 18:9 18:10 18:12 18:13^2 18:15 18:18 18:19^2 18:20 18:22 18:24^2 18:25^2 18:26 18:29^2

18:30 18:31^4 18:32^2 18:36^4 18:38 18:40^2 18:41^2 18:42 18:44 18:46^2 19:2^2 19:6 19:7 19:8^2 19:9 19:10^2 19:13 19:14^2 19:15 19:16^3 19:17^2 19:19^2 19:21^2 20:1 20:2 20:4 20:6 20:7^2 20:9 20:10 20:11 20:13 20:14^2 20:15^3 20:17^3 20:19^3 20:20 20:21 20:22^3 20:23^3 20:24 20:26 20:27^3 20:28^4 20:29^2 20:30 20:31^3 20:32 20:35^3 20:36 20:39^2 20:40 20:41^2 20:42 20:43 21:1^2 21:2^2 21:3 21:4^2 21:7^2 21:10 21:11 21:13^4 21:15^2 21:16^2 21:17 21:18^2 21:19 21:20 21:22^4 21:23^2 21:24^2 21:25 21:26 21:28 22:2^2 22:3^4 22:4 22:5^2 22:6^2 22:7^2 22:8^3 22:9^2 22:10^3 22:11^2 22:13^3 22:15

22:16 22:18 22:19^2 22:22 22:23 22:24^2 22:26^2 22:27^2 22:28 22:29^2 22:30^2 22:31^2 22:32^2 22:33^2 22:34^4 22:35^2 22:36 22:38^2 22:39^5 22:41^3 22:42 22:43^2 22:44 22:45^5 22:46^3 22:48 22:49 22:50 22:51^3 22:52^5 22:53

2 KI

1:1 1:2^3 1:3^5 1:6^2 1:7 1:8 1:9^3 1:10^2 1:11^2 1:12^2 1:13^4 1:14 1:15^2 1:16^3 1:17^4 1:18^5 2:3 2:5 2:7^2 2:9 2:11^2 2:12^2 2:13^2 2:14^2 2:15^2 2:16 2:19^2 2:21 2:22 2:23 2:24^3 3:1^3 3:2^2 3:3^2 3:4^2 3:5^2 3:6 3:7^2 3:8 3:9^4 3:10^2 3:11^6 3:12^3 3:13^5 3:14^3 3:15 3:16 3:18 3:19^2 3:20 3:24 3:25^2

3:26^2 4:1^3 4:2 4:3 4:7^2 4:9 4:13 4:16^2 4:17 4:21^2 4:22^3 4:25^2 4:27^2 4:28 4:29 4:30 4:31 4:34 4:38^2 4:39 4:40^2 4:42^4 4:44 5:1^3 5:2^2 5:3 5:4^2 5:5^5 5:6^2 5:7^2 5:8^2 5:9^2 5:11 5:12^2 5:14^3 5:15^2 5:17 5:18^3 5:20^2 5:22^4 5:23^3 5:27 6:1 6:6 6:8 6:9^2 6:10^3 6:11^4 6:12 6:15^2 6:17^3 6:18 6:20^2 6:21 6:23^2 6:24 6:25^4 6:26 6:27^2 6:30 6:31^2 6:32^2 6:33 7:1^4 7:2 7:3 7:4 7:5^3 7:6^7 7:8 7:9 7:10^3 7:12^2 7:13^4 7:14 7:15 7:16^4 7:17^2 7:18^4 7:19 8:2^3 8:3^2 8:4^2 8:6 8:7^2 8:8^3 8:9^4

8:11 8:12 8:16^6 8:18^5 8:20 8:21 8:22 8:23^5 8:24 8:25^5 8:26^2 8:27^6 8:28^2 8:29^5 9:1^3 9:2^2 9:3 9:5^2 9:6^2 9:7^5 9:8 9:9^5 9:10 9:11 9:13 9:14^4 9:15^3 9:16 9:17 9:20^2 9:21^3 9:22 9:25^2 9:26^4 9:27^2 9:28 9:29^2 9:30 9:33 9:35^2 9:36^3 9:37^3 10:1 10:3 10:5 10:6^2 10:8^2 10:10^3 10:11^3 10:13^5 10:14^2 10:15 10:17 10:19^2 10:21^3 10:22 10:23^6 10:24^2 10:25^4 10:26^2 10:27^2 10:28 10:29^2 10:30^3 10:31^3 10:32 10:33 10:34^5 11:1 11:2^3 11:3 11:4^3 11:5^3 11:6^2 11:7^3 11:10 11:11^2 11:13^3 11:14 11:15^3 11:18^4 11:19^5 11:20 12:1^2 12:2 12:4^4 12:5^2

12:6[2] 12:7[3] 12:8[2] 12:9[3] 12:10 12:11[4] 12:12[3] 12:13[6] 12:14 12:16 12:17 12:18[5] 12:19[5] 12:20 12:21[3] 13:1[4] 13:2[3] 13:3[5] 13:4[2] 13:5[2] 13:6[2] 13:7[2] 13:8[5] 13:10[3] 13:11[3] 13:12[6] 13:13 13:14[3] 13:16 13:17[2] 13:18 13:19 13:20[2] 13:21[3] 13:22[2] 13:23 13:24 13:25[7] 14:1[5] 14:2 14:3 14:6[3] 14:7[3] 14:8[3] 14:9[2] 14:10 14:11[2] 14:13[6] 14:14[2] 14:15[6] 14:16 14:17[5] 14:18[5] 14:20 14:21[2] 14:23[5] 14:24[3] 14:25[8] 14:26 14:27[3] 14:28[5] 14:29 15:1[4] 15:2 15:3 15:5[2] 15:6[5] 15:7 15:8[3] 15:9[3] 15:10 15:11[5] 15:12[2] 15:13[3] 15:14[2] 15:15[5] 15:17[3] 15:18[3] 15:19[2] 15:20[7] 15:21[5] 15:23[3] 15:24[3] 15:25[4] 15:26[5] 15:27[3] 15:28[3]

15:29[4] 15:30[4] 15:31[5] 15:32[5] 15:33 15:34 15:35[2] 15:36[6] 15:37[2] 15:38 16:1[4] 16:2 16:3[4] 16:5[3] 16:6 16:7[7] 16:8[3] 16:9[3] 16:10[3] 16:13 16:14[3] 16:15[4] 16:17[2] 16:18[2] 16:19[5] 16:20 17:1[3] 17:2[2] 17:3 17:4[4] 17:5 17:6[4] 17:7[5] 17:8[4] 17:9[2] 17:14 17:16[2] 17:17 17:18[2] 17:19[2] 17:20[3] 17:21[2] 17:22[2] 17:23[2] 17:24[4] 17:25[2] 17:26[6] 17:27[4] 17:28 17:29[2] 17:30[3] 17:31 17:32[4] 17:33 17:34 17:36[2] 17:39[2] 18:1[5] 18:2 18:3 18:4 18:5[3] 18:7 18:8 18:9[5] 18:10[4] 18:11[3] 18:12[2] 18:13[3] 18:14[6] 18:15[2] 18:16[4] 18:17 18:18[2] 18:19 18:21[2] 18:23 18:24[3] 18:26[2] 18:28 18:29 18:30[2] 18:31[4] 18:32[3] 18:33[5] 18:34[4]

18:35[3] 18:37[3] 19:1 19:2 19:3[2] 19:4[2] 19:5 19:6[3] 19:8 19:9[2] 19:10[3] 19:11 19:12[2] 19:13[5] 19:14[3] 19:15[3] 19:16 19:17[2] 19:18 19:19 19:20[3] 19:21[2] 19:22 19:23[5] 19:24[2] 19:25 19:26[2] 19:29[2] 19:30[2] 19:31[4] 19:32 19:35[2] 19:36 19:37[2] 20:1 20:4 20:5[3] 20:6[3] 20:7 20:8 20:9 20:11 20:12[2] 20:13[2] 20:16 20:18[3] 20:19 20:20[5] 21:2[3] 21:3[2] 21:4[2] 21:5[3] 21:6 21:7[4] 21:8[2] 21:9 21:11 21:12[2] 21:13[2] 21:14[2] 21:15 21:16 21:17[5] 21:18[2] 21:19[2] 21:20 21:22[2] 21:23 21:24[2] 21:25[5] 21:26 22:1[2] 22:2[2] 22:3[4] 22:4[3] 22:5[7] 22:7 22:8[2] 22:9[3] 22:11[2] 22:12[3] 22:13[4] 22:14[4] 22:15 22:16 22:17

22:18[3] 23:1[2] 23:2[6] 23:3 23:4[7] 23:5[3] 23:6[3] 23:7[2] 23:8[7] 23:9[3] 23:10[2] 23:11[5] 23:12[6] 23:13[7] 23:14 23:15 23:16[3] 23:17[4] 23:18[2] 23:19[3] 23:20 23:21 23:22[5] 23:23 23:24[3] 23:25 23:26[2] 23:27[2] 23:28[5] 23:29[2] 23:30[2] 23:31[2] 23:32 23:33[4] 23:34 23:35[4] 23:36[2] 23:37 24:1 24:2[6] 24:3[3] 24:5[5] 24:7[5] 24:8[2] 24:9 24:10[2] 24:11 24:12[4] 24:13[6] 24:14[3] 24:15 24:16[2] 24:17 24:18[2] 24:19 24:20[2] 25:1[3] 25:2 25:3[2] 25:4[2] 25:5[2] 25:6 25:7[3] 25:8[6] 25:9[2] 25:10[3] 25:11[4] 25:12[3] 25:13[4] 25:14 25:15[3] 25:16[2] 25:17[3] 25:18[2] 25:19[7] 25:20[2] 25:21[3] 25:22[4] 25:23[6] 25:24[2] 25:25[3] 25:26[2] 25:27[8] 25:28 25:29 25:30[2]

1 CH

1:5 1:6 1:7 1:8 1:9[2] 1:12 1:17 1:19 1:23 1:28 1:29 1:31 1:32[2] 1:33[2] 1:34 1:35 1:36 1:37 1:38 1:39 1:40[2] 1:41[2] 1:42[2] 1:43[4] 1:44[2] 1:45[2] 1:46[3] 1:47 1:48 1:49 1:50[3] 1:51 1:54 2:1 2:3[6] 2:4 2:5 2:6[2] 2:7[2] 2:8 2:9 2:10[2] 2:16 2:17 2:18[3] 2:21[2] 2:22 2:23[3] 2:24 2:25[2] 2:26 2:27[2] 2:28[2] 2:29[2] 2:30 2:31[3] 2:32[2] 2:38[2] 2:42[5] 2:43 2:44 2:45[2] 2:47 2:49[4] 2:50[4] 2:51[2] 2:52[2] 2:53[2] 2:54[3] 2:55[4] 3:1[3] 3:2[4] 3:3 3:5[2] 3:9[2] 3:15 3:16 3:17 3:19[2] 3:21[5] 3:22[2] 3:23 3:24 4:1 4:2

4:3[3] 4:4[5] 4:5 4:6 4:7 4:8[2] 4:10 4:11[2] 4:12[2] 4:13[2] 4:14[2] 4:15[2] 4:16 4:17[2] 4:18[5] 4:19[3] 4:20[2] 4:21[5] 4:22 4:24 4:26 4:27 4:31 4:34 4:35[3] 4:37[5] 4:38 4:39[2] 4:40[2] 4:41[2] 4:42[4] 4:43 5:1[4] 5:2 5:3[2] 5:4 5:6[2] 5:7 5:8[3] 5:9[2] 5:10[2] 5:11[2] 5:13[2] 5:14[8] 5:15[4] 5:16 5:17[4] 5:18[3] 5:20 5:21[4] 5:22 5:23[2] 5:24[5] 5:25[3] 5:26[6] 6:1 6:2 6:3[2] 6:15 6:16 6:17[2] 6:18 6:19[2] 6:20 6:22 6:25 6:26 6:28 6:29 6:31[2] 6:32[3] 6:33[4] 6:34[4] 6:35[4] 6:36[4] 6:37[4] 6:38[4] 6:39[2] 6:40[3] 6:41[3] 6:42[3] 6:43[3] 6:44[4] 6:45[3] 6:46[3] 6:47[4] 6:48[4]

6:49[4] 6:50 6:54[4] 6:55 6:56[2] 6:57[3] 6:60[2] 6:61[6] 6:62[9] 6:63[7] 6:64 6:65[9] 6:66[6] 6:67[2] 6:70[5] 6:71[4] 6:72[2] 6:74[2] 6:76[2] 6:77[4] 6:78[3] 6:80[2] 7:1 7:2[5] 7:3[3] 7:4[2] 7:5[2] 7:6 7:7[4] 7:8[2] 7:9[4] 7:10[2] 7:11[3] 7:12[2] 7:13[2] 7:14[2] 7:15[2] 7:16[2] 7:17[4] 7:19 7:20 7:21 7:29[4] 7:30 7:31[2] 7:33[2] 7:34 7:35 7:36 7:38 7:39 7:40[5] 8:3 8:6[4] 8:8 8:9 8:10 8:11 8:12 8:13[4] 8:16 8:18 8:21 8:25 8:27 8:28 8:29 8:34 8:35 8:38 8:39 8:40[4] 9:1[2] 9:3[6] 9:4[7] 9:5 9:6[2] 9:7[5] 9:8[6] 9:9[2] 9:10 9:11[7] 9:12[8] 9:13[5] 9:14[6] 9:15[3] 9:16[6]

9:18[2] 9:19[10] 9:20 9:21[4] 9:23[4] 9:26[2] 9:27 9:28[2] 9:29[2] 9:30[8] 9:31[3] 9:32[3] 9:33[2] 9:34 9:35 9:40 9:41 9:44 10:1 10:2 10:3 10:7 10:9 10:10[2] 10:12[2] 10:13[3] 10:14[2] 11:3[2] 11:4 11:5[3] 11:6 11:7 11:8 11:9 11:10[2] 11:11[2] 11:12[2] 11:13[2] 11:14 11:15[4] 11:17[3] 11:18[4] 11:19[2] 11:20[2] 11:21 11:22[4] 11:23[2] 11:24 11:26[4] 11:28 11:30 11:31[3] 11:32[2] 11:34[2] 11:35[2] 11:37 11:38[2] 11:39[2] 11:41 11:42[2] 11:43 11:44 11:45 11:46 12:1[3] 12:2[3] 12:3[2] 12:7[2] 12:8[4] 12:14[4] 12:15 12:16[2] 12:17 12:18[3] 12:19[3] 12:20[3] 12:21[2] 12:22 12:23[3] 12:24 12:25[3] 12:26[2] 12:37 12:28[2] 12:29[6] 12:30[4] 12:31[2]

12:32[4] 12:33[3] 12:34 12:35 12:36 12:37[6] 12:38[3] 12:40[2] 13:1 13:2[3] 13:3[2] 13:4 13:5[3] 13:6 13:7[3] 13:9 13:10 13:12[2] 13:13[2] 13:14[3] 14:1[2] 14:2 14:4 14:8 14:9 14:10 14:11[3] 14:14 14:15[3] 14:16 14:17[2] 15:1[2] 15:2[2] 15:3 15:4 15:5[2] 15:6[2] 15:7[2] 15:8[2] 15:9[2] 15:10[2] 15:12[4] 15:14[2] 15:15[3] 15:16[2] 15:17[6] 15:18 15:19 15:22 15:24 15:25[5] 15:26[2] 15:27[3] 15:28[3] 15:29[4] 16:1[2] 16:2[2] 16:3[4] 16:4[3] 16:6[2] 16:7 16:9 16:10 16:12 16:13[2] 16:15 16:16[2] 16:18[2] 16:26 16:28 16:29 16:33[2] 16:35 16:36 16:37[2] 16:38 16:39 16:40[2] 16:42[2] 17:1[3] 17:3 17:6[3] 17:7 17:8 17:9 17:11 17:17[2]

17:18 17:21[2] 17:24[3] 17:27 18:1[2] 18:3 18:4 18:5[3] 18:7[2] 18:8[2] 18:9[3] 18:10[3] 18:11 18:12[3] 18:15[2] 18:16[2] 18:17[2] 19:1[2] 19:2[4] 19:3[2] 19:6[6] 19:7[2] 19:8[2] 19:9[2] 19:10[2] 19:11[3] 19:12 19:13[2] 19:15 19:16[2] 19:18[2] 19:19[2] 20:1[3] 20:2[3] 20:3[3] 20:4[2] 20:5[2] 20:6[2] 20:7 20:8[2] 21:2[2] 21:3 21:5[3] 21:8 21:9 21:12[4] 21:13[2] 21:14 21:15[3] 21:16[2] 21:18[2] 21:19[2] 21:21 21:22 21:25 21:26 21:28 21:29[2] 21:30[4] 22:1[2] 22:2[2] 22:3 22:5[2] 22:6 22:7 22:8 22:9 22:10 22:11[2] 22:12 22:13 22:14[4] 22:15[3] 22:16 22:17 22:18 22:19[5] 23:1 23:2 23:3 23:4[3] 23:6 23:7 23:8 23:9[3] 23:10[2] 23:12

23:13 23:14[3] 23:15 23:16[2] 23:17[2] 23:18[2] 23:19[2] 23:20[2] 23:21[2] 23:22 23:23 23:24[7] 23:25 23:26 23:27 23:28[7] 23:29 23:32[7] 24:1[3] 24:3[4] 24:4[9] 24:5[7] 24:6[5] 24:19[3] 24:20[6] 24:21[2] 24:22[3] 24:23 24:24[4] 24:25[3] 24:26[2] 24:27 24:28 24:29 24:30[3] 24:31[4] 25:1[6] 25:2[4] 25:3[3] 25:4[2] 25:5[2] 25:6[4] 25:7[2] 26:1[5] 26:2 26:4 26:6[2] 26:7 26:8[3] 26:10[2] 26:11 26:12[2] 26:13 26:15 26:16 26:19[3] 26:20[4] 26:21[3] 26:22[3] 26:23 26:24[3] 26:26[2] 26:27[2] 26:28[5] 26:29 26:30[5] 26:31[5] 26:32[3] 27:1[5] 27:2 27:3[4] 27:4[2] 27:5[2] 27:7 27:9 27:10[2] 27:11 27:12 27:13 27:14[2] 27:15 27:16[5] 27:17[2] 27:18[5] 27:19[2] 27:20[6] 27:21[5]

27:22[4] 27:23[2] 27:24[3] 27:25[2] 27:26[3] 27:27 27:28 27:29 27:31 27:32 27:34[2] 28:1[5] 28:2[4] 28:3 28:4[6] 28:5[3] 28:8[4] 28:9[3] 28:11[7] 28:12[10] 28:13[6] 28:14[7] 28:15[4] 28:16[2] 28:17 28:18[5] 28:19 28:20[3] 28:21[5] 29:2[8] 29:3[4] 29:4[5] 29:5[4] 29:6[6] 29:7[6] 29:8[3] 29:10 29:12 29:14[2] 29:16 29:17 29:18[5] 29:20 29:22 29:23[2] 29:24 29:25 29:26 29:28 29:29[4] 29:30

2 CH

1:1 1:2[3] 1:3[3] 1:4 1:5[3] 1:6 1:9 1:11 1:12 1:13 1:16 1:17[4] 2:1 2:3 2:4[2] 2:6 2:8 2:10[4] 2:11 2:12 2:13 2:14[6] 2:15 2:16 2:17 2:18[2] 3:1[2] 3:2[2] 3:3[2] 3:4[3] 3:6 3:8

3:9[2] 3:10 3:11[4] 3:12[3] 3:13 3:14 3:15[3] 3:16 3:17[2] 4:1 4:2[2] 4:3[2] 4:5[5] 4:7 4:8 4:9[2] 4:10 4:11 4:12[3] 4:13[2] 4:16[2] 4:17 4:18 4:19 4:20 4:21 4:22[5] 5:1[3] 5:2[9] 5:3 5:4 5:5 5:6 5:7[4] 5:8 5:9[2] 5:10[2] 5:11 5:12[5] 5:13 5:14[3] 6:2 6:3[2] 6:4 6:5[3] 6:7[3] 6:9 6:10[4] 6:11[2] 6:12[3] 6:13[3] 6:14 6:16[2] 6:17 6:18 6:19 6:21[2] 6:25 6:27[2] 6:28 6:29[2] 6:30[2] 6:32 6:33 6:37 6:38 6:42[9] 7:1[2] 7:2[2] 7:3[3] 7:5[2] 7:6[2] 7:7[3] 7:8[2] 7:9 7:10 7:11[2] 7:12 7:18 7:20[2] 7:22[3] 8:1[2] 8:2 8:6[2] 8:7[2] 8:8[2] 8:9[5]

8:10 8:11[6] 8:12 8:13[4] 8:14[4] 8:15 8:16[5] 8:17 8:18[4] 9:1[4] 9:3[2] 9:4[4] 9:5[2] 9:6[2] 9:9[3] 9:10[2] 9:11[3] 9:12 9:13[2] 9:14[2] 9:15[2] 9:16[4] 9:17 9:18[2] 9:20[9] 9:21[2] 9:22 9:23[2] 9:24[2] 9:26[2] 9:28[2] 9:29[6] 9:31 10:2[3] 10:4 10:13 10:14 10:15[3] 10:16 10:17[2] 10:18 10:19 11:1[2] 11:2[2] 11:3[2] 11:4[2] 11:11[2] 11:13 11:16[4] 11:17[3] 11:18[4] 11:20 11:21 11:22 11:23[2] 12:1 12:2[2] 12:3 12:5[3] 12:6 12:7[2] 12:8[2] 12:9[5] 12:10[5] 12:11 12:12 12:13[2] 12:15[3] 12:16 13:1 13:2[2] 13:3[3] 13:5[2] 13:6[3] 13:7[2] 13:8[3] 13:9[5] 13:10 13:11[2] 13:12[2] 13:15[2] 13:16 13:17 13:18[3] 13:20 13:22[3] 14:1

14:2 14:3 14:4 14:5[2] 14:8[4] 14:9 14:10 14:14 14:15 15:1[2] 15:2 15:4[2] 15:5 15:6 15:8[6] 15:9[3] 15:10 15:11 15:12 15:13 15:15 15:16 15:17[2] 15:18 15:19[2] 16:1[4] 16:2[5] 16:3 16:4[3] 16:5 16:6 16:7[5] 16:9[2] 16:10[2] 16:11[3] 16:12 16:13 16:14[2] 17:2[3] 17:3 17:4[2] 17:6[2] 17:7[2] 17:9[3] 17:10[2] 17:11 17:12 17:13[3] 17:14[5] 17:16[2] 17:17[2] 18:3[2] 18:4[2] 18:5[2] 18:6[2] 18:7[3] 18:8[2] 18:9[5] 18:10[2] 18:11 18:12[3] 18:15 18:17 18:18[2] 18:19 18:21 18:22 18:23[2] 18:25[2] 18:26[2] 18:28[2] 18:29[2] 18:30[3] 18:31[2] 18:32[2] 18:33[3] 18:34[2] 19:1 19:2 19:3 19:4 19:5 19:7[3] 19:8[6] 19:9 19:10 19:11[4]

20:1[2] 20:4[3] 20:5[2] 20:6[2] 20:7[2] 20:10[3] 20:11 20:14[8] 20:15[2] 20:16[3] 20:17 20:18 20:19[5] 20:20[2] 20:21 20:22 20:23[4] 20:25 20:26[3] 20:27[2] 20:28 20:29[3] 20:30 20:31 20:32[2] 20:33 20:34[6] 20:35[2] 20:37[2] 21:1 21:2[3] 21:3[3] 21:4[3] 21:6[5] 21:7[2] 21:8 21:9 21:10[2] 21:11[2] 21:12[4] 21:13[6] 21:15[2] 21:16[2] 21:17 21:19[5] 21:20[2] 22:1[4] 22:2 22:3[2] 22:4[3] 22:5[3] 22:6[5] 22:7[4] 22:8[4] 22:9[2] 22:10[3] 22:11[5] 22:12 23:1[6] 23:2[4] 23:3[3] 23:4[4] 23:5[3] 23:6[3] 23:9[2] 23:10[2] 23:12[2] 23:13[2] 23:14[3] 23:15 23:17[2] 23:18[6] 23:19[2] 23:20[5] 23:21 24:1 24:2[2] 24:4 24:5[3] 24:6[8] 24:7[4] 24:8[2] 24:9 24:11 24:12[5] 24:13 24:14[5]

24:15 24:16 24:17[2] 24:18[2] 24:20[3] 24:21[3] 24:23[5] 24:24[3] 24:25[4] 24:26[2] 24:27[5] 25:1 25:2 25:4 25:5 25:6[3] 25:7[2] 25:9[3] 25:10 25:11[3] 25:12[3] 25:13[3] 25:14[3] 25:15[3] 25:16 25:17[4] 25:18[2] 25:20[3] 25:21[2] 25:23[6] 25:24[2] 25:25[5] 25:26[4] 25:28 26:1[2] 26:3 26:4 26:5[2] 26:6[3] 26:8 26:9 26:11[5] 26:12[4] 26:16[2] 26:17 26:18[2] 26:19 26:21[3] 26:22[3] 26:23 27:1 27:2[2] 27:3[3] 27:4 27:5[6] 27:7[4] 27:9 28:1 28:2[2] 28:3[4] 28:5[5] 28:6[2] 28:7[2] 28:8[2] 28:9[2] 28:10 28:11[2] 28:12[7] 28:15[2] 28:16 28:18[3] 28:19[2] 28:20 28:21[6] 28:23[5] 28:24[7] 28:25[2] 28:26[4] 28:27[2] 29:1 29:2 29:3[3] 29:5[3] 29:6[2] 29:7[2] 29:8 29:10

29:12[11] 29:13[4] 29:14[4] 29:15[3] 29:16[5] 29:17[5] 29:18[2] 29:19 29:20[2] 29:21[2] 29:25[4] 29:26 29:27[2] 29:29 29:30[2] 29:31[2] 29:32 29:35[3] 30:1[2] 30:5[2] 30:6[7] 30:7 30:8 30:10 30:11[2] 30:12[4] 30:13 30:15[2] 30:16[4] 30:17[2] 30:18[2] 30:19[2] 30:21[2] 30:22[2] 30:24[2] 30:25[4] 30:26[3] 31:1[3] 31:2[3] 31:3[2] 31:4[2] 31:5[5] 31:6[4] 31:7 31:10[3] 31:11 31:13[4] 31:14[3] 31:15 31:16[2] 31:17[2] 31:18 31:19[4] 31:21[2] 32:1 32:3 32:4[2] 32:5 32:6[3] 32:7 32:8[3] 32:9[3] 32:10 32:11[3] 32:13[4] 32:14[3] 32:15[5] 32:17[6] 32:18 32:19[5] 32:20 32:21[6] 32:22[4] 32:23[2] 32:26[4] 32:27 32:28[2] 32:29 32:30[3] 32:31[4] 32:32[6] 32:33[4] 33:2[3] 33:3 33:4 33:5[3] 33:6[3]

33:7[3] 33:8[3] 33:9[2] 33:11[3] 33:12 33:13 33:14[4] 33:15[5] 33:16[2] 33:18[7] 33:19[2] 33:22 33:25[2] 34:2[2] 34:3[2] 34:4[3] 34:5 34:6 34:7 34:8[5] 34:9[6] 34:10[4] 34:11 34:12[8] 34:13[4] 34:14[3] 34:15[2] 34:17[3] 34:19 34:20[3] 34:21[4] 34:22[4] 34:23 34:24 34:25 34:26[3] 34:28 34:29 34:30[6] 34:31 34:32[3] 34:33[3] 35:1 35:2[2] 35:3[2] 35:4[4] 35:5[5] 35:6[2] 35:7[3] 35:8[2] 35:9 35:12[3] 35:14[3] 35:15[2] 35:16[3] 35:17[2] 35:18[3] 35:19[2] 35:20 35:21 35:22[3] 35:24[3] 35:25 35:26[3] 35:27[2] 36:1 36:3[3] 36:4 36:5 36:6 36:7[3] 36:8[4] 36:9 36:10[2] 36:12[2] 36:13 36:14[3] 36:15 36:16[2] 36:17[2] 36:18[6] 36:19[2] 36:20[2] 36:21[2] 36:22[6] 36:23[4]

EZR

1:1[6] 1:2[3] 1:3[3] 1:4[2] 1:5[3] 1:6 1:7[4] 1:8[3] 1:9[3] 1:10[2] 1:11[3] 2:1[4] 2:2[3] 2:3 2:4 2:5 2:6[3] 2:7 2:8 2:9 2:10 2:11 2:12 2:13 2:14 2:15 2:16[2] 2:17 2:18 2:19 2:20 2:21 2:22 2:23 2:24 2:25 2:26 2:27 2:28 2:29 2:30 2:31 2:32 2:33 2:34 2:36[3] 2:37 2:38 2:39 2:40[3] 2:41 2:42[7] 2:43[3] 2:44[3] 2:45[3] 2:46[3] 2:47[3] 2:48[3] 2:49[3] 2:50[3] 2:51[3] 2:52[3] 2:53[3] 2:54[2] 2:55[4] 2:56[3] 2:57[5] 2:58 2:59 2:60[3] 2:61[7] 2:63 2:65 2:68[4] 2:69[3] 2:70 3:1 3:2[6] 3:3[2] 3:4[2] 3:5[4] 3:6[3] 3:7[5] 3:8[8] 3:9[3]

3:10[5] 3:11[2] 3:12[3] 3:13[4] 4:1[3] 4:2[3] 4:3[5] 4:4[3] 4:5[4] 4:6[3] 4:7[4] 4:9 4:10[2] 4:11 4:13 4:15[4] 4:17 4:19 4:22 4:23 4:24[5] 5:1[3] 5:2[4] 5:4 5:5[2] 5:6 5:8[2] 5:10[2] 5:11[3] 5:12[3] 5:13[3] 5:14[7] 5:15 5:16[2] 5:17[2] 6:1 6:2 6:3[2] 6:4[3] 6:5[4] 6:7[5] 6:8[5] 6:9[4] 6:10[4] 6:12 6:14[7] 6:15[3] 6:16[5] 6:17[4] 6:18[2] 6:19[2] 6:20[2] 6:21[5] 6:22[6] 7:1[4] 7:2[3] 7:3[3] 7:4[3] 7:5[4] 7:6[3] 7:7[4] 7:8 7:9[3] 7:10 7:11[5] 7:12[4] 7:13[4] 7:14[3] 7:15 7:16[4] 7:17[2] 7:18[2] 7:19[3] 7:20[2] 7:21[4] 7:22[4] 7:23[4] 7:24[3] 7:25[2] 7:26[3] 7:27[2] 7:28[2] 8:1[3] 8:2[6] 8:3[5] 8:4[3] 8:5[3]

8:6[3] 8:7[3] 8:8[3] 8:9[3] 8:10[3] 8:11[3] 8:12[3] 8:13[2] 8:14[2] 8:15[2] 8:16 8:17 8:18[6] 8:19[2] 8:20[3] 8:21[2] 8:22[3] 8:23 8:24[3] 8:25[2] 8:26[2] 8:27[3] 8:28 8:29[5] 8:30[2] 8:31[5] 8:33[6] 8:34 8:35[3] 8:36 9:1[3] 9:2[3] 9:3[2] 9:4[4] 9:7[4] 9:9[3] 9:11[2] 9:12 9:14 9:15[2] 10:1[3] 10:2[5] 10:3[3] 10:4 10:6[5] 10:7 10:8[2] 10:9[5] 10:10 10:11[2] 10:13[2] 10:14[3] 10:15[2] 10:16[5] 10:17 10:18[4] 10:19 10:20[2] 10:21[2] 10:22[2] 10:23 10:24[2] 10:25[3] 10:26[2] 10:27[2] 10:28[2] 10:29[2] 10:30[2] 10:31[2] 10:33[2] 10:34[2] 10:43[2] 10:44

NE

1:2[2] 1:2[3] 1:3[2] 1:4 1:5 1:6[4] 1:9[2] 1:11[3] 2:1 2:2

2:3 2:4 2:5 2:8[4] 2:9 2:10[3] 2:13[2] 2:14 2:15 2:17 2:18[2] 2:20 3:1[2] 3:2[2] 3:3 3:4[5] 3:5 3:6[2] 3:7[3] 3:8[4] 3:9[3] 3:10[2] 3:11[3] 3:12[3] 3:13 3:14[3] 3:15[7] 3:16[5] 3:17[3] 3:18[3] 3:19[3] 3:20[4] 3:21[6] 3:22 3:23[2] 3:24[3] 3:25[4] 3:27 3:29[3] 3:30[3] 3:31[3] 3:32 4:2[3] 4:4 4:7 4:8 4:9 4:10[2] 4:14[2] 4:15 4:16[3] 4:17 4:19 4:20 4:21[2] 4:23[2] 5:1[2] 5:3 5:5[2] 5:7 5:9[3] 5:10 5:11[3] 5:12[2] 5:14[3] 5:15[4] 5:16 5:17 5:18[3] 6:1 6:2[2] 6:7 6:8 6:10[5] 6:14 6:15 6:16 6:17[2] 7:2 7:3[3] 7:5[2] 7:6[4] 7:7[3] 7:8 7:9 7:10 7:11[3]

7:12 7:13 7:14 7:15 7:16 7:17 7:18 7:19 7:20 7:21[2] 7:22 7:23 7:24 7:25 7:26 7:27 7:28 7:29 7:30 7:31 7:32 7:33 7:34 7:35 7:36 7:37 7:38 7:39[3] 7:40 7:41 7:42 7:43[4] 7:44 7:45[6] 7:46[3] 7:47[3] 7:48[3] 7:49[3] 7:50[3] 7:51[3] 7:52[3] 7:53[3] 7:54[3] 7:55[3] 7:56[2] 7:57[4] 7:58[3] 7:59[5] 7:60 7:61 7:62[3] 7:63[6] 7:65 7:67 7:70[3] 7:71[5] 7:72[3] 7:73[2] 8:1[2] 8:2[2] 8:3[2] 8:4 8:5 8:8 8:9 8:10 8:13[3] 8:14[2] 8:15 8:16[6] 8:17[5] 8:18[2] 9:1[2] 9:2[2] 9:3[3] 9:4 9:6[2] 9:7[3] 9:8 9:9 9:10 9:11 9:12 9:14 9:15 9:17[2] 9:18

9:19[2] 9:22[5] 9:23 9:24[2] 9:25 9:27[4] 9:28 9:30[2] 9:32[2] 9:37 9:38 10:1 10:9[2] 10:14 10:28[3] 10:29[2] 10:30 10:31[3] 10:32[3] 10:33[4] 10:34[3] 10:35[4] 10:36[6] 10:37[9] 10:38[3] 10:39[6] 11:1[3] 11:3[3] 11:4[13] 11:5[7] 11:6 11:7[8] 11:9[3] 11:10[2] 11:11[7] 11:12[7] 11:13[5] 11:14[3] 11:15[5] 11:16[5] 11:17[6] 11:20[3] 11:22[9] 11:24[4] 11:25[2] 11:30 11:31 11:35 11:36 12:1 12:7[3] 12:12[4] 12:13[2] 12:14[2] 12:15[2] 12:16[2] 12:17[3] 12:18[2] 12:19[2] 12:20[2] 12:21[2] 12:22[3] 12:23[5] 12:24[4] 12:25 12:26[5] 12:27[3] 12:28[3] 12:29[3] 12:31[2] 12:33[2] 12:35[7] 12:36[2] 12:37[4] 12:38[3] 12:39[3] 12:40[3] 12:43 12:44[3] 12:45[4] 12:46[4] 12:47[4] 13:1[3] 13:2 13:4[3] 13:5[2] 13:6[3]

13:7[3] 13:8[2] 13:9[2] 13:10 13:11 13:12 13:13[3] 13:14 13:15 13:16[3] 13:17 13:19[2] 13:20[2] 13:22 13:23[3] 13:24[2] 13:25 13:26[2] 13:28[3] 13:29[2] 13:30

ES

1:1 1:2 1:3[3] 1:4[2] 1:5[2] 1:6[4] 1:7[2] 1:8 1:10[2] 1:14 1:15 1:16 1:17 1:18[3] 1:19 1:21 1:22[2] 2:1 2:3[4] 2:4 2:5[3] 2:6[2] 2:8[3] 2:9[4] 2:11[2] 2:12[4] 2:13[2] 2:14[2] 2:15[5] 2:16 2:17 2:18 2:20 2:21[2] 2:23[2] 3:1 3:5 3:6[3] 3:7 3:8 3:9[3] 3:10 3:12[4] 3:13[2] 3:14 4:1 4:5 4:6 4:7[3] 4:8[2] 4:9 4:11[2] 5:1[2] 5:2 5:3 5:6[2] 5:8 5:9 5:11[4] 5:14 6:1[2] 6:2[3]

6:4 6:9[3] 6:10 6:11 6:13[2] 7:2[2] 7:7 7:8[3] 7:9[2] 8:1 8:2 8:3 8:5 8:6 8:7 8:9 8:11[2] 8:12[2] 8:13 8:15[5] 8:17[3] 9:1[2] 9:2[2] 9:3[3] 9:5 9:10[3] 9:11 9:12[2] 9:15 9:16 9:17[3] 9:18[2] 9:19[4] 9:20 9:21[2] 9:22[2] 9:24[2] 9:26[3] 9:28[2] 9:29[2] 9:30[3] 9:31[2] 9:32[2] 10:1 10:2[7] 10:3[3]

JOB

1:1 1:3[3] 1:5[2] 1:6 1:10 1:12 1:15 1:16 1:17 1:19 1:21[2] 2:1 2:7[2] 2:10[2] 2:11 3:5[2] 3:6[2] 3:9[2] 3:10 3:11 3:14 3:18 3:25 4:6 4:9[2] 4:10[3] 4:11 4:13 4:15 4:19 5:1 5:5 5:6[2] 5:12 5:13 5:15 5:17

5:20 5:21[2] 5:22[2] 5:23[2] 5:25 5:26 6:3 6:4[2] 6:6 6:10 6:12[2] 6:14 6:15 6:16 6:17 6:18 6:19[2] 6:22 6:23 6:26 7:1 7:2 7:3 7:4[2] 7:5 7:8 7:11[2] 7:20 8:2 8:6 8:8[2] 8:9 8:10 8:13 8:17 8:19[2] 8:22 9:2 9:3 9:6 9:8 9:9 9:19[2] 9:23 9:24[2] 9:28 10:1[2] 10:3[2] 10:4 10:5 10:7 10:15 10:18 10:21[2] 10:22[3] 11:2[2] 11:6[2] 11:20[2] 12:4 12:5 12:6 12:7 12:8 12:9 12:10[2] 12:12 12:18 12:20[2] 12:21 12:22[2] 12:24[3] 13:4[2] 13:6 13:12 13:26 13:27 14:1[3] 14:4 14:5 14:7 14:9 14:12 14:14 14:15 14:18 14:19[3] 14:21

15:5 15:8 15:11 15:13 15:14 15:20 15:22[2] 15:23 15:26 15:27 15:30[2] 15:34[2] 16:5 16:11 16:16 17:5 17:6 17:7 17:11 17:12 17:16 18:2 18:4 18:5[2] 18:7 18:13[2] 18:14[2] 18:15 18:18 18:21[2] 19:7 19:9 19:11 19:17 19:20 19:21 19:28 19:29[2] 20:3[2] 20:4 20:5[2] 20:8 20:11[2] 20:14 20:15 20:16 20:17 20:20 20:21 20:22[2] 20:23 20:24 20:25[2] 20:28[2] 20:29 21:9 21:12 21:14 21:16 21:17 21:20[2] 21:21 21:24 21:25 21:28[2] 21:30[2] 21:33 22:4 22:6 22:9 22:11 22:12[2] 22:14 22:16 22:18 22:20 22:24[2] 22:25 22:30[2] 23:12[2] 23:15 24:3 24:4[2] 24:6 24:8[2] 24:9[2] 24:12[2]

24:13 24:15 24:17[3] 24:18 24:22 24:24[3] 25:3 25:4 25:6 26:9 26:11 26:14[3] 27:3 27:8 27:11 27:13[3] 27:15 27:21 27:22 27:23 28:2[2] 28:3[2] 28:4 28:5 28:6[3] 28:12 28:13 28:16 28:17[2] 28:18[3] 28:19 28:20 28:21[2] 28:24 28:26 28:28 29:4[2] 29:6 29:10 29:13 29:17[2] 29:24 30:1 30:2 30:6[2] 30:8[2] 30:12 30:14 30:16 30:18[2] 30:27 30:31 31:2[2] 31:3 31:7 31:13[2] 31:16 31:19 31:20 31:23 31:29 31:31[2] 31:34[2] 31:37 31:40[3] 32:2[4] 32:5 32:6 32:7 32:8 32:12 32:18 33:3[2] 33:4[2] 33:6 33:8 33:13[2] 33:15 33:16 33:19 33:25 33:30 34:8 34:10 34:11 34:16 34:19[2]

34:21 34:22[2] 34:26 34:27 34:28[2] 34:34 34:36 35:7 35:8 35:9[4] 35:11[2] 35:12[2] 36:6 36:8 36:16[2] 36:17 36:19 36:26 36:27 36:29[2] 36:30 37:1 37:2[2] 37:3 37:4 37:6 37:7 37:9[2] 37:10[2] 37:12 37:14 37:15 37:16[2] 37:19 37:22 37:23 37:24 38:1 38:3 38:4 38:7 38:8 38:13[3] 38:16[2] 38:17[3] 38:18 38:21 38:22[2] 38:23[2] 38:24[2] 38:25[2] 38:26[2] 38:27 38:28 38:29[2] 38:30 38:31[2] 38:32 38:34 38:37 38:39 38:41 39:1 39:5 39:7[2] 39:8 39:17 39:20 39:24 39:25 39:28 40:6 40:7 40:11 40:16 40:17 40:18[2] 40:19[2] 40:20 40:21 40:22 41:6 41:9[2] 41:13 41:14 41:18 41:19[2]

41:20[2] 41:21 41:23 41:24 41:25 41:26 41:29 41:31 41:34 42:4 42:5 42:7 42:8 42:10 42:11[3] 42:12[2] 42:14[3] 42:15 42:17

PS

1:1[3] 1:2 1:3 1:5 1:6[2] 2:2 2:6 2:8[2] 2:9 2:10 3:2 3:3 3:4 3:6[2] 3:7 4:*title* 4:1 4:2 4:5 4:6 5:*title* 5:2 5:5 5:7 5:8 5:10 6:*title* 6:5 6:7[2] 6:8[2] 7:*title* 7:6[2] 7:7 7:9 7:10 7:13 7:17 8:*title* 8:2[3] 8:3 8:4[2] 8:6 8:7 8:8[3] 9:*title* 9:9 9:12 9:13[2] 9:14[2] 9:16 9:18 9:20 10:1 10:3 10:4 10:5 10:7 10:8 10:14 10:15 10:16 10:17 10:18 11:*title*

11:4 11:6 12:*title* 12:1 12:5[2] 12:6[2] 13:*title* 13:3 14:*title* 14:2 14:4 14:5 14:6 14:7[3] 15:*title* 16:*title* 16:4 16:5[2] 16:11[2] 17:*title* 17:1 17:4[3] 17:8[2] 17:12 17:14[3] 18:*title*[5] 18:2 18:4[2] 18:5[2] 18:6 18:7 18:8[2] 18:10 18:11 18:12 18:13 18:15[4] 18:16 18:18 18:20 18:21 18:24 18:30 18:34 18:35 18:40 18:43[2] 18:44 18:45 18:46 19:*title* 19:1 19:4 19:5 19:6[2] 19:7[2] 19:8[2] 19:9[2] 19:11 19:14[2] 20:*title* 20:1[3] 20:2 20:5 20:6 20:7 21:*title* 21:2 21:3[2] 21:4[2] 21:7 21:9 21:10 21:12 22:*title* 22:1 22:3 22:6[2] 22:9 22:12 22:14[2] 22:15 22:16 22:20 22:21 22:22 22:23[2]

22:24 22:25 22:27[2] 23:*title* 23:3 23:4[2] 23:5 23:6[2] 24:*title* 24:3 24:5 24:6 24:7 24:8 24:9 24:10[3] 25:*title* 25:5 25:6 25:7 25:10 25:14 25:15 25:17[2] 25:22 26:*title* 26:5 26:7[2] 26:8 26:10 27:*title* 27:1[2] 27:4[4] 27:5[2] 27:6 27:9 27:11 27:12 27:13[2] 27:14 28:*title* 28:2 28:3 28:4[2] 28:5[2] 28:6 28:8 29:*title* 29:2 29:3[2] 29:4[3] 29:5[2] 29:7[2] 29:8[2] 29:9[2] 30:*title*[2] 30:4[2] 31:*title* 31:2 31:4 31:5 31:8 31:10 31:12 31:13 31:15 31:19 31:20[3] 31:22 31:24 32:*title* 32:4 32:5 32:6 32:7 33:2 33:4 33:5[2] 33:6[3] 33:7 33:8[2] 33:10[3] 33:11[2] 33:13 33:14[2] 33:16 33:18

34:*title* 34:6 34:7 34:11 34:15 34:16[2] 34:17 34:18[2] 34:19[2] 34:20 34:22[2] 35:*title* 35:2 35:5 35:6 35:12 35:27 35:28[2] 36:*title*[2] 36:1[2] 36:3 36:7[2] 36:8[3] 36:9 36:11[2] 36:12 37:*title* 37:1[2] 37:4 37:7[2] 37:11 37:14 37:16 37:17 37:18 37:19 37:20[2] 37:22[2] 37:23 37:28 37:30[2] 37:31[2] 37:37 37:38 37:39[3] 38:*title* 38:3[2] 38:5 38:8[2] 38:10 39:*title* 39:4 39:8 39:10 40:*title* 40:2[2] 40:5 40:7[2] 40:12 40:15 41:*title* 41:1 41:2 41:3 41:5 41:9 41:13 42:*title* 42:4[2] 42:5 42:6[2] 42:7 42:8 42:9[2] 42:11 43:2[3] 43:4 43:5 44:*title* 44:1 44:3 44:14 44:15 44:16[2] 44:19[2] 44:20 44:21

45:*title*[2] 45:1[2] 45:2 45:4 45:5 45:6 45:7 45:8[2] 45:9 45:12 45:13 45:14 45:16 46:*title* 46:2 46:4[3] 46:5 46:7[2] 46:8 46:9 46:11[2] 47:*title* 47:1 47:4 47:5 47:7 47:8 47:9[4] 48:*title* 48:1[2] 48:2[3] 48:6 48:7 48:8[3] 48:9[2] 48:10[2] 48:11[2] 49:*title* 49:1 49:3[3] 49:5[2] 49:6 49:7 49:8 49:15 49:16 49:19 50:*title* 50:1 50:2[2] 50:9[2] 50:10 50:11[2] 50:13[2] 50:15 50:23 51:*title* 51:1 51:12 51:14[2] 51:17 51:18 51:19 52:*title* 52:1 52:5[3] 52:7 52:8[2] 53:*title* 53:2 53:3 53:4 53:5 53:6[3] 54:*title* 54:2 54:7 55:*title* 55:3[4] 55:4 55:10 55:14 55:19 55:21 55:23 56:*title* 56:13

57:*title*
57:1
57:3
57:4
58:*title*
58:1
58:2
58:4
58:5
58:6
58:8^{2}
58:10
59:*title*
59:2
59:5^{2}
59:9
59:10
59:12^{2}
59:13
59:16^{3}
59:17
60:*title*^{3}
60:3
60:4
60:6
60:7
60:8
60:11
61:*title*
61:2
61:4
61:5
62:*title*
62:3
62:7
62:8^{2}
63:*title*^{2}
63:7
63:9
63:11
64:*title*
64:1
64:2^{3}
64:5
64:6^{2}
64:9^{2}
65:*title*
65:4^{2}
65:5^{4}
65:7^{3}
65:8
65:9^{2}
65:12
66:2
66:3
66:5^{2}
66:8
66:15^{2}
66:19
67:7
68:*title*
68:2
68:5^{2}
68:8^{3}
68:10
68:11
68:12
68:13
68:15^{3}
68:17^{2}
68:19
68:20
68:21^{2}
68:22
68:23^{2}
68:24
68:26
68:27^{3}
68:29
68:30^{4}
68:31
68:32
68:33^{2}
68:35^{2}
69:*title*
69:3
69:4
69:6^{2}
69:9^{2}
69:12
69:13^{2}
69:14^{2}
69:16
69:18
69:20
69:24
69:26
69:28^{2}
69:30
69:35
69:36
70:*title*
70:3
70:4^{4}
70:6^{2}
70:9
70:16^{3}
70:20
70:22
70:24
72:4^{2}
72:7
72:8
72:10^{3}
72:13
72:15^{2}
72:16^{4}
72:18
72:20^{2}
73:*title*
73:1
73:3
73:10
73:15
73:17
73:26
74:*title*
74:1
74:2^{2}
74:4
74:7
74:8
74:11
74:12^{2}
74:13
74:14
74:17
74:19^{3}
74:20^{3}
74:23^{2}
75:*title*
75:3
75:8^{4}
75:9
75:10^{2}
76:*title*
76:3
76:4
76:5^{2}
76:6
76:9
76:10^{2}
76:12^{2}
77:*title*
77:2
77:5
77:10^{2}
77:11^{2}
77:12^{2}
77:15
77:18
77:20
78:*title*
78:1
78:2
78:4
78:7
78:9^{2}
78:10
78:12^{3}
78:14
78:15
78:16
78:23
78:24^{2}
78:27
78:28
78:31^{3}
78:38
78:41
78:43
78:45
78:49
78:51^{2}
78:54
78:55
78:60
78:65^{2}
78:67^{2}
78:68
78:72^{2}
79:*title*
79:2^{4}
79:9^{2}
79:10^{2}
79:11^{2}
79:13
80:*title*
80:1
80:4^{2}
80:5
80:7
80:8
80:10
80:13^{2}
80:14
80:16
80:17^{2}
80:19
81:*title*
81:1
81:4^{2}
81:5
81:7^{2}
81:10^{2}
81:11
81:15
81:16^{2}
82:*title*
82:1
82:2
82:4^{2}
82:5^{2}
82:6^{2}
82:7
83:*title*
83:4
83:6^{2}
83:7
83:8
83:9
83:12
84:*title*
84:1
84:2
84:3
84:5
84:6
84:7
84:8^{2}
84:9
84:10^{2}
84:12
85:*title*
85:1
85:2
85:3
85:4
85:11
85:13
86:*title*
86:4
86:6
86:7
86:14
86:15
86:16
87:*title*
87:2
87:3^{2}
87:4
87:5
88:*title*^{2}
88:1
88:3
88:9
88:12
89:*title*
89:1^{2}
89:5
89:6
89:7^{2}
89:8
89:9
89:14
89:15
89:17
89:18
89:19
89:22
89:26
89:27
89:29
89:34
89:39
89:42
89:43
89:45
89:48
89:50^{2}
89:51
90:*title*^{2}
90:3
90:8
90:10
90:11
90:17^{3}
91:1^{2}
91:2
91:3
91:8
92:3
92:4
92:7
92:9
92:10
92:11
92:13^{2}
93:2
93:4^{2}
94:2
94:4
94:7
94:11
94:12
94:13
94:16
94:19
94:20
94:21
94:22
95:1
95:4
95:7^{2}
95:8
96:5
96:7
96:9
96:12
97:1
97:2
97:5^{3}
97:7
97:8^{2}
97:10^{3}
97:12
98:2
98:3^{3}
98:5
98:6
98:8
100:*title*
100:3
101:*title*
101:1
101:3
101:6
101:8^{2}
102:*title*
102:5^{2}
102:6^{2}
102:10
102:15^{2}
102:17
102:19
102:20
102:21
102:24
102:25^{3}
102:26
102:28
103:*title*
103:7
103:15
103:17
103:20
103:21
103:22
104:3^{2}
104:5
104:7
104:11
104:12
104:13
104:14^{2}
104:15
104:16^{3}
104:20
104:24
104:30
104:31
104:34
104:35
105:2
105:3
105:5
105:6^{2}
105:11^{2}
105:16
105:19
105:20
105:21^{2}
105:23
105:27
105:30
105:31
105:33
105:35
105:36
105:38
105:40
105:44^{2}
106:2
106:5^{2}
106:7
106:10^{2}
106:11
106:16
106:17
106:20
106:22
106:25
106:28
106:32
106:38^{3}
106:40
106:41
106:45
106:46
106:48
107:2^{2}
107:3
107:6
107:7
107:8
107:10
107:11^{2}
107:13
107:14
107:15
107:16^{2}
107:17^{2}
107:18^{2}
107:19
107:21
107:22
107:24
107:26
107:28
107:31
107:32^{2}
107:34
107:37
107:43
108:*title*
108:7
108:8
108:12
109:*title*
109:1
109:2^{2}
109:3
109:10
109:14^{2}
109:15
109:20^{2}
109:24
109:31
110:*title*
110:2^{3}
110:3^{4}
110:4
110:5
110:7
111:1
111:2^{2}
111:4
111:5
111:6^{2}
111:7
111:10^{2}
112:2
112:4
112:7
112:10
113:1^{2}
113:2
113:3^{2}
113:7^{2}
113:8
113:9
114:1^{3}
114:7^{2}
114:8
115:4
115:10
115:12^{3}
115:15
115:16
116:3^{2}
116:4
116:9
116:13^{2}
116:14
116:15^{2}
116:16
116:17^{2}
116:18
116:19^{2}
117:2
118:3
118:10
118:11
118:12^{2}
118:15^{3}
118:16^{2}
118:17
118:19
118:20
118:22
118:26^{3}
119:1
119:7
119:13
119:14
119:18
119:27^{2}
119:29
119:30
119:32
119:33
119:35
119:43^{2}
119:46
119:52
119:53
119:54
119:61
119:62
119:63^{2}
119:64
119:72^{2}
119:84
119:88
119:96
119:108
119:111
119:115
119:116
119:119
119:120^{2}
119:123
119:130
119:134
119:136
119:144
119:147
119:152
119:160
119:161
119:164
119:172
120:*title*
120:4^{2}
120:5
121:*title*
122:*title*^{2}
122:1
122:4^{3}
122:5^{3}
122:6
122:9^{2}
123:*title*
123:2^{4}
123:4^{2}
124:*title*^{2}
124:7^{2}
124:8
125:*title*
125:3^{2}
125:5
126:*title*
126:1
127:*title*
127:2
127:3^{2}
127:4^{2}
127:5
128:*title*
128:2
128:3
128:5^{3}
129:*title*
129:4
129:8^{2}
130:*title*
130:1
130:2
131:*title*^{2}
131:2
132:*title*
132:2
132:3
132:5
132:6^{2}
132:8
132:10
132:11^{2}
132:17
133:*title*
133:2
133:3^{2}
134:*title*
134:1^{2}
134:3
135:1^{2}
135:2^{3}
135:7^{2}
135:8^{2}
135:9
135:11^{3}
135:15^{2}
135:19^{2}
135:20
135:21
136:2
136:3
136:14
136:19
136:20
136:26
137:1
137:3^{4}
137:6
137:7^{2}
137:8
138:*title*
138:4^{2}
138:5^{2}
138:7^{2}
138:8
139:*title*
139:9^{2}
139:15
139:16
139:17
140:*title*
140:4
140:6
140:7^{2}
140:8
140:9^{2}
140:12^{2}
141:*title*
141:2
141:3
141:4
141:9^{2}
142:*title*
142:5
142:7
143:*title*
143:5^{2}
143:10
143:11
143:12
144:*title*
144:3^{3}
144:7^{2}
144:8
144:9
144:11^{2}
144:12
144:13
145:*title*
145:5^{3}
145:6^{2}
145:7^{2}
145:8^{2}
145:11^{3}
145:12^{2}
145:15
145:16
145:19
145:21
146:3
146:8
146:9
147:2
147:4
147:5
147:10^{2}
147:13
147:14
148:3
148:4
148:5
148:11^{2}
148:13
148:14^{2}
149:1
149:2
149:6
149:8
150:1
150:3

PR

1:1^{3}
1:2
1:3
1:5
1:6
1:7^{2}
1:8^{2}
1:9
1:17
1:19^{3}
1:21^{2}
1:25
1:29
1:30
1:31
1:32^{2}
1:33
2:5^{2}
2:6
2:8^{2}
2:12
2:13^{2}
2:14
2:17^{2}
2:19^{2}
2:20^{2}
2:22
3:2
3:3
3:4
3:9
3:11^{2}
3:14^{2}
3:16
3:17
3:18
3:25^{3}
3:27
3:31
3:33^{3}
3:35
4:1
4:3
4:5
4:9^{2}
4:10
4:11
4:13
4:14^{2}
4:17^{2}
4:18
4:19
4:21
4:23^{2}
4:26
5:3
5:6
5:7
5:8
5:10
5:13
5:14
5:15^{2}
5:16
5:18
5:20
5:21^{2}
5:22
5:23
6:2^{2}
6:3
6:5^{2}
6:9
6:10
6:20
6:23^{2}
6:24^{2}
6:26^{2}
6:31
6:34^{2}
7:2
7:3
7:6
7:7
7:10^{2}
7:16^{2}
7:18
7:20
7:21
7:22
7:24
7:27
8:2^{2}
8:3
8:4
8:5
8:6^{2}
8:8
8:12
8:13
8:16
8:20^{3}
8:22^{2}
8:26^{2}
8:27
8:28
8:29
8:31^{2}
8:34
8:35
9:3
9:5^{2}
9:6
9:10^{2}
9:11
9:14^{2}
9:18
10:1^{2}
10:2
10:3^{2}
10:4
10:6^{2}
10:7^{2}
10:11^{3}
10:13^{3}
10:14
10:15
10:16^{2}
10:17
10:19
10:20^{2}
10:21^{2}
10:22
10:23
10:24^{2}
10:27^{2}
10:28^{2}
10:29^{2}
10:31
10:32^{2}
11:3^{2}
11:4
11:5
11:6
11:7
11:8
11:11^{2}
11:12^{2}
11:13
11:14
11:20
11:21
11:22
11:23^{2}
11:26
11:29
11:30^{2}
12:2^{2}
12:3
12:5^{2}
12:6^{2}
12:7
12:8
12:10^{2}
12:11
12:12^{2}
12:13^{2}
12:14^{2}
12:15
12:18^{2}
12:19
12:20^{2}
12:23
12:24
12:25
12:26
12:27
12:28
13:2^{2}
13:4^{2}
13:8
13:9^{2}
13:12
13:14^{3}
13:15
13:20
13:22
13:23^{2}
13:25^{2}
14:3^{3}
14:4
14:7^{2}
14:8^{2}
14:11^{2}
14:12
14:13
14:17
14:19
14:20
14:23
14:24^{2}
14:26^{2}
14:27^{3}
14:28^{3}
14:29^{2}
14:30^{2}
14:33^{2}
15:2^{2}
15:3
15:4
15:6^{2}
15:7^{2}
15:8^{2}
15:9
15:11^{2}
15:13
15:14^{2}
15:15^{2}
15:16
15:17
15:19^{3}
15:21^{2}
15:22
15:23
15:24
15:25^{2}
15:26^{2}
15:27
15:28^{2}
15:29
15:30
15:31
15:33^{2}
16:1^{2}
16:2
16:4
16:6
16:10
16:11
16:13
16:14^{2}
16:15^{2}
16:17
16:19
16:21
16:22^{2}
16:23
16:25
16:26
16:31^{2}
16:33
17:1
17:2
17:6^{2}
17:8
17:12
17:14
17:16
17:18^{2}
17:21
17:23^{2}
17:24^{2}
17:27^{2}
17:28
18:4^{2}
18:5
18:7
18:8^{2}
18:10
18:12
18:14
18:15^{2}
18:19
18:20^{2}
18:21
18:22
19:3
19:6
19:7
19:11
19:12
19:13^{2}
19:14
19:19
19:21
19:22
19:23
19:27
19:28
19:29
20:2^{2}
20:4
20:5^{2}
20:8
20:10
20:12
20:15^{2}
20:16
20:17
20:24
20:27^{3}
20:29^{2}
20:30^{2}
21:1^{2}
21:2
21:4
21:5^{2}
21:6^{2}
21:7
21:8
21:9
21:10
21:12
21:13
21:15
21:16^{3}
21:20
21:22^{2}
21:25
21:27
21:31^{2}
22:2
22:4
22:5
22:8
22:9
22:11^{2}
22:12^{2}
22:14^{2}
22:15^{2}
22:17
22:21^{3}
22:23
22:26^{2}
23:3
23:6
23:9^{2}
23:10
23:12
23:17
23:20
23:24^{2}
23:29
23:34^{2}
24:2
24:5
24:6
24:9
24:10
24:14
24:15
24:19
24:20
24:22
24:23
24:30^{3}
24:33
25:1^{3}
25:2^{2}
25:3
25:6^{2}
25:7
25:11^{2}
25:12^{2}
25:13^{3}
25:14
25:17
25:19^{2}
25:22
25:24
26:6
26:7^{2}
26:9^{2}
26:12^{2}
26:22^{2}
27:1
27:6^{2}
27:9
27:10
27:13
27:16
27:17
27:19
27:20
27:23
27:25
27:26
28:2^{2}
28:7
28:17
28:19
28:21^{2}
28:24
28:25
29:6
29:7
29:20^{2}
29:25
30:1^{2}
30:2
30:3
30:4
30:5
30:7
30:9
30:17
30:19^{5}
30:20
30:27
30:33^{3}
31:1
31:2^{2}
31:5
31:6^{2}
31:8
31:9
31:11^{2}
31:12
31:16
31:21
31:22
31:23
31:26
31:27^{2}
31:31^{2}

EC

1:1^{2}
1:2^{2}
1:3
1:8
1:10
1:11^{2}
1:13
1:14
1:16
1:17
2:2^{2}
2:3^{2}
2:5^{2}
2:6
2:7
2:8^{5}
2:10
2:11
2:16^{2}
2:17
2:20
2:22^{3}
2:24
2:26
3:8^{2}
3:10
3:13^{2}
3:16^{2}
3:18^{2}
3:19
3:20
3:21^{2}
4:1^{2}
4:4^{2}
4:6
4:8^{2}
4:14
4:16^{3}
5:1^{2}
5:3^{2}
5:6
5:7
5:8^{2}
5:9
5:11
5:12^{2}
5:15^{2}
5:18^{2}
5:19
5:20^{2}
6:2
6:3
6:7
6:9^{3}
6:12
7:1^{2}
7:2^{3}
7:3
7:4^{4}
7:5^{2}
7:6^{2}
7:8
7:9
7:12
7:13
7:14^{2}
7:15
7:18^{2}
7:25^{3}
8:1^{2}
8:2^{2}
8:3
8:4
8:6
8:8
8:10
8:11^{2}
8:14^{2}
8:15^{2}
8:17
9:1
9:3^{3}
9:5
9:9^{3}
9:11^{2}
9:12
9:17^{2}
9:18
10:1
10:4
10:12^{2}
10:13^{3}
10:14
10:15^{2}
10:17
10:18
10:20
11:3
11:5^{3}
11:8
11:9^{3}
12:1
12:3^{2}
12:4^{3}
12:5
12:8
12:10
12:11^{2}
12:12^{2}
12:13^{2}

CA

1:1
1:2
1:3^{2}
1:5^{3}
1:6
1:7
1:8
1:9
1:10^{2}
1:11^{2}
1:13
1:14^{2}
1:17^{2}
2:1^{2}
2:3
2:5
2:7^{2}
2:8
2:12^{3}
2:14^{2}
2:17
3:4
3:5^{2}
3:6^{3}
3:7
3:8
3:9^{2}
3:10^{5}
3:11^{4}
4:1
4:2
4:3^{2}
4:4^{2}
4:6^{2}
4:8^{3}
4:9^{2}
4:10
4:11^{2}
4:13
4:14
4:15^{2}
5:2^{2}
5:4
5:5
5:7
5:8^{2}
5:12^{2}
5:13
5:15^{2}
5:16
6:2
6:5
6:6
6:7
6:9^{2}
6:11^{2}
6:12
6:13
7:1^{3}
7:2
7:4^{3}
7:5
7:7
7:8^{3}
7:9^{2}
7:13
8:1
8:2^{3}
8:4
8:6
8:7
8:9^{2}
8:11
8:14

ISA

1:1^{4}
1:4^{2}
1:6
1:8^{2}
1:9
1:10^{4}
1:11^{7}
1:13
1:15
1:16
1:19
1:20
1:21
1:23^{2}
1:24^{4}
1:26
1:28^{2}
1:29
1:31
2:1
2:2^{2}
2:3^{6}
2:5^{2}
2:6^{2}
2:7^{4}
2:8^{2}
2:10^{2}
2:11^{2}
2:12^{2}
2:13^{2}
2:16
2:17^{2}
2:19^{4}
2:20^{2}
2:21^{4}
2:22
3:1^{3}
3:2
3:3
3:6^{3}
3:7
3:8
3:9
3:10
3:11
3:12
3:14^{2}
3:15^{2}
3:16
3:17^{3}
3:18
3:20
3:22
3:24^{6}
4:1
4:2^{3}
4:4^{5}
4:5^{2}
4:6
5:1
5:2
5:3
5:7^{4}
5:8
5:9^{2}
5:10^{2}
5:12^{2}
5:15
5:16
5:17
5:18
5:19^{2}
5:22
5:23
5:24^{4}
5:25^{2}
5:26
5:27^{2}
5:29
5:30
6:3^{2}
6:4^{2}
6:5^{4}
6:6
6:8
6:10
6:12
7:1^{7}
7:2^{3}
7:3^{3}
7:4^{4}
7:5
7:6^{2}
7:8^{2}
7:9^{2}
7:11
7:13
7:16
7:17
7:18^{3}
7:19^{2}
7:20^{2}
7:22
7:25^{3}
8:2
8:4^{3}
8:6
8:7^{2}
8:8^{2}
8:9
8:11
8:13
8:14^{4}
8:17
8:18
8:22
9:1^{4}
9:2^{2}
9:4^{4}
9:5^{2}
9:6
9:7^{5}
9:9^{2}
9:11
9:13
9:16^{2}
9:18^{2}
9:19^{3}
9:20
10:2
10:3
10:5
10:6^{2}
10:10^{3}
10:12^{4}
10:13^{2}
10:14
10:16^{2}
10:17
10:18^{2}
10:19^{2}
10:20^{4}
10:21
10:22^{2}
10:23^{2}
10:24^{3}
10:26^{4}
10:27
10:29
10:30
10:31
10:32^{3}
10:33^{2}
10:34
11:1^{3}
11:2^{6}
11:3^{4}
11:4^{3}
11:5^{2}
11:8
11:9^{2}
11:10^{2}
11:11^{2}
11:12^{3}
11:13^{2}
11:14^{3}
11:15
11:16^{3}
12:3^{2}
12:6^{3}
13:1^{2}
13:2
13:4^{6}
13:5^{2}
13:6
13:8
13:9^{2}
13:10
13:11^{2}
13:12
13:13^{4}
13:18
13:19^{2}
13:21^{2}
13:22
14:1
14:2^{2}
14:4
14:5^{2}
14:8
14:9^{2}
14:11
14:12
14:13^{3}
14:14
14:15
14:17
14:18^{2}
14:19^{3}
14:20
14:21^{2}
14:22
14:23^{3}
14:24
14:27
14:29^{2}
14:30
14:32^{7}
15:1^{3}
15:3
15:4
15:5^{4}
15:6
15:7
15:8
15:9^{4}
16:1^{3}
16:2^{3}
16:3
16:4^{2}
16:5
16:6^{3}
16:7
16:8^{3}
16:9^{2}
16:10
16:14^{2}
17:1
17:2
17:3^{4}
17:4^{2}
17:5
17:6^{3}
17:7
17:8
17:9^{2}
17:10^{3}
17:11^{2}
17:12^{4}
17:13^{2}
17:14^{2}
18:1
18:2
18:3
18:4^{2}
18:6^{3}
18:7^{5}
19:1^{4}

19:3 19:4^2 19:6 19:7 19:11^5 19:12 19:13^3 19:16^4 19:17^4 19:18^4 19:19^2 19:20^3 19:22 19:23 19:24 19:25^2 20:1 20:2 20:4^2 20:5^2 20:6^2 21:1^2 21:3^3 21:4 21:7^3 21:9^3 21:10^4 21:11^4 21:13 21:14^2 21:15 21:16^2 21:17^5 22:1^2 22:2 22:4^3 22:5^6 22:6 22:7 22:8^3 22:9^3 22:10 22:11 22:12 22:14^2 22:15 22:18^2 22:20 22:21^2 22:22^2 22:24^4 22:25 23:1^3 23:2^2 23:3^3 23:4 23:5 23:6 23:7 23:8 23:9^3 23:10 23:12 23:13 23:14 23:15^2 23:17^3 24:2^2 24:4 24:6 24:8^3 24:10 24:11 24:13^2 24:15^3 24:16 24:17 24:18^4 24:21^2 24:23 25:1 25:2^3 25:3 25:4 25:5^3 25:6^6 25:7

25:8 25:10 25:11^2 25:12^2 26:1 26:6^2 26:7^2 26:8^3 26:9 26:10^2 26:11 26:13 26:15 26:17 26:18 26:19 26:21^2 27:2 27:5 27:6^2 27:7 27:8 27:9^2 27:11 27:12^3 27:13^2 28:1^4 28:2^2 28:3^2 28:4 28:5^4 28:6 28:7^3 28:8 28:13 28:14 28:17 28:21 28:22 28:24 28:28 28:29 29:4^3 29:5^2 29:6^3 29:7^2 29:8 29:10 29:11^2 29:13 29:14^2 29:16^3 29:18^4 29:19 29:21 29:22 29:23^4 30:1^2 30:2^2 30:3^2 30:5 30:6^5 30:9 30:11^3 30:12 30:14^3 30:15 30:17^3 30:18 30:19 30:20^2 30:22^4 30:23^3 30:25^2 30:26^6 30:27^2 30:28^3 30:29^3 30:30^3 30:31 30:32 30:33^3 31:1 31:2^2 31:4^4 31:5 31:6

31:7^2 31:8^2 31:9 32:2^2 32:3^2 32:4^2 32:6^2 32:7 32:13^2 32:14^3 32:17^2 32:20 33:2 33:3^2 33:4^2 33:6^3 33:7 33:12 33:15^3 33:16^2 33:19^2 33:20^3 33:21 33:23 34:1 34:2 34:3 34:4 34:5 34:6^5 34:8^3 34:11^2 34:13 34:14^3 34:16^3 35:2^4 35:4 35:5^2 35:6 35:7^2 35:8 35:10 36:1^3 36:2^3 36:4 36:6^2 36:8 36:9^3 36:11 36:13^2 36:15^2 36:16^4 36:17^2 36:18^5 36:19^3 36:20^3 36:22^3 37:1 37:2^2 37:3^3 37:4^2 37:5 37:6^3 37:8 37:9 37:10^3 37:11 37:12^2 37:13^4 37:14^2 37:16^4 37:17 37:18^2 37:19 37:20 37:21^3 37:22^2 37:23 37:24^5 37:25^2 37:26 37:27^2 37:30^2 37:31^2 37:32^4 37:33 37:36^2

37:37 37:38^2 38:1 38:4 38:5 38:6^3 38:8^2 38:9^3 38:10^4 38:11^2 38:12 38:13 38:15 38:16 38:17 38:20^2 38:21 38:22 39:1^2 39:2^3 39:5^2 39:7^3 39:8 40:2 40:3^2 40:5^2 40:6 40:7 40:8 40:9 40:12^2 40:13 40:14^2 40:15^2 40:21 40:22 40:23 40:26 40:28^3 41:5 41:6 41:8 41:9 41:10 41:12 41:14^2 41:16 41:17 41:18^3 41:20^2 41:21 41:22 41:24^2 41:25 41:28 42:5 42:6^2 42:7 42:9 42:10 42:11^2 42:13 42:22 42:25^2 43:3 43:6 43:13 43:14 43:15 43:18 43:20 43:22 43:23 43:24 43:28 44:5^2 44:6^2 44:9 44:11 44:12 44:13^2 44:14 44:19^2 44:21 44:23 44:25 44:26^3

44:28 45:1 45:2^2 45:3^3 45:6 45:9 45:11^3 45:13 45:14^4 45:15 45:16^2 45:19^2 45:20^2 45:22 45:23 45:25 46:3^2 46:6 46:7 46:9 47:1^2 47:4^2 47:5^2 47:7 47:8 47:9^3 47:12 47:13 47:14 48:1^7 48:2^3 48:3 48:10 48:13 48:17 48:18 48:19 48:20^3 48:21 49:1^2 49:2 49:5 49:6^3 49:7^3 49:8^2 49:9 49:10 49:12 49:15 49:16 49:17 49:19^2 49:23 49:25^2 49:26 50:1^2 50:4 50:10^2 50:11^2 51:1 51:3^2 51:4 51:7^2 51:9^2 51:10^2 51:11 51:12^3 51:13^4 51:15 51:16^2 51:17^4 51:18 51:20^4 51:22^5 51:23 52:2^2 52:7^2 52:9 52:10^3 52:11^3 52:12 52:14 53:1 53:2 53:3^2 53:4 53:5

53:6 53:8^3 53:10 53:11^2 53:12 54:1^2 54:2^2 54:4^2 54:5^3 54:6 54:9^2 54:10 54:12^3 54:13^2 54:17^3 55:3 55:5^2 55:11 55:12 55:13^2 56:2 56:3 56:4 56:5^2 56:6^3 56:7^2 56:8 56:9 57:3^2 57:4^2 57:6 57:10^2 57:11^2 57:14^2 57:15^3 57:17^2 57:19 58:1 58:2^3 58:3 58:4 58:6 58:8 58:9^2 58:11 58:12^4 58:13 58:14^3 59:5 59:6^2 59:7 59:8 59:13 59:17^2 59:19^3 59:21^5 60:1 60:3 60:5^2 60:6^3 60:7^3 60:9^3 60:10 60:11 60:13^3 60:14^5 60:15 60:16^3 60:20 60:21^2 61:1^2 61:2^3 61:3^5 61:4 61:5 61:6^3 61:10^2 62:2 62:3^3 62:6 62:8^2 62:9 62:10 62:11^3 62:12 63:1 63:3

63:4^2 63:7^4 63:9^2 63:11^2 63:12 63:14 63:15^4 63:16 63:17 63:18 64:4 64:7^2 64:8 65:1^2 65:3 65:4 65:7 65:9^3 65:10^2 65:14^3 65:16^2 65:19^2 65:20 65:21 65:22^3 65:23^2 66:1 66:2 66:5 66:6^2 66:7 66:11^2 66:12 66:14 66:15 66:16 66:19 66:20^3 66:21 66:24

JER

1:1^4 1:2^5 1:3^8 1:4 1:5 1:8 1:11^2 1:13 1:14^2 1:15^5 1:16 1:18^2 2:1 2:2^3 2:3 2:4^4 2:6^7 2:10 2:13 2:16^2 2:18^4 2:19 2:20 2:21 2:26 2:27 2:28^2 2:31^2 2:34^2 2:36^2 3:4 3:6 3:8 3:9 3:14^2 3:16^2 3:17^3 3:18^4 3:19^2 3:20 3:21^2 3:23^2 3:24

3:25 4:1 4:3 4:4^5 4:7 4:8 4:9^2 4:11^2 4:16 4:17 4:19^2 4:21 4:26 4:29 4:30 4:31^5 5:1 5:4^2 5:5^2 5:6^2 5:11^2 5:14 5:15 5:20 5:22 5:24 5:27^2 5:28^3 6:1^5 6:2 6:4 6:6^2 6:9^2 6:10 6:11^4 6:12 6:13^3 6:14^2 6:17 6:19 6:22 6:23 6:24 6:25 6:26 6:29 7:2^3 7:3^2 7:4^3 7:12 7:15^2 7:17^2 7:18 7:19 7:20^2 7:21^2 7:22^2 7:24 7:25^2 7:28 7:29 7:30 7:31^3 7:32^3 7:33^3 7:34^6 8:1^8 8:2^2 8:3^3 8:5 8:6 8:7^2 8:8^2 8:9 8:11^2 8:12 8:14 8:15 8:16^3 8:19^4 8:21^2 8:22^2 9:1^3 9:2^2 9:4 9:6 9:7^2

9:10^4 9:11^2 9:12 9:14 9:15^3 9:17 9:19^2 9:20^2 9:22 9:26^2 10:1 10:2^2 10:3^4 10:5 10:7^2 10:8 10:9^4 10:13^3 10:15^2 10:16^4 10:17^2 10:18 10:20 10:22^3 10:23 11:2^3 11:3^2 11:4^2 11:6^3 11:7^2 11:8^2 11:9^2 11:10^3 11:12^3 11:13^3 11:16^3 11:17^5 11:18 11:19 11:20 11:21^3 11:22 11:23^2 12:1^2 12:3 12:4^2 12:5^2 12:6 12:7^2 12:9 12:12^3 12:13^3 12:14^2 12:16^2 13:2 13:3 13:4 13:8 13:9^2 13:10 13:11^3 13:12 13:13^2 13:16 13:18 13:19^2 13:22 13:24 13:25 13:27 14:1 14:2 14:8^2 14:9 14:14^2 14:16^2 14:17 14:19 14:30 14:21 14:22 15:1 15:3^2 15:4^4 15:7^2 15:8^2 15:9

15:10^3 15:11^2 15:15 15:16^2 15:17^2 15:21^4 16:1 16:4^4 16:5 16:7 16:8 16:9^7 16:12 16:13 16:14^3 16:15^2 16:16^2 16:18 16:19^2 17:1^5 17:8 17:10 17:11 17:12 17:13^2 17:15 17:16 17:17 17:18 17:19^4 17:20^3 17:21 17:22 17:24 17:25^4 17:26^4 17:27^2 18:4^2 18:5 18:6^2 18:8 18:10 18:11^2 18:12 18:13 18:14^2 18:17 18:18 18:21^2 18:23 19:1^4 19:2^3 19:3^5 19:4^2 19:5 19:6^3 19:7^4 19:8 19:9^3 19:10 19:11 19:13^6 19:14 19:15^2 20:1^2 20:2^2 20:3 20:4^3 20:5^4 20:8 20:9 20:10 20:12 20:13^2 20:18 21:1^2 21:2^2 21:4^4 21:6^2 21:7^6 21:8^2 21:10^2 21:11^3 21:12^5 21:13^2 21:14 22:1^2

22:2^3 22:3^2 22:4^2 22:6^2 22:9 22:11^4 22:16 22:18^2 22:19^2 22:23^2 22:24^2 22:25^5 22:29 22:30^2 23:1 23:2^2 23:3^2 23:7^3 23:8^3 23:9^4 23:10^3 23:12 23:13 23:14^3 23:15^3 23:16^5 23:17 23:18 23:19^2 23:20^2 23:22 23:26^3 23:33 23:34 23:36^4 23:38^3 23:39 24:1^6 24:4 24:5^4 24:8^3 24:9 25:1^6 25:2^2 25:3^4 25:5 25:6 25:7 25:8 25:9^2 25:10^6 25:11 25:12^2 25:14^2 25:15^2 25:16 25:18 25:19 25:20^5 25:21 25:22^3 25:24^2 25:25^3 25:26^4 25:27^3 25:28 25:29^2 25:30 25:31 25:32^2 25:33^3 25:34^3 25:35 25:36^4 25:37^2 25:38^3 26:1^4 26:2^2 26:3^3 26:5 26:6 26:7 26:8 26:9^2 26:10^4 26:13^2 26:15

26:16 26:17^3 26:18^6 26:19^2 26:20^4 26:22 26:23^2 26:24^3 27:1^4 27:3^7 27:4^2 27:6^3 27:7^2 27:8^3 27:9 27:11^2 27:12^3 27:13 27:14^2 27:16^2 27:17 27:18^5 27:19^2 27:20^4 27:21^6 28:1^8 28:2^4 28:3^2 28:4^5 28:5^3 28:6 28:7 28:8^4 28:9^2 28:11^5 28:13^2 28:14^6 28:16 29:1^2 29:2 29:3^5 29:4^2 29:5 29:7 29:8^3 29:11^2 29:14 29:16^4 29:17 29:18 29:20 29:21^8 29:22^3 29:25^3 29:26^2 29:27 29:28 29:29 29:30 29:31 30:2 30:3 30:5^3 30:7^2 30:8^2 30:10 30:11^2 30:14^3 30:15 30:16 30:17 30:18 30:19^2 30:21^2 30:23^2 30:24^2 31:1^2 31:2 31:3 31:4 31:1^2 31:2 31:3 31:4 31:5 31:7^2 31:8

31:9 31:10 31:11 31:12^4 31:14 31:16 31:19 31:21 31:23^5 31:27^4 31:31^2 31:32^2 31:33 31:34^2 31:35^3 31:36 31:37^2 31:38^2 31:40^4 32:1^3 32:2^3 32:3^3 32:4^5 32:6 32:7^2 32:8^5 32:9^2 32:11 32:12^7 32:14^3 32:15^2 32:16^2 32:18^3 32:19^3 32:20 32:21^2 32:23 32:24^4 32:25 32:26 32:27 32:28^3 32:30^4 32:31^2 32:32^7 32:35^3 32:36^3 32:37 32:39^2 32:43 32:44^5 33:1^2 33:4^4 33:5 33:6 33:7^2 33:9^2 33:10^2 33:11^{10} 33:12^2 33:13^6 33:14^2 33:15 33:17^2 33:19 33:20^2 33:22^3 33:23 33:25 33:26^3 34:1^3 34:2^4 34:3^3 34:4^3 34:5 34:6 34:7^4 34:9^2 34:10 34:12 34:13^5 34:14 34:17 34:18 34:19^4 34:20^4 34:21^5

34:22 35:1^3 35:2^3 35:3^3 35:4^9 35:5^3 35:6 35:8^2 35:11^5 35:12 35:13^4 35:14^2 35:16^3 35:17^3 35:18^4 35:19^3 36:1^3 36:2^2 36:3 36:4^4 36:5 36:6^4 36:8^2 36:9^4 36:10^7 36:11^4 36:12^4 36:13 36:14^5 36:16 36:20^2 36:21^3 36:24 36:26^3 36:27^2 36:28 36:29^2 36:30^3 36:31^2 36:32^4 37:1^5 37:2^2 37:3^2 37:5^2 37:6 37:7^3 37:10 37:11^2 37:12^3 37:13^4 37:15 37:17^2 37:19 37:20 37:21^4 38:1^4 38:3^2 38:4^4 38:6^3 38:7^2 38:8 38:10 38:11 38:13^2 38:14 38:16 38:17^3 38:18^3 38:19 38:20 38:22^2 38:23^3 38:24 38:28 39:1^3 39:2^2 39:3^5 39:4^5 39:5^3 39:6^4 39:8^2 39:9^3 39:10^4 39:11^2 39:13^2 39:14^4 39:15^2

39:16^2 39:17^2 40:1^2 40:2 40:5^5 40:6 40:7^6 40:8^5 40:9^4 40:11^4 40:12^2 40:13^2 40:14^3 40:15^2 40:16^3 41:1^5 41:2^4 41:3 41:5 41:6^2 41:7^3 41:8^4 41:9^5 41:10^4 41:11^4 41:12 41:13^2 41:14 41:15 41:16^6 41:17 41:18^5 42:1^3 42:2 42:6^2 42:7 42:8^2 42:9 42:10 42:11^4 42:13 42:14^3 42:15^4 42:16 42:17 42:18^3 42:19 42:21 43:1^2 43:2^2 43:3^2 43:4^4 43:5^4 43:6^4 43:7^2 43:8 43:9^3 43:10^3 43:11 43:12^3 43:13^4 44:1^2 44:2^3 44:3 44:6^2 44:7^3 44:8^3 44:9^7 44:11^2 44:12^3 44:13 44:14^4 44:15 44:16 44:17^5 44:18 44:19 44:21^3 44:22^3 44:23 44:24^2 44:25^3 44:26^5 44:27^3 44:28^5 44:30^6 45:1^5

45:2 46:1 46:2^6 46:10^5 46:11 46:12 46:13^2 46:16 46:17 46:18 46:20 46:21^3 46:22 46:24^3 46:25^3 46:26^5 46:27 46:28^2 47:1 47:2^2 47:3^6 47:4^3 47:5 47:6 48:1^2 48:2 48:3 48:5^3 48:10 48:13^3 48:15^2 48:16 48:18 48:19 48:24^2 48:25 48:27 48:28 48:29^2 48:31 48:32^3 48:33 48:34^3 48:36 48:38 48:41 48:43 48:44^2 48:45^7 48:46 48:47^2 49:2^2 49:3 49:6^2 49:7 49:8^2 49:12^2 49:16^3 49:18^2 49:19^2 49:20^3 49:21^2 49:22^3 49:25^2 49:26^2 49:27^2 49:28^3 49:30^2 49:32 49:33 49:34^4 49:35^3 49:36^2 49:39 50:1 50:3 50:4^2 50:7^2 50:8^4 50:9^2 50:11 50:12 50:13^2 50:15 50:16^2 50:17^2 50:18^4

50:20^2 50:21^2 50:22^2 50:23 50:25^4 50:26 50:27 50:28^5 50:29 50:30 50:31 50:33^3 50:34^2 50:35 50:37 50:38 50:39^2 50:40 50:41 50:42 50:43^4 50:44^2 50:45^3 50:46^2 51:1 51:2 51:4 51:5^4 51:6^3 51:7 51:10 51:11^4 51:12^2 51:13 51:14 51:16^3 51:18^2 51:19^4 51:20 51:23 51:24 51:26 51:27 51:28^2 51:29^2 51:30 51:31 51:32 51:33^4 51:34 51:35 51:41 51:42 51:43 51:44^2 51:45^3 51:47^2 51:49^2 51:51 51:53 51:54^2 51:55^2 51:56^2 51:57 51:58^2 51:59^4 51:63^2 51:64 52:1^2 52:2 52:3^2 52:4^3 52:5 52:6^2 52:7^4 52:8^2 52:10^3 52:11^3 52:12^5 52:13^3 52:14^3 52:15^6 52:16^3 52:17^4 52:18 52:19^3

52:20^2 52:21^2 52:22^3 52:24^2 52:25^9 52:26^2 52:27^3 52:29 52:30^3 52:31^8 52:32 52:33 52:34^4

LA

1:1 1:3^2 1:4 1:5 1:6 1:7^4 1:12 1:14 1:15^2 1:21 2:1^3 2:2^3 2:3 2:4^2 2:5 2:6^3 2:7^4 2:8^2 2:10^3 2:11^3 2:12 2:13^2 2:14 2:15^3 2:17^2 2:18^3 2:19^4 2:20^2 2:21 2:22 3:1 3:6 3:13 3:22 3:26 3:32 3:33 3:34 3:35^2 3:38^2 3:39 3:45 3:48^3 3:51^2 3:55 3:58 3:62 3:64 3:65 3:66 4:1^2 4:2^3 4:3 4:4^2 4:6^5 4:7 4:9^2 4:10^3 4:12^3 4:13^4 4:16^2 4:19 4:20^3 4:21^2 4:22^3 5:8 5:9^3 5:10 5:11 5:12

5:15 5:18[2] 5:21

EZE

1:1[3] 1:2[2] 1:3[4] 1:4[5] 1:5[3] 1:7[3] 1:8 1:10[5] 1:11 1:13[4] 1:14[2] 1:16[3] 1:18 1:20 1:21 1:22[3] 1:24[5] 1:26[4] 1:27[5] 1:28[7] 2:2 2:3[2] 2:6[4] 2:8 2:9 3:1[2] 3:3 3:4[2] 3:5[3] 3:6[2] 3:7[2] 3:10 3:11[2] 3:12[2] 3:13[4] 3:14[2] 3:15[2] 3:16[2] 3:17[2] 3:22 3:23[2] 3:25 3:26 4:1 4:3[2] 4:4[3] 4:5[4] 4:6[2] 4:7 4:8 4:9 4:11 4:12 4:13 4:14[2] 4:16[2] 5:1 5:2[2] 5:4[3] 5:5 5:7 5:8[2] 5:9 5:10[2] 5:12[2] 5:14 5:16[2] 6:1 6:2[2] 6:3[2] 6:5[2] 6:7 6:9 6:11[2] 6:12 6:13 7:1 7:2[3] 7:4 7:7[2]

7:9 7:11[5] 7:13 7:16[3] 7:19[3] 7:20[3] 7:21[2] 7:23[2] 7:24[2] 7:26 7:27[2] 8:1[3] 8:2[4] 8:3[6] 8:4[2] 8:5[3] 8:6[2] 8:7 8:8 8:10[3] 8:11[6] 8:12[4] 8:14[2] 8:15 8:16[4] 8:17[2] 9:2 9:3[3] 9:4[3] 9:8[2] 9:9[4] 10:1[3] 10:2 10:3 10:4[4] 10:5[2] 10:7 10:8 10:9[2] 10:10 10:12 10:14[4] 10:15 10:17 10:18[2] 10:19[4] 10:20[2] 10:21[2] 10:22[2] 11:1[5] 11:2 11:4 11:5[3] 11:7[3] 11:9[2] 11:10 11:11 11:12 11:13[3] 11:14 11:15[4] 11:17[2] 11:19[2] 11:21 11:22[2] 11:23[3] 11:24[2] 11:25 12:1 12:2[2] 12:3 12:6 12:8 12:9[2] 12:10 12:13 12:16 12:17 12:18 12:19[7] 12:21 12:22[2] 12:23 12:24 12:26 12:27[4] 12:28

13:1 13:2[4] 13:5[2] 13:9[4] 13:16[2] 13:17[3] 13:18[2] 13:19[2] 13:21 13:22[2] 13:23 14:1[2] 14:2 14:3[3] 14:4[4] 14:5 14:6 14:7[5] 14:8 14:9 14:10[3] 14:11 14:12 14:13[2] 14:15 15:1 15:2[2] 15:3 15:4[2] 15:6[2] 16:1 16:2 16:3[2] 16:5 16:7 16:8 16:13 16:15 16:16 16:17[3] 16:20 16:22 16:25 16:26 16:27[3] 16:29 16:30 16:31 16:32 16:35 16:36[2] 16:39 16:41 16:43 16:45 16:49[4] 16:51 16:53[4] 16:56 16:57[4] 16:60 16:63 17:1 17:2[2] 17:3[2] 17:4[3] 17:5[2] 17:6 17:7 17:9 17:11 17:12 17:13[3] 17:14 17:16 17:22[3] 17:23[4] 17:24 18:1 18:2 18:4[2] 18:6[2] 18:10[2] 18:11 18:15[2] 18:17 18:19

18:20[4] 18:25[2] 18:29[3] 18:30 18:31 18:32 19:1 19:3 19:4 19:5 19:7 19:9[2] 19:10 19:11[2] 19:14[2] 20:1[4] 20:2 20:3[4] 20:4[2] 20:5[3] 20:6[3] 20:7[2] 20:8[4] 20:9[2] 20:10[2] 20:13 20:15 20:17 20:18 20:22 20:27[2] 20:28 20:30[2] 20:31[3] 20:32 20:34 20:35 20:36[2] 20:37 20:38[2] 20:39 20:40[5] 20:41 20:42 20:44 20:45 20:46[2] 20:47[2] 20:49 21:1 21:2[2] 21:3[2] 21:4 21:5 21:6[2] 21:8 21:9 21:10 21:11 21:12[3] 21:14[3] 21:15 21:18 21:19[5] 21:20 21:21[3] 21:25 21:28[2] 21:29[2] 21:30 21:31[2] 21:32 22:1 22:2 22:3 22:6 22:7 22:9 22:12 22:13 22:15 22:16 22:17 22:18[4] 22:19 22:20 22:21

22:22 22:23 22:24[2] 22:25 22:29 22:31 23:1 23:2[2] 23:3 23:4 23:6 23:7 23:8 23:9[2] 23:12 23:14 23:15[4] 23:17 23:19[2] 23:20[2] 23:21[2] 23:23[2] 23:24 23:26 23:27 23:28[2] 23:29 23:31 23:32 23:33[2] 23:36 23:39 23:42[2] 23:46[2] 23:48 23:49 24:1[2] 24:2[4] 24:5[2] 24:6 24:7[2] 24:11[3] 24:12 24:15 24:16[2] 24:17[2] 24:20 24:21[3] 24:22 24:25[3] 25:1 25:2 25:3[3] 25:4 25:5 25:7 25:8 25:9[2] 25:10 25:12 25:13 25:14 25:16 26:1[2] 26:2[2] 26:4[2] 26:5[2] 26:7[2] 26:9 26:10[5] 26:11 26:12[3] 26:13[2] 26:14 26:15[2] 26:16 26:17 26:18 26:20[4] 27:1 27:2 27:3[3] 27:4 27:5[2] 27:6[6] 27:7 27:8

27:9[2] 27:10[4] 27:11 27:12[3] 27:13[2] 27:14[2] 27:15[3] 27:16[3] 27:17[2] 27:18[4] 27:21 27:22[2] 27:23 27:24[3] 27:25[3] 27:26 27:27[5] 27:28[2] 27:29 27:31 27:32 27:33[4] 27:34[2] 27:35 28:1 28:2[5] 28:5 28:6 28:7[2] 28:8[2] 28:9 28:10[2] 28:11 28:12[3] 28:13[3] 28:14[3] 28:16[6] 28:17[2] 28:18[4] 28:20 28:21 28:22 28:23 28:24[2] 28:25[2] 29:1[2] 29:2[2] 29:3[2] 29:4[4] 29:5[3] 29:6[3] 29:7 29:8 29:9 29:10[3] 29:11[2] 29:12[2] 29:13 29:14[3] 29:15 29:16[2] 29:17[2] 29:18[2] 29:19[2] 29:20[2] 29:21[4] 30:1 30:2 30:3[2] 30:5 30:6[2] 30:7[2] 30:9 30:10[3] 30:11 30:12[2] 30:13[4] 30:15[2] 30:17[2] 30:18[2] 30:20 30:21[3] 30:22[2] 30:24[3] 30:25[6] 31:1[2] 31:2[2]

31:3 31:4 31:5[3] 31:6[2] 31:7 31:8[2] 31:9[3] 31:11[2] 31:12[3] 31:13[2] 31:14[4] 31:15 31:16[4] 31:17 31:18[4] 32:1[2] 32:2[3] 32:3 32:4[2] 32:6 32:8 32:9 32:10 32:11[2] 32:12[4] 32:13[2] 32:15[2] 32:16 32:17[2] 32:18[4] 32:20[2] 32:21[2] 32:22 32:23[3] 32:24[3] 32:25[4] 32:26[2] 32:27[4] 32:28 32:30[3] 32:32[2] 33:2[4] 33:4 33:5 33:7[2] 33:9 33:10[2] 33:11[2] 33:12[5] 33:15 33:16 33:17[2] 33:20[2] 33:21[3] 33:22 33:23 33:24[3] 33:27 33:28[2] 33:29 33:30[3] 33:32 34:1 34:2[3] 34:5 34:6 34:7 34:8 34:9 34:12 34:13[2] 34:14[2] 34:18[2] 34:25[2] 34:26 34:27[5] 34:28 34:29[2] 34:30 34:31 35:1 35:2 35:5[4] 35:11 35:12 35:15[3]

36:1[4] 36:3[3] 36:4[3] 36:5[3] 36:6[2] 36:8[2] 36:10[2] 36:12 36:15[2] 36:16 36:17[3] 36:20[2] 36:21 36:22[2] 36:23 36:24 36:26[2] 36:30[3] 36:32 36:34 36:35 36:37[2] 36:38[2] 37:1[4] 37:3 37:4 37:8 37:9 37:11[2] 37:12[2] 37:13 37:15 37:16[4] 37:18 37:19[4] 37:21 37:22 37:23[2] 37:26[2] 37:28 38:1 38:2[3] 38:3 38:4[2] 38:5 38:6[2] 38:8[4] 38:11 38:12[2] 38:13 38:14[2] 38:15[2] 38:16 38:17[2] 38:18 38:19[2] 38:20[4] 38:23 39:1[2] 39:2[2] 39:3[2] 39:4[3] 39:7 39:9 39:10[2] 39:11[5] 39:12[2] 39:13 39:14[3] 39:15 39:16 39:17[3] 39:18[9] 39:19 39:20 39:22 39:23[2] 39:25[2] 39:27[2] 39:28 39:29 40:1[4] 40:2[3] 40:3[2] 40:4[2] 40:5[3] 40:6[2]

40:7[2] 40:8 40:9[2] 40:10[2] 40:11[3] 40:13[2] 40:14[2] 40:15[4] 40:18[2] 40:19[2] 40:20 40:21 40:22 40:23 40:38 40:39 40:40[2] 40:41 40:42[2] 40:43 40:44[3] 40:45[2] 40:46[4] 40:48[3] 40:49 41:1 41:2[2] 41:3[2] 41:5[2] 41:6[2] 41:7[2] 41:8[3] 41:9[2] 41:10 41:11[2] 41:12 41:14[3] 41:15[2] 41:19[2] 41:20 41:21[4] 41:22[2] 41:25[2] 41:26[2] 42:2 42:4[2] 42:5 42:6 42:7 42:8 42:10[2] 42:11 42:12[2] 42:14 42:15 43:2[4] 43:3 43:4[2] 43:5 43:6 43:7[8] 43:8 43:9[2] 43:10[3] 43:11[2] 43:12[3] 43:13[2] 43:18[2] 43:19[2] 43:20[3] 43:21[2] 43:22 43:23 43:25 44:1[2] 44:2 44:3[3] 44:4[3] 44:5[5] 44:6[2] 44:7 44:8[2] 44:9[2] 44:11 44:12 44:13[2]

44:14[2] 44:15[3] 44:17[2] 44:22[3] 44:30[6] 44:31[2] 45:1[2] 45:2 45:3[3] 45:4[2] 45:5[3] 45:6[3] 45:7[7] 45:8[2] 45:9 45:11[3] 45:13[6] 45:14[5] 45:15[4] 45:16 45:17[3] 45:18 45:19[7] 45:20 45:21[2] 45:22 45:23[2] 45:24[2] 45:25[2] 46:1[2] 46:2[4] 46:3[2] 46:5 46:6 46:7 46:8[2] 46:9[6] 46:10 46:11 46:13[2] 46:14[3] 46:16 46:17[3] 46:18[3] 46:19[2] 46:21[2] 46:22[3] 46:23 46:24[3] 47:1[5] 47:2[2] 47:6[2] 47:7 47:9 47:10 47:12 47:13 47:15[2] 47:16[3] 47:17[2] 47:18 47:19 47:21 47:22[2] 48:1[5] 48:2 48:3 48:4 48:5 48:6 48:7 48:8[4] 48:9[2] 48:10 48:11[3] 48:12[2] 48:13 48:14[2] 48:17 48:18[2] 48:19[2] 48:20 48:21[5] 48:22[5] 48:23 48:24 48:25

48:26 48:27 48:28[2] 48:29 48:30 48:31[6] 48:32[3] 48:33[3] 48:34[3] 48:35

DA

1:1[4] 1:2[7] 1:3[5] 1:4 1:5[2] 1:6[2] 1:7[5] 1:8[3] 1:9 1:10[2] 1:11 1:13[3] 1:15[2] 1:16 1:18[2] 1:20[2] 1:21 2:1[2] 2:6 2:7 2:8 2:12 2:14[2] 2:16 2:18[4] 2:19 2:20 2:23[2] 2:24[2] 2:25[2] 2:27 2:28 2:30 2:32[3] 2:33[3] 2:34 2:35 2:37[2] 2:38[4] 2:39 2:41[4] 2:42[3] 2:43 2:44[2] 2:45 2:47[4] 2:48[3] 2:49[4] 3:1[3] 3:2[2] 3:3[2] 3:5[2] 3:6 3:7[2] 3:10[2] 3:11 3:12[2] 3:15[4] 3:17 3:19[2] 3:21 3:22 3:23 3:24 3:25[3] 3:26[4] 3:27[2] 3:28 3:29 3:30 4:5 4:6[2] 4:8[2]

4:9[3] 4:10[2] 4:11 4:12[3] 4:13 4:15[5] 4:17[4] 4:18[2] 4:21[2] 4:22 4:23[5] 4:24 4:25[3] 4:26 4:27 4:29[3] 4:30[3] 4:32[3] 4:33 4:34 4:35[3] 4:36 4:37 5:1 5:2 5:3[3] 5:4[6] 5:5[4] 5:6 5:7[2] 5:10[2] 5:11[4] 5:12[3] 5:13[4] 5:14[2] 5:15 5:16[2] 5:21[3] 5:23[4] 5:24 5:26 5:29 5:30 6:2 6:5 6:7[4] 6:8 6:12[4] 6:13[3] 6:14 6:15 6:16 6:17[2] 6:18 6:19 6:20 6:23[3] 6:24[3] 6:26[2] 6:27 6:28[2] 7:1[4] 7:2 7:5[2] 7:6[2] 7:7 7:8[2] 7:9[2] 7:11[2] 7:12 7:13[3] 7:15[2] 7:16[3] 7:17 7:18 7:19[3] 7:20[3] 7:22[2] 7:24 7:25[2] 7:27[3] 7:28 8:1[2] 8:2[2] 8:4 8:5 8:6

8:7 8:8 8:9[2] 8:10[3] 8:11[2] 8:12 8:13 8:15 8:16 8:17[2] 8:19 8:20 8:21 8:22 8:23 8:25 8:26 9:1[5] 9:2[4] 9:6 9:7[4] 9:8 9:10 9:11[2] 9:13 9:15 9:16 9:17 9:20[2] 9:21 9:23 9:24 9:25 9:26[2] 9:27[2] 10:1[3] 10:4[3] 10:5 10:6[4] 10:9[2] 10:10 10:13[4] 10:16[2] 10:17 10:18 10:20[2] 10:21 11:1 11:2 11:4 11:5[2] 11:6[4] 11:7[4] 11:8[3] 11:9 11:10 11:11[2] 11:13: 11:14[2] 11:15[2] 11:17[2] 11:19 11:20[2] 11:21 11:22[2] 11:24 11:25[2] 11:26[2] 11:30 11:31 11:35[3] 11:36 11:37[2] 11:38 11:40[3] 11:41[3] 11:42 11:43[3] 11:44[2] 11:45 12:1[2] 12:2[2] 12:3 12:4 12:5[4] 12:6[2] 12:7[2]

12:8 12:9 12:10 12:13

HO

1:1[7] 1:2[4] 1:3 1:4[4] 1:5[2] 1:6 1:7 1:10[4] 1:11[4] 2:2 2:4 2:10[2] 2:12 2:13 2:15[5] 2:17[2] 2:18[4] 3:1[4] 3:2[3] 3:4 3:5 4:1[4] 4:3[3] 4:6[2] 4:8 4:12 4:13 4:19 5:1[2] 5:2 5:4[2] 5:5 5:9[2] 5:10 5:12 5:13 5:14 6:5 6:6 6:8 6:9[2] 6:10[2] 6:11 7:1[3] 7:5[2] 7:10 7:12 7:16[2] 8:1 8:4 8:6 8:10[2] 8:12 8:13 9:4[2] 9:5[2] 9:6 9:7[3] 9:8[3] 9:9 9:15[2] 9:16 10:1[2] 10:4 10:5[3] 10:6 10:8[2] 10:9[2] 10:13[2] 10:14 10:15[2] 11:1 11:4[2] 11:5 11:6 11:9[2] 11:11[3] 11:12 12:5

12:7 12:9[2] 12:10 12:11 12:12 12:13 13:2[4] 13:3[2] 13:4 13:5 13:8[2] 13:10 13:12 13:13[3] 13:14 13:15[2] 14:2 14:3 14:7 14:9

JOE

1:1[2] 1:2[2] 1:3 1:5[2] 1:6[2] 1:8 1:9 1:11 1:12[2] 1:13[3] 1:14[2] 1:15 1:16 1:18[2] 1:19[2] 1:20[3] 2:1[2] 2:2[5] 2:3 2:4[2] 2:5[4] 2:7 2:11 2:13[2] 2:16[2] 2:17 2:22[2] 2:23 2:24 2:26 2:27 2:30 2:31 2:32 3:1 3:2 3:4 3:6 3:7 3:8[2] 3:9 3:12 3:14[3] 3:16[4] 3:18[4] 3:19

AM

1:1[7] 1:2[2] 1:3[2] 1:4[2] 1:5[4] 1:6 1:7 1:8 1:9 1:10 1:11 1:12 1:13[3] 1:14[3]

2:1[3] 2:2[2] 2:4[2] 2:5 2:6[2] 2:7[3] 2:8[2] 2:9 2:10[2] 2:11[3] 2:13 2:15 3:1[2] 3:2[2] 3:4 3:9[2] 3:12[5] 3:13[2] 3:14[3] 3:15 4:1[2] 4:5[2] 4:6[2] 4:10[2] 4:11[2] 4:13[2] 5:1 5:2 5:3 5:4 5:6 5:8[3] 5:11[3] 5:14 5:15[2] 5:16[2] 5:18[2] 5:20 5:22 5:23[2] 5:25 5:26[2] 5:27 6:1[3] 6:2 6:3 6:4[4] 6:5[2] 6:6 6:7 6:8[2] 6:10[4] 6:12 6:13 6:14[4] 7:1[2] 7:2[2] 7:8 7:9[3] 7:10[4] 7:11 7:12 7:14 7:16[2] 7:17 8:1 8:2[2] 8:3 8:4 8:5[2] 8:6[2] 8:8 8:10 8:11[3] 8:12 8:14[2] 9:1[5] 9:3[2] 9:5[2] 9:6[2] 9:7[4] 9:8[3] 9:9 9:10 9:11[2] 9:12[2] 9:13

9:14[3] 9:15

OB

1 3[2] 6 7 8[3] 9[2] 11 12[4] 13[4] 14[3] 15 17 18[5] 19[5] 20[6] 21

JON

1:1[2] 1:3[2] 1:5[2] 1:8 1:9 1:10 1:17 2:1 2:2[3] 2:3 2:4 2:6 2:9[2] 3:1 3:3[2] 3:5[3] 3:6 3:7 3:10 4:2[2] 4:5[3] 4:6 4:8

MIC

1:1[3] 1:3[2] 1:5[5] 1:6[2] 1:7[3] 1:9 1:10 1:11[4] 1:12[2] 1:13[4] 1:14[2] 1:15[2] 2:1 2:4 2:5 2:7[2] 2:8 2:9 2:11[2] 2:12[6] 2:13 3:1[3] 3:3 3:7 3:8[4] 3:9[4] 3:12[2] 4:1[3] 4:2[6] 4:4[2] 4:5[2] 4:8[4] 4:10[3] 4:12 4:13[2] 5:1[2]

5:2[3] 5:3[2] 5:4[4] 5:6[2] 5:7[3] 5:8[4] 5:10 5:11 5:12 5:13[3] 5:14 6:2 6:4[4] 6:5[3] 6:6 6:7[5] 6:8 6:9 6:10[2] 6:11 6:12 6:13 6:14 6:16[4] 7:1 7:2 7:4[2] 7:5 7:6 7:7 7:9 7:10 7:13[2] 7:14[3] 7:15[3] 7:17[4] 7:18[2] 7:19 7:20

NA

1:1[3] 1:3 1:4 1:6 1:7 1:8 1:11 1:14[3] 1:15 2:2[2] 2:3[2] 2:6 2:7 2:8[2] 2:9[4] 2:10 2:11[2] 2:13[2] 3:1 3:2[5] 3:3[3] 3:4[4] 3:5 3:10 3:11 3:12 3:13[2] 3:16 3:18 3:19[2]

HAB

1:2 1:6 1:7 1:13 1:14 1:15 2:8[5] 2:9 2:11[2] 2:13[2] 2:14[2]

2:16
2:17^{6}
2:18^{2}
2:19
3:1
3:2^{2}
3:3
3:4^{2}
3:7^{3}
3:8
3:9
3:10
3:11^{2}
3:13^{3}
3:14
3:15
3:16
3:17
3:18

ZEP

1:1^{8}
1:3^{2}
1:4^{3}
1:5
1:7^{2}
1:8
1:10
1:11
1:14^{3}
1:15^{5}
1:16
1:18^{3}
2:2^{2}
2:3^{2}
2:5^{4}
2:7^{3}
2:8^{3}
2:9^{6}
2:10^{2}
2:11^{2}
2:14^{3}
3:8
3:9
3:10^{2}
3:11^{3}
3:12^{2}
3:13
3:14^{2}
3:15^{2}
3:17
3:18^{2}
3:20

HAG

1:1^{6}
1:2
1:3
1:5
1:7
1:9^{2}
1:11
1:12^{5}
1:14^{9}
1:15^{2}
2:1^{2}
2:2^{4}
2:3
2:4^{3}
2:5
2:6
2:7^{2}
2:8
2:9^{4}
2:10^{3}
2:11
2:12
2:13
2:14
2:15
2:16^{2}
2:17
2:18^{2}
2:20^{2}
2:21
2:22^{4}
2:23^{3}

ZEC

1:1^{4}
1:3^{3}
1:4
1:6^{2}
1:7^{5}
1:11
1:12^{3}
1:14
1:16
1:17
1:21^{2}
2:4
2:5^{2}
2:6^{2}
2:7
2:8^{2}
2:9
2:10^{2}
2:11^{2}
2:13
3:1
3:2
3:4
3:5
3:6
3:7
3:9^{2}
3:10
4:1
4:2^{2}
4:3
4:6^{2}
4:8
4:9^{3}
4:10^{3}
4:11
4:12
4:14
5:3
5:4^{4}
5:7^{2}
5:8^{2}
5:9
5:11
6:1
6:5^{2}
6:9
6:10^{7}
6:11^{2}
6:12^{3}
6:13^{2}
6:14^{2}
6:15^{3}
7:1^{3}
7:2
7:3^{2}
7:4^{2}
7:5
7:8
7:9
7:10
7:12^{2}
7:13
8:1^{2}
8:2
8:3^{4}
8:4^{2}
8:5^{2}
8:6^{4}
8:7
8:8
8:9^{5}
8:10
8:11^{2}
8:12
8:13^{2}
8:14^{2}
8:15
8:16
8:17
8:18^{2}
8:19^{6}
8:20^{2}
8:21^{2}
8:22
8:23^{5}
9:1^{6}
9:3
9:6
7:7
9:8^{3}
9:9^{3}
9:10
9:11^{2}
9:12
9:13
9:14
9:15^{2}
9:16^{2}
10:1^{3}
10:3^{2}
10:4^{4}
10:5
10:6^{2}
10:7
10:10^{4}
10:11^{3}
11:2^{2}
11:3^{5}
11:4
11:6^{3}
11:7^{2}
11:9
11:11^{2}
11:12
11:13^{3}
11:15
11:16
12:1^{4}
12:2
12:3
12:4^{2}
12:5^{3}
12:6^{3}
12:7^{5}
12:8^{3}
12:10^{4}
12:11^{2}
12:12^{4}
12:13^{3}
13:1^{2}
13:2^{4}
13:3
13:4
13:6
13:7
14:1^{2}
14:2^{2}
14:3
14:4^{4}
14:5^{4}
14:8^{2}
14:10^{3}
14:13^{2}
14:14
14:15^{5}
14:16^{3}
14:17^{3}
14:18^{2}
14:19^{3}
14:20
14:21^{4}

MAL

1:1^{2}
1:3
1:4^{2}
1:5
1:6
1:7
1:8
1:9
1:10
1:11^{3}
1:12
1:13^{2}
1:14
2:2
2:3
2:4
2:5
2:6
2:7^{2}
2:8^{3}
2:10
2:11^{2}
2:12^{3}
2:13
2:14^{2}
2:15^{2}
2:16^{2}
2:17^{2}
3:1^{2}
3:2
3:3^{2}
3:4^{2}
3:5
3:6
3:7^{2}
3:10^{2}
3:11^{2}
3:12
3:14
3:16
3:17
4:1
4:1^{2}
4:2^{2}
4:4
4:5^{2}
4:6^{2}

MT

1:1^{4}
1:3
1:5^{2}
1:6^{2}
1:16^{2}
1:18^{2}
1:20^{3}
1:22
1:24
2:1^{2}
2:2
2:4^{2}
2:5
2:6^{3}
2:7
2:12
2:13
2:15^{3}
2:16^{2}
2:19
2:20
2:21
2:22^{3}
3:1
3:2
3:3^{3}
3:4
3:6
3:7^{2}
3:9
3:10
3:13
3:14
3:16^{2}
4:1^{2}
4:3
4:4^{2}
4:5
4:6
4:8^{2}
4:13
4:15^{4}
4:16
4:17
4:18
4:19
4:21
4:23^{3}
4:25
5:3
5:9
5:10
5:11
5:13^{2}
5:14
5:19^{3}
5:20^{2}
5:21^{2}
5:22^{3}
5:27
5:29
5:30
5:31
5:32
5:33
5:35
5:37
5:42
5:45
6:1^{2}
6:2
6:5^{2}
6:8
6:16
6:22^{2}
6:23
6:26
6:27
6:28
6:29
6:30^{2}
6:32
6:33
6:34
7:4
7:5^{2}
7:9
7:15
7:16^{2}
7:21^{2}
7:24
7:26
7:27
8:6
8:11
8:12^{2}
8:14
8:20^{2}
8:21
8:26
8:27
8:28^{2}
8:29
8:30
8:31
8:32^{2}
8:33
8:34
9:2^{3}
9:3
9:6^{2}
9:9
9:14
9:15
9:16
9:20^{2}
9:22
9:27
9:34
9:35
9:38
10:1^{2}
10:2^{2}
10:3
10:5^{2}
10:6^{2}
10:7
10:14^{2}
10:15^{2}
10:16
10:17
10:20
10:22
10:23^{2}
10:25^{2}
10:29
10:30
10:31
10:36
10:37^{2}
10:38
10:41^{2}
10:42^{3}
11:1
11:2^{2}
11:10
11:11^{2}
11:12^{2}
11:19^{3}
11:20
11:22
11:24^{2}
11:25
11:27
11:29
12:1
12:4
12:8^{2}
12:23
12:24
12:28^{2}
12:31
12:32
12:34^{3}
12:35^{3}
12:36
12:38^{2}
12:39
12:40^{2}
12:41^{2}
12:42^{3}
12:43
12:45
12:50
13:1
13:5
13:11^{2}
13:14
13:15
13:18
13:19
13:21
13:22^{2}
13:24
13:27
13:30
13:31^{2}
13:32^{2}
13:33^{2}
13:35
13:36^{2}
13:37
13:38^{2}
13:39
13:40
13:41^{2}
13:42^{2}
13:43
13:44
13:45
13:46
13:47^{2}
13:49
13:50^{2}
13:52^{2}
13:58
14:1^{2}
14:6
14:8
14:13^{2}
14:20
14:24
14:25
14:27
14:29
14:31
14:33^{2}
14:34
14:35^{2}
14:36
15:1
15:2
15:3
15:6^{2}
15:7
15:9
15:11
15:14
15:18
15:19
15:21
15:22^{3}
15:24^{2}
15:27
15:29
15:31
15:37
15:39
16:3^{2}
16:4
16:6^{3}
16:8
16:9
16:10
16:11^{3}
16:12^{5}
16:13^{2}
16:14
16:16
16:18
16:19^{2}
16:21
16:23^{2}
16:27^{2}
16:28^{2}
17:5
17:9
17:12^{2}
17:13
17:18
17:20^{2}
17:22^{2}
17:25^{4}
17:26
17:27
18:1
18:2
18:3
18:4
18:6
18:7
18:10^{2}
18:11
18:12
18:13^{2}
18:14^{2}
18:16
18:19^{2}
18:20
18:23^{2}
18:27
18:28
19:1
19:7
19:8^{2}
19:10
19:12^{2}
19:14^{2}
19:23
19:24^{2}
19:28^{3}
20:1
20:8
20:11
20:12
20:13
20:18
20:20^{2}
20:22^{2}
20:23^{2}
20:25
20:28
20:30
20:31
21:1
21:3
21:5^{2}
21:9^{2}
21:11^{2}
21:12^{3}
21:13^{2}
21:15
21:16^{2}
21:17
21:23
21:25^{2}
21:26
21:31^{3}
21:32
21:34^{2}
21:37
21:39
21:40
21:42
21:43
21:45
22:2
22:5
22:13
22:16^{2}
22:27
22:28
22:29
22:30
22:31
22:32^{5}
22:35
22:42^{2}
23:4
23:5^{2}
23:7
23:13
23:15
23:16
23:22
23:23^{2}
23:25^{3}
23:26
23:27^{2}
23:28
23:29^{2}
23:30^{2}
23:31
23:32
23:33^{2}
23:34^{2}
23:35^{3}
23:39
24:1
24:3^{4}
24:6^{2}
24:8
24:9
24:12
24:14
24:15^{2}
24:17
24:21
24:27^{3}
24:29^{2}
24:30^{5}
24:31^{2}
24:32
24:36^{2}
24:37^{2}
24:39^{2}
24:43
24:44
24:50^{2}
24:51
25:1
25:2
25:8
25:13
25:14
25:19
25:21
25:23
25:30
25:31^{2}
25:34^{2}
25:40
25:45^{2}
26:2^{2}
26:3^{2}
26:6
26:7
26:13
26:14
26:15
26:17^{2}
26:21
26:22
26:24^{3}
26:27
26:28^{2}
26:29^{2}
26:30
26:31^{2}
26:33
26:37
26:45^{2}
26:47^{2}
26:51^{2}
26:53
26:56
26:61
26:63
26:64^{3}
26:65
26:66
26:67
26:69
26:71
26:73
26:75
27:1
27:3
27:5
27:6
27:8
27:9^{4}
27:11
27:12
27:19
27:21
27:24^{2}
27:27^{2}
27:29^{2}
27:32
27:33
27:37
27:40
27:42
27:43
27:47
27:48
27:51
27:52
27:53
27:54
27:56^{2}
27:57
27:58
27:60
27:62
28:1^{2}
28:2
28:4
28:11
28:19^{3}
28:20

MK

1:1^{3}
1:3^{2}
1:4^{2}
1:5^{4}
1:6
1:7
1:9^{2}
1:10
1:13
1:14^{2}
1:15
1:16
1:17
1:19
1:24^{2}
1:25
1:26
1:29^{2}
1:30^{2}
1:34
2:3^{2}
2:4
2:5
2:6
2:9
2:10^{2}
2:14^{2}
2:17
2:18^{4}
2:19
2:21
2:23
2:26^{2}
2:28^{2}
3:5
3:9
3:11
3:17^{3}
3:18
3:21
3:22
3:28
3:29
3:35
4:4
4:5
4:10
4:11^{2}
4:19^{3}
4:26
4:28
4:30
4:31
4:32^{2}
4:37
4:38
4:41
5:1^{2}
5:2^{2}
5:7
5:8
5:10
5:11
5:17
5:22^{2}
5:23
5:25
5:26
5:27
5:29^{2}
5:30
5:34
5:35
5:36
5:37
5:38^{2}
5:40
5:42^{2}
6:3^{3}
6:6
6:11
6:14
6:15
6:21
6:22^{2}
6:23^{2}
6:24
6:25
6:29
6:33
6:37
6:43^{2}
6:44
6:47
6:48
6:50
6:52
6:53
6:54
6:56
7:1
7:2
7:3
7:4^{2}
7:5
7:6
7:7
7:8^{3}
7:9
7:13^{2}
7:14
7:15
7:20
7:21^{2}
7:24
7:25
7:26
7:28
7:29
7:31^{4}
7:35
8:3
8:8
8:10
8:11
8:15^{4}
8:19
8:20
8:23
8:27
8:28
8:30
8:31^{3}
8:33^{2}
8:38^{5}
9:1^{3}
9:7
9:9
9:12^{2}
9:13
9:17
9:21
9:24
9:25
9:26
9:31^{2}
9:35^{2}
9:36
9:37
9:39
9:41
9:42
9:47
10:1^{2}
10:4
10:5
10:6
10:10
10:14^{2}
10:15
10:23
10:24
10:25^{2}
10:26
10:33
10:35
10:38^{2}
10:39^{2}
10:44^{2}
10:45
10:46^{3}
10:47^{2}
10:48
10:49
11:1^{2}
11:3
11:5
11:9
11:10^{2}
11:13
11:14
11:15^{2}
11:17^{3}
11:19
11:29
11:30^{2}
11:32
12:2^{2}
12:8
12:9
12:10
12:13^{2}
12:14^{2}
12:22
12:23
12:24
12:26^{4}
12:27^{2}
12:28^{2}
12:29
12:34
12:35
12:38
12:44^{2}
13:1^{3}
13:3
13:7^{2}
13:8
13:13
13:14^{2}
13:15
13:19
13:25
13:26
13:27^{2}
13:28
13:32
13:34
13:35
14:1^{2}
14:2
14:3^{3}
14:4
14:9^{2}
14:10
14:12
14:13^{2}
14:14
14:18
14:20
14:21^{3}
14:23
14:24
14:25^{3}
14:26
14:27
14:41^{2}
14:43
14:47^{2}
14:54
14:61
14:62^{3}
14:64
14:65
14:66^{2}
14:67
14:69
14:70
14:71
15:2
15:3
15:9
15:12
15:17
15:18
15:21^{2}
15:22
15:26^{2}
15:32
15:35
15:36
15:38
15:39
15:40^{2}
15:43^{2}
15:45
15:46^{2}
15:47
16:1
16:2^{2}
16:3
16:6
16:9^{2}
16:11
16:12
16:14
16:19

LU

1:1
1:2
1:3
1:4
1:5^{6}
1:6
1:8
1:9^{2}
1:10^{2}
1:11^{3}
1:15
1:16^{2}
1:17^{3}
1:19
1:23
1:26
1:27
1:29
1:32^{2}
1:33^{2}
1:35^{3}
1:38
1:39
1:40
1:41
1:42
1:43
1:44
1:45
1:48
1:51
1:52
1:54
1:59
1:61
1:65
1:66^{2}
1:68
1:69^{2}
1:70
1:71
1:74^{2}
1:75
1:76^{2}
1:77^{2}
1:78
1:79^{2}
1:80
2:2
2:4^{5}
2:9^{2}
2:10
2:11
2:13
2:21^{2}
2:22^{2}
2:23
2:24^{2}
2:25
2:27
2:31
2:32
2:33
2:34
2:35
2:36^{4}
2:37
2:38
2:39
2:40
2:41
2:42
2:43
2:46
3:1^{8}
3:2^{2}
3:3^{2}
3:4^{4}
3:6
3:7^{2}
3:8^{2}
3:9
3:14
3:15
3:16
3:23^{9}
3:24^{5}
3:25^{4}
3:26^{5}
3:27^{5}
3:28^{5}
3:29^{5}
3:30^{5}
3:31^{5}
3:32^{5}
3:33^{5}
3:34^{5}
3:35^{5}
3:36^{5}
3:37^{5}
3:38^{4}
4:1
4:2
4:3
4:4
4:5^{2}
4:6
4:9^{2}
4:14^{2}
4:15
4:17
4:18^{2}
4:19
4:20
4:22
4:25^{2}
4:26^{2}
4:27^{2}
4:29^{2}
4:30
4:31
4:33
4:34^{2}
4:35^{2}
4:37
4:38
4:40
4:41^{2}
4:43
4:44
5:1^{2}
5:2
5:3^{2}
5:6
5:9
5:10
5:12
5:15
5:17^{4}
5:19
5:24^{2}
5:27
5:29^{2}
5:33^{2}
5:34
5:36^{2}
6:1
6:2
6:4
6:5^{2}
6:13
6:15
6:16
6:17^{5}
6:19
6:20
6:22
6:26
6:30^{2}
6:34
6:35
6:42
6:44^{2}
6:45^{6}
6:49
7:1
7:3^{2}
7:7
7:11
7:12^{3}
7:18^{2}
7:19
7:21
7:24
7:27
7:28^{2}
7:29
7:30^{2}
7:31
7:34^{2}
7:35
7:36
7:37
7:38
7:39
7:42
7:44
8:1^{2}
8:2^{2}
8:4
8:5
8:10^{2}
8:11
8:12
8:13
8:14
8:21
8:22
8:23
8:24
8:25
8:26
8:27
8:28
8:29^{2}
8:32
8:33
8:35^{2}
8:36
8:37^{2}
8:38
8:41
8:42
8:43^{2}
8:44^{2}
8:46
8:48
8:49
8:51
9:2
9:5
9:7^{2}
9:8^{3}
9:9
9:11^{3}
9:17
9:19
9:20
9:22^{2}
9:26^{5}
9:27^{3}
9:29
9:31
9:35
9:36
9:38
9:43
9:44^{2}
9:45
9:46
9:47
9:52
9:55^{2}
9:56
9:58^{2}
9:60
9:62
10:2
10:6
10:7
10:9
10:10
10:11^{3}
10:19
10:21
10:22
10:30
10:34
10:35
10:36
11:1
11:5
11:6
11:8
11:11^{2}
11:15^{2}
11:16
11:20^{2}
11:24
11:26
11:27
11:28
11:29
11:30
11:31^{4}
11:32^{2}
11:34^{3}
11:36^{3}
11:39^{2}
11:41
11:42^{2}
11:44
11:45
11:46
11:47
11:48
11:49^{2}
11:50^{3}
11:51^{3}
11:52
11:53
11:54
12:1^{4}
12:4
12:6
12:7
12:8^{2}
12:9
12:10
12:13
12:15^{2}
12:16
12:20
12:25
12:27
12:28
12:29
12:30^{2}
12:31
12:39
12:40
12:42
12:44
12:46
12:48^{3}
12:51
12:56^{2}
12:57
13:1
13:7
13:10
13:11
13:14
13:15
13:16
13:18
13:19^{3}
13:20
13:21
13:25
13:27
13:28^{2}
13:29
13:31
13:33
13:35
14:1^{2}
14:5
14:8^{2}
14:10
14:14
14:15^{2}
14:18
14:19
14:21^{2}
14:24^{2}
14:28
14:32
14:33
15:4^{2}
15:8
15:10^{2}
15:12^{2}
15:15
15:17
15:19
15:26
16:2
16:4
16:5
16:6
16:7
16:8^{2}
16:9^{2}
16:15
16:16
16:17
16:20
16:24
16:28
17:2
17:6
17:7
17:11
17:15
17:20^{3}
17:21
17:22^{3}
17:24^{2}
17:25
17:26^{3}
17:28
17:29
17:30
18:3
18:8
18:12
18:16^{2}
18:17
18:24
18:25
18:29
18:31
18:34
18:37
18:38
18:39
19:3
19:8
19:9
19:10
19:11
19:22
19:29^{2}
19:31
19:34
19:37^{3}
19:38
19:39
19:44
19:46^{2}
19:47
20:1
20:4^{2}
20:6
20:10^{2}
20:13
20:15^{2}
20:17
20:20^{2}
20:21^{2}
20:26
20:27
20:32
20:33
20:34
20:36^{2}
20:37^{3}
20:38^{2}
20:39
20:42
20:45
20:46
21:3
21:4^{3}
21:5
21:9
21:16
21:17
21:18
21:21
21:22
21:24^{3}
21:25
21:26
21:27
21:30
21:31
21:34
21:35
21:36
21:37
22:1
22:3^{2}
22:6
22:7
22:10
22:11
22:16
22:18^{2}
22:19
22:21
22:22
22:23
22:24
22:25
22:30
22:39
22:44
22:47
22:48
22:50^{2}
22:52
22:53
22:55
22:58
22:59^{2}
22:61
22:66
22:69^{3}
22:70
22:71
23:1
23:3
23:6
23:8^{2}
23:11
23:15
23:17
23:22
23:23^{2}
23:26
23:27^{2}
23:28
23:35
23:37
23:38^{2}
23:39
23:41
23:45
23:51^{4}
23:52
24:1
24:3
24:7^{2}
24:10
24:13
24:14
24:17
24:18
24:19
24:22
24:23
24:24
24:25
24:31
24:35^{2}
24:36
24:42^{2}
24:44

24:47
24:48
24:49^2

JOH

1:4
1:7
1:8
1:12
1:13^6
1:14^3
1:15^2
1:16
1:18
1:19
1:22
1:23^2
1:24
1:29^2
1:30
1:34
1:35
1:36
1:40
1:42
1:44^2
1:45^3
1:46
1:47
1:49^2
1:51^2
2:1^2
2:3
2:6^3
2:8
2:9^2
2:11^2
2:14
2:15^2
2:16
2:17
2:21^2
2:25
3:1^2
3:3
3:5^3
3:6^2
3:8
3:10
3:12
3:13
3:14
3:18^2
3:22
3:25
3:29^2
3:31^2
3:34
3:36
4:5^2
4:7
4:9^3
4:10^2
4:13
4:14^2
4:22
4:30
4:32
4:34
4:39^3
4:42^2
4:46
4:47^2
4:52
4:54
5:1
5:3^3
5:4^2
5:19
5:25^2
5:27
5:29^2
5:30^2
5:31
5:32^2
5:36^2
5:37
5:39
5:42
5:44
5:46
6:1^2
6:4
6:7^2
6:8
6:11
6:13
6:14
6:18
6:22
6:25
6:26
6:27
6:28
6:29
6:33
6:35
6:38
6:39
6:40
6:42
6:45^2
6:46
6:48
6:51^2
6:53^2
6:58
6:60
6:62
6:64
6:65
6:66
6:68
6:69
6:70
6:71^3
7:2
7:7
7:13^2
7:14
7:17^3
7:18
7:19
7:22^2
7:23
7:25
7:28
7:31
7:36
7:37
7:38^2
7:39
7:40^2
7:41
7:42^4
7:43
7:44
7:48^2
7:50
7:52^2
8:1
8:12^2
8:13
8:14
8:17
8:18^2
8:23^2
8:26^2
8:27
8:28^2
8:34
8:39
8:40
8:41^2
8:42
8:44^4
8:46^2
8:47^2
8:52
8:54
8:59^2
9:3
9:4
9:5
9:6^2
9:7
9:11
9:16^2
9:17
9:18
9:21
9:22
9:23
9:31
9:32
9:33
9:35
9:40
10:2
10:5
10:7
10:14
10:16
10:18^2
10:20
10:21^2
10:22
10:25
10:26
10:28
10:29
10:32
10:35
10:36^2
10:37
10:39
10:41
11:1^2
11:4^2
11:8
11:9
11:11
11:13^3
11:19
11:22
11:27
11:37^2
11:39
11:40
11:42
11:45
11:46
11:49
11:51
11:52
11:55
12:2
12:3^4
12:4
12:7
12:9
12:11^2
12:13^3
12:15
12:16
12:17
12:21^2
12:23
12:24
12:30
12:31^2
12:34^3
12:36
12:38^2
12:41
12:42^2
12:43^2
12:49
13:1^2
13:2
13:18
13:21
13:22
13:23
13:24
13:26
13:29^2
13:31
14:10
14:17
14:21
14:30
15:4
15:15
15:16
15:19^3
15:26^2
16:2
16:4
16:5
16:8^3
16:9
16:10
16:11^2
16:13^2
16:14
16:15
16:17
16:19
16:21
16:25
16:33
17:6
17:7
17:12^2
17:14^2
17:15
17:16^2
17:24
18:3
18:5
18:7
18:9
18:12
18:15
18:17
18:18
18:19^2
18:22^2
18:23
18:25
18:26^2
18:28
18:32
18:33
18:34
18:36^2
18:37
18:39
19:2
19:3
19:5
19:7
19:14
19:17
19:19^2
19:20
19:21^3
19:25^2
19:29
19:32^2
19:34
19:36
19:38^5
19:39
19:40^2
19:42
20:1
20:2
20:12
20:19^2
20:24
20:25^2
20:30
20:31
21:1
21:2^3
21:6^2
21:9
21:10
21:11
21:12
21:15
21:16
21:17
21:24

AC

1:1
1:3^3
1:4^2
1:6
1:8
1:9
1:11
1:13^2
1:14
1:15^2
1:16
1:17
1:18
1:19
1:20
1:21
1:22^2
1:24^2
1:25
2:1
2:2
2:3^2
2:5
2:10^2
2:11
2:13
2:14
2:15
2:17
2:18
2:19
2:20
2:21
2:22^4
2:23
2:24^2
2:28^2
2:29
2:30^2
2:31^2
2:33^3
2:36
2:37
2:38^4
2:42
2:46
3:1
3:2^2
3:5
3:6^2
3:10
3:12
3:13^5
3:15
3:16
3:18
3:19^2
3:21^3
3:22
3:24
3:25^3
3:26
4:1
4:4^2
4:6^2
4:8^2
4:9
4:10^3
4:11^2
4:13^2
4:15
4:18
4:19
4:21
4:22
4:25
4:26
4:27^2
4:30
4:31
4:32^5
4:33^2
4:34^2
4:36^3
5:2
5:3^2
5:7
5:9^2
5:12
5:13
5:14
5:15
5:16
5:17
5:19
5:20
5:21^2
5:24^2
5:30
5:31
5:32
5:34
5:35
5:36
5:37^2
5:38
5:39
5:40
5:41
6:1^2
6:2^2
6:3^2
6:4
6:5^3
6:7^3
6:8
6:9^5
6:14
6:15
7:2
7:3
7:4^2
7:8
7:10^3
7:11
7:16^4
7:17
7:22
7:23
7:24
7:29
7:30^3
7:31
7:32^4
7:34
7:35
7:36
7:37^2
7:40^3
7:41
7:42^4
7:43^2
7:44
7:45^3
7:46
7:49
7:52^4
7:53
7:55^3
7:56^2
7:58
8:1
8:3
8:5
8:7
8:9
8:10
8:11
8:12^2
8:14
8:16^2
8:18
8:20
8:21
8:22^2
8:23^3
8:24
8:25^2
8:26
8:27^4
8:32
8:34^3
8:37
8:39^2
9:1
9:2^2
9:11^2
9:13
9:15
9:20
9:24
9:26
9:27
9:29
9:31^2
9:33
9:36
10:1
10:3^2
10:7^2
10:12^3
10:22^3
10:28
10:31
10:32
10:33
10:34^2
10:36^2
10:38^2
10:39^2
10:41
10:42^2
10:43
10:45^2
10:48
11:1
11:2
11:5
11:6^2
11:16
11:20^2
11:21
11:22^2
11:23^2
11:24^2
11:28^2
11:30
12:1
12:2
12:3
12:4
12:5
12:7
12:10
12:11^5
12:12^2
12:13
12:17
12:18
12:20
12:22^2
12:23^2
12:24
13:1
13:5^2
13:7^2
13:10^4
13:11
13:12
13:15^3
13:16
13:17^4
13:18
13:19
13:20
13:21^4
13:22
13:23
13:24^2
13:25
13:26^3
13:27
13:28
13:29
13:31
13:34
13:36
13:38
13:39
13:40
13:42
13:43^2
13:44
13:46^2
13:47^2
13:48
13:49
13:50^2
13:51
14:1^3
14:3
14:4
14:5^2
14:6^2
14:11^2
14:13
14:14
14:15
14:19
14:22^2
14:26
14:27
15:1
15:2
15:3
15:4^2
15:5^3
15:6
15:7
15:10
15:11
15:14
15:15
15:16
15:17
15:18
15:20
15:21
15:22
15:23
15:26
15:35
15:36
15:40
16:1
16:2
16:3
16:4
16:6^2
16:9
16:12^2
16:13
16:14^4
16:16
16:17^2
16:18^2
16:19
16:26
16:27^2
16:32
16:33
16:36
16:39
16:40^2
17:1
17:2
17:4^3
17:5^2
17:6
17:7
17:8
17:9^2
17:10
17:11
17:12^3
17:13^3
17:18^3
17:22^2
17:24
17:26^4
17:27
17:28
17:29
17:30
17:32^3
18:3
18:8^2
18:11
18:12
18:14
18:15^3
18:17^2
18:18
18:23
18:25^3
18:26
19:4
19:5
19:8^2
19:9^2
19:10^2
19:11
19:12
19:13^2
19:14^2
19:16
19:17
19:19^3
19:20
19:22
19:25
19:27
19:28^2
19:29
19:31^2
19:33
19:34^2
19:35^4
19:37^2
19:40
20:4^4
20:6
20:7
20:11
20:16
20:17
20:19^2
20:24^4
20:25
20:26
20:27
20:28
20:30
20:31
20:32
20:35
20:38
21:5
21:6
21:8^3
21:11
21:12
21:13
21:14
21:16^3
21:20^2
21:21
21:26^3
21:27
21:28
21:30
21:31
21:32
21:35^2
21:36
21:39^2
22:3^3
22:5
22:8
22:9
22:10
22:11^2
22:12
22:14^2
22:15
22:16
22:18
22:20^2
22:30
23:5^2
23:6^2
23:9
23:10
23:11^2
23:12
23:16
23:17
23:20
23:21
23:23
23:27^2
23:29^4
23:34^2
24:4
24:5^3
24:7
24:8^2
24:10
24:14
24:15^2
24:16
24:21
24:22^2
24:23
24:25
24:26
25:2
25:8
25:9
25:11^2
25:15
25:16
25:18
25:19^2
25:20^3
25:21
25:23^3
25:24
25:25
25:26
26:2
26:4
26:5
26:6^2
26:7
26:9^2
26:10
26:13
26:16^2
26:18^2
26:20^2
26:22
26:25
26:26^2
26:31^2
27:1
27:2^3
27:5^2
27:6
27:8
27:10^2
27:11
27:12
27:19
27:21
27:22^3
27:23
27:25
27:29
27:30^2
27:32
27:34^2
27:35
27:36
27:41
27:42
27:44
28:2^2
28:3^2
28:7^2
28:8^3
28:11
28:15
28:16
28:17^3
28:18
28:19
28:20
28:21^3
28:22
28:23^3
28:27^2
28:28
28:31

RO

1:1^2
1:3^2
1:4^2
1:6
1:7
1:8
1:9^2
1:10
1:12
1:16^3
1:17
1:18^2
1:19
1:20^2
1:23
1:24
1:25
1:27^2
1:29
1:30^2
1:32^2
2:2
2:3
2:4^2
2:5^3
2:9^2
2:11
2:13^2
2:15
2:16
2:17
2:18
2:19^2
2:20^4
2:23
2:24
2:25
2:26
2:29^3
3:1
3:2
3:3
3:5
3:7
3:12
3:13
3:14
3:17
3:18
3:20^2
3:21
3:22^2
3:23^2
3:25^2
3:26
3:27^2
3:28
3:29^3
4:4^2
4:6
4:11^4
4:12^4
4:13^2
4:14^2
4:16^5
4:17
4:18
4:19
4:20
5:2^2
5:5
5:10
5:14^2
5:15^2
5:16
5:17^3
5:18^3
5:19
6:3
6:4^2
6:5^2
6:6
6:13^2
6:16^2
6:17^2
6:18
6:19^3
6:20
6:21
6:23^2
7:2
7:4
7:5
7:6^2
7:8
7:22
7:23^2
7:24
7:25^2
8:2^3
8:3
8:4
8:5^2
8:7
8:9^3
8:10^2
8:11
8:13
8:14^2
8:15^2
8:16
8:17
8:18
8:19^3
8:20
8:21^3
8:23^2
8:27^2
8:29
8:33
8:34
8:35
8:39
9:4^2
9:5
9:6^2
9:7
9:8^3
9:9
9:11^3
9:16^3
9:21
9:22
9:23^2
9:24^2
9:26
9:27^3
9:29
9:30
9:31^2
9:32
9:33
10:2
10:3^2
10:4
10:5
10:6
10:8
10:13
10:14
10:15^3
10:17
10:18
10:20
11:1^4
11:2
11:4^2
11:5
11:6^2
11:8
11:12^4
11:13
11:14
11:15^3
11:17^3
11:20
11:22
11:24
11:25^2
11:26
11:29
11:33^3
11:34
11:36
12:1
12:2^2
12:3^2
12:5
12:6
12:13
12:16^2
12:17
12:20
12:21
13:1^2
13:2
13:3^2
13:4^2
13:10
13:11
13:12^2
14:7
14:9
14:10
14:12^2
14:14
14:16
14:17
14:18
14:20
14:23^2
15:1
15:2
15:3
15:4
15:5
15:6
15:7
15:8^2
15:12
15:13^2
15:14^2
15:15^2
15:16^3
15:18^2
15:19^3
15:21
15:26
15:27
15:29^3
15:30
15:31
15:32
15:33
16:1
16:2^3
16:4
16:5
16:7
16:10
16:11^2
16:16
16:18
16:20^2
16:23^2
16:24
16:25^3
16:26^3

1 CO

1:1^2
1:2^2
1:4
1:6
1:7
1:8
1:9
1:10
1:11^3
1:12^5
1:13
1:14
1:16
1:17^3
1:18^2
1:19^2
1:20^2
1:21^2
1:24^2
1:25^2
1:27^2
1:28
1:30^2
2:1^3
2:4^3
2:5^2
2:6^3
2:7
2:8^3
2:9
2:10
2:11^4
2:12^3
2:14^2
2:15
2:16^2
3:4^2
3:10
3:13
3:16^2
3:17^2
3:19
3:20
4:1^5
4:3^2
4:5^3
4:6^2
4:13^2
4:16
4:17
4:19
4:20
4:21
5:4^2
5:5^2
5:8^2
5:10^2
6:1
6:4
6:9^2
6:10
6:11^3
6:12
6:15^3
6:19^2
7:4^2
7:6
7:7
7:19^2
7:23
7:25^2
7:31
7:33
7:34^2
7:36
7:40
8:3
8:4
8:6
8:7
8:9
8:10
9:2
9:5
9:7^3
9:9^2
9:10
9:12^2
9:13^2
9:14
9:15
9:16
9:17
9:18
10:4
10:5
10:7
10:8
10:9^2
10:10^2
10:11
10:16^5
10:17
10:18^2
10:21^5
10:27
10:29^2
10:30
10:31
10:32
10:33
11:1^2
11:3^3
11:7^2
11:8^2
11:10
11:12^2
11:16
11:18
11:22
11:23
11:24
11:25
11:27^3
11:28^2
11:32
12:3
12:4
12:5
12:6
12:7
12:8^2
12:9
12:10^4
12:12
12:15^2
12:16^2
12:18
12:21^2
12:22
12:23
12:27
12:10^4
12:29
12:30
13:1^2
13:2
13:13
14:10^2
14:11
14:12^2
14:16^2
14:21
14:24^2
14:25^2
14:26
14:32
14:33^3
14:36
14:37
15:3
15:5^2
15:6^2
15:7^2
15:8^4
15:9^2
15:10^2
15:12
15:13
15:15^2
15:19
15:20
15:21
15:32
15:34
15:37^2
15:39^5
15:40^2
15:41^3
15:42
15:47
15:49^2
15:50
15:52
15:56^2
15:58
16:1
16:2^2
16:10
16:15^3
16:17^2
16:19
16:21
16:23

2 CO

1:1^3
1:3^3
1:4
1:5
1:6
1:7^3
1:8^3
1:9
1:11
1:12^2
1:14
1:16^2
1:19
1:20^2
1:22
1:24
2:3^2
2:4^2
2:6
2:9
2:10
2:11^2
2:12
2:13
2:14
2:15
2:16^2
2:17^4
3:1^2
3:2
3:3^4
3:5^3
3:6^3
3:7^4
3:8
3:9^2
3:10
3:12
3:13^2
3:14
3:17
3:18^2
4:2^4
4:4^5
4:6^5
4:7^3
4:10^2
4:11
4:13
4:15^2
4:17
5:1^2
5:4
5:5
5:9
5:10
5:11
5:14
5:18^2
5:19
5:21
6:1
6:2^2
6:4
6:7^3
6:16^2
7:1^2
7:4^2
7:6
7:10^2
7:11
7:12
7:13
7:14
7:15
8:1^3
8:2^3
8:3
8:4
8:5
8:8^3
8:9
8:11^2
8:16
8:17
8:19^3
8:21^2
8:23^4
8:24^2
9:2^3
9:3
9:4
9:5^2
9:7
9:10
9:12^2
9:13^2
9:14
10:1
10:2
10:4^2
10:5^2
10:7
10:8
10:12
10:13^2
10:14
10:15^2
10:16
11:7
11:8
11:10^3
11:13
11:14
11:15
11:17
11:20
11:22
11:23
11:24
11:26^2
11:28
11:30
11:31
11:32
12:1
12:2
12:3
12:5^2
12:6^2
12:7^2
12:9
12:11
12:12
12:17^2
12:18
12:21
13:1
13:3
13:4^2
13:11^3
13:14^3

GA

1:1
1:2
1:4
1:6
1:7
1:10
1:11
1:12^2
1:13^2
1:14^2
1:19
1:21
1:22
2:2
2:4
2:5
2:6
2:7^2
2:8
2:9
2:12
2:14^2
2:15
2:16^5
2:17
2:20^2
2:21
3:2^3
3:5^2
3:9
3:10^3
3:11
3:12
3:13
3:14^2
3:15
3:16^5
3:17^2
3:18^2
3:19^2
3:20
3:21
3:22
3:26
3:27
4:1
4:2
4:3
4:4^2
4:5
4:6
4:7
4:9
4:11
4:13
4:14
4:15
4:19
4:20
4:23^2
4:26
4:28
4:30^2
4:31^2
5:1
5:4^2
5:5
5:8
5:11
5:15
5:16
5:18
5:19
5:21^2
5:22
5:26
6:1
6:2
6:8^2
6:10^2
6:12
6:14
6:16
6:17
6:18

EPH

1:1^2
1:3
1:4
1:5^2
1:6^2
1:7^2
1:9
1:10^2
1:11^2
1:12

1:13^{3} 1:14^{3} 1:15 1:16 1:17^{4} 1:18^{4} 1:19^{2} 1:23 2:2^{4} 2:3^{4} 2:7 2:8^{2} 2:9 2:12^{2} 2:13 2:14 2:15^{2} 2:19^{2} 2:20 2:22 3:1 3:2^{3} 3:4 3:5 3:6^{2} 3:7^{3} 3:8^{2} 3:9^{2} 3:10 3:12 3:14 3:15 3:16 3:19^{2} 4:1^{2} 4:3^{2} 4:4 4:6 4:7^{3} 4:9 4:12^{4} 4:13^{7} 4:14^{2} 4:16^{3} 4:17 4:18^{3} 4:23 4:25 4:29 4:30^{2} 5:1 5:4 5:5^{2} 5:6^{3} 5:8 5:9 5:11 5:12^{2} 5:17 5:20 5:21 5:23^{3} 5:26 5:30^{3} 5:33 6:4 6:5 6:6^{2} 6:8 6:9 6:10 6:11^{2} 6:12^{2} 6:13 6:14 6:15^{2} 6:16^{2} 6:17^{3} 6:19

PHP

1:1 1:3 1:4 1:6^{2} 1:7^{3} 1:8 1:10 1:11^{2} 1:12 1:14 1:15^{2} 1:16 1:17^{2} 1:19^{2} 1:22 1:25 1:27^{3} 1:28^{3} 1:29 2:1^{2} 2:2^{2} 2:3 2:4 2:6 2:7^{3} 2:8 2:10^{2} 2:11 2:13 2:15 2:16 2:17 2:19 2:22 2:26 2:30 3:2^{3} 3:5^{5} 3:8 3:9^{3} 3:10^{2} 3:11 3:12 3:14^{2} 3:17 3:18^{3} 4:2 4:3 4:7 4:8 4:9 4:10 4:11 4:15 4:18^{2} 4:22 4:23

COL

1:1^{2} 1:3 1:4^{2} 1:5^{2} 1:6^{2} 1:7^{2} 1:9 1:10^{2} 1:12^{2} 1:13^{2} 1:14 1:15^{2} 1:18 1:20 1:22 1:23 1:24^{2} 1:25^{2} 1:27^{3} 2:2^{6} 2:3 2:5 2:8^{2} 2:9 2:10 2:11^{3} 2:12^{2} 2:13 2:14^{2} 2:15 2:16^{3} 2:17^{2} 2:18^{2} 2:19 2:20 2:22 2:23^{3} 3:1 3:6^{2} 3:8 3:10 3:12^{3} 3:14 3:15 3:16 3:17 3:22 3:24 3:25 4:3^{2} 4:9 4:11 4:12^{3} 4:16 4:18

1 TH

1:1 1:2 1:3^{4} 1:4 1:5 1:6^{3} 1:8 1:9^{2} 2:2 2:3^{2} 2:4 2:5 2:6^{4} 2:8^{2} 2:9^{2} 2:11 2:12 2:13^{4} 2:14^{3} 2:19^{2} 3:2^{2} 3:6 3:13 4:1 4:3 4:4 4:5 4:6 4:9 4:12 4:15^{2} 4:16^{2} 5:1 5:2 5:5^{4} 5:8^{3} 5:18 5:22 5:23^{2} 5:28

2 TH

1:1 1:3 1:4 1:5^{4} 1:8 1:9^{2} 1:11^{3} 1:12^{2} 2:1 2:2 2:3^{2} 2:4 2:7^{2} 2:8^{2} 2:9 2:10^{2} 2:13^{3} 2:14^{2} 3:1 3:5 3:6^{2} 3:8 3:16 3:17 3:18

1 TI

1:1^{2} 1:5^{4} 1:7 1:9^{2} 1:11 1:14 1:15^{2} 1:20 2:1^{2} 2:3 2:4 2:7 3:1 3:2^{2} 3:3 3:5^{2} 3:6 3:7^{2} 3:8 3:9 3:10 3:12 3:13 3:15^{2} 3:16^{2} 4:1 4:3 4:5 4:6^{4} 4:8^{2} 4:9 4:10^{2} 4:12 4:14^{2} 5:8 5:9 5:10 5:17 5:18 5:22 5:25 6:1^{2} 6:2 6:3 6:4 6:5^{8} 6:10^{2} 6:11 6:12 6:13 6:14 6:15 6:20

2 TI

1:1^{3} 1:3 1:4 1:6^{2} 1:7^{4} 1:8^{6} 1:10 1:11 1:13^{2} 1:15 1:16^{2} 1:18 2:2 2:3 2:4 2:6 2:8^{2} 2:9 2:14^{2} 2:15 2:17 2:18 2:19^{2} 2:20^{4} 2:22 2:24 2:25 2:26^{2} 3:2 3:3 3:4^{2} 3:5 3:6 3:7 3:8 3:10 3:11 3:14^{2} 3:16 3:17 4:2 4:5 4:6 4:8 4:15 4:17^{2} 4:18

TIT

1:1^{4} 1:2 1:3 1:6^{2} 1:7 1:8^{2} 1:10 1:12^{2} 1:14 2:3 2:5 2:7 2:8^{2} 2:10 2:11 2:13 2:14 3:2 3:4 3:5^{3} 3:7 3:11

PHM

1 4 5 6^{2} 7 9 13 14 20 25

HEB

1:2 1:3^{4} 1:5 1:6 1:7^{2} 1:8^{2} 1:9 1:10^{2} 1:13 1:14 2:2 2:4 2:6^{2} 2:7 2:9^{2} 2:10 2:11 2:12 2:14^{3} 2:15 2:16^{2} 2:17 3:1^{2} 3:3 3:5 3:6 3:8 3:12 3:13^{2} 3:14^{2} 3:16 3:19 4:1^{3} 4:3 4:4 4:6 4:8 4:9 4:11 4:12^{5} 4:13 4:14 4:15 4:16^{2} 5:2 5:4 5:6 5:7 5:9 5:10^{2} 5:11^{2} 5:12^{4} 5:13 5:14^{2} 6:1^{4} 6:2^{7} 6:4^{2} 6:5^{2} 6:6 6:9 6:10 6:11^{2} 6:12 6:16 6:17^{2} 6:19 6:20 7:1^{3} 7:2^{4} 7:3^{3} 7:4 7:5^{7} 7:6 7:7 7:8 7:10 7:11^{2} 7:12^{2} 7:13^{2} 7:14^{2} 7:15 7:16^{2} 7:17 7:18 7:19 7:21 7:22 7:23 7:28 8:1^{3} 8:2^{2} 8:3 8:5^{2} 8:6 8:8^{2} 8:9^{2} 8:10 9:1 9:3 9:4^{2} 9:5^{2} 9:6 9:7 9:8 9:10 9:11^{2} 9:12 9:13^{4} 9:14 9:15^{4} 9:16^{2} 9:17^{2} 9:19^{2} 9:20 9:21 9:22 9:23 9:24^{2} 9:25 9:26^{3} 9:28 10:1^{2} 10:2 10:3 10:4^{2} 10:7^{2} 10:10^{2} 10:12 10:18 10:19 10:21 10:22 10:23 10:25^{2} 10:26 10:27 10:29^{4} 10:31 10:32 10:33 10:34^{2} 10:35 10:36^{2} 10:39^{3} 11:1^{2} 11:3^{2} 11:4 11:6 11:7^{4} 11:9^{2} 11:11 11:12 11:13 11:15 11:18 11:21^{2} 11:22^{3} 11:23^{2} 11:24 11:25^{2} 11:26^{2} 11:27 11:28 11:30 11:32^{6} 11:33 11:34^{4} 11:36^{2} 11:38^{2} 12:1 12:2^{3} 12:3 12:5^{2} 12:9^{2} 12:10 12:11 12:13 12:15^{3} 12:16 12:17 12:19^{2} 12:22^{2} 12:23^{3} 12:24^{3} 12:27^{2} 13:7^{2} 13:11 13:15^{2} 13:20^{3} 13:22 13:24

JAS

1:1^{2} 1:3 1:5^{2} 1:6 1:7 1:9 1:10 1:11^{2} 1:12 1:13 1:14 1:17^{2} 1:18^{4} 1:20^{2} 1:21 1:22 1:23 1:24 1:25^{2} 2:1^{3} 2:4 2:5^{2} 2:9 2:10 2:11 2:12 2:15 2:16 2:23 3:4 3:6^{3} 3:7^{5} 3:8 3:9 3:10 3:13^{2} 3:17 3:18^{2} 4:1 4:4^{3} 4:10 4:11^{4} 5:3 5:4^{5} 5:5 5:7^{2} 5:8 5:10^{3} 5:11^{4} 5:14^{2} 5:15 5:16 5:17 5:19 5:20^{2}

1 PE

1:1 1:2^{4} 1:3^{2} 1:5 1:7^{3} 1:8 1:9^{2} 1:10^{2} 1:11^{3} 1:13^{2} 1:15 1:17^{2} 1:19^{2} 1:20 1:22 1:23^{3} 1:24^{2} 1:25 2:2 2:4^{2} 2:7 2:8^{2} 2:9^{2} 2:10 2:12 2:13 2:14^{2} 2:15^{2} 2:16^{2} 2:25 3:1 3:3^{5} 3:4^{4} 3:7^{2} 3:8^{2} 3:12^{2} 3:13 3:14 3:15 3:16^{2} 3:17 3:20^{2} 3:21^{4} 3:22 4:2^{3} 4:3^{3} 4:4^{2} 4:7 4:8 4:10^{2} 4:11^{2} 4:13 4:14^{4} 4:15 4:17^{3} 4:19^{2} 5:1^{3} 5:2^{2} 5:4 5:5 5:6 5:10 5:12 5:14

2 PE

1:1^{2} 1:2^{2} 1:3 1:4 1:8 1:11 1:12 1:16^{2} 1:19 1:20^{2} 1:21^{2} 2:2^{2} 2:3^{2} 2:4 2:5^{2} 2:6 2:7 2:9^{2} 2:10^{2} 2:12 2:13 2:14 2:15^{3} 2:16 2:17 2:18^{2} 2:19^{3} 2:20 2:21 3:1 3:2^{4} 3:4^{2} 3:5^{4} 3:7^{2} 3:8 3:10 3:11 3:12^{2} 3:14 3:15 3:16 3:17 3:18

1 JO

1:1^{2} 1:5 1:7 2:2 2:5 2:10 2:14 2:15 2:16^{5} 2:17 2:19^{3} 2:21 2:27^{2} 2:29 3:1^{2} 3:2 3:4 3:8^{3} 3:9^{2} 3:10^{3} 3:12 3:16 3:19 3:22 3:23 4:1 4:2^{2} 4:3^{2} 4:4 4:5^{2} 4:6^{4} 4:7^{2} 4:9 4:13 4:14 4:15 4:17 5:1^{2} 5:2 5:3 5:4 5:5 5:9^{4} 5:10^{2} 5:12 5:13^{4} 5:15 5:18^{2} 5:19 5:20

2 JO

3 4 9^{2} 11 13

3 JO

3 6 7 10 11 12^{2}

JUDE

1^{2} 3 4^{2} 5^{2} 6 7 8 9 10 11^{3} 12^{2} 13^{2} 14^{2} 15^{2} 16 17^{2} 21^{2} 22 23 24

RE

1:1 1:2^{5} 1:3 1:5^{3} 1:7^{2} 1:9^{3} 1:10 1:13^{2} 1:14 1:15 1:16 1:18^{2} 1:20^{2} 2:1^{3} 2:5 2:6 2:7^{4} 2:8 2:9^{2} 2:10^{3} 2:11 2:12 2:14^{2} 2:15 2:16 2:17 2:18^{3} 2:21 2:22 2:23 2:24 2:27^{3} 3:1^{2} 3:5^{2} 3:7^{2} 3:9^{2} 3:10^{2} 3:12^{5} 3:14^{4} 3:16 3:17 3:18^{2} 4:1 4:4 4:5^{3} 4:6^{3} 4:8^{2} 5:1 5:5^{4} 5:6^{4} 5:7^{2} 5:8^{3} 5:9 5:11^{3} 6:1^{3} 6:5 6:6^{3} 6:7 6:8^{2} 6:9^{2} 6:11 6:12 6:13^{2} 6:14 6:15^{2} 6:16^{2} 6:17 7:1^{2} 7:2 7:3 7:4^{4} 7:5^{6} 7:6^{6} 7:7^{6} 7:8^{6} 7:9 7:13 7:14^{2} 7:15 7:17^{2} 8:1 8:3 8:4^{3} 8:5 8:7 8:8 8:9^{2} 8:10^{2} 8:11^{3} 8:12^{5} 8:13^{5} 9:1 9:2^{4} 9:3^{2} 9:4^{2} 9:5 9:7^{2} 9:8^{2} 9:9^{4} 9:11 9:13 9:15 9:16^{3} 9:17^{5} 9:18^{2} 9:20^{5} 9:21^{4} 10:1 10:7^{3} 10:8 10:10 11:1 11:4 11:5 11:6 11:7 11:8 11:9 11:11 11:13^{3} 11:15^{3} 11:18 11:19^{2} 12:1 12:4^{2} 12:5 12:6 12:10^{3} 12:11^{2} 12:12^{2} 12:14^{2} 12:15^{2} 12:16 12:17^{3} 13:1^{3} 13:2^{2} 13:3 13:8^{3} 13:10 13:11 13:12 13:13 13:14^{2} 13:15^{3} 13:17^{2} 13:18^{2} 14:2^{3} 14:5 14:6 14:7^{2} 14:8^{3} 14:10^{6} 14:11^{2} 14:12^{3} 14:14 14:15^{2} 14:17 14:18^{2} 14:19^{3} 14:20^{2} 15:1 15:2^{4} 15:3^{4} 15:5^{2} 15:6 15:7^{3} 15:8^{2} 16:1^{3} 16:2 16:3 16:4 16:5 16:6 16:7 16:9 16:10^{2} 16:11^{3} 16:12^{2} 16:13^{6} 16:14^{5} 16:17^{2} 16:19^{4} 16:21^{4} 17:1^{2} 17:2^{3} 17:3^{2} 17:4^{2} 17:5^{2} 17:6^{3} 17:7^{2} 17:8^{3} 17:12 17:14^{2} 17:17 17:18 18:2^{3} 18:3^{6} 18:4^{3} 18:9^{2} 18:10 18:11 18:12^{5} 18:13 18:15^{2} 18:18 18:19 18:22^{4} 18:23^{4} 18:24^{3} 19:1 19:2 19:5 19:6^{3} 19:7 19:8 19:9^{2} 19:10^{4} 19:12 19:13 19:15^{4} 19:16^{2} 19:17^{2} 19:18^{6} 19:19 19:20^{2} 19:21^{2} 20:1 20:4^{3} 20:5 20:6^{2} 20:7 20:8^{3} 20:9^{3} 20:10 20:12^{2} 20:14 20:15^{2} 21:2 21:3^{2} 21:6^{3} 21:9^{2} 21:10 21:11 21:12^{3} 21:14^{3} 21:16 21:17^{2} 21:18^{3} 21:19^{3} 21:21^{2} 21:22 21:23^{3} 21:24^{3} 21:25 21:26 21:27 22:1^{5} 22:2^{7} 22:3^{2} 22:5 22:6 22:7^{2} 22:8 22:9^{3} 22:10^{2} 22:14 22:16 22:17 22:18^{2} 22:19^{5} 22:21

OUR

2257

GE

1:26^{2} 5:29^{2} 19:31 19:32^{2} 19:34 23:6 24:60 29:26 31:1^{2} 31:14 31:15 31:16^{2} 31:32 33:12 34:9 34:14 34:16 34:17 34:21 34:31 37:26 37:27^{3} 41:12 42:13 42:21 42:32^{2} 43:4 43:7^{2} 43:8 43:18^{2} 43:21^{3} 43:22^{3} 43:28 44:8 44:25 44:26^{2} 44:31 46:34^{2} 47:8 47:18^{4} 47:19^{3} 47:25

EX

1:10 3:18 5:3 5:8 5:21 8:10 8:27 10:9^{6} 10:25 10:26^{2} 12:27 17:3^{2} 34:9^{2}

LE

25:20

NU

11:6^{2} 13:33 14:3^{2} 20:3 20:4 20:15^{2} 20:16 21:5 27:3 27:4^{2} 31:49 31:50 32:16^{2} 32:17 32:18 32:19 32:26^{4} 32:32 36:2 36:3^{2} 36:4

DE

1:6 1:19 1:20 1:25 1:28^{2} 1:41 2:1 2:8 2:29 2:33 2:36 2:37 3:3^{2} 4:7 5:2 5:3 5:24 5:25 5:27^{2} 6:4 6:20 6:22 6:23 6:24^{2} 6:25^{2} 21:7^{2} 21:20^{2} 26:3 26:7^{5} 26:15 29:15 29:18 29:29^{2} 31:17 32:3 32:27 32:31^{2}

JOS

2:11 2:13 2:14^{2} 2:19 2:20 2:24 5:13 7:9 9:11^{2} 9:12^{3} 9:13^{2} 9:24 17:4 18:6 21:2 22:19 22:24 22:25 22:27^{5} 22:28^{2} 22:29 24:17^{3} 24:18 24:24

JG

6:13 9:3 10:10 11:2 11:6 11:8 11:24 13:23 16:23^{3} 16:24^{4} 18:5 19:19 21:7 21:18 21:22

RU

2:20 3:2 4:3

1 SA

2:2 4:3 5:7 5:10 5:11 7:8 7:20^{2} 9:6 9:7 9:8 12:10 12:19 14:9 14:10 16:16 17:9 17:46 20:29 23:20 25:14 25:17 30:23

2 SA

7:22 10:12 12:18 18:12 19:9 19:43 22:32

1 KI

1:11 1:43 1:47 8:21 8:40 8:53 8:57^{2} 8:58^{2} 8:59 8:61 8:65 12:4 12:10 20:31^{2}

2 KI

7:9 18:22 19:19 22:13

1 CH

12:17 12:19 13:2^{2} 13:3 15:13 16:14 16:35 17:20 19:13^{2} 28:2 28:8 29:10 29:13 29:15^{2} 29:16 29:18

2 CH

2:4 2:5 6:31 10:4^{2} 10:10 13:10 13:11 13:12 14:7 14:11 19:7 20:6 20:7 20:9 20:12^{2} 28:13^{3} 29:6^{2} 29:9^{4} 32:8^{2} 32:11 34:21

EZR

4:3 5:12 7:27 8:17 8:18 8:21^{3} 8:22 8:23 8:25 8:30 8:31 8:33 9:6^{3} 9:7^{4} 9:8^{4} 9:9^{3} 9:10 9:13^{4} 9:15 10:2 10:3^{2} 10:14^{3}

NE

4:4 4:9^{2} 4:11 4:15 4:20

4:23 5:2[2] 5:3 5:4 5:5[8] 5:8[2] 5:9[2] 6:1 6:16[2] 6:18[4] 8:10 9:9 9:16 9:32[6] 9:34[4] 9:36 9:37[3] 9:38 10:29 10:30[2] 10:32 10:33 10:34[3] 10:35 10:36[6] 10:37[5] 10:38 10:39 13:2 13:4 13:18 13:27

JOB

8:9 17:16 22:20 28:22 37:19

PS

8:1 8:9 12:4[3] 17:11 18:31 20:5[2] 20:7 22:4 33:20[3] 33:21 35:21 40:3 44:1[2] 44:5 44:7 44:9 44:13 44:18[2] 44:20[2] 44:24[2] 44:25[2] 44:26 46:1 46:7 46:11 47:3 47:4 47:6 48:1 48:8 48:14[2] 50:3 59:11 60:10 60:12 65:3 65:5 66:8 66:9[2] 66:11 66:12 67:6 68:19 68:20 74:9 77:13 78:3 78:5 79:4 79:9[2] 79:10 79:12 80:6[2] 81:1 81:3 84:9 85:4 85:9 85:12 89:17 89:18[2] 90:1 90:8[2] 90:9[2] 90:10 90:12[2] 90:14 90:17[3] 92:13 92:23 95:1 95:6 95:7 98:3 99:5 99:8 99:9[2] 103:10[2] 103:12 103:14 105:7 106:6 106:7 106:47 108:11 108:13 113:5 115:3 116:5 118:23 122:2 122:9 123:2[2] 123:4 124:1 124:2 124:4 124:5 124:7 124:8 126:2[2] 126:4 135:2 136:23 137:2 141:7 144:12[2] 144:13[3] 144:14[2] 147:1 147:5 147:7

PR

1:13 7:18

CA

1:16 1:17[2] 2:9 2:12 2:15 7:13 8:8

ISA

1:10 3:6 4:1[3] 20:6 25:9 26:8 26:12 26:13 28:15 33:2 33:20 33:22[3] 35:2 36:7 37:20 38:20 40:3 40:8 42:17 47:4 52:10 53:1 53:3 53:4[2] 53:5[3] 55:7 58:3 59:12[4] 59:13 61:2 61:6 63:16[3] 63:17 63:18 64:6[2] 64:7 64:8[2] 64:11[4]

JER

3:22 3:23 3:24[2] 3:25[6] 5:19 5:24 6:24 8:14 9:18[2] 9:19 9:21[2] 11:21 12:4 14:7[2] 14:20[2] 14:22 16:10[3] 16:19 17:12 18:12 20:10 21:13 23:6 23:36 26:16 26:19 31:6 33:16 35:6 35:8[5] 35:10 36:15 37:3 42:2 42:6[2] 42:20[2] 43:2 44:17[4] 44:19 44:25 46:16 50:28 51:10[2] 51:51

LA

3:40 3:41[2] 3:44 3:46 4:17[3] 4:18[5] 4:19 4:20 5:1 5:2[2] 5:3 5:4[2] 5:5 5:7 5:9[2] 5:10 5:15[2] 5:16 5:17[2] 5:21

EZE

33:10[2] 33:21 37:11[3] 40:1

DA

1:13 3:17 9:6[3] 9:8[3] 9:9 9:10 9:12 9:13[3] 9:14 9:15 9:16[2] 9:17 9:18[3]

HO

7:5 14:2 14:3[2]

JOE

1:16

AM

6:13

MIC

2:4 4:5 4:11 5:5[2] 5:6[2] 7:17 7:19 7:20

ZEC

1:6[2] 9:7

MAL

2:10

MT

3:9 6:9 6:11 6:12 8:17 20:33 21:42 23:30 25:8 27:25

MK

9:40 11:10 12:11 12:29

LU

1:55 1:71 1:72 1:73 1:74 1:75 1:78 1:79 3:8 7:5 11:2 11:3 11:4 13:26 17:5 17:10 23:41 24:40 24:22 24:32

JOH

3:11 4:12 4:20 6:31 7:51 8:39 8:53 9:20 11:11 11:48 12:38 14:23 19:7

AC

2:8 2:11 2:39 3:12 3:13 3:25 5:30 7:2 7:11 7:12 7:15 7:19[2] 7:38 7:39 7:44 7:45[2] 13:17 14:17 15:10 15:25 15:26 15:36 16:20 17:20 17:28 19:25 19:27 20:21 21:5[2] 21:6 21:7 21:15 22:14 24:6 24:7 26:5 26:6 26:7 27:10 27:19 28:17 28:25

RO

1:3 1:7 3:5 4:1 4:12 4:24 4:25[2] 5:1 5:5 5:11 5:21 6:6 6:11 6:23 7:5 7:25 8:16 8:23 8:26 8:39 9:10 10:16 12:7 13:11 15:4 15:6 16:1 16:9 16:18 16:20 16:24

1 CO

1:1 1:2 1:3 1:7 1:8 1:9 1:10 2:7 4:12 5:4[2] 5:7 6:11 9:1 9:10[2] 10:1 10:6 10:11 12:23 12:24 15:3 15:14 15:31 15:57 16:12 16:23

2 CO

1:1 1:2 1:3 1:4 1:5 1:7 1:8 1:11 1:12 1:15 1:18 1:22 3:2[2] 3:5 4:3 4:6 4:10 4:11 4:16 4:17 5:1 5:2 5:12 6:11[2] 7:3 7:4 7:5 7:12 7:14 8:9 8:22 8:23 8:24 9:3 10:4 10:8 10:13 10:14 10:15[2] 10:16 11:31

GA

1:3 1:4[2] 2:4 3:24 6:14 6:18

EPH

1:2 1:3 1:14 1:17 2:3[2] 2:14 3:11 3:14 5:20 6:22 6:24

PHP

1:2 3:20 3:21 4:20 4:23

COL

1:1 1:2 1:3 1:7 3:4

1 TH

1:1 1:2 1:3 1:5 2:1 2:2 2:3 2:4 2:8 2:9 2:19[2] 2:20 3:2[2] 3:5 3:7 3:9 3:11[3] 3:13[2] 5:9 5:23 5:28

2 TH

1:1 1:2 1:8 1:10 1:11 1:12[2] 2:1[2] 2:14[2] 2:15 2:16[2] 3:6 3:12 3:14 3:18

1 TI

1:1[2] 1:2 1:12 1:14 2:3 6:3 6:14

2 TI

1:2 1:8 1:9 1:10 4:15

TIT

1:3 1:4 2:10 2:13 3:4 3:6

PHM

1[2] 2[2] 3 25

HEB

1:3 3:1 3:14 4:14 4:15 7:14 10:22[2] 10:23 12:2 12:9 12:10 12:29 13:15 13:20 13:23

JAS

2:1 2:21 3:6

1 PE

1:3 2:24 4:3

2 PE

1:1 1:2 1:8 1:11 1:14 1:16 3:15[2] 3:18

1 JO

1:1[2] 1:3 1:9[2] 2:2 3:5 3:16 3:17[2] 3:19 3:20[2] 3:21 4:10 4:17 5:4

2 JO

12

3 JO

12 14

JUDE

4[2] 17 21 25

RE

1:5 5:10 6:10 7:3 7:10 7:12 11:8 11:15 12:10[3] 19:1 19:5 22:21

OUT

4480, *1537*

GE

2:9 2:10 2:19 2:23 3:19 3:24 4:14 4:16 8:10 8:19 9:10 10:11 10:14 12:1 12:4 13:1 14:8 14:17 15:4 15:7 15:14 17:6 19:5 19:6 19:8 19:12 19:14[2] 19:24 19:29 19:30 21:10 21:17 21:21 22:11 22:15 23:4 23:8 24:11 24:13 24:15 24:29 24:44 24:63 25:25 25:26 26:8 27:3 27:30 28:10 28:16 29:2 30:16[2] 31:13 31:33 32:25 34:1 34:6 34:7 34:24[2] 34:26[2] 35:9 35:11 37:14 37:21 37:22 37:23 37:28 38:28[2] 38:29 38:30 39:12 39:15 39:18 40:14 40:15 40:17 41:2 41:3 41:14 41:18 41:33 41:45 41:46 42:2 43:23 43:31 44:4 44:8[2] 44:16 44:28 45:1 45:19 45:24 45:25 46:26 47:1 47:10 47:30 48:12 48:14 48:22 49:20 50:24

EX

1:5 1:10[2] 2:10 2:11 2:13 2:19 3:2 3:4 3:8[2] 3:10 3:11 3:12 3:17 3:20 4:7 4:9 5:10 6:1 6:6[3] 6:7 6:11 6:13 6:26 6:27 7:2 7:4 7:5 7:15 7:19 8:6 8:12 8:13[3] 8:16 8:17 8:29 8:30 9:15 9:29 9:33 10:5 10:6 10:11 10:12 10:18 10:21 11:1 11:4 11:6 11:8[3] 11:10 12:5 12:15 12:17 12:21 12:22 12:33 12:39[2] 12:41 12:42 12:46 12:51 13:3[3] 13:4 13:8 13:9 13:14 13:16 13:18 14:8 14:10 14:11 14:16 14:21 14:26 14:30 14:45 14:53 15:12 15:20 15:22 16:1 16:4 16:6 16:27 16:29 17:3 17:6 17:9 17:14 18:1 18:7 18:9[2] 18:10[2] 18:21 18:25 19:1 19:3 19:17 20:2[2] 21:2 21:3[2] 21:4 21:5 21:7 21:11 21:27 22:6 22:7 23:13 23:15 23:16 23:28 23:29 23:30 23:31 24:16 25:32[3] 25:33 25:35 28:35 29:23 29:46 32:1[2] 32:4 32:7 32:8[2] 32:11 32:12 32:19 32:23 32:24 32:27 32:32 32:33 33:1 33:2 33:7 33:8 33:11 34:11 34:18 34:24 34:34[2] 37:7 37:8 37:9 37:18[3] 37:19 37:21

LE

1:1 1:15 2:14 4:12[2] 4:18 4:25 4:30 4:34 5:9 5:15 5:18 6:6 6:12 6:13 7:14 7:35 8:26 8:33 9:9 9:23 9:24 10:2 10:4 10:5 10:7 10:14 11:45 13:12 13:20 13:25 13:56[4] 14:3 14:8 14:38 14:41 14:43 14:45 14:53 15:2 15:16 15:25 16:17 16:18 17:3 17:13 18:24 18:25 18:28[2] 19:36 20:22 20:23 21:12 22:33 23:17 23:43 24:10 24:23 25:12 25:28 25:30 25:31 25:33 25:38 25:42 25:51 25:54 25:55 26:6 26:13 26:33 26:45 27:21

NU

1:1 3:9 5:2 5:3 5:4 5:23 5:25 6:19 9:1 10:12 10:33 10:34 11:15 11:20[2] 11:24 11:26 12:4[2] 12:12 12:14 12:15 13:16 13:17 14:44 15:41 16:13 16:14 16:27 16:35 16:37 16:46 17:9 18:29[2] 20:5 20:8 20:10 20:11 20:16 20:18 20:20 21:5 21:13 21:23 21:26 21:28 21:32[2] 21:33 22:5[2] 22:11[2] 22:23 22:32 22:36 23:7 23:22 24:7 24:8 24:17[3] 24:19 26:4 27:17[2] 27:21 28:26 30:2 30:6 30:12 31:5 31:27 31:28 31:36 32:11 32:21 32:23 32:24 33:1 33:2[2] 33:3 33:12 33:38 33:52 33:55 34:5 34:7 34:8 34:9 34:10 34:12 34:25

DE

1:22 1:24 1:27 1:33 1:44 2:14 2:23 2:26 2:32 3:1 3:8 4:12 4:15 4:20[2] 4:33 4:34 4:36[2] 4:37[2] 4:38 4:45 4:46 5:4 5:6 5:15[2] 5:22 5:23 5:24 5:26 6:12 6:19 6:21 6:23 7:1 7:8[2] 7:19[2] 7:22 8:3 8:7 8:9 8:14 8:15 9:3 9:4[2] 9:5 9:7 9:10 9:12[2] 9:14 9:16 9:17 9:21 9:26 9:28[2] 9:29[2] 10:4 11:10 11:23 11:28 12:3 12:5 12:27 13:5[3] 13:10 13:13 15:11 15:13 15:14[3] 16:1 16:3[2] 16:6 17:18 18:5 18:6 18:12 20:1[2] 21:19 22:21 22:24 23:4 23:10 23:23 24:1 24:2 24:3 24:5 24:9 24:11 25:4 25:6 25:11 25:17 25:19 26:4 26:8 26:13 27:18 28:6 28:7 28:19 28:25 28:38 28:57 29:7 29:20 29:21 29:25 29:28 30:4 31:2 31:21 32:13 32:39 33:18 33:27

JOS

1:8 2:1 2:2 2:3 2:5 2:7 2:10 2:19 3:10 3:12[2] 4:2[2] 4:3 4:4 4:8 4:16 4:17 4:18 4:19 4:20 5:4[2] 5:5[2] 5:6 6:1 6:10 6:22[2] 6:23[2] 6:25 7:23[2] 8:3 8:5 8:6 8:14 8:17 8:18[2] 8:19[2] 8:22 8:26 9:12 9:26 10:22[2] 10:23 10:24 11:4 13:6 13:12 14:7 14:11 14:12 15:3 15:4 15:7 15:9 15:11[3] 15:63 16:2 16:3 16:6 16:7 16:8[2] 16:10 17:12 17:13 17:18 18:4 18:12 18:14 18:15[2] 19:9 19:12 19:13 19:17 19:24 19:27 19:32 19:34 19:40 19:47 20:2 20:8[3] 21:3 21:4[4] 21:5[3] 21:6[4] 21:7[3] 21:9[2] 21:16 21:17 21:20 21:23 21:25 21:27 21:28 21:30 21:32 21:34 21:36 21:38 22:9 22:31 22:32 23:5 23:9 23:13 24:5 24:6 24:10 24:12 24:17 24:18 24:32

JG

1:16 1:19[2] 1:21 1:24 1:27 1:28 1:29 1:30 1:31 1:32 1:33 2:1 2:3 2:12 2:15 2:16 2:17 2:18 2:21 2:23 3:10 3:19 3:20 3:22[2] 3:24 4:6 4:14 4:18 4:22 5:4[2] 5:14[3] 5:28 6:8 6:9[3] 6:19 6:20 6:21[2] 6:30 6:38 7:23[3] 8:34 9:4 9:15 9:17 9:20[2] 9:27 9:29 9:33 9:35

9:38 9:39 9:41 9:42 9:43 10:12 11:2 11:3 11:5 11:7 11:13 11:24 11:34 11:36 12:2 13:5 14:9 14:12 14:14^{2} 14:18 15:17 16:14 16:20^{2} 16:21 16:25 17:7 17:8 18:2 18:11^{2} 18:14 18:17 19:1 19:16 19:23 19:24 19:27 19:30 20:1 20:10 20:14 20:15 20:20 20:21 20:25 20:28 20:31 20:33^{3} 20:34 20:38 20:40 20:42 21:16 21:21^{2} 21:24

RU

1:7 1:13 1:21 1:22 2:6 2:17 2:22 4:3

1 SA

1:3 1:15 1:16 2:3 2:5 2:8 2:10 2:28 3:3 4:1 4:3^{2} 4:8 4:12 4:13 4:16^{2} 5:10 7:3 7:6 7:8 7:11 7:14 8:8 8:18 8:20 9:11 9:14 9:16^{2} 9:26 10:18^{3} 10:19 11:2 11:3 11:5 11:7 11:10 12:6 12:8 12:10 12:11 13:10 13:17 13:23 14:11 14:48 15:6 16:16 17:4^{2} 17:8 17:23 17:34 17:35^{2} 17:37^{3} 17:40 17:51 18:5 18:6 18:11 18:13 18:16 19:3 19:8 19:10 20:11^{2} 20:21 20:35 20:36 20:41 21:5 23:13 23:15 23:23 24:2 24:7 24:8 24:14 24:15 24:21 25:5 25:14 25:29^{2} 25:37 26:4 26:19 26:20 26:24 27:1 28:1 28:3 28:9 28:13 28:17 29:6 30:16^{2}

2 SA

1:2 1:3 2:12 2:13 2:23 3:18^{2} 3:25 3:26 4:4 4:9 5:2 5:13 5:24 6:3 6:4 6:20 7:6 7:9 7:12 8:1 9:5 10:3 10:8 10:16 11:8 11:13 11:17 11:23 12:7 12:11 13:9^{3} 13:17 14:16^{2} 15:11 15:24 15:35 16:5 16:7 17:1 17:21 18:3 18:4 18:6 19:9^{3} 19:19 20:7^{2} 20:8 20:10 20:12 20:13 20:16 20:22 21:10 21:17 22:1^{2} 22:7 22:9 22:15 22:17 22:46 23:4 23:16^{2} 23:21 23:29 24:4 24:7 24:16 24:20

1 KI

1:29 1:39 2:27 2:37 2:42 2:46 3:7 4:23 4:33 5:6 5:12 6:1 6:8 7:13 7:47 8:1 8:8 8:9 8:10 8:16^{2} 8:19 8:21 8:41 8:42 8:44 8:51 8:53 9:7^{2} 9:9 9:12 9:24 10:28 10:29^{2} 11:12 11:18^{2} 11:29 11:31 11:32 11:34 11:35 12:25 12:28 13:1 13:3 13:5 14:15 14:21 14:24 15:12 15:17 16:2 17:19 17:23 18:28 18:44 19:13 20:16 20:17^{3} 20:18^{2} 20:19 20:21 20:24 20:31 20:39 20:42 21:10 21:13 21:26 22:3 22:32 22:34 22:35 22:46

2 KI

2:23 2:24 3:6 4:4 4:5 4:18 4:21 4:37 4:39 4:40^{2} 4:41 5:2^{2} 5:11 5:27 6:7 6:27^{2} 7:12^{2} 7:16 7:20 8:3 9:2 9:15 9:19 9:21^{2} 9:24 9:30 9:32 10:3 10:9 10:25 10:26 10:28 11:8 11:9 12:11^{4} 12:12 13:5 13:25^{2} 14:27 16:3 16:7^{2} 17:7 17:8 17:18 17:20 17:23^{2} 17:36^{2} 17:39 18:18 18:29 18:31 18:33 18:34 18:35^{2} 19:9 19:19 19:27 19:31^{2} 19:35 20:4 20:6 21:2 21:7 21:8 21:15 23:4 23:6 23:8 23:16 23:18 23:27 24:3 24:7 24:12 24:13 24:20 25:7 25:19 25:21 25:27

1 CH

5:18 6:60 6:61^{2} 6:62^{3} 6:63^{3} 6:65^{3} 6:66 6:70 6:71 6:72 6:74 6:76 6:77 6:78 6:80 7:11 9:28 11:2 11:18^{2} 11:23 12:2 12:17 13:7 14:8 14:15 14:17 15:25 15:29 16:33 17:21^{2} 18:1 19:3 19:6^{3} 19:9 19:10 20:1 20:2 20:3 21:16 21:21 26:14 26:27 27:1 28:18

2 CH

1:10 1:16 1:17^{2} 2:2 2:8 2:14 2:16 4:18 5:2 5:9 5:10 5:11 6:5 6:9 6:32 6:34 7:20^{2} 7:22 8:11 9:28^{2} 10:2 11:13 11:16 12:3 12:7 12:13 13:9 14:5 14:8^{2} 14:9 14:10 15:2 15:5 15:8^{2} 15:9^{3} 15:17 16:1 16:2 16:7 17:6 18:20 18:21^{2} 18:31 18:33 19:2 19:3 19:4 20:4 20:7 20:10 20:11 20:17 20:21 21:15 21:19 22:7 23:2 23:7 23:8 23:11 23:14 24:5 24:6 25:6 25:10 25:15 26:11 26:18 26:20^{2} 28:3 28:9 28:21^{2} 29:5 29:7 29:16^{2} 30:6 30:25 31:1^{2} 32:11 32:13 32:14^{2} 32:15^{2} 32:17^{2} 33:2 33:8 33:15^{2} 34:14 34:21 34:25 34:33 35:20 35:24

EZR

1:7 2:1 3:8 5:14^{2} 6:4 6:5 6:21 7:20 7:28 8:35 9:5 10:1

NE

1:9 2:13 3:25 3:26 3:27 4:2 4:5 5:13^{2} 6:8 7:6 8:17 9:7 9:15 9:18 9:27 12:27 12:28 12:29 12:44 13:8 13:14

ES

2:9 2:13 2:23 3:15 4:1 4:11 5:2 7:8^{2} 8:4 8:14 8:15 9:4

JOB

1:17 1:21 3:11 3:24 5:5 5:6 6:17 8:10 8:19 9:6 9:8 9:10 9:14 10:7 10:10 10:18 11:7^{2} 11:13 12:15 12:22 13:9 14:4 14:12 14:18 14:19 15:13 15:22 15:25 15:30 16:13 16:20 18:4 18:5 18:6 18:18 19:7 20:15 20:25^{2} 21:17 22:16 24:4 24:12^{2} 24:24 26:7 27:21 27:22 27:23 28:2^{2} 28:3 28:4 28:5 28:10 28:27 29:6 29:7 29:16 29:17 29:19 29:25 30:16 30:24 31:7 31:8 31:12 31:34 32:11 32:13 33:6 33:21 35:9 36:16 36:26 37:1 37:2 37:9^{2} 37:18 37:22 37:23 38:1 38:8 38:13 38:29 39:3 39:5 40:6 41:1 41:19^{2} 41:20^{2} 41:21

PS

3:4 5:10 8:2 9:5 10:5 10:16 14:7 15:5 17:1 18:6 18:8^{2} 18:14^{2} 18:16 18:42 18:45 19:4 19:5 20:2 21:8^{2} 22:7 22:9 22:14^{2} 25:15 25:17 25:22 27:12 31:4 31:12 34:6 34:17 34:19 35:3 37:14 40:2^{2} 42:4 43:3 44:2^{2} 44:20 44:21 45:8^{2} 50:2 50:9^{2} 51:1 51:9 52:5^{2} 53:6 54:7 55:23 58:6 59:7 60:6 60:8 60:10 62:8 64:6 66:12 68:6 68:31^{2} 68:33 68:35 69:14^{2} 69:24 69:28 71:4^{2} 71:6 73:7 73:10 74:11 75:8^{2} 77:17^{2} 78:15 78:16 78:20 78:55 78:65 79:6 80:8^{2} 80:11 80:13 81:5 81:10 81:16 82:4 82:5 84:2 85:5 85:11 88:9 89:19 89:34 94:12 97:10 102 *title* 104:2 104:14 104:35 105:41 107:3 107:6 107:13 107:14 107:19 107:28 108:7 108:9 109:10 109:13 109:14 110:2 111:2 113:7^{2} 114:1 118:26 119:18 119:43 121:8 124:7 128:5 130:1 132:5 134:3 135:7 136:6 142:2 142:7 143:11 144:6 144:7 144:14 147:18

PR

1:23 1:24 2:6 2:22 3:10 4:23 5:15^{2} 6:9 8:12 9:1 10:31 11:8 12:13 13:9 15:2 15:28 17:14 17:23 20:5 20:20 21:16 22:10^{2} 24:20 25:1 25:2 25:19 26:20 28:11 30:17 31:18 31:20

EC

1:13 3:11 4:14 7:24 7:25 7:27 7:29 8:3 8:17^{2} 12:3 12:9 12:10

CA

3:6 4:16 8:11

ISA

2:3 5:2 5:25 8:8 9:12 9:17 9:21 10:4 11:1^{2} 11:16 12:3 12:6 13:9 13:13 14:19 14:26 14:27 14:29 15:4 15:5 16:2 16:4 16:8 16:10^{2} 18:2 18:7 19:23 21:11 22:16^{2} 23:11 24:18 26:16 26:17 26:19 26:21 28:7^{2} 28:27 29:4^{4} 29:9 29:10 29:18^{2} 30:11^{2} 30:13 30:14 31:3 34:3^{2} 34:11 34:16 35:6 36:16 36:18 36:19 36:20^{2} 37:28 37:32^{2} 38:6 40:12 40:22^{2} 40:26 42:5^{2} 42:7^{2} 43:13 43:25 44:13^{3} 44:22 45:12 45:23 46:6 46:7 48:1 48:3 48:21^{2} 51:17 51:22 52:11^{2} 52:12 53:2 53:8 53:12 55:11 55:12 57:4 57:14 58:7 58:10 59:5 59:21^{3} 62:10 62:12 63:11 65:2 65:9^{2} 66:5 66:11 66:20

JER

1:5 1:10 1:14 2:6 2:13 3:18 4:1 4:16 5:6^{2} 6:1^{2} 6:4 6:7^{2} 6:11 6:12 7:15^{2} 7:18 7:20 7:22 7:25 8:1^{2} 9:8 9:18 9:19^{2} 10:3 10:12 10:13 10:17 10:18 10:22 10:25 11:4 11:7 12:3 12:8 12:14^{2} 12:15 14:16 15:1 15:6 15:21^{2} 16:9 16:13 16:14 16:16 17:8 17:16 17:19 17:22 18:21 18:23 19:13 20:3 20:8 20:18 21:9 21:12^{2} 22:3 22:11 22:14 22:26 22:28 23:3 23:7 23:8 23:16 23:39 24:5 26:23 27:10 27:15 30:7 30:19 31:32 31:37 32:4 32:17 32:21^{2} 32:29 32:37 32:43 34:3 34:13^{2} 36:6 36:11 36:21 36:30 37:4 37:5 37:12 37:17 37:21 38:8 38:10 38:13 38:18 38:23^{2} 39:4^{2} 39:7 39:14 40:12 44:7 44:17^{2} 44:18 44:19^{2} 44:25 44:28 46:20 47:2 48:15 48:31 48:44 48:45 49:5 49:20 50:3 50:8^{2} 50:28 50:45 51:6 51:15 51:16 51:25 51:34 51:44 51:45 51:55 52:3 52:7 52:11 52:25 52:27 52:31

LA

1:10 2:4 2:8 2:12 2:19^{2} 3:7 3:8 3:38 3:55 4:1 4:3 4:11 5:8

EZE

1:4^{3} 1:5 1:13 3:25 4:12 5:2 5:8 5:12 5:14 9:8 10:7 10:19 11:7 11:9 11:17 11:19 12:5 12:12 12:14 13:2 13:17 13:21 13:23 14:9 14:13 14:19 15:7 16:5 16:15 16:27 16:36 19:14 20:8 20:9 20:10 20:13 20:14 20:21 20:28 20:32^{2} 20:34^{4} 20:38^{2} 20:41^{2} 21:3 21:4 21:5 21:19 21:31 22:15 22:22 22:31 23:26 23:34 23:48 24:6^{2} 24:12 25:7^{2} 25:13 25:16 27:6 27:33 28:16 29:4 29:7 30:13 30:22 30:25 31:4 31:11 32:3 32:7 32:21 33:21 34:11 34:12^{3} 34:13 34:25 34:27 35:3 35:7 35:11 36:5 36:20 36:24 36:26 37:1 37:12 37:13 37:23 38:8 38:12 38:15 39:3^{2} 39:10^{2} 39:14 39:27 39:29 42:11 42:14 43:6 43:11 43:23 43:25 44:3 45:14 45:15^{3} 46:9 46:18^{2} 46:20 47:1 47:2^{2} 47:8 47:12 48:19 48:30

DA

2:34 2:45 3:15 3:17 5:2 5:3 5:13 6:23^{2} 7:17 7:24 7:25 8:4 8:7 8:9 8:22 9:15 11:7 11:41 11:44^{2}

HO

1:11 2:2 2:10 2:15 2:17 2:18 4:2 5:10 7:5 9:15 10:11 11:1 11:11^{2} 12:8 12:13 13:3^{2}

JOE

1:16 2:28 2:29 3:7 3:16

AM

3:4 3:12^{2} 4:3 4:11 5:3 5:6 5:8 6:4^{2} 6:10^{2} 7:11 8:8 9:3 9:6 9:7 9:15

OB

6 8^{2}

JON

1:4 2:1 2:2 2:4 2:10 5:3

MIC

1:3 2:9 2:13 4:6 4:9 4:10 5:2 5:10 5:12 5:13 5:14 6:4^{2} 7:2 7:15 7:17

NA

1:6 1:11 1:14 2:2 2:9

HAB

1:2 2:11^{2} 3:4 3:13 3:14

ZEP

1:4 1:17 2:4 2:13 3:11 3:15 3:19

HAG

2:5 2:16^{2}

ZEC

1:21 2:3 2:13 3:2 4:1 4:12 5:9 6:1 6:12 8:10 8:23 9:4 9:7 9:11 10:4^{4} 10:10^{2} 11:6 13:2^{2} 14:8

MAL

2:8 2:12 2:13 3:10

MT

2:6 2:15 3:5 3:16 4:4 5:13 5:26 5:29 7:4^{2} 7:5^{4} 7:22 8:12 8:16 8:28 8:29 8:31 8:32 8:34^{2} 9:17 9:32 9:33 9:34 10:1 10:8 10:14 11:7 11:8 11:9 12:11 12:14 12:24 12:26 12:27^{2} 12:28 12:34 12:35^{2} 12:43 12:44 13:1 13:41 13:52 14:13 14:26 14:29 14:35 15:11 15:17 15:18 15:19 15:22 17:5 17:18 17:19 17:21 18:9 18:28 20:1 20:3 20:5 20:6 20:30 21:12 21:16 21:17 21:33 21:39 21:41 22:10 22:16 24:1 24:17 24:27 25:6 25:8 26:30 26:51 26:55 26:71 26:75 27:23 27:32 27:53 27:60

MK

1:5 1:10 1:23 1:25 1:26 1:29 1:34 1:35 1:39 1:45 3:5 3:15 3:21 3:22 3:23 3:31 4:3 4:32 5:2^{2} 5:8 5:10 5:13 5:14 5:17 5:30 5:40 6:1 6:12 6:13 6:33 6:34 6:49 6:54 7:12 7:15 7:19 7:20 7:21 7:26 7:29 7:30 8:23 8:27 9:7 9:18 9:24 9:25 9:26 9:28 9:38 9:47 10:21 10:46 10:47 11:11 11:15 11:19 12:1 12:8 13:1 13:15 14:26 14:48 14:68 15:13 15:14 15:20 15:21 15:39

15:46 16:8 16:9 16:17

LU

1:22 1:42 1:74 2:1 2:4 4:14 4:22 4:29 4:33 4:35^{2} 4:36 4:37 4:38 4:41^{2} 5:2 5:3^{2} 5:4 5:17 5:36 6:12 6:17 6:19 6:22 6:42^{4} 6:45^{2} 7:24 7:25 7:26 8:2 8:3^{3} 8:4 8:5 8:12 8:27 8:28 8:29 8:31 8:33 8:35^{2} 8:38 8:46 8:54 9:5 9:35 9:38 9:39 9:40 9:49 10:10 10:35 11:14^{2} 11:15 11:18 11:19^{2} 11:20 11:24^{2} 11:54 12:54 13:28 13:31 13:32 13:33 14:5 14:7 14:21 14:23 14:35 15:28 16:4 17:24 17:29 19:22 19:40 19:45 20:12 20:15 21:21 21:37 22:39 22:52 22:62 23:18 23:26 24:31 24:50

JOH

1:46 2:8 2:15^{2} 4:30 4:47 4:54 6:37 7:38 7:41 7:42 7:52 8:9 8:59 9:22 9:34 9:35 10:3 10:9 10:28 10:29 10:39 11:11 11:31 11:55 12:17 12:31 12:34 12:42 13:1 13:30 13:31 15:19 16:2 16:27 17:6 17:8 17:15 18:16 18:29 18:39 19:6 19:12 19:15 19:34 20:2

AC

1:9 1:18 1:21 2:5 2:17 2:18 3:19 4:15 5:6 5:9 5:16 6:3 7:3 7:4 7:10 7:12 7:19 7:21 7:36 7:40 7:45 7:57 7:58 8:7 8:9 8:39 9:1 9:28 10:45 12:9 12:10 12:11 12:17 13:17 13:42 13:50 14:14 14:19 15:14 15:24 16:13 16:18^{2} 16:27^{2} 16:30 16:37^{2} 16:39^{2} 16:40 17:2 17:5 19:12 19:16 19:28 19:33 19:34 21:5 21:28 21:30 21:38 22:18 22:23 23:6 24:7 27:19 27:29 27:30^{2} 27:38 27:42 28:3 28:21 28:23^{2}

RO

2:18 3:12 11:24 11:26 11:33 13:11

1 CO

5:7 5:10 9:9 14:36 15:8

2 CO

1:8 1:16 2:4 4:6 6:17 8:11 12:2 12:3

GA

2:4 4:15 4:30

EPH

4:29

PHP

1:12 2:12

COL

2:14 3:8

1 TH

1:8

2 TH

2:7

1 TI

1:5 5:18 6:7

2 TI

1:17 2:22 2:26 3:11 4:2 4:17

HEB

3:16 5:2 7:5 7:14 8:9 11:8^{2} 11:15 11:34 12:13

JAS

2:25 3:10 3:13

1 PE

2:9

2 PE

2:9 3:5

1 JO

2:19^{2} 4:1 4:18

3 JO

10

JUDE

5 13 23

RE

1:16 2:5 3:5 3:12^{2} 3:16 4:5 5:7 5:9 6:4 6:14 7:14 8:4 9:2 9:3 9:17 9:18 10:10 11:2 11:5 11:7 12:9^{3} 12:15 12:16 13:1 13:11 14:10 14:15 14:17 14:18 14:20 16:1^{2} 16:2 16:3 16:4 16:7 16:8 16:10 16:12 16:13^{3} 16:17^{2} 16:21 17:8 18:4 19:5 19:15 19:21 20:7 20:8 20:9 20:12 21:2 21:3 21:10 22:1 22:19^{2}

SHALL

GE

1:29 2:23 2:24^{2} 3:1 3:3 3:4 3:5 3:15 3:16 3:18 4:7 4:12 4:14^{2} 4:15 4:24 5:29 6:3^{2} 6:15 6:17 6:19 6:20 6:21 8:22 9:2 9:3 9:4 9:6 9:11^{2} 9:13 9:14^{2} 9:15 9:16 9:25 9:26 9:27^{2} 12:3 12:12^{2} 12:13 13:16 15:4^{2} 15:5 15:8 15:13^{2} 15:14 15:16 16:10 16:12 17:5^{2} 17:6 17:10^{2} 17:11 17:12 17:13 17:14 17:15 17:16 17:17^{2} 17:19 17:20 17:21 18:5 18:10 18:12 18:13 18:14 18:17 18:18^{2} 18:19 18:25 18:27 18:29 18:30 18:31 18:32 19:2 19:20 20:7 20:13 21:10 21:12 22:14 22:17 22:18 23:6 23:9 24:7 24:14^{3} 24:43 24:55 25:23^{3} 25:32 26:2 26:4 26:11 26:22 27:12 27:33 27:37 27:39 27:40 27:46 28:14^{2} 28:21 28:22 29:15 30:3 30:15 30:24 30:30 30:31 30:32 30:33^{3} 31:8^{2} 32:4 32:8 32:19 32:28 34:10^{2} 34:11 34:12 34:23 34:30^{2} 35:10^{2} 35:11^{2} 37:10 37:20 37:30 38:18 40:13 40:14 40:19^{3} 41:16 41:27 41:30^{3} 41:31^{2} 41:36^{2} 41:40 41:44 42:15^{2} 42:16 42:20^{2} 42:33 42:34^{2} 42:38^{2} 43:3 43:5 43:16 44:10^{2} 44:16^{3} 44:17 44:23 44:29 44:31^{2} 44:32 44:34^{2} 45:6 45:13^{2} 45:18 46:4 46:33^{3} 46:34 47:19 47:23 47:24^{3} 48:5 48:6^{2} 48:19^{4} 48:20 48:21 49:1 49:8^{3} 49:9 49:10^{2} 49:12 49:13^{3} 49:16 49:17^{2} 49:19^{2} 49:20^{2} 49:25^{2} 49:26 49:27^{3} 50:17 50:25

EX

1:16^{2} 1:22^{2} 2:7 3:12^{2} 3:13^{3} 3:18^{2} 3:21^{2} 3:22^{3} 4:8 4:9^{2} 4:15 4:16^{3} 4:21 5:7 5:8^{2} 5:11 5:18^{2} 5:19 6:1^{2} 6:7 6:12 6:30 7:1 7:2 7:4 7:5 7:9^{2} 7:17 7:18^{3} 8:3^{2} 8:4 8:9 8:11^{2} 8:21 8:22 8:23 8:26^{2} 8:27 8:28 9:3 9:4^{2} 9:5 9:9^{2} 9:19^{4} 9:29^{2} 10:5^{3} 10:6 10:7 10:8 10:14 10:26^{2} 11:1^{2} 11:5 11:6^{2} 11:7 11:8 11:9 12:2^{2} 12:3 12:4 12:5^{2} 12:6^{2} 12:7^{2} 12:8^{2} 12:10^{2} 12:11^{2} 12:13^{2} 12:14^{3} 12:15^{3} 12:16^{3} 12:17^{2} 12:18 12:19^{2} 12:20^{2} 12:22^{2} 12:24 12:25^{2} 12:26^{2} 12:27 12:43 12:44 12:45 12:46^{2} 12:47 12:48^{3} 12:49 13:3 13:5^{2} 13:6 13:7^{3} 13:9 13:11^{3} 13:12 13:14 13:16 13:19 14:2 14:4 14:13 14:14^{2} 14:16 14:17 14:18 15:9^{2} 15:14^{2} 15:15^{3} 15:16^{2} 15:18 15:24 16:4 16:5^{3} 16:6 16:7 16:8^{2} 16:12^{3} 16:25 16:26^{2} 17:4 17:6 18:19 18:22^{5} 18:23 19:5 19:6 19:12 19:13^{4} 20:23^{2} 21:2^{2} 21:3^{2} 21:4^{2} 21:5 21:6^{4} 21:7 21:8^{2} 21:9 21:10 21:11 21:12 21:13 21:15 21:16 21:17 21:19^{3} 21:20 21:21 21:22^{2} 21:26 21:27 21:28^{3} 21:29^{2} 21:30 21:31 21:32^{3} 21:33^{2} 21:34^{2} 21:35^{2} 21:36^{2} 22:1^{2} 22:2 22:3^{2} 22:4 22:5^{4} 22:6 22:7 22:8 22:9^{3} 22:11^{3} 22:12 22:13 22:14 22:15 22:16 22:17 22:19 22:20 22:22 22:24^{2} 22:27^{2} 22:30 22:31^{3} 23:11 23:15 23:17 23:18 23:23 23:25^{2} 23:26 23:28 23:33 24:2^{3} 25:2 25:3 25:9 25:10^{2} 25:12 25:15^{2} 25:16 25:17 25:19 25:20^{3} 25:21 23:23 25:27 25:31^{2} 25:32 25:34 25:35 25:36^{2} 25:37 25:38 25:39 26:2^{2} 26:3^{2} 26:6 26:8^{2} 26:12 26:13 26:16^{2} 26:17 26:20 26:24^{4} 26:25 26:28 26:31 26:32 26:33 26:37 27:1^{2} 27:2 27:7^{2} 27:8 27:9 27:10^{2} 27:11 27:12 27:13 27:14 27:15 27:16^{2} 27:17 27:18 27:19 27:21^{2} 28:4^{2} 28:5 28:6 28:7^{2} 28:8 28:12 28:16^{3} 28:17^{2} 28:18 28:20 28:21^{2} 28:28 28:29 28:30^{2} 28:32^{2} 28:35^{2} 28:37 28:38^{3} 28:42 28:43^{2} 29:9 29:10 29:15 29:19 29:21 29:26 29:28^{2} 29:29 29:30 29:32 29:33^{2} 29:34 29:37^{2} 29:42 29:43 29:46 30:2^{4} 30:4 30:7^{2} 30:8 30:9^{2} 30:10^{2} 30:12 30:13^{2} 30:14 30:15^{2} 30:19 30:20 30:21^{3} 30:25 30:29 30:31 30:32^{3} 30:33 30:34 30:36 30:37^{2} 30:38^{2} 31:11 31:13 31:14^{3} 31:15 31:16 32:1 32:13 32:23 32:30 32:34 33:14 33:16^{2} 33:20 33:22 33:23 34:3 34:10 34:13 34:20 34:23 34:24 34:25 35:2^{3} 35:3 35:10 40:9 40:10 40:15

LE

1:2 1:3 1:4^{2} 1:5^{2} 1:6 1:7 1:8 1:9^{2} 1:10 1:11^{2} 1:12^{2} 1:13^{2} 1:14 1:15^{2} 1:16 1:17^{3} 2:1^{2} 2:2^{3} 2:3 2:4 2:5 2:7 2:8 2:9^{2} 2:10 2:11^{3} 2:12^{2} 2:16 3:1 3:2^{2} 3:3 3:4 3:5 3:6 3:7 3:8^{2} 3:9^{2} 3:10 3:11 3:12 3:13^{2} 3:14 3:15 3:16 3:17 4:2^{2} 4:4^{2} 4:5 4:6 4:7^{2} 4:8 4:9 4:10 4:12^{2} 4:14 4:15^{2} 4:16 4:17 4:18^{2} 4:19 4:20^{4} 4:21 4:23 4:24 4:25^{2} 4:26^{3} 4:28 4:29 4:30^{2} 4:31^{4} 4:32 4:33 4:34^{2} 4:35^{4} 5:1 5:2 5:3^{2} 5:4^{2} 5:5^{3} 5:6^{2} 5:7 5:8^{3} 5:9^{2} 5:13^{3} 5:11^{3} 5:12^{2} 5:13^{3} 5:15 5:16^{4} 5:17 5:18^{3} 6:4^{2} 6:5^{2} 6:6 6:7^{2} 6:9 6:10^{3} 6:11 6:12^{4} 6:13^{2} 6:14 6:15^{2} 6:16^{3} 6:17 6:18^{3} 6:20 6:21 6:22^{2} 6:23^{2} 6:25 6:26^{2} 6:27^{2} 6:28^{2} 6:29 6:30^{2} 7:2^{2} 7:4 7:5 7:6 7:7 7:8 7:9 7:10 7:11 7:12 7:13 7:14^{2} 7:15^{2} 7:16^{2} 7:17 7:18^{4} 7:19^{3} 7:20 7:21^{2} 7:23 7:24 7:25 7:26 7:27 7:29 7:30^{2} 7:31^{2} 7:32 7:33 8:31 8:32 8:33^{2} 8:35 9:6 10:7 10:9 10:13 10:14 10:15^{2} 11:2 11:3 11:4 11:8^{2} 11:9^{2} 11:10 11:11^{3} 11:12 11:13^{2} 11:20 11:23 11:24^{2} 11:25 11:26 11:27 11:28 11:29 11:31 11:32^{3} 11:33^{2} 11:34^{2} 11:35^{3} 11:36^{2} 11:37 11:38 11:39 11:40^{2} 11:41^{2} 11:42 11:43^{2} 11:44^{3} 11:45 12:2^{2} 12:3 12:4^{2} 12:5^{2} 12:6 12:7^{2} 12:8^{3} 13:2^{2} 13:3^{2} 13:4 13:5^{2} 13:6^{3} 13:7 13:8 13:9 13:10 13:11^{2} 13:13^{2} 13:14 13:15 13:16 13:17^{2} 13:20 13:21 13:22 13:23 13:25^{2} 13:26 13:27^{2} 13:28 13:30^{2} 13:31 13:32 13:33^{3} 13:34^{3} 13:36^{2} 13:37 13:39 13:43 13:44 13:45^{3} 13:46^{4} 13:49 13:50 13:51 13:52^{2} 13:53 13:54^{2} 13:55 13:56 13:58^{2} 14:2^{2} 14:3^{2} 14:4 14:5 14:6^{2} 14:7^{3} 14:8^{3} 14:9^{6} 14:10 14:11 14:12 14:13^{2} 14:14^{2} 14:15 14:16^{2} 14:17 14:18^{2} 14:19^{2} 14:20^{3} 14:21 14:22 14:23 14:24^{2} 14:25^{2} 14:26 14:27 14:28 14:29 14:30 14:31 14:35 14:36^{2} 14:37 14:38 14:39^{2} 14:40^{2} 14:41^{2} 14:42^{3} 14:44 14:45^{2} 14:46 14:47^{2} 14:48^{2} 14:49 14:50 14:51 14:52 14:53^{2} 15:3 15:4 15:5 15:6 15:7 15:8 15:9 15:10^{2} 15:11 15:12^{2} 15:13^{2} 15:14 15:15^{2} 15:16 15:17 15:18^{2} 15:19^{2} 15:20^{2} 15:21 15:22 15:23 15:24^{2} 15:25^{2} 15:26^{2} 15:27^{2} 15:28^{2} 15:29 15:30^{2} 15:31 16:3 16:4^{5} 16:5 16:6 16:7 16:8 16:9 16:10 16:11^{3} 16:12 16:13 16:14^{2} 16:15 16:16^{2} 16:17 16:18^{2} 16:19 16:20 16:21^{2} 16:22^{2} 16:23^{2} 16:24 16:25 16:26 16:27^{2} 16:28^{2} 16:29^{2} 16:30 16:31^{2} 16:32^{4} 16:33^{3} 16:34 17:4^{2} 17:6 17:7^{2} 17:9 17:12^{2} 17:13 17:14^{2} 17:15^{2} 17:16 18:3^{2} 18:4 18:5^{2} 18:6 18:23 18:26^{2} 18:29^{2} 18:30 19:2 19:3 19:5 19:6^{2} 19:7 19:8^{2} 19:11 19:12 19:13 19:15 19:19^{2} 19:20^{2} 19:21 19:22^{2} 19:23^{5} 19:24 19:25 19:26^{2} 19:27 19:28 19:30 19:33 19:34 19:35 19:36 19:37 20:2^{2} 20:8 20:9^{2} 20:10 20:11^{2} 20:12^{2} 20:13^{2} 20:14 20:15^{2} 20:16^{2} 20:17^{3} 20:18^{3} 20:19 20:20^{3} 20:21^{2} 20:22 20:23 20:24 20:25^{2} 20:26 20:27^{3} 21:1 21:4 21:5^{2} 21:6^{2} 21:7^{2} 21:8 21:9 21:10 21:11 21:12 21:13 21:14^{2} 21:15 21:18 21:21^{2} 21:22 21:23 22:3 22:4 22:6^{2} 22:7^{2} 22:8 22:9 22:10^{2} 22:11^{2} 22:13^{2} 22:14^{2} 22:15 22:19 22:20^{2} 22:21^{2} 22:22 22:23 22:24^{2} 22:25^{2} 22:27^{2} 22:28 22:30^{2} 22:31 22:32 23:2 23:3^{2} 23:4 23:7 23:8^{2} 23:10^{2} 23:11^{2} 23:12 23:13^{2} 23:14^{2} 23:15^{2} 23:16^{2} 23:17^{3} 23:18^{2} 23:19 23:20^{2} 23:21^{3} 23:24 23:25^{2} 23:27^{3} 23:28 23:29^{2} 23:31^{2} 23:32^{3} 23:34 23:35^{2} 23:36^{4} 23:37 23:39^{3} 23:40^{2} 23:41^{3} 23:42^{2} 24:3^{2} 24:4 24:5 24:8 24:9^{2} 24:15 24:16^{3} 24:17 24:18 24:19 24:20 24:21^{2} 24:22 25:2 25:4 25:6 25:7 25:8 25:9 25:10^{4} 25:11^{2} 25:12^{2} 25:13 25:14 25:15 25:17 25:18^{2} 25:19^{2} 25:20^{3} 25:21 25:22^{2} 25:23 25:24 25:25 25:28^{3} 25:30^{2} 25:31^{2} 25:33 25:40^{2} 25:41^{3} 25:42 25:44^{2} 25:45^{2} 25:46^{3} 25:50^{3} 25:51^{2} 25:52^{2} 25:53^{2} 25:54 26:1^{2} 26:2 26:4^{2} 26:5^{3} 26:6^{3} 26:7^{2} 26:8^{3} 26:10 26:11 26:12 26:15 26:16^{3} 26:17^{3} 26:20^{3} 26:22^{2} 26:25^{2} 26:26^{3} 26:29^{2} 26:30 26:32 26:33 26:34^{2} 26:35 26:36^{3} 26:37^{2} 26:38^{2}

26:39^2
26:40
26:43^3
27:2^2
27:3^2
27:4
27:5
27:6^2
27:7
27:8^3
27:9
27:10^3
27:11
27:12^2
27:13
27:14^4
27:15^2
27:16^3
27:17
27:18^2
27:19^2
27:20
27:21^2
27:23^2
27:24
27:25^2
27:26
27:27^4
27:28^2
27:29^3
27:31
27:32
27:33^4

NU

1:3
1:4
1:5
1:50^3
1:51^3
1:52
1:53^2
2:2^2
2:3^2
2:5^2
2:7
2:9
2:10^2
2:12^2
2:14
2:16
2:17^2
2:18^2
2:20^2
2:22
2:24
2:25^2
2:27^2
2:29
2:31
3:7
3:8
3:10^2
3:12
3:13
3:23
3:24
3:25
3:29
3:30
3:31
3:32
3:35
3:36
3:38^2
3:45
4:4
4:5^2
4:6^3
4:7^2
4:8^2
4:9
4:10^2
4:11^2
4:12^2
4:13
4:14^2
4:15^3
4:19
4:20
4:25
4:26
4:27^2
4:28
4:32
5:3^2
5:6
5:7^2
5:8
5:9
5:10^2
5:15^3
5:16
5:17^2
5:18^2
5:19
4:21^2
5:22^2
5:23
5:24^2
5:25^2
5:26^2
5:27^5
5:28^2
5:30^2
5:31^2
6:2
6:3^3
6:4
6:5^3
6:6
6:7
6:9^2
6:10
6:11^2
6:12^3
6:13
6:14
6:16^2
6:17^2
6:18^2
6:19^2
6:20
6:21
6:23
6:27
7:11
8:2
8:10
8:11
8:12
8:14
8:15
8:24
8:25^2
8:26^2
9:3^2
9:10^2
9:11
9:12^2
9:13^2
9:14^3
10:3
10:4
10:5
10:6^2
10:7^2
10:8^2
10:9^3
10:10
10:32^3
11:4
11:17
11:18^3
11:19
11:22^2
11:23
12:8
13:2
14:13
14:21
14:23^2
14:24
14:27
14:29
14:30
14:31
14:32
14:33
14:34^2
14:35^2
14:41
14:43
15:4
15:9
15:11
15:12^2
15:13
15:14
15:15^2
15:16
15:19^2
15:20^2
15:21
15:24^2
15:25^3
15:26
15:27
15:28^2
15:29
15:30
15:31^2
15:35^2
15:39
16:7^2
16:7^2
16:22
16:28
16:30
16:38
17:3
17:5^3
17:13^2
18:1^2
18:2
18:3^2
18:4^2
18:5
18:7^3
18:9^3
18:10^2
18:11
18:12
18:13^3
18:14
18:15
18:18
18:23^3
18:24
18:26
18:27
18:28
18:29
18:30
18:31
18:32^2
19:3^2
19:4
19:5^2
19:6
19:7^4
19:8^2
19:9^2
19:10^2
19:11
19:12^3
19:13^2
19:14
19:16
19:17^2
19:18
19:19^3
19:20^3
19:21^3
19:22^2
20:8
20:12
20:24^2
20:26^2
21:8^2
22:4
22:6
22:8
22:11
22:20
22:35
22:38
23:8^2
23:9^2
23:19^2
23:23
23:24^2
24:7^4
24:8^2
24:9
24:14
24:17^5
24:18^3
24:19^3
24:20
24:22^2
24:23
24:24^4
25:13
26:53
26:54
26:55^2
26:56
26:65
27:8
27:9
27:10
27:11^3
27:21^4
28:2
28:3
28:7
28:11
28:14
28:15
28:17
28:18^2
28:19^2
28:20^2
28:23
28:24^2
28:25^2
28:26^2
28:27
28:31^2
29:1^2
29:2
29:3
29:7^3
29:8^2
29:9
29:12^3
29:13^2
29:14
29:17
29:18
29:21
29:24
29:27
29:30
29:33
29:35^2
29:36
29:37
29:39
30:2^2
30:4^3
30:5^2
30:7^2
30:8^2
30:9
30:11^2
30:12^2
30:15^2
31:4
31:23^4
31:24^3
32:6^2
32:11
32:15
32:17
32:22^2
32:26
32:29^2
32:30
33:52
33:53
33:54^5
33:55^3
33:56^2
34:2
34:3^2
34:4^3
34:5^2
34:6^2
34:7^2
34:8^2
34:9^3
34:10
34:11^3
34:12^3
34:13
34:17
34:18
35:2
35:3^2
35:4^2
35:5^3
35:6^4
35:7^8
35:8^6
35:11
35:12
35:13^2
35:14^3
35:15
35:16
35:17
35:18
35:19^2
35:21^2
35:24
35:25^2
35:26
35:27
35:28
35:29
35:30^2
35:31^2
35:32
35:33
35:34
36:3^3
36:4^3
36:6
36:7^2
36:8
36:9^3

DE

1:17^3
1:22^2
1:28
1:30
1:35
1:36
1:38^2
1:39^2
2:4
2:6^2
2:25^2
2:29
3:18
3:19
3:20
3:21
3:22^2
3:28^2
4:2^2
4:6
4:10
4:22
4:25^3
4:26^3
4:27^3
4:28
5:25
5:27^2
5:32^2
5:33^2
6:6
6:8
6:10^2
6:14
6:16
6:17
6:25
7:1
7:2
7:5^2
7:12^2
7:14
7:16^2
7:19
7:23^2
7:24^2
7:25
8:1
8:19^2
8:20
9:3^2
11:8
11:13^2
11:18
11:19
11:22
11:23
11:24^3
11:25^3
11:29
11:31^2
11:32
12:1
12:2^2
12:3^2
12:4
12:5^2
12:6
12:7^2
12:8
12:11^3
12:12
12:14
12:16^2
12:18
12:20
12:22
12:26
12:27
12:29
13:4^2
13:5
13:8
13:9
13:11^2
13:16^2
13:17
14:1
14:6
14:7
14:8
14:9^2
14:11
14:12
14:19
14:21
14:23
14:24
14:25
14:29^2
15:2^2
15:3
15:4^2
15:6
15:10^2
15:11
15:16
15:17
15:18^2
15:20
15:22
16:2
16:4^2
16:6
16:7
16:8
16:15^2
16:16^3
16:17
16:18
17:6^2
17:7
17:8
17:9^2
17:10^2
17:11^3
17:12
17:13
17:15
17:16^2
17:17^2
17:18^2
17:19^2
18:1^2
18:2
18:3^2
18:6
18:7
18:8
18:10
18:15
18:18^2
18:19^2
18:20^3
18:21
19:4
19:5
19:12
19:13
19:15^2
19:17^2
19:18
19:19
19:20^2
19:21^2
20:2^2
20:3
20:5
20:8^2
20:9^2
20:11^4
21:2^2
21:3^2
21:4^2
21:5^2
21:6
21:7
21:8
21:12
21:13^3
21:14
21:16
21:17
21:19
21:20
21:21^2
21:23
22:2
22:5^2
22:15
22:16
22:17
22:18
22:19^2
22:21^2
22:22
22:24^2
22:25
22:29^2
22:30
23:1
23:2^2
23:3^2
23:8
23:10^2
23:11^3
23:13
23:14
23:16^2
23:17
23:22
24:5^4
24:6
24:7
24:8^2
24:11
24:13
24:15
24:16^3
24:19
24:20
24:21
25:1
25:2^2
25:5^2
25:6^2
25:8
25:9^3
25:10
25:12
25:19
26:1
26:2
26:3
26:4
27:2
27:4^2
27:12
27:13
27:14
27:15
27:16
27:17
27:18
27:19
27:20
27:21
27:22
27:23
27:24
27:25
27:27
28:1
28:2
28:4
28:5
28:7^2
28:8^2
28:9
28:10^2
28:11
28:12
28:13
28:15^2
28:17
28:18
28:20
28:21
28:22^2
28:23^2
28:24^2
28:25
28:26^2
28:28
28:29
28:30
28:31^4
28:32^3
28:33
28:35
28:36
28:37
28:38
28:39
28:40
28:41
28:42
28:43
28:44^2
28:45^2
28:46
28:48^2
28:49
28:50
28:51^2
28:52^2
28:53
28:54^2
28:55^2
28:56
28:57^3
28:60
28:62
28:63^2
28:64
28:65^2
28:66
28:68^3
29:19
29:20^3
29:21
29:22^3
29:24
29:25
30:1
30:12
30:13
30:16
30:18^2
31:3
31:4
31:5
31:11
31:17^3
31:18
31:20^2
31:21^3
32:2^2
32:20
32:22^2
32:24
32:25
32:35^2
32:36
32:37
32:42
32:46
32:47
33:3
33:10^2
33:12^3
33:17
33:19^3
33:22
33:25^2
33:27^2
33:28^3
33:29

JOS

1:3
1:4
1:5
1:8
1:11
1:14^2
1:15
1:18
2:5
2:14
2:19^5
3:3
3:4
3:8
3:10
3:13^4
4:3^2
4:7^2
4:21
4:22
6:3
6:4^3
6:5^4
6:10^3
6:17^2
6:19
6:26^2
7:8
7:9^2
7:14^7
7:15^2
7:25
8:2
8:4
8:5
8:7
8:8^3
9:7
9:23
10:8
10:25
14:9
14:12
15:4
17:18^2
18:4^2
18:5^3
18:6
20:3
20:4^3
20:5
20:6^3
22:22
22:25
22:28
22:34
23:5^2
23:10
23:12
23:13
23:15^2
23:16^2
24:27^2

JG

1:1
1:2
2:2^2
2:3^2
4:9^2
4:20
5:11^2
5:24^2
6:15
6:37
7:4^5
7:11
7:17^2
8:23^2
9:33
10:18
11:9
11:24
11:31^2
13:5^3
13:7
13:8^2
13:12^2
13:15
13:22
14:16
15:3
15:18
16:2
16:7
16:11
16:17
18:5
18:10
20:9
20:18^2
20:23
20:28^2
21:1
21:5
21:7
21:11^2
21:16
21:22

RU

1:16
2:2
2:9
3:1
3:3
3:4^2
3:13
4:12
4:15

1 SA

1:11
1:28
2:9^2
2:10^4
2:25^2
2:30
2:31
2:32^2
2:33^3
2:34^3
2:35^2
2:36^3
3:9
3:11
3:14
4:8
5:7
5:8
6:2^2
6:3^2
6:4^2
6:5^2
6:9
6:20
8:9
8:11^2
8:17
8:18^2
9:7
9:13^2
9:17
9:19
10:2
10:3
10:5^2
10:27
11:7
11:9^2
11:10
11:12
11:13
12:12
12:14
12:15
12:17
12:25^2
13:14
14:10
14:37
14:39
14:45^2
15:33
16:16^2
17:9
17:25
17:26
17:27
17:36
17:47
18:25
19:6
20:7
20:10
20:31
20:32
21:15
23:2
23:17
23:20
23:23
24:4
24:12
24:13
24:20
25:6
25:11
25:29^2
25:30^3
25:31^2
26:10^3
27:1^3
27:12
28:8
28:10
28:11
28:15
28:19
29:9
30:8^2
30:23
30:24^2

2 SA

2:1^2
2:26^2
3:12
3:39
4:11
5:8^2
5:19
5:24
6:9
6:22
7:10
7:12
7:13
7:14
7:15
7:16
9:10^2
9:11^2
11:11
12:5
12:6
12:10
12:11
12:14
12:23^2
13:13
14:7^2
14:10
14:17
14:18
15:8
15:10
15:14
15:15
15:21
15:25
15:35
15:36
16:3
16:10
16:20
16:21^2
17:2
17:3
17:6
17:10
17:12^3
17:13
17:21
17:22
19:37
19:38^2
20:6
20:18
20:21
21:2^2
21:4
21:17
22:4
22:44
22:45^2
22:46^2
23:4
23:6
23:7
24:13^2

1 KI

1:13^2
1:17^2
1:20
1:21^3
1:24^2
1:30
1:33^2
1:52^3
2:4
2:24
2:32
2:33^2
2:37^2
2:44
2:45^2
3:5
3:12
3:13
5:5
5:6
5:9
8:19^2
8:25
8:29
8:30
8:33
8:38
8:42^2
8:44
8:47
8:59
9:3
9:5
9:6
9:7
9:8^3
9:9
11:2^2
11:32
11:38
12:10
12:24
12:26
12:27^2
13:2^3
13:3^2
13:22
13:32
14:3^2
14:5^2
14:11^2
14:12
14:13^2
14:14^2
14:15^3
14:16
16:4^2
17:1
17:4
17:14^2
18:12^3
18:24
18:31
19:17^3
20:6^3
20:10
20:14
20:23
20:25
20:28
20:36
20:39
20:40
20:42
21:19
21:23
21:24^2
22:6^3
22:12
22:15^3
22:16
22:20

2 KI

1:2
2:9
2:10^2
2:16
2:21
3:8
3:17^3
3:19^2
4:2
4:10^2
4:23
4:43^2
5:8
5:10
5:17
5:27
6:8
6:15
6:21^2
6:27
6:31
7:1
7:4^3
7:12
7:18
8:1
8:8
8:9
8:10
9:8
9:10^2
9:36
9:37^2
10:4
10:10
10:18
10:19^2
10:24
10:30
11:5^2
11:6^2
11:7
11:8
12:5
14:6^2
15:12
16:15
17:12
17:35
17:36^3
17:37^2
17:38^2
17:39^2
18:22
18:29
18:30
19:6
19:7^2
19:10^2
19:29^3
19:30
19:31^2
19:32
19:33^2
20:8^2
20:9
20:17^2
20:18^3
21:12
21:14
22:17^2
22:18
22:20
23:27
25:24

1 CH

11:6
11:19
12:17
13:12
14:10
14:15
16:30
16:33
17:9^{24}
17:11^2
17:12
17:13
17:14
17:27
21:12
22:9^3
22:10^2
23:26
28:6
28:21^2

2 CH

1:7
1:12
2:8
2:9
2:14
6:9^2
6:16
6:21
6:24
6:29^3
7:14
7:15
7:16
7:18
7:19
7:21^2
7:22
8:11
10:10
11:4
12:7
12:8
13:12
15:7
18:5^2
18:11
18:14^3
18:15
18:19
19:9
19:10^3
19:11^2
20:16
20:17
20:20^2
23:3
23:4^2
23:5^2
23:6^2
23:7^2
25:4^3
25:8
25:9
26:18
28:13
30:9^2
32:11
32:12
32:15
32:17
33:4
34:25^2
34:26
34:28
35:3

EZR

4:21
6:8
6:11
6:12
7:18
7:20
7:21
7:24
9:10

NE

2:6
2:8
4:3
4:11
4:12
4:20
5:8
6:7
6:9
9:29
10:38^2
10:39
13:25
13:27

ES

1:15
1:17^3
1:18^2
1:20^3
4:11^2
4:14^2
5:3
5:6^2
5:8
6:6
6:9
6:11
7:2^2
8:6
9:12^2

JOB

1:21
2:10^2
4:17^2
5:19^2
5:20
5:23
5:24
5:25
7:4
7:7
7:8
7:9
7:10^2
7:13^2
7:20
7:21^2
8:2
8:10
8:13
8:14^2
8:15^4
8:18
8:19
8:22^2
9:14
9:19
9:20^2
9:31^2
10:21
11:3
11:17
11:19^2
11:20^3
12:2
12:7^2
12:8^2
13:11
13:16^2
13:18
13:19
14:6
14:12
14:14
14:22^2
15:21
15:22
15:24^2
15:29^3
15:30^3
15:31
15:32^2
15:33^2
15:34^2
16:3
16:22^2
17:5
17:8^2
17:9^2
17:15
17:16
18:4^2
18:5^2
18:6^2
18:7^2
18:9^2
18:11^2
18:12^2
18:13^2
18:14^2
18:15^2
18:16^2
18:17^2
18:18
18:19
18:20
19:25
19:26
19:27^2
20:7^2
20:8^3
20:9^2
20:10^2
20:11
20:15^2
20:16^2
20:17
20:18^4
20:20^2
20:21^2
20:22^2
20:23^2
20:24^2
20:26^3
20:27^2
20:28^2
21:19
21:20^2
21:22
21:26^2
21:30
21:31^2
21:32^2
21:33^2
22:21
22:25
22:27
22:28^2
22:29
22:30
23:10
24:15
24:20^4
27:4
27:6
27:13
27:14
27:15^2
27:17^2
27:19^2
27:22
27:23
28:12
28:15
28:17
28:18
28:19^2
29:18^2
31:14^2
33:3^2
33:7^2
33:25^2
33:26^2
33:28
33:33
34:11
34:15^2
34:17
34:20^3
34:24
36:4
36:11
36:12^2
37:19
37:20^2
38:11
38:15
40:2
40:4
41:6^2
41:9
42:8

PS

1:3^3
1:5
1:6
2:4^2
2:5
2:8
5:4
5:5
6:5
7:7
7:8
7:16^2
9:3
9:7
9:8^2
9:17
9:18^2
10:6^2
11:6^2
12:3
13:2^2
13:5
14:7^2
15:1^2
15:5
16:4
16:8
16:9
17:3
17:15
18:3
18:43
18:44^2
18:45
19:13^2
21:1^2
21:7
21:8^2
21:9^2
22:25
22:26^3
22:27^2
22:29^2
22:30^2
22:31^2
23:1
23:6
24:3^2
24:5
24:7
24:9
25:12^2
25:13^2
25:15
26:1
27:1^2
27:3
27:5^3
27:6
27:14
28:5
30:6
30:9^2
31:24
32:6^2
32:10^2
33:17
33:21
34:1
34:2^2
34:10
34:21^2
34:22

35:9[2]
35:10
35:28
36:8
36:9
36:12
37:2
37:4
37:5
37:6
37:9[2]
37:10[2]
37:11[2]
37:13
37:15[2]
37:17
37:18
37:19[2]
37:20[4]
37:22[2]
37:24
37:28
37:29
37:31
37:34
37:38[2]
37:40[2]
39:6
40:3[2]
41:2
41:5
41:8
42:2
42:5
42:8
42:11
43:5
44:6
44:21
45:4
45:11
45:12[2]
45:14[2]
45:15[2]
45:16
45:17
46:4
46:5[2]
47:3
47:4
49:3[2]
49:5
49:11
49:14[3]
49:15
49:17[2]
49:19[2]
50:3[4]
50:4
50:6
51:7[2]
51:13
51:14
51:15
51:19
52:5[2]
52:6[2]
53:6[2]
54:5
55:16
55:17
55:19
55:22[2]
55:23
56:7
56:9
57:3[2]
58:9
58:10[2]
58:11
59:10[2]
60:12[2]
61:7
62:2
62:3[2]
62:6
63:3
63:5[2]
63:9
63:10[2]
63:11[3]
64:5
64:7[2]
64:8[2]
64:9[3]
64:10[3]
65:1
65:2
65:4
66:3
66:4[3]
67:6[2]
67:7[2]
68:13
68:21
68:29
68:31[2]
69:31
69:32[2]
69:36[2]
71:6
71:15
71:23
71:24
72:2
72:3
72:4[3]
72:5
72:6
72:7
72:8
72:9[2]
72:10[2]
72:11[2]
72:12
72:13[2]
72:14[2]
72:15[4]
72:16[3]
72:17[4]
73:27
74:10[2]
75:2
75:8
75:10
76:10
76:12
79:5
80:3
80:7
80:19
81:9
82:7
85:11[2]
85:12[2]
85:13[2]
86:9
87:5[2]
87:6
87:7
88:10
88:11
88:12
88:13
89:2
89:5
89:12
89:14
89:15
89:16[2]
89:17
89:21[2]
89:22
89:24[2]
89:26
89:28
89:36
89:37
89:46
89:48[2]
91:1
91:3
91:4[2]
91:7[2]
91:10[2]
91:11
91:12
91:15
92:7
92:9[2]
92:10
92:11[2]
92:12[2]
92:13
92:14[2]
94:3[2]
94:4
94:7[2]
94:9[2]
94:10[2]
94:15[2]
94:20
94:23[3]
96:10[2]
96:12
96:13
98:9
101:3
101:4
101:6[2]
101:7[2]
102:15
102:16[2]
102:18[3]
102:26[3]
102:28[2]
103:16
104:12
104:31[2]
104:34
107:42[2]
107:43
108:13[2]
109:7
110:2
110:3
110:5
110:6[3]
110:7[2]
112:2[2]
112:3
112:6[2]
112:7
112:8
132:12[2]
132:16
132:18
137:4
137:8
137:9
138:4
138:5
138:7
139:10[2]
139:11[2]
140:11
140:13[2]
141:5[4]
142:7
143:2
144:5
145:4[2]
145:6
145:7[2]
145:10[2]
145:11
145:21
146:9
148:6

PR

1:5
1:9
1:13[2]
1:28[2]
1:31
1:32[2]
1:33[3]
2:11[2]
2:21[2]
2:22[2]
3:2
3:6
3:8
3:10[2]
3:22
3:23
3:24
3:26[2]
3:35[2]
4:6[2]
4:8[2]
4:9[2]
4:10
4:12
5:22[2]
5:23[2]
6:11
6:15[2]
6:22[3]
6:29
6:31[2]
6:33[2]
8:6
8:7
8:17
8:35
9:11[2]
10:7
10:8
10:9
10:10
10:24[2]
10:27
10:28[2]
10:29
10:30[2]
10:31
11:3[2]
11:5[2]
11:6[2]
11:7
11:9
11:15
11:18
11:21[2]
11:25[2]
11:26[2]
11:27
11:28[2]
11:29[2]
11:31
12:3[2]
12:6
12:7
12:8[2]
12:11
12:13
12:14[2]
12:19
12:21[2]
12:24[2]
13:2[2]
13:3
13:4
13:9
13:11[2]
13:13
13:18[2]
13:20[2]
13:21
13:25
14:3
14:11[2]
14:14[2]
14:22
14:26
15:10
15:27
16:3
16:5
16:20
16:21
17:2[2]
17:5
17:11
17:13
18:20
18:21
19:5[2]
19:9[2]
19:15
19:16
19:19
19:21
19:23[2]
20:4
20:17
20:20
20:21
20:22
21:7
21:13[2]
21:15
21:16
21:17[2]
21:18
21:28
22:5
22:8[2]
22:9
22:10[2]
22:11
22:13
22:14
22:15
22:16
22:18
22:29[2]
23:11
23:13
23:15
23:16
23:18
23:21[2]
23:24[2]
23:25[2]
23:33[2]
23:35
24:4
24:8
24:12
24:14[2]
24:16
24:20[2]
24:22
24:24[2]
24:25[2]
24:26
24:34
25:4
25:5
25:22
26:2
26:26
26:27
27:14
27:18[2]
28:2
28:8
28:9
28:10[2]
28:13[2]
28:14
28:16
28:17
28:18[2]
28:19[2]
28:20[2]
28:22
28:23
28:25
28:26
28:27[2]
29:1
29:14
29:16
29:17[2]
29:21
29:23[2]
29:25
30:17[2]
31:11
31:25
31:30

EC

1:9[2]
1:11[2]
2:16
2:18
2:19[2]
2:21
3:14
3:17
3:22[2]
4:12
4:15
4:16
5:10
5:15[2]
5:16
5:20
6:4
6:12
7:18
7:26[2]
8:1
8:5
8:7[2]
8:8
8:12
8:13[2]
8:15
8:17[2]
9:5
10:8[2]
10:9[2]
10:14[2]
10:20[2]
11:2
11:3
11:4[2]
11:6[2]
11:8
12:3[2]
12:4[3]
12:5[5]
12:7[2]
12:14

CA

1:13
5:3[2]
7:8[2]
8:8[2]

ISA

1:18[2]
1:19
1:20
1:27
1:28[2]
1:29[2]
1:30
1:31[3]
2:2[4]
2:3[3]
2:4[5]
2:11[3]
2:12[2]
2:17[3]
2:18
2:19
2:20
3:4
3:5[2]
3:6
3:7
3:10[2]
3:11[2]
3:24[2]
3:25
3:26[2]
4:1
4:2[2]
4:3[2]
4:4[2]
4:5
4:6
5:5[2]
5:6[2]
5:9
5:10[2]
5:14
5:15[2]
5:16[2]
5:17[2]
5:24[2]
5:26
5:27[3]
5:28
5:29[5]
5:30
6:8
6:13[4]
7:7[2]
7:8
7:9
7:14[3]
7:15
7:16[2]
7:17
7:18[2]
7:19[2]
7:20[2]
7:21[2]
7:22[4]
7:23[3]
7:24[2]
7:25[3]
8:4[2]
8:7
8:8[4]
8:9[3]
8:10[2]
8:12
8:14
8:15
8:19
8:21[4]
8:22[2]
9:1
9:5
9:6[2]
9:7
9:9
9:11
9:12
9:17[2]
9:18[3]
9:19[2]
9:20[4]
9:21
10:3
10:4[2]
10:11
10:15[2]
10:16[2]
10:17[2]
10:18[2]
10:19
10:20[3]
10:21
10:22
10:23
10:24[2]
10:25
10:26[2]
10:27[3]
10:32[2]
10:33[3]
10:34[2]
11:1[2]
11:2
11:3[2]
11:4[3]
11:5
11:6[3]
11:7[3]
11:8[2]
11:9[2]
11:10[4]
11:11[3]
11:12[2]
11:13[4]
11:14[4]
11:15[3]
11:16[2]
12:3
12:4
13:6
13:7[2]
13:8[5]
13:9
13:10[3]
13:13
13:14[2]
13:15[2]
13:16[2]
13:17[2]
13:18[3]
13:19
13:20[4]
13:21[4]
13:22[2]
14:1[2]
14:2[4]
14:3[2]
14:10
14:16
14:20
14:24[2]
14:25
14:27[2]
14:29[2]
14:30[3]
14:31[2]
14:32[2]
15:2[2]
15:3[2]
15:4[4]
15:5[4]
15:6
15:7
15:9
16:2[2]
16:5[2]
16:6
16:7[3]
16:10[3]
16:11
16:12[3]
16:14
17:1
17:2[3]
17:3[2]
17:4[3]
17:5[2]
17:6
17:7[2]
17:8[2]
17:9[2]
17:11
17:13[4]
18:5
18:6[3]
18:7
19:1[3]
19:2
19:3[2]
19:4
19:5[2]
19:6[3]
19:7
19:8[3]
19:9
19:10
19:15
19:16[2]
19:17[2]
19:18[2]
19:19
19:20[4]
19:21[4]
19:22[5]
19:23[3]
19:24
19:25
20:4
20:5
20:6[2]
21:13
21:16
21:17
22:7[3]
22:13
22:14
22:18
22:19
22:20
22:21
22:22[4]
22:23
22:24
22:25[2]
23:5
23:7
23:15[3]
23:17[3]
23:18[3]
24:2
24:3
24:9[2]
24:13[2]
24:14[3]
24:18[3]
24:20[4]
24:21[2]
24:22[3]
24:23[2]
25:2
25:3[2]
25:5
25:6
25:8
25:9
25:10[2]
25:11[2]
25:12
26:1
26:6
26:11[2]
26:14[2]
26:19[3]
26:21[2]
27:1[2]
27:5
27:6[2]
27:9[2]
27:10[3]
27:11
27:12[3]
27:13[4]
28:2
28:3
28:4
28:5
28:9[2]
28:15[2]
28:16
28:17[2]
28:18[4]
28:19[3]
28:21[2]
29:2[2]
29:4[3]
29:5[3]
29:7
29:8[2]
29:14[2]
29:16[3]
29:17[2]
29:18[2]
29:19[2]
29:22[2]
29:23[2]
29:24[2]
30:2
30:6
30:7
30:13
30:14[3]
30:15[2]
30:16[2]
30:17[2]
30:19[2]
30:20[2]
30:21
30:22
30:23[3]
30:24
30:25
30:26[2]
30:28[2]
30:29
30:30[2]
30:31
30:32[3]
31:3
31:4
31:7
31:8[4]
31:9[2]
32:1[2]
32:2
32:3[2]
32:4[2]
32:5
32:8
32:10[3]
32:12
32:13
32:14[3]
32:16
32:17
32:18
32:19[2]
33:1
33:4[2]
33:6
33:7[2]
33:11[3]
33:12[2]
33:14[2]
33:16[4]
33:17[2]
33:18
33:20[4]
33:21[2]
33:24[2]
34:3[3]
34:4[3]
34:5[2]
34:7[2]
34:9[2]
34:10[4]
34:11[3]
34:12[3]
34:13[2]
34:14[3]
34:15[2]
34:16[2]
34:17[2]
35:1
35:2[3]
35:5[2]
35:6[2]
35:7[2]
35:8[5]
35:9[4]
35:10[3]
36:7
36:14
36:15
37:6
37:7
37:10[2]
37:30[2]
37:31
37:32[2]
37:33
37:34[2]
38:7
38:10
38:11[2]
38:15[2]
38:19[2]
38:21
38:22
39:6[2]
39:7[3]
39:8
40:4[3]
40:5[2]
40:6
40:8
40:10
40:11[3]
41:20
41:24[2]
41:25
41:30[2]
41:31[4]
41:11[3]
41:12
41:16[2]
41:22
41:25[3]
41:27
42:1
42:2
42:3[3]
42:4[2]
42:13[4]
42:17[2]
43:2[2]
43:10
43:13
43:17[2]
43:19[2]
43:20
43:21
44:4
44:5[3]
44:7[3]
44:9
44:11[3]
44:15
44:19[2]
44:26
44:28[2]
45:1
45:9
45:13[2]
45:14[3]
45:16[2]
45:17[2]
45:23[3]
45:24[3]
45:25[2]
46:7[2]
46:10
46:13[2]
47:3[2]
47:7
47:8[2]
47:9[2]
47:11[3]
47:13
47:14[4]
47:15[3]
48:14
48:15
49:5[2]
49:7
49:9[4]
49:10[4]
49:11
49:12
49:17[2]
49:19[2]
49:20
49:22[2]
49:23[3]
49:24
49:25[2]
49:26[2]
50:7[2]
50:9[3]
50:11[2]
51:3[2]
51:4
51:5[3]
51:6[3]
51:8[3]
51:11[4]
51:12[2]
51:19[2]
52:1
52:3
52:6[2]
52:8[4]
52:10
52:12
52:13[2]
52:15[4]
53:2[2]
53:8
53:10[2]
53:11[4]
53:12
54:3
54:5
54:10[3]
54:13[2]
54:14
54:15[3]
54:17[2]
55:3
55:5
55:11[4]
55:12[3]
55:13[4]
56:5
56:7[2]
56:12
57:2
57:12
57:13[4]
57:14
58:4
58:8[4]
58:9[2]
58:10
58:11
58:12[2]
59:6[2]
59:8
59:19[3]
59:20
59:21
60:2[3]
60:3
60:4[2]
60:5[3]
60:6[4]
60:7[3]
60:9
60:10[2]
60:11[2]
60:12[2]
60:13
60:14[3]
60:18
60:19[3]
60:20[4]
60:21[2]
60:22
61:4[3]
61:5[2]
61:6[4]
61:7[4]
61:9[2]
61:10
62:2[2]
62:4[2]
62:5[2]
62:6
62:8
62:9[2]
62:12
63:3
64:5
65:9[2]
65:10
65:12
65:13[6]
65:14[3]
65:15[2]
65:16[2]
65:17
65:19
65:20[3]
65:21[2]
65:22[3]
65:23
65:24
65:25[4]
66:5[2]
66:8[2]
66:9[2]
66:12[2]
66:13
66:14[3]
66:16
66:17
66:18[2]
66:19
66:20
66:22[2]
66:23[2]
66:24[4]

JER

1:7
1:14
1:15[2]
1:19[2]
2:3[2]
2:19[2]
2:24
2:35
3:1[2]
3:15
3:16[6]
3:17[3]
3:18[2]
3:19
4:2[2]
4:7
4:9[4]
4:10
4:11
4:12
4:13[2]
4:14
4:21
4:27
4:28
4:29[3]
5:6[4]
5:7
5:9[2]
5:12[2]
5:13[2]
5:14
5:17[4]
5:19[3]
5:29[2]
6:3[3]
6:9
6:10
6:11
6:12
6:15[2]
6:16
6:21[2]
6:22
6:23
6:26
6:30
7:20[3]
7:23
7:32[2]
7:33[2]
7:34
8:1
8:2[3]
8:3
8:4[2]
8:10
8:12[2]
8:13[3]
8:17
9:7
9:9[2]
9:22[2]
10:10[2]
10:11[2]
10:15
10:21[2]
11:4
11:11[2]
11:12[2]
11:22[2]
11:23
12:4[2]
12:12[2]
12:13[3]
12:15
12:16[2]
13:10
13:12[3]
13:17[2]
13:18
13:19[4]
13:21[2]
13:27
14:13[2]
14:15[2]
14:16[2]
15:2[2]
15:5[3]
15:11
15:12
15:14
15:20[2]
16:4[6]
16:6[3]
16:7[2]
16:10[2]
16:13
16:14
16:16[2]
16:19[2]
16:20
16:21
17:4
17:6[3]
17:8[5]
17:11[2]
17:13[2]
17:14[2]
17:24
17:25[2]
17:26
17:27[2]
18:7
18:9
18:14
18:16
18:18
18:20
19:2
19:3
19:6
19:8
19:9[2]
19:11
19:13
20:4[4]
20:5
20:6
20:10[2]
20:11[5]
21:3
21:6
21:7[2]
21:9[3]
21:10[2]
21:13[2]
21:14
22:4
22:5
22:7
22:8[2]
22:9
22:10
22:11
22:12[2]
22:18[2]
22:19
22:22[2]
22:26
22:27
22:30[2]
23:3
23:4[3]
23:5[2]
23:6[3]
23:7
23:8
23:12[2]
23:17[2]
23:19
23:20[2]
23:24
23:26
23:32
23:33
23:34
23:35
23:36[2]
23:38
23:40
24:7[2]
24:9
25:11[2]
25:12
25:14
25:16
25:26
25:28[2]
25:29
25:30[3]
25:31
25:32[2]
25:33[3]
25:34
25:35
25:36
26:9[2]
26:15
26:18[2]
27:4
27:7[2]
27:8
27:9
27:11
27:14
27:16
27:22[2]
28:9
28:14
29:7
29:12[2]
29:13[2]
29:21
29:22
29:32[2]
30:3
30:7
30:8[2]
30:9
30:10[3]
30:16[3]
30:18[2]
30:19[3]
30:20[2]
30:21[3]
30:22
30:23
30:24[2]
31:1
31:5[2]
31:6[2]
31:8
31:9[2]
31:12[4]
31:13
31:14
31:16[2]
31:17
31:18
31:22
31:23[2]
31:24
31:28
31:29
31:30[2]
31:33[2]
31:34[2]
31:36
31:38
31:39[2]
31:40[2]
32:3
32:4[4]
32:5[3]
32:7
32:15
32:28
32:29
32:36
32:38
32:40
32:43
32:44
33:9[3]
33:10[2]
33:11[2]
33:12
33:13
33:15
33:16[3]
33:17
33:18
34:2
34:3[2]
34:5
34:20
34:22
35:6
35:7[2]
35:15
35:19
36:29[2]
36:30[2]
37:7[2]
37:8
37:9[2]
37:19
38:2[4]
38:3[2]
38:17[2]
38:18[2]
38:20[3]
38:22[2]
38:23
39:12
39:16
39:18
40:9
40:15
42:4[2]
42:5
42:14
42:16[4]
42:17[3]
42:18[4]
42:20
42:22
43:10
43:11
43:12[3]
43:13[2]
44:12[4]
44:14[3]
44:26
44:27
44:28[3]
44:29[2]
46:6
46:10[2]
46:14
46:18
46:19
46:22[2]
46:23
46:24[2]
46:26
46:27[2]
47:2[4]
47:3
48:2
48:3
48:5
48:7
48:8[4]
48:9
48:12[2]
48:13
48:18[2]
48:26[2]
48:30[2]
48:31
48:33[2]
48:34
48:36[2]
48:37[2]
48:38
48:39[2]
48:40[2]
48:41
48:42
48:43
48:44[2]
48:45[2]
49:2[3]
49:3
49:4
49:5[2]
49:10
49:12
49:13[2]
49:17[3]
49:18[2]
49:19
49:20[2]
49:22[2]
49:26[2]
49:27
49:28
49:29[3]
49:32
49:33[2]
49:36[2]
49:39
50:3[4]
50:4[2]
50:5[2]
50:9[4]
50:10[2]
50:12[3]
50:13[3]
50:16[2]
50:19[2]
50:20[3]
50:30[2]
50:32[3]
50:34
50:36[2]
50:37[2]
50:38
50:39[4]
50:40[2]
50:41[2]
50:42[3]
50:44
50:45[2]
51:2[3]
51:4
51:14
51:18
51:26
51:29[2]
51:31
51:33
51:35[2]
51:37
51:38[2]
51:44[2]
51:46[3]
51:47[2]
51:48[2]
51:49
51:52
51:53
51:56
51:57
51:58[4]
51:62[2]
51:63
51:64[3]

LA

1:21
2:13[3]
2:20[2]
4:15
4:20
4:21
5:21

EZE

2:5
3:18
3:19
3:20[3]
3:21
3:25[2]
4:3[2]
4:7
4:13
4:16[2]
5:4
5:10[2]
5:11
5:12[3]
5:13[2]
5:15[2]
5:16[2]
5:17[2]
6:2
6:4[2]
6:6[2]
6:7[2]
6:8[2]
6:9[3]
6:10
6:11
6:12[3]
6:13[2]
6:14
7:4[3]
7:9[2]
7:11[2]
7:13[3]
7:15[2]
7:16[2]
7:17[2]
7:18[3]
7:19[4]
7:21
7:22[2]
7:24[2]
7:25[2]
7:26[4]
7:27[4]
8:18
9:10
11:10[2]
11:11[2]
11:12
11:16
11:18[2]
11:20
12:11[2]
12:12[4]
12:13[3]
12:15[2]
12:16
12:19
12:20[3]
12:23
12:24
12:25[3]
12:28[2]
13:9[5]
13:11[4]
13:12
13:13
13:14[4]
13:21[2]
13:23[2]
14:8
14:10[2]
14:16[3]
14:18[2]
14:20[2]
14:22[5]
14:23[2]
15:3

15:5 15:7[3] 16:16[2] 16:39[4] 16:40 16:41 16:42 16:44 16:53 16:55[3] 17:9[3] 17:10[3] 17:15[3] 17:16 17:17 17:18 17:20 17:21[3] 17:23[3] 17:24 18:3 18:4 18:9 18:13[4] 18:17[2] 18:18 18:19 18:20[5] 18:21[2] 18:22[2] 18:24[3] 18:26 18:27 18:28[2] 18:30 19:14 20:11 20:13 20:20 20:21 20:31 20:32 20:38[2] 20:40 20:42[2] 20:43[2] 20:44 20:47[3] 20:48[2] 21:4 21:5 21:7[6] 21:12[3] 21:13 21:19 21:23 21:24 21:25 21:26 21:27 21:29 21:30 22:5 22:14 22:21 22:22[2] 23:24[3] 23:25[5] 23:26 23:29[4] 23:45 23:47[2] 23:49[3] 24:12 24:14[2] 24:16 24:21 24:22[2] 24:23[3] 24:24[2] 24:25 24:26 24:27[2] 25:4[3] 25:5 25:11 25:13

25:14[2] 25:17[2] 26:2 26:4 26:5[2] 26:6[2] 26:8[2] 26:9 26:10[3] 26:11[3] 26:12[3] 26:13 26:15 26:16[4] 26:17 26:18[2] 26:19[3] 26:20[3] 27:27 27:28 27:29[2] 27:30[4] 27:31[2] 27:32 27:34 27:35[3] 27:36 28:7[2] 28:8 28:18 28:19 28:22[3] 28:23[2] 28:24[2] 28:25[3] 28:26[4] 29:4 29:6 29:9[2] 29:11[3] 29:12 29:14 29:15[3] 29:16[3] 29:19[2] 29:21 30:3 30:4[5] 30:5 30:6[3] 30:7[2] 30:8[2] 30:9[2] 30:11[2] 30:13 30:16[3] 30:17[2] 30:18[5] 30:19 30:21 30:24 30:25[4] 30:26 31:11 31:13[2] 31:16 32:3 32:6 32:7[2] 32:9 32:10[3] 32:11 32:12[2] 32:13 32:15[4] 32:16[3] 32:20 32:21 32:27[2] 32:29 32:31[2] 32:32 33:4 33:5[2] 33:8 33:9 33:12[3]

33:13[4] 33:15[2] 33:16[2] 33:18 33:19 33:25 33:26 33:27[2] 33:28[3] 33:29 33:33 34:10 34:14[3] 34:22 34:23[3] 34:25 34:26 34:27[4] 34:28[4] 34:29 34:30 35:6[2] 35:8 35:9[2] 35:10 35:15 36:7 36:8 36:9 36:10[2] 36:11[2] 36:12 36:23[2] 36:25 36:27 36:28[2] 36:30 36:31[2] 36:33[2] 36:34 36:35 36:36 36:38[2] 37:5 37:6[2] 37:13 37:14[4] 37:17 37:18 37:19 37:20 37:22[3] 37:23[2] 37:24[3] 37:25[3] 37:26 37:27[2] 37:28[2] 38:8 38:10[2] 38:13 38:16[2] 38:18[3] 38:19 38:20[4] 38:21 38:23 39:6 39:7 39:9[3] 39:10[3] 39:11[4] 39:12 39:13[3] 39:14[2] 39:15 39:16[2] 39:18 39:19 39:20 39:21 39:22 39:23 39:28 40:4 42:13[2] 42:14[4]

43:7 43:12 43:13[3] 43:14[2] 43:15[2] 43:16 43:17[4] 43:18 43:21 43:22 43:24[2] 43:25 43:26[2] 43:27[2] 44:2[4] 44:3[3] 44:9 44:10 44:11[3] 44:12 44:13[2] 44:14 44:15[2] 44:16[3] 44:17[3] 44:18[3] 44:19[3] 44:20[2] 44:21 44:22[2] 44:23 44:24[4] 44:25 44:26 44:27 44:28[2] 44:29[2] 44:30[2] 44:31 45:1[5] 45:2 45:3 45:4[3] 45:6[2] 45:7[2] 45:8[3] 45:10 45:11[2] 45:12[2] 45:13[2] 45:14 45:16 45:17[2] 45:19 45:20 45:21[2] 45:22 45:23 45:24 45:25 46:1[3] 46:2[6] 46:3 46:4[2] 46:5[2] 46:6[2] 46:7[2] 46:8[3] 46:9[5] 46:10[2] 46:11 46:12[5] 46:15 46:16[2] 46:17[3] 46:18 46:20[2] 46:24 47:8 47:9[7] 47:10[4] 47:11[2] 47:12[5] 47:13[3] 47:14[2] 47:15 47:17

47:18 47:20 47:21 47:22[5] 47:23[2] 48:8[3] 48:9[2] 48:10[2] 48:11 48:12 48:13[2] 48:14 48:15[2] 48:16 48:17 48:18[3] 48:19 48:20[2] 48:21[3] 48:22 48:23 48:24 48:28 48:29 48:31 48:35

DA

1:10 2:5[2] 2:6 2:9 2:28 2:29 2:30 2:39[2] 2:40[2] 2:41[2] 2:42 2:43[2] 2:44[5] 2:45 3:6 3:10[2] 3:15[2] 3:29[2] 4:25[5] 4:26 4:32[4] 5:7[3] 6:5 6:7[2] 6:12[2] 6:26[2] 7:14[2] 7:17 7:18 7:23[4] 7:24[4] 7:25[3] 7:26[2] 7:27[2] 8:13 8:14 8:17 8:19[2] 8:22 8:23 8:24[4] 8:25[5] 8:26 9:25[2] 9:26[4] 9:27[2] 10:14 10:20 11:2[3] 11:3[2] 11:4[4] 11:5[3] 11:6[5] 11:7[5] 11:8[2] 11:9[2] 11:10[4] 11:11[4] 11:12[3] 11:13[3] 11:14[3] 11:15[3] 11:16[4] 11:17[4] 11:18[4] 11:19[2] 11:20[2] 11:21[3] 11:22[2] 11:23[3] 11:24[4] 11:25[4] 11:26[3] 11:27[4] 11:28[3] 11:29[2] 11:30[4] 11:31[4] 11:32[2] 11:33[2] 11:34[3] 11:35 11:36[5] 11:37[2] 11:38[2] 11:39[4] 11:40[4] 11:41[3] 11:42[3] 11:43[2] 11:44[2] 11:45[2] 12:1[4] 12:2 12:3 12:4[2] 12:6 12:7[3] 12:8 12:10[4] 12:11[2]

HO

1:5 1:10[3] 1:11[3] 2:6 2:7[5] 2:10 2:12 2:15 2:16 2:17 2:21[2] 2:22[2] 2:23 3:4 3:5[2] 4:3[3] 4:5 4:9 4:10[3] 4:13[2] 4:14 4:19 5:5[2] 5:6[2] 5:7 5:9[2] 5:14 6:2 6:3[2] 6:4[2] 7:12 7:16[2] 8:1 8:2 8:3 8:6 8:7[3] 8:8 8:10 8:11 8:13 8:14 9:2[2] 9:3[3] 9:4[5] 9:6[4] 9:7 9:11 9:12 9:13 9:16 9:17 10:2[3] 10:3 10:5[2] 10:6[3] 10:8[3] 10:10[2] 10:11[2] 10:14[2] 10:15[2] 11:5[2] 11:6[2] 11:8[4] 11:10[4] 11:11 12:8 12:14[2] 13:3 13:8 13:13 13:14 13:15[5] 13:16[4] 14:3 14:5 14:6[2] 14:7[3] 14:8 14:9[4]

JOE

1:15 2:2 2:3 2:4 2:5 2:6[2] 2:7[4] 2:8[3] 2:9[4] 2:10[4] 2:11 2:19 2:20[2] 2:24[2] 2:26[2] 2:27[2] 2:28[4] 2:31 2:32[5] 3:1 3:8 3:15[2] 3:16[2] 3:17[3] 3:18[6] 3:19[2] 3:20

AM

1:2[2] 1:4 1:5 1:7 1:8 1:10 1:12 1:14 1:15 2:2[2] 2:5 2:14[3] 2:15[3] 2:16 3:5 3:6[2] 3:11[3] 3:12 3:14[2] 3:15[2] 4:2 4:3[2] 5:2 5:3[2] 5:4 5:5[2] 5:6 5:9 5:11[2] 5:13 5:14 5:16[3] 5:17 5:20 6:7[2] 6:9[2] 6:10[4] 6:12 6:14 7:2 7:3 7:5 7:6 7:9[2] 7:11[2] 7:17[4] 8:3[4] 8:8[3] 8:9 8:12[3] 8:13 8:14 9:1[2] 9:2 9:3 9:4 9:5[4] 9:9 9:10[2] 9:13[3] 9:14[3] 9:15

OB

3 8 9 10 15[2] 16[4] 17[3] 18[3] 19[3] 20[2] 21[2]

JO

1:11 1:12 3:4

MIC

1:4[2] 1:7[3] 1:14 1:15 2:3[2] 2:4 2:5 2:6[2] 2:10 2:11 2:12 2:13 3:4 3:6[6] 3:7[2] 3:12[2] 4:1[4] 4:2[2] 4:3[4] 4:4[2] 4:7 4:8[2] 4:10 4:12 5:1 5:2 5:3 5:4[3] 5:5[4] 5:6[2] 5:7 5:8 5:9[2] 5:10 6:6[2] 6:7 6:9 6:11 6:14 6:16 7:4 7:8[2] 7:9 7:10[4] 7:11 7:12 7:13 7:16[2] 7:17[4]

NA

1:8 1:9 1:10 1:12[2] 1:15 2:3[2] 2:4[4] 2:5[4] 2:6[2] 2:7[3] 2:8[3] 2:13[2] 3:7[3] 3:12[2] 3:13[2] 3:15[3] 3:18 3:19

HAB

1:2 1:6 1:7 1:8[3] 1:9[3] 1:10[4] 1:11[2] 1:12 1:17 2:1 2:3 2:4 2:6 2:7[3] 2:8 2:11[2] 2:13[2] 2:14 2:16[2] 2:17 2:19 3:17[6]

ZEP

1:8 1:10[2] 1:12 1:13[3] 1:14 1:17[2] 1:18[3] 2:3 2:4[3] 2:5 2:6 2:7[4] 2:9[3] 2:10 2:11 2:12 2:14[5] 3:8 3:10 3:12 3:13[4] 3:16

HAG

2:7 2:9 2:12 2:13[2] 2:15 2:22

ZEC

1:16[2] 1:17[3] 2:4 2:9[2] 2:11[2] 2:12[2] 3:9 3:10 4:7 4:9 4:10[2] 5:3[2] 5:4[3] 5:11 6:12[2] 6:13[5] 6:14 6:15[3] 8:3 8:4 8:5 8:8[2] 8:12[4] 8:13[2] 8:16 8:19 8:20[2] 8:21 8:22 8:23[3] 9:1[2] 9:2 9:4 9:5[5] 9:6 9:7[2] 9:8 9:10[3] 9:14[4] 9:15[4] 9:16[2] 9:17 10:1 10:5[3] 10:6 10:7[4] 10:8 10:9[2] 10:10 10:11[5] 10:12 11:6 11:16[3] 11:17[3] 12:2 12:3 12:5[2] 12:6[2] 12:7 12:8[3] 12:9 12:10[3] 12:11 12:12 13:1 13:2[2] 13:3[4] 13:4[3] 13:5 13:6[2] 13:7 13:8[3] 13:9[2] 14:1 14:2[3] 14:3 14:4[4] 14:5[4] 14:6[2] 14:7[4] 14:8[3] 14:9[2] 14:10[2] 14:11[3] 14:12[4] 14:13[4] 14:14[2] 14:15[2] 14:16[2] 14:17[2] 14:18 14:19 14:20[2] 14:21[3]

MAL

1:4[2] 1:5[2] 1:11[3] 2:2 2:4 3:1[3] 3:2 3:3[2] 3:4 3:7 3:10 3:11[2] 3:12[2] 3:17 3:18 4:1[4] 4:2[2] 4:3[3] 4:6

MT

1:21[2] 1:23[3] 2:6[2] 2:23 3:11 4:4 4:6[2] 5:4 5:5 5:6 5:7 5:8 5:9 5:11[2] 5:13 5:18 5:19[5] 5:20[2] 5:21[2] 5:22[5] 5:31 5:32[2] 5:39 5:41 6:4 6:6 6:7 6:18 6:22 6:23 6:25[3] 6:30 6:31[3] 6:33 6:34 7:2[2] 7:7[3] 7:8 7:11 7:16 7:20 7:21 7:26 8:8 8:11[2] 8:12[2] 9:15[2] 9:18 9:21 10:11 10:14 10:15 10:18 10:19[3] 10:21[2] 10:22[2] 10:23 10:25 10:26[2] 10:29 10:32 10:33 10:36 10:39[2] 10:41[2] 10:42[2] 11:6 11:10 11:16 11:22 11:24 11:29 12:11[2] 12:18 12:19[2] 12:20[2] 12:21 12:25 12:26 12:27 12:31[2] 12:32[2] 12:36[2] 12:39 12:40 12:41[2] 12:42[2] 12:45 12:50 13:12[3] 13:14[4] 13:40 13:41[2] 13:42[2] 13:43 13:49[2] 13:50[2] 15:5 15:6 15:13 15:14 16:4 16:18 16:19[2] 16:22 16:25[2] 16:26[2] 16:27[2] 16:28 17:11 17:12 17:17[2] 17:20[3] 17:22 17:23[2] 18:3 18:4 18:5 18:6 18:15[2] 18:17 18:18[4] 18:19[3] 18:21 18:35 19:5[3] 19:9[2] 19:16 19:23 19:27 19:28[2] 19:29[2] 19:30[2] 20:7 20:16 20:18[2] 20:19[2] 20:22 20:23[2] 20:26 20:32 21:2 21:3 21:13 21:21[3] 21:22[2] 21:25 21:26 21:41 21:43 22:44[3] 22:9 22:13 22:24 22:28 23:11 23:12[4] 23:14 23:16[2] 23:18 23:20 23:21 23:22 23:34[2] 23:36 23:39[2] 24:2[2] 24:3[2] 24:5[2] 24:6 24:7[2] 24:9[3] 24:10[3] 24:11[2] 24:12[2] 24:13[2] 24:14[2] 24:15 24:21[2] 24:22 24:23 24:24[3] 24:26 24:27 24:29[4] 24:30[3] 24:31[2] 24:33 24:34 24:35[2] 24:37 24:39 24:40[2] 24:41[2] 24:46 24:47 24:48 24:49 24:50 24:51[2] 25:1 25:29[3] 25:30 25:31[2] 25:32[2] 25:33 25:34 25:37 25:40 25:41 25:44 25:45 25:46 26:13[2] 26:21 26:23 26:31[2] 26:33 26:48 26:52 26:53 26:54 26:64 27:22 27:64 28:7 28:10

MK

1:2 1:8 2:20[2] 3:28[2] 3:29 3:35 4:22 4:24[2] 4:25[2] 4:30[2] 5:23 5:28 6:11[2] 6:24 6:37 7:11[2] 8:12 8:35[2] 8:36[2] 8:37 8:38[2] 9:1 9:19[2] 9:31[2] 9:35 9:37[2] 9:39 9:41[2] 9:42 9:43 9:45 9:49[2] 10:7 10:8 10:11 10:12 10:15[2] 10:17 10:23 10:30 10:31 10:33[2] 10:34[5] 10:35 10:39[2] 10:40 10:43[2] 10:44 11:2 11:17 11:23[5] 11:24 11:31 11:32 12:7 12:9 12:15[2] 12:23[2] 12:25 12:40 13:2[2] 13:4[3] 13:6[2] 13:7[2] 13:8[3] 13:9[3] 13:11[3] 13:12[3] 13:13[3] 13:14 13:19[2] 13:21 13:22[2] 13:24[2] 13:25[2] 13:26 13:27[2] 13:29 13:30 13:31[2] 14:9[2] 14:13 14:14[2] 14:18 14:27[2] 14:29 14:32 14:44 14:62 15:12 16:3 16:7 16:16[2] 16:17[3] 16:18[4]

LU

1:13 1:14 1:15[3] 1:16 1:17 1:18 1:20[2] 1:32[3] 1:33[2] 1:34 1:35[4] 1:37 1:45 1:48 1:60 1:66 2:10 2:12[2] 2:23 2:34 2:35 3:5[4] 3:6 3:10 3:12 3:14 3:16 4:4 4:7 4:10 4:11 5:35[2] 5:37 6:21[2] 6:22[3] 6:25[2] 6:26 6:35[2] 6:37[3] 6:38[3] 6:39 6:40 7:7 7:23 7:27 7:31 8:17[2] 8:18[2] 8:50 9:24[2] 9:26[3] 9:27 9:41 9:44 9:48[3] 10:6[2] 10:12 10:14 10:19 10:25 10:42 11:5[2] 11:7 11:9[3] 11:10 11:11 11:12 11:13 11:18 11:19 11:22 11:29 11:30 11:31 11:32[2] 11:36 11:49 11:51 12:2[2] 12:3[2] 12:5 12:8[2] 12:9 12:10[3] 12:11[2] 12:12 12:17 12:20[2] 12:22[2] 12:29[2] 12:31 12:37[2] 12:38 12:42 12:43 12:45 12:47 12:48[2] 12:52 12:53 13:3 13:5 13:8 13:18 13:20 13:24 13:25 13:26 13:27 13:28[2] 13:29 13:30[2] 13:32 13:35[2] 14:5 14:11[2] 14:15 14:24 14:34 15:7 16:3 16:12 17:10 17:21 17:22[2] 17:23 17:24 17:26 17:30 17:31 17:33[4] 17:34[3] 17:35[2] 17:36[2] 18:7 18:8 18:14[2] 18:17[2] 18:18 18:24 18:30 18:31 18:32[2] 18:33[2] 18:41 19:26[2] 19:30 19:31 19:43[2] 19:44[2] 20:5 20:13 20:15 20:16[2] 20:18[2] 20:35 20:47 21:6[2] 21:7[2] 21:8 21:9 21:10 21:11[2] 21:12 21:13 21:14 21:15 21:16[2] 21:17 21:18 21:20 21:23 21:24[3] 21:25 21:26 21:27 21:32 21:33 21:35 21:36 22:10 22:11[2] 22:12 22:18 22:26 22:34 22:49 22:69 23:29 23:30 23:31

JOH

1:51 3:12 3:36 4:13 4:14[4] 4:21 4:23 4:25[2] 4:28 4:29 4:43 4:47 6:5 6:27 6:28 6:35[2] 6:37 6:45 6:51 6:57 6:58 6:62 6:68 7:17 7:34[2] 7:35 7:36[2] 7:38 7:41 8:12 8:21[2] 8:24[2] 8:28 8:32[2] 8:33 8:36[2] 8:51 8:52 8:55 9:21 10:9[2] 10:16 10:28 11:12 11:23 11:24 11:25 11:26 11:48 12:25[2] 12:26 12:27 12:31 12:48 13:21 13:26 13:32[2] 13:33 13:35 13:38 14:12[2] 14:13 14:14 14:16 14:17 14:19 14:20 14:21 14:26 15:7[2] 15:8 15:10 15:16 15:26 15:27 16:2 16:4 16:13[3] 16:14[3] 16:15[2] 16:16[2] 16:17[2] 16:19[2] 16:20[4] 16:22 16:23[2] 16:24 16:25[2] 16:26 16:32[2] 16:33 17:20 18:11 19:15 19:24 19:36 19:37 20:25 21:6 21:18 21:21 21:23

AC 1:5 1:8[2] 1:11 2:17[4] 2:18 2:20 2:21[3] 2:26 2:37 2:38 2:39 3:19 3:20 3:22[3] 3:23[2] 3:25 4:16 5:9 6:14[2] 7:3 7:7[2] 7:37[2] 8:33 9:6 10:6 10:32 10:43 11:14[2] 11:16 13:22 13:41 15:11 15:27 15:29 18:10 19:39 20:22 20:25 20:29 20:30 21:11[2] 22:10[2] 23:3 24:15 24:22 26:2 27:22 27:25 27:34 28:26[3]

RO 1:17 2:12[2] 2:13 2:16 2:26 2:27 3:3 3:5 3:6 3:20 3:30 4:1 4:18 4:24 5:9 5:10 5:17 5:19 6:1[2] 6:2 6:5 6:8 6:14 6:15 7:3 7:7 7:24 8:11 8:13[2] 8:18 8:21 8:31 8:32 8:33 8:35[2] 8:39 9:7 9:9 9:12 9:14 9:20 9:26[2] 9:27 9:30 9:33 10:5 10:6 10:7 10:11 10:13[2] 10:14[3] 10:15 11:15 11:22 11:24 11:26[3] 11:27 11:35 13:2 14:4 14:10 14:11[2] 14:12 15:12[3] 15:21[2] 15:29 16:20

1 CO 1:8 3:8 3:13[4] 3:14 3:15[3] 3:17 4:5 4:17 4:21 6:2[2] 6:3 6:5 6:9 6:10 6:13 6:15 6:16 7:28 8:10 8:11 9:11 11:22[2] 11:27[2] 12:15 12:16 13:8[3] 13:10 13:12 14:6[2] 14:7 14:8 14:9[2] 14:11[2] 14:16 15:22 15:24[2] 15:26 15:28[2] 15:29 15:37 15:49 15:51[2] 15:52[3] 15:54[3] 16:3 16:4 16:5 16:12

2 CO 1:7 1:13 3:8 3:16[2] 4:14[2] 5:3 6:16 6:18 9:6[2] 10:15 11:10 11:15 12:6 12:20[2] 13:1 13:4 13:6 13:11

GA 2:16 3:8 3:11 3:12 4:30 5:2 5:10 5:16 5:21 6:4 6:5 6:7 6:8[2] 6:9

EPH 5:14 5:31[3] 6:8 6:16 6:21

PHP 1:19 1:20[2] 1:22 1:25 2:23 2:24 3:15 3:21 4:7 4:9 4:19

COL 3:4[2] 3:24 3:25 4:7 4:9

1 TH 4:15 4:16[2] 4:17[2] 5:3

2 TH 1:7 1:9 1:10 2:3 2:8[3] 2:11 3:3

1 TI 2:15 3:5 4:1 6:15

2 TI 2:2 2:11 2:12 2:21 3:1 3:2 3:9[2] 3:12 3:13 4:1 4:3 4:4[2] 4:8 4:18

TIT 3:12

PHM 2

HEB 1:5 1:11[2] 1:12[2] 1:14 2:3 3:11 4:3 4:5 6:6 8:10 8:11[2] 9:14 9:28 10:27 10:29 10:30 10:37 10:38[2] 11:18 11:32 12:9 12:14 12:20 12:25 13:6

JAS 1:5 1:7 1:10 1:11 1:12 1:25 2:10 2:12 2:13 3:1 4:10 4:14 4:15 5:1 5:3[2] 5:15[3] 5:20[2]

1 PE 2:6 2:12 2:20 4:5 4:8 4:13 4:17 4:18 5:1 5:4[2]

2 PE 1:8 1:10 1:11 2:1[2] 2:2[2] 2:3 2:12 2:13 3:3 3:10[3] 3:11 3:12[2]

1 JO 2:18 2:24[2] 2:27 2:28 3:2[4] 3:19 4:15 5:16[3]

2 JO 1:2

3 JO 14

RE 1:7[2] 1:19 2:10[2] 2:11 2:23 2:27[2] 3:4 3:5 3:10 3:12 5:10 6:17 7:15 7:16[2] 7:17[3] 9:6[4] 10:7 10:9[2] 11:2 11:3 11:7[3] 11:8 11:9[2] 11:10[2] 11:15 13:8 13:10 14:10[2] 15:4[2] 17:8[2] 17:13 17:14[2] 17:16[3] 17:17 18:7 18:8[2] 18:9[2] 18:11 18:15 18:21[2] 18:22[3] 18:23[2] 19:15 20:6[2] 20:7 20:8 20:10 21:3[2] 21:4[3] 21:7[2] 21:8 21:24 21:25[2] 21:26 21:27 22:3[2] 22:4[2] 22:5[2] 22:12 22:18[2] 22:19[2]

SHALT

GE 2:17[2] 3:14 3:15 3:16 3:17[2] 3:18 3:19[2] 4:7[2] 4:12 6:14 6:15 6:16[3] 6:18 6:19 6:21 7:2 12:2 15:15 16:11 17:4 17:9 17:15 17:19 20:7[2] 20:13 21:23 21:30 24:3 24:4 24:7 24:8 24:37 24:38 24:40 24:41[2] 27:10 27:40[2] 28:1 28:6 28:14 28:22 28:27 28:31 28:50[2] 28:52 32:18 35:17 37:8[2] 40:13 41:40 43:9 45:10[2] 47:30 49:4 50:5

EX 3:14 3:15 3:18 4:9 4:12 4:15 4:16 4:17[2] 4:22 6:1 7:2 7:9 7:15[2] 7:16 7:17 9:15 9:28 12:46 13:5 13:6 13:8 13:10 13:12 13:13[3] 13:14 15:17 17:6 18:20[2] 18:21 18:23 19:3 19:6 19:12 19:24 20:3 20:4 20:5 20:7 20:9 20:10 20:13 20:14 20:15 20:16 20:17[2] 20:22 20:24[2] 20:25 20:26 21:1 21:14 21:23 22:18 22:21 22:25[2] 22:26 22:28 22:29[2] 22:30[2] 23:1 23:2[2] 23:3 23:4 23:5 23:6 23:8 23:9 23:10[2] 23:11[2] 23:12[2] 23:14 23:15[2] 23:18 23:19[2] 23:22 23:24[2] 23:27 23:31 23:32 25:11[3] 25:11 25:13 25:14 25:16 25:17 25:18[2] 25:21[2] 25:23 25:24 25:25[2] 25:26 25:28 25:29[2] 25:30 25:31 25:37 26:1[2] 26:4[2] 26:5[2] 26:6 26:7[2] 26:9[2] 26:10 26:11 26:14 26:15 26:17 26:18 26:19 26:22 26:23 26:26 26:29[2] 26:30 26:31 26:32 26:33 26:34 26:35[2] 26:36 26:37[2] 27:1 27:2[2] 27:3[2] 27:4[2] 27:5 27:6 27:8 27:9 27:20 28:2 28:3 28:9 28:11[2] 28:12 28:13 28:14 28:15[3] 28:17 28:22 28:23[2] 28:24 28:25 28:26[2] 28:27[2] 28:30 28:31 28:33 28:36 28:37 28:39[3] 28:40[3] 28:41[2] 28:42 29:1 29:2 29:3 29:4[2] 29:5 29:6 29:7 29:8 29:9[2] 29:10 29:11 29:12 29:13 29:14 29:15 29:16[2] 29:17 29:18 29:19 29:20 29:21 29:22 29:24[2] 29:25 29:26 29:27 29:31 29:34 29:35[2] 29:36[2] 29:37 29:38 29:39[3] 29:41[2] 30:1[2] 30:3[2] 30:4 30:5 30:6 30:16[2] 30:18[3] 30:25 30:26 30:29 30:30 30:31 30:35 30:36 30:37 33:21 33:23 34:14 34:17 34:18[2] 34:20[3] 34:21[3] 34:22 34:24 34:25 34:26[2] 40:2 40:3 40:4[2] 40:5 40:6 40:7[2] 40:8 40:9[2] 40:10 40:11 40:12 40:13 40:14 40:15

LE 2:6 2:8 2:13[3] 2:14 2:15 6:21[2] 6:27 9:3 13:55 13:57 13:58 17:8 18:7[2] 18:8 18:9 18:10 18:11 18:12 18:13 18:14[2] 18:15[2] 18:16 18:17[2] 18:18 18:19 18:20 18:21[2] 18:22 18:23 19:9[2] 19:10[3] 19:12 19:13 19:14[2] 19:15[2] 19:16[2] 19:17[2] 19:18[2] 19:19[2] 19:27 19:32 19:34 20:2 20:16 20:19 21:8 23:22[3] 24:5 24:6 24:7 24:15 25:3[2] 25:4 25:5 25:8 25:9 25:15 25:16[2] 25:17 25:35 25:37 25:39 25:43[2] 25:44

NU 1:49 1:50 3:9 3:10 3:15 3:41 3:46[2] 3:48 4:28 4:29 4:30 7:5 8:7 8:8 8:9[2] 8:10 8:12 8:13 8:14 8:15 8:26 10:2 11:23 14:15 15:5 15:6 15:7 15:10 17:3 17:4 17:10 18:10 18:15[2] 18:16 18:17[3] 18:20[2] 18:30 20:8[2] 20:18 20:20 20:34 21:12[2] 21:20 22:35 23:5 23:13[2] 26:54[2] 27:7[2] 27:8 27:13 27:20 28:3 28:4[2] 28:7 28:8[2] 28:21 31:2 31:30

DE 1:37 2:28 3:2 3:27 3:28 4:25 4:29[2] 4:30 4:40 5:7 5:8 5:9 5:11 5:13 5:14 5:17 5:18 5:19 5:20 5:21[2] 5:31 6:5 6:7[2] 6:8 6:9 6:11 6:13[2] 6:18 6:21 7:2[2] 7:3[3] 7:11 7:14 7:16[2] 7:17 7:18[2] 7:21 7:24 7:25 7:26[2] 8:2 8:5 8:6 8:9[2] 8:10 8:18 9:3 10:2 10:20[3] 11:1 11:20 11:29 12:5 12:14[2] 12:18 12:20 12:21[2] 12:22 12:24[2] 12:25[2] 12:26 12:27[2] 12:31 12:32 13:3 13:5 13:8[3] 13:9 13:10 13:12 13:14 13:15 13:16[2] 13:18 14:3 14:21[2] 14:22 14:23 14:25[2] 14:26[3] 14:27 14:28[2] 15:1 15:6[3] 15:7 15:8[2] 15:10 15:11 15:12 15:13 15:14[2] 15:15 15:17[2] 15:19[2] 15:20 15:21 15:22 15:23[2] 16:2 16:3[2] 16:6 16:7[2] 16:8[2] 16:9 16:10[2] 16:11 16:12[2] 16:13 16:14 16:15[2] 16:18 16:19[2] 16:20 16:21[2] 16:22 17:1 17:5[2] 17:7 17:8 17:9 17:10[2] 17:11[2] 17:12 17:14[3] 17:15[2] 18:4 18:9 18:13 18:14 18:22 19:2 19:3 19:7 19:9[2] 19:13 19:14[2] 19:19 20:12 20:13 20:14[2] 20:15 20:16 20:17 20:19[3] 20:20[2] 21:9[2] 21:12 21:13 21:14[3] 21:21 21:23 22:1[2] 22:2[2] 22:3[3] 22:4[2] 22:6 22:7 22:8 22:9 22:10 22:11 22:12 22:21 22:22 22:24 22:26 23:6 23:7[2] 23:12[2] 23:13[3] 23:15 23:16 23:18 23:19 23:20 23:21[2] 23:22 23:23 23:24 23:25 24:4 24:7 24:10 24:11 24:12 24:13 24:14 24:15 24:17 24:18 24:19 24:20 24:21 24:22 25:4 25:12 25:13 25:14 25:15[2] 25:19[2] 26:2[4] 26:3 26:5 26:10 26:11 26:13 26:16 27:2 27:3 27:4 27:5[2] 27:6[2] 27:7[2] 27:8 27:10 28:1 28:2 28:3[2] 28:6[2] 28:9 28:12[2] 28:13[2] 28:14 28:16[2] 28:19[2] 28:25[2] 28:29[3] 28:30[5] 28:31[2] 28:33 28:34[2] 28:36[2] 28:37 28:38[2] 28:39[2] 28:40[2] 28:41[2] 28:43 28:44[2] 28:48 28:49 28:53 28:64 28:65 28:66[2] 28:67[4] 28:68 30:1 30:2[2] 30:5 30:8 30:10 30:17 31:2 31:3 31:7 31:11 31:16 31:23 32:52[2] 33:29 34:4

JOS 1:6 1:8[2] 2:18[2] 3:8 6:3 8:2 11:6 17:17 17:18[2]

JG 4:20 6:14 6:16 6:23 6:26 7:5 7:11 9:33[2] 11:2 11:30 13:3 13:5 13:7

RU 2:21 3:4[3]

1 SA 2:16 2:32 3:9 9:16 10:2 10:3[2] 10:4 10:5[2] 10:6[2] 10:8[3] 14:44 16:3[2] 16:16 18:21 19:11 20:2 20:8 20:14 20:15 20:18 20:19[2] 20:31 22:16 22:23 23:17 24:20 26:25[2] 28:1 28:2 28:19 30:8

2 SA 3:13 5:2[2] 5:6 5:23 5:24 7:5 7:8 7:12 9:7 9:10 10:11 11:25 12:13 13:13 15:33 15:35 18:3 18:20[3] 19:23 19:38

1 KI 2:37[2] 2:42 5:6 5:9[3] 8:19 8:44 11:37[2] 12:10[2] 13:17 14:5 17:4 19:16[2] 20:5 20:13 20:34 20:39 21:19[2] 22:11 22:22 22:25[2]

2 KI 1:4[2] 1:6[2] 2:16[2] 4:4[3] 4:16 5:10 6:22 7:2[2] 7:19[2] 8:13 9:7 10:5 13:18 13:19 19:11 20:1 20:5 20:9 20:18 22:20

1 CH 11:2[2] 11:5 14:15[2] 17:4 17:7 19:12 21:22 22:8 22:13

2 CH 28:3 2:16[2] 6:9 6:34 7:17 10:10[2] 16:9 18:10 18:21[2] 18:24[2] 21:15 34:28

EZR 4:13 4:15 4:16 7:20

ES 4:13 6:13[2]

JOB 5:21[2] 5:22[2] 5:23 5:24[3] 5:25 5:26 7:21 11:15[3] 11:16 11:17[2] 11:18[3] 11:19 14:15 17:4 22:23[2] 22:24 22:25 22:26[2] 22:27[2] 22:28 22:29 35:14 38:11

PS 2:9[2] 5:3 5:6 12:7[2] 17:3 21:9 21:10 21:12[2] 31:20[2] 32:7[2] 32:8 36:8 37:3[2] 37:10 37:34 50:15 51:6 51:19 55:23 59:8[2] 65:3 67:4 71:20[2] 71:21 73:20 73:24 76:10 81:9 82:8 89:2 91:4 91:5 91:8 91:13[2] 92:10 102:12 102:13 102:26[2] 102:27 112:9 112:10[3] 115:14 116:12 118:7 118:17 118:20 119:6 119:7 119:9 119:27 119:32 119:33 119:34[2] 119:42 119:44 119:88 119:117 119:144 119:146 119:165 119:171 119:172 119:175 120:3[2] 121:4 121:6 121:7[2] 121:8 122:2 122:6 125:1 125:3 125:5[2] 126:5 126:6 127:5[2] 128:2[2] 128:5 128:6 130:3 130:8 138:7 142:7

PR 2:5 2:9 3:4 3:23 3:24[2] 4:12 9:12[2] 20:13 22:24 23:8 23:14[2] 23:34 23:35 24:6 25:22 27:27

EC 11:1 12:1

ISA 1:26 12:1 14:4 14:15 14:20 17:10 17:11 22:18 23:12[2] 25:5 29:4[2] 29:6 30:19 30:22[2] 30:23 33:1[3] 33:19 37:11 38:1 39:7 41:12[2] 41:15[2]

41:16[2] 43:2 44:21 44:26 44:28 47:1 47:5 47:11[3] 47:12 49:18 49:20 49:21 49:23 51:22 53:10 54:3 54:4[4] 54:14[3] 54:17 55:5 58:9[2]
58:11 58:12[2] 58:13 58:14 60:5 60:16[3] 60:18 62:2 62:3 62:4[2] 62:12
JER 1:7[2] 2:36 2:37[2] 3:19[2] 4:1 4:2
4:30 5:19 7:27[2] 7:28 8:4 13:12 13:13 14:17 15:2 15:19[2] 16:2[2] 16:8 16:10 16:11 17:4 18:22 19:10 19:11 20:6[3] 21:8 22:15
22:22 22:23 23:33 23:37 25:27 25:28 26:4 26:8 28:13 28:16 29:24 31:4[3] 31:5 34:3[3] 34:4 34:5 34:14 36:6 36:29 37:17 38:17
38:18 38:23[3] 38:24 38:26 39:17 39:18 40:16 45:4 46:11[2] 48:2 48:7 49:12[2] 51:26 51:61[2] 51:62 51:63 51:64
LA 4:21[2]
EZE 2:4 2:7 3:18 3:25 3:26[2] 3:27 4:3 4:4[2] 4:5 4:6 4:7[2] 4:8 4:9[2] 4:10[3] 4:11[2] 4:12[2] 4:15 5:2[3] 5:3
8:6 8:13 8:15 12:3 12:4[2] 12:6[2] 16:41 16:43 16:61[2] 16:62 21:7 21:32[3] 22:2 22:16[2] 23:32[2] 23:33 23:34[2] 24:13 24:16 24:27[2] 25:7
26:14[2] 26:21[2] 27:34 27:36[2] 28:8 28:9 28:10 28:19[2] 29:5[2] 31:18[2] 32:28[2] 33:7 33:8 33:14 35:4[2] 35:12 35:15 36:12[2] 36:14 36:15[2] 38:8
38:9[2] 38:10 38:11 38:14 38:15 38:16 39:4 39:5 43:19 43:20[2] 43:21 43:22 43:23 43:24 43:25 44:6 45:3 45:18 45:20 46:13[2] 46:14
DA 4:26 5:16[2] 12:13
HOS 2:16[2] 2:20 3:3[3] 4:5 4:6 13:4
AM 7:17
OB 10
MIC 1:14 2:5 4:10[4] 4:13 5:12 5:13 6:14[3] 6:15[5]
NA 3:11[3]
HAB 2:7
ZEP 3:11[2] 3:15
ZEC 2:11 3:7[2] 4:7 4:9 13:3
MT 1:21 4:7 4:10[2] 5:21 5:26 5:27 5:33[2] 5:36 5:43 6:5 7:5 11:23 12:37[2] 16:19[2] 17:27 19:18[4] 19:19 19:21 22:37 22:39 26:34 26:75
MK 6:23 10:21 12:30 12:31 14:30 14:72
LU 1:13 1:14 1:20 1:31[2] 1:76[2] 4:8[2] 4:12 5:10 6:42 10:15 10:27 10:28 12:59 13:9 14:10 14:14[2] 17:4 17:8 18:22 22:34 22:61 23:43
JOH 1:33 1:42 1:50 13:7 13:8 13:36 21:18[2]
AC 2:28 13:11 13:35 16:31 22:15 23:5 25:12 25:22
RO 2:3 7:7 10:9[3] 11:22 12:20 13:3 13:9[6]
1 CO 7:16[2] 9:9 16:14
GA 5:14
1 TI 4:6 4:16 5:18
HEB 1:12
JAS 2:8
3 JO 1:6
RE 2:10 3:3[2] 16:5 18:14

SHE

1931, *846*

GE 2:23 3:6 3:12 3:20 4:1 4:2 4:17 4:22 4:25[2] 8:9 11:30 12:14 12:16 12:18 12:19 15:9 16:1 16:4[2] 16:5 16:6 16:8 16:13[2] 16:16 18:15 19:26 19:33 19:35 19:38 20:2 20:3 20:5 20:12[2] 20:16 21:7 21:9 21:10 21:14 21:15 21:16[3] 21:19 22:20 22:24 24:14[2] 24:16 24:18 24:19 24:20
24:24[2] 24:25 24:36 24:44 24:45 24:46[2] 24:47 24:55 24:58 24:64 24:65[2] 24:67 25:2 25:21 25:22[2] 25:26 26:7[3] 26:9 27:16 27:17 27:42 29:9 29:12 29:32 29:33[2] 29:34 29:35[2] 30:1 30:3[2] 30:4 30:6 30:8 30:9 30:11 30:13 30:15 30:17 30:18 30:20 30:21 30:23 30:24 30:35 31:38 32:14 32:15 34:1 35:8
35:16 35:17 35:18[2] 36:12 36:14 38:3 38:4[2] 38:5[2] 38:14[3] 38:15 38:16[2] 38:17 38:18[2] 38:19 38:24 38:25[3] 38:26 38:28 38:29 39:7 39:10 39:12 39:13 39:14 39:16 39:17 39:19 45:23 46:25 46:18
EX 1:16 2:2[2] 2:3[3] 2:5[2] 2:6[3] 2:7 2:10[3] 2:22 2:26 6:20 6:23 6:25 21:4 21:7 21:8 21:11
LE 12:2[2] 12:4[2] 12:5[3] 12:6 12:7 12:8[3] 15:19 15:20[2] 15:22 15:23 15:25 15:26[2] 15:28[3] 15:29 18:7 18:9 18:11 18:12 18:13 18:14 18:15 18:19 19:20[2] 20:17 20:18 21:9[3] 22:12 22:13 26:43
NU 5:13[2] 5:14[2] 5:27 5:28 12:10 12:14 22:25 22:27 22:28 22:33 26:59 30:4[2] 30:5 30:6[3] 30:7 30:8[2] 30:10 30:11
DE 21:12 21:13[2] 21:14 22:19 22:21[2] 22:24 22:29 24:2[2] 24:4 25:6 25:57[2]
JOS 2:6[2] 2:8 2:9 2:15[2] 2:16 2:21[3] 6:17 6:22 6:23 6:25[3] 15:18[3]
JG 1:14[3] 1:15 4:4 4:5 4:6 4:9 4:18 4:19 5:24 5:25[2] 5:26[4] 5:29 8:31 11:34 11:36 11:37 11:38 11:39[2] 13:9 13:14 14:3 14:6 14:17[3] 15:2 16:8 16:9 16:14 16:15 16:16 16:18 16:19[4] 16:20 19:3 20:5
RU 1:3 1:6[3] 1:7[2] 1:9 1:15 1:18[3] 1:20 2:2 2:3 2:7[3] 2:10 2:13 2:14[2] 2:15 2:16 2:17[2] 2:18[5] 2:19[2] 2:23 3:5 3:6 3:7 3:9 3:14[2] 3:15[2] 3:16[3] 3:17 3:18 4:13[2]
1 SA 1:7[3] 1:10 1:11 1:12 1:13[2] 1:18 1:20 1:22 1:23 1:24[2] 1:26 2:5 2:19 2:21 4:19[2] 4:20[2] 4:21 4:22 18:19 18:21 19:14 25:3 25:19[2] 25:20[3] 25:23 25:35 25:36 25:41 25:42 28:12 28:14 28:24 28:25
2 SA 4:4 6:16 11:4[3] 11:26 11:27 12:24 13:2 13:8 13:9 13:10 13:11 13:12 13:14 13:16 13:18 14:4 14:5 14:11 14:27 20:17 20:18 21:8[2]
1 KI 1:17 1:22 1:28 2:13 2:14 2:16 2:19 2:20 2:21 3:19 3:20 3:26 3:27 10:1 10:2[3] 10:6 10:10 10:13[3] 14:5[2] 14:6 14:17 15:13 17:11 17:12 17:15[2] 17:18 21:8 21:9 21:11
2 KI 2:24 4:2 4:5[2] 4:6 4:7 4:8 4:9 4:12 4:13 4:14 4:15 4:16 4:21 4:22 4:23 4:24 4:25 4:26 4:27[2] 4:28 4:36 4:37 5:2 5:3 6:28 6:29 8:2 8:3 8:6[2] 9:30 9:31 9:34 11:1 11:13 11:14 11:16[2] 22:14 22:15
1 CH 1:32 2:21 2:26 2:29 2:35 2:49 4:17 7:14 7:16 7:23 15:29
2 CH 9:1[3] 9:5 9:9 9:12[4] 15:16 22:10 22:11[2] 23:12 23:13[3] 23:15 34:22 34:23 36:21[2]
ES 1:15 1:17 1:19 2:1 2:7 2:9 2:10 2:12 2:13 2:14[4] 2:15 2:17 2:20 4:4 4:8 5:2 5:12
JOB 1:3 39:16 39:18[2] 39:28 39:29 39:30 42:12
PS 45:14 46:5 68:12 80:11 84:3
PR 1:20 1:21[2] 3:15 3:18 4:6[2] 4:8[2] 4:9[2] 4:13 7:11 7:12 7:13 7:21[2] 7:26 8:2 8:3 9:1 9:2[3] 9:3[2] 9:4 9:13 9:14 9:16 12:4 23:22 23:25 23:28 30:20 30:23 31:12 31:13 31:14[2] 31:15 31:16[2] 31:17 31:18 31:19 31:20[2] 31:21 31:22 31:24 31:25 31:26 31:27 31:30
CA 2:7 3:5 6:9[2] 6:10 8:4 8:5 8:8[2] 8:9[2]
ISA 3:26 8:3 23:3 23:17 40:2 49:15 51:18[2] 66:7[3] 66:8
JER 2:1 3:6 3:7[2] 3:9 4:17 6:6 6:7 11:15 15:9[3] 33:16 46:24 50:9 50:12 50:14 50:15[2] 50:29[2] 51:8 51:9 51:42 51:53
LA 1:1[3] 1:2[2] 1:3[2] 1:4 1:7 1:8[2] 1:9[3] 1:10
EZE 5:6 16:46 16:48 16:49 19:2[2] 19:3 19:5[3] 19:10 19:11[2] 19:12[2] 19:13 19:14 25:5[2] 25:7[3] 25:8 25:9 25:10 25:11 25:12 25:13 25:14[2] 25:16[2] 25:17 25:18 25:19[2] 25:20 25:43 24:7[2] 24:12 26:2[3] 26:17 32:20
DA 11:6[2] 11:17
HO 1:6 1:8[2] 2:2 2:3 2:5[2] 2:6 2:7[4] 2:8 2:12 2:13[3] 2:15[2] 13:16
AM 5:2[2]
MIC 1:7 1:11 1:13 5:3 7:10
NA 2:7 2:10[2] 3:10[2]
ZEP 2:15 3:2[4]
ZEC 9:4
MAL 2:14
MT 1:18 1:21 1:25 8:15 9:18 9:21 12:42 14:7 14:8 14:11 15:23 15:25 15:27 20:21 22:28 26:10 26:12[2]
MK 1:31 5:23[2] 5:26 5:27 5:28 5:29[2] 5:42 6:19 6:24[2] 6:25 7:26 7:28 7:30[2] 10:12 12:23 12:42 12:44[2] 14:3 14:6 14:8[3] 14:9 14:67[2] 16:10
LU 1:29[2] 1:36 1:42 1:45 1:57[2] 2:6 2:7 2:36 2:37 2:38 4:39 7:12 7:37 7:39 7:44 7:47 8:42 8:47[5] 8:50 8:52 8:53 8:55 10:39 10:40 11:31 13:13 15:8[2] 15:9[2] 18:3 18:5 20:33 21:4[2]
JOH 8:11 11:20 11:27 11:28[2] 11:29[2] 11:31[2] 11:32 12:7 16:21[3] 20:2 20:11[2] 20:13 20:14[2] 20:15 20:16 20:18
AC 5:8 5:10 9:36 9:37 9:39 9:40[3] 12:14[2] 12:15 16:14 16:15[3] 16:18
RO 7:2 7:3[5] 16:2[2]
1 CO 7:11 7:12 7:28 7:34[3] 7:36 7:39[2] 7:40[2] 11:5
GA 4:27
EPH 5:33
1 TI 2:15 5:5 5:6[2] 5:10[5]
HEB 11:31
JAS 2:25
RE 2:21 6:13 12:2 12:5 12:6 12:14[2] 14:8 18:6[2] 18:7[2] 18:8 18:19 19:8

THAT

834 or 2088, or 3588, *1565* or *3754*

GE 1:4 1:10 1:12 1:18 1:20[2] 1:21[2] 1:25[2] 1:26 1:28 1:30 1:31 2:3 2:4[2] 2:9 2:11 2:12 2:13 2:14[2] 2:17 2:19 3:5 3:6 3:7 3:11 3:13[2] 3:14 4:3 4:8 4:14 5:1 5:5 6:2 6:3 6:4 6:5[2] 6:6 6:7 6:17 6:21 6:22 7:2 7:4 7:5 7:8 7:10 7:14 7:16 7:19 7:21[2] 7:22 7:23 8:1 8:11 8:17[2] 9:2 9:3 9:10[2] 9:12 9:14 9:16[2] 9:17 9:18 10:11 11:2 11:7 12:1 12:3 12:5[2] 12:11 12:12 12:13 12:14[2] 12:18 12:20 13:1 13:6[2] 13:10 13:14 13:16 14:2 14:5 14:7 14:10 14:13 14:14 14:17 14:23[3] 14:24 15:4 15:7 15:8 15:13[2] 15:14 15:17[2] 16:2 16:4 16:5 16:10 16:13[2] 17:12[2] 17:13 17:14 17:17[2] 17:18 17:23 17:24 18:17 18:18 18:19[3] 18:25[3] 19:5[2] 19:11[2] 19:14 19:17 19:21 19:25 19:29 19:32 19:33 19:34[2] 19:35 20:6 20:7[2] 20:9[2] 20:10 20:13 20:16 21:3 21:6[2] 21:7[2] 21:12 21:22[3] 21:23[2] 21:30 21:31 22:4 22:6 22:8 22:9 22:14 23:4 23:6

23:8 23:9 23:10 23:11 23:15 23:17 23:18 23:20 24:2 24:3 24:6 24:7 24:9 24:11 24:14^{4} 24:15 24:22 24:30 24:32 24:36 24:43 24:49 24:52 24:54 24:55 24:56 24:65 24:66 25:5 25:11 25:18 25:26 25:30 26:1 26:5 26:8 26:11 26:12 26:21 26:22 26:28 26:29^{2} 26:32 27:1 27:4 27:7 27:8 27:10 27:19 27:20 27:21 27:25 27:30 27:31 27:33 27:40 27:45 28:3 28:4 28:6^{2} 28:7 28:8 28:11^{2} 28:15 28:18 28:19^{2} 28:20 28:21 28:22 29:2 29:7 29:10 29:12 29:13 29:19 29:21 29:23 29:25 29:31 29:33 30:1 30:3 30:9 30:15 30:16 30:25^{2} 30:27

30:33^{2} 30:35 30:88 30:41^{2} 31:1^{2} 31:5 31:6 31:10^{2} 31:12 31:16 31:19 31:20^{2} 31:21 31:22 31:24 31:26 31:27 31:29 31:32 31:35 31:36 31:37 31:39 31:43 31:52^{2} 32:2 32:5 32:7 32:13^{2} 32:19 32:20 32:21 32:22 32:23 32:25 32:29 32:32 33:9 33:11 33:13 33:14 33:15 33:16 34:5^{5} 34:14^{2} 34:15 34:24^{2} 34:25 34:28^{2} 34:29 35:1 35:2^{2} 35:5 35:6 35:17 35:18 35:20 35:22^{2} 36:7 36:16 36:17 36:18 36:24^{2} 36:29 36:30 36:31 36:40 37:4 37:10 37:22^{2} 37:23^{2} 38:1^{2} 38:9^{3} 38:14 38:16^{2} 38:18 38:21^{2} 38:22 38:24 38:26 38:27 38:28 38:29 38:30 39:3^{3} 39:4 39:5^{4}

39:6 39:7 39:8 39:10 39:11 39:13 39:14 39:15^{2} 39:18 39:19 39:22 39:23^{2} 40:1 40:7 40:15 40:16 40:20 41:1 41:8^{2} 41:15^{2} 41:21 41:24 41:27 41:31 41:32 41:35 41:36^{2} 41:53 41:57 42:1 42:2^{2} 42:5 42:6 42:14^{2} 42:16 42:21 42:23 42:28 42:29 42:33 42:34^{2} 42:35 43:7 43:8 43:12 43:14 43:15 43:18^{2} 43:21 43:25 44:2 44:7 44:15^{2} 44:17 44:21 44:30 44:31^{2} 44:34 45:1 45:8 45:10 45:11 45:12^{2} 45:13 45:15 45:24 46:1 46:26 46:32 46:34 47:1 47:13 47:14 47:17 47:18^{2} 47:19^{2} 47:24 47:26 47:29 48:1 48:10 48:17 48:20 49:1^{2} 49:15^{2} 49:17^{2} 49:25

49:26 49:28 49:29 49:30 49:32 50:14 50:15

EX

1:5 1:6 1:10 1:21 1:22 2:2 2:7 2:11 2:12^{2} 2:13 2:18 2:20^{2} 2:23 3:8 3:10 3:11^{2} 3:12 3:16 3:18 3:19 3:20 3:21 3:22 4:2 4:5^{2} 4:8 4:9 4:14 4:21^{2} 4:23 4:24 4:31^{2} 5:1 5:2 5:9 5:19 5:22 6:7 6:11 6:26 6:27 6:29^{2} 7:2^{2} 7:4 7:5 7:13 7:16 7:17 7:18 7:19^{2} 7:20^{2} 7:21 7:25 8:1 8:8^{2} 8:9 8:10^{2} 8:15 8:16 8:20 8:22^{2} 8:28 8:29 9:1 9:4 9:6 9:13 9:14^{2} 9:15 9:16 9:17 9:19 9:20 9:21 9:22 9:28

9:29 9:30 9:34 10:1 10:2^{3} 10:3 10:5^{2} 10:6 10:7^{2} 10:8 10:11^{2} 10:12 10:13 10:15 10:17 10:20 10:21 10:25 10:28 11:5^{2} 11:7^{2} 11:8^{2} 11:9 11:10 12:8 12:10 12:15 12:16 12:19^{2} 12:22^{2} 12:25 12:27 12:29^{3} 12:33 12:36 12:37 12:41 12:42 12:44 12:48 12:49^{2} 12:51 13:5 13:8 13:9 13:12^{3} 13:14 13:15^{2} 13:17^{2} 14:2 14:4^{3} 14:5^{2} 14:12^{3} 14:15 14:18 14:20 14:21 14:24 14:25^{2} 14:26 14:28 14:30 14:31 15:7 15:26^{2} 16:4 16:5^{2} 16:6 16:7^{2} 16:8 16:10 16:12 16:13 16:14 16:18 16:22 16:23^{4} 16:25 16:27 16:29 16:32 17:2 17:3 17:6 17:11 17:16 18:1^{2}

18:8^{2} 18:11 18:13 18:14^{2} 18:17 18:18 18:19 18:20 18:22 18:24 19:8 19:9 19:12 19:16^{3} 20:4^{3} 20:5 20:6 20:7 20:10 20:11 20:12 20:17 20:20^{2} 20:22 20:26 21:12^{2} 21:14 21:15 21:16 21:17 21:19 21:22 21:26 21:28 21:29 21:35 21:36 22:2 22:6^{2} 22:11 22:13 22:16 22:20 22:25 22:26 22:27^{2} 22:31 23:5 23:11 23:12 23:13 23:22 24:12 25:2^{2} 25:8 25:9 25:14 25:21 25:26 25:28 25:33 25:35 25:37 25:40 26:5 26:10 26:11 26:12^{2} 26:13^{2} 26:33 27:5 27:20 28:1 28:3^{3} 28:4 28:28^{2} 28:32 28:35 28:37 28:38^{2} 28:41 28:43 29:1 29:13^{3} 29:21 29:22^{2} 29:23

29:27 29:30^{2} 29:32 29:38 29:46^{3} 30:6 30:12 30:13^{2} 30:14^{2} 30:16 30:20 30:21 30:29 30:30 30:38 31:6^{3} 31:7 31:11 31:13^{3} 31:14^{2} 32:1^{2} 32:10^{2} 32:13 32:18^{3} 32:19 32:21 32:22 32:23 32:25 32:28 32:29 32:30 33:5 33:7 33:8 33:13^{3} 33:16^{3} 33:17 33:22 34:1 34:3 34:7 34:10 34:11 34:19^{2} 34:29^{2} 34:32 34:34 34:35 35:1 35:10 35:22 35:24 35:25^{2} 35:34 35:35^{2} 36:1 36:4 36:8 36:18 36:19 37:8 37:13 38:15 38:22 38:24 38:25 38:26^{2} 39:5 39:7 39:21^{2} 39:23 39:32 39:42 40:4 40:9 40:13 40:15 40:16 40:17 40:37

LE

1:5 1:8

1:12 1:17 2:8 2:10 3:3^{2} 3:4 3:5 3:9^{2} 3:10 3:14^{2} 3:15 3:17 4:3 4:5 4:8^{2} 4:9 4:16 4:18 4:35 5:3 5:4 5:5^{3} 5:8 5:11 5:13 5:16 6:2 6:3^{2} 6:4^{3} 6:5 6:7 6:18 6:22 6:26 6:27 7:3 7:4^{2} 7:7 7:8 7:9^{3} 7:14 7:15 7:16 7:18^{2} 7:19^{2} 7:20^{3} 7:21^{2} 7:24^{2} 7:25 7:27^{2} 7:29 7:30 7:33 7:36 8:10 8:16 8:25 8:26 8:31 8:32 8:35 8:38 9:1 9:5 9:6 9:19 10:3^{2} 10:10 10:11 10:12^{2} 10:20 11:2 11:3 11:4^{2} 11:9 11:10^{2} 11:12 11:20 11:21 11:26 11:27 11:28 11:29 11:31 11:34^{2} 11:36 11:39

11:40^{2} 11:41 11:42 11:43^{2} 11:44 11:45 11:46^{2} 11:47^{2} 12:7 13:4 13:7 13:8 13:12 13:13 13:17 13:24 13:31^{2} 13:33 13:37 13:39 13:41 13:47 13:50 13:51 13:52 13:54 13:55 13:57 14:4 14:5 14:6 14:7 14:8^{3} 14:9 14:11^{2} 14:14 14:16 14:17^{2} 14:18^{2} 14:19 14:25 14:27 14:28^{2} 14:29^{2} 14:31 14:32 14:35 14:36^{3} 14:40 14:41 14:43 14:46^{2} 14:47^{2} 15:4 15:6^{2} 15:7^{2} 15:8^{2} 15:9 15:10^{2} 15:11 15:12 15:13 15:20^{2} 15:22 15:28 15:31^{2} 15:32 15:33 16:2^{2} 16:13^{3} 16:15^{2} 16:16 16:18 16:26 16:28 16:29^{2} 16:30^{2} 17:3^{2} 17:4^{2} 17:5^{2} 17:8 17:9 17:10^{4} 17:11 17:12 17:13^{2} 17:15^{3}

18:6 18:26 18:28^{2} 18:29 18:30^{2} 19:8^{2} 19:13 19:20 19:25 19:31 19:34 20:2^{2} 20:3 20:5^{2} 20:6^{2} 20:9 20:10^{2} 20:11 20:14 20:22 20:24 20:25 20:26 20:27^{2} 21:2^{2} 21:3 21:7 21:10^{2} 21:17 21:18^{2} 21:19 21:20 21:21 21:23 22:2^{2} 22:3^{2} 22:4 22:8 22:11 22:18 22:20 22:23^{2} 22:24 22:33 23:12 23:14 23:15 23:21 23:23 23:28 23:29^{2} 23:30^{2} 23:42 23:43^{2} 24:2 24:7 24:12 24:14^{2} 24:16^{2} 24:17 24:18 24:21^{2} 24:23 25:5 25:6 25:7 25:11^{2} 25:25 25:27 25:28^{2} 25:30^{2} 25:33 25:35 25:36 25:39 25:44 25:45^{2} 25:47 25:48 25:49 25:50^{2} 25:51 26:13 26:15^{2} 26:16 26:17 26:25

26:36 26:39 26:40 26:41 26:44 26:45 27:8 27:9 27:15 27:18 27:19 27:23 27:28^{2}

NU

1:3 1:5 1:20 1:21 1:22^{2} 1:23 1:24 1:25 1:26 1:27 1:28 1:29 1:30 1:31 1:32 1:33 1:34 1:35 1:36 1:37 1:38 1:39 1:40 1:41 1:42 1:43 1:44 1:45^{2} 1:46 1:50 1:51 1:53 1:54 2:4 2:5 2:6 2:8 2:9 2:10 2:11 2:13 2:15 2:16 2:19 2:21 2:23 2:24 2:26 2:27 2:28 2:30 2:31 2:32 2:34 3:1 3:6 3:12 3:13 3:22^{2} 3:32 3:34 3:36 3:38^{2} 3:39 3:43 3:46 3:49^{2} 3:51 4:3 4:15

4:16 4:19 4:23 4:25 4:26 4:30 4:35 4:36 4:37^{2} 4:38 4:39 4:40 4:41^{2} 4:42 4:43 4:44 4:45 4:46 4:47 4:48 5:2^{2} 5:3 5:6^{2} 5:17 5:18 5:19 5:22 5:24^{2} 5:27^{2} 6:4 6:6 6:11^{2} 6:12 6:20 6:21^{2} 7:1 7:2^{2} 7:5 7:9 7:10 7:12 7:88 7:89 8:11 8:15 8:17 8:19 8:20 8:22 8:24 9:4 9:5 9:6^{3} 9:7 9:13^{2} 9:14 9:15 9:17 9:21^{2} 9:22 10:2 10:5 10:6 10:9 10:10 10:11 10:32 10:35^{2} 11:1 11:4 11:11 11:12 11:13 11:16 11:17 11:20 11:21 11:25^{2} 11:26 11:29^{2} 11:32^{3} 11:34^{2} 12:14 13:2 13:18 13:19^{2} 13:28

13:31 13:32^{2} 14:1 14:2 14:3 14:6 14:14^{4} 14:23 14:29 14:35 14:37 14:38 14:42 14:45 15:12 15:13 15:15 15:16 15:19 15:23^{2} 15:24 15:26 15:28 15:29^{3} 15:30^{2} 15:31 15:32 15:33 15:38^{2} 15:39^{2} 15:40 16:7 16:9 16:11 16:13^{2} 16:14 16:21 16:28 16:30^{2} 16:31^{2} 16:32 16:33 16:34 16:35 16:37 16:39 16:40^{2} 16:42 16:45 16:49^{2} 17:5 17:8 17:10 18:2 18:3 18:5 18:7 18:11 18:13 18:15 18:16 18:23 19:2 19:3 19:8 19:9 19:10^{2} 19:11 19:13^{2} 19:14^{2} 19:16 19:18^{2} 19:20^{2} 19:21^{3} 19:22 20:3 20:4 20:14 20:29 21:1 21:7 21:8^{2} 21:9 21:13 21:15 21:16 21:20

21:27 21:29 21:32 22:2 22:4^{2} 22:6^{3} 22:19 22:20 22:24 22:28 22:34 22:35^{2} 22:36 22:38^{2} 22:40 22:41^{2} 23:12 23:19^{2} 23:26^{2} 23:27 23:28 24:1 24:9^{2} 24:13 24:19^{2} 24:20 25:4 25:5 25:9 25:11 25:14^{2} 25:15 26:1 26:2 26:7 26:9 26:10 26:18 26:22 26:25 26:27 26:34 26:37 26:41 26:43 26:47 26:50 26:54 26:57 26:62 26:63 27:3 27:11 27:14 27:17 27:20 29:40 30:2 30:5 30:7 30:8^{2} 30:9 30:14 30:15 31:8 31:17 31:18 31:20 31:23^{2} 31:26 31:27 31:35 31:36 31:42 31:43 31:52 32:1 32:9 32:11 32:13 32:24 32:32 33:55 33:56 34:2 35:2 35:6

35:8^{2} 35:11 35:12 35:15^{2} 35:16 35:20 35:21^{2} 35:23 35:32^{2} 35:33^{2} 36:8^{2}

DE

1:3^{2} 1:9 1:16^{2} 1:17 1:18 1:19 1:30 1:31^{2} 1:35 1:36 1:39 1:41 1:44 1:46 2:6^{2} 2:17 2:20 2:25 2:28^{2} 2:30 2:31 2:34 2:36 3:4 3:8 3:9 3:12 3:18^{2} 3:19 3:21^{2} 3:23 3:24 3:25^{2} 4:1 4:2 4:3 4:4 4:5 4:7 4:8 4:10^{4} 4:14^{2} 4:15 4:17 4:18^{2} 4:21^{2} 4:22^{3} 4:26 4:32^{2} 4:34 4:35^{2} 4:36 4:39 4:40^{2} 4:42^{2} 5:1 5:5 5:8^{3} 5:9 5:10 5:11 5:14^{2} 5:15^{2} 5:16^{2} 5:21 5:23 5:24 5:26 5:27^{2} 5:28^{2} 5:29^{3} 5:31

5:33^{3} 6:1 6:2^{2} 6:3^{3} 6:18^{3} 6:23 6:24 7:4 7:6 7:9^{2} 7:10^{2} 7:12 7:15 7:16 7:20 7:25 8:1 8:3^{3} 8:5 8:7 8:11 8:13 8:15 8:16^{2} 8:18^{2} 8:19 9:3 9:4 9:5 9:6 9:7 9:8 9:11 9:14 9:19 9:21 9:24 10:1 10:2 10:8 10:10 10:11 10:14 10:21 11:6 11:8 11:9^{2} 11:14^{2} 11:15 11:16 11:17^{2} 11:18 11:21 11:25 11:29 12:1 12:3 12:7 12:8 12:10 12:11 12:12 12:13^{2} 12:14 12:18^{2} 12:19 12:23 12:25^{2} 12:28^{2} 12:30^{3} 13:3^{2} 13:5^{2} 13:10 13:14 13:15^{2} 13:17 13:18 14:2 14:6^{2} 14:7^{2} 14:9^{2} 14:19 14:21^{3} 14:22 14:23 14:24 14:26

14:27 14:29 15:2 15:3 15:8 15:9 15:10^{2} 15:14 15:15 15:18 15:19 16:3 16:6 16:11^{2} 16:12 16:13 16:14 16:20^{2} 17:1 17:2 17:4 17:5^{5} 17:6 17:9 17:10^{2} 17:12^{3} 17:14 17:16^{2} 17:17 17:18^{2} 17:19 17:20^{3} 18:3 18:8 18:10^{2} 18:12 18:16^{2} 18:17 18:18 18:19 18:20^{2} 18:22 19:3 19:4 19:5 19:10 19:11 19:12 19:13 19:14 19:15 19:16 20:4 20:5 20:6 20:7 20:8 20:9 20:11^{2} 20:14 20:16 20:18 20:20^{2} 21:2 21:3^{2} 21:4 21:6^{3} 21:9 21:11 21:13 21:15 21:16^{2} 21:17 21:18 21:21 21:23^{3} 22:5^{2} 22:7^{2} 22:8 22:18^{2} 22:21 22:22 22:23 22:24^{2} 22:25 22:28 22:29

23:1 23:8 23:10^{2} 23:13 23:14 23:16 23:19 23:20^{2} 23:23 24:1 24:4^{2} 24:7 24:8^{2} 24:9 24:13 24:14^{2} 24:18 24:19 24:22 25:1 25:2 25:6^{2} 25:9^{2} 25:10 25:11 25:15 25:16^{2} 25:18 25:19 26:2^{2} 26:3^{2} 26:9 26:11 26:12 26:14 26:15 26:18 26:19 27:2 27:3^{2} 27:4 27:15 27:16 27:17 27:18 27:19 27:20 27:21 27:22 27:23 27:24 27:25 27:26 28:1 28:7 28:8 28:10 28:13 28:15 28:20 28:23^{2} 28:34 28:35 28:43 28:54 28:55 28:57 28:58^{2} 28:63 29:2 29:6^{2} 29:9^{2} 29:11 29:12 29:13^{2} 29:15^{2} 29:18 29:19 29:20^{2} 29:21 29:22^{4} 29:23^{2} 29:27 29:29 30:2 30:3 30:6

30:7 30:12^2 30:13^2 30:14 30:16^2 30:17 30:18^2 30:19^2 30:20^4 31:5 31:6 31:8 31:12^3 31:13 31:14^2 31:17^3 31:18^2 31:19 31:20 31:21 31:25 31:26 31:28 31:29 32:6 32:13 32:17 32:18^2 32:21 32:27 32:29^3 32:35 32:36 32:39^2 32:41 32:42 32:48 32:49 33:11^3 33:13 33:16^2 33:20 34:1 34:12

JOS

1:1 1:3^2 1:7^2 1:8^2 1:16 1:18^2 2:3 2:5 2:9^3 2:10 2:12 2:13^2 2:14 2:19 2:23 3:2 3:4 3:7^2 3:8 3:10^2 3:13^3 3:15^2 3:16^3 3:17 4:1 4:6^2 4:7 4:10^2 4:11 4:14 4:16^2 4:18^2 4:24^3 5:1^2 5:2 5:4^2 5:5^2 5:6^4 5:8

5:12 5:13 6:5 6:7 6:8 6:9 6:15^2 6:17^3 6:20^2 6:21 6:22^2 6:23^2 6:24 6:25 6:26^2 7:14 7:15^3 7:24 7:26 8:5^2 8:8 8:9 8:11 8:13^2 8:14^2 8:16 8:17 8:18^2 8:20^2 8:21^2 8:22^2 8:24 8:25^3 8:27 8:29^2 8:33^3 8:34 8:35^2 9:2 9:9 9:10^2 9:16^3 9:24 9:26 9:27 10:1 10:4 10:6 10:10 10:11 10:14^2 10:20 10:24 10:27 10:28^2 10:30 10:32^2 10:35^4 10:37^3 10:39 10:40 11:1 11:2 11:4 11:10 11:11 11:13^2 11:15 11:16 11:17 11:19 11:20^3 11:21 11:23 11:26 12:4 12:6 12:7 13:2 13:4 13:9^2 13:16^2 13:17 13:22 13:25 14:4 14:6

14:8 14:9 14:11 14:12^2 14:14 15:2 15:4 15:7^2 15:8 15:16 15:17 15:18 15:46 16:1 16:10 17:7 17:12 17:13 17:16 18:6 18:8^2 18:13 18:14 18:16 19:8 19:10 19:11 19:21 20:3^2 20:4^3 20:6^2 20:9^2 21:26 21:44 22:2^2 22:10 22:16^3 22:18^2 22:20 22:23 22:27^3 22:28^2 22:29^2 22:30 22:31 22:34 23:1^2 23:3^2 23:4^2 23:6^2 23:7^2 23:10 23:11 23:12 23:13 23:14 23:15 24:5 24:8 24:15 24:16 24:17 24:20 24:22 24:25 24:26 24:29 24:31^2 24:33

JG

1:1 1:3 1:9 1:10 1:12 1:14 1:17 1:21 1:28 1:29 1:35 2:4 2:5 2:7^2

2:10 2:12 2:14^2 2:16 2:18 2:19 2:20 2:22 3:2 3:3 3:18 3:19^2 3:22 3:24 3:27 3:29 3:30 4:2 4:4 4:9 4:12 4:13 4:15 4:20 4:23 5:1 5:5 5:7^2 5:9 5:10^2 5:13 5:14 5:18 5:21 5:30 5:31 6:3 6:8 6:9 6:11 6:17 6:21 6:22 6:25^3 6:27^2 6:28^2 6:30^2 6:31^2 6:32 6:37 6:40 7:1^2 7:2 7:4 7:5^2 7:6 7:7 7:9 7:11 7:13^3 7:15 7:17 7:18 7:19^2 8:1 8:3 8:4 8:5 8:6 8:10^2 8:11 8:15^2 8:21 8:24 8:26^3 8:28 8:31 8:33 9:2^3 9:6 9:7 9:16 9:24 9:25^2 9:28 9:32 9:33^2

9:34 9:35 9:38^2 9:41 9:42 9:44^2 9:45^2 9:46 9:47 9:48^2 9:49 9:54 9:55 10:4 10:8^2 10:9 10:18 11:4 11:5 11:6 11:8 11:12 11:21 11:24 11:26^2 11:31 11:35^2 11:36 11:37 11:39 11:40 12:3 12:5^2 12:6 12:14 13:8 13:10 13:11 13:13 13:14^2 13:16 13:17 13:20 13:21

1 KI

2:29 2:31 2:37^2 2:39 2:41 2:42^2 2:43 2:44 2:46 3:4^2 3:6 3:8 3:9 3:10 3:12 3:13^2 3:16 3:18^2 3:23 3:27 3:65 4:12 4:29 4:33 5:1 5:3 5:4 5:6^4 5:7 5:9 5:15 5:16 6:1 6:6 6:7 6:17 6:21 6:27 7:3

7:18 7:19 7:29 7:40 7:41 7:42 7:48 7:51 8:1 8:4 8:5^2 8:8 8:10 8:11 8:12 8:16^2 8:18 8:19 8:20 8:23 8:24 8:25^3 8:27 8:29^2 8:36 8:40^2 8:41 8:43^4 8:46^2 8:47 8:50^2 8:52^2 8:54 8:56 8:58 8:59 8:60 8:64 8:66 9:2 9:3 9:4 9:8 9:11 9:16 9:19 9:20 9:21 9:23^2 9:25 9:27 10:2^2 10:4 10:6 10:8 10:11 10:13 10:14 10:15 10:27 11:4 11:7 11:10^2 11:17 11:19 11:21^3 11:22 11:25 11:27 11:28 11:29^2 11:30 11:33^2 11:36 11:37 11:38^3 11:41 11:42 12:3 12:6^2 12:8 12:9 12:10^2 12:13 12:15 12:16 12:18

12:20 12:22^2 13:2 13:3 13:4^3 13:6 13:9 13:10 13:11^2 13:14 13:17 13:18 13:20^2 13:21 13:23 13:26 13:31 14:1 14:2^2 14:5 14:6 14:8 14:9 14:10^2 14:11^2 14:14 14:22 14:25 14:28 14:29 15:5^2 15:7 15:11 15:12 15:17 15:18^2 15:19 15:21 15:23 15:29^2 15:31 16:4 16:7 16:11^2 16:14 16:16^2 16:18^2 16:20 16:22^2 16:25 16:27 16:30 16:31 16:33 17:3 17:4 17:5 17:7 17:10 17:12^2 17:14 17:17^2 17:24^2 18:1 18:4 18:5 18:7 18:9 18:10 18:12 18:17^2 18:18 18:24 18:26 18:27 18:29^2 18:30 18:36^4 18:37^3 18:38 18:44^2 18:45 19:1 19:3 19:4 19:8 19:13

19:17^3 20:4 20:6 20:9 20:10 20:11^2 20:12 20:13 20:16 20:25 20:26 20:28 20:29 20:30 20:31 20:37 20:41 21:1 21:2 21:3 21:5 21:8 21:10 21:13 21:14^2 21:16^2 21:21^2 21:24^2 21:27 22:2 22:3 22:7 22:13^2 22:14 22:16^2 22:17 22:18 22:20^2 22:25 22:31 22:32 22:33^2 22:35 22:39^2 22:43 22:45 22:53

2 KI

1:2 1:3 1:4 1:6^3 2:1 2:3^2 2:5^2 2:8 2:9 2:11 2:13 2:14 2:16 3:2 3:5 3:9 3:10 3:11 3:14 3:15 3:17^2 3:20 3:21^2 3:24 3:26^2 3:27 4:1 4:4 4:6 4:8^2 4:9 4:10 4:11 4:17^2 4:18 4:22

4:25^2 4:40 4:41 4:42 4:43 5:3 5:4 5:6 5:7^2 5:8^3 5:15 5:18 5:20 6:9 6:12^2 6:13 6:16^2 6:17 6:20^2 6:22 6:24 6:28 6:29 6:30 7:9 7:12 7:13^2 7:19 8:3 8:4 8:5 8:6^2 8:10 8:12 8:13^2 8:14 8:15^2 8:23 9:7 9:8 9:22 9:25 9:37 10:1 10:3 10:5^2 10:7 10:9 10:10^2 10:11 10:17 10:19 10:21^2 10:22 10:24 10:25 10:29^2 10:30^2 10:34 10:36 11:1 11:2 11:5^2 11:6 11:7 11:8 11:9^3 11:10 11:15 11:17 12:2 12:4^4 12:6 12:9^2 12:10^3 12:12 12:13 12:14 12:18^2 12:19 13:2 13:5 13:8 13:11 13:12 13:21 14:3

14:5 14:6 14:9^3 14:10 14:14 14:22 14:24 14:26 14:27 14:28 15:3 15:4^3 15:5 15:6 15:9 15:16^2 15:18 15:19 15:21 15:24 15:26 15:28 15:31 15:34^2 15:36 16:2 16:6 16:8 16:10 16:11 16:16 16:17 16:18 17:2^2 17:9 17:14 17:15^3 17:25 17:38 18:1 18:3^2 18:4 18:5^2 18:9 18:10 18:12 18:14 18:15 18:16 18:20 18:21 18:22 18:26 18:27^2 18:32 18:35^2 19:1 19:4 19:8 19:19^2 19:20 19:21 19:25^2 19:29 19:30 19:31 19:33 19:35^2 19:37 20:3 20:4 20:8^2 20:9^2 20:12^2 20:13^2 20:15^2 20:17^3 20:18 21:2 21:8^2 21:11 21:12 21:15 21:16 21:17^2 21:20 21:21^2

21:24 22:2 22:3 22:4 22:5 22:7 22:9^3 22:11 22:13^3 22:15 22:17 22:19 23:3 23:4 23:5 23:7 23:8 23:10 23:11 23:12 23:13 23:15^2 23:16 23:17^3 23:18 23:19^2 23:20 23:22 23:24^3 23:25 23:26 23:28 23:32^2 23:33 23:37^2 24:3 24:4 24:5 24:7 24:9^2 24:10 24:16 24:19^2 24:20 25:1 25:10 25:11^2 25:13^2 25:19^2 25:22 25:23 25:25^2 25:27^2 25:28

1 CH

1:43 2:9 2:24 2:55 4:10^5 4:21 4:23 4:33 4:43 5:18 5:20 6:10^2 6:31 6:33 6:49 6:61 7:21^2 7:40 9:1 9:16 9:28 9:31 9:33 10:5 10:7^3 10:8 10:11 10:13 10:14

10:17 10:19 10:31 12:1 12:8 12:15 12:20 12:22 12:24 12:32 12:38 13:2^3 13:4 13:6 13:11 13:12 13:14 14:2 14:8 14:11 14:15 15:12^2 15:13 15:26^2 15:27 15:29 16:1 16:7 16:10 16:12 16:30 16:32 16:35 16:39 16:40 16:41 16:42 17:1 17:2 17:3 17:5 17:7 17:8 17:10^2 17:11^2 17:16 17:24 17:25 17:27 18:1 18:7 18:11 19:1 19:3^2 19:6 19:9 19:10 19:13 19:14 19:15 19:16^2 19:19 20:1^2 20:3 20:4^2 21:2 21:5^2 21:10 21:12^2 21:15 21:17^3 21:18 21:22^2 21:23 21:24 21:28^2 21:29 22:2 22:5 22:12 22:13 22:19 23:13 23:24 23:25 23:29^2 23:32

25:7^2 26:6 26:28 27:1 27:6 27:26 27:28 27:29^2 28:1 28:8 28:9 28:12 28:14 28:17 28:18 29:8 29:9 29:11 29:14 29:16 29:17 29:21 29:22 29:27 29:30

2 CH

1:3 1:5 1:7 1:10^2 1:11 1:12 1:13 1:15 2:6 2:7^2 2:10 2:12 2:17 3:1 3:4 3:15 3:17^2 4:11 4:19 4:20 4:21 5:1^3 5:5 5:6 5:9 5:11 5:13 5:14 6:1 6:4 6:5^2 6:6 6:8 6:10 6:11 6:14 6:15 6:16^2 6:20^2 6:31 6:33^3 6:34 6:40 7:7 7:10 7:11 7:13 7:15 7:16 7:17 7:21^2 8:2 8:6^2 8:7 8:10 8:11 8:18 9:1^2

9:3 9:6 9:12 9:13 9:14 9:23 9:27 10:2 10:4 10:6 10:8^2 10:9^2 10:10^2 10:15 10:16 10:17 10:18^2 11:1 11:13 12:2 12:3 12:5 12:7 12:8 12:10 12:12 13:5 13:9^2 13:15 13:18 14:2 14:8^2 14:11 14:13^2 15:5^2 15:8 15:9 15:13 15:18^2 16:1 16:2 16:3 16:5 16:7 17:10^2 18:2 18:6 18:12 18:13 18:15 18:16 18:17 18:19^2 18:24 18:30 18:31 18:32^2 18:33 18:34 19:2 19:3 19:10^2 20:1 20:2 20:6 20:12 20:21 20:29 20:32 20:37 21:6 21:7 21:16 21:17^2 21:19 22:1 22:8^2 22:10 22:11^2 23:4 23:6 23:8^3 23:9 23:14 23:16 23:19 23:21

24:2 24:4 24:5 24:7 24:9 24:11^2 24:20 24:23 24:26 25:2 25:3^2 25:5 25:10 25:12 25:13 25:14^2 25:16^2 25:18^3 25:19 25:20 25:24 25:27 26:2 26:4 26:7 26:11 26:13 26:17 26:18 27:2^2 28:1 28:7 28:9^2 28:12 28:15 28:16 28:22 28:23 29:2^2 29:6 29:10 29:11 29:16 29:24 29:29 29:34 29:36 30:1 30:3 30:5 30:6 30:8 30:9^2 30:14 30:17^2 30:19 30:21 30:22 30:25^3 31:1 31:4^2 31:6 31:10 31:16 31:19^2 31:20 31:21 32:2 32:4 32:5 32:7 32:9 32:10 32:14^3 32:18^2 32:21 32:23 32:26 32:31^3 33:2 33:8^2 33:13 33:15 33:18 33:19 33:22 33:25

34:2 34:4^2 34:9^2 34:10^2 34:12 34:13 34:14 34:16 34:17 34:21^4 34:22^2 34:23 34:24 34:25 34:28 34:30 34:32 34:33^2 35:3 35:6 35:7 35:12 35:17^2 35:18^2 35:21 35:22 35:24^2 35:26 36:5 36:8 36:9 36:12 36:17 36:20 36:22^2

EZR

1:1 1:4 1:6^2 1:11 2:1 2:62 2:63 3:5^2 3:7 3:8 3:12 3:13 4:1 4:10 4:11 4:12 4:13 4:15^2 4:16 4:17 4:19^2 4:21 4:22 5:1 5:4 5:5 5:6 5:8 5:10^2 5:11 5:12 5:14 5:15 5:16 5:17 6:2 6:8^2 6:9 6:10 6:11 6:12 7:11 7:13^2 7:16 7:17 7:18 7:19 7:21

7:24 7:25^3 8:1 8:15 8:17 8:21 8:22^2 8:34 8:35 9:2 9:4^2 9:8 9:12 9:13^2 9:14 10:3 10:5 10:6 10:7 10:8^2 10:13 10:17 10:18 10:19

NE

1:2^2 1:3 1:4 1:5^2 1:6 1:8 1:9 2:1 2:5^2 2:7 2:8^2 2:10 2:12 2:14 2:16 2:17^2 2:18 2:19 3:15 3:16 3:25 3:26 3:27 4:1^2 4:3 4:7^3 4:10 4:12 4:15^2 4:16^2 4:17^2 4:18 4:22 4:23 5:2^2 5:3^2 5:4^2 5:9 5:11 5:12 5:13 5:14^2 5:15 5:17^2 5:18 5:19 6:1^3 6:2 6:3 6:6^2 6:9 6:11 6:12^2 6:13^3 6:14 6:16^3 7:2 7:5 7:6^2

7:64 7:65 7:72 8:1 8:2 8:3^2 8:9 8:12 8:14 8:15 8:17^2 9:6^2 9:10 9:11 9:15 9:17 9:18 9:21 9:23 9:24 9:28 9:29 9:32 9:33 9:35 9:36 10:1 10:28 10:30 10:31^2 10:36 10:37^2 10:39 11:2 11:3 11:6 11:12 11:19 11:23 12:1 12:31 12:38 12:40 12:43^2 12:44^2 13:1^2 13:2 13:3 13:7 13:10^2 13:14 13:17 13:19^4 13:21 13:22^4 13:23

ES

1:2 1:5 1:8 1:10 1:13 1:16 1:17 1:19^2 1:22^2 2:2 2:3 2:7 2:8 2:10 2:12 2:14 2:15 2:17 3:1 3:2 3:4^2 3:5 3:6 3:7^4 3:9^2 3:12^2 3:14^2

4:1 4:7^2 4:8^2 4:11 4:13 4:16 4:17 5:1 5:2^2 5:4 5:5^2 5:8 5:9^2 5:12 5:14 6:1 6:2^2 6:3 6:4 6:8^3 6:9 6:10 6:13 6:14 7:5 7:7 7:10 8:1 8:3 8:6 8:9^3 8:11 8:13^2 8:14 9:1^4 9:5 9:11^2 9:15 9:16^2 9:18 9:19 9:20 9:21 9:22 9:24 9:25^2 9:26 9:27 9:28^2

JOB

1:1^2 1:3 1:5^2 1:8^2 1:10 1:11 1:12 2:3^2 2:4 2:11 2:13 3:4 3:6 3:7 3:8 3:12 3:15 3:20 3:25 4:4 4:8 4:19 5:1 5:11^2 5:12 5:24 5:25 6:2 6:6 6:7 6:8^3 6:9^2 6:11^2 6:14 6:26

7:7 7:8 7:9 7:12 8:13 8:15 8:17^2 8:18 8:20 8:22 9:16 9:26 9:28 9:32 9:33 10:3^2 10:6^2 10:7^2 10:9 10:13 10:18 10:20 11:5 11:6^3 11:16 12:5^2 12:6 12:9 13:5 13:9 13:13 13:18 13:19 13:28 14:1 14:5 14:6 14:7^2 14:13^2 15:7 15:9^2 15:14^2 15:17 15:22 15:23 15:31 16:3 16:21 17:3 17:5 17:9 18:20^2 18:21 19:3 19:4 19:6 19:8 19:15 19:23^2 19:24 19:25^2 20:5 20:18 20:20 20:26 20:29 21:13^2 21:15 21:18 21:22 21:29 21:30 22:2 22:3^2 23:10 23:11 23:13 23:14^2 24:1 24:7 24:13 24:21 25:4 25:6 26:2^2 26:3 27:5

27:7 27:11 27:15 27:18 28:11 28:28 29:2 29:12^2 29:13 29:25 30:1 30:23 30:25 30:31 31:6 31:12 31:15 31:28 31:29 31:31 31:34 31:35^3 31:38 32:5 32:12^2 32:20 33:12 33:17 33:20 33:21^2 33:27 34:2 34:9 34:10 34:17^2 34:19 34:23 34:25 34:28 34:30 34:32 34:36 35:2 36:2 36:4 36:9 36:10 36:16 36:24 36:32 37:2 37:7 37:12 37:20 37:24 37:34 38:2 38:13^2 38:20^2 38:35 39:2 39:12 39:15^2 39:24 40:2^2 40:8 40:11 40:12 40:14 40:19 40:23 41:10 41:11 41:16 41:17^2 41:26 42:2 42:3^2 42:7^2 42:8 42:11^2 46:5

PS

1:1 1:3

2:4 2:12 3:1^2 3:6 4:3^2 4:6 4:7 5:4 5:6 5:11^2 7:1 7:4^2 7:6 7:8 8:2 8:4^2 9:10^2 9:13^2 9:14 9:15 9:17 9:20 10:2 10:10 10:18 11:2 11:5 12:3 12:5 13:4 14:1 14:2 14:3 14:7 15:2 15:3 15:4^2 15:5^2 16:3 16:4 17:1 17:2 17:3 17:5 17:7^2 17:9 17:12 18:*title* 18:12 18:30 18:32 18:34 18:36 18:38 18:39 18:40^2 18:47 18:48 20:6 21:8 22:3 22:7 22:8 22:9 22:23 22:25 22:26 22:29^2 22:31^2 24:1 24:4 24:6^2 25:3 25:12^2 25:14 26:7 27:4^2 28:1 30:3 30:12 31:4 31:6 31:11 31:15 31:19^2 31:24 32:6

32:10 32:11 33:18^2 34:7 34:8^2 34:9 34:10 34:12^2 34:16 34:18 34:21 34:22 35:1^2 35:3 35:4^2 35:8^2 35:10^2 35:11 35:14 35:19^2 35:20 35:26^2 35:27 35:28 36:4 36:10 37:9 37:13 37:16 37:22 37:37 38:12^2 38:13 38:14 38:19 38:20^2 39:1 39:4 39:13 40:4^2 40:12 40:14^2 40:15 40:16 41:1 41:7 41:8 41:10 41:11 42:4 44:5 44:7 44:13 44:16 45:14 46:10 48:13 49:6 49:9 49:10 49:11 49:12 49:20^2 50:4 50:5 50:16 50:21 50:22 50:23 51:4 51:8 52:7 53:1 53:2^2 53:3 53:5 53:6 54:4 55:6 55:12^3 55:18 55:19 56:1 56:2 56:13 57:2 57:3

57:4 58:4 58:8 58:11^2 59:1 59:13^2 60:4^2 60:5 60:12 61:2 61:5 61:8 62:11 63:9 63:11^2 64:4 64:8 65:2 65:4 65:5 65:8 66:16 67:2 68:1 68:4 68:11 68:12 68:18 68:20 68:23 68:28 68:30 68:33^2 68:35 69:4^3 69:6^2 69:9 69:10 69:12 69:14 69:22 69:23 69:31 69:32 69:34 69:35 69:36 70:2^2 70:3 70:4 70:6 70:10 70:13^2 70:18 70:24 72:6 72:9 72:12 73:25 73:27^2 73:28 74:3 74:9 74:18^2 74:23 75:1 76:11^2 77:4 77:14 78:4 78:5 78:6 78:7 78:8 78:11 78:20 78:35 78:39^2 78:44 78:53 78:60 78:65 79:4 79:6^2 79:11 80:1^2 80:12

80:13 80:15 81:5 81:13 83:2 83:4 83:16 83:18^2 84:4 84:11 84:12 85:6 85:9^2 85:12 86:2 86:5 86:17 87:4 87:5 87:6 88:4^2 88:5 89:7 89:10 89:15 89:19 89:23 89:34 89:35 89:41 89:48 90:9 90:12 90:14 91:1 91:5 91:6^2 92:7 92:11 92:13 92:15 93:1 94:9^2 94:10^2 94:11 94:13 95:10 95:11 96:10^2 96:12 97:7^2 97:10 98:8 99:6 99:7 99:8 100:3^2 101:3 101:5 101:6^2 101:7^2 101:8 102:4 102:8 102:11 102:20 103:1 103:5 103:6 103:11 103:13 103:14 103:17 103:18 103:20^2 103:21 104:5 104:9^2 104:14 104:15 104:26 104:27 104:28 105:3 105:5 105:19 105:34

105:45 106:3^2 106:4 106:5^3 106:8 106:10 106:20 106:25 106:31 106:32 106:33 106:40 106:41 106:46 107:7 107:8 107:15 107:21 107:23^2 107:29 107:31 107:34 107:36 107:38 108:6 108:13 109:11 109:15 109:16^2 109:20 109:27^3 109:31 111:2 111:5 111:6 111:10 112:1^2 113:6 113:8 114:5^2 114:6 115:8^2 115:11 115:13 115:17 118:2 118:3 118:4^2 118:7^2 118:13 118:26 119:2^2 119:5 119:11 119:17 119:18 119:20 119:21 119:42 119:53 119:57 119:63^2 119:71^2 119:73 119:74 119:75^2 119:77 119:79^2 119:80 119:84 119:101 119:106 119:116 119:118 119:125 119:132 119:138 119:148 119:150 119:152 119:162 120:5^2 120:6 121:3 121:4 122:3 122:6

123:1 123:2 123:4 125:1 125:4^2 126:1 126:5 126:6 127:1 127:5 128:1^2 128:4^2 129:5 129:7 130:4 130:6^2 131:2 132:12 133:2^2 133:3 134:3 135:2 135:5^3 135:6 135:18^2 135:20 136:5 136:6 136:7 136:10 137:3^2 137:8 137:9 138:8 139:14 139:21^2 140:9 140:10^2 140:12^2 141:4 141:10 142:4 142:7^2 143:3 143:7 143:12 144:3^2 144:4 144:10 144:12^2 144:13^2 144:14^2 144:15^3 145:14^2 145:18^2 145:19 145:20 146:4 146:5 146:6 146:8 147:11^2 148:4 149:2 149:6

PR

1:12 1:19 1:29 2:2 2:7 2:12 2:19 2:20 2:27 3:13^2 3:18^2 4:18 4:22 5:2^2 5:6 5:13 6:11 6:17 6:18^2

6:19^2 6:29 6:32 7:5 7:23 8:9^2 8:11 8:17^2 8:21^2 8:29 8:32 8:34 8:36^2 9:4 9:7^2 9:16 9:18^2 10:4 10:5^3 10:9^2 10:10 10:13^2 10:17^2 10:18^2 10:19 10:26 11:12 11:13 11:15^2 11:17 11:18 11:19 11:20 11:24^2 11:25 11:26^2 11:27^2 11:28 11:29 11:30 12:1 12:4 12:8 12:9^2 12:11^2 12:15 12:17 12:18 12:20 12:22 13:3^2 13:6 13:7^2 13:11 13:13 13:18^2 13:20 13:23 13:24^2 14:2^2 14:6 14:13 14:17 14:21^2 14:22^2 14:29^2 14:31^2 14:33^2 14:35 15:5 15:9 15:10^2 15:12 15:14 15:15 15:18 15:21 15:24 15:27^2 15:31 15:32^2 16:5 16:13 16:17 16:20 16:22 16:25

16:26 16:29 16:32^3 17:2 17:5 17:8 17:9^2 17:15^2 17:19^2 17:20^2 17:21 17:24 17:25 17:27 17:28 18:2 18:9^2 18:13 18:17 18:21 18:24^2 19:1^2 19:2^2 19:5 19:6 19:8^2 19:9 19:16^2 19:17^2 19:20 19:21 19:23 19:25 19:26^2 19:27 20:8 20:16 20:19^2 20:25 21:5 21:6 21:16 21:17^2 21:21 21:28 22:5 22:8 22:9 22:11 22:14 22:16^2 22:19 22:21^3 22:26^2 23:5 23:6 23:22 23:24 23:25 23:30^2 23:34^2 24:8 24:11^2 24:12^2 24:21 24:24 24:25 24:26 24:34 25:7^2 25:10 25:13 25:18 25:20^2 25:28^2 26:6 26:8^2 26:10 26:16 26:17^2 26:19 26:24 26:27 26:28 27:8^2 27:10 27:11^2

27:13 27:14 27:18 28:3 28:4 28:5 28:6^2 28:7 28:8^2 28:9 28:11 28:13 28:14^2 28:16^2 28:17 28:18 28:19^2 28:20 28:21 28:22^2 28:23^2 28:25^2 28:26 28:27^2 29:1^2 29:3 29:4 29:5 29:14 29:18 29:20 29:21 29:27 30:5 30:11 30:12 30:15 30:16^2 30:17 30:23 31:1 31:3 31:6^2 31:11 31:18 31:30

EC

1:9^3 1:11^2 1:13 1:14 1:15^2 1:16 1:17 1:18 2:3 2:6 2:7 2:8 2:9 2:11^3 2:12 2:13 2:14 2:15 2:16 2:17 2:18 2:21 2:24^3 2:26^3 3:2 3:9^2 3:11^2 3:12 3:13 3:14 3:15 3:16^2 3:18^3 3:19^2 3:21^2 3:22^3 4:1

4:3 4:4 4:10 4:14 4:15 4:16^2 5:1 5:4 5:5^2 5:6 5:8 5:10^2 5:11 5:16^2 5:18^2 6:2^2 6:3^3 6:8 6:10^3 6:11 7:2 7:10 7:11 7:12 7:13 7:14 7:15^2 7:18^2 7:20 7:21 7:22 7:24 7:29 8:2 8:7 8:8^3 8:9 8:12^2 8:14^2 8:15 8:16^2 8:17^2 9:1^2 9:2^4 9:3^2 9:4 9:5 9:6 9:9 9:11 9:12^2 9:15 9:17 10:1 10:3^2 10:8 10:9 10:20 11:4^2 11:5 11:6 11:8 11:9 12:3 12:5 12:10

CA

1:7 2:7 2:14 2:15 3:3 3:4^2 3:5 3:6 4:1 4:2 4:5 4:16 5:2 5:7 5:8^2 5:9 6:1

6:5 6:9 6:10 6:13 7:3 7:9^2 8:1 8:4 8:5^2 8:10 8:12 8:13

ISA

1:4 1:28 1:29 1:30 2:1 2:2 2:8 2:11 2:12^2 2:13 2:14 2:17 2:20 3:7 3:10 3:15 3:18 3:24 4:1 4:2 4:3 5:2 5:4 5:6 5:8^3 5:11^3 5:14 5:16 5:18 5:19^2 5:20^3 5:21 5:22 5:30 6:1 6:4 7:1 7:8 7:15 7:16 7:17^2 7:18^3 7:20 7:21 7:22^2 7:23 7:25 8:6 8:11 8:17 8:19^3 8:21 9:2^2 9:9 9:13 9:15 9:16 10:1^2 10:2^2 10:12 10:14 10:15^3 10:19 10:20^3 10:24 10:27^2 10:32^2 11:10 11:11^2 11:16 12:1

12:4^2 12:21 12:25 12:32 13:3 13:8 13:14 13:15^2 14:3 14:6 14:16^3 14:17^2 14:19^2 14:26^2 14:28 14:29 15:7 15:9 16:2 16:3 16:12^2 16:13^2 16:14 17:4^2 17:5 17:7 17:8 17:9 17:12 17:14^2 18:2 19:3 19:7 19:8^2 19:9^2 19:10 19:13 19:16 19:17 19:18 19:19 19:21 19:23 19:24 20:1 20:6^2 21:3 21:10 21:14^2 22:1 22:2 22:3 22:7 22:8 22:9 22:11 22:12 22:16^3 22:20^2 22:25^2 23:1 23:2 23:13 23:15^2 23:16^2 23:17 23:18 24:6 24:8 24:9 24:10 24:18^2 24:21^3 25:7 25:9 25:11 26:1 26:2 26:5 26:17 26:20 27:1^2 27:2 27:5 27:6 27:7^2 27:9

27:11^2 27:12^2 27:13^2 28:1 28:4 28:5 28:6^2 28:8 28:9 28:13 28:14 28:16 28:19 28:20^2 28:21 29:4 29:5 29:7^3 29:8 29:11^2 29:12 29:15 29:16^2 29:18 29:20 29:21^2 29:24^2 30:1^3 30:2 30:5 30:6 30:8 30:9^2 30:14^2 30:16 30:18^2 30:23^2 30:26 31:1 31:2 31:3^2 31:7 32:3^2 32:9 32:11 32:20^2 33:1 33:13^2 33:15^4 33:17 33:18 33:19 33:20 33:24 34:1^2 35:4 36:1 36:5 36:6 36:11 36:12^2 36:20^2 36:22 37:1 37:4 37:6 37:8 37:16 37:20^2 37:26^2 37:30 37:31 37:32 37:34 37:38 38:3 38:7^2 38:13 38:18 38:22 39:1 39:2^2 39:4^2 39:6^3 39:7 40:2^2 40:3

40:9^2 40:11 40:20^4 40:22^2 40:23 40:26^2 40:28 40:29 40:31 41:3 41:7^3 41:11^2 41:12^2 41:20^2 41:23^2 41:24 41:26^3 41:27 41:28 42:5^5 42:7 42:8 42:10^2 42:11 42:16^2 42:17^2 42:18 42:19^2 43:1^2 43:7 43:8^2 43:9 43:10^2 43:12 43:13 43:25 43:26 44:2 44:3 44:7 44:8 44:9^2 44:10 44:13 44:18^2 44:20 44:24^4 44:25^2 44:26^2 44:27 44:28 45:3^2 45:6^2 45:9^2 45:10 45:15 45:16 45:18^2 45:19 45:20^3 45:21 45:23 45:24 46:5 46:10 46:11 46:12 47:7 47:8^3 47:13 48:4 48:8^3 48:9 48:16 48:17 48:18 49:5 49:6^2 49:9^3 49:10 49:15 49:17 49:19 49:20 49:23^2 49:25 49:26^2

50:2 50:4^2 50:6 50:7 50:8 50:9 50:10^3 50:11^3 51:1^2 51:2 51:6 51:7 51:9 51:10 51:12^3 51:13 51:14^3 51:15 51:16 51:18^2 51:22 51:23^3 52:5^2 52:6^3 52:7^5 52:11 53:2 53:15 54:1^2 54:9^2 54:10 54:16^2 54:17^2 55:1^2 55:2^3 55:5^2 55:10 55:11^2 55:13 56:2^3 56:3 56:4^2 56:5 56:6^2 56:8 56:11 57:1 57:11 57:13 57:15^2 57:19^2 58:2 58:5 58:6^2 58:7^4 58:12 59:1 59:2 59:5^2 59:15^2 59:16^2 59:20 59:21 60:8 60:11 60:12 60:14^2 60:15 60:16 60:21 61:1 61:2 61:3^3 61:9^2 61:11 62:1 62:6 62:9^2 63:1^3 63:2 63:5 63:7 63:8 63:11^2 63:12 63:13^2 64:1

64:2 64:4 64:5^2 64:7^2 65:1^3 65:2 65:3^2 65:5 65:8 65:10 65:11^6 65:12 65:16^2 65:18 65:20 65:24 66:1 66:2 66:3^4 66:4 66:5^3 66:6 66:10^2 66:11^2 66:17 66:18 66:19^2 66:23 66:24

JER

1:1 1:7 1:17 2:2 2:3 2:5 2:6^3 2:8^2 2:11 2:13 2:17 2:19^2 2:24^2 2:28 3:1 3:6 3:9 3:13 3:16 3:17 3:18 4:4 4:9^2 4:11 4:14 4:16 4:31^3 5:1^2 5:6 5:7 5:19 5:22 5:24 5:26 6:10 6:11 6:15^2 6:27 7:1^2 7:2 7:7 7:8 7:18 7:22 7:23^2 7:25 7:28 7:32 8:3 8:10 8:12 8:13 8:16^2 8:19

9:1^2 9:2^2 9:10 9:12^3 9:17^3 9:18 9:24^3 9:25 9:26^2 10:4 10:11 10:18 10:23^2 10:25^2 11:1 11:3 11:4 11:5 11:7 11:13 11:14 11:17 11:19^2 11:20^2 11:21^2 12:1 12:4 12:14 12:17 13:4 13:6 13:11 13:12 13:13 13:15 13:20^2 13:23 13:24 13:26 14:1 14:8 14:9 14:15 14:18^2 14:22 15:4 15:9 15:10 15:13 15:15 15:18 16:3^3 16:10 16:12 16:13 16:14 16:15^2 16:21 17:4 17:5 17:7 17:8 17:11 17:13^2 17:16 17:18 17:20 17:23 18:4 18:8^2 18:10 18:14 18:16 18:19 18:20 19:2 19:6 19:7 19:8 19:9 19:10 19:11 19:15^2 20:1 20:2 20:3 20:6

20:12 20:16 20:17 20:18 21:2 21:4 21:7 21:9^3 21:12^2 22:2^2 22:5 22:10 22:13^2 22:14 22:21 22:23 22:25 22:26 22:30 23:1 23:2 23:5 23:7 23:14 23:16 23:17^2 23:24 23:25 23:26 23:28^2 23:29 23:30 23:31 23:32 23:34^2 23:39 24:2 24:3 24:5 24:7 24:8^2 24:10 25:1^2 25:3 25:5 25:7 25:12^2 25:13^2 25:16 25:23 25:24 25:30 25:31 25:33 26:2 26:3 26:8^2 26:12 26:13 26:15 26:20 26:24 27:5 27:8^3 27:10 27:11 27:13 27:14 27:15^2 27:16 27:18 27:19 27:21 27:22 28:1 28:3 28:4 28:5 28:6 28:7 28:8 28:9 28:12 28:14 29:1 29:2 29:4

29:6^2 29:8 29:10 29:11 29:16^4 29:17 29:25 29:26^3 29:31 29:32 30:1 30:2 30:3^2 30:4 30:7^2 30:8^2 30:13 30:16^3 30:19 30:20 30:21 31:4 31:6 31:8 31:10 31:11 31:17 31:19^2 31:24 31:27 31:28 31:30 31:31 31:32^2 31:33 31:37 31:38 32:1 32:7 32:8^2 32:9 32:11^2 32:12^2 32:14 32:23 32:24 32:29 32:31^2 32:35 32:39 32:40^2 32:42 33:2 33:9^2 33:10 33:11^2 33:13 33:14^2 33:15 33:20 33:21 33:22 33:24 33:26 34:7 34:8^2 34:9^2 34:10^2 34:13 34:18 34:20 34:21 35:7 35:8 35:10 35:11 35:17 35:18 36:1 36:2 36:3^3 36:6 36:7 36:8 36:9^2 36:13

36:23^3 36:24 36:25 36:27 36:28 36:31 37:5 37:7 37:10 37:11 37:15 37:18 37:20 37:21^2 38:1 38:2^2 38:4 38:5 38:6 38:7 38:9 38:14 38:16^2 38:19 38:21 38:22 38:25 38:26 38:27 38:28 39:4 39:9^4 39:14 39:16 39:17 40:1^2 40:6 40:7^2 40:10 40:11^4 40:13 40:14 40:15 41:1 41:2 41:3^2 41:5 41:7^2 41:8 41:9 41:10^2 41:11^2 41:12 41:13^2 41:14 41:16^2 42:3^2 42:10 42:12 42:16 42:17^2 42:19 42:20 42:22 43:1 43:3 43:5 43:6 43:10 43:13 44:1 44:2 44:3^2 44:4 44:8^4 44:10 44:12 44:13 44:14^2 44:15^3 44:16 44:20 44:21 44:22 44:24 44:25 44:26^2

44:27 44:28^2 44:29^3 44:30^2 45:1 45:4^2 46:7 46:9^2 46:10 46:13 46:25 46:26 47:1^2 47:2^2 47:4^2 48:9 48:10^2 48:12^2 48:17^2 48:18 48:19^2 48:20 48:28^2 48:35^2 48:36 48:41 48:44^2 48:45 49:2^2 49:4 49:5^2 49:8 49:12 49:13 49:16^2 49:17 49:19^3 49:20^2 49:22 49:26 49:31 49:32 49:34 49:37 49:39 50:1 50:4 50:5 50:7 50:10 50:12 50:13 50:14 50:16 50:20 50:21 50:28 50:29^2 50:30 50:31 50:33 50:34 50:37 50:44^3 50:45^2 51:1^2 51:2 51:3^2 51:4 51:7 51:12 51:13 51:24 51:31 51:32 51:39 51:44 51:46^2 51:47 51:48 51:50 51:52 51:60^2 51:62^2 51:63 51:64 52:2^2

52:3 52:4 52:14 52:15^3 52:17^2 52:19 52:20 52:25^2 52:31 52:32

LA

1:1^2 1:6 1:7 1:8 1:10^2 1:12 1:16 1:17 1:21^3 2:4 2:13 2:15^2 2:16 2:17^2 2:19 2:22^2 3:1 3:6 3:7 3:22 3:25^2 3:26 3:27 3:30 3:37 3:44 3:57 3:62 4:5^2 4:6 4:9^2 4:12 4:13 4:14 4:17 4:18 4:21 5:8 5:16

EZE

1:18 1:23 1:25 1:26 1:28^2 2:2^2 2:3 2:5 2:8 3:1 3:2 3:3 3:8 3:10 3:13 3:15 3:16 3:21 3:26 3:27^2 4:4 4:9 4:12 4:14 4:17 5:5 5:6 5:7^2 5:9 5:13 5:14^2

5:15 6:6 6:7 6:8^2 6:9 6:10^3 6:12^3 6:13 6:14 7:4 7:7 7:9^3 7:13 7:15^2 7:16 7:27 8:1 8:3 8:4 8:6^2 8:9 8:13 8:17 9:1 9:4^3 9:8 10:1 10:6 10:7^2 10:12 10:15 10:20^2 11:2 11:5 11:10 11:12^2 11:13 11:20 11:24 11:25 12:4 12:6 12:10 12:12^2 12:14 12:15 12:16^2 12:19^3 12:20^2 12:22^2 12:25 12:27^2 13:2^2 13:3 13:6 13:9^3 13:11 13:14^3 13:15^2 13:18^2 13:19^3 13:21 13:22 13:23^2 14:4^2 14:5 14:7 14:8^2 14:9 14:10 14:11^2 14:15^2 14:17^2 14:19 14:22^3 14:23^2 15:7 16:5^2 16:15 16:21 16:24 16:25 16:27 16:31^2 16:32 16:33 16:34

16:37^3 16:38 16:44 16:45 16:46^2 16:47 16:52^2 16:54^3 16:57 16:62 16:63^2 17:7 17:8^3 17:9 17:14^3 17:15^2 17:16 17:19^2 17:20 17:21^2 17:24 18:2 18:4 18:5 18:8^2 18:10^2 18:11 18:14 18:15 18:17^2 18:18 18:19 18:20 18:21^2 18:22^2 18:23^2 18:24^4 18:26 18:27^2 18:28 18:32 19:5 19:9 19:11 19:14 20:1 20:6^2 20:9 20:12^3 20:14 20:15 20:20^2 20:22 20:23 20:24^3 20:25 20:26^5 20:27 20:32^2 20:38^2 20:42 20:43 20:44 20:48 21:4 21:5^2 21:7 21:10 21:11 21:14 21:15 21:19 21:20 21:23^2 21:26^2 21:29 22:3 22:4 22:5^2 22:9 22:10 22:14 22:16 22:22 22:24 22:30^2 23:7

23:13 23:14 23:37 23:40 23:43 23:44 23:45 23:48 23:49 24:8 24:11^3 24:19 24:21 24:24^2 24:26^3 24:27^2 25:5 25:7 25:10 25:11 25:12 25:17 26:1 26:2^2 26:6 26:17^2 26:18 26:19 26:20^3 27:3 27:7^2 27:8 27:27 27:29 28:3 28:8 28:9^2 28:13 28:14 28:15 28:17 28:18 28:19 28:22 28:23 28:24^3 28:25 28:26^2 29:3 29:6 29:9 29:12^2 29:15 29:16 29:18 29:21^2 30:5 30:6 30:7^2 30:8 30:9 30:12 30:20 30:22 30:25 30:26 31:1 31:9^2 31:14^3 31:16^2 31:17^3 31:18 32:1 32:8 32:15^3 32:17 32:18 32:20 32:21 32:24 32:25^2 32:27 32:28 32:29^2 32:30^2 32:32 33:5

33:11 33:12^2 33:13 33:14 33:15 33:16^2 33:19 33:21^2 33:22 33:24 33:27^3 33:28 33:29 33:30 33:32 33:33 34:2 34:3 34:4^4 34:10 34:12^2 34:16^4 34:19^2 34:27^2 34:30^2 35:4 35:5 35:7^2 35:8 35:9 35:12 35:15 36:3 36:4^2 36:7 36:11 36:18 36:23 36:28 36:30 36:31 36:33 36:34 36:35 36:36^3 36:38 37:6 37:9 37:13 37:14 37:25 37:28 38:7 38:8 38:10 38:11^2 38:12^3 38:14 38:16 38:17 38:18 38:19 38:20^3 38:22 38:23 39:4 39:6^2 39:7 39:9 39:10^3 39:11 39:12 39:13 39:14 39:15 39:17^2 39:21^2 39:22^2 39:26 39:28 40:1 40:4^2 40:6 40:10^2 40:12^2 40:20 40:21

40:22 40:24 40:34 40:37 40:39 40:41 40:47 40:48^2 40:49 41:6 41:9^2 41:11^2 41:12 41:17 41:18 41:19 41:22 42:1 42:7 42:8 42:12 42:13 43:1 43:3^2 43:8 43:10 43:11^2 43:19 43:21 44:3 44:5 44:7 44:8 44:9 44:10 44:14 44:15 44:17 44:18 44:22^2 44:25 44:27 44:30 44:31 45:11 45:13 45:20^2 45:22 46:1 46:2 46:4 46:8 46:9^2 46:12 46:18 46:20 46:24 47:2 47:3 47:5^2 47:9 47:12 47:22^2 48:9 48:10 48:11 48:12 48:15 48:18 48:19 48:22 48:23 48:35

DA

1:3 1:5 1:8^2 1:13 1:16 1:18 1:20^2 2:8 2:9 2:10^2

2:11^2 2:13 2:16 2:18^2 2:21 2:25 2:28 2:29 2:30^3 2:34^2 2:35^2 2:40 2:45^2 2:46 2:47 3:3^2 3:5^2 3:7^2 3:8 3:10^2 3:11 3:15^2 3:17 3:18 3:19 3:20 3:28^2 3:29^2 4:1 4:2 4:6 4:9^2 4:17^2 4:19 4:20 4:22 4:25^2 4:26^2 4:30 4:32 4:34 4:37 5:2 5:3 5:5 5:6 5:13 5:14^2 5:15 5:16 5:17^3 5:19 5:21^2 5:25 5:29 6:2 6:7 6:8 6:10 6:12^2 6:13 6:15^2 6:17 6:21 6:22 6:23 6:25 6:26 7:7 7:14^2 7:16 7:20^3 7:22 7:24 8:1 8:2 8:4^2 8:6 8:7 8:13 8:21 8:22 9:2 9:4^2 9:7^3 9:11^2

9:12 9:13 9:15 9:16 9:17 9:25 9:26 9:27 10:1 10:7 10:11 10:12 10:16 10:21^2 11:3 11:6^3 11:16 11:24 11:26 11:30 11:31 11:32 11:33 11:36^2 12:1^5 12:2 12:3^2 12:5^2 12:7^2 12:11^2 12:12

HO

1:1 2:3 2:5^2 2:6 2:8 2:10 2:12 2:16^2 2:18 2:21 2:23 4:3 4:4 4:6 4:14 5:9 5:10 6:5 6:8 7:2 7:7 8:3 8:4 9:4 9:10 9:12 10:5 10:10 10:11 11:3 11:4 12:8 12:9 13:2 13:3^2 13:8 13:10 14:7

JOE

1:1 1:4^3 2:5 2:11 2:16 2:17 2:25 2:26 2:27^2 2:28

2:38 3:1 3 3: 6 3: 17 3: 18^2 3: 21

AM

1:5 1:8 1:13 2:7 2:13 2:15^3 2:16^2 3:1 3:12 3:14^2 4:1 4:2^2 4:13^2 5:3^2 5:8^2 5:9^2 5:10^2 5:13 5:14 5:15 5:18 6:1 6:3 6:4 6:5 6:6 6:8 6:9 6:10^2 7:2 8:3^2 8:4 8:5 8:8 8:9^2 8:11 8:13 8:14 9:1^3 9:5^2 9:6^2 9:8 9:11^2 9:12^2 9:13^2

OB

3^2 7^2 8 9 11^2 12 14^2 20

JON

1:2 1:4 1:5 1:6 1:7 1:10 1:11 1:12 2:8 2:9^2 3:2^2 3:8 3:9 3:10^3

4:2 4:6 4:7 4:8^2 4:11

MIC

1:1 1:2 1:4 2:1 2:4 2:5 2:6^2 2:7^2 2:8 3:4 3:5^3 3:6 3:9 4:1 4:6 4:7^2 4:11 5:2 5:3 5:7 5:10^2 6:5 6:10 6:16 7:3 7:5 7:10 7:11^2 7:12 7:13 7:18

NA

1:5 1:7 1:11 1:14 1:15^2 2:1 3:4 3:7^2 3:8^2 3:19

HAB

1:3 1:6^2 1:8 1:13^2 1:14 2:2^2 2:6^3 2:7^2 2:8 2:9^3 2:12 2:13 2:15^3 2:17 2:18^2 2:19 3:8 3:16

ZEP

1:5^4 1:6^2 1:8 1:9 1:10^2 1:11 1:12 1:15 1:17

1:18 2:5 2:15^3 3:1 3:6^3 3:8^2 3:9 3:11^2 3:16 3:18 3:19^4 3:20^2

HAG

1:2 1:6 1:9 1:11 2:3 2:5 2:13 2:14 2:18 2:22 2:23

ZEC

1:8 1:9 1:10 1:11 1:13 1:14 1:15 1:19 1:21 2:3 2:7 2:8 2:9 2:11^2 3:2 3:4 3:7 3:8 3:9^2 3:10 4:1^2 4:4 4:5 4:9 4:14 5:3^4 5:4 5:5^2 5:6 5:7 5:10 6:4 6:7 6:8 6:15^2 7:1 7:11 7:13 7:14 8:9^3 8:10 8:13^2 8:16 8:17 8:20 8:23^3 9:7 9:8^2 9:12 9:16 11:1 11:5 11:9^4 11:10 11:11^3 11:13

11:14 11:16^5 11:17 12:3^2 12:4 12:6 12:7 12:8^3 12:9^3 12:10 12:11 12:14 13:1 13:2^2 13:3^3 13:4^2 13:7 13:8 14:4 14:6 14:7 14:8^2 14:9 14:12 14:13^2 14:15 14:16^2 14:17 14:18^2 14:19 14:20 14:21^2

MAL

1:6 1:7 1:9 1:10 1:12 2:4^2 2:12^2 2:13 2:15 2:16^2 2:17 3:3 3:5^2 3:10^2 3:14^2 3:15^2 3:16^3 3:17^2 3:18^2 4:1^3 4:2 4:3

MT

1:6 1:20 1:22 2:2 2:6 2:8 2:12 2:15 2:16^2 2:17 2:22 2:23 3:3 3:9 3:11 4:3 4:4 4:12 4:14 4:17 4:24^2 5:4 5:14 5:15 5:16

5:17 5:21 5:22 5:23 5:27 5:28 5:29[2] 5:30[2] 5:32[2] 5:33 5:38 5:39 5:42[2] 5:43 5:44[2] 5:45 6:1 6:2 6:4 6:5 6:7 6:16 6:18 6:23[2] 6:29 6:32 7:1 7:3[2] 7:6 7:8[3] 7:11 7:12 7:13 7:14 7:19 7:21[3] 7:23 7:25 7:26 7:27 8:4 8:8 8:10 8:11 8:16[2] 8:17 8:24 8:27 8:28[2] 8:33 8:34 9:6[2] 9:12[3] 9:13 9:16 9:22 9:26 9:28 9:30 9:31 9:38 10:14 10:15 10:19 10:20 10:22 10:25[2] 10:26[2] 10:27[2] 10:34 10:37[2] 10:38 10:39[2] 10:40[3] 10:41[2] 11:3 11:8 11:11[2] 11:15 11:24 11:28 12:1 12:2 12:3 12:5 12:6 12:10

12:11 12:16 12:17 12:22 12:30[2] 12:36[2] 12:45 12:48 13:2 13:12 13:17 13:19 13:20[2] 13:22[2] 13:23[2] 13:28 13:32 13:35 13:37 13:39 13:41 13:44[2] 13:46 13:47 13:52 13:53 13:54 14:1 14:15 14:20 14:21 14:33 14:35[3] 14:36 15:4 15:11[2] 15:12 15:17 15:28 15:30 15:31 15:37 15:38 16:1 16:11 16:12 16:13 16:14 16:15 16:18 16:20[2] 16:21[2] 16:23[2] 17:10 17:12 17:13 17:18 17:24 17:27[2] 18:6 18:7[2] 18:10[2] 18:11 18:12 18:13[2] 18:14 18:16 18:19[2] 18:25 18:28 18:28 18:31 18:32[2] 18:34 19:1 19:4 19:12 19:13 19:16 19:17 19:21 19:22 19:23 19:28 19:29 19:30 20:1

20:7 20:9 20:10 20:14 20:21 20:22[2] 20:23 20:25[2] 20:30 20:32 20:33 21:4 21:9[3] 21:12[2] 21:15 21:31 21:32 21:34 21:45 22:3 22:16 22:21 22:23 22:31 22:34 22:46 23:3 23:12 23:13 23:17 23:18 23:19 23:21[2] 23:22[2] 23:26[2] 23:31 23:35 23:37 23:39 24:2 24:4 24:6 24:13 24:19[2] 24:20 24:24 24:32 24:33 24:36 24:38[2] 24:43 24:46 24:47 24:48 24:50[2] 25:3 25:9 25:10 25:16 25:17 25:18 25:20 25:22 25:24 25:25 25:26 25:29[3] 26:2 26:4 26:12 26:13 26:16[2] 26:17 26:21 26:23 26:24[2] 26:29 26:41 26:46 26:48[2] 26:52 26:54 26:55 26:56 26:57 26:63 26:68

26:71 26:73 27:3 27:4[2] 27:8 27:9[2] 27:14 27:15 27:17 27:18 27:19 27:20 27:21 27:24[2] 27:31 27:33 27:35 27:39 27:40 27:46 27:54[2] 27:62 27:63[2] 27:64 28:2 28:7 28:10 28:11

MK

1:9 1:14 1:22 1:27 1:32[2] 1:34 1:36 1:38 1:45 2:1 2:2 2:8 2:10[2] 2:11 2:12 2:15 2:16 2:17[2] 2:21 2:23 2:24 2:25 3:2 3:9 3:10 3:12 3:14[2] 3:20 3:24 3:25 3:29 4:1 4:8 4:9 4:10 4:11 4:12 4:15 4:22 4:24 4:25[3] 4:28 4:31 4:32 4:37 4:38 4:40 4:41 5:4 5:7 5:10 5:12 5:14[2] 5:15 5:16[2]

5:18[2] 5:23 5:26 5:29[2] 5:30 5:32 5:36 5:38 5:40 5:43[2] 6:2 6:5 6:8 6:10 6:11 6:12 6:13 6:14 6:15[2] 6:20 6:21 6:22 6:25 6:36 6:44 6:55[2] 6:56 7:2 7:9 7:11 7:15[2] 7:18 7:20[2] 7:26 7:32 7:34 7:36 8:8 8:9 8:21 8:25 8:27 8:29 8:30 8:31 8:32 8:33[2] 9:1[2] 9:7 9:9 9:10 9:11 9:12 9:13 9:18 9:23 9:25 9:26 9:30 9:31 9:32 9:33 9:37 9:39 9:40 9:42[2] 9:43 9:45 10:13[2] 10:17 10:18 10:22 10:23 10:24 10:29 10:31 10:35 10:36 10:37 10:38[2] 10:39[2] 10:42 10:47 10:48 10:52[2] 11:3 11:5

11:9[3] 11:10 11:16 11:23[2] 11:24 11:25 11:32 12:2 12:12 12:14 12:15 12:17[2] 12:19 12:26 12:28 12:34[2] 12:35 12:41 12:43 12:44 13:2 13:11[3] 13:13 13:14[2] 13:15 13:16 13:17[2] 13:18 13:20 13:24 13:25 13:28 13:29 13:30 13:32 14:4 14:9 14:12 14:20 14:21[2] 14:25[2] 14:28 14:35 14:42 14:44[2] 14:47 14:58 14:69 14:70 14:72 15:5 15:6 15:7 15:9 15:10 15:11 15:12 15:29[2] 15:32[2] 15:35 15:39 15:42 16:1 16:4 16:7 16:10 16:11 16:12 16:16[2] 16:17

LU

1:4 1:7 1:8 1:19 1:20 1:21 1:22 1:23 1:35 1:41 1:45 1:49 1:50

1:57 1:59 1:61 1:65 1:66 1:71[2] 1:74[2] 1:79 2:1[2] 2:6[2] 2:18 2:20 2:23 2:24 2:26 2:35 2:38[2] 2:46 2:47 2:49[2] 3:7 3:8 3:11[3] 3:13 3:20 3:21 4:3 4:4 4:6 4:18 4:20 4:26 4:29 4:40 4:41 4:42 4:45[2] 5:1 5:3 5:7[2] 5:9 5:24[2] 5:29 5:31[2] 5:36 6:1 6:4 6:5 6:6 6:7 6:12 6:18 6:21[2] 6:23 6:24 6:25[2] 6:28 6:29[2] 6:30[2] 6:31 6:32 6:38 6:40 6:41[2] 6:42[3] 6:42[3] 6:48 6:49[3] 7:3 7:4 7:6 7:9 7:10[2] 7:11 7:14 7:15 7:16[2] 7:19 7:20 7:21[2] 7:22 7:28[2] 7:29 7:36 7:37 7:39 7:43

7:49[2] 8:1 8:8 8:10 8:12 8:14 8:15 8:16 8:17[2] 8:18 8:22 8:31 8:34 8:36 8:38 8:40 8:41 8:45 8:46 8:47 8:53 9:5[2] 9:7[3] 9:8[2] 9:10 9:11 9:12 9:17 9:18 9:19 9:20 9:21 9:32[2] 9:37 9:39 9:45[2] 9:48[2] 9:50 9:51 9:54 9:57 10:2 10:9 10:11 10:12[3] 10:16[4] 10:20 10:21[2] 10:23 10:24 10:31 10:36 10:37 10:38 10:40[2] 10:42 11:1 11:4 11:10[3] 11:11 11:13 11:18 11:23[2] 11:26 11:27 11:28 11:33 11:35 11:38 11:40[3] 11:44 11:48 11:50 11:52 11:54 12:1 12:2[2] 12:3 12:4[3] 12:9 12:10 12:13 12:26 12:27 12:30 12:33[2] 12:36[2]

12:37 12:39 12:42 12:43 12:44[2] 12:45 12:46 12:47 12:58 12:51 12:56 12:58 13:1[2] 13:2 13:4[2] 13:9 13:14 13:17 13:23 13:32 13:33 13:34 13:35 14:1 14:9 14:10[3] 14:11 14:12 14:15[2] 14:17 14:21 14:23 14:24 14:29 14:31 14:32[2] 14:35 15:4 15:7[2] 15:10 15:12 15:14 15:15 15:16 15:29 15:31 15:32 16:1 16:2 16:4 16:9 16:10[3] 16:12[2] 16:15 16:16 16:18 16:22 16:24 16:25 16:26[2] 16:27 16:28 17:1 17:2[2] 17:9[2] 17:10 17:11 17:12 17:14 17:15 17:18 17:24 17:27 17:29 17:31[2] 17:34 18:1 18:3 18:8 18:9 18:11 18:12 18:14[2] 18:15 18:19 18:22 18:24[2]

18:26 18:29 18:31 18:35 18:37 18:39 18:41[2] 19:4[2] 19:7[2] 19:10 19:11 19:15[2] 19:21[2] 19:22[3] 19:23 19:24[2] 19:26[3] 19:27 19:32 19:37 19:38 19:40 19:43 19:45[2] 20:1 20:6 20:7 20:10 20:14 20:17 20:18[2] 20:19 20:20[2] 20:21 20:27 20:28 20:35 20:37 20:40 20:41 21:3 21:4 21:6 21:8 21:20 21:21 21:22 21:23[2] 21:30 21:31 21:34 21:35 21:36[2] 21:37[2] 22:8 22:9 22:21 22:22 22:23 22:25 22:26[3] 22:27[4] 22:30 22:31 22:32 22:34[2] 22:36[2] 22:37[2] 22:40 22:47 22:63 22:64 22:70 23:2 23:7[2] 23:14 23:23 23:24 23:25 23:26 23:29 23:48[2] 23:49 23:53 29:54 24:10 24:12

24:13 24:15 24:16 24:17 24:21 24:23[2] 24:25 24:33 24:37 24:39 24:44 24:45 24:47

JOH

1:3 1:7 1:8[2] 1:9[2] 1:12 1:15 1:21 1:22[2] 1:25 1:31 1:33 1:34 1:39 1:48 2:9 2:10 2:14 2:16 2:17 2:18 2:20 2:25 3:2[2] 3:6[2] 3:7 3:8 3:11[2] 3:13 3:15 3:16[2] 3:17 3:18[2] 3:19 3:20 3:21[3] 3:26 3:28[2] 3:29 3:31[3] 3:32 3:33[2] 3:36[2] 4:1 4:5 4:9 4:10 4:11 4:14[2] 4:15 4:18 4:19 4:20 4:24 4:25 4:26 4:27 4:29 4:32 4:34 4:36[4] 4:37 4:38 4:39[2] 4:40 4:42 4:44 4:45 4:47[2] 4:50 4:53 4:54

5:6[2] 5:10 5:11 5:12 5:13[2] 5:15 5:18 5:20[2] 5:23[2] 5:24[2] 5:25 5:28 5:29[2] 5:32[2] 5:34 5:36[3] 5:40 5:42 5:44 5:45[2] 6:2[2] 6:5 6:7 6:11 6:12 6:13 6:14[3] 6:15 6:18 6:22[2] 6:23 6:24 6:27 6:28 6:29 6:30 6:32 6:35[2] 6:36 6:37[2] 6:38 6:39 6:40[2] 6:42 6:45 6:46 6:47 6:48 6:50 6:51 6:56 6:57 6:58[2] 6:61 6:63[2] 6:64[2] 6:65 6:66 6:69[2] 6:71 7:3[2] 7:4 7:7 7:16 7:18[3] 7:23 7:26 7:28 7:32 7:33 7:35 7:36 7:37 7:38 7:39[2] 7:42 7:50 8:5 8:6 8:7 8:12 8:16 8:17 8:18[2] 8:24[2] 8:25 8:26

8:27 8:28[2] 8:29[2] 8:37 8:38[2] 8:40 8:47 8:48 8:50 8:52 8:54[2] 9:2 9:3 9:4 9:8[2] 9:11 9:13 9:16 9:17 9:18[2] 9:22[2] 9:24[2] 9:25 9:29 9:30 9:31 9:32[2] 9:35 9:36 9:37 9:39[2] 9:40 10:1 10:2 10:8 10:10[2] 10:12 10:17 10:21 10:25 10:33 10:38[2] 10:41 11:2 11:4[2] 11:6 11:7 11:11[2] 11:13 11:15 11:16 11:17 11:20 11:22 11:24 11:25 11:27 11:29 11:30 11:31 11:37 11:39 11:40 11:41 11:42[3] 11:44 11:49 11:50[3] 11:51[3] 11:52[3] 11:56 11:57[2] 12:2 12:6 12:9[2] 12:10 12:11 12:12[2] 12:13 12:16[2] 12:17 12:18[2] 12:20 12:23 12:25[2] 12:29[2] 12:34

12:35 12:36 12:38 12:39 12:40 12:44[2] 12:45[2] 12:46 12:48[3] 12:50 13:1 13:3[2] 13:5 13:10 13:15 13:16[2] 13:18[2] 13:19[2] 13:20[3] 13:21 13:24 13:27 13:29[3] 13:34 13:35 14:3 14:9 14:10[3] 14:11 14:12[2] 14:13[2] 14:16 14:20[2] 14:21[3] 14:22 14:24 14:29 14:31[2] 15:2[3] 15:5 15:8 15:11[2] 15:12 15:13 15:15 15:16[3] 15:17 15:18 15:20 15:21 15:23 15:25[2] 16:1 16:2[2] 16:4[2] 16:5 16:7 16:13 16:15[2] 16:17 16:18 16:19[2] 16:20 16:21 16:23 16:24 16:26[2] 16:27 16:30[3] 16:32 16:33 17:1 17:2 17:3 17:7 17:8[2] 17:11 17:12[2] 17:13 17:15[2] 17:19 17:21[4] 17:22 17:23[3] 17:24[2] 17:25 17:26

18:4 18:8 18:9 18:13 18:14[2] 18:15 18:16 18:17 18:28 18:32 18:36 18:37[3] 18:39[2] 19:4[2] 19:8 19:10 19:11 19:13[2] 19:21 19:24 19:27 19:28[2] 19:31[4] 19:33 19:35[3] 19:36 19:38 20:3 20:7 20:8 20:9 20:14 20:18[2] 20:29 20:31[3] 21:3 21:4 21:7[2] 21:12 21:14[2] 21:15 21:16 21:17 21:20 21:22[2] 21:23 21:24 21:25[2]

AC

1:1 1:2 1:4 1:8 1:16 1:19[2] 1:21 1:22[2] 1:25[2] 2:6 2:14 2:16 2:20 2:21 2:24 2:25 2:29 2:30[2] 2:31 2:36[2] 2:39 2:41 2:44 3:2 3:10[2] 3:11 3:17 3:18 3:19 3:23[2] 3:24 4:2 4:5 4:10 4:13[2]

4:16[2] 4:17[2] 4:21 4:23 4:24[2] 4:29 4:30 4:32[2] 4:34[2] 5:5 5:9 5:15[2] 5:17 5:21[2] 5:28 5:32 5:33 5:40 5:41 6:2 6:14 6:15 7:5 7:6[2] 7:7 7:12 7:16 7:19 7:24 7:25 7:27 7:36 7:37 7:38 7:44[2] 7:45 8:1 8:4 8:7[2] 8:8 8:9 8:11 8:14 8:15 8:18 8:19 8:20 8:24 8:26 8:31 8:37 8:39 9:2 9:12 9:14 9:17[2] 9:20 9:21[4] 9:22 9:23 9:26 9:27 9:35 9:37 9:38[2] 9:43 10:2 10:7 10:14 10:15 10:22 10:27 10:28[3] 10:33[2] 10:34 10:35 10:37 10:38 10:43[2] 10:45 10:47 11:1[2] 11:2 11:9 11:16 11:17 11:19

11:22 11:23 11:26 11:28 12:1 12:9 12:10 12:11 12:15 12:19 12:25 13:1[2] 13:16 13:20 13:27 13:28 13:29 13:32 13:33 13:34 13:38 13:39 13:40 13:42 13:46 13:47 14:1 14:6 14:9 14:15[2] 14:17 14:18 14:21 14:22 14:27 15:2 15:4 15:5 15:7[2] 15:11 15:17 15:19 15:20[2] 15:21 15:24 15:26 15:29 15:39 16:2 16:3 16:4 16:10 16:12[2] 16:14 16:19 16:26 16:27 16:32 16:38 17:3[2] 17:6 17:7 17:11 17:13 17:22 17:24[2] 17:27 17:29 17:31[2] 18:2 18:5 18:7 18:14 18:21 18:28[2] 19:1 19:4[2] 19:9 19:10 19:12 19:16[2] 19:18 19:22 19:23 19:25 19:26[2] 19:27[2]

19:31 19:34 19:35[2] 19:36 20:18 20:20 20:22 20:23[2] 20:24 20:25 20:26 20:29 20:31 20:34[2] 20:35 20:38 21:1 21:4 21:8 21:11 21:12 21:21[2] 21:22 21:23 21:24[3] 21:25[2] 21:26 21:28 21:29 21:31 21:35 21:38[2] 22:2 22:6 22:9[2] 22:11[2] 22:14[2] 22:17 22:19[2] 22:20 22:22 22:24[2] 22:25[2] 22:26 22:29 23:2 23:4 23:5 23:6 23:8 23:9 23:12 23:14 23:15 23:19 23:20 23:21 23:22 23:24 23:27 23:30 23:34 24:2[2] 24:4[2] 24:9 24:10[2] 24:11[2] 24:14 24:15 24:21 24:22 24:23 24:26[2] 25:3 25:4[2] 25:16 25:24 25:25[2] 25:26 26:5 26:8 26:9 26:18[2] 26:20 26:23[3] 26:26 26:27

26:29[2]
26:30
27:1
27:10
27:13
27:20
27:24
27:25
27:27
27:33
27:43
27:44
28:1
28:6
28:8
28:16
28:17
28:19
28:20
28:21
28:22
28:25
28:28[2]
28:30

RO

1:7
1:8
1:9
1:11
1:12[2]
1:13[2]
1:15
1:16
1:19
1:20[2]
1:21
1:26
1:27[2]
1:32[2]
2:1[2]
2:2
2:3[2]
2:4
2:8
2:9
2:10
2:18
2:19
2:21[2]
2:22[2]
2:23
2:28
2:29
3:2
3:4
3:8[2]
3:9
3:11[2]
3:12
3:19[2]
3:22
3:24
3:25
3:26
3:28
4:1
4:4
4:5[2]
4:9
4:11[3]
4:12
4:13
4:16[3]
4:18[2]
4:21
4:23
4:24
5:3
5:8
5:12
5:14[2]
5:16
5:20
5:21
6:1
6:2
6:3
6:4
6:6[3]
6:7
6:8
6:9
6:10[2]
6:12
6:13
6:16
6:17[2]
7:1[2]
7:3[2]
7:4[2]
7:6[2]
7:13[3]
7:14
7:15[3]
7:16[2]
7:17[2]
7:18[3]
7:19[2]
7:20[3]
7:21
7:24
8:3
8:4
8:5[2]
8:8
8:9
8:11[3]
8:16
8:17[2]
8:18
8:22
8:24
8:25
8:27
8:28[2]
8:29
8:32
8:33
8:34[3]
8:37
8:38
9:2
9:3
9:8
9:11[2]
9:16[3]
9:17[2]
9:20[2]
9:23
9:26
9:30
9:32
10:1
10:2
10:4
10:6
10:7
10:8
10:9[2]
10:12
10:15
10:19
10:20[2]
11:7
11:8[2]
11:10
11:11
11:19
11:25[2]
11:31
11:32
11:33[3]
11:34[2]
12:1
12:2[2]
12:3[3]
12:6
12:7
12:8[4]
12:9
12:15[2]
13:1
13:2
13:3
13:4[2]
13:8
13:11[2]
14:1
14:2
14:3[3]
14:4
14:6[4]
14:9
14:13
14:14[2]
14:18
14:22
14:23
15:1
15:3
15:4
15:6
15:8
15:9
15:12
15:13
15:14
15:15
15:16[2]
15:19
15:21
15:29
15:30
15:31[3]
15:32
16:2[2]
16:5
16:11
16:18
16:25

1 CO

1:2[2]
1:5
1:7
1:8
1:10[3]
1:11
1:12
1:14
1:15
1:18
1:21[2]
1:26
1:28
1:29
1:31[2]
2:5
2:6[2]
2:9
2:12[2]
2:15
2:16
3:7[3]
3:8[2]
3:11
3:16
3:18
3:20
4:2
4:3
4:4
4:6[3]
4:7
4:8
4:9
5:1[2]
5:2[2]
5:3
5:5
5:6
5:7
5:11
5:12[2]
5:13
6:2
6:3[2]
6:5[2]
6:6
6:8
6:9
6:15
6:16
6:17
6:18[2]
6:19
7:5[2]
7:7[2]
7:12
7:13
7:22[2]
7:25
7:26
7:29[2]
7:30[3]
7:31
7:32[2]
7:33[2]
7:34[2]
7:35[8]
7:36
7:37[2]
7:38[2]
7:40
8:1
8:2
8:4[3]
8:5
8:9
9:3
9:9
9:10[4]
9:13
9:14
9:15[2]
9:18[2]
9:19
9:20[4]
9:21[3]
9:22[2]
9:23
9:24[2]
9:25
9:26[2]
10:1
10:4
10:12
10:13[2]
10:19[2]
10:20[2]
10:25
10:27
10:28
10:30
10:33
11:2
11:3
11:5[2]
11:13
11:14
11:17[2]
11:18
11:19
11:22
11:23[2]
11:29
11:32
11:34
12:2
12:3[3]
12:11
12:25[2]
12:28
13:2
13:10[2]
14:1
14:2
14:3
14:4[2]
14:5[5]
14:11[3]
14:13[3]
14:16
14:21
14:22[3]
14:23[2]
14:24
14:25
14:27
14:30
14:31
14:37[2]
15:3[2]
15:4[2]
15:5[2]
15:6
15:7
15:9
15:12[2]
15:15[2]
15:20
15:23
15:26
15:27
15:28[2]
15:36
15:37[2]
15:46[3]
15:48[2]
15:50
15:54
15:58
16:2
16:4
16:6[2]
16:10
16:11
16:15[2]
16:16[2]
16:17
16:18
16:19

2 CO

1:4
1:7
1:8
1:9
1:10
1:11
1:12
1:14
1:15
1:17[2]
1:23
1:24
2:1
2:2
2:3
2:4[2]
2:5
2:7
2:8
2:9
2:15[2]
3:5
3:7
3:10[2]
3:11[2]
3:12
3:13[2]
4:7
4:10
4:11
4:14
4:15
5:1
5:3
5:4[3]
5:5
5:6
5:9
5:10[2]
5:12
5:14
5:15[2]
5:19
5:21
6:1
6:3
6:15
7:3
7:6[2]
7:7
7:8
7:9[3]
7:11
7:12[3]
7:16
8:2
8:4
8:6[2]
8:7
8:9[2]
8:11[2]
8:12[2]
8:13[2]
8:14[3]
8:15
8:20
9:2
9:3
9:4
9:5[2]
9:8
9:10
10:2
10:5
10:7[2]
10:9
10:11
10:12
10:15
10:17[2]
10:18
11:2
11:3
11:4
11:7
11:9
11:12[3]
11:16
11:17
11:18
11:28[2]
11:31
12:4
12:8
12:9
12:13
12:19
12:20
12:21
13:2
13:5
13:6[2]
13:7[3]

GA

1:4
1:6[2]
1:7
1:8
1:9
1:11
1:13
1:16
1:23
2:2
2:4[2]
2:5
2:7
2:8
2:9[2]
2:10
2:12
2:13
2:14
2:16[2]
2:19
3:1
3:5
3:7
3:8
3:10
3:11
3:12
3:13
3:14[2]
3:17[3]
3:22[2]
3:24
3:25[2]
4:1
4:5[2]
4:9
4:15
4:17
4:21
4:22
4:27[2]
4:29[2]
5:2
5:3[2]
5:7
5:8
5:10[2]
5:15
5:17[2]
5:21
5:24
6:6[2]
6:7
6:8[2]
6:13
6:14

EPH

1:4
1:10
1:12
1:13[2]
1:17
1:18
1:21[2]
1:23
2:2
2:7
2:8
2:10
2:11[2]
2:12
2:16
2:17
2:18
3:3
3:6
3:8
3:10
3:13
3:16
3:17[2]
3:19
3:20[3]
4:1
4:9[2]
4:10[3]
4:14
4:16
4:17
4:18
4:21
4:22
4:24
4:28[3]
4:29[2]
5:5
5:13
5:14
5:15
5:26
5:27[2]
5:28
5:33
6:3
6:5
6:8
6:9
6:11
6:12
6:19[2]
6:20
6:21
6:22[2]
6:24

PHP

1:6
1:9
1:10[3]
1:12
1:13
1:17
1:19
1:20[2]
1:25
1:26
1:27[2]
1:28
2:2
2:10
2:11[2]
2:15
2:16[2]
2:19
2:22
2:24
2:25
2:26
2:28[2]
3:4
3:8
3:9
3:10
3:12[2]
3:18
3:21
4:2
4:10
4:11
4:14
4:15
4:17
4:22

COL

1:9
1:10
1:16[2]
1:18
1:19
1:21
1:24
1:28
2:1
2:2
2:14
3:9
3:10
3:24
3:25
4:1[2]
4:3
4:4
4:5
4:6
4:8
4:12
4:13[2]
4:16[2]
4:17

1 TH

1:7[2]
1:8
2:1
2:2
2:10
2:12
2:13
2:16
3:3[2]
3:4
3:6
3:10[2]
4:1
4:3
4:4
4:6[2]
4:8
4:9
4:10
4:11
4:12[3]
4:13
4:14
4:15
5:1
5:2
5:4[2]
5:7
5:10
5:14
5:15
5:21
5:24
5:27

2 TH

1:3
1:4[2]
1:5
1:6
1:8[2]
1:10[2]
1:11
1:12
2:2[2]
2:3[2]
2:4[4]
2:5
2:6
2:8
2:10[2]
2:11
2:12
3:1
3:2
3:4
3:6[2]
3:8
3:10
3:11
3:12[2]
3:14[2]

1 TI

1:3[2]
1:8
1:9
1:10[2]
1:12
1:15
1:16
1:18
1:20
2:1
2:2[2]
2:8
2:9
3:4
3:13
3:15
4:1
4:8[2]
4:10
4:14
4:15
4:16
5:3
5:4
5:5
5:6
5:7
5:14
5:16[3]
5:17
5:18
5:20[2]
5:21
5:25
6:1
6:2
6:5
6:9
6:14
6:17[2]
6:18[2]
6:19
6:20

2 TI

1:3
1:4
1:5[2]
1:6
1:12[3]
1:14
1:15
1:18[2]
2:1
2:2
2:4[2]
2:6
2:8
2:10
2:14
2:15
2:18
2:19[2]
2:22
2:23
2:25
2:26
3:1
3:3
3:8
3:12
3:15
3:17
4:8
4:13
4:16
4:17[2]

TIT

1:2
1:5[2]
1:9
1:13
1:14
1:15
1:16
2:2
2:3
2:4
2:5
2:8[3]
2:10
2:11
2:12
2:13
2:14
3:4
3:7
3:8[2]
3:10
3:11[2]
3:13
3:14
3:15[2]

PHM

6
8
12
13
14
15
18
21
22

HEB

2:3
2:6[2]
2:8[2]
2:9
2:11
2:14[3]
2:17
2:18[2]
3:2
3:4
3:10
3:16
3:17
3:18[2]
3:19
4:2
4:6
4:10
4:11
4:13
4:14[2]
4:16
5:1
5:2[2]
5:4
5:5
5:7[2]
5:9
5:12
5:13
5:14
6:7
6:8
6:9
6:10
6:11
6:12
6:18
6:19
7:2
7:5[2]
7:6
7:8[2]
7:11
7:14
7:15
7:21
7:25
8:3
8:4[2]
8:5
8:7
8:9
8:10
8:13[2]
9:4[2]
9:8
9:9[2]
9:11
9:15[2]
9:23
9:25
9:28
10:2
10:4
10:9
10:14
10:15
10:16
10:20
10:23
10:26
10:28
10:30
10:33
10:34
10:36
10:37
10:39
11:3[2]
11:4
11:5[2]
11:6[4]
11:13
11:14[2]
11:15
11:16
11:17
11:18
11:19
11:28
11:31
11:35
11:40
12:1
12:2
12:3
12:10
12:13
12:17
12:18[2]
12:19[2]
12:20
12:21
12:24[2]
12:25[4]
12:27[3]
13:3
13:6
13:9[2]
13:12
13:15
13:17[4]
13:19
13:20[2]
13:21
13:23
13:24

JAS

1:3
1:4
1:5
1:6
1:7[2]
1:9
1:10
1:12[2]
1:18
2:3
2:5
2:7
2:11
2:12
2:13
2:19
2:20
2:24
3:1
3:3
3:6
3:17
3:18
4:1
4:3
4:4
4:5[2]
4:17
5:1
5:11[2]
5:12
5:13
5:14
5:16
5:17[2]
5:20

1 PE

1:4
1:7
1:10
1:11
1:12[2]
1:13
1:18
1:21[2]
1:22
2:2
2:3
2:6
2:9
2:12
2:14[2]
2:15
2:21
2:23
2:24
3:1
3:3
3:7
3:9[2]
3:10[2]
3:12
3:13
3:15[2]
3:16[2]
3:17
3:18
3:20
4:1
4:2
4:4
4:5
4:6[2]
4:11
4:13
4:15[2]
4:17[2]
4:19
5:1
5:4
5:6
5:9[2]
5:10
5:12
5:13
5:14

2 PE

1:1
1:3[2]
1:4[2]
1:8
1:9[2]
1:14
1:15
1:19[2]
1:20
2:1
2:4
2:6
2:8
2:10
2:12
2:13
2:14
2:17
2:18
2:22
3:2
3:3
3:4
3:5
3:6
3:8
3:9[2]
3:10[3]
3:11
3:13
3:14[2]
3:15
3:16[2]

1 JO

1:1
1:2
1:3[2]
1:4
1:5
1:6
1:8
1:10
2:1
2:3
2:4
2:5
2:6
2:9
2:10
2:11[2]
2:13[2]
2:14
2:15
2:16
2:17
2:19[2]
2:21
2:22[3]
2:23
2:24
2:25
2:26
2:27
2:28
2:29[2]
3:1
3:2
3:3
3:5
3:7
3:8[2]
3:10
3:11[2]
3:12
3:14[2]
3:15
3:19
3:22
3:23
3:24[2]
4:2[2]
4:3[4]
4:4[2]
4:6[2]
4:7
4:8
4:9[2]
4:10[2]
4:13
4:14
4:15
4:16[2]
4:17
4:18
4:20
4:21
5:1[4]
5:2
5:3
5:4
5:5[3]
5:6[2]
5:7
5:8
5:10[3]
5:11
5:12[2]
5:13[4]
5:14[2]
5:15[2]
5:16[2]
5:18[3]
5:19
5:20[4]

2 JO

1
4
5[2]
6[2]
7
8[2]
9
11
12

3 JO

2
3
4
7
8
10
11[4]
12

JUDE

1
3
5[2]
15
18
24

RE

1:2
1:3[2]
1:5
1:9
1:12
1:18
2:1
2:6
2:7[2]
2:10
2:11[2]
2:14
2:15
2:17[3]
2:20
2:22
2:23
2:25
2:26
2:29
3:1[3]
3:2
3:5
3:6
3:7[4]
3:9
3:10
3:11[2]
3:12
3:13
3:15
3:17
3:18[4]
3:21
3:22
4:3
4:9
4:10[2]
5:1
5:7
5:12
5:13[2]
5:14
6:2
6:4[3]
6:5
6:8
6:9
6:10
6:11[2]
6:16
7:1
7:15
8:3
9:4
9:5[2]
9:17
9:20
10:6[4]
11:1
11:6
11:7
11:10[2]
11:18[3]
12:6
12:9
12:12[2]
12:13
12:14
12:15
13:6
13:8
13:10[2]
13:13
13:14[3]
13:15[2]
13:17[2]
13:18
14:3
14:6
14:7
14:8
14:12
14:13
14:15
14:16
14:18
15:2
15:4
16:12
16:14
16:15
17:1
17:7
17:8[3]
17:11
17:14
17:18
18:4[2]
18:10
18:14
18:16[2]
18:19[2]
18:21
18:24
19:4
19:5
19:8
19:10
19:11
19:12
19:15
19:17
19:18[2]
19:19
19:20[3]
19:21
20:2
20:3[2]
20:4
20:6
20:10
20:11
21:5
21:6
21:7
21:10
21:15
21:17
21:27
22:7
22:11[3]
22:14[2]
22:17[2]
22:18[2]

THE

3588

GE

1:1[3]
1:2[6]
1:4[3]
1:5[5]
1:6[4]
1:7[5]
1:8[4]
1:9[3]
1:10[3]
1:11[4]
1:12[2]
1:13[2]
1:14[4]
1:15[3]
1:16[5]
1:17[3]
1:18[4]
1:19[3]
1:20[4]
1:21
1:22[3]
1:23[3]
1:24[3]
1:25[3]
1:26[7]
1:27
1:28[6]
1:29[4]
1:30[3]
1:31[3]
2:1[3]
2:2[2]
2:3
2:4[7]
2:5[6]
2:6[3]
2:7[4]
2:8[2]
2:9[7]
2:10
2:11[3]
2:12[2]
2:13[4]
2:14[4]
2:15[3]
2:16[3]
2:17[3]
2:18[2]
2:19[5]
2:20[3]
2:21[2]
2:22[3]
2:25
3:1[5]
3:2[5]
3:3[4]
3:4[2]
3:5
3:6[4]
3:7
3:8[9]
3:9
3:10
3:11
3:12[3]
3:13[4]
3:14[4]
3:15
3:16
3:17[4]
3:18[2]
3:19[2]
3:20
3:21
3:22[3]
3:23[3]
3:24[5]
4:1
4:2
4:3[3]
4:4[3]
4:6
4:7
4:8
4:9
4:10[2]
4:11
4:12[2]

4:13 4:14^{3} 4:15^{2} 4:16^{4} 4:17^{3} 4:19^{4} 4:20 4:21^{2} 4:22 4:26^{2} 5:1^{4} 5:2 5:4 5:5 5:8 5:11 5:14 5:17 5:20 5:23 5:27 5:29^{2} 5:31 6:1^{2} 6:2^{2} 6:3 6:4^{4} 6:5^{2} 6:6^{2} 6:7^{6} 6:8^{2} 6:9 6:11^{2} 6:12^{2} 6:13^{3} 6:14^{2} 6:15^{5} 6:16^{4} 6:17^{3} 6:18 6:19 6:20 7:1^{2} 7:2^{2} 7:3^{5} 7:4^{3} 7:5 7:6^{2} 7:7^{3} 7:8 7:9^{3} 7:10^{3} 7:11^{8} 7:12^{2} 7:13^{4} 7:14^{2} 7:15^{2} 7:16 7:17^{6} 7:18^{4} 7:19^{4} 7:20^{2} 7:21^{2} 7:22^{2} 7:23^{7} 7:24^{2} 8:1^{4} 8:2^{4} 8:3^{5} 8:4^{5} 8:5^{7} 8:6^{3} 8:7^{2} 8:8^{3} 8:9^{7} 8:10^{2} 8:11^{4} 8:12 8:13^{10} 8:14^{4} 8:16 8:17^{3} 8:19^{2} 8:20^{2} 8:21^{4} 8:22 9:1

9:2^{7} 9:3 9:4^{2} 9:5^{4} 9:6 9:7 9:10^{5} 9:11^{2} 9:12^{2} 9:13^{2} 9:14^{3} 9:15 9:16^{4} 9:17^{3} 9:18^{3} 9:19^{2} 9:21 9:22^{2} 9:23 9:26 9:27 9:28 9:29 10:1^{3} 10:2 10:3 10:4 10:5^{2} 10:6 10:7^{2} 10:8 10:9^{3} 10:10^{2} 10:11 10:12 10:16^{3} 10:17^{3} 10:18^{5} 10:19^{2} 10:20 10:21^{4} 10:22 10:23 10:25^{2} 10:29 10:30 10:31 10:32^{5} 11:1 11:2^{2} 11:4^{2} 11:5^{4} 11:6^{2} 11:8^{4} 11:9^{6} 11:10^{2} 11:27 11:28^{2} 11:29^{5} 11:31^{3} 11:32 12:1 12:3 12:4 12:5^{3} 12:6^{5} 12:7^{2} 12:8^{6} 12:9 12:10^{2} 12:12 12:14^{2} 12:15^{2} 12:17 13:1 13:3^{3} 13:4^{5} 13:6 13:7^{5} 13:9^{5} 13:10^{5} 13:11^{3} 13:12^{3} 13:13^{2} 13:14 13:15 13:16^{4}

13:17^{3} 13:18 14:1 14:2 14:3^{2} 14:4 14:5^{5} 14:6^{2} 14:7^{3} 14:8^{7} 14:9 14:10^{3} 14:11 14:13^{3} 14:15 14:16^{3} 14:17^{5} 14:18^{2} 14:19 14:20 14:21^{3} 14:22^{4} 14:24^{3} 15:1^{2} 15:2 15:4^{2} 15:5 15:6 15:7^{2} 15:10^{2} 15:11^{2} 15:12 15:16^{3} 15:17 15:18^{5} 15:19^{3} 15:20^{3} 15:21^{4} 16:2^{2} 16:3^{2} 16:5 16:7^{5} 16:8 16:9^{2} 16:10^{2} 16:11^{3} 16:12 16:13^{2} 16:14 17:1^{2} 17:8^{2} 17:11^{2} 17:12 17:14 17:21 17:23^{3} 17:24 17:25 17:26 17:27^{3} 18:1^{5} 18:2^{2} 18:4 18:6^{2} 18:7 18:8^{2} 18:9 18:10^{2} 18:11 18:13 18:14^{3} 18:16^{2} 18:17 18:18^{2} 18:19^{3} 18:20^{2} 18:21 18:22^{2} 18:23^{2} 18:24^{3} 18:25^{6} 18:26^{3} 18:27 18:28^{2} 18:30 18:31 18:32

18:33 19:1^{2} 19:2 19:4^{5} 19:5 19:6^{2} 19:8 19:9^{2} 19:10^{3} 19:11^{4} 19:12^{2} 19:13^{3} 19:14 19:15^{4} 19:16^{5} 19:17^{2} 19:19 19:21 19:22^{2} 19:23^{2} 19:24^{2} 19:25^{4} 19:27^{3} 19:28^{5} 19:29^{6} 19:30 19:31^{5} 19:33 19:34^{3} 19:35 19:36 19:37^{2} 19:38^{4} 20:1 20:3 20:5 20:6 20:7 20:8^{2} 20:11 20:12^{2} 20:16 20:18^{3} 21:1^{2} 21:2 21:3 21:8^{2} 21:9^{2} 21:10 21:11 21:12 21:13^{2} 21:14^{3} 21:15^{4} 21:16^{2} 21:17^{5} 21:18 21:19^{2} 21:20^{2} 21:21^{2} 21:22 21:23^{2} 21:28 21:32^{3} 21:33^{3} 21:34 22:2^{2} 22:3^{4} 22:4^{2} 22:5^{2} 22:6^{3} 22:9^{4} 22:10 22:11^{2} 22:12 22:13^{2} 22:14^{3} 22:15^{3} 22:16^{2} 22:17^{5} 22:18^{2} 22:21 23:1^{2} 23:2^{2} 23:3 23:5 23:6

23:7^{3} 23:8 23:9^{2} 23:10^{5} 23:11^{4} 23:12^{2} 23:13^{4} 23:15 23:16^{4} 23:17^{6} 23:18^{3} 23:19^{4} 23:20^{8} 24:1 24:3^{6} 24:5^{3} 24:7^{2} 24:8 24:9^{2} 24:10^{4} 24:11^{4} 24:13^{4} 24:14^{2} 24:15 24:16^{2} 24:17 24:20^{2} 24:21^{2} 24:22^{2} 24:24^{2} 24:26^{2} 24:27^{4} 24:28 24:29^{2} 24:30^{6} 24:31^{3} 24:32^{4} 24:35 24:37^{2} 24:39 24:40 24:42 24:43^{2} 24:44^{3} 24:45 24:46 24:47^{3} 24:48^{3} 24:49^{2} 24:50^{2} 24:51 24:52^{2} 24:53 24:54^{2} 24:55^{2} 24:56 24:57 24:60^{2} 24:61^{3} 24:62^{3} 24:63^{3} 24:64 24:65^{3} 24:66 25:3 25:4^{2} 25:6^{3} 25:7^{2} 25:8 25:9^{4} 25:10^{2} 25:11^{2} 25:12^{2} 25:13^{3} 25:16 25:17^{3} 25:18 25:19 25:20^{4} 25:21^{2} 25:22^{2} 25:23^{5} 25:25 25:27^{2} 25:29 25:32

26:1^{4} 26:2^{2} 26:3 26:4^{3} 26:7^{4} 26:8 26:10 26:12^{2} 26:13 26:14 26:15^{3} 26:17 26:18^{5} 26:19 26:20^{4} 26:21 26:22^{3} 26:24^{3} 26:25^{2} 26:26 26:28 26:29^{2} 26:31 26:32^{2} 26:33^{2} 26:34^{4} 27:2 27:3 27:5 27:7 27:9^{2} 27:15 27:16^{4} 27:17^{3} 27:20 27:22^{3} 27:27^{4} 27:28^{3} 27:30 27:34 27:39^{3} 27:40 27:41^{2} 27:46^{4} 28:1 28:2^{2} 28:4^{2} 28:5^{2} 28:6 28:8 28:9^{3} 28:11^{2} 28:12^{3} 28:13^{4} 28:14^{8} 28:16 28:17^{2} 28:18^{3} 28:19^{3} 28:21 28:22 29:1^{3} 29:2^{3} 29:3^{6} 29:5 29:6 29:7^{2} 29:8^{4} 29:10^{5} 29:13 29:14 29:16^{4} 29:20 29:22^{2} 29:23 29:25 29:26^{2} 29:27 29:31 29:32 29:33 29:35 30:2^{2} 30:13 30:14^{2} 30:16^{2}

30:17 30:19 30:24 30:27 30:30 30:32^{5} 30:33^{2} 30:35^{5} 30:36 30:37^{3} 30:38^{5} 30:39^{2} 30:40^{6} 30:41^{6} 30:42^{3} 30:43 31:1 31:2 31:3^{2} 31:4 31:5 31:8^{4} 31:9 31:10^{4} 31:11 31:12^{2} 31:13^{3} 31:16 31:18^{2} 31:19 31:20 31:21^{2} 31:22 31:23 31:24 31:25^{2} 31:26 31:29^{2} 31:33 31:34^{3} 31:35^{2} 31:38 31:39 31:40^{3} 31:42^{4} 31:46 31:48 31:49 31:53^{4} 31:54^{2} 31:55 32:1 32:2 32:3^{2} 32:6 32:7^{3} 32:8^{2} 32:9 32:10^{3} 32:11^{4} 32:12^{2} 32:16 32:17 32:19^{3} 32:20 32:21^{2} 32:22 32:23 32:24^{2} 32:25^{2} 32:26 32:30^{2} 32:31 32:32^{6} 33:1^{2} 33:2 33:3 33:5^{3} 33:6 33:8 33:10 33:13^{3} 33:14^{2} 33:15^{2} 33:17^{2} 33:18^{2}

33:19^{2} 34:1^{3} 34:2^{3} 34:3^{3} 34:5 34:6 34:7^{3} 34:8 34:10 34:12 34:13 34:19^{3} 34:20^{2} 34:21^{2} 34:22 34:24^{2} 34:25^{4} 34:26^{2} 34:27^{3} 34:28^{2} 34:29 34:30^{4} 35:1 35:2 35:3^{2} 35:4^{2} 35:5^{3} 35:6^{2} 35:7^{2} 35:8 35:12^{2} 35:13 35:14 35:15^{2} 35:17 35:19 35:20 35:21 35:22 35:23 35:24 35:25 35:26^{2} 35:27 35:28 35:29 36:1 36:2^{6} 36:5^{2} 36:6^{4} 36:7 36:9^{3} 36:10^{5} 36:11 36:12 36:13^{2} 36:14^{3} 36:15^{3} 36:16^{3} 36:17^{4} 36:18^{3} 36:19 36:20^{3} 36:21^{4} 36:22 36:23 36:24^{4} 36:25^{2} 36:26 36:27 36:28 36:29^{2} 36:30^{2} 36:31^{3} 36:32^{2} 36:33 36:34 36:35^{3} 36:37 36:38 36:39^{4} 36:40^{2} 36:43^{4} 37:1^{2} 37:2^{5} 37:3 37:5

37:7 37:8 37:9^{3} 37:10 37:11 37:13 37:14^{2} 37:15^{2} 37:17 37:22 37:24 37:27 37:28^{2} 37:29^{2} 37:30 37:31^{3} 37:32 37:35 37:36^{2} 38:7^{3} 38:9^{2} 38:10^{2} 38:12^{2} 38:14 38:16 38:17 38:19 38:20^{4} 38:21^{3} 38:22^{2} 38:24 38:25^{2} 38:27 38:28^{2} 38:30 39:1^{3} 39:2^{3} 39:3^{2} 39:5^{7} 39:6 39:8 39:11^{3} 39:14 39:17 39:19 39:20^{3} 39:21^{4} 39:22^{5} 39:23^{4} 40:1^{3} 40:2^{4} 40:3^{5} 40:4^{2} 40:5^{5} 40:6 40:7 40:9 40:10^{2} 40:11^{2} 40:12^{2} 40:13 40:15^{3} 40:16^{2} 40:17^{3} 40:18^{2} 40:19 40:20^{4} 40:21^{2} 40:22 40:23 41:1^{2} 41:2 41:3^{4} 41:4^{2} 41:5 41:6 41:7^{2} 41:8^{3} 41:9 41:10^{3} 41:11 41:12^{2} 41:14 41:17^{2} 41:18 41:19 41:20^{3}

41:21 41:23 41:24^{3} 41:25 41:26^{3} 41:27^{3} 41:28 41:29 41:30^{4} 41:31^{2} 41:32^{2} 41:33 41:34^{4} 41:35^{3} 41:36^{5} 41:37^{3} 41:38 41:40 41:41 41:43^{3} 41:44 41:45^{2} 41:46^{2} 41:47^{2} 41:48^{8} 41:49^{2} 41:50^{2} 41:51^{2} 41:52^{3} 41:53^{2} 41:54^{3} 41:55^{3} 41:56^{7} 41:57 42:5^{3} 42:6^{5} 42:7 42:9^{3} 42:12^{2} 42:13^{3} 42:15 42:16 42:18 42:19^{2} 42:21 42:22 42:25 42:26 42:27 42:29 42:30^{4} 42:32^{2} 42:33^{4} 42:34 42:35 42:38^{3} 43:1^{2} 43:2 43:3 43:5 43:6 43:7^{2} 43:8 43:9 43:11^{3} 43:12^{2} 43:13 43:14 43:15 43:16 43:17^{3} 43:18^{3} 43:19^{3} 43:20 43:21^{2} 43:23 43:24^{2} 43:25 43:26^{3} 43:27 43:32^{3} 43:33^{3} 44:1^{2} 44:2^{4} 44:3^{2} 44:4^{2} 44:8^{2}

44:11 44:12^{2} 44:13 44:14 44:16^{2} 44:17^{2} 44:22 44:24 44:26 44:28 44:29 44:30^{2} 44:31^{3} 44:32^{2} 44:33^{2} 44:34^{2} 45:2^{2} 45:6^{3} 45:7 45:8 45:10 45:12 45:16 45:17 45:18^{4} 45:19 45:20^{2} 45:21^{3} 45:23^{2} 45:24 45:25 45:26 45:27^{3} 46:1 46:2^{2} 46:3 46:5^{2} 46:6 46:8^{2} 46:9 46:10^{2} 46:11 46:12^{3} 46:13 46:14 46:15^{2} 46:16 46:17^{2} 46:18 46:19 46:20^{2} 46:21 46:22^{2} 46:23 46:24 46:25^{2} 46:26^{2} 46:27^{3} 46:28 46:31 46:32 46:34^{2} 47:1^{2} 47:4^{4} 47:6^{4} 47:9^{8} 47:11^{4} 47:13^{5} 47:14^{5} 47:15^{4} 47:17^{4} 47:18^{2} 47:19 47:20^{4} 47:21^{3} 47:22^{3} 47:23^{2} 47:24^{3} 47:25 47:26^{4} 47:27^{2} 47:28^{2} 47:29 47:31 48:2 48:3

48:5 48:6 48:7^{4} 48:10 48:12 48:14^{2} 48:15 48:16^{5} 48:17 48:18 48:21 48:22^{2} 49:1 49:3^{3} 49:8 49:9 49:10^{3} 49:11^{3} 49:13^{2} 49:16 49:17^{3} 49:19 49:22 49:24^{5} 49:25^{5} 49:26^{7} 49:27^{3} 49:28 49:29^{3} 49:30^{5} 49:32^{4} 49:33^{2} 50:2^{2} 50:3^{2} 50:4^{2} 50:5 50:7^{4} 50:8^{2} 50:10 50:11^{6} 50:13^{5} 50:15 50:17^{4} 50:19 50:23^{3} 50:24 50:25

EX

1:1^{2} 1:5^{2} 1:7^{2} 1:9^{2} 1:10 1:12^{3} 1:13^{2} 1:14 1:15^{6} 1:16^{3} 1:17^{3} 1:18^{3} 1:19^{4} 1:20^{2} 1:21 1:22 2:1 2:2 2:3^{3} 2:5^{5} 2:6^{3} 2:7^{2} 2:8^{2} 2:9^{2} 2:10^{2} 2:12^{2} 2:13^{3} 2:14 2:15^{2} 2:16^{2} 2:17 2:19^{3} 2:20 2:21 2:23^{4} 2:25

3:1^{6} 3:2^{5} 3:3 3:4^{3} 3:5 3:6^{4} 3:7^{2} 3:8^{9} 3:9^{4} 3:10 3:11 3:12 3:13^{2} 3:14 3:15^{5} 3:16^{3} 3:17^{8} 3:18^{5} 3:19 3:20 3:21^{2} 3:22 4:1 4:2 4:3^{2} 4:4^{2} 4:5^{4} 4:6 4:8^{4} 4:9^{7} 4:10 4:11^{5} 4:13 4:14^{3} 4:16 4:19^{2} 4:20^{2} 4:21^{2} 4:22 4:24^{3} 4:25 4:26 4:27^{3} 4:28^{3} 4:29^{2} 4:30^{5} 4:31^{3} 5:1^{2} 5:2^{2} 5:3^{5} 5:4^{2} 5:5^{2} 5:6^{3} 5:7 5:8 5:9 5:10^{3} 5:12^{2} 5:13 5:14^{2} 5:15 5:16 5:17 5:18 5:19^{2} 5:20 5:21^{3} 5:22 6:1 6:2 6:3 6:4^{2} 6:5^{3} 6:6^{4} 6:7^{3} 6:8^{3} 6:9 6:10 6:11 6:12^{2} 6:13^{4} 6:14^{4} 6:15^{3} 6:16^{4} 6:17 6:18^{3} 6:19^{2}

6:20^{2} 6:21 6:22 6:24^{3} 6:25^{4} 6:26^{3} 6:27 6:28^{3} 6:29^{2} 6:30 7:1 7:2 7:3 7:4^{2} 7:5^{3} 7:6 7:8 7:10 7:11^{3} 7:13 7:14^{2} 7:15^{4} 7:16^{3} 7:17^{5} 7:18^{6} 7:19^{3} 7:20^{8} 7:21^{7} 7:22^{2} 7:24^{4} 7:25^{2} 8:1^{2} 8:3^{2} 8:4 8:5^{5} 8:6^{3} 8:7^{2} 8:8^{4} 8:9^{2} 8:10 8:11 8:12^{2} 8:13^{6} 8:15 8:16^{4} 8:17^{5} 8:18 8:19^{3} 8:20^{4} 8:21^{3} 8:22^{5} 8:24^{5} 8:25 8:26^{5} 8:27^{2} 8:28^{2} 8:29^{4} 8:30 8:31 8:32 9:1^{3} 9:3^{8} 9:4^{4} 9:5^{3} 9:6^{5} 9:7^{4} 9:8^{4} 9:9^{2} 9:10 9:11^{5} 9:12^{3} 9:13^{4} 9:14 9:15 9:16 9:18 9:19^{3} 9:20^{4} 9:21^{3} 9:22^{4} 9:23^{5} 9:24^{2} 9:25^{6} 9:26^{2} 9:27 9:28 9:29^{5}

9:30 9:31^{5} 9:32^{2} 9:33^{5} 9:34^{3} 9:35^{3} 10:1^{2} 10:2^{2} 10:3^{2} 10:4 10:5^{6} 10:6^{5} 10:7^{2} 10:8 10:9 10:10 10:11 10:12^{6} 10:13^{5} 10:14^{3} 10:15^{11} 10:16 10:17 10:18 10:19^{4} 10:20^{2} 10:21^{2} 10:22 10:23 10:24 10:25 10:26^{2} 10:27 11:1 11:2^{2} 11:3^{9} 11:4^{2} 11:5^{7} 11:6 11:7^{3} 11:8 11:9^{2} 11:10^{2} 12:1^{2} 12:2^{3} 12:3^{3} 12:4^{5} 12:5^{3} 12:6^{5} 12:7^{4} 12:8 12:9 12:10^{2} 12:11 12:12^{5} 12:13^{5} 12:14 12:15^{3} 12:16^{2} 12:17^{2} 12:18^{5} 12:19^{2} 12:21^{2} 12:22^{8} 12:23^{8} 12:25^{2} 12:27^{7} 12:28^{2} 12:29^{8} 12:30^{2} 12:31^{2} 12:33^{3} 12:34 12:35^{3} 12:36^{5} 12:37 12:39 12:40^{2} 12:41^{6} 12:42^{4} 12:43^{3} 12:46^{2} 12:47 12:48^{3} 12:49 12:50^{2} 12:51^{4}

13:1 13:2^{3} 13:3^{3} 13:4 13:5^{7} 13:6^{2} 13:8 13:9^{2} 13:11^{3} 13:12^{4} 13:13 13:14^{2} 13:15^{8} 13:16 13:17^{5} 13:18^{6} 13:19^{2} 13:20^{2} 13:21^{2} 13:22^{4} 14:1 14:2^{3} 14:3^{3} 14:4^{2} 14:5^{4} 14:7 14:8^{4} 14:9^{3} 14:10^{4} 14:11 14:12^{4} 14:13^{4} 14:14 14:15^{2} 14:16^{4} 14:17^{2} 14:18^{2} 14:19^{4} 14:20^{6} 14:21^{5} 14:22^{5} 14:23^{3} 14:24^{8} 14:25^{4} 14:26^{4} 14:27^{8} 14:28^{5} 14:29^{4} 14:30^{5} 14:31^{5} 15:1^{5} 15:2 15:3^{2} 15:4^{2} 15:5^{2} 15:6 15:7 15:8^{6} 15:9^{2} 15:10^{2} 15:11 15:12 15:13 15:14^{2} 15:15^{3} 15:16^{2} 15:17^{3} 15:18 15:19^{8} 15:20^{3} 15:21^{3} 15:22^{3} 15:23^{2} 15:24 15:25^{4} 15:26^{4} 15:27 16:1^{6} 16:2^{3} 16:3^{6} 16:4^{2} 16:5 16:6^{3} 16:7^{4} 16:8^{6} 16:9^{3}

16:10^{6} 16:11 16:12^{4} 16:13^{5} 16:14^{5} 16:15^{3} 16:16^{3} 16:17 16:19 16:20 16:21 16:22^{3} 16:23^{5} 16:24 16:25^{2} 16:26^{2} 16:27^{2} 16:28 16:29^{5} 16:30^{2} 16:31^{3} 16:32^{5} 16:33 16:34^{2} 16:35^{3} 16:36 17:1^{6} 17:2^{2} 17:3^{2} 17:4 17:5^{4} 17:6^{5} 17:7^{6} 17:9^{3} 17:10^{2} 17:12^{6} 17:13^{2} 17:14^{3} 17:15 17:16^{2} 18:1^{2} 18:3^{2} 18:4^{4} 18:5^{2} 18:7 18:8^{5} 18:9^{4} 18:10^{7} 18:11^{2} 18:12 18:13^{5} 18:14^{3} 18:15 18:16 18:17 18:19^{2} 18:20^{2} 18:21 18:22^{2} 18:24 18:25 18:26^{2} 19:1^{5} 19:2^{3} 19:3^{4} 19:4 19:5 19:6^{2} 19:7^{3} 19:8^{5} 19:9^{5} 19:10^{2} 19:11^{5} 19:12^{4} 19:13^{2} 19:14^{3} 19:15^{2} 19:16^{7} 19:17^{4} 19:18^{4} 19:19^{2} 19:20^{6} 19:21^{3} 19:22^{3} 19:23^{3} 19:24^{4}

19:25 20:2^{3} 20:4^{3} 20:5^{5} 20:7^{3} 20:8 20:10^{3} 20:11^{5} 20:12^{2} 20:18^{7} 20:20 20:21^{2} 20:22^{2} 21:1 21:2 21:4 21:5 21:6^{2} 21:7 21:9 21:19 21:22^{2} 21:26^{2} 21:28^{3} 21:29^{2} 21:30 21:32^{2} 21:34^{4} 21:35^{3} 21:36^{2} 22:3 22:4 22:5^{2} 22:6^{4} 22:7^{2} 22:8^{4} 22:9^{3} 22:11^{2} 22:12 22:14 22:15 22:17 22:20 22:21 22:24 22:26 22:28^{2} 22:29^{2} 22:30 22:31^{2} 23:1 23:5 23:6 23:7^{2} 23:8^{4} 23:9^{2} 23:10 23:11^{4} 23:12^{3} 23:13 23:14 23:15^{3} 23:16^{7} 23:17^{2} 23:18^{3} 23:19^{4} 23:20^{2} 23:23^{6} 23:25^{2} 23:26 23:27 23:28^{3} 23:29^{3} 23:30 23:31^{7} 24:1^{2} 24:2^{2} 24:3^{7} 24:4^{5} 24:6^{3} 24:7^{5} 24:8^{5} 24:9 24:10^{2} 24:11^{2}

24:12[2] 24:13 24:14 24:15[2] 24:16[6] 24:17[7] 24:18[4] 25:1 25:2 25:3 25:6 25:7[2] 25:9[4] 25:10[3] 25:12[8] 25:14[5] 25:15[3] 25:16 25:17[2] 25:18[2] 25:19[6] 25:20[5] 25:21[4] 25:22[5] 25:23[3] 25:25 25:26[3] 25:27[4] 25:28[2] 25:29 25:30 25:31[2] 25:32[5] 25:33[3] 25:34 25:35[5] 25:36 25:37 25:38[2] 25:40 26:1 26:2[3] 26:3 26:4[7] 26:5[6] 26:6[2] 26:7 26:8[3] 26:9[3] 26:10[6] 26:11[3] 26:12[6] 26:13[7] 26:14 26:15 26:16 26:17[2] 26:18[3] 26:19 26:20[3] 26:22[2] 26:23[3] 26:24[2] 26:26[2] 26:27[7] 26:28[3] 26:29[3] 26:30[3] 26:32 26:33[8] 26:34[4] 26:35[9] 26:36[2] 26:37 27:1[2] 27:2[3] 27:3 27:4[2] 27:5[5] 27:6 27:7[5] 27:8 27:9[4] 27:10[3] 27:11[3] 27:12[3] 27:13[3]

27:14[2] 27:15 27:16[2] 27:17[2] 27:18[4] 27:19[6] 27:20[3] 27:21[7] 28:1[2] 28:3[2] 28:4[2] 28:6 28:7[2] 28:8[4] 28:9[2] 28:10[3] 28:11[5] 28:12[5] 28:14[3] 28:15[3] 28:16[2] 28:17[2] 28:18 28:19 28:20 28:21[5] 28:22 28:23[4] 28:24[4] 28:25[5] 28:26[5] 28:27[6] 28:28[8] 28:29[5] 28:30[7] 28:31[2] 28:32[4] 28:33[2] 28:34[2] 28:35[2] 28:36[2] 28:37[2] 28:38[4] 28:39[3] 28:41 28:42[2] 28:43[4] 29:1[2] 29:3[3] 29:4[3] 29:5[8] 29:6[3] 29:7 29:9[2] 29:10[4] 29:11 29:12[7] 29:13[7] 29:14[3] 29:15[2] 29:16[2] 29:17[2] 29:18[4] 29:19[3] 29:20[9] 29:21[4] 29:22[10] 29:23[3] 29:24[3] 29:25[3] 29:26[3] 29:27[6] 29:28[4] 29:29 29:30[3] 29:31[3] 29:32[7] 29:33 29:34[5] 29:36 29:37[2] 29:38[2] 29:39[3] 29:40[3] 29:41[5] 29:42[4] 29:43[2]

29:44[4] 29:45 29:46[3] 30:2[5] 30:3[3] 30:4[4] 30:5 30:6[5] 30:7 30:8[2] 30:10[5] 30:11 30:12[3] 30:13[4] 30:14 30:15[3] 30:16[7] 30:17 30:18[3] 30:20[4] 30:22 30:24[2] 30:25[2] 30:26[4] 30:27[3] 30:28[2] 30:30 30:31 30:32 30:34 30:35[2] 30:36[3] 30:37[3] 31:1 31:2[3] 31:3 31:6[3] 31:7[7] 31:8[3] 31:9[2] 31:10[5] 31:11[2] 31:12 31:13[2] 31:14 31:15[4] 31:16[3] 31:17[3] 31:18 32:1[5] 32:2[2] 32:3[2] 32:4 32:5 32:6[2] 32:7[2] 32:8[2] 32:11[2] 32:12[4] 32:13 32:14[2] 32:15[6] 32:16[5] 32:17[3] 32:18[3] 32:19[5] 32:20[4] 32:22[2] 32:23[2] 32:24 32:25 32:26[4] 32:27[2] 32:28[3] 32:29 32:30[3] 32:31 32:33 32:34[3] 32:35[3] 33:1[4] 33:2[6] 33:3[2] 33:4 33:5[3] 33:6[2] 33:7[9]

33:8[3] 33:9[5] 33:10[4] 33:11[4] 33:12 33:16[3] 33:17 33:19[2] 33:21 33:22 34:1[4] 34:2[4] 34:3[2] 34:4[4] 34:5[4] 34:6[3] 34:7[7] 34:8 34:10[4] 34:11[6] 34:12[3] 34:14 34:15[2] 34:18[4] 34:19 34:20[2] 34:21 34:22[4] 34:23[3] 34:24[3] 34:25[5] 34:26[4] 34:27[2] 34:28[5] 34:29[3] 34:30[2] 34:31[2] 34:32[2] 34:33[3] 34:35[4] 35:1[4] 35:2[2] 35:3 35:4[4] 35:5[2] 35:8[2] 35:9[2] 35:10 35:11 35:12[5] 35:13[2] 35:14[4] 35:15[7] 35:16 35:17[5] 35:18[4] 35:19[6] 35:20[3] 35:21[5] 35:22 35:24[2] 35:25 35:26 35:27[3] 35:28[3] 35:29[4] 35:30[5] 35:31 35:32 35:33 35:34[2] 35:35[4] 36:1[4] 36:2[4] 36:3[5] 36:4[3] 36:5[4] 36:6[4] 36:7[2] 36:8[2] 36:9[3] 36:10 36:11[4] 36:12[5] 36:13[2] 36:14[2] 36:15[3]

36:17[6] 36:18 36:19 36:20 36:21[2] 36:22[2] 36:23[2] 36:24 36:25[3] 36:27[2] 36:28[3] 36:29[2] 36:31[3] 36:32[6] 36:33[4] 36:34[3] 36:37 36:38 37:1[4] 37:3[3] 37:5[5] 37:6[3] 37:7[2] 37:8[5] 37:9[5] 37:10[4] 37:12 37:13[3] 37:14[5] 37:15[2] 37:16[2] 37:17[3] 37:18[5] 37:19[3] 37:20 37:21[4] 37:22 37:24 37:25[6] 37:26[3] 37:27[4] 37:28 37:29[4] 38:1[4] 38:2[4] 38:3[8] 38:4[2] 38:5[3] 38:6 38:7[5] 38:8[7] 38:9[4] 38:10[2] 38:11[4] 38:12[3] 38:13 38:14[3] 38:15[2] 38:16[2] 38:17[7] 38:18[8] 38:19 38:20[3] 38:21[8] 38:22[4] 38:23 38:24[8] 38:25[4] 38:26[2] 28:27[5] 38:28[2] 38:29[2] 38:30[8] 38:31[8] 39:1[4] 39:2 39:3[5] 39:4 39:5[4] 39:6 39:7[4] 39:8[3] 39:9[3] 39:10[2] 39:11 39:12 39:13

39:14[5] 39:15[2] 39:16[3] 39:17[4] 39:18[5] 39:19[5] 39:20[6] 39:21[8] 39:22[2] 39:23[4] 39:24[2] 39:25[5] 39:26[3] 39:29 39:30[4] 39:31[2] 39:32[6] 39:33[2] 39:34[4] 39:35[4] 39:36[3] 39:37[5] 39:38[5] 39:39[2] 39:40[9] 39:41[5] 39:42[3] 39:43[2] 40:1 40:2[5] 40:3[4] 40:4[4] 40:5[7] 40:6[6] 40:7[4] 40:8[3] 40:9[3] 40:10[9] 40:11 40:12[3] 40:13[2] 40:15 40:16 40:17[5] 40:18[3] 40:19[5] 40:20[6] 40:21[7] 40:22[6] 40:23[3] 40:24[5] 40:25[3] 40:26[4] 40:27 40:28[3] 40:29[8] 40:30[4] 40:32[4] 40:33[6] 40:34[5] 40:35[6] 40:36[3] 40:37[2] 40:38[5]

LE

1:1[3] 1:2[5] 1:3[5] 1:4[2] 1:5[9] 1:6 1:7[5] 1:8[7] 1:9[3] 1:10[3] 1:11[5] 1:12[4] 1:13[5] 1:14[2] 1:15[6] 1:16[4] 1:17[6] 2:1

2:2[8] 2:3[4] 2:4 2:7 2:8[4] 2:9[4] 2:10[3] 2:11 2:12[4] 2:13[2] 2:14[2] 2:16[6] 3:1[2] 3:2[7] 3:3[6] 3:4[6] 3:5[5] 3:6[2] 3:7 3:8[5] 3:9[10] 3:10[6] 3:11[5] 3:12 3:13[6] 3:14[5] 3:15[6] 3:16[6] 3:17 4:1 4:2[3] 4:3[4] 4:4[8] 4:5[4] 4:6[6] 4:7[15] 4:8[7] 4:9[6] 4:10[5] 4:11[2] 4:12[4] 4:13[6] 4:14[5] 4:15[7] 4:16[5] 4:17[4] 4:18[13] 4:19 4:20[3] 4:21[4] 4:22 4:23 4:24[5] 4:25[7] 4:26[4] 4:27[3] 4:28 4:29[5] 4:30[7] 4:31[7] 4:32 4:33[4] 4:34[8] 4:35[10] 5:1 5:2 5:3 5:4[6] 5:7[2] 5:8[2] 5:9[8] 5:10[3] 5:11 5:12[5] 5:13[3] 5:14 5:15[6] 5:16[7] 5:17[2] 5:18[4] 5:19 6:1 6:2 6:4 6:5[3] 6:6[3]

6:7[2] 6:8 6:9[8] 6:10[6] 6:11[2] 6:12[6] 6:13[2] 6:14[5] 6:15[8] 6:16[5] 6:17[2] 6:18[4] 6:19 6:20[5] 6:21[3] 6:22[2] 6:23 6:24 6:25[6] 6:26[5] 6:27[3] 6:28 6:29[2] 6:30[5] 7:1[2] 7:2[5] 7:3[4] 7:4[6] 7:5[3] 7:6[2] 7:7[3] 7:8[4] 7:9[5] 7:10 7:11[3] 7:12 7:13[2] 7:14[5] 7:15[4] 7:16[4] 7:17[4] 7:18[4] 7:19[2] 7:20[4] 7:21[5] 7:22 7:23 7:24[3] 7:25[4] 7:28 7:29[5] 7:30[6] 7:31[4] 7:32[3] 7:33[5] 7:34[6] 7:35[8] 7:36[3] 7:37[8] 7:38[5] 8:1 8:2[3] 8:3[4] 8:4[5] 8:5[3] 8:7[6] 8:8[4] 8:9[5] 8:10[2] 8:11[3] 8:12 8:13 8:14[5] 8:15[7] 8:16[6] 8:17[3] 8:18[4] 8:19[2] 8:20[4] 8:21[6] 8:22[3] 8:23[4] 8:24[6] 8:25[8] 8:26[4] 8:27

8:28[3] 8:29[4] 8:30[3] 8:31[6] 8:32[2] 8:33[4] 8:34 8:35[5] 8:36[2] 9:1[2] 9:2 9:3[3] 9:4[2] 9:5[4] 9:6[4] 9:7[5] 9:8[3] 9:9[8] 9:10[7] 9:11[3] 9:12[3] 9:13[4] 9:14[4] 9:15[5] 9:16[2] 9:17[4] 9:18[5] 9:19[8] 9:20[4] 9:21[3] 9:22[3] 9:23[6] 9:24[5] 10:1 10:2[2] 10:3[2] 10:4[4] 10:5 10:6[4] 10:7[6] 10:8 10:9[2] 10:11[4] 10:12[4] 10:13[3] 10:14[3] 10:15[6] 10:16[3] 10:17[5] 10:18[3] 10:19[4] 11:2[4] 11:3[3] 11:4[5] 11:5[3] 11:6[3] 11:7[3] 11:9[4] 11:10[4] 11:12 11:13[4] 11:14[2] 11:16[4] 11:17[3] 11:18[3] 11:19[4] 11:20 11:22[4] 11:24[2] 11:25[2] 11:26[3] 11:27 11:28[2] 11:29[5] 11:30[5] 11:31 11:32 11:38 11:39[2] 11:40[4] 11:41 11:42[2] 11:44[2] 11:45[2] 11:46[5] 11:47[3]

12:1 12:2[3] 12:3[2] 12:4[3] 12:5 12:6[6] 12:7[3] 12:8[4] 13:1 13:2[5] 13:3[9] 13:4[6] 13:5[6] 13:6[6] 13:7[4] 13:8[4] 13:9[2] 13:10[5] 13:11[2] 13:12[5] 13:13[3] 13:15[3] 13:16[2] 13:17[4] 13:18[2] 13:19[3] 13:20[5] 13:21[3] 13:22[2] 13:23[2] 13:24[2] 13:25[7] 13:26[4] 13:27[5] 13:28[5] 13:29[2] 13:30[5] 13:31[7] 13:32[6] 13:33[3] 13:34[7] 13:35[2] 13:36[4] 13:37[3] 13:38 13:39[4] 13:40 13:41 13:42 13:43 13:44 13:45[2] 13:46[2] 13:47[2] 13:48 13:49[6] 13:50[3] 13:51[7] 13:52[2] 13:53[5] 13:54[3] 13:55[5] 13:56[7] 13:57[4] 13:58[3] 13:59[3] 14:1 14:2[4] 14:3[5] 14:4 14:5[2] 14:6[8] 14:7[3] 14:8 14:9 14:10[2] 14:11[6] 14:12[3] 14:13[8] 14:14[8] 14:15[3] 14:16[4] 14:17[9] 14:18[6] 14:19[3] 14:20[5]

14:22[2] 14:23[5] 14:24[6] 14:25[9] 14:26[3] 14:27[3] 14:28[9] 14:29[5] 14:30[3] 14:31[5] 14:32[2] 14:33 14:34[3] 14:35[3] 14:36[7] 14:37[5] 14:38[5] 14:39[5] 14:40[4] 14:41[3] 14:42[2] 14:43[4] 14:44[4] 14:45[6] 14:46[3] 14:47[2] 14:48[7] 14:49 14:50[2] 14:51[8] 14:52[8] 14:53[4] 14:54 14:55 14:57 15:1 15:2 15:4 15:5 15:6[2] 15:7[3] 15:8[2] 15:9 15:10[2] 15:11[2] 15:12[2] 15:14[6] 15:15[5] 15:16 15:17[2] 15:18[2] 15:19 15:21 15:22 15:23 15:24 15:25[5] 15:26[3] 15:27 15:29[5] 15:30[6] 15:31 15:32 15:33[2] 16:1[4] 16:2[7] 16:3 16:4[3] 16:5[3] 16:6 16:7[5] 16:8[4] 16:9[2] 16:10[5] 16:11[4] 16:12[3] 16:13[7] 16:14[5] 16:15[8] 16:16[6] 16:17[4] 16:18[8] 16:19[3] 16:20[5] 16:21[8] 16:22[3] 16:23[4]

16:24[4] 16:25[3] 16:26[3] 16:27[7] 16:28 16:29[3] 16:30 16:32[5] 16:33[7] 16:34[2] 17:1 17:2[3] 17:3[3] 17:4[6] 17:5[9] 17:6[9] 17:8[2] 17:9[3] 17:10[2] 17:11[6] 17:12 17:13[3] 17:14[7] 17:15 18:1 18:2[2] 18:3[4] 18:4 18:5 18:6 18:7[2] 18:8 18:9[2] 18:10 18:11 18:12 18:13 18:14 18:15 18:16 18:17 18:18 18:21[3] 18:24 18:25[3] 18:27[3] 18:28[2] 18:29 18:30 19:1 19:2[3] 19:3 19:4 19:5 19:6[4] 19:7 19:8[2] 19:9[3] 19:10[2] 19:12[2] 19:13[2] 19:14[3] 19:15[4] 19:16[2] 19:18[2] 19:21[4] 19:22[5] 19:23[2] 19:24[3] 19:25[4] 19:26 19:27[2] 19:28[2] 19:29[2] 19:30 19:31 19:32[4] 19:34[3] 19:36[2] 19:37 20:1 20:2[5] 20:4[3] 20:6 20:7 20:8 20:10[3]

20:11 20:15 20:16[2] 20:17 20:18 20:19 20:22 20:23[2] 20:24 20:25 20:26 21:1[4] 21:5 21:6[4] 21:8[2] 21:9[2] 21:10[3] 21:12[5] 21:15 21:16 21:17 21:21[5] 21:22[3] 21:23[3] 21:24 22:1 22:2[3] 21:3[4] 21:4[3] 21:6[2] 21:7[2] 21:8 21:9 21:10[3] 21:11 21:12[2] 21:13 21:14[4] 21:15[3] 21:16[2] 21:17 21:18[4] 21:19[3] 21:21 21:22[3] 21:24 21:25 21:26 21:27[3] 21:29 21:30[3] 21:31 21:32[2] 21:33[2] 23:1 23:2[3] 23:3[4] 23:4[2] 23:5[3] 23:6[4] 23:7 23:8[2] 23:9 23:10[5] 23:11[5] 23:12[3] 23:13[4] 23:14 23:15[5] 23:16[3] 23:17[2] 23:18[4] 23:19[2] 23:20[7] 23:21 23:22[5] 23:23 23:24[4] 23:25 23:26 23:27[2] 23:28 23:30 23:32[2] 23:33 23:34[4] 23:35

23:36[3] 23:37[3] 23:38[3] 23:39[7] 23:40[5] 23:41[3] 23:43[3] 23:44[3] 24:1 24:2[3] 24:3[7] 24:4[3] 24:6[2] 24:7[2] 24:8[2] 24:9[3] 24:10[4] 24:11[5] 24:12[2] 24:13 24:14[2] 24:15 24:16[7] 24:22[2] 24:23[4] 25:1 25:2[4] 25:3 25:4[3] 25:5[2] 25:6[2] 25:7[2] 25:8[2] 25:9[6] 25:10[3] 25:11 25:12[3] 25:13 25:15[4] 25:16[7] 25:17 25:18 25:19 25:20 25:21 25:22[3] 25:23[2] 25:24[2] 25:26 25:27[4] 25:28[3] 25:30[4] 25:31[5] 25:32[5] 25:33[8] 25:34[2] 25:38[3] 25:40 25:41 25:42 25:44 25:45[2] 25:46 25:47[3] 25:50[5] 25:51[2] 25:52[2] 25:53 25:54 25:55[3] 26:1 26:2 26:4[3] 26:5[4] 26:6[3] 26:7 26:8 26:10[2] 26:13[3] 26:16[2] 26:19 26:20[2] 26:25[4] 26:26 26:29[2] 26:30 26:31

26:32 26:33 26:34[2] 26:36[2] 26:38[2] 26:39 26:40 26:41[2] 26:42 26:43[2] 26:44[2] 26:45[5] 26:46[4] 27:1 27:2[3] 27:3[3] 27:5[2] 27:6[2] 27:7 27:8[3] 27:9[2] 27:10 27:11[2] 27:12[2] 27:14[3] 27:15[2] 27:16[2] 27:17 27:18[6] 27:19[3] 27:20[2] 27:21[5] 27:22[2] 27:23[5] 27:24[5] 27:25[3] 27:26[4] 27:28[3] 27:30[8] 27:31 27:32[6] 27:33 27:34[3]

NU

1:1[8] 1:2[5] 1:4 1:5[4] 1:6 1:7 1:8 1:9 1:10[3] 1:11 1:12 1:13 1:14 1:15 1:16[3] 1:18[6] 1:19[2] 1:20[4] 1:21 1:22[4] 1:23 1:24[4] 1:25 1:26[4] 1:27 1:28[4] 1:29 1:30[4] 1:31 1:32[4] 1:33 1:34[4] 1:35 1:36[4] 1:37 1:38[4] 1:39 1:40[4] 1:41 1:42[4]

1:43 1:44[2] 1:45[2] 1:47[2] 1:48 1:49[3] 1:50[6] 1:51[5] 1:52 1:53[7] 1:54[2] 2:1 2:2[4] 2:3[7] 2:5[3] 2:7[3] 2:9 2:10[6] 2:12[4] 2:14[4] 2:16[2] 2:17[6] 2:18[6] 2:20[4] 2:22[4] 2:24[2] 2:25[6] 2:27[4] 2:29[4] 2:31 2:32[3] 2:33[3] 2:34[3] 3:1[3] 3:2[3] 3:3[4] 3:4[5] 3:5 3:6[2] 3:7[6] 3:8[7] 3:9[2] 3:10 3:11 3:12[6] 3:13[6] 3:14[2] 3:15[2] 3:16[2] 3:17 3:18[2] 3:19 3:20[4] 3:21[6] 3:22[2] 3:23[3] 3:24[5] 3:25[11] 3:26[9] 3:27[10] 3:28[4] 3:29[4] 3:30[6] 3:31[8] 3:32[7] 3:33[5] 3:34[2] 3:35[7] 3:36[5] 3:37[2] 3:38[9] 3:39[4] 3:40[5] 3:41[9] 3:42[3] 3:43[2] 3:44 3:45[7] 3:46[4] 3:47[4] 3:48[4] 3:49[2] 3:50[5] 3:51[4] 4:1 4:2[4]

4:3[4] 4:4[5] 4:5[3] 4:6[2] 4:7[5] 4:8[2] 4:9[3] 4:10 4:11[2] 4:12[2] 4:13[2] 4:14[8] 4:15[9] 4:16[12] 4:17 4:18[4] 4:19 4:20 4:21 4:22[3] 4:23[4] 4:24[3] 4:25[10] 4:26[9] 4:27[4] 4:28[8] 4:29[2] 4:30[4] 4:31[7] 4:32[4] 4:33[8] 4:34[5] 4:35[4] 4:37[7] 4:38[2] 4:39[4] 4:40 4:41[6] 4:42[3] 4:43[4] 4:45[5] 4:46[3] 4:47[6] 4:49[4] 5:1 5:2[3] 5:3[2] 5:4[4] 5:5 5:6[2] 5:7[2] 5:8[7] 5:9[3] 5:10 5:11 5:12 5:13[2] 5:14[2] 5:15[2] 5:16[2] 5:17[6] 5:18[9] 5:19[3] 5:21[6] 5:22[2] 5:23[2] 5:24[5] 5:25[6] 5:26[6] 5:27[4] 5:28 5:29 5:30[4] 5:31 6:1 6:2[2] 6:4[4] 6:5[7] 6:6[2] 6:7 6:8[2] 6:9[3] 6:10[5] 6:11[4] 6:12[4] 6:13[6]

6:14[3] 6:16[2] 6:17[4] 6:18[10] 6:19[7] 6:20[5] 6:21[5] 6:22 6:23 6:24 6:25 6:26 6:27 7:1[5] 7:2[4] 7:3[3] 7:4 7:5[4] 7:6[3] 7:7 7:8[4] 7:9[3] 7:10[5] 7:11[3] 7:12[3] 7:13[3] 7:15 7:16 7:17[3] 7:18[2] 7:19[3] 7:21 7:22 7:23[3] 7:24[3] 7:25[3] 7:27 7:28 7:29[3] 7:30[3] 7:31[3] 7:33 7:34 7:35[3] 7:36[3] 7:37[3] 7:39 7:40 7:41[3] 7:42[3] 7:43[3] 7:45 7:46 7:47[3] 7:48[3] 7:49[3] 7:51 7:52 7:53[3] 7:54[3] 7:55[3] 7:57 7:58 7:59[3] 7:60[3] 7:61[3] 7:63 7:64 7:65[3] 7:66[3] 7:67[3] 7:69 7:70 7:71[3] 7:72[3] 7:73[3] 7:75 7:76 7:77[3] 7:78[3] 7:79[3] 7:81 7:82 7:83[3] 7:84[4] 7:85[3]

7:86^{5} 7:87^{7} 7:88^{9} 7:89^{6} 8:1 8:2^{3} 8:3^{3} 8:4^{6} 8:5 8:6^{2} 8:9^{5} 8:10^{4} 8:11^{5} 8:12^{7} 8:13^{2} 8:14^{3} 8:15^{4} 8:16^{3} 8:17^{4} 8:18^{3} 8:19^{10} 8:20^{6} 8:21^{2} 8:22^{5} 8:23 8:24^{4} 8:25^{2} 8:26^{4} 9:1^{5} 9:2^{2} 9:3^{3} 9:4^{2} 9:5^{6} 9:6^{2} 9:7^{3} 9:8 9:9 9:10^{3} 9:11^{2} 9:12^{3} 9:13^{5} 9:14^{7} 9:15^{9} 9:16^{2} 9:17^{6} 9:18^{7} 9:19^{5} 9:20^{6} 9:21^{5} 9:22^{3} 9:23^{9} 10:1 10:2^{4} 10:3^{4} 10:4^{2} 10:5^{2} 10:6^{3} 10:7 10:8^{3} 10:9^{3} 10:10^{5} 10:11^{6} 10:12^{4} 10:13^{3} 10:14^{5} 10:15^{4} 10:16^{4} 10:17^{4} 10:18^{3} 10:19^{4} 10:20^{4} 10:21^{4} 10:22^{4} 10:23^{4} 10:24^{4} 10:25^{6} 10:26^{4} 10:27^{4} 10:28^{2} 10:29^{5} 10:31 10:32^{2} 10:33^{6} 10:34^{3} 10:35 10:36 11:1^{7}

11:2^{3} 11:3^{4} 11:4^{2} 11:5^{6} 11:7^{3} 11:8^{3} 11:9^{4} 11:10^{4} 11:11^{2} 11:12^{2} 11:16^{6} 11:17^{3} 11:18^{3} 11:20 11:21 11:22^{4} 11:23^{2} 11:24^{7} 11:25^{4} 11:26^{9} 11:27 11:28^{2} 11:29^{2} 11:30^{2} 11:31^{7} 11:32^{4} 11:33^{6} 11:34^{2} 11:35 12:1 12:2^{2} 12:3^{4} 12:4^{3} 12:5^{5} 12:6 12:8^{2} 12:9^{2} 12:10^{2} 12:11 12:12 12:13 12:14^{2} 12:15^{2} 12:16^{2} 13:1 13:2^{2} 13:3^{4} 13:4^{2} 13:5^{2} 13:6^{2} 13:7^{2} 13:8^{2} 13:9^{2} 13:10^{2} 13:11^{3} 13:12^{2} 13:13^{2} 13:14^{2} 13:15^{2} 13:16^{4} 13:17^{2} 13:18^{2} 13:19 13:20^{6} 13:21^{2} 13:22^{2} 13:23^{3} 13:24^{4} 13:25 13:26^{6} 13:27^{2} 13:28^{4} 13:29^{10} 13:30 13:31^{2} 13:32^{5} 13:33^{3} 14:1^{2} 14:2^{3} 14:3^{2} 14:5^{3} 14:6^{3} 14:7^{3} 14:8 14:9^{4} 14:10^{6} 14:11^{2}

14:12 14:13^{2} 14:14 14:15^{2} 14:16^{3} 14:17 14:18^{6} 14:19^{2} 14:20 14:21^{3} 14:22 14:23 14:24 14:25^{6} 14:26 14:27^{2} 14:28 14:30^{3} 14:31 14:33^{2} 14:34^{3} 14:35 14:36^{4} 14:37^{4} 14:38^{4} 14:39^{2} 14:40^{5} 14:41^{2} 14:42 14:43^{5} 14:44^{5} 14:45^{2} 15:1 15:2^{2} 15:3^{4} 15:4^{2} 15:5^{2} 15:6 15:7^{2} 15:8 15:10 15:12 15:13^{2} 15:14 15:15^{4} 15:16 15:17 15:18^{2} 15:19^{3} 15:20^{3} 15:21^{2} 15:22 15:23^{4} 15:24^{6} 15:25^{5} 15:26^{4} 15:27 15:28^{3} 15:29^{2} 15:30^{4} 15:31^{2} 15:32^{3} 15:33 15:35^{4} 15:36^{3} 15:37 15:38^{4} 15:39^{2} 15:41^{3} 16:1^{5} 16:2^{3} 16:3^{4} 16:5 16:7^{3} 16:9^{6} 16:10^{2} 16:11 16:12 16:13 16:14 16:15 16:16 16:17 16:18^{3} 16:19^{7} 16:20

16:22^{3} 16:23 16:24^{2} 16:25 16:26^{2} 16:27^{2} 16:28 16:29^{3} 16:30^{4} 16:31 16:32^{2} 16:33^{3} 16:34^{2} 16:35^{2} 16:36 16:37^{5} 16:38^{4} 16:39^{3} 16:40^{5} 16:41^{5} 16:42^{6} 16:43^{2} 16:44 16:46^{4} 16:47^{5} 16:48^{3} 16:49^{2} 16:50^{4} 17:1 17:2^{3} 17:3^{3} 17:4^{3} 17:5^{3} 17:6^{2} 17:7^{3} 17:8^{4} 17:9^{3} 17:10^{3} 17:11 17:12 17:13^{2} 18:1^{4} 18:2^{3} 18:3^{5} 18:4^{5} 18:5^{5} 18:6^{6} 18:7^{3} 18:8^{5} 18:9 18:10 18:11^{3} 18:12^{7} 18:13^{2} 18:15^{4} 18:16^{3} 18:17^{5} 18:18^{3} 18:19^{5} 18:20^{2} 18:21^{5} 18:22^{3} 18:23^{5} 18:24^{5} 18:25 18:26^{5} 18:27^{4} 18:28^{4} 18:29^{3} 18:30^{6} 18:31^{2} 18:32^{3} 19:1 19:2^{4} 19:3^{2} 19:4^{3} 19:5 19:6^{4} 19:7^{4} 19:8 19:9^{5} 19:10^{5} 19:11 19:12^{4} 19:13^{4} 19:14^{3}

19:16 19:17^{2} 19:18^{4} 19:19^{5} 19:20^{5} 19:21^{2} 19:22^{2} 20:1^{5} 20:2 20:3^{2} 20:4^{2} 20:6^{7} 20:7 20:8^{5} 20:9^{2} 20:10^{2} 20:11^{3} 20:12^{4} 20:13^{3} 20:14^{2} 20:15 20:16^{2} 20:17^{7} 20:18 20:19 20:22^{2} 20:23^{3} 20:24^{3} 20:27^{3} 20:28^{3} 20:29^{2} 21:1^{4} 21:2 21:3^{5} 21:4^{6} 21:5^{2} 21:6^{3} 21:7^{5} 21:8 21:9 21:10 21:11^{2} 21:12 21:13^{6} 21:14^{5} 21:15^{4} 21:16^{3} 21:18^{7} 21:20^{3} 21:21 21:22^{5} 21:23 21:24^{5} 21:25^{3} 21:26^{4} 21:27 21:28^{3} 21:29 21:31^{2} 21:32^{2} 21:33^{3} 21:34^{2} 22:1^{2} 22:2^{2} 22:3^{2} 22:4^{6} 22:5^{6} 22:6 22:7^{4} 22:8^{2} 22:10 22:11^{2} 22:12 22:13^{3} 22:14 22:16 22:18^{3} 22:29 22:20^{2} 22:21^{2} 22:22^{3} 22:23^{9} 22:24^{3} 22:25^{5} 22:26^{4} 22:27^{4}

22:28^{3} 22:29 22:30 22:31^{5} 22:32^{2} 22:33 22:34^{3} 22:35^{5} 22:36^{2} 22:38 22:40 22:41^{4} 23:3 23:5 23:6 23:7^{3} 23:8 23:9^{5} 23:10^{5} 23:12 23:13 23:14^{2} 23:15 23:16 23:17^{2} 23:19 23:21^{2} 23:22 23:24^{4} 23:26 23:28 24:1^{2} 24:2 24:3^{2} 24:4^{3} 24:6^{5} 24:7 24:8^{2} 24:11 24:13^{3} 24:14 24:15^{2} 24:16^{5} 24:17^{2} 24:19 24:20^{2} 24:21 24:22 24:24 25:1^{2} 25:2^{3} 25:3^{2} 25:4^{7} 25:5 25:6^{8} 25:7^{4} 25:8^{6} 25:9 25:10 25:11^{4} 25:13^{2} 25:14^{5} 25:15^{3} 25:16 25:17 25:18^{5} 26:1^{4} 26:2^{3} 26:3^{2} 26:4^{5} 26:5^{6} 26:6^{4} 26:7^{2} 26:8 26:9^{4} 26:10^{2} 26:11 26:12^{7} 26:13^{4} 26:14^{2} 26:15^{7} 26:16^{3} 26:17^{4} 26:18^{2} 26:19^{2} 26:20^{7}

26:21^{5} 26:22 26:23^{5} 26:24^{4} 26:25 26:26^{7} 26:27^{2} 26:28 26:29^{5} 26:30^{5} 26:31^{4} 26:32^{4} 26:33^{3} 26:34 26:35^{7} 26:36^{3} 26:37^{3} 26:38^{7} 26:39^{4} 26:40^{5} 26:41 26:42^{4} 26:43^{2} 26:44^{7} 26:45^{5} 26:46 26:47^{2} 26:48^{5} 26:49^{4} 26:50 26:51^{2} 26:52 26:53^{2} 26:54^{2} 26:55^{3} 26:56^{2} 26:57^{7} 26:58^{12} 26:59^{2} 26:61 26:62^{2} 26:63^{3} 26:64^{3} 26:65^{4} 27:1^{8} 27:2^{6} 27:3^{4} 27:4^{2} 27:5 27:6 27:7^{2} 27:8 27:11^{2} 27:12^{3} 27:14^{6} 27:15 27:16^{4} 27:17^{2} 27:18^{3} 27:19^{2} 27:20^{2} 27:21^{5} 27:22^{3} 27:23^{2} 28:1 28:2 28:3^{3} 28:4^{3} 28:5 28:6 28:7^{6} 28:8^{5} 28:9^{3} 28:10^{2} 28:11^{3} 28:13 28:14^{4} 28:15^{3} 28:16^{4} 28:17^{2} 28:18 28:19^{2} 28:21 28:23^{2} 28:24^{5} 28:25 28:26^{3}

28:27^{3} 28:29 28:30 28:31 29:1^{4} 29:2^{2} 29:4 29:5 29:6^{4} 29:7 29:8^{2} 29:10 29:11^{4} 29:12^{3} 29:13^{2} 29:14^{2} 29:15 29:16^{2} 29:17^{2} 29:18^{4} 29:19^{3} 29:20^{2} 29:21^{4} 29:22 29:23^{2} 29:24^{4} 29:25^{2} 29:26^{2} 29:27^{4} 29:28 29:29^{2} 29:30^{4} 29:31 29:32^{2} 29:33^{4} 29:34 29:35 29:36^{2} 29:37^{4} 29:38 29:39 29:40^{2} 30:1^{5} 30:2 30:3 30:5^{2} 30:7 30:8^{2} 30:12^{3} 30:13 30:14 30:16^{3} 31:1 31:2^{2} 31:3^{4} 31:4^{2} 31:5 31:6^{6} 31:7^{3} 31:8^{4} 31:9^{3} 31:11^{2} 31:12^{8} 31:13^{4} 31:14^{4} 31:15 31:16^{6} 31:17 31:18 31:19^{3} 31:21^{6} 31:22^{6} 31:23^{5} 31:24^{2} 31:25 31:26^{5} 31:27^{3} 31:28^{6} 31:29^{2} 31:30^{8} 31:31^{2} 31:32^{4} 31:36^{2} 31:37^{2} 31:38^{2} 31:39^{2} 31:40^{2}

31:41^{4} 31:42^{2} 31:43^{2} 31:47^{5} 31:48^{3} 31:49^{2} 31:50^{2} 31:51^{2} 31:52^{5} 31:53 31:54^{7} 32:1^{5} 32:2^{5} 32:4^{3} 32:6^{2} 32:7^{4} 32:8 32:9^{6} 32:10^{2} 32:11^{2} 32:12^{4} 32:13^{5} 32:14^{2} 32:15 32:17^{4} 32:18 32:20 32:21 32:22^{4} 32:23 32:25^{2} 32:26 32:27 32:28^{5} 32:29^{5} 32:30 32:31^{3} 32:32^{3} 32:33^{12} 32:34 32:37 32:38 32:39^{3} 32:40 32:41^{2} 32:42 33:1^{4} 33:2^{2} 33:3^{8} 33:4^{3} 33:5 33:6^{2} 33:8^{4} 33:10 33:11^{2} 33:12 33:14 33:15 33:16 33:36 33:37^{2} 33:38^{8} 33:40^{5} 33:44 33:47 33:48^{2} 33:49 33:50^{2} 33:51^{2} 33:52^{2} 33:53^{6} 33:54^{7} 33:55^{8} 34:1 34:2^{5} 34:3^{4} 34:4^{4} 34:5^{4} 34:6^{2} 34:7 34:8^{3} 34:9^{2} 34:11^{5} 34:12^{4} 34:13^{5} 34:14 34:15^{3}

34:16 34:17^{5} 34:18 34:19^{4} 34:20^{3} 34:21^{2} 34:22^{3} 34:23^{5} 34:24^{4} 34:25^{4} 34:26^{4} 34:27^{4} 34:28^{4} 34:29^{4} 35:1^{2} 35:2^{5} 35:3^{2} 35:4^{5} 35:5^{9} 35:6^{3} 35:7^{2} 35:8^{4} 35:9 35:10^{2} 35:11 35:12^{3} 35:14 35:15^{3} 35:16 35:17 35:18 35:19^{2} 35:21^{2} 35:24^{3} 35:25^{9} 35:26^{3} 35:27^{5} 35:28^{7} 35:30^{2} 35:31 35:32^{4} 35:33^{5} 35:34^{3} 36:1^{10} 36:2^{5} 36:3^{7} 36:4^{6} 36:5^{5} 36:6^{5} 36:7^{5} 36:8^{5} 36:9^{3} 36:10^{2} 36:11 36:12^{5} 36:13^{6}

DE

1:1^{4} 1:2 1:3^{6} 1:4^{3} 1:5 1:6 1:7^{12} 1:8^{3} 1:10^{2} 1:11 1:14 1:15 1:16^{2} 1:17^{5} 1:18 1:19^{4} 1:20^{3} 1:21^{3} 1:22 1:23 1:24^{2} 1:25^{3} 1:26^{2} 1:27^{4} 1:28^{4} 1:30 1:31^{3}

1:32 1:33 1:34^{2} 1:36^{3} 1:37 1:38 1:40^{3} 1:41^{3} 1:42 1:43^{3} 1:44 1:45^{2} 1:46 2:1^{4} 2:2 2:4^{3} 2:7^{3} 2:8^{5} 2:9^{3} 2:10^{2} 2:11^{2} 2:12^{4} 2:13^{2} 2:14^{6} 2:15^{3} 2:16^{2} 2:17 2:18 2:19^{4} 2:20 2:21^{2} 2:22^{2} 2:23^{2} 2:24^{2} 2:25^{4} 2:26 2:27^{3} 2:29^{4} 2:30 2:31 2:33 2:34^{3} 2:35^{3} 2:36^{5} 2:37^{6} 3:1^{2} 3:2^{2} 3:3^{2} 3:4^{2} 3:6 3:7^{3} 3:8^{4} 3:9^{2} 3:10^{3} 3:11^{5} 3:12^{4} 3:13^{5} 3:14^{3} 3:16^{3} 3:17^{5} 3:18^{3} 3:20^{3} 3:21^{3} 3:22 3:23 3:25 3:26^{2} 3:27 3:28 3:29 4:1^{4} 4:2^{3} 4:3^{3} 4:4 4:5^{2} 4:6^{2} 4:7 4:9^{2} 4:10^{6} 4:11^{3} 4:12^{5} 4:14^{2} 4:15^{4} 4:16^{2} 4:17^{4} 4:18^{5}

4:19^{6} 4:20^{2} 4:21^{2} 4:23^{4} 4:24 4:25^{4} 4:26 4:27^{4} 4:28 4:29 4:30^{2} 4:31^{2} 4:32^{5} 4:33^{3} 4:34^{2} 4:35 4:36^{2} 4:39^{2} 4:40^{2} 4:41 4:42 4:43^{5} 4:44^{2} 4:45^{4} 4:46^{4} 4:47^{3} 4:48^{2} 4:49^{4} 5:1 5:2 5:3 5:4^{4} 5:5^{5} 5:6^{3} 5:8^{3} 5:9^{5} 5:11^{3} 5:12^{2} 5:14^{3} 5:15^{4} 5:16^{3} 5:22^{7} 5:23^{5} 5:24^{3} 5:25^{2} 5:26^{4} 5:27^{2} 5:28^{5} 5:31^{4} 5:32^{3} 5:33^{3} 6:1^{5} 6:2^{2} 6:3^{2} 6:4 6:5 6:7 6:9 6:10^{2} 6:12^{3} 6:13 6:14^{2} 6:15^{5} 6:16 6:17^{2} 6:18^{4} 6:19 6:20^{4} 6:21 6:22 6:23 6:24^{2} 6:25 7:1^{9} 7:2 7:4^{2} 7:6^{4} 7:7^{2} 7:8^{5} 7:9^{2} 7:11^{3} 7:12^{3} 7:13^{5} 7:15^{2} 7:16^{2} 7:18

7:19^{8} 7:20^{2} 7:21 7:22^{3} 7:23 7:25^{3} 8:1^{3} 8:2^{3} 8:3^{2} 8:5 8:6^{2} 8:7 8:10^{2} 8:11 8:14^{3} 8:15 8:16 8:17 8:18 8:19 8:20^{4} 9:2^{3} 9:3^{2} 9:4^{4} 9:5^{5} 9:6 9:7^{5} 9:8^{2} 9:9^{6} 9:10^{9} 9:11^{5} 9:12^{2} 9:13 9:15^{4} 9:16^{3} 9:17 9:18^{4} 9:19^{3} 9:20^{2} 9:21^{4} 9:22 9:23^{4} 9:24^{2} 9:25^{3} 9:26 9:27 9:28^{4} 10:1^{3} 10:2^{4} 10:3^{3} 10:4^{10} 10:5^{4} 10:6^{3} 10:8^{6} 10:9^{2} 10:10^{4} 10:11^{3} 10:12^{3} 10:13^{2} 10:14^{4} 10:15 10:16 10:17 10:18^{3} 10:19^{2} 10:20 10:22^{2} 11:1 11:2 11:3^{2} 11:4^{4} 11:5 11:6^{5} 11:7^{2} 11:8^{2} 11:9^{2} 11:10^{2} 11:11^{2} 11:12^{7} 11:13 11:14^{3} 11:17^{5} 11:19 11:20 11:21^{5} 11:22

11:23 11:24^{5} 11:25^{4} 11:27^{2} 11:28^{3} 11:29^{4} 11:30^{7} 11:31^{2} 11:32 12:1^{4} 12:2^{4} 12:3^{2} 12:4 12:5^{2} 12:6 12:7^{2} 12:8 12:9^{3} 12:10^{2} 12:11^{3} 12:12^{2} 12:14^{2} 12:15^{6} 12:16 12:17^{2} 12:18^{5} 12:19^{2} 12:20 12:21^{3} 12:22^{4} 12:23^{5} 12:24 12:25^{2} 12:26^{2} 12:27^{8} 12:28^{2} 12:29^{2} 12:31^{3} 13:2^{2} 13:3^{3} 13:4 13:5^{7} 13:6^{2} 13:7^{6} 13:9^{2} 13:10^{3} 13:12 13:13^{2} 13:14 13:15^{6} 13:16^{6} 13:17^{3} 13:18^{4} 14:1^{3} 14:2^{4} 14:4^{4} 14:5^{7} 14:6^{4} 14:7^{7} 14:8^{3} 14:9 14:12^{3} 14:13^{3} 14:15^{4} 14:16^{3} 14:17^{3} 14:18^{4} 14:21^{2} 14:22^{2} 14:23^{5} 14:24^{4} 14:25^{3} 14:26 14:27 14:28^{3} 14:29^{6} 15:1 15:2^{3} 15:4^{3} 15:5^{2} 15:6 15:7 15:9^{3} 15:10 15:11^{2} 15:12

15:14 15:15^{2} 15:17 15:18 15:19^{4} 15:20^{3} 15:21 15:22^{4} 15:23^{2} 16:1^{5} 16:2^{6} 16:3^{5} 16:4^{3} 16:5^{2} 16:6^{6} 16:7^{3} 16:8^{2} 16:9^{3} 16:10^{4} 16:11^{7} 16:13 16:14^{4} 16:15^{5} 16:16^{6} 16:17^{2} 16:18^{2} 16:19^{4} 16:20^{2} 16:21^{2} 16:22 17:1^{2} 17:2^{3} 17:3^{2} 17:4 17:6^{2} 17:7^{5} 17:8^{2} 17:9^{4} 17:10^{2} 17:11^{6} 17:12^{5} 17:13 17:14^{3} 17:15 17:16^{3} 17:18^{3} 17:19^{3} 17:20^{5} 18:1^{5} 18:2 18:3^{6} 18:4^{3} 18:5^{3} 18:6^{3} 18:7^{4} 18:8 18:9^{3} 18:10 18:12^{2} 18:13 18:14 18:15^{2} 18:16^{5} 18:17 18:20^{2} 18:21^{2} 18:22^{6} 19:1^{3} 19:2^{2} 19:3^{2} 19:4^{2} 19:5^{5} 19:6^{4} 19:8^{2} 19:9 19:10 19:12^{3} 19:13 19:14^{2} 19:15^{3} 19:17^{5} 19:18^{2} 19:19 20:1^{2} 20:2^{3} 20:4

20:5^{3} 20:6 20:7 20:8^{2} 20:9^{4} 20:11 20:13^{3} 20:14^{7} 20:15^{2} 20:16^{2} 20:17^{7} 20:18 20:19^{4} 20:20^{2} 21:1^{3} 21:2 21:3^{4} 21:4^{4} 21:5^{5} 21:6^{4} 21:8 21:9^{3} 21:10 21:11 21:13 21:15^{3} 21:16^{5} 21:17^{6} 21:18^{2} 21:19^{2} 21:20 21:21 21:23^{2} 22:4 22:5^{2} 22:6^{7} 22:7^{2} 22:9^{2} 22:12 22:15^{7} 22:16^{2} 22:17^{4} 22:18 22:19^{2} 22:20^{2} 22:21^{4} 22:22^{3} 22:23 22:24^{4} 22:25^{3} 22:26^{2} 22:27^{2} 22:29^{2} 23:1^{3} 23:2^{4} 23:3^{4} 23:4^{2} 23:5^{4} 23:8^{3} 23:9 23:10^{2} 23:11^{2} 23:12 23:14^{2} 23:15 23:17^{2} 23:18^{5} 23:20^{2} 23:21^{2} 23:23 23:25^{2} 24:3^{2} 24:4^{3} 24:6^{2} 24:7 24:8^{3} 24:9^{2} 24:11^{2} 24:12 24:13^{3} 24:15^{2} 24:16^{4} 24:17^{3} 24:18 24:19^{6} 24:20^{4} 24:21^{4}

24:22 25:1^{3} 25:2^{2} 25:4^{2} 25:5^{3} 25:6^{2} 25:7^{4} 25:8 25:9^{2} 25:10 25:11^{4} 25:15^{2} 25:16 25:17 25:18^{2} 25:19^{4} 26:1^{2} 26:2^{6} 26:3^{4} 26:4^{4} 26:5 26:6 26:7^{2} 26:8 26:10^{4} 26:11^{3} 26:12^{7} 26:13^{6} 26:14^{3} 26:15 26:16 26:17 26:18 26:19 27:1^{3} 27:2^{3} 27:3^{4} 27:5 27:6^{3} 27:7 27:8^{2} 27:9^{4} 27:10^{2} 27:11^{2} 27:12 27:14^{2} 27:15^{6} 27:16 27:17 27:18^{3} 27:19^{3} 27:20 27:21 27:22^{3} 27:23 27:24 27:25 27:26^{2} 28:1^{4} 28:2^{2} 28:3^{2} 28:4^{5} 28:7 28:8^{4} 28:9^{3} 28:10^{3} 28:11^{6} 28:12^{4} 28:13^{5} 28:14^{3} 28:15^{2} 28:16^{2} 28:18^{4} 28:20^{2} 28:21^{3} 28:22^{2} 28:23 28:24^{2} 28:25^{3} 28:26^{3} 28:27^{5} 28:28 28:29 28:30 28:32 28:33 28:34

28:35^{5} 28:36 28:37 28:38^{2} 28:39^{3} 28:40 28:42 28:43 28:44^{2} 28:45^{2} 28:47^{2} 28:48 28:49^{4} 28:50^{3} 28:51^{3} 28:52 28:53^{3} 28:54^{3} 28:55^{3} 28:56^{4} 28:57 28:58^{2} 28:59^{2} 28:60 28:61^{2} 28:62^{3} 28:63^{3} 28:64^{4} 28:65^{2} 28:67^{3} 28:68^{2} 29:1^{6} 29:2^{2} 29:3^{2} 29:4 29:5 29:6 29:7^{2} 29:8^{3} 29:9 29:10^{2} 29:11^{2} 29:12^{2} 29:15 29:16^{2} 29:18^{2} 29:19^{2} 29:20^{5} 29:21^{5} 29:22^{5} 29:23^{8} 29:24^{2} 29:25^{3} 29:27^{3} 29:28 29:29^{3} 30:1^{4} 30:2 30:3^{3} 30:4^{2} 30:5^{2} 30:6^{3} 30:7 30:8^{2} 30:9^{5} 30:10^{4} 30:13^{2} 30:14 30:16^{3} 30:18 30:20^{4} 31:2 31:3^{2} 31:4^{3} 31:5^{2} 31:6 31:7^{3} 31:8 31:9^{6} 31:10^{4} 31:11^{2} 31:12^{3} 31:13^{2} 31:14^{5} 31:15^{6} 31:16^{4} 31:18

31:19^{2} 31:20 31:21^{2} 31:22^{2} 31:23^{4} 31:24 31:25^{4} 31:26^{5} 31:27 31:28 31:29^{5} 31:30^{3} 32:1 32:2^{6} 32:3^{2} 32:4 32:5 32:6 32:7^{2} 32:8^{7} 32:9^{2} 32:10^{2} 32:12 32:13^{6} 32:14^{4} 32:15 32:18 32:19^{2} 32:22^{4} 32:24^{3} 32:25^{5} 32:26 32:27^{3} 32:30 32:32^{2} 32:33^{2} 32:35^{2} 32:36 32:38^{2} 32:42^{5} 32:43 32:44^{4} 32:46^{2} 32:47 32:48 32:49^{3} 32:50 32:51^{5} 32:52^{2} 33:1^{3} 33:3 33:4^{2} 33:5^{3} 33:7^{2} 33:8 33:11^{2} 33:12^{4} 33:13^{4} 33:14^{4} 33:15^{4} 33:16^{8} 33:17^{7} 33:19^{5} 33:20^{3} 33:21^{6} 33:23^{4} 33:26^{3} 33:27^{3} 33:28 33:29^{3} 34:1^{5} 34:2^{3} 34:3^{4} 34:4^{2} 34:5^{5} 34:6 34:8^{3} 34:9^{4} 34:10 34:11^{4} 34:12^{2}

JOS

1:1^{5} 1:2^{2} 1:3 1:4^{8} 1:5 1:6 1:7^{3} 1:8 1:9 1:10^{2} 1:11^{4} 1:12^{3} 1:13^{4} 1:14^{2} 1:15^{6} 1:17 2:1^{2} 2:2^{3} 2:3^{3} 2:4^{2} 2:5^{4} 2:6^{4} 2:7^{4} 2:8 2:9^{5} 2:10^{6} 2:11 2:12 2:14^{3} 2:15^{3} 2:16^{3} 2:17 2:18^{2} 2:19^{3} 2:21^{2} 2:22^{4} 2:23^{3} 2:24^{4} 3:1^{2} 3:2^{2} 3:3^{6} 3:4 3:5^{2} 3:6^{7} 3:7^{2} 3:8^{5} 3:9^{3} 3:10^{8} 3:11^{4} 3:12 3:13^{10} 3:14^{5} 3:15^{7} 3:16^{6} 3:17^{7} 4:1^{2} 4:2 4:3^{4} 4:4^{2} 4:5^{6} 4:7^{6} 4:8^{8} 4:9^{6} 4:10^{6} 4:11^{6} 4:12^{4} 4:13^{2} 4:14^{3} 4:15 4:16^{3} 4:17 4:18^{9} 4:19^{4} 4:21 4:23^{4} 4:24^{5} 5:1^{10} 5:2^{3} 5:3^{3} 5:4^{5} 5:5^{4} 5:6^{8} 5:7 5:8^{2} 5:9^{4} 5:10^{5} 5:11^{5} 5:12^{7} 5:14^{3}

5:15^{3} 6:1 6:2^{3} 6:3^{2} 6:4^{5} 6:5^{7} 6:6^{6} 6:7^{4} 6:8^{8} 6:9^{7} 6:10^{2} 6:11^{5} 6:12^{4} 6:13^{9} 6:14^{3} 6:15^{6} 6:16^{6} 6:17^{5} 6:18^{3} 6:19^{4} 6:20^{11} 6:21^{3} 6:22^{4} 6:23^{2} 6:24^{7} 6:25^{2} 6:26^{4} 6:27^{2} 7:1^{10} 7:2^{3} 7:3^{2} 7:4^{2} 7:5^{5} 7:6^{5} 7:7^{3} 7:9^{4} 7:10 7:11 7:12^{2} 7:13^{4} 7:14^{8} 7:15^{3} 7:16^{2} 7:17^{5} 7:18^{4} 7:19 7:20 7:21^{4} 7:22^{2} 7:23^{4} 7:24^{5} 7:25 7:26^{4} 8:1^{3} 8:2^{3} 8:3 8:4^{3} 8:5^{3} 8:6^{2} 8:7^{3} 8:8^{4} 8:9^{2} 8:10^{4} 8:11^{4} 8:12^{2} 8:13^{8} 8:14^{5} 8:15^{2} 8:16^{2} 8:17 8:18^{4} 8:19^{3} 8:20^{6} 8:21^{5} 8:22^{3} 8:23 8:24^{8} 8:25 8:26^{2} 8:27^{4} 8:29^{6} 8:30 8:31^{6} 8:32^{4} 8:33^{10} 8:34^{5} 8:35^{4}

9:1^{11} 9:3 9:5 9:6^{2} 9:7^{2} 9:9^{3} 9:10^{2} 9:11^{2} 9:12 9:13 9:14^{3} 9:15^{2} 9:16 9:17^{2} 9:18^{6} 9:19^{3} 9:20 9:21^{3} 9:23 9:24^{4} 9:26^{2} 9:27^{4} 10:1 10:2^{2} 10:4 10:5^{7} 10:6^{5} 10:7^{2} 10:8 10:10^{2} 10:11^{4} 10:12^{7} 10:13^{6} 10:14^{3} 10:15 10:17 10:18^{2} 10:19^{2} 10:20^{2} 10:21^{3} 10:22^{3} 10:23^{6} 10:24^{5} 10:25 10:26^{2} 10:27^{6} 10:28^{6} 10:30^{8} 10:32^{6} 10:35^{3} 10:37^{6} 10:39^{6} 10:40^{6} 10:41 10:42 10:43 11:1^{2} 11:2^{7} 11:3^{10} 11:4^{2} 11:5 11:6 11:7^{2} 11:8^{3} 11:9 11:10^{3} 11:11^{3} 11:12^{6} 11:13 11:14^{5} 11:15^{2} 11:16^{8} 11:17^{2} 11:19^{3} 11:20^{2} 11:21 11:22^{3} 11:23^{3} 12:1^{9} 12:2^{8} 12:3^{9} 12:4^{3} 12:5^{4} 12:6^{8} 12:7^{7} 12:8^{12}

12:9^{2} 12:10^{2} 12:11^{2} 12:12^{2} 12:13^{2} 12:14^{2} 12:15^{2} 12:16^{2} 12:17^{2} 12:18^{2} 12:19^{2} 12:20^{2} 12:21^{2} 12:22^{2} 12:23^{4} 12:24^{2} 13:1 13:2^{3} 13:3^{9} 13:4^{6} 13:5^{4} 13:6^{5} 13:7^{2} 13:8^{4} 13:9^{6} 13:10^{4} 13:11^{2} 13:12^{3} 13:13^{6} 13:14^{3} 13:15^{2} 13:16^{6} 13:17 13:19^{2} 13:21^{6} 13:22^{4} 13:23^{7} 13:24^{2} 13:25^{3} 13:26 13:27^{6} 13:28^{3} 13:29^{4} 13:30^{2} 13:31^{5} 13:32^{3} 13:33^{2} 14:1^{9} 14:2^{4} 14:3^{3} 14:4^{3} 14:5^{3} 14:6^{6} 14:7^{3} 14:8^{3} 14:9^{2} 14:10 14:11 14:12^{5} 14:13 14:14^{4} 14:15^{3} 15:1^{7} 15:2^{3} 15:3^{2} 15:4^{3} 15:5^{7} 15:6^{5} 15:7^{8} 15:8^{13} 15:9^{7} 15:10^{3} 15:11^{6} 15:12^{5} 15:13^{6} 15:14^{2} 15:15^{2} 15:17^{2} 15:19^{2} 15:20^{3} 15:21^{4} 15:32 15:33 15:46 15:47^{3} 15:48

15:61 15:62 15:63^{5} 16:1^{5} 16:2 16:3^{5} 16:4 16:5^{5} 16:6^{5} 16:8^{7} 16:9^{5} 16:10^{3} 17:1^{4} 17:2^{10} 17:3^{5} 17:4^{7} 17:5^{2} 17:6^{3} 17:7^{4} 17:8^{3} 17:9^{9} 17:10^{3} 17:11^{4} 17:12^{3} 17:13^{2} 17:14^{2} 17:15^{4} 17:16^{6} 17:17 17:18^{3} 18:1^{5} 18:2 18:3^{3} 18:4^{2} 18:5^{3} 18:6^{2} 18:7^{7} 18:8^{4} 18:9^{3} 18:10^{3} 18:11^{6} 18:12^{7} 18:13^{6} 18:14^{7} 18:15^{5} 18:16^{11} 18:17^{4} 18:18 18:19^{8} 18:20^{5} 18:21^{4} 18:28^{2} 19:1^{5} 19:8^{5} 19:9^{8} 19:10^{3} 19:11^{2} 19:12^{2} 19:13 19:14^{4} 19:16^{2} 19:17^{2} 19:22^{2} 19:23^{4} 19:24^{3} 19:27^{4} 19:29^{6} 19:31^{3} 19:32^{3} 19:33 19:34^{4} 19:35 19:39^{4} 19:40^{3} 19:41 19:46 19:47^{6} 19:48^{3} 19:49^{3} 19:50^{4} 19:51^{12} 20:1 20:2^{2} 20:3^{2} 20:4^{6} 20:5^{2}

20:6^{5} 20:7 20:8^{6} 20:9^{6} 21:1^{9} 21:2^{4} 21:3^{4} 21:4^{9} 21:5^{6} 21:6^{6} 21:7^{4} 21:8^{4} 21:9^{4} 21:10^{5} 21:11^{4} 21:12^{4} 21:13^{3} 21:17 21:19^{3} 21:20^{6} 21:21 21:23 21:25 21:26^{3} 21:27^{5} 21:28 21:30 21:32^{2} 21:33^{2} 21:34^{5} 21:36 21:38^{2} 21:40^{4} 21:41^{4} 21:43^{2} 21:44^{2} 21:45^{2} 22:1^{3} 22:2^{2} 22:3^{3} 22:4^{5} 22:5^{5} 22:7^{3} 22:8 22:9^{10} 22:10^{5} 22:11^{8} 22:12^{3} 22:13^{7} 22:14^{3} 22:15^{4} 22:16^{5} 22:17^{3} 22:18^{3} 22:19^{8} 22:20^{3} 22:21^{5} 22:22^{3} 22:23^{2} 22:24 22:25^{3} 22:27^{3} 22:28^{3} 22:29^{4} 22:30^{8} 22:31^{10} 22:32^{8} 22:33^{5} 22:34^{4} 23:1 23:3^{2} 23:4^{2} 23:5^{2} 23:6^{4} 23:7 23:8 23:9 23:10 23:11 23:12 23:13^{2} 23:14^{4} 23:15^{3} 23:16^{5} 24:1^{2} 24:2^{6}

24:3^{3} 24:6^{3} 24:7^{4} 24:8^{3} 24:9^{2} 24:11^{8} 24:12^{3} 24:13 24:14^{5} 24:15^{7} 24:16^{2} 24:17^{5} 24:18^{5} 24:19^{2} 24:20 24:21^{2} 24:22^{2} 24:23^{2} 24:24^{2} 24:25 24:26^{4} 24:27^{3} 24:28 24:29^{3} 24:30^{3} 24:31^{6} 24:32^{6} 24:33

JG

1:1^{4} 1:2^{2} 1:3 1:4^{3} 1:5^{2} 1:8^{4} 1:9^{5} 1:10^{2} 1:11^{2} 1:13 1:15^{2} 1:16^{7} 1:17^{3} 1:18^{3} 1:19^{5} 1:20 1:21^{4} 1:22^{2} 1:23^{3} 1:24^{3} 1:25^{6} 1:26^{5} 1:27^{5} 1:28 1:29^{2} 1:30^{3} 1:31^{2} 1:32^{4} 1:33^{6} 1:34^{4} 1:35^{3} 1:36^{4} 2:1^{2} 2:2 2:4^{4} 2:5 2:6^{3} 2:7^{7} 2:8^{3} 2:9^{4} 2:10^{2} 2:11^{3} 2:12^{5} 2:13 2:14^{4} 2:15^{4} 2:16^{2} 2:17^{3} 2:18^{7} 2:19 2:20^{2} 2:21 2:22^{2} 2:23^{2} 3:1^{3}

3:2^{3} 3:3^{5} 3:4^{3} 3:5^{2} 3:7^{5} 3:8^{4} 3:9^{5} 3:10^{3} 3:11^{2} 3:12^{7} 3:13^{2} 3:14^{2} 3:15^{6} 3:17 3:18^{3} 3:19 3:21 3:22^{6} 3:23^{3} 3:24^{2} 3:25^{3} 3:26 3:27^{3} 3:28^{3} 3:30^{2} 3:31^{2} 4:1^{3} 4:2^{4} 4:3^{3} 4:4 4:5^{2} 4:6^{4} 4:7^{2} 4:9^{3} 4:11^{5} 4:12 4:13^{3} 4:14^{3} 4:15^{3} 4:16^{6} 4:17^{6} 4:18 4:20^{2} 4:21^{3} 4:22^{2} 4:23^{2} 4:24^{3} 5:1 5:2^{3} 5:3^{2} 5:4^{4} 5:5^{3} 5:6^{5} 5:7^{2} 5:8 5:9^{3} 5:10 5:11^{9} 5:13^{4} 5:14^{2} 5:15^{3} 5:16^{4} 5:17 5:18^{3} 5:19^{3} 5:20 5:21^{2} 5:22^{4} 5:23^{8} 5:24^{3} 5:26^{3} 5:28^{3} 5:30^{3} 5:31^{2} 6:1^{5} 6:2^{5} 6:3^{4} 6:4^{2} 6:5 6:6^{3} 6:7^{3} 6:8^{4} 6:9^{3} 6:10^{3} 6:11^{4} 6:12^{3} 6:13^{5}

6:14^{3} 6:15 6:16^{2} 6:19^{3} 6:20^{4} 6:21^{11} 6:22^{2} 6:23 6:24^{2} 6:25^{5} 6:26^{6} 6:27^{3} 6:28^{7} 6:29 6:30^{4} 6:33^{5} 6:34^{2} 6:37^{4} 6:38^{4} 6:39^{3} 6:40^{2} 7:1^{7} 7:2^{3} 7:3^{3} 7:4^{5} 7:5^{4} 7:6^{3} 7:7^{4} 7:8^{4} 7:9^{3} 7:10 7:11^{4} 7:12^{7} 7:13^{2} 7:14^{3} 7:15^{6} 7:16^{2} 7:17^{2} 7:18^{4} 7:19^{8} 7:20^{7} 7:21 7:22^{6} 7:23^{2} 7:24^{4} 7:25^{5} 8:1^{2} 8:2^{3} 8:3 8:4 8:5^{2} 8:6^{2} 8:7^{3} 8:8^{2} 8:9 8:10^{3} 8:11^{4} 8:12^{2} 8:13^{2} 8:14^{3} 8:15^{2} 8:16^{4} 8:17^{3} 8:18 8:19^{2} 8:20 8:21^{2} 8:22^{2} 8:23 8:24 8:25 8:26^{4} 8:28^{3} 8:29 8:32^{3} 8:33 8:34^{3} 8:35^{2} 9:1^{3} 9:2^{3} 9:3^{2} 9:4 9:5^{2} 9:6^{4} 9:7 9:8^{2} 9:9^{2}

9:10^{2} 9:11^{2} 9:12^{2} 9:13^{2} 9:14^{2} 9:15^{4} 9:16 9:17 9:18^{2} 9:20^{4} 9:23^{2} 9:24^{4} 9:25^{3} 9:26^{2} 9:27^{3} 9:28^{4} 9:30^{4} 9:31^{2} 9:32^{2} 9:33^{4} 9:34 9:35^{5} 9:36^{5} 9:37^{3} 9:38 9:39 9:40^{2} 9:42^{3} 9:43^{4} 9:44^{7} 9:45^{4} 9:46^{4} 9:47^{2} 9:48^{3} 9:49^{5} 9:51^{5} 9:52^{3} 9:53 9:55 9:56 9:57^{4} 10:1^{2} 10:4 10:6^{11} 10:7^{6} 10:8^{5} 10:9^{2} 10:10^{2} 10:11^{6} 10:12^{3} 10:14^{2} 10:15^{2} 10:16^{3} 10:17^{2} 10:18^{3} 11:1^{2} 11:2 11:3 11:4 11:5^{3} 11:6 11:7 11:8^{3} 11:9^{3} 11:10^{2} 11:11^{3} 11:12^{2} 11:13^{3} 11:14^{2} 11:15^{3} 11:16^{2} 11:17^{3} 11:18^{8} 11:19^{2} 11:21^{5} 11:22^{3} 11:23^{2} 11:24 11:25 11:26^{2} 11:27^{4} 11:28^{3} 11:29^{3} 11:30^{2} 11:31^{3} 11:32^{2} 11:33^{4}

11:35 11:36^{3} 11:37 11:38 11:39 11:40^{3} 12:1^{2} 12:2 12:3^{2} 12:4^{4} 12:5^{4} 12:6^{2} 12:7^{2} 12:12^{2} 12:13 12:15^{5} 13:1^{6} 13:2^{2} 13:3^{3} 13:5^{4} 13:6^{2} 13:7^{3} 13:8^{3} 13:9^{4} 13:10^{3} 13:11^{3} 13:12 13:13^{3} 13:14 13:15^{2} 13:16^{4} 13:17^{2} 13:18^{2} 13:19^{2} 13:20^{7} 13:21^{3} 13:23 13:24^{3} 13:25^{3} 14:1^{2} 14:2^{2} 14:3^{2} 14:4^{3} 14:5 14:6^{2} 14:7 14:8^{4} 14:9^{3} 14:10^{2} 14:12^{2} 14:14^{4} 14:15^{3} 14:16 14:17^{4} 14:18^{4} 14:19^{3} 15:1^{2} 15:3 15:4 15:5^{6} 15:6^{4} 15:8^{2} 15:9 15:10 15:11^{3} 15:12^{2} 15:13 15:14^{4} 15:16^{2} 15:17 15:18^{4} 15:19^{2} 15:20^{2} 16:2^{5} 16:3^{5} 16:4 16:5^{3} 16:8^{2} 16:9^{4} 16:12^{2} 16:13^{2} 16:14^{5} 16:18^{3} 16:19 16:20^{2} 16:21^{2} 16:22

16:23^{2} 16:24^{2} 16:25^{2} 16:26^{4} 16:27^{4} 16:28^{2} 16:29^{4} 16:30^{5} 16:31^{2} 17:2^{2} 17:3^{3} 17:4^{3} 17:5 17:7 17:8^{3} 17:10^{2} 17:11^{3} 17:12^{3} 17:13 18:1^{3} 18:2^{4} 18:3^{4} 18:6^{2} 18:7^{6} 18:9^{2} 18:10 18:11 18:13^{2} 18:14^{2} 18:15^{4} 19:16^{4} 18:17^{10} 18:18^{5} 18:19 18:20^{6} 18:21^{3} 18:22^{4} 18:23 18:24 18:25^{2} 18:26 18:27^{5} 18:28 18:29^{6} 18:30^{8} 18:31^{2} 19:1 19:2 19:3^{2} 19:4 19:5^{3} 19:6^{2} 19:7 19:8^{3} 19:9^{4} 19:10 19:11^{3} 19:12^{2} 19:14 19:15 19:16^{3} 19:17^{3} 19:18^{3} 19:19 19:20^{2} 19:21 19:22^{8} 19:23^{3} 19:25^{5} 19:26^{5} 19:27^{7} 19:28^{2} 19:29 19:30^{3} 20:1^{4} 20:2^{5} 20:3^{3} 20:4^{3} 20:5^{2} 20:6^{2} 20:8 20:9 20:10^{3} 20:11^{2} 20:12^{2} 20:13^{5} 20:14^{3}

20:15^{3} 20:17 20:18^{5} 20:19^{2} 20:20^{2} 20:21^{3} 20:22^{4} 20:23^{5} 20:24^{3} 20:25^{4} 20:26^{5} 20:27^{4} 20:28^{4} 20:30^{3} 20:31^{8} 20:32^{5} 20:33^{3} 20:34 20:35^{4} 20:36^{4} 20:37^{5} 20:38^{2} 20:39^{4} 20:40^{5} 20:41^{2} 20:42^{6} 20:43^{2} 20:45^{3} 20:46 20:47^{3} 20:48^{7} 21:1 21:2^{2} 21:4^{2} 21:5^{5} 21:6 21:7 21:8^{4} 21:9^{2} 21:10^{7} 21:11 21:12^{3} 21:13^{3} 21:14 21:15^{3} 21:16^{3} 21:18 21:19^{5} 21:20^{2} 21:21^{4} 21:22 21:23^{2} 21:24

RU

1:1^{4} 1:2^{5} 1:4^{5} 1:5 1:6^{3} 1:7^{3} 1:8^{2} 1:9^{2} 1:13^{2} 1:17 1:19 1:20 1:21^{3} 1:22^{3} 2:1 2:2^{2} 2:3^{4} 2:4^{3} 2:5 2:6^{4} 2:7^{4} 2:9^{4} 2:10 2:11^{2} 2:12^{2} 2:14^{3} 2:15 2:16 2:17 2:18 2:19 2:20^{4} 2:21 2:23^{2} 3:2 3:3^{2} 3:4 3:6 3:7^{2} 3:8 3:10^{3} 3:11 3:13^{6} 3:14^{2} 3:15^{2} 3:16 3:18^{3} 4:1^{2} 4:2^{2} 4:3^{2} 4:4^{2} 4:5^{7} 4:6 4:7 4:8 4:9^{3} 4:10^{7} 4:11^{6} 4:12^{3} 4:13 4:14^{2} 4:16 4:17^{3} 4:18

1 SA

1:1^{4} 1:2^{4} 1:3^{4} 1:4 1:5 1:6 1:7^{2} 1:9^{3} 1:10 1:11^{2} 1:12 1:15 1:16 1:17 1:18 1:19^{3} 1:20^{2} 1:21^{3} 1:22^{2} 1:23^{2} 1:24^{3} 1:25 1:26^{2} 1:27 1:28^{3} 2:1^{2} 2:2 2:3 2:4^{2} 2:5 2:6^{2} 2:7 2:8^{3} 2:9^{2} 2:10^{6} 2:11^{3} 2:12^{2} 2:13^{4} 2:14^{4} 2:15^{4} 2:16 2:17^{5} 2:18 2:19 2:20^{3} 2:21^{3} 2:22^{4} 2:24 2:25^{4}

2:26^{2} 2:27^{2} 2:28^{4} 2:29^{2} 2:30^{3} 2:31^{2} 2:32 2:33^{3} 2:36 3:1^{4} 3:3^{4} 3:4 3:6 3:7^{3} 3:8^{4} 3:10 3:11^{2} 3:13 3:14^{2} 3:15^{9} 3:17^{3} 3:18 3:19^{2} 3:20 3:21^{4} 4:1^{3} 4:2^{4} 4:3^{9} 4:4^{8} 4:5^{5} 4:6^{9} 4:7^{2} 4:8^{5} 4:9 4:10 4:11^{2} 4:12^{2} 4:13^{5} 4:14^{4} 4:16^{3} 4:17^{4} 4:18^{4} 4:19^{2} 4:20^{2} 4:21^{3} 4:22^{2} 5:1^{2} 5:2^{3} 5:3^{4} 5:4^{8} 5:5^{2} 5:6^{3} 5:7^{8} 5:8^{8} 5:9^{5} 5:10^{5} 5:11^{6} 5:12^{4} 6:1^{4} 6:2^{5} 6:3^{2} 6:4^{4} 6:5^{2} 6:6^{2} 6:7^{2} 6:8^{5} 6:9 6:10^{2} 6:11^{6} 6:12^{9} 6:13^{2} 6:14^{6} 6:15^{9} 6:16^{3} 6:17^{3} 6:18^{10} 6:19^{7} 6:20 6:21^{4} 7:1^{7} 7:2^{4} 7:3^{6} 7:4^{2} 7:5 7:6^{3} 7:7^{6} 7:8^{4}

7:9^{3} 7:10^{4} 7:11^{2} 7:12^{2} 7:13^{6} 7:14^{6} 7:15 7:17 8:2^{2} 8:4 8:5 8:6^{2} 8:8^{2} 8:9^{2} 8:10^{3} 8:11^{2} 8:14 8:15 8:17 8:18 8:19^{2} 8:20 8:21^{4} 8:22^{2} 9:1^{4} 9:2^{2} 9:3^{3} 9:4^{4} 9:5^{2} 9:7^{3} 9:8^{3} 9:9 9:10^{2} 9:11^{3} 9:12^{3} 9:13^{4} 9:14^{3} 9:15 9:16^{3} 9:17^{2} 9:18^{2} 9:19^{2} 9:20 9:21^{5} 9:22^{2} 9:23^{2} 9:24^{3} 9:25^{4} 9:26^{4} 9:27^{4} 10:1 10:2^{4} 10:3 10:5^{4} 10:6^{2} 10:10^{2} 10:11^{4} 10:12^{2} 10:13 10:14 10:16^{3} 10:17^{2} 10:18^{5} 10:19 10:20^{2} 10:21^{3} 10:22^{4} 10:23^{2} 10:24^{3} 10:25^{5} 10:27 11:1^{2} 11:2 11:3^{2} 11:4^{5} 11:5^{5} 11:6 11:7^{5} 11:8^{2} 11:9^{5} 11:10 11:11^{6} 11:12^{3} 11:13 11:14^{2} 11:15^{4} 12:2

12:3 12:5 12:6^{3} 12:7^{3} 12:8^{2} 12:9^{7} 12:10^{3} 12:11^{2} 12:12^{3} 12:13^{2} 12:14^{5} 12:16 12:17^{3} 12:18^{4} 12:19^{2} 12:20^{3} 12:22^{2} 12:23^{3} 12:24 13:2^{2} 13:3^{6} 13:4^{3} 13:5^{3} 13:6^{3} 13:7^{3} 13:8^{2} 13:9 13:10 13:11^{3} 13:12 13:13^{3} 13:14^{3} 13:15 13:16^{2} 13:17^{5} 13:18^{5} 13:19^{3} 13:20^{2} 13:21^{5} 13:22^{3} 13:23^{3} 14:4^{4} 14:2^{2} 14:3^{5} 14:4^{7} 14:5^{3} 14:6^{4} 14:10 14:11^{5} 14:12^{4} 14:15^{6} 14:16^{2} 14:17 14:18^{3} 14:19^{5} 14:20^{2} 14:21^{5} 14:22^{3} 14:23^{2} 14:24^{4} 14:25^{2} 14:26^{5} 14:27^{4} 14:28^{4} 14:29 14:30^{3} 14:31^{2} 14:32^{5} 14:33^{3} 14:34^{4} 14:35^{4} 14:36^{3} 14:37^{2} 14:38^{2} 14:39^{2} 14:40^{2} 14:41^{2} 14:43^{2} 14:45^{4} 14:46^{2} 14:47^{4} 14:48^{2} 14:49^{6} 14:50^{5} 14:51^{3} 14:52^{2} 15:1^{4}

15:2^2 15:4 15:5 15:6^5 15:7 15:8^5 15:9^6 15:10^2 15:11 15:12 15:13^3 15:14^3 15:15^7 15:16 15:17^3 15:18^3 15:19^5 15:20^6 15:21^5 15:22^4 15:23^3 15:24^3 15:25 15:26^3 15:27 15:28^2 15:29 15:30^2 15:31 15:32^3 15:33 15:35 16:1^2 16:2^2 16:3 16:4^3 16:5^3 16:6 16:7^6 16:8 16:9 16:10 16:11^2 16:12 16:13^4 16:14^3 16:16 16:18^3 16:19 16:23^2 17:1 17:2^4 17:3^3 17:4^2 17:5^2 17:7 17:8 17:10^2 17:11 17:12^3 17:13^6 17:14^2 17:16 17:17 17:18 17:19^3 17:20^6 17:21^2 17:22^4 17:23^5 17:24^2 17:25^3 17:26^5 17:27^2 17:28^4 17:30^3 17:31 17:34 17:36^4 17:37^6 17:40^2 17:41^3 17:42 17:43^2 17:44^5 17:45^4 17:46^9

17:47^3 17:48^3 17:49^3 17:50^3 17:51^3 17:52^7 17:53^2 17:54^2 17:55^3 17:56^2 17:57^4 17:58^2 18:1^2 18:4 18:5^4 18:6^3 18:7 18:8^2 18:10^4 18:11^2 18:12 18:13 18:14 18:17^3 18:18 18:19^2 18:20 18:21^4 18:22^2 18:23 18:24 18:25^5 18:26^2 18:27^3 18:28 18:29 18:30^3 19:2 19:3 19:4 19:5^2 19:6^2 19:8 19:9^2 19:10^4 19:11 19:13 19:15^2 19:16^2 19:20^4 19:21 19:23 19:24 20:3 20:5^4 20:6 20:8 20:11^2 20:12 20:13^2 20:14^2 20:15^4 20:16^3 20:18 20:19^3 20:20 20:21^4 20:22^3 20:23^2 20:24^3 20:25^2 20:27^4 20:29^2 20:30^3 20:31^2 20:34^3 20:36^2 20:37^5 20:38^2 20:39^2 20:40 20:41^3 20:42^4 21:1^2 21:2^3 21:4^2 21:5^5

21:6^4 21:7^4 21:8 21:9^5 21:10 21:11^3 21:12 21:13^2 21:14 21:15 22:1 22:3 22:4^3 22:5^4 22:6 22:7 22:8 22:9^4 22:10^3 22:11^5 22:13 22:14^2 22:15^2 22:16 22:17^8 22:18^4 22:19^6 22:20^2 22:21 22:22^3 23:1^2 23:2^3 23:3^2 23:4^3 23:5^2 23:6 23:8 23:9^2 23:10 23:11^2 23:12^3 23:14^2 23:15 23:16 23:17 23:18^2 23:19^4 23:20^2 23:21 23:23^4 23:24^3 23:25^2 23:26^2 23:27^2 23:28 24:1^2 24:2^2 24:3^4 24:4^4 24:6^4 24:7 24:8^3 24:10^3 24:11^2 24:12^2 24:13^3 24:14 24:15 24:18 24:19 24:20 24:21 24:22 25:1^2 25:2 25:3^5 25:4 25:5 25:7 25:8 25:9 25:10 25:13 25:14^2 25:15^2 25:16^2 25:20^3

25:21 25:22^3 25:23^2 25:24 25:25 25:26^2 25:27 25:28^4 25:29^5 25:30^2 25:31 25:32 25:34^3 25:36^2 25:37^2 25:38 25:39^5 25:40 25:41^3 25:42 25:44 26:1^2 26:2^2 26:3^4 26:5^3 26:6^3 26:7^4 26:8^3 26:9 26:10^2 26:11^4 26:12^3 26:13^2 26:14^3 26:15^3 26:16^4 26:19^7 26:20^5 26:21 26:22^2 26:23^3 26:24^2 27:1^3 27:2^2 27:3^2 27:5^2 27:6 27:7^3 27:8^6 27:9^5 27:10^6 27:11^3 28:1 28:3^2 28:4 28:5^2 28:6^2 28:8^2 28:9^3 28:10^2 28:11 28:12^2 28:13^3 28:14 28:15 28:16 28:17^3 28:18^3 28:19^7 28:20^4 28:21 28:22 28:23^3 28:24^2 29:1^2 29:2^3 29:3^6 29:4^6 29:6^4 29:7^2 29:8^2 29:9^3 29:10^2 29:11^4 30:1^3 30:2 30:3

30:4 30:5^3 30:6^4 30:7^3 30:8 30:9^2 30:10 30:11 30:14^4 30:15 30:16^5 30:17^3 30:18 30:20^2 30:21^4 30:22^2 30:23^2 30:24^2 30:26^5 30:29^4 30:31 31:1^3 31:2^2 31:3^3 31:7^7 31:8^3 31:9^4 31:10^2 31:11^2 31:12^4

2 SA

1:1^2 1:2^3 1:3 1:4^4 1:5 1:6^2 1:10^2 1:11 1:12^4 1:13^2 1:14 1:15 1:16 1:18^4 1:20^5 1:21^3 1:22^6 1:25^3 1:26 1:27^2 2:1^3 2:2^2 2:3 2:4^3 2:5^2 2:6 2:7 2:8^2 2:9 2:10 2:11^2 2:12^3 2:13^9 2:14 2:15^2 2:16 2:17^2 2:19^2 2:21 2:22 2:23^6 2:24^4 2:26^3 2:27^2 2:28 2:29 2:30 2:31 2:32 3:1^3 3:2 3:3^5 3:4^4

3:5 3:6^3 3:7 3:8^3 3:9 3:10^3 3:12 3:14 3:15 3:17 3:18^5 3:19^3 3:20 3:21 3:22 3:23^3 3:24 3:25 3:26 3:27^3 3:28^3 3:29^3 3:30 3:31^2 3:32^3 3:33 3:34 3:35^2 3:36^3 3:37^3 3:38 3:39^3 4:2^6 4:3 4:4 4:5^5 4:6^3 4:7^2 4:8^6 4:9^3 4:11 4:12^3 5:1 5:2^2 5:3^3 5:6^6 5:7^3 5:8^7 5:9^2 5:10 5:12 5:14 5:17^3 5:18^2 5:19^4 5:20^3 5:22^2 5:23^2 5:24^6 5:25^2 6:1 6:2^5 6:3^4 6:4^3 6:5^2 6:6^2 6:7^3 6:8^3 6:9^3 6:10^5 6:11^5 6:12^6 6:13^2 6:14 6:15^5 6:16^4 6:17^5 6:18^3 6:19^4 6:20^5 6:21^4 6:22 6:23^2 7:1^2 7:2^3 7:3^2

7:4^2 7:5 7:6^2 7:7^3 7:8^3 7:9^3 7:10 7:11^2 7:13 7:14 7:18 7:19 7:23^2 7:25 7:26^3 7:29^2 8:1^3 8:2^2 8:3^2 8:4 8:5^2 8:6^2 8:7^2 8:9 8:11 8:12^3 8:13^2 8:14 8:16^3 8:17^4 8:18^3 9:1 9:2^2 9:3^4 9:4^4 9:5^2 9:6^2 9:7 9:9 9:10^2 9:11^4 9:12 9:13 10:1^2 10:2^4 10:3^3 10:4^2 10:5^2 10:6^4 10:7^2 10:8^6 10:9^4 10:10^4 10:11^2 10:12^3 10:13^3 10:14^4 10:15 10:16^4 10:17 10:18^4 10:19^3 11:1^3 11:2^4 11:3^4 11:5 11:6 11:7^2 11:8^2 11:9^3 11:11^3 11:12 11:13 11:14^2 11:15^3 11:16 11:17^5 11:18^2 11:19^4 11:20^3 11:21^4 11:22 11:23^5 11:24^4 11:25^3 11:26

11:27^3 12:1^3 12:2 12:4^4 12:5^3 12:6 12:7^3 12:8 12:9^6 12:10^3 12:11^2 12:12 12:13^2 12:14^3 12:15^2 12:16 12:17^2 12:18^6 12:19^2 12:20^3 12:21^2 12:22^2 12:24 12:25^3 12:26^2 12:27 12:28^4 12:29 12:30^4 12:31^5 13:1^2 13:3 13:4 13:5 13:6^2 13:8 13:10^4 13:13^2 13:15 13:16 13:17 13:18^2 13:23 13:25 13:26 13:27 13:29^2 13:30^2 13:31^2 13:32^5 13:33^3 13:34^4 13:35^2 13:36^2 13:37 13:39 14:1^2 14:2 14:3^2 14:4^3 14:5 14:6^3 14:7^4 14:8^2 14:9^4 14:10 14:11^5 14:12^2 14:13^4 14:14 14:15^5 14:16^4 14:17^4 14:18^5 14:19^8 14:20^2 14:21^2 14:22^4 14:24^2 14:25^2 14:26^3 14:28 14:29^2 14:30 14:32^2 14:33^5

15:2^4 15:3 15:4 15:6^3 15:7^2 15:8^2 15:9 15:10^3 15:12^3 15:13^2 15:14^3 15:15^3 15:16^3 15:17^2 15:18^4 15:19^3 15:21^4 15:22^2 15:23^7 15:24^6 15:25^5 15:27^4 15:28^2 15:29 15:30^2 15:31 15:32^3 15:34^2 15:35^3 15:37 16:1^3 16:2^7 16:3^4 16:4 16:5^3 16:6^3 16:8^6 16:9^3 16:10^2 16:11 16:12^2 16:13 16:14^2 16:15^2 16:16^3 16:18^2 16:19 16:21^2 16:22^3 16:23^3 17:2^2 17:3^3 17:4^2 17:5 17:7 17:8^2 17:9^2 17:10 17:11^2 17:12^3 17:13 17:14^8 17:15^2 17:16^4 17:17 17:19^2 17:20^4 17:21^2 17:22^2 17:23 17:24 17:25^2 17:26 17:27^4 17:29^3 18:1 18:2^8 18:3^2 18:4^4 18:5^5 18:6^4 18:7^2 18:8^5 18:9^7 18:11^2 18:12^4

18:13 18:14^3 18:16^3 18:17 18:18^2 18:19^3 18:20 18:21 18:22 18:23^2 18:24^5 18:26^4 18:27^6 18:28^6 18:29^3 18:30 18:31^2 18:32^4 18:33^3 19:1 19:2^4 19:3^2 19:4^2 19:5^6 19:7^2 19:8^7 19:9^7 19:10 19:11^6 19:12^2 19:13^2 19:14^4 19:15^3 19:16^2 19:17^3 19:18^3 19:19^4 19:20^3 19:22^2 19:24^5 19:25^2 19:26 19:27^2 19:28^2 19:29^2 19:30^2 19:31 19:32 19:33 19:34^2 19:35^2 19:36^2 19:38 19:39^3 19:40^4 19:41^5 19:42^4 19:43^7 20:1^2 20:2^2 20:3^4 20:4^2 20:5^2 20:6 20:7^4 20:8^2 20:9^2 20:10^4 20:12^6 20:13^3 20:14^2 20:15^4 20:16 20:17^2 20:18 20:19^2 20:21^6 20:22^6 20:23^4 20:24^2 20:25 20:26 21:1^4 21:2^8 21:3^4 21:4

21:5^3 21:6^3 21:6^3 21:7^5 21:8^7 21:9^7 21:10^5 21:11^2 21:12^6 21:13^3 21:14^4 21:15^2 21:16^3 21:17^4 21:18^4 21:19^5 21:20 21:21^2 21:22^3 22:1^6 22:2 22:3^2 22:4 22:5^2 22:6^2 22:7 22:8^2 22:10 22:11^2 22:12 22:13 22:14^2 22:16^8 22:19^2 22:21^2 22:22^2 22:25 22:26^2 22:27^2 22:28^2 22:29 22:31^2 22:32 22:36 22:41 22:42 22:43^4 22:44^2 22:47^2 22:48 22:49 22:50 22:51 23:1^6 23:2^2 23:3^3 23:4^5 23:6 23:7^3 23:8^7 23:9^5 23:10^4 23:11^5 23:12^4 23:13^6 23:14^2 23:15^3 23:16^6 23:17^2 23:18^3 23:19 23:20^3 23:21^3 23:22^2 23:23^2 23:23^2 23:24^3 23:25^2 23:26^3 23:27^2 23:28^2 23:29^3 23:30^2 23:31^2 23:32^2 23:33^3

23:34^5 23:35^2 23:36^2 23:37^3 23:39 24:2^7 24:3^6 24:4^8 24:5^4 24:6 24:7^5 24:8^2 24:9^6 24:10^3 24:11^4 24:12 24:14^3 24:15^4 24:16^9 24:17^3 24:18^3 24:19^2 24:20^3 24:21^5 24:22^2 24:23^3 24:24^4 24:25^4

1 KI

1:2^3 1:3^2 1:4^3 1:5 1:7^2 1:8^4 1:9^4 1:10^2 1:11^2 1:12 1:14 1:15^5 1:16^2 1:17 1:18 1:19^5 1:20^3 1:21 1:22^2 1:23^5 1:25^4 1:26^2 1:27^3 1:28^2 1:29^2 1:30 1:31^2 1:32^4 1:33^2 1:34^3 1:36^4 1:37^3 1:38^5 1:39^4 1:40^4 1:41^4 1:42^2 1:44^7 1:45^4 1:46^2 1:47^3 1:48^2 1:49 1:50^2 1:51^3 1:52 1:53 2:1 2:2^2 2:3^3 2:4^2 2:5^7 2:6 2:7^2 2:8^4

2:9 2:10 2:11 2:12 2:13^2 2:15^3 2:17^2 2:18 2:19^2 2:20 2:21 2:22^4 2:23 2:24^2 2:25^2 2:26^4 2:27^4 2:28^4 2:29^4 2:30^4 2:31^3 2:32^6 2:33^3 2:34^2 2:35^5 2:36 2:37^2 2:38^3 2:39^2 2:42^4 2:43^3 2:44^3 2:45^2 2:46^4 3:1^4 3:2^3 3:3^2 3:4^2 3:5 3:8 3:10^2 3:11 3:13 3:15^3 3:16 3:17^2 3:18^3 3:19 3:21^2 3:22^6 3:23^6 3:24^2 3:25^4 3:26^5 3:27^3 3:28^4 4:2^3 4:3^3 4:4^3 4:5^4 4:6^3 4:7 4:8 4:9 4:10^2 4:11^3 4:12^2 4:13^4 4:14 4:15 4:16 4:17 4:19 4:19^6 4:20^2 4:21^5 4:23 4:24^4 4:25 4:28^3 4:29^2 4:30^4 4:31^2 4:33^3 4:34^2 5:1 5:3^5

5:4 5:5^3 5:6 5:7^2 5:8 5:9^2 5:12 5:13 5:14 5:15 5:16^4 5:17^3 5:18^2 6:1^8 6:2^5 6:3^8 6:4 6:5^6 6:6^8 6:7^2 6:8^7 6:9^2 6:10^2 6:11^2 6:13 6:14 6:15^8 6:16^6 6:17^2 6:18^2 6:19^5 6:20^4 6:21^3 6:22^4 6:23 6:24^8 6:25^2 6:26^3 6:27^{12} 6:28 6:29^2 6:30^2 6:31^4 6:32^3 6:33^3 6:34^5 6:35 6:36 6:37^5 6:38^6 7:2^6 7:3 7:5^2 7:6^5 7:7^4 7:8^2 7:9^5 7:10 7:11 7:12^6 7:14 7:16^6 7:17^5 7:18^5 7:19^4 7:20^6 7:21^7 7:22^4 7:23^2 7:24^3 7:25^5 7:26^2 7:27^3 7:28^4 7:29^4 7:30^3 7:31^6 7:32^5 7:33^3 7:34^3 7:35^7 7:36^4 7:37 7:38 7:39^8 7:40^6 7:41^{10}

7:42^4 7:43 7:44 7:45^5 7:46^3 7:47^3 7:48^6 7:48^6 7:49^7 7:50^{12} 7:51^{10} 8:1^{10} 8:2^4 8:3^3 8:4^8 8:6^9 8:7^6 8:8^5 8:9^5 8:10^5 8:11^6 8:12^2 8:14^3 8:15 8:16^2 8:17^3 8:18 8:19^2 8:20^6 8:21^4 8:22^4 8:25 8:27^2 8:28^3 8:29^2 8:30 8:31 8:32^2 8:33 8:34^2 8:36^2 8:37^2 8:38 8:39^2 8:40^2 8:43^2 8:44^3 8:46^3 8:47^2 8:48^3 8:51 8:52^2 8:53^3 8:54^3 8:55 8:56^2 8:57 8:59^5 8:60^3 8:61 8:62 8:63^5 8:64^{13} 8:65^3 8:66^5 9:1^4 9:2^2 9:3 9:5^2 9:7 9:8 9:9^3 9:10^5 9:11^2 9:12 9:13 9:14 9:15^5 9:16^2 9:17 9:18^2 9:19^2 9:20^3 9:21^2 9:22 9:23^4 9:24

9:25^5 9:26^3 9:27^3 10:1^4 10:3 10:4^2 10:5^5 10:6 10:7^3 10:9^3 10:10^2 10:11 10:12^5 10:13 10:14 10:15^6 10:17^3 10:18^2 10:19^6 10:20^4 10:21^4 10:22^3 10:23^2 10:24 10:26^2 10:27^3 10:28^2 10:29^3 11:1^2 11:2^3 11:4^2 11:5^4 11:6^3 11:7^4 11:9^2 11:10 11:11^2 11:12 11:13 11:14^3 11:15^3 11:19^4 11:20^2 11:21^2 11:23 11:25^2 11:26^2 11:27^4 11:28^4 11:29^4 11:30 11:31^4 11:32^2 11:33^6 11:34^2 11:35 11:36 11:39 11:40 11:41^4 11:42 11:43 12:2^2 12:3 12:4 12:5 12:6 12:8^3 12:9 12:10 12:12^4 12:13^3 12:14^2 12:15^7 12:16^4 12:17^2 12:18 12:19 12:20^3 12:21^5 12:22 12:23^4 12:25 12:27^3 12:28^2 12:29^2 12:30^2

12:31^3 12:32^8 12:33^6 13:1^3 13:2^7 13:3^5 13:4^4 13:5^7 13:6^7 13:7^2 13:8^2 13:9^3 13:10 13:11^4 13:12 13:13^2 13:14^2 13:17^3 13:18^2 13:20^4 13:21^6 13:22^4 13:23^2 13:24^5 13:25^6 13:26^9 13:27 13:28^7 13:29^6 13:31^2 13:32^7 13:33^5 13:34^3 14:1 14:2^2 14:3 14:4 14:5^2 14:6^2 14:7^2 14:8^2 14:10^4 14:11^6 14:12^2 14:13^3 14:14^2 14:15^4 14:16 14:17^3 14:18^4 14:19^5 14:20 14:21^4 14:22^2 14:24^5 14:25 14:26^6 14:27^5 14:28^5 14:29^5 14:31 15:1^2 15:2 15:3^3 15:4 15:5^4 15:6 15:7^5 15:8 15:9 15:10 15:11^2 15:12^3 15:13 15:14^2 15:15^4 15:18^{10} 15:20^4 15:22^2 15:23^7 15:24 15:25^2 15:26^3 15:27^3 15:28 15:29^4 15:30^2

15:31^5 15:33^2 15:34^3 16:1^3 16:2^2 16:3^4 16:4^5 16:5^5 16:7^{10} 16:8^2 16:9 16:10 16:11 16:12^4 16:13^3 16:14^5 16:15^3 16:16^5 16:18^4 16:19^3 16:20^5 16:21^3 16:22^3 16:23 16:24^6 16:25^2 16:26^3 16:27^5 16:29^3 16:30^3 16:31^4 16:32 16:33^2 16:34^6 17:1^3 17:2^2 17:3 17:4^2 17:5^3 17:6^4 17:7^2 17:8^2 17:10^3 17:12 17:14^6 17:15 17:16^4 17:17^4 17:20^2 17:21^2 17:22^4 17:23^3 17:24^3 18:1^4 18:3^2 18:4^2 18:5^3 18:6 18:7 18:9 18:10^2 18:12^3 18:13^3 18:15 18:18^2 18:19^3 18:20^2 18:21^3 18:22^2 18:23 18:24^5 18:25^2 18:26^3 18:28 18:29^3 18:30^4 18:31^5 18:32^4 18:33^5 18:34^4 18:35^3 18:36^4 18:37 18:38^8 18:39^5 18:40 18:42^2

18:43 18:44[3] 18:45[2] 18:46[3] 19:1[2] 19:2[2] 19:4 19:6 19:7[4] 19:8[2] 19:9[2] 19:10[3] 19:11[11] 19:12[4] 19:13[2] 19:14[3] 19:15[2] 19:16[2] 19:17[2] 19:18 19:19[2] 19:20 19:21[3] 20:1 20:2 20:3 20:4 20:5 20:6 20:7[3] 20:8[2] 20:9[4] 20:10[3] 20:11 20:12[3] 20:13[2] 20:14[5] 20:15[5] 20:16[3] 20:17[3] 20:19[4] 20:20[3] 20:21[3] 20:22[5] 20:23[4] 20:24 20:25[2] 20:26[3] 20:27[4] 20:28[7] 20:29[5] 20:30[4] 20:31[3] 20:32 20:33[2] 20:34 20:35[5] 20:36[2] 20:37 20:38[3] 20:39[4] 20:40 20:41[3] 20:42 20:43 21:1[2] 21:2 21:3[2] 21:4[3] 21:6 21:7[3] 21:8[3] 21:9[2] 21:10 21:11[5] 21:12 21:13[5] 21:15[2] 21:16[2] 21:17[3] 21:18 21:19[4] 21:20[2] 21:21 21:22[5] 21:23[3] 21:24[5]

21:25[2] 21:26[3] 21:28[3] 21:29[2] 22:2[3] 22:3[3] 22:4 22:5[3] 22:6[5] 22:7 22:8[4] 22:9[2] 22:10[5] 22:11[3] 22:12[3] 22:13[5] 22:14[2] 22:15[5] 22:16[3] 22:17[2] 22:18 22:19[4] 22:20 22:21 22:22[2] 22:23[3] 22:24[4] 22:26[4] 22:27[2] 22:28 22:29[2] 22:30[4] 22:31[2] 22:32[3] 22:33[3] 22:34[5] 22:35[7] 22:36[3] 22:37[2] 22:38[5] 22:39[7] 22:41[2] 22:42 22:43[6] 22:44 22:45[5] 22:46[4] 22:48 22:49[2] 22:50 22:51[2] 22:52[4] 22:53

2 KI

1:1 1:2 1:3[6] 1:4 1:5 1:6[3] 1:8 1:9[3] 1:10 1:11 1:12 1:13[3] 1:14[2] 1:15[3] 1:16[2] 1:17[4] 1:18[5] 2:1 2:2[2] 2:3[3] 2:4[2] 2:5[3] 2:6[2] 2:7[2] 2:8 2:12[2] 2:13[2] 2:14[4] 2:15[4] 2:16[2]

2:19[5] 2:21[4] 2:22[2] 2:23[2] 2:24[3] 3:1[2] 3:2[3] 3:3[2] 3:4[2] 3:5[2] 3:6 3:7[2] 3:8[2] 3:9[5] 3:10[3] 3:11[5] 3:12[4] 3:13[6] 3:14[3] 3:15[3] 3:16 3:17 3:18[3] 3:20[4] 3:21[3] 3:22[6] 3:23[2] 3:24[4] 3:25[5] 3:26[3] 3:27 4:1[5] 4:2[2] 4:4 4:5[2] 4:6[2] 4:7[3] 4:10 4:11 4:13[3] 4:15 4:16 4:17[2] 4:18[2] 4:18[2] 4:21[3] 4:22[3] 4:25[2] 4:26 4:27[5] 4:29[2] 4:30[3] 4:31[4] 4:32[2] 4:33[2] 4:34[4] 4:35[3] 4:37 4:38[6] 4:39[2] 4:40[3] 4:41[3] 4:42[4] 4:43[2] 4:44[2] 5:1[3] 5:2[2] 5:3[5] 5:4[2] 5:6[7] 5:7[2] 5:8[3] 5:9[2] 5:11[4] 5:12 5:13 5:14[3] 5:15[2] 5:16 5:17 5:18[5] 5:20[3] 5:21 5:22[2] 5:24[3] 5:26 5:27

6:1[3] 6:5[2] 6:6[3] 6:8 6:9[3] 6:10[3] 6:11[3] 6:12[3] 6:14 6:15[3] 6:17[4] 6:18[2] 6:19[3] 6:20[3] 6:21 6:23[2] 6:25 6:26[2] 6:27[3] 6:28 6:29 6:30[5] 6:31[2] 6:32[8] 6:33[3] 7:1[4] 7:2[3] 7:3[2] 7:4[5] 7:5[5] 7:6[9] 7:7[2] 7:8[2] 7:9[2] 7:10[5] 7:11[2] 7:12[7] 7:13[5] 7:14[3] 7:15[4] 7:16[5] 7:17[8] 7:18[3] 7:19[2] 7:20[2] 8:1[3] 8:2[5] 8:3[5] 8:4[4] 8:5[4] 8:6[7] 8:7[2] 8:8[3] 8:10 8:11 8:12[3] 8:13 8:15 8:16[3] 8:18[6] 8:19 8:20 8:21[5] 8:22[2] 8:23[5] 8:24 8:25[3] 8:26 8:27[7] 8:28[3] 8:29[4] 9:1[3] 9:2[2] 9:3[3] 9:4[3] 9:5[2] 9:6[6] 9:7[7] 9:8[2] 9:9[5] 9:10[3] 9:11[2] 9:12 9:13[2] 9:14[2] 9:15[3] 9:17[2]

9:18[3] 9:19 9:20[4] 9:21[2] 9:22 9:24 9:25[4] 9:26[7] 9:27[5] 9:28 9:29[2] 9:31 9:32 9:33[2] 9:35[3] 9:36[5] 9:37[4] 10:1[2] 10:3 10:5[5] 10:6[6] 10:7[2] 10:8[5] 10:9 10:10[6] 10:11 10:12[2] 10:13[6] 10:14[2] 10:15[2] 10:16 10:17[2] 10:18 10:19[4] 10:21[3] 10:22[2] 10:23[6] 10:24[2] 10:25[9] 10:26[2] 10:27[2] 10:29[3] 10:30[4] 10:31[3] 10:32[2] 10:33[5] 10:34[5] 10:36 11:1[2] 11:2[4] 11:3[3] 11:4[10] 11:5[4] 11:6[5] 11:7[5] 11:8[3] 11:9[6] 11:10[4] 11:11[8] 11:12[4] 11:13[6] 11:14[7] 11:15[10] 11:16[4] 11:17[6] 11:18[8] 11:19[14] 11:20[5] 12:1 12:2[3] 12:3[3] 12:4[11] 12:5[3] 12:6[4] 12:7[6] 12:8[4] 12:9[11] 12:10[6] 12:11[9] 12:12[4] 12:13[5] 12:14[3] 12:15[2] 12:16[4] 12:18[6] 12:19[5] 12:20

12:21[3] 13:1[3] 13:2[4] 13:3[5] 13:4[4] 13:5[4] 13:6[3] 13:7[3] 13:8[5] 13:10[2] 13:11[4] 13:12[5] 13:13 13:14[3] 13:16[3] 13:17[5] 13:18[3] 13:19 13:20[5] 13:21[4] 13:22 13:23 13:25[6] 14:1[3] 14:3[2] 14:4[3] 14:5[2] 14:6[9] 14:7[2] 14:8[2] 14:9[4] 14:11 14:12 14:13[5] 14:14[6] 14:15[5] 14:16 14:17[2] 14:18[5] 14:20 14:21 14:22 14:23[3] 14:24[4] 14:25[9] 14:26[2] 14:27[4] 14:28[5] 14:29 15:1 15:3[2] 15:4[3] 15:5[7] 15:6[5] 15:7 15:8[2] 15:9[4] 15:10[2] 15:11[5] 15:12[4] 15:13[2] 15:14[2] 15:15[5] 15:16[2] 15:17[2] 15:18[4] 15:19[3] 15:20[5] 15:21[5] 15:23[2] 15:24[4] 15:25[4] 15:26[5] 15:27[2] 15:28[4] 15:29[2] 15:30[4] 15:31[5] 15:32[3] 15:33 15:34[2] 15:35[6] 15:36[5] 15:37[3] 15:38 16:1[3] 16:2[2]

16:3[7] 16:4[2] 16:6[2] 16:7[4] 16:8[6] 16:9[3] 16:10[5] 16:11[2] 16:12[5] 16:13[2] 16:14[9] 16:15[13] 16:16 16:17[5] 16:18[7] 16:19[5] 16:20 17:1[2] 17:2[3] 17:4[3] 17:5[2] 17:6[5] 17:7[4] 17:8[5] 17:9[5] 17:11[4] 17:12 17:13[5] 17:14[2] 17:15[2] 17:16[3] 17:17[3] 17:18[2] 17:19[3] 17:20[3] 17:21[3] 17:22[2] 17:23[2] 17:24[4] 17:25[3] 17:26[9] 17:27[5] 17:28[2] 17:29[3] 17:30[3] 17:31[3] 17:32[5] 17:33[3] 17:34[5] 17:35 17:36[2] 17:37[4] 17:38 17:39[2] 17:41 18:1[2] 18:2 18:3[2] 18:4[5] 18:5[2] 18:6[2] 18:7[2] 18:8[5] 18:9[2] 18:10[3] 18:11[4] 18:12[4] 18:13[2] 18:14[2] 18:15[5] 18:16[6] 18:17[5] 18:18[6] 18:19[2] 18:20 18:21 18:22 18:23 18:24[2] 18:25[2] 18:26[6] 18:27[2] 18:28[4] 18:29 18:30[4] 18:31[2] 18:32

18:33[4] 18:34[2] 18:35[3] 18:36[2] 18:37[6] 19:1[2] 19:2[6] 19:3[2] 19:4[7] 19:5 19:6[4] 19:7 19:8 19:10[2] 19:11 19:12[3] 19:13[4] 19:14[6] 19:15[5] 19:16[2] 19:17[2] 19:18[2] 19:19[3] 19:20[2] 19:21[5] 19:22 19:23[9] 19:24[2] 19:26[5] 19:28 19:29[4] 19:30[2] 19:31[2] 19:32[2] 19:33[3] 19:35[5] 19:37[3] 20:1[3] 20:2[2] 20:4[3] 20:5[6] 20:6[2] 20:7 20:8[5] 20:9[4] 20:10[2] 20:11[4] 20:12 20:13[6] 20:14 20:15 20:16[2] 20:17[2] 20:18[3] 20:19[2] 20:20[6] 21:2[6] 21:3[2] 21:4[3] 21:5[4] 21:6[3] 21:7[4] 21:8[3] 21:9[3] 21:10[2] 21:10[2] 21:11 21:12 21:13[3] 21:14[2] 21:15 21:16[2] 21:17[5] 21:18[2] 21:19 21:20[2] 21:21[2] 21:22[3] 21:23[2] 21:24[4] 21:25[5] 21:26 22:1 22:2[5] 22:3[7] 22:4[7] 22:5[12]

22:6 22:7 22:8[7] 22:9[10] 22:10[4] 22:11[4] 22:12[6] 22:13[6] 22:14[7] 22:15[2] 22:16[5] 22:17 22:18[4] 22:19[3] 22:20[2] 23:1[2] 23:2[13] 23:3[6] 23:4[13] 23:5[9] 23:6[9] 23:7[6] 23:8[12] 23:9[5] 23:10[3] 23:11[11] 23:12[11] 23:13[11] 23:14[3] 23:15[6] 23:16[8] 23:17[5] 23:18[2] 23:19[6] 23:20[3] 23:21[5] 23:22[5] 23:23[2] 23:24[12] 23:25[2] 23:26[3] 23:27[2] 23:28[5] 23:29[2] 23:30[3] 23:31 23:32[2] 23:33[2] 23:34[2] 23:35[9] 23:36 23:37[2] 24:2[8] 24:3[3] 24:4[2] 24:5[6] 24:7[5] 24:8 24:9[2] 24:10[2] 24:11 24:12[4] 24:13[9] 24:14[6] 24:15[4] 24:16[2] 24:17 24:18 24:19[2] 24:20[3] 25:1[4] 25:2[2] 25:3[6] 25:4[10] 25:5[4] 25:6[2] 25:7[2] 25:8[6] 25:9[4] 25:10[5] 25:11[9] 25:12[4] 25:13[9] 25:14[5] 25:15[4] 25:16[5] 25:17[8]

25:18[6] 25:19[11] 25:20[2] 25:21[2] 25:22[4] 25:23[8] 25:24[4] 25:25[6] 25:26[4] 25:27[7] 25:28[2] 25:29 25:30[2]

1 CH

1:5 1:6 1:7 1:8 1:9[2] 1:10 1:12 1:14[3] 1:15[3] 1:16[3] 1:17 1:19[3] 1:23 1:27 1:28 1:29 1:31 1:32[2] 1:33[2] 1:34 1:35 1:36 1:37 1:38 1:39 1:40[2] 1:41[2] 1:42[2] 1:43[5] 1:44 1:45[2] 1:46[3] 1:48 1:49 1:50[3] 1:51 1:54 2:1 2:3[6] 2:4 2:5 2:6 2:7[3] 2:8 2:9 2:10 2:13[2] 2:14[2] 2:15[2] 2:16 2:17[2] 2:18 2:21[2] 2:22 2:23[4] 2:24 2:25[3] 2:26 2:27[2] 2:28[2] 2:29[2] 2:30 2:31[3] 2:32[2] 2:33[2] 2:42[5] 2:43 2:44 2:45[2] 2:47

2:49[4] 2:50[4] 2:51[2] 2:52[2] 2:53[7] 2:54[5] 2:55[7] 3:1[5] 3:2[5] 3:3[2] 3:5 3:9[3] 3:15[5] 3:16 3:17 3:19[2] 3:21[5] 3:22[2] 3:23 3:24 4:1 4:2[3] 4:3[2] 4:4[5] 4:5 4:6 4:7 4:8[2] 4:10 4:11[2] 4:12[2] 4:13[2] 4:14[2] 4:15[3] 4:16 4:17[2] 4:18[5] 4:19[5] 4:20[2] 4:21[7] 4:22[2] 4:23[2] 4:24 4:26 4:27 4:31 4:33 4:34 4:35[3] 4:37[5] 4:38 4:39[3] 4:40 4:41[2] 4:42[2] 4:43[2] 5:1[7] 5:3[2] 5:4 5:6 5:7[2] 5:8[3] 5:9[4] 5:10[4] 5:11[2] 5:12[2] 5:13 5:14[4] 5:15[3] 5:16 5:17[2] 5:18[4] 5:19 5:20[2] 5:22[2] 5:23[3] 5:24[3] 5:25[4] 5:26[7] 6:1 6:2 6:3[2] 6:10[2] 6:15[2] 6:16 6:17[2]

6:18 6:19[3] 6:22 6:25 6:26 6:28[2] 6:29 6:31[4] 6:32[5] 6:33[4] 6:34[4] 6:35[4] 6:36[4] 6:37[4] 6:38[4] 6:39[2] 6:40[3] 6:41[3] 6:42[3] 6:43[3] 6:44[5] 6:45[3] 6:46[3] 6:47[4] 6:48[3] 6:49[6] 6:50 6:54[4] 6:55[2] 6:56[4] 6:57[2] 6:60 6:61[4] 6:62[5] 6:63[4] 6:64[2] 6:65[6] 6:66[3] 6:67 6:70[4] 6:71[3] 6:72 6:74 6:76 6:77[3] 6:78[4] 6:80 7:1 7:2[2] 7:3[2] 7:4 7:5 7:6 7:7[2] 7:8[2] 7:9[2] 7:10[2] 7:11[2] 7:12[2] 7:13[2] 7:14[3] 7:15[3] 7:16[2] 7:17[4] 7:19 7:20 7:21 7:24[2] 7:28[4] 7:29[3] 7:30 7:31[2] 7:33[2] 7:34 7:35 7:36 7:38 7:39 7:40[5] 8:1[2] 8:2[2] 8:3 8:6[4] 8:8 8:10 8:12[2]

8:13[3] 8:16 8:18 8:21 8:25 8:27 8:28 8:29 8:34 8:35 8:38 8:39[3] 8:40[2] 9:1[2] 9:2[4] 9:3[3] 9:4[6] 9:5[2] 9:6 9:7[4] 9:8[6] 9:9[2] 9:10 9:11[7] 9:12[8] 9:13[4] 9:14[5] 9:15[3] 9:16[7] 9:17[2] 9:18[3] 9:19[12] 9:20[3] 9:21[4] 9:22[2] 9:23[6] 9:24[2] 9:26[3] 9:27[3] 9:28[2] 9:29[8] 9:30[4] 9:31[6] 9:32[3] 9:33[4] 9:34 9:35 9:40 9:41 9:44 10:1[3] 10:2[3] 10:3[3] 10:5 10:7[3] 10:8[3] 10:9[5] 10:10[2] 10:11 10:12[4] 10:13[2] 10:14[3] 11:2 11:3[5] 11:4[3] 11:5[3] 11:6[2] 11:7[2] 11:8[3] 11:9 11:10[4] 11:11[4] 11:12[3] 11:13[3] 11:14[3] 11:16[6] 11:16[2] 11:17[3] 11:18[6] 11:19[2] 11:20[3] 11:21[3] 11:22[2] 11:23[3] 11:24[3] 11:25[2]

11:26[4] 11:27[2] 11:28[3] 11:29[2] 11:30[3] 11:31[3] 11:32[2] 11:33[2] 11:34[4] 11:35[3] 11:36[2] 11:37[2] 11:38[2] 11:39[4] 11:40[2] 11:41[2] 11:42[3] 11:44[3] 11:45[2] 11:46[3] 11:47 12:1[3] 12:2[2] 12:3[5] 12:4[4] 12:5 12:6 12:7 12:8[7] 12:9[3] 12:10[2] 12:11[2] 12:12[2] 12:13[2] 12:14[4] 12:15[4] 12:16[2] 12:17 12:18[2] 12:19[4] 12:20 12:21[3] 12:22 12:23[6] 12:24[2] 12:25[2] 12:26 12:27[2] 12:29[5] 12:30[2] 12:31 12:32[3] 12:35 12:37[5] 12:38 13:1 13:2[4] 13:3[2] 13:4[4] 13:5[2] 13:6[3] 13:7[3] 13:9[3] 13:10[3] 13:11 13:12 13:13[4] 13:14[4] 14:2 14:4 14:8[2] 14:9[2] 14:10[2] 14:11[2] 14:13[2] 14:14 14:15[4] 14:16[2] 14:17[3] 15:1[2] 15:2[5] 15:3[2] 15:4[2] 15:5[2] 15:6[2] 15:7[2]

15:8[2] 15:9[2] 15:10[2] 15:11[2] 15:12[6] 15:13[3] 15:14[4] 15:15[6] 15:16[4] 15:17[5] 15:18[2] 15:19 15:21 15:22[2] 15:23 15:24[4] 15:25[6] 15:26[4] 15:27[6] 15:28[4] 15:29[5] 16:1[3] 16:2[5] 16:4[4] 16:5 16:6[3] 16:7[2] 16:8[2] 16:10[2] 16:11 16:12 16:14[2] 16:15 16:16 16:17 16:18[2] 16:23[2] 16:24 16:25 16:26[4] 16:28[3] 16:29[4] 16:30[2] 16:31[4] 16:32[3] 16:33[5] 16:34 16:35 16:36[3] 16:37[4] 16:38 16:39[5] 16:40[5] 16:41[2] 16:42 16:43 17:1[4] 17:3[2] 17:4 17:5 17:6 17:7[3] 17:8[3] 17:9[2] 17:10[3] 17:16[2] 17:17 17:18 17:21 17:23 17:24[3] 17:27 18:1[3] 18:2 18:3 18:4 18:5[2] 18:6[2] 18:7[2] 18:8[3] 18:9 18:11[5] 18:12[3] 18:13[2] 18:15[3] 18:16[3]

18:17[5] 19:1[2] 19:2[5] 19:3[3] 19:4 19:5[3] 19:6[2] 19:7[2] 19:8[2] 19:9[6] 19:10[3] 19:11[4] 19:12[2] 19:13[2] 19:14[3] 19:15[3] 19:16[6] 19:17[3] 19:18[4] 19:19[4] 20:1[6] 20:2[2] 20:3[4] 20:4[4] 20:5[4] 20:6[2] 20:7 20:8[3] 21:2[3] 21:3[2] 21:4 21:5[3] 21:6 21:8 21:9 21:10 21:11 21:12[8] 21:13[3] 21:14 21:15[7] 21:16[5] 21:17 21:18[5] 21:19[3] 21:20 21:21[2] 21:22[5] 21:23[5] 21:24[2] 21:25 21:26[3] 21:27[3] 21:28[3] 21:29[6] 21:30[3] 22:1[4] 22:2[3] 22:3[4] 22:4 22:5[2] 22:6 22:7[2] 22:8[3] 22:10 22:11[3] 22:12[3] 22:13[2] 22:14[2] 22:16[5] 22:17 22:18[5] 22:17 22:18[5] 22:19[10] 23:2[3] 23:3[2] 23:4[3] 23:5[2] 23:6 23:7 23:8[2] 23:9[3] 23:10[2] 23:11[2] 23:12

23:13[3] 23:14[2] 23:15 23:16[2] 23:17[3] 23:18[2] 23:19[5] 23:20[3] 23:21[2] 23:22 23:33 23:24[9] 23:25 23:26[3] 23:27[2] 23:28[10] 23:29[4] 23:30 23:31[6] 23:32[10] 24:1[3] 24:2 24:3[2] 24:4[6] 24:5[5] 24:6[10] 24:7[2] 24:8[2] 24:9[2] 24:10[2] 24:11[2] 24:12[2] 24:13[2] 24:14[2] 24:15[2] 24:16[2] 24:17[2] 24:18[2] 24:19[6] 24:20[4] 24:21[2] 24:22[2] 24:23[5] 24:24[2] 24:25[2] 24:26[2] 24:27 24:29 24:30[4] 24:31[7] 25:1[6] 25:2[5] 25:3[3] 25:4 25:5[4] 25:6[6] 25:7[3] 25:8[4] 25:9[2] 25:10 25:11 25:12 25:13 25:14 25:15 25:16 25:17 25:18 25:19 25:21 25:22 25:23 25:24 25:25 25:26 25:27 25:28 25:29 25:30 25:31 26:1[5] 26:2[5] 26:3[3] 26:4[6] 26:5[3] 26:6

26:7 26:8[2] 26:10[4] 26:11[4] 26:12[5] 26:13[3] 26:14 26:15 26:16[4] 26:18 26:19[4] 26:20[5] 26:21[4] 26:22[4] 26:23[4] 26:24[2] 26:26[7] 26:27[3] 26:28[5] 26:29[2] 26:30[5] 26:31[6] 26:32[4] 27:1[6] 27:2[3] 27:3[5] 27:4[3] 27:5[4] 27:6[2] 27:7[3] 27:8[3] 27:9[4] 27:10[4] 27:11[4] 27:12[4] 27:13[4] 27:14[4] 27:15[3] 27:16[6] 27:17[2] 27:18[2] 27:19[2] 27:20[4] 27:21[3] 27:23[3] 27:23[4] 27:24[4] 27:25[8] 27:26[4] 27:27[6] 27:28[5] 27:29[5] 27:30[4] 27:31[4] 27:32[2] 27:33[3] 27:34[3] 28:1[15] 28:2[6] 28:4[6] 28:5[4] 28:8[6] 28:9[4] 28:10[2] 28:11[8] 28:12[10] 28:13[10] 28:15[7] 28:16[2] 28:17[4] 28:18[7] 28:19[2] 28:20[5] 28:21[7] 29:1[5] 29:2[5] 29:3[3] 29:4[3] 29:5[4] 29:6[6] 29:7[2] 29:8[5] 29:9[3] 29:10[2] 29:11[8] 29:15

29:17[2] 29:18[3] 29:19[2] 29:20[6] 29:21[3] 29:22[5] 29:23[2] 29:24[4] 29:25[2] 29:26 29:27 29:29[8] 29:30[3]

2 CH

1:1[2] 1:2[4] 1:3[7] 1:4[2] 1:5[6] 1:6[4] 1:9[2] 1:11 1:12[2] 1:13[3] 1:14[2] 1:15[3] 1:16[2] 1:17[3] 2:1[2] 2:2 2:3 2:4[8] 2:5 2:6 2:7 2:9 2:10 2:11[2] 2:12[3] 2:14[3] 2:15[4] 2:17[3] 2:18 3:1[6] 3:2[3] 3:3[6] 3:4[7] 3:5 3:6[2] 3:7[6] 3:8[5] 3:9[3] 3:10 3:11[8] 3:12[6] 3:13 3:14 3:15[3] 3:16[4] 3:17[9] 4:1[3] 4:2 4:3[2] 4:4[5] 4:5[4] 4:6[5] 4:7[3] 4:8[3] 4:9[5] 4:10[4] 4:11[5] 4:12[10] 4:13[4] 4:14 4:16[5] 4:17[3] 4:18[2] 4:19[5] 4:20[3] 4:21[3] 4:22[11] 5:1[9] 5:2[10] 5:3[4]

5:4[3] 5:5[7] 5:6[2] 5:7[9] 5:8[6] 5:9[6] 5:10[4] 5:11[3] 5:12[4] 5:13[7] 5:14[5] 6:1[2] 6:3[3] 6:5[3] 6:7[3] 6:8 6:9[2] 6:10[7] 6:11[4] 6:12[4] 6:13[3] 6:14[2] 6:16 6:18[2] 6:19[3] 6:20[2] 6:21 6:22 6:23[2] 6:24[2] 6:25[3] 6:26 6:27[2] 6:28[2] 6:30[2] 6:31 6:32 6:33[3] 6:34[2] 6:35 6:37[2] 6:38[3] 6:39 6:40 6:41 6:42[2] 7:1[6] 7:2[6] 7:3[8] 7:4[3] 7:5[3] 7:6[6] 7:7[10] 7:8[4] 7:9[4] 7:10[5] 7:11[5] 7:12 7:13[2] 7:15 7:18 7:20 7:21 7:22[2] 8:1[3] 8:2[2] 8:4[2] 8:5[2] 8:6[5] 8:7[6] 8:8[2] 8:9 8:10[2] 8:11[7] 8:12[4] 8:13[8] 8:14[8] 8:15[4] 8:16[7] 8:17[2] 8:18[3] 9:1[2] 9:3[3] 9:4[5] 9:5 9:6[3] 9:8[2]

9:9[2] 9:10[2] 9:11[6] 9:12[2] 9:13 9:14[2] 9:15 9:16[2] 9:17 9:18[4] 9:19[4] 9:20[5] 9:21[3] 9:22[2] 9:23[3] 9:25[2] 9:26[5] 9:27[3] 9:29[9] 9:31 10:2[3] 10:4 10:5 10:6 10:8[3] 10:9 10:10[2] 10:12[4] 10:13[3] 10:14[2] 10:15[7] 10:16[4] 10:17[2] 10:18[2] 10:19 11:1[2] 11:2[3] 11:3 11:4[3] 11:11 11:13[2] 11:14[3] 11:15[3] 11:16[3] 11:17[3] 11:18[4] 11:20 11:21 11:22[2] 11:23 12:1[3] 12:2[2] 12:3[4] 12:4 12:5[4] 12:6[3] 12:7[4] 12:8[3] 12:9[6] 12:10[5] 12:11[5] 12:12[2] 12:13[3] 12:14 12:15[4] 12:16 13:1 13:2 13:3[2] 13:5[2] 13:6[3] 13:7[2] 13:8[4] 13:9[7] 13:10[5] 13:11[7] 13:12 13:13 13:14[4] 13:15[2] 13:16 13:18[3] 13:19[3] 13:20[2] 13:22[4] 14:1[2] 14:2[2]

14:3[5] 14:4[3] 14:5[4] 14:6[2] 14:7[2] 14:9 14:10[2] 14:11 14:12[3] 14:13[3] 14:14[4] 14:15 15:1[2] 15:2 15:3 15:4 15:5[2] 15:8[9] 15:9[2] 15:10[3] 15:11[3] 15:12 15:13 15:14 15:15[2] 15:16[3] 15:17[2] 15:18[2] 15:19[2] 16:1[3] 16:2[4] 16:4[3] 16:6[3] 16:7[5] 16:8[3] 16:9[4] 16:10[3] 16:11[3] 16:12[3] 16:13 16:14[3] 17:2[3] 17:3[2] 17:4[2] 17:5[2] 17:6[3] 17:7[2] 17:9[5] 17:10[4] 17:11[2] 17:13[2] 17:14[4] 17:15 17:16[2] 17:18 17:19[3] 18:2 18:3 18:4[3] 18:5[2] 18:6 18:7[5] 18:8[2] 18:9[4] 18:10[2] 18:11[4] 18:12[4] 18:13 18:14[2] 18:15[4] 18:16[2] 18:17 18:18[4] 18:19 18:30[2] 18:21[2] 18:22[3] 18:23[4] 18:25[4] 18:26[2] 18:27 18:28[2] 18:29[4] 18:30[4] 18:31[4] 18:32[3] 18:33[4]

18:34[6] 19:1 19:2[5] 19:3[2] 19:4[2] 19:5[2] 19:6[3] 19:7[3] 19:8[6] 19:9[2] 19:10 19:11[9] 20:1[3] 20:2 20:3 20:4[3] 20:5[4] 20:6[2] 20:7[2] 20:9 20:10[2] 20:13 20:14[9] 20:15[2] 20:16[4] 20:17[3] 20:18[4] 20:19[6] 20:20[3] 20:21[5] 20:22[2] 20:23[3] 20:24[4] 20:25[3] 20:26[6] 20:27[2] 20:28[2] 20:29[4] 20:30 20:31 20:32[3] 20:33[3] 20:34[6] 20:36 20:37[3] 21:1 21:2[2] 21:3[2] 21:4[3] 21:6[6] 21:7[3] 21:8[2] 21:9[3] 21:10[4] 21:11[2] 21:12[4] 21:13[5] 21:14 21:15 21:16[5] 21:17[3] 21:18 21:19[2] 21:20[3] 22:1[6] 22:2 22:3[2] 22:4[2] 22:5[2] 22:6[3] 22:7[4] 22:8[4] 22:9[4] 22:10[3] 22:11[8] 22:12[2] 23:1[7] 23:2[4] 23:3[6] 23:4[5] 23:5[7] 23:6[7] 23:7[4] 23:8[6] 23:9[3] 23:10[8] 23:11[4]

23:12[6] 23:13[8] 23:14[8] 23:15[3] 23:16[3] 23:17[4] 23:18[11] 23:19[4] 23:20[14] 23:21[4] 24:2[4] 24:4 24:5[6] 24:6[9] 24:7[5] 24:8[4] 24:9[4] 24:10[3] 24:11[7] 24:12[7] 24:13[3] 24:14[8] 24:16[2] 24:17[4] 24:18[2] 24:19 24:20[7] 24:21[5] 24:22[3] 24:23[8] 24:24[4] 24:26[2] 24:27[7] 25:2[2] 25:3[2] 25:4[7] 25:5 25:7[3] 25:8[2] 25:9[5] 25:10 25:11[2] 25:12[5] 25:13[3] 25:14[4] 25:15[4] 25:16[3] 25:17[3] 25:18[3] 25:19 25:20[2] 25:21[2] 25:22 25:23[6] 25:24[7] 25:25[2] 25:26[4] 25:27[2] 25:28 26:1[2] 26:2 26:4[2] 26:5[3] 26:6[5] 26:7[3] 26:8[2] 26:9[4] 26:10[4] 26:11[6] 26:12[4] 26:13[2] 26:14 26:15[2] 26:16[4] 26:17[2] 26:18[6] 26:19[6] 26:20[3] 26:21[7] 26:22[4] 26:23[3] 27:1 27:2[5] 27:3[4] 27:4[2] 27:5[7] 27:6

27:7[4] 27:9 28:1[2] 28:2[2] 28:3[7] 28:4[2] 28:5[5] 28:6[2] 28:7[4] 28:8[2] 28:9[3] 28:10[2] 28:11[3] 28:12[7] 28:13[2] 28:14[5] 28:15[5] 28:16 28:17 28:18[7] 28:19[2] 28:21[6] 28:22[2] 28:23[4] 28:24[7] 28:25 28:26[3] 28:27[3] 29:1 29:2[2] 29:3[5] 29:4[3] 29:5[4] 29:6[4] 29:7[5] 29:8[2] 29:9 29:10 29:11 29:12[11] 29:13[2] 29:14[2] 29:15[6] 29:16[12] 29:17[10] 29:18[7] 29:19[3] 29:20[5] 29:21[6] 29:22[10] 29:23[4] 29:24[5] 29:25[8] 29:26[4] 29:27[7] 29:28[4] 29:29 29:30[6] 29:31[4] 29:32[4] 29:33 29:34[7] 29:35[7] 29:36[3] 30:1[4] 30:2[4] 30:3[2] 30:4[3] 30:6[9] 30:7 30:8[3] 30:9[2] 30:10[2] 30:12[6] 30:13[2] 30:14[3] 30:15[8] 30:16[6] 30:17[6] 30:18[3] 30:19[3] 30:20[2] 30:21[6] 30:22[5] 30:23 30:24[3] 30:25[6]

30:26[3] 30:27[3] 31:1[6] 31:2[7] 31:3[9] 31:4[6] 31:5[6] 31:6[3] 31:7[4] 31:8[3] 31:9[3] 31:10[7] 31:11[2] 31:12[5] 31:13[5] 31:14[8] 31:15[4] 31:16[2] 31:17[4] 31:18[2] 31:19[8] 31:20 31:21[4] 32:1[2] 32:3[3] 32:4[5] 32:5[3] 32:6[4] 32:7[2] 32:8[3] 32:10 32:11[3] 32:12 32:13[3] 32:14 32:15 32:16 32:17[4] 32:18[4] 32:19[6] 32:20[3] 32:21[7] 32:22[5] 32:23[2] 32:24[2] 32:25 32:26[5] 32:28 32:30[3] 32:31[5] 32:32[7] 32:33[4] 33:2[6] 33:3[2] 33:4[3] 33:5[4] 33:6[5] 33:7[3] 33:8[6] 33:9[4] 33:10 33:11[5] 33:12[2] 33:13 33:14[6] 33:15[9] 33:16[3] 33:17[3] 33:18[8] 33:19[3] 33:22[3] 33:23 33:25[4] 34:2[5] 34:3[7] 34:4[6] 34:5[2] 34:6 34:7[5] 34:8[10] 34:9[7] 34:10[9] 34:11[3] 34:12[8] 34:13[3] 34:14[6] 34:15[6]

34:16[3] 34:17[7] 34:18[4] 34:19[3] 34:20[5] 34:21[7] 34:22[2] 34:23[2] 34:24[5] 34:25 34:26[4] 34:27[2] 34:28[4] 34:29[2] 34:30[13] 34:31[5] 34:32[3] 34:33[6] 35:1[4] 35:2[4] 35:3[6] 35:4[3] 35:5[8] 35:6[4] 35:7[5] 35:8[6] 35:9[2] 35:10[4] 35:11[4] 35:12[7] 35:13[4] 35:14[7] 35:15[6] 35:16[6] 35:17[3] 35:18[6] 35:19[2] 35:20 35:21 35:22[3] 35:23[2] 35:24[2] 35:25[3] 35:26[4] 35:27[2] 36:1[3] 36:3[2] 36:4 36:5[2] 36:7[3] 36:8[4] 36:9[2] 36:10[4] 36:12[5] 36:13 36:14[7] 36:15 36:16[3] 36:17[4] 36:18[7] 36:19[4] 36:20[3] 36:21[4] 36:22[6] 36:23[4]

EZR

1:1[6] 1:2[3] 1:3[3] 1:4[3] 1:5[6] 1:7[5] 1:8[3] 1:9 1:11[2] 2:1[4] 2:2[3] 2:3 2:4 2:5 2:6[2] 2:7 2:8 2:8

2:10 2:11 2:12 2:13 2:14 2:15 2:16 2:17 2:18 2:19 2:20 2:21 2:22 2:23 2:24 2:25 2:26 2:27 2:28 2:29 2:30 2:31[2] 2:32 2:33 2:34 2:35 2:36[3] 2:37 2:38 2:39 2:40[3] 2:41[2] 2:42[8] 2:43[4] 2:44[3] 2:45[3] 2:46[3] 2:47[3] 2:48[3] 2:49[3] 2:50[3] 2:51[3] 2:52[3] 2:53[3] 2:54[2] 2:55[4] 2:56[3] 2:57[4] 2:58[2] 2:60[3] 2:61[7] 2:62 2:63[2] 2:64 2:68[5] 2:69[2] 2:70[6] 3:1[4] 3:2[7] 3:3[3] 3:4[4] 3:5[5] 3:6[6] 3:7[4] 3:8[13] 3:9[5] 3:10[9] 3:11[6] 3:12[4] 3:13[8] 4:1[5] 4:2[3] 4:3[5] 4:4[4] 4:5[2] 4:6[3] 4:7[6] 4:8[3] 4:9[19] 4:10[6] 4:11[5] 4:12[6] 4:13[4] 4:14[3] 4:15[5]

4:16[3] 4:17[6] 4:18 4:20 4:22[2] 4:23[3] 4:24[4] 5:1[6] 5:2[4] 5:3[2] 5:4[2] 5:5[4] 5:6[6] 5:7 5:8[5] 5:10[3] 5:11[3] 5:12[5] 5:13[3] 5:14[6] 5:15[3] 5:16[3] 5:15[2] 5:16[3] 5:17[4] 6:1[4] 6:2[3] 6:3[10] 6:4[2] 7:5[5] 7:6[3] 7:7[5] 7:8[5] 7:9[4] 7:10[3] 7:12 7:13[2] 7:14[8] 7:15[5] 7:19[7] 7:17[3] 7:18[4] 7:19[5] 7:20[6] 7:21[5] 7:22[7] 7:1[4] 7:2[3] 7:3[3] 7:4[3] 7:5[5] 7:6[5] 7:7[8] 7:8[3] 7:9[5] 7:10[2] 7:11[8] 7:12[3] 7:13 7:14 7:15[3] 7:16[6] 7:17[2] 7:18[4] 7:19[2] 7:20[2] 7:21[7] 7:23[6] 7:24 7:25[4] 7:26[3] 7:27[4] 7:28[4] 8:1[4] 8:2[3] 8:3[3] 8:4[2] 8:5[2] 8:6[2] 8:7[2] 8:8[2] 8:9[2] 8:10[2] 8:11[2] 8:12[2] 8:13 8:14

8:15[4] 8:17[5] 8:18[4] 8:19 8:20[4] 8:21 8:22[5] 8:24[2] 8:25[6] 8:28[5] 8:29[7] 8:30[7] 8:31[7] 8:33[11] 8:34 8:35[4] 8:36[6] 9:1[14] 9:2[4] 9:3 9:4[4] 9:5[2] 9:6 9:7[6] 9:8 9:9[4] 9:11[5] 9:12[2] 9:14 10:1[2] 10:2[4] 10:3[4] 10:5[2] 10:6[4] 10:7[2] 10:8[4] 10:9[8] 10:10[2] 10:11[4] 10:12 10:13 10:14[4] 10:15[3] 10:16[8] 10:17[3] 10:18[4] 10:19 10:20 10:21 10:22 10:23[2] 10:24[2] 10:25 10:26 10:27 10:28 10:29 10:30 10:31 10:33 10:34 10:43

NE

1:1[5] 1:2[5] 1:3[5] 1:4 1:5 1:6[4] 1:7[3] 1:8[2] 1:9[3] 1:11[4] 2:1[5] 2:2 2:3[5] 2:4[2] 2:5[3] 2:6[3] 2:7[4] 2:8[9] 2:9[5] 2:10[5] 2:12[2]

2:13[6] 2:14[4] 2:15[5] 2:16[7] 2:17[3] 2:18[2] 2:19[5] 2:20 3:1[6] 3:2[2] 3:3[6] 3:4[5] 3:5[2] 3:6[7] 3:7[6] 3:8[5] 3:9[3] 3:10[2] 3:11[5] 3:12[3] 3:13[7] 3:14[6] 3:15[12] 3:16[8] 3:17[4] 3:18[3] 3:19[6] 3:20[7] 3:21[6] 3:22[3] 3:23[2] 3:24[5] 3:25[8] 3:26[5] 3:27[3] 3:28[2] 3:29[4] 3:30[3] 3:31[7] 3:32[5] 4:1[2] 4:2[4] 4:3 4:4 4:5 4:6[4] 4:7[5] 4:10[3] 4:11[2] 4:12 4:13[4] 4:14[5] 4:15 4:16[9] 4:17[3] 4:18[2] 4:19[6] 4:20[2] 4:21[5] 4:22[4] 4:23[2] 5:1[2] 5:3 5:4 5:5 5:7[2] 5:8[2] 5:9[3] 5:11[5] 5:12 5:13[3] 5:14[7] 5:15[4] 5:16[2] 5:17[2] 5:18[3] 6:1[5] 6:2[3] 6:3 6:4 6:5 6:6[3] 6:7 6:9 6:10[8] 6:11 6:14[5]

6:15[3] 6:16 6:17[2] 6:18[4] 7:1[5] 7:2[2] 7:3[4] 7:4[3] 7:5[5] 7:6[4] 7:7[3] 7:8 7:9 7:10 7:11[2] 7:12 7:13 7:14 7:15 7:16 7:17 7:18 7:19 7:20 7:21 7:22 7:23 7:24 7:25 7:26 7:27 7:28 7:29 7:30 7:31 7:32 7:33[2] 7:34[2] 7:35 7:36 7:37 7:38 7:39[3] 7:40 7:41 7:42 7:43[3] 7:44[2] 7:45[7] 7:46[4] 7:47[3] 7:48[3] 7:49[3] 7:50[3] 7:51[3] 7:52[3] 7:53[3] 7:54[3] 7:55[3] 7:56[2] 7:57[4] 7:58[3] 7:59[4] 7:60[2] 7:62[3] 7:63[6] 7:64 7:65[2] 7:66 7:70 7:71[4] 7:72[2] 7:73[8] 8:1[7] 8:2[5] 8:3[5] 8:6[5] 8:7[4] 8:8[4] 8:10[4] 8:11[3] 8:12[2] 8:13[9] 8:14[5] 8:15 8:16[8] 8:17[6]

8:18[7] 9:1[2] 9:2[2] 9:3[5] 9:4[3] 9:5[2] 9:9[4] 9:7[4] 9:8[7] 9:9[2] 9:10 9:11[6] 9:12[3] 9:14 9:15[2] 9:19[6] 9:21 9:22[4] 9:23[3] 9:24[7] 9:27[3] 9:28[2] 9:29 9:30[3] 9:32[6] 9:35 9:36[3] 9:37 10:1[2] 10:8 10:9[3] 10:14[2] 10:28[10] 10:29[3] 10:30[2] 10:31[7] 10:32[3] 10:33[10] 10:34[10] 10:35[4] 10:36[6] 10:37[10] 10:38[10] 10:39[13] 11:1[5] 11:2[2] 11:3[7] 11:4[9] 11:5[7] 11:6 11:7[8] 11:9[3] 11:10[2] 11:11[7] 11:12[6] 11:13[5] 11:14[2] 11:15[5] 11:16[5] 11:17[9] 11:18[2] 11:19[2] 11:20[4] 11:21[2] 11:22[10] 11:23[2] 11:24[5] 11:25[5] 11:27 11:28 11:30[3] 11:31 11:35 11:36 12:1[4] 12:7[3] 12:8[2] 12:9 12:12[3] 12:22[6] 12:23[7] 12:24[5] 12:25[3] 12:26[7] 12:27[4] 12:28[4] 12:29[3]

12:30[5] 12:31[5] 12:32 12:35[7] 12:36[3] 12:37[7] 12:38[7] 12:39[7] 12:40[4] 12:41 12:42 12:43[3] 12:44[12] 12:45[6] 12:46[2] 12:47[8] 13:1[6] 13:2[2] 13:3[2] 13:4[4] 13:5[12] 13:6[3] 13:7[9] 13:8[2] 13:9[5] 13:10[5] 13:11[2] 13:12[5] 13:13[6] 13:14[2] 13:15[3] 13:16[2] 13:17[2] 13:18 13:19[6] 13:20 13:21[2] 13:22[4] 13:24[3] 13:28[4] 13:29[4] 13:30[3] 13:31[2]

ES

1:1 1:2[3] 1:3[4] 1:4[2] 1:5[6] 1:6 1:7[3] 1:8[4] 1:9[3] 1:10[6] 1:11[5] 1:12[3] 1:13[4] 1:14[5] 1:15[4] 1:16[3] 1:17[3] 1:18[4] 1:19[5] 1:20[2] 1:21[5] 1:22[3] 2:1 2:2[2] 2:3[9] 2:4[5] 2:5[4] 2:6[2] 2:7 2:8[6] 2:9[5] 2:11[2] 2:12[5] 2:13[4] 2:14[9] 2:15[8] 2:16[3] 2:17[4] 2:18[4] 2:19[3]

2:20 2:21[4] 2:22[3] 2:23[4] 3:1[3] 3:2[3] 3:3[3] 3:6[4] 3:7[6] 3:8[4] 3:9[5] 3:10[4] 3:11[3] 3:12[9] 3:13[6] 3:14[2] 3:15[6] 4:1[2] 4:2[2] 4:3[2] 4:4 4:5 4:6[3] 4:7[4] 4:8[4] 4:9 4:11[8] 4:13[2] 4:14[2] 4:16[3] 5:1[8] 5:2[7] 5:3[3] 5:4[3] 5:5[3] 5:6[4] 5:8[4] 5:9 5:11[6] 5:12[4] 5:13[2] 5:14[6] 6:1[4] 6:2[4] 6:3[2] 6:4[6] 6:5[3] 6:6[4] 6:7[3] 6:8[5] 6:9[8] 6:10[5] 6:11[6] 6:12 6:13[2] 6:14[2] 7:1[2] 7:2[5] 7:3[2] 7:4[2] 7:5[2] 7:6[3] 7:7[5] 7:8[10] 7:9[6] 7:10[2] 8:1[5] 8:2[2] 8:3[4] 8:4[2] 8:5[8] 8:6[2] 8:7[6] 8:8[6] 8:9[10] 8:10[2] 8:11[5] 8:12[4] 8:13[3] 8:14[4] 8:15[3] 8:16 8:17[6] 9:1[10] 9:2[4] 9:3[7] 9:4[2]

9:5[3] 9:6[2] 9:10[5] 9:11[3] 9:12[7] 9:13[3] 9:14[2] 9:15[4] 9:16[3] 9:17[4] 9:18[5] 9:19[5] 9:20[3] 9:21[4] 9:22[4] 9:23 9:24[6] 9:25[3] 9:26[2] 9:27 9:28[2] 9:29[3] 9:30[4] 9:31[4] 9:32[2] 10:1[4] 10:2[7] 10:3[4]

JOB

1:1 1:3[3] 1:5[3] 1:6[2] 1:7[3] 1:8[2] 1:9 1:10[2] 1:12[3] 1:14[2] 1:15[4] 1:16[3] 1:17[5] 1:19[4] 1:20 1:21[4] 2:1[3] 2:2[3] 2:3[2] 2:4 2:6 2:7[3] 2:8 2:10[2] 2:11[3] 2:13 3:3[2] 3:4 3:5[3] 3:6[4] 3:8 3:9[4] 3:10 3:11[3] 3:12[2] 3:14 3:17[2] 3:18[3] 3:19[2] 3:20 3:22 3:24 3:25 4:1 4:3 4:4 4:6 4:7 4:8 4:9[2] 4:10[6] 4:11[2] 4:13[2] 4:15 4:16

4:19^{2} 5:1 5:2^{2} 5:3 5:4 5:5^{3} 5:6^{2} 5:7 5:10^{2} 5:12^{2} 5:13^{3} 5:14^{3} 5:15^{4} 5:16 5:17^{3} 5:20^{2} 5:21^{2} 5:22^{2} 5:23^{4} 5:25^{2} 6:2 6:3^{2} 6:4^{4} 6:5^{2} 6:6 6:7 6:8 6:10^{2} 6:12 6:14^{2} 6:15 6:16^{2} 6:18 6:19^{2} 6:23^{2} 6:26 6:27 7:1 7:2^{2} 7:4^{3} 7:8 7:9^{2} 7:11^{2} 7:21^{2} 8:1 8:2 8:3 8:5 8:6 8:8^{2} 8:11^{2} 8:13^{2} 8:16 8:17^{2} 8:19^{2} 8:20 8:22^{2} 9:5 9:6^{2} 9:7^{2} 9:8^{3} 9:9^{2} 9:13 9:22^{2} 9:23^{3} 9:24^{5} 9:26^{3} 9:31 10:1 10:3^{3} 10:5 10:9 10:18^{2} 10:19^{2} 10:21^{2} 10:22^{2} 11:1 11:2 11:6 11:7 11:9^{3} 11:17^{2} 11:20^{4} 12:2 12:4 12:5

12:6 12:7^{3} 12:8^{3} 12:9^{2} 12:10^{2} 12:11^{2} 12:12 12:15^{2} 12:16^{2} 12:17 12:18 12:19 12:20^{4} 12:21^{2} 12:22 12:23^{2} 12:24^{4} 12:25 13:2 13:3 13:6 13:19 13:25 13:26 13:27^{2} 14:5 14:7 14:8 14:8^{4} 14:9 14:10 14:11^{3} 14:12 14:13 14:14 14:15 14:18^{2} 14:19^{6} 15:1 15:2 15:5^{2} 15:7^{2} 15:8 15:10 15:11 15:15 15:19 15:20^{3} 15:21 15:22 15:23 15:24 15:25 15:26 15:29^{2} 15:30^{2} 15:33^{2} 15:34^{2} 16:5 16:10 16:11^{3} 16:13 16:15 16:16 16:22 17:1 17:5 17:6 17:8^{2} 17:9 17:11 17:12^{2} 17:13^{2} 17:14 17:16^{3} 18:1 18:4^{2} 18:5^{3} 18:6 18:7 18:9^{3} 18:10^{2} 18:13^{2} 18:14 18:17^{2} 18:18

18:21^{3} 19:9 19:17 19:20 19:21 19:24 19:25^{2} 19:28^{2} 19:29^{3} 20:1 20:3^{2} 20:5^{4} 20:6^{2} 20:8 20:9 20:10 20:11^{2} 20:14 20:16^{2} 20:17^{3} 20:18 20:19 20:22^{2} 20:23 20:24^{2} 20:25^{2} 20:27^{2} 20:28^{2} 20:29^{2} 21:7 21:9 21:13^{3} 21:13 21:14 21:15 21:16^{2} 21:17^{2} 21:18^{2} 21:20^{2} 21:21^{2} 21:25 21:26^{2} 21:27 21:28^{4} 21:29 21:30^{3} 21:32^{2} 21:33^{2} 22:1 22:3 22:6 22:7^{2} 22:8^{3} 22:9^{2} 22:12^{3} 22:13 22:14 22:15 22:17 22:18^{2} 22:19^{2} 22:20^{2} 22:22 22:23 22:24^{3} 22:25 22:26 22:28 22:29 22:30^{3} 23:5 23:7 23:9^{2} 23:10 23:12^{2} 23:14 23:16 23:17^{2} 24:1 24:2 24:3^{2} 24:4^{4} 24:5^{2} 24:6^{3} 24:7^{2} 24:8^{3}

24:9^{3} 24:10^{2} 24:12^{3} 24:13^{3} 24:14^{4} 24:15^{3} 24:16^{3} 24:17^{4} 24:18^{4} 24:19^{2} 24:20^{2} 24:21^{2} 24:22 24:24^{3} 25:1 25:5^{2} 25:6 26:2 26:3 26:5^{2} 26:7^{3} 26:8^{2} 26:9 26:10^{2} 26:11 26:12^{2} 26:13^{2} 26:14 27:2 27:3^{2} 27:7^{2} 27:8^{2} 27:10 27:11^{2} 27:13^{3} 27:14 27:16^{2} 27:17^{3} 27:18 27:19 27:20 27:21 28:1 28:2^{2} 28:3^{2} 28:4^{4} 28:5 28:6^{2} 28:7 28:8^{2} 28:9^{3} 28:10 28:11^{2} 28:12 28:13^{3} 28:14^{2} 28:15 28:16^{3} 28:17^{3} 28:18 28:19 28:20 28:21^{3} 28:22 28:23^{2} 28:24^{3} 28:25^{3} 28:26^{3} 28:28^{2} 29:2 29:4^{2} 29:5 29:6 29:7^{3} 29:8^{2} 29:9 29:10^{2} 29:11^{2} 29:12^{2} 29:13^{2} 29:15^{2} 29:16^{2} 29:17^{3} 29:18 29:19^{2} 29:23^{2}

29:23^{2} 29:24 29:25^{2} 30:1 30:2 30:3 30:4 30:6^{4} 30:7^{2} 30:8 30:11 30:12^{2} 30:14 30:15 30:16 30:17 30:18^{2} 30:19 30:22 30:23 30:24 30:25 30:27 30:28^{2} 30:31 31:2 31:3^{2} 31:7 31:11 31:13 31:15^{2} 31:16^{3} 31:17 31:20 31:21^{2} 31:22 31:24 31:26^{2} 31:28^{2} 31:29 31:31 31:32^{3} 31:34^{2} 31:35 31:37 31:38 31:39^{2} 31:40 32:2^{4} 32:5 32:6^{2} 32:8^{2} 32:9 32:18 33:3 33:4^{3} 33:6 33:8 33:11 33:15^{2} 33:16 33:18^{2} 33:19 33:22^{2} 33:24 33:25 33:28^{2} 33:30^{3} 34:3^{2} 34:8 34:10 34:11 34:12 34:13^{2} 34:16 34:19^{4} 34:20^{2} 34:21 34:22 34:25 34:26 34:28^{4} 34:30^{2} 34:36 35:5^{2} 35:8

35:9^{4} 35:10 35:11^{3} 35:12 35:13 36:6^{3} 36:7^{2} 36:12 36:13 36:14 36:15 36:16 36:17^{2} 36:19 36:20 36:26 36:27^{2} 36:28 36:29^{3} 36:30^{2} 36:31 36:32^{2} 36:33^{3} 37:2^{2} 37:3^{3} 37:4 37:6^{4} 37:7 37:8 37:9^{3} 37:10^{3} 37:11 37:12^{3} 37:14 37:15 37:16^{3} 37:17^{2} 37:18 37:21^{3} 37:22 37:23 38:1^{2} 38:4^{2} 38:5^{2} 38:6^{2} 38:7^{2} 38:8^{2} 38:9^{2} 38:12^{2} 38:13^{3} 38:14 38:15^{2} 38:16^{4} 38:17^{3} 38:18^{2} 38:19^{2} 38:20^{3} 38:21 38:22^{4} 38:23^{2} 38:24^{3} 38:25^{2} 38:26^{2} 38:27^{3} 38:28^{2} 38:29^{2} 38:30^{3} 38:31^{2} 38:33^{3} 38:34 38:36^{2} 38:37^{2} 38:38^{2} 38:39^{4} 38:40 38:41 39:1^{4} 39:2^{2} 39:5^{3} 39:6^{2} 39:7^{4} 39:8^{2} 39:9 39:10^{3} 39:13^{3} 39:14^{2}

39:15^{2} 39:18 39:19 39:20 39:21^{2} 39:22 39:23^{3} 39:24^{3} 39:25^{5} 39:26^{2} 39:27 39:28^{4} 39:29 39:30 40:1 40:2 40:3 40:6^{2} 40:11 40:12 40:13 40:16 40:17 40:19^{2} 40:20^{3} 40:21^{3} 40:22^{3} 41:6^{2} 41:8 41:9^{2} 41:11 41:13 41:14 41:18^{2} 41:23 41:24 41:25 41:26^{4} 41:28 41:29 41:30 41:31^{2} 41:32 41:34 42:1 42:5^{2} 42:7^{4} 42:8 42:9^{5} 42:10^{3} 42:11^{2} 42:12^{2} 42:14^{6} 42:15^{2}

PS

1:1^{6} 1:2^{2} 1:3 1:4^{3} 1:5^{4} 1:6^{5} 2:1^{2} 2:2^{4} 2:4^{2} 2:7^{2} 2:8^{3} 2:10 2:11 2:12^{2} 3:3 3:4 3:5 3:7^{3} 3:8 4:*title* 4:3^{2} 4:5^{2} 4:6 4:7 5:*title* 5:2 5:3^{2} 5:5 5:6^{2}

5:7 5:10 5:12 6:*title* 6:5 6:6 6:8^{2} 6:9^{2} 7:*title*^{3} 7:5^{3} 7:6^{2} 7:7^{2} 7:8^{2} 7:9^{5} 7:10 7:11^{2} 7:13^{2} 7:15 7:17^{3} 8:*title* 8:1^{2} 8:2^{3} 8:3^{3} 8:4 8:5 8:6 8:7^{2} 8:8^{6} 8:9 9:*title* 9:4 9:5^{2} 9:7 9:8^{2} 9:9^{2} 9:11^{2} 9:12^{2} 9:13 9:14^{2} 9:15^{3} 9:16^{4} 9:17^{2} 9:18^{3} 9:19 9:20 10:2^{3} 10:3^{3} 10:4^{2} 10:8^{5} 10:9^{2} 10:10 10:12 10:13 10:14^{3} 10:15^{3} 10:16^{2} 10:17^{2} 10:18^{4} 11:*title* 11:1 11:2^{3} 11:3^{2} 11:4^{3} 11:5^{3} 11:6^{2} 11:7^{2} 12:*title* 12:1^{3} 12:3^{2} 12:5^{5} 12:6^{2} 12:8^{2} 13:*title* 13:3 13:6 14:*title* 14:1 14:2^{2} 14:4^{2} 14:5^{2} 14:6^{3} 14:7^{3} 15:2 15:4 15:5 16:2 16:3^{3}

16:5^{2} 16:6 16:7^{2} 16:8 16:11 17:1 17:2 17:3 17:4^{4} 17:8^{3} 17:9 17:11 17:13 17:14^{2} 18:*title*^{9} 18:2^{2} 18:3 18:4^{2} 18:5^{2} 18:6 18:7^{3} 18:9 18:10^{2} 18:11 18:12 18:13^{3} 18:15^{5} 18:18^{2} 18:20^{2} 18:21^{2} 18:24^{2} 18:25 18:26^{2} 18:27 18:28 18:30^{2} 18:31 18:35 18:39 18:40 18:41 18:42^{4} 18:43^{4} 18:44 18:45 18:46^{2} 18:47 18:48 18:49 19:*title* 19:1^{3} 19:4^{3} 19:6^{4} 19:7^{6} 19:8^{6} 19:9^{4} 19:10 19:13 19:14^{2} 20:*title* 20:1^{4} 20:2 20:5^{2} 20:6^{2} 20:7^{2} 20:9 21:*title* 21:1 21:2 21:3 21:7^{4} 21:9^{3} 21:10^{2} 21:12 22:*title* 22:1 22:2^{2} 22:3 22:6 22:7^{2} 22:8 22:9 22:10 22:14 22:15 22:16^{2} 22:20^{3}

22:21^{3} 22:22^{2} 22:23^{3} 22:24^{2} 22:25 22:26^{2} 22:27^{5} 22:28^{4} 22:29 22:30 23:1 23:2 23:3 23:4^{2} 23:5 23:6^{3} 24:1^{4} 24:2^{2} 24:3^{2} 24:5^{3} 24:6 24:7 24:8^{2} 24:9 24:10^{2} 25:5^{2} 25:7 25:8^{2} 25:9^{2} 25:11^{2} 25:12^{2} 25:13 25:14^{2} 25:15^{2} 25:17 26:1 26:5^{2} 26:7 26:8^{2} 26:12^{2} 27:1^{3} 27:2 27:4^{6} 27:5^{2} 27:6 27:10 27:12 27:13^{4} 27:14^{2} 28:1 28:2 28:3^{2} 28:4^{2} 28:5^{3} 28:6^{2} 28:7 28:8^{2} 29:1^{2} 29:2^{4} 29:3^{5} 29:4^{4} 29:5^{5} 29:7^{3} 29:8^{5} 29:9^{4} 29:10^{3} 29:11^{2} 30:*title*^{2} 30:3^{2} 30:4^{2} 30:5 30:8 30:9^{2} 30:12 31:*title* 31:4 31:6 31:8^{2} 31:13 31:15 31:17^{2} 31:18^{2} 31:19 31:20^{3} 31:21 31:22 31:23^{4}

31:24 32:2^{2} 32:3 32:4 32:5^{2} 32:6 32:8 32:9^{2} 32:10^{2} 32:11 33:1^{2} 33:2^{2} 33:4^{2} 33:5^{3} 33:6^{5} 33:7^{3} 33:8^{4} 33:10^{5} 33:11^{3} 33:12^{3} 33:13^{2} 33:14^{3} 33:16 33:18^{2} 33:20 34:1 34:2^{2} 34:3 34:4 34:6 34:7^{2} 34:8^{2} 34:9 34:10^{2} 34:11^{2} 34:15^{3} 34:16^{4} 34:17^{2} 34:18 34:19^{3} 34:21^{2} 34:22^{2} 35:3^{2} 35:5^{3} 35:6^{2} 35:9 35:10^{3} 35:12 35:15 35:17 35:18 35:19 35:20 35:27^{2} 35:28 36:*title*^{3} 36:1^{2} 36:3 36:5^{2} 36:6 36:7^{2} 36:8^{2} 36:9 36:10 36:11^{2} 36:12 37:1 37:2^{2} 37:3^{2} 37:4^{2} 37:5 37:6^{2} 37:7^{2} 37:9^{2} 37:10 37:11^{3} 37:12^{2} 37:13 37:14^{3} 37:16 37:17^{4} 37:18^{3} 37:19^{2} 37:20^{4} 37:21^{2} 37:22 37:23

37:24 37:25 37:28^{3} 37:29^{2} 37:30^{2} 37:31 37:32^{2} 37:33 37:34^{3} 37:35 37:37^{3} 37:38^{3} 37:39^{4} 37:40^{2} 38:6 38:8 38:10 38:12 38:20 39:*title* 39:1 39:3 39:4 39:8^{2} 39:10 40:*title* 40:1 40:2 40:3 40:4^{2} 40:7^{2} 40:9 40:10 40:12 40:16 40:17 41:*title* 41:1^{2} 41:2^{3} 41:3^{2} 41:13 42:*title*^{2} 42:1^{2} 42:2 42:4^{3} 42:5 42:6^{3} 42:7 42:8^{4} 42:9^{2} 42:11 43:1 43:2^{3} 43:4^{2} 43:5 44:*title*^{2} 44:1 44:2 44:3^{2} 44:8 44:10 44:11 44:14^{3} 44:15 44:16^{2} 44:19^{2} 44:20 44:21^{2} 44:22^{2} 44:25^{2} 45:*title*^{2} 45:1^{3} 45:2 45:5^{3} 45:6 45:7 45:8 45:9 45:11 45:12^{3} 45:13 45:14^{2} 45:15 45:16 45:17 46:*title*^{2} 46:2^{4}

46:3^{3} 46:4^{5} 46:5 46:6^{3} 46:7^{2} 46:8^{3} 46:9^{6} 46:10^{2} 46:11^{2} 47:*title*^{2} 47:1 47:2^{2} 47:3^{2} 47:4 47:5^{2} 47:7^{2} 47:8^{2} 47:9^{6} 48:*title* 48:1^{3} 48:2^{6} 48:4 48:7 48:8^{3} 48:9 48:10^{2} 48:11 48:12 48:13 49:*title*^{2} 49:1 49:3 49:4 49:5^{2} 49:6 49:8 49:10^{2} 49:12 49:14^{4} 49:15^{2} 49:16 49:19 49:20 50:1^{6} 50:2 50:4^{2} 50:6 50:10^{2} 50:11^{4} 50:12^{2} 50:13^{2} 50:14 50:15 50:16 50:23 51:*title*^{2} 51:1 51:6^{2} 51:8 51:12 51:17 51:18 51:19 52:*title*^{3} 52:1 52:5^{2} 52:6 52:7^{2} 52:8^{2} 53:*title* 53:1 53:2 53:4 53:5 53:6^{2} 54:*title*^{2} 54:2 54:4 55:*title* 55:3^{4} 55:4 55:7 55:8 55:9 55:10^{2} 55:11 55:14

55:16 55:18 55:21 55:22^{2} 55:23 56:*title*^{2} 56:7 56:10 56:13^{2} 57:*title*^{2} 57:1 57:3 57:4 57:5^{2} 57:6 57:9^{2} 57:10^{2} 57:11^{2} 58:*title* 58:2 58:3^{2} 58:4^{2} 58:5 58:6^{2} 58:8^{2} 58:9 58:10^{4} 58:11^{2} 59:*title*^{2} 59:2 59:3 59:5^{2} 59:6 59:8 59:10 59:12^{2} 59:13^{2} 59:14 59:16^{2} 59:17 60:*title*^{2} 60:2^{2} 60:3 60:4 60:6 60:7 60:9 60:11 61:*title* 61:2^{3} 61:3 61:4 61:5 61:6 62:*title* 62:7 62:9 63:*title* 63:2 63:6 63:7 63:9^{2} 63:10 63:11^{2} 64:*title* 64:1 64:2^{4} 64:4 64:6^{2} 64:9 64:10^{3} 65:*title* 65:1 65:4^{2} 65:5^{4} 65:6 65:7^{5} 65:8^{3} 65:9^{2} 65:10^{3} 65:11 65:12^{3} 65:13^{2} 66:*title* 66:2 66:3 66:4

66:5^{2} 66:6^{2} 66:8 66:7^{2} 66:8 66:11 66:15 66:18 66:19 67:*title* 67:3^{2} 67:4^{3} 67:5^{2} 67:6 67:7^{2} 68:*title* 68:2^{3} 68:3 68:4 68:5^{2} 68:6^{2} 68:7 68:8^{5} 68:10 68:11^{3} 68:12 68:13^{2} 68:14 68:15^{3} 68:16^{2} 68:17^{3} 68:18^{2} 68:19^{2} 68:20^{3} 68:21^{2} 68:22^{3} 68:23^{3} 68:24^{2} 68:25^{3} 68:26^{3} 68:27^{3} 68:30^{6} 68:32^{2} 68:33 68:34 68:35 69:*title* 69:1 69:2 69:4 69:9^{2} 69:12^{3} 69:13^{2} 69:14^{2} 69:15^{3} 69:16 69:26 69:28^{3} 69:30 69:31 69:32 69:33^{2} 69:34^{2} 69:35 69:36 70:*title* 71:4^{4} 71:6 71:8 71:9 71:15^{2} 71:16^{2} 71:20^{2} 71:22^{2} 71:24 72:1^{2} 72:3^{3} 72:4^{5} 72:5 72:6^{2} 72:7^{2} 72:8^{3} 72:9^{2} 72:10^{3} 72:12^{2} 72:13^{3} 72:15

72:16^{6} 72:17 72:18^{2} 72:19 72:20^{2} 73:3^{3} 73:9^{2} 73:11 73:12^{2} 73:14 73:15 73:17 73:26 73:28 74:1 74:2 74:3^{3} 74:4 74:5 74:6 74:7^{2} 74:8^{2} 74:10^{2} 74:12^{2} 74:13^{4} 74:14^{3} 74:15^{2} 74:16^{4} 74:17^{2} 74:18^{2} 74:19^{4} 74:20^{4} 74:21^{2} 74:22 74:23^{2} 75:*title* 75:2 75:3^{3} 75:4^{3} 75:6^{3} 75:7 75:8^{7} 75:9 75:10^{4} 76:*title* 76:3^{5} 76:4 76:5^{2} 76:6 76:8 76:9^{2} 76:10^{2} 76:11 76:12^{3} 77:*title* 77:2^{3} 77:5^{2} 77:6 77:7 77:10^{3} 77:11^{2} 77:13 77:14^{2} 77:15 77:16^{3} 77:17^{2} 77:18^{5} 77:19 77:20 78:1 78:4^{3} 78:6^{2} 78:7 78:9^{2} 78:10 78:12^{3} 78:13^{2} 78:14^{2} 78:15^{3} 78:16 78:17^{2} 78:19 78:20^{3} 78:21 78:23^{2} 78:24 78:25

78:26^{2} 78:27^{2} 78:28 78:31^{3} 78:35 78:40^{2} 78:41 78:42^{2} 78:43 78:46^{2} 78:48 78:49 78:50 78:51^{3} 78:52 78:53 78:54 78:55^{2} 78:56 78:60^{2} 78:61 78:62 78:63 78:64 78:65 78:66 78:67^{2} 78:68^{2} 78:69 78:70 78:71 78:72^{2} 79:1 79:2^{6} 79:6^{2} 79:9 79:10^{4} 79:11^{3} 80:*title* 80:1 80:4 80:5 80:8 80:9 80:10^{4} 80:11^{2} 80:12 80:13^{4} 80:15^{2} 80:16 80:17^{2} 81:*title* 81:1 81:2^{3} 81:3^{3} 81:4^{3} 81:5 81:6^{2} 81:7^{2} 81:10^{2} 81:15^{2} 81:16^{3} 82:1^{3} 82:2^{2} 82:3^{2} 82:4^{3} 82:5^{2} 82:6 82:7 82:8 83:2 83:4 83:6^{3} 83:7^{2} 83:8 83:9^{2} 83:10 83:12 83:13^{2} 83:14^{3} 83:18^{2} 84:*title*^{2} 84:2^{3} 84:3^{2} 84:5^{2} 84:6^{3} 84:9

84:10^{2} 84:11^{2} 84:12 85:*title*^{2} 85:1 85:2 85:3 85:8 85:11 85:12 85:13 86:4 86:6 86:7 86:8 86:13 86:14^{2} 86:16 87:*title* 87:1 87:2^{3} 87:5 87:6^{2} 87:7^{2} 88:*title*^{2} 88:3 88:4 88:5^{3} 88:6^{2} 88:10^{2} 88:11 88:12^{2} 88:13 89:*title* 89:1^{2} 89:2 89:5^{3} 89:6^{5} 89:7^{2} 89:9^{3} 89:11^{4} 89:12^{2} 89:14 89:15^{3} 89:16 89:17 89:18^{2} 89:19 89:22^{2} 89:25^{2} 89:26 89:27^{2} 89:29 89:32 89:34 89:36 89:37 89:39^{2} 89:41 89:42 89:43^{2} 89:44 89:45 89:48^{2} 89:50^{3} 89:51 89:52 90:*title* 90:2^{3} 90:4 90:5 90:6^{2} 90:8 90:10 90:11 90:15^{2} 90:17^{4} 91:1^{4} 91:2 91:3^{3} 91:5^{2} 91:6^{2} 91:8^{2} 91:9^{2} 91:13^{3} 92:*title* 92:1

PR

EC

CA

ISA

8:6 8:7[4] 8:8[3] 8:10 8:11[2] 8:13 8:14[3] 8:16[2] 8:17[2] 8:18[3] 8:19[2] 8:20[2] 8:22 9:1[7] 9:2[4] 9:3[4] 9:4[4] 9:5 9:6[4] 9:7[4] 9:8 9:9[3] 9:10[2] 9:11[2] 9:12[2] 9:13[2] 9:14 9:15[4] 9:16 9:17 9:18[5] 9:19[6] 9:20[3] 10:2[4] 10:3[2] 10:4[2] 10:5[2] 10:6[5] 10:10[2] 10:12[5] 10:13[4] 10:14[5] 10:15[4] 10:16[3] 10:17 10:18 10:19[2] 10:20[4] 10:21[3] 10:22[3] 10:23[3] 10:24[3] 10:25 10:26[5] 10:27[2] 10:29 10:31 10:32[3] 10:33[5] 10:34[2] 11:1 11:2[7] 11:3[4] 11:4[7] 11:5[2] 11:6[7] 11:7[4] 11:8[5] 11:9[5] 11:10[2] 11:11[5] 11:12[5] 11:13[2] 11:14[5] 11:15[5] 11:16[3] 12:2 12:3 12:4[2] 12:5[2] 12:6[2] 13:1[2] 13:2[6] 13:4[6] 13:5[4] 13:6[3] 13:9[4]

13:10[4] 13:11[6] 13:12 13:13[5] 13:14 13:15 13:17 13:18[3] 13:19[3] 13:20[2] 13:21 13:22[2] 14:1[3] 14:2[4] 14:3[3] 14:4[3] 14:5[5] 14:7 14:8[2] 14:9[5] 14:11[4] 14:12[3] 14:13[5] 14:14[3] 14:15[2] 14:16[2] 14:17[3] 14:18[2] 14:19[3] 14:20 14:21[4] 14:22[3] 14:23[3] 14:24 14:25 14:26[4] 14:27 14:28 14:29[2] 14:30[3] 14:31 14:32[4] 15:1[3] 15:2 15:3 15:4 15:5[2] 15:6[3] 15:7[3] 15:8[4] 15:9[3] 16:1[6] 16:2[3] 16:3[4] 16:4[6] 16:5[2] 16:6 16:7 16:8[7] 16:9[3] 16:10[3] 16:12 16:13[2] 16:14 17:1 17:2 17:3[6] 17:4[2] 17:5[4] 17:6[5] 17:7 17:8[4] 17:9 17:10[2] 17:11[4] 17:12[5] 17:13[6] 17:14[3] 18:1[2] 18:2[3] 18:3[3] 18:4[2] 18:4[6] 18:5[6] 18:6[9] 18:7[7] 19:1[5]

19:2[2] 19:3[6] 19:4[4] 19:5[3] 19:6[3] 19:7[5] 19:8[3] 19:10 19:11[6] 19:12 19:13[4] 19:14[2] 19:15 19:16[3] 19:17[3] 19:18[4] 19:19[5] 19:20[4] 19:21[4] 19:22[2] 19:23[4] 19:24[3] 19:25 20:1[2] 20:2[4] 20:3 20:4[4] 20:6[2] 21:1[5] 21:2[3] 21:3[3] 21:4 21:5[3] 21:6 21:8[2] 21:9[2] 21:10[3] 21:11[3] 21:12[3] 21:13[2] 21:14[2] 21:15[4] 21:16[3] 21:17[5] 22:1[3] 22:2 22:3 22:4[2] 22:5[4] 22:6[2] 22:7[2] 22:8[4] 22:9[4] 22:10[3] 22:11[4] 22:12 22:14[2] 22:15[2] 22:17 22:18[2] 22:20 22:21[2] 22:22[2] 22:24[5] 22:25[5] 23:1[2] 23:2[4] 23:3[3] 23:4[3] 23:5[2] 23:6 23:8[3] 23:9[4] 23:11[5] 23:13[6] 23:15[2] 23:16 23:17[6] 23:18[2] 24:1[4] 24:2[10] 24:3[2] 24:4[4] 24:5[5] 24:6[4] 24:7[3] 24:8[4]

24:10 24:11[3] 24:12[2] 24:13[6] 24:14[3] 24:15[6] 24:16[5] 24:17[3] 24:18[9] 24:19[3] 24:20[2] 24:21[6] 24:22[2] 24:23[3] 25:3[3] 25:4[7] 25:5[6] 25:6[3] 25:7[3] 25:8[4] 25:9 25:10[3] 25:11[2] 25:12[4] 26:1 26:2[3] 26:4[2] 26:5[3] 26:6[5] 26:7[4] 26:8[3] 26:9[4] 26:10[4] 26:11[2] 26:15[4] 26:17 26:18[3] 26:19[3] 26:20 26:21[4] 27:1[4] 27:3 27:4 27:6[2] 27:7 27:8[2] 27:9[5] 27:10[4] 27:11[2] 27:12[4] 27:13[6] 28:1[4] 28:2[3] 28:3[2] 28:4[5] 28:5[2] 28:6[2] 28:7[4] 28:9[2] 28:12[3] 28:13[2] 28:14[2] 28:15 28:16 28:17[6] 28:18 28:19[2] 28:20[2] 28:21[2] 28:22[2] 28:24[2] 28:25[6] 28:27[4] 28:28 28:29 29:1 29:4[4] 29:5[3] 29:6[2] 29:7[2] 29:8[2] 29:10[4] 29:11[2] 29:12 29:13[2] 29:14[2] 29:15[2]

29:16[3] 29:17 29:18[5] 29:19[4] 29:20[2] 29:21[2] 29:22[2] 29:23[4] 30:1[2] 30:2[2] 30:3[2] 30:6[8] 30:7 30:8 30:9[2] 30:10[2] 30:11[3] 30:12 30:14[5] 30:15[2] 30:16 30:17[3] 30:18[2] 30:19[2] 30:20[3] 30:21[3] 30:22 30:23[4] 30:24[5] 30:25[3] 30:26[11] 30:27[3] 30:28[6] 30:29[4] 30:30[4] 30:31[3] 30:32 30:33[6] 31:1[2] 31:2[3] 31:3[2] 31:4[6] 31:5 31:6 31:8[4] 31:9[2] 32:2[3] 32:3[2] 32:4[4] 32:5[2] 32:6[6] 32:7[4] 32:8 32:10[2] 32:12[3] 32:13[3] 32:14[4] 32:15[3] 32:16[2] 32:17[2] 32:19[2] 32:20[3] 33:2 33:3[5] 33:4[3] 33:5 33:6[3] 33:7 33:8[4] 33:9 33:10 33:12[3] 33:14[3] 33:15 33:16 33:17[2] 33:18[3] 33:20[3] 33:21 33:22[3] 33:23[4] 33:24 34:1[3] 34:2[3] 34:3 34:4 34:5

34:6[7] 34:7[3] 34:8[4] 34:9[3] 34:10 34:11[6] 34:12[2] 34:13 34:14[6] 34:15[2] 34:16[2] 34:17 35:1[4] 35:2[5] 35:3[2] 35:5[4] 35:6[5] 35:7[3] 35:8[3] 35:9 35:10[2] 36:1[2] 36:2[5] 36:3[3] 36:4[2] 36:6 36:7 36:8 36:9[2] 36:10[2] 36:11[5] 36:12[2] 36:13[4] 36:14 36:15[4] 36:16[2] 36:18[5] 36:19[2] 36:20[2] 36:21 36:22[6] 37:1[2] 37:2[6] 37:3[2] 37:4[7] 37:5 37:6[4] 37:7 37:8 37:10[2] 37:11 37:12[3] 37:13[4] 37:14[6] 37:15 37:16[4] 37:17[2] 37:18[2] 37:19[2] 37:20[3] 37:21[2] 37:22[5] 37:23 37:24[9] 37:25[3] 37:27[5] 37:29 37:30[4] 37:31[2] 37:32[2] 37:33[2] 37:34[3] 37:36[5] 37:38[3] 38:1[3] 38:2[2] 38:4[2] 38:5[2] 38:6[2] 38:7[2] 38:8[4] 38:9 38:10[4] 38:11[6] 38:15 38:16

38:17 38:18[2] 38:19[4] 38:20[5] 38:21 38:22[3] 39:1 39:2[6] 39:3 39:5[2] 39:6[2] 39:7[2] 39:8[2] 40:2 40:3[5] 40:4[2] 40:5[4] 40:6[4] 40:7[5] 40:8[3] 40:9[2] 40:10 40:11 40:12[7] 40:13[2] 40:14[2] 40:15[4] 40:16 40:19[2] 40:21[3] 40:22[4] 40:23[3] 40:24[2] 40:25 40:26 40:27 40:28[5] 40:29 40:30[2] 40:31 41:1 41:2[4] 41:3 41:4[5] 41:5[3] 41:7[5] 41:8 41:9[3] 41:10 41:13 41:14[2] 41:15[2] 41:16[4] 41:17[3] 41:18[4] 41:19[9] 41:20[3] 41:21[2] 41:22[2] 41:23 41:25[4] 41:26 41:27 42:1 42:2 42:3 42:4[2] 42:5[4] 42:6[3] 42:7[4] 42:8 42:9 42:10[6] 42:11[7] 42:12[2] 42:13 42:15[2] 42:16 42:17 42:19 42:20 42:21[2] 42:23 42:24[2] 42:25[2] 43:1 43:2[4]

43:3[2] 43:5[2] 43:6[4] 43:8[2] 43:9[2] 43:10 43:11 43:12 43:13 43:14[4] 43:15[2] 43:16[3] 43:17[3] 43:18[2] 43:19[2] 43:20[6] 43:23 43:24 43:28[3] 44:2[2] 44:3 44:4[2] 44:5[4] 44:6[5] 44:7[2] 44:11 44:12[3] 44:13[5] 44:14[5] 44:16[2] 44:17 44:19[4] 44:23[3] 44:24[5] 44:25[2] 44:26[4] 44:27 44:28 45:1[4] 45:2[3] 45:3[3] 45:5 45:6[4] 45:7[2] 45:8[3] 45:9[4] 45:10 45:11[3] 45:12[2] 45:13 45:14[3] 45:15 45:17 45:18[4] 45:19[3] 45:20[2] 45:21 45:22[2] 45:23 45:24 45:25[2] 46:1[3] 46:2 46:3[4] 46:6[2] 46:7 46:9 46:10[3] 46:11[2] 47:1[3] 47:2[4] 47:4[2] 47:5[2] 47:6 47:7 47:8 47:9[3] 47:12 47:13[4] 47:14[3] 48:1[5] 48:2[3] 48:3[2] 48:5 48:7[2] 48:8 48:10

48:12[2] 48:13[2] 48:14[2] 48:16[3] 48:17[4] 48:18[2] 48:19[2] 48:20[4] 48:21[5] 48:22[2] 49:1[3] 49:2 49:4 49:5[4] 49:6[5] 49:7[5] 49:8[3] 49:9[2] 49:10[2] 49:12[3] 49:13 49:14 49:15 49:16 49:18 49:19[3] 49:20[3] 49:22[3] 49:23[3] 49:24[3] 49:25[5] 49:26[2] 50:1[2] 50:2[2] 50:3 50:4[4] 50:5 50:6[2] 50:7 50:9[2] 50:10[4] 50:11[2] 51:1[4] 51:3[4] 51:4 51:5[2] 51:6[4] 51:7[2] 51:8[2] 51:9[4] 51:10[6] 51:11[2] 51:12 51:13[8] 51:14[2] 51:15[3] 51:16[4] 51:17[5] 51:18[3] 51:19[2] 51:20[5] 51:22[5] 51:23[3] 52:1[3] 52:2[2] 52:3 52:4[2] 52:5[2] 52:7[2] 52:8[3] 52:9 52:10[6] 52:11[3] 52:12[2] 52:14 52:15 53:1[2] 53:5 53:6[2] 53:7 53:8[3] 53:9[2] 53:10[3] 53:11 53:12[6] 54:1[5] 54:2[2]

54:3[4] 54:5[4] 54:6 54:8 54:9[3] 54:10[4] 54:13[2] 54:16[4] 54:17[4] 55:1 55:3 55:4[2] 55:5[2] 55:6 55:7[3] 55:8 55:9[2] 55:10[5] 55:11 55:12[4] 55:13[5] 56:1 56:2[3] 56:3[5] 56:4[3] 56:6[6] 56:8[2] 56:9[2] 57:1[3] 57:3[4] 57:4 57:5[4] 57:6[2] 57:8[2] 57:9 57:10[2] 57:13[2] 57:14[3] 57:15[6] 57:16[2] 57:17[2] 57:19[3] 57:20[2] 57:21 58:1 58:2[2] 58:3 58:4 58:5 58:6[4] 58:7[3] 58:8[3] 58:9[5] 58:10[3] 58:11 58:12[5] 58:13[4] 58:14[6] 59:1 59:5 59:6 59:8 59:10[3] 59:13[2] 59:14 59:15 59:17 59:18 59:19[8] 59:20[2] 59:21[4] 60:1[2] 60:2[4] 60:3[2] 60:5[4] 60:6[4] 60:7[3] 60:8 60:9[5] 60:10 60:11[2] 60:12 60:13[6] 60:14[6] 60:16[5] 60:19[3] 60:20[2]

60:21[3] 60:22 61:1[7] 61:2[3] 61:3[5] 61:4[4] 61:5[2] 61:6[5] 61:7 61:8 61:9[4] 61:10[3] 61:11[5] 62:1[2] 62:2[3] 62:3[3] 62:4 62:5[2] 62:6 62:7 62:8[3] 62:9[2] 62:10[6] 62:11[4] 62:12[3] 63:1 63:2 63:3[2] 63:4[2] 63:6[2] 63:7[8] 63:9[2] 63:11[3] 63:12[2] 63:13[2] 63:14[3] 63:15[2] 63:17 63:18 64:1[2] 64:2[4] 64:3 64:4[4] 64:6 64:8[2] 65:2 65:4[2] 65:5 65:7[4] 65:8[2] 65:10[2] 65:11[2] 65:12[2] 65:13 65:15 65:16[5] 65:17 65:19[2] 65:20[2] 65:21 65:22[3] 65:23[3] 65:25[6] 66:1[5] 66:2 66:5[2] 66:6[3] 66:8 66:9[3] 66:11[2] 66:12[3] 66:14[2] 66:15 66:16[3] 66:17[5] 66:19[4] 66:20[5] 66:21 66:22[3] 66:23 66:24[2]

JER

1:1[4] 1:2[5] 1:3[7] 1:4[2] 1:5[3] 1:7 1:8 1:9[2] 1:10[2] 1:11[2] 1:12 1:13[5] 1:14[4] 1:15[8] 1:16 1:18[6] 1:19 2:1[2] 2:2[5] 2:3[3] 2:4[4] 2:5 2:6[4] 2:7[2] 2:8[5] 2:9 2:10 2:12 2:13 2:15 2:16[2] 2:17[2] 2:18[5] 2:19[2] 2:20 2:21 2:22 2:23 2:24[2] 2:26[2] 2:27 2:28[2] 2:29 2:31[2] 2:33 2:34[3] 2:37 3:1[2] 3:2[5] 3:3 3:4 3:5 3:6[4] 3:8[2] 3:9[2] 3:10 3:11[2] 3:12[3] 3:13[3] 3:14 3:16[5] 3:17[6] 3:18[5] 3:19[2] 3:20 3:21[3] 3:22 3:23[4] 3:24 3:25[3] 4:1[2] 4:2[2] 4:3[2] 4:4[3] 4:5[3] 4:6[2] 4:7[3] 4:8[2] 4:9[7] 4:10[2] 4:11[3] 4:16[2] 4:17 4:19[3] 4:20 4:21[3] 4:23[2] 4:24[2]

4:25[2] 4:26[4] 4:27[2] 4:28[2] 4:29[4] 4:31[3] 5:1[3] 5:2 5:3 5:4[3] 5:5[6] 5:6[2] 5:7[2] 5:8 5:9 5:10 5:11[4] 5:12 5:13[2] 5:14 5:15 5:17 5:18 5:19 5:20 5:22[5] 5:24[5] 5:28[7] 5:29 5:30 5:31[3] 6:1[3] 6:2 6:3 6:4[3] 6:6[3] 6:9[3] 6:10[2] 6:11[7] 6:12[3] 6:13[3] 6:14[2] 6:15[2] 6:16[4] 6:17[2] 6:19 6:20 6:21[4] 6:22[4] 6:23 6:24 6:25[4] 6:26 6:29[5] 6:30 7:1[2] 7:2[5] 7:3[2] 7:4[6] 7:6[3] 7:7 7:11 7:12[2] 7:13 7:14 7:15 7:17[2] 7:18[5] 7:19[2] 7:20[5] 7:21[2] 7:22[2] 7:23 7:24[2] 7:25[3] 7:28[2] 7:29[2] 7:30[3] 7:31[4] 7:32[5] 7:33[5] 7:34[9] 8:1[10] 8:2[5] 8:3[3] 8:4 8:6[2]

8:7[8] 8:8[4] 8:9[3] 8:10[4] 8:11[2] 8:12[2] 8:13[5] 8:14[3] 8:16[6] 8:17 8:19[4] 8:20[2] 8:21[2] 8:22[2] 9:1[2] 9:2 9:3[3] 9:5 9:6[2] 9:7[2] 9:9 9:10[8] 9:11 9:12[4] 9:13 9:14 9:15[2] 9:16 9:17[2] 9:19 9:20[3] 9:21[3] 9:22[5] 9:23[4] 9:24[3] 9:25[3] 9:26[5] 10:1[2] 10:2[5] 10:3[7] 10:5 10:7[2] 10:8 10:9[5] 10:10[5] 10:11[4] 10:12[3] 10:13[5] 10:14 10:15[2] 10:16[4] 10:17[2] 10:18[3] 10:21[2] 10:22[4] 10:23 10:25[2] 11:1[2] 11:2[3] 11:3[3] 11:4[3] 11:5 11:6[4] 11:7[2] 11:8[2] 11:9[3] 11:10[3] 11:11 11:12[3] 11:13[3] 11:14 11:15 11:16[3] 11:17[4] 11:18 11:19[4] 11:20[2] 11:21[4] 11:22[3] 11:23[2] 12:1[2] 12:3[2] 12:4[5] 12:5[3] 12:6 12:7[2] 12:8

12:9[3] 12:11 12:12[8] 12:13[2] 12:14[3] 12:16[3] 12:17 13:1 13:2[2] 13:3[3] 13:4[2] 13:5 13:6[2] 13:7[4] 13:8[2] 13:9[3] 13:10 13:11[5] 13:12 13:13[6] 13:14[3] 13:15 13:16[3] 13:17 13:18[3] 13:19[2] 13:20[2] 13:22 13:23[2] 13:24[3] 13:25[2] 13:27[3] 14:1[3] 14:2[3] 14:3[2] 14:4[3] 14:5[2] 14:6[3] 14:8[3] 14:9 14:10[2] 14:11 14:12[3] 14:13[2] 14:14[3] 14:15[2] 14:16[4] 14:17 14:18[6] 14:19 14:20 14:21 14:22[3] 15:1 15:2[7] 15:3[7] 15:4[2] 15:6 15:7[2] 15:8[6] 15:9[4] 15:10 15:11[4] 15:12[2] 15:13 15:16 15:17[2] 15:19[3] 15:20 15:21[4] 16:1[2] 16:3[3] 16:4[6] 16:5[3] 16:6[2] 16:7[2] 16:8 16:9[8] 16:10[2] 16:11 16:12 16:14[5] 16:15[5] 16:16[3] 16:18 16:19[4] 16:21

17:1[4] 17:2[2] 17:3[2] 17:4 17:5[3] 17:6[4] 17:7[3] 17:8[3] 17:9 17:10[4] 17:11[2] 17:12[2] 17:13[4] 17:15[2] 17:16 17:17 17:18 17:19[7] 17:20[3] 17:21[3] 17:22[2] 17:24[4] 17:25[4] 17:26[8] 17:27[5] 18:1[2] 18:2 18:3[2] 18:4[4] 18:5[2] 18:6[3] 18:8 18:10 18:11[3] 18:12 18:13[3] 18:14[4] 18:15 18:17[4] 18:18[6] 18:19 18:21[4] 18:23 19:1[5] 19:2[5] 19:3[5] 19:4[2] 19:5 19:6[5] 19:7[7] 19:8 19:9[4] 19:10[3] 19:11 19:12[2] 19:13[6] 19:14[4] 19:15[3] 20:1[4] 20:2[5] 20:3[3] 20:4[5] 20:5[6] 20:8[2] 20:10 20:11 20:12[3] 20:13[5] 20:14[2] 20:15 20:16[5] 20:17 20:18 21:1[5] 21:2[2] 21:4[6] 21:6 21:7[10] 21:8[3] 21:9[4] 21:10[3] 21:11[4] 21:12[5] 21:13[3] 21:14[3] 22:1[3] 22:2[3]

22:3[7] 22:4[2] 22:5 22:6[3] 22:7 22:8 22:9[2] 22:10 22:11[2] 22:12 22:16[3] 22:18[2] 22:19[2] 22:20 22:22 22:23[2] 22:24[3] 22:25[5] 22:27 22:29[2] 22:30[2] 23:1[3] 23:2[4] 23:3 23:4 23:5[3] 23:6 23:7[5] 23:8[4] 23:9[3] 23:10[4] 23:11 23:12[3] 23:13 23:14[3] 23:15[5] 23:16[5] 23:17[2] 23:18[2] 23:19[3] 23:20[4] 23:22 23:23 23:24[2] 23:25 23:26[3] 23:28[4] 23:29[2] 23:30[2] 23:31[2] 23:32[2] 23:33[4] 23:34[5] 23:35[2] 23:36[5] 23:37[3] 23:38[7] 23:39 24:1[6] 24:2[2] 24:3[3] 24:4[2] 24:5[4] 24:7 24:8[5] 24:9[2] 24:10[4] 25:1[5] 25:2[4] 25:3[5] 25:4[2] 25:5[3] 25:6 25:7[2] 25:8 25:9[5] 25:10[10] 25:11 25:12[4] 25:13 25:14 25:15[3] 25:16 25:17[4] 25:18[3] 25:20[7] 25:21

25:22[5] 25:23 25:24[4] 25:25[4] 25:26[7] 25:27[3] 25:28[2] 25:29[4] 25:30[4] 25:31[6] 25:32[3] 25:33[6] 25:34[3] 25:35[3] 25:36[5] 25:37[3] 25:38[3] 26:1[4] 26:2[6] 26:3[2] 26:4 26:5[2] 26:6[2] 26:7[5] 26:8[5] 26:9[5] 26:10[7] 26:11[4] 26:12[4] 26:13[4] 26:15[2] 26:16[6] 26:17[4] 26:18[7] 26:19[4] 26:20[4] 26:21[3] 26:22[2] 26:23[4] 26:24[4] 27:1[4] 27:2 27:3[8] 27:4[2] 27:5[4] 27:6[4] 27:7 27:8[9] 27:9 27:11[4] 27:12[2] 27:13[6] 27:14[3] 27:15[2] 27:16[5] 27:17 27:18[8] 27:19[6] 27:20[2] 27:21[7] 27:22[2] 28:1[12] 28:2[4] 28:3[2] 28:4[5] 28:5[8] 28:6[5] 28:7[2] 28:8 28:9[5] 28:10[3] 28:11[7] 28:12[7] 28:13[2] 28:14[5] 28:15[3] 28:16[4] 28:17[3] 29:1[8] 29:2[6] 29:3[3] 29:4[2] 29:5 29:7[4] 29:8[3] 29:9

29:10
29:11^{2}
29:14^{5}
29:15
29:16^{5}
29:17^{4}
29:18^{6}
29:19^{3}
29:20^{3}
29:21^{5}
29:22^{4}
29:23
29:24
29:25^{6}
29:26^{6}
29:28
29:29^{3}
29:30^{2}
29:31^{3}
29:32^{5}
30:1^{2}
30:2^{2}
30:3^{5}
30:4^{2}
30:5
30:7
30:8
30:9
30:10^{2}
30:11
30:12
30:14^{3}
30:15
30:17
30:18^{5}
30:19
30:21^{2}
30:23^{4}
30:24^{4}
31:1^{4}
31:2^{4}
31:3
31:4
31:5^{2}
31:6^{3}
31:7^{4}
31:8^{6}
31:9
31:10^{3}
31:11^{2}
31:12^{6}
31:13^{2}
31:14^{3}
31:15
31:16^{4}
31:17
31:18^{2}
31:19
31:20
31:21^{2}
31:22^{2}
31:23^{5}
31:24
31:25
31:27^{6}
31:28
31:29^{2}
31:30
31:31^{4}
31:32^{5}
31:33^{3}
31:34^{4}
31:35^{8}
31:36^{2}
31:37^{5}
31:38^{7}
31:39^{2}
31:40^{9}
32:1^{4}
32:2^{5}
32:3^{3}
32:4^{4}
32:5^{2}
32:6^{2}
32:7^{2}
32:8^{9}
32:9^{2}
32:10^{3}
32:11^{3}
32:12^{12}
32:14^{3}
32:15^{2}
32:16^{4}
32:17^{2}
32:18^{6}
32:19^{3}
32:20
32:21
32:24^{8}
32:25^{4}
32:26^{2}
32:27^{2}
32:28^{4}
32:29^{2}
32:30^{5}
32:31
32:32^{5}
32:33^{2}
32:34
32:35^{4}
32:36^{7}
32:39
32:42^{2}
32:43^{2}
32:44^{10}
33:1^{5}
33:2^{4}
33:4^{7}
33:5^{2}
33:6
33:7^{3}
33:9^{5}
33:10^{3}
33:11^{16}
33:12^{2}
33:13^{12}
33:14^{4}
33:15^{2}
33:16^{2}
33:17^{3}
33:18^{2}
33:19^{2}
33:20^{3}
33:21^{2}
33:22^{5}
33:23^{2}
33:24^{2}
33:25^{2}
33:26^{2}
34:1^{6}
34:2^{5}
34:3^{2}
34:4^{4}
34:5^{4}
34:6
34:7^{3}
34:8^{4}
34:10^{3}
34:11^{2}
34:12^{3}
34:13^{5}
34:14
34:15
34:16^{2}
34:17^{7}
34:18^{5}
34:19^{8}
34:20^{6}
34:21^{4}
34:22^{2}
35:1^{4}
35:2^{5}
35:3^{4}
35:4^{11}
35:5^{3}
35:6
35:7
35:8^{2}
35:11^{5}
35:12^{2}
35:13^{5}
35:14^{2}
35:15^{2}
35:16^{3}
35:17^{4}
35:18^{5}
35:19^{3}
36:1^{3}
36:2^{4}
36:3^{2}
36:4^{4}
36:5^{2}
36:6^{8}
36:7^{4}
36:8^{6}
36:9^{7}
36:10^{13}
36:11^{5}
36:12^{9}
36:13^{4}
36:14^{9}
36:16^{2}
36:18
36:19
36:20^{8}
36:21^{8}
36:22^{4}
36:23^{6}
36:24
36:25^{2}
36:26^{7}
36:27^{6}
36:28^{3}
36:29^{2}
36:30^{6}
36:31^{3}
36:32^{6}
37:1^{3}
37:2^{5}
37:3^{6}
37:4
37:5
37:6^{3}
37:7^{3}
37:8
37:9^{2}
37:10^{2}
37:11^{2}
37:12^{3}
37:13^{6}
37:14^{2}
37:15^{4}
37:16^{2}
37:17^{5}
37:19
37:20^{3}
37:21^{8}
38:1^{6}
38:2^{5}
38:3^{3}
38:4^{8}
38:5^{2}
38:6^{6}
38:7^{6}
38:8^{2}
38:9^{5}
38:10^{4}
38:11^{5}
38:12^{2}
38:13^{3}
38:14^{6}
38:16^{3}
38:17^{4}
38:18^{3}
38:19^{3}
38:20^{2}
38:21^{2}
38:22^{4}
38:23^{3}
38:25^{3}
38:26
38:27^{3}
38:28^{3}
39:1^{2}
39:2^{5}
39:3^{6}
39:4^{9}
39:5^{3}
39:6^{4}
39:8^{5}
39:9^{7}
39:10^{6}
39:11^{2}
39:13^{3}
39:14^{5}
39:15^{4}
39:16^{3}
39:17^{3}
39:18^{2}
40:1^{4}
40:2^{3}
40:3^{2}
40:4^{2}
40:5^{7}
40:6^{2}
40:7^{7}
40:8^{6}
40:9^{5}
40:10
40:11^{6}
40:12^{2}
40:13^{4}
40:14^{4}
40:15^{4}
40:16^{2}
41:1^{7}
41:2^{7}
41:3^{3}
41:4
41:5^{2}
41:6^{2}
41:7^{6}
41:8
41:9^{5}
41:10^{9}
41:11^{5}
41:12^{3}
41:13^{4}
41:14^{2}
41:15^{2}
41:16^{10}
41:17
41:18^{5}
42:1^{7}
42:2^{2}
42:3^{3}
42:4^{3}
42:5^{3}
42:6^{4}
42:7^{2}
42:8^{6}
42:9^{2}
42:10
42:11^{2}
42:13^{2}
42:14^{3}
42:15^{4}
42:16^{3}
42:17^{5}
42:18^{3}
42:19
42:20^{3}
42:21^{3}
42:22^{4}
43:1^{4}
43:2^{4}
43:3^{2}
43:4^{7}
43:5^{5}
43:6^{7}
43:7^{3}
43:8^{2}
43:9^{5}
43:10^{3}
43:11^{3}
43:12^{3}
43:13^{5}
44:1^{4}
44:2^{4}
44:4
44:6^{2}
44:7
44:8^{4}
44:9^{7}
44:11^{2}
44:12^{9}
44:13^{4}
44:14^{4}
44:15^{4}
44:16^{3}
44:17^{3}
44:18^{3}
44:19
44:20^{4}
44:21^{6}
44:22^{3}
44:23^{3}
44:24^{5}
44:25^{3}
44:26^{7}
44:27^{4}
44:28^{5}
44:29
44:30^{4}
45:1^{6}
45:2^{2}
45:3
45:4
45:5
46:1^{4}
46:2^{4}
46:3
46:4^{3}
46:5
46:6^{4}
46:7
46:8^{4}
46:9^{6}
46:10^{6}
46:11
46:12^{4}
46:13^{4}
46:14
46:15
46:16^{3}
46:17
46:18^{4}
46:20
46:21^{3}
46:22
46:23^{2}
46:24^{4}
46:25^{3}
46:26^{5}
46:27^{6}
46:28^{2}
47:1^{4}
47:2^{7}
47:3^{5}
47:4^{6}
47:5
47:6
47:7^{2}
48:1^{2}
48:2
48:5^{3}
48:6^{2}
48:8^{4}
48:9
48:10^{2}
48:12^{2}
48:13
48:14
48:15^{3}
48:16
48:17^{2}
48:18
48:19
48:21
48:24^{2}
48:25^{2}
48:26
48:28^{5}
48:29^{2}
48:30
48:31
48:32^{4}
48:33^{3}
48:34^{2}
48:35^{2}
48:36^{2}
48:37^{2}
48:38^{3}
48:39
48:40
48:41^{3}
48:42
48:43^{3}
48:44^{6}
48:45^{7}
48:46
48:47^{4}
49:1^{2}
49:2^{4}
49:3
49:4
49:5
49:6^{3}
49:7^{2}
49:8^{2}
49:12^{2}
49:13^{2}
49:14^{3}
49:15
49:16^{7}
49:17
49:18^{3}
49:19^{4}
49:20^{5}
49:21^{5}
49:22^{3}
49:23
49:25^{2}
49:26^{2}
49:27^{2}
49:28^{4}
49:29
49:31^{2}
49:32^{3}
49:34^{5}
49:35^{3}
49:36^{3}
49:37^{2}
49:38^{3}
49:39^{3}
50:1^{5}
50:2
50:3
50:4^{4}
50:5^{2}
50:6
50:7^{4}
50:8^{5}
50:9
50:10
50:11
50:12^{2}
50:13^{2}
50:14^{2}
50:15^{2}
50:16^{4}
50:17^{2}
50:18^{4}
50:20^{3}
50:21^{3}
50:22
50:23^{3}
50:24
50:25^{6}
50:26
50:27^{2}
50:28^{5}
50:29^{4}
50:30^{2}
50:31^{2}
50:32
50:33^{3}
50:34^{2}
50:35^{3}
50:36
50:37^{2}
50:38
50:39^{5}
50:40^{2}
50:41^{3}
50:42^{4}
50:43^{2}
50:44^{4}
50:45^{6}
50:46^{4}
51:1^{2}
51:2
51:3
51:4^{3}
51:5^{2}
51:6^{3}
51:7^{4}
51:9
51:10^{3}
51:11^{9}
51:12^{7}
51:13
51:14
51:15^{3}
51:16^{5}
51:17
51:18^{2}
51:19^{4}
51:20
51:21^{2}
51:22^{2}
51:23^{2}
51:24^{2}
51:25^{3}
51:26
51:27^{7}
51:28^{6}
51:29^{3}
51:30
51:31
51:32^{3}
51:33^{4}
51:34
51:35^{3}
51:36
51:39
51:40
51:41^{3}
51:42^{3}
51:44^{2}
51:45^{3}
51:46^{3}
51:47^{3}
51:48^{5}
51:49^{3}
51:50^{2}
51:51^{2}
51:52^{3}
51:53^{2}
51:54^{2}
51:55^{2}
51:56^{2}
51:57^{2}
51:58^{5}
51:59^{6}
51:60
51:63
51:64^{2}
52:1
52:2^{2}
52:3^{3}
52:4^{4}
52:5^{2}
52:6^{7}
52:7^{11}
52:8^{4}
52:9^{3}
52:10^{3}
52:11^{2}
52:12^{6}
52:13^{6}
52:14^{5}
52:15^{10}
52:16^{4}
52:17^{9}
52:18^{6}
52:19^{9}
52:20^{4}
52:21^{3}
52:22^{4}
52:23^{2}
52:24^{6}
52:25^{13}
52:26^{3}
52:27^{2}
52:28^{2}
52:29
52:30^{5}
52:31^{7}
52:32^{2}
52:33
52:34^{3}

LA

1:1^{3}
1:2
1:3^{2}
1:4^{2}
1:5^{4}
1:6^{2}
1:7^{4}
1:9
1:10^{2}
1:11
1:12^{2}
1:13
1:14^{2}
1:15^{5}
1:16^{2}
1:17
1:18
1:19^{2}
1:20
2:1^{5}
2:2^{7}
2:3^{2}
2:4^{2}
2:5^{2}
2:6^{6}
2:7^{7}
2:8^{5}
2:9^{4}
2:10^{5}
2:11^{7}
2:12^{3}
2:13
2:15^{4}
2:16^{2}
2:17^{3}
2:18^{3}
2:19^{7}
2:20^{5}
2:21^{6}
2:22^{2}
3:3
3:12
3:13
3:24
3:25^{2}
3:26^{2}
3:27
3:29
3:31
3:32
3:33
3:34^{2}
3:35^{3}
3:36
3:37
3:38^{2}
3:39
3:40
3:41
3:45
3:48^{2}
3:50
3:51
3:53
3:58
3:64
3:66^{2}
4:1^{5}
4:2^{4}
4:3^{5}
4:4^{3}
4:5
4:6^{5}
4:8
4:9^{3}
4:10^{4}
4:11^{2}
4:12^{7}
4:13^{5}
4:14
4:15
4:16^{5}
4:19^{4}
4:20^{4}
4:21^{2}
4:22
5:6^{2}
5:9^{2}
5:10
5:11^{3}
5:12
5:13^{3}
5:14^{3}
5:15
5:16
5:18^{2}

EZE

1:1^{7}
1:2^{3}
1:3^{8}
1:4^{5}
1:5^{3}
1:7^{3}
1:8
1:10^{7}
1:12
1:13^{6}
1:14^{2}
1:15^{3}
1:16^{4}
1:19^{5}
1:20^{5}
1:21^{5}
1:22^{6}
1:23^{3}
1:24^{6}
1:25
1:26^{7}
1:27^{5}
1:28^{10}
2:2
2:3
3:1
3:4
3:5
3:11^{3}
3:12^{3}
3:13^{5}
3:14^{4}
3:15^{2}
3:16^{3}
3:17^{2}
3:18^{3}
3:19
3:21^{2}
3:22^{3}
3:23^{5}
3:24
3:26
3:27
4:1
4:2
4:3^{2}
4:4^{4}
4:5^{5}
4:6^{2}
4:7
4:8
4:9^{2}
4:13^{3}
4:16
5:1
5:2^{5}
5:4^{4}
5:5^{3}
5:6^{2}
5:7^{4}
5:8^{4}
5:9
5:10^{6}
5:11
5:12^{4}
5:13
5:14^{2}
5:15^{2}
5:16^{2}
5:17^{2}
6:1^{2}
6:2
6:3^{7}
6:5^{2}
6:6^{2}
6:7^{3}
6:8^{3}
6:9^{2}
6:10
6:11^{6}
6:12^{3}
6:13^{4}
6:14^{3}
7:1^{2}
7:2^{5}
7:3
7:4^{2}
7:5
7:6
7:7^{6}
7:9^{2}
7:10^{3}
7:12^{5}
7:13^{4}
7:14^{3}
7:15^{6}
7:16^{2}
7:19^{5}
7:20^{2}
7:21^{4}
7:22
7:23^{2}
7:24^{4}
7:26^{4}
7:27^{6}
8:1^{7}
8:2^{4}
8:3^{10}
8:4^{4}
8:5^{7}
8:6^{2}
8:7^{3}
8:8^{2}
8:9
8:10^{3}
8:11^{4}
8:12^{7}
8:14^{4}
8:16^{12}
8:17^{4}
9:1
9:2^{4}
9:3^{7}
9:4^{8}
9:5^{2}
9:6^{3}
9:7^{4}
9:8
9:9^{7}
9:11^{3}
10:1^{5}
10:2^{5}
10:3^{6}
10:4^{10}
10:5^{5}
10:6^{4}
10:7^{4}
10:8^{2}
10:9^{5}
10:10
10:11^{2}
10:12^{2}
10:13
10:14^{8}
10:15^{3}
10:16^{5}
10:17^{2}
10:18^{5}
10:19^{8}
10:20^{4}
10:21^{2}
10:22^{3}
11:1^{8}
11:2
11:3^{2}
11:5^{4}
11:6^{2}
11:7^{5}
11:8^{2}
11:9^{2}
11:10^{3}
11:11^{3}
11:12^{3}
11:13^{2}
11:14^{2}
11:15^{4}
11:16^{4}
11:17^{4}
11:18^{2}
11:19
11:21^{2}
11:22^{4}
11:23^{7}
11:24^{4}
11:25^{3}
12:1^{2}
12:2
12:5
12:6^{3}
12:7^{3}
12:8^{3}
12:9^{2}
12:10^{3}
12:12^{4}
12:13^{2}
12:14
12:15^{3}
12:16^{5}
12:17^{2}
12:19^{6}
12:20^{3}
12:21^{2}
12:22^{2}
12:23^{3}
12:24
12:25^{4}
12:26^{2}
12:27^{3}
12:28^{3}
13:1^{2}
13:2^{3}
13:3^{2}
13:4^{2}
13:5^{6}
13:6^{3}
13:7
13:8^{2}
13:9^{6}
13:12^{2}
13:13
13:14^{5}
13:15^{2}
13:16^{2}
13:17
13:18^{5}
13:19^{2}
13:20^{4}
13:21
13:22^{4}
13:23
14:1
14:2^{2}
14:3
14:4^{6}
14:5
14:6^{2}
14:7^{4}
14:8^{2}
14:9^{3}
14:10^{4}
14:11^{2}
14:12^{2}
14:13^{3}
14:14
14:15^{2}
14:16^{2}
14:17
14:18
14:20
14:21^{5}
14:22
14:23
15:1^{2}
15:2^{3}
15:4^{4}
15:5
15:6^{6}
15:7
15:8^{2}
16:1^{2}
16:3^{2}
16:4
16:5^{3}
16:7^{2}
16:8^{2}
16:14^{2}
16:15
16:16^{2}
16:19
16:21
16:22
16:23
16:25
16:26
16:27^{8}
16:28^{3}
16:29
16:30^{2}
16:31
16:34
16:35^{2}
16:36^{3}
16:41^{2}
16:43^{2}
16:44
16:45
16:48
16:49^{3}
16:53^{4}
16:56
16:57^{4}
16:58
16:59^{3}
16:60
16:62
16:63
17:1^{2}
17:2
17:3^{3}
17:4
17:5^{2}
17:6
17:7
17:9^{5}
17:10^{2}
17:11^{2}
17:12^{4}
17:13^{3}
17:14
17:15
17:16^{4}
17:17
17:18^{2}
17:19
17:21^{2}
17:22^{4}
17:23^{4}
17:24^{8}
18:1^{2}
18:2^{3}
18:3
18:4^{5}
18:6^{3}
18:7^{3}
18:9
18:10
18:11
18:12^{3}
18:15^{3}
18:16^{3}
18:17^{2}
18:19^{4}
18:20^{11}
18:21
18:23^{2}
18:24^{3}
18:25^{2}
18:27
18:29^{3}
18:30
18:32^{2}
19:1
19:3
19:4^{2}
19:6^{2}
19:7^{3}
19:8^{2}
19:9^{2}
19:10
19:11^{3}
19:12^{3}
19:13
19:14
20:1^{6}
20:2^{2}
20:3^{3}
20:4
20:5^{6}
20:6^{3}
20:7^{3}
20:8^{4}
20:9^{2}
20:10^{2}
20:12
20:13^{3}
20:14
20:15^{3}
20:17
20:18^{2}
20:19
20:20
20:21^{2}
20:22^{2}
20:23^{3}
20:26^{4}
20:27^{2}
20:28^{4}
20:29^{2}
20:30^{3}
20:31^{2}
20:32^{3}
20:33
20:34^{2}
20:35^{2}
20:36^{3}
20:37^{3}
20:38^{4}
20:39
20:40^{6}
20:41^{3}
20:42^{4}
20:44^{2}
20:45^{2}
20:46^{4}
20:47^{8}
20:48
21:1^{2}
21:2^{2}
21:3^{4}
21:4^{4}
21:5
21:6
21:7^{2}
21:8^{2}
21:9
21:10
21:11^{2}
21:12^{2}
21:13^{3}
21:14^{6}
21:15^{3}
21:16^{2}
21:17
21:18^{2}
21:19^{5}
21:20^{3}
21:21^{6}
21:22^{5}
21:23
21:24^{2}
21:26^{4}
21:28^{6}
21:29^{2}
21:30^{2}
21:31^{2}
21:32^{4}
22:1^{2}
22:2
22:3^{3}
22:4
22:6
22:7^{4}
22:9^{2}
22:12
22:13
22:14^{2}
22:15^{2}
22:16^{3}
22:17
22:18^{4}
22:19^{2}
22:20^{3}
22:21^{2}
22:22^{4}
22:23^{2}
22:24^{2}
22:25^{4}
22:26^{3}
22:27^{2}
22:28^{2}
22:29^{4}
22:30^{3}
22:31^{2}
23:1^{2}
23:2
23:3
23:4^{2}
23:5^{2}
23:7
23:8
23:9^{3}
23:10
23:12
23:14^{3}
23:15^{2}
23:17^{2}
23:19^{3}
23:20^{2}
23:21^{3}
23:22
23:23^{3}
23:25^{2}
23:27
23:28^{3}
23:29
23:30
23:31
23:32
23:33^{2}
23:34^{2}
23:35
23:36
23:37
23:38
23:39^{2}
23:42^{3}
23:44^{2}
23:45^{3}
23:46
23:47
23:48
23:49^{2}
24:1^{6}
24:2^{3}
24:3^{2}
24:4^{4}
24:5^{4}
24:6^{3}
24:7^{3}
24:8
24:9^{3}
24:10^{3}
24:11^{4}
24:12
24:14^{2}
24:15^{2}
24:16
24:17^{3}
24:18^{3}
24:19
24:20^{2}
25:21^{5}
25:22
25:24
25:25^{3}
25:27
25:1^{2}
25:2
25:3^{6}
25:4^{2}
25:5^{2}
25:6^{3}
25:7^{4}
25:8^{3}
25:9^{4}
25:10^{5}
25:11
25:12^{2}
25:13^{2}
25:14^{2}
25:15^{3}
25:16^{5}
25:17
26:1^{5}
26:2^{2}
26:3^{2}
26:4^{2}
26:5^{5}
26:6^{3}
26:7^{2}
26:8^{3}
26:10^{5}
26:11^{3}
26:12^{2}
26:13^{2}
26:14^{3}
26:15^{6}
26:16^{3}
26:17
26:18^{4}
26:19^{3}
26:20^{7}
26:21
27:1^{2}
27:3^{4}
27:4^{2}
27:6^{4}
27:7
27:8
27:9^{4}
27:10
27:11^{2}
27:12
27:13
27:14
27:15^{2}
27:16^{2}
27:17
27:18^{4}
27:21
27:22
27:23
27:25^{3}
27:26^{3}
27:27^{5}
27:28^{3}
27:29^{5}
27:30
27:32^{3}
27:33^{4}
27:34^{5}
27:35^{2}
27:36^{2}
28:1^{2}
28:2^{6}
28:6^{2}
28:7^{3}
28:8^{4}
28:9
28:10^{4}
28:11^{2}
28:12^{3}
28:13^{11}
28:14^{4}
28:15
28:16^{4}
28:17
28:18^{5}
28:19
28:20^{2}
28:22^{3}
28:23^{4}
28:24^{2}
28:25^{2}
28:26
29:1^{6}
29:3^{3}
29:4^{3}
29:5^{7}
29:6
29:8
29:9^{3}
29:10^{3}
29:12^{7}
29:13^{4}
29:14^{3}
29:15^{4}
29:16^{3}
29:17^{6}
29:18
29:19^{3}
29:20
29:21^{6}
30:1^{2}
30:2
30:3^{5}
30:4^{2}
30:5^{4}
30:6^{5}
30:7^{4}
30:8
30:9^{2}
30:10^{3}
30:11^{5}
30:12^{7}
30:13^{4}
30:15^{2}
30:17^{2}
30:18^{3}
30:19
30:20^{6}
30:21^{2}
30:22^{3}
30:23^{3}
30:24^{3}
30:25^{7}
30:26^{4}
31:1^{6}
31:3^{2}
31:4^{4}
31:5^{3}
31:6^{3}
31:7
31:8^{5}
31:9^{3}
31:10^{2}
31:11^{3}
31:12^{8}
31:13^{4}
31:14^{8}
31:15^{8}
31:16^{7}
31:17^{3}
31:18^{8}
32:1^{6}
32:2^{3}
32:3
32:4^{6}
32:5^{2}
32:6^{3}
32:7^{4}
32:8^{2}
32:9^{3}
32:10
32:11^{3}
32:12^{6}
32:13^{4}
32:14
32:15^{3}
32:16^{4}
32:17^{5}
32:18^{6}
32:19
32:20^{3}
32:21^{4}
32:22
32:23^{5}
32:24^{6}
32:25^{7}
32:26^{3}
32:27^{6}
32:28^{3}
32:29^{3}
32:30^{6}
32:31^{2}
32:32^{6}
33:1^{2}
33:2^{4}
33:3^{4}
33:4^{4}
33:5^{2}
33:6^{3}
33:7^{2}
33:8^{2}
33:9
33:10
33:11^{4}
33:12^{9}
33:13
33:14
33:15^{3}
33:17^{3}
33:18
33:19
33:20^{2}
33:21^{5}
33:22^{4}
33:23^{2}
33:24^{3}
33:25^{3}
33:26
33:27^{8}
33:28^{3}
33:29^{2}
33:30^{6}
33:31
34:1^{2}
34:2^{6}
34:3^{3}
34:4
34:5^{2}
34:6^{3}
34:7^{2}
34:8^{3}
34:9^{2}
34:10^{4}
34:11
34:12^{2}
34:13^{6}
34:14^{2}
34:15
34:16^{2}
34:17^{3}
34:18^{4}
34:20^{3}
34:21
34:24^{2}
34:25^{4}
34:26^{2}
34:27^{5}
34:28^{3}
34:29^{3}
34:30^{3}
34:31^{2}
35:1^{2}
35:3
35:4
35:5^{6}
35:6
35:8
35:9
35:10
35:11
35:12^{2}
35:14^{2}
35:15^{3}
36:1^{3}
36:2^{3}
36:3^{5}
36:4^{11}
36:5^{4}
36:6^{8}
36:7^{2}
36:10^{3}
36:11
36:13
36:14
36:15^{5}
36:16^{2}
36:17^{2}
36:18^{2}
36:19^{2}
36:20^{3}
36:21^{2}
36:22^{3}
36:23^{5}
36:24
36:28
36:29
36:30^{5}
36:32
36:33^{3}
36:34^{2}
36:35^{2}
36:36^{4}
36:37^{2}
36:38^{4}
37:1^{6}
37:2
37:4^{2}
37:5
37:6
37:7
37:8^{3}
37:9^{4}
37:10
37:11
37:12^{2}
37:13
37:14^{2}
37:15^{2}
37:16^{3}
37:18
37:19^{5}
37:20
37:21^{3}
37:22^{2}
37:25
37:26
37:28^{3}
38:1^{2}
38:2^{2}
38:3^{2}
38:6^{2}
38:8^{5}
38:9
38:10^{2}
38:12^{5}
38:13^{2}
38:14
38:15
38:16^{3}
38:17^{2}
38:18^{3}
38:19^{2}
38:20^{13}
38:21
38:22
38:23^{2}
39:1^{2}
39:2^{3}
39:4^{5}
39:5^{2}
39:6^{2}
39:7^{4}
39:8^{2}
39:9^{8}
39:10^{4}
39:11^{7}
39:12^{2}
39:13^{4}
39:14^{5}
39:15^{4}
39:16^{3}
39:17^{3}
39:18^{5}
39:20
39:21^{2}
39:22^{2}
39:23^{4}

39:25^{3} 39:27^{2} 39:28 39:29^{2} 40:1^{10} 40:2^{4} 40:3^{2} 40:4^{3} 40:5^{7} 40:6^{7} 40:7^{5} 40:8^{2} 40:9^{5} 40:10^{3} 40:11^{5} 40:12^{4} 40:13^{4} 40:14^{3} 40:15^{6} 40:16^{3} 40:17^{3} 40:18^{6} 40:19 40:20^{5} 40:21^{7} 40:22^{4} 40:23^{5} 40:24^{4} 40:25^{3} 40:26^{2} 40:27^{3} 40:28^{3} 40:29^{4} 40:30 40:31^{4} 40:32^{3} 40:33^{4} 40:34^{4} 40:35 40:36^{6} 40:37^{4} 40:38^{5} 40:39^{5} 40:40^{6} 40:41^{2} 40:42^{5} 40:43^{3} 40:44^{11} 40:45^{5} 40:46^{9} 40:47^{3} 40:48^{5} 40:49^{5} 41:1^{6} 41:2^{8} 41:3^{5} 41:4^{4} 41:5^{4} 41:6^{6} 41:7^{9} 41:8^{4} 41:9^{5} 41:10^{3} 41:11^{7} 41:12^{7} 41:13^{4} 41:14^{5} 41:15^{9} 41:16^{7} 41:17^{3} 41:19^{7} 41:20^{4} 41:21^{8} 41:22^{7} 41:23^{2} 41:24^{3} 41:25^{5} 41:26^{5} 42:1^{7} 42:2^{3} 42:3^{4} 42:4^{2} 42:5^{5} 42:6^{6} 42:7^{6} 42:8^{4} 42:9^{3}

42:10^{7} 42:11^{4} 42:12^{8} 42:13^{11} 42:14^{4} 42:15^{3} 42:16^{3} 42:17^{2} 42:18^{2} 42:19^{2} 42:20^{3} 43:1^{3} 43:2^{5} 43:3^{7} 43:4^{6} 43:5^{5} 43:6^{2} 43:7^{7} 43:8 43:9^{2} 43:10^{3} 43:11^{11} 43:12^{7} 43:13^{10} 43:14^{7} 43:15^{2} 43:16^{2} 43:17^{4} 43:18^{4} 43:19^{4} 43:20^{5} 43:21^{5} 43:22^{4} 43:23 43:24^{3} 43:25 43:26 43:27^{4} 44:1^{4} 44:2^{3} 44:3^{7} 44:4^{7} 44:5^{8} 44:6^{3} 44:7^{2} 44:8 44:9^{2} 44:10 44:11^{6} 44:12^{2} 44:13^{2} 44:14^{3} 44:15^{8} 44:17^{4} 44:19^{5} 44:21 44:22^{2} 44:23^{4} 44:27^{5} 44:29^{3} 44:30^{6} 44:31 45:1^{7} 45:2^{2} 45:3^{4} 45:4^{7} 45:5^{5} 45:6^{5} 45:7^{17} 45:8^{4} 45:9^{2} 45:11^{8} 45:12 45:13^{2} 45:14^{4} 45:15^{3} 45:16^{3} 45:17^{10} 45:18^{5} 45:19^{11} 45:20^{3} 45:21^{9} 45:22^{3} 45:23^{3} 45:25^{10} 46:1^{8} 46:2^{10}

46:3^{6} 46:4^{4} 46:5^{3} 46:6^{2} 46:7 46:8^{4} 46:9^{14} 46:10^{2} 46:11^{4} 46:12^{6} 46:13^{2} 46:14^{4} 46:15^{3} 46:16^{3} 46:17^{2} 46:18^{2} 46:19^{7} 46:20^{7} 46:21^{4} 46:22^{2} 46:23 46:24^{5} 47:1^{12} 47:2^{6} 47:3^{5} 47:4^{5} 47:5 47:6^{2} 47:7^{4} 47:8^{5} 47:9^{2} 47:10^{3} 47:11^{2} 47:12^{6} 47:13^{4} 47:14 47:15^{5} 47:16^{3} 47:17^{6} 47:18^{5} 47:19^{5} 47:20^{4} 47:21 47:22^{4} 47:23^{2} 48:1^{7} 48:2^{3} 48:3^{3} 48:4^{3} 48:5^{3} 48:6^{3} 48:7^{3} 48:8^{9} 48:9^{2} 48:10^{8} 48:11^{4} 48:12^{3} 48:13^{5} 48:14^{3} 48:15^{6} 48:16^{5} 48:17^{6} 48:18^{7} 48:19^{2} 48:20^{4} 48:21^{18} 48:22^{9} 48:23^{4} 48:24^{3} 48:25^{3} 48:26^{3} 48:27^{3} 48:28^{6} 48:29^{3} 48:30^{3} 48:31^{4} 48:32 48:33 48:34 48:35^{3}

DA

1:1^{2} 1:2^{7} 1:3^{5} 1:4^{4} 1:5^{5} 1:6 1:7^{3} 1:8^{5} 1:9^{2} 1:10^{5} 1:11^{2} 1:13^{4} 1:15^{4} 1:16^{2} 1:18^{5} 1:19^{2} 1:20^{2} 1:21 2:1^{2} 2:2^{7} 2:3^{2} 2:4^{4} 2:5^{5} 2:6^{4} 2:7^{3} 2:8^{3} 2:9^{4} 2:10^{4} 2:11^{3} 2:12^{2} 2:13^{2} 2:14^{3} 2:15^{4} 2:16^{3} 2:17 2:18^{3} 2:19^{2} 2:20 2:21^{3} 2:22^{3} 2:23 2:24^{6} 2:25^{4} 2:26^{3} 2:27^{9} 2:28^{3} 2:30^{3} 2:31 2:34 2:35^{11} 2:36^{3} 2:37 2:38^{5} 2:39 2:40 2:41^{5} 2:42^{3} 2:43 2:44^{3} 2:45^{11} 2:46 2:47 2:48^{4} 2:49^{5} 3:1^{4} 3:2^{13} 3:3^{12} 3:5^{4} 3:6^{2} 3:7^{8} 3:8 3:9 3:10^{3} 3:11 3:12^{3} 3:13 3:14 3:15^{5} 3:16 3:17 3:18 3:19^{2} 3:20^{2} 3:21^{2} 3:22^{4} 3:23^{2} 3:24^{4} 3:25^{5} 3:26^{5}

3:27^{4} 3:28^{2} 3:29 3:30^{2} 4:1^{2} 4:2^{2} 4:5^{2} 4:6^{3} 4:7^{6} 4:8^{5} 4:9^{5} 4:10^{4} 4:11^{5} 4:12^{7} 4:13 4:14^{3} 4:15^{8} 4:17^{10} 4:18^{5} 4:19^{5} 4:20^{4} 4:21^{5} 4:22^{2} 4:23^{10} 4:24^{4} 4:25^{5} 4:26^{3} 4:27 4:28 4:29^{3} 4:30^{5} 4:31^{3} 4:32^{4} 4:33^{3} 4:34^{3} 4:35^{5} 4:36^{2} 4:37 5:1^{2} 5:2^{4} 5:3^{4} 5:4 5:5^{8} 5:6^{2} 5:7^{9} 5:8^{4} 5:10^{5} 5:11^{8} 5:12^{3} 5:13^{5} 5:14^{2} 5:15^{5} 5:16^{4} 5:17^{4} 5:18 5:19 5:21^{6} 5:23^{4} 5:24^{2} 5:25 5:26^{2} 5:27 5:28 5:29^{2} 5:30^{2} 5:31^{2} 6:1^{2} 6:2^{2} 6:3^{3} 6:4^{2} 6:5 6:6 6:7^{7} 6:8^{4} 6:9^{2} 6:10 6:12^{7} 6:13^{4} 6:14^{3} 6:15^{5} 6:16^{3} 6:17^{5} 6:18^{2} 6:19^{3} 6:20^{4} 6:21

6:22 6:23^{3} 6:24^{6} 6:25 6:26^{3} 6:27^{2} 6:28^{3} 7:1^{4} 7:2^{3} 7:3 7:4^{4} 7:5^{2} 7:6^{2} 7:7^{4} 7:8^{4} 7:9^{5} 7:10^{2} 7:11^{5} 7:12^{2} 7:13^{4} 7:15^{2} 7:16^{3} 7:17 7:18^{4} 7:19^{4} 7:20^{2} 7:21^{2} 7:22^{6} 7:23^{3} 7:24^{2} 7:25^{4} 7:26^{2} 7:27^{7} 7:28^{3} 8:1^{3} 8:2^{3} 8:3^{4} 8:4 8:5^{5} 8:6^{3} 8:7^{5} 8:8^{3} 8:9^{3} 8:10^{4} 8:11^{4} 8:12^{3} 8:13^{5} 8:14 8:15^{3} 8:16^{2} 8:17^{3} 8:18 8:19^{4} 8:20^{2} 8:21^{4} 8:22 8:23^{3} 8:24^{2} 8:25 8:26^{4} 8:27^{2} 9:1^{6} 9:2^{7} 9:3 9:4^{3} 9:6^{3} 9:7^{3} 9:9 9:10^{3} 9:11^{4} 9:12 9:13^{2} 9:14^{3} 9:15 9:16 9:17^{2} 9:18 9:20^{3} 9:21^{5} 9:23^{4} 9:24^{3} 9:25^{6} 9:26^{7} 9:27^{8} 10:1^{5} 10:4^{4}

10:6^{4} 10:7^{3} 10:9^{3} 10:10 10:11 10:12 10:13^{4} 10:14^{2} 10:15 10:16^{3} 10:17 10:18 10:20^{2} 10:21 11:1^{2} 11:2^{3} 11:4 11:5^{2} 11:6^{7} 11:7^{3} 11:8^{2} 11:9^{2} 11:11^{5} 11:12 11:13^{3} 11:14^{4} 11:15^{5} 11:16 11:17^{2} 11:18^{2} 11:19 11:20^{2} 11:21^{3} 11:22^{3} 11:23 11:24^{4} 11:25^{4} 11:26 11:27^{2} 11:28 11:29^{4} 11:30^{3} 11:31^{3} 11:32^{2} 11:33^{2} 11:35^{2} 11:36^{3} 11:37^{2} 11:38 11:39^{2} 11:40^{7} 11:41^{3} 11:42^{2} 11:43^{4} 11:44^{2} 11:45^{3} 12:1^{3} 12:2^{2} 12:3^{3} 12:4^{4} 12:5^{6} 12:6^{4} 12:7^{5} 12:8 12:9^{3} 12:10^{3} 12:11^{3} 12:12 12:13^{3}

HO

1:1^{6} 1:2^{6} 1:3 1:4^{5} 1:5^{2} 1:6 1:7^{2} 1:10^{7} 1:11^{4} 2:3 2:4 2:5 2:9^{2} 2:10 2:12^{2} 2:13^{2} 2:14 2:15^{4} 2:16 2:17 2:18^{9} 2:20 2:21^{3} 2:22^{4} 2:23 3:1^{4} 3:3 3:4 3:5^{4} 4:1^{6} 4:3^{6} 4:4 4:5^{3} 4:6 4:8 4:10 4:11 4:12 4:13^{4} 4:14 4:15^{2} 4:16 4:19 5:1 5:2 5:4^{3} 5:5 5:6 5:7 5:8^{2} 5:9^{2} 5:10^{2} 5:11 5:12 5:13 5:14 6:1 6:2 6:3^{5} 6:4 6:5^{3} 6:6 6:7 6:9^{2} 6:10^{2} 6:11 7:1^{4} 7:3^{2} 7:4^{2} 7:5^{2} 7:6^{2} 7:8 7:10^{2} 7:12^{2} 7:16^{4} 8:1^{3} 8:3^{2} 8:6^{2} 8:7^{4} 8:8 8:10^{3} 8:12 8:13^{2} 8:14 9:2^{3} 9:3 9:4^{4} 9:5^{4} 9:6 9:7^{6} 9:8^{3} 9:9 9:10^{3} 9:11^{3} 9:13 9:15 9:16 9:17 10:1^{3} 10:3 10:4^{2}

10:5^{5} 10:7^{2} 10:8^{6} 10:9^{3} 10:10 10:11 10:12 10:13^{2} 10:14^{2} 10:15 11:4 11:5^{2} 11:6 11:7 11:9^{4} 11:10^{3} 11:11^{2} 11:12^{2} 12:1^{2} 12:2 12:3^{2} 12:4 12:5^{2} 12:7 12:9^{4} 12:10^{3} 12:11^{2} 12:12 12:13 13:2^{4} 13:3^{7} 13:4^{2} 13:5^{2} 13:7 13:8^{2} 13:12 13:13^{3} 13:14^{2} 13:15^{4} 13:16 14:1 14:2^{2} 14:3^{2} 14:5^{2} 14:6 14:7^{4} 14:9^{4}

JOE

1:1^{3} 1:2^{2} 1:4^{6} 1:5 1:6^{2} 1:7 1:8 1:9^{6} 1:10^{5} 1:11^{4} 1:12^{8} 1:13^{4} 1:14^{6} 1:15^{4} 1:16^{2} 1:17^{4} 1:18^{3} 1:19^{6} 1:20^{6} 2:1^{5} 2:2^{4} 2:3^{2} 2:4^{2} 2:5^{4} 2:6 2:7 2:8 2:9^{4} 2:10^{5} 2:11^{3} 2:12 2:13^{2} 2:14 2:15 2:16^{7} 2:17^{7} 2:18 2:19^{2} 2:20^{3} 2:21 2:22^{6} 2:23^{6} 2:24^{2} 2:25^{5} 2:26^{2} 2:27^{2} 2:29^{2} 2:30^{2} 2:31^{5} 2:32^{5} 3:1 3:2^{2} 3:4 3:6^{3} 3:7 3:8^{4} 3:9^{3} 3:10 3:12^{3} 3:13^{4} 3:14^{4} 3:15^{3} 3:16^{7} 3:17 3:18^{6} 3:19^{2} 3:21

AM

1:1^{6} 1:2^{4} 1:3^{2} 1:4^{2} 1:5^{7} 1:6^{3} 1:7^{2} 1:8^{5} 1:9^{4} 1:10^{2} 1:11^{3} 1:12 1:13^{4} 1:14^{5} 1:15 2:1^{4} 2:2^{3} 2:3^{4} 2:4^{5} 2:5 2:6^{4} 2:7^{7} 2:8^{3} 2:9^{4} 2:10^{4} 2:11 2:12^{2} 2:14^{4} 2:15^{2} 2:16^{2} 3:1^{3} 3:2^{2} 3:4 3:5^{2} 3:6^{3} 3:7^{2} 3:8^{2} 3:9^{8} 3:10 3:11^{2} 3:12^{6} 3:13^{3} 3:14^{6} 3:15^{5} 4:1^{3} 4:2^{2} 4:3^{3} 4:5^{2} 4:6 4:7^{3} 4:8 4:9^{2} 4:10^{5} 4:11^{2} 4:13^{7} 5:2 5:3^{3} 5:4^{2} 5:6^{2} 5:7 5:8^{9} 5:9^{4} 5:10 5:11 5:12^{3} 5:13 5:14^{2} 5:15^{5} 5:16^{5} 5:17 5:18^{4} 5:19^{2} 5:20^{2} 5:22 5:23^{2} 5:25 5:26^{2} 5:27^{2} 6:1^{3} 6:2^{2} 6:3^{2} 6:4^{5} 6:5^{2} 6:6^{2} 6:7^{2} 6:8^{5} 6:10^{6} 6:11^{3} 6:12^{2} 6:14^{5} 7:1^{6} 7:2^{2} 7:3^{2} 7:4^{3} 7:6^{2} 7:7 7:8^{3} 7:9^{4} 7:10^{4} 7:11 7:12 7:13^{2} 7:15^{3} 7:16^{3} 7:17^{3} 8:1 8:2^{2} 8:3^{3} 8:4^{3} 8:5^{5} 8:6^{4} 8:7^{2} 8:8^{2} 8:9^{4} 8:10^{2} 8:11^{5} 8:12^{4} 8:13 8:14^{2} 9:1^{8} 9:3^{4} 9:4 9:5^{3} 9:6^{7} 9:7^{5} 9:8^{7} 9:9^{3} 9:10^{3} 9:11^{3} 9:12^{3} 9:13^{7} 9:14^{4} 9:15

OB

1^{4} 2 3^{4} 4^{3} 5 6 7^{3} 8^{3} 9^{2} 11^{4} 12^{5} 13^{4} 14^{2} 15^{3} 16 17 18^{5} 19^{6} 20^{6} 21^{3}

JON

1:1^{3} 1:3^{5} 1:4^{4} 1:5^{6} 1:6 1:7 1:9^{4} 1:10^{4} 1:11^{2} 1:12^{2} 1:13^{3} 1:14 1:15^{2} 1:16^{3} 1:17^{3} 2:1^{2} 2:2^{2} 2:3^{4} 2:5^{4} 2:6^{3} 2:7 2:9^{2} 2:10^{3} 3:1^{3} 3:2 3:3^{2} 3:4 3:5^{3} 3:6 3:7^{2} 3:8 3:10 4:2^{2} 4:4 4:5^{5} 4:6^{2} 4:7^{3} 4:8^{3} 4:9 4:10^{3}

MIC

1:1^{4} 1:2^{2} 1:3^{3} 1:4^{4} 1:5^{5} 1:6^{4} 1:7^{6} 1:8^{2} 1:9 1:10^{2} 1:11^{2} 1:12^{3} 1:13^{6} 1:14^{2} 1:15 1:16 2:1^{2} 2:3 2:4 2:5^{2} 2:7^{3} 2:8^{2} 2:9 2:11^{2} 2:12^{5} 2:13^{4} 3:1 3:2^{2} 3:3^{3} 3:4 3:5^{2} 3:6^{3} 3:7^{2} 3:8^{2} 3:9^{2} 3:11^{5} 3:12^{4} 4:1^{7} 4:2^{7} 4:4^{2} 4:5^{3} 4:6 4:7 4:8^{6} 4:10^{4} 4:12^{4} 4:13^{3} 5:1^{2} 5:2 5:3^{3} 5:4^{7} 5:5^{2} 5:6^{5} 5:7^{6} 5:8^{6} 5:10^{2} 5:11 5:13^{2} 5:14 5:15 6:1^{3} 6:2^{3} 6:4^{2} 6:5^{3} 6:6^{2} 6:7^{3} 6:8 6:9^{4} 6:10^{4} 6:11^{2} 6:12^{2} 6:14^{2} 6:15 6:16^{5} 7:1^{4} 7:2^{2} 7:3^{3} 7:4^{3} 7:5 7:6^{5} 7:7^{2} 7:8 7:9^{3} 7:10^{3} 7:11^{2} 7:12^{3} 7:13^{2} 7:14^{4} 7:15^{2} 7:16 7:17^{3} 7:18^{2} 7:19^{2} 7:20^{3}

NA

1:1^{4} 1:2^{3} 1:3^{7} 1:4^{3} 1:5^{4} 1:6^{2} 1:7^{2} 1:8 1:9^{2} 1:11 1:12 1:14^{4} 1:15^{3} 2:1^{2} 2:2^{4} 2:3^{5} 2:4^{4} 2:5^{2} 2:6^{3} 2:7 2:9^{4} 2:10^{3} 2:11^{7} 2:12 2:13^{5} 3:1^{2} 3:2^{6} 3:3^{3} 3:4^{4} 3:5^{3} 3:8^{4} 3:10^{2} 3:11 3:12^{3} 3:13^{3} 3:14^{3} 3:15^{5} 3:16^{3} 3:17^{5} 3:18^{2} 3:19^{2}

HAB

1:1^{2} 1:4^{3} 1:5 1:6^{4} 1:8^{3} 1:9^{3} 1:10^{2} 1:13^{2} 1:14^{3} 1:15 1:17 2:1 2:2^{2} 2:3^{2} 2:4 2:8^{5} 2:9 2:11^{4} 2:13^{4} 2:14^{6} 2:16^{2} 2:17^{5} 2:18^{4} 2:19^{3} 2:20^{2} 3:1 3:2^{4} 3:3^{2} 3:4^{2} 3:5 3:6^{4} 3:7^{3} 3:8^{4} 3:9^{3} 3:10^{4} 3:11^{3} 3:12^{2} 3:13^{6} 3:14^{2} 3:15^{2} 3:16^{3} 3:17^{8} 3:18^{2} 3:19^{2}

ZEP

1:1^{8} 1:2^{2} 1:3^{8} 1:4^{5} 1:5^{3} 1:6^{2} 1:7^{5} 1:8^{4} 1:9^{2} 1:10^{5} 1:11 1:12^{2} 1:13 1:14^{6} 1:16^{3} 1:17^{2} 1:18^{5} 2:2^{7} 2:3^{4} 2:4 2:5^{8} 2:6 2:7^{6} 2:8^{3} 2:9^{6} 2:10^{2} 2:11^{5} 2:13 2:14^{9} 2:15 3:1 3:2^{2} 3:3^{2} 3:4^{2} 3:5^{3} 3:6 3:8^{7} 3:9^{3} 3:10^{2} 3:11 3:12^{3} 3:13 3:14 3:15^{4} 3:17^{2} 3:18^{2} 3:20^{3}

HAG

1:1^{11} 1:2^{4} 1:3^{2} 1:5 1:7 1:8^{3} 1:9 1:10^{2} 1:11^{8} 1:12^{12} 1:13^{4} 1:14^{11} 1:15^{4} 2:1^{6} 2:2^{5} 2:4^{5} 2:5 2:6^{5} 2:7^{2} 2:8^{3} 2:9^{4} 2:10^{6} 2:11^{3} 2:12^{2} 2:13 2:14 2:15^{2} 2:16^{2} 2:17^{2} 2:18^{5} 2:19^{6} 2:20^{4} 2:21^{2} 2:22^{7} 2:23^{4}

ZEC

1:1^{7} 1:2 1:3^{3} 1:4^{3} 1:5 1:6^{2} 1:7^{9} 1:8^{2} 1:9 1:10^{4} 1:11^{5} 1:12^{3} 1:13^{2} 1:14^{2} 1:15^{2} 1:16^{2} 1:17^{2} 1:19^{2} 1:20 1:21^{4} 2:2^{2} 2:3 2:4 2:5^{3} 2:6^{6} 2:7 2:8^{4} 2:9 2:10^{2} 2:11^{3} 2:12^{2} 2:13 3:1^{3} 3:2^{4} 3:3 3:4 3:5^{2} 3:6^{2} 3:7 3:8^{2} 3:9^{4} 3:10^{3} 4:1 4:2^{3} 4:3^{4} 4:4 4:5 4:6^{3} 4:7 4:8^{2} 4:9^{3} 4:10^{6} 4:11^{3} 4:12^{2} 4:14^{3} 5:2^{2} 5:3^{3} 5:4^{7} 5:5 5:6 5:7^{2} 5:8^{4} 5:9^{5} 5:10^{2} 5:11 6:1 6:2^{2} 6:3^{2} 6:4 6:5^{5} 6:6^{5} 6:7^{4} 6:8^{2} 6:9^{2} 6:10^{4} 6:11^{3} 6:12^{5} 6:13^{4} 6:14^{4} 6:15^{5} 7:1^{5} 7:2^{2} 7:3^{5} 7:4^{2} 7:5^{4} 7:7^{6} 7:8^{2} 7:9 7:10^{4} 7:11 7:12^{5} 7:13 7:14^{3} 8:1^{2} 8:2 8:3^{5} 8:4^{2} 8:5^{3} 8:6^{4} 8:7^{3} 8:8 8:9^{8} 8:10 8:11^{3} 8:12^{5} 8:13 8:14^{2} 8:15 8:16^{3} 8:17 8:18^{2} 8:19^{11} 8:20^{2} 8:21^{3} 8:22^{2} 8:23^{3} 9:1^{8} 9:3^{3} 9:4^{2} 9:5 9:6^{2} 9:8 9:9 9:10^{7} 9:11^{2} 9:12 9:13^{2} 9:14^{5} 9:15^{3} 9:16^{3} 9:17^{2} 10:1^{5} 10:2^{2} 10:3^{5} 10:4^{3} 10:5^{5} 10:6^{3} 10:7 10:9 10:10^{2} 10:11^{7} 10:12^{2} 11:1 11:2^{4} 11:3^{4} 11:4^{3} 11:5 11:6^{6} 11:7^{5} 11:9^{2} 11:10 11:11^{4} 11:13^{6} 11:14 11:15^{2} 11:16^{4} 11:17^{3} 12:1^{8} 12:2^{2} 12:3^{2} 12:4^{3} 12:5^{3} 12:6^{5} 12:7^{6} 12:8^{5} 12:9 12:10^{3} 12:11^{2} 12:12^{5} 12:13^{3} 12:14 13:1^{2} 13:2^{7} 13:3^{2} 13:4 13:6 13:7^{5} 13:8^{3} 13:9^{3} 14:1^{3} 14:2^{7} 14:3^{2} 14:4^{9} 14:5^{8} 14:6 14:7 14:8^{2} 14:9^{2} 14:10^{6} 14:12^{3} 14:13^{3} 14:14^{2} 14:15^{6} 14:16^{4} 14:17^{4} 14:18^{5} 14:19^{3} 14:20^{7} 14:21^{4}

MAL

1:1^{3} 1:2^{2} 1:3^{2} 1:4^{5} 1:5^{2} 1:6 1:7^{2} 1:8^{3} 1:9 1:10^{2} 1:11^{7} 1:12^{3} 1:13^{4} 1:14^{4} 2:2 2:3 2:4 2:5 2:6 2:7^{4} 2:8^{4} 2:9^{2} 2:10 2:11^{3} 2:12^{6} 2:13^{3} 2:14^{3} 2:15^{3} 2:16^{3} 2:17^{4} 3:1^{5} 3:2 3:3^{2} 3:4^{3} 3:5^{7} 3:6 3:7^{2} 3:10^{4} 3:11^{5} 3:12 3:13 3:14 3:15 3:16^{3} 3:17 3:18^{2} 4:1^{4} 4:2^{2} 4:3^{4} 4:4^{2} 4:5^{4} 4:6^{6}

MT

1:1^{4} 1:6^{3} 1:11 1:16 1:17^{3} 1:18^{2} 1:20^{3}

THE—*continued*

1:22[2] 1:24[2] 2:1[3] 2:2[2] 2:3 2:4[2] 2:5 2:6[3] 2:7[2] 2:8 2:9[4] 2:10 2:11[2] 2:13[4] 2:14 2:15[3] 2:16[5] 2:17 2:19 2:20[3] 2:21[2] 2:22[2] 2:23 3:1[2] 3:2 3:3[5] 3:4 3:5 3:7[2] 3:10[4] 3:11 3:12[2] 3:16[3] 4:1[3] 4:3[2] 4:4 4:5[3] 4:6 4:7 4:8[4] 4:10 4:11 4:13[2] 4:14 4:15[5] 4:16[2] 4:17 4:18[2] 4:21 4:22 4:23[3] 4:24 5:1 5:3[2] 5:5[2] 5:7 5:8 5:9[2] 5:10 5:12 5:13[3] 5:14[2] 5:15 5:17[2] 5:18 5:19[4] 5:20[3] 5:21 5:22[2] 5:23 5:24 5:25[5] 5:26 5:32 5:33 5:35[3] 5:39 5:40 5:45[5] 5:46[2] 5:47 6:2[3] 6:5[4] 6:7 6:13[3] 6:16 6:22[3]

6:23 6:24[4] 6:25[2] 6:26[2] 6:28[2] 6:30[3] 6:32 6:33 6:34[5] 7:3[2] 7:4 7:5[2] 7:6 7:12[2] 7:13[3] 7:14[2] 7:19 7:21[2] 7:25[3] 7:26 7:27[4] 7:28 7:29 8:1 8:4[2] 8:6 8:8[2] 8:11[2] 8:12[2] 8:13[2] 8:15 8:16[2] 8:17 8:18 8:20[4] 8:22 8:24[3] 8:26[2] 8:27[3] 8:28[4] 8:29 8:31[2] 8:32[4] 8:33[3] 8:34 9:2[3] 9:3 9:6[3] 9:8 9:9 9:10 9:11 9:13 9:14[2] 9:15[5] 9:16[2] 9:17[3] 9:20 9:22 9:23[3] 9:24 9:25[3] 9:26 9:28[2] 9:33[3] 9:34[3] 9:35[4] 9:37[2] 9:38[2] 10:2[4] 10:3[2] 10:4 10:5[3] 10:6[2] 10:7 10:8[3] 10:10 10:13 10:14 10:15[2] 10:16 10:17 10:18 10:20 10:21[5] 10:22 10:23[2]

10:24[2] 10:25[4] 10:27[2] 10:28[2] 10:29 10:30 10:35[2] 10:41[2] 10:42 11:2[2] 11:5[7] 11:7[3] 11:11[2] 11:12[4] 11:13[2] 11:16 11:19 11:20 11:21 11:22 11:23 11:24[2] 11:25 11:27[5] 12:1[3] 12:2[2] 12:4[3] 12:5[5] 12:6 12:7 12:8[2] 12:10 12:11 12:12 12:13[2] 12:14 12:17 12:18 12:19 12:21 12:22 12:23 12:24[3] 12:28[2] 12:29 12:31[2] 12:32[3] 12:33[3] 12:34[3] 12:35[3] 12:36 12:38[2] 12:39[2] 12:40[4] 12:41[3] 12:42[6] 12:43 12:45[2] 12:46 12:50[2] 13:1[3] 13:2[2] 13:4[2] 13:6 13:7 13:10 13:11[2] 13:14 13:18[2] 13:19[4] 13:20[3] 13:21 13:22[5] 13:23[2] 13:24 13:25 13:26[3] 13:27[2] 13:28 13:29[2] 13:30[5] 13:31 13:32[5] 13:33[2] 13:34 13:35[3] 13:36[5]

13:37[2] 13:38[8] 13:39[7] 13:40[3] 13:41 13:43[3] 13:44[2] 13:45 13:47[2] 13:48[2] 13:49[5] 13:50 13:52 13:55 14:1[2] 14:2[2] 14:5 14:6 14:9[2] 14:10 14:11 14:12 14:13[2] 14:15[3] 14:19[7] 14:20 14:22[2] 14:23[2] 14:24[4] 14:25[3] 14:26[2] 14:28 14:29[2] 14:30 14:32[2] 14:33[2] 14:34 14:35 14:36 15:2[2] 15:3 15:4 15:6 15:9 15:10 15:11[2] 15:12 15:14[4] 15:17[3] 15:18[3] 15:19 15:20 15:21 15:22 15:24[2] 15:26 15:27[2] 15:29 15:31[6] 15:32[2] 15:33 15:35[2] 15:36[4] 15:37 15:39[2] 16:1[2] 16:2 16:3[6] 16:4[2] 16:5 16:6[3] 16:9[2] 16:10[2] 16:11[3] 16:12[4] 16:13[2] 16:14[2] 16:16[3] 16:18 16:19[2] 16:20 16:21[2] 16:23 16:26 16:27[2] 16:28 17:2[2]

17:5 17:6 17:9[4] 17:10 17:12 17:13[2] 17:14 17:15[2] 17:18[2] 17:19 17:22 17:23 17:25[3] 17:26 17:27[2] 18:1[4] 18:2 18:3 18:4[2] 18:6[2] 18:7[2] 18:10 18:11 18:12 18:13 18:14 18:16 18:17[2] 18:20 18:23 18:26 18:27[2] 18:28[2] 18:30 18:34 19:1 19:3 19:4 19:8[2] 19:10[2] 19:12 19:13 19:14 19:17 19:20 19:21 19:22 19:23 19:24[2] 19:28[4] 19:30 20:1[2] 20:2 20:3[2] 20:4 20:5 20:6[2] 20:7 20:8[5] 20:9 20:10 20:11[2] 20:12[2] 20:16[2] 20:17[2] 20:18[3] 20:19[2] 20:20 20:21[3] 20:22[2] 20:23 20:24[2] 20:25[2] 20:28 20:30 20:31[2] 21:1 21:2 21:3 21:4 21:5[2] 21:6 21:7[2] 21:8[3] 21:9[5] 21:10 21:11[2]

21:12[5] 21:13 21:14[3] 21:15[5] 21:16 21:17 21:18[2] 21:19[2] 21:20[2] 21:21[2] 21:23[4] 21:25 21:26 21:28 21:30 21:31[5] 21:32[3] 21:34[4] 21:35 21:36 21:38[3] 21:39 21:40[2] 21:41 21:42[7] 21:43[2] 21:45 21:46 22:2 22:3 22:4 22:6 22:7 22:8 22:9[2] 22:10[2] 22:11[2] 22:13[2] 22:15 22:16[3] 22:19 22:21[2] 22:23[2] 22:25 22:26[3] 22:27 22:28[2] 22:29[2] 22:30[2] 22:31[2] 22:32[6] 22:33 22:34[2] 22:36[2] 22:37 22:38 22:39 22:40[2] 22:41 22:42 22:44 23:1 23:2[2] 23:5 23:6[3] 23:7 23:9 23:13 23:14 23:15 23:16[3] 23:17[3] 23:18[2] 23:19[3] 23:20 23:21 23:22 23:23[3] 23:25[3] 23:26[2] 23:29[4] 23:30[3] 23:31[2] 23:32 23:33 23:35[6] 23:37

23:39[2] 24:1[3] 24:3[5] 24:6 24:8 24:12 24:13[2] 24:14[3] 24:15[3] 24:16 24:17 24:18 24:20[2] 24:21[2] 24:22 24:24 24:26[2] 24:27[5] 24:28[2] 24:29[6] 24:30[6] 24:31[2] 24:32 24:33 24:36 24:37[3] 24:38[4] 24:39[3] 24:40[3] 24:41[3] 24:43[3] 24:44 24:49 24:50 24:51 25:1[2] 25:4 25:5 25:6 25:8[2] 25:9 25:10[3] 25:11 25:13[3] 25:14 25:16[2] 25:18 25:19 25:21 25:23 25:24 25:25 25:27 25:28 25:30 25:31[3] 25:32 25:33[3] 25:34[4] 25:37 25:40[2] 25:41[2] 25:45 25:46 26:2[2] 26:3[6] 26:5[2] 26:6[2] 26:9 26:10 26:11 26:13 26:14[2] 26:17[4] 26:18[3] 26:19[2] 26:20 26:23[2] 26:24[2] 26:26 26:27 26:28[2] 26:29 26:30 26:31[3] 26:34 26:35

26:36 26:37 26:40 26:41[2] 26:42 26:44[2] 26:45[3] 26:47[3] 26:51 26:52[2] 26:54 26:55[2] 26:56[3] 26:57[3] 26:58[3] 26:59[2] 26:60 26:61 26:62 26:63[4] 26:64[3] 26:65 26:67 26:69 26:71 26:72 26:74[2] 26:75[2] 27:1[3] 27:2[3] 27:3[2] 27:4 27:5[2] 27:6[4] 27:7 27:8 27:9[4] 27:10[2] 27:11[4] 27:12 27:14 27:15[2] 27:19 27:20[2] 27:21[2] 27:23[2] 27:24[2] 27:25 27:27[4] 27:29[2] 27:30[2] 27:31 27:35 27:37[2] 27:38[2] 27:40[3] 27:41[2] 27:42[2] 27:43 27:44[2] 27:45[3] 27:46 27:49 27:50 27:51[6] 27:52[2] 27:53[2] 27:54[3] 27:56[2] 27:57 27:58[2] 27:59 27:60[3] 27:61[2] 27:62[4] 27:64[2] 27:66[2] 28:1[5] 28:2[4] 28:4 28:5[2] 28:6[2] 28:7 28:8 28:9 28:11[4] 28:12[2]

28:14 28:15[2] 28:16 28:19[4] 28:20[2]

MK

1:1[3] 1:2 1:3[4] 1:4[3] 1:5[2] 1:7 1:8 1:10[3] 1:12[2] 1:13[3] 1:14[2] 1:15[3] 1:16[2] 1:19[2] 1:20[2] 1:21[2] 1:22 1:24 1:26 1:27 1:28 1:29[2] 1:31[2] 1:33[2] 1:34 1:35 1:38 1:42 1:44 1:45 2:1 2:2[2] 2:3 2:4[5] 2:5[2] 2:6 2:9[2] 2:10[3] 2:12 2:13[2] 2:14[2] 2:16 2:17[2] 2:18[4] 2:19[4] 2:20[2] 2:21[3] 2:22[4] 2:23[3] 2:24[2] 2:26[5] 2:27[2] 2:28[2] 3:1 3:2 3:3[2] 3:4 3:5[3] 3:6[2] 3:7 3:9 3:11 3:17[3] 3:18[2] 3:20 3:22[3] 3:27 3:28 3:29 3:32 3:35[2] 4:1[5] 4:4[3] 4:6 4:7 4:10[2] 4:11[2]

4:14[2] 4:15[3] 4:16 4:17 4:18 4:19[4] 4:20 4:26[2] 4:27 4:28[5] 4:29[3] 4:30 4:31[3] 4:32[3] 4:33 4:35[3] 4:36[2] 4:37[2] 4:38[2] 4:39[3] 4:41[2] 5:1[4] 5:2[2] 5:3 5:4[2] 5:5[2] 5:7 5:8 5:10 5:11 5:12[2] 5:13[5] 5:14[3] 5:15[2] 5:16[2] 5:18[2] 5:19 5:21[2] 5:22[2] 5:23 5:27 5:29 5:30 5:31 5:33[2] 5:35[2] 5:36[3] 5:37 5:38[4] 5:39 5:40[4] 5:41[2] 5:42[2] 6:2[2] 6:3[3] 6:6 6:7 6:11[2] 6:14[2] 6:15 6:16 6:22[4] 6:23 6:24[2] 6:25[3] 6:26 6:27[2] 6:28[2] 6:30 6:33 6:35[2] 6:36[2] 6:39 6:41[4] 6:43[2] 6:44 6:45[3] 6:47[4] 6:48[4] 6:49 6:51[2] 6:52[2] 6:53[2] 6:54 6:56[3] 7:1[2] 7:3[4]

7:4[2] 7:5[3] 7:7 7:8[3] 7:9 7:10 7:13 7:14 7:15[2] 7:17[3] 7:18 7:19[2] 7:20[2] 7:21 7:23 7:24 7:26[2] 7:27[3] 7:28[3] 7:29 7:30[2] 7:31[4] 7:33 7:35 7:36[2] 7:37[2] 8:1 8:2 8:3 8:4 8:6[4] 8:8 8:10 8:11 8:13[2] 8:14[2] 8:15[3] 8:19 8:20 8:23[3] 8:26[2] 8:27[2] 8:28[2] 8:29 8:31[3] 8:33[2] 8:34 8:35[2] 8:36 8:38[3] 9:1 9:7 9:9[3] 9:10[2] 9:11 9:12 9:14 9:15 9:16 9:17 9:20[2] 9:22[2] 9:24[2] 9:25[2] 9:26 9:27 9:28 9:31[3] 9:33[2] 9:34[2] 9:35[2] 9:36 9:42 9:43 9:44 9:45 9:46 9:47 9:48 9:50 10:2 10:5 10:6[2] 10:10[2] 10:14[2] 10:15 10:17

10:19 10:21[2] 10:23 10:24[2] 10:25[2] 10:29 10:30 10:31 10:32[2] 10:33[4] 10:34 10:35 10:37 10:38[2] 10:39[2] 10:41 10:42 10:44 10:45 10:46[2] 10:48 10:49 10:51 10:52 11:1 11:2 11:3 11:4[2] 11:5 11:7 11:8[3] 11:9[2] 11:10[4] 11:11[3] 11:12 11:13 11:15[5] 11:16 11:17 11:18[2] 11:19 11:20[3] 11:21 11:23 11:27[4] 11:30 11:32 12:1 12:2[5] 12:4 12:7[2] 12:8 12:9[4] 12:10[4] 12:11 12:12[2] 12:13[2] 12:14[2] 12:17[2] 12:18 12:20 12:21[2] 12:22[2] 12:23[2] 12:24[2] 12:25[2] 12:26[6] 12:27[4] 12:28[2] 12:29[3] 12:30[2] 12:31 12:32[2] 12:33[4] 12:34 12:35[3] 12:36 12:37 12:38[2] 12:39[3] 12:41[3] 12:43 13:1 13:3[2] 13:4 13:7 13:8

13:9 13:10 13:11 13:12[4] 13:13[2] 13:14[3] 13:15[2] 13:16 13:18 13:19[2] 13:20[3] 13:22 13:24[2] 13:25[2] 13:26[2] 13:27[4] 13:28 13:29 13:32[3] 13:33 13:34[2] 13:35[4] 14:1[4] 14:2[2] 14:3[3] 14:4 14:5 14:7 14:8 14:9 14:10[2] 14:12[3] 14:13 14:14[5] 14:16[2] 14:17[2] 14:20[2] 14:21[2] 14:23 14:24 14:25[3] 14:26 14:27[2] 14:30 14:31 14:35[2] 14:38[2] 14:39 14:41[4] 14:43[4] 14:47 14:49[2] 14:51 14:52 14:53[4] 14:54[4] 14:55[2] 14:60[2] 14:61[4] 14:62[3] 14:63 14:64 14:65[2] 14:66[3] 14:68[2] 14:72[4] 15:1[4] 15:2[2] 15:3 15:7 15:8 15:9[2] 15:10 15:11[2] 15:12[2] 15:14 15:15 15:16[3] 15:18 15:19 15:20 15:21 15:22[2] 15:25 15:26[3] 15:27[2] 15:28[2]

15:29 15:30 15:31[2] 15:32[2] 15:33[3] 15:34 15:37 15:38[4] 15:39[3] 15:40[2] 15:42[4] 15:43[2] 15:44 15:45[2] 15:46[3] 15:47 16:1[2] 16:2[6] 16:4 16:5[2] 16:6 16:8 16:9[2] 16:12 16:13 16:14 16:15[2] 16:16[3] 16:18 16:19[2] 16:20[2]

LU

1:2[2] 1:3 1:4 1:5[4] 1:6[2] 1:8[2] 1:9[4] 1:10[3] 1:11[3] 1:13 1:15[3] 1:16[2] 1:17[8] 1:18 1:19[2] 1:20 1:21[2] 1:22 1:23 1:25[2] 1:26[2] 1:27[2] 1:28[2] 1:30 1:32[4] 1:33 1:34 1:35[5] 1:36 1:38[3] 1:39 1:40 1:41[3] 1:42 1:43 1:44[2] 1:45 1:46 1:48 1:51[2] 1:52 1:53[2] 1:58 1:59[3] 1:65 1:66[2] 1:67 1:68 1:69 1:70[2] 1:71 1:72

1:73 1:74 1:75 1:76[4] 1:77 1:78[2] 1:79[2] 1:80[3] 2:1 2:4[3] 2:6 2:7 2:8[2] 2:9[4] 2:10 2:11[2] 2:12 2:13[2] 2:14 2:15[3] 2:16 2:17 2:18 2:20[2] 2:21[4] 2:22[3] 2:23[4] 2:24[2] 2:25[3] 2:26[2] 2:27[6] 2:31 2:32[2] 2:34 2:35 2:36[2] 2:37 2:39[2] 2:40[2] 2:41[2] 2:42[2] 2:43[2] 2:44 2:46[3] 2:50 3:1[4] 3:2[4] 3:3[3] 3:4[7] 3:5[2] 3:6 3:7[2] 3:9[4] 3:10 3:14 3:15[2] 3:16[2] 3:17[2] 3:18 3:19[2] 3:21[2] 3:22 3:23[2] 3:24[5] 3:25[5] 3:26[5] 3:27[5] 3:28[5] 3:29[5] 3:30[5] 3:31[5] 3:32[5] 3:33[5] 3:34[5] 3:35[5] 3:36[5] 3:37[5] 3:38[4] 4:1[3] 4:2 4:3[2] 4:5[3] 4:6[2] 4:8 4:9[2] 4:12 4:13[2]

4:14[3] 4:16[2] 4:17[4] 4:18[7] 4:19[2] 4:20[4] 4:22 4:25[3] 4:27[3] 4:28 4:29[3] 4:30 4:31 4:33 4:34 4:35[2] 4:36 4:37[2] 4:38 4:39 4:40 4:41 4:42 4:43 4:44 5:1[3] 5:2[2] 5:3[4] 5:4 5:5[2] 5:7[2] 5:9[2] 5:10 5:13 5:14 5:15 5:16 5:17[3] 5:19[4] 5:21[2] 5:24[3] 5:27 5:32 5:33[3] 5:34[3] 5:35[2] 5:36[4] 5:37[3] 5:39 6:1[4] 6:2[2] 6:4[3] 6:5[2] 6:6 6:7[2] 6:8[3] 6:9 6:10[2] 6:15 6:16[2] 6:17[3] 6:19 6:20 6:22 6:23[2] 6:26 6:29[2] 6:33 6:35[4] 6:38 6:39[3] 6:40 6:41[2] 6:42[4] 6:45[4] 6:46 6:48[3] 6:49[3] 7:1[2] 7:3[2] 7:6[2] 7:9 7:10[2] 7:11 7:12[4] 7:13 7:14

7:17 7:18 7:20 7:22[7] 7:24[4] 7:28[2] 7:29[3] 7:30[2] 7:31 7:32 7:33 7:34 7:36[2] 7:37[2] 7:38[2] 7:39 7:41[2] 7:44[2] 7:45 7:47 7:50 8:1[3] 8:3 8:5[3] 8:7 8:10[2] 8:11[3] 8:12[3] 8:13[2] 8:15[2] 8:16 8:19 8:21 8:22[2] 8:23 8:24[3] 8:25 8:26[2] 8:27[2] 8:29[5] 8:31 8:32 8:33[5] 8:34 8:35[3] 8:36 8:37[4] 8:38[2] 8:39 8:40 8:41 8:42 8:44 8:45 8:47[2] 8:49[3] 8:51[4] 8:54 9:2[2] 9:5 9:6[2] 9:7[2] 9:8 9:10[2] 9:11[2] 9:12[4] 9:16[4] 9:18 9:19[2] 9:20 9:22[3] 9:24 9:25 9:26[2] 9:27 9:29 9:32 9:34 9:35 9:36 9:37[2] 9:38 9:42[3] 9:43 9:44[2] 9:47 9:48

9:51 9:52 9:56 9:57 9:58[2] 9:60[2] 9:62[2] 10:1 10:2[4] 10:4 10:6 10:7[2] 10:9[2] 10:10[2] 10:11[2] 10:13 10:14 10:17[2] 10:19[2] 10:20 10:21 10:22[5] 10:23[2] 10:26 10:27 10:31 10:32[2] 10:35[3] 10:36 11:7 11:13 11:14[3] 11:15[2] 11:20[2] 11:24 11:26[2] 11:27[3] 11:28 11:29[3] 11:30[2] 11:31[7] 11:32[3] 11:33 11:34[3] 11:35 11:36[2] 11:38 11:39[4] 11:42[2] 11:43[3] 11:44 11:45 11:46 11:47[2] 11:48 11:49 11:50[4] 11:51[4] 11:52 11:53[2] 12:1[3] 12:3[3] 12:4 12:7 12:8[2] 12:9 12:10[2] 12:11 12:12[2] 12:13[2] 12:15[2] 12:16 12:22 12:23[2] 12:24[2] 12:26 12:27 12:28[3] 12:30[2] 12:31 12:32 12:33 12:36 12:37 12:38[2] 12:39[3] 12:40

12:42
12:45
12:46^{2}
12:48
12:49
12:53^{10}
12:54^{2}
12:55
12:56^{3}
12:58^{6}
12:59
13:1
13:2
13:4
13:7^{2}
13:10^{2}
13:14^{5}
13:15^{3}
13:16
13:17^{2}
13:18
13:19^{3}
13:20
13:21
13:22
13:24
13:25^{4}
13:28^{2}
13:29^{5}
13:31^{2}
13:32
13:33
13:34
13:35^{3}
14:1^{3}
14:2
14:3^{2}
14:5
14:7
14:8
14:9
14:10^{2}
14:13^{4}
14:14^{2}
14:15
14:18
14:21^{8}
14:22
14:23^{3}
14:28
14:29
14:32
14:34
14:35^{2}
15:1
15:2
15:4^{2}
15:8
15:9
15:10^{2}
15:12^{2}
15:13
15:16^{2}
15:21
15:22^{2}
15:23
15:25^{2}
15:26
15:27
15:30
16:3^{2}
16:4
16:5
16:8^{4}
16:9
16:10
16:11^{2}
16:13^{4}
16:14
16:15
16:16^{3}
16:17
16:21^{3}
16:22^{3}
16:24
16:29
16:30
16:31^{2}
17:1
17:2
17:5^{2}
17:6^{3}
17:7
17:9
17:11
17:14
17:17
17:20^{3}
17:21
17:22^{4}
17:24^{4}
17:26^{3}
17:27^{3}
17:28
17:29
17:30^{2}
17:31^{3}
17:34^{2}
17:35^{2}
17:36^{3}
17:37^{2}
18:6^{2}
18:8^{2}
18:10^{3}
18:11
18:12
18:13
18:14
18:16
18:17
18:20
18:22
18:24
18:25
18:27
18:29
18:30
18:31^{3}
18:32
18:33
18:34
18:35
18:36
18:39
18:43
19:2^{2}
19:3
19:5
19:8^{3}
19:10
19:11
19:15^{2}
19:16
19:18
19:23
19:24
19:29^{2}
19:30^{2}
19:31
19:33^{3}
19:34
19:35
19:36
19:37^{5}
19:38^{4}
19:39^{2}
19:40
19:41
19:42
19:43
19:44^{2}
19:45
19:46
19:47^{5}
19:48
20:1^{6}
20:2
20:4
20:6
20:9
20:10^{5}
20:13^{2}
20:14^{3}
20:15^{3}
20:16
20:17^{4}
20:19^{4}
20:20^{2}
20:21^{2}
20:25^{2}
20:26
20:27
20:29
20:30
20:31^{2}
20:32
20:33
20:34
20:35^{2}
20:36^{4}
20:37^{6}
20:38^{2}
20:39
20:42^{2}
20:45^{2}
20:46^{5}
20:47
21:1^{2}
21:4^{2}
21:5
21:6^{2}
21:8
21:9
21:12
21:20
21:21^{3}
21:22
21:23
21:24^{5}
21:25^{6}
21:26^{2}
21:27
21:29^{2}
21:31
21:35^{2}
21:36
21:37
21:38^{3}
22:1^{2}
22:2^{2}
22:3^{2}
22:4
22:6^{2}
22:7^{2}
22:8
22:10^{2}
22:11^{5}
22:13
22:14^{2}
22:16
22:17
22:18^{3}
22:20^{2}
22:21^{2}
22:22
22:24
22:25^{2}
22:26
22:30
22:31
22:34
22:37^{2}
22:39
22:40
22:44
22:47
22:48
22:49
22:50^{2}
22:53^{2}
22:54
22:55^{2}
22:56
22:59
22:60
22:61^{4}
22:63
22:64
22:66^{4}
22:67
22:69^{3}
22:70
23:1
23:2
23:3^{2}
23:4^{2}
23:5^{2}
23:6
23:10
23:12
23:13^{3}
23:14
23:17
23:19
23:23^{2}
23:26^{2}
23:29^{5}
23:30^{2}
23:31
23:33^{5}
23:35^{3}
23:36
23:37^{2}
23:38^{2}
23:39
23:40^{2}
23:41
23:44^{3}
23:45^{4}
23:46
23:47
23:48^{2}
23:49
23:51^{4}
23:52
23:54^{2}
23:55^{2}
23:56^{2}
24:1^{5}
24:2^{2}
24:3^{2}
24:5^{3}
24:7^{3}
24:9^{3}
24:10^{2}
24:12^{2}
24:18^{2}
24:19
24:20
24:21
24:22
24:24^{2}
24:25
24:27^{3}
24:28
24:29
24:32^{2}
24:33^{2}
24:35
24:36
24:44^{4}
24:45
24:46^{2}
24:49^{2}
24:53

JOH

1:1^{4}
1:2
1:4^{2}
1:5^{2}
1:7^{2}
1:9^{2}
1:10^{3}
1:12
1:13^{3}
1:14^{4}
1:17
1:18^{3}
1:19^{2}
1:20
1:23^{5}
1:24
1:29^{4}
1:32
1:33^{4}
1:34
1:35
1:36
1:37
1:39
1:40
1:41^{2}
1:42
1:43
1:44
1:45^{3}
1:48
1:49^{2}
1:50
1:51^{2}
2:1^{2}
2:2
2:3
2:5
2:6^{3}
2:7^{2}
2:8^{2}
8:9^{8}
2:10^{2}
2:13
2:14^{2}
2:15^{5}
2:17
2:18
2:20
2:21
2:22^{3}
2:23^{3}
3:1^{2}
3:2
3:3
3:4
3:5^{2}
3:6^{2}
3:8^{3}
3:13
3:14^{3}
3:16
3:17^{3}
3:18^{2}
3:19^{2}
3:20^{2}
3:21
3:22
3:25
3:26
3:28
3:29^{5}
3:31^{2}
3:34^{2}
3:35^{2}
3:36^{3}
4:1^{2}
4:5
4:6^{2}
4:8
4:9^{3}
4:10
4:11^{2}
4:12
4:14^{2}
4:15
4:17
4:19
4:20
4:21^{2}
4:22
4:23^{4}
4:25
4:27
4:28^{3}
4:29
4:30
4:31
4:33
4:34
4:35
4:39^{3}
4:40
4:42^{4}
4:45^{4}
4:46
4:47
4:49
4:50^{2}
4:52^{3}
4:53^{3}
4:54
5:1
5:2^{2}
5:3^{2}
5:4^{5}
5:7^{3}
5:9^{3}
5:10^{2}
5:11
5:14
5:15^{2}
5:16^{2}
5:18^{3}
5:19^{3}
5:20^{2}
5:21^{3}
5:22^{2}
5:23^{4}
5:25^{3}
5:26^{2}
5:27
5:28^{3}
5:29^{2}
5:30^{2}
5:32
5:33
5:36^{4}
5:37
5:39
5:42
5:44
5:45
6:1^{2}
6:4^{2}
6:10^{3}
6:11^{4}
6:12
6:13^{2}
6:14^{2}
6:16
6:17
6:18
6:19^{2}
6:21^{3}
6:22^{5}
6:23^{2}
6:24
6:25^{2}
6:26^{2}
6:27^{3}
6:28
6:29
6:31
6:32
6:33^{2}
6:35
6:37
6:38
6:39^{2}
6:40^{3}
6:41^{2}
6:42
6:44^{2}
6:45^{2}
6:46^{2}
6:49
6:50
6:51^{4}
6:52
6:53^{2}
6:54
6:57^{2}
6:59
6:62
6:63^{3}
6:64
6:67
6:68
6:69^{2}
6:71^{2}
7:1
7:2
7:3
7:4
7:7^{2}
7:10
7:11^{2}
7:12^{2}
7:13
7:14^{3}
7:15
7:17
7:18
7:19^{2}
7:20
7:22^{2}
7:23^{3}
7:24
7:26^{2}
7:28
7:31
7:32^{4}
7:35^{4}
7:37^{2}
7:38
7:39^{2}
7:40^{2}
7:41
7:42^{3}
7:43
7:45^{2}
7:46
7:47
7:48^{2}
7:49
8:1
8:2^{3}
8:3^{2}
8:4
8:5
8:6
8:8
8:9^{4}
8:10
8:12^{3}
8:13
8:15
8:16
8:17
8:18
8:20^{2}
8:22
8:25^{2}
8:26^{2}
8:27
8:28
8:29
8:32^{2}
8:34
8:35^{3}
8:36
8:39
8:40
8:41
8:44^{5}
8:45
8:46
8:48
8:52^{2}
8:53
8:57
8:59^{2}
9:3
9:4^{2}
9:5^{3}
9:6^{5}
9:7
9:8
9:11
9:13
9:14^{2}
9:15
9:16^{2}
9:17
9:18^{2}
9:22^{3}
9:24^{2}
9:30
9:32^{2}
9:35
10:1^{3}
10:2^{3}
10:3^{2}
10:4
10:5
10:7^{2}
10:8
10:9
10:10
10:11^{3}
10:12^{6}
10:13^{2}
10:14
10:15^{3}
10:19
10:21^{3}
10:22^{2}
10:23
10:24^{2}
10:25
10:31
10:33
10:35^{2}
10:36^{3}
10:37
10:38^{2}
10:40
11:1
11:2
11:4^{2}
11:6
11:8
11:9^{3}
11:10
11:15
11:17
11:19
11:20
11:24^{2}
11:25^{2}
11:27^{3}
11:28
11:30
11:31^{3}
11:33^{2}
11:36
11:37^{2}
11:38
11:39^{2}
11:40
11:41^{3}
11:42
11:45^{2}
11:46
11:47^{2}
11:48
11:49
11:50^{2}
11:52
11:54^{2}
11:55^{3}
11:56^{2}
11:57^{2}
12:1^{2}
12:2
12:3^{4}
12:5
12:6^{2}
12:7
12:8
12:9^{2}
12:10
12:11
12:12^{2}
12:13^{3}
12:16
12:17^{2}
12:18
12:19^{2}
12:20
12:21
12:23^{2}
12:24
12:29
12:31^{2}
12:32
12:34^{3}
12:35^{2}
12:36^{2}
12:38^{4}
12:42^{3}
12:43^{2}
12:46
12:47^{2}
12:48^{3}
12:49
12:50
13:1^{5}
13:2^{2}
13:3
13:5^{2}
13:16
13:18
13:22
13:26^{2}
13:27
13:28
13:29^{3}
13:30
13:31
13:33
13:38
14:4
14:5
14:6^{4}
14:8
14:9^{2}
14:10^{5}
14:11^{3}
14:12
14:13^{2}
14:16
14:17^{2}
14:19
14:22
14:24^{2}
14:26^{3}
14:27
14:28
14:30
14:31^{3}
15:1^{2}
15:3
15:4^{2}
15:5^{3}
15:6
15:9
15:15
15:16
15:18
15:19^{5}
15:20^{2}
15:24
15:25
15:26^{4}
15:27
16:2^{2}
16:3
16:4^{2}
16:7^{2}
16:8
16:11
16:13
16:15
16:16
16:17
16:20
16:21^{3}
16:23
16:24^{2}
16:26
16:27
16:28^{4}
16:32^{2}
16:33^{2}
17:1
17:3
17:4^{2}
17:5^{2}
17:6^{2}
17:8
17:9
17:11^{2}
17:12^{3}
17:13
17:14^{4}
17:15^{2}
17:16^{2}
17:18^{2}
17:19
17:21
17:22
17:23
17:24^{2}
17:25
17:26
18:1^{2}
18:2
18:3
18:6
18:9
18:10^{2}
18:11^{2}
18:12^{3}
18:13
18:14^{2}
18:15^{3}
18:16^{3}
18:17^{2}
18:18
18:19
18:20^{4}
18:22^{3}
18:23
18:24
18:26^{3}
18:27
18:28^{3}
18:31
18:32
18:33^{4}
18:35
18:36
18:37^{3}
18:38
18:39^{3}
19:2
19:3
19:5^{3}
19:6
19:7^{2}
19:8
19:9
19:11
19:12
19:13^{3}
19:14^{4}
19:15
19:17^{2}
19:18
19:19^{4}
19:20^{3}
19:21^{5}
19:23^{3}
19:24^{2}
19:25^{2}
19:26
19:27
19:28
19:30^{2}
19:31^{5}
19:32^{4}
19:34
19:36
19:38^{3}
19:39
19:40^{4}
19:41^{2}
19:42^{2}
20:1^{5}
20:2^{3}
20:3
20:4^{2}
20:5
20:6^{2}
20:7^{2}
20:8
20:9^{2}
20:10
20:11^{2}
20:12^{5}
20:15
20:18^{2}
20:19^{7}
20:20^{2}
20:22
20:24
20:25^{6}
20:26^{2}
20:30
20:31^{2}
21:1^{2}
21:2
21:4^{3}
21:6^{4}
21:7^{3}
21:8^{2}
21:10
21:11^{2}
21:12^{2}
21:14^{2}
21:16
21:17^{2}
21:20
21:23
21:24
21:25^{3}

AC

1:1
1:2^{3}
1:3^{2}
1:4^{2}
1:5
1:6
1:7^{2}
1:8^{3}
1:12
1:13^{2}
1:14^{2}
1:15^{3}
1:16^{2}
1:18^{2}
1:19^{2}
1:20
1:21^{2}
1:22
1:24
1:26^{2}
2:1
2:2
2:4^{2}
2:6
2:9
2:10
2:11
2:14
2:15^{2}
2:16
2:17
2:19
2:20^{3}
2:21^{2}
2:22
2:23
2:24
2:25
2:28
2:29
2:30^{2}
2:31
2:33^{4}
2:34^{2}
2:36
2:37^{2}
2:39^{2}
2:41
2:42
2:43
2:46
2:47^{3}
3:1^{3}
3:2^{3}
3:3
3:6
3:7
3:8
3:9
3:10^{2}
3:11^{3}
3:12
3:13^{3}
3:14^{2}
3:15^{2}
3:16^{2}
3:18
3:19^{3}
3:21^{4}
3:22^{2}
3:23
3:24
3:25^{5}
4:1^{5}
4:2^{3}
4:3
4:4^{3}
4:5
4:6^{3}
4:7
4:8^{2}
4:9^{2}
4:10^{3}
4:11^{3}
4:13
4:14
4:15
4:17
4:18
4:19
4:20
4:21
4:22
4:23
4:24
4:25^{3}
4:26^{4}
4:27^{2}
4:30
4:31^{3}
4:32^{2}
4:33^{3}
4:34^{2}
4:35
4:36^{3}
4:37^{2}
5:2^{2}
5:3^{3}
5:5
5:6
5:7
5:8
5:9^{4}
5:10^{2}
5:11
5:12^{3}
5:13^{2}
5:14^{2}
5:15^{4}
5:16
5:17^{3}
5:18^{2}
5:19^{3}
5:20^{3}
5:21^{7}
5:22^{2}
5:23^{3}
5:24^{4}
5:25^{3}
5:26^{3}
5:27^{2}
5:29
5:30
5:32
5:33
5:34^{4}
5:37^{2}
5:40^{2}
5:41^{2}
5:42
6:1^{5}
6:2^{4}
6:3
6:4^{2}
6:5^{3}
6:6
6:7^{5}
6:8
6:9^{3}
6:10^{2}
6:12^{4}
6:13
6:14
6:15^{2}
7:1
7:2
7:3
7:4^{2}
7:7
7:8^{3}
7:9
7:10
7:11
7:13
7:16^{3}
7:17^{3}
7:19^{2}
7:22^{2}
7:23
7:24
7:26
7:28
7:29
7:30^{2}
7:31^{3}
7:32^{4}
7:33^{2}
7:34
7:35^{4}
7:36^{3}
7:37^{2}
7:38^{5}
7:40
7:41^{2}
7:42^{5}
7:43^{2}
7:44^{3}
7:45^{4}
7:46
7:48^{2}
7:49^{2}
7:51
7:52^{4}
7:53^{2}
7:54
7:55^{3}
7:56^{3}
7:58^{2}
8:1^{3}
8:3
8:4
8:5
8:6^{2}
8:9^{2}
8:10^{3}
8:12^{3}
8:13
8:14^{2}
8:15
8:16^{2}
8:17
8:18^{2}
8:19
8:20
8:21
8:22
8:23^{2}
8:24
8:25^{4}
8:26^{4}
8:27^{2}
8:28
8:29
8:30
8:32^{3}
8:33
8:34^{2}
8:35
8:36
8:37
8:38^{3}
8:39^{4}
8:40
9:1^{3}
9:2
9:4
9:5^{2}
9:6^{2}
9:7
9:8^{2}
9:10
9:11^{3}
9:14
9:15^{3}
9:17^{4}
9:19
9:20^{2}
9:21
9:22^{2}
9:23
9:24
9:25^{2}
9:26
9:27^{4}
9:29^{3}
9:30
9:31^{5}
9:32
9:33
9:35
9:38
9:39^{3}
9:40
9:41
9:42
10:1^{2}
10:2
10:3^{2}
10:6
10:7
10:9^{4}
10:11^{2}
10:12^{2}
10:15^{2}
10:16
10:17^{2}
10:19^{2}
10:21^{2}
10:22^{3}
10:23
10:24
10:30
10:31
10:32^{2}
10:36^{2}
10:37
10:38^{2}
10:39^{2}
10:40
10:41^{2}
10:42^{2}
10:43
10:44^{2}
10:45^{4}
10:47
10:48^{2}
11:1^{3}
11:2
11:4^{2}
11:5
11:6^{3}
11:9
11:11
11:12^{2}
11:15^{2}
11:16^{3}
11:17^{2}
11:18
11:19^{3}
11:20^{2}
11:21^{3}
11:22^{2}
11:23^{2}
11:24^{2}
11:26^{2}
11:28^{3}
11:29^{2}
11:30^{2}
12:1^{2}
12:2^{2}
12:3^{2}
12:4
12:5
12:6^{4}
12:7^{4}
12:8
12:9
12:10^{5}
12:11^{5}
12:12^{3}
12:13^{2}
12:14^{2}
12:16
12:17^{4}
12:18
12:19
12:20^{2}
12:22^{2}
12:23^{4}
12:24
13:1^{2}
13:2^{3}
13:4
13:5^{3}
13:6
13:7^{3}
13:8^{3}
13:9
13:10^{3}
13:11^{4}
13:12^{3}
13:14^{2}
13:15^{6}
13:17^{3}
13:18^{2}
13:19
13:20^{2}
13:21^{3}
13:22
13:24^{2}
13:26^{2}
13:27^{2}
13:29
13:30
13:31
13:32^{2}
13:33^{2}
13:34^{2}
13:36
13:38
13:39
13:40
13:42^{4}
13:43^{3}
13:44^{3}
13:45^{2}
13:46^{2}
13:47^{4}
13:48^{3}
13:49^{3}
13:50^{4}
13:51
13:52^{2}
14:1^{4}
14:2^{3}
14:3^{2}
14:4^{4}
14:5^{2}
14:6
14:7
14:9
14:11^{4}
14:12
14:13^{3}
14:14^{2}
14:15^{2}
14:18
14:19^{2}
14:20^{3}
14:21
14:22^{4}
14:23
14:25
14:26^{2}
14:27^{3}
14:28
15:1^{2}
15:2
15:3^{4}
15:4^{2}
15:5^{3}
15:6
15:7^{3}
15:8^{2}
15:10^{2}
15:11^{2}
15:12^{2}
15:14^{2}
15:15^{2}
15:16^{2}
15:17^{4}
15:18^{2}
15:19
15:21
15:22^{3}
15:23^{3}
15:24
15:26
15:27
15:28
15:30^{2}
15:31
15:32
15:33^{2}
15:35^{2}
15:36^{2}
15:38
15:39^{2}
15:40^{2}
15:41
16:1
16:2
16:3
16:4^{3}
16:5^{2}
16:6^{3}
16:7
16:9
16:10^{3}
16:11
16:12
16:13^{3}
16:14^{3}
16:15
16:17^{4}
16:18^{3}
16:19^{3}
16:20
16:22^{2}
16:23
16:24^{2}
16:25
16:26^{3}
16:27^{4}
16:31
16:32^{2}
16:33^{2}
16:35^{2}
16:36^{3}
16:38^{2}
16:39
16:40^{3}
17:1
17:2
17:3
17:4^{2}
17:5^{5}
17:6^{3}
17:7
17:8^{3}
17:9
17:10^{2}
17:11^{2}
17:13^{3}
17:14^{2}
17:15
17:16
17:17^{4}
17:18^{3}
17:21
17:22
17:23
17:24
17:26^{4}
17:27
17:29^{2}
17:30
17:31^{3}
17:32^{2}
17:34^{2}
18:3
18:4^{3}
18:5^{2}
18:6
18:7
18:8^{4}
18:9^{2}
18:11
18:12^{3}
18:13
18:14
18:16
18:17^{4}
18:18
18:19^{2}
18:22
18:23^{2}
18:24
18:25^{6}
18:26^{2}
18:27^{2}
18:28^{2}
19:1
19:2
19:4^{2}
19:5^{2}
19:6
19:7
19:8^{4}
19:9^{3}
19:10^{3}
19:11
19:12^{3}
19:13^{3}
19:14
19:15
19:16^{2}
19:17^{3}
19:19
19:20
19:21
19:23
19:24
19:25
19:27^{3}
19:28
19:29^{2}
19:30^{2}
19:31^{2}
19:32^{2}
19:33^{4}
19:34^{2}
19:35^{6}
19:38^{2}
19:41
20:1^{2}
20:3
20:4
20:6
20:7^{4}
20:8
20:9
20:12
20:15^{3}
20:16^{2}
20:17^{2}
20:18
20:19^{3}
20:21^{2}
20:22^{2}
20:23
20:24^{4}
20:25
20:26
20:27
20:28^{4}
20:29
20:31
20:32
20:35^{3}
20:38^{2}
21:1
21:3^{2}
21:4
21:5^{2}
21:7
21:8^{4}
21:9
21:11^{5}
21:13^{2}
21:14^{2}
21:16
21:17
21:18^{2}
21:19
21:20^{2}
21:21^{3}
21:22
21:24
21:25
21:26^{5}
21:27^{4}
21:28^{4}
21:29^{2}
21:30^{4}
21:31^{2}
21:32^{2}
21:33
21:34^{4}
21:35^{4}
21:36^{2}
21:37^{2}
21:38
21:39
21:40^{4}
22:2^{2}
22:3^{4}
22:4
22:5^{4}
22:7
22:9^{2}
22:10
22:11^{2}
22:12^{2}
22:13
22:14^{2}
22:16^{2}
22:17
22:20^{2}
22:21
22:22
22:23
22:24^{2}
22:25
22:26^{2}
22:27
22:28
22:29
22:30^{4}
23:1
23:2^{2}
23:3^{2}
23:5^{2}
23:6^{6}
23:7^{3}
23:8^{2}
23:9^{2}
23:10^{3}
23:11^{2}
23:12
23:14
23:15^{2}
23:16
23:17^{2}
23:18^{2}
23:19^{2}
23:20^{2}
23:22^{2}
23:23^{2}
23:24
23:26
23:27

THE—*continued*

4:12[5] 4:13 4:14[2] 4:15 4:16 5:2[2] 5:3 5:6 5:7 5:8 5:9 5:10 5:12[3] 5:13 6:1[3] 6:2[3] 6:4[2] 6:5[3] 6:6 6:7[2] 6:10 6:11[3] 6:12 6:15 6:16 6:17[2] 6:18 6:19[2] 6:20[2] 7:1[3] 7:3 7:4[3] 7:5[6] 7:6 7:7[2] 7:10 7:11[5] 7:12[2] 7:13 7:15 7:16[2] 7:17 7:18[2] 7:19[3] 7:21[2] 7:25 7:26 7:27

7:28[5] 8:1[6] 8:2[3] 8:4 8:5[4] 8:6 8:7 8:8[4] 8:9[5] 8:10[3] 8:11[3] 8:13 9:1 9:2[5] 9:3[3] 9:4[6] 9:5[2] 9:6[3] 9:7[4] 9:8[4] 9:9[3] 9:10 9:12[2] 9:13[5] 9:14[3] 9:15[5] 9:16[2] 9:17 9:18 9:19[5] 9:20[2] 9:21[3] 9:22 9:23[3] 9:24[4] 9:25 9:26[5] 9:27 9:28[2] 10:1[4] 10:2 10:4 10:5 10:7[2] 10:8 10:9[2] 10:10[3] 10:11

10:12 10:15 10:16[2] 10:19[2] 10:20 10:21 10:23 10:25[4] 10:26[2] 10:27 10:29[4] 10:30[2] 10:31[2] 10:32 10:34 10:36[2] 10:38 10:39[2] 11:1[2] 11:2 11:3[2] 11:7[4] 11:9[3] 11:12[4] 11:13[2] 11:17 11:19 11:21[2] 11:22[2] 11:23 11:24 11:25[2] 11:26[4] 11:27[2] 11:28[3] 11:29[2] 11:30 11:31[2] 11:32[2] 11:33 11:34[5] 11:37 11:38[2] 11:39 12:1[2] 12:2[6] 12:5[3] 12:6

12:7 12:9 12:11[2] 12:12[2] 12:13 12:14 12:15 12:17 12:18 12:19[3] 12:20 12:21 12:22[3] 12:23[4] 12:24[3] 12:26[2] 12:27 13:3 13:4 13:6 13:7[3] 13:8 13:9 13:10 13:11[4] 13:12[2] 13:13 13:15[2] 13:17 13:19[2] 13:20[5] 13:22 13:24[2] 13:*sub.*

JAS

1:1[2] 1:3 1:6[2] 1:7 1:9 1:10[3] 1:11[6] 1:12[3] 1:17

1:18 1:20[2] 1:21 1:22 1:23 1:25[2] 1:27[3] 2:1[2] 2:3[2] 2:5[2] 2:6[2] 2:7 2:8[2] 2:9 2:10 2:11 2:12 2:16 2:19 2:21 2:23[2] 2:25[2] 2:26[2] 3:1 3:2[2] 3:3 3:4[2] 3:5 3:6[4] 3:7 3:8 3:9[2] 3:10 3:11 3:12 3:14 3:17 3:18 4:4[4] 4:5[2] 4:6[2] 4:7 4:10[3] 4:11[4] 4:14 4:15 5:3[2]

5:4[5] 5:5 5:6 5:7[6] 5:8[2] 5:9[2] 5:10[3] 5:11[4] 5:12 5:14[4] 5:15[3] 5:16 5:17[2] 5:18[3] 5:19 5:20[2]

1 PE

1:1 1:2[4] 1:3[3] 1:5[2] 1:7[2] 1:9[2] 1:10[2] 1:11[3] 1:12[4] 1:13[4] 1:17[2] 1:19 1:20[2] 1:21 1:23[3] 1:23 1:24[4] 1:25[4] 2:2[2] 2:3 2:6 2:7[5] 2:8 2:9 2:10 2:11 2:12[2]

2:13[2] 2:14[2] 2:15[2] 2:16 2:17[2] 2:18[2] 2:24 2:25 3:1[4] 3:3 3:4[4] 3:5[2] 3:7[3] 3:12[5] 3:15[2] 3:17 3:18[4] 3:19 3:20[3] 3:21[6] 3:22 4:1[3] 4:2[4] 4:3[3] 4:4 4:5[2] 4:6[3] 4:7 4:8 4:10[3] 4:11 4:12 4:14[2] 4:17[4] 4:18[3] 4:19[2] 5:1[3] 5:2[2] 5:3 5:4 5:5[3] 5:6 5:8 5:9[3] 5:10 5:12 5:13

2 PE

1:1 1:2 1:3 1:4[3] 1:8 1:10 1:11 1:12 1:16 1:17[2] 1:18 1:19[2] 1:20 1:21[3] 2:1[2] 2:2 2:4 2:5[5] 2:6 2:7[2] 2:9[4] 2:10[2] 2:11 2:12 2:13[2] 2:15[4] 2:16[3] 2:17 2:18[2] 2:19[2] 2:20[6] 2:21[2] 2:22[4] 3:2[5] 3:3 3:4[4] 3:5[5] 3:6 3:7[4] 3:8 3:9 3:10[8] 3:12[4] 3:15 3:16

3:17[2] 3:18

1 JO

1:1[2] 1:2[2] 1:3 1:5 1:6 1:7[3] 1:8 2:1[2] 2:2[3] 2:4 2:5 2:7[4] 2:8[2] 2:9 2:10 2:13[3] 2:14[3] 2:15[6] 2:16[8] 2:17[3] 2:18[2] 2:20 2:21[2] 2:22[3] 2:23[5] 2:24[4] 2:25 2:27[2] 3:1[3] 3:2 3:4[3] 3:8[6] 3:10[3] 3:11[2] 3:13 3:14 3:16[2] 3:17 3:19 3:23 3:24

4:1[2] 4:2[2] 4:3[2] 4:4 4:5[3] 4:6[2] 4:9[2] 4:10 4:14[4] 4:15 4:16 4:17 5:1 5:2 5:3 5:4[3] 5:5[2] 5:6[2] 5:7[3] 5:9[3] 5:10[3] 5:11 5:12[2] 5:13[4] 5:14 5:15 5:19 5:20[2]

2 JO

1[4] 2 3[4] 4 5 6[2] 7[2] 9[4] 13

3 JO

1[3] 3[3] 5 6 7 8 9[2] 10[2] 12 14

JUDE

1[2] 3[3] 4[2] 5[3] 6[3] 7[2] 8 9[4] 11[3] 12 13[2] 14[2] 17[2] 18 19 20 21[2] 23[3] 24 25

RE

1:1 1:2[2] 1:3[2] 1:4[2] 1:5[6] 1:7 1:8[4] 1:9[4] 1:10[2] 1:11[3] 1:12 1:13[5] 1:15

1:16 1:17[2] 1:18 1:19[3] 1:20[8] 2:1[5] 2:5 2:6[2] 2:7[5] 2:8[4] 2:9[2] 2:10 2:11[3] 2:12[3] 2:14[2] 2:15[2] 2:16 2:17[4] 2:18[3] 2:19[2] 2:23[2] 2:24[2] 2:26[2] 2:27 2:28 2:29[2] 3:1[4] 3:2 3:5[2] 3:6[2] 3:7[3] 3:9 3:10[4] 3:12[4] 3:13[2] 3:14[7] 3:18[2] 3:20[2] 3:22[2] 4:1 4:2[2] 4:3 4:4[2] 4:5[3] 4:6[4] 4:7[4] 4:8

4:9 4:10[3] 5:1[3] 5:2[2] 5:3[2] 5:4 5:5[6] 5:6[7] 5:7[3] 5:8[4] 5:9[2] 5:10 5:11[5] 5:12 5:13[5] 5:14[2] 6:1[4] 6:3[2] 6:4 6:5[2] 6:6[4] 6:7[3] 6:8[4] 6:9[4] 6:10 6:12[3] 6:13[2] 6:14 6:15[9] 6:16[5] 6:17 7:1[7] 7:2[6] 7:3[4] 7:4[3] 7:5[3] 7:6[3] 7:7[3] 7:8[3] 7:9[2] 7:10[2] 7:11[5] 7:13 7:14[2] 7:15[2] 7:16[3] 7:17[3]

8:1[2] 8:2 8:3[4] 8:4[5] 8:5[4] 8:6[2] 8:7[3] 8:8[4] 8:9[5] 8:10[4] 8:11[5] 8:12[10] 8:13[6] 9:1[4] 9:2[7] 9:3[4] 9:4[3] 9:5 9:7[3] 9:8[2] 9:9[2] 9:11[4] 9:13[3] 9:14[4] 9:15[2] 9:16[4] 9:17[5] 9:18[4] 9:20[3] 10:1 10:2[2] 10:4[2] 10:5[3] 10:6[5] 10:7[5] 10:8[6] 10:9[2] 10:10[2] 11:1[3] 11:2[4] 11:4[4] 11:6[2] 11:7[2] 11:8[2] 11:9 11:10[2] 11:11

11:13[6] 11:14[2] 11:15[3] 11:16 11:18[6] 11:19[2] 12:1[2] 12:4[5] 12:6[2] 12:7[2] 12:9[4] 12:10[3] 12:11[4] 12:12[4] 12:13[4] 12:14[4] 12:15[3] 12:16[5] 12:17[5] 13:1[4] 13:2[4] 13:3[2] 13:4[4] 13:7 13:8[5] 13:10[5] 13:11 13:12[4] 13:13[2] 13:14[7] 13:15[6] 13:18[3] 14:1 14:2[3] 14:3[5] 14:4[3] 14:5 14:6[3] 14:7[3] 14:8[2] 14:9[2] 14:10[8] 14:11[3] 14:12[4] 14:13[3] 14:14[2] 14:15[5] 14:16[3]

14:17 14:18[5] 14:19[6] 14:20[5] 15:1[2] 15:2[5] 15:3[4] 15:5[3] 15:6[3] 15:7[3] 15:8[5] 16:1[5] 16:2[5] 16:3[4] 16:4[2] 16:5[2] 16:6 16:7 16:8 16:9 16:10[3] 16:11 16:12[6] 16:13[6] 16:14[5] 16:16 16:17[4] 16:18 16:19[6] 16:20 16:21[4] 17:1[4] 17:2[5] 17:3[2] 17:4 17:5[3] 17:6[5] 17:7[5] 17:8[7] 17:9[3] 17:10 17:11[3] 17:12[2] 17:13 17:14[2] 17:15[2] 17:16[3]

17:17[2] 17:18[3] 18:1 18:2[3] 18:3[7] 18:6 18:8 18:9[3] 18:10 18:11[2] 18:12 18:14 18:15[2] 18:17 18:18 18:19 18:21 18:22[2] 18:23[6] 18:24[2] 19:1 19:2[3] 19:4[3] 19:5 19:6[4] 19:7[2] 19:8[2] 19:9[3] 19:10[3] 19:13 19:14 19:15[3] 19:17[5] 19:18[5] 19:19[4] 19:20[4] 19:21[4] 20:1[2] 20:2[2] 20:3[3] 20:4[4] 20:5[4] 20:6[2] 20:7 20:8[6] 20:9[5] 20:10[4]

20:11[2] 20:12[5] 20:13[3] 20:14[2] 20:15[2] 21:1[2] 21:2 21:3 21:4 21:5 21:6[4] 21:8[4] 21:9[5] 21:10[2] 21:11 21:12[4] 21:13[4] 21:14[5] 21:15[3] 21:16[8] 21:17[3] 21:18[3] 21:19[7] 21:20[8] 21:21[3] 21:22[3] 21:23[6] 21:24[4] 21:25 21:26[2] 21:27 22:1[2] 22:2[8] 22:3[2] 22:5[2] 22:6[3] 22:7[2] 22:8[2] 22:9[2] 22:10[3] 22:13[4] 22:14[3] 22:16[4] 22:17[3] 22:18[3] 22:19[5] 22:21

THEE

4571

GE

3:11[2] 3:15 3:16 3:17 3:18 4:7 4:12 6:14 6:18[2] 6:19 6:20 6:21[2] 7:1 7:2 8:16 8:17 12:1[2] 12:2 12:3[2] 12:12[2] 12:13[2] 13:8 13:9 13:15 13:17 15:7 16:2 16:5[2] 16:6 17:2 17:4 17:6[2]

17:7[4] 17:8 17:9 17:10 17:16 17:18 17:19 17:20 17:21 18:3 18:10 18:14 18:25[2] 19:5 19:9 19:17 19:21 19:22 20:6[2] 20:7 20:9 20:15 20:16 21:12 21:17 21:22 21:23 22:2[2] 22:17 23:6 23:11[2] 23:13 23:15 24:2

24:3 24:7 24:8 24:12 24:14 24:17 24:23 24:40 24:41 24:43 24:45 24:50 24:51 25:30 26:2 26:3 26:24 26:28[2] 26:29[2] 27:3 27:4 27:7 27:8 27:10 27:19 27:21 27:25 27:28 27:29[3] 27:37 27:42 27:45[2] 28:2 28:3

28:4[2] 28:13 28:14 28:15[3] 28:22 29:18 29:19 29:25 29:27 30:2 30:14 30:15 30:16 30:26[2] 30:27 30:29 30:30 30:31 31:3 31:12 31:13 31:16 31:27 31:32 31:35 31:38 31:39 31:41 31:42 31:44 31:48 31:49 31:50 31:51

31:52 32:6 32:9 32:11 32:12 32:17[3] 32:26 32:29 33:5 33:10 33:11[2] 33:12 33:14 33:15 35:1 35:11 35:12[2] 37:10 37:13 37:14 37:16 38:16[2] 38:17 38:18 38:25 38:29 39:9 40:13 40:14[2] 40:19[3] 41:15 41:39 41:41 41:44

42:37[2] 43:4 43:9[2] 43:29 44:8 44:18 44:32 44:33 45:11 46:3 46:4[2] 47:4 47:5 47:6 47:29[2] 48:2 48:4[4] 48:5[2] 48:9 48:20[2] 48:22 49:8 49:25[2] 50:5 50:6 50:17[3]

EX

2:7[2] 2:9 2:14 3:10 3:12[3]

3:18 4:1 4:5 4:8 4:12 4:13 4:14[2] 4:16 4:18 4:23 5:3 6:29 7:1 7:2 7:15 7:16 8:4 8:9[2] 8:11 8:21 8:29 9:15 9:16[2] 9:30 10:17 10:28 11:8[2] 12:24 12:48 13:5[2] 13:7[2] 13:9[2] 13:11[3] 13:14

14:12 15:7 15:11[2] 15:17 15:26[2] 17:5 17:6 18:6 18:14 18:18[2] 18:19[2] 18:22[2] 18:23 19:9[3] 19:24[2] 20:2 20:4 20:12 20:24[2] 21:13 22:25 23:5 23:7 23:15 23:20[3] 23:23[2] 23:25 23:27[2] 23:28[2] 23:29[2] 23:30 23:31 23:33[2] 24:12

25:9 25:16 25:21 25:22[3] 25:40 26:30 27:8 27:20 28:1 29:35 29:42 30:6 30:23 30:34 30:36 30:37 31:6 31:11 32:4 32:7 32:8 32:10 32:21 32:32 32:34[2] 33:2 33:3[2] 33:5[4] 33:12 33:13[2] 33:14[2] 33:17 33:18 33:19[2]

33:22[2] 34:1 34:3 34:9 34:10 34:11[2] 34:12 34:15 34:17 34:18 34:24 34:27

LE

9:2 10:9 10:14 10:15 19:13 19:19 19:33 21:8 24:2 25:6[2] 25:8[2] 25:15 25:35[2] 25:36 25:39[2] 25:40[2] 25:41 25:47[2]

NU

5:19 5:20 5:21 6:24[2] 6:25[2] 6:26[2] 10:2 10:3 10:4 10:29 10:31 10:32 10:35[2] 11:15 11:16 11:17[3] 11:23 12:11 12:13 14:12 14:15 14:17 14:19 16:10[2] 18:1[2] 18:2[4] 18:4 18:7 18:8 18:9 18:10 18:11[2]

18:12 18:19[4] 19:2 20:17 21:7 21:29 22:6 22:8 22:9 22:16[2] 22:17[2] 22:20[2] 22:28 22:29 22:30 22:32 22:33 22:34 22:35 22:37[3] 22:38 23:3 23:11 23:13 23:26 23:27[2] 24:9[2] 24:10 24:11[2] 24:14 24:22 27:12 27:18

DE

1:21[2] 1:31 1:38 2:7[2] 2:9 2:19 2:25[4] 2:31 3:25 3:26 3:27 4:21 4:23 4:30 4:31[2] 4:32 4:35 4:36[3] 4:37 4:38[3] 4:40[4] 5:6 5:8 5:12 5:15[2] 5:16[3] 5:27 5:28 5:31[2] 6:2 6:3[2] 6:6

6:10[2] 6:12 6:15[2] 6:17 6:18 6:19 6:20 7:1[2] 7:2 7:4 7:6 7:11 7:12 7:13[4] 7:15[3] 7:16[2] 7:19 7:20 7:22[2] 7:23 7:24 7:25 8:1 8:2[3] 8:3[4] 8:4 8:5 8:7 8:10 8:11 8:14 8:15[2] 8:16[4] 8:18

9:3[2] 9:4[2] 9:5 9:6 9:12 9:14 10:1[2] 10:10 10:12 10:13 10:21 10:22 11:29 12:1 12:7 12:14 12:15 12:20 12:21[3] 12:25[2] 12:28[3] 12:29 12:30 13:1 13:2 13:5[3] 13:6 13:7[2] 13:10[2] 13:12 13:17[3] 13:18 14:2 14:24[3]

14:27 14:29[2] 15:4[2] 15:5 15:6[3] 15:7 15:9[2] 15:10 15:11 15:12[3] 15:13 15:14 15:15[2] 15:16[4] 15:18[5] 16:1 16:4 16:5 16:9 16:10 16:15 16:17 16:18[2] 16:20 16:21[2] 16:22 17:2 17:4 17:8[2] 17:9 17:10[2] 17:11[3] 17:14 17:15[3]

18:9 18:12 18:14[2] 18:15[2] 18:18 19:1 19:2[2] 19:3[2] 19:7 19:8 19:9[2] 19:10[2] 19:13 19:14 20:1[2] 20:11[4] 20:12[2] 20:14 20:15 20:16 20:17 20:20 21:1 21:23 22:2[2] 22:6 22:7[2] 22:12 23:4 23:5[2] 23:9 23:13 23:14[4] 23:15

23:16 23:20 23:21[2] 23:22 24:4 24:11 24:13[2] 24:15[2] 24:18[2] 24:19 24:22 25:3 25:15 25:17 25:18[3] 25:19[2] 26:1 26:2 26:11 26:16 26:18[2] 26:19 27:2[2] 27:3[2] 27:10 28:1[2] 28:2[2] 28:7[2] 28:8[3] 28:9[2] 28:10 28:11[2] 28:12 28:13[2]

28:14 28:15[3] 28:20 28:21[2] 28:22[2] 28:23 28:24 28:25 28:27 28:28 28:29 28:31 28:35 28:36[2] 28:37 28:43[2] 28:44 28:45[4] 28:46 28:48[2] 28:49 28:51[2] 28:52[3] 28:53[2] 28:55 28:57 28:60[2] 28:61 28:64 28:65 28:66 28:68[2] 29:12 29:13[3] 30:1[3] 30:2[3] 30:3[2] 30:4[2] 30:5[3] 30:7[2] 30:8 30:9[2] 30:11[2] 30:14 30:15 30:16[2] 31:3 31:6[3] 31:8[4] 31:23 31:26 32:6[3] 32:7[2] 32:18[2] 32:49 32:52 33:10 33:27 33:29[2] 34:4

JOS

1:5[4] 1:7 1:9[2] 1:17[2] 2:3 2:14 2:18 2:19 3:7[2] 5:2 7:10 7:13 7:19 7:25 8:1 8:2 9:25 10:8 13:6 14:6 17:15[2]

JG

1:3 1:24[2] 3:19 3:20 4:6 4:7 4:9 4:14 4:19 4:20 4:22 5:14 6:12 6:14 6:16 6:18[3] 6:23 6:39 7:2 7:4[6] 7:9 9:31 9:32 9:33 10:10 10:15[2] 11:8 11:17 11:19 11:24 11:27 11:36 12:1[2] 13:4 13:15[3] 13:17 14:15 14:16 15:2 15:12[2] 15:13[3] 16:5 16:6[2] 16:9 16:10 16:12 16:14 16:15 16:20 16:28[2] 17:2 17:3 17:10 18:3 18:5 18:19 18:23 18:24 18:25 19:6 19:8 19:11 19:20

RU

1:10 1:16[2] 1:17 2:4 2:9 2:12 2:19 2:22 3:1[2] 3:3[3] 3:4[2] 3:11 3:13[3] 3:15 4:4[3] 4:8 4:12 4:14 4:15[3]

1 SA

1:8 1:14 1:17 1:23 1:26 2:2 2:15 2:20 2:34 2:36 3:9 3:17[4] 8:7[2] 8:8 9:3 9:16 9:17 9:18 9:19[2] 9:20 9:23[3] 9:24[2] 9:26 9:27 10:1 10:2 10:3 10:4[2] 10:6 10:7[3] 10:8[3] 10:15 11:1 11:3 11:5 11:10 13:13 13:14 14:7[2] 14:36 14:40 15:1 15:16 15:17 15:18 15:23 15:25 15:26[2] 15:28 15:30 16:1 16:2 16:3[2] 16:15 16:16[2] 16:22 17:37 17:45 17:46[3] 18:17 18:22[2] 19:2[2] 19:3[2] 19:4 19:17 20:4 20:8 20:9[3] 20:10 20:12[2] 20:13[4] 20:21[2] 20:22[2] 20:23 20:29[2] 20:37 20:42 21:1 21:2[2] 22:3 22:5 23:11 23:12 23:17[2] 23:27 24:4[2] 24:10[3] 24:11[2] 24:12[3] 24:13 24:15 24:17 24:19 25:6 25:8[2] 25:24 25:25 25:26 25:28[2] 25:29 25:30[2] 25:31 25:32 25:34 25:40[2] 26:6 26:8 26:11 26:15 26:19[2] 26:21 26:23 27:5 28:2 28:8[2] 28:10 28:11 28:15 28:16 28:18 28:19 28:22[2] 29:6[2] 29:8 29:10 30:7 30:15

2 SA

1:4 1:9 1:16 1:26 2:21[3] 2:22[2] 3:12[2] 3:13[2] 3:21 3:24 3:25 5:2 5:24 7:3 7:8 7:9[2] 7:11[3] 7:12 7:15 7:16 7:20 7:22[2] 7:23 7:24 7:26 7:27[2] 7:29[2] 9:7[2] 10:3[2] 10:11[2] 11:12 11:20 11:25 12:7[2] 12:8[2] 12:11 12:12 12:14 13:5[3] 13:6 13:13[3] 13:20 13:24 13:25 13:26[2] 14:2 14:5 14:8 14:10[2] 14:11 14:12 14:17 14:18[2] 14:19 14:32[2] 15:3 15:7 15:20[2] 15:26 15:31 15:35 16:4 16:8 16:9 16:21 17:3 17:11 18:11 18:12 18:14 18:22 18:31 18:32 18:33 19:6 19:7[3] 19:21[2] 19:33 19:37[2] 19:38[2] 19:41 20:16 20:21 20:30 20:50 24:10 24:12[3] 24:13[2] 24:17 24:21 24:23 24:24

1 KI

1:12[2] 1:13 1:14 1:30 2:4 2:8[2] 2:14 2:16 2:17[2] 2:18 2:20[3] 2:26[2] 2:36 2:42[2] 2:43 3:5 3:6[2] 3:12[5] 3:13[2] 5:6 6:12 6:26 8:13[2] 8:23 8:25 8:27 8:28 8:33[3] 8:35 8:40 8:43[2] 8:46 8:47 8:48[2] 8:50[2] 8:52 9:4 9:5 10:8 10:9[3] 10:11[2] 10:31[2] 10:35 10:37 10:38[4] 12:4 12:10 12:28 13:2[3] 13:7 13:8 13:16[3] 13:18 13:21 13:22 14:2[2] 14:3[2] 14:5 14:6 14:7[2] 14:8 14:9[2] 14:12 15:19[2] 16:2[2] 17:3[2] 17:4 17:9[2] 17:10 17:11 17:13 17:18 17:21 18:10[2] 18:12[3] 18:41 18:44[2] 19:7 19:20[3] 20:5 20:6 20:22 20:25 20:31 20:32 20:34[2] 20:35 20:36 20:37 21:2[3] 21:3 21:4 21:6[3] 21:7 21:14 21:20 21:21 22:5 22:13 22:16 22:18 22:23 22:24

2 KI

1:10 1:12 1:13 2:2[2] 2:4[2] 2:6[2] 2:9[3] 2:10[2] 2:16 2:19 3:13[2] 3:14[2] 4:2 4:3 4:4 4:10 4:13 4:22 4:24 4:26[2] 4:29 4:30 5:6[2] 5:10 5:13[2] 5:15 5:17 5:22 5:26[2] 5:27 6:1 6:2 6:3 6:7 6:17 6:18 6:27[2] 6:28 7:13 8:4 8:9 8:14 9:3[2] 9:5[2] 9:6 9:11 9:12 9:18 9:19 9:26 14:10[2] 18:23[2] 18:26 18:27 19:9 19:10 19:19 19:21[3] 19:28 19:29 20:3[2] 20:5 20:6 20:14 20:18 22:19 22:20

1 CH

11:2 12:18[2] 14:15 16:18 17:2 17:7 17:8[3] 17:10[2] 17:11 17:13 17:18 17:20[2] 17:21 17:24 17:25 17:27[2] 19:3[2] 19:12[2] 21:8 21:10[3] 21:11 21:12 21:23[2] 22:9 22:11[2] 22:12[2] 22:15 22:16 28:9[2] 28:10 28:20[3] 28:21[2] 29:12 29:13 29:14[2] 29:15 29:16 29:17 29:18

2 CH

1:7 1:11 1:12[4] 2:11 2:16 6:2 6:14[2] 6:16 6:18 6:19 6:24[2] 6:26 6:31 6:33[2] 6:34 6:36 6:37 6:38 6:39 6:40 7:17[2] 7:18 9:7 9:8[3] 10:4 10:5 10:10 14:11[3] 16:3[2] 18:3 18:4 18:12 18:15 18:17 18:22 18:23 19:2 19:3 20:2 20:6 20:8 20:9 20:12 25:7 25:8 25:9 25:16 25:19[2] 26:18 34:27 34:28 35:21[4]

EZR

4:12 5:10 7:13 7:18 7:19 9:6 9:15[2] 10:4[2]

NE

1:5 1:6[2] 1:7 1:8 1:11[2] 4:5[2] 6:7 6:10[2] 9:6 9:8 9:10 9:18 9:26[2] 9:27 9:28[3] 9:32 9:35

ES

3:11[2] 5:3 5:6 7:2 9:12

JOB

1:11 1:15 1:16 1:17 1:19 2:5 4:2 4:5[2] 4:7 5:1 5:19[2] 5:20 5:23 7:20[2] 8:6 8:8 8:10[2] 8:18 8:22 10:3 10:9 10:13 11:3 11:5 11:6[2] 11:18 11:19[2] 12:7[2] 12:8[3] 13:20 14:3 14:5 14:15 15:6[2] 15:11[2] 15:12 15:17 16:3 17:3 18:4 22:4[3] 22:10[2] 22:11 22:21 22:22 22:27 22:28 26:3 30:20 33:1 33:7[2] 33:12 33:32 33:33 35:3 35:4[2] 36:2 36:4 36:16 36:17 36:18[2] 38:3 38:17 38:34 38:35 39:9 39:10 40:4 40:7 40:14[2] 40:15 41:3[2] 41:4 42:2 42:4[2] 42:5[2] 42:7

PS

2:7 2:8 5:2 5:3 5:4 5:10 5:11[2] 6:5[2] 7:1 7:7 9:1 9:2 9:10[2] 10:14 16:1 16:2 17:6 17:7 18:1 18:29 18:49 20:1[2] 20:2[2] 20:4 21:4 21:8 21:11 22:4 22:5[2] 22:10 22:19 22:22 22:25 22:27 25:1 25:2 25:3 25:5 25:16 25:20 25:21 27:8 28:1 28:2 30:1 30:2 30:8 30:9 30:12[2] 31:1 31:14 31:17 31:19[2] 31:22 32:5 32:6 32:8[3] 32:9 33:22 35:10 35:18[2] 36:9 36:10 37:4 37:34 38:9[2] 38:15 39:5 39:7 39:12 40:5 40:16[2] 41:4 42:1 42:6 43:4 44:5 44:17 45:2 45:4 45:5 45:7 45:8 45:14 45:17 49:18 50:7 50:8 50:12 50:15 50:17 50:21 51:4[2] 51:13 52:5[4] 52:9 53:5 54:6 55:22 55:23 56:3 56:9 56:12 57:1 57:9[2] 59:9 59:17 60:4 61:2 62:12 63:1[3] 63:2 63:3 63:4 63:5 63:6[2] 63:8 65:1[2] 65:2 65:4 66:3 66:4[2] 66:13 66:15 67:3[2] 67:5[2] 68:29 69:5 69:6[2] 69:9 69:13 69:19 70:4[2] 71:1 71:6[2] 71:14 71:19 71:22[2] 71:23 72:5 73:22 73:23 73:25[2] 73:27[2] 74:22 74:23 75:1[2] 76:10 77:16[2] 79:6 79:11 79:12 79:13 80:14 80:18 81:7[3] 81:8 81:9 81:10 81:16 83:2 83:5 84:4 84:5 84:12 85:6 86:2 86:3 86:4 86:5 86:7 86:8 86:9 86:12 86:14 87:3 87:7 88:1 88:2 88:9[2] 88:10 88:13[2] 89:8[2] 90:8 90:13 91:3 91:4 91:7 91:10 91:11[2] 91:12 94:20 101:1 102:1 102:28 103:4 104:27 105:11 108:3[2] 114:5 116:4 116:7 116:17 116:19 118:21 118:25[2] 118:28[2] 119:7 119:10 119:11 119:62 119:63 119:74 119:76 119:79 119:108 119:120 119:126 119:146 119:164 119:168 119:169 119:170 119:175 120:3[2] 121:3 121:6 121:7 122:6 122:8 123:1 128:2 128:5 130:1 130:4 134:4 135:9 137:5 137:6 137:8 138:1[2] 138:4 139:12[2] 139:14 139:15 139:18 139:20 139:21[2] 141:1 141:2 141:8[2] 142:5 143:6[2] 143:8[2] 143:9 144:9[2] 145:1 145:2 145:10 145:15 147:13 147:14

PR

1:10 2:1 2:11[2] 2:12 2:16 3:2 3:3 3:28 3:29 3:20 4:6[2] 4:8[2] 4:9 4:11[2] 4:24[2] 4:25 5:17 5:19 6:22[3] 6:24 6:25 7:1 7:5 7:15[2] 9:8[2] 20:22 22:18 22:19[2] 22:20 22:21[2] 22:27 23:1 23:7[2] 23:11 23:22 23:25 25:7 25:8 25:10 25:16 25:17[2] 25:22 27:2 29:17 30:6 30:7 30:9 30:10

EC

2:1 7:21 8:2 9:9 10:4 10:16 11:9

CA

1:3 1:4[3] 1:9 1:11 4:7 6:1 6:13 7:5 7:12 7:13 8:1[2] 8:2[3] 8:5[4]

ISA

1:25 2:10 3:12[2] 7:5 7:11 7:17 8:1 9:3 10:24[2] 12:1 12:6 14:3 14:8 14:9[3] 14:10 14:11[2] 14:16[3] 14:29 16:4 16:9[3] 19:12 22:1 22:3 22:15 22:16 22:17[2] 22:18 22:19[2] 24:17 25:1 25:3[2] 26:3[2] 26:8[2] 26:9[2] 26:13[2] 26:16 26:20 29:3[3] 29:11 29:12 30:19[2] 30:21 30:22 33:1[3] 33:2 36:8[2] 36:11 36:12 37:9 37:10 37:22[3] 37:29 37:30 38:3[2] 38:6 38:7 38:18[2] 38:19 39:3 39:7 40:9 41:9[4] 41:10[4] 41:11[2] 41:12[2] 41:14 41:15 42:5[3] 43:1[4] 43:2[3] 43:3 43:4[2] 43:5[2] 43:23[2] 44:2[3] 44:8 44:21 44:22 44:24 45:2 45:3[2] 45:4[2] 45:5 45:14[5] 47:3 47:5 47:9[2] 47:10 47:11[3] 47:13[2] 47:15[2] 48:5[2] 48:6 48:9[2] 48:10[2] 48:17[2] 49:6 49:7 49:8[4] 49:15 49:16 49:17[2] 49:18[3] 49:19 49:23 49:25 49:26 51:16 51:19[3] 51:23 52:1 52:14 54:6 54:7[2] 54:8[2] 54:9[2] 54:10[2] 54:14 54:15 54:17[2] 55:5[3] 57:8 57:12 57:13 58:8 58:9 58:11 58:12 58:14[2] 59:12 59:21 60:1 60:2[2] 60:4 60:5[2] 60:6 60:7[2] 60:9 60:10[3] 60:11 60:12 60:13 60:14[4] 60:15[2] 60:19[2] 62:4 62:5[2] 64:4 64:5 64:7 64:9 64:11 65:15

JER

1:5[4] 1:7[2] 1:8[2] 1:10 1:17[2] 1:18 1:19[4] 2:2 2:17 2:19[3] 2:21 2:22[2] 2:28[2] 2:31 2:35 3:19[2] 3:22 4:14 4:18 4:30[2] 5:7 6:8[2] 6:23 6:26[2] 6:27 7:16 7:27[2] 10:6 10:7[3] 10:25 11:15 11:17[2] 11:20 12:1[2] 12:3 12:5[2] 12:6[3] 13:1 13:6 13:12 13:20 13:21[3] 13:27 14:7 14:20 14:22 15:2 15:5[2] 15:6[2] 15:11 15:14 15:19[2] 15:20[6] 15:21[2] 16:2 16:10 16:19 17:4[2] 17:13 17:16[2] 18:2 18:20 18:23 19:2 19:10 20:4 20:12 20:15 21:2 21:13 22:6 22:7 22:21 22:23 22:24 22:25 22:26[2] 23:33 23:37 25:15 26:2 27:2 28:8 28:15 28:16 29:22 29:26 30:2[2] 30:10 30:11[6] 30:14[3] 30:15 30:16[3] 30:17[3] 31:3[2] 31:4 31:21[2] 31:23 32:7[2] 32:8 32:17 32:20 32:25 33:3[2] 34:3 34:4 34:5[3] 34:14[3] 36:2[3] 36:19 36:28 37:18 37:20[3] 38:4 38:10 38:14 38:15[2] 38:16[2] 38:20[4] 38:22 38:25[5] 39:12 39:16 39:17 39:18[2] 40:4[6] 40:5 40:14 40:15[3] 42:2[2] 42:5 43:2 43:3 44:16 45:2 45:5 46:14[2] 46:27 46:28[5] 48:2 48:18 48:27 48:32 48:43 48:46 49:5[2] 49:9 49:15 49:16[2] 50:21 50:24 50:31[2] 50:42 51:14[2] 51:20[2] 51:21[2] 51:22[3] 51:23[3] 51:25[4] 51:26 51:36

LA

1:22 2:13[5] 2:14[2] 2:15 2:16 2:17 3:57 4:21 4:22 5:21

EZE

2:2 2:3 2:4 2:6 2:8[2] 3:3 3:4 3:6[2] 3:7 3:10 3:11 3:17 3:22 3:25[2] 3:27 4:1 4:3[2] 4:5 4:6 4:8[2] 4:9[2] 4:15 5:1[3] 5:8[2] 5:9 5:10[3] 5:11 5:12[3] 5:14[2] 5:15[2] 5:17[3] 7:3[4] 7:4[3] 7:6 7:7 7:8[4] 7:9[2] 8:6 8:13 8:15 12:3 12:6 12:9 16:4 16:5[3] 16:6[4] 16:7 16:8[5] 16:9[3] 16:10[3] 16:11 16:14 16:17 16:19[2] 16:23 16:24[2] 16:27[3] 16:33 16:34[3] 16:37 16:38[2] 16:39[3] 16:40[3] 16:41[2] 16:42[2] 16:44 16:57 16:59 16:60[2] 16:61 16:62 16:63 20:47[2] 21:3[2] 21:4 21:7 21:16 21:19 21:29[3] 21:30 21:31[3] 22:4 22:5[2] 22:6 22:7[3]

22:9^3 22:10^2 22:11 22:12 22:13 22:14 22:15^3 23:22^2 23:24^3 23:25^2 23:26 23:27 23:28 23:29 23:30 24:2 24:13^2 24:14 24:16 24:17 24:26^2 25:4^3 25:7^5 26:3^2 26:8^3 26:10 26:14 26:15 26:17^2 26:19^3 26:20^2 26:21 27:5 27:7 27:8 27:9^2 27:10 27:15 27:21 27:25 27:26^2 27:27^2 27:30 27:31^2 27:32^2 27:34 27:35 27:36 28:3 28:4 28:7 28:8 28:9^2 28:13 28:14 28:15 28:16^3 28:17^3 28:18^4 28:19^2 28:22^2 29:3 29:4 29:5^3 29:7^2 29:8^2 29:10 29:21 32:3^2 32:4^4 32:6 32:7 32:8 32:10^2 32:11 33:7 33:30 33:31^2 35:3^3 35:6^3 35:9 35:11 35:14 35:15 36:12 36:15 37:16 37:18 38:3 38:4^2 38:6 38:7 38:9 38:13 38:15 38:16^2 38:17 39:1 39:2^4 39:4^2 40:4 44:5

DA

1:12 1:13 2:23^3 2:29^2 2:31 2:37 2:38 2:39^2 3:12 3:16 3:18 4:9^2 4:18 4:19^2 4:25^4 4:26 4:27 4:31^2 4:32^3 5:10 5:14^2 5:16 5:23 6:7 6:12 6:13 6:16 6:20 6:22 8:19 9:7^2 9:8 9:15 9:16 9:18 9:22 9:23 10:11^2 10:14 10:19 10:20 10:21 11:2

HO

1:2 2:19^2 2:20 3:3 4:5 4:6 5:8 6:4^2 6:11 8:2 8:5 11:8^4 11:9 12:9 13:5 13:10 13:11 14:3

JOE

1:19 1:20 3:11 4:12^2 5:17

AM

6:10 7:2 7:5 7:10 7:12

OB

2 3 4 5^2 7^5 10 15

JON

1:8 1:11 1:14^3 2:7 2:9 3:2 4:2^2 4:3

MIC

1:13 1:15 1:16^3 2:11 2:12 4:8 4:9^2 4:10 4:11 5:2 5:10 5:13 5:14 6:3^2 6:4^3 6:8^2 6:13^3 6:14 6:15 6:16 7:12 7:17 7:18

NA

1:11 1:12^2 1:13 1:14 1:15 2:13 3:5 3:6^3 3:7^3 3:13 3:14 3:15^3 3:19^2

HAB

1:2 2:7^2 2:8 2:16 2:17 3:10

ZEP

2:5 3:11 3:12 3:15 3:17^3 3:18 3:19

HAG

2:23^3

ZEC

1:9 2:10 2:11^2 3:2^2 3:4^2 3:7 3:8 9:9 9:11 9:12 9:13 11:15 14:1 14:5

MAL

1:7 1:8 2:14 3:8 3:13

MT

1:20 2:6 2:13 3:14 4:6^2 4:9 4:10 5:23 5:25^2 5:26 5:29^3 5:30^3 5:39 5:40 5:41 5:42^2 6:2 6:4 6:6 6:18 6:23 8:13 8:19 8:29 9:2 9:5 9:22 11:10 11:21^2 11:23 11:24 11:25 12:38 12:47 14:4 14:28 15:28 16:17 16:18 16:19 16:22^2 16:23 17:4 17:27 18:8^3 18:9^3 18:15^3 18:16^2 18:17 18:22 18:26 18:29 18:32 18:33 18:27 20:13 20:14 21:5 21:19 21:23 23:27 25:21 25:23 25:24 25:37^3 25:38^3 25:39^2 25:44^2 26:17 26:33 26:34 26:35^2 26:62 26:63 26:68 26:73 27:13

MK

1:2 1:24^2 1:37 2:5 2:9 3:32 5:7^2 5:19^2 5:23 5:31 5:34 5:41 6:18 6:22 6:23 8:33 9:5 9:17 9:25 9:34 9:43^2 9:45^2 9:47^2 10:28 10:49 10:51 10:52 11:14 11:28 14:30 14:31^2 14:36 14:60 15:4

LU

1:3 1:13 1:19^2 1:28 1:35^3 1:48 4:6 4:8 4:10^2 4:11 4:34^2 5:20 5:23 5:24 6:29 6:30 7:7 7:14 7:20 7:27 7:40 7:47 7:50 8:20 8:28^2 8:39 8:45^2 8:48 9:33 9:38 9:57 9:61 10:13^2 10:21 10:35 11:7 11:27 11:35 11:36 12:20 12:58^3 12:59 13:31^2 13:34 14:9^2 14:10^3 14:12^2 14:14 14:18 14:19 15:18 15:29 16:2 16:27 17:3 17:4^2 17:19 18:11 18:28 18:41 18:42 19:21 19:22 19:43^4 19:44^3 20:2 22:11 22:32 22:33 22:34 22:64 23:43 23:48

JOH

1:48^2 1:50^2 2:4 3:3 3:5 3:7 3:11 3:26 4:10^2 4:26 5:10 5:12 5:14 6:30 7:20 8:10 8:11 9:21 9:37 10:33 11:8 11:22 11:28 11:40 11:41 13:8 13:37 13:38 16:30 17:1 17:3 17:4 17:5 17:7 17:8 17:11 17:13 17:21 17:25^2 18:26 18:30 18:34 18:35 19:10^2 19:11^2 21:3 21:15 21:16 21:17 21:18^3 21:20 21:22 21:23

AC

3:6 5:9 7:3^2 7:27 7:34 7:35 8:20 8:22 8:34 9:5 9:6 9:17 9:34 10:6 10:19 10:20 10:22^2 10:32 10:33^2 11:14 12:9 13:11 13:33 13:47 16:18 17:32 18:10^3 21:21 21:23 21:24 21:37 21:39 22:10^2 22:14 22:18 22:19 22:21 23:3 23:18^2 23:20 23:21 23:30^2 23:35 24:2 24:4^2 24:8 24:14 24:19 24:25 25:26 26:2 26:3^2 26:14 26:16^3 26:17^2 26:24 27:24 28:21^2

RO

2:4 2:27 4:17 9:17^2 10:8 11:21 11:22 13:4 15:3 15:9

1 CO

4:7 8:10 12:21

2 CO

6:2^2 12:9

GA

3:8

EPH

5:14 6:3

PHP

4:3

1 TI

1:3 1:18^2 3:14^2 4:14^2 4:16 5:21 6:13 6:21

2 TI

1:3 1:4 1:5^2 1:6^2 1:14 2:7 3:15 3:17 4:1 4:11 4:13 4:21

TIT

1:5^2 2:15 3:12 3:15

PHM

4 7 8 9 10 11^2 16 18^2 19 20 21 23

HEB

1:5 1:9 2:12 5:5 6:14^2 8:5 13:5^2

JAS

2:18

2 JO

5^2 13

3 JO

3 13 14^3

JUDE

9

RE

2:4 2:5 2:10 2:14 2:16 2:20 3:3^2 3:8 3:9 3:10 3:16 3:18 4:1 11:17^2 14:15 15:4^2 17:1 17:7 18:14^2 18:22^3 18:23^2 21:9

THEIR

846

GE

1:21 1:25 5:2 6:20 7:14 8:19 9:23^3 10:5^2 10:20^2 10:30 10:31^2 10:32 11:7 12:5 13:6 14:6 14:11 14:24 17:7 17:8 17:9 17:23 18:20 18:22 18:26 19:10 19:33 19:34 19:36 20:8 24:52 24:59 25:13 25:16^2 26:18 31:43 31:53 32:15 33:2 33:6 34:13 34:18 34:20^2 34:21 34:23^2 34:27 34:28^3 34:29^3 35:4^3 36:7^2 36:19 36:30 36:40^3 36:43^2 37:2 37:4 37:12 37:16 37:21 37:22 37:25^2 37:32 40:1 42:6 42:24 42:25 42:26 42:28 42:29 42:35^2 42:36 43:2 43:11 43:15 43:24^2 43:26 43:27 43:28 44:3 44:11 44:13 45:25 45:27 46:5^3 46:6^2 46:32^3 47:1^2 47:4 47:9 47:12 47:17^2 47:22^2 47:30 48:6^2 49:5 49:6^4 49:7^2 49:28 50:8^3 50:15 50:17

EX

1:11 1:14^2 2:11 2:16 2:17 2:18 2:23 2:24 3:7^3 4:5 4:31^2 5:4 5:5 5:6 5:10 5:21 6:4 6:6 6:14 6:16 6:17 6:19 6:25 6:26 7:11 7:12 7:19^4 7:22 8:7 8:18 8:26 10:7 10:23 12:3 12:34^4 12:42 12:51 13:20 14:10 14:22^2 14:25 14:26^2 14:29^2 16:1^2 17:1 18:7 18:23 19:7 19:10 19:14 21:32 22:23 23:24^3 23:26 23:27 23:32 23:33 25:20^3 25:34^2 25:36^2 25:40 26:21 26:25 26:29 26:32 26:37 27:10^2 27:11^2 27:12^2 27:14^2 27:15^2 27:16^2 27:17^2 27:18 27:21 28:10^2 28:12 28:20 28:21 28:38 28:42 29:10 29:15 29:19 29:20^2 29:25 29:28^2 29:45 29:46^2 30:12 30:19^2 30:21^3 31:16 32:3 32:4 32:15 32:25^2 32:32 32:34 33:6 34:13^3 34:15^2 34:16^4 35:17 35:18 35:25 36:26 36:30 36:34 36:36 36:38^4 37:9^3 37:22^2 38:10^3 38:11^3 38:12^3 38:14^2 38:15^2 38:17^2 38:19^2 38:28 39:13 39:14 39:15^3 40:31^2 40:36 40:38

LE

4:15 6:17 7:34 7:36 7:38 8:14 8:16 8:18 8:22 8:24^3 8:25 8:28 9:24 10:5 10:19^2 11:8^2 11:11^2 11:21 11:27 11:35 11:36 11:37 11:38 13:38 13:39 15:31^2 16:16^3 16:21^3 16:22 16:27^3 16:34 17:5 17:7^2 18:3 18:6 18:9 18:10 18:29 20:4 20:5 20:11 20:12 20:13 20:16 20:17 20:18 20:19 20:20 20:24 20:27 21:5^3 21:6^3 21:17 22:16 22:25 23:4 23:18^2 24:14 25:32 25:33 25:34^2 25:45 26:4 26:13 26:20 26:36^2 26:39^2 26:40^2 26:41^3 26:43^2 26:44^2 26:45^3

NU

1:2^4 1:3 1:16 1:17 1:18^4 1:20^4 1:22^4 1:24^3 1:26^3 1:28^3 1:30^3 1:32^3 1:34^3 1:36^3 1:38^3 1:40^3 1:42^3 1:45 1:47 1:52^2 2:2 2:3 2:4 2:9 2:10 2:16 2:17 2:18 2:24 2:25 2:31 2:32^2 2:34^3 3:10 3:15^2 3:17 3:18 3:19 3:20^2 3:31 3:37^3 3:39 3:40 3:45 4:2^2 4:22^2 4:26^2 4:27^3 4:28 4:29^2 4:31^2 4:32^6 4:33 4:34^2 4:36 4:38^2 4:40^2 4:42^2 4:44 4:46^2 5:3 5:7 6:15^2 7:2 7:3 7:7 7:8 7:9 7:10 7:11 7:87 8:7^2 8:10 8:12 8:21 8:22 8:26^2 9:17 9:18 9:20 9:22 9:23 10:6^2 10:12 10:13 10:14 10:18 10:22 10:25 10:28 11:10 11:12 11:33 13:2 13:4 13:33 14:1 14:5 14:6 14:9 14:23 15:25^3 15:38^2 16:15 16:22 16:26 16:27^2 16:32^2 16:38 16:45 17:2^3 17:3 17:6^3 17:10 18:11 18:17^2 18:20 18:21 18:23 20:6 20:8^2 20:11 20:18 21:2 21:3 21:18 22:7 24:2 24:8 25:2^2 25:18 26:2 26:12 26:15 26:20 26:23 26:26 26:28 26:35 26:37 26:38 26:41 26:42^2 26:44 26:48 26:50 26:55 26:57 26:59 27:5 27:7^2 27:14 27:19 28:2 28:14 28:20 28:28 28:31 29:3 29:6^2 29:9 29:11 29:14 29:18^3 29:19 29:21^3 29:24^3 29:27^3 29:30^3 29:33^3 29:37^3 30:9 31:9^4 31:10^2 31:29 32:17 32:38 33:1 33:2^4 33:4^2 33:12 33:52^3 34:14^4 34:15 35:2 35:3^3 35:7 36:3 36:4^2 36:6 36:11 36:12^2

DE

1:8 1:25 2:5 2:9 2:12 2:21 2:22 2:23 4:10 4:37 4:38 5:29 7:5^4 7:10 7:16 7:24^2 7:25 9:5 9:14 9:27^2 10:6 10:11 10:15 11:4^2 11:6^3 11:9 12:2 12:3^4 12:29 12:30^2 12:31^4 13:13 14:8^2 18:2^2 18:18 19:1^2 20:18^2 21:5 21:6 23:3 23:6^2 23:8 29:8 29:17^2 29:25 29:28 29:7 29:11 29:13 29:19 29:20 29:21^2 29:28 32:5 32:8 32:20 32:21 32:27 32:29 32:30 32:31 32:32^3 32:33 32:35^2 32:36 32:37^2 32:38^2 33:29

JOS

1:6 3:14 4:6 4:18 4:21 5:1 5:6 5:7^2 5:8 7:6 7:8^2 7:11 7:12^3 7:16 8:13 8:19 8:33^2 9:4 9:5^2 9:14 9:16 9:17^2 10:5 10:13 10:19 10:24 10:40 10:42 11:4 11:6^2 11:9^2 11:13 11:17 11:20 11:21 11:23^2 12:1 12:7 13:8 13:14 13:15 13:16 13:23 13:24 13:25 13:28^2 13:29 13:30 13:31 13:33 14:2 14:4^3 15:1 15:2 15:5 15:12 15:20 15:32 15:36 15:41 15:44 15:46 15:51 15:54 15:57 15:59 15:60 15:62 16:4 16:5^2 16:8 16:9 17:2^2 17:4 18:2 18:5^2 18:7^2 18:10 18:11^2 18:12 18:20 18:21 18:24 18:28^2 19:1^2 19:2 19:6 19:7 19:8 19:9 19:10^2 19:11 19:15 19:16^2 19:17 19:18 19:22^2 19:23^2 19:24 19:25 19:30 19:31^2 19:32 19:33 19:38 19:39^2 19:40 19:41 19:47 19:48^2 19:49 21:3^2 21:7 21:8 21:19 21:20 21:26 21:33^2 21:40^2 21:41 21:42 21:43 21:44^4 22:6 22:7^2 22:9 22:14 23:1 23:2^4 23:5 23:7 24:1^3 24:8

JG

1:4 1:7^3 2:2 2:3 2:4 2:10 2:12

2:14^{2} 2:17^{2} 2:18^{2} 2:19^{3} 2:20 2:22 3:4 3:6^{5} 3:7 3:25 5:18 5:20 5:22 6:5^{3} 6:9 7:2 7:6^{3} 7:8^{2} 7:12 7:19 7:20^{2} 8:3 8:10 8:21 8:26 8:28 8:33 8:34^{2} 9:3 9:24^{2} 9:26 9:27^{2} 9:57 10:12 12:2 13:20 14:17 14:19 15:13 16:18 16:23 16:24 16:25 18:1 18:2^{2} 18:8^{2} 18:14 18:16 18:23 18:26 18:29 19:14 19:21 19:22 20:13 20:22 20:33^{2} 20:42 21:2 21:6 21:22^{2} 21:23^{2}

RU

1:9 1:14

1 SA

1:19 2:20 2:26 2:33 5:9 6:6 6:7 6:10 6:11 6:13^{2} 8:9 9:22 9:16 10:4 10:12 10:21 11:4 12:9 14:30 14:46 15:24 17:1 17:18^{2} 17:51 17:53 18:27 21:13 22:17^{2} 23:5 25:12 28:1 28:23 29:1 30:2 30:3^{3} 30:4 31:9 31:13

2 SA

1:23^{2} 2:26 3:18 3:30 4:12^{2} 5:21 7:10 7:23 7:24 10:3 10:4^{3} 10:18 12:30 13:31 13:36 15:11 15:36 16:8 18:28 20:2 20:3 22:46 23:17 23:19

1 KI

2:4^{2} 2:15 2:33 4:8 4:27 7:26 7:31 7:33^{4} 8:7 8:23 8:25 8:35 8:37^{2} 8:44 8:45^{3} 8:48^{5} 8:49^{3} 8:50 8:66 9:9 9:21 10:5 10:29 11:2 11:8 12:16 12:27 13:11 13:12 14:15^{2} 14:22^{2} 14:27 14:30 15:16 15:32 16:2 16:13 16:26 18:28 18:37 18:39 19:21 20:6 20:23 20:24 20:25 20:32^{2} 22:10

2 KI

1:14 3:24 3:27 5:24 6:20 6:22 6:23 7:7^{4} 7:15 8:12^{4} 8:21 10:7 11:12 13:3 13:5 14:12 16:15^{2} 17:7 17:9^{2} 17:14^{3} 17:15 17:16 17:17^{2} 17:19 17:23 17:25 17:29^{2} 17:31 17:33 17:34^{2} 17:40 17:41^{4} 18:12 18:27^{2} 18:35 18:36 18:37 19:17 19:18 19:26 21:8 21:14^{2} 21:15 22:7 22:17 23:2 23:3^{2} 23:9 23:14 25:21 25:23^{2} 25:24

1 CH

1:29 3:9 3:19 4:1 4:27 4:31 4:32 4:33^{3} 4:38^{3} 4:39 4:41^{3} 4:42 5:7^{2} 5:9 5:10^{2} 5:13^{2} 5:15 5:16 5:20^{2} 5:21^{2} 5:22 5:24^{2} 5:25 6:19 6:32^{2} 6:33 6:44 6:48 6:54^{3} 6:57 6:60^{2} 6:62 6:63 6:64 6:65 6:66 7:2^{2} 7:4^{2} 7:5^{2} 7:7^{2} 7:9^{3} 7:11 7:21 7:22 7:28 7:30 7:32 7:40 8:28 8:32 9:1 9:2^{2} 9:6 9:9^{3} 9:13^{2} 9:17 9:19 9:22^{3} 9:23 9:25^{2} 9:26 9:32 9:34 9:38^{2} 10:7 10:9 10:10 10:12 11:19^{2} 11:21 12:30 12:32^{2} 12:39 13:2 13:8 14:12 15:15 15:16 15:17 15:18 16:21 16:38 17:9 17:22 19:4^{2} 19:7 20:2 21:16 23:3^{2} 23:11 23:22 23:24^{2} 23:28 23:32 24:2 24:3^{2} 24:4^{2} 24:19^{3} 24:30 24:31^{2} 25:1 25:3 25:6 25:7 26:6 26:8^{2} 26:13 27:1^{2} 28:15 28:19 29:18 29:20^{2} 29:21

2 CH

1:17 3:13^{2} 4:4 4:7 4:16 4:20 5:8 5:12^{2} 5:13 6:14 6:16 6:25 6:26 6:28^{2} 6:34 6:35^{3} 6:36 6:37 6:38^{5} 6:39^{3} 7:3 7:6^{2} 7:10 7:14^{3} 7:22 8:8 8:14^{3} 9:4^{2} 9:6 10:16 11:13 11:14^{2} 11:16^{2} 13:10 13:16 13:18 14:4 15:4 15:12^{3} 15:15^{2} 17:14 18:9 19:4 19:10 20:13^{3} 20:27 20:33^{3} 21:3 22:5 24:18^{2} 24:24^{2} 25:4 25:5 25:10 25:15 25:20 26:11 26:13 28:6 28:8 28:15 29:6^{2} 29:15 29:23 29:24 29:30 29:34 30:7 30:16^{2} 30:22 30:27^{2} 31:1 31:2 31:6 31:15^{2} 31:16^{4} 31:17^{3} 31:18^{5} 31:19 32:13 32:17 33:17 34:5 34:6 34:25 34:30 34:32 34:33^{2} 35:2 35:10^{2} 35:11 35:15^{2} 35:25 36:15 36:17^{2}

EZR

1:6 2:59^{2} 2:61 2:62 2:65^{2} 2:66^{2} 2:67^{2} 2:69 2:70^{2} 3:8^{2} 3:9^{2} 3:10 3:12 4:5 4:7 4:9 4:17 4:23 5:3 5:5 5:8 5:10 6:12 6:13 6:18^{2} 6:20 6:22 7:13 7:16 7:17^{2} 8:1 8:19 8:24 8:26 9:1 9:2^{2} 9:11^{2} 9:12^{4} 10:16^{2} 10:19^{3}

NE

2:18 3:5^{3} 3:18 3:23 4:3 4:4^{2} 4:5^{2} 4:13^{4} 4:15 5:1^{2} 5:5 5:6 5:8 5:11^{4} 5:14 5:15 6:6 6:9 6:14 6:16 7:61^{2} 7:63 7:64 7:67^{2} 7:68^{2} 7:69 7:73^{2} 8:6^{3} 8:7 8:12 8:15 8:16 9:2^{2} 9:3^{3} 9:4 9:6 9:9 9:11 9:15^{2} 9:16 9:17^{3} 9:20^{2} 9:21^{2} 9:23^{2} 9:24^{2} 9:26 9:27^{3} 9:28 9:29 9:35^{2} 9:37 10:10 10:28^{3} 10:29^{2} 10:30 11:3 11:9 11:12 11:14^{2} 11:19 11:25 11:30 11:31 12:7 12:9 12:24 12:27 12:42 12:45 13:11 13:13^{2} 13:24 13:25^{3}

ES

1:17^{2} 1:20 1:22 2:3 2:12 3:8 3:12 8:9^{3} 8:11 8:13 9:2^{2} 9:5 9:10 9:15 9:16^{4} 9:22 9:27^{3} 9:28 9:31^{3}

JOB

1:4^{2} 1:5^{2} 1:13 1:18 2:12^{3} 3:8 3:15 4:21 5:5 5:12^{2} 5:13 5:15 6:17 6:18 8:4 8:8 8:10 11:3 11:20 12:18 14:12 15:18 15:35 16:10 17:2 17:4 19:12 19:15 20:10 21:8^{4} 21:9 21:10^{2} 21:11^{2} 21:13 21:16^{2} 21:17 21:29 22:6 22:18 24:5^{2} 24:11^{2} 24:18 24:23 27:23 29:9^{2} 29:10^{3} 29:23 29:25 30:2 30:4 30:9^{2} 30:12 31:16 31:39 33:16 34:24 34:25 36:9^{2} 36:10 36:11^{2} 36:14 36:15 36:20 37:8 38:15 38:40 39:3^{2} 39:4 40:12 40:13 40:22 42:15^{2}

PS

2:3^{2} 2:12 4:7^{2} 5:9^{4} 5:10^{2} 5:11 7:7 9:5 9:6 9:10 9:15 10:17 11:2^{2} 11:6 16:4^{3} 17:7 17:10^{2} 17:11 17:14^{3} 18:45 19:3 19:4^{2} 21:10^{2} 21:12 22:13 26:10 28:3 28:4^{4} 28:8 33:15^{2} 33:19 34:5 34:15 34:17 35:6 35:7 35:16 35:17 35:21 35:25 36:7 37:14 37:15^{3} 37:18 37:39 40:15 44:1 44:3^{2} 44:12 49:6^{2} 49:8 49:10 49:11^{5} 49:13^{4} 49:14^{2} 55:9 55:15 55:23 56:5 57:4 58:4 58:6^{2} 59:7^{2} 59:12^{3} 62:4 64:3^{3} 64:8 65:7 68:27^{2} 69:22^{2} 69:23^{2} 69:25^{2} 69:27 70:3 72:14^{2} 73:4^{2} 73:7^{2} 73:9^{2} 73:17 73:20 74:4 74:8 76:5^{2} 78:4 78:5 78:6 78:7 78:8^{2} 78:12 78:18^{2} 78:28^{2} 78:29 78:30^{3} 78:33^{2} 78:35^{2} 78:36^{2} 78:37 78:38 78:44^{2} 78:46^{2} 78:47 78:48^{2} 78:50^{2} 78:51 78:53 78:55 78:57 78:58^{2} 78:63^{2} 78:64^{2} 79:3 79:10 79:12^{2} 81:12^{2} 81:14^{2} 81:15 83:11^{2} 83:16 85:2 89:17 89:32^{2} 90:10 90:16 91:12 93:3^{2} 94:23^{2} 95:10 98:8 99:8 102:17 102:28 104:11 104:12 104:17 104:21^{2} 104:22 104:27 104:29^{2} 105:14 105:24 105:25 105:29^{2} 105:30^{2} 105:31 105:32 105:33^{3} 105:35^{2} 105:36^{2} 105:37 106:11 106:15^{2} 106:18 106:20 106:21 106:25 106:27 106:29 106:32 106:35 106:36 106:37^{2} 106:38^{2} 106:39^{2} 106:42^{2} 106:43^{2} 106:44^{2} 107:5 107:6^{2} 107:12 107:13^{2} 107:14 107:17^{2} 107:18 107:19^{2} 107:20 107:26 107:27 107:28^{2} 107:30 107:38 109:10^{2} 109:13 109:25 109:29 115:2 115:4 115:7 115:9^{2} 115:10^{2} 115:11^{2} 119:70 119:118 123:2 124:3 124:6 125:3 125:4 125:5 129:3 132:12 135:12 135:17 136:21 140:2 140:3^{2} 140:9 141:4 141:5 141:6 141:10 144:8 144:11 144:12 145:15 145:19 147:3 147:4 149:2 149:5 149:6^{2} 149:8^{2}

PR

1:6 1:15 1:16 1:18^{2} 1:22 1:31^{2} 2:15 4:16 4:22 8:21 9:15 10:15 11:6 11:20 14:24 17:6 18:19 20:29 21:12 22:23 23:11 24:2^{2} 24:22 25:27 29:13 29:16 30:5 30:11^{2} 30:12^{2} 30:13^{2} 30:14 30:25 30:26

EC

2:3 3:11 4:1 4:9 5:11 5:13 9:3 9:6^{3}

ISA

2:4^{2} 2:7^{4} 2:8^{3} 3:4 3:8^{2} 3:9^{3} 3:10 3:12 3:16 3:17 3:18^{4} 5:12 5:13^{2} 5:14^{3} 5:17 5:21^{2} 5:24^{2} 5:25 5:27^{2} 5:28^{3} 5:29 6:10^{5} 6:13 8:12 8:19 8:21^{2} 9:17^{2} 10:2 10:5 10:13 10:25 10:29 11:7 11:14 13:8 13:10 13:11^{2} 13:16^{4} 13:18^{2} 13:20 13:21 13:22^{2} 14:1 14:2^{2} 14:9 14:21 14:25 15:2 15:3^{2} 15:4 16:10^{2} 18:2 18:7 20:4 20:5^{2} 21:14 24:14 25:11^{2} 26:11 26:14 26:21 28:25 29:13^{4} 29:14^{2} 29:15^{2} 29:19 30:6^{2} 30:7 30:26 31:3 31:4 33:2 33:7 33:9 33:23 33:24 34:2 34:3^{4} 34:4 34:7^{2} 35:10 36:12^{2} 36:20 36:21 36:22 37:18 37:19 37:27 40:24 40:26 40:31 41:1 41:17 41:29^{2} 42:11 42:15 43:9 43:14 44:9^{2} 44:18^{2} 44:25 45:12 45:20 46:1 47:9 49:9 49:22^{2} 49:23^{2} 49:26^{2} 50:2 50:3 51:7 51:11 52:15 53:11 54:17 55:12 56:7^{2} 56:11 57:2 57:8 58:1^{2} 58:2 59:5 59:6^{4} 59:7^{3} 59:8 59:18 60:8 60:9^{2} 60:10 60:11 61:6 61:7^{2} 61:8 61:9^{2} 62:6 63:3 63:6 63:8 63:9 63:10 65:2 65:4 65:6 65:7^{2} 65:22 65:23 66:3^{3} 66:5^{2} 66:18^{2} 66:24^{2}

JER

1:8 1:16^{2} 1:17 2:11^{2} 2:26^{4} 2:27^{3} 3:17 3:21^{2} 3:24^{4} 4:16 5:3 5:4 5:5 5:6^{3} 5:16 5:24 5:27 5:31 6:3^{2} 6:10 6:12^{2} 6:19 6:23 6:27 7:18 7:19 7:24^{2} 7:26^{3} 7:28^{2} 7:30 7:31^{2} 8:1 8:7 8:10^{2} 8:12 8:19 9:3^{2} 9:5 9:8 9:14^{2} 9:16 10:7 10:9 10:15 10:21 11:8^{2} 11:10^{2} 11:12 11:14 11:18 11:22^{2} 11:23 12:2^{2} 12:14 13:10 14:3^{4} 14:4 14:6 14:10^{3} 14:11 14:12 14:14 14:16^{4} 15:7 15:8 15:9 16:3^{2} 16:4 16:7^{2} 16:15^{2} 16:17^{2} 16:18^{3} 17:1 17:2^{3} 17:23^{2} 17:25 18:8 18:15 18:16 18:17 18:21^{6} 18:22 18:23^{3} 19:4 19:5 19:7^{3} 19:9^{4} 19:15 20:4 20:5 20:11 21:7^{2} 22:9 23:3 23:8 23:10^{2} 23:11 23:12^{2} 23:16 23:22^{2} 23:26 23:27 23:31 23:32^{2} 24:5 24:7^{2} 24:9 24:10 25:12 25:14^{2} 25:36 25:38 26:3 27:4 27:8 27:11^{2} 29:23 30:3 30:9^{2} 30:10 30:20^{2} 30:21^{2} 31:12 31:13^{2} 31:17 31:23 31:32 31:33^{3} 31:34^{2} 32:18 32:22 32:30^{2} 32:32^{4} 32:34 32:35^{2} 32:38 32:39 32:40 32:44 33:8^{2} 33:12 33:20 33:26 34:14 34:16 34:20^{3} 34:21^{2} 35:14 35:16 36:3^{2} 36:6 36:7 36:15 36:24 36:31 37:7 38:18 38:19 38:23 40:7 40:8 40:9 41:5^{3} 41:8 42:17 43:1^{2} 44:3 44:5^{2} 44:9 44:12 44:15 46:5 46:10 46:21^{2} 46:25^{2} 46:26 46:27 47:3 47:5 48:12 48:13 48:33 48:34 48:44 49:1 49:3 49:7 49:20 49:21 49:29^{5} 49:32^{3} 49:35 49:37^{2} 50:4 50:5 50:6^{2} 50:7^{2} 50:9 50:27^{2} 50:34^{2} 50:37^{2} 50:38 50:42 50:45 51:5 51:18 51:24 51:30^{2} 51:39^{2} 51:55 51:56

LA

1:11 1:14 1:19^{2} 1:22 2:10^{2} 2:12^{3} 2:15^{2} 2:16 2:18 2:20 3:14 3:46 3:60^{2} 3:61^{2} 3:62 3:63^{3} 3:64 3:65 4:3 4:7 4:8^{3} 4:10^{2} 4:14 4:20 5:7 5:8 5:12 5:14

EZE

1:5 1:7^{2} 1:8^{4} 1:9 1:10 1:11^{3} 1:13 1:16^{3} 1:17 1:18^{2} 1:20 1:22 1:23^{2} 1:24^{2} 1:26 2:3 2:6^{3} 2:7^{2} 3:8^{2} 3:9 4:4 4:5 4:12 4:13 4:17 5:10 5:16 6:5 6:9^{4} 6:13^{4} 6:14 7:11 7:18 7:19^{7} 7:20^{2} 7:24^{2} 7:27^{2} 8:16^{2} 8:17 9:10^{2} 10:8 10:10 10:11 10:12^{4} 10:16 10:19 10:21 10:22^{2} 11:19 11:20 11:21^{4} 11:22 12:3^{2} 12:4^{2} 12:5 12:6 12:7 12:16 12:19^{2} 13:2 13:3 13:17 14:3^{4} 14:5^{2} 14:10 14:11^{2} 14:14^{2} 14:20^{2} 14:22 14:23^{2} 16:39 16:40 16:45^{2} 16:47^{2} 16:53 16:55^{2} 19:4 19:7^{2} 19:8^{2} 20:4 20:8 20:16^{2} 20:18^{3} 20:24^{2} 20:26 20:28^{4} 20:30 21:6 21:14 21:15^{3} 21:28 21:29 22:6 22:10 22:26 22:31^{2} 23:3^{3} 23:4 23:7 23:8 23:15^{3} 23:17 23:20 23:24 23:30 23:36 23:37^{3} 23:39^{2} 23:42^{2} 23:45 23:47^{4} 24:25^{5} 24:4^{2} 25:4^{2} 26:10 26:16^{3} 26:17 27:9 27:11 27:29 27:30^{2} 27:32 27:35^{2} 28:7 28:25 28:26 29:7^{2} 29:14 29:16 30:11 30:13 31:6^{2} 31:14^{4} 32:2 32:10 32:14^{2} 32:24^{2} 32:25^{2} 32:26 32:27^{5} 32:29 32:30^{3} 33:2^{2} 33:17 33:29 33:31^{3} 34:10^{2} 34:13 34:14 34:23 34:24 34:27^{2} 34:30 35:5^{2} 36:5^{2} 36:7 36:12 36:17^{4} 36:18 36:19^{2} 36:23 37:10 37:20 37:21 37:23^{5} 37:25^{3} 37:27 38:16 39:22 39:23^{2} 39:24^{2} 39:26^{3} 39:27 39:28^{2} 40:16 40:22^{3} 40:41 40:44 41:16 42:4 42:11^{3} 42:14 43:7^{4} 43:8^{4} 43:9^{2} 43:10 43:11 44:10^{2} 44:12^{2} 44:13^{2} 44:18^{2} 44:19^{2} 44:20^{3} 44:22 44:28^{2} 45:4 45:8 46:16 46:18 47:10^{2} 47:12 48:29 48:34

DA

1:15 1:16 2:30 3:21^{4}

3:27^{2} 3:28^{2} 3:29 4:21 6:24^{3} 7:12^{2} 8:23 9:7 11:8^{3} 11:32

HO

1:7 2:5 2:17 3:5^{2} 4:7 4:8^{2} 4:9^{2} 4:12^{3} 4:18 4:19 5:4^{2} 5:5 5:6^{2} 5:7 5:15^{2} 7:2^{3} 7:3^{2} 7:6^{2} 7:7^{2} 7:10 7:12 7:14^{2} 7:15 7:16^{3} 8:4^{2} 8:13^{2} 9:4^{3} 9:6^{2} 9:9^{2} 9:10 9:11 9:12 9:15^{3} 9:16^{2} 10:2^{3} 10:8 10:10 11:3 11:4 11:6 11:11 12:11 13:2^{2} 13:6^{2} 13:8 13:16^{2} 14:4

JOE

1:3^{2} 1:17 2:6 2:7 2:10 2:17 2:22 3:6 3:13 3:15 3:19 3:21

AM

1:13 1:15 2:4^{2} 2:8 3:10 4:1 5:12 6:2 6:4 7:11 8:7 9:4 9:15^{2}

OB

12 13^{5} 17

JON

1:2 2:8 3:8 3:10^{2} 4:11^{2}

MIC

2:1^{2} 2:9^{2} 2:12 2:13 3:2^{3} 3:3^{2} 3:4 3:5^{2} 3:7 4:3^{2} 4:13^{2} 6:12^{2} 6:16 7:4 7:13 7:16^{4} 7:17 7:19

NA

2:2 2:5 2:7 3:3^{2} 3:17

HAB

1:7^{2} 1:8^{3} 1:9 1:15^{2} 1:16^{4} 1:17 2:15 3:11 3:14

ZEP

1:9 1:12^{2} 1:13^{2} 1:17^{2} 1:18^{2} 2:7^{2} 2:8 2:10 2:14 3:6^{3} 3:7^{2} 3:13

HAG

1:12^{2} 1:14 2:14 2:22

ZEC

1:21 2:9 5:6 5:9 7:2 7:11 7:12 8:8 8:12 9:16 10:2 10:5 10:6 10:7^{3} 10:9 11:3 11:5 11:6 11:8 11:16 12:5^{2} 12:12^{2} 12:13^{2} 12:14 14:12^{6}

MAL

4:6

MT

1:21 2:11 2:12 3:6 4:6 4:20 4:21^{2} 4:22 4:23 6:2 6:5 6:7 6:14 6:15 6:16 7:6 7:16 7:20 8:22 8:33 8:34 9:2 9:4 9:29 9:30 9:35 10:17 10:21 11:1 11:5 11:16 12:9 12:25 13:15^{5} 13:43 13:54 13:58 14:4 15:2 15:8^{3} 15:27 17:6 17:8 17:25 18:10 18:31 18:35 19:12 20:4 20:8 20:31 20:34^{2} 21:7 21:8 21:41 22:5 22:7 22:16 22:18 22:22 23:3 23:4 23:5^{3} 25:1 25:3 25:4^{2} 25:7 26:43 26:67 27:39

MK

1:5 1:18 1:19 1:20 1:23 1:39 2:5 2:6 3:4 3:5 4:12 4:15 5:17 6:6 6:8^{2} 6:26 6:52 7:3 7:6^{2} 8:3 9:44 9:46 9:48 10:42 11:4 11:7 11:8 12:12 12:15 12:44 13:12 14:40 14:46 14:56 14:59 14:65 15:19 15:29 16:14

LU

1:16 1:20 1:51 1:52 1:66 1:77 2:8 2:39 2:44 3:15 4:11 4:15 4:29 5:2 5:6 5:7 5:11 5:15 5:20 5:22 5:30 6:1 6:8 6:17 6:22 6:23 6:26 7:21 8:3 8:12 8:25 9:47 9:60 11:17 11:48 12:36 12:42 13:1 14:4 16:4 16:8 17:13 19:32 19:35 19:36 19:40 20:23 20:26 21:1 21:4 21:12 22:66 23:25 24:5 24:11 24:16 24:31 24:45

JOH

3:19 4:38 8:9 10:39 11:19 11:46 12:40^{4} 13:12 15:22 15:25 17:19 17:20 18:8 19:3 19:31 20:10

AC

1:9 1:19 1:26 2:37 2:45 2:46 4:5 4:23 4:24 4:29 5:18 6:1 6:6 7:19 7:34 7:39 7:41 7:54 7:57 7:58 7:60 8:17 8:36 9:24 10:9 11:18 12:17 12:20^{2} 12:25 13:3 13:5 13:18 13:19 13:22 13:27 13:33 13:50 13:51 14:2 14:3 14:5 14:11 14:13 14:14 14:16 15:3 15:9 15:13 15:22 15:26 16:19 16:22 16:24 16:33 17:21 17:26 18:3 19:18 19:19 21:21 21:24 22:22 22:23 22:30 23:16 23:28 23:29 25:19 26:18 27:13 27:43 28:6 28:27^{5}

RO

1:21^{2} 1:24^{2} 1:26 1:27^{2} 1:28 2:15^{3} 3:3 3:13^{3} 3:15 3:16 3:18 10:3 10:18^{2} 11:9 11:10^{2} 11:11 11:12 11:18 11:24 11:27 11:30 13:7 15:27^{3} 16:4 16:5 16:18

1 CO

3:19 8:7 8:12 14:35 16:19

2 CO

3:14 3:15 5:19 6:16 8:2^{3} 8:3^{2} 8:5 8:14^{2} 9:14 11:15

GA

2:13

EPH

4:17 4:18 5:24^{2} 5:28^{2}

PHP

2:21 3:19^{2}

COL

2:2

1 TH

2:15 2:16 5:13

2 TH

3:12

1 TI

3:11 3:12^{2} 4:2 5:4 5:12 6:1

2 TI

2:3 2:17 3:8 4:3 4:4 4:16

TIT

1:12 1:15 2:4^{2} 2:5 2:9 3:13

HEB

2:10 2:15 3:10 5:14 7:5 8:9 8:10^{2} 8:12^{3} 10:16^{2} 10:17 11:16 11:35 12:10 13:7

JAS

1:27 3:3

1 PE

3:5 3:12 3:14 4:14 4:19

2 PE

2:2 2:3 2:8 2:12 2:13 3:3 3:16

3 JO

6

JUDE

6^{2} 13 15^{2} 16^{2} 18

RE

2:22 3:4 4:4 4:10 6:11^{2} 6:14 7:3 7:9 7:11 7:14 7:17 9:4 9:5 9:7^{2} 9:8 9:9 9:10^{2} 9:17 9:18 9:19^{4} 9:20 9:21^{4} 10:3 10:4 11:5^{2} 11:6 11:7 11:8 11:9^{2} 11:11 11:12 11:16^{2} 12:8 12:11^{2} 13:16^{2} 14:1 14:2 14:5 14:11 14:13^{2} 15:6 16:10 16:11^{3} 17:13 17:17^{2} 18:11 18:19 19:19 19:21 20:4^{2} 20:12 20:13 21:3 21:4 21:8 21:24 22:4

THEM

846

GE

1:14 1:15 1:17 1:22 1:26 1:27 1:28 2:1 2:19^{2} 3:7 3:21 5:2 6:1 6:2 6:4 6:7 6:13^{2} 6:19 6:20 6:21 7:3 9:1 9:19 10:1 11:3 11:6 11:8 11:9 11:29 11:31 12:3 13:6 14:8 14:14 14:15^{2} 14:24 15:5 15:10 15:11 15:13 18:2 18:8 18:16 19:1 19:3^{2} 19:5 19:6 19:8^{2} 19:9 19:10 19:12 19:13 19:17 19:18 20:14 21:27 21:31 22:6 22:8 23:8 24:28 24:53 24:56 24:60 25:6 25:26 26:15 26:18^{2} 26:27 26:30 26:31 27:9 27:13 27:14 27:15 28:11 29:4 29:5 29:6 29:7 29:9^{2} 30:14 30:35 30:37 30:40 30:42 31:5 31:9 31:32 31:33 31:34^{2} 31:55 32:2 32:4 32:16 32:23^{2} 33:3 33:13 34:14 34:21^{3} 34:23 35:4 35:5 36:7 37:6 37:13 37:17^{2} 37:18 37:22 37:26 39:14 40:3 40:4^{2} 40:5 40:6^{2} 40:8^{2} 40:11 40:17 40:22 41:3 41:6 41:8^{2} 41:19 41:21^{2} 41:23 41:27 41:30 41:35^{2} 42:7^{4} 42:9^{2} 42:12 42:14 42:17 42:18 42:22 42:23^{2} 42:24^{4} 42:25^{2} 42:27 42:28 42:29 42:36 43:2 43:11 43:16 43:23 43:24 43:27 43:32 43:34 44:4^{2} 44:6^{2} 44:15 45:1 45:15 45:21^{2} 45:22 45:24 45:26 45:27 47:2 47:6^{3} 47:11 47:17^{2} 47:20 47:21 47:22^{2} 47:24 48:6 48:9^{2} 48:10^{3} 48:12 48:13^{2} 48:16^{2} 48:20 49:7^{2} 49:28^{3} 49:29^{2} 50:12 50:19 50:21^{2}

EX

1:7 1:10^{2} 1:11^{2} 1:12 1:14 1:16 1:17 1:18 1:19 1:21 2:17^{2} 2:25 3:8^{2} 3:9 3:13^{2} 3:16 3:22 4:20 5:4 5:5 5:7 5:8 5:9 5:13 5:14 5:21 6:1^{2} 6:3 6:4^{2} 6:13 7:5 7:6 7:13 7:22 8:2 8:14 8:15 8:19 9:2^{2} 9:12 9:17 9:19 9:27 10:2 10:8 10:10 10:14^{2} 10:19 10:27 12:3 12:16 12:21 12:33 12:36 12:38 12:42 13:17 13:31^{3} 14:3 14:4 14:7 14:9^{2} 14:10 14:13 14:17 14:19^{2} 14:20 14:22 14:23 14:25^{2} 14:28^{2} 14:29 15:5 15:7^{2} 15:9^{2} 15:10 15:12 15:13 15:15 15:16 15:17^{2} 15:19 15:21 15:25^{2} 16:3 16:4 16:12 16:15 16:16 16:20^{2} 16:23 17:2 17:8^{2} 17:11 17:16 18:20^{2} 18:21 18:22 18:25 19:10^{2} 19:21 19:22 19:24 19:25 20:5^{3} 20:6 20:11 21:1 21:34 22:11 22:23 23:23 23:24^{2} 23:29 23:30 23:31 23:32 24:12 24:14 25:3 25:8^{2} 25:12 25:13 25:14 25:18 25:28^{2} 25:29 25:40 26:1 26:24 26:37^{2} 27:6 28:9 28:11 28:14 28:25 28:26 28:27 28:33 28:40^{2} 28:41^{4} 28:42 29:1^{2} 29:2 29:3^{2} 29:4 29:8 29:9^{2} 29:13^{2} 29:17 29:22 29:24 29:25^{2} 29:29 29:30 29:33 29:35 29:46^{2} 30:5 30:12^{3} 30:13 30:14 30:21 30:29^{2} 30:30 31:5 32:2^{2} 32:3 32:4 32:8^{2} 32:10^{2} 32:12^{3} 32:13 32:18^{3} 32:19 32:21 32:24^{2} 32:25 32:27 32:31 32:34 34:31^{2} 34:32 34:33 35:1^{2} 35:23 35:26 35:29 35:33 35:35^{2} 36:8^{2} 36:14 36:29 36:36^{2} 37:4 37:7 37:15 37:28 38:6 38:25 38:28 39:7 39:18 39:19 39:20 39:43 40:12 40:14 40:15

LE

1:12 2:12 3:4 3:10 3:15 3:16 4:2 4:9 4:10 4:20^{2} 4:35 5:8 6:10 6:17 6:18 7:4 7:5 7:7 7:34 7:35 7:36^{2} 8:6 8:10 8:11 8:13^{3} 8:26 8:27 8:28^{2} 9:2 9:7 9:13 9:14 9:22 10:1^{2} 10:2 10:3 10:4 10:5 10:11 10:17 11:1 11:4^{2} 11:9 11:22 11:24 11:25 11:26 11:28 11:31 11:32 11:33 11:42 11:43 13:58 14:6 14:12 14:23 14:24 14:40 14:42 14:45 14:51 15:2 15:14 15:15 15:29 15:31 16:4 16:7 16:16 16:21 16:23 16:28 17:2 17:5^{2} 17:7 17:8 17:16 18:2 18:5 18:29 19:2 19:10 19:31^{2} 19:37 20:6 20:8 20:11^{2} 20:12^{2} 20:13^{2} 20:16 20:18 20:22 20:23 20:27^{2} 21:1 21:23 22:3 22:9 22:16^{2} 22:18 22:22 22:25 22:31 23:2 23:10 23:20 23:22 23:43 24:6 24:12 25:2 25:18 25:31 25:44 25:45 25:46^{2} 25:51 26:3 26:36^{2} 26:39 26:41^{2} 26:43^{2} 26:44^{4} 27:2

NU

1:3 1:19 1:21 1:22 1:23 1:25 1:27 1:29 1:31 1:33 1:35 1:37 1:39 1:41 1:43 1:47 1:49 2:4 2:13 2:15 2:19 2:21 2:23 2:26 2:28 2:30 3:6 3:15 3:16 3:22^{2} 3:32 3:34 3:43 3:47 3:48 3:49^{2} 3:51 4:8 4:12^{3} 4:19^{2} 4:23 4:26 4:27 4:29 4:30 4:36 4:40 4:44 4:48 5:3 5:4 5:12 5:23 6:2 6:16 6:19 6:20 6:23 6:27 7:1^{2} 7:2 7:3 7:5^{2} 7:6 7:9 7:13 7:19 7:25 7:31 7:37 7:43 7:49 7:55 7:61 7:67 7:73 7:19 8:6 8:7^{5} 8:8 8:13 8:15^{2} 8:16 8:17 8:20 8:21^{3} 8:22 9:8 10:2^{2} 10:3 10:33^{2} 10:34 10:35 11:1^{2} 11:3 11:4 11:12^{2} 11:16^{2} 11:17 11:21 11:22^{4} 11:24 11:25 11:26^{2} 11:28 11:29 11:31 11:32 12:9 13:2 13:3 13:17^{2} 13:26^{2} 14:2 14:6 14:9^{2} 14:10 14:11 14:12^{2} 14:13 14:14^{2} 14:16^{2} 14:23 14:28 14:31 14:40 14:45^{2} 15:2 15:18 15:25 15:26 15:29 15:38^{2} 15:39 16:3^{3} 16:7 16:9 16:15^{2} 16:17 16:18 16:19 16:21 16:28 16:30^{2} 16:31 16:32 16:33^{2} 16:34^{2} 16:38^{3} 16:45 16:46 16:49 17:2 17:4 17:8 17:11 17:12^{2} 17:18 17:20 17:24 17:26^{2} 17:30 19:9 19:10 20:6 20:8 20:10 20:12 20:13 20:21 20:25 20:26 20:28 21:1 21:3 21:16 21:30^{2} 21:33 22:6^{2} 22:8 22:11^{3} 22:12 22:20 23:11 23:13^{4} 23:21 23:22 23:25^{2} 23:27 24:8 24:10 25:4 25:8 25:11 25:17 26:3 26:7 26:10 26:18 26:22 26:25 26:27 26:34 26:37 26:41 26:43 26:47 26:50 26:62^{2} 26:64 26:64^{2} 27:3 27:7^{2} 27:17^{4} 28:2 28:3 28:31 30:12^{3} 30:14^{2} 30:15^{2} 31:3 31:6^{2} 31:8 31:13 31:15 31:27^{2} 31:30 31:36 31:47 31:51 32:7 32:8 32:9 32:13 32:15 32:17 32:19 32:20 32:28 32:29^{2} 32:33 32:41 33:4 33:51 33:55 33:56 34:2 35:2

35:3 35:5 35:6 35:7 35:8[2] 35:10 35:15 36:6

DE

1:3 1:8[2] 1:13 1:15 1:29 1:39 1:42 2:5 2:6[2] 2:9 2:11 2:12[4] 2:14 2:15[2] 2:19[2] 2:20 2:21[3] 2:22[2] 2:23 3:4 3:6 3:14 3:20 3:22 3:28 4:1 4:3 4:6 4:7 4:9 4:10 4:13 4:14 4:19[2] 4:31 4:37 5:1[3] 5:9[3] 5:10 5:22[2] 5:29[2] 5:30 5:31[3] 6:1 6:7[2] 6:8 6:9 7:2[5] 7:3 7:5 7:9 7:10[2] 7:11 7:12 7:15[2] 7:16 7:17 7:18 7:20 7:21 7:22 7:23 7:24 7:25 8:19[2] 9:3[4] 9:4[2] 9:5 9:10 9:12[2] 9:14 9:17[2] 9:28[5] 10:2 10:4 10:11 10:15[2] 11:4[2] 11:6 11:9 11:16 11:18 11:19[2] 11:20 11:21 11:22 12:3 12:18 12:22[2] 12:29[2] 12:30 13:2 13:17 14:7[2] 17:3 17:5 17:19 18:2 18:3 18:12 18:18[2] 19:1 19:9 20:1[2] 20:3[2] 20:17 20:19[4] 20:20 21:5 21:8 21:10[2] 21:18 22:1[2] 22:4[2] 22:19 22:22 22:24[2] 23:8 24:8 25:1 25:5 25:13 25:16 26:13 27:2 27:3 27:4 27:5 27:26 28:13 28:14 28:25[2] 28:26 28:31 28:32 28:39[2] 28:41 28:55 28:57 28:61 29:1 29:2 29:7 29:9 29:17 29:25[2] 29:26[2] 29:28[2] 30:1 30:7 30:17 30:20 31:2 31:3 31:4[2] 31:5[2] 31:6 31:7[2] 31:10 31:16[3] 31:17[4] 31:20[2] 31:21[3] 31:23 31:28 32:11 32:19 32:20 32:21[2] 32:23[2] 32:24 32:26[2] 32:28 32:30[2] 32:35 32:38 32:41 32:46 33:2[2] 33:11[2] 33:17 33:27

JOS

1:2 1:6 1:14 1:15 2:4 2:5[2] 2:6[2] 2:7[2] 2:8 2:15 2:16 2:21 2:22[2] 2:23 4:3[3] 4:5 4:7 4:8[3] 4:12 5:1 5:5 5:6 5:7[2] 6:6 6:8 6:13 6:23 6:26 7:2 7:5[3] 7:11 7:21[2] 7:23[3] 7:24 7:25[2] 8:3 8:4 8:5 8:6[2] 8:9 8:11 8:12 8:15 8:16 8:20 8:22[3] 8:24 8:33[3] 8:35 9:5 9:8 9:11[2] 9:15[4] 9:16[2] 9:18[2] 9:19[2] 9:20[3] 9:21[4] 9:22[2] 9:26[3] 9:27 10:1 10:8[3] 10:9 10:10[4] 10:11 10:18 10:19[3] 10:20[2] 10:24 10:25 10:26[3] 10:27[2] 10:28 10:39 10:41 11:4 11:6[2] 11:7[2] 11:8[5] 11:9 11:11 11:12[3] 11:13 11:14 11:17 11:20[2] 11:21 12:6 13:6 13:8[2] 13:12 13:14 13:22[2] 13:33 14:1 14:3 14:12 15:63 17:4 17:13 17:15 18:1 18:4[2] 18:7 18:8 18:10 19:9[2] 19:47 19:49 20:4[2] 20:9 21:2 21:11 21:21 21:42 21:44[2] 22:2 22:4 22:6[2] 22:7[2] 22:8 22:12 22:15 22:30 22:32 22:33 23:2 23:5[2] 23:7[3] 23:12[2] 23:16 24:5 24:7[2] 24:8[2] 24:11 24:12 24:13 24:25

JG

1:1 1:4 1:22 1:25 1:28 1:29 1:30 1:32 1:33 1:34 2:3 2:10 2:12[3] 2:14[3] 2:15[2] 2:16[2] 2:17 2:18[5] 2:19[2] 2:21 2:22 2:23[2] 3:1 3:2 3:4 3:8 3:9 3:15 3:23 3:25 3:27 3:28 4:2 5:14 5:21 5:30 5:31 6:1 6:2 6:3 6:4 6:8 6:9 6:20 6:35 7:1 7:4[2] 7:6 7:17 7:24 8:2 8:4 8:8 8:10 8:11 8:12 8:16 8:19 8:20 8:23 8:24 8:25 8:34 9:1 9:7 9:8 9:9 9:11 9:13 9:24 9:25 9:33 9:38 9:43[3] 9:44 9:49[2] 9:51[2] 9:57 10:7 10:16 11:9 11:11 11:14 11:21 11:24 11:25 11:26 11:32[2] 11:33 11:35 12:2 12:3 13:1 14:9[2] 14:12 14:14 14:18 14:19[2] 15:3[2] 15:5 15:7 15:8 15:11[2] 15:12 16:3[3] 16:8 16:12 16:23 16:25 16:26 17:4 18:1[2] 18:2 18:4 18:6 18:7 18:8 18:9 18:18 18:21 18:27 18:31 19:6 19:8 19:14 19:15 19:23[2] 19:24[3] 19:25 20:13 20:20 20:25 20:28 20:32 20:34 20:40 20:41 20:42[3] 20:43[2] 20:45[3] 20:48 21:6 21:7[2] 21:10 21:12 21:13 21:14[2] 21:15 21:16 21:17 21:18 21:19 21:22[3] 21:23[3]

RU

1:4 1:5 1:6 1:9 1:13[2] 1:19 1:20 2:9 2:16[2]

1 SA

2:8[3] 2:10 2:16 2:23 2:26 2:30 2:34 3:13 5:6[3] 5:8 6:6 6:7 6:10 6:12 6:15 7:10 7:11 8:7 8:8 8:9[3] 8:11 8:12 8:14[2] 8:16 8:21 8:22 9:4[2] 9:11 9:12 9:14 9:20 9:22[3] 9:26 10:5 10:6 10:10 10:18 11:2 11:7[2] 11:8 11:11 11:12 12:5 12:8 12:9[2] 13:16 13:19 14:8 14:9 14:10 14:11 14:12 14:21 14:22 14:32[2] 14:34[3] 14:36[2] 14:37 14:47 14:48[2] 15:3 15:4 15:6 15:9 15:15 15:18 16:5 16:20 17:3 17:8 17:23[2] 17:24 17:31 17:36 17:39[2] 17:40 18:16 18:27 19:8 19:20 20:11 20:21 20:40 21:13 22:2 22:4 22:11 23:5 23:26 24:7 24:22 25:7[2] 25:14 25:15 25:16 25:18 25:20 25:43 26:12[2] 26:13 26:14 27:5 30:2 30:8[2] 30:17[2] 30:19[2] 30:21 30:22[2] 30:27[3] 30:28[3] 30:29[3] 30:30[3] 30:31 31:7 31:12 31:13

2 SA

1:10 1:11 1:18 2:5 2:7 2:14 2:36 4:7 4:9 4:12[2] 5:3 5:19 5:21 5:23[2] 6:22 7:10[2] 7:21 8:1 8:2[2] 8:4 8:7 10:4 10:5 10:9 10:10 10:16 10:19 11:23 12:11 12:17 12:31 13:9 13:10 13:11 13:30 14:6 14:36[2] 16:1 17:9 17:17 17:18 17:20[2] 17:22 18:1 18:4 18:14 18:31 19:3 19:28 20:3[3] 20:8 20:19 21:2[3] 21:6[2] 21:7 21:9[2] 21:10[2] 21:12[2] 21:13 22:15[2] 22:18 22:23 22:28 22:31 22:38[2] 22:39[2] 22:40 22:41 22:42 22:43[3] 22:49 23:6 23:7 23:18 24:1 24:12

1 KI

1:20 1:33 1:40 2:7 2:32 5:3 5:9[4] 5:14 5:18 6:12 6:15 6:16 6:32[2] 6:34 7:6[2] 7:15 7:25 7:37 7:46 8:21 8:34 8:35 8:36 8:37 8:44 8:46[3] 8:47[2] 8:48 8:50[4] 8:52 8:53 9:6 9:7 9:9[3] 9:13 9:21 10:17 10:29 11:2 11:18 11:24 12:5 12:7[3] 12:9 12:10 12:14 12:16 12:17 12:28 13:11 13:12 14:15 14:23 14:27 14:28[2] 15:18[2] 15:22 18:4[2] 18:6 18:13 18:23[2] 18:26 18:27 18:28 18:40[5] 19:2 19:21 20:15 20:18[2] 20:19 20:20 20:23 20:25 20:27[2] 21:8 21:11[2] 22:6 22:10 22:11 22:13 22:17

2 KI

1:2 1:3 1:5 1:7 1:12 2:11 2:12 2:16 2:18 2:24[3] 3:9 3:10 3:13 3:21 3:24 4:31 4:33 4:39[2] 4:44 5:12 5:22 5:23[2] 5:24[2] 6:4 6:11 6:16 6:18 6:19[2] 6:21[3] 6:22[2] 6:23[2] 6:33 7:10 7:12 9:11 9:15 9:17 9:18 9:19 9:20 10:1 10:6[2] 10:7[2] 10:8 10:14[4] 10:18 10:22 10:25[3] 10:26 10:29 10:32 11:4[4] 11:5 11:9 11:15 12:5[2] 12:7 12:11 13:3 13:4 13:7[2] 13:17 13:18 13:23[4] 14:27 15:29 16:17 17:6 17:7 17:9 17:10 17:11 17:12 17:15[4] 17:16 17:18 17:20[3] 17:21 17:22 17:24 17:25[2] 17:26[2] 17:27[2] 17:28 17:29 17:32[2] 17:35[4] 18:11 18:12[2] 18:13 18:19 18:23 18:27 19:6 19:11 19:12 19:18 20:13[3] 20:15 21:3 21:8[2] 21:9 21:14 21:21 21:24 22:5[2] 22:7 22:9 22:15 23:4[2] 23:5 23:12[2] 23:16 23:19 23:20 24:2 24:3 24:16 24:20 25:13 25:19 25:20 25:21[2] 25:22 25:24[2]

1 CH

2:6 2:23 2:53 4:21 4:41 4:42 5:11 5:20[3] 5:25 5:26[2] 6:55 6:67 6:78 7:3 7:4 7:9 7:40 8:6 8:7 8:8 8:32 9:20 9:25 9:27[2] 9:28[2] 9:29 10:7 10:12 11:3 11:14 11:20 12:15 12:17[2] 12:18[2] 12:19 12:29 12:32 12:34 12:39 12:40 13:2 14:8 14:10[2] 14:11 14:14[3] 15:2 15:12 15:18 16:10 16:21 16:41 16:42 17:9[2] 18:1 18:4 18:7 18:11 19:4[2] 19:5 19:6 19:10 19:16 19:17[2] 20:3 21:2 21:6 21:10 23:6 23:22 23:31 24:3 24:6 24:19 25:7 26:30 26:31 27:23 27:26 29:8

2 CH

2:2 2:11 2:17 2:18 3:10 3:15 3:16[2] 4:4 4:6[2] 4:7 4:8 4:9 4:17 5:12[2] 6:25[2] 6:26 6:27 6:28 6:34 6:36[3] 6:38 7:6 7:19 7:20[2] 7:22[4] 8:2 8:8[2] 8:18 9:8[2] 9:16 10:7[2] 10:9 10:10 10:13 10:14 10:16 10:17 11:11 11:12 11:14 11:16 11:23 12:5 12:7[2] 12:10 12:11[2] 13:7 13:9 13:13[2] 13:16 13:17 14:7 14:9 14:11 14:13 14:14[2] 15:4 15:6 15:9 15:15[2] 16:8 16:9 17:8[2] 17:9 17:14 18:5 18:9[2] 18:16 18:31 19:2 19:4 19:9 19:10 20:1 20:10[2] 20:12 20:16[2] 20:17 20:23 20:25[2] 20:27[2] 21:3 22:8 22:12 23:3 23:8 23:14 24:5 24:13 24:17 24:19[3] 24:20 24:23 25:5[3] 25:10 25:12[2] 25:13 25:14[3] 25:20 26:9 26:14 27:5 28:5[2] 28:8 28:9[3] 28:12 28:13 28:15[7] 28:23[2] 29:3 29:4 29:5 29:8 29:21 29:23 29:24 29:34 30:7 30:9[2] 30:10[2] 30:12 30:14 30:17 30:18 31:1 31:6 31:7 31:11 32:1 32:6[2] 32:18[2] 32:22 32:26 33:3 33:8 33:11 33:15 33:22 33:25 34:4[4] 34:12 34:21 34:23 35:2 35:11 35:13 35:15 35:25 36:7 36:15 36:17[2] 36:20

EZR

1:5 1:6 1:7 1:8 1:9 1:11 2:63 2:65 3:3 3:7[2] 4:2 4:3 4:4 4:5 4:20 4:23 5:1 5:2[2] 5:3[2] 5:4 5:5 5:9 5:10 5:12 5:14 5:15 6:5 6:9 6:20 6:21 6:22[2] 7:17 7:24 7:25[2] 8:1 8:13 8:14 8:15 8:17[2] 8:20 8:22[2] 8:24 8:25 8:28 8:29[2] 8:30 8:33 10:3 10:6 10:10 10:14[2] 10:15 10:16 10:44

NE

1:2 1:5 1:9[3] 2:9 2:10 2:17 2:18 2:20[2] 3:2 3:4[3] 3:5 3:7 3:9 3:10 3:27 3:29 4:4 4:8 4:9[2] 4:11[2] 4:12 4:14 4:16 4:21 4:23 5:2 5:5 5:7[2] 5:8 5:10 5:11[2] 5:12[3] 5:15 6:3 6:4 6:8 6:17 7:3[3] 7:5 7:65 8:8 8:10[2] 8:12 8:16 8:17 9:1 9:6 9:10 9:11 9:12[2] 9:13[2] 9:14[2] 9:15[4] 9:17[2] 9:18 9:19[4] 9:20[2] 9:21 9:22[2] 9:23 9:24[3] 9:26[2] 9:27[5] 9:28[4] 9:29[3] 9:30[3] 9:31[2] 9:34 9:35[2] 10:31 11:23 12:9 12:24 12:27 12:29 12:31 12:32 12:36 12:37 12:38[3] 12:40 12:43 12:44 12:47 13:2[2] 13:10 13:11[2] 13:13 13:15 13:17 13:21[2] 13:25[4] 13:29 13:30

ES

1:7 2:3 2:15 3:4[2] 3:8 3:11 3:13 4:7 4:8 4:15 5:8 5:11 8:11[2] 8:17 9:1[3] 9:2[2] 9:3 9:5 9:21 9:22[2] 9:23 9:24[3] 9:26 9:27[2] 9:28 9:31

JOB

1:4 1:5[2] 1:6 1:14 1:15[2] 1:16 1:17 2:1 3:8 4:19 4:21 5:4 6:19 8:4 9:5 12:15 12:23[2] 12:24 12:25 14:21 15:19 17:4 20:15[2] 21:8 21:9 21:17 21:26 21:29 22:17 22:19 22:20 24:5 24:12 24:17[2] 26:8 29:22 29:24 30:5 30:31 32:8 34:25 34:26 36:7 36:9 36:13 36:31 37:4 37:12 37:15 37:21 39:4 39:14 39:15[2] 40:13 41:16 42:9 42:15

PS

2:4 2:5[2] 2:9[2] 5:6 5:10[3] 5:11[3] 6:10 7:1 9:6 9:10 9:12 9:13 9:20 10:2 10:5 12:7[2] 15:4 17:7[2] 18:14[2] 18:17 18:37 18:38 18:40 18:41[2] 18:42[2] 19:4 19:11[2] 19:13 21:9[3] 21:12[2] 22:4 22:18 22:25 24:6 24:9 25:3 25:14[2] 28:1 28:4[3] 28:5[2] 28:9[2] 29:6 31:6 31:15 31:17 31:19[2] 31:20[2] 33:6 33:18[2] 33:19 34:7[2] 34:9 34:16[2] 34:17 34:18 34:19 34:20 34:22 35:1[2] 35:3 35:4[2] 35:5[2] 35:6 35:19[2] 35:20 35:25[2] 35:26[2] 35:27[2] 36:8 36:10 37:40[4] 39:6 40:5 40:14[2] 40:15 41:10 42:4 43:3[2] 44:2[2] 44:3[2] 44:5 44:7 44:13 48:6 49:7 49:14[2] 50:21 53:3 53:5[2] 54:3 54:4 54:5 55:15[3] 55:19 55:23 57:4 58:7[2] 58:8 58:9 59:1 59:8 59:11[3] 59:12 59:13[3] 59:14[2] 59:15 60:4 62:10 63:11 64:5 64:6 64:7 64:8 65:3 65:5 65:9 68:1 68:2 68:3[2] 68:17 68:18 68:25 69:6 69:9 69:11 69:14 69:22 69:24[2] 69:27 69:28 70:2[2] 70:3 71:13[2] 73:6[2] 73:10 73:18[2] 73:27 74:8 75:8[2] 78:4 78:5 78:6[2] 78:11 78:13 78:14 78:15 78:24[2] 78:25 78:27 78:29 78:31[2] 78:34 78:38 78:42 78:45[3] 78:49[2] 78:52 78:53

78:54 78:55^{2} 78:66 78:72^{2} 79:3 79:4 80:5^{2} 81:12 81:16 82:4 83:4 83:8 83:9 83:13 83:15^{2} 83:17^{2} 84:5 84:7 84:11 85:8 85:9 86:5 86:14 87:4 88:4 88:8 89:7 89:9 89:11 89:12 89:23 90:5 94:23^{3} 97:10 99:3 99:6^{2} 99:7^{2} 99:8^{2} 101:3 102:26^{2} 103:11 103:13 103:17 103:18 104:8 104:12 104:22 104:24 104:27 104:28 105:3 105:14 105:24 105:27 105:32 105:37 105:38^{2} 105:40 105:44 106:8 106:9 106:10^{3} 106:11 106:15 106:25^{2} 106:26^{2} 106:27 106:29 106:34 106:36 106:41^{3} 106:42 106:43 106:45 106:46^{2} 107:3 107:5 107:6 107:7 107:13 107:14 107:19 107:20^{2} 107:22 107:28 107:30 107:32

107:34 107:38 107:40 109:10 109:15^{2} 109:20 109:25 109:28^{2} 109:29 111:2 111:5 111:6 115:8^{3} 115:13 118:4 118:7^{2} 118:10 118:11 118:12 118:19 119:63^{2} 119:84 119:93 119:118 119:129 119:152 119:165 119:167 125:4 125:5 126:1 126:2 127:5 129:5 129:6 132:12 135:18^{3} 136:11 139:16 139:17 139:18 139:21 139:22^{2} 140:9 140:10^{2} 143:7 143:12 144:6^{2} 145:15 145:18 145:19^{2} 145:20 146:8 147:11 147:18 147:20 148:5 148:6 148:13 149:3^{2} 149:5 149:9

PR

1:12 1:15 1:32^{2} 2:7 3:3^{2} 3:18 3:21 3:27 4:21^{2} 4:22 5:6 5:13 5:17 6:21^{2} 7:3^{2} 8:8 8:9 8:17 10:26 11:3^{2} 11:6 12:6 12:20 12:26 14:3 14:22 19:7 20:10 20:12 20:26 21:6 21:7 22:2 22:5 22:18 22:21 22:23 22:26^{2} 24:1 24:11 24:21 24:22 24:25^{2} 25:13 27:3 28:4 28:13 30:5 30:7 30:27 31:29

EC

2:5 2:10 2:14 3:12 3:18 3:19 4:16 5:11^{2} 7:11 7:12 8:11 8:12 9:1 9:5 9:11 9:12 10:15 11:8 12:1

CA

3:4 4:2 5:3 6:6

ISA

1:14 1:23 1:31 2:9 3:4 3:9 3:12 4:2 5:8 5:11^{2} 5:18 5:20 5:21 5:22 5:25^{2} 5:26 5:27^{2} 5:30 6:13 7:19 7:20 8:7 8:12 8:15 8:19 8:20 9:2 9:10 9:13 9:16^{2} 10:1 10:6 10:10 10:15 10:18 10:20 10:22 11:6 11:14^{2} 13:2 13:3 13:8 13:15 13:17 14:1^{2} 14:2^{4} 14:18 14:20 14:22 14:25 16:4 17:2 17:13 17:4^{2} 18:6^{2} 19:3 19:4 19:12^{2} 19:20^{2} 19:22^{2} 23:1 23:13 23:18 24:8 24:9 25:11 26:5 26:11 26:14 26:16 27:4^{2} 27:5 27:6 27:11^{5} 28:1 28:6 28:9 28:13 29:1 29:15 30:5 30:6 30:8 30:22 30:28 31:1 31:2 31:4 32:3^{2} 33:4 34:2^{2} 34:7 34:16 34:17^{2} 35:1 35:4 36:1 36:4 36:8 37:6 37:11 37:12 37:19 38:21 39:2^{3} 39:4 40:11 40:22 40:24^{2} 40:26 40:29 41:1^{2} 41:2 41:3 41:12^{3} 41:15 41:16^{3} 41:17^{2} 41:22^{5} 41:27 41:28^{2} 42:5^{2} 42:7 42:9 42:11 42:12 42:16^{4} 42:22 43:9^{3} 44:7^{2} 44:9 44:11^{2} 45:8 45:16 45:22^{2} 47:6^{2} 47:14 48:3^{2} 48:5^{2} 48:6 48:7^{2} 48:13 48:14 48:21^{2} 49:9 49:10^{4} 49:18^{2} 49:26 50:6 50:9 51:8^{2} 51:17 51:23^{2} 52:4 52:5^{2} 52:15 54:2 56:5^{2} 56:7^{2} 57:6 57:8 57:13^{2} 59:8 59:12 59:20 59:21 60:9 60:14 61:1 61:3^{2} 61:7 61:8 61:9^{2} 62:12 63:3^{2} 63:6 63:7 63:9^{4} 63:10 63:11 63:12^{2} 63:13 63:19 65:1^{2} 65:8 65:21^{2} 65:23 66:4 66:19^{2} 66:21

JER

1:16 1:17^{2} 2:3 2:13 2:25 2:28 2:37 3:2 4:12 5:3^{2} 5:5 5:6^{2} 5:7^{2} 5:13^{2} 5:14 5:19 6:10 6:13^{2} 6:15^{2} 6:18 6:21 6:30^{2} 7:16 7:22^{2} 7:23 7:25 7:27^{2} 7:28 7:31 7:33 8:2 8:3^{2} 8:4 8:9 8:10^{2} 8:12 8:13^{3} 8:19 9:2 9:7^{2} 9:9 9:10 9:13 9:14 9:15^{2} 9:16^{3} 9:18 9:22 9:25 10:2 10:5^{2} 10:11 10:14 10:16 10:18 11:3 11:4^{2} 11:5 11:6 11:7 11:8^{2} 11:10 11:11^{2} 11:12 11:14^{2} 11:20 11:22 11:23 12:2 12:3^{2} 12:4 12:6 12:14^{2} 12:15^{3} 13:10^{2} 13:12 13:13 13:14^{2} 13:19 13:20 13:21 13:24 14:10 14:12^{2} 14:13 14:14^{3} 14:15 14:16^{3} 14:17^{2} 14:18 15:1^{2} 15:2 15:3 15:4 15:7^{2} 15:8 15:9 15:10 15:16 15:19^{2} 16:3^{2} 16:5 16:6^{2} 16:7^{3} 16:8 16:11^{3} 16:15^{2} 16:16^{2} 16:21^{2} 17:11^{2} 17:18^{4} 17:20 18:8 18:10 18:15 18:17^{2} 18:19 18:20^{2} 18:22 18:23^{2} 19:7^{2} 19:9^{2} 19:11^{2} 20:4^{2} 20:5^{3} 20:12 21:3 21:4 21:7^{2} 22:7 22:9 22:25^{2} 23:2^{2} 23:3^{2} 23:4^{2} 23:8 23:12^{2} 23:14 23:15^{2} 23:17 23:21 23:22 23:32^{4} 23:33 24:1 24:5 24:6^{6} 24:7 24:8 24:9^{2} 24:10^{2} 25:4 25:6^{2} 25:9^{3} 25:10 25:14^{2} 25:16 25:18 25:26 25:27 25:28 25:30^{2} 25:31 26:2 26:3 26:4 26:5 26:19 27:2 27:3 27:4 27:8 27:15 27:17 27:18^{2} 27:22^{3} 28:3 28:13 29:5^{2} 29:9 29:17^{2} 29:18^{3} 29:19^{2} 29:21^{2} 29:22 29:23 29:28^{2} 29:31 30:3 30:9 30:16 30:19^{4} 30:20 30:21 31:4 31:5 31:8^{3} 31:9^{2} 31:13^{2} 31:28^{2} 31:32^{3} 31:34^{2} 32:13 32:14 32:18 32:22^{2} 32:23^{2} 32:33^{2} 32:37^{4} 32:39^{3} 32:40^{3} 32:41^{3} 32:42^{2} 32:44 33:5 33:6^{2} 33:7 33:8 33:9 33:11^{2} 33:13 33:24^{2} 33:26 34:8 34:9 34:10^{2} 34:11 34:13 34:16 34:20^{2} 34:21 34:22 35:2^{3} 35:4 35:5 35:15^{2} 35:16 35:17^{3} 36:3 36:6 36:13 36:14 36:18^{2} 36:25 36:26 36:31^{2} 36:32 37:5 37:10 38:4 38:11 38:26 38:27 39:4 39:5 39:10 40:7 40:9 40:10 40:14 41:5 41:6^{3} 41:7^{2} 41:8^{2} 41:9 41:10 41:18 42:17^{2} 43:1 43:9 43:10^{2} 43:12^{2} 44:4 44:13 44:21 44:27^{2} 44:30 45:5 46:5 46:15 46:21 46:25 46:26 47:2 48:39 49:2 49:11 49:20^{2} 49:32 49:36 49:37^{4} 50:6^{2} 50:7^{2} 50:20 50:21 50:27^{2} 50:28 50:33^{3} 50:43 50:45^{2} 51:1^{2} 51:17 51:19 51:39 51:40 52:3 52:17 52:25 52:26^{2} 52:27^{2}

LA

1:13 1:22 2:2 2:17 2:21 3:20 3:25 3:64 3:65^{2} 3:66 4:4 4:15 4:16^{2}

EZE

1:18 1:19 1:20 1:21 2:4^{2} 2:5 2:6 2:7 3:4 3:6 3:9 3:11^{3} 3:13 3:15^{2} 3:17 3:25^{2} 3:26 3:27 4:6 4:9 4:13 5:2 5:3 5:4^{3} 5:6 5:12 5:13^{2} 5:16 6:2 6:10 6:12 6:14 7:11^{2} 7:16^{2} 7:18 7:19 7:20 7:22 7:27^{2} 8:11^{2} 8:18 9:1 9:2 9:7 9:8 10:1 10:2 10:13 10:16^{2} 10:17 10:19^{2} 11:4 11:5 11:16^{3} 11:19^{2} 11:20 11:21 11:22^{2} 11:24 11:25 12:10^{2} 12:11 12:12 12:14 12:15^{2} 12:16 12:19 12:23^{2} 12:28 13:2 13:6 13:11 13:15 13:17 13:20^{3} 14:3 14:4^{2} 15:7^{3} 16:17 16:18^{2} 16:19 16:20 16:21^{3} 16:27 16:28 16:33 16:36 16:37^{4} 16:50 16:53 16:54 16:61 17:12^{2} 18:19 18:24 18:26 19:12 20:3 20:4^{3} 20:5^{3} 20:6^{3} 20:7 20:8^{2} 20:9^{2} 20:10^{2} 20:11^{3} 20:12^{3} 20:13^{3} 20:14 20:15^{3} 20:17^{3} 20:19 20:21^{4} 20:22 20:23^{3} 20:25 20:26^{2} 20:27 20:28^{2} 20:29 20:38^{2} 20:40^{2} 21:23 21:29 22:26 22:28^{2} 22:30 22:31^{2} 23:4 23:6 23:7^{2} 23:12 23:15 23:16^{2} 23:17^{2} 23:22 23:23^{3} 23:27 23:28^{2} 23:36 23:37^{2} 23:43 23:45 23:46^{2} 23:47^{2} 24:3 24:5 24:20 24:25 24:27 25:2 25:10 25:12 25:17^{2} 26:20^{2} 27:31 28:8 28:18 28:24 28:25 28:26^{2} 29:12 29:14 29:15 29:16 29:21 30:5 30:9 30:23 30:26 31:14 31:16 31:17 31:18 32:10 32:12 32:13^{2} 32:15 32:18^{2} 32:20 32:21 32:22 32:23 32:24^{2} 32:25^{3} 32:26 32:28 32:29^{2} 32:30^{2} 32:31 32:32 33:2 33:6 33:7 33:10 33:21 33:17 33:25 33:27 33:31 33:32^{3} 33:33 34:2 34:3 34:4 34:6 34:10^{2} 34:11 34:12 34:13^{4} 34:14 34:15 34:16 34:20 34:21 34:23^{8} 34:24 34:25 34:26 34:27^{2} 34:28^{2} 34:29 34:30 35:11^{2} 35:12 35:13 36:18 36:19^{2} 36:20 36:23 36:27 36:37^{2} 37:2 37:4 37:8^{3} 37:10 37:12 37:17 37:19^{3} 37:21^{3} 37:22^{2} 37:23^{2} 37:24^{2} 37:26^{5} 37:27 37:28 38:4^{2} 38:5^{2} 38:7 38:8 38:11^{2} 38:15 38:17 39:6 39:7 39:9 39:10^{2} 39:12 39:13^{2} 39:18 39:21 39:23^{2} 39:24^{2} 39:26 39:27^{3} 39:28^{3} 39:29 40:4 40:22 40:26 41:25 42:9 42:11 42:12 43:8^{2} 43:10 43:11^{2} 43:24^{3} 44:11^{2} 44:12^{2} 44:14 44:17 44:19 44:23 44:28^{2} 45:15 46:10 46:17 46:18 46:20 46:23^{2} 46:24 48:10 48:12 48:18

DA

1:4 1:5^{2} 1:12 1:14^{2} 1:16 1:17 1:18^{2} 1:19^{2} 1:20^{2} 2:3 2:21 2:34 2:35^{2} 2:38 3:14 3:20 3:27 4:7 4:19 5:3 5:23 6:2 6:24^{3} 7:8 7:16 7:21 7:24 8:9 8:10 9:4^{2} 9:7 10:7 11:7 11:24 11:30 11:34 11:35^{3} 11:39 12:2

HO

1:6 1:7^{2} 1:10^{2} 2:5 2:7^{3} 2:12^{2} 2:13 2:18^{2} 2:23 4:9^{2} 4:12^{2} 4:16 5:2 5:4 5:5 5:6 5:7 5:10^{2} 6:5^{2} 6:8 7:2 7:7 7:12^{3} 7:13^{3} 8:4 8:5 8:10 8:13 9:2 9:4 9:6^{3} 9:12^{3} 9:14^{2} 9:15^{3} 9:17 10:9 10:10^{2} 11:2^{2} 11:3^{2} 11:4^{3} 11:6 11:7 11:11 13:2^{2} 13:7^{2} 13:8^{3} 13:14^{2} 14:4 14:9^{2}

JOE

2:3^{5} 2:4 2:10 2:17^{2} 3:2^{2} 3:6 3:7^{2} 3:8 3:9

AM

1:6 2:4 2:9 4:3 4:9 5:8 5:11^{2} 5:22 6:1 6:7 7:8 8:2 8:3 9:1^{5} 9:2^{2} 9:3^{2} 9:4^{2} 9:6 9:14^{2} 9:15^{2}

OB

11 18^{2}

JON

1:3 1:5 1:9 1:10 1:12 1:13 3:5^{2} 3:7 3:8 3:10

MIC

2:1 2:2^{2} 2:6^{2} 2:8 2:12 2:13^{3} 3:2 3:3^{2} 3:4^{2} 3:6 4:4 4:7 4:12 5:3 6:11 7:13 7:14

NA

1:7 2:2 2:10 2:11 3:18

HAB

1:10 1:12^{2} 1:13 1:14 1:15^{3} 1:16 2:7 2:17 3:16

ZEP

1:5^{2} 1:6 1:13 1:18^{2} 2:7 2:9^{2} 2:11 3:7 3:8 3:11 3:13 3:18 3:19

HAG

2:22

ZEC

1:3 1:21 2:9 3:5 6:6 6:10 6:11 6:13 7:14^{2} 8:8 9:8 9:14 9:15 9:16 10:1 10:3 10:5 10:6^{5} 10:8^{3} 10:9 10:10^{4} 10:12 11:5^{3} 11:6 11:8 11:12 11:13^{2} 12:8^{2} 13:9^{3} 14:8^{2} 14:13 14:17 14:21

MAL

1:4 2:2 2:5 2:17 3:3 3:7 3:16 3:17 4:1^{2}

MT

2:4 2:7 2:8 2:9 3:7 4:16 4:19 4:21 4:24 5:2 5:19 5:21 5:27 5:33 5:44^{3} 5:46 6:1 6:8 6:26 7:6 7:11 7:12 7:16 7:20 7:23 7:24 7:26 7:29 8:4 8:10 8:15 8:26 8:30 8:32 8:33 9:12 9:15^{3} 9:18 9:24 9:28 9:30 9:36 10:1^{2} 10:5 10:18 10:21 10:25 10:26 10:28 10:29 11:4 11:5 11:11 11:25 12:3 12:4 12:11 12:15 12:16 12:25 12:27 12:39 13:3 13:4 13:7 13:10 13:11 13:13 13:14 13:15 13:17^{2} 13:24 13:28^{2} 13:29 13:30^{2} 13:31 13:33 13:34 13:37 13:39 13:41 13:42 13:51 13:52 13:54 13:57 14:6 14:9 14:16^{2} 14:18 14:25 14:27 15:3 15:10 15:14 15:30^{3} 15:32 15:34 15:36 16:1 16:2 16:4 16:6 16:8 16:12 16:15 17:1 17:2 17:3 17:5 17:7 17:9 17:11 17:12 17:13 17:20 17:22 17:27^{2} 18:2 18:8^{2} 18:12 18:17 18:19 18:20 19:2 19:4^{3} 19:8 19:11 19:13^{2} 19:14 19:15 19:26^{2} 19:28 20:2 20:4 20:6 20:7 20:8 20:12 20:13 20:17 20:23^{2} 20:25^{3} 20:31 20:32 20:34 21:2^{3} 21:3^{2} 21:6 21:7 21:8 21:12^{2} 21:13 21:14 21:16 21:17 21:21 21:24 21:27 21:31^{2} 21:36 21:37 21:42 21:45 22:1 22:3 22:4 22:6^{2} 22:20 22:21 22:29 22:35 22:41 22:43 23:4^{2} 23:13 23:26 23:30 23:31 23:34^{3} 23:37 24:2 24:4 24:16 24:19^{2} 24:39 24:45 25:2 25:3 25:9 25:14 25:16 25:19 25:20 25:22 25:32 25:34 25:40 25:41 25:45 26:10 26:15 26:19 26:22 26:27 26:31 26:36 26:38 26:40 26:43 26:44 26:45 26:48 26:51 26:70 26:71 26:73 27:6 27:7 27:10 27:17 27:21 27:22 27:26 27:35 27:47 27:48 27:65 28:9 28:10 28:16 28:18 28:19 28:20

MK

1:17 1:20 1:22 1:31 1:32 1:38 1:44 2:2^{2} 2:8

2:12 2:14 2:17 2:19^{3} 2:20 2:25 2:26 2:27 3:4 3:5 3:12 3:14 3:17 3:23^{2} 3:33 3:34 4:2^{2} 4:9 4:11^{2} 4:12 4:13 4:21 4:24 4:33 4:34 4:35 4:40 5:10 5:12 5:13 5:16 5:19^{2} 5:38 5:39 5:40^{2} 5:43 6:4 6:5 6:7^{2} 6:8 6:10 6:11 6:13 6:22 6:31 6:33^{2} 6:34^{2} 6:36 6:37^{3} 6:38 6:39 6:41^{3} 6:46 6:48^{4} 6:50^{2} 6:51 7:6 7:9 7:14 7:18 7:36^{2} 8:1 8:3^{2} 8:5 8:6^{2} 8:7^{2} 8:9 8:13 8:14 8:15

8:17 8:21 8:27 8:29 8:30 8:31 8:34 9:1^{2} 9:2^{2} 9:3 9:4 9:7 9:9 9:12 9:14^{2} 9:16 9:29 9:31 9:33 9:35 9:36^{2} 10:1 10:3 10:5 10:6 10:11 10:13^{2} 10:14^{2} 10:16^{3} 10:24^{2} 10:27 10:32^{2} 10:36 10:38 10:39 10:40 10:42^{4} 11:2 11:5^{2} 11:6^{2} 11:8 11:16^{2} 11:17 11:22 11:24^{2} 11:29 11:33 12:1 12:4 12:6 12:12 12:15 12:16 12:17 12:23 12:24 12:28^{2} 12:38 12:43 13:5 13:9 13:12 13:14 13:17^{2} 14:10 14:13 14:16 14:20 14:22 14:23

14:24 14:27 14:34 14:37 14:40 14:41 14:44 14:47 14:48 14:52 14:69^{2} 14:70 15:6 15:7 15:8 15:9 15:11 15:12 15:14 15:15 15:24 15:35 16:6 16:10 16:12 16:13 16:14^{2} 16:15 16:17 16:18 16:19 16:20

LU

1:2 1:22^{2} 1:50 1:52 1:65 1:66^{2} 1:79 2:7 2:9^{2} 2:10 2:15 2:17 2:18 2:19 2:20 2:34 2:38 2:46^{2} 2:49 2:50 2:51^{2} 3:11 3:13 3:14 3:16 4:6 4:18 4:20 4:21 4:22 4:23 4:26 4:27 4:30 4:31

4:39 4:40^{3} 4:41^{2} 4:42 4:43 5:2 5:7 5:14 5:17 5:22 5:25 5:29 5:31 5:34^{2} 5:35 5:36 6:1 6:2 6:3 6:4 6:5 6:9 6:10 6:13 6:17 6:19 6:27 6:28^{2} 6:30 6:31 6:32^{2} 6:33 6:34 6:39 6:47 7:6 7:19 7:22 7:38^{2} 7:42^{2} 7:44 8:21 8:22 8:31 8:32^{3} 8:34 8:36 8:37 8:54 8:56 9:1 9:2 9:3 9:5 9:10 9:11^{3} 9:13^{2} 9:14 9:15 9:16 9:17 9:18 9:20 9:21^{2} 9:23 9:34 9:45 9:46^{2} 9:48 9:54

9:55 9:56 9:61 10:1 10:2 10:9 10:18 10:21 10:24^{2} 10:35 11:2 11:5 11:13 11:15 11:17 11:19 11:31 11:44^{2} 11:47 11:48 11:49^{2} 11:52 11:53 12:4 12:6 12:15 12:16 12:24 12:37^{2} 12:38 12:42 13:2 13:4 13:14 13:23 13:32 13:34 14:5 14:7 14:10 14:15 14:17 14:19 14:23 14:25 15:1 15:3 15:4 15:6 15:12^{2} 16:15 16:28 16:29^{2} 16:30 17:14^{2} 17:15 17:20 17:23^{2} 17:27 17:29 17:37 18:1 18:7 18:8 18:15^{2} 18:16^{2} 18:29 18:31 18:34 19:13^{2}

19:24 19:27^{2} 19:32 19:33 19:40 19:45^{2} 19:46 20:3 20:8 20:15 20:17 20:19 20:23 20:25 20:33 20:34 20:41 21:8 21:10 21:21^{3} 21:23^{2} 21:26 21:29 21:35 22:4 22:6 22:10 22:13 22:15 22:19 22:23 22:24^{2} 22:25^{3} 22:35 22:36 22:38 22:40 22:41 22:45 22:46 22:47 22:50 22:52^{3} 22:55 22:58 22:67 22:70 23:1 23:14 23:17 23:20 23:22 23:23 23:25 23:28 23:34 23:35 23:51 24:1 24:4 24:5 24:10 24:11^{2} 24:13 24:15 24:17 24:18 24:19 24:24 24:25

24:27 24:29 24:30^{2} 24:33^{2} 24:34 24:35 24:36^{2} 24:38 24:40 24:41 24:43 24:44 24:46 24:50^{2} 24:51^{2}

JOH

1:12^{2} 1:22 1:26 1:38^{2} 1:39 2:7^{2} 2:8 2:15 2:16 2:19 2:20 2:24 3:22 4:32 4:34 4:40 4:52 5:11 5:17 5:19 5:21 5:39 6:2 6:7^{2} 6:11 6:13^{2} 6:17 6:20 6:26 6:29 6:31 6:32 6:35 6:43 6:53 6:61 6:70 7:6 7:9 7:16 7:21 7:25 7:33 7:44 7:45 7:47 7:50^{2} 8:2 8:6 8:7 8:12 8:14

8:21 8:23 8:25 8:27 8:28 8:34 8:39 8:42 8:47 8:58 8:59 9:15 9:16 9:19 9:20 9:27 9:30 9:41 10:1 10:4 10:6^{2} 10:7 10:8 10:12 10:16 10:20 10:25 10:27 10:28^{2} 10:29^{2} 10:32 10:34 10:35 11:11 11:14 11:19 11:37 11:44 11:46^{2} 11:49^{2} 12:2 12:20 12:23 12:35 12:36 12:37 12:40 13:1 13:5 13:12 13:17 13:29 14:21 15:6^{2} 15:22 15:24 16:4 16:12 16:19 16:31 17:6 17:8^{2} 17:9^{2} 17:10 17:12^{3} 17:14^{2} 17:15^{2} 17:17 17:18 17:20

17:22 17:23^{2} 17:26^{3} 18:4 18:5^{2} 18:6 18:7 18:9 18:18 18:21^{2} 18:29 18:31 18:38 19:4 19:5 19:6 19:15 19:16 19:24 20:2 20:13 20:17 20:19 20:20 20:21 20:22^{2} 20:23 20:24 20:25 20:26 21:3 21:5 21:6 21:10 21:12 21:13

AC

1:3 1:4^{2} 1:7 1:10 1:16 2:3^{2} 2:4 2:6 2:11 2:14 2:38 2:41 2:45 3:2 3:5^{2} 3:8 3:11 4:1 4:3^{2} 4:4 4:7 4:8 4:13 4:14 4:15 4:16^{2} 4:17 4:18^{2} 4:19 4:21^{3} 4:23

4:24 4:32^{2} 4:33 4:34^{2} 4:35 5:5 5:9 5:13^{2} 5:15^{2} 5:16 5:18 5:19 5:21 5:22 5:24 5:25 5:26 5:27^{3} 5:32 5:33 5:35 5:38 5:40^{2} 6:2 6:6 6:9 7:6^{2} 7:24 7:25 7:26^{2} 7:34 7:36 7:39 7:42 7:43 7:52 8:3 8:5 8:7 8:11 8:14 8:15 8:16 8:17 8:18 8:25^{2} 9:2 9:21^{2} 9:27 9:28 9:38 9:39^{2} 9:40 10:7 10:8^{2} 10:20^{2} 10:23^{3} 10:24 10:28 10:44 10:46 10:48 11:3 11:4 11:12 11:15 11:17 11:20 11:21

11:23 11:28 12:10 12:17^{2} 12:20 12:21 12:25 13:2 13:3^{2} 13:8 13:13 13:15 13:17 13:19 13:20 13:21 13:22 13:27 13:31 13:42 13:43^{2} 13:50 13:51 14:5^{2} 14:18 14:22 14:23^{2} 14:27 15:2^{2} 15:4 15:5^{2} 15:7 15:8^{2} 15:9 15:12 15:14 15:19 15:20 15:21 15:23 15:32 15:37 15:38^{3} 15:39 16:4 16:7 16:10 16:19 16:20 16:22^{2} 16:23^{3} 16:24 16:25 16:30 16:33 16:34^{2} 16:37^{2} 16:39^{3} 16:40 17:2^{2} 17:4 17:5^{2} 17:6 17:9 17:12 17:16 17:17 17:18 17:33

17:34 18:2 18:3 18:6 18:11 18:16 18:19 18:20 18:21 18:26 18:27 19:2 19:3 19:6^{2} 19:9 19:12^{2} 19:13^{2} 19:16^{3} 19:17 19:19^{3} 19:22 19:38 20:1 20:2 20:6 20:7 20:18 20:30 20:32 20:34 20:36 21:1 21:7 21:16 21:19 21:23 21:24^{3} 21:26^{2} 21:32 21:40 22:2 22:5 22:11 22:19 22:20 22:30 23:2 23:10^{2} 23:21^{2} 23:24 23:27 23:31 24:21 24:22 25:5 25:6 25:11 26:10 26:11^{4} 26:13 26:18^{2} 26:20 26:30 27:9 27:10 27:21 27:24 27:33 27:35

27:42 27:43 28:3 28:14 28:17 28:23 28:27

RO

1:19^{2} 1:24 1:26 1:28 1:32^{2} 2:2 2:3 2:7 2:8 2:19 3:2 3:19 3:22 4:11^{2} 4:12 5:14 7:1 8:1 8:28^{2} 8:30^{3} 9:25 9:26 10:2 10:5 10:15 10:19 10:20^{2} 11:8 11:9 11:11 11:12^{2} 11:14^{2} 11:15^{2} 11:17^{2} 11:22 11:23 11:27 11:32 12:14 12:15^{2} 15:3 15:26 15:27^{2} 15:28 15:31 16:10 16:11 16:14 16:15 16:17^{2}

1 CO

1:2 1:11 1:18 1:21 1:24

2:6 2:9 2:10 2:14 4:19 5:12^{2} 5:13 6:4 6:13 6:15 7:8 7:9 7:36 8:9 9:3 9:20^{2} 9:21^{2} 10:4 10:5 10:7 10:8 10:9 10:10 10:11 10:27 11:2 11:22 12:18 14:10 14:22^{4} 14:34 14:35 15:20 16:3 16:18

2 CO

1:4 2:3 2:13 2:15^{2} 4:3 4:4^{2} 5:12 5:15 5:19 6:16^{2} 6:17 8:22 8:24 9:2 9:13 11:8 11:12 12:17 13:2

GA

1:17 2:2^{2} 2:12 2:14 3:10 3:12^{2} 3:22 4:5

4:8 4:15 4:17 6:10 6:16

EPH

2:10 2:17 4:18 5:7 5:11 5:12 6:4 6:5 6:9 6:24

PHP

1:28 2:1 3:8 3:17

COL

2:15 3:7 3:19 4:5 4:13^{2}

1 TH

2:16 4:12 4:13 4:14 4:15 4:17 5:3 5:12 5:13 5:14

2 TH

1:6 1:8 1:10 2:10 2:11 3:12

1 TI

1:10 1:16 1:18 3:7 3:10 4:3 4:15 4:16^{2} 5:4 5:16^{3}

5:20 6:2^{3} 6:17

2 TI

2:14^{2} 2:19 2:22 2:25 3:11 3:14 4:8

TIT

1:13 1:15 2:9 3:1 3:13 3:15

HEB

1:12 1:14 2:1 2:3 2:4 2:11 2:15 2:18 3:17 3:18 4:2^{3} 4:8 5:2 5:9 5:14 6:6 6:7 6:12 6:16 7:6 7:8 7:25^{2} 8:8 8:9^{3} 8:10^{2} 9:10 9:28 10:14 10:16^{2} 10:33 10:39^{2} 11:6 11:13^{3} 11:16 11:28 11:31 12:9 12:11 12:19 13:3^{3} 13:7 13:9 13:17 13:24

JAS

1:12 2:5 2:16^{2} 2:25 3:18 5:3 5:4 5:11 5:14

1 PE

1:11 1:12 2:7 2:8 2:14^{2} 3:7 3:12 4:4 4:6 4:17 4:19

2 PE

1:1 1:12 2:1 2:4^{2} 2:6^{2} 2:8 2:10 2:11 2:18 2:19 2:20 2:21^{2} 2:22 3:16

1 JO

2:26 4:4 4:5 5:16

3 JO

9 10^{2}

JUDE

1 5 7 11 15 23

RE

2:2^{3} 2:9 2:14 2:15

2:16 2:22 2:27 3:9^{2} 3:10 4:8 5:8 5:11 5:13 6:8 6:9 6:10 6:11^{2} 7:4 7:14 7:15 7:16 7:17^{2} 8:2 8:12 9:3 9:4 9:5^{2} 9:6 9:11 9:16 9:17^{2} 9:19 10:4 11:1 11:5^{2} 11:6 11:7^{3} 11:10^{2} 11:11^{3} 11:12^{2} 11:18^{2} 12:4 12:10 12:12 13:6 13:7 13:12 13:14^{2} 14:6 14:9 14:13 15:1 15:2^{2} 16:2 16:6 16:14 16:16 17:14 18:14 19:15 19:18^{2} 19:20^{2} 20:4^{3} 20:8 20:9 20:10 20:11 20:13 21:3^{2} 21:14 21:24 22:5 22:8 22:9

THEY

1992, *846*

GE

2:4 2:24 2:25 3:7 3:8 4:8 5:2 6:2^{2} 6:4 6:19

7:14 7:15 7:16 7:23^{2} 8:17 9:2 9:23 11:2^{2} 11:3^{2} 11:4 11:6^{2} 11:7

11:8 11:31^{2} 12:5^{3} 12:12^{2} 12:20 13:6^{2} 13:11 14:4 14:7 14:8 14:10 14:11

14:12 15:13 15:14^{2} 15:16 18:5 18:8 18:9 18:19 18:21 19:2 19:3^{2} 19:4

19:5 19:8 19:9^{2} 19:11^{2} 19:16 19:17 19:33 19:35 20:11 20:17 21:30 21:31

21:32^{2} 22:6 22:8 22:9 22:19 24:19 24:41 24:54^{2} 24:57 24:58 24:59 24:60

24:61 25:18 25:25 26:18 26:20 26:21 26:22 26:28 26:30 26:31^{2} 26:32 29:2

29:3 29:4 29:5 29:6 29:8^{2} 29:20 30:38 30:41 31:23 31:37 31:43 31:46^{2}

31:54 32:18 33:4 33:6^{2} 33:7 34:5 34:7^{2} 34:8 34:14 34:22 34:23 34:25

34:26 34:27 34:28 34:29 34:30 34:31 35:4 35:5^{2} 35:16 36:7^{2} 37:4 37:5

37:8 37:16 37:17 37:18^{2} 37:19 37:23 37:24 37:25^{2} 37:28^{2} 37:31 37:32^{2} 38:21

39:22 40:4 40:5 40:6 40:8 40:15 41:2 41:14 41:18 41:21^{3} 41:43 42:7

42:8 42:10 42:13 42:20 42:21 42:23 42:26 42:28 42:29 42:35^{3} 43:2^{2} 43:7

43:15 43:18^{2} 43:19^{2} 43:24 43:25^{3} 43:26 43:28^{2} 43:32 43:33 43:34 44:1 44:4

44:7 44:13 44:14 45:3 45:4 45:24 45:25 45:27 46:6^{2} 46:28 46:32^{2}

47:1^{2} 47:2 47:4 47:14 47:17 47:18 47:22 47:25 47:27 48:5 48:9

49:6^{2} 49:26 49:31^{2} 50:8 50:10^{2} 50:11 50:15 50:16 50:17^{2} 50:18 50:26

EX

1:10^{2} 1:11^{2} 1:12^{3} 1:14^{2} 1:19 2:16 2:18 2:19 2:23 3:13

3:18 4:1[2] 4:5 4:8[2] 4:9 4:18 4:31[2] 5:1 5:3 5:8[3] 5:9 5:10 5:16 5:19 5:20[2] 5:21 6:4 6:9 6:27 7:6 7:7 7:10 7:11 7:12[2] 7:16 7:17 7:19 7:24 8:1 8:8 8:9 8:11 8:14 8:17 8:18 8:20 8:21 9:1 9:10 9:13 9:19 9:32 10:3 10:5[2] 10:6[2] 10:7 10:8 10:11 10:12 10:14[2] 10:15[2] 10:23 12:3 12:7[2] 12:8[2] 12:28 12:33[2] 12:35 12:36[3] 12:39[4] 12:50 13:17 13:20 14:2 14:3 14:4 14:5 14:10 14:11 14:15 14:17 14:25 15:5 15:10 15:16 15:22[2] 15:23[3] 15:27[2] 16:1 16:4 16:5[3] 16:10 16:15 16:18[2] 16:20 16:21 16:22

16:24 16:27 16:32 16:35[3] 17:4 17:7 17:12 18:7[2] 18:11 18:16[2] 18:20[2] 18:22[3] 18:26[3] 19:1 19:2 19:13 19:14 19:17 19:21 20:18 20:19 21:28 21:35 23:11 23:33[2] 24:2 24:7 24:10 24:11 25:2 25:10 25:15 25:37[2] 26:24[3] 26:25 27:8 27:20 28:3 28:4[2] 28:5 28:6 28:20 28:21 28:28 28:30 28:38 28:41 28:42 28:43[4] 29:33[2] 29:46 30:4 30:12 30:13 30:15 30:20[4] 30:21[4] 30:29 30:30 31:6 31:11 32:4 32:6 32:8[2] 32:13 32:15 32:17 32:20 32:22 32:23 32:24 32:35 33:4 34:15 34:30 35:21[2] 35:22 35:25 36:3[2] 36:4 36:5 36:6 36:7 36:29 39:1 39:3 39:4

39:6 39:7 39:9 39:10 39:13 39:15 39:16 39:17 39:18 39:19 39:20 39:21 39:24 39:25 39:27 39:30 39:31 39:32 39:33 39:43[2] 40:15 40:32[3] 40:37

LE

2:12 4:13 4:14 4:24 4:33 6:16 6:20 7:2[2] 8:28 9:5 9:13 9:20 9:24 10:2 10:5 10:7 10:14 10:15 10:19 11:8 11:10 11:11 11:13[3] 11:28 11:31 11:32 11:35 11:42 13:54 14:36 14:40[2] 14:41[2] 14:42 15:18 15:31[2] 16:1 16:27 17:5[2] 17:7[2] 18:17 19:20 20:12 20:13 20:14[2] 20:16 20:17 20:19 20:20[2] 20:21 20:23 20:27 21:5[2] 21:6[3] 21:7[2] 22:2[3] 22:9[3] 22:11 22:15[2] 22:16 22:18 22:25 23:17[3] 23:18 23:20 24:2 24:9 24:11 24:12 24:23 24:31[2] 25:42[2] 25:45[2] 25:46 25:55 26:7 26:17 26:26 26:36 26:37[2] 26:39[2] 26:40[3] 26:41 26:43[2] 26:44 27:11

NU

1:1 1:18[2] 1:46 1:50[2] 1:54 2:2 2:3 2:16 2:17[2] 2:24 2:31[2] 2:34[2] 3:4[2] 3:6 3:7 3:8 3:9 3:10 3:13 3:31 4:5 4:7 4:8 4:9[2] 4:10 4:11 4:12[2] 4:13 4:14[3] 4:15[2] 4:19[2] 4:20[2] 4:25 4:26 4:37 4:41 4:49[2] 5:2 5:3 5:7 5:9 6:7 6:27 7:3[2] 7:5 7:9 7:11 8:11 8:16 8:21 8:22 8:24 8:25 9:1 9:4 9:5 9:6[2] 9:11

9:12[2] 9:18[2] 9:20[2] 9:21[2] 9:22 9:23[3] 10:3 10:4 10:6 10:8 10:10 10:13 10:21 10:28 10:33 10:34 11:13 11:16 11:17 11:21 11:25 11:26[2] 11:32[2] 11:34 12:2 12:4 12:5 13:2 13:18 13:19[3] 13:21 13:22 13:23[3] 13:25 13:26 13:27 13:31 13:32[9] 14:4 14:7 14:9 14:11 14:12 14:14[2] 14:23 14:27 14:31 14:32 14:35[2] 14:40 14:44 15:25 15:32 15:33 15:34 15:38[2] 16:2 16:3 16:16 16:18 16:22 16:27 16:29 16:30 16:33[2] 16:34 16:37 16:38[3] 16:39[2] 16:42 16:45 16:49 17:5 17:9 17:10 18:2 18:3[3] 18:4 18:6 18:9 18:12 18:13 18:15 18:17 18:21 18:22 18:23[2]

18:24[2] 19:2 19:17 20:2 20:6 20:27 20:29 21:3 21:4 21:6 21:11 21:12 21:13 21:16 21:18 21:27 21:32 21:33 21:35[2] 22:3 22:5[2] 22:6 22:7 22:12 22:14 22:15 22:16 22:39 24:6 25:2 25:18[2] 26:9 26:10 26:41 26:50 26:55 26:57 26:61 26:62 26:63 26:64 26:65 27:2 27:21[2] 28:19 28:31 29:8 29:13 30:9 31:7[2] 31:8[2] 31:10[2] 31:11 31:12 31:49 31:52 32:1 32:5 32:9[3] 32:11 32:12 32:16 32:30[2] 32:38 33:3 33:6 33:7[2] 33:8 33:9[2] 33:10 33:11 33:12 33:13 33:14 33:15 33:16 33:17 33:18 33:19 33:20 33:21 33:22 33:23 33:24 33:25 33:26 33:27

33:28 33:29 33:30 33:31 33:32 33:33 33:34 33:35 33:36 33:37 33:41 33:42 33:43 33:44 33:45 33:46 33:47 33:48 33:49 34:29 35:2 35:3 35:12 36:2 36:3[2] 36:4 36:6[2] 36:12

DE

1:22 1:24 1:25 1:39[2] 2:4 2:12 2:15 2:21 2:22 3:20 4:9 4:10[3] 4:45 4:46 4:47 5:28[3] 5:29 5:31 6:8 7:4[2] 7:20 7:23 9:12[2] 9:14 9:29 10:5 10:7 10:11 11:4 11:18 11:30 12:30 12:31[2] 14:7[2] 14:12 14:19 15:6 16:16 16:18 17:5 17:9 17:10[2] 17:11[3] 18:1 18:2 18:3 18:8 18:17[2] 19:14 20:8 20:9 20:11 20:18[2] 20:20 21:2

21:6 21:7 21:15 21:18 21:20 22:17 22:19 22:21 22:22 22:24 22:28 23:3 23:4[2] 25:1[2] 25:12 28:7 28:10 28:22 28:41 28:46 28:60 29:22 29:25 29:26[2] 31:12[2] 31:16 31:17[2] 31:18[2] 31:20[2] 31:21 31:24 31:30 32:5[2] 32:7 32:16[2] 32:17[2] 32:20 32:21[2] 32:24 32:27 32:28 32:29[3] 32:37 33:3 33:9 33:10[2] 33:11 33:17[2] 33:19[3]

JOS

1:15 1:16 2:1 2:3 2:4 2:7[2] 2:8 2:13 2:21 2:22 2:24 3:1[2] 3:3 3:6 3:7 3:13 3:15 4:8 4:9 4:14[2] 4:16 4:18 4:20 5:4 5:5 5:6 5:7[2] 5:8[3] 5:11 5:12[2] 6:5 6:11 6:14[2] 6:15[2]

6:19 6:20 6:21 6:23 6:24[2] 7:3[2] 7:4 7:5 7:11[3] 7:12 7:21 7:22 7:23 7:24 7:25 7:26 8:5 8:6[3] 8:9 8:13 8:14 8:15 8:16 8:17 8:19[2] 8:20[2] 8:21 8:22[3] 8:23 8:24[3] 8:29 8:31 8:33 9:2 9:4[2] 9:6 9:8 9:9 9:13 9:16[4] 9:24 9:26 10:2 10:5 10:11[4] 10:20 10:23 10:24[2] 10:26 10:27[2] 10:34 10:35 10:36 10:37 10:39 11:4 11:5 11:7 11:8[2] 11:11 11:14[3] 11:19 11:20[2] 14:4 14:5 16:10 17:4 17:10 17:13 17:16[2] 17:18[2] 18:4[2] 18:5 19:2 19:49 19:50 19:51 20:2 20:4 20:5 20:7 20:8 21:2 21:9 21:11 21:12 21:13

21:20 21:21 21:27 21:43 22:6 22:9 22:10 22:15[2] 22:28 23:12 23:13 24:1 24:2 24:7 24:8 24:22 24:30 24:32 24:33

JG

1:4 1:5[3] 1:6 1:7 1:10 1:16 1:17 1:19 1:20 1:22 1:24 1:25[2] 1:28 1:32 1:34 1:35 2:3 2:5[2] 2:9 2:12 2:13 2:14 2:15[2] 2:17[4] 2:19[2] 2:22 3:4 3:6 3:12 3:24[2] 3:25[3] 3:26 3:28 3:29 4:12 4:24 5:7 5:8 5:11[2] 5:14 5:19 5:20 5:23 5:30[2] 6:3 6:4 6:5[4] 6:29[3] 6:35 7:11 7:19[2] 7:20 7:21 7:25[3] 8:1 8:5 8:18[2] 8:19 8:24[2] 8:25[2] 8:28 8:35 9:3 9:4

9:7 9:8 9:9 9:25 9:27 9:31 9:34 9:36 9:41 9:42 9:46 9:51 9:55 10:4 10:8 10:16 11:2 11:6 11:13 11:17 11:18 11:21 11:22 12:4 12:6[2] 14:9 14:11[2] 14:13 14:14 14:15 15:6 15:10 15:11 15:12 15:13[2] 16:2 16:7 16:11 16:23 16:24[2] 16:25[3] 16:30 17:4 18:2[3] 18:3[3] 18:5 18:7[2] 18:8 18:9 18:12[2] 18:13 18:15 18:19 18:21 18:22 18:23[2] 18:26 18:27[2] 18:28[2] 18:29 18:31 19:4 19:5 19:8[2] 19:11 19:14[2] 19:15 19:21 19:22 19:25[2] 20:5 20:6 20:10[3] 20:22 20:31 20:32 20:34 20:36[3] 20:38 20:39[2] 20:41 20:42[2] 20:43 20:45[2] 20:48[2] 21:5 21:8

21:12[2] 21:14[3] 21:17 21:19 21:20 21:23[2] 21:24

RU

1:2 1:4[2] 1:7 1:9 1:10 1:11 1:13 1:14 1:19[4] 1:22 2:4 2:9[2] 2:21 2:22 4:2 4:17

1 SA

1:9[2] 1:19 1:25 2:4 2:5[2] 2:12 2:14 2:15 2:20 2:22 2:26 2:27 2:30 2:34 4:2[2] 4:4 4:6[2] 4:7[2] 4:9 4:10 5:2 5:3[2] 5:4 5:7 5:8[2] 5:9[2] 5:10[2] 5:11 6:4[2] 6:6[2] 6:11 6:12 6:13[2] 6:14 6:16 6:18 6:19 6:21 7:6 7:7 7:10 7:11 7:13 8:2 8:6 8:7[3] 8:8[3] 8:19 9:4[4] 9:5 9:10 9:11[2] 9:12 9:13 9:14[2] 9:20 9:25

9:26[2] 9:27 10:2 10:4 10:5 10:10 10:14 10:21 10:22 10:23 10:27 11:5[2] 11:7 11:9[2] 11:11[2] 11:15[2] 12:4 12:5 12:9[2] 12:10 12:21 13:5 13:6 13:21 14:9 14:10 14:11 14:13 14:15 14:16 14:17 14:20 14:21 14:22[2] 14:25 14:30 14:31 14:33[2] 14:35 14:36 15:3 15:6 15:9 15:15 15:18 16:6 17:11 17:19 17:31 17:51 17:53 18:6 18:7 18:8[2] 18:20 18:27 18:30 19:1 19:8 19:20[2] 19:31[2] 19:22 19:24 20:11 20:41 21:11 22:1 22:4 22:11 22:17 23:1[2] 23:12 23:13 23:18 23:24 23:25 23:28 25:7 25:8 25:9 25:11 25:13 25:16 25:26 25:29 25:41 25:43

26:12[2] 26:19[3] 27:10 28:4 28:8 28:25[2] 29:5 30:2 30:4 30:10 30:11[2] 30:12 30:16[2] 30:19 30:20 30:21[3] 30:22[2] 30:24 31:7[2] 31:8 31:9 31:10[2] 31:13

2 SA

1:12[2] 1:23[3] 2:3 2:4[3] 2:13 2:16[2] 2:24 2:28 2:29 2:32[2] 3:11 3:21 3:23 3:32 4:6[3] 4:7[2] 4:8 4:12[2] 5:3 5:8 5:17 5:21 6:3 6:4 6:6 6:13 6:17 7:10 8:14 9:2 10:5 10:6 10:13 10:14 10:15 10:16 10:19[2] 11:10 11:20 12:18 12:19 12:20 13:9 13:30 13:32 14:6 14:7[2] 14:11[2] 15:24 15:29 15:30 15:36 16:22 17:8[2] 17:10 17:17[2] 17:18[2] 17:20[4] 17:21[2] 17:22

17:29 18:3[2] 18:17 19:3 19:8 19:14 19:17 20:3 20:7 20:8 20:14 20:15[2] 20:18[3] 20:22[2] 21:5 21:9[2] 21:13 21:14[2] 21:18 21:19 22:39[2] 22:42 22:45 22:46 23:6 23:7 23:9 24:3 24:5 24:6[2] 24:7 24:8[2] 24:13 24:17

1 KI

1:1 1:3 1:7 1:23 1:25 1:32 1:39 1:41 1:44 1:45 1:53 2:7 2:39 3:22 3:24 3:28[2] 4:21 4:27 4:28 5:1 5:6 5:12 5:14 5:17 5:18 6:8 6:10 6:27 7:28 7:47 8:1 8:4 8:8[3] 8:9 8:25 8:26 8:30 8:33 8:35[2] 8:36 8:40[2] 8:42 8:43 8:46[2] 8:47[2] 8:50[2] 8:51 8:52 8:66

9:8 9:9[2] 9:12 9:22 9:28 10:25 10:29 11:2[2] 11:18[3] 11:24 11:29 11:33 11:41 12:3 12:7[2] 12:8 12:13 12:20 12:24 12:27 13:11 13:13 13:20 13:25 13:27 13:30 14:15 14:18 14:19 14:22[2] 14:23 14:24 14:29 15:7 15:8 15:22 15:23 15:31 16:5 16:13[2] 16:14 16:17 16:20 16:27 18:6 18:10[2] 18:26[3] 18:28 18:29 18:34[2] 18:39[2] 18:40 19:10 19:14 19:21 20:6[2] 20:12 20:15 20:16 20:17 20:18[2] 20:20 20:23[2] 20:25 20:29 20:32 20:33 21:12 21:13 21:14 22:1 22:6 22:32[2] 22:33 22:37 22:38 22:39 22:45 22:48

2 KI

1:6 1:8 1:18 2:2 2:4 2:6 2:7 2:8[2] 2:9 2:11 2:14 2:15[2] 2:16 2:17[3] 2:18 2:20 3:9 3:21 3:22 3:23[2] 3:24[3] 3:25[3] 3:26 3:27 4:39 4:40[4] 4:42 4:43[2] 4:44 5:23 5:24 6:4[2] 6:14 6:16[2] 6:18 6:20[4] 6:22 6:23[2] 6:25 7:3 7:4[2] 7:5[2] 7:6 7:7 7:8 7:9 7:10[3] 7:11 7:12[3] 7:13[2] 7:14 7:15 8:23 9:12 9:13 9:21 9:27 9:33 9:35[2] 9:36 9:37 10:4 10:7 10:8 10:13 10:14 10:16 10:20 10:21 10:24 10:25 10:26 10:27 10:34 10:35 11:2 11:7 11:9 11:12[2] 11:16 11:17 11:18 11:19 11:20 12:10[2] 12:11[2] 12:14 12:15[3] 12:19 12:21 13:5

13:6 13:8 13:9 13:12 13:20 13:21[3] 14:12 14:15 14:18 14:19[2] 14:20 14:28 15:6 15:7 15:11 15:15 15:16 15:21 15:26 15:31 15:36 16:5 16:18 16:19 17:8 17:9 17:10 17:11 17:12 17:14 17:15[3] 17:16 17:17 17:19 17:21 17:22 17:24 17:25 17:26[3] 17:28[2] 17:29 17:32 17:33[2] 17:34[3] 17:40[2] 17:41 18:10 18:12 18:17[3] 18:18 18:20 18:27 18:34 18:35 19:3 19:18[2] 19:26[2] 19:31 19:35[2] 19:37 20:7 20:14[2] 20:15[2] 20:18[2] 20:20 21:8 21:9 21:14 21:15 21:17 21:25 22:7 22:14 22:17[2] 22:19 22:20 23:1 23:8 23:9 23:28 24:5 25:1 25:6[2] 25:7 25:14[2] 25:23[2] 25:26

44:14[2] 46:6 46:12 46:15 46:16 46:17 46:21[2] 46:22 46:23[2] 48:2 48:32 48:34 48:39 48:45 49:9[3] 49:12 49:23[2] 49:29[3] 50:3[2] 50:4[2] 50:5 50:6[3] 50:7 50:9 50:16[2] 50:20 50:33 50:36[2] 50:37[2] 50:38[2] 50:42[3] 51:2 51:4 51:14 51:18[2] 51:24 51:26 51:30[3] 51:32 51:38[2] 51:39 51:57 51:58 51:64 52:7 52:9 52:18[2]

LA

1:2 1:6 1:8 1:10 1:11[2] 1:14 1:19[2] 1:21[3] 2:7 2:8 2:10[2] 2:12[2] 2:14 2:15 2:16[2] 2:19[2] 3:6 3:23 3:53 4:2 4:3 4:5[2] 4:7[2] 4:8 4:9[2] 4:10 4:12 4:14[2] 4:15[4] 4:16[2] 4:18 4:19[2] 5:11 5:13

EZE

1:5 1:7 1:8[2] 1:9[3] 1:10[3] 1:12[4] 1:16 1:17[4] 1:18[2] 1:20 1:24[3] 1:25 2:3 2:4 2:5[4] 2:6 2:7[3] 3:6 3:7 3:9 3:11[2] 3:15 3:25 3:26 3:27 4:16 4:17 5:6[2] 5:12 5:13 5:17 6:9[4] 6:10 6:11 6:13 6:14 7:13 7:14 7:16 7:18 7:19[2] 7:20 7:21 7:22 7:24 7:25 7:26 7:27 8:6 8:9 8:12 8:13 8:16 8:17[4] 8:18 9:2 9:6 9:7 9:8 9:9 10:10 10:11[7] 10:12 10:17[2] 10:19 10:20 10:22 11:7 11:15 11:16 11:18[2] 11:20[2] 12:2[2] 12:3[2] 12:4 12:11 12:12 12:15 12:16[3] 12:19 12:23 12:27 13:6[3] 13:9[3] 13:10 13:15 13:21 14:5 14:10 14:11 14:14 14:15 14:16[2] 14:18[2] 14:20[2] 14:22 14:23 15:7 15:8 16:33[2] 16:37 16:39[2] 16:40[2] 16:41 16:47 16:50 16:51 16:52[2] 17:15 17:21 17:23 18:22 19:4 19:9[2] 20:8[3] 20:9 20:12 20:13[3] 20:16 20:20 20:21[2] 20:24 20:25 20:26[2] 20:27 20:28[4] 20:38[2] 20:49 21:7 21:23 21:29[2] 22:7[3] 22:9[2] 22:10[2] 22:12 22:18[2] 22:20 22:25[3] 22:26[2] 22:29 23:3[3] 23:4[2] 23:8[2] 23:10[2] 23:13 23:17 23:24[2] 23:25[3] 23:26 23:29 23:37[3] 23:38[2] 23:39[3] 23:40 23:43 23:44[3] 23:45[2] 23:47 23:49 24:14 24:25 24:27 25:3 25:4[3] 25:11 25:13 25:14[2] 25:17 26:4 26:6 26:12[3] 26:16[2] 26:17 27:5[2] 27:6 27:10[2] 27:11[2] 27:12 27:13[2] 27:14 27:15 27:16 27:17[2] 27:21[2] 27:22[2] 27:29 27:30 27:31[2] 27:32 27:35 28:3 28:7[2] 28:8 28:16 28:17 28:19 28:22 28:23 28:24 28:25[2] 28:26[3] 29:6 29:7[2] 29:9 29:13 29:14 29:15 29:16[2] 29:20 29:21 30:4 30:6[2] 30:7 30:8 30:11 30:19 30:25 30:26 31:14 31:17[2] 32:3 32:10 32:12 32:15 32:16[2] 32:20 32:21[2] 32:24 32:25[2] 32:26 32:27[3] 32:29 32:30[2] 33:24 33:27[2] 33:29[2] 33:31[5] 33:32[2] 33:33 34:5[3] 34:10 34:12 34:14[2] 34:19[2] 34:22 34:25 34:27 34:28[2] 34:29 34:30[2] 35:8 35:12[2] 35:15 36:3 36:7 36:8 36:11 36:12 36:13 36:17 36:18[2] 36:19 36:20[4] 36:21 36:35 36:38 37:2 37:9 37:10 37:11 37:17 37:19 37:21 37:22[2] 37:23[3] 37:24[2] 37:25[3] 37:26 37:27 38:8 38:23 39:6 39:9[2] 39:10[3] 39:11[2] 39:12 39:14[2] 39:16 39:23[2] 39:26[3] 39:28 40:10 40:22 40:38 40:41 40:42[2] 40:49 41:6[3] 42:6 42:11[2] 42:13[2] 42:14[4] 43:7 43:8[2] 43:9[2] 43:10 43:11[3] 43:18 43:22[2] 43:24 43:25 43:26[2] 44:7 44:10 44:11[3] 44:12[2] 44:13[3] 44:15[2] 44:16[3] 44:17[3] 44:18[2] 44:19[5] 44:20[2] 44:21 44:22[2] 44:23 44:24[4] 44:25[2] 44:26 44:29 45:8 46:6 46:10[2] 46:15 46:20[2] 47:9 47:10 47:11 47:12 47:22[2] 48:14 48:19

DA

1:4 1:5 1:16 1:19 2:2 2:7 2:13 2:18 2:43[2] 2:46 3:3 3:9 3:12 3:13 3:24 3:25 3:28 4:6 4:7 4:25[3] 4:26 4:32[2] 5:3 5:4 5:8 5:15[2] 5:20 5:21 5:23 5:29 6:4 6:12 6:13 6:16 6:22 6:23 6:24[3] 7:5 7:12 7:13 7:25 7:26 9:7 9:11 10:7 11:2 11:6[2] 11:14 11:21 11:22 11:25 11:26 11:27 11:31[2] 11:33[2] 11:34[2] 12:3[2]

HO

1:11 2:4 2:8 2:17 2:21 2:22 2:23 4:2 4:4 4:7[2] 4:8[2] 4:10[3] 4:12 4:13 4:14[3] 4:18 4:19 5:4[2] 5:6[2] 5:7[2] 5:15[2] 6:7[2] 6:9 7:1 7:2[2] 7:3 7:4 7:6[2] 7:7 7:10 7:11[2] 7:12 7:13[3] 7:14[4] 7:15 7:16[2] 8:1 8:4[4] 8:5 8:7[2] 8:8 8:9 8:10[2] 8:12 8:13[2] 9:3[2] 9:4[2] 9:6 9:9 9:10[2] 9:12 9:16[2] 9:17[2] 10:1 10:2 10:3 10:4 10:8 10:9 10:10 11:2[3] 11:3 11:4 11:5 11:7 11:10 11:11 12:1 12:8 12:11[2] 13:2[2] 13:3 13:6[3] 13:16 14:7[2]

JOE

1:18 2:4 2:5 2:7[4] 2:8[3] 2:9[4] 2:17 3:2 3:3[2] 3:8 3:19

AM

1:3 1:6 1:9 1:13[2] 2:4 2:6 2:8[2] 3:3 3:10 4:8 5:10[2] 5:12[3] 5:16[2] 6:2 6:6 6:7 6:9 6:14 7:2 8:3 8:12[2] 8:14[2] 9:2[2] 9:3[2] 9:4 9:12 9:14[3] 9:15

OB

5[3] 7 16[4] 18 19[3]

JON

1:7[2] 1:8 1:11 1:13 1:14 1:15 2:8 3:10

MIC

1:5 1:7 1:16 2:1 2:2[2] 2:6[3] 2:12 2:13 3:3 3:4[2] 3:5 3:7 3:10 3:11 4:3[2] 4:4 4:12[2] 5:1 5:4 5:6 5:15 7:1 7:2[2] 7:3[2] 7:4 7:16 7:17[3]

NA

1:10[3] 1:12[2] 2:4[3] 2:5[2] 2:8[2] 3:3 3:7 3:10 3:12[2] 3:17[2]

HAB

1:7 1:8 1:9[2] 1:10[3] 1:15[3] 1:16 1:17 2:7 3:10 3:11 3:14

ZEP

1:11 1:13[2] 1:17[2] 2:4 2:7[2] 2:8 2:10[2] 3:3 3:4 3:7 3:9 3:12 3:13 3:19

HAG

1:14 2:14

ZEC

1:4 1:5[2] 1:6[2] 1:10 1:11 1:15 2:9 3:5 3:8 4:10[2] 5:9[2] 6:7[2] 6:15 7:2 7:11[2] 7:12[2] 7:13[2] 7:14[2] 8:8[2] 9:15[3] 9:16 10:2[3] 10:5[2] 10:6 10:7 10:8[2] 10:9[2] 10:12 11:5 11:6 11:12 12:2 12:6 12:10[3] 13:2 13:4 13:9[2] 14:12 14:13 14:21

MAL

1:4[2] 1:7 3:3 3:15[2] 3:16 3:17 4:3

MT

1:11 1:12 1:18 1:23 2:5 2:9[3] 2:10[2] 2:11[4] 2:12[2] 2:13 2:18 2:20 4:6 4:18 4:20 4:22 4:24 5:4[2] 5:5 5:6[2] 5:7 5:8 5:9 5:10 5:12 5:16 6:2[2] 6:5[3] 6:7[2] 6:16[3] 6:26[3] 6:28[3] 7:6 7:15 8:16 8:29 8:32[2] 8:33 8:34[2] 9:2 9:8 9:11 9:12[2] 9:15 9:17 9:24 9:28 9:31[2] 9:32[2] 9:36 10:17[2] 10:19 10:23 10:25[2] 10:36 11:7 11:8 11:18 11:19 11:20 11:21 12:2 12:3 12:10[2] 12:14 12:16 12:24 12:27 12:36 12:41 12:45 13:5[3] 13:6[3] 13:13[3] 13:15[2] 13:16[2] 13:41 13:48 13:51 13:54 13:56 13:57 14:5 14:13 14:15 14:16 14:17 14:20[2] 14:21 14:26[2] 14:32 14:33 14:34[2] 14:35 14:36 15:2[2] 15:9 15:12 15:14 15:18 15:31[2] 15:32[2] 15:34 15:37[2] 15:38 16:5 16:7 16:12 16:14 16:20 16:28 17:6 17:8[2] 17:9 17:12[2] 17:14 17:16 17:22 17:23[2] 17:24[2] 18:19 18:31 19:5 19:6 19:7 19:11 19:25 20:4 20:7 20:9[2] 20:10[3] 20:11[2] 20:18 20:22 20:24 20:25 20:29 20:30 20:31[2] 20:33 20:34 21:1 21:7 21:15 21:20 21:25 21:27 21:31 21:34 21:36 21:37 21:38 21:39 21:41 21:45 21:46[3] 22:3 22:5 22:8 22:10 22:15 22:16 22:19 22:21 22:22[2] 22:28 22:30 22:33 22:34 22:42 23:3[2] 23:4[2] 23:5[2] 23:25 24:9 24:24 24:26 24:30 24:31 24:38 25:3 25:5 25:10[2] 25:44 26:4 26:5 26:8 26:15 26:19 26:21 26:22 26:26 26:30[2] 26:50 26:52 26:57 26:60 26:66 26:67 26:73 27:4 27:7 27:9[2] 27:13 27:15 27:16 27:17 27:18 27:20 27:21 27:22 27:23 27:28 27:29[3] 27:30 27:31[2] 27:32[3] 27:33 27:34 27:35[3] 27:36 27:39 27:47 27:54[2] 27:66 28:8 28:9[2] 28:10[2] 28:11 28:12[2] 28:15[2] 28:17[2]

MK

1:5 1:16 1:18 1:20 1:21 1:22 1:27[3] 1:29[2] 1:30 1:32 1:34 1:36 1:37[2] 1:45 2:3 2:4[4] 2:8 2:12 2:15 2:16 2:17[2] 2:18 2:19[2] 2:20 2:23 2:24 2:25 3:2[2] 3:4 3:6 3:8[2] 3:9 3:10 3:11 3:12 3:13 3:14 3:19 3:20 3:21[2] 3:28 3:30 3:32 4:10 4:12[3] 4:15[2] 4:16[2] 4:17 4:18 4:20 4:33 4:34 4:36[2] 4:38 4:41 5:1 5:13 5:14[2] 5:15[2] 5:16 5:17 5:40 5:42 6:3 6:8 6:12 6:13 6:29 6:30[2] 6:31 6:32 6:34 6:36[2] 6:37 6:38[2] 6:40 6:42 6:43 6:44 6:49[2] 6:50 6:51 6:52 6:53[2] 6:54[2] 6:55 6:56[2] 7:2[2] 7:3 7:4[4] 7:7 7:15 7:32 7:36[2] 8:2 8:3 8:5 8:6 8:7 8:8[2] 8:9 8:14 8:16 8:19 8:20 8:22 8:28 8:30 9:1 9:4 9:6 9:8[2] 9:9[3] 9:10 9:11 9:13[2] 9:15 9:18[2] 9:20 9:30 9:31 9:32 9:34[2] 10:4 10:8[2] 10:13 10:23 10:26 10:32[4] 10:33 10:34 10:37 10:39 10:41 10:42 10:46 10:49 11:1 11:4[2] 11:6[2] 11:7 11:9[2] 11:12 11:15 11:18[2] 11:20[2] 11:27 11:31 11:32 11:33 12:3 12:4 12:5 12:6 12:8 12:12[3] 12:13 12:14[2] 12:16[2] 12:17 12:18 12:23 12:25[2] 12:26 12:43 12:44 13:9 13:11 13:26 14:1 14:2 14:5 14:11[2] 14:12 14:16 14:18 14:19 14:22 14:23 14:26[2] 14:31 14:32 14:40 14:46 14:50 14:53 14:64 14:70 15:4 15:6 15:13 15:14 15:16 15:17 15:19 15:20[2] 15:21 15:22 15:23 15:24[2] 15:25 15:27 15:29 15:32 15:35 16:1 16:2 16:3 16:4[2] 16:5[2] 16:6 16:8[4] 16:10 16:11[2] 16:12 16:13[2] 16:14[2] 16:17[2] 16:18[4] 16:20

LU

1:2 1:6 1:7[2] 1:22 1:58 1:59[2] 1:61 1:62 1:63 1:66 2:6 2:9 2:16 2:17[2] 2:18 2:20 2:22 2:39[2] 2:42 2:43[2] 2:44[2] 2:45[2] 2:46 2:48[2] 2:50 4:2 4:11 4:28[2] 4:29 4:32 4:36[2] 4:38 4:40 4:41 5:6[2] 5:7[4] 5:9 5:11[2] 5:18 5:19[2] 5:26[2] 5:31[2] 5:33 5:35 6:3 6:7 6:11[2] 6:18[2] 6:22 6:39 6:44 7:4[2] 7:10 7:14 7:16 7:20 7:25 7:31 7:32 7:42 7:49 8:10[2] 8:12[2] 8:13[3] 8:14[2] 8:15 8:16 8:22 8:23[2] 8:24[2] 8:25[2] 8:26 8:31 8:32 8:34[2] 8:35[2] 8:36 8:37 8:40 8:45 8:53 8:56 9:6 9:10[2] 9:11 9:12 9:13 9:14 9:15 9:17 9:19 9:27 9:32[3] 9:33 9:34[2] 9:36[2] 9:37 9:40 9:43[2] 9:45[3] 9:52 9:53 9:54 9:56 9:57 10:7 10:8 10:10 10:13 10:38 11:19 11:26 11:28 11:29 11:32 11:33 11:48 11:49 11:54 12:1 12:4 12:11 12:24 12:27[3] 12:36 12:48 13:2 13:4 13:29 14:1 14:4 14:6 14:7 14:12 14:14 14:18 15:25 16:4 16:9 16:14 16:15 16:26[2] 16:28 16:29 16:30 16:31[2] 17:1 17:13 17:14[2] 17:21 17:23 17:27[4] 17:28[6] 17:37 18:9 18:15[2] 18:24 18:26 18:33 18:34[2] 18:37 18:39 18:43 19:7[2] 19:11[2] 19:25 19:32 19:33 19:34 19:35[3] 19:36 19:37 19:42 19:44 19:48 20:5 20:6 20:7[2] 20:10 20:11 20:12 20:13[2] 20:14 20:15 20:16[2] 20:19[2] 20:20[3] 20:21 20:24 20:26[2] 20:27 20:31 20:35 20:36[2] 20:40 20:41 21:3 21:7 21:12 21:16 21:24 21:27 21:30 22:2[2] 22:5 22:9 22:13[2] 22:23 22:25 22:28 22:35 22:38 22:49[2] 22:54 22:64[2] 22:65 22:70 22:71 23:2 23:5 23:12 23:18 23:21 23:23 23:24 23:25 23:26[3] 23:29 23:30 23:31 23:33[2] 23:34[3] 23:56 24:1[2] 24:2 24:3 24:4 24:5[2] 24:8 24:11 24:14 24:15 24:16 24:19 24:23[3] 24:24 24:28[2] 24:29 24:31[2] 24:32 24:33 24:35 24:36 24:37[2] 24:41 24:42 24:45 24:52

JOH

1:21 1:22 1:24 1:25 1:37 1:38 1:39 2:3[2] 2:7 2:8 2:12 2:20 2:23 3:21 3:23 3:26 4:24 4:30 4:35 4:40 4:45 4:52 5:12 5:23 5:25 5:29[2] 5:39[2] 6:2 6:9 6:11 6:12 6:13 6:14 6:15 6:19[3] 6:21[2] 6:23 6:24 6:25[2] 6:28 6:30 6:34 6:42 6:45 6:60 6:63[2] 6:64 7:25 7:26 7:30 7:39 7:40 7:45 7:52 8:3 8:4 8:6[2] 8:7 8:9 8:19 8:25 8:27 8:33 8:39 8:41 8:59 9:8 9:10 9:12 9:13 9:17 9:18 9:19

9:22 9:24 9:26 9:28 9:34[2] 9:35 9:39[2] 10:4 10:5[2] 10:6[2] 10:10[2] 10:16 10:25 10:27 10:28 10:39 11:13 11:31 11:34 11:41 11:42 11:53 11:56[2] 11:57 12:2 12:9[2] 12:10 12:12[2] 12:16[2] 12:18 12:37 12:39 12:40 12:42[2] 12:43 15:6 15:20[4] 15:21[2] 15:22[2] 15:24[2] 15:25 16:2
16:3[2] 16:9 16:18 16:19 17:3 17:6[2] 17:7 17:8[2] 17:9 17:11 17:13 17:14 17:15[2] 17:16 17:19 17:21[2] 17:22 17:23 17:24[2] 18:5 18:6 18:7 18:18 18:21 18:25 18:28[4] 18:30 18:40 19:2 19:3 19:6 19:15 19:16 19:18 19:23 19:24[3] 19:29 19:31 19:33[2] 19:37[2] 19:40 19:42
20:2[2] 20:4 20:9 20:13[3] 20:20 20:23[2] 20:29 21:3[3] 21:5 21:6[2] 21:8 21:9[2] 21:15 21:25

AC

1:4 1:6[2] 1:9 1:10 1:12 1:13[2] 1:23 1:24 1:26 2:1 2:2 2:4 2:7 2:18 2:37[2] 2:41 2:42 2:46 3:2 3:10[2] 4:1 4:2 4:3 4:7[2] 4:13[5]
4:14 4:15[2] 4:17 4:18 4:21[3] 4:23 4:24[2] 4:29 4:31[4] 4:32 5:12 5:15 5:16 5:17 5:21[3] 5:22 5:24 5:26[2] 5:27[2] 5:33[2] 5:40[4] 5:41[2] 5:42 6:5 6:6[3] 6:10 6:11 6:12 7:6 7:7[2] 7:19[2] 7:25 7:26 7:35 7:41 7:52 7:54[3] 7:57 7:59 8:1 8:4 8:10
8:11 8:12[2] 8:14 8:15[2] 8:16 8:17[2] 8:36[2] 8:38 8:39 9:2 9:8 9:24 9:26 9:27 9:30 9:37[2] 9:38 9:39 10:9 10:10 10:22 10:24 10:39 10:45 10:46 10:48 11:2 11:18[2] 11:19 11:20 11:22 11:23 11:26 11:30 12:10[3] 12:15[2] 12:16[2] 12:19 12:20 12:25 13:2 13:3[2]
13:4[2] 13:5[3] 13:6[2] 13:13 13:14[2] 13:17 13:27[3] 13:28[2] 13:29[2] 13:45 13:48 13:51 14:1 14:3 14:6 14:7 14:11 14:12 14:14 14:18[2] 14:21[2] 14:23[3] 14:24[2] 14:25[3] 14:26[2] 14:27[2] 14:28 15:2 15:3[2] 15:4[3] 15:11 15:13 15:20 15:23 15:30[4] 15:31[2] 15:33[2] 15:36 15:39 16:3 16:4[2] 16:6
16:7[2] 16:8 16:19 16:23[2] 16:31 16:32 16:37[2] 16:38[3] 16:39 16:40[3] 17:1[2] 17:6[2] 17:8[2] 17:9[2] 17:11 17:13 17:15[2] 17:19 17:27[2] 17:32 18:3 18:6 18:20 18:26 19:2 19:3 19:4 19:5[2] 19:6 19:10 19:16 19:19 19:26 19:28[2] 19:29 19:32 19:33 19:34 20:8 20:12 20:18 20:37
20:38[2] 21:5 21:6 21:12 21:20[3] 21:21[2] 21:22 21:24[2] 21:25[2] 21:27 21:29[2] 21:30 21:31 21:32[2] 22:2[2] 22:9[2] 22:18 22:19 22:22 22:23 22:24 22:25 22:29 23:4 23:12[2] 23:13 23:14 23:20 23:21[3] 23:24 23:28 23:30 23:32 23:33 24:12 24:13[2] 24:14 24:15 24:19 24:20 25:7 25:14
25:17 25:18 26:5 26:10 26:18 26:20 26:30 26:31[2] 27:1 27:12 27:13[2] 27:17[3] 27:18 27:27 27:28[2] 27:29 27:30[2] 27:36[2] 27:38[2] 27:39[3] 27:40[2] 27:41 27:43 27:44 28:1[2] 28:2 28:4 28:6[3] 28:10 28:15 28:17 28:18 28:21 28:23 28:25[2] 28:27[2] 28:28

RO

1:20 1:21[2] 1:22 1:28 1:32 3:9[2] 3:12[2] 3:13 3:17 4:7 4:11 4:14 4:17 5:17 8:5[2] 8:8 8:14 8:23 9:6 9:7[2] 9:8 9:26 9:32[2] 10:1 10:2 10:3 10:14[5] 10:15[2] 10:16 10:18 11:3[2] 11:8[2] 11:10 11:11[2] 11:20 11:23[2] 11:28[2] 11:31 13:2 13:6 15:21[2] 15:27 16:18

1 CO

2:8[2] 2:14[2] 3:20 7:8 7:9 7:14 7:29[2] 7:30[6] 7:31 8:11 9:13[2] 9:14 9:24 9:25 10:4 10:5 10:6 10:11 10:18 10:20 10:33 11:19 12:19 12:20 13:8[2] 14:7 14:21 14:23 14:34 14:35 15:10 15:11 15:18 15:23 15:29[2] 15:35 15:48[2] 16:4 16:15 16:17 16:18

2 CO

5:15 6:16 8:3 8:5 8:23 9:4 9:5 9:13 10:10 10:12 11:12[2] 11:22[3] 11:23 12:21

GA

1:23 1:24 2:4 2:6[2] 2:7 2:9[2] 2:10 2:12 2:14 3:7 3:9 4:17[2] 5:12 5:21 5:24 6:12[2] 6:13[2]

EPH

4:14 5:31

PHP

3:18 4:2 4:22

COL

1:10 1:20 3:21 4:9

1 TH

1:9 2:14 2:15 2:16 5:3[2] 5:7[2]

2 TH

2:10[2] 2:11 2:12 3:12

1 TI

1:3 1:7[2] 1:20 2:15 3:13 5:7 5:11[2] 5:12 5:13[2] 5:17 5:24 5:25 6:2[3] 6:9 6:10 6:17 6:18[2] 6:19

2 TI

1:15 2:10 2:14 2:16 2:23 2:26 3:6 3:8 4:3[2] 4:4

TIT

1:10 1:11 1:13 1:16[3] 2:3 2:4 2:10 3:8 3:9 3:14

HEB

1:4 3:11[2] 3:14 2:11 3:10 3:11 3:16 3:18 3:19 4:3 4:5 4:6 6:6[2] 7:5[2] 7:23[2] 8:9 8:10 8:11 9:15 10:1 10:2 11:13 11:14[2] 11:15[3] 11:16 11:23 11:29 11:30 11:35 11:37[3] 11:38 11:40 12:10 12:19 12:20 12:25 13:10 13:17[3] 13:24

JAS

2:7 2:12 3:3 3:4[2] 4:1 5:15

1 PE

1:12 2:8 2:12[3] 3:1 3:2 3:10 3:16[2] 4:4 4:6

2 PE

1:8 1:21 2:3 2:10[2] 2:12 2:13[3] 2:14 2:18[2] 2:19[2] 2:20[2] 2:21 3:4 3:5 3:16[2]

1 JO

2:19[7] 4:1 4:5[2]

2 JO

1

3 JO

7

JUDE

10[3] 11 12[2] 15 18 19

RE

1:3 1:7 1:15 2:2 2:9 2:22 2:24 2:27 3:4[2] 3:9 4:4 4:8[2] 4:11 5:9 6:4 6:9 6:10 6:11[2] 7:13 7:14 7:15 7:16 8:7 8:11 9:4 9:5[2] 9:8 9:9 9:10 9:11 9:19 9:20
9:21 11:2 11:3 11:6 11:7 11:9 11:10 11:11 11:12[2] 11:18 12:6 12:11[2] 13:4[2] 14:3 14:4[2] 14:5 14:11 14:12 14:13 15:3 16:4 16:6[2] 16:9 16:10 16:14 16:15 17:8[2] 17:14 18:9 18:18 18:19 19:3 19:9 20:4[2] 20:6 20:9 20:13 21:3 21:26 21:27 22:4 22:5[2] 22:14[2]

THOU

859, *4771*

GE

2:16 2:17[2] 3:9 3:11[3] 3:12 3:13 3:14[2] 3:15 3:16 3:17[3] 3:18 3:19[2] 4:6 4:7[3] 4:10 4:11 4:12[2] 4:14 6:14 6:15 6:16[3] 6:18 6:19 6:21[2] 7:1 7:2 8:16 10:19 10:30 12:2 12:11 12:13 12:18 12:19 13:9[2] 13:10 13:14 13:15
14:23 15:2 15:3 15:5 15:15 16:8 16:11 16:13 17:1 17:4 17:8 17:9 17:15 17:19 18:5 18:15 18:23 18:24 18:28 19:12[2] 19:15 19:17[2] 19:19 19:21 19:22 19:34 20:3 20:4 20:6 20:7[2] 20:9[3] 20:10 20:13 21:22 21:23[2] 21:26 21:29 21:30 22:2
22:12[2] 22:16 22:18 23:6[2] 23:13 24:3 24:4 24:5 24:6 24:7 24:8 24:14[2] 24:23 24:31[2] 24:37 24:38 24:40 24:41[2] 24:42 24:44 24:47 24:58 24:60 25:18 26:9 26:10[2] 26:16 26:29[2] 27:10 27:18 27:19 27:20 27:21 27:24 27:32 27:33 27:36 27:38 27:40[2]
27:43 27:45 28:1 28:3 28:4 28:6 28:13 28:14 28:15 28:22 29:14 29:15 29:25[2] 29:27 30:15[2] 30:16 30:26 30:29 30:30 30:31 31:13[2] 31:24 31:26 31:27 31:28 31:29 31:30[2] 31:31 31:32[2] 31:36 31:37 31:39 31:41 31:42 31:43 31:44[2] 31:50[2] 31:52 32:10
32:12 32:17[2] 32:18 32:26 32:28 32:29 33:8 33:9 33:10 35:1 35:17 37:8[2] 37:10 37:15 38:16[2] 38:17[2] 38:23 38:29 39:9 39:17 40:13[2] 41:15 41:39 41:40[2] 43:4 43:5 43:8 43:9 44:3 44:4 44:18 44:21 44:23 45:10[4] 45:11[2] 45:19 45:30 47:6 47:8
47:25 47:30[2] 48:6 49:3 49:4[3] 49:6[2] 49:8 49:9 50:5

EX

2:13 2:14[2] 3:5 3:10 3:12 3:14 3:15 3:18[2] 4:9[2] 4:10 4:12 4:13 4:15 4:16 4:17[2] 4:21[2] 4:22 4:23 4:25 4:26 5:15 5:22[2] 5:23 6:1 6:29 7:2 7:9
7:15[2] 7:16[2] 7:17 8:2 8:10 8:21 8:22 9:2 9:14 9:15 9:17[2] 9:19 9:29 10:2 10:3 10:4 10:7 10:25 10:28[2] 10:29 10:44 10:46 13:5 13:6 13:8 13:10 13:12[2] 13:13[4] 13:14 14:11[2] 14:15 14:16 15:7[2] 15:10 15:12 15:13[3] 15:16 15:17[2] 15:26
17:3 17:5 17:6 18:14 18:17 18:18[3] 18:19[2] 18:20 18:21 18:23[2] 19:3 19:6 19:12 19:23 19:24[2] 20:3 20:4 20:5 20:7 20:9 20:10[2] 20:13 20:14 20:15 20:16 20:17[2] 20:19 20:22 20:24 20:25[4] 20:26 21:1 21:2 21:14 21:23 22:18 22:21 22:23 22:25[3]
22:26[2] 22:28 22:29[2] 22:30[2] 23:1 23:2[2] 23:3 23:4[2] 23:5[2] 23:6 23:7 23:8 23:9 23:10 23:11[2] 23:12[2] 23:14 23:15[3] 23:16[2] 23:18 23:19[2] 23:22 23:24[2] 23:27 23:30 23:31 23:32 23:33 24:1 24:12 25:11[2] 25:12 25:13 25:14 25:16 25:17 25:18[2] 25:21[2] 25:23
25:24 25:25[2] 25:26 25:28 25:29[2] 25:30 25:31 25:37 25:40 26:1[2] 26:4[2] 26:5[2] 26:6 26:7[2] 26:9 26:10 26:11 26:14 26:15 26:17 26:18 26:19 26:22 26:23 26:26 26:29[2] 26:30 26:31 26:32 26:33[2] 26:34 26:35[2] 26:36 26:37[2] 27:1 27:2[2] 27:3[2] 27:4[2] 27:5
27:6 27:8 27:9 27:20 28:1 28:2 28:3 28:9 28:11[2] 28:12 28:13 28:14 28:15[3] 28:17 28:22 28:23 28:24 28:25 28:26[2] 28:27 28:30 28:31 28:33 28:36 28:37 28:39[3] 28:40[3] 28:41 28:42 29:1 29:2 29:3 29:4 29:5 29:6 29:7 29:8 29:9[2] 29:10
29:11 29:12 29:13 29:14 29:15 29:16[2] 29:17 29:18 29:19 29:20 29:21 29:22 29:24 29:25 29:26 29:27 29:31 29:34 29:35[2] 29:36[4] 29:37 29:38 29:39[2] 29:41 30:1[2] 30:3[2] 30:4[2] 30:5 30:6 30:12[3] 30:16 30:18[3] 30:23 30:25 30:26 30:29 30:30 30:31 30:35
30:36 30:37 31:13 32:7 32:11 32:13 32:21 32:22 32:32[2] 33:1[2] 33:3 33:12[5] 33:16 33:17[2] 33:20 33:21 33:23 34:1 34:10 34:11 34:12[2] 34:14 34:15[2] 34:16 34:17 34:18[3] 34:20[4] 34:21[3] 34:22 34:24 34:25 34:26[2] 34:27 40:2 40:3 40:4[2] 40:5 40:6 40:7
40:8 40:9 40:10 40:11 40:12 40:13 40:14 40:15[2]

LE

1:2 2:4 2:6 2:8 2:13[3] 2:14[2] 2:15 6:21[2] 6:27 8:3 9:3 10:9 10:14 13:55 13:57 13:58 17:8 18:7[2] 18:8 18:9 18:10 18:11 18:12 18:13 18:14[2] 18:15[2] 18:16 18:17[2]
18:18 18:19 18:20 18:21[2] 18:22 18:23 19:9[2] 19:10[3] 19:12 19:13 19:14 19:15[2] 19:16[2] 19:17[2] 19:18[2] 19:19[2] 19:27 19:32 19:34 20:2 20:16 21:8 22:23 23:22[4] 24:5 24:6 24:7 24:15 25:3[2] 25:4 25:5 25:8 25:9 25:14 25:15 25:16[2] 25:17 25:35 25:36
25:37 25:39 25:43 25:44 27:12

NU

1:3 1:49 1:50 3:9 3:10 3:15 3:41 3:47[2] 3:48 4:23 4:29 4:30 5:19[2] 5:20[2] 7:5 8:2 8:7 8:8 8:9[2] 8:10 8:12 8:13 8:14 8:15 8:26 10:2[2] 10:29 10:31[2] 10:32 11:11[2] 11:12[2]
11:15 11:16 11:17 11:18 11:21 11:23 11:29 13:2 13:27 14:13 14:14[3] 14:15 14:17 14:19 15:5 15:6 15:7 15:8 15:10 16:11 16:13[2] 16:14[2] 16:15 16:16[2] 16:17 16:22 16:37 17:2 17:3 17:4 17:10 18:1[2] 18:2[2] 18:7 18:10 18:15[2] 18:16
18:17[2] 18:20[2] 18:30 20:8[4] 20:14 20:18 20:20 21:2 21:29 21:34[2] 22:6[2] 22:12[2] 22:17 22:20 22:28 22:29 22:30 22:32 22:34 22:35 22:37 23:5 23:11[2] 23:13[2] 23:18 23:27 24:10 24:11 24:12 24:21 26:54[2] 27:7[2] 27:8 27:13[2] 27:20 28:3 28:4[2] 28:7 28:8

28:21
31:2
31:26
31:30

DE

1:14
1:31
1:37
2:4
2:7
2:18
2:19
2:28
2:31
2:37
3:2^{2}
3:21
3:24
3:27
3:28
4:9
4:10
4:19^{2}
4:25
4:29^{3}
4:33
4:35
4:36
4:33
4:40^{2}
5:7
5:8
5:9
5:11
5:13
5:14^{3}
5:15
5:17
5:18
5:19
5:20
5:21^{2}
5:27^{2}
5:31^{2}
6:2^{2}
6:5
6:7^{5}
6:8
6:9
6:10
6:11^{4}
6:12
6:13
6:18^{2}
6:21
7:1^{2}
7:2^{2}
7:3^{3}
7:6
7:11
7:14
7:15
7:16^{2}
7:17
7:18
7:19
7:21
7:22
7:24^{2}
7:25^{2}
7:26^{4}
8:2^{2}
8:3
8:5
8:6
8:9^{3}
8:10^{2}
8:11
8:12
8:13
8:14
8:17
8:18
8:19
9:1
9:2^{2}
9:3
9:4
9:5
9:6
9:7^{2}
9:12
9:26^{2}
9:28
9:29
10:2^{2}
10:20^{3}
11:1
11:10^{2}
11:14
11:15
11:19^{4}
11:20
11:29^{2}
12:5
12:13^{2}
12:14^{2}
12:15
12:17^{2}
12:18^{4}
12:19^{2}
12:20^{2}
12:21^{2}
12:22
12:23^{2}
12:24^{2}
12:25^{2}
12:26^{2}
12:27^{2}
12:28
12:29^{2}
12:30^{2}
12:31
12:32
13:2
13:3
13:5
13:6^{2}
13:8^{3}
13:9
13:10
13:12
13:14
13:15
13:16
13:18
14:2
14:3
14:21^{4}
14:22
14:23^{2}
14:24
14:25
14:26^{4}
14:27
14:28
14:29
15:1
15:3
15:5
15:6^{3}
15:7
15:8
15:9
15:10^{3}
15:11
15:12
15:13^{2}
15:14^{2}
15:15^{2}
15:17^{2}
15:18^{2}
15:19^{2}
15:20^{2}
15:21
15:22
15:23^{2}
16:2
16:3^{5}
16:4
16:5
16:6^{2}
16:7^{2}
16:8^{2}
16:9^{2}
16:10^{2}
16:11^{2}
16:12^{3}
16:13^{2}
16:14^{2}
16:15^{2}
16:18
16:19^{2}
16:20^{2}
16:21^{2}
16:22
17:1
17:4
17:5
17:7
17:8
17:9
17:10^{2}
17:11^{2}
17:12
17:14
17:15^{3}
18:4
18:9^{2}
18:13
18:14
18:16
18:21
18:22
19:1
19:2
19:3
19:7
19:9^{2}
19:13
19:14^{2}
19:19
20:1^{2}
20:10
20:12
20:13
20:14^{2}
20:15
20:16
20:17
20:19^{4}
20:20^{3}
21:8
21:9^{2}
21:10^{2}
21:11
21:12
21:13
21:14^{5}
21:21
21:22
22:1^{2}
22:2^{3}
22:3^{5}
22:4^{2}
22:6^{2}
22:8^{3}
22:9^{2}
22:10
22:11
22:12^{2}
22:21
22:22
22:24
22:26
23:6
23:7^{3}
23:12^{2}
23:13^{3}
23:15
23:16
23:18
23:19
23:20^{3}
23:21^{2}
23:22
23:23^{3}
23:24^{3}
23:25^{3}
24:4
24:7
24:8
24:10^{2}
24:11^{2}
24:12
24:13
24:14
24:15
24:17
24:18^{2}
24:19^{2}
24:20^{2}
24:21
24:22^{2}
25:4
25:12
25:13
25:14
25:15^{2}
25:18
25:19^{3}
26:1
26:2^{2}
26:3
26:5
26:10^{2}
26:11^{2}
26:12
26:13^{2}
26:14
26:15^{2}
26:16
26:17
26:18
26:19
27:2
27:3^{3}
27:4
27:5^{2}
27:6^{3}
27:7
27:8
27:9
27:10
28:1
28:2
28:3^{2}
28:6^{4}
28:8
28:9
28:10
28:12^{2}
28:13^{3}
28:14
28:15
28:16^{2}
28:19^{4}
28:20^{4}
28:21
28:22
28:24
28:25
28:27
28:29^{3}
28:30^{4}
28:31^{2}
28:33^{2}
28:34^{2}
28:36^{3}
28:37
28:38
28:39
28:40^{2}
28:41^{2}
28:43
28:44^{2}
28:45^{2}
28:47
28:48
28:49
28:51
28:52
28:53
28:58^{2}
28:60
28:61
28:62
28:63
28:64^{2}
28:65
28:66
28:67^{4}
28:68
29:12
30:1
30:2
30:5
30:6
30:8
30:10^{2}
30:12
30:13
30:14
30:16^{2}
30:17
30:18
30:19
30:20^{4}
31:2
31:3
31:7^{2}
31:11
31:14
31:16
31:23
32:14
32:15^{3}
32:18
32:50
32:52^{2}
33:7
33:8^{2}
33:23
33:29^{2}
34:4

JOS

1:2
1:6
1:7^{4}
1:8^{4}
1:9^{2}
1:16^{2}
1:18
2:17
2:18^{3}
2:20^{2}
3:8
3:13
5:15
6:3
7:7
7:9
7:10
7:13
7:19
7:25
8:1
8:2^{2}
10:12^{2}
11:6
13:1
13:6
14:6
14:9
14:12
15:18
15:19
17:14
17:15
17:17^{2}
17:18^{2}

JG

1:14
1:15
4:8^{2}
4:9
4:20
4:22
5:4^{2}
5:12
5:16
5:21
6:4
6:12
6:14
6:16
6:17
6:18
6:23
6:26
6:36^{2}
6:37^{2}
7:5
7:10^{2}
7:11
8:1^{3}
8:18
8:21
8:22^{3}
9:8
9:10
9:12
9:14
9:32
9:33^{3}
9:36
9:38^{2}
10:15
11:2^{2}
11:8
11:12^{2}
11:23
11:24
11:25
11:27
11:30
11:31
11:32
11:33
11:35^{2}
11:36
12:1
12:5
13:3^{2}
13:5
13:7
13:8
13:11
13:16^{3}
13:18
14:3
14:16^{2}
15:2
15:11^{2}
15:18
16:6
16:10^{2}
16:13^{3}
16:15^{2}
17:2^{2}
17:9
18:3^{2}
18:19
18:23
18:25
19:9
19:17^{2}

RU

1:15
1:16^{2}
1:17
2:8
2:9^{2}
2:10
2:11^{3}
2:12
2:13^{2}
2:14
2:19^{2}
2:21
2:22
3:1
3:4^{3}
3:5
3:9^{2}
3:10^{3}
3:11^{2}
3:15
3:16
3:18
4:4^{2}
3:5^{2}
3:6
3:11

1 SA

1:8^{2}
1:11
1:14
1:17
1:23
2:16
2:32
3:5
3:6
3:8
3:9
3:17
4:20
8:5
9:16
9:21
9:27
10:2^{3}
10:3^{2}
10:4
10:5^{3}
10:6
10:7
10:8^{3}
12:4^{2}
13:11^{2}
13:13^{2}
13:14
14:37
14:43
14:44
15:1
15:7
15:13
15:17^{2}
15:19
15:23
15:26
15:28
16:1
16:3^{2}
16:4
16:16
17:29^{4}
17:33^{2}
17:43
17:45^{2}
17:52
17:56
17:58^{2}
18:17
18:21
19:3
19:5^{2}
19:11^{2}
19:17
20:2
20:8^{3}
20:13
20:14
20:15
20:18
20:19^{3}
20:21
20:23
20:30^{2}
20:31
21:1
21:9^{2}
22:12
22:13^{2}
22:16^{2}
22:18
22:23^{2}
23:17
24:4
24:9
24:11^{2}
24:14
24:17^{2}
24:18^{3}
24:19
24:20
24:21^{2}
25:6
25:7
25:17
25:25
25:31
25:33
25:34
26:11
26:14^{2}
26:15^{2}
26:16
26:25^{2}
27:8
28:1^{3}
28:2
28:9^{2}
28:12^{2}
28:13
28:15^{2}
28:16
28:18
28:19
28:21
28:22^{3}
29:4
29:6
29:7
29:8
29:9
30:8
30:13^{2}
30:15^{2}

2 SA

1:3
1:5
1:8
1:13
1:14
1:25
1:26
2:20
2:26^{2}
2:27
3:7
3:8
3:13^{3}
3:21
3:24^{2}
3:25^{2}
3:34
5:2
5:6^{2}
5:19
5:22
5:23
5:24^{2}
5:25
7:5
7:8
7:9
7:12
7:18
7:19
7:20
7:21
7:22
7:23
7:24^{2}
7:25^{2}
7:27
7:28^{2}
7:29
9:2
9:7
9:8
9:10^{2}
10:3
10:11
11:10
11:11
11:19
11:21
11:25^{2}
12:7
12:9^{2}
12:10
12:12
12:13
12:14
12:21^{3}
13:4^{2}
13:12
13:13
13:16
14:11
14:13
15:2
15:19^{2}
15:20^{2}
15:27
15:33^{2}
15:34^{2}
15:35^{3}
16:2
16:7^{2}
16:8^{3}
16:10
16:17
16:21
17:3
17:6
17:8
17:11
18:3^{3}
18:11^{2}
18:13
18:20^{3}
18:21
18:22^{2}
19:5
19:6^{3}
19:7
19:13^{2}
19:14
19:19
19:22
19:25
19:28
19:29^{2}
19:30
19:38
20:4
20:6
20:9
20:17
20:19^{2}
21:4
21:17^{2}
22:3
22:26^{3}
22:27^{2}
22:28^{2}
22:29
22:36
22:37
22:40^{2}
22:41
22:44^{2}
22:49
24:13

1 KI

1:6
1:11
1:12
1:13
1:14
1:16
1:17
1:18
1:20
1:24
1:27
1:42
2:2
2:3^{3}
2:5
2:8
2:9^{3}
2:13
2:15
2:22
2:26^{3}
2:31
2:37^{3}
2:42^{3}
2:43
2:44^{2}
3:6^{3}
3:7
3:8
3:11
3:13
3:14
5:3
5:6^{3}
5:8
5:9^{3}
6:12^{2}
8:18
8:19
8:24^{2}
8:25^{2}
8:26
8:28
8:29^{2}
8:30^{3}
8:32
8:33
8:34^{2}
8:36^{3}
8:39^{4}
8:40
8:43
8:44^{2}
8:45
8:46
8:48
8:49
8:51
8:53^{3}
9:3^{2}
9:4
9:13
11:11
11:22^{2}
11:37
11:38
12:4
12:7
12:10^{3}
13:8
13:9
13:14
13:17^{2}
13:18
13:21
14:2
14:5
14:6^{2}
14:8
14:9
14:12
16:2
17:4
17:13
17:18^{2}
17:20
17:24
18:7
18:9
18:11
18:14
18:17
18:18^{2}
18:36
18:37^{2}
19:9
19:13
19:15
19:16^{2}
20:5
20:9
20:13^{2}
20:14
20:22
20:25
20:34
20:36^{2}
20:39
20:42
21:5
21:7
21:10
21:19^{3}
21:20^{2}
21:22
21:29
22:4^{2}
22:11^{2}
22:16
22:19
22:22
22:25^{2}
22:28
22:30

2 KI

1:4^{2}
1:6^{3}
1:9
1:16^{3}
2:3
2:5
2:10^{2}
2:23^{2}
3:7^{2}
4:1
4:2
4:4^{3}
4:7
4:13^{2}
4:16^{2}
4:23
4:29
4:40
5:6
5:8
5:10
5:13
5:25
6:9
6:12
6:22^{3}
7:2
7:19
8:1^{2}
8:10
8:12^{3}
8:13
8:14
9:2
9:7
9:18
9:19
9:25
10:5^{2}
10:30
13:17^{2}
13:19^{4}
14:10^{4}
17:26
18:14
18:19
18:20^{3}
18:21
18:23
18:24
19:6
19:10
19:11^{2}
19:15^{3}
19:19^{3}
19:20
19:22^{2}
19:23
19:25^{2}
19:28
20:1
20:5
20:9
20:18
20:19
22:18
22:19^{2}
22:20
23:17

1 CH

4:10^{2}
11:2^{3}
11:5
12:18
14:10
14:15^{2}
17:4
17:7^{2}
17:8
17:11
17:16
17:17
17:18
17:19
17:21
17:22^{2}
17:23^{2}
17:25^{2}
17:26
17:27
19:3
19:12
21:22
22:8^{3}
22:11
22:12
22:13^{2}
22:14
28:3^{2}
28:9^{4}
28:20
29:10
29:11
29:12
29:17

2 CH

1:8
1:9
1:11^{2}
2:3
2:16^{2}
6:8
6:9
6:15^{2}
6:16^{2}
6:17
6:20^{2}
6:21^{2}
6:23
6:25^{2}
6:26
6:27^{3}
6:30^{3}
6:31
6:33
6:34^{2}
6:35
6:36
6:38^{2}
6:39
6:41
7:17
9:6
10:4
10:7
10:10^{3}
13:4
14:11
16:7
16:8
16:9^{2}
18:3^{2}
18:10
18:12
18:15
18:21^{2}
18:24^{2}
18:27
18:29
18:33
19:2
19:3
20:6^{2}
20:7
20:9
20:10
20:11
20:12
20:15
20:37
21:12
21:15
24:6
25:8
25:15
25:16^{3}
25:19^{5}
26:18
34:26
34:27^{2}
34:28
35:21

EZR

4:13
4:15
4:16
7:14
7:16
7:17
7:19
7:20
7:25
9:11
9:13
9:14^{2}
9:15
10:12

NE

1:6
1:7
1:8
1:10
2:2
2:4
2:5
2:6
5:12
6:6^{3}
6:7
6:8^{2}
6:14
9:6^{4}
9:7
9:8
9:10^{2}
9:11^{2}
9:12
9:13
9:15
9:17
9:19
9:20
9:21
9:22
9:23^{2}
9:24
9:27^{3}
9:28^{3}
9:29
9:30^{2}
9:31^{2}
9:33^{2}
9:34
9:35^{2}
9:36
9:37

ES

3:3
4:3
4:14^{3}
5:3
5:14^{2}
6:10^{2}
6:13^{2}

JOB

1:7
1:8
1:10^{2}
2:2
2:3^{2}
2:9
2:10
4:2
4:3^{2}
4:4
4:5^{2}
5:6
5:17
5:21^{2}
5:22^{2}
5:23
5:24^{2}
5:25
5:26
5:27
7:12
7:14
7:17^{2}
7:18
7:19
7:20^{2}
7:21^{2}
8:2
8:5
8:6
9:12
9:28
9:31
10:2
10:3^{2}
10:4^{2}
10:6
10:7
10:8
10:9^{2}
10:10
10:11
10:12
10:13
10:14^{2}
10:15
10:16^{2}
10:17
10:18
11:3
11:4
11:7^{2}
11:8^{2}
11:13
11:15^{2}
11:16
11:17^{2}
11:18^{3}
11:19
13:22^{2}
13:24
13:25^{2}
13:26
13:27^{2}
14:3
14:5
14:13^{3}
14:15^{2}
14:16^{2}
14:17
14:19^{2}
14:20^{2}
15:4
15:5
15:7^{2}
15:8^{2}
15:9^{2}
15:13
16:3
16:7
16:8
16:18
17:4^{2}
17:14^{2}
20:4
22:3^{2}
22:6
22:7^{2}
22:9
22:11
22:13
22:15
22:23^{3}
22:24
22:25
22:26
22:27^{2}
22:28
22:29
26:2^{2}
26:3^{2}
26:4
30:20^{2}
30:21^{2}
30:22^{2}
30:23
31:24
33:5
31:8
33:12
33:13
33:32
34:16
34:17
34:18
34:32
34:33^{3}
35:2^{2}
35:3
35:5
35:6^{3}
35:7^{2}
35:8
35:14^{3}
36:17
36:21
36:23
36:24
37:6
37:15
37:16
37:18
38:3
38:4^{2}
38:5
38:11
38:12
38:16^{2}
38:17
38:18^{2}
38:20^{2}
38:21^{2}
38:22^{2}
38:31
38:32^{2}
38:33^{2}
38:34
38:35
38:39
39:1^{2}
39:2^{2}
39:10
39:11^{2}
39:12
39:13
39:19^{2}
39:20
40:7
40:8^{3}
40:9^{2}
41:1^{2}
41:2
41:4
41:5^{2}
41:7
42:2
42:4

PS

2:7
2:9^{2}
3:7^{2}
4:1
4:6
4:7
4:8
5:3
5:4
5:5
5:6
5:10
5:11
5:12^{2}
6:3
7:6
7:7
8:2^{2}
8:3
8:4^{2}
8:5
8:6^{2}
9:2
9:4^{2}
9:5^{3}
9:6^{2}
9:10
9:13
10:1^{2}
10:13
10:14^{3}
10:15^{2}
10:17^{3}
12:7^{2}
13:1^{2}
16:2^{2}
16:5
16:10^{2}
16:11
17:3^{3}
17:6
17:7
17:14
18:25^{2}
18:26^{2}
18:27
18:28
18:35
18:36
18:39^{2}
18:40
18:43^{2}
18:48^{2}
19:12
21:2
21:3^{2}
21:4
21:5
21:6^{2}
21:9
21:10
21:12^{2}
21:13
22:1^{2}
22:2
22:3^{2}
22:4
22:9^{2}
22:10
22:15
22:19
22:21
23:4
23:5^{2}
25:5
25:7
25:17
27:8
27:9
28:1
30:1
30:2
30:3^{2}
30:7^{2}
30:10
30:11^{2}
31:2
31:3
31:4
31:5
31:7^{2}
31:8
31:14
31:19^{2}
31:20^{2}
31:22
32:5
32:6
32:7^{3}
32:8
35:17
35:22
36:6
36:8
37:1
37:10
37:34
38:15
39:5
39:9
39:11^{2}
40:5
40:6^{3}
40:9
40:11
40:17
41:2
41:3
41:10
41:11
41:12
42:5^{3}
42:9
42:11^{3}
43:2^{3}
43:5^{2}
44:1
44:2^{2}
44:3
44:4
44:7
44:9
44:10
44:11
44:12
44:13
44:14
44:19
44:23
44:24
45:2
45:7
45:11
45:16
48:7
49:16
49:18
50:15
50:16^{2}
50:17
50:18^{2}
50:19
50:20^{2}
50:21^{2}
51:4^{3}
51:6^{2}
51:8
51:14
51:15
51:16^{2}
51:17
51:18
51:19
52:1
52:3
52:4^{2}
52:9
53:5
55:13
55:23
56:2
56:8^{2}
56:13^{2}
57:5
57:11
59:5
59:8^{2}
59:16
60:1^{3}
60:2^{2}
60:3^{2}
60:4
60:8
60:10^{2}
61:3
61:5^{2}
61:6
62:5
62:12
63:1
63:7
65:2
65:3
65:4
65:5
65:8
65:9^{4}
65:10^{4}
65:11
66:3
66:10^{2}
66:11^{2}
66:12^{2}
67:4
68:7^{2}
68:9^{2}
68:10
68:18^{3}
68:28
68:30
68:35
69:5
69:19
69:26^{2}
70:5
71:3^{2}
71:5^{2}
71:6
71:7
71:17
71:20
71:21
71:22
71:23
73:18^{2}
73:20^{2}
73:23
73:24
73:27
74:1
74:2^{3}
74:11

17:19, 17:20, 21:20, 21:21, 21:22, 21:24, 21:37, 21:38, 22:7, 22:8^{2}, 22:14, 22:15^{2}, 22:16, 22:26, 22:27, 23:3^{2}, 23:4, 23:5, 23:11^{2}, 23:19, 23:20, 23:21, 23:22^{2}, 24:4, 24:10, 24:11, 25:9, 25:10, 25:12^{2}, 25:22, 26:1, 26:14, 26:15^{2}, 26:16, 26:24, 26:27^{2}, 26:28, 26:29, 27:24, 28:22

RO

2:1^{5}, 2:3^{2}, 2:4, 2:17, 2:19, 2:21^{4}, 2:22^{4}, 2:23^{2}, 2:25^{2}, 3:4^{2}, 7:7, 9:19, 9:20^{2}, 10:9^{2}, 11:17, 11:18^{2}, 11:19, 11:20, 11:22^{2}, 11:24, 12:30, 13:3^{2}, 13:4, 13:9^{6}, 14:4, 14:10^{2}, 14:15, 14:22

1 CO

4:7^{5}, 7:16^{4}, 7:21^{2}, 7:27^{2}, 7:28^{2}, 9:9, 14:16^{2}, 14:17, 15:36^{2}, 15:37^{2}

GA

2:14^{2}, 4:7, 4:27^{2}, 5:14, 6:1

EPH

5:14, 6:3

COL

4:17^{2}

1 TI

1:3, 1:18, 3:15^{2}, 4:6^{3}, 4:12, 4:16, 5:18, 5:21, 6:11, 5:12, 5:14

2 TI

1:6, 1:8, 1:13, 1:15, 1:18, 2:1, 2:2^{2}, 2:3, 3:10, 3:14^{3}, 3:15, 4:5, 4:13, 4:15

TIT

1:5, 2:1, 3:8

PHP

5, 12, 15, 17, 19, 21

HEB

1:5, 1:9, 1:10, 1:11, 1:12^{2}, 2:6^{2}, 2:7^{2}, 2:8, 5:5, 5:6, 7:17, 7:21, 8:5, 10:5^{2}, 10:6, 10:8, 12:5^{2}

JAS

2:3^{2}, 2:8, 2:11^{3}, 2:18, 2:19^{2}, 2:20, 2:22, 4:11^{2}, 4:12

JOH

2, 3, 5^{2}, 6^{2}

RE

1:11, 1:19, 1:20^{2}, 2:2^{2}, 2:4, 2:5^{2}, 2:6^{2}, 2:9, 2:10^{2}, 2:13^{2}, 2:14, 2:15, 2:20, 3:1^{2}, 3:3^{3}, 3:4, 3:8, 3:10, 3:11, 3:15^{2}, 3:16, 3:17^{2}, 3:18^{3}, 4:11^{2}, 5:9^{2}, 6:6, 6:10, 7:14, 10:11, 11:17, 11:18, 15:3, 15:4, 16:5^{2}, 16:6, 17:7, 17:8, 17:12, 17:15, 17:16, 17:18, 18:14, 18:20, 19:10, 22:9

THY

4674 or *4675*

GE

3:10, 3:14^{2}, 3:15, 3:16^{2}, 3:17^{3}, 3:19, 4:6, 4:9, 4:10, 4:11, 4:14, 6:18, 7:1, 8:16, 12:1, 12:2, 12:7, 12:13, 12:18, 12:19, 13:8, 13:15, 13:16^{2}, 14:20, 15:1, 15:5, 15:13, 15:15, 15:18, 16:5, 16:6, 16:9, 16:10, 16:11, 17:5, 17:7^{2}, 17:8, 17:9, 17:10, 17:12, 17:13, 17:15, 17:19, 18:3, 18:9, 18:10, 19:12, 19:15, 19:17, 19:18^{2}, 20:6, 20:13, 20:16, 21:12^{3}, 21:13, 22:2, 22:12, 22:16, 22:17^{2}, 22:18, 22:20, 23:6^{2}, 23:11, 23:15, 24:2, 24:5, 24:7, 24:14^{3}, 24:17, 24:19, 24:23, 24:40, 24:43, 24:44, 24:46, 24:51, 24:60, 25:23^{2}, 25:31, 26:3^{2}, 26:4^{3}, 26:9, 26:10, 26:24^{2}, 27:3, 27:6, 27:9, 27:10, 27:13, 27:19^{2}, 27:20, 27:29, 27:31, 27:32, 27:35, 27:37, 27:39, 27:40^{2}, 27:42, 27:44, 27:45, 28:2^{2}, 28:4, 28:13^{2}, 28:14^{2}, 29:15, 29:18, 30:14, 30:15, 30:27, 30:28, 30:29, 30:31, 30:32, 31:33, 31:34, 31:3, 31:8^{2}, 31:13, 31:30, 31:31, 31:32, 31:37^{2}, 31:38^{2}, 31:41^{2}, 32:4, 32:5, 32:6, 32:9^{2}, 32:10, 32:12, 32:18, 32:20, 32:27, 32:28, 32:29, 33:5, 33:10^{3}, 35:1, 35:10^{3}, 35:11, 35:12, 37:10^{2}, 37:13, 37:14, 37:32, 38:8^{2}, 38:11, 38:13, 38:18^{3}, 38:24, 39:19, 40:13, 40:19^{2}, 41:40, 42:10, 42:11, 42:13, 43:28, 44:7, 44:8, 44:9, 44:16, 44:18^{2}, 44:21, 44:23, 44:24, 44:27, 44:30, 44:31^{2}, 44:32, 44:33, 45:9, 45:10^{4}, 45:11, 46:3, 46:30, 46:34, 47:3, 47:4^{2}, 47:5^{2}, 47:6, 47:15, 47:29^{2}, 48:1, 48:2, 48:4, 48:5, 48:6, 48:11^{2}, 48:18, 48:22, 49:4, 49:8^{3}, 49:18, 49:25, 49:26, 50:6, 50:16, 50:17^{2}, 50:18

EX

2:9, 2:13, 3:5^{2}, 3:6, 3:18, 4:6, 4:7, 4:9, 4:10, 4:12, 4:14, 4:15, 4:16, 4:19, 4:23^{2}, 5:15, 5:16^{2}, 5:23^{2}, 7:1^{2}, 7:2, 7:9, 7:19, 8:2, 8:3^{5}, 8:4^{2}, 8:5, 8:9^{3}, 8:10, 8:11^{3}, 8:16, 8:21^{3}, 8:23, 9:3, 9:14, 9:15, 9:19, 9:30, 10:2^{2}, 10:4, 10:6^{4}, 10:29, 11:8, 12:24, 13:5, 13:7, 13:8, 13:9, 13:11, 13:13, 13:14, 14:16, 15:6^{2}, 15:7, 15:8, 15:10, 15:12, 15:13^{3}, 15:16, 15:17, 15:26, 17:5, 18:6^{2}, 20:2, 20:5, 20:7, 20:9, 20:10^{8}, 20:12^{4}, 20:16, 20:17^{3}, 20:24^{3}, 20:25, 20:26, 22:26, 22:28, 22:29^{3}, 22:30, 23:6, 23:10, 23:11^{3}, 23:12^{2}, 23:13, 23:16^{2}, 23:17, 23:19^{2}, 23:25^{2}, 23:26^{2}, 23:31, 23:33, 28:1, 28:2, 28:4, 28:41, 29:12, 29:26, 32:4, 32:7, 32:8, 32:11^{2}, 32:12^{2}, 32:13, 32:32, 33:1, 33:5, 33:13^{4}, 33:15, 33:16^{3}, 33:18, 34:9, 34:10, 34:16^{2}, 34:19, 34:20, 34:24^{3}, 34:26^{2}

LE

2:5, 2:7, 2:13^{3}, 2:14^{2}, 5:15, 5:18, 6:6, 9:7^{2}, 10:9, 10:13^{2}, 10:14^{3}, 10:15^{4}, 16:2, 18:7^{3}, 18:8^{2}, 18:9^{3}, 18:10^{2}, 18:11^{3}, 18:12^{2}, 18:13^{2}, 18:14, 18:15^{2}, 18:16^{2}, 18:20, 18:21^{2}, 19:9^{2}, 19:10^{2}, 19:12, 19:13, 19:14, 19:15, 19:16^{2}, 19:17^{2}, 19:18^{2}, 19:19^{2}, 19:27, 19:29, 19:32, 20:19^{2}, 21:8, 21:17, 23:22^{2}, 24:47, 25:3^{2}, 25:4^{2}, 25:5^{2}, 25:6^{4}, 25:7^{2}, 25:11, 25:15, 25:17, 25:25, 25:35, 25:36^{2}, 25:37^{2}, 25:39, 25:43, 25:44^{2}, 25:53, 27:2, 27:3^{2}, 27:4, 27:5, 27:6^{2}, 27:7, 27:8, 27:13, 27:15, 27:16, 27:17, 27:18, 27:19, 27:23, 27:25, 27:27

NU

5:19, 5:20, 5:21^{3}, 5:22^{3}, 11:11^{2}, 11:12, 11:15, 14:13, 14:14, 14:19, 14:20, 16:10, 16:11, 16:16, 18:1^{3}, 18:2^{3}, 18:3, 18:7, 18:8, 18:9, 18:11^{3}, 18:19^{3}, 18:20, 20:8, 20:14, 20:16, 20:17^{2}, 20:19, 21:22^{2}, 21:34, 22:32, 23:3, 23:15, 24:5^{2}, 24:11, 24:12, 24:14, 24:21^{2}, 27:13^{2}, 31:2, 31:49, 32:4, 32:5^{2}, 32:25, 32:27, 32:31

DE

1:21^{2}, 1:31, 2:7^{4}, 2:27, 2:30^{2}, 3:2, 3:24^{5}, 4:3, 4:9^{5}, 4:10, 4:19, 4:21, 4:23, 4:24, 4:25, 4:29^{3}, 4:30, 4:31^{2}, 4:37, 4:40^{3}, 5:6, 5:9, 5:11, 5:12, 5:13, 5:14^{10}, 5:15^{2}, 5:16^{5}, 5:20, 5:21^{3}, 6:2^{5}, 6:3, 6:5^{3}, 6:7, 6:9^{2}, 6:10^{2}, 6:13, 6:15^{2}, 6:18, 6:20, 6:21, 7:1, 7:2, 7:3^{2}, 7:4, 7:6^{2}, 7:9, 7:12^{2}, 7:13^{7}, 7:16, 7:18, 7:19^{2}, 7:20, 7:21, 7:22, 7:23, 7:25, 8:2, 8:3, 8:4^{2}, 8:5, 8:6, 8:7, 8:10, 8:11, 8:13^{4}, 8:14, 8:16^{2}, 8:18^{2}, 8:19, 9:3^{2}, 9:4, 9:5^{3}, 9:6^{2}, 9:7, 9:12, 9:26^{2}, 9:27, 9:29^{3}, 10:9, 10:11, 10:12^{5}, 10:13, 10:14, 10:15, 10:20, 10:21^{2}, 10:22^{2}, 11:1, 11:10^{2}, 11:12^{2}, 11:14^{2}, 11:15^{2}, 11:20, 11:29, 12:1, 12:7, 12:13, 12:14^{2}, 12:15^{3}, 12:17^{8}, 12:18^{8}, 12:20^{4}, 12:21^{5}, 12:25, 12:26^{2}, 12:27^{4}, 12:28^{2}, 12:29, 12:31, 13:5, 13:6^{7}, 13:10, 13:12^{2}, 13:16, 13:17, 13:18^{2}, 14:2, 14:21^{2}, 14:22, 14:23^{6}, 14:24^{2}, 14:25, 14:26^{3}, 14:27, 14:28, 14:29^{2}, 15:3, 15:4, 15:5, 15:6, 15:7^{5}, 15:9^{2}, 15:10^{2}, 15:11^{4}, 15:12, 15:14^{4}, 15:15, 15:17^{2}, 15:18, 15:19^{5}, 15:20^{2}, 15:21, 15:22, 16:1^{2}, 16:2, 16:3, 16:4, 16:5^{2}, 16:6, 16:7^{2}, 16:8, 16:10^{3}, 16:11^{7}, 16:13^{2}, 16:14^{6}, 16:15^{2}, 16:16^{2}, 16:17, 16:18^{3}, 16:20, 16:21, 16:22, 17:1^{2}, 17:2^{3}, 17:5, 17:8^{2}, 17:12, 17:14, 17:15^{3}, 18:4^{3}, 18:5^{2}, 18:6, 18:9, 18:12, 18:13, 18:14, 18:15^{2}, 18:16, 19:1^{2}, 19:2^{2}, 19:3^{2}, 19:8^{4}, 19:9, 19:10^{2}, 19:14^{2}, 20:1, 20:13, 20:14, 20:16, 20:17, 21:1, 21:2^{2}, 21:6, 21:8^{2}, 21:10, 21:11, 21:13, 21:23^{2}, 22:1^{2}, 22:2^{2}, 22:3, 22:4, 22:5, 22:7, 22:8, 22:9^{3}, 22:12, 22:17, 23:5^{3}, 23:6, 23:7, 23:13, 23:14^{3}, 23:16, 23:18^{2}, 23:19, 23:20^{2}, 23:21^{2}, 23:23^{3}, 23:24^{3}, 23:25^{2}, 24:4, 24:9, 24:10, 24:13, 24:14^{4}, 24:18, 24:19^{2}, 24:21, 25:3, 25:13, 25:15^{2}, 25:16, 25:19^{2}, 26:1, 26:2^{3}, 26:3, 26:4, 26:5, 26:10^{2}, 26:11, 26:12, 26:13^{3}, 26:15^{2}, 26:16^{2}, 26:17, 26:19, 27:2, 27:3^{2}, 27:5, 27:6^{2}, 27:7, 27:9, 27:10, 28:1^{2}, 28:2, 28:4^{5}, 28:7, 28:8^{2}, 28:9, 28:11^{4}, 28:12, 28:13, 28:15, 28:17^{2}, 28:18^{4}, 28:20, 28:23^{2}, 28:24, 28:26, 28:29, 28:31^{2}, 28:32^{2}, 28:33^{2}, 28:35^{2}, 28:36^{2}, 28:40, 28:42^{2}, 28:45, 28:46, 28:47, 28:48, 28:51^{4}, 28:52^{6}, 28:53^{3}, 28:55, 28:57, 28:58, 28:59^{2}, 28:62, 28:64, 28:65, 28:66^{2}, 29:5^{2}, 29:11^{4}, 29:12^{2}, 29:13, 30:1, 30:2^{3}, 30:3^{3}, 30:4, 30:5^{3}, 30:6^{4}, 30:7, 30:9^{5}, 30:10^{3}, 30:14^{2}, 30:16^{2}, 30:19, 30:20^{4}, 31:3, 31:6, 31:11, 31:12^{2}, 31:14, 31:16, 31:27^{2}, 32:6, 32:7^{2}, 32:50^{2}, 33:3^{3}, 33:8^{3}, 33:9^{2}, 33:10^{2}, 33:18^{2}, 33:25^{3}, 33:26, 33:27, 33:29^{2}, 34:4

JOS

1:5, 1:8^{2}, 1:9, 1:17, 1:18^{2}, 2:18^{4}, 2:19, 5:15^{2}, 7:9, 7:10, 8:1, 8:18, 9:8, 9:9^{2}, 9:24^{2}, 10:6^{2}, 14:9^{2}, 24:12^{2}

JG

1:3, 5:12, 5:14, 6:14, 6:17, 6:25^{2}, 6:26, 6:30, 7:10, 8:15, 8:22^{2}, 9:38, 9:54, 11:10, 11:17, 11:19, 11:24, 11:36^{2}, 13:12, 13:16, 13:17^{2}, 14:3, 14:13, 14:15^{2}, 15:2, 15:18, 16:6, 16:15, 17:10, 18:19^{2}, 18:25^{3}, 19:19^{2}, 19:20

RU

1:10, 1:15^{2}, 1:16^{2}, 2:11^{4}, 2:12, 2:13, 2:14, 3:3, 3:9, 3:12, 3:17, 4:12, 4:15^{2}

1 SA

1:8, 1:14, 1:17, 1:18, 1:26, 2:1, 2:16, 2:27, 2:28, 2:29, 2:30, 2:31, 2:34, 3:9, 3:10, 4:17, 8:5^{2}, 9:20^{2}, 10:2, 12:19^{2}, 13:13^{2}, 13:14, 14:7, 14:28, 15:15, 15:21, 15:24, 15:30, 15:33^{2}, 16:11, 16:16, 16:19, 17:17^{2}, 17:18, 17:29, 17:32, 17:34, 17:36, 17:44, 17:55, 17:58, 19:11, 20:1, 20:3^{2}, 20:4, 20:6, 20:7, 20:8^{3}, 20:10, 20:15, 20:18, 20:22, 20:30, 20:31, 20:42, 22:14^{2}, 22:15, 22:16, 22:22, 22:23, 23:10, 23:11^{2}, 23:20, 24:9, 24:11^{2}, 24:16, 25:7, 25:8^{3}, 25:26, 25:28, 25:29, 25:33, 25:35^{2}, 26:15^{2}, 26:17, 26:24, 27:5, 28:1, 28:2, 28:17, 28:19, 28:21^{2}, 28:22, 29:6^{2}, 29:8, 29:10, 31:4

2 SA

1:16^{3}, 1:19, 1:26, 2:21^{2}, 2:22, 3:8, 3:12, 3:25^{2}, 3:34^{2}, 4:8, 5:1, 6:21, 7:9, 7:12^{4}, 7:16^{2}, 7:19^{2}, 7:20, 7:21^{2}, 7:23^{3}, 7:24, 7:25, 7:26^{2}, 7:27^{2}, 7:28^{2}, 7:29^{3}, 9:2, 9:7^{2}, 9:8, 9:9, 9:10^{4}, 9:11, 10:3, 11:8^{2}, 11:10, 11:11, 11:21, 11:24^{2}, 11:25, 12:8^{3}, 12:9, 12:10, 12:11^{3}, 12:13, 13:5^{2}, 13:7, 13:20^{3}, 13:24^{2}, 13:35, 14:6, 14:11^{2}, 14:15, 14:17, 14:19, 14:20, 14:22^{2}, 14:31, 15:2, 15:3, 15:8, 15:15, 15:19, 15:20, 15:21, 15:27, 15:34^{3}, 16:3, 16:4, 16:8^{2}, 16:17^{3}, 16:19^{2}, 16:21^{2}, 17:8^{2}, 17:10, 18:28, 18:29, 19:5^{6}, 19:6, 19:7^{2}, 19:14, 19:19, 19:20, 19:26^{2}, 19:27, 19:28, 19:29, 19:35, 19:36, 19:37^{2}, 20:6, 22:36^{2}, 22:50, 24:3, 24:10, 24:13^{2}, 24:23

1 KI

1:2, 1:13, 1:14, 1:17, 1:19, 1:26^{2}, 1:27, 1:30, 1:47^{2}, 2:3, 2:4, 2:6, 2:7^{2}, 2:21, 2:37, 2:38, 2:39, 2:44, 3:6, 3:7, 3:8^{2}, 3:9^{3}, 3:12, 3:13, 3:14^{2}, 3:22^{2}, 3:23^{2}, 5:3^{2}, 5:6^{2}, 5:8, 6:12, 8:19^{2}, 8:23, 8:24^{2}, 8:25^{2}, 8:26^{2}, 8:28, 8:29, 8:30^{3}, 8:32, 8:33^{2}, 8:34, 8:35, 8:36^{4}, 8:38, 8:39, 8:41^{2}, 8:42^{3}, 8:43^{4}, 8:44^{2}, 8:48, 8:49, 8:50, 8:51, 8:52^{2}, 8:53, 9:3^{2}, 9:4, 9:5^{2}, 10:7, 10:8^{3}, 10:9, 11:11, 11:12^{3}, 11:13, 11:37, 12:4^{2}, 12:7, 12:9, 12:10, 12:28, 13:6, 13:21, 13:22^{2}, 14:9, 14:12, 15:19^{2}, 16:3, 17:12, 17:13, 17:19, 17:23, 17:24, 18:8, 18:9, 18:10, 18:11, 18:12, 18:14, 18:18, 18:31, 18:36^{2}, 18:44, 19:2, 19:10^{2}, 19:14^{2}, 19:15, 19:16, 20:3^{4}, 20:5^{4}, 20:6, 20:9, 20:31, 20:32, 20:33, 20:34, 20:39^{2}, 20:40^{2}, 20:42^{3}, 21:2, 21:5, 21:6, 21:19, 21:21, 22:4^{2}, 22:13, 22:23, 22:30, 22:49

2 KI

1:10, 1:12, 1:13^{2}, 1:14, 2:2, 2:3^{2}, 2:4, 2:5^{2}, 2:6, 2:9, 2:16^{2}, 3:7^{2}, 3:13^{2}, 4:1^{2}, 4:3, 4:4, 4:7^{2}, 4:24, 4:26, 4:29^{2}, 4:30, 4:36, 5:8, 5:10, 5:15, 5:17^{2}, 5:18^{2}, 5:25, 5:27, 6:3, 6:12, 6:22^{2}, 6:28, 6:29, 8:9, 8:13, 9:1, 9:7, 9:22, 10:5, 10:15, 10:30, 14:9, 14:10, 15:12, 16:7^{2}, 18:23, 18:24, 18:26, 18:27, 19:4^{3}, 19:10, 19:22, 19:23, 19:27^{4}, 19:28^{4}, 20:3, 20:5^{3}, 20:6, 20:17, 20:18

22:9 22:19 22:20[2]

1 CH

10:4 11:1[2] 11:2 12:18[2] 16:35[2] 17:11[4] 17:17 17:18[2] 17:19 17:21[2] 17:22 17:23 17:24[2] 17:25[2] 17:26 17:27 19:3 21:8 21:12 21:17 22:11 22:12 28:6 28:9 28:21 29:13 29:17 29:18 29:19[3]

2 CH

1:9 1:10 2:8[2] 2:10 2:14[2] 6:2 6:9[2] 6:14 6:15[2] 6:16[2] 6:17[2] 6:19[2] 6:20[2] 6:21[3] 6:23 6:24[2] 6:25 6:26 6:27[4] 6:29 6:30 6:31 6:32[4] 6:33[4] 6:34[2] 6:38 6:39[2] 6:41[4] 6:42 7:12 7:17 7:18[2] 9:5 9:6 9:7[3] 9:8[3] 10:4[2] 10:7 10:9 10:10 14:11 16:3[2] 16:7 18:3 18:12 18:22 18:29 20:7[2] 20:8 20:9[2] 20:11 20:37 21:12[2] 21:13[2] 21:14[4] 21:15[2] 25:18 34:16 34:27 34:28[2]

EZR

4:11 4:15 7:14 7:18 7:19 7:20 7:25[2] 7:26 9:10 9:11 9:14

NE

1:6[2] 1:7 1:8 1:10[4] 1:11[4] 2:2 2:5[2] 2:6 9:5 9:8 9:14[2] 9:16 9:17 9:18 9:19 9:20[2] 9:25 9:26[2] 9:27 9:28 9:29[3] 9:30[2] 9:31 9:32 9:34[3] 9:35 13:22

ES

3:8 4:14[2] 5:3 5:6[2] 7:2[2] 7:3 9:12[2]

JOB

1:11 1:12 1:18[2] 2:5 4:4 4:6[4] 5:24[2] 5:25 5:26 5:27 8:2 8:4 8:5 8:6 8:7[2] 8:21[2] 10:5[2] 10:12 10:17 11:3 11:14 11:15 11:16 11:18 13:21 13:24 14:13 15:5 15:10 15:12 15:13[2] 21:14 22:3 22:5 22:6 22:23 22:25 22:27[2] 22:28 30:21 33:5 33:6 33:8 33:31 33:33 34:33 35:4 35:6 35:8[2] 36:16 36:19 37:17 38:3 38:11 38:12 38:21 38:34 39:9 39:11 39:12[2] 39:26 39:27 40:7 40:11 41:5 42:7

PS

2:8 3:8[2] 4:6 5:5 5:7[4] 5:8[2] 5:11 6:1 6:4 8:1[2] 8:3[2] 8:6 8:9 9:1 9:2 9:3 9:10 9:14[2] 9:19 10:5 10:14 13:1 13:5[2] 15:1[2] 16:11[2] 17:2 17:4 17:5 17:7[2] 17:8 17:13 17:14[2] 17:15[2] 18:15[2] 18:35[3] 18:49 19:11 19:13 19:14 20:3[2] 20:4 20:5[2] 21:1[2] 21:5 21:6 21:8 21:12 21:13 22:22 23:4[2] 24:6 25:4[2] 25:5 25:6[2] 25:7[2] 25:11 26:3[2] 26:7 26:8 27:8 27:9[2] 27:11 28:2 28:9 30:7[2] 30:9 31:1 31:3 31:7 31:15 31:16[3] 31:19 31:20 32:4 33:22 34:13[2] 35:3 35:24 35:28[2] 36:5[2] 36:6[2] 36:7[2] 36:8[2] 36:9 36:10[2] 37:5 37:6[2] 38:1[2] 38:2 39:10 39:12 40:5[2] 40:8[2] 40:10[5] 40:11[3] 40:16 41:12 42:3 42:7[3] 42:10 43:3[4] 44:2 44:3[2] 44:5 44:8 44:12[2] 44:17 44:18 44:22 44:24 44:26 45:2 45:3[4] 45:4[2] 45:6[2] 45:7[2] 45:8 45:9[2] 45:10 45:11[2] 45:12 45:16[2] 45:17 48:9 48:10[3] 48:11 50:7 50:8[2] 50:9[2] 50:14 50:16 50:19[2] 50:20 51:1[2] 51:4 51:9 51:11[2] 51:12[2] 51:13 51:14 51:15 51:18 52:2 52:5 52:9[2] 54:1[2] 54:5 54:6 55:22 56:8[2] 56:12 57:1 57:5 57:10[2] 57:11 59:11 59:16[2] 60:3 60:5[2] 61:4[2] 61:5 61:8 63:2[2] 63:3 63:4 63:7 63:8 65:4[3] 65:8 65:11[2] 66:3[2] 66:4 66:13 67:2[2] 68:7 68:10[2] 68:23[2] 68:24 68:28[2] 68:29 68:35 69:7 69:13[2] 69:16[2] 69:17[2] 69:24 69:27 69:29 70:4 71:2 71:8[2] 71:15[2] 71:16 71:17 71:18[2] 71:19 71:22 71:24 72:1[2] 72:2[2] 73:15 73:24 73:28 74:1 74:2 74:3 74:4 74:7[2] 74:10 74:11[3] 74:13 74:18 74:19[2] 74:21 75:1[2] 76:6 76:7 77:11 77:12[2] 77:13 77:14 77:15 77:18 77:19[3] 77:20 79:1 79:2[2] 79:5 79:6 79:8 79:9[2] 79:10 79:11 79:13[3] 80:2 80:3 80:4 80:7 80:15 80:16 80:17[2] 80:18 80:19 81:10[2] 83:1 83:3[2] 83:15[2] 83:16 84:1 84:4 84:10 85:1 85:2 85:3 85:6 85:7[2] 86:2 86:4 86:8 86:9 86:11[3] 86:12 86:13 86:16[2] 88:5 88:7[2] 88:11[2] 88:12[2] 88:14 88:15 88:16[2] 89:1 89:2 89:4[2] 89:5[2] 89:8 89:10 89:12 89:13[2] 89:14[2] 89:15 89:16[2] 89:17 89:19 89:39 89:46 89:49[2] 89:50 90:4 90:7 90:8 90:9 90:11[2] 90:13 90:14 90:16[3] 91:4 91:7[2] 91:9 91:10 91:11 91:12 92:1 92:2[2] 92:4[2] 92:5[2] 93:2 93:5 94:5 94:12 94:18 94:19 97:8 99:3 102:2 102:10 102:12 102:14 102:15 102:24 102:25 102:27 102:28 103:3 103:4 103:5[2] 104:7[2] 104:13 104:24[2] 104:29 104:30 106:4[2] 106:5[2] 106:7[2] 106:47[2] 108:4[2] 108:5 108:6[2] 109:1 109:21[2] 109:26 109:27 109:28 110:1 110:2 110:3[3] 110:5 115:1[3] 116:7 116:16[2] 119:4 119:5 119:6 119:7 119:8 119:9 119:10 119:11 119:12 119:13 119:14 119:15[2] 119:16[2] 119:17[2] 119:18 119:19 119:20 119:21 119:22 119:23[2] 119:24 119:25 119:26 119:27[2] 119:28 119:29 119:30 119:31 119:32 119:33 119:34 119:35 119:36 119:37 119:38[3] 119:39 119:40[2] 119:41[3] 119:42 119:43[2] 119:44 119:45 119:47 119:48[2] 119:49 119:50 119:51 119:52 119:53 119:54 119:55[2] 119:56 119:57 119:58[2] 119:59 119:60 119:61 119:62 119:63 119:64[2] 119:65[2] 119:66 119:67 119:68 119:69 119:70 119:71 119:72 119:73[2] 119:74 119:75 119:76[3] 119:77[2] 119:78[2] 119:79 119:80 119:81[2] 119:82 119:83 119:84 119:85 119:86 119:87 119:88[2] 119:89 119:90 119:91 119:92 119:93 119:94 119:95 119:96 119:97 119:98 119:99 119:100 119:101 119:102 119:103 119:104 119:105 119:106 119:107 119:108 119:109 119:110 119:111 119:112 119:113 119:114 119:115 119:116 119:117 119:118 119:119 119:120 119:123[2] 119:124[3] 119:125[2] 119:126 119:127 119:128 119:129 119:130 119:131 119:132 119:133 119:134 119:135[3] 119:136 119:137 119:138 119:139 119:140[2] 119:141 119:142[2] 119:143 119:144[2] 119:145 119:146 119:147 119:148 119:149[2] 119:150 119:151 119:152 119:153 119:154 119:155 119:156[2] 119:157 119:158 119:159[2] 119:160[2] 119:161 119:162 119:163 119:164 119:165 119:166[2] 119:167 119:168[2] 119:169 119:170 119:171 119:172[2] 119:173 119:174[2] 119:175 119:176[2] 121:3 121:5[3] 121:7 121:8[2] 122:2 122:7[2] 122:9 128:3[3] 128:5 128:6 132:8[2] 132:9[2] 132:10 132:11[2] 132:12[2] 135:13[2] 137:9 138:2[6] 138:4 138:7 138:8 139:7 139:10[2] 139:14 139:16 139:17 139:20 140:13[2] 142:7 143:1[2] 143:2[2] 143:5[2] 143:7 143:8 143:10[2] 143:11[2] 143:12[2] 144:5 145:1 145:2 145:4[2] 145:5[2] 145:6[2] 145:7[2] 145:10[2] 145:11[2] 145:13[2] 146:10 147:12 147:13[2] 147:14

PR

1:8[2] 1:9[2] 1:14 1:15 2:3 2:10 3:3 3:6 3:8 3:9 3:10[2] 3:22[2] 3:23[2] 3:24 3:26[2] 3:28 3:29 4:7 4:10 4:12 4:13 4:23 4:26[2] 4:27 5:2 5:8 5:9 5:10[2] 5:11[2] 5:16 5:18 6:1[2] 6:2[2] 6:3[2] 6:9 6:11[2] 6:20[2] 6:21 7:3 7:4 7:15 9:11[2] 16:3[2] 19:18[2] 19:20 22:18 22:19 22:25 22:27 22:28 23:2 23:8 23:9 23:16 23:22[2] 23:25[2] 24:6 24:10 24:12 24:13 24:14[2] 24:27 24:28[2] 24:34[2] 25:8 25:9[2] 25:17[2] 27:10[3] 27:23[2] 27:26 27:27[3] 29:17[2] 30:32 31:3[2] 31:8 31:9

EC

5:1 5:2[2] 5:6[3] 7:9 7:17 7:21 9:7[4] 9:8[2] 9:9[4] 9:10[2] 10:4 10:16[2] 10:17[2] 10:20[2] 11:1 11:6 11:9[2] 11:10[2] 12:1

CA

1:2 1:3[2] 1:4 1:7[2] 1:8[2] 1:10[2] 2:14[4] 4:1[2] 4:2 4:3[4] 4:4 4:5 4:10[2] 4:11[3] 4:13 5:9[2] 6:1[2] 6:5 6:6 6:7[2] 7:1[2] 7:2[2] 7:3 7:4[2] 7:7[2] 7:8[2] 7:9 8:5 8:13

ISA

1:22[2] 1:23 1:25[2] 1:26[2] 2:6 3:6 3:12 3:25[2] 4:1 6:7[2] 7:3 7:11 7:17[2] 8:8 10:22 10:27[2] 10:30 14:3[2] 14:9 14:11[2] 14:19 14:20[2] 14:30[2] 16:3 16:9[2] 17:10[2] 17:11 19:12 20:2[3] 22:2 22:3 22:7 22:18[2] 22:19[2] 22:21[3] 23:10 25:1[2] 25:12 26:8[2] 26:9 26:11 26:13 26:16 26:17 26:19[2] 26:20[2] 29:4[3] 29:5 30:19 30:20[2] 30:22[2] 30:23 33:6 33:23 36:8 36:9 36:11 37:4[3] 37:10 37:23 37:24 37:28[4] 37:29[4] 38:3 38:5[4] 38:17 38:18 38:19 39:6 39:7 40:9 41:10 41:13[2] 41:14 43:1 43:3[2] 43:4 43:5 43:23[2] 43:24[2] 43:25[2] 43:27[2] 44:3 44:22[2] 44:24 44:27 44:28 45:3 45:4 45:9 47:2 47:3[2] 47:6 47:7 47:9 47:10[3] 47:12[2] 47:13 47:15[2] 48:4[2] 48:17[2] 48:18[2] 48:19[2] 49:16 49:17[2] 49:19[3] 49:22[2] 49:23[3] 49:25 49:26[2] 51:13 51:15 51:16 51:22[2] 51:23[2] 52:1[2] 52:2 52:7 52:8 54:2[3] 54:3 54:4[2] 54:5[2] 54:6 54:8 54:11[2] 54:12[3] 54:13[2] 54:15 55:5 57:6[2] 57:7 57:8[2] 57:9[2] 57:10 57:11 57:12[2] 57:13 58:1 58:7[2] 58:8[3] 58:10[3] 58:11[2] 58:13[2] 58:14 59:21[4] 60:1 60:3[2] 60:4[3] 60:9[2] 60:10 60:11 60:14 60:16[2] 60:17 60:18[4] 60:19[3] 60:20[3] 60:21 62:2[2] 62:3 62:4[3] 62:5[2] 62:6 62:8[2] 62:11 63:2 63:14 63:15[6] 63:16 63:17[3] 63:18[2] 63:19 64:1 64:2[2] 64:3 64:5 64:7[2] 64:8 64:9 64:10 64:12 66:9

JER

1:9 1:17 2:2 2:16 2:17 2:19[2] 2:20[2] 2:23 2:25 2:28[4] 2:33[2] 2:34 2:36 2:37 3:2[2] 3:13[2] 4:7[2] 4:14 4:18[3] 4:30[3] 5:7 5:14 5:17[7] 10:6 10:17 10:25[2] 11:13[2] 11:16 11:20 11:21 12:1 12:6[2] 13:1 13:4 13:20 13:22[2] 13:25[2] 13:26[3] 13:27[2] 14:7 14:9 14:19 14:21[3] 15:11 15:13[4] 15:15[2] 15:16[3] 15:17 17:3[4] 18:20 18:23 20:3 20:4 20:6 20:12 22:2[2] 22:7 22:15 22:17 22:20[2] 22:21[3] 22:22[3] 22:23 22:25 22:26 27:2 27:13 28:6 29:25 30:8[2] 30:10 30:12[2] 30:13 30:14[2] 30:15[2] 30:17 31:4 31:7 31:16[2] 31:17 31:21 32:17 32:21 32:23[2] 34:5 37:18 38:16 38:17 38:20 38:22[2] 38:23[2] 39:18[2] 40:2 42:2 42:3 42:5 45:5 46:12[2] 46:15 46:27 47:6 48:7[2] 48:18[2] 48:32[3] 48:46[2] 49:4 49:11[2] 49:16[2] 50:31 51:13 51:36

LA

1:10 2:13 2:14[2] 3:23 3:55 4:22 5:19

EZE

2:1 2:8 3:3[2] 3:8[2] 3:9 3:11 3:19 3:21 3:26[2] 3:27 4:3 4:4 4:6 4:7 4:8 4:9 4:10 4:15 5:1 5:3 5:11 6:2 6:11 7:3 7:8 7:9 9:8[2] 11:15[3] 12:3 12:4 12:6[2] 12:18[2] 13:4 13:17[2] 16:3[4] 16:4[2] 16:5 16:6[2] 16:7 16:8[2] 16:9 16:11[2] 16:12 16:13 16:14[2] 16:15[2] 16:16[2] 16:17 16:18 16:20[3] 16:22[3] 16:23 16:25[4] 16:26[2] 16:27 16:29 16:33[3] 16:34 16:36[6] 16:37[3] 16:39[3] 16:43[2] 16:45 16:46[3] 16:47 16:48[2] 16:49 16:51[2] 16:52[4] 16:53 16:55 16:56[3] 16:57[2] 16:58 16:61[4] 16:63[2] 19:2 19:10[2] 19:11 20:46[2] 21:2[2] 21:6 21:12 21:16 21:30 21:32 22:4[3] 22:12 22:13[2] 22:15 23:21[3] 23:22 23:25[5] 23:26[2] 23:27[2] 23:28 23:29[4] 23:31 23:32 23:33 23:35[3] 23:40 24:13[2] 24:14[2] 24:16 24:17[3] 24:27 25:1 25:4[2] 25:6 26:8 26:9[2] 26:10[2] 26:11[3] 26:12[7] 26:13[2] 26:15 26:18[2] 27:4[3] 27:5 27:6 27:7 27:8[3] 27:9[2] 27:10[2] 27:11[4] 27:12[2] 27:13[2] 27:14 27:15 27:16[3] 27:17[2] 27:18[2] 27:19[2] 27:20 27:21 27:22[2] 27:23 27:24[2] 27:25 27:26 27:27[10] 27:28 27:33[3] 27:34[2] 28:4[2] 28:5[4] 28:7[2] 28:13[3] 28:15 28:16 28:17[3] 28:18[2] 28:21 29:2 29:4[6] 29:5 29:7 29:10 31:2 32:2[2] 32:5[2] 32:6 32:8 32:9 32:10 32:12 33:2 33:9 33:12 33:17 33:30 33:31 33:32 35:2 35:4 35:8[3] 35:9 35:11 35:12 36:13 36:14 36:15 37:18 38:2 38:4 38:7 38:9 38:10 38:13 38:15 39:3[3] 39:4

DA

1:12 1:13 2:4 2:28[3] 2:29[3] 2:30 3:12 3:18 4:22[2] 4:25 4:26 4:27[2] 4:32 5:10[2] 5:11[4] 5:16 5:17[2] 5:18 5:23[5] 5:26 5:28 6:16 6:20 9:5[2] 9:6[2] 9:11[2] 9:13 9:15 9:16[5] 9:17[3] 9:18[2] 9:19[3] 9:23 9:24[2] 10:12[3] 10:14 11:14 12:1[2] 12:9 12:13[2]

HO

2:6 4:4 4:5 4:6[2] 6:5 8:1 8:5 9:1 10:13[2] 10:14[2] 12:6[2] 12:9 13:4 13:10[3] 13:14[2] 14:1 14:8

JOE

2:17 3:11

AM

3:11[2] 4:12 5:23[2] 6:10 7:16 7:17[4] 8:14 9:15

OB

4 7[2] 9 10[2] 12 15

JON

1:6 1:8 2:3[2] 2:4[2]

MIC

1:11 1:16[2] 4:9 4:13 5:10[2] 5:11[2] 5:13[2] 5:14[2] 6:1 6:8 6:9 6:13 6:14 7:4[2] 7:5[2] 7:10 7:11 7:14[2] 7:15

THY—*continued* 1773

NA
1:13 1:14^{3} 1:15^{2} 2:1^{3} 2:13^{3} 3:2^{2} 3:5^{4} 3:8^{2} 3:9 3:9^{2} 3:11 3:12 3:13 3:13^{3} 3:14 3:16 3:17^{2} 3:18^{3} 3:19^{3}

HAB
1:13 2:10^{2} 2:15 2:16^{2}

ZEP
1:7 3:11^{2} 3:15 3:17

ZEC
3:8 9:9 9:11^{2} 9:13^{2} 11:1^{2} 14:1

MAL
1:6 1:8^{2} 2:14^{3}

MT
1:20 4:6 4:7 4:10 5:23^{2} 5:24^{4} 5:29^{3} 5:30^{3} 5:36 5:39 5:40^{2} 5:43 6:3^{2} 6:4 6:6^{4} 6:9 6:10^{2} 6:17 6:18^{2} 6:22 6:23 7:3 7:4 7:5 7:22^{3} 8:4 8:13 9:2 9:5 9:6 9:14 9:18 9:22 11:10^{2} 11:26 12:2 12:37^{2} 12:47^{2} 13:27 15:2 15:4 15:28 17:16 18:8^{2} 18:15^{2} 18:33 19:19^{3} 20:14 20:21^{2} 21:5 22:37^{4} 22:39 22:44 23:37 24:3 25:21 25:23 25:25 26:18 26:42 26:52 26:73

MK
1:2^{2} 1:25 1:44^{2} 2:5 2:9^{2} 2:11^{2} 2:18 3:32^{2} 5:9 5:19 5:23 5:34^{2} 5:35 6:18 7:5 7:10^{2} 7:29^{2} 9:18 9:38 9:43 9:45 10:19 10:21 10:37^{3} 10:52^{2} 12:30^{5} 12:31 12:36 14:70

LU
1:13 1:31 1:36 1:38 1:42 1:44 1:61 2:29^{2} 2:30 2:32 2:35 2:48 4:8 4:11 4:12 4:23 4:35 5:5 5:14 5:20 5:23 5:24 6:10 6:29^{2} 6:30 6:41 6:42^{2} 7:27^{2} 7:48 7:50 8:20^{2} 8:30 8:48 8:49 9:40 9:41 9:49 10:17 10:21 10:27^{6} 11:2^{3} 11:34^{2} 11:36 12:20 13:26 13:34 14:12^{4} 15:19^{2} 15:21^{2} 15:27 15:29 15:30^{2} 15:32 16:1 16:2 16:6 16:7 16:25^{2} 17:3 17:19^{2} 18:20^{2} 18:42^{2} 19:5 19:16 19:18 19:20 19:39 19:42^{2} 19:44^{2} 20:43 22:32^{2} 23:42 23:46

JOH
4:16 4:18 4:42 4:50^{2} 4:51 4:53 5:8 5:10 5:11 5:12 7:3 8:13 8:19 11:23 12:15 12:28 13:37 13:38 17:1^{3} 17:2 17:6^{2} 17:12 17:13 17:14 17:17^{2} 17:26 18:11 19:26 19:27 20:27^{2} 21:18

AC
2:28 2:35^{2} 3:25 4:25 4:27 4:28^{2} 4:29^{2} 4:30 5:9 7:3^{2} 7:32 7:33^{2} 8:20 8:21 8:22 8:23 9:13 9:14 9:15 9:17 9:34 10:4 10:31 11:14 12:8^{2} 14:10 16:31 18:9 22:13 22:16 22:18 22:20 23:5 24:2 24:4 24:25 26:16

RO
2:5 2:17 2:23 2:25 3:4 4:18 8:36 9:7 10:8^{2} 10:9 11:3 13:9 14:10^{2} 14:15^{3} 14:21 15:9

1 CO
7:16^{2} 14:16 15:55^{2}

GA
3:16 5:14

EPH
6:2

1 TI
4:12 4:15 5:23 6:20

2 TI
1:4 1:5^{2} 4:5 4:9 4:21 4:22

PHM
2 5 6 7 13 14^{2} 21

HEB
1:8^{2} 1:9^{2} 1:12 1:13 2:7 2:12 10:7 10:9 11:18

JAS
2:8 2:18^{2}

2 JO
4 13

3 JO
2 6

RE
2:2^{3} 2:4 2:5 2:9 2:13 2:19^{3} 3:1 3:2 3:8 3:9 3:11 3:15 3:18 4:11 5:9 10:9^{2} 11:17 11:18^{3} 14:15 14:18 15:3^{2} 15:4^{2} 16:7 18:10 18:14 18:23^{2} 19:10^{2} 22:9^{2}

TO *1519*

GE
1:14 1:16^{2} 1:17 1:18^{2} 1:29 1:30^{3} 2:5 2:9^{2} 2:10 2:15^{2} 2:19 2:20^{2} 2:21 3:6^{2} 3:7 3:12 3:16 3:18 3:21 3:22 3:23 3:24 4:3 4:4 4:5 4:7 4:11 4:14 4:23 4:26^{2} 6:1 6:4 6:16 6:17 6:19 6:20 6:21 6:22 7:2 7:3 7:4 7:10 8:1 8:6 8:8 8:11 8:13 9:8 9:10 9:11 9:14 9:15 9:20 10:8 10:19 10:21 11:2 11:3^{2} 11:4 11:5 11:6^{2} 11:7 11:8 11:21 12:5 12:10 12:11^{2} 12:12 12:14 12:19 13:3 13:6 13:9^{2} 13:15 14:1 14:7 14:10 14:17 14:21 14:22 14:23 15:3 15:5 15:6 15:7 15:15 15:17 16:2 16:3^{3} 16:6 16:7 16:9 16:16 17:1 17:7^{2} 17:8 18:2 18:5 18:7 18:10 18:11 18:14 18:16 18:19 18:21 18:25 18:27 18:31 19:1^{2} 19:5 19:8 19:9^{3} 19:10 19:11 19:13 19:17^{2} 19:19 19:20 19:27 19:29 19:30 19:31 19:34 20:3 20:6 20:13 20:16 21:2 21:3 21:6 21:17 21:22 21:23^{2} 21:26 22:1 22:5 22:9 22:10 22:14 22:19 22:20 22:23 23:2 23:7^{2} 23:8 23:16 24:4 24:5 24:8 24:9 24:10 24:11^{2} 24:13 24:14^{2} 24:15^{2} 24:16^{2} 24:17 24:20 24:21 24:22 24:23 24:25 24:27 24:30 24:32 24:33 24:36 24:37 24:38 24:41 24:43^{3} 24:44 24:48 24:49 24:52^{2} 24:53^{3} 24:56 24:63 24:65 25:8 25:11 25:13 25:16 25:20^{2} 25:22 25:24 25:30 25:32^{3} 25:33 26:4 26:7^{2} 26:8 26:11 26:23 26:26 26:27 26:31 26:32 26:34 26:35 27:1 27:3 27:4 27:5^{3} 27:8 27:9 27:10 27:11 27:12 27:14 27:20 27:25^{2} 27:29^{2} 27:30 27:37 27:40 27:42^{2} 27:43 27:45 27:46 28:2 28:4 28:5 28:6^{2} 28:7 28:9 28:11 28:12 28:13 28:14^{2} 28:15 28:20 28:21 29:10 29:13^{3} 29:14 29:19 29:20 29:23^{2} 29:25^{2} 29:26 29:28 29:29^{2} 30:4 30:9 30:14 30:15 30:16 30:18 30:22 30:24 30:25^{2} 30:32 30:33 30:34 30:38^{2} 30:41 31:3 31:4 31:7 31:9 31:10 31:18^{2} 31:19 31:20 31:24^{2} 31:26^{2} 31:28 31:29^{2} 31:31 31:32 31:35 31:36 31:51 31:52 31:54 32:3 32:5 32:6^{3} 32:8 32:9 32:13 32:30 33:3^{2} 33:4 33:8 33:11 33:14 33:17 33:18 34:1 34:4 34:6 34:7 34:8 34:12 34:14^{2} 34:16^{2} 34:17 34:19 34:21 34:22^{2} 34:25 34:30^{3} 35:1 35:2 35:6 35:12^{2} 35:16^{2} 35:17 35:18 35:19 35:22 35:26 36:4 36:12^{2} 36:14 36:40 36:43 37:7 37:8 37:9 37:10^{5} 37:12 37:13 37:14^{2} 37:17 37:18 37:19 37:22^{2} 37:23 37:25^{3} 37:27 37:28 37:32 37:35^{2} 38:1^{2} 38:8 38:9^{2} 38:11 38:12 38:13^{2} 38:14^{2} 38:15 38:16 38:20 38:22 38:23 38:24 38:25 38:26 38:27 38:28 38:29 39:1 39:3 39:5 39:7 39:8 39:10^{4} 39:11^{2} 39:13 39:14^{2} 39:15 39:17^{2} 39:18 39:19^{2} 39:22 39:23^{2} 40:1 40:5 40:8 40:9 40:20 40:22 41:1 41:8 41:11 41:12^{4} 41:13^{2} 41:24 41:25 41:28 41:32 41:36 41:43 41:45 41:52 41:54 41:55^{2} 41:57^{2} 42:3 42:5 42:6^{2} 42:7 42:9 42:10 42:12 42:21 42:24 42:25^{3} 42:27 42:28 42:30 42:35 42:37^{2} 42:38 43:2 43:6 43:7 43:15 43:16 43:19 43:20 43:21^{2} 43:22 43:23 43:26^{2} 43:30 43:33^{2} 44:2 44:7 44:11 44:13 44:14 44:24 44:29 44:30 44:31^{2} 44:32 44:33 44:34 45:1 45:4 45:5 45:7^{2} 45:8 45:9 45:11 45:17 45:21 45:22^{2} 45:23 45:27 46:1 46:3 46:5 46:18 46:22 46:28 46:29^{2} 46:32 46:33 47:4 47:6 47:12 47:21^{2} 47:24 48:1 48:4 48:7 48:11 48:12 48:17 48:22 49:4^{2} 49:15 49:28 49:29 50:2 50:7 50:10 50:11 50:14 50:20^{3} 50:24^{3}

EX
1:10 1:11 1:13 1:15 1:16 1:21 2:1 2:4^{2} 2:5^{2} 2:7^{2} 2:8 2:11 2:13 2:14 2:15 2:16 2:18^{2} 2:21 2:23 3:1^{3} 3:4 3:6 3:8^{2} 3:13 3:16 3:18^{2} 3:21 4:8^{2} 4:9 4:14 4:16^{2} 4:18^{2} 4:20 4:21 4:23 4:24^{2} 4:25 4:27^{2} 5:2 5:7 5:8 5:10 5:12 5:14 5:16 5:17 5:21^{3} 5:23^{3} 6:1 6:3 6:4 6:7^{2} 6:8^{4} 6:15 6:16 6:17 6:19 6:20 6:23 6:25^{2} 6:26^{2} 6:27^{2} 6:28 7:1 7:14 7:15 7:17 7:18 7:20 7:23 7:24 8:2 8:5 8:9 8:10^{2} 8:13 8:18 8:20 8:22 8:23 8:25 8:26^{2} 8:27 8:28 8:29^{3} 8:31 9:2 9:5 9:8 9:16 9:18^{2} 10:3 10:4^{2} 10:5 10:10 10:26 10:28 12:2 12:3^{2} 12:4^{2} 12:13^{2} 12:14 12:16 12:21 12:23^{3} 12:24^{2} 12:25^{2} 12:26 12:29 12:35 12:37 12:41^{2} 12:42^{2} 12:48 12:49 12:51 13:5 13:6 13:10 13:11 13:14 13:15^{2} 13:17^{2} 13:21^{2} 14:2^{2} 14:12 14:13^{3} 14:20^{2} 14:21 14:23 14:24 14:27 15:21 15:23 15:26^{2} 15:27^{2} 16:3^{3} 16:5 16:8^{2} 16:10 16:13 16:15^{2} 16:16^{2} 16:18 16:21 16:22 16:23^{3} 16:25^{3} 16:27^{2} 16:28 16:32 16:33 16:34 16:35 17:1^{2} 17:3 17:4 17:9 17:10^{2} 17:11 17:16 18:7 18:8 18:9 18:12 18:13^{2} 18:14^{2} 18:15 18:18 18:19 18:21 18:23^{2} 18:24 19:2 19:3 19:10^{2} 19:12^{2} 19:13 19:16 19:17 19:20 19:21 19:22 19:23 19:24 20:5 20:8 20:20 21:6 21:7 21:8 21:12 21:14 21:15 21:16 21:17 21:19 21:29^{3} 21:31 21:36 22:5 22:7 22:8 22:9 22:10 22:16 22:17^{2} 22:18 22:19 22:25^{2} 22:26 22:27 22:29 22:31 23:1 23:2^{3} 23:4 23:5 23:20^{2} 23:24 23:27 24:4 24:12 24:14 25:7 25:9 25:20 25:25 25:27 25:29 25:35 26:3^{2} 26:7 26:13 26:28 26:30 27:3 27:5 27:7 27:20^{2} 27:21 28:3 28:8 28:10 28:11 28:14 28:21^{2} 28:35 28:36 28:42 28:43 29:1^{2} 29:10 29:29^{2} 29:30 29:33^{2} 29:35^{2} 29:36 29:41^{2} 29:42 29:44^{2} 30:1 30:4 30:15 30:16 30:18 30:20^{3} 30:21^{3} 30:37^{2} 30:38 31:4^{2} 31:5^{2} 31:10 31:11 31:14 31:15^{2} 31:16 32:1 32:5^{2} 32:6^{2} 32:12^{2} 32:13 32:14 32:19 32:20 32:27 32:28 32:29^{2} 32:30 33:1^{2} 33:5 33:7 33:8 33:9 33:11 33:19 33:22 34:2 34:7 34:12 34:24 34:29 34:30 34:34 34:35 35:2^{3} 35:9 35:19^{2} 35:21 35:27 35:29^{2} 35:32^{2} 35:33^{2} 35:35 36:1^{3} 36:2^{2} 36:3 36:5 36:6 36:7 36:12 36:18 36:29^{2} 36:33^{2} 36:34 37:2 37:3 37:5 37:9^{2} 37:14 37:15 37:16 37:21 37:27^{2} 37:29 38:5 38:7 38:18 38:21^{2} 38:26 38:30 39:1 39:3 39:4 39:5 39:7 39:14^{3} 39:26 39:30^{2} 39:31 39:32 39:37 39:41^{2} 39:42 40:4 40:5 40:16 40:17 40:30 40:35

LE
1:11 1:9 1:14 2:2^{4} 2:13 4:2 4:3 4:5 4:16 4:23 4:27 4:28 4:35 5:4^{2} 5:7 5:10 5:11 5:12^{2} 5:17 6:2 6:4 6:5 6:25 6:30 7:8 7:35 7:36 7:38 8:4 8:5 8:12 8:15 8:31 8:34^{2} 9:1 9:4 9:16 10:7 10:15 10:17^{2} 10:19 11:1 11:7 11:8 11:21 11:31 11:37 11:45 11:47 12:2 12:8 13:12 13:15 13:19 13:59^{2} 14:1 14:7 14:8 14:11 14:14 14:17 14:18 14:19 14:21^{2} 14:22 14:25 14:28 14:29^{2} 14:31^{2} 14:32^{2} 14:34 14:35 14:36^{2} 14:38 14:41 14:49 14:57 15:1 15:13 15:14 15:28 15:29 16:10^{3} 16:17 16:27 16:30 16:32 16:34 17:4 17:5 17:11^{2} 18:4 18:6^{3} 18:14 18:17 18:18^{3} 18:19 18:20 18:21 18:23^{2} 19:4 19:11 19:20^{2} 19:24 19:29 19:31 19:32 20:2^{2} 20:3^{2} 20:5 20:6 20:9 20:10 20:11 20:12 20:13 20:15 20:16 20:22 20:24 20:27 21:4 21:10 21:11 21:14 21:17 21:21^{2} 21:24 22:2 22:8 22:16 22:18 22:21^{2} 22:33 23:9 23:11 23:20 23:22 23:28 23:37^{2} 23:43 24:2^{2} 24:16^{2} 24:17 24:19 24:20 24:21 24:23 25:9 25:15 25:16^{3} 25:25 25:26^{2} 25:27 25:28^{2} 25:30 25:38^{2} 25:39 25:46 25:47 25:50^{2} 26:1 26:5 26:8 26:21 26:37 26:44^{2} 27:8 27:14 27:16 27:17 27:18 27:19 27:20 27:24^{2} 27:25 27:27^{2} 27:29

NU
1:3^{2} 1:18 1:20^{3} 1:22^{3} 1:24^{3} 1:26^{3} 1:28^{3} 1:30^{3} 1:32^{3} 1:34^{3} 1:36^{3} 1:38^{3} 1:40^{3} 1:42^{3} 1:45^{2} 1:50 1:51^{2} 1:54 2:10

2:18 2:34[2] 3:3 3:7 3:8 3:9 3:10 3:16 3:20 3:22 3:34 3:38 3:46 3:48[2] 3:51 4:3 4:7 4:11[2] 4:14[2] 4:15[2] 4:16[2] 4:19[2] 4:20 4:23[2] 4:24 4:30 4:31 4:33 4:37 4:41 4:45 4:47 4:49[3] 5:1 5:8[2] 5:15 5:19 5:20 5:21[2] 5:22[3] 5:24 5:26 5:27[2] 5:29 6:2[2] 6:4 6:10[2] 6:21 7:1 7:5[3] 7:7 7:89 8:1 8:12 8:15 8:19[4] 8:20 8:21 8:22 8:24 8:26 9:3[2] 9:5 9:12 9:13 9:14[2] 9:20[2] 10:3 10:7 10:8 10:9 10:10 10:11 10:13 10:14 10:18 10:22 10:28 10:30[2] 10:31[2] 10:33 10:35 11:4 11:13 11:14 11:16 11:18[2]

11:22[2] 11:23 11:25 12:8[2] 13:16 13:17 13:21 13:26[4] 13:30 13:31 13:32 14:3[2] 14:4 14:7 14:14[2] 14:16 14:20 14:22 14:25 14:28 14:29 14:30 14:36[2] 14:38 14:44 15:3 15:12[3] 15:24 15:28 15:34 15:35 15:39 15:41 16:5[2] 16:7 16:9[4] 16:10 16:12 16:13 16:16 16:28 16:31 16:33 16:40[3] 16:42 17:2[2] 17:5[2] 17:6 17:8 17:10 18:6[2] 18:7 18:8 18:11[2] 18:16[2] 18:19 18:24[2] 18:28 20:5[3] 20:8 20:12 20:17[2] 20:21 21:3 21:4 21:5 21:7 21:8 21:9 21:15 21:16 21:18 21:19[2] 21:20 21:23[2] 21:29 21:32 21:33 21:34 22:2 22:5[2] 22:11 22:13[2] 22:14 22:16[2] 22:18 22:20

22:23 22:26 22:30 22:32 22:36 22:37[3] 22:38 22:40[2] 22:41 23:3[2] 23:11 23:12 23:14 23:17 23:20 23:23 24:1[2] 24:2 24:10 24:11[2] 24:12 24:13 24:14 24:25 25:1 25:2 26:1 26:2[2] 26:18 26:22 26:25 26:27 26:37 26:43 26:47 26:50 26:53 26:54[4] 26:55 26:56 26:59 27:7 27:8 27:11 27:14 28:2 28:7 28:22 28:30 29:5 29:9[2] 29:14 29:15 29:18 29:21 29:24 29:27 29:30 29:33 29:37 29:40 30:2[2] 30:13 30:14 31:4 31:6[3] 31:13 31:16 31:21 31:27 31:28 31:36 31:50 31:52 32:2 32:6[2] 32:8 32:14 32:19 32:20 32:27 32:29 32:33[2] 32:39 33:2[2] 33:14 33:35

33:53 33:54[3] 33:56[2] 34:4[5] 34:8 34:9 34:10 34:11 34:12 34:13[2] 34:14[2] 34:18 34:29 35:2 35:3 35:5 35:6 35:7 35:8 35:11 35:16 35:17 35:18 35:21 35:24 35:25 35:30[2] 35:31 35:32[2] 36:2[3] 36:3[2] 36:5 36:6[2] 36:7[2] 36:9[2]

DE

1:3 1:5 1:7[2] 1:8[2] 1:9 1:14 1:19 1:27[2] 1:28 1:30 1:33[3] 1:35 1:36[2] 1:38 1:41[2] 1:45 2:4 2:15 2:16 2:18 2:22 2:24 2:25 2:27 2:31[2] 2:32 2:34 3:1[2] 3:3 3:7 3:8 3:12 3:24[3] 3:28 4:1 4:5 4:9 4:10 4:13 4:14[2] 4:19 4:20 4:25[2] 4:26[2] 4:30 4:34[2] 4:36 4:38[3]

5:4 5:5 5:12 5:15 5:23 5:31 5:32[3] 6:1[2] 6:2 6:3 6:10[4] 6:19 6:20 6:23 6:24[2] 6:25 7:1 7:6 7:9 7:10[4] 7:11 7:12[2] 7:13 7:24 7:25 8:1 8:2[3] 8:3 8:6[2] 8:16 8:18 9:1[2] 9:4 9:5 9:6 9:7 9:8[2] 9:9 9:10 9:11 9:18[2] 9:19 9:20 9:22 9:23 9:27[2] 9:28[2] 10:4 10:6 10:7 10:8[4] 10:10 10:11 10:12[4] 10:13 10:15 10:20 11:4[2] 11:8 11:9[2] 11:10 11:11 11:13[3] 11:16 11:21 11:22[4] 11:25 11:28 11:29[2] 11:31[2] 11:32 12:1[2] 12:5 12:9[2] 12:10 12:13 12:14[2] 12:15 12:19 12:20 12:21 12:29 12:30 12:31[2] 12:32 13:2 13:3

13:5[3] 13:9[2] 13:10 13:12 13:17 13:18[2] 14:23[2] 14:24[2] 15:4 15:5[2] 15:11[2] 15:15 15:18 16:2 16:6 16:8 16:9[3] 16:11 16:17 17:6[2] 17:7[2] 17:10[3] 17:11[4] 17:12 17:16[4] 17:17[2] 17:19[3] 17:20[3] 18:5[2] 18:8 18:9 18:10 18:14 18:16 18:19 18:20[2] 18:32 19:2 19:3 19:5 19:8 19:9[3] 19:14 19:16 19:19 20:1 20:4[2] 20:5[2] 20:9 20:10 20:18 20:19[2] 21:1 21:5[2] 21:10 21:11 21:12 21:16 21:22[2] 22:2 22:4 22:6 22:7 22:14 22:16 22:21[2] 22:22 22:27 23:2 23:3 23:4 23:14[2] 23:19 23:20[2] 23:21 23:22 24:1 24:3 24:4[2] 24:5 24:6[2] 24:8[2] 24:10 24:11 24:16[3] 24:17 24:18

24:19 24:22 25:2[4] 25:5 25:7[3] 25:8 25:11 25:19 26:2 26:3 26:5 26:8 26:13[3] 26:14[2] 26:16 26:17[4] 26:18 26:19 27:12 27:13 27:18 27:23 27:26 28:1[3] 28:7 28:11 28:12[2] 28:13[2] 28:14[4] 28:15[3] 28:20 28:21 28:25 28:31[2] 28:44[2] 28:45 28:50 28:55 28:56 28:58 28:63[7] 29:1 29:4[3] 29:8[2] 29:13[4] 29:18 29:19[3] 29:21 29:22 29:27 29:29 30:1[2] 30:2 30:6 30:10 30:12 30:14 30:18[2] 30:19 30:20[4] 31:4[2] 31:7[2] 31:11 31:12 31:13[2] 31:16 31:21 31:24 31:28 31:29[2] 32:8[2] 32:13 32:16[2] 32:17[3] 32:21[4] 32:26 32:30 32:35 32:40 32:41 32:43[2] 32:45 32:46[2] 32:47 33:7 33:9 33:17

33:24 34:1 34:4 34:5 34:10 34:11[4]

JOS

1:1 1:2[2] 1:5 1:6 1:7[4] 1:8[2] 1:11 1:12[3] 1:18 2:1 2:2[2] 2:3[2] 2:5 2:6 2:7 2:16 2:20 2:23 3:1 3:2 3:5 3:7 3:8 3:13 3:14[2] 4:1 4:6 4:8 4:10[2] 4:11 4:13 4:18 4:21 4:23 5:1 5:8 5:13 5:14 6:5 6:8 6:15 6:16 6:17 6:20 6:25 7:2 7:3[2] 7:6 7:7[3] 7:13 7:14[2] 7:19 8:1 8:2 8:3 8:5 8:8 8:9 8:10 8:12 8:14[2] 8:16 8:20[3] 8:23 8:24 8:34 9:1 9:2 9:3 9:6[2] 9:10[3] 9:11[2] 9:12 9:13 9:16[2] 9:20 9:24[2]

9:25 10:1[3] 10:6 10:10[2] 10:11[2] 10:12 10:13 10:15 10:18 10:19 10:20 10:21[2] 10:24 10:25 10:27 10:28 10:32[2] 10:33 10:35[2] 10:37[2] 10:38 10:39[5] 10:43 11:1[4] 11:2 11:3[3] 11:5 11:6 11:11 11:14 11:17 11:20 11:23[2] 12:3[2] 12:7[2] 13:1 13:3 13:4 13:15 13:24 13:31 14:4 14:7 14:11[2] 14:12 15:1 15:3[6] 15:6[2] 15:7 15:8 15:9[2] 15:10[2] 15:11[2] 15:12[2] 15:13[2] 15:15 15:16[2] 15:17 15:18[2] 15:20 16:1 16:2[2] 16:3[2] 16:5 16:6[2] 16:7[3] 17:1 17:4[2] 17:5 17:7 17:8 17:13[2] 17:14 17:15 17:17[2] 18:3 18:4[2] 18:6[2] 18:8[2] 18:9[2] 18:10 18:11 18:12 18:13[2] 18:15 18:16[4]

18:17[2] 18:19 18:20 18:21 18:28 19:1[2] 19:8[2] 19:10 19:11[2] 19:12[2] 19:13[4] 19:14 19:16 19:17[2] 19:22 19:23 19:24 19:26[2] 19:27[4] 19:29[4] 19:31 19:32[2] 19:33 19:34[5] 19:39 19:40 19:47 19:48 19:49 19:50 20:2 21:2[2] 21:12 21:13[2] 21:21 21:27 21:32 21:33 21:38 21:43 21:44 21:45 22:5[6] 22:7 22:9[3] 22:10 22:12[2] 22:13[2] 22:15[2] 22:16 22:18[2] 22:23[3] 22:24[2] 22:26 22:27[2] 22:28[3] 22:29 22:31[2] 22:32 22:33[2] 23:1 23:4 23:6[4] 23:7 23:9 23:12 23:14 23:15 23:16 24:1 24:4 24:5 24:9 24:15 24:16 24:22 24:29 24:33

JG

1:1 1:7 1:9

1:12[2] 1:13 1:14[3] 1:23 1:28[2] 1:34[2] 1:36 2:1[2] 2:4 2:6 2:12 2:19[3] 2:22 3:1 3:2 3:4[2] 3:6[2] 3:9 3:10 3:18 3:27 3:28 4:5 4:7 4:9 4:10 4:12 4:17 4:18[2] 4:19 4:22 5:3 5:11 5:16 5:23[2] 5:26[2] 5:29 5:30[2] 6:5 6:7 6:11 6:22 6:25 6:29 6:31 6:35 7:2 7:3 7:5 7:6 7:9 7:10[2] 7:11 7:17 7:20 7:22[2] 7:25 8:1 8:3 8:4 8:8 8:27 8:33 8:35[2] 9:1 9:3 9:7 9:8 9:9 9:10 9:11 9:13 9:16 9:21 9:24 9:26 9:29[2] 9:31 9:33 9:36 9:43 9:48 9:49 9:50 9:51[2] 9:52 9:53

10:9 10:12 10:18[2] 11:3 11:4 11:5 11:8 11:9 11:10 11:12[2] 11:16 11:20 11:24 11:27 11:33 11:34[2] 11:35 11:36[2] 11:39[2] 11:40 12:1[2] 12:3 12:5 13:5 13:7[2] 13:9 13:11 13:12 13:17 13:20 13:21[2] 13:23 13:25 14:1 14:2 14:3 14:5[2] 14:8[2] 14:9 14:10 14:11[2] 14:15[4] 14:17[2] 14:19[2] 14:20 15:1[3] 15:2 15:4 15:6 15:10[4] 15:11[2] 15:12 15:17 16:1 16:3 16:4 16:5 16:6[2] 16:8 16:16 16:19 16:21 16:22 16:23[2] 16:25 17:3[2] 17:4 17:8[3] 17:9 17:11 17:13 18:1 18:2[4] 18:7[2] 18:8 18:9[3] 18:10 18:14[2] 18:15 18:17 18:19[2] 18:22 18:30 19:1[2] 19:2 19:3[3] 19:5[2]

19:7 19:8 19:9[3] 19:12 19:13[2] 19:14 19:15[3] 19:18[3] 19:22 19:25[2] 19:27 20:1 20:3 20:4[2] 20:5 20:8 20:9 20:10[3] 20:13[2] 20:14[2] 20:18[2] 20:20[2] 20:21 20:23 20:25 20:28[2] 20:31[3] 20:36 20:39 20:40[2] 20:47 20:48[3] 21:1 21:2 21:3[2] 21:4 21:5[3] 21:7 21:8[4] 21:12 21:13[3] 21:18 21:21[2] 21:22 21:23 21:24[3]

RU

1:1[2] 1:7 1:8 1:12 1:16 1:17 1:18 1:19[3] 1:22 2:2 2:3 2:8 2:10 2:12 2:15 2:17 2:18 2:19[2] 2:20[2] 2:23 3:2 3:3 3:6 3:7 3:8 3:11 3:13[2] 3:16[2] 3:17 4:1 4:4[2] 4:5 4:6 4:7[2] 4:10[2] 4:15 4:17

1 SA

1:3[2] 1:4[2] 1:6 1:7 1:8[2] 1:12 1:19[2] 1:20 1:21 1:25 1:28[2] 2:6 2:8[2] 2:10 2:11[2] 2:15[2] 2:16 2:19[3] 2:20 2:24 2:28[4] 2:29 2:33[2] 2:35 2:36[2] 3:2[2] 3:3 3:6 3:8 3:11 3:15 3:17 3:19 3:20[2] 3:21 4:1 4:3 4:4 4:9 4:12 4:16 4:18 4:19 5:3 5:4[2] 5:10[5] 5:11 5:12 6:2[2] 6:3[2] 6:4[2] 6:7 6:9[2] 6:10 6:12[3] 6:13 6:16 6:18[2] 6:20[2] 6:21[2] 7:1 7:2 7:5 7:6 7:7 7:8[2] 7:10 7:14 7:16[2] 7:17 8:1 8:4 8:5 8:6 8:8 8:11 8:12[3] 8:13[2] 8:14 8:15[2] 8:16 8:19 8:22 9:3 9:5[2]

9:6 9:7[2] 9:8[2] 9:9[2] 9:10 9:11[2] 9:12[3] 9:13[2] 9:14[2] 9:16[2] 9:17 9:18 9:19[2] 9:21 9:26[2] 9:27[2] 10:1 10:2[2] 10:3[3] 10:5[3] 10:8[4] 10:9[2] 10:10 10:11[2] 10:13 10:14[3] 10:17 10:20 10:21 10:24 10:25 10:26 11:3[2] 11:4 11:9[2] 11:10 11:11 11:12 11:13[2] 11:14[2] 11:15 12:3 12:7[2] 12:17 12:20 12:22 12:23 13:2 13:4 13:5 13:7 13:8[2] 13:9 13:10[2] 13:12 13:13 13:14 13:17 13:18[3] 13:20[2] 13:21 13:22 13:23 14:1[2] 14:4 14:6[3] 14:7 14:9 14:12 14:19 14:20 14:21 14:25 14:26 14:27 14:30 14:31 14:43 14:45 14:46 15:1[2] 15:2 15:5 15:6 15:7 15:11 15:12[3]

15:13 15:15 15:16 15:21 15:22[2] 15:27 15:28 15:32 15:34[3] 15:35 16:1 16:2[2] 16:3 16:4 16:5[3] 16:6 16:9 16:10 16:12[2] 16:13 16:16[2] 16:17 16:21 16:22 16:23 17:1[2] 17:8[3] 17:9 17:13[2] 17:15 17:17[2] 17:20[2] 17:23 17:25 17:26[2] 17:27 17:32 17:33[5] 17:39 17:40 17:43 17:44[3] 17:45[3] 17:46 17:48[3] 17:49 17:52[3] 17:54 17:58 18:1 18:2 18:4[4] 18:6[2] 18:8 18:10 18:11 18:17[2] 18:18 18:19[3] 18:21[2] 18:23[2] 18:25[3] 18:26 18:27[2] 18:30 19:1[2] 19:2[2] 19:4 19:5 19:7 19:10[2] 19:11[4] 19:14 19:15[2] 19:18[3] 19:20 19:22[2] 19:23[2] 20:5[2] 20:6 20:8 20:9 20:10 20:13[2] 20:17 20:18[2] 20:19

20:21 20:24 20:27[3] 20:28[2] 20:29 20:30 20:33[2] 20:35 20:37 20:38 20:40 20:41 20:42 21:1[2] 21:2 21:6 21:7 21:10 21:11 21:14 21:15 22:1[2] 22:3 22:8 22:9[2] 22:11[2] 22:13 22:15[2] 22:17[2] 22:18 23:3 23:4 23:5 23:6[3] 23:7 23:8[4] 23:9 23:10[3] 23:13 23:15 23:16 23:18 23:19[2] 23:20[3] 23:23[2] 23:24 23:25 23:26[2] 24:1 24:2 24:3[2] 24:4 24:5 24:6 24:7 24:8 24:9 24:10 24:11 24:16 24:17 25:1 25:5[2] 25:6[3] 25:8[2] 25:9[2] 25:14 25:17 25:22 25:23 25:26[2] 25:29[2] 25:30[3] 25:32[2] 25:33 25:34 25:35[2] 25:36 25:37 25:38 25:39[3] 25:40[5] 25:41[2] 25:44 26:1 26:2[2] 26:5

26:6[5] 26:7 26:8[2] 26:9 26:10 26:13 26:14[3] 26:15[3] 26:16 26:20[2] 26:23[3] 26:25[2] 27:1 27:4 27:8 27:9 27:10 27:11[2] 27:12 28:1[2] 28:2[2] 28:7[2] 28:8 28:9[2] 28:10[2] 28:12 28:14 28:15[2] 28:17[3] 28:19 29:1 29:4[3] 29:5 29:9[2] 29:11[3] 30:1[2] 30:3 30:4 30:7[2] 30:9 30:11 30:12 30:13[2] 30:14 30:15[3] 30:19[2] 30:21[5] 30:22 30:24 30:26[2] 30:27[3] 30:28[3] 30:29[3] 30:30[3] 30:31[5] 31:8[2] 31:9 31:10 31:11 31:12

2 SA

1:1 1:2[3] 1:14[2] 1:26 2:1 2:8 2:10 2:12 2:14 2:15 2:19[2] 2:21[3] 2:22[2] 2:23[3] 2:24 2:26 2:29 2:30 3:5 3:6 3:7 3:8[3] 3:9[3]

3:10[3] 3:12[2] 3:14[2] 3:16 3:17 3:19[3] 3:20[2] 3:23 3:24 3:25[3] 3:27[2] 3:31[2] 3:35[3] 3:37 3:39 4:2 4:3 4:4 4:5 4:8[2] 4:10 5:1 5:2 5:3[2] 5:4 5:6 5:8 5:11 5:13 5:17[2] 5:19 5:20 5:24 5:25 6:2 6:6[2] 6:8 6:9 6:19[3] 6:20[3] 6:21 7:1 7:3 7:4 7:5 7:6 7:7 7:8 7:11[2] 7:17[2] 7:19 7:21[2] 7:22 7:23[5] 7:24[3] 7:27[2] 7:29 8:1 8:2[3] 8:3 8:5 8:6 8:7 8:10[2] 9:9[3] 9:10 9:11 10:1 10:2 10:3 10:4 10:5 10:14 10:16 10:17 10:19[2] 11:1[2] 11:2[2] 11:6 11:8[2] 11:9 11:11[3] 11:12[2] 11:13[2] 11:14[2] 11:16 11:27

12:4[3] 12:5 12:6 12:9[3] 12:10 12:14[2] 12:17[2] 12:18[2] 12:20 12:22 12:23[2] 12:27 12:29 13:1 13:2[2] 13:4 13:5 13:6 13:7[2] 13:8[2] 13:10 13:11 13:12 13:13 13:23 13:24 13:25 13:30[2] 13:33[2] 13:36 13:37 13:38 13:39 14:2[2] 14:3 14:4[2] 14:6 14:7 14:8 14:10 14:11[2] 14:15 14:16 14:17 14:19[2] 14:20[3] 14:22[2] 14:23[2] 14:24[2] 14:25[2] 14:29[3] 14:31 14:32[3] 14:33[3] 15:1 15:2 15:3 15:5[2] 15:6[2] 15:7 15:8 15:9 15:13 15:14 15:15 15:16 15:19[2] 15:22 15:26 15:28 15:29 15:32[3] 15:34 15:35 16:2[2] 16:3 16:4 16:5 16:10 16:11[2] 16:15 16:16 16:17[2] 16:21 17:6 17:9 17:11[2]

17:13 17:14[2] 17:15 17:17 17:18 17:20[3] 17:21 17:23[2] 17:24 17:25[2] 17:27[2] 17:29 18:11 18:17 18:18 18:21 18:22 18:24 18:28 18:32 18:33 19:5 19:8 19:11[6] 19:12 19:13[2] 19:15[5] 19:16 19:18 19:19 19:20[2] 19:21 19:22[2] 19:25[3] 19:26 19:28 19:31 19:34 19:37 19:38 19:40 19:41 19:42 20:1[2] 20:2 20:3 20:4 20:5 20:6 20:7 20:9[2] 20:10[2] 20:13 20:14 20:15 20:18 20:19 20:21 20:22[2] 21:2[2] 21:9 21:10 21:16 21:17 21:18 21:20 21:22 22:4 22:7 22:21 22:25[2] 22:31 22:35 22:40 22:42 22:44 22:51[2] 23:5 23:9 23:10 23:13 23:16 23:21 23:23 23:37 24:1 24:2[2]

24:4 24:6[4] 24:7[4] 24:8 24:13[2] 24:15 24:16[2] 24:18 24:19 24:21[2]

1 KI

1:3 1:4 1:5 1:8 1:21 1:23 1:31[2] 1:33[2] 1:35 1:38[2] 1:44 1:47 1:48 1:51 1:52 1:53[3] 2:3[2] 2:5[2] 2:6[2] 2:7 2:8[4] 2:9[2] 2:13 2:14 2:17 2:19 2:21[2] 2:23 2:24 2:26[2] 2:28 2:30 2:32 2:39 2:40[3] 2:41 2:44[3] 3:4[2] 3:5 3:6 3:7 3:9[2] 3:11 3:12 3:14 3:15[2] 3:18 3:21 3:25 3:28 4:10 4:11 4:12[2] 4:13[2] 4:15 4:24 4:25 4:28 4:34 5:2 5:5 5:6[2] 5:7 5:8[2] 5:9 5:10 5:11[2] 5:14 5:17 5:18 6:1 6:3 6:11

6:12 6:19 6:38 7:7 7:8 7:14[3] 7:16 7:18 7:23 7:32 7:36 7:41 7:42 7:45 7:50 8:6 8:10 8:11 8:13 8:16[2] 8:17 8:18 8:25[2] 8:28[4] 8:30 8:32[3] 8:33 8:36 8:39[2] 8:43[3] 8:44 8:46 8:52 8:53 8:54 8:56 8:58 8:61[2] 8:64 9:1[3] 9:3 9:4[2] 9:5 9:8 9:10 9:11 9:12 9:14 9:15 9:19 9:21 9:28[2] 10:1 10:2[2] 10:6 10:9[2] 10:10 10:13 10:14 10:16 10:17 10:24[2] 10:27[2] 11:2 11:4 11:11 11:13 11:15[2] 11:17 11:18[2] 11:19 11:21[2] 11:22[2] 11:24 11:25 11:29 11:31[4] 11:33[2] 11:36 11:37 11:38 11:40 12:1[3] 12:2 12:5 12:7 12:9

12:11 12:12[2] 12:14[2] 12:16[2] 12:18[4] 12:20 12:21[4] 12:23 12:24[4] 12:25 12:27[2] 12:28[2] 12:30 13:1 13:4[2] 13:5 13:10 13:11 13:17[2] 13:20 13:22 13:23[2] 13:26 13:27 13:29[3] 13:31[2] 13:32 13:34[2] 14:2[3] 14:3 14:4[3] 14:5[2] 14:6[2] 14:8 14:9[2] 14:12 14:13 14:15[2] 14:16 14:17[2] 14:18 14:21[2] 14:22 14:24 14:25 15:4[2] 15:17[2] 15:18 15:21[2] 15:25 15:26 15:27[2] 15:29[2] 15:30 15:33 15:34 16:1 16:2[3] 16:7 16:8 16:11[2] 16:12 16:13[2] 16:15 16:18[2] 16:19[2] 16:21 16:23 16:26[3] 16:29 16:31[3] 16:33[2] 16:34 17:1 17:4 17:7 17:9[3] 17:10[3] 17:11[2] 17:15 17:16 17:17 17:18[4] 17:24 18:1[2] 18:2 18:5

18:6 18:9 18:10 18:12 18:15 18:16[2] 18:17 18:19 18:27 18:29[2] 18:31 18:36 18:40 18:42[3] 18:43 18:44 18:45[2] 18:46 19:2[2] 19:3[2] 19:9 19:10 19:14 19:15[2] 19:16[2] 19:17 19:20 20:2 20:4 20:6 20:9 20:12 20:22 20:26[3] 20:30 20:31 20:33[2] 20:35 20:42 20:43[2] 21:1 21:2 21:3 21:4 21:5 21:8 21:10 21:14 21:15[3] 21:16[4] 21:17 21:18[2] 21:20[2] 21:22[2] 21:25 21:26 21:27 21:28 22:2[2] 22:4[2] 22:5 22:6 22:12 22:13 22:15[2] 22:17 22:24 22:25 22:26 22:29 22:32[2] 22:33 22:36[2] 22:37 22:41 22:42 22:48[2] 22:51 22:52 22:53[2]

2 KI

1:3[3] 1:6[2] 1:7 1:9 1:10 1:16[2] 1:17 2:1 2:2[2] 2:3[2] 2:4[2] 2:5[2] 2:6 2:7 2:9 2:11 2:15[3] 2:18 2:20 2:22 2:25[2] 3:1 3:3 3:5 3:7[2] 3:10 3:12 3:13[4] 3:15 3:20 3:21[2] 3:23 3:24 3:26 3:27 4:1 4:5 4:6 4:8[3] 4:10 4:12 4:13[3] 4:14 4:16 4:17 4:18[2] 4:19[2] 4:20 4:22 4:23[2] 4:24 4:25[3] 4:26 4:27[3] 4:29 4:31 4:35 4:37 4:38 4:39 4:40[2] 4:44 5:5 5:6[2] 5:7 5:8[2] 5:10 5:11 5:13 5:14 5:15 5:16 5:17 5:18 5:21 5:22 5:24 5:26[3] 6:4 6:7 6:10 6:18[2] 6:19[2] 6:20 6:22 6:23 6:24 6:28[2] 6:30 6:31

6:32[3] 7:1 7:3 7:5[2] 7:6[2] 7:8 7:9 7:10 7:11 7:12[2] 7:16 7:17[2] 7:18[3] 8:1 8:3[2] 8:5[5] 8:7 8:9[2] 8:14[3] 8:15 8:16 8:17 8:19[2] 8:21 8:25 8:26 8:28 8:29[2] 9:1 9:2 9:4 9:5[2] 9:10 9:11[2] 9:12 9:15[3] 9:16[2] 9:17 9:18[3] 9:19[2] 9:22 9:23 9:25 9:26 9:27[2] 9:28 9:29 9:30 9:32[2] 9:35 10:1[3] 10:2 10:5 10:6[4] 10:7[3] 10:9[2] 10:12 10:13 10:15[3] 10:17[3] 10:19[3] 10:21 10:24 10:25[4] 10:29[2] 10:30 10:31[2] 10:32 11:4 11:9[3] 11:10 11:11 11:13 11:19 11:21 12:1 12:4[2] 12:5 12:8[2] 12:11 12:12[4] 12:14 12:15 12:17[2] 12:18 12:20 13:1

13:2 13:7 13:16 13:21 14:2 14:3 14:5 14:8 14:9[4] 14:10 14:11 14:12[2] 14:13 14:14 14:16 14:19[2] 14:22 14:23 14:24 14:25 14:28 15:1 15:2 15:3 15:4 15:9 15:12 15:13 15:16 15:17 15:18 15:19 15:20[2] 15:23 15:24 15:27 15:28 15:29 15:32 15:33 15:34 15:37 16:1 16:2 16:3[2] 16:5[2] 16:6[2] 16:7 16:8 16:9 16:10[4] 16:11 16:12 16:15 16:16 17:1 17:4[2] 17:5 17:11[2] 17:13[2] 17:14 17:17 17:23 17:26 17:31 17:35[2] 17:17 17:36 17:37 18:1[2] 18:2 18:3 18:4 18:6 18:8 18:9 18:14[2] 18:16 18:17[2] 18:18[2] 18:19 18:22 18:23[2] 18:25[2] 18:26 18:27[4] 18:29

18:31[2] 18:32 18:37 19:1 19:2 19:3[2] 19:4 19:5 19:6 19:7[2] 19:9 19:10 19:11 19:16 19:20[2] 19:21 19:23[2] 19:25[2] 19:35 19:37 20:1 20:2 20:4[2] 20:10 21:1 21:6[2] 21:7[2] 21:8[3] 21:9 21:11 21:14 21:15 21:16[2] 21:19 22:1 22:2[2] 22:3[2] 22:4 22:5[2] 22:6 22:8 22:9 22:11 22:13 22:15 22:17 22:18[3] 23:3[2] 23:4 23:5[5] 23:6 23:8 23:9 23:10[2] 23:11 23:15[2] 23:16 23:19[4] 23:20 23:23 23:25 23:29 23:30 23:31 23:32 23:33 23:34[2] 23:35[4] 23:36 23:37 24:2[2] 24:3[2] 24:7 24:8 24:9 24:12 24:15[2] 24:16 24:17 24:18 24:19 24:20 25:1 25:6[2] 25:7 25:11 25:12

25:13 25:20 25:23[2] 25:24[3] 25:25 25:26 25:27[2] 25:28

1 CH

1:10 2:21 2:23 2:35 4:27 4:35 4:39[2] 4:42 5:1 5:2[2] 5:18[3] 5:20 5:26 6:19 6:32 6:49[2] 6:56 6:57 6:62 6:64 7:2 7:11 7:15 7:21 7:22 7:23 7:40[2] 8:6 9:1 9:9 9:22 9:25[2] 9:27 9:29 9:32[2] 10:4 10:8 10:9[2] 10:11 10:12 10:13 11:1 11:3[3] 11:4 11:5 11:10[2] 11:13 11:15[2] 11:18[2] 11:21 11:23 11:25 11:31 12:1[2] 12:8 12:15 12:16 12:17[4] 12:18 12:19[4] 12:20[2] 12:22[2] 12:23[6] 12:24 12:31 12:32 12:36 12:38[3] 13:2 13:3 13:5 13:6[4] 13:9 13:10 13:11

13:12 13:13[2] 14:1[2] 14:8 14:11 14:15 14:16 15:2[2] 15:3[2] 15:14 15:15[2] 15:16[3] 15:19 15:21 15:25 15:26 15:29[2] 16:3[2] 16:4 16:5 16:7 16:15 16:17[2] 16:20[2] 16:21 16:23 16:25[2] 16:33 16:35 16:37 16:38 16:40[3] 16:41[2] 16:43[2] 17:1[2] 17:3[2] 17:4 17:5[2] 17:6[2] 17:10 17:11[2] 17:15[2] 17:17[2] 17:18 17:19 17:20 17:21 17:24 17:25 17:27 18:1 18:3 18:5 18:7 18:10[3] 19:1 19:2[4] 19:3[4] 19:5 19:6[2] 19:7 19:15 19:16 19:19 20:1 20:2 20:3 20:4 21:1 21:2[4] 21:3 21:4 21:6 21:11 21:12[2] 21:15[2] 21:17 21:18[2] 21:21[3] 21:22 21:23 21:24 21:25 21:30 22:2[3] 22:4

22:5 22:6 22:7[2] 22:8 22:9 22:13 22:17 22:19[4] 23:4 23:5 23:11 23:13[3] 23:28 23:30[2] 23:31[2] 24:3 24:4 24:7[2] 24:8[2] 24:9[2] 24:10[2] 24:11[2] 24:12[2] 24:13[2] 24:14[2] 24:15[2] 24:16[2] 24:17[2] 24:18[2] 24:19[2] 25:1[2] 25:2 25:3[2] 25:5[2] 25:6 25:9[2] 25:10 25:11 25:12 25:13 25:14 25:15 25:16 25:17 25:18 25:19 25:20 25:21 25:22 25:23 25:24 25:25 25:26 25:27 25:28 25:29 25:30 25:31 26:12 26:13 26:14 26:15[2] 26:16 26:27 26:31 26:32 27:1 27:23 27:24 28:1 28:2 28:4[2] 28:5 28:6 28:7 28:10 28:11 28:15 28:20 29:2[2] 29:3[2] 29:4 29:8 29:9 29:20 29:22

2 CH

1:2[3] 1:3 1:4 1:6 1:8 1:11 1:13[2] 2:1 2:2 2:3[3] 2:4[5] 2:6[2] 2:7[2] 2:8 2:9[2] 2:10 2:11 2:12 2:14[4] 2:16[3] 2:18[3] 3:1 3:2 3:4 3:8[2] 3:11[2] 3:12[2] 4:2 4:6 4:7 4:11 4:12[2] 4:13 4:16 5:2 5:7 5:11 5:13[3] 5:14 6:4 6:5 6:6 6:7 6:8[2] 6:16[3] 6:19[3] 6:20 6:22 6:23 6:24 6:25[2] 6:31 6:33[2] 6:34 6:38 7:3 7:6 7:7 7:10[2] 7:11 7:12[2] 7:13 7:17 7:18 7:20 7:21 8:1 8:2[2] 8:3 8:6 8:8 8:13 8:14[4] 8:17[2] 8:18[2] 9:1[2] 9:5 9:8[4] 9:11[2] 9:12[2] 9:13 9:14 9:16 9:18[2] 9:21

9:23 9:26 10:1[3] 10:2 10:3 10:6[2] 10:7[2] 10:9[2] 10:11 10:12[2] 10:15 10:16[3] 10:18[4] 11:1[3] 11:2 11:3 11:4 11:13 11:14 11:16[3] 11:18 11:22[2] 12:1 12:2 12:4[2] 12:5[3] 12:7 12:10 12:13[3] 12:14 13:1 13:5[4] 13:8 13:9 13:11 13:12 13:13 13:15 14:4[2] 14:15 15:2 15:5[2] 15:9 15:12 15:13 16:1[2] 16:2 16:5 16:7 16:9[2] 16:12[2] 17:4 17:5 17:7[7] 17:14 17:15 18:2[4] 18:3 18:4 18:5[2] 18:11 18:12[2] 18:14[3] 18:15[2] 18:16 18:17 18:23 18:24 18:25[2] 18:28 18:29[2] 18:31[3] 18:32 18:33 19:1[2] 19:2[2] 19:3 19:4 19:6 19:8 19:10 20:1[2] 20:3 20:4[2] 20:6 20:7 20:11[3]

20:12 20:16 20:17[2] 20:18 20:19 20:21 20:22[3] 20:23[2] 20:24 20:25 20:27[3] 20:28 20:31 20:36[3] 20:37[2] 21:3 21:4 21:6 21:7[3] 21:11 21:12 21:13[2] 21:19 21:20 22:1 22:2 22:3 22:4 22:5 22:6[2] 22:7[2] 22:8[2] 22:9[2] 23:2 23:7 23:8[3] 23:9 23:10 23:12 23:13 23:15 23:17 23:18 24:1 24:4[2] 24:5[3] 24:6[2] 24:9[2] 24:11[2] 24:12[3] 24:14[2] 24:17 24:19[2] 24:22 24:23[2] 25:1 25:3[2] 25:5[3] 25:7[2] 25:8 25:9[3] 25:10[3] 25:11 25:13 25:14[2] 25:16[2] 25:17 25:18[4] 25:19[2] 25:21 25:22[2] 25:23[2] 25:24 25:27[2] 26:2 26:3 26:4 26:5 26:8[2] 26:11[2] 26:13 26:14 26:15[2] 26:16[2] 26:18[3] 26:19 26:20

26:23 27:1 27:2 27:8 28:1 28:5 28:7 28:8 28:9 28:10 28:13[3] 28:15[5] 28:16 28:23 28:25[2] 29:1 29:2 29:8[3] 29:10 29:11[2] 29:15[2] 29:16[2] 29:17[2] 29:18 29:20 29:21 29:24 29:25 29:27 29:30 29:32 29:34 30:1[4] 30:2 30:3 30:5[3] 30:6[2] 30:7 30:10[2] 30:11 30:13 30:16 30:17 30:19[2] 30:20 30:22 30:23 30:24[2] 30:27 31:1[2] 31:2[4] 31:3 31:4 31:7 31:10[2] 31:11 31:14 31:15[4] 31:16 31:17 31:18 31:19[3] 31:21 32:1 32:2 32:3 32:5 32:6[2] 32:8[2] 32:9 32:11[2] 32:13 32:14 32:15 32:17[2] 32:18[2] 32:20 32:21 32:23[2] 32:24 32:25 32:30 32:31[2] 33:1 33:6[3] 33:7[2] 33:8[2]

33:9[2] 33:10[2] 33:11 33:13 33:14 33:16 33:18 33:21 34:1 34:2[2] 34:3[2] 34:7 34:8 34:9[2] 34:10[2] 34:11[3] 34:15[2] 34:16[2] 34:17 34:19 34:21 34:22[3] 34:23 34:25 34:26 34:28[2] 34:31[3] 34:32[3] 34:33 35:2 35:4[2] 35:5 35:6 35:7[2] 35:8[2] 35:10 35:12[2] 35:13 35:15 35:16[3] 35:18 35:20 35:21[3] 35:22 35:23 35:24 35:25 35:26 36:2 36:4[2] 36:5 36:6[2] 36:7 36:9 36:10 36:11 36:15 36:18 36:20[2] 36:21[2] 36:23

EZR

1:2 1:3 1:5[2] 2:68[2] 3:1 3:2 3:4 3:6 3:7[4] 3:8 3:9 3:10 4:2[2] 4:3[2] 4:5 4:8 4:12 4:14 4:17[2] 4:21[2] 4:22[2] 4:23[2] 5:2 5:3[3] 5:5[2] 5:8 5:9[2] 5:10 5:13 5:17[3] 6:5 6:8 6:9 6:12[4] 6:13 6:14[2] 6:17 6:21 6:22 7:6 7:8 7:9[3] 7:10[3] 7:14[2] 7:18[3] 7:20 7:21 7:22[3] 7:24 7:26[8] 7:27 7:28 8:15[2] 8:17 8:21 8:22[2] 8:30[2] 8:31 8:32 8:36 9:1[2] 9:6[2] 9:7[4] 9:8[3] 9:9[4] 9:11[2] 9:12 10:3[3] 10:5[2] 10:8 10:10 10:13 10:16

NE

1:1 1:4 1:9 1:11[2] 2:1[2] 2:4 2:6 2:7 2:8[3] 2:9 2:10 2:11 2:12 2:13 2:14[2] 2:16[5] 2:19 3:2 3:5 3:16 3:19[2] 3:21 3:31 4:1 4:5 4:6 4:7[2] 4:8[3] 4:10 4:11 4:12 4:14[2] 4:15[3] 4:16 4:19[2] 4:22 5:5 5:8 5:11 5:12 5:13 5:14 5:19 6:1 6:2 6:3 6:6[2] 6:7[7] 6:10[2] 6:11 6:14 6:16 6:19[2] 7:1 7:3 7:5 7:6[2] 7:63 7:70 7:71 8:1[2] 8:6 8:7 8:8 8:12[4] 8:13 8:15 9:8 9:12 9:15[2] 9:16 9:17[5] 9:19[2] 9:20 9:23[2] 9:26[2] 9:27 9:28 9:36 10:29[3] 10:31 10:32 10:33 10:34[2] 10:35 10:36[2] 10:37 10:38 11:1[2] 11:2 11:3 11:17 12:22 12:24[3] 12:27[3] 12:44 12:45 13:3 13:5[2] 13:7 13:10 13:13[2] 13:19[2] 13:22[2] 13:24 13:26 13:27[2] 13:28

ES

1:1 1:6 1:7 1:8[3] 1:9 1:11[3] 1:12 1:13 1:15 1:16[3] 1:17 1:20[2] 1:21 1:22[3] 2:3 2:8[3] 2:9[2] 2:11 2:12[4] 2:13 2:14 2:15 2:18[2] 2:21 2:22 3:4[2] 3:6[2] 3:7[3] 3:8 3:9[2] 3:11[3] 3:12[5] 3:13[5] 3:14 3:15 4:4[2] 4:5[3] 4:6 4:7[3] 4:8[6] 4:11[4] 4:12 4:13 4:14[2] 4:16 4:17 5:1 5:2 5:3 5:5[2] 5:6 5:8[3] 5:12 5:14[2] 6:1 6:3 6:4[2] 6:6[4] 6:7 6:8 6:9[4] 6:10[2] 6:11 6:12[2] 6:13 6:14 7:1 7:2 7:4[3] 7:5 7:7[2] 8:3 8:5 8:6[2] 8:7 8:9[6] 8:11[7] 8:13[2] 9:1[3] 9:2 9:13[3] 9:14 9:19 9:21 9:22[3] 9:23 9:24[3] 9:27[2] 9:29 9:30 9:31 10:3

JOB

1:4[2] 1:5 1:6 1:7 1:11 1:15 1:16 1:17 1:19 2:1[2] 2:2 2:3 2:5 2:8 2:11[3] 3:8 3:20 3:23 4:2 4:12 4:14 4:20 5:1 5:4 5:11[2] 5:26 6:7 6:9 6:14 6:18 6:24 6:26 7:1 7:3[2] 7:4 7:5 7:9 7:10 7:20 8:5[2] 8:8 8:22 9:14 9:15 9:18 9:19 9:26 10:19 10:21 11:16 12:3 12:4 12:5 12:8 12:22 12:24 13:3[2] 13:6 13:12 13:23 13:25 13:26 14:15 14:18 14:21 15:8 15:20 15:24 15:28 16:8 16:11 16:12 17:5 17:14[2] 17:16 18:11 18:14 19:3 19:17 19:20[2] 20:2 20:3 20:6 20:10 20:18 20:23 21:4 21:13 21:30[2] 21:31 21:32 22:3[2] 22:7[2] 22:14 22:19 22:23 23:2 23:3 24:5 24:7 24:10 24:12 24:17 24:21 25:5 26:4 26:10 28:3 28:11 28:24 28:25 28:28 29:7 29:10 29:11 29:12 29:13 29:15[2] 29:16 30:1 30:6 30:10 30:21 30:22[2] 30:23[2] 30:24 30:29[2] 30:31 31:3[2] 31:5 31:7 31:11 31:12 31:16 31:23 31:24 31:28 31:30[2] 31:32 31:36 31:39 32:1 32:10 32:11[2] 32:19 32:22 33:1 33:6 33:22 33:23 33:24 33:25 33:30[2] 33:32[2] 34:4 34:11[2] 34:16 34:18[3] 34:19 34:28 34:31 34:33 35:2 35:9 36:2 36:3 36:6 36:10 36:27 36:32 37:6[3] 37:15 38:12 38:14 38:20[2] 38:26[2] 38:27[3] 38:34 38:37 38:40 39:9 39:11 39:17 39:21 40:19 41:10 41:13 41:16 41:17 41:31 41:32[2] 42:7 42:8

PS

4:*title* 5:*title* 5:1 6:*title* 6:6 7:2 7:6 7:8[2] 7:9 7:17[2] 8:*title* 8:6 9:*title* 9:2 9:6 9:8 9:11 9:20 10:9 10:14 10:17 10:18 11:*title* 12:*title* 13:*title* 14:*title* 14:2 15:3 15:4 15:5 16:2 16:3[2] 16:10 17:11 17:14 18:*title* 18:3 18:20[2] 18:24[2] 18:30 18:34 18:38 18:40 18:50[4] 19:*title* 19:4 19:5 19:10 20:*title* 20:4 21:*title* 21:11 22:*title* 22:7 22:11 22:15 22:19 22:29 22:30 23:2 25:7 27:2 27:4[2] 27:13 28:1[2] 28:3 28:4[3] 29:6 29:9 30:1 30:3 30:7 30:8 30:9 30:12[2] 31:*title* 31:2[2] 31:11 32:10 33:10 33:11 33:13 33:16 33:18 33:19[2] 34:9 34:16 35:4[2] 35:11 35:12 35:23 35:24 35:26 36:*title* 36:2 36:3[2] 36:10 36:12 37:5 37:7 37:8 37:14 37:32 37:34 38:*title* 38:17 38:22 39:*title* 39:1 39:4 39:11 40:*title* 40:4 40:5 40:8 40:12 40:13[2] 40:14 41:*title* 41:6[2] 41:13 42:*title* 42:4 43:3 44:*title* 44:7 44:9 44:10 44:13[2] 44:20 44:25 45:*title* 45:17 46:*title* 46:9 47:*title* 47:6 48:1 48:10 48:13 49:*title* 49:4 49:7 49:10 49:11 49:18 49:19 50:4[2] 50:8 50:11[2] 50:19 50:22 50:23 51:*title*[2] 51:1 51:6 51:8 52:*title*[2] 52:3 53:*title* 53:2 53:5 54:*title*[2] 54:2 55:*title* 55:1 55:2 56:*title* 57:*title* 58:*title* 58:5 58:7 59:*title*[2] 59:4 59:5[2] 60:*title*[2] 60:1 60:2 60:3 60:4 61:*title* 61:2 62:*title*[2] 62:4 62:9 62:12[2] 63:2 63:9 64:*title* 64:3 64:8 65:*title* 65:4 65:8 66:*title* 66:4 66:8 66:9 66:12 66:19 67:*title* 67:1 68:*title* 68:4 68:16 68:33 69:*title* 69:10 69:11 69:16 69:20 69:21 69:23 69:26 70:*title*[3] 70:1[2] 70:2 71:1 71:2 71:3 71:13 71:18[2] 72:3 72:8 72:15 73:1[2] 73:10 73:16 73:24 73:28[2] 74:7 74:14[2] 75:*title* 75:4 75:9 76:*title* 76:7 76:8 76:9[2] 76:11 76:12 77:*title*[2] 77:2 77:6 77:9 78:1[2] 78:4[2] 78:5 78:6[2] 78:10 78:13[2] 78:16 78:24 78:25 78:26 78:48[2] 78:50[2] 78:52 78:54[2] 78:55 78:58[2] 78:63 78:66 78:71 78:72 79:2 79:3 79:4[2] 79:11[2] 79:13 80:*title* 80:3 80:5 80:7 80:9 80:19 81:*title* 81:11 82:3 83:9[2] 83:12 83:17 84:*title* 84:7 84:10 85:*title* 85:4 85:5 85:8[2] 86:5 86:6 86:11 87:4 88:*title* 88:10 88:15 89:1 89:4 89:7[2] 89:8 89:19 89:29 89:33 89:39 89:40 89:41 89:42 89:43 89:44[2] 90:2 90:3 90:11 90:12 90:15 91:11 92:1[2] 92:2 92:15 94:1[2] 94:2 95:1 95:7 96:2 96:4[2] 96:13 98:9 100:5 101:3 102:4 102:5 102:13 102:18 102:20[3] 102:21 102:22 103:8 103:10 103:17 103:18[3] 104:9 104:11 104:14 104:15[2] 104:23 104:26 104:29 104:33 105:8 105:10 105:13[2] 105:14 105:22 105:25[2] 105:39 106:8 106:23 106:26 106:27[2] 106:29 106:45 106:46 106:47[2] 106:48 107:4 107:7 107:8 107:12 107:15 107:21 107:23 107:26[2] 107:27 107:31 107:36 107:38 107:40 109:*title* 109:12 109:16 109:26 109:31 111:4 112:9 113:3 113:6 113:9[2] 115:16 116:17 118:8[2] 118:9[2] 118:19 119:4 119:5 119:9 119:25 119:27 119:31 119:35 119:36 119:38 119:41 119:42 119:49 119:58 119:60 119:62 119:76 119:91 119:95 119:103 119:112 119:121 119:126 119:128 119:132 119:135 119:149 119:154 119:156 119:159 119:169 119:170 121:3 122:4 124:6 125:4 127:2[3] 130:2 132:4[2] 132:17 133:1 133:2 135:7 136:3 136:4 136:5 136:6 136:7 136:8 136:9 136:10 136:13 136:14 136:16 136:17 136:25 137:6 137:7 137:8 139:*title* 139:12 140:*title* 140:4 140:11 141:4[2] 143:1 143:3[2] 143:8[2] 143:9 143:10 144:1[2] 144:4 144:11 144:14 145:3 145:4 145:8 145:9 145:12[2] 145:18 146:7 147:1 147:6 147:9[2] 147:18 149:7 149:8 149:9 150:2

PR

1:2[2] 1:3 1:4[3] 1:6 1:16[2] 2:2 2:7 2:12 2:13 2:14 2:16 3:2 3:8 3:15 3:18 3:22 3:27[2] 3:28 3:32 4:1 4:8 4:9[2] 4:16 4:20 4:22 4:27 5:1 5:5 5:13 6:4[2] 6:6 6:10 6:18 6:24 6:26 6:29 6:30 7:8 7:15[2] 7:21 7:22[2] 7:23 7:24 7:25 7:27[2] 8:4 8:7 8:9[2] 8:11[2] 8:13 8:21 8:29 9:4 9:7 9:9 9:15 9:16 10:3 10:16[2] 10:23[2] 10:26[3] 10:29[2] 11:1 11:17 11:18 11:19[2] 11:20 11:24 11:29 12:4 12:6 12:8 12:20 12:21 12:22 13:5 13:14 13:18 13:19[2] 13:21 13:22 13:25 14:8 14:15 14:22 14:23 14:27 14:29 14:34 15:8 15:18 15:21 15:24 15:26 15:28 16:5 16:7 16:12[2] 16:16[3] 16:17 16:19[2] 16:23 16:24[2] 16:30[2] 16:32 17:4[2] 17:15 17:16[2] 17:21 17:23 17:25[2] 17:26 18:5 18:9 18:18 18:19 19:6 19:7 19:10 19:11 19:23 19:24 19:27[2] 20:2 20:3 20:10 20:13 20:17 20:25[2] 21:3[2] 21:5[2] 21:6 21:7 21:9 21:15[3] 21:20 21:25 22:1 22:7 22:9 22:16[3] 22:19[2] 22:20 22:21 22:25 22:27 23:1 23:2[2] 23:4 23:7 23:12 23:21 23:30 24:1 24:8 24:9 24:11[2] 24:12[2] 24:13 24:20 24:21 24:23[2] 24:25 24:29[4] 24:33 25:2[2] 25:8[3] 25:9 25:10 25:13 25:20 25:21[2] 25:24 25:25 25:27[2] 26:4 26:5 26:8 26:11 26:15[2] 26:17 26:21[3] 27:1 27:4 27:7 27:14 27:19[2] 27:21 27:23[2] 27:24 28:10 28:17[2] 28:20 28:21 28:22 29:7 29:12 29:15[2] 29:27[2] 30:14 30:17 30:23 31:3 31:4 31:6 31:8 31:15[2] 31:19 31:20[2] 31:25 31:27

EC

1:5 1:6 1:11 1:13[3] 1:16 1:17[2] 2:1 2:3 2:6 2:11 2:12 2:14 2:15[2] 2:16 2:20[2] 2:21 2:26[5] 3:1[2] 3:2[4] 3:3[4] 3:4[4] 3:5[4] 3:6[4] 3:7[4] 3:8[2] 3:10[2] 3:11 3:12[2] 3:14 3:15 3:20 3:21 3:22 4:10[2] 4:14 5:1[3] 5:2 5:4 5:6[2] 5:11 5:12 5:13 5:15 5:18[3] 5:19[4] 6:2[2] 6:6 6:8 7:2[5] 7:9 7:11 7:12 7:14 7:25[4] 7:27 8:1 8:2 8:3 8:6 8:8[2] 8:9 8:11 8:14[2] 8:15[3] 8:16[2] 8:17[3] 9:1 9:2[8] 9:3 9:4[2] 9:10 9:11[6] 10:1 10:3 10:10[2] 10:15[2] 10:16 11:2[2] 11:7 12:5 12:7 12:12

CA

1:7 1:9 2:3 2:4 3:11 4:6[2] 5:2 5:5[2] 5:6 6:2[3] 6:11[2] 7:7[2] 7:8 7:9 7:12 8:2 8:11 8:13[2] 8:14

ISA

1:11 1:12 1:14 1:16 1:17 2:2 2:3[2] 2:19 2:20[3] 2:21[2] 2:22 3:4 3:8 3:10 3:12 3:13[2] 3:15 3:24 4:1 4:3 5:1 5:4 5:5[2] 5:8[2] 5:22[2] 5:26 7:1[2] 7:3 7:7 7:13 7:15 7:16 7:18 7:21 7:22 7:23 8:2[2] 8:4 8:8 8:10 8:11 8:12[2] 8:14[2] 8:19 8:20[3] 8:21 8:22 9:2 9:7[2] 9:16 10:2[2] 10:3 10:6[7] 10:7 10:11 10:12 10:20 10:26 10:27 10:28[2] 10:30 10:31 11:10 11:11[2] 11:16 13:5 13:9 13:10 13:11 13:14 13:16 13:18 13:20 13:22 14:1 14:2 14:3[2] 14:9 14:11 14:12 14:15[2] 14:16 14:19 14:24 15:1[4] 15:2[3] 15:7 16:1[2] 16:4 16:10 16:12[3] 17:4 17:7[2] 17:8 17:11[2] 17:12[3] 18:1 18:2 18:6 18:7 19:3[4] 19:14 19:18 19:19[2] 19:21 19:22 19:23 20:4 20:6 21:2 21:11 21:14 21:16 22:1 22:4 22:5 22:7 22:8 22:10 22:12[4] 22:13 22:20 22:21[2] 22:23 22:24 23:1 23:6 23:7 23:9[2] 23:11 23:12 23:13 23:15[2] 23:17[2] 23:18[2] 24:2 24:9 24:16 24:18 24:20 25:2 25:4[2] 25:11 25:12[2] 26:5[2] 26:8[2] 26:10 26:14 26:21 27:6 27:7 27:9 27:12 27:13 28:1[2] 28:2 28:6[3] 28:9 28:11 28:12[2] 28:17[2] 28:19 28:20 28:21 28:24 29:1[3] 29:11 29:12 29:14 29:15 29:20 29:24 30:1[2] 30:2[3] 30:4 30:6 30:7[2] 30:8 30:10[2] 30:11 30:13[2] 30:14[2] 30:21[2] 30:28[3] 30:29[2] 30:30 31:1[2] 31:4 31:9 32:4 32:5 32:6[4] 32:7 33:1[3] 33:4 34:1 34:2 34:5 34:10 34:12 34:14 34:17 35:4 35:10 36:1 36:2 36:4 36:6 36:7[3] 36:8[2] 36:10 36:11 36:12[4]

8:23
9:10^2
9:12^2
10:1
10:6
11:9
11:13
11:17
12:9^2
13:1^2
13:2
13:3
13:4^2
13:5
13:8
14:2
14:5
14:6
14:7^2
14:10
14:13
14:16^4
14:17
14:18
14:19

MAL

1:1
2:2^3
2:5
2:8
2:15
2:16
3:1
3:5^2
3:10
3:14
3:16
4:6^2

MT

1:11
1:12
1:17
1:18
1:19^2
1:20
2:1
2:2
2:8
2:12
2:13^2
2:16
2:19
2:22
3:5
3:7^3
3:9^3
3:11
3:13^2
3:14^2
3:15^2
4:1
4:3
4:16
4:17^2
5:13^2
5:17^2
5:22
5:23
5:24
5:25^2
5:28
5:39
5:41
5:42
5:44
5:45
6:1^2
6:5
6:16
6:18
6:24
6:30^2
7:2
7:4
7:5
7:8
7:11^2
7:12^2
7:13
7:15
7:18
7:20
7:21
7:22
7:28
8:4
8:9^3
8:10
8:25
8:28
8:29^2
8:31
8:33
8:34
9:2
9:5^2
9:6^2
9:7
9:10
9:13^2
9:14
9:16
9:24
9:28^2
9:29
9:32
10:1^2
10:6
10:13
10:17
10:21^3
10:22
10:28^2
10:34^2
10:35
10:42
11:1^3
11:5
11:7^2
11:8
11:9
11:14
11:15
11:20
11:23
11:27
12:1
12:2
12:4
12:10
12:12
12:13
12:18
12:25
12:32
12:39
12:42
12:46^2
12:47
13:3
13:9
13:11^2
13:12
13:13
13:17^2
13:30^2
13:31^2
13:43
13:48
13:53
14:4
14:5
14:7
14:9
14:11^2
14:15
14:16
14:18
14:19^4
14:22^2
14:23
14:29^2
14:30
15:1
15:5
15:20
15:26^3
15:31^4
15:32
15:33
15:35
15:36^2
16:3
16:5^2
16:11
16:21
16:22
16:27
17:4
17:9
17:14^2
17:16
17:17
17:19
17:20
17:24^2
17:27
18:7
18:8^2
18:9^2
18:11
18:17^2
18:21
18:24
18:25^3
18:34
19:1
19:3
19:5
19:7^2
19:8
19:10
19:11
19:12
19:14
19:21
19:24^2
20:1
20:15
20:18^2
20:19^4
20:20
20:22^2
20:23^3
20:28^3
21:1
21:9
21:14
21:15
21:19
21:21
21:28^2
21:30
21:33
21:34
21:43
21:44
21:46
22:3^2
22:5^2
22:8
22:9
22:11
22:13
22:17
22:23
22:34
22:46
23:1^2
23:4
23:5
23:7
23:13
23:15
23:23^2
23:34
24:1
24:6
24:9
24:17
24:18
24:19
24:21
24:31
24:43
24:45
24:49^2
25:1
25:6
25:9
25:10^2
25:11
25:15^4
25:27^2
25:45
26:1
26:2
26:8
26:9
26:16
26:17^2
26:18
26:22
26:26
26:27
26:45
26:49
26:53
26:55^2
26:57
26:58
26:59^2
26:61^2
26:73
26:74^2
27:1^2
27:2
27:3
27:4^2
27:6
27:7
27:14
27:15
27:19
27:24
27:26
27:31
27:32
27:33
27:34
27:46
27:48
27:49
27:51
27:58^2
27:60
28:1^2
28:8
28:9
28:14
28:20

MK

1:7
1:9
1:17
1:24^2
1:34
1:40^2
1:44^2
1:45^3
2:2
2:9^3
2:10^2
2:15
2:17^2
2:18
2:23^2
2:26^2
3:4^4
3:7
3:9
3:10
3:14
3:15^3
3:21
4:1
4:3
4:4
4:9
4:11
4:21^2
4:23
4:24
4:25
4:33
4:34
4:41
5:7
5:14
5:15
5:16
5:17^2
5:19
5:20
5:32
5:37
5:38
5:40
5:43
6:2
6:7
6:18
6:21
6:27
6:28^2
6:31
6:34
6:36
6:37^2
6:39
6:41^3
6:45^3
6:46
6:53
6:55
7:2
7:4
7:5
7:11^2
7:12
7:16
7:27^2
7:30
7:32
7:34
7:37^2
8:1
8:2
8:3
8:6^3
8:7
8:13
8:14
8:22^2
8:26^2
8:31
8:32
9:5^2
9:6
9:14
9:15
9:18
9:22
9:23
9:32
9:33
9:35
9:41^2
9:43^2
9:45^2
9:47^2
10:1^3
10:2^2
10:4^2
10:7
10:12
10:13
10:14
10:17
10:21
10:24
10:25^2
10:28
10:30
10:32^2
10:33^3
10:40^3
10:41
10:42^2
10:45^3
10:46
10:47
10:49
10:50
11:1
11:7
11:13
11:15^2
11:21
11:23
11:27^2
11:28
12:1^2
12:2
12:12
12:13
12:14^2
12:17^2
12:23
12:33^2
12:36
12:38
13:5
13:9^2
13:12^3
13:14
13:15
13:16
13:17^2
13:21
13:22
13:27
13:29
13:34^3
14:1
14:5
14:8^2
14:10
14:11
14:14
14:19^2
14:21
14:22
14:23
14:32^2
14:33^2
14:40
14:45
14:48
14:53
14:55^2
14:64
14:65^4
14:69^2
14:70
14:71^2
14:72
15:1
15:8^2
15:15^2
15:18
15:20
15:21
15:23
15:36^2
15:38
15:45
16:8
16:9

LU

1:1
1:3^2
1:8
1:9^2
1:16
1:17^4
1:19^2
1:20
1:23^2
1:25
1:27^2
1:38
1:41
1:43^2
1:49
1:50
1:55^3
1:56
1:59^2
1:62
1:72^3
1:73
1:76
1:77
1:79^3
2:1
2:3
2:5
2:10
2:14
2:15^3
2:22^4
2:23
2:24^2
2:27
2:29
2:32
2:38
2:39^2
2:41
2:42
2:44
2:45
2:46
2:51
3:7^4
3:8^3
3:11
3:12
3:14
3:16
3:21
3:23
4:6
4:9
4:10
4:16^2
4:18^7
4:19
4:20
4:21
4:31
4:34^2
4:41
4:43
5:1
5:7
5:11
5:12
5:14^2
5:15^2
5:17^2
5:18^2
5:21
5:23^2
5:24^2
5:26
5:32^2
6:1
6:2
6:4^2
6:6
6:8
6:9^4
6:11
6:12^3
6:17
6:19
6:26
6:27
6:29
6:30
6:31^2
6:33^2
6:34^4
6:35
6:38
6:42
6:47^2
7:2
7:4
7:6
7:7
7:8^2
7:10
7:11
7:12
7:15^2
7:19
7:22
7:24^2
7:25
7:26
7:31
7:32^2
7:36
7:38
7:40
7:42
7:43
7:44
7:45
7:47
7:49
7:50
8:1
8:4
8:10^2
8:14
8:18^2
8:19
8:20
8:22
8:24
8:25
8:27
8:28
8:29
8:31
8:32
8:35^2
8:37
8:39
8:40
8:49
8:51
8:53
8:55
9:1
9:2^2
9:9
9:10
9:12
9:13
9:14
9:16^3
9:17
9:18
9:21
9:23
9:28^2
9:33^2
9:37
9:40
9:42
9:45
9:51^3
9:52
9:53
9:54
9:56^3
9:57
9:58
9:59
9:62
10:5
10:6
10:7
10:15^2
10:19
10:22^2
10:24^2
10:25
10:29
10:30
10:34^2
10:35
10:38
10:40^2
11:1
11:4
11:6^2
11:10
11:13^2
11:14
11:17
11:26
11:27
11:29
11:30
11:31
11:37^2
11:42^2
11:46
11:53
11:54
12:1
12:5
12:12
12:13
12:17
12:19
12:21
12:25
12:26
12:28
12:32
12:37^2
12:39
12:41
12:42
12:45^3
12:47
12:48
12:49
12:50
12:51
12:54
12:55
12:58^3
13:12
13:14
13:15
13:24^2
13:25^3
13:26
13:32^2
13:33^2
14:1^2
14:3
14:6
14:7
14:8
14:9
14:17^2
14:18
14:19
14:21
14:23
14:26
14:28^2
14:29^2
14:30^2
14:31^2
14:35
15:1
15:12^2
15:14
15:15^3
15:17^2
15:18
15:19
15:20
15:21
15:22
15:24
15:25
15:29
16:3
16:4
16:7
16:9
16:11
16:13
16:17^2
16:21
16:22
16:26^2
16:27
17:3
17:4
17:7
17:11^2
17:14
17:18^2
17:22
17:23
17:31
17:33
18:1^3
18:10
18:13
18:14
18:16
18:18
18:25^2
18:30
18:31
18:33
18:35
18:40
19:3
19:4^2
19:5^2
19:7
19:8
19:9
19:10^2
19:11
19:12^2
19:14
19:15^3
19:19
19:24
19:28
19:29^2
19:35
19:37
19:45
19:47
19:48
20:1
20:9^3
20:10
20:16
20:18
20:19
20:22
20:27
20:30
20:33
20:35
20:46
21:7
21:9
21:12
21:13
21:14
21:16^2
21:21
21:23
21:28^2
21:29
21:31
21:34
21:36^3
21:38^2
22:5
22:6
22:15
22:23
22:31
22:33^2
22:39
22:44
22:45
22:47
22:52
23:2^3
23:4^2
23:5
23:7
23:8^2
23:12
23:15
23:20^2
23:25
23:30^3
23:32^2
23:33
23:36
23:43
23:48
23:51
23:56
24:4
24:5
24:9
24:11
24:12
24:13
24:15
24:17
24:18
24:20^2
24:21
24:24
24:25
24:26^2
24:29
24:30^2
24:32^2
24:33
24:34
24:46^2
24:50
24:51
24:52

JOH

1:7
1:8
1:12^3
1:19
1:22
1:27
1:31
1:33
1:38
1:42
1:47
2:2
2:4
2:7
2:12
2:13
3:2
3:13
3:17
3:20
3:21
3:23
3:26^2
3:33
4:5^3
4:7
4:8
4:10^2
4:11
4:15
4:20
4:23
4:28
4:32
4:33^2
4:34^2
4:35
4:38
4:52
5:1
5:7
5:10
5:16
5:18
5:26^2
5:27
5:35
5:36
5:40
5:45
6:6
6:11^2
6:15
6:17
6:24
6:31
6:35
6:37^2
6:38
6:44
6:52
6:68
7:1
7:4^2
7:19
7:20
7:24
7:25
7:30
7:32
7:45
7:50
8:6
8:26^3
8:27
8:31
8:33
8:37
8:40
8:41
8:56
8:59
9:11
9:13
9:26^2
10:3
10:10
10:18^2
10:24
10:29
10:31
10:38
11:7
11:8
11:15
11:19^2
11:31
11:38
11:45
11:46
11:53^2
11:54
11:55^2
11:56
12:1
12:5
12:10
12:12^2
12:13
12:20
12:21
12:29
12:38
12:47^2
13:2
13:3
13:5^2
13:6
13:10^2
13:12
13:14
13:15
13:19
13:24
13:26^2
13:29
13:33
13:35
14:2
14:18
14:21
14:26
14:29^2
15:25
16:5
16:10
16:12^2
16:13
16:16
16:17
16:19
16:28
16:32
17:1
17:4
17:11
18:6
18:13^2
18:14
18:20
18:31^3
18:36
18:37
19:4
19:7
19:10^2
19:12
19:16
19:20
19:21
19:23
19:27
19:29
19:33
19:39
19:40
20:2^2
20:3
20:4
20:8
20:15
20:16
20:17^3
20:21
20:27
21:1
21:6
21:9
21:11
21:14
21:15
21:16
21:21
21:22
21:23

AC

1:1
1:3^2
1:6
1:7
1:16
1:19
1:22
1:25
2:4
2:7
2:12
2:14
2:17
2:21
2:27
2:28
2:30^2
2:37
2:38^4
2:39^2
2:45
2:46
2:47
3:2
3:3
3:5
3:12
3:13
3:14
3:23
3:26
4:5
4:9
4:10
4:15
4:16^2
4:17
4:18
4:19
4:23
4:24
4:28^2
5:2
5:3^3
5:9
5:13
5:14
5:20
5:21^2
5:28
5:29
5:31^3
5:32
5:33^2
5:34
5:35^2
5:36^3
5:38
5:39
5:40
5:41
5:42
6:4^2
6:7
6:10
6:12
6:13
7:5^3
7:7
7:13
7:14
7:17
7:19
7:23
7:26
7:30
7:31
7:33
7:34
7:35^2
7:38^2
7:39
7:40
7:42^2
7:43
7:44
7:46
7:54
7:60
8:2
8:3
8:5
8:10^2
8:11
8:24
8:25
8:27^2
8:29
8:30
8:32
8:36
8:38
8:40
9:2^2
9:4
9:5
9:6
9:10
9:13
9:14
9:15
9:23
9:24
9:26^3
9:27^2
9:29
9:30^2
9:32^2
9:35
9:37
9:38^3
9:40
9:43
10:2^2
10:3
10:5
10:6
10:8
10:9
10:11
10:13
10:21
10:22^2
10:28
10:32
10:33^2
10:36
10:40^2
10:42^3
10:43
10:48^2
11:2
11:3
11:5
11:13
11:15
11:18
11:19
11:20
11:25^2
11:26
11:28
11:29^2
11:30
12:1
12:3
12:4^4
12:10
12:11
12:12
12:13
12:17^2
12:19^2
12:20
13:2
13:4
13:5
13:7
13:8
13:10
13:11
13:13^2
13:14
13:19
13:22^2
13:23
13:24
13:25
13:26
13:31
13:34^2
13:35
13:42
13:43^2
13:44
13:46^2
13:47
13:48
14:1
14:3
14:5^2
14:9
14:11
14:16
14:20
14:21^3
14:22
14:23
14:24
14:26^2
15:2
15:4
15:5
15:6
15:10^2
15:12
15:14
15:15
15:19
15:22^2
15:24
15:25
15:28^3
15:29
15:30
15:34
15:37
15:38^2
16:1
16:3
16:4
16:6
16:7^2
16:8
16:9
16:10^2
16:11^2
16:12
16:13
16:15^2
16:16^2
16:18^2
16:20
16:21^2
16:22
16:23
16:30
16:32
16:36^2
16:39
17:1
17:5^2
17:7
17:14^2
17:15^2
17:16
17:18
17:20
17:21^2
17:23
17:25
17:26
17:29
17:30
18:1
18:2
18:5
18:7
18:9
18:10
18:12
18:13^2
18:14
18:15
18:19
18:20
18:22
18:24
18:26
18:27^2
19:1^2
19:13
19:17
19:21^2
19:27
19:36^2
19:40
20:1
20:3^2
20:6
20:7^2
20:13^2
20:14
20:15
20:16^2
20:17
20:18
20:20
20:21^2
20:24
20:26
20:27
20:28^2
20:30
20:31
20:32^3
20:34
20:35^4
21:1
21:3
21:4^2
21:7
21:12^2
21:13^4
21:15
21:17
21:21^3
21:23
21:25
21:26
21:31
21:33
21:34
21:37
21:39
22:2
22:3
22:5^3
22:6
22:9
22:10
22:12
22:17^2
22:24
22:25
22:30
23:1
23:3^3
23:9
23:10^3
23:14
23:15^3
23:17
23:18^3
23:19
23:20^2
23:22
23:23^2
23:29^3
23:30^3
23:31
23:32^2
23:33^2
23:35
24:2
24:6^3
24:8
24:10
24:11^2
24:16
24:17^2
24:19
24:23^2
24:25
24:27
25:1
25:3^2
25:6
25:9^2
25:10^2
25:11
25:13
25:15
25:16^5
25:17
25:19
25:20
25:21^3
25:22
25:24
25:25^2
25:26^2
25:27^3
26:1
26:3^2
26:7
26:9^2
26:10
26:11
26:12
26:14^2
26:16
26:18^3
26:20^2
26:21
26:22
26:23
26:28
26:29
27:2
27:3^2
27:5
27:12^4
27:16
27:21
27:22
27:27
27:30
27:31^2
27:33
27:34
27:35^2
27:39
27:40
27:42
27:43^2
27:44^2
28:4
28:6
28:8^2
28:13^2
28:14
28:15
28:16^2
28:17
28:19^2
28:20^2
28:22
28:23^2

RO

1:1
1:3
1:4^2
1:5
1:7^3
1:10
1:11^2
1:13
1:14^4
1:15^2
1:16^3
1:17
1:22
1:23^2
1:24^2
1:28^3
1:30
2:2^2
2:4
2:6^2
2:7
2:10^3
2:16
3:15
3:19
3:25^2
3:26
4:1
4:2
4:4
4:5

4:8 4:9 4:12 4:13^2 4:16^4 4:18 4:20 4:21 4:22 4:23 4:24 5:7 5:10 5:14^2 5:16 5:18 6:2 6:11 6:16^3 6:19^3 6:22 7:1 7:2 7:3^2 7:4^3 7:5 7:10^2 7:18 7:23 8:1 8:6^2 8:7 8:12^2 8:15 8:18 8:20 8:23 8:27 8:28^3 8:29^2 8:31 8:33 8:38 8:39 9:3 9:4 9:11 9:15 9:20 9:21 9:22^3 9:26 9:30 9:31 10:1 10:2 10:3 10:4 10:6 10:7 10:19 10:21 11:1 11:2 11:4^2 11:5 11:11 11:13 11:14 11:23 11:24 11:25 11:35 11:36^2 12:2 12:3^5 12:6^3 12:9 12:10 12:13^2 12:16 12:17 13:2 13:3^2 13:4^2 13:7^5 13:8 13:10 13:11 13:14 14:1 14:4^2 14:6^3 14:7^2 14:9 14:11^2 14:12 14:13 14:14^3 14:18 14:21^2 14:22 15:1^2 15:2 15:5^2 15:7 15:8 15:9 15:12 15:14 15:15 15:16 15:17 15:18^2 15:20 15:21 15:22 15:23 15:24^3 15:25 15:26 15:27 15:28 15:30 16:17 16:25^4 16:26^2 16:27 16:*sub.*

1 CO

1:1 1:2^2 1:17^2 1:18 1:19 1:21 1:27^2 1:28^2 2:1 2:2 2:6 2:12 3:2 3:5 3:8 3:10 3:18 3:22 4:5 4:6^3 4:7 4:8 4:9^3 4:14 4:18 4:19 5:5 5:9 5:11^2 5:12^2 6:1 6:2 6:3 6:4^2 6:5^2 6:6 6:7^2 6:16 7:1 7:2 7:5 7:8 7:9 7:11 7:12^2 7:13 7:15 7:17 7:25 7:26 7:27 7:32 7:39^2 8:2 8:6 8:8 8:9 8:10^2 8:13^2 9:2 9:3 9:4^2 9:5 9:6 9:15 9:20 9:21^3 9:25 9:26^2 9:27 10:6 10:7^2 10:13^3 10:15 10:19 10:20^2 10:22 10:27^2 10:31 10:32^3 11:2 11:6 11:7 11:10 11:15 11:16 11:20 11:23^3 11:29 11:33 12:3 12:7^2 12:8^2 12:9^2 12:10^5 12:11 12:13 12:21 12:22 12:23 12:24 13:3^2 13:12 14:3 14:6 14:8 14:9 14:12 14:22^2 14:28^2 14:30 14:32 14:34^2 14:35 14:37 14:39 15:3 15:4 15:9 15:24 15:34^2 15:38 15:54 15:57 16:1 16:3 16:7 16:12^2 16:15 16:16 16:*sub.*

2 CO

1:2 1:4 1:8 1:12 1:13 1:15 1:16^3 1:17 1:23 2:1 2:3 2:6 2:7 2:9 2:10^2 2:12^2 2:14 2:16^2 3:1^2 3:3 3:4 3:5 3:7 3:13 3:16 3:18 4:2 4:3 4:6^2 4:15 5:2 5:8^2 5:10 5:12^2 5:13 5:18^2 5:19^2 5:20 5:21 7:3^2 7:9 7:10^2 7:11 7:14^2 8:1^2 8:3 8:4 8:5 8:7 8:8 8:10^2 8:11 8:12^2 8:13 8:16 8:19 8:24 9:1^3 9:2 9:5 9:8^2 9:9 9:10 9:11^2 10:2^2 10:4 10:5 10:6 10:13^3 10:14 10:15 10:16^3 11:1 11:2^2 11:7 11:8 11:9^2 11:15 11:32 12:1^2 12:2 12:4 12:6^2 12:7^2 12:11 12:13^2 12:14^4 13:1 13:2^2 13:3 13:7 13:10^3 13:*sub.*

GA

1:3 1:4 1:5 1:10 1:16 1:17^2 1:18^2 2:1 2:2 2:3 2:4 2:5 2:6^4 2:8 2:9^2 2:10 2:11^3 2:14^2 2:17 2:19 3:5 3:6 3:10 3:16^3 3:18 3:19 3:22 3:24 3:29 4:5 4:9^2 4:15 4:18 4:20^2 4:21 4:24 4:25 5:3^2 5:13 5:17 6:3 6:8^2 6:12^2 6:13 6:16

EPH

1:1^2 1:2 1:5^2 1:6 1:7 1:9 1:11 1:12 1:16 1:19^2 1:21 1:22^2 2:2^2 2:7 2:15 2:17^2 3:2 3:7 3:9 3:10 3:11 3:16^2 3:18 3:19 3:20^2 4:3 4:7 4:14^2 4:16 4:19 4:22 4:27 4:28^2 4:29 4:32 5:2 5:12 5:19^2 5:21 5:24 5:27 5:28 6:4 6:5^2 6:7^2 6:11 6:13^2 6:16 6:19 6:20 6:21 6:23

PHP

1:1 1:7 1:16^2 1:19 1:20 1:21^3 1:23 1:24 1:26 1:28^2 1:29 1:30 2:6 2:11 2:13 2:19 2:23 2:25^3 2:30 3:1^3 3:7 3:13 3:21^2 4:11 4:12^6 4:17 4:18 4:19 4:*sub.*

COL

1:2 1:3 1:4 1:9^2 1:11 1:12 1:20 1:22 1:23 1:25^3 1:26 1:27 1:29 2:2 2:14^2 2:17 2:20 2:22 2:23 3:9 3:15 3:16 3:17 3:21 3:22 3:33 4:3 4:4 4:6 4:10 4:17^2 4:*sub.*

1 TH

1:2 1:7 1:8^2 1:9^2 1:10^2 2:2 2:4 2:8 2:15 2:16^3 2:17 3:1 3:2^2 3:4 3:5 3:6^2 3:9 3:12 3:13 4:1^2 4:4 4:9 4:11^3 4:13 4:17 5:9^2 5:12 5:13 5:15

2 TH

1:3 1:6^2 1:7 1:10^2 1:12 2:13^3 2:14 3:7 3:8 3:9^2 3:*sub.*

1 TI

1:3 1:4 1:7 1:10 1:11 1:15 1:16^2 1:18 1:20 2:4 2:6 2:12^3 3:2^2 3:3 3:5 3:8 3:13 3:14 3:15 4:1 4:3^3 4:4 4:8 4:13^3 4:15^2 5:4^2 5:11 5:13^3 5:14^2 5:17 5:18^2 5:19 5:24 6:3^3 6:16 6:20 6:*sub.*

2 TI

1:1 1:2 1:4 1:5 1:8 1:9^2 1:10 1:12 2:2^2 2:4 2:8 2:14 2:15^2 2:20 2:24 2:25 3:2 3:7^2 3:15 3:16 4:3 4:6 4:8 4:9 4:10 4:11 4:12 4:14 4:16 4:18 4:21

TIT

1:1 1:3 1:4 1:7^2 1:9^2 1:14 2:3 2:4^3 2:5^2 2:6 2:9^2 2:11 3:1^5 3:2^2 3:5 3:7 3:8 3:12^3 3:14 3:*sub.*

PHM

2^2 8 11^3 13 16 19 *sub.*

HEB

1:5^2 1:13 1:14 2:1^2 2:3 2:4 2:5 2:10 2:11 2:15 2:17^3 2:18 3:2 3:5 3:7 3:13 3:15 3:18^2 4:1 4:6 4:7^2 4:9 4:11 4:12 4:13 4:16 5:1 5:3 5:5^2 5:7 5:11^2 5:12 5:14^2 6:5 6:6^3 6:8 6:10^2 6:11 6:13 6:16 6:17 6:18^2 7:2 7:5^2 7:13 7:23 7:25^3 7:27 8:3^2 8:4 8:5^3 8:9^2 8:10^2 8:11 8:12 8:13 9:9 9:11 9:13 9:14^2 9:19^2 9:24 9:26 9:27 9:28 10:1 10:2 10:7 10:9 10:15 10:19 10:20 10:24^2 10:31 10:32 10:39 11:6^2 11:7 11:8 11:11 11:15 11:16 11:19 11:20 11:24^2 11:25^2 11:29 11:32 11:34 11:35 12:11 12:19 12:22 12:23^3 12:24^2 13:2 13:8 13:10 13:14 13:15^2 13:16^2 13:18 13:19^2 13:21^2 13:*sub.*

JAS

1:1 1:5 1:12 1:19^3 1:21 1:26 1:27^2 2:3^2 2:5 2:8 2:9 2:16 3:2 3:10 3:17 4:2 4:5 4:7 4:8^2 4:9^2 4:12^2 4:13^2 4:15 4:17^3 5:16 5:17

1 PE

1:1 1:2 1:3 1:4 1:5 1:12 1:13^2 1:14 1:17 2:4 2:5^2 2:8 2:13^2 2:15 2:18^3 2:23 2:24 3:1 3:7 3:15^2 3:18^2 4:2^2 4:3 4:4 4:5^2 4:6^3 4:9 4:10 4:11 4:12 4:13 4:19^2 5:1 5:3 5:5^2 5:11

2 PE

1:1 1:3 1:5^2 1:6^3 1:7^2 1:10 1:12 1:13 1:15 1:17 2:4^2 2:8 2:9^3 2:10 2:12 2:13 2:17 2:21^2 2:22^3 3:9^2 3:13 3:15 3:16 3:18

1 JO

1:9^2 2:6 3:5 3:16 4:10 4:14 4:16 5:11 5:14

2 JO

8 12^3

3 JO

4 5^2 8^2 9 13 14^2

JUDE

1 3^2 4 7 13 15^2 24^2 25

RE

1:1^2 1:4^2 1:6 1:8 1:12 1:13 2:7^2 2:12 2:14^3 2:17^2 2:19 2:20^4 2:21 2:23 2:26 2:27 3:2 3:7 3:9^2 3:10 3:18 3:20 3:21^2 4:3 4:8 4:9 4:11 5:2^2 5:3^2 5:4^3 5:5^2 5:9^3 5:12 6:1 6:4^2 6:8 6:16 6:17 7:2^3 7:10 7:14 8:2 8:6 8:13^2 9:1 9:5 9:6 9:9 9:10 9:14 9:15 10:4 10:5 10:7^2 11:6^4 11:9 11:10 11:12 11:13 11:17 11:18 11:19 12:2 12:4^3 12:5^2 12:12 12:14 12:15 12:17 13:3 13:4 13:5 13:6 13:7^3 13:12 13:14^3 13:15 13:16 13:17^3 14:4 14:6^2 14:7 14:15^2 14:18 15:8 16:1 16:6 16:8 16:9 16:14^2 16:19 17:17^2 18:6^2 18:17 19:7 19:8 19:10 19:17 19:19 20:8^3 20:12 20:13 21:10 21:15 21:17 21:23 22:6 22:8 22:12 22:14 22:16

UNTO

1519

GE

1:9 1:28 2:19 2:22 2:24 3:1 3:2 3:4 3:6 3:9 3:13 3:14 3:16 3:17 3:19^2 3:21 4:3 4:4 4:5 4:6 4:7 4:9 4:10 4:12 4:13 4:15 4:18 4:19 4:23^2 6:1 6:4 6:13 6:20 6:21 7:1 7:5 7:9 7:15 8:9^2 8:12 8:15 8:20 9:1 9:8 9:17 9:24 9:25 10:1 10:19^2 10:21 10:25 10:30 11:4 11:31 12:1^2 12:4 12:6 12:7^2 12:8^2 12:11 12:18 13:3 13:4 13:8 13:10 13:14 13:17 13:18 14:6 14:14 14:15 14:21 14:22 15:1 15:4 15:5 15:7 15:9 15:10 15:13 15:18^2 16:2^2 16:3 16:4 16:6 16:8 16:10 16:11 16:13 17:1 17:7 17:8 17:9 17:15 17:17 17:18 17:21 17:23 18:1 18:6 18:7^2 18:9 18:10 18:13 18:14 18:21 18:27 18:29 18:30 18:31 18:33 19:3 19:5^2 19:6 19:8^2 19:12 19:14^2 19:16 19:18 19:19 19:20 19:21 19:31^2 19:34 19:37 19:38 20:5 20:6 20:9^2 20:10 20:13 20:14 20:16^2 20:17 21:1 21:3 21:5 21:7 21:8 21:10 21:12^2 21:14 21:17 21:22 21:23^2 21:27 21:29 21:30 22:1 22:3 22:5 22:7 22:11 22:12 22:15 22:19 22:20 23:3 23:5 23:13 23:14 23:15 23:16 23:18 23:20 24:2 24:3 24:4 24:5^3 24:6 24:7^3 24:10 24:12 24:14 24:20 24:24^2 24:25 24:29 24:30 24:36 24:38^2 24:39 24:40 24:42 24:45^2 24:47 24:48 24:50 24:54 24:56 24:58 24:60 24:65 25:5 25:6^2 25:12 25:17 25:18 25:23 25:33 26:1 26:2 26:3^2 26:4 26:9 26:10 26:16 26:24 26:27 26:29 26:32 26:33 26:35 27:1^2 27:6^2 27:13 27:18 27:19 27:20 27:21 27:22 27:26 27:31 27:32 27:34 27:37^2 27:38 27:39 27:42 28:1 28:4 28:5 28:9 28:22 29:4 29:5 29:6 29:15 29:20 29:21^2 29:23 29:24 29:25 29:30 29:34 30:1 30:3 30:4 30:14 30:15 30:16 30:17 30:25^2 30:27 30:29 30:30 30:40 31:3 31:4 31:5 31:11 31:12 31:13^2 31:14 31:16 31:24 31:29 31:39 31:43^3 31:46 31:52 31:55 32:3 32:4 32:9^2 32:10 32:16 32:18 32:19 32:27 32:32 33:1^3 33:9 33:13 33:14^2 33:16 34:1 34:3^2 34:4 34:6 34:9^2 34:11^3 34:12 34:14^2 34:15 34:16 34:17 34:20 34:22 34:23 34:24^2 35:1^3 35:2 35:3 35:4 35:7 35:9 35:10 35:11 35:17 35:20 35:27^3 35:29 36:5 37:2 37:4 37:6 37:10 37:13^2 37:18 37:22 37:23 37:26 37:29 37:30 37:35 37:36 38:2 38:8^2 38:9 38:12 38:14 38:16^8 38:18 39:8 39:10 39:14^4 39:17^3 39:19 40:6 40:8^2 40:12 40:13 40:14^2 40:16 40:20 40:21 41:8 41:9 41:13 41:14 41:15 41:17 41:24 41:25 41:28^2 41:32 41:38 41:39 41:40 41:41 41:44 41:50^2 41:55^2 41:56 42:1 42:7^3 42:9 42:10 42:12 42:14^2 42:18 42:20 42:22 42:23 42:25 42:28^2 42:29^3 42:31 42:33 42:34 42:36 42:37 43:2 43:3^2 43:5 43:8 43:9 43:11 43:13 43:23 43:29^2 43:32 43:34 44:4^2 44:6 44:7 44:8 44:10 44:15 44:16 44:17 44:18 44:20 44:21^2 44:22 44:23 44:24 44:27 44:32^3 45:1 45:3 45:4 45:9^2 45:10 45:12 45:17^3 45:18 45:24 45:25 45:27 46:1 46:2 46:15 46:18 46:20^2 46:25^2 46:28^2 46:29 46:30

46:31[4] 46:34 47:2 47:3[2] 47:4 47:5[2] 47:8 47:9[2] 47:15 47:17 47:18[2] 47:19 47:23 47:24 47:26 47:29 47:31[2] 48:2 48:3[2] 48:4 48:5[2] 48:7 48:9[2] 48:10 48:11 48:13 48:15 48:17 48:18 48:21[2] 49:1 49:2 49:6 49:10 49:11[2] 49:13 49:15 49:26 49:28 49:29[2] 50:4 50:12 50:15 50:16 50:17[3] 50:19 50:20 50:21 50:24[2]

EX

1:9 1:10 1:18 1:19[2] 2:9 2:10 2:11 2:20 2:23 2:25 3:2 3:4 3:8[3] 3:9 3:10 3:11[2] 3:12 3:13[4] 3:14[3] 3:15[4] 3:16[2] 3:17[2] 3:18 4:1[2] 4:2 4:4 4:5 4:6 4:9 4:10[2] 4:11 4:15 4:16 4:18[2]

4:19 4:21 4:22 4:23 4:30 5:1 5:3 5:4[2] 5:15 5:16 5:21 5:22 6:1 6:2[2] 6:3[3] 6:6 6:8 6:9[2] 6:10 6:11 6:12 6:13[4] 6:28 6:29[3] 6:30 7:1 7:2 7:4 7:7 7:8[2] 7:9[2] 7:10 7:13 7:14 7:15[2] 7:16[2] 7:19[2] 7:22 8:1[3] 8:5 8:8 8:9 8:10 8:12 8:15 8:16[2] 8:19 8:20[2] 9:1[2] 9:8[2] 9:12[2] 9:13[2] 9:22 9:27 9:29[2] 9:33 10:1[2] 10:3[2] 10:5 10:6 10:7[2] 10:8[2] 10:9 10:10 10:12 10:21 10:24 10:25 10:28 11:1 11:5 11:8[2] 11:9[2] 12:1 12:2 12:3 12:4 12:14 12:21 12:23 12:26 12:29 12:36 12:42 12:43 12:49 13:1

13:2 13:3 13:5 13:8 13:9 13:11 13:12 13:14 14:1 14:2 14:10 14:11 14:13 14:15[3] 14:22 14:24 14:26 14:29 15:1[2] 15:11 15:13 15:25 16:1 16:3 16:4 16:6 16:9[2] 16:10 16:11 16:12 16:15 16:20 16:23[2] 16:25 16:28 16:33 16:35 17:2 17:4[2] 17:5 17:9 17:14 18:5 18:6[2] 18:8 18:13 18:14 18:15[2] 18:16 18:17 18:19[2] 18:22 18:26 19:3[2] 19:4[2] 19:5 19:6[2] 19:8 19:9[3] 19:10[2] 19:12 19:14 19:15 19:21[2] 19:23 19:24[2] 19:25[2] 20:4 20:5 20:6 20:19 20:20 20:21 20:22[2] 20:23 20:24[2] 20:26 21:6[2] 21:8 21:9 21:11 21:31 21:32 21:34 22:7 22:8[2] 22:9

22:10 22:11 22:12 22:17 22:20[2] 22:23 22:26 22:27 22:29 22:31 23:13 23:14 23:22[2] 23:23 23:27 23:31[2] 23:33 24:1[2] 24:5 24:12 24:14[3] 24:16 25:1 25:2 25:22 25:25 25:33 25:34 26:24 26:33 27:21 28:1[2] 28:3[2] 28:4 28:12 28:28 28:29 28:35 28:41 28:42 28:43[3] 29:1[2] 29:4 29:17[2] 29:18[2] 29:25 29:28 29:34 29:35 29:41 29:42 30:3 30:10 30:11 30:12 30:14 30:15 30:16 30:17 30:20 30:22 30:23 30:30 30:31[2] 30:32 30:34[2] 30:36 30:37 30:38 31:1 31:12 31:13 31:14 31:18 32:1[2] 32:2[2] 32:3 32:7 32:9 32:13[2] 32:14 32:17 32:19 32:21[2] 32:23 32:24 32:25

32:26[2] 32:27 32:30[2] 32:31 32:33 32:34[2] 33:1[4] 33:3 33:5[3] 33:7 33:8 33:11[2] 33:12[2] 33:15 33:17 34:1[2] 34:2 34:4[2] 34:7 34:15 34:16 34:25 34:26 34:27 34:31[2] 34:34 35:1 35:4 35:5 35:22 35:29 35:30 36:2 36:3 36:5 36:10[2] 36:13 37:26 38:4 39:21 39:31 39:33 40:1 40:12 40:13 40:15 40:32

LE

1:1[2] 1:2[3] 1:9 1:13 1:15 1:17 2:1 2:2 2:8[3] 2:9 2:11 2:12 2:14 2:16 3:3 3:5 3:6 3:9 3:11 3:14 4:1 4:2 4:3 4:4 4:12 4:31 4:35 5:6 5:7 5:8 5:12 5:14 5:16 5:18 6:1 6:2

6:5 6:6[2] 6:8 6:9 6:11 6:15 6:17 6:19 6:20 6:21 6:22 6:24 6:25 7:5 7:11 7:14 7:18 7:20 7:21 7:22 7:23 7:25 7:28 7:29[3] 7:32 7:34[2] 7:35 7:38 8:1 8:3 8:4 8:5 8:7 8:21 8:28 8:31 9:2 9:3 9:4 9:6 9:7[2] 9:8 9:9 9:12 9:13 9:18 9:23 10:3 10:4 10:6[3] 10:8 10:11 10:12[3] 10:19 11:1[2] 11:2 11:4 11:5 11:6 11:10 11:11 11:12 11:20 11:23 11:26 11:27 11:28 11:29 11:35 11:38 12:1 12:2 12:6[2] 13:1 13:2 13:9 13:16[2] 13:49 14:1 14:2 14:23[2] 14:33[2] 15:1 15:2[2] 15:14[2] 15:26 15:29[2]

16:1 16:2[2] 16:18 16:22 16:29 16:31 16:34 17:1 17:2[4] 17:4[3] 17:5[4] 17:6 17:7[2] 17:8 17:9[2] 17:12 17:14 18:1 18:2[2] 18:19 19:1 19:2[2] 19:4 19:5 19:21[2] 19:23 19:25 19:34 20:1 20:2 20:3 20:4 20:16 20:24[2] 20:26 21:1[3] 21:2[2] 21:3[2] 21:6 21:7 21:8 21:16 21:17 21:23[2] 21:24[2] 22:1 22:2 22:3[2] 22:12 22:13 22:14[2] 22:15 22:17 22:18[4] 22:21 22:22[2] 22:24 22:26 22:27 22:29 23:1 23:2[2] 23:6 23:8 23:9 23:10[4] 23:12 23:13 23:14 23:15 23:16[2] 23:17 23:18[2] 23:21 23:22 23:23 23:24 23:25 23:26 23:27[2] 23:32[2] 23:33 23:34[2] 23:36[3] 23:37 23:38 23:39

23:41 23:44 24:1 24:2 24:3 24:7 24:9 24:11 24:13 24:15 25:1 25:2[3] 25:4 25:5 25:8[2] 25:10[4] 25:11 25:12 25:13 25:14 25:15[2] 25:16 25:27[2] 25:28 25:39 25:40 25:41[2] 25:47 25:49 25:50[2] 25:51 25:52[2] 25:55 26:1 26:5[2] 26:9 26:14 26:16 26:18 26:21[2] 26:23 26:24 26:27 26:28 26:31 26:40 26:41 27:1 27:2[2] 27:3 27:5 27:6 27:9[2] 27:11 27:13 27:14 27:15 27:16 27:18[2] 27:19 27:21 27:22 27:23[3] 27:24 27:28[2] 27:30 27:32

NU

1:1 1:48 1:50 2:1[2] 2:5 3:5 3:6 3:9[2] 3:11 3:13 3:14 3:40 3:44 3:48 3:51 4:1[2]

4:9 4:17[2] 4:19[2] 4:21 4:27 4:30 4:35 4:39 4:43 4:47 5:1 5:4 5:5 5:6 5:7[2] 5:8[2] 5:9 5:11 5:12[2] 5:15 5:19 5:21 6:1 6:2[3] 6:5 6:6 6:8 6:12 6:13 6:14 6:17 6:21 6:22 6:23[3] 6:25 7:4 7:5 7:6 7:7 7:8[2] 7:9[2] 7:11 7:89[2] 8:1 8:2[2] 8:4[3] 8:5 8:7 8:12 8:13 8:16[2] 8:19 8:20[2] 8:22 8:23 8:24 8:26 9:1 9:4 9:7 9:8 9:9 9:10[2] 9:12 9:14 9:21 10:1 10:4 10:29[2] 10:30 10:32[2] 10:36 11:2[2] 11:11 11:12[3] 11:13[2] 11:16[3] 11:18 11:20 11:23[2] 11:25[2] 11:26 11:29 11:35 12:4[4] 12:6[2] 12:11

12:13 12:14 13:1 13:2 13:17 13:21 13:22 13:23 13:26[3] 13:27 13:32 14:2 14:3 14:7 14:11 14:13 14:16 14:18 14:19 14:23 14:26[2] 14:28 14:35 14:39 14:40 14:44 14:45 15:1 15:2[3] 15:3 15:4 15:7 15:8 15:10 15:13 15:14 15:17 15:18[2] 15:19 15:21 15:22 15:24 15:25 15:33[2] 15:35 15:37 15:38 15:39 15:40 16:3 16:5[3] 16:8 16:9[2] 16:15 16:16 16:19[2] 16:20[2] 16:23 16:24 16:25 16:26 16:30 16:32 16:36 16:37 16:38 16:40 16:44 16:46[2] 16:50[2] 17:1 17:2 17:6 17:9 17:10 17:12 17:13 18:1 18:2[2] 18:4[2] 18:7 18:8[2] 18:9 18:10 18:11 18:12 18:13

18:15 18:17 18:19[2] 18:20 18:24[2] 18:25 18:26 18:27 18:28 18:30[2] 19:1 19:2 19:3 19:10[2] 19:21 20:5 20:6[2] 20:7 20:8[2] 20:10 20:12 20:14 20:16 20:18 20:19 20:22 20:23 20:24[2] 20:25 20:26 21:2 21:7 21:8 21:16 21:17 21:21 21:24[2] 21:26 21:29 21:30[2] 21:34[2] 22:4 22:5 22:7[2] 22:8[2] 22:9 22:10[2] 22:12 22:13 22:14 22:16 22:17[2] 22:18 22:19 22:20[3] 22:25 22:28[2] 22:29 22:30[3] 22:32 22:34 22:35[2] 22:36 22:37[3] 22:38[2] 22:39 23:1 23:3 23:4 23:5 23:6 23:11[2] 23:13[2] 23:15 23:16 23:17 23:18 23:25 23:26 23:27[2] 23:28 23:29 24:10 24:11 24:12[2] 24:14 25:2

25:3 25:4 25:5[2] 25:6 25:8 25:10 25:12 25:16 26:1[2] 26:52 26:53 26:59 26:60 27:4 27:6 27:7 27:8[2] 27:9 27:10 27:11[2] 27:12[2] 27:13 27:15 27:18 28:1 28:2[3] 28:3[2] 28:6 28:7 28:8 28:11 28:13[2] 28:14[3] 28:15 28:19[2] 28:24 28:26 28:27 28:28[2] 28:29 28:31 29:1 29:2 29:6[2] 29:8[2] 29:12 29:13 29:14 29:36 29:39 30:1 30:2 30:3 31:1 31:2 31:3[2] 31:12[3] 31:15 31:21 31:25 31:28 31:29 31:30 31:41 31:43 31:47 31:48 31:49 32:2[2] 32:5 32:6 32:9 32:11[3] 32:16 32:17 32:18 32:20 32:25 32:29 32:31 32:33[2] 32:38 32:40 33:7 33:9 33:49 33:50

33:51[2] 33:56[2] 34:1 34:2[2] 34:5 34:8 34:11 34:13 34:16 34:17 34:29 35:1 35:2[2] 35:4 35:6 35:8 35:9 35:10[2] 35:12 35:25 35:29 36:2 36:4 36:8 36:11 36:13

DE

1:1 1:2 1:3[3] 1:6 1:7[3] 1:8[2] 1:9 1:17 1:20[3] 1:21 1:22 1:24 1:25 1:29 1:35 1:39 1:41 1:42[2] 1:43 1:44 1:45 1:46 2:1 2:2 2:4 2:5 2:9[2] 2:12[2] 2:14 2:17 2:19 2:22 2:23 2:26 2:27 2:29 2:31 2:35 2:36[2] 2:37[4] 3:2[3] 3:6 3:8 3:10 3:12 3:13 3:14[2] 3:15 3:16[4] 3:17 3:20[3] 3:21[2] 3:26[2] 4:1[2] 4:2 4:4 4:7

4:10 4:11 4:12 4:13 4:15[2] 4:19[2] 4:20 4:21 4:23 4:26 4:30 4:31 4:32 4:35 4:42 4:45 4:48 4:49 5:1 5:9[2] 5:10 5:22[2] 5:23 5:27[2] 5:28[3] 5:31 6:7 6:10 6:18 6:21 6:23 7:2 7:3[2] 7:6[2] 7:8 7:12[2] 7:13 7:16 7:18[2] 7:19 7:23 7:25 8:1 8:18 8:20 9:3 9:5 9:7 9:10 9:12 9:13 9:19 9:26 9:27 10:1[3] 10:3 10:4[2] 10:7 10:8[2] 10:10 10:11[3] 11:3[2] 11:4[3] 11:5 11:6 11:9[2] 11:12 11:13 11:21 11:22 11:24 11:25 11:29 12:4 12:5[2] 12:7 12:11 12:18 12:26 12:31[2] 13:2 13:3 13:4 13:7[2] 13:8[2] 13:17 14:2[2]

14:7 14:8 14:10 14:19 14:21[3] 14:25 15:2 15:5 15:6 15:8 15:9[2] 15:10[2] 15:11 15:12 15:14 15:16 15:17[2] 15:18 15:19 15:21 16:1 16:2 16:7 16:9 16:10[2] 16:15 16:21 17:1[2] 17:5 17:9[2] 17:12[2] 17:14 17:16 18:2 18:3 18:6 18:12 18:14[2] 18:15[3] 18:17 18:18[2] 18:19 19:5 19:8[2] 19:19[2] 20:2 20:3[2] 20:5 20:6 20:7 20:8[2] 20:9 20:10[2] 20:11[2] 20:14 20:15 20:18 21:2 21:3 21:4 21:5 21:6 21:8[2] 21:11 21:13 21:18 21:19[2] 21:20 22:1 22:2[2] 22:5[2] 22:13 22:15[2] 22:19 22:23 22:24 22:26 22:29 23:5[2] 23:15[2] 23:18 23:20[2] 23:21 23:23 23:24 24:9 24:11

24:13 24:15[2] 25:1 25:3 25:5[3] 25:7[2] 25:8 25:9[2] 25:16 25:17 26:1 26:2 26:3[5] 26:7 26:11[2] 26:12 26:13[2] 26:15 26:17 26:19 27:2 27:3 27:5 27:6 27:9 27:14 27:15 28:1 28:2 28:8 28:9[2] 28:11 28:12[3] 28:13 28:15 28:20 28:21 28:26[2] 28:31 28:32 28:35 28:36 28:45 28:60 28:64 28:68[2] 29:2[5] 29:4 29:7[2] 29:8 29:11 29:13[4] 29:21 29:24 29:26 29:29[2] 30:2 30:4 30:10[2] 30:12 30:13 30:14 30:18 30:20[2] 31:1 31:2[2] 31:4[2] 31:5[2] 31:7[4] 31:9[2] 31:14 31:16 31:18 31:20[2] 31:23 31:28 32:3 32:17 32:22 32:43 32:46[2] 32:48 32:49 32:50[2] 32:52 33:2 33:7

33:9 33:19 33:26 33:29[2] 34:1[2] 34:2 34:3 34:4[5] 34:6 34:9 34:10

JOS

1:1 1:2 1:3[2] 1:4[2] 1:6[2] 1:15 1:17[2] 1:18 2:3 2:4 2:7 2:8 2:9 2:10 2:12[2] 2:16 2:17 2:18 2:21 2:22 2:24 3:4 3:5 3:6 3:7 3:9 3:15 4:1 4:5[2] 4:7 4:8[2] 4:9 4:10 4:12 4:13 4:15 4:18[2] 4:21 5:2 5:6[2] 5:9[2] 5:13[2] 5:14[2] 5:15 6:2 6:6 6:7 6:8 6:16 6:19 6:22[2] 6:25 7:2 7:3 7:5 7:9 7:10 7:19[2] 7:22 7:23[2] 7:24 7:26 8:1[2] 8:2[2] 8:5 8:18 8:24 8:27[2] 8:28 8:29 8:30 8:31

9:3 9:6[2] 9:7 9:8[2] 9:9 9:11 9:12 9:15 9:17 9:18 9:19[2] 9:20 9:21[2] 9:22 9:25[2] 9:26 9:27 10:3[4] 10:4 10:6 10:8 10:9 10:10 10:11 10:14 10:15 10:22 10:23 10:24[2] 10:25 10:28 10:29 10:30[2] 10:31 10:34 10:36 10:41[2] 10:43 11:6 11:8[3] 11:9 11:14 11:17 11:23[2] 12:1 12:2 12:3 12:5 12:6 12:7[2] 13:1 13:3 13:4 13:5 13:6[2] 13:7 13:9 13:10 13:11 13:14[2] 13:15 13:24[2] 13:25 13:26 13:27 13:29 13:31 13:33[2] 14:3 14:4 14:6[3] 14:10 14:13 14:14 15:3 15:4 15:5 15:8 15:9 15:10[2] 15:11[2] 15:13 15:18[2] 15:46 15:47 15:63 16:1

16:2
16:3
16:5
16:6
16:8
16:10
17:7
17:9
17:14
17:17
18:3
18:10
18:18
19:10
19:12
19:28
19:33
20:1
20:2
20:4^{2}
20:6^{3}
21:1^{3}
21:2
21:3
21:8
21:27
21:34
21:43^{2}
21:44
21:45
22:2
22:3
22:4^{3}
22:5
22:6
22:7^{2}
22:8^{2}
22:9
22:10
22:13
22:15^{2}
22:19
22:21
22:24
22:31
22:32
23:1
23:2
23:3
23:4^{2}
23:5
23:7
23:8^{2}
23:9
23:11
23:12^{2}
23:13
23:14
23:16
24:2
24:4^{2}
24:6^{2}
24:7
24:10
24:11
24:15
24:19
24:21
24:22
24:23
24:24
24:27^{4}
24:28

JG

1:3
1:14
1:20
1:21
1:24
1:25
1:33
2:1^{2}
2:3
2:4
2:5
2:6
2:10
2:12
2:15
2:17^{2}
2:19
2:20
3:3
3:4
3:9
3:13
3:15^{2}
3:17
3:19
3:20^{2}
3:26
3:28
4:3
4:6
4:7
4:8
4:11
4:13
4:14
4:16
4:18^{2}
4:19
4:20
4:21
4:22
5:3
5:18
6:4
6:6
6:7
6:8^{2}
6:10
6:11
6:12^{2}
6:13
6:15
6:16
6:17
6:18
6:19
6:20
6:23^{2}
6:24^{2}
6:25
6:26
6:27
6:30
6:31
6:35^{3}
6:36
6:39
7:2
7:4^{4}
7:5^{2}
7:7^{2}
7:8
7:9^{2}
7:11^{2}
7:13^{2}
7:17
7:19
7:22
7:24^{2}
8:1
8:2
8:5^{2}
8:6
8:8
8:9
8:14
8:15^{2}
8:18
8:20
8:22
8:23
8:24
8:27
8:35
9:1
9:5
9:7^{3}
9:8
9:9
9:11
9:12
9:13
9:14
9:15
9:16
9:31
9:36
9:38
9:40
9:48
9:52^{2}
9:54^{2}
9:55
9:56
10:4
10:10
10:11
10:14
10:15^{3}
11:2
11:6
11:7^{2}
11:8
11:9
11:10
11:12
11:13^{3}
11:14
11:15
11:16
11:17^{2}
11:19^{2}
11:22^{2}
11:28
11:29
11:30
11:32
11:33
11:34
11:35
11:36^{2}
11:37
11:39
12:1
12:2
12:3
12:5
12:6
13:3^{2}
13:5
13:6
13:7
13:8^{2}
13:9
13:10^{3}
13:11^{2}
13:12
13:13^{2}
13:15
13:16^{2}
13:17
13:18
13:19
13:22
13:23
14:3^{2}
14:10
14:12^{2}
14:13
14:14
14:15^{2}
14:16^{2}
14:18^{2}
14:19
15:7
15:12^{3}
15:13
15:14
15:19
16:1
16:5^{2}
16:7
16:9
16:10
16:11
16:12
16:13^{2}
16:14
16:15
16:16
16:17^{2}
16:18
16:23
16:26
16:28
17:2
17:3^{2}
17:4
17:9^{2}
17:10^{2}
17:11
18:1^{2}
18:2
18:3
18:4
18:5
18:6
18:8^{2}
18:10
18:12
18:13^{2}
18:14
18:15
18:18^{3}
18:23^{2}
18:24
18:25
18:26
18:27^{2}
18:29
19:2
19:3
19:5
19:6
19:9
19:11
19:12
19:13
19:18
19:21
19:23^{2}
19:24^{2}
19:25
19:28^{2}
19:30
20:1
20:14
20:26
20:32
20:36
20:42
20:45^{2}
20:47
21:1
21:5
21:12
21:13
21:22^{4}
21:23

RU

1:7
1:8
1:10^{2}
1:14
1:15^{2}
1:18
1:20
2:2^{2}
2:3
2:4
2:5
2:8
2:9
2:10
2:11^{3}
2:13^{2}
2:14
2:19
2:20^{3}
2:21
2:22
2:23
3:1
3:3
3:5^{2}
3:6
3:13
3:17
4:1
4:3
4:8
4:9^{2}
4:12
4:13
4:14
4:15
4:16

1 SA

1:3
1:5
1:10
1:11^{2}
1:14
1:21
1:22
1:23
1:24
1:26
2:10
2:11
2:14
2:16
2:20
2:22
2:23
2:25
2:27^{3}
2:28
2:34
3:1
3:5
3:7
3:9
3:14
3:17^{2}
4:3
4:7
4:8
4:9
4:16
4:20
5:1
5:5
5:8^{2}
6:5
6:12
6:14
6:15
6:17
6:18^{2}
7:3^{3}
7:5
7:8
7:9^{2}
7:14
7:17
8:4
8:5
8:6
8:7^{3}
8:8^{2}
8:9^{2}
8:10
8:22^{3}
9:6
9:10
9:11
9:16
9:17
9:19
9:23^{2}
9:24
10:2
10:7
10:8
10:11
10:14
10:15
10:16
10:17
10:18
10:19
11:1
11:3^{2}
11:7
11:9^{2}
11:10^{2}
11:12
12:1^{3}
12:2
12:5
12:6
12:8
12:10
12:12
12:17
12:18
12:19^{3}
12:20
13:12
13:15
13:17^{2}
14:1
14:4
14:6
14:7
14:8^{2}
14:9^{2}
14:10^{2}
14:11
14:12
14:17
14:18
14:19^{2}
14:23
14:33
14:34
14:35^{2}
14:36^{2}
14:40^{3}
14:41
14:45
14:52
15:1^{2}
15:6
15:10
15:11
15:13
15:15
15:16^{2}
15:20
15:21
15:24
15:26
15:28
15:32
16:1
16:3^{2}
16:5
16:7
16:10
16:11^{2}
16:15
16:17
16:19
16:20
17:8^{2}
17:13
17:17
17:18
17:28
17:34
17:37
17:39
17:41
17:43
17:44
17:46
17:52^{2}
17:55
18:1
18:8
18:18
18:19
19:4^{2}
19:6
19:11
19:17^{2}
20:2
20:4
20:5^{2}
20:11
20:12^{2}
20:21
20:22
20:27
20:29
20:30^{2}
20:31
20:32
20:36
20:40^{2}
21:1
21:2^{2}
21:5
21:8
21:11
21:14
22:2
22:3
22:5
22:7
22:8
22:13
22:15
22:17
22:22
23:2
23:3
23:17^{2}
23:27
24:4^{3}
24:6^{2}
24:16
24:19
24:21
24:22^{2}
25:5
25:6
25:7
25:8
25:11
25:13
25:15
25:16
25:19
25:21
25:22
25:27^{2}
25:31^{2}
25:34
25:35
25:40^{2}
26:1
27:2
27:5
27:6^{2}
27:8
28:1
28:7
28:8^{2}
28:9
28:11
28:13^{2}
28:14
28:15
28:18
28:21^{4}
28:22
28:23
29:3^{3}
29:4^{4}
29:6^{3}
29:8^{2}
30:13
30:15
30:17
30:24
30:25
30:26
31:1

2 SA

1:3^{2}
1:4
1:5
1:7
1:9
1:10
1:13
1:14
1:16
1:26
2:1^{2}
2:5^{4}
2:6
3:2
3:7
3:8
3:12
3:16
3:21^{2}
3:24
3:38
4:8
4:9
5:1
5:6^{2}
5:14
5:19
6:10
6:12
6:21
6:23
7:2
7:4
7:8
7:9
7:17
7:20
7:24
7:27
7:28
8:10
8:11
8:15
9:2^{2}
9:3^{2}
9:4^{2}
9:6
9:7
9:9^{2}
9:11
9:12
10:2
10:3^{3}
10:5
10:13
11:4^{2}
11:7
11:10^{3}
11:11
11:16
11:19
11:20^{2}
11:23^{3}
11:25^{2}
12:1^{3}
12:3
12:4^{2}
12:8
12:11
12:13^{2}
12:14
12:15
12:18^{2}
12:19
12:21
12:31^{2}
13:4^{2}
13:5^{2}
13:6
13:10
13:11^{2}
13:13
13:14
13:15
13:16^{3}
13:17
13:20
13:22
13:25
13:26
13:28
13:29
13:35
13:39
14:2
14:3
14:5
14:8
14:9
14:10
14:12
14:15^{2}
14:18
14:21
14:27
14:30
14:31^{2}
14:32
15:2
15:3
15:4
15:7^{2}
15:9
15:14
15:15
15:25
15:26
15:27
15:33^{2}
15:34
15:36
16:2
16:3
16:4
16:9
16:10
16:16^{2}
16:18
16:21^{2}
16:22
17:1
17:3
17:6
17:7
17:11
17:15
17:20
17:21
18:2
18:4
18:11
18:12
18:18
18:20
18:21
18:23
18:24
18:26
18:28
18:30
18:32
19:2
19:7^{2}
19:8
19:11
19:14
19:18^{2}
19:22
19:23^{2}
19:25
19:27
19:28
19:29
19:30^{2}
19:33
19:34^{2}
19:35
19:37
19:38
19:39
19:41
20:2
20:3^{2}
20:8
20:14
20:16
20:17^{2}
20:21
20:22^{2}
21:2^{2}
21:3
21:4
21:6^{2}
21:8
21:17
22:1
22:42
22:45^{2}
22:50^{2}
22:51
23:10
23:13
23:16
23:19
24:3^{2}
24:9
24:10
24:11
24:12^{2}
24:13^{2}
24:14
24:17
24:18^{2}
24:21
24:22^{2}
24:23^{2}
24:24
24:25

1 KI

1:2
1:11
1:13^{3}
1:15^{2}
1:16
1:17^{2}
1:27
1:30
1:33
1:42
1:51
1:53
2:5^{2}
2:7
2:9
2:14
2:16
2:17
2:18
2:19^{3}
2:20
2:22
2:26^{2}
2:27
2:28
2:29
2:30
2:31
2:36
2:38
2:39
2:42^{3}
3:2
3:6
3:11
3:12
3:13
3:16
3:26
4:12
4:21
4:27
4:28
4:33
5:1
5:3
5:5^{3}
5:6^{2}
5:7
5:9^{2}
6:12
6:24
7:8
7:9
7:48
8:1
8:2
8:5
8:6
8:8
8:15
8:18^{2}
8:19
8:26
8:28^{2}
8:29
8:33
8:34^{2}
8:40
8:44
8:46
8:47
8:48^{3}
8:52^{4}
8:54
8:56
8:58
8:59
8:63
8:65
8:66
9:2
9:3
9:8
9:13
9:16
9:21
9:24
9:25
10:5
10:12
10:13
11:2^{3}
11:8
11:9
11:11
11:14
11:18
11:22
11:24
11:35
11:36
11:38^{2}
11:40
12:3
12:5
12:7^{2}
12:9
12:10^{5}
12:15^{2}
12:16^{2}
12:19
12:20
12:22
12:23^{2}
12:27^{2}
12:28
12:30
12:32^{2}
12:33
13:1
13:2
13:6
13:7
13:8
13:11
13:12
13:13
13:14
13:15
13:18^{3}
13:20
13:21
13:22
13:26^{3}
13:34
14:5^{2}
14:27
15:19
15:20
15:29
17:1
17:2
17:5
17:8
17:13^{2}
17:18^{2}
17:19
17:20
17:21
17:23
18:1
18:2
18:5^{3}
18:15
18:17
18:19
18:20^{2}
18:21
18:22
18:25
18:30^{3}
18:31
18:40
18:41
18:44
19:2
19:5
19:8
19:9^{2}
19:13
19:15
19:18
19:20
19:21^{2}
20:2
20:5
20:6
20:7
20:8^{2}
20:9
20:10^{2}
20:12
20:13
20:22
20:23
20:25
20:28
20:31
20:34
20:35
20:36
20:39^{2}
20:40
20:42
21:2^{2}
21:3
21:5
21:6^{3}
21:7
21:8
21:11^{2}
21:19^{2}
21:25
22:3
22:4
22:5
22:6
22:8
22:13^{2}
22:14
22:15
22:16
22:18
22:22
22:24
22:26
22:30
22:34
22:38
22:49

2 KI

1:2
1:3
1:5^{2}
1:6^{4}
1:7
1:9^{2}
1:11^{2}
1:12
1:13
1:15^{2}
1:16
2:2^{2}
2:3
2:4
2:5
2:6
2:9
2:10
2:16
2:18^{2}
2:19
2:21
2:22
2:23^{2}
3:3
3:4
3:13^{2}
3:26
4:1^{2}
4:2
4:6^{2}
4:9
4:13^{2}
4:16
4:17
4:19
4:22
4:25
4:26
4:33
4:36
4:38
4:42
5:1
5:3
5:5
5:6
5:7
5:10
5:13
5:14
5:17^{2}
5:19
5:25
5:26
5:27^{2}
6:1
6:2
6:9
6:11
6:15
6:18
6:19
6:21
6:26
6:28^{2}
6:29
6:33
7:4
7:5
7:10
7:12
7:15
7:20
8:1
8:3
8:6
8:8
8:10^{2}
8:12
8:22
9:1
9:5
9:6
9:11^{2}
9:20
10:1
10:6
10:10
10:17
10:18
10:19
10:22
10:23
10:27
10:30^{2}
11:15
12:7
13:4
13:14
13:15^{2}
13:18
13:23^{2}
14:6
14:7
14:13
14:25
15:5
15:12^{2}
16:6
16:9
17:12
17:23
17:32
17:34
17:41
18:4
18:8
18:11
18:14
18:19
18:21
18:22
18:26
18:27
18:32
19:3
19:6
19:9
19:29
20:1^{2}
20:2
20:5
20:8
20:11
20:12
20:13
20:14^{3}
20:16
20:17^{2}
20:19
21:15
22:6
22:8
22:13^{2}
22:14
22:15
22:17
22:20
23:1
23:4
23:5
23:6
23:21
23:25
23:35
24:7
25:2
25:8
25:17
25:24

1 CH

1:19
2:3
2:9
2:19
3:1
3:4
3:5
4:31
4:33
4:39
4:41
4:43
5:1
5:8
5:9
5:11
5:23^{2}
5:26^{2}
6:48
6:61
6:63
6:67
6:71
6:72
7:28
10:9
10:14
11:1
11:2
12:8
12:16
12:17^{3}
12:18
12:40
13:2^{4}
13:5
13:9
14:10
14:14
15:2
15:3
15:12^{2}
16:8
16:9^{2}
16:16
16:18
16:28^{2}
16:29^{2}
16:34
16:40
17:2
17:5
17:7
17:15
17:26
18:3
18:11
19:2
19:3^{2}
19:11
19:14
20:8
21:5
21:8
21:9
21:10
21:11
21:13
21:15
21:17
21:18
21:22
21:23
21:26
22:7
22:8
22:9
22:13
22:25
22:26
22:31^{2}
26:6
28:1
28:3
28:6
29:1
29:5
29:12
29:17
29:18
29:19
29:21^{2}
29:22
29:24

2 CH

1:2
1:5
1:7^{2}
1:8^{2}
1:9
1:12
2:15
3:1
5:2
5:3
5:6
5:7
5:9
6:14
6:17
6:19
6:20
6:21
6:25
6:27
6:30^{2}
6:31
6:34
6:36
6:37
6:38
6:40
7:8
7:10
7:12
7:15
7:21^{2}
8:11
8:12
8:15
8:16
9:12
9:26
9:28
10:4^{2}
10:7
10:9
10:10^{3}
10:15
10:16
10:19
11:3
11:14
11:16
11:23
12:5
13:7
13:10
13:11
13:14
14:7
14:9
14:11
14:13
15:2
15:4
15:11
15:14
15:19
16:4
16:7
17:3
17:16
18:3
18:4
18:5
18:7^{2}
18:14
18:17
18:20
18:23
18:29
19:4
20:9
20:15
20:21
20:24
20:26
20:28
20:33
21:10
23:3
23:14
24:5
24:6
24:11
24:17
24:19
24:20
24:23
25:12
25:13
25:14
25:15^{2}
25:16^{2}
26:18^{2}
26:21
27:5
28:9^{2}
28:10
28:13
28:16
28:20
28:21
28:23
28:35
29:7
29:11
29:30
29:31
30:1
30:5
30:6
30:8
30:9^{2}
30:10
30:17
30:21
30:22
30:27
31:6
31:16
32:9^{2}
32:13
32:18
32:23
32:24^{2}
32:25
32:31
33:2
33:13
33:17
33:18
33:22
34:4
34:6
34:25
34:26
35:1
35:3^{2}
35:8^{2}
35:9
35:12
35:22
36:13

EZR

1:8
1:11
2:1^{3}
2:69
3:3
3:5
3:6
3:7^{2}
3:8^{2}
3:11
4:1
4:2^{2}
4:3^{3}
4:6
4:7
4:11^{2}
4:12^{2}
4:13
4:15
4:17^{2}
4:18
4:20
4:23
4:24
5:1^{2}
5:3
5:4
5:6
5:7^{2}
5:8
5:9
5:12
5:14
5:15
6:5^{2}
6:8
6:10
6:21
6:22
7:7
7:11
7:12
7:15
7:22
7:26
7:28
8:17^{3}
8:22
8:25
8:26
8:28^{3}
8:30
8:31
8:35^{2}
8:36
9:4
9:5
9:6
9:7
9:9
9:11
9:12^{2}
10:1
10:2
10:4
10:7^{2}
10:9
10:10
10:11

NE

1:3
1:9^{3}
2:1
2:2
2:3
2:4
2:5^{3}
2:6
2:7
2:8
2:17
2:18
2:20
3:1^{2}
3:2
3:4^{3}
3:5
3:7^{2}
3:8^{3}
3:9
3:10^{2}

3:18
3:24[2]
4:1[2]
4:6
4:7
4:11
4:16
4:18
4:20
4:22
4:26
4:27
4:34[2]
4:35
4:36[4]
5:13
5:15
5:17
6:2
6:6
6:15[2]
6:16
6:19
6:20
6:21
6:25[2]
6:26
7:5
7:10
7:16
7:26
8:1[3]
8:6
8:7
8:13
8:14[2]
8:17
9:3
9:4
9:6
9:7[3]
9:25
9:26
10:1
10:11[4]
10:12
10:15
10:16
10:19[2]
10:20
11:18
12:7

HO

1:1
1:2
1:4
1:6
1:10[2]
2:1
2:14
2:19[2]
2:20
2:23
3:1
3:3
4:12
4:15
5:4
5:12
5:14
6:3[2]
6:4[2]
7:7
7:13[2]
7:14
8:2
8:11
9:4[2]
9:10
9:17
10:1
10:6
10:15
11:2
11:4
12:4
12:14
13:7
14:1
14:2
14:5

JOE

1:14
1:20
2:13
2:14
2:19
3:3

AM

1:5
2:7
3:7
4:6
4:8[2]
4:9
4:10[2]
4:11
4:12[2]
4:13
5:4
5:15
5:18
5:25
6:2
6:10
6:14
7:1
7:4
7:8
7:12
7:15[2]
8:1
8:2
9:7

OB

15
20

JON

1:1
1:3[2]
1:5
1:6
1:8
1:9
1:10
1:11[3]
1:12[2]
1:14
1:16
2:1
2:2
2:7
2:9
2:10
3:1
3:2[2]
3:3
3:6
3:8
3:10
4:2[2]
4:8
4:9

MIC

1:9[2]
1:12
1:15[2]
2:11
3:4
3:6[2]
3:8
4:1
4:13[2]
5:2
5:3
5:4
6:3
6:5
6:9
7:7
7:8
7:10
7:15
7:18
7:20

NA

3:13

HAB

1:2
1:10
1:11
1:16[2]
2:1
2:5[2]
2:7
2:15[2]
2:16
2:19
3:13
3:16

ZEP

1:1
2:5
2:11

HAG

1:1
1:9
1:13
2:20

ZEC

1:1
1:3[3]
1:4[2]
1:6
1:7
1:9
1:14
1:19
2:2
2:4
2:5
2:8
2:11
3:2
3:4[2]
3:6
4:2
4:5
4:6[2]
4:7
4:8
4:9
4:11
4:12
5:2
5:3
5:5
5:11
6:4
6:5
6:8
6:9
6:12
6:15
7:1
7:2
7:4
7:5[2]
7:8
8:3
8:11
8:15
8:18
9:9
9:10
9:12
11:7
11:12
11:13[2]
11:15[2]
12:2
13:3
13:6
14:5
14:10[3]
14:17
14:20
14:21

MAL

1:6
1:8
1:9
1:11[2]
1:14
2:2
2:4
2:12
3:3
3:4
3:7[2]
4:2
4:4

MT

1:17
1:20[2]
1:24
2:5
2:11
3:7
3:9[2]
3:10
3:11
3:13
3:15
3:16
4:6
4:7
4:9
4:10
4:11
4:19
4:24
5:1
5:15
5:18
5:20
5:22
5:26
5:28
5:32
5:33
5:34
5:39
5:44
6:2
6:5
6:8
6:16[2]
6:18[2]
6:25
6:27
6:29
6:33
6:34
7:6
7:7
7:11
7:14
7:21
7:23
7:24
7:26
8:4[2]
8:5
8:7
8:10
8:11
8:13[2]
8:15
8:16
8:18
8:19
8:20
8:21
8:22
8:26
8:32
9:2
9:6
9:8
9:9
9:11
9:12
9:15
9:16
9:18
9:24
9:28[2]
9:29
9:37
10:1
10:15
10:23
10:42[2]
11:3
11:4
11:7
11:9
11:11
11:16[2]
11:17
11:21[2]
11:22
11:23
11:24
11:25
11:27
11:28
11:29
12:2
12:3
12:6
12:11
12:20
12:22
12:25
12:28
12:31[3]
12:36
12:39
12:45
12:47
12:48
13:2
13:3
13:10[2]
13:11[2]
13:17
13:24[2]
13:27
13:28[2]
13:31
13:33[2]
13:34[2]
13:36[2]
13:37
13:44
13:45
13:47
13:51[2]
13:52[3]
13:57
14:2
14:4
14:16
14:17
14:22
14:25
14:27
14:28
14:31
14:35
15:3
15:8
15:10
15:12
15:15[2]
15:22
15:24
15:28[2]
15:29
15:30
15:32
15:33
15:34
16:2
16:4
16:8
16:15
16:17[2]
16:18
16:19
16:21[2]
16:22
16:23[2]
16:24
16:28
17:3
17:4
17:11[2]
17:12[2]
17:13
17:20[4]
17:22
17:26[2]
17:27
18:1
18:2
18:3
18:7
18:10
18:13
18:17[2]
18:18
18:19
18:22[2]
18:23
18:24
18:31
18:32
18:34
18:35
19:3[2]
19:4
19:7
19:8
19:9
19:10
19:11
19:13
19:14
19:16
19:17
19:18
19:20
19:21
19:23[3]
19:24
19:26
19:27
19:28[2]
20:1
20:4
20:6
20:7[2]
20:8[2]
20:12
20:14[2]
20:17
20:18[2]
20:21[2]
20:22
20:23
20:25
20:28
20:32
20:33
21:1[2]
21:2[2]
21:3
21:5
21:13
21:16[2]
21:19
21:21[3]
21:23
21:24
21:25
21:27
21:31[3]
21:32
21:36
21:37
21:40
21:41[2]
21:42
21:43
22:1
22:2
22:4
22:12
22:16
22:17
22:19
22:20
22:21[4]
22:24
22:25
22:26
22:29
22:31
22:37
22:39
22:42
22:43
22:44
23:13
23:14
23:15
23:16
23:23
23:25
23:27[2]
23:28
23:29
23:31
23:34
23:35
23:36
23:37
23:38
23:39
24:2
24:3
24:4
24:13
24:14
24:19
24:23
24:26
24:27
24:34
24:47
25:1
25:8
25:12
25:14
25:15
25:20
25:21
25:22
25:23
25:26
25:28
25:29
25:34
25:36
25:39
25:40[4]
25:41
25:44
25:45
26:1
26:3
26:7
26:10
26:13
26:14
26:15[2]
26:17
26:18
26:21
26:22
26:24
26:25
26:29
26:31
26:33
26:34[2]
26:35
26:36[2]
26:38[2]
26:40[2]
26:45
26:50
26:52
26:58
26:62
26:63
26:64[2]
26:68
26:69
26:71
26:73
26:75
27:8
27:11
27:13
27:15
27:17[2]
27:19
27:21[2]
27:22[2]
27:26
27:27
27:33
27:45
27:53
27:55
27:62
27:64
27:65
28:5
28:10
28:11
28:12
28:18[2]
28:20

MK

1:5
1:13
1:17
1:31
1:32
1:37
1:38
1:40
1:41
1:44[2]
2:2
2:3
2:4
2:5
2:8
2:11
2:13
2:14
2:16
2:17
2:18
2:19
2:24
2:25
2:27
3:3
3:4
3:5
3:8
3:13[2]
3:23[2]
3:28[2]
3:31
3:32
4:1
4:2
4:9
4:11[3]
4:13
4:21
4:24[2]
4:33
4:34
4:35[2]
4:38
4:39
4:40
5:1
5:8
5:11
5:19
5:21[3]
5:31
5:34
5:36
5:39
5:41[2]
6:2
6:4
6:7
6:10
6:11
6:18
6:22
6:23[2]
6:24
6:25
6:30
6:31
6:33
6:35
6:37[2]
6:38
6:45
6:48[2]
6:50
6:51
7:1
7:6
7:9
7:14[3]
7:18
7:27[2]
7:28
7:29
7:31
7:32
7:34
8:1[2]
8:12[2]
8:17
8:19
8:21
8:22
8:27
8:29[2]
8:34[2]
9:1
9:4
9:13[2]
9:17
9:19
9:21
9:23
9:25
9:29
9:31
9:35
9:36
9:41
10:1
10:3
10:5
10:11
10:14[2]
10:15
10:18
10:20
10:21
10:23
10:24
10:28
10:29
10:32
10:33[2]
10:35
10:36
10:37[2]
10:38
10:39[2]
10:42
10:45
10:49
10:51[3]
10:52
11:1
11:2
11:3
11:5
11:6
11:11
11:14
11:17
11:21
11:22
11:23[2]
11:24
11:28
11:29
11:33[2]
12:1
12:4
12:6
12:9
12:13
12:14
12:15
12:16[2]
12:17
12:18
12:19[2]
12:24
12:26
12:32
12:34
12:38
12:43[3]
13:1
13:2
13:13
13:19
13:30
13:37[2]
14:9
14:10[2]
14:12
14:13
14:16
14:18
14:19
14:20
14:24
14:25
14:27
14:29
14:30[2]
14:34[2]
14:36
14:37
14:41
14:48
14:61
14:65
14:72
15:2
15:6
15:8
15:9
15:11
15:12[2]
15:14
15:15
15:22
15:41[2]
15:43
15:44
15:46
16:2
16:6
16:7
16:12
16:13
16:14
16:15
16:19

LU

1:2
1:3
1:11
1:13
1:18
1:19[2]
1:22[2]
1:26
1:28
1:30
1:32
1:34
1:35
1:38
1:61
1:74
1:77
1:80
2:4
2:10
2:11
2:12
2:15[2]
2:20
2:26
2:34
2:38
2:48
2:49
2:50
2:51
3:2
3:8[2]
3:9
3:11
3:12
3:13
3:14
3:16
3:18
4:3
4:5
4:6[2]
4:8
4:9
4:12
4:17
4:21
4:23[2]
4:24
4:26[3]
4:29
4:31
4:40
4:42
4:43
5:4
5:5
5:7
5:10
5:14
5:20
5:22
5:24[2]
5:27
5:31
5:33
5:34
5:36
6:2
6:5
6:9
6:10
6:13
6:23
6:24
6:25[2]
6:26
6:27
6:29
6:35
6:38
6:39
7:2
7:3
7:6
7:7
7:8
7:9[2]
7:13
7:14
7:19
7:20[2]
7:21
7:22
7:24
7:26
7:28
7:32[2]
7:40[2]
7:43
7:44
7:47
7:48
8:3
8:10
8:21
8:22[2]
8:25
8:39[2]
8:47
8:48
9:3
9:11
9:12
9:13
9:20
9:33
9:43
9:48
9:50
9:57
9:58
9:59
9:60
9:62
10:2
10:9[2]
10:11
10:12
10:13[2]
10:17
10:18
10:19
10:20
10:21[2]
10:23
10:26
10:28
10:29
10:35
10:36
10:37
10:41
11:1
11:2
11:5[3]
11:8
11:9[2]
11:13
11:17
11:24
11:27
11:30
11:39
11:41
11:42
11:43
11:44
11:45
11:46
11:47
11:51[2]
11:52
11:53
12:1
12:4
12:5
12:8
12:10
12:11[2]
12:13
12:14
12:15
12:16
12:20
12:22[2]
12:27
12:31
12:36[2]
12:37
12:41[2]
12:44
12:48
13:2
13:7
13:8
13:12
13:14
13:18[2]
13:23[2]
13:24
13:25[2]
13:31
13:32
13:34
13:35[2]
14:3
14:7
14:10
14:14
14:16
14:18
14:23
14:25
15:1
15:3
15:7
15:10
15:15
15:16
15:18
15:21
15:27
15:31
16:1[2]
16:2
16:5[3]
16:6
16:7
16:9
16:15
16:28
16:29
16:30
16:31
17:1[2]
17:5
17:6
17:7
17:8
17:14[2]
17:19
17:22
17:24
17:37[2]
18:1
18:3
18:7
18:9
18:13
18:15
18:16[2]
18:17
18:19
18:22[2]
18:29[2]
18:31[2]
18:32
18:35
18:40
18:41
18:42
18:43
19:5
19:8
19:9
19:13
19:15
19:17
19:22
19:24
19:25
19:26[2]
19:31
19:32
19:33
19:39
19:40
19:42
19:46
20:2
20:3
20:8
20:15
20:20
20:22
20:23
20:25[3]
20:28[2]
20:34
20:36
20:38
20:41
20:42
20:45
21:3
21:4
21:10
21:23
21:32
22:4
22:6
22:9
22:10
22:11[2]
22:13
22:15
22:16
22:18
22:19
22:22
22:25
22:29[2]
22:33
22:35
22:36
22:37
22:38
22:40
22:43
22:46
22:47
22:49
22:52
22:61
22:67
22:70
23:1
23:7
23:14[2]
23:15
23:17
23:18
23:22
23:25
23:28
23:42
23:43[2]
23:52
24:1[2]
24:5
24:6
24:9
24:10
24:12
24:17
24:18
24:19[2]
24:25
24:27
24:28
24:36[2]
24:38
24:41
24:44[2]
24:46

JOH

1:11
1:22[2]
1:25
1:29
1:33
1:38[2]
1:39
1:41
1:43
1:45
1:46[2]
1:48[2]
1:49
1:50[2]
1:51[2]
2:3
2:4
2:5[2]
2:7
2:8[2]
2:10
2:16
2:18[2]
2:19
2:22
2:24
3:2
3:3[2]
3:4
3:5
3:7
3:9
3:10
3:11
3:26[2]
3:34
4:7
4:8
4:9
4:10
4:11
4:13
4:15
4:16
4:17
4:19
4:21
4:25
4:26[2]
4:30
4:32
4:34
4:35
4:36
4:40
4:42
4:45
4:47
4:48
4:49
4:50[2]
4:52
4:53
5:6
5:8
5:10
5:11
5:12
5:14[2]
5:19[2]
5:22
5:24[2]
5:25
5:29[2]
5:33[2]
6:5[2]
6:8
6:12
6:13
6:16
6:19
6:20
6:23
6:25
6:26
6:27[2]
6:28
6:29
6:30
6:32[2]
6:33
6:34
6:35
6:36
6:43
6:45
6:47
6:53[2]
6:61
6:63
6:65[3]
6:67
7:3
7:6
7:8[2]
7:9
7:10[2]
7:21
7:22
7:26
7:33[2]
7:35
7:37
7:45
7:50
7:52
7:53
8:1
8:2
8:3
8:4
8:7
8:9
8:10
8:11
8:12
8:13
8:14
8:19
8:21
8:23
8:24
8:25[3]
8:28
8:34
8:39[2]
8:42
8:48
8:51
8:52
8:55
8:57
8:58[2]
9:7
9:10
9:11
9:12
9:15
9:17
9:24
9:29
9:30
9:34
9:35
9:37
9:40
9:41
10:1
10:6[2]
10:7[2]
10:24
10:26
10:28
10:35
10:41
11:3
11:4
11:8
11:11
11:14
11:15
11:16
11:18
11:21
11:23
11:24
11:25
11:27
11:29
11:31
11:32
11:34
11:39
11:40[2]
11:44
11:49
11:54
12:16
12:24
12:25
12:27
12:32
12:35
12:50
13:1[2]
13:6
13:7
13:8
13:9
13:12
13:16
13:20
13:21
13:25
13:27
13:28
13:29
13:33
13:34
13:36
13:37
13:38
14:3
14:5
14:6[2]
14:8
14:9
14:10
14:12[2]
14:22[3]
14:23[2]
14:25
14:26
14:27[2]
14:28[3]
15:3
15:7
15:11
15:15
15:20
15:21
15:22
15:26
16:1
16:3
16:4
16:6
16:7[2]
16:12
16:14
16:15
16:17
16:19
16:10
16:23
16:25
16:26
16:29
16:33
17:6
17:8
17:26
18:4
18:5
18:6
18:11
18:15
18:16[2]
18:17
18:21
18:24
18:25
18:28
18:29
18:30[2]
18:31[2]
18:33
18:35
18:37[2]
18:38[3]
18:39[2]
19:4
19:5
19:6
19:9
19:10[2]
19:11
19:14
19:15
19:16
19:26
19:27
20:1
20:2
20:10
20:13[2]
20:15[2]
20:16[2]
20:17[3]
20:18
20:19[2]
20:20
20:21
20:22
20:23
20:25[2]
20:26
20:28
20:29
21:3[2]
21:5
21:6
21:7[2]
21:10
21:12
21:15[2]
21:16[2]
21:17[4]
21:18
21:19
21:22
21:23

AC

1:2
1:7
1:8[2]
1:12
1:19

1:22 2:3 2:14^{2} 2:29^{2} 2:34 2:37 2:38 2:39 2:41 3:5 3:10 3:11 3:12 3:14 3:20 3:22^{4} 3:25 3:26 4:1 4:3 4:8 4:10 4:17 4:19^{3} 4:23 4:29 4:35 5:4^{2} 5:8 5:9 5:16 5:35 5:38 6:2 7:2 7:3 7:13 7:26 7:31 7:37^{3} 7:38 7:40 7:41 7:44 7:46 8:1 8:5 8:6 8:14 8:20

8:26^{3} 8:29 8:35 8:36 9:1 9:2 9:4 9:6 9:11 9:15^{2} 9:17 9:21 9:27 9:34 9:38 10:3 10:4 10:7 10:8 10:9 10:11 10:15 10:19 10:21 10:28^{2} 10:29 10:32 10:36 10:41 10:42 11:4 11:7 11:11^{2} 11:13 11:17 11:18 11:19 11:20 11:21 11:22 11:23 11:24 11:26 11:27 11:29 12:5 12:8^{2} 12:10^{2} 12:15 12:17^{3}

12:21 13:4 13:6 13:15 13:20 13:21 13:22 13:23 13:31 13:32^{2} 13:33 13:36 13:38^{2} 13:41 13:47 13:51 14:3 14:6^{2} 14:13 14:15^{2} 14:18 14:27 15:2 15:3 15:7 15:8 15:13 15:18 15:20 15:23 15:25^{2} 15:33 15:36 15:39 15:40 16:10 16:13 16:14 16:17 16:19 16:25 16:32 16:37 16:38 17:2 17:3 17:5 17:6 17:10 17:15^{2}

17:18 17:19 17:23 17:29 17:31 17:34 18:2 18:6^{2} 18:14 18:21 18:26^{2} 19:2^{2} 19:3^{3} 19:4 19:12 19:22 19:24 19:30 19:31 19:33 20:1 20:6 20:7 20:13 20:18 20:20 20:22 20:24 20:27 20:28 20:34 20:38 21:1^{3} 21:2 21:8 21:11 21:18 21:20 21:31 21:32 21:37^{2} 21:39 21:40^{2} 22:1 22:4 22:5^{2} 22:6 22:7^{2} 22:8 22:10

22:13^{2} 22:15 22:18 22:20 22:21^{2} 22:22 22:25 22:27 23:3 23:15^{2} 23:17^{2} 23:18^{2} 23:21 23:23 23:24 23:26 24:2 24:4 24:8 24:10^{2} 24:14 24:23 25:6 25:11^{2} 25:12^{2} 25:13 25:14 25:21 25:22 25:26 26:1 26:6 26:7 26:11 26:14 26:16^{2} 26:17 26:18 26:19 26:20 26:22 26:23 26:28 26:32^{2} 27:1 27:3 27:8 27:10 27:21 27:40

28:17 28:19 28:21 28:25 28:26 28:28^{2} 28:30

RO

1:1 1:10 1:11 1:13 1:16 1:19 1:26 2:5 2:8 2:14 3:2 3:7 3:22 4:3 4:6 4:11 5:4 5:15 5:16 5:18 5:21^{3} 6:10^{2} 6:11^{2} 6:13^{3} 6:16^{2} 6:19^{2} 6:22 7:4 7:5 7:10 7:13 7:16 9:12 9:17 9:19 9:21^{2} 9:23 9:26 9:29 10:3 10:10^{2} 10:12 10:18 10:20 10:21 11:4 11:8 11:9 11:11 11:27 11:35 12:1 12:3 12:19 13:1 14:6 14:8^{2} 15:8 15:9 15:15 15:19 15:23 15:25^{2} 15:27 15:29 15:32 16:1 16:4 16:5 16:19^{2}

1 CO

1:2 1:3 1:8 1:9 1:11 1:18 1:23^{2} 1:24 1:30 2:1 2:7 2:10 2:14 3:1^{4} 3:10 4:9 4:11 4:13 4:17 4:21 5:5 5:9 5:11 6:12 6:17 7:1 7:3 7:10 7:27 8:1 8:4 8:7 9:2 9:11 9:15 9:16 9:17 9:19 9:20 10:2 10:11 10:28^{2} 11:13 11:14 11:17 11:23 11:34 12:2 12:21 12:31 14:2 14:3 14:6 14:11^{2} 14:21 14:26 14:34 14:36 14:37 15:1^{2} 15:2 15:3 15:6 15:28^{2} 16:3 16:5 16:9 16:11 16:12 16:16

2 CO

1:1 1:13 1:15 1:16 1:20 1:23 2:3 2:4^{2} 2:12 2:14 2:15 2:16^{2} 3:15 4:4 4:11 5:5 5:11 5:12 5:15^{2} 5:19^{3} 6:11 6:13 6:18 7:12^{2} 8:2 8:5 8:17 9:5 9:12 9:13^{3} 9:15 10:13 10:14 11:9 12:9 12:17 12:19 12:20

GA

1:2 1:6 1:8 1:9 1:17 1:20 1:22 2:2 2:7^{2} 2:9^{3} 2:14 2:19 3:8 3:23 3:24 4:8 4:13 5:2 5:4 5:13 6:6 6:10^{2} 6:11 6:14^{2} 6:*sub.*

EPH

1:5 1:9 1:14 1:15 1:17 2:10 2:16 2:18 2:21 3:3 3:5 3:7 3:8 3:10 3:14 3:20 3:21 4:7 4:8 4:13^{2} 4:16 4:19 4:29 4:30 5:10 5:20 5:22^{2} 5:24 5:31 6:5 6:9 6:13 6:19 6:22 6:*sub.*

PHP

1:2 1:11 1:12^{2} 1:29 2:8 2:19 2:27 2:30 3:10 3:11 3:13 3:15 3:21^{2} 4:5 4:6 4:16 4:20

COL

1:2 1:6 1:8 1:10 1:11 1:12 1:20 2:2 3:18 3:20 3:23 4:3 4:7 4:8 4:9 4:10 4:11^{2}

1 TH

1:1^{2} 1:5 1:9 2:1 2:2 2:8^{2} 2:9^{2} 2:12 2:18 3:6 3:11 4:7^{2} 4:8 4:9 4:15^{2} 5:1 5:15 5:23 5:27 5:*sub.*

2 TH

1:1 1:2 2:1 3:9

1 TI

1:2 1:6 1:17 1:18 1:20 2:4 3:14^{2} 3:16 4:7 4:8 4:16^{2} 6:16

2 TI

1:12 1:14 1:16 1:18^{2} 2:9 2:15 2:16 2:21^{2} 2:24 3:9 3:11 3:15 3:17 4:4 4:8 4:9 4:10^{2} 4:18 4:*sub.*

TIT

1:3 1:15^{2} 1:16 2:9 2:14 3:2 3:5 3:8 3:12 3:13

PHM

1 13 16 19 21 22

HEB

1:1 1:2 1:5 1:8 2:3 2:5 2:10 2:12 2:17 3:6 3:14 4:2^{2} 4:13 4:16 5:4 5:5 5:7 5:9 6:1 6:6 6:7 6:8 6:11 6:17 7:3 7:4 7:19 7:21 7:25 8:5 9:20 9:27 9:28^{2} 10:24 10:29 10:30 10:39 11:4 11:26 12:2 12:4 12:5^{2} 12:9 12:11 12:18^{2} 12:22^{2} 13:6 13:7 13:13 13:22

JAS

1:23 2:2 2:3 2:16 2:23 4:6 5:7

1 PE

1:2^{2} 1:3 1:5 1:7 1:10 1:12^{5} 1:13 1:22 1:25 2:4 2:7^{2} 2:14^{2} 2:24 2:25 3:5 3:7^{2} 3:12 3:19 3:22 4:7 4:12 4:19 5:5 5:10 5:12

2 PE

1:2 1:3^{2} 1:4 1:11 1:16 1:19 2:4 2:9 2:21 2:22 3:1 3:7 3:12 3:15^{2} 3:16

1 JO

1:2^{2} 1:3 1:4 1:5 2:1 2:7 2:8 2:12 2:13^{3} 2:14^{2} 2:21 2:26 3:14 5:13 5:16^{3} 5:17

2 JO

1 5 10 12^{2}

2 JO

1 9 13

JUDE

2 3^{3} 6 11 21 24

RE

1:1^{3} 1:4 1:5 1:6 1:11^{8} 1:13 1:15 1:17 2:1 2:5 2:7 2:8 2:10 2:11 2:14 2:16 2:17 2:18^{2} 2:20 2:23 2:24^{2} 2:26 2:29 3:1 3:6 3:13 3:14 3:22 4:3 4:6 5:5 5:10 5:13^{2} 6:2 6:4 6:8 6:11^{2} 6:13 7:10 7:12 7:13 7:14 7:17 8:3 9:1 9:3 9:7^{2} 9:10 9:19 10:4 10:8 10:9^{3} 10:11 11:1 11:2 11:3 11:12 11:18 12:5 12:11 12:12 12:13 13:2 13:4^{2} 13:5^{2} 13:7 13:15 14:4 14:6 14:13 14:14 14:20 15:7 16:8 16:14 16:19 17:1^{2} 17:7 17:13 17:15 17:17 18:5 18:6 18:18 19:1 19:9^{3} 19:10 19:17 20:4 21:5 21:6^{2} 21:9 21:11 21:18 22:6^{2} 22:9 22:10 22:16 22:18^{2}

UP

4605,*507*

GE

2:6 2:21 4:8 7:11 7:17 8:7 8:13 13:1 13:10 13:14 14:22 17:22 18:2 18:16 19:1 19:2 19:14 19:27 19:28 19:30 20:18 21:14 21:16 21:18 21:32 22:3^{2} 22:4 22:13^{2} 22:19 23:3 23:7 24:16 24:54 24:63 24:65 25:8 25:17 25:34 26:23 26:31 27:38 28:12 28:18^{2} 29:11 31:10 31:12 31:17 31:21 31:35 31:45 31:55 32:22 33:1 33:5 35:1 35:3 35:13 35:14 35:29 37:25 37:28 37:35 38:8 38:12 38:13 39:15 39:16 39:18 40:13 40:19 40:20 41:2 41:3 41:4 41:5 41:6 41:18 41:19 41:20 41:21 41:22 41:23 41:27 41:34 41:35 41:44 41:48^{3} 43:2 43:15 43:29 44:4 44:17 44:24 44:30 44:33 44:34 45:9 45:25 46:4 46:5 46:29 46:31 47:14 48:17 49:4^{2} 49:9^{2} 49:33^{2} 50:5 50:6 50:7^{2} 50:9 50:14 50:23 50:25

EX

1:8 1:10 2:17 2:23 3:8 3:17 7:12 7:20 8:3 8:4 8:5 8:6 8:7 8:20 9:10 9:13 9:16 9:32 10:12 10:14 12:6 12:30 12:31 12:34 12:38 13:18 13:19 14:10 14:16 15:7 16:13 16:14 16:23 16:24 16:33 16:34 17:3 17:10 17:11 17:12 19:3 19:12 19:13 19:20^{2} 19:23 19:24^{2} 20:25 20:26 22:2 24:1 24:2 24:4 24:9 24:12 24:13^{2} 24:15 24:18 26:15 26:30 26:33 29:27 32:1^{2} 32:4 32:6^{2} 32:8 32:23 32:30 33:1^{2} 33:3 33:5 33:8 33:10 33:12 33:15 34:2 34:3 34:4^{2} 34:24 35:21 35:26 36:2 36:20 40:2 40:8^{2} 40:17 40:18^{3} 40:21 40:28 40:33^{2} 40:36 40:37^{2}

LE

6:10 9:22 11:45 13:4 13:5 13:11 13:21 13:26 13:31 13:33 13:37 13:42 13:50 13:54 14:38 14:46 19:32 20:16 22:30 26:1^{2} 30:38

NU

1:51 6:26 7:1 9:15 9:17 9:21^{2} 9:22 10:11 10:21 10:35 11:32 13:17^{2} 13:21 13:30 13:31^{2} 13:32^{2} 14:1 14:13 14:36 14:37 14:40^{3} 14:42 14:44 15:19 15:20 16:2 16:3 16:12 16:13 16:14 16:24 16:25 16:27 16:30 16:32 16:34 16:37 16:45 17:4 17:7 19:9^{2} 20:4 20:5 20:11 20:25 20:27 21:3 21:5 21:17 21:33 22:4^{2} 22:13 22:14 22:20 22:21 22:41 23:7 23:18^{2} 23:24^{2} 24:2 24:3 24:8 24:9 24:15 24:20 24:21 24:23 24:25 25:4 25:7 26:10 27:12 31:52 32:9 32:11 32:14 33:38

DE

1:21 1:22 1:24 1:26 1:28^{2} 1:41^{2} 1:42 1:43 2:13 2:24 3:1 3:27^{2} 4:19 5:5 6:7 8:14 9:1 9:9 9:23 10:1 10:3 11:6 11:17 11:18 11:19 14:25 14:28 16:22 17:8 17:20 18:15 18:18 19:11 19:15 19:16 20:1 22:4 22:14 22:19 23:14 24:5 25:7^{2} 25:9 27:2 27:4 27:5 28:7 28:33 28:43 29:22 30:12 31:5 31:16 32:11 32:17 32:30 32:34^{2} 32:36 32:38 32:40 32:49 32:50 33:2 34:1

JOS

2:6 2:8 2:10 3:6^{2} 3:16 4:5 4:8 4:9 4:16 4:17 4:18^{2} 4:19 4:23^{2} 5:1 5:7 6:1 6:5 6:6 6:12 6:13 6:20 6:26^{2} 7:2^{2} 7:3^{2} 7:4 7:10 7:13 7:16 8:1 8:3 8:7 8:10^{2} 8:11 8:14 8:20 8:31 9:4 10:4 10:5 10:6 10:9 10:10 10:12 10:33 10:36 11:6 11:17 12:7 12:8 15:3^{2} 15:6^{2} 15:7^{2} 15:8^{2} 15:15 16:1 17:5 18:1 18:11 18:12^{2} 18:17 19:10 19:11 19:12^{2} 19:47 20:5 22:12 22:33 24:17 24:26 24:32

JG

1:1 1:2 1:3 1:4 1:16 1:22 1:36 2:1^{2} 2:4 2:16 2:18 3:9 3:15 4:5 4:10^{2} 4:12 4:14 6:3^{2} 6:5 6:8 6:13 6:21 6:35 6:38 7:1 8:8 8:11 8:13 8:20 8:28 9:7 9:18 9:32 9:33 9:34 9:35 9:43 9:48 9:51 11:2 11:13 11:16 11:31 11:37 12:3 13:20 14:2 14:19 15:5 15:6 15:9 15:10^{2} 15:11^{4} 15:13 16:3 16:5 16:8 16:18^{2} 16:29 16:31 18:9 18:12 18:17 18:30 18:31 19:5 19:7 19:9 19:10 19:17 19:27 19:28^{3} 19:30 20:3 20:9 20:18^{3} 20:19 20:23^{3} 20:26 20:28 20:30 20:31 20:33 20:38 20:40^{2} 21:2 21:5^{2} 21:8 21:19

RU

1:9 1:14 2:15 2:18 3:14 4:1 4:5 4:10

1 SA

1:3 1:5 1:6 1:7 1:9 1:19 1:21 1:22^{2} 1:24 2:6 2:7 2:8^{2} 2:14

2:19 2:35 5:12 6:9 6:10 6:13 6:20 6:21 7:1 7:7 7:10 8:8 9:11 9:13[2] 9:14[2] 9:19 9:24 9:26 10:3 10:18 10:25 11:1 11:4 12:6 13:5 13:15 14:9 14:10[2] 14:12[2] 14:13 14:21 14:46 15:2 15:6 15:11 15:12 15:34 16:13 17:20 17:23 17:25[2] 19:15 20:38 21:12 22:8 23:11 23:12 23:19 23:29 24:7 24:16 24:22 25:5 25:13 25:35 26:19 27:8 28:8 28:11[2] 28:14 28:15 28:25 29:9 29:10[2] 29:11[2] 30:4

2 SA

2:1[3] 2:2 2:3 2:22 2:27 2:32 3:10 3:32 4:4 4:12 5:8 5:17 5:19[2] 5:22 5:23 6:2 6:12 6:15 7:6 7:12 12:3 12:11 12:17 13:29 13:34 13:36 14:14 15:2 15:20 15:24 15:30[4] 17:16 17:21 18:9 18:18 18:24[2] 18:28[2] 18:29 18:31 18:33 19:34 20:2 20:3 20:15 20:19[2] 20:20 20:21 21:6 21:8 21:13 22:9 22:49 23:1 23:8 23:18 24:9 24:11 24:18 24:19 24:22

1 KI

1:35 1:40 1:45 1:49 2:19 2:33 3:15 6:8 7:21[2] 8:1 8:3 8:4[2] 8:20 8:35 8:54 9:16 9:24 10:5 10:29 11:14 11:15 11:23 11:26 11:27 12:8 12:10 12:18 12:24 12:27 12:28[2] 13:4 13:29 14:1 14:10 14:15 14:16 14:25 15:4 15:17 16:17 16:32 16:34 17:7 17:19 18:38 18:41 18:42[2] 18:43[2] 18:44 18:46 20:1 20:22 20:26 20:33 21:16 21:21 21:25 22:6 22:12 22:20 22:29 22:35 22:38

2 KI

1:3 1:4 1:6[2] 1:7 1:9 1:13 1:14 1:16 2:1 2:11 2:13 2:16 2:23[4] 3:7 3:8 3:21 3:22 3:24 4:21 4:29 4:34 4:35 4:36 4:37 6:7 6:24 7:5 8:12 9:1 9:2 9:8 9:25 9:27 9:32 10:1 12:10[2] 12:17[2] 13:21 14:10 14:11 14:26 15:4 15:16 16:5 16:7[2] 16:9 17:3 17:4 17:5[2] 17:7 17:10 17:36 18:9 18:13 18:17[2] 18:25[2] 19:4 19:14 19:22 19:23 19:24 19:26 19:28 20:5 20:6 20:8 20:17 21:3[2] 22:4 23:2 23:9 23:29 24:1 24:10 25:4 25:6 25:27

1 CH

5:2 5:4 5:5 11:6 11:11 11:20 13:6[2] 14:2 14:8 14:10[2] 14:11 14:14 15:3 15:12 15:14 15:16 15:25 15:28 17:5 17:11 21:1 21:16 21:18[2] 21:19 21:27 25:5 26:16 28:2

2 CH

1:4 1:6 1:17 2:16 3:17 5:2 5:4 5:5[2] 5:13 6:10 6:26 7:13 7:20 8:11 9:4 10:8 10:10 10:18 11:4 12:2 12:9 13:4 13:6 16:1 17:6 18:2 18:5 18:11 18:14 18:19 18:28 18:34 20:16 20:19 20:23 21:4 21:9 21:16 21:17 24:7 24:23 25:14 25:19 25:21 26:16 26:19 28:9 28:12 28:15 28:24 29:7 29:20 30:7 30:27 32:5[2] 32:25 33:3 33:14 33:19 34:30 35:20 36:6 36:15 36:22 36:23

EZR

1:1 1:3 1:5[2] 1:11[2] 2:1 2:59 2:63 2:68 3:2 4:2 4:12[2] 4:13 4:16 4:23 5:2 5:3 5:9 5:11 6:1 6:11 7:6 7:7 7:9 7:13 7:28 8:1 9:5 9:6[2] 9:9 10:6 10:10

NE

2:1 2:15 2:17 2:18 3:1 3:3 3:6 3:13 3:14 3:15 3:19 3:31 3:32 4:3 4:7 4:14 5:2 6:1 6:10 7:1 7:5 7:6 7:61 7:65 8:5 8:6 9:3 9:4 9:5 9:18 10:38 12:1 12:31 12:37[2]

ES

2:7 2:20 5:9 7:7

JOB

1:5 1:7 1:16 2:2 2:12[2] 3:8 3:10 3:11 4:15 5:5[2] 5:11 5:18 6:3 6:4 7:9 8:11 9:7 10:15 10:18 11:10 11:15 11:20 12:14 12:15 13:19 14:10 14:11 14:17[2] 15:30 16:4 16:8 16:12 17:8 18:16 19:8 19:12 20:6 20:15 20:27 21:19 22:22 22:23 22:24 22:26 22:29 24:22 26:8 27:7 27:16 28:4 28:5 29:8 30:4 30:12 30:20 30:22 30:28 31:14 31:18 31:21 31:29 33:5 34:7 36:13 37:7 37:20 38:3 38:8 38:10 38:34 39:4 39:18 39:27 39:30 40:7 40:23[2] 41:10 41:15 41:25 42:8

PS

3:1 3:3 4:6 5:3 7:6 9:13 10:12 14:4 15:3 16:4 17:5 17:7 18:8 18:35 18:39 18:48[2] 20:5 21:9 22:15 24:4 24:7[2] 24:9[2] 25:1 27:2 27:5 27:6 27:10 27:12 28:2 28:5 28:9 30:1 30:3 31:8 31:19 33:7 35:2 35:11 35:23 35:25 39:6 40:2 40:5 40:12 41:8 41:9 41:10 44:5 47:5 53:4 54:3 56:1 56:2 57:3 57:8 59:1 59:15 63:4 69:9 69:15 69:29 71:6 71:20 74:3 74:4 74:5 74:8 74:15 74:23 75:3 75:4 75:5 75:7 77:9 78:21 78:38 78:48 80:2 81:3 81:12 83:2 86:4 87:6 88:8 88:15 89:2 89:4 89:42 90:5 90:6 91:12 92:11 93:3[2] 94:2 94:16[2] 94:18 97:3 102:10 102:16 104:8 105:35 106:9 106:17 106:18 106:26 106:30 107:25 107:26 109:23 110:7 113:7 119:48 119:117 121:1 122:4 123:1 124:2 124:3 127:2[2] 129:6 132:3 134:2 139:8 139:21 140:10 141:2 143:8 144:12 145:14 147:2 147:3 147:6

PR

1:12 2:3 2:7 3:20 7:1 8:23 8:30 10:12 10:14 13:22 15:1 15:18 16:27 21:20 22:6 23:8 24:16 25:7 26:9 26:24 28:25 29:21 29:22 30:4 30:13 30:31 30:32 31:28

EC

2:26 3:2 3:3 4:10[2] 4:15 10:4 10:12 12:4

CA

2:7 2:10 3:5 4:2 4:12 5:5 6:6 7:8 7:12 7:13 8:4 8:5[2]

ISA

1:2 1:6 2:3 2:4 2:12 2:13 2:14 3:13 3:14 5:5 5:6 5:11 5:13 5:24 5:26 6:1 7:1 7:6 8:7[2] 8:16 9:11 9:18[2] 10:15[2] 10:24 10:26[2] 10:28 10:29 10:30 11:12 11:16 13:2 13:14 13:17 14:4 14:8 14:9[2] 14:22 15:2 15:5[3] 15:7 18:3 19:5 19:6 21:2 22:1 23:4[2] 23:13[2] 23:18 24:10 24:14 24:18 24:22 25:8 26:11 27:9 28:4 28:7 28:21 30:26 32:9 32:13 33:3 33:10 33:12 34:3 34:10 34:13 35:9 36:1 36:10[2] 37:4 37:14 37:23 37:24 37:25 37:27 37:29 38:22 39:6 40:9[3] 40:15 40:26 40:31 41:2 41:25 42:2 42:11 42:13 42:15[2] 43:6 44:4 44:11 44:26 44:27 45:8 45:13 45:20 47:13 48:13 49:6 49:18 49:19 49:21 49:22[2] 49:23 50:2 50:9 51:6 51:8 51:17 51:18 52:8 53:2 55:13[2] 57:7 57:8[2] 57:14[3] 57:20 58:1 58:12 59:19 60:4 60:7 60:10 61:1 61:4 62:10[2] 63:11 64:7 64:11

JER

1:17 2:6 2:24 3:2 3:6 4:3 4:6 4:7 4:13 4:29 5:10 5:17[3] 6:1 6:4 7:13 7:16 7:25 7:29 9:10[2] 9:12 9:18 9:21 10:17 10:20 10:25 11:7 11:13 11:14 12:17 13:19 13:20 14:2 14:6 15:9 16:14 16:15 18:7 18:15 18:21 20:9 21:2 22:20[2] 22:22 23:4 23:7 23:8 23:10 24:6 25:32 26:5 26:10 26:17 27:22 29:15 29:19 29:22 30:9 30:13 31:6 31:21 31:28 31:40 32:2 32:3 32:33 33:1 33:15 34:21 35:11 35:15 36:5 36:20 37:10 37:11 38:10 38:13[2] 39:2 39:5 39:15 42:10 45:4 46:4 46:7 46:8[2] 46:9 46:11 47:2 47:6 48:5 48:15 48:44 49:5 49:14 49:19 49:22 49:28 49:31 50:2 50:9 50:21 50:26 50:32 50:38 50:41 50:44 51:2 51:3 51:9 51:11 51:12[2] 51:14 51:27[2] 51:34 51:36 51:42 51:44 51:53 52:7 52:9 52:31

LA

1:14[2] 1:19 2:2 2:5[2] 2:7 2:10 2:16 2:17 2:19 2:22 3:41 3:62 3:63 4:5 5:12

EZE

1:13 1:19[2] 1:20 1:21[2] 3:14 4:14 7:11 8:3 8:5[2] 8:11 9:3 10:4 10:15 10:16[2] 10:17[2] 10:19[2] 11:1 11:22 11:23 11:24[2] 13:5[2] 13:10 14:3 14:4 14:7 14:40 17:9[2] 17:14 17:17 17:24 18:6 18:12 18:15 19:1 19:3 19:6 19:12[2] 20:5[2] 20:6 20:15 20:24 20:28 20:42 21:15 21:22 22:30 23:8 23:22 23:27 23:46 23:47 26:3[2] 26:8 26:17 26:19 27:2 27:32 28:2 28:5 28:12[2] 28:14 28:17 29:4 30:21 31:4 31:10[2] 31:14[2] 32:2 32:3 33:25 34:4 34:16 34:18 34:23 34:29 36:3[2] 36:7 36:13 37:6 37:8 37:10 37:12 37:13 38:11 38:16 38:18 39:2 39:15 40:6 40:22 40:26 40:31 40:34 40:37 40:40 40:49 41:16 43:5 43:24 44:12 47:14

DA

2:21 2:44 3:1 3:2 3:3[2] 3:5 3:7 3:12 3:14 3:18 3:22 3:24 4:17 4:34 5:19 5:20 5:23 6:23[2] 7:3 7:4 7:5 7:8[2] 7:20 8:3[2] 8:8 8:22[2] 8:23 8:25 8:26 8:27 9:24 10:5 11:2[2] 11:3 11:4[2] 11:6 11:7 11:10[2] 11:12 11:14 11:15 11:20 11:21 11:23 11:25[2] 12:1 12:4 12:7 12:9 12:11

HO

1:11 2:6 2:15 4:8 4:15 4:19 6:1 6:2 8:4 8:7 8:8 8:9 9:6 9:12 9:16 10:4 10:8 10:12 11:8 13:12 13:15[2] 13:16

JOE

1:6 1:10 1:12 1:20 2:9 2:20[2] 3:9[2] 3:12

AM

1:6 1:9 1:13 2:10 2:11 3:1 3:5 3:10 4:10 5:1 5:2 6:8 6:10 6:14 7:1 7:4 8:4 8:8 8:10 8:14 9:2 9:5 9:7 9:11[3] 9:15

OB

1 6 14 21

JON

1:2 1:3 1:6 1:12 1:15 1:17 2:6 4:6 4:10

MIC

2:4 2:8 2:13[2] 3:10 4:2 4:3 5:3 5:9 5:14 6:4 6:14 7:3 7:6

NA

1:4 1:9 2:1 2:7 3:3 3:15

HAB

1:3 1:6 1:9 1:15 2:4 2:6 2:7 3:10 3:16

ZEP

2:4 3:8

HAG

1:8 1:14

ZEC

1:18 1:21[2] 2:1 2:13 5:1 5:5 5:7 5:9[2] 6:1 6:12 9:3 9:13 9:16 10:11 10:12 11:16 11:17 14:10 14:13 14:16 14:17 14:18[2] 14:19

MAL

3:15 3:17 4:1 4:2

MT

3:9 3:12 3:16 4:1 4:5 4:6 4:8 4:16 5:1 6:19 6:20 9:6 9:16 10:17 10:19 10:21[2] 11:5 12:42 13:4 13:5 13:6 13:7 13:26 13:28 13:29[2] 14:12 14:19 14:20 14:23 15:13 15:29 15:37 16:9 16:10 16:24 17:1 17:8 17:27[2] 19:20 20:17 20:18 22:7 22:24 23:13 23:32 24:9 24:43 26:52 27:37 27:50

MK

1:10 1:31 1:35 2:4 2:9 2:11 2:12 2:21 3:13 3:26 4:4 4:5 4:6 4:7 4:8 4:27 4:32 5:29 6:29 6:40 6:43 6:51 7:34 8:8 8:19 8:20 8:24 8:25 8:34 9:2 9:27 10:16 10:21 10:32 10:33 11:20 12:19 13:9 13:11 13:12 13:16 14:42 14:60 15:37 15:39 15:41 16:18 16:19

LU

1:66 1:69 2:4 2:28 2:42 3:5 3:6[2] 3:8 3:20 3:25 3:29 4:11 5:23 5:24 5:25[2] 5:28 6:8 6:20 7:15 7:16 8:6 8:7 8:8 8:37 9:16 9:17 9:23 9:28 9:51 10:25 10:34 11:27 11:31 11:32 12:19 12:21 13:11 13:25 14:10 16:23 17:6 17:13 18:10 18:13 18:21 18:31 19:4 19:5 19:20 19:21 19:22 19:28 20:28 21:1 21:12 21:28[2] 22:45 23:5 23:46 24:33 24:50 24:51

JOH

2:7 2:13 2:17 2:19 2:20 3:13 3:14[2] 4:14 4:35 5:1 5:8 5:9 5:11 5:12 5:21 6:3 6:5 6:12 6:39 6:40 6:44 6:54 6:62 7:8[2] 7:10[2] 7:14 8:7 8:10 8:28 8:59 10:1 10:31 11:31 11:41 11:55 12:20 12:32 12:34 13:18 17:1 18:11 18:30 19:30 21:11

AC

1:2 1:9 1:10 1:11[2] 1:13 1:15 1:22 2:14[2]

2:24 2:30 2:32 3:1 3:6 3:7 3:8 3:13 3:22 3:26 4:24 4:26

5:5 5:6 5:10 5:17 5:30 5:34 5:36 5:37 6:12 6:13 7:20 7:21

7:37 7:42 7:43 7:55 8:31 8:39 9:40 9:41 10:4 10:9 10:16 10:26^{2}

10:40 11:2 11:10 11:28 12:7^{2} 12:23 13:1 13:16 13:22 13:31 13:33 13:34

13:43 13:50 14:2 14:11 14:20 15:2 15:5 15:7 15:16 16:22 17:13 18:22

20:9 20:11 20:32 21:4 21:12 21:15^{2} 21:27 22:3 22:13 22:22 24:11 24:12

25:9 25:18 26:10 26:30 27:15 27:17 27:27 27:40^{2}

RO

1:24 1:26

2:5 4:24 6:4 8:11^{2} 8:32 9:17 10:7 14:4 15:16

1 CO

4:6

4:18 4:19 5:2 6:14^{2} 8:1 10:7 13:4 15:15^{2} 15:24 15:35 15:54

2 CO

2:7 4:14^{2} 5:4 9:5 12:2 12:4 12:14

GA

1:17

1:18 2:1 2:2 3:23

EPH

2:6 4:8 4:10 4:15 6:4

COL

1:5 1:24 2:7 2:18

1 TH

2:16 4:17

1 TI

2:8 3:6 3:16 4:6 5:10 6:19

2 TI

1:6 4:8

HEB

1:12 5:7 7:27^{2} 11:17^{2} 11:19 12:12 12:15

JAS

4:10 5:15

1 PE

1:13 1:21 2:5^{2}

2 PE

1:13 3:1 3:10

1 JO

3:17

JUDE

12 20

RE

4:1 8:4 8:7^{2} 10:4 10:5 10:9 10:10 11:12^{2} 12:5

12:16 13:1 13:11 14:11 15:1 16:12 18:21 19:3 20:3 20:9 20:13^{2}

UPON

5921, *1909*

GE

1:2^{2} 1:11 1:15 1:17 1:25 1:26 1:28 1:29 1:30 2:5 2:21 3:14 4:15 4:26 6:12^{2} 6:17 7:3 7:4 7:6 7:8 7:10 7:12 7:14 7:17 7:18^{2} 7:19 7:21^{2} 7:23 7:24 8:4 8:17^{2} 8:19 9:2^{3} 9:16^{2} 9:17 9:23 11:4 11:8 11:9 12:8 12:11 15:11 15:12 16:5 17:17 18:6 18:19 18:25 18:31 19:3 19:9 19:16^{2} 19:23 19:24 19:25 22:2 22:6 22:9 22:12 22:17 24:15 24:16 24:18 24:30 24:47 24:61 26:7 26:10

26:25 27:12 27:13 27:15 27:16 28:11 28:18 29:2 29:3 29:32 30:3 31:10 31:12 31:17 31:34 31:35 31:46 31:54 32:31^{2} 32:32 34:25 34:27 35:5 35:20 37:22 37:27 37:34 38:28 38:29 38:30 39:5 39:7 40:6 40:17 41:3 41:5 41:17 41:42 42:1 42:21 43:18 43:30 44:21 45:14^{2} 45:15 46:4 47:31 48:2 48:14^{2} 48:17 48:18 50:1^{2} 50:23

EX

1:16 2:25 3:6 3:12 3:22^{2} 4:9^{2} 4:20 4:31 5:3 5:8 5:9 5:21 7:4

7:5 7:17 7:19^{5} 8:3^{2} 8:4^{2} 8:5 8:7 8:14 8:18^{2} 8:21^{3} 9:3^{6} 9:9^{2} 9:10^{2} 9:11^{2} 9:14^{3} 9:19^{2} 9:22 9:23^{2} 9:33 10:6 10:12 10:13 11:1^{2} 11:5 12:13^{2} 12:23 12:33 12:34 13:9 13:16 14:4^{2} 14:17^{4} 14:18^{3} 14:22 14:26^{3} 14:29 14:30 14:31 15:9 15:15 15:16 15:19 15:26^{2} 16:14 17:6 18:8 19:11 19:16 19:18 19:20 19:22 19:24 20:5 20:12 20:25 21:14 21:19 21:22 21:30 22:3 22:25 24:11 24:16 25:11 25:21 25:22 25:30 26:4 26:7

26:32^{2} 26:34 27:2 27:4 27:7 28:8 28:12^{2} 28:22 28:23 28:26 28:29 28:30^{2} 28:33 28:34 28:35 28:36 28:37^{2} 28:38^{2} 28:41 28:43^{2} 29:5 29:6^{2} 29:7 29:8 29:10 29:12 29:13^{2} 29:15 29:16 29:18 29:19 29:20^{5} 29:21^{5} 29:22 29:25 29:38 30:1 30:4 30:7 30:8 30:10^{2} 30:32 30:33 31:18 32:16 32:20 32:21 32:29^{3} 32:34 33:16 33:21 34:1 34:7^{2} 34:28 34:35 35:3 36:17^{2} 37:3^{2} 37:13 37:16 37:27 39:5 39:15 39:19 39:24 39:25 39:30 39:31 39:43

40:4 40:13 40:19 40:20 40:22 40:23 40:29 40:38

LE

1:4 1:5 1:7^{2} 1:8^{2} 1:11 1:12 1:13 1:17^{3} 2:1 2:2 2:9 2:15 3:2^{2} 3:3 3:5^{2} 3:8^{2} 3:9 3:10 3:11 3:13^{2} 3:14 3:15 3:16 4:4 4:7 4:8 4:9 4:10 4:15 4:18 4:19 4:24 4:25 4:26 4:29 4:30 4:31 4:33 4:34 4:35 5:9 5:11 6:9 6:10 6:12^{2} 6:13 6:15^{2} 6:27 7:2 7:5 7:20 7:31 8:7^{2} 8:8 8:9^{3} 8:11 8:12 8:13^{2}

8:14 8:15^{2} 8:16^{2} 8:18 8:19 8:21 8:22 8:23^{3} 8:24^{4} 8:25 8:26 8:27^{2} 8:28 8:30^{5} 9:9 9:10 9:12 9:13 9:14 9:17 9:18 9:20^{2} 9:24 10:6 10:7 11:20 11:21^{2} 11:27 11:29 11:32 11:37 11:38 11:41 11:42^{3} 11:44 11:46 13:25 13:27 13:29 13:30 13:43 13:45 13:50 14:7 14:14^{3} 14:17^{4} 14:18 14:20 14:25^{3} 14:28^{4} 14:29 14:48 15:8 15:9 15:20^{2} 15:22 15:24 15:26 16:2^{2} 16:4 16:8 16:9 16:13^{2} 16:14 16:15 16:18 16:19 16:21^{2} 16:22

16:25 17:6 17:11 18:25 19:17 19:19 19:28 20:9 20:11 20:12 20:13 20:16 20:27 21:5 21:10 21:12 22:3 22:22 23:37 24:4 24:6 24:7 24:14 25:21 25:37 26:21 26:25 26:30 26:35 26:36 26:37

NU

1:53 4:7 4:8 4:10 4:11 4:14^{2} 4:25 5:14^{2} 5:15 5:25 5:26 5:30^{2} 6:5 6:7 6:19 6:25 6:26 6:27 7:9 7:89 8:7 8:10 8:12 8:24 8:25 9:15 9:18 9:19 9:20 9:22 10:34 11:9^{2} 11:11 11:17^{2} 11:25^{2}

11:26 11:29 11:31 12:3 12:10 12:11 13:23 14:18 14:36 14:37 15:31 15:32 15:38 15:39 16:3 16:4 16:7 16:22 16:33 16:45 17:2 17:3 18:5 18:17 18:26 19:2 19:13^{2} 19:15 19:18^{4} 19:19 19:20 20:6 20:26 20:28 21:8^{2} 21:9 21:15 22:22 22:30 23:4 24:2 27:18 27:20 27:23 30:14 31:27 33:4 35:22 35:23

DE

1:36 2:25 4:7 4:10 4:13 4:26 4:30 4:32 4:36 4:39 4:40 5:9 6:8 6:9 6:22^{3} 7:6 7:7

7:15^{2} 7:16 7:22 8:4 11:12 11:18 11:20^{2} 11:21 11:25^{2} 11:29^{2} 12:1 12:2^{2} 12:16 12:20 12:24 12:27^{2} 13:9 13:17 14:2 15:23 17:7 17:18 19:5 19:10 21:23 22:6^{2} 22:8 22:12 22:14 22:19 23:13 23:19^{2} 23:20^{2} 24:15^{2} 26:6 27:3 27:5 27:8 27:12 27:13 28:8 28:15 28:20 28:24 28:45 28:46^{2} 28:48 28:56 28:60 28:61 29:5^{2} 29:20 29:22 29:27 30:1 30:3 30:7 30:18 31:17 32:2^{2} 32:23^{2} 32:24 32:35 32:42 33:10 33:16^{2} 33:26 33:28

33:29 34:9

JOS

1:3 2:6 2:8 2:9 2:15^{2} 2:19^{2} 3:13 3:16 4:5 7:6^{2} 7:10 8:7 8:20 8:32 9:4 9:5^{2} 9:20 10:11 10:12 10:13 10:18 10:24^{2} 10:26 11:4 11:7 12:2 13:9 19:34 20:8 23:15^{2} 24:7

JG

3:10 3:16 3:22 3:23 4:16 6:14 6:20 6:26 6:28 6:34 6:37 6:39^{2} 6:40 7:5 7:6 7:25 8:21 9:5 9:18 9:24^{2} 9:33 9:44 9:49 9:53 9:57^{2} 11:29 11:37 11:38 12:1 13:19

14:6 14:17 14:19 15:12 15:14^{2} 15:16 16:3 16:9 16:12 16:14 16:17 16:19 16:20 16:26 16:27 16:29 16:30^{2} 18:25 19:14 19:20 19:27 19:28 20:5 20:37 20:41 20:48

RU

3:3 3:15 4:7 4:10

1 SA

1:9 1:11 2:8 2:10 2:28 2:34 4:12 4:13 4:19 5:3 5:4^{2} 5:6 5:7^{2} 6:8 6:11 7:10 9:16 9:24 9:25 10:1 10:6 10:10 11:2 11:6 13:12 13:13 14:1 14:13^{2} 14:25 14:32 15:19 15:27 16:13

16:16 16:23 17:5 17:6 17:38 17:39 17:49 17:51 18:4 18:10 18:17^{2} 19:9 19:20 19:23 20:9 20:25^{2} 20:31 21:13 22:17 22:18^{2} 24:2 24:12 24:13 24:24^{2} 25:39 25:42 26:12 28:18 28:23 30:14^{3} 30:16 30:17 31:2 31:4 31:5

2 SA

1:2 1:6^{2} 1:9^{2} 1:10^{2} 1:15 1:16 1:19 1:21 1:24 4:11 5:20 5:23 6:3 6:8 9:8 11:2^{2} 11:21 11:23 11:24 12:16 12:18 13:29 14:7 15:14 15:32 16:1 16:8 16:22 17:2 17:12^{2} 17:14

18:9 18:17 18:28 20:8 20:12 21:10^{2} 22:7 22:11^{2} 22:28 22:34 24:15 24:16 24:20

1 KI

1:13 1:17 1:20 1:24 1:30 1:33 1:35 1:38 1:44 1:47 2:5 2:12 2:25 2:29 2:30 2:32^{2} 2:33^{6} 2:34 2:37 2:44 2:46 3:4 3:26 5:5 6:32^{3} 6:35 7:2^{2} 7:3 7:16 7:17 7:18^{2} 7:19 7:20^{2} 7:22 7:25^{2} 7:29 7:31 7:38 7:41 7:42 8:31 8:32 8:36 9:5^{2} 9:9 9:25^{2} 10:20 12:4 12:9 12:32 12:33^{2} 13:2^{3} 13:3

13:29 14:10 17:14 17:19 17:20 17:21 18:1 18:26 18:28 18:42 19:11 19:19 20:30 20:31 20:38 21:4 21:21 21:27 21:29 22:17

2 KI

2:9 2:16 3:15 3:22 3:27 4:4^{2} 4:5^{2} 4:21 4:29 4:31 4:32 4:33 4:34^{5} 4:35 5:23 6:26 6:30^{2} 7:6 7:9 7:17 7:20 8:1 9:25 9:37 10:5 10:6 10:15 11:12 12:11 13:13 13:16^{3} 13:18 16:13 16:15^{2} 16:17 18:21^{2} 18:23 19:7 21:12 22:16^{2} 22:20 23:6 23:16 23:20^{2} 24:3

25:6 25:17^{2}

1 CH

1:10 5:16 6:49 9:27 10:4 12:8 12:18 12:19 13:11 14:11 14:14 14:17 15:13 15:15 15:27 16:8 16:40 19:17 20:2 21:14 21:16 21:26^{2} 22:8 28:2 28:5 28:19 29:25

2 CH

1:6 4:4^{2} 4:13 4:14 6:13^{2} 6:16 6:20^{2} 6:22 6:23 6:27 7:3^{2} 7:22 9:19 10:4 10:9 10:11 12:7 13:4 13:10 13:11 13:18 14:14 15:1 15:5 17:10 18:16 18:18 18:23 19:2 19:7 19:10^{2} 20:9 20:12 20:14

22:8 23:11 23:20 24:7 24:9 24:18 24:20 24:22 24:27 25:18 25:28 26:15 26:16 26:20 28:11 28:15 29:8 29:22^{2} 29:23 29:24 29:27 32:8 32:12 32:25^{2} 32:26 33:11 34:4 34:5 34:21 34:24^{2} 34:25 34:28^{2} 35:3 35:16 36:17^{2}

EZR

3:3^{2} 5:5 6:19 7:6 7:9^{2} 7:17 7:24 7:26 7:28 8:18 8:22 8:31 9:5 9:13

NE

2:8 2:12 2:18 4:4 4:12 4:19 5:4 5:18 5:19 6:1 6:14 8:2 8:4 8:16

9:1 9:4 9:10 9:13 9:32 9:33 10:34 12:31^{2} 12:38 13:18^{2}

ES

1:6 2:15 2:17 3:13 4:5 5:1 6:8^{2} 7:8 8:7^{2} 8:12^{2} 8:14 8:17 9:2 9:3 9:13 9:25 9:27^{3} 10:1^{2}

JOB

1:12 1:15 1:17 1:19 1:20 2:11 2:12 2:13 3:4 3:5 3:6 3:25 4:5 4:14 5:10^{2} 6:28 7:1 7:8 7:17 8:9 8:15 9:8 9:33 10:1 10:3 10:16 10:17 12:4 12:21 13:11 13:27 14:3 14:22 15:26^{2} 15:29

16:9^{2} 16:10^{2} 16:13 16:14^{2} 16:15 18:8 18:15 19:21^{2} 19:25 20:4 20:22 20:23^{2} 20:25 21:5 21:9 21:17 22:28 24:23 25:3 26:7 26:9 27:9 27:10 27:22 28:9 29:3 29:4 29:13 29:19 29:22 30:12 30:14^{2} 30:15 30:16^{2} 30:22 30:30 31:1 31:10 31:36 33:7 33:15^{2} 33:19 33:27 34:14 34:21 34:23 36:28 36:30 37:12 38:5 38:24 39:28 40:4 41:8 41:30 41:33

PS

2:6 3:7 3:8 4:1 4:4 4:6 5:*title* 6:*title* 6:2 7:5

US

2248

24:17^2
24:18
24:27^2

JG

1:1
1:24
6:13^6
8:1^2
8:21
8:22^2
9:8
9:10
9:12
9:14
11:8
11:10
11:15^2
11:19
11:24
12:1
13:8^2
13:15
13:23^3
14:15^2
15:10^2
15:11^2
16:5
16:24
16:25
18:19^2
18:25
19:11
19:13
19:28
20:3
20:8^2
20:13
20:18
20:32^2
20:39
21:1
21:22

RU

2:20

1 SA

4:3^5
4:7
4:8^2
5:7^2
5:10^2
5:11
6:2
6:9^3
6:20
7:8^2
7:12
8:5^2
8:6
8:19
8:20^2
9:5^2
9:6^2
9:8
9:9
9:10
9:27
10:16
10:19
10:27
11:1
11:3^2
11:10
11:12
11:14
12:4^2
12:10
12:12
12:19
14:1
14:6^2
14:9
14:10^2
14:12
14:17
14:36^3
17:9
20:11
20:42
21:5
23:19
25:7
25:15
25:16
25:40
26:11
27:11
29:4^2
29:9
30:22
30:23^3

2 SA

2:14
5:2
10:12
11:23
13:25
13:26
15:14^2
15:19
15:20
17:5
17:5
18:3^5
19:9^2
19:10^2
19:42^2
19:43
20:6^2
21:4
21:5^2
21:6
21:17
24:14

1 KI

3:8
5:6
8:57^3
12:4
12:9
12:10
18:23
18:26
20:23
20:31

2 KI

1:6
4:9
4:10^3
4:13
6:1
6:2^3
6:11
6:16
7:4^3
7:6^2
7:9
7:12
7:13
9:5
9:12
10:5
14:8
18:26
18:30
18:32
19:19
22:13^2

1 CH

13:2^2
13:3^2
15:13
16:35^2
19:13

2 CH

10:4
10:9
10:10
13:10
13:12
14:7^2
14:11
20:9
20:11^3
20:12
25:17
29:10
32:7
32:8^2
32:11
34:21

EZR

4:2^2
4:3^2
4:12
4:14
4:18
5:11
5:17
8:17
8:18^2
8:21
8:22
8:23
8:31^2
9:8^3
9:9^4
9:13^3
9:44^2
10:3
10:14

NE

2:17
2:18
2:19^2
2:20
4:12^2
4:15^2
4:20^2
4:22
4:23
5:8
5:10
5:17^2
6:2
6:7
6:9
6:10^2
6:16
9:32
9:33
9:37
10:32
13:18

JOB

9:33^2
15:9
15:10
21:14
22:17
31:15
34:4^3
34:37
35:11^2
37:19

PS

2:3^2
4:6^2
12:4
17:11
19:9
33:22
34:3
44:1
44:7^2
44:9
44:10^2
44:11^2
44:13^2
44:14
44:17
44:19^2
44:23
44:26
46:7
46:11
47:3
47:4
54:*title*
60:1^3
60:3
60:10
60:11
62:8
65:5
66:10^2
66:11
66:12
67:1^2
67:6
67:7
68:19
68:28
74:1
74:8
74:9
78:3
79:4
79:8^2
79:9^2
80:2
80:3
80:6
80:7
80:18
80:19
83:4
83:12
85:4^2
85:5
85:6
85:7^2
85:13
90:12
90:14
90:15^2
90:17^2
95:1^2
95:2
95:6^2
100:3
103:10^2
103:12
106:47^2
108:11
108:12
115:1^2
115:12^2
117:2
118:27
119:4
122:1
123:2
123:3^2
124:2
124:3^2
124:4
124:6
126:3
136:23
136:24
137:3^5

PR

1:11
1:12
1:14
7:18^2

EC

1:10
12:13

CA

2:15
5:9
7:11^2
7:12^2

ISA

1:9
1:18
2:3^2
2:5
4:1
6:8
7:6^3
8:10
9:6
14:8
14:10
17:14^2
22:13
25:9
26:12^2
26:13
28:15
29:15^2
30:10^2
30:11
30:15
33:3
33:14^2
33:21
33:22
36:11
36:15
36:17
37:20
40:1
41:22^2
43:9
43:26
50:8
53:6
59:9^2
59:11
59:12^2
63:7
63:16^2
63:17
64:6
64:7^2
64:12

JER

2:6^2
2:27
3:25
4:5
4:8
4:13
5:12
5:19
5:24^2
6:4^2
6:5^2
6:24
6:26
8:8
8:14^4
9:18
9:19
11:19^2
14:7
14:9^2
14:19^2
14:21^2
16:10
18:18^3
21:2^4
21:13
26:16
29:15
29:28
31:6
35:6
35:8
35:9
35:10
35:11
36:17
37:3
37:9
38:16
38:25^2
40:10
41:8
42:2^2
42:3
42:5^2
42:6
42:20^2
43:3^4
44:16
46:16
48:2
50:5
51:9
51:10

LA

3:40
3:41
3:43
3:45
3:46
3:47
4:17^2
4:19^2
5:1
5:4
5:8^2
5:16
5:20^2
5:21
5:22^2

EZE

8:12
11:3
11:15
24:19^2
33:10
33:24
35:12
37:18

DA

1:12
2:23
3:17^2
9:7
9:8
9:10
9:11
9:12^3
9:13
9:14
9:16

HO

6:1^3
6:2^2
6:3
10:3
10:8^2
12:4
14:2
14:3

AM

4:1
6:13
9:10

OB

1

JON

1:7
1:8^2
1:11
1:14^2

MIC

3:11^2
4:2^2
5:1
5:6
7:19

ZEC

1:6^2
8:21

MAL

1:2
1:9
2:10

MT

1:23
3:15
6:11
6:12
6:13^2
8:25
8:29
8:31^2
9:27
13:36
13:56
15:15
15:23
17:4^2
20:7
20:12
20:30
20:31
21:25
21:38^2
22:17
22:25
24:3
25:8
25:9
25:11
26:46
26:63
26:68
27:4
27:25
27:49

MK

1:24
1:38
4:35
5:12
6:3
9:5^2
9:22^2
9:38^2
9:40
10:35
10:37
12:7
12:19
13:4
14:15
14:42
15:36
16:3

LU

1:1
1:2
1:69
1:71
1:74
1:78
2:15^2
2:48
4:34^2
7:5
7:16
7:20
8:22
9:33^2
9:49
9:50^2
10:11
10:17
11:1
11:3
11:4^4
11:45
12:41
13:25
15:23
16:26^2
17:13
19:14
20:2
20:6
20:14
20:22
20:28
22:8
22:67
23:18
23:30^2
23:39
24:22
24:24
24:29
24:32^3

JOH

1:14
1:22
2:18
4:12
4:25
6:34
6:52
8:5
9:34
10:24^2
11:7
11:15
11:16
11:50
14:8^2
14:9
14:22
14:31
16:17
17:21
18:31
19:24

AC

1:17
1:21^2
1:22^2
2:29
3:4
3:12
5:28
6:14
7:27
7:38
7:40^3
10:41
10:42
11:13
11:15
11:17
13:33
13:47
14:11
14:17
15:7
15:8
15:9
15:24
15:25
15:28
15:36
16:9
16:10
16:14
16:15^2
16:16
16:17^2
16:21
16:37^4
17:27
20:5
20:14
21:5
21:11
21:16
21:17
21:18
23:9
24:4
24:7
25:24
27:2
27:6
27:7
27:20
28:2^2
28:7^2
28:10^2
28:15^2

RO

3:8
4:16
4:24
5:5
5:8^2
6:3
8:4
8:18
8:26
8:31^2
8:32^2
8:34
8:35
8:37
8:39
9:24
9:29
12:6^2
12:7
13:12^2
13:13
14:7
14:12
14:13
14:19
15:2
15:7
16:6

1 CO

1:18
1:30
2:10
2:12
4:1
4:6
4:8
4:9
5:7
5:8
6:14
7:15
8:6
8:8
10:8
10:9
15:32
15:57
16:16

2 CO

1:4
1:5
1:8
1:10^2
1:11^2
1:14
1:19
1:20
1:21^2
1:22
2:11
2:14^2
3:3
3:6
4:7
4:12
4:14^2
4:17
5:5^2
5:14
5:18^2
5:19
5:20
5:21
6:12
7:1
7:2
7:6
7:7
7:9
8:4^2
8:5
8:7
8:19^2
8:20^2
9:11
10:2
10:8
10:13

GA

1:4
1:23
2:4
3:13^2
3:24
4:26
5:1
5:25
5:26
6:9
6:10

EPH

1:3
1:4
1:5
1:6
1:8
1:9
2:4
2:5
2:6^2
2:7
2:14
3:20
4:7
5:2^2

PHP

3:15
3:16^2
3:17

COL

1:2
1:8
1:13^2
2:14^2
4:3^2

1 TH

1:6
1:9
1:10
2:13
2:15
2:16
2:18
3:6^4
4:1
4:7
4:8
5:6^2
5:8
5:9
5:10
5:25

2 TH

1:7
2:2
2:16^2
3:1
3:6
3:7
3:9

1 TI

6:8
6:17

2 TI

1:7
1:9^3
1:14
2:12
2:12
2:14^2
3:6
3:15

HEB

1:2
2:3
4:1^2
4:2
4:11
4:14
4:16
6:1
6:18
6:20
7:26
9:12
9:24
10:15
10:20
10:22
10:23
10:24
11:40^2
12:1^4
12:9
12:10
12:28
13:13
13:15
13:18

JAS

1:18
3:3
4:5

1 PE

1:3
1:12
2:21^2
3:18
3:21
4:1
4:3
4:17
5:10

2 PE

1:1
1:3^2
1:4
3:2

1 JO

1:2
1:3
1:7
1:8
1:9^2
1:10
2:19^5
2:25
3:1^2
3:16
3:18
3:20
3:21
3:23
3:24^2
4:6^2
4:7
4:9
4:10
4:11
4:12^2
4:13^2
4:16
4:19
5:11
5:14
5:15
5:20

2 JO

2^2

3 JO

9
10

RE

1:5^2
1:6
5:9
5:10
6:16^2
19:7

WAS

1961, *2258*

GE

1:2^2
1:3
1:4
1:7
1:9
1:10
1:11
1:12^2
1:15
1:18
1:21
1:24
1:25
1:30
1:31
2:5^2
2:10
2:19
2:20
2:23
3:1
3:6
3:10
3:20
3:23
4:2
4:5
4:18
4:19
4:20
4:21
4:22
4:26
5:24
5:32
6:5^2
6:9
6:11
6:12
7:6^2
7:12
7:17^2
7:22
7:23
8:1
8:2
8:11
8:13
9:19
9:21
10:9
10:10
10:19
10:25^2
10:30
11:1
11:10
11:29
11:30
12:4
12:6
12:10^2
12:11
12:14^2
12:15
12:18
13:2
13:6^2
13:7
13:10
13:14
14:10
14:14
14:18
15:12
15:17
16:1
16:4
16:5
16:14
16:16
17:1
17:24
17:25
17:26
18:10
18:15
19:22
19:23
20:16
21:3
21:5
21:8^2
21:11
21:15
21:20
22:20
22:24
23:1
23:17^2
24:1
24:15
24:16
24:29
24:33
24:36
24:67
25:1
25:8
25:10
25:17
25:20
25:21
25:26
25:27^2
25:29
25:30
26:1^2
26:7
26:8
26:28
26:34
27:1
27:30
28:7
28:11
28:17
28:19
29:2
29:12
29:16
29:17
29:23
29:31
29:33
29:34
30:2
30:29
30:30
30:37
31:1^2
31:2
31:22
31:31
31:36
31:39
31:40
31:48
32:7^2
32:24
32:25
34:19
34:24
34:28^2
34:29
35:3
35:4
35:5
35:8^2
35:16
35:17
35:18
35:19
35:29
36:12
36:22
36:24
36:32
36:35
36:39^2
37:1
37:2^2
37:3
37:15
37:23^2
37:24^2
37:29
38:1
38:2
38:5
39:6
38:7
38:12
38:13
38:14^2
38:16
38:21^2
38:22
38:24
38:25
38:29
38:30
39:1
39:2^3
39:3
39:5
39:6
39:11
39:13
39:19
39:20
39:21
39:22
39:23^2
40:2
40:3
40:9
40:10
40:11
40:15
40:16^2
40:17
40:20
41:7
41:8^2
41:10
41:12
41:13
41:24
41:32
41:37
41:46
41:48
41:49
41:53
41:54^2
41:55
41:56
41:57
42:1
42:5
42:6^2
42:27
42:35
43:1
43:12^2
43:18
43:21
43:26
43:34
44:3
44:12
44:14
45:8
45:16
47:13^2
47:14
47:18
47:28
48:7
48:14^2
49:7^2
49:15^2
49:26
49:32
49:33
50:9
50:11
50:15
50:26

EX

1:5
1:7
1:14
1:15
2:2
2:11
2:12
2:21
3:2
3:6
4:6
4:7
4:14
5:13
5:19
6:3
7:7
7:15
7:21^2
7:22
8:15
8:19
8:24
9:7^2
9:11
9:24^2
9:25
9:26
9:31^3
9:33
9:35
10:13
10:15
10:22
11:3
11:6
11:29
11:30^3
11:34
11:39
11:40
13:17
14:5^2
14:20
15:23
16:14
16:15
16:20
16:24
16:31^2
17:1
18:3
18:4^2
18:11
19:16
19:18
20:21
22:13
24:10
24:17
24:18
25:40
26:30
27:8
29:33
31:17
32:16
33:7
33:8
34:28
34:34
35:23
35:24
36:7
36:9
36:12
36:15^2
36:21
37:1
37:6
37:10
37:22
37:25^3
38:1^2
38:18^2
38:21
38:23
38:24^2
38:25
38:29
39:4
39:5^2
39:9^2
39:10^2
39:19
39:23
39:32
40:17
40:35
40:36
40:37
40:38^2

LE

4:10
6:2
6:3
6:4
6:27
8:4
8:10
8:16
8:21
8:25
8:26
8:29
8:30
9:8
9:15
9:18
10:16^2
10:18
10:20
13:18
14:6
14:48
15:10
16:27
17:15
19:20
21:10
24:10
24:11
25:33
25:50
25:51
27:24

NU

1:44
3:16
3:21
3:27
3:33
3:35
6:12
7:9
7:10
7:12
7:13^2
7:17
7:19
7:23
7:25^2
7:29
7:31
7:35
7:37^2
7:41
7:43
7:47

7:49[2]
7:53
7:55
7:59
7:61[2]
7:65
7:67[2]
7:71
7:73
7:77
7:79[2]
7:83
7:84[2]
7:86
7:88[2]
7:89[2]
8:4[2]
9:14
9:15[2]
9:16
9:17
9:20[2]
9:21[4]
9:22
10:11
10:14
10:15
10:16
10:17
10:18
10:19
10:20
10:22
10:23
10:24
10:25[2]
10:26
10:27
10:34
11:1
11:2
11:4
11:7
11:8
11:10[2]
11:18
11:25
11:26
11:33[3]
12:3
12:9
12:10
12:15[2]
13:20
13:22
13:24
14:16
15:34
16:15
16:31
16:42
16:47
16:48
16:50
18:6
18:8
19:13
20:1
20:2
20:13
20:29
21:4
21:24
21:26
21:35
22:3[2]
22:4
22:14
22:22[2]
22:26
22:27
22:30[2]
22:36
24:10
24:20
25:3
25:8
25:11
25:13
25:14[3]
25:15[3]
25:18
26:46
26:59
26:60
26:62
26:64
26:65
27:3
27:13
28:6
31:14
31:16
31:26
31:32
31:36[2]
31:37
31:38
31:39
31:40
31:41
31:43
31:52
32:1
32:10
32:13[2]
32:39
33:14
33:39
35:23
35:25
35:26
36:2

DE

1:34
1:37
2:14
2:15
2:20
2:36
3:3
3:4
3:8
3:11[2]
3:13
3:26
4:21
4:35
8:2
8:15
9:8
9:9
9:10
9:19[2]
9:20
9:21
9:28
10:6
11:6
20:6
21:15
22:27
26:5
29:7
29:15[2]
29:27
32:12
32:50
33:5
33:16
33:21
34:7[2]
34:9

JOS

1:5
1:17
2:2
2:5
2:15
3:7
4:10
5:1
5:13
6:1
6:21
6:24
6:27[2]
7:1
7:16
7:17
7:18
7:22
7:26
8:11
8:13
8:17
8:25
8:29
8:33
8:35
9:5
9:10
9:24
10:2[2]
10:14
10:17
11:10
11:11
12:4
13:1
13:16
13:23[2]
13:25
13:29
13:30
13:33
14:2
14:7[2]
14:11[2]
14:15[2]
15:1[2]
15:2
15:5[2]
15:9[2]
15:11
15:12
15:15
16:5[2]
17:1[2]
17:2
17:7
17:9
17:10[2]
18:1
18:12
18:14[2]
18:15
18:17
18:19
18:20[2]
19:1
19:9[2]
19:10
19:18
19:25
19:33
19:41
21:10
22:14
22:17
24:26
24:33

JG

1:10
1:11
1:17
1:19
1:22
1:23
1:28
1:36
2:14
2:15
2:18
2:19
2:20
3:8
3:17
3:20
3:24
3:25
3:27
3:30
3:31
4:1
4:2
4:11
4:12
4:16
4:17
4:21
4:22
5:8[2]
5:14
5:15
6:3
6:6
6:11
6:21
6:22
6:27
6:28[5]
6:30
6:34
6:35
6:38
6:40[2]
7:8
7:13[2]
7:15
8:3[2]
8:11
8:13
8:20
8:26[2]
8:28[2]
8:31
8:32
8:33
9:5
9:6
9:26
9:30
9:44
9:45
9:47
9:51
9:55
10:2
10:5
10:7
10:9
10:16
11:1[2]
11:5
11:18
11:34
11:39
12:5
12:7
12:10
12:12
12:15
13:2[3]
13:6[2]
13:9
13:16
13:21
14:4
14:8
14:19
14:20
15:14
15:18
15:19
16:2
16:4
16:9
16:16
16:20
16:22
16:27
16:29
17:1[2]
17:6[2]
17:7[2]
17:11[2]
17:12
18:1
18:7
18:20
18:28[3]
18:29[2]
18:31
19:1[2]
19:2
19:10
19:11
19:15
19:16
19:26[2]
19:27
19:29
19:30[2]
20:1
20:3
20:4
20:27
20:34[2]
20:38
20:41
21:25[2]

RU

1:1
1:2
1:3
1:4
1:5
1:7
1:18
1:19
2:1
2:3[2]
2:5
2:6
2:14
2:15
2:17
2:18
3:7
3:8
4:3
4:7[2]
4:9[2]
4:13

1 SA

1:1[2]
1:2
1:4
1:10
1:13
1:18
1:20
1:24
2:13[2]
2:17
2:22
2:26
3:1[2]
3:2
3:3[2]
3:7
3:19
3:20
4:2
4:6
4:10[2]
4:11
4:15
4:18
4:19[2]
4:21
5:3
5:4[2]
5:6
5:7
5:9[2]
5:11[2]
6:1
6:4
6:9
6:14
6:15
7:2[2]
7:10
7:13
7:14
7:17[2]
8:1
8:2
9:1[2]
9:2[3]
9:5
9:9
9:10
9:24
10:9
10:20
10:21[2]
10:23
11:6
11:11
12:8
12:12
12:15
13:3
13:4
13:7
13:19
13:22[2]
14:3
14:4[2]
14:5
14:14
14:15[2]
14:18
14:19
14:20[2]
14:25
14:27
14:35
14:39
14:42
14:43
14:50[2]
14:51[2]
14:52[2]
15:9[2]
15:12
16:12
16:23[3]
17:3
17:4
17:5[2]
17:12[2]
17:14
17:20
17:24
17:28
17:40
17:42
17:50
17:51
18:1
18:4
18:5
18:6
18:8
18:10
18:12[3]
18:14
18:15
18:19
18:28
18:29
18:30
19:7
19:8
19:9
19:16
19:19
19:20
19:21
19:23
20:19
20:24
20:27[2]
20:30
20:33
20:34
20:37
20:41
21:1
21:6[3]
21:7[2]
21:12
22:2[3]
22:4
22:6
22:9
22:22
23:7[2]
23:13[2]
23:15[2]
24:1[2]
24:3
25:2[3]
25:3[4]
25:7
25:20
25:21
25:36[2]
25:37
25:39
25:44
26:4
26:12
26:16
26:21
26:24
27:4[2]
27:7
28:3
28:5
28:14
28:20[2]
28:21
30:3
30:6[2]
30:9[2]
30:10
30:19
30:25
31:3
31:4
31:5

2 SA

1:1
1:2
1:10[4]
1:26
2:10
2:11[2]
2:16
2:17[2]
2:18
2:32
3:1
3:2
3:6
3:7
3:8
3:22[2]
3:23
3:26
3:27
3:35
3:37
4:1
4:2[2]
4:4[3]
5:2
5:4
5:10
5:13
6:3
6:4
6:7
6:8
6:9
6:12
6:13
6:14
6:20
6:21
7:9
7:19
8:16[2]
8:17
8:18
9:2[2]
9:6
9:12
9:13
10:9
10:17
11:1
11:2
11:4
11:7
11:26
11:27
12:3
12:4[2]
12:5
12:15
12:18[2]
12:19
12:21
12:22
12:30
13:1
13:2[2]
13:3[2]
13:6
13:8
13:15
13:19
13:21
13:38
13:39[2]
14:1
14:6
14:25[2]
14:26[2]
14:27[2]
15:2
15:5
15:12
15:17
15:30
15:32
16:1
16:5
16:16
16:23[2]
17:6
17:19
17:22
17:23[2]
17:25[2]
17:27
18:6
18:7
18:8
18:9[2]
18:14
18:29
18:33
19:1
19:2[2]
19:16
19:18
19:25
19:32
19:39
20:1
20:8
20:10
20:13
20:17
20:20
20:23[2]
20:24[2]
20:25
20:26
21:1
21:7
21:11
21:14
21:16
21:18[2]
21:19[2]
21:20[3]
22:8
22:10
22:11
22:19
22:24
22:42
23:1
23:2
23:8
23:9
23:10
23:11[2]
23:14[2]
23:16
23:18
23:19[2]
23:23
23:24
24:1
24:2
24:11
24:16
24:25[2]

1 KI

1:1
1:4
1:6
1:15[2]
1:23
2:10
2:12
2:26
2:29
2:34
2:41[2]
2:46
3:2
3:4
3:12
3:15
3:17
3:18[3]
3:21[2]
3:26
3:28
4:1
4:4
4:5[2]
4:6[2]
4:15
4:16
4:19[3]
4:22
4:31[2]
5:1
5:12[2]
5:14
6:2
6:3[2]
6:6[3]
6:7[3]
6:8
6:17
6:18[3]
6:20[2]
6:22
6:24
6:25
6:26
6:37
6:38[2]
7:1
7:2
7:3
7:4
7:5
7:6[2]
7:7
7:8
7:10
7:12
7:14[3]
7:16[3]
7:20
7:22[2]
7:23[2]
7:24
7:25
7:26[2]
7:27
7:28
7:29
7:31[2]
7:32
7:33
7:35
7:38
7:47
7:48
7:51
8:9
8:17
8:18[2]
8:34
8:37
8:64[3]
9:1
9:25
10:2[2]
10:3
10:5
10:6
10:7
10:14
10:19
10:20
10:21
11:4[3]
11:9[2]
11:14
11:15[2]
11:20
11:21
11:25
11:26
11:27
11:28[2]
11:30
11:40
11:42
11:43
12:2[2]
12:15
12:18
12:20[2]
12:21
13:5
13:6[2]
13:9
13:17
13:24[2]
13:26
14:6
14:8
14:21[2]
14:28
14:30
14:31[2]
15:2
15:3
15:5
15:6
15:7
15:10
15:11
15:14
15:16
15:22
15:23
15:24
15:32
16:6
16:9
16:18
16:28
17:1
17:10
17:11
17:17[2]
18:2
18:3
18:4
18:7
18:13
18:26[3]
18:29[2]
18:30
18:38
18:45[2]
18:46
19:6
19:11[2]
19:12
19:13
19:19
20:12
20:16
20:29[2]
20:36
20:40[2]
20:41
21:1
21:11
21:15[2]
21:16
21:25
22:13
22:33
22:35
22:37
22:42[2]
22:43
22:47[2]
22:50

2 KI

1:2[2]
1:7
1:8
2:17
2:23
3:4
3:5
3:9
3:20[2]
3:26
3:27
4:8[2]
4:18[2]
4:31
4:32[2]
4:36
4:38
4:41
5:1[3]
5:8
5:11
5:14
6:5[2]
6:11
6:13
6:15
6:17
6:25[2]
6:26
7:5
7:7
7:10
7:15
7:16
8:5
8:6
8:7[2]
8:11
8:17
8:18
8:24
8:26[2]
8:27
8:29
9:15
9:16
9:21
9:30
9:34
10:5[2]
10:12
10:15
10:21[2]
10:22
10:30
10:36
11:1
11:2
11:3
11:14
11:16
11:20
11:21
12:1
12:2
12:6
12:9
12:10[8]
12:12
12:13
12:16[2]
12:18
13:2
13:3
13:11
13:13
13:14
13:19
13:21
13:23
14:2[2]
14:3
14:5
14:9[3]
14:12
14:16
14:20
14:21
14:24
14:25
14:26[2]
15:2[2]
15:3
15:5[2]
15:9
15:12
15:18
15:24
15:27
15:33[2]
15:34
15:38
16:2[2]
16:8
16:10
16:12
16:14
16:20
17:2
17:7
17:18[2]
17:23
17:25
18:2[2]
18:3
18:5
18:7
18:9
18:10
18:15
18:18
18:36
18:37
19:2
19:8
19:37
20:1
20:4
20:13[2]
21:1[3]
21:2
21:15
21:16
21:18
21:19[2]
21:20
21:26
22:1[2]
22:2
22:7[2]
22:9
22:19
23:2
23:3
23:11
23:15
23:22
23:23
23:25
23:26
23:31[2]
23:32
23:36[2]
23:37
24:8[2]
24:9
24:10
24:18[2]
24:19
25:2
25:3
25:4
25:13
25:16
25:17[2]
25:19
25:21
25:30

1 CH

1:19[2]
1:39
1:43
1:44
1:45
1:46[2]
1:47
1:48
1:49
1:50[2]
2:3
2:17
2:19
2:21
2:24
2:26[2]
2:29
2:34
2:42
2:45[2]
2:49
3:10
4:3
4:9
4:11
4:40
4:41
5:1[2]
5:2
5:6
5:7
5:20
5:22
6:54
7:2
7:9
7:15[2]
7:16
7:24
7:25
7:40
8:29
8:34
8:37
9:17
9:20[2]
9:21
9:27
9:31
9:35
9:40
10:3
10:4
10:5
11:2
11:6
11:9
11:12[2]
11:13[2]
11:16[2]
11:18
11:20
11:21[2]
11:23
11:25
12:3
12:14
12:18
12:22
12:27
12:40
13:4
13:10
13:11
13:12
14:2
14:8
15:22[2]
15:27
16:39
17:13
17:17
18:15
18:16
18:17
19:10
19:17
20:1
20:2
20:4
20:5[2]
20:6[3]
21:5
21:6
21:7
21:15
21:20
21:30
22:7
23:1
23:3
23:8
23:11
23:13
23:16
24:21
24:25
24:29
25:1
25:7
26:1
26:10
26:20
26:24
26:28
26:31
27:2
27:3
27:4[2]
27:5
27:6[2]
27:7
27:8
27:9
27:10
27:11
27:12
27:13
27:14
27:15
27:16
27:24
27:25[2]
27:26
27:27[2]
27:28[2]
27:29[2]
27:30[2]
27:31[2]
27:32[2]
27:33[2]
27:34[2]
29:27

2 CH

1:1[2]
1:3[2]
1:6
1:11
1:13
2:14
3:3[2]
3:4[3]
3:6
3:8
3:9
3:11[2]
3:12[2]
3:15[2]
4:3[2]
4:4
4:5
4:6
4:11
4:19
5:1
5:3
5:10
5:13
6:7
6:8[2]
7:7[2]
8:16[3]
9:1[2]
9:2
9:4
9:5
9:6
9:9
9:13
9:19
9:20
9:31
10:2
10:15
10:18
11:1
12:13[2]
12:16
13:2[2]
13:7
13:13
13:14
14:1
14:2
14:5
14:14
15:4
15:5
15:6
15:8
15:9
15:15
15:17
15:19
16:3
16:6
16:10[2]
16:12[2]
16:14
17:3
17:6
17:15
17:16
17:18
18:14
18:32
20:25
20:26
20:29
20:30
20:31[2]
20:32
21:1
21:3
21:4
21:5
21:6
21:17[2]
21:20
22:2[2]
22:3
22:6
22:7[2]
22:8
22:9
22:10
22:11
22:12
23:15
23:18
23:19
23:21
24:1[2]
24:2
24:4
24:11[2]
24:13
24:15[2]
25:1[2]
25:2
25:3
25:10[2]
25:14
25:15
25:18[3]
25:22
26:1
26:3[2]
26:4
26:13
26:15[2]
26:16[2]
26:19[2]
26:20
26:21[3]
27:1[2]
27:2
27:8
28:1[2]
28:5
28:7
28:9[3]
29:1[2]
29:2
29:6
29:8
29:25
29:28
29:32
29:34
29:35
29:36
30:5
30:12
30:17
30:18
30:26[2]
30:27
31:1
31:12[2]
31:14
31:20
32:2[2]
32:4
32:5
32:14
32:15
32:21
32:23
32:24
32:25[2]
32:31[2]
33:1
33:2
33:12
33:13[2]
33:19[2]
33:20
33:21
33:22
34:1
34:2
34:3
34:9
34:14
34:16
34:17
34:27
34:30
35:10
35:16
35:18
35:19
35:24
35:26
36:2
36:5[2]
36:8
36:9[2]
36:10
36:11
36:12
36:16

EZR

1:6
2:61
2:64
3:1
3:3
3:6
3:11
3:12
3:13
4:7
4:14
4:15
4:20
4:23
5:5
5:7
5:11
5:14[2]
5:17
6:1
6:2[2]
6:15[2]
7:6
7:8
7:28[2]
8:22
8:23
8:31
8:33[3]
8:34
8:35
10:9

NE

1:1
1:11
2:1
2:2
2:10
2:11
2:12
2:14[2]
2:18
3:16
3:25
4:1
4:3
4:6
4:15
4:18
5:1
5:6
5:14
5:18[3]
6:1
6:6
6:10
6:13
6:15
6:16
6:18
7:1
7:2
7:4
7:7
7:63
7:64
7:66
7:72
8:1
8:3
8:5
8:17
8:18
10:29
11:9[2]
11:11
11:14
11:17
11:22
11:23
11:24
12:8
12:37
12:43
13:1
13:4
13:5
13:6
13:13[2]
13:26[2]
13:28

ES

1:2
1:8
1:10
1:11
1:12
1:13
1:14
2:1[2]
2:5[2]
2:7
2:8[2]
2:12
2:13
2:15
2:16
2:20
2:22
2:23[3]
3:4
3:5
3:12[2]
3:14
3:15[2]
4:1
4:3
4:4
4:5[2]
4:6
4:8
5:2[2]
5:9
6:2
6:4
7:6
7:7
7:8[2]

7:10 8:1 8:9 8:13 8:14 8:15 9:1 9:4 9:11 9:14 9:22 9:32 10:3

JOB

1:1^3 1:3^2 1:5 1:6 1:13 1:16 1:17 1:18 2:1 2:11 2:13 3:3^2 3:25 3:26^2 4:4 4:12 4:16^2 8:7 15:7 15:19 16:12 17:6 20:4 22:16 23:17 29:4^2 29:5 29:13 29:14 29:15^2 29:16 29:19 29:20^2 30:2 30:25^2 31:18 31:23 31:25 32:1 32:2^2 32:3 32:5^2 32:6 32:12 33:27 42:7

PS

4:1 7:4 18:7 18:9 18:12 18:17 18:23 18:41 22:9 22:10 30:7 31:11 31:13 32:4 33:9 35:13 37:36 38:13 38:14 39:2 39:3^2 39:9 50:21 51:5 53:5 55:12^2 55:13 55:18 55:21 63:*title* 66:14 66:17 68:8 68:9 68:11 68:14 69:10 69:12 69:20 73:3 73:16 73:21^2 73:22^2 74:5 76:8 77:3^2 77:18 78:8 78:21^2 78:30 78:35 78:37 78:59 78:62 79:3 81:4 87:5 87:6 95:10 97:8 105:17 105:18 105:37 105:38 106:9 106:11 106:18 106:30 106:31 106:38 106:40 107:12 114:2 114:3 116:6 116:10 119:67 119:158 122:1 124:1 124:2 124:3 126:2 139:15^2 139:16 142:*title* 142:3 142:4

PR

4:3 5:14 8:23^2 8:24 8:25 8:27 8:30^2 23:35 24:31^2

EC

1:10 1:12 2:3 2:9 2:10 2:11^2 2:15 2:24 3:16^2 4:1 5:6 7:23 9:14 9:15 12:7 12:9 12:10^2

CA

2:3 2:4 3:4 5:6 6:12 8:10 8:11

ISA

1:21 6:4 7:2^2 9:1 10:14 10:26 11:16 14:28 21:3 21:14 22:14 22:25 23:13 26:16 28:13 36:3 36:21 36:22 37:2 37:8 37:38 38:1 38:8 38:9 38:20 39:1 39:2^3 41:28^2 43:10 43:12 43:13 47:6 48:8 48:16 49:20 50:2^2 50:5 52:14 53:3 53:5^3 53:7^2 53:8^3 53:9 53:12 57:17^2 59:15 59:16^2 59:17 63:3 63:5^2 63:8 63:10 65:1 65:2

JER

2:2 2:3 3:21 4:23 4:25 4:26 7:12 8:16 11:19 13:7^2 13:20 14:4 14:5 14:6 15:9 15:16 17:16 18:4 20:1 20:2 20:7 20:8 20:9^2 20:14 22:15 22:16^2 25:1 26:20 26:21 26:24 28:1 31:11 31:15 31:18 31:19^3 31:26 31:32 32:1 32:2^2 32:8 32:9 32:11^2 33:1 35:4^2 35:23^3 37:5 37:11 37:13^3 37:16 38:6^2 38:7 38:27 38:28^3 39:2 39:15 40:5 41:7 41:9 44:6^2 46:2 46:5 46:21 48:13 48:27^2 49:12 49:21 51:5 51:59 52:1^2 52:2 52:5 52:6^2 52:8 52:12 52:17 52:19^2 52:20 52:21^2 52:22^2 52:27 52:34

LA

1:1^2 2:5 2:12 3:10 3:14 4:6 4:7 4:20 5:10

EZE

1:1 1:2 1:3 1:4 1:5 1:7 1:12 1:13^2 1:16^2 1:20^3 1:21 1:22 1:25^2 1:26^3 1:28^2 2:9^2 2:10^2 3:3 3:14 3:22 8:3 8:4 8:14 9:2 9:3^2 9:8 10:1 10:4^2 10:5 10:7^2 10:9 10:13 10:14^2 10:17 10:19 10:21 10:22 11:22 13:7 13:10 15:5 16:3 16:4 16:8 16:13 16:14 16:15 16:19 16:36 16:45 16:49 16:56 16:57 17:7 17:8 19:4 19:5 19:7 19:8 19:10 19:11 19:12 21:22 22:10 23:5 23:11 23:13 23:17^2 23:18^2 23:40 23:42 23:43 24:18 25:3^2 26:2 27:7^2 27:12 27:16 27:18 27:20 28:13^2 28:15 28:17 29:18^2 30:22 31:3^2 31:5 31:7^2 31:8 32:15 32:25 33:22^4 33:24 34:4^4 34:6 34:8 34:16^4 35:10 35:15 36:17 36:23 36:35 36:36 37:1^2 37:7^2 37:8 40:1^2 40:2 40:3^2 40:6^2 40:7^2 40:9 40:12^2 40:13 40:18 40:21 40:22^2 40:23 40:25 40:27 40:29 40:33 40:36 40:40 40:43 40:44^2 40:47 40:48 40:49 41:1 41:2 41:6 41:7^2 41:9^4 41:10 41:11^3 41:12^3 41:15 41:18^2 41:19^2 41:22 42:1^2 42:2^2 42:3^2 42:4 42:6 42:7^2 42:8 42:9 42:11 42:12 43:2 43:3 44:1 44:5^3 46:19^2 46:21 46:23^2 47:5 48:35

DA

1:4 1:19 2:1 2:3 2:12 2:14 2:19 2:26 2:31^2 2:32 2:34 2:35^2 2:45 3:1 3:19^3 3:22 3:24 3:27 4:4 4:8 4:10 4:11 4:12^2 4:19^2 4:20 4:21 4:31 4:33^3 4:36^2 5:2 5:3 5:6 5:9^2 5:11 5:13 5:20^2 5:21^4 5:24^2 5:25 5:30 6:2 6:3^2 6:4^2 6:10 6:14 6:17 6:22 6:23^3 7:4^3 7:6 7:7 7:9^2 7:10 7:11 7:14 7:15 7:19 7:20 7:22 8:2^2 8:3 8:4 8:5 8:6 8:7^3 8:8^2 8:11^2 8:12 8:17 8:18^2 8:26 8:27^2 9:1 9:20 9:21 10:1^4 10:2 10:4 10:6 10:8^2 10:9 10:19 12:1^2 12:6 12:7

HO

1:10 2:3 2:7 7:1 9:8 10:14 11:1 11:4 12:13 13:6

AM

1:1 2:9^2 4:7 7:1 7:14^3

JON

1:4^2 1:5^2 1:11 1:13 1:17 2:6 3:3 4:1 4:2^2 4:6 4:7

NA

3:8^3 3:9 3:10

HAB

3:2 3:3 3:4^2 3:8^3 3:9 3:14

ZEP

3:18 3:19

HAG

2:15 2:18

ZEC

1:15 3:3 5:7 5:9 7:7 7:14 8:2^2 8:9 8:10^2 10:2 10:3 11:11^2 11:13 13:6

MAL

1:2 1:13 2:5^2 2:6^2 3:16

MT

1:16 1:18^3 1:19 1:22^2 2:1 2:3 2:9 2:15^2 2:16^2 2:17^2 2:18 2:19 2:22 2:23 3:3 3:4 3:16 4:1 4:2 4:12 4:14 5:1 5:21 5:27 6:29 7:25 7:27 8:1 8:3 8:5 8:13 8:14 8:16 8:17 8:23 8:24^2 8:26 8:28 8:30 8:33 9:20 9:22 9:28 9:33^2 9:36 10:3 11:14 12:3 12:4 12:9 12:10 12:13 12:17 12:22 12:40 13:6 13:19 13:26 13:33 13:35 13:47 13:48 13:54 14:6 14:9 14:11 14:14 14:15 14:23^2 14:24^2 14:29 14:30 15:28 15:37 16:20 17:2^2 17:18 17:25 18:11 18:24 18:27 18:31^2 18:34^2 19:8 20:8 21:4^2 21:10^2 21:23^2 21:25 21:33 22:7 22:10 22:12 22:31 22:35 22:46 24:21 25:6 25:10 25:25 25:35^3 25:36^2 25:42^2 25:43 26:3 26:6 26:20 26:56 26:71^2 27:1 27:3 27:8 27:9^3 27:12 27:15 27:19 27:24 27:35 27:45 27:51 27:54 27:56 27:57^2 27:61 27:63 28:2 28:3 28:5

MK

1:6 1:9 1:13^2 1:14 1:23 1:33 1:42 1:45 2:1^2 2:2 2:3 2:4 2:25 2:27 3:1 3:5 4:1 4:6^2 4:10 4:15 4:22 4:35 4:36 4:37 4:38 4:39 5:2 5:5 5:11 5:14^2 5:15 5:16 5:18 5:21^2 5:26 5:29^2 5:33 5:36 5:39 5:40 5:42 6:2 6:14^2 6:20 6:21 6:26 6:34 6:35 6:47^2 6:48 6:52 6:55 7:17 7:26 7:30 7:32 7:35 8:8 8:25 9:2 9:7 9:26 9:28 9:33 10:1 10:14 10:17 10:22 10:47 11:11 11:12 11:13 11:18 11:19 11:27 11:30 11:32 12:11 13:19 14:1 14:4 14:32 14:45 14:49 14:66 15:7 15:25 15:26 15:28^2 15:33^2 15:38 15:39 15:40 15:41 15:42^2 15:46 15:47 16:1 16:4^2 16:6 16:9 16:11 16:14 16:19

LU

1:5^3 1:7 1:9 1:12 1:26 1:27^2 1:29 1:36 1:41 1:64 1:66 1:67 1:80 2:2^2 2:4 2:6 2:7 2:13 2:17 2:20 2:21^3 2:25^4 2:26 2:36^2 2:37 2:40 2:42 2:51 3:21 3:23^2 3:24^5 3:25^5 3:26^5 3:27^5 3:28^5 3:29^5 3:30^5 3:31^5 3:32^5 3:33^5 3:34^5 3:35^5 3:36^5 3:37^5 3:38^4 4:1 4:16 4:17^2 4:25^2 4:26^2 4:27 4:29 4:32 4:33 4:38 4:40 4:41 4:42 5:3 5:9 5:10 5:12 5:17^2 5:18 5:29 5:36 6:3 6:6^2 6:10 6:13 6:16 6:48 6:49 7:2^2 7:4 7:6 7:12^3 7:15 7:37 7:41 8:5 8:6 8:20 8:24 8:29^2 8:32 8:34 8:35 8:36^2 8:40 8:41 8:47^2 8:53 8:56 9:7^4 9:8 9:17 9:18 9:29^2 9:36^2 9:42 9:45 9:51 9:53 10:32 10:33 10:36 10:40 11:1 11:14^3 11:30 11:50 12:27 13:10 13:11^2 13:13 13:21 14:2 14:30 15:6 15:20 15:24^2 15:25 15:28 15:30 15:32^3 16:1^2 16:19^2 16:20^2 16:22^2 17:10 17:15 17:16 17:20 17:26 17:28 18:2 18:3 18:23^2 18:24 18:34 18:35 18:40 19:2^3 19:3^2 19:4 19:7 19:10 19:11 19:15 19:22 19:29 19:37 19:41 20:4 20:6 20:7 21:5 21:37 22:14 22:22 22:23 22:24 22:37 22:39 22:40 22:41 22:44 22:45 22:47 22:53 22:56 22:59 22:66 23:7 23:8^2 23:19 23:25 23:38 23:44^2 23:45^2 23:47^2 23:50^2 23:51 23:53^2 23:54 23:55 24:6 24:10 24:12 24:13 24:18 24:19 24:23 24:35 24:44 24:51

JOH

1:1^3 1:2 1:3^2 1:4^2 1:6^2 1:8^2 1:9 1:10^2 1:14 1:15^2 1:17 1:28 1:30 1:39 1:40 1:44 2:1^2 2:2 2:9^2 2:13 2:17 2:20 2:22 2:23 2:25 3:1 3:23^2 3:24 3:26 4:6 4:45 4:46^2 4:47^2 4:51 4:53 4:54 5:1 5:4 5:5 5:9^2 5:10 5:13^2 5:15 5:18 5:35 6:4 6:10 6:16 6:17^2 6:21 6:22 6:24 6:62 6:71 7:2 7:12 7:30 7:39^2 7:42 7:43 8:4 8:9 8:20 8:44 8:56 8:58 9:1 9:2 9:8 9:13 9:14 9:16 9:19 9:20 9:22 9:24 9:25 9:32^2 10:19 10:22^2 11:1 11:2^2 11:6^2 11:15 11:18 11:20 11:30^2 11:32^2 11:33 11:38 11:39 11:41 11:44^2 11:55 12:1 12:2 12:3 12:5 12:6^2 12:9 12:12 12:16 12:17 12:21 13:1 13:3 13:5 13:12 13:21 13:23 13:30 13:31 16:4 17:5 17:12 18:1 18:10 18:13^2 18:14^2 18:15 18:16 18:18 18:28 18:37 18:40 19:8 19:14 19:19 19:20^3 19:23 19:29 19:31^2 19:32 19:33 19:41^3 19:42 20:1 20:7 20:14 20:24 21:4^2 21:7^2 21:11 21:12 21:14 21:17

AC

1:2 1:9 1:16 1:17 1:19 1:22 1:23 1:26 2:1 2:6 2:16 2:24 2:26 2:31 3:2 3:10 3:11 3:13 3:20 4:3 4:4 4:11 4:14 4:21 4:22^2 4:31 4:33 4:34 4:35 4:36 5:4^3 5:7^2 5:36 6:1 7:2 7:4 7:9 7:12 7:13^2 7:20^2 7:21 7:22^2 7:23 7:24 7:29 7:38 7:58 8:1^3 8:8 8:9^2 8:13 8:16 8:18 8:28 8:32^2 8:33 8:40 9:9 9:10 9:18 9:19^2 9:24 9:26^2 9:28 9:33 9:36^2 9:37 9:38^2 9:39^2 9:42 10:1 10:4 10:7 10:16^2 10:18 10:20 10:22 10:25 10:29 10:30 10:37 10:38 10:42 10:45 11:2 11:5 11:10 11:11 11:17 11:21 11:22 11:23 11:24^2 12:5^2 12:6 12:9^2 12:11 12:12 12:15 12:18^2 12:20^2 12:23 12:25 13:1^2 13:6 13:7 13:12 13:29 13:31 13:32 13:36 13:43 13:46 13:49 14:4 14:5 14:12 14:13 15:5 15:37 15:39 16:1^3 16:2 16:3 16:13 16:15 16:19 16:26 16:33 16:35 17:1 17:2 17:13 17:16 17:34 18:3 18:5^2 18:12 18:14 18:25 18:27^2 18:28 19:1 19:16 19:17^2 19:29 19:32 19:34 20:1 20:3 20:9^2 20:11 20:14 20:20 21:3 21:8 21:11 21:30 21:31 21:33 21:35^2 21:37 21:40 22:3 22:6 22:17^2 22:20^2 22:28 22:29^2 22:30 23:5 23:7 23:12 23:27^2 23:30 23:31 23:34^2 24:2 24:24 25:1 25:7 25:15 25:19 25:23^3 26:4 26:19 26:26 26:27 27:8 27:9^3 27:12 27:15 27:20 27:25 27:27 27:33 27:39 27:41 27:42 28:1 28:6 28:7 28:9 28:16 28:17 28:18 28:19

RO

1:3 1:13 1:21 1:27 4:3 4:9 4:10^2 4:13 4:18 4:19 4:20 4:21 4:22 4:23^2 4:25^2 5:13 5:14 5:16^2 6:4 6:17 7:8 7:9 7:10 7:13 8:3 8:20 9:12 9:25 9:26 10:20^2 15:8 15:20 15:21 16:25

1 CO

1:6 1:13 2:3 2:4 7:20 10:4 10:5 11:9 11:29 13:11 15:4 15:5 15:6 15:7 15:8 15:10^3 15:45^2 15:46 16:12 16:17 16:*sub.*

2 CO

1:15 1:17 1:18 1:19^3 2:6

2:12 3:7[2] 3:10 3:11 5:19 7:7 7:13 8:9 8:11 8:19 9:2 11:5 11:9[3] 11:25[2] 11:33 12:4 12:7 12:13 13:4 13:*sub.*

GA
1:11 1:12 1:22 2:3[2] 2:7[2] 2:8 2:9 2:10 2:11[2] 2:13 3:6 3:17[3] 3:19[3] 3:24 4:4 4:14 4:23[3] 4:28 4:29[2]

EPH
3:5 3:7

PHP
2:5 2:7 2:26 2:27 2:30 2:*sub.*

COL
1:23 2:14[2]

1 TH
2:1 2:3 2:*sub.*

2 TH
1:10 2:5 2:*sub.*

1 TI
1:11 1:13 1:14 2:13 2:14[2] 3:16 4:14 4:*sub.*

2 TI
1:9 1:14 1:16 1:17 2:8 3:9 4:17 4:*sub*[2]

TIT
3:*sub.*

PHM
11

HEB
2:2 2:3 2:9 3:2[2] 3:3 3:5 3:10 3:17[2] 4:2 4:6 4:15 5:4 5:7[2] 6:18 7:4 7:10 7:11 7:20 7:22 7:28 8:5[2] 8:6 9:2[2] 9:4 9:8[2] 9:9 9:18 9:23 9:28 10:29 11:4 11:5[2] 11:8 11:11[2] 11:17 11:18 11:19 11:21 11:23[3] 11:24 11:38 12:2 12:17 12:20 12:21

JAS
1:24 2:21 2:22 2:23[3] 2:25 5:17

1 PE
1:11 1:12 1:20[2] 2:22 2:23 3:20 4:6

2 PE
1:9 2:16 2:22 3:6

1 JO
1:1 1:2[3] 3:5 3:8 3:12 4:9

JUDE
3[2]

RE
1:4 1:8 1:9 1:10 1:16 1:18 2:8 2:13 4:1[2] 4:2[2] 4:3[2] 4:6 4:7[2] 4:8 5:3 5:4 5:11 5:12 6:2 6:4[3] 6:8[2] 6:12 7:2 8:1 8:3[2] 8:7[2] 8:8 8:12[2] 9:1 9:3 9:4 9:5[2] 9:9 9:10 9:18 10:1[2] 10:4 10:10[2] 11:1 11:8 11:13 11:19 12:4[2] 12:5[2] 12:7 12:8 12:9[2] 12:13 12:17 13:2 13:3 13:5[2] 13:7[2] 13:12 14:5 14:16 14:20 15:5 15:8[2] 16:8 16:10 16:12 16:18[2] 16:19 16:21 17:4 17:5 17:8[2] 17:11 18:1 18:16 18:24 19:8 19:11 19:13 19:20 20:4 20:10 20:11 20:12 20:15[2] 21:1 21:11 21:18[2] 21:19 21:21[2] 22:2

WE

587, *2249*

GE
3:2 11:4 13:8 19:2 19:5 19:9 19:13 19:32 19:34 20:13 24:25 24:50 24:57 26:16 26:22 26:28 26:29 26:32 29:4 29:5 29:8[2] 29:27 31:15 31:49 32:6 34:14 34:15 34:16[4] 34:17 37:7 37:20[2] 37:26 37:32 38:23 40:8 41:11[2] 41:12 41:38 42:2 42:11 42:21[3] 42:31 42:32 43:4 43:5 43:7[2] 43:8[3] 43:10 43:18 43:20 43:21[3] 43:22[2] 4:8[3] 4:9 4:16[5] 4:20 4:22 4:24[2] 4:26[4] 46:34 47:3 47:4[2] 47:15 47:18 47:19[4] 47:25 50:15 50:17 50:18

EX
1:9 3:18[2] 5:3 8:26 10:9[3] 10:25 10:26[3] 12:33 14:5 14:12[3] 15:24 16:3[2] 16:7 16:8 17:2 19:8 20:19[2] 24:3 24:7 24:14 32:1 32:23 33:16

LE
25:20[2]

NU
9:7[3] 10:29[2] 10:31 10:32 11:5[2] 11:13 11:20 12:11[2] 13:27 13:28 13:30 13:31[2] 13:32[2] 13:33 14:2 14:7 14:40[2] 16:12 16:14 17:12[3] 17:13 20:3 20:4 20:10 20:15 20:16[2] 20:17[5] 20:19 21:7[2] 21:22[4] 21:30[2] 22:6 31:50 32:5 32:16 32:17[2] 32:18 32:19 32:31 32:32

DE
1:19[3] 1:22[3] 1:28[3] 1:41[2] 2:1 2:2 2:8[2] 2:13 2:14[2] 2:33 2:34[2] 2:35[2] 3:1 3:3 3:4[2] 3:6[2] 3:7 3:8 3:12 3:29 4:7 5:24[2] 5:25[3] 5:26 5:27 6:21 6:25 12:8 18:21 26:7 29:7 29:8 29:16[2] 29:29 30:12 30:13

JOS
1:16[2] 1:17[2] 2:10 2:11 2:14 2:17 2:18 2:19 2:20 4:23 5:1 6:17 7:7 8:5 8:6[2] 9:6 9:7 9:8 9:9 9:11 9:12[2] 9:13 9:19[2] 9:20[3] 9:22 9:24 9:25 10:4 22:17 22:23 22:24 22:26 22:27 22:28[2] 22:29 22:31 24:15 24:16 24:17[2] 24:18 24:21 24:22 24:24[2]

JG
1:3 1:24[2] 8:6 8:15 8:25 9:28[2] 9:38 10:10[2] 10:15[2] 11:6 11:8 11:10 11:19 11:24 12:1 13:8 13:12[2] 13:15 13:17 13:22[2] 14:13 14:15[2] 15:10 15:12[2] 15:13[2] 16:2 16:5[3] 18:5[3] 18:9[2] 19:12[2] 19:18 19:22 20:8[2] 20:9[2] 20:10 20:13 21:7[3] 21:16 21:18 21:22[2]

RU
1:10 4:11

1 SA
5:8 6:2[2] 6:4 6:9 7:6 8:19 8:20 9:6 9:7[3] 9:22[2] 10:14[2] 11:1 11:3[2] 11:10 11:12 12:10[3] 12:19[2] 14:8[2] 14:9[2] 14:10 14:12 15:15 16:11 17:9 17:10 20:42 23:3[2] 25:7 25:8 25:15[4] 25:16 30:14[2] 30:22[2]

2 SA
5:1 7:22 11:23 12:18[2] 13:25 14:7[2] 14:14 15:14 16:20 17:2 17:6 17:12[2] 17:18 19:6 19:10 19:42 19:43[2] 20:1[2] 21:4 21:5 21:6

1 KI
3:18[2] 8:47 12:4 12:9 12:16[2] 17:12 18:5[2] 20:23[2] 20:25[2] 20:31 22:3 22:7 22:8 22:15[2]

2 KI
2:16 3:8 3:11 6:1 6:2[2] 6:15 6:28[2] 6:29[2] 7:3[2] 7:4[7] 7:9[4] 7:10 7:12[2] 10:4 10:5[2] 10:13[2] 18:22 18:26

1 CH
11:1 12:18 13:3 15:13 16:35 17:20 29:13 29:14[2] 29:15 29:16

2 CH
2:16[2] 6:37[2] 10:4 10:9 10:16[2] 13:10 13:11 14:7[2] 14:11[2] 18:3 18:5 18:6 18:7 18:14 20:9 20:12[2] 25:9 28:13 29:18 29:19 31:10

EZR
4:2[2] 4:3 4:14[2] 4:16 5:4 5:8 5:9 5:10[2] 5:11 7:24 8:15 8:21 8:22 8:23 8:31 8:32 9:7[2] 9:9 9:10[2] 9:14 9:15[3] 10:2 10:4 10:12 10:13[2]

NE
1:6 1:7 2:17[2] 2:20 4:1 4:4 4:6 4:9 4:10 4:11 4:15 4:19 4:21 5:2[3] 5:3[2] 5:4 5:5 5:8 5:12[2] 5:16 9:33 9:36[2] 9:37 9:38 10:30 10:31[2] 10:32 10:34 10:37 10:39 13:27

ES
1:15 7:4[2]

JOB
2:10[2] 4:2 5:27 8:9 9:32 15:9 18:2 18:3 19:28 21:14 21:15[3] 28:23 31:31[2] 32:13 36:26 37:5 37:19[2] 38:35

PS
12:4 20:5[2] 20:7 20:8 20:9 21:13 33:21 33:22 35:25[2] 36:9 44:1 44:5[2] 44:8 44:17[2] 44:20 44:22[2] 46:2 48:8[2] 48:9 55:14 60:12 65:4 66:6 66:12 74:9 75:1[2] 78:3 78:4 79:4 79:8 79:13[2] 80:3 80:7 80:14 80:18[2] 80:19 90:7[2] 90:9 90:10 90:12 90:14 90:15 95:7 100:3[2] 103:14 106:6[3] 108:13 115:18 118:24 118:26 123:3 124:7 126:1 126:3 129:8 132:6 137:1

PR
1:13[2] 24:12

CA
1:4[3] 1:11 6:1 6:13 8:8[3] 8:9[2]

ISA
1:9[2] 2:3 4:1 5:19[2] 9:10[2] 14:10 16:6 20:6[2] 22:13 24:16 25:9[3] 26:1 26:8 26:13 26:17 26:18[4] 28:15[4] 30:16[2] 33:2 36:7 36:11 38:20 41:22 41:23[2] 41:26[2] 42:24 46:5 51:23 53:2[2] 53:3[2] 53:4 53:5 53:6[2] 56:12 58:3[2] 59:9[2] 59:10[5] 59:11[2] 59:12 63:19 64:3 64:5[2] 64:6[2] 64:9[2] 64:8[2] 64:9[2]

JER
2:31[2] 3:22 3:25[3] 4:13 5:12 5:17 6:24 7:10 8:8 8:14[2] 8:15 8:20 9:19[3] 13:12 14:7 14:9 14:19 14:20[2] 14:22 15:2 16:10 18:12[2] 20:10[3] 26:19 30:5 35:6 35:8[2] 35:9 35:10 35:11[2] 36:16 38:4 38:25 41:8 42:2[2] 42:3[2] 42:5 42:6[3] 42:13 42:14[3] 42:20 44:16 44:17[4] 44:18[2] 44:19[2] 44:25[2] 48:14 48:29 50:7 51:9 51:51[2]

LA
2:16[4] 3:22 3:42 4:17 4:18 4:20[2] 5:3 5:4 5:5 5:6 5:7 5:9 5:16 5:21

EZE
11:3 20:32 21:10 33:10[2] 33:24 35:10 37:11

DA
2:4 2:7 2:23 2:36 3:16 3:17 3:18 3:24 6:5[2] 9:5 9:6 9:8 9:9 9:10 9:11 9:13[2] 9:14 9:15[2] 9:18

HO
6:2 6:3[2] 8:2 10:3[2] 14:2 14:3[2]

AM
6:10 6:13 8:5[2] 8:6

OB
1

JON
1:6 1:7 1:8 1:11 1:14[2] 3:9

MIC
2:4 4:2 4:5 5:5

HAB
1:12

ZEC
1:11 8:23[2]

MAL
1:4[2] 1:6 1:7 2:10[2] 2:17 3:7 3:8 3:13 3:14[2] 3:15

MT
2:2 3:9 6:12 6:31 7:22 8:25 8:29 9:14 11:3 11:17 12:38 13:28 14:17 15:33 16:7 17:19 17:27 19:27[2] 20:18 20:22 21:25 21:26[2] 21:27 22:16 23:30[2] 25:37 25:38 25:39 25:44 26:17 26:65 27:42 27:63 28:13 28:14

MK
1:24 2:12 4:30[2] 4:38 5:9 5:12 6:37 8:16 9:28 9:38[2] 10:28 10:33 10:35[2] 10:37 10:39 11:31 11:32 11:33 12:14 12:15[2] 14:12 14:58 14:63 15:32

LU
1:71 1:74 3:8 3:10 3:12 3:14 4:23 4:34 5:5 5:26 7:19 7:20 7:32[2] 8:24 9:12 9:13[2] 9:49[2] 9:54 10:11 11:4 13:26 15:32 17:10[2] 18:28 18:31 19:14 20:5 20:6 20:21 22:8 22:9 22:49 22:71[2] 23:2 23:41[2] 24:21

JOH
1:14 1:16 1:22 1:41 1:45 3:2 3:11[3] 4:22[2] 4:42[2] 6:5 6:28[2] 6:30 6:40 6:68 6:69 7:27 7:35 8:33 8:41[2] 8:48 8:52 9:20 9:21[2] 9:24 9:28 9:29[2] 9:31 9:40 9:41 10:33 11:16 11:47 11:48 12:21 12:34 13:29 14:5[2] 14:23 16:18 16:30[2] 17:11 17:22 18:30 19:7 19:15 20:2 20:25 21:3 21:24

AC
2:8[2] 2:11 2:32 2:37 3:12 3:15 4:9 4:12 4:16[2] 4:20[2] 5:23[3] 5:28 5:29 5:32 6:2 6:3 6:4 6:11 6:14 7:40 10:33 10:39 10:47 11:12 13:32 13:46 14:15 14:22 15:10 15:11[2] 15:19 15:20 15:24[2] 15:27 15:36 16:10 16:11 16:12 16:13[2] 16:16 16:28 17:19 17:20 17:28[2] 17:29[2] 17:32 19:2 19:13 19:21 19:40[2] 20:6[2] 20:13 20:14 20:15[3] 21:1[2] 21:2 21:3[2] 21:4 21:5[4] 21:6[2] 21:7[2] 21:8[2] 21:10 21:12[2] 21:14 21:15 21:16 21:17 21:23[2] 21:25 23:9 23:14[3] 23:15 24:2 24:3 24:5 24:6 24:8 26:14 27:1 27:2 27:3 27:4[2] 27:5[2] 27:7[2] 27:15 27:16 27:18 27:19 27:20 27:26 27:27 27:29 27:37 28:10 28:11 28:12 28:13[2] 28:14[2] 28:16 28:21 28:22[2]

RO
1:5 2:2 3:5 3:8[2] 3:9[2] 3:19 3:28 3:31[2] 4:1 4:9 4:24 5:1 5:2[2] 5:3 5:6 5:8 5:9 5:10[3] 5:11[2] 6:1[2] 6:2 6:4[2] 6:5[2] 6:6 6:8[2] 6:15[2] 7:4 7:5 7:6[3] 7:7 7:14 8:12 8:15 8:16 8:17[2] 8:22 8:23 8:24 8:25[3] 8:26[3] 8:28 8:31 8:36[2] 8:37 9:14 9:29 9:30 10:8 12:4 12:5 13:11 14:8[6] 14:10 15:1 15:4

1 CO
1:22 2:6 2:7 2:12[2] 2:13 2:16 3:9 4:8 4:9 4:10[3] 4:11 4:12[2] 4:13[2] 6:3 8:1[2] 8:4 8:6[2] 8:8[4] 9:4 9:5 9:6 9:11[2] 9:12[3] 9:25 10:6 10:16[2] 10:17[2] 10:22[2] 11:16 11:31[2] 11:32[3] 12:13[3] 12:23[2] 13:9[2] 13:12 15:11 15:15[2] 15:19[2] 15:30 15:32 15:49[2] 15:51[2] 15:52

2 CO
1:4[2] 1:6[3] 1:8[3] 1:9[2] 1:10 1:12 1:13 1:14 1:24 2:11 2:15 2:16 2:17[2] 3:1[2] 3:4 3:5 3:12[2] 3:18

4:1^3 4:5 4:7 4:8^2 4:11 4:13^2 4:16 4:18 5:1^2 5:2 5:3 5:4^2 5:6^3 5:7 5:8 5:9^2 5:10 5:11^2 5:12 5:13^2 5:14 5:16^3 5:20^2 5:21 6:1 6:9 7:2^3 7:5^2 7:13^2 7:14 8:1 8:4 8:5 8:6 8:18 8:22^2 9:4 10:2 10:3^2 10:7 10:11^4 10:13 10:14^3 10:15 11:4 11:6 11:12 11:21 12:18^2 12:19^3 13:4^2 13:6 13:7^2 13:8 13:9^3

GA

1:8^2 1:9 2:4 2:5 2:9 2:10 2:15 2:16^2 2:17^2 3:14 3:23 3:24 3:25 4:3^2 4:5 4:28 4:31 5:5 5:25 6:9^2 6:10

EPH

1:4 1:7 1:11 1:12 2:3 2:5 2:10^2 2:18 3:12 3:20 4:13 4:14 4:25 5:30 6:12

PHP

3:3 3:16 3:20

COL

1:3 1:4 1:9 1:14 1:28^2

1 TH

1:2 1:5 1:8 1:9 2:2^2 2:4 2:5 2:6 2:7 2:8 2:9^2 2:10 2:11 2:13 2:17 2:18 3:1^2 3:3 3:4^3 3:6 3:7 3:8 3:9^2 3:10 3:12 4:1 4:2 4:6 4:10 4:11 4:14 4:15^2 4:17^2 5:5 5:10^2 5:12 5:14

2 TH

1:3 1:4 1:11 2:1 2:13 3:2 3:4^2 3:6 3:7 3:8^2 3:9 3:10^2 3:11 3:12

1 TI

1:8 2:2 4:10 6:7^2

2 TI

2:11^2 2:12^3 2:13

TIT

2:12 3:3 3:5 3:7

PHM

7

HEB

2:1^3 2:3^2 2:5 2:8 2:9 3:6^2 3:14^2 3:19 4:3 4:13 4:14 4:15^2 4:16 5:11 6:3 6:9^2 6:11 6:18 6:19 7:19 8:1^2 9:5 10:10 10:26^2 10:30 10:39 11:3 12:1 12:9^3 12:10 12:25^2 12:28^2 13:6 13:10 13:14^2 13:18^2

JAS

1:18 3:1 3:2 3:3^2 3:9^2 4:13 4:15 5:11 5:17

1 PE

2:24 4:3

2 PE

1:16^2 1:18^2 1:19 3:13

1 JO

1:1^3 1:2 1:3^2 1:4 1:5 1:6^3 1:7^2 1:8^3 1:9 1:10^3 2:1 2:3^3 2:5^2 2:18 2:28 3:1 3:2^5 3:11 3:14^3 3:16^2 3:19^2 3:21 3:22^3 3:23 3:24 4:6^2 4:9 4:10 4:11 4:12 4:13^2 4:14 4:16 4:17^2 4:19 4:21 5:2^2 5:3 5:9 5:14^2 5:15^5 5:18 5:19^2 5:20^3

2 JO

4 5^2 6 8^3

3 JO

8^2 12 14

RE

5:10 7:3 11:17

WERE

1961, *2258*

GE

1:5 1:7^2 1:8 1:13 1:19 1:23 1:31 2:1 2:4 2:25 3:7^2 4:8 5:4 5:5 5:8 5:11 5:14 5:17 5:20 5:23 5:27 5:31 6:1 6:2 6:4^2 7:10 7:11^2 7:18 7:19 7:20 7:23^2 8:2 8:3 8:5 8:7 8:8 8:9 8:11 8:13 9:18 9:23 9:29 10:1 10:5 10:18 10:21 10:29 10:31 11:32 13:13 14:3 14:5 14:13 14:17 17:23 17:27 18:11 19:11 19:36 20:8 21:16 23:1 23:17^2 23:20 24:10 24:32 24:54 24:63 25:3 25:4 25:24^2 26:35 27:1 27:15 27:23 27:42 29:2 29:3 30:35^2 30:42^2 31:10 31:19 34:5^2 34:7^2 34:14 34:25 35:2 35:4^2 35:5 35:6 35:22 35:26 35:28 36:5 36:7^2 36:11 36:12 36:13 36:14 36:15 36:16 36:18 36:22 36:23 36:25 37:7 37:27 38:27 39:20 39:22 40:5 40:6 40:7 40:10 41:21 41:48 41:50 41:53 42:28 42:35 43:18 43:34 44:3 44:4 45:3 46:12 46:15 46:20 46:21 46:22^2 46:25 46:26 46:27^3 46:31 48:5 48:10 49:24 50:3 50:4 50:20

EX

1:5 1:7 1:12 3:6 5:12 5:14 5:19 6:4 6:16 6:18 6:20 7:20^3 7:25 8:18 9:26 9:32^2 9:34 10:6 10:8 10:11 10:14^2 12:33 12:37 12:39 14:10 14:11 14:21 14:22 14:29 15:8^2 15:23 15:25 15:27 17:12^2 19:1 19:2^2 19:16 21:3 21:29 22:21 23:9 24:10^2 28:32 32:3 32:15^3 32:16 32:25 34:1 34:30 35:22 35:25 36:6 36:9 36:15 36:29 36:30^2 36:36 36:38 37:9 37:13 37:14 37:16 37:17 37:20 37:22 37:25 38:2 38:9 38:10^2 38:11^2 38:12 38:14 38:15 38:16 38:17^2 38:19 38:20 38:25 38:27 39:13 39:14 40:37

LE

8:28 10:12 10:16 14:35 18:27 18:28 18:30 19:34 26:37

NU

1:1 1:16 1:20 1:21^2 1:22^2 1:23^2 1:24 1:25^2 1:26 1:27^2 1:28 1:29^2 1:30 1:31^2 1:32 1:33^2 1:34 1:35^2 1:36 1:37^2 1:38 1:39^2 1:40 1:41^2 1:42 1:43^2 1:44 1:45^3 1:46^2 1:47 2:4^2 2:6^2 2:8^2 2:9^2 2:11^2 2:13^2 2:15^2 2:16^2 2:19^2 2:21^2 2:23^2 2:24^2 2:26^2 2:28^2 2:30^2 2:31^2 2:32^3 2:33 3:3 3:17 3:22^3 3:28 3:34^2 3:39^2 3:43^2 3:49^2 3:51 4:36^2 4:37^2 4:38 4:40^2 4:41 4:42 4:44^2 4:45 4:46 4:48^2 4:49^2 6:12 7:2^3 7:13 7:86 7:87 7:88 8:21 9:1 9:6^2 9:15 9:22 10:28 11:26^2 11:29 11:31^3 12:3 12:8 13:3 13:4 13:22 13:33^2 14:3 14:6 14:29 14:38 15:26 15:32 16:34 16:39^2 16:49 18:27 19:18 21:32 22:3 22:22 22:29 22:40 23:22 24:8 25:5 25:6 25:9 26:7^2 26:9 26:18 26:19 26:20 26:21 26:22 26:25 26:27 26:28 26:33 26:34 26:37 26:40 26:41^2 26:43^2 26:47^2 26:50^2 26:51 26:54 26:57 26:62^3 26:63 31:5 31:8 31:38 31:39 31:40 31:48 33:9 33:38 36:11 36:12

DE

1:41 2:11 2:14^2 2:15 2:16 3:5 3:32 4:46 4:47 5:5 5:29 6:21 7:7^2 8:25 9:15 10:2 10:29 24:9 25:17 25:18 28:62 28:67^2 29:17 31:24 31:30 32:27 32:29 33:5 34:8

JOS

2:4 2:7 2:8 2:10 2:22 3:15^2 3:16 3:17 4:1 4:7^2 4:11 4:18^2 4:23^2 5:1^3 5:4 5:5^2 5:6^2 5:7 5:8 6:23 7:12 8:7 8:11 8:14 8:15 8:16^3 8:22 8:24^2 8:25 8:35 9:1 9:10 9:13 9:16 9:17 9:24 10:1 10:2 10:11^2 10:20 10:26 10:28 10:30 10:32 10:35^2 10:39 11:2 11:5 11:11 11:19 11:20 11:22 13:21 13:22 13:31 14:4 14:12^2 15:4 15:7 15:11 15:21 16:8 16:9 17:2 17:5 17:9 17:13 18:12 18:14 18:19 18:21 19:8 19:22 19:33 20:9 21:4 21:10 21:19 21:26 21:33 21:40^2 21:41 21:42^2 22:9 22:30 24:15

JG

2:10 2:12 2:15 3:4 3:19 3:24 3:25 4:13 5:6 5:15^2 5:16 5:18 5:22 6:5 6:33 7:1^2 7:6 7:11 7:12 7:19^2 8:4 8:10^2 8:18^2 8:19 8:21 8:24 8:26 9:29 9:34 9:35 9:36 9:40 9:43 9:44 9:47 9:48^2 10:8 10:17 11:3 11:33 12:2 13:23 15:14 16:2 16:7 16:9 16:11 16:12 16:23 16:27^2 16:30^2 17:2 17:4 18:3 18:7^2 18:16 18:17 18:22^3 18:26 18:27 18:30 19:10 19:11 19:14 19:16 19:22 19:27 20:3 20:11 20:15^2 20:16 20:17^2 20:31 20:36 20:41 20:44 20:46^2 21:9^2 21:13

RU

1:13 1:19 4:11

1 SA

1:3 2:5^2 2:12 2:27 4:3 4:4 4:7 4:11 4:15 4:19 5:4 5:12 6:13 6:15 7:7^2 7:10 7:13 7:14 8:2 9:3 9:4 9:5 9:14 9:20 9:25 9:27 10:14 10:16 11:8 11:9 11:11^2 13:2^2 13:4 13:6^2 13:8 13:11 13:15 13:16 13:22 14:2^2 14:14 14:17^2 14:20 14:21^2 14:24 14:26 14:27 14:28 14:31 14:41 14:49^2 16:6 17:1 17:2 17:11 17:13 17:19 17:31 18:26 19:16 20:9 21:5 22:2 22:6^2 22:11 23:13 23:24 25:1 25:2 25:7^2 25:15^4 25:16^2 25:40 25:43 26:12 27:2 27:8 29:4 30:1 30:2 30:3 30:4 30:5 30:16 30:21^2 30:27^3 30:28^3 30:29^3 30:30^3 30:31 31:7^3

2 SA

1:11 1:12 1:23^4 2:3 2:4 2:18 2:24 3:2 3:5 3:20 3:23 3:31 3:34 4:1 4:2 4:3 5:13 5:14 6:2 8:7 8:17 8:18 9:12 9:21 10:8 10:12 10:13 10:16 10:19 12:1 12:31 13:18^2 13:30 14:27 15:4 15:11 15:14 15:16 15:21 15:22 15:24 16:6 16:14 16:22 16:29 18:1 18:7 19:9 19:17 19:28 19:43 20:3 20:8 20:14 20:15 20:18 20:25 21:9 21:13 21:22 22:9 22:13 22:16 22:18 22:23 24:9^2

1 KI

1:8 1:41 1:49^2 2:5 2:11 3:16 3:18 4:2 4:4 4:20 4:28 4:32 5:3 5:14 5:16 6:1 6:24 6:31 6:32 6:34^3 7:4 7:5 7:6 7:9 7:11 7:17 7:18 7:19^2 7:20 7:24^2 7:25 7:28 7:29^3 7:30 7:31 7:32^2 7:33 7:34^2 7:41^2 7:42 7:45 7:47 8:4 8:5^2 8:8^2 8:10 8:47 9:20^2 9:21 9:22 9:23^2 10:12 10:19 10:21^3 11:29 12:1 12:8 12:10 12:21 12:31 14:4 14:9 14:20 14:24 15:14 15:18 16:15 16:16 16:21 16:25 16:30 16:33 20:1 20:15 20:23 20:27^2 20:30 21:8 21:11 22:43 22:48

2 KI

2:3 2:5 2:8 2:9 2:15 2:22 3:14 3:21^2 4:6 4:38 4:40 5:3 6:20^2 7:3 7:5 7:10 9:5 10:4 10:6 10:29^2 11:2 11:9 11:10 12:3 12:13 13:21 14:4 14:14 15:4 15:16^2 15:35 16:17 17:2 17:9 17:15 18:5 18:17 19:12 19:18 19:26^3 19:35 21:11 23:4 23:7 23:8^2 23:12 23:13^2 23:16 23:19 23:20 23:24^2 24:16 25:4 25:5 25:10 25:11 25:13 25:15 25:19^3 25:25 25:26 25:28

1 CH

1:19 1:23 1:51 2:3 2:4 2:9 2:16 2:25 2:27 2:28 2:33 2:42 2:50 3:1^2 3:4 3:5 3:9 3:15 3:19 3:24 4:3 4:6 4:7 4:14 4:17 4:20^2 4:21 4:23 4:24 4:31 4:32 4:33^2 4:38 4:41 4:43 5:3 5:7 5:9 5:13 5:17 5:18 5:20^3 5:24 6:18 6:48 6:49 6:60 6:61^2 6:63 6:71 6:77 6:78 7:1 7:2 7:4 7:7 7:11 7:16 7:17 7:19 7:21 7:28 7:40^2 8:3 8:8 8:10 8:13 8:28 8:35 8:38 8:39 8:40 9:1^3 9:2 9:9 9:17 9:18 9:19^2 9:22^3 9:24 9:25^2 9:26^2 9:29 9:31 9:32 9:33^2 9:34 9:41 9:44 10:7^2 11:4 11:13 11:26 12:1 12:2 12:8^2 12:14 12:20 12:21^2 12:23 12:24 12:27 12:31 12:32^3 12:33 12:38 12:39 12:40 14:12 15:19 15:23 15:24 16:19 16:41^2 16:42 18:7 18:16 18:17 19:5^2 19:9^2 19:14 19:15 19:16^2 19:19 20:2 20:3 20:4 20:5 20:6 20:8 21:16 21:29 22:2 23:3 23:4^2 23:5 23:7 23:9 23:10^2 23:11 23:14 23:15 23:17^2 23:24^2 23:27 24:4^3 24:5^2 24:19 24:20 24:26 24:30 25:5 25:6 25:7^2 25:9 25:10 25:11 25:12 25:13 25:14 25:15 25:16 25:17 25:18 25:19 25:20 25:21 25:22 25:23 25:24 25:25 25:26 25:27 25:28 25:29 25:30 25:31 26:2 26:4 26:6^2 26:7 26:8 26:11 26:12 26:17 26:21 26:22 26:26 26:29 26:30 26:31^2 26:32 27:1 27:2 27:4 27:5 27:7 27:8 27:9 27:10 27:11 27:12 27:13 27:14 27:15 27:22 27:28 27:29 27:31 29:8 29:15

2 CH

2:17^2 3:11 3:13

4:3 4:4 4:12^{2} 4:13 4:19 4:22 5:5 5:6 5:9^{2} 5:11^{3} 5:12 5:13 8:7^{2} 8:8 8:9 8:10 9:11 9:18^{2} 9:20^{3} 10:1 10:8 10:10 11:1 11:13 12:3 12:5 12:15 13:13 13:18 14:8 14:13^{2} 15:5 15:17 16:8 17:10 17:13 18:30 20:22^{2} 20:24 20:25 20:33 20:37^{2} 21:2 21:13 21:16 22:4 22:6 22:11 23:8^{2} 23:9 23:14 24:14 24:25 25:12 25:24 26:12 26:17 28:6 28:15^{2} 28:23 29:29 29:31 29:32 29:33 29:34^{2} 29:35 30:8 30:14 30:15 30:17^{2} 30:21 31:1 31:6 31:13 31:15 31:19^{3} 32:3 32:9 32:13 32:18 32:19 34:4 34:12 34:13^{3} 34:32 34:33 35:3 35:7^{2} 35:14 35:15 35:17 35:18 36:20

EZR

1:6 1:11^{2} 2:58 2:59^{2} 2:62^{3} 2:65^{2} 2:66 3:1 3:5 3:8 3:12 5:1 5:2 5:6 5:10 5:14 6:1 6:20^{2} 6:21 8:3 8:20 8:35 9:1 9:4 9:9 10:15 10:16 10:18

NE

1:2 1:9 2:13^{2} 4:7^{2} 4:16 5:2 5:3 5:4 5:8 5:15 5:16 5:17 5:18 6:16^{2} 6:18 7:1 7:4^{2} 7:60 7:61^{2} 7:64^{2} 7:67 7:73 8:3 8:12 8:13 8:17 9:1 9:17 9:25 9:26 10:1 10:8 11:6 11:12 11:18 11:19 11:20 11:21 11:22 11:36 12:7 12:9 12:12 12:23 12:25 12:26 12:44 12:46 13:10 13:13

ES

1:5^{2} 1:6^{2} 2:7 2:8 2:9 2:12 2:14 2:19 2:21 2:23 3:1 3:2 3:3 3:6 3:12^{2} 3:13 6:1 6:14 8:9 8:11 9:11 9:15 9:16 9:18 9:20

JOB

1:2 1:5 1:13 1:14 1:18 4:7 6:2 6:20^{2} 9:15 9:21 16:4 19:20 19:23^{2} 19:24 21:4 22:16 28:5 29:2 29:5 30:3 30:5 30:7 30:8^{2} 31:20 31:28 32:4 32:15 33:21 34:35 39:16 42:15

PS

14:2 14:5 14:7 17:12 18:7 18:8 18:11 18:15^{2} 18:17 18:22 18:27 18:38 22:5^{2} 33:6 34:5^{2} 35:13 39:12 45:9 46:6 48:4 48:5 50:12 53:2 53:5 53:6 55:18 55:21^{3} 68:25 68:33 73:2 77:16^{2} 78:29 78:30 78:37 78:39 78:57 78:63 80:10^{2} 81:6 90:2 105:12 106:35 106:36 106:39 106:42 106:43 119:5 126:1 139:16^{2} 148:5

PR

8:24^{2} 8:25 8:31

EC

2:7 2:9 4:1 7:10 8:10

CA

1:6 5:4 6:13

ISA

5:18 5:25 7:23 10:15 14:2 26:18 26:20 27:13 30:4 30:5 33:3 37:12 37:19 37:27^{3} 37:36 41:5 41:11 42:24 46:1^{2} 51:13 52:14 53:3 63:19

JER

1:1 4:25 4:26 5:8 6:15 8:12^{2} 9:1 11:13 14:3 14:4 15:16 20:2 22:24 22:26 24:1 24:2 26:9 29:1 29:2 30:14 30:15 31:2 31:15 34:5 34:7 34:8 34:15 36:16 36:24 36:28 36:32 37:15 37:21 40:1^{2} 40:4 40:6 40:7^{2} 40:11^{2} 40:12 40:13 41:2 41:3^{2} 41:7 41:8 41:9 41:10 41:11 41:13^{3} 41:16 41:18 42:8 42:16 43:5 44:17 49:2 50:11 50:33 52:7 52:14 52:17 52:20 52:22 52:23^{2} 52:25^{2} 52:30 52:32

LA

2:4 2:6 4:5 4:7^{3} 4:10 5:12

EZE

1:1 1:7 1:9 1:11^{3} 1:16 1:18^{3} 1:19^{2} 1:20 1:21^{2} 1:23 1:27 7:13 8:16 9:6 9:8 10:1 10:12 10:15 10:17 10:19 10:20 14:14 14:16 14:18 14:20 16:47 16:50 17:6 19:12 20:9 20:24 20:25 22:6 23:2 23:3 23:4^{3} 23:6 23:7 23:42 27:8^{3} 27:9^{2} 27:10 27:11^{2} 27:13 27:15^{2} 27:17 27:19 27:21 27:22 27:23 27:24 29:13 31:5 31:8^{2} 31:9 31:15 31:17 32:27 32:29 34:5^{2} 36:19 36:31 37:2^{2} 40:7 40:10^{2} 40:12 40:15 40:16^{3} 40:17^{2} 40:21^{2} 40:25 40:26^{2} 40:29 40:30 40:31^{2} 40:33^{2} 40:34^{2} 40:37^{2} 40:38 40:39 40:40^{2} 40:41 40:42 40:43 40:44 40:49 41:2 41:6 41:8 41:9 41:11 41:16 41:20 41:21 41:22 41:25^{3} 41:26 42:3 42:5^{2} 42:6 42:8^{2} 42:10 42:11^{2} 42:12 43:3 46:22^{2} 47:3 47:4^{2} 47:5 47:7

DA

1:6 1:20 2:34 2:42 3:8 3:20 3:21^{2} 3:27 4:10 4:12 4:21 4:33 5:3 5:6 5:9 5:12 6:18 7:4 7:7 7:8^{2} 7:9 7:10 7:12 7:19 7:20 8:3 10:3 10:5 10:7 10:12

HO

2:23 4:7 5:10 8:12 9:10 12:8 13:6^{2}

AM

4:7 4:8 4:11

OB

7

JON

1:5^{2} 1:10 2:5

MIC

1:13

NA

3:9 3:10^{2}

HAB

3:6

HAG

2:16^{3}

ZEC

1:8^{2} 6:1 6:2 7:3 8:9 8:13 10:2

MT

1:11 1:12 2:11 2:13 2:16 3:6 3:16 4:18 4:24^{3} 5:12 7:28 8:16^{2} 8:32 9:25 9:30 9:31 9:36 11:20 11:21 12:1 12:3 12:4 12:23 13:2 13:6 13:54 13:57 14:20 14:21 14:26 14:32 14:33 14:34 14:35 14:36 15:1 15:12 15:30 15:37 15:38 16:5 17:6 17:14 17:23 17:24 18:6^{3} 18:31 19:12^{2} 19:13 19:25 20:9 20:24 21:1 21:15 22:3 22:8^{2} 22:25 22:33 22:34 22:41 24:24 24:37 24:38^{2} 25:2^{2} 25:3 25:10 26:22 26:26 26:43 26:51 26:57 26:71 27:17 27:33 27:38 27:44 27:52 27:54^{2} 27:55 28:11^{2} 28:12 28:15

MK

1:5 1:16 1:19 1:22 1:27 1:29 1:32^{2} 1:34 1:36 2:2 2:6 2:12 2:15 2:25 2:26 4:10 4:33 4:34 4:36 5:13^{2} 5:15 5:40 5:42 6:2 6:3 6:13 6:31 6:34 6:42 6:44 6:50 6:51 6:54 6:55 6:56^{2} 7:35 7:37 8:8 8:9 9:4 9:6 9:9 9:15 9:32 9:42^{2} 10:24 10:26 10:32^{3} 11:12 12:14 12:20 12:41 13:22 14:4 14:11 14:21 14:35 14:40 14:53 15:32 15:40 15:44 16:5 16:8^{2}

LU

1:2 1:6 1:7 1:10 1:23 1:44 1:65 2:6^{2} 2:8 2:9 2:15 2:18 2:21 2:22 2:33 2:47 2:48 3:15^{2} 3:21 4:2 4:20^{2} 4:25 4:27 4:28 4:32 4:36 5:2^{2} 5:7 5:9 5:10 5:17^{2} 5:26^{2} 6:3 6:4 6:11 6:18^{2} 7:10 7:20 7:21 7:24 7:39 8:1 8:4^{2} 8:23 8:30 8:33 8:35^{2} 8:37 8:38 8:40 8:45 8:56 9:10 9:14 9:17 9:18 9:30 9:32^{3} 9:37 9:43 11:29 11:52 12:1 13:1 13:2 13:4 13:17^{2} 14:7 14:17 14:24 16:14 16:16 17:2^{2} 17:9 17:12 17:14 17:17 17:27 18:9 18:34 19:32 19:33 19:48 20:29 22:5 22:44 22:49 22:52 22:55 23:5 23:6 23:12^{2} 23:23 23:32 23:33 23:39 23:48 24:4 24:5 24:10 24:16 24:21 24:22 24:24 24:31 24:33 24:35 24:37 24:44 24:53

JOH

1:3 1:13 1:24^{2} 1:28 2:6 3:19 3:23 4:8 4:40 5:35 6:2 6:11 6:12 6:19 6:22^{2} 6:26 6:64 6:65 7:10^{2} 8:33 8:39 8:42 9:10 9:33 9:40 9:41 10:6 10:41 11:25 11:31 11:52 11:57 12:12 12:16 12:20 13:1 14:2 15:19 16:19 17:6 18:30 18:36 19:11 19:28 19:36^{2} 20:19^{2} 20:20 20:26 21:2 21:6 21:8^{2} 21:9 21:11

AC

1:6 1:13 1:15 2:1 2:2 2:4 2:5 2:6 2:7 2:8 2:14^{2} 2:37 2:41^{2} 2:43 2:44 3:10 4:6^{2} 4:13 4:26 4:27 4:31^{2} 4:32 4:34^{2} 5:12^{2} 5:14 5:16^{2} 5:17^{2} 5:21 5:33 5:36 5:37 5:41 6:1 6:7 6:10 7:16 7:30 7:54 8:1 8:4 8:7^{3} 8:12 8:13 8:14 8:15 8:16 8:39 9:2 9:8 9:19 9:21 9:23 9:26 9:31^{2} 10:12 10:17 10:18 10:26 10:27 10:38 10:45 11:1 11:2 11:10 11:11 11:19 11:20^{2} 11:26 12:3 12:10 12:12 12:16 13:1 13:5 13:42 13:45^{2} 13:48^{2} 13:52 14:6 14:27 15:4^{2} 15:10 15:30 15:33 16:2 16:3 16:4^{2} 16:5 16:6 16:7 16:12 16:14 16:26^{3} 16:32 16:38 17:11^{2} 17:12 17:14 17:21 18:3 18:5 18:8 18:14 19:3 19:5 19:7 19:9 19:12 19:14 19:21 19:28 19:31 19:32 20:8^{2} 20:12 20:16 20:18 20:34 21:1 21:5 21:8 21:17 21:18 21:24 21:27^{2} 21:30 21:38 22:5 22:9^{2} 22:11 23:6 23:9 23:13 24:9 25:17 26:10 26:14 26:29 26:31 27:4 27:7 27:11 27:17 27:27 27:30 27:36 27:37 27:39^{2} 28:1 28:7 28:9 28:10 28:14 28:17 28:24

RO

1:21 3:2 4:2 4:17 5:6 5:8 5:10^{2} 5:19 6:3^{2} 6:17 6:20^{2} 7:5^{2} 7:6 9:3 9:25 9:32 11:7 11:19 11:20 15:4^{2} 16:7

1 CO

1:9 1:13 3:2 4:9 5:3 6:11 7:7 7:14 9:15 10:1 10:2 10:5 10:6 10:7 10:9 10:10 11:5 12:2 12:17^{4} 12:19^{2} 15:11

2 CO

1:8 3:14 5:1 5:14 7:5^{4} 7:8 7:9^{2} 7:13 8:3 11:17 12:12 12:13 13:2

GA

1:17 1:22 2:2 2:6 2:12 3:16 3:23 4:3^{2} 4:5 5:12

EPH

1:13 2:1 2:3 2:5 2:12 2:13 2:17^{2} 5:8

PHP

3:7 3:12 4:18

COL

1:16^{2} 1:21

2 TH

1:5 1:7 2:2^{2} 2:4 2:7 2:8^{2} 3:4 3:7

2 TH

3:10

TIT

3:3

PHM

14

HEB

2:15 3:5 4:3 5:8 6:4^{2} 7:11 7:21 7:23^{2} 8:4 9:6 9:9 9:15 10:32 10:33^{2} 11:3^{2} 11:13^{2} 11:23 11:29 11:30 11:34 11:35 11:37^{4}

JAS

5:3

1 PE

1:18 2:8 2:10 2:21 2:24 2:25 3:20^{2}

2 PE

1:16 1:18 1:21 2:1 2:18 3:2 3:4 3:5

1 JO

2:19^{2} 3:12

JUDE

4 17

RE

1:14^{2} 4:1 4:4 4:5 4:6 4:8 4:11 6:1 6:9 6:11^{2} 6:14 7:4^{2} 7:5^{3} 7:6^{3} 7:7^{3} 7:8^{3} 8:2 8:5 8:7 8:8 8:9^{2} 8:10 8:11 9:2 9:7^{4} 9:8 9:9 9:10 9:15^{2} 9:16 9:17 9:19 9:20 10:1 11:13^{2} 11:15 11:18 11:19 12:9 12:14 13:2 13:3 14:3^{2} 14:4^{2} 15:2 15:8 16:9 16:18^{2} 16:20 17:8 18:14 18:15 18:19 18:23^{2} 18:24 19:6 19:12^{2} 19:14 19:20 19:21^{2} 20:4 20:5 20:12^{3} 20:13^{3} 20:14 21:1 21:19 21:21^{2} 22:2

WITH

5973, *4862*

GE

3:6 3:12 4:8 5:22 5:24 6:3 6:9 6:11 6:13^{2} 6:14 6:16 6:18^{2} 6:19 7:13 7:23 8:1 8:16 8:17 8:18 9:3 9:8 9:9 9:10^{2} 9:11 9:12 11:31 12:4 12:13 12:17 13:1 13:5 14:2 14:5 14:8 14:9^{2} 14:13 14:17 14:24 15:14 15:18 16:6 16:11 17:3 17:4 17:12 17:13 17:19 17:21 17:22 17:23 17:27 18:11 18:16 18:23 18:25 18:33 19:1 19:9 19:11 19:30 19:32 19:33 19:34^{2} 19:35 19:36 20:16 21:6 21:10 21:19 21:20 21:22 21:23 22:3 22:5 23:4^{2} 23:8 23:16 24:15 24:32 24:40 24:45 24:49 24:54 24:55 24:58 25:30 26:3 26:8 26:10 26:15 26:20^{2} 26:24 26:28^{2} 27:15 27:34 27:35 27:37 27:44 28:4 28:15 28:20 29:6 29:9 29:14 29:19 29:25 29:27 29:30 30:8 30:15 30:16^{2} 30:20^{2} 30:29 30:33 31:3 31:5 31:6 31:21 31:23 31:25 31:26 31:27 31:32^{2} 31:36

31:38 31:42 31:50 32:4 32:6 32:7 32:9 32:10 32:11 32:15 32:20 32:24 32:25 32:28^2 33:1 33:5 33:7 33:10 33:11 33:13^2 33:15^2 34:5 34:6 34:7 34:8 34:9 34:10 34:16 34:20 34:21 34:22 34:23 34:26 34:31 35:2 35:3 35:6 35:13 35:14 35:15 35:22 37:2^3 37:14^2 37:25 38:14 38:24 38:25 39:2 39:3 39:7 39:8 39:10 39:12 39:14^2 39:18 39:21 39:23 40:4 40:7 40:14 41:6 41:10 41:12 41:23 41:27 42:4 42:6 42:13 42:24 42:25 42:26 42:32 42:33 42:38^2 43:3 43:4 43:5 43:6 43:8 43:16^2 43:19 43:32^2 43:34 44:1 44:9 44:10 44:16

44:23 44:26^2 44:29 44:30 44:31^2 44:33 44:34 45:1 45:5 45:15 45:23^2 46:1 46:4 46:6 46:7^2 46:15 46:26 47:12 47:17 47:29 47:30 48:1 48:12 48:21 48:22^2 49:12^2 49:25 49:29 49:30 50:7 50:9 50:10 50:13 50:14

EX

1:1 1:7 1:10 1:11 1:13 1:14^2 1:20 2:3^2 2:21 2:24^3 3:2 3:8 3:12 3:17 3:18 3:20 4:12 4:15^2 5:3^3 5:15 6:1^2 6:4 6:6^2 7:11 7:17 7:22 8:2 8:5 8:7 8:17 8:18 9:9 9:10 9:15 9:24 10:9^6 10:10 10:24 10:26^2 12:8^2 12:9^4 12:10 12:11 12:22 12:38 12:48 13:5 13:7^2 13:9

13:13 13:19^2 14:6 14:8 14:11 15:8 15:10 15:19^2 15:20^2 16:3 16:12 16:18 16:20 16:31 17:2^2 17:3 17:5 17:8 17:9^2 17:10 17:13 17:16 18:5 18:6 18:12 18:18 18:19 18:22 19:9 19:17 19:24 20:19^2 20:22 20:23 21:3 21:6 21:8 21:9 21:14 21:18^2 21:20 21:22 21:29 22:14 22:15 22:16 22:19 22:24 22:30^3 23:1 23:5 23:11^2 23:18 23:32^2 24:2 24:3 24:8 24:14 25:2 25:11 25:13 25:14 25:20 25:22^2 25:24 25:28^2 25:33^2 25:34 25:39 26:1^2 26:6 26:29^2 26:31 26:32 26:36 26:37 27:2 27:6 27:8 27:16 27:17 28:1 28:3 28:6 28:11^2 28:15 28:21^2

28:28 28:41 29:2^2 29:3 29:4 29:5 29:9 29:12 29:14 29:21^2 29:34 29:40^2 29:43 30:3 30:5 30:6 30:10 30:20 30:28 30:34 30:36 31:3 31:6 31:8 31:9 31:18^2 32:4 32:11 33:3 33:9 33:12 33:14 33:15 33:16 33:22 34:3 34:5 34:10 34:12 34:15 34:20 34:25 34:27^2 34:28 34:29^2 34:31 34:32 34:33 34:34 34:35 35:12 35:14 35:16 35:23 35:24 35:25 35:31 35:35 36:8 36:13 36:34^2 36:35 36:36 36:38^2 37:2 37:4 37:9^2 37:11 37:15 37:26 37:28 38:2 38:6 38:7 38:17 38:23 39:3 39:6 39:14 39:21 39:23 39:37^2 40:3 40:12 40:14

LE

1:12 1:13 1:16 1:17 2:2 2:4^2 2:5 2:7 2:11 2:13^2 2:16 3:4 3:10 3:15 4:9 4:11^2 4:12 4:20^3 4:25 4:30 4:34 5:4^2 5:15 5:16 5:18 6:6 6:10 6:16 6:17 6:21 7:4 7:10 7:12^4 7:13 7:17 7:19 7:24 7:30 8:1 8:6 8:7^3 8:13 8:15 8:17 8:30^2 8:31 8:32 9:4 9:11 9:13 10:9 10:14 10:15^2 10:16 10:43^2 10:44 10:57 14:10 14:16 14:21 14:27 14:31 14:37 14:52^6 15:3 15:17 15:18^2 15:24 15:33 16:3 16:4^2 16:10 16:14^2 16:15^2 16:18 16:24 17:13 17:15 18:20^2 18:22^2 18:23 19:13 19:19^2 19:20 19:22

19:26 19:33 19:34 20:2 20:5 20:10^2 20:11 20:12 20:13^2 20:14 20:15 20:18 20:20 20:24 20:27 21:9 22:6 22:8 22:11 22:14 23:13 23:17 23:18^2 23:20^2 23:23 25:6 25:23 25:35^2 25:36 25:40 25:41 25:43 25:45 25:46 25:50 25:52 25:53^2 25:54 26:9 26:39 26:42^3 26:44

NU

1:2 1:4 1:5 2:2 2:17 2:31 3:1 4:5 4:8 4:11 4:12 4:32^2 5:7 5:13^2 5:17 5:19^2 5:20 5:21 5:23 6:15^2 6:20 7:13 7:19 7:25 7:31 7:37 7:43 7:49 7:55 7:61 7:67 7:73 7:79 7:87 7:89 8:8^2 8:26 9:11 10:3 10:4 10:8

10:9 10:10 10:29 10:32 11:15 11:16 11:17^2 11:18 11:33 12:8 13:23 13:27 13:31 14:8 14:9 14:10 14:12 14:21 14:24 14:27 14:43 15:4 15:5 15:6 15:9^2 15:14 15:15 15:16 15:24 15:35 15:36 16:2 16:10 16:13 16:14 16:18 16:22 16:30 17:4 17:13 18:1^2 18:2^2 18:7 18:11^2 18:19^2 19:4 19:5 19:12 19:16 20:3 20:11 20:13 20:18 20:20^2 21:18 21:24 22:7 22:8 22:9 22:12 22:13 22:14 22:20 22:21 22:22 22:27 22:35^2 22:39 22:40 23:13 23:17 23:21 24:8 25:1 25:14 25:18 26:3 26:10 27:21 28:5 28:9 28:12^2 28:13 28:20 28:28 29:3 29:9

29:14 30:2 30:8 30:10 31:6 31:8 31:10 31:14^2 31:17 31:18 31:23 31:35 32:19 32:29 32:30 32:33 33:1 33:3 34:2 34:12 35:7 35:16 35:17 35:18 35:21 35:23 35:25

DE

1:16 1:37 2:5 2:7 2:9 2:19 2:24 2:26 3:5 3:13 3:26 3:27 4:11^2 4:21 4:23 4:29^2 4:37 4:40^2 5:2 5:3^2 5:4 5:16 5:22 5:23 5:24 5:29^2 5:33 6:3^2 6:5^3 6:18 6:21 7:2 7:3 7:5^2 7:8 7:9 7:23 7:25 8:3 8:16 9:8 9:10^2 9:15 9:20 9:21 9:26 10:9 10:12^2 10:14 10:22 11:2 11:9 11:10 11:13^2 12:3 12:12

12:23 12:25^2 12:28^2 13:3^2 13:10 13:15^2 13:16 14:27 14:29 15:3 15:16 15:19 16:3 16:4 16:10 16:18 17:5 17:19 18:1 18:6 18:11 18:13 19:5^2 19:13 20:1 20:4 20:12 20:13 20:20 21:3 21:21 22:2 22:3^3 22:6 22:7 22:9 22:10 22:21 22:22^2 22:23 22:24 22:25^2 22:28 22:29 23:4^2 23:11 23:16 23:23 23:25 24:5 24:12 25:3 25:11 26:5 26:8^5 26:9 26:15 26:16^2 27:1 27:2 27:3 27:4 27:14 27:20 27:21 27:22 27:23 28:22^7 28:27^4 28:28 28:30 28:32 28:35 28:40 28:47^2 28:68 29:1^2 29:10 29:12^2 29:14 29:15^4 29:25 30:2^2 30:6^2 30:10^2 31:6 31:7

31:8 31:16^2 31:20 31:23 31:27 32:12 32:14^2 32:15 32:16^2 32:21^4 32:22 32:24^4 32:25 32:34 32:39 32:42^2 32:43 33:2 33:8^2 33:17 33:20 33:21^2 33:23^2 33:24 34:4

JOS

1:5^2 1:9 1:17^2 2:6 2:14 2:19 3:7^2 4:3 4:8 5:6 5:13 6:4 6:5^2 6:8 6:9^2 6:10 6:13^2 6:16 6:17 6:20^2 6:21 6:24 6:27 7:12 7:15^2 7:24 7:25^3 8:1 8:5 8:11 8:24 8:35 9:2^3 9:6 9:7 9:11^2 9:15^2 9:16 10:1 10:4^2 10:7 10:10 10:11^2 10:15 10:20 10:24 10:28 10:29 10:30 10:31 10:32 10:34 10:35 10:36 10:37 10:38 10:39 10:43

11:4 11:6 11:7 11:9 11:10 11:11^2 11:12 11:14 11:18 11:19 11:21 13:8 13:21 13:22 14:4 14:8 14:12 15:32 15:36 15:41 15:44 15:45 15:46 15:47^2 15:51 15:54 15:57 15:59 15:60 15:62 15:63 16:9 18:24 18:28 19:15 19:16 19:22 19:30 19:31 19:38 19:46 19:47 19:48 21:2 21:8 21:11 21:13^2 21:14^2 21:15^2 21:16^3 21:17^2 21:18^2 21:19 21:21^2 21:22^2 21:23^2 21:24^2 21:25^2 21:26 21:27^2 21:28^2 21:29^2 21:30^2 21:31^2 21:32^3 21:33 21:34^2 21:35^2 21:36^2 21:37^2 21:38^2 21:39^2 21:41 21:42 22:5^2 22:8^8 22:14 22:15 22:18 22:24 22:27^3 22:30 23:4 23:12 24:6 24:8

24:12^2 24:25

JG

1:3^3 1:8 1:16 1:17 1:18^3 1:19 1:21 1:22 1:25 2:1 2:2 2:18 3:27 3:31 4:6 4:7 4:8^2 4:9^2 4:10^2 4:13 4:15 4:18 5:15 5:26 6:5 6:12 6:13 6:16 6:17 6:26 6:39 7:1 7:2 7:4^3 7:5 7:10 7:11 7:16 7:18^2 7:19 8:1^2 8:4 8:7^2 8:10 8:15 8:16 9:1^2 9:16 9:19^2 9:23 9:26 9:32 9:33 9:34 9:35 9:38 9:39 9:44 9:45 9:48^2 9:52 11:3 11:6 11:8 11:11 11:12 11:33 11:34^2 11:38 11:39 12:1^2 12:2 12:4 13:9 13:19 14:7 14:11 14:15 14:18 15:1 15:5

15:6 15:8 15:13 15:14 15:16^2 16:3 16:7 16:8 16:9 16:11 16:13 16:14^3 16:15 16:16 16:21 16:29^2 16:30^2 17:2 17:10 17:11 18:4 18:7 18:11 18:16 18:17^2 18:19 18:23 18:25 18:27^2 18:28 19:3 19:4 19:5 19:10^2 19:19 19:20 19:24 19:29 20:1 20:37 20:38 20:40 20:43 20:48 21:5 21:10^2 21:12

RU

1:6 1:7 1:8^3 1:10 1:11 1:18 1:20 1:22 2:4 2:6 2:19^2 2:22 2:23 3:1 3:2

1 SA

1:24^2 2:4 2:13^2 2:18 2:19 2:22 2:26^2 2:29 3:14 3:19 4:4 4:5 4:8 4:12^2 4:19 5:6 5:7 5:8

5:9 5:12 6:11 6:15 6:19 7:3 7:10 9:3 9:5 9:19 9:24 9:25 10:5 10:6 10:7 10:26 11:1 11:2 11:7 11:10 12:2 12:7 12:20 12:24 13:2^2 13:4 13:5 13:15 13:16 13:22^3 14:2 14:7 14:17 14:18 14:20 14:21^4 14:27 14:28 14:32 14:33 14:34^2 14:43 14:45 15:6 15:8 15:25 15:26 15:30 16:1 16:2 16:5 16:16 16:18 16:19 16:20 16:23 17:5 17:7 17:9 17:19 17:20 17:23 17:25 17:28 17:32 17:33 17:37 17:38^2 17:39 17:43 17:45^3 17:47 17:50^2 17:57 18:1 18:6^3 18:10 18:11 18:12 18:14 18:22 18:28 19:3 19:8^2 19:9^2 19:10 19:13

19:16 20:5 20:8^2 20:13^2 20:16 20:35^2 20:41 21:1 21:8 22:2 22:3 22:4 22:6 22:8 22:17 22:19^2 22:23^2 23:5^2 23:6 23:19 23:23^2 24:7 24:8 24:18 25:7 25:15 25:16 25:25 25:26 25:29 25:31 25:33 25:39 25:42 26:2 26:6^2 26:8 27:2^2 27:3^3 27:5 28:1^2 28:8 28:12 28:14^2 28:19^2 28:23 29:2 29:3 29:4^3 29:6 29:8 29:9 29:10^2 30:1 30:3 30:4 30:9 30:14 30:21 30:22^2 30:23 31:5

2 SA

1:2 1:11 1:17 1:21 1:24 2:3^2 2:23 3:8 3:12^2 3:13 3:16 3:17 3:20^2 3:21 3:22^2 3:23 3:27 3:31^2 5:3 5:10 6:2^2

6:12 6:14^2 6:15^2 7:3 7:7^2 7:9 7:12 7:14 7:22 7:29 8:2^3 8:10^2 8:11 10:13 10:17 10:19 11:1 11:4 11:5 11:9 11:11 11:13 11:17 12:3 12:9^2 12:11 12:17 12:24 12:30 13:11 13:14 13:18 13:20 13:24 13:26^2 13:27 13:28 13:31 14:2 14:17 14:19 15:11 15:12 15:14^2 15:19^2 15:20^2 15:22 15:23 15:24 15:27 15:30 15:31 15:32 15:33 15:35 15:36 16:1 16:10 16:14 16:15 16:17 16:18 16:21 16:23^2 17:2 17:8 17:10 17:12 17:16 17:22 17:24 17:29 18:1 18:2 18:5^2 18:14 18:27 19:4 19:7 19:17^2 19:22 19:25 19:31 19:33^2 19:34 19:36^2 19:37

19:38 19:40 19:41 20:8 20:9 20:15 20:16 21:15^2 21:16 21:17 21:18 21:19 21:26^2 21:27^2 22:40 23:5^2 23:6 23:7^2 23:9 23:21^2 24:2

1 KI

1:1 1:7^2 1:8 1:14 1:21 1:22 1:23 1:31 1:33 1:34 1:37^2 1:40^3 1:41 1:44 1:49 1:51 2:4^2 2:8^3 2:9 2:10 2:32 2:43 3:1 3:6 3:16 3:17 3:18 4:13 5:6 6:8 6:9 6:10 6:12 6:15^3 6:16 6:18 6:20 6:21^2 6:22^2 6:28 6:29 6:30 6:32 6:35 6:36 7:2 7:3 7:5 7:7 7:9 7:12 7:14 7:18 7:26 7:31 7:49 8:5 8:9 8:15^2 8:21 8:23^2 8:24

8:25 8:46 8:47 8:48 8:54 8:55 8:57^2 8:61 8:62 8:65 9:11 9:16 9:27 10:1 10:2^2 10:18 10:22 10:26 11:1 11:4 11:9 11:16 11:17 11:18 11:21 11:22 11:29 11:38 11:43 12:6 12:8^2 12:10 12:11^3 12:14^2 12:18 12:21 13:7 13:8 13:15 13:16^3 13:18 13:19 14:3 14:6 14:8 14:20 14:22 14:31^2 15:3 15:8 15:14 15:19 15:20 15:22^2 15:24^2 16:2 16:6 16:7 16:13 16:17 16:18 16:26 16:28 17:18 17:20 18:4 18:13 18:28 18:32 18:33 18:35 18:45 19:1 19:10 19:14 19:19^2 19:21 20:1 20:20 20:21 20:34^2 20:38 21:8^2 21:13 22:4 22:11 22:13

41:15 41:16 42:6 42:8 42:11 43:6 43:12 43:13 44:8 44:25[2] 46:4 46:10 46:22[2] 46:25 46:28 47:5 48:7 48:32 48:33 48:39 49:2 49:3 49:20 50:5 50:39 51:5 51:14[2] 51:16 51:20[2] 51:21[2] 51:22[3] 51:23[3] 51:28 51:32 51:34 51:40 51:42 51:45 51:58 51:59 52:13 52:14 52:22 52:32

LA

1:2 1:16 2:1 2:4 2:10 2:11 3:5 3:9 3:15[2] 3:16[2] 3:30 3:41 3:43 3:44 3:48 4:9[2] 4:14 5:6 5:9

EZE

1:15 2:6 3:3 3:4 3:10 3:22 3:24 3:25 3:26 4:12 4:16[2] 4:17 5:2[2] 5:11[2] 5:12[2] 6:9[2] 6:11[2] 7:15 7:18 7:27 8:11 8:16 8:17 9:1[2] 9:2[2] 9:3 9:7 9:11 10:2[2] 10:4 10:6 10:7 11:6 11:13 12:7 12:12 12:18[3] 12:19[2] 13:10 13:11 13:13 13:14 13:15 13:22 14:11 16:8 16:9[2] 16:10[4] 16:11 16:13 16:16 16:17 16:26 16:28[2] 16:36[2] 16:37[2] 16:40[2] 16:41 16:59 16:60 16:62 17:3 17:7 17:12 17:13 17:16 17:17 17:20 17:21 18:7 18:16 19:4 19:11 20:6 20:7 20:15 20:18 20:31 20:33 20:34[3] 20:35 20:36[2] 20:39[2] 20:40 20:41 20:44 21:6[2] 21:21 21:22 21:24 22:7 22:11 22:14 22:28 22:31 23:6 23:7[4] 23:8 23:10 23:14 23:15 23:16 23:17[2] 23:23 23:24[2] 23:25 23:29 23:30 23:33[3] 23:37 23:40 23:42[2] 23:43[2] 23:47[3] 24:4 24:7 24:12 24:16 24:26 25:6[2] 25:10 25:15 25:17 26:7[4] 26:8 26:9 26:11 26:16 26:20[3] 26:27 27:9 27:11 27:12 27:14 27:16 27:21 27:22[2] 27:24 27:31[2] 27:33 28:4[2] 28:16 28:26 30:5 30:11[2] 30:24 31:3[2] 31:4 31:11 31:14 31:16 31:17[2] 31:18[2] 32:2[2] 32:3 32:4 32:5 32:6 32:7 32:18 32:19 32:21 32:24 32:25[2] 32:27[2] 32:28[2] 32:29[3] 32:30[4] 32:32[2] 33:25 33:31 34:3 34:4[2] 34:16 34:18[2] 34:19[2] 34:21[3] 34:25 34:29 34:30 35:8[2] 35:13 36:5[2] 36:37 36:38 37:6 37:19[2] 37:23[3] 37:26[2] 37:27 38:4[2] 38:5[2] 38:6 38:9 38:13 38:15 38:22[2] 38:23 39:4 39:9 39:10 39:14 39:20[3] 40:3 40:4[2] 41:13 41:15 41:16 41:18 42:16[2] 42:17 42:18 42:19 43:2 43:22 44:17 44:18 44:19 45:2 46:14 46:23 47:22 48:20 48:34

DA

1:2 1:8[2] 1:9 1:13 1:19 2:5 2:11 2:14 2:18 2:22 2:41 2:43[3] 4:15[3] 4:23[3] 4:25[2] 4:32 4:33 5:7 5:16 5:21[3] 5:29 6:14 6:17[2] 6:20 7:7 7:13 7:19 7:21 8:7 8:18 9:3 9:15 9:22 9:26 9:27 10:5 10:7 10:13 10:17 10:20 10:21 11:3 11:7 11:8[2] 11:11[3] 11:13[2] 11:17[2] 11:23[2] 11:25[2] 11:28 11:30 11:34[2] 11:38[2] 11:39[2] 11:40[3] 11:44

HO

2:2 2:3 2:6 2:7 2:13 2:18[3] 4:1 4:3[2] 4:4 4:5 4:14[2] 4:18 5:5 5:6[2] 5:7 6:8 7:3[2] 7:5[2] 7:14 9:8 11:4[2] 11:12[4] 12:1 12:2 12:3 12:4 13:3 13:16 14:2 14:8

JOE

1:8 2:12[4] 2:20 2:24 2:26 3:2 3:4 3:18[2]

AM

1:3 1:11 1:13 1:14[2] 2:2[3] 2:3 3:15 4:2[2] 4:5 4:9 4:10 5:8 5:14 6:6 6:7 6:8 6:10 6:11[2] 6:12 7:7 7:9 8:3 9:1

OB

7

JON

1:3 2:6 2:9 3:6 3:8

MIC

1:7 2:4 2:8 2:10 3:5 3:10[2] 5:1 5:6 6:2[2] 6:6[2] 6:7[2] 6:8 6:11[2] 6:15 7:2 7:3 7:14

NA

1:8 2:3 2:7 2:12[2] 3:12

HAB

1:15 2:6 2:12 2:14 2:16 2:19 3:9 3:13 3:14 3:15 3:16

ZEP

1:3 1:4 1:8 1:9 1:12 3:8 3:9 3:14 3:17[2]

HAG

1:6[2] 1:12 1:13 2:4 2:5 2:7 2:12 2:17[3]

ZEC

1:2 1:6 1:9 1:13[2] 1:14[2] 1:15 1:16 1:19 2:1 2:3 2:7 3:3 3:4 3:5 4:1 4:2 4:4 4:5 4:7 4:10 5:4 5:5 5:10 6:4 7:14 8:2[2] 8:4 8:23[2] 9:4 9:8 9:13 9:14 9:15 10:5 10:9 10:11 11:10 12:3 12:4[3] 13:6 14:5 14:18

MAL

1:8 2:3 2:4 2:5 2:6 2:13[4] 2:14 2:16 2:17 3:9 4:2 4:4 4:6

MT

1:18 1:23 2:3 2:10 2:11 3:11[3] 3:12 4:21 4:24[2] 5:22 5:25 5:28 5:41 7:2[2] 8:11 8:16[2] 8:28 8:29 9:10 9:11 9:15 9:20 9:32 9:36 11:7 12:3 12:4 12:22 12:30 12:41 12:42 12:45 12:46 12:47 13:15[3] 13:20 13:29 13:56 14:7 14:9 14:14 14:24 15:8[2] 15:20 15:22 15:30 15:32 16:1 16:27 17:3 17:17 18:9 18:16 18:26 18:27 18:29 19:10 19:26[2] 20:2 20:13 20:15 20:20 20:22[2] 20:23[2] 20:24 21:2 21:25 22:10 22:16 22:25 22:37[3] 23:4 23:30 24:19 24:30 24:31 24:49 24:51 25:3 25:4 25:10 25:16 25:19 25:27 25:31 26:11 26:15 26:18 26:20 26:23 26:29 26:35 26:36 26:37 26:38 26:40 26:47[2] 26:51 26:52 26:55[2] 26:58 26:67 26:69 26:71 26:72 27:7 27:19 27:22 27:34 27:38 27:41 27:44 27:46 27:48 27:50 27:54 28:8 28:12 28:20

MK

1:6[2] 1:8[2] 1:13 1:20 1:23 1:24 1:26 1:27 1:29 1:32 1:36 1:41 2:15 2:16[2] 2:19[2] 2:25 2:26 3:5 3:6 3:7 3:14 4:10 4:16 4:24 4:30 4:33 4:36 5:2 5:3 5:4 5:5 5:7[2] 5:15 5:16 5:18[2] 5:24 5:40 5:42 6:3 6:9 6:13 6:22 6:25 6:26 6:34 6:50 7:2[2] 7:5 7:6 8:2 8:4 8:10 8:11 8:14 8:34 8:38 9:1 9:2 9:4[2] 9:8 9:10[2] 9:14 9:16 9:18 9:19 9:24 9:47 9:49[2] 9:50 10:27[3] 10:30 10:38[2] 10:39 10:41 10:46 11:11 11:31 12:30[4] 12:33[4] 13:17 13:26 14:7 14:14 14:17 14:18 14:20 14:31 14:33 14:43[2] 14:48[2] 14:49 14:53 14:54 14:58 14:65 14:67 15:1 15:7 15:17 15:19 15:23 15:27 15:28 15:31 15:32 15:34 15:37 15:41 16:10 16:14 16:17 16:20[2]

LU

1:15 1:25 1:28 1:30 1:36 1:37 1:39 1:41 1:42 1:51 1:53 1:56 1:58 1:66 1:67 2:5[2] 2:13 2:16 2:36 2:37 2:40 2:48 2:51 2:52 3:14 3:16[3] 3:17 4:28 4:32 4:33 4:34 4:36 4:38 4:40 5:9 5:10 5:18 5:19 5:26 5:29 5:30 5:34 5:36 6:3 6:4 6:11[2] 6:17 6:18 6:38 7:6 7:11 7:12 7:24 7:29 7:36 7:38[3] 7:44[2] 7:46[2] 7:49 8:1 8:7 8:13 8:14 8:15 8:16 8:22 8:23 8:28[2] 8:29 8:37 8:38 8:45 9:18 9:30 9:32[3] 9:41 9:49 10:17 10:27[4] 11:7 11:20 11:23[2] 11:31 11:32 11:37 11:46[3] 12:13 12:25 12:46 12:47 12:48 12:50 12:58 13:1 13:14 14:9 14:10 14:15 14:18 14:25 14:31[2] 15:2 15:6 15:9 15:13 15:16 15:17 15:29 15:30 15:31 16:21 17:15 17:20 18:7 18:11 18:27[2] 19:7 19:23 19:37 19:44 20:1 20:5 21:5 21:20 21:23 21:25 21:27 21:34 22:4 22:11 22:14 22:15[2] 22:21 22:28 22:33 22:48 22:49 22:52 22:53 22:56 22:59 23:9 23:11 23:18 23:23 23:32 23:35 23:43 23:46 23:55 24:1 24:10 24:15 24:24 24:29[2] 24:30 24:32 24:33 24:44 24:49 24:52

JOH

1:1 1:2 1:26 1:31 1:33[2] 1:39 2:4 2:7 3:2 3:22 3:26 4:6 4:9 4:11 4:27[2] 4:40 5:18 6:3 6:13 6:22 6:66 7:33 8:6 8:29 8:38[2] 9:6 9:37 9:40 11:2[2] 11:16 11:31 11:33 11:43 11:44[2] 11:54 12:2 12:3[2] 12:8 12:17 12:35 12:40[2] 13:5 13:8 13:18 13:33 14:9 14:16 14:17 14:23 14:25 14:27 14:30 15:27 16:4 16:32 17:5[3] 17:12 17:24 18:1 18:2 18:3 18:5 18:18 18:22 18:26 19:3 19:15[2] 19:18 19:29 19:32 19:34 19:40 20:7 20:24 20:26 21:3 21:8

AC

1:4 1:5[2] 1:14[3] 1:17 1:18 1:21 1:22 1:26 2:4[2] 2:14 2:28 2:29 2:30 2:40 2:46[2] 2:47 3:4 3:8 3:10 3:25 4:8 4:13 4:14 4:24 4:27 4:29 4:31[2] 4:32 4:33 5:1 5:12 5:16 5:17[2] 5:21 5:23 5:26 5:28 5:31 6:9 7:9[2] 7:19 7:38[2] 7:45 7:48 7:54 7:57[2] 7:60 8:6 8:7[3] 8:11 8:13 8:20[3] 8:31 8:37 9:7 9:17 9:19 9:28 9:39[2] 9:43 10:2 10:6 10:23 10:27 10:35 10:38[3] 10:41 10:45 10:46 11:2 11:3 11:12 11:16[2] 11:21 11:23 11:26 12:2 12:6 12:17 12:20[2] 12:25 13:1 13:7 13:9 13:16 13:17 13:31 13:45 13:52[2] 14:4[2] 14:5 14:8 14:13 14:15 14:17 14:18 14:20 14:23 14:27 14:28 15:2 15:4 15:22[2] 15:24 15:25[2] 15:32 15:35 15:37 15:38[2] 16:3 16:11 16:16 16:28 16:34 17:2 17:4 17:5 17:11 17:15 17:17[4] 17:23 17:24 17:25 17:34 18:2 18:3 18:8 18:10 18:12 18:14 18:18 18:19 18:20 19:4 19:6 19:21 19:26 19:29[2] 19:33 19:34 19:38 20:9 20:18 20:19[2] 20:24 20:28 20:31 20:34 20:36 21:1 21:5 21:7 21:8 21:16[3] 21:18 21:24[2] 21:26 21:29 21:33 21:36 21:40 22:9 22:11 22:22 22:25 22:28 23:15 23:19 23:21 23:27 23:32 24:1[2] 24:3 24:7 24:12 24:18[2] 24:24 24:26 25:5 25:12 25:23[2] 25:24[2] 26:8 26:9 26:12 26:13 26:24 26:30 27:2 27:10 27:18 27:19 27:24 27:39 27:41 28:10[2] 28:11 28:14 28:16 28:20[2] 28:27[3] 28:31

RO

1:4 1:9 1:12 1:27 1:29 2:11 3:13 5:1 6:4 6:6 6:8[2] 7:18 7:21 7:25[2] 8:16 8:17[2] 8:18 8:25 8:26 8:32 9:14 9:22 10:9 10:10[2] 11:17 12:8[3] 12:10 12:15[2] 12:18 12:21 14:15[2] 14:20 15:6 15:10 15:13 15:14 15:24 15:30 15:32[2] 15:33 16:14 16:15 16:16 16:20 16:24

1 CO

1:2 1:17 2:1 2:3 2:4 2:13 3:2[2] 3:9 3:19 4:3 4:8 4:12 4:21 5:4 5:8[3] 5:9 5:10[3] 5:11 6:6 6:7 6:9 6:20 7:5 7:12 7:13 7:23 7:24 8:7 9:13 9:23 10:5 10:13 10:20 11:5 11:32 12:26[2] 12:30 13:1 14:5[2] 14:6 14:15[4] 14:16 14:18 14:19 14:21 14:23 14:39 15:10 15:32 15:35 16:4 16:6 16:7 16:10 16:11 16:12 16:14 16:16 16:19 16:20 16:21 16:23 16:24

2 CO

1:1 1:12 1:17 1:21 2:1 2:4 2:7 3:3[2] 3:18 4:14 5:1 5:2 5:8 6:1 6:14[3] 6:15[2] 6:16 7:3 7:4 7:8 7:15 8:4 8:18 8:19[2] 8:22 9:4 10:2 10:12 11:1[2] 11:2 11:4 11:9 11:25 11:32 12:16 12:18 13:4 13:11 13:12 13:14

GA

1:2 1:16 1:18 2:1[2] 2:3 2:5 2:12 2:13[2] 2:20 3:9 4:18 4:20 4:25 4:30 5:1 5:24 6:11 6:18

EPH

1:3 1:13 2:5 2:19 3:12 3:16 3:18 3:19 4:2[2] 4:14 4:19 4:25 4:28 4:31 5:6 5:7 5:11 5:18[2] 5:26 6:2 6:3 6:5 6:6 6:7 6:9 6:14 6:15 6:18[2] 6:23 6:24

PHP

1:1 1:4 1:11 1:20 1:23 1:25 1:27 2:6 2:12 2:17 2:18 2:22[2] 2:23 2:29 4:3[3] 4:6 4:9 4:14 4:15 4:21 4:23

COL

1:9 1:11[2] 2:4 2:5 2:7 2:11 2:12[2] 2:13 2:19 2:20 2:22 3:1 3:3 3:4 3:9 3:16 3:22 4:2 4:6[2] 4:9 4:18

1 TH

1:6 2:2 2:4 2:17 3:4 3:13 4:11 4:14 4:16[3] 4:17[2] 4:18 5:3 5:10 5:26 5:28

2 TH

1:6 1:7[2] 1:9 1:11 2:5 2:8[2] 2:9 2:10 3:1 3:8 3:10 3:12 3:14 3:16 3:17 3:18

1 TI

1:10 1:14 2:9[2] 2:10 2:11

2:15, 3:4, 3:6, 4:2, 4:3, 4:4, 4:14, 5:2, 6:6, 6:10, 6:21

2 TI

1:3, 1:4, 1:9, 2:4, 2:10, 2:11^{2}, 2:12, 2:22, 3:6^{2}, 4:2, 4:11^{2}, 4:13, 4:16, 4:17, 4:22

TIT

2:15, 3:15^{2}

PHM

19, 13, 25

HEB

1:9, 2:4^{2}, 2:7, 2:9, 3:10, 3:17^{2}, 4:2, 4:13, 4:15, 5:2, 5:7, 7:21, 8:8^{3}, 8:9, 8:10, 9:4, 9:11, 9:19, 9:21, 9:22, 9:23^{2}, 9:24, 9:25, 10:1, 10:16, 10:22^{2}, 11:7, 11:9^{2}, 11:25, 11:31^{2}, 11:37, 12:1^{2}, 12:7, 12:14, 12:17, 12:18, 12:20, 12:28, 13:3, 13:5, 13:9^{3}, 13:12, 13:16, 13:17^{2}, 13:23, 13:25

JAS

1:6, 1:11, 1:13, 1:17, 1:18, 1:21, 2:1, 2:2, 2:22, 3:4, 3:13^{2}, 4:4, 5:14

1 PE

1:7, 1:8, 1:12, 1:18, 1:19, 1:22, 2:15, 2:18, 2:20, 3:2, 3:6, 3:7, 3:15, 4:1, 4:4, 4:13, 5:5, 5:13, 5:14

2 PE

1:1, 1:18, 2:3, 2:6, 2:7, 2:8, 2:13^{2}, 2:14, 2:16, 2:17, 2:20, 3:6, 3:8, 3:10^{2}, 3:12, 3:17

1 JO

1:1, 1:2, 1:3^{3}, 1:6, 1:7, 2:1, 2:19

2 JO

2, 3, 12

3 JO

10, 13

JUDE

9, 12, 14, 23, 24

RE

1:7, 1:12, 1:13^{2}, 2:12, 2:16, 2:22, 2:23, 2:27, 3:4, 3:17, 3:18, 3:20^{2}, 3:21^{2}, 4:1, 5:1, 5:2, 5:12, 6:8^{5}, 6:10, 6:11, 7:2, 7:9, 7:10, 8:3, 8:4, 8:5, 8:7, 8:8, 8:13, 9:19, 10:1, 10:3, 11:6, 12:1, 12:2, 12:5, 12:9, 12:17^{2}, 13:4, 13:7, 13:10^{2}, 14:1, 14:2, 14:4, 14:7, 14:9, 14:10, 14:15, 14:18, 15:2, 15:6, 15:8, 16:8, 16:9, 17:1, 17:2^{2}, 17:4, 17:6^{3}, 17:12, 17:14^{2}, 17:16, 18:1, 18:2, 18:3, 18:8, 18:9, 18:16, 18:21, 19:2, 19:13, 19:15^{2}, 19:17, 19:20^{3}, 19:21^{2}, 20:4, 20:6, 21:3^{3}, 21:8, 21:9, 21:15, 21:16, 21:19, 22:12, 22:21

YE

859, *5210*

GE

3:1, 3:3, 3:4, 3:5^{2}, 4:23, 9:4, 9:7, 17:10, 17:11, 18:5^{2}, 19:2, 19:8, 22:5, 24:49, 26:27, 29:4, 29:5, 29:7, 31:6, 32:4, 32:19, 32:20, 34:9, 34:10^{2}, 34:11, 34:12, 34:15, 34:17, 34:30, 40:7, 42:1, 42:7, 42:9^{2}, 42:12, 42:14, 42:15^{2}, 42:16^{2}, 42:19^{2}, 42:20, 42:22, 42:33, 42:34^{2}, 42:36^{2}, 42:38, 43:3, 43:5, 43:6^{2}, 43:7, 43:27, 43:29, 44:4, 44:5, 44:10, 44:15, 44:19, 44:23, 44:27, 44:29^{2}, 45:4, 45:5, 45:9, 45:13^{2}, 45:17, 45:18, 45:19, 45:24, 46:34^{2}, 47:23, 47:24, 49:2, 50:17, 50:20, 50:21, 50:25

EX

1:16^{2}, 1:18, 1:22^{2}, 2:18, 2:20, 3:12, 3:18, 3:21, 3:22^{2}, 4:15, 5:4, 5:5, 5:7, 5:8^{2}, 5:11, 5:14, 5:17^{2}, 5:18, 5:19, 5:21, 6:7, 8:25, 8:28^{2}, 9:28, 9:30, 10:2, 10:11^{2}, 10:24, 11:7, 12:3, 12:5, 12:6, 12:10^{2}, 12:11^{2}, 12:13, 12:14^{2}, 12:15^{2}, 12:17^{2}, 12:18, 12:20^{2}, 12:22, 12:24, 12:25^{2}, 12:26, 12:27, 12:31^{2}, 12:32, 12:46, 13:3, 13:4, 13:19, 14:13^{3}, 14:14, 15:21, 16:3, 16:6, 16:7^{2}, 16:8, 16:12^{3}, 16:16, 16:23^{2}, 16:25, 16:26, 16:28, 16:29, 17:2^{2}, 19:4, 19:5^{2}, 19:6, 19:12, 20:20, 20:22, 20:23^{2}, 22:21, 22:22, 22:31^{3}, 23:9^{2}, 23:25, 24:1, 24:14, 25:2, 25:3, 25:9, 25:19, 30:9^{2}, 30:32, 30:37, 31:13^{2}, 31:14, 32:30, 33:5, 34:13, 35:1, 35:3, 35:5

LE

1:2, 2:11^{2}, 2:12, 3:17, 7:23, 7:24, 7:26, 7:32, 8:32, 8:33, 8:35^{2}, 9:3, 9:6, 10:6, 10:7^{2}, 10:9^{2}, 10:10, 10:11, 10:13, 10:14, 10:17, 10:18, 11:2, 11:3, 11:4, 11:8^{2}, 11:9^{2}, 11:11^{2}, 11:13, 11:21, 11:22, 11:24, 11:33, 11:39, 11:42, 11:43^{2}, 11:44^{3}, 11:45, 14:34, 15:31, 16:29, 16:30, 16:31, 17:14, 18:3^{4}, 18:4, 18:5, 18:24, 18:26, 18:28, 18:30^{3}, 19:2, 19:3, 19:4, 19:5^{2}, 19:6, 19:9, 19:11, 19:12, 19:15, 19:19, 19:23^{2}, 19:25, 19:26^{2}, 19:27, 19:28, 19:30, 19:33, 19:34, 19:35, 19:36, 19:37, 20:7, 20:8, 20:15, 20:22, 20:23, 20:24, 20:25^{2}, 20:26^{2}, 22:19, 22:20, 22:24^{2}, 22:25, 22:28, 22:29, 22:30, 22:31, 22:32, 23:2, 23:3, 23:4, 23:6, 23:7^{2}, 23:8^{2}, 23:10^{2}, 23:12^{2}, 23:14^{2}, 23:15^{2}, 23:16^{2}, 23:17, 23:18, 23:19, 23:21^{2}, 23:22, 23:24, 23:25^{2}, 23:27, 23:28, 23:31, 23:32^{2}, 23:35, 23:36^{3}, 23:37, 23:38, 23:39^{2}, 23:40^{2}, 23:41^{2}, 23:42, 24:22, 25:2, 25:9, 25:10^{3}, 25:11, 25:12, 25:13, 25:14, 25:17, 25:18^{2}, 25:19, 25:20, 25:22^{2}, 25:23, 25:24, 25:44, 25:45, 25:46^{2}, 26:1^{2}, 26:2, 26:3, 26:5, 26:6, 26:7, 26:10, 26:12, 26:13, 26:14, 26:15^{3}, 26:16, 26:17^{2}, 26:18, 26:21, 26:23, 26:25^{2}, 26:26, 26:27, 26:29^{2}, 26:34, 26:35, 26:37, 26:38

NU

1:2, 4:18, 4:27, 4:32, 5:3^{2}, 6:23, 9:3^{2}, 9:14, 10:5, 10:6, 10:7^{2}, 10:9^{4}, 10:10, 11:18^{3}, 11:19, 11:20, 12:4, 12:8, 13:2, 13:20, 14:9^{2}, 14:28, 14:30, 14:31^{2}, 14:34^{3}, 14:41, 14:42, 14:43^{2}, 15:2, 15:12^{2}, 15:14, 15:15, 15:18, 15:19^{2}, 15:20^{3}, 15:21, 15:22, 15:29, 15:39^{3}, 15:40, 16:3^{2}, 16:7^{2}, 16:8, 16:10, 16:11, 16:17, 16:26, 16:28, 16:30, 16:41, 18:3, 18:5, 18:7, 18:26^{2}, 18:28^{3}, 18:29, 18:30, 18:31^{2}, 18:32^{4}, 19:3, 20:4, 20:5, 20:8, 20:10, 20:12^{2}, 20:24, 21:5, 21:17, 22:19, 25:5, 27:8, 27:9, 27:10, 27:11, 27:14, 28:2, 28:3, 28:11, 28:18, 28:19, 28:20, 28:23, 28:24, 28:25^{2}, 28:26^{3}, 28:27, 28:31, 29:1^{2}, 29:2, 29:7^{3}, 29:8, 29:12^{3}, 29:13, 29:17, 29:35^{2}, 29:36, 29:39, 31:4, 31:15, 31:19, 31:23^{2}, 31:24^{3}, 32:6, 32:7, 32:14, 32:15^{2}, 32:20^{2}, 32:22, 32:23^{2}, 32:29, 33:51, 33:52, 33:53, 33:54^{4}, 33:55^{3}, 34:2, 34:6, 34:7, 34:8, 34:10, 34:13, 34:18, 35:2, 35:4, 35:5, 35:6^{3}, 35:7^{2}, 35:8^{3}, 35:10, 35:11, 35:13^{2}, 35:14^{2}, 35:31, 35:32, 35:33^{2}, 35:34

DE

1:6, 1:10, 1:11, 1:14, 1:17^{3}, 1:18, 1:19, 1:20, 1:22, 1:26, 1:27, 1:31^{2}, 1:32, 1:33, 1:39, 1:41^{3}, 1:42, 1:43, 1:45, 1:46^{2}, 2:3, 2:4^{2}, 2:6^{4}, 2:24, 3:18, 3:19, 3:20, 3:22, 4:1, 4:2^{3}, 4:4, 4:5^{2}, 4:11, 4:12^{2}, 4:14^{2}, 4:15^{2}, 4:16, 4:20, 4:22, 4:23, 4:25, 4:26^{3}, 4:27, 4:28, 5:1, 5:5, 5:23^{2}, 5:24, 5:28, 5:32^{2}, 5:33^{4}, 6:1^{2}, 6:3, 6:14, 6:16^{2}, 6:17, 7:5^{2}, 7:7^{2}, 7:12, 7:25, 8:1^{2}, 8:19, 8:20^{2}, 9:7^{2}, 9:8, 9:16^{2}, 9:18, 9:21, 9:22, 9:23^{2}, 9:24, 10:19^{2}, 11:2, 11:5, 11:8^{3}, 11:9, 11:10, 11:11, 11:13, 11:16, 11:17, 11:18, 11:19, 11:22, 11:23, 11:25, 11:27, 11:28^{2}, 11:31^{2}, 11:32, 12:1^{2}, 12:2^{2}, 12:3^{2}, 12:4, 12:5, 12:6, 12:7^{4}, 12:8, 12:9, 12:10^{2}, 12:11^{2}, 12:12^{2}, 12:16^{2}, 13:3, 13:4^{2}, 13:13, 14:1^{2}, 14:4, 14:6, 14:7, 14:8, 14:9^{2}, 14:10, 14:11, 14:12, 14:20, 14:21, 17:16, 18:15, 19:19, 20:2, 20:3^{2}, 20:18, 22:24^{2}, 23:4, 24:8, 24:9, 25:17, 27:2, 27:4^{2}, 27:12, 28:62^{2}, 28:63, 28:68, 29:2, 29:6^{3}, 29:7, 29:9^{2}, 29:10, 29:16^{2}, 29:17, 29:18^{2}, 31:5, 31:13^{2}, 31:19, 31:27, 31:29^{2}, 32:1, 32:3, 32:6, 32:43, 32:46, 32:47^{2}, 32:51^{2}

JOS

1:11, 1:14, 1:15, 2:5, 2:10^{3}, 2:12, 2:13, 2:14, 2:16, 3:3^{2}, 3:4^{3}, 3:8^{2}, 3:10, 4:3^{3}, 4:6, 4:7, 4:17, 4:22, 4:23, 4:24, 6:3^{2}, 6:4, 6:5, 6:10^{2}, 6:18^{3}, 6:22, 7:12, 7:13, 7:14, 8:2, 8:4^{2}, 8:7, 8:8^{3}, 9:6, 9:7, 9:8^{2}, 9:11, 9:22^{2}, 9:23, 10:19, 10:25, 18:3, 18:6, 22:2, 22:3, 22:4, 22:16^{3}, 22:18^{2}, 22:19, 22:24, 22:25^{2}, 22:27, 22:31^{2}, 23:3, 23:5, 23:6^{2}, 23:7, 23:8, 23:11, 23:12, 23:13, 23:14, 23:16^{2}, 24:6, 24:7, 24:8, 24:11, 24:13^{5}, 24:14, 24:15^{2}, 24:19, 24:20, 24:22^{2}, 24:27

JG

2:2^{4}, 5:2, 5:3^{2}, 5:9, 5:10^{2}, 5:23^{2}, 6:10^{2}, 6:31^{2}, 7:17, 7:18, 8:15, 8:18, 8:19, 8:24, 9:7, 9:15, 9:16^{3}, 9:18, 9:19^{2}, 9:48, 10:12, 10:13, 10:14, 11:7^{3}, 11:9, 11:26, 12:2, 12:3^{2}, 12:4, 14:12, 14:13^{2}, 14:15, 14:18^{2}, 15:7, 15:10, 15:11, 18:6, 18:8, 18:9, 18:10^{2}, 18:14^{2}, 18:18, 18:24^{3}, 19:24, 20:7, 20:11^{2}, 21:21, 21:22^{2}

RU

1:8, 1:9, 1:11, 1:13^{2}, 1:21, 4:2, 4:9, 4:10

1 SA

2:23, 2:24, 2:29, 4:9^{2}, 6:3^{2}, 6:5^{2}, 6:6, 6:8, 6:21, 7:3, 8:17, 8:18^{2}, 8:22, 9:13^{3}, 9:19, 10:14, 10:19^{2}, 10:24, 11:9^{2}, 11:10, 12:1, 12:5, 12:11, 12:12^{2}, 12:13^{2}, 12:14^{2}, 12:15, 12:17^{2}, 12:20, 12:21^{2}, 12:25^{3}, 14:34, 14:38, 14:40, 15:6, 15:32, 17:8^{2}, 17:9, 17:25, 18:25, 21:14^{2}, 21:15, 22:7, 22:13, 23:21^{2}, 23:23, 25:6, 25:13, 26:16^{2}, 27:10, 29:10, 30:23

2 SA

1:21, 1:24, 2:5^{2}, 2:6, 2:7, 3:38, 7:7, 11:15, 11:20^{3}, 11:21, 13:28, 15:10^{2}, 15:36^{2}, 16:10, 19:10, 19:11, 19:12^{3}, 19:13, 19:22^{2}, 19:42, 19:43^{2}, 21:3, 21:4, 24:2

1 KI

1:34, 1:35, 1:45, 9:6^{2}, 11:2, 12:6, 12:9, 12:24, 18:18, 18:21, 18:24, 18:25, 20:28, 20:33, 22:3

2 KI

1:3, 1:5, 2:3, 2:5, 2:16, 3:17^{4}, 3:19, 6:2, 6:17, 6:19, 6:32, 7:1, 9:11, 10:6^{3}, 10:8, 10:9, 10:13, 11:5, 11:6, 11:8^{2}, 12:7, 17:12, 17:13, 17:27, 17:35, 17:36^{3}, 17:37^{2}, 17:38^{2}, 17:39, 18:19, 18:22^{2}, 18:31^{2}, 18:32, 19:6, 19:10, 19:29^{2}, 22:13, 22:18

1 CH

12:17^{2}, 15:12^{3}, 15:13, 16:9, 16:10, 16:13^{2}, 16:15, 16:19, 16:23, 16:28, 16:35, 17:6, 22:19, 28:8

2 CH

7:19, 10:6, 10:9, 11:4, 12:5, 13:5, 13:8^{2}, 13:9, 13:11, 13:12^{2}, 15:2^{4}, 15:7, 18:14, 18:25, 18:27, 18:30, 19:6^{2}, 19:9, 19:10^{2}, 20:15^{2}, 20:16^{2}, 20:17^{2}, 20:20^{3}, 23:4, 23:7, 24:6, 24:20^{3}, 28:9, 28:10, 28:11, 28:13^{2}, 29:5, 29:8, 29:11, 29:31, 30:6, 30:7^{2}, 30:8, 30:9^{2}, 32:10^{2}, 32:12, 32:13, 34:23, 34:26

EZR

4:2, 4:3, 4:18, 4:21, 4:22, 6:6, 6:8, 7:25, 8:28, 8:29^{2}, 9:11, 9:12, 10:10

NE

1:8, 1:9, 2:17, 2:19^{2}, 2:20, 4:12, 4:14, 4:20^{2}, 5:7, 5:8, 5:9^{2}, 5:11, 8:10, 8:11, 13:17, 13:18, 13:21^{2}, 13:25

ES

4:16, 8:8

JOB

6:21^{2}, 6:26, 6:27^{2}, 12:2, 13:2, 13:4^{2}, 13:5, 13:7, 13:8^{2}, 13:9, 13:10, 16:2, 16:4, 17:10, 18:2, 19:2, 19:3^{3}, 19:5, 19:21, 19:22, 19:28, 19:29^{2}, 21:27, 21:28, 21:29^{3}, 21:34, 27:12^{2}, 32:6, 32:11, 32:13, 34:2^{2}, 34:10, 34:18, 42:7, 42:8

PS

2:10^{2}, 2:12, 4:2^{3}, 6:8, 11:1, 14:2, 22:23^{3}, 24:7^{3}, 24:9^{2}, 27:8, 29:1, 30:4, 31:23, 31:24, 32:9, 32:11^{2}, 33:1, 34:9, 34:11, 47:1, 47:7, 48:13^{2}, 49:1^{2}, 50:22, 58:1^{3}, 58:2^{2}, 62:3^{3}, 62:8, 66:1, 66:8, 66:16, 68:13^{2}, 68:16^{2}, 68:26, 68:32, 68:34, 82:2, 82:6, 82:7, 90:3, 94:8^{3}, 95:7, 96:7, 97:7, 97:10, 97:12, 99:5, 100:1, 100:3, 103:20, 103:21^{3}, 104:35, 105:2, 105:3, 105:6^{2}, 105:45, 106:1, 106:48, 111:1, 112:1, 113:1^{2}, 113:9, 114:6^{3}, 115:11, 115:15, 116:19, 117:1^{2}, 117:2, 119:115, 134:1^{2}, 135:1^{2}, 139:19, 146:1, 146:10, 147:1, 147:20, 148:1^{2}, 148:2^{2}, 148:3^{2}, 148:4^{2}, 148:7, 148:14, 149:1, 149:9, 150:1, 150:6

PR

1:22, 1:23, 1:24, 1:25, 4:1, 4:2, 5:7, 7:24, 8:5^{2}, 8:32

CA

1:5, 2:7^{2}, 3:3, 3:5^{2}, 3:11, 5:8^{2}, 6:13, 8:4

ISA

1:5^{2}, 1:10^{2}, 1:12, 1:15^{2}, 1:16, 1:19, 1:20, 1:29^{2}, 1:30, 2:3, 2:5, 2:22, 3:10, 3:14, 3:15, 6:9^{2}, 7:9, 7:13^{2}, 8:9^{4}, 8:12^{2}, 10:3^{3}, 12:3, 12:4, 13:2, 13:6, 16:1, 16:7, 18:2, 18:3^{3}

19:11
21:5
21:12[2]
21:13[2]
22:9[2]
22:10[2]
22:11[2]
22:14
23:1
23:2
23:6[2]
23:14
24:15
25:2
25:4
25:19
27:2
27:12[2]
28:12
28:14
28:15
28:18
28:22
28:23
29:1
29:9
30:12
30:15[2]
30:16[2]
30:17[2]
30:21[3]
30:22
30:29
31:6
32:9[2]
32:10[2]
32:11[2]
32:20
33:11[2]
33:13[2]
34:1[2]
34:16
35:3
36:4
36:7
36:13
36:16[2]
37:6
37:10
37:30[2]
40:1[2]
40:2
40:3
40:18[2]
40:21[3]
40:25
41:14
41:23
41:24
42:10
42:17
42:18[3]
43:10[2]
43:12
43:18
43:19
44:8[2]
44:23[3]
44:26
45:8
45:11
45:17
45:19
45:20
45:21
45:22
46:5
46:8
46:12
48:1
48:6
48:14
48:16[2]
48:20[4]
49:1
50:1
50:11[4]
51:1[4]
51:7[3]
52:3[2]
52:9
52:11[5]
52:12
55:1[2]
55:2[2]
55:6[2]
55:12
56:1
56:9[2]
56:12
57:3
57:4[3]
57:14[2]
58:3
58:4[3]
58:6
61:6[3]
61:7
62:6
62:10
62:11
65:11
65:12[3]
65:13[3]
65:14
65:15
65:18
66:1
66:5
66:10[3]
66:11[2]
66:12[2]
66:13
66:14

JER

2:4
2:7[2]
2:12[2]
2:29[2]
2:31
3:13
3:16
3:20
3:22
4:4
4:5[2]
4:10
4:16
5:1[2]
5:10
5:14
5:19[3]
5:22[2]
5:31
6:1
6:4
6:6
6:16[2]
6:18
7:2
7:4
7:5[2]
7:6
7:8
7:9[2]
7:12
7:13[3]
7:14
7:23[2]
8:8
9:4[2]
9:17
9:20
10:1
10:11
11:2
11:4
11:6
11:13
12:9
13:15
13:16
13:17
13:23
14:13[2]
16:12[2]
16:13[3]
17:4
17:20[2]
17:22[2]
17:24
17:27
18:6
18:11
18:13
19:3
20:13
21:3
21:4
21:11
22:3
22:4
22:5
22:10
22:26[2]
22:30
23:2
23:17
23:20
23:35
23:36[2]
23:38[3]
25:3
25:4
25:5
25:7[2]
25:8
25:27
25:28
25:29[2]
25:34[3]
26:4
26:5
26:11
26:12
26:15[3]
27:4
27:9[2]
27:10
27:13
27:14
27:15[2]
29:5
29:6[2]
29:7
29:8
29:12[2]
29:13[2]
29:15
29:19
29:20[2]
29:26
29:28
30:6
30:22
30:24
31:6
31:7[2]
31:10
32:5[2]
32:36
32:43
33:10
33:20
34:14
34:15[2]
34:16
34:17
35:5
35:6[2]
35:7[4]
35:13
35:14
35:15[3]
35:18
36:19
37:7
37:10
37:18
40:3
40:10[3]
42:9
42:10
42:11
42:13
42:14[2]
42:16[3]
42:18[3]
42:19[2]
42:20
42:21
42:22
44:2
44:3
44:7
44:8[4]
44:9
44:20[2]
44:22
44:23[2]
44:25[3]
44:26
44:29
46:3
46:4
46:9[2]
46:14[2]
48:14
48:17[2]
48:20
48:26
48:28
49:3
49:5
49:8
49:14
49:28
49:30
50:2
50:11[4]
50:14
50:29
50:45
51:3[2]
51:27
51:45[2]
51:46
51:50

LA

1:12
4:15

EZE

5:7
6:3
6:7
6:8[2]
6:13
7:4
7:9
9:5[2]
9:7
11:5
11:6[2]
11:7
11:8
11:10[2]
11:11
11:12[2]
11:17
12:20
12:22
13:2
13:5
13:7[3]
13:8
13:9
13:11
13:12
13:14[3]
13:18[2]
13:19
13:20[2]
13:21
13:22
13:23
14:8
14:22[2]
14:23[2]
15:7
17:12
17:21
18:2
18:3
18:19
18:25
18:31[3]
18:32
20:3
20:7
20:18
20:20
20:29
20:30[2]
20:31[3]
20:32
20:34
20:38
20:39[4]
20:41
20:42
20:43[4]
20:44[2]
21:24[3]
22:19
22:21
22:22[2]
23:40
23:49[2]
24:21
24:22[2]
24:23[2]
24:24[2]
25:5
30:2
33:10
33:11[3]
33:20[2]
33:25[2]
33:26[4]
34:3[4]
34:4[6]
34:7
34:9
34:18[2]
34:19[2]
34:21[2]
34:31
35:9
35:13
36:1
36:3[2]
36:4
36:6
36:8[2]
36:9
36:11[3]
36:22[2]
36:23
36:25
36:27
36:28[2]
36:30
36:31
37:4
37:5
37:6[2]
37:13
37:14[2]
39:17
39:18
39:19[3]
39:20
44:6
44:7[2]
44:8[2]
44:28
44:30
45:1[2]
45:6
45:10
45:13
45:14
45:20
45:21
47:13
47:14
47:18
47:21
47:22
47:23
48:8
48:9
48:20
48:29

DA

1:10
2:5[2]
2:6
2:8[2]
2:9[3]
3:5[2]
3:14
3:15[5]
3:26

HO

1:9
1:10
2:1
4:1
4:15[2]
4:18
5:1[4]
5:8
9:5
10:13[3]
14:3

JOE

1:2[2]
1:3
1:5[2]
1:11[3]
1:13[3]
1:14
2:1
2:12
2:19
2:22
2:23
2:26
2:27
3:4[3]
3:5
3:6[2]
3:7
3:9
3:11
3:13
3:17

AM

2:11
2:12
3:13
4:1
4:3[2]
4:5
4:6
4:8
4:9
4:10
4:11[2]
5:1
5:4[2]
5:6
5:7
5:11[5]
5:14[2]
5:22
5:25
5:26[2]
6:2[2]
6:3
6:12
6:13
8:4
9:7

OB

1
16

MIC

1:2
1:10[2]
1:11
2:3[2]
2:6
2:8
2:9[2]
2:10
3:1
3:6[2]
3:9
6:1
6:2[2]
6:5
6:9
6:16[2]
7:5[2]

NA

1:9
2:9

HAB

1:5[2]

ZEP

1:11
2:3[3]
2:12[2]
3:8
3:20[3]

HAG

1:4
1:6[6]
1:9[3]
2:3
2:4
2:5[2]
2:17

ZEC

1:3
1:4[2]
2:9
3:10
6:15[2]
7:5[2]
7:6[3]
7:7
8:9
8:13[2]
8:15
8:16[2]
9:12
10:1
11:2
11:12
14:5[3]

MAL

1:2
1:5
1:6
1:7[3]
1:8[2]
1:10
1:12[2]
1:13[4]
2:1
2:2[3]
2:4
2:8[3]
2:9
2:13
2:14
2:16
2:17[3]
3:1[2]
3:6
3:7[2]
3:8[2]
3:9[2]
3:10
3:12
3:13
3:14
3:18
4:2
4:3
4:4

MT

2:8
3:2
3:3
5:11
5:13
5:14
5:20
5:21
5:27
5:33
5:38
5:49
5:43
5:45
5:46[2]
5:47[2]
5:48
6:1[2]
6:7
6:8[3]
6:9
6:14
6:15
6:16
6:24
6:25[3]
6:26
6:28
6:30
6:32
6:33
7:1
7:2[3]
7:6
7:7
7:11
7:12[2]
7:13
7:16
7:20
7:23
8:26[2]
9:4
9:6
9:13
9:28
9:38
10:5
10:7
10:8
10:11[2]
10:12
10:14
10:16
10:18
10:19[2]
10:20
10:22
10:23[2]
10:27[3]
10:31[2]
11:4
11:7
11:8
11:9
11:14
11:17[2]
11:28
11:29
12:3
12:5
12:7[2]
12:34
13:14[2]
13:17[2]
13:18
13:29[2]
13:30
13:51
14:16
15:3
15:5
15:6
15:7
15:16
15:17
15:34
16:2
16:3[3]
16:8[3]
16:9[2]
16:10
16:11[2]
16:15
17:5
17:20[2]
18:3[2]
18:10
18:12
18:18[2]
18:35
19:4
19:28[2]
20:4
20:6
20:7[2]
20:22[3]
20:23
20:25
20:32
21:2
21:3
21:5
21:13
21:16
21:21[3]
21:22[2]
21:24
21:25
21:28
21:32[4]
21:42
22:9[2]
22:18[2]
22:29
22:31
22:42
23:3
23:8[2]
23:10
23:13[3]
23:14[3]
23:15[2]
23:16
23:17
23:19
23:23[2]
23:24
23:25
23:27
23:28[2]
23:29
23:31[2]
23:32
23:33[3]
23:34[2]
23:35
23:37
23:39[2]
24:2
24:6[2]
24:9
24:15
24:20
24:32
24:33[2]
24:42
24:44[2]
25:6
25:9
25:13
25:30
25:34
25:35[3]
25:36[3]
25:40[2]
25:41
25:42[2]
25:43[2]
25:45[2]
26:2
26:10
26:11[2]
26:15
26:27
26:31
26:36
26:38
26:40
26:41
26:55[2]
26:64
26:65
26:66
27:17
27:21
27:24
27:65[2]
28:5[2]
28:13
28:19

MK

1:3
1:15
1:17
2:8
2:10
2:25
4:13[2]
4:24[2]
4:40[2]
5:39
6:10[2]
6:11
6:31
6:37
6:38
7:8[2]
7:9[2]
7:11
7:12
7:13[2]
7:18[2]
8:5
8:17[4]
8:18[3]
8:19
8:20
8:21
8:29
9:16
9:33
9:41
9:50
10:36
10:38[3]
10:39[2]
10:42
11:2[2]
11:3[2]
11:5
11:17
11:24[4]
11:25[2]
11:26
11:31
12:10
12:15
12:24[2]
12:26
12:27
13:7[2]
13:9[2]
13:11[4]
13:13
13:14
13:18
13:23
13:28
13:29[2]
13:33[2]
13:35[2]
14:6
14:7[4]
14:13
14:14
14:27
14:32
14:34
14:38[2]
14:48
14:49
14:62
14:64[2]
14:71
15:9
15:12[2]
16:6
16:7
16:15

LU

2:12
2:49
3:4
4:23
5:22
5:24
5:30
5:34
6:2
6:3
6:20
6:21[4]
6:22
6:23
6:24
6:25[2]
6:31[2]
6:32[2]
6:33[2]
6:34[3]
6:35[2]
6:36
6:37[3]
6:38
6:46
7:22
7:24
7:25
7:26
7:32[2]
7:33
7:34
8:18
9:4
9:5
9:13
9:20
9:55[2]
10:2
10:5
10:8
10:10
10:11
10:23
10:24[2]
11:2
11:5
11:9
11:13
11:18
11:39
11:40
11:41
11:42[2]
11:43
11:44
11:46[3]
11:47
11:48[3]
11:52[3]
12:1
12:3[2]
12:5
12:7
12:11[3]
12:12
12:22[2]
12:24
12:26[2]
12:28
12:29[4]
12:30
12:31
12:33
12:36
12:40[2]
12:51
12:54[2]
12:55[2]
12:56[3]
12:57
13:2
13:3[2]
13:4
13:5[2]
13:25[2]
13:26
13:27[2]
13:28
13:32
13:34
13:35
16:9
16:11
16:12
16:13
16:15
17:6[2]
17:10[2]
17:22[2]
19:30[2]
19:31[2]
19:33
19:46
20:5
20:23
21:6
21:8[2]
21:9
21:14
21:16
21:17
21:20
21:30
21:31[3]
21:36[2]
22:10
22:11
22:26
22:28
22:30
22:35
22:40
22:46[2]
22:51
22:52
22:53
22:67
22:88
22:70
23:14[2]
23:15
24:5
24:17[2]
24:38
24:39
24:41
24:48
24:49[2]

JOH

1:26
1:38
1:51
3:7
3:11
3:12[2]
3:28
4:20
4:21
4:22[2]
4:32
4:35
4:38[2]
4:48[2]
5:20
5:33
5:34
5:35
5:37
5:38[2]
5:39[2]
5:40[2]
5:42
5:43[2]
5:44
5:45
5:46[2]
5:47[2]
6:26[3]
6:29
6:36
6:53[2]
6:62
6:67
7:8
7:19
7:21
7:22
7:23
7:28[3]
7:34[2]
7:36[2]
7:45
7:47
8:14
8:15
8:19[3]
8:21[2]
8:22
8:23[2]
8:24[3]
8:28[2]
8:31[2]
8:32
8:33
8:36
8:37[2]
8:38[2]
8:39[2]
8:40
8:41
8:42
8:43[2]
8:44[2]
8:45
8:46
8:47[2]
8:49
8:54
8:55
9:19
9:27[3]
9:30
9:41[3]
10:20
10:25
10:26[2]
10:32
10:34
10:36
10:38[2]
11:15
11:34
11:39
11:49
11:56
12:8[2]
12:19[2]
12:35
12:36[2]
13:10
13:11
13:12
13:13[2]
13:14
13:15
13:17[3]
13:19
13:33[2]
13:34[2]
13:35[2]
14:1
14:3
14:4[2]
14:7[3]
14:13
14:14
14:15
14:17
14:19[2]
14:20[2]
14:24
14:28[3]
14:29
15:3
15:4[2]
15:5[2]
15:7[3]
15:8[2]
15:9
15:10[2]
15:12
15:14[2]
15:16[3]
15:17
15:18
15:19[2]
15:27[2]
16:1
16:4
16:10
16:12
16:16[2]
16:17[2]
16:19[3]
16:20[2]
16:22
16:23[2]
16:24[2]
16:26
16:27
16:31
16:32
16:33[2]
18:4
18:7
18:8
18:29
18:31
18:39[2]
19:4
19:6
19:35
20:22
20:23[2]
20:31[2]
21:5
21:6
21:10

AC

1:4
1:5
1:8[2]
1:11[3]
2:14[2]
2:15
2:22[2]
2:23
2:33
2:36
2:38
3:12[3]
3:13
3:14
3:16
3:17
3:19
3:22
3:25
4:7
4:8
4:10
4:19
5:8
5:9
5:25
5:28[2]
5:30
5:35[2]
5:39[2]
6:3
7:4
7:26[2]
7:37
7:42[2]
7:43[2]
7:49
7:51[3]
7:52
8:24[2]
10:21[2]
10:28
10:29
10:37
11:16
13:15[2]
13:16
13:25
13:39
13:41[2]
13:46
14:15[2]
15:1[2]
15:7
15:10
15:24
15:29[4]
16:15
17:22[2]
17:23
18:14
18:15
19:2[2]
19:3
19:15
19:25
19:26
19:35
19:36
19:37
19:39
20:18
20:25
20:34
20:35
21:13
22:1
22:3
23:15[2]
25:24
27:21
27:31
27:33
28:26[2]

RO

1:6
1:11
6:3
6:11
6:12
6:13
6:14
6:16[4]
6:17[2]
6:18
6:19
6:20[2]
6:21[2]
6:22
7:1
7:4[2]
8:9
8:13[4]
8:15[2]
9:26
11:2
11:25[2]
11:30
12:1
12:2[2]
13:5
13:6
13:14
14:1
15:6
15:7
15:10
15:11[2]
15:13
15:14
15:30
16:2[2]
16:17

1 CO

1:5
1:7
1:8
1:9
1:10[2]
1:13
1:26
1:30
3:2[2]
3:3[2]
3:4
3:5
3:9[2]
3:16[2]
3:17
3:23
4:6
4:8[4]
4:10[3]
4:15[2]
4:16
4:21
5:2
5:4
5:6
5:7[2]
5:10
5:12
6:2[2]
6:3
6:4
6:7[3]
6:8
6:9
6:11[3]
6:15
6:16
6:19[3]
6:20
7:1
7:5[2]
7:23[2]
7:35
8:12[2]
9:1
9:2
9:13
9:24[2]
10:1
10:7
10:10
10:13[2]
10:15
10:20
10:21[2]
10:27
10:31[2]
11:1
11:2
11:17
11:18
11:20
11:22[2]
11:25[2]
11:26[2]
11:33
11:34
12:2[3]
12:27
14:1
14:5[2]
14:9[3]
14:12[3]
14:18
14:20
14:23
14:26
14:31
15:1[2]
15:2[3]
15:11
15:17
15:58
16:2
16:3
16:6
16:13
16:15
16:16
16:18
16:20

2 CO

1:7[2]
1:11
1:13[2]
1:14[2]
1:15
1:24
2:4[2]
2:7
2:8
2:9
2:10
3:2
3:3
5:12
5:20
6:1
6:11
6:12[2]
6:13
6:14
6:16
6:17
6:18
7:3
7:9[4]
7:11[2]
7:15
8:7[2]
8:9[2]
8:11
8:13
8:24
9:3
9:4
9:5
9:8
10:7
11:1
11:4[4]
11:7
11:19[2]
11:20
12:11
12:13
12:19
12:20
13:3
13:5[3]
13:6
13:7[2]
13:9

GA

1:6
1:9
1:10
1:13
3:1
3:2
3:3[2]
3:4
3:7
3:26
3:28
3:29[2]
4:6
4:8[2]
4:9[3]
4:10
4:12[2]
4:13
4:14
4:15[2]
4:17
4:21[2]
5:2
5:4
5:7
5:10
5:13
5:15[2]
5:16
5:17[2]
5:18[2]
6:1
6:2
6:11

EPH

1:13[4]
1:18
2:2
2:5
2:8
2:11
2:12
2:13
2:19
2:22
3:2
3:4[2]
3:13
3:17
3:19
4:1
4:4
4:17
4:20
4:21
4:22
4:24

4:26 4:30 4:32 5:1 5:5 5:7 5:8 5:15 5:17 6:4 6:9 6:11 6:13 6:16 6:21 6:22

PHP

1:7 1:10[2] 1:12 1:27 1:30 2:2[2] 2:12 2:15[2] 2:18 2:22 2:26 2:28 3:15 3:17 4:9 4:10[2] 4:14[2] 4:15[2] 4:16

COL

1:4 1:5 1:6 1:7 1:9 1:10 1:23[2] 2:1 2:6[2] 2:7 2:10 2:11 2:12 2:20[2] 3:1 3:3 3:4 3:7 3:8 3:9 3:13 3:15 3:17 3:23 3:24 4:1 4:6 4:10 4:12 4:16

1 TH

1:5 1:6 1:7 1:9 2:2 2:5 2:8 2:9 2:10 2:11 2:12 2:13[3] 2:14[2] 2:19 2:20 3:4 3:6 3:8 4:1[3] 4:2 4:3 4:9[2] 4:10[2] 4:11 4:12[2] 4:13 5:1 5:4 5:5 5:11

2 TH

1:4 1:5[2] 1:12 2:2 2:5 2:6 2:15 3:4 3:6 3:7 3:13

HEB

3:7 3:15 4:7 5:11 5:12[2] 6:10[2] 6:12 10:25 10:29 10:32[2] 10:33[2] 10:34[2] 10:36[3] 12:3 12:4 12:5 12:7 12:8[2] 12:17 12:18 12:22 12:25 13:5 13:23

JAS

1:2 1:4 1:22 2:3 2:4 2:6 2:7 2:8[2] 2:9[2] 2:12 2:16[2] 2:24 3:14 4:2[5] 4:3[3] 4:4[2] 4:5 4:8[2] 4:13 4:14 4:15 4:16 5:1 5:3 5:5[2] 5:6 5:8 5:9 5:11 5:12 5:16

1 PE

1:6[2] 1:8[3] 1:15 1:16 1:17 1:18[2] 1:22 2:2 2:3 2:5 2:9[2] 2:15 2:20[4] 2:21[2] 2:24 2:25 3:1 3:6[2] 3:7 3:8 3:9[2] 3:13 3:14[2] 3:17 4:4 4:7 4:13[2] 4:14[2] 5:4 5:5 5:10 5:12 5:14

2 PE

1:4 1:8 1:10[2] 1:12 1:15 1:19[2] 3:1 3:11 3:14[2] 3:17[3]

1 JO

1:3 2:1 2:7[2] 2:13[3] 2:14[3] 2:18 2:20[2] 2:21[2] 2:24[3] 2:27[3] 2:29[2] 3:5 3:11 3:15 4:2 4:3 4:4 5:13[3]

2 JO

6[2]

3 JO

12

JUDE

3 5 17 20

RE

2:10[2] 2:25 12:12[2] 18:4[2] 18:20 19:5[2] 19:18

YOU

5209

GE

1:12 1:29 9:2 9:3[2] 9:7 9:9 9:10[2] 9:11 9:12 9:15 17:10 17:11 17:12 18:4 19:2 19:7 19:8 19:14 22:5 23:4[2] 23:9 26:27 27:45 31:29 34:8 34:9 34:10[2] 34:15[2] 34:16[2] 35:2 37:6 40:8 41:55 42:2 42:14 42:16[2] 42:22 42:34 42:38 43:3 43:5 43:14 43:23[2] 44:17 44:23 45:4 45:5 45:7 45:8 45:12 45:17 45:18 45:19 46:33 47:16 47:23[2] 48:21 49:1 50:4 50:20 50:21 50:24 50:25

EX

3:13 3:14 3:15 3:16[2] 3:17 3:19 3:20 4:15 5:4 5:10 5:11 5:18 5:21 6:6[3] 6:7[3] 6:8[2] 7:4 7:9 8:28 9:8 9:28 10:5[2] 10:10[3] 10:16 10:24 11:1[2] 11:9 12:2[2] 12:13[5] 12:14 12:16[2] 12:21 12:22 12:23 12:25 12:26 12:31 12:49 13:3 13:19[2] 14:13 14:14 16:4 16:6 16:8 16:15 16:23 16:29[2] 16:32[2] 18:10 19:4[2] 20:20 20:22 20:23 22:24 23:13 24:8 24:14[2] 26:33 29:42 30:36 31:13[2] 31:14 31:29 35:2 35:5 35:10

LE

1:2 8:33 8:34 9:4 9:6 10:7 10:17 11:4 11:5 11:6 11:7 11:8 11:10 11:11 11:12 11:20 11:23 11:26 11:27 11:28 11:29 11:31 11:35 11:38 11:45 14:34 16:29[2] 16:30[2] 16:31 16:34 17:8 17:10 17:11 17:12[2] 17:13 18:3 18:6 18:24 18:26 18:27 18:28[2] 18:30 19:23 19:25 19:28 19:34[3] 19:36 20:8 20:14 20:22[2] 20:23 20:24[3] 20:25 20:26 21:8 22:20 22:25 22:32 22:33 23:10 23:11 23:15 23:21 23:27 23:28 23:32 23:36 23:40 25:2 25:6 25:10 25:11 25:12 25:21 25:38[2] 25:44 25:45[2] 25:46 26:1[2] 26:4 26:6 26:7 26:8[3] 26:9[4] 26:11[2] 26:12 26:13[2] 26:16[2] 26:17[4] 26:18 26:21 26:22[3] 26:24[2] 26:25[2] 26:26 26:28[2] 26:30 26:33[2] 26:36 26:38 26:39

NU

1:4 1:5 9:8 9:10 9:14 10:8 10:9 10:10 10:29 11:18 11:20[2] 12:6 13:17 14:25[2] 14:28 14:29 14:30 14:32 14:42 14:43[2] 15:2 15:14[2] 15:15[2] 15:16[2] 15:18 15:23 15:39 15:41 16:3 16:6 16:7 16:8 16:9[3] 16:17 16:24 16:26 16:45 17:4 17:5 18:4 18:6 18:7 18:26 18:27 20:10 22:8 22:13[2] 22:19 25:18[2] 28:19 28:22 28:30 28:31 29:1 29:5 29:8 32:21 32:23 32:24 32:29[2] 32:30[2] 33:52 33:53 33:55[2] 33:56 34:2 34:7 34:17 35:11[2] 35:12 35:29

DE

1:7 1:8 1:9[2] 1:10 1:11[3] 1:13[2] 1:15 1:17 1:18 1:20 1:22 1:23 1:29 1:30[3] 1:33[2] 1:40[2] 1:42 1:43 1:44[3] 1:45 2:3 2:4 2:5 2:13 3:18[2] 3:19 3:20[2] 3:22 4:1[2] 4:2[2] 4:3 4:4 4:5 4:8 4:12 4:13[2] 4:14 4:15 4:16 4:20[2] 4:23[2] 4:26 4:27[2] 4:34 5:4 5:5[2] 5:30 5:32 5:33[2] 6:1 6:14 6:15 6:20 7:4 7:7[2] 7:8[3] 7:14 7:21 8:19 9:8[2] 9:9 9:10 9:16[2] 9:19[2] 9:23[2] 9:24 9:25 10:4 10:15 11:4 11:5 11:8 11:13 11:14 11:17[2] 11:22 11:23 11:25[4] 11:26 11:27 11:28 11:31 11:32 12:9 12:10[2] 12:11 12:12 12:32 13:1 13:3 13:5[3] 13:7 13:11 13:13 13:14 14:7 14:8 14:10 14:19 15:4 15:7 16:11 17:2 17:7 17:16 18:10 19:19 19:20 20:4[2] 20:18 21:9 21:21 22:21 22:24 23:4 23:10 23:16 24:7 24:8 26:11 27:1 27:4 28:54 28:55 28:63[6] 28:68 29:4 29:5[2] 29:10 29:14 29:18[2] 29:22 30:18 30:19[2] 31:5 31:19 31:27 31:29[2] 32:38 32:46 32:47

JOS

1:3 1:11[2] 1:13[3] 1:14 1:15[2] 2:9[2] 2:10 2:11 2:12[2] 2:16[2] 3:4 3:5 3:10[2] 3:11 3:12 4:2 4:3[2] 4:5[2] 4:6 4:23 5:9 6:10 6:16 7:12[2] 7:13 8:8 9:7 9:11 9:12 9:22 9:23 9:24[3] 18:3 18:4 18:6 18:7 18:8 20:2[2] 22:2[2] 22:4[2] 22:5 22:16 22:19 22:25 22:27 22:28 23:3[2] 23:4 23:5[2] 23:7 23:9[3] 23:10[3] 23:12[2] 23:13[3] 23:14[2] 23:15[5] 23:16[3] 24:5 24:7 24:8[3] 24:9 24:10[2] 24:11 24:12[2] 24:13 24:15[2] 24:20[3] 24:22 24:23 24:27

JG

2:1[3] 2:3[2] 6:8[2] 6:9[4] 6:10 7:7 8:2 8:3 8:5 8:19 8:23[3] 8:24 9:2[4] 9:7 9:15 9:17[2] 9:19 10:11 10:12[2] 10:13 10:14 12:2 14:12[2] 15:7 19:9[2] 19:23 19:24 20:12 20:21

RU

1:8 1:9[2] 2:4 2:7

1 SA

4:9 6:3[2] 6:4 6:5 6:21 7:3[2] 7:5 8:11 8:18[2] 9:12 9:13 10:2 10:15 10:18[2] 10:19 11:2 11:10[2] 12:1 12:2[3] 12:3 12:5 12:7[2] 12:11 12:12 12:13 12:14 12:15 12:17 12:23[2] 12:24 14:9 14:12 14:29 15:6[2] 17:8[2] 17:47 18:23 22:3 22:7[2] 22:8[2] 23:22 23:23 25:5 25:19 30:24 30:26

2 SA

1:21 1:24 2:6[2] 3:17 3:31 4:11 7:23 13:28[2] 15:27 15:28 16:10 16:20 17:21 18:2 18:4 18:22 20:16 21:3 21:4

1 KI

1:33 9:6 11:2 12:11[3] 12:14[2] 12:28 18:25 20:7 22:28

2 KI

1:6 1:7[2] 2:18 5:7 6:19 7:12 10:2[3] 10:23 11:5 11:7 17:13 17:36 17:37 17:38 17:39 18:27 18:29[2] 18:30 18:32[2] 22:15 22:18 25:24

1 CH

12:17 13:2 22:18[2] 28:8

2 CH

7:19 10:11[3] 10:14[2] 12:5 13:8[2] 13:9 13:12 15:2[3] 19:6 19:7 19:10[2] 19:11 20:15 20:17[2] 23:4 24:20 28:10[3] 28:11 29:11 30:6 30:8 30:9 32:11 32:14 32:15[3] 34:23 34:26 36:23

EZR

1:3 4:2 5:3 5:9 7:21 7:24

NE

1:8 1:9 4:12 5:10 5:11 6:3 13:21 13:27

ES

8:8

JOB

6:28 6:29 12:2 12:3[2] 13:2 13:9 13:10 13:11[2] 16:4[2] 16:5 17:10[2] 27:5 27:11 32:6 32:12[2] 32:21 42:8[3]

PS

34:11 50:22 62:3 82:6 115:14[2] 118:26 127:2 129:8[2]

PR

1:23[3] 1:27 4:2 8:4

CA

2:7 3:5 5:8 8:4

ISA

1:15 1:16 5:3 5:5 7:13 7:14 8:19 21:10 22:14 28:19 29:11 30:11 30:13 30:16 30:18[2] 30:20 31:7 32:11[2] 33:11 35:4 36:12 36:14[2] 36:15 36:17 36:18 40:21 41:24 42:9 42:23 43:12 46:4[2] 50:1 50:10 51:2 51:12 59:2[2] 61:6 65:12 66:5[2] 66:13

JER

2:7 2:9 3:12 3:14[3] 3:15[2] 4:8 4:15 4:18 4:25 6:17 7:3 7:7 7:13[2] 7:14 7:15 7:23[2] 7:25 8:17[2] 10:1 11:4 14:13 14:14 15:14 16:13[2] 18:6 18:11[2] 21:4 21:5 21:8 21:9 21:14 23:2 23:16[2] 23:17 23:33 23:38 23:39[4] 23:40 25:3 25:4 25:5 25:6 25:27 26:4 26:5 26:13 26:14 26:15 27:9 27:10[3] 27:14[2] 27:15[2] 27:16[2] 29:7 29:8[2] 29:9 29:10[3] 29:11[2] 29:12 29:14[5] 29:16 29:21 29:27 29:31[2] 34:16 34:17[2] 34:21 35:14 35:15[2] 35:18 37:7[2] 37:10 37:19[2] 38:5 40:3 40:9 42:4[4] 42:10[5] 42:11[3] 42:12[3] 42:16[2] 42:18 42:19[2] 42:21[2] 44:4 44:7[2] 44:10 44:11 44:23 44:29[3] 49:3 49:30[3] 49:31 50:12

LA

1:12 1:18

EZE

5:7[2] 5:16[2] 5:17 6:3 6:7 6:9 11:7 11:8 11:9[3] 11:10 11:11 11:12 11:15 11:17[3] 11:19 13:8 13:12 13:15 13:18 14:22 14:23 18:30 18:31[2] 20:3 20:20 20:31[2] 20:33 20:34[2] 20:35[2] 20:36 20:37[2] 20:38 20:39 20:41[4] 20:42 20:44 22:19 22:20[3] 22:21[2] 22:22 23:49 24:24 33:20 33:30 34:3 34:17 34:18 36:2 36:3[2] 36:7 36:9[2] 36:10 36:11[2] 36:12 36:13 36:23 36:24[3] 36:25[2] 36:26[3] 36:27[2] 36:29[2] 36:32 36:33[2] 36:36 37:5 37:6[4] 37:12[2] 37:13 37:14[2] 39:17 39:19 43:27 44:6 45:9 47:14 47:21 47:22[5]

DA

2:9 3:4 3:15 4:1 6:2

JOE

2:19[2] 2:20 2:23[2] 2:25[2] 2:26 3:13

AM

2:10[2] 2:13 3:1 3:2[2] 4:2[2] 4:5 4:6 4:7 4:9 4:10 4:11 5:1 5:14 5:18[2] 5:27 6:14[2]

JON

1:12[2]

MIC

1:2 1:11 2:4 2:10 3:1[2] 3:6[2] 3:9

HAB

1:5

ZEP

2:2[2] 2:5

HAG

1:4 1:6 1:10 1:13 2:3 2:4[2] 2:5[2] 2:15 2:17 2:19

ZEC

1:3 2:6 2:8[2] 4:9 6:7 6:15 7:10 8:13 8:14 8:17 8:23[2] 9:12 11:7 11:9

MAL

1:2 1:6 1:9 1:10[2] 2:1 2:2 2:3 2:4 2:9 3:5 3:7 3:10[2] 3:12 4:2 4:5

MT

3:7 3:9 3:11[2] 4:19 5:11[3] 5:12 5:18 5:20 5:22 5:28 5:32 5:34 5:39 5:44[5] 5:46 6:2 6:5 6:14 6:16 6:25 6:27 6:29 6:30 6:33 7:2 7:6 7:7[2] 7:9 7:12 7:15 7:23 8:10 8:11 9:29 10:13 10:14 10:15 10:16 10:17[2] 10:19[2] 10:20 10:23[2] 10:27 10:40 10:42 11:9 11:11 11:17[2] 11:21 11:22[2] 11:24 11:28 11:29 12:6 12:11 12:28 12:31 12:36 13:11 13:17 15:7 16:11 16:28 17:12 17:17[2]

17:20^2
18:3
18:10
18:13
18:18
18:19^2
18:35
19:8
19:9
19:23
19:24
19:28
20:4
20:26^2
20:27
20:32
21:2
21:3
21:21
21:24^2
21:27
21:31^2
21:32
21:43^2
22:31
23:3
23:11
23:13
23:14
23:15
23:16
23:23
23:25
23:25
23:27
23:29
23:34
23:35
23:36
23:38
23:39
24:2
24:4
24:9^2
24:23
24:25
24:26
24:34
24:47
25:9
25:12^2
25:34
25:40
25:45
26:11
26:13
26:15
26:21^2
26:29^2
26:32
26:55
26:64
27:17
27:21
28:7^2
28:14
28:20^2

MK

1:8^2
1:17
3:28
4:11
4:24^2
6:11^3
7:6
7:14
8:12
9:1
9:13
9:19^2
9:41^2
10:3
10:5
10:15
10:29
10:36
10:43^2
10:44
11:2
11:3
11:23
11:24
11:25
11:29^2
11:33
12:43
13:5
13:9
13:11^3
13:21
13:23
13:30
13:36
13:37
14:7
14:9
14:13
14:15
14:18^2
14:25
14:28
14:49
15:9
16:7^2

LU

2:10
2:11
2:12
3:7
3:8
3:13
3:16^2
4:24
4:25
6:9
6:22^3
6:24
6:25^2
6:26^2
6:27^2
6:28^2
6:31
6:32
6:33
6:38^2
6:47
7:9
7:26
7:28
7:32^2
8:10
9:5
9:27
9:41^2
9:48
10:3
10:6
10:8^2
10:9
10:10
10:11^2
10:12
10:13
10:14
10:16^2
10:19^2
10:20
10:24
11:8
11:9^3
11:11
11:20
11:41
11:42
11:43
11:44
11:46
11:47
11:51
11:52
12:4
12:5^2
12:8
12:11
12:12
12:14
12:22
12:25
12:27
12:28
12:31
12:32
12:37
12:44
12:51
13:3
13:5
13:15
13:24
13:25^2
13:27^2
13:28
13:35^2
14:5
14:24
14:28
14:33
15:4
15:7
15:10
16:9^2
16:12
16:26^2
17:6
17:7
17:10
17:21
17:23
17:34
18:8
18:14
18:17
18:29
19:26
19:30
19:31
19:40
20:3
20:8
21:3
21:12^3
21:13
21:15
21:16
21:32
21:34
22:10
22:12
22:15
22:16
22:18
22:19
22:20
22:26
22:27
22:29
22:31^2
22:35
22:37
22:53
22:67
22:68
23:14
24:6
24:36
24:44^2
24:49

JOH

1:26
1:51
2:5
3:12^2
4:35
4:38
5:19
5:24
5:25
5:38
5:42^2
5:45^2
6:26
6:27
6:32^3
6:36
6:47
6:53^2
6:61
6:63
6:64
6:65
6:70^2
7:7
7:19^2
7:22
7:33
8:7
8:24
8:25
8:26
8:32
8:34
8:36
8:37
8:40
8:45
8:46
8:51
8:58
9:27
10:1
10:7
10:25
10:26
10:32
12:8
12:24
12:35^2
13:12
13:15^2
13:16
13:18
13:19
13:20
13:21^2
13:33^2
13:34^2
14:2^2
14:3^2
14:9
14:10
14:12
14:16^2
14:17^2
14:18^2
14:20
14:25^2
14:26^2
14:27^3
14:28^2
14:29
14:30
15:3
15:4
15:7^2
15:9
15:11^2
15:12
15:14
15:15^3
15:16^3
15:17
15:18^2
15:19^2
15:20^2
15:21
15:26
16:1
16:2^2
16:3
16:4^4
16:5
16:6
16:7^4
16:12
16:13^2
16:14
16:15
16:20
16:22^2
16:23^2
16:25^3
16:26^2
16:27
16:33
18:8
18:39^2
19:4
20:19
20:21^2
20:26

AC

1:7
1:8
1:11
2:14
2:22^2
2:29
2:38
2:39
3:14
3:16
3:20
3:22^2
3:26^3
4:10^2
4:11
4:19
5:28
5:38
6:3
7:37
7:43
10:29
13:26^2
13:32
13:34
13:38^2
13:40
13:41
13:46^2
14:15^2
15:24
15:25
15:27
15:28
16:36
17:3
17:23
18:14
18:21
19:13
20:18
20:20^3
20:26
20:27
20:28
20:29
20:32^3
20:35
22:1
22:25
23:15
24:21
25:5
25:26
26:8
27:22^2
27:34^2
28:20^3
28:28

RO

1:7
1:8
1:9
1:10
1:11^2
1:12^2
1:13^3
1:15
2:24
6:14
6:17
8:9
8:10
8:11^2
10:19^2
11:13
12:1
12:3
12:14
12:18
15:5
15:13
15:14
15:15^2
15:22
15:23
15:24^3
15:28
15:29
15:30
15:32^2
15:33
16:1
16:2
16:16
16:17
16:19
16:20
16:21
16:22
16:23^2
16:24
16:25

1 CO

1:3
1:4
1:6
1:8
1:10^2
1:11
1:12
1:13
1:14
2:1^2
2:2
2:3
3:1
3:2
3:3
3:16
3:18
4:3
4:6
4:8
4:14^2
4:15
4:16
4:17^2
4:18
4:19
4:21
5:1
5:2
5:9
5:11
6:1
6:2
6:5
6:7
6:11
6:19
7:5
7:28
7:32
7:35
9:2
9:11
9:12
9:23
10:13^2
10:27^2
10:28
11:2^2
11:3
11:14
11:17^2
11:18
11:19^2
11:22^3
11:23
11:24
11:30
12:1
12:3
12:21
12:31
14:6^3
14:25
14:26
14:36^2
14:37
15:1^2
15:2
15:3
15:12
15:51
16:2
16:5
16:6
16:7^2
16:10
16:12
16:13
16:15
16:19^2
16:20
16:23
16:24

2 CO

1:2
1:7
1:8
1:12
1:13
1:15
1:16^3
1:18
1:19
1:21
1:23
2:1
2:2
2:3^3
2:4^2
2:5
2:8
2:9
3:1^2
4:12
4:14
5:12^2
5:20^2
6:1
6:11
6:17
6:18
7:3^2
7:4^2
7:7
7:8^2
7:11
7:12^3
7:13
7:14^2
7:15^2
7:16
8:1
8:6
8:10
8:16
8:17
8:22
8:23
9:1
9:2
9:3
9:4
9:5
9:8
9:14^3
10:1^3
10:2
10:9
10:13
10:14^2
10:15
10:16
11:2^3
11:6
11:7
11:8
11:9^2
11:11
11:20^4
12:11
12:12
12:13
12:14^3
12:15^2
12:16^2
12:17
12:18
12:19
12:20^2
12:21
13:1
13:2^2
13:3
13:4
13:5
13:11
13:13
13:14

GA

1:3
1:6
1:7
1:8^2
1:9
1:11
1:20
2:5
3:1^2
3:2
3:5^2
3:27
4:11^2
4:12
4:13
4:15
4:16
4:17^2
4:18
4:19
4:20^2
5:2^2
5:4^2
5:7
5:8
5:10^2
5:12
5:21^2
6:11
6:12
6:13

EPH

1:2
1:16^2
1:17
2:1
2:17
3:1
3:13
3:16
4:1
4:6
4:31
4:32
5:3
5:6
5:33
6:13
6:21
6:22

PHP

1:2
1:3
1:4
1:6
1:7^2
1:8
1:24
1:25
1:26
1:27
1:28
1:26
2:5
2:13
2:17
2:19
2:25
2:26
3:1
3:15
3:18
4:9
4:18
4:21
4:22
4:23

COL

1:2
1:3
1:5
1:6^2
1:7
1:9
1:21
1:22
1:24
1:25
1:27
2:1
2:4
2:5
2:8
2:13^2
2:16
2:18
3:13
3:16
4:7
4:8
4:9
4:10
4:12
4:13
4:14
4:16
4:18

2 TH

1:1
1:2
1:5
1:8
1:9
2:1
2:2
2:6
2:7
2:8^2
2:9
2:10
2:11
2:12
2:13
2:17
2:18
3:2^2
3:4^2
3:5
3:6^2
3:7
3:9
3:11
3:12^2
4:1^2
4:2
4:4
4:6
4:9
4:10
4:11
4:13
4:15
5:1
5:4
5:12^4
5:14
5:18
5:23
5:24
5:27
5:28

2 TH

1:2
1:3
1:4
1:6
1:7
1:10
1:11^2
1:12
2:1
2:3
2:5^2
2:13^2
2:14
2:17
3:1
3:3^2
3:4^2
3:6
3:7
3:8
3:9
3:10^2
3:11
3:16^2
3:18

2 TI

4:22

TIT

2:8
3:15

PHM

3
6
22

HEB

3:12
3:13
4:1
5:12
6:9
6:11
9:20
12:5
12:7
12:15
13:7^2
13:17^2
13:19^2
13:21^2
13:22^2
13:23
13:24^2
13:25

JAS

1:5
1:26
2:6^2
2:16
3:13
4:1
4:7
4:8
4:10
5:1
5:4
5:6
5:13
5:14
5:19

1 PE

1:2
1:4
1:10
1:12^2
1:13
1:15
1:20
1:25
2:7
2:9
2:11
2:12
3:13
3:15^2
3:16
4:4
4:12^2
4:14
4:15
5:1
5:2
5:5
5:6
5:7
5:10^2
5:12
5:13^2
5:14

2 PE

1:2
1:8^2
1:11
1:12
1:13^2
1:16
2:1
2:3
2:13
3:2
3:15

1 JO

1:2
1:3
1:4
1:5
2:1
2:8^2
2:12^2
2:13^3
2:14^3
2:21
2:24^2
2:26^2
2:27^4
3:7
3:13
4:4
5:13

2 JO

3
10
12^2

JUDE

2
3^3
5
12
18
24^2

RE

1:4
2:10
2:13
2:23
2:24^2
12:12
18:6
18:20
22:16
22:21

A Concise Dictionary

of the Words in the

Hebrew Bible

---

with their Renderings in the King James Version

PREFACE

THIS work, although prepared as a companion to the Main Concordance, is paged separately, in the belief that a brief and simple Dictionary of the Biblical Hebrew and Chaldee will be useful to students and others, who do not care at all times to consult a more copious and elaborate Lexicon. It will be particularly serviceable to many who are unable to turn conveniently and rapidly, amid the perplexities and details of foreign characters with which the pages of Gesenius and Fürst bristle, to the fundamental and essential points of information that they are seeking. Even scholars will find here, not only all of a strictly verbal character which they most frequently want in ordinary consultation of a lexicon, but numerous original suggestions, relations, and distinctions, carefully made and clearly put, which are not unworthy of their attention, especially in the affinities of roots and the classification of meanings. The portable form and moderate cost of the book, it is hoped, will facilitate its use with all classes. The vocabulary is complete as to the ground-forms that actually occur in the biblical text (or *Kethib*), with the pointing that properly belongs to them. Their designation by numbers will especially aid those who are not very familiar with the original language, and the Anglicizing and pronunciation of the words will not come amiss to multitudes who have some acquaintance with it. The addition of the renderings in the common version will greatly contribute to fixing and extending the varied significations and applications of the Hebrew and Chaldee words, as well as to correcting their occasionally wrong translations. On this account, as well as for the sake of precision and to prevent repetition, the use of the same terms in the preceding definitions has been avoided wherever practicable. The design of the volume, being purely *lexical,* does not include grammatical, archæological, or exegetical details, which would have swelled its size and encumbered its plan. By observing the subjoined directions, in the associated use of the Main Concordance, the reader will have substantially a Concordance-Dictionary of the Authorized/King James Version and the Hebrew Bible.

PLAN OF THE DICTIONARY

ALL the original words are treated in their alphabetical Hebrew order, and are numbered regularly from the first to the last, each being known throughout by its appropriate number. This renders reference easy without recourse to the Hebrew characters.

Immediately after each word is given its exact equivalent in English letters, according to the system of transliteration laid down in the scheme here following, which is substantially that adopted in the Common English Version, only more consistently and uniformly carried out; so that the word could readily be turned back again into Hebrew from the form thus given it.

Next follows the precise pronunciation, according to the usual English mode of sounding syllables, so plainly indicated that none can fail to apprehend and apply it. The most approved sounds are adopted, as laid down in the annexed scheme of articulation, and in such a way that any good Hebraist would immediately recognize the word if so pronounced, notwithstanding the minor variations current among scholars in this respect.

Then ensues a tracing of the etymology, radical meaning, and applied signification of the word, justly but tersely analyzed and expressed, with any other important peculiarities in this regard.

In the case of proper names, the same method is pursued, and at this point the regular mode of Anglicizing it, after the general style of the Common English Version, is given, and a few words of explanation are added to identify it.

Finally (after the punctuation-mark :—) are given all the different renderings of the word in the Authorized/King James Version, arranged in the alphabetical order of the leading terms, and conveniently condensed according to the explanations given below.

By searching out these various renderings in the Main Concordance, to which this Dictionary is designed as a companion, and noting the passages to which the same number corresponding to that of any given Hebrew word is attached in the marginal column, the reader, whether acquainted with the original language or not, will obtain a complete *Hebrew Concordance* also, expressed in the words of the Common English Version. This is an advantage which no other Concordance or Lexicon affords.

HEBREW ARTICULATION

THE following explanations are sufficient to show the method of transliterating Hebrew words into English adopted in this *Dictionary.*

The Hebrew is read *from right to left.* The Alphabet consists of 22 letters (and their variations), which are all regarded as *consonants,* being enunciated by the aid of certain "points" or marks, mostly beneath the letters, and which serve as *vowels.* There is no distinction of *capitals, italics,* etc.

The letters are as follows:

No.	Form	Name		Transliteration and Power
1.	א	'Aleph	*(aw´-lef)*	' unappreciable
2.	ב	Bêyth	*(bayth)*	**b**
3.	ג	Gîymel	*(ghee´-mel)*	**g** hard = γ
4.	ד	Dâleth	*(daw´-leth)*	**d**
5.	ה	Hê'	*(hay)*	**h,** often quies- [cent
6.	ו	Vâv	*(vawv)*	**v,** or **w** quies- [cent
7.	ז	Zayin	*(zah´-yin)*	**z, as in** *zeal*
8.	ח	Chêyth	*(khayth)*	German **ch** = χ [(nearly *kh*)
9.	ט	Têyth	*(tayth)*	**ṭ** = ת [cent
10.	י	Yôwd	*(yode)*	**y,** often quies-
11.	כ, final ך	Kaph	*(caf)*	**k** = ק
12.	ל	Lâmed	*(law´-med)*	**l**
13.	מ, final ם	Mêm	*(mame)*	**m**
14.	נ, final ן	Nûwn	*(noon)*	**n**
15.	ס	Çâmek	*(saw´-mek)*	**ç** = *s* sharp = שׂ
16.	ע	'Ayin	*(ah´-yin)*	' peculiar *
17.	פּ, final ף	Phê'	*(fay)*	**ph** = *f* = φ
	פ	Pê'	*(pay)*	**p**
18.	צ, final ץ	Tsâdêy	*(tsaw-day´)*	**ts**
19.	ק	Qôwph	*(cofe)*	**q** = *k* = כ
20.	ר	Rêysh	*(raysh)*	**r**
21.	שׂ	Sîyn	*(seen)*	**s** sharp = ס = σ
	שׁ	Shîyn	*(sheen)*	**sh**
22.	ת	Thâv	*(thawv)*	**th,** as in THin
	תּ	Tâv	*(tawv)*	**t** = ט = τ [= ϑ

*The letter *'Ayin,* owing to the difficulty experienced by Occidentals in pronouncing it accurately (it is a deep guttural sound, like that made in *gargling*), is generally neglected (i.e. passed over silently) in reading. We have represented it to the eye (but not exactly to the ear) by the Greek *rough breathing* (for distinctness and typographical convenience, a reversed *apostrophe*) in order to distinguish it from *'Âleph,* which is likewise treated as silent being similarly represented by the Greek *smooth breathing* (the *apostrophe*).

The *vowel-points* are the following:

Form*	Name		Representation and Power
(ָ)	Qâmêts	*(caw-mates´)*	**â,** as in *All*
(ַ)	Pattach	*(pat´-takh)*	**a,** as in *mAn, (fār)*
(ֲ)	Sh^e^vâ'-Pattach	*(she-vaw´ pat´-takh)*	**ă,** as in *hAt*
(ֵ)	Tsêrêy	*(tsay-ray´)*	**ê,** as in *thEy* = η
(ֶ)	Çegôwl	*(seg-ole´)*	**e,** as in *thEir*; **e,** as in *mEn* = ε
(ֱ)	Sh^e^vâ'-Çegôwl	*(she-vaw´ seg-ole)*	**ĕ,** as in *mEt*
(ְ)	Sh^e^vâ'†	*(she-vaw´)*	^e^ obscure, as in [*avErage*; silent, as *e* in *madE*
(ִ)	Chîyriq	*(khee´-rik)*	**î,** as in *machIne* ‡; **i,** as in *supplIant,* [(*mĭsery, hit*)
(ֹ)	Chôwlem §	*(kho´-lem)*	**ô,** as in *no* = ω
(ָ)	Short Qâmêts ‖		**o,** as in *nor* = ο
(ֳ)	Sh^e^vâ'-Qâmêts	*(she-vaw´ caw-mates´)*	**ŏ,** as in *not*
(וּ)	Shûwrêq *	*(shoo-rake´)*	**û,** as in *crUel*
(ֻ)	Qĭbbûts *	*(kib´-boots)*	**u,** as in *fUll, rūde*

* The parenthesis-marks ( ) are given here in order to show the place of the vowel-points, whether below, above, or in the middle of the letter.

† *Silent Sh^e^vâ'* is not represented by any mark in our method of transliteration, as it is understood whenever there is no other vowel-point.

‡ *Chîyriq* is thus long only when it is followed by a quiescent *yôwd* (either expressed or implied).

§ *Chôwlem* is written *fully* only over *Vâv,* which is then quiescent (*w*); but when used "defectively" (without the *Vâv*) it may be written either over the left-hand corner of the letter to which it belongs, or over the right-hand corner of the following one.

‖ Short *Qâmêts* is found only in *unaccented syllables ending with a consonant sound.*

A point in the bosom of a letter is called *Dâgêsh´,* and is of two kinds, which must be carefully distinguished.

a. Dâgêsh *lenê* occurs only in the letters בּ, גּ, דּ, כּ, פּ, תּ, (technically vocalized *B^e^gad´-K^e^phath´,*) when they *begin* a clause or sentence, or are preceded by a consonant *sound;* and simply has the effect of removing their aspiration.†

b. Dâgêsh *fortè* may occur in any letter except א, ה, ח, ע or ר; it is equivalent to *doubling* the letter, and at the same time it removes the aspiration of a B^e^gad-K^e^phath letter.‡

The *Maqqêph´* (־), like a *hyphen,* unites words only for purposes of pronunciation (by removing the primary accent from all except the last of them), but does not affect their meaning or their grammatical construction.

* *Shûwrêq* is written only in the bosom of *Vâv.* Sometimes it is said to be "defectively" written (without the *Vâv*), and then takes the form of *Qibbûts,* which in such cases is called *vicarious.*

† In our system of transliteration Dâgêsh *lenè* is represented only in the letters פּ and תּ, because elsewhere it does not affect the pronunciation (with most Hebraists).

‡ A point in the bosom of ה is called *Mappîyq (mappeek´).* It occurs only in the final vowelless letter of a few words, and we have represented it by *hh. A Dâgêsh fortè* in the bosom of ו may easily be distinguished from the vowel *Shûwrêq* by noticing that in the former case the letter has a proper vowel-point accompanying it.

It should be noted that both kinds of Dâgêsh are often omitted in writing (being then said to be *implied*), but (in the case at least of Dâgêsh *fortè*) the word is (by most Hebraists) pronounced the same as if it were present.

ABBREVIATIONS EMPLOYED

abb. = abbreviated, abbreviation
absol. = absolute, absolutely
abstr. = abstract, abstractly
act. = active, actively
adj. = adjective, adjectively
adv. = adverb, adverbial, adverbially
aff. = affix, affixed
affin. = affinity
appar. = apparent, apparently
arch. = architecture, architectural, architecturally
art. = article.
artif. = artificial, artificially
Ass. = Assyrian
A. V. = Authorized Version
Bab. = Babylon, Babylonia, Babylonian
caus. = causative, causatively
Chald. = Chaldaism, Chaldee
collat. = collateral, collaterally
collect. = collective, collectively
comp. = compare, comparative, comparatively, comparison
concr. = concrete, concretely
conjec. = conjecture, conjectural, conjecturally
conjug. = conjugation, conjugational, conjugationally
conjunc. = conjunction, conjunctional, conjunctionally
constr. = construct, construction, constructive, constructively
contr. = contracted, contraction
correl. = correlated, correlation, correlative, correlatively
corresp. = corresponding, correspondingly
def. = definite, definitely
denom. = denominative, denominatively
der. = derivation, derivative, derivatively
desc. = descendant, descendants
E. = East, Eastern
e.g. = *exempli gratiâ* for example
Eg. = Egypt, Egyptian, Egyptians
ellip. = ellipsis, elliptical, elliptically
equiv. = equivalent, equivalently
err. = erroneous, erroneously, error
esp. = especial, especially
etym. = etymology, etymological, etymologically
euphem. = euphemism, euphemistic, euphemistically
euphon. = euphonically, euphonious

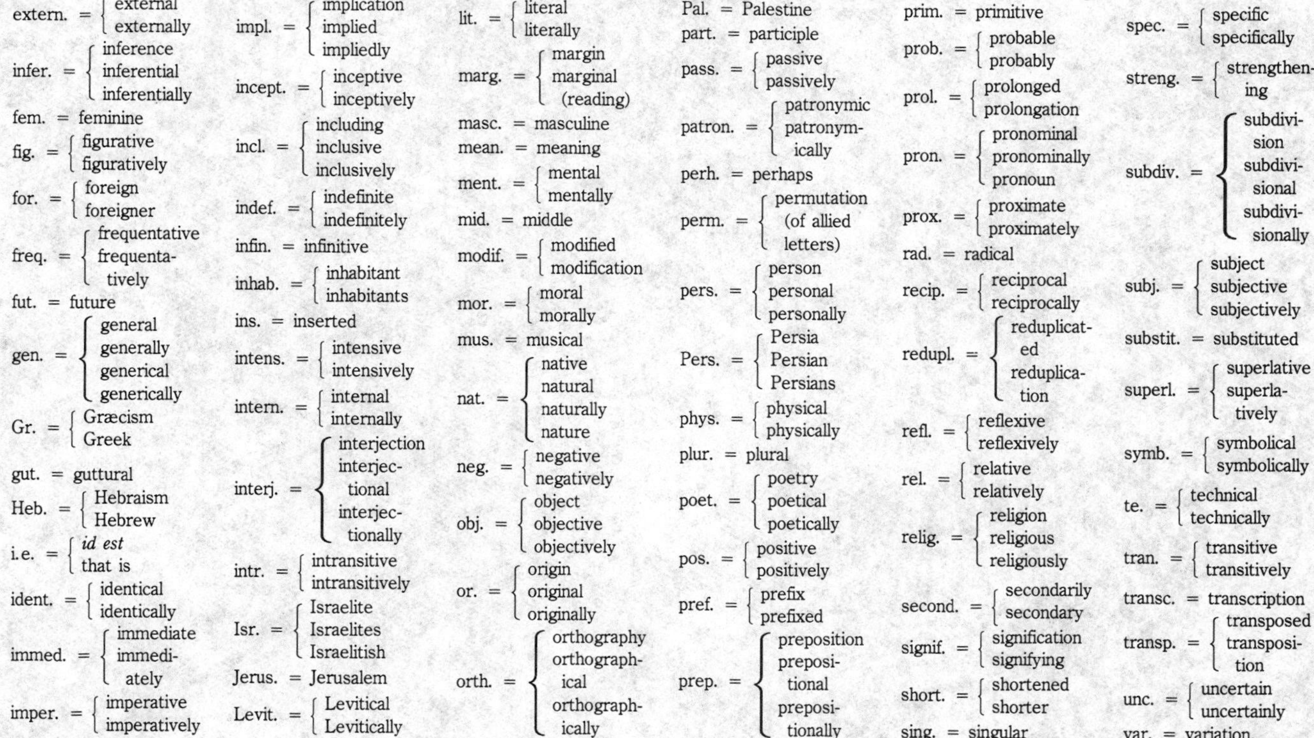

extern. = external / externally
infer. = inference / inferential / inferentially
fem. = feminine
fig. = figurative / figuratively
for. = foreign / foreigner
freq. = frequentative / frequentatively
fut. = future
gen. = general / generally / generical / generically
Gr. = Græcism / Greek
gut. = guttural
Heb. = Hebraism / Hebrew
i.e. = *id est* / that is
ident. = identical / identically
immed. = immediate / immediately
imper. = imperative / imperatively
impl. = implication / implied / impliedly
incept. = inceptive / inceptively
incl. = including / inclusive / inclusively
indef. = indefinite / indefinitely
infin. = infinitive
inhab. = inhabitant / inhabitants
ins. = inserted
intens. = intensive / intensively
intern. = internal / internally
interj. = interjection / interjectional / interjectionally
intr. = intransitive / intransitively
Isr. = Israelite / Israelites / Israelitish
Jerus. = Jerusalem
Levit. = Levitical / Levitically
lit. = literal / literally
marg. = margin / marginal (reading)
masc. = masculine
mean. = meaning
ment. = mental / mentally
mid. = middle
modif. = modified / modification
mor. = moral / morally
mus. = musical
nat. = native / natural / naturally / nature
neg. = negative / negatively
obj. = object / objective / objectively
or. = origin / original / originally
orth. = orthography / orthographical / orthographically
Pal. = Palestine
part. = participle
pass. = passive / passively
patron. = patronymic / patronymically
perh. = perhaps
perm. = permutation (of allied letters)
pers. = person / personal / personally
Pers. = Persia / Persian / Persians
phys. = physical / physically
plur. = plural
poet. = poetry / poetical / poetically
pos. = positive / positively
pref. = prefix / prefixed
prep. = preposition / prepositional / prepositionally
prim. = primitive
prob. = probable / probably
prol. = prolonged / prolongation
pron. = pronominal / pronominally / pronoun
prox. = proximate / proximately
rad. = radical
recip. = reciprocal / reciprocally
redupl. = reduplicated / reduplication
refl. = reflexive / reflexively
rel. = relative / relatively
relig. = religion / religious / religiously
second. = secondarily / secondary
signif. = signification / signifying
short. = shortened / shorter
sing. = singular
spec. = specific / specifically
streng. = strengthening
subdiv. = subdivision / subdivisional / subdivisionally
subj. = subject / subjective / subjectively
substit. = substituted
superl. = superlative / superlatively
symb. = symbolical / symbolically
te. = technical / technically
tran. = transitive / transitively
transc. = transcription
transp. = transposed / transposition
unc. = uncertain / uncertainly
var. = variation.

SIGNS EMPLOYED

+ *(addition)* denotes a rendering in the KJV of one or more Hebrew words in connection with the one under consideration.

× *(multiplication)* denotes a rendering in the KJV that results from an idiom peculiar to the Hebrew.

° *(degree)*, appended to a Hebrew word, denotes a vowel-pointing corrected from that of the text. (This mark is set in Hebrew Bibles over syllables in which the vowels of the margin have been inserted instead of those properly belonging to the text.)

( ) *(parenthesis)*, in the renderings from the KJV, denotes a word or syllable sometimes given in connection with the principal word to which it is annexed.

[ ] *(bracket)*, in the rendering from the KJV, denotes the inclusion of an additional word in the Hebrew.

Italics, at the end of a rendering from the KJV, denote an explanation of the variations from the usual form.

Hebrew and Chaldee Dictionary of The Old Testament

א

1. אָב **'âb,** *awb;* a prim. word; *father* in a lit, and immed., or fig, and remote application):—chief, (fore-) father ([-less]), × patrimony, principal. Comp. names in "Abi-".

2. אַב **'ab** (Chald.), *ab;* corresp. to 1:—father.

3. אֵב **'êb,** *abe;* from the same as 24; a *green* plant:—greenness, fruit.

4. אֵב **'êb** (Chald), *abe;* corresp. to 3:—fruit.
אֹב **'ôb.** See 178.

5. אֲבַגְתָא **'Ăbagthâ',** *ab-ag-thaw´;* of for. or.; *Abagtha,* a eunuch of Xerxes:—Abagtha.

6. אָבַד **'âbad,** *aw-bad´;* a prim. root; prop. to *wander* away, i.e. *lose* oneself; by impl. to *perish* (caus. *destroy*):—break, destroy (-uction), + not escape, fail, lose, (cause to, make) perish, spend, × and surely, take, be undone, × utterly, be void of, have no way to flee.

7. אֲבַד **'ăbad** (Chald.), *ab-ad´;* corresp. to 6:—destroy, perish.

8. אֹבֵד **'ôbêd,** *o-bade´;* act. part. of 6; (concr.) *wretched* or (abstr.) *destruction:*—perish.

9. אֲבֵדָה **'ăbêdâh,** *ab-ay-daw´;* from 6; concr. something *lost;* abstr. *destruction,* i.e. Hades:—lost. Comp. 10.

10. אֲבַדֹּה **'ăbaddôh,** *ab-ad-do´;* the same as 9, miswritten for 11; a *perishing:*—destruction.

11. אֲבַדּוֹן **'ăbaddôwn,** *ab-ad-done´;* intens. from 6; abstr. a *perishing;* concr. Hades:—destruction.

12. אַבְדָן **'abdân,** *ab-dawn´;* from 6; a *perishing:*—destruction.

13. אָבְדָן **'obdân.** *ob-dawn´;* from 6; a *perishing:*—destruction.

14. אָבָה **'âbâh,** *aw-baw´;* a prim. root; to *breathe* after, i.e. (fig.) to *be acquiescent:*—consent, rest content, will, be willing.

15. אָבֶה **'âbeh,** *aw-beh´;* from 14; *longing:*—desire.

16. אֵבֶה **'êbeh,** *ay-beh´;* from 14 (in the sense of *bending* towards); the *papyrus:*—swift.

17. אֲבוֹי **'ăbôwy,** *ab-o´ee;* from 14 (in the sense of *desiring*); *want:*—sorrow.

18. אֵבוּס **'êbûwç,** *ay-booce´;* from 75; a *manger* or *stall:*—crib.

19. אִבְחָה **'ibchâh,** *ib-khaw´;* from an unused root (appar. mean. to *turn*); *brandishing* of a sword:—point.

20. אֲבַטִּיחַ **'ăbaṭṭîyach,** *ab-at-tee´-akh;* of uncert, der.; a *melon* (only plur.):—melon.

21. אֲבִי **'Ăbîy,** *ab-ee´;* from 1; *fatherly; Abi,* Hezekiah's mother:—Abi.

22. אֲבִיאֵל **'Ăbîy'êl,** *ab-ee-ale´;* from 1 and 410; *father* (i.e. *possessor*) *of God; Abiel,* the name of two Isr.:—Abiel.

23. אֲבִיאָסָף **'Ăbîy'âçâph,** *ab-ee-aw-sawf´;* from 1 and 622; *father of gathering* (i.e. *gatherer*); *Abiasaph,* an Isr.:—Abiasaph.

24. אָבִיב **'âbîyb,** *aw-beeb´;* from an unused root (mean to *be tender*); *green,* i.e. a young *ear* of grain; hence the name of the month *Abib* or Nisan:—Abib, ear, green ears of corn.

25. אֲבִי גִבְעוֹן **'Ăbîy Gib'ôwn,** *ab-ee´ ghib-one´;* from 1 and 1391; *father* (i.e. *founder*) *of Gibon; Abi-Gibon,* perh. an Isr.:—father of Gibeon.

26. אֲבִיגַיִל **'Ăbîgayil,** *ab-ee-gah´-yil,* or shorter אֲבִיגַל **'Ăbîygal,** *ab-ee-gal´;* from 1 and 1524; *father* (i.e. *source*) *of joy; Abigail* or *Abigal,* the name of two Israelitesses:—Abigal.

27. אֲבִידָן **'Ăbîydân,** *ab-ee-dawn´;* from 1 and 1777; *father of judgment* (i.e. *judge*); *Abidan,* an Isr.:—Abidan.

28. אֲבִידָע **'Ăbiydâ',** *ab-ee-daw´;* from 1 and 3045; *father of knowledge* (i.e. *knowing*); *Abida,* a son of Abraham by Keturah:—Abida, Abidah.

29. אֲבִיָּה **'Ăbîyâh,** *ab-ee-yaw´;* or prol. אֲבִיָּהוּ **'Ăbîyâhûw,** *ab-ee-yah´-hoo;* from 1 and 3050; *father* (i.e. *worshipper*) *of Jah; Abijah,* the name of several Isr. men and two Israelitesses:—Abiah, Abijah.

30. אֲבִיהוּא **'Ăbîyhûw',** *ab-ee-hoo´;* from 1 and 1931; *father* (i.e. *worshipper*) of *Him* (i.e. *God*); *Abihu,* a son of Aaron:—Abihu.

31. אֲבִיהוּד **'Ăbîyhûwd,** *ab-ee-hood´;* from 1 and 1935; *father* (i.e. *possessor*) *of renown; Abihud,* the name of two Isr.:—Abihud.

32. אֲבִיהַיִל **'Ăbîyhayil,** *ab-ee-hah´-yil;* or (more correctly) אֲבִיחַיִל **'Ăbîychayil,** *ab-ee-khah´-yil;* from 1 and 2428; *father* (i.e. *possessor*) *of might, Abihail* or *Abichail,* the name of three Isr. and two Israelitesses:—Abihail.

33. אֲבִי הָעֶזְרִי **'Ăbîy hâ-'Ezrîy,** *ab-ee´-haw-ez-ree´;* from 44 with the art. inserted; *father of the Ezrite;* an *Abiezrite* or descendant of Abiezer:—Abiezrite.

34. אֶבְיוֹן **'ebyôwn,** *eb-yone´;* from 14, in the sense of *want* (espec. in feeling); *destitute:*—beggar, needy, poor (man).

35. אֲבִיּוֹנָה **'abîyôwnâh,** *ab-ee-yo-naw´;* from 14; provocative of *desire;* the *caper* berry (from its *stimulative* taste):—desire.
אֲבִיחַיִל **'Ăbîychayil.** See 32.

36. אֲבִיטוּב **'Ăbîytûwb,** *ab-ee-toob´;* from 1 and 2898; *father of goodness* (i.e. *good*); *Abitub,* an Isr.:—Abitub.

37. אֲבִיטַל **'Ăbîytâl,** *ab-ee-tal´;* from 1 and 2919; *father of dew* (i.e. *fresh*); *Abital,* a wife of King David:—Abital.

38. אֲבִיָּם **'Ăbîyâm,** *ab-ee-yawm´;* from 1 and 3220; *father of* (the) *sea* (i.e. *seaman*); *Abijam* (or Abijah), a king of Judah:—Abijam.

39. אֲבִימָאֵל **'Ăbîymâ'êl,** *ab-ee-maw-ale´;* from 1 and an elsewhere unused (prob. for.) word; *father of Mael* (appar. some Arab tribe); *Abimael,* a son of Joktan:—Abimael.

40. אֲבִימֶלֶךְ **'Ăbîymelek,** *ab-ee-mel´-ek;* from 1 and 4428; *father of* (the) *king; Abimelek,* the name of two Philistine kings and of two Isr.:—Abimelech.

41. אֲבִינָדָב **'Ăbîynâdâb,** *ab-ee-naw-dawb´;* from 1 and 5068; *father of generosity* (i.e. *liberal*); *Abinadab,* the name of four Isr.:—Abinadab.

42. אֲבִינֹעַם **'Ăbiynô'am,** *ab-ee-no´-am;* from 1 and 5278; *father of pleasantness* (i.e. *gracious*); *Abinoam,* an Isr.:—Abinoam.
אֲבִינֵר **'Ăbîynêr.** See 74.

43. אֶבְיָסָף **'Ebyâçâph,** *eb-yaw-sawf´;* contr. from 23; *Ebjasaph,* an Isr.:—Ebiasaph.

44. אֲבִיעֶזֶר **'Ăbîy'ezer,** *ab-ee-ay´-zer;* from 1 and 5829; *father of help* (i.e. *helpful*); *Abiezer,* the name of two Isr.:—Abiezer.

45. אֲבִי־עַלְבוֹן **'Ăbîy-'albôwn,** *ab-ee-al-bone´;* from 1 and an unused root of unc. der.; prob. *father of strength* (i.e. *valiant*); *Abialbon,* an Isr.:—Abialbon.

46. אָבִיר **'âbîyr,** *aw-beer´;* from 82; *mighty* (spoken of God):—mighty (one).

47. אַבִּיר **'abbîyr,** *ab-beer´;* for 46:—angel, bull, chiefest, mighty (one), stout [-hearted], strong (one), valiant.

48. אֲבִירָם **'Ăbîyrâm,** *ab-ee-rawm´;* from 1 and 7311; *father of height* (i.e. *lofty*); *Abiram,* the name of two Isr.:—Abiram.

49. אֲבִישַׁג **'Ăbîyshag,** *ab-ee-shag´;* from 1 and 7686; *father of error* (i.e. *blundering*); *Abishag,* a concubine of David:—Abishag.

50. אֲבִישׁוּעַ **'Ăbîyshûwac,** *ab-ee-shoo´-ah;* from 1 and 7771; *father of plenty* (i.e. *prosperous*); *Abishua,* the name of two Isr.:—Abishua.

51. אֲבִישׁוּר **'Ăbîyshûwr,** *ab-ee-shoor´;* from 1 and 7791; *father of* (the) *wall* (i.e. perh. *mason*); *Abishur,* an Isr.:—Abishur.

52. אֲבִישַׁי **'Ăbîyshay,** *ab-ee-shah´ee;* or (shorter) אַבְשַׁי **'Abshay,** *ab-shah´ee;* from 1 and 7862; *father of a gift* (i.e. prob. *generous*); *Abishai,* an Isr.:—Abishai.

53. אֲבִישָׁלוֹם **'Abîyshâlôwm,** *ab-ee-shaw-lome´;* or (short.) אַבְשָׁלוֹם **Abshâlôwm,** *ab-shaw-lome´;* from 1 and 7965; *father of peace* (i.e. *friendly*); *Abshalom,* a son of David; also (the fuller form) a later Isr.:—Abishalom, Absalom.

54. אֶבְיָתָר **'Ebyâthâr,** *eb-yaw-thawr´;* contr. from 1 and 3498; *father of abundance* (i.e. *liberal*); *Ebjathar,* an Isr.:—Abiathar.

55. אָבַךְ **'âbak,** *aw-bak´;* a prim. root; prob. to *coil* upward:—mount up.

56. אָבַל **'âbal,** *aw-bal´;* a prim. root; to *bewail:*—lament, mourn.

57. אָבֵל **'âbêl,** *aw-bale´;* from 56; *lamenting:*—mourn (er, -ing).

58. אָבֵל **'âbêl,** *aw-bale´;* from an unused root (mean. to *be grassy*); a *meadow:*—plain. Comp. also the prop. names beginning with Abel-.

59. אָבֵל **'Âbêl,** *aw-bale´;* from 58; a *meadow; Abel,* the name of two places in Pal.:—Abel.

60. אֵבֶל **'êbel,** *ay´-bel;* from 56; *lamentation:*—mourning.

61. אֲבָל **'ăbâl,** *ab-awl´;* appar. from 56 through the idea of *negation; nay,* i.e. *truly* or *yet:*—but, indeed, nevertheless, verily.

62. אָבֵל בֵּית־מַעֲכָה **'Âbêl Bêyth-Ma'âkâh,** *aw-bale´ bayth ma-a-kaw´;* from 58 and 1004 and 4601; *meadow of Beth-Maakah; Abel of Beth-maakah,* a place in Pal.:—Abel-beth-maachah, Abel of Beth-maachah.

63. אָבֵל הַשִּׁטִּים **'Âbêl hash-Shiṭṭîym,** *aw-bale´ hash-shit-teem´,* from 58 and the plur. of 7848, with the art. ins.; *meadow of the acacias; Abel hash-Shittim,* a place in Pal.:—Abel-shittim.

64. אָבֵל כְּרָמִים **'Âbêl Kᵉrâmiym,** *aw-bale´ ker-aw-meem´;* from 58 and the plur. of 3754; *meadow of vineyards; Abel-Keramim,* a place in Pal.:—plain of the vineyards.

65. אָבֵל מְחוֹלָה **'Âbêl Mᵉchôwlâh,** *aw-bale´ mekh-o-law´;* from 58 and 4246; *meadow of dancing; Abel-Mecholah,* a place in Pal.:—Abel-meholah.

66. אָבֵל מַיִם **'Âbêl Mayim,** *aw-bale´ mah´-yim;* from 58 and 4325; *meadow of water; Abel-Majim,* a place in Pal.:—Abel-maim.

67. אָבֵל מִצְרַיִם **'Âbêl Mitsrayim,** *aw-bale´ mits-rah´-yim;* from 58 and 4714; *meadow of Egypt; Abel-Mitsrajim,* a place in Pal.:—Abel-mizraim.

68. אֶבֶן **'eben,** *eh´-ben;* from the root of 1129 through the mean. to *build; a stone:*— + carbuncle, + mason, + plummet, [chalk-, hail-, bead-, sling-] stone (-ny), (divers) weight (-s).

69. אֶבֶן **'eben** (Chald.), *eh´-ben;* corresp. to 68:—stone.

70. אֹבֶן **'ôben,** *o´-ben;* from the same as 68; *a pair of stones* (only dual); a potter's *wheel* or a midwife's *stool* (consisting alike of two horizontal disks with a support between):—wheel, stool.

71. אֲבָנָה **'Ăbânâh,** *ab-aw-naw´;* perh. fem. of 68; *stony; Abanah,* a river near Damascus:—Abana. Comp. 549.

72. אֶבֶן הָעֵזֶר **'Eben hâ-'êzer,** *eh´-ben haw-e´-zer;* from 68 and 5828 with the art. ins.; *stone of the help; Eben-ha-Ezer,* a place in Pal.:—Ebenezer.

73. אַבְנֵט **'abnêt,** *ab-nate´;* of uncert. deriv.; a *belt:*—girdle.

74. אַבְנֵר **'Abnêr,** *ab-nare´;* or (fully) אֲבִינֵר **'Ăbîynêr,** *ab-ee-nare´;* from 1 and 5216; *father of light* (i.e. *enlightening*); *Abner,* an Isr.:—Abner.

75. אָבַס **'âbaç,** *aw-bas´;* a prim. root; to *fodder:*—fatted, stalled.

76. אֲבַעְבֻּעָה **'ăba'bû'âh,** *ab-ah-boo-aw´;* (by re-dupl.) from an unused root (mean. to *belch* forth); an inflammatory *pustule* (as *eruption*):—blains.

77. אֶבֶץ **'Ebets,** *eh´-bets;* from an unused root prob. mean. to *gleam; conspicuous; Ebets,* a place in Pal.:—Abez.

78. אִבְצָן **'Ibtsân,** *ib-tsawn¡;* from the same as 76; *splendid; Ibtsan,* an Isr.:—Ibzan.

79. אָבַק **'âbaq,** *aw-bak´;* a prim. root; prob. to *float* away (as vapor), but used only as denom. from 80; to *bedust,* i.e. *grapple:*—wrestle.

80. אָבָק **'âbâq,** *aw-bawk´;* from root of 79; light *particles* (as *volatile*):—(small) dust, powder.

81. אֲבָקָה **'ăbâqâh,** *âb-aw-kaw´;* fem. of 80:—powder.

82. אָבַר **'âbar,** *aw-bar´;* a prim. root; to *soar:*—fly.

83. אֵבֶר **'êber,** *ay-ber´;* from 82; a *pinion:*—[long-] wing (-ed).

84. אֶבְרָה **'ebrâh,** *eb-raw´;* fem. of 83:—feather, wing.

85. אַבְרָהָם **'Abrâhâm,** *ab-raw-hawm´;* contr. from 1 and an unused root (prob. mean. *to be populous*); *father of a multitude; Abraham,* the later name of Abram:—Abraham.

86. אַבְרֵךְ **'abrêk,** *ab-rake´;* prob. an Eg. word mean. *kneel:*—bow the knee.

87. אַבְרָם **'Abrâm,** *ab-rawm´;* contr. from 48; *high father; Abram,* the original name of Abraham:—Abram.

אַבְשַׁי **'Abshay.** See 52.

אַבְשָׁלוֹם **'Abshâlôwm.** See 53.

88. אֹבֹת **'ôbôth,** *o-both´;* plur. of 178; water-*skins; Oboth,* a place in the Desert:—Oboth.

89. אָגֵא **'Âgê'** *aw-gay´;* of uncert. der. [comp. 90]; *Agè,* an Isr.:—Agee.

90. אֲגַג **'Ăgag,** *ag-ag´;* or אֲגָג **'Ăgâg,** *ag-awg´;* of uncert. der. [comp. 89]; *flame; Agag,* a title of Amalekitish kings:—Agag.

91. אֲגָגִי **'Ăgâgîy,** *ag-aw-ghee´;* patrial or patron. from 90; an *Agagite* or descendant (subject) of Agag:—Agagite.

92. אֲגֻדָּה **'ăguddâh,** *ag-ood-daw´;* fem. pass. part. of an unused root (mean. to *bind*); a *band, bundle, knot,* or *arch:*—bunch, burden, troop.

93. אֱגוֹז **'ĕgôwz,** *eg-oze´;* prob. of Pers. or.; a *nut:*—nut.

94. אָגוּר **'Âgûwr,** *aw-goor´;* pass. part. of 103; *gathered* (i.e. *received* among the sages); *Agur,* a fanciful name for Solomon:—Agur.

95. אֲגוֹרָה **'ăgôwrâh,** *ag-o-raw´;* from the same as 94; prop. something *gathered,* i.e. perh. a *grain* or *berry;* used only of a small (silver) *coin:*—piece [of] silver.

96. אֶגֶל **'egel,** *eh´-ghel;* from an unused root (mean. to *flow* down or together as drops); a *reservoir:*—drop.

97. אֶגְלַיִם **'Eglayim,** *eg-lah´-yim;* dual of 96; a *double pond; Eglajim,* a place in Moab:—Eglaim.

98. אֲגַם **'ăgam,** *ag-am´;* from an unused root (mean. to *collect* as water); a *marsh;* hence a *rush* (as growing in swamps); hence a *stockade* of reeds:—pond, pool, standing [water].

99. אָגֵם **'âgêm,** *aw-game´;* prob. from the same as 98 (in the sense of *stagnant* water); fig. *sad:*—pond.

100. אַגְמוֹן **'agmôwn,** *ag-mone´;* from the same as 98; a marshy *pool* [others from a different root, a *kettle*]; by impl. a *rush* (as growing there); collect. a *rope* of rushes:—bulrush, caldron, hook, rush.

101. אַגָּן **'aggân,** *ag-gawn´;* prob. from 5059; a *bowl* (as *pounded* out hollow):—basin, cup, goblet.

102. אַגָּף **'aggâph,** *ag-gawf´;* prob. from 5062 (through the idea of *impending*); a *cover* or *heap;* i.e. (only plur.) *wings* of an army. or *crowds* of troops:—bands.

103. אָגַר **'âgar,** *aw-gar´;* a prim. root; to *harvest:*—gather.

104. אִגְּרָא **'igg^{e}râ'** (Chald.) *ig-er-aw´;* of Pers. or.; an *epistle* (as carried by a state courier or postman):—letter.

105. אֲגַרְטָל **'ăgarṭâl,** *ag-ar-tawl´;* of uncert. der.; a *basin:*—charger.

106. אֶגְרֹף **'egrôph,** *eg-rofe´;* from 1640 (in the sense of *grasping*); the *cleanched* hand:—fist.

107. אִגֶּרֶת **'iggereth,** *ig-eh´-reth;* fem. of 104; an *epistle:*—letter.

108. אֵד **'êd,** *ade;* from the same as 181 (in the sense of *enveloping*); a *fog:*—mist, vapor.

109. אָדַב **'âdab,** *aw-dab´;* a prim. root; to *languish:*—grieve.

110. אַדְבְּאֵל **'Adb^{e}'êl,** *ad-beh-ale´;* prob. from 109 (in the sense of *chastisement*) and 410; *disciplined of God;* Adbeël, a son of Ishmael:—Adbeel.

111. אֲדַד **'Ădad,** *ad-ad´;* prob. an orth. var. for 2301; *Adad* (or Hadad), an Edomite:—Hadad.

112. אִדּוֹ **'Iddôw,** *id-do;* of uncert. der.; *Iddo,* an Isr.:—Iddo.

אֱדוֹם **'Ědôwm.** See 123.

אֱדוֹמִי **'Ědôwmîy.** See 30.

113. אָדוֹן **'âdôwn,** *aw-done´,* or (short.) אָדֹן **'âdôn,** *aw-done´;* from an unused root (mean to *rule*); *sovereign,* i.e. *controller* (human or divine):—lord, master, owner. Comp. also names beginning with "Adoni-".

114. אַדּוֹן **'Addôwn,** *ad-done´;* prob. intens. for 113; *powerful; Addon,* appar. an Isr.:—Addon.

115. אֲדוֹרַיִם **'Ădôwrayim,** *ad-o-rah´im;* dual from 142 (in the sense of *eminence*); *double mound; Adorajim,* a place in Pal.:—Adoraim.

116. אֱדַיִן **'ědayin** (Chald.), *ed-ah´-yin;* of uncert. der.; *then* (of time):—now, that time, then.

117. אַדִּיר **'addîyr,** *ad-deer´;* from 142; *wide* or (gen.) *large;* fig. *powerful:*—excellent, famous, gallant, glorious, goodly, lordly, mighty (-ier, one), noble, principal, worthy.

118. אֲדַלְיָא **'Ădalyâ',** *ad-al-yaw´;* of Pers. der.; *Adalja,* a son of Haman:—Adalia.

119. אָדַם **'âdam,** *aw-dam´;* to *show blood* in the face), i.e. *flush* or turn rosy:—be (dyed, made) red (ruddy).

120. אָדָם **'âdâm,** *aw-dawm´;* from 119; *ruddy,* i.e. a *human being* (an individual or the species, *mankind,* etc.):—× another, + hypocrite, + common sort, × low, man (mean, of low degree), person.

121. אָדָם **'Âdâm,** *aw-dawm´;* the same as 120; *Adam,* the name of the first man, also of a place in Pal.:—Adam.

122. אָדֹם **'âdôm,** *aw-dome´;* from 119; *rosy:*—red, ruddy.

123. אֱדֹם **'Ědôm,** *ed-ome´;* or (fully) אֱדוֹם **'Êdôwm,** *ed-ome´;* from 122; *red* [see Gen. 25 : 25]; *Edom,* the elder twin-brother of Jacob; hence the region (Idumaea) occupied by him:—Edom, Edomites, Idumea.

124. אֹדֶם **'ôdem,** *o´-dem;* from 119; *redness,* i.e. the *ruby, garnet,* or some other red gem:—sardius.

125. אֲדַמְדָּם **'ădamdâm,** *ad-am-dawm´;* redupl. from 119; *reddish:*—(somewhat) reddish.

126. אַדְמָה **'Admâh,** *ad-maw´;* contr. for 127; *earthy; Admah,* a place near the Dead Sea:—Admah.

127. אֲדָמָה **'ădâmâh,** *ad-aw-maw´;* from 119; *soil* (from its gen. *redness*):—country, earth, ground, husband [-man] (-ry), land.

128. אֲדָמָה **'Ădâmâh,** *ad-aw-maw´;* the same as 127; *Adamah,* a place in Pal.:—Adamah.

אַדְמוֹנִי **'admôwnîy.** See 132.

129. אֲדָמִי **Ădâmîy,** *ad-aw-mee´;* from 127; *earthy; Adami,* a place in Pal.:—Adami.

130. אֱדֹמִי **'Ědômîy,** *ed-o-mee´;* or (fully) אֱדוֹמִי, **Ědôwmîy,** *ed-o-mee´;* patron. from 123; an *Edomite,* or desc. from (or inhab. of) Edom:—Edomite. See 726.

131. אֲדֻמִּים **'Ădummîym,** *ad-oom-meem´;* plur. of 121; *red* spots; *Adummim,* a pass in Pal.:—Adummim.

132. אַדְמֹנִי **'admônîy,** *ad-mo-nee´,* or (fully) אַדְמוֹנִי **'admôwnîy,** *ad-mo-nee´;* from 119; *reddish* (of the hair or the complexion):—red, ruddy.

133. אַדְמָתָא **'Admâthâ',** *ad-maw-thaw´;* prob. of Pers. der.; *Admatha,* a Pers. nobleman:—Admatha.

134. אֶדֶן **'eden,** *eh´den;* from the same as 113 (in the sense of *strength*); a *basis* (of a building, a column, etc.):—foundation, socket.

אָדֹן **'âdôn.** See 118.

135. אַדָּן **'Addân,** *ad-dawn´;* intens. from the same as 134; *firm; Addan,* an Isr.:—Addan.

136. אֲדֹנָי **'Ădônây,** *ad-o-noy´;* an emphatic form of 113; the *Lord* (used as a prop. name of God only):—(my) Lord.

137. אֲדֹנִי־בֶזֶק **'Ădônîy-Bezeq,** *ad-o´´-nee-beh´-zek;* from 113 and 966; *lord of Bezek; Adoni-Bezek,* A Canaanitish king:—Adonibezek.

138. אֲדֹנִיָּה **'Ădônîyâh,** *ad-o-nee-yaw´;* or (prol.) אֲדֹנִיָּהוּ **'Ădônîyâhûw,** *ad-o-nee-yaw´-hoo;* from 113 and 3050; *lord* (i.e. worshipper) of Jah; *Adonijah,* the name of three Isr.:—Adonijah.

139. אֲדֹנִי־צֶדֶק **'Ădônîy-Tsedeq,** *ad-o´´-nee-tseh´-dek;* from 113 and 6664; *lord of justice; Adoni-Tsedek,* a Canaanitish king:—Adonizedec.

140. אֲדֹנִיקָם **'Ădônîyqâm,** *ad-o-nee-kawm´;* from 113 and 6965; *lord of rising* (i.e. *high*)*: Adonikam,* the name of one or two Isr.:—Adonikam

141. אֲדֹנִירָם **'Ădôniyrâm,** *ad-o-nee-rawm´;* from 113 and 7311*; lord of height; Adoniram,* an Isr.:—Adoniram.

142. אָדַר **'âdar,** *aw-dar´:* a prim. root; to *expand,* i.e. *be great* or (fig.) *magnificent:*—(become) glorious, honourable.

143. אֲדָר **'Ădâr,** *ad-awr´;* prob. of for. der.; perh. mean. *fire; Adar,* the 12th Heb. month:—Adar.

144. אֲדָר **'Ădâr** (Chald.), *ad-awr´;* corresp. to 143:—Adar.

145. אֶדֶר **'eder,** *eh´-der;* from 142; *amplitude,* i.e. (concr.) a *mantle;* also (fig.) *splendor:*—goodly, robe.

146. אַדָּר **'Addâr,** *ad-dawr´;* intens. from 142; *ample; Addar,* a place in Pal.; also an Isr.:—Addar.

147. אִדַּר **'iddar** (Chald.), *id-dar´;* intens. from a root corresp. to 142; *ample,* i.e. a threshing-*floor:*—threshingfloor.

148. אֲדַרְגָּזֵר **'ădargâzêr** (Chald), *ad-ar´´-gaw-zare´;* from the same as 147, and 1505; a *chief diviner,* or *astrologer:*—judge.

149. אַדְרַזְדָּא **'adrazdâ'** (Chald.), *ad-raz-daw´;* prob. of Pers. or.; *quickly* or *carefully:*—diligently.

150. אֲדַרְכֹּן **'ădarkôn,** *ad-ar-kone´;* of Pers. or.; a *daric* or Pers. coin:—dram.

151. אֲדֹרָם **'Ădôrâm,** *ad-o-rawm´;* contr. for 141; *Adoram* (or Adoniram), an Isr.:—Adoram.

152. אַדְרַמֶּלֶךְ **'Adrammelek,** *ad-ram-meh´-lek;* from 142 and 4428; *splendor of* (the) *king; Adrammelek,* the name of an Assyr. idol, also of a son of Sennacherib:—Adrammelech.

153. אֶדְרָע **'edra'** (Chald.), *ed-raw´;* an orth. var. for 1872; an *arm,* i.e. (fig.) *power:*—force.

154. אֶדְרֶעִי **'edre'îy,** *ed-reh´-ee;* from the equivalent of 153; *mighty; Edrei,* the name of two places in Pal.:—Edrei.

155. אַדֶּרֶת **'addereth,** *ad-deh´-reth;* fem. of 117; something *ample* (as a *large* vine, a *wide* dress); also the same as 145:—garment, glory, goodly, mantle, robe.

156. אָדַשׁ **'âdash,** *aw-dash´;* a prim. root; to *tread* out (grain):—thresh.

157. אָהַב **'âhab,** *aw-hab´;* or אָהֵב **'âhêb,** *aw-habe´;* a prim. root; to *have affection* for (sexually or otherwise):—(be-) love (-d, -ly, -r), like, friend.

158. אַהַב **'ahab,** *ah´-hab;* from 157; *affection* (in a good or a bad sense):—love (-r).

159. אֹהַב **'ôhab,** *o'hab;* from 157; mean. the same as 158:—love.

160. אַהֲבָה **'ahăbâh,** *ă-hab-aw´;* fem. of 158 and mean. the same:—love.

161. אֹהַד **'Ôhad,** *o´-had;* from an unused root mean. to *be united; unity; Ohad,* an Isr.:—Ohad.

162. אֲהָהּ **'ăhâhh,** *ă-haw´;* appar. a prim. word expressing *pain* exclamatorily; *Oh!:*—ah, alas.

163. אַהֲוָא **'Ahăvâ',** *ă-hav-aw´;* prob. of for. or.; *Ahava,* a river of Babylonia:—Ahava.

164. אֵהוּד **'Êhûwd,** *ay-hood';* from the same as 161; *united; Ehud,* the name of two or three Isr.:—Ehud.

165. אֱהִי **'ĕhîy,** *e-hee';* appar. an orth. var. for 346; *where:*—I will be (Hos. 13:10, 14) [*which is often the rendering of the same Heb. form from* 1961].

166. אָהַל **'âhal,** *aw-hal´;* a prim. root; to *be clear:*—shine.

167. אָהַל **'âhal,** *aw-hal´;* a denom. from 168; to *tent:*—pitch (remove) a tent.

168. אֹהֶל **'ôhel,** *o´-hel;* from 166; a *tent* (as *clearly* conspicuous from a distance):—covering, (dwelling) (place), home, tabernacle, tent.

169. אֹהֶל **'Ôhel,** *o´-hel;* the same as 168; *Ohel,* an Isr.:—Ohel.

170. אָהֳלָה **'Ohŏlâh,** *ŏ-hol-aw´;* in form a fem. of 168, but in fact for אָהֳלָהּ **'Ohŏlâhh,** *ŏ-hol-aw´;* from 168; *her tent* (i.e. idolatrous *sanctuary*); *Oholah,* a symbol. name for Samaria:—Aholah.

171. אָהֳלִיאָב **'Ohŏlîy'âb,** *ŏ´´-hol-e-awb´;* from 168 and 1; *tent of* (his) *father; Oholiab,* an Isr.:—Aholiab.

172. אָהֳלִיבָה **'Ohŏlîybâh,** *ŏ´´-hol-ee-baw´;* (similarly with 170) for אָהֳלִיבָהּ **'Ohŏlîybâhh,** *ŏ´´-hol-e-baw´;* from 168; *my tent* (is) *in her; Oholibah,* a symbol. name for Judah:—Aholibah.

173. אָהֳלִיבָמָה **'Ohŏlîybâmâh,** *ŏ´´-hol-e-baw-maw´;* from 168 and 1116; *tent of* (the) *height; Oholibamah,* a wife of Esau:—Aholibamah.

174. אֲהָלִים **ăhâlîym,** *â-haw-leem´;* or (fem.) אֲהָלוֹת **'ăhâlôwth,** *ă-haw-loth´* (only used thus in the plur.); of for. or.; *aloe* wood (i.e. sticks):—(tree of lign-) aloes.

175. אַהֲרוֹן **'Ahărôwn,** *ă-har-one´;* of uncert. deriv.; *Aharon,* the brother of Moses:—Aaron.

176. אוֹ **'ôw,** *o;* presumed to be the "constr." or genitival form of אַו **'av,** *av,* short. for 185; *desire* (and so prob. in Prov. 31 : 4); hence (by way of alternative) *or,* also *if:*—also, and, either, if, at the least, × nor, or, otherwise, then, whether.

177. אוּאֵל **'Ûw'êl,** *oo-ale´;* from 176 and 410; *wish of God; Uel,* an Isr.:—Uel.

178. אוֹב **'ôwb,** *obe;* from the same as 1 (appar. through the idea of *prattling* a father's name); prop. a *mumble,* i.e. a water-*skin* (from its hollow sound); hence a *necromancer* (ventriloquist, as from a jar):—bottle, familiar spirit.

179. אוֹבִיל **'Ôwbîyl,** *o-beel´;* prob. from 56; *mournful; Obil,* an Ishmaelite:—Obil.

180. אוּבָל **'ûwbâl,** *oo-bawl´;* or (short.) אֻבָל **'ûbâl,** *oo-bawl´;* from 2986 (in the sense of 2988); a *stream:*—river.

181. אוּד **'ûwd,** *ood;* from an unused root mean. to *rake* together; a *poker* (for *turning* or *gathering* embers):—(fire-) brand.

182. אוֹדוֹת **'ôwdôwth,** *o-dōth´;* or (short.) אֹדוֹת **'ôdôwth,** *o-dōth´* (only thus in the plur.); from the same as 181; *turnings* (i.e. *occasions*); (adv.) on *account* of:—(be-) cause, concerning, sake.

183. אָוָה **'âvâh,** *aw-vaw´;* a prim. root; to *wish* for:—covet, (greatly) desire, be desirous, long, lust (after).

184. אָוָה **'âvâh,** *aw-vaw´;* a prim. root; to *extend* or *mark* out:—point out.

185. אַוָּה **'avvâh,** *av-vaw´;* from 183; *longing:*—desire, lust after, pleasure.

186. אוּזַי **'Ûwzay,** *oo-zah´ee;* perh. by perm. for 5813, *strong; Uzai,* an Isr.:—Uzai.

187. אוּזָל **'Ûwzâl,** *oo-zâwl´;* of uncert. der.; *Uzal,* a son of Joktan:—Uzal.

188. אוֹי **'ôwy,** *ō´ee;* prob. from 183 (in the sense of *crying* out after); *lamentation;* also interj. *Oh!:*—alas, woe.

189. אֱוִי **'Ĕvîy,** *ev-ee´;* prob. from 183; *desirous; Evi,* a Midianitish chief:—Evi.

אוֹיֵב **'ôwyêb.** See 341.

190. אוֹיָה **'ôwyâh,** *o-yaw´;* fem. of 188:—woe.

191. אֱוִיל **'ĕvîyl,** *ev-eel´;* from an unused root (mean. to be *perverse*); (fig.) *silly:*—fool (-ish) (man).

192. אֱוִיל מְרֹדַךְ **'Ĕvîyl Merôdak,** *ev-eel´ mer-o-dak´;* of Chald. deriv. and prob. mean. *soldier of Merodak; Evil-Merodak,* a Babylonian king:—Evil-merodach.

193. אוּל **'ûwl,** *ool;* from an unused root mean. to *twist,* i.e. (by impl.) *be strong;* the *body (as being rolled* together); also *powerful:*—mighty, strength.

194. אוּלַי **'ûwlay,** *oo-lah´ee;* or (short.) אֻלַי **'ûlay,** *oo-lah´ee;* from 176; *if not;* hence *perhaps:*—if so be, may be, peradventure, unless.

195. אוּלַי **'Ûwlay,** *oo-lah´ee:* of Pers. der.; the *Ulai* (or Eulæus), a river of Persia:—Ulai.

196. אֱוִלִי **'ĕvîlîy,** *ev-ee-lee´;* from 191; *silly, foolish;* hence (mor.) *impious:*—foolish.

197. אוּלָם **'ûwlâm,** *oo-lawm´;* or (short.) אֻלָם **'ûlâm,** *oo-lawm´;* from 481 (in the sense of *tying*); a *vestibule* (as *bound* to the building):—porch.

198. אוּלָם **'Ûwlâm,** *oo-lawm´;* appar. from 481 (in the sense of *dumbness*); *solitary; Ulam,* the name of two Isr.:—Ulam.

199. אוּלָם **'ûwlâm,** *oo-lawm´;* appar. a variation of 194; *however* or *on the contrary:*—as for, but, howbeit, in very deed, surely, truly, wherefore.

200. אִוֶּלֶת **'ivveleth,** *iv-veh´-leth;* from the same as 191; *silliness:*—folly, foolishly (-ness).

201. אוֹמָר **'Ôwmâr,** *o-mawr´;* from 559; *talkative; Omar,* a grandson of Esau:—Omar.

202. אוֹן **'ôwn,** *ōne;* prob. from the same as 205 (in the sense of *effort,* but successful); *ability, power,* (fig.) *wealth:*—force, goods, might, strength, substance.

203. אוֹן **'Ôwn,** *ōne;* the same as 202; *On,* an Isr.:—On.

204. אוֹן **'Ôwn,** *ōne;* or (short.) אֹן **'Ôn,** *ōne;* of Eg. der.; *On,* a city of Egypt:—On.

205. אָוֶן **'âven,** *aw´-ven;* from an unused root perh. mean. prop. to *pant* (hence to *exert* oneself, usually in vain; to *come to naught*); strictly *nothingness;* also *trouble, vanity, wickedness;* spec. an *idol:*—affliction, evil, false, idol, iniquity, mischief, mourners (-ing), naught, sorrow, unjust, unrighteous, vain, vanity, wicked (-ness.) Comp. 369.

206. אָוֶן **'Âven,** *aw´-ven;* the same as 205; *idolatry; Aven,* the contemptuous synonym of three places, one in Coœle-Syria, one in Egypt (On), and one in Pal. (Bethel):—Aven. See also 204, 1007.

207. אוֹנוֹ **'Ôwnôw,** *o-no´;* or (short.) אֹנוֹ **'Ônôw,** *o-no´;* prol. from 202; *strong; Ono,* a place in Pal.:—Ono.

208. אוֹנָם **'Ôwnâm,** *o-nawm´;* a var. of 209; *strong; Onam,* the name of an Edomite and of an Isr.:—Onam.

209. אוֹנָן **'Ôwnân,** *o-nawn´;* a var. of 207; *strong; Onan,* a son of Judah:—Onan.

210. אוּפָז **'Ûwphâz,** *oo-fawz´;* perh. a corruption of 211; *Uphaz,* a famous gold region:—Uphaz.

211. אוֹפִיר **'Ôwphîyr,** *o-feer´;* or (short.) אֹפִיר **'Ôphîyr,** *o-feer´;* and אוֹפִר **'Ôwphîr,** *o-feer´;* of uncert. deriv.; *Ophir,* the name of a son of Joktan, and of a gold region in the East:—Ophir.

212. אוֹפָן **'ôwphân,** *o-fawn´;* or (short.) אֹפָן **'ôphân,** *o-fawn´;* from an unused root mean. to *revolve;* a *wheel:*—wheel.

אוֹפִר **'Ôwphîr.** see 211.

213. אוּץ **'ûwts,** *oots;* a prim. root; to *press;* (by impl.) to *be close, hurry, withdraw:*—(make) haste (-n, -y), labor, be narrow.

214. אוֹצָר **'ôwtsâr,** *o-tsaw´;* from 686; a *depository:*—armory, cellar, garner, store (-house), treasure (-house) (-y).

215. אוֹר **'ôwr,** *ore;* a prim. root; *to be* (caus. *make*) *luminous* (lit. and metaph.):—× break of day, glorious, kindle, (be, en-, give, show) light (-en, -ened), set on fire, shine.

216. אוֹר **'ôwr,** *ore;* from 215; *illumination* or (concr.) *luminary* (in every sense, including *lightning, happiness,* etc.):—bright, clear, + day, light (-ning), morning, sun.

217. אוּר **'ûwr,** *oor;* from 215; *flame,* hence (in the plur.) the *East* (as being the region of light):—fire, light. See also 224.

218. אוּר **'Ûwr,** *oor;* the same as 217; *Ur,* a place in Chaldæa; also an Isr.:—Ur.

219. אוֹרָה **'ôwrâh,** *o-raw´;* fem. of 216; *luminousness,* i.e. (fig.) *prosperity;* also a plant (as being *bright*):—herb light.

220. אֲוֵרָה **'ăvêrâh,** *av-ay-raw´;* by transp. for 723; a *stall:*—cote.

221. אוּרִי **'Ûwrîy,** *oo-ree´;* from 217; *fiery; Uri,* the name of three Isr.:—Uri.

222. אוּרִיאֵל **'Ûwrîy'êl,** *oo-ree-ale´;* from 217 and 410; *flame of God; Uriel,* the name of two Isr.:—Uriel.

223. אוּרִיָּה **'Ûwrîyâh,** *oo-ree-yaw´;* or (prol.) אוּרִיָּהוּ **'Ûwrîyâhûw,** *oo-ree-yaw´-hoo;* from 217 and 3050; *flame of Jah; Urijah,* the name of one Hittite and five Isr.:—Uriah, Urijah.

224. אוּרִים **'Ûwrîym,** *oo-reem´;* plur. of 217; *lights; Urim,* the oracular brilliancy of the figures in the high-priest's breastplate:—Urim.

אוֹרְנָה **'Owrenâh.** See 728.

225. אוּת **'ûwth,** *ooth;* a prim. root; prop. to *come,* i.e. (impl.) to *assent:*—consent.

226. אוֹת **'ôwth,** *ōth;* prob. from 225 (in the sense of *appearing*); a *signal* (lit. or fig.), as a *flag, beacon, monument, omen, prodigy, evidence,* etc.:—mark, miracle, (en-) sign, token.

227. אָז **'âz,** *awz;* a demonstrative adv.; *at that time* or *place;* also as a conj., *therefore:*—beginning, for, from, hitherto, now, of old, once, since, then, at which time, yet.

228. אֲזָא **'ăzâ'** (Chald.), *az-aw´;* or אֲזָה **'ăzăh** (Chald.), *az-aw´;* to *kindle;* (by impl.) to *heat:*—heat, hot.

229. אֶזְבַּי **'Ezbay,** *ez-bah´ee;* prob. from 231; *hyssop-like; Ezbai,* an Isr.:—Ezbai.

230. אֲזַד **'ăzad** (Chald.), *az-awd´;* of uncert. der.; *firm:*—be gone.

231. אֵזוֹב **'êzôwb,** *ay-zobe´;* prob. of for. der.; *hyssop:*—hyssop.

232. אֵזוֹר **'êzôwr,** *ay-zore´;* from 246; something *girt;* a *belt,* also a *band:*—girdle.

233. אֲזַי **'ăzay,** *az-ah´ee;* prob. from 227; *at that time:*—then.

234. אַזְכָּרָה **'azkârâh,** *az-kaw-raw´;* from 2142; a *reminder;* spec. *remembrance-offering:*—memorial.

235. אָזַל **'âzal,** *aw-zal´;* a prim. root; to *go away;* hence to *disappear:*—fail, gad about, go to and fro [*but in Ezek.* 27:19 *the word is rendered* by *many* "from Uzal," *by others* "yarn"], be gone (spent).

236. אֲזַל **'ăzal** (Chald.), *az-al´;* the same as 235; to *depart:*—go (up).

237. אֶזֶל **'ezel,** *eh´-zel;* from 235; *departure; Ezel,* a memorial stone in Pal.:—Ezel.

238. אָזַן **'âzan,** *aw-zan´;* a prim. root; prob. to *expand;* but used only as a denom. from 241; to *broaden out the ear* (with the hand), i.e. (by impl.) to *listen:*—give (perceive by the) ear, hear (-ken). See 239.

239. אָזַן **'âzan,** *aw-zan´;* a prim. root [rather ident. with 238 through the idea of *scales* as if two ears]; to *weigh,* i.e. (fig.) *ponder:*—give good heed.

240. אָזֵן **'âzên,** *aw-zane´;* from 238; a *spade* or *paddle* (as having a *broad* end):—weapon.

241. אֹזֶן **'ôzen,** *o´-zen;* from 238; *broadness,* i.e. (concr.) the *ear* (from its form in man):— + advertise, audience, + displease, ear, hearing, + show.

242. אֻזֵּן שֶׁאֱרָה **'Uzzên She'ĕrâh,** *ooz-zane´ sheh-er-aw´;* from 238 and 7609; *plat of Sheerah* (i.e. settled by him); *Uzzen-Sheërah,* a place in Pal.:—Uzzen-sherah.

243. אַזְנוֹת תָּבוֹר **'Aznôwth Tâbôwr,** *aznōth´ taw-bore´;* from 238 and 8396; *flats* (i.e. *tops*) *of Tabor* (i.e. situated on it); *Aznoth-Tabor,* a place in Pal.:—Aznoth-tabor.

244. אָזְנִי **'Oznîy,** *oz-nee´;* from 241; *having* (quick) *ears; Ozni,* an Isr.; also an *Oznite* (collect.), his desc.:—Ozni, Oznites.

245. אֲזַנְיָה **'Ăzanyâh,** *az-an-yaw´;* from 238 and 3050; *heard* by *Jah; Azanjah,* an Isr.:—Azaniah.

246. אֲזִקִּים **'ăziqqîym,** *az-ik-keem´;* a var. for 2131; *manacles:*—chains.

247. אָזַר **'âzar,** *aw-zar´;* a prim. root; to *belt:*—bind (compass) about, gird (up, with).

248. אֶזְרוֹעַ **'ezrôwa',** *ez-ro´-ă;* a var. for 2220; the *arm:*—arm.

249. אֶזְרָח **'ezrâch,** *ez-rawkh´;* from 2224 (in the sense of *springing up*); a spontaneous *growth,* i.e. *native* (tree or persons):—bay tree, (home-) born (in the land), of the (one's own) country (nation).

250. אֶזְרָחִי **'Ezrâchîy,** *ez-raw-khee´;* patron. from 2246; an *Ezrachite* or desc. of Zerach:—Ezrahite.

251. אָח **'âch,** *awkh;* a prim. word; a *brother* (used in the widest sense of literal relationship and metaph. affinity or resemblance [like 1]:—another, brother (-ly), kindred, like, other. Comp. also the prop. names beginning with "Ah-" or "Ahi-".

252. אַח **'ach** (Chald.), *akh;* corresp. to 251:—brother.

253. אָח **'âch,** *awkh;* a var. for 162; *Oh!* (expressive of grief or surprise):—ah, alas.

254. אָח **'âch,** *awkh;* of uncert. der.; a fire-*pot* or chafing-dish:—hearth.

255. אֹחַ **'ôach,** *o´-akh;* prob. from 253; a *howler* or lonesome wild animal:—doleful creature.

256. אַחְאָב **'Ach'âb,** *akh-awb´;* once (by contr.) אֶחָב **'Echâb** (Jer. 29 : 22), *ekh-awb´;* from 251 and 1; *brother* [i.e. *friend*] *of* (his) *father; Achab,* the name of a king of Israel and of a prophet at Babylon:—Ahab.

257. אַחְבָּן **'Achbân,** *akh-bawn´;* from 251 and 995; *brother* (i.e. *possessor*) *of understanding; Achban,* an Isr.:—Ahban.

258. אָחַד **'âchad,** *aw-khad´;* perh. a prim. root; to *unify,* i.e. (fig.) *collect* (one's thoughts):—go one way or other.

259. אֶחָד **'echâd,** *ekh-awd´;* a numeral from 258; prop. *united,* i.e. *one;* or (as an ordinal) *first:*—a, alike, alone, altogether, and, any (-thing), apiece, a certain [dai-] ly, each (one), + eleven, every, few, first, + highway, a man, once, one, only, other, some, together.

260. אָחוּ **'âchûw,** *aw´-khoo;* of unc. (perh. Eg.) der.; a *bulrush* or any marshy grass (particularly that along the Nile):—flag, meadow.

261. אֵחוּד **'Êchûwd,** *ay-khood´;* from 258; *united; Echud,* the name of three Isr.:—Ehud.

262. אַחְוָה **'achvâh,** *akh-vaw´;* from 2331 (in the sense of 2324); an *utterance:*—declaration.

263. אַחֲוָה **'achăvâh** (Chald.), *akh-av-aw´;* corresp. to 262; *solution* (of riddles):—showing.

264. אַחֲוָה **'achăvâh,** *akh-av-aw´;* from 251; *fraternity:*—brotherhood.

265. אֲחוֹחַ **'Ăchôwach,** *akh-o´-akh;* by redupl. from 251; *brotherly; Achoach,* an Isr.:—Ahoah.

266. אֲחוֹחִי **'Ăchôwchîy,** *akh-o-khee´;* patron. from 264; an *Achochite* or desc. of Achoach:—Ahohite.

267. אֲחוּמַי **'Ăchûwmay,** *akh-oo-mah´ee;* perh. from 251 and 4325; *brother* (i.e. *neighbour*) *of water; Achumai,* an Isr.:—Ahumai.

268. אָחוֹר **'âchôwr,** *aw-khore´;* or (short.) אָחֹר **'âchôr,** *aw-khore´;* from 299; the *hinder* part; hence (adv.) *behind, backward;* also (as facing north) the *West:*—after (-ward), back (part, -side, -ward), hereafter, (be-) hind (-er part), time to come, without.

269. אָחוֹת **'achôwth,** *aw-khōth´;* irreg. fem. of 251; a *sister* (used very widely [like 250], lit. and fig.):—(an-) other, sister, together.

270. אָחַז **'âchaz,** *aw-khaz´;* a prim. root; to *seize* (often with the accessory idea of holding in possession):— + be affrighted, bar, (catch, lay, take) hold (back), come upon, fasten, handle, portion, (get, have or take) possess (-ion).

271. אָחָז **'Âchâz,** *aw-khawz´;* from 270; *possessor; Achaz,* the name of a Jewish king and of an Isr.:—Ahaz.

272. אֲחֻזָּה **'ăchuzzâh,** *akh-ooz-zaw´;* fem. pass. part. from 270; something *seized,* i.e. a *possession* (esp. of land):—possession.

273. אַחְזַי **'Achzay,** *akh-zah´ee;* from 270; *seizer; Achzai,* an Isr.:—Ahasai.

274. אֲחַזְיָה **'Ăchazyâh,** *akh-az-yaw´;* or (prol.) אֲחַזְיָהוּ **'Ăchazyâhûw,** *akh-az-yaw´-hoo;* from 270 and 3050; *Jah has seized; Achazjah,* the name of a Jewish and an Isr. king:—Ahaziah.

275. אֲחֻזָּם **Ăchuzzâm,** *akh-ooz-zawm´;* from 270; *seizure; Achuzzam,* an Isr.:—Ahuzam.

276. אֲחֻזַּת **'Ăchuzzath,** *akh-ooz-zath´;* a var. of 272; *possession; Achuzzath,* a Philistine:—Ahuzzath.

277. אֲחִי **'Ăchîy,** *akh-ee´;* from 251; *brotherly; Achi,* the name of two Isr.:—Ahi.

278. אֵחִי **'Êchîy,** *ay-khee´;* prob. the same as 277; *Echi,* an Isr.:—Ehi.

279. אֲחִיאָם **'Ăchîy'âm,** *akh-ee-awm´;* from 251 and 517; *brother of* the *mother* (i.e. *uncle*); *Achiam,* an Isr.:—Ahiam.

280. אֲחִידָה **'ăchîydâh** (Chald.), *akh-ee-daw´;* corresp. to 2420, an *enigma:*—hard sentence.

281. אֲחִיָּה **'Ăchiyâh,** *akh-ee-yaw´;* or (prol.) אֲחִיָּהוּ **'Ăchîyâhûw,** *akh-ee-yaw´-hoo;* from 251 and 3050; *brother* (i.e. *worshipper*) *of Jah; Achijah,* the name of nine Isr.:—Ahiah, Ahijah.

282. אֲחִיהוּד **'Ăchîyhûwd,** *akh-ee-hood´;* from 251 and 1935; *brother* (i.e. *possessor*) *of renown; Achihud,* an Isr.:—Ahihud.

283. אַחְיוֹ **'Achyôw,** *akh-yo´;* prol. from 251; *brotherly; Achio,* the name of three Isr.:—Ahio.

284. אֲחִיחֻד **'Ăchîychûd,** *akh-ee-khood´;* from 251 and 2330; *brother of a riddle* (i.e. *mysterious*); *Achichud,* an Isr.:—Ahihud.

285. אֲחִיטוּב **'Ăchîyṭûwb,** *akh-ee-toob´;* from 251 and 2898; *brother of goodness; Achitub,* the name of several priests:—Ahitub.

286. אֲחִילוּד **'Ăchîylûwd,** *akh-ee-lood´;* from 251 and 3205; *brother of* one *born; Achilud, an Isr.:—Ahilud.*

287. אֲחִימוֹת **'Ăchîymôwth,** *akh-ee-mōth´;* from 251 and 4191; *brother of death; Achimoth,* an Isr.:—Ahimoth.

288. אֲחִימֶלֶךְ **'Ăchîymelek,** *akh-ee-meh´-lek;* from 251 and 4428; *brother of* (the) *king; Achimelek,* the name of an Isr. and of a Hittite:—Ahimelech.

289. אֲחִימַן **'Ăchîyman,** *akh-ee-man´;* or אֲחִימָן **'Ăchîymân,** *akh-ee-mawn´;* from 251 and 4480; *brother of a portion* (i.e. *gift*); *Achiman,* the name of an Anakite and of an Isr.:—Ahiman.

290. אֲחִימַעַץ **'Ăchîyma'ats,** *akh-ee-mah´-ats;* from 251 and the equiv. of 4619; *brother of anger; Achimaats,* the name of three Isr.:—Ahimaaz.

291. אַחְיָן **'Achyân,** *akh-yawn´;* from 251; *brotherly; Achjan,* an Isr.:—Ahian.

292. אֲחִינָדָב **'Ăchîynâdâb,** *akh-ee-naw-dawb´;* from 251 and 5068; *brother of liberality; Achinadab,* an Isr.:—Ahinadab.

293. אֲחִינֹעַם **'Ăchîynô'am,** *akh-ee-no´-am;* from 251 and 5278; *brother of pleasantness; Achinoam,* the name of two Israelitesses:—Ahinoam.

294. אֲחִיסָמָךְ **'Ăchîyçâmâk,** *akh-ee-saw-mawk´;* from 251 and 5564; *brother of support; Achisamak,* an Isr.:—Ahisamach.

295. אֲחִיעֶזֶר **'Ăchîy'ezer,** *akh-ee-eh´-zer;* from 251 and 5828; *brother of help; Achiezer,* the name of two Isr.:—Ahiezer.

296. אֲחִיקָם **'Ăchîyqâm,** *akh-ee-kawm´;* from 251 and 6965; *brother of rising* (i.e. *high*); *Achikam,* an Isr.:—Ahikam.

297. אֲחִירָם **'Ăchîyrâm,** *akh-ee-rawm´;* from 251 and 7311; *brother of height* (i.e. *high*); *Achiram,* an Isr.:—Ahiram.

298. אֲחִירָמִי **'Ăchîyrâmîy,** *akh-ee-raw-mee´;* patron. from 297; an *Achiramite* or desc. (collect.) of Achiram:—Ahiramites.

299. אֲחִירַע **'Ăchîyra',** *akh-ee-rah´;* from 251 and 7451; *brother of wrong; Achira,* an Isr.:—Ahira.

300. אֲחִישַׁחַר **'Achîyshachar,** *akh-ee-shakh´-ar;* from 251 and 7837; *brother of* (the) *dawn; Achishachar,* an Isr.:—Ahishar.

301. אֲחִישָׁר **'Ăchîyshâr,** *akh-ee-shawr´;* from 251 and 7891; *brother of* (the) *singer; Achishar,* an Isr: Ahishar.

302. אֲחִיתֹפֶל **'Ăchîythôphel,** *akh-ee-tho´-fel;* from 251 and 8602; *brother of folly; Achithophel,* an Isr.:—Ahithophel.

303. אַחְלָב **'Achlâb,** *akh-lawb´;* from the same root as 2459; *fatness* (i.e. *fertile*); *Achlab,* a place in Pal.:—Ahlab.

304. אַחְלַי **'Achlay,** *akh-lah´ee;* the same as 305; *wishful; Achlai,* the name of an Israelitess and of an Isr.:—Ahlai.

305. אַחֲלַי **'achălay,** *akh-al-ah´ee;* or אַחֲלֵי **'achălêy,** *akh-al-ay´:* prob. from 253 and a var. of 3863; *would that!:*—O that, would God.

306. אַחְלָמָה **'achlâmâh,** *akh-law´-maw;* perh. from 2492 (and thus *dream-stone*); a gem, prob, the *amethyst:*—amethyst.

307. אַחְמְתָא **'Achmᵉthâ',** *akh-me-thaw´;* of Pers. der.; *Achmetha* (i.e. *Ecbatana*), the summer capital of Persia:—Achmetha.

308. אֲחַסְבַּי **'Ăchaçbay,** *akh-as-bah´ee;* of uncert. der.; *Achasbai,* an Isr.:—Ahasbai.

309. אָחַר **'âchar,** *aw-khar´;* a prim. root; to *loiter* (i.e. *be behind*); by impl. to *procrastinate:*—continue, defer, delay, hinder, be late (slack), stay (there), tarry (longer).

310. אַחַר **'achar,** *akh-ar´;* from 309; prop. the *hind* part; gen. used as an adv. or conj., *after* (in various senses):—after (that, -ward), again, at, away from, back (from, -side), behind, beside, by, follow (after, -ing), forasmuch, from, hereafter, hinder end, + out (over) live, + persecute, posterity, pursuing, remnant, seeing, since, thence [-forth], when, with.

311. אַחַר **'achar** (Chald.), *akh-ar´;* corresp. to 310; *after:*—[here-] after.

312. אַחֵר **'achêr,** *akh-air´;* from 309; prop. *hinder;* gen. *next, other,* etc.:—(an-) other (man), following, next, strange.

313. אַחֵר **'Achêr,** *akh-air´;* the same as 312; *Acher,* an Isr.:—Aher.

314. אַחֲרוֹן **'achărôwn,** *akh-ar-one´;* or (short.) אַחֲרֹן **'achărôn,** *akh-ar-one´;* from 309; *hinder:* gen. *late* or *last;* spec. (as facing the east) *western:*—after (-ward), to come, following, hind (-er, -ermost, -most), last, latter, rereward, ut(ter)most.

315. אַחְרַח **'Achrach,** *akh-rakh;* from 310 and 251, *after* (his) *brother: Achrach,* an Isr.:—Aharah.

316. אֲחַרְחֵל **'Ăcharchêl,** *akh-ar-kale´;* from 310 and 2426; *behind* (the) *intrenchment* (i.e. *safe*); *Acharchel,* an Isr.:—Aharhel.

317. אָחֳרִי **'ochŏrîy** (Chald.), *okh-or-ee´;* from 311; *other:* (an-) other.

318. אָחֳרֵין **'ochŏrêyn** (Chald.), *okh-or-ane´;* or (short.) אָחֳרֵן **'ochŏrên** (Chald.), *okh-or-ane´;* from 317; *last:*—at last.

319. אַחֲרִית **'achărîyth,** *akh-ar-eeth´;* from 310; the *last* or *end,* hence the *future;* also *posterity:*—(last, latter) end (time), hinder (utter) -most, length, posterity, remnant, residue, reward.

320. אַחֲרִית **'achărîyth** (Chald.), *akh-ar-eeth´;* from 311; the same as 319; *later:*—latter.

321. אָחֳרָן **ochŏrân** (Chald.), *okh-or-awn´;* from 311; the same as 317; *other:*—(an-) other.

אָחֳרֵן **'ochŏrên.** See 318.

322. אֲחֹרַנִּית **'ăchôranniyth,** *akh-o-ran-neeth´;* prol. from 268; *backwards:*—back (-ward, again).

323. אֲחַשְׁדַּרְפַּן **'ăchashdarpan,** *akh-ash-dar-pan´:* of Pers. der.; a *satrap* or governor of a main province (of Persia):—lieutenant.

324. אֲחַשְׁדַּרְפַּן **'ăchashdarpan** (Chald.), *akh-ash-dar-pan´;* corresp. to 323:—prince.

325. אֲחַשְׁוֵרוֹשׁ **Ăchashvêrôwsh,** *akh-ash-vay-rōsh´;* or (short.) אַחַשְׁרֹשׁ **'Achashrôsh,** *akh-ash-rōsh´* (Esth. 10:1); of Pers. or.; *Achashverosh* (i.e. Ahasuerus or Artaxerxes, but in this case Xerxes), the title (rather than name) of a Pers. king:—Ahasuerus.

326. אֲחַשְׁתָּרִי **'ăchashtârîy,** *akh-ash-taw-ree´;* prob. of Pers. der.; an *achastarite* (i.e. courier); the designation (rather than name) of an Isr.:—Haakashtari *[includ. the art.].*

327. אֲחַשְׁתָּרָן **'ăchastârân,** *akh-ash-taw-rawn´;* of Pers. or.; a *mule:*—camel.

328. אַט **’aṭ,** *at;* from an unused root perh. mean. to *move softly;* (as a noun) a *necromancer* (from their soft incantations), (as an adv.) *gently:*—charmer, gently, secret, softly.

329. אָטָד **’âṭâd,** *aw-tawd´;* from an unused root prob. mean. to *pierce* or *make fast;* a *thorn*-tree (espec. the *buckthorn*):—Atad, bramble, thorn.

330. אֵטוּן **’êṭûwn,** *ay-toon´;* from an unused root (prob. mean. to *bind*); prop. *twisted* (yarn), i.e. *tapestry:*—fine linen.

331. אָטַם **’âṭam,** *aw-tam´;* a prim. root; to *close* (the lips or ears); by anal. to *contract* (a window by bevelled jambs):—narrow, shut, stop.

332. אָטַר **âṭar,** *aw-tar´;* a prim. root; to *close* up:—shut.

333. אָטֵר **Âṭêr,** *aw-tare´;* from 332; *maimed; Ater,* the name of three Isr.:—Ater.

334. אִטֵּר **’iṭṭêr,** *it-tare´;* from 332; *shut* up, i.e. *impeded* (as to the use of the right hand)— + left-handed.

335. אַי **’ay,** *ah´ee;* perh. from 370; *where ?* hence *how ?:*—how, what, whence, where, whether, which (way).

336. אִי **’îy,** *ee;* prob. ident. with 335 (through the idea of a *query*); *not:*—island (Job 22 : 30).

337. אִי **’îy,** *ee;* short. from 188; *alas!:*—woe.

338. אִי **’îy,** *ee;* prob. ident. with 337 (through the idea of a *doleful* sound); a *howler* (used only in the plural), i.e. any solitary wild creature:—wild beast of the islands.

339. אִי **’îy,** *ee:* from 183; prop. a *habitable* spot (as *desirable*); dry *land,* a *coast,* an *island:*—country, isle, island.

340. אָיַב **’âyab,** *aw-yab´;* a prim. root; to *hate* (as one of an opposite tribe or party); hence to be *hostile:*—be an enemy.

341. אֹיֵב **’ôyêb,** *o-yabe´;* or (fully) אוֹיֵב **’ôwyêb,** *o-yabe´;* act. part. of 340; *hating;* an *adversary:*—enemy, foe.

342. אֵיבָה **’êybâh,** *ay-baw´;* from 340; *hostility:*—enmity, hatred.

343. אֵיד **’êyd,** *ade;* from the same as 181 (in the sense of *bending* down); *oppression;* by impl. *misfortune, ruin:*—calamity, destruction.

344. אַיָּה **’ayâh,** *ah-yaw´;* perh. from 337; the *screamer,* i.e. a *hawk:*—kite, vulture.

345. אַיָּה **’Ayâh,** *ah-yaw´;* the same as 344; *Ajah,* the name of two Isr.:—Aiah, Ajah.

346. אַיֵּה **’ayêh,** *ah-yay´;* prol. from 335; *where?:*—where.

347. אִיּוֹב **’Îyôwb,** *ee-yobe´;* from 340; *hated* (i.e. *persecuted*); *Ijob,* the patriarch famous for his patience:—Job.

348. אִיזֶבֶל **’Îyzebel,** *ee-zeh´-bel;* from 336 and 2083; *chaste; Izebel,* the wife of king Ahab:—Jezebel.

349. אֵיךְ **’êyk,** *ake;* also אֵיכָה **’êykâh,** *ay-kaw´;* and אֵיכָכָה **’êykâkâh,** *ay-kaw´-kah;* prol. from 335; *how? or how!;* also *where:*—how, what.

350. אִי־כָבוֹד **’Îy-kâbôwd,** *ee-kaw-bode´;* from 336 and 3519; (there is) *no glory,* i.e. *inglorious; Ikabod,* a son of Phineas:—I-chabod.

351. אֵיכֹה **’êykôh,** *ay-kō;* prob. a var. for 349, but not as an interrogative; *where:*—where.

אֵיכָה **’êykâh;** אֵיכָכָה **’êykâkâh.** See 349.

352. אַיִל **’ayîl,** *ah´-yil;* from the same as 193; prop. *strength;* hence anything *strong;* spec. a *chief* (politically); also a *ram* (from his strength); a *pilaster* (as a strong support); an *oak* or other strong tree:—mighty (man), lintel, oak, post, ram, tree.

353. אֱיָל **’ĕyâl,** *eh-yawl´;* a var. of 352; *strength.*—strength.

354. אַיָּל **’ayâl,** *ah-yawl´;* an intens. form of 352 (in the sense of *ram*); a *stag* or male deer:—hart.

355. אַיָּלָה **’ayâlâh,** *ah-yaw-law´;* fem. of 354; a *doe* or female deer:—hind.

356. אֵילוֹן **’Êylôwn,** *ay-lone´;* or (short.) אֵלוֹן **’Êlôwn,** *ay-lone´;* or אֵילֹן **’Êylôn,** *ay-lone´;* from 352; *oak-grove; Elon,* the name of a place in Pal., and also of one Hittite, two Isr.:—Elon.

357. אַיָּלוֹן **’Ayâlôwn,** *ah-yaw-lone´;* from 354. *deer-field; Ajalon,* the name of five places in Pal.:—Aijalon, Ajalon.

358. אֵילוֹן בֵּית חָנָן **’Êylôwn Bêyth Chânân,** *ay-lone´ bayth-chawnawn´;* from 356, 1004, and 2603; *oak-grove of* (the) *house of favor; Elon of Beth-chanan,* a place in Pal.:—Elon-beth-hanan.

359. אֵילוֹת **’Êylôwth,** *ay-lōth´;* or אֵילַת **’Êylath,** *ay-lath´;* from 352; *trees* or a *grove* (i.e. palms); *Eloth* or *Elath,* a place on the Red Sea:—Elath, Eloth.

360. אֱיָלוּת **’ĕyâlûwth,** *eh-yaw-looth´;* fem. of 353; *power;* by impl. *protection:*—strength.

361. אֵילָם **’êylâm,** *ay-lawm´;* or (short.) אֵלָם **’êlâm,** *ay-lawm´;* or (fem.) אֵלַמָּה **’êlammâh,** *ay-lam-maw´;* prob. from 352; a *pillar-space* (or colonnade), i.e. a *pale* (or portico):—arch.

362. אֵילִם **’Êylîm,** *ay-leem´;* plur. of 352: palm-*trees; Elim,* a place in the Desert:—Elim.

363. אִילָן **’îylân** (Chald.), *ee-lawn´;* corresp. to 356; a *tree:*—tree.

364. אֵיל פָּארָן **’Êyl Pâ’rân,** *ale paw-rawn´;* from 352 and 6290; *oak of Paran; El-Paran,* a portion of the district of Paran:—El-paran.

אֵילֹן **’Êylôn.** See 356.

365. אַיֶּלֶת **’ayeleth,** *ah-yeh´-leth;* the same as 355; a *doe:*—hind, Aijeleth.

אַיִם **’ayim.** See 368.

366. אָיֹם **’âyôm,** *aw-yome´;* from an unused root (mean. to *frighten*); *frightful:*—terrible.

367. אֵימָה **’êymâh,** *ay-maw´;* or (short.) אֵמָה **’êmah,** *ay-maw´;* from the same as 366; *fright;* concr. an *idol* (as a bugbear):—dread. fear, horror, idol, terrible, terror.

368. אֵימִים **’Êymîym,** *ay-meem´; plur. of 367; terrors; Emim,* an early Canaanitish (or Moabitish) tribe:—Emims.

369. אַיִן **’ayin,** *ah´-yin;* as if from a prim. root mean. to *be nothing* or *not exist;* a *nonentity;* gen. used as a neg. particle:—else, except, fail [father-] less, be gone, in [-curable], neither, never, no (where), none, nor (any, thing), not, nothing, to nought, past, un [-searchable], well-nigh, without, Comp. 370.

370. אַיִן **’ayin,** *ah-yin´;* prob. ident. with 369 in the sense of *query* (comp. 336);—*where?* (only in connection with prep. pref., *whence*):—whence, where.

371. אִין **’îyn,** *een;* appar. a short. form of 369; but (like 370) interrog.; is it *not?:*—not

372. אִיעֶזֶר **’Îy‘ezer,** *ee-eh´-zer;* from 336 and 5828; *helpless; Iezer,* an Isr.:—Jeezer.

373. אִיעֶזְרִי **’Îy‘ezrîy,** *ee-ez-ree´;* patron. from 372; an *Iezrite* or desc. of Iezer:—Jezerite.

374. אֵיפָה **’êyphâh,** *ay-faw´;* or (short.) אֵפָה **’êphâh,** *ay-faw´;* of Eg. der.; an *ephah* or measure for grain; hence a *measure* in gen.:—ephah, (divers) measure (-s).

375. אֵיפֹה **’êyphôh,** *ay-fō´;* from 335 and 6311; *what place?* also (of time) *when?;* or (of means) *how?:*—what manner, where.

376. אִישׁ **’îysh,** *eesh;* contr. for 582 [or perh. rather from an unused root mean. to *be extant*]; a *man* as an individual or a male person; often used as an adjunct to a more definite term (and in such cases frequently not expressed in translation):—also, another, any (man), a certain, + champion, consent, each, every (one), fellow, [foot-, husband-] man, (good-, great, mighty) man, he, high (degree), him (that is), husband, man [-kind], + none, one, people, person, + steward, what (man) soever, whoso (-ever), worthy. Comp. 802.

377. אִישׁ **’îysh,** *eesh;* denom. from 376; to *be a man,* i.e. act in a manly way:—show (one) self a man.

378. אִישׁ־בֹּשֶׁת **’Îysh-Bôsheth,** *eesh-bō´-sheth;* from 376 and 1322; *man of shane; Ish-Bosheth,* a son of King Saul:—Ish-bosheth.

379. אִישְׁהוֹד **’Îyshhôwd** *eesh-hode´;* from 376 and 1935; *man of renown; Ishod,* an Isr.:—Ishod.

380. אִישׁוֹן **’îyshôwn,** *ee-shone´;* dimin. from 376; the *little man* of the eye; the *pupil* or *ball;* hence the *middle* (of night):—apple [of the eye], black, obscure.

אִישׁ־חַי **’Îysh-Chay.** See 381.

381. אִישׁ־חַיִל **’Îysh-Chayil,** *eesh-khah´-yil;* from 376 and 2428; *man of might;* by defect. transcription (2 Sam. 23 : 20) אִישׁ־חַי **’Îsh-Chay,** *eesh-khah´ee;* as if from 376 and 2416; *living man; Ish-chail* (or *Ish-chai*), an Isr.:—a valiant man.

382. אִישׁ־טוֹב **'Îysh-Tôwb,** *eesh-tobe´;* from 376 and 2897; *man of Tob; Ish-Tob,* a place in Pal.:—Ish-tob.

אִישַׁי **'Îshay.** See 3448.

אִיתוֹן **'îthôwn.** See 2978.

383. אִיתַי **'îythay** (Chald.), *ee-thah´ee;* corresp. to 3426; prop. *entity;* used only as a particle of affirmation, there *is:*—art thou, can, do ye, have it be, there is (are), × we will not.

384. אִיתִיאֵל **'Îythîy'êl,** *eeth-ee-ale´;* perh. from 837 and 410; *God has arrived; Ithiel,* the name of an Isr., also of a symb. person:—Ithiel.

385. אִיתָמָר **'Îythâmâr,** *eeth-aw-mawr´;* from 339 and 8558; *coast of* the *palm*-tree; *Ithamar,* a son of Aaron:—Ithamar.

386. אֵיתָן **'êythân,** *ay-thawn´;* or (short.) אֵתָן **'êthân,** *ay-thawn´;* from an unused root (mean. to *continue*); *permanence;* hence (concr.) *permanent;* spec. a *chieftain:*—hard, mighty, rough, strength, strong.

387. אֵיתָן **'Êythân,** *ay-thawn´;* the same as 386; *permanent; Ethan,* the name of four Isr.:—Ethan.

388. אֵיתָנִים **'Êythânîym,** *ay-thaw-neem´;* plur. of 386; always with the art.; the *permanent* brooks; *Ethanim,* the name of a month:—Ethanim.

389. אַךְ **'ak,** *ak;* akin to 403; a particle of affirmation, *surely;* hence (by limitation) *only:*—also, in any wise, at least, but, certainly, even, howbeit, nevertheless, notwithstanding, only, save, surely of a surety, truly, verily, + wherefore, yet (but).

390. אַכַּד **'Akkad,** *ak-kad´;* from an unused root prob. mean. to *strengthen;* a *fortress; Accad,* a place in Bab.:—Accad.

391. אַכְזָב **'akzâb,** *ak-zawb´;* from 3576; *falsehood;* by impl. *treachery:*—liar, lie.

392. אַכְזִיב **'Akzîyb,** *ak-zeeb´;* from 391; *deceitful* (in the sense of a winter-torrent which *fails* in summer); *Akzib,* the name of two places in Pal.:—Achzib.

393. אַכְזָר **'akzâr,** *ak-zawr´;* from an unused root (appar. mean. to *act harshly*); *violent;* by impl. *deadly;* also (in a good sense) *brave:*—cruel, fierce.

394. אַכְזָרִי **'akzârîy,** *ak-zaw-ree´;* from 393; *terrible:*—cruel (one).

395. אַכְזְרִיּוּת **'akz^{e}rîyûwth,** *ak-ze-ree-ooth´;* from 394; *fierceness:*—cruel.

396. אֲכִילָה **'ăkîylâh,** *ak-ee-law´;* fem. from 398; something *eatable,* i.e. *food:*—meat.

397. אָכִישׁ **'Âkîysh,** *aw-keesh´;* of uncert. der.; *Akish,* a Philistine king:—Achish.

398. אָכַל **'âkal,** *aw-kal´;* a prim. root; to *eat* (lit. or fig.):—× at all, burn up, consume, devour (-er, up), dine, eat (-er, up), feed (with), food, × freely, × in . . . wise (-deed, plenty), (lay) meat, × quite.

399. אֲכַל **'ăkal** (Chald.), *ak-al´;* corresp. to 398:—+ accuse, devour, eat.

400. אֹכֶל **'ôkel,** *o´-kel;* from 398; *food:*—eating, food, meal [-time], meat, prey, victuals.

401. אֻכָל **'Ûkâl,** *oo-kawl´;* or אֻכָּל **'Ukkâl,** *ook-kawl´;* appar. from 398: *devoured; Ucal,* a fancy name:—Ucal.

402. אָכְלָה **'oklâh,** *ok-law´;* fem. of 401; *food:*—consume, devour, eat, food, meat.

403. אָכֵן **'âkên,** *aw-kane´;* from 3559 [comp. 3651]; *firmly;* fig. *surely;* also (advers.) *but:*—but, certainly, nevertheless, surely, truly, verily.

404. אָכַף **'akaph,** *aw-kaf´;* a prim. root; appar. mean. to *curve* (as with a burden); to *urge:*—crave.

405. אֶכֶף **'ekeph,** *eh´-kef;* from 404; a *load;* by impl. a *stroke* (others *dignity*):—hand.

406. אִכָּר **'ikkâr,** *ik-kawr´;* from an unused root mean. to *dig;* a *farmer:*—husbandman, ploughman.

407. אַכְשָׁף **'Akshâph,** *ak-shawf´;* from 3784; *fascination; Acshaph,* a place in Pal.:—Achshaph.

408. אַל **'al,** *al;* a neg. particle [akin to 3808]; *not* (the qualified negation, used as a deprecative); once (Job 24 : 25) as a noun, *nothing:*—nay, neither, + never, no, nor, not, nothing [worth], rather than.

409. אַל **'al** (Chald.), *al;* corresp. to 408:—not.

410. אֵל **'êl,** *ale;* short. from 352; *strength;* as adj. *mighty;* espec. the *Almighty* (but used also of any *deity*):—God (god), × goodly, × great, idol, might (-y one), power, strong. Comp. names in "-el."

411. אֵל **'êl,** *ale;* a demonstr. particle (but only in a plur. sense) *these* or *those:*—these, those, Comp. 428.

412. אֵל **'êl** (Chald.), *ale;* corresp. to 411:—these.

413. אֵל **'êl,** *ale;* (but used only in the shortened constr. form אֶל **'el,** *el*); a prim. particle, prop. denoting motion *towards,* but occasionally used of a quiescent position, i.e. *near, with* or *among;* often in general, *to:*—about, according to, after, against, among, as for, at, because (-fore, -side), both . . . and, by, concerning, for, from, × hath, in (-to), near, (out) of, over, through, to (-ward), under, unto, upon, whether, with (-in).

414. אֵלָא **'Êlâ',** *ay-law´;* a var. of 424; *oak; Ela,* an Isr.:—Elah.

415. אֵל אֱלֹהֵי יִשְׂרָאֵל **'Êl 'ĕlôhêy Yisrâ'êl,** *ale el-o-hay´ yis-raw-ale´;* from 410 and 430 and 3478; the *mighty God of Jisrael; El-Elohi-Jisrael,* the title given to a consecrated spot by Jacob:—El-elohe-israel.

416. אֵל בֵּית־אֵל **'Êl Bêyth-'Êl,** *ale bayth-ale´;* from 410 and 1008; the *God of Bethel; El-Bethel,* the title given to a consecrated spot by Jacob:—El-beth-el.

417. אֶלְגָּבִישׁ **'elgâbîysh,** *el-gaw-beesh´;* from 410 and 1378; *hail* (as if a *great pearl*):—great hail [-stones].

418. אַלְגּוּמִּים **'algûwmmîym,** *al-goom-meem´;* by transp. for 484; sticks of *algum* wood:—algum [trees].

419. אֶלְדָּד **'Eldâd,** *el-dâd´;* from 410 and 1730; *God has loved; Eldad,* an Isr.:—Eldad.

420. אֶלְדָּעָה **'Eldâ'âh,** *el-daw-aw´;* from 410 and 3045; *God of knowledge; Eldaah,* a son of Midian:—Eldaah.

421. אָלָה **'âlâh,** *aw-law´;* a prim. root [rather ident. with 422 through the idea of *invocation*]; to *bewail:*—lament.

422. אָלָה **'âlâh,** *aw-law´;* a prim. root; prop. to *adjure,* i.e. (usually in a bad sense) *imprecate:*—adjure, curse, swear.

423. אָלָה **'âlâh,** *aw-law´;* from 422; an *imprecation:*—curse, cursing, execration, oath, swearing.

424. אֵלָה **'êlâh,** *ay-law´;* fem. of 352; an *oak* or other strong tree:—elm, oak, teil tree

425. אֵלָה **Êlâh,** *ay-law´;* the same as 424; *Elah,* the name of an Edomite, of four Isr., and also of a place in Pal.:—Elah.

426. אֱלָהּ **'ĕlâhh** (Chald.), *el-aw´;* corresp. to 433; *God:*—God, god.

427. אַלָּה **'allâh,** *al-law´;* a var. of 424:—oak.

428. אֵלֶּה **'êl-leh,** *ale´-leh;* prol. from 411; *these* or *those:*—an- (the) other; one sort, so, some, such, them, these (same), they, this, those, thus, which, who (-m).

429. אֵלֶּה **'êlleh** (Chald.), *ale-leh;* corresp. to 428:—these.

אֱלֹהַּ **'ĕlôahh.** see 433.

430. אֱלֹהִים **'ĕlôhîym,** *el-o-heem´;* plur. of 433; *gods* in the ordinary sense; but spec. used (in the plur. thus, esp. with the art.) of the supreme *God;* occasionally applied by way of deference to *magistrates;* and sometimes as a superlative:—angels, × exceeding, God (gods) (-dess, -ly), × (very) great, judges, × mighty.

431. אֲלוּ **'ălûw** (Chald.), *al-oo´;* prob. prol. from 412; *lo!:*—behold.

432. אִלּוּ **'illûw,** *il-loo´;* prob. from 408; *nay,* i.e. (softened) *if:*—but if, yea though.

433. אֱלוֹהַּ **'ĕlôwahh,** *el-o´-ah;* rarely (short.) אֱלֹהַּ **'ĕlôahh,** *el-o´-ah; prob. prol. (emphat.) from 410; a deity* or the *Deity:*—God, god. See 430.

434. אֱלוּל **'ĕlûwl,** *el-ool´;* for 457; good for *nothing:*—thing of nought.

435. אֱלוּל **'Ĕlûwl,** *el-ool´;* prob. of for. der.; *Elul,* the sixth Jewish month:—Elul.

436. אֵלוֹן **'êlôwn,** *ay-lone´;* prol. from 352; an *oak* or other strong tree:—plain. See also 356.

437. אַלּוֹן **'allôwn,** *al-lone´;* a var. of 436:—oak.

438. אַלּוֹן **'Allôwn,** *al-lone´;* the same as 437; *Allon,* an Isr., also a place in Pal:—Allon.

439. אַלּוֹן בָּכוּת **'Allôwn Bâkûwth,** *al-lone´ baw-kooth´;* from 437 and a var. of 1068; *oak of weeping; Allon-Bakuth,* a monumental tree:—Allon-bachuth.

440. אֵלוֹנִי **'Êlôwnîy,** *ay-lo-nee´;* or rather (short.) אֵלֹנִי **'Êlônîy,** *ay-lo-nee´;* patron. from 438; an *Elonite* or desc. (collect.) of Elon:—Elonites.

441. אַלּוּף **'allûwph,** *al-loof´;* or (short.) אַלֻּף **'allûph,** *al-loof´;* from 502; *familiar;* a *friend,* also *gentle;* hence a *bullock* (as being tame; applied, although masc., to a *cow*); and so a *chieftain* (as notable like neat cattle):—captain, duke, (chief) friend, governor, guide, ox.

442. אָלוּשׁ **'Âlûwsh,** *aw-loosh´;* of uncert. der.; *Alush,* a place in the Desert:—Alush.

443. אֶלְזָבָד **'Elzâbâd,** *el-zaw-bawd´;* from 410 and 2064; *God has bestowed; Elzabad,* the name of two Isr.:—Elzabad.

444. אָלַח **'âlach,** *aw-lakh´;* a prim. root; to *muddle,* i.e. (fig. and intrans.) to *turn* (morally) *corrupt:*—become filthy.

445. אֶלְחָנָן **'Elchânân,** *el-khaw-nawn´;* from 410 and 2603; *God* (is) *gracious; Elchanan,* an Isr.:—Elkanan.

אֵלִי **'Êlîy.** See 1017.

446. אֱלִיאָב **'Ĕlîy'âb,** *el-ee-awb´;* from 410 and 1; *God of* (his) *father; Eliab,* the name of six Isr.:—Eliab.

447. אֱלִיאֵל **'Ĕlîy'êl,** *el-ee-ale´;* from 410 repeated; *God of* (his) *God; Eliel,* the name of nine Isr.:—Eliel.

448. אֱלִיאָתָה **'Ĕlîy'âthâh,** *el-ee-aw-thaw´;* or (contr.) אֱלִיָּתָה **'Ĕlîyâthâh,** *el-ee-yaw-thaw´;* from 410 and 225; *God of* (his) *consent; Eliathah,* an Isr.:—Eliathah.

449. אֱלִידָד **'Ĕlîydâd,** *el-ee-dawd´;* from the same as 419; *God of* (his) *love, Elidad,* an Isr.:—Elidad.

450. אֶלְיָדָע **'Elyâdâ',** *el-yaw-daw´;* from 410 and 3045; *God* (is) *knowing: Eljada,* the name of two Isr. and of an Aramaean leader:—Eliada.

451. אַלְיָה **'alyâh,** *al-yaw´;* from 422 (in the orig. sense of *strength*); the *stout* part, i.e. the fat *tail* of the Oriental sheep:—rump.

452. אֵלִיָּה **'Êlîyâh,** *ay-lee-yaw´;* or prol. אֵלִיָּהוּ **'Êlîyâhûw,** *ay-lee-yaw´-hoo;* from 410 and 3050; *God of Jehovah; Elijah,* the name of the famous prophet and of two other Isr.:—Elijah, Eliah.

453. אֱלִיהוּ **'Ĕlîyhûw,** *el-ee-hoo´;* or (fully) אֱלִיהוּא **'Ĕlîyhûw',** *el-ee-hoo´;* from 410 and 1931; *God of him; Elihu,* the name of one of Job's friends, and of three Isr.:—Elihu.

454. אֶלְיְהוֹעֵינַי **'Elyᵉhôw'êynay,** *el-ye-ho-ay-nah´ee;* or (short.) אֶלְיוֹעֵינַי **'Elyôw'êynay,** *el-yo-ay-nah´ee;* from 413 and 3068 and 5869; *towards Jehovah* (are) *my eyes; Eljehoenai* or *Eljoenai,* the name of seven Isr.:—Elihoenai, Elionai.

455. אֶלְיַחְבָּא **'Elyachbâ',** *el-yakh-baw´;* from 410 and 2244; *God will hide; Eljachba,* an Isr.:—Eliahbah.

456. אֱלִיחֹרֶף **'Ĕlîychôreph,** *el-ee-kho´-ref;* from 410 and 2779; *God of autumn; Elichoreph,* an Isr.:—Elihoreph.

457. אֱלִיל **'ĕlîyl,** *el-eel´;* appar. from 408; good for *nothing,* by anal. *vain* or *vanity;* spec. an *idol:*—idol, no value, thing of nought.

458. אֱלִימֶלֶךְ **'Ĕlîymelek,** *el-ee-meh´-lek;* from 410 and 4428; *God of* (the) *king; Elimelek,* an Isr.—Elimelech.

459. אִלֵּין **'illêyn** (Chald.), *il-lane´;* or shorter אִלֵּן **'illên,** *il-lane´;* prol. from 412; *these:*—the, these.

460. אֶלְיָסָף **'Elyâçâph,** *el-yaw-sawf´;* from 410 and 3254; *God* (is) *gatherer; Eljasaph,* the name of two Isr.:—Eliasaph.

461. אֱלִיעֶזֶר **'Ĕlîy'ezer,** *el-ee-eh´-zer;* from 410 and 5828; *God of help; Eliezer,* the name of a Damascene and of ten Isr.:—Eliezer.

462. אֱלִיעֵינַי **'Ĕlîy'êynay,** *el-ee-ay-nah´ee;* prob. contr. for 454; *Elienai,* an Isr.:—Elienai.

463. אֱלִיעָם **'Ĕlîy'âm,** *el-ee-awm´;* from 410 and 5971; *God of* (the) *people; Eliam,* an Isr.:—Eliam.

464. אֱלִיפַז **'Ĕlîyphaz,** *el-ee-faz´;* from 410 and 6337; *God of gold; Eliphaz,* the name of one of Job's friends, and of a son of Esau:—Eliphaz.

465. אֱלִיפָל **'Ĕlîyphâl,** *el-ee-fawl´;* from 410 and 6419; *God of judgment; Eliphal,* an Isr.:—Eliphal.

466. אֱלִיפְלֵהוּ **'Ĕlîyphᵉlêhûw,** *el-ee-fe-lay´-hoo;* from 410 and 6395; *God of his distinction; Eliphelehu,* an Isr.:—Elipheleh.

467. אֱלִיפֶלֶט **'Ĕlîypheleṭ** *el-ee-feh´-let;* or (short.) אֶלְפֶּלֶט **'Ĕlpeleṭ,** *el-peh´-let:* from 410 and 6405; *God of deliverance; Eliphelet* or *Elpelet,* the name of six Isr.:—Eliphalet, Eliphelet, Elpalet.

468. אֱלִיצוּר **'Ĕlêytsûwr,** *el-ee-tsoor´;* from 410 and 6697; *God of* (the) *rock; Elitsur,* an Isr.:—Elizur.

469. אֱלִיצָפָן **'Ĕlîytsâphân,** *el-ee-tsaw-fawn´;* or (short.) אֶלְצָפָן **'Eltsâphân,** *el-tsaw-fawn´;* from 410 and 6845; *God of treasure; Elitsaphan* or *Eltsaphan,* an Isr.:—Elizaphan, Elzaphan.

470. אֱלִיקָא **'Ĕlîyqâ',** *el-ee-kaw´;* from 410 and 6958; *God of rejection; Elika,* an Isr.:—Elika.

471. אֶלְיָקִים **'Elyâqîym,** *el-yaw-keem´;* from 410 and 6965; *God of raising; Eljakim,* the name of four Isr.:—Eliakim.

472. אֱלִישֶׁבַע **'Ĕlîysheba',** *el-ee-sheh´-bah;* from 410 and 7651 (in the sense of 7650); *God of* (the) *oath; Elisheba,* the wife of Aaron:—Elisheba.

473. אֱלִישָׁה **'Ĕlîyshâh,** *el-ee-shaw´;* prob. of for. der.; *Elishah,* a son of Javan:—Elishah.

474. אֱלִישׁוּעַ **'Ĕlîyshûwa',** *el-ee-shoo´-ah;* from 410 and 7769; *God of supplication* (or *of riches*); *Elishua,* a son of King David:—Elishua.

475. אֶלְיָשִׁיב **'Elyâshîyb,** *el-yaw-sheeb´;* from 410 and 7725; *God will restore; Eljashib,* the name of six Isr.:—Eliashib.

476. אֱלִישָׁמָע **'Ĕlîyshâmâ',** *el-ee-shaw-maw´;* from 410 and 8085; *God of hearing; Elishama,* the name of seven Isr.:—Elishama.

477. אֱלִישָׁע **'Ĕlîyshâ',** *el-ee-shaw´;* contr. for 474; *Elisha,* the famous prophet:—Elisha.

478. אֱלִישָׁפָט **'Ĕlîyshâphât,** *el-ee-shaw-fawt´;* from 410 and 8199; *God of judgment; Elishaphat,* an Isr.:—Elishaphat.

אֱלִיָּתָה **Ĕlîyâthâh.** See 448.

479. אִלֵּךְ **'illêk** (Chald.), *il-lake´;* prol. from 412; *these:*—these, those.

480. אַלְלַי **'alᵉlay,** *al-le-lah´ee;* by redupl. from 421; *alas!:*—woe.

481. אָלַם **'âlam,** *aw-lam´;* a prim. root; to *tie* fast; hence (of the mouth) to be *tongue-tied:*—bind, be dumb, put to silence.

482. אֵלֶם **'êlem,** *ay´-lem;* from 481; *silence* (i.e. mute justice):—congregation. Comp. 3128.

אֵלָם **'êlâm.** See 361.

אֻלָם **'âlûm.** See 485.

483. אִלֵּם **'illêm,** *il-lame´;* from 481; *speechless:*—dumb (man).

484. אַלְמֻגִּים **'almuggiym,** *al-moog-gheem´;* prob. of for. der. (used thus only in the plur.); *almug* (i.e. prob. sandal-wood) sticks:—almug trees. Comp. 418.

485. אֲלֻמָּה **'ălummâh,** *al-oom-maw´;* or (masc.) אָלֻם **'âlûm,** *aw-loom´;* pass. part. of 481; something *bound;* a *sheaf:*—sheaf.

486. אַלְמוֹדָד **'Almôwdâd,** *al-mo-dawd´;* prob. of for. der.:—*Almodad,* a son of Joktan:—Almodad.

487. אַלַּמֶּלֶךְ **'Allammelek,** *al-lam-meh´-lek;* from 427 and 4428; *oak of* (the) *king; Allammelek,* a place in Pal.:—Alammelech.

488. אַלְמָן **'almân,** *al-mawn´;* prol. from 481 in the sense of *bereavement; discarded* (as a divorced person):—forsaken.

489. אַלְמֹן **'almôn,** *al-mone´;* from 481 as in 488; *bereavement:*—widowhood.

490. אַלְמָנָה **'almânâh,** *al-maw-naw´;* fem. of 488; a *widow;* also a *desolate place:*—*desolate house (palace), widow.*

491. אַלְמָנוּת **'almânûwth,** *al-maw-nooth´;* fem. of 488; concr. a *widow;* abstr. *widowhood:*—widow, widowhood.

492. אַלְמֹנִי **'almônîy,** *al-mo-nee´;* from 489 in the sense of *concealment; some* one (i.e. *so and so,* without giving the name of the person or place):—one, and such.
אִלֵּן **'illên.** See 459.
אֵלֹנִי **'Êlônîy.** See 440.

493. אֶלְנַעַם **'Elna'am,** *el-nah´-am;* from 410 and 5276; *God* (is his) *delight; Elnaam,* an Isr.:—Elnaam.

494. אֶלְנָתָן **'Elnâthân,** *el-naw-thawn´;* from 410 and 5414; *God* (is the) *giver; Elnathan,* the name of four Isr.:—Elnathan.

495. אֶלָּסָר **'Ellâçâr,** *el-law-sawr´;* prob. of for. der.; *Ellasar,* an early country of Asia:—Ellasar.

496. אֶלְעָד **'El'âd,** *el-awd´;* from 410 and 5749; *God has testified; Elad,* an Isr.:—Elead.

497. אֶלְעָדָה **'El'âdâh,** *el-aw-daw´;* from 410 and 5710; *God has decked; Eladah,* an Isr.:—Eladah.

498. אֶלְעוּזַי **'El'ûwzay,** *el-oo-zah´ee;* from 410 and 5756 (in the sense of 5797); *God* (is) *defensive; Eluzai,* an Isr.:—Eluzai.

499. אֶלְעָזָר **'El'âzâr,** *el-aw-zawr´;* from 410 and 5826; *God* (is) *helper; Elazar,* the name of seven Isr.:—Eleazar.

500. אֶלְעָלֵא **'El'âlê',** *el-aw-lay´;* or (more properly) אֶלְעָלֵה **'El'âlêh,** *el-aw-lay´;* from 410 and 5927; *God* (is) *going up; Elale* or *Elaleh,* a place east of the Jordan:—Elealeh.

501. אֶלְעָשָׂה **'El'âsâh,** *el-aw-saw´;* from 410 and 6213; *God has made; Elasah,* the name of four Isr.:—Elasah, Eleasah.

502. אָלַף **'âlaph,** *aw-lof´;* a prim. root, to *associate* with; hence to *learn* (and caus. to *teach*):—learn, teach, utter.

503. אָלַף **'âlaph,** *aw-laf´;* denom. from 505; caus. to *make a thousandfold:*—bring forth thousands.

504. אֶלֶף **'eleph,** *eh´-lef;* from 502; a *family;* also (from the sense of *yoking* or *taming*) an *ox* or *cow:*—family, kine, oxen.

505. אֶלֶף **'eleph,** *eh-lef;* prop. the same as 504; hence (an ox's head being the first letter of the alphabet, and this eventually used as a numeral) a *thousand:*—thousand.

506. אֲלַף **'ălaph** (Chald.), *al-af´;* or אֶלֶף **'eleph,** (Chald.), *eh´-lef;* corresp. to 505:—thousand.

507. אֶלֶף **'Eleph,** *eh´-lef;* the same as 505; *Eleph,* a place in Pal.:—Eleph.
אַלֻּף **'allûph.** See 441.
אֱלִפֶּלֶט **'Elpelet.** See 467.

508. אֶלְפַּעַל **'Elpa'al,** *el-pah´-al;* from 410 and 6466; *God* (is) *act; Elpaal,* an Isr.:—Elpaal.

509. אָלַץ **'âlats,** *aw-lats´;* a prim. root; to *press:*—urge.
אֶלְצָפָן **'Eltsâphân.** See 469.

510. אַלְקוּם **'alqûwm,** *al-koom´;* prob. from 408 and 6965; a *non-rising* (i.e. *resistlessness*):—no rising up.

511. אֶלְקָנָה **'Elqânâh,** *el-kaw-naw´;* from 410 and 7069; *God has obtained; Elkanah.* the name of seven Isr.:—Elkanah.

512. אֶלְקֹשִׁי **'Elqôshîy,** *el-ko-shee´;* patrial from a name of uncert. der.; an *Elkoshite* or native of Elkosh:—Elkoshite.

513. אֶלְתּוֹלַד **'Eltôwlad,** *el-to-lad´;* prob. from 410 and a masc. form of 8435 [comp. 8434]; *God* (is) *generator; Eltolad,* a place in Pal.:—Eltolad.

514. אֶלְתְּקֵא **'Elteqê,** *el-te-kay´;* or (more prop.) אֶלְתְּקֵה **'Elteqêh,** *el-te-kay´;* of uncert. der.; *Eltekeh* or *Elteke,* a place in Pal.:—Eltekeh.

515. אֶלְתְּקֹן **'Elteqôn,** *el-te-kone´;* from 410 and 8626; *God* (is) *straight; Eltekon,* a place in Pal.:—Eltekon.

516. אַל תַּשְׁחֵת **'Al tashchêth,** *al tash-kayth´;* from 408 and 7843; *Thou must not destroy;* prob. the opening words of a popular song:—Al-taschith.

517. אֵם **'êm,** *ame;* a prim. word; a *mother* (as the *bond* of the family); in a wide sense (both lit. and fig.) [like 1]:—dam, mother, × parting.

518. אִם **'îm,** *eem;* a prim. particle; used very widely as demonstr., *lo!;* interrog., *whether?;* or conditional, *if, although;* also *Oh that!, when;* hence as a neg., *not:*—(and, can-, doubtless, if, that) (not), + but, either, + except, + more (-over if, than), neither, nevertheless, nor, oh that, or, + save (only, -ing), seeing, since, sith, + surely (no more, none, not), though, + of a truth, + unless, + verily, when, whereas, whether, while, + yet.

519. אָמָה **'âmâh,** *aw-maw´;* appar. a prim. word; a *maid-servant* or female slave:—(hand-) bondmaid (-woman,) maid (-servant).
אֵמָה **'êmâh.** See 361.

520. אַמָּה **'ammâh,** *am-maw´;* prol. from 517; prop. a *mother* (i.e. *unit*) of measure, or the *fore-arm* (below the elbow), i.e. a *cubit;* also a door-*base* (as a *bond* of the entrance):—cubit, + hundred [*by exchange for* 3967], measure, post.

521. אַמָּה **'ammâh** (Chald.), *am-maw´;* corresp. to 520:—cubit.

522. אַמָּה **'Ammâh,** *am-maw´;* the same as 520; *Ammah,* a hill in Pal.:—Ammah.

523. אֻמָּה **'ummâh,** *oom-maw´;* from the same as 517; a *collection,* i.e. community of persons:—nation, people.

524. אֻמָּה **'ummâh** (Chald.), *oom-maw´;* corresp. to 523:—nation.

525. אָמוֹן **'âmôwn,** *aw-mone´;* from 539, prob. in the sense of *training; skilled,* i.e. an architect [like 542]:—one brought up.

526. אָמוֹן **'Âmôwn,** *aw-mone´;* the same as 525; *Amon,* the name of three Isr.:—Amon.

527. אָמוֹן **'âmôwn,** *aw-mone´;* a var. for 1995; a *throng* of people:—multitude.

528. אָמוֹן **'Âmôwn,** *aw-mone´;* of Eg. der.; *Amon* (i.e. Ammon or Amn), a deity of Egypt (used only as an adjunct of 4996):—multitude, populous.

529. אֵמוּן **'êmûwn,** *ay-moon´;* from 539; *established,* i.e. (fig.) *trusty;* also (abstr.) *trustworthiness:*—faith (-ful), truth.

530. אֱמוּנָה **'ĕmûwnâh,** *em-oo-naw´;* or (short.) אֱמֻנָה **'ĕmûnâh,** *em-oo-naw´;* fem. of 529; lit. *firmness;* fig. *security;* mor. *fidelity:*—faith (-ful, -ly, -ness, [man]), set office, stability, steady, truly, truth, verily.

531. אָמוֹץ **'Âmôwts,** *aw-mohts´;* from 553; *strong; Amots,* an Isr.:—Amoz.

532. אָמִי **'Âmîy,** *aw-mee´;* an abbrev. for 526; *Ami,* an Isr.:—Ami.
אֲמִינוֹן **'Ămîynôwn.** See 550.

533. אַמִּיץ **'ammîyts,** *am-meets´;* or (short.) אַמִּץ **'ammîts,** *am-meets´;* from 553; *strong* or (abstr.) *strength:*—courageous, mighty, strong (one).

534. אָמִיר **'âmîyr,** *aw-meer´;* appar. from 559 (in the sense of *self-exaltation*); a *summit* (of a tree or mountain):—bough, branch.

535. אָמַל **'âmal,** *aw-mal´;* a prim. root; to *droop;* by impl. to *be sick,* to *mourn:*—languish, be weak, wax feeble.

536. אֻמְלַל **'umlal,** *oom-lal´;* from 535; *sick:*—weak.

537. אֲמֵלָל **'ămêlâl,** *am-ay-lawl´;* from 535; *languid:*—feeble.

538. אֲמָם **'Ămâm,** *am-awm´;* from 517; *gathering*-spot; *Amam,* a place in Pal.:—Amam.

539. אָמַן **âman,** *aw-man´;* a prim. root; prop. to *build up* or *support;* to *foster* as a parent or nurse; fig. to *render* (or *be*) *firm* or faithful, to *trust* or believe, to be *permanent* or quiet; mor. to *be true* or certain; once (Isa. 30 : 21; by interch. for 541) to *go to the right hand:*—hence assurance, believe, bring up, establish, + fail, be faithful (of long continuance, stedfast, sure, surely, trusty, verified), nurse, (-ing father), (put), trust, turn to the right.

540. אֲמַן **'ăman** (Chald.), *am-an´;* corresp. to 539:—believe, faithful, sure.

541. אָמַן **'âman,** *aw-man´;* denom. from 3225; to take the *right hand* road:—turn to the right. See 539.

542. אָמָן **'âmân,** *aw-mawn´;* from 539 (in the sense of *training*); an *expert:*—cunning workman.

543. אָמֵן **'âmên,** *aw-mane´;* from 539; *sure;* abstr. *faithfulness;* adv. *truly:*—Amen, so be it, truth.

544. אֹמֶן **'ômen,** *oh-men´;* from 539; *verity:*—truth.

545. אָמְנָה **'omnâh,** *om-naw´;* fem. of 544 (in the spec. sense of *training*); *tutelage:*—brought up.

546. אָמְנָה **'omnâh,** *om-naw´;* fem. of 544 (in its usual sense); adv. *surely:*—indeed.

547. אֹמְנָה **'ômᵉnâh,** *o-me-naw´;* fem. act. part. of 544 (in the orig. sense of *supporting*); a *column:*—pillar.

548. אֲמָנָה **'ămânâh,** *am-aw-naw´;* fem. of 543; something *fixed,* i.e. a *covenant,* an *allowance:*—certain portion, sure.

549. אֲמָנָה **'Ămânâh,** *am-aw-naw´;* the same as 548; *Amanah,* a mountain near Damascus:—Amana.

אֱמֻנָה **'ĕmûnâh.** See 530.

550. אַמְנוֹן **'Ămnôwn,** *am-nohn´;* or אֲמִינוֹן **'Ămîynôwn,** *am-ee-nohn´;* from 539; *faithful; Amnon* (or Aminon), a son of David:—Amnon.

551. אָמְנָם **'omnâm,** *om-nawm´;* adv. from 544; *verily:*—indeed, no doubt, surely, (it is, of a) true (-ly, -th).

552. אֻמְנָם **'umnâm,** *oom-nawm´;* an orth. var. of 551:—in (very) deed; of a surety.

553. אָמַץ **'âmats,** *aw-mats´;* a prim. root; to *be alert,* phys. (on foot) or ment. (in courage):—confirm, be courageous (of good courage, stedfastly minded, strong, stronger), establish, fortify, harden, increase, prevail, strengthen (self), make strong (obstinate, speed).

554. אָמֹץ **'âmôts,** *aw-mohts´;* prob. from 553; of a *strong* color, i.e. *red* (others *fleet*):—bay.

555. אֹמֶץ **'ômets,** *o´-mets;* from 553; *strength:*—stronger.

אַמִּץ **'ammîts.** See 533.

556. אַמְצָה **'amtsâh,** *am-tsaw´;* from 553; *force:*—strength.

557. אַמְצִי **'Amtsîy,** *am-tsee´;* from 553; *strong; Amtsi,* an Isr.:—Amzi.

558. אֲמַצְיָה **'Ămatsyâh,** *am-ats-yaw´;* or אֲמַצְיָהוּ **'Ămatsyâhûw,** *am-ats-yaw´-hoo;* from 553 and 3050; *strength of Jah; Amatsjah,* the name of four Isr.:—Amaziah.

559. אָמַר **'âmar,** *aw-mar´;* a prim. root; to *say* (used with great latitude):—answer, appoint, avouch, bid, boast self, call, certify, challenge, charge, + (at the, give) command (ment), commune, consider, declare, demand, × desire, determine, × expressly, × indeed, × intend, name, × plainly, promise, publish, report, require, say, speak (against, of), × still, × suppose, talk, tell, term, × that is, × think, use [speech], utter, × verily, × yet.

560. אֲמַר **'ămar** (Chald.), *am-ar´;* corresp. to 559:—command, declare, say, speak, tell.

561. אֵמֶר **'êmer,** *ay´-mer; from 559; something said:*—answer, × appointed unto him, saying, speech, word.

562. אֹמֶר **'ômer,** *o´-mer;* the same as 561:—promise, speech, thing, word.

563. אִמַּר **'immar** (Chald.), *im-mar´;* perh. from 560 (in the sense of *bringing forth*); a *lamb:*—lamb.

564. אִמֵּר **'Immêr,** *im-mare´;* from 559; *talkative; Immer,* the name of five Isr.:—Immer.

565. אִמְרָה **'imrâh,** *im-raw´;* or אֶמְרָה **'emrâh,** *em-raw´;* fem. of 561, and mean. the same:—commandment, speech, word.

566. אִמְרִי **'Imrîy,** *im-ree´;* from 564; *wordy; Imri,* the name of two Isr.:—Imri.

567. אֱמֹרִי **'Ĕmôrîy,** *em-o-ree´;* prob. a patron. from an unused name derived from 559 in the sense of *publicity,* i.e. prominence; thus a *mountaineer;* an *Emorite,* one of the Canaanitish tribes:—Amorite.

568. אֲמַרְיָה **'Ămaryâh,** *am-ar-yaw´;* or (prol.) אֲמַרְיָהוּ **'Ămaryâhûw,** *am-ar-yaw´-hoo;* from 559 and 3050; *Jah has said* (i.e. promised); *Amarjah,* the name of nine Isr.:—Amariah.

569. אַמְרָפֶל **'Amrâphel,** *am-raw-fel´;* of uncert. (perh. for.) der.; *Amraphel,* a king of Shinar:—Amraphel.

570. אֶמֶשׁ **'emesh,** *eh´-mesh;* time *past,* i.e. *yesterday* or *last night:*—former time, yesterday (-night).

571. אֱמֶת **'emeth,** *eh´-meth;* contr. from 539; *stability;* fig. *certainty, truth, trustworthiness:*—assured (-ly), establishment, faithful, right, sure, true (-ly, -th), verity.

572. אַמְתַּחַת **'amtachath,** *am-takh´-ath;* from 4969; prop. something *expansive,* i.e. a *bag:*—sack.

573. אֲמִתַּי **'Ămittay,** *am-it-tah´ee;* from 571; *veracious; Amittai,* an Isr.:—Amittai.

574. אֵמְתָנִי **'emtânîy** (Chald.), *em-taw-nee´;* from a root corresp. to that of 4975; well-*loined* (i.e. burly) or *mighty:*—terrible.

575. אָן **ân,** *awn;* or אָנָה **'ânâh,** *aw´-naw;* contr. from 370; *where?;* hence *whither?, when?;* also *hither* and *thither:*— + any (no) whither, now, where, whither (-soever).

אֹן **'Ôn.** See 204.

576. אֲנָא **'ănâ'** (Chald.), *an-aw´;* or אֲנָה **'ănâh** (Chald.), *an-aw´;* corresp. to 589; *I:*—I, as for me.

577. אָנָּא **'ânnâ',** *awn´-naw;* or אָנָּה **'ânnâh,** *awn´-naw;* appar. contr. from 160 and 4994: *oh now!:*—I (me) beseech (pray) thee, O.

אֲנָה **'ănâh.** See 576.

אָנָה **'ânâh.** See 575.

578. אָנָה **'ânâh,** *aw-naw´;* a prim. root; to *groan:*—lament, mourn.

579. אָנָה **'ânâh,** *aw-naw´;* a prim. root [perh. rather ident. with 578 through the idea of *contraction* in anguish]; to *approach;* hence to *meet* in various senses:—befall, deliver, happen, seek a quarrel.

אָנָּה **'ânnâh.** See 577.

580. אֲנוּ **'ănûw,** *an-oo´;* contr. for 587; *we:*—we.

אנוֹ **Ônôw.** See 207.

581. אִנּוּן **'innûwn** (Chald.), *in-noon´;* or (fem.) אִנִּין **'innîyn** (Chald.), *in-neen´;* corresp. to 1992; *they:*— × are, them, these.

582. אֱנוֹשׁ **'ĕnôwsh,** *en-oshe´;* from 605; prop. a *mortal* (and thus differing from the more dignified 120); hence a *man* in gen. (singly or collect.):—another, × [blood-] thirsty, certain, chap [-man], divers, fellow, × in the flower of their age, husband, (certain, mortal) man, people, person, servant, some (× of them), + stranger, those, + their trade. It is often unexpressed in the Engl. version, especially when used in apposition with another word. Comp. 376.

583. אֱנוֹשׁ **'Ĕnôwsh,** *en-ohsh´;* the same as 582; *Enosh,* a son of Seth:—Enos.

584. אָנַח **'ânach,** *aw-nakh´;* a prim. root; to *sigh:*—groan, mourn, sigh.

585. אֲנָחָה **'ănâchâh,** *an-aw-khaw´;* from 584; *sighing:*—groaning, mourn, sigh.

586. אֲנַחְנָא **'ănachnâ'** (Chald.), *an-akh´-naw;* or אֲנַחְנָה **'ănachnâh** (Chald.), *an-akh-naw´;* corresp. to 587; *we:*—we.

587. אֲנַחְנוּ **'ănachnûw,** *an-akh´-noo,* appar. from 595; *we:*—ourselves, us, we.

588. אֲנָחֲרָת **'Ănâchărâth,** *an-aw-kha-rawth´;* prob. from the same root as 5170; a *gorge* or narrow pass; *Anacharath,* a place in Pal.:—Anaharath.

589. אֲנִי **'ănîy,** *an-ee´;* contr. from 595; *I:*—I, (as for) me, mine, myself, we, × which, × who.

590. אֳנִי **'ŏnîy,** *on-ee´;* prob. from 579 (in the sense of *conveyance*); a *ship* or (collect.) a *fleet:*—galley, navy (of ships).

591. אֳנִיָּה **'ŏnîyâh,** *on-ee-yaw´;* fem. of 590; a *ship:*—ship ([-men]).

592. אֲנִיָּה **'ănîyâh,** *an-ee-yaw´;* from 578; *groaning:*—lamentation, sorrow.

אִנִּין **'innîyn.** See 581.

593. אֲנִיעָם **'Ănîy'âm,** *an-ee-awm´;* from 578 and 5971; *groaning* of (the) *people; Aniam,* an Isr.:—Aniam.

594. אֲנָךְ **'ănâk,** *an-awk´;* prob. from an unused root mean. to *be narrow;* according to most a plumb-*line,* and to others a *hook:*—plumb-line.

595. אָנֹכִי **'ânôkîy,** *aw-no-kee´* (sometimes *aw-no´-kee*); a prim. pron.; *I:*—I, me, × which.

596. אָנַן **'ânan,** *aw-nan´;* a prim. root; to *mourn,* i.e. *complain:*—complain.

597. אָנַס **'ânaç,** *aw-nas´;* to *insist:*—compel.

598. אֲנַס **'ănaç** (Chald.), *an-as´;* corresp. to 597; fig. to *distress:*—trouble.

599. אָנַף **'ânaph,** *aw-naf´;* a prim. root; to *breathe* hard, i.e. *be enraged:*—be angry (displeased).

600. אֱנַף **'ănaph** (Chald.), *an-af´;* corresp. to 639 (only in the plur. as a sing.); the *face:*—face, visage.

601. אֲנָפָה **'ănâphâh,** *an-aw-faw´;* from 599; an unclean bird, perh. the *parrot* (from its *irascibility*):—heron.

602. אָנַק **'ânaq,** *aw-nak´;* a prim. root; to *shriek:—cry, groan.*

603. אֲנָקָה **'ănâqâh,** *an-aw-kaw´,* from 602; *shrieking:*—crying out, groaning, sighing.

604. אֲנָקָה **'ănâqâh,** *an-aw-kaw´;* the same as 603; some kind of lizard, prob. the *gecko* (from its *wail*):—ferret.

605. אָנַשׁ **'ânash,** *aw-nash´;* a prim. root; to *be frail, feeble,* or (fig.) *melancholy:*—desperate (-ly wicked), incurable, sick, woeful.

606. אֱנָשׁ **'ĕnâsh** (Chald.), *en-awsh´;* or אֱנַשׁ **'ĕnash** (Chald.), *en-ash´;* corresp. to 582; a *man:*—man, + whosoever.

אַנְתְּ **'ant.** See 859.

607. אַנְתָּה **'antâh** (Chald.), *an-taw´;* corresp. to 859; *thou:*—as for thee, thou.

608. אַנְתּוּן **'antûwn** (Chald.), *an-toon´;* plur. of 607; *ye:*—ye.

609. אָסָא **'Âça',** *aw-saw´;* of uncert. der.; *Asa,* the name of a king and of a Levite:—Asa.

610. אָסוּךְ **'âçûwk,** *aw-sook´;* from 5480; *anointed,* i.e. an oil-*flask:*—pot.

611. אָסוֹן **'âçôwn,** *aw-sone´;* of uncert. der.; *hurt:*—mischief.

612. אֵסוּר **'êçûwr,** *ay-soor´;* from 631; a *bond* (espec. *manacles* of a prisoner):—band, + prison.

613. אֱסוּר **'ĕçûwr** (Chald.), *es-oor´;* corresp. to 612:—band, imprisonment.

614. אָסִיף **'âçîyph,** *aw-seef´;* or אָסִף **'âçîph,** *aw-seef´;* from 622; *gathered,* i.e. (abstr.) a *gathering* in of crops:—ingathering.

615. אָסִיר **'âçîyr,** *aw-sere´;* from 631; *bound,* i.e. a *captive:*—(those which are) bound, prisoner.

616. אַסִּיר **'aççîyr,** *as-sere´;* for 615:—prisoner.

617. אַסִּיר **'Aççîyr,** *as-sere´;* the same as 616; *prisoner; Assir,* the name of two Isr.:—Assir.

618. אָסָם **'âçâm,** *aw-sawm´;* from an unused root mean. to *heap* together; a *storehouse* (only in the plur.):—barn, storehouse.

619. אַסְנָה **'Açnâh,** *as-naw´;* of uncert. der.; *Asnah,* one of the Nethinim:—Asnah.

620. אָסְנַפַּר **'Oçnappar,** *os-nap-par´;* of for. der.; *Osnappar,* an Assyrian king:—Asnapper.

621. אָסְנַת **'Âçᵉnath,** *aw-se-nath´;* of Eg. der.; *Asenath,* the wife of Joseph:—Asenath.

622. אָסַף **'âçaph,** *aw-saf´;* a prim. root; to *gather* for any purpose; hence to *receive, take away,* i.e. remove (destroy, leave behind, put up, restore, etc.):—assemble, bring, consume, destroy, fetch, gather (in, together, up again), × generally, get (him), lose, put all together, receive, recover [another from leprosy], (be) rereward, × surely, take (away, into, up), × utterly, withdraw.

623. אָסָף **'Âçâph,** *aw-sawf´;* from 622; *collector; Asaph,* the name of three Isr., and of the family of the first:—Asaph.

אָסִף **'âçîph.** See 614.

624. אָסֻף **'âçûph,** *aw-soof´;* pass. part. of 622; *collected* (only in the plur.), i.e. a *collection* (of offerings):—threshold, Asuppim.

625. אֹסֶף **'ôçeph,** *o´-sef;* from 622; a *collection* (of fruits):—gathering.

626. אֲסֵפָה **'ăçêphâh,** *as-ay-faw´;* from 622; a *collection* of people (only adv.):— × together.

627. אֲסֻפָּה **'ăçuppâh,** *as-up-paw´;* fem. of 624; a *collection* of (learned) men (only in the plur.):—assembly.

628. אַסְפְּסֻף **'açpᵉçûph,** *as-pes-oof´;* by redupl. from 624; *gathered up together,* i.e. a promiscuous *assemblage* (of people):—mixt multitude.

629. אָסְפַּרְנָא **'oçparnâ'** (Chald.). *os-par-naw´;* of Pes. der.; *diligently:*—fast, forthwith, speed (-ily)

630. אַסְפָּתָא **'Açpâthâ',** *as-paw-thaw´;* of Pers. der.; *Aspatha,* a son of Haman:—Aspatha.

631. אָסַר **'âçar,** *aw-sar´;* a prim. root; to *yoke* or *hitch;* by anal. to *fasten* in any sense, to *join* battle:—bind, fast, gird, harness, hold, keep, make ready, order, prepare, prison (-er), put in bonds, set in array, tie.

632. אֱסָר **'ĕçâr,** *es-awr´;* or אִסָּר **"iççâr,** *is-saw´;* from 631; an *obligation* or *vow* (of abstinence):—binding, bond.

633. אֱסָר **'ĕçâr** (Chald.), *es-awr´;* corresp. to 632 in a legal sense; an *interdict:*—decree.

634. אֵסַר־חַדּוֹן **'Êçar-Chaddôwn,** *ay-sar´ chad-dohn´;* of for. der.; *Esarchaddon,* an Assyr. king:—Esar-haddon.

635. אֶסְתֵּר **'Eçtêr,** *es-tare´;* of Pers. der.; *Ester,* the Jewish heroine:—Esther.

636. אָע **'â'** (Chald.), *aw;* corresp. to 6086; a *tree* or *wood:*—timber, wood.

637. אַף **'aph,** *af;* a prim. particle; mean. *accession* (used as an adv. or conj.); *also* or *yea;* adversatively *though:*—also, + although, and (furthermore, yet), but, even, + how much less (more, rather than), moreover, with, yea.

638. אַף **'aph** (Chald.), *af:* corresp. to 637:—also.

639. אַף **'aph,** *af;* from 599; prop. the *nose* or *nostril;* hence the *face,* and occasionally a *person;* also (from the rapid breathing in passion) *ire:*—anger (-gry), + before, countenance, face, + forbearing, forehead, + [long-] suffering, nose, nostril, snout, × worthy, wrath.

640. אָפַד **'âphad,** *aw-fad´;* a prim. root [rather a denom. from 646]; to *gird* on (the ephod):—bind, gird.

אֵפֹד **'êphôd.** See 646.

641. אֵפֹד **'Êphôd,** *ay-fode´;* the same as 646 short.; *Ephod,* an Isr.:—Ephod.

642. אֲפֻדָּה **'êphuddâh,** *ay-food-daw´;* fem. of 646; a *girding* on (of the ephod); hence gen. a *plating* (of metal):—ephod, ornament.

643. אַפֶּדֶן **'appeden,** *ap-peh´-den;* appar. of for. der.; a *pavilion* or palace-tent:—palace.

644. אָפָה **'âphâh,** *aw-faw´;* a prim. root; to *cook,* espec. to *bake:*—bake, (-r, [-meats]).

אֵפָה **'êphâh.** See 374.

645. אֵפוֹ **'ephôw,** *ay-fo´;* or אֵפוֹא **'êphôw',** *ay-fo´;* from 6311; strictly a demonstrative particle, *here;* but used of time, *now* or *then:*—here, now, where?

646. אֵפוֹד **'êphôwd,** *ay-fode´;* rarely אֵפֹד **'êphôd,** *ay-fode;´;* prob. of for. der.; a *girdle;* spec. the *ephod* or high-priest's shoulder piece; also gen. an *image:*—ephod.

647. אֲפִיחַ **'Ăphîyach,** *af-ee´-akh;* perh. from 6315; *breeze; Aphiach,* an Isr.:—Aphiah.

648. אָפִיל **'âphîyl,** *aw-feel´;* from the same as 651 (in the sense of *weakness*): *unripe:*—not grown up.

649. אַפַּיִם **'Appayim,** *ap-pah´-yim;* dual of 639; *two nostrils; Appajim,* an Isr.:—Appaim.

650. אָפִיק **'âphîyq,** *aw-feek´;* from 622; prop. *containing,* i.e. a *tube;* also a *bed* or *valley* of a stream; also a *strong* thing or a *hero:*—brook, channel, mighty, river, + scale, stream, strong piece.

אֹפִיר **'Ôphîyr.** See 211.

651. אָפֵל **'âphêl,** *aw-fale´;* from an unused root mean. to *set* as the sun; *dusky:*—very dark.

652. אֹפֶל **ôphel,** *o´-fel;* from the same as 651; *dusk:*—darkness, obscurity, privily.

653. אֲפֵלָה **'ăphêlâh,** *af-ay-law´;* fem. of 651; *duskiness,* fig. *misfortune;* concr. *concealment:*—dark, darkness, gloominess, × thick.

654. אֶפְלָל **'Ephlâl,** *ef-lawl´;* from 6419; *judge; Ephlal,* an Isr.:—Ephlal.

655. אֹפֶן **'ôphen,** *o´-fen;* from an unused root mean. to *revolve;* a *turn,* i.e. a *season:*— + fitly.

אֹפָן **'ôphân.** See 212.

656. אָפֵס **'âphêç,** *aw-face´;* a prim. root; to *disappear,* i.e. *cease:*—be clean gone (at an end, brought to nought), fail.

657. אֶפֶס **'epheç,** *eh´-fes;* from 656; *cessation,* i.e. an *end* (espec. of the earth); often used adv. *no further;* also (like 6466) the *ankle* (in the dual), as being the extremity of the leg or foot:—ankle, but (only), end, howbeit, less than nothing, nevertheless (where), no, none (be-

side), not (any, -withstanding), thing of nought, save (-ing), there, uttermost part, want, without (cause).

658. אֶפֶס דַּמִּים **'Epheç Dammîym,** *eh´-fes dam-meem´;* from 657 and the plur. of 1818; *boundary of blood*-drops; *Ephes-Dammim,* a place in Pal.:—Ephes-dammim.

659. אֵפַע **'êpha',** *eh´-fah;* from an unused root prob. mean. to *breathe;* prop. a *breath,* i.e. *nothing:*—of nought.

660. אֶפְעֶה **'eph'eh,** *ef-eh´;* from 659 (in the sense of *hissing*); an *asp* or other venomous serpent:—viper.

661. אָפַף **'âphaph,** *aw-faf´;* a prim. root; to *surround:*—compass.

662. אָפַק **'âphaq,** *aw-fak´;* a prim. root; to *contain,* i.e. (reflex.) *abstain:*—force (oneself), restrain.

663. אֲפֵק **'Ăphêq,** *af-ake´;* or אֲפִיק **'Ăphîyq,** *af-eek´;* from 662 (in the sense of *strength*); *fortress; Aphek* (or *Aphik*), the name of three places in Pal.:—Aphek, Aphik.

664. אֲפֵקָה **'Ăphêqâh,** *af-ay-kaw´;* fem. of 663; *fortress; Aphekah,* a place in Pal.:—Aphekah.

665. אֵפֶר **'êpher,** *ay´-fer;* from an unused root mean. to *bestrew; ashes:*—ashes.

666. אֲפֵר **'ăphêr,** *af-ayr´;* from the same as 665 (in the sense of *covering*); a *turban:*—ashes.

667. אֶפְרֹחַ **'ephrôach,** *ef-ro´-akh;* from 6524 (in the sense of *bursting* the shell); the *brood* of a bird:—young (one).

668. אַפִּרְיוֹן **'appiryôwn,** *ap-pir-yone´;* prob. of Eg. der.; a *palanquin:*—chariot.

669. אֶפְרַיִם **'Ephrayim,** *ef-rah´-yim;* dual of a masc. form of 672; *double fruit; Ephrajim,* a son of Joseph; also the tribe descended from him, and its territory:—Ephraim Ephraimites

670. אֲפָרְסַי **'Ăphârᵉçay** (Chald.), *af-aw-re-sah´-ee;* of for. or. (only in the plur.); an *Apharesite* or inhabitant of an unknown region of Assyria:—Apharsite.

671. אֲפָרְסְכַי **'Ăpharçᵉkay** (Chald.), *af-ar-sek-ah´ee;* or אֲפָרְסַתְכַי **'Ăpharçathkay** (Chald.), *af-ar-sath-kah´ee;* of for. or. (only in the plur.); an *Apharsekite* or *Apharsathkite,* an unknown Assyrian tribe:—Apharsachites, Apharsathchites.

672. אֶפְרָת **'Ephrâth,** *ef-rawth´;* or אֶפְרָתָה **'Ephrâthâh,** *ef-raw´-thaw;* from 6509; *fruitfulness; Ephrath,* another name for Bethlehem; once (Psa. 132 : 6) perh. for *Ephraim;* also of an Israelitish woman:—Ephrath, Ephratah.

673. אֶפְרָתִי **'Ephrâthîy,** *ef-rawth-ee´;* patrial from 672; an *Ephrathite* or an *Ephraimite:*—Ephraimite, Ephrathite.

674. אַפְּתֹם **'appᵉthôm** (Chald.), *ap-pe-thome´;* of Pers. or.; *revenue;* others *at the last:*—revenue.

675. אֶצְבּוֹן **'Etsbôwn,** *ets-bone´;* or אֶצְבֹּן **'Etsbôn,** *ets-bone´;* of uncert. der.; *Etsbon,* the name of two Isr.:—Ezbon.

676. אֶצְבַּע **'etsba',** *ets-bah´;* from the same as 6648 (in the sense of *grasping*); some thing to *seize* with, i.e. a *finger;* by anal. a *toe:*—finger, toe.

677. אֶצְבַּע **'etsba'** (Chald.), *ets-bah´;* corresp. to 676:—finger, toe.

678. אָצִיל **'âtsîyl,** *aw-tseel´;* from 680 (in its secondary sense of *separation*); an *extremity* (Isa. 41: 9), also a *noble:*—chief man, noble.

679. אַצִּיל **'atstsîyl,** *ats-tseel´;* from 680 (in its primary sense of *uniting*); a *joint* of the hand (i.e. *knuckle*); also (accord. to some) a *partywall (Ezek. 41 : 8):—[arm] hole, great.*

680. אָצַל **'âtsal,** *aw-tsal´;* a prim. root; prop. to *join;* used only as a denom. from 681; to *separate;* hence to *select, refuse, contract:*—keep, reserve, straiten, take.

681. אֵצֶל **'êtsel,** *ay-tsel;* from 680 (in the sense of *joining*); a *side;* (as a prep.) *near:*—at, (hard) by, (from) (beside), near (unto), toward, with. See also 1018.

682. אָצֵל **'Âtsêl,** *aw-tsale´;* from 680; *noble; Atsel,* the name of an Isr., and of a place in Pal.:—Azal, Azel.

683. אֲצַלְיָהוּ **'Ătsalyâhûw,** *ats-al-yaw´-hoo;* from 680 and 3050 prol.; *Jah has reserved; Atsaljah,* an Isr.:—Azaliah.

684. אֹצֶם **'Ôtsem,** *o´-tsem;* from an unused root prob. mean. to *be strong; strength* (i.e. *strong*); *Otsem,* the name of two Isr.:—Ozem.

685. אֶצְעָדָה **'ets'âdâh,** *ets-aw-daw´;* a var. from 6807; prop. a *step-chain;* by anal. a *bracelet:*—bracelet, chain.

686. אָצַר **'âtsar,** *aw-tsar;* a prim. root; to *store* up:—(lay up in) store, (make) treasure (-r).

687. אֵצֶר **'Êtser,** *ay´-tser;* from 686; *treasure; Etser,* an Idumæan:—Ezer.

688. אֶקְדָּח **'eqdâch,** *ek-dawkh´;* from 6916; *burning,* i.e. a *carbuncle* or other fiery gem:—carbuncle.

689. אַקּוֹ **'aqqôw,** *ak-ko´;* prob. from 602; *slender,* i.e. the *ibex:*—wild goat.

690. אֲרָא **'Ărâ',** *ar-raw´;* prob. for 738; *lion; Ara,* an Isr.:—Ara.

691. אֶרְאֵל **'er'êl,** *er-ale´;* prob. for 739; a *hero* (collect.):—valiant one.

692. אַרְאֵלִי **'Ar'êlîy,** *ar-ay-lee´;* from 691; *heroic; Areli* (or an *Arelite,* collect.)an Isr. and his desc.:—Areli, Arelites.

693. אָרַב **'ârab,** *aw-rab´;* a prim. root; to *lurk:*—(lie in) ambush (-ment), lay (lie in) wait.

694. אֲרָב **'Ărâb,** *ar-awb´;* from 693; *ambush; Arab,* a place in Pal.:—Arab.

695. אֶרֶב **'ereb,** *eh´-reb;* from 693; *ambuscade:*—den, lie in wait.

696. אֹרֶב **'ôreb,** *o´-reb;* the same as 695:—wait.

אַרְבֵּאל **'Arbê'l.** See 1009.

697. אַרְבֶּה **'arbeh,** *ar-beh´;* from 7235; a *locust* (from its rapid *increase*):—grasshopper, locust.

698. אָרֳבָה **'orŏbâh,** *or-ob-aw´;* fem. of 696 (only in the plur.); *ambuscades:*—spoils.

699. אֲרֻבָּה **'ărubbâh,** *ar-oob-baw´;* fem. part. pass. of 693 (as if for *lurking*); a *lattice;* (by impl.) a *window, dove-cot* (because of the pigeon-holes), *chimney* (with its apertures for smoke), *sluice* (with openings for water):—chimney, window.

700. אֲרֻבּוֹת **'Ărubbôwth,** *ar-oob-both;* plur. of 699; *Arubboth,* a place in Pal.:—Aruboth.

701. אַרְבִּי **'Arbîy,** *ar-bee´;* patrial from 694; an *Arbite* or native of Arab:—Arbite.

702. אַרְבַּע **'arba',** *ar-bah´;* masc. אַרְבָּעָה **'arbâ'âh,** *ar-baw-aw´;* from 7251; *four:*—four.

703. אַרְבַּע **'arba'** (Chald.), *ar-bah´;* corresp. to 702:—four.

704. אַרְבַּע **'Arba',** *ar-bah´;* the same as 702; *Arba,* one of the Anakim:—Arba.

אַרְבָּעָה **'arbâ'âh.** See 702.

705. אַרְבָּעִים **'arbâ'îym,** *ar-baw-eem´;* multiple of 702; *forty:*—forty.

706. אַרְבַּעְתַּיִם **'arba'tayim,** *ar-bah-tah´-yim;* dual of 702; *fourfold:*—fourfold.

707. אָרַג **'ârag,** *aw-rag´;* a prim. root; to *plait* or *weave:*—weaver (-r).

708. אֶרֶג **'ereg,** *eh-reg;* from 707; a *weaving;* a *braid;* also a *shuttle:*—beam, weaver's shuttle.

709. אַרְגֹּב **'Argôb,** *ar-gobe´;* from the same as 7263; *stony; Argob,* a district of Pal.:—Argob.

710. אַרְגְּוָן **'argᵉvân,** *arg-ev-awn´;* a var. for 713; *purple:*—purple.

711. אַרְגְּוָן **'argᵉvân** (Chald.), *arg-ev-awn´;* corresp. to 710:—scarlet.

712. אַרְגָּז **'argâz,** *ar-gawz´;* perh. from 7264 (in the sense of being *suspended*); a *box* (as a pannier):—coffer.

713. אַרְגָּמָן **'argâmân,** *ar-gaw-mawn´;* of for. or.; *purple* (the color or the dyed stuff):—purple.

714. אַרְדְּ **'Ard,** *ard;* from an unused root prob. mean. to *wander; fugitive; Ard,* the name of two Isr.:—Ard.

715. אַרְדּוֹן **'Ardôwn,** *ar-dohn´;* from the same as 714; *roaming; Ardon,* an Isr.:—Ardon.

716. אַרְדִּי **'Ardîy,** *ar-dee´;* patron. from 714; an *Ardite* (collect.) or desc. of Ard:—Ardites.

717. אָרָה **'ârâh,** *aw-raw´;* a prim. root; to *pluck:*—gather, pluck.

718. אֲרוּ **'ărûw** (Chald.), *ar-oo´;* prob. akin to 431; *lo!:*—behold, lo.

719. אַרְוַד **'Arvad,** *ar-vad´;* prob. from 7300; a refuge for the *roving; Arvad,* an island city of Pal.:—Arvad.

720. אֲרוֹד **'Ărôwd,** *ar-ode´;* an orth. var. of 719; *fugitive; Arod,* an Isr.:—Arod.

721. אַרְוָדִי **'Arvâdîy,** *ar-vaw-dee´;* patrial from 719; an *Arvadite* or citizen of Arvad:—Arvadite.

722. אֲרוֹדִי **'Ărôwdîy,** *ar-o-dee´;* patron. from 721; an *Arodite* or desc. of Arod:—Arodi, Arodites.

723. אֻרְוָה **'urvâh,** *oor-vaw´;* or, אֲרָיָה **'ărâyâh,** *ar-aw-yah´;* from 717 (in the sense of *feeding*); a *herding-place* for an animal:—stall.

724. אֲרוּכָה **'ărûwkâh,** *ar-oo-kaw´;* or אֲרֻכָה **'ărûkâh,** *ar-oo-kaw´;* fem. pass. part. of 748 (in the sense of *restoring* to soundness); *wholeness* (lit. or fig.):—health, made up, perfected.

725. אֲרוּמָה **'Ărûwmâh,** *ar-oo-maw´;* a var. of 7316; *height; Arumah,* a place in Pal.:—Arumah.

726. אֲרוֹמִי° **'Ărôwmîy,** *ar-o-mee´;* a clerical error for 130; an *Edomite* (as in the marg.):—Syrian.

727. אָרוֹן **'ârôwn,** *aw-rone´;* or אָרֹן **'ârôn,** *aw-rone´;* from 717 (in the sense of *gathering*); a *box:*—ark, chest, coffin.

728. אֲרַוְנָה **'Ăravnâh,** *ar-av-naw´;* or (by transp.) אוֹרְנָה° **'Ôwrnâh,** *ore-naw´;* or אַרְנִיָּה° **'Arnîyah,** *ar-nee-yaw´;* all by orth. var. for 771; *Aravnah* (or *Arnijah* or *Ornah*), a Jebusite:—Araunah.

729. אָרַז **'âraz,** *aw-raz´;* a prim. root; to be *firm;* used only in the pass. participle as a denom. from 730; of *cedar:*—made of cedar.

730. אֶרֶז **'erez,** *eh´-rez;* from 729; a *cedar* tree (from the tenacity of its roots):—cedar (tree).

731. אַרְזָה **'arzâh,** *ar-zaw´;* fem. of 730; *cedar* wainscoting:—cedar work.

732. אָרַח **'ârach,** *aw-rakh´;* a prim. root; to *travel:*—go, wayfaring (man).

733. אָרַח **'Ârach,** *aw-rakh´;* from 732; *wayfaring; Arach,* the name of three Isr.:—Arah.

734. אֹרַח **'ôrach,** *o´-rakh;* from 732; a well trodden *road* (lit. or fig.); also a *caravan:*—manner, path, race, rank, traveller, troop, [by-, high-] way.

735. אֹרַח **'ôrach** (Chald.), *o´-rakh;* corresp. to 734; a *road:*—way.

736. אֹרְחָה **'ôrᵉchâh,** *o-rekh-aw´;* fem. act. part. of 732; a *caravan:*—(travelling) company.

737. אֲרֻחָה **'ărûchâh,** *ar-oo-khaw´;* fem. pass. part. of 732 (in the sense of *appointing*); a *ration* of food:—allowance, diet, dinner, victuals.

738. אֲרִי **'ărîy,** *ar-ee´;* or (prol.) אַרְיֵה **'aryêh,** *ar-yay´;* from 717 (in the sense of *violence*); a *lion:*—(young) lion, + pierce [*from the marg.*].

739. אֲרִיאֵל **'ărîy'êl,** *ar-ee-ale´;* or אֲרִאֵל **'ărî'êl,** *ar-ee-ale´;* from 738 and 410; *lion of God,* i.e. *heroic:*—lionlike men.

740. אֲרִיאֵל **'Ărî'êl,** *ar-ee-ale´;* the same as 739; *Ariel,* a symb. name for Jerusalem, also the name of an Isr.:—Ariel.

741. אֲרִאֵיל **'ărî'êyl,** *ar-ee-ale´;* either by transposition for 739 or, more prob., an orth. var. for 2025; the *altar* of the Temple:—altar.

742. אֲרִידַי **'Ărîyday,** *ar-ee-dah´-ee;* of Pers. or.; *Aridai,* a son of Haman:—Aridai.

743. אֲרִידָתָא **'Ărîydâthâ',** *ar-ee-daw-thaw´;* of Pers. or.; *Aridatha,* a son of Haman:—Aridatha.

אַרְיֵה **'aryêh.** See 738.

744. אַרְיֵה **'aryêh** (Chald.), *ar-yay´;* corresp. to 738:—lion.

745. אַרְיֵה **'Aryêh,** *ar-yay´;* the same as 738; *lion; Arjeh,* an Isr.:—Arieh.

אֲרָיָה **'ărâyâh.** See 723.

746. אַרְיוֹךְ **'Ăryôwk,** *ar-yoke´;* of for. or.; *Arjok,* the name of two Babylonians:—Arioch.

747. אֲרִיסַי **'Ărîyçay,** *ar-ee-sah´-ee;* of Pers. or.; *Arisai,* a son of Haman:—Arisai.

748. אָרַךְ **'ârak,** *aw-rak´;* a prim. root; to *be* (caus. *make*) *long* (lit. or fig.):—defer, draw out, lengthen, (be, become, make, pro-) long, + (out-, over-) live, tarry (long).

749. אֲרַךְ **'ărak** (Chald.), *ar-ak´;* prop. corresp. to 748, but used only in the sense of *reaching* to a given point; to *suit:*—be meet.

750. אָרֵךְ **'ârêk** *aw-rake´;* from 748; *long:*—long [-suffering, -winged], patient, slow [to anger].

751. אֶרֶךְ **'Erek,** *eh´-rek;* from 748; *length; Erek,* a place in Bab.:—Erech.

752. אָרֹךְ **'âtôk,** *aw-roke´;* from 748; *long:*—long.

753. אֹרֶךְ **'ôrek,** *o´-rek;*from 748; *length:*— + for ever, length, long.

754. אַרְכָּא **'arkâ'** (Chald.), *ar-kaw´;* or אַרְכָּה **'arkâh** (Chald.), *arkaw´;* from 749; *length:*—lengthening, prolonged.

755. אַרְכֻבָה **'arkûbâh** (Chald.), *ar-koo-baw´* from an unused root corresp. to 7392 (in the sense of *bending* the knee); the *knee:*—knee.

אֲרֻכָה **'ărûkâh.** See 724.

756. אַרְכְּוָי **'Arkᵉvay** (Chald.), *ar-kev-ah´ee;* patrial from 751; an *Arkevite* (collect.) or native of Erek:—Archevite.

757. אַרְכִּי **'Arkîy,** *ar-kee´;* patrial from another place (in Pal.) of similar name with 751; an *Arkite* or native of Erek:—Archi, Archite.

758. אֲרָם **'Ărâm,** *arawm´;* from the same as 759; the *highland; Aram* or Syria, and its inhabitants; also the name of a son of Shem, a grandson of Nahor, and of an Isr.:—Aram, Mesopotamia, Syria, Syrians.

759. אַרְמוֹן **'armôwn,** *ar-mone´;* from an unused root (mean. to *be elevated*); a *citadel* (from its *height*):—castle, palace. Comp. 2038.

760. אֲרַם צוֹבָה **'Ăram Tsôbâh,** *ar-am´ tso-baw´;* from 758 and 6678; *Aram of Tsoba* (or Cœle-Syria):—Aram-zobah.

761. אֲרַמִּי **'Ărammîy,** *ar-am-mee´;* patrial from 758; an *Aramite* or Aramæan:—Syrian, Aramitess.

762. אֲרָמִית **'Ărâmîyth,** *ar-aw-meeth´;* fem. of 761; (only adv.) *in Aramœan:*—in the Syrian language (tongue), in Syriack.

763. אֲרַם נַהֲרַיִם **'Ăram Nahărayim,** *ar-am´ nah-har-ah´-yim;* from 758 and the dual of 5104; *Aram of* (the) *two rivers* (Euphrates and Tigris) or Mesopotamia:—Aham-naharaim, Mesopotamia.

764. אַרְמֹנִי **'Armônîy,** *ar-mo-nee´;* from 759; *palatial; Armoni,* an Isr.:—Armoni.

765. אֲרָן **'Ărân,** *ar-awn´;* from 7442; *stridulous; Aran,* an Edomite:—Aran.

766. אֹרֶן **'ôren,** *o´-ren;* from the same as 765 (in the sense of *strength*); the *ash* tree (from its toughness):—ash.

767. אֹרֶן **'Ôren,** *o´-ren;* the same as 766; *Oren,* an Isr.:—Oren.

אָרֹן **'ârôn.** See 727.

768. אַרְנֶבֶת **'arnebeth,** *ar-neh´-beth;* of uncert. der.; the *hare:*—hare.

769. אַרְנוֹן **'Arnôwn,** *ar-nohn´;* or אַרְנֹן **'Arnôn,** *ar-nohn´;* from 7442; a *brawling* stream; the *Arnon,* a river east of the Jordan; also its territory:—Arnon.

אַרְנִיָּה° **'Arnîyah.** See 728.

770. אַרְנָן **'Arnân,** *ar-nawn´;* prob. from the same as 769; *noisy; Arnan,* an Isr.:—Arnan.

771. אָרְנָן **'Ornân,** *or-nawn´;* prob. from 766; *strong; Ornan,* a Jebusite:—Ornan. See 728.

772. אֲרַע **'ăra'** (Chald.), *ar-ah´;* corresp. to 776; the *earth;* by impl. (fig.) *low:*—earth, inferior.

773. אַרְעִית **'ar'îyth** (Chald.), *arh-eeth´;* fem. of 772; the *bottom:*—bottom.

774. אַרְפָּד **'Arpâd.** *ar-pawd´;* from 7502; *spread* out: *Arpad,* a place in Syria:—Arpad, Arphad.

775. אַרְפַּכְשַׁד **'Arpakshad,** *ar-pak-shad´;* prob of for. or.; *Arpakshad,* a son of Noah; also the region settled by him:—Arphaxad.

776. אֶרֶץ **'erets,** *eh´-rets;* from an unused root prob. mean. to *be firm;* the *earth* (at large, or partitively a *land*):— × common, country, earth, field, ground, land, × nations, way, + wilderness, world.

777. אַרְצָא **'artsâ',** *ar-tsaw´;* from 776; *earthiness; Artsa,* an Isr.:—Arza.

778. אֲרַק **'ăraq** (Chald.), *ar-ak´;* by transmutation for 772; the *earth:*—earth.

779. אָרַר **'ârar,** *aw-rar´;* a prim. root; to *execrate;*— × bitterly curse.

780. אֲרָרַט **'Ărâraṭ,** *ar-aw-rat´;* of for. or.; *Ararat* (or rather Armenia):—Ararat, Armenia.

781. אָרַשׂ **'âras,** *aw-ras´;* a prim. root; to *engage* for matrimony:—betroth, espouse.

782. אֲרֶשֶׁת **'ăresheth,** *ar-eh´-sheth;* from 781 (in the sense of *desiring* to possess); a *longing* for:—request.

783. אַרְתַּחְשַׁשְׁתָּא **'Artachshashtâ',** *ar-takh-shash-taw´;* or אַרְתַּחְשַׁשְׁתְּא **'Artachshasht',** *ar-takh-shasht´;* or by perm. אַרְתַּחְשַׁסְתְּא **'Artachshaçt,** *ar-takh-shast´;* of for. or.; *Artachshasta* (or Artaxerxes), a title (rather than name) of several Pers. kings:—Artaxerxes.

784. אֵשׁ **'êsh,** *aysh;*a prim. word; *fire* (lit. or fig.):—burning, fiery, fire, flaming, hot.

785. אֵשׁ **'êsh** (Chald.), *aysh;* corresp. to 784:—flame.

786. אִשׁ **'îsh,** *eesh;* ident. (in or. and formation) with 784; *entity;* used only adv., there *is* or *are:*—are there, none can. Comp. 3426.

787. אשׁ **'ôsh** (Chald.), *ohsh;* corresp. (by transp. and abb.) to 803; a *foundation:*—foundation.

788. אַשְׁבֵּל **'Ashbêl,** *ash-bale´;* prob. from the same as 7640; *flowing; Ashbel,* an Isr.:—Ashbel.

789. אַשְׁבֵּלִי **'Ashbêlîy,** *ash-bay-lee´;* patron. from 788; an *Ashbelite* (collect.) or desc. of Ashbel:—Ashbelites.

790. אֶשְׁבָּן **'Eshbân,** *esh-bawn´;* prob. from the same as 7644; *vigorous; Eshban,* an Idumæan:—Eshban.

791. אַשְׁבֵּעַ **'Ashbêa',** *ash-bay´-ah;* from 7650; *adjurer; Asbeä,* an Isr.:—Ashbea.

792. אֶשְׁבַּעַל **'Eshba'al,** *esh-bah´-al;* from 376 and 1168; *man of Baal; Eshbaal* (or Ishbosheth), a son of King Saul:—Eshbaal.

793. אֶשֶׁד **'eshed,** *eh´-shed;* from an unused root mean. to *pour;* an *outpouring:*—stream.

794. אֲשֵׁדָה **'ăshêdâh,** *ash-ay-daw´;* fem. of 793; a *ravine:*—springs.

795. אַשְׁדּוֹד **'Ashdôwd,** *ash-dode´;* from 7703; *ravager; Ashdod,* a place in Pal.:—Ashdod.

796. אַשְׁדּוֹדִי **'Ashdôwdîy,** *ash-do-dee´;* patrial from 795; an *Ashdodite* (often collect.) or inhabitant of Ashdod:—Ashdodites, of Ashdod.

797. אַשְׁדּוֹדִית **'Ashdôwdîyth,** *ash-do-deeth´;* fem. of 796; (only adv.) *in the language of Ashdod:*—in the speech of Ashdod.

798. אַשְׁדּוֹת הַפִּסְגָּה **'Ashdôwth hap-Piçgâh,** *ash-doth´hap-pis-gaw´;* from the plur. of 794 and 6449 with the art. interposed; *ravines of the Pisgah; Ashdoth-Pisgah,* a place east of the Jordan:—Ashdoth-pisgah.

799. אֶשְׁדָּת **'eshdâth,** *esh-dawth´;* from 784 and 1881; a *fire-law:*—fiery law.

800. אֶשָּׁה **'eshshâh,** *esh-shaw´;* fem. of 784; *fire:*—fire.

801. אִשֶּׁה **'ishshâh,** *ish-shaw´;* the same as 800, but used in a liturgical sense; prop. a *burnt-offering;* but occasionally of any *sacrifice:*—(offering, sacrifice), (made) by fire.

802. אִשָּׁה **'ishshâh,** *ish-shaw´;* fem. of 376 or 582; irregular plur. נָשִׁים **nâshîym,** *naw-sheem´;* a *woman* (used in the same wide sense as 582):—[adulter]ess, each, every, female, × many, + none, one, + together, wife, woman. Often unexpressed in English.

803. אֲשׁוּיָה° **'ăshûwyâh,** *ash-oo-yah´;* fem. pass. part. from an unused root mean. to *found; foundation:*—foundation.

804. אַשּׁוּר **'Ashshûwr,** *ash-shoor´;* or אַשֻּׁר **'Ashshûr,** *ash-shoor´;* appar. from 833 (in the sense of *successful*); *Ashshur,* the second son of Shem; also his desc. and the country occupied by them (i.e. Assyria), its region and its empire:—Asshur, Assur, Assyria, Assyrians. See 838.

805. אֲשׁוּרִי **'Ăshûwrîy,** *ash-oo-ree´;* or אַשּׁוּרִי **'Ashshûwrîy,** *ash-shoo-ree´;* from a patrial word of the same form as 804; an *Ashurite* (collect.) or inhab. of Ashur, a district in Pal.:—Asshurim, Ashurites.

806. אַשְׁחוּר **'Ashchûwr,** *ash-khoor´;* prob. from 7835; *black; Ashchur,* an Isr.:—Ashur.

807. אֲשִׁימָא **'Ăshîymâ',** *ash-ee-maw´;* of for. or.; *Ashima,* a deity of Hamath:—Ashima.

אֲשֵׁירָה **'ăshêyrah.** See 842.

808. אָשִׁישׁ **'âshîysh,** *aw-sheesh´;* from the same as 784 (in the sense of *pressing* down firmly; comp. 803); a (ruined) *foundation:*—foundation.

809. אֲשִׁישָׁה **'ăshîyshâh,** *ash-ee-shaw´;* fem. of 808; something closely *pressed* together, i.e. a *cake* of raisins or other comfits:—flagon.

810. אֶשֶׁךְ **'eshek,** *eh´-shek;* from an unused root (prob. mean. to *bunch* together); a *testicle* (as a *lump*):—stone.

811. אֶשְׁכּוֹל **'eshkôwl,** *esh-kole´;* or אֶשְׁכֹּל **'eshkôl,** *esh-kole´;* prob. prol. from 810; a *bunch of grapes* or other fruit:—cluster (of grapes).

812. אֶשְׁכֹּל **'Eshkôl,** *esh-kole´;* the same as 811; *Eshcol,* the name of an Amorite, also of a valley in Pal.:—Eshcol.

813. אַשְׁכְּנַז **'Ashkᵉnaz,** *ash-ken-az´;* of for. or.; *Ashkenaz,* a Japhethite, also his desc.:—Ashkenaz.

814. אֶשְׁכָּר **'eshkâr,** *esh-cawr´;* for 7939; a *gratuity:*—gift, present.

815. אֵשֶׁל **'êshel,** *ay´-shel;* from a root of uncert. signif.; a *tamarisk* tree; by extens. a *grove* of any kind:—grove, tree.

816. אָשַׁם **'âsham,** *aw-sham´;* or אָשֵׁם **'âshêm,** *aw-shame´;* a prim. root; to *be guilty;* by impl. to *be punished* or *perish:*— × certainly, be (-come, made) desolate, destroy, × greatly, be (-come, found, hold) guilty, offend (acknowledge offence), trespass.

817. אָשָׁם **âshâm,** *aw-shawm´;* from 816; *guilt;* by impl. a *fault;* also a *sin-offering:*—guiltiness, (offering for) sin, trespass (offering).

818. אָשֵׁם **'âshêm,** *aw-shame´;* from 816; *guilty;* hence *presenting a sin-offering:*—one which is faulty, guilty.

819. אַשְׁמָה **'ashmâh,** *ash-maw´;* fem. of 817; *guiltiness,* a *fault,* the *presentation of a sin-offering:*—offend, sin, (cause of) trespass (-ing, offering).

אַשְׁמוּרָה **'ashmûrâh.** See 821.

820. אַשְׁמָן **'ashmân,** *ash-mawn´;* prob. from 8081; a *fat* field:—desolate place.

821. אַשְׁמֻרָה **'ashmûrâh,** *ash-moo-raw´;* or אַשְׁמוּרָה **'ashmûwrâh,** *ash-moo-raw´;* or אַשְׁמֹרֶת **'ashmôreth,** *ash-mo´-reth;* (fem.) from 8104; a night *watch:*—watch.

822. אֶשְׁנָב **'eshnâb,** *esh-nawb´;* appar. from an unused root (prob. mean. to *leave interstices*); a latticed *window:*—casement, lattice.

823. אַשְׁנָה **'Ashnâh,** *ash-naw´;* prob. a var. for 3466; *Ashnah,* the name of two places in Pal.:—Ashnah.

824. אֶשְׁעָן **'Esh'ân,** *esh-awn´;* from 8172; *support; Eshan,* a place in Pal.:—Eshean.

825. אַשָּׁף **'ashshâph,** *ash-shawf´;* from an unused root (prob. mean. to *lisp,* i.e. *practice enchantment*); a *conjurer:*—astrologer.

826. אַשָּׁף **'ashshâph** (Chald.), *ash-shawf´;* corresp. to 825:—astrologer.

827. אַשְׁפָּה **'ashpâh,** *ash-paw´;* perh. (fem.) from the same as 825 (in the sense of *covering*); a *quiver* or arrow-case:—quiver.

828. אַשְׁפְּנַז **'Ashpᵉnaz,** *ash-pen-az´;* of for. or.; *Asphenaz,* a Bab. eunuch:—Ashpenaz.

829. אֶשְׁפָּר **'eshpâr,** *esh-pawr´;* of uncert. der.: a measured *portion:*—good piece (of flesh).

830. אַשְׁפֹּת **'ashpôth,** *ash-poth´;* or אַשְׁפּוֹת **'ashpôwth,** *ash-pohth´;* or (contr.) שְׁפֹת **'shᵉphôth,** *shef-ohth´;* plur. of a noun of the same form as 827, from 8192 (in the sense of *scraping*); a heap of *rubbish* or *filth:*—dung (hill).

831. אַשְׁקְלוֹן **'Ashqᵉlôwn,** *ash-kel-one´;* prob. from 8254 in the sense of *weighing*-place (i.e. *mart*); *Ashkelon,* a place in Pal.:—Ashkelon, Askalon.

832. אֶשְׁקְלוֹנִי **'Eshqᵉlôwnîy,** *esh-kel-o-nee´;* patrial from 831; an *Ashkelonite* (collect.) or inhab. of Ashkelon:—Eshkalonites.

833. אָשַׁר **'âshar,** *aw-shar´;* or אָשֵׁר **'âshêr,** *aw-share´;* a prim. root; to *be straight* (used in the widest sense, espec. to *be level, right,*

happy); fig. to *go forward, be honest, prosper:*—(call, be) bless (-ed, happy), go, guide, lead, relieve.

834. אֲשֶׁר **'âsher,** *ash-er´;* a prim. rel. pron. (of every gend. and numb.); *who, which, what, that;* also (as adv. and conjunc.) *when, where, how, because, in order that,* etc.:— × after, × alike, as (soon as), because, × every, for, + forasmuch, + from whence, + how (-soever), × if, (so) that ([thing] which, wherein), × though, + until, + whatsoever, when, where (+ -as, -in, -of, -on, -soever, -with), which, whilst, + whither (-soever), who (-m, -soever, -se). As it is indeclinable, it is often accompanied by the personal pron. expletively, used to show the connection.

835. אֶשֶׁר **'esher,** *eh´-sher;* from 833; *happiness;* only in masc. plur. constr. as interjec., how *happy!:*—blessed, happy.

836. אָשֵׁר **'Âshêr,** *aw-share´;* from 833; *happy; Asher,* a son of Jacob, and the tribe descended from him, with its territory; also a place in Pal.:—Asher.

837. אֹשֶׁר **'ôsher,** *o´-sher;* from 833; *happiness:*—happy.

838. אָשֻׁר **'âshûr,** *aw-shoor´;* or אַשֻּׁר **'ashshûr,** *ash-shoor´;* from 833 in the sense of *going;* a *step:*—going, step.

839. אֲשֻׁר **'ăshûr,** *ash-oor´;* contr. for 8391; the *cedar* tree or some other light elastic wood:—Ashurite.

אַשֻּׁר **'Ashshûr.** See 804, 838.

840. אֲשַׂרְאֵל **'Ăsar'êl,** *as-ar-ale´;* by orth. var. from 833 and 410; *right of God; Asarel,* an Isr.:—Asareel.

841. אֲשַׂרְאֵלָה **'Ăsar'êlâh,** *as-ar-ale´-aw;* from the same as 840; *right towards God; Asarelah,* an Isr.:—Asarelah. Comp. 3480.

842. אֲשֵׁרָה **'ăshêrâh,** *ash-ay-raw´;* or אֲשֵׁירָה **'ăshêyrâh,** *ash-ay-raw´;* from 833; *happy; Asherah* (or Astarte) a Phœnician goddess; also an *image* of the same:—grove. Comp. 6253.

843. אָשֵׁרִי **'Âshêrîy,** *aw-shay-ree´;* patron. from 836; an *Asherite* (collect.) or desc. of Asher:—Asherites.

844. אַשְׂרִיאֵל **'Asrîy'êl,** *as-ree-ale´;* an orth. var. for 840; *Asriel,* the name of two Isr.:—Ashriel, Asriel.

845. אַשְׂרִאֵלִי **'Asrî'êlîy,** *as-ree-ale-ee´;* patron. from 844; an *Asrielite* (collect.) or desc. of Asriel:—Asrielites.

846. אֻשַּׁרְנָא **'ushsharnâ'** (Chald.), *oosh-ar-naw´;* from a root corresp. to 833; a *wall* (from its uprightness):—wall.

847. אֶשְׁתָּאֹל **'Eshtâ'ôl,** *esh-taw-ole´;* or אֶשְׁתָּאוֹל **'Eshtâ'ôwl,** *esh-taw-ole´;* prob. from 7592; *intreaty; Eshtaol,* a place in Pal.:—Eshtaol.

848. אֶשְׁתָּאֻלִי **'Eshtâ'ûlîy,** *esh-taw-oo-lee´;* patrial from 847; an *Eshtaolite* (collect.) or inhab. of Eshtaol:—Eshtaulites.

849. אֶשְׁתַּדּוּר **'eshtaddûwr** (Chald.), *esh-tad-dure´;* from 7712 (in a bad sense); *rebellion:*—sedition.

850. אֶשְׁתּוֹן **'Eshtôwn,** *esh-tone´;* prob. from the same as 7764; *restful; Eshton,* an Isr.:—Eshton.

851. אֶשְׁתְּמֹעַ **'Eshtᵉmôa',** *esh-tem-o´-ah;* or אֶשְׁתְּמוֹעַ **'Eshtᵉmôwa',** *esh-tem-o´-ah;* or אֶשְׁתְּמֹה **'Eshtᵉmôh,** *esh-tem-o´;* from 8085 (in the sense of *obedience*); *Eshtemoa* or *Eshtemoh,* a place in Pal.:—Eshtemoa, Eshtemoh.

אַתְּ° **ath.** See 859.

852. אָת **'âth** (Chald.), *awth;* corresp. to 226; a *portent:*—sign.

853. אֵת **'êth,** *ayth;* appar. contr. from 226 in the demonstr. sense of *entity;* prop. *self* (but gen. used to point out more def. the object of a verb or prep., *even* or *namely*):—[*as such unrepresented in English.*]

854. אֵת **'êth,** *ayth;* prob. from 579; prop. *nearness* (used only as a prep. or adv.), *near;* hence gen. *with, by, at, among,* etc.:—against, among, before, by, for, from, in (-to), (out) of, with. Often with another prep. prefixed.

855. אֵת **'êth,** *ayth;* of uncert. der.; a *hoe* or other digging implement:—coulter, plowshare.

אַתָּ **'attâ.** See 859.

אָתָא **'âthâ',** See 857.

856. אֶתְבַּעַל **'Ethba'al,** *eth-bah´-al;* from 854 and 1168; *with Baal; Ethbaal,* a Phœnician king:—Ethbaal.

857. אָתָה **'âthâh,** *aw-thaw´;* or אָתָא **'âthâ',** *aw-thaw´;* a prim. root [collat. to 225 contr.]; to *arrive:*—(be-, things to) come (upon), bring.

858. אָתָה **'âthâh** (Chald.), *aw-thaw´;* or אָתָא **'âthâ'** (Chald.), *aw-thaw´;* corresp. to 857:—(be-) come, bring.

859. אַתָּה **'attâh,** *at-taw´;* or (short.) אַתָּ **'attâ,** *at-taw´;* or אַתְּ° **'ath,** *ath;* fem. (irreg.) sometimes אַתִּי **'attîy,** *at-tee´;* plur. masc. אַתֶּם **'attem,** *at-tem´;* fem. אַתֶּן **'atten,** *at-ten´;* or אַתֵּנָה **'attênâh,** *at-tay´-naw;* or אַתֵּנָּה **'attênnâh,** *at-tane´-naw;* a prim. pron. of the sec. pers.; *thou* and *thee,* or (plur.) *ye* and *you:*—thee, thou, ye, you.

860. אָתוֹן **'athôwn,** *aw-thone´;* prob. from the same as 386 (in the sense of *patience);* a female *ass* (from its docility):—(she) ass.

861. אַתּוּן **'attûwn** (Chald.), *at-toon´;* prob. from the corresp. to 784; prob. a *fire-place,* i.e. *furnace:*—furnace.

862. אַתּוּק **'attûwq,** *at-tooke´;* or אַתִּיק **'attîyq,** *at-teek´;* from 5423 in the sense of *decreasing;* a *ledge* or offset in a building:—gallery.

אַתִּי **'attîy.** See 859.

863. אִתַּי **'Ittay,** *it-tah´ee;* or אִיתַי **'Iythay,** *ee-thah´ee;* from 854; *near; Ittai* or *Ithai,* the name of a Gittite and of an Isr.:—Ithai, Ittai.

864. אֵתָם **'Êthâm,** *ay-thawm´;* of Eg. der.; *Etham,* a place in the Desert:—Etham.

אַתֶּם **'attem.** See 859.

865. אֶתְמוֹל **'ethmôwl,** *eth-mole´;* or אִתְמוֹל **'ithmôwl,** *ith-mole´;* or אֶתְמוּל **'ethmûwl,** *eth-mool´;* prob. from 853 or 854 and 4136; *heretofore;* def. *yesterday:*— + before (that) time, + heretofore, of late (old), + times past, yester[day].

אַתֶּן **atten.** See 859.

866. אֶתְנָה **'êthnâh,** *eth-naw´;* from 8566; a *present* (as the price of harlotry):—reward.

אַתֵּנָה **'attênâh,** or אַתֵּנָּה **'attênnâh.** See 859.

867. אֶתְנִי **'Ethnîy,** *eth-nee´;* perh. from 866; *munificence; Ethni,* an Isr.:—Ethni.

868. אֶתְנַן **'ethnan,** *eth-nan´;* the same as 866; a *gift* (as the price of harlotry or idolatry):—hire, reward.

869. אֶתְנַן **'Ethnan,** *eth-nan´;* the same as 868 in the sense of 867; *Ethnan,* an Isr.:—Ethnan.

870. אֲתַר **'ăthar** (Chald.), *ath-ar´;* from a root corresp. to that of 871; a *place;* (adv.) *after:*—after, place.

871. אֲתָרִים **'Ăthârîym,** *ath-aw-reem´;* plur. from an unused root (prob. mean. to *step*); *places; Atharim,* a place near Pal.:—spies.

ב

872. בְּאָה **bᵉ'âh,** *bĕ-aw;* from 935; an *entrance* to a building:—entry.

873. בִּאוּשׁ **bî'ûwsh** (Chald.) *be-oosh´;* from 888; *wicked:*—bad.

874. בָּאַר **'bâ'ar,** *baw-ar´;* a prim. root; to *dig;* by anal. to *engrave;* fig. to *explain:*—declare, (make) plain (-ly).

875. בְּאֵר **bᵉ'êr,** *bĕ-ayr´;* from 874; a *pit;* espec. a *well:*—pit, well.

876. בְּאֵר **Bᵉ'êr,** *bĕ-ayr´;* the same as 875; *Beër,* a place in the Desert, also one in Pal.:—Beer.

877. בֹּאר **bô'r,** *bore;* from 874; a *cistern:*—cistern.

878. בְּאֵרָא **Bᵉ'êrâ',** *bĕ-ay-raw´;* from 875; a *well; Beëra,* an Isr.:—Beera.

879. בְּאֵר אֵלִים **Bᵉ'êr 'Êlîym,** *bĕ-ayr´ ay-leem´;* from 875 and the plur. of 410; *well of heroes; Beër-Elim,* a place in the Desert:—Beer-elim.

880. בְּאֵרָה **Bᵉ'êrâh,** *bĕ-ay-raw´;* the same as 878; *Beërah,* an Isr.:—Beerah.

881. בְּאֵרוֹת **Bᵉ'êrôwth,** *bĕ-ay-rohth´;* fem. plur. of 875; *wells; Beëroth,* a place in Pal.:—Beeroth.

882. בְּאֵרִי **'Bᵉ'êrîy,** *bĕ-ay-ree´;* from 875; *fountained; Beëri,* the name of a Hittite and of an Isr.:—Beeri.

883. בְּאֵר לַחַי רֹאִי **Bᵉ'êr la-Chay Rô'îy,** *bĕ-ayr´ lakh-ah´ee ro-ee´;* from 875 and 2416

(with pref.) and 7203; *well of a living* (One) *my Seer; Beër-Lachai-Roï,* a place in the Desert:—Beer-lahai-roi.

884. בְּאֵר שֶׁבַע **B^e'êr Sheba',** *bĕ-ayr´ sheh´-bah;* from 875 and 7651 (in the sense of 7650); *well of an oath; Beër-Sheba,* a place in Pal.:—Beer-shebah.

885. בְּאֵרֹת בְּנֵי־יַעֲקָן **B^{e}êrôth B^{e}nêy-Ya'ăqan,** *bĕ-ay-roth´ bĕ-nay´ yah-a-can´;* from the fem. plur. of 875, and the plur. contr. of 1121, and 3292; *wells of* (the) *sons of Jaakan; Beeroth-Bene-Jaakan,* a place in the Desert:—Beeroth of the children of Jaakan.

886. בְּאֵרֹתִי **B^e'êrôthîy,** *bĕ-ay-ro-thee´;* patrial from 881; a *Beërothite* or inhab. of Beëroth:—Beerothite.

887. בָּאַשׁ **bâ'ash,** *baw-ash´;* a prim. root; to *smell* bad; fig. to *be offensive* morally:—(make to) be abhorred (had in abomination, loathsome, odious), (cause a, make to) stink (-ing savour), × utterly.

888. בְּאֵשׁ **b^e'êsh** (Chald.), *bĕ-aysh´;* corresp. to 887:—displease.

889. בְּאֹשׁ **'b^e'ôsh,** *bĕ-oshe´;* from 877; a *stench:*—stink.

890. בָּאְשָׁה **bo'shâh,** *bosh-aw´;* fem. of 889; *stink-weed* or any other noxious or useless plant:—cockle.

891. בְּאֻשִׁים **b^e'ûshîym,** *bĕ-oo-sheem´;* plur. of 889; *poison-berries:*—wild grapes.

892. בָּבָה **bâbâh,** *baw-baw´;* fem. act. part. of an unused root mean. to *hollow* out; something *hollowed* (as a *gate*), i.e. the *pupil* of the eye:—apple [of the eye].

893. בֵּבַי **Bêbay,** *bay-bah´ee;* prob. of for. or.; *Bebai,* an Isr.:—Bebai.

894. בָּבֶל **Bâbel,** *baw-bel´;* from 1101; *confusion; Babel* (i.e. Babylon), including Babylonia and the Bab. empire:—Babel, Babylon.

895. בָּבֶל **Bâbel** (Chald.), *baw-bel´;* corresp. to 894:—Babylon.

896. בַּבְלִי **Bablîy** (Chald.), *bab-lee´;* patrial from 895; a *Babylonian:*—Babylonia.

897. בַּג **bag,** *bag;* a Pers. word; *food:*—spoil [*from the marg. for* 957.]

898. בָּגַד **bâgad,** *baw-gad´;* a prim. root; to *cover* (with a garment); fig. to *act covertly;* by impl. to *pillage:*—deal deceitfully (treacherously, unfaithfully), offend, transgress (-or), (depart), treacherous (dealer, -ly, man), unfaithful (-ly, man), × very.

899. בֶּגֶד **beged,** *begh´-ed;* from 898; a *covering,* i.e. clothing; also *treachery* or *pillage:*—apparel, cloth (-es, -ing), garment, lap, rag, raiment, robe, × very [treacherously], vesture, wardrobe.

900. בֹּגְדוֹת **'bôg^{e}dôwth,** *bohg-ed-ôhth;* fem. plur. act. part. of 898; *treacheries:*—treacherous.

901. בָּגוֹד **bâgôwd,** *baw-gode´;* from 898; *treacherous:*—treacherous.

902. בִּגְוַי **Bigvay,** *big-vah´ee;* prob. of for. or.; *Bigvai,* an Isr.:—Bigvai.

903. בִּגְתָא **Bigthâ',** *big-thaw´;* of Pers. der.; *Bigtha,* a eunuch of Xerxes:—Bigtha.

904. בִּגְתָן **Bigthân,** *big-thawn´;* or בִּגְתָנָא **Bigthânâ',** *big-thaw´-naw;* of similar deriv. to 903; *Bigthan* or *Bigthana,* a eunuch of Xerxes:—Bigthan, Bigthana.

905. בַּד **bad,** *bad;* from 909; prop. *separation;* by impl. a *part* of the body, *branch* of a tree, *bar* for carrying; fig. *chief* of a city; espec. (with prep. pref.) as adv., *apart, only, besides:*—alone, apart, bar, besides, branch, by self, of each alike, except, only, part, staff, strength.

906. בַּד **bad,** *bad;* perh. from 909 (in the sense of *divided* fibres); flaxen *thread* or yarn; hence a *linen* garment:—linen.

907. בַּד **bad,** *bad;* from 908; a *brag* or *lie;* also a *liar:*—liar, lie.

908. בָּדָא **bâdâ',** *baw-daw';* a prim. root; (fig.) to *invent:*—devise, feign.

909. בָּדַד **bâdad,** *baw-dad´;* a prim. root; to *divide,* i.e. (reflex.) *be solitary:*—alone.

910. בָּדָד **bâdâd,** *baw-dawd´;* from 909; *separate;* adv. *separately:*—alone, desolate, only, solitary.

911. בְּדַד **B^{e}dad,** *bed-ad´;* from 909; *separation; Bedad,* an Edomite:—Bedad.

912. בֵּדְיָה **Bêd^{e}yâh,** *bay-dĕ-yaw´;* prob. shortened for 5662; *servant of Jehovah; Bedejah,* an Isr.:—Bedeiah.

913. בְּדִיל **b^{e}dîyl,** *bed-eel´;* from 914; *alloy (because removed* by smelting); by anal. *tin:*— + plummet, tin.

914. בָּדַל **bâdal,** *baw-dal´;* a prim. root; to *divide* (in var. senses lit. or fig., *separate, distinguish, differ, select,* etc.):—(make, put) difference, divide (asunder), (make) separate (self, -ation), sever (out), × utterly.

915. בָּדָל **bâdâl,** *baw-dawl´;* from 914; a *part:*—piece.

916. בְּדֹלַח **b^{e}dôlach,** *bed-o´-lakh;* prob. from 914; something in *pieces,* i.e. *bdellium,* a (fragrant) gum (perh. *amber*); others a *pearl:*—bdellium.

917. בְּדָן **B^{e}dan,** *bed-awn´;* prob. short. for 5658; *servile; Bedan,* the name of two Isr.:—Bedan.

918. בָּדַק **bâdaq,** *baw-dak´;* a prim. root; to *gap* open; used only as a denom. from 919; to *mend* a breach:—repair.

919. בֶּדֶק **bedeq,** *beh´-dek;* from 918; a *gap* or *leak* (in a building or a ship):—breach, + calker.

920. בִּדְקַר **Bidqar,** *bid-car´;* prob. from 1856 with prep. pref.; *by stabbing,* i.e. *assassin; Bidkar,* an Isr.:—Bidkar.

921. בְּדַר **b^{e}dar** (Chald.), *bed-ar´;* corresp. (by transp.) to 6504; to *scatter:*—scatter.

922. בֹּהוּ **bôhûw,** *bo-hoo;* from an unused root (mean. to *be empty*); a *vacuity,* i.e. (superficially) an undistinguishable *ruin:*—emptiness, void.

923. בַּהַט **bahaṭ,** *bah´-hat;* from an unused root (prob. mean. to *glisten*); white *marble* or perh. *alabaster:*—red [marble].

924. בְּהִילוּ **b^{e}hîylûw** (Chald.), *bĕ-hee-loo´;* from 927; a *hurry;* only adv. *hastily:*—in haste.

925. בָּהִיר **bâhîyr,** *baw-here´;* from an unused root (mean. to *be bright*); *shining:*—bright.

926. בָּהַל **bâhal,** *baw-hal´;* a prim. root; to *tremble* inwardly (or *palpitate*), i.e. (fig.) *be* (caus. *make*) (suddenly) *alarmed* or *agitated;* by impl. to *hasten* anxiously:—be (make) affrighted (afraid, amazed, dismayed, rash), (be, get, make) haste (-n, -y, -ily), (give) speedy (-ily), thrust out, trouble, vex.

927. בְּהַל **b^{e}hal** (Chald.), *bĕhal´;* corresp. to 926; to *terrify, hasten:*—in haste, trouble.

928. בֶּהָלָה **behâlâh,** *beh-haw-law´;* from 926; *panic, destruction:*—terror, trouble.

929. בְּהֵמָה **b^{e}hêmâh,** *bĕ-hay-maw´;* from an unused root (prob. mean. to be *mute*); prop. a *dumb* beast; espec. any large quadruped or *animal* (often collect.):—beast, cattle.

930. בְּהֵמוֹת **b^{e}hemôwth,** *bĕ-hay-mōhth´;* in form a plur. of 929, but really a sing. of Eg. der.; a *water-ox,* i.e. the *hippopotamus* or Nile-horse:—Behemoth.

931. בֹּהֶן **bôhen,** *bo´-hen;* from an unused root appar. mean. to be *thick;* the *thumb* of the hand or *great toe* of the foot:—thumb, great toe.

932. בֹּהַן **Bôhan,** *bo´-han;* an orth. var. of 931; *thumb; Bohan,* an Isr.:—Bohan.

933. בֹּהַק **bôhaq,** *bo´-hak;* from an unused root mean. to *be pale;* white *scurf:*—freckled spot.

934. בֹּהֶרֶת **bôhereth,** *bo-heh´-reth;* fem. act. part. of the same as 925; a *whitish* spot on the skin:—bright spot.

935. בּוֹא **bôw',** *bo;* a prim. root; to *go* or *come* (in a wide variety of applications):—abide, apply, attain, × be, befall, + besiege, bring (forth, in, into, to pass), call, carry, × certainly, (cause, let, thing for) to come (against, in, out, upon, to pass), depart, × doubtless again, + eat, + employ, (cause to) enter (in, into, -tering, -trance, -try), be fallen, fetch, + follow, get, give, go (down, in, to war), grant, + have, × indeed, [in-]vade, lead, lift [up], mention, pull in, put, resort, run (down), send, set, × (well) stricken [in age], × surely, take (in), way.

בּוּב **bûwb.** See 892, 5014.

936. בּוּז **bûwz,** *booz;* a prim. root; to *disrespect:*—contemn, despise, × utterly.

937. בּוּז **bûwz,** *booz;* from 936; *disrespect:*—contempt (-uously), despised, shamed.

938. בּוּז **Bûwz,** *booz;* the same as 937; *Buz,* the name of a son of Nahor, and of an Isr.:—Buz.

939. בּוּזָה **bûwzâh,** *boo-zaw´;* fem. pass. part. of 936; something *scorned;* an object of *contempt:*—despised.

940. בּוּזִי **Bûwzîy,** *boo-zee´;* patron. from 938; a *Buzite* or desc. of Buz:—Buzite.

941. בּוּזִי **Bûwzîy,** *boo-zee´;* the same as 940, *Buzi,* an Isr.:—Buzi.

942. בַּוַּי **Bavvay,** *bav-vah´ee;* prob. of Pers. or.; *Bavvai,* an Isr.:—Bavai.

943. בּוּךְ **bûwk,** *book;* a prim. root; to *involve* (lit. or fig.):—be entangled (perplexed).

944. בּוּל **bûwl,** *bool;* for 2981; *produce* (of the earth, etc.):—food, stock.

945. בּוּל **Bûwl,** *bool;* the same as 944 (in the sense of *rain*); *Bul,* the eighth Heb. month:—Bul.

בּוּם **bûwm.** See 1116.

946. בּוּנָה **Bûwnâh,** *boo-naw´;* from 995; *discretion; Bunah,* an Isr.:—Bunah.

בּוּנִי **Bûwnîy.** See 1138.

947. בּוּס **bûwç,** *boos;* a prim. root; to *trample* (lit. or fig.):—loath, tread (down, under [foot]), be polluted.

948. בּוּץ **bûwts,** *boots;* from an unused root (of the same form) mean. to *bleach,* i.e. (intrans.) *be white;* prob. *cotton* (of some sort):—fine (white) linen.

949. בּוֹצֵץ **Bôwtsêts,** *bo-tsates´;* from the same as 948; *shining; Botsets,* a rock near Michmash:—Bozez.

950. בּוּקָה **bûwqâh,** *boo-kaw´;* fem. pass. part. of an unused root (mean. to *be hollow*); *emptiness* (as adj.):—empty.

951. בּוֹקֵר **bôwkêr,** *bo-kare´;* prop. act. part. from 1239 as denom. from 1241; a *cattle tender:*—herdman.

952. בּוּר **bûwr,** *boor;* a prim. root; to *bore,* i.e. (fig.) *examine:*—declare.

953. בּוֹר **bôwr,** *bore;* from 952 (in the sense of 877); a pit *hole* (espec. one used as a *cistern* or *prison*):—cistern, dungeon, fountain, pit, well.

954. בּוּשׁ **bûwsh,** *boosh;* a prim. root; prop. to *pale,* i.e. by impl. to *be ashamed;* also (by impl.) to *be disappointed,* or *delayed:*—(be, make, bring to, cause, put to, with, a-) shame (-d), be (put to) confounded (-fusion), become dry, delay, be long.

955. בּוּשָׁה **bûwshâh,** *boo-shaw´;* fem. part. pass. of 954; *shame:*—shame.

956. בּוּת **bûwth** (Chald.), *booth;* appar. denom. from 1005; to *lodge* overnight:—pass the night.

957. בַּז **baz,** *baz;* from 962; *plunder:*—booty, prey, spoil (-ed).

958. בָּזָא **bâzâ',** *baw-zaw´;* a prim. root; prob. to *cleave:*—spoil.

959. בָּזָה **bâzâh,** *baw-zaw´;* a prim. root; to *disesteem:*—despise, disdain, contemn (-ptible), + think to scorn, vile person.

960. בָּזֹה **bâzôh,** *baw-zo´;* from 959; *scorned:*—despise.

961. בִּזָּה **bizzâh,** *biz-zaw´;* fem. of 957; *booty:*—prey, spoil.

962. בָּזַז **bâzaz,** *baw-zaz´;* a prim. root; to *plunder:*—catch, gather, (take) for a prey, rob (-ber), spoil, take (away, spoil), × utterly.

963. בִּזָּיוֹן **bizzâyôwn,** *biz-zaw-yone´;* from 959:—*disesteem:*—contempt.

964. בִּזְיוֹתְיָה **bizyôwth**e**yâh,** *biz-yo-thĕ-yaw´;* from 959 and 3050; *contempts of Jah; Bizjothjah,* a place in Pal.:—Bizjothjah.

965. בָּזָק **bâzâq,** *baw-zawk´;* from an unused root mean. to *lighten;* a *flash* of lightning:—flash of lightning.

966. בֶּזֶק **Bezeq,** *beh´-zek;* from 965; *lightning; Bezek,* a place in Pal.:—Bezek.

967. בָּזַר **bâzar,** *baw-zar´;* a prim. root; to *disperse:*—scatter.

968. בִּזְתָא **Bizthâ',** *biz-thaw´;* of Pers. or.; *Biztha,* a eunuch of Xerxes:—Biztha.

969. בָּחוֹן **bâchôwn', baw-khone´;** from 974; an *assayer* of metals:—tower.

970. בָּחוּר **bâchûwr,** *baw-khoor´;* or בָּחֻר **bâchûr,** *baw-khoor´;* part. pass. of 977; prop. *selected,* i.e. a *youth* (often collect.):—(choice) young (man), chosen, × hole.

בְּחוּרוֹת **b**e**chûwrôwth.** See 979.

בַּחוּרִים **Bachûwrîym.** See 980.

971. בַּחִין° **bachîyn,** *bakh-een´;* another form of 975; a watch-*tower* of besiegers:—tower.

972. בָּחִיר **bâchîyr,** *baw-kheer´;* from 977; *select:*—choose, chosen one, elect.

973. בָּחַל **bâchal,** *baw-khal´;* a prim. root; to *loathe:*—abhor, get hastily [*from the marg. for* 926].

974. בָּחַן **bâchan,** *baw-khan´;* a prim. root; to *test* (espec. metals); gen. and fig. to *investigate:*—examine, prove, tempt, try (trial).

975. בַּחַן **bachan,** *bakh´-an;* from 974 (in the sense of keeping a *look-out*); a watch-*tower:*—tower.

976. בֹּחַן **bôchan,** *bo´-khan;* from 974; *trial:*—tried.

977. בָּחַר **bâchar,** *baw-khar´;* a prim. root; prop. to *try,* i.e. (by impl.) *select:*—acceptable, appoint, choose (choice), excellent, join, be rather, require.

בָּחֻר **bâchûr.** See 970.

978. בַּחֲרוּמִי **Bachărûwmîy,** *bakh-ar-oo-mee´;* patrial from 980 (by transp.); a *Bacharumite* or inhab. of Bachurim:—Baharumite.

979. בְּחֻרוֹת **b**e**chûrôwth,** *bekh-oo-rothe´;* or בְּחוּרוֹת **b**e**chûwrôwth,** *bekh-oo-roth´;* fem. plur. of 970; also (masc. plur.) בְּחֻרִים **b**e**chûrîym,** *bekh-oo-reem´; youth* (collect. and abstr.):—young men, youth.

980. בַּחֻרִים **Bachûrîym,** *bakh-oo-reem´;* or בַּחוּרִים **Bachûwrîym,** *bakh-oo-reem´;* masc. plur. of 970; *young men; Bachurim,* a place in Pal.:—Bahurim.

981. בָּטָא **bâṭâ',** *baw-taw´;* or בָּטָה **bâṭâh,** *baw-taw´;* a prim. root; to *babble;* hence to *vociferate* angrily:—pronounce, speak (unadvisedly).

982. בָּטַח **bâṭach,** *baw-takh´;* a prim. root; prop. to *hie* for refuge [but not so *precipitately* as 2620]; fig. to *trust,* be *confident* or *sure:*—be bold (confident, secure, sure), careless (one, woman), put confidence, (make to) hope, (put, make to) trust.

983. בֶּטַח **beṭach,** *beh´-takh;* from 982; prop. a place of *refuge;* abstr. *safety,* both the fact *(security)* and the feeling *(trust);* often (adv. with or without prep.) *safely:*—assurance, boldly, (without) care (-less), confidence, hope, safe (-ly, -ty), secure, surely.

984. בֶּטַח **Beṭach,** *beh´-takh;* the same as 983; *Betach,* a place in Syria:—Betah.

985. בִּטְחָה **biṭchâh,** *bit-khaw´;* fem. of 984; *trust:*—confidence.

986. בִּטָּחוֹן **biṭṭâchôwn,** *bit-taw-khone´;* from 982; *trust:*—confidence, hope.

987. בַּטֻּחוֹת **baṭṭûchôwth,** *bat-too-khōth´;* fem. plur. from 982; *security:*—secure.

988. בָּטֵל **bâṭêl,** *baw-tale´;* a prim. root; to *desist* from labor:—cease.

989. בְּטֵל **b**e**ṭêl** (Chald.), *bet-ale´;* corresp. to 988; to *stop:*—(cause, make to), cease, hinder.

990. בֶּטֶן **beṭen,** *beh´-ten;* from an unused root prob. mean. to *be hollow;* the *belly,* espec. the *womb;* also the *bosom* or *body* of anything:—belly, body, + as they be born, + within, womb.

991. בֶּטֶן **Beṭen,** *beh´-ten;* the same as 990; *Beten,* a place in Pal.:—Beten.

992. בֹּטֶן **bôṭen,** *bo´-ten;* from 990; (only in plur.) a *pistachio*-nut (from its form):—nut.

993. בְּטֹנִים **B**e**ṭônîym,** *bet-o-neem´;* prob. plur. from 992; *hollows: Betonim,* a place in Pal.:—Betonim.

994. בִּי **bîy,** *bee;* perh. from 1158 (in the sense of *asking*); prop. a *request;* used only adv. (always with "my Lord"); *Oh that!; with leave,* or *if it please:*—alas, O, oh.

995. בִּין **bîyn,** *bene;* a prim. root; to *separate* mentally (or *distinguish*), i.e. (gen.) *understand:*—attend, consider, be cunning, diligently, direct, discern, eloquent, feel, inform, instruct, have intelligence, know, look well to, mark, perceive, be prudent, regard, (can) skill (-ful), teach, think, (cause, make to, get, give, have) understand (-ing), view, (deal) wise (-ly, man).

996. בֵּין **bêyn,** *bane* (sometimes in the plur. masc. or fem.); prop. the constr. contr. form of an otherwise unused noun from 995; a *distinction;* but used only as a prep., *between* (repeated before each noun, often with other particles); also as a conj., *either . . . or:*—among, asunder, at, between (-twixt . . . and), + from (the widest), × in, out of, whether (it be . . . or), within.

997. בֵּין **bêyn** (Chald.), *bane;* corresp. to 996:—among, between.

998. בִּינָה **bîynâh,** *bee-naw´;* from 995; *understanding:*—knowledge, meaning, × perfectly, understanding, wisdom.

999. בִּינָה **bîynâh** (Chald.), *bee-naw´;* corresp. to 998:—knowledge.

1000. בֵּיצָה **bêytsâh,** *bay-tsaw´;* from the same as 948; an *egg* (from its whiteness):—egg.

1001. בִּירָא **bîyrâ'** (Chald.), *bee-raw´;* corresp. to 1002; a *palace:*—palace.

1002. בִּירָה **bîyrâh,** *bee-raw´;* of for. or.; a *castle* or *palace:*—palace.

1003. בִּירָנִית **bîyrânîyth,** *bee-raw-neeth´;* from 1002; a *fortress:*—castle.

1004. בַּיִת **bayith,** *bah´-yith;* prob. from 1129 abbrev.; a *house* (in the greatest var. of applications, espec. *family,* etc.):—court, daughter, door, + dungeon, family, + forth of, × great as would contain, hangings. home[born], [winter]house (-hold), inside (-ward), palace, place, + prison, + steward, + tablet, temple, web, + within (-out).

1005. בַּיִת **bayith** (Chald.), *bah-yith;* corresp. to 1004:—house.

1006. בַּיִת **Bayith,** *bah´-yith;* the same as 1004; *Bajith,* a place in Pal.:—Bajith.

1007. בֵּית אָוֶן **Bêyth 'Âven,** *bayth aw´-ven;* from 1004 and 205; *house of vanity; Beth-Aven,* a place in Pal.:—Beth-aven.

1008. בֵּית־אֵל **Bêyth-'Êl,** *bayth-ale´;* from 1004 and 410; *house of God; Beth-El,* a place in Pal.:—Beth-el.

1009. בֵּית אַרְבֵּאל **Bêyth 'Arbê'l,** *bayth arbale´;* from 1004 and 695 and 410; *house of God's ambush; Beth-Arbel,* a place in Pal.:—Beth-Arbel.

1010. בֵּית בַּעַל מְעוֹן **Bêyth Ba'al Meʿôwn,** *bayth bah´-al mĕ-own´;* from 1004 and 1168 and 4583; *house of Baal* of (the) *habitation of* [appar. by transp.]; or (shorter)
בֵּית מְעוֹן **Bêyth Meʿôwn,** *bayth mĕown´;* *house of habitation of* (Baal); *Beth-Baal-Meön,* a place in Pal.:—Beth-baal-meon. Comp. 1186 and 1194.

1011. בֵּית בִּרְאִי **Bêyth Birʾîy,** *bayth bir-ee´;* from 1004 and 1254; *house of a creative* one; *Beth-Biri,* a place in Pal.:—Beth-birei.

1012. בֵּית בָּרָה **Bêyth Bârâh,** *bayth baw-raw´;* prob. from 1004 and 5679; *house of* (the) *ford; Beth-Barah,* a place in Pal.:—Beth-barah.

1013. בֵּית־גָּדֵר **Bêyth-Gâdêr,** *bayth-gaw-dare´;* from 1004 and 1447; *house of* (the) *wall; Beth-Gader,* a place in Pal.:—Beth-gader.

1014. בֵּית גָּמוּל **Bêyth Gâmûwl,** *bayth gaw-mool´;* from 1004 and the pass. part. of 1576; *house of* (the) *weaned; Beth-Gamul,* a place E. of the Jordan:—Beth-gamul.

1015. בֵּית דִּבְלָתַיִם **Bêyth Diblâthayim,** *bayth dib-law-thah´-yim;* from 1004 and the dual of 1690; *house of* (the) *two figcakes; Beth-Diblathajim,* a place E. of the Jordan:—Beth-diblathaim.

1016. בֵּית־דָּגוֹן **Bêyth-Dâgôwn,** *bayth-daw-gohn´;* from 1004 and 1712; *house of Dagon; Beth-Dagon,* the name of two places in Pal.:—Beth-dagon.

1017. בֵּית הָאֱלִי **Bêyth hâ-'Ělîy,** *bayth haw-el-ee´;* patrial from 1008 with the art. interposed; a *Beth-elite,* or inhab. of Bethel:—Bethelite.

1018. בֵּית הָאֵצֶל **Bêyth hâ-'êtsel,** *bayth haw-ay´-tsel;* from 1004 and 681 with the art. interposed; *house of the side; Beth-ha-Etsel,* a place in Pal.:—Beth-ezel.

1019. בֵּית הַגִּלְגָּל **Bêyth hag-Gilgâl,** *bayth hag-gil-gawl´;* from 1004 and 1537 with the article interposed; *house of the Gilgal* (or *rolling*); *Beth-hag-Gilgal,* a place in Pal.:—Beth-gilgal.

1020. בֵּית הַיְשִׁימוֹת **Bêyth ha-Yeshîy-môwth,** *bayth hah-yesh-ee-mōth´;* from 1004 and the plur. of 3451 with the art. interposed; *house of the deserts; Beth-ha-Jeshimoth,* a town E. of the Jordan:—Beth-jeshimoth.

1021. בֵּית הַכֶּרֶם **Bêyth hak-Kerem,** *bayth hak-keh´-rem;* from 1004 and 3754 with the art. interposed; *house of the vineyard; Beth-hak-Kerem,* a place in Pal.:—Beth-haccerem.

1022. בֵּית הַלַּחְמִי **Bêyth hal-Lachmîy,** *bayth hal-lakh-mee´;* patrial from 1035 with the art. ins.; a *Beth-lechemite,* or native of Bethlechem:—Bethlehemite.

1023. בֵּית הַמֶּרְחָק **Bêyth ham-Merchâq,** *bayth ham-mer-khawk´;* from 1004 and 4801 with the art. interposed; *house of the breadth; Beth-ham-Merchak,* a place in Pal.:—place that was far off.

1024. בֵּית הַמַּרְכָּבוֹת **Bêyth ham-Markâbôwth,** *bayth ham-mar-kaw-both´;* or (short.) בֵּית מַרְכָּבוֹת **Bêyth Mar-kâbôwth,** *bayth mar-kaw-both´;* from 1004 and the plur. of 4818 (with or without the art. interposed); *place of* (the) *chariots: Beth-ham-Markaboth* or *Beth-Markaboth,* a place in Pal.:—Beth-marcaboth.

1025. בֵּית הָעֵמֶק **Bêyth hâ-ʿÊmeq,** *bayth haw-Ay´-mek;* from 1004 and 6010 with the art. interposed; *house of the valley; Beth-ha-Emek,* a place in Pal.:—Beth-emek.

1026. בֵּית הָעֲרָבָה **Bêyth hâ-ʿĂrâbah,** *bayth haw-ar-aw-baw´;* from 1004 and 6160 with the art. interposed; *house of the Desert, Beth-ha-Arabah,* a place in Pal.:—Beth-arabah.

1027. בֵּית הָרָם **Bêyth hâ-Râm,** *bayth haw-rawm´;* from 1004 and 7311 with the art. interposed; *house of the height; Beth-ha-Ram,* a place E. of the Jordan:—Beth-aram.

1028. בֵּית הָרָן **Bêyth hâ-Rân,** *bayth haw-rawn´;* prob. for 1027; *Beth-ha Ran,* a place E. of the Jordan:—Beth-haran.

1029. בֵּית הַשִּׁטָּה **Bêyth hash-Shiṭṭâh,** *bayth hash-shit-taw´;* from 1004 and 7848 with the art. interposed; *house of the acacia; Beth-hash-Shittah,* a place in Pal.:—Beth-shittah.

1030. בֵּית הַשִּׁמְשִׁי **Bêyth hash-Shimshîy,** *bayth hash-shim-shee´;* patrial from 1053 with the art. inserted; a *Beth-shimshite,* or inhab. of Bethshemesh:—Bethshemite.

1031. בֵּית חָגְלָה **Bêyth Choglâh,** *bayth chog-law´;* from 1004 and the same as 2295; *house of a partridge; Beth-Choglah,* a place in Pal.:—Beth-hoglah.

1032. בֵּית חוֹרוֹן **Bêyth Chôwrôwn,** *bayth kho-rone´;* from 1004 and 2356; *house of hollowness; Beth-Choron,* the name of two adjoining places in Pal.:—Beth-horon.
בֵּית חָנָן **Bêyth Chânân.** See 358.

1033. בֵּית כַּר **Bêyth Kar,** *bayth kar;* from 1004 and 3733; *house of pasture; Beth-Car,* a place in Pal.:—Beth-car.

1034. בֵּית לְבָאוֹת **Bêyth Lebâ'ôwth,** *bayth leb-aw-ōth´;* from 1004 and the plur. of 3833; *house of lionesses; Beth-Lebaoth,* a place in Pal.:—Beth-lebaoth. Comp. 3822.

1035. בֵּית לֶחֶם **Bêyth Lechem,** *bayth leh´-khem;* from 1004 and 3899; *house of bread; Beth-Lechem,* a place in Pal.:—Beth-lehem.

1036. בֵּית לְעַפְרָה **Bêyth le-'Aphrâh,** *bayth lĕ-af-raw´;* from 1004 and the fem. of 6083 (with prep. interposed); *house to* (i.e. *of*) *dust; Beth-le-Aphrah,* a place in Pal.:—house of Aphrah.

1037. בֵּית מִלּוֹא **Bêyth Millôw',** *bayth millo´;* or בֵּית מִלֹּא **Bêyth Millô',** *bayth mil-lo´* from 1004 and 4407; *house of* (the) *rampart; Beth-Milo,* the name of two citadels:—house of Millo.

1038. בֵּית מַעֲכָה **Bêyth Maʿâkâh,** *bayth mah-ak-aw;* from 1004 and 4601; *house of Maakah; Beth-Maakah,* a place in Pal.:—Beth-maachah.

1039. בֵּית נִמְרָה **Bêyth Nimrâh,** *bayth nimraw´;* from 1004 and the fem. of 5246; *house of* (the) *leopard; Beth-Nimrah,* a place east of the Jordan:—Beth-nimrah. Comp. 5247.

1040. בֵּית עֶדֶן **Bêyth ʿÊden,** *bayth ay´-den;* from 1004 and 5730; *house of pleasure; Beth-Eden,* a place in Syria:—Beth-eden.

1041. בֵּית עַזְמָוֶת **Bêyth ʿAzmâveth,** *bayth az-maw´-veth;* from 1004 and 5820; *house of Azmaveth,* a place in Pal.:—Beth-az-maveth. Comp. 5820.

1042. בֵּית עֲנוֹת **Bêyth ʿĂnôwth,** *bayth anōth´;* from 1004 and a plur. from 6030; *house of replies; Beth-Anoth,* a place in Pal.:—Beth-anoth.

1043. בֵּית עֲנָת **Bêyth ʻĂnâth,** *bayth an-awth´;* an orth. var. for 1042; *Beth-Anath,* a place in Pal.:—Beth-anath.

1044. בֵּית עֵקֶד **Bêyth ʻÊqed,** *bayth ay´-ked;* from 1004 and a deriv. of 6123; *house of* (the) *binding* (for sheep-shearing); *Beth-Eked,* a place in Pal.:—shearing-house.

1045. בֵּית עַשְׁתָּרוֹת **Bêyth ʻAshtârôwth,** *bayth ash-taw-rōth´;* from 1004 and 6252; *house of Ashtoreths; Beth-Ashtaroth,* a place in Pal.:—house of Ashtaroth. Comp. 1203, 6252.

1046. בֵּית פֶּלֶט **Bêyth Peleṭ,** *bayth peh´-let;* from 1004 and 6412; *house of escape; Beth-Palet,* a place in Pal.:—Beth-palet.

1047. בֵּית פְּעוֹר **Bêyth Peʻôwr,** *bayth pĕ-ore´;* from 1004 and 6465; *house of Peor; Beth-Peor,* a place E. of the Jordan:—Beth-peor.

1048. בֵּית פַּצֵּץ **Bêyth Patstsêts,** *bayth pats-tsates´;* from 1004 and a der. from 6327; *house of dispersion; Beth-Patstets,* a place in Pal.:—Beth-pazzez.

1049. בֵּית צוּר **Bêyth Tsûwr,** *bayth tsoor´;* from 1004 and 6697; *house of* (the) *rock; Beth-Tsur,* a place in Pal.:—Beth-zur.

1050. בֵּית רְחוֹב **Bêyth Rechôwb,** *bayth rĕ-khobe´;* from 1004 and 7339; *house of* (the) *street; Beth-Rechob,* a place in Pal.:—Beth-rehob.

1051. בֵּית רָפָא **Bêyth Râphâʼ,** *bayth raw-faw´;* from 1004 and 7497; *house of* (the) *giant; Beth-Rapha,* an Isr.:—Beth-rapha.

1052. בֵּית שְׁאָן **Bêyth Sheʼân,** *bayth shĕ-awn´;* or בֵּית שָׁן **Bêyth Shân,** *bayth shawn´;* from 1004 and 7599; *house of ease; Beth-Shean* or *Beth-Shan,* a place in Pal.:—Beth-shean, Beth-Shan.

1053. בֵּית שֶׁמֶשׁ **Bêyth Shemesh,** *bayth sheh´-mesh;* from 1004 and 8121; *house of* (the) *sun; Beth-Shemesh,* a place in Pal.:—Beth-shemesh.

1054. בֵּית תַּפּוּחַ **Bêyth Tappûwach,** *bayth tap-poo´-akh;* from 1004 and 8598; *house of* (the) *apple; Beth-Tappuach,* a place in Pal.:—Beth-tappuah.

1055. בִּיתָן **bîythân,** *bee-thawn´;* prob. from 1004; a *palace* (i.e. *large house*):—palace.

1056. בָּכָא **Bâkâʼ,** *baw-kaw´;* from 1058; *weeping; Baca,* a valley in Pal.:—Baca.

1057. בָּכָא **bâkâʼ,** *baw-kaw´;* the same as 1056; the *weeping* tree (some gum-distilling tree, perh. the *balsam*):—mulberry tree.

1058. בָּכָה **bâkâh,** *baw-kaw´;* a prim. root; to *weep;* gen. to *bemoan:*— × at all, bewail, complain, make lamentation, × more, mourn, × sore, × with tears, weep.

1059. בֶּכֶה **bekeh,** *beh´-keh;* from 1058; a *weeping:*— × sore.

1060. בְּכוֹר **bekôwr,** *bek-ore´;* from 1069; *first-born;* hence *chief:*—eldest (son), first-born (-ling).

1061. בִּכּוּר **bikkûwr,** *bik-koor´;* from 1069; the *first-fruits* of the crop:—first fruit (-ripe [fig.]), hasty fruit.

1062. בְּכוֹרָה **bekôwrâh,** *bek-o-raw´;* or (short.) בְּכֹרָה **bekôrâh,** *bek-o-raw´;* fem. of 1060; the *firstling* of man or beast; abstr. *primogeniture:*—birthright, firstborn (-ling).

1063. בִּכּוּרָה **bikkûwrâh,** *bik-koo-raw´;* fem. of 1061; the *early* fig:—firstripe (fruit).

1064. בְּכוֹרַת **Bekôwrath,** *bek-o-rath´;* fem. of 1062; *primogeniture; Bekorath,* an Isr.:—Bechorath.

1065. בְּכִי **bekîy,** *bek-ee´;* from 1058; a *weeping;* by analogy, a *dripping:*—overflowing, × sore, (continual) weeping, wept.

1066. בֹּכִים **Bôkîym,** *bo-keem´;* plur. act. part. of 1058; (with the art.) the *weepers; Bo-kim,* a place in Pal.:—Bochim.

1067. בְּכִירָה **bekîyrâh,** *bek-ee-raw´;* fem. from 1069; the *eldest* daughter:—firstborn.

1068. בְּכִית **bekîyth,** *bek-eeth´;* from 1058; a *weeping:*—mourning.

1069. בָּכַר **bâkar,** *baw-kar´;* a prim. root; prop. to *burst* the womb, i.e. (caus.) *bear* or *make early fruit* (of woman or tree); also (as denom. from 1061) to *give the birthright:*—make firstborn, be firstling, bring forth first child (new fruit).

1070. בֶּכֶר **beker,** *beh´-ker;* from 1069 (in the sense of *youth*); a young *camel:*—dromedary.

1071. בֶּכֶר **Beker,** *beh´-ker;* the same as 1070; *Beker,* the name of two Isr.:—Becher.

1072. בִּכְרָה **bikrâh,** *bik-raw´;* fem. of 1070; a young *she-camel:*—dromedary.

בְּכֹרָה **bekôrâh.** See 1062.

1073. בַּכֻּרָה **bakkûrâh,** *bak-koo-raw´;* by orth. var. for 1063; a *first-ripe* fig:—first-ripe.

1074. בֹּכְרוּ **Bôkerûw,** *bo-ker-oo´;* from 1069; *first-born; Bokeru,* an Isr.:—Bocheru.

1075. בִּכְרִי **Bikrîy,** *bik-ree´;* from 1069; *youthful; Bikri,* an Isr.:—Bichri.

1076. בַּכְרִי **Bakrîy,** *bak-ree´;* patron. from 1071; a *Bakrite* (collect.) or desc. of Beker:—Bachrites.

1077. בַּל **bal,** *bal;* from 1086; prop. a *failure;* by impl. *nothing;* usually (adv.) *not* at all; also *lest:*—lest, neither, no, none (that . . .), not (any), nothing.

1078. בֵּל **Bêl,** *bale;* by contr. for 1168; *Bel,* the Baal of the Babylonians:—Bel.

1079. בָּל **bâl** (Chald.), *bawl;* from 1080; prop. *anxiety,* i.e. (by impl.) the *heart* (as its seat):—heart.

1080. בְּלָא **belâʼ** (Chald.), *bel-aw´;* corresp. to 1086 (but used only in a mental sense); to *afflict:*—wear out.

1081. בַּלְאֲדָן **Balʼădân,** *bal-ad-awn´;* from 1078 and 113 (contr.); *Bel* (is his) *lord; Baladan,* the name of a Bab. prince:—Baladan.

1082. בָּלַג **bâlag,** *baw-lag´;* a prim. root; to *break off* or *loose* (in a favorable or unfavorable sense), i.e. *desist* (from grief) or *invade* (with destruction):—comfort, (recover) strength (-en).

1083. בִּלְגָּה **Bilgâh,** *bil-gaw´;* from 1082; *desistance; Bilgah,* the name of two Isr.:—Bilgah.

1084. בִּלְגַּי **Bilgay,** *bil-gah´ee;* from 1082; *desistant; Bilgai,* an Isr.:—Bilgai.

1085. בִּלְדַּד **Bildad,** *bil-dad´;* of uncert. der.; *Bildad,* one of Job's friends:—Bildad.

1086. בָּלָה **bâlâh,** *baw-law´;* a prim. root; to *fail;* by impl. to *wear out, decay* (caus. *consume, spend*):—consume, enjoy long, become (make, wax) old, spend, waste.

1087. בָּלֶה **bâleh,** *baw-leh´;* from 1086; *worn out:*—old.

1088. בָּלָה **Bâlâh,** *baw-law´;* fem. of 1087; *failure; Balah,* a place in Pal.:—Balah.

1089. בָּלַהּ **bâlahh,** *baw-lah´;* a prim. root [rather by transp. for 926]; to *palpitate;* hence (caus.) to *terrify:*—trouble.

1090. בִּלְהָה **Bilhâh,** *bil-haw´;* from 1089; *timid; Bilhah,* the name of one of Jacob's concubines; also of a place in Pal.:—Bilhah.

1091. בַּלָּהָה **ballâhâh,** *bal-law-haw´;* from 1089; *alarm;* hence *destruction:*—terror, trouble.

1092. בִּלְהָן **Bilhân,** *bil-hawn´;* from 1089; *timid; Bilhan,* the name of an Edomite and of an Isr.:—Bilhan.

1093. בְּלוֹ **belôw** (Chald.), *bel-o´;* from a root corresp. to 1086; *excise* (on articles consumed):—tribute.

1094. בְּלוֹא **belôwʼ,** *bel-o´;* or (fully) בְּלוֹי **belôwy,** *bel-o´ee;* from 1086; (only in plur. constr.) *rags:*—old.

1095. בֵּלְטְשַׁאצַּר **Bêlṭeshaʼtstsar,** *bale-tesh-ats-tsar´;* of for. der.; *Belteshatstsar,* the Bab. name of Daniel:—Belteshazzar.

1096. בֵּלְטְשַׁאצַּר **Bêlṭeshaʼtstsar** (Chald.), *bale-tesh-ats-tsar´;* corresp. to 1095:—Belteshazzar.

1097. בְּלִי **belîy,** *bel-ee´;* from 1086; prop. *failure,* i.e. *nothing* or *destruction;* usually (with prep.) *without, not yet, because not, as long as,* etc.:—corruption, ig[norantly], for lack of, where no . . . is, so that no, none, not, un[awares], without.

1098. בְּלִיל **belîyl,** *bel-eel´;* from 1101; *mixed,* i.e. (spec.) *feed* (for cattle):—corn, fodder, provender.

1099. בְּלִימָה **belîymâh,** *bel-ee-mah´;* from 1097 and 4100; (as indef.) *nothing whatever:*—nothing.

1100. בְּלִיַּעַל **b^elîya‘al,** *bel-e-yah´-al;* from 1097 and 3276; *without profit, worthlessness;* by extens. *destruction, wickedness* (often in connection with 376, 802, 1121, etc.):—Belial, evil, naughty, ungodly (men), wicked.

1101. בָּלַל **bâlal,** *baw-lal´;* a prim. root; to *overflow* (spec. with oil); by impl. to *mix;* also (denom. from 1098) to *fodder:*—anoint, confound, × fade, mingle, mix (self), give provender, temper.

1102. בָּלַם **bâlam,** *baw-lam´;* a prim. root; to *muzzle:*—be held in.

1103. בָּלַס **bâlaç,** *baw-las´;* a prim. root; to *pinch* sycamore figs (a process necessary to ripen them):—gatherer.

1104. בָּלַע **bâla‘,** *baw-lah´;* a prim. root; to *make away with* (spec. by *swallowing*); gen. to *destroy:*—cover, destroy, devour, eat up, be at end, spend up, swallow down (up).

1105. בֶּלַע **bela‘,** *beh´-lah;* from 1104; a *gulp;* fig. *destruction:*—devouring, that which he hath swallowed up.

1106. בֶּלַע **Bela‘,** *beh´-lah;* the same as 1105; *Bela,* the name of a place, also of an Edomite and of two Isr.:—Bela.

1107. בִּלְעֲדֵי **bil‘ădêy,** *bil-ad-ay´;* or בַּלְעֲדֵי **bal‘ădêy,** *bal-ad-ay´;* constr. plur. from 1077 and 5703; *not till,* i.e. (as prep. or adv.) *except, without, besides:*—beside, not (in), save, without.

1108. בַּלְעִי **Bal‘îy,** *bel-ee´;* patronym. from 1106: a *Belaite* (collect.) or desc. of Bela:—Belaites.

1109. בִּלְעָם **Bil‘âm,** *bil-awm´;* prob. from 1077 and 5971; *not* (of the) *people,* i.e. *foreigner; Bilam,* a Mesopotamian prophet; also a place in Pal.:—Balaam, Bileam.

1110. בָּלַק **bâlaq,** *baw-lak´;* a prim. root; to *annihilate:*—(make) waste.

1111. בָּלָק **Bâlâq,** *baw-lawk´;* from 1110; *waster; Balak,* a Moabitish king:—Balak.

1112. בֵּלְשַׁאצַּר **Bêlsha’tstsar,** *bale-shats-tsar´;* or בֵּלְאשַׁצַּר **Bêl’shatstsar,** *bale-shats-tsar´;* of for. or. (comp. 1095); *Belshatstsar,* a Bab. king:—Belshazzar.

1113. בֵּלְשַׁאצַּר **Bêlsha’tstsar** (Chald.), *bale-shats-tsar´;* corresp. to 1112; —Belshazzar.

1114. בִּלְשָׁן **Bilshân,** *bil-shawn´;* of uncert. der.; *Bilshan,* an Isr.:—Bilshan.

1115. בִּלְתִּי **biltîy,** *bil-tee´;* constr. fem. of 1086 (equiv. to 1097); prop. a *failure of,* i.e. (used only as a neg. particle, usually with prep. pref.) *not, except, without, unless, besides, because not, until,* etc.:—because un[satiable], beside, but, + continual, except, from, lest, neither, no more, none, not, nothing, save, that no, without.

1116. בָּמָה **bâmâh,** *baw-maw´;* from an unused root (mean. to *be high*); an *elevation:*—height, high place, wave.

1117. בָּמָה **Bâmâh,** *baw-maw´;* the same as 1116; *Bamah,* a place in Pal.:—Bamah. See also 1120.

1118. בִּמְהָל **Bimhâl,** *bim-hawl´;* prob. from 4107 with prep. pref.; *with pruning; Bimhal,* an Isr.:—Bimhal.

1119. בְּמוֹ **b^emôw,** *bem-o´;* prol. for prep. pref.; *in, with, by,* etc.:—for, in, into, through.

1120. בָּמוֹת **Bâmôwth,** *baw-mōth´;* plur. of 1116; *heights;* or (fully) בָּמוֹת בַּעַל **Bâmôwth Ba‘al,** *baw-mōth´; bah´-al;* from the same and 1168; *heights of Baal; Bamoth* or *Bamoth-Baal,* a place E. of the Jordan:—Bamoth, Bamoth-baal.

1121. בֵּן **bên,** *bane;* from 1129; a *son* (as a *builder* of the family name), in the widest sense (of lit. and fig. relationship, including *grandson, subject, nation, quality* or *condition,* etc., [like 1, 251, etc.]):— + afflicted, age, [Ahoh-] [Ammon-] [Hachmon-] [Lev-]ite, [anoint-]ed one, appointed to, (+) arrow, [Assyr-] [Babylon-] [Egypt-] [Grec-]ian, one born, bough, branch, breed, + (young) bullock, + (young) calf, × came up in, child, colt, × common, × corn, daughter, × of first, + firstborn, foal, + very fruitful, + postage, × in, + kid, + lamb, (+) man, meet, + mighty, + nephew, old, (+) people, + rebel, + robber, × servant born, × soldier, son, + spark, + steward, + stranger, × surely, them of, + tumultuous one, + valiant[-est], whelp, worthy, young (one), youth.

1122. בֵּן **Bên,** *bane;* the same as 1121; *Ben,* an Isr.:—Ben.

1123. בֵּן **bên** (Chald.), *bane;* corresp. to 1121:—child, son, young.

1124. בְּנָא **b^enâ’** (Chald.), *ben-aw´;* or בְּנָה **b^enâh** (Chald.), *ben-aw´;* corresp. to 1129; to *build:*—build, make.

1125. בֶּן־אֲבִינָדָב **Ben-’Âbîynâdâb,** *ben-ab-ee´´-naw-dawb´;* from 1121 and 40; (the) *son of Abinadab; Ben-Abinadab,* an Isr.:—the son of Abinadab.

1126. בֶּן־אוֹנִי **Ben-’Ôwnîy,** *ben-o-nee´;* from 1121 and 205; *son of my sorrow; Ben-Oni,* the original name of Benjamin:—Ben-oni.

1127. בֶּן־גֶּבֶר **Ben-Geber,** *ben-gheh´-ber;* from 1121 and 1397; *son of* (the) *hero; Ben-Geber,* an Isr.:—the son of Geber.

1128. בֶּן־דֶּקֶר **Ben-Deqer,** *ben-deh´-ker;* from 1121 and a der. of 1856; *son of piercing* (or *of a lance*); *Ben-Deker,* an Isr.:—the son of Dekar.

1129. בָּנָה **bânâh,** *baw-naw´;* a prim. root; to *build* (lit. and fig.):—(begin to) build (-er), obtain children, make, repair, set (up), × surely.

1130. בֶּן־הֲדַד **Ben-Hădad,** *ben-had-ad´;* from 1121 and 1908; *son of Hadad; Ben-Hadad,* the name of several Syrian kings:—Ben-hadad.

1131. בִּנּוּי **Binnûwy,** *bin-noo´ee;* from 1129; *built* up; *Binnui,* an Isr.:—Binnui.

1132. בֶּן־זוֹחֵת **Ben-Zôwehêth,** *ben-zo-khayth´;* from 1121 and 2105; *son of Zocheth; Ben-Zocheth,* an Isr.:—Ben-zoketh.

1133. בֶּן־חוּר **Ben-Chûwr,** *ben-khoor´;* from 1121 and 2354; *son of Chur; Ben-Chur,* an Isr.:—the son of Hur.

1134. בֶּן־חַיִל **Ben-Chayil,** *ben-khah´-yil;* from 1121 and 2428; *son of might; Ben-Chail,* an Isr.:—Ben-hail.

1135. בֶּן־חָנָן **Ben-Chânañ,** *ben-khaw-nawn´;* from 1121 and 2605; *son of Chanan; Ben-Chanan,* an Isr.:—Ben-hanan.

1136. בֶּן־חֶסֶד **Ben-Cheçed,** *ben-kheh´-sed;* from 1121 and 2617; *son of kindness; Ben-Chesed,* an Isr.:—the son of Hesed.

1137. בָּנִי **Bânîy,** *baw-nee´;* from 1129; *built; Bani,* the name of five Isr.:—Bani.

1138. בֻּנִּי **Bunnîy,** *boon-nee´;* or (fuller) בּוּנִי **Bûwnîy,** *boo-nee´;* from 1129; *built; Bunni* or *Buni,* an Isr.:—Bunni.

1139. בְּנֵי־בְרַק **B^enêy-B^eraq,** *ben-ay´-ber-ak´;* from the plur. constr. of 1121 and 1300; *sons of lightning, Bene-berak,* a place in Pal.:—Bene-barak.

1140. בִּנְיָה **binyâh,** *bin-yaw´;* fem. from 1129; a *structure:*—building.

1141. בְּנָיָה **B^enâyâh,** *ben-aw-yaw´;* or (prol.) בְּנָיָהוּ **B^enâyâhûw,** *ben-aw-yaw´-hoo;* from 1129 and 3050; *Jah has built; Benajah,* the name of twelve Isr.:—Benaiah.

1142. בְּנֵי יַעֲקָן **B^enêy Ya‘ăqân,** *ben-ay´ yah-ak-awn´;* from the plur. of 1121 and 3292; *sons of Yaakan; Bene-Jaakan,* a place in the Desert:—Bene-jaakan.

1143. בֵּנַיִם **bênayim,** *bay-nah´-yim;* dual of 996; a *double interval,* i.e. the space between two armies:— + champion.

1144. בִּנְיָמִין **Binyâmîyn,** *bin-yaw-mene´;* from 1121 and 3225; *son of* (the) *right hand; Binjamin,* youngest son of Jacob; also the tribe descended from him, and its territory:—Benjamin.

1145. בֶּן־יְמִינִי **Ben-y^emîynîy,** *ben-yem-ee-nee´;* sometimes (with the art. ins.) בֶּן־הַיְמִינִי **Ben-ha-y^emînîy,** *ben-hah-yem-ee-nee´;* with 376 ins. (1 Sam. 9: 1) בֶּן־אִישׁ יְמִינִי **Ben-’Îysh Y^emîynîy,** *ben-eesh´ yem-ee-nee´;* *son of a man of Jemini;* or short. (1 Sam. 9: 4; Esth. 2 : 5) אִישׁ יְמִינִי **’Îysh Y^emîynîy,** *eesh yem-ee-nee´;* *a man of Jemini;* or (1 Sam. 20 : 1) simply יְמִינִי **Y^emînîy,** *yem-ee-nee´;* *a Jeminite;* (plur. בְּנֵי יְמִינִי **B^enîy Y^emîynîy,** *ben-ay´ yem-ee-nee´;*) patron. from 1144; a *Benjaminite,* or descendant of Benjamin:—Benjamite, of Benjamin.

1146. בִּנְיָן **binyân,** *bin-yawn´;* from 1129; an *edifice:*—building.

1147. בִּנְיָן **binyân** (Chald.), *bin-yawn´;* corresp. to 1146:—building.

1148. בְּנִינוּ **B^enîynûw,** *ben-ee-noo´;* prob. from 1121 with pron. suff.; *our son; Beninu,* an Isr.:—Beninu.

1149. בְּנַס **b^e^naç** (Chald.), *ben-as´;* of uncert. affin.; to *be enraged:*—be angry.

1150. בִּנְעָא **Bin'â',** *bin-aw´;* or בִּנְעָה **Bin'âh,** *bin-aw´;* of uncert. der.; *Bina* or *Binah,* an Isr.:—Binea, Bineah.

1151. בֶּן־עַמִּי **Ben-'Ammîy,** *ben-am-mee´;* from 1121 and 5971 with pron. suff.; *son of my people; Ben-Ammi,* a son of Lot:—Ben-ammi.

1152. בְּסוֹדְיָה **B^e^çôwd^e^yâh,** *bes-o-deh-yaw´;* from 5475 and 3050 with prep. pref.; *in* (the) *counsel of Jehovah; Besodejah,* an Isr.:—Besodeiah.

1153. בְּסַי **B^e^çay,** *bes-ah´-ee;* from 947; *domineering; Besai,* one of the Nethinim:—Besai.

1154. בֶּסֶר **bêçer,** *beh´-ser;* from an unused root mean. to *be sour;* an *immature* grape:—unripe grape.

1155. בֹּסֶר **bôçer,** *bo´-ser;* from the same as 1154:—sour grape.

1156. בְּעָא **b^e^'â'** (Chald.), *beh-aw´;* or בְּעָה **b^e^'âh** (Chald.), *beh-aw´;* corresp. to 1158; to *seek* or *ask:*—ask, desire, make [petition], pray, request, seek.

1157. בְּעַד **b^e^'ad,** *beh-ad´;* from 5704 with prep. pref.; *in up to* or *over against;* gen. *at, beside, among, behind, for,* etc.:—about, at, by (means of), for, over, through, up (-on), within.

1158. בָּעָה **bâ'âh,** *baw-aw´;* a prim. root; to *gush* over i.e. to *swell;* (fig.) to *desire* earnestly; by impl. to *ask:*—cause, inquire, seek up, swell out, boil.

1159. בָּעוּ **bâ'ûw** (Chald.), *baw-oo´;* from 1156; a *request:*—petition.

1160. בְּעוֹר **B^e^'ôwr,** *beh-ore´;* from 1197 (in the sense of *burning*); a *lamp, Beör,* the name of the father of an Edomitish king; also of that of Balaam:—Beor.

1161. בִּעוּתִים **bi'ûwthîym,** *be-oo-theme´;* masc. plur. from 1204; *alarms:*—terrors.

1162. בֹּעַז **Bô'az,** *bo´-az;* from an unused root of uncert. mean.; *Boaz,* the ancestor of David; also the name of a pillar in front of the temple:—Boaz.

1163. בָּעַט **bâ'aṭ,** *baw-at´;* a prim. root; to *trample* down, i.e. (fig.) *despise:*—kick.

1164. בְּעִי **b^e^'îy,** *beh-ee´;* from 1158; a *prayer:*—grave.

1165. בְּעִיר **b^e^'îyr,** *beh-ere´;* from 1197 (in the sense of *eating*): cattle:—beast, cattle.

1166. בָּעַל **bâ'al,** *baw-al´;* a prim. root; to *be master;* hence (as denom. from 1167) to *marry:*—Beulah have dominion (over), be husband, marry (-ried, × wife).

1167. בַּעַל **ba'al,** *bah´-al;* from 1166; a *master;* hence a *husband,* or (fig.) *owner* (often used with another noun in modifications of this latter sense):— + archer, + babbler, + bird, captain, chief man, + confederate, + have to do, + dreamer, those to whom it is due, + furious, those that are given to it, great, + hairy, he that hath it, have, + horseman, husband, lord, man, + married, master, person, + sworn, they of.

1168. בַּעַל **Ba'al,** *bah´-al;* the same as 1167; *Baal,* a Phœnician deity:—Baal, [*plur.*] Baalim.

1169. בְּעֵל **b^e^'êl** (Chald.), *beh-ale´;* corresp. to 1167:— + chancellor.

1170. בַּעַל בְּרִית **Ba'al B^e^rîyth,** *bah´-al ber-eeth´;* from 1168 and 1285; *Baal of* (the) *covenant; Baal-Berith,* a special deity of the Shechemites:—Baal-berith.

1171. בַּעַל גָּד **Ba'al Gâd,** *bah´-al gawd;* from 1168 and 1409; *Baal of Fortune; Baal-Gad,* a place in Syria:—Baal-gad.

1172. בַּעֲלָה **ba'ălâh,** *bah-al-aw´;* fem. of 1167; a *mistress:*—that hath, mistress.

1173. בַּעֲלָה **Ba'ălâh,** *bah-al-aw´;* the same as 1172; *Baalah,* the name of three places in Pal.:—Baalah.

1174. בַּעַל הָמוֹן **Ba'al Hâmôwn,** *bah´-al haw-mone´; from 1167 and 1995; possessor of a multitude; Baal-Hamon,* a place in Pal.:—Baal-hamon.

1175. בְּעָלוֹת **B^e^'âlôwth,** *beh-aw-lōth´;* plur. of 1172; *mistresses; Beäloth,* a place in Pal.:—Bealoth, in Aloth [*by mistake for a plur. from* 5927 *with prep. pref.*].

1176. בַּעַל זְבוּב **Ba'al Z^e^bûwb,** *bah´-al zeb-oob´;* from 1168 and 2070; *Baal of* (the) *Fly; Baal-Zebub,* a special deity of the Ekronites—Baal-zebub.

1177. בַּעַל חָנָן **Ba'al Chânân,** *bah´-al khaw-nawn´;* from 1167 and 2603; *possessor of grace; Baal-Chanan,* the name of an Edomite, also of an Isr.:—Baal-hanan.

1178. בַּעַל חָצוֹר **Ba'al Châtsôwr,** *bah´-al khaw-tsore´;* from 1167 and a modif. of 2691; *possessor of a village; Baal-Chatsor,* a place in Pal.:—Baal-hazor.

1179. בַּעַל חֶרְמוֹן **Ba'al Chermôwn,** *bah´-al kher-mone´;* from 1167 and 2768; *possessor of Hermon; Baal-Chermon,* a place in Pal.:—Baal-hermon.

1180. בַּעֲלִי **Ba'ălîy,** *bah-al-ee´;* from 1167 with-pron. suff.; *my master; Baali,* a symbolical name for Jehovah:—Baali.

1181. בַּעֲלֵי בָמוֹת **Ba'ălêy Bâmôwth,** *bah-al-ay´ baw-mōth´;* from the plur. of 1168 and the plur. of 1116; *Baals of* (the) *heights; Baale-Bamoth,* a place E. of the Jordan:—lords of the high places.

1182. בְּעֶלְיָדָע **B^e^'elyâdâ',** *beh-el-yaw-daw´;* from 1168 and 3045; *Baal has known; Beëljada,* an Isr.:—Beeliada.

1183. בְּעַלְיָה **B^e^'alyâh,** *beh-al-yaw´;* from 1167 and 3050; *Jah* (is) *master; Bealjah,* an Isr.:—Bealiah.

1184. בַּעֲלֵי יְהוּדָה **Ba'ălêy Y^e^hûwdâh,** *bah-al-ay´ yeh-hoo-daw´;* from the plur. of 1167 and 3063; *masters of Judah; Baale-Jehudah,* a place in Pal.:—Baale of Judah.

1185. בַּעֲלִיס **Ba'ălîç,** *bah-al-ece´;* prob. from a der. of 5965 with prep. pref.; *in exultation; Baalis,* an Ammonitish king:—Baalis.

1186. בַּעַל מְעוֹן **Ba'al M^e^'ôwn,** *bah-al meh-one´;* from 1168 and 4583; *Baal of* (the) *habitation* (of) [comp. 1010]; *Baal-Meön,* a place E. of the Jordan:—Baal-meon.

1187. בַּעַל פְּעוֹר **Ba'al P^e^'ôwr,** *bah´-al peh-ore´;* from 1168 and 6465; *Baal of Peor; Baal-Peör,* a Moabitish deity:—Baal-peor.

1188. בַּעַל פְּרָצִים **Ba'al P^e^râtsîym,** *bah´-al per-aw-tseem´;* from 1167 and the plur. of 6556; *possessor of breaches; Baal-Pera-tsim,* a place in Pal.:—Baal-perazim.

1189. בַּעַל צְפוֹן **Ba'al Ts^e^phôwn,** *bah´-al-tsef-one´;* from 1168 and 6828 (in the sense of *cold*) [according to others an Eg. form of *Typhon,* the destroyer]; *Baal of winter; Baal-Tse-phon,* a place in Egypt:—Baal-zephon.

1190. בַּעַל שָׁלִשָׁה **Ba'al Shâlîshâh,** *bah´-al shaw-lee-shaw´;* from 1168 and 8031; *Baal of Shalishah; Baal-Shalishah,* a place in Pal.:—Baal-shalisha.

1191. בַּעֲלָת **Ba 'ălâth,** *bah-al-awth´;* a modif. of 1172; *mistresship; Baalath,* a place in Pal.:—Baalath.

1192. בַּעֲלַת בְּאֵר **Ba'ălath B^e^'êr,** *bah-al-ath´ beh-ayr´;* from 1172 and 875; *mistress of a well; Baalath-Beër,* a place in Pal.:—Baalath-beer.

1193. בַּעַל תָּמָר **Ba'al Tâmâr,** *bah´-al taw-mawr´,* from 1167 and 8558; *possessor of* (the) *palm-tree; Baal-Tamar,* a place in Pal.:—Baal-tamar.

1194. בְּעֹן **B^e^'ôn,** *beh-ohn´;* prob. a contr. of 1010; *Beön,* a place E. of the Jordan:—Beon.

1195. בַּעֲנָא **Ba'ănâ',** *bah-an-aw´;* the same as 1196; *Baana,* the name of four Isr.:—Baana, Baanah.

1196. בַּעֲנָה **Ba'ănâh,** *bah-an-aw´;* from a der. of 6031 with prep. pref.; *in affliction:—Baanah,* the name of four Isr.:—Baanah.

1197. בָּעַר **bâ'ar,** *baw-ar´;* a prim. root; to *kindle,* i.e. *consume* (by fire or by eating); also (as denom. from 1198) to *be (-come) brutish:*—be brutish, bring (put, take) away, burn, (cause to) eat (up), feed, heat, kindle, set ([on fire]), waste.

1198. בַּעַר **ba'ar,** *bah´-ar;* from 1197; prop. *food* (as *consumed*); i.e. (by exten.) of cattle *brutishness;* (concr.) *stupid:*—brutish (person), foolish.

1199. בָּעֲרָא **Bâ'ărâ',** *bah-ar-aw´;* from 1198; *brutish; Baara,* an Israelitish woman:—Baara.

1200. בְּעֵרָה **b^e^'êrâh,** *bĕ-ay-raw´;* from 1197; a *burning:*—fire.

1201. בַּעְשָׁא **Baʻshâʼ,** *bah-shaw´;* from an unused root mean. to *stink; offensiveness: Basha,* a king of Israel:—Baasha.

1202. בַּעֲשֵׂיָה **Baʻăsêyâh,** *bah-as-ay-yaw´;* from 6213 and 3050 with prep. pref.; *in* (the) *work of Jah; Baasejah,* an Isr.:—Baaseiah.

1203. בְּעֶשְׁתְּרָה **Beʻeshterâh,** *beh-esh-ter-aw´;* from 6251 (as sing. of 6252) with prep. pref.; *with Ashtoreth; Beështerah,* a place E. of the Jordan:—Beeshterah.

1204. בָּעַת **bâʻath,** *baw-ath´;* a prim. root; to *fear:*—affright, be (make) afraid, terrify, trouble.

1205. בְּעָתָה **beʻâthâh,** *beh-aw-thaw´;* from 1204; *fear:*—trouble.

1206. בֹּץ **bôts,** *botse;* prob. the same as 948; *mud* (as *whitish* clay):—mire.

1207. בִּצָּה **bitstsâh,** *bits-tsaw´;* intens. from 1206; a *swamp:*—fen. mire (-ry place).

1208. בָּצוֹר° **bâtsowr,** *baw-tsore´;* from 1219; *inaccessible,* i.e. *lofty:*—vintage [*by confusion with* 1210].

1209. בֵּצַי **Bêtsay,** *bay-tsah´ee;* perh. the same as 1153; *Betsai,* the name of two Isr.:—Bezai.

1210. בָּצִיר **bâtsîyr,** *baw-tseer´;* from 1219; *clipped,* i.e. the *grape crop:*—vintage.

1211. בֶּצֶל **betsel,** *beh´-tsel;* from an unused root appar. mean. to *peel;* an *onion:*—onion.

1212. בְּצַלְאֵל **Betsalʼêl,** *bets-al-ale´;* prob. from 6738 and 410 with prep. pref.; *in* (the) *shadow* (i.e. protection) *of God; Betsalel;* the name of two Isr.:—Bezaleel.

1213. בַּצְלוּת **Batslûwth,** *bats-looth´;* or בַּצְלִית **Batslîyth,** *bats-leeth´;* from the same as 1211; a *peeling; Batsluth* or *Batslith;* an Isr.:—Bazlith, Bazluth.

1214. בָּצַע **bâtsaʻ,** *baw-tsah´;* a prim. root to *break* off, i.e. (usually) *plunder;* fig. to *finish,* or (intrans.) *stop:*—(be) covet (-ous), cut (off), finish, fulfill, gain (greedily), get, be given to [covetousness], greedy, perform, be wounded.

1215. בֶּצַע **betsaʻ,** *beh´-tsah;* from 1214; *plunder;* by extens. *gain* (usually unjust):—covetousness, (dishonest) gain, lucre, profit.

1216. בָּצֵק **bâtsêq,** *baw-tsake´;* a prim. root; perh. to *swell* up, i.e. *blister:*—swell.

1217. בָּצֵק **bâtsêq,** *baw-tsake´;* from 1216; *dough* (as *swelling* by fermentation):—dough, flour.

1218. בָּצְקַת **Botsqath,** *bots-cath´;* from 1216; a *swell* of ground; *Botscath,* a place in Pal.:—Bozcath, Boskath.

1219. בָּצַר **bâtsar,** *baw-tsar´;* a prim. root; to *clip* off; spec. (as denom. from 1210) to *gather* grapes; also to *be isolated* (i.e. *inaccessible* by height or fortification):—cut off, (de-) fenced, fortify, (grape) gather (-er), mighty things, restrain, strong, wall (up), withhold.

1220. בֶּצֶר **betser,** *beh´-tser;* from 1219; strictly a *clipping,* i.e. *gold* (as *dug* out):—gold defence.

1221. בֶּצֶר **Betser,** *beh´-tser;* the same as 1220. an *inaccessible* spot; *Betser,* a place in Pal.; also an Isr.:—Bezer.

1222. בְּצַר **betsar,** *bets-ar´;* another form for 1220; *gold:*—gold.

1223. בָּצְרָה **botsrâh,** *bots-raw´;* fem. from 1219; an *enclosure,* i.e. *sheep-fold:*—Bozrah.

1224. בָּצְרָה **Botsrâh,** *bots-raw´;* the same as 1223; *Botsrah,* a place in Edom:—Bozrah.

1225. בִּצָּרוֹן **bitstsârôwn,** *bits-tsaw-rone´;* masc. intens. from 1219; a *fortress:*—stronghold.

1226. בַּצֹּרֶת **batstsôreth,** *bats-tso´-reth;* fem. intens. from 1219; *restraint* (of rain), i.e. *drought:*—dearth, drought.

1227. בַּקְבּוּק **Baqbûwq,** *bak-book´;* the same as 1228; *Bakbuk,* one of the *Nethinim:*—Bakbuk.

1228. בַּקְבֻּק **baqbûk,** *bak-book´;* from 1238; a *bottle* (from the gurgling in *emptying*):—bottle, cruse.

1229. בַּקְבֻּקְיָה **Baqbukyâh,** *bak-book-yaw´;* from 1228 and 3050; *emptying* (i.e. *wasting*) *of Jah; Bakbukjah,* an Isr.:—Bakbukiah.

1230. בַּקְבַּקַּר **Baqbaqqar,** *bak-bak-kar´;* redupl. from 1239; *searcher; Bakbakkar,* an Isr.:—Bakbakkar.

1231. בֻּקִּי **Buqqîy,** *book-kee´;* from 1238; *wasteful; Bukki,* the name of two Isr.:—Bukki.

1232. בֻּקִּיָּה **Buqqîyâh,** *book-kee-yaw´;* from 1238 and 3050; *wasting of Jah; Bukkijah,* an Isr.:—Bukkiah.

1233. בְּקִיעַ **beqîyaʻ,** *bek-ee´-ah;* from 1234; a *fissure:*—breach, cleft.

1234. בָּקַע **bâqaʻ,** *baw-kah´;* a prim. root; to *cleave;* gen. to *rend, break, rip* or *open:*—make a breach, break forth (into, out, in pieces, through, up), be ready to burst, cleave (asunder), cut out, divide, hatch, rend (asunder), rip up, tear, win.

1235. בֶּקַע **beqâʻ,** *beh´-kah;* from 1234; a *section* (half) of a shekel, i.e. a *beka* (a weight and a coin):—bekah, half a shekel.

1236. בִּקְעָא **biqʻâʼ** (Chald.), *bik-aw´;* corresp. to 1237:—plain.

1237. בִּקְעָה **biqʻâh,** *bik-aw´;* from 1234; prop. a *split,* i.e. a wide level *valley* between mountains:—plain, valley.

1238. בָּקַק **bâqaq,** *baw-kah´;* a prim. root; to *pour* out, i.e. to *empty,* fig. to *depopulate;* by anal. to *spread* out (as a fruitful vine):—(make) empty (out), fail, × utterly, make void.

1239. בָּקַר **bâqar,** *baw-kar´;* a prim. root; prop. to *plough,* or (gen.) *break* forth, i.e. (fig.) to *inspect, admire, care for, consider:*—(make) inquire (-ry), (make) search, seek out.

1240. בְּקַר **beqar** (Chald.), *bek-ar´;* corresp. to 1239:—inquire, make search.

1241. בָּקָר **bâqâr,** *baw-kaw´;* from 1239; a *beeve* or animal of the ox kind of either gender (as used for *ploughing*); collect, a *herd:*—beeve, bull (+ -ock), + calf, + cow, great [cattle], + heifer, herd, kine, ox.

1242. בֹּקֶר **bôqer,** *bo´-ker;* from 1239; prop. *dawn* (as the *break* of day); gen. *morning:*—(+) day, early, morning, morrow.

1243. בַּקָּרָה **baqqârâh,** *bak-kaw-raw´;* intens. from 1239; a *looking after:*—seek out.

1244. בִּקֹּרֶת **biqqôreth,** *bik-ko -reth;* from 1239; prop. *examination,* i.e. (by impl.) *punishment:*—scourged.

1245. בָּקַשׁ **bâqash,** *baw-kash´;* a prim. root; to *search* out (by any method, spec. in worship or prayer); by impl. to *strive after:*—ask, beg, beseech, desire, enquire, get, make inquisition, procure, (make) request, require, seek (for).

1246. בַּקָּשָׁה **baqqâshâh,** *bak-kaw-shaw´;* from 1245; a *petition:*—request.

1247. בַּר **bar** (Chald.), *bar;* corresp. to 1121; a *son, grandon,* etc.:— × old, son.

1248. בַּר **bar,** *bar;* borrowed (as a title) from 1247; the *heir* (apparent to the throne):—son.

1249. בַּר **bar,** *bar;* from 1305 (in its various senses); *beloved;* also *pure, empty:*—choice, clean, clear, pure.

1250. בָּר **bâr,** *bawr;* or בַּר **bar,** *bar;* from 1305 (in the sense of *winnowing*): *grain* of any kind (even while standing in the field); by extens. the open *country:*—corn, wheat.

1251. בַּר **bar** (Chald.), *bar;* corresp. to 1250; a *field:*—field.

1252. בֹּר **bôr,** *bore;* from 1305; *purity:*—cleanness, pureness.

1253. בֹּר **bôr,** *bore;* the same as 1252; vegetable *lye* (from its *cleansing*); used as a *soap* for washing, or a *flux* for metals:— × never so, purely.

1254. בָּרָא **bârâʼ,** *baw-raw´;* a prim. root; (absol.) to *create;* (qualified) to *cut* down (a wood), *select, feed* (as formative processes):—choose, create (creator), cut down, dispatch, do, make (fat).

1255. בְּרֹאדַךְ בַּלְאֲדָן **Berôʼdak Balʼădân,** *ber-o-dak´ bal-ad-awn´;* a var. of 4757; *Berodak-Baladan,* a Bab. king:—Berodach-baladan.

בִּרְאִי **Birʼîy.** See 1011.

1256. בְּרָאיָה **Berâʼyâh,** *ber-aw-yaw´;* from 1254 and 3050; *Jah has created; Berajah,* an Isr.:—Beraiah.

1257. בַּרְבֻּר **barbûr,** *bar-boor´;* by redupl. from 1250; a *fowl* (as fattened on *grain*):—fowl.

1258. בָּרַד **bârad,** *baw-rad´;* a prim. root, to *hail:*—hail.

1259. בָּרָד **bârâd,** *baw-rawd´;* from 1258; *hail:*—hail ([stones]).

1260. בֶּרֶד **Bered,** *beh´-red;* from 1258; *hail; Bered,* the name of a place south of Pal., also of an Isr.:—Bered.

1261. בָּרֹד **bârôd,** *baw-rode´;* from 1258; *spotted* (as if with *hail*):—grisled.

1262. בָּרָה **bârâh,** *baw-raw´;* a prim. root; to *select;* also (as denom. from 1250) to *feed;* also (as equiv. to 1305) to *render clear* (Eccl. 3 : 18):—choose, (cause to) eat, manifest, (give) meat.

1263. בָּרוּךְ **Bârûwk,** *baw-rook´;* pass. part. from 1288; *blessed; Baruk,* the name of three Isr.:—Baruch.

1264. בְּרוֹם **b^{e}rôwm,** *ber-ome´;* prob. of for. or. *damask* (stuff of variegated thread):—rich apparel.

1265. בְּרוֹשׁ **b^{e}rôwsh,** *ber-ōsh´;* of uncert. der.; a *cypress* (?) tree; hence a *lance* or a *musical* instrument (as made of that wood):—fir (tree).

1266. בְּרוֹת **b^{e}rôwth,** *ber-ōth´;* a var. of 1265; the *cypress* (or some elastic tree):—fir.

1267. בָּרוּת **bârûwth,** *baw-rooth´;* from 1262; *food:*—meat.

1268. בֵּרוֹתָה **Bêrôwthâh,** *bay-ro-thaw´;* or בֵּרֹתַי **Bêrôthay,** *bay-ro-thah´ee;* prob. from 1266; *cypress* or *cypresslike; Berothah* or *Berothai,* a place north of Pal.:—Berothah, Berothai.

1269. בִּרְזוֹת° **Birzôwth,** *beer-zoth´;* prob. fem. plur. from an unused root (appar. mean. to *pierce*); *holes; Birzoth,* an Isr.:—Birzavith [*from the marg.*].

1270. בַּרְזֶל **barzel,** *bar-zel´;* perh. from the root of 1269; *iron* (as *cutting*) by extens. an iron *implement:*—(ax) head, iron.

1271. בַּרְזִלַּי **Barzillay,** *bar-zil-lah´ee;* from 1270; *iron* hearted; *Barzillai,* the name of three Isr.:—Barzillai.

1272. בָּרַח **bârach,** *baw-rakh´;* a prim. root; to *bolt,* i.e. flg. to *flee* suddenly:—chase (away); drive away, fain, flee (away), put to flight, make haste, reach, run away, shoot.

בָּרִחַ **bârîach.** See 1281.

1273. בַּרְחֻמִי **Barchûmîy,** *bar-khoo-mee´;* by transp. for 978; a *Barchumite,* or native of *Bachurim:*—Barhumite.

1274. בְּרִי **b^{e}rîy,** *ber-ee´;* from 1262; *fat:*—fat.

1275. בֵּרִי **Bêrîy,** *bay-ree´;* prob. by contr. from 882; *Beri,* an Isr.:—Beri.

1276. בֵּרִי **Bêrîy,** *bay-ree´;* of uncert. der.; (only in the plur. and with the art.) the *Berites,* a place in Pal.:—Berites.

1277. בָּרִיא **bârîy',** *baw-ree´;* from 1254 (in the sense of 1262); *fatted* or *plump:*—fat ([fleshed], -ter), fed, firm, plenteous, rank.

1278. בְּרִיאָה **b^{e}rîy'âh,** *ber-ee-aw´;* fem. from 1254; a *creation,* i.e. a *novelty:*—new thing.

1279. בִּרְיָה **biryâh,** *beer-yaw´;* fem. from 1262; *food:*—meat.

1280. בְּרִיחַ **b^{e}rîyach,** *ber-ee´-akh;* from 1272; a *bolt:*—bar, fugitive.

1281. בָּרִיחַ **bârîyach,** *baw-ree´-akh;* or (short.) בָּרִחַ **bârîach,** *baw-ree´-akh;* from 1272; a *fugitive,* i.e. the *serpent* (as *fleeing*), and the constellation by that name:—crooked, noble, piercing.

1282. בָּרִיחַ **Bârîyach,** *baw-ree´-akh;* the same as 1281; *Bariach,* an Isr.:—Bariah.

1283. בְּרִיעָה **B^{e}rîy'âh,** *ber-ee´-aw;* appar. from the fem. of 7451 with prep. pref.; *in trouble; Beriah,* the name of four Isr.:—Beriah.

1284. בְּרִיעִי **B^{e}rîy'îy,** *ber-ee-ee´;* patron. from 1283; a *Beriite* (collect.) or desc. of Beriah:—Beerites.

1285. בְּרִית **b^{e}rîyth,** *ber-eeth´;* from 1262 (in the sense of *cutting* [like 1254]); a *compact* (because made by passing between *pieces* of flesh):—confederacy, [con-]feder[-ate], covenant, league.

1286. בְּרִית **B^{e}rîyth,** *ber-eeth´;* the same as 1285; *Berith,* a Shechemitish deity:—Berith.

1287. בֹּרִית **bôrîyth,** *bo-reeth´;* fem. of 1253; vegetable *alkali:*—sope.

1288. בָּרַךְ **bârak,** *baw-rak´;* a prim. root; to *kneel;* by impl. to *bless* God (as an act of adoration), and (vice-versa) man (as a benefit); also (by euphemism) to *curse* (God or the king, as treason):— × abundantly, × altogether, × at all, blaspheme, bless, congratulate, curse, × greatly, × indeed, kneel (down), praise, salute, × still, thank.

1289. בְּרַךְ **b^{e}rak** (Chald.), *ber-ak´;* corresp. to 1288:—bless, kneel.

1290. בֶּרֶךְ **berek,** *beh´-rek;* from 1288; a *knee:*—knee.

1291. בֶּרֶךְ **berek** (Chald.), *beh´-rek;* corresp. to 1290:—knee.

1292. בָּרַכְאֵל **Bârak'êl,** *baw-rak-ale´;* from 1288 and 410, *God has blessed; Barakel,* the father of one of Job's friends:—Barachel.

1293. בְּרָכָה **B^{e}râkâh,** *ber-aw-kaw´;* from 1288; *benediction;* by impl. *prosperity:*—blessing, liberal, pool, present.

1294. בְּרָכָה **B^{e}râkâh,** *ber-aw-kaw´;* the same as 1293; *Berakah,* the name of an Isr., and also of a valley in Pal.:—Berachah.

1295. בְּרֵכָה **b^{e}rêkâh,** *ber-ay-kaw´;* from 1288; a *reservoir* (at which camels *kneel* as a resting place):—(fish-) pool.

1296. בֶּרֶכְיָה **Berekyâh,** *beh-rek-yaw´;* or בֶּרֶכְיָהוּ **Berekyâhûw,** *beh-rek-yaw´-hoo;* from 1290 and 3050; *knee* (i.e. *blessing*) of *Jah; Berekjah,* the name of six Isr.:—Berachiah, Berechiah.

1297. בְּרַם **b^{e}ram, (Chald.)** *ber-am´;* perh. from 7313 with prep. pref.; prop. *highly,* i.e. *surely;* but used adversatively, *however:*—but, nevertheless, yet.

1298. בֶּרַע **Bera',** *beh´-rah;* of uncert. der.; *Bera,* a Sodomitish king:—Bera.

1299. בָּרַק **bâraq,** *baw-rak´;* a prim. root; to *lighten* (lightning):—cast forth.

1300. בָּרָק **bârâq,** *baw-rawk´;* from 1299; *lightning;* by anal. a *gleam;* concr. a *flashing* sword:—bright, glitter (-ing, sword), lightning.

1301. בָּרָק **Bârâq,** *baw-rawk´;* the same as 1300; *Barak,* an Isr.:—Barak.

1302. בַּרְקוֹס **Barqôwç,** *bar-kose´;* of uncert. der.; *Barkos,* one of the Nethimim:—Barkos.

1303. בַּרְקָן **barqân,** *bar-kawn´;* from 1300; a *thorn* (perh. as burning *brightly*):—brier.

1304. בָּרֶקֶת **bâreqeth,** *baw-reh´-keth;* or בָּרְקַת **bâr^{e}kath,** *baw-rek-ath´;* from 1300; a gem (as *flashing*), perh. the *emerald:*—carbuncle.

1305. בָּרַר **bârar,** *baw-rar´;* a prim. root; to *clarify* (i.e. *brighten*), *examine, select:*—make bright, choice, chosen, cleanse (be clean), clearly, polished, (shew self) pure (-ify), purge (out).

1306. בִּרְשַׁע **Birsha',** *beer-shah´;* prob. from 7562 with prep. pref.; *with wickedness; Birsha,* a king of Gomorrah:—Birsha.

1307. בֵּרֹתִי **Bêrôthîy,** *bay-ro-thee´;* patrial from 1268; a *Berothite,* or inhabitant of Berothai:—Berothite.

1308. בְּשׂוֹר **B^{e}sôwr,** *bes-ore´;* from 1319; *cheerful; Besor,* a stream of Pal.:—Besor.

1309. בְּשׂוֹרָה *bes-o-raw´;* or (short.) בְּשֹׂרָה **b^{e}sôrâh,** *bes-o-raw´;* fem. from 1319; glad *tidings;* by impl. *reward for good news:*—reward for tidings.

1310. בָּשַׁל **bâshal,** *baw-shal´;* a prim. root; prop. to *boil* up; hence to *be done* in cooking; fig. to *ripen:*—bake, boil, bring forth, is ripe, roast, seethe, sod (be sodden).

1311. בָּשֵׁל **bâshêl,** *baw-shale´;* from 1310; *boiled:*— × at all, sodden.

1312. בִּשְׁלָם **Bishlâm,** *bish-lawm´;* of for. der.; *Bishlam,* a Pers.:—Bishlam.

1313. בָּשָׂם **bâsâm,** *baw-sawm´;* from an unused root mean. to *be fragrant;* [comp. 5561] the *balsalm* plant:—spice.

1314. בֶּשֶׂם **besem,** *beh´-sem;* or בֹּשֶׂם **bôsem,** *bo´-sem;* from the same as 1313; *fragrance;* by impl. *spicery;* also the *balsam* plant:—smell, spice, sweet (odour).

1315. בָּשְׂמַת **Bosmath,** *bos-math´;* fem. of 1314 (the second form); *fragrance; Bosmath,* the name of a wife of Esau, and of a daughter of Solomon:—Bashemath, Basmath.

1316. בָּשָׁן **Bâshân,** *baw-shawn´;* of uncert. der.; *Bashan* (often with the art.), a region E. of the Jordan:—Bashan.

1317. בָּשְׁנָה **boshnâh,** *bosh-naw´;* fem. from 954, *shamefulness:*—shame.

1318. בָּשַׁס **bâshaç,** *baw-shas´;* a prim. root; to *trample* down:—tread.

1319. בָּשַׂר **bâsar,** *baw-sar´;* a prim. root; prop. to *be fresh,* i.e. *full* (*rosy,* fig. *cheerful*); to *announce* (glad news):—messenger, preach, publish, shew forth, (bear, bring, carry, preach, good, tell good) tidings.

1320. בָּשָׂר **bâsâr,** *baw-sawr´;* from 1319; *flesh* (from its *freshness*); by extens. *body, person;* also (by euphem.) the *pudenda* of a man:—body, [fat, lean] flesh [-ed], kin, [man-] kind, + nakedness, self, skin.

1321. בְּשַׂר **b**e**sar** (Chald.), *bes-ar´;* corresp. to 1320:—flesh.

בְּשׂרָה **b**e**sôrâh.** See 1309.

1322. בֹּשֶׁת **bôsheth,** *bo´-sheth;* from 954; *shame* (the feeling and the condition, as well as its cause); by impl. (spec.) an *idol:*—ashamed, confusion, + greatly, (put to) shame (-ful thing).

1323. בַּת **bath,** *bath;* from 1129 (as fem. of 1121); a *daughter* (used in the same wide sense as other terms of relationship, lit. and fig.):—apple [of the eye], branch, company, daughter, × first, × old, + owl, town, village.

1324. בַּת **bath,** *bath;* prob. from the same as 1327; a *bath* or Heb. measure (as a means of *division*) of liquids:—bath.

1325. בַּת **bath** (Chald.), *bath;* corresp. to 1324:—bath.

1326. בָּתָה **bâthâh,** *baw-thaw´;* prob. an orth. var. for 1327; *desolation:*—waste.

1327. בַּתָּה **battâh,** *bat-taw´;* fem. from an unused root (mean. to *break* in pieces); *desolation:*—desolate.

1328. בְּתוּאֵל **B**e**thûw'êl,** *beth-oo-ale´;* appar. from the same as 1326 and 410; *destroyed of God; Bethuel,* the name of a nephew of Abraham, and of a place in Pal.:—Bethuel. Comp. 1329.

1329. בְּתוּל **B**e**thûwl,** *beth-ool´;* for 1328; *Bethul* (i.e. *Bethuel*), a place in Pal.:—Bethuel.

1330. בְּתוּלָה **b**e**thûwlâh,** *beth-oo-law´;* fem. pass. part. of an unused root mean. to *separate;* a *virgin* (from her *privacy*); sometimes (by continuation) a *bride;* also (fig.) a *city* or *state:*—maid, virgin.

1331. בְּתוּלִים **b**e**thûwlîym,** *beth-oo-leem´;* masc. plur. of the same as 1330; (collect. and abstr.) *virginity;* by impl. and concr. the *tokens* of it:— × maid, virginity.

1332. בִּתְיָה **Bithyâh,** *bith-yaw´;* from 1323 and 3050; *daughter* (i.e. worshipper) *of Jah; Bithjah,* an Eg. woman:—Bithiah.

1333. בָּתַק **bâthaq,** *baw-thak´;* a prim. root; to *cut* in pieces:—thrust through.

1334. בָּתַר **bâthar,** *baw-thar´;* a prim. root, to *chop* up:—divide.

1335. בֶּתֶר **bether,** *beh´-ther;* from 1334; a *section:*—part, piece.

1336. בֶּתֶר **Bether,** *beh´-ther;* the same as 1335; *Bether,* a (craggy) place in Pal.:—Bether.

1337. בַּת רַבִּים **Bath Rabbîym,** *bath rab-beem´;* from 1323 and a masc. plur. from 7227; the *daughter* (i.e. *city*) *of Rabbah:*—Bath-rabbim.

1338. בִּתְרוֹן **Bithrôwn,** *bith-rone´;* from 1334; (with the art.) the *craggy* spot; *Bithron,* a place E. of the Jordan:—Bithron.

1339. בַּת־שֶׁבַע **Bath-Sheba',** *bath-sheh´-bah;* from 1323 and 7651 (in the sense of 7650); *daughter of an oath; Bath-Sheba,* the mother of Solomon:—Bath-sheba.

1340. בַּת־שׁוּעַ **Bath-Shûwa',** *bath-shoo´-ah;* from 1323 and 7771; *daughter of wealth; Bath-shuä,* the same as 1339:—Bath-shua.

ג

1341. גֵּא **gê',** *gay;* for 1343; *haughty:*—proud.

1342. גָּאָה **gâ'âh,** *gaw-aw´;* a prim. root; to *mount* up; hence in gen. to *rise,* (fig.) be *majestic:*—gloriously, grow up, increase, be risen, triumph.

1343. גֵּאֶה **gê'eh,** *gay-eh´;* from 1342; *lofty;* fig. *arrogant:*—proud.

1344. גֵּאָה **gê'âh,** *gay-aw´;* fem. from 1342; *arrogance:*—pride.

1345. גְּאוּאֵל **G**e**'ûw'êl,** *gheh-oo-ale´;* from 1342 and 410; *majesty of God; Geüel,* an Isr.:—Geuel.

1346. גַּאֲוָה **ga'ăvâh,** *gah-av-aw´;* from 1342; *arrogance* or *majesty;* by impl. (concr.) *ornament:*—excellency, haughtiness, highness, pride, proudly, swelling.

1347. גָּאוֹן **gâ'ôwn,** *gaw-ohn´;* from 1342; the same as 1346:—arrogancy, excellency (-lent), majesty, pomp, pride, proud, swelling.

1348. גֵּאוּת **gê'ûwth,** *gay-ooth´;* from 1342; the same as 1346:—excellent things, lifting up, majesty, pride, proudly, raging.

1349. גַּאֲיוֹן **ga'ăyôwn,** *gah-ăh-yone´;* from 1342: *haughty:*—proud.

1350. גָּאַל **gâ'al,** *gaw-al´;* a prim. root, to *redeem* (according to the Oriental law of kinship), i.e. to *be the next of kin* (and as such to *buy back* a relative's property, *marry* his widow, etc.):— × in any wise, × at all, avenger, deliver, (do, perform the part of near, next) kinsfolk (-man), purchase, ransom, redeem (-er), revenger.

1351. גָּאַל **gâ'al,** *gaw-al´;* a prim. root, [rather ident. with 1350, through the idea of *freeing,* i.e. *repudiating*]; to *soil* or (fig.) *descrate:*—defile, pollute, stain.

1352. גֹּאֶל **gô'el,** *go´-el;* from 1351; *profanation:*—defile.

1353. גְּאֻלָּה **g**e**ullâh,** *gheh-ool-law´;* fem. pass. part. of 1350; *redemption* (including the right and the object); by impl. *relationship:*—kindred, redeem, redemption, right.

1354. גַּב **gab,** *gab;* from an unused root mean. to *hollow* or *curve;* the *back* (as *rounded* [comp. 1460 and 1479]; by anal. the *top* or *rim,* a *boss,* a *vault, arch* of eye, *bulwarks,* etc.:—back, body, boss, eminent (higher) place, [eye] brows, nave, ring.

1355. גַּב **gab** (Chald.), *gab;* corresp. to 1354:—back.

1356. גֵּב **gêb,** *gabe;* from 1461; a *log* (as *cut* out); also *well* or *cistern* (as *dug*):—beam, ditch, pit.

1357. גֵּב **gêb,** *gabe;* prob. from 1461 [comp. 1462]; a *locust* (from its *cutting*):—locust.

1358. גֹּב **gôb** (Chald.), *gobe;* from a root corresp. to 1461; a *pit* (for wild animals) (as *cut* out):—den.

1359. גֹּב **Gôb,** *gobe;* or (fully) גּוֹב **Gôwb,** *gobe´;* from 1461; *pit; Gob,* a place in Pal.:—Gob.

1360. גֶּבֶא **gebe,** *geh´-beh;* from an unused root mean. prob. to *collect;* a *reservoir;* by anal. a *marsh:*—marsh, pit.

1361. גָּבַהּ **gâbahh,** *gaw-bah´;* a prim. root; to *soar,* i.e. *be lofty;* fig. to *be haughty:*—exalt, be haughty, be (make) high (-er), lift up, mount up, be proud, raise up great height, upward.

1362. גָּבָהּ **gâbâhh,** *gaw-bawh´;* from 1361; *lofty* (lit. or fig.):—high, proud.

1363. גֹּבַהּ **gôbahh,** *go´-bah;* from 1361; *elation, grandeur, arrogance:*—excellency, haughty, height, high, loftiness, pride.

1364. גָּבֹהַּ **gâbôahh,** *gaw-bo´-ah;* or (fully) גָּבוֹהַּ **gâbôwahh,** *gaw-bo´-ah;* from 1361; *elevated* (or *elated*), *powerful, arrogant:*—haughty, height, high (-er), lofty, proud, × exceeding proudly.

1365. גַּבְהוּת **gabhûwth,** *gab-hooth´;* from 1361; *pride:*—loftiness, lofty.

1366. גְּבוּל **g**e**bûwl,** *gheb-ool´;* or (short.) גְּבֻל **g**e**bûl,** *gheb-ool´;* from 1379; prop. a *cord* (as *twisted*), i.e. (by impl.) a *boundary;* by extens. the *territory* inclosed:—border, bound, coast, × great, landmark, limit, quarter, space.

1367. גְּבוּלָה **g**e**bûwlâh,** *gheb-oo-law´;* or (short.) גְּבֻלָה **g**e**bûlâh,** *gheb-oo-law´;* fem. of 1366; a *boundary, region:*—border, bound, coast, landmark, place.

1368. גִּבּוֹר **gibbôwr,** *ghib-bore´;* or (short.) גִּבֹּר **gibbôr,** *ghib-bore´;* intens. from the same as 1397; *powerful;* by impl. *warrior, tyrant:*—champion, chief, × excel, giant, man, mighty (man, one), strong (man), valiant man.

1369. גְּבוּרָה **g**e**bûwrâh,** *gheb-oo-raw´;* fem. pass. part. from the same as 1368; *force* (lit. or fig.); by impl. *valor, victory:*—force, mastery, might, mighty (act, power), power, strength.

1370. גְּבוּרָה **gᵉbûwrâh** (Chald.), *gheb-oo-raw´;* corresp. to 1369; *power:*—might.

1371. גִּבֵּחַ **gibbêach,** *ghib-bay´-akh;* from an unused root mean. to *be high* (in the forehead); *bald* in the forehead:—forehead bald.

1372. גַּבַּחַת **gabbachath,** *gab-bakh´-ath;* from the same as 1371; *baldness* in the forehead; by anal. a *bare spot* on the right side of cloth:—bald forehead, × without.

1373. גַּבַּי **Gabbay,** *gab-bah´ee;* from the same as 1354; *collective:*—*Gabbai,* an Isr.:—Gabbai.

1374. גֵּבִים **Gêbîym,** *gay-beem´;* plur. of 1356; *cisterns; Gebim,* a place in Pal.:—Gebim.

1375. גְּבִיעַ **gᵉbîyaʻ,** *gheb-ee´-ah;* from an unused root (mean. to *be convex*); a *goblet;* by anal. the *calyx* of a flower:—house, cup, pot.

1376. גְּבִיר **gᵉbîyr,** *gheb-eer´;* from 1396, a *master:*—lord.

1377. גְּבִירָה **gᵉbîyrâh,** *gheb-ee-raw´;* fem. of 1376; a *mistress:*—queen.

1378. גָּבִישׁ **gâbîysh,** *gaw-beesh´;* from an unused root (prob. mean. to *freeze*); *crystal* (from its resemblance to *ice*):—pearl.

1379. גָּבַל **gâbal,** *gaw-bal´;* a prim. root; prop. to *twist* as a rope; only (as a denom. from 1366) to *bound* (as by a line):—be border, set (bounds about).

1380. גְּבַל **Gᵉbal,** *gheb-al´;* from 1379 (in the sense of a *chain* of hills); a *mountain; Gebal,* a place in Phœnicia:—Gebal.

1381. גְּבָל **Gᵉbâl,** *gheb-awl´;* the same as 1380; *Gebal,* a region in Idumæa:—Gebal.
גְּבֻלָה **gᵉbûlâh.** See 1367.

1382. גִּבְלִי **Giblîy,** *ghib-lee´;* patrial from 1380; a *Gebalite,* or inhab. of Gebal:—Giblites, stone-squarer.

1383. גַּבְלֻת **gablûth,** *gab-looth´;* from 1379; a twisted *chain* or *lace:*—end.

1384. גִּבֵּן **gibbên,** *gib-bane´;* from an unused root mean. to be *arched* or *contracted; hunch-backed:*—crookbackt.

1385. גְּבִנָה **gᵉbînah,** *gheb-ee-naw´;* fem. from the same as 1384; *curdled* milk:—cheese.

1386. גַּבְנֹן **gabnôn,** *gab-nohn´;* from the same as 1384; a *hump* or *peak* of hills:—high.

1387. גֶּבַע **Gebaʻ,** *gheh´-bah;* from the same as 1375, a *hillock; Geba,* a place in Pal.:—Gaba, Geba, Gibeah.

1388. גִּבְעָא **Gibʻâʼ,** *ghib-aw´;* by perm. for 1389; a *hill; Giba,* a place in Pal.:—Gibeah.

1389. גִּבְעָה **gibʻâh,** *ghib-aw´;* fem. from the same as 1387; a *hillock:*—hill, little hill.

1390. גִּבְעָה **Gibʻâh,** *ghib-aw´;* the same as 1389; *Gibah;* the name of three places in Pal.:—Gibeah, the hill.

1391. גִּבְעוֹן **Gibʻôwn,** *ghib-ohn´;* from the same as 1387; *hilly; Gibon,* a place in Pal.:—Gibeon.

1392. גִּבְעֹל **gibʻôl,** *ghib-ole´;* prol. from 1375; the *calyx* of a flower:—bolled.

1393. גִּבְעֹנִי **Gibʻônîy,** *ghib-o-nee´;* patrial from 1391 a *Gibonite,* or inhab. of Gibon:—Gibeonite.

1394. גִּבְעַת **Gibʻath,** *ghib-ath´;* from the same as 1375; *hilliness; Gibath:*—Gibeath.

1395. גִּבְעָתִי **Gibʻâthîy,** *ghib-aw-thee´;* patrial from 1390; a *Gibathite,* or inhab. of Gibath:—Gibeathite.

1396. גָּבַר **gâbar,** *gaw-bar´;* a prim. root; to *be strong;* by impl. to *prevail, act insolently:*—exceed, confirm, be great, be mighty, prevail, put to more [strength], strengthen, be stronger, be valiant.

1397. גֶּבֶר **geber,** *gheh´-ber;* from 1396; prop. a *valiant* man or *warrior;* gen. a *person* simply:—every one, man, × mighty.

1398. גֶּבֶר **Geber,** *gheh´-ber;* the same as 1397; *Geber,* the name of two Isr.:—Geber.

1399. גְּבַר **gᵉbar,** *gheb-ar´;* from 1396; the same as 1397; a person:—man.

1400. גְּבַר **gᵉbar** (Chald.), *gheb-ar´;* corresp. to 1399:—certain, man.

1401. גִּבָּר **gibbâr** (Chald.), *ghib-bawr´;* intens. of 1400; *valiant,* or *warrior:*—mighty.

1402. גִּבָּר **Gibbâr,** *ghib-bawr´;* intens. of 1399; *Gibbar,* an Isr.:—Gibbar.
גְּבֻרָה **gᵉbûrâh.** See 1369.

1403. גַּבְרִיאֵל **Gabrîyʼêl,** *gab-ree-ale´;* from 1397 and 410; *man of God; Gabriel,* an archangel:—Gabriel.

1404. גְּבֶרֶת **gᵉbereth,** *gheb-eh´-reth;* fem. of 1376; *mistress:*—lady, mistress.

1405. גִּבְּתוֹן **Gibbᵉthôwn,** *ghib-beth-one´;* in tens. from 1389; a *hilly* spot; *Gibbethon,* a place in Pal.:—Gibbethon.

1406. גָּג **gâg,** *gawg;* prob. by redupl. from 1342; a *roof;* by anal. the *top* of an altar:—roof (of the house), (house) top (of the house).

1407. גַּד **gad,** *gad;* from 1413 (in the sense of *cutting*); *coriander* seed (from its furrows):—coriander.

1408. גַּד **Gad,** *gad;* a var. of 1409; *Fortune,* a Bab. deity:—that troop.

1409. גָּד **gâd,** *gawd;* from 1464 (in the sense of *distributing*); *fortune:*—troop.

1410. גָּד **Gâd,** *gawd;* from 1464; *Gad,* a son of Jacob, includ. his tribe and its territory; also a prophet:—Gad.

1411. גְּדָבָר **gᵉdâbâr** (Chald.), *ghed-aw-bawr´;* corresp. to 1489; a *treasurer:*—treasurer.

1412. גֻּדְגֹּדָה **Gudgôdâh,** *gud-go´-daw;* by redupl. from 1413 (in the sense of *cutting*) *cleft; Gudgodah,* a place in the Desert:—Gudgodah.

1413. גָּדַד **gâdad,** *gaw-dad´;* a prim. root [comp. 1464]; to *crowd;* also to *gash* (as if by *pressing* into):—assemble (selves by troops), gather (selves together, self in troops), cut selves.

1414. גְּדַד **gᵉdad** (Chald.), *ghed-ad´;* corresp. to 1413; to *cut* down:—hew down.
גְּדֻדָה **gᵉdûdâh.** See 1417.

1415. גָּדָה **gâdâh,** *gaw-daw´;* from an unused root (mean. to *cut* off); a *border* of a river (as *cut* into by the stream):—bank.
גַּדָּה **Gaddâh.** See 2693.

1416. גְּדוּד **gᵉdûwd,** *ghed-ood´;* from 1413; a *crowd* (espec. of soldiers):—army, band (of men), company, troop (of robbers).

1417. גְּדוּד **gᵉdûwd,** *ghed-ood´;* or (fem.) גְּדֻדָה **gᵉdûdâh,** *ghed-oo-daw´;* from 1413; a *furrow* (as *cut*):—furrow.

1418. גְּדוּדָה **gᵉdûwdâh,** *ghed-oo-daw´;* fem. part. pass. of 1413; an *incision:*—cutting.

1419. גָּדוֹל **gâdôwl,** *gaw-dole´;* or (short.) גָּדֹל **gâdôl,** *gaw-dole´;* from 1431; *great* (in any sense); hence *older;* also *insolent:*— + aloud, elder (-est), + exceeding (-ly), + far, (man of) great (man, matter, thing, -er, -ness), high, long, loud, mighty, more, much, noble, proud thing, × sore, (×) very.

1420. גְּדוּלָה **gᵉdûwlâh,** *ghed-oo-law´;* or (short.) גְּדֻלָּה **gᵉdullâh,** *ghed-ool-law´;* or (less accurately) גְּדוּלָּה **gᵉdûwllâh,** *ghed-ool-law´;* fem. of 1419; *greatness;* (concr.) *mighty acts:*—dignity, great things (-ness), majesty.

1421. גִּדּוּף **giddûwph,** *ghid-doof´;* or (short.) גִּדֻּף **giddûph,** *ghid-doof´;* and (fem.) גִּדּוּפָה **giddûphâh,** *ghid-doo-faw´;* or גִּדֻּפָה **giddûphâh,** *ghid-doo-faw´;* from 1422, *vilification:*—reproach, reviling.

1422. גְּדוּפָה **gᵉdûwphâh,** *ghed-oo-faw´;* fem. pass. part. of 1442; a *revilement:*—taunt.
גְּדוֹר **Gᵉdôwr.** See 1446.

1423. גְּדִי **gᵉdîy,** *ghed-ee´;* from the same as 1415; a young *goat* (from *browsing*):—kid.

1424. גָּדִי **Gâdîy,** *gaw-dee´;* from 1409; *fortunate; Gadi,* an Isr.:—Gadi.

1425. גָּדִי **Gâdîy,** *gaw-dee´;* patron. from 1410; a *Gadite* (collect.) or desc. of Gad:—Gadites, children of Gad.

1426. גַּדִּי **Gaddîy,** *gad-dee´;* intens. for 1424; *Gaddi,* an Isr.:—Gaddi.

1427. גַּדִּיאֵל **Gaddîyʼêl,** *gad-dee-ale´;* from 1409 and 410; *fortune of God; Gaddiel,* an Isr.:—Gaddiel.

1428. גִּדְיָה° **gidyâh,** *ghid-yaw´;* or גַּדְיָה° **gadyâh,** *gad-yaw´;* the same as 1415; a river *brink:*—bank.

1429. גְּדִיָּה **gᵉdîyâh,** *ghed-ee-yaw´;* fem. of 1423; a young female *goat:*—kid.

1430. גָּדִישׁ **gâdîysh,** *gaw-deesh´;* from an unused root (mean. to *heap* up); a *stack* of sheaves; by anal. a *tomb:*—shock (stack) (of corn), tomb.

1431. גָּדַל **gâdal,** *gaw-dal´;* a prim. root; prop. to *twist* [comp. 1434], i.e. to *be* (caus. *make*) *large* (in various senses, as in body, mind, estate or honor, also in pride):—advance, boast, bring up, exceed, excellent, be (-come, do, give, make, wax), great (-er, come to . . estate, + things), grow (up), increase, lift up, magnify (-ifical), be much set by, nourish (up), pass, promote, proudly [spoken], tower.

1432. גָּדֵל **gâdêl,** *gaw-dale´;* from 1431; *large* (lit. or fig.):—great, grew.

1433. גֹּדֶל **gôdel,** *go´-del;* from 1431; *magnitude* (lit. or fig.):—greatness, stout (-ness).

1434. גְּדִל **gᵉdîl,** *ghed-eel´;* from 1431 (in the sense of *twisting*); *thread,* i.e. a *tassel* or *festoon:*—fringe, wreath.

1435. גִּדֵּל **Giddêl,** *ghid-dale´;* from 1431; *stout; Giddel,* the name of one of the Nethinim, also of one of "Solomon's servants":—Giddel.

גָּדֹל **gâdôl.** See 1419.

גְּדֻלָּה **gᵉdullâh.** See 1420.

1436. גְּדַלְיָה **Gᵉdalyâh,** *ghed-al-yaw´;* or (prol.) גְּדַלְיָהוּ **Gᵉdalyâhûw,** *ghed-al-yaw´-hoo;* from 1431 and 3050; *Jah has become great; Gedaljah,* the name of five Isr.:—Gedaliah.

1437. גִּדַּלְתִּי **Giddaltîy,** *ghid-dal´-tee;* from 1431; *I have made great; Giddalti,* an Isr.:—Giddalti.

1438. גָּדַע **gâdaʻ,** *gaw-dah´;* a prim. root; to *fell* a tree; gen. to *destroy* anything:—cut (asunder, in sunder, down, off), hew down.

1439. גִּדְעוֹן **Gidʻôwn,** *ghid-ohn´;* from 1438; *feller* (i.e. *warrior*): *Gidon,* an Isr.:—Gideon.

1440. גִּדְעֹם **Gidʻôm,** *ghid-ohm´;* from 1438; a *cutting* (i.e. *desolation*); *Gidom,* a place in Pal.:—Gidom.

1441. גִּדְעֹנִי **Gidʻônîy,** *ghid-o-nee´;* from 1438; *warlike* [comp. 1439]; *Gidoni,* an Isr.:—Gideoni.

1442. גָּדַף **gâdaph,** *gaw-daf´;* a prim. root; to *hack* (with words), i.e. *revile:*—blaspheme, reproach.

גִּדּוּף **giddûph,** and

גִּדּוּפָה **giddûphâh.** See 1421.

1443. גָּדַר **gâdar,** *gaw-dar´;* a prim. root; to *wall* in or around:—close up, fence up, hedge, inclose, make up [a wall], mason, repairer.

1444. גֶּדֶר **geder,** *gheh´-der;* from 1443; a *circumvallation:*—wall.

1445. גֶּדֶר **Geder,** *gheh´-der;* the same as 1444: *Geder,* a place in Pal.:—Geder.

1446. גְּדֹר **Gᵉdor,** *ghed-ore´;* or (fully) גְּדוֹר **Gᵉdôwr,** *ghed-ore´;* from 1443; *inclosure; Gedor,* a place in Pal.; also the name of three Isr.:—Gedor.

1447. גָּדֵר **gâdêr,** *gaw-dare´;* from 1443; a *circumvallation;* by impl. an *inclosure:*—fence, hedge, wall.

1448. גְּדֵרָה **gᵉdêrâh,** *ghed-ay-raw´;* fem. of 1447; *inclosure* (espec. for flocks):— [sheep-] cote (fold) hedge, wall.

1449. גְּדֵרָה **Gᵉdêrâh,** *ghed-ay-raw´;* the same as 1448; (with the art.) *Gederah,* a place in Pal.:—Gederah, hedges.

1450. גְּדֵרוֹת **Gᵉdêrôwth,** *ghed-ay-rohth´;* plur. of 1448; *walls; Gederoth,* a place in Pal.:—Gederoth.

1451. גְּדֵרִי **Gᵉdêrîy,** *ghed-ay-ree´;* patrial from 1445; a *Gederite,* or inhab. of Geder:—Gederite.

1452. גְּדֵרָתִי **Gᵉdêrâthîy,** *ghed-ay-raw-thee´;* patrial from 1449; a *Gederathite,* or inhab. of Gederah:—Gederathite.

1453. גְּדֵרֹתַיִם **Gᵉdêrôthayim,** *ghed-ay-ro-thah´-yim;* dual of 1448; *double wall; Gederothajim,* a place in Pal.:—Gederothaim.

1454. גֵּה **gêh,** *gay;* prob. a clerical error for 2088; *this:*—this.

1455. גָּהָה **gâhâh,** *gaw-haw´;* a prim. root; to *remove* (a bandage from a wound, i.e. *heal* it):—cure.

1456. גֵּהָה **gêhâh,** *gay-haw´;* from 1455; a *cure:*—medicine.

1457. גָּהַר **gâhar,** *gaw-har´;* a prim. root; to *prostrate* oneself:—cast self down, stretch self.

1458. גַּו **gav,** *gav;* another form for 1460; the *back:*—back.

1459. גַּו **gav** (Chald.), *gav;* corresp. to 1460; the *middle:*—midst, same, there- (where-) in.

1460. גֵּו **gêv** *gave;* from 1342 [corresp. to 1354]; the *back;* by anal. the *middle:*— + among, back, body.

1461. גּוּב **gûwb,** *goob;* a prim. root; to *dig:*—husbandman.

1462. גּוֹב **gôwb,** *gobe;* from 1461; the *locust* (from its *grubbing* as a larve):—grasshopper, × great.

1463. גּוֹג **Gôwg,** *gohg;* of uncert. der.; *Gog,* the name of an Isr., also of some northern nation:—Gog.

1464. גּוּד **gûwd,** *goode;* a prim. root [akin to 1413]; to *crowd* upon, i.e. *attack:*—invade, overcome.

1465. גֵּוָה **gêvâh,** *gay-vaw´;* fem. of 1460; the *back,* i.e. (by extens.) the *person:*—body.

1466. גֵּוָה **gêvâh,** *gay-vaw´;* the same as 1465; *exaltation;* (fig.) *arrogance:*—lifting up, pride.

1467. גֵּוָה **gêvâh** (Chald.), *gay-vaw´;* corresp. to 1466:—pride.

1468. גּוּז **gûwz,** *gooz;* a prim. root [comp. 1494]; prop. to *shear* off; but used only in the (fig.) sense of *passing* rapidly:—bring, cut off.

1469. גּוֹזָל **gôwzâl,** *go-zawl´;* or (short.) גֹּזָל **gôzâl,** *go-zawl´;* from 1497; a *nestling* (as being comparatively *nude* of feathers):—young (pigeon).

1470. גּוֹזָן **Gôwzân,** *go-zawn´;* prob. from 1468; a *quarry* (as a place of *cutting* stones); *Gozan,* a province of Assyria:—Gozan.

1471. גּוֹי **gôwy,** *go´ee;* rarely (short.) גֹּי **gôy,** *go´-ee;* appar. from the same root as 1465 (in the sense of *massing*); a foreign *nation;* hence a *Gentile;* also (fig.) a *troop* of animals, or a *flight* of locusts:—Gentile, heathen, nation, people.

1472. גְּוִיָּה **gᵉvîyâh,** *ghev-ee-yaw´;* prol. for 1465; a *body,* whether alive or dead:—(dead) body, carcase, corpse.

1473. גּוֹלָה **gôwlâh,** *go-law´;* or (short.) גֹּלָה **gôlah,** *go-law´;* act. part. fem. of 1540; *exile;* concr. and coll. *exiles:*—(carried away), captive (-ity), removing.

1474. גּוֹלָן **Gôwlân,** *go-lawn´;* from 1473; *captive; Golan,* a place east of the Jordan:—Golan.

1475. גּוּמָּץ **gûwmmâts,** *goom-mawts´;* of uncert. der.; a *pit:*—pit.

1476. גּוּנִי **Gûwnîy,** *goo-nee´;* prob. from 1598; *protected; Guni,* the name of two Isr.:—Guni.

1477. גּוּנִי **Gûwnîy,** *goo-nee´;* patron. from 1476; a *Gunite* (collect. with art. pref.) or desc. of Guni:—Gunites.

1478. גָּוַע **gâvaʻ,** *gaw-vah´;* a prim. root; to *breathe* out, i.e. (by impl.) *expire:*—die, be dead, give up the ghost, perish.

1479. גּוּף **gûwph,** *goof;* a prim. root; prop. to *hollow* or *arch,* i.e. (fig.) *close;* to *shut:*—shut.

1480. גּוּפָה **gûwphâh,** *goo-faw´;* from 1479; a *corpse* (as *closed* to sense):—body.

1481. גּוּר **gûwr,** *goor;* a prim. root; prop. to *turn* aside from the road (for a lodging or any other purpose), i.e. *sojourn* (as a guest); also to *shrink, fear* (as in a *strange* place); also to *gather* for hostility (as *afraid*):—abide, assemble, be afraid, dwell, fear, gather (together), inhabitant, remain, sojourn, stand in awe, (be) stranger, × surely.

1482. גּוּר **gûwr,** *goor;* or (short.) גֻּר **gûr,** *goor;* perh. from 1481; a *cub* (as still *abiding* in the lair), espec. of the lion:—whelp, young one.

1483. גּוּר **Gûwr,** *goor;* the same as 1482; *Gur,* a place in Pal.:—Gur.

1484. גּוֹר **gôwr,** *gore;* or (fem.) גֹּרָה **gôrah,** *go-raw´;* a var. of 1482:—whelp.

1485. גּוּר־בַּעַל **Gûwr-Baʻal,** *goor-bah´-al;* from 1481 and 1168; *dwelling of Baal; Gur-Baal,* a place in Arabia:—Gur-baal.

1486. גּוֹרָל **gôwrâl,** *go-rawl´;* or (short.) גֹּרָל **gôral,** *go-ral´;* from an unused root mean. to *be rough* (as stone); prop. a *pebble,* i.e. a *lot* (small stones being used for that purpose); fig. a *portion* or *destiny* (as if determined by lot):—lot.

1487. גּוּשׁ **gûwsh,** *goosh;* or rather (by perm.) גִּישׁ° **gîysh,** *gheesh;* of uncert. der.; a *mass* of earth:—clod.

1488. גֵּז **gêz,** *gaze;* from 1494; a *fleece* (as *shorn*); also mown *grass:*—fleece, mowing, mown grass.

1489. גִּזְבָּר **gizbâr,** *ghiz-bawr´;* of for. der.: *treasurer:*—treasurer.

1490. גִּזְבָּר **gizbâr** (Chald.), *ghiz-bawr´;* corresp. to 1489:—treasurer.

1491. גָּזָה **gâzâh,** *gaw-zaw´;* a prim. root [akin to 1468]; to *cut* off, i.e. *portion* out:—take.

1492. גַּזָּה **gazzâh,** *gaz-zaw´;* fem. from 1494; a *fleece:*—fleece.

1493. גִּזוֹנִי **Gizôwnîy,** *ghee-zo-nee´;* patrial from the unused name of a place appar. in Pal.; a *Gizonite* or inhab. of Gizoh:—Gizonite.

1494. גָּזַז **gâzaz,** *gaw-zaz´;* a prim. root [akin to 1468]; to *cut* off; spec. to *shear* a flock, or *shave* the hair; fig. to *destroy* an enemy:—cut off (down), poll, shave, ([sheep-]) shear (-er).

1495. גָּזֵז **Gâzêz** *gaw-zaze´;* from 1494; *shearer; Gazez,* the name of two Isr.:—Gazez.

1496. גָּזִית **gâzîyth,** *gaw-zeeth´;* from 1491; something *cut,* i.e. *dressed* stone:—hewed, hewn stone, wrought.

1497. גָּזַל **gâzal,** *gaw-zal´;* a prim. root; to *pluck* off; spec. to *flay, strip* or *rob:*—catch, consume, exercise [robbery], pluck (off), rob, spoil, take away (by force, violence), tear.

1498. גָּזֵל **gâzêl,** *gaw-zale´;* from 1497; *robbery,* or (concr.) *plunder:*—robbery, thing taken away by violence.

1499. גֵּזֶל **gêzel,** *ghe´-zel;* from 1497; *plunder,* i.e. *violence:*—violence, violent preverting.

גֹּזָל **gôzâl.** See 1469.

1500. גְּזֵלָה **g^ezêlâh,** *ghez-ay-law´;* fem. of 1498 and mean. the same:—that (he had robbed) [which he took violently away], spoil, violence.

1501. גָּזָם **gâzâm,** *gaw-zawm´;* from an unused root mean. to *devour;* a kind of *locust:*—palmerworm.

1502. גַּזָּם **Gazzâm,** *gaz-zawm´;* from the same as 1501; *devourer:*—*Gazzam,* one of the Nethinim:—Gazzam.

1503. גֶּזַע **geza',** *geh-zah;* from an unused root mean. to *cut* down (trees); the *trunk* or *stump* of a tree (as felled or as planted):—stem, stock.

1504. גָּזַר **gâzar,** *gaw-zar´;* a prim. root; to *cut* down or off; (fig.) to *destroy, divide, exclude* or *decide:*—cut down (off), decree, divide, snatch.

1505. גְּזַר **g^ezar** (Chald.), *ghez-ar´;* corresp. to 1504; to *quarry; determine:*—cut out, soothsayer.

1506. גֶּזֶר **gezer,** *gheh´-zer;* from 1504; something *cut* off; a *portion:*—part, piece.

1507. גֶּזֶר **Gezer,** *gheh´-zer;* the same as 1506; *Gezer,* a place in Pal.:—Gazer, Gezer.

1508. גִּזְרָה **gizrâh,** *ghiz-raw´;* fem. of 1506; the *figure* or person (as if *cut* out); also an *inclosure* (as *separated*):—polishing, separate place.

1509. גְּזֵרָה **g^ezêrâh,** *ghez-ay-raw´;* from 1504; a *desert* (as *separated*):—not inhabited.

1510. גְּזֵרָה **g^ezêrâh** (Chald.), *ghez-ay-raw´;* from 1505 (as 1504); a *decree:*—decree.

1511. גִּזְרִי **Gizrîy** (in the marg.), *ghiz-ree´;* patrial from 1507; a *Gezerite* (collect.) or inhab. of Gezer; but better (as in the text) by transp. גִּרְזִי° **Girzîy,** *gher-zee´;* patrial of 1630; a *Girzite* (collect.) or member of a native tribe in Pal.:—Gezrites.

גִּחוֹן **Gîchôwn.** See 1521.

1512. גָּחוֹן **gâchôwn,** *gaw-khone´;* prob. from 1518; the external *abdomen, belly* (as the *source* of the fœtus [comp. 1521]):—belly.

גֵּחֲזִי **Gêchăzîy.** See 1522.

גָּחֹל **gâchol.** See 1513.

1513. גֶּחֶל **gechel,** *geh´-khel;* or (fem.) גַּחֶלֶת **gacheleth,** *gah-kheh´-leth;* from an unused root mean. to *glow* or *kindle;* an *ember:*—(burning) coal.

1514. גַּחַם **Gacham,** *gah´-kham;* from an unused root mean. to *burn; flame; Gacham,* a son of Nahor:—Gaham.

1515. גַּחַר **Gachar,** *gah´-khar;* from an unused root mean. *to hide; lurker; Gachar,* one of the Nethinim:—Gahar.

גֹּי **gôy.** See 1471.

1516. גַּיְא **gay',** *gah´ee;* or (short.) גַּי **gay,** *gah´ee;* prob. (by transm.) from the same root as 1466 (abbrev.); a *gorge* (from its *lofty* sides; hence narrow, but not a gully or winter-torrent):—valley.

1517. גִּיד **gîyd,** *gheed;* prob. from 1464; a *thong* (as *compressing*); by anal. a *tendon:*—sinew.

1518. גִּיחַ **gîyach,** *ghee´-akh;* or (short.) גֹּחַ **gôach,** *go´-akh;* a prim. root; to *gush* forth (as water), gen. to *issue:*—break forth, labor to bring forth, come forth, draw up, take out.

1519. גִּיחַ **gîyach** (Chald.), *ghee´-akh;* or (short.) גּוּחַ **gûwach** (Chald.), *goo´-akh;* corresp. to 1548; to *rush* forth:—strive.

1520. גִּיחַ **Gîyach,** *ghee´-akh;* from 1518; a *fountain; Giach,* a place in Pal.:—Giah.

1521. גִּיחוֹן **Gîychôwn,** *ghee-khone´;* or (short.) גִּחוֹן **Gîchôwn,** *ghee-khone´;* from 1518; *stream; Gichon,* a river of Paradise; also a valley (or pool) near Jerusalem:—Gihon.

1522. גֵּיחֲזִי **Gêychăzîy,** *gay-khah-zee´;* or גֵּחֲזִי **Gêchăzîy,** *gay-khah-zee´;* appar-from 1516 and 2372; *valley of a visionary; Gechazi,* the servant of Elisha:—Gehazi.

1523. גִּיל **gîyl,** *gheel;* or (by perm.) גּוּל° **gûwl,** *gool;* a prim. root; prop. to *spin* round (under the influence of any violent emotion), i.e. usually *rejoice,* or (as *cringing*) *fear:*—be glad, joy, be joyful, rejoice.

1524. גִּיל **gîyl,** *gheel;* from 1523; a *revolution* (of time, i.e. an *age*); also *joy:*— × exceedingly, gladness, × greatly, joy, rejoice (-ing), sort.

1525. גִּילָה **gîylâh,** *ghee-law´;* or גִּילַת **gîylath,** *ghee-lath´;* fem. of 1524; *joy:*—joy, rejoicing.

גִּילֹה **Gîylôh.** See 1542.

1526. גִּילֹנִי **Gîylônîy,** *ghee-lo-nee´;* patrial from 1542; a *Gilonite* or inhab. of Giloh:—Gilonite.

1527. גִּינַת **Gîynath,** *ghee-nath´;* of uncert. der.; *Ginath,* an Isr.:—Ginath.

1528. גִּיר **gîyr** (Chald.), *gheer;* corresp. to 1615; *lime:*—plaster.

גֵּיר **gêyr.** See 1616.

1529. גֵּישָׁן **Gêyshân,** *gay-shawn´;* from the same as 1487; *lumpish; Geshan,* an Isr.:—Geshan.

1530. גַּל **gal,** *gal;* from 1556; something *rolled,* i.e. a *heap* of stone or dung (plur. *ruins*); by anal. a *spring* of water (plur. *waves*):—billow, heap, spring, wave.

1531. גֹּל **gôl,** *gole;* from 1556; a *cup* for oil (as *round*):—bowl.

גְּלָא **g^elâ'.** See 1541.

1532. גַּלָּב **gallâb,** *gal-lawb´;* from an unused root mean. to *shave;* a *barber:*—barber.

1533. גִּלְבֹּעַ **Gilbôa',** *ghil-bo´-ah;* from 1530 and 1158; *fountain of ebullition; Gilboa,* a mountain of Pal.:—Gilboa.

1534. גַּלְגַּל **galgal,** *gal-gal´;* by redupl. from 1556; a *wheel;* by anal. a *whirlwind;* also *dust* (as *whirled*):—heaven, rolling thing, wheel.

1535. גַּלְגַּל **galgal** (Chald.), *gal-gal´;* corresp. to 1534; a *wheel;*—wheel.

1536. גִּלְגָּל **gilgâl,** *ghil-gawl´;* a var. of 1534:—wheel.

1537. גִּלְגָּל **Gilgâl,** *ghil-gawl´;* the same as 1536 (with the art. as a prop. noun); *Gilgal.* the name of three places in Pal.:—Gilgal. See also 1019.

1538. גֻּלְגֹּלֶת **gulgôleth,** *gul-go´-leth;* by redupl. from 1556; a *skull* (as *round*); by impl. a *head* (in enumeration of persons):—head, every man, poll, skull.

1539. גֶּלֶד **geled,** *ghe´-led;* from an unused root prob. mean. to *polish;* the (human) *skin* (as *smooth*):—skin.

1540. גָּלָה **gâlâh,** *gaw-law´;* a prim. root; to *denude* (espec. in a disgraceful sense); by impl. to *exile* (captives being usually *stripped*); fig. to *reveal:*— + advertise, appear, bewray, bring, (carry, lead, go) captive (into captivity), depart, disclose, discover, exile, be gone, open, × plainly, publish, remove, reveal, × shamelessly, shew, × surely, tell, uncover.

1541. גְּלָה **g^elah** (Chald.), *ghel-aw´;* or גְּלָא **g^elâ'** (Chald.), *ghel-aw´;* corresp. to 1540:—bring over, carry away, reveal.

גֹּלָה **gôlâh.** See 1473.

1542. גִּלֹה **Gîlôh,** *ghee-lo´;* or (fully) גִּילֹה **Gîylôh,** *ghee-lo´;* from 1540; *open; Giloh,* a place in Pal.:—Giloh.

1543. גֻּלָּה **gullâh,** *gool-law´;* fem. from 1556; a *fountain, bowl* or *globe* (all as *round*):—bowl, pommel, spring.

1544. גִּלּוּל **gillûwl,** *ghil-lool´;* or (short.) גִּלֻּל **gillûl,** *ghil-lool´;* from 1556; prop. a *log* (as *round*); by impl. an *idol;*—idol.

1545. גְּלוֹם **g**e**lôwm,** *ghel-ome´;* from 1563; *clothing* (as *wrapped*):—clothes.

1546. גָּלוּת **gâlûwth.** *gaw-looth´;* fem. from 1540; *captivity;* concr. *exiles* (collect.):—(they that are carried away) captives (-ity.)

1547. גָּלוּת **gâlûwth** (Chald.), *gaw-looth´;* corresp. to 1546:—captivity.

1548. גָּלַח **gâlach,** *gaw-lakh´;* a prim. root; prop. to *be bald,* i.e. (caus.) to *shave;* fig. to *lay waste:*—poll, shave (off).

1549. גִּלָּיוֹן **gillâyôwn,** *ghil-law-yone´;* or גִּלְיוֹן **gilyôwn,** *ghil-yone´;* from 1540; a *tablet* for writing (as *bare*); by anal. a *mirror* (as a *plate*):—glass, roll.

1550. גָּלִיל **gâlîyl,** *gaw-leel´;* from 1556; a *valve* of a folding door (as *turning*); also a *ring* (as *round*):—folding, ring.

1551. גָּלִיל **Gâlîyl,** *gaw-leel´;* or (prol.) גָּלִילָה **Gâlîylâh,** *gaw-lee-law´;* the same as 1550; a *circle* (with the art.); *Galil* (as a special *circuit*) in the North of Pal.:—Galilee.

1552. גְּלִילָה **g**e**lîylâh,** *ghel-ee-law´;* fem. of 1550; a *circuit* or *region:*—border, coast, country.

1553. גְּלִילוֹת **G**e**lîylôwth,** *ghel-ee-lowth´;* plur. of 1552; *circles; Geliloth,* a place in Pal.:—Geliloth.

1554. גַּלִּים **Gallîym,** *gal-leem´;* plur. of 1530; *springs; Gallim,* a place in Pal.:—Gal-lim.

1555. גָּלְיַת **Golyath,** *gol-yath´;* perh. from 1540; *exile; Goljath,* a Philistine:—Goliath.

1556. גָּלַל **gâlal,** *gaw-lal´;* a prim. root; to *roll* (lit. or fig.):—commit, remove, roll (away, down, together), run down, seek occasion, trust, wallow.

1557. גָּלָל **gâlâl,** *gaw-lawl´;* from 1556; *dung* (as in *balls*):—dung.

1558. גָּלָל **gâlâl,** *gaw-lawl´;* from 1556; a *circumstance* (as *rolled* around); only used adv., on *account* of:—because of, for (sake).

1559. גָּלָל **Gâlâl,** *gaw-lawl´;* from 1556, in the sense of 1560; *great; Galal,* the name of two Isr.:—Galal.

1560. גְּלָל **g**e**lâl** (Chald.), *ghel-awl´;* from a root corresp. to 1556; *weight* or *size* (as if *rolled*):—great.

1561. גֵּלֶל **gêlel,** *gay´-lel;* a var. of 1557; *dung* (plur. *balls* of dung):—dung.

1562. גִּלֲלַי **Gîlălay,** *ghe-lal-ah´ee;* from 1561; *dungy; Gilalai,* an Isr.:—Gilalai.

1563. גָּלַם **gâlam,** *gaw-lam´;* a prim. root; to *fold:*—wrap together.

1564. גֹּלֶם **gôlem,** *go´-lem;* from 1563; a *wrapped* (and unformed *mass,* i.e. as the *embryo*):—substance yet being unperfect.

1565. גַּלְמוּד **galmûwd,** *gal-mood´;* prob. by prol. from 1563; *sterile* (as *wrapped* up too hard); fig. *desolate:*—desolate, solitary.

1566. גָּלַע **gâla‘,** *gaw-lah´;* a prim. root; to *be obstinate:*—(inter-) meddle (with).

1567. גַּלְעֵד **Gal‘êd,** *gal-ade´;* from 1530 and 5707; *heap of testimony; Galed,* a memorial cairn E. of the Jordan:—Galeed.

1568. גִּלְעָד **Gil‘âd,** *ghil-awd´;* prob. from 157; *Gilad,* a region E. of the Jordan; also the name of three Isr.:—Gilead, Gileadite.

1569. גִּלְעָדִי **Gil‘âdîy,** *ghil-aw-dee´;* patron. from 1568; a *Giladite* or desc. of Gilad:—Gileadite.

1570. גָּלַשׁ **gâlash,** *gaw-lash´;* a prim. root; prob. to *caper* (as a goat):—appear.

1571. גַּם **gam,** *gam;* by contr. from an unused root mean. to *gather;* prop. *assemblage;* used only adv. *also, even, yea, though;* often repeated as correl, *both . . . and:*—again, alike, also, (so much) as (soon), both (so) . . . and, but, either . . . or, even, for all, (in) likewise (manner), moreover, nay . . . neither, one, then (-refore), though, what, with, yea.

1572. גָּמָא **gâmâ’,** *gaw-maw´;* a prim. root (lit. or fig.) to *absorb:*—swallow, drink.

1573. גֹּמֶא **gôme’,** *go´-meh;* from 1572; prop. an *absorbent,* i.e. the *bulrush* (from its *porosity*); spec. the *papyrus:*—(bul-) rush.

1574. גֹּמֶד **gômed,** *go´-med;* from an unused root appar. mean. to *grasp;* prop. a *span:*—cubit.

1575. גַּמָּד **gammâd,** *gam-mawd´;* from the same as 1574; a *warrior* (as *grasping* weapons):—Grammadims.

1576. גְּמוּל **g**e**mûwl,** *ghem-ool´;* from 1580; *treatment,* i.e. an *act* (of good or ill); by impl. *service* or *requital:*— + as hast served, benefit, desert, deserving, that which he hath given, recompence, reward.

1577. גָּמוּל **gâmûwl,** *gaw-mool´;* pass. part. of 1580; *rewarded; Gamul,* an Isr.:—Gamul. See also 1014.

1578. גְּמוּלָה **g**e**mûwlâh,** *ghem-oo-law´;* fem. of 1576; mean. the same:—deed, recompence, such a reward.

1579. גִּמְזוֹ **Gimzôw,** *ghim-zo´;* of uncert. der.; Gimzo, a place in Pal.:—Gimzo.

1580. גָּמַל **gâmal,** *gaw-mal´;* a prim. root; to *treat* a person (well or ill), i.e. *benefit* or *requite;* by impl. (of *toil*) to *ripen,* i.e. (spec.) to *wean:*—bestow on, deal bountifully, do (good), recompense, requite, reward, ripen, + serve, wean, yield.

1581. גָּמָל **gâmâl,** *gaw-mawl´;* appar. from 1580 (in the sense of *labor* or *burden-bearing*): a *camel:*—camel.

1582. גְּמַלִּי **G**e**malliy,** *ghem-al-lee´;* prob. from 1581; *camel-driver; Gemalli,* an Isr.:—Gemalli.

1583. גַּמְלִיאֵל **Gamliy’el,** *gam-lee-ale´;* from 1580 and 410; *reward of God; Gamliel,* an Isr.:—Gamaliel.

1584. גָּמַר **gâmar,** *gaw-mar´;* a prim. root; to *end* (in the sense of *completion* or *failure*):—cease, come to an end, fail, perfect, perform.

1585. גְּמַר **g**e**mar** (Chald.), *ghem-ar´;* corresp. to 1584:—perfect.

1586. גֹּמֶר **Gômer,** *go´-mer;* from 1584; *completion; Gomer,* the name of a son of Japheth and of his desc.; also of a Hebrewess:—Gomer.

1587. גְּמַרְיָה **G**e**maryâh,** *ghem-ar-yaw´;* or גְּמַרְיָהוּ **G**e**maryâhûw,** *ghem-ar-yaw´-hoo;* from 1584 and 3050; *Jah has perfected; Gemarjah,* the name of two Isr.:—Gemariah.

1588. גַּן **gan,** *gan;* from 1598; a *garden* (as *fenced*):—garden.

1589. גָּנַב **gânab,** *gaw-nab´;* a prim. root; to *thieve* (lit. or fig.); by impl. to *deceive:*—carry away, × indeed, secretly bring, steal (away), get by stealth.

1590. גַּנָּב **gannâb,** *gaw-nab´;* from 1589; a *stealer:*—thief.

1591. גְּנֵבָה **g**e**nêbâh,** *ghen-ay-baw´;* from 1589; *stealing,* i.e. (concr.) something *stolen:*—theft.

1592. גְּנֻבַת **G**e**nûbath,** *ghen-oo-bath´* from 1589, *theft; Genubath,* an Edomitish prince:—Genubath.

1593. גַּנָּה **gannâh,** *gan-naw´;* fem. of 1588; a *garden:*—garden.

1594. גִּנָּה **ginnâh,** *ghin-naw´;* another form for 1593:—garden.

1595. גֶּנֶז **genez,** *geh´-nez;* from an unused root mean. to *store; treasure;* by impl. a *coffer:*—chest, treasury.

1596. גְּנַז **g**e**naz** (Chald.), *ghen-az´;* corresp. to 1595; *treasure:*—treasure.

1597. גִּנְזַךְ **ginzak,** *ghin-zak´;* prol. from 1595; a *treasury:*—treasury.

1598. גָּנַן **gânan,** *gaw-nan´;* a prim. root; to *hedge* about, i.e. (gen.) *protect:*—defend.

1599. גִּנְּתוֹן **Ginn**e**thôwn,** *ghin-neth-ōne;* or גִּנְּתוֹ **Ginn**e**thôw,** *ghin-neth-o´;* from 1598; *gardener; Ginnethon* or *Ginnetho,* an Isr.:—Ginnetho, Ginnethon.

1600. גָּעָה **gâ‘âh,** *gaw-aw´;* a prim. root; to *bellow* (as cattle):—low.

1601. גֹּעָה **Gô‘âh,** *go-aw´;* fem. act. part. of 1600; *lowing; Goah,* a place near Jerus.:—Goath.

1602. גָּעַל **gâʻal,** *gaw-al´;* a prim. root; to *detest;* by impl. to *reject:*—abhor, fail, lothe, vilely cast away.

1603. גַּעַל **Gaʻal,** *gah´-al;* from 1602; *loathing; Gaal,* an Isr.:—Gaal.

1604. גֹּעַל **gôʻal,** *go´-al;* from 1602; *abhorrence:*—loathing.

1605. גָּעַר **gâʻar,** *gaw-ar´;* a prim. root; to *chide:*—corrupt, rebuke, reprove.

1606. גְּעָרָה **geʻârâh,** *gheh-aw-raw;* from 1605; a *chiding:*—rebuke (-ing), reproof.

1607. גָּעַשׁ **gâʻash,** *gaw-ash´;* a prim. root to *agitate* violently:—move, shake, toss, trouble.

1608. גַּעַשׁ **Gaʻash,** *ga´-ash;* from 1607; a *quaking; Gaash,* a hill in Pal.:—Gaash.

1609. גַּעְתָּם **Gaʻtâm,** *gah-tawm´;* of uncert. der.; *Gatam,* an Edomite:—Gatam.

1610. גַּף **gaph,** *gaf;* from an unused root mean. to *arch;* the *back;* by extens. the *body* of self:—+ highest places, himself.

1611. גַּף **gaph** (Chald.), *gaf;* corresp. to 1610:—a *wing:*—wing.

1612. גֶּפֶן **gephen,** *gheh´-fen;* from an unused root mean. to *bend; a vine* (as *twining*), esp. the grape:—vine, tree.

1613. גֹּפֶר **gôpher,** *go´-fer;* from an unused root, prob. mean. to *house in;* a kind of tree or wood (as used for *building*), appar. the *cypress:*—gopher.

1614. גָּפְרִית **gophrîyth,** *gof-reeth´;* prob. fem. of 1613; prop. cypress-*resin;* by anal. *sulphur* (as equally inflammable):—brimstone.

1615. גִּר **gîr,** *gheer;* perh. from 3564; *lime* (from being *burned* in a kiln:—chalk [-stone].

1616. גֵּר **gêr,** *gare;* from 1481; prop. a *guest;* by impl. a *foreigner:*—alien, sojourner, stranger.
גֻּר **gûr.** See 1482.

1617. גֵּרָא **Gêrâʼ,** *gay-raw´;* perh. from 1626; a *grain; Gera,* the name of six Isr.:—Gera.

1618. גָּרָב **gârâb,** *gaw-rawb´;* from an unused root mean. to *scratch; scurf* (from *itching*):—scab, scurvy.

1619. גָּרֵב **Gârêb,** *gaw-rabe´;* from the same as 1618; *scabby; Gareb,* the name of an Isr., also of a hill near Jerus.:—Gareb.

1620. גַּרְגַּר **gargar,** *gar-gar´;* by redupl. from 1641; a *berry* (as if a pellet of *rumination*):—berry.

1621. גַּרְגְּרוֹת **gargerôwth,** *gar-gher-owth´;* fem. plur. from 1641; the *throat* (as used in *rumination*):—neck.

1622. גִּרְגָּשִׁי **Girgâshîy,** *ghir-gaw-shee´;* patrial from an unused name [of uncert. der.]; a *Girgashite,* one of the native tribes of Canaan:—Girgashite, Girgasite.

1623. גָּרַד **gârad,** *gaw-rad´;* a prim. root; to *abrade:*—scrape.

1624. גָּרָה **gârâh,** *gaw-raw´;* a prim. root; prop. to *grate,* i.e. (fig.) to *anger:*—contend, meddle, stir up, strive.

1625. גֵּרָה **gêrâh,** *gay-raw´;* from 1641; the *cud* (as *scraping* the throat):—cud.

1626. גֵּרָה **gêrâh,** *gay-raw´;* from 1641 (as in 1625); prop. (like 1620) a *kernel* (round as if *scraped*), i.e. a *gerah* or small weight (and coin):—gerah.
גֹּרָה **gôrâh.** See 1484.

1627. גָּרוֹן **gârôwn,** *gaw-rone´;* or (short.) גָּרֹן **gârôn,** *gaw-rone´;* from 1641; the *throat* [comp. 1621] (as *roughened* by swallowing):—× aloud, mouth, neck, throat.

1628. גֵּרוּת **gêrûwth,** *gay-rooth´;* from 1481; a (temporary) *residence:*—habitation.

1629. גָּרַז **gâraz,** *gaw-raz´;* a prim. root; to *cut* off:—cut off.

1630. גְּרִזִים **Gerîzîym,** *gher-ee-zeem´;* plur. of an unused noun from 1629 [comp. 1511], *cut* up (i.e. *rocky*); *Gerizim,* a mountain of Pal.:—Gerizim.

1631. גַּרְזֶן **garzen,** *gar-zen´;* from 1629; an *axe:*—ax.

1632. גָּרֹל° **gârôl,** *gaw-role´;* from the same as 1486; *harsh:*—man of great [*as in the marg. which reads* 1419].
גֹּרָל **gôrâl.** See 1486.

1633. גָּרַם **gâram,** *gaw-ram´;* a prim. root; to *be spare* or *skeleton-like;* used only as a denom. from 1634; (caus.) to *bone,* i.e. *denude* (by extens. *craunch*) the bones:—gnaw the bones, break.

1634. גֶּרֶם **gerem,** *gheh´-rem;* from 1633; a *bone* (as the *skeleton* of the body); hence *self,* i.e. (fig.) *very:*—bone, strong, top.

1635. גֶּרֶם **gerem** (Chald.), *gheh´-rem;* corresp. to 1634; a *bone:*—bone.

1636. גַּרְמִי **Garmîy,** *gar-mee´;* from 1634; *bony,* i.e. *strong:*—Garmite.

1637. גֹּרֶן **gôren,** *go´-ren;* from an unused root mean. to *smooth;* a threshing-*floor* (as made *even*); by anal. any open *area:*—(barn, corn, threshing-) floor, (threshing-, void) place.
גָּרֹן **gârôn.** See 1627.

1638. גָּרַס **gâraç** *gaw-ras´;* a prim. root; to *crush;* also (intrans. and fig.) to *dissolve:*—break.

1639. גָּרַע **gâraʻ,** *gaw-rah´;* a prim. root; to *scrape* off; by impl. to *shave, remove, lessen* or *withhold:*—abate, clip, (di-) minish, do (take) away, keep back, restrain, make small, withdraw.

1640. גָּרַף **gâraph,** *gaw-raf´;* a prim. root; to *bear* off violently:—sweep away.

1641. גָּרַר **gârar,** *gaw-rar´;* a prim. root; to *drag* off roughly; by impl. to *bring up* the cud (i.e. *ruminate*); by anal. to *saw:*—catch, chew, × continuing, destroy, saw.

1642. גְּרָר **Gerâr,** *gher-awr´;* prob. from 1641; a *rolling* country; *Gerar,* a Philistine city:—Gerar.

1643. גֶּרֶשׂ **geres,** *gheh´-res;* from an unused root mean. to *husk;* a *kernel* (collect.), i.e. *grain:*—beaten corn.

1644. גָּרַשׁ **gârash,** *gaw-rash´;* a prim. root; to *drive* out from a possession; espec. to *expatriate* or *divorce:*—cast up (out), divorced (woman), drive away (forth, out), expel, × surely put away, trouble, thrust out.

1645. גֶּרֶשׁ **geresh,** *gheh´-resh;* from 1644; *produce* (as if *expelled*):—put forth.

1646. גְּרֻשָׁה **gerûshâh,** *gher-oo-shaw´;* fem. pass. part. of 1644; (abstr.) *dispossession:*—exaction.

1647. גֵּרְשֹׁם **Gêreshôm,** *gay-resh-ome´;* for 1648; *Gereshom,* the name of four Isr.:—Gershom.

1648. גֵּרְשׁוֹן **Gêreshown,** *gay-resh-one´;* or גֵּרְשׁוֹם **Gêreshôwm,** *gay-resh-ome´;* from 1644; a *refugee; Gereshon* or *Gereshom,* an Isr.:—Gershon, Gershom.

1649. גֵּרְשֻׁנִּי **Gereshunnîy,** *gay-resh-oon-nee´;* patron. from 1648; a *Gereshonite* or desc. of Gereshon:—Gershonite, sons of Gershon.

1650. גְּשׁוּר **Geshûwr,** *ghesh-oor´;* from an unused root (mean. to *join*); *bridge; Geshur,* a district of Syria:—Geshur, Geshurite.

1651. גְּשׁוּרִי **Geshûwrîy,** *ghe-shoo-ree´;* patrial from 1650; a *Geshurite* (also collect.) or inhab. of Geshur:—Geshuri, Geshurites.

1652. גָּשַׁם **gâsham,** *gaw-sham´;* a prim. root; to *shower* violently:—(cause to) rain.

1653. גֶּשֶׁם **geshem,** *gheh´-shem;* from 1652; a *shower:*—rain, shower.

1654. גֶּשֶׁם **Geshem,** *gheh´-shem;* or (prol.) גַּשְׁמוּ **Gashmûw,** *gash-moo´;* the same as 1653; *Geshem* or *Gashmu,* an Arabian:—Geshem, Gashmu.

1655. גֶּשֶׁם **geshem** (Chald.), *gheh´-shem;* appar. the same as 1653; used in a peculiar sense, the *body* (prob. for the [fig.] idea of a *hard* rain):—body.

1656. גֹּשֶׁם **gôshem,** *go´-shem;* from 1652; equiv. to 1653:—rained upon.
גַּשְׁמוּ **Gashmûw.** See 1654.

1657. גֹּשֶׁן **Gôshen,** *go´-shen;* prob. of Eg. or.; *Goshen,* the residence of the Isr. in Egypt; also a place in Pal.:—Goshen.

1658. גִּשְׁפָּא **Gishpâʼ,** *ghish-paw´;* of uncert. der.; *Gishpa,* an Isr.:—Gispa.

1659. גָּשַׁשׁ **gâshash,** *gaw-shash´;* a prim. root; appar. to *feel* about:—grope.

1660. גַּת **gath,** *gath;* prob. from 5059 (in the sense of *treading* out grapes); a wine-*press* (or vat for holding the grapes in pressing them):—(wine-) press (fat).

1661. גַּת **Gath,** *gath;* the same as 1660; *Gath,* a Philistine city:—Gath.

1662. גַּת־הַחֵפֶר **Gath-ha-Chêpher,** *gath-hah-khay´-fer;* or (abridged) גִּתָּה־חֵפֶר **Gittâh-Chêpher,** *ghit-taw-khay´-fer;* from 1660 and 2658 with the art. ins.; *wine-press of (the) well; Gath-Chepher,* a place in Pal.:—Gath-kephr, Gittah-kephr.

1663. גִּתִּי **Gittîy,** *ghit-tee´;* patrial from 1661; a *Gittite* or inhab. of Gath:—Gittite.

1664. גִּתַּיִם **Gittayim,** *ghit-tah´-yim;* dual of 1660; *double wine-press; Gittajim,* a place in Pal.:—Gittaim.

1665. גִּתִּית **Gittîyth,** *ghit-teeth´;* fem. of 1663; a *Gittite* harp:—Gittith.

1666. גֶּתֶר **Gether,** *gheh´-ther;* of uncert. der.; *Gether,* a son of Aram, and the region settled by him:—Gether.

1667. גַּת־רִמּוֹן **Gath-Rimmôwn,** *gath-rim-mone´;* from 1660 and 7416; *wine-press of* (the) *pomegranate; Gath-Rimmon,* a place in Pal.:—Gath-rimmon.

ד

1668. דָא **dâ'** (Chald.), *daw;* corresp. to 2088; *this:*—one . . . another, this.

1669. דָּאַב **dâ'ab,** *daw-ab´;* a prim. root; to *pine:*—mourn, sorrow (-ful).

1670. דְּאָבָה **de'âbâh,** *dĕh-aw-baw´;* from 1669; prop. *pining;* by anal. *fear:*—sorrow.

1671. דְּאָבוֹן **de'âbôwn,** *dĕh-aw-bone´;* from 1669; *pining:*—sorrow.

1672. דָּאַג **dâ'ag,** *daw-ag´;* a prim. root; *be anxious:*—be afraid (careful, sorry), sorrow, take thought.

1673. דֹּאֵג **Dô'êg,** *do-ayg´;* or (fully) דּוֹאֵג **Dôw'êg,** *do-ayg´;* act. part. of 1672; *anxious; Doëg,* an Edomite:—Doeg.

1674. דְּאָגָה **de'âgâh,** *dĕh-aw-gaw´;* from 1672; *anxiety:*—care (-fulness), fear, heaviness, sorrow.

1675. דָּאָה **dâ'âh,** *daw-aw´;* a prim. root; to *dart,* i.e. *fly* rapidly:—fly.

1676. דָּאָה **dâ'âh,** *daw-aw´;* from 1675; the *kite* (from its rapid *flight*):—vulture. See 7201.

1677. דֹּב **dôb,** *dobe; or (fully)* דּוֹב **dôwb,** *dobe;* from 1680; the *bear* (as slow):—bear.

1678. דֹּב **dôb** (Chald.), *dobe;* corresp. to 1677:—bear.

1679. דֹּבֶא **dôbe',** *do´-beh;* from an unused root (comp. 1680) (prob. mean. to *be sluggish,* i.e. *restful*); *quiet:*—strength.

1680. דָּבַב **dâbab,** *daw-bab´;* a prim. root (comp. 1679); to *move* slowly, i.e. *glide:*—cause to speak.

1681. דִּבָּה **dibbâh,** *dib-baw´;* from 1680 (in the sense of *furtive* motion); *slander:*—defaming, evil report, infamy, slander.

1682. דְּבוֹרָה **debôwrâh,** *deb-o-raw´;* or (short.) דְּבֹרָה **debôrâh,** *deb-o-raw´;* from 1696 (in the sense of *orderly* motion); the *bee* (from its *systematic* instincts):—bee.

1683. דְּבוֹרָה **Debôwrâh,** *deb-o-raw´;* or (short.) דְּבֹרָה **Debôrâh,** *deb-o-raw´;* the same as 1682; *Deborah,* the name of two Hebrewesses:—Deborah.

1684. דְּבַח **debach** (Chald.), *deb-akh´;* corresp. to 2076; to *sacrifice* (an animal):—offer [sacrifice].

1685. דְּבַח **debach** (Chald.), *deb-akh´;* from 1684; a *sacrifice:*—sacrifice.

1686. דִּבְיוֹן **dibyôwn,** *dib-yone´* in the marg. for the textural reading. חֶרְיוֹן° **cheryôwn,** *kher-yone´;* both (in the plur. only and) of uncert. der.; prob. some cheap vegetable, perh. a bulbous root:—dove's dung.

1687. דְּבִיר **debîyr,** *deb-eer´;*or (short.) דְּבִר **debîr,** *deb-eer´;* from 1696 (appar. in the sense of *oracle*); the *shrine* or innermost part of the sanctuary:—oracle.

1688. דְּבִיר **Debîyr,** *deb-eer´;* or (short.) דְּבִר **Debîr** (Josh. 13 : 26 [but see 3810]), *deb-eer´;* the same as 1687; *Debir,* the name of an Amoritish king and of two places in Pal.:—Debir.

1689. דִּבְלָה **Diblâh,** *dib-law´;* prob. an orth. err. for 7247; *Diblah,* a place in Syria:—Diblath.

1690. דְּבֵלָה **debêlâh,** *deb-ay-law´;* from an unused root (akin to 2082) prob. mean. to *press* together; a *cake* of pressed figs:—cake (lump) of figs.

1691. דִּבְלַיִם **Diblayim,** *dib-lah´-yim;* dual from the masc. of 1690; *two cakes; Diblajim,* a symbol. name:—Diblaim.

דִּבְלָתַיִם **Diblâthayim.** See 1015.

1692. דָּבַק **dâbaq,** *daw-bak´;* a prim. root; prop. to *impinge,* i.e. *cling* or *adhere;* fig. to *catch* by pursuit:—abide, fast, cleave (fast together), follow close (hard, after), be joined (together), keep (fast), overtake, pursue hard, stick, take.

1693. דְּבַק **debaq** (Chald.), *deb-ak´;* corresp. to 1692; to *stick* to:—cleave.

1694. דֶּבֶק **debeq,** *deh´-bek;* from 1692; a *joint;* by impl. *solder:*—joint, solder.

1695. דָּבֵק **dâbêq,** *daw-bake´;* from 1692; *adhering:*—cleave, joining, stick closer.

1696. דָּבַר **dâbar,** *daw-bar´;* a prim. root; perh. prop. to *arrange;* but used fig. (of words) to *speak;* rarely (in a destructive sense) to *subdue:*—answer, appoint, bid, command, commune, declare, destroy, give, name, promise, pronounce, rehearse, say, speak, be spokesman, subdue, talk, teach, tell, think, use [entreaties], utter, × well, × work.

1697. דָּבָר **dâbâr,** *daw-bawr´;* from 1696; a *word;* by impl. a *matter* (as *spoken* of) or *thing;* adv. a *cause:*—act, advice, affair, answer, × any such (thing), + because of, book, business, care, case, cause, certain rate, + chronicles, commandment, × commune (-ication), + concern [-ing], + confer, counsel, + dearth, decree, deed, × disease, due, duty, effect, + eloquent, errand, [evil favoured-] ness, + glory, + harm, hurt, + iniquity, + judgment, language, + lying, manner, matter, message, [no] thing, oracle, × ought, × parts, + pertaining, + please, portion, + power, promise, provision, purpose, question, rate, reason, report, request, × (as hast) said, sake, saying, sentence, + sign, + so, some [uncleanness], somewhat to say, + song, speech, × spoken, talk, task, + that, × there done, thing (concerning), thought, + thus, tidings, what [-soever], + wherewith, which, word, work.

1698. דֶּבֶר **deber,** *deh´-ber;* from 1696 (in the sense of *destroying*); a *pestilence:*—murrain, pestilence, plague.

1699. דֹּבֶר **dôber,** *do´-ber;* from 1696 (in its original sense); a *pasture* (from its *arrangement* of the flock):—fold, manner.

דְּבִר **debîr** or **Debîr.** See 1687, 1688.

1699´. דִּבֵּר **dibbêr,** *dib-bare´;* for 1697:—word.

1700. דִּבְרָה **dibrâh,** *dib-raw´;* fem. of 1697; a *reason, suit* or *style:*—cause, end, estate, order, regard.

1701. דִּבְרָה **dibrâh** (Chald.), *dib-raw´;* corresp. to 1700:—intent, sake.

דְּבֹרָה **debôrâh** or **Debôrâh.** See 1682, 1683.

1702. דֹּבְרָה **dôberâh,** *do-ber-aw´;* fem. act. part. of 1696 in the sense of *driving* [comp. 1699]; a *raft:*—float.

1703. דַּבָּרָה **dabbârâh,** *dab-baw-raw´;* intens. from 1696; a *word:*—word.

1704. דִּבְרִי **Dibrîy,** *dib-ree´;* from 1697; *wordy; Dibri,* an Isr.:—Dibri.

1705. דָּבְרַת **Dâberath,** *daw-ber-ath´;* from 1697 (perh. in the sense of 1699); *Daberath,* a place in Pal.:—Dabareh, Daberath.

1706. דְּבַשׁ **debash,** *deb-ash´;* from an unused root mean. to *be gummy; honey* (from its *stickiness*); by anal. *syrup:*—honey ([-comb]).

1707. דַּבֶּשֶׁת **dabbesheth,** *dab-beh´-sheth;* intens. from the same as 1706; a sticky *mass,* i.e. the *hump* of a camel:—hunch [of a camel].

1708. דַּבֶּשֶׁת **Dabbesheth,** *dab-beh´-sheth;* the same as 1707; *Dabbesheth,* a place in Pal.:—Dabbesheth.

1709. דָּג **dâg,** *dawg;* or (fully) דָּאג° **dâ'g** (Neh. 13 : 16) *dawg;* from 1711; a *fish* (as *prolific*), or perh. rather from 1672 (as *timid*); but still better from 1672 (in the sense of *squirming,* i.e. moving by the vibratory action of the tail); a *fish* (often used collect.):—fish.

1710. דָּגָה **dâgâh,** *daw-gaw´;* fem. of 1709, and mean. the same:—fish.

1711. דָּגָה **dâgâh,** *daw-gaw´;* a prim. root; to *move rapidly;* used only as a denom. from 1709; to *spawn,* i.e. *become numerous:*—grow.

1712. דָּגוֹן **Dâgôwn,** *daw-gohn´;* from 1709; the *fish-god; Dagon,* a Philistine deity:—Dagon.

1713. דָּגַל **dâgal,** *daw-gal´;* a prim. root; to *flount,* i.e. *raise a flag;* fig. to *be conspicuous:*—(set up, with) banners, chiefest.

1714. דֶּגֶל **degel,** *deh´-gel;* from 1713; a *flag:*—banner, standard.

1715. דָּגָן **dâgân,** *daw-gawn´;* from 1711; prop. *increase,* i.e. *grain:*—corn ([floor]), wheat.

1716. דָּגַר **dâgar,** *daw-gar´;* a prim. root; to *brood* over eggs or young:—gather, sit.

1717. דַּד **dad,** *dad;* appar. from the same as 1730; the *breast* (as the seat of *love,* or from its shape):—breast, teat.

1718. דָּדָה **dâdâh,** *daw-daw´;* a doubtful root; to *walk gently:*—go (softly, with).

1719. דְּדָן **Dᵉdân,** *ded-awn´;* or (prol.) דְּדָנֶה **Dᵉdâneh** (Ezek. 25 : 13), *deh-daw´-neh;* of uncert. der.; *Dedan,* the name of two Cushites and of their territory:—Dedan.

1720. דְּדָנִים **Dᵉdânîym,** *ded-aw-neem´;* plur. of 1719 (as patrial); *Dedanites,* the desc. or inhab. of Dedan:—Dedanim.

1721. דֹּדָנִים **Dôdânîym,** *do-daw-neem´;* or (by orth. err.) רֹדָנִים **Rôdânîym** (1 Chron. 1 : 7), *ro-daw-neem´;* a plur. of uncert. der.; *Dodanites,* or desc. of a son of Javan:—Dodanim.

1722. דְּהַב **dᵉhab** (Chald.), *deh-hab´;* corresp. to 2091; *gold:*—gold (-en).

1723. דַּהֲוָא° **Dahăvâ'** (Chald.), *dah-hav-aw´;* of uncert. der.; *Dahava,* a people colonized in Samaria:—Dehavites.

1724. דָּהַם **dâham,** *daw-ham´;* a prim. root (comp. 1740); to *be dumb,* i.e. (fig.) *dumbfounded:*—be astonished.

1725. דָּהַר **dâhar,** *daw-har´;* a prim. root; to *curvet* or move irregularly:—pranse.

1726. דַּהֲהַר **dahăhar,** *dah-hah-har´;* by redupl. from 1725; a *gallop:*—pransing.

דּוֹאֵג **Dôw'êg.** See 1673.

1727. דּוּב **dûwb,** *doob;* a prim. root; to *mope,* i.e. (fig.) *pine:*—sorrow.

דּוֹב **dôwb.** See 1677.

1728. דַּוָּג **davvâg,** *dav-vawg´;* an orth. var. of 1709 as a denom. [1771]; a *fisherman:*—fisher.

1729. דּוּגָה **dûwgâh,** *doo-gaw´;* fem. from the same as 1728; prob. *fishery,* i.e. a *hook* for fishing:—fish [hook].

1730. דּוֹד **dôwd,** *dode;* or (short.) דֹּד **dôd,** *dode;* from an unused root mean. prob. to *boil,* i.e. (fig.) to *love;* by impl. a *love-token, lover, friend;* spec. an *uncle:*—(well-) beloved, father's brother, love, uncle.

1731. דּוּד **dûwd,** *dood;* from the same as 1730; a *pot* (for *boiling*); also (by resemblance of shape) a *basket:*—basket, caldron, kettle, (seething) pot.

1732. דָּוִד **Dâvîd,** *daw-veed´;* rarely (fully) דָּוִיד **Dâvîyd,** *daw-veed´;* from the same as 1730; *loving; David,* the youngest son of Jesse.—David.

1733. דּוֹדָה **dôwdâh,** *do-daw´;* fem. of 1730; an *aunt:*—aunt, father's sister, uncle's wife.

1734. דּוֹדוֹ **Dôwdôw,** *do-do´;* from 1730; *loving; Dodo,* the name of three Isr.:—Dodo.

1735. דּוֹדָוָהוּ **Dôwdâvâhûw,** *do-daw-vaw´-hoo;* from 1730 and 3050; *love of Jah; Dodavah,* an Isr.:—Dodavah.

1736. דּוּדַי **dûwday,** *doo-dah´-ee;* from 1731; a *boiler* or *basket;* also the *mandrake* (as *aphrodisiac*):—basket, mandrake.

1737. דּוֹדַי **Dôwday,** *do-dah´ee;* formed like 1736; *amatory; Dodai,* an Isr.:—Dodai.

1738. דָּוָה **dâvâh,** *daw-vaw´;* a prim. root; to *be sick* (as if in menstruation):—infirmity.

1739. דָּוֶה **dâveh,** *daw-veh´;* from 1738; *sick* (espec. in menstruation):—faint, menstruous cloth, she that is sick, having sickness.

1740. דּוּחַ **dûwach,** *doo´-akh;* a prim. root; to *thrust* away; fig. to *cleanse:*—cast out, purge, wash.

1741. דְּוַי **dᵉvay,** *dev-ah´ee;* from 1739; *sickness;* fig. *loathing:*—languishing, sorrowful.

1742. דַּוָּי **davvây,** *dav-voy´;* from 1739; *sick;* fig. *troubled:*—faint.

דָּוִיד **Dâvîyd.** See 1732.

1743. דּוּךְ **dûwk,** *dook;* a prim. root; to *bruise* in a mortar:—beat.

1744. דּוּכִיפַת **dûwkîyphath,** *doo-kee-fath´;* of uncert. der.; the *hoopoe* or else the *grouse:*—lapwing.

1745. דּוּמָה **dûwmâh,** *doo-maw´;* from an unused root mean. to *be dumb* (comp. 1820); *silence;* fig. *death:*—silence.

1746. דּוּמָה **Dûwmâh,** *doo-maw´;* the same as 1745; *Dumah,* a tribe and region of Arabia:—Dumah.

1747. דּוּמִיָּה **dûwmîyâh,** *doo-me-yaw´;* from 1820; *stillness;* adv. *silently;* abstr. *quiet, trust:*—silence, silent, waiteth.

1748. דּוּמָם **dûwmâm,** *doo-mawm´;* from 1826; *still;* adv. *silently:*—dumb, silent, quietly wait.

דּוּמֶשֶׂק° **Dûwmesheq.** See 1833.

1749. דּוֹנַג **dôwnag,** *do-nag´;* of uncert. der.; *wax:*—wax.

1750. דּוּץ **dûwts,** *doots;* a prim. root; to *leap:*—be turned.

1751. דּוּק **dûwq** (Chald.), *dook;* corresp. to 1854; to *crumble:*—be broken to pieces.

1752. דּוּר **dûwr,** *dure;* a prim. root; prop. to *gyrate* (or move in a circle), i.e. to *remain:*—dwell.

1753. דּוּר **dûwr** (Chald.), *dure;* corresp. to 1752; to *reside:*—dwell.

1754. דּוּר **dûwr,** *dure;* from 1752; a *circle, ball* or *pile:*—ball, turn, round about.

1755. דּוֹר **dôwr,** *dore;* or (short.) דֹּר **dôr,** *dore;* from 1752; prop. a *revolution* of time, i.e. an *age* or generation; also a *dwelling:*—age, × evermore, generation, [n-]ever, posterity.

1756. דּוֹר **Dôwr,** *dore;* or (by perm.) דֹּאר **Dô'r** (Josh. 17 : 11; 1 Kings 4 : 11), *dore;* from 1755; *dwelling; Dor,* a place in Pal.:—Dor.

1757. דּוּרָא **Dûwrâ'** (Chald.), *doo-raw´;* prob. from 1753; *circle* or *dwelling; Dura,* a place in Bab.:—Dura.

1758. דּוּשׁ **dûwsh,** *doosh;* or דּוֹשׁ **dôwsh,** *dōsh;* or דִּישׁ **dîysh,** *deesh;* a prim. root; to *trample* or *thresh:*—break, tear, thresh, tread out (down), at grass [Jer. 50 : 11, *by mistake for* 1877].

1759. דּוּשׁ **dûwsh** (Chald.), *doosh;* corresp. to 1758; to *trample:*—tread down.

1760. דָּחָה **dâchâh,** *daw-khaw´;* or דָּחַח **dâchach** (Jer. 23 : 12), *daw-khakh´;* a prim. root; to *push* down:—chase, drive away (on), overthrow, outcast, × sore, thrust, totter.

1761. דַּחֲוָה **dachăvâh** (Chald.), *dakh-av-aw´;* from the equiv. of 1760; prob. a musical *instrument* (as being *struck*):—instrument of music.

1762. דְּחִי **dᵉchîy,** *deh-khee´;* from 1760; a *push,* i.e. (by impl.) a *fall:*—falling.

1763. דְּחַל **dᵉchal** (Chald.), *dek-khal´;* corresp. to 2119; to *slink,* i.e. (by impl.) to *fear,* or (caus.) *be formidable:*—make afraid, dreadful, fear, terrible.

1764. דֹּחַן **dôchan,** *do´-khan;* of uncert. der.; *millet:*—millet.

1765. דָּחַף **dâchaph,** *daw-khaf´;* a prim. root; to *urge,* i.e. *hasten:*—(be) haste (-ned), pressed on.

1766. דָּחַק **dâchaq,** *daw-khak´;* a prim. root; to *press,* i.e. *oppress:*—thrust, vex.

1767. דַּי **day,** *dahee;* of uncert. der.; *enough* (as noun or adv.), used chiefly with prep. in phrases:—able, according to, after (ability), among, as (oft as), (more than) enough, from, in, since, (much as is) sufficient (-ly), too much, very, when.

1768. דִּי **dîy** (Chald.), *dee;* appar. for 1668; *that,* used as rel., conj., and espec. (with prep.) in adv. phrases; also as a prep. *of:*— × as, but, for (-asmuch +), + now, of, seeing, than, that, therefore, until, + what (-soever), when, which, whom, whose.

1769. דִּיבוֹן **Dîybôwn,** *dee-bone´;* or (short.) דִּיבֹן **Dîybôn,** *dee-bone´;* from 1727; *pining:—Dibon,* the name of three places in Pal.:—Dibon. [*Also, with* 1410 *added,* Dibon-gad.]

1770. דִּיג **dîyg,** *deeg;* denom. from 1709; to *fish:*—fish.

1771. דַּיָּג **dayâg,** *dah-yawg´;* from 1770; a *fisherman:*—fisher.

1772. דַּיָּה **dayâh,** *dah-yaw´;* intens. from 1675; a *falcon* (from its *rapid* flight):—vulture.

1773. דְּיוֹ **deyôw,** *deh-yo´;* of uncert. der.; *ink:*—ink.

1774. דִּי זָהָב **Dîy zâhâb,** *dee zaw-hawb´;* as if from 1768 and 2091; *of gold; Dizahab,* a place in the Desert:—Dizahab.

1775. דִּימוֹן **Dîymôwn,** *dee-mone´;* perh. for 1769; *Dimon,* a place in Pal.:—Dimon.

1776. דִּימוֹנָה **Dîymôwnâh,** *dee-mo-naw´;* fem. of 1775; *Dimonah,* a place in Pal.:—Dimonah.

1777. דִּין **dîyn,** *deen;* or (Gen. 6 : 3) דּוּן **dûwn,** *doon;* a prim. root [comp. 113]; to *rule;* by impl. to *judge* (as umpire); also to *strive* (as at law):—contend, execute (judgment), judge, minister judgment, plead (the cause), at strife, strive.

1778. דִּין **dîyn** (Chald.), *deen;* corresp. to 1777; to *judge:*—judge.

1779. דִּין **dîyn,** *deen;* or (Job 19 : 29) דּוּן **dûwn,** *doon;* from 1777; *judgment* (the suit, justice, sentence or tribunal); by impl. also *strife:*—cause, judgment, plea, strife.

1780. דִּין **dîyn** (Chald.), *deen;* corresp. to 1779:—judgment.

1781. דַּיָּן **dayân,** *dah-yawn´;* from 1777; a *judge* or *advocate:*—judge.

1782. דַּיָּן **dayân** (Chald.), *dah-yawn´;* corresp. to 1781:—judge.

1783. דִּינָה **Dîynâh,** *dee-naw´;* fem. of 1779; *justice; Dinah,* the daughter of Jacob:—Dinah.

1784. דִּינַי **Dîynay** (Chald.), *dee-nah´ee;* patrial from an uncert. prim.; a *Dinaite* or inhab. of some unknown Ass. province:—Dinaite.

דִּיפַת **Dîyphath.** See 7384.

1785. דָּיֵק **dâyêq,** *daw-yake´;* from a root corresp. to 1751; a *battering*-tower:—fort.

1786. דַּיִשׁ **dayîsh,** *dah´-yish;* from 1758; *threshing*-time:—threshing.

1787. דִּישׁוֹן **Dîyshôwn,** דִּישֹׁן **Dîyshôn,** דִּשׁוֹן **Dîshôwn,** or דִּשֹׁן **Dîshôn,** *dee-shone´;* the same as 1788; *Dishon,* the name of two Edomites:—Dishon.

1788. דִּישֹׁן **dîyshôn,** *dee-shone´;* from 1758; the *leaper,* i.e. an *antelope:*—pygarg.

1789. דִּישָׁן **Dîyshân,** *dee-shawn´;* another form of 1787; *Dishan,* an Edomite:—Dishan, Dishon.

1790. דַּךְ **dak,** *dak;* from an unused root (comp., 1794); *crushed,* i.e. (fig.) *injured:*—afflicted, oppressed.

1791. דֵּךְ **dêk** (Chald.), *dake;* or דָּךְ **dâk** (Chald.), *dawk;* prol. from 1668; *this:*—the same, this.

1792. דָּכָא **dâkâ',** *daw-kaw´;* a prim. root (comp. 1794); to *crumble;* trans. to *bruise* (lit. or fig.):—beat to pieces, break (in pieces), bruise, contrite, crush, destroy, humble, oppress, smite.

1793. דַּכָּא **dakkâ',** *dak-kaw´;* from 1792; *crushed* (lit. *powder* or fig. *contrite*):—contrite, destruction.

1794. דָּכָה **dâkâh,** *daw-kaw´;* a prim. root (comp. 1790, 1792); to *collapse* (phys. or mentally):—break (sore), contrite, crouch.

1795. דַּכָּה **dakkâh,** *dak-kaw´;* from 1794 like 1793; *mutilated:*— + wounded.

1796. דֳּכִי **dŏkîy,** *dok-ee´;* from 1794; a *dashing* of surf:—wave.

1797. דִּכֵּן **dikkên** (Chald.), *dik-kane´;* prol. from 1791; *this:*—same, that, this.

1798. דְּכַר **dekar** (Chald.), *dek-ar´;* corresp. to 2145; prop. a *male,* i.e. of sheep:—ram.

1799. דִּכְרוֹן **dikrôwn** (Chald.), *dik-rone´;* or דָּכְרָן **dokrân,** *dok-rawn´* (Chald.); corresp. to 2146; a *register:*—record.

1800. דַּל **dal,** *dal;* from 1809; prop. *dangling,* i.e. (by impl.) *weak* or *thin:*—lean, needy, poor (man), weaker.

1801. דָּלַג **dâlag,** *daw-lag´;* a prim. root; to *spring:*—leap.

1802. דָּלָה **dâlâh,** *daw-law´;* a prim. root *(comp. 1809); prob. to dangle,* i.e. to *let down* a bucket (for *drawing* out water); fig. to *deliver:*—draw (out), × enough, lift up.

1803. דַּלָּה **dallâh,** *dal-law´;* from 1802; prop. something *dangling,* i.e. a loose *thread* or *hair;* fig. *indigent:*—hair, pining sickness, poor (-est sort).

1804. דָּלַח **dâlach,** *daw-lakh´;* a prim. root; to *roil* water:—trouble.

1805. דְּלִי **delîy,** *del-ee´;* or דֳּלִי **dŏlîy,** *dol-ee´;* from 1802; a *pail* or *jar* (for *drawing* water):—bucket.

1806. דְּלָיָה **Delâyâh,** *del-aw-yaw´;* or (prol.) דְּלָיָהוּ **Delâyâhhûw,** *del-aw-yaw´-hoo;* from 1802 and 3050; *Jah has delivered; Delajah,* the name of five Isr.:—Dalaiah, Delaiah.

1807. דְּלִילָה **Delîylâh,** *del-ee-law´;* from 1809; *languishing:—Delilah,* a Philistine woman:—Delilah.

1808. דָּלִיָּה **dâlîyâh,** *daw-lee-yaw´;* from 1802; something *dangling,* i.e. a *bough:*—branch.

1809. דָּלַל **dâlal,** *daw-lal´;* a prim. root (comp. 1802); to *slacken* or *be feeble;* fig. to *be oppressed:*—bring low, dry up, be emptied, be not equal, fail, be impoverished, be made thin.

1810. דִּלְעָן **Dil'ân,** *dil-awn´;* of uncert. der.; *Dilan,* a place in Pal.:—Dilean.

1811. דָּלַף **dâlaph,** *daw-laf´;* a prim. root; to *drip;* by impl. to *weep:*—drop through, melt, pour out.

1812. דֶּלֶף **deleph,** *deh´-lef;* from 1811; a *dripping:*—dropping.

1813. דַּלְפוֹן **Dalphôwn,** *dal-fone´;* from 1811; *dripping, Dalphon,* a son of Haman:—Dalphon.

1814. דָּלַק **dâlaq,** *daw-lak´;* a prim. root; to *flame* (lit. or fig.):—burning, chase, inflame, kindle, persecute (-or), pursue hotly.

1815. דְּלַק **delaq** (Chald.), *del-ak´;* corresp. to 1814:—burn.

1816. דַּלֶּקֶת **dalleqeth,** *dal-lek´-keth;* from 1814; a *burning* fever:—inflammation.

1817. דֶּלֶת **deleth,** *deh´-leth;* from 1802; something *swinging,* i.e. the *valve* of a door:—door (two-leaved), gate, leaf, lid. [In Psa. 141:3, *dâl,* irreg.]

1818. דָּם **dâm,** *dawm;* from 1826 (comp. 119); *blood* (as that which when shed causes *death*) of man or an animal; by anal. the *juice* of the grape; fig. (espec. in the plur.) *bloodshed* (i.e. *drops* of blood):—blood (-y, -guiltiness, [-thirsty]), + innocent.

1819. דָּמָה **dâmâh,** *daw-maw´;* a prim. root; to *compare;* by impl. to *resemble, liken, consider:*—compare, devise, (be) like (-n), mean, think, use similitudes.

1820. דָּמָה **dâmâh,** *daw-maw´;* a prim. root; to *be dumb* or *silent;* hence to *fail* or *perish;* trans. to *destroy:*—cease, be cut down (off), destroy, be brought to silence, be undone, × utterly.

1821. דְּמָה **demâh** (Chald.), *dema-aw´;* corresp. to 1819; to *resemble:*—be like.

1822. דֻּמָּה **dummâh,** *doom-maw´;* from 1820; *desolation;* concr. *desolate:*—destroy.

1823. דְּמוּת **demûwth,** *dem-ooth´;* from 1819; *resemblance;* concr. *model, shape;* adv. *like:*—fashion, like (-ness, as), manner, similitude.

1824. דְּמִי **demîy,** *dem-ee´;* or דֳּמִי **dŏmîy,** *dom-ee´;* from 1820; *quiet:*—cutting off, rest, silence.

1825. דִּמְיוֹן **dimyôwn,** *dim-yone´;* from 1819; *resemblance:*— × like.

1826. דָּמַם **dâmam,** *daw-mam´;* a prim. root [comp. 1724, 1820]; to *be dumb;* by impl. to *be astonished,* to *stop;* also to *perish:*—cease, be cut down (off), forbear, hold peace, quiet self, rest, be silent, keep (put to) silence, be (stand), still, tarry, wait.

1827. דְּמָמָה **demâmâh,** *dem-aw-maw´;* fem. from 1826; *quiet:*—calm, silence, still.

1828. דֹּמֶן **dômen,** *do´-men;* of uncert. der.; *manure:*—dung.

1829. דִּמְנָה **Dimnâh,** *dim-naw´;* fem. from the same as 1828; a *dung-heap; Dimnah,* a place in Pal.:—Dimnah.

1830. דָּמַע **dâma',** *daw-mah´;* a prim. root; to *weep:*— × sore, weep.

1831. דֶּמַע **dema',** *deh´-mah;* from 1830; a *tear;* fig. *juice:*—liquor.

1832. דִּמְעָה **dim'âh,** *dim-aw´;* fem. of 1831; *weeping:*—tears.

1833. דְּמֶשֶׁק **d^{e}mesheq,** *dem-eh´-shek;* by orth. var. from 1834; *damask* (as a fabric of Damascus):—in Damascus.

1834. דַּמֶּשֶׂק **Dammeseq,** *dam-meh´-sek;* or דּוּמֶשֶׂק° **Dûwmeseq,** *doo-meh´-sek;* or דַּרְמֶשֶׂק **Darmeseq,** *dar-meh´-sek;* of for. or.; *Damascus,* a city of Syria:—Damascus.

1835. דָּן **Dan,** *dawn;* from 1777; *judge; Dan,* one of the sons of Jacob; also the tribe descended from him, and its territory; likewise a place in Pal. colonized by them:—Dan.

1836. דֵּן **dên** (Chald.), *dane;* an orth. var. of 1791; *this:*—[afore-] time, + after this manner, here [-after], one . . . another, such, there [-fore], these, this (matter), + thus, where [-fore], which.

דָּנִאֵל **Dânî'êl.** See 1841.

1837. דַּנָּה **Dannâh,** *dan-naw´;* of uncert. der.; *Dannah,* a place in Pal.:—Dannah.

1838. דִּנְהָבָה **Dinhâbâh,** *din-haw-baw´;* of uncert. der.; *Dinhabah,* an Edomitish town:—Dinhaban.

1839. דָּנִי **Dânîy,** *daw-nee´:* patron. from 1835; a *Danite* (often collect.) or desc. (or inhab.) of Dan:—Danites, of Dan.

1840. דָּנִיֵּאל **Dânîyê'l,** *daw-nee-yale´;* in Ezek. דָּנִאֵל **Dânî'êl,** *daw-nee-ale´;* from 1835 and 410; *judge of God; Daniel* or *Danijel,* the name of two Isr.:—Daniel.

1841. דָּנִיֵּאל **Dânîyê'l** (Chald.), *daw-nee-yale´;* corresp. to 1840; *Danijel,* the Heb. prophet:—Daniel.

1842. דָּן יַעַן **Dân Ya'an,** *dawn yah´-an;* from 1835 and (appar.) 3282; *judge of purpose; Dan-Jaan,* a place in Pal.:—Dan-jaan.

1843. דֵּעַ **dêa',** *day´-ah;* from 3045; *knowledge:*—knowledge, opinion.

1844. דֵּעָה **dê'âh,** *day-aw´;* fem. of 1843; *knowledge:*—knowledge.

1845. דְּעוּאֵל **D^e'ûw'êl,** *deh-oo-ale´;* from 3045 and 410; *known of God; Deüel,* an Isr.:—Deuel.

1846. דָּעַךְ **dâ'ak,** *daw-ak´; a prim. root; to be extinguished:* fig. to *expire* or *be dried up:*—be extinct, consumed, put out, quenched.

1847. דַּעַת **da'ath,** *dah´-ath;* from 3045; *knowledge:*—cunning, [ig-] norantly, know (-ledge), [un-] awares (wittingly).

1848. דֳּפִי **dŏphîy,** *dof´-ee;* from an unused root (mean. to *push* over); a *stumbling*-block:—slanderest.

1849. דָּפַק **dâphaq,** *daw-fak´;* a prim. root; to *knock;* by anal. to *press* severely:—beat, knock, overdrive.

1850. דָּפְקָה **Dophqâh,** *dof-kaw´;* from 1849; a *knock; Dophkah,* a place in the Desert:—Dophkah.

1851. דַּק **daq,** *dak;* from 1854; *crushed,* i.e. (by impl.) *small* or *thin:*—dwarf, lean [-fleshed], very little thing, small, thin.

1852. דֹּק **dôq,** *doke;* from 1854; something *crumbling,* i.e. *fine* (as a *thin* cloth):—curtain.

1853. דִּקְלָה **Diqlâh,** *dik-law´;* of for. or.; *Diklah,* a region of Arabia:—Diklah.

1854. דָּקַק **dâqaq,** *daw-kak´;* a prim. root [comp. 1915]; to *crush* (or intrans.) *crumble:*—beat in pieces (small), bruise, make dust, (into) × powder, (be, very) small, stamp (small).

1855. דְּקַק **d^{e}qaq** (Chald.), *dek-ak´;* corresp. to 1854; to *crumble* or (trans.) *crush:*—break to pieces.

1856. דָּקַר **dâqar,** *daw-kar´;* a prim. root; to *stab;* by anal. to *starve;* fig. to *revile:*—pierce, strike (thrust) through, wound.

1857. דֶּקֶר **Deqer,** *deh´-ker;* from 1856; a *stab; Deker,* an Isr.:—Dekar.

1858. דַּר **dar,** *dar;* appar. from the same as 1865; prop. a *pearl* (from its sheen as rapidly *turned*); by anal. *pearl-stone,* i.e. mother-of-pearl or alabaster:— × white.

1859. דָּר **dâr** (Chald.), *dawr;* corresp. to 1755; an *age:*—generation.

דֹּר **dôr.** See 1755.

1860. דְּרָאוֹן **d^{e}râ'ôwn,** *der-aw-one´;* or דֵּרָאוֹן **dêra'ôwn,** *day-raw-one´;* from an unused root (mean. to *repulse*); an object of *aversion:*—abhorring, contempt.

1861. דָּרְבוֹן **dorbôwn,** *dor-bone´* [also *dor-bawn´*] of uncert. der.; a *goad:*—goad.

1862. דַּרְדַּע **Darda',** *dar-dah´;* appar. from 1858 and 1843; *pearl of knowledge; Darda,* an Isr.:—Darda.

1863. דַּרְדַּר **dardar,** *dar-dar´;* of uncert. der.; a *thorn:*—thistle.

1864. דָּרוֹם **dârôwm,** *daw-rome´;* of uncert. der.; the *south;* poet. the *south wind:*—south.

1865. דְּרוֹר **d^{e}rôwr,** *der-ore´;* from an unused root (mean. to *move rapidly*); *freedom;* hence *spontaneity* of outflow, and so *clear:*—liberty, pure.

1866. דְּרוֹר **d^{e}rôwr,** *der-ore´;* the same as 1865, applied to a bird; the *swift,* a kind of swallow:—swallow.

1867. דָּרְיָוֶשׁ **Dâr^{e}yâvêsh,** *daw-reh-yaw-vaysh´;* of Pers. or.; *Darejavesh,* a title (rather than name) of several Persian kings:—Darius.

1868. דָּרְיָוֶשׁ **Dâr^{e}yâvêsh** (Chald.), *daw-reh-yaw-vaysh´;* corresp. to 1867:—Darius.

1869. דָּרַךְ **dârak,** *daw-rak´;* a prim. root; to *tread;* by impl. to *walk;* also to *string* a bow (by treading on it in bending):—archer, bend, come, draw, go (over), guide, lead (forth), thresh, tread (down), walk.

1870. דֶּרֶךְ **derek,** *deh´-rek;* from 1869; a *road* (as *trodden*); fig. a *course* of life or *mode* of action, often adv.:—along, away, because of, + by, conversation, custom, [east-] ward, journey, manner, passenger, through, toward, [high-] [path-] way [-side], whither [-soever].

1871. דַּרְכְּמוֹן **dark^{e}môwn,** *dar-kem-one´;* of Pers. or.; a *"drachma,"* or coin:—dram.

1872. דְּרָע **d^{e}râ'** (Chald.), *der-aw´;* corresp. to 2220; an *arm:*—arm.

1873. דָּרַע **Dâra',** *daw-rah´;* prob. contr. from 1862; *Dara,* an Isr.:—Dara.

1874. דַּרְקוֹן **Darqôwn,** *dar-kone´;* of uncert. der.; *Darkon,* one of "Solomon's servants":—Darkon.

1875. דָּרַשׁ **dârash,** *daw-rash´;* a prim. root; prop. to *tread* or *frequent;* usually to *follow* (for pursuit or search); by impl. to *seek* or *ask;* spec. to *worship:*—ask, × at all, care for, × diligently, inquire, make inquisition, [necro-] mancer, question, require, search, seek [for, out], × surely.

1876. דָּשָׁא **dâshâ',** *daw-shaw´;* a prim. root; to *sprout:*—bring forth, spring.

1877. דֶּשֶׁא **deshe',** *deh´-sheh;* from 1876; a *sprout;* by anal. *grass:*—(tender) grass, green, (tender) herb.

1878. דָּשֵׁן **dâshên,** *daw-shane´;* a prim. root; to *be fat;* trans. to *fatten* (or regard as fat); spec. to *anoint;* fig. to *satisfy;* denom. (from 1880) to *remove* (fat) *ashes* (of sacrifices):—accept, anoint, take away the (receive) ashes (from), make (wax) fat.

1879. דָּשֵׁן **dâshên,** *daw-shane´;* from 1878; *fat;* fig. *rich, fertile:*—fat.

1880. דֶּשֶׁן **deshen,** *deh´-shen;* from 1878; the *fat;* abstr. *fatness,* i.e. (fig.) *abundance;* spec. the (fatty) *ashes* of sacrifices:—ashes, fatness.

1881. דָּת **dâth,** *dawth;* of uncert. (perh. for.) der.: a royal *edict* or statute:—commandment, commission, decree, law, manner.

1882. דָּת **dâth** (Chald.), *dawth;* corresp. to 1881; decree, law.

1883. דֶּתֶא **dethe'** (Chald.), *deh´-thay;* corresp. to 1877:—tender grass.

1884. דְּתָבָר **d^{e}thâbâr** (Chald.), *deth-aw-bawr´;* of Pers. or.; mean. one *skilled in law;* a *judge:*—counsellor.

1885. דָּתָן **Dâthân,** *daw-thawn´;* of uncert. der.; *Dathan,* an Isr.:—Dathan.

1886. דֹּתָן **Dôthân,** *do´-thawn;* or (Chaldaizing dual)

דֹּתַיִן **Dôthayin** (Gen. 37 : 17), *do-thah´-yin;* of uncert. der.; *Dothan,* a place in Pal.:—Dothan.

ה

1887. הֵא **hê',** *hay;* a prim. particle; *lo!:*—behold, lo.

1888. הֵא **hê'** (Chald.), *hay;* or הָא **hâ'** (Chald.), *haw;* corresp. to 1887:—even, lo.

1889. הֶאָח **heâch,** *heh-awkh´;* from 1887 and 253, *aha!:*—ah, aha, ha.

הָארָרִי **Hâ'rârîy.** See 2043.

1890. הַבְהָב **habhâb,** *hab-hawb´;* by redupl. from 3051; *gift* (in sacrifice), *i.e. holocaust:*—offering.

1891. הָבַל **hâbal,** *haw-bal´;* a prim. root; to *be vain* in act, word, or expectation; spec. to *lead astray:*—be (become, make) vain.

1892. הֶבֶל **hebel,** *heh´-bel;* or (rarely in the abs.) הֲבֵל **hăbêl,** *hab-ale´;* from 1891; *emptiness* or *vanity;* fig. something *transitory* and *unsatisfactory;* often used as an adv.:— × altogether, vain, vanity.

1893. הֶבֶל **Hebel,** *heh´-bel;* the same as 1892; *Hebel,* the son of Adam:—Abel.

1894. הֹבֶן **hôben,** *ho´-ben;* only in plur., from an unused root mean. to *be hard; ebony:*—ebony.

1895. הָבַר **hâbar,** *haw-bar´;* a prim. root of uncert. (perh. for.) der.; to *be a horoscopist:*— + (astro-) loger.

1896. הֵגֵא **Hêgê',** *hay-gay´;* or (by perm.) הֵגַי **Hêgay,** *hay-gah´ee;* prob. of Pers. or.; *Hege* or *Hegai,* a eunuch of Xerxes:—Hegai, Hege.

1897. הָגָה **hâgâh,** *haw-gaw´;* a prim. root [comp. 1901]; to *murmur* (in pleasure or anger); by impl. to *ponder:*—imagine, meditate, mourn, mutter, roar, × sore, speak, study, talk, utter.

1898. הָגָה **hâgâh,** *haw-gaw´;* a prim. root; to *remove;*—stay, take away.

1899. הֶגֶה **hegeh,** *heh´-geh;* from 1897; a *muttering* (in sighing, thought, or as thunder):—mourning, sound, tale.

1900. הָגוּת **hâgûwth,** *haw-gooth´;* from 1897; *musing:*—meditation.

1901. הָגִיג **hâgîyg,** *haw-gheeg´;* from an unused root akin to 1897; prop. a *murmur,* i.e. *complaint:*—meditation, musing.

1902. הִגָּיוֹן **higgâyôwn,** *hig-gaw-yone´;* intens. from 1897; a *murmuring* sound, i.e. a musical notation (prob. similar to the modern *affettuoso* to indicate solemnity of movement); by impl. a *machination:*—device, Higgaion, meditation, solemn sound.

1903. הָגִין **hâgîyn,** *haw-gheen´;* of uncert. der.; perh. *suitable* or *turning:*—directly.

1904. הָגָר **Hâgâr,** *haw-gawr´;* of uncert. (perh. for.) der.; *Hagar,* the mother of Ishmael:—Hagar.

1905. הַגְרִי **Hagrîy,** *hag-ree´;* or (prol.) הַגְרִיא **Hagrî',** *hag-ree´;* perh. patron. from 1904; a *Hagrite* or member of a certain Arabian clan:—Hagarene, Hagarite, Haggeri.

1906. הֵד **hêd,** *hade;* for 1959; a *shout:*—sounding again.

1907. הַדָּבָר **haddâbâr** (Chald.), *had-daw-bawr´;* prob. of for. or.; a *vizier:*—counsellor.

1908. הֲדַד **Hădad,** *had-ad´;* prob. of for. or. [comp. 111]; *Hadad,* the name of an idol, and of several kings of Edom:—Hadad.

1909. הֲדַדְעֶזֶר **Hădad'ezer,** *had-ad-eh´-zer;* from 1908 and 5828; *Hadad* (is his) *help; Hadadezer,* a Syrian king:—Hadadezer. Comp. 1928.

1910. הֲדַדְרִמּוֹן **Hădadrimmôwn,** *had-ad-rim-mone´;* from 1908 and 7417; *Hadad-Rimmon,* a place in Pal.:—Hadad-rimmon.

1911. הָדָה **hâdâh,** *haw-daw´;* a prim. root [comp. 3034]; to *stretch forth* the hand:—put.

1912. הֹדּוּ **Hôdûw,** *ho´-doo;* of for. or.; *Hodu* (i.e. Hindû-stan):—India.

1913. הֲדוֹרָם **Hădôwrâm,** *had-o-rawm´;* or הֲדֹרָם **Hădôrâm,** *had-o-rawm´;* prob. of for. der.; *Hadoram,* a son of Joktan, and the tribe descended from him:—Hadoram.

1914. הִדַּי **Hidday,** *hid-dah´ee;* of uncert. der.; *Hiddai,* an Isr.:—Hiddai.

1915. הָדַךְ **hâdak,** *haw-dak´;* a prim. root [comp. 1854]; to *crush* with the foot:—tread down.

1916. הֲדֹם **hădôm,** *had-ome´;* from an unused root mean. to *stamp* upon; a *footstool:*—[foot-] stool.

1917. הַדָּם **haddâm** (Chald.), *had-dawm´;* from a root corresp. to that of 1916; something *stamped* to pieces, i.e. a *bit:*—piece.

1918. הֲדַס **hădaç,** *had-as´;* of uncert. der.; the *myrtle:*—myrtle (tree).

1919. הֲדַסָּה **Hădaççâh,** *had-as-saw´;* fem. of 1918, *Hadassah* (or Esther):—Hadassah.

1920. הָדַף **hâdaph,** *haw-daf´;* a prim. root; to *push* away or down:—cast away (out), drive, expel, thrust (away).

1921. הָדַר **hâdar,** *haw-dar´;* a prim. root; to *swell* up (lit. or fig., act. or pass.); by impl. to *favor* or *honour, be high* or *proud:*—countenance, crooked place, glorious, honour, put forth.

1922. הֲדַר **hădar** (Chald.), *had-ar´;* corresp. to 1921; to *magnify* (fig.):—glorify, honour.

1923. הֲדַר **hădar** (Chald.), *had-ar´;* from 1922; *magnificence:*—honour, majesty.

1924. הֲדַר **Hădar,** *had-ar´;* the same as 1926; *Hadar,* an Edomite:—Hadar.

1925. הֶדֶר **heder,** *heh´-der;* from 1921; *honour;* used (fig.) for the *capital* city (Jerusalem):—glory.

1926. הָדָר **hâdâr,** *haw-dawr´;* from 1921; *magnificience,* i.e. ornament or splendor:—beauty, comeliness, excellency, glorious, glory, goodly, honour, majesty.

1927. הֲדָרָה **hădârâh,** *had-aw-raw´;* fem. of 1926; *decoration:*—beauty, honour.

הֲדֹרָם **Hădôrâm.** See 1913.

1928. הֲדַרְעֶזֶר **Hădar'ezer,** *had-ar-eh´-zer;* from 1924 and 5828; *Hadar* (i.e. *Hadad,* 1908) is his *help; Hadarezer* (i.e. Hadadezer, 1909), a Syrian king:—Hadarezer.

1929. הָהּ **hâhh,** *haw;* a short. form of 162; *ah!* expressing grief:—woe worth.

1930. הוֹ **hôw,** *ho;* by perm. from 1929; *oh!:*—alas.

1931. הוּא **hûw',** *hoo;* of which the fem. (beyond the Pentateuch) is הִיא **hîy',** *he;* a prim. word, the third pers. pron. sing., *he* (*she* or *it*); only expressed when emphatic or without a verb; also (intens.) *self,* or (esp. with the art.) the *same;* sometimes (as demonstr.) *this* or *that;* occasionally (instead of copula) *as* or *are:*—he, as for her, him (-self), it, the same, she (herself), such, that (. . . it), these, they, this, those, which (is), who.

1932. הוּא **hûw'** (Chald.), *hoo;* or (fem.) הִיא **hîy'** (Chald.), *he;* corresp. to 1931:— × are, it, this.

1933. הָוָא **hâvâ',** *haw-vaw´;* or הָוָה **hâvâh,** *haw-vaw´;* a prim. root [comp. 183, 1961] supposed to mean prop. to *breathe;* to *be* (in the sense of existence):—be, × have.

1934. הֲוָא **hăvâ'** (Chald.), *hav-aw´;* or הֲוָה **hăvâh** (Chald.), *hav-aw´;* corresp. to 1933; to *exist;* used in a great variety of applications (especially in connection with other words):—be, become, + behold, + came (to pass), + cease, + cleave, + consider, + do, + give, + have + judge, + keep, + labour, + mingle (self), + put, + see, + seek, + set, + slay, + take heed, tremble, + walk, + would.

1935. הוֹד **hôwd,** *hode;* from an unused root; *grandeur* (i.e. an imposing form and appearance):—beauty, comeliness, excellency, glorious, glory, goodly, honour, majesty.

1936. הוֹד **Hôwd,** *hode;* the same as 1935; *Hod,* an Isr.:—Hod.

1937. הוֹדְוָה **Hôwdᵉvâh,** *ho-dev-aw´;* a form of 1938; *Hodevah* (or Hodevjah), an Isr.:—Hodevah.

1938. הוֹדַוְיָה **Hôwdavyâh,** *ho- dav-yaw´;* from 1935 and 3050; *majesty of Jah; Hodavjah,* the name of three Isr.:—Hodaviah.

1939. הוֹדַיְוָהוּ **Howdayᵉvâhûw,** *ho-dah-yeh-vaw´-hoo;* a form of 1938; *Hodajvah,* an Isr.:—Hodaiah.

1940. הוֹדִיָּה **Hôwdîyâh,** *ho-dee-yaw´;* a form for the fem. of 3064; a *Jewess:*—Hodiah.

1941. הוֹדִיָּה **Hôwdîyâh,** *ho-dee-yaw´;* a form of 1938; *Hodijah,* the name of three Isr.:—Hodijah.

הָוָה **hâvâh.** See 1933.

הָוָה **hâvâh.** See 1934.

1942. הַוָּה **havvâh,** *hav-vaw´;* from 1933 (in the sense of eagerly *coveting* and *rushing* upon; by impl. of *falling*); *desire;* also *ruin:*—calamity, iniquity, mischief, mischievous (thing), naughtiness, naughty, noisome, perverse thing, substance, very wickedness.

1943. הֹוָה **hôvâh,** *ho-vaw´;* another form for 1942; *ruin:*—mischief.

1944. הוֹהָם **Hôwhâm,** *ho-hawm´;* of uncert. der.; *Hoham,* a Canaanitish king:—Hoham.

1945. הוֹי **hôwy,** *hoh´ee;* a prol. form of 1930 [akin to 188]; *oh!:*—ah, alas, ho, O, woe.

1946. הוּךְ **hûwk** (Chald.), *hook;* corresp. to 1981; to *go;* caus. to *bring:*—bring again, come, go (up).

1947. הוֹלֵלָה **hôwlêlâh,** *ho-lay-law´;* fem. act. part. of 1984; *folly:*—madness.

1948. הוֹלֵלוּת **hôwlêlûwth,** *ho-lay-looth´;* from act. part. of 1984; *folly:*—madness.

1949. הוּם **hûwm,** *hoom;* a prim. root [comp. 2000]; to *make an uproar,* or *agitate* greatly:—destroy, move, make a noise, put, ring again.

1950. הוֹמָם **Hôwmâm,** *ho-mawm´;* from 2000; *raging; Homam,* an Edomitish chieftain:—Homam. Comp. 1967.

1951. הוּן **hûwn,** *hoon;* a prim. root; prop. to *be naught,* i.e. (fig.) to *be* (caus. *act*) *light:*—be ready.

1952. הוֹן **hôwn,** *hone;* from the same as 1951 in the sense of 202; *wealth;* by impl. *enough:*—enough, + for nought, riches, substance, wealth.

1953. הוֹשָׁמָע **Hôwshâmâʻ,** *ho-shaw-maw´;* from 3068 and 8085; *Jehovah has heard; Hoshama,* an Isr.:—Hoshama.

1954. הוֹשֵׁעַ **Hôwshêaʻ,** *ho-shay´-ah;* from 3467; *deliverer; Hosheă,* the name of five Isr.:—Hosea, Hoshea, Oshea.

1955. הוֹשַׁעְיָה **Hôwshaʻyâh,** *ho-shah-yaw´;* from 3467 and 3050; *Jah has saved; Hoshajah,* the name of two Isr.:—Hoshaiah.

1956. הוֹתִיר **Hôwthîyr,** *ho-theer´;* from 3498; *he has caused to remain; Hothir,* an Isr.:—Hothir.

1957. הָזָה **hâzâh,** *haw-zaw´;* a prim. root [comp. 2372]; to *dream:*—sleep.

1958. הִי **hîy,** *he;* for 5092; *lamentation:*—woe.

הִיא **hîy'.** See 1931, 1932.

1959. הֵידָד **hêydâd,** *hay-dawd´;* from an unused root (mean. to *shout*); *acclamation:*—shout (-ing).

1960. הֻיְּדָה **huyᵉdâh,** *hoo-yed-aw´;* from the same as 1959; prop. an *acclaim,* i.e. a *choir* of singers:—thanksgiving.

1961. הָיָה **hâyâh,** *haw-yaw´;* a prim. root [comp. 1933]; to *exist,* i.e. *be* or *become, come to pass* (always emphatic, and not a mere copula or auxiliary):—beacon, × altogether, be (-come, accomplished, committed, like), break, cause, come (to pass), continue, do, faint, fall, + follow, happen, × have, last, pertain, quit (one-) self, require, × use.

1962. הַיָּה **hayâh,** *hah-yaw´;* another form for 1943; *ruin:*—calamity.

1963. הֵיךְ **hêyk,** *hake;* another form for 349; *how?:*—how.

1964. הֵיכָל **hêykâl,** *hay-kawl´;* prob. from 3201 (in the sense of *capacity*); a large public building, such as a *palace* or *temple:*—palace, temple.

1965. הֵיכַל **hêykal** (Chald.), *hay-kal´;* corresp. to 1964:—palace, temple.

1966. הֵילֵל **hêylêl,** *hay-lale´;* from 1984 (in the sense of *brightness*); the *morning-star:*—lucifer.

1967. הֵימָם **Hêymâm,** *hay-mawm´;* another form for 1950; *Hemam,* an Idumæan:—Hemam.

1968. הֵימָן **Hêymân,** *hay-mawn´;* prob. from 539; *faithful; Heman,* the name of at least two Isr.:—Heman.

1969. הִין **hîyn,** *heen;* prob. of Eg. or.; a *hin* or liquid measure:—hin.

1970. הָכַר **hâkar,** *haw-kar´;* a prim. root; appar. to *injure:*—make self strange.

1971. הַכָּרָה **hakkârâh,** *hak-kaw-raw´;* from 5234; *respect,* i.e. partiality:—shew.

הַל **hal.** See 1973.

1972. הָלָא **hâlâ',** *haw-law´;* prob. denom. from 1973; to *remove* or be *remote:*—cast far off.

1973. הָלְאָה **hâlᵉâh,** *haw-leh-aw´;* from the prim. form of the art. [הַל **hal**]; *to the distance,* i.e. *far away;* also (of time) *thus far:*—back, beyond, (hence-) forward, hitherto, thenceforth, yonder.

1974. הִלּוּל **hillûwl,** *hil-lool´;* from 1984 (in the sense of *rejoicing*); a *celebration* of thanksgiving for harvest:—merry, praise.

1975. הַלָּז **hallâz,** *hal-lawz´;* from 1976; *this* or *that:*—side, that, this.

1976. הַלָּזֶה **hallâzeh,** *hal-law-zeh´;* from the art. [see 1973] and 2088; *this very:*—this.

1977. הַלֵּזוּ **hallêzûw,** *hal-lay-zoo´;* another form of 1976; *that:*—this.

1978. הָלִיךְ **hâlîyk,** *haw-leek´;* from 1980; a *walk,* i.e. (by impl.) a *step:*—step.

1979. הֲלִיכָה **hălîykâh,** *hal-ee-kaw´;* fem. of 1978; a *walking;* by impl. a *procession* or *march,* a *caravan:*—company, going, walk, way.

1980. הָלַךְ **hâlak,** *haw-lak´;* akin to 3212; a prim. root; to *walk* (in a great variety of applications, lit. and fig.):—(all) along, apace, behave (self), come, (on) continually, be conversant, depart, + be eased, enter, exercise (self), + follow, forth, forward, get, go (about, abroad, along, away, forward, on, out, up and down), + greater, grow, be wont to haunt, lead, march, × more and more, move (self), needs, on, pass (away), be at the point, quite, run (along), + send, speedily, spread, still, surely, + tale-bearer, + travel (-ler), walk (abroad, on, to and fro, up and down, to places), wander, wax, [way-] faring man, × be weak, whirl.

1981. הֲלַךְ **hălak** (Chald.), *hal-ak´;* corresp. to 1980 [comp. 1946]; to *walk:*—walk.

1982. הֵלֶךְ **hêlek,** *hay´-lek;* from 1980; prop. a *journey,* i.e. (by impl.) a *wayfarer;* also a *flowing:*— × dropped, traveller.

1983. הֲלָךְ **hălâk** (Chald.), *hal-awk´;* from 1981; prop. a *journey,* i.e. (by impl.) *toll* on goods at a road:—custom.

1984. הָלַל **hâlal,** *haw-lal´;* a prim. root; to *be clear* (orig. of sound, but usually of color); to *shine;* hence to *make a show,* to *boast;* and thus to *be* (clamorously) *foolish;* to *rave;* causat. to *celebrate;* also to *stultify:*—(make) boast (self), celebrate, commend, (deal, make), fool (-ish, -ly), glory, give [light], be (make, feign self) mad (against), give in marriage, [sing, be worthy of] praise, rage, renowned, shine.

1985. הִלֵּל **Hillêl,** *hil-layl´;* from 1984; *praising* (namely God); *Hillel,* an Isr:—Hillel.

1986. הָלַם **hâlam,** *haw-lam´;* a prim. root; to *strike* down; by impl. to *hammer, stamp, conquer, disband:*—beat (down), break (down), overcome, smite (with the hammer).

1987. הֶלֶם **Hêlem,** *hay´-lem;* from 1986; *smiter; Helem,* the name of two Isr.:—Helem.

1988. הֲלֹם **hălôm,** *hal-ome´;* from the art. [see 1973]; *hither:*—here, hither (-[to]), thither.

1989. הַלְמוּת **halmûwth,** *hal-mooth´;* from 1986; a *hammer* (or *mallet*):—hammer.

1990. הָם **Hâm,** *hawm;* of uncert. der.; *Ham,* a region of Pal.:—Ham.

1991. הֵם **hêm,** *haym;* from 1993; *abundance,* i.e. *wealth:*—any of theirs.

1992. הֵם **hêm,** *haym;* or (prol.) הֵמָּה **hêmâh.** *haym´-maw;* masc. plur. from 1931; *they* (only used when emphatic):—it, like, × (how, so) many (soever, more as) they (be), (the) same, × so, × such, their, them, these, they, those, which, who, whom, withal, ye.

1993. הָמָה **hâmâh,** *haw-maw´;* a prim. root [comp. 1949]; to *make a loud sound* (like Engl. "hum"); by impl. to *be in great commotion* or *tumult,* to *rage, war, moan, clamor:*—clamorous, concourse, cry aloud, be disquieted, loud, mourn, be moved, make a noise, rage, roar, sound, be troubled, make in tumult, tumultuous, be in an uproar.

1994. הִמּוֹ **himmôw** (Chald.), *him-mo´;* or (prol.) הִמּוֹן **himmôwn** (Chald.) *him-mone´;* corresp. to 1992; *they:*— × are, them, those.

1995. הָמוֹן **hâmôwn,** *haw-mone´;* or הָמֹן **hâmôn** (Ezek. 5 : 7), *haw-mone´;* from 1993; a *noise, tumult, crowd;* also *disquietude, wealth:*—abundance, company, many, multitude, multiply, noise, riches, rumbling, sounding, store, tumult.

הַמֹּלֶכֶת **ham-môleketh.** See 4447.

1996. הֲמוֹן גּוֹג **Hămôwn Gôwg,** *ham-one´; gohg;* from 1995 and 1463; the *multitude of Gog;* the fanciful name of an emblematic place in Pal.:—Hamon-gog.

1997. הֲמוֹנָה **Hămôwnâh,** *ham-o-naw´;* fem. of 1995; *multitude; Hamonah,* the same as 1996:—Hamonah.

הֲמוּנֵךְ° **hămûwnêk.** See 2002.

1998. הֶמְיָה **hemyâh,** *hem-yaw´;* from 1993; *sound:*—noise.

1999. הֲמֻלָּה **hămullâh,** *ham-ool-law´;* or (too fully) הֲמוּלָּה **hămûwllâh** (Jer. 11 : 16), *ham-ool-law´;* fem. pass. part. of an unused root mean. to *rush* (as rain with a windy roar); a *sound:*—speech, tumult.

הַמֶּלֶךְ **ham-melek.** See 4429.

2000. הָמַם **hâmam,** *haw-mam´;* a prim. root [comp. 1949, 1993]; prop. to *put in commotion;* by impl. *to disturb, drive, destroy:*—break, consume, crush, destroy, discomfit, trouble, vex.

הָמָן **hâmôn.** See 1995.

2001. הָמָן **Hâmân,** *haw-mawn´;* of for. der.; *Haman,* a Pers. vizier:—Haman.

2002. הַמְנִיךְ **hamnîyk** (Chald.), *ham-neek´;* but the text is הֲמוּנֵךְ° **hămûwnêk,** *ham-oo-nayk´;* of for. or.; a *necklace:*—chain.

2003. הָמָס **hâmâç,** *haw-mawce´;* from an unused root appar. mean. to *crackle;* a dry *twig* or *brushwood:*—melting.

2004. הֵן **hên,** *hane;* fem. plur. from 1931; *they* (only used when emphatic):— × in, such like, (with) them, thereby, therein, (more than) they, wherein, in which, whom, withal.

2005. הֵן **hên,** *hane;* a prim. particle; *lo!;* also (as expressing surprise) *if:*—behold, if, lo, though.

2006. הֵן **hên** (Chald.), *hane;* corresp. to 2005: *lo!* also *there* [-fore], [un-] *less, whether, but, if:*—(that) if, or, whether.

2007. הֵנָּה **hênnâh,** *hane´-naw;* prol. for 2004; *themselves* (often used emphat. for the copula, also in indirect relation):— × in, × such (and such things), their, (into) them, thence, therein, these, they (had), on this side, those, wherein.

2008. הֵנָּה **hênnâh,** *hane´-naw;* from 2004; *hither* or *thither* (but used both of place and time):—here, hither [-to], now, on this (that) side, + since, this (that) way, thitherward, + thus far, to . . . fro, + yet.

2009. הִנֵּה **hinnêh,** *hin-nay´;* prol. for 2005; *lo!:*—behold, lo, see.

2010. הֲנָחָה **hănâchâh,** *han-aw-khaw´;* from 5117; *permission* of rest, i.e. *quiet:*—release.

2011. הִנֹּם **Hinnôm,** *hin-nome´;* prob. of for. or.; *Hinnom,* appar. a Jebusite:—Hinnom.

2012. הֵנַע **Hêna‘,** *hay-nah´;* prob. of for. der. *Hena,* a place appar. in Mesopotamia:—Hena.

2013. הָסָה **hâçâh,** *haw-saw´;* a prim. root; to *hush:*—hold peace (tongue), (keep) silence, be silent, still.

2014. הֲפֻגָה **hăphûgâh,** *haf-oo-gaw´;* from 6313; *relaxation:*—intermission.

2015. הָפַךְ **haphak,** *haw-fak´;* a prim. root; to *turn* about or over; by impl. to *change, overturn, return, pervert:*— × become, change, come, be converted, give, make [a bed], overthrow (-turn), perverse, retire, tumble, turn (again, aside, back, to the contrary, every way).

2016. הֶפֶךְ **hephek,** *heh´-fek;* or הֵפֶךְ **hêphek,** *hay´-fek;* from 2015; a *turn,* i.e. the *reverse:*—contrary.

2017. הֹפֶךְ **hôphek,** *ho´-fek;* from 2015; an *upset,* i.e. (abstr.) *perversity:*—turning of things upside down.

2018. הֲפֵכָה **hăphêkâh,** *haf-ay-kaw´;* fem. of 2016; *destruction:*—overthrow.

2019. הֲפַכְפַּךְ **hăphakpak,** *haf-ak-pak´;* by redupl. from 2015; *very perverse:*—froward.

2020. הַצָּלָה **hatstsâlâh,** *hats-tsaw-law´;* from 5337; *rescue:*—deliverance.

2021. הֹצֶן **hôtsen,** *ho´-tsen;* from an unused root mean. appar. to *be sharp* or *strong;* a *weapon* of war:—chariot.

2022. הַר **har,** *har;* a short. form of 2042; a *mountain* or *range* of hills (sometimes used fig.):—hill (country), mount (-ain), × promotion.

2023. הֹר **Hôr,** *hore;* another form for 2022; *mountain; Hor,* the name of a peak in Idumæa and of one in Syria:—Hor.

2024. הָרָא **Hârâ’,** *haw-raw´;* perh. from 2022; *mountainousness; Hara,* a region of Media:—Hara.

2025. הַרְאֵל **har’êl,** *har-ale´;* from 2022 and 410; *mount of God;* fig. the *altar* of burnt-offering:—altar. Comp. 739.

2026. הָרַג **hârag,** *haw-rag´;* a prim. root; to *smite* with deadly intent:—destroy, out of hand, kill, murder (-er), put to [death], make [slaughter], slay (-er), × surely.

2027. הֶרֶג **hereg,** *heh´-reg;* from 2026; *slaughter:*—be slain, slaughter.

2028. הֲרֵגָה **hărêgâh,** *har-ay-gaw´;* fem. of 2027; *slaughter:*—slaughter.

2029. הָרָה **hârâh,** *haw-raw´;* a prim. root; to *be* (or *become*) *pregnant, conceive* (lit. or fig.):—been, be with child, conceive, progenitor.

2030. הָרֶה **hâreh,** *haw-reh´;* or הָרִי **hârîy** (Hos. 14 : 1), *haw-ree´;* from 2029; *pregnant:*—(be, woman) with child, conceive, × great.

2031. הַרְהֹר **harhôr** (Chald.), *har-hor´;* from a root corresp. to 2029; a mental *conception:*—thought.

2032. הֵרוֹן **hêrôwn,** *hay-rone´;* or הֵרָיוֹן **hêrâyôwn,** *hay-raw-yone´;* from 2029; *pregnancy:*—conception.

2033. הֲרוֹרִי **Hărôwrîy,** *har-o-ree´;* another form for 2043; a *Harorite* or mountaineer:—Harorite.

2034. הֲרִיסָה **hărîyçâh,** *har-ee-saw´;* from 2040; something *demolished:*—ruin.

2035. הֲרִיסוּת **hărîyçûwth,** *har-ee-sooth´;* from 2040; *demolition:*—destruction.

2036. הֹרָם **Hôrâm,** *ho-rawm´;* from an unused root (mean. to *tower* up); *high; Horam,* a Canaanitish king:—Horam.

2037. הָרֻם **Hârûm,** *haw-room´;* pass. part. of the same as 2036; *high; Harum,* an Isr.:—Harum.

2038. הַרְמוֹן **harmôwn,** *har-mone´;* from the same as 2036; a *castle* (from its height):—palace.

2039. הָרָן **Hârân,** *haw-rawn´;* perh. from 2022; *mountaineer; Haran,* the name of two men:—Haran.

2040. הָרַס **hâraç,** *haw-ras´;* a prim. root; to *pull* down or in pieces, *break, destroy:*—beat down, break (down, through), destroy, overthrow, pluck down, pull down, ruin, throw down, × utterly.

2041. הֶרֶס **hereç,** *heh´-res;* from 2040; *demolition:*—destruction.

2042. הָרָר **hârâr,** *haw-rawr´;* from an unused root mean. to *loom* up; a *mountain:*—hill, mount (-ain).

2043. הֲרָרִי **Hărârîy** *hah-raw-ree´;* or הָרָרִי **Hârârîy** (2 Sam. 23 : 11), *haw-raw-ree´;* or הָאֲרָרִי **Hâ’rârîy** (2 Sam 23 : 34, last clause), *haw-raw-ree´;* appar. from 2042; a *mountaineer:*—Hararite.

2044. הָשֵׁם **Hâshêm,** *haw-shame´;* perh. from the same as 2828; *wealthy; Hashem,* an Isr.:—Hashem.

2045. הַשְׁמָעוּת **hâshmâ‘ûwth,** *hashmaw-ooth´;* from 8085; *announcement:*—to cause to hear.

2046. הִתּוּךְ **hittûwk,** *hit-took´;* from 5413; a *melting:*—is melted.

2047. הֲתָךְ **Hăthâk,** *hath-awk´;* prob. of for. or.; *Hathak,* a Pers. eunuch:—Hatach.

2048. הָתַל **hâthal,** *haw-thal´;* a prim. root; to *deride;* by impl. to *cheat:*—deal deceitfully, deceive, mock.

2049. הָתֹל **hâthôl,** *haw-thole´;* from 2048 (only in plur. collect.) a *derision:*—mocker.

2050. הָתַת **hâthath',** *haw-thath';* a prim. root; prop. to *break* in upon, i.e. to *assail:*—imagine mischief.

ו

2051. וְדָן **Vᵉdân,** *ved-awn';* perh. for 5730; *Vedan* (or Aden), a place in Arabia:—Dan also.

2052. וָהֵב **Vâhêb,** *vaw-habe';* of uncert. der.; *Vaheb,* a place in Moab:—what he did.

2053. וָו **vâv,** *vaw;* prob. a *hook* (the name of the sixth Heb. letter):—hook.

2054. וָזָר **vâzâr,** *vaw-zawr';* presumed to be from an unused root mean. to *bear* guilt; *crime:*— × strange.

2055. וַיְזָתָא **Vayᵉzâthâ',** *vah-yez-aw'-thaw;* of for. or.; *Vajezatha,* a son of Haman:—Vajezatha.

2056. וָלָד **vâlâd,** *vaw-lawd';* for 3206; a *boy:*—child.

2057. וַנְיָה **Vanyâh,** *van-yaw';* perh. for 6043; *Vanjah,* an Isr.:—Vaniah.

2058. וָפְסִי **Vophçîy,** *vof-see';* prob. from 3254; *additional; Vophsi,* an Isr.:—Vophsi.

2059. וַשְׁנִי **Vashnîy,** *vash-nee';* prob. from 3461; *weak; Vashni,* an Isr.:—Vashni.

2060. וַשְׁתִּי **Vashtîy,** *vash-tee';* of Pers. or.; *Vashti,* the queen of Xerxes:—Vashti.

ז

2061. זְאֵב **zᵉ'êb,** *zeh-abe';* from an unused root mean. to *be yellow;* a *wolf:*—wolf.

2062. זְאֵב **Zᵉ'êb,** *zeh-abe';* the same as 2061; *Zeëb,* a Midianitish prince:—Zeeb.

2063. זֹאת **zô'th,** *zothe';* irreg. fem. of 2089; *this* (often used adv.):—hereby (-in, -with), it, likewise, the one (other, same), she, so (much), such (deed), that, therefore, these, this (thing), thus.

2064. זָבַד **zâbad,** *zaw-bad';* a prim. root; to *confer:*—endure.

2065. זֶבֶד **zebed,** *zeh'-bed;* from 2064; a *gift:*—dowry.

2066. זָבָד **Zâbâd,** *zaw-bawd';* from 2064; *giver; Zabad,* the name of seven Isr.:—Zabad.

2067. זַבְדִּי **Zabdîy,** *zab-dee';* from 2065; *giving; Zabdi,* the name of four Isr.:—Zabdi.

2068. זַבְדִּיאֵל **Zabdîy'êl,** *zab-dee-ale';* from 2065 and 410; *gift of God; Zabdiel,* the name of two Isr.:—Zabdiel.

2069. זְבַדְיָה **Zᵉbadyâh,** *zeb-ad-yaw';* or זְבַדְיָהוּ **Zᵉbadyâhûw,** *zeb-ad-yaw'-hoo;* from 2064 and 3050; *Jah has given; Zebadjah,* the name of nine Isr.:—Zebadiah.

2070. זְבוּב **zᵉbûwb,** *zeb-oob';* from an unused root (mean. to *flit*); a *fly* (espec. one of a stinging nature):—fly.

2071. זָבוּד **Zâbûwd,** *zaw-bood';* from 2064; *given; Zabud,* an Isr.:—Zabud.

2072. זַבּוּד **Zabbûwd,** *zab-bood';* a form of 2071; *given; Zabbud,* an Isr.:—Zabbud.

2073. זְבוּל **zᵉbûwl,** *ze-bool';* or זְבֻל **zᵉbûl,** *zeb-ool';* from 2082; a *residence:*—dwell in, dwelling, habitation.

2074. זְבוּלוּן **Zᵉbûwlûwn,** *zeb-oo-loon';* or זְבֻלוּן **Zᵉbûlûwn,** *zeb-oo-loon';* or זְבוּלֻן **Zᵉbûwlûn,** *zeb-oo-loon';* from 2082; *habitation; Zebulon,* a son of Jacob; also his territory and tribe:—Zebulun.

2075. זְבוּלֹנִי **Zᵉbûwlônîy,** *zeb-oo-lo-nee';* patron. from 2074; a *Zebulonite* or desc. of Zebulun:—Zebulonite.

2076. זָבַח **zâbach,** *zaw-bakh'; a prim. root; to slaughter* an animal (usually in sacrifice):—kill, offer, (do) sacrifice, slay.

2077. זֶבַח **zebach,** *zeh'-bakh;* from 2076; prop. a *slaughter,* i.e. the *flesh* of an animal; by impl. a *sacrifice* (the victim or the act):—offer (-ing), sacrifice.

2078. זֶבַח **Zebach,** *zeh'-bakh;* the same as 2077; *sacrifice; Zebach,* a Midianitish prince:—Zebah.

2079. זַבַּי **Zabbay,** *zab-bah'ee;* prob. by orth. err. for 2140; *Zabbai* (or Zaccai), an Isr.:—Zabbai.

2080. זְבִידָה **Zᵉbîydâh,** *zeb-ee-daw';* fem. from 2064; *giving; Zebidah,* an Israelitess:—Zebudah.

2081. זְבִינָא **Zᵉbîynâ',** *zeb-ee-naw';* from an unused root (mean. to *purchase*); *gainfulness; Zebina,* an Isr.:—Zebina.

2082. זָבַל **zâbal,** *zaw-bal';* a prim. root; appar. prop. to *inclose,* i.e. to *reside:*—dwell with.

2083. זְבֻל **Zᵉbûl,** *zeb-ool';* the same as 2073; *dwelling; Zebul,* an Isr.:—Zebul. Comp. 2073.
זְבֻלוּן **Zᵉbûlûwn.** See 2074.

2084. זְבַן **zᵉban** (Chald.), *zeb-an';* corresp. to the root of 2081; to *acquire* by purchase:—gain.

2085. זָג **zâg,** *zawg;* from an unused root prob. mean. to *inclose;* the *skin* of a grape:—husk.

2086. זֵד **zêd,** *zade';* from 2102; *arrogant:*—presumptuous, proud.

2087. זָדוֹן **zâdôwn,** *zaw-done';* from 2102; *arrogance:*—presumptuously, pride, proud (man).

2088. זֶה **zeh,** *zeh;* a prim. word; the masc. demonst. pron., *this* or *that:*—he, × hence, × here, it (-self), × now, × of him, the one . . . the other, × than the other, (× out of) the (self) same, such (an one) that, these, this (hath, man), on this side . . . on that side, × thus, very, which. Comp. 2063, 2090, 2097, 2098.

2089. זֶה **zeh** (1 Sam. 17 : 34), *zeh;* by perm. for 7716; a *sheep:*—lamb.

2090. זֹה **zôh,** *zo;* for 2088; *this* or *that:*—as well as another, it, this, that, thus and thus.

2091. זָהָב **zâhâb,** *zaw-hawb';* from an unused root mean. to *shimmer; gold;* fig. something *gold-colored* (i.e. *yellow*), as *oil,* a *clear sky:*—gold (-en), fair weather.

2092. זָהַם **zâham,** *zaw-ham';* a prim. root; to *be rancid,* i.e. (trans.) to *loathe:*—abhor.

2093. זַהַם **Zaham,** *zah'-ham;* from 2092; *loathing; Zaham,* an Isr.:—Zaham.

2094. זָהַר **zâhar,** *zaw-har;* a prim. root; to *gleam;* fig. to *enlighten* (by caution):—admonish, shine, teach, (give) warn (-ing).

2095. זְהַר **zᵉhar** (Chald.), *zeh-har';* corresp. to 2094; (pass.) *be admonished:*—take heed.

2096. זֹהַר **zôhar,** *zo'-har;* from 2094; *brilliancy:*—brightness.

2097. זוֹ **zôw,** *zo;* for 2088; *this* or *that:*—that, this.

2098. זוּ **zûw,** *zoo;* for 2088; *this* or *that:*—that this, × wherein, which, whom.

2099. זִו **Zîv,** *zeev';* prob. from an unused root mean. to *be prominent;* prop. *brightness* [comp. 2122], i.e. (fig.) the month of *flowers; Ziv* (corresp. to Ijar or May):—Zif.

2100. זוּב **zûwb,** *zoob;* a prim. root; to *flow* freely (as water), i.e. (spec.) to *have* a (sexual) *flux;* fig. to *waste* away; also to *overflow:*—flow, gush out, have a (running) issue, pine away, run.

2101. זוֹב **zôwb,** *zobe;* from 2100; a seminal or menstrual *flux:*—issue.

2102. זוּד **zûwd,** *zood;* or (by perm.) זִיד **zîyd,** *zeed;* a prim. root; to *seethe;* fig. to *be insolent:*—be proud, deal proudly, presume, (come) presumptuously, sod.

2103. זוּד **zûwd** (Chald.), *zood;* corresp. to 2102; to *be proud:*—in pride.

2104. זוּזִים **Zûwzîym,** *zoo-zeem';* plur. prob. from the same as 2123; *prominent; Zuzites,* an aboriginal tribe of Pal.:—Zuzims.

2105. זוֹחֵת **Zôwchêth,** *zo-khayth';* of uncert. or.; *Zocheth,* an Isr.:—Zoheth.

2106. זָוִית **zâvîyth,** *zaw-veeth';* appar. from the same root as 2099 (in the sense of *prominence*); an *angle* (as *projecting*), i.e. (by impl.) a *corner-column* (or *anta*):—corner (stone).

2107. זוּל **zûwl,** *zool;* a prim. root [comp. 2151]; prob. to *shake* out, i.e. (by impl.) to *scatter* profusely; fig. to *treat lightly:*—lavish, despise.

2108. זוּלָה **zûwlâh,** *zoo-law';* from 2107; prop. *scattering,* i.e. *removal;* used adv. *except:*—beside, but, only, save.

2109. זוּן **zûwn** *zoon;* a prim. root; perh. prop. to *be plump,* i.e. (trans.) to *nourish:*—feed.

2110. זוּן **zûwn** (Chald.), *zoon;* corresp. to 2109:—feed.

2111. זוּעַ **zûwâʻ,** *zoo´-ah;* a prim. root; prop. to *shake* off, i.e. (fig.) to *agitate* (as with fear):—move, tremble, vex.

2112. זוּעַ **zûwaʻ** (Chald.), *zoo´-ah;* corresp. to 2111; to *shake* (with fear):—tremble.

2113. זְוָעָה **zᵉvâʻâh,** *zev-aw-aw´;* from 2111; *agitation, fear:*—be removed, trouble, vexation. Comp. 2189.

2114. זוּר **zûwr,** *zoor;* a prim. root; to *turn* aside (espec. for lodging); hence to *be a foreigner, strange, profane;* spec. (act. part.) to *commit adultery:*—(come from) another (man, place), fanner, go away, (e-) strange (-r, thing, woman).

2115. זוּר **zûwr,** *zoor;* a prim. root [comp. 6695]; to *press* together, *tighten:*—close, crush, thrust together.

2116. זוּרֶה **zûwreh,** *zoo-reh´;* from 2115; *trodden* on:—that which is crushed.

2117. זָזָא **zâzâʼ,** *zaw-zaw´;* prob. from the root of 2123; *prominent; Zaza,* an Isr.:—Zaza.

2118. זָחַח **zâchach,** *zaw-khakh´;* a prim. root; to *shove* or *displace:*—loose.

2119. זָחַל **zâchal,** *zaw-khal´;* a prim. root; to *crawl;* by impl. to *fear:*—be afraid, serpent, worm.

2120. זֹחֶלֶת **Zôcheleth,** *zo-kheh´-leth;* fem. act. part. of 2119; *crawling* (i.e. *serpent*); *Zocheleth,* a boundary stone in Pal.:—Zoheleth.

2121. זֵידוֹן **zêydôwn,** *zay-dohn´;* from 2102; *boiling* of water, i.e. *wave:*—proud.

2122. זִיו **zîyv** (Chald.), *zeev;* corresp. to 2099; (fig.) *cheerfulness:*—brightness, countenance.

2123. זִיז **zîyz,** *zeez;* from an unused root appar. mean. to *be conspicuous; fulness* of the breast; also a moving *creature:*—abundance, wild beast.

2124. זִיזָא **Zîyzâʼ,** *zee-zaw´;* appar. from the same as 2123; *prominence, Ziza,* the name of two Isr.:—Ziza.

2125. זִיזָה **Zîyzâh,** *zee-zaw´;* another form for 2124; *Zizah,* an Isr.:—Zizah.

2126. זִינָא **Zîynâʼ,** *zee-naw´;* from 2109; well *fed;* or perh. an orth. err. for 2124; *Zina,* an Isr.:—Zina.

2127. זִיעַ **Zîyaʻ,** *zee´-ah;* from 2111; *agitation; Zia,* an Isr.:—Zia.

2128. זִיף **Zîyph,** *zeef;* from the same as 2203; *flowing; Ziph,* the name of a place in Pal.; also of an Isr.:—Ziph.

2129. זִיפָה **Zîyphâh,** *zee-faw´;* fem. of 2128; a *flowing; Ziphah,* an Isr.:—Ziphah.

2130. זִיפִי **Zîyphîy,** *zee-fee´;* patrial from 2128; a *Ziphite* or inhab. of Ziph:—Ziphim, Ziphite.

2131. זִיקָה **zîyqâh** (Isa. 50 : 11), *zee-kaw´* (fem.); and זִק **zîq,** *zeek;* or זֵק **zêq,** *zake;* from 2187; prop. what *leaps* forth, i.e. *flash* of fire, or a burning *arrow;* also (from the orig. sense of the root) a *bond:*—chain, fetter, firebrand, spark.

2132. זַיִת **zayith,** *zah´-yith;* prob. from an unused root [akin to 2099]; an *olive* (as yielding *illuminating* oil), the tree, the branch or the berry:—olive (tree, -yard), Olivet.

2133. זֵיתָן **Zêythân,** *zay-thawn´;* from 2132; *olive* grove, *Zethan,* an Isr.:—Zethan.

2134. זַךְ **zak,** *zak;* from 2141; *clear:*—clean, pure.

2135. זָכָה **zâkâh,** *zaw-kaw´;* a prim. root [comp. 2141]; to *be translucent;* fig to *be innocent:*—be (make) clean, cleanse, be clear, count pure.

2136. זָכוּ **zâkûw** (Chald.) *zaw-koo´;* from a root corresp. to 2135; *purity:*—innocency.

2137. זְכוּכִית **zᵉkûwkîyth,** *zek-oo-keeth´;* from 2135; prop. *transparency,* i.e. *glass:*—crystal.

2138. זָכוּר **zâkûwr,** *zaw-koor´;* prop. pass. part. of 2142, but used for 2145; a *male* (of man or animals):—males, men-children.

2139. זַכּוּר **Zakkûwr,** *zak-koor´;* from 2142; *mindful; Zakkur,* the name of seven Isr.:—Zaccur, Zacchur.

2140. זַכַּי **Zakkay,** *zak-kah´ee;* from 2141; *pure; Zakkai,* an Isr.:—Zaccai.

2141. זָכַךְ **zâkak,** *zaw-kak´;* a prim. root [comp. 2135]; to *be transparent* or *clean* (phys. or mor.):—be (make) clean, be pure (-r).

2142. זָכַר **zâkar,** *zaw-kar´;* a prim. root; prop. to *mark* (so as to be recognized), i.e. to *remember;* by impl. to *mention;* also (as denom. from 2145) to *be male:*— × burn [incense], × earnestly, be male, (make) mention (of), be mindful, recount, record (-er), remember, make to be remembered, bring (call, come, keep, put) to (in) remembrance, × still, think on, × well.

2143. זֵכֶר **zêker,** *zay´-ker;* or זֶכֶר **zeker,** *zeh´-ker,* from 2142; a *memento,* abstr. *recollection* (rarely if ever); by impl. *commemoration:*—memorial, memory, remembrance, scent.

2144. זֶכֶר **Zeker,** *zeh´-ker;* the same as 2143; *Zeker,* an Isr.:—Zeker.

2145. זָכָר **zâkâr,** *zaw-kawr´;* from 2142; prop. *remembered,* i.e. a *male* (of man or animals, as being the most noteworthy sex):— × him, male, man (child, -kind).

2146. זִכְרוֹן **zikrôwn,** *zik-rone´;* from 2142; a *memento* (or memorable thing, day or writing):—memorial, record.

2147. זִכְרִי **Zikrîy,** *zik-ree´;* from 2142; *memorable; Zicri,* the name of twelve Isr.:—Zichri.

2148. זְכַרְיָה **Zᵉkaryâh,** *zek-ar-yaw´;* or זְכַרְיָהוּ **Zᵉkaryâhûw,** *zek-ar-yaw´-hoo;* from 2142 and 3050; *Jah has remembered; Zecarjah,* the name of twenty-nine Isr.:—Zachariah, Zechariah.

2149. זֻלּוּת **zullûwth,** *zool-looth´;* from 2151; prop. a *shaking,* i.e. perh. a *tempest:*—vilest.

2150. זַלְזַל **zalzal,** *zal-zal´;* by redupl. from 2151; *tremulous,* i.e. a *twig:*—sprig.

2151. זָלַל **zâlal,** *zaw-lal´;* a prim. root [comp. 2107]; to *shake* (as in the wind), i,.e. to *quake;* fig. to *be loose* morally, *worthless* or *prodigal:*—blow down, glutton, riotous (eater), vile.

2152. זַלְעָפָה **zalʻâphâh,** *zal-aw-faw´;* or זִלְעָפָה **zilʻâphâh,** *zil-aw-faw´;* from 2196; a *glow* (of wind or anger); also a *famine* (as *consuming*):—horrible, horror, terrible.

2153. זִלְפָּה **Zilpâh,** *zil-paw;* from an unused root appar. mean. to *trickle,* as myrrh; fragrant *dropping; Zilpah,* Leah's maid:—Zilpah.

2154. זִמָּה **zimmâh,** *zim-maw´;* or זַמָּה **zammâh,** *zam-maw´;* from 2161; a *plan,* espec. a bad one:—heinous crime, lewd (-ly, -ness), mischief, purpose, thought, wicked (device, mind, -ness).

2155. זִמָּה **Zimmâh,** *zim-maw´;* the same as 2154; *Zimmah,* the name of two Isr.:—Zimmah.

2156. זְמוֹרָה **zᵉmôwrâh,** *zem-o-raw´;* or זְמֹרָה **zᵉmôrâh,** *zem-o-raw´;* (fem.); and זְמֹר **zᵉmôr,** *zem-ore´;* (masc.): from 2168; a *twig* (as *pruned*):—vine, branch, slip.

2157. זַמְזֹם **Zamzôm,** *zam-zome´;* from 2161; *intriguing;* a *Zamzumite,* or native tribe of Pal.:—Zamzummim.

2158. זָמִיר **zâmîyr,** *zaw-meer´;* or זָמִר **zâmîr,** *zaw-meer´;* and (fem.) זְמִרָה **zᵉmîrâh,** *zem-ee-raw´;* from 2167; a *song* to be accompanied with instrumental music:—psalm (-ist), singing, song.

2159. זָמִיר **zâmîyr,** *zaw-meer´;* from 2168; a *twig* (as *pruned*):—branch.

2160. זְמִירָה **Zᵉmîyrâh,** *zem-ee-raw´;* fem. of 2158, *song; Zemirah,* an Isr.:—Zemira.

2161. זָמַם **zâmam,** *zaw-mam´;* a prim. root; to *plan,* usually in a bad sense:—consider, devise, imagine, plot, purpose, think (evil).

2162. זָמָם **zâmâm,** *zaw-mawm´;* from 2161; a *plot:*—wicked device.

2163. זָמַן **zâman,** *zaw-man´;* a prim. root; to *fix* (a time):—appoint.

2164. זְמַן **zᵉman** (Chald.), *zem-an´;* corresp. to 2163; to *agree* (on a time and place):—prepare.

2165. זְמָן **zᵉmân,** *zem-awn´;* from 2163; an *appointed* occasion:—season, time.

2166. זְמָן **zᵉmân** (Chald.), *zem-awn´;* from 2165; the same as 2165:—season, time.

2167. זָמַר **zâmar,** *zaw-mar´;* a prim, root [perh. ident. with 2168 through the idea of *striking* with the fingers]; prop. to *touch* the strings or parts of a musical instrument, i.e. *play* upon it; to make *music,* accompanied by the voice; hence to *celebrate* in song and music:—give praise, sing forth praises, psalms.

2168. זָמַר **zâmar,** *zaw-mar´;* a prim. root [comp. 2167, 5568, 6785]; to *trim* (a vine):—prune.

2169. זֶמֶר **zemer,** *zeh´-mer;* appar. from 2167 or 2168; a *gazelle* (from its lightly *touching* the ground):—chamois.

2170. זְמָר **zᵉmâr** (Chald.), *zem-awr´;* from a root corresp. to 2167; instrumental *music:*—musick.

זָמִר **zâmîr.** See 2158.

זְמֹר **zᵉmôr.** See 2156.

2171. זַמָּר **zammâr** (Chald.), *zam-mawr´;* from the same as 2170; an instrmental *musician:*—singer.

2172. זִמְרָה **zimrâh,** *zim-raw´;* from 2167; a *musical* piece or *song* to be accompanied by an instrument:—melody, psalm.

2173. זִמְרָה **zimrâh,** *zim-raw´;* from 2168; *pruned* (i.e. *choice*) fruit:—best fruit.

זְמִרָה **zᵉmîrâh.** See 2158.

זְמֹרָה **zᵉmôrâh.** See 2156.

2174. זִמְרִי **Zimrîy,** *zim-ree´;* from 2167; *musical; Zimri,* the name of five Isr., and of an Arabian tribe:—Zimri.

2175. זִמְרָן **Zimrân,** *zim-rawn´;* from 2167; *musical; Zimran,* a son of Abraham by Keturah:—Zimran.

2176. זִמְרָת **zimrâth,** *zim-rawth´;* from 2167; instrumental *music;* by impl. *praise:*—song.

2177. זַן **zan,** *zan;* from 2109; prop. *nourished* (or fully *developed*), i.e. a *form* or *sort:*—divers kinds, × all manner of store.

2178. זַן **zan** (Chald.), *zan;* corresp. to 2177; *sort:*—kind.

2179. זָנַב **zânab,** *zaw-nab´;* a prim. root mean. to *wag;* used only as a denom. from 2180; to *curtail,* i.e. *cut* off the rear:—smite the hindmost.

2180. זָנָב **zânâb,** *zaw-nawb´;* from 2179 (in the orig. sense of *flapping*); the *tail* (lit. or fig.):—tail.

2181. זָנָה **zânâh,** *zaw-naw´;* a prim. root [highly *fed* and therefore *wanton*]; to *commit adultery* (usually of the female, and less often of simple fornication, rarely of involuntary ravishment); fig. to *commit idolatry* (the Jewish people being regarded as the spouse of Jehovah):—(cause to) commit fornication, × continually, × great, (be an, play the) harlot, (cause to be, play the) whore, (commit, fall to) whoredom, (cause to) go a-whoring, whorish.

2182. זָנוֹחַ **Zânôwach,** *zaw-no´-akh;* from 2186; *rejected; Zanoach,* the name of two places in Pal.:—Zanoah.

2183. זָנוּן **zânûwn,** *zaw-noon´;* from 2181; *adultery;* fig. *idolatry:*—whoredom.

2184. זְנוּת **zᵉnûwth,** *zen-ooth´;* from 2181; *adultery,* i.e. (fig.) *infidelity, idolatry:*—whoredom.

2185. זֹנוֹת **zônôwth,** *zo-noth´;* regarded by some as if from 2109 or an unused root, and applied to military *equipments;* but evidently the fem. plur. act. part. of 2181; *harlots:*—armour.

2186. זָנַח **zânach,** *zaw-nakh´;* a prim. root mean. to *push* aside, i.e. *reject, forsake, fail:*—cast away (off), remove far away (off).

2187. זָנַק **zânaq,** *zaw-nak´;* a prim. root; prop. to *draw together* the feet (as an animal about to dart upon its prey), i.e. to *spring* forward:—leap.

2188. זֵעָה **zêʻâh,** *zay-aw´;* from 2111 (in the sense of 3154); *perspiration:*—sweat.

2189. זַעֲוָה **zaʻăvâh,** *zah-av-aw´;* by transp. for 2113; *agitation, maltreatment:*— × removed, trouble.

2190. זַעֲוָן **Zaʻăvân,** *zah-av-awn´;* from 2111; *disquiet: Zaavan,* an Idumæan:—Zaavan.

2191. זְעֵיר **zeʻêyr,** *zeh-ayr´;* from an unused root [akin (by perm.) to 6819], mean. to *dwindle; small:*—little.

2192. זְעֵיר **zᵉʻêyr** (Chald.), *zeh-ayr´;* corresp. to 2191:—*little.*

2193. זָעַךְ **zâʻak,** *zaw-ak´;* a prim. root; to *extinguish:*—be extinct.

2194. זָעַם **zâʻam,** *zaw-am´;* a prim. root; prop. to *foam* at the mouth, i.e. to *be enraged:*—abhor, abominable, (be) angry, defy, (have) indignation.

2195. זַעַם **zaʻam,** *zah´-am;* from 2194; strictly *froth* at the mouth, i.e. (fig.) *fury* (espec. of God's displeasure with sin):—angry, indignation, rage.

2196. זָעַף **zâʻaph,** *zaw-af´;* a prim. root; prop. to *boil* up, i.e. (fig.) to *be peevish* or *angry:*—fret, sad, worse liking, be wroth.

2197. זַעַף **zaʻaph,** *zah´-af;* from 2196; *anger:*—indignation, rage (-ing), wrath.

2198. זָעֵף **zâʻêph,** *zaw-afe´;* from 2196; *angry:*—displeased.

2199. זָעַק **zâʻaq,** *zaw-ak´;* a prim. root; to *shriek* (from anguish or danger); by anal. (as a herald) to *announce* or *convene* publicly:—assemble, call (together), (make a) cry (out), come with such a company, gather (together), cause to be proclaimed.

2200. זְעִק **zᵉʻîq** (Chald.), *zeh´-eek;* corresp. to 2199; to *make an outcry:*—cry.

2201. זַעַק **zaʻaq,** *zah´-ak;* and (fem.) זְעָקָה **zᵉʻâqâh,** *zeh-aw-kaw´;* from 2199; a *shriek* or *outcry:*—cry (-ing).

2202. זִפְרֹן **Ziphrôn,** *zi-frone´;* from an unused root (mean. to *be fragrant*); *Ziphron,* a place in Pal.:—Ziphron.

2203. זֶפֶת **zepheth,** *zeh´-feth;* from an unused root (mean. to *liquify*); *asphalt* (from its tendency to *soften* in the sun):—pitch.

זִק **zîq,** or זֵק **zêq.** See 2131.

2204. זָקֵן **zâqên,** *zaw-kane´;* a prim. root; to *be old:*—aged man, be (wax) old (man).

2205. זָקֵן **zâqên,** *zaw-kane´;* from 2204; *old:*—aged, ancient (man), elder (-est), old (man, men and . . . women), senator.

2206. זָקָן **zâqân,** *zaw-kawn´;* from 2204; the *beard* (as indicating *age*):—beard.

2207. זֹקֶן **zôqen,** *zo´-ken;* from 2204; old *age:*—age.

2208. זָקֻן **zâqûn,** *zaw-koon´;* prop. pass. part. of 2204 (used only in the plur. as a noun); *old* age:—old age.

2209. זִקְנָה **ziqnâh,** *zik-naw´;* fem. of 2205; old *age:*—old (age).

2210. זָקַף **zâqaph,** *zaw-kaf´;* a prim. root; to *lift,* i.e. (fig.) *comfort:*—raise (up).

2211. זְקַף **zᵉqaph** (Chald.), *zek-af´;* corresp. to 2210; to *hang,* i.e. *impale:*—set up.

2212. זָקַק **zâqaq,** *zaw-kak´;* a prim. root; to *strain,* (fig.) *extract, clarify:*—fine, pour down, purge, purify, refine.

2213. זֵר **zêr,** *zare;* from 2237 (in the sense of *scattering*); a *chaplet* (as *spread* around the top), i.e. (spec.) a border *moulding:*—crown.

2214. זָרָא **zârâʼ,** *zaw-raw´;* from 2114 (in the sense of *estrangement*) [comp. 2219]; *disgust:*—loathsome.

2215. זָרַב **zârab,** *zaw-rab´;* a prim. root; to *flow* away:—wax warm.

2216. זְרֻבָּבֶל **Zᵉrubbâbel,** *zer-oob-baw-bel´;* from 2215 and 894; *descended of* (i.e. from) *Babylon,* i.e. born there; *Zerubbabel,* an Isr.:—Zerubbabel.

2217. זְרֻבָּבֶל **Zᵉrubbâbel** (Chald.), *zer-oob-baw-bel´;* corresp. to 2216:—Zerubbabel.

2218. זֶרֶד **Zered,** *zeh´-red;* from an unused root mean. to *be exuberant* in growth; lined with *shrubbery; Zered,* a brook E. of the Dead Sea:—Zared, Zered.

2219. זָרָה **zârâh,** *zaw-raw´;* a prim. root [comp. 2114; to *toss* about; by impl. to *diffuse, winnow:*—cast away, compass, disperse, fan, scatter (away), spread, strew, winnow.

2220. זְרוֹעַ **zᵉrôwaʻ,** *zer-o´-ah;* or (short.) זְרֹעַ **zᵉrôaʻ,** *zer-o-ah;* and (fem.) זְרוֹעָה **zᵉrôwʻâh,** *zer-o-aw´;* or זְרֹעָה **zᵉrôʻâh,** *zer-o-aw´;* from 2232; the *arm* (as *stretched* out), or (of animals) the *foreleg;* fig. *force:*—arm, + help, mighty, power, shoulder, strength.

2221. זְרוּעַ **zêrûwaʻ,** *zay-roo´-ah;* from 2232; something *sown,* i.e. a *plant:*—sowing, thing that is sown.

2222. זַרְזִיף **zarzîyph,** *zar-zeef´;* by redupl. from an unused root mean. to *flow;* a *pouring rain:*—water.

זְרוֹעָה **zᵉrôwʻâh.** See 2220.

2223. זַרְזִיר **zarzîyr,** *zar-zeer´;* by redupl. from 2115; prop. tightly *girt,* i.e. prob. a *racer,* or some fleet animal (as being *slender* in the waist):— + greyhound.

2224. זָרַח **zârach,** *zaw-rakh´;* a prim. root; prop, to *irradiate* (or shoot forth beams), i.e. to *rise* (as the sun); spec. to *appear* (as a symptom of leprosy):—arise, rise (up), as soon as it is up.

2225. זֶרַח **zerach,** *zeh´-rakh;* from 2224; a *rising* of light:—rising.

2226. זֶרַח **Zerach,** *zeh´-rakh;* the same as 2225: *Zerach,* the name of three Isr., also of an Idumæan and an Ethiopian prince:—Zarah, Zerah.

2227. זַרְחִי **Zarchîy,** *zar-khee´;* patron. from 2226; a *Zarchite* or desc. of Zerach:—Zarchite.

2228. זְרַחְיָה **Zᵉrachyâh,** *zer-akh-yaw´;* from 2225 and 3050; *Jah has risen; Zerachjah,* the name of two Isr.:—Zerahiah.

2229. זָרַם **zâram,** *zaw-ram´;* a prim. root; to *gush* (as water):—carry away as with a flood, pour out.

2230. זֶרֶם **zerem,** *zeh´-rem;* from 2229; a *gush* of water:—flood, overflowing, shower, storm, tempest.

2231. זִרְמָה **zirmâh,** *zir-maw´;* fem. of 2230; a *gushing* of fluid (semen):—issue.

2232. זָרַע **zâraʻ,** *zaw-rah´;* a prim. root; to *sow;* fig. to *disseminate, plant, fructify:*—bear, conceive seed, set with, sow (-er), yield.

2233. זֶרַע **zeraʻ,** *zeh´-rah;* from 2232; *seed;* fig. *fruit, plant, sowing-time, posterity:*— × carnally, child, fruitful, seed (-time), sowing-time.

2234. זְרַע **zᵉraʻ** (Chald.) *zer-ah´;* corresp. to 2233; *posterity:*—seed.

זֵרֹעַ **zᵉrôaʻ.** See 2220.

2235. זֵרֹעַ **zêrôaʻ,** *zay-ro´-ah;* or זֵרָעֹן **zêrâʻôn,** *zay-raw-ohn´;* from 2232; something *sown* (only in the plur.), i.e. a *vegetable* (as food):—pulse.

זְרֹעָה **zᵉrʻôâh.** See 2220.

2236. זָרַק **zâraq,** *zaw-rak´;* a prim. root; to *sprinkle* (fluid or solid particles):—be here and there, scatter, sprinkle, strew.

2237. זָרַר **zârar,** *zaw-rar´;* a prim. root [comp. 2114]; perh. to *diffuse,* i.e. (spec.) to *sneeze:*—sneeze.

2238. זֶרֶשׁ **Zeresh,** *zeh´-resh;* of Pers. or.; *Zeresh,* Haman's wife:—Zeresh.

2239. זֶרֶת **zereth,** *zeh´-reth;* from 2219; the *spread* of the fingers, i.e. a *span:*—span.

2240. זַתּוּא **Zattûwʼ,** *zat-too´;* of uncert. der.; *Zattu,* an Isr.:—Zattu.

2241. זֵתָם **Zêthâm,** *zay-thawm´;* appar. a var. for 2133; *Zetham,* an Isr.:—Zetham.

2242. זֵתַר **Zêthar,** *zay-thar´;* of Pers. or.; *Zethar,* a eunuch of Xerxes:—Zethar.

ח

2243. חֹב **chôb,** *khobe;* by contr. from 2245; prop. a *cherisher,* i.e. the *bosom:*—bosom.

2244. חָבָא **châbâʼ,** *khaw-baw´;* a prim. root [comp. 2245]; to *secrete:*— × held, hide (self), do secretly.

2245. חָבַב **châbab,** *khaw-bab´;* a prim. root [comp. 2244, 2247]; prop. to *hide* (as in the bosom), i.e. to *cherish* (with affection):—love.

2246. חֹבָב **Chôbâb,** *kho-bawb´;* from 2245; *cherished; Chobab,* father-in-law of Moses:—Hobab.

2247. חָבָה **châbah,** *khaw-bah´;* a prim. root [comp. 2245]; to *secrete:*—hide (self).

2248. חֲבוּלָה **chăbûwlâh** (Chald.), *khab-oo-law´;* from 2255; prop. *overthrown,* i.e. (morally) *crime:*—hurt.

2249. חָבוֹר **Châbôwr,** *khaw-bore´;* from 2266; *united; Chabor,* a river of Assyria:—Habor.

2250. חַבּוּרָה **chabbûwrâh,** *khab-boo-raw´;* or חַבֻּרָה **chabbûrâh,** *khab-boo-raw´;* or חֲבֻרָה **chăbûrâh,** *khab-oo-raw´;* from 2266; prop. *bound* (with stripes), i.e. a *weal* (or black-and-blue mark itself):—blueness, bruise, hurt, stripe, wound.

2251. חָבַט **châbaṭ** *khaw-bat´;* a prim. root; to *knock* out of off:—beat (off, out), thresh.

2252. חֲבַיָּה **Chăbayâh,** *khab-ah-yaw´;* or חֳבָיָה **Chăbâyâh,** *khab-aw-yaw´;* from 2247 and 3050; *Jah has hidden; Chabajah,* an Isr.:—Habaiah.

2253. חֶבְיוֹן **chebyôwn,** *kheb-yone´;* from 2247; a *concealment:*—hiding.

2254. חָבַל **châbal,** *khaw-bal´;* a prim. root; to *wind* tightly (as a rope), i.e. to *bind;* spec. by a *pledge;* fig. to *pervert, destroy;* also to *writhe* in pain (espec. of parturition):— × at all, band, bring forth, (deal) corrupt (-ly) destroy, offend, lay to (take a) pledge, spoil, travail, × very, withhold.

2255. חֲבַל **chăbal** (Chald.), *khab-al´;* corresp. to 2254; to *ruin:*—destroy, hurt.

2256. חֶבֶל **chebel,** *kheh´-bel;* or חֵבֶל **chêbel,** *khay´-bel;* from 2254; a *rope* (as *twisted*), espec. a measuring *line;* by impl. a *district* or *inheritance* (as *measured*); or a *noose* (as of *cords*); fig. a *company* (as if *tied* together); also a *throe* (espec. of parturition); also *ruin:*—band, coast, company, cord, country, destruction, line, lot, pain, pang, portion, region, rope, snare, sorrow, tackling.

2257. חֲבַל **chăbal** (Chald.), *khab-al´;* from 2255; *harm* (personal or pecuniary):—damage, hurt.

2258. חֲבֹל **chăbôl,** *khab-ole´;* or (fem.) חֲבֹלָה **chăbôlâh,** *khab-o-law´;* from 2254; a *pawn* (as security for debt):—pledge.

2259. חֹבֵל **chôbêl,** *kho-bale´;* act. part. from 2254 (in the sense of handling *ropes*); a *sailor:*—pilot, shipmaster.

2260. חִבֵּל **chibbêl,** *khib-bale´;* from 2254 (in the sense of furnished with *ropes*); a *mast:*—mast.

2261. חֲבַצֶּלֶת **chăbatstseleth,** *khab-ats-tseh´-leth;* of uncert. der.; prob. *meadow-saffron:*—rose.

2262. חֲבַצַּנְיָה **Chăbatstsanyâh,** *khab-ats-tsan-yaw´;* of uncert. der.; *Chabatstsanjah,* a Rechabite:—Habazaniah.

2263. חָבַק **châbaq,** *khaw-bak´;* a prim. root; to *clasp* (the hands or in embrace):—embrace, fold.

2264. חִבֻּק **chibbûq,** *khib-book´;* from 2263; a *clasping* of the hands (in idleness):—fold.

2265. חֲבַקּוּק **Chăbaqqûwq,** *khab-ak-kook´;* by redupl. from 2263; *embrace; Chabakkuk,* the prophet:—Habakkuk.

2266. חָבַר **châbar,** *khaw-bar´;* a prim. root; to *join* (lit. or fig.); spec. (by means of spells) to *fascinate:*—charm (-er), be compact, couple (together), have fellowship with, heap up, join (self, together), league.

2267. חֶבֶר **cheber,** *kheh´-ber;* from 2266; a *society;* also a *spell:*— + charmer (-ing), company, enchantment, × wide.

2268. חֶבֶר **Cheber,** *heh´-ber;* the same as 2267; *community; Cheber,* the name of a Kenite and of three Isr.:—Heber.

2269. חֲבַר **chăbar** (Chald.), *khab-ar´;* from a root corresp. to 2266; an *associate:*—companion, fellow.

2270. חָבֵר **châbêr,** *khaw-bare´;* from 2266; an *associate:*—companion, fellow, knit together.

2271. חַבָּר **chabbâr,** *khab-bawr´;* from 2266; a *partner:*—companion.

2272. חֲבַרְבֻּרָה **chăbarbûrâh,** *khab-ar-boo-raw´;* by redupl. from 2266; a *streak* (like a *line),* as on the tiger:—spot.

2273. חַבְרָה **chabrâh** (Chald.), *khab-raw´;* fem. of 2269; an *associate:*—other.

2274. חֶבְרָה **chebrâh,** *kheb-raw´;* fem. of 2267; *association:*—company.

2275. חֶבְרוֹן **Chebrôwn,** *kheb-rone´;* from 2267; seat of *association; Chebron,* a place in Pal., also the name of two Isr.:—Hebron.

2276. חֶבְרוֹנִי **Chebrôwnîy,** *kheb-ro-nee´;* or חֶבְרֹנִי **Chebrônîy,** *kheb-ro-nee´;* patron. from 2275; *Chebronite* (collect.), an inhab. of Chebron:—Hebronites.

2277. חֶבְרִי **Chebrîy,** *kheb-ree´;* patron. from 2268; a *Chebrite* (collect.) or desc. of Cheber:—Heberites.

2278. חֲבֶרֶת **chăbereth,** *khab-eh´-reth;* fem. of 2270; a *consort:*—companion.

2279. חֹבֶרֶת **chôbereth,** *kho-beh´-reth;* fem. act. part. of 2266; a *joint:*—which coupleth, coupling.

2280. חָבַשׁ **châbash,** *khaw-bash´;* a prim. root; to *wrap* firmly (espec. a turban, compress, or *saddle*); fig. to *stop,* to *rule:*—bind (up), gird about, govern, healer, put, saddle, wrap about.

2281. חָבֵת **châbêth,** *khaw-bayth´;* from an unused root prob. mean. to *cook* [comp. 4227]; something *fried,* prob. a griddle-*cake:*—pan.

2282. חַג **chag,** *khag;* or חָג **châg,** *khawg;* from 2287; a *festival,* or a *victim* therefor:—(solemn) feast (day), sacrifice, solemnity.

2283. חָגָא **châgâ',** *khaw-gaw´;* from an unused root mean. to *revolve* [comp. 2287]; prop. *vertigo,* i.e. (fig.) *fear:*—terror.

2284. חָגָב **châgâb,** *khaw-gawb´;* of uncert. der.; a *locust:*—locust.

2285. חָגָב **Châgâb,** *khaw-gawb´;* the same as 2284; *locust; Chagab,* one of the Nethinim:—Hagab.

2286. חֲגָבָא **Chăgâbâ',** *khag-aw-baw´;* or חֲגָבָה **Chăgâbâh,** *khag-aw-baw´;* fem. of 2285; *locust; Chagaba* or *Chagabah,* one of the Nethinim:—Hagaba, Hagabah.

2287. חָגַג **châgag,** *khaw-gag´;* a prim. root [comp. 2283, 2328; prop. to move in a *circle,* i.e. (spec.) to *march* in a sacred procession, to *observe* a festival; by impl. to *be giddy:*—celebrate, dance, (keep, hold) a (solemn) feast (holiday), reel to and fro.

2288. חָגָו **chăgâv,** *khag-awv´;* from an unused root mean. to take *refuge;* a *rift* in rocks:—cleft.

2289. חָגוֹר **châgôwr,** *khaw-gore´;* from 2296; *belted:*—girded with.

2290. חֲגוֹר **chăgôwr,** *khag-ore´;* or חֲגֹר **chăgôr,** *khag-ore´;* and (fem.) חֲגוֹרָה **chăgôwrâh,** *khag-o-raw´;* or חֲגֹרָה **chăgôrâh,** *khag-o-raw´;* from 2296; a *belt* (for the waist):—apron, armour, gird (-le).

2291. חַגִּי **Chaggîy,** *khag-ghee´;* from 2287; *festive; Chaggi,* an Isr.; also (patron.) a *Chaggite,* or desc. of the same:—Haggi, Haggites.

2292. חַגַּי **Chaggay,** *khag-gah´ee;* from 2282; *festive; Chaggai,* a Heb. prophet:—Haggai.

2293. חַגִּיָּה **Chaggîyâh,** *khag-ghee-yaw´;* from 2282 and 3050; *festival of Jah; Chaggijah,* an Isr.:—Haggiah.

2294. חַגִּית **Chaggiyîth,** *khag-gheeth´;* fem. of 2291; *festive; Chaggith,* a wife of David:—Haggith.

2295. חָגְלָה **Choglâh,** *khog-law´;* of uncert. der.; prob. a *partridge; Choglah,* an Israelitess:—Hoglah. See also 1031.

2296. חָגַר **châgar,** *khaw-gar´;* a prim. root; to *gird* on (as a belt, armor, etc.):—be able to put on, be afraid, appointed, gird, restrain, × on every side.

2297. חַד **chad,** *khad;* abridged from 259; *one:*—one.

2298. חַד **chad** (Chald.), *khad;* corresp. to 2297; as card. *one;* as art. *single;* as ord. *first;* adv. *at once:*—a, first, one, together.

2299. חַד **chad,** *khad;* from 2300; *sharp:*—sharp.

2300. חָדַד **châdad,** *khaw-dad´;* a prim. root; to *be* (caus. *make*) *sharp* or (fig.) *severe:*—be fierce, sharpen.

2301. חֲדַד **Chădad,** *khad-ad´;* from 2300; *fierce; Chadad,* an Ishmaelite:—Hadad.

2302. חָדָה **châdâh,** *khaw-daw´;* a prim. root; to *rejoice:*—make glad, be joined, rejoice.

2303. חַדּוּד **chaddûwd,** *khad-dood´;* from 2300; a *point:*—sharp.

2304. חֶדְוָה **chedvâh,** *khed-vaw´;* from 2302; *rejoicing:*—gladness, joy.

2305. חֶדְוָה **chedvâh** (Chald.), *khed-vaw´;* corresp. to 2304:—*joy.*

2306. חֲדִי **chădîy** (Chald.), *khad-ee´;* corresp. to 2373; a *breast:*—breast.

2307. חָדִיד **Châdîyd,** *khaw-deed´;* from 2300; a *peak; Chadid,* a place in Pal.:—Hadid.

2308. חָדַל **châdal,** *khaw-dal´;* a prim. root; prop. to *be flabby,* i.e. (by impl.) *desist;* (fig.) *be lacking* or *idle:*—cease, end, fail, forbear, forsake, leave (off), let alone, rest, be unoccupied, want.

2309. חֶדֶל **chedel,** *kheh´-del;* from 2308; *rest,* i.e. the state of the *dead:*—world.

2310. חָדֵל **châdêl,** *khaw-dale´;* from 2308; *vacant,* i.e. *ceasing* or *destitute:*—he that forbeareth, frail, rejected.

2311. חַדְלַי **Chadlay,** *khad-lah´ee;* from 2309; *idle; Chadlai,* an Isr.:—Hadlai.

2312. חֵדֶק **hêdeq,** *khay´-dek;* from an unused root mean. to *sting;* a *prickly* plant:—brier, thorn.

2313. חִדֶּקֶל **Chiddeqel,** *khid-deh´-kel;* prob. of for. or.; the *Chiddekel* (or Tigris) river:—Hiddekel.

2314. חָדַר **châdar,** *khaw-dar´;* a prim. root; prop. to *inclose* (as a room), i.e. (by anal.) to *beset* (as in a siege):—enter a privy chamber.

2315. חֶדֶר **cheder,** *kheh´-der;* from 2314; an *apartment* (usually lit.):—([bed] inner) chamber, innermost (-ward) part, parlour, + south, × within.

2316. חֲדַר **Chădar,** *khad-ar´;* another form for 2315; *chamber; Chadar,* an Ishmaelite:—Hadar.

2317. חַדְרָךְ **Chadrâk,** *khad-rawk´;* of uncert. der.; *Chadrak,* a Syrian deity:—Hadrach.

2318. חָדַשׁ **châdash,** *khaw-dash´;* a prim. root; to *be new;* caus. to *rebuild:*—renew, repair.

2319. חָדָשׁ **châdâsh,** *khaw-dawsh´;* from 2318; *new:*—fresh, new thing.

2320. חֹדֶשׁ **chôdesh,** *kho´-desh;* from 2318; the *new* moon; by impl. a *month:*—month (-ly), new moon.

2321. חֹדֶשׁ **Chôdesh,** *kho´-desh;* the same as 2320; *Chodesh,* an Israelitess:—Hodesh.

2322. חֲדָשָׁה **Chădâshâh,** *khad-aw-shaw´;* fem. of 2319; *new; Chadashah,* a place in Pal.:—Hadashah.

2323. חֲדַת **chădath** (Chald.), *khad-ath´;* corresp. to 2319; *new:*—new.

2324. חֲוָא **chăva'** (Chald.), *khav-aw´;* corresp. to 2331; to *show:*—shew.

2325. חוּב **chûwb,** *khoob;* also חָיַב **châyab,** *khaw-yab´;* a prim. root; prop. perh. to *tie,* i.e. (fig. and reflex.) to *owe,* or (by impl.) to *forfeit:*—make endanger.

2326. חוֹב **chôwb,** *khobe;* from 2325; *debt:*—debtor.

2327. חוֹבָה **chôwbâh,** *kho-baw´;* fem. act. part. of 2247; *hiding* place; *Chobah,* a place in Syria:—Hobah.

2328. חוּג **chûwg,** *khoog;* a prim. root [comp. 2287]; to describe a *circle:*—compass.

2329. חוּג **chûwg,** *khoog;* from 2328; a *circle:*—circle, circuit, compass.

2330. חוּד **chûwd,** *khood;* a prim. root; prop. to *tie* a knot, i.e. (fig.) to *propound* a riddle:—put forth.

2331. חָוָה **châvâh,** *khaw-vah´;* a prim. root; [comp. 2324, 2421]; prop. to *live;* by impl. (intens.) to *declare* or *show:*—show.

2332. חַוָּה **Chavvâh,** *khav-vaw´;* causat. from 2331; *life-giver; Chavvah* (or Eve), the first woman:—Eve.

2333. חַוָּה **chavvâh,** *khav-vaw´;* prop. the same as 2332 (*life-giving,* i.e. *living-place*); by impl. an encampment or *village:*—(small) town.

2334. חַוּוֹת יָעִיר **Chavvôwth Yâ'îyr,** *khav-vothe´; yaw-eer´;* from the plur. of 2333 and a modification of 3265; *hamlets of Jair,* a region of Pal.:—[Bashan-] Havoth-jair.

2335. חוֹזַי **Chôwzay,** *kho-zah´ee;* from 2374; *visionary; Chozai,* an Isr.:—the seers.

2336. חוֹחַ **chôwach,** *kho´-akh;* from an unused root appar. mean. to *pierce;* a *thorn;* by anal. a *ring* for the nose:—bramble, thistle, thorn.

2337. חָוָח châvâch, *khaw-vawkh´;* perh. the same as 2336; a *dell* or *crevice* (as if *pierced* in the earth):—thicket.

2338. חוּט **chûwṭ** (Chald.), *khoot;* corresp. to the root of 2339, perh. as a denom.; to *string* together, i.e. (fig.) to *repair:*—join.

2339. חוּט **chûwṭ,** *khoot;* from an unused root prob. mean. to *sew;* a *string;* by impl. a measuring *tape:*—cord, fillet, line, thread.

2340. חִוִּי **Chivvîy,** *khiv-vee´;* perh. from 2333; a *villager;* a *Chivvite,* one of the aboriginal tribes of Pal.:—Hivite.

2341. חֲוִילָה **Chăvîylâh,** *khav-ee-law´;* prob. from 2342; *circular; Chavilah,* the name of two or three eastern regions; also perh. of two men:—Havilah.

2342. חוּל **chûwl,** *khool;* or חִיל **chîyl,** *kheel;* a prim. root; prop. to *twist* or *whirl* (in a circular or spiral manner), i.e. (spec.) to *dance,* to *writhe* in pain (espec. of parturition) or fear; fig. to *wait,* to *pervert:*—bear, (make to) bring forth, (make to) calve, dance, drive away, fall grievously (with pain), fear, form, great, grieve, (be) grievous, hope, look, make, be in pain, be much (sore) pained, rest, shake, shapen, (be) sorrow (-ful), stay, tarry, travail (with pain), tremble, trust, wait carefully (patiently), be wounded.

2343. חוּל **Chûwl,** *khool;* from 2342; a *circle; Chul,* a son of Aram; also the region settled by him:—Hul.

2344. חוֹל **chôwl,** *khole;* from 2342; *sand* (as *round* or whirling particles):—sand.

2345. חוּם **chûwm,** *khoom;* from an unused root mean. to *be warm,* i.e. (by impl.) *sunburnt* or *swarthy* (blackish):—brown.

2346. חוֹמָה **chôwmâh,** *kho-maw´;* fem. act. part. of an unused root appar. mean. to *join;* a *wall* of protection:—wall, walled.

2347. חוּס **chûwç** *khoos;* a prim. root; prop. to *cover,* i.e. (fig.) to *compassionate:*—pity, regard, spare.

2348. חוֹף **chôwph,** *khofe;* from an unused root mean. to *cover;* a *cove* (as a *sheltered* bay):—coast [of the sea], haven, shore, [sea-] side.

2349. חוּפָם **Chûwphâm,** *khoo-fawm´;* from the same as 2348; *protection: Chupham,* an Isr.:—Hupham.

2350. חוּפָמִי **Chûwphâmîy,** *khoo-faw-mee´;* patron. from 2349; a *Chuphamite* or desc. of Chupham:—Huphamites.

2351. חוּץ **chûwts,** *khoots;* or (short.) חֻץ **chûts,** *khoots;* (both forms fem. in the plur.) from an unused root mean. to *sever;* prop. *separate* by a wall, i.e. *outside, outdoors:*—abroad, field, forth, highway, more, out (-side, -ward), street, without.

חוֹק **chôwq.** See 2436.

חוּקֹק **Chûwqôq.** See 2712.

2352. חוּר **chûwr,** *khoor;* or (short.) חֻר **chûr,** *khoor;* from an unused root prob. mean. to *bore;* the *crevice* of a serpent; the *cell* of a prison:—hole.

2353. חוּר **chûwr,** *khoor;* from 2357; *white* linen:—white.

2354. חוּר **Chûwr.** *khoor;* the same as 2353 or 2352; *Chur,* the name of four Isr. and one Midianite:—Hur.

2355. חוֹר **chôwr,** *khore;* the same as 2353; *white* linen:—network. Comp. 2715.

2356. חוֹר **chôwr,** *khore;* or (short.) חֹר **chôr,** *khore;* the same as 2352; a *cavity, socket, den:*—cave, hole.

2357. חָוַר **châvar,** *khaw-var´;* a prim. root; to *blanch* (as with shame):—wax pale.

2358. חִוָּר **chivvâr** (Chald.), *khiv-vawr´;* from a root corresp. to 2357; *white:*—white.

חוֹרוֹן **Chôwrôwn.** See 1032.

חוֹרִי **chôwrîy.** See 2753.

2359. חוּרִי **Chûwrîy,** *khoo-ree´;* prob. from 2353; *linen*-worker; *Churi,* an Isr.:—Huri.

2360. חוּרַי **Chûwray,** *khoo-rah´ee;* prob. an orth. var. for 2359; *Churai,* an Isr.:—Hurai.

2361. חוּרָם **Chûwrâm,** *khoo-rawm´;* prob. from 2353; *whiteness,* i.e. noble; *Churam,* the name of an Isr. and two Syrians:—Huram. Comp. 2438.

2362. חַוְרָן **Chavrân,** *khav-rawn´;* appar. from 2357 (in the sense of 2352); *cavernous; Chavran,* a region E. of the Jordan:—Hauran.

2363. חוּשׁ **chûwsh,** *koosh;* a prim. root; to *hurry;* fig. to *be eager* with excitement or enjoyment:—(make) haste (-n), ready.

2364. חוּשָׁה **Chûwshâh,** *khoo-shaw´;* from 2363; *haste; Chushah,* an Isr.:—Hushah.

2365. חוּשַׁי **Chûwshay,** *khoo-shah´ee;* from 2363; *hasty; Chushai,* an Isr.:—Hushai.

2366. חוּשִׁים **Chûwshîym,** *khoo-sheem´;* or חֻשִׁים **Chûshîym,** *khoo-shem´;* or חֻשִׁם **Chûshîm,** *khoo-sheem´;* plur. from 2363; *hasters; Chushim,* the name of three Isr.:—Hushim.

2367. חוּשָׁם **Chûwshâm,** *khoo-shawm´;* or חֻשָׁם **Chûshâm,** *khoo-shawm´;* from 2363; *hastily; Chusham,* an Idumæan:—Husham.

2368. חוֹתָם **chôwthâm,** *kho-thawm´;* or חֹתָם **chôthâm,** *kho-thawm´;* from 2856; a *signature*-ring:—seal, signet.

2369. חוֹתָם **Chôwthâm,** *kho-thawm´,* the same as 2368; *seal; Chotham,* the name of two Isr.:—Hotham, Hothan.

2370. חֲזָא **chăzâ'** (Chald.), *khaz-aw´;* or חֲזָה **chăzâh** (Chald.), *khaz-aw´;* corresp. to 2372; to *gaze* upon; mentally to *dream, be usual* (i.e. *seem*):—behold, have [a dream], see, be wont.

2371. חֲזָאֵל **Chăzâ'êl,** *khaz-aw-ale´;* or חֲזָהאֵל **Chăzâh'êl,** *khaz-aw-ale´;* from 2372 and 410; *God has seen; Chazaël,* a king of Syria:—Hazael.

2372. חָזָה **châzâh,** *khaw-zaw´;* a prim. root; to *gaze* at; mentally to *perceive, contemplate* (with pleasure); spec. to *have a vision of:*—behold, look, prophesy, provide, see.

2373. חָזֶה **châzeh,** *khaw-zeh´;* from 2372; the *breast* (as most *seen* in front):—breast.

2374. חֹזֶה **chôzeh,** *kho-zeh´;* act. part. of 2372; a *beholder* in vision; also a *compact* (as *looked upon* with approval):—agreement, prophet, see that, seer, [star-] gazer.

חֲזָהאֵל **Chăzâh'êl.** See 2371.

2375. חֲזוֹ **Chăzow,** *khaz-o´;* from 2372; *seer; Chazo,* a nephew of Abraham:—Hazo.

2376. חֵזֶו **chêzev** (Chald.), *khay´-zev;* from 2370; a *sight:*—look, vision.

2377. חָזוֹן **châzôwn,** *khaw-zone´;* from 2372; a *sight* (mentally) i.e. a *dream, revelation,* or *oracle:*—vision.

2378. חָזוֹת **châzôwth,** *khaw-zooth´;* from 2372; a *revelation:*—vision.

2379. חֲזוֹת **chăzôwth** (Chald.), *khaz-oth´;* from 2370; a *view:*—sight.

2380. חָזוּת **châzûwth,** *khaw-zooth´;* from 2372; a *look;* hence (fig.) striking *appearance, revelation,* or (by impl.) *compact:*—agreement, notable (one), vision.

2381. חֲזִיאֵל **Chăzîy'êl,** *khaz-ee-ale´;* from 2372 and 410; *seen of God; Chaziel,* a Levite:—Haziel.

2382. חֲזָיָה **Chăzâyâh,** *khaz-aw-yaw´;* from 2372 and 3050; *Jah has seen; Chazajah,* an Isr.:—Hazaiah.

2383. חֶזְיוֹן **Chezyôwn,** *khez-yone´;* from 2372; *vision; Chezjon,* a Syrian:—Hezion.

2384. חִזָּיוֹן **chizzâyôwn,** *khiz-zaw-yone´;* from 2372; a *revelation,* espec. by *dream:*—vision.

2385. חֲזִיז **châzîyz,** *khaw-zeez´;* from an unused root mean. to *glare;* a *flash* of lightning:—bright cloud, lightning.

2386. חֲזִיר **chăzîyr,** *khaz-eer´;* from an unused root prob. mean. to *inclose;* a *hog* (perh. as *penned*):—boar, swine.

2387. חֵזִיר **Chêzîyr,** *khay-zeer´;* from the same as 2386; perh. *protected; Chezir,* the name of two Isr.:—Hezir.

2388. חָזַק **châzaq,** *khaw-zak´;* a prim. root; to *fasten* upon; hence to *seize, be strong* (fig. *courageous,* causat. *strengthen, cure, help, repair, fortify*), *obstinate;* to *bind, restrain, conquer:*—aid, amend, × calker, catch, cleave, confirm, be constant, constrain, continue, be of good (take) courage (-ous, -ly), encourage (self), be established, fasten, force, fortify, make hard, harden, help, (lay) hold (fast), lean, maintain, play the man, mend, become (wax) mighty, prevail, be recovered, repair, retain, seize, be (wax) sore, strengten (self), be stout, be (make, shew, wax) strong (-er), be sure, take (hold), be urgent, behave self valiantly, withstand.

2389. חָזָק **châzâq,** *khaw-zawk´;* from 2388; *strong* (usu. in a bad sense, *hard, bold, violent*):—harder, hottest, + impudent, loud, mighty, sore, stiff [-hearted], strong (-er).

2390. חָזֵק **châzêq,** *khaw-zake´;* from 2388; *powerful:*— × wax louder- stronger.

2391. חֵזֶק **chêzeq,** *khay´-zek;* from 2388; *help:*—strength.

2392. חֹזֶק **chôzeq,** *kho´-zek;* from 2388; *power:*—strength.

2393. חֶזְקָה **chezqâh,** *khez-kaw´;* fem. of 2391; prevailing *power:*—strength (-en self), (was) strong.

2394. חָזְקָה **chozqâh,** *khoz-kaw´;* fem. of 2392; *vehemence* (usu. in a bad sense):—force, mightily, repair, sharply.

2395. חִזְקִי **Chizqîy,** *khiz-kee´;* from 2388; *strong; Chizki,* an Isr.:—Hezeki.

2396. חִזְקִיָּה **Chizqîyâh,** *khiz-kee-yaw´;* or חִזְקִיָּהוּ **Chizqîyâhûw,** *khiz-kee-yaw´-hoo;* also יְחִזְקִיָּה **Y**e**chizqîyâh,** *yekh-iz-kee-yaw´;* or יְחִזְקִיָּהוּ **Y**e**chizqîyâhûw,** *yekh-iz-kee-yaw´-hoo;* from 2388 and 3050; *strengthened of Jah; Chizkijah,* a king of Judah, also the name of two other Isr.:—Hezekiah, Hizkiah, Hizkijah. Comp. 3169.

2397. חָח **châch,** *khawkh;* once (Ezek. 29 : 4) חָחִי **chăchîy,** *khakh-ee´;* from the same as 2336; a *ring* for the nose (or lips):—bracelet, chain, hook.

חָחִי **châchîy.** See 2397.

2398. חָטָא **châtâ',** *khaw-taw´;* a prim. root; prop. to *miss;* hence (fig. and gen.) to *sin;* by infer. to *forfeit, lack, expiate, repent,* (causat.) *lead astray, condemn:*—bear the blame, cleanse, commit [sin], by fault, harm he hath done, loss, miss, (make) offend (-er), offer for sin, purge, purify (self), make reconciliation, (cause, make) sin (-ful, -ness), trespass.

2399. חֵטְא **chêt',** *khate;* from 2398; a *crime* or its *penalty:*—fault, × grievously, offence, (punishment of) sin.

2400. חַטָּא **chattâ',** *khat-taw´;* intens. from 2398; a *criminal,* or one accounted *guilty:*—offender, sinful, sinner.

2401. חֲטָאָה **chătâ'âh,** *khat-aw-aw´;* fem. of 2399; an *offence,* or a *sacrifice* for it:—sin (offering), sinful.

2402. חַטָּאָה **chattâ'âh** (Chald.), *khat-taw-aw´;* corresp. to 2401; an *offence,* and the *penalty* or *sacrifice* for it:—sin (offering).

2403. חַטָּאָה **chattâ'âh,** *khat-taw-aw´;* or חַטָּאת **chattâ'th,** *khat-tawth´;* from 2398; an *offence* (sometimes habitual *sinfulness*), and its penalty, occasion, sacrifice, or expiation; also (concr.) an *offender:*—punishment (of sin), purifying (-fication for sin), sin (-ner, offering).

2404. חָטַב **châtab,** *khaw-tab´;* a prim. root; to *chop* or *carve* wood:—cut down, hew (-er), polish.

2405. חֲטֻבָה **chătûbâh,** *khat-oo-baw´;* fem. pass. part. of 2404; prop. a *carving;* hence a *tapestry* (as figured):—carved.

2406. חִטָּה **chittâh,** *khit-taw´;* of uncert. der.; *wheat,* whether the grain or the plant:—wheat (-en).

2407. חַטּוּשׁ **Chattûwsh,** *khat-toosh´;* from an unused root of uncert. signif.; *Chattush,* the name of four or five Isr.:—Hattush.

2408. חֲטִי **chătîy** (Chald.), *khat-ee´;* from a root corresp. to 2398; an *offence:*—sin.

2409. חַטָּיָא **chattâyâ'** (Chald.), *khat-taw-yaw´;* from the same as 2408; an *expiation:*—sin offering.

2410. חֲטִיטָא **Chătîyta',** *khat-ee-taw´;* from an unused root appar. mean. to *dig* out; *explorer; Chatita,* a temple porter:—Hatita.

2411. חַטִּיל **Chattîyl,** *khat-teel´;* from an unused root appar. mean. to *wave; fluctuating; Chattil,* one of "Solomon's servants":—Hattil.

2412. חֲטִיפָא **Chătîyphâ',** *khat-ee-faw´;* from 2414; *robber; Chatipha,* one of the Nethinim:—Hatipha.

2413. חָטַם **châtam,** *khaw-tam´;* a prim. root; to *stop:*—refrain.

2414. חָטַף **châtaph,** *khaw-taf´;* a prim. root; to *clutch;* hence to *seize* as a prisoner:—catch.

2415. חֹטֶר **chôter,** *kho´-ter;* from an unused root of uncert. signif.; a *twig:*—rod.

2416. חַי **chay,** *khah´ee;* from 2421; *alive;* hence *raw* (flesh); *fresh* (plant, water, year), *strong,* also (as noun, espec. in the fem. sing. and masc. plur.) *life* (or living thing), whether lit. or fig.:— + age, alive, appetite, (wild) beast, company, congregation, life (-time), live (-ly), living (creature, thing), maintenance, + merry, multitude, + (be) old, quick, raw, running, springing, troop.

2417. חַי **chay** (Chald.), *khah´ee;* from 2418; *alive;* also (as noun in plur.) *life:*—life, that liveth, living.

2418. חֲיָא **chăyâ'** (Chald.), *khah-yaw´;* or חֲיָה **chăyâh** (Chald.), *khah-yaw´;* corresp. to 2421; to *live:*—live, keep alive.

2419. חִיאֵל **Chîy'êl,** *khee-ale´;* from 2416 and 410; *living of God; Chiel,* an Isr.:—Hiel.

חָיָב **châyab.** See 2325.

2420. חִידָה **chîydâh,** *khee-daw´;* from 2330; a *puzzle;* hence a *trick, conundrum,* sententious *maxim:*—dark saying (sentence, speech), hard question, proverb, riddle.

2421. חָיָה **châyâh,** *khaw-yaw´;* a prim. root [comp. 2331, 2424]; to *live* whether lit. or fig.; causat, to *revive:*—keep (leave, make) alive, × certainly, give (promise) life, (let, suffer to) live, nourish up, preserve (alive), quicken, recover, repair, restore (to life), revive, (× God) save (alive, life, lives), × surely, be whole.

2422. חָיֶה **châyeh,** *khaw-yeh´;* from 2421; *vigorous:*—lively.

2423. חֵיוָא **chêyvâ'** (Chald.), *khay-vaw´;* from 2418; an *animal:*—beast.

2424. חַיּוּת **chayûwth,** *khah-yooth´;* from 2421; *life:*— × living.

2425. חָיַי **châyay,** *khaw-yah´ee;* a prim. root [comp. 2421]; to *live;* causat. to *revive:*—live, save life.

2426. חֵיל **chêyl,** *khale;* or (short.) חֵל **chêl,** *khale;* a collat. form of 2428; an *army;* also (by anal.) an *intrenchment:*—army, bulwark, host, + poor, rampart, trench, wall.

חִיל **chîyl.** See 2342.

2427. חִיל **chîyl,** *kheel;* and (fem.) חִילָה **chîylâh,** *khee-law´;* from 2342; a *throe* (espec. of childbirth):—pain, pang, sorrow.

2428. חַיִל **chayil,** *khah´-yil;* from 2342; prob. a *force,* whether of men, means or other resources; an *army, wealth, virtue, valor, strength:*—able, activity, (+) army, band of men (soldiers), company, (great) forces, goods, host, might, power, riches, strength, strong, substance, train, (+) valiant (-ly), valour, virtuous (-ly), war, worthy (-ily).

2429. חַיִל **chayil** (Chald.), *khah´-yil;* corresp. to 2428; an *army,* or *strength:*—aloud, army, × most [mighty], power.

2430. חֵילָה **chêylâh,** *khay-law´;* fem. of 2428; an *intrenchment:*—bulwark.

2431. חֵילָם **Chêylâm,** *khay-lawm´;* or חֵלָאם **Chêl'âm,** *khay-lawm´;* from 2428; *fortress; Chelam,* a place E. of Pal.:—Helam.

2432. חִילֵן **Chîylên,** *khee-lane´;* from 2428; *fortress; Chilen,* a place in Pal.:—Hilen.

2433. חִין **chîyn,** *kheen;* another form for 2580; *beauty:*—comely.

2434. חַיִץ **chayits,** *khah´-yits;* another form for 2351; a *wall:*—wall.

2435. חִיצוֹן **chîytsôwn,** *khee-tsone´;* from 2434; prop. the (outer) *wall side;* hence *exterior;* fig. *secular* (as opposed to sacred):—outer, outward, utter, without.

2436. חֵיק **chêyq,** *khake,* or חֵק **chêq,** *khake;* and חוֹק **chôwq,** *khoke;* from an unused root, appar. mean. to *inclose;* the *bosom* (lit. or fig.):—bosom, bottom, lap, midst, within.

2437. חִירָה **Chîyrâh,** *khee-raw´; from 2357 in the sense of splendor; Chirah,* an Adullamite:—Hirah.

2438. חִירָם **Chîyrâm,** *khee-rawm´,* or חִירוֹם **Chîyrôwm,** *khee-rome´;* another form of 2361; *Chiram* or *Chirom,* the name of two Tyrians:—Hiram, Huram.

2439. חִישׁ **chîysh,** *kheesh;* another form for 2363; to *hurry:*—make haste.

2440. חִישׁ **chîysh,** *kheesh;* from 2439; prop. a *hurry;* hence (adv.) *quickly:*—soon.

2441. חֵךְ **chêk,** *khake;* prob. from 2596 in the sense of *tasting;* prop. the *palate* or inside of the mouth; hence the *mouth* itself (as the organ of speech, taste and kissing):—(roof of the) mouth, taste.

2442. חָכָה **châkâh,** *khaw-kaw´;* a prim. root [appar. akin to 2707 through the idea of *piercing*]; prop. to *adhere* to; hence to await:—long, tarry, wait.

2443. חַכָּה **chakkâh,** *khak-kaw´;* prob. from 2442; a *hook* (as *adhering*):—angle, hook.

2444. חֲכִילָה **Chakîylâh,** *khak-ee-law´;* from the same as 2447; *dark; Chakilah,* a hill in Pal.:—Hachilah.

2445. חַכִּים **chakkîym** (Chald.), *khak-keem´;* from a root corresp. to 2449; *wise,* i.e. a *Magian:*—wise.

2446. חֲכַלְיָה **Chăkalyâh,** *khak-al-yaw´;* from the base of 2447 and 3050; *darkness* of *Jah; Chakaljah,* an Isr.:—Hachaliah.

2447. חַכְלִיל **chaklîyl,** *khak-leel´;* by redupl. from an unused root appar. mean. to *be dark;* darkly *flashing* (only of the eyes); in a good sense, *brilliant* (as stimulated by wine):—red.

2448. חַכְלִלוּת **chaklîlûwth,** *khak-lee-looth´;* from 2447; *flash* (of the eyes); in a bad sense, *blearedness:*—redness.

2449. חָכַם **châkam,** *khaw-kam´;* a prim. root, to *be wise* (in mind, word or act):— × exceeding, teach wisdom, be (make self, shew self) wise, deal (never so) wisely, make wiser.

2450. חָכָם **châkâm,** *khaw-kawm´;* from 2449; *wise,* (i.e. intelligent, skilful or artful):—cunning (man), subtil, ([un-]), wise ([hearted], man).

2451. חָכְמָה **chokmâh,** *khok-maw´;* from 2449; *wisdom* (in a good sense):—skillful, wisdom, wisely, wit.

2452. חָכְמָה **chokmâh (Chald.),** *khok-maw´;* corresp. to 2451; *wisdom:*—wisdom.

2453. חַכְמוֹנִי **Chakmôwnîy,** *khak-mo-nee´;* from 2449; *skilful; Chakmoni,* an Isr.:—Hachmoni, Hachmonite.

2454. חָכְמוֹת **chokmôwth,** *khok-mōth´;* or חַכְמוֹת **chakmôwth,** *khak-mōth´;* collat. forms of 2451; *wisdom:*—wisdom, every wise [woman].

חֵל **chêl.** See 2426.

2455. חֹל **chôl,** *khole;* from 2490; prop. *exposed;* hence *profane:*—common, profane (place), unholy.

2456. חָלָא **châlâ',** *khaw-law´;* a prim. root [comp. 2470]; to *be sick:*—be diseased.

2457. חֶלְאָה **chel'âh,** *khel-aw´;* from 2456; prop. *disease;* hence *rust:*—scum.

2458. חֶלְאָה **Chel'âh,** *khel-aw´;* the same as 2457; *Chelah,* an Israelitess:—Helah.

2459. חֶלֶב **cheleb,** *kheh´-leb;* or חֵלֶב **chêleb,** *khay´-leb;* from an unused root mean. to *be fat; fat,* whether lit. or fig.; hence the *richest* or *choice* part:— × best, fat (-ness), × finest, grease, marrow.

2460. חֵלֶב **Chêleb,** *khay´-leb;* the same as 2459; *fatness; Cheleb,* an Isr.:—Heleb.

2461. חָלָב **châlâb,** *khaw-lawb´;* from the same as 2459; *milk* (as the *richness* of kine):— + cheese, milk, sucking,

2462. חֶלְבָּה **Chelbâh,** *khel-baw´;* fem. of 2459; *fertility: Chelbah,* a place in Pal.:—Helbah.

2463. חֶלְבּוֹן **Chelbôwn,** *khel-bone´;* from 2459; *fruitful; Chelbon,* a place in Syria:—Helbon.

2464. חֶלְבְּנָה **chelbᵉnâh,** *khel-ben-aw´;* from 2459; *galbanam,* an odorous gum (as if *fatty*):—galbanum.

2465. חֶלֶד **cheled,** *kheh´-led;* from an unused root appar. mean. to *glide* swiftly; *life* (as a *fleeting* portion of time); hence the *world* (as *transient*):—age, short time, world.

2466. חֵלֶד **chêled,** *khay´-led;* the same as 2465; *Cheled,* an Isr.:—Heled.

2467. חֹלֶד **chôled,** *kho´-led;* from the same as 2465; a *weasel* (from its *gliding* motion):—weasel.

2468. חֻלְדָּה **Chuldâh,** *khool-daw´;* fem. of 2467; *Chuldah,* an Israelitess:—Huldah.

2469. חֶלְדַּי **Chelday,** *khel-dah´-ee;* from 2466; *worldliness; Cheldai,* the name of two Isr.:—Heldai.

2470. חָלָה **châlâh,** *khaw-law´;* a prim. root [comp. 2342, 2470, 2490]; prop. to *be rubbed* or *worn;* hence (fig.) to *be weak, sick, afflicted;* or (causat.) to *grieve, make sick;* also to *stroke* (in flattering), *entreat:*—beseech, (be) diseased, (put to) grief, be grieved, (be) grievous, infirmity, intreat, lay to, put to pain, × pray, make prayer, be (fall, make) sick, sore, be sorry, make suit (× supplication), woman in travail, be (become) weak, be wounded.

2471. חַלָּה **challâh,** *khal-law´;* from 2490; a *cake* (as usually *punctured*):—cake.

2472. חֲלוֹם **chălôwm,** *khal-ome´;* or (short.) חֲלֹם **chălôm,** *khal-ome´;* from 2492; a *dream:*—dream (-er).

2473. חֹלוֹן **Chôlôwn,** *kho-lone´;* or (short.) חֹלֹן **Chôlôn,** *kho-lone´;* prob. from 2344; *sandy; Cholon,* the name of two places in Pal.:—Holon.

2474. חַלּוֹן **challôwn,** *khal-lone´;* a *window* (as *perforated*):—window.

2475. חֲלוֹף **chălôwph,** *khal-ofe´;* from 2498, prop. *surviving;* by impl. (collect.) *orphans:*— × destruction.

2476. חֲלוּשָׁה **chălûwshâh,** *khal-oo-shaw´;* fem. pass. part. of 2522; *defeat:*—being overcome.

2477. חֲלַח **Chălach,** *khal-akh´;* prob. of for. or.; *Chalach,* a region of Assyria:—Halah.

2478. חַלְחוּל **Chalchûwl,** *khal-khool´;* by redupl. from 2342; *contorted; Chalchul,* a place in Pal.:—Halhul.

2479. חַלְחָלָה **chalchâlâh,** *khal-khaw-law´;* fem. from the same as 2478; *writhing* (in childbirth); by impl. *terror:*—(great, much) pain.

2480. חָלַט **châlaṭ,** *khaw-lat´;* a prim. root; to *snatch* at:—catch.

2481. חֲלִי **chălîy,** *khal-ee´;* from 2470; a *trinket* (as *polished*):—jewel, ornament.

2482. חֲלִי **Chălîy,** *hhal-ee´;* the same as 2481; *Chali,* a place in Pal.:—Hali.

2483. חֳלִי **chŏlîy,** *khol-ee´;* from 2470; *malady, anxiety, calamity:*—disease, grief, (is) sick (-ness).

2484. חֶלְיָה **chelyâh,** *khel-yaw´;* fem. of 2481; a *trinket:*—jewel.

2485. חָלִיל **châlîyl,** *khaw-leel´;* from 2490; a *flute* (as *perforated*):—pipe.

2486. חָלִילָה **châlîylâh,** *khaw-lee´-law;* or חָלִלָה **châlîlâh,** *khaw-lee´-law;* a directive from 2490; lit. *for a profaned* thing; used (interj.) *far be it!:*—be far, (× God) forbid.

2487. חֲלִיפָה **chălîyphâh,** *khal-ee-faw´;* from 2498; *alternation:*—change, course.

2488. חֲלִיצָה **chălîytsâh,** *khal-ee-tsaw´;* from 2502; *spoil:*—armour.

2489. חֵלְכָא **chêlᵉkâ',** *khay-lek-aw´;* or חֵלְכָה **chêlᵉkâh,** *khay-lek-aw´;* appar. from an unused root prob. mean. to *be dark* or (fig.) *unhappy;* a *wretch,* i.e. unfortunate:—poor.

2490. חָלַל **châlal,** *khaw-lal´;* a prim. root [comp. 2470]; prop. to *bore,* i.e. (by impl.) to *wound,* to *dissolve;* fig. to *profane* (a person, place or thing), to *break* (one's word), to *begin* (as if by an "opening wedge"); denom. (from 2485) to *play* (the flute):—begin (× men began), defile, × break, defile, × eat (as common things), × first, × gather the grape thereof, × take inheritance, pipe, player on instruments, pollute, (cast as) profane (self), prostitute, slay (slain), sorrow, stain, wound.

2491. חָלָל **châlâl,** *khaw-lawl´;* from 2490; *pierced* (espec. to death); fig. *polluted:*—*kill, profane, slain (man),* × *slew, (deadly) wounded.*

חָלִלָה **châlîlâh.** See 2486.

2492. חָלַם **châlam,** *khaw-lam´;* a prim. root; prop. to *bind* firmly, i.e. (by impl.) to *be* (causat. to *make*) *plump;* also (through the fig. sense of *dumbness*) to *dream:*—(cause to) dream (-er), be in good liking, recover.

2493. חֵלֶם **chêlem** (Chald.), *khay´-lem;* from a root corresp. to 2492; a *dream:*—dream.

2494. חֵלֶם **Chêlem,** *khay´-lem;* from 2492; a *dream; Chelem,* an Isr.:—Helem. Comp. 2469.

2495. חַלָּמוּת **challâmûwth,** *khal-law-mooth´;* from 2492 (in the sense of *insipidity*); prob. *purslain:*—egg.

2496. חַלָּמִישׁ **challâmîysh,** *khal-law-meesh´;* prob. from 2492 (in the sense of *hardness*); *flint:*—flint (-y), rock.

2497. חֵלֹן **Chêlôn,** *khay-lone´;* from 2428; *strong Chelon,* an Isr.:—Helon

2498. חָלַף **châlaph,** *khaw-laf´;* a prim. root; prop. to *slide* by i.e. (by impl.) to *hasten* away, *pass* on, *spring* up, *pierce* or *change:*—abolish, alter change, cut onf, go on forward, grow up, be over, pass (away, on, through), renew, sprout, strike through.

2499. חֲלַף **chălaph** (Chald.), *khal-af´;* corresp. to 2498; to *pass* on (of time):—pass.

2500. חֵלֶף **chêleph,** *khay´-lef;* from 2498; prop. *exchange;* hence (as prep.) *instead* of:—× for.

2501. חֶלֶף **Cheleph,** *kheh´-lef;* the same as 2500; *change; Cheleph,* a place in Pal.:—Heleph.

2502. חָלַץ **châlats,** *khaw-lats´* a prim. root; to *pull* off; hence (hntens.) to *strip,* (reflex.) to *depart;* by impl. to *deliver, equip* (for fight); *present, strengthen:*—arm (self), (go, ready) armed (× man, soldier), deliver, draw out, make fat, loose, (ready) prepared, put off, take away, withdraw self.

2503. חֶלֶץ **Chelets,** *kheh´-lets;* or חֵלֶץ **Chêlets,** *khay´-lets;* from 2502; perh. *strength; Chelets,* the name of two Isr.:—Helez.

2504. חָלָץ **châlâts,** *khaw-lawts´;* from 2502 (in the sense of *strength*); only in the dual; the *loins* (as the seat of vigor):—loins, reins.

2505. חָלַק **châlaq,** *khaw-lak´;* a prim. root; to *be smooth* (fig.); by impl. (as smooth stones were used for *lots*) to *apportion* or *separate:*—deal, distribute, divide, flatter, give, (have, im-) part (-ner), take away a portion, receive, separate self, (be) smooth (-er).

2506. חֵלֶק **chêleq,** *khay´-lek;* from 2505; prop. *smoothness* (of the tongue); also an *allotment:*—flattery, inheritance, part, × partake, portion.

2507. חֵלֶק **Chêleq,** *khay´-lek;* the same as 2506; *portion; Chelek,* an Isr.:—Helek.

2508. חֲלָק **chălâq** (Chald.), *khal-awk´;* from a root corresp. to 2505; a *part:*—portion.

2509. חָלָק **châlâq,** *khaw-lawk´;* from 2505; *smooth* (espec. of tongue):—flattering, smooth.

2510. חָלָק **Châlâq,** *khaw-lawk´;* the same as 2509; *bare; Chalak,* a mountain of Idumæa:—Halak.

2511. חַלָּק **challâq,** *khal-lawk´;* from 2505; *smooth:*—smooth.

2512. חַלֻּק **challûq,** *khal-look´;* from 2505; *smooth:*—smooth.

2513. חֶלְקָה **chelqâh,** *khel-kaw´;* fem. of 2506; prop. *smoothness;* fig. *flattery;* also an *allotment:*—field, flattering (-ry), ground, parcel, part, piece of land ([ground]), plat, portion, slippery place, smooth (thing).

2514. חֲלַקָּה **chălaqqâh,** *khal-ak-kaw´;* fem. from 2505; *flattery:*—flattery.

2515. חֲלֻקָּה **chăluqqâh,** *khal-ook-kaw´;* fem. of 2512; a *distribution:*—division.

2516. חֶלְקִי **Chelqîy,** *khel-kee´;* patron. from 2507; a *Chelkite* or desc. of Chelek:—Helkites.

2517. חֶלְקַי **Chelqay,** *khel-kah´ee;* from 2505; *apportioned; Chelkai,* an Isr.:—Helkai.

2518. חִלְקִיָּה **Chilqîyâh,** *khil-kee-yaw´;* or חִלְקִיָּהוּ **Chilqîyâhûw,** *khil-kee-yaw´-hoo;* from 2506 and 3050; *portion* of *Jah; Chilhijah,* the name of eight Isr.:—Hilkiah.

2519. חֲלַקְלַקָּה **chălaqlaqqâh,** *khal-ak-lak-kaw´;* by redupl. from 2505; prop. something *very smooth;* i.e. a *treacherous* spot; fig. *blandishment:*—flattery, slippery.

2520. חֶלְקַת **Chelqath,** *khel-kath´;* a form of 2513; *smoothness; Chelkath,* a place in Pal.:—Helkath.

2521. חֶלְקַת הַצֻּרִים **Chelqath hats-Tsûrîym,** *khel-kath´ hats-tsoo-reem´;* from 2520 and the plur. of 6697, with the art. inserted; *smoothness of the rocks; Chelkath Hatstsurim,* a place in Pal.:—Helkath-hazzurim.

2522. חָלַשׁ **châlash,** *khaw-lash´;* a prim. root; to *prostrate;* by impl. to *overthrow, decay:*—discomfit, waste away, weaken.

2523. חַלָּשׁ **challâsh,** *khal-lawsh´;* from 2522; *frail:*—weak.

2524. חָם **châm,** *khawm;* from the same as 2346; a *father-in-law* (as in *affinity*):—father in law.

2525. חָם **châm,** *khawm;* from 2552; *hot:*—hot, warm.

2526. חָם **Châm,** *khawm;* the same as 2525; *hot* (from the tropical habitat); *Cham,* a son of Noah; also (as a patron.) his desc. or their country:—Ham.

2527. חֹם **chôm,** *khome;* from 2552; *heat:*—heat, to be hot (warm).

2528. חֱמָא **chĕmâ'** (Chald.), *khem-aw´;* or חֲמָה **chămâh** (Chald.), *kham-aw´;* corresp. to 2354; *anger:*—fury.
חֱמָא **chêmâ'.** See 2534.

2529. חֶמְאָה **chem'âh,** *khem-aw´;* or (short.) חֵמָה **chêmâh,** *khay-maw´;* from the same root as 2346; curdled *milk* or *cheese:*—butter.

2530. חָמַד **châmad,** *khaw-mad´;* a prim. root; to *delight* in:—beauty, greatly beloved, covet, delectable thing, (× great) delight, desire, goodly, lust, (be) pleasant (thing), precious (thing).

2531. חֶמֶד **chemed,** *kheh´-med;* from 2530; *delight:*—desirable, pleasant.

2532. חֶמְדָּה **chemdâh,** *khem-daw´;* fem. of 2531; *delight:*—desire, goodly, pleasant, precious.

2533. חֶמְדָּן **Chemdân,** *khem-dawn´;* from 2531; *pleasant; Chemdan,* an Idumæan:—Hemdan.

2534. חֵמָה **chêmâh,** *khay-maw´;* or (Dan. 11 : 44) חֵמָא **chêmâ',** *khay-maw´;* from 3179; *heat;* fig. *anger, poison* (from its *fever*):—anger, bottles, hot displeasure, furious (-ly, -ry), heat, indignation, poison, rage, wrath (-ful). See 2529.

2535. חַמָּה **chammâh,** *kham-maw´;* from 2525; *heat;* by impl. the *sun:*—heat, sun.

2536. חַמּוּאֵל **Chammûw'êl,** *kham-moo-ale´;* from 2535 and 410; *anger of God; Chammuel,* an Isr.:—Hamuel.

2537. חֲמוּטַל **Chămûwṭal,** *kham-oo-tal´;* or חֲמִיטַל **Chămîyṭal,** *kham-ee-tal´;* from 2524 and 2919; *father-in-law of dew; Chamutal* or *Chamital,* an Israelitess:—Hamutal.

2538. חָמוּל **Châmûwl,** *khaw-mool´;* from 2550; *pitied; Chamul,* an Isr.:—Hamul.

2539. חָמוּלִי **Châmûwlîy,** *khaw-moo-lee´;* patron. from 2538: a *Chamulite* (collect.) or desc. of Chamul:—Hamulites.

2540. חַמּוֹן **Chammôwn,** *kham-mone´;* from 2552; *warm spring; Chammon,* the name of two places in Pal.:—Hammon.

2541. חָמוֹץ **châmôwts,** *khaw-motse´;* from 2556; prop. *violent;* by impl. a *robber:*—oppressed.

2542. חַמּוּק **chammûwq,** *kham-mook´;* from 2559; a *wrapping,* i.e. *drawers:*—joints.

2543. חֲמוֹר **chămôwr,** *kham-ore´;* or (short.) חֲמֹר **chămôr,** *kham-ore;* from 2560; a male *ass* (from its dun *red*):—(he) ass.

2544. חֲמוֹר **Chămôwr,** *kham-ore´;* the same as 2543; *ass; Chamor,* a Canaanite:—Hamor.

2545. חֲמוֹת **chămôwth,** *kham-ōth´;* or (short.) חֲמֹת **chămôth,** *kham-ōth´;* fem. of 2524; a *mother-in-law:*—mother in law.

2546. חֹמֶט **chômeṭ,** *kho´-met;* from an unused root prob. mean. to *lie low;* a *lizard* (as *creeping*):—snail.

2547. חֻמְטָה **Chumṭâh,** *khoom-taw´;* fem. of 2546; *low; Chumtah,* a place in Pal.:—Humtah.

2548. חָמִיץ **châmîyts,** *khaw-meets´;* from 2556; *seasoned,* i.e. *salt* provender:—clean.

2549. חֲמִישִׁי **châmîyshîy,** *kham-ee-shee´;* or חֲמִשִׁי **chămishshîy,** *kham-ish-shee´;* ord. from 2568; *fifth;* also a *fifth:*—fifth (part).

2550. חָמַל **châmal,** *khaw-mal´;* a prim. root; to *commiserate;* by impl. to *spare:*—have compassion, (have) pity, spare.

2551. חֶמְלָה **chemlâh,** *khem-law´;* from 2550; *commiseration:*—merciful, pity.

2552. חָמַם **châmam,** *khaw-mam´;* a prim. root; to *be hot* (lit. or fig.):—enflame self, get (have) heat, be (wax) hot, (be, wax) warm (self, at).

2553. חַמָּן **chammân,** *kham-mawn´;* from 2535; a *sun*-pillar:—idol, image.

2554. חָמַס **châmaç,** *khaw-mas´;* a prim. root; to *be violent;* by impl. to *maltreat:*—make bare, shake off, violate, do violence, take away violently, wrong, imagine wrongfully.

2555. חָמָס **châmâç,** *khaw-mawce´;* from 2554; *violence;* by impl. *wrong;* by meton. unjust *gain:*—cruel (-ty), damage, false, injustice, × oppressor, unrighteous, violence (against, done), violent (dealing), wrong.

2556. חָמֵץ **châmêts,** *khaw-mates´;* a prim. root; to *be pungent;* i.e. in taste (*sour,* i.e. lit. *fermented,* or fig. *harsh*), in color (*dazzling*):—cruel (man), dyed, be grieved, leavened.

2557. חָמֵץ **châmêtz,** *khaw-mates´;* from 2556; *ferment,* (fig.) *extortion:*—leaven, leavened (bread).

2558. חֹמֶץ **chômets,** *kho´-mets;* from 2556; *vinegar:*—vinegar.

2559. חָמַק **châmaq,** *khaw-mak´;* a prim. root; prop. to *enwrap;* hence to *depart* (i.e. turn about):—go about, withdraw self.

2560. חָמַר **châmar,** *khaw-mar´;* a prim. root; prop. to *boil* up; hence to *ferment* (with scum); to *glow* (with redness); as denom. (from 2564) to *smear* with pitch:—daub, foul, be red, trouble.

2561. חֶמֶר **chemer,** *kheh´-mer;* from 2560; *wine* (as *fermenting*):— × pure, red wine.

2562. חֲמַר **chămar** (Chald.), *kham-ar´;* corresp. to 2561; *wine:*—wine.

חֲמֹר **chămôr.** See 2543.

2563. חֹמֶר **chômer,** *kho´-mer;* from 2560; prop. a *bubbling* up, i.e. of water, a *wave;* of earth, *mire* or *clay* (cement); also a *heap;* hence a *chomer* or dry measure:—clay, heap, homer, mire, motion, mortar.

2564. חֵמָר **chêmâr,** *khay-mawr´;* from 2560; *bitumen* (as *rising* to the surface):—slime (-pit).

2565. חֲמֹרָה **chămôrâh,** *kham-o-raw´;* from 2560 [comp. 2563]; a *heap:*—heap.

2566. חַמְרָן **Chamrân,** *kham-rawn´;* from 2560; *red; Chamran,* an Idumæan:—Amran.

2567. חָמַשׁ **châmash,** *khaw-mash´;* a denom. from 2568; to *tax a fifth:*—take up the fifth part.

2568. חָמֵשׁ **châmêsh,** *khaw-maysh´;* masc. חֲמִשָּׁה **chămishshâh,** *kham-ish-shaw´;* a prim. numeral; *five:*—fif [-teen], fifth, five (× apiece).

2569. חֹמֶשׁ **chômesh,** *kho´-mesh;* from 2567; a *fifth* tax:—fifth part.

2570. חֹמֶשׁ **chômesh,** *kho´-mesh;* from an unused root prob. mean. to *be stout;* the *abdomen* (as *obese*):—fifth [rib].

2571. חָמֻשׁ **châmûsh,** *khaw-moosh´;* pass. part. of the same as 2570; *staunch,* i.e. able bodied *soldiers:*—armed (men), harnessed.

חֲמִשָּׁה **chămishshâh.** See 2568.

חֲמִשִּׁי **chămishshîy.** See 2549.

2572. חֲמִשִּׁים **chămishshîym,** *kham-ish-sheem´;* multiple of 2568; *fifty:*—fifty.

2573. חֵמֶת **chêmeth,** *khay´-meth;* from the same as 2346; a skin *bottle* (as *tied* up):—bottle.

2574. חֲמָת **Chămâth,** *kham-awth´;* from the same as 2346; *walled; Chamath,* a place in Syria:—Hamath, Hemath.

חַמֹּת **chămôth.** See 2545.

2575. חַמַּת **Chammath,** *kham-math´;* a var. for the first part of 2576; *hot* springs; *Chammath,* a place in Pal.:—Hammath.

2576. חַמֹּת דֹּאר **Chammôth Dôʼr,** *kham-moth´ dore;* from the plur. of 2535 and 1756; *hot* springs of *Dor; Chammath-Dor,* a place in Pal.:—Hamath-Dor.

2577. חֲמָתִי **Chămâthîy,** *kham-aw-thee´;* patrial from 2574; a *Chamathite* or native of *Chamath:*—Hamathite.

2578. חֲמַת צוֹבָה **Chămath Tsôwbâh,** *kham-ath´ tso-baw´;* from 2574 and 6678; *Chamath of Tsobah; Chamath-Tsobah;* prob. the same as 2574:—Hamath-Zobah.

2579. חֲמַת רַבָּה **Chămath Rabbâh,** *kham-ath´ rab-baw´;* from 2574 and 7237; *Chamath of Rabbah; Chamath-Rabbah,* prob. the same as 2574.

2580. חֵן **chên,** *khane;* from 2603; *graciousness,* i.e. subj. *(kindness, favor)* or objective *(beauty):*—favour, grace (-ious), pleasant, precious, [well-] favoured.

2581. חֵן **Chên,** *khane;* the same as 2580; *grace; Chen,* a fig. name for an Isr.:—Hen.

2582. חֵנָדָד **Chênâdâd,** *khay-naw-dawd´;* prob. from 2580 and 1908; *favor of Hadad; Chenadad,* an Isr.:—Henadad.

2583. חָנָה **chânâh,** *khaw-naw´;* a prim. root [comp. 2603]; prop. to *incline;* by impl. to *decline* (of the slanting rays of evening); spec. to *pitch* a tent; gen. to *encamp* (for abode or siege):—abide (in tents), camp, dwell, encamp, grow to an end, lie, pitch (tent), rest in tent.

2584. חַנָּה **Channâh,** *khan-naw´;* from 2603; *favored; Channah,* an Israelitess:—Hannah.

2585. חֲנוֹךְ **Chănôwk,** *khan-oke´;* from 2596; *initiated; Chanok,* an antediluvian patriach:—Enoch.

2586. חָנוּן **Chânûwn,** *khaw-noon´;* from 2603; *favored; Chanun,* the name of an Ammonite and of two Isr.:—Hanun.

2587. חַנּוּן **channûwn,** *khan-noon´;* from 2603; *gracious:*—gracious.

2588. חָנוּת **chânûwth,** *khaw-nooth´;* from 2583; prop. a *vault* or *cell* (with an arch); by impl. a *prison:*—cabin.

2589. חַנּוֹת **channôwth,** *khan-nōth´;* from 2603 (in the sense of *prayer*); *supplication:*—be gracious, intreated.

2590. חָנַט **chânaṭ,** *khaw-nat´;* a prim. root; to *spice;* by impl. to *embalm;* also to *ripen:*—embalm, put forth.

2591. חִנְטָא **chinṭâʼ** (Chald.), *khint-taw´;* corresp. to 2406; *wheat:*—wheat.

2592. חַנִּיאֵל **Chănnîyʼêl,** *khan-nee-ale´;* from 2603 and 410; *favor of God; Channiel,* the name of two Isr.:—Hanniel.

2593. חָנִיךְ **chânîyk,** *kaw-neek´;* from 2596; *initiated;* i.e. *practised:*—trained.

2594. חֲנִינָה **chănîynâh,** *khan-ee-naw´;* from 2603; *graciousness:*—favour.

2595. חֲנִית **chănîyth,** *khan-eeth´;* from 2583; a *lance* (for *thrusting,* like *pitching* a tent):—javelin, spear.

2596. חָנַךְ **chânak,** *khaw-nak´;* a prim. root; prop. to *narrow* [comp. 2614]; fig. to *initiate* or *discipline:*—dedicate, train up.

2597. חֲנֻכָּא **chănukkâʼ** (Chald.), *chan-ook-kaw´;* corresp. to 2598; *consecration:*—dedication.

2598. חֲנֻכָּה **chănukkâh,** *khan-ook-kaw´;* from 2596; *initiation,* i.e. *consecration:*—dedicating (-tion).

2599. חֲנֹכִי **Chănôkîy,** *khan-o-kee´;* patron. from 2585; a *Chanokite* (collect.) or desc. of Chanok:—Hanochites.

2600. חִנָּם **chinnâm,** *khin-nawm´;* from 2580; *gratis,* i.e. devoid of cost, reason or advantage:—without a cause (cost, wages), causeless, to cost nothing, free (-ly), innocent, for nothing (nought), in vain.

2601. חֲנַמְאֵל **Chănamʼêl,** *khan-am-ale´;* prob. by orth. var. for 2606; *Chanamel,* an Isr.:—Hanameel.

2602. חֲנָמָל **chănâmâl,** *khan-aw-mawl´;* of uncert. der.; perh. the *aphis* or plant-louse:—frost.

2603. חָנַן **chânan,** *khaw-nan´;* a prim. root [comp. 2583]; prop. to *bend* or stoop in kindness to an inferior; to *favor, bestow;* causat. to *implore* (i.e. move to favor by petition):—beseech, × fair, (be, find, shew) favour (-able), be (deal, give, grant (gracious (-ly), intreat, (be) merciful, have (shew) mercy (on, upon), have pity upon, pray, make supplication, × very.

2604. חֲנַן **chănan** (Chald.), *khan-an´;* corresp. to 2603; to *favor* or (causat.) to *entreat:*—shew mercy, make supplication.

2605. חָנָן **Chânân,** *khaw-nawn´;* from 2603; *favor; Chanan,* the name of seven Isr.:—Canan.

2606. חֲנַנְאֵל **Chănanʼêl,** *khan-an-ale´;* from 2603 and 410; *God has favored; Chananel,* prob. an Isr., from whom a tower of Jerusalem was named:—Hananeel.

2607. חֲנָנִי **Chănânîy,** *khan-aw-nee´;* from 2603; *gracious; Chanani,* the name of six Isr.:—Hanani.

2608. חֲנַנְיָה **Chănanyâh,** *khan-an-yaw´;* or חֲנַנְיָהוּ **Chănanyâhûw,** *khan-an-yaw´-hoo;* from 2603 and 3050; *Jah has favored; Chananjah,* the name of thirteen Isr.:—Hananiah.

2609. חָנֵס **Chânêç,** *khaw-nace´;* of Eg. der.; *Chanes,* a place in Egypt:—Hanes.

2610. חָנֵף **chânêph,** *khaw-nafe´;* a prim. root; to *soil,* espec. in a moral sense:—corrupt, defile, × greatly, pollute, profane.

2611. חָנֵף **chânêph,** *khaw-nafe´;* from 2610; *soiled* (i.e. with sin), *impious:*—hypocrite (-ical).

2612. חֹנֶף **chôneph,** *kho´-nef;* from 2610; moral *filth,* i.e. *wickedness:*—hypocrisy.

2613. חֲנֻפָה **chănûphâh,** *khan-oo-faw´;* fem. from 2610; *impiety:*—profaneness.

2614. חָנַק **chânaq,** *khaw-nak´;* a prim. root [comp. 2596]; to *be narrow;* by impl. to *throttle,* or (reflex.) to *choke* oneself to death (by a rope):—hang self, strangle.

2615. חַנָּתֹן **Channâthôn,** *khan-naw-thone´;* prob. from 2603; *favored; Channathon,* a place in Pal.:—Hannathon.

2616. חָסַד **châçad,** *khaw-sad´;* a prim. root; prop. perh. to *bow* (the neck only [comp. 2603] in courtesy to an equal), i.e. to *be kind;* also (by euphem. [comp. 1288], but rarely) to *reprove:*—shew self merciful, put to shame.

2617. חֶסֶד **cheçed,** *kheh´-sed;* from 2616; *kindness;* by impl. (towards God) *piety;* rarely (by opp.) *reproof,* or (subject.) *beauty:*—favour, good deed (-liness, -ness), kindly, (loving-) kindness, merciful (kindness), mercy, pity, reproach, wicked thing.

2618. חֶסֶד **Cheçed** *kheh´-sed;* the same as 2617; *favor; Chesed,* an Isr.:—Hesed.

2619. חֲסַדְיָה **Chăçadyâh,** *khas-ad-yaw´;* from 2617 and 3050; *Jah has favored; Chasadjah,* an Isr.:—Hasadiah.

2620. חָסָה **châçâh,** *khaw-saw´;* a prim. root; to *flee* for protection [comp. 982]; fig. to *confide* in:—have hope, make refuge, (put) trust.

2621. חֹסָה **Chôçâh,** *kho-saw´;* from 2620; *hopeful; Chosah,* an Isr.; also a place in Pal.:—Hosah.

2622. חָסוּת **châçûwth,** *khaw-sooth´;* from 2620; *confidence:*—trust.

2623. חָסִיד **châçîyd,** *khaw-seed´;* from 2616; prop. *kind,* i.e. (religiously) *pious* (a saint):—godly (man), good, holy (one), merciful, saint, [un-] godly.

2624. חֲסִידָה **chăçîydâh,** *khas-ee-daw´;* fem. of 2623; the *kind* (maternal) bird, i.e. a *stork:*—× feather, stork.

2625. חָסִיל **châçîyl,** *khaw-seel´;* from 2628; the *ravager,* i.e. a *locust:*—caterpillar.

2626. חֲסִין **chăçîyn,** *khas-een´;* from 2630; prop. *firm,* i.e. (by impl.) *mighty:*—strong.

2627. חַסִּיר **chaççîyr** (Chald.), *khas-seer´;* from a root corresp. to 2637; *deficient:*—wanting.

2628. חָסַל **châçal,** *khaw-sal´;* a prim. root; to *eat* off:—consume.

2629. חָסַם **châçam,** *khaw-sam´;* a prim. root; to *muzzle;* by anal. to *stop* the nose:—muzzle, stop.

2630. חָסַן **châçan,** *khaw-san´;* a prim. root; prop. to *(be) compact;* by impl. to *hoard:*—lay up.

2631. חֲסַן **chăçan** (Chald.), *khas-an´;* corresp. to 2630; to *hold* in occupancy:—possess.

2632. חֵסֶן **chêçen** (Chald.), *khay´-sen;* from 2631; *strength:*—power.

2633. חֹסֶן **chôçen,** *kho´-sen;* from 2630; *wealth:*—riches, strength, treasure.

2634. חָסֹן **châçôn,** *khaw-sone´;* from 2630; *powerful:*—strong.

2635. חֲסַף **chăçaph** (Chald.), *khas-af´;* from a root corresp. to that of 2636; a *clod:*—clay.

2636. חַסְפַּס **chaçpaç,** *khas-pas´;* redupl. from an unused root mean. appar. to *peel;* a *shred* or *scale:*—round thing.

2637. חָסֵר **châçêr,** *khaw-sare´;* a prim. root to *lack;* by impl. to *fail, want, lessen:*—be abated, bereave, decrease, (cause to) fail, (have) lack, make lower, want.

2638. חָסֵר **châçêr,** *khaw-sare´;* from 2637; *lacking;* hence *without:*—destitute, fail, lack, have need, void, want.

2639. חֶסֶר **cheçer,** *kheh´-ser; from 2637; lack;* hence *destitution:*—poverty, want.

2640. חֹסֶר **chôçer,** *kho´-ser;* from 2637; *poverty:*—in want of.

2641. חַסְרָה **Chaçrâh,** *khas-raw´;* from 2637; *want:*—*Chasrah,* an Isr.:—Hasrah.

2642. חֶסְרוֹן **cheçrôwn,** *khes-rone´;* from 2637; *deficiency:*—wanting.

2643. חַף **chaph,** *khaf;* from 2653 (in the moral sense of *covered* from soil); *pure:*—innocent.

2644. חָפָא **châphâ',** *khaw-faw´;* an orth. var. of 2645; prop. to *cover,* i.e. (in a sinister sense) to *act covertly:*—do secretly.

2645. חָפָה **châphâh,** *khaw-faw´;* a prim. root [comp. 2644, 2653]; to *cover;* by impl. to *veil,* to *incase, protect:*—ceil, cover, overlay.

2646. חֻפָּה **chuppâh,** *khoop-paw´;* from 2645; a *canopy:*—chamber, closet, defence.

2647. חֻפָּה **Chuppâh,** *khoop-paw´;* the same as 2646; *Chuppah,* an Isr.:—Huppah.

2648. חָפַז **châphaz,** *khaw-faz´;* a prim. root; prop. to *start* up suddenly, i.e. (by impl.) to *hasten* away, to *fear:*—(make) haste (away), tremble.

2649. חִפָּזוֹן **chîppâzôwn,** *khip-paw-zone´;* from 2648; *hasty flight:*—haste.

2650. חֻפִּים **Chuppîym,** *khoop-peem´;* plur. of 2646 [comp. 2349]; *Chuppim,* an Isr.:—Huppim.

2651. חֹפֶן **chôphen,** *kho´-fen;* from an unused root of uncert. signif.; a *fist* (only in the dual):—fists, (both) hands, hand [-full].

2652. חָפְנִי **Chophnîy,** *khof-nee´;* from 2651; perh. *pugilist; Chopni,* an Isr.:—Hophni.

2653. חֹפַף **chôphaph,** *khaw-faf´;* a prim. root [comp. 2645, 3182]; to *cover* (in protection):—cover.

2654. חָפֵץ **châphêts,** *khaw-fates´;* a prim. root; prop. to *incline* to; by impl. (lit. but rarely) to *bend;* fig. to *be pleased* with, *desire:*— × any at all, (have, take) delight, desire, favour, like, move, be (well) pleased, have pleasure, will, would.

2655. חָפֵץ **châphêts,** *khaw-fates´;* from 2654; *pleased* with:—delight in, desire, favour, please, have pleasure, whosoever would, willing, wish.

2656. חֵפֶץ **chêphets,** *khay´-fets;* from 2654; *pleasure;* hence (abstr.) *desire;* concr. a *valuable* thing; hence (by extens.) a *matter* (as something in mind):—acceptable, delight (-some), desire, things desired, matter, pleasant (-ure), purpose, willingly.

2657. חֶפְצִי בָּהּ **Chephtsîy bâhh,** *khef-tsee´; baw;* from 2656 with suffixes; *my delight* (is) *in her; Cheptsi-bah,* a fanciful name for Pal.:—Hephzi-bah.

2658. חָפַר **châphar,** *khaw-far´;* a prim. root; prop. to *pry* into; by impl. to *delve,* to *explore:*—dig, paw, search out, seek.

2659. חָפֵר **châphêr,** *khaw-fare´;* a prim. root [perh. rath. the same as 2658 through the idea of *detection*]; to *blush;* fig. to *be ashamed, disappointed;* causat. to *shame, reproach:*—be ashamed, be confounded, be brought to confusion (unto shame), come (be put to) shame, bring reproach.

2660. חֵפֶר **Chêpher,** *khay´-fer;* from 2658 or 2659; a *pit* or *shame; Chepher,* a place in Pal.; also the name of three Isr.:—Hepher.

2661. חֲפֹר **chăphôr,** *khaf-ore´;* from 2658; a *hole;* only in connection with 6512, which ought rather to be joined as one word, thus חֲפַרְפֵּרָה **chăpharpêrâh,** *khaf-ar-pay-raw´;* by redupl. from 2658; a *burrower,* i.e. prob. a *rat:*— + mole.

2662. חֶפְרִי **Chephrîy,** *khef-ree´;* patron. from 2660; a *Chephrite* (collect.) or desc. of *Chepher:*—Hepherites.

2663. חֲפָרַיִם **Chăphârayîm,** *khaf-aw-rah´-yim;* dual of 2660; *double pit; Chapharajim,* a place in Pal.:—Haphraim.

חֲפַרְפֵּרָה **chăpharpêrâh.** See 2661.

2664. חָפַשׂ **châphas,** *khaw-fas´;* a prim. root; to *seek;* causat. to *conceal* oneself (i.e. let be sought), or *mask:*—change, (make) diligent (search), disguise self, hide, search (for, out).

2665. חֵפֶשׂ **chêphes,** *khay´-fes;* from 2664; something *covert,* i.e. a *trick:*—search.

2666. חָפַשׁ **châphash,** *khaw-fash´;* a prim. root; to *spread* loose, fig. to *manumit:*—be free.

2667. חֹפֶשׁ **Chôphesh,** *kho´-fesh;* from 2666; something *spread* loosely, i.e. a *carpet:*—precious.

2668. חֻפְשָׁה **chuphshâh,** *khoof-shaw´;* from 2666; *liberty* (from slavery):—freedom.

2669. חָפְשׁוּת **chôphshûwth,** *khof-shooth´;* and חָפְשִׁית **chophshîyth,** *khof-sheeth´;* from 2666; *prostration* by sickness (with 1004, a *hospital*):—several.

2670. חָפְשִׁי **chophshîy,** *khof-shee´;* from 2666; *exempt* (from bondage, tax or care):—free, liberty.

2671. חֵץ **chêts,** *khayts;* from 2686; prop. a *piercer,* i.e. an *arrow;* by impl. a *wound;* fig. (of God) thunder-*bolt;* (by interchange for 6086) the *shaft* of a spear:— + archer, arrow, dart, shaft, staff, wound.

חֻץ **chûts.** See 2351.

2672. חָצַב **châtsab,** *khaw-tsab´;* or חָצֵב **châtsêb,** *khaw-tsabe´;* a prim. root; to *cut* or carve (wood, stone or other material); by impl. to *hew, split, square, quarry, engrave:*—cut, dig, divide, grave, hew (out, -er), make, mason.

2673. חָצָה **châtsâh,** *khaw-tsaw´;* a prim. root [comp. 2686]; to *cut* or *split* in two; to *halve:*—divide, × live out half, reach to the midst, part.

2674. חָצוֹר **Châtsôwr,** *khaw-tsore´;* a collect. form of 2691; *village; Chatsor,* the name (thus simply) of two places in Pal. and of one in Arabia:—Hazor.

2675. חָצוֹר חֲדַתָּה **Châtsôwr Chădattâh,** *khaw-tsore´ khad-at-taw´;* from 2674 and a Chaldaizing form of the fem. of 2319 [comp. 2323]; *new Chatsor,* a place in Pal.:—Hazor, Hadattah [*as if two places*].

2676. חָצוֹת **châtsôwth,** *khaw-tsoth´;* from 2673; the *middle* (of the night):—mid [-night].

2677. חֵצִי **chêtsîy,** *khay-tsee´;* from 2673; the *half* or *middle:*—half, middle, mid [-night], midst, part, two parts.

2678. חִצִּי **chitstsîy,** *khits-tsee´;* or חֵצִי **chêtsîy,** *chay-tsee´;* prol. from 2671; an *arrow:*—arrow.

2679. חֲצִי הַמְּנֻחוֹת **Chătsîy ham-Mᵉnûchôwth,** *chat-tsee´ ham-men-oo-khoth´;* from 2677 and the plur. of 4496, with the art. interposed; *midst of the resting-places; Chatsi-ham-Menuchoth,* an Isr.—half of the Manahethites.

2680. חֲצִי הַמְּנַחְתִּי **Chătsîy ham-Mᵉnachtîy,** *khat-see´ ham-men-akh-tee´;* patron. from 2679; a *Chatsi-ham-Menachtite* or desc. of Chatsi-ham-Menuchoth:—half of the Manahethites.

2681. חָצִיר **châtsîyr,** *khaw-tseer´;* a collat. form of 2691; a *court* or *abode:*—court.

2682. חָצִיר **châtsîyr,** *khaw-tseer´;* perh. orig. the same as 2681, from the *greenness* of a court-yard; *grass;* also a *leek* (collect.):—grass, hay, herb, leek.

2683. חֵצֶן **chêtsen,** *khay´-tsen;* from an unused root mean. to hold *firmly;* the *bosom* (as *comprised* between the arms):—bosom.

2684. חֹצֶן **chôtsen,** *kho´-tsen;* a collat. form of 2683, and mean. the same:—arm, lap.

2685. חֲצַף **chătsaph** (Chald.), *khats-af´;* a prim. root; prop. to *shear* or cut close; fig. to *be severe:*—hasty, be urgent.

2686. חָצַץ **châtsats,** *khaw-tsats´;* a prim. root [comp. 2673]; prop. to *chop* into, pierce or sever; hence to *curtail,* to *distribute* (into ranks); as denom. from 2671, to *shoot* an arrow:—archer, × bands, cut off in the midst.

2687. חָצָץ **châtsâts,** *khaw-tsawts´;* from 2687; prop. something *cutting;* hence *gravel* (as *grit*); also (like 2671) an *arrow:*—arrow, gravel (stone).

2688. חַצְצוֹן תָּמָר **Chatsᵉtsôwn Tâmâr,** *khats-ets-one´ taw-mawr´;* or חַצֲצֹן תָּמָר **Chatsătsôn Tâmâr,** *khats-ats-one´ taw-mawr´;* from 2686 and 8558; *division* [i.e. perh. *row*] *of* (the) *palm-tree; Chatsetson-tamar,* a place in Pal.:—Hazezon-tamar.

2689. חֲצֹצְרָה **chătsôtsᵉrâh,** *khats-o-tser-aw´;* by redupl. from 2690; a *trumpet* (from its *sundered* or quavering note):—trumpet (-er).

2690. חָצַר **châtsar,** *khaw-tsar´;* a prim. root; prop. to *surround* with a stockade, and thus *separate* from the open country; but used only in the redupl. form. חֲצֹצֵר **chătsôtsêr,** *khast-o-tsare´;* or (2 Chron. 5 : 12) חֲצֹרֵר **chătsôrêr,** *hhats-o-rare´;* as dem. from 2689; to *trumpet,* i.e. blow on that instrument:—blow, sound, trumpeter.

2691. חָצֵר **châtsêr,** *khaw-tsare´;* (masc. and fem.); from 2690 in its original sense; a *yard* (as *inclosed* by a fence); also a *hamlet* (as similarly *surrounded* with walls):—court, tower, village.

2692. חֲצַר אַדָּר **Chătsar Addâr,** *khats-ar´ ad-dawr´;* from 2691 and 146; (the) *village of Addar; Chatsar-Addar,* a place in Pal.:—Hazar-addar.

2693. חֲצַר גַּדָּה **Chătsar Gaddâh,** *khats-ar´ gad-daw´;* from 2691 and a fem. of 1408; (the) *village of* (female) *Fortune; Chatsar-Gaddah,* a place in Pal.:—Hazar-gaddah.

2694. חֲצַר הַתִּיכוֹן **Chătsar hat-Tîykôwn,** *khats-ar´ hat-tee-kone´;* from 2691 and 8484 with the art. interposed; *village of the middle; Chatsar-hat-Tikon,* a place in Pal.:—Hazar-hatticon.

2695. חֶצְרוֹ **Chetsrôw,** *khets-ro´;* by an orth. var. for 2696; *inclosure; Chetsro,* an Isr.:—Hezro, Hezrai.

2696. חֶצְרוֹן **Chetsrôwn,** *khets-rone´;* from 2691; *court-yard; Chetsron,* the name of a place in Pal.; also of two Isr.:—Hezron.

2697. חֶצְרוֹנִי **Chetsrôwnîy,** *khets-ro-nee´;* patron. from 2696; a *Chetsronite* or (collect.) desc. of Chetsron:—Hezronites.

2698. חֲצֵרוֹת **Chătsêrowth,** *khats-ay-roth´;* fem. plur. of 2691; *yards; Chatseroth,* a place in Pal.:—Hazeroth.

2699. חֲצֵרִים **Chătsêrîym,** *khats-ay-reem´;* plur. masc. of 2691; *yards; Chatserim,* a place in Pal.:—Hazerim.

2700. חֲצַרְמָוֶת **Chătsarmâveth,** *khats-ar-maw´-veth;* from 2691 and 4194; *village of death; Chatsarmaveth,* a place in Arabia:—Hazarmaveth.

2701. חֲצַר סוּסָה **Chătsar Çûwçâh,** *khats-ar´ soo-saw´;* from 2691 and 5484; *village of cavalry; Chatsar-Susah,* a place in Pal.:—Hazar-susah.

2702. חֲצַר סוּסִים **Chătsar Çûwçîym,** *khats-ar´ soo-seem´;* from 2691 and the plur. of 5483; *village of horses; Chatsar-Susim,* a place in Pal.:—Hazar-susim.

2703. חֲצַר עֵינוֹן **Chătsar ʽÊynôwn,** *khats-ar´ ay-none;* from 2691 and a der. of 5869; *village of springs; Chatsar-Enon,* a place in Pal.:—Hazar-enon.

2704. חֲצַר עֵינָן **Chătsar ʽÊynân,** *khats-ar´ ay-nawn´;* from 2691 and the same as 5881; *village of springs; Chatsar-Enan,* a place in Pal.:—Hazar-enan.

2705. חֲצַר שׁוּעָל **Chătsar Shûwʽâl,** *khats-ar´ shoo-awl´;* from 2691 and 7776; *village of* (the) *fox; Chatsar-Shual,* a place in Pal.:—Hazar-shual.

חֵק **chêq.** See 2436.

2706. חֹק **chôq,** *khoke;* from 2710; an *enactment;* hence an *appointment* (of time, space, quantity, labor or usage):—appointed, bound, commandment, convenient, custom, decree (-d), due, law, measure, × necessary, ordinance (-nary), portion, set time, statute, task.

2707. חָקָה **châqah,** *khaw-kaw´;* a prim. root; to *carve;* by impl. to *delineate;* also to *intrench:*—carved work, portrayed, set a print.

2708. חֻקָּה **chuqqâh,** *khook-kaw´;* fem. of 2706, and mean. substantially the same:—appointed, custom, manner, ordinance, site, statute.

2709. חֲקוּפָא **Chăqûwphâʼ,** *khah-oo-faw´;* from an unused root prob. mean. to *bend; crooked; Chakupha,* one of the Nethinim:—Hakupha.

2710. חָקַק **châqaq,** *khaw-kak´;* a prim. root; prop. to *hack,* i.e. *engrave* (Judg. 5 : 14, to *be a scribe* simply); by impl. to *enact* (laws being *cut* in stone or metal tablets in primitive times) or (gen.) *prescribe:*—appoint, decree, governor, grave, lawgiver, note, pourtray, print, set.

2711. חֵקֶק **chêqeq,** *khay´-kek;* from 2710; an *enactment,* a *resolution:*—decree, thought.

2712. חֻקֹּק **Chuqqôq,** *khook-koke´;* or (fully) חוּקוֹק **Chûwqôq,** *khoo-koke´;* from 2710; *appointed; Chukkok* or *Chukok,* a place in Pal.:—Hukkok, Hukok.

2713. חָקַר **châqar,** *khaw-kar´;* a prim. root; prop. to *penetrate;* hence to *examine* intimately:—find out, (make) search (out), seek (out), sound, try.

2714. חֵקֶר **chêqer,** *khay´-ker;* from 2713; *examination, enumeration, deliberation:*—finding out, number, [un-] search (-able, -ed out, -ing).

2715. חֹר **chôr,** *khore;* or (fully) חוֹר **chôwr,** *khore;* from 2787; prop. *white* or *pure* (from the *cleansing* or *shining* power of fire [comp. 2751]); hence (fig.) *noble* (in rank):—noble.

חֻר **chûr.** See 2352.

2716. חֶרֶא **chere',** *kheh´-reh;* from an unused (and vulg.) root prob. mean. to *evacuate* the bowels; *excrement:*—dung. Also חֲרִי° **chărîy,** *khar-ee´.*

2717. חָרַב **chârab,** *khaw-rab´;* or חָרֵב **chârêb,** *khaw-rabe´;* a prim. root; to *parch* (through drought), i.e. (by anal.) to *desolate, destroy, kill:*—decay, (be) desolate, destroy (-er), (be) dry (up), slay, × surely, (lay, lie, make) waste.

2718. חֲרַב **chărab** (Chald.), *khar-ab´;* a root corresp. to 2717; to *demolish:*—destroy.

2719. חֶרֶב **chereb,** *kheh´-reb;* from 2717; *drought;* also a *cutting* instrument (from its *destructive* effect), as a *knife, sword,* or other sharp implement:—axe, dagger, knife, mattock, sword, tool.

2720. חָרֵב **chârêb,** *khaw-rabe´;* from 2717; *parched* or *ruined:*—desolate, dry, waste.

2721. חֹרֶב **chôreb,** *kho´-reb;* a collat. form of 2719; *drought* or *desolation:*—desolation, drought, dry, heat, × utterly, waste.

2722. חֹרֵב **Chôrêb,** *kho-rabe´;* from 2717; *desolate; Choreb,* a (gen.) name for the Sinaitic mountains:—Horeb.

2723. חָרְבָּה **chorbâh,** *khor-baw´;* fem. of 2721; prop. *drought,* i.e. (by impl.) a *desolation:*—decayed place, desolate (place, -tion), destruction, (laid) waste (place).

2724. חָרָבָה **chârâbâh,** *khaw-raw-baw´;* fem. of 2720; a *desert:*—dry (ground, land).

2725. חֲרָבוֹן **chărâbôwn,** *khar-aw-bone´;* from 2717; parching *heat:*—drought.

2726. חַרְבוֹנָא **Charbôwnâ',** *khar-bo-naw´;* or חַרְבוֹנָה **Charbôwnâh,** *khar-bo-naw´;* of Pers. or.; *Charbona* or *Charbonah,* a eunuch of Xerxes:—Harbona, Harbonah.

2727. חָרַג **chârag,** *khaw-rag´;* a prim. root; prop. to *leap* suddenly, i.e. (by impl.) to *be dismayed:*—be afraid.

2728. חַרְגֹּל **chargôl,** *khar-gole´;* from 2727; the *leaping* insect, i.e. a *locust:*—beetle.

2729. חָרַד **chârad,** *khaw-rad´;* a prim. root; to *shudder* with terror; hence to *fear;* also to *hasten* (with anxiety):—be (make) afraid, be careful, discomfit, fray (away), quake, tremble.

2730. חָרֵד **chârêd,** *khaw-rade´;* from 2729; *fearful;* also *reverential:*—afraid, trembling.

2731. חֲרָדָה **chărâdâh,** *khar-aw-daw´;* fem. of 2730; *fear, anxiety:*—care, × exceedingly, fear, quaking, trembling.

2732. חֲרָדָה **Chărâdâh,** *khar-aw-daw´;* the same as 2731; *Charadah,* a place in the Desert:—Haradah.

2733. חֲרֹדִי **Chărôdîy,** *khar-o-dee´;* patrial from a deriv. of 2729 [comp. 5878]; a *Charodite,* or inhab. of *Charod:*—Harodite.

2734. חָרָה **chârâh,** *khaw-raw´;* a prim. root [comp. 2787]; to *glow* or grow warm; fig. (usually) to *blaze* up, of anger, zeal, jealousy:—be angry, burn, be displeased, × earnestly, fret self, grieve, be (wax) hot, be incensed, kindle, × very, be wroth. See 8474.

2735. חֹר הַגִּדְגָּד **Chôr hag-Gidgâd,** *khore hag-ghid-gawd´;* from 2356 and a collat. (masc.) form of 1412, with the art. interposed; *hole of the cleft; Chor-hag-Gidgad,* a place in the Desert:—Hor-hagidgad.

2736. חַרְהֲיָה **Charhăyâh,** *khar-hah-yaw´;* from 2734 and 3050; *fearing Jah; Charhajah,* an Isr.:—Harhaiah.

2737. חָרוּז **chârûwz,** *khaw-rooz´;* from an unused root mean. to *perforate;* prop. *pierced,* i.e. a *bead* of pearl, gems or jewels (as strung):—chain.

2738. חָרוּל **chârûwl,** *khaw-rool´;* or (short.) חָרֻל **chârûl,** *khaw-rool´;* appar. pass. part. of an unused root prob. mean. to *be prickly;* prop. *pointed,* i.e. a *bramble* or other thorny weed:—nettle.

חֹרוֹן **chôrôwn.** See 1032, 2772.

2739. חֲרוּמַף **chărûwmaph,** *khar-oo-maf´;* from pass. part. of 2763 and 639; *snubnosed; Charumaph,* an Isr.:—Harumaph.

2740. חָרוֹן **chârôwn,** *khaw-rone´;* or (short.) חָרֹן **chârôn,** *khaw-rone´;* from 2734; a *burning* of anger:—sore displeasure, fierce (-ness), fury, (fierce) wrath (-ful).

2741. חֲרוּפִי **Chărûwphîy,** *khar-oo-fee´;* a patrial from (prob.) a collat. form of 2756; a *Charuphite* or inhab. of Charuph (or Chariph):—Haruphite.

2742. חָרוּץ **chârûwts,** *khaw-roots´;* or חָרֻץ **chârûts,** *khaw-roots´;* pass. part. of 2782; prop. *incised* or (act.) *incisive;* hence (as noun masc. or fem.) a *trench* (as dug), *gold* (as mined), a *threshing-sledge* (having sharp teeth); (fig.) *determination;* also *eager:*—decision, diligent, (fine) gold, pointed things, sharp, threshing instrument, wall.

2743. חָרוּץ **Chârûwts,** *khaw-roots´;* the same as 2742; *earnest; Charuts,* an Isr.:—Haruz.

2744. חַרְחוּר **Charchûwr,** *khar-khoor´;* a fuller form of 2746; *inflammation; Charchur,* one of the Nethinim:—Harhur.

2745. חַרְחַס **Charchaç** *khar-khas´;* from the same as 2775; perh. *shining; Charchas,* an Isr.:—Harbas.

2746. חַרְחֻר **charchûr,** *khar-khoor´:* from 2787; *fever* (as *hot*):—extreme burning.

2747. חֶרֶט **chereṭ,** *kheh´-ret;* from a prim. root mean. to *engrave;* a *chisel* or *graver;* also a *style* for writing:—graving tool, pen.

חָרִט **chârîṭ.** See 2754.

2748. חַרְטֹם **charṭôm,** *khar-tome´;* from the same as 2747; a *horoscopist* (as *drawing* magical lines or circles):—magician.

2749. חַרְטֹם **charṭôm** (Chald.), *khar-tome´;* the same as 2748:—magician.

2750. חֳרִי **chŏrîy,** *khor-ee´;* from 2734; a *burning* (i.e. intense) anger:—fierce, × great, heat.

חֲרִי° **chărîy.** See 2716.

2751. חֹרִי **chôrîy,** *kho-ree´;* from the same as 2353; *white* bread:—white.

2752. חֹרִי **Chôrîy,** *kho-ree´;* from 2356; *cave-dweller* or troglodyte; a *Chorite* or aboriginal Idumæan:—Horims, Horites.

2753. חֹרִי **Chôrîy,** *kho-ree´;* or חוֹרִי **Chôwrîy,** *kho-ree´;* the same as 2752; *Chori,* the name of two men:—Hori.

2754. חָרִיט **chârîyṭ,** *khaw-reet´;* or חָרִט **chârîṭ,** *khaw-reet´;* from the same as 2747; prop. *cut* out (or *hollow*), i.e. (by impl.) a *pocket:*—bag, crisping pin.

2755. חֲרֵי־יוֹנִים **chărêy-yôwnîym,** *khar-ay´-yo-neem´;* from the plur. of 2716 and the plur. of 3123; *excrements of doves* [or perh. rather the plur. of a single word חֲרָאיוֹן **chârâ'yôwn,** *khar-aw-yone´;* of similar or uncert. deriv.], prob. a kind of vegetable:—doves' dung.

2756. חָרִיף **Chârîyph,** *khaw-reef´;* from 2778; *autumnal; Chariph,* the name of two Isr.:—Hariph.

2757. חָרִיץ **chârîyts,** *khaw-reets´;* or חָרִץ **chârîts,** *khaw-reets´;* from 2782; prop. *incisure* or (pass.) *incised* [comp. 2742]; hence a *threshing-sledge* (with *sharp* teeth): also a *slice* (as cut):— + cheese, harrow.

2758. חָרִישׁ **chârîysh,** *khaw-reesh´;* from 2790; *ploughing* or its season:—earing (time), ground.

2759. חֲרִישִׁי **chărîyshîy,** *khar-ee-shee´;* from 2790 in the sense of *silence; quiet,* i.e. *sultry* (as noun fem. the *sirocco* or hot east wind):—vehement.

2760. חָרַךְ **chârak,** *khaw-rak´;* a prim. root; to *braid* (i.e. to *entangle* or snare) or *catch* (game) in a net:—roast.

2761. חֲרַךְ **chărak** (Chald.), *khar-ak´;* a root prob. allied to the equiv. of 2787; to *scorch:*—singe.

2762. חֶרֶךְ **cherek,** *kheh´-rek;* from 2760; prop. a *net,* i.e. (by anal.) *lattice:*—lattice.
חָרֻל **chârûl.** See 2738.

2763. חָרַם **charam,** *khaw-ram´;* a prim. root; to *seclude;* spec. (by a ban) to *devote* to relig. uses (espec. destruction); phys. and reflex. to be *blunt* as to the nose:—make accursed, consecrate, (utterly) destroy, devote, forfeit, have a flat nose, utterly (slay, make away).

2764. חֵרֶם **chêrem,** *khay´-rem;* or (Zech. 14 : 11) חֶרֶם **cherem,** *kheh´-rem;* from 2763; phys. (as *shutting in*) a *net* (either lit. or fig.); usually a *doomed* object; abstr. *extermination:*—(ac-) curse (-d, -d thing), dedicated thing, things which should have been utterly destroyed, (appointed to) utter destruction, devoted (thing), net.

2765. חֳרֵם **Chŏrêm,** *khor-ame´;* from 2763; *devoted; Chorem,* a place in Pal.:—Horem.

2766. חָרִם **Chârîm,** *khaw-reem´;* from 2763; *snub-nosed; Charim,* an Isr.:—Harim.

2767. חָרְמָה **Chormâh,** *khor-maw´;* from 2763; *devoted; Chormah,* a place in Pal.:—Hormah.

2768. חֶרְמוֹן **Chermôwn,** *kher-mone´;* from 2763; *abrupt; Chermon,* a mount of Pal.:—Hermon.

2769. חֶרְמוֹנִים **Chermôwnîym,** *kher-mo-neem´;* plur. of 2768; *Hermons,* i.e. its peaks:—the Hermonites.

2770. חֶרְמֵשׁ **chermêsh,** *kher-mashe´;* from 2763; a *sickle* (as *cutting*):—sickle.

2771. חָרָן **Chârân,** *kaw-rawn´;* from 2787; *parched; Charan,* the name of a man and also of a place:—Haran.
חָרֹן **chârôn.** See 2740.

2772. חֹרֹנִי **Chêrônîy,** *kho-ro-nee´;* patrial from 2773; a *Choronite* or inhab. of Choronaim:—Horonite.

2773. חֹרֹנַיִם **Chôrônayim,** *kho-ro-nah´-yim;* dual of a deriv. from 2356; *double cave-town; Choronajim,* a place in Moab:—Horonaim.

2774. חַרְנֶפֶר **Charnepher,** *khar-neh´-fer;* of uncert. der.; *Charnepher,* an Isr.:—Harnepher.

2775. חֶרֶס **chereç** *kheh´-res;* or (with a directive enclitic) חַרְסָה **charçâh,** *khar´-saw;* from an unused root mean. to *scrape;* the *itch;* also [perh. from the mediating idea of 2777] the *sun:*—itch, sun.

2776. חֶרֶס **Chereç,** *kheh´-res;* the same as 2775; *shining; Cheres,* a mount. in Pal.:—Heres.

2777. חַרְסוּת **charçûwth,** *khar-sooth´;* from 2775 (appar. in the sense of a red *tile* used for scraping); a *potsherd,* i.e. (by impl.) a *pottery;* the name of a gate at Jerus.:—east.

2778. חָרַף **châraph,** *khaw-raf´;* a prim. root; to *pull* off, i.e. (by impl.) to *expose* (as by *stripping*); spec. to *betroth* (as if a surrender); fig. to carp at, i.e. *defame;* denom. (from 2779) to spend the *winter:*—betroth, blaspheme, defy, jeopard, rail, reproach, upbraid.

2779. חֹרֶף **chôreph,** *kho´-ref;* from 2778; prop. the *crop* gathered, i.e. (by impl.) the *autumn* (and winter) season; fig. *ripeness* of age:—cold, winter ([-house]), youth.

2780. חָרֵף **Chârêph,** *khaw-rafe´;* from 2778; *reproachful; Chareph,* an Isr.:—Hareph.

2781. חֶרְפָּה **cherpâh,** *kher-paw´;* from 2778; *contumely, disgrace,* the *pudenda:*—rebuke, reproach (-fully), shame.

2782. חָרַץ **chârats,** *khaw-rats´;* a prim. root; prop. to *point* sharply, i.e. (lit.) to *wound;* fig. to *be alert,* to *decide:*—bestir self, decide, decree, determine, maim, move.

2783. חֲרַע **chărats** (Chald.), *khar-ats´;* from a root corresp. to 2782 in the sense of *vigor;* the *loin* (as the seat of strength):—loin.
חָרֻץ **chârûts.** See 2742.

2784. חַרְצֻבָּה **chartsubbâh,** *khar-tsoob-baw´;* of uncert. der.; a *fetter;* fig. a *pain:*—band.
חָרִץ **chârîts.** See 2757.

2785. חַרְצַן **chartsan,** *khar-tsan´;* from 2782; a *sour* grape (as *sharp* in taste):—kernel.

2786. חָרַק **châraq,** *khaw-rak´;* a prim. root; to *grate* the teeth:—gnash.

2787. חָרַר **chârar,** *khaw-rar´;* a prim. root; to *glow,* i.e. lit. (to *melt, burn, dry* up) or fig. (to *show* or *incite passion:*—be angry, burn, dry, kindle.

2788. חָרֵר **chârêr,** *khaw-rare´;* from 2787; *arid:*—parched place.

2789. חֶרֶשׂ **cheres,** *kheh´-res;* a collat. form mediating between 2775 and 2791; a piece of *pottery:*—earth (-en), (pot-) sherd, + stone.

2790. חָרַשׁ **chârash,** *khaw-rash´;* a prim. root; to *scratch,* i.e. (by impl.) to *engrave, plough;* hence (from the use of tools) to *fabricate* (of any material); fig. to *devise* (in a bad sense); hence (from the idea of secrecy) to be *silent,* to *let alone;* hence (by impl.) to *be deaf* (as an accompaniment of dumbness):— × altogether, cease, conceal, be deaf, devise, ear, graven, imagine, leave off speaking, hold peace, plow (-er, -man), be quiet, rest, practise secretly, keep silence, be silent, speak not a word, be still, hold tongue, worker.

2791. חֶרֶשׁ **cheresh,** *kheh´-resh;* from 2790; magical *craft;* also *silence:*—cunning, secretly.

2792. חֶרֶשׁ **Cheresh,** *kheh´-resh;* the same as 2791:—*Cheresh,* a Levite:—Heresh.

2793. חֹרֶשׁ **chôresh,** *kho´-resh;* from 2790; a *forest* (perh. as furnishing the material for fabric):—bough, forest, shroud, wood.

2794. חֹרֵשׁ **chôrêsh,** *kho-rashe´;* act. part. of 2790; a *fabricator* or mechanic:—artificer.

2795. חֵרֵשׁ **chêrêsh,** *khay-rashe´;* from 2790; *deaf* (whether lit. or spir.):—deaf.

2796. חָרָשׁ **chârâsh,** *khaw-rawsh´;* from 2790; a *fabricator* of any material:—artificer, (+) carpenter, craftsman, engraver, maker, + mason, skilful, (+) smith, worker, workman, such as wrought.

2797. חַרְשָׁא **Charshâ',** *khar-shaw´;* from 2792; *magician; Charsha,* one of the Nethinim:—Harsha.

2798. חֲרָשִׁים **Chărâshîym,** *khar-aw-sheem´;* plur. of 2796; *mechanics,* the name of a valley in Jerus.:—Charashim, craftsmen.

2799. חֲרֹשֶׁת **chărôsheth,** *khar-o´-sheth;* from 2790; mechanical *work:*—carving, cutting.

2800. חֲרֹשֶׁת **Chărôsheth,** *khar-o´-sheth;* the same as 2799; *Charosheth,* a place in Pal.:—Harosheth.

2801. חָרַת **chârath,** *khaw-rath´;* a prim. root; to *engrave:*—graven.

2802. חֶרֶת **Chereth,** *kheh´-reth;* from 2801 [but equiv. to 2793]; *forest; Chereth,* a thicket in Pal.:—Hereth.

2803. חָשַׁב **châshab,** *khaw-shab´;* a prim. root; prop. to *plait* or interpenetrate, i.e. (lit.) to *weave* or (gen.) to *fabricate;* fig. to *plot* or contrive (usually in a malicious sense); hence (from the mental effort) to *think, regard, value, compute:*—(make) account (of), conceive, consider, count, cunning (man, work, workman), devise, esteem, find out, forecast, hold, imagine, impute, invent, be like, mean, purpose, reckon (-ing be made), regard, think.

2804. חֲשַׁב **chăshab** (Chald.), *khash-ab´;* corresp. to 2803; to *regard:*—repute.

2805. חֵשֶׁב **chêsheb,** *khay´-sheb;* from 2803; a *belt* or strap (as being interlaced):—curious girdle.

2806. חַשְׁבַּדָּנָה **Chashbaddânâh,** *khash-bad-daw´-naw;* from 2803 and 1777; *considerate judge; Chasbaddanah,* an Isr.:—Hasbadana.

2807. חֲשֻׁבָה **Chăshûbâh,** *khash-oo-baw´;* from 2803; *estimation; Chashubah,* an Isr.:—Hashubah.

2808. חֶשְׁבּוֹן **cheshbôwn,** *khesh-bone´;* from 2803; prop. *contrivance;* by impl. *intelligence:*—account, device, reason.

2809. חֶשְׁבּוֹן **Cheshbôwn,** *khesh-bone´;* the same as 2808; *Cheshbon,* a place E. of the Jordan:—Heshbon.

2810. חִשָּׁבוֹן **chishshâbôwn,** *khish-shaw-bone´;* from 2803; a *contrivance,* i.e. actual (a warlike *machine*) or mental (a *machination*):—engine, invention.

2811. חֲשַׁבְיָה **Chăshabyâh,** *khash-ab-yaw´;* or חֲשַׁבְיָהוּ **Chăshabyâhûw,** *khash-ab-yaw´-hoo;* from 2803 and 3050; *Jah has regarded; Chashabjah,* the name of nine Isr.:—Hashabiah.

2812. חֲשַׁבְנָה **Chăshabnâh,** *khash-ab-naw´;* fem. of 2808; *inventiveness; Chash-nah,* an Isr.:—Hashabnah.

2813. חֲשַׁבְנְיָה **Chăshabnᵉyâh,** *khash-ab-neh-yaw´;* from 2808 and 3050; *thought of Jah; Chashabnejah,* the name of two Isr.:—Hashabniah.

2814. חָשָׁה **châshâh,** *khaw-shaw´;* a prim. root; to *hush* or keep quiet:—hold peace, keep silence, be silent, (be) still.

2815. חַשּׁוּב **Chashshûwb,** *khash-shoob´;* from 2803; *intelligent; Chashshub,* the name of two or three Isr.:—Hashub, Hasshub.

2816. חֲשׁוֹךְ **chăshôwk** (Chald.), *khash-oke´;* from a root corresp. to 2821; the *dark:*—darkness.

2817. חֲשׂוּפָא **Chăsûwphâ',** *khas-oo-faw´;* or חֲשֻׂפָא **Chăsûphâ',** *khas-oo-faw´;* from 2834; *nakedness; Chasupha,* one of the Nethinim:—Hashupha, Hasupha.

חָשׁוּק **châshûwq.** See 2838.

2818. חֲשַׁח **chăshach** (Chald.), *khash-akh´;* a collat. root to one corresp. to 2363 in the sense of *readiness;* to *be necessary* (from the idea of *convenience*) or (transit.) to *need:*—careful, have need of.

2819. חַשְׁחוּת **chashchûwth,** *khash-khooth´;* from a root corresp. to 2818; *necessity:*—be needful.

חֲשֵׁיכָה **chăshêykâh.** See 2825.

חֻשִׁים **Chûshîym.** See 2366.

2820. חָשַׂךְ **châsak,** *khaw-sak´;* a prim. root; to *restrain* or (reflex.) *refrain;* by impl. to *refuse, spare, preserve;* also (by interch. with 2821) to *observe:*—assuage, × darken, forbear, hinder, hold back, keep (back), punish, refrain, reserve, spare, withhold.

2821. חָשַׁךְ **châshak,** *khaw-shak´;* a prim. root; to *be dark* (as *withholding* light); transit. to *darken:*—be black, be (make) dark, darken, cause darkness, be dim, hide.

2822. חֹשֶׁךְ **chôshek,** *kho-shek´;* from 2821; the *dark;* hence (lit.) *darkness;* fig. *misery, destruction, death, ignorance, sorrow, wickedness:*—dark (-ness), night, obscurity.

2823. חָשֹׁךְ **châshôk,** *khaw-shoke´;* from 2821; *dark* (fig. i.e. *obscure*):—mean.

2824. חֶשְׁכָה **cheshkâh,** *khesh-kaw´;* from 2821; *darkness:*—dark.

2825. חֲשֵׁכָה **chăshêkâh,** *khash-ay-kaw´;* or חֲשֵׁיכָה **chăshêkâh,** *khash-ay-kaw´;* from 2821; *darkness;* fig. *misery:*—darkness.

2826. חָשַׁל **châshal,** *khaw-shal´;* a prim. root; to *make* (intrans. *be*) *unsteady,* i.e. *weak:*—feeble.

2827. חֲשַׁל **chăshal** (Chald.), *khash-al´;* a root corresp. to 2826; to *weaken,* i.e. *crush:*—subdue.

2828. חָשֻׁם **Châshûm,** *khaw-shoom´;* from the same as 2831; *enriched; Chashum,* the name of two or three Isr.:—Hashum.

חֻשָׁם **Chûshâm.** See 2367.

חֻשִׁם **Chûshîm.** See 2366.

2829. חֶשְׁמוֹן **Cheshmôwn,** *khesh-mone´;* the same as 2831; *opulent; Cheshmon,* a place in Pal.:—Heshmon.

2830. חַשְׁמַל **chashmal,** *khash-mal´;* of uncert. der.; prob. *bronze* or polished spectrum metal:—amber.

2831. חַשְׁמַן **chashmân,** *khash-man´;* from an unused root (prob. mean. *firm* or *capacious* in resources); appar. *wealthy:*—princes.

2832. חַשְׁמֹנָה **Chashmônâh,** *khash-mo-naw´;* fem. of 2831; *fertile; Chasmonah,* a place in the Desert:—Hashmonah.

2833. חֹשֶׁן **chôshen,** *kho´-shen;* from an unused root prob. mean. to *contain* or *sparkle;* perh. a *pocket* (as holding the Urim and Thummim), or *rich* (as containing gems), used only of the *gorget* of the highpriest:—breastplate.

2834. חָשַׂף **châsaph,** *khaw-saf´;* a prim. root; to *strip* off, i.e. gen. to *make naked* (for exertion or in disgrace), to *drain* away or *bail* up (a liquid):—make bare, clean, discover, draw out, take, uncover.

2835. חָשִׂף **châsîph,** *khaw-seef´;* from 2834; prop. *drawn off,* i.e. separated; hence a small *company* (as divided from the rest):—little flock.

2836. חָשַׁק **châshaq,** *khaw-shak´;* a prim. root; to *cling,* i.e. *join,* (fig.) to *love, delight* in; ellipt. (or by interch. for 2820) to *deliver:*—have a delight, (have a) desire, fillet, long, set (in) love.

2837. חֵשֶׁק **chêsheq,** *khay´-shek;* from 2836; *delight:*—desire, pleasure.

2838. חָשֻׁק **châshûq,** *khaw-shook´;* or חָשׁוּק **châshûwq,** *khaw-shook´;* pass. part. of 2836; *attached,* i.e. a fence-*rail* or rod connecting the posts or pillars:—fillet.

2839. חִשֻּׁק **chishshûq,** *khish-shook´;* from 2836; *conjoined,* i.e. a wheel-*spoke* or rod connecting the hub with the rim:—felloe.

2840. חִשֻּׁר **chishshûr,** *khish-shoor´;* from an unused root mean. to *bind* together; *combined,* i.e. the *nave* or hub of a wheel (as holding the spokes together):—spoke.

2841. חַשְׁרָה **chashrâh,** *khash-raw´;* from the same as 2840; prop. a *combination* or gathering, i.e. of watery *clouds:*—dark.

חֲשֻׂפָא **Chăsûphâ'.** See 2817.

2842. חָשַׁשׁ **châshash,** *khaw-shash´;* by var. for 7179; dry *grass:*—chaff.

2843. חֻשָׁתִי **Chûshâthîy,** *khoo-shaw-thee´;* patron. from 2364; a *Chushathite* or desc. of Chushah:—Hushathite.

2844. חַת **chath,** *khath;* from 2865; concr. *crushed;* also *afraid;* abstr. *terror:*—broken, dismayed, dread, fear.

2845. חֵת **Chêth,** *khayth;* from 2865; *terror; Cheth,* an aboriginal Canaanite:—Heth.

2846. חָתָה **châthâh,** *khaw-thaw´;* a prim. root; to lay *hold* of; espec. to *pick* up fire:—heap, take (away).

2847. חִתָּה **chittâh,** *khit-taw´;* from 2865; *fear:*—terror.

2848. חִתּוּל **chittûwl,** *khit-tool´;* from 2853; *swathed,* i.e. a *bandage:*—roller.

2849. חַתְחַת **chathchath,** *khath-khath´;* from 2844; *terror:*—fear.

2850. חִתִּי **Chittîy,** *khit-tee´;* patron. from 2845; a *Chittite,* or desc. of Cheth:—Hittite, Hittites.

2851. חִתִּית **chittîyth,** *khit-teeth´;* from 2865; *fear:*—terror.

2852. חָתַךְ **châthak,** *khaw-thak´;* a prim. root; prop. to *cut* off, i.e. (fig.) to *decree:*—determine.

2853. חָתַל **châthal,** *khaw-thal´;* a prim. root; to *swathe:*— × at all, swaddle.

2854. חֲתֻלָּה **chăthullâh,** *khath-ool-law´;* from 2853; a *swathing* cloth (fig.):—swaddling band.

2855. חֶתְלֹן **Chethlôn,** *kheth-lone´;* from 2853; *enswathed; Chethlon,* a place in Pal.:—Hethlon.

2856. חָתַם **châtham,** *khaw-tham´;* a prim. root; to *close* up; espec. to *seal:*—make an end, mark, seal (up), stop.

2857. חֲתַם **chătham** (Chald.), *khath-am´;* a root corresp. to 2856; to *seal:*—seal.

חֹתָם **chôthâm.** See 2368.

2858. חֹתֶמֶת **chôthemeth,** *kho-the-meth;* fem. act. part. of 2856; a *seal:*—signet.

2859. חָתַן **châthan,** *khaw-than´;* a prim. root; to *give* (a daughter) *away* in marriage; hence (gen.) to *contract affinity* by marriage:—join in affinity, father in law, make marriages, mother in law, son in law.

2860. חָתָן **châthân,** *khaw-thawn´;* from 2859; a *relative* by marriage (espec. through the bride); fig. a *circumcised* child (as a species of religious espousal):—bridegroom, husband, son in law.

2861. חֲתֻנָּה **chăthunnâh,** *khath-oon-naw´;* from 2859; a *wedding:*—espousal.

2862. חָתַף **châthaph,** *khaw-thaf´;* a prim. root; to *clutch:*—take away.

2863. חֶתֶף **chetheph,** *kheh´-thef;* from 2862; prop. *rapine;* fig. *robbery:*—prey.

2864. חָתַר **châthar,** *khaw-thar´;* a prim. root; to *force* a passage, as by burglary; fig. with oars:—dig (through), row.

2865. חָתַת **châthath,** *khaw-thath´;* a prim. root; prop. to *prostrate;* hence to *break* down, either (lit.) by violence, or (fig.) by confusion and fear:—abolish, affright, be (make) afraid, amaze, beat down, discourage, (cause to) dismay, go down, scare, terrify.

2866. חֲתַת **chăthath,** *khath-ath´;* from 2865; *dismay:*—casting down.

2867. חֲתַת **Chăthath,** *khath-ath´;* the same as 2866; *Chathath,* an Isr.:—Hathath.

ט

2868. טְאֵב **ṭeʼêb** (Chald.), *teh-abe´;* a prim. root; to *rejoice:*—be glad.

2869. טָב **ṭâb** (Chald.), *tawb;* from 2868; the same as 2896; *good:*—fine, good.

2870. טָבְאֵל **ṭâbeʼêl,** *taw-beh-ale´;* from 2895 and 410; *pleasing* (to) *God; Tabeël,* the name of a Syrian and of a Persian:—Tabeal, Tabeel.

2871. טָבוּל **ṭâbûwl,** *taw-bool´;* pass. part. of 2881; prop. *dyed,* i.e. a *turban* (prob. as of *colored* stuff):—dyed attire.

2872. טַבּוּר **ṭabbûwr,** *tab-boor´;* from an unused root mean. to *pile* up; prop. *accumulated;* i.e. (by impl.) a *summit:*—middle, midst.

2873. טָבַח **ṭâbach,** *taw-bakh´;* a prim. root; to *slaughter* (animals or men):—kill, (make) slaughter, slay.

2874. טֶבַח **ṭebach,** *teh´-bakh;* from 2873; prop. something *slaughtered;* hence a *beast* (or *meat,* as butchered); abstr. *butchery* (or concr. a place of slaughter):— × beast, slaughter, × slay, × sore.

2875. טֶבַח **Ṭebach,** *teh´-bakh;* the same as 2874; *massacre; Tebach,* the name of a Mesopotamian and of an Isr.:—Tebah.

2876. טַבָּח **ṭabbâch,** *tab-bawkh´;* from 2873; prop. a *butcher;* hence a *lifeguardsman* (because acting as executioner); also a *cook* (as usually slaughtering the animal for food):—cook, guard.

2877. טַבָּח **ṭabbâch** (Chald.), *tab-bawkh´;* the same as 2876; a *lifeguardsman:*—guard.

2878. טִבְחָה **ṭibchâh,** *tib-khaw´;* fem. of 2874 and mean. the same:—flesh, slaughter.

2879. טַבָּחָה **ṭabbâchâh,** *tab-baw-khaw´;* fem. of 2876; a female *cook:*—cook.

2880. טִבְחַת **Ṭibchath,** *tib-khath´;* from 2878; *slaughter; Tibchath,* a place in Syria:—Tibhath.

2881. טָבַל **ṭâbal,** *taw-bal´;* a prim. root; to *dip:*—dip, plunge.

2882. טְבַלְיָהוּ **Ṭebalyâhûw,** *teb-al-yaw´-hoo;* from 2881 and 3050; *Jah has dipped; Tebaljah,* an Isr.:—Tebaliah.

2883. טָבַע **ṭâbaʻ,** *taw-bah´;* a prim. root; to *sink:*—drown, fasten, settle, sink.

2884. טַבָּעוֹת **Ṭabbâʻôwth,** *tab-baw-othe´;* plur. of 2885; *rings; Tabbaoth,* one of the Nethinim:—Tabbaoth.

2885. טַבַּעַת **ṭabbaʻath,** *tab-bah´-ath;* from 2883; prop. a *seal* (as *sunk* into the wax), i.e. *signet* (for sealing); hence (gen.) a *ring* of any kind:—ring.

2886. טַבְרִמּוֹן **Ṭabrimmôwn,** *tab-rim-mone´;* from 2895 and 7417; *pleasing* (to) *Rimmon; Tabrimmon,* a Syrian:—Tabrimmon.

2887. טֵבֵת **Ṭêbeth,** *tay´-beth;* prob. of for. der.; *Tebeth,* the tenth Heb. month:—Tebeth.

2888. טַבַּת **Ṭabbath,** *tab-bath´;* of uncert. der.; *Tabbath;* a place E. of the Jordan:—Tabbath.

2889. טָהוֹר **ṭâhôwr,** *taw-hore´;* or טָהֹר **ṭahôr,** *taw-hore´;* from 2891; *pure* (in a phys., chem., cerem. or moral sense):—clean, fair, pure (-ness).

2890. טְהוֹר **ṭehôwr,** *teh-hore´;* from 2891; *purity:*—pureness.

2891. טָהֵר **ṭâhêr,** *taw-hare´;* a prim. root; prop. to *be bright;* i.e. (by impl.) to *be pure* (phys. *sound, clear, unadulterated;* Levit. *uncontaminated;* mor. *innocent* or *holy*):—be (make, make self, pronounce) clean, cleanse (self), purge, purify (-ier, self).

2892. טֹהַר **ṭôhar,** *to´-har;* from 2891; lit. *brightness;* ceremon. *purification:*—clearness, glory, purifying.

2893. טָהֳרָה **ṭohŏrâh,** *toh-or-aw´;* fem. of 2892; cerem. *purification;* moral *purity:*— × is cleansed, cleansing, purification (-fying).

2894. טוּא **ṭûwʼ,** *too;* a prim. root; to *sweep away:*—sweep.

2895. טוֹב **ṭowb,** *tobe;* a prim. root, to *be* (trans. *do* or *make*) *good* (or *well*) in the widest sense:—be (do) better, cheer, be (do, seem) good, (make), goodly, × please, (be, do, go, play) well.

2896. טוֹב **ṭôwb,** *tobe;* from 2895; *good* (as an adj.) in the widest sense; used likewise as a noun, both in the masc. and the fem., the sing. and the plur. (*good,* a *good* or *good* thing, a *good* man or woman; the *good, goods* or *good* things, *good* men or women), also as an adv. (*well*):—beautiful, best, better, bountiful, cheerful, at ease, × fair (word), (be in) favour, fine, glad, good (deed, -lier, liest, -ly, -ness, -s), graciously, joyful, kindly, kindness, liketh (best), loving, merry, × most, pleasant, + pleaseth, pleasure, precious, prosperity, ready, sweet, wealth, welfare, (be) well ([-favoured]).

2897. טוֹב **Ṭôwb,** *tobe;* the same as 2896; *good; Tob,* a region appar. E. of the Jordan:—Tob.

2898. טוּב **ṭûwb,** *toob;* from 2895; *good* (as a noun), in the widest sense, espec. *goodness* (superl. concr. the *best*), *beauty, gladness, welfare:*—fair, gladness, good (-ness, thing, -s), joy, go well with.

2899. טוֹב אֲדֹנִיָּהוּ **Ṭôwb Ădônîyâhûw,** *tobe ado-nee-yah´-hoo;* from 2896 and 138; *pleasing* (to) *Adonijah; Tob-Adonijah,* an Isr.:—Tob-adonijah.

2900. טוֹבִיָּה **Ṭôwbîyâh,** *to-bee-yaw´;* or טוֹבִיָּהוּ **Ṭôwbîyâhûw,** *to-bee-yaw´-hoo;* from 2896 and 3050; *goodness of Jehovah; Tobijah,* the name of three Isr. and of one Samaritan:—Tobiah, Tobijah.

2901. טָוָה **ṭâvâh,** *taw-vaw´;* a prim. root; to *spin:*—spin.

2902. טוּחַ **ṭûwach,** *too´-akh;* a prim. root; to *smear,* espec. with lime:—daub, overlay, plaister, smut.

2903. טוֹפָפָה **ṭôwphâphâh,** *to-faw-faw´;* from an unused root mean. to *go around* or *bind;* a *fillet* for the forehead:—frontlet.

2904. טוּל **ṭûwl,** *tool;* a prim. root; to *pitch* over or *reel;* hence (transit.) to *cast* down or out:—carry away, (utterly) cast (down, forth, out), send out.

2905. טוּר **ṭûwr,** *toor;* from an unused root mean. to *range* in a reg. manner; a *row;* hence a *wall:*—row.

2906. טוּר **ṭûwr** (Chald.), *toor;* corresp. to 6697; a *rock* or hill:—mountain.

2907. טוּשׂ **ṭûws,** *toos;* a prim. root; to *pounce* as a bird of prey:—haste.

2908. טְוָת **ṭevâth** (Chald.), *tev-awth´;* from a root corresp. to 2901; *hunger* (as *twisting*):—fasting.

2909. טָחָה **ṭâchâh,** *taw-khaw´;* a prim. root; to *stretch* a bow, as an *archer:*—[bow-] shot.

2910. טֻחָה **ṭûwchâh,** *too-khaw´;* from 2909 (or 2902) in the sense of *overlaying;* (in the plur. only) the *kidneys* (as being *covered*); hence (fig.) the inmost *thought:*—inward parts.

2911. טְחוֹן **ṭechôwn,** *tekh-one´;* from 2912; a hand *mill;* hence a *millstone:*—to grind.

2912. טָחַן **ṭâchan,** *taw-khan´;* a prim. root; to *grind* meal; hence to *be a concubine* (that being their employment):—grind (-er).

2913. טַחֲנָה **ṭachănâh,** *takh-an-aw´;* from 2912; a hand *mill;* hence (fig.) *chewing:*—grinding.

2914. טְחֹר **ṭechôr,** *tekh-ore´;* from an unused root mean. to *burn;* a *boil* or ulcer (from the inflammation), espec. a tumor in the anus or pudenda (the piles):—emerod.

2915. טִיחַ **ṭîyach,** *tee´-akh;* from (the equiv. of) 2902; mortar or *plaster:*—daubing.

2916. טִיט **ṭîyṭ,** *teet;* from an unused root mean. appar. to *be sticky* [rath. perh. a denom. from 2894, through the idea of dirt to be *swept* away]; *mud* or *clay;* fig. *calamity:*—clay, dirt, mire.

2917. טִין **ṭîyn** (Chald.), *teen;* perh. by interch. for a word corresp. to 2916; *clay:*—miry.

2918. טִירָה **ṭîyrâh,** *tee-raw´;* fem. of (an equiv. to) 2905; a *wall;* hence a *fortress* or a *hamlet:*—(goodly) castle, habitation, palace, row.

2919. טַל **ṭal,** *tal;* from 2926; *dew* (as *covering* vegetation):—dew.

2920. טַל **ṭal** (Chald.), *tal;* the same as 2919:—dew.

2921. טָלָא **ṭâlâʼ,** *taw-law´;* a prim. root; prop. to *cover* with pieces; i.e. (by impl.) to *spot* or *variegate* (as tapestry):—clouted, with divers colours, spotted.

2922. טְלָא **ṭᵉlâ',** *tel-aw´;* appar. from 2921 in the (orig.) sense of *covering* (for protection); a *lamb* [comp. 2924]:—lamb.

2923. טְלָאִים **Ṭᵉlâ'îym,** *tel-aw-eem´;* from the plur. of 2922; *lambs; Telaim,* a place in Pal.:—Telaim.

2924. טָלֶה **ṭâleh,** *taw-leh´;* by var. for 2922; a *lamb:*—lamb.

2925. טַלְטֵלָה **ṭalṭêlâh,** *tal-tay-law´;* from 2904; *overthrow* or *rejection:*—captivity.

2926. טָלַל **ṭâlal,** *taw-lal´;* a prim. root; prop. to *strew* over, i.e. (by impl.) to *cover* in or *plate* (with beams):—cover.

2927. טְלַל **ṭᵉlal** (Chald.), *tel-al´;* corresp. to 2926; to *cover* with shade:—have a shadow.

2928. טֶלֶם **Ṭelem,** *teh´-lem;* from an unused root mean. to *break* up or treat violently; *oppression; Telem,* the name of a place in Idumæa, also of a temple doorkeeper:—Telem.

2929. טַלְמוֹן **Ṭalmôwn,** *tal-mone´;* from the same as 2728; *oppressive; Talmon,* a temple doorkeeper:—Talmon.

2930. טָמֵא **ṭâmê',** *taw-may´;* a prim. root; to *be foul,* espec. in a cerem. or mor. sense *(contaminated):*—defile (self), pollute (self), be (make, make self, pronounce) unclean, × utterly.

2931. טָמֵא **ṭâmê',** *taw-may´;* from 2930; *foul* in a relig. sense:—defiled, + infamous, polluted (-tion), unclean.

2932. טֻמְאָה **ṭum'âh,** *toom-aw´;* from 2930; relig. *impurity:*—filthiness, unclean (-ness).

2933. טָמָה **ṭâmâh,** *taw-maw´;* a collat. form of 2930; to *be impure* in a relig. sense:—be defiled, be reputed vile.

2934. טָמַן **ṭâman,** *taw-man´;* a prim. root; to *hide* (by *covering* over):—hide, lay privily, in secret.

2935. טֶנֶא **ṭene',** *teh´-neh;* from an unused root prob. mean. to *weave;* a *basket* (of interlaced osiers):—basket.

2936. טָנַף **ṭânaph,** *taw-naf´;* a prim. root; to *soil:*—defile.

2937. טָעָה **ṭâ'âh,** *taw-aw´;* a prim. root; to *wander;* causat. to *lead astray:*—seduce.

2938. טָעַם **ṭâ'am,** *taw-am´;* a prim. root; to *taste;* fig. to *perceive:*— × but, perceive, taste.

2939. טְעַם **ṭᵉ'am** (Chald.), *teh-am´;* corresp. to 2938; to *taste;* causat. to *feed:*—make to eat, feed.

2940. טַעַם **ṭa'am,** *tah´-am;* from 2938; prop. a *taste,* i.e. (fig.) *perception;* by impl. *intelligence;* transit, a *mandate:*—advice, behaviour, decree, discretion, judgment, reason, taste, understanding.

2941. טַעַם **ṭa'am** (Chald.), *tah´-am;* from 2939; prop. a *taste,* i.e. (as in 2940) a judicial *sentence;*—account, × to be commanded, commandment, matter.

2942. טְעֵם **ṭᵉ'êm** (Chald.), *teh-ame´;* from 2939; and equiv. to 2941; prop. *flavor;* fig. *judgment* (both subj. and obj.); hence *account* (both subj. and obj.):— + chancellor, + command, commandment, decree, + regard, taste, wisdom.

2943. טָעַן **ṭâ'an,** *taw-an´;* a prim. root; to *load* a beast:—lade.

2944. טָעַן **ṭâ'an,** *taw-an´;* a prim. root; to *stab:*—thrust through.

2945. טַף **ṭaph,** *taf;* from 2952 (perh. referring to the *tripping* gait of children); a *family* (mostly used collect. in the sing.):—(little) children (ones), families.

2946. טָפַח **ṭâphach,** *taw-fakh´;* a prim. root; to *flatten* out or *extend* (as a tent); fig. to *nurse* a child (as *promotive* of growth); or perh. a denom. from 2947, from *dandling* on the palms:—span, swaddle.

2947. טֵפַח **ṭêphach,** *tay´-fakh;* from 2946; a *spread* of the hand, i.e. a *palm-breadth* (not "span" of the fingers); archit. a *corbel* (as a supporting palm):—coping, hand-breadth.

2948. טֹפַח **ṭôphach,** *to´-fakh;* from 2946 (the same as 2947):—hand-breadth (broad).

2949. טִפֻּח **ṭippûch,** *tip-pookh´;* from 2946; *nursing:*—span long.

2950. טָפַל **ṭâphal,** *taw-fal´;* a prim. root; prop. to *stick* on as a patch; fig. to *impute* falsely:—forge (-r), sew up.

2951. טִפְסַר **ṭiphçar,** *tif-sar´;* of for. der.; a military *governor:*—captain.

2952. טָפַף **ṭâphaph,** *taw-faf´;* a prim. root; appar. to *trip* (with short steps) coquettishly:—mince.

2953. טְפַר **ṭᵉphar** (Chald.), *tef-ar´;* from a root corresp. to 6852, and mean. the same as 6856; a finger-*nail;* also a *hoof* or *claw:*—nail.

2954. טָפַשׁ **ṭâphash,** *taw-fash´;* a prim. root; prop. appar. to *be thick;* fig. to *be stupid:*—be fat.

2955. טָפַת **Ṭâphath,** *taw-fath´;* prob. from 5197; a *dropping* (of ointment); *Taphath,* an Israelitess:—Taphath.

2956. טָרַד **ṭârad,** *taw-rad´;* a prim. root; to *drive* on; fig. to *follow* close:—continual.

2957. טְרַד **ṭᵉrad** (Chald.), *ter-ad´;* corresp. to 2956; to *expel:*—drive.

2958. טְרוֹם **ṭᵉrôwm,** *ter-ome´;* a var. of 2962; *not yet:*—before.

2959. טָרַח **ṭârach,** *taw-rakh´;* a prim. root; to *overburden:*—weary.

2960. טֹרַח **ṭôrach,** *to´-rakh;* from 2959; a *burden:*—cumbrance, trouble.

2961. טָרִי **ṭârîy,** *taw-ree´;* from an unused root appar. mean. to *be moist;* prop. *dripping;* hence *fresh* (i.e. recently made such):—new, putrefying.

2962. טֶרֶם **ṭerem,** *teh´-rem;* from an unused root appar. mean. to *interrupt* or *suspend;* prop. *non-occurrence;* used adv. *not yet* or *before:*—before, ere, not yet.

2963. טָרַף **ṭâraph,** *taw-raf´;* a prim. root; to *pluck* off or *pull* to pieces; causat. to *supply* with food (as in morsels):—catch, × without doubt, feed, ravin, rend in pieces, × surely, tear (in pieces).

2964. טֶרֶף **ṭereph,** *teh´-ref;* from 2963; something *torn,* i.e. a fragment, e.g. a *fresh* leaf, *prey, food:*—leaf, meat, prey, spoil.

2965. טָרָף **ṭârâph,** *taw-rawf´;* from 2963; recently *torn* off, i.e. *fresh:*—pluckt off.

2966. טְרֵפָה **ṭᵉrêphâh,** *ter-ay-faw´;* fem. (collect.) of 2964; *prey,* i.e. flocks devoured by animals:—ravin, (that which was) torn (of beasts, in pieces).

2967. טַרְפְּלַי **Ṭarpᵉlay** (Chald.), *tar-pel-ah´ee;* from a name of for. der.; a *Tarpelite* (collect.) or inhab. of Tarpel, a place in Assyria:—Tarpelites.

י

2968. יָאַב **yâ'ab,** *yaw-ab´;* a prim. root; to *desire:*—long.

2969. יָאָה **yâ'âh,** *yaw-aw´;* a prim. root; to *be suitable:*—appertain.

יְאוֹר **yᵉ'ôwr.** See 2975.

2970. יַאֲזַנְיָה **Ya'ăzanyâh,** *yah-as-an-yaw´;* or יַאֲזַנְיָהוּ **Ya'ăzanyâhûw,** *yah-az-an-yaw´-hoo;* from 238 and 3050; *heard of Jah; Jaazanjah,* the name of four Isr.:—Jaazaniah. Comp. 3153.

2971. יָאִיר **Yâ'îyr,** *yaw-ere´;* from 215; *enlightener; Jaïr,* the name of four Isr.:—Jair.

2972. יָאִרִי **Yâ'irîy,** *yaw-ee-ree´;* patron. from 2971; a *Jaïrite* or desc. of Jair:—Jairite.

2973. יָאַל **yâ'al,** *yaw-al´;* a prim. root; prop. to *be slack,* i.e. (fig.) *to be foolish:*—dote, be (become, do) foolish (-ly).

2974. יָאַל **yâ'al,** *yaw-al´;* a prim. root [prob. rather the same as 2973 through the idea of mental *weakness*]; prop. to *yield,* espec. *assent;* hence (pos.) to *undertake* as an act of volition:—assay, begin, be content, please, take upon, × willingly, would.

2975. יְאֹר **yᵉ'ôr,** *yeh-ore´;* of Eg. or.; a *channel,* e.g. a fosse, canal, shaft; spec. the *Nile,* as the one river of Egypt, including its collat. trenches; also the *Tigris,* as the main river of Assyria:—brook, flood, river, stream.

2976. יָאַשׁ **yâ'ash,** *yaw-ash´;* a prim. root; to *desist,* i.e. (fig.) to *despond:*—(cause to) despair, one that is desperate, be no hope.

2977. יֹאשִׁיָּה **Yô'shîyâh,** *yo-shee-yaw´;* or יֹאשִׁיָּהוּ **Yô'shîyâhûw,** *yo-she-yaw´-hoo;* from the same root as 803 and 3050; *founded of Jah; Joshijah,* the name of two Isr.:—Josiah.

2978. יְאִתוֹן° **y^e'îthôwn,** *yeh-ee-thone´;* from 857; an *entry:*—entrance.

2979. יְאָתְרַי **y^eâth^eray,** *yeh-aw-ther-ah´ee* from the same as 871; *stepping; Jeätherai,* an Isr.:—Jeaterai.

2980. יָבַב **yâbab,** *yaw-bab;* a prim. root; to *bawl:*—cry out.

2981. יְבוּל **y^ebûwl,** *yeb-ool´;* from 2986; *produce,* i.e. a *crop* or (fig.) *wealth:*—fruit, increase.

2982. יְבוּס **Y^ebûwç,** *yeb-oos´;* from 947; *trodden,* i.e. threshing-place; *Jebus,* the aboriginal name of Jerus.:—Jebus.

2983. יְבוּסִי **Yebûwçîy,** *yeb-oo-see´;* patrial from 2982; a *Jebusite* or inhab. of Jebus:—Jebusite(-s).

2984. יִבְחַר **Yibchar,** *yib-khar´;* from 977; *choice; Jibchar,* an Isr.:—Ibhar.

2985. יָבִין **Yâbîyn,** *yaw-bene´;* from 995; *intelligent; Jabin,* the name of two Canaanitish kings:—Jabin.

יָבֵישׁ **Yâbêysh.** See 3003.

2986. יָבַל **yâbal,** *yaw-bal´;* a prim. root; prop. to *flow;* causat. to *bring* (espec. with pomp):—bring (forth), carry, lead (forth).

2987. יְבַל **y^ebal** (Chald.), *yeb-al´;* corresp. to 2986; to *bring:*—bring, carry.

יֹבֵל **yôbêl.** See 3104.

2988. יָבָל **yâbâl,** *yaw-bawl´;* from 2986; a *stream:*—[water-] course, stream.

2989. יָבָל **Yâbâl,** *yaw-bawl´;* the same as 2988; *Jabal,* an antediluvian:—Jabal.

יֹבֵל **yôbêl.** See 3104.

2990. יַבֵּל **yabbêl,** *yab-bale´;* from 2986; having *running* sores:—wen.

2991. יִבְלְעָם **Yibl^e'âm,** *yib-leh-awm´;* from 1104 and 5971; *devouring people; Jibleäm,* a place in Pal.:—Ibleam.

2992. יָבַם **yâbam,** *yaw-bam´;* a prim. root of doubtful mean.; used only as a denom. from 2993; to *marry* a (deceased) brother's widow:—perform the duty of a husband's brother, marry.

2993. יָבָם **yâbâm,** *yaw-bawm´;* from (the orig. of) 2992; a *brother-in-law:*—husband's brother.

2994. יְבֵמֶת **y^ebêmeth,** *yeb-ay´-meth;* fem. part. of 2992; a *sister-in-law:*—brother's wife, sister in law.

2995. יַבְנְאֵל **Yabn^e'êl,** *yab-neh-ale´;* from 1129 and 410; *built of God; Jabneël,* the name of two places in Pal.:—Jabneel.

2996. יַבְנֶה **Yabneh,** *yab-neh´;* from 1129; a *building; Jabneh,* a place in Pal.:—Jabneh.

2997. יִבְנְיָה **Yibn^eyâh,** *yib-neh-yaw´;* from 1129 and 3050; *built of Jah; Jibnejah,* an Isr.:—Ibneiah.

2998. יִבְנִיָּה **Yibnîyâh,** *yib-nee-yaw´;* from 1129 and 3050; *building of Jah; Jibnijah,* an Isr.:—Ibnijah.

2999. יַבֹּק **Yabbôq,** *yab-boke´;* prob. from 1238; *pouring* forth; *Jabbok,* a river E. of the Jordan:—Jabbok.

3000. יְבֶרֶכְיָהוּ **Y^eberekyâhûw,** *yeb-eh-rek-yaw´-hoo;* from 1288 and 3050; *blessed of Jah; Jeberekjah,* an Isr.:—Jeberechiah.

3001. יָבֵשׁ **yâbêsh,** *yaw-bashe´;* a prim. root; to *be ashamed, confused* or *disappointed;* also (as failing) to *dry* up (as water) or *wither* (as herbage):—be ashamed, clean, be confounded, (make) dry (up), (do) shame (-fully), × utterly, wither (away).

3002. יָבֵשׁ **yâbêsh,** *yaw-bashe´;* from 3001: *dry:*—dried (away), dry.

3003. יָבֵשׁ **Yâbêsh,** *yaw-bashe´;* the same as 3002 (also יָבֵישׁ **Yâbêysh,** *yaw-bashe´;* often with the addition of 1568, i.e. *Jabesh of Gilad*); *Jabesh,* the name of an Isr. and of a place in Pal.:—Jabesh ([-Gilead]).

3004. יַבָּשָׁה **yabbâshâh,** *yab-baw-shaw´;* from 3001; *dry* ground:—dry (ground, land).

3005. יִבְשָׂם **Yibsâm,** *yib-sawm´;* from the same as 1314; *fragrant; Jibsam,* an Isr.:—Jibsam.

3006. יַבֶּשֶׁת **yabbesheth,** *yab-beh´-sheth;* a var. of 3004; *dry* ground:—dry land.

3007. יַבֶּשֶׁת **yabbesheth** (Chald.), *yab-beh´-sheth;* corresp. to 3006; *dry* land:—earth.

3008. יִגְאָל **Yig'âl,** *yig-awl´;* from 1350; *avenger; Jigal,* the name of three Isr.:—Igal, Igeal.

3009. יָגַב **yâgab,** *yaw-gab´;* a prim. root; to *dig* or plough:—husbandman.

3010. יָגֵב **yâgêb,** *yaw-gabe´;* from 3009; a ploughed *field:*—field.

3011. יָגְבְּהָה **Yogb^ehâh,** *yog-beh-haw´;* fem. from 1361; *hillock; Jogbehah,* a place E. of the Jordan:—Jogbehah.

3012. יִגְדַּלְיָהוּ **Yigdalyâhûw,** *yig-dal-yaw´-hoo;* from 1431 and 3050; *magnified of Jah; Jigdaljah,* an Isr.:—Igdaliah.

3013. יָגָה **yâgâh,** *yaw-gaw´;* a prim. root; to *grieve:*—afflict, cause grief, grieve, sorrowful, vex.

3014. יָגָה **yâgâh,** *yaw-gaw´;* a prim. root [prob. rather the same as 3013 through the common idea of *dissatisfaction*]; to *push* away:—be removed.

3015. יָגוֹן **yâgôwn,** *yaw-gohn´;* from 3013; *affliction:*—grief, sorrow.

3016. יָגוֹר **yâgôwr,** *yaw-gore´;* from 3025; *fearful:*—afraid, fearest.

3017. יָגוּר **Yâgûwr,** *yaw-goor´;* prob. from 1481; a *lodging; Jagur,* a place in Pal.:—Jagur.

3018. יְגִיעַ **y^egîya',** *yeg-ee´-ah;* from 3021; *toil;* hence a *work, produce, property* (as the result of labor):—labour, work.

3019. יָגִיעַ **yâgîya',** *yaw-ghee´-ah;* from 3021; *tired:*—weary.

3020. יָגְלִי **Yoglîy,** *yog-lee´;* from 1540; *exiled; Jogli,* an Isr.:—Jogli.

3021. יָגַע **yâga',** *yaw-gah´;* a prim. root; prop. to *gasp;* hence to *be exhausted,* to *tire,* to *toil:*—faint, (make to) labour, (be) weary.

3022. יָגָע **yâgâ',** *yaw-gaw´;* from 3021; *earnings* (as the product of toil):—that which he laboured for.

3023. יָגֵעַ **yâgêa',** *yaw-gay´-ah;* from 3021; *tired;* hence (trans.) *tiresome:*—full of labour, weary.

3024. יְגִעָה **y^egî'âh,** *yeg-ee-aw´;* fem. of 3019; *fatigue:*—weariness.

3025. יָגֹר **yâgôr,** *yaw-gore´;* a prim. root; to *fear:*—be afraid, fear.

3026. יְגַר שָׂהֲדוּתָא **Y^egar Sahădûwthâ'** (Chald.), *yegar´ sah-had-oo-thaw´;* from a word derived from an unused root (mean. to *gather*) and a der. of a root corresp. to 7717; *heap of the testimony; Jegar-Sahadutha,* a cairn E. of the Jordan:—Jegar-Sahadutha.

3027. יָד **yâd,** *yawd;* a prim. word; a *hand* (the *open* one [indicating *power, means, direction,* etc.], in distinction from 3709, the *closed* one); used (as noun, adv., etc.) in a great variety of applications, both lit. and fig., both proximate and remote [as follow]:—(+ be) able, × about, + armholes, at, axletree, because of, beside, border, × bounty, + broad, [broken-] handed, × by, charge, coast, + consecrate, + creditor, custody, debt, dominion, × enough, + fellowship, force, × from, hand [-staves, -y work], × he, himself, × in, labour, + large, ledge, [left-] handed, means, × mine, ministry, near, × of, × order, ordinance, × our, parts, pain, power, × presumptuously, service, side, sore, state, stay, draw with strength, stroke, + swear, terror, × thee, × by them, × themselves, × thine own, × thou, through, × throwing, + thumb, times, × to, × under, × us, × wait on, [way-] side, where, + wide, × with (him, me, you), work, + yield, × yourselves.

3028. יַד **yad,** (Chald.), *yad;* corresp. to 3027:—hand, power.

3029. יְדָא **y^edâ'** (Chald.), *yed-aw´;* corresp. to 3034; to *praise:*—(give) thank (-s).

3030. יִדְאֲלָה **Yidălâh,** *yid-al-aw´;* of uncert. der. *Jidalah,* a place in Pal.:—Idalah.

3031. יִדְבָּשׁ **Yidbâsh,** *yid-bawsh´;* from the same as 1706; perh. *honeyed; Jidbash,* an Isr.:—Idbash.

3032. יָדַד **yâdad,** *yaw-dad´;* a prim. root; prop. to *handle* [comp. 3034], i.e. to *throw,* e.g. lots:—cast.

3033. יְדִדוּת **yᵉdîdûwth,** *yed-ee-dooth´;* from 3039; prop. *affection;* concr. a *darling* object:—dearly beloved.

3034. יָדָה **yâdâh,** *yaw-daw´;* a prim. root; used only as denom. from 3027; lit. to *use* (i.e. hold out) *the hand;* phys. to *throw* (a stone, an arrow) at or away; espec. to *revere* or *worship* (with extended hands); intens. to *bemoan* (by wringing the hands):—cast (out), (make) confess (-ion), praise, shoot, (give) thank (-ful, -s, -sgiving).

3035. יִדּוֹ **Yiddôw,** *yid-do´;* from 3034; *praised; Jiddo,* an Isr.:—Iddo.

3036. יָדוֹן **Yâdôwn,** *yaw-done´;* from 3034; *thankful; Jadon,* an Isr.:—Jadon.

3037. יַדּוּעַ **Yaddûwaʻ,** *yad-doo´-ah;* from 3045; *knowing; Jadduä,* the name of two Isr.:—Jaddua.

3038. יְדוּתוּן **Yᵉdûwthûwn,** *yed-oo-thoon´;* or יְדֻתוּן **Yᵉdûthûwn,** *yed-oo-thoon´;* or יְדִיתוּן **Yᵉdîythûwn,** *yed-ee-thoon´;* prob. from 3034; *laudatory; Jeduthun,* an Isr.:—Jeduthun.

3039. יְדִיד **yᵉdîyd,** *yed-eed´;* from the same as 1730; *loved:*—amiable, (well-) beloved, loves.

3040. יְדִידָה **Yᵉdîydâh,** *yed-ee-daw´;* fem. of 3039; *beloved; Jedidah,* an Israelitess:—Jedidah.

3041. יְדִידְיָה **Yᵉdîydᵉyâh,** *yed-ee-deh-yaw´;* from 3039 and 3050; *beloved of Jah; Jedidejah,* a name of Solomon:—Jedidiah.

3042. יְדָיָה **Yᵉdâyâh,** *yed-aw-yaw´;* from 3034 and 3050; *praised of Jah; Jedajah,* the name of two Isr.:—Jedaiah.

3043. יְדִיעֲאֵל **Yᵉdîyʻăʼêl,** *yed-ee-ah-ale´;* from 3045 and 410; *knowing God; Jediaël,* the name of three Isr.:—Jediael.

3044. יִדְלָף **Yidlâph,** *yid-lawf´;* from 1811; *tearful; Jidlaph,* a Mesopotamian:—Jidlaph.

3045. יָדַע **yâdaʻ,** *yaw-dah´;* a prim. root; to *know* (prop. to ascertain by *seeing*); used in a great variety of senses, fig., lit., euphem. and infer. (including *observation, care, recognition,* and causat. *instruction, designation, punishment,* etc.) [as follow]:—acknowledge, acquaintance (-ted with), advise, answer, appoint, assuredly, be aware, [un-] awares, can [-not], certainly, for a certainty, comprehend, consider, × could they, cunning, declare, be diligent, (can, cause to) discern, discover, endued with, familiar friend, famous, feel, can have, be [ig-] norant, instruct, kinsfolk, kinsman, (cause to, let, make) know, (come to give, have, take) knowledge, have [knowledge], (be, make, make to be, make self) known, + be learned, + lie by man, mark, perceive, privy to, × prognosticator, regard, have respect, skilful, shew, can (man of) skill, be sure, of a surety, teach, (can) tell, understand, have [understanding], × will be, wist, wit, wot.

3046. יְדַע **yᵉdaʻ** (Chald.), *yed-ah´;* corresp. to 3045:—certify, know, make known, teach.

3047. יָדָע **Yâdâʻ,** *yaw-daw´;* from 3045; *knowing; Jada,* an Isr.:—Jada.

3048. יְדַעְיָה **Yᵉdaʻyâh,** *yed-ah-yaw´;* from 3045 and 3050; *Jah has known; Jedajah,* the name of two Isr.:—Jedaiah.

3049. יִדְּעֹנִי **yiddᵉʻônîy,** *yid-deh-o-nee´;* from 3045; prop. a *knowing* one; spec. a *conjurer;* (by impl.) a *ghost:*—wizard.

3050. יָהּ **Yâhh,** *yaw;* contr. for 3068, and mean. the same; *Jah,* the sacred name:—Jah, the Lord, most vehement. Cp. names in "-iah," "-jah."

3051. יָהַב **yâhab,** *yaw-hab´;* a prim. root; to *give* (whether lit. or fig.); gen. to *put;* imper. (reflex.) *come:*—ascribe, bring, come on, give, go, set, take.

3052. יְהַב **yᵉhab** (Chald.), *yeh-hab´;* corresp. to 3051:—deliver, give, lay, + prolong, pay, yield.

3053. יְהָב **yᵉhâb,** *yeh-hawb´;* from 3051; prop. what is *given* (by Providence), i.e. a *lot:*—burden.

3054. יָהַד **yâhad,** *yaw-had´;* denom. from a form corresp. to 3061; to *Judaize,* i.e. become Jewish:—become Jews.

3055. יְהֻד **Yᵉhûd,** *yeh-hood´;* a briefer form of one corresp. to 3061; *Jehud,* a place in Pal.:—Jehud.

3056. יֶהְדַי **Yehday,** *yeh-dah´ee;* perh. from a form corresp. to 3061; *Judaistic; Jehdai,* an Isr.:—Jehdai.

3057. יְהֻדִיָּה **Yᵉhûdîyâh,** *yeh-hoo-dee-yaw´;* fem. of 3064; *Jehudijah,* a Jewess:—Jehudijah.

3058. יֵהוּא **Yêhûwʼ,** *yay-hoo´;* from 3068 and 1931; *Jehovah* (is) *He; Jehu,* the name of five Isr.:—Jehu.

3059. יְהוֹאָחָז **Yᵉhowʼâchâz,** *yeh-ho-aw-khawz´;* from 3068 and 270; *Jehovah-seized; Jehoächaz,* the name of three Isr.:—Jehoahaz. Comp. 3099.

3060. יְהוֹאָשׁ **Yᵉhôwʼâsh,** *yeh-ho-awsh´;* from 3068 and (perh.) 784; *Jehovah-fired; Jehoäsh,* the name of two Isr. kings:—Jehoash Comp. 3101.

3061. יְהוּד **Yᵉhûwd** (Chald.), *yeh-hood´;* contr. from a form corresp. to 3063; prop. *Judah,* hence *Judæa:*—Jewry, Judah, Judea.

3062. יְהוּדָאִי **Yᵉhûwdâʼîy** (Chald.), *yeh-hoo-daw-ee´;* patrial from 3061; a *Jehudaïte* (or Judaite), i.e. Jew:—Jew.

3063. יְהוּדָה **Yᵉhûwdâh,** *yeh-hoo-daw´;* from 3034; *celebrated; Jehudah* (or Judah), the name of five Isr.; also of the tribe descended from the first, and of its territory:—Judah.

3064. יְהוּדִי **Yᵉhûwdîy,** *yeh-hoo-dee´;* patron. from 3063; a *Jehudite* (i.e. Judaite or Jew), or desc. of Jehudah (i.e. Judah):—Jew.

3065. יְהוּדִי **Yᵉhûwdîy,** *yeh-hoo-dee´;* the same as 3064; *Jehudi,* an Isr.:—Jehudi.

3066. יְהוּדִית **Yᵉhûwdîyth,** *yeh-hoo-deeth´;* fem. of 3064; the *Jewish* (used adv.) language:—in the Jews' language.

3067. יְהוּדִית **Yᵉhûwdîyth,** *yeh-hoo-deeth´;* the same as 3066; *Jewess; Jehudith,* a Canaanitess:—Judith.

3068. יְהֹוָה **Yᵉhôvâh,** *yeh-ho-vaw´;* from 1961; (the) self-*Existent* or Eternal; *Jeho-vah,* Jewish national name of God:—Jehovah, the Lord. Comp. 3050, 3069.

3069. יְהֹוִה **Yᵉhôvîh,** *yeh-ho-vee´;* a var. of 3068 [used after 136, and pronounced by Jews as 430, in order to prevent the repetition of the same sound, since they elsewhere pronounce 3068 as 136]:—God.

3070. יְהֹוָה יִרְאֶה **Yᵉhôvâh yireh,** *yeh-ho-vaw´ yir-eh´;* from 3068 and 7200; *Jehovah will see* (to it); *Jehovah-Jireh,* a symbolical name for Mt. Moriah:—Jehovah-jireh.

3071. יְהֹוָה נִסִּי **Yᵉhôvâh niççîy,** *yeh-ho-vaw´ nis-see´;* from 3068 and 5251 with pron. suffix.; *Jehovah* (is) *my banner; Jehovah-Nissi,* a symbolical name of an altar in the Desert.—Jehovah-nissi.

3072. יְהֹוָה צִדְקֵנוּ **Yᵉhôvâh tsidqênûw,** *yeh-ho-vaw´ tsid-kay´-noo;* from 3068 and 6664 with pron. suffix.; *Jehovah* (is) *our right; Jehovah-Tsidkenu,* a symbolical epithet of the Messiah and of Jerus.:—the Lord our righteousness.

3073. יְהֹוָה שָׁלוֹם **Yᵉhôvâh shâlôwm,** *yeh-ho-vaw´ shaw-lome´;* from 3068 and 7965; *Jehovah* (is) *peace; Jehovah-Shalom,* a symbolical name of an altar in Pal.:—Jehovah-shalom.

3074. יְהֹוָה שָׁמָּה **Yᵉhôvâh shâmmâh,** *yeh-ho-vaw´ shawm´-maw;* from 3068 and 8033 with directive enclitic; *Jehovah* (is) *thither; Jehovah-Shammah,* a symbol. title of Jerus.:—Jehovah-shammah.

3075. יְהוֹזָבָד **Yᵉhôwzâbâd,** *yeh-ho-zaw-bawd´;* from 3068 and 2064; *Jehovah-endowed; Jehozabad,* the name of three Isr.:—Jehozabad. Comp. 3107.

3076. יְהוֹחָנָן **Yᵉhôwchânân,** *yeh-ho-khaw-nawn´;* from 3068 and 2603; *Jehovah-favored; Jehochanan,* the name of eight Isr.:—Jehohanan, Johanan. Comp. 3110.

3077. יְהוֹיָדָע **Yᵉhôwyâdâʻ,** *yeh-ho-yaw-daw´;* from 3068 and 3045; *Jehovah-known; Jehojada,* the name of three Isr.:—Jehoiada. Comp. 3111.

3078. יְהוֹיָכִין **Yᵉhôwyâkîyn,** *yeh-ho-yaw-keen´;* from 3068 and 3559; *Jehovah will establish; Jehojakin,* a Jewish king:—Jehoiachin. Comp. 3112.

3079. יְהוֹיָקִים **Yᵉhôwyâqîym,** *yeh-ho-yaw-keem´;* from 3068 abbrev. and 6965; *Jehovah will raise; Jehojakim,* a Jewish king:—Jehoiakim. Comp. 3113.

3080. יְהוֹיָרִיב **Yᵉhôwyârîyb,** *yeh-ho-yaw-reeb´;* from 3068 and 7378; *Jehovah will contend; Jehojarib,* the name of two Isr.:—Jehoiarib. Comp. 3114.

3081. יְהוּכַל **Yᵉhûwkal,** *yeh-hoo-kal´;* from 3201; *potent; Jehukal,* an Isr.:—Jehucal. Comp. 3116.

3082. יְהוֹנָדָב **Yᵉhôwnâdâb,** *yeh-ho-naw-dawb´;* from 3068 and 5068; *Jehovah-largessed; Jehonadab,* the name of an Isr. and of an Arab:—Jehonadab, Jonadab. Comp. 3122.

3083. יְהוֹנָתָן **Yᵉhôwnâthân,** *yeh-ho-naw-thawn´;* from 3068 and 5414; *Jehovah-given; Jehonathan,* the name of four Isr.:—Jonathan. Comp. 3129.

3084. יְהוֹסֵף **Yᵉhôwçêph,** *yeh-ho-safe´;* a fuller form of 3130; *Jehoseph* (i.e. Joseph), a son of Jacob:—Joseph.

3085. יְהוֹעַדָּה **Yᵉhôwʻaddâh,** *yeh-ho-ad-daw´;* from 3068 and 5710; *Jehovah-adorned; Jehoäddah,* an Isr.:—Jehoada.

3086. יְהוֹעַדִּין **Yᵉhôwʻaddîyn,** *yeh-ho-ad-deen´;* or יְהוֹעַדָּן **Yᵉhôwʻaddân,** *yeh-ho-ad-dawn´;* from 3068 and 5727; *Jehovah-pleased; Jehoäddin* or *Jehoäddan,* an Israelitess:—Jehoaddan.

3087. יְהוֹצָדָק **Yᵉhôwtsâdâq,** *yeh-ho-tsaw-dawk´;* from 3068 and 6663; *Jehovah-righted; Jehotsadak,* an Isr.:—Jehozadek, Josedech. Comp. 3136.

3088. יְהוֹרָם **Yᵉhôwrâm,** *yeh-ho-rawm´;* from 3068 and 7311; *Jehovah-raised; Jehoram,* the name of a Syrian and of three Isr.:—Jehoram, Joram. Comp. 3141.

3089. יְהוֹשֶׁבַע **Yᵉhôwshebaʻ,** *yeh-ho-sheh´-bah;* from 3068 and 7650; *Jehovah-sworn; Jehosheba,* an Israelitess:—Jehosheba. Comp. 3090.

3090. יְהוֹשַׁבְעַת **Yᵉhôwshabʻath,** *yeh-ho-shab-ath´;* a form of 3089; *Jehoshabath,* an Israelitess:—Jehoshabeath.

3091. יְהוֹשׁוּעַ **Yᵉhôwshûwaʻ,** *yeh-ho-shoo´-ah;* or יְהוֹשֻׁעַ **Yᵉhôwshûʻa,** *yeh-ho-shoo´-ah;* from 3068 and 3467; *Jehovah-saved; Jehoshuä* (i.e. Joshua), the Jewish leader:—Jehoshua, Jehoshuah, Joshua. Comp. 1954, 3442.

3092. יְהוֹשָׁפָט **Yᵉhôwshâphâṭ,** *yeh-ho-shaw-fawt´;* from 3068 and 8199; *Jehovah-judged; Jehoshaphat,* the name of six Isr.; also of a valley near Jerus.:—Jehoshaphat. Comp. 3146.

3093. יָהִיר **yâhîyr,** *yaw-here´;* prob. from the same as 2022; *elated;* hence *arrogant:*—haughty, proud.

3094. יְהַלֶּלְאֵל **Yᵉhallelʼêl,** *yeh-hal-lel-ale´;* from 1984 and 410; *praising God; Jehallelel,* the name of two Isr.:—Jehaleleel, Jehalelel.

3095. יַהֲלֹם **yahălôm,** *yah-hal-ome´;* from 1986 (in the sense of *hardness*); a precious stone, prob. *onyx:*—diamond.

3096. יַהַץ **Yahats,** *yah´-hats;* or יַהְצָה **Yahtsâh,** *yah´-tsaw;* or (fem.) יַהְצָה **Yahtsâh,** *yah-tsaw´;* from an unused root mean. to *stamp;* perh. *threshing*-floor; *Jahats* or *Jahtsah,* a place E. of the Jordan:—Jahaz, Jahazah, Jahzah.

3097. יוֹאָב **Yôwʼâb,** *yo-awb´;* from 3068 and 1; *Jehovah-fathered; Joäb,* the name of three Isr.:—Joab.

3098. יוֹאָח **Yôwʼâch,** *yo-awkh´;* from 3068 and 251; *Jehovah-brothered; Joach,* the name of four Isr.:—Joah.

3099. יוֹאָחָז **Yôwʼâchâz,** *yo-aw-khawz´;* a form of 3059; *Joächaz,* the name of two Isr.:—Jehoahaz, Joahaz.

3100. יוֹאֵל **Yôwʼêl,** *yo-ale´;* from 3068 and 410; *Jehovah* (is his) *God; Joël,* the name of twelve Isr.:—Joel.

3101. יוֹאָשׁ **Yôwʼâsh,** *yo-awsh´;* or יֹאָשׁ **Yôʼâsh** (2 Chron. 24 : 1), *yo-awsh´;* a form of 3060; *Joäsh,* the name of six Isr.:—Joash.

3102. יוֹב **Yôwb,** *yobe;* perh. a form of 3103, but more prob. by err. transc. for 3437; *Job,* an Isr.:—Job.

3103. יוֹבָב **Yôwbâb,** *yo-bawb´;* from 2980; *howler; Jobab,* the name of two Isr. and of three foreigners:—Jobab.

3104. יוֹבֵל **yôwbêl,** *yo-bale´;* or יֹבֵל **yôbêl,** *yo-bale´;* appar. from 2986; the *blast* of a horn (from its *continuous* sound); spec. the *signal* of the silver trumpets; hence the instrument itself and the festival thus introduced:—jubile, ram's horn, trumpet.

3105. יוּבַל **yûwbal,** *yoo-bal´;* from 2986; a *stream:*—river.

3106. יוּבָל **Yûwbâl,** *yoo-bawl´;* from 2986; *stream; Jubal,* an antediluvian:—Jubal.

3107. יוֹזָבָד **Yôwzâbâd,** *yo-zaw-bawd´;* a form of 3075; *Jozabad,* the name of ten Isr:—Josabad, Jozabad.

3108. יוֹזָכָר **Yôwzâkâr,** *yo-zaw-kawr´;* from 3068 and 2142; *Jehovah-remembered; Jozacar,* an Isr.:—Jozacar.

3109. יוֹחָא **Yôwchâʼ,** *yo-khaw´;* prob. from 3068 and a var. of 2421; *Jehovah-revived; Jocha,* the name of two Isr.:—Joha.

3110. יוֹחָנָן **Yôwchânân,** *yo-khaw-nawn´;* a form of 3076; *Jochanan,* the name of nine Isr.:—Johanan.

יוּטָה **Yûwṭâh.** See 3194.

3111. יוֹיָדָע **Yôwyâdâʻ,** *yo-yaw-daw´;* a form of 3077; *Jojada,* the name of two Isr.:—Jehoiada, Joiada.

3112. יוֹיָכִין **Yôwyâkîyn,** *yo-yaw-keen´;* a form of 3078; *Jojakin,* an Isr. king:—Jehoiachin.

3113. יוֹיָקִים **Yôwyâqîym,** *yo-yaw-keem´;* a form of 3079; *Jojakim,* an Isr.:—Joiakim. Comp. 3137.

3114. יוֹיָרִיב **Yôwyârîyb,** *yo-yaw-reeb´;* a form of 3080; *Jojarib,* the name of four Isr.:—Joiarib.

3115. יוֹכֶבֶד **Yôwkebed,** *yo-keh´-bed;* from 3068 contr. and 3513; *Jehovah-gloried; Jokebed,* the mother of Moses:—Jochebed.

3116. יוּכַל **Yûwkal,** *yoo-kal´;* a form of 3081; *Jukal,* an Isr.:—Jucal.

3117. יוֹם **yôwm,** *yome;* from an unused root mean. to *be hot;* a *day* (as the *warm* hours), whether lit. (from sunrise to sunset, or from one sunset to the next), or fig. (a space of time defined by an associated term), [often used adv.]:—age, + always, + chronicles, continually (-ance), daily, ([birth-], each, to) day, (now a, two) days (agone), + elder, × end, + evening, + (for) ever (-lasting, -more), × full, life, as (so) long as (. . . live), (even) now, + old, + outlived, + perpetually, presently, + remaineth, × required, season, × since, space, then, (process of) time, + as at other times, + in trouble, weather, (as) when, (a, the, within a) while (that), × whole (+ age), (full) year (-ly), + younger.

3118. יוֹם **yôwm** (Chald.), *yome;* corresp. to 3117; a *day:*—day (by day), time.

3119. יוֹמָם **yôwmâm,** *yo-mawm´;* from 3117; *daily:*—daily, (by, in the) day (-time).

3120. יָוָן **Yâvân,** *yaw-vawn´;* prob. from the same as 3196; *effervescing* (i.e. hot and active); *Javan,* the name of a son of Japheth, and of the race (*Ionians,* i.e. Greeks) descended from him, with their territory; also of a place in Arabia:—Javan.

3121. יָוֵן **yâvên,** *yaw-ven´;* from the same as 3196; prop. *dregs* (as *effervescing*); hence *mud:*—mire, miry.

3122. יוֹנָדָב **Yôwnâdâb,** *yo-naw-dawb´;* a form of 3082; *Jonadab,* the name of an Isr. and of a Rechabite:—Jonadab.

3123. יוֹנָה **yôwnâh,** *yo-naw´;* prob. from the same as 3196; a *dove* (appar. from the *warmth* of their mating):—dove, pigeon.

3124. יוֹנָה **Yônâh,** *yo-naw´;* the same as 3123; *Jonah,* an Isr.:—Jonah.

3125. יְוָנִי **Yᵉvânîy,** *yev-aw-nee´;* patron. from 3121; a *Jevanite,* or desc. of Javan:—Grecian.

3126. יוֹנֵק **yôwnêq,** *yo-nake´;* act. part. of 3243; a *sucker;* hence a *twig* (of a tree felled and sprouting):—tender plant.

3127. יוֹנֶקֶת **yôwneqeth,** *yo-neh´-keth;* fem. of 3126; a *sprout:*—(tender) branch, young twig.

3128. יוֹנַת אֵלֶם רְחֹקִים **yôwnath ʼêlem rᵉchôqîym,** *yo-nath´ ay´-lem rekh-o-kheem´;* from 3123 and 482 and the plur. of 7350; *dove of* (the) *silence* (i.e. *dumb* Israel) *of* (i.e. among) *distances* (i.e. strangers); the title of a ditty (used for a name of its melody):—Jonath-elem-rechokim.

3129. יוֹנָתָן **Yôwnâthân,** *yo-naw-thawn´;* a form of 3083; *Jonathan,* the name of ten Isr.:—Jonathan.

3130. יוֹסֵף **Yôwçêph,** *yo-safe´;* fut. of 3254; *let him add* (or perh. simply act. part. *adding*); *Joseph,* the name of seven Isr.:—Joseph. Comp. 3084.

3131. יוֹסִפְיָה **Yôwçiphyâh,** *yo-sif-yaw´;* from act. part. of 3254 and 3050; *Jah* (is) *adding; Josiphjah,* an Isr.:—Josiphiah.

3132. יוֹעֵאלָה **Yôwʻêʼlâh,** *yo-ay-law´;* perh. fem. act. part. of 3276; *furthermore; Joelah,* an Isr.:—Joelah.

3133. יוֹעֵד **Yôwʻêd,** *yo-ade´;* appar. act. part. of 3259; *appointer; Joed,* an Isr.:—Joed.

3134. יוֹעֶזֶר **Yôwʻezer,** *yo-eh´-zer;* from 3068 and 5828; *Jehovah* (is his) *help; Joezer,* an Isr.:—Joezer.

3135. יוֹעָשׁ **Yôwʻâsh,** *yo-awsh´;* from 3068 and 5789; *Jehovah-hastened; Joash,* the name of two Isr.:—Joash.

3136. יוֹצָדָק **Yôwtsâdâq,** *yo-tsaw-dawk´;* a form of 3087; *Jotsadak,* an Isr.:—Jozadak.

3137. יוֹקִים **Yôwqîym,** *yo-keem´;* a form of 3113; *Jokim,* an Isr.:—Jokim.

3138. יוֹרֶה **yôwreh,** *yo-reh´;* act. part. of 3384; *sprinkling;* hence a *sprinkling* (or autumnal showers):—first rain, former [rain].

3139. יוֹרָה **Yôwrâh,** *yo-raw´;* from 3384; *rainy; Jorah,* an Isr.:—Jorah.

3140. יוֹרַי **Yôwray,** *yo-rah´-ee;* from 3384; *rainy; Jorai,* an Isr.:—Jorai.

3141. יוֹרָם **Yôwrâm,** *yo-rawm´;* a form of 3088; *Joram,* the name of three Isr. and one Syrian:—Joram.

3142. יוּשַׁב חֶסֶד **Yûwshab Cheçed,** *yoo-shab´ kheh´-sed;* from 7725 and 2617; *kindness will be returned; Jushab-Chesed,* an Isr.:—Jushab-heshed.

3143. יוֹשִׁבְיָה **Yôwshîbyâh,** *yo-shib-yaw´;* from 3427 and 3050; *Jehovah will cause to dwell; Joshibjah,* an isr.:—Josibiah.

3144. יוֹשָׁה **Yôwshâh,** *yo-shaw´;* prob. a form of 3145; *Joshah,* an Isr.:—Joshah.

3145. יוֹשַׁוְיָה **Yôwshavyâh,** *yo-shav-yaw´;* from 3068 and 7737; *Jehovah-set; Joshavjah,* an Isr.:—Joshaviah. Comp. 3144.

3146. יוֹשָׁפָט **Yôwshâphâṭ,** *yo-shaw-fawt´;* a form of 3092; *Joshaphat,* an Isr.:—Joshaphat.

3147. יוֹתָם **Yôwthâm,** *yo-thawm´;* from 3068 and 8535; *Jehovah* (is) *perfect; Jotham,* the name of three Isr.:—Jotham.

3148. יוֹתֵר **yôwthêr,** *yo-thare´;* act. part. of 3498; prop. *redundant;* hence *over and above,* as adj., noun, adv. or conj. [as follows]:—better, more (-over), over, profit.

3149. יְזַוְאֵל° **Y^{e}zav'êl,** *yez-av-ale´;* from an unused root (mean. to *sprinkle*) and 410; *sprinkled of God; Jezavel,* an Isr.:—Jeziel [*from the marg.*].

3150. יִזִּיָּה **Yizzîyâh,** *yiz-zee-yaw´;* from the same as the first part of 3149 and 3050; *sprinkled of Jah; Jizzijah,* an Isr.:—Jeziah.

3151. יָזִיז **Yâzîyz** *yaw-zeez´;* from the same as 2123; *he will make prominent; Jaziz,* an Isr.:—Jaziz.

3152. יִזְלִיאָה **Yizlîy'ah,** *yiz-lee-aw´;* perh. from an unused root (mean. to *draw up*); *he will draw out; Jizliah,* an Isr.:—Jezliah.

3153. יְזַנְיָה **Y^{e}zanyâh,** *yez-an-yaw´;* or יְזַנְיָהוּ **Y^{e}zanyâhûw,** *yez-an-yaw´-hoo;* prob. for 2970; *Jezanjah,* an Isr.:—Jezaniah.

3154. יֶזַע **yezaʻ,** *yeh´-zah;* from an unused root mean. to *ooze; sweat,* i.e. (by impl.) a *sweating* dress:—any thing that causeth sweat.

3155. יִזְרָח **Yizrâch,** *yiz-rawkh´;* a var. for 250; a *Jizrach* (i.e. Ezrachite or Zarchite) or desc. of Zerach:—Izrahite.

3156. יִזְרַחְיָה **Yizrachyâh,** *yiz-rakh-yaw´;* from 2224 and 3050; *Jah will shine; Jizrachjah,* the name of two Isr.:—Izrahiah, Jezrahiah.

3157. יִזְרְעֶאל **Yizr^{e}ʻê'l,** *yiz-reh-ale´;* from 2232 and 410; *God will sow; Jizreël,* the name of two places in Pal. and of two Isr.:—Jezreel.

3158. יִזְרְעֵאלִי **Yizr^{e}ʻê'lîy,** *yiz-reh-ay-lee´;* patron. from 3157; a *Jizreëlite* or native of Jizreel:—Jezreelite.

3159. יִזְרְעֵאלִית **Yizr^{e}ʻê'lîyth,** *yiz-reh-ay-leeth´;* fem. of 3158; a *Jezreëlitess:*—Jezreelitess.

3160. יְחֻבָּה **Y^{e}chubbâh,** *yekh-oob-baw´;* from 2247; *hidden; Jechubbah,* an Isr.:—Jehubbah.

3161. יָחַד **yâchad,** *yaw-khad´;* a prim. root; to *be* (or become) *one:*—join, unite.

3162. יַחַד **yachad,** *yakh´-ad;* from 3161; prop. a *unit,* i.e. (adv.) *unitedly:*—alike, at all (once), both, likewise, only, (al-) together, withal.

3163. יַחְדוֹ **Yachdôw,** *yakh-doe´;* from 3162 with pron. suffix; *his unity,* i.e. (adv.) *together; Jachdo,* an Isr.:—Jahdo.

3164. יַחְדִּיאֵל **Yachdîy'êl,** *yakh-dee-ale´;* from 3162 and 410; *unity of God; Jachdiël,* an Isr.:—Jahdiel.

3165. יֶחְדְּיָהוּ **Yechdîyâhûw,** *yekh-dee-yaw´-hoo;* from 3162 and 3050; *unity of Jah; Jechdijah,* the name of two Isr.:—Jehdeiah.

יְחַוְאֵל **Y^{e}chav'êl.** See 3171.

3166. יַחֲזִיאֵל **Yachăzîy'êl,** *yahk-az-ee-ale´;* from 2372 and 410; *beheld of God; Jachaziël,* the name of five Isr.:—Jahaziel, Jahziel.

3167. יַחְזְיָה **Yachz^{e}yâh,** *yakh-zeh-yaw´;* from 2372 and 3050; *Jah will behold; Jachzejah,* an Isr.:—Jahaziah.

3168. יְחֶזְקֵאל **Y^{e}chezqê'l,** *yekh-ez-kale´;* from 2388 and 410; *God will strengthen; Jechezkel,* the name of two Isr.:—Ezekiel, Jehezekel.

3169. יְחִזְקִיָּה **Y^{e}chizqîyâh,** *yekh-iz-kee-yaw´;* or יְחִזְקִיָּהוּ **Y^{e}chizqîyâhûw,** *yekh-iz-kee-yaw´-hoo;* from 3388 and 3050; *strengthened of Jah; Jechizkijah,* the name of five Isr.:—Hezekiah, Jehizkiah. Comp. 2396.

3170. יַחְזֵרָה **Yachzêrâh,** *yakh-zay-raw´;* from the same as 2386; perh. *protection; Jachzerah,* an Isr.:—Jahzerah.

3171. יְחִיאֵל **Y^{e}chîy'êl,** *yekh-ee-ale´;* or (2 Chron. 29 : 14) יְחַוְאֵל° **Y^{e}chav'êl,** *yekh-av-ale´;* from 2421 and 410; *God will live; Jechiël* (or *Jechavel*), the name of eight Isr.:—Jehiel.

3172. יְחִיאֵלִי **Y^{e}chîy'êlîy,** *yekh-ee-ay-lee´;* patron. from 3171; a *Jechiëlite* or desc. of Jechiel:—Jehieli.

3173. יָחִיד **yâchîyd,** *yaw-kheed´;* from 3161; prop. *united,* i.e. *sole;* by impl. *beloved;* also *lonely:* (fem.) the *life* (as not to be replaced):—darling, desolate, only (child, son), solitary.

3174. יְחִיָּה **Y^{e}chîyâh,** *yekh-ee-yaw´;* from 2421 and 3050; *Jah will live; Jechijah,* an Isr.:—Jehiah.

3175. יָחִיל **yâchîyl,** *yaw-kheel´;* from 3176; *expectant:*—should hope.

3176. יָחַל **yâchal,** *yaw-chal´;* a prim. root; to *wait;* by impl. to *be patient, hope:*—(cause to, have, make to) hope, be pained, stay, tarry, trust, wait.

3177. יַחְלְאֵל **Yachl^{e}'êl,** *yakh-leh-ale´;* from 3176 and 410; *expectant of God; Jachleël,* an Isr.:—Jahleel.

3178. יַחְלְאֵלִי **Yachl^{e}'êlîy,** *yakh-leh-ay-lee´;* patron. from 3177; a *Jachleëlite* or desc. of Jachleel.:—Jahleelites.

3179. יָחַם **yâcham,** *yaw-kham´;* a prim. root; prob. to *be hot;* fig. to *conceive:*—get heat, be hot, conceive, be warm.

3180. יַחְמוּר **yachmûwr,** *yakh-moor´;* from 2560; a kind of *deer* (from the color; comp. 2543):—fallow deer.

3181. יַחְמַי **Yachmay,** *yakh-mah´-ee;* prob. from 3179; *hot; Jachmai,* an Isr.:—Jahmai.

3182. יָחֵף **yâchêph,** *yaw-khafe´;* from an unused root mean. to *take off the shoes; unsandalled:*—barefoot, being unshod.

3183. יַחְצְאֵל **Yachts^{e}'êl,** *yakh-tseh-ale´;* from 2673 and 410; *God will allot; Jachtseël,* an Isr.:—Jahzeel. Comp. 3185.

3184. יַחְצְאֵלִי **Yachts^{e}'êlîy,** *yakh-tseh-ay-lee´;* patron. from 3183; a *Jachtseëlite* (collect.) or desc. of Jachtseel:—Jahzeelites.

3185. יַחְצִיאֵל **Yachtsîy'êl,** *yakh-tsee-ale´;* from 2673 and 410; *allotted of God; Jachtsiël,* an Isr.:—Jahziel. Comp. 3183.

3186. יָחַר **yâchar,** *yaw-khar´;* a prim. root; to *delay:*—tarry longer.

3187. יָחַשׂ **yâchas,** *yaw-khas´;* a prim. root; to *sprout;* used only as denom. from 3188; to *enroll* by pedigree:—(number after, number throughout the) genealogy (to be reckoned), be reckoned by genealogies.

3188. יַחַשׂ **yachas,** *yakh´-as;* from 3187; a *pedigree* or family list (as *growing* spontaneously):—genealogy.

3189. יַחַת **Yachath,** *yakh´-ath;* from 3161; *unity; Jachath,* the name of four Isr.:—Jahath.

3190. יָטַב **yâṭab,** *yaw-tab´;* a prim. root; to *be* (causat.) *make well,* lit. (*sound, beautiful*) or fig. (*happy, successful, right*):—be accepted, amend, use aright, benefit, be (make) better, seem best, make cheerful, be comely, + be content, diligent (-ly), dress, earnestly, find favour, give, be glad, do (be, make) good ([-ness]), be (make) merry, please (+ well), shew more [kindness], skilfully, × very small, surely, make sweet, thoroughly, tire, trim, very, be (can, deal, entreat, go, have) well [said, seen].

3191. יְטַב **yeṭab** (Chald.), *yet-ab´;* corresp. to 3190:—seem good.

3192. יָטְבָה **Yoṭbâh,** *yot-baw´;* from 3190; *pleasantness; Jotbah,* a place in Pal.:—Jotbah.

3193. יָטְבָתָה **Yoṭbâthâh,** *yot-baw´-thaw;* from 3192; *Jotbathah,* a place in the Desert:—Jotbath, Jotbathah.

3194. יֻטָּה **Yuṭṭah,** *yoot-taw´;* or יוּטָה **Yûwṭâh,** *yoo-taw´;* from 5186; *extended; Juttah* (or *Jutah*), a place in Pal.:—Juttah.

3195. יְטוּר **Yeṭûwr,** *yet-oor´;* prob. from the same as 2905; *encircled* (i.e. inclosed); *Jetur,* a son of Ishmael:—Jetur.

3196. יַיִן **yayin,** *yah´-yin;* from an unused root mean. to *effervesce; wine* (as fermented); by impl. *intoxication:*—banqueting, wine, wine [-bibber].

3197. יַךְ **yak,** *yak;* by err. transc. for 3027; a *hand* or *side:*—[way-] side.

יָכוֹל **yâkôwl.** See 3201.

יְכוֹנְיָה **Yekôwneyâh.** See 3204.

3198. יָכַח **yâkach,** *yaw-kahh´;* a prim. root; to *be right* (i.e. correct); recip. to *argue;* causat. to *decide, justify* or *convict:*—appoint, argue, chasten, convince, correct (-ion), daysman, dispute, judge, maintain, plead, reason (together), rebuke, reprove (-r), surely, in any wise.

יְכִילְיָה **Yekîyleyâh.** See 3203.

3199. יָכִין **Yâkîyn,** *yaw-keen´;* from 3559; *he* (or *it*) *will establish; Jakin,* the name of three Isr. and of a temple pillar:—Jachin.

3200. יָכִינִי **Yâkîynîy,** *yaw-kee-nee´;* patron. from 3199; a *Jakinite* (collect.) or desc. of Jakin:—Jachinites.

3201. יָכֹל **yâkôl,** *yaw-kole´;* or (fuller) יָכוֹל **yâkôwl,** *yaw-kole´;* a prim. root; to *be able,* lit. (*can, could*) or mor. (*may, might*):—be able, any at all (ways), attain, can (away with, [-not]), could, endure, might, overcome, have power, prevail, still, suffer.

3202. יְכֵל **yekêl** (Chald.), *yek-ale´;* or יְכִיל **yekîyl** (Chald.), *yek-eel´;* corresp. to 3201:—be able, can, couldest, prevail.

3203. יְכָלְיָה **Yekolyâh,** *yek-ol-yaw´;* and יְכָלְיָהוּ **Yekolyâhûw,** *yek-ol-yaw´-hoo;* or (2 Ch. 26 : 3) יְכִילְיָה° **Yekîyleyâh,** *yek-ee-leh-yaw´;* from 3201 and 3050; *Jah will enable; Jekoljah* or *Jekiljah,* an Israelitess:—Jecholiah, Jecoliah.

3204. יְכָנְיָה **Yekonyâh,** *yek-on-yaw´;* and יְכָנְיָהוּ **Yekonyâhûw,** *yek-on-yaw´-hoo;* or (Jer. 27 : 20) יְכוֹנְיָה° **Yekôwneyâh,** *yek-o-neh-yaw´;* from 3559 and 3050; *Jah will establish; Jekonjah,* a Jewish king:—Jeconiah. Comp. 3659.

3205. יָלַד **yâlad,** *yaw-lad´;* a prim. root; to *bear* young; causat. to *beget;* med. to *act as midwife;* spec. to *show lineage:*—bear, beget, birth ([-day]), born, (make to) bring forth (children, young), bring up, calve, child, come, be delivered (of a child), time of delivery, gender, hatch, labour, (do the office of a) midwife, declare pedigrees, be the son of, (woman in, woman that) travail (-eth, -ing woman).

3206. יֶלֶד **yeled,** *yeh´-led;* from 3205; something *born,* i.e. a *lad* or *offspring:*—boy, child, fruit, son, young man (one).

3207. יַלְדָּה **yaldâh,** *yal-daw´;* fem. of 3206; a *lass:*—damsel, girl.

3208. יַלְדוּת **yaldûwth,** *yal-dooth´;* abstr. from 3206; *boyhood* (or *girlhood*):—childhood, youth.

3209. יִלּוֹד **yillôwd,** *yil-lode´;* pass. from 3205; *born:*—born.

3210. יָלוֹן **Yâlôwn,** *yaw-lone´;* from 3885; *lodging; Jalon,* an Isr.:—Jalon.

3211. יָלִיד **yâlîyd,** *yaw-leed´;* from 3205; *born:*—([home-]) born, child, son.

3212. יָלַךְ **yâlak,** *yaw-lak´;* a prim. root [comp. 1980]; to *walk* (lit. or fig.); causat. to *carry* (in various senses):— × again, away, bear, bring, carry (away), come (away), depart, flow, + follow (-ing), get (away, hence, him), (cause to, make) go (away, -ing, -ne, one's way, out), grow, lead (forth), let down, march, prosper, + pursue, cause to run, spread, take away ([-journey]), vanish, (cause to) walk (-ing), wax, × be weak.

3213. יָלַל **yâlal,** *yaw-lal´;* a prim. root; to *howl* (with a wailing tone) or *yell* (with a boisterous one):—(make to) howl, be howling.

3214. יְלֵל **yelêl,** *yel-ale´;* from 3213; a *howl;*—howling.

3215. יְלָלָה **yelâlâh,** *yel-aw-law´;* fem. of 3214; a *howling:*—howling.

3216. יָלַע **yâla',** *yaw-lah´;* a prim. root; to *blurt* or utter inconsiderately:—devour.

3217. יַלֶּפֶת **yallepheth,** *yal-leh´-feth;* from an unused root appar. mean. to *stick* or *scrape; scurf* or *tetter:*—scabbed.

3218. יֶלֶק **yeleq,** *yeh´-lek;* from an unused root mean. to *lick* up; a *devourer;* spec. the young *locust:*—cankerworm, caterpillar.

3219. יַלְקוּט **yalqûwṭ,** *yal-koot´;* from 3950; a travelling *pouch* (as if for gleanings):—scrip.

3220. יָם **yâm,** *yawm;* from an unused root mean. to *roar;* a *sea* (as breaking in *noisy* surf) or large body of water; spec. (with the art.) the *Mediterranean;* sometimes a large *river,* or an artificial *basin;* locally, the *west,* or (rarely) the *south:*—sea (× -faring man, [-shore]), south, west (-ern, side, -ward).

3221. יָם **yâm** (Chald.), *yawm;* corresp. to 3220:—sea.

3222. יֵם **yêm,** *yame;* from the same as 3117; a *warm* spring:—mule.

3223. יְמוּאֵל **Yemûw'êl,** *yem-oo-ale´;* from 3117 and 410; *day of God; Jemuel,* an Isr.:—Jemuel.

3224. יְמִימָה **Yemîymâh,** *yem-ee-maw´;* perh. from the same as 3117; prop. *warm,* i.e. *affectionate;* hence *dove* [comp. 3123]; *Jemimah,* one of Job's daughters:—Jemimah.

3225. יָמִין **yâmîyn,** *yaw-meen´;* from 3231; the *right* hand or side (leg, eye) of a person or other object (as the *stronger* and more dexterous); locally, the *south:*— + left-handed, right (hand, side), south.

3226. יָמִין **Yâmîyn,** *yaw-meen´;* the same as 3225; *Jamin,* the name of three Isr.:—Jamin. See also 1144.

3227. יְמִינִי **yemîynîy,** *yem-ee-nee´;* for 3225; *right:*—(on the) right (hand).

3228. יְמִינִי **Yemîynîy,** *yem-ee-nee´;* patron. from 3226; a *Jeminite* (collect.) or desc. of Jamin:—Jaminites. See also 1145.

3229. יִמְלָא **Yimlâ',** *yeem-law´;* or יִמְלָה **Yimlâh,** *yim-law´;* from 4390; *full; Jimla* or *Jimlah,* an Isr.:—Imla, Imlah.

3230. יַמְלֵךְ **Yamlêk,** *yam-lake´;* from 4427; *he will make king; Jamlek,* an Isr.:—Jamlech.

3231. יָמַן **yâman,** *yaw-man´;* a prim. root; to *be* (phys.) *right* (i.e. firm); but used only as denom. from 3225 and transit., to *be right-handed* or *take the right-hand* side:—go (turn) to (on, use) the right hand.

3232. יִמְנָה **Yimnâh,** *yim-naw´;* from 3231; *prosperity* (as betokened by the *right* hand); *Jimnah,* the name of two Isr.; also (with the art.) of the posterity of one of them:—Imna, Imnah, Jimnah, Jimnites.

3233. יְמָנִי **yemânîy,** *yem-aw-nee´;* from 3231; *right* (i.e. at the right hand):—(on the) right (hand).

3234. יִמְנָע **Yimnâ',** *yim-naw´;* from 4513; *he will restrain; Jimna,* an Isr.:—Imna.

3235. יָמַר **yâmar,** *yaw-mar´;* a prim. root; to *exchange;* by impl. to *change places:*—boast selves, change.

3236. יִמְרָה **Yimrâh,** *yim-raw´;* prob. from 3235; *interchange; Jimrah,* an Isr.:—Imrah.

3237. יָמַשׁ **yâmash,** *yaw-mash´;* a prim. root; to *touch:*—feel.

3238. יָנָה **yânâh,** *yaw-naw´;* a prim. root; to *rage* or *be violent:* by impl. to *suppress,* to *maltreat:*—destroy, (thrust out by) oppress (-ing, -ion, -or), proud, vex, do violence.

3239. יָנוֹחַ **Yânôwach,** *yaw-no´-akh;* or (with enclitic) יָנוֹחָה **Yânôwchâh,** *yaw-no´-khaw;* from 3240; *quiet; Janoäch* or *Janochah,* a place in Pal.:—Janoah, Janohah.

יָנוּם **Yânûm.** See 3241.

3240. יָנַח **yânach,** *yaw-nakh´;* a prim. root; to *deposit;* by impl. to *allow to stay:*—bestow, cast down, lay (down, up), leave (off), let alone (remain), pacify, place, put, set (down), suffer, withdraw, withhold. (The Hiphil forms with the *dagesh* are here referred to, in accordance with the older grammarians; but if any distinction of the kind is to be made, these should rather be referred to 5117, and the others here.)

3241. יָנִים° **Yânîym,** *yaw-neem´;* from 5123; *asleep; Janim,* a place in Pal.:—Janum [*from the marg.*].

3242. יְנִיקָה **y^enîyqâh,** *yen-ee-kaw´;* from 3243; a *sucker* or sapling:—young twig.

3243. יָנַק **yânaq,** *yaw-nak´;* a prim. root; to *suck;* causat. to *give milk:*—milch, nurse (-ing mother), give, make to) suck (-ing child, -ling).

3244. יַנְשׁוּף **yanshûwph,** *yan-shoof´;* or יַנְשׁוֹף **yanshôwph,** *yan-shofe´;* appar. from 5398; an unclean (aquatic) bird; prob. the *heron* (perh. from its *blowing* cry, or because the *night*-heron is meant [comp. 5399]):—(great) owl.

3245. יָסַד **yâçad,** *yaw-sad´;* a prim. root; to *set* (lit. or fig.); intens. to *found;* reflex. to *sit* down together, i.e. *settle, consult:*—appoint, take counsel, establish, (lay the, lay for a) found (-ation), instruct, lay, ordain, set, × sure.

3246. יְסֻד **y^eçûd,** *yes-ood´;* from 3245; a *foundation* (fig. i.e. *beginning*):— × began.

3247. יְסוֹד **y^eçôwd,** *yes-ode´;* from 3245; a *foundation* (lit. or fig.):—bottom, foundation, repairing.

3248. יְסוּדָה **y^eçûwdâh,** *yes-oo-daw´;* fem. of 3246; a *foundation:*—foundation.

3249. יָסוּר **yâçûwr,** *yaw-soor´;* from 5493; *departing:*—they that depart.

3250. יִסּוֹר **yiççôwr,** *yis-sore´;* from 3256; a *reprover:*—instruct.

3251. יָסַךְ **yâçak,** *yaw-sak´;* a prim. root; to *pour* (intrans.):—be poured.

3252. יִסְכָּה **Yiçkâh,** *yis-kaw´;* from an unused root mean. to *watch; observant; Jiskah,* sister of Lot:—Iscah.

3253. יִסְמַכְיָהוּ **Yiçmakyâhûw,** *yis-mak-yaw-hoo´;* from 5564 and 3050; *Jah will sustain; Jismakjah,* an Isr.:—Ismachiah.

3254. יָסַף **yâçaph,** *yaw-saf´;* a prim. root; to *add* or *augment* (often adv. to *continue* to do a thing):— add, × again, × any more, × cease, × come more, + conceive again, continue, exceed, × further, × gather together, get more, give moreover, × henceforth, increase (more and more), join, × longer (bring, do, make, much, put), × (the, much, yet) more (and more), proceed (further), prolong, put, be [strong-] er, × yet, yield.

3255. יְסַף **y^eçaph** (Chald.), *yes-af´;* corresp. to 3254:—add.

3256. יָסַר **yâçar,** *yaw-sar´;* a prim. root; to *chastise,* lit. (with blows) or fig. (with words); hence to *instruct:*—bind, chasten, chastise, correct, instruct, punish, reform, reprove, sore, teach.

3257. יָע **yâʻ,** *yaw;* from 3261; a *shovel:*—shovel.

3258. יַעְבֵּץ **Yaʻbêts,** *yah-bates´;* from an unused root prob. mean. to *grieve; sorrowful; Jabets,* the name of an Isr., and also of a place in Pal.:—Jabez.

3259. יָעַד **yâʻad,** *yaw-ad´;* a prim. root; to *fix* upon (by agreement or appointment); by impl. to *meet* (at a stated time), to *summon* (to trial), to *direct* (in a certain quarter or position), to *engage* (for marriage):—agree, (make an) appoint (-ment, a time), assemble (selves), betroth, gather (selves, together), meet (together), set (a time).

יֶעְדּוֹ **Yeʻdôw.** See 3260.

3260. יֶעְדִּי **Yeʻdîy,** *yed-ee´;* from 3259; *appointed; Jedi,* an Isr.:—Iddo [*from the marg.*] See 3035.

3261. יָעָה **yâʻâh,** *yaw-aw´;* a prim. root; appar. to *brush* aside:—sweep away.

3262. יְעוּאֵל **Y^eʻûwʻêl,** *yeh-oo-ale´;* from 3261 and 410; *carried away of God; Jeüel,* the name of four Isr.;—Jehiel, Jeiel, Jeuel. Comp 3273.

3263. יְעוּץ **Y^eʻûwts,** *yeh-oots´;* from 5779; *counsellor; Jeüts,* an Isr.:—Jeuz.

3264. יָעוֹר **yâʻôwr,** *yaw-ore´;* a var. of 3293; a *forest:*—wood.

3265. יָעוּר **Yâʻûwr,** *yaw-oor´;* appar. pass. part of the same as 3293; *wooded; Jaür,* an Isr.:—Jair [*from the marg.*].

3266. יְעוּשׁ **Y^eʻûwsh,** *yeh-oosh´;* from 5789; *hasty; Jeüsh,* the name of an Edomite and of four Isr.:—Jehush, Jeush. Comp. 3274.

3267. יָעַז **yâʻaz,** *yaw-az´;* a prim. root; to be *bola* or *obstinate:*—fierce.

3268. יַעֲזִיאֵל **Yaʻăzîyʼêl,** *yah-az-ee-ale´;* from 3267 and 410; *emboldened of God; Jaaziël,* an Isr.:—Jaaziel.

3269. יַעֲזִיָּהוּ **Yaʻăzîyâhûw,** *yah-az-ee-yaw´hoo;* from 3267 and 3050; *emboldened of Jah; Joazijah,* an Isr.:—Jaaziah.

3270. יַעֲזֵיר **Yaʻăzêyr,** *yah-az-ayr´;* or יַעְזֵר **Yaʻzêr,** *yah-zare´;* from 5826; *helpful; Jaazer* or *Jazer,* a place E. of the Jordan:—Jaazer, Jazer.

3271. יָעַט **yâʻaṭ,** *yaw-at´;* a prim. root; to *clothe:*—cover.

3272. יְעַט **y^eʻaṭ** (Chald.), *yeh-at´;* corresp. to 3289; to *counsel;* reflex. to *consult:*—counsellor, consult together.

3273. יְעִיאֵל **Y^eʻîyʼêl,** *yeh-ee-ale´;* from 3261 and 410; *carried away of God; Jeïel,* the name of six Isr.:—Jeiel, Jehiel. Comp. 3262.

יָעִיר **Yâʻîyr.** See 3265.

3274. יְעִישׁ **Y^eʻîysh,** *yeh-eesh´;* from 5789; *hasty: Jeïsh,* the name of an Edomite and of an Isr.:—Jeush [*from the marg.*]. Comp. 3266.

3275. יַעְכָּן **Yaʻkân,** *yah-kawn´;* from the same as 5912; *troublesome; Jakan,* an Isr.:—Jachan.

3276. יָעַל **yâʻal,** *yaw-al´;* a prim. root; prop. to *ascend;* fig. to *be valuable* (obj. *useful,* subj. *benefited*):— × at all, set forward, can do good, (be, have) profit (-able).

3277. יָעֵל **yâʻêl,** *yaw-ale´;* from 3276; an *ibex* (as *climbing*):—wild goat.

3278. יָעֵל **Yâʻêl,** *yaw-ale´;* the same as 3277; *Jaël,* a Canaanite:—Jael.

3279. יַעֲלָא **Yaʻălâʼ,** *yah-al-aw´;* or יַעֲלָה **Yaʻălâh,** *yah-al-aw´;* the same as 3280 or direct from 3276; *Jaala* or *Jaalah,* one of the Nethinim:—Jaala, Jaalah.

3280. יַעֲלָה **yaʻălâh,** *yah-al-aw´;* fem. of 3277:—roe.

3281. יַעְלָם **Yaʻlâm,** *yah-lawm´;* from 5956; *occult; Jalam,* an Edomite:—Jalam.

3282. יַעַן **yaʻan,** *yah´-an;* from an unused root mean. to *pay attention;* prop. *heed;* by impl. *purpose* (sake or account); used adv. to indicate the *reason* or cause:—because (that), forasmuch (+ as), seeing then, + that, + whereas, + why.

3283. יָעֵן **yâʻên,** *yaw-ane´;* from the same as 3282; the *ostrich* (prob. from its *answering* cry:—ostrich.

3284. יַעֲנָה **yaʻănâh,** *yah-an-aw´;* fem. of 3283, and mean. the same:— + owl.

3285. יַעֲנַי **Yaʻănay,** *yah-an-ah´ee;* from the same as 3283; *responsive; Jaanai,* an Isr.:—Jaanai.

3286. יָעַף **yâʻaph,** *yaw-af´;* a prim. root; to *tire* (as if from wearisome *flight*):—faint, cause to fly, (be) weary (self).

3287. יָעֵף **yâʻêph,** *yaw-afe´;* from 3286; *fatigued;* fig. *exhausted:*—faint, weary.

3288. יְעָף **y^eʻâph,** *yeh-awf´;* from 3286; *fatigue* (adv. utterly *exhausted*):—swiftly.

3289. יָעַץ **yâʻats,** *yaw-ats´;* a prim. root; to *advise;* reflex. to *deliberate* or *resolve:*—advertise, take advice, advise (well), consult, (give take) counsel (-lor), determine, devise, guide, purpose.

3290. יַעֲקֹב **Yaʻăqôb,** *yak-ak-obe´;* from 6117; *heel*-catcher (i.e. supplanter); *Jaakob,* the Israelitish patriarch:—Jacob.

3291. יַעֲקֹבָה **Yaʻăqôbâh,** *yah-ak-o´-baw;* from 3290; *Jaakobah,* an Isr.:—Jaakobah.

3292. יַעֲקָן **Yaʻăqân,** *yah-ak-awn´;* from the same as 6130; *Jaakan,* an Idumæan:—Jaakan. Comp. 1142.

3293. יַעַר **ya'ar,** *yah´-ar;* from an unused root prob. mean. to *thicken* with verdure; a *copse* of bushes; hence a *forest;* hence *honey* in the *comb* (as hived in trees):—[honey-] comb, forest, wood.

3294. יַעְרָה **Ya'râh,** *yah-raw´;* a form of 3295; *Jarah,* an Isr.:—Jarah.

3295. יַעֲרָה **ya'ărâh,** *yah-ar-aw´;* fem. of 3293, and mean. the same:—[honey-] comb, forest.

3296. יַעֲרֵי אֹרְגִים **Ya'ărêy 'Orᵉgîym,** *yah-ar-ay´ o-reg-eem´;* from the plur. of 3293 and the masc. plur. part. act. of 707; *woods of weavers; Jaare-Oregim,* an Isr.:—Jaare-oregim.

3297. יְעָרִים **Yᵉ'ârîym,** *yeh-aw-reem´;* plur. of 3293; *forests; Jeärim,* a place in Pal.:—Jearim. Comp. 7157.

3298. יַעֲרֶשְׁיָה **Ya'ăreshyâh,** *yah-ar-esh-yaw´;* from an unused root of uncert. signif. and 3050; *Jaareshjah,* an Isr.:—Jaresiah.

3299. יַעֲשׂוּ **Ya'ăsûw,** *yah-as-oo´;* from 6213; *they will do; Jaasu,* an Isr.:—Jaasau.

3300. יַעֲשִׂיאֵל **Ya'ăsîy'êl,** *yah-as-ee-ale´;* from 6213 and 410; *made of God; Jaasiel,* an Isr.:—Jaasiel, Jasiel.

3301. יִפְדְּיָה **Yiphdᵉyâh,** *yif-deh-yaw´;* from 6299 and 3050; *Jah will liberate; Jiphdejah,* an Isr.:—Iphedeiah.

3302. יָפָה **yâphâh,** *yaw-faw´;* a prim. root; prop. to *be bright,* i.e. (by impl.) *beautiful:*—be beautiful, be (make self) fair (-r), deck.

3303. יָפֶה **yâpheh,** *yaw-feh´;* from 3302; *beautiful* (lit. or fig.):— + beautiful, beauty, comely, fair (-est, one), + goodly, pleasant, well.

3304. יְפֵה־פִיָּה **yᵉphêh-phîyah,** *yef-eh´ fee-yaw´;* from 3302 by redupl.; *very beautiful:*—very fair.

3305. יָפוֹ **Yâphô,** *yaw-fo´;* or יָפוֹא **Yâphôw'** (Ezra 3 : 7), *yaw-fo´;* from 3302; *beautiful; Japho,* a place in Pal.:—Japha, Joppa.

3306. יָפַח **yâphach,** *yaw-fakh´;* a prim. root; prop. to *breathe* hard, i.e. (by impl.) to *sigh:*—bewail self.

3307. יָפֵחַ **yâphêach,** *yaw-fay´-akh;* from 3306; prop. *puffing,* i.e. (fig.) *meditating:*—such as breathe out.

3308. יֳפִי **yŏphîy,** *yof-ee´;* from 3302; *beauty:*—beauty.

3309. יָפִיעַ **Yâphîya',** *yaw-fee´-ah;* from 3313; *bright; Japhia,* the name of a Canaanite, an Isr., and a place in Pal.:—Japhia.

3310. יַפְלֵט **Yaphlêṭ,** *yaf-late´;* from 6403; *he will deliver; Japhlet,* an Isr.:—Japhlet.

3311. יַפְלֵטִי **Yaphlêṭîy,** *yaf-lay-tee´;* patron. from 3310; a *Japhletite* or desc. of Japhlet:—Japhleti.

3312. יְפֻנֶּה **Yᵉphunneh,** *yef-oon-neh´;* from 6437; *he will be prepared; Jephunneh,* the name of two Isr.:—Jephunneh.

3313. יָפַע **yâpha',** *yaw-fah´;* a prim. root; to *shine:*—be light, shew, self, (cause to) shine (forth).

3314. יִפְעָה **yiph'âh,** *yif-aw´;* from 3313; *splendor* or (fig.) *beauty:*—brightness.

3315. יֶפֶת **Yepheth,** *yeh´-feth;* from 6601; *expansion; Jepheth,* a son of Noah; also his posterity:—Japheth.

3316. יִפְתָּח **Yiphtâch,** *yif-tawkh´;* from 6605; *he will open; Jiphtach,* an Isr.; also a place in Pal.:—Jephthah, Jiphtah.

3317. יִפְתַּח־אֵל **Yiphtach-'êl,** *yif-tach-ale´;* from 6605 and 410; *God will open; Jiphtach-el,* a place in Pal.:—Jiphthah-el.

3318. יָצָא **yâtsâ',** *yaw-tsaw´;* a prim. root; to *go* (causat. *bring*) *out,* in a great variety of applications, lit. and fig., direct and proxim.:— × after, appear, × assuredly, bear out, × begotten, break out, bring forth (out, up), carry out, come (abroad, out, thereat, without), + be condemned, depart (-ing, -ure), draw forth, in the end, escape, exact, fail, fall (out), fetch forth (out), get away (forth, hence, out), (able to, cause to, let) go abroad (forth, on, out), going out, grow, have forth (out), issue out, lay (lie) out, lead out, pluck out, proceed, pull out, put away, be risen, × scarce, send with commandment, shoot forth, spread, spring out, stand out, × still, × surely, take forth (out), at any time, × to [and fro], utter.

3319. יְצָא **yᵉtsâ'** (Chald.), *yets-aw´;* corresp. to 3318:—finish.

3320. יָצַב **yâtsab,** *yaw-tsab´;* a prim. root; to *place* (any thing so as to stay); reflex. to *station, offer, continue:*—present selves, remaining, resort, set (selves), (be able to, can, with-) stand (fast, forth, -ing, still, up).

3321. יְצֵב **yᵉtsêb** (Chald.), *yets-abe´;* corresp. to 3320; to *be firm;* hence to *speak surely:*—truth.

3322. יָצַג **yâtsag,** *yaw-tsag´;* a prim. root; to *place* permanently:—establish, leave, make, present, put, set, stay.

3323. יִצְהָר **yitshâr,** *yits-hawr´;* from 6671; *oil* (as producing *light*); fig. *anointing:*— + anointed, oil.

3324. יִצְהָר **Yitshâr,** *yits-hawr´;* the same as 3323; *Jitshar,* an Isr.:—Izhar.

3325. יִצְהָרִי **Yitshârîy,** *yits-haw-ree´;* patron. from 3324; a *Jitsharite* or desc. of Jitshar:—Izeharites, Izharites.

3326. יָצוּעַ **yâtsûwa',** *yaw-tsoo´-ah;* pass. part. of 3331; *spread,* i.e. a *bed;* (arch.) an *extension,* i.e. *wing* or *lean-to* (a single story or collect.):—bed, chamber, couch.

3327. יִצְחָק **Yitschâq,** *yits-khawk´;* from 6711; *laughter* (i.e. *mockery*); *Jitschak* (or Isaac), son of Abraham:—Isaac. Comp. 3446.

3328. יִצְחַר **Yitschar,** *yits-khar´;* from the same as 6713; *he will shine; Jitschar,* an Isr.:—and Zehoar [*from the marg.*].

3329. יָצִיא **yâtsîy',** *yaw-tsee´;* from 3318; *issue,* i.e. offspring:—those that came forth.

3330. יַצִּיב **yatstsîyb** (Chald.), *yats-tseeb´;* from 3321; *fixed, sure;* concr. *certainty:*—certain (-ty), true, truth.

יָצִיעַ **yâtsîya'.** See 3326.

3331. יָצַע **yâtsa',** *yaw-tsah´;* a prim. root; to *strew* as a surface:—make [one's] bed, × lie, spread.

3332. יָצַק **yâtsaq,** *yaw-tsak´;* a prim. root; prop. to *pour* out (trans. or intrans.); by impl. to *melt* or *cast* as metal; by extens. to *place* firmly, to *stiffen* or grow hard:—cast, cleave fast, be (as) firm, grow, be hard, lay out, molten, overflow, pour (out), run out, set down, stedfast.

3333. יְצֻקָה **yᵉtsûkâh,** *yets-oo-kaw´;* pass. part. fem. of 3332; *poured* out, i.e. *run* into a mould:—when it was cast.

3334. יָצַר **yâtsar,** *yaw-tsar´;* a prim. root; to *press* (intrans.), i.e. *be narrow;* fig. *be in distress:*—be distressed, be narrow, be straitened (in straits), be vexed.

3335. יָצַר **yâtsar,** *yaw-tsar´;* prob. identical with 3334 (through the *squeezing* into shape); ([comp. 3331]), to *mould* into a form; espec. as a *potter;* fig. to *determine* (i.e. form a resolution):— × earthen, fashion, form, frame, make (-r), potter, purpose.

3336. יֵצֶר **yêtser,** *yay´-tser;* from 3335; a *form;* fig. *conception* (i.e. purpose):—frame, thing framed, imagination, mind, work.

3337. יֵצֶר **Yêtser,** *yay´-tser;* the same as 3336; *Jetser,* an Isr.:—Jezer.

3338. יָצֻר **yâtsûr,** *yaw-tsoor´;* pass. part. of 3335; *structure,* i.e. limb or part:—member.

3339. יִצְרִי **Yitsrîy,** *yits-ree´;* from 3335; *formative; Jitsri,* an Isr.:—Isri.

3340. יִצְרִי **Yitsrîy,** *yits-ree´;* patron. from 3337; a *Jitsrite* (collect.) or desc. of Jetser:—Jezerites.

3341. יָצַת **yâtsath,** *yaw-tsath´;* a prim. root; to *burn* or *set on fire;* fig. to *desolate:*—burn (up), be desolate, set (on) fire ([fire]), kindle.

3342. יֶקֶב **yeqeb,** *yeh´-keb;* from an unused root mean. to *excavate;* a *trough* (as dug out); spec. a wine-*vat* (whether the lower one, into which the juice drains; or the upper, in which the grapes are crushed):—fats, presses, press-fat, wine (-press).

3343. יְקַבְצְאֵל **Yᵉqabtsᵉ'êl,** *yek-ab-tseh-ale´;* from 6908 and 410; *God will gather; Jekabtseël,* a place in Pal.:—Jekabzeel. Comp. 6909.

3344. יָקַד **yâqad,** *yaw-kad´;* a prim. root; to *burn:*—(be) burn (-ing), × from the hearth, kindle.

3345. יְקַד **yᵉqad** (Chald.), *yek-ad´;* corresp. to 3344:—burning.

3346. יְקֵדָא **yᵉqêdâʼ** (Chad.), *yek-ay-daw´;* from 3345; a *conflagration:*—burning.

3347. יָקְדְעָם **Yoqdᵉʻâm,** *yok-deh-awm´;* from 3344 and 5971; *burning of* (the) *people; Jokdeäm,* a place in Pal.:—Jokdeam.

3348. יָקֶה **Yâqeh,** *yaw-keh´;* from an unused root prob. mean. to *obey; obedient; Jakeh,* a symbolical name (for Solomon):—Jakeh.

3349. יִקָּהָה **yiqqâhâh,** *yik-kaw-haw´;* from the same as 3348; *obedience:*—gathering, to obey.

3350. יְקוֹד **yᵉqôwd,** *yek-ode´;* from 3344; a *burning:*—burning.

3351. יְקוּם **yᵉqûwm,** *yek-oom´;* from 6965; prop. *standing* (extant), i.e. by impl. a *living thing:*—(living) substance.

3352. יָקוֹשׁ **yâqôwsh,** *yaw-koshe´;* from 3369; prop. *entangling;* hence a *snarer:*—fowler.

3353. יָקוּשׁ **yâqûwsh,** *yaw-koosh´;* pass. part. of 3369; prop. *entangled,* i.e. by impl. (intrans.) a *snare,* or (trans.) a *snarer:*—fowler, snare.

3354. יְקוּתִיאֵל **Yᵉqûwthîyʼêl,** *yek-ooth-ee´-ale;* from the same as 3348 and 410; *obedience of God; Jekuthiël,* an Isr.:—Jekuthiel.

3355. יָקְטָן **Yoqṭân,** *yok-tawn´;* from 6994; *he will be made little; Joktan,* an Arabian patriarch:—Joktan.

3356. יָקִים **Yâqîym,** *yaw-keem´;* from 6965; *he will raise; Jakim,* the name of two Isr.:—Jakim. Comp. 3079.

3357. יַקִּיר **yaqqîyr,** *yak-keer´;* from 3365; *precious:*—dear.

3358. יַקִּיר **yaqqîyr** (Chald.) *yak-keer´;* corresp. to 3357:—noble, rare.

3359. יְקַמְיָה **Yᵉqamyâh,** *yek-am-yaw´;* from 6965 and 3050; *Jah will rise; Jekamjah,* the name of two Isr.:—Jekamiah. Comp. 3079.

3360. יְקַמְעָם **Yᵉqamʻâm,** *yek-am´-awm;* from 6965 and 5971; (the) *people will rise; Jekamam,* an Isr.:—Jekameam. Comp. 3079, 3361.

3361. יָקְמְעָם **Yoqmᵉʻâm,** *yok-meh-awm´;* from 6965 and 5971; (the) *people will be raised; Jokmeäm,* a place in Pal.:—Jokmeam. Comp. 3360, 3362.

3362. יָקְנְעָם **Yoqnᵉʻâm,** *yok-neh-awm´;* from 6969 and 5971; (the) *people will be lamented; Jokneäm,* a place in Pal.:—Jokneam.

3363. יָקַע **yâqaʻ,** *yaw-kah´;* a prim. root; prop. to *sever* oneself, i.e. (by impl.) to *be dislocated;* fig. to *abandon;* causat. to *impale* (and thus allow to drop to pieces by *rotting*):—be alienated, depart, hang (up), be out of joint.

3364. יָקַץ **yâqats,** *yaw-kats´;* a prim. root; to *awake* (intrans.):—(be) awake (-d).

יָקַף **yâqaph.** See 5362.

3365. יָקַר **yâqar,** *yaw-kar´;* a prim. root; prop. appar. to *be heavy,* i.e. (fig.) *valuable;* causat. to *make rare* (fig. to *inhibit*):—be (make) precious, be prized, be set by, withdraw.

3366. יְקָר **yᵉqâr,** *yek-awr´;* from 3365; *value,* i.e. (concr.) *wealth;* abstr. *costliness, dignity:*—honour, precious (things), price.

3367. יְקָר **yᵉqâr** (Chald.), *yek-awr´;* corresp. to 3366:—glory, honour.

3368. יָקָר **yâqâr,** *yaw-kawr´;* from 3365; *valuable* (obj. or subj.):—brightness, clear, costly, excellent, fat, honourable women, precious, reputation.

3369. יָקֹשׁ **yâqôsh,** *yaw-koshe´;* a prim. root; to *ensnare* (lit. or fig.):—fowler (lay a) snare.

3370. יָקְשָׁן Yoqshân, *yok-shawn* from 3369; *insidious; Jokshan,* an Arabian patriarch:—Jokshan.

3371. יָקְתְאֵל **Yoqthᵉʼêl,** *yok-theh-ale´;* prob. from the same as 3348 and 410; *veneration of God* [comp. 3354]; *Joktheël,* the name of a place in Pal., and of one in Idumæa:—Joktheel.

יָרָא **yârâʼ.** See 3384.

3372. יָרֵא **yârêʼ,** *yaw-ray´;* a prim. root; to *fear;* mor. to *revere;* caus. to *frighten:*—affright, be (make) afraid, dread (-ful), (put in) fear (-ful, -fully, -ing). (be had in) reverence (-end), × see, terrible (act, -ness, thing).

3373. יָרֵא **yârêʼ,** *yaw-raw´;* from 3372; *fearing;* mor. *reverent:*—afraid, fear (-ful).

3374. יִרְאָה **yirʼâh,** *yir-aw´;* fem. of 3373; *fear* (also used as infin.); mor. *reverence:*— × dreadful, × exceedingly, fear (-fulness).

3375. יִרְאוֹן **Yirôwn,** *yir-ohn´;* from 3372; *fearfulness; Jiron,* a place in Pal.:—Iron.

3376. יִרְאִיָּיה **Yirʼîyâyh,** *yir-ee-yaw´;* from 3373 and 3050; *fearful of Jah; Jirijah,* an Isr.:—Irijah.

3377. יָרֵב **Yârêb,** *yaw-rabe´;* from 7378; *he will contend; Jareb,* a symbolical name for Assyria:—Jareb. Comp. 3402.

3378. יְרֻבַּעַל **Yᵉrubbaʻal,** *yer-oob-bah´-al;* from 7378 and 1168; *Baal will contend; Jerubbaal,* a symbol. name of Gideon:—Jerubbaal.

3379. יָרָבְעָם **Yârobʻâm,** *yaw-rob-awm´;* from 7378 and 5971; (the) *people will contend; Jarobam,* the name of two Isr. kings:—Jeroboam.

3380. יְרֻבֶּשֶׁת **Yᵉrubbesheth,** *yer-oob-beh´-sheth;* from 7378 and 1322; *shame* (i.e. the idol) *will contend; Jerubbesheth,* a symbol. name for Gideon:—Jerubbesheth.

3381. יָרַד **yârad,** *yaw-rad´;* a prim. root; to *descend* (lit. to *go downwards;* or conventionally to a lower region, as the shore, a boundary, the enemy, etc.; or fig. to *fall*); causat. to *bring down* (in all the above applications):— × abundantly, bring down, carry down, cast down, (cause to) come (-ing) down, fall (down), get down, go (-ing) down (-ward), hang down, × indeed, let down, light (down), put down (off), (cause to, let) run down, sink, subdue, take down.

3382. יֶרֶד **Yered,** *yeh´-red;* from 3381; a *descent; Jered,* the name of an antediluvian, and of an Isr.:—Jared.

3383. יַרְדֵּן **Yardên,** *yar-dane´;* from 3381; a *descender; Jarden,* the principal river of Pal.:—Jordan.

3384. יָרָה **yârâh,** *yaw-raw´;* or (2 Chr. 26 : 15) יָרָא **yârâʼ,** *yaw-raw´;* a prim. root; prop. to *flow* as water (i.e. to *rain*); trans. to *lay* or *throw* (espec. an arrow. i.e. to *shoot*); fig. to *point* out (as if by *aiming* the finger), to *teach:*— (+) archer, cast, direct, inform, instruct, lay, shew, shoot, teach (-er, -ing), through.

3385. יְרוּאֵל **Yᵉrûwʼêl,** *yer-oo-ale´;* from 3384 and 410; *founded of God; Jeruel,* a place in Pal.:—Jeruel

3386. יָרוֹחַ **Yârôwach,** *yaw-ro´-akh;* perh. denom. from 3394; (born at the) new *moon; Jaroäch,* an Isr.:—Jaroah.

3387. יָרוֹק **yârôwq,** *yaw-roke´;* from 3417; *green,* i.e. an herb:—green thing.

3388. יְרוּשָׁא **Yᵉrûwshâʼ,** *yer-oo-shaw´;* or יְרוּשָׁה **Yᵉrûwshâh,** *yer-oo-shaw´;* fem. pass. part. of 3423; *possessed; Jerusha* or *Jerushah,* an Israelitess:—Jerusha, Jerushah.

3389. יְרוּשָׁלַםִ **Yᵉrûwshâlaim,** *yer-oo-shaw-lah´-im;* rarely יְרוּשָׁלַיִם **Yᵉrûwshâlayim,** *yer-oo-shaw-lah´-yim;* a dual (in allusion to its two main hills [the true pointing, at least of the former reading, seems to be that of 3390]); prob. from (the pass. part. of) 3384 and 7999; *founded peaceful; Jerushalaïm* or *Jerushalem,* the capital city of Pal.:—Jerusalem.

3390. יְרוּשְׁלֵם **Yᵉrûwshâlêm** (Chald.), *yer-oo-shaw-lame´;* corresp. to 3389:—Jerusalem.

3391. יֶרַח **yerach,** *yeh´-rakh;* from an unused root of uncert. signif.; a *lunation,* i.e. *month:*—month, moon.

3392. יֶרַח **Yerach,** *yeh´-rakh;* the same as 3391; *Jerach,* an Arabian patriarch:—Jerah.

3393. יְרַח **yᵉrach** (Chald.), *yeh-rakh´;* corresp. to 3391; a *month:*—month.

3394. יָרֵחַ **yârêach,** *yaw-ray´-akh;* from the same as 3391; the *moon:*—moon.

יְרֵחוֹ **Yᵉrêchôw.** See 3405.

3395. יְרֹחָם **Yᵉrôchâm,** *yer-o-khawm´;* from 7355; *compassionate; Jerocham,* the name of seven or eight Isr.:—Jeroham.

3396. יְרַחְמְאֵל **Yᵉrachmᵉʼêl,** *yer-akh-meh-ale´;* from 7355 and 410; *God will compassionate; Jerachmeël,* the name of three Isr.:—Jerahmeel.

3397. יְרַחְמְאֵלִי **Yᵉrachmᵉʼêlîy,** *yer-akh-meh-ay-lee´;* patron. from 3396; a *Jerachmeëlite* or desc. of Jerachmeel:—Jerahmeelites.

3398. יַרְחָע **Yarchâʻ,** *yar-khaw´;* prob. of Eg. or.; *Jarcha,* an Eg.:—Jarha.

3399. יָרַט **yâraṭ,** *yaw-rat´;* a prim. root; to *precipitate* or *hurl* (*rush*) headlong; (intrans.) to *be rash:*—be perverse, turn over.

3400. יְרִיאֵל **Yᵉrîyʼêl,** *yer-ee-ale´;* from 3384 and 410; *thrown of God; Jeriël,* an Isr.:—Jeriel. Comp. 3385.

3401. יָרִיב **yârîyb,** *yaw-rebe´;* from 7378; lit. *he will contend;* prop. adj. *contentious;* used as noun, an *adversary:*—that contend (-eth), that strive.

3402. יָרִיב **Yârîyb,** *yaw-rebe´;* the same as 3401; *Jarib,* the name of three Isr.:—Jarib.

3403. יְרִיבַי **Yᵉrîybay,** *yer-eeb-ah´ee;* from 3401; *contentious; Jeribai,* an Isr.:—Jeribai.

3404. יְרִיָּה **Yᵉrîyâh,** *yer-ee-yaw´;* or יְרִיָּהוּ **Yᵉrîyâhûw,** *yer-ee-yaw´-hoo;* from 3384 and 3050; *Jah will throw; Jerijah,* an Isr.:—Jeriah, Jerijah.

3405. יְרִיחוֹ **Yᵉrîychôw,** *yer-ee-kho´;* or יְרֵחוֹ **Yᵉrêchôw** *yer-ay-kho´;* or var. (1 Kings 16 : 34) יְרִיחֹה **Yᵉrîychôh,** *yer-ee-kho´;* perh. from 3394; *its month;* or else from 7306; *fragrant; Jericho* or *Jerecho,* a place in Pal.:—Jericho.

3406. יְרִימוֹת **Yᵉrîymôwth,** *yer-ee-mohth´;* or יְרֵימוֹת **Yᵉrêymôwth,** *yer-ay-mohth´;* or יְרֵמוֹת **Yᵉrêmôwth,** *yer-ay-mohth´;* fem. plur. from 7311; *elevations; Jerimoth* or *Jeremoth,* the name of twelve Isr.:—Jeremoth, Jerimoth, and Ramoth [*from the marg.*].

3407. יְרִיעָה **yᵉrîyʻâh,** *yer-ee-aw´;* from 3415; a *hanging* (as *tremulous*):—curtain.

3408. יְרִיעוֹת **Yᵉrîyʻôwth,** *yer-ee-ohth´;* plur. of 3407; *curtains; Jerioth,* an Israelitess:—Jerioth.

3409. יָרֵךְ **yârêk,** *yaw-rake´;* from an unused root mean. to *be soft;* the *thigh* (from its fleshy *softness*); by euphem. the *generative parts;* fig. a *shank, flank, side:*— × body, loins, shaft, side, thigh.

3410. יַרְכָא **yarkâʼ** (Chald.), *yar-kaw´;* corresp. to 3411; a *thigh:*—thigh.

3411. יְרֵכָה **yᵉrêkâh,** *yer-ay-kaw´;* fem. of 3409; prop. the *flank;* but used only fig., the *rear* or *recess:*—border, coast, part, quarter, side.

3412. יַרְמוּת **Yarmûwth,** *yar-mooth´;* from 7311; *elevation; Jarmuth,* the name of two places in Pal.:—Jarmuth.

יְרֵמוֹת **Yᵉrêmôwth.** See 3406.

3413. יְרֵמַי **Yᵉrêmay,** *yer-ay-mah´ee;* from 7311; *elevated; Jeremai,* an Isr.:—Jeremai.

3414. יִרְמְיָה **Yirmᵉyâh,** *yir-meh-yaw´;* or יִרְמְיָהוּ **Yirmᵉyâhûw,** *yir-meh-yaw´-hoo;* from 7311 and 3050; *Jah will rise; Jirmejah,* the name of eight or nine Isr.:—Jeremiah.

3415. יָרַע **yâraʻ,** *yaw-rah´;* a prim. root; prop. to *be broken* up (with any violent action), i.e. (fig.) to *fear:*—be grievous [*only Isa.* 15 : 4; *the rest belong* to 7489].

3416. יִרְפְּאֵל **Yirpᵉʼêl,** *yir-peh-ale´;* from 7495 and 410; *God will heal; Jirpeël,* a place in Pal.:—Irpeel.

3417. יָרַק **yâraq,** *yaw-rak´;* a prim. root; to *spit:*— × but, spit.

3418. יֶרֶק **yereq,** *yeh´-rek;* from 3417 (in the sense of *vacuity* of color); prop. *pallor,* i.e. hence the yellowish *green* of young and sickly vegetation; concr. *verdure,* i.e. grass or vegetation:—grass, green (thing).

3419. יָרָק **yârâq,** *yaw-rawk´;* from the same as 3418; prop. *green;* concr. a *vegetable:*—green, herbs.

יַרְקוֹן **Yarqôwn.** See 4313.

3420. יֵרָקוֹן **yêrâqôwn,** *yay-raw-kone´;* from 3418; *paleness,* whether of persons (from fright), or of plants (from drought):—mildew, paleness.

3421. יָרְקְעָם **Yorqᵉʻâm,** *yor-keh-awm´;* from 7324 and 5971; *people will be poured forth; Jorkeäm,* a place in Pal.:—Jorkeam.

3422. יְרַקְרַק **yᵉraqraq,** *yer-ak-rak´;* from the same as 3418; *yellowishness:*—greenish, yellow.

3423. יָרַשׁ **yârash,** *yaw-rash´;* or יָרֵשׁ **yârêsh,** *yaw-raysh´;* a prim. root; to *occupy* (by *driving* out previous tenants, and *possessing* in their place); by impl. to *seize,* to *rob,* to *inherit;* also to *expel,* to *impoverish,* to *ruin:*—cast out, consume, destroy, disinherit, dispossess, drive (-ing) out, enjoy, expel, × without fail, (give to, leave for) inherit (-ance, -or), + magistrate, be (make) poor, come to poverty, (give to, make to) possess, get (have) in (take) possession, seize upon, succeed, × utterly.

3424. יְרֵשָׁה **yᵉrêshâh,** *yer-ay-shaw´;* from 3423; *occupancy:*—possession.

3425. יְרֻשָּׁה **yᵉrushshâh,** *yer-oosh-shaw´;* from 3423; something *occupied;* a *conquest;* also a *patrimony:*—heritage, inheritance, possession.

3426. יֵשׁ **yêsh,** *yaysh;* perh. from an unused root mean. to *stand* out, or *exist; entity;* used adv. or as a copula for the substantive verb (1961); there *is* or *are* (or any other form of the verb to *be,* as may suit the connection):—(there) are, (he, it, shall, there, there may, there shall, there should) be, thou do, had, hast, (which) hath, (I, shalt, that) have, (he, it, there) is, substance, it (there) was, (there) were, ye will, thou wilt, wouldest.

3427. יָשַׁב **yâshab,** *yaw-shab´;* a prim. root; prop. to *sit* down (spec. as judge. in ambush, in quiet); by impl. to *dwell,* to *remain:* causat. to *settle,* to *marry:*— (make to) abide (-ing), continue, (cause to, make to) dwell (-ing), ease self, endure, establish, × fail, habitation, haunt, (make to) inhabit (-ant), make to keep [house], lurking, × marry (-ing), (bring again to) place, remain, return, seat, set (-tle), (down-) sit (-down, still, -ting down, -ting [place] -uate), take, tarry.

3428. יֶשֶׁבְאָב **Yeshebʼâb,** *yeh-sheb-awb´;* from 3427 and 1; *seat of (his) father; Jeshebab,* an Isr.:—Jeshebeab.

3429. יֹשֵׁב בַּשֶּׁבֶת **Yôshêb bash-Shebeth,** *yo-shabe´ bash-sheh´-beth;* from the act. part. of 3427 and 7674, with a prep. and the art. interposed; *sitting in the seat; Josheb-bash-Shebeth,* an Isr.:—that sat in the seat.

3430. יִשְׁבּוֹ בְּנֹב **Yishbôw bᵉ-Nôb,** *yish-bo´ beh-nobe;* from 3427 and 5011, with a pron. suffix and a prep. interposed; *his dwelling* (is) *in Nob; Jishbo-be-Nob,* a Philistine:—Ishbi-benob [*from the marg.*].

3431. יִשְׁבַּח **Yishbach,** *yish-bakh´;* from 7623; *he will praise; Jishbach,* an Isr.:—Ishbah.

3432. יָשֻׁבִי **Yâshûbîy,** *yaw-shoo-bee´;* patron. from 3437; a *Jashubite,* or desc. of Jashub:—Jashubites.

3433. יָשֻׁבִי לֶחֶם **Yâshûbîy Lechem,** *yaw-shoo´-bee leh´-khem;* from 7725 and 3899; *returner of bread; Jashubi-Lechem,* an Isr.:—Jashubi-lehem. [Prob. the text should be pointed יֹשְׁבֵי לֶחֶם **Yôshᵉbêy Lechem,** *yo-sheh-bay´ leh´-khem,* and rendered "(they were) inhabitants of Lechem," i.e. of Bethlehem (by contraction). Comp. 3902.]

3434. יָשָׁבְעָם **Yâshobʻâm,** *yaw-shob-awm´;* from 7725 and 5971; *people will return; Jashobam,* the name of two or three Isr.:—Jashobeam.

3435. יִשְׁבָּק **Yishbâq,** *yish-bawk´;* from an unused root corresp. to 7662; *he will leave; Jishbak,* a son of Abraham:—Ishbak.

3436. יָשְׁבְּקָשָׁה **Yoshbᵉqâshâh,** *yosh-bek-aw-shaw´;* from 3427 and 7186; a *hard seat; Joshbekashah,* an Isr.:—Joshbekashah.

3437. יָשׁוּב **Yâshûwb,** *yaw-shoob´;* or יָשִׁיב **Yâshîyb,** *yaw-sheeb´;* from 7725; *he will return; Jashub,* the name of two Isr.:—Jashub.

3438. יִשְׁוָה **Yishvâh,** *yish-vaw´;* from 7737; *he will level; Jishvah,* an Isr.:—Ishvah, Isvah.

3439. יְשׁוֹחָיָה **Yᵉshôwchâyâh,** *yesh-o-khaw-yaw´;* from the same as 3445 and 3050; *Jah will empty; Jeshochajah,* an Isr.:—Jeshoaiah.

3440. יִשְׁוִי **Yishvîy,** *yish-vee´;* from 7737; *level; Jishvi,* the name of two Isr.:—Ishuai, Ishvi, Isui, Jesui.

3441. יִשְׁוִי **Yishvîy,** *yish-vee´;* patron. from 3440; a *Jishvite* (collect.) or desc. of Jishvi:—Jesuites.

3442. יֵשׁוּעַ **Yêshûwaʻ,** *yay-shoo´-ah;* for 3091; *he will save; Jeshua,* the name of ten Isr., also of a place in Pal.:—Jeshua.

3443. יֵשׁוּעַ **Yêshûwaʻ** (Chald.), *yay-shoo´-ah;* corresp. to 3442:—Jeshua.

3444. יְשׁוּעָה **yᵉshûwʻâh,** *yesh-oo´-aw;* fem. pass. part. of 3467; something *saved,* i.e. (abstr.) *deliverance;* hence *aid, victory, prosperity:*—deliverance, health, help (-ing), salvation, save, saving (health), welfare.

3445. יֶשַׁח **yeshach,** *yeh´-shakh;* from an unused root mean. to *gape* (as the empty stomach); *hunger:*—casting down.

3446. יִשְׂחָק **Yischâq,** *yis-khawk´;* from 7831; *he will laugh; Jischak,* the heir of Abraham:—Isaac. Comp. 3327.

3447. יָשַׁט **yâshaṭ,** *yaw-shat´;* a prim. root; to *extend:*—hold out.

3448. יִשַׁי **Yîshay,** *yee-shah´-ee;* by Chald. אִישַׁי **'Îyshay,** *ee-shah´ee;* from the same as 3426; *extant; Jishai,* David's father:—Jesse.

יָשִׁיב **Yâshîyb.** See 3437.

3449. יִשִּׁיָּה **Yishshîyâh,** *yish-shee-yaw´;* or יִשִּׁיָּהוּ **Yishshîyâhûw,** *yish-shee-yaw´-hoo;* from 5383 and 3050; *Jah will lend; Jishshijah,* the name of five Isr.:—Ishiah, Isshiah, Ishijah, Jesiah.

3450. יְשִׂימָאֵל **Yᵉsîymi'êl,** *yes-eem-ee-ale´;* from 7760 and 410; *God will place; Jesimiël,* an Isr.:—Jesimiel.

3451. יְשִׁימָה° **yᵉshîymâh,** *yesh-ee-maw´;* from 3456; *desolation:*—let death seize [*from the marg.*].

3452. יְשִׁימוֹן **yᵉshîymôwn,** *yesh-ee-mone´;* from 3456; a *desolation:*—desert, Jeshimon, solitary, wilderness.

יְשִׁימוֹת **yᵉshîymôwth.** See 1020, 3451.

3453. יָשִׁישׁ **yâshîysh,** *yaw-sheesh´;* from 3486; an *old* man:—(very) aged (man), ancient, very old.

3454. יְשִׁישַׁי **Yᵉshîyshay,** *yesh-ee-shah´ee;* from 3453; *aged; Jeshishai,* an Isr.:—Jeshishai.

3455. יָשַׂם **yâsam,** *yaw-sam´;* a prim root; to *place;* intrans. to *be placed:*—be put (set).

3456. יָשַׁם **yâsham,** *yaw-sham´;* a prim. root; to *lie waste:*—be desolate.

3457. יִשְׁמָא **Yishmâ',** *yish-maw´;* from 3456; *desolate; Jishma,* an Isr.:—Ishma.

3458. יִשְׁמָעֵאל **Yishmâ'ê'l,** *yish-maw-ale´; from 8085 and 410; God will hear; Jishmaël,* the name of Abraham's oldest son, and of five Isr.:—Ishmael.

3459. יִשְׁמְעֵאלִי **Yishmâ'ê'lîy,** *yish-maw-ay-lee´;* patron. from 3458; a *Jishmaëlite* or desc. of Jishmael:—Ishmaelite.

3460. יִשְׁמַעְיָה **Yishma'yâh,** *yish-mah-yaw´;* or יִשְׁמַעְיָהוּ **Yishma'yâhûw,** *yish-mah-yaw´-hoo;* from 8085 and 3050; *Jah will hear; Jishmajah,* the name of two Isr.:—Ishmaiah.

3461. יִשְׁמְרַי **Yishmᵉray,** *yish-mer-ah´ee;* from 8104; *preservative; Jishmerai,* an Isr.:—Ishmerai.

3462. יָשֵׁן **yâshên,** *yaw-shane´;* a prim. root; prop. to *be slack* or *languid,* i.e. (by impl.) *sleep* (fig. to *die*); also to *grow old, stale* or *inveterate:*—old (store), remain long, (make to) sleep.

3463. יָשֵׁן **yâshên,** *yaw-shane´;* from 3462; *sleepy:*—asleep, (one out of) sleep (-eth, -ing), slept.

3464. יָשֵׁן **Yâshên,** *yaw-shane´;* the same as 3463; *Jashen,* an Isr.:—Jashen.

3465. יָשָׁן **yâshân,** *yaw-shawn´;* from 3462; *old:*—old.

3466. יְשָׁנָה **Yᵉshânâh,** *yesh-aw-naw´;* fem. of 3465; *Jeshanah,* a place in Pal.:—Jeshanah.

3467. יָשַׁע **yâsha',** *yaw-shah´;* a prim. root; prop. to *be open, wide* or *free,* i.e. (by impl.) to *be safe;* causat. to *free* or *succor:*— × at all, avenging, defend, deliver (-er), help, preserve, rescue, be safe, bring (having) salvation, save (-iour), get victory.

3468. יֶשַׁע **yesha',** *yeh´-shah;* or יֵשַׁע **yêsha',** *yay´-shah;* from 3467; *liberty, deliverance, prosperity:*—safety, salvation, saving.

3469. יִשְׁעִי **Yish'îy,** *yish-ee´;* from 3467; *saving; Jishi,* the name of four Isr.:—Ishi.

3470. יְשַׁעְיָה **Yᵉsha'yâh,** *yesh-ah-yaw´;* or יְשַׁעְיָהוּ **Yᵉsha'yâhûw,** *yesh-ah-yaw´-hoo;* from 3467 and 3050; *Jah has saved; Jeshajah,* the name of seven Isr.:—Isaiah, Jesaiah, Jeshaiah.

3471. יָשְׁפֵה **yâshᵉphêh,** *yaw-shef-ay´;* from an unused root mean. to *polish;* a gem supposed to be *jasper* (from the resemblance in name):—jasper.

3472. יִשְׁפָּה **Yishpâh,** *yish-paw´;* perh. from 8192; *he will scratch; Jishpah,* an Isr.:—Ispah.

3473. יִשְׁפָּן **Yishpân,** *yish-pawn´;* prob. from the same as 8227; *he will hide; Jishpan,* an Isr.:—Ishpan.

3474. יָשַׁר **yâshar,** *yaw-shar´;* a prim. root; to *be straight* or *even;* fig. to *be* (causat. to *make*) *right, pleasant, prosperous:*—direct, fit, seem good (meet), + please (well), be (esteem, go) right (on), bring (look, make, take the) straight (way), be upright (-ly).

3475. יֵשֶׁר **Yêsher,** *yay´-sher;* from 3474; the *right; Jesher,* an Isr.:—Jesher.

3476. יֹשֶׁר **yôsher,** *yo´-sher;* from 3474; the *right:*—equity, meet, right, upright (-ness).

3477. יָשָׁר **yâshâr,** *yaw-shawr´;* from 3474; *straight* (lit. or fig.):—convenient, equity, Jasher, just, meet (-est), + pleased well right (-eous), straight, (most) upright (-ly, -ness).

3478. יִשְׂרָאֵל **Yisrâ'êl,** *yis-raw-ale´;* from 8280 and 410; *he will rule as God; Jisraël,* a symbolical name of Jacob; also (typically) of his posterity:—Israel.

3479. יִשְׂרָאֵל **Yisrâ'êl** (Chald.), *yis-raw-ale´* corresp. to 3478:—Israel.

3480. יְשַׂרְאֵלָה **Yᵉsar'êlâh,** *yes-ar-ale´-aw;* by var. from 3477 and 410 with directive enclitic; *right towards God; Jesarelah,* an Isr.:—Jesharelah. Comp. 841

3481. יִשְׂרְאֵלִי **Yisrᵉ'êlîy,** *yis-reh-ay-lee´;* patron. from 3478; a *Jisreëlite* or desc. of Jisrael:—of Israel, Israelite.

3482. יִשְׂרְאֵלִית **Yisrᵉ'êlîyth,** *yis-reh-ay-leeth´;* fem. of 3481; a *Jisreëlitess* or female desc. of Jisrael:—Israelitish.

3483. יִשְׁרָה **yishrâh,** *yish-raw´;* fem. of 3477; *rectitude:*—uprightness.

3484. יְשֻׁרוּן **Yᵉshûrûwn,** *yesh-oo-roon´;* from 3474; *upright; Jeshurun,* a symbol. name for Israel:—Jeshurun.

3485. יִשָּׂשכָר **Yissâˢkâr,** *yis-saw-kawr´* (strictly *yis-saws-kawr´*); from 5375 and 7939; *he will bring a reward; Jissaskar,* a son of Jacob:—Issachar.

3486. יָשֵׁשׁ **yâshêsh,** *yaw-shaysh´;* from an unused root mean. to *blanch; gray*-haired, i.e. an *aged* man:—stoop for age.

3487. יַת **yath** (Chald.), *yath;* corresp. to 853; a sign of the object of a verb: + whom.

3488. יְתִב **yᵉthîyb** (Chald.), *yeth-eeb´;* corresp. to 3427; to *sit* or *dwell:*—dwell, (be) set, sit.

3489. יָתֵד **yâthêd,** *yaw-thade´;* from an unused root mean. to *pin* through or fast; a *peg:*—nail, paddle, pin, stake.

3490. יָתוֹם **yâthôwm,** *yaw-thome´;* from an unused root mean. to *be lonely;* a *bereaved* person:—fatherless (child), orphan.

3491. יָתוּר **yâthûwr,** *yaw-thoor´;* pass. part. of 3498; prop. what is *left,* i.e. (by impl.) a *gleaning:*—range.

3492. יַתִּיר **Yattîyr,** *yat-teer´;* from 3498; *redundant; Jattir,* a place in Pal.:—Jattir.

3493. יַתִּיר **yattîyr** (Chald.) *yat-teer´;* corresp. to 3492; *preeminent;* adv. *very:*—exceeding (-ly), excellent.

3494. יִתְלָה **Yithlâh,** *yith-law´;* prob. from 8518; it *will hang,* i.e. be high; *Jithlah,* a place in Pal.:—Jethlah.

3495. יִתְמָה **Yithmâh,** *yith-maw´;* from the same as 3490; *orphanage; Jithmah,* an Isr.:—Ithmah.

3496. יַתְנִיאֵל **Yathnîy'êl,** *yath-nee-ale´;* from an unused root mean. to *endure,* and 410; *continued of God; Jathniël,* an Isr.:—Jathniel.

3497. יִתְנָן **Yithnân,** *yith-nawn´;* from the same as 8577; *extensive; Jithnan,* a place in Pal.:—Ithnan.

3498. יָתַר **yâthar,** *yaw-thar´;* a prim. rot; to *jut* over or *exceed;* by impl. to *excel;* (intrans.) to *remain* or *be left;* causat. to *leave, cause to abound, preserve:*—excel, leave (a remnant), left behind, too much, make plenteous, preserve, (be, let) remain (-der, -ing, -nant), reserve, residue, rest.

3499. יֶתֶר **yether,** *yeh´-ther;* from 3498; prop. an *overhanging,* i.e. (by impl.) an *excess, superiority, remainder;* also a small *rope* (as hanging free):— + abundant, cord, exceeding, excellency (-ent), what they leave, that hath left, plentifully, remnant, residue, rest, string, with.

3500. יֶתֶר **Yether,** *yeh´-ther;* the same as 3499 *Jether,* the name of five or six Isr. and of one Midianite:—Jether, Jethro. Comp. 3503.

3501. יִתְרָא **Yithrâ',** *yith-raw´;* by var. for 3502; *Jithra,* an Isr. (or Ishmaelite):—Ithra.

3502. יִתְרָה **yithrâh,** *yith-raw´;* fem. of 3499; prop. *excellence,* i.e. (by impl.) *wealth:*—abundance, riches.

3503. יִתְרוֹ **Yithrôw,** *yith-ro´;* from 3499 with pron. suffix; *his excellence; Jethro,* Moses' father-in-law:—Jethro. Comp. 3500.

3504. יִתְרוֹן **yithrôwn,** *yith-rone´;* from 3498; *preeminence, gain:*—better, excellency (-leth), profit (-able).

3505. יִתְרִי **Yithrîy,** *yith-ree´;* patron. from 3500; a *Jithrite* or desc. of Jether:—Ithrite.

3506. יִתְרָן **Yithrân,** *yith-rawn´;* from 3498; *excellent; Jithran;* the name of an Edomite and of an Isr.:—Ithran.

3507. יִתְרְעָם **Yithreʿâm,** *yith-reh-awm´;* from 3499 and 5971; *excellence of people; Jithreäm,* a son of David:—Ithream.

3508. יֹתֶרֶת **yôthereth,** *yo-theh´-reth;* fem. act. part. of 3498; the *lobe* or *flap* of the liver (as if redundant or outhanging):—caul.

3509. יְתֵת **Yethêth,** *yeh-thayth´;* of uncert. der.; *Jetheth,* an Edomite:—Jetheth.

כ

3510. כָּאַב **kâ'ab,** *kaw-ab´;* a prim. root; prop. to feel *pain;* by impl. to *grieve;* fig. to *spoil:*—grieving, mar, have pain, make sad (sore), (be) sorrowful.

3511. כְּאֵב **ke'êb,** *keh-abe´;* from 3510; *suffering* (phys. or mental), *adversity:*—grief, pain, sorrow.

3512. כָּאָה **kâ'âh,** *kaw-aw´;* a prim. root; to *despond:* causat. to *deject:*—broken, be grieved, make sad.

3513. כָּבַד **kâbad,** *kaw-bad´;* or כָּבֵד **kâbêd,** *kaw-bade´;* a prim. root; to *be heavy,* i.e. in a bad sense *(burdensome, severe, dull)* or in a good sense *(numerous, rich, honorable);* causat. to *make weighty* (in the same two senses):—abounding with, more grievously afflict, boast, be chargeable, × be dim, glorify, be (make) glorious (things), glory, (very) great, be grievous, harden, be (make) heavy, be heavier, lay heavily, (bring to, come to, do, get, be had in) honour (self), (be) honourable (man), lade, × more be laid, make self many, nobles, prevail, promote (to honour), be rich, be (go) sore, stop.

3514. כֹּבֶד **kôbed,** *ko´-bed;* from 3513; *weight, multitude, vehemence:*—grievousness, heavy, great number.

3515. כָּבֵד **kâbêd,** *kaw-bade´;* from 3513; *heavy;* fig. in a good sense *(numerous)* or in a bad sense *(severe, difficult, stupid):*—(so) great, grievous, hard (-ened), (too) heavy (-ier), laden, much, slow, sore, thick.

3516. כָּבֵד **kâbêd,** *kaw-bade´;* the same as 3515; the *liver* (as the *heaviest* of the viscera):—liver.

כָּבֹד **kâbôd.** See 3519.

3517. כְּבֵדֻת **kebêdûth,** *keb-ay-dooth´;* fem. of 3515; *difficulty:*— × heavily.

3518. כָּבָה **kâbâh,** *kaw-baw´;* a prim. root; to *expire* or (causat.) to *extinguish* (fire, light, anger):—go (put) out, quench.

3519. כָּבוֹד **kâbôwd,** *kaw-bode´;* rarely כָּבֹד **kâbôd,** *kaw-bode´;* from 3513; prop. *weight;* but only fig. in a good sense, *splendor* or *copiousness:*—glorious (-ly), glory, honour (-able).

3520. כְּבוּדָּה **kebûwddâh,** *keb-ood-daw´;* irreg. fem. pass. part. of 3513; *weightiness,* i.e. *magnificence, wealth:*—carriage, all glorious, stately.

3521. כָּבוּל **Kâbûwl,** *kaw-bool´;* from the same as 3525 in the sense of *limitation; sterile; Cabul,* the name of two places in Pal.:—Cabul.

3522. כַּבּוֹן **Kabbôwn,** *kab-bone´;* from an unused root mean. to *heap* up; *hilly; Cabbon,* a place in Pal.:—Cabbon.

3523. כְּבִיר **kebîyr,** *keb-eer;* from 3527 in the orig. sense of *plaiting;* a *matrass* (of intertwined materials):—pillow.

3524. כַּבִּיר **kabbîyr,** *kab-beer´;* from 3527; *vast,* whether in extent (fig. of power, *mighty,* of time, *aged*), or in number, *many:*— + feeble, mighty, most, much, strong, valiant.

3525. כֶּבֶל **kebel,** *keh´-bel;* from an unused root mean. to *twine* or braid together; a *fetter:*—fetter.

3526. כָּבַס **kâbaç,** *kaw-bas´;* a prim. root; to *trample;* hence to *wash* (prop. by stamping with the feet), whether lit. (including the *fulling* process) or fig.:—fuller, wash (-ing).

3527. כָּבַר **kâbar,** *kaw-bar´;* a prim. root; prop. to *plait* together, i.e. (fig.) to *augment* (espec. in number or quantity, to *accumulate*):—in abundance, multiply.

3528. כְּבָר **kebâr,** *keb-awr´;* from 3527; prop. *extent* of time, i.e. a *great while;* hence *long ago, formerly, hitherto:*—already, (seeing that which), now.

3529. כְּבָר **Kebâr,** *keb-awr´;* the same as 3528; *length; Kebar,* a river of Mesopotamia:—Chebar. Comp. 2249.

3530. כִּבְרָה **kibrâh,** *kib-raw´;* fem. of 3528; prop. *length,* i.e. a *measure* (of uncert. dimension):— × little.

3531. כְּבָרָה **kebârâh,** *keb-aw-raw´;* from 3527 in its orig. sense; a *sieve* (as netted):—sieve.

3532. כֶּבֶשׂ **kebes,** *keh-bes´;* from an unused root mean. to *dominate;* a *ram (just old enough to butt):*—lamb, sheep.

3533. כָּבַשׁ **kâbash,** *kaw-bash´;* a prim. root; to *tread* down; hence neg. to *disregard;* pos. to *conquer, subjugate, violate:*—bring into bondage, force, keep under, subdue, bring into subjection.

3534. כֶּבֶשׁ **kebesh,** *keh´-besh;* from 3533; a *footstool* (as trodden upon):—footstool.

3535. כִּבְשָׂה **kibsâh,** *kib-saw´;* or כַּבְשָׂה **kabsâh,** *kab-saw´;* fem. of 3532; a *ewe:*—(ewe) lamb.

3536. כִּבְשָׁן **kibshân,** *kib-shawn´;* from 3533; a smelting *furnace* (as *reducing* metals):—furnace.

3537. כַּד **kad,** *kad;* from an unused root mean. to *deepen;* prop. a *pail;* but gen. of earthenware; a *jar* for domestic purposes:—barrel, pitcher.

3538. כְּדַב **kedab** (Chald.), *ked-ab´;* from a root corresp. to 3576; *false:*—lying.

3539. כַּדְכֹּד **kadkôd,** *kad-kode´;* from the same as 3537 in the sense of *striking fire* from a metal forged; a *sparkling* gem, prob. the ruby:—agate.

3540. כְּדָרְלָעֹמֶר **Kedorlâʿômer,** *ked-or-law-o´-mer;* of for. or.; *Kedorlaomer,* an early Pers. king:—Chedorlaomer.

3541. כֹּה **kôh,** *ko;* from the prefix *k* and 1931; prop. *like this,* i.e. by impl. (of manner) *thus* (or *so*); also (of place) *here* (or *hither*); or (of time) *now:*—also, here, + hitherto, like, on the other side, so (and much), such, on that manner, (on) this (manner, side, way, way and that way), + mean while, yonder.

3542. כָּה **kâh** (Chald.), *kaw;* corresp. to 3541:—hitherto.

3543. כָּהָה **kâhâh,** *kaw-haw´;* a prim. root; to *be weak,* i.e. (fig.) to *despond* (causat. *rebuke*), or (of light, the eye) to *grow dull:*—darken, be dim, fail, faint, restrain, × utterly.

3544. כֵּהֶה **kêheh,** *kay-heh´;* from 3543; *feeble, obscure:*—somewhat dark, darkish, wax dim, heaviness, smoking.

3545. כֵּהָה **kêhâh,** *kay-haw´;* fem. of 3544; prop. a *weakening;* fig. *alleviation,* i.e. cure:—healing.

3546. כְּהַל **kehal** (Chald.), *keh-hal´;* a root corresp. to 3201 and 3557; to *be able:*—be able, could.

3547. כָּהַן **kâhan,** *kaw-han´;* a prim. root, appar. mean. to *mediate* in religious services; but used only as denom. from 3548; to *officiate* as a priest; fig. to *put on regalia:*—deck, be (do the office of a, execute the, minister in the) priest ('s office).

3548. כֹּהֵן **kôhên,** *ko-hane´;* act. part. of 3547; lit. one *officiating,* a *priest;* also (by courtesy) an *acting priest* (although a layman):—chief ruler, × own, priest, prince, principal officer.

3549. כָּהֵן **kâhên** (Chald.), *kaw-hane´;* corresp. to 3548:—priest.

3550. כְּהֻנָּה **kehunnâh,** *keh-hoon-naw´;* from 3547; *priesthood:*—priesthood, priest's office.

3551. כַּו **kav** (Chald.), *kav;* from a root corresp. to 3854 in the sense of *piercing;* a *window* (as a perforation):—window.

3552. כּוּב **Kûwb,** *koob;* of for. der.; *Kub,* a country near Egypt:—Chub.

3553. כּוֹבַע **kôwbaʻ,** *ko´-bah;* from an unused root mean. to be *high* or *rounded;* a *helmet* (as *arched*):—helmet. Comp. 6959.

3554. כָּוָה **kâvâh,** *kaw-vaw´;* a prim. root; prop. to *prick* or *penetrate;* hence to *blister* (as smarting or eating into):—burn.

כּוֹחַ **kôwach.** See 3581.

3555. כְּוִיָּה **kᵉvîyâh,** *kev-ee-yaw´;* from 3554; a *branding:*—burning.

3556. כּוֹכָב **kôwkâb,** *ko-kawb´;* prob. from the same as 3522 (in the sense of *rolling*) or 3554 (in the sense of *blazing*); a *star* (as *round* or as *shining*); fig. a *prince:*—star ([-gazer]).

3557. כּוּל **kûwl,** *kool;* a prim. root; prop. to *keep in;* hence to *measure;* fig. to *maintain* (in various senses):—(be able to, can) abide, bear, comprehend, contain, feed, forbearing, guide, hold (-ing in), nourish (-er), be present, make provision, receive, sustain, provide sustenance (victuals).

3558. כּוּמָז **kûwmâz,** *koo-mawz´;* from an unused root mean. to *store* away; a *jewel* (prob. gold beads):—tablet.

3559. כּוּן **kûwn,** *koon;* a prim. root; prop. to *be erect* (i.e. stand perpendicular); hence (causat.) to *set up,* in a great variety of applications, whether lit. *(establish, fix, prepare, apply),* or fig. *(appoint, render sure, proper or prosperous):*—certain (-ty), confirm, direct, faithfulness, fashion, fasten, firm, be fitted, be fixed, frame, be meet, ordain, order, perfect, (make) preparation, prepare (self), provide, make provision, (be, make) ready, right, set (aright, fast, forth), be stable, (e-) stablish, stand, tarry, × very deed.

3560. כּוּן **Kûwn,** *koon;* prob. from 3559; *established; Kun,* a place in Syria:—Chun.

3561. כַּוָּן **kavvân,** *kav-vawn´;* from 3559; something *prepared,* i.e. a sacrificial *wafer:*—cake.

3562. כּוֹנַנְיָהוּ **Kôwnanyâhûw,** *ko-nan-yaw´-hoo;* from 3559 and 3050; *Jah has sustained; Conanjah,* the name of two Isr.:—Conaniah, Cononiah. Comp. 3663.

3563. כּוֹס **kôwç,** *koce;* from an unused root mean. to *hold* together; a *cup* (as a container), often fig. a *lot* (as if a potion); also some unclean bird, prob. an *owl* (perh. from the cup-like cavity of its eye):—cup, (small) owl. Comp. 3599.

3564. כּוּר **kûwr,** *koor;* from an unused root mean. prop. to *dig* through; a *pot* or *furnace* (as if excavated):—furnace. Comp. 3600.

כּוֹר **kôwr.** See 3733.

3565. כּוֹר עָשָׁן **Kôwr ʻÂshân,** *kore aw-shawn´;* from 3564 and 6227; *furnace of smoke; Cor-Ashan,* a place in Pal.:—Chor-ashan.

3566. כּוֹרֶשׁ **Kôwresh,** *ko´-resh;* or (Ezra 1 : 1 [last time], 2) כֹּרֶשׁ **Kôresh,** *ko´-resh;* from the Pers.; *Koresh* (or Cyrus), the Pers. king:—Cyrus.

3567. כּוֹרֶשׁ **Kôwresh** (Chald.), *ko´-resh;* corresp. to 3566:—Cyrus.

3568. כּוּשׁ **Kûwsh,** *koosh;* prob. of for. or.; *Cush* (or Ethiopia), the name of a son of Ham, and of his territory; also of an Isr.:—Chush, Cush, Ethiopia.

3569. כּוּשִׁי **Kûwshîy,** *koo-shee´;* patron. from 3568; a *Cushite,* or desc. of Cush:—Cushi, Cushite, Ethiopian (-s).

3570. כּוּשִׁי **Kûwshîy,** *koo-shee´;* the same as 3569; *Cushi,* the name of two Isr.:—Cushi.

3571. כּוּשִׁית **Kûwshîyth,** *koo-sheeth´;* fem. of 3569; a *Cushite woman:*—Ethiopian.

3572. כּוּשָׁן **Kûwshân,** *koo-shawn´;* perh. from 3568; *Cushan,* a region of Arabia:—Cushan.

3573. כּוּשַׁן רִשְׁעָתַיִם **Kûwshan Rishʻâthâyim,** *koo-shan´rish-aw-thah´-yim;* appar. from 3572 and the dual of 7564; *Cushan of double wickedness; Cushan-Rishathajim,* a Mesopotamian king:—Chushan-rishathayim.

3574. כּוֹשָׁרָה **kôwshârâh,** *ko-shaw-raw´;* from 3787; *prosperity;* in plur. *freedom:*— × chain.

3575. כּוּת **Kûwth,** *kooth;* or (fem.) כּוּתָה **Kûwthâh,** *koo-thaw´;* of for. or.; *Cuth* or *Cuthah,* a province of Assyria:—Cuth.

3576. כָּזַב **kâzab,** *kaw-zab´;* a prim. root; to *lie* (i.e. *deceive*), lit. or fig.:—fail, (be found a, make a) liar, lie, lying, be in vain.

3577. כָּזָב **kâzâb,** *kaw-zawb´;* from 3576; *falsehood;* lit. (*untruth*) or fig. *(idol)*:—deceitful, false, leasing, + liar, lie, lying.

3578. כֹּזְבָא **Kôzᵉbâʼ,** *ko-zeb-aw´;* from 3576; *fallacious; Cozeba,* a place in Pal.:—Choseba.

3579. כָּזְבִּי **Kozbîy,** *koz-bee´;* from 3576; *false; Cozbi,* a Midianitess:—Cozbi.

3580. כְּזִיב **Kᵉzîyb,** *kez-eeb´; from 3576; falsified; Kezib,* a place in Pal.:—Chezib.

3581. כֹּחַ **kôach,** *ko´-akh;* or (Dan. 11 : 6) כּוֹחַ **kôwach,** *ko´-akh;* from an unused root mean. to *be firm; vigor,* lit. (*force,* in a good or a bad sense) or fig. *(capacity, means, produce);* also (from its hardiness) a large *lizard:*—ability, able, chameleon, force, fruits, might, power (-ful), strength, substance, wealth.

3582. כָּחַד **kâchad,** *kaw-khad´;* a prim. root; to *secrete,* by act or word; hence (intens.) to *destroy:*—conceal, cut down (off), desolate, hide.

3583. כָּחַל **kâchal,** *kaw-khal´;* a prim. root; to *paint* (with stibium):—paint.

3584. כָּחַשׁ **kâchash,** *kaw-khash´;* a prim. root; to *be untrue,* in word (to *lie, feign, disown*) or deed (to *disappoint, fail, cringe*):—deceive, deny, dissemble, fail, deal falsely, be found liars, (be-) lie, lying, submit selves.

3585. כַּחַשׁ **kachash,** *kakh´-ash;* from 3584; lit. a *failure* of flesh, i.e. *emaciation;* fig. *hypocrisy:*—leanness, lies, lying.

3586. כֶּחָשׁ **kechâsh,** *kekh-awsh´;* from 3584; *faithless:*—lying.

3587. כִּי **kîy,** *kee;* from 3554; a *brand* or *scar:*—burning.

3588. כִּי **kîy,** *kee;* a prim. particle [the full form of the prepositional prefix] indicating *causal* relations of all kinds, antecedent or consequent; (by impl.) very widely used as a rel. conj. or adv. [as below]; often largely modified by other particles annexed:—and, + (forasmuch, inasmuch, where-) as, assured [-ly], + but, certainly, doubtless, + else, even, + except, for, how, (because, in, so, than) that, + nevertheless, now, rightly, seeing, since, surely, then, therefore, + (al-) though, + till, truly, + until, when, whether, while, who, yea, yet,

3589. כִּיד **kîyd,** *keed;* from a prim, root mean. to *strike:* a *crushing;* fig. *calamity:*—destruction.

3590. כִּידוֹד **kîydôwd,** *kee-dode´;* from the same as 3589 [comp. 3539]; prop. something *struck* off, i.e. a *spark* (as struck):—spark.

3591. כִּידוֹן **kîydôwn,** *kee-dohn´;* from the same as 3589; prop. something to *strike* with, i.e. a *dart* (perh. smaller than 2595):—lance, shield, spear, target.

3592. כִּידוֹן **Kîydôwn,** *kee-dohn´;* the same as 3591; *Kidon,* a place in Pal.:—Chidon.

3593. כִּידוֹר **kîydôwr,** *kee-dore´;* of uncert. der.; perh. *tumult:*—battle.

3594. כִּיּוּן **Kîyûwn,** *kee-yoon´;* from 3559; prop. a *statue,* i.e. idol; but used (by euphemism) for some heathen deity (perh. corresp. to Priapus or Baal-peor):—Chiun.

3595. כִּיּוֹר **kîyôwr,** *kee-yore´;* or כִּיֹּר **kîyôr,** *kee-yore´;* from the same as 3564; prop. something *round* (as *excavated* or *bored*), i.e. a chafing-*dish* for coals or a *caldron* for cooking; hence (from similarity of form) a *washbowl;* also (for the same reason) a *pulpit* or platform:—hearth, laver, pan, scaffold.

3596. כִּילַי **kîylay,** *kee-lah´ee;* or כֵּלַי **kêlay,** *kay-lah´ee;* from 3557 in the sense of *withholding; niggardly:*—churl.

3597. כֵּילַף **kêylaph,** *kay-laf´;* from an unused root mean. to *clap* or strike with noise; a *club* or sledge-hammer:—hammer.

3598. כִּימָה **Kîymâh,** *kee-maw´;* from the same as 3558; a *cluster* of stars, i.e. the *Pleiades:*—Pleiades, seven stars.

3599. כִּיס **kîyç,** *keece;* a form for 3563; a *cup;* also a *bag* for money or weights:—bag, cup, purse.

3600. כִּיר **kîyr,** *keer;* a form for 3564 (only in the dual); a cooking *range* (consisting of two parallel stones, across which the boiler is set):—ranges for pots.

כִּיֹּר **kîyôr.** See 3595.

3601. כִּישׁוֹר **kîyshôwr,** *kee-shore´;* from 3787; lit. a *director,* i.e. the *spindle* or shank of a distaff (6418), by which it is twirled:—spindle.

3602. כָּכָה **kâkâh,** *kaw´-kaw;* from 3541; *just so,* referring to the previous or following context:—after that (this) manner, this matter, (even) so, in such a case, thus.

3603. כִּכָּר **kikkâr,** *kik-kawr´;* from 3769; a *circle,* i.e. (by impl.) a circumjacent *tract* or region, espec. the *Ghôr* or valley of the Jordan; also a (round) *loaf;* also a *talent* (or large [round] coin):—loaf, morsel, piece, plain, talent.

3604. כִּכַּר **kikkêr** (Chald.), *kik-kare´;* corresp. to 3603; a *talent:*—talent.

3605. כֹּל **kôl,** *kole;* or (Jer. 33 : 8)° כּוֹל **kôwl,** *kole;* from 3634; prop. the *whole;* hence *all, any* or *every* (in the sing. only, but often in a plur. sense):—(in) all (manner, [ye]), altogether, any (manner), enough, every (one, place, thing), howsoever, as many as, [no-] thing, ought, whatsoever, (the) whole, whoso (-ever).

3606. כֹּל **kôl** (Chald.), *kole;* corresp. to 3605:—all, any, + (forasmuch) as, + be- (for this) cause, every, + no (manner, -ne), + there (where) -fore, + though, what (where, who) -soever, (the) whole.

3607. כָּלָא **kâlâ',** *kaw-law´;* a prim. root; to *restrict,* by act (*hold* back or in) or word (*prohibit):*—finish, forbid, keep (back), refrain, restrain, retain, shut up, be stayed, withhold.

3608. כֶּלֶא **kele',** *keh´-leh;* from 3607; a *prison:*—prison. Comp. 3610, 3628.

3609. כִּלְאָב **Kil'âb,** *kil-awb´;* appar. from 3607 and 1; *restraint of* (his) *father; Kilab,* an Isr.:—Chileab.

3610. כִּלְאַיִם **kil'ayim,** *kil-ah´-yim;* dual of 3608 in the original sense of *separation; two heterogeneities:*—divers seeds (-e kinds), mingled (seed).

3611. כֶּלֶב **keleb,** *keh´-leb;* from an unused root mean. to *yelp,* or else to *attack;* a *dog;* hence (by euphemism) a male *prostitute:*—dog.

3612. כָּלֵב **Kâlêb,** *kaw-labe´;* perh. a form of 3611, or else from the same root in the sense of *forcible; Caleb,* the name of three Isr.:—Caleb.

3613. כָּלֵב אֶפְרָתָה **Kâlêb 'Ephrâthâh,** *kaw-labe´ ef-raw´-thaw;* from 3612 and 672; *Caleb-Ephrathah,* a place in Eg. (if the text is correct):—Caleb-ephrathah.

3614. כָּלִבּוֹ° **Kâlibbôw,** *kaw-lib-bo´;* prob. by err. transc. for כָּלֵבִי **Kâlêbîy,** *kaw-lay-bee´;* patron. from 3612; a *Calebite* or desc. of Caleb:—of the house of Caleb.

3615. כָּלָה **kâlâh,** *kaw-law´;* a prim. root; to *end,* whether intrans. (to *cease, be finished, perish*) or trans. (to *complete, prepare, consume*):—accomplish, cease, consume (away), determine, destroy (utterly), be (when . . . were) done, (be an) end (of), expire, (cause to) fail, faint, finish, fulfil, × fully, × have, leave (off), long, bring to pass, wholly reap, make clean riddance, spend, quite take away, waste.

3616. כָּלֶה **kâleh,** *kaw-leh´;* from 3615; *pining:*—fail.

3617. כָּלָה **kâlâh,** *kaw-law´;* from 3615; a *completion;* adv. *completely;* also *destruction:*—altogether, (be, utterly) consume (-d), consummation (-ption), was determined, (full, utter) end, riddance.

3618. כַּלָּה **kallâh,** *kal-law´;* from 3634; a *bride* (as if *perfect*); hence a *son's wife:*—bride, daughter-in-law, spouse.

כְּלוּא **kᵉlûw'.** See 3628.

3619. כְּלוּב **kᵉlûb,** *kel-oob´;* from the same as 3611; a bird-*trap* (as furnished with a *clap*-stick or treadle to spring it); hence a *basket* (as resembling a wicker cage):—basket, cage.

3620. כְּלוּב **Kᵉlûwb,** *kel-oob´;* the same as 3619; *Kelub,* the name of two Isr.:—Chelub.

3621. כְּלוּבַי **Kᵉlûwbay,** *kel-oo-bay´ee;* a form of 3612; *Kelubai,* an Isr.:—Chelubai.

3622. כְּלוּהַי **Kᵉlûwhay,** *kel-oo-hah´ee;* from 3615; *completed; Keluhai,* an Isr.:—Chelluh.

3623. כְּלוּלָה **kᵉlûwlâh,** *kel-oo-law´;* denom. pass. part. from 3618; *bridehood* (only in the plur.):—espousal.

3624. כֶּלַח **kelach,** *keh´-lakh;* from an unused root mean. to *be complete; maturity:*—full (old) age.

3625. כֶּלַח **Kelach,** *keh´-lakh;* the same as 3624; *Kelach,* a place in Assyria:—Calah.

3626. כָּל־חֹזֶה **Kol-Chôzeh,** *kol-kho-zeh´;* from 3605 and 2374; *every seer; Col-Chozeh,* an Isr.:—Col-hozeh.

3627. כְּלִי **kᵉlîy,** *kel-ee´;* from 3615; something *prepared,* i.e. any *apparatus* (as an implement, utensil, dress, vessel or weapon):—armour ([-bearer]), artillery, bag, carriage, + furnish, furniture, instrument, jewel, that is made of, × one from another, that which pertaineth, pot, + psaltery, sack, stuff, thing, tool, vessel, ware, weapon, + whatsoever.

3628. כְּלִיא **kᵉlîy',** *kel-ee´;* or כְּלוּא **kᵉlûw',** *kel-oo´;* from 3607 [comp. 3608]; a *prison:*—prison.

3629. כִּלְיָה **kilyâh,** *kil-yaw´;* fem. of 3627 (only in the plur.); a *kidney* (as an essential *organ*); fig. the *mind* (as the interior self):—kidneys, reins.

3630. כִּלְיוֹן **Kilyôwn,** *kil-yone´;* a form of 3631; *Kiljon,* an Isr.:—Chilion.

3631. כִּלָּיוֹן **killâyôwn,** *kil-law-yone´;* from 3615; *pining, destruction:*—consumption, failing.

3632. כָּלִיל **kâlîyl,** *kaw-leel´;* from 3634; *complete;* as noun, the *whole* (spec. a sacrifice *entirely consumed*); as adv. *fully:*—all, every whit, flame, perfect (-ion), utterly, whole burnt offering (sacrifice), wholly.

3633. כַּלְכֹּל **Kalkôl,** *kal-kole´;* from 3557; *sustenance; Calcol,* an Isr.:—Calcol, Chalcol.

3634. כָּלַל **kâlal,** *kaw-lal´;* a prim. root; to *complete:*—(make) perfect.

3635. כְּלַל **kᵉlal** (Chald.), *kel-al´;* corresp. to 3634; to *complete:*—finish, make (set) up.

3636. כְּלָל **Kᵉlâl,** *kel-awl´;* from 3634; *complete; Kelal,* an Isr.:—Chelal.

3637. כָּלַם **kâlam,** *kaw-lawm´;* a prim. root; prop. to *wound;* but only fig., to *taunt* or *insult:*—be (make) ashamed, blush, be confounded, be put to confusion, hurt, reproach, (do, put to) shame.

3638. כִּלְמָד **Kilmâd,** *kil-mawd´;* of for. der.; *Kilmad,* a place appar. in the Assyrian empire:—Chilmad.

3639. כְּלִמָּה **kᵉlimmâh,** *kel-im-maw´;* from 3637; *disgrace:*—confusion, dishonour, reproach, shame.

3640. כְּלִמּוּת **kᵉlimmûwth,** *kel-im-mooth´;* from 3639; *disgrace:*—shame.

3641. כַּלְנֶה **Kalneh,** *kal-neh´;* or כַּלְנֵה **Kalnêh,** *kal-nay´;* also כַּלְנוֹ **Kalnôw,** *kal-no´;* of for. der.; *Calneh* or *Calno,* a place in the Assyrian empire:—Calneh, Calno. Comp. 3656.

3642. כָּמַהּ **kâmahh,** *kaw-mah´;* a prim. root; to *pine* after:—long.

3643. כִּמְהָם **Kimhâm,** *kim-hawm´;* from 3642; *pining; Kimham,* an Isr.:—Chimham.

3644. כְּמוֹ **kᵉmôw,** *kem-o´;* or כָּמוֹ **kâmôw,** *kaw-mo´;* a form of the pref. *k,* but used separately [comp. 3651]; *as, thus, so:*—according to, (such) as (it were, well as), in comparison of, like (as, to, unto), thus, when, worth.

3645. כְּמוֹשׁ **Kᵉmôwsh,** *kem-oshe´;* or (Jer. 48 : 7) כְּמִישׁ° **Kᵉmîysh,** *kem-eesh´;* from an unused root mean. to *subdue;* the *powerful; Kemosh,* the god of the Moabites:—Chemosh.

3646. כַּמֹּן **kammôn,** *kam-mone´;* from an unused root mean. to *store* up or *preserve;* *"cummin"* (from its use as a *condiment*):—cummin.

3647. כָּמַס **kâmaç,** *kaw-mas´;* a prim. root; to *store* away, i.e. (fig.) in the memory:—lay up in store.

3648. כָּמַר **kâmar,** *kaw-mar´;* a prim. root; prop. to *intertwine* or *contract,* i.e. (by impl.) to *shrivel* (as with heat); fig. to *be* deeply *affected* with passion (love or pity):—be black, be kindled, yearn.

3649. כָּמָר **kâmâr,** *kaw-mawr´;* from 3648; prop. an *ascetic* (as if *shrunk* with self-maceration), i.e. an idolatrous *priest* (only in plur.):—Chemarims, (idolatrous) priests.

3650. כִּמְרִיר **kimrîyr,** *kim-reer´;* redupl. from 3648; *obscuration* (as if from *shrinkage* of light), i.e. an *eclipse* (only in plur.):—blackness.

3651. כֵּן **kên,** *kane;* from 3559; prop. *set* upright; hence (fig. as adj.) *just;* but usually (as adv. or conj.) *rightly* or *so* (in various applications to manner, time and relation; often with other particles):— + after that (this, -ward, -wards), as . . . as, + [for-] asmuch as yet, + be (for which) cause, + following, howbeit, in (the) like (manner, -wise), × the more, right, (even) so, state, straightway, such (thing), surely, + there (where) -fore, this, thus, true, well, × you.

3652. כֵּן **kên** (Chald.), *kane;* corresp. to 3651; *so:*—thus.

3653. כֵּן **kên,** *kane;* the same as 3651, used as a noun; a *stand,* i.e. pedestal or station:—base, estate, foot, office, place, well.

3654. כֵּן **kên,** *kane;* from 3661 in the sense of *fastening;* a *gnat* (from infixing its sting; used only in plur. [and irreg. in Exod. 8 : 17, 18, Heb. 13 : 14]):—lice, × manner.

3655. כָּנָה **kânâh,** *kaw-naw´;* a prim. root; to *address* by an additional name; hence, to *eulogize:*—give flattering titles, surname (himself).

3656. כַּנֶּה **Kanneh,** *kan-neh´;* for 3641; *Canneh,* a place in Assyria:—Canneh

3657. כַּנָּה **kannâh,** *kan-naw´;* from 3661; a *plant* (as *set*):— × vineyard.

3658. כִּנּוֹר **kinnôwr,** *kin-nore´;* from an unused root mean. to *twang;* a *harp:*—harp.

3659. כָּנְיָהוּ **Konyâhûw,** *kon-yaw´-hoo;* for 3204; *Conjah,* an Isr. king:—Coniah.

3660. כְּנֵמָא **kᵉnêmâʼ** (Chald.), *ken-ay-maw´;* corresp. to 3644; *so* or *thus:*—so, (in) this manner (sort), thus.

3661. כָּנַן **kânan,** *kaw-nan´;* a prim. root; to *set out, i.e. plant:*— × vineyard.

3662. כְּנָנִי **Kᵉnânîy,** *ken-aw-nee´;* from 3661; *planted; Kenani,* an Isr.:—Chenani.

3663. כְּנַנְיָה **Kᵉnanyâh,** *ken-an-yaw´;* or כְּנַנְיָהוּ **Kᵉnanyâhûw,** *ken-an-yaw´-hoo;* from 3661 and 3050; *Jah has planted; Kenanjah,* an Isr.:—Chenaniah.

3664. כָּנַס **kânaç,** *kaw-nas´;* a prim. root; to *collect;* hence, to *enfold:*—gather (together), heap up, wrap self.

3665. כָּנַע **kânaʻ,** *kaw-nah´;* a prim. root; prop. to *bend* the knee; hence to *humiliate, vanquish:*—bring down (low), into subjection, under, humble (self), subdue.

3666. כִּנְעָה **kinʻâh,** *kin-aw´;* from 3665 in the sense of *folding* [comp. 3664]; a *package:*—wares.

3667. כְּנַעַן **Kᵉnaʻan,** *ken-ah´-an;* from 3665; *humiliated; Kenaan,* a son of Ham; also the country inhabited by him:—Canaan, merchant, traffick.

3668. כְּנַעֲנָה **Kᵉnaʻănâh,** *ken-ah-an-aw´;* fem. of 3667; *Kenaanah,* the name of two Isr.:—Chenaanah.

3669. כְּנַעֲנִי **Kᵉnaʻănîy,** *ken-ah-an-ee´;* patrial from 3667; a *Kenaanite* or inhabitant of Kenaan; by impl. a *pedlar* (the Canaanites standing for their neighbors the Ishmaelites, who conducted mercantile caravans):—Canaanite, merchant, trafficker.

3670. כָּנַף **kânaph,** *kaw-naf´;* a prim. root; prop. to *project* laterally, i.e. prob. (reflex.) to *withdraw:*—be removed.

3671. כָּנָף **kânâph,** *kaw-nawf´;* from 3670; an *edge* or *extremity;* spec. (of a bird or army) a *wing,* (of a garment or bed-clothing) a *flap,* (of the earth) a *quarter,* (of a building) a *pinnacle:*— + bird, border, corner, end, feather [-ed], × flying, + (one an-) other, overspreading, × quarters, skirt, × sort, uttermost part, wing ([-ed]).

3672. כִּנְּרוֹת **Kinnᵉrôwth,** *kin-ner-ōth;* or כִּנֶּרֶת **Kinnereth,** *kin-neh´-reth;* respectively plur. and sing. fem. from the same as 3658; perh. *harp*-shaped; *Kinneroth* or *Kinnereth,* a place in Pal.:—Chinnereth, Chinneroth, Cinneroth.

3673. כָּנַשׁ **kânash** (Chald.), *kaw-nash´;* corresp. to 3664; to *assemble:*—gather together.

3674. כְּנָת **kᵉnâth,** *ken-awth´;* from 3655; a *colleague* (as having the same title):—companion.

3675. כְּנָת **kᵉnâth** (Chald.), *ken-awth´;* corresp. to 3674:—companion.

3676. כֵּס **kêç,** *kace;* appar. a contr. for 3678, but prob. by err. transc. for 5251:—sworn.

3677. כֶּסֶא **keçeʼ,** *keh´-seh;* or כֶּסֶה **keçeh,** *keh´-seh;* appar. from 3680; prop. *fulness* or the *full moon,* i.e. its festival:—(time) appointed.

3678. כִּסֵּא **kiççêʼ,** *kis-say´;* or כִּסֵּה **kiççêh,** *kis-say´;* from 3680; prop. *covered,* i.e. a *throne* (as *canopied*):—seat, stool, throne.

3679. כַּסְדַּי **Kaçday,** *kas-dah´ee;* for 3778:—Chaldean.

3680. כָּסָה **kâçâh,** *kaw-saw´;* a prim. root; prop. to *plump,* i.e. *fill up* hollows; by impl. to *cover* (for clothing or secrecy):—clad self, close, clothe, conceal, cover (self), (flee to) hide, overwhelm. Comp. 3780.

כֶּסֶה **keçeh.** See 3677.

כִּסֵּה **kiççêh.** See 3678.

3681. כָּסוּי **kâçûwy,** *kaw-soo´ee;* pass. part. of 3680; prop. *covered,* ie. (as noun) a *covering:*—covering.

3682. כְּסוּת **kᵉçûwth,** *kes-ooth´;* from 3680; a *cover (garment); fig. a veiling:*—covering, raiment, vesture.

3683. כָּסַח **kâçach,** *kaw-sakh´;* a prim. root; to *cut off:*—cut down (up).

3684. כְּסִיל **kᵉçîyl,** *kes-eel´;* from 3688; prop. *fat,* i.e. (fig.) stupid or *silly:*—fool (-ish).

3685. כְּסִיל **Kᵉçîyl,** *kes-eel´;* the same as 3684; any notable *constellation;* spec. *Orion* (as if a *burly* one):—constellation, Orion.

3686. כְּסִיל **Kᵉçîyl,** *kes-eel´;* the same as 3684; *Kesil,* a place in Pal.:—Chesil.

3687. כְּסִילוּת **kᵉçîylûwth,** *kes-eel-ooth´;* from 3684; *silliness:*—foolish.

3688. כָּסַל **kâçal,** *kaw-sal´;* a prim. root; prop. to *be fat,* i.e. (fig.) *silly:*—be foolish.

3689. כֶּסֶל **keçel,** *keh´-sel;* from 3688; prop. *fatness,* i.e. by impl. (lit.) the *loin* (as the seat of the leaf *fat*) or (gen.) the *viscera;* also (fig.) *silliness* or (in a good sense) *trust:*—confidence, flank, folly, hope, loin.

3690. כִּסְלָה **kiçlâh,** *kis-law´;* fem. of 3689; in a good sense, *trust;* in a bad one, *silliness:*—confidence, folly.

3691. כִּסְלֵו **Kîçlêv,** *kis-lave´;* prob. of for. or.; *Kisleu,* the 9th Heb. month:—Chisleu.

3692. כִּסְלוֹן **Kiçlôwn,** *kis-lone´;* from 3688; *hopeful; Kislon,* an Isr.—Chislon.

3693. כְּסָלוֹן **Kᵉçâlôwn,** *kes-aw-lone´;* from 3688; *fertile; Kesalon,* a place in Pal.:—Chesalon.

3694. כְּסֻלּוֹת **Kᵉçullôwth,** *kes-ool-lōth´;* fem. plur. of pass. part. of 3688; *fattened, Kesulloth,* a place in Pal.:—Chesulloth.

3695. כַּסְלֻחִים **Kaçlûchîym,** *kas-loo´-kheem;* a plur. prob. of for. der.; *Casluchim,* a people cognate to the Eg.:—Casluhim.

3696. כִּסְלֹת תָּבֹר **Kiçlôth Tâbôr,** *kis-lōth´ taw-bore´;* from the fem. plur. of 3689 and 8396; *flanks of Tabor; Kisloth-Tabor,* a place in Pal.:—Chisloth-tabor.

3697. כָּסַם **kâçam,** *kaw-sam´;* a prim. root; to *shear:*— × only, poll. Comp. 3765.

3698. כֻּסֶּמֶת **kuççemeth,** *koos-seh´-meth;* from 3697; *spelt* (from its bristliness as if just *shorn*):—fitches, rie.

3699. כָּסַס **kâçaç,** *kaw-sas´;* a prim. root; to *estimate:*—make count.

3700. כָּסַף **kâçaph,** *kaw-saf´;* a prim. root; prop. to become *pale,* i.e. (by impl.) to *pine* after; also to *fear:*—[have] desire, be greedy, long, sore.

3701. כֶּסֶף **keçeph,** *keh´-sef;* from 3700; *silver* (from its *pale* color); by impl. *money:*—money, price, silver (-ling).

3702. כְּסַף **kᵉçaph** (Chald.), *kes-af´;* corresp. to 3701:—money, silver.

3703. כָּסִפְיָא **Kâçiphyâʼ,** *kaw-sif-yaw´;* perh. from 3701; *silvery; Casiphja,* a place in Bab.:—Casiphia.

3704. כֶּסֶת **keçeth,** *keh´-seth;* from 3680; a *cushion* or pillow (as *covering* a seat or bed):—pillow.

3705. כְּעַן **kᵉʻan** (Chald.), *keh-an´;* prob. from 3652; *now:*—now.

3706. כְּעֶנֶת **keʻeneth** (Chald.), *keh-eh´-neth;* or כְּעֶת **keʻeth** (Chald.), *keh-eth´;* fem. of 3705; *thus* (only in the formula "and *so forth*"):—at such a time.

3707. כָּעַס **kâʻac,** *kaw-as´;* a prim. root; to *trouble;* by impl. to *grieve, rage, be indignant:*—be angry, be grieved, take indignation, provoke (to anger, unto wrath), have sorrow, vex, be wroth.

3708. כַּעַס **kaʻaç,** *kah´-as;* or (in Job) כַּעַשׂ **kaʻas,** *kah´-as;* from 3707; *vexation:*—anger, angry, grief, indignation, provocation, provoking, × sore, sorrow, spite, wrath.

כְּעֶת **keʻeth.** See 3706.

3709. כַּף **kaph,** *kaf;* from 3721; the hollow *hand* or palm (so of the *paw* of an animal, of the *sole,* and even of the *bowl* of a dish or sling, the *handle* of a bolt, the *leaves* of a palm-tree); fig. *power:*—branch, + foot, hand ([-ful], -dle, [-led]), hollow, middle, palm, paw, power, sole, spoon.

3710. כֵּף **kêph,** *kafe;* from 3721; a hollow *rock:*—rock.

3711. כָּפָה **kâphâh,** *kaw-faw´;* a prim. root; prop. to *bend,* i.e. (fig.) to *tame* or subdue:—pacify.

3712. כִּפָּה **kippâh,** *kip-paw´;* fem. of 3709; a *leaf* of a palm-tree:—branch.

3713. כְּפוֹר **kephôwr,** *kef-ore´;* from 3722; prop. a *cover,* i.e. (by impl.) a *tankard* (or *covered* goblet); also white *frost* (as *covering* the ground):—bason, hoar (-y) frost.

3714. כָּפִיס **kâphîyç,** *kaw-fece´;* from an unused root mean. to *connect;* a *girder:*—beam.

3715. כְּפִיר **kephîyr,** *kef-eer´;* from 3722; a *village* (as *covered* in by walls); also a young *lion* (perh. as *covered* with a mane):—(young) lion, village. Comp. 3723.

3716. כְּפִירָה **Kephîyrâh,** *kef-ee-raw´;* fem. of 3715; the *village* (always with the art.); *Kephirah,* a place in Pal.:—Chephirah.

3717. כָּפַל **kâphal,** *kaw-fal´;* a prim. root; to *fold* together; fig. to *repeat:*—double.

3718. כֶּפֶל **kephel,** *keh´-fel;* from 3717; a *duplicate:*—double.

3719. כָּפַן **kâphan,** *kaw-fan´;* a prim. root; to *bend:*—bend.

3720. כָּפָן **kâphân,** *kaw-fawn´;* from 3719; *hunger* (as making to *stoop* with emptiness and pain):—famine.

3721. כָּפַף **kâphaph,** *kaw-faf´;* a prim. root; to *curve:*—bow down (self).

3722. כָּפַר **kâphar,** *kaw-far´;* a prim. root; to *cover* (spec. with bitumen); fig. to *expiate* or *condone,* to *placate* or *cancel:*—appease, make (an) atonement, cleanse, disannul, forgive, be merciful, pacify, pardon, to *pitch,* purge (away), put off, (make) reconcile (-liation).

3723. כָּפָר **kâphâr,** *kaw-fawr´;* from 3722; a *village* (as *protected* by walls):—village. Comp. 3715.

3724. כֹּפֶר **kôpher,** *ko´-fer;* from 3722; prop. a *cover,* i.e. (lit.) a *village* (as *covered* in); (spec.) *bitumen* (as used for *coating*), and the *henna* plant (as used for *dyeing*); fig. a *redemption-*price:—bribe, camphire, pitch, ransom, satisfaction, sum of money, village.

3725. כִּפֻּר **kippûr,** *kip-poor´;* from 3722; *expiation* (only in plur.):—atonement.

3726. כְּפַר הָעַמּוֹנִי **Kephar hâ-ʻAmmôwnîy,** *kef-ar´ haw-am-mo-nee´;* from 3723 and 5984, with the art. interposed; *village of the Ammonite; Kefar-ha-Ammoni,* a place in Pal.:—Chefar-haamonai.

3727. כַּפֹּרֶת **kappôreth,** *kap-po´-reth;* from 3722; a *lid* (used only of the *cover* of the sacred Ark):—mercy seat.

3728. כָּפַשׁ **kâphash,** *kaw-fash´;* a prim. root; to *tread* down; fig. to *humiliate:*—cover.

3729. כְּפַת **kephath** (Chald.), *kef-ath´;* a root of uncert. correspondence; to *fetter:*—bind.

3730. כַּפְתֹּר **kaphtôr,** *kaf-tore´;* or (Am. 9 : 1) כַּפְתּוֹר **kaphtôwr,** *kaf-tore´;* prob. from an unused root mean. to *encircle;* a *chaplet;* but used only in an architectonic sense, i.e. the *capital* of a column, or a wreath-like *button* or *disk* on the candelabrum:—knop, (upper) lintel.

3731. כַּפְתֹּר **Kaphtôr,** *kaf-tore´;* or (Am. 9 : 7) כַּפְתּוֹר **Kaphtôwr,** *kaf-tore´;* appar. the same as 3730; *Caphtor* (i.e. a *wreath*-shaped island), the original seat of the Philistines:—Caphtor.

3732. כַּפְתֹּרִי **Kaphtôrîy,** *kaf-to-ree´;* patrial from 3731; a *Caphtorite* (collect.) or native of Caphtor:—Caphthorim, Caphtorim (-s).

3733. כַּר **kar,** *kar;* from 3769 in the sense of *plumpness;* a *ram* (as *full-grown* and *fat*), including a *battering-ram* (as *butting*); hence a *meadow* (as *for sheep*); also a *pad* or camel's saddle (as *puffed out*):—captain, furniture, lamb, (large) pasture, ram. See also 1033, 3746.

3734. כֹּר **kôr,** *kore;* from the same as 3564; prop. a deep round *vessel,* i.e. (spec.) a *cor* or measure for things dry:—cor, measure. Chald. the same.

3735. כָּרָא **kârâʼ** (Chald.), *kaw-raw´;* prob. corresp. to 3738 in the sense of *piercing* (fig.); to *grieve:*—be grieved.

3736. כַּרְבֵּל **karbêl,** *kar-bale´;* from the same as 3525; to *gird* or *clothe:*—clothed.

3737. כַּרְבְּלָא **karbelâʼ** (Chald.), *kar-bel-aw´;* from a verb corresp. to that of 3736; a *mantle:*—hat.

3738. כָּרָה **kârâh,** *kaw-raw´;* a prim. root; prop. to *dig;* fig. to *plot;* gen. to *bore* or open:—dig, × make (a banquet), open.

3739. כָּרָה **kârâh,** *kaw-raw´;* usually assigned as a prim. root, but prob. only a special application of 3738 (through the common idea of *planning* implied in a bargain); to *purchase:*—buy, prepare.

3740. כֵּרָה **kêrâh,** *kay-raw´;* from 3739; a *purchase:*—provision.

3741. כָּרָה **kârâh,** *kaw-raw´;* fem. of 3733; a *meadow:*—cottage.

3742. כְּרוּב **kerûwb,** *ker-oob´;* of uncert. der.; a *cherub* or imaginary figure:—cherub, [*plur.*] cherubims.

3743. כְּרוּב **Kerûwb,** *ker-oob´;* the same as 3742; *Kerub,* a place in Bab.:—Cherub.

3744. כָּרוֹז **kârôwz** (Chald.), *kaw-roze´;* from 3745; a *herald:*—herald.

3745. כְּרַז **keraz** (Chald.), *ker-az´;* prob. of Greek or. (κηρύσσω); to *proclaim:*—make a proclamation.

3746. כָּרִי **kârîy,** *kaw-ree´;* perh. an abridged plur. of 3733 in the sense of *leader* (of the flock); a *life-guardsman:*—captains, Cherethites [*from the marg.*].

3747. כְּרִית **Kerîyth,** *ker-eeth´;* from 3772; a *cut; Kerith,* a brook of Pal.:—Cherith.

3748. כְּרִיתוּת **kerîythûwth,** *ker-ee-thooth´;* from 3772; a *cutting* (of the matrimonial bond), i.e. *divorce:*—divorce (-ment).

3749. כַּרְכֹּב **karkôb,** *kar-kobe´;* expanded from the same as 3522; a *rim* or top margin:—compass.

3750. כַּרְכֹּם **karkôm,** *kar-kome´;* prob. of for. or.; the *crocus:*—saffron.

3751. כַּרְכְּמִישׁ **Karkemîysh,** *kar-kem-eesh´;* of for. der.; *Karkemish,* a place in Syria:—Carchemish.

3752. כַּרְכַּס **Karkaç,** *kar-kas´;* of Pers. or.; *Karkas,* a eunuch of Xerxes:—Carcas.

3753. כַּרְכָּרָה **karkârâh,** *kar-kaw-raw´;* from 3769; a *dromedary* (from its *rapid* motion as if dancing):—swift beast.

3754. כֶּרֶם **kerem,** *keh´-rem;* from an unused root of uncert. mean.; a *garden* or *vineyard:*—vines, (increase of the) vineyard (-s), vintage. See also 1021.

3755. כֹּרֵם **kôrêm,** *ko-rame´;* act. part. of an imaginary denom. from 3754; a *vinedresser:*—vine dresser [*as one or two words*].

3756. כַּרְמִי **Karmîy,** *kar-mee´;* from 3754; *gardener; Karmi,* the name of three Isr.:—Carmi.

3757. כַּרְמִי **Karmîy,** *kar-mee´;* patron. from 3756; a *Karmite* or desc. of *Karmi:*—Carmites.

3758. כַּרְמִיל **karmîyl,** *kar-mele´;* prob. of for. or.; *carmine,* a deep red:—crimson.

3759. כַּרְמֶל **karmel,** *kar-mel´;* from 3754; a planted *field* (garden, orchard, vineyard or park); by impl. garden *produce:*—full (green) ears (of corn), fruitful field (place), plentiful (field).

3760. כַּרְמֶל **Karmel,** *kar-mel´;* the same as 3759; *Karmel,* the name of a hill and of a town in Pal.:—Carmel, fruitful (plentiful) field, (place).

3761. כַּרְמְלִי **Karmᵉlîy,** *kar-mel-ee´;* patron from 3760; a *Karmelite* or inhab. of Karmel (the town):—Carmelite.

3762. כַּרְמְלִית **Karmᵉlîyth,** *kar-mel-eeth´;* fem of 3761; a *Karmelitess* or female in hab. of Karmel:—Carmelitess.

3763. כְּרָן **Kᵉrân,** *ker-awn´;* of uncert. der.: *Keran,* an aboriginal Idumæan:—Cheran.

3764. כָּרְסֵא **korçêʼ** (Chald.), *kor-say´;* corresp. to 3678; a *throne:*—throne.

3765. כִּרְסֵם **kirçêm,** *kirsame´;* from 3697; to *lay waste:*—waste.

3766. כָּרַע **kâraʻ,** *kaw-rah´;* a prim. root; to *bend* the knee; by impl. to *sink,* to *prostrate:*—bow (down, self), bring down (low), cast down, couch, fall, feeble, kneeling, sink, smite (stoop) down, subdue, × very.

3767. כָּרָע **kârâʻ,** *kaw-raw´;* from 3766; the *leg* (from the knee to the ankle) of men or locusts (only in the dual):—leg.

3768. כַּרְפַּס **karpaç,** *kar-pas´;* of for. or.; *byssus* or fine vegetable wool:—green.

3769. כָּרַר **kârar,** *kaw-rar´;* a prim. root; to *dance* (i.e. *whirl*):—dance (-ing).

3770. כְּרֵשׂ **kᵉrês,** *ker-ace´;* by var. from 7164; the *paunch* or belly (as *swelling* out):—belly.

כֹּרֶשׁ **Kôresh.** See 3567.

3771. כַּרְשְׁנָא **Karshᵉnâʼ,** *kar-shen-aw´;* of for. or.; *Karshena,* a courtier of Xerxes:—Carshena.

3772. כָּרַת **kârath,** *kaw-rath´;* a prim. root; to *cut* (off, down or asunder); by impl. to *destroy* or *consume;* spec. to *covenant* (i.e. make an alliance or bargain, orig. by cutting flesh and passing between the pieces):—be chewed, be con-[feder-] ate, covenant, cut (down, off), destroy, fail, feller, be freed, hew (down), make a league ([covenant]), × lose, perish, × utterly, × want.

3773. כָּרֻתָה **kârûthâh,** *kaw-rooth-aw´;* pass. part. fem. of 3772; something *cut,* i.e. a hewn *timber:*—beam.

3774. כְּרֵתִי **Kᵉrêthîy,** *ker-ay-thee´;* prob. from 3772 in the sense of *executioner;* a *Kerethite* or *life-guardsman* [comp. 2876] (only collect. in the sing. as plur.):—Cherethims, Cherethites.

3775. כֶּשֶׂב **keseb,** *keh´-seb;* appar. by transp. for 3532; a young *sheep:*—lamb, sheep.

3776. כִּשְׂבָּה **kisbâh,** *kis-baw´;* fem. of 3775; a young *ewe:*—lamb.

3777. כֶּשֶׂד **Kesed,** *keh´-sed;* from an unused root of uncert. mean.; *Kesed,* a relative of Abraham:—Chesed.

3778. כַּשְׂדִּי **Kasdîy,** *kas-dee´* (occasionally with enclitic כַּשְׂדִּימָה **Kasdîymâh,** *kas-dee´-maw; towards* the *Kasdites:*—into Chaldea), patron. from 3777 (only in the plur.); a *Kasdite;* or desc. of Kesed; by impl. a *Chaldæan* (as if so descended); also an *astrologer* (as if proverbial of that people):—Chaldeans, Chaldees, inhabitants of Chaldea.

3779. כַּשְׂדַּי **Kasday** (Chald.), *kas-dah´ee;* corresp. to 3778; a *Chaldæan* or inhab. of Chaldæa; by impl. a *Magian* or professional astrologer:—Chaldean.

3780. כָּשָׂה **kâsâh,** *kaw-saw´;* a prim. root; to *grow fat* (i.e. be *covered* with flesh):—be covered. Comp. 3680.

3781. כַּשִּׁיל **kashshîyl,** *kash-sheel´;* from 3782; prop. a *feller,* i.e. an *axe:*—ax.

3782. כָּשַׁל **kâshal,** *kaw-shal´;* a prim. root; to *totter* or *waver* (through weakness of the legs, espec. the ankle); by impl. to *falter, stumble,* faint or fall:—bereave [*from the marg.*], cast down, be decayed, (cause to) fail, (cause, make to) fall (down, -ing), feeble, be (the) ruin (-ed, of), (be) overthrown, (cause to) stumble, × utterly, be weak.

3783. כִּשָּׁלוֹן **kishshâlôwn,** *kish-shaw-lone´* from 3782; prop. a *tottering,* i.e. *ruin:*—fall.

3784. כָּשַׁף **kâshaph,** *kaw-shaf´;* a prim. root; prop. to *whisper* a spell, i.e. to *inchant* or practise magic:—sorcerer, (use) witch (-craft).

3785. כֶּשֶׁף **kesheph,** *keh´-shef;* from 3784; *magic:*—sorcery, witchcraft.

3786. כַּשָּׁף **kashshâph,** *kash-shawf´;* from 3784; a *magician:*—sorcerer.

3787. כָּשֵׁר **kâshêr,** *kaw-share´;* a prim. root prop. to be *straight* or *right;* by impl. to *be acceptable;* also to *succeed* or prosper:—direct, be right, prosper.

3788. כִּשְׁרוֹן **kishrôwn,** *kish-rone´;* from 3787; *success, advantage:*—equity, good, right.

3789. כָּתַב **kâthab,** *kaw-thab´;* a prim. root; to *grave;* by impl. to *write* (describe, inscribe, prescribe, subscribe):—describe, record, prescribe, subscribe, write (-ing, -ten).

3790. כְּתַב **kᵉthab** (Chald.), *keth-ab´;* corresp. to 3789:—write (-ten).

3791. כָּתָב **kâthâb,** *kaw-thawb´;* from 3789; something *written,* i.e. a *writing, record* or *book:*—register, scripture, writing.

3792. כְּתָב **kᵉthâb** (Chald.), *keth-awb´;* corresp. to 3791:—prescribing, writing (-ten).

3793. כְּתֹבֶת **kᵉthôbeth,** *keth-o´-beth;* from 3789; a *letter* or other *mark* branded on the skin:— × any [mark].

3794. כִּתִּי **Kittîy,** *kit-tee´;* or כִּתִּיִּי **Kittîyîy,** *kit-tee-ee´;* patrial from an unused name denoting Cyprus (only in the plur.); a *Kittite* or Cypriote; hence an *islander* in gen., i.e. the Greeks or Romans on the shores opposite Pal.:—Chittim, Kittim.

3795. כָּתִית **kâthîyth,** *kaw-theeth´;* from 3807; *beaten,* i.e. pure (oil):—beaten.

3796. כֹּתֶל **kôthel,** *ko´-thel;* from an unused root mean. to *compact;* a *wall* (as *gathering* inmates):—wall.

3797. כְּתַל **kᵉthal** (Chald.), *keth-al´;* corresp. to 3796:—wall.

3798. כִּתְלִישׁ **Kithlîysh,** *kith-leesh´;* from 3796 and 376; *wall of a man; Kithlish,* a place in Pal.:—Kithlish.

3799. כָּתַם **kâtham,** *kaw-tham´;* a prim. root; prop. to *carve* or *engrave,* i.e. (by impl.) to *inscribe* indelibly:—mark.

3800. כֶּתֶם **kethem,** *keh´-them;* from 3799; prop. something *carved* out, i.e. *ore;* hence *gold* (pure as originally minded):—([most] fine, pure) gold (-en wedge).

3801. כְּתֹנֶת **kᵉthôneth,** *keth-o´-neth;* or כֻּתֹּנֶת **kuttôneth,** *koot-to´-neth;* from an unused root mean. to *cover* [comp. 3802]: a *shirt:*—coat, garment, robe.

3802. כָּתֵף **kâthêph,** *kaw-thafe´;* from an unused root mean. to *clothe;* the *shoulder* (proper, i.e. upper end of the arm; as being the spot where the garments hang); fig. *side-piece* or lateral projection of anything:—arm, corner, shoulder (-piece), side, undersetter.

3803. כָּתַר **kâthar,** *kaw-thar´;* a prim. root; to *enclose;* hence (in a friendly sense) to *crown,* (in a hostile one) to *besiege;* also to *wait* (as restraining oneself):—beset round, compass about, be crowned inclose round, suffer.

3804. כֶּתֶר **kether,** *keh´-ther;* from 3803; prop. a *circlet,* i.e. a *diadem:*—crown.

3805. כֹתֶרֶת **kôthereth,** *ko-theh´-reth;* fem. act. part. of 3803; the *capital* of a column:—chapiter.

3806. כָּתַשׁ **kâthash,** *kaw-thash´;* a prim. root; to *butt* or *pound:*—bray.

3807. כָּתַת **kâthath,** *kaw-thath´;* a prim. root; to *bruise* or violently *strike:*—beat (down, to pieces), break in pieces, crushed, destroy, discomfit, smite, stamp.

ל

3808. לֹא **lôʼ** *lo;* or לוֹא **lôwʼ,** *lo;* or לֹה **lôh** (Deut. 3 : 11), *lo;* a prim. particle; *not* (the simple or abs. negation); by impl. *no;* often used with other particles (as follows):— × before, + or else, ere, + except, ig [-norant], much, less, nay, neither, never, no ([-ne], -r, [-thing]), (× as though . . . , [can-], for) not (out of), of nought, otherwise, out of, + surely, + as truly as, + of a truth, + verily, for want, + whether, without.

3809. לָא **lâʼ** (Chald.), *law;* or לָה **lâh** (Chald.) (Dan. 4 :32), *law;* corresp. to 3808:—or even, neither, no (-ne, -r), ([can-]) not, as nothing, without.

לָא **lûʼ.** See 3863.

3810. לֹא דְבָר **Lôʼ Debar,** *lo deb-ar´;* or לוֹ דְבָר **Lôw Debar** (2 Sam. 9 : 4, 5), *lo deb-ar´;* or לִדְבִר **Lidbîr** (Josh. 13 : 26), *lid-beer´* [prob. rather לֹדְבַר° **Lôdebar,** *lo-deb-ar´*]; from 3808 and 1699; *pastureless; Lo-Debar,* a place in Pal.:—Debir, Lo-debar.

3811. לָאָה **lâʼâh,** *law-aw´;* a prim. root; to *tire;* (fig.) to *be* (or *make*) *disgusted:*—faint, grieve, lothe, (be, make) weary (selves).

3812. לֵאָה **Lêʼâh,** *lay-aw´;* from 3811; *weary; Leah,* a wife of Jacob:—Leah.

לְאוֹם **leʼowm.** See 3816.

3813. לָאַט **lâʼaṭ,** *law-at´;* a prim. root; to *muffle:*—cover.

3814. לָאט **lâʼṭ,** *lawt;* from 3813 (or perh. for act. part. of 3874); prop. *muffled,* i.e. *silently:*—softly.

3815. לָאֵל **Lâʼêl,** *law-ale´;* from the prep. pref. and 410; (belonging) *to God; Laël* an Isr.:—Lael.

3816. לְאֹם **leôm,** *leh-ome´;* or לְאוֹם **leʼôwm,** *leh-ome´;* from an unused root mean. to *gather;* a *community:*—nation, people.

3817. לְאֻמִּים **Leʼummîym,** *leh-oom-meem´;* plur. of 3816; *communities; Leüm mim,* an Arabian:—Leummim.

3818. לֹא עַמִּי **Lôʼ ʻAmmîy,** *lo am-mee´;* from 3808 and 5971 with pron. suffix; *not my people; Lo-Ammi,* the symbol. name of a son of Hosea:—Lo-ammi.

3819. לֹא רֻחָמָה **Lôʼ Rûchâmâh,** *lo roo-khaw-maw´;* from 3808 and 7355; *not pitied; Lo-Ruchamah,* the symbol. name of a daughter of Hosea:—Lo-ruhamah.

3820. לֵב **lêb,** *labe;* a form of 3824; the *heart;* also used (fig.) very widely for the feelings, the will and even the intellect; likewise for the *centre* of anything:— + care for, comfortably, consent, × considered, courag [-eous], friend [-ly], ([broken-], [hard-], [merry-], [stiff-], [stout-], double) heart ([-ed]), × heed, × I, kindly, midst, mind (-ed), × regard ([-ed)], × themselves, × unawares, understanding, × well, willingly, wisdom.

3821. לֵב **lêb** (Chald.), *labe;* corresp. to 3820:—heart.

3822. לְבָאוֹת **Lebâʼôwth,** *leb-aw-ōth´;* plur. of 3833; *lionesses; Lebaoth,* a place in Pal.:—Lebaoth. See also 1034.

3823. לָבַב **lâbab,** *law-bab´;* a prim. root; prop. to *be enclosed* (as if with *fat*); by impl. (as denom. from 3824) to *unheart,* i.e. (in a good sense) *transport* (with love), or (in a bad sense) *stultify;* also (as denom. from 3834) to *make cakes:*—make cakes, ravish, be wise.

3824. לֵבָב **lêbâb,** *lay-bawb´;* from 3823; the *heart* (as the most interior organ); used also like 3820:— + bethink themselves, breast, comfortably, courage, ([faint], [tender-] heart ([-ed]), midst, mind, × unawares, understanding.

3825. לְבַב **lebab** (Chald.), *leb-ab´;* corresp. to 3824:—heart.

לְבִבָה **lebîbâh.** See 3834.

3826. לִבָּה **libbâh,** *lib-baw´;* fem. of 3820; the *heart:*—heart.

3827. לַבָּה **labbâh,** *lab-baw´;* for 3852; *flame:*—flame.

3828. לְבוֹנָה **lebôwnâh,** *leb-o-naw´;* or לְבֹנָה **lebonâh,** *leb-o-naw´;* from 3836; *frankincense* (from its *whiteness* or perh. that of its smoke):—(frank-) incense.

3829. לְבוֹנָה **Lebôwnâh,** *leb-o-naw´;* the same as 3828; *Lebonah,* a place in Pal.: Lebonah.

3830. לְבוּשׁ **lebûwsh,** *leb-oosh´;* or לְבֻשׁ **lebûsh,** *leb-oosh´;* from 3847; a *garment* (lit. or fig.); by impl. (euphem.) a *wife:*—apparel, clothed with, clothing, garment, raiment, vestment, vesture.

3831. לְבוּשׁ **lebûwsh** (Chald.), *leb-oosh´;* corresp. to 3830:—garment.

3832. לָבַט **lâbaṭ,** *law-bat´;* a prim. root; to *overthrow;* intrans. to *fall:*—fall.

לֻבִּי **Lubbîy.** See 3864.

3833. לָבִיא **lâbîyʼ,** *law-bee´;* or (Ezek. 19 : 2) לְבִיָּא **lebîyâʼ,** *leb-ee-yaw´;* irreg. masc. plur. לְבָאִים **lebâʼîym,** *leb-aw-eem´;* irreg. fem. plur. לְבָאוֹת **lebâʼôwth,** *leb-aw-ōth´;* from an unused root mean. to *roar;* a *lion* (prop. a lioness as the fiercer [although not a *roarer;* comp. 738]):—(great, old, stout) lion, lioness, young [lion].

3834. לָבִיבָה **lâbîybâh,** *law-bee-baw´;* or rather לְבִבָה **lebîbâh,** *leb-ee-baw´;* from 3823 in its orig. sense of *fatness* (or perh. of *folding*); a *cake* (either as *fried* or *turned*):—cake.

3835. לָבַן **lâban,** *law-ban´;* a prim. root; to *be* (or be*come*) *white;* also (as denom. from 3843) to *make bricks:*—make brick, be (made, make) white (-r).

3836. לָבָן **lâbân,** *law-bawn´;* or (Gen. 49 : 12) לָבֵן **lâbên,** *law-bane´;* from 3835; *white:*—white.

3837. לָבָן **Lâbân,** *law-bawn´;* the same as 3836; *Laban,* a Mesopotamian; also a place in the Desert:—Laban.

לַבֵּן **Labbên.** See 4192.

3838. לְבָנָא **Lebânâʼ,** *leb-aw-naw´;* or לְבָנָה **Lebânâh,** *leb-aw-naw´;* the same as 3842; *Lebana* or *Lebanah,* one of the Nethinim:—Lebana, Lebanah.

3839. לִבְנֶה **libneh,** *lib-neh´;* from 3835; some sort of *whitish tree, perh. the storax:*—poplar.

3840. לִבְנָה **libnâh,** *lib-naw´;* from 3835; prop. *whiteness,* i.e. (by impl.) *transparency:*—paved.

3841. לִבְנָה **Libnâh,** *lib-naw´;* the same as 3839; *Libnah,* a place in the Desert and one in Pal.:—Libnah.

3842. לְבָנָה **lebânâh,** *leb-aw-naw´;* from 3835; prop. (the) *white,* i.e. the *moon:*—moon. See also 3838.

3843. לְבֵנָה **lebênâh,** *leb-ay-naw´;* from 3835; a *brick* (from the *whiteness* of the clay):—(altar of) brick, tile.

לְבֹנָה **lebônâh.** See 3828.

3844. לְבָנוֹן **Lebânôwn,** *leb-aw-nohn´;* from 3825; (the) *white* mountain (from its snow); *Lebanon,* a mountain range in Pal.:—Lebanon.

3845. לִבְנִי **Libnîy,** *lib-nee´;* from 3835; *white; Libni,* an Isr.:—Libni.

3846. לִבְנִי **Libnîy,** *lib-nee´;* patron. from 3845; a *Libnite* or desc. of Libni (collect.):—Libnites.

3847. לָבַשׁ **lâbash,** *law-bash´;* or לָבֵשׁ **lâbêsh,** *law-bashe´;* a prim. root; prop. *wrap* around, i.e. (by impl.) to *put on* a garment or *clothe* (oneself, or another), lit. or fig.:—(in) apparel, arm, array (self), clothe (self), come upon, put (on, upon), wear.

3848. לְבַשׁ **lebash** (Chald.), *leb-ash´;* corresp. to 3847:—clothe.

לְבֻשׁ **lebûsh.** See 3830.

3849. לֹג **lôg,** *lohg;* from an unused root appar. mean. to *deepen* or *hollow* [like 3537]; a *log* or measure for liquids:—log [of oil].

3850. לֹד **Lôd,** *lode;* from an unused root of uncert. signif.; *Lod,* a place in Pal.:—Lod.

לִדְבִר **Lidbîr.** See 3810.

3851. לַהַב **lahab,** *lah´-hab;* from an unused root mean. to *gleam;* a *flash;* fig. a sharply polished *blade* or *point* of a weapon:—blade, bright, flame, glittering.

3852. לֶהָבָה **lehâbâh,** *leh-aw-baw´;* or לַהֶבֶת **lahebeth,** *lah-eh´-beth;* fem. of 3851, and mean. the same:—flame (-ming), head [of a spear].

3853. לְהָבִים **Lehâbîym,** *leh-haw-beem´;* plur. of 3851; *flames; Lehabim,* a son of Mizrain, and his descend.:—Lehabim.

3854. לַהַג **lahag,** *lah´-hag;* from an unused root mean. to *be eager;* intense mental *application:*—study.

3855. לַהַד **Lahad,** *lah´-had;* from an unused root mean. to *glow* [comp. 3851] or else to *be earnest* [comp. 3854]; *Lahad,* an Isr.:—Lahad.

3856. לָהַהּ **lâhahh,** *law-hah´;* a prim. root mean. prop. to *burn,* i.e. (by impl.) to *be rabid* (fig. *insane*); also (from the *exhaustion* of frenzy) to *languish:*—faint, mad.

3857. לָהַט **lâhaṭ,** *law-hat´;* a prim. root; prop. to *lick,* i.e. (by impl.) to *blaze:*—burn (up), set on fire, flaming, kindle.

3858. לַהַט **lahaṭ,** *lah´-hat;* from 3857; a *blaze;* also (from the idea of *enwrapping*) *magic* (as *covert*):—flaming, enchantment.

3859. לָהַם **lâham,** *law-ham´;* a prim. root; prop. to *burn* in, i.e. (fig.) to *rankle:*—wound.

3860. לָהֵן **lâhên,** *law-hane´;* from the pref. prep. mean. *to* or *for* and 2005; pop. *for if;* hence *therefore:*—for them [*by mistake for prep. suffix*].

3861. לָהֵן **lâwhên** (Chald.), *law-hane´;* corresp. to 3860; *therefore;* also *except:*—but, except, save, therefore, wherefore.

3862. לַהֲקָה **lahăqâh,** *lah-hak-aw´;* prob. from an unused root mean. to *gather;* an *assembly:*—company.

לוֹא **lôw'.** See 3808.

3863. לוּא **lûw',** *loo;* or לֻא **lû',** *loo;* or לוּ **lûw,** *loo;* a conditional particle; *if;* by impl. (interj. as a wish) *would that!:*—if (haply), peradventure, I pray thee, though, I would, would God (that).

3864. לוּבִי **Lûwbîy,** *loo-bee´;* or לֻבִּי **Lubbîy** (Dan. 11 : 43), *loob-bee´;* patrial from a name prob. derived from an unused root mean. to *thirst,* i.e. a *dry* region; appar. a *Libyan* or inhab. of interior Africa (only in plur.):—Lubim (-s), Libyans.

3865. לוּד **Lûwd,** *lood;* prob. of for. der.; *Lud,* the name of two nations:—Lud, Lydia.

3866. לוּדִי **Lûwdîy,** *loo-dee´;* or לוּדִיִּי **Lûwdîyîy,** *loo-dee-ee´;* patrial from 3865; a *Ludite* or inhab. of Lud (only in plur.):—Ludim, Lydians.

3867. לָוָה **lâvâh,** *law-vaw´;* a prim. root; prop. to *twine,* i.e. (by impl.) to *unite,* to *remain;* also to *borrow* (as a form of *obligatin*) or (caus.) to *lend:*—abide with, borrow (-er), cleave, join (self), lend (-er).

3868. לוּז **lûwz,** *looz;* a prim. root; to *turn* aside [comp. 3867, 3874 and 3885], i.e. (lit.) to *depart,* (fig.) *be perverse:*—depart, froward, perverse (-ness).

3869. לוּז **lûwz,** *looz;* prob. of for. or; some kind of *nut*-tree, perh. the *almond:*—hazel.

3870. לוּז **Lûwz,** *looz;* prob. from 3869 (as growing there); *Luz,* the name of two places in Pal.:—Luz.

3871. לוּחַ **lûwach,** *loo´-akh;* or לֻחַ **lûach,** *loo´-akh;* from a prim. root; prob. mean. to *glisten;* a *tablet* (as *polished*), of stone, wood or metal:—board, plate, table.

3872. לוּחִית **Lûwchîyth,** *loo-kheeth´;* or לֻחוֹת° **Lûchôwth** (Jer. 48 : 5), *loo-khoth´;* from the same as 3871; *floored; Luchith,* a place E. of the Jordan:—Luhith.

3873. לוֹחֵשׁ **Lôwchêsh,** *lo-khashe´;* act. part. of 3907; (the) *enchanter; Lochesh,* an Isr.:—Hallohesh, Haloshesh [*includ. the art.*].

3874. לוּט **lûwṭ,** *loot;* a prim. root; to *wrap* up:—cast, wrap.

3875. לוֹט **lôwṭ,** *lote;* from 3874; a *veil:*—covering.

3876. לוֹט **Lôwṭ,** *lote;* the same as 3875; *Lot,* Abraham's nephew:—Lot.

3877. לוֹטָן **Lôwṭân,** *lo-tawn´;* from 3875; *covering; Lotan,* an Idumæan:—Lotan.

3878. לֵוִי **Lêvîy,** *lay-vee´;* from 3867; *attached; Levi,* a son of Jacob:—Levi. See also 3879, 3881.

3879. לֵוִי **Lêvîy** (Chald.), *lay-vee´;* corresp. to 3880:—Levite.

3880. לִוְיָה **livyâh,** *liv-yaw´;* from 3867; something *attached,* i.e. a *wreath:*—ornament.

3881. לֵוִיִּי **Lêvîyîy,** *lay-vee-ee´;* or לֵוִי **Lêvîy,** *lay-vee´;* patron. from 3878; a *Leviite* or desc. of Levi:—Levite.

3882. לִוְיָתָן **livyâthân,** *liv-yaw-thawn´;* from 3867; a *wreathed* animal, i.e. a *serpent* (espec. the *crocodile* or some other large sea-monster); fig. the constellation of the *dragon;* also as a symbol of *Bab:*—leviathan, mourning.

3883. לוּל **lûwl,** *lool;* from an unused root mean. to *fold* back; a *spiral* step:—winding stair. Comp. 3924.

3884. לוּלֵא **lûwlê',** *loolay´;* or לוּלֵי **lûwlêy,** *loo lay´;* from 3863 and 3808; *if not:*—except, had not, if (. . . not), unless, were it not that.

3885. לוּן **lûwn,** *loon;* or לִין **lîyn,** *leen;* a prim. root; to *stop* (usually over night); by impl. to *stay* permanently; hence (in a bad sense) to be *obstinate* (espec. in words, to *complain*):—abide (all night), continue, dwell, endure, grudge, be left, lie all night, (cause to) lodge (all night, in, -ing, this night), (make to) murmur, remain, tarry (all night, that night).

3886. לוּעַ **lûwa',** *loo´-ah;* a prim. root; to *gulp;* fig. to *be rash:*—swallow down (up).

3887. לוּץ **lûwts,** *loots;* a prim. root; prop. to *make mouths* at, i.e. to *scoff:* hence (from the effort to pronounce a foreign language) to *interpret,* or (gen.) *intercede:*—ambassador, have in derision, interpreter, make a mock, mocker, scorn (-er, -ful), teacher.

3888. לוּשׁ **lûwsh,** *loosh;* a prim. root; to *knead:*—knead.

3889. לוּשׁ° **Lûwsh,** *loosh;* from 3888; *kneading; Lush,* a place in Pal.:—Laish [*from the marg.*]. Comp. 3919.

3890. לְוָת **levâth** (Chald.), *lev-awth´;* from a root corresp. to 3867; prop. *adhesion,* i.e. (as prep.) *with:*— × thee.

לֻחוֹת **Lûchôwth.** See 3872.

לָז **lâz,** and

לָזֶה **lâzeh.** See 1975 and 1976.

3891. לְזוּת **lezûwth,** *lez-ooth´;* from 3868; *perverseness:*—perverse.

3892. לַח **lach,** *lakh;* from an unused root mean. to *be new; fresh,* i.e. unused or undried:—green, moist.

3893. לֵחַ **lêach,** *lay´-akh;* from the same as 3892; *freshness,* i.e. vigor:—natural force.

לֻחַ **lûach.** See 3871.

3894. לָחוּם **lâchûwm,** *law-khoom´;* or לָחֻם **lâchûm,** *law-khoom´;* pass. part. of 3898; prop. *eaten,* i.e. *food;* also *flesh,* i.e. *body:*—while . . . is eating, flesh.

3895. לְחִי **lechîy,** *lekh-ee´;* from an unused root mean. to *be soft;* the *cheek* (from its *fleshiness*); hence the *jaw*-bone:—cheek (bone), jaw (bone).

3896. לֶחִי **Lechîy,** *lekh´-ee;* a form of 3895; *Lechi,* a place in Pal.:—Lehi. Comp. also 7437.

3897. לָחַךְ **lâchak,** *law-khak´;* a prim. root; to *lick:*—lick (up).

3898. לָחַם **lâcham,** *law-kham´;* a prim. root; to *feed* on; fig. to *consume;* by impl. to *battle* (as *destruction*):—devour, eat, × ever, fight (-ing), overcome, prevail, (make) war (-ring).

3899. לֶחֶם **lechem,** *lekh´-em;* from 3898; *food* (for man or beast), espec. *bread,* or *grain* (for making it):—([shew-]) bread, × eat, food, fruit, loaf, meat, victuals. See also 1036.

3900. לְחֶם **lechem** (Chald.), *lekh-em´;* corresp. to 3899:—feast.

3901. לָחֶם **lâchem,** *law-khem´;* from 3898; *battle:*—war.

לָחֻם **lâchûm.** See 3894.

3902. לַחְמִי **Lachmîy,** *lakh-mee´;* from 3899; *foodful; Lachmi,* a Philis.; or rather prob. a brief form (or perh. err. transc.) for 1022:—Lahmi. See also 3433.

3903. לַחְמָס **Lachmâç,** *lakh-maws´;* prob. by err. transc. for לַחְמָם° **Lachmâm,** *lakh-mawm´;* from 3899; *food-like; Lachmam* or *Lachmas,* a place in Pal.:—Lahmam.

3904. לְחֵנָה **lechênâh** (Chald.), *lekh-ay-naw´;* from an unused root or uncert. mean.; a *concubine:*—concubine.

3905. לָחַץ **lâchats,** *law-khats´;* a prim. root; prop. to *press,* i.e. (fig.) to *distress:*—afflict, crush, force, hold fast, oppress (-or), thrust self.

3906. לַחַץ **lachats,** *lakh´-ats;* from 3905; *distress:*—affliction, oppression.

3907. לָחַשׁ **lâchash,** *law-khash´;* a prim. root; to *whisper;* by impl. to *mumble* a spell (as a magician):—charmer, whisper (together).

3908. לַחַשׁ **lachash,** *lakh´-ash;* from 3907; prop. a *whisper,* i.e. by impl. (in a good sense) a private *prayer,* (in a bad one) an *incantation;* concr. an *amulet:*—charmed, earring, enchantment, orator, prayer.

3909. לָט **lâṭ,** *lawt;* a form of 3814 or else part. from 3874; prop. *covered,* i.e. *secret;* by impl. *incantation;* also *secrecy* or (adv.) *covertly:*—enchantment, privily, secretly, softly.

3910. לֹט **lôṭ,** *lote;* prob. from 3874; a gum (from its *sticky* nature), prob. *ladanum:*—myrrh.

3911. לְטָאָה **leṭâ'âh,** *let-aw-aw´;* from an unused root mean. to *hide;* a kind of *lizard* (from its *covert* habits):—lizard.

3912. לְטוּשִׁם **Leṭûwshîm,** *let-oo-sheem´;* masc. plur. of pass. part. of 3913; *hammered* (i.e. *oppressed*) ones; *Letushim,* an Arabian tribe:—Letushim.

3913. לָטַשׁ **lâṭash,** *law-tash´;* a prim. root; prop. to *hammer* out (an edge), i.e. to *sharpen:*—instructer, sharp (-en), whet.

3914. לֹיָה **lôyâh,** *lo-yaw´;* a form of 3880; a *wreath:*—addition.

3915. לַיִל **layil,** *lah´-yil;* or (Isa. 21 : 11) לֵיל **lêyl,** *lale;* also לַיְלָה **lay^elâh,** *lah´-yel-aw;* from the same as 3883; prop. a *twist* (away of the light), i.e. *night;* fig. *adversity:*—([mid-]) night (season).

3916. לֵילְיָא **leyl^eyâ'** (Chald.), *lay-leh-yaw´;* corresp. to 3915:—night.

3917. לִילִית **lîylîyth,** *lee-leeth´;* from 3915; a *night* spectre:—screech owl.

3918. לַיִשׁ **layish,** *lay´-yish;* from 3888 in the sense of *crushing;* a lion (from his destructive *blows*):—(old) lion.

3919. לַיִשׁ **Layish,** *lah´-yish;* the same as 3918; *Laïsh,* the name of two places in Pal.:—Laish. Comp. 3889.

3920. לָכַד **lâkad,** *law-kad´;* a prim. root; to *catch* (in a net, trap or pit); gen. to *capture* or occupy; also to *choose* (by lot); fig. to *cohere:*—× at all, catch (self), be frozen, be holden, stick together, take.

3921. לֶכֶד **leked,** *leh´-ked;* from 3920; something to *capture* with, i.e. a *noose:*—being taken.

3922. לֵכָה **lêkâh,** *lay-kaw´;* from 3212; a *journey; Lekah,* a place in Pal.:—Lecah.

3923. לָכִישׁ **Lâchîysh,** *law-keesh´;* from an unused root of uncert. mean.; *Lakish,* a place in Pal.:—Lachish.

3924. לֻלָאָה **lûlâ'âh,** *loo-law-aw´;* from the same as 3883; a *loop:*—loop.

3925. לָמַד **lâmad,** *law-mad´;* a prim. root; prop. to *goad,* i.e. (by impl.) to *teach* (the rod being an Oriental *incentive*):—[un-] accustomed, × diligently, expert, instruct, learn, skilful, teach (-er, -ing).

לִמֻּד **limmûd.** See 3928.

3926. לְמוֹ **l^emôw,** *lem-o´;* a prol. and separable form of the pref. prep.; *to* or *for:*—at, for, to, upon.

3927. לְמוּאֵל **L^emûw'êl,** *lem-oo-ale´;* or לְמוֹאֵל **L^emôw'êl,** *lem-o-ale´;* from 3926 and 410; (belonging) *to God; Lemuël* or *Lemoël,* a symbol. name of Solomon:—Lemuel.

3928. לִמּוּד **limmûwd,** *lim-mood´;* or לִמֻּד **limmûd,** *lim-mood´;* from 3925; *instructed:*—accustomed, disciple, learned, taught, used.

3929. לֶמֶךְ **Lemek,** *leh´-mek;* from an unused root of uncert. mean.; *Lemek,* the name of two antediluvian patriarchs:—Lamech.

3930. לֹעַ **lôaʻ,** *lo´ah* friom 3886; the *gullet:*—throat.

3931. לָעַב **lâʻab,** *law-ab´;* a prim. root; to *deride:*—mock.

3932. לָעַג **lâʻag,** *law-ag´;* a prim. root; to *deride;* by impl. (as if imitating a foreigner) to *speak unintelligibly:*—have in derision, laugh (to scorn), mock (on), stammering.

3933. לַעַג **laʻag,** *lah´-ag;* from 3932; *derision, scoffing:*—derision, scorn (-ing).

3934. לָעֵג **lâʻêg,** *law-ayg´;* from 3932; a *buffoon;* also a *foreigner:*—mocker, stammering.

3935. לַעְדָּה **Laʻdâh,** *lah-daw´;* from an unused root of uncert. mean.; *Ladah,* an Isr.:—Laadah.

3936. לַעְדָּן **Laʻdân,** *lah-dawn´;* from the same as 3935; *Ladan,* the name of two Isr.:—Laadan.

3937. לָעַז **lâʻaz,** *law-az´;* a prim. root; to *speak in a foreign tongue:*—strange language.

3938. לָעַט **lâʻaṭ,** *law-at´;* a prim. root; to *swallow* greedily; causat. to *feed:*—feed.

3939. לַעֲנָה **laʻănâh,** *lah-an-aw´;* from an unused root supposed to mean to *curse; wormwood* (regarded as *poisonous,* and therefore *accursed*):—hemlock, wormwood.

3940. לַפִּיד **lappîyd,** *lap-peed´;* or לַפִּד **lappîd,** *lap-peed´;* from an unused root prob. mean. to *shine;* a *flambeau, lamp* or *flame:*—(fire-) brand, (burning) lamp, lightning, torch.

3941. לַפִּידוֹת **Lappîydôwth,** *lap-pee-dōth´;* fem. plur. of 3940; *Lappidoth,* the husband of Deborah:—Lappidoth.

3942. לִפְנַי **liphnay,** *lif-nah´ee;* from the pref. prep. (*to* or *for*) and 6440; *anterior:*—before.

3943. לָפַת **lâphath,** *law-fath´;* a prim. root; prop. to *bend,* i.e. (by impl.) to *clasp;* also (reflex.) to *turn* around or aside:—take hold, turn aside (self).

3944. לָצוֹן **lâtsôwn,** *law-tsone´;* from 3887; *derision:*—scornful (-ning).

3945. לָצַץ **lâtsats,** *law-tsats´;* a prim. root; to *deride:*—scorn.

3946. לַקּוּם **Laqqûwm** *lak-koom´;* from an unused root thought to mean to *stop* up by a barricade; perh. *fortification; Lakkum,* a place in Pal.:—Lakum.

3947. לָקַח **lâqach,** *law-kakh´;* a prim. root; to *take* (in the widest variety of applications):—accept, bring, buy, carry away, drawn, fetch, get, infold, × many, mingle, place, receive (-ing), reserve, seize, send for, take (away, -ing, up), use, win.

3948. לֶקַח **leqach,** *leh´-kakh;* from 3947; prop. something *received,* i.e. (mentally) *instruction* (whether on the part of the teacher or hearer); also (in an act. and sinister sense) *inveiglement:*—doctrine, learning, fair speech.

3949. לִקְחִי **Liqchîy,** *lik-khee´;* from 3947; *learned; Likchi,* an Isr.:—Likhi.

3950. לָקַט **lâqaṭ,** *law-kat´;* a prim. root; prop. to *pick* up, i.e. (gen.) to *gather;* spec. to *glean:*—gather (up), glean.

3951. לֶקֶט **leqeṭ,** *leh´-ket;* from 3950; the *gleaning:*—gleaning.

3952. לָקַק **lâqaq,** *law-kak´;* a prim. root; to *lick* or *lap:*—lap, lick.

3953. לָקַשׁ **lâqash,** *law-kash´;* a prim. root; to *gather* the *after* crop:—gather.

3954. לֶקֶשׁ **leqesh,** *leh´-kesh;* from 3953; the *after crop:*—latter growth.

3955. לְשַׁד **l^eshad,** *lesh-ad´;* from an unused root of uncert. mean.; appar. *juice,* i.e. (fig.) *vigor;* also a sweet or fat *cake:*—fresh, moisture.

3956. לָשׁוֹן **lâshôwn,** *law-shone´;* or לָשֹׁן **lâshôn,** *law-shone´;* also (in plur.) fem. לְשֹׁנָה **l^eshônâh** *lesh-o-naw´;* from 3960; the *tongue* (of man or animals), used lit. (as the instrument of licking, eating, or speech), and fig. (speech, an ingot, a fork of flame, a cove of water):— + babbler, bay, + evil speaker, language, talker, tongue, wedge.

3957. לִשְׁכָּה **lishkâh,** *lish-kaw´;* from an unused root of uncert. mean.; a *room* in a building (whether for storage, eating, or lodging):—chamber, parlour. Comp. 5393.

3958. לֶשֶׁם **leshem,** *leh´-shem;* from an unused root of uncert. mean.; a *gem,* perh. the *jacinth:*—ligure.

3959. לֶשֶׁם **Leshem,** *leh´-shem;* the same as 3958; *Leshem,* a place in Pal.:—Leshem.

3960. לָשַׁן **lâshan,** *law-shan´;* a prim. root; prop. to *lick;* but used only as a denom. from 3956; to *wag the tongue,* i.e. to *calumniate:*—accuse, slander.

3961. לִשָּׁן **lishshân** (Chald.) *lish-shawn´;* corresp. to 3956; *speech,* i.e. a *nation:*—language.

3962. לֶשַׁע **Leshaʻ,** *leh´-shah;* from an unused root thought to mean to *break* through; a boiling *spring; Lesha,* a place prob. E. of the Jordan:—Lasha.

3963. לֶתֶךְ **lethek,** *leh´-thek;* from an unused root of uncert. mean.; a *measure* for things dry:—half homer.

מ

-מַ **ma-,** or

-מָ **mâ-.** See 4100.

3964. מָא **mâ'** (Chald.) *maw;* corresp. to 4100; (as indef.) *that:*— + what.

3965. מַאֲבוּס **ma'ăbûwç,** *mah-ab-ooce´;* from 75; a *granary:*—storehouse.

3966. מְאֹד **m^e'ôd,** *meh-ode´;* from the same as 181; prop. *vehemence,* i.e. (with or without prep.) *vehemently;* by impl. *wholly, speedily,* etc. (often with other words as an intensive or superlative; espec. when repeated):—diligently, especially, exceeding (-ly), far, fast, good, great (-ly), × louder and louder, might (-ily, -y), (so) much, quickly, (so) sore, utterly, very (+ much, sore), well.

3967. מֵאָה **mê'âh,** *may-aw´;* or מֵאיָה **mê'yâh,** *may-yaw´;* prob. a prim. numeral; a *hundred;* also as a multiplicative and a fraction:—hundred ([-fold], -th), + sixscore.

3968. מֵאָה **Mêʼâh,** *may-aw´;* the same as 3967; *Meäh,* a tower in Jerus.:—Meah.

3969. מְאָה **mᵉʼâh** (Chald.), *meh-aw´;* corresp. to 3967:—hundred.

3970. מַאֲוַי **maʼăvay,** *mah-av-ah´eee;* from 183; a *desire:*—desire.
מוֹאל **môwʼl.** See 4136.

3971. מאוּם **mʼûwm,** *moom;* usually מוּם **mûwm,** *moom;* as if pass. part. from an unused root prob. mean. to *stain;* a *blemish* (phys. or mor.):—blemish, blot, spot.

3972. מְאוּמָה **mᵉʼûwmâh,** *meh-oo´-maw;* appar. a form of 3971; prop. a *speck* or *point,* i.e. (by impl.) *something;* with neg. *nothing:*—fault, + no (-ught), ought, somewhat, any ([no-]) thing.

3973. מָאוֹס **mâʼôwç,** *maw-oce´;* from 3988; *refuse:*—refuse.

3974. מָאוֹר **mâʼôwr,** *maw-ore´;* or מָאֹר **mâʼôr,** *maw-ore´;* also (in plur.) fem. מְאוֹרָה **mᵉʼôwrâh,** *meh-o-raw´;* or מְאֹרָה **mᵉʼôrâh,** *meh-o-raw´;* from 215; prop. a *luminous* body or *luminary,* i.e. (abstr.) *light* (as an element); fig. *brightness,* i.e. *cheerfulness;* spec. a *chandelier:*—bright, light.

3975. מְאוּרָה **mᵉʼûwrâh,** *meh-oo-raw´;* fem. pass. part, of 215; something *lighted,* i.e. an *aperture;* by impl. a *crevice* or *hole* of a serpent):—den.

3976. מֹאזֵן **môʼzên,** *mo-zane´;* from 239; (only in the dual) a pair of *scales:*—balances.

3977. מֹאזֵן **môʼzên** (Chald.) *mo-zane´;* corresp. to 3976:—balances.
מֵאיָה **mêʼyâh.** See 3967.

3978. מַאֲכָל **maʼăkâl,** *mah-ak-awl´;* from 398; an *eatable* (includ. provender, flesh and fruit):—food, fruit, ([bake-]) meat (-s), victual.

3979. מַאֲכֶלֶת **maʼăkeleth,** *mah-ak-eh´-leth;* from 398; something to *eat* with, i.e. a *knife:*—knife.

3980. מַאֲכֹלֶת **maʼăkôleth,** *mah-ak-o´-leth;* from 398; something *eaten* (by fire), i.e. *fuel:*—fuel.

3981. מַאֲמָץ **maʼămâts,** *mah-am-awts´;* from 553; *strength,* i.e. (plur.) *resources:*—force.

3982. מַאֲמַר **maʼămar,** *mah-am-ar´;* from 559; something (authoritatively) *said,* i.e. an *edict:*—commandment, decree.

3983. מֵאמַר **mêʼmar** (Chald.), *may-mar´;* corresp. to 3982:—appointment, word.

3984. מָאן **mâʼn** (Chald.), *mawn;* prob. from a root corresp. to 579 in the sense of an *inclosure* by sides; a *utensil:*—vessel.

3985. מָאֵן **mâʼên,** *maw-ane´;* a prim. root; to *refuse:*—refuse, × utterly.

3986. מָאֵן **mâʼên,** *maw-ane´;* from 3985; *unwilling:*—refuse.

3987. מֵאֵן **mêʼên,** *may-ane´;* from 3985; *refractory:*—refuse.

3988. מָאַס **mâʼaç,** *maw-as´;* a prim. root; to *spurn;* also (intrans.) to *disappear:*—abhor, cast away (off), contemn, despise, disdain, (become) loathe (-some), melt away, refuse, reject, reprobate, × utterly, vile person.

3989. מַאֲפֶה **mâʼăpheh,** *mah-af-eh´;* from 644; something *baked,* i.e. a *batch:*—baken

3990. מַאֲפֵל **maʼăphêl,** *mah-af-ale´;* from the same as 651; something *opaque:*—darkness.

3991. מַאְפֵלְיָה° **maʼphêlᵉyâh,** *mah-af-ay-leh-yaw´;* prol. fem. of 3990; *opaqueness;*—darkness.

3992. מָאַר **mâʼar,** *maw-ar´,* a prim. root; to *be bitter* or (causat.) to *embitter,* i.e. *be painful:*—fretting, picking.
מָאֹר **mâʼôr.** See 3974.

3993. מַאֲרָב **maʼărâb,** *mah-ar-awb´;* from 693; an *ambuscade:*—lie in ambush, ambushment, lurking place, lying in wait.

3994. מְאֵרָה **mᵉʼêrâh,** *meh-ay-raw´;* from 779; an *execration:*—curse.
מְאֹרָה **mᵉʼôrâh.** See 3974.

3995. מִבְדָּלָה **mibdâlâh,** *mib-daw-law´;* from 914; a *separation,* i.e. (concr.) a *separate* place:—separate.

3996. מָבוֹא **mâbôwʼ,** *maw-bo´;* from 935; an *entrance* (the place or the act); spec. (with or without 8121) *sunset* or the *west;* also (adv. with prep.) *towards:*—by which came, as cometh, in coming, as men enter into, entering, entrance into, entry, where goeth, going down, + westward. Comp. 4126.

3997. מְבוֹאָה **mᵉbôwʼâh,** *meb-o-aw´;* fem. of 3996; a *haven:*—entry.

3998. מְבוּכָה **mᵉbûwkâh,** *meb-oo-kaw´;* from 943; *perplexity:*—perplexity.

3999. מַבּוּל **mabbûwl,** *mab-bool´;* from 2986 in the sense of *flowing;* a *deluge:*—flood.

4000. מָבוֹן **mâbôwn,** *maw-bone´;* from 995; *instructing:*—taught.

4001. מְבוּסָה **mᵉbûwçâh,** *meb-oo-saw´;* from 947; a *trampling:*—treading (trodden) down (under foot).

4002. מַבּוּעַ **mabbûwaʻ,** *mab-boo´-ah;* from 5042; a *fountain:*—fountain, spring.

4003. מְבוּקָה **mᵉbûwqâh,** *meb-oo-kah´;* from the same as 950; *emptiness:*—void.

4004. מִבְחוֹר **mibchôwr,** *mib-khore´;* from 977; *select,* i.e. well fortified:—choice.

4005. מִבְחָר **mibchâr,** *mib-khawr´;* from 977; *select,* i.e. best:—choice (-st), chosen.

4006. מִבְחָר **Mibchâr,** *mib-khawr´;* the same as 4005; *Mibchar,* an Isr.:—Mibhar.

4007. מַבָּט **mabbâṭ,** *mab-bawt´;* or מֶבָּט **mebbâṭ,** *meb-bawt´;* from 5027; something *expected,* i.e. (abstr.) *expectation:*—expectation.

4008. מִבְטָא **mibṭâʼ,** *mib-taw´;* from 981; a rash *utterance* (hasty vow):—(that which . . .) uttered (out of).

4009. מִבְטָח **mibṭâch,** *mib-tawkh´;* from 982; prop. a *refuge,* i.e. (obj.) *security,* or (subj.) *assurance:*—confidence, hope, sure, trust.

4010. מַבְלִיגִית **mablîygîyth,** *mab-leeg-eeth´;* from 1082; *desistance* (or rather *desolation*):—comfort self.

4011. מִבְנֶה **mibneh,** *mib-neh´;* from 1129; a *building:*—frame.

4012. מְבֻנַּי **Mᵉbunnay,** *meb-oon-nah´ee;* from 1129; *built* up; *Mebunnai,* an Isr.:—Mebunnai.

4013. מִבְצָר **mibtsâr,** *mib-tsawr´;* also (in plur.) fem. (Dan. 11 : 15) מִבְצָרָה **mibtsârâh,** *mib-tsaw-raw´;* from 1219; a *fortification, castle,* or *fortified* city; fig. a *defender:*—(de-, most) fenced, fortress, (most) strong (hold).

4014. מִבְצָר **Mibtsâr,** *mib-tsawr´;* the same as 4013: *Mibtsar,* an Idumæan:—Mibzar.
מִבְצָרָה **mibtsârâh.** See 4013.

4015. מִבְרָח **mibrâch,** *mib-rawkh´;* from 1272; a *refugee:*—fugitive.

4016. מָבֻשׁ **mâbûsh,** *maw-boosh´;* from 954; (plur.) the (male) *pudenda:*—secrets.

4017. מִבְשָׂם **Mibsâm,** *mib-sawm´;* from the same as 1314; *fragrant; Mibsam,* the name of an Ishmaelite and of an Isr.:—Mibsam.

4018. מְבַשְּׁלָה **mᵉbashshᵉlâh,** *meb-ash-shel-aw´;* from 1310; a cooking *hearth:*—boiling-place.
מַג **Mâg.** See 7248, 7249.

4019. מַגְבִּישׁ **Magbîysh,** *mag-beesh´;* from the same as 1378; *stiffening; Magbish,* an Isr., or a place in Pal.:—Magbish.

4020. מִגְבָּלָה **migbâlâh,** *mig-baw-law´;* from 1379; a *border:*—end.

4021. מִגְבָּעָה **migbâʻâh,** *mig-baw-aw´;* from the same as 1389; a *cap* (as *hemispherical*):—bonnet.

4022. מֶגֶד **meged,** *meh´-ghed;* from an unused root prop. mean. to *be eminent;* prop. a *distinguished* thing; hence something *valuable,* as a product or fruit:—pleasant, precious fruit (thing).

4023. מְגִדּוֹן **Mᵉgiddôwn** (Zech. 12 : 11), *meg-id-dōne´;* or מְגִדּוֹ **Mᵉgiddôw,** *meg-id-do´;* from 1413; *rendezvous; Megiddon* or *Megiddo,* a place in Pal.:—Megiddo, Megiddon.

4024. מִגְדּוֹל **Migdôwl,** *mig-dole´;* or מִגְדֹּל **Migdôl,** *mig-dole´;* prob. of Eg. or.; *Migdol,* a place in Eg.:—Migdol, tower.

4025. מַגְדִּיאֵל **Magdîyʼêl,** *mag-dee-ale´;* from 4022 and 410; *preciousness of God; Magdiël,* an Idumæan:—Magdiel.

4026. מִגְדָּל **migdâl,** *mig-dawl´;* also (in plur.) fem. מִגְדָּלָה **migdâlâh,** *mig-daw-law´;* from 1431; a *tower* (from its size or height); by anal.

a *rostrum;* fig. a (pyramidal) *bed* of flowers:—castle, flower, pulpit, tower. Comp. the names following.

מִגְדֹּל **Migdôl.** See 4024.

מִגְדָּלָה **migdâlâh.** See 4026.

4027. מִגְדַּל־אֵל **Migdal-'Êl,** *mig-dal-ale´;* from 4026 and 410; *tower of God; Migdal-El,* a place in Pal.:—Migdal-el.

4028. מִגְדַּל־גָּד **Migdal-Gâd,** *migdal-gawd´;* from 4026 and 1408; *tower of Fortune; Migdal-Gad,* a place in Pal.:—Migdal-gad.

4029. מִגְדַּל־עֵדֶר **Migdal-'Êder,** *mig-dal´-ay´-der;* from 4026 and 5739; *tower of a flock; Migdal-Eder,* a place in Pal.:—Migdal-eder, tower of the flock.

4030. מִגְדָּנָה **migdânâh,** *mig-daw-naw´;* from the same as 4022; *preciousness,* i.e. a *gem:*—precious thing, present.

4031. מָגוֹג **Mâgôwg,** *maw-gogue´;* from 1463; *Magog,* a son of Japheth; also a barbarous northern region:—Magog.

4032. מָגוֹר **mâgôwr,** *maw-gore´;* or (Lam. 2 : 22) מָגוּר **mâgûwr,** *maw-goor´;* from 1481 in the sense of *fearing;* a *fright* (obj. or subj.):—fear, terror. Comp. 4036.

4033. מָגוּר **mâgûwr,** *maw-goor´;* or מָגֻר **mâgûr,** *maw-goor´;* from 1481 in the sense of *lodging;* a temporary *abode;* by extens. a permanent *residence:*—dwelling, pilgrimage, where sojourn, be a stranger. Comp. 4032.

4034. מְגוֹרָה **m**e**gôwrâh,** *meg-o-raw´;* fem. of 4032; *affright:*—fear.

4035. מְגוּרָה **m**e**gûwrâh,** *meg-oo-raw´;* fem. of 4032 or of 4033; a *fright;* also a *granary:*—barn, fear.

4036. מָגוֹר מִסָּבִיב **Mâgôwr miç-Çâbîyb,** *maw-gore´ mis-saw-beeb´;* from 4032 and 5439 with the prep. inserted; *affright from around; Magor-mis-Sabib,* a symbol. name of Pashur:—Magor-missabib.

4037. מַגְזֵרָה **magzêrâh,** *mag-zay-raw´;* from 1504; a *cutting* implement, i.e. a *blade:*—axe.

4038. מַגָּל **maggâl,** *mag-gawl´;* from an unused root mean. to *reap;* a *sickle:*—sickle.

4039. מְגִלָּה **m**e**gillâh,** *meg-il-law´;* from 1556; a *roll:*—roll, volume.

4040. מְגִלָּה **m**e**gillâh** (Chald.), *meg-il-law´;* corresp. to 4039:—roll.

4041. מְגַמָּה **m**e**gammâh,** *meg-am-maw´;* from the same as 1571; prop. *accumulation,* i.e. *impulse* or *direction:*—sup up.

4042. מָגַן **mâgan,** *maw-gan´;* a denom. from 4043; prop. to *shield; encompass* with; fig. to *rescue,* to *hand* safely *over* (i.e. *surrender*):—deliver.

4043. מָגֵן **mâgên,** *maw-gane´;* also (in plur.) fem. מְגִנָּה **m**e**ginnâh,** *meg-in-naw´;* from 1598; a *shield* (i.e. the small one or *buckler*); fig. a *protector;* also the scaly *hide* of the crocodile:—× armed, buckler, defence, ruler, + scale, shield.

4044. מְגִנָּה **m**e**ginnâh,** *meg-in-naw´;* from 4042; a *covering* (in a bad sense), i.e. *blindness* or obduracy:—sorrow. See also 4043.

4045. מִגְעֶרֶת **mig'ereth,** *mig-eh´-reth;* from 1605; *reproof* (i.e. curse):—rebuke.

4046. מַגֵּפָה **maggêphâh,** *mag-gay-faw´;* from 5062; a *pestilence;* by anal. *defeat:*—(× be) plague (-d), slaughter, stroke.

4047. מַגְפִּיעָשׁ **Magpîy'âsh,** *mag-pee-awsh´;* appar. from 1479 or 5062 and 6211; *exterminator of* (the) *moth; Magpiash,* an Isr.:—Magpiash.

4048. מָגַר **mâgar,** *maw-gar´;* a prim. root; to *yield up;* intens. to *precipitate:*—cast down, terror.

4049. מְגַר **m**e**gar** (Chald.), *meg-ar´;* corresp. to 4048; to *overthrow:*—destroy.

4050. מְגֵרָה **m**e**gêrâh,** *meg-ay-raw´;* from 1641; a *saw:*—axe, saw.

4051. מִגְרוֹן **Migrôwn,** *mig-rone´;* from 4048; *precipice; Migron,* a place in Pal.:—Migron.

4052. מִגְרָעָה **migrâ'âh,** *mig-raw-aw´;* from 1639; a *ledge* or offset:—narrowed rest.

4053. מִגְרָפָה **migrâphâh,** *mig-raw-faw´;* from 1640; something *thrown off* (by the spade), i.e. a *clod:*—clod.

4054. מִגְרָשׁ **migrâsh,** *mig-rawsh´;* also (in plur.) fem. (Ezek. 27 : 28) מִגְרָשָׁה **migrâshâh,** *mig-raw-shaw´;* from 1644; a *suburb* (i.e. open country whither flocks are *driven* for pasture); hence the *area* around a building, or the *margin* of the sea:—cast out, suburb.

4055. מַד **mad,** *mad;* or מֵד **mêd,** *made;* from 4058; prop. *extent,* i.e. *height;* also a *measure;* by impl. a *vesture* (as measured); also a *carpet:*—armour, clothes, garment, judgment, measure, raiment, stature.

4056. מַדְבַּח **madbach** (Chald.), *mad-bakh´;* from 1684; a sacrificial *altar:*—altar.

4057. מִדְבָּר **midbâr,** *mid-bawr´;* from 1696 in the sense of *driving;* a *pasture* (i.e. open field, whither cattle are driven); by impl. a *desert;* also *speech* (including its organs):—desert, south, speech, wilderness.

4058. מָדַד **mâdad,** *maw-dad´;* a prim. root; prop. to *stretch;* by impl. to *measure* (as if by *stretching* a line); fig. to *be extended:*—measure, mete, stretch self.

4059. מִדַּד **middad,** *mid-dad´;* from 5074; *flight:*—be gone.

4060. מִדָּה **middâh,** *mid-daw´;* fem. of 4055; prop. *extension,* i.e. height or breadth; also a *measure* (including its standard); hence a *portion* (as measured) or a *vestment;* spec. *tribute* (as measured):—garment, measure (-ing, meteyard, piece, size, (great) stature, tribute, wide.

4061. מִדָּה **middâh** (Chald.), *mid-daw´;* or מִנְדָּה **mindâh** (Chald.), *min-daw´;* corresp. to 4060; *tribute* in money:—toll, tribute.

4062. מַדְהֵבָה **madhêbâh,** *mad-hay-baw´;* perh. from the equiv. of 1722; *gold-making,* i.e. *exactress:*—golden city.

4063. מֶדֶו **medev,** *meh´-dev;* from an unused root mean. to *stretch;* prop. *extent,* i.e. *measure;* by impl. a *dress* (as measured):—garment.

4064. מַדְוֶה **madveh,** *mad-veh´;* from 1738; *sickness:*—disease.

4065. מַדּוּחַ **maddûwach,** *mad-doo´-akh;* from 5080; *seduction:*—cause of banishment.

4066. מָדוֹן **mâdôwn,** *maw-dohn´;* from 1777; a *contest* or quarrel:—brawling, contention (-ous), discord, strife. Comp. 4079, 4090.

4067. מָדוֹן **mâdôwn,** *maw-dohn´;* from the same as 4063; *extensiveness,* i.e. height:—stature.

4068. מָדוֹן **Mâdôwn,** *maw-dohn´;* the same as 4067; *Madon,* a place in Pal.:—Madon.

4069. מַדּוּעַ **maddûwa',** *mad-doo-´-ah;* or מַדֻּעַ **maddûa',** *mad-doo´-ah;* from 4100 and the pass. part. of 3045; *what* (is) *known?;* i.e. (by impl.) (adv.) *why?:*—how, wherefore, why.

4070. מְדוֹר **m**e**dôwr** (Chald.), *med-ore´;* or מְדֹר **m**e**dôr** (Chald.), *med-ore´;* or מְדָר **m**e**dâr** (Chald.), *med-awr´;* from 1753; a *dwelling:*—dwelling.

4071. מְדוּרָה **m**e**dûwrâh,** *med-oo-raw´;* or מְדֻרָה **m**e**dûrâh,** *med-oo-raw´;* from 1752 in the sense of *accumulation;* a *pile* of fuel:—pile (for fire).

4072. מִדְחֶה **midcheh,** *mid-kheh´;* from 1760; *overthrow:*—ruin.

4073. מְדַחְפָה **m**e**dachphâh,** *med-akh-faw´;* from 1765; a *push,* i.e. ruin:—overthrow.

4074. מָדַי **Mâday,** *maw-dah´ee;* of for. der.; *Madai,* a country of central Asia:—Madai, Medes, Media.

4075. מָדַי **Mâday,** *maw-dah´ee;* patrial from 4074; a *Madian* or native of Madai:—Mede.

4076. מָדַי **Mâday** (Chald.), *maw-dah´ee;* corresp. to 4074:—Mede (-s).

4077. מָדַי **Mâday** (Chald.), *maw-dah´ee;* corresp. to 4075:—Median.

4078. מַדַּי **madday,** *mad-dah´ee;* from 4100 and 1767; *what* (is) *enough,* i.e. *sufficiently:*—sufficiently.

4079. מִדְיָן **midyân,** *mid-yawn´;* a var. for 4066:—brawling, contention (-ous).

4080. מִדְיָן **Midyân,** *mid-yawn´;* the same as 4079; *Midjan,* a son of Abraham; also his country and (collect.) his descend.:—Midian, Midianite.

4081. מִדִּין **Middîyn,** *mid-deen´;* a var. for 4080:—Middin.

4082. מְדִינָה **mᵉdîynâh,** *med-ee-naw´;* from 1777; prop. a *judgeship,* i.e. *jurisdiction;* by impl. a *district* (as ruled by a judge); gen. a *region:*—(× every) province.

4083. מְדִינָה **mᵉdîynâh** (Chald.), *med-ee-naw´;* corresp. to 4082:—province.

4084. מִדְיָנִי **Midyânîy,** *mid-yaw-nee´;* patron. or patrial from 4080; a *Midjanite* or descend. (native) of Midjan:—Midianite. Comp. 4092.

4085. מְדֹכָה **mᵉdôkâh,** *med-o-kaw´;* from 1743; a *mortar:*—mortar.

4086. מַדְמֵן **Madmên,** *mad-mane´;* from the same as 1828; *dunghill; Madmen,* a place in Pal.:—Madmen.

4087. מַדְמֵנָה **madmênâh,** *mad-may-naw´;* fem. from the same as 1828; a *dunghill:*—dunghill.

4088. מַדְמֵנָה **Madmênâh,** *mad-may-naw´;* the same as 4087; *Madmenah,* a place in Pal.:—Madmenah.

4089. מַדְמַנָּה **Madmannâh,** *mad-man-naw´;* a var. for 4087; *Madmannah,* a place in Pal.:—Madmannah.

4090. מְדָן **mᵉdân,** *med-awn´;* a form of 4066:—discord, strife.

4091. מְדָן **Mᵉdân,** *med-awn´;* the same as 4090; *Medan,* a son of Abraham:—Medan.

4092. מְדָנִי **Mᵉdânîy,** *med-aw-nee´;* a var. of 4084:—Midianite.

4093. מַדָּע **maddâʻ,** *mad-daw´;* or מַדַּע **maddaʻ,** *mad-dah´;* from 3045; *intelligence* or *consciousness:*—knowledge, science, thought.

מֹדָע **môdâʻ.** See 4129.

מַדֻּעַ **madûaʻ.** See 4069.

4094. מַדְקָרָה **madqârâh,** *mad-kaw-raw´;* from 1856; a *wound:*—piercing.

מְדֹר **mᵉdôr.** See 4070.

4095. מַדְרֵגָה **madrêgâh,** *mad-ray-gaw´;* from an unused root mean. to *step;* prop. a *step;* by impl. a *steep* or inaccessible place:—stair, steep place.

מְדֻרָה **mᵉdûrâh.** See 4071.

4096. מִדְרָךְ **midrâk,** *mid-rawk´;* from 1869; a *treading,* i.e. a place for stepping on:—[foot-] breadth.

4097. מִדְרָשׁ **midrâsh,** *mid-rawsh´;* from 1875; prop. an *investigation,* i.e. (by impl.) a *treatise* or elaborate compilation:—story.

4098. מְדֻשָּׁה **mᵉdushshâh,** *med-oosh-shaw´;* from 1758; a *threshing,* i.e. (concr. and fig.) *down-trodden* people:—threshing.

4099. מְדָתָא **Mᵉdâthâ,** *med-aw-thaw´;* of Pers. or.; *Medatha,* the father of Haman:—Hammedatha [*includ. the art.*].

4100. מָה **mâh,** *maw;* or מַה **mah,** *mah;* or מָ־ **mâ,** *maw;* or מַ־ **ma,** *mah;* also מֶה **meh,** *meh;* a prim. particle; prop. interrog. *what?* (includ. *how? why? when?*); but also exclam. *what!* (includ. *how!*), or indef. *what* (includ. *whatever,* and even rel. *that which*); often used with prefixes in various adv. or conj. senses:—how (long, oft, [-soever]), [no-] thing, what (end, good, purpose, thing), whereby (-fore, -in, -to, -with), (for) why.

4101. מָה **mâh** (Chald.), *maw;* corresp. to 4100:—how great (mighty), that which, what (-soever), why.

4102. מָהַהּ **mâhahh,** *maw-hah´;* appar. a denom. from 4100; prop. to *question* or hesitate, i.e. (by impl.) to *be reluctant:*—delay, linger, stay selves, tarry.

4103. מְהוּמָה **mᵉhûwmâh,** *meh-hoo-maw´;* from 1949; *confusion* or uproar:—destruction, discomfiture, trouble, tumult, vexation, vexed.

4104. מְהוּמָן **Mᵉhûwmân** *meh-hoo-mawn´;* of Pers. or.; *Mehuman,* a eunuch of Xerxes:—Mehuman.

4105. מְהֵיטַבְאֵל **Mᵉhêyṭabʼêl,** *meh-hay-tab-ale´;* from 3190 (augmented) and 410; *bettered of God; Mehetabel,* the name of an Edomitish man and woman:—Mehetabeel, Mehetabel.

4106. מָהִיר **mâhîyr,** *maw-here´;* or מָהִר **mâhîr,** *maw-here´;* from 4116; *quick;* hence *skilful:*—diligent, hasty, ready.

4107. מָהַל **mâhal,** *maw-hal´;* a prim. root; prop. to *cut down* or *reduce,* i.e. by impl. to *adulterate:*—mixed.

4108. מַהְלֵךְ **mahlêk,** *mah-lake´;* from 1980; a *walking* (plur. collect.), i.e. *access:*—place to walk.

4109. מַהֲלָךְ **mahălâk,** *mah-hal-awk´;* from 1980; a *walk,* i.e. a *passage* or a *distance:*—journey, walk.

4110. מַהֲלָל **mahălâl,** *mah-hal-awl´;* from 1984; *fame:*—praise.

4111. מַהֲלַלְאֵל **Mahălalʼêl,** *mah-hal-al-ale´;* from 4110 and 410; *praise of God; Mahalalel,* the name of an antediluvian patriarch and of an Isr.:—Mahalaleel.

4112. מַהֲלֻמָּה **mahălummâh,** *mah-hal-oom-maw´;* from 1986; a *blow:*—stripe, stroke.

4113. מַהֲמֹרָה **mahămôrâh,** *mah-ham-o-raw´;* from an unused root of uncert. mean.; perh. an *abyss:*—deep pit.

4114. מַהְפֵּכָה **mahpêkâh,** *mah-pay-kaw´;* from 2015; a *destruction:*—when . . . overthrew, overthrow (-n).

4115. מַהְפֶּכֶת **mahpeketh,** *mah-peh´-keth;* from 2015; a *wrench,* i.e. the *stocks:*—prison, stocks.

4116. מָהַר **mâhar,** *maw-har´;* a prim. root; prop. to *be liquid* or *flow* easily, i.e. (by impl.); *to hurry* (in a good or a bad sense); often used (with another verb) adv. *promptly:*—be carried headlong, fearful, (cause to make, in, make) haste (-n, -ily, (be) hasty, (fetch, make ready) × quickly, rash, × shortly, (be so) × soon, make speed, × speedily, × straightway, × suddenly, swift.

4117. מָהַר **mâhar,** *maw-har´;* a prim. root (perh. rather the same as 4116 through the idea of *readiness* in assent): to *bargain* (for a wife), i.e. to *wed:*—endow, × surely.

4118. מַהֵר **mahêr,** *mah-hare´;* from 4116; prop. *hurrying;* hence (adv.) *in a hurry:*—hasteth, hastily, at once, quickly, soon, speedily, suddenly.

מָהִר **mâhîr.** See 4106.

4119. מֹהַר **môhar,** *mo´-har;* from 4117; a *price* (for a wife):—dowry.

4120. מְהֵרָה **mᵉhêrâh,** *meh-hay-raw´;* fem. of 4118; prop. a *hurry;* hence (adv.) *promptly:*—hastily, quickly, shortly, soon, make (with) speed (-ily), swiftly.

4121. מַהֲרַי **Mahăray,** *mah-har-ah´ee;* from 4116; *hasty; Maharai,* an Isr.:—Maharai.

4122. מַהֵר שָׁלָל חָשׁ בַּז **Mahêr Shâlâl Châsh Baz,** *mah-hare´ shaw-lawl´ khawsh baz;* from 4118 and 7998 and 2363 and 957; *hasting* (is he [the enemy] to the) *booty, swift* (to the) *prey; Maher-Shalal-Chash-Baz;* the symbol. name of the son of Isaiah:—Maher-shalal-hash-baz.

4123. מַהֲתַלָּה **mahăthallâh,** *mah-hath-al-law´;* from 2048; a *delusion:*—deceit.

4124. מוֹאָב **Môwʼâb,** *mo-awb;* from a prol. form of the prep. pref. *m-* and 1; *from* (her [the mother's]) *father; Moäb,* an incestuous son of Lot; also his territory and desc.:—Moab.

4125. מוֹאָבִי **Môwʼâbîy,** *mo-aw-bee´;* fem. מוֹאָבִיָּה **Môwʼâbîyâh,** *mo-aw-bee-yaw´;* or מוֹאָבִית **Môwâbîyth,** *mo-aw-beeth´;* patron. from 4124; a *Moäbite* or *Moäbitess,* i.e. a desc. from Moab:—(woman) of Moab, Moabite (-ish, -ss).

מוֹאל **môwʼl.** See 4136.

4126. מוֹבָא **môwbâʼ,** *mo-baw´;* by transp. for 3996; an *entrance:*—coming.

4127. מוּג **mûwg,** *moog;* a prim. root; to *melt,* i.e. lit. (to *soften,* flow down, *disappear*), or fig. (to *fear, faint*):—consume, dissolve, (be) faint (-hearted), melt (away), make soft.

4128. מוּד **mûwd,** *mood;* a prim. root; to *shake:*—measure.

4129. מוֹדַע **môwdaʻ,** *mo-dah´;* or rather מֹדָע **môdâʻ,** *mo-daw´;* from 3045; an *acquaintance:*—kinswoman.

4130. מוֹדַעַת **môwdaʻath,** *mo-dah´-ath;* from 3045; *acquaintance:*—kindred.

4131. מוֹט **môwṭ,** *mote;* a prim. root; to *waver;* by impl. to *slip, shake, fall:*—be carried, cast, be out of course, be fallen in decay, × exceedingly, fall (-ing down), be (re-) moved, be ready shake, slide, slip.

4132. מוֹט **môwṭ,** *mote;* from 4131; a *wavering,* i.e. *fall;* by impl. a *pole* (as shaking); hence a *yoke* (as essentially a bent pole):—bar, be moved, staff, yoke.

4133. מוֹטָה **môwṭah,** *mo-taw´;* fem. of 4132; a *pole;* by impl. an ox-*bow;* hence a *yoke* (either lit. or fig.):—bands, heavy, staves, yoke.

4134. מוּךְ **mûwk,** *mook;* a prim. root; to *become thin,* i.e. (fig.) *be impoverished:*—be (waxen) poor (-er).

4135. מוּל **mûwl,** *mool;* a prim. root; to *cut* short, i.e. *curtail* (spec. the prepuce, i.e. to *circumcise*); by impl. to *blunt;* fig. to *destroy:*—circumcise (-ing, selves), cut down (in pieces), destroy, × must needs.

4136. מוּל **mûwl,** *mool;* or מוֹל **môwl** (Deut. 1 : 1), *mole;* or מוֹאל **môw'l** (Neh. 12 : 38), *mole;* or מֻל **mûl** (Num. 22 : 5), *mool;* from 4135; prop. *abrupt,* i.e. a *precipice;* by impl. the *front;* used only adv. (with prep. pref.) *opposite:*—(over) against, before, [fore-] front, from, [God-] ward, toward, with.

4137. מוֹלָדָה **Môwlâdâh,** *mo-law-daw´;* from 3205; *birth; Moladah,* a place in Pal.:—Moladah.

4138. מוֹלֶדֶת **môwledeth,** *mo-leh´-deth;* from 3205; *nativity* (plur. *birth-place*); by impl. *lineage, native country;* also *offspring, family:*—begotten, born, issue, kindred, native (-ity).

4139. מוּלָה **mûwlâh,** *moo-law´;* from 4135; *circumcision:*—circumcision.

4140. מוֹלִיד **Môwlîyd,** *mo-leed´;* from 3205; *genitor; Molid,* an Isr.:—Molid.

מוּם **muwm.** See 3971.

מוֹמֻכָן° **Môwmûkân.** See 4462.

4141. מוּסָב **mûwçâb,** *moo-sawb´;* from 5437; a *turn,* i.e. *circuit* (of a building):—winding about.

4142. מוּסַבָּה **mûwçabbâh,** *moo-sab-baw´;* or מֻסַבָּה **mûçabbâh,** *moo-sab-baw´;* fem. of 4141; a *reversal,* i.e. the *backside* (of a gem), *fold* (of a double-leaved door), *transmutation* (of a name):—being changed, inclosed, be set, turning.

4143. מוּסָד **mûwçad,** *moo-sawd´;* from 3245; a *foundation:*—foundation.

4144. מוֹסָד **môwçâd,** *mo-sawd´;* from 3245; a *foundation:*—foundation.

4145. מוּסָדָה **mûwçâdâh,** *moo-saw-daw´;* fem. of 4143; a *foundation;* fig. an *appointment:*—foundation, grounded. Comp. 4328.

4146. מוֹסָדָה **môwçâdâh,** *mo-saw-daw´;* or מֹסָדָה **môçâdâh** *mo-saw-daw´;* fem. of 4144; a *foundation:*—foundation.

4147. מוֹסֵר **môwçêr,** *mo-sare´;* also (in plur.) fem. מוֹסֵרָה **môwçêrâh,** *mo-say-raw´;* or מֹסְרָה **môçᵉrâh,** *mo-ser-aw´;* from 3256; prop. *chastisement,* i.e. (by impl.) a *halter;* fig. *restraint:*—band, bond.

4148. מוּסָר **mûwçâr,** *moo-sawr´;* from 3256; prop. *chastisement;* fig. *reproof. warning* or *instruction;* also *restraint:*—bond, chastening ([-eth]), chastisement, check, correction, discipline, doctrine, instruction, rebuke.

4149. מוֹסֵרָה **Môwçêrâh,** *mo-say-raw´;* or (plur.) מֹסֵרוֹת **Môçᵉrôwth,** *mo-ser-othe´;* fem. of 4147; *correction* or *corrections; Moserah* or *Moseroth,* a place in the Desert:—Mosera, Moseroth.

4150. מוֹעֵד **môw'êd,** *mo-ade´;* or מֹעֵד **mô'êd** *mo-ade´;* or (fem.) מוֹעָדָה **môw'âdâh** (2 Chron. 8 : 13), *mo-aw-daw´;* from 3259; prop. an *appointment,* i.e. a fixed *time* or season; spec. a *festival;* conventionally a *year;* by implication, an *assembly* (as convened for a definite purpose); technically the *congregation;* by extension, the *place of meeting;* also a *signal* (as appointed beforehand):—appointed (sign, time), (place of, solemn) assembly, congregation, (set, solemn) feast, (appointed, due) season, solemn (-ity), synagogue, (set) time (appointed).

4151. מוֹעָד **môw'âd,** *mo-awd´;* from 3259; prop. an *assembly* [as in 4150]; fig. a *troop:*—appointed time.

4152. מוּעָדָה **mûw'âdâh,** *moo-aw-daw´;* from 3259; an *appointed* place, i.e. *asylum:*—appointed.

4153. מוֹעַדְיָה **Môw'adyâh,** *mo-ad-yaw´;* from 4151 and 3050; *assembly of Jah; Moädjah,* an Isr.:—Moadiah. Comp. 4573.

4154. מוּעֶדֶת **mûw'edeth,** *moo-ay´-deth;* fem. pass. part. of 4571; prop. *made to slip,* i.e. *dislocated:*—out of joint.

4155. מוּעָף **mûw'âph,** *moo-awf´;* from 5774; prop. *covered,* i.e. *dark;* abstr. *obscurity,* i.e. *distress:*—dimness.

4156. מוֹעֵצָה **môw'êtsâh,** *mo-ay-tsaw´;* from 3289; a *purpose:*—counsel, device.

4157. מוּעָקָה **mûw'âqâh,** *moo-aw-kaw´;* from 5781; *pressure,* i.e. (fig.) *distress:*—affliction.

4158. מוֹפַעַת° **Môwpha'ath** (Jer. 48 : 21), *mo-fah´-ath;* or מֵיפַעַת **mêypha'ath,** *may-fah´-ath;* or מֵפַעַת **mêpha'ath,** *may-fah´-ath;* from 3313; *illuminative; Mophaath* or *Mephaath,* a place in Pal.:—Mephaath.

4159. מוֹפֵת **môwphêth,** *mo-faith´;* or מֹפֵת **môphêth,** *mo-faith´;* from 3302 in the sense of *conspicuousness;* a *miracle;* by impl. a *token* or *omen:*—miracle, sign, wonder (-ed at).

4160. מוּץ **mûwts,** *moots;* a prim. root; to *press,* i.e. (fig.) to *oppress:*—extortioner.

4161. מוֹצָא **môwtsâ',** *mo-tsaw´;* or מֹצָא **môtsâ,** *mo-tsaw´;* from 3318; a *going forth,* i.e. (the act) an *egress,* or (the place) an *exit:* hence a *source* or *product;* spec. *dawn,* the *rising* of the sun (the *East*), *exportation, utterance,* a *gate,* a *fountain,* a *mine,* a *meadow* (as producing grass):—brought out, bud, that which came out, east, going forth, goings out, that which (thing that) is gone out, outgoing, proceeded out, spring, vein, [water-] course [springs].

4162. מוֹצָא **môwtsâ',** *mo-tsaw´;* the same as 4161; *Motsa,* the name of two Isr.:—Moza.

4163. מוֹצָאָה **môwtsâ'âh,** *mo-tsaw-aw´;* fem. of 4161; a family *descent;* also a *sewer* [marg.; comp. 6675]:—draught house; going forth.

4164. מוּצַק **mûwtsaq,** *moo-tsak´;* or מוּצָק **mûwtsâq,** *moo-tsawk´;* from 3332; *narrowness;* fig. *distress:*—anguish, is straitened, straitness.

4165. מוּצָק **mûwtsâq,** *moo-tsawk´;* from 5694; prop. *fusion,* i.e. lit. a *casting* (of metal); fig. a *mass* (of clay):—casting, hardness.

4166. מוּצָקָה **mûwtsâqâh,** *moo-tsaw-kaw´;* or מֻצָקָה **mûtsâqâh,** *moo-tsaw-kaw´;* from 3332; prop. something *poured* out, i.e. a *casting* (of metal); by impl. a tube (as cast):—when it was cast, pipe.

4167. מוּק **mûwq,** *mook;* a prim. root; to *jeer,* i.e. (intens.) *blaspheme:*—be corrupt.

4168. מוֹקֵד **môwqêd,** *mo-kade´;* from 3344; a *fire* or *fuel;* abstr. a *conflagration:*—burning, hearth.

4169. מוֹקְדָה° **môwqᵉdâh,** *mo-ked-aw´;* fem. of 4168; *fuel:*—burning.

4170. מוֹקֵשׁ **môwqêsh,** *mo-kashe´;* or מֹקֵשׁ **môqêsh,** *mo-kashe´;* from 3369; a *noose* (for catching animals) (lit. or fig.); by impl. a *hook* (for the nose):—be ensnared, gin, (is) snare (-d), trap.

4171. מוּר **mûwr,** *moor; a prim. root; to alter;* by impl. to *barter,* to *dispose of:*— × at all, (ex-) change, remove.

4172. מוֹרָא **môwrâ',** *mo-raw´;* or מֹרָא **môrâ',** *mo-raw´;* or מוֹרָה **môrâh** (Psa. 9 : 20), *mo-raw´;* from 3372; *fear;* by impl. a *fearful* thing or deed:—dread, (that ought to be) fear (-ed), terribleness, terror.

4173. מוֹרַג **môwrag,** *mo-rag´;* or מֹרַג **môrag,** *mo-rag´;* from an unused root mean. to *triturate;* a threshing *sledge:*—threshing instrument.

4174. מוֹרָד **môwrâd,** *mo-rawd´;* from 3381; a *descent;* arch. an ornamental *appendage,* perh. a *festoon:*—going down, steep place, thin work.

4175. מוֹרֶה **môwreh,** *mo-reh´;* from 3384; an *archer;* also *teacher* or *teaching;* also the *early rain* [see 3138]:—(early) rain.

4176. מוֹרֶה **Môwreh,** *mo-reh´;* or מֹרֶה **Môreh,** *mo-reh´;* the same as 4175; *Moreh,* a Canaanite; also a hill (perh. named from him):—Moreh.

4177. מוֹרָה **môwrâh,** *mo-raw´;* from 4171 in the sense of *shearing;* a *razor:*—razor.

4178. מוֹרָט **môwraṭ,** *mo-rawt`;* from 3399; *obstinate,* i.e. independent:—peeled.

4179. מוֹרִיָּה **Môwrîyâh,** *mo-ree-yaw´;* or מֹרִיָּה **Môrîyâh,** *mo-ree-yaw´;* from 7200 and 3050; *seen of Jah; Morijah,* a hill in Pal.:—Moriah.

4180. מוֹרָשׁ **môwrâsh,** *mo-rawsh´;* from 3423; a *possession;* fig. *delight:*—possession, thought.

4181. מוֹרָשָׁה **môwrâshâh,** *mo-raw-shaw´;* fem. of 4180; a *possession:*—heritage, inheritance, possession.

4182. מוֹרֶשֶׁת גַּת **Môwresheth Gath,** *mo-reh´-sheth gath;* from 3423 and 1661; *possession of Gath; Moresheth-Gath,* a place in Pal.:—Moresheth-gath.

4183. מוֹרַשְׁתִּי **Morashtîy,** *mo-rash-tee´;* patrial from 4182; a *Morashtite* or inhab. of Moresheth-Gath:—Morashthite.

4184. מוּשׁ **mûwsh,** *moosh;* a prim. root; to *touch:*—feel, handle.

4185. מוּשׁ **mûwsh,** *moosh;* a prim. root [perh. rather the same as 4184 through the idea of receding by *contact*]; to *withdraw* (both lit. and fig., whether intrans. or trans.):—cease, depart, go back, remove, take away.

4186. מוֹשָׁב **môwshâb,** *mo-shawb´;* or מֹשָׁב **môshâb,** *mo-shawb´;* from 3427; a *seat;* fig. a *site;* abstr. a *session;* by extension an *abode* (the place or the time); by impl. *population:*—assembly, dwell in, dwelling (-place), wherein (that) dwelt (in), inhabited place, seat, sitting, situation, sojourning.

4187. מוּשִׁי **Mûwshîy,** *moo-shee´;* or מֻשִּׁי **Mushshîy,** *mush-shee´;* from 4184; *sensitive; Mushi,* a Levite:—Mushi.

4188. מוּשִׁי **Mûwshîy,** *moo-shee´;* patron. from 4187; a *Mushite* (collect.) or desc. of Mushi:—Mushites.

4189. מוֹשְׁכָה **môwsh^{e}kâh,** *mo-shek-aw´;* act part. fem. of 4900; something *drawing,* i.e. (fig.) a *cord:*—band.

4190. מוֹשָׁעָה **môwshâʽâh,** *mo-shaw-aw´;* from 3467; *deliverance:*—salvation.

4191. מוּת **mûwth,** *mooth;* a prim. root; to *die* (lit. or fig.); causat. to *kill:*— × at all, × crying, (be) dead (body, man, one), (put to, worthy of) death, destroy (-er), (cause to, be like to, must) die, kill, necro [-mancer], × must needs, slay, × surely, × very suddenly, × in [no] wise.

4192. מוּת **Mûwth** (Psa. 48 : 14), *mooth;* or מוּת לַבֵּן **Mûwth lab-bên,** *mooth labbane´;* from 4191 and 1121 with the prep. and art. interposed; *"To die for the son",* prob. the title of a popular song:—death, Muthlabben.

4193. מוֹת **môwth** (Chald.), *mohth;* corresp. to 4194; *death:*—death.

4194. מָוֶת **mâveth,** *maw´-veth;* from 4191; *death* (nat. or violent); concr. the *dead,* their place or state *(hades);* fig. *pestilence, ruin:*—(be) dead ([-ly]), death, die (-d).

מוּת לַבֵּן **Mûwth lab-bên.** See 4192.

4195. מוֹתָר **môwthar,** *mo-thar´;* from 3498; lit. *gain;* fig. *superiority:*—plenteousness, preeminence, profit.

4196. מִזְבֵּחַ **mizbêach,** *miz-bay´-akh;* from 2076; an *altar:*—altar.

4197. מֶזֶג **mezeg,** *meh´-zeg;* from an unused root mean. to *mingle* (water with wine); *tempered* wine:—liquor.

4198. מָזֶה **mâzeh,** *maw-zeh´;* from an unused root mean. to *suck* out; *exhausted:*—burnt.

4199. מִזָּה **Mizzâh,** *miz-zaw´;* prob. from an unused root mean. to *faint* with fear; *terror; Mizzah,* an Edomite:—Mizzah.

4200. מֶזֶו **mezev,** *meh´-zev;* prob. from an unused root mean. to *gather* in; a *granary:*—garner.

4201. מְזוּזָה **m^{e}zûwzâh,** *mez-oo-zaw´;* or מְזֻזָה **m^{e}zûzâh,** *mez-oo-zaw´;* from the same as 2123; a *door-post* (as *prominent*):—(door, side) post.

4202. מָזוֹן **mâzôwn,** *maw-zone´;* from 2109; *food:*—meat, victual.

4203. מָזוֹן **mâzôwn,** (Chald.), *maw-zone´;* corresp. to 4202:—meat.

4204. מָזוֹר **mâzôwr,** *maw-zore´;* from 2114 in the sense of *turning aside* from truth; *treachery,* i.e. a *plot:*—wound.

4205. מָזוֹר **mâzôwr,** *maw-zore´;* or מָזֹר **mâzôr,** *maw-zore´;* from 2115 in the sense of *binding* up; a *bandage,* i.e. remedy; hence a *sore* (as needing a compress):—bound up, wound.

מְזֻזָה **m^{e}zûzâh.** See 4201.

4206. מָזִיחַ **mâzîyach,** *maw-zee´-akh;* or מֵזַח **mêzach,** *may-zakh´;* from 2118; a *belt* (as movable):—girdle, strength.

4207. מַזְלֵג **mazlêg,** *maz-layg´;* or (fem.) מִזְלָגָה **mizlâgâh,** *miz-law-gaw´;* from an unused root mean. to *draw* up; a *fork:*—fleshhook.

4208. מַזָּלָה **mazzâlâh,** *maz-zaw-law´;* appar. from 5140 in the sense of *raining;* a *constellation,* i.e. Zodiacal sign (perh. as affecting the weather):—planet. Comp. 4216.

4209. מְזִמָּה **m^{e}zimmâh,** *mez-im-maw´;* from 2161; a *plan,* usually evil (*machination*), sometimes good *(sagacity):*—(wicked) device, discretion, intent, witty invention, lewdness, mischievous (device), thought, wickedly.

4210. מִזְמוֹר **mizmôwr,** *miz-more´;* from 2167; prop. instrumental *music;* by impl. a *poem* set to notes:—psalm.

4211. מַזְמֵרָה **mazmêrâh,** *maz-may-raw´;* from 2168; a *pruning-knife:*—pruning-hook.

4212. מְזַמְּרָה **m^{e}zamm^{e}râh,** *mez-am-mer-aw´;* from 2168; a *tweezer* (only in the plur.):—snuffers.

4213. מִזְעָר **mizʽâr,** *miz-awr´;* from the same as 2191; *fewness;* by impl. as superl. *diminutiveness:*—few, × very.

מָזֹר **mâzôr.** See 4205.

4214. מִזְרֶה **mizreh,** *miz-reh´;* from 2219; a winnowing *shovel* (as scattering the chaff):—fan.

4215. מְזָרֶה **m^{e}zâreh,** *mez-aw-reh´;* appar. from 2219; prop. a *scatterer,* i.e. the north *wind* (as dispersing clouds; only in plur.):—north.

4216. מַזָּרָה **mazzârâh,** *maz-zaw-raw´;* appar. from 5144 in the sense of *distinction;* some noted *constellation* (only in the plur.), perh. collect. the *zodiac:*—Mazzoroth. Comp. 4208.

4217. מִזְרָח **mizrâch,** *miz-rawkh´;* from 2224; *sunrise,* i.e. the *east:*—east (side, -ward), (sun-) rising (of the sun).

4218. מִזְרָע **mizrâʽ,** *miz-raw´;* from 2232; a planted *field:*—thing sown.

4219. מִזְרָק **mîzrâq,** *miz-rawk´;* from 2236; a *bowl* (as if for sprinkling):—bason, bowl.

4220. מֵחַ **mêach,** *may´-akh;* from 4229 in the sense of *greasing; fat;* fig. *rich:*—fatling (one).

4221. מֹחַ **môach,** *mo´-akh;* from the same as 4220; *fat,* i.e. marrow:—marrow.

4222. מָחָא **mâchâʼ,** *maw-khaw´;* a prim. root; to *rub* or *strike* the hands together (in exultation):—clap.

4223. מְחָא **m^{e}châʼ** (Chald.), *mekh-aw´;* corresp. to 4222; to *strike* in pieces; also to *arrest;* spec. to *impale:*—hang, smite, stay.

4224. מַחֲבֵא **machăbêʼ,** *makh-ab-ay´;* or מַחֲבֹא **machăbôʼ,** *makh-ab-o´;* from 2244; a *refuge:*—hiding (lurking) place.

4225. מַחְבֶּרֶת **machbereth,** *makh-beh´-reth;* from 2266; a *junction,* i.e. seam or sewed piece:—coupling.

4226. מְחַבְּרָה **m^{e}chabb^{e}râh,** *mekh-ab-ber-aw´;* from 2266; a *joiner,* i.e. brace or cramp:—coupling, joining.

4227. מַחֲבַת **machăbath,** *makh-ab-ath´;* from the same as 2281; a *pan* for baking in:—pan.

4228. מַחֲגֹרֶת **machăgôreth,** *makh-ag-o´-reth;* from 2296; a *girdle:*—girding.

4229. מָחָה **mâchâh,** *maw-khaw´;* a prim. root; prop. to *stroke* or *rub;* by impl. to *erase;* also to *smooth* (as if with oil), i.e. *grease* or make fat; also to *touch,* i.e. reach to:—abolish, blot out, destroy, full of marrow, put out, reach unto, × utterly, wipe (away, out).

4230. מְחוּגָה **m^{e}chûwgâh,** *mekh-oo-gaw´;* from 2328; an instrument for marking a circle, i.e. *compasses:*—compass.

4231. מָחוֹז **mâchôwz,** *maw-khoze´;* from an unused root mean. to *enclose;* a *harbor* (as *shut* in by the shore):—haven.

4232. מְחוּיָאֵל **M^{e}chûwyâʼêl,** *mekh-oo-yaw-ale´;* or מְחִיָּאֵל° **M^{e}chîyyâʼêl,** *mekh-ee-yaw-ale´;* from 4229 and 410; *smitten of God; Mechujael* or *Mechijael,* an antediluvian patriarch:—Mehujael.

4233. מַחֲוִים **Machăvîym** *makh-av-eem´;* appar. a patrial, but from an unknown place (in the plur. only for a sing.); a *Machavite* or inhab. of some place named Machaveh:—Mahavite.

4234. מָחוֹל **mâchôwl,** *maw-khole´;* from 2342; a (round) *dance:*—dance (-cing).

4235. מָחוֹל **Mâchôwl,** *maw-khole´;* the same as 4234; *dancing; Machol,* an Isr.:—Mahol.

מְחוֹלָה **m^{e}chôwlâh.** See 65, 4246.

4236. מַחֲזֶה **machăzeh,** *makh-az-eh´;* from 2372; a *vision:*—vision.

4237. מֶחֱזָה **mechĕzâh,** *mekh-ez-aw´;* from 2372; a *window:*—light.

4238. מַחֲזִיאוֹת **Machăzîyʼôwth,** *makh-az-ee-oth´;* fem. plur. from 2372; *visions; Machazioth,* an Isr.—Mahazioth.

4239. מְחִי **m^{e}chîy,** *mekh-ee´;* from 4229; a *stroke;* i.e. battering-*ram:*—engines.

4240. מְחִידָא **Mᵉchîydâʼ,** *mekh-ee-daw´;* from 2330; *junction; Mechida,* one of the Nethinim:—Mehida.

4241. מִחְיָה **michyâh,** *mikh-yaw´;* from 2421; *preservation of life;* hence *sustenance;* also the live flesh, i.e. the *quick:*—preserve life, quick, recover selves, reviving, sustenance, victuals.

מְחִייָאֵל° **Mᵉchîyyâʼêl.** See 4332.

4242. מְחִיר **mᵉchîyr,** *mekh-eer´;* from an unused root mean. to *buy; price, payment, wages:*—gain, hire, price, sold, worth.

4243. מְחִיר **Mᵉchîyr,** *mekh-eer´;* the same as 4242; *price; Mechir,* an Isr.:—Mehir.

4244. מַחְלָה **Machlâh,** *makh-law´;* from 2470; *sickness; Machlah,* the name appar. of two Israelitesses—Mahlah.

4245. מַחֲלֶה **machăleh,** *makh-al-eh´;* or (fem.) מַחֲלָה **machălâh,** *makk-al-aw´;* from 2470; *sickness:*—disease, infirmity, sickness.

4246. מְחֹלָה **mᵉchôwlâh,** *mekh-o-law´;* fem. of 4234; a *dance:*—company, dances (-cing).

4247. מְחִלָּה **mᵉchillâh,** *mekh-il-law´;* from 2490; a *cavern* (as if excavated):—cave.

4248. מַחְלוֹן **Machlôwn,** *makh-lone´;* from 2470; *sick; Machlon,* an Isr.:—Mahlon.

4249. מַחְלִי **Machlîy,** *makh-lee´;* from 2470; *sick; Machli,* the name of two Isr.:—Mahli.

4250. מַחְלִי **Machlîy,** *makh-lee´;* patron. from 4249; a *Machlite* or (collect.) desc. of Machli:—Mahlites.

4251. מַחְלֻי **machlûy,** *makh-loo´ee;* from 2470; a *disease:*—disease.

4252. מַחֲלָף **machălâph,** *makh-al-awf´;* from 2498; a (sacrificial) *knife* (as *gliding* through the flesh):—knife.

4253. מַחְלָפָה **machlâphâh,** *makh-law-faw´;* from 2498; a *ringlet* of hair (as *gliding* over each other):—lock.

4254. מַחֲלָצָה **machălâtsâh,** *makh-al-aw-tsaw´;* from 2502; a *mantle* (as easily *drawn off*):—changeable suit of apparel, change of raiment.

4255. מַחְלְקָה **machlᵉqâh** (Chald.), *makh-lek-aw´;* corresp. to 4256; a *section* (of the Levites):—course.

4256. מַחֲלֹקֶת **machălôqeth,** *makh-al-o´-keth;* from 2505; a *section* (of Levites, people or soldiers):—company, course, division, portion. See also 5555.

4257. מַחֲלַת **machălath,** *makh-al-ath´;* from 2470; *sickness; Machalath,* prob. the title (initial word) of a popular song:—Mahalath.

4258. מַחֲלַת **Machălath,** *makh-al-ath´;* the same as 4257; *sickness; Machalath,* the name of an Ishmaelitess and of an Israelitess:—Mahalath.

4259. מְחֹלָתִי **Mᵉchôlâthîy,** *mekh-o-law-thee´;* patrial from 65; a *Meholathite* or inhab. of Abel-Mecholah:—Mecholathite.

4260. מַחֲמָאָה **machămâʼâh,** *makh-am-aw-aw´;* a denom. from 2529; something *buttery* (i.e. unctuous and pleasant), as (fig.) *flattery:*—× than butter.

4261. מַחְמָד **machmâd,** *makh-mawd´;* from 2530; *delightful;* hence a *delight,* i.e. object of affection or desire:—beloved, desire, goodly, lovely, pleasant (thing).

4262. מַחְמֻד **machmûd,** *makh-mood´;* or מַחְמוּד° **machmûwd,** *makh-mood´;* from 2530; *desired;* hence a *valuable:*—pleasant thing.

4263. מַחְמָל **machmâl,** *makh-mawl´;* from 2550; prop. *sympathy;* (by paronomasia with 4261) *delight:*—pitieth.

4264. מַחֲנֶה **machăneh,** *makh-an-eh´;* from 2583; an *encampment* (of travellers or troops); hence an *army,* whether lit. (of soldiers) or fig. (of dancers, angels, cattle, locusts, stars; or even the sacred courts):—army, band, battle, camp, company, drove, host, tents.

4265. מַחֲנֵה־דָן **Machănêh-Dân,** *makh-an-ay´-dawn;* from 4264 and 1835; *camp of Dan; Machaneh-Dan,* a place in Pal.:—Mahaneh-dan.

4266. מַחֲנַיִם **Machănayim,** *makh-an-ah´-yim;* dual of 4264; *double camp; Machanajim,* a place in Pal.:—Mahanaim.

4267. מַחֲנַק **machănaq,** *makh-an-ak´;* from 2614; *choking:*—strangling.

4268. מַחֲסֶה **machăçeh,** *makh-as-eh´;* or מַחְסֶה **machçeh,** *makh-seh´;* from 2620; a *shelter* (lit. or fig.):—hope, (place of) refuge, shelter, trust.

4269. מַחְסוֹם **machçôwm,** *makh-sohm´;* from 2629; a *muzzle:*—bridle.

4270. מַחְסוֹר **machçôwr,** *makh-sore´;* or מַחְסֹר **machçôr,** *makh-sore´;* from 2637; *deficiency;* hence *impoverishment:*—lack, need, penury, poor, poverty, want.

4271. מַחְסֵיָה **Machçêyâh,** *makh-say-yaw´;* from 4268 and 3050; *refuge of* (i.e. *in*) *Jah; Machsejah,* an Isr.:—Maaseiah.

4272. מָחַץ **mâchats,** *maw-khats´;* a prim. root; to *dash* asunder; by impl. to *crush, smash* or violently *plunge;* fig. to *subdue* or *destroy:*—dip, pierce (through), smite (through), strike through, wound.

4273. מַחַץ **machats,** *makh´-ats;* from 4272; a *contusion:*—stroke.

4274. מַחְצֵב **machtsêb,** *makh-tsabe´;* from 2672; prop. a *hewing;* concr. a *quarry:*—hewed (-n).

4275. מֶחֱצָה **mechĕtsâh,** *mekh-ets-aw´;* from 2673; a *halving:*—half.

4276. מַחֲצִית **machătsîyth,** *makh-ats-eeth´;* from 2673; a *halving* or the *middle:*—half (so much), mid [-day].

4277. מָחַק **mâchaq,** *maw-khak´;* a prim. root; to *crush:*—smite off.

4278. מֶחְקָר **mechqâr,** *mekh-kawr´;* from 2713; prop. *scrutinized,* i.e. (by impl.) a *recess:*—deep place.

4279. מָחָר **mâchar,** *maw-khar´;* prob. from 309; prop. *deferred,* i.e. the *morrow;* usually (adv.) *tomorrow;* indef. *hereafter:*—time to come, tomorrow.

4280. מַחֲרָאָה **machărâʼâh,** *makh-ar-aw-aw´;* from the same as 2716; a *sink:*—draught house.

4281. מַחֲרֵשָׁה **machărêshâh,** *makh-ar-ay-shaw´;* from 2790; prob. a *pick*-axe:—mattock.

4282. מַחֲרֶשֶׁת **machăresheth,** *makh-ar-eh´-sheth;* from 2790; prob. a *hoe:*—share.

4283. מָחֳרָת **mochŏrâth,** *mokh-or-awth´;* or מָחֳרָתָם **mochŏrâthâm** (1 Sam. 30 : 17), *mokh-or-aw-thawm´;* fem. from the same as 4279; the *morrow* or (adv.) *tomorrow:*—morrow, next day.

4284. מַחֲשָׁבָה **machăshâbâh,** *makh-ash-aw-baw´;* or מַחֲשֶׁבֶת **machăshebeth,** *makh-ash-eh´-beth;* from 2803; a *contrivance,* i.e. (concr.) a *texture, machine,* or (abstr.) *intention, plan* (whether bad, a *plot;* or good, *advice*):—cunning (work), curious work, device (-sed), imagination, invented, means, purpose, thought.

4285. מַחְשָׁךְ **machshâk,** *makh-shawk´;* from 2821; *darkness;* concr. a *dark place:*—dark (-ness, place).

4286. מַחְשֹׂף **machsôph,** *makh-sofe´;* from 2834; a *peeling:*—made appear.

4287. מַחַת **Machath,** *makh´-ath;* prob. from 4229; *erasure; Machath,* the name of two Isr.:—Mahath.

4288. מְחִתָּה **mᵉchittâh,** *mekh-it-taw´;* from 2846; prop. a *dissolution;* concr. a *ruin,* or (abstr.) *consternation:*—destruction, dismaying, ruin, terror.

4289. מַחְתָּה **machtâh,** *makh-taw´;* the same as 4288 in the sense of *removal;* a *pan* for live coals:—censer, firepan, snuffdish.

4290. מַחְתֶּרֶת **machtereth,** *makh-teh´-reth;* from 2864; a *burglary;* fig. *unexpected examination:*—breaking up, secret search.

4291. מְטָא **mᵉṭâʼ** (Chald.), *met-aw´;* or מְטָה **mᵉṭâh** (Chald.), *met-aw´;* appar. corresp. to 4672 in the intrans. sense of being found *present;* to *arrive, extend* or *happen:*—come, reach.

4292. מַטְאֲטֵא **maṭʼăṭêʼ,** *mat-at-ay´;* appar. a denom. from 2916; a *broom* (as removing *dirt* [comp. Engl. "to dust", i.e. remove dust]):—besom.

4293. מַטְבֵּחַ **maṭbêach,** *mat-bay´-akh;* from 2873; *slaughter:*—slaughter.

4294. מַטֶּה **maṭṭeh,** *mat-teh´;* or (fem.) מַטָּה **maṭṭâh,** *mat-taw´;* from 5186; a *branch* (as *extending*); fig. a *tribe;* also a *rod,* whether for chastising (fig. *correction*), ruling (a *sceptre*), throwing (a *lance*), or walking (a *staff;* fig. a *support* of life, e.g. bread):—rod, staff, tribe.

4295. מַטָּה **maṭṭâh,** *mat´-taw;* from 5786 with directive enclitic appended; *downward, below* or *beneath;* often adv. with or without prefixes:—beneath, down (-ward), less, very low, under (-neath).

4296. מִטָּה **miṭṭâh,** *mit-taw´;* from 5186; a *bed* (as *extended*) for sleeping or eating; by anal. a *sofa, litter* or *bier:*—bed ([-chamber]), bier.

4297. מֻטֶּה **muṭṭeh,** *moot-teh´;* from 5186; a *stretching,* i.e. *distortion* (fig. *iniquity*):—perverseness.

4298. מֻטָּה **muṭṭâh,** *moot-taw´;* from 5186; *expansion:*—stretching out.

4299. מַטְוֶה **maṭveh,** *mat-veh´;* from 2901; something *spun:*—spun.

4300. מְטִיל **m**e**ṭîyl,** *met-eel´;* from 2904 in the sense of *hammering* out; an iron *bar* (as *forged*):—bar.

4301. מַטְמוֹן **maṭmôwn,** *mat-mone´;* or מַטְמֹן **maṭmôn,** *mat-mone´;* or מַטְמֻן **maṭmûn,** *mat-moon´;* from 2934; a *secret* storehouse; hence a *secreted* valuable (buried); gen. *money:*—hidden, riches, (hid) treasure (-s).

4302. מַטָּע **maṭṭâʻ,** *mat-taw´;* from 5193; something *planted,* i.e. the place (a *garden* or vineyard), or the thing (a *plant,* fig. of men); by impl. the act, *planting:*—plant (-ation, -ing).

4303. מַטְעַם **maṭʻam,** *mat-am´;* or (fem.) מַטְעַמָּה **maṭʻammâh,** *mat-am-maw´;* from 2938; a *delicacy:*—dainty (meat), savoury meat.

4304. מִטְפַּחַת **miṭpachath,** *mit-pakh´-ath;* from 2946; a wide *cloak* (for a woman):—vail, wimple.

4305. מָטַר **mâṭar,** *maw-tar´;* a prim. root; to *rain:*—(cause to) rain (upon).

4306. מָטָר **mâṭâr,** *maw-tawr´;* from 4305; *rain:*—rain.

4307. מַטָּרָא **maṭṭârâʼ,** *mat-taw-raw´;* or מַטָּרָה **maṭṭârâh,** *mat-taw-raw´;* from 5201; a *jail* (as a *guard*-house); also an *aim* (as being closely *watched*):—mark, prison.

4308. מַטְרֵד **Maṭrêd,** *mat-rade´;* from 2956; *propulsive; Matred,* an Edomitess:—Matred.

4309. מַטְרִי **Maṭrîy,** *mat-ree´;* from 4305; *rainy; Matri,* an Isr.:—Matri.

4310. מִי **mîy,** *me;* an interrog. pron. of persons, as 4100 is of things, *who?* (occasionally, by a peculiar idiom, of things); also (indef.) *whoever;* often used in oblique construction with pref. or suff.:—any (man), × he, × him, + O that! what, which, who (-m, -se, -soever), + would to God.

4311. מֵידְבָא **Mêyd**e**bâʼ,** *may-deb-aw´;* 4325 and 1679; *water of quiet; Medeba,* a place in Pal.:Medeba.

4312. מֵידָד **Mêydâd,** *may-dawd´;* from 3032 in the sense of *loving; affectionate; Medad,* an Isr.:—Medad.

4313. מֵי הַיַּרְקוֹן **Mêy hay-Yarqôwn,** *may hah´´ee-yar-kone´;* from 4325 and 3420 with the art. interposed; *water of the yellowness; Me-haj-Jarkon,* a place in Pal.:—Me-jarkon.

4314. מֵי זָהָב **Mêy Zâhâb,** *may-zaw-hawb´;* from 4325 and 2091, *water of gold; Me-Zahab,* an Edomite:—Mezahab.

4315. מֵיטָב **mêyṭab,** *may-tawb´;* from 3190; the *best* part:—best.

4316. מִיכָא **Mîykâʼ,** *mee-kaw´;* a var. for 4318; *Mica,* the name of two Isr.:—Micha.

4317. מִיכָאֵל **Mîykâʼêl,** *me-kaw-ale´;* from 4310 and (the pref. der. from) 3588 and 410; *who* (is) *like God?; Mikael,* the name of an archangel and of nine Isr.:—Michael.

4318. מִיכָה **Mîykâh,** *mee-kaw´;* an abbrev. of 4320; *Micah,* the name of seven Isr.:—Micah, Micaiah, Michah.

4319. מִיכָהוּ° **Mîykâhûw,** *me-kaw´-hoo;* a contr. for 4321; *Mikehu,* an Isr. prophet:—Micaiah (2 Chron. 18 : 8).

4320. מִיכָיָה **Mîykâyâh,** *me-kaw-yaw´;* from 4310 and (the pref. der. from) 3588 and 3050; *who* (is) *like Jah?; Micajah,* the name of two Isr.:—Micah, Michaiah. Comp. 4318.

4321. מִיכָיְהוּ **Mîykây**e**hûw,** *me-kaw-yeh-hoo´;* or מִכָיְהוּ **Mikây**e**huw** (Jer. 36 : 11), *me-kaw-yeh-hoo´;* abbrev. for 4322; *Mikajah,* the name of three Isr.:—Micah, Micaiah, Michaiah.

4322. מִיכָיָהוּ **Mîykâyâhûw,** *me-kaw-yaw´-hoo;* for 4320; *Mikajah,* the name of an Isr. and an Israelitess:—Michaiah.

4323. מִיכָל **mîykâl,** *me-kawl´;* from 3201; prop. a *container,* i.e. a *streamlet:*—brook.

4324. מִיכָל **Mîykâl,** *me-kawl´;* appar. the same as 4323; *rivulet; Mikal,* Saul's daughter:—Michal.

4325. מַיִם **mayim,** *mah´-yim;* dual of a prim. noun (but used in a sing. sense); *water;* fig. *juice;* by euphem. *urine, semen:*— + piss, wasting, water (-ing, [-course, -flood, -spring]).

4326. מִיָּמִן **Mîyâmîn,** *me-yaw-meen´;* a form for 4509; *Mijamin,* the name of three Isr.:—Miamin, Mijamin.

4327. מִין **mîyn,** *meen;* from an unused root mean. to *portion* out; a *sort,* i.e. *species:*—kind. Comp. 4480.

4328. מְיֻסָּדָה° **m**e**yuççâdâh,** *meh-yoos-saw-daw´;* prop. fem. pass. part. of 3245; something *founded,* i.e. a *foundation:*—foundation.

4329. מֵיסָךְ **mêyçâk,** *may-sawk´;* from 5526; a *portico* (as *covered*):—covert.

מֵיפַעַת **Mêyphaʻath.** See 4158.

4330. מִיץ **mîyts,** *meets;* from 4160; *pressure:*—churning, forcing, wringing.

4331. מֵישָׁא **Mêyshâʼ,** *may-shaw´;* from 4185; *departure; Mesha,* a place in Arabia; also an Isr.:—Mesha.

4332. מִישָׁאֵל **Mîyshâʼêl,** *mee-shaw-ale´;* from 4310 and 410 with the abbrev. insep. rel. [see 834] interposed; *who* (is) *what God* (is)?; *Mishaël,* the name of three Isr.:—Mishael.

4333. מִישָׁאֵל **Mîyshâʼêl** (Chald.), *mee-shaw-ale´;* corresp. to 4332; *Mishaël,* an Isr.:—Mishael.

4334. מִישׁוֹר **mîyshôwr,** *mee-shore´;* or מִישֹׁר **mîyshôr,** *mee-shore´;* from 3474; a *level,* i.e. a *plain* (often used [with the art. pref.] as a prop. name of certain districts); fig. *concord:* also *straightness,* i.e. (fig.) *justice* (sometimes adv. *justly*):—equity, even place, plain, right (-eously), (made) straight, uprightness.

4335. מֵישַׁךְ **Mêyshak,** *may-shak´; borrowed from 4336; Meshak,* an Isr.:—Meshak.

4336. מֵישַׁךְ **Mêyshak** (Chald.), *may-shak´;* of for. or. and doubtful signif.; *Meshak,* the Bab. name of 4333:—Meshak.

4337. מֵישַׁע **Mêyshâʻ,** *may-shah´;* from 3467; *safety; Mesha,* an Isr.:—Mesha.

4338. מֵישַׁע **Mêyshaʻ,** *may-shaw´;* a var. for 4337; *safety; Mesha,* a Moabite:—Mesha.

4339. מֵישָׁר **mêyshâr,** *may-shawr´;* from 3474; *evenness,* i.e. (fig.) *prosperity* or *concord;* also *straightness,* i.e. (fig.) *rectitude* (only in plur. with sing. sense; often adv.):—agreement, aright, that are equal, equity, (things that are) right (-eously, things), sweetly, upright (-ly, -ness).

4340. מֵיתָר **mêythâr,** *may-thawr´;* from 3498; a *cord* (of a tent) [comp. 3499] or the *string* (of a bow):—cord, string.

4341. מַכְאֹב **makʼôb,** *mak-obe´;* sometimes מַכְאוֹב **makʼôwb,** *mak-obe´;* also (fem. Isa. 53 : 3) מַכְאֹבָה **makʼôbâh,** *mak-o-baw´;* from 3510; *anguish* or (fig.) *affliction:*—grief, pain, sorrow.

4342. מַכְבִּיר **makbîyr,** *mak-beer´;* trans. part. of 3527; *plenty:*—abundance.

4343. מַכְבֵּנָא **Makbênâʼ,** *mak-bay-naw´;* from the same as 3522; *knoll; Macbena,* a place in Pal. settled by him:—Machbenah.

4344. מַכְבַּנַּי **Makbannay,** *mak-ban-nah´ee;* patrial from 4343; a *Macbannite* or native of Macbena:—Machbanai.

4345. מַכְבֵּר **makbêr,** *mak-bare´;* from 3527 in the sense of *covering* [comp. 3531]; a *grate:*—grate.

4346. מַכְבָּר **makbâr,** *mak-bawr´;* from 3527 in the sense of *covering;* a cloth (as *netted* [comp. 4345]):—thick cloth.

4347. מַכָּה **makkâh,** *mak-kaw´;* or (masc.) מַכֶּה **makkeh,** *mak-keh´;* (plur. only) from 5221; a *blow* (in 2 Chron. 2 : 10, of the flail); by impl. a *wound;* fig. *carnage,* also *pestilence:*—beaten, blow, plague, slaughter, smote, × sore, stripe, stroke, wound ([-ed]).

4348. מִכְוָה **mikvâh,** *mik-vaw´;* from 3554; a *burn:*—that burneth, burning.

4349. מָכוֹן **mâkôwn,** *maw-kone´;* from 3559; prop. a *fixture,* i.e. a *basis;* gen. a *place,* esp. as an *abode:*—foundation, habitation, (dwelling-, settled) place.

4350. מְכוֹנָה **m^{e}kôwnâh,** *mek-o-naw´;* or מְכֹנָה **m^{e}kônâh,** *mek-o-naw´;* fem. of 4349; a *pedestal,* also a *spot:*—base.

4351. מְכוּרָה **m^{e}kûwrâh,** *mek-oo-raw´;* or מְכֹרָה **m^{e}kôrâh,** *mek-o-raw´;* from the same as 3564 in the sense of *digging; origin* (as if a mine):—birth, habitation, nativity.

4352. מָכִי **Mâkîy,** *maw-kee´;* prob. from 4134; *pining; Maki,* an Isr.:—Machi.

4353. מָכִיר **Mâkîyr,** *maw-keer´;* from 4376; *salesman; Makir,* an Isr.:—Machir.

4354. מָכִירִי **Mâkîyrîy,** *maw-kee-ree´;* patron. from 4353; a *Makirite* or descend. of Makir:—of Machir.

4355. מָכַךְ **mâkak,** *maw-kak´;* a prim. root; to *tumble* (in ruins); fig. to *perish:*—be brought low, decay.

4356. מִכְלָאָה **miklâ'âh,** *mik-law-aw´;* or מִכְלָה **miklâh,** *mik-law´;* from 3607; a *pen* (for flocks):—([sheep-]) fold. Comp. 4357.

4357. מִכְלָה **miklâh,** *mik-law´;* from 3615; *completion* (in plur. concr. adv. *wholly*):—perfect. Comp. 4356.

4358. מִכְלוֹל **miklôwl,** *mik-lole´;* from 3634; *perfection* (i.e. concr. adv. *splendidly*):—most gorgeously, all sorts.

4359. מִכְלָל **miklâl,** *mik-lawl´;* from 3634; *perfection* (of beauty):—perfection.

4360. מִכְלֻל **miklûl,** *mik-lool´;* from 3634; something *perfect,* i.e. a splendid *garment:*—all sorts.

4361. מַכֹּלֶת **makkôleth,** *mak-ko-leth;* from 398; *nourishment:*—food.

4362. מִכְמַן **mikman,** *mik-man´;* from the same as 3646 in the sense of *hiding; treasure* (as *hidden*):—treasure.

4363. מִכְמָס **Mikmâç** (Ezra 2 : 27; Neh. 7 : 31), *mik-maws´;* or מִכְמָשׁ **Mikmâsh,** *mik-mawsh´;* or מִכְמַשׁ **Mikmash** (Neh. 11 : 31), *mik-mash´;* from 3647; *hidden Mikmas* or *Mikmash,* a place in Pal.:—Mikmas, Mikmash.

4364. מַכְמָר **makmâr,** *mak-mawr´;* or מִכְמֹר **mikmôr,** *mik-more´;* from 3648 in the sense of *blackening* by heat; a (hunter's) *net* (as *dark* from concealment):—net.

4365. מִכְמֶרֶת **mikmereth,** *mik-meh´-reth;* or מִכְמֹרֶת **mikmôreth,** *mik-mo´-reth;* fem. of 4364; a (fisher's) *net:*—drag, net.

מִכְמָשׁ **Mikmâsh.** See 4363.

4366. מִכְמְתָת **Mikm^{e}thâth,** *mik-meth-awth´;* appar. from an unused root mean. to *hide; concealment; Mikmethath,* a place in Pal.:—Michmethath.

4367. מַכְנַדְבַי **Maknadbay,** *mak-nad-bah´ee;* from 4100 and 5068 with a particle interposed; *what* (is) *like* (a) *liberal* (man)?; *Maknadbai,* an Isr.:—Machnadebai.

מְכֹנָה **m^{e}kônâh.** See 4350.

4368. מְכֹנָה **M^{e}kônâh,** *mek-o-naw´;* the same as 4350; a *base; Mekonah,* a place in Pal.:—Mekonah.

4369. מְכֻנָה **m^{e}kûnâh,** *mek-oo-naw´;* the same as 4350; a *spot:*—base.

4370. מִכְנָס **miknâç,** *mik-nawce´;* from 3647 in the sense of *hiding;* (only in dual) *drawers* (from *concealing* the private parts):—breeches.

4371. מֶכֶס **mekeç,** *meh´-kes;* prob. from an unused root mean. to *enumerate;* an *assessment* (as based upon a *census*):—tribute.

4372. מִכְסֶה **mikçeh,** *mik-seh´;* from 3680; a *covering,* i.e. weather-*boarding:*—covering.

4373. מִכְסָה **mikçâh,** *mik-saw´;* fem. of 4371; an *enumeration;* by impl. a *valuation:*—number, worth.

4374. מְכַסֶּה **m^{e}kaççeh,** *mek-as-seh´;* from 3680; a *covering,* i.e. *garment;* spec. a *coverlet* (for a bed), an *awning* (from the sun); also the *omentum* (as covering the intestines):—clothing, to cover, that which covereth.

4375. מַכְפֵּלָה **Makpêlâh,** *mak-pay-law´;* from 3717; a *fold; Makpelah,* a place in Pal.:—Machpelah.

4376. מָכַר **mâkar,** *maw-kar´;* a prim. root; to *sell,* lit. (as merchandise, a daughter in marriage, into slavery), or fig. (to *surrender*):— × at all, sell (away, -er, self).

4377. מֶכֶר **meker,** *meh´-ker;* from 4376; *merchandise;* also *value:*—pay, price, ware.

4378. מַכָּר **makkâr,** *mak-kawr´;* from 5234; an *acquaintance:*—acquaintance.

4379. מִכְרֶה **mikreh,** *mik-reh´;* from 3738; a *pit* (for salt):—[salt-] pit.

4380. מְכֵרָה **m^{e}kêrâh,** *mek-ay-raw´;* prob. from the same as 3564 in the sense of *stabbing;* a *sword:*—habitation.

מְכֹרָה **m^{e}kôrâh.** See 4351.

4381. מִכְרִי **Mikrîy,** *mik-ree´;* from 4376; *salesman; Mikri,* an Isr.—Michri.

4382. מְכֵרָתִי **M^{e}kêrâthîy,** *mek-ay-raw-thee´;* patrial from an unused name (the same as 4380) of a place in Pal.; a *Mekerathite,* or inhab. of Mekerah:—Mecherathite.

4383. מִכְשׁוֹל **mikshôwl,** *mik-shole´;* or מִכְשֹׁל **mikshôl,** *mik-shole´;* masc. from 3782; a *stumbling-block,* lit. or fig. (*obstacle, enticement* [spec. an idol], *scruple*):—caused to fall, offence, × [no-] thing offered, ruin, stumbling-block.

4384. מַכְשֵׁלָה **makshêlâh,** *mak-shay-law´;* fem. from 3782; a *stumbling-block,* but only fig. (*fall, enticement* [idol]):—ruin, stumbling-block.

4385. מִכְתָּב **miktâb,** *mik-tawb´;* from 3789; a thing *written,* the *characters,* or a *document* (letter, copy, edict, poem):—writing.

4386. מְכִתָּה **m^{e}kittâh,** *mek-it-taw´;* from 3807; a *fracture:*—bursting.

4387. מִכְתָּם **miktâm,** *mik-tawm´;* from 3799; an *engraving,* i.e. (techn.) a *poem:*—Michtam.

4388. מַכְתֵּשׁ **maktêsh,** *mak-taysh´;* from 3806; a *mortar;* by anal. a *socket* (of a tooth):—hollow place, mortar.

4389. מַכְתֵּשׁ **Maktêsh,** *mak-taysh´;* the same as 4388; *dell;* the *Maktesh,* a place in Jerus.:—Maktesh.

מֻל **mûl.** See 4136.

4390. מָלֵא **mâlê',** *maw-lay´;* or מָלָא **mâlâ'** (Esth. 7 : 5), *maw-law´;* a prim. root, to *fill* or (intrans.) *be full* of, in a wide application (lit. and fig.):—accomplish, confirm, + consecrate, be at an end, be expired, be fenced, fill, fulfil, (be, become, × draw, give in, go) fully (-ly, -ly set, tale), [over-] flow, fulness, furnish, gather (selves, together), presume, replenish, satisfy, set, space, take a [hand-] full, + have wholly.

4391. מְלָא **m^{e}lâ'** (Chald.), *mel-aw´;* corresp. to 4390; to *fill:*—fill, be full.

4392. מָלֵא **mâlê',** *maw-lay´;* from 4390; *full* (lit. or fig.) or *filling* (lit.); also (concr.) *fulness;* adv. *fully:*— × she that was with child, fill (-ed, -ed with), full (-ly), multitude, as is worth.

4393. מְלֹא **m^{e}lô',** *mel-o´;* rarely מְלוֹא **m^{e}lôw',** *mel-o´;* or מְלוֹ **m^{e}lôw** (Ezek. 41 : 8), *mel-o´;* from 4390; *fulness* (lit. or fig.):— × all along, × all that is (there-) in, fill, (× that whereof . . . was) full, fulness, [hand-] full, multitude.

מִלֹּא **Millô'.** See 4407.

4394. מִלֻּא **millû',** *mil-loo´;* from 4390; a *fulfilling* (only in plur.), i.e. (lit.) a *setting* (of gems), or (techn.) *consecration* (also concr. a dedicatory *sacrifice*):—consecration, be set.

4395. מְלֵאָה **m^{e}lê'âh,** *mel-ay-aw´;* fem. of 4392; something *fulfilled,* i.e. *abundance* (of produce):—(first of ripe) fruit, fulness.

4396. מִלֻּאָה **millû'âh,** *mil-loo-aw´;* fem. of 4394; a *filling,* i.e. *setting* (of gems):—inclosing, setting.

4397. מַלְאָךְ **mal'âk,** *mal-awk´;* from an unused root mean. to *despatch* as a deputy; a *messenger;* spec. of God, i.e. an *angel* (also a prophet, priest or teacher):—ambassador, angel, king, messenger.

4398. מַלְאַךְ **mal'ak** (Chald.), *mal-ak´;* corresp. to 4397; an *angel:*—angel.

4399. מְלָאכָה **m^{e}lâ'kâh,** *mel-aw-kaw´;* from the same as 4397; prop. *deputyship,* i.e. ministry; gen. *employment* (never servile) or work (abstr. or concr.); also *property* (as the result of *labor*):—business, + cattle, + industrious, occupation, (+ -pied), + officer, thing (made), use, (manner of) work ([-man], -manship).

4400. מַלְאֲכוּת **mal'ăkûwth,** *mal-ak-ooth´;* from the same as 4397; a *message:*—message.

4401. מַלְאָכִי **Mal'âkîy,** *mal-aw-kee´;* from the same as 4397; *ministrative; Malaki,* a prophet:—Malachi.

4402. מִלֵּאת **millê'th,** *mil-layth´;* from 4390; *fulness,* i.e. (concr.) a *plump* socket (of the eye):— × fitly.

4403. מַלְבּוּשׁ **malbûwsh,** *mal-boosh´;* or מַלְבֻּשׁ **malbûsh,** *mal-boosh´;* from 3847; a *garment,* or (collect.) *clothing:*—apparel, raiment, vestment.

4404. מַלְבֵּן **malbên,** *mal-bane´;* from 3835 (denom.); a *brick-kiln:*—brickwork.

4405. מִלָּה **millâh,** *mil-law´;* from 4448 (plur. masc. as if from מִלֶּה **milleh,** *mil-leh´;* a *word;* collect. a *discourse;* fig. a *topic:*— + answer, by-word, matter, any thing (what) to say, to speak (-ing), speak, talking, word.

4406. מִלָּה **millâh** (Chald.), *mil-law´;* corresp. to 4405; a *word, command, discourse,* or *subject:*—commandment, matter, thing, word.
מִלוֹ **m**e**lôw.** See 4393.
מִלוֹא **m**e**lôw'.** See 4393.

4407. מִלּוֹא **millôw',** *mil-lo´;* or מִלֹּא **mil-lô'** (2 Kings 12 : 20), *mil-lo´;* from 4390; a *rampart* (as *filled* in), i.e. the *citadel:*—Millo. See also 1037.

4408. מַלּוּחַ **mallûwach,** *mal-loo´-akh;* from 4414; *sea-purslain* (from its *saltness*):—mallows.

4409. מַלּוּךְ **Mallûwk,** *mal-luke´;* or מַלּוּכִי° **Mallûwkîy** (Neh. 12 : 14), *mal-loo-kee´;* from 4427; *regnant; Malluk,* the name of five Isr.:—Malluch, Melichu [*from the marg.*].

4410. מְלוּכָה **m**e**lûwkâh,** *mel-oo-kaw´;* fem. pass. part. of 4427; something *ruled,* i.e. a *realm:*—kingdom, king's, × royal.

4411. מָלוֹן **mâlôwn,** *maw-lone´;* from 3885; a *lodgment,* i.e. *caravanserai* or *encampment:*—inn, place where . . . lodge, lodging (place).

4412. מְלוּנָה **m**e**lûwnâh,** *mel-oo-naw´;* fem. from 3885; a *hut,* a *hammock:*—cottage, lodge.

4413. מַלּוֹתִי **Mallôwthîy,** *mal-lo´-thee;* appar. from 4448; *I have talked* (i.e. *loquacious*):—*Mallothi,* an Isr.:—Mallothi.

4414. מָלַח **mâlach,** *maw-lakh´;* a prim. root; prop. to *rub* to pieces or pulverize; intrans. to *disappear* as dust; also (as denom. from 4417) to *salt* whether intern. (to *season* with salt) or extern. (to *rub* with salt):— × at all, salt, season, temper together, vanish away.

4415. מְלַח **m**e**lach** (Chald.), *mel-akh´;* corresp. to 4414; to *eat* salt, i.e. (gen.) *subsist:*— + have maintenance.

4416. מְלַח **m**e**lach** (Chald.), *mel-akh´;* from 4415; *salt:*— + maintenance, salt.

4417. מֶלַח **melach,** *meh´-lakh;* from 4414; prop. *powder,* i.e. (spec.) *salt* (as easily pulverized and dissolved:—salt ([-pit]).

4418. מָלָח **mâlâch,** *maw-lawkh´;* from 4414 in its orig. sense; a *rag* or old garment:—rotten rag.

4419. מַלָּח **mallâch,** *mal-lawkh´;* from 4414 in its second. sense; a *sailor* (as following "the salt"):—mariner.

4420. מְלֵחָה **m**e**lêchâh,** *mel-ay-khaw´;* from 4414 (in its denom. sense); prop. *salted* (i.e. land [776 being understood]), i.e. a *desert:*—barren land (-ness), salt [land].

4421. מִלְחָמָה **milchâmâh,** *mil-khaw-maw´;* from 3898 (in the sense of *fighting*); a *battle* (i.e. the *engagement*); gen. *war* (i.e. *war-fare*):—battle, fight, (-ing), war ([-rior]).

4422. מָלַט **mâlaṭ,** *maw-lat´;* a prim. root; prop. to *be smooth,* i.e. (by impl.) to *escape* (as if by *slipperiness); causat. to release* or *rescue;* spec. to *bring forth* young, *emit* sparks:—deliver (self), escape, lay, leap out, let alone, let go, preserve, save, × speedily, × surely.

4423. מֶלֶט **meleṭ,** *meh´-let;* from 4422, *cement* (from its plastic *smoothness*):—clay.

4424. מְלַטְיָה **M**e**laṭyâh,** *mel-at-yaw´;* from 4423 and 3050; (whom) *Jah has delivered; Melatjah,* a Gibeonite:—Melatiah.

4425. מְלִילָה **m**e**lîylâh,** *mel-ee-law´;* from 4449 (in the sense of *cropping* [comp. 4135]); a *head* of grain (as *cut* off):—ear.

4426. מְלִיצָה **m**e**lîytsâh,** *mel-ee-tsaw´;* from 3887; an *aphorism;* also a *satire:*—interpretation, taunting.

4427. מָלַךְ **mâlak,** *maw-lak´;* a prim. root; to *reign;* incept. to *ascend the throne;* causat. to *induct* into royalty; hence (by impl.) to *take counsel:*—consult, × indeed, be (make, set a, set up) king, be (make) queen, (begin to, make to) reign (-ing), rule, × surely.

4428. מֶלֶךְ **melek,** *meh´-lek;* from 4427; a *king:*—king, royal.

4429. מֶלֶךְ **Melek,** *meh´-lek;* the same as 4428; *king; Melek,* the name of two Isr.:—Melech, Hammelech [*by includ. the art.*].

4430. מֶלֶךְ **melek** (Chald.), *meh´-lek;* corresp. to 4428; a *king:*—king, royal.

4431. מְלַךְ **m**e**lak** (Chald.), *mel-ak´;* from a root corresp. to 4427 in the sense of *consultation; advice:*—counsel.

4432. מֹלֶךְ **Môlek,** *mo´-lek;* from 4427; *Molek* (i.e. king), the chief deity of the Ammonites:—Molech. Comp. 4445.

4433. מַלְכָּא **malkâ'** (Chald.), *mal-kaw´;* corresp. to 4436; a *queen:*—queen.

4434. מַלְכֹּדֶת **malkôdeth,** *mal-ko´-deth;* from 3920; a *snare:*—trap.

4435. מִלְכָּה **Milkâh,** *mil-kaw´;* a form of 4436; *queen; Milcah,* the name of a Hebrewess and of an Isr.:—Milcah.

4436. מַלְכָּה **malkâh,** *mal-kaw´;* fem. of 4428; a *queen:*—queen.

4437. מַלְכוּ **malkûw** (Chald.), *mal-koo´;* corresp. to 4438; *dominion* (abstr. or concr.):—kingdom, kingly, realm, reign.

4438. מַלְכוּת **malkûwth,** *mal-kooth´;* or מַלְכֻת **malkûth,** *mal-kooth´;* or (in plur.) מַלְכֻיָּה **malkûyâh,** *mal-koo-yâh´;* from 4427; a *rule;* concr. a *dominion:*—empire, kingdom, realm, reign, royal.

4439. מַלְכִּיאֵל **Malkîy'êl,** *mal-kee-ale´;* from 4428 and 410; *king of* (i.e. appointed by) *God; Malkiël,* an Isr.:—Malchiel.

4440. מַלְכִּיאֵלִי **Malkîy'êlîy,** *mal-kee-ay-lee´;* patron. from 4439; a *Malkiëlite* or desc. of Malkiel:—Malchielite.

4441. מַלְכִּיָּה **Malkîyâh,** *mal-kee-yaw´;* or מַלְכִּיָּהוּ **Malkîyâhûw** (Jer. 38 : 6), *mal-kee-yaw´-hoo;* from 4428 and 3050; *king of* (i.e. appointed by) *Jah; Malkijah,* the name of ten Isr.:—Malchiah, Malchijah.

4442. מַלְכִּי־צֶדֶק **Malkîy-Tsedeq,** *mal-kee-tseh´-dek;* from 4428 and 6664; *king of right; Malki-Tsedek,* an early king in Pal.:—Melchizedek.

4443. מַלְכִּירָם **Malkîyrâm,** *mal-kee-rawm´;* from 4428 and 7311; *king of* a *high* one (i.e. of exaltation); *Malkiram,* an Isr.:—Malchiram.

4444. מַלְכִּישׁוּעַ **Malkîyshûwa',** *mal-kee-shoo´-ah;* from 4428 and 7769; *king of wealth; Malkishua,* an Isr.:—Malchishua.

4445. מַלְכָּם **Malkâm,** *mal-kawm´;* or מִלְכּוֹם **Milkôwm,** *mil-kome´;* from 4428 for 4432; *Malcam* or *Milcom,* the national idol of the Ammonites:—Malcham, Milcom.

4446. מְלֶכֶת **m**e**leketh,** *mel-eh´-keth;* from 4427; a *queen:*—queen.

4447. מֹלֶכֶת **Môleketh,** *mo-leh´-keth;* fem. act. part. of 4427; *queen; Moleketh,* an Israelitess:—Hammoleketh [*includ. the art.*].

4448. מָלַל **mâlal,** *maw-lal´;* a prim. root; to *speak* (mostly poet.) or *say:*—say, speak, utter.

4449. מְלַל **m**e**lal** (Chald.), *mel-al´;* corresp. to 4448; to *speak:*—say, speak (-ing).

4450. מִלֲלַי **Milălay,** *mee-lal-ah´-ee;* from 4448; *talkative; Milalai,* an Isr.:—Milalai.

4451. מַלְמָד **malmâd,** *mal-mawd´;* from 3925; a *goad* for oxen:—goad.

4452. מָלַץ **mâlats,** *maw-lats´;* a prim. root; to be *smooth,* i.e. (fig.) *pleasant:*—be sweet.

4453. מֶלְצָר **meltsâr,** *mel-tsawr´;* of Pers. der.; the *butler* or other officer in the Bab. court:—Melzar.

4454. מָלַק **mâlaq,** *maw-lak´;* a prim. root; to *crack* a joint; by impl. to *wring* the neck of a fowl (without separating it):—wring off.

4455. מַלְקוֹחַ **malqôwach,** *mal-ko´-akh;* from 3947; trans. (in dual) the *jaws* (as taking food); intrans. *spoil* [and captives] (as taken):—booty, jaws, prey.

4456. מַלְקוֹשׁ **malqôwsh,** *mal-koshe´;* from 3953; the spring *rain* (comp. 3954); fig. *eloquence:*—latter rain.

4457. מֶלְקָח **melqâch,** *mel-kawkh´;* or מַלְקָח **malqâch,** *mal-kawkh´;* from 3947; (only in dual) *tweezers:*—snuffers, tongs.

4458. מֶלְתָּחָה **meltâchâh,** *mel-taw-khaw´;* from an unused root mean. to *spread* out; a *wardrobe* (i.e. room where clothing is *spread*):—vestry.

4459. מַלְתָּעָה **maltâ'âh,** *mal-taw-aw´;* transp. for 4973; a *grinder,* i.e. back *tooth:*—great tooth.

4460. מַמְּגֻרָה **mamm^{e}gûrâh,** *mam-meg-oo-raw´;* from 4048 (in the sense of *depositing*); a *granary:*—barn.

4461. מֵמַד **mêmad,** *may-mad´;* from 4058; a *measure:*—measure.

4462. מְמוּכָן **M^{e}mûwkân,** *mem-oo-kawn´;* or (transp.) מוֹמֻכָן° **Môwmûkân** (Esth. 1 : 16), *mo-moo-kawn´;* of Pers. der.; *Memucan* or *Momucan,* a Pers. satrap:—Memucan.

4463. מָמוֹת **mâmôwth,** *maw-mothe´;* from 4191; a mortal *disease;* concr. a *corpse:*—death.

4464. מַמְזֵר **mamzêr,** *mam-zare´;* from an unused root mean. to *alienate;* a *mongrel,* i.e. born of a Jewish father and a heathen mother:—bastard.

4465. מִמְכָּר **mimkâr,** *mim-kawr´;* from 4376; *merchandise;* abstr. a *selling:*— × ought, (that which cometh of) sale, that which . . . sold, ware.

4466. מִמְכֶּרֶת **mimkereth,** *mim-keh´-reth;* fem. of 4465; a *sale:*— + sold as.

4467. מַמְלָכָה **mamlâkâh,** *mam-law-kaw´;* from 4427; *dominion,* i.e.(abstr.) the estate (*rule*) or (concr.) the country (*realm*):—kingdom, king's, reign, royal.

4468. מַמְלָכוּת **mamlâkûwth,** *mam-law-kooth´;* a form of 4467 and equiv. to it:—kingdom, reign.

4469. מַמְסָךְ **mamçâk,** *mam-sawk´;* from 4537; *mixture,* i.e. (spec.) wine *mixed* (with water or spices):—drink-offering, mixed wine.

4470. מֶמֶר **memer,** *meh´-mer;* from an unused root mean. to *grieve; sorrow:*—bitterness.

4471. מַמְרֵא **Mamrê',** *mam-ray´;* from 4754 (in the sense of *vigor*); *lusty; Mamre,* an Amorite:—Mamre.

4472. מַמְרֹר **mamrôr,** *mam-rore´;* from 4843; a *bitterness,* i.e. (fig.) calamity:—bitterness.

4473. מִמְשַׁח **mimshach,** *mim-shakh´;* from 4886, in the sense of *expansion; outspread* (i.e. with outstretched wings):—anointed.

4474. מִמְשָׁל **mimshâl,** *mim-shawl´;* from 4910; a *ruler* or (abstr.) *rule:*—dominion, that ruled.

4475. מֶמְשָׁלָה **memshâlâh,** *mem-shaw-law´;* fem. of 4474; *rule;* also (concr. in plur.) a *realm* or a *ruler:*—dominion, government, power, to rule.

4476. מִמְשָׁק **mimshâq,** *mim-shawk´;* from the same as 4943; a *possession:*—breeding.

4477. מַמְתַּק **mamtaq,** *mam-tak´;* from 4985; something *sweet* (lit. or fig.):—(most) sweet.

4478. מָן **mân,** *mawn;* from 4100; lit. a *whatness* (so to speak), i.e. *manna* (so called from the question about it):—manna.

4479. מָן **mân** (Chald.), *mawn;* from 4101; *who* or *what* (prop. interrog., hence also indef. and rel.):—what, who (-msoever, + so).

4480. מִן **min,** *min;* or מִנִּי **minnîy,** *min-nee´;* or מִנֵּי **minnêy** (constr. plur.), *minn-nay´;* (Isa. 30 : 11); for 4482; prop. a *part* of; hence (prep.), *from* or *out of* in many senses (as follows):—above, after, among, at, because of, by (reason of), from (among), in, × neither, × nor, (out) of, over, since, × then, through, × whether, with.

4481. מִן **min** (Chald.), *min;* corresp. to 4480:—according, after, + because, + before, by, for, from, × him, × more than, (out) of, part, since, × these, to, upon, + when.

4482. מֵן **mên,** *mane;* from an unused root mean. to *apportion;* a *part;* hence a musical *chord* (as parted into strings):—in [the same] (Psa. 68 : 23), stringed instrument (Psa. 150 : 4), whereby (Psa. 45 : 8 [*defective plur.*]).

4483. מְנָא **m^{e}nâ'** (Chald.), *men-aw´;* or מְנָה **m^{e}nâh** (Chald.), *men-aw´;* corresp. to 4487; to *count appoint:*—number, ordain, set.

4484. מְנֵא **menê'** (Chald.), *men-ay´;* pass. part. of 4483; *numbered:*—Mene.

4485. מַנְגִּינָה **mangîynâh,** *man-ghee-naw´;* from 5059; a *satire:*—music.

מִנְדָּה **mindâh.** See 4061.

4486. מַנְדַּע **manda'** (Chald.), *man-dah´;* corresp. to 4093; *wisdom* or *intelligence:*—knowledge, reason, understanding.

מְנָה **m^{e}nâh.** See 4483.

4487. מָנָה **mânâh,** *maw-naw´;* a prim. root; prop. to *weigh* out; by impl. to *allot* or constitute officially; also to *enumerate* or enroll:—appoint, count, number, prepare, set, tell.

4488. מָנֶה **mâneh,** *maw-neh´;* from 4487; prop. a fixed *weight* or measured amount, i.e. (techn.) a *maneh* or mina:—maneh, pound.

4489. מֹנֶה **môneh,** *mo-neh´;* from 4487; prop. something *weighed* out, i.e. (fig.) a *portion* of time, i.e. an *instance:*—time.

4490. מָנָה **mânâh,** *maw-naw´;* from 4487; prop. something *weighed* out, i.e. (gen.) a *division;* spec. (of food) a *ration;* also a *lot:*—such things as belonged, part, portion.

4491. מִנְהָג **minhâg,** *min-hawg´;* from 5090; the *driving* (of a chariot):—driving.

4492. מִנְהָרָה **minhârâh,** *min-haw-raw´;* from 5102; prop. a *channel* or fissure, i.e. (by impl.) a *cavern:*—den.

4493. מָנוֹד **mânôwd,** *maw-node´;* from 5110; a *nodding* or *toss* (of the head in derision):—shaking.

4494. מָנוֹחַ **mânôwach,** *maw-no´-akh;* from 5117; *quiet,* i.e. (concr.) a *settled spot,* or (fig.) a *home:*—(place of) rest.

4495. מָנוֹחַ **Mânôwach,** *maw-no´-akh;* the same as 4494; *rest; Manoäch,* an Isr.:—Manoah.

4496. מְנוּחָה **m^{e}nûwchâh,** *men-oo-khaw´;* or מְנֻחָה **m^{e}nûchâh,** *men-oo-khaw´;* fem. of 4495; *repose* or (adv.) *peacefully;* fig. *consolation* (spec. *matrimony*); hence (concr.) an *abode:*—comfortable, ease, quiet, rest (-ing place), still.

4497. מָנוֹן **mânôwn,** *maw-nohn´;* from 5125; a *continuator,* i.e. *heir:*—son.

4498. מָנוֹס **mânôwç,** *maw-noce´;* from 5127; a *retreat* (lit. or fig.); abstr. a *fleeing:*— × apace, escape, way to flee, flight, refuge.

4499. מְנוּסָה **m^{e}nuwçâh,** *men-oo-saw´;* or מְנֻסָה **m^{e}nûçâh,** *men-oo-saw´;* fem. of 4498; *retreat:*—fleeing, flight.

4500. מָנוֹר **mânôwr,** *maw-nore´;* from 5214; a *yoke* (prop. for *ploughing*), i.e. the *frame* of a loom:—beam.

4501. מְנוֹרָה **m^{e}nôwrâh,** *men-o-raw´;* or מְנֹרָה **m^{e}nôrâh,** *men-o-raw´;* fem. of 4500 (in the orig. sense of 5216); a *chandelier:*—candlestick.

4502. מִנְּזָר **minn^{e}zâr,** *min-ez-awr´;* from 5144; a *prince:*—crowned.

4503. מִנְחָה **minchâh,** *min-khaw´;* from an unused root mean. to *apportion,* i.e. *bestow;* a *donation;* euphem. *tribute;* spec. a sacrificial *offering* (usually bloodless and voluntary):—gift, oblation, (meat) offering, present, sacrifice.

4504. מִנְחָה **minchâh** (Chald.), *min-khaw´;* corresp. to 4503; a sacrificial *offering:*—oblation, meat offering.

מְנֻחָה **m^{e}nûchâh.** See 4496.

מְנֻחוֹת **M^{e}nûchôwth.** See 2679.

4505. מְנַחֵם **M^{e}nachêm,** *men-akh-ame´;* from 5162; *comforter; Menachem,* an Isr.:—Menahem.

4506. מָנַחַת **Mânachath,** *maw-nakh´-ath;* from 5117; *rest; Manachath,* the name of an Edomite and of a place in Moab:—Manahath.

מְנַחְתִּי **M^{e}nachtîy.** See 2680.

4507. מְנִי **M^{e}nîy,** *men-ee´;* from 4487; the *Apportioner,* i.e. Fate (as an idol):—number.

מִנִּי **minnîy.** See 4480, 4482.

4508. מִנִּי **Minnîy,** *min-nee´;* of for. der.; *Minni,* an Armenian province:—Minni.

מְנָיוֹת **m^{e}nâyôwth.** See 4521.

4509. מִנְיָמִין **Minyâmîyn,** *min-yaw-meen´;* from 4480 and 3225; *from* (the) *right hand; Minjamin,* the name of two Isr.:—Miniamin. Comp. 4326.

4510. מִנְיָן **minyân** (Chald.), *min-yawn´;* from 4483; *enumeration:*—number.

4511. מִנִּית **Minnîyth,** *min-neeth´;* from the same as 4482; *enumeration; Minnith,* a place E. of the Jordan:—Minnith.

4512. מִנְלֶה **minleh,** *min-leh´;* from 5239; *completion,* i.e. (in produce) *wealth:*—perfection.

מְנֻסָה **menûçâh.** See 4499.

4513. מָנַע **mânaʻ,** *maw-nah´;* a prim. root; to *debar* (neg. or pos.) from benefit or injury:—deny, keep (back), refrain, restrain, withhold.

4514. מַנְעוּל **manʻûwl,** *man-ool´;* or מַנְעֻל **manʻûl,** *man-ool´;* from 5274; a *bolt:*—lock.

4515. מַנְעָל **manʻâl,** *man-awl´;* from 5274; a *bolt:*—shoe.

4516. מַנְעַם **manʻam,** *man-am´;* from 5276; a *delicacy:*—dainty.

4517. מְנַעְנַע **menaʻnaʻ,** *men-ah-ah´;* from 5128; a *sistrum* (so called from its *rattling* sound):—cornet.

4518. מְנַקִּית **menaqqîyth,** *men-ak-keeth´;* from 5352; a *sacrificial basin* (for holding blood):—bowl.

מְנֹרָה **menôrâh.** See 4501.

4519. מְנַשֶּׁה **Menashsheh,** *men-ash-sheh´;* from 5382; *causing to forget; Menashsheh,* a grandson of Jacob, also the tribe desc. from him, and its territory:—Manasseh.

4520. מְנַשִּׁי **Menashshîy,** *men-ash-shee´;* from 4519; a *Menashshite* or desc. of Menashsheh:—of Manasseh, Manassites.

4521. מְנָת **menâth,** *men-awth´;* from 4487; an *allotment* (by courtesy, law or providence):—portion.

4522. מַס **maç,** *mas;* or מִס **miç,** *mees;* from 4549; prop. a *burden* (as causing to *faint*), i.e. a *tax* in the form of forced *labor:*—discomfited, levy, task [-master], tribute (-tary).

4523. מָס **mâç,** *mawce;* from 4549; *fainting,* i.e. (fig.) *disconsolate:*—is afflicted.

4524. מֵסַב **mêçab,** *may-sab´;* plur. masc. מְסִבִּים **meçibbîym,** *mes-ib-beem´;* or fem. מְסִבּוֹת **meçibbôwth,** *mes-ib-bohth´;* from 5437; a *divan* (as *enclosing* the room); abstr. (adv.) *around:*—that compass about, (place) round about, at table.

מֻסַבָּה **mûçabbâh.** See 4142.

4525. מַסְגֵּר **maçgêr,** *mas-gare´;* from 5462; a *fastener,* i.e. (of a person) a *smith,* (of a thing) a *prison:*—prison, smith.

4526. מִסְגֶּרֶת **miçgereth,** *mis-gheh´-reth;* from 5462; something *enclosing,* i.e. a *margin* (of a region, of a panel); concr. a *stronghold:*—border, close place, hole.

4527. מַסַּד **maççad,** *mas-sad´;* from 3245; a *foundation:*—foundation.

מֹסָדָה **môçâdâh.** See 4146.

4528. מִסְדְּרוֹן **miçderôwn,** *mis-der-ohn´;* from the same as 5468; a *colonnade* or internal portico (from its *rows* of pillars):—porch.

4529. מָסָה **mâçâh,** *maw-saw´;* a prim. root; to *dissolve:*—make to consume away, (make to) melt, water.

4530. מִסָּה **miççâh,** *mis-saw´;* from 4549 (in the sense of *flowing*); *abundance,* i.e. (adv.) *liberally:*—tribute.

4531. מַסָּה **maççâh,** *mas-saw´;* from 5254; a *testing,* of men (judicial) or of God (querulous):—temptation, trial.

4532. מַסָּה **Maççâh,** *mas-saw´;* the same as 4531; *Massah,* a place in the Desert:—Massah.

4533. מַסְוֶה **maçveh,** *mas-veh´;* appar. from an unused root mean. to *cover;* a *veil:*—vail.

4534. מְסוּכָה **meçûwkâh,** *mes-oo-kaw´;* for 4881; a *hedge:*—thorn hedge.

4535. מַסָּח **maççâch,** *mas-sawkh´;* from 5255 in the sense of *staving* off; a *cordon,* (adv.) or (as a) military *barrier:*—broken down.

4536. מִסְחָר **miçchâr,** *mis-khawr´;* from 5503; *trade:*—traffic.

4537. מָסַךְ **mâçak,** *maw-sak´;* a prim. root; to *mix,* espec. wine (with spices):—mingle.

4538. מֶסֶךְ **meçek,** *meh´-sek;* from 4537; a *mixture,* i.e. of wine with spices:—mixture.

4539. מָסָךְ **mâçâk,** *maw-sawk´;* from 5526; a *cover,* i.e. *veil:*—covering, curtain, hanging.

4540. מְסֻכָּה **meçukkâh,** *mes-ook-kaw´;* from 5526; a *covering,* i.e. garniture:—covering.

4541. מַסֵּכָה **maççêkâh,** *mas-say-kaw´;* from 5258; prop. a *pouring* over, i.e. *fusion* of metal (espec. a *cast* image); by impl. a *libation,* i.e. league; concr. a *coverlet* (as if *poured* out):—covering, molten (image), vail.

4542. מִסְכֵּן **miçkên,** *mis-kane´;* from 5531; *indigent:*—poor (man).

4543. מִסְכְּנָה **miçkenâh,** *mis-ken-aw´;* by transp. from 3664; a *magazine:*—store (-house), treasure.

4544. מִסְכֵּנֻת **miçkênûth,** *mis-kay-nooth´;* from 4542; *indigence:*—scarceness.

4545. מַסֶּכֶת **maççeketh,** *mas-seh´-keth;* from 5259 in the sense of *spreading* out; something *expanded,* i.e. the *warp* in a loom (as *stretched* out to receive the woof):—web.

4546. מְסִלָּה **meçillâh,** *mes-il-law´;* from 5549; a *thoroughfare* (as *turnpiked*), lit. or fig.; spec. a *viaduct,* a *staircase:*—causeway, course, highway, path, terrace.

4547. מַסְלוּל **maçlûwl,** *mas-lool´;* from 5549; a *thoroughfare* (as turnpiked):—highway.

4548. מַסְמֵר **maçmêr,** *mas-mare´;* or מִסְמֵר **miçmêr,** *mis-mare´;* also (fem.) מַסְמְרָה **maçmerâh,** *mas-mer-aw´;* or מִסְמְרָה **miçmerâh,** *mis-mer-aw´;* or even מַשְׂמְרָה **masmerâh** (Eccles. 12 : 11), *mas-mer-aw´;* from 5568; a *peg* (as *bristling* from the surface):—nail.

4549. מָסַס **mâçaç,** *maw-sas´;* a prim. root; to *liquefy;* fig. to *waste* (with disease), to *faint* (with fatigue, fear or grief):—discourage, faint, be loosed, melt (away), refuse, × utterly.

4550. מַסַּע **maççaʻ,** *mas-sah´;* from 5265; a *departure* (from *striking* the tents), i.e. march (not necessarily a single day's travel); by impl. a *station* (or point of *departure*):—journey (-ing).

4551. מַסָּע **maççâʻ,** *mas-saw´;* from 5265 in the sense of *projecting;* a *missle* (spear or arrow); also a *quarry* (whence stones are, as it were, *ejected*):—before it was brought, dart.

4552. מִסְעָד **miçʻâd,** *mis-awd´;* from 5582; a *balustrade* (for stairs):—pillar.

4553. מִסְפֵּד **miçpêd,** *mis-pade´;* from 5594; a *lamentation:*—lamentation, one mourneth, mourning, wailing.

4554. מִסְפּוֹא **miçpôwʼ,** *mis-po´;* from an unused root mean. to *collect; fodder:*—provender.

4555. מִסְפָּחָה **miçpâchâh,** *mis-paw-khaw´;* from 5596; a *veil* (as *spread* out):—kerchief.

4556. מִסְפַּחַת **miçpachath,** *mis-pakh´-ath;* from 5596; *scurf* (as *spreading* over the surface):—scab.

4557. מִסְפָּר **miçpâr,** *mis-pawr´;* from 5608; a *number,* def. (arithmetical) or indef. (large, *innumerable;* small, a *few*); also (abstr.) *narration:*— + abundance, account, × all, × few, [in-] finite, (certain) number (-ed), tale, telling, + time.

4558. מִסְפָּר **Miçpâr,** *mis-pawr´;* the same as 4557; *number; Mispar,* an Isr.:—Mizpar. Comp. 4559.

מֹסֵרוֹת **Môçerowth.** See 4149.

4559. מִסְפֶּרֶת **Miçpereth,** *mis-peh´-reth;* fem. of 4557; *enumeration; Mispereth,* an Isr.:—Mispereth. Comp. 4458.

4560. מָסַר **mâçar,** *maw-sar´;* a prim. root; to *sunder,* i.e. (trans.) *set apart,* or (reflex.) *apostatize:*—commit, deliver.

4561. מֹסָר **môçâr,** *mo-sawr´;* from 3256; *admonition*—instruction.

4562. מָסֹרֶת **mâçôreth,** *maw-so´-reth;* from 631; a *band:*—bond.

4563. מִסְתּוֹר **miçtôwr,** *mis-tore´;* from 5641; a *refuge:*—covert.

4564. מַסְתֵּר **maçtêr,** *mas-tare´;* from 5641; prop. a *hider,* i.e. (abstr.) a hiding, i.e. *aversion:*—hid.

4565. מִסְתָּר **miçtâr** *mis-tawr´;* from 5641; prop. a *concealer,* i.e. a *covert:*—secret (-ly, place).

מְעָא **meʻâʼ,** See 4577.

4566. מַעְבָּד **ma'bâd,** *mah-bawd´;* from 5647; an *act:*—work.

4567. מַעְבָד **ma'bâd** (Chald.), *mah-bawd´;* corresp. to 4566; an *act:*—work.

4568. מַעֲבֶה **ma'ăbeh,** *mah-ab-eh´;* from 5666; prop. *compact* (part of soil), i.e. *loam:*—clay.

4569. מַעֲבָר **ma'ăbâr,** *mah-ab-awr´;* or fem. מַעֲבָרָה **ma'ăbârâh,** *mah-ab-aw-raw´;* from 5674; a *crossing*-place (of a river, a *ford;* of a mountain, a *pass*); abstr. a *transit,* i.e. (fig.) *overwhelming:*—ford, place where . . . pass, passage.

4570. מַעְגָּל **ma'gâl,** *mah-gawl´;* or fem. מַעְגָּלָה **ma'gâlâh,** *mah-gaw-law´;* from the same as 5696; a *track* (lit. or fig.); also a *rampart* (as *circular*):—going, path, trench, way ([-side]).

4571. מָעַד **mâ'ad,** *maw-ad´;* a prim. root; to *waver:*—make to shake, slide, slip.

מֹעֵד **mô'êd.** See 4150.

4572. מַעֲדַי **Ma'ăday,** *mah-ad-ah´ee;* from 5710; *ornamental; Maadai,* an Isr.:—Maadai.

4573. מַעַדְיָה **Ma'adyâh,** *mah-ad-yaw´;* from 5710 and 3050; *ornament of Jah; Maadjah,* an Isr.:—Maadiah. Comp. 4153.

4574. מַעֲדָן **ma'ădân,** *mah-ad-dawn´;* or (fem.) מַעֲדַנָּה **ma'ădannâh,** *mah-ad-an-naw´;* from 5727; a *delicacy* or (abstr.) *pleasure* (adv. *cheerfully*):—dainty, delicately, delight.

4575. מַעֲדַנָּה **ma'ădannâh,** *mah-ad-an-naw´;* by transp. from 6029; a *bond,* i.e. *group:*—influence.

4576. מַעְדֵּר **ma'dêr,** *mah-dare´;* from 5737; a (weeding) *hoe:*—mattock.

4577. מְעָה **me'âh** (Chald.), *meh-aw´;* or מְעָא **me'â'** (Chald.), *meh-aw´;* corresp. to 4578; only in plur. the *bowels:*—belly.

4578. מֵעֶה **mê'âh,** *may-aw´;* from an unused root prob. mean. to *be soft;* used only in plur. the *intestines,* or (collect.) the *abdomen,* fig. *sympathy;* by impl. a *vest;* by extens. the *stomach,* the *uterus* (or of men, the seat of generation), the *heart* (fig.):—belly, bowels, × heart, womb.

4579. מֵעָה **mê'âh,** *may-aw´;* fem. of 4578; the *belly,* i.e. (fig.) interior:—gravel.

4580. מָעוֹג **mâ'ôwg,** *maw-ogue´;* from 5746; a *cake* of bread (with 3934 a *table-buffoon,* i.e. *parasite*):—cake, feast.

4581. מָעוֹז **mâ'ôwz,** *maw-oze´* (also מָעוּז **mâ'ûwz,** *maw-ooz´*); or מָעֹז **mâ'ôz,** *maw-oze´* (also מָעֻז **mâ'ûz,** *maw-ooz´*); from 5810; a *fortified* place; fig. a *defence:*—force, fort (-ress), rock, strength (-en), (× most) strong (hold).

4582. מָעוֹךְ **Mâ'ôwk,** *maw-oke´;* from 4600; *oppressed; Maok,* a Philistine:—Maoch.

4583. מָעוֹן **mâ'ôwn,** *maw-ohn´;* or מָעִין° **mâ'îyn** (1 Chron. 4 : 41), *maw-een´;* from the same as 5772; an *abode,* of God (the Tabernacle or the Temple), men (their home) or animals (their lair); hence a *retreat* (asylum):—den, dwelling ([-]) place), habitation.

4584. מָעוֹן **Mâ'ôwn,** *maw-ohn´;* the same as 4583; a *residence; Maon,* the name of an Isr. and of a place in Pal.:—Maon, Maonites. Comp. 1010, 4586.

4585. מְעוֹנָה **me'ôwnâh,** *meh-o-naw´;* or מְעֹנָה **me'ônâh,** *meh-o-naw´;* fem. of 4583, and mean. the same:—den, habitation, (dwelling) place, refuge.

4586. מְעוּנִי **Me'ûwnîy,** *meh-oo-nee´;* or מְעִינִי° **Me'îynîy,** *meh-ee-nee´;* prob. patrial from 4584; a *Meünite,* or inhab. of Maon (only in plur.):—Mehunim (-s), Meunim.

4587. מְעוֹנֹתַי **Me'ôwnôthay,** *meh-o-no-thah´ee;* plur. of 4585; *habitative; Meonothai,* an Isr.:—Meonothai.

4588. מָעוּף **mâ'ûwph,** *maw-oof´;* from 5774 in the sense of *covering* with shade [comp. 4155]; *darkness:*—dimness.

4589. מָעוֹר **mâ'ôwr,** *maw-ore´;* from 5783; *nakedness,* i.e. (in plur.) the *pudenda:*—nakedness.

מָעֹז **mâ'ôz.** See 4583.

מָעֻז **mâ'ûz.** See 4583.

4590. מַעַזְיָה **Ma'azyâh,** *mah-az-yaw´;* or מַעַזְיָהוּ **Ma'azyâhûw,** *mah-az-yaw´-hoo;* prob. from. 5756 (in the sense of *protection*) and 3050; *rescue of Jah; Maazjah,* the name of two Isr.:—Maaziah.

4591. מָעַט **mâ'aṭ,** *maw-at´;* a prim. root; prop. to *pare* off, i.e. *lessen;* intrans. to *be* (or caus. to *make*) *small* or *few* (or fig. *ineffective*):—suffer to decrease, diminish, (be, × borrow a, give, make) few (in number, -ness), gather least (little), be (seem) little, (× give the) less, be minished, bring to nothing.

4592. מְעַט **me'aṭ,** *meh-at´;* or מְעָט **me'âṭ,** *meh-awt´;* from 4591; a *little* or *few* (often adv. or compar.):—almost, (some, very) few (-er, -est), lightly, little (while), (very) small (matter, thing), some, soon, × very.

4593. מָעֹט **mâ'ôṭ,** *maw-ote´;* pass. adj. of 4591; *thinned* (as to the edge), i.e. *sharp:*—wrapped up.

4594. מַעֲטֶה **ma'ăṭeh,** *mah-at-eh´;* from 5844; a *vestment:*—garment.

4595. מַעֲטָפָה **ma'ăṭâphâh,** *mah-at-aw-faw´;* from 5848; a *cloak:*—mantle.

4596. מְעִי **me'îy,** *meh-ee´;* from 5753; a *pile* of rubbish (as *contorted*), i.e. a *ruin* (comp. 5856):—heap.

4597. מָעַי **Mâ'ai,** *maw-ah´ee;* prob. from 4578; *sympathetic; Maai,* an Isr.:—Maai.

4598. מְעִיל **me'îyl,** *meh-eel´;* from 4603 in the sense of *covering;* a *robe* (i.e. upper and outer *garment*):—cloke, coat, mantle, robe.

מֵעִים **mê'îym.** See 4578.

מְעִין **me'îyn** (Chald.). See 4577.

4599. מַעְיָן **ma'yân** *mah-yawn´;* or מַעְיְנוֹ **ma'yenôw** (Psa. 114 : 8), *mah-yen-o´;* or (fem.) מַעְיָנָה **ma'yânâh,** *mah-yaw-naw´;* from 5869 (as a denom. in the sense of a *spring*); a *fountain* (also collect.), fig. a *source* (of satisfaction):—fountain, spring, well.

מְעִינִי° **Me'îynîy.** See 4586.

4600. מָעַךְ **mâ'ak,** *maw-ak´;* a prim. root; to *press,* i.e. to *pierce, emasculate, handle:*—bruised, stuck, be pressed.

4601. מַעֲכָה **Ma'ăkâh,** *mah-ak-aw´;* or מַעֲכָת **Ma'ăkâth** (Josh. 13 : 13), *mah-ak-awth´;* from 4600; *depression; Maakah* (or *Maakath*), the name of a place in Syria, also of a Mesopotamian, of three Isr., and of four Israelitesses and one Syrian woman:—Maachah, Maachathites. See also 1038.

4602. מַעֲכָתִי **Ma'ăkâthîy,** *mah-ak-aw-thee´;* patrial from 4601; a *Maakathite,* or inhab. of Maakah:—Maachathite.

4603. מָעַל **mâ'al,** *maw-al´;* a prim. root; prop. to *cover* up; used only fig. to *act covertly,* i.e. *treacherously:*—transgress, (commit, do a) tresspass (-ing).

4604. מַעַל **ma'al,** *mah´-al;* from 4603; *treachery,* i.e. sin:—falsehood, grievously, sore, transgression, trespass, × very.

4605. מַעַל **ma'al,** *mah´-al;* from 5927; prop. the *upper* part, used only adv. with pref. *upward, above, overhead, from the top,* etc.:—above, exceeding (-ly), forward, on (× very) high, over, up (-on, -ward), very.

מֵעַל **mê'al.** See 5921.

4606. מֵעָל **mê'âl** (Chald.), *may-awl´;* from 5954; (only in plur. as sing.) the *setting* (of the sun):—going down.

4607. מֹעַל **mô'al,** *mo´-al;* from 5927; a *raising* (of the hands):—lifting up.

4608. מַעֲלֶה **ma'ăleh,** *mah-al-eh´;* from 5927; an *elevation,* i.e. (concr.) *acclivity* or *platform;* abstr. (the relation or state) a *rise* or (fig.) *priority:*—ascent, before, chiefest, cliff, that goeth up, going up, hill, mounting up, stairs.

4609. מַעֲלָה **ma'ălâh,** *mah-al-aw´;* fem. of 4608; *elevation,* i.e. the act (lit. a *journey* to a higher place, fig. a *thought* arising), or (concr.) the condition (lit. a *step* or *grade*-mark, fig. a *superiority* of station); spec. a climactic *progression* (in certain Psalms):—things that come up, (high) degree, deal, go up, stair, step, story.

4610. מַעֲלֵה עַקְרַבִּים **Ma'ălêh 'Aqrabbîym,** *mah-al-ay´ ak-rab-beem´;* from 4608 and (the plur. of) 6137; *Steep of Scorpions,* a place in the Desert:—Maaleh-accrabim, the ascent (going up) of Akrabbim.

4611. מַעֲלָל **ma'ălâl,** *mah-al-awl´;* from 5953; an *act* (good or bad):—doing, endeavour, invention, work.

4612. מַעֲמָד **ma'ămâd,** *mah-am-awd´;* from 5975; (fig.) a *position:*—attendance, office, place, state.

4613. מָעֳמָד **mo'ŏmâd,** *moh-om-awd´;* from 5975; lit. a *foothold:*—standing.

4614. מַעֲמָסָה **ma'ămâçâh,** *mah-am-aw-saw´;* from 6006; *burdensomeness:*—burdensome.

4615. מַעֲמָק **ma'ămâq,** *mah-am-awk´;* from 6009; a *deep:*—deep, depth.

4616. מַעַן **ma'an,** *mah´-an;* from 6030; prop. *heed,* i.e. *purpose;* used on adv., *on account of* (as a motive or an aim), teleologically *in order that:*—because of, to the end (intent) that, for (to, . . . 's sake), + lest, that, to.

4617. מַעֲנֶה **ma'ăneh,** *mah-an-eh´;* from 6030; a *reply* (favorable or contradictory):—answer, × himself.

4618. מַעֲנָה **ma'ănâh,** *mah-an-aw´;* from 6031; in the sense of *depression* or *tilling;* a *furrow:*— + acre, furrow.

מְעֹנָה **meʼônâh.** See 4585.

4619. מַעַץ **Ma'ats,** *mah´-ats;* from 6095; *closure; Maats,* an Isr.:—Maaz.

4620. מַעֲצֵבָה **ma'ătsêbâh,** *mah-ats-ay-baw´;* from 6087; *anguish:*—sorrow.

4621. מַעֲצָד **ma'ătsâd,** *mah-ats-awd´;* from an unused root mean. to *hew;* an *axe:*—ax, tongs.

4622. מַעְצוֹר **ma'tsôwr,** *mah-tsore´;* from 6113; obj. a *hindrance:*—restraint.

4623. מַעְצָר **ma'tsâr,** *mah-tsawr´;* from 6113; sub,. *control:*—rule.

4624. מַעֲקֶה **ma'ăqeh,** *mah-ak-eh´;* from an unused root mean. to *repress;* a *parapet:*—battlement.

4625. מַעֲקָשׁ **ma'ăqâsh,** *mah-ak-awsh´;* from 6140; a *crook* (in a road):—crooked thing.

4626. מַעַר **ma'ar,** *mah´-ar;* from 6168; a *nude* place, i.e. (lit.) the *pudenda,* or (fig.) a vacant *space:*—nakedness, proportion.

4627. מַעֲרָב **ma'ărâb,** *mah-ar-awb´;* from 6148, in the sense of *trading; traffic;* by impl. mercantile *goods:*—market, merchandise.

4628. מַעֲרָב **ma'ărâb,** *mah-ar-awb´;* or (fem.) מַעֲרָבָה **ma'ărâbâh,** *mah-ar-aw-baw´;* from 6150, in the sense of *shading;* the *west* (as the region of the *evening* sun):—west.

4629. מַעֲרֶה **ma'ăreh,** *mah-ar-eh´;* from 6168; a *nude* place, i.e. a *common:*—meadows.

4630. מַעֲרָה° **ma'ărâh,** *mah-ar-aw´;* fem. of 4629; an *open* spot:—army [*from the marg.*].

4631. מְעָרָה **meʼârâh,** *meh-aw-raw´;* from 5783; a *cavern* (as dark):—cave, den, hole.

4632. מְעָרָה **Meʼârâh,** *meh-aw-raw´;* the same as 4631; *cave; Meärah,* a place in Pal.:—Mearah.

4633. מַעֲרָךְ **ma'ărâk,** *mah-ar-awk´;* from 6186; an *arrangement* i.e. (fig.) mental *disposition:*—preparation.

4634. מַעֲרָכָה **ma'ărâkâh,** *mah-ar-aw-kaw´;* fem. of 4633; an *arrangement;* concr. a *pile;* spec. a military *array:*—army, fight, be set in order, ordered place, rank, row.

4635. מַעֲרֶכֶת **ma'ăreketh,** *mah-ar-eh´-keth;* from 6186; an *arrangement,* i.e. (concr.) a *pile* (of loaves):—row, shewbread.

4636. מַעֲרֹם **ma'ărôm** , *mah-ar-ome´;* from 6191, in the sense of *stripping; bare:*—naked.

4637. מַעֲרָצָה **ma'ărâtsâh,** *mah-ar-aw-tsaw´;* from 6206; *violence:*—terror.

4638. מַעֲרָת **Ma'ărâth,** *mah-ar-awth´;* a form of 4630; *waste; Maarath,* a (place in Pal.:—Maarath.

4639. מַעֲשֶׂה **ma'ăseh,** *mah-as-eh´;* from 6213; an *action* (good or bad); gen. a *transaction;* abstr. *activity;* by impl. a *product* (spec. a *poem*) or (gen.) *property:*—act, art, + bakemeat, business, deed, do (-ing), labour, thing made, ware of making, occupation, thing offered, operation, possession, × well, ([handy-, needle-, net-]) work, (-ing, -manship), wrought.

4640. מַעֲשַׂי **Ma'say,** *mah-as-ah´ee;* from 6213; *operative; Maasai,* an Isr.:—Maasiai.

4641. מַעֲשֵׂיָה **Ma'ăsêyâh,** *mah-as-ay-yaw´;* or מַעֲשֵׂיָהוּ **Ma'ăsêyâhûw,** *mah-as-ay-yaw´-hoo;* from 4639 and 3050; *work of Jah; Maasejah,* the name of sixteen Isr.:—Masseiah.

4642. מַעֲשַׁקָּה **ma'ăshaqqâh,** *mah-ash-ak-kaw´;* from 6231; *oppression:*—oppression, × oppressor.

4643. מַעֲשֵׂר **ma'ăsêr,** *mah-as-ayr´;* or מַעֲשַׂר **ma'ăsar,** *mah-as-ar´;* and (in plur.) fem. מַעַשְׂרָה **ma'asrâh,** *mah-as-raw´;* from 6240; a *tenth;* espec. a *tithe:*—tenth (part), tithe (-ing).

4644. מֹף **Môph** *mofe;* of Eg. or.; *Moph,* the capital of Lower Egypt:—Memphis. Comp. 5297.

מְפִבֹשֶׁת **Mephîbôsheth.** See 4648.

4645. מִפְגָּע **miphgâ',** *mif-gaw´;* from 6293; an *object of attack:*—mark.

4646. מַפָּח **mappâch,** *map-pawkh´;* from 5301; a *breathing out* (of life), i.e. expiring:—giving up.

4647. מַפֻּחַ **mappûach,** *map-poo´-akh;* from 5301; the *bellows* (i.e. *blower*) of a forge:—bellows.

4648. מְפִיבֹשֶׁת **Mephîybôsheth,** *mef-ee-bo´-sheth;* or מְפִבֹשֶׁת **Mephîbôsheth,** *mef-ee-bo´-sheth;* prob. from 6284 and 1322; *dispeller of shame* (i.e. of Baal); *Mephibosheth,* the name of two Isr.:—Mephibosheth.

4649. מֻפִּים **Muppîym,** *moop-peem´;* a plur. appar. from 5130; *wavings; Muppim,* an Isr.:—Muppim. Comp. 8206.

4650. מֵפִיץ **mêphîyts,** *may-feets´;* from 6327; a *breaker,* i.e. mallet:—maul.

4651. מַפָּל **mappâl,** *map-pawl´;* from 5307; a *falling* off, i.e. chaff; also something *pendulous,* i.e. a flap:—flake, refuse.

4652. מִפְלָאָה **miphlâ'âh,** *mif-law-aw´;* from 6381; a *miracle:*—wondrous work.

4653. מִפְלַגָּה **miphlaggâh,** *mif-lag-gaw´;* from 6385; a *classification:*—division.

4654. מַפָּלָה **mappâlâh,** *map-paw-law´;* or מַפֵּלָה **mappêlâh,** *map-pay-law´;* from 5307; something *fallen,* i.e. a *ruin:*—ruin (-ous).

4655. מִפְלָט **miphlâṭ,** *mif-lawt´;* from 6403; an *escape:*—escape.

4656. מִפְלֶצֶת **miphletseth,** *mif-leh´-tseth;* from 6426; a *terror,* i.e. an idol:—idol.

4657. מִפְלָשׂ **miphlâs,** *mif-lawce´;* from an unused root mean. to *balance;* a *poising:*—balancing.

4658. מַפֶּלֶת **mappeleth,** *map-peh´-leth;* from 5307; *fall,* i.e. *decadence;* concr. a *ruin;* spec. a *carcase:*—carcase, fall, ruin.

4659. מִפְעָל **miph'âl,** *mif-awl´;* or (fem.) מִפְעָלָה **miph'âlâh,** *mif-aw-law´;* from 6466; a *performance:*—work.

4660. מַפָּץ **mappâts,** *map-pawts´;* from 5310; a *smiting* to pieces:—slaughter.

4661. מַפֵּץ **mappêts,** *map-pates´;* from 5310; a *smiter,* i.e. a war *club:*—battle ax.

4662. מִפְקָד **miphqâd,** *mif-kawd´;* from 6485; an *appointment,* i.e. *mandate;* concr. a designated *spot;* spec. a *census:*—appointed place, commandment, number.

4663. מִפְקָד **Miphqâd,** *mif-kawd´;* the same as 4662; *assignment; Miphkad,* the name of a gate in Jerus.:—Miphkad.

4664. מִפְרָץ **miphrâts,** *mif-rawts´;* from 6555; a *break* (in the shore), i.e. a *haven:*—breach.

4665. מִפְרֶקֶת **miphreketh,** *mif-reh´-keth;* from 6561; prop. a *fracture,* i.e. *joint (vertebra)* of the neck:—neck.

4666. מִפְרָשׂ **miphrâs,** *mif-rawce´;* from 6566; an *expansion:*—that which . . . spreadest forth, spreading.

4667. מִפְשָׂעָה **miphsâ'âh,** *mif-saw-aw´;* from 6585; a *stride,* i.e. (by euphem.) the *crotch:*—buttocks.

מֹפֵת **môphêth.** See 4159.

4668. מַפְתֵּחַ **maphtêach,** *maf-tay´-akh;* from 6605; an *opener,* i.e. a *key:*—key.

4669. מִפְתָּח **miphtâch,** *mif-tawkh´;* from 6605; an *aperture,* i.e. (fig.) *utterance:*—opening.

4670. מִפְתָּן **miphtân,** *mif-tawn´;* from the same as 6620; a *stretcher,* i.e. a *sill:*—threshold.

4671. מֹץ **môts,** *motes;* or מוֹץ **môwts** (Zeph. 2 : 2), *motes;* from 4160; *chaff* (as *pressed* out, i.e. *winnowed* or [rather] threshed loose):—chaff.

4672. מָצָא **mâtsâ'**, *maw-tsaw´;* a prim. root; prop. to *come* forth to, i.e. *appear* or *exist;* trans. to *attain,* i.e. *find* or *acquire;* fig. to *occur, meet* or *be present:*— + be able, befall, being, catch, × certainly (cause to) come (on, to, to hand), deliver, be enough (cause to) find (-ing, occasion, out), get (hold upon), × have (here), be here, hit, be left, light (up-) on, meet (with), × occasion serve, (be) present, ready, speed, suffice, take hold on.

מֹצָא **môtsâ'**. See 4161.

4673. מַצָּב **matstsâb,** *mats-tsawb´;* from 5324; a fixed *spot;* fig. an *office,* a military *post:*—garrison, station, place where . . . stood.

4674. מֻצָּב **mutstsâb,** *moots-tsawb´;* from 5324; a *station,* i.e. military *post:*—mount.

4675. מַצָּבָה **matstsâbâh,** *mats-tsaw-baw´;* or מִצָּבָה **mitstsâbâh,** *mits-tsaw-baw´;* fem. of 4673; a military *guard:*—army, garrison.

4676. מַצֵּבָה **matstsêbâh,** *mats-tsay-baw´;* fem. (causat.) part. of 5324; something *stationed,* i.e. a *column* or (memorial *stone*); by anal. an *idol:*—garrison, (standing) image, pillar.

4677. מְצֹבָיָה **M^{e}tsôbâyâh,** *mets-o-baw-yaw´;* appar. from 4672 and 3050; *found of Jah; Metsobajah,* a place in Pal.:—Mesobaite.

4678. מַצֶּבֶת **matstsebeth,** *mats-tseh´-beth;* from 5324; something *stationary,* i.e. a monumental *stone;* also the *stock* of a tree:—pillar, substance.

4679. מְצַד **m^{e}tsad,** *mets-ad´;* or מְצָד **m^{e}tsâd,** *mets-awd´;* or (fem.) מְצָדָה **m^{e}tsâdâh,** *mets-aw-daw´;* from 6679; a *fastness* (as a *covert* of ambush):—castle, fort, (strong) hold, munition.

מְצֻדָה **m^{e}tsûdâh.** See 4686.

4680. מָצָה **mâtsâh,** *maw-tsaw´;* a prim. root; to *suck* out; by impl. to *drain,* to *squeeze* out:—suck, wring (out).

4681. מֹצָה **Môtsâh,** *mo-tsaw´;* act. part. fem. of 4680; *drained; Motsah,* a place in Pal.:—Mozah.

4682. מַצָּה **matstsâh,** *mats-tsaw´;* from 4711 in the sense of *greedily* devouring for sweetness; prop. *sweetness;* concr. *sweet* (i.e. not soured or bittered with yeast); spec. an *unfermented cake* or loaf, or (ellipt.) the festival of *Passover* (because no leaven was then used):—unleavened (bread, cake), without leaven.

4683. מַצָּה **matstsâh,** *mats-tsaw´;* from 5327; a *quarrel:*—contention, debate, strife.

4684. מַצְהָלָה **matshâlâh,** *mats-haw-law´;* from 6670; a *whinnying* (through impatience for battle or lust):—neighing.

4685. מָצוֹד **mâtsôwd,** *maw-tsode´;* or (fem.) מְצוֹדָה **m^{e}tsôwdâh,** *mets-o-daw´;* or מְצֹדָה **m^{e}tsôdâh,** *mets-o-daw´;* from 6679; a *net* (for *capturing* animals or fishes); also (by interch. for 4679) a *fastness* or (besieging) *tower:*—bulwark, hold, munition, net, snare.

4686. מָצוּד **mâtsûwd,** *maw-tsood´;* or (fem.) מְצוּדָה **m^{e}tsûwdâh,** *mets-oo-daw´;* or מְצֻדָה **m^{e}tsûdâh,** *mets-oo-daw´;* for 4685; a *net,* or (abstr.) *capture;* also a *fastness:*—castle, defence, fort (-ress), (strong) hold, be hunted, net, snare, strong place.

4687. מִצְוָה **mitsvâh,** *mits-vaw´;* from 6680; a *command,* whether human or divine (collect. the *Law*):—(which was) commanded (-ment), law, ordinance, precept.

4688. מְצוֹלָה **m^{e}tsôwlâh,** *mets-o-law´;* or מְצֹלָה **m^{e}tsôlâh,** *mets-o-law´;* also מְצוּלָה **m^{e}tsûwlâh,** *mets-oo-law´;* or מְצֻלָה **m^{e}tsûlâh,** *mets-oo-law´;* from the same as 6683; a *deep* place (of water or mud):—bottom, deep, depth.

4689. מָצוֹק **mâtsôwq,** *maw-tsoke´;* from 6693; a *narrow* place, i.e. (abstr. and fig.) *confinement* or *disability:*—anguish, distress, straitness.

4690. מָצוּק **mâtsûwq,** *maw-tsook´;* or מָצֻק **mâtsûq,** *maw-tsook´;* from 6693; something *narrow,* i.e. a *column* or *hill*top:—pillar, situate.

4691. מְצוּקָה **m^{e}tsûwqâh,** *mets-oo-kaw´;* or מְצֻקָה **m^{e}tsûqâh,** *mets-oo-kaw´;* fem. of 4690; *narrowness,* i.e. (fig.) *trouble:*—anguish, distress.

4692. מָצוֹר **mâtsôwr,** *maw-tsore´;* or מָצוּר **mâtsûwr,** *maw-tsoor´;* from 6696; something *hemming* in, i.e. (obj.) a *mound* (of besiegers), (abstr.) a *siege,* (fig.) *distress;* or (subj.) a *fastness:*—besieged, bulwark, defence, fenced, fortress, siege, strong (hold), tower.

4693. מָצוֹר **mâtsôwr,** *maw-tsore´;* the same as 4692 in the sense of a *limit; Egypt* (as the *border* of Pal.):—besieged places, defence, fortified.

4694. מְצוּרָה **m^{e}tsûwrâh,** *mets-oo-raw´;* or מְצֻרָה **m^{e}tsûrâh,** *mets-oo-raw´;* fem. of 4692; a *hemming* in, i.e. (obj.) a *mound* (of siege), or (subj.) a *rampart* (of protection), (abstr.) *fortification:* fenced (city,) fort, munition, strong hold.

4695. מַצּוּת **matstsûwth,** *mats-tsooth´;* from 5327; a *quarrel:*—that contended.

4696. מֵצַח **mêtsach,** *may´-tsakh;* from an unused root mean. to be *clear,* i.e. *conspicuous;* the *forehead* (as *open* and *prominent*):—brow, forehead, + impudent.

4697. מִצְחָה **mitschâh,** *mits-khaw´;* from the same as 4696; a *shin-piece* of armour (as *prominent*), only plur.:—greaves.

מְצֹלָה **m^{e}tsôlah.** See 4688.

מְצֻלָה **m^{e}tsûlâh.** See 4688.

4698. מְצִלָּה **m^{e}tsillâh,** *mets-il-law´;* from 6750; a *tinkler,* i.e. a *bell:*—bell.

4699. מְצֻלָּה **m^{e}tsullâh,** *mets-ool-law´;* from 6751; *shade:*—bottom.

4700. מְצֵלֶת **m^{e}tsêleth,** *mets-ay´-leth;* from 6750; (only dual) double *tinklers,* i.e. cymbals:—cymbals.

4701. מִצְנֶפֶת **mitsnepheth,** *mits-neh´-feth;* from 6801; a *tiara,* i.e. official *turban* (of a king or high priest):—diadem, mitre.

4702. מַצָּע **matstsâ',** *mats-tsaw´;* from 3331; a *couch:*—bed.

4703. מִצְעָד **mits'âd,** *mits-awd´;* from 6805; a *step;* fig. *companionship:*—going, step.

4704. מִצְּעִירָה **mitsts^e'îyrâh,** *mits-tseh-ee-raw´;* fem. of 4705; prop. *littleness:* concr. *diminutive:*—little.

4705. מִצְעָר **mits'âr,** *mits-awr´;* from 6819, *petty* (in size or number); adv. a *short* (time):—little one, (while), small.

4706. מִצְעָר **Mits'âr,** *mits-awr´;* the same as 4705; *Mitsar,* a peak of Lebanon:—Mizar.

4707. מִצְפֶּה **mitspeh,** *mits-peh´;* from 6822; an *observatory,* espec. for military purposes:—watch tower.

4708. מִצְפֶּה **Mitspeh,** *mits-peh´;* the same as 4707; *Mitspeh,* the name of five places in Pal.:—Mizpeh, watch tower. Comp. 4709.

4709. מִצְפָּה **Mitspah,** *mits-paw´;* fem. of 4708; *Mitspah,* the name of two places in Pal.:—Mitspah. [This seems rather to be only an orth. var. of 4708 when "in pause".]

4710. מִצְפֻּן **mitspûn,** *mits-poon´;* from 6845; a *secret* (place or thing, perh. *treasure*):—hidden thing.

4711. מָצַץ **mâtsats,** *maw-tsats´;* a prim. root; to *suck:*—milk.

מְצָקָה **mûtsâqâh.** See 4166.

4712. מֵצַר **mêtsar,** *may-tsar´;* from 6896; something *tight,* i.e. (fig.) *trouble:*—distress, pain, strait.

מָצֻק **mâtsûq.** See 4690.

מְצֻקָה **m^{e}tsûqâh.** See 4691.

מְצֻרָה **m^{e}tsûrâh.** See 4694.

4713. מִצְרִי **Mitsrîy,** *mits-ree´;* from 4714; a *Mitsrite,* or inhab. of Mitsrajim:—Egyptian, of Egypt.

4714. מִצְרַיִם **Mitsrayim,** *mits-rah´-yim;* dual of 4693; *Mitsrajim,* i.e. Upper and Lower Egypt:—Egypt, Egyptians, Mizraim.

4715. מִצְרֵף **mitsrêph,** *mits-rafe´;* from 6884; a *crucible:*—fining pot.

4716. מַק **maq,** *mak;* from 4743; prop. a *melting,* i.e. *putridity:*—rottenness, stink.

4717. מַקָּבָה **maqqâbâh,** *mak-kaw-baw-´;* from 5344; prop. a *perforatrix,* i.e. a *hammer* (as *piercing*):—hammer.

4718. מַקֶּבֶת **maqqebeth,** *mak-keh´-beth;* from 5344; prop. a *perforator,* i.e. a *hammer* (as *piercing*); also (intrans.) a *perforation,* i.e. a *quarry:*—hammer, hole.

4719. מַקֵּדָה **Maqqêdâh,** *mak-kay-daw´;* from the same as 5348 in the denom. sense of *herding* (comp. 5349); *fold; Makkedah,* a place in Pal.:—Makkedah.

4720. מִקְדָּשׁ **miqdâsh,** *mik-dawsh´;* or מִקְּדָשׁ **miqq^{e}dâsh** (Exod. 15 : 17), *mik-ked-awsh´;* from 6942; a *consecrated* thing or place, espec. a *palace, sanctuary* (whether of Jehovah or of idols) or *asylum:*—chapel, hallowed part, holy place, sanctuary.

4721. מַקְהֵל **maqhêl,** *mak-hale´;* or (fem.) מַקְהֵלָה **maqhêlâh,** *mak-hay-law´;* from 6950; an *assembly:*—congregation.

4722. מַקְהֵלֹת **Maqhêlôth,** *mak-hay-loth´;* plur. of 4721 (fem.); *assemblies; Makheloth,* a place in the Desert:—Makheloth.

4723. מִקְוֶה **miqveh,** *mik-veh´;* or מִקְוֵה **miqvêh** (1 Kings 10 : 28), *mik-vay´;* or מִקְוֵא° **miqvê'** (2 Chron. 1 : 16), *mik-vay´;* from 6960; something *waited* for, i.e. *confidence* (obj. or subj.); also a *collection,* i.e. (of water) a *pond,* or (of men and horses) a *caravan* or *drove:*—abiding, gathering together, hope, linen yarn, plenty [of water], pool.

4724. מִקְוָה **miqvâh,** *mik-vaw´;* fem. of 4723; a *collection,* i.e. (of water) a *reservoir:*—ditch.

4725. מָקוֹם **mâqôwm,** *maw-kome´;* or מָקֹם **mâqôm,** *maw-kome´;* also (fem.) מְקוֹמָה **m**e**qôwmâh,** *mek-o-mah´;* or מְקֹמָה **m**e**qômâh,** *mek-o-mah´;* from 6965; prop. a *standing,* i.e. a *spot;* but used widely of a *locality* (gen. or spec.); also (fig.) of a *condition* (of body or mind):—country, × home, × open, place, room, space, × whither [-soever].

4726. מָקוֹר **mâqôwr,** *maw-kore´;* or מָקֹר **mâqôr,** *maw-kore´;* from 6979; prop. something *dug,* i.e. a (gen.) *source* (of water, even when naturally flowing; also of tears, blood [by euphem. of the female *pudenda*]; fig. of happiness, wisdom, progeny):—fountain, issue, spring, well (-spring).

4727. מִקָּח **miqqâch,** *mik-kawkh´;* from 3947; *reception:*—taking.

4728. מַקָּחָה **maqqâchâh,** *mak-kaw-khaw´;* from 3947; something *received,* i.e. *merchandise* (purchased):—ware.

4729. מִקְטָר **miqṭâr,** *mik-tawr´;* from 6999; something to *fume* (incense) on, i.e. a *hearth* place:—to burn . . . upon.

מְקַטְּרָה **m**e**qaṭṭ**e**râh.** See 6999.

4730. מִקְטֶרֶת **miqṭereth,** *mik-teh´-reth;* fem. of 4729; something to *fume* (incense) in, i.e. a *coal-pan:*—censer.

4731. מַקֵּל **maqqêl,** *mak-kale´;* or (fem.) מַקְּלָה **maqq**e**lâh,** *mak-kel-aw´;* from an unused root mean. appar. to *germinate;* a *shoot,* i.e. *stick* (with leaves on, or for walking, striking, guiding, divining):—rod, ([hand-]) staff.

4732. מִקְלוֹת **Miqlôwth,** *mik-lohth´* (or perh. *mik-kel-ohth´*); plur. of (fem.) 4731; *rods; Mikloth,* a place in the Desert:—Mikloth.

4733. מִקְלָט **miqlâṭ,** *mik-lawt´;* from 7038 in the sense of *taking* in; an *asylum* (as a *receptacle*):—refuge.

4734. מִקְלַעַת **miqla'ath,** *mik-lah´-ath;* from 7049; a *sculpture* (prob. in bass-relief):—carved (figure), carving, graving.

מָקֹם **mâqôm.** See 4725.

מְקֹמָה **m**e**qômâh.** See 4725.

4735. מִקְנֶה **miqneh,** *mik-neh´;* from 7069; something *bought,* i.e. *property,* but only live *stock;* abstr. *acquisition:*—cattle, flock, herd, possession, purchase, substance.

4736. מִקְנָה **miqnâh,** *mik-naw´;* fem. of 4735; prop. a *buying,* i.e. *acquisition;* concr. a piece of *property* (land or living); also the *sum* paid:—(he that is) bought, possession, piece, purchase.

4737. מִקְנֵיָהוּ **Miqnêyâhûw,** *mik-nay-yaw´-hoo;* from 4735 and 3050; *possession of Jah; Miknejah,* an Isr.:—Mikneiah.

4738. מִקְסָם **miqçâm,** *mik-sawm´;* from 7080; an *augury:*—divination.

4739. מָקַץ **Mâqats,** *maw-kats´;* from 7112; *end; Makats,* a place in Pal:—Makaz.

4740. מַקְצוֹעַ **maqtsôwa',** *mak-tso´-ah;* or מַקְצֹעַ **maqtsôa',** *mak-tso´-ah;* or (fem.) מַקְצֹעָה **maqtsô'âh,** *mak-tso-aw´;* from 7106 in the denom. sense of *bending.* an *angle* or recess:—corner, turning.

4741. מַקְצֻעָה **maqtsû'âh,** *mak-tsoo-aw´;* from 7106; a *scraper,* i.e. a carving *chisel:*—plane.

4742. מְקֻצְעָה **m**e**quts'âh,** *mek-oots-aw´;* from 7106 in the denom. sense of *bending;* an *angle:*—corner.

4743. מָקַק **mâqaq,** *maw-kak´;* a prim. root; to *melt;* fig. to *flow, dwindle, vanish:*—consume away, be corrupt, dissolve, pine away.

מָקֹר **mâqôr.** See 4726.

4744. מִקְרָא **miqrâ',** *mik-raw´;* from 7121; something *called* out, i.e. a public *meeting* (the act, the persons, or the place); also a *rehearsal:*—assembly, calling, convocation, reading.

4745. מִקְרֶה **miqreh,** *mik-reh´;* from 7136; something *met* with i.e. an *accident* or *fortune:*—something befallen, befalleth, chance, event, hap (-peneth).

4746. מְקָרֶה **m**e**qâreh,** *mek-aw-reh´;* from 7136; prop. something *meeting,* i.e. a *frame* (of timbers):—building.

4747. מְקֵרָה **m**e**qêrâh,** *mek-ay-raw´;* from the same as 7119; a *cooling* off:— × summer.

מֹקֵשׁ **môqêsh.** See 4170.

4748. מִקְשֶׁה **miqsheh,** *mik-sheh´;* from 7185 in the sense of *knotting* up round and hard; something *turned* (rounded), i.e. a *curl* (of tresses):— × well [set] hair.

4749. מִקְשָׁה **miqshâh,** *mik-shaw´;* fem. of 4748; *rounded* work, i.e. moulded by *hammering (repoussé):*—beaten (out of one piece, work), upright, whole piece.

4750. מִקְשָׁה **miqshâh,** *mik-shaw´;* denom. from 7180; lit. a *cucumbered* field, i.e. a *cucumber* patch:—garden of cucumbers.

4751. מַר **mar,** *mar;* or (fem.) מָרָה **mârâh,** *maw-raw´;* from 4843; *bitter* (lit. or fig.); also (as noun) *bitterness,* or (adv.) *bitterly:*— + angry, bitter (-ly, -ness), chafed, discontented, × great, heavy.

4752. מַר **mar,** *mar;* from 4843 in its orig. sense of *distillation;* a *drop:*—drop.

4753. מֹר **môr,** *more;* or מוֹר **môwr,** *more;* from 4843; *myrrh* (as *distilling* in drops, and also as *bitter*):—myrrh.

4754. מָרָא **mârâ',** *maw-raw´;* a prim. root; to *rebel;* hence (through the idea of *maltreating*) to *whip,* i.e. *lash* (self with wings, as the ostrich in running):—be filthy, lift up self.

4755. מָרָא **Mârâ',** *maw-raw´;* for 4751 fem.; *bitter; Mara,* a symbol. name of Naomi:—Mara.

4756. מָרֵא **mârê'** (Chald.), *maw-ray´;* from a root corresp. to 4754 in the sense of *domineering;* a *master:*—lord, Lord.

מֹרָא **môrâ'.** See 4172.

4757. מְרֹאדַךְ בַּלְאֲדָן **M**e**rô'dak Bal'âdân,** *mer-o-dak´ bal-aw-dawn´;* of for. der.; *Merodak-Baladan,* a Bab. king:—Merodach-baladan. Comp. 4781.

4758. מַרְאֶה **mar'eh,** *mar-eh´;* from 7200; a *view* (the act of seeing); also an *appearance* (the thing seen), whether (real) a *shape* (espec. if handsome, *comeliness;* often plur. the *looks*), or (mental) a *vision:*— × apparently, appearance (-reth), × as soon as beautiful (-ly), countenance, fair, favoured, form, goodly, to look (up) on (to), look [-eth], pattern, to see, seem, sight, visage, vision.

4759. מַרְאָה **mar'âh,** *mar-aw´;* fem. of 4758; a *vision;* also (causat.) a *mirror:*—looking glass, vision.

4760. מֻרְאָה **mur'âh,** *moor-aw´;* appar. fem. pass. causat. part. of 7200; something *conspicuous,* i.e. the *craw* of a bird (from its *prominence*):—crop.

מְרָאוֹן° **M**e**r'ôwn.** See 8112.

4761. מַרְאָשָׁה **mar'âshâh,** *mar-aw-shaw´;* denom. from 7218; prop. *headship,* i.e. (plur. for collect.) *dominion:*—principality.

4762. מַרְאֵשָׁה **Mar'êshâh,** *mar-ay-shaw´;* or מַרֵשָׁה **Marêshâh,** *mar-ay-shaw´;* formed like 4761; *summit; Mareshah,* the name of two Isr. and of a place in Pal.:—Mareshah.

4763. מְרַאֲשָׁה **m**e**ra'ăshâh** *mer-ah-ash-aw´;* formed like 4761; prop. a *headpiece,* i.e. (plur. for adv.) *at* (or *as*) the *head-rest* (or pillow):—bolster, head, pillow. Comp. 4772.

4764. מֵרָב **Mêrâb,** *may-rawb´;* from 7231; *increase; Merab,* a daughter of Saul:—Merab.

4765. מַרְבַד **marbad,** *mar-bad´;* from 7234; a *coverlet:*—covering of tapestry.

4766. מַרְבֶּה **marbeh,** *mar-beh´;* from 7235; prop. *increasing;* as noun, *greatness,* or (adv.) *greatly:*—great, increase.

4767. מִרְבָּה **mirbâh,** *meer-baw´;* from 7235; *abundance,* i.e. a great quantity:—much.

4768. מַרְבִּית **marbîyth,** *mar-beeth´;* from 7235; a *multitude;* also *offspring;* spec. *interest* (on capital):—greatest part, greatness, increase, multitude.

4769. מַרְבֵּץ **marbêts,** *mar-bates´;* from 7257; a *reclining* place, i.e. *fold* (for flocks):—couching place, place to lie down.

4770. מַרְבֵּק **marbêq,** *mar-bake´;* from an unused root mean. to *tie* up; a *stall* (for cattle):—× fat (-ted), stall.

מֹרַג **môrag.** See 4173.

4771. מַרְגּוֹעַ **margôwaʻ,** *mar-go´-ah;* from 7280; a *resting* place:—rest.

4772. מַרְגְּלָה **margelâh,** *mar-ghel-aw´;* denom. from 7272; (plur. for collect.) a *footpiece,* i.e. (adv.) *at the foot,* or (direct.) the *foot* itself:—feet. Comp. 4763.

4773. מַרְגֵּמָה **margêmâh,** *mar-gay-maw´;* from 7275; a *stone*-heap:—sling.

4774. מַרְגֵּעָה **margêʻâh,** *mar-gay-aw´;* from 7280; *rest:*—refreshing.

4775. מָרַד **mârad,** *maw-rad´;* a prim. root; to *rebel:*—rebel (-lious).

4776. מְרַד **merad** (Chald.), *mer-ad´;* from a root corresp. to 4775; *rebellion:*—rebellion.

4777. מֶרֶד **mered,** *meh´-red;* from 4775; *rebellion:*—rebellion.

4778. מֶרֶד **Mered,** *meh´-red;* the same as 4777; *Mered,* an Isr.:—Mered.

4779. מָרָד **mârâd** (Chald.), *maw-rawd´;* from the same as 4776; *rebellious:*—rebellious.

4780. מַרְדּוּת **mardûwth,** *mar-dooth´;* from 4775; *rebelliousness:*— × rebellious.

4781. מְרֹדָךְ **Merôdâk,** *mer-o-dawk´;* of for. der.; *Merodak,* a Bab. idol:—Merodach. Comp. 4757.

4782. מָרְדְּכַי **Mordekay,** *mor-dek-ah´ee;* of for. der.; *Mordecai,* an Isr.:—Mordecai.

4783. מֻרְדָּף **murdâph,** *moor-dawf´;* from 7291; *persecuted:*—persecuted.

4784. מָרָה **mârâh,** *maw-raw´;* a prim. root; to *be* (caus. *make*) *bitter* (or unpleasant); (fig.) to *rebel* (or resist; causat. to *provoke*):—bitter, change, be disobedient, disobey, grievously, provocation, provoke (-ing), (be) rebel (against, -lious).

4785. מָרָה **Mârâh,** *maw-raw´;* the same as 4751 fem.; *bitter; Marah,* a place in the Desert:—Marah.

מֹרֶה **Môreh.** See 4175.

4786. מֹרָה **môrâh,** *mo-raw´;* from 4843; *bitterness,* i.e. (fig.) *trouble:*—grief.

4787. מָרָּה **morrâh,** *mor-raw´;* a form of 4786; *trouble:*—bitterness.

4788. מָרוּד **mârûwd,** *maw-rood´;* from 7300 in the sense of *maltreatment;* an *outcast;* (abstr.) *destitution:*—cast out, misery.

4789. מֵרוֹז **Mêrôwz,** *may-roze´;* of uncert. der.; *Meroz,* a place in Pal.:—Meroz.

4790. מְרוֹחַ **merôwach,** *mer-o-akh´;* from 4799; *bruised,* i.e. *emasculated:*—broken.

4791. מָרוֹם **mârôwm,** *maw-rome´;* from 7311; *ltitude,* i.e. concr. (an *elevated place*), abstr. *(elevation),* fig. *(elation),* or adv. *(aloft):*—(far) above, dignity, haughty, height, (most, on) high (one, place), loftily, upward.

4792. מֵרוֹם **Mêrôwm,** *may-rome´;* formed like 4791; *height; Merom,* a lake in Pal.:—Merom.

4793. מֵרוֹץ **mêrôwts,** *may-rotes´;* from 7323; a *run* (the trial of speed):—race.

4794. מְרוּצָה **merûwtsâh,** *mer-oo-tsaw´;* or מְרֻצָה **merûtsâh,** *mer-oo-tsaw´;* fem. of 4793; a *race* (the act), whether the manner or the progress:—course, running. Comp. 4835.

4795. מָרוּק **mârûwq,** *maw-rook´;* from 4838; prop. *rubbed;* but used abstr., a *rubbing* (with perfumery):—purification.

מְרוֹר **merôwr.** See 4844.

מְרוֹרָה **merôwrâh.** See 4846.

4796. מָרוֹת **Mârôwth,** *maw-rohth´;* plur. of 4751 fem.; *bitter* springs; *Maroth,* a place in Pal.:—Maroth.

4797. מִרְזַח **mirzach,** *meer-zakh´;* from an unused root mean. to *scream;* a *cry,* i.e. (of joy), a *revel:*—banquet.

4798. מַרְזֵחַ **marzêach,** *mar-zay´-akh;* formed like 4797; a *cry,* i.e. (of grief) a *lamentation:*—mourning.

4799. מָרַח **mârach,** *maw-rakh´;* a prim. root; prop. to *soften* by rubbing or pressure; hence (medicinally) to *apply* as an emollient:—lay for a plaister.

4800. מֶרְחָב **merchâb,** *mer-khawb´;* from 7337; *enlargement,* either lit. (an *open space,* usually in a good sense), or fig. *(liberty):*—breadth, large place (room).

4801. מֶרְחָק **merchâq,** *mer-khawk´;* from 7368; *remoteness,* i.e. (concr.) a *distant* place; often (adv.) *from afar:*— (a, dwell in, very) far (country, off). See also 1023.

4802. מַרְחֶשֶׁת **marchesheth,** *mar-kheh´-sheth;* from 7370; a *stew*-pan:—fryingpan.

4803. מָרַט **mâraṭ,** *maw-rat´;* a prim. root; to *polish;* by impl. to *make bald* (the head), to *gall* (the shoulder); also, to *sharpen:*—bright, furbish, (have his) hair (be) fallen off, peeled, pluck off (hair.)

4804. מְרַט **meraṭ** (Chald.), *mer-at´;* corresp. to 4803; to *pull* off:—be plucked.

4805. מְרִי **merîy,** *mer-ee´;* from 4784; *bitterness,* i.e. (fig.) *rebellion;* concr. *bitter,* or *rebellious:*—bitter, (most) rebel (-ion, -lious).

4806. מְרִיא **merîy',** *mer-ee´;* from 4754 in the sense of *grossness,* through the idea of *domineering* (comp. 4756); *stall-fed;* often (as noun) a *beeve:*—fat (fed) beast (cattle, -ling).

4807. מְרִיב בַּעַל **Merîyb Baʻal,** *mer-eeb´ bah´-al;* from 7378 and 1168; *quarreller of Baal; Merib-Baal,* an epithet of Gideon:—Merib-baal. Comp. 4810.

4808. מְרִיבָה **merîybâh,** *mer-ee-baw´;* from 7378; *quarrel:*—provocation, strife.

4809. מְרִיבָה **Merîybâh,** *mer-ee-baw´;* the same as 4808; *Meribah,* the name of two places in the Desert:—Meribah.

4810. מְרִי בַעַל **Merîy Baʻal,** *mer-ee´ bah´-al;* from 4805 and 1168; *rebellion of* (i.e. *against*) *Baal; Meri-Baal,* an epithet of Gideon:—Meri-baal. Comp. 4807.

4811. מְרָיָה **Merâyâh,** *mer-aw-yaw´;* from 4784; *rebellion; Merajah,* an Isr.:—Meraiah. Comp. 3236.

מֹרִיָּה **Môrîyâh.** See 4179.

4812. מְרָיוֹת **Merâyôwth,** *mer-aw-yohth´;* plur. of 4811; *rebellious; Merajoth,* the name of two Isr.:—Meraioth.

4813. מִרְיָם **Miryâm,** *meer-yawm´;* from 4805; *rebelliously; Mirjam,* the name of two Israelitesses:—Miriam.

4814. מְרִירוּת **merîyrûwth,** *mer-ee-rooth´;* from 4843; *bitterness,* i.e. (fig.) *grief:*—bitterness.

4815. מְרִירִי **merîyrîy,** *mer-ee-ree´;* from 4843; *bitter,* i.e. *poisonous:*—bitter.

4816. מֹרֶךְ **môrek,** *mo´-rek;* perh. from 7401; *softness,* i.e. (fig.) *fear:*—faintness.

4817. מֶרְכָּב **merkâb,** *mer-kawb´;* from 7392; a *chariot;* also a *seat* (in a vehicle):—chariot, covering, saddle.

4818. מֶרְכָּבָה **merkâbâh,** *mer-kaw-baw´;* fem. of 4817; a *chariot:*—chariot. See also 1024.

4819. מַרְכֹּלֶת **markôleth,** *mar-ko´-leth;* from 7402; a *mart:*—merchandise.

4820. מִרְמָה **mirmâh,** *meer-maw´;* from 7411 in the sense of *deceiving; fraud:*—craft, deceit (-ful, -fully), false, feigned, guile, subtilly, treachery.

4821. מִרְמָה **Mirmâh,** *meer-maw´;* the same as 4820; *Mirmah,* an Isr.:—Mirma.

4822. מְרֵמוֹת **Merêmôwth,** *mer-ay-mohth´;* plur. from 7311; *heights; Meremoth,* the name of two Isr.:—Meremoth.

4823. מִרְמָס **mirmâç,** *meer-mawce´;* from 7429; *abasement* (the act or the thing):—tread (down) -ing, (to be) trodden (down) under foot.

4824. מֵרֹנֹתִי **Mêrônôthîy,** *may-ro-no-thee´;* patrial from an unused noun; a *Meronothite,* or inhab. of some (otherwise unknown) Meronoth:—Meronothite.

4825. מֶרֶס **Mereç,** *meh´-res;* of for. der.; *Meres,* a Pers.:—Meres.

4826. מַרְסְנָא **Marçenâ',** *mar-sen-aw´;* of for. der.,; *Marsena,* a Pers.:—Marsena.

4827. מֵרַע **mêraʽ,** *may-rah´;* from 7489; used as (abstr.) noun, *wickedness:*—do mischief.

4828. מֵרֵעַ **mêrêaʽ,** *may-ray´-ah;* from 7462 in the sense of *companionship;* a *friend:*—companion, friend.

4829. מִרְעֶה **mirʽeh,** *meer-eh´;* from 7462 in the sense of *feeding; pasture* (the place or the act); also the *haunt* of wild animals:—feeding place, pasture.

4830. מִרְעִית **mirʽîyth,** *meer-eeth´;* from 7462 in the sense of *feeding; pasturage;* concr. a *flock:*—flock, pasture.

4831. מַרְעֲלָה **Marʽălâh,** *mar-al-law´;* from 7477; perh. *earthquake; Maralah,* a place in Pal.:—Maralah.

4832. מַרְפֵּא **marpêʼ,** *mar-pay´;* from 7495; prop. *curative,* i.e. lit. (concr.) a *medicine,* or (abstr.) a *cure;* fig. (concr.) *deliverance,* or (abstr.) *placidity:*—([in-]) cure (-able), healing (-lth), remedy, sound, wholesome, yielding.

4833. מִרְפָּשׂ **mirpâs,** *meer-paws´;* from 7515; *muddled* water:—that which . . . have fouled.

4834. מָרַץ **mârats,** *maw-rats´;* a prim. root; prop. to *press,* i.e. (fig.) to be *pungent* or vehement; to *irritate:*—embolden, be forcible, grievous, sore.

4835. מְרֻצָה **merûtsâh,** *mer-oo-tsaw´;* from 7533; *oppression:*—violence. See also 4794.

4836. מַרְצֵעַ **martsêaʽ,** *mar-tsay´-ah;* from 7527; an *awl:*—aul.

4837. מַרְצֶפֶת **martsepheth,** *mar-tseh´-feth;* from 7528; a *pavement:*—pavement.

4838. מָרַק **mâraq,** *maw-rak´;* a prim. root; to *polish;* by impl. to *sharpen;* also to *rinse:*—bright, furbish, scour.

4839. מָרָק **mârâq,** *maw-rawk´;* from 4838; *soup* (as if a *rinsing*):—broth. See also 6564.

4840. מֶרְקָח **merqâch,** *mer-kawkh´;* from 7543; a *spicy* herb:— × sweet.

4841. מֶרְקָחָה **merqâchâh,** *mer-kaw-khaw´,* fem. of 4840; abstr. a *seasoning* (with spicery); concr. an *unguent-kettle* (for preparing spiced oil):—pot of ointment, × well.

4842. מִרְקַחַת **mirqachath,** *meer-kakh´-ath;* from 7543; an aromatic *unguent;* also an *unguent-pot:*—prepared by the apothecaries' art, compound, ointment.

4843. מָרַר **mârar,** *maw-rar´;* a prim. root; prop. to *trickle* [see 4752]; but used only as a denom. from 4751; to *be* (causat. *make*) *bitter* (lit. or fig.):—(be, be in, deal, have, make) bitter (-ly, -ness), be moved with choler, (be, have sorely, it) grieved (-eth), provoke, vex.

4844. מְרֹר **merôr,** *mer-ore´;* or מְרוֹר **merôwr,** *mer-ore´;* from 4843; a *bitter* herb:—bitter (-ness).

4845. מְרֵרָה **merêrâh,** *mer-ay-raw´;* from 4843; *bile* (from its bitterness):—gall.

4846. מְרֹרָה **merôrâh,** *mer-o-raw´;* or מְרוֹרָה **merôwrâh,** *mer-o-raw´;* from 4843; prop. *bitterness;* concr. a *bitter thing;* spec. *bile;* also *venom* (of a serpent):—bitter (thing), gall.

4847. מְרָרִי **Merârîy,** *mer-aw-ree´;* from 4843; *bitter; Merari,* an Isr.:—Merari. See also 4848.

4848. מְרָרִי **Merârîy,** *mer-aw-ree´;* from 4847; a *Merarite* (collect.), or desc. of Merari:—Merarites.

מָרֵשָׁה **Mârêshâh.** See 4762.

4849. מִרְשַׁעַת **mirshaʽath,** *meer-shah´-ath;* from 7561; a female *wicked doer:*—wicked woman.

4850. מְרָתַיִם **Merâthayim,** *mer-aw-thah´-yim;* dual of 4751 fem.; *double bitterness; Merathajim,* an epithet of Babylon:—Merathaim.

4851. מַשׁ **Mash,** *mash;* of for. der.; *Mash,* a son of Aram, and the people desc. from him:—Mash.

4852. מֵשָׁא **Mêshâʼ,** *may-shaw´;* of for. der.; *Mesha,* a place in Arabia:—Mesha.

4853. מַשָּׂא **massâʼ,** *mas-saw´;* from 5375; a *burden;* spec. *tribute,* or (abstr.) *porterage;* fig. an *utterance,* chiefly a *doom,* espec. *singing;* mental, *desire:*—burden, carry away, prophecy, × they set, song, tribute.

4854. מַשָּׂא **Massâʼ,** *mas-saw´;* the same as 4853; *burden; Massa,* a son of Ishmael:—Massa.

4855. מַשָּׁא **mashshâʼ,** *mash-shaw´;* from 5383; a *loan;* by impl. *interest* on a debt:—exaction, usury.

4856. מַשֹּׂא **massôʼ,** *mas-so´;* from 5375; *partiality* (as a *lifting* up):—respect.

4857. מַשְׁאָב **mashʼâb,** *mash-awb´;* from 7579; a *trough* for cattle to drink from:—place of drawing water.

מְשֹׁאָה **meshôʼâh.** See 4875.

4858. מַשָּׂאָה **massâʼâh,** *mas-saw-aw´;* from 5375; a *conflagration* (from the *rising* of smoke):—burden.

4859. מַשָּׁאָה **mashshâʼâh,** *mash-shaw-aw´;* fem. of 4855; a *loan:*— × any [-thing], debt.

מַשֻּׁאָה **mashshûʼâh.** See 4876.

4860. מַשָּׁאוֹן **mashshâʼôwn,** *mash-shaw-ohn´;* from 5377; *dissimulation:*—deceit.

4861. מִשְׁאָל **Mishʼâl,** *mish-awl´;* from 7592; *request; Mishal,* a place in Pal.:—Mishal, Misheal. Comp. 4913.

4862. מִשְׁאָלָה **mishʼâlâh,** *mish-aw-law´;* from 7592; a *request:*—desire, petition.

4863. מִשְׁאֶרֶת **mishʼereth,** *mish-eh´-reth;* from 7604 in the orig. sense of *swelling;* a *kneading-trough* (in which the dough *rises*):—kneading trough, store.

4864. מַשְׂאֵת **masʼêth,** *mas-ayth´;* from 5375; prop. (abstr.) a *raising* (as of the hands in prayer), or *rising* (of flame); fig. an *utterance;* concr. a *beacon* (as *raised*); a *present* (as taken), *mess,* or *tribute;* fig. a *reproach* (as a burden):—burden, collection, sign of fire, (great) flame, gift, lifting up, mess, oblation, reward.

מֹשָׁב **môshâb. See 4186.**

מְשֻׁבָה **meshûbâh.** See 4878.

4865. מִשְׁבְּצָה **mishbetsâh,** *mish-bets-aw´;* from 7660; a *brocade;* by anal. a (reticulated) *setting* of a gem:—ouch, wrought.

4866. מִשְׁבֵּר **mishbêr,** *mish-bare´;* from 7665; the *orifice* of the womb (from which the fœtus *breaks* forth):—birth, breaking forth.

4867. מִשְׁבָּר **mishbâr,** *mish-bawr´;* from 7665; a *breaker* (of the sea):—billow, wave.

4868. מִשְׁבָּת **mishbâth,** *mish-bawth´;* from 7673; *cessation,* i.e. destruction:—sabbath.

4869. מִשְׂגָּב **misgâb,** *mis-gawb´;* from 7682; prop. a *cliff* (or other *lofty* or *inaccessible* place); abstr. *altitude;* fig. a *refuge:*—defence, high fort (tower), refuge. 4869; *Misgab,* a place in Moab:—Misgab.

4870. מִשְׁגֶּה **mishgeh,** *mis-gay´;* from 7686; an *error:*—oversight.

4871. מָשָׁה **mâshâh,** *maw-shaw´;* a prim. root; to *pull* out (lit. or fig.):—draw (out).

4872. מֹשֶׁה **Môsheh,** *mo-sheh´;* from 4871; *drawing* out (of the water), i.e. *rescued; Mosheh,* the Isr. lawgiver:—Moses.

4873. מֹשֶׁה **Môsheh** (Chald.), *mo-sheh´;* corresp. to 4872:—Moses.

4874. מַשֶּׁה **mashsheh,** *mash-sheh´;* from 5383; a *debt:*— + creditor.

4875. מְשׁוֹאָה **meshôwʼâh,** *mesh-o-aw´;* or מְשֹׁאָה **meshôʼâh,** *mesh-o-aw´;* from the same as 7722; (a) *ruin,* abstr. (the act) or concr. (the wreck):—desolation, waste.

4876. מַשּׁוּאָה **mashshûwʼâh,** *mash-shoo-aw´;* or מַשֻּׁאָה **mashshûʼâh,** *mash-shoo-aw´;* for 4875; *ruin:*—desolation, destruction.

4877. מְשׁוֹבָב **Meshôwbâb,** *mesh-o-bawb´;* from 7725; *returned; Meshobab,* an Isr.:—Meshobab.

4878. מְשׁוּבָה **meshûwbâh,** *mesh-oo-baw´;* or מְשֻׁבָה **meshûbâh,** *mesh-oo-baw´;* from 7725; *apostasy:*—backsliding, turning away.

4879. מְשׁוּגָה **meshûwgâh,** *mesh-oo-gaw´;* from an unused root mean. to *stray; mistake:*—error.

4880. מָשׁוֹט **mâshôwṭ,** *maw-shote´;* or מִשּׁוֹט **mishshôwṭ,** *mish-shote´;* from 7751; an *oar:*—oar.

4881. מְשׂוּכָה° **mesûwkâh,** *mes-oo-kaw´;* or מְשֻׂכָה **mesûkâh,** *mes-oo-kaw´;* from 7753; a *hedge:*—hedge.

4882. מְשׁוּסָה° **meshûwçâh,** *mesh-oo-saw´;* from an unused root mean. to *plunder; spoilation:*—spoil.

4883. מַשּׂוֹר **massôwr,** *mas-sore´;* from an unused root mean. to *rasp;* a *saw:*—saw.

4884. מְשׂוּרָה **m^{e}sûwrâh,** *mes-oo-raw´;* from an unused root mean. appar. to *divide;* a *measure* (for liquids):—measure.

4885. מָשׂוֹשׂ **mâsôws,** *maw-soce´;* from 7797; *delight,* concr. (the cause or object) or abstr. (the feeling):—joy, mirth, rejoice.

4886. מָשַׁח **mâshach,** *maw-shakh´;* a prim. root; to *rub* with oil, i.e. to *anoint;* by impl. to *consecrate;* also to *paint:*—anoint, paint.

4887. מְשַׁח **m^{e}shach** (Chald.), *mesh-akh´;* from a root corresp. to 4886; *oil:*—oil.

4888. מִשְׁחָה **mishchâh,** *meesh-khaw´;* or מָשְׁחָה **moshchâh,** *mosh-khaw´;* from 4886; *unction* (the act); by impl. a consecratory *gift:*—(to be) anointed (-ing), ointment.

4889. מַשְׁחִית **mashchîyth,** *mash-kheeth´;* from 7843; *destructive,* i.e. (as noun) *destruction,* lit. (spec. a *snare*) or fig. *(corruption):*—corruption, (to) destroy (-ing), destruction, trap, × utterly.

4890. מִשְׂחָק **mischâq,** *mis-khawk´;* from 7831; a *laughing-stock:*—scorn.

4891. מִשְׁחָר **mishchâr,** *mish-khawr´;* from 7836 in the sense of day *breaking; dawn:*—morning.

4892. מַשְׁחֵת **mashchêth,** *mash-khayth´;* for 4889; *destruction:*—destroying.

4893. מִשְׁחָת **mishchâth,** *mish-khawth´;* or מָשְׁחָת **moshchâth,** *mosh-khawth´;* from 7843; *disfigurement:*—corruption, marred.

4894. מִשְׁטוֹחַ **mishṭôwach,** *mish-to´-akh;* or מִשְׁטַח **mishṭach,** *mish-takh´;* from 7849; a *spreading*-place:—(to) spread (forth, -ing, upon).

4895. מַשְׂטֵמָה **masṭêmâh,** *mas-tay-maw´;* from the same as 7850; *enmity:*—hatred.

4896. מִשְׁטָר **mishṭâr,** *mish-tawr´;* from 7860; *jurisdiction:*—dominion.

4897. מֶשִׁי **meshîy,** *meh´-shee;* from 4871; *silk* (as *drawn* from the cocoon):—silk.

מֻשִׁי **Mûshîy.** See 4187.

4898. מְשֵׁיזַבְאֵל **M^{e}shêyzab'êl,** *mesh-ay-zab-ale´;* from an equiv. to 7804 and 410; *delivered of God; Meshezabel,* an Isr.:—Meshezabeel.

4899. מָשִׁיחַ **mâshîyach,** *maw-shee´-akh;* from 4886; *anointed;* usually a *consecrated* person (as a king, priest, or saint); spec. the *Messiah:*—anointed, Messiah.

4900. מָשַׁךְ **mâshak,** *maw-shak´;* a prim. root; to *draw,* used in a great variety of applications (includ. to *sow,* to *sound,* to *prolong,* to *develop,* to *march,* to *remove,* to *delay,* to *be tall,* etc.):—draw (along, out), continue, defer, extend, forbear, × give, handle, make (pro-, sound) long, × sow, scatter, stretch out.

4901. מֶשֶׁךְ **meshek,** *meh´-shek;* from 4900; a *sowing;* also a *possession:*—precious, price.

4902. מֶשֶׁךְ **Meshek,** *meh´-shek;* the same in form as 4901, but prob. of for. der.; *Meshek,* a son of Japheth, and the people desc. from him:—Mesech, Meshech.

4903. מִשְׁכַּב **mishkab** (Chald.), *mish-kab´;* corresp. to 4904; a *bed:*—bed.

4904. מִשְׁכָּב **mishkâb,** *mish-kawb´;* from 7901; a *bed* (fig. a *bier*); abstr. *sleep;* by euphem. carnal *intercourse:*—bed ([-chamber]), couch, lieth (lying) with.

מְשֻׂכָה **m^{e}sûkâh.** See 4881.

4905. מַשְׂכִּיל **maskîyl,** *mas-keel´;* from 7919; *instructive,* i.e. a *didactic* poem:—Maschil.

מַשְׁכִּים **mashkîym.** See 7925.

4906. מַשְׂכִּית **maskîyth,** *mas-keeth´;* from the same as 7906; a *figure* (carved on stone, the wall, or any object); fig. *imagination:*— conceit, image (-ry), picture, × wish.

4907. מִשְׁכַּן **mishkan** (Chald.), *mish-kan´;* corresp. to 4908; *residence:*—habitation.

4908. מִשְׁכָּן **mishkân,** *mish-kawn´;* from 7931; a *residence* (includ. a shepherd's *hut,* the *lair* of animals, fig. the *grave;* also the *Temple*); spec. the *Tabernacle* (prop. its wooden walls):—dwelleth, dwelling (place), habitation, tabernacle, tent.

4909. מַשְׂכֹּרֶת **maskôreth,** *mas-koh´-reth;* from 7936; *wages* or a *reward:*—reward, wages.

4910. מָשַׁל **mâshal,** *maw-shal´;* a prim. root; to *rule:*—(have, make to have) dominion, governor, × indeed, reign, (bear, cause to, have) rule (-ing, -r), have power.

4911. מָשַׁל **mâshal,** *maw-shal´;* denom. from 4912; to *liken,* i.e. (trans.) to use figurative language (an allegory, adage, song or the like); intrans. to *resemble:*—be (-come) like, compare, use (as a) proverb, speak (in proverbs), utter.

4912. מָשָׁל **mâshâl,** *maw-shawl´;* appar. from 4910 in some orig. sense of *superiority* in mental action; prop. a pithy *maxim,* usually of a metaphorical nature; hence a *simile* (as an adage, poem, discourse):—byword, like, parable, proverb.

4913. מָשָׁל **Mâshâl,** *maw-shawl´;* for 4861; *Mashal,* a place in Pal.:—Mashal.

4914. מְשֹׁל **m^{e}shôwl,** *mesh-ol´;* from 4911; a *satire:*—byword.

4915. מֹשֶׁל **môshel,** *mo´-shel;* (1) from 4910; *empire;* (2) from 4911; a *parallel:*—dominion, like.

מִשְׁלוֹשׁ **mishlôwsh.** See 7969.

4916. מִשְׁלוֹחַ **mishlôwach,** *mish-lo´-akh;* or מִשְׁלֹחַ **mishlôach,** *mish-lo´-akh;* also מִשְׁלָח **mishlâch,** *mish-lawkh´;* from 7971; a *sending* out, i.e. (abstr.) *presentation* (favorable), or *seizure* (unfavorable); also (concr.) a place of *dismissal,* or a *business* to be discharged:—to lay, to put, sending (forth), to set.

4917. מִשְׁלַחַת **mishlachath,** *mish-lakh´-ath;* fem. of 4916; a *mission,* i.e. (abstr. and favorable) *release,* or (concr. and unfavorable) an *army:*—discharge, sending.

4918. מְשֻׁלָּם **M^{e}shullâm,** *mesh-ool-lawm´;* from 7999; *allied; Meshullam,* the name of seventeen Isr.:—Meshullam.

4919. מְשִׁלֵּמוֹת **M^{e}shillêmôwth,** *mesh-il-lay-mohth´;* plur. from 7999; *reconciliations:—Meshillemoth,* an Isr.:—Meshillemoth. Comp. 4921.

4920. מְשֶׁלֶמְיָה **M^{e}shelemyâh,** *mesh-eh-lem-yaw´;* or מְשֶׁלֶמְיָהוּ **M^{e}shelemyâhûw,** *mesh-eh-lem-yaw´-hoo;* from 7999 and 3050; *ally of Jah; Meshelemjah,* an Isr.:—Meshelemiah.

4921. מְשִׁלֵּמִית **M^{e}shillêmîyth,** *mesh-il-lay-meeth´;* from 7999; *reconciliation; Meshillemith,* an Isr.:—Meshillemith. Comp. 4919.

4922. מְשֻׁלֶּמֶת **M^{e}shullemeth,** *mesh-ool-leh´-meth;* fem. of 4918; *Meshullemeth,* an Israelitess:—Meshullemeth.

4923. מְשַׁמָּה **m^{e}shammâh,** *mesh-am-maw´;* from 8074; a *waste* or *amazement:*—astonishment, desolate.

4924. מַשְׁמָן **mashmân,** *mash-mawn´;* from 8080; *fat,* i.e. (lit. and abstr.) *fatness; but usually (fig. and concr.) a rich* dish, a *fertile* field, a *robust* man:—fat (one, -ness, -test, -test place).

4925. מִשְׁמַנָּה **Mishmannâh,** *mish-man-naw´;* from 8080; *fatness; Mashmannah,* an Isr.:—Mishmannah.

4926. מִשְׁמָע **mishmâʻ,** *mish-maw´;* from 8085; a *report:*—hearing.

4927. מִשְׁמָע **Mishmâʻ,** *mish-maw´;* the same as 4926; *Mishma,* the name of a son of Ishmael, and of an Isr.:—Mishma.

4928. מִשְׁמַעַת **mishmaʻath,** *mish-mah´-ath;* fem. of 4926; *audience,* i.e. the royal *court;* also *obedience,* i.e. (concr.) a *subject:*—bidding, guard, obey.

4929. מִשְׁמָר **mishmâr,** *mish-mawr´;* from 8104; a *guard* (the man, the post, or the *prison*); fig. a *deposit;* also (as observed) a *usage* (abstr.), or an *example* (concr.):—diligence, guard, office, prison, ward, watch.

4930. מַשְׂמְרָה **masm^{e}râh,** *mas-mer-aw´;* for 4548 fem.; a *peg:*—nail.

4931. מִשְׁמֶרֶת **mishmereth,** *mish-meh´-reth;* fem. of 4929; *watch,* i.e. the act *(custody)* or (concr.) the *sentry,* the *post;* obj. *preservation,* or (concr.) *safe;* fig. *observance,* i.e. (abstr.) *duty,* or (obj.) a *usage* or *party:*—charge, keep, to be kept, office, ordinance, safeguard, ward, watch.

4932. מִשְׁנֶה **mishneh,** *mish-neh´;* from 8138; prop. a *repetition,* i.e. a *duplicate* (*copy* of a document), or a *double* (in amount); by impl. a *second* (in order, rank, age, quality or location):—college, copy, double, fatlings, next, second (order), twice as much.

4933. מְשִׁסָּה **m^{e}shiççâh,** *mesh-is-saw´;* from 8155; *plunder:*—booty, spoil.

4934. מִשְׁעוֹל **mishʻôwl,** *mish-ole´;* from the same as 8168; a *hollow,* i.e. a narrow passage:—path.

4935. מִשְׁעִי **mishʻîy,** *mish-ee´;* prob. from 8159; *inspection:*—to supple.

4936. מִשְׁעָם **Mishʻâm,** *mish-awm´;* appar. from 8159; *inspection; Misham,* an Isr.:—Misham.

4937. מִשְׁעֵן **mishʻên,** *mish-ane´;* or מִשְׁעָן **mishʻân,** *mish-awn´;* from 8172; a *support* (concr.), i.e. (fig.) a *protector* or *sustenance:*—stay.

4938. מִשְׁעֵנָה **mishʻênâh,** *mish-ay-naw´;* or מִשְׁעֶנֶת **mishʻeneth,** *mish-eh´-neth;* fem. of 4937; *support* (abstr.). i.e. (fig.) *sustenance* or (concr.) a *walking-stick:*—staff.

4939. מִשְׂפָּח **mispâch,** *mis-pawkh´;* from 5596; *slaughter:*—oppression.

4940. מִשְׁפָּחָה **mishpâchâh,** *mish-paw-khaw´;* from 8192 [comp. 8198]; a *family,* i.e. circle of relatives; fig. a *class* (of persons), a *species* (of animals) or *sort* (of things); by extens. a *tribe or people:*—family, kind (-red).

4941. מִשְׁפָּט **mishpâṭ,** *mish-pawt´;* from 8199; prop. a *verdict* (favorable or unfavorable) pronounced judicially, espec. a *sentence* or formal decree (human or [partic.] divine *law,* individual or collect.), includ. the act, the place, the suit, the crime, and the penalty; abstr. *justice,* includ. a partic. *right,* or *privilege* (statutory or customary), or even a *style:*— + adversary, ceremony, charge, × crime, custom, desert, determination, discretion, disposing, due, fashion, form, to be judged, judgment, just (-ice, -ly), (manner of) law (-ful), manner, measure, (due) order, ordinance, right, sentence, usest, × worthy, + wrong.

4942. מִשְׁפָּת **mishpâth,** *mish-pawth´;* from 8192; a *stall* for cattle (only dual):—burden, sheepfold.

4943. מֶשֶׁק **mesheq,** *meh´-shek;* from an unused root mean. to *hold; possession:*— + steward.

4944. מַשָּׁק **mashshâq,** *mash-shawk´;* from 8264; a *traversing,* i.e. rapid *motion:*—running to and fro.

4945. מַשְׁקֶה **mashqeh,** *mash-keh´;* from 8248; prop. *causing to drink, i.e. a butler;* by impl. (intrans.) *drink* (itself); fig. a *well-watered* region:—butler (-ship), cupbearer, drink (-ing), fat pasture, watered.

4946. מִשְׁקוֹל **mishqôwl,** *mish-kole´;* from 8254; *weight:*—weight.

4947. מַשְׁקוֹף **mashqôwph,** *mash-kofe´;* from 8259 in its orig. sense of *overhanging;* a *lintel:*—lintel, upper door post.

4948. מִשְׁקָל **mishqâl,** *mish-kawl´;* from 8254; *weight* (numerically estimated); hence, *weighing* (the act):—(full) weight.

4949. מִשְׁקֶלֶת **mishqeleth,** *mish-keh´-leth´;* or מִשְׁקֹלֶת **mishqôleth,** *mish-ko´-leth;* fem. of 4948 or 4947; a *weight,* i.e. a *plummet* (with line attached):—plummet.

4950. מִשְׁקָע **mishqâʻ,** *mish-kaw´;* from 8257; a *settling* place (of water), i.e. a pond:—deep.

4951. מִשְׂרָה **misrâh,** *mis-raw´;* from 8280; *empire:*—government.

4952. מִשְׁרָה **mishrâh,** *mish-raw´;* from 8281 in the sense of *loosening; maceration,* i.e. steeped *juice:*—liquor.

4953. מַשְׁרוֹקִי **mashrôwqîy** (Chald.), *mash-ro-kee´;* from a root corresp. to 8319; a (musical) *pipe* (from its *whistling* sound):—flute.

4954. מִשְׁרָעִי **Mishrâʻîy,** *mish-raw-ee´;* patrial from an unused noun from an unused root; prob. mean. to *stretch* out; *extension;* a *Mishraite,* or inhab. (collect.) of Mishra:—Mishraites.

4955. מִשְׂרָפָה **misrâphâh,** *mis-raw-faw´;* from 8813; *combustion,* i.e. *cremation* (of a corpse), or *calcination* (of lime):—burning.

4956. מִשְׂרְפוֹת מַיִם **Misrᵉphôwth mayim,** *mis-ref-ohth´ mah´-yim;* from the plur. of 4955 and 4325; *burnings of water; Misrephoth-Majim,* a place in Pal.:—Misrephoth-mayim.

4957. מַשְׂרֵקָה **Masrêqâh,** *mas-ray-kaw´;* a form for 7796 used denom.; *vineyard; Masrekah,* a place in Idumæa:—Masrekah.

4958. מַשְׂרֵת **masrêth,** *mas-rayth´;* appar. from an unused root mean. to *perforate,* i.e. hollow out, a *pan:*—pan.

4959. מָשַׁשׁ **mâshash,** *maw-shash´;* a prim. root; to *feel* of; by impl. to *grope:*—feel, grope, search.

4960. מִשְׁתֶּה **mishteh,** *mish-teh´;* from 8354; *drink;* by impl. *drinking* (the act); also (by impl.), a *banquet* or (gen.) feast:—banquet, drank, drink, feast ([-ed], -ing).

4961. מִשְׁתֵּה **mishteh** (Chald.), *mish-teh´;* corresp. to 4960; a *banquet:*—banquet.

4962. מַת **math,** *math;* from the same as 4970; prop. an *adult* (as of full length); by impl. a *man* (only in the plur.):— + few, × friends, men, persons, × small.

4963. מַתְבֵּן **mathbên,** *math-bane´;* denom. from 8401; *straw* in the heap:—straw.

4964. מֶתֶג **metheg,** *meh´-theg;* from an unused root mean. to *curb;* a *bit:*—bit, bridle.

4965. מֶתֶג הָאַמָּה **Metheg hâ-'Ammâh,** *meh´-theg haw-am-maw´;* from 4964 and 520 with the art. interposed; *bit of the metropolis; Metheg-ha-Ammah* an epithet of Gath:—Metheg-ammah.

4966. מָתוֹק **mâthôwq,** *maw-thoke´;* or מָתוּק **mâthûwq,** *maw-thook´;* from 4985; *sweet:*—sweet (-er, -ness).

4967. מְתוּשָׁאֵל **Mᵉthûwshâ'êl,** *meth-oo-shaw-ale´;* from 4962 and 410, with the rel. interposed; *man who* (is) *of God; Methushaël,* an antediluvian patriarch:—Methusael.

4968. מְתוּשֶׁלַח **Mᵉthûwshelach,** *meth-oo-sheh´-lakh;* from 4962 and 7973; *man of a dart; Methushelach,* an antediluvian patriarch:—Methuselah.

4969. מָתַח **mâthach,** *maw-thakh´;* a prim. root; to *stretch* out:—spread out.

4970. מָתַי **mâthay,** *maw-thah´ee;* from an unused root mean. to *extend;* prop. *extent* (of time); but used only adv. (espec. with other particles pref.), *when* (either rel. or interrog.):—long, when.

מְתִים **mᵉthîym.** See 4962.

4971. מַתְכֹּנֶת **mathkôneth,** *math-ko´-neth;* or מַתְכֻּנֶת **mathkûneth,** *math-koo´-neth;* from 8505 in the transferred sense of *measuring; proportion* (in size, number or ingredients):—composition, measure, state, tale.

4972. מַתְּלָאָה **mattᵉlâ'âh,** *mat-tel-aw-aw´;* from 4100 and 8513; *what a trouble!:*—what a weariness.

4973. מְתַלְּעָה **mᵉthallᵉʻâh,** *meth-al-leh-aw´;* contr. from 3216; prop. a *biter,* i.e. a *tooth:*—cheek (jaw) tooth, jaw.

4974. מְתֹם **mᵉthôm,** *meth-ohm´;* from 8552; *wholesomeness;* also (adv.) *completely:*—men [*by reading* 4962], soundness.

מֶתֶן **Methen.** See 4981.

4975. מֹתֶן **môthen,** *mo´-then;* from an unused root mean. to *be slender;* prop. the *waist* or small of the back; only in plur. the *loins:*— + greyhound, loins, side.

4976. מַתָּן **mattân,** *mat-tawn´;* from 5414; a *present:*—gift, to give, reward.

4977. מַתָּן **Mattân,** *mat-tawn´;* the same as 4976; *Mattan,* the name of a priest of Baal, and of an Isr.:—Mattan.

4978. מַתְּנָא **mattᵉnâ'** (Chald.), *mat-ten-aw´;* corresp. to 4979:—gift.

4979. מַתָּנָה **mâttânâh,** *mat-taw-naw´;* fem. of 4976; a *present;* spec. (in a good sense) a sacrificial *offering,* (in a bad sense) a *bribe:*—gift.

4980. מַתָּנָה **Mattânâh,** *mat-taw-naw´;* the same as 4979; *Mattanah,* a place in the Desert:—Mattanah.

4981. מִתְנִי **Mithnîy,** *mith-nee´;* prob. patrial from an unused noun mean. *slenderness;* a *Mithnite,* or inhab. of Methen:—Mithnite.

4982. מַתְּנַי **Mattᵉnay,** *mat-ten-ah´ee;* from 4976; *liberal; Mattenai,* the name of three Isr.:—Mattenai.

4983. מַתַּנְיָה **Mattanyâh,** *mat-tan-yaw´;* or מַתַּנְיָהוּ **Mattanyâhûw,** *mat-tan-yaw´-hoo;* from 4976 and 3050; *gift of Jah; Mattanjah,* the name of ten Isr.:—Mattaniah.

מָתְנַיִם **mothnayim.** See 4975.

4984. מִתְנַשֵּׂא **mithnassê'**, *mith-nas-say´*; from 5375; (used as abstr.) supreme *exaltation:*—exalted.

4985. מָתַק **mâthaq**, *maw-thak´*; a prim. root; to *suck;* by impl. to *relish,* or (intrans.) *be sweet:*—be (made, × take) sweet.

4986. מֶתֶק **metheq**, *meh´-thek;* from 4985; fig. *pleasantness* (of discourse):—sweetness.

4987. מֹתֶק **môtheq**, *mo´-thek;* from 4985; *sweetness;*—sweetness.

4988. מָתָק **mâthâq**, *maw-thawk´; from 4985; a dainty,* i.e. (gen.) *food:*—feed sweetly.

4989. מִתְקָה **Mithqâh**, *mith-kaw´;* fem. of 4987; *sweetness; Mithkah,* a place in the Desert:—Mithcah.

4990. מִתְרְדָת **Mithrᵉdâth**, *mith-red-awth´;* of Pers. origin; *Mithredath,* the name of two Persians:—Mithredath.

4991. מַתָּת **mattâth**, *mat-tawth´;* fem. of 4976 abbrev.; a *present:*—gift, reward.

4992. מַתַּתָּה **Mattattâh**, *mat-tat-taw´;* for 4993; *gift of Jah; Mattattah,* an Isr.:—Mattathah.

4993. מַתִּתְיָה **Mattithyâh**, *mat-tith-yaw* or מַתִּתְיָהוּ **Mattithyâhûw**, *mat-tith-yaw´-hoo;* from 4991 and 3050; *gift of Jah; Mattithjah,* the name of four Isr.:—Mattithiah.

נ

4994. נָא **nâ'**, *naw;* a prim. particle of incitement and entreaty, which may usually be rendered *I pray, now* or *then;* added mostly to verbs (in the Imperat. or Fut.), or to interj., occasionally to an adv. or conj.:—I beseech (pray) thee (you), go to, now, oh.

4995. נָא **nâ'**, *naw;* appar. from 5106 in the sense of *harshness* from refusal; prop. *tough,* i.e. *uncooked* (flesh):—raw.

4996. נֹא **Nô'**, *no;* of Eg. origin; *No* (i.e. *Thebes*), the capital of Upper Egypt:—No. Comp. 528.

4997. נֹאד **nô'd**, *node;* or נֹאוד **nô'wd**, *node;* also (fem.) נֹאדָה **nô'dâh**, *no-daw´;* from an unused root of uncert. signif.; a (skin or leather) *bag* (for fluids):—bottle.

נְאַדְרַי **ne'dârîy.** See 142.

4998. נָאָה **nâ'âh**, *naw-aw´;* a prim. root; prop. to *be at home,* i.e. (by impl.) to be *pleasant* (or *suitable*), i.e. *beautiful:*—be beautiful, become, be comely.

4999. נָאָה **nâ'âh**, *naw-aw´;* from 4998; a *home;* fig. a *pasture:*—habitation, house, pasture, pleasant place.

5000. נָאוֶה **nâ'veh**, *naw-veh´;* from 4998 or 5116; *suitable,* or *beautiful:*—becometh, comely, seemly.

5001. נָאַם **nâ'am**, *naw-am´;* a prim. root; prop. to *whisper,* i.e. (by impl.) to *utter* as an oracle:—say.

5002. נְאֻם **nᵉ'ûm**, *neh-oom´;* from 5001; an *oracle:*—(hath) said, saith.

5003. נָאַף **nâ'aph**, *naw-af´;* a prim. root; to *commit adultery;* fig. to *apostatize:*—adulterer (-ess), commit (-ing) adultery, woman that breaketh wedlock.

5004. נִאֻף **nî'ûph**, *nee-oof´;* from 5003; *adultery:*—adultery.

5005. נַאֲפוּף **na'ăphûwph**, *nah-af-oof´;* from 5003; *adultery:*—adultery.

5006. נָאַץ **nâ'ats**, *naw-ats´;* a prim. root; to *scorn;* or (Eccles. 12 : 5); by interch. for 5132, to *bloom:*—abhor, (give occasion to) blaspheme, contemn, despise, flourish, × great, provoke.

5007. נְאָצָה **nᵉ'âtsâh**, *neh-aw-tsaw´;* or נֶאָצָה **ne'âtsâh**, *neh-aw-tsaw´;* from 5006; *scorn:*—blasphemy.

5008. נָאַק **nâ'aq**, *naw-ak´;* a prim. root; to *groan:*—groan.

5009. נְאָקָה **nᵉ'âqâh**, *neh-aw-kaw´;* from 5008; a *groan:*—groaning.

5010. נָאַר **nâ'ar**, *naw-ar´;* a prim. root; to *reject:*—abhor, make void.

5011. נֹב **Nôb**, *nobe;* the same as 5108; *fruit; Nob,* a place in Pal.:—Nob.

5012. נָבָא **nâbâ'**, *naw-baw´;* a prim. root; to *prophesy,* i.e. speak (or sing) by inspiration (in prediction or simple discourse):—prophesy (-ing) make self a prophet.

5013. נְבָא **nᵉbâ'** (Chald.), *neb-aw´;* corresp. to 5012:—prophesy.

5014. נָבַב **nâbab**, *naw-bab´;* a prim. root; to *pierce;* to *be hollow,* or (fig.) *foolish:*—hollow, vain.

5015. נְבוֹ **Nᵉbôw**, *neb-o´;* prob. of for. der.; *Nebo,* the name of a Bab. deity, also of a mountain in Moab, and of a place in Pal.:—Nebo.

5016. נְבוּאָה **nᵉbûw'âh**, *neb-oo-aw´;* from 5012; a *prediction* (spoken or written):—prophecy.

5017. נְבוּאָה **nᵉbûw'âh** (Chald.), *neb-oo-aw;* corresp. to 5016; inspired *teaching:*—prophesying.

5018. נְבוּזַרְאֲדָן **Nᵉbûwzarădân**, *neb-oo-zar-ad-awn´;* of for. or.; *Nebuzaradan,* a Bab. general:—Nebuzaradan.

5019. נְבוּכַדְנֶאצַּר **Nᵉbûwkadne'tstsar**, *neb-oo-kad-nets-tsar´;* or נְבֻכַדְנֶאצַּר **Nᵉbûkadne'tstsar** (2 Kings 24 : 1, 10), *neb-oo-kad-nets-tsar´;* or נְבוּכַדְנֶצַּר **Nᵉbûwkadnetstsar** (Esth. 2 : 6; Dan. 1 : 18), *neb-oo-kad-nets-tsar´;* or נְבוּכַדְרֶאצַּר **Nᵉbûwkadre'tstsar**, *neb-oo-kad-rets-tsar´;* or נְבוּכַדְרֶאצּוֹר° **Nᵉbûwkadre'tstsôwr** (Ezra 2 : 1; Jer. 49 : 28), *neb-oo-kad-rets-tsore´;* of for. der.; *Nebukadnetstsar* (or *-retstar,* or *-retstsor*), king of Babylon—Nebuchadnezzar, Nebuchadrezzar.

5020. נְבוּכַדְנֶצַּר **Nᵉbûwkadnetstsar** (Chald.), *neb-oo-kad-nets-tsar´;* corresp. to 5019:—Nebuchadnezzar.

5021. נְבוּשַׁזְבָּן **Nᵉbûwshazbân**, *neb-oo-shaz-bawn´;* of for. der.; *Nebushazban,* Nebuchadnezzar's chief eunuch:—Nebushazban.

5022. נָבוֹת **Nâbôwth**, *naw-both´;* fem. plur. from the same as 5011; *fruits; Naboth,* an Isr.:—Naboth.

5023. נְבִזְבָּה **nᵉbizbâh** (Chald), *neb-iz-baw´;* of uncert. der.; a *largess:*—reward.

5024. נָבַח **nâbach**, *naw-bakh´;* a prim. root; to *bark* (as a dog):—bark.

5025. נֹבַח **Nôbach**, *no´-bach;* from 5024; a *bark; Nobach,* the name of an Isr., and of a place E. of the Jordan:—Nobah.

5026. נִבְחַז **Nibchaz**, *nib-khaz´;* of for. or.; *Nibchaz,* a deity of the Avites:—Nibhaz.

5027. נָבַט **nâbaṭ**, *naw-bat´;* a prim. root; to *scan,* i.e. look intently at; by impl. to *regard* with pleasure, favor or care:—(cause to) behold, consider, look (down), regard, have respect, see.

5028. נְבָט **Nᵉbâṭ**, *neb-awt´;* from 5027; *regard; Nebat,* the father of Jeroboam I:—Nebat.

5029. נְבִיא **nᵉbîy'** (Chald.), *neb-ee´;* corresp. to 5030; a *prophet:*—prophet.

5030. נָבִיא **nâbîy'**, *naw-bee´;* from 5012; a *prophet* or (gen.) *inspired* man:—prophecy, that prophesy, prophet.

5031. נְבִיאָה **nᵉbîy'âh**, *neb-ee-yaw´;* fem. of 5030; a *prophetess* or (gen.) *inspired* woman; by impl. a *poetess;* by association a *prophet's wife:*—prophetess.

5032. נְבָיוֹת **Nᵉbâyôwth**, *neb-aw-yoth´;* or נְבָיֹת **Nᵉbâyôth**, *neb-aw-yoth´;* fem. plur. from 5107; *fruitfulness; Nebajoth,* a son of Ishmael, and the country settled by him:—Nebaioth, Nebajoth.

5033. נֵבֶךְ **nêbek**, *nay´-bek;* from an unused root mean. to *burst* forth; a *fountain:*—spring.

5034. נָבֵל **nâbêl**, *naw-bale´;* a prim. root; to *wilt;* gen. to *fall* away, *fail, faint;* fig. to *be foolish* or (mor.) *wicked;* causat. to *despise, disgrace:*—disgrace, dishonour, lightly esteem, fade (away, -ing), fall (down, -ling, off), do foolishly, come to nought, × surely, make vile, wither.

5035. נֶבֶל **nebel**, *neh´-bel;* or נֵבֶל **nêbel**, *nay´-bel;* from 5034; a skin-*bag* for liquids (from *collapsing* when empty); hence, a *vase* (as similar in shape when full); also a *lyre* (as having a body of like form):—bottle, pitcher, psaltery, vessel, viol.

5036. נָבָל **nâbâl**, *na-bawl´;* from 5034; *stupid; wicked* (espec. *impious*):—fool (-ish, -ish man, -ish woman), vile person.

5037. נָבָל **Nâbâl**, *naw-bawl´;* the same as 5036; *dolt; Nabal,* an Isr.:—Nabal.

5038. נְבֵלָה **nᵉbêlâh**, *neb-ay-law´;* from 5034; a *flabby* thing, i.e. a *carcase* or *carrion* (human or bestial, often collect.); fig. an *idol:*— (dead) body, (dead) carcase, dead of itself, which died, (beast) that (which) dieth of itself.

5039. נְבָלָה **n^{e}bâlâh,** *neb-aw-law´;* fem of 5036; *foolishness,* i.e. (mor.) *wickedness;* concr. a *crime;* by extens. *punishment:*—folly, vile, villany.

5040. נַבְלוּת **nablûwth,** *nab-looth´;* from 5036; prop. *disgrace,* i.e. the (female) *pudenda:*—lewdness.

5041. נְבַלָּט **N^{e}ballâṭ,** *neb-al-lawt´;* appar. from 5036 and 3909; *foolish secrecy; Neballat,* a place in Pal.:—Neballat.

5042. נָבַע **nâba',** *naw-bah´;* a prim. root; to *gush* forth; fig. to *utter* (good or bad words); spec. to *emit* (a foul odor):—belch out, flowing, pour out, send forth, utter (abundantly).

5043. נֶבְרְשָׁא **nebr^{e}shâ'** (Chald.), *neb-reh-shaw´;* from an unused root mean. to *shine;* a *light;* plur. (collect.) a *chandelier:*—candlestick.

5044. נִבְשָׁן **Nibshân,** *nib-shawn´;* of uncert. der.; *Nibshan,* a place in Pal.:—Nibshan.

5045. נֶגֶב **negeb,** *neh´-gheb;* from an unused root mean. to *be parched;* the *south* (from its drought); spec. the *Negeb* or southern district of Judah, occasionally, *Egypt* (as south to Pal.):—south (country, side, -ward).

5046. נָגַד **nâgad,** *naw-gad´;* a prim. root; prop. to *front,* i.e. stand boldly out opposite; by impl. (causat.), to *manifest;* fig. to *announce* (always by word of mouth to one present); spec. to *expose, predict, explain, praise:*—bewray, × certainly, certify, declare (-ing), denounce, expound, × fully, messenger, plainly, profess, rehearse, report, shew (forth), speak, × surely, tell, utter.

5047. נְגַד **n^{e}gad** (Chald.), *neg-ad´;* corresp. to 5046; to *flow* (through the idea of *clearing* the way):—issue.

5048. נֶגֶד **neged,** *neh´-ghed;* from 5046; a *front,* i.e. part opposite; spec. a *counterpart,* or mate; usually (adv., espec. with prep.) *over against* or *before:*—about, (over) against, × aloof, × far (off), × from, over, presence, × other side, sight, × to view.

5049. נֶגֶד **neged** (Chald.), *neh´-ghed;* corresp. to 5048; *opposite:*—toward.

5050. נָגַהּ **nâgahh,** *naw-găh´;* a prim. root; to *glitter;* causat. to *illuminate:*—(en-) lighten, (cause to) shine.

5051. נֹגַהּ **nôgahh,** *no´-găh;* from 5050; *brilliancy* (lit. or fig.):—bright (-ness), light, (clear) shining.

5052. נֹגַהּ **Nôgahh,** *no´-găh;* the same as 5051; *Nogah,* a son of David:—Nogah.

5053. נֹגַהּ **nôgahh** (Chald.), *no´-găh;* corresp. to 5051; *dawn:*—morning.

5054. נְגֹהָה **n^{e}gôhâh,** *neg-o-haw´;* fem. of 5051; *splendor:*—brightness.

5055. נָגַח **nâgach,** *naw-gakh´;* a prim. root; to *but* with the horns; fig. to *war* against:—gore, push (down, -ing).

5056. נַגָּח **naggâch,** *nag-gawkh´;* from 5055; *butting,* i.e. *vicious:*—used (wont) to push.

5057. נָגִיד **nâgîyd,** *naw-gheed´;* or נָגִד **nâgîd,** *naw-gheed´;* from 5046; a *commander* (as occupying the *front*), civil, military or religious; gen. (abstr. plur.); *honorable* themes:—captain, chief, excellent thing, (chief) governor, leader, noble, prince, (chief) ruler.

5058. נְגִינָה **n^{e}gîynâh,** *neg-ee-naw´;* or נְגִינַת **n^{e}gîynath** (Psa. 61 : title), *neg-ee-nath´;* from 5059; prop. instrumental *music;* by impl. a stringed *instrument;* by extens. a *poem* set to music; spec. an *epigram:*—stringed instrument, musick, Neginoth [*plur.*], song.

5059. נָגַן **nâgan,** *naw-gan´;* a prim. root; prop. to *thrum,* i.e. *beat* a tune with the fingers; espec. to *play* on a stringed instrument; hence (gen.) to *make music:*—player on instruments, sing to the stringed instruments, melody, ministrel, play (-er. -ing).

5060. נָגַע **nâga',** *naw-gah´;* a prim. root; prop. to *touch,* i.e. *lay the hand upon* (for any purpose; euphem., to *lie with* a woman); by impl. to *reach* (fig. to *arrive, acquire*); violently, to *strike* (punish, defeat, destroy, etc.):—beat, (× be able to) bring (down), cast, come (nigh), draw near (nigh), get up, happen, join, near, plague, reach (up), smite, strike, touch.

5061. נֶגַע **nega',** *neh´-gah;* from 5060; a *blow* (fig. *infliction*); also (by impl.) a *spot* (concr. a *leprous* person or dress):—plague, sore, stricken, stripe, stroke, wound.

5062. נָגַף **nâgaph,** *naw-gaf´;* a prim. root; to *push, gore, defeat, stub* (the toe), *inflict* (a disease):—beat, dash, hurt, plague, slay, smite (down), strike, stumble, × surely, put to the worse.

5063. נֶגֶף **negeph,** *neh´-ghef;* from 5062; a *trip* (of the foot); fig. an *infliction* (of disease):—plague, stumbling.

5064. נָגַר **nâgar,** *naw-gar´;* a prim. root; to *flow;* fig. to *stretch* out; causat. to *pour* out or down; fig. to *deliver* over:—fall, flow away, pour down (out), run, shed, split, trickle down.

5065. נָגַשׂ **nâgas,** *naw-gas´;* a prim. root; to *drive* (an animal, a workman, a debtor, an army); by impl. to *tax, harass, tyrannize:*—distress, driver, exact (-or), oppress (-or), × raiser of taxes, taskmaster.

5066. נָגַשׁ **nâgash,** *naw-gash´;* a prim. root; to *be* or *come* (causat. *bring*) *near* (for any purpose); euphem. to *lie with* a woman; as an enemy, to *attack;* relig. to *worship;* causat. to *present;* fig. to *adduce* an argument; by reversal, to *stand back:*—(make to) approach (nigh), bring (forth, hither, near), (cause to) come (higher, near, nigh), give place, go hard (up), (be, draw, go) near (nigh), offer, overtake, present, put, stand.

5067. נֵד **nêd,** *nade;* from 5110 in the sense of *piling* up; a *mound,* i.e. *wave:*—heap.

5068. נָדַב **nâdab,** *naw-dab´;* a prim. root; to *impel;* hence to *volunteer* (as a soldier), to *present* spontaneously:—offer freely, be (give, make, offer self) willing (-ly).

5069. נְדַב **n^{e}dab** (Chald.), *ned-ab´;* corresp. to 5068; *be* (or *give*) *liberal (-ly):*—(be minded of . . . own) freewill (offering), offer freely (willingly).

5070. נָדָב **Nâdâb,** *naw-dawb´;* from 5068; *liberal; Nadab,* the name of four Isr.:—Nadab.

5071. נְדָבָה **n^{e}dâbâh,** *ned-aw-baw´;* from 5068; prop. (abstr.) *spontaneity,* or (adj.) *spontaneous; also (concr.) a spontaneous* or (by infer., in plur.) *abundant* gift:—free (-will) offering, freely, plentiful, voluntary (-ily, offering), willing (-ly, offering).

5072. נְדַבְיָה **N^{e}dabyâh,** *ned-ab-yaw´;* from 5068 and 3050; *largess of Jah; Nedabjah,* an Isr.:—Nedabiah.

5073. נִדְבָּךְ **nidbâk** (Chald.), *nid-bawk´;* from a root mean. to *stick;* a *layer* (of building materials):—row.

5074. נָדַד **nâdad,** *naw-dad´;* a prim. root; prop. to *wave* to and fro (rarely to *flap* up and down); fig. to *rove, flee,* or (caus.) to *drive* away:—chase (away), × could not, depart, flee (× apace, away), (re-) move, thrust away, wander (abroad, -er, -ing).

5075. נְדַד **n^{e}dad** (Chald.), *ned-ad´;* corresp. to 5074; to *depart:*—go from.

5076. נָדֻד **nâdûd,** *naw-dood´;* pass. part. of 5074; prop. *tossed;* abstr. a *rolling* (on the bed):—tossing to and fro.

5077. נָדָה **nâdâh,** *naw-daw´;* or נָדָא° **nâdâ'** (2 Kings 17 : 21), *naw-daw´;* a prim. root; prop. to *toss;* fig. to *exclude,* i.e. banish, postpone, prohibit:—cast out, drive, put far away.

5078. נֵדֶה **nêdeh,** *nay´-deh;* from 5077 in the sense of freely *flinging* money; a *bounty* (for prostitution):—gifts.

5079. נִדָּה **niddâh,** *nid-daw´;* from 5074; prop. *rejection;* by impl. *impurity,* espec. personal (menstruation) or moral (idolatry, incest):— × far, filthiness, × flowers, menstruous (woman), put apart, × removed (woman), separation, set apart, unclean (-ness, thing, with filthiness).

5080. נָדַח **nâdach,** *naw-dakh´;* a prim. root; to push *off;* used in a great variety of applications, lit. and fig. (to expel, mislead, strike, inflict, etc.):—banish, bring, cast down (out), chase, compel, draw away, drive (away, out, quite), fetch a stroke, force, go away, outcast, thrust away (out), withdraw.

5081. נָדִיב **nâdîyb,** *naw-deeb´;* from 5068; prop. *voluntary,* i.e. generous; hence, *magnanimous;* as noun, a *grandee* (sometimes a *tyrant*):—free, liberal (things), noble, prince, willing ([hearted]).

5082. נְדִיבָה **n^{e}dîybâh,** *ned-ee-baw´;* fem. of 5081; prop. *nobility,* i.e. reputation:—soul.

5083. נָדָן **nâdân,** *naw-dawn´;* prob. from an unused root mean. to *give;* a *present* (for prostitution):—gift.

5084. נָדָן **nâdân,** *naw-dawn´;* of uncert. der.; a *sheath* (of a sword):—sheath.

5085. נִדְנֶה **nidneh** (Chald.), *nid-neh´;* from the same as 5084; a *sheath;* fig. the *body* (as the receptacle of the soul):—body.

5086. נָדַף **nâdaph,** *naw-daf´;* a prim. root; to *shove* asunder, i.e. *disperse:*—drive (away, to and fro), thrust down, shaken, tossed to and fro.

5087. נָדַר **nâdar,** *naw-dar´;* a prim. root; to *promise* (pos., to do or give something to God):—(make a) vow.

5088. נֶדֶר **neder,** *neh´-der;* or נֵדֶר **nêder,** *nay´-der;* from 5087; a *promise* (to God); also (concr.) a thing *promised:*—vow ([-ed]).

5089. נֹהַּ **nôahh,** *no´-ăh;* from an unused root mean. to *lament; lamentation:*—wailing.

5090. נָהַג **nâhag,** *naw-hag´;* a prim. root; to *drive* forth (a person, an animal or chariot), i.e. *lead, carry away;* reflex. to *proceed* (i.e. impel or guide oneself); also (from the *panting* induced by effort), to *sigh:*—acquaint, bring (away), carry away, drive (away), lead (away, forth), (be) guide, lead (away, forth).

5091. נָהָה **nâhâh,** *naw-haw´;* a prim. root; to *groan,* i.e. *bewail;* hence (through the idea of *crying* aloud) to *assemble* (as if on proclamation):—lament, wail.

5092. נְהִי **n**e**hîy,** *neh-hee´;* from 5091; an *elegy:*—lamentation, wailing.

5093. נִהְיָה **nihyâh,** *nih-yaw´;* fem. of 5092; *lamentation:*—doleful.

5094. נְהִיר° **n**e**hîyr** (Chald.), *neh-heere´;* or נְהִירוּ **n**e**hîyrûw** (Chald.), *neh-hee-roo´;* from the same as 5105; *illumination,* i.e. (fig.) wisdom:—light.

5095. נָהַל **nâhal,** *naw-hal´;* a prim. root; prop. to run with a *sparkle,* i.e. *flow;* hence (trans.) to *conduct,* and (by infer.) to *protect, sustain:*—carry, feed, guide, lead (gently, on).

5096. נַהֲלָל **Nahălâl,** *năh-hal-awl´;* or נַהֲלֹל **Nahălôl,** *năh-hal-ole´;* the same as 5097; *Nahalal* or *Nahalol,* a place in Pal.:—Nahalal, Nahallal, Nahalol.

5097. נַהֲלֹל **nahălôl,** *năh-hal-ole´;* from 5095; *pasture:*—bush.

5098. נָהַם **nâham,** *naw-ham´;* a prim. root; to *growl:*—mourn, roar (-ing).

5099. נַהַם **naham,** *năh´-ham;* from 5098; a *snarl:*—roaring.

5100. נְהָמָה **n**e**hâmâh,** *neh-haw-maw´;* fem. of 5099; *snarling:*—disquietness, roaring.

5101. נָהַק **nâhaq,** *naw-hak´;* a prim. root; to *bray* (as an ass), *scream* (from hunger):—bray.

5102. נָהַר **nâhar,** *naw-har´;* a prim. root; to *sparkle,* i.e. (fig.) *be cheerful;* hence (from the *sheen* of a running stream) to *flow,* i.e. (fig.) *assemble:*—flow (together), be lightened.

5103. נְהַר **n**e**har** (Chald.), *neh-har´;* from a root corresp. to 5102; a *river,* espec. the Euphrates:—river, stream.

5104. נָהָר **nâhâr,** *naw-hawr´;* from 5102; a *stream* (includ. the *sea;* espec. the Nile, Euphrates, etc.); fig., *prosperity:*—flood, river.

5105. נְהָרָה **n**e**hârâh,** *neh-haw-raw´;* from 5102 in its orig. sense; *daylight:*—light.

5106. נוּא **nûw',** *noo;* a prim. root; to *refuse, forbid, dissuade,* or *neutralize:*—break, disallow, discourage, make of none effect.

5107. נוּב **nûwb,** *noob;* a prim. root; to *germinate,* i.e. (fig.) to (causat. *make*) *flourish;* also (of words), to *utter:*—bring forth (fruit), make cheerful, increase.

5108. נוֹב° **nôwb,** *nobe;* or נֵיב **nêyb,** *nabe;* from 5107; *produce,* lit, or fig.:—fruit.

5109. נוֹבַי° **Nôwbay,** *no-bah´ee;* from 5108; *fruitful; Nobai,* an Isr.:—Nebai [*from the marg.*].

5110. נוּד **nûwd,** *nood;* a prim. root; to *nod,* i.e. waver, fig. to *wander, flee, disappear;* also (from *shaking* the head in sympathy), to *console, deplore,* or (from *tossing* the head in scorn) *taunt:*—bemoan, flee, get, mourn, make to move, take pity, remove, shake, skip for joy, be sorry, vagabond, way, wandering.

5111. נוּד **nûwd** (Chald.), *nood;* corresp. to 5116; to *flee:*—get away.

5112. נוֹד **nôwd,** *node* [only defect. נֹד **nôd,** *node*]; from 5110; *exile:*—wandering.

5113. נוֹד **Nôwd,** *node;* the same as 5112; *vagrancy; Nod,* the land of Cain:—Nod.

5114. נוֹדָב **Nôwdâb,** *no-dawb´;* from 5068; *noble; Nodab,* an Arab tribe:—Nodab.

5115. נָוָה **nâvâh,** *naw-vaw´;* a prim. root; to *rest* (as at home); causat. (through the implied idea of *beauty* [comp. 5116]), to *celebrate* (with praises):—keep at home, prepare an habitation.

5116. נָוֶה **nâveh,** *naw-veh´;* or (fem.) נָוָה **nâvâh,** *naw-vaw´;* from 5115; (adj.) *at home;* hence (by impl. of satisfaction) *lovely;* also (noun) a *home,* of God (temple), men (residence), flocks (pasture), or wild animals *(den):*—comely, dwelling (place), fold, habitation, pleasant place, sheepcote, stable, tarried.

5117. נוּחַ **nûwach,** *noo´-akh;* a prim. root; to *rest,* i.e. *settle* down; used in a great variety of applications, lit. and fig., intrans., trans. and causat. (to *dwell, stay, let fall, place, let alone, withdraw, give comfort,* etc.):—cease, be confederate, lay, let down, (be) quiet, remain, (cause to, be at, give, have, make to) rest, set down. Comp. 3241.

5118. נוּחַ **nûwach,** *noo´-akh;* or נוֹחַ **nôwach,** *no´-akh;* from 5117; *quiet:*—rest (-ed, -ing place).

5119. נוֹחָה **Nôwchâh,** *no-chaw´;* fem. of 5118; *quietude; Nochah,* an Isr.:—Nohah.

5120. נוּט **nûwṭ,** *noot;* to *quake:*—be moved.

5121. נָוִית° **Nâvîyth,** *naw-veeth´;* from 5115; *residence; Navith,* a place in Pal.:—Naioth [*from the marg.*].

5122. נְוָלוּ **n**e**vâlûw** (Chald.), *nev-aw-loo´;* or נְוָלִי **n**e**vâlîy** (Chald), *nev-aw-lee´;* from an unused root prob. mean. to be *foul;* a *sink:*—dunghill.

5123. נוּם **nûwm,** *noom;* a prim. root; to *slumber* (from drowsiness):—sleep, slumber.

5124. נוּמָה **nûwmâh,** *noo-maw´;* from 5123; *sleepiness:*—drowsiness.

5125. נוּן **nûwn,** *noon;* a prim. root; to *resprout,* i.e. propagate by shoots; fig. to *be perpetual:*—be continued.

5126. נוּן **Nûwn,** *noon;* or נוֹן **Nôwn** (1 Chron. 7 : 27), *nohn;* from 5125; *perpetuity; Nun* or *Non,* the father of Joshua:—Non, Nun.

5127. נוּס **nûwç,** *noos;* a prim. root; to *flit,* i.e. *vanish* away (subside, escape; causat. chase, impel, deliver):— × abate, away, be displayed, (make to) flee (away, -ing), put to flight, × hide, lift up a standard.

5128. נוּעַ **nûwaʻ,** *noo´-ah;* a prim. root; to *waver,* in a great variety of applications, lit. and fig. (as subjoined):—continually, fugitive, × make to [go] up and down, be gone away, (be) move (-able, -d), be promoted, reel, remove, scatter, set, shake, sift, stagger, to and fro, be vagabond, wag, (make) wander (up and down).

5129. נוֹעַדְיָה **Nôwʻadyâh,** *no-ad-yaw´;* from 3259 and 3050; *convened of Jah; Noädjah,* the name of an Isr., and a false prophetess:—Noadiah.

5130. נוּף **nûwph,** *noof;* a prim. root; to *quiver* (i.e. *vibrate* up and down, or *rock* to and fro); used in a great variety of applications (includ. sprinkling, beckoning, rubbing, bastinadoing, sawing, waving, etc.):—lift up, move, offer, perfume, send, shake, sift, strike, wave.

5131. נוֹף **nôwph,** *nofe;* from 5130; *elevation:*—situation. Comp. 5297.

5132. נוּץ **nûwts,** *noots;* a prim. root; prop. to *flash;* hence, to *blossom* (from the brilliancy of color); also, to *fly* away (from the quickness of motion):—flee away, bud (forth).

5133. נוֹצָה **nôwtsâh,** *no-tsaw´;* or נֹצָה **nôtsâh,** *no-tsaw´;* fem. act. part. of 5327 in the sense of *flying;* a *pinion* (or wing feather); often (collect.) *plunge:*—feather (-s), ostrich.

5134. נוּק **nûwq,** *nook;* a prim. root; to *suckle:*—nurse.

5135. נוּר **nûwr** (Chald.), *noor;* from an unused root (corresp. to that of 5216) mean. to *shine; fire:*—fiery, fire.

5136. נוּשׁ **nûwsh,** *noosh;* a prim. root; to *be sick,* i.e. (fig.) *distressed:*—be full of heaviness.

5137. נָזָה **nâzâh,** *naw-zaw´;* a prim. root; to *spirt,* i.e. *besprinkle* (espec. in expiation):—sprinkle.

5138. נָזִיד **nâzîyd,** *naw-zeed´;* from 2102; something *boiled,* i.e. *soup:*—pottage.

5139. נָזִיר **nâzîyr,** *naw-zeer´;* or נָזִר **nâzîr,** *naw-zeer´;* from 5144; *separate,* i.e. consecrated (as *prince,* a *Nazirite*); hence (fig. from the latter) an *unpruned* vine (like an unshorn Nazirite):—Nazarite [*by a false alliteration with Nazareth*], separate (-d), vine undressed.

5140. נָזַל **nâzal,** *naw-zal´;* a prim. root; to *drip,* or *shed* by trickling:—distil, drop, flood, (cause to) flow (-ing), gush out, melt, pour (down), running water, stream.

5141. נֶזֶם **nezem,** *neh´-zem;* from an unused root of uncert. mean.; a nose-*ring;*—earring, jewel.

5142. נְזַק **nᵉzaq** (Chald.), *nez-ak´;* corresp. to the root of 5143; to *suffer* causat. *inflict*) *loss:*—have (en-) damage, hurt (-ful).

5143. נֵזֶק **nêzeq,** *nay´-zek;* from an unused root mean. to *injure; loss:*—damage.

5144. נָזַר **nâzar,** *naw-zar´;* a prim. root; to *hold aloof,* i.e. (intrans.) *abstain* (from food and drink, from impurity, and even from divine worship [i.e. *apostatize*]); spec. to *set apart* (to sacred purposes), i.e. *devote:*—consecrate, separate (-ing, self).

5145. נֶזֶר **nezer,** *neh´-zer;* or נֵזֶר **nêzer,** *nay´-zer;* from 5144; prop. something *set apart,* i.e. (abstr.) *dedication* (of a priest or Nazirite); hence (concr.) unshorn *locks;* also (by impl.) a *chaplet* (espec. of royalty):—consecration, crown, hair, separation.

5146. נֹחַ **Nôach,** *no´-akh;* the same as 5118; *rest; Noăch,* the patriarch of the flood:—Noah.

5147. נַחְבִּי **Nachbîy,** *nakh-bee´;* from 2247; *occult; Nachbi,* an Isr.:—Nakbi.

5148. נָחָה **nâchâh,** *naw-khaw´;* a prim. root; to *guide;* by impl. to *transport* (into exile, or as colonists):—bestow, bring, govern, guide, lead (forth), put, straiten.

5149. נְחוּם **Nᵉchûwm,** *neh-khoom´;* from 5162; *comforted; Nechum,* an Isr.:—Nehum.

5150. נִחוּם **nichûwm,** *nee-khoom´;* or נִחֻם **nichûm,** *nee-khoom´;* from 5162; prop. *consoled;* abstr. *solace:*—comfort (-able), repenting.

5151. נַחוּם **Nachûwm,** *nakh-oom´;* from 5162; *comfortable; Nachum,* an Isr. prophet:—Nahum.

5152. נָחוֹר **Nâchôwr,** *naw-khore´;* from the same as 5170; *snorer; Nachor,* the name of the grandfather and a brother of Abraham:—Nahor.

5153. נָחוּשׁ **nâchûwsh,** *naw-khoosh´;* appar. pass. part. of 5172 (perh. in the sense of *ringing,* i.e. bell-metal; or from the *red* color of the throat of a serpent [5175, as denom.] when hissing); *coppery,* i.e. (fig.) hard:—of brass.

5154. נְחוּשָׁה **nᵉchûwshâh,** *nekh-oo-shaw´;* or נְחֻשָׁה **nᵉchûshâh,** *nekh-oo-shaw´;* fem. of 5153; *copper:*—brass, steel. Comp. 5176.

5155. נְחִילָה **nᵉchîylah,** *nekh-ee-law´;* prob. denom. from 2485, a *flute:*—[*plur.*] Nehiloth.

5156. נְחִיר **nᵉchîyr,** *nekh-eer´;* from the same as 5170; a *nostril:*—[*dual*] nostrils.

5157. נָחַל **nâchal,** *naw-khal´;* a prim. root; to *inherit* (as a [fig.] mode of descent), or (gen.) to *occupy;* causat. to *bequeath,* or (gen.) *distribute, instate:*—divide, have ([inheritance]), take as an heritage, (cause to, give to, make to) inherit, (distribute for, divide [for, for an, by], give for, have, leave for, take [for]) inheritance, (have in, cause to be made to) possess (-ion).

5158. נַחַל **nachal,** *nakh´-al;* or (fem.) נַחְלָה **nachlâh** (Psa. 124 : 4), *nahk´-law;* or נַחֲלָה **nachălâh** (Ezek. 47 : 19, 48 : 28), *nakh-al-aw´;* from 5157 in its orig. sense; a *stream,* espec. a winter *torrent;* (by impl.) a (narrow) *valley* (in which a brook runs); also a *shaft* (of a mine):—brook, flood, river, stream, valley.

5159. נַחֲלָה **nachălâh,** *nakh-al-aw´;* from 5157 (in its usual sense); prop. something *inherited,* i.e. (abstr.) *occupancy,* or (concr.) an *heirloom;* gen. an *estate, patrimony* or *portion:*—heritage, to inherit, inheritance, possession. Comp. 5158.

5160. נַחֲלִיאֵל **Nachălîy'êl,** *nakh-al-ee-ale´;* from 5158 and 410; *valley of God; Nachaliël,* a place in the Desert:—Nahaliel.

5161. נֶחֱלָמִי **Nechĕlâmîy,** *nekh-el-aw-mee´;* appar. a patron. from an unused name (appar. pass. part. of 2492); *dreamed;* a *Nechelamite,* or descend. of Nechlam:—Nehelamite.

5162. נָחַם **nâcham,** *naw-kham´;* a prim. root; prop. to *sigh,* i.e. *breathe* strongly; by impl. to be *sorry,* i.e. (in a favorable sense) to *pity, console,* or (reflex.) *rue;* or (unfavorably) to *avenge* (oneself):—comfort (self), ease [one's self], repent (-er, -ing, self).

5163. נַחַם **Nacham,** *nakh´-am;* from 5162; *consolation; Nacham,* an Isr.:—Naham.

5164. נֹחַם **nôcham,** *no´-kham;* from 5162; *ruefulness,* i.e. desistance:—repentance.

5165. נֶחָמָה **nechâmâh,** *nekh-aw-maw´;* from 5162; *consolation:*—comfort.

5166. נְחֶמְיָה **Nᵉchemyâh,** *nekh-em-yaw´;* from 5162 and 3050; *consolation of Jah; Nechemjah,* the name of three Isr.:—Nehemiah.

5167. נַחֲמָנִי **Nachămânîy,** *nakh-am-aw-nee´;* from 5162; *consolatory; Nachamani,* an Isr.:—Nahamani.

5168. נַחְנוּ **nachnûw,** *nakh-noo´;* for 587; *we:*—we.

5169. נָחַץ **nâchats,** *naw-khats´;* a prim. root; to *be urgent:*—require haste.

5170. נַחַר **nachar,** *nakh´-ar;* and (fem.) נַחֲרָה **nachărâh,** *nakh-ar-aw´;* from an unused root mean. to *snort* or *snore;* a *snorting:*—nostrils, snorting.

5171. נַחֲרַי **Nachăray,** *nakh-ar-ah´ee;* or נַחְרַי **Nachray,** *nakh-rah´ee;* from the same as 5170; *snorer; Nacharai* or *Nachrai,* an Isr.:—Naharai, Nahari.

5172. נָחַשׁ **nâchash,** *naw-khash´;* a prim. root; prop. to *hiss,* i.e. *whisper* a (magic) spell; gen. to *prognosticate:*— × certainly, divine, enchanter, (use) × enchantment, learn by experience, × indeed, diligently observe.

5173. נַחַשׁ **nachash,** *nakh´-ash;* from 5172; an *incantation* or *augury:*—enchantment.

5174. נְחָשׁ **nᵉchâsh** (Chald.) *nekh-awsh´;* corresp. to 5154; *copper:*—brass.

5175. נָחָשׁ **nâchâsh,** *naw-khawsh´;* from 5172; a *snake* (from its *hiss*):—serpent.

5176. נָחָשׁ **Nâchâsh,** *naw-khawsh´;* the same as 5175; *Nachash,* the name of two persons appar. non-Isr.:—Nahash.

נְחֻשָׁה **nᵉchûshâh.** See 5154.

5177. נַחְשׁוֹן **Nachshôwn,** *nakh-shone´;* from 5172; *enchanter; Nachshon,* an Isr.:—Naashon, Nahshon.

5178. נְחֹשֶׁת **nᵉchôsheth,** *nekh-o´-sheth;* for 5154; *copper;* hence, something made of that metal, i.e. *coin,* a *fetter;* fig. *base* (as compared with gold or silver):—brasen, brass, chain, copper, fetter (of brass), filthiness, steel.

5179. נְחֻשְׁתָּא **Nᵉchushtâ',** *nekh-oosh-taw´;* from 5178; *copper; Nechusta,* an Israelitess:—Nehushta.

5180. נְחֻשְׁתָּן **Nᵉchushtân,** *nekh-oosh-tawn´;* from 5178; something made *of copper,* i.e. the copper *serpent* of the Desert:—Nehushtan.

5181. נָחַת **nâchath,** *naw-khath´;* a prim. root; to *sink,* i.e. *descend;* causat., to *press* or *lead* down:—be broken, (cause to) come down, enter, go down, press sore, settle, stick fast.

5182. נְחַת **nᵉchath** (Chald.), *nekh-ath´;* corresp. to 5181; to *descend;* causat., to *bring away, deposit, depose:*—carry, come down, depose, lay up, place.

5183. נַחַת **nachath,** *nakh´-ath;* from 5182; a *descent,* i.e. imposition, unfavorable *(punishment)* or favorable *(food);* also (intrans.; perh. from 5117), *restfulness:*—lighting down, quiet (-ness), to rest, be set on.

5184. נַחַת **Nachath,** *nakh´-ath;* the same as 5183; *quiet; Nachath,* the name of an Edomite and of two Isr.:—Nahath.

5185. נָחֵת **nâchêth,** *naw-khayth´;* from 5181; *descending;*—come down.

5186. נָטָה **nâṭâh,** *naw-taw´;* a prim. root; to *stretch* or spread out; by impl. to *bend* away (includ. mor. deflection); used in a great variety of application (as follows):— + afternoon, apply, bow (down, -ing), carry aside, decline, deliver, extend, go down, be gone, incline, intend, lay, let down, offer, outstretched, overthrown, pervert, pitch, prolong, put away, shew, spread (out), stretch (forth, out), take (aside), turn (aside, away), wrest, cause to yield.

5187. נְטִיל **neṭîyl,** *net-eel´;* from 5190; *laden:*—that bear.

5188. נְטִיפָה **neṭîyphâh,** *net-ee-faw´;* from 5197; a *pendant* for the ears (espec. of pearls):—chain, collar.

5189. נְטִישָׁה **neṭîyshâh,** *net-ee-shaw´;* from 5203; a *tendril* (as an offshoot):—battlement, branch, plant.

5190. נָטַל **nâṭal,** *naw-tal´;* a prim root; to *lift;* by impl. to *impose:*—bear, offer, take up.

5191. נְטַל **neṭal** (Chald.), *net-al´;* corresp. to 5190; to *raise:*—take up.

5192. נֵטֶל **nêṭel,** *nay´-tel;* from 5190; a *burden:*—weighty.

5193. נָטַע **nâṭaʻ,** *naw-tah´;* a prim. root; prop. to *strike* in, i.e. *fix;* spec. to *plant* (lit. or fig.):—fastened, plant (-er).

5194. נֶטַע **neṭaʻ,** *neh´-tah;* from 5193; a *plant;* collect., a *plantation;* abstr., a *planting:*—plant.

5195. נָטִיעַ **nâṭiaʻ,** *naw-tee´-ah;* from 5193; a *plant:*—plant.

5196. נְטָעִים **Neṭâʻîym,** *net-aw-eem´;* plur. of 5194; *Netaïm,* a place in Pal.:—plants.

5197. נָטַף **nâṭaph,** *naw-taf´;* a prim. root; to *ooze,* i.e. *distil* gradually, by impl. to *fall in drops;* fig. to *speak* by inspiration:—drop (-ping), prophesy (-et).

5198. נָטָף **nâṭâph,** *naw-tawf´;* from 5197; a *drop;* spec., an aromatic *gum* (prob. *stacte*):—drop, stacte.

5199. נְטֹפָה **Neṭôphâh,** *net-o-faw´;* from 5197; *distillation; Netophah,* a place in Pal.:—Netophah.

5200. נְטֹפָתִי **Neṭôphâthîy,** *net-o-faw-thee´;* patron. from 5199; a *Netophathite,* or inhab. of Netophah:—Netophathite.

5201. נָטַר **nâṭar,** *naw-tar´;* a prim. root; to *guard;* fig. to *cherish* (anger):—bear grudge, keep (-er), reserve.

5202. נְטַר **neṭar** (Chald.), *net-ar´;* corresp. to 5201; to *retain:*—keep.

5203. נָטַשׁ **nâṭash,** *naw-tash´;* a prim. root; prop. to *pound,* i.e. *smite;* by impl. (as if beating out, and thus expanding) to *disperse;* also, to *thrust* off, down, out or upon (includ. *reject, let alone, permit, remit,* etc.):—cast off, drawn, let fall, forsake, join [battle], leave (off), lie still, loose, spread (self) abroad, stretch out, suffer.

5204. נִי **nîy,** *nee;* a doubtful word; appar. from 5091; *lamentation:*—wailing.

5205. נִיד **nîyd,** *need;* from 5110; *motion* (of the lips in speech):—moving.

5206. נִידָה **nîydâh,** *nee-daw´;* fem. of 5205; *removal,* i.e. exile:—removed.

5207. נִיחוֹחַ **nîychôwach,** *nee-kho´-akh;* or נִיחֹחַ **nîychôach,** *nee-kho´-akh;* from 5117; prop. *restful,* i.e. *pleasant;* abstr. *delight:*—sweet (odour).

5208. נִיחוֹחַ **nîychôwach** (Chald.), *nee-kho´-akh;* or (shorter) נִיחֹחַ **nîychôach** (Chald.), *nee-kho´-akh;* corresp. to 5207; *pleasure:*—sweet odour (savour).

5209. נִין **nîyn,** *neen;* from 5125; *progeny:*—son.

5210. נִינְוֵה **Nîynevêh,** *nee-nev-ay;* of for. or.; *Nineveh,* the capital of Assyria:—Nineveh.

5211. נִיס° **nîyç,** *neece;* from 5127; *fugitive:*—that fleeth.

5212. נִיסָן **Nîyçân,** *nee-sawn´;* prob. of for. or.; *Nisan,* the first month of the Jewish sacred year:—Nisan.

5213. נִיצוֹץ **nîytsôwts,** *nee-tsotes´;* from 5340; a *spark:*—spark.

5214. נִיר **nîyr,** *neer;* a root prob. ident. with that of 5216, through the idea of the *gleam* of a fresh furrow; to *till* the soil:—break up.

5215. נִיר **nîyr,** *neer;* or נִר **nîr,** *neer;* from 5214; prop. *ploughing,* i.e. (concr.) freshly *ploughed* land:—fallow ground, ploughing, tillage.

5216. נִיר **nîyr,** *neer;* or נִר **nîr,** *neer;* also נֵיר **nêyr,** *nare;* or נֵר **nêr,** *nare;* or (fem.) נֵרָה **nêrâh,** *nay-raw´;* from a prim. root [see 5214; 5135] prop. mean. to *glisten;* a *lamp* (i.e. the burner) or *light* (lit. or fig.):—candle, lamp, light.

5217. נָכָא **nâkâʼ,** *naw-kaw´;* a prim. root; to *smite,* i.e. *drive* away:—be viler.

5218. נָכֵא **nâkêʼ,** *naw-kay´;* or נָכָא **nâkâʼ,** *naw-kaw´;* from 5217; *smitten,* i.e. (fig.) *afflicted:*—broken, stricken, wounded.

5219. נְכֹאת **nekôʼth,** *nek-oth´;* from 5218; prop. a *smiting,* i.e. (concr.) an aromatic *gum* [perh. *styrax*] (as *powdered*):—spicery (-ces).

5220. נֶכֶד **neked,** *neh´-ked;* from an unused root mean. to *propagate; offspring:*—nephew, son's son.

5221. נָכָה **nâkâh,** *naw-kaw´;* a prim. root; to *strike* (lightly or severely, lit. or fig.):— beat, cast forth, clap, give [wounds], × go forward, × indeed, kill, make [slaughter], murderer, punish, slaughter, slay (-er, -ing), smite (-r, -ing), strike, be stricken, (give) stripes, × surely, wound.

5222. נֵכֶה **nêkeh,** *nay-keh´;* from 5221; a *smitter,* i.e. (fig.) *traducer:*—abject.

5223. נָכֶה **nâkeh,** *naw-keh´;* *smitten,* i.e. (lit.) maimed, or (fig.) dejected:—contrite, lame.

5224. נְכוֹ **Nekôw,** *nek-o´;* prob. of Eg. or.; *Neko* an Eg. king:—Necho. Comp. 6549.

5225. נָכוֹן **Nâkôwn,** *naw-kone´;* from 3559; *prepared; Nakon,* prob. an Isr.:—Nachon.

5226. נֵכַח **nêkach,** *nay´-kakh;* from an unused root mean. to *be straightforward;* prop. the *fore* part; used adv., *opposite:*—before, over against.

5227. נֹכַח **nôkach,** *no´-kakh;* from the same as 5226; prop., the *front* part; used adv. (espec. with prep.), *opposite, in front of, forward, in behalf of:*—(over) against, before, direct [-ly], for, right (on).

5228. נָכֹחַ **nâkôach,** *naw-ko´-akh;* from the same as 5226; *straightforward,* i.e. (fig.), *equitable, correct,* or (abstr.), *integrity:*—plain, right, uprightness.

5229. נְכֹחָה **nekôchâh,** *nek-o-khaw´;* fem. of 5228; prop. *straightforwardness,* i.e. (fig.) *integrity,* or (concr.) a *truth:*—equity, right (thing), uprightness.

5230. נָכַל **nâkal,** *naw-kal´;* a prim. root; to *defraud,* i.e. *act treacherously:*—beguile, conspire, deceiver, deal subtilly.

5231. נֵכֶל **nêkel,** *nay´-kel;* from 5230; *deceit:*—wile.

5232. נְכַס **nekaç** (Chald.), *nek-as´;* corresp. to 5233:—goods.

5233. נֶכֶס **nekeç,** *neh´-kes;* from an unused root mean. to *accumulate; treasure:*—riches, wealth.

5234. נָכַר **nâkar,** *naw-kar´;* a prim. root; prop. to *scrutinize,* i.e. look intently at; hence (with *recognition* implied), to *acknowledge, be acquainted with, care for, respect, revere,* or (with *suspicion* implied), to *disregard, ignore, be strange* toward, *reject, resign, dissimulate* (as if ignorant or disowning):—acknowledge, × could, deliver, discern, dissemble, estrange, feign self to be another, know, take knowledge (notice), perceive, regard, (have) respect, behave (make) self strange (-ly).

5235. נֶכֶר **neker,** *neh´-ker;* or נֹכֶר **nôker,** *no´-ker;* from 5234; something *strange,* i.e. unexpected *calamity:*—strange.

5236. נֵכָר **nêkâr,** *nay-kawr´;* from 5234; *foreign,* or (concr.) a *foreigner,* or (abstr.) *heathendom:*—alien, strange (+ -er).

5237. נָכְרִי **nokrîy,** *nok-ree´;* from 5235 (second form); *strange,* in a variety of degrees and applications *(foreign, non-relative, adulterous, different, wonderful):*—alien, foreigner, outlandish, strange (-r, woman).

5238. נְכֹת **nekôth,** *nek-ōth´;* prob. for 5219; *spicery,* i.e. (gen.) *valuables:*—precious things.

5239. נָלָה **nâlâh,** *naw-law´;* appar. a prim. root; to *complete:*—make an end.

5240. נְמִבְזֶה **nemibzeh,** *nem-ib-zeh´;* from 959; *despised:*—vile.

5241. נְמוּאֵל **Nemûwʼêl,** *nem-oo-ale´;* appar. for 3223; *Nemuel,* the name of two Isr.:—Nemuel.

5242. נְמוּאֵלִי **Nᵉmûwʼêlîy,** *nem-oo-ay-lee´;* from 5241; a *Nemuelite,* or desc. of Nemuel:—Nemuelite.

5243. נָמַל **nâmal,** *naw-mal´;* a prim. root; to *become clipped* or (spec.) *circumcised:*—(branch to) be cut down (off), circumcise.

5244. נְמָלָה **nᵉmâlâh,** *nem-aw-law´;* fem. from 5243; an *ant* (prob. from its almost *bisected* form):—ant.

5245. נְמַר **nᵉmar** (Chald.), *nem-ar´;* corresp. to 5246:—leopard.

5246. נָמֵר **nâmêr,** *naw-mare´;* from an unused root mean. prop. to *filtrate,* i.e. *be limpid* [comp. 5247 and 5249]; and thus to *spot* or *stain* as if by dripping; a *leopard* (from its stripes):—leopard.

נִמְרֹד **Nimrôd.** See 5248.

5247. נִמְרָה **Nimrâh,** *nim-râw´;* from the same as 5246; *clear* water; *Nimrah,* a place E. of the Jordan:—Nimrah. See also 1039, 5249.

5248. נִמְרוֹד **Nimrôwd,** *nim-rode´;* or נִמְרֹד **Nimrôd,** *nim-rode´;* prob. of for. or.; *Nimrod,* a son of Cush:—Nimrod.

5249. נִמְרִים **Nimrîym,** *nim-reem´;* plur. of a masc. corresp. to 5247; *clear* waters; *Nimrim,* a place E. of the Jordan:—Nimrim. Comp. 1039.

5250. נִמְשִׁי **Nimshîy,** *nim-shee´;* prob. from 4871; *extricated; Nimshi,* the (grand-) father of Jehu:—Nimshi.

5251. נֵס **nêç,** *nace;* from 5264; a *flag;* also a *sail;* by impl. a *flagstaff;* gen. a *signal;* fig. a *token:*—banner, pole, sail, (en-) sign, standard.

5252. נְסִבָּה **nᵉçibbâh,** *nes-ib-baw´;* fem. part. pass. of 5437; prop. an *environment,* i.e. *circumstance* or *turn* of affairs:—cause.

5253. נָסַג **nâçag,** *naw-sag´;* a prim. root; to *retreat:*—departing away, remove, take (hold), turn away.

נְסָה **nᵉçâh.** See 5375.

5254. נָסָה **nâçâh,** *naw-saw´;* a prim. root; to *test;* by impl. to *attempt:*—adventure, assay, prove, tempt, try.

5255. נָסַח **nâçach,** *naw-sakh´;* a prim. root; to *tear* away:—destroy, pluck, root.

5256. נְסַח **nᵉçach** (Chald.), *nes-akh´;* corresp. to 5255:—pull down.

5257. נְסִיךְ **nᵉçîyk,** *nes-eek´;* from 5258; prop. something *poured* out, i.e. a *libation;* also a molten *image;* by impl. a *prince* (as *anointed*)—drink offering, duke, prince (-ipal).

5258. נָסַךְ **nâçak,** *naw-sak´;* a prim. root; to *pour* out, espec. a libation, or to *cast* (metal); by anal. to *anoint* a king:—cover, melt, offer, (cause to) pour (out), set (up).

5259. נָסַךְ **nâçak,** *naw-sak´;* a prim. root [prob. identical with 5258 through the idea of fusion]; to *interweave,* i.e. (fig.) to *overspread:*—that is spread.

5260. נְסַךְ **nᵉçak** (Chald.), *nes-ak´;* corresp. to 5258; to *pour* out a libation:—offer.

5261. נְסַךְ **nᵉçak** (Chald.), *nes-ak´;* corresp. to 5262; a *libation:*—drink offering.

5262. נֶסֶךְ **neçek,** *neh´-sek;* or נֵסֶךְ **nêçek,** *nay´-sek;* from 5258; a *libation;* also a *cast idol:*—cover, drink offering, molten image.

נִסְמָן **niçmân.** See 5567.

5263. נָסַס **nâçaç,** *naw-sas´;* a prim. root; to *wane,* i.e. *be sick.*

5264. נָסַס **nâçaç** *naw-sas´;* a prim. root; to *gleam* from afar, i.e. to *be conspicuous* as a signal; or rather perh. a denom. from 5251 [and ident. with 5263, through the idea of a flag as *fluttering* in the wind]; to *raise a beacon:*—lift up as an ensign, standard bearer.

5265. נָסַע **nâçaʻ,** *naw-sah´;* a prim. root; prop. to *pull* up, espec. the tent-pins, i.e. *start* on a journey:—cause to blow, bring, get, (make to) go (away, forth, forward, onward, out), (take) journey, march, remove, set aside (forward), × still, be on his (go their) way.

5266. נָסַק **nâçaq,** *naw-sak´;* a prim. root; to *go* up:—ascend.

5267. נְסַק **nᵉçaq** (Chald.), *nes-ak´;* corresp. to 5266:—take up.

5268. נִסְרֹךְ **Niçrôk,** *nis-roke´;* of for. or.; *Nisrok,* a Bab. idol:—Nisroch.

5269. נֵעָה **Nêʻâh,** *nay-aw´;* from 5128; *motion; Neäh,* a place in Pal.:—Neah.

5270. נֹעָה **Nôʻâh,** *no-aw´;* from 5128; *movement; Noäh,* an Israelitess:—Noah.

5271. נָעוּר **nâʻûwr,** *naw-oor´;* or נָעֻר **nâʻûr,** *naw-oor´;* and (fem.) נְעֻרָה **nᵉʻûrâh,** *neh-oo-raw´;* prop. pass. part. from 5288 as denom.; (only in plur. collect. or emphat.) *youth,* the state *(juvenility)* or the persons (*young* people):—childhood, youth.

5272. נְעִיאֵל **Nᵉʻîyʼêl,** *neh-ee-ale´;* from 5128 and 410; *moved of God; Neïel,* a place in Pal.:—Neiel.

5273. נָעִים **nâʻîym,** *naw-eem´;* from 5276; *delightful* (obj. or subj., lit. or fig.):—pleasant (-ure), sweet.

5274. נָעַל **nâʻal,** *naw-al´;* a prim. root; prop. to *fasten* up, i.e. with a bar or cord; hence (denom. from 5275), to *sandal,* i.e. furnish with slippers:—bolt, inclose, lock, shod, shut up.

5275. נַעַל **naʻal,** *noh´-al;* or (fem.) נַעֲלָה **naʻălâh,** *nah-al-aw´;* from 5274; prop. a sandal *tongue;* by extens. a *sandal* or slipper (sometimes as a symbol of occupancy, a refusal to marry, or of something valueless):—dryshod, (pair of) shoe ([-latchet], -s).

5276. נָעֵם **nâʻêm,** *naw-ame´;* a prim. root; to *be agreeable* (lit. or fig.):—pass in beauty, be delight, be pleasant, be sweet.

5277. נַעַם **Naʻam,** *nah´-am;* from 5276; *pleasure; Naam,* an Isr.:—Naam.

5278. נֹעַם **noʻam,** *no´-am;* from 5276; *agreeableness,* i.e. *delight, suitableness, splendor* or *grace:*—beauty, pleasant (-ness).

5279. נַעֲמָה **Naʻămâh,** *nah-am-aw´;* fem. of 5277; *pleasantness; Naamah,* the name of an antediluvian woman, of an Ammonitess, and of a place in Pal.:—Naamah.

5280. נַעֲמִי **Naʻâmîy,** *nah-am-ee´;* patron. from 5283; a *Naamanite,* or desc. of Naaman (collect.):—Naamites.

5281. נָעֳמִי **Noʻŏmîy,** *nŏ-om-ee´;* from 5278; *pleasant; Noömi,* an Israelitess:—Naomi.

5282. נַעֲמָן **naʻămân,** *nah-am-awn´;* from 5276; *pleasantness* (plur. as concr.):—pleasant.

5283. נַעֲמָן **Naʻămân,** *nah-am-awn´;* the same as 5282; *Naaman,* the name of an Isr. and of a Damascene:—Naaman.

5284. נַעֲמָתִי **Naʻămâthîy,** *nah-am-aw-thee´;* patrial from a place corresp. in name (but not ident.) with 5279; a *Naamathite,* or inhab. of Naamah:—Naamathite

5285. נַעֲצוּץ **naʻătsûwts,** *nah-ats-oots´;* from an unused root mean. to *prick;* prob. a *brier;* by impl. a *thicket* of thorny bushes:—thorn.

5286. נָעַר **nâʻar,** *naw-ar´;* a prim. root; to *growl:*—yell.

5287. נָעַר **nâʻar,** *naw-ar´;* a prim. root [prob. ident. with 5286, through the idea of the *rustling* of mane, which usually accompanies the lion's roar]; to *tumble* about:—shake (off, out, self), overthrow, toss up and down.

5288. נַעַר **naʻar,** *nah´-ar;* from 5287; (concr.) a *boy* (as active), from the age of infancy to adolescence; by impl. a *servant;* also (by interch. of sex), a *girl* (of similar latitude in age):—babe, boy, child, damsel [*from the marg.*], lad, servant, young (man).

5289. נַעַר **naʻar,** *nah´-ar;* from 5287 in its der. sense of *tossing* about; a *wanderer:*—young one.

5290. נֹעַר **nôʻar,** *no´-ar;* from 5287; (abstr.) *boyhood* [comp. 5288]:—child, youth.

נָעֻר **nâʻûr.** see 5271.

5291. נַעֲרָה **naʻărâh,** *nah-ar-aw´;* fem. of 5288; a *girl* (from infancy to adolescence):—damsel, maid (-en), young (woman).

5292. נַעֲרָה **Naʻărâh,** *nah-ar-aw´;* the same as 5291; *Naarah,* the name of an Israelitess, and of a place in Pal.:—Naarah, Naarath.

נְעֻרָה **nᵉʻûrâh.** See 5271.

5293. נַעֲרַי **Naʻăray,** *nah-ar-ah´ee;* from 5288; *youthful; Naarai,* an Isr.:—Naarai.

5294. נְעַרְיָה **Nᵉʻaryâh,** *neh-ar-yaw´;* from 5288 and 3050; *servant of Jah; Neärjah,* the name of two Isr.:—Neariah.

5295. נַעֲרָן **Naʻărân,** *nah-ar-awn´;* from 5288; *juvenile; Naaran,* a place in Pal.:—Naaran.

5296. נְעֹרֶת **n^eʿôreth,** *neh-o´-reth;* from 5287; something *shaken* out, i.e. *tow* (as the refuse of flax):—tow.

נַעֲרָתָה **Naʿărâthâh.** See 5292.

5297. נֹף **Nôph,** *nofe;* a var. of 4644; *Noph,* the capital of Upper Egypt:—Noph.

5298. נֶפֶג **Nepheg,** *neh´-feg;* from an unused root prob. mean. to *spring* forth; a *sprout; Nepheg,* the name of two Isr.:—Nepheg.

5299. נָפָה **nâphâh,** *naw-faw´;* from 5130 in the sense of *lifting;* a *height;* also a *sieve:*—border, coast, region, sieve.

5300. נְפוּשְׁסִים° **N^ephûwsh^eçîym,** *nef-oo-shes-eem´;* for 5304; *Nephushesim,* a Temple-servant:—Nephisesim [*from the marg.*].

5301. נָפַח **nâphach,** *naw-fakh´;* a prim. root; to *puff,* in various applications (lit. to *inflate, blow* hard, *scatter, kindle, expire;* fig. to *disesteem*):—blow, breath, give up, cause to lose [life], seething, snuff.

5302. נֹפַח **Nôphach,** *no´-fakh;* from 5301; a *gust; Nophach,* a place in Moab:—Nophah.

5303. נְפִיל **n^ephîyl,** *nef-eel´;* or נְפִל **n^ephîl,** *nef-eel´;* from 5307; prop., a *feller,* i.e. a *bully* or *tyrant:*—giant.

5304. נְפִיסִים° **N^ephîyçîym,** *nef-ee-seem´;* plur. from an unused root mean. to *scatter; expansions; Nephisim,* a Temple-servant:—Nephusim [*from the marg.*].

5305. נָפִישׁ **Nâphîysh,** *naw-feesh´;* from 5314; *refreshed; Naphish,* a son of Ishmael, and his posterity:—Naphish.

5306. נֹפֶךְ **nôphek,** *no´-fek;* from an unused root mean. to *glisten; shining;* a gem, prob. the *garnet:*—emerald.

5307. נָפַל **nâphal,** *naw-fal´;* a prim. root; to *fall,* in a great variety of applications (intrans. or causat., lit. or fig.):—be accepted, cast (down, self, [lots], out), cease, die, divide (by lot), (let) fail, (cause to, let, make, ready to) fall (away, down, -en, -ing), fell (-ing), fugitive, have [inheritamce], inferior, be judged [*by mistake for* 6419], lay (along), (cause to) lie down, light (down), be (× hast) lost, lying, overthrow, overwhelm, perish, present (-ed, -ing), (make to) rot, slay, smite out, × surely, throw down.

5308. נְפַל **n^ephal** (Chald.), *nef-al´;* corresp. to 5307:—fall (down), have occasion.

5309. נֶפֶל **nephel,** *neh´-fel;* or נֵפֶל **nêphel,** *nay´-fel;* from 5307; something *fallen,* i.e. an *abortion:*—untimely birth.

נְפִל **n^ephîl.** See 5303.

5310. נָפַץ **nâphats,** *naw-fats´;* a prim. root; to *dash* to pieces, or *scatter:*—be beaten in sunder, break (in pieces), broken, dash (in pieces), cause to be discharged, dispersed, be overspread, scatter.

5311. נֶפֶץ **nephets,** *neh´-fets;* from 5310; a *storm* (as dispersing):—scattering.

5312. נְפַק **n^ephaq** (Chald.), *nef-ak´;* a prim. root to *issue;* causat., to *bring out:*—come (go, take) forth (out).

5313. נִפְקָא **niphqâʾ** (Chald.), *nif-kaw´;* from 5312; an *outgo,* i.e. expense:—expense.

5314. נָפַשׁ **nâphash,** *naw-fash´;* a prim. root; to *breathe;* pass, to *be breathed* upon, i.e. (fig.) *refreshed* (as if by a current of air):—(be) refresh selves (-ed).

5315. נֶפֶשׁ **nephesh,** *neh´-fesh;* from 5314; prop. a *breathing* creature, i.e. *animal* or (abstr.) *vitality;* used very widely in a lit., accommodated or fig. sense (bodily or mental):—any, appetite, beast, body, breath, creature, × dead (-ly), desire, × [dis-] contented, × fish, ghost, + greedy, he, heart (-y), (hath, × jeopardy of) life (× in jeopardy), lust, man, me, mind, mortality, one, own, person, pleasure, (her-, him-, my-, thy-) self, them (your) -selves, + slay, soul, + tablet, they, thing, (× she) will, × would have it.

5316. נֶפֶת **nepheth,** *neh´-feth;* for 5299; a *height:*—country.

5317. נֹפֶת **nôpheth,** *no´-feth;* from 5130 in the sense of *shaking* to pieces; a *dripping* i.e. of *honey* (from the comb):—honeycomb.

5318. נֶפְתּוֹחַ **Nephtôwach,** *nef-to´-akh;* from 6605; *opened,* i.e. a *spring; Nephtoäch,* a place in Pal.:—Neptoah.

5319. נַפְתּוּל **naphtûwl,** *naf-tool´;* from 6617; prop. *wrestled;* but used (in the plur.) trans., a *struggle:*—wrestling.

5320. נַפְתֻּחִים **Naphtûchîym,** *naf-too-kheem;* plur. of for. or.; *Naphtuchim,* an Eg. tribe:—Naptuhim.

5321. נַפְתָּלִי **Naphtâlîy,** *naf-taw-lee´;* from 6617; *my wrestling; Naphtali,* a son of Jacob, with the tribe descended from him, and its territory:—Naphtali.

5322. נֵץ **nêts,** *nayts;* from 5340; a *flower* (from its *brilliancy*); also a *hawk* (from its *flashing* speed):—blossom, hawk.

5323. נָצָא **nâtsâʾ,** *naw-tsaw´;* a prim. root; to *go away:*—flee.

5324. נָצַב **nâtsab,** *naw-tsab´;* a prim. root; to *station,* in various applications (lit. or fig.):—appointed, deputy, erect, establish, × Huzzah [*by mistake for a prop. name*], lay, officer, pillar, present, rear up, set (over, up), settle, sharpen, stablish, (make to) stand (-ing, still, up, upright), best state.

נְצִב **n^etsîb.** See 5333.

5325. נִצָּב **nitstsâb,** *nits-tsawb´;* pass. part. of 5324; *fixed,* i.e. a *handle:*—haft.

5326. נִצְבָה **nitsbâh** (Chald.), *nits-baw´;* from a root corresp. to 5324; *fixedness,* i.e. *firmness:*—strength.

5327. נָצָה **nâtsâh,** *naw-tsaw´;* a prim. root; prop. to *go forth,* i.e. (by impl.) to *be expelled,* and (consequently) *desolate;* causat. to *lay waste;* also (spec.), to *quarrel:*—be laid waste, ruinous, strive (together).

נֹצָה **nôtsâh.** See 5133.

5328. נִצָּה **nitstsâh,** *nits-tsaw´;* fem. of 5322; a *blossom:*—flower.

בְּצוּרָה **n^etsûwrâh.** See 5341.

5329. נָצַח **nâtsach,** *naw-tsakh´;* a prim. root; prop. to *glitter* from afar, i.e. to be *eminent* (as a superintendent, espec. of the Temple services and its music); also (as denom. from 5331), to *be permanent:*—excel, chief musician (singer), oversee (-r), set forward.

5330. נְצַח **n^etsach** (Chald.), *nets-akh´;* corresp. to 5329; to *become chief:*—be preferred.

5331. נֶצַח **netsach,** *neh´-tsakh;* or נֵצַח **nêtsach,** *nay´-tsakh;* from 5329; prop. a *goal,* i.e. the bright object at a distance travelled towards; hence (fig.) *splendor,* or (subj.) *truthfulness,* or (obj.) *confidence;* but usually (adv.), *continually* (i.e. to the most distant point of view):—alway (-s), constantly, end, (+ n-) ever (more), perpetual, strength, victory.

5332. נֵצַח **Nêtsach,** *nay´-tsakh;* prob. ident. with 5331, through the idea of *brilliancy* of color; *juice* of the grape (as blood red):—blood, strength.

5333. נְצִיב **n^etsîyb,** *nets-eeb´;* or בְּצִב **n^etsîb,** *nets-eeb´;* from 5324; something *stationary,* i.e. a *prefect,* a military *post,* a *statue:*—garrison, officer, pillar.

5334. נְצִיב **N^etsîyb,** *nets-eeb´;* the same as 5333; *station; Netsib,* a place in Pal.:—Nezib.

5335. נְצִיחַ **n^etsîyach,** *nets-ee´-akh;* from 5329; *conspicuous; Netsiach,* a Temple-servant:—Neziah.

5336. נָצִיר° **nâtsîyr,** *naw-tsere´;* from 5341; prop. *conservative;* but used pass., *delivered:*—preserved.

5337. נָצַל **nâtsal,** *naw-tsal´;* a prim. root; to *snatch* away, whether in a good or a bad sense:— × at all, defend, deliver (self), escape, × without fail, part, pluck, preserve, recover, rescue, rid, save, spoil, strip, × surely, take (out).

5338. נְצַל **n^etsal** (Chald.), *nets-al´;* corresp. to 5337; to *extricate:*—deliver, rescue.

5339. נִצָּן **nitstsân,** *nits-tsawn´;* from 5322; a *blossom:*—flower.

5340. נָצַץ **nâtsats,** *naw-tsats´;* a prim. root; to *glare,* i.e. *be bright*-colored:—sparkle.

5341. נָצַר **nâtsar,** *naw-tsar´;* a prim. root; to *guard,* in a good sense (to *protect, maintain, obey,* etc.) or a bad one (to *conceal,* etc.):—besieged, hidden thing, keep (-er, -ing), monument, observe, preserve (-r), subtil, watcher (-man).

5342. נֵצֶר **nêtser,** *nay´-tser;* from 5341 in the sense of *greenness* as a striking color; a *shoot:* fig. a *descendant:*—branch.

5343. נְקֵא **n^{e}qê'** (Chald.), *nek-ay´;* from a root corresp. to 5352; *clean:*—pure.

5344. נָקַב **nâqab,** *naw-kab´;* a prim. root; to *puncture,* lit. (to *perforate,* with more or less violence) or fig. (to *specify, designate, libel*):—appoint, blaspheme, bore, curse, express, with holes, name, pierce, strike through.

5345. נֶקֶב **neqeb,** *neh´-keb;* a *bezel* (for a gem):—pipe.

5346. נֶקֶב **Neqeb,** *neh´-keb;* the same as 5345; *dell; Nekeb,* a place in Pal.:—Nekeb.

5347. נְקֵבָה **n^{e}qêbâh,** *nek-ay-baw´;* from 5344; *female* (from the sexual form):—female, woman.

5348. נָקֹד **nâqôd,** *naw-kode´;* from an unused root mean. to *mark* (by *puncturing* or *branding*); *spotted:*—speckled.

5349. נֹקֵד **nôqêd,** *no-kade´;* act. part. from the same as 5348; a *spotter* (of sheep or cattle), i.e. the owner or tender (who thus marks them):—herdman, sheepmaster.

5350. נִקֻּד **niqqud,** *nik-kood´;* from the same as 5348; a *crumb* (as *broken* to spots); also a *biscuit* (as *pricked*):—cracknel, mouldy.

5351. נְקֻדָּה **n^{e}quddâh,** *nek-ood-daw´;* fem. of 5348; a *boss:*—stud.

5352. נָקָה **nâqâh,** *naw-kaw´;* a prim. root; to *be* (or *make*) *clean* (lit. or fig.); by impl. (in an adverse sense) to *be bare,* i.e. *extirpated:*—acquit × at all, × altogether, be blameless, cleanse, (be) clear (-ing), cut off, be desolate, be free, be (hold) guiltless, be (hold) innocent, × by no means, be quit, be (leave) unpunished, × utterly, × wholly.

5353. נְקוֹדָא **N^{e}qôwdâ',** *nek-o-daw´;* fem. of 5348 (in the fig. sense of *marked*); *distinction; Nekoda,* a Temple-servant:—Nekoda.

5354. נָקַט **nâqaṭ,** *naw-kat´;* a prim. root; to *loathe:*—weary.

5355. נָקִי **nâqîy,** *naw-kee´;* or נָקִיא **nâqîy'** (Joel 4 : 19; Jonah 1 : 14), *naw-kee´;* from 5352; *innocent:*—blameless, clean, clear, exempted, free, guiltless, innocent, quit.

5356. נִקָּיוֹן **niqqâyôwn,** *nik-kaw-yone´;* or נִקָּיֹן **niqqâyôn,** *nik-kaw-yone´;* from 5352; *clearness* (lit. or fig.):—cleanness, innocency.

5357. נָקִיק **nâqîyq,** *naw-keek´;* from an unused root mean. to *bore;* a *cleft:*—hole.

5358. נָקַם **nâqam,** *naw-kam´;* a prim. root; to *grudge,* i.e. *avenge* or *punish:*—avenge (-r, self), punish, revenge (self), × surely, take vengeance.

5359. נָקָם **nâqâm,** *naw-kawm´;* from 5358; *revenge:*— + avenged, quarrel, vengeance.

5360. נְקָמָה **n^{e}qâmâh,** *nek-aw-maw´;* fem. of 5359; *avengement,* whether the act or the passion:— + avenge, revenge (-ing), vengeance.

5361. נָקַע **nâqa',** *naw-kah´;* a prim. root; to *feel aversion:*—be alienated.

5362. נָקַף **nâqaph,** *naw-kaf´;* a prim. root; to *strike* with more or less violence *(beat, fell, corrode);* by impl. (of attack) to *knock together,* i.e *surround* or *circulate:*—compass (about, -ing), cut down, destroy, go round (about), inclose, round.

5363. נֹקֶף **nôqeph,** *no´-kef;* from 5362; a *threshing* (of olives):—shaking.

5364. נִקְפָּה **niqpâh,** *nik-paw´;* from 5362; prob. a *rope* (as *encircling*):—rent.

5365. נָקַר **nâqar,** *naw-kar´;* a prim. root; to *bore (penetrate, quarry):*—dig, pick out, pierce, put (thrust) out.

5366. נְקָרָה **n^{e}qârâh,** *nek-aw-raw´;* from 5365; a *fissure:*—cleft, clift.

5367. נָקַשׁ **nâqash,** *naw-kash´;* a prim. root; to *entrap* (with a noose), lit. or fig.:—catch. (lay a) snare.

5368. נְקַשׁ **n^{e}qash** (Chald.), *nek-ash´;* corresp. to 5367; but used in the sense of 5362; to *knock:*—smote.

נֵר **nêr,** נִר **nîr.** See 5215, 5216.

5369. נֵר **Nêr,** *nare;* the same as 5216; *lamp; Ner,* an Isr.:—Ner.

5370. נֵרְגַל **Nêrgal,** *nare-gal´;* of for. or.; *Nergal,* a Cuthite deity:—Nergal.

5371. נֵרְגַל שַׁרְאֶצֶר **Nêrgal Shar'etser,** *nare-gal´ shar-eh´-tser;* from 5370 and 8272; *Nergal-Sharetser,* the name of two Bab.:—Nergal-sharezer.

5372. נִרְגָּן **nirgân,** *neer-gawn´;* from an unused root mean. to *roll* to pieces; a *slanderer:*—talebearer, whisperer.

5373. נֵרְדְּ **nêrd,** *nayrd;* of for. or.; *nard,* an aromatic:—spikenard.

נֵרָה **nêrâh.** See 5216.

5374. נֵרִיָּה **Nêrîyâh,** *nay-ree-yaw´;* or נֵרִיָּהוּ **Nêrîyâhûw,** *nay-ree-yaw´-hoo;* from 5216 and 3050; *light of Jah; Nerijah,* an Isr.:—Neriah.

5375. נָשָׂא **nâsâ',** *naw-saw´;* or נָסָה **nâçâh** (Psa. 4 : 6 [7], *naw-saw´;* a prim. root; to *lift,* in a great variety of applications, lit. and fig., absol. and rel. (as follows):—accept, advance, arise, (able to, [armour], suffer to) bear (-er, up), bring (forth), burn, carry (away), cast, contain, desire, ease, exact, exalt (self), extol, fetch, forgive, furnish, further, give, go on, help, high, hold up, honourable (+ man), lade, lay, lift (self) up, lofty, marry, magnify, × needs, obtain, pardon, raise (up), receive, regard, respect, set (up), spare, stir up, + swear, take (away, up), × utterly, wear, yield.

5376. נְשָׂא **n^{e}sâ'** (Chald.), *nes-aw´;* corresp. to 5375:—carry away, make insurrection, take.

5377. נָשָׁא **nâshâ',** *naw-shaw´;* a prim. root; to *lead astray,* i.e. (mentally) to *delude,* or (morally) to *seduce:*—beguile, deceive, × greatly, × utterly.

5378. נָשָׁא **nâshâ',** *naw-shaw´;* a prim. root [perh. ident. with 5377; through the idea of *imposition*]; to *lend* on interest; by impl. to *dun* for debt:— × debt, exact, give of usury.

נָשִׂא **nâsî'.** See 5387.

נְשֻׂאָה **n^{e}sû'âh.** See 5385.

5379. נִשֵּׂאת **nissê'th,** *nis-sayth´;* pass. part. fem. of 5375; something *taken,* i.e. a *present:*—gift.

5380. נָשַׁב **nâshab,** *naw-shab´;* a prim. root; to *blow;* by impl. to *disperse:*— (cause to) blow, drive away.

5381. נָשַׂג **nâsag,** *naw-sag´;* a prim. root; to *reach* (lit. or fig.):—ability, be able, attain (unto), (be able to, can) get, lay at, put, reach, remove, wax rich, × surely, (over-) take (hold of, on, upon).

5382. נָשָׁה **nâshâh,** *naw-shaw´;* a prim. root; to *forget;* fig., to *neglect;* causat., to *remit, remove:*—forget, deprive, exact.

5383. נָשָׁה **nâshâh,** *naw-shaw´;* a prim. root [rather ident. with 5382, in the sense of 5378]; to *lend* or (by reciprocity) *borrow* on security or interest:—creditor, exact, extortioner, lend, usurer, lend on (taker of) usury.

5384. נָשֶׁה **nâsheh,** *naw-sheh´;* from 5382, in the sense of *failure; rheumatic* or *crippled* (from the incident to Jacob):—which shrank.

5385. נְשׂוּאָה **n^{e}sûw'âh,** *nes-oo-aw´;* or rather נְשֻׂאָה **n^{e}sû'âh,** *nes-oo-aw´;* fem. pass. part. of 5375; something *borne,* i.e. a *load:*—carriage.

5386. נְשִׁי **n^{e}shîy,** *nesh-ee´;* from 5383; a *debt:*—debt.

5387. נָשִׂיא **nâsîy',** *naw-see´;* or נָשִׂא **nâsî',** *naw-see´;* from 5375; prop. an *exalted* one, i.e. a *king* or *sheik;* also a rising *mist:*—captain, chief, cloud, governor, prince, ruler, vapour.

5388. נְשִׁיָּה **n^{e}shîyâh,** *nesh-ee-yaw´;* from 5382; *oblivion:*—forgetfulness.

נָשִׁים **nâshîym.** See 802.

5389. נָשִׁין **nâshîyn** (Chald.), *naw-sheen´;* irreg. plur. fem. of 606:—women.

5390. נְשִׁיקָה **n^{e}shîyqâh,** *nesh-ee-kaw´;* from 5401; a *kiss:*—kiss.

5391. נָשַׁךְ **nâshak,** *naw-shak´;* a prim. root; to *strike* with a sting (as a serpent); fig.; to *oppress* with interest on a loan:—bite, lend upon usury.

5392. נֶשֶׁךְ **neshek,** *neh´-shek;* from 5391; *interest* on a debt:—usury.

5393. נִשְׁכָּה **nishkâh,** *nish-kaw´;* for 3957; a *cell:*—chamber.

5394. נָשַׁל **nâshal,** *naw-shal´;* a prim. root; to *pluck* off, i.e. *divest, eject,* or *drop:*—cast (out), drive, loose, put off (out), slip.

5395. נָשַׁם **nâsham,** *naw-sham´;* a prim. root; prop. to *blow* away, i.e. *destroy:*—destroy.

5396. נִשְׁמָא **nishmâ'** (Chald.), *nish-maw´;* corresp. to 5397; vital *breath:*—breath.

5397. נְשָׁמָה **neshâmâh,** *nesh-aw-maw´;* fr. 5395; a *puff,* i.e. *wind,* angry or vital *breath,* divine *inspiration, intellect.* or (concr.) an *animal:*—blast, (that) breath (-eth), inspiration, soul, spirit.

5398. נָשַׁף **nâshaph,** *naw-shaf´;* a prim. root; to *breeze,* i.e. *blow* up fresh (as the wind):—blow.

5399. נֶשֶׁף **nesheph,** *neh´-shef;* from 5398; prop. a *breeze,* i.e. (by impl.) *dusk* (when the evening breeze prevails):—dark, dawning of the day (morning), night, twilight.

5400. נָשַׂק **nâsaq,** *naw-sak´;* a prim. root; to *catch* fire:—burn, kindle.

5401. נָשַׁק **nâshaq,** *naw-shak´;* a prim. root [ident. with 5400, through the idea of *fastening* up; comp. 2388, 2836]; to *kiss,* lit. or fig. *(touch);* also (as a mode of *attachment*), to *equip* with weapons:—armed (men), rule, kiss, that touched.

5402. נֶשֶׁק **nesheq,** *neh´-shek;* or נֵשֶׁק **nêsheq,** *nay´-shek;* from 5401; military *equipment,* i.e. (collect.) *arms* (offensive or defensive), or (concr.) an *arsenal:*—armed men, armour (-y), battle, harness, weapon.

5403. נְשַׁר **neshar** (Chald.), *nesh-ar´;* corresp. to 5404; an *eagle:*—eagle.

5404. נֶשֶׁר **nesher,** *neh´-sher;* from an unused root mean. to *lacerate;* the *eagle* (or other large bird of prey):—eagle.

5405. נָשַׁת **nâshath,** *naw-shath´;* a prim. root; prop. to *eliminate,* i.e. (intrans.) to *dry* up:—fail.
נְתִבָה **nethîbâh.** See 5410.

5406. נִשְׁתְּוָן **nishtevân,** *nish-tev-awn´;* prob. of Pers. or.; an *epistle:*—letter.

5407. נִשְׁתְּוָן **nishtevân** (Chald.), *nish-tev-awn´;* corresp. to 5406:—letter.
נָתוּן° **Nathûwn.** See 5411.

5408. נָתַח **nâthach,** *naw-thakh´;* a prim. root; to *dismember:*—cut (in pieces), divide, hew in pieces.

5409. נֵתַח **nêthach,** *nay´-thakh;* from 5408; a *fragment:*—part, piece.

5410. נָתִיב **nâthîyb,** *naw-theeb´;* or (fem.) נְתִיבָה **nethîybâh,** *neth-ee-baw´;* or נְתִבָה **nethîbâh** (Jer. 6 : 16), *neth-ee-baw´;* from an unused root mean. to *tramp;* a (beaten) *track:*—path ([-way]), × travel [-er], way.

5411. נָתִין **Nâthîyn,** *naw-theen´;* or נָתוּן° **Nâthûwn** (Ezra 8 : 17), *maw-thoon´* (the prop. form, as pass. part.) from 5414; one *given,* i.e. (in the plur. only) the *Nethinim,* or Temple-servants (as *given* up to that duty):—Nethinims.

5412. נְתִין **Nethîyn (Chald.),** *netheen´;* corresp. to 5411:—Nethinims.

5413. נָתַךְ **nâthak,** *naw-thak´;* a prim. root; to *flow* forth (lit. or fig.); by impl. to *liquefy:*—drop, gather (together), melt, pour (forth, out).

5414. נָתַן **nâthan** *naw-than´;* a prim. root; to *give,* used with great latitude of application (*put, make,* etc.):—add, apply, appoint, ascribe, assign, × avenge, × be ([healed]), bestow, bring (forth, hither), cast, cause, charge, come, commit consider, count, + cry, deliver (up), direct, distribute do, × doubtless, × without fail, fasten, frame, × get, give (forth, over, up), grant, hang (up), × have, × indeed, lay (unto charge, up), (give) leave, lend, let (out), + lie, lift up, make, + O that, occupy, offer, ordain, pay, perform, place, pour, print, × pull, put (forth), recompense, render, requite, restore, send (out), set (forth), shew, shoot forth (up). + sing, + slander, strike, [sub-] mit, suffer, × surely, × take, thrust, trade, turn, utter, + weep, × willingly, + withdraw, + would (to) God, yield.

5415. נְתַן **nethan** (Chald.), *neth-an´;* corresp. to 5414; *give:*—bestow, give, pay.

5416. נָתָן **Nâthân,** *naw-thawn´;* from 5414; *given; Nathan,* the name of five Isr.:—Nathan.

5417. נְתַנְאֵל **Nethanê'l,** *neth-an-ale´;* from 5414 and 410; *given of God; Nethanel,* the name of ten Isr.:—Nethaneel.

5418. נְתַנְיָה **Nethanyâh,** *neth-an-yaw´;* or נְתַנְיָהוּ **Nethanyâhûw,** *neth-an-yaw´-hoo;* from 5414 and 3050; *given of Jah; Nethanjah,* the name of four Isr.:—Nethaniah.

5419. נְתַן־מֶלֶךְ **Nethan-Melek,** *neth-an´ meh´-lek;* from 5414 and 4428; *given of* (the) *king; Nethan-Melek,* an Isr.:—Nathan-melech.

5420. נָתַס **nâthaç,** *naw-thas´;* a prim. root; to *tear* up:—mar.

5421. נָתַע **nâtha',** *naw-thah´;* for 5422; to *tear* out:—break.

5422. נָתַץ **nâthats,** *naw-thats';* a prim. root; to *tear* down:—beat down, break down (out), cast down, destroy, overthrow, pull down, throw down.

5423. נָתַק **nâthaq,** *naw-thak´;* a prim. root; to *tear* off:—break (off), burst, draw (away), lift up, pluck (away, off), pull (out), root out.

5424. נֶתֶק **netheq,** *neh´-thek;* from 5423; *scurf:*—(dry) scall.

5425. נָתַר **nâthar,** *naw-thar´;* a prim. root; to *jump,* i.e. *be* violently *agitated;* causat., to *terrify, shake* off, *untie:*—drive asunder, leap, (let) loose, × make, move, undo.

5426. נְתַר **nethar** (Chald.), *neth-ar´;* corresp. to 5425:—shake off.

5427. נֶתֶר **nether,** *neh´-ther;* from 5425; mineral *potash* (so called from *effervescing* with acid):—nitre.

5428. נָתַשׁ **nâthash,** *naw-thash´;* a prim. root; to *tear* away:—destroy, forsake, pluck (out, up, *by* the roots), pull up, root out (up), × utterly.

ס

5429. סְאָה **çe'âh,** *seh-aw´;* from an unused root mean. to *define;* a *seäh,* or certain measure (as *determinative*) for grain:—measure.

5430. סְאוֹן **çe'ôwn,** *seh-own´;* from 5431; perh. a military *boot* (as a protection from *mud*):—battle.

5431. סָאַן **çâ'an,** *saw-an´;* a prim. root; to *be miry;* used only as denom. from 5430; to *shoe,* i.e. (act. part.) a *soldier* shod:—warrior.

5432. סַאסְּאָה° **ça'çe'âh,** *sah-seh-aw´;* for 5429; *measurement,* i.e. *moderation:*—measure.

5433. סָבָא **çâbâ',** *saw-baw´;* a prim. root; to *quaff* to satiety, i.e. *become tipsy:*—drunkard, fill self, Sabean, [wine-] bibber.

5434. סְבָא **Çebâ',** *seb-aw´;* of for. or.; *Seba,* a son of Cush, and the country settled by him:—Seba.

5435. סֹבֶא **çôbe',** *so´-beh;* from 5433; *potation,* concr. *(wine),* or abstr. *(carousal):*—drink, drunken, wine.

5436. סְבָאִי **Çebâ'îy,** *seb-aw-ee´;* patrial from 5434; a *Sebaite,* or inhab. of Seba:—Sabean.

5437. סָבַב **çâbab,** *saw-bab´;* a prim. root; to *revolve, surround* or *border;* used in various applications, lit and fig. (as follows):—bring, cast, fetch, lead, make, walk, × whirl, × round about, be about on every side, apply, avoid, beset (about), besiege, bring again, carry (about), change, cause to come about, × circuit, (fetch a) compass (about, round), drive, environ, × on every side, beset (close, come, compass, go, stand) round about, remove, return, set, sit down, turn (self) (about, aside, away, back).

5438. סִבָּה **çibbâh,** *sib-baw´;* from 5437; a (providential) *turn* (of affairs):—cause.

5439. סָבִיב **çâbîyb,** *saw-beeb´;* or (fem.) סְבִיבָה **çebîybâh,** *seb-ee-baw´;* from 5437; (as noun) a *circle, neighbor,* or *environs;* but chiefly (as adv., with or without prep.) *around:*—(place, round) about, circuit, compass, on every side.

5440. סָבַךְ **çâbak,** *saw-bak´;* a prim. root; to *entwine:*—fold together, wrap.

5441. סֹבֶךְ **çôbek,** *so´-bek;* from 5440; a *copse:*—thicket.

5442. סְבָךְ **çebâk,** *seb-awk´;* from 5440; a *copse:*—thick (-et).

5443. סַבְּכָא **çabbekâ'** (Chald.), *sab-bek-aw´;* or שַׂבְּכָא **sabbekâ'** (Chald.), *sab-bek-aw´;* from a root corresp. to 5440; a *lyre:*—sackbut.

5444. סִבְּכַי **Çibbekay,** *sib-bek-ah´ee;* from 5440; *copse-like; Sibbecai,* an Isr.:—Sibbecai, Sibbechai.

5445. סָבַל **çâbal,** *saw-bal´;* a prim. root; to *carry* (lit. or fig.), or (reflex.) *be burdensome;* spec. to *be gravid:*—bear, be a burden, carry, strong to labour.

5446. סְבַל **çebal** (Chald.), *seb-al´;* corresp. to 5445; to *erect:*—strongly laid.

5447. סֵבֶל **çêbel,** *say´-bel;* from 5445; a *load* (lit. or fig.):—burden, charge.

5448. סֹבֶל **çôbel,** *so´-bel* [only in the form סֻבָּל **çubbâl,** *soob-bawl´*]; from 5445; a *load* (fig.):—burden.

5449. סַבָּל **çabbâl,** *sab-bawl´;* from 5445; a *porter:*—(to bear, bearer of) burden (s).

5450. סְבָלָה **çᵉbâlâh,** *seb-aw-law´;* from 5447; *porterage:*—burden.

5451. סִבֹּלֶת **çibbôleth,** *sib-bo-leth;* for 7641; an *ear* of grain:—Sibboleth.

5452. סְבַר **çᵉbar** (Chald.), *seb-ar´;* a prim. root; to *bear in mind,* i.e. *hope:*—think.

5453. סִבְרַיִם **Çibrayim,** *sib-rah´-yim;* dual from a root corresp. to 5452; *double hope; Sibrajim,* a place in Syria:—Sibraim.

5454. סַבְתָּא **Çabtâ,** *sab-taw´;* or סַבְתָּה **Çabtâh,** *sab-taw´;* prob. of for. der.; *Sabta* or *Sabtah,* the name of a son of Cush, and the country occupied by his posterity:—Sabta, Sabtah.

5455. סַבְתְּכָא **Çabtᵉkâ',** *sab-tek-aw´;* prob. of for. der.; *Sabteca,* the name of a son of Cush, and the region settled by him:—Sabtecha, Sabtechah.

5456. סָגַד **çâgad,** *saw-gad´;* a prim. root; to *prostrate* oneself (in homage):—fall down.

5457. סְגִד **çᵉgîd** (Chald.), *seg-eed´;* corresp. to 5456:—worship.

5458. סְגוֹר **çᵉgôwr,** *seg-ore´;* from 5462; prop. *shut up,* i.e. the *breast* (as inclosing the heart); also *gold* (as generally *shut* up safely):—caul, gold.

5459. סְגֻלָּה **çᵉgullâh,** *seg-ool-law´;* fem. pass. part. of an unused root mean. to *shut* up; *wealth* (as closely *shut* up):—jewel, peculiar (treasure), proper good, special.

5460. סְגַן **çᵉgan** (Chald.), *seg-an´;* corresp. to 5461:—governor.

5461. סָגָן **çâgân,** *saw-gawn´;* from an unused root mean. to *superintend;* a *præfect* of a province:—prince, ruler.

5462. סָגַר **çâgar,** *saw-gar´;* a prim. root; to *shut* up; fig. to *surrender:*—close up, deliver (up), give over (up), inclose, × pure, repair, shut (in, self, out, up, up together), stop, × straitly.

5463. סְגַר **çᵉgar** (Chald.), *seg-ar´;* corresp. to 5462:—shut up.

5464. סַגְרִיד **çagrîyd,** *sag-reed´;* prob. from 5462 in the sense of *sweeping* away; a pouring rain:—very rainy.

5465. סַד **çad,** *sad;* from an unused root mean. to *estop;* the *stocks:*—stocks.

5466. סָדִין **çâdîyn,** *saw-deen´;* from an unused root mean. to *envelop;* a *wrapper,* i.e. *shirt:*—fine linen, sheet.

5467. סְדֹם **Çᵉdôm,** *sed-ome´;* from an unused root mean. to *scorch; burnt* (i.e. *volcanic* or *bituminous*) district; *Sedom,* a place near the Dead Sea:—Sodom.

5468. סֶדֶר **çeder,** *seh´-der;* from an unused root mean. to *arrange; order:*—order.

5469. סַהַר **çahar,** *sah´-har;* from an unused root mean. to *be round; roundness:*—round.

5470. סֹהַר **çôhar,** *so´-har;* from the same as 5469; a *dungeon* (as *surrounded* by walls):—prison.

5471. סוֹא **Çôw',** *so;* of for. der.; *So,* an Eg. king:—So.

5472. סוּג **çûwg,** *soog;* a prim. root; prop. to *flinch,* i.e. (by impl.) to *go back,* lit. (to *retreat*) or fig. (to *apostatize*):—backslider, drive, go back, turn (away, back).

5473. סוּג **çûwg,** *soog;* a prim. root [prob. rather ident. with 5472 through the idea of *shrinking* from a hedge; comp. 7735]; to *hem* in, i.e. *bind:*—set about.

סוּג° **çûwg.** See 5509.

5474. סוּגַר **çûwgar,** *soo-gar´;* from 5462; an *inclosure,* i.e. *cage* (for an animal):—ward.

5475. סוֹד **çôwd,** *sode;* from 3245; a *session,* i.e. *company* of persons (in close deliberation); by impl. *intimacy, consultation,* a *secret:*—assembly, counsel, inward, secret (counsel).

5476. סוֹדִי **Çôwdîy,** *so-dee´;* from 5475; a *confidant; Sodi,* an Isr.:—Sodi.

5477. סוּחַ **Çûwach,** *soo´-akh;* from an unused root mean. to *wipe* away; *sweeping; Suäch, an Isr.:—Suah.*

5478. סוּחָה **çûwchâh,** *soo-khaw´;* from the same as 5477; something *swept* away, i.e. *filth:*—torn.

סוּט **çûwṭ.** See 7750.

5479. סוֹטַי **Çôwṭay,** *so-tah´ee;* from 7750; *roving; Sotai,* one of the Nethinim:—Sotai.

5480. סוּךְ **çûwk,** *sook;* a prim. root; prop. to *smear* over (with oil), i.e. *anoint:*—anoint (self), × at all.

סוֹלְלָה **çôwlᵉlâh.** See 5550.

5481. סוּמְפּוֹנְיָה **çûwmpôwnᵉyâh** (Chald.), *soom-po-neh-yaw´;* or סוּמְפֹּנְיָה **çûwmpônᵉyâh** (Chald.), *soom-po-neh-yaw´;* or סִיפֹנְיָא° **çîyphônᵉyâ'** (Dan. 3 : 10) (Chald.), *see-fo-neh-yaw´;* of Greek origin (συμφωνία) a *bagpipe* (with a double pipe):—dulcimer.

5482. סְוֵנֵה **Çᵉvênêh,** *sev-ay-nay´* [rather to be written סְוֵנָה **Çᵉvênâh,** *sev-ay´-naws;* for סְוֵן **Çᵉvên,** *sev-ane´;* i.e. *to Seven*]; of Eg. der.; *Seven,* a place in Upper Eg.:—Syene.

5483. סוּס **çûwç,** *soos;* or סֻס **çûç,** *soos;* from an unused root mean. to *skip* (prop. for joy): a *horse* (as leaping); also a *swallow* (from its rapid *flight*):—crane, horse ([-back, -hoof]). Comp. 6571.

5484. סוּסָה **çûwçâh,** *soo-saw´;* fem. of 5483; a *mare:*—company of horses.

5485. סוּסִי **Çûwçîy,** *soo-see´;* from 5483; *horse-like; Susi,* an Isr.:—Susi.

5486. סוּף **çûwph,** *soof;* a prim. root; to *snatch* away, i.e. *terminate:*—consume, have an end, perish, × be utterly.

5487. סוּף **çûwph** (Chald.), *soof;* corresp. to 5486; to *come to an end:*—consumme, fulfil.

5488. סוּף **çûwph,** *soof;* prob. of Eg. or.; a *reed,* espec. the *papyrus:*—flag. Red [sea], weed. Comp. 5489.

5489. סוּף **Çûwph,** *soof;* for 5488 (by ellipsis of 3220); the *Reed (Sea):*—Red sea.

5490. סוֹף **çôwph,** *sofe;* from 5486; a *termination:*—conclusion, end, hinder part.

5491. סוֹף **çôwph** (Chald.), *sofe;* corresp. to 5490:—end.

5492. סוּפָה **çûwphâh,** *soo-faw´;* from 5486; a *hurricane:*—Red Sea, storm, tempest, whirlwind, Red sea.

5493. סוּר **çûwr,** *soor;* or שׂוּר **sûwr** (Hos. 9 : 12), *soor;* a prim. root; to *turn* off (lit. or fig.):—be [-head], bring, call back, decline, depart, eschew, get [you], go (aside), × grievous, lay away (by), leave undone, be past, pluck away, put (away, down), rebel, remove (to and fro), revolt, × be sour, take (away, off), turn (aside, away, in), withdraw, be without.

5494. סוּר **çûwr,** *soor;* prob. pass. part. of 5493; *turned* off, i,.e. *deteriorated:*—degenerate.

5495. סוּר **Çûwr,** *soor;* the same as 5494; *Sur,* a gate of the Temple:—Sur.

5496. סוּת **çûwth,** *sooth;* perh. denom. from 7898; prop. to *prick,* i.e. (fig.) stimulate; by impl. to *seduce:*—entice, move, persuade, provoke, remove, set on, stir up, take away.

5497. סוּת **çûwth,** *sooth;* prob. from the same root as 4533; *covering,* i.e. *clothing:*—clothes.

5498. סָחַב **çâchab,** *saw-khab´;* a prim. root; to *trail* along:—draw (out), tear.

5499. סְחָבָה **çᵉchâbâh,** *seh-khaw-baw´;* from 5498; a *rag:*—cast clout.

5500. סָחָה **çâchâh,** *saw-khaw´;* a prim. root; to *sweep* away:—scrape.

5501. סְחִי **çᵉchîy,** *seh-khee´;* from 5500; *refuse* (as *swept* off):—offscouring.

סָחִישׁ **çâchîysh.** See 7823.

5502. סָחַף **çâchaph,** *saw-khaf´;* a prim. root; to *scrape* off:—sweep (away).

5503. סָחַר **çâchar,** *saw-khar´;* a prim. root; to *travel* round (spec. as a *pedlar*); intens. to *palpitate:*—go about, merchant (-man), occupy with, pant, trade, traffick.

5504. סַחַר **çachar,** *sakh´-ar;* from 5503; *profit* (from trade):—merchandise.

5505. סָחַר **çâchar,** *saw-khar´;* from 5503; an *emporium;* abstr. *profit* (from trade):—mart, merchandise.

5506. סְחֹרָה **çechôrâh,** *sekh-o-raw´;* from 5503; *traffic:*—merchandise.

5507. סֹחֵרָה **çôchêrâh,** *so-khay-raw´;* prop. act. part. fem. of 5503; something *surrounding* the person, i,e, a *shield:*—buckler.

5508. סֹחֶרֶת **çôchereth,** *so-kheh´-reth;* similar to 5507; prob. a (black) *tile* (or *tessara*) for laying borders with:—black marble.

סֵט **çêṭ.** See 7750.

5509. סִיג **çîyg,** *seeg;* or סוּג° **çûwg** (Ezek. 22: 18), *soog;* from 5472 in the sense of *refuse; scoria:*—dross.

5510. סִיוָן **Çîyvân,** *see-vawn´;* prob. of Pers. or.; *Sivan,* the third Heb. month:—Sivan.

5511. סִיחוֹן **Çîychôwn,** *see-khone´;* or סִיחֹן **Çîychôn,** *see-khone´;* from the same as 5477; *tempestuous; Sichon,* an Amoritish king:—Sihon.

5512. סִין **Çîyn,** *seen;* of uncert. der.; *Sin,* the name of an Eg. town and (prob.) desert adjoining:—Sin.

5513. סִינִי **Çîynîy,** *see-nee´;* from an otherwise unknown name of a man; a *Sinite,* or descend. of one of the sons of Canaan:—Sinite.

5514. סִינַי **Çîynay,** *see-nah´ee;* of uncert. der.; *Sinai,* a mountain of Arabia:—Sinai.

5515. סִינִים **Çîynîym,** *see-neem´;* plur. of an otherwise unknown name; *Sinim,* a distant Oriental region:—Sinim.

5516. סִיסְרָא **Çîyçerâ',** *see-ser-aw´;* of uncert. der.; *Sisera,* the name of a Canaanitish king and of one of the Nethinim:—Sisera.

5517. סִיעָא **Çîy'â',** *see-ah´;* or סִיעֲהָא **Çîy'ăhâ',** *see-ah-haw´;* from an unused root mean. to *converse; congregation; Sia,* or *Siaha,* one of the Nethinim:—Sia, Siaha.

סִיפֹנְיָא° **çîyphôneyâ'.** See 5481.

5518. סִיר **çîyr,** *seer;* or (fem.) סִירָה **çîyrâh,** *see-raw´;* or סִרָה **çirâh** (Jer. 52 : 18), *see-raw´;* from a prim. root mean. to *boil* up; a *pot;* also a *thorn* (as springing up rapidly); by impl. a *hook:*—caldron, fishhook, pan, ([wash-]) pot, thorn.

5519. סָךְ **çâk,** *sawk;* from 5526; prop. a *thicket* of men, i.e. a *crowd:*—multitude.

5520. סֹךְ **çôk,** *soke;* from 5526; a *hut* (as of *entwined* boughs); also a *lair:*—covert, den, pavilion, tabernacle.

5521. סֻכָּה **çukkâh,** *sook-kaw´;* fem. of 5520; a *hut* or *lair:*—booth, cottage, covert, pavilion, tabernacle, tent.

5522. סִכּוּת **çikkûwth,** *sik-kooth´;* fem. of 5519; an (idolatrous) *booth:*—tabernacle.

5523. סֻכּוֹת **Çukkôwth,** *sook-kohth´;* or סֻכֹּת **Çukkôth,** *sook-kohth´;* plur. of 5521; *booths; Succoth,* the name of a place in Egypt and of three in Pal.:—Succoth.

5524. סֻכּוֹת בְּנוֹת **Çukkôwth benôwth,** *sook-kohth´ ben-ohth´;* from 5523 and the (irreg.) plur. of 1323; *booths of (the) daughters; brothels,* i.e. idolatrous *tents* for impure purposes:—Succoth-benoth.

5525. סֻכִּי **Çukkîy,** *sook-kee´;* patrial from an unknown name (perh. 5520); a *Sukkite,* or inhab. of some place near Eg. (i.e. *hut-dwellers*):—Sukkiims.

5526. סָכַךְ **çâkak,** *saw-kak´;* or שָׂכַךְ **sâkak** (Exod. 33 : 22), *saw-kak´;* a prim. root; prop. to *entwine* as a screen; by impl. to *fence* in, *cover* over, (fig.) *protect:*—cover, defence, defend, hedge in, join together, set, shut up.

5527. סְכָכָה **Çekâkâh,** *sek-aw-kaw´;* from 5526; *inclosure; Secacah,* a place in Pal.:—Secacah.

5528. סָכַל **çâkal,** *saw-kal´;* for 3688; to *be silly:*—do (make, play the, turn into) fool (-ish, -ishly, -ishness).

5529. סֶכֶל **çekel,** *seh´-kel;* from 5528; *silliness;* concr. and collect. *dolts:*—folly.

5530. סָכָל **çâkâl,** *saw-kawl´;* from 5528; *silly:*—fool (-ish), sottish.

5531. סִכְלוּת **çiklûwth,** *sik-looth´;* or שִׂכְלוּת **siklûwth** (Eccl. 1 : 17), *sik-looth´;* from 5528; *silliness:*—folly, foolishness.

5532. סָכַן **çâkan,** *saw-kan´;* a prim. root; to *be familiar* with; by impl. to *minister* to, *be serviceable* to, to *cherish, be customary:*—acquaint (self), be advantage, × ever, (be, [un-]) profit (-able), treasure, be wont.

5533. סָכַן **çâkan,** *saw-kan´;* prob. a denom. from 7915; prop. *to cut,* i.e. *damage;* also to *grow* (caus. *make*) *poor:*—endanger, impoverish.

5534. סָכַר **çâkar,** *saw-kar´;* a prim. root; to *shut* up; by impl. to *surrender:*—stop, give over. See also 5462; 7936.

5535. סָכַת **çâkath,** *saw-kath´;* a prim. root; to *be silent;* by impl. to *observe* quietly:—take heed.

סֻכֹּת **Çukkôth.** See 5523.

5536. סַל **çal,** *sal;* from 5549; prop. a willow *twig* (as *pendulous*), i.e. an *osier,* but only as woven into a *basket:*—basket.

5537. סָלָא **çâlâ',** *saw-law´;* a prim. root; to *suspend* in a balance, i.e. *weigh:*—compare.

5538. סִלָּא **Çillâ',** *sil-law´;* from 5549; an *embankment; Silla,* a place in Jerus.:—Silla.

5539. סָלַד **çâlad,** *saw-lad´;* a prim. root; prob. to *leap* (with joy), i.e. *exult:*—harden self.

5540. סֶלֶד **Çeled,** *seh´-led;* from 5539; *exultation; Seled,* an Isr.:—Seled.

5541. סָלָה **çâlâh,** *saw-law´;* a prim. root; to *hang* up, i.e. *weigh,* or (fig.) *contemn:*—tread down (under foot), value.

5542. סֶלָה **çelâh,** *seh´-law;* from 5541; *suspension* (of music), i.e. *pause:*—Selah.

5543. סַלּוּ **Çallûw,** *sal-loo´;* or סַלּוּא **Çallûw',** *sal-loo´;* or סָלוּא **Çâlûw',** *saw-loo´;* or סַלַּי **Çallay,** *sal-lah´ee;* from 5541; *weighed; Sallu* or *Sallai,* the name of two Isr.:—Sallai, Sallu, Salu.

5544. סִלּוֹן **çillôwn,** *sil-lone´;* or סַלוֹן **çallôwn,** *sal-lone´;* from 5541; a *prickle* (as if *pendulous*):—brier, thorn.

5545. סָלַח **çâlach,** *saw-lakh´;* a prim. root; to *forgive:*—forgive, pardon, spare.

5546. סַלָּח **çallâch,** *sal-lawkh´;* from 5545; *placable:*—ready to forgive.

סַלַּי **Çallay.** See 5543.

5547. סְלִיחָה **çelîychâh,** *sel-ee-khaw´;* from 5545; *pardon:*—forgiveness, pardon.

5548. סַלְכָה **Çalkâh,** *sal-kaw´;* from an unused root mean. to *walk; walking; Salcah,* a place E. of the Jordan:—Salcah, Salchah.

5549. סָלַל **çâlal,** *saw-lal´;* a prim. root; to *mound* up (espec. a turnpike); fig. to *exalt;* reflex, to *oppose* (as by a dam):—cast up, exalt (self), extol, make plain, raise up.

5550. סֹלְלָה **çôlelâh,** *so-lel-aw´;* or סוֹלְלָה **çôwlelâh,** *so-lel-aw´;* act. part. fem. of 5549, but used pass.; a military *mound,* i.e. *rampart* of besiegers:—bank, mount.

5551. סֻלָּם **çullâm,** *sool-lawm´;* from 5549; a *stair-case:*—ladder.

5552. סַלְסִלָּה **çalçillâh,** *sal-sil-law´;* from 5541; a *twig* (as *pendulous*):—basket.

5553. סֶלַע **çela',** *seh´-lah;* from an unused root mean. to be *lofty;* a craggy *rock,* lit. or fig. (a *fortress*):—(ragged) rock, stone (-ny), strong hold.

5554. סֶלַע **Çela',** *seh´-lah;* the same as 5553; *Sela,* the rock-city of Idumæa:—rock, Sela (-h).

5555. סֶלַע הַמַּחְלְקוֹת **Çela' ham-machlequôwth,** *seh´-lah ham-makh-lek-ōth´;* from 5553 and the plur. of 4256 with the art. interposed; *rock of the divisions; Sela-ham-Mach-lekoth,* a place in Pal.:—Sela-hammalekoth.

5556. סָלְעָם **çol'âm,** *sol-awm´;* appar. from the same as 5553 in the sense of *crushing* as with a rock, i.e. consuming; a kind of *locust* (from it *destructiveness*):—bald locust.

5557. סָלַף **çâlaph,** *saw-laf´;* a prim. root; prop. to *wrench,* i.e. (fig.) to *subvert:*—overthrow, pervert.

5558. סֶלֶף **çeleph,** *seh´-lef;* from 5557; *distortion,* i.e. (fig.) *viciousness:*—perverseness.

5559. סְלִק **çelîq** (Chald.), *sel-eek´;* a prim. root; to *ascend:*—come (up).

5560. סֹלֶת **çôleth,** *so´-leth;* from an unused root mean. to *strip; flour* (as *chipped* off):—(fine) flour, meal.

5561. סַם **çam,** *sam;* from an unused root mean. to *smell* sweet; an *aroma:*—sweet (spice).

5562. סַמְגַּר נְבוֹ **Çamgar Nᵉbôw,** *sam-gar´ neb-o´;* of for. or.; *Samgar-Nebo,* a Bab. general:—Samgar-nebo.

5563. סְמָדַר **çᵉmâdar,** *sem-aw-dar´;* of uncert. der.; a vine *blossom;* used also adv. *abloom:*—tender grape.

5564. סָמַךְ **çâmak,** *saw-mak´;* a prim. root; to *prop* (lit. or fig.); reflex. to *lean* upon or *take hold* of (in a favorable or unfavorable sense):—bear up, establish, (up-) hold, lay, lean, lie hard, put, rest self, set self, stand fast, stay (self), sustain.

5565. סְמַכְיָהוּ **Çᵉmakyâhûw,** *sem-ak-yaw´-hoo;* from 5564 and 3050; *supported of Jah; Semakjah,* an Isr.:—Semachiah.

5566. סֶמֶל **çemel,** *seh´-mel;* or סֵמֶל **çêmel,** *say´-mel;* from an unused root mean. to *resemble;* a *likeness:*—figure, idol, image.

5567. סָמַן **çâman,** *saw-man´;* a prim. root; to *designate:*—appointed.

5568. סָמַר **çâmar,** *saw-mar´;* a prim. root; to *be erect,* i.e. *bristle* as hair:—stand up, tremble.

5569. סָמָר **çâmâr,** *saw-mawr´;* from 5568; *bristling,* i.e. *shaggy:*—rough.

5570. סְנָאָה **Çᵉnâ'âh,** *sen-aw-aw´;* from an unused root mean. to *prick; thorny; Senaah,* a place in Pal.:—Senaah, Hassenaah [*with the art.*].

סְנֻאָה **çᵉnû'âh.** See 5574.

5571. סַנְבַלַּט **Çanballaṭ,** *san-bal-lat´;* of for. or.; *Sanballat,* a Pers. satrap of Samaria:—Sanballat.

5572. סְנֶה **çᵉneh,** *sen-eh´;* from an unused root mean. to *prick;* a *bramble:*—bush.

5573. סֶנֶה **Çeneh,** *seh´-neh;* the same as 5572; *thorn; Seneh,* a crag in Pal.:—Seneh.

סַנָּה **Çannâh.** See 7158.

5574. סְנוּאָה **Çᵉnûw'âh,** *sen-oo-aw´;* or סְנֻאָה **Çᵉnû'âh,** *sen-oo-aw´;* from the same as 5570; *pointed;* (used with the art. as a prop. name) *Senuah,* the name of two Isr.:—Hasenuah [*includ. the art.*], Senuah.

5575. סַנְוֵר **çanvêr,** *san-vare´;* of uncert. der.; (in plur.) *blindness:*—blindness.

5576. סַנְחֵרִיב **Çanchêrîyb,** *san-khay-reeb´;* of for. or.; *Sancherib,* an Ass. king:—Sennacherib.

5577. סַנְסִן **çançin,** *san-seen´;* from an unused root mean. to be *pointed;* a *twig* (as *tapering*):—bough.

5578. סַנְסַנָּה **Çançannâh,** *san-san-naw´;* fem. of a form of 5577; a *bough; Sansannah,* a place in Pal.:—Sansannah.

5579. סְנַפִּיר **çᵉnappîyr,** *sen-ap-peer´;* of uncert. der.; a *fin* (collect.):—fins.

5580. סָס **çâç,** *sawce;* from the same as 5483; a *moth* (from the *agility* of the fly):—moth.

סֻס **çûç.** See 5483.

5581. סִסְמַי **Çiçmay,** *sis-mah´ee;* of uncert. der.; *Sismai,* an Isr.:—Sisamai.

5582. סָעַד **çâ'ad,** *saw-ad´;* a prim. root; to *support* (mostly fig.):—comfort, establish, hold up, refresh self, strengthen, be upholden.

5583. סְעַד **çᵉ'ad** (Chald.), *seh-ad´;* corresp. to 5582; to *aid:*—helping.

5584. סָעָה **çâ'âh,** *saw-aw´;* a prim. root; to *rush:*—storm.

5585. סָעִיף **çâ'îyph,** *saw-eef´;* from 5586; a *fissure* (of rocks); also a *bough* (as *subdivided*):—(outmost), branch, clift, top.

5586. סָעַף **çâ'aph,** *saw-af´;* a prim. root; prop. to *divide* up; but used only as denom. from 5585; to *disbranch* (a tree):—top.

5587. סָעִף **çâ'îph,** *saw-eef´;* or שָׂעִף **sâ'îph,** *saw-eef´;* from 5586; *divided* (in mind), i.e. (abstr.) a *sentiment:*—opinion.

5588. סֵעֵף **çê'êph,** *say-afe´;* from 5586; *divided* (in mind), i.e. (concr.) a *skeptic:*—thought.

5589. סְעַפָּה **çᵉ'appâh,** *seh-ap-paw´;* fem. of 5585; a *twig* or *branch:*—bough. Comp. 5634.

5590. סָעַר **çâ'ar,** *saw-ar´;* a prim. root; to *rush* upon; by impl. to *toss* (trans. or intrans., lit. or fig.):—be (toss with) tempest (-uous), be sore troubled, come out as a (drive with the, scatter with a) whirlwind.

5591. סַעַר **ça'ar,** *sah´-ar;* or (fem.) סְעָרָה **çᵉ'ârâh,** *seh-aw-raw´;* from 5590; a *hurricane:*—storm (-y), tempest, whirlwind.

5592. סַף **çaph,** *saf;* from 5605; in its original sense of *containing;* a *vestibule* (as a *limit*); also a *dish* (for holding blood or wine):—bason, bowl, cup, door (post), gate, post, threshold.

5593. סַף **Çaph,** *saf;* the same as 5592; *Saph,* a Philistine:—Saph. Comp. 5598.

5594. סָפַד **çâphad,** *saw-fad´;* a prim. root; prop. to *tear* the hair and *beat* the breasts (as Orientals do in grief); gen. to *lament;* by impl. to *wail:*—lament, mourn (-er), wail.

5595. סָפָה **çâphâh,** *saw-faw´;* a prim. root; prop. to *scrape* (lit. to *shave;* but usually fig.) together (i.e. to *accumulate* or *increase*) or away (i.e. to *scatter, remove* or *ruin;* intrans. to *perish*):—add, augment, consume, destroy, heap, join, perish, put.

5596. סָפַח **çâphach,** *saw-fakh´;* or שָׂפַח **sâphach** (Isa. 3 : 17), *saw-fakh´;* a prim. root; prop. to *scrape* out, but in certain peculiar senses (of *removal* or *association*):—abiding, gather together, cleave, put, smite with a scab.

5597. סַפַּחַת **çappachath,** *sap-pakh´-ath;* from 5596; the *mange* (as making the hair fall off):—scab.

5598. סִפַּי **Çippay,** *sip-pah´ee;* from 5592; *bason-like; Sippai,* a Philistine:—Sippai. Comp. 5593.

5599. סָפִיחַ **çâphîyach,** *saw-fee´-akh;* from 5596; something (spontaneously) *falling* off, i.e. a *self-sown* crop; fig. a *freshet:*—(such) things as (which) grow (of themselves), which groweth of its own accord (itself).

5600. סְפִינָה **çᵉphîynâh,** *sef-ee-naw´;* from 5603; a (sea-going) *vessel* (as *ceiled* with a deck):—ship.

5601. סַפִּיר **çappîyr,** *sap-peer´;* from 5608; a *gem* (perh. as used for *scratching* other substances), prob. the *sapphire:*—sapphire.

5602. סֵפֶל **çêphel,** *say´-fel;* from an unused root mean. to *depress;* a *basin* (as *deepened* out):—bowl, dish.

5603. סָפַן **çâphan,** *saw-fan´;* a prim. root; to *hide* by covering; spec. to *roof* (pass. part. as noun, a *roof*) or *wainscot;* fig. to *reserve:*—cieled, cover, seated.

5604. סִפֻּן **çippûn,** *sip-poon´;* from 5603; a *wainscot:*—cieling.

5605. סָפַף **çâphaph,** *saw-faf´;* a prim. root; prop. to *snatch* away, i.e. *terminate;* but used only as denom. from 5592 (in the sense of a *vestibule*), to *wait at* the *threshold:*—be a doorkeeper.

5606. סָפַק **çâphaq,** *saw-fak´;* or שָׂפַק **sâphaq** (1 Kings 20 : 10; Job 27 : 23; Isa. 2 : 6), *saw-fak´;* a prim. root; to *clap* the hands (in token of compact, derision, grief, indignation or punishment); by impl. of satisfaction, to *be enough;* by impl. of excess, to *vomit:*—clap, smite, strike, suffice, wallow.

5607. סֵפֶק **çêpheq,** *saw´-fek;* or שֶׂפֶק **sepheq** (Job 20 : 22; 36 : 18), *seh´-fek;* from 5606; *chastisement;* also *satiety:*—stroke, sufficiency.

5608. סָפַר **çâphar,** *saw-far´;* a prim. root; prop. to *score* with a mark as a tally or record, i.e. (by impl.) to *inscribe,* and also to *enumerate;* intens. to *recount,* i.e. *celebrate:*—commune, (ac-) count, declare, number, + penknife, reckon, scribe, shew forth, speak, talk, tell (out), writer.

5609. סְפַר **çᵉphar** (Chald.), *sef-ar´;* from a root corresp. to 5608; a *book:*—book, roll.

5610. סְפָר **çᵉphâr,** *sef-awr´;* from 5608; a *census:*—numbering.

5611. סְפָר **Çᵉphâr,** *sef-awr´;* the same as 5610; *Sephar,* a place in Arabia:—Sephar.

5612. סֵפֶר **çêpher,** *say´-fer;* or (fem.) סִפְרָה **çiphrâh** (Psa. 56 : 8 [9], *sif-raw´;* from 5608; prop. *writing* (the art or a document); by impl. a *book:*—bill, book, evidence, × learn [-ed] (-ing), letter, register, scroll.

5613. סָפֵר **çâphêr** (Chald.), *saw-fare´;* from the same as 5609; a *scribe* (secular or sacred):—scribe.

5614. סְפָרָד **Çᵉphârâd,** *sef-aw-rawd´;* of for. der.; *Sepharad,* a region of Ass.:—Sepharad.

סִפְרָה **çiphrâh.** See 5612.

5615. סְפֹרָה **çᵉphôrâh,** *sef-o-raw´;* from 5608; a *numeration:*—number.

5616. סְפַרְוִי **Çᵉpharvîy,** *sef-ar-vee´;* patrial from 5617; a *Sepharvite* or inhab. of Sepharvain:—Sepharvite.

5617. סְפַרְוַיִם **Çᵉpharvayim** (dual), *sef-ar-vah´-yim;* or סְפָרִים° **Çᵉphârîym** (plur.), *sef-aw-reem´;* of for. der.; *Sepharvajim* or *Sepharim,* a place in Ass.:—Sepharvaim.

5618. סֹפֶרֶת **Çôphereth,** *so-feh´-reth;* fem. act. part. of 5608; a *scribe* (prop. female); *Sophereth,* a temple servant:—Sophereth.

5619. סָקַל **çâqal,** *saw-kal´;* a prim. root; prop. to *be weighty;* but used only in the sense of *lapidation* or its contrary (as if a *de*lapidation):—(cast, gather out, throw) stone (-s), × surely.

5620. סַר **çar,** *sar;* from 5637 contr.; *peevish:*—heavy, sad.

5621. סָרָב **çârâb,** *saw-rawb´;* from an unused root mean. to *sting;* a thistle:—brier.

5622. סַרְבַּל **çarbal** (Chald.), *sar-bal´;* of uncert. der.; a *cloak:*—coat.

5623. סַרְגּוֹן **Çargôwn,** *sar-gōne´;* of for. der.; *Sargon,* an Ass. king:—Sargon.

5624. סֶרֶד **Çered,** *seh´-red;* from a prim. root mean. to *tremble; trembling; Sered,* an Isr.:—Sered.

5625. סַרְדִּי **Çardîy,** *sar-dee´;* patron. from 5624; a *Seredite* (collect.) or desc. of Sered:—Sardites.

5626. סִרָה **Çîrâh,** *see-raw´;* from 5493; *departure; Sirah,* a cistern so-called:—Sirah. See also 5518.

5627. סָרָה **çârâh,** *saw-raw´;* from 5493; *apostasy, crime;* fig. *remission:*— × continual, rebellion, revolt ([-ed]), turn away, wrong.

5628. סָרַח **çârach,** *saw-rakh´;* a prim. root; to *extend* (even to *excess*):—exceeding, hand, spread, stretch self, banish.

5629. סֶרַח **çerach,** *seh´-rakh;* from 5628; a *redundancy:*—remnant.

5630. סִרְיֹן **çiryôn,** *sir-yone´;* for 8302; a coat of *mail:*—brigandine.

5631. סָרִיס **çârîyç,** *saw-reece´;* or סָרִס **çârîç,** *saw-reece´;* from an unused root mean. to *castrate;* a *eunuch;* by impl. *valet* (espec. of the female apartments), and thus a *minister* of state:—chamberlain, eunuch, officer. Comp. 7249.

5632. סָרֵךְ **çârêk** (Chald.), *saw-rake´;* of for. or.; an *emir:*—president.

5633. סֶרֶן **çeren,** *seh´-ren;* from an unused root of unc. mean.; an *axle;* fig. a *peer:*—lord, plate.

5634. סַרְעַפָּה **çar'appâh,** *sar-ap-paw´;* for 5589; a *twig:*—bough.

5635. סָרַף **çâraph,** *saw-raf´;* a prim. root; to *cremate,* i.e. to *be* (near) *of kin* (such being privileged to kindle the pyre):—burn.

5636. סַרְפָּד **çarpâd,** *sar-pawd´;* from 5635; a *nettle* (as stinging like a *burn*):—brier.

5637. סָרַר **çârar,** *saw-rar´;* a prim. root; to *turn* away, i.e. (morally) *be refractory:*— × away, backsliding, rebellious, revolter (-ing), slide back, stubborn, withdrew.

5638. סְתָו° **çᵉthâv,** *seth-awv´;* from an unused root mean. to *hide; winter* (as the dark season):—winter.

5639. סְתוּר **Çᵉthûwr,** *seth-oor´;* from 5641; *hidden; Sethur,* an Isr.:—Sethur.

5640. סָתַם **çâtham,** *saw-tham´;* or שָׂתַם **sâtham** (Num. 24 : 15), *saw-tham´;* a prim. root; to *stop* up; by impl. to *repair;* fig. to *keep secret:*—closed up, hidden, secret, shut out (up), stop.

5641. סָתַר **çâthar,** *saw-thar´;* a prim. root; to *hide* (by covering), lit. or fig.:—be absent, keep close, conceal, hide (self), (keep) secret, × surely.

5642. סְתַר **çᵉthar** (Chald.), *seth-ar´;* corresp. to 5641; to *conceal;* fig. to *demolish:*—destroy, secret thing.

5643. סֵתֶר **çêther,** *say´-ther;* or (fem.) סִתְרָה **çithrâh** (Deut. 32 : 38), *sith-raw´;* from 5641; a *cover* (in a good or a bad, a lit. or a fig. sense):—backbiting, covering, covert, × disguise [-th], hiding place, privily, protection, secret (-ly, place).

5644. סִתְרִי **Çithrîy,** *sith-ree´;* from 5643; *protective; Sithri,* an Isr.:—Zithri.

ע

5645. עָב **'âb,** *awb* (masc. and fem.); from 5743; prop. an *envelope,* i.e. *darkness* (or *density,* 2 Chron. 4 : 17); spec. a (scud) *cloud;* also a *copse:*—clay, (thick) cloud, × thick, thicket. Comp. 5672.

5646. עָב **'âb,** *awb;* or עֹב **'ôb,** *obe;* from an unused root mean. to *cover;* prop. equiv. to 5645; but used only as an arch. term, an *architrave* (as *shading* the pillars):—thick (beam, plant).

5647. עָבַד **'âbad,** *aw-bad´;* a prim. root; to *work* (in any sense); by impl. to *serve, till,* (caus.) *enslave,* etc.:— × be, keep in bondage, be bondmen, bond-service, compel, do, dress, ear, execute, + husbandman, keep, labour (-ing man), bring to pass, (cause to, make to) serve (-ing, self), (be, become) servant (-s), do (use) service, till (-er), transgress *[from margin],* (set a) work, be wrought, worshipper.

5648. עֲבַד **'ăbad** (Chald.), *ab-ad´;* corresp. to 5647; to *do, make, prepare, keep,* etc.:— × cut, do, execute, go on, make, move, work.

5649. עֲבַד **'ăbad** (Chald.), *ab-ad´;* from 5648; a *servant:*—servant.

5650. עֶבֶד **'ebed,** *eh´-bed;* from 5647; a *servant:*— × bondage, bondman, [bond-] servant, (man-) servant.

5651. עֶבֶד **'Ebed,** *eh´-bed;* the same as 5650; *Ebed,* the name of two Isr.:—Ebed.

5652. עֲבָד **'ăbâd,** *ab-awd´;* from 5647; a *deed:*—work.

5653. עַבְדָּא **'Abdâ',** *ab-daw´;* from 5647; *work; Abda,* the name of two Isr.:—Abda.

5654. עֹבֵד אֱדוֹם **'Obêd 'Ĕdôwm,** *o-bade´ ed-ome´;* from the act. part. of 5647 and 123; *worker of Edom; Obed-Edom,* the name of five Isr.:—Obed-edom.

5655. עַבְדְאֵל **'Abdᵉ'êl,** *ab-deh-ale´;* from 5647 and 410; *serving God; Abdeël,* an Isr.:—Abdeel. Comp. 5661.

5656. עֲבֹדָה **'ăbôdâh,** *ab-o-daw´;* or עֲבוֹדָה **'ăbôwdâh,** *ab-o-daw´;* from 5647; *work* of any kind:—act, bondage, + bondservant, effect, labour, ministering (-try), office, service (-ile, -itude), tillage, use, work, × wrought.

5657. עֲבֻדָּה **'ăbuddâh,** *ab-ood-daw´;* pass. part. of 5647; something *wrought,* i.e. (concr.) *service:*—household, store of servants.

5658. עַבְדוֹן **'Abdôwn,** *ab-dohn´;* from 5647; *servitude; Abdon,* the name of a place in Pal. and of four Isr.:—Abdon. Comp. 5683.

5659. עַבְדוּת **'abdûwth,** *ab-dooth´;* from 5647; *servitude:*—bondage.

5660. עַבְדִּי **'Abdîy,** *ab-dee´;* from 5647; *serviceable; Abdi,* the name of two Isr.:—Abdi.

5661. עַבְדִיאֵל **'Abdîy'êl,** *ab-dee-ale´;* from 5650 and 410; *servant of God; Abdiël,* an Isr.:—Abdiel. Comp. 5655.

5662. עֹבַדְיָה **'Ôbadyâh,** *o-bad-yaw´;* or עֹבַדְיָהוּ **'Ôbadyâhûw,** *o-bad-yaw´-hoo;* act. part. of 5647 and 3050; *serving Jah; Obadjah,* the name of thirteen Isr.:—Obadiah.

5663. עֶבֶד מֶלֶךְ **'Ebed Melek,** *eh´-bed meh´-lek;* from 5650 and 4428; *servant of a king; Ebed-Melek,* a eunuch of king Zedekeah:—Ebed-melech.

5664. עֲבֵד נְגוֹ **'Ăbêd Nᵉgôw,** *ab-ade´; neg-o´;* the same as 5665; *Abed-Nego,* the Bab. name of one of Daniel's companions:—Abed-nego.

5665. עֲבֵד נְגוֹא **'Ăbêd Nᵉgôw'** (Chald.), *ab-ade´ neg-o´;* of for. or.; *Abed-Nego,* the name of Azariah:—Abed-nego.

5666. עָבָה **'âbâh,** *aw-baw´;* a prim. root; to *be dense:*—be (grow) thick (-er).

5667. עֲבוֹט **'ăbôwṭ,** *ab-ote´;* or עֲבֹט **'ăbôṭ,** *ab-ote´;* from 5670; a *pawn:*—pledge.

5668. עָבוּר **'âbûwr,** *aw-boor´;* or עָבֻר **'âbûr,** *aw-boor´;* pass. part. of 5674; prop. *crossed,* i.e. (abstr.) *transit;* used only adv. on *account* of, in *order* that:—because of, for (. . . 's sake), (intent) that, to.

5669. עָבוּר **'âbûwr,** *aw-boor´;* the same as 5668; *passed,* i.e. *kept* over; used only of *stored* grain:—old corn.

5670. עָבַט **'âbaṭ,** *aw-bat´;* a prim. root; to *pawn;* caus. to *lend* (on security); fig. to *entangle:*—borrow, break [*ranks*], fetch *[a pledge],* lend, × surely.

5671. עַבְטִיט **'abṭîyṭ,** *ab-teet´;* from 5670; something *pledged,* i.e. (collect.) *pawned* goods:—thick clay [*by a false etym.*].

5672. עֲבִי **'ăbîy,** *ab-ee´;* or עֳבִי **'ŏbîy,** *ob-ee´;* from 5666; *density,* i.e. *depth* or *width:*—thick (-ness). Comp. 5645.

5673. עֲבִידָה **'ăbîydâh** (Chald.), *ab-ee-daw´;* from 5648; *labor* or *business:*—affairs, service, work.

5674. עָבַר **'âbar,** *aw-bar´;* a prim. root; to *cross* over; used very widely of any *transition* (lit. or fig.; trans., intrans. intens. or causat.); spec. to *cover* (in copulation):—alienate, alter, × at all, beyond, bring (over, through), carry over, (over-) come (on, over), conduct (over), convey over, current, deliver, do away, enter, escape, fail, gender, get over, (make) go (away, beyond, by, forth, his way, in, on, over, through), have away (more), lay, meddle, overrun, make partition, (cause to, give, make to, over) pass (-age, along, away, beyond, by, -enger, on, out, over, through), (cause to, make) + proclaim (-amation), perish, provoke to anger, put away, rage, + raiser of taxes, remove, send over, set apart, + shave, cause to (make) sound, × speedily, × sweet smelling, take (away), (make to) transgress (-or), translate, turn away, [way-] faring man, be wrath.

5675. עֲבַר **'ăbar** (Chald.), *ab-ar´;* corresp. to 5676:—beyond, this side.

5676. עֵבֶר **'êber,** *ay´-ber;* from 5674; prop. a region *across;* but used only adv. (with or without a prep.) on the *opposite* side (espec. of the Jordan; usually mean. the *east*):— × against, beyond, by, × from, over, passage, quarter, (other, this) side, straight.

5677. עֵבֶר **'Êber,** *ay´-ber;* the same as 5676; *Eber,* the name of two patriarchs and four Isr.:—Eber, Heber.

5678. עֶבְרָה **'ebrâh,** *eb-raw´;* fem. of 5676; an *outburst* of passion:—anger, rage, wrath.

5679. עֲבָרָה **'ăbârâh,** *ab-aw-raw´;* from 5674; a *crossing*-place:—ferry, plain [*from the marg.*].

5680. עִבְרִי **'Ibrîy,** *ib-ree´;* patron. from 5677; an *Eberite* (i.e. Hebrew) or desc. of Eber:—Hebrew (-ess, woman).

5681. עִבְרִי **'Ibrîy,** *ib-ree´;* the same as 5680; *Ibri,* an Isr.:—Ibri.

5682. עֲבָרִים **'Ăbârîm,** *ab-aw-reem´;* plur. of 5676; regions *beyond; Abarim,* a place in Pal.:—Abarim, passages.

5683. עֶבְרֹן **'Ebrôn,** *eb-rone´;* from 5676; *transitional; Ebron,* a place in Pal.:—Hebron. Perh. a clerical error for 5658.

5684. עֶבְרֹנָה **'Ebrônâh,** *eb-raw-naw´;* fem. of 5683; *Ebronah,* a place in the Desert:—Ebronah.

5685. עָבַשׁ **'âbash,** *aw-bash´;* a prim. root; to *dry* up:—be rotten.

5686. עָבַת **'âbath,** *aw-bath´;* a prim. root; to *interlace,* i.e. (fig.) to *pervert:*—wrap up.

5687. עָבֹת **'âbôth,** *aw-both´;* or עָבוֹת **'âbôwth,** *aw-both´;* from 5686; *intwined,* i.e. *dense:*—thick.

5688. עֲבֹת **'ăbôth,** *ab-oth´;* or עֲבוֹת **'ăbôwth,** *ab-oth´;* or (fem.) עֲבֹתָה **'ăbôthâh,** *ab-oth-aw´;* the same as 5687; something *intwined,* i.e. a *string, wreath* or *foliage:*—band, cord, rope, thick bough (branch), wreathen (chain).

5689. עָגַב **'âgab,** *aw-gab´;* a prim. root; to *breathe* after, i.e. to *love* (sensually):—dote, lover.

5690. עֶגֶב **'egeb,** *eh´-gheb;* from 5689; *love* (concr.), i.e. *amative* words:—much love, very lovely.

5691. עֲגָבָה **'ăgâbâh,** *ag-aw-baw´;* from 5689; *love* (abstr.), i.e. *amorousness:*—inordinate love.

5692. עֻגָּה **'uggâh,** *oog-gaw´;* from 5746; an *ashcake* (as *round*):—cake (upon the hearth).

עָגוֹל **'âgôwl.** See 5696.

5693. עָגוּר **'âgûwr,** *aw-goor´;* pass. part. [but with act. sense] of an unused root mean. to *twitter;* prob. the *swallow:*—swallow.

5694. עָגִיל **'âgîyl,** *aw-gheel´;* from the same as 5696; something *round,* i.e. a *ring* (for the ears):—earring.

5695. עֵגֶל **'êgel,** *ay´-ghel;* from the same as 5696; a (male) *calf* (as *frisking* round), espec. one nearly grown (i.e. a *steer*):—bullock, calf.

5696. עָגֹל **'âgôl,** *aw-gole´;* or עָגוֹל **'âgôwl,** *aw-gole´;* from an unused root mean. to *revolve, circular:*—round.

5697. עֶגְלָה **'eglâh,** *eg-law´;* fem. of 5695; a (female) *calf,* espec. one nearly grown (i.e. a *heifer*):—calf, cow, heifer.

5698. עֶגְלָה **'Eglâh,** *eg-law´;* the same as 5697; *Eglah,* a wife of David:—Eglah.

5699. עֲגָלָה **'ăgâlâh,** *ag-aw-law´;* from the same as 5696; something *revolving,* i.e. a wheeled *vehicle:*—cart, chariot, wagon.

5700. עֶגְלוֹן **'Eglôwn,** *eg-lawn´;* from 5695; *vituline; Eglon,* the name of a place in Pal. and of a Moabitish king:—Eglon.

5701. עָגַם **'âgam,** *aw-gam´;* a prim. root; to *be sad:*—grieve.

5702. עָגַן **'âgan,** *aw-gan´;* a prim. root; to *debar,* i.e. from marriage:—stay.

5703. עַד **'ad,** *ad;* from 5710; prop. a (peremptory) *terminus,* i.e. (by impl.) *duration,* in the sense of *advance* or *perpetuity* (substantially as a noun, either with or without a prep.):—eternity, ever (-lasting, -more), old, perpetually, + world without end.

5704. עַד **'ad,** *ad;* prop. the same as 5703 (used as a prep., adv. or conj.; especially with a prep.); *as far* (or *long,* or *much*) *as,* whether of space (*even unto*) or time (*during, while, until*) or degree (*equally with*):—against, and, as, at, before, by (that), even (to), for (-asmuch as), [hither-] to, + how long, into, as long (much) as, (so) that, till, toward, until, when, while, (+ as) yet.

5705. עַד **'ad** (Chald.), *ad;* corresp. to 5704; × and, at, for, [hither-] to, on, till, (un-) to, until, within.

5706. עַד **'ad,** *ad;* the same as 5703 in the sense of the *aim* of an attack; *booty:*—prey.

5707. עֵד **'êd,** *ayd;* from 5749 contr.; concr. *a witness;* abstr. *testimony;* spec. a *recorder,* i.e. *prince:*—witness.

5708. עֵד **'êd,** *ayd;* from an unused root mean. to *set* a period [comp. 5710, 5749]; the *menstrual* flux (as periodical); by impl. (in plur.) *soiling:*—filthy.

עֹד **'ôd.** See 5750.

5709. עֲדָא **'ădâ'** (Chald.), *ad-aw´;* or עֲדָה **'ădâh** (Chald.), *ad-aw´;* corresp. to 5710:—alter, depart, pass (away), remove, take (away).

עֹדֵד **'Ôdêd.** See 5752.

5710. עָדָה **'âdâh,** *aw-daw´;* a prim. root; to *advance,* i.e. *pass* on or *continue;* causat. to *remove;* spec. to *bedeck* (i.e. bring an ornament upon):—adorn, deck (self), pass by, take away.

5711. עָדָה **'Âdâh,** *aw-daw´;* from 5710; *ornament; Adah,* the name of two women:—Adah.

5712. עֵדָה **'êdâh,** *ay-daw´;* fem. of 5707 in the orig. sense of *fixture;* a stated *assemblage* (spec. a *concourse,* or gen. a *family* or *crowd*):—assembly, company, congregation, multitude, people, swarm. Comp. 5713.

5713. עֵדָה **'êdâh,** *ay-daw´;* fem. of 5707 in its techn. sense; *testimony:*—testimony, witness. Comp. 5712.

5714. עִדּוֹ **'Iddôw,** *id-do´;* or עִדּוֹא **'Iddôw',** *id-do´;* or עִדִּיא° **'Iddiy',** *id-dee´;* from 5710; *timely; Iddo* (or *Iddi*), the name of five Isr.:—Iddo. Comp. 3035, 3260.

5715. עֵדוּת **'êdûwth,** *ay-dooth´;* fem. of 5707; *testimony:*—testimony, witness.

5716. עֲדִי **'ădîy,** *ad-ee´;* from 5710 in the sense of *trappings; finery;* gen. an *outfit;* spec. a *headstall:*— × excellent, mouth, ornament.

5717. עֲדִיאֵל **'Ădîy'êl,** *ad-ee-ale´;* from 5716 and 410; *ornament of God; Adiël,* the name of three Isr.:—Adiel.

5718. עֲדָיָה **'Ădâyâh,** *ad-aw-yaw´;* or עֲדָיָהוּ **'Ădâyâhûw,** *ad-aw-yaw´-hoo;* from 5710 and 3050; *Jah has adorned; Adajah,* the name of eight Isr.:—Adaiah.

5719. עָדִין **'âdîyn,** *aw-deen´;* from 5727; *voluptuous:*—given to pleasures.

5720. עָדִין **'Âdîyn,** *aw-deen´;* the same as 5719; *Adin,* the name of two Isr.:—Adin.

5721. עֲדִינָא **'Ădîynâ',** *ad-een-naw´;* from 5719; *effeminacy; Adina,* an Isr.:—Adina.

5722. עֲדִינוֹ **'ădîynôw,** *ad-ee-no´;* prob. from 5719 in the orig. sense of *slender* (i.e. a *spear*); *his spear:*—Adino.

5723. עֲדִיתַיִם **'Ădîythayim,** *ad-ee-thah´-yim;* dual of a fem. of 5706; *double prey; Adithajim,* a place in Pal.:—Adithaim.

5724. עַדְלַי **'Adlay,** *ad-lah´ee;* prob. from an unused root of uncert. mean.; *Adlai,* an Isr.:—Adlai.

5725. עֲדֻלָּם **'Ădullâm,** *ad-ool-lawn´;* prob. from the pass. part. of the same as 5724; *Adullam,* a place in Pal.:—Adullam.

5726. עֲדֻלָּמִי **'Ădullâmîy,** *ad-ool-law-mee´;* patrial from 5725; an *Adullamite* or native of Adullam:—Adullamite.

5727. עָדַן **'âdan,** *aw-dan´;* a prim. root; to be *soft* or *pleasant;* fig. and reflex. to *live voluptuously:*—delight self.

5728. עֲדֶן **'ăden,** *ad-en´;* or עֲדֶנָּה **'ădennâh,** *ad-en´-naw;* from 5704 and 2004; *till now:*—yet.

5729. עֶדֶן **'Eden,** *eh´-den;* from 5727; *pleasure; Eden,* a place in Mesopotamia:—Eden.

5730. עֵדֶן **'êden.** *ay´-den;* or (fem.) עֶדְנָה **'ednâh,** *ed-naw´;* from 5727; *pleasure:*—delicate, delight, pleasure. See also 1040.

5731. עֵדֶן **'Êden,** *ay´-den;* the same as 5730 (masc.); *Eden,* the region of Adam's home:—Eden.

5732. עִדָּן **'iddân** (Chald.), *id-dawn´;* from a root corresp. to that of 5708; a set *time;* techn. a *year:*—time.

5733. עַדְנָא **'Adnâ',** *ad-naw´;* from 5727; *pleasure; Adna,* the name of two Isr.:—Adna.

5734. עַדְנָה **'Adnâh,** *ad-naw´;* from 5727; *pleasure; Adnah,* the name of two Isr.:—Adnah.

5735. עֲדְעָדָה **'Ăd'âdâh,** *ad-aw-daw´;* from 5712; *festival; Adadah,* a place in Pal.:—Adadah.

5736. עָדַף **'âdaph,** *aw-daf´;* a prim. root; to *be* (causat. *have*) *redundant:*—be more, odd number, be (have) over (and above), overplus, remain.

5737. עָדַר **'âdar,** *aw-dar´;* a prim. root; to *arrange,* as a battle, a vineyard (to *hoe*); hence to *muster,* and so to *miss* (or find *wanting*):—dig, fail, keep (rank), lack.

5738. עֶדֶר **'Eder,** *eh´-der;* from 5737; an *arrangement* (i.e. drove), *Eder,* an Isr.:—Ader.

5739. עֵדֶר **'êder,** *ay´-der;* from 5737; an *arrangement,* i.e. *muster* (of animals):—drove, flock, herd.

5740. עֵדֶר **'Êder,** *ay´-der;* the same as 5739; *Eder,* the name of an Isr. and of two places in Pal.:—Edar, Eder.

5741. עַדְרִיאֵל **'Adrîy'êl,** *ad-ree-ale´;* from 5739 and 410; *flock of God; Adriel,* an Isr.:—Adriel.

5742. עָדָשׁ **'âdâsh,** *aw-dawsh´;* from an unused root of uncert. mean.; a *lentil:*—lentile.

עַוָּא **'Avvâ'.** See 5755.

5743. עוּב **'ûwb,** *oob;* a prim. root; to be *dense* or *dark,* i.e. to *becloud:*—cover with a cloud.

5744. עוֹבֵד **'Ôwbêd,** *o-bade´;* act. part. of 5647; *serving; Obed,* the name of five Isr.:—Obed.

5745. עוֹבָל **'Ôwbâl,** *o-bawl´;* of for. der.; *Obal,* a son of Joktan:—Obal.

5746. עוּג **'ûwg,** *oog;* a prim, root; prop. to *gyrate;* but used only as denom. from 5692; to *bake* (round cakes on the hearth):—bake.

5747. עוֹג **'Ôwg,** *ogue;* prob. from 5746; *round; Og,* a king of Bashan:—Og.

5748. עוּגָב **'ûwgâb,** *oo-gawb´;* or עֻגָּב **'ûggâb,** *oog-gawb´;* from 5689 in the orig. sense of *breathing;* a *reed*-instrument of music:—organ.

5749. עוּד **'ûwd,** *ood;* a prim. root; to *duplicate* or *repeat;* by impl. to *protest, testify* (as by reiteration); intens. to *encompass, restore* (as a sort of reduplication):—admonish, charge, earnestly, lift up, protest, call (take) to record, relieve, rob, solemnly, stand upright, testify, give warning, (bear, call to, give, take to) witness.

5750. עוֹד **'ôwd,** *ode;* or עֹד **'ôd,** *ode;* from 5749; prop. *iteration* or *continuance;* used only adv. (with or without prep.), *again, repeatedly, still, more:*—again, × all life long, at all, besides, but, else, further (-more), henceforth, (any) longer, (any) more (-over), × once, since, (be) still, when, (good, the) while (having being), (as, because, whether, while) yet (within).

5751. עוֹד **'ôwd** (Chald.), *ode;* corresp. to 5750:—while.

5752. עוֹדֵד **'Ôwdêd,** *o-dade´;* or עֹדֵד **'Ôdêd,** *o-dade´;* from 5749; *reiteration; Oded,* the name of two Isr.:—Oded.

5753. עָוָה **'âvâh,** *aw-vaw´;* a prim. root; to *crook,* lit. or fig. (as follows):—do amiss, bow down, make crooked, commit iniquity, pervert, (do) perverse (-ly), trouble, × turn, do wickedly, do wrong.

5754. עַוָּה **'avvâh,** *av-vaw´;* intens. from 5753 abbrev.; *overthrow:*— × overturn.

5755. עִוָּה **'Ivvâh,** *iv-vaw´;* or עַוָּא **'Avvâ'** (2 Kings 17 : 24), *av-vaw´;* for 5754; *Ivvah* or *Avva,* a region of Ass.:—Ava, Ivah.

עָוֹון **'âvôwn.** See 5771.

5756. עוּז **'ûwz,** *ooz;* a prim. root; to *be strong;* causat. to *strengthen,* i.e. (fig.) to *save* (by flight):—gather (self, self to flee), retire.

5757. עַוִּי **'Avvîy,** *av-vee´;* patrial from 5755; an *Avvite* or native of Avvah (only plur.):—Avims, Avites.

5758. עִוְיָא **'ivyâ'** (Chald.), *iv-yaw´;* from a root corresp. to 5753; *perverseness:*—iniquity.

5759. עֲוִיל **'ăvîyl,** *av-eel´;* from 5764; a *babe:*—young child, little one.

5760. עֲוִיל **'ăvîyl,** *av-eel´;* from 5765; *perverse* (morally):—ungodly.

5761. עַוִּים **'Avvîym,** *av-veem´;* plur. of 5757; *Avvim* (as inhabited by Avvites), a place in Pal. (with the art. pref.):—Avim.

5762. עֲוִית **'Ăvîyth,** *av-veeth´;* or [perh. עַיּוֹת° **'Ayôwth,** *ah-yōth´,* as if plur. of 5857] עַיּוּת° **'Ayûwth,** *ah-yōth´;* from 5753; *ruin; Avvith* (or *Avvoth*), a place in Pal.:—Avith.

5763. עוּל **'ûwl,** *ool;* a prim. root; to *suckle,* i.e. *give milk:*—milch, (ewe great) with young.

5764. עוּל **'ûwl,** *ool;* from 5763; a *babe:*—sucking child, infant.

5765. עָוַל **'âval,** *aw-val´;* a prim. root; to *distort* (morally):—deal unjustly, unrighteous.

עוֹל **'ôwl.** See 5923.

5766. עֶוֶל **'evel,** *eh´-vel;* or עָוֶל **'âvel,** *aw´-vel;* and (fem.) עַוְלָה **'avlâh,** *av-law´;* or עוֹלָה **'ôwlâh,** *o-law´;* or עֹלָה **'ôlâh,** *o-law´;* from 5765; (moral) *evil:*—iniquity, perverseness, unjust (-ly), unrighteousness (-ly), wicked (-ness).

5767. עַוָּל **'avvâl,** *av-vawl´;* intens. from 5765; *evil* (morally):—unjust, unrighteous, wicked.

עוֹלָה **'ôwlâh.** See 5930.

5768. עוֹלֵל **'ôwlêl,** *o-lale´;* or עֹלָל **'ôlâl,** *o-lawl´;* from 5763; a *suckling:*—babe, (young) child, infant, little one.

5769. עוֹלָם **'ôwlâm,** *o-lawm´;* or עֹלָם **'ôlâm,** *o-lawm´;* from 5956; prop. *concealed,* i.e. the *vanishing* point; gen. time *out of mind* (past or fut.), i.e. (practically) *eternity;* freq. adv. (espec. with prep. pref.) *always:*—always (-s), ancient (time), any more, continuance, eternal, (for, [n-]) ever (-lasting, -more, of old), lasting, long (time), (of) old (time), perpetual, at any time, (beginning of the) world (+ without end). Comp. 5331, 5703.

5770. עָוַן° **'âvan,** *aw-van´;* denom. from 5869; to *watch* (with jealousy):—eye.

5771. עָוֹן **'âvôn,** *aw-vone´;* or עָווֹן **'âvôwn** (2 Kings 7 : 9; Psa. 51 : 5 [7]), *aw-vone´;* from 5753; *perversity,* i.e. (moral) *evil:*—fault, iniquity, mischief, punishment (of iniquity), sin.

5772. עוֹנָה **'ôwnâh,** *o-naw´;* from an unused root appar. mean. to *dwell* together; (sexual) *cohabitation:*—duty of marriage.

5773. עַוְעֶה **'av'eh,** *av-eh´;* from 5753; *perversity:*— × perverse.

5774. עוּף **'ûwph,** *oof;* a prim, root; to *cover* (with wings or obscurity); hence (as denom. from 5775) to *fly;* also (by impl. of dimness) to *faint* (from the darkness of swooning):—brandish, be (wax) faint, flee away, fly (away—, × set, shine forth, weary.

5775. עוֹף **'ôwph,** *ofe;* from 5774; a *bird* (as *covered* with feathers, or rather as *covering* with wings), often collect.:—bird, that flieth, flying, fowl.

5776. עוֹף **'ôwph** (Chald), *ofe;* corresp. to 5775:—fowl.

5777. עוֹפֶרֶת **'owphereth,** *o-feh´-reth;* or עֹפֶרֶת **'ôphereth,** *o-feh´-reth;* fem. part. act. of 6080; *lead* (from its *dusty* color):—lead.

5778. עוֹפַי° **'Ôwphay,** *o-fah´-ee;* from 5775; *birdlike; Ephai,* an Isr.:—Ephai [*from marg.*].

5779. עוּץ **'ûwts,** *oots;* a prim. root; to *consult:*—take advice ([counsel] together).

5780. עוּץ **'Ûwts,** *oots;* appar. from 5779; *consultation; Uts,* a son of Aram, also a Seirite, and the regions settled by them:—Uz.

5781. עוּק **'ûwq,** *ook;* a prim. root; to *pack:*—be pressed.

5782. עוּר **'ûwr,** *oor;* a prim. root [rather ident. with 5783 through the idea of *opening* the eyes]; to *wake* (lit. or fig.):—(a-) wake (-n, up), lift up (self), × master, raise (up), stir up (self).

5783. עוּר **'ûwr,** *oor;* a prim. root; to *(be) bare:*— be made naked.

5784. עוּר **'ûwr** (Chald.), *oor; chaff* (as the *naked* husk):—chaff.

5785. עוֹר **'ôwr,** *ore;* from 5783; *skin* (as *naked*); by impl. *hide, leather:*—hide, leather, skin.

5786. עָוַר **'âvar,** *aw-var´;* a prim. root [rather denom. from 5785 through the idea of a *film* over the eyes]; to *blind:*—blind, put out. See also 5895.

5787. עִוֵּר **'ivvêr,** *iv-vare´;* intens. from 5786; *blind* (lit. or fig.):—blind (men, people).

עוֹרֵב **'ôwrêb.** See 6159.

5788. עִוָּרוֹן **'ivvârôwn,** *iv-vaw-rone´;* and (fem.) עַוֶּרֶת **'avvereth,** *av-veh´-reth;* from 5787; *blindness:*—blind (-ness).

5789. עוּשׁ **'uwsh,** *oosh;* a prim. root; to *hasten:*—assemble self.

5790. עוּת **'ûwth,** *ooth;* for 5789; to *hasten,* i.e. *succor:*—speak in season.

5791. עָוַת **'âvath,** *aw-vath´;* a prim. root; to *wrest:*—bow self, (make) crooked, falsifying, overthrow, deal perversely, pervert, subvert, turn upside down.

5792. עַוָּתָה **'avvâthâh,** *av-vaw-thaw´;* from 5791; *oppression:*—wrong.

5793. עוּתַי **'Ûwthay,** *oo-thah´-ee;* from 5790: *succoring; Uthai,* the name of two Isr.:—Uthai.

5794. עַז **'az,** *az;* from 5810; *strong, vehement, harsh:*—fierce, + greedy, mighty, power, roughly, strong.

5795. עֵז **'êz,** *aze;* from 5810; a she-*goat* (as *strong*), but masc. in plur. (which also is used ellipt. for *goats' hair*):—(she) goat, kid.

5796. עֵז **'êz** (Chald.), *aze;* corresp. to 5795:—goat.

5797. עֹז **'ôz,** *oze;* or (fully) עוֹז **'ôwz,** *oze;* from 5810; *strength* in various applications (*force, security, majesty, praise*):—boldness, loud, might, power, strength, strong.

5798. עֻזָּא **'Uzzâ',** *ooz-zaw´;* or עֻזָּה **'Uzzâh,** *ooz-zaw´;* fem. of 5797; *strength; Uzza* or *Uzzah,* the name of five Isr.:—Uzza, Uzzah.

5799. עֲזָאזֵל **'ăzâ'zêl,** *az-aw-zale´;* from 5795 and 235; *goat of departure;* the *scapegoat:*—scapegoat.

5800. עָזַב **'âzab,** *aw-zab´;* a prim. root; to *loosen,* i.e. *relinquish, permit,* etc.:—commit self, fail, forsake, fortify, help, leave (destitute, off), refuse, × surely.

5801. עִזָּבוֹן **'izzâbôwn,** *iz-zaw-bone´* from 5800 in the sense of *letting go* (for a price, i.e. *selling*); *trade, i.e. the place (mart)* or the payment (*revenue*):—fair, ware.

5802. עַזְבּוּק **'Azbûwq,** *az-book´;* from 5794 and the root of 950; *stern depopulator; Azbuk,* an Isr.:—Azbuk.

5803. עַזְגָּד **'Azgâd,** *az-gawd´;* from 5794 and 1409; *stern troop; Azgad,* an Isr.:—Azgad.

5804. עַזָּה **'Azzâh,** *az-zaw´;* fem. of 5794; *strong; Azzah,* a place in Pal.:—Azzah, Gaza.

5805. עֲזוּבָה **'ăzûwbâh,** *az-oo-baw´;* fem. pass. part. of 5800; *desertion* (of inhabitants):—forsaking.

5806. עֲזוּבָה **'Ăzûwbâh,** *az-oo-baw´;* the same as 5805; *Azubah,* the name of two Israelitesses:—Azubah.

5807. עֱזוּז **'ĕzûwz,** *ez-ooz´;* from 5810; *forcibleness:*—might, strength.

5808. עִזּוּז **'izzûwz,** *iz-zooz´;* from 5810; *forcible;* collect. and concr. an *army:*—power, strong.

5809. עַזּוּר **'Azzûwr,** *az-zoor´;* or עַזֻּר **'Azzûr,** *az-zoor´;* from 5286; *helpful: Azzur,* the name of three Isr.:—Azur, Azzur.

5810. עָזַז **'âzaz,** *aw-zaz´;* a prim. root; to *be stout* (lit. or fig.):—harden, impudent, prevail, strengthen (self), be strong.

5811. עָזָז **'Âzâz,** *aw-zawz´;* from 5810; *strong; Azaz,* an Isr.:—Azaz.

5812. עֲזַזְיָהוּ **'Ăzazyâhûw,** *az-az-yaw´-hoo;* from 5810 and 3050; *Jah has strengthened; Azazjah,* the name of three Isr.:—Azaziah.

5813. עֻזִּי **'Uzzîy,** *ooz-zee´;* from 5810; *forceful; Uzzi,* the name of six Isr.:—Uzzi.

5814. עֻזִּיָּא **'Uzzîyâ',** *ooz-zee-yaw´;* perh. for 5818; *Uzzija,* an Isr.:—Uzzia.

5815. עֲזִיאֵל **'Ăzîy'êl,** *az-ee-ale´;* from 5756 and 410; *strengthened of God; Aziël,* an Isr.:—Aziel. Comp. 3268.

5816. עֻזִּיאֵל **'Uzzîy'êl,** *ooz-zee-ale´;* from 5797 and 410; *strength of God; Uzziël,* the name of six Isr.:—Uzziel.

5817. עָזִּיאֵלִי **'Ozzîy'êlîy,** *oz-zee-ay-lee´;* patron. from 5816; an *Uzziëlite* (collect.) or desc. of Uzziel:—Uzzielites.

5818. עֻזִּיָּה **'Uzzîyâh,** *ooz-zee-yaw´;* or עֻזִּיָּהוּ **'Uzzîyâhûw,** *ooz-zee-yaw´-hoo;* from 5797 and 3050; *strength of Jah; Uzzijah,* the name of five Isr.:—Uzziah.

5819. עֲזִיזָא **'Ăzîyzâ',** *az-ee-zaw´;* from 5756; *strengthfulness; Aziza,* an Isr.:—Aziza.

5820. עַזְמָוֶת **'Azmâveth,** *az-maw´-veth;* from 5794 and 4194; *strong* one *of death; Azmaveth,* the name of three Isr. and of a place in Pal.:—Azmaveth. See also 1041.

5821. עַזָּן **'Azzân,** *az-zawn´;* from 5794; *strong* one; *Azzan,* an Isr.:—Azzan.

5822. עָזְנִיָּה **'oznîyâh,** *oz-nee-yaw´;* prob. fem. of 5797; prob. the *sea-eagle* (from its *strength*):—ospray.

5823. עָזַק **'âzaq,** *aw-zak´;* a prim. root; to *grub* over:—fence about.

5824. עִזְקָא **'izqâ'** (Chald.), *iz-kaw´;* from a root corresp. to 5823; a *signet*-ring (as engraved):—signet.

5825. עֲזֵקָה **'Ăzêqâh,** *az-ay-kaw´;* from 5828; *tilled; Azekah,* a place in Pal.:—Azekah.

5826. עָזַר **'âzar,** *aw-zar´;* a prim. root; to *surround,* i.e. *protect* or *aid:*—help, succour.

5827. עֶזֶר **'Ezer,** *eh´-zer;* from 5826; *help; Ezer,* the name of two Isr.:—Ezer. Comp. 5829.

5828. עֵזֶר **'êzer,** *ay´-zer;* from 5826; *aid:*—help.

5829. עֵזֶר **'Êzer,** *ay´-zer;* the same as 5828; *Ezer,* the name of four Isr.:—Ezer. Comp. 5827.

עַזֻּר **'Azzûr.** See 5809.

5830. עֶזְרָא **'Ezrâ',** *ez-raw´;* a var. of 5833; *Ezra,* an Isr.:—Ezra.

5831. עֶזְרָא **'Ezrâ'** (Chald.), *ez-raw´;* corresp. to 5830; *Ezra,* an Isr.:—Ezra.

5832. עֲזַרְאֵל **'Ăzar'êl,** *az-ar-ale´;* from 5826 and 410; *God has helped; Azarel,* the name of five Isr.:—Azarael, Azareel.

5833. עֶזְרָה **'ezrâh,** *ex-raw´;* or עֶזְרָת **'ezrâth** (Psa. 60 : 11 [13], 108 : 12 [13]), *ez-rawth´;* fem. of 5828; *aid:*—help (-ed, -er).

5834. עֶזְרָה **'Ezrâh,** *ez-raw´;* the same as 5833; *Ezrah,* an Isr.:—Ezrah.

5835. עֲזָרָה **'ăzârâh,** *az-aw-raw´* from 5826 in its orig. mean. of *surrounding;* an *inclosure;* also a *border:*—court, settle.

5836. עֶזְרִי **'Ezrîy,** *ez-ree´;* from 5828; *helpful; Ezri,* an Isr.:—Ezri.

5837. עַזְרִיאֵל **'Azrîy'êl,** *az-ree-ale´;* from 5828 and 410; *help of God; Azriël,* the name of three Isr.:—Azriel.

5838. עֲזַרְיָה **'Ăzaryâh,** *az-ar-yaw´;* or עֲזַרְיָהוּ **'Ăzaryâhûw,** *az-ar-yaw´-hoo;* from 5826 and 3050; *Jah has helped; Azarjah,* the name of nineteen Isr.:—Azariah.

5839. עֲזַרְיָה **'Ăzaryâh** (Chald.), *az-ar-yaw´;* corresp. to 5838; *Azarjah,* one of Daniel's companions:—Azariah.

5840. עַזְרִיקָם **'Azrîyqâm,** *az-ree-kawm´;* from 5828 and act. part. of 6965; *help of an enemy; Azrikam,* the name of four Isr.:—Azrikam.

5841. עַזָּתִי **'Azzâthîy,** *az-zaw-thee´;* patrial from 5804; an *Azzathite* or inhab. of Azzah:—Gazathite, Gazite.

5842. עֵט **'êṭ,** *ate;* from 5860 (contr.) in the sense of *swooping,* i.e. *side-long stroke;* a *stylus* or marking stick:—pen.

5843. עֵטָא **'êṭâ'** (Chald.), *ay-taw´;* from 3272; *prudence:*—counsel.

5844. עָטָה **'âṭâh,** *aw-taw´;* a prim. root; to *wrap,* i.e. *cover, veil, clothe* or *roll:*—array, self, be clad, (put a) cover (-ing, self), fill, put on, × surely, turn aside.

5845. עֲטִין **'ăṭîyn,** *at-een´;* from an unused root mean. appar. to *contain;* a *receptacle* (for milk, i.e. *pail;* fig. *breast*):—breast.

5846. עֲטִישָׁה **'ăṭîyshâh,** *at-ee-shaw´;* from an unused root mean. to *sneeze; sneezing:*—sneezing.

5847. עֲטַלֵּף **'ăṭallêph,** *at-al-lafe´;* of uncert. der.; a *bat:*—bat.

5848. עָטַף **'âṭaph,** *aw-taf´;* a prim. root; to *shroud,* i.e. *clothe* (whether trans. or reflex.); hence (from the idea of *darkness*) to *languish:*—cover (over), fail, faint, feebler, hide self, be overwhelmed, swoon.

5849. עָטַר **'âṭar,** *aw-tar´;* a prim. root; to *encircle* (for attack or protection); espec. to *crown* (lit. or fig.):—compass, crown.

5850. עֲטָרָה **'ăṭârâh,** *at-aw-raw´;* from 5849; a *crown:*—crown.

5851. עֲטָרָה **'Ăṭârâh,** *at-aw-raw´;* the same as 5850; *Atarah,* an Israelitess:—Atarah.

5852. עֲטָרוֹת **'Ăṭârôwth,** *at-aw-rōth´;* or עֲטָרֹת **'Ăṭârôth,** *at-aw-rōth´;* plur. of 5850; *Ataroth,* the name (thus simply) of two places in Pal.:—Ataroth.

5853. עַטְרוֹת אַדָּר **'Aṭrôwth 'Addâr,** *at-rōth´ ad-dawr´;* from the same as 5852 and 146; *crowns of Addar; Atroth-Addar,* a place in Pal.:—Ataroth-adar (-addar).

5854. עַטְרוֹת בֵּית יוֹאָב **'Aṭrôwth bêyth Yôw'âb,** *at-rōth´ bayth yo-awb´;* from the same as 5852 and 1004 and 3097; *crowns of the house of Joäb; Atroth-beth-Joäb,* a place in Pal.:—Ataroth the house of Joab.

5855. עַטְרוֹת שׁוֹפָן **'Aṭrôwth Shôwphân,** *at-rōth´ sho-fawn´;* from the same as 5852 and a name otherwise unused [being from the same as 8226] mean. *hidden; crowns of Shophan; Atroth-Shophan,* a place in Pal.:—Atroth, Shophan [*as if two places*].

5856. עִי **'îy,** *ee;* from 5753; a *ruin* (as if overturned):—heap.

5857. עַי **'Ay,** *ah´ee;* or (fem.) עַיָּא **'Ayâ'** (Neh. 11 : 31), *ah-yaw´;* or עַיָּת **'Ayâth** (Isa. 10 : 28), *ah-yawth´;* for 5856; *Ai, Aja* or *Ajath,* a place in Pal.:—Ai, Aija, Aijath, Hai.

5858. עֵיבָל **'Êybâl,** *ay-bawl´;* perh. from an unused root prob. mean. to *be bald; bare; Ebal,* a mountain of Pal.:—Ebal.

עַיָּה **'Ayâh.** See 5857.

5859. עִיּוֹן **'Iyôwn,** *ee-yone´;* from 5856; *ruin; Ijon,* a place in Pal.:—Ijon.

5860. עִיט **'îyṭ,** *eet;* a prim. root; to *swoop* down upon (lit. or fig.):—fly, rail.

5861. עַיִט **'ayiṭ,** *ah´-yit;* from 5860; a *hawk* or other bird of prey:—bird, fowl, ravenous (bird).

5862. עֵיטָם **'Êyṭâm,** *ay-tawm´;* from 5861; *hawk-ground; Etam,* a place in Pal.:—Etam.

5863. עִיֵּי הָעֲבָרִים **'Iyêy hâ-'Ăbârîym,** *ee-yay´ haw-ab-aw-reem´;* from the plur. of 5856 and the plur. of the act. part. of 5674 with the art. interposed; *ruins of the passers; Ije-ha-Abarim,* a place near Pal.:—Ije-abarim.

5864. עִיִּים **'Iyîym,** *ee-yeem´;* plur. of 5856; *ruins; Ijim,* a place in the Desert:—Iim.

5865. עֵילוֹם **'êylôwm,** *ay-lome´;* for 5769:—ever.

5866. עִילַי **'Îylay,** *ee-lah´ee;* from 5927; *elevated; Ilai,* an Isr.:—Ilai.

5867. עֵילָם **'Êylâm,** *ay-lawm´;* or עוֹלָם° **'Ôwlâm** (Ezra 10 : 2; Jer. 49 : 36), *o-lawm´;* prob. from 5956; *hidden,* i.e. *distant; Elam,* a son of Shem, and his descend., with their country; also of six Isr.:—Elam.

5868. עֲיָם **'ăyâm,** *ah-yawm´;* of doubtful or. and authenticity; prob. mean. *strength:*—mighty.

5869. עַיִן **'ayin,** *ah´-yin;* prob. a prim. word; an *eye* (lit. or fig.); by anal. a *fountain* (as the *eye* of the landscape):—affliction, outward appearance, + before, + think best, colour, conceit, + be content, countenance, + displease, eye ([-brow], [-d], -sight), face, + favour, fountain, furrow [*from the marg.*], × him, + humble, knowledge, look, (+ well), × me, open (-ly), + (not) please, presence, + regard, resemblance, sight, × thee, × them, + think, × us, well, × you (-rselves).

5870. עַיִן **'ayin (Chald.),** *ah´-yin;* corresp. to 5869; an *eye:*—eye.

5871. עַיִן **'Ayin,** *ah´-yin;* the same as 5869; *fountain; Ajin,* the name (thus simply) of two places in Pal.:—Ain.

5872. עֵין גֶּדִי **'Êyn Gedîy,** *ane geh´-dee;* from 5869 and 1423; *fountain of a kid; En-Gedi,* a place in Pal.:—En-gedi.

5873. עֵין גַּנִּים **'Êyn Gannîym,** *ane ganneem´;* from 5869 and the plur. of 1588; *fountain of gardens; En-Gannim,* a place in Pal.:—En-gannim.

5874. עֵין־דֹּאר **'Êyn-Dô'r,** *ane-dore´;* or עֵין דּוֹר **'Êyn Dôwr,** *ane dore;* or עֵין־דֹּר **'Êyn-Dôr,** *ane-dore´;* from 5869 and 1755; *fountain of dwelling; En-Dor,* a place in Pal.:—En-dor.

5875. עֵין הַקּוֹרֵא **'Êyn haq-Qôwrê',** *ane hak-ko-ray´;* from 5869 and the act. part. of 7121; *fountain of One calling; En-hak-Korè;* a place near Pal.:—En-hakhore.

עֵינוֹן **'Êynôwn.** See 2703.

5876. עֵין חַדָּה **'Êyn Chaddâh,** *ane khad-daw´;* from 5869 and the fem. of a der. from 2300; *fountain of sharpness; En-Chaddah,* a place in Pal.:—En-haddah.

5877. עֵין חָצוֹר **'Êyn Châtsôwr,** *ane khaw-tsore´;* from 5869 and the same as 2674; *fountain of a village; En-Chatsor,* a place in Pal.:—En-hazor.

5878. עֵין חֲרֹד **'Êyn Chărôd,** *ane khar-ode´;* from 5869 and a der. of 2729; *fountain of trembling; En-Charod,* a place in Pal.:—well of Harod.

5879. עֵינַיִם **'Êynayim,** *ay-nah´-yim;* or עֵינָם **'Êynâm,** *ay-nawm´;* dual of 5869; *double fountain; Enajim* or *Enam,* a place in Pal.:—Enaim, openly (Gen. 38 : 21).

5880. עֵין מִשְׁפָּט **'Êyn Mishpâṭ,** *ane mish-pawt´;* from 5869 and 4941; *fountain of judgment; En-Mishpat,* a place near Pal.:—En-mishpat.

5881. עֵינָן **'Êynân,** *ay-nawn´;* from 5869; *having eyes; Enan,* an Isr.:—Enan. Comp. 2704.

5882. עֵין עֶגְלַיִם **'Êyn 'Eglayim,** *ane eg-lah´-yim;* from 5869 and the dual of 5695; *fountain of two calves; En-Eglajim,* a place in Pal.:—En-eglaim.

5883. עֵין רֹגֵל **'Êyn Rôgêl,** *ane ro-gale´;* from 5869 and the act. part. of 7270; *fountain of a traveller; En-Rogel,* a place near Jerus.:—En-rogel.

5884. עֵין רִמּוֹן **'Êýn Rimmôwn,** *ane rim-mone´;* from 5869 and 7416; *fountain of a pomegranate; En-Rimmon,* a place in Pal.:—En-rimmon.

5885. עֵין שֶׁמֶשׁ **'Êyn Shemesh,** *ane sheh´-mesh;* from 5869 and 8121; *fountain of* the *sun; En-Shemesh,* a place in Pal.:—En-Shemesh.

5886. עֵין תַּנִּים **'Êyn Tannîym,** *ane tan-neem´;* from 5869 and the plur. of 8565; *fountain of jackals; En-Tannim,* a pool near Jerus:—dragon well.

5887. עֵין תַּפּוּחַ **'Êyn Tappûwach,** *ane tap-poo´-akh;* from 5869 and 8598; *fountain of an apple*-tree; *En-Tappuäch,* a place in Pal.:—En-tappuah.

5888. עָיֵף **'âyêph,** *aw-yafe´;* a prim. root; to *languish:*—be wearied.

5889. עָיֵף **'âyêph,** *aw-yafe´;* from 5888; *languid:*—faint, thirsty, weary.

5890. עֵיפָה **'êyphâh,** *ay-faw´;* fem. from 5774; *obscurity* (as if from *covering*):—darkness.

5891. עֵיפָה **'Êyphâh,** *ay-faw´;* the same as 5890; *Ephah,* the name of a son of Midian, and of the region settled by him; also of an Isr. and of an Israelitess:—Ephah.

5892. עִיר **'îyr,** *eer;* or (in the plur.) עָר **'âr,** *awr;* or עָיַר **'âyar** (Judg. 10 : 4), *aw-yar´;* from 5782 a *city* (a place guarded by *waking* or a watch) in the widest sense (even of a mere *encampment* or *post*):—Ai [*from marg.*], city, court [*from marg.*], town.

5893. עִיר **'Îyr,** *eer;* the same as 5892; *Ir,* an Isr.:—Ir.

5894. עִיר **'îyr** (Chald.), *eer;* from a root corresp. to 5782; a *watcher,* i.e. an *angel* (as guardian):—watcher.

5895. עַיִר **'ayir,** *ah´-yeer;* from 5782 in the sense of *raising* (i.e. *bearing* a burden); prop. a young *ass* (as just broken to a load); hence an ass-*colt:*—(ass) colt, foal, young ass.

5896. עִירָא **'Îyrâ',** *ee-raw´;* from 5782; *wakefulness; Ira,* the name of three Isr.:—Ira.

5897. עִירָד **'Îyrâd,** *ee-rawd´;* from the same as 6166; *fugitive; Irad,* an antediluvian:—Irad.

5898. עִיר הַמֶּלַח **'Îyr ham-Melach,** *eer ham-meh´-lakh;* from 5892 and 4417 with the art. of substance interp.; *city of (the) salt; Ir-ham-Melach,* a place near Pal.:—the city of salt.

5899. עִיר הַתְּמָרִים **'Îyr hat-Temârîym,** *eer hat-tem-aw-reem´;* from 5892 and the plur. of 8558 with the art. interp.; *city of the palmtrees; Ir-hat-Temarim,* a place in Pal.:—the city of palmtrees.

5900. עִירוּ **'Îyrûw,** *ee-roo´;* from 5892; a *citizen; Iru,* an Isr.:—Iru.

5901. עִירִי **'Îyrîy,** *ee-ree´;* from 5892; *urbane; Ira,* an Isr.:—Iri.

5902. עִירָם **'Îryâm,** *ee-rawm´;* from 5892; *citywise; Iram,* an Idumæan:—Iram.

5903. עֵירֹם **'êyrôm,** *ay-rome´;* or עֵרֹם **'êrôm,** *ay-rome´;* from 6191; *nudity:*—naked (-ness).

5904. עִיר נָחָשׁ **'Îyr Nâchâsh,** *eer naw-khawsh´;* from 5892 and 5175; *city of a serpent; Ir-Nachash,* a place in Pal.:—Ir-nahash.

5905. עִיר שֶׁמֶשׁ **'Îyr Shemesh,** *eer sheh´-mesh;* from 5892 and 8121; *city of the sun; Ir-Shemesh,* a place in Pal.:—Ir-shemesh.

5906. עַיִשׁ **'Ayish,** *ah´-yish;* or עָשׁ **'Âsh,** *awsh;* from 5789; the constellation of the Great *Bear* (perh. from its *migration* through the heavens):—Arcturus.

עַיָת **'Ayâth.** See 5857.

5907. עַכְבּוֹר **'Akbôwr,** *ak-bore´;* prob. for 5909; *Akbor,* the name of an Idumæan and two Isr.:—Achbor.

5908. עַכָּבִישׁ **'akkâbîysh,** *ak-kaw-beesh´;* prob. from an unused root in the lit. sense of *entangling;* a *spider* (as *weaving* a network):—spider.

5909. עַכְבָּר **'akbâr,** *ak-bawr´;* prob. from the same as 5908 in the secondary sense of *attacking;* a *mouse* (as *nibbling*):—mouse.

5910. עַכּוֹ **'Akkôw,** *ak-ko´;* appar. from an unused root mean. to *hem* in; *Akko* (from its situation on a *bay*):—Accho.

5911. עָכוֹר **'Âkôwr,** *aw-kore´;* from 5916; *troubled; Akor,* the name of a place in Pal.:—Achor.

5912. עָכָן **'Âkân,** *aw-kawn´;* from an unused root mean. to *trouble; troublesome; Akan,* an Isr.:—Achan. Comp. 5917.

5913. עָכַס **'âkaç,** *aw-kas´;* a prim. root; prop. to *tie,* spec. with fetters; but used only as denom. from 5914; to *put on anklets:*—make a tinkling ornament.

5914. עֶכֶס **'ekeç,** *eh´-kes;* from 5913; a *fetter;* hence an *anklet:*—stocks, tinkling ornament.

5915. עַכְסָה **'Akçâh,** *ak-saw´;* fem. of 5914; *anklet; Aksah,* an Israelitess:—Achsah.

5916. עָכַר **'âkar,** *aw-kar´;* a prim. root; prop. to *roil* water; fig. to *disturb* or *afflict:*—trouble, stir.

5917. עָכָר **'Âkâr,** *aw-kawr´;* from 5916; *troublesome; Akar,* an Isr.:—Achar. Comp. 5912.

5918. עָכְרָן **'Okrân,** *ok-rawn´;* from 5916; *muddler; Okran,* an Isr.:—Ocran.

5919. עַכְשׁוּב **'akshûwb,** *ak-shoob´;* prob. from an unused root mean. to *coil;* an *asp* (from lurking *coiled* up):—adder.

5920. עַל **'al,** *al;* from 5927; prop. the *top;* spec. the *Highest* (i.e. *God*); also (adv.) *aloft, to Jehovah:*—above, high, most High.

5921. עַל **'al,** *al;* prop. the same as 5920 used as a prep. (in the sing. or plur., often with pref., or as conj. with a particle following); *above, over, upon,* or *against* (yet always in this last relation with a downward aspect) in a great variety of applications (as follow):—above, according to (-ly), after, (as) against, among, and, × as, at, because of, beside (the rest of), between, beyond the time, × both and, by (reason of), × had the charge of, concerning for, in (that), (forth, out) of, (from) (off), (up-) on, over, than, through (-out), to, touching, × with.

5922. עַל **'al** (Chald.), *al;* corresp. to 5921:—about, against, concerning, for, [there-] fore, from, in, × more, of, (there-, up-) on, (in-) to, + why with.

5923. עֹל **'ôl,** *ole;* or עוֹל **'ôwl,** *ole;* from 5953; a *yoke* (as *imposed* on the neck), lit. or fig.:—yoke.

5924. עֵלָּא **'êllâ'** (Chald.), *ale-law´;* from 5922; *above:*—over.

5925. עֻלָּא **'Ullâ',** *ool-law´;* fem. of 5923; *burden; Ulla,* an Isr.:—Ulla.

5926. עִלֵּג **'illêg,** *il-layg´;* from an unused root mean. to *stutter; stuttering:*—stammerer.

5927. עָלָה **'âlâh,** *aw-law´;* a prim. root; to *ascend,* intrans. *(be high)* or act. *(mount);* used in a great variety of senses, primary and secondary, lit. and fig. (as follow):—arise (up). (cause to) ascend up, at once, break [*the day*] (up), bring (up), (cause to) burn, carry up, cast up, + shew, climb (up), (cause to, make to) come (up), cut off, dawn, depart, exalt, excel, fall, fetch up, get up, (make to) go (away, up), grow (over), increase, lay, leap, levy, lift (self) up, light, [make] up, × mention, mount up, offer, make to pay, + perfect, prefer, put (on), raise, recover, restore, (make to) rise (up), scale, set (up), shoot forth (up), (begin to) spring (up), stir up, take away (up), work.

5928. עֲלָה **'ălâh** (Chald.), *al-aw´;* corresp. to 5930; a *holocaust:*—burnt offering.

5929. עָלֶה **'âleh,** *aw-leh´;* from 5927; a *leaf* (as *coming up* on a tree); collect. *foliage:*—branch, leaf.

5930. עֹלָה **'ôlâh,** *o-law´;* or עוֹלָה **'ôwlâh,** *o-law´;* fem. act. part of 5927; a *step* or (collect. *stairs,* as *ascending*); usually a *holocaust* (as *going up* in smoke):—ascent, burnt offering (sacrifice), go up to. See also 5766.

5931. עִלָּה **'illâh** (Chald.), *il-law´;* fem. from a root corresp. to 5927; a *pretext* (as *arising* artificially):—occasion.

5932. עַלְוָה **'alvâh,** *al-vaw´;* for 5766; moral *perverseness:*—iniquity.

5933. עַלְוָה **'Alvâh,** *al-vaw´;* or עַלְיָה **'Alyâh,** *al-yaw´;* the same as 5932; *Alvah* or *Aljah,* an Idumæan:—Aliah, Alvah.

5934. עָלוּם **'âlûwm,** *aw-loom´;* pass. part. of 5956 in the denom. sense of 5958; (only in plur. as abstr.) *adolescence;* fig. *vigor:*—youth.

5935. עַלְוָן **'Alvân,** *al-vawn´;* or עַלְיָן **'Alyân,** *al-yawn´;* from 5927; *lofty; Alvan* or *Aljan,* an Idumæan:—Alian, Alvan.

5936. עֲלוּקָה **'ălûwqâh,** *al-oo-kaw´;* fem. pass. part. of an unused root mean. to *suck;* the *leech:*—horse-leech.

5937. עָלַז **'âlaz,** *aw-laz´;* a prim. root; to *jump* for joy, i.e. *exult:*—be joyful, rejoice, triumph.

5938. עָלֵז **'âlêz,** *aw-laze´;* from 5937; *exultant:*—that rejoiceth.

5939. עֲלָטָה **'ălâṭâh,** *al-aw-taw´;* fem. from an unused root mean. to *cover; dusk:*—dark, twilight.

5940. עֱלִי **'ĕlîy,** *el-ee´;* from 5927; a *pestle* (as *lifted*):—pestle.

5941. עֵלִי **'Êlîy,** *ay-lee´;* from 5927; *lofty; Eli,* an Isr. high-priest:—Eli.

5942. עִלִּי **'illîy,** *il-lee´;* from 5927; *high,* i.e. compar.:—upper.

5943. עִלַּי **'illay** (Chald.), *il-lah´ee;* corresp. to 5942; *supreme* (i.e. *God*):—(most) high.
עַלְיָה° **'Alyâh.** See 5933.

5944. עֲלִיָּה **'ălîyâh,** *al-ee-yaw´;* fem. from 5927; something *lofty,* i.e. a *stair-way;* also a *second-story* room (or even one on the roof); fig. the *sky:*—ascent, (upper) chamber, going up, loft, parlour.

5945. עֶלְיוֹן **'elyôwn,** *el-yone´;* from 5927; an *elevation,* i.e. (adj.) *lofty* (compar.); as title, the *Supreme:*—(Most, on) high (-er, -est), upper (-most).

5946. עֶלְיוֹן **'elyôwn** (Chald.), *el-yone´;* corresp. to 5945; the *Supreme:*—Most high.

5947. עַלִּיז **'allîyz,** *al-leez´;* from 5937; *exultant:*—joyous, (that) rejoice (-ing).

5948. עֲלִיל **'ălîyl,** *al-eel´;* from 5953 in the sense of *completing;* prob. a *crucible* (as *working* over the metal):—furnace.

5949. עֲלִילָה **'ălîylâh,** *al-ee-law´;* or עֲלִלָה **'ălîlâh,** *al-ee-law´;* from 5953 in the sense of *effecting;* an *exploit* (of God), or a *performance* (of man, often in a bad sense); by impl. an *opportunity:*—act (-ion), deed, doing, invention, occasion, work.

5950. עֲלִילִיָּה **'ălîylîyâh,** *al-ee-lee-yaw´;* for 5949; (miraculous) *execution:*—work.
עַלְיָן **'Alyân.** See 5935.

5951. עֲלִיצוּת **'ălîytsûwth,** *al-ee-tsooth´;* from 5970; *exultation:*—rejoicing.

5952. עַלִּית **'allîyth,** *al-leeth´;* from 5927; a *second-story* room:—chamber. Comp. 5944.

5953. עָלַל **'âlal,** *aw-lal´;* a prim. root; to *effect* thoroughly; spec. to *glean* (also fig.); by impl. (in a bad sense) to *overdo,* i.e. maltreat, be saucy to, pain, impose (also lit.):—abuse, affect, × child, defile, do, glean, mock, practise, throughly, work (wonderfully).

5954. עֲלַל **'ălal** (Chald.), *al-al´;* corresp. to 5953 (in the sense of *thrusting* oneself in), to *enter;* caus. to *introduce:*—bring in, come in, go in.
עֹלָל **'ôlâl.** See 5768.
עֲלִלָה **'ălîlâh.** See 5949.

5955. עֹלֵלָה **'ôlêlâh,** *o-lay-law´;* fem. act. part. of 5953; only in plur. *gleanings;* by extens. *gleaning-time:*—(gleaning) (of the) grapes, grapegleanings.

5956. עָלַם **'âlam,** *aw-lam´;* a prim. root; to *veil* from sight, i.e. *conceal* (lit. or fig.):— × any ways, blind, dissembler, hide (self), secret (thing).

5957. עָלַם **'âlam** (Chald.), *aw-lam´;* corresp. to 5769; *remote* time, i.e. the *future* or *past* indefinitely; often adv. *forever:*—for([n-]) ever (lasting), old.

5958. עֶלֶם **'elem,** *eh´-lem;* from 5956; prop. something *kept out of sight* [comp. 5959], i.e. a *lad:*—young man, stripling.
עֹלָם **'ôlâm.** See 5769.

5959. עַלְמָה **'almâh,** *al-maw´;* fem. of 5958; a *lass* (as *veiled* or private):—damsel, maid, virgin.

5960. עַלְמוֹן **'Almôwn,** *al-mone´;* from 5956; *hidden; Almon,* a place in Pal. See also 5963.

5961. עֲלָמוֹת **'Ălâmôwth,** *al-aw-mōth´;* plur. of 5959; prop. *girls,* i.e. the *soprano* or female voice, perh. *falsetto:*—Alamoth.
עַלְמוּת **'almûwth.** See 4192.

5962. עַלְמִי **'Almîy** (Chald.), *al-mee´;* patrial from a name corresp. to 5867 contr.; an *Elamite* or inhab. of Elam:—Elamite.

5963. עַלְמֹן דִּבְלָתָיְמָה **'Almôn Diblâthâyᵉmâh,** *al-mone´ dib-law-thaw´-yem-aw;* from the same as 5960 and the dual of 1690 [comp. 1015] with enclitic of direction; *Almon towards Diblathajim; Almon-Diblathajemah,* a place in Moab:—Almon-diblathaim.

5964. עָלֶמֶת **'Âlemeth,** *aw-leh´-meth;* from 5956; a *covering; Alemeth,* the name of a place in Pal. and of two Isr.:—Alameth, Alemeth.

5965. עָלַס **'âlaç,** *aw-las´;* a prim. root; to *leap* for joy, i.e. *exult, wave* joyously:— × peacock, rejoice, solace self.

5966. עָלַע **'âla',** *aw-lah´;* a prim. root; to *sip* up:—suck up.

5967. עֲלַע **'ăla'** (Chald.), *al-ah´;* corresp. to 6763; a *rib:*—rib.

5968. עָלַף **'âlaph,** *aw-laf´;* a prim. root; to *veil* or *cover;* fig. to *be languid:*—faint, overlaid, wrap self.

5969. עֻלְפֶּה **'ulpeh,** *ool-peh´;* from 5968; an *envelope,* i.e. (fig.) *mourning:*—fainted.

5970. עָלַץ **'âlats,** *aw-lats´;* a prim. root; to *jump* for joy, i.e. *exult:*—be joyful, rejoice, triumph.

5971. עַם **'am,** *am;* from 6004; a *people* (as a congregated *unit*); spec. a *tribe* (as those of Israel); hence (collect.) *troops* or *attendants;* fig. a *flock:*—folk, men, nation, people.

5972. עַם **'am** (Chald.), *am;* corresp. to 5971:—people.

5973. עִם **'îm,** *eem;* from 6004; adv. or prep. *with* (i.e. in *conjunction* with), in varied applications; spec. *equally with;* often with prep. pref. (and then usually unrepresented in English):—accompanying, against, and, as (× long as), before, beside, by (reason of), for all, from (among, between), in, like, more than, of, (un-) to, with (-al).

5974. עִם **'îm** (Chald.), *eem;* corresp. to 5973:—by, from, like, to (-ward), with.

5975. עָמַד **'âmad,** *aw-mad´;* a prim. root; to *stand,* in various relations (lit. and fig., intrans. and trans.):—abide (behind), appoint, arise, cease, confirm, continue, dwell, be employed, endure, establish, leave, make, ordain, be [over], place, (be) present (self), raise up, remain, repair, + serve, set (forth, over, -tle, up), (make to, make to be at a, with-) stand (by, fast, firm, still, up), (be at a) stay (up), tarry.

5976. עָמַד **'âmad,** *aw-mad´;* for 4571; to *shake:*—be at a stand.

5977. עֹמֶד **'ômed,** *o´-med;* from 5975 ; a *spot* (as being *fixed*):—place, (+ where) stood, upright.

5978. עִמָּד **'immâd,** *im-mawd´;* prol. for 5973; along *with:*—against, by, from, in, + me, + mine, of, + that I take, unto, upon, with (-n).
עַמֻּד **'ammûd.** See 5982.

5979. עֶמְדָּה **'emdâh,** *em-daw´;* from 5975; a *station,* i.e. domicile:—standing.

5980. עֻמָּה **'ummâh,** *oom-maw´;* from 6004; *conjunction,* i.e. *society;* mostly adv. or prep. (with prep. pref.) *near, beside, along with:*—(over) against, at, beside, hard by, in points.

5981. עֻמָּה **'Ummâh,** *oom-maw´;* the same as 5980; *association; Ummah,* a place in Pal.:—Ummah.

5982. עַמּוּד **'ammûwd,** *am-mood´;* or עַמֻּד **'ammûd,** *am-mood´;* from 5975; a *column* (as *standing*); also a *stand,* i.e. platform:— × apiece, pillar.

5983. עַמּוֹן **'Ammôwn,** *am-mone´;* from 5971; *tribal,* i.e. *inbred; Ammon,* a son of Lot; also his posterity and their country:—Ammon, Ammonites.

5984. עַמּוֹנִי **'Ammôwnîy,** *am-mo-nee´;* patron. from 5983; an *Ammonite* or (adj.) *Ammonitish:*—Ammonite (-s).

5985. עַמּוֹנִית **'Ammôwnîyth,** *am-mo-neeth´;* fem. of 5984; an *Ammonitess:*—Ammonite (-ss).

5986. עָמוֹס **'Âmôwç,** *aw-moce´;* from 6006; *burdensome; Amos,* an Isr. prophet:—Amos.

5987. עָמוֹק **'Âmôwq,** *aw-moke´;* from 6009; *deep; Amok,* an Isr.:—Amok.

5988. עַמִּיאֵל **'Ammîy'êl,** *am-mee-ale´;* from 5971 and 410; *people of God; Ammiël,* the name of three or four Isr.:—Ammiel.

5989. עַמִּיהוּד **'Ammîyhûwd,** *am-mee-hood´;* from 5971 and 1935; *people of splendor; Ammihud,* the name of three Isr.:—Ammihud.

5990. עַמִּיזָבָד **'Ammîyzâbâd,** *am-mee-zaw-bawd´;* from 5971 and 2064; *people of endowment; Ammizabad,* an Isr.:—Ammizabad.

5991. עַמִּיחוּר° **'Ammîychûwr,** *am-mee-khoor´;* from 5971 and 2353; *people of nobility; Ammichur,* a Syrian prince:—Ammihud [*from the marg.*].

5992. עַמִּינָדָב **'Ammîynâdâb,** *am-mee-naw-dawb´;* from 5971 and 5068; *people of liberality; Amminadab,* the name of four Isr.:—Amminadab.

5993. עַמִּי נָדִיב **'Ammîy Nâdîyb,** *am-mee´ naw-deeb´;* from 5971 and 5081; *my people* (is) *liberal; Ammi-Nadib,* prob. an Isr.:—Amminadib.

5994. עֲמִיק **'âmîyq** (Chald.), *am-eek´;* corresp. to 6012; *profound,* i.e. unsearchable:—deep.

5995. עָמִיר **'âmîyr,** *aw-meer´;* from 6014; a *bunch* of grain:—handful, sheaf.

5996. עַמִּישַׁדַּי **'Ammîyshadday,** *am-mee-shad-dah´ee;* from 5971 and 7706; *people of* (the) *Almighty; Ammishaddai,* an Isr.:—Ammishaddai.

5997. עָמִית **'âmîyth,** *aw-meeth´;* from a prim. root mean. to *associate; companionship;* hence (concr.) a *comrade* or kindred man:—another, fellow, neighbour.

5998. עָמַל **'âmal,** *aw-mal´;* a prim. root; to *toil,* i.e. *work severely* and with irksomeness:—[take] labour (in).

5999. עָמָל **'âmâl,** *aw-mawl´;* from 5998; *toil,* i.e. *wearing effort;* hence *worry,* wheth. of body or mind:—grievance (-vousness), iniquity, labour, mischief, miserable (-sery), pain (-ful), perverseness, sorrow, toil, travail, trouble, wearisome, wickedness.

6000. עָמָל **'Âmâl,** *aw-mawl´;* the same as 5999; *Amal,* an Isr.:—Amal.

6001. עָמֵל **'âmêl,** *aw-male´;* from 5998; *toiling* concr. a *laborer;* fig. *sorrowful:*—that laboureth, that is a misery, had taken [labour], wicked, workman.

6002. עֲמָלֵק **'Ămâlêq,** *am-aw-lake´;* prob. of for. or.; *Amalek,* a descend. of Esau; also his posterity and their country:—Amalek.

6003. עֲמָלֵקִי **'Ămâlêqîy,** *am-aw-lay-kee´;* patron. from 6002; an *Amalekite* (or collect. the *Amalekites*) or desc. of Amalek:—Amalekite (-s).

6004. עָמַם **'âmam,** *aw-mam´;* a prim. root; to *associate;* by impl. to *overshadow* (by *huddling* together):—become dim, hide.

6005. עִמָּנוּאֵל **'Immânûw'êl,** *im-maw-noo-ale´;* from 5973 and 410 with suff. pron. ins.; *with us* (is) *God; Immanuel,* a typ. name of Isaiah's son:—Immanuel.

6006. עָמַס **'âmaç,** *aw-mas´;* or עָמַשׂ **'âmas,** *aw-mas´;* a prim. root; to *load,* i.e. *impose* a burden (or fig. infliction):—be borne, (heavy) burden (self), lade, load, put.

6007. עֲמַסְיָה **'Ămaçyâh,** *am-as-yaw´;* from 6006 and 3050; *Jah has loaded; Amasjah,* an Isr.:—Amasiah.

6008. עַמְעָד **'Am'âd,** *am-awd´;* from 5971 and 5703; *people of time; Amad,* a place in Pal:—Amad.

6009. עָמַק **'âmaq,** *aw-mak´;* a prim, root; to *be* (causat, *make*) *deep* (lit. or fig.):—(be, have, make, seek) deep (-ly), depth, be profound.

6010. עֵמֶק **'êmeq,** *ay´-mek;* from 6009; a *vale* (i.e. broad *depression*):—dale, vale, valley [*often used as a part of proper names*]. See also 1025.

6011. עֹמֶק **'ômeq,** *o´-mek;* from 6009; *depth:*—depth.

6012. עָמֵק **'âmêq,** *aw-make´;* from 6009; *deep* (lit. or fig.):—deeper, depth, strange.

6013. עָמֹק **'âmôq,** *aw-moke´;* from 6009; *deep* (lit. or fig.):— (× exceeding) deep (thing)

6014. עָמַר **'âmar,** *aw-mar´;* a prim. root; prop. appar. to *heap;* fig. to *chastise* (as if *piling* blows); spec. (as denom. from 6016) to *gather* grain:—bind sheaves, make merchandise of.

6015. עֲמַר **'ămar** (Chald.), *am-ar´;* corresp. to 6785; *wool:*—wool.

6016. עֹמֶר **'ômer,** *o´-mer;* from 6014; prop. a *heap,* i.e. a *sheaf;* also an *omer,* as a dry measure:—omer, sheaf.

6017. עֲמֹרָה **'Ămôrâh,** *am-o-raw´;* from 6014; a (ruined) *heap; Amorah,* a place in Pal.:—Gomorrah.

6018. עָמְרִי **'Omrîy,** *om-ree´;* from 6014; *heaping; Omri,* an Isr.:—Omri.

6019. עַמְרָם **'Amrâm,** *am-rawm´;* prob. from 5971 and 7311; *high people; Amram,* the name of two Isr.:—Amram.

6020. עַמְרָמִי **'Amrâmîy,** *am-raw-mee´;* patron. from 6019; an *Amramite* or desc. of Amram:—Amramite.

עָמַשׂ **'âmas.** See 6006.

6021. עֲמָשָׂא **'Ămâsâ',** *am-aw-saw´;* from 6006; *burden; Amasa,* the name of two Isr.:—Amasa.

6022. עֲמָשַׂי **'Ămâsay,** *am-aw-sah´ee;* from 6006; *burdensome; Amasai,* the name of three Isr.:—Amasai.

6023. עֲמַשְׁסַי **'Ămashçay,** *am-ash-sah´ee;* prob. from 6006; *burdensome; Amashsay,* an Isr.:—Amashai.

6024. עֲנָב **'Ănâb,** *an-awb´;* from the same as 6025; *fruit; Anab,* a place in Pal.:—Anab.

6025. עֵנָב **'ênâb,** *ay-nawb´;* from an unused root prob. mean. to *bear* fruit; a *grape:*—(ripe) grape, wine.

6026. עָנַג **'ânag,** *aw-nag´;* a prim. root; to be *soft* or pilable, i.e. (fig.) *effeminate* or luxurious:—delicate (-ness), (have) delight (self), sport self.

6027. עֹנֶג **'ôneg,** *o´-neg;* from 6026; *luxury:*—delight, pleasant.

6028. עָנֹג **'ânôg,** *aw-nogue´;* from 6026; *luxurious:*—delicate.

6029. עָנַד **'ânad,** *aw-nad´;* a prim. root; to *lace* fast:—bind, tie.

6030. עָנָה **'ânâh,** *aw-naw´;* a prim. root; prop. to *eye* or (gen.) to *heed,* i.e. *pay attention;* by impl. to *respond;* by extens. to *begin* to speak; spec. to *sing, shout, testify, announce:*—give account, afflict [*by mistake for* 6031], (cause to, give) answer, bring low [*by mistake for* 6031], cry, hear, Leannoth, lift up, say, × scholar, (give a) shout, sing (together by course), speak, testify, utter, (bear) witness. See also 1042, 1043.

6031. עָנָה **'ânâh,** *aw-naw´;* a prim. root [possibly rather ident. with 6030 through the idea of *looking* down or *browbeating*]; to *depress* lit. or fig., trans. or intrans. (in various applications, as follow):—abase self, afflict (-ion, self), answer [*by mistake for* 6030], chasten self, deal hardly with, defile, exercise, force, gentleness, humble (self), hurt, ravish, sing [*by mistake for* 6030], speak [*by mistake for* 6030], submit self, weaken, × in any wise.

6032. עֲנָה **'ănâh** (Chald.), *an-aw´;* corresp. to 6030:—answer, speak.

6033. עֲנָה **'ănâh** (Chald.), *an-aw´;* corresp. to 6031:—poor.

6034. עֲנָה **'Ănâh,** *an-aw´;* prob. from 6030; an *answer; Anah,* the name of two Edomites and one Edomitess:—Anah.

6035. עָנָו **'ânâv,** *aw-nawv´;* or [by intermixture with 6041] עָנָיו **'ânâyv,** *aw-nawv´;* from 6031; *depressed* (fig.), in mind (*gentle*) or circumstances (*needy,* espec. *saintly*):—humble, lowly, meek, poor°. Comp. 6041.

6036. עָנוּב **'Ânûwb,** *aw-noob´;* pass. part. from the same as 6025; *borne* (as fruit); *Anub,* an Isr.:—Anub.

6037. עַנְוָה **'anvâh,** *an-vaw´;* fem. of 6035; *mildness* (royal), also (concr.) *oppressed:*—gentleness, meekness.

6038. עֲנָוָה **'ănâvâh,** *an-aw-vaw´;* from 6035; *condescension,* human and subj. (*modesty*), or divine and obj. (*clemency*):—gentleness, humility, meekness.

6039. עֱנוּת **'ênûwth,** *en-ooth´;* from 6031; *affliction:*—affliction.

6040. עֳנִי **'ônîy,** *on-ee´;* from 6031; *depression,* i.e. misery:—afflicted (-ion), trouble.

6041. עָנִי **'ânîy,** *aw-nee´;* from 6031; *depressed,* in mind or circumstances [practically the same as 6035; although the marg. constantly disputes this, making 6035 subj. and 6041 obj.]:—afflicted, humble°, lowly°, needy, poor.

6042. עֻנִּי **'Unnîy,** *oon-nee´;* from 6031; *afflicted; Unni,* the name of two Isr.:—Unni.

6043. עֲנָיָה **'Ânâyâh,** *an-aw-yaw´;* from 6030; *Jah has answered; Anajah,* the name of two Isr.:—Anaiah.

עָנָיו **'ânâyv.** See 6035.

6044. עָנִים **'Ânîym,** *aw-neem´;* for plur. of 5869; *fountains; Anim,* a place in Pal.:—Anim.

6045. עִנְיָן **'inyân,** *in-yawn´;* from 6031; *ado,* i.e. (gen.) *employment* or (spec.) an *affair:*—business, travail.

6046. עָנֵם **'Ânêm,** *aw-name´;* from the dual of 5869; *two fountains; Anem,* a place in Pal.:—Anem.

6047. עֲנָמִים **'Ănâmîm,** *an-aw-meem´;* as if plur. of some Eg. word; *Anamim,* a son of Mizraim and his desc., with their country:—Anamim.

6048. עֲנַמֶּלֶךְ **'Ănammelek,** *an-am-meh´-lek;* of for. or.; *Anammelek,* an Assyrian deity:—Anammelech.

6049. עָנַן **'ânan,** *aw-nan´;* a prim. root; to *cover;* used only as denom. from 6051, to *cloud* over; fig. to *act covertly,* i.e. practise magic:—× bring, enchanter, Meonemin, observe (-r of) times, soothsayer, sorcerer.

6050. עֲנַן **'ănan** (Chald.), *an-an´;* corresp. to 6051:—cloud.

6051. עָנָן **'ânân,** *aw-nawn´;* from 6049; a *cloud* (as *covering* the sky), i.e. the *nimbus* or thunder-cloud:—cloud (-y).

6052. עָנָן **'Ânân,** *aw-nawn´;* the same as 6051; *cloud; Anan,* an Isr.:—Anan.

6053. עֲנָנָה **'ănânâh,** *an-aw-naw´;* fem. of 6051; *cloudiness:*—cloud.

6054. עֲנָנִי **'Ănânîy,** *an-aw-nee´;* from 6051; *cloudy; Anani,* an Isr.:—Anani.

6055. עֲנַנְיָה **'Ănanyâh,** *an-an-yaw´;* from 6049 and 3050; *Jah has covered; Ananjah,* the name of an Isr. and of a place in Pal.:—Ananiah.

6056. עֲנַף **'ănaph** (Chald.), *an-af´;* or עֶנֶף **'eneph** (Chald.), *eh´-nef;* corresp. to 6057:—bough, branch.

6057. עָנָף **'ânâph,** *aw-nawf´;* from an unused root mean. to *cover;* a *twig* (as *covering* the limbs):—bough, branch.

6058. עָנֵף **'ânêph,** *aw-nafe´;* from the same as 6057; *branching:*—full of branches.

6059. עָנַק **'ânaq,** *aw-nak´;* a prim. root; prop. to *choke;* used only as denom. from 6060, to *collar,* i.e. adorn with a necklace; fig. to *fit out* with supplies:—compass about as a chain, furnish, liberally.

6060. עָנָק **'ânâq,** *aw-nawk´;* from 6059; a *necklace* (as if *strangling*):—chain.

6061. עָנָק **'Ânâq,** *aw-nawk´;* the same as 6060; *Anak,* a Canaanite:—Anak.

6062. עֲנָקִי **'Ânâqîy,** *an-aw-kee´;* patron. from 6061; an *Anakite* or desc. of Anak:—Anakim.

6063. עָנֵר **'Ânêr,** *aw-nare´;* prob. for 5288; *Aner,* an Amorite, also a place in Pal.:—Aner.

6064. עָנַשׁ **'ânash,** *aw-nash´;* a prim. root; prop. to *urge;* by impl. to *inflict* a penalty, spec. to *fine:*—amerce, condemn, punish, × surely.

6065. עֲנַשׁ **'ănash** (Chald.), *an-ash´;* corresp. to 6066; a *mulct:*—confiscation.

6066. עֹנֶשׁ **'ônesh,** *o´-nesh;* from 6064; a *fine:*—punishment, tribute.

עֶנֶת **'eneth.** See 3706.

6067. עֲנָת **'Ânâth,** *an-awth´;* from 6030; *answer; Anath,* an Isr.:—Anath.

6068. עֲנָתוֹת **'Ânâthôwth,** *an-aw-thōth´;* plur. of 6067; *Anathoth,* the name of two Isr., also of a place in Pal.:—Anathoth.

6069. עַנְתֹתִי **'Anthôthîy,** *an-tho-thee´;* or עַנְּתוֹתִי **'Annethôwthîy,** *an-ne-tho-thee´;* patrial from 6068; an *Antothite* or inhab. of Anathoth:—of Anathoth, Anethothite, Anetothite, Antothite.

6070. עַנְתֹתִיָּה **'Anthôthîyâh,** *an-tho-thee-yaw´;* from the same as 6068 and 3050; *answers of Jah; Anthothijah,* an Isr.:—Antothijah.

6071. עָסִיס **'âçîyç,** *aw-sees´;* from 6072; *must* or fresh grape-juice (as just *trodden* out):—juice, new (sweet) wine.

6072. עָסַס **'âçaç,** *aw-sas´; a prim. root; to squeeze* out juice; fig. to *trample:*—tread down.

6073. עֳפֶא **'ŏphe',** *of-eh´;* from an unused root mean. to *cover;* a *bough* (as covering the tree):—branch.

6074. עֳפִי **'ŏphîy** (Chald.), *of-ee´;* corresp. to 6073; a *twig,* bough, i.e. (collect.) *foliage:*—leaves.

6075. עָפַל **'âphal,** *aw-fal´;* a prim. root; to *swell;* fig. *be elated:*—be lifted up, presume.

6076. עֹפֶל **'ôphel,** *o´-fel;* from 6075; a *turior;* also a *mound,* i.e. fortress:—emerod, fort, strong hold, tower.

6077. עֹפֶל **'Ôphel,** *o´-fel;* the same as 6076; *Ophel,* a ridge in Jerus.:—Ophel.

6078. עָפְנִי **'Ophnîy,** *of-nee´;* from an unused noun [denoting a place in Pal.; from an unused root of uncert. mean.[; an *Ophnite* (collect.) or inhab. of Ophen:—Ophni.

6079. עַפְעַף **'aph'aph,** *af-af´;* from 5774; an *eyelash* (as *fluttering*); fig. morning *ray:*—dawning, eye-lid.

6080. עָפַר **'âphar,** *aw-far´;* a prim. root; mean. either to *be gray* or perh. rather to *pulverize;* used only as denom. from 6083; to *be dust:*—cast [dust].

6081. עֵפֶר **'Êpher,** *ay´-fer;* prob. a var. of 6082; *gazelle; Epher,* the name of an Arabian and of two Isr.:—Epher.

6082. עֹפֶר **'ôpher,** *o´-fer;* from 6080; a *fawn* (from the *dusty* color):—young roe [hart].

6083. עָפָר **'âphâr,** *aw-fawr´;* from 6080; *dust* (as *powdered* or *gray*); hence *clay, earth, mud:*—ashes, dust, earth, ground, morter, powder, rubbish.

עַפְרָה **'Aphrâh.** See 1035.

6084. עָפְרָה **'Ophrâh,** *of-raw´;* fem. of 6082; *female fawn; Ophrah,* the name of an Isr and of two places in Pal.:—Ophrah.

6085. עֶפְרוֹן **'Ephrôwn,** *ef-rone´;* from the same as 6081; *fawn-like; Ephron,* the name of a Canaanite and of two places in Pal.:—Ephron, Ephrain [*from the marg.*].

עֹפֶרֶת **'ôphereth.** See 5777.

6086. עֵץ **'êts,** *ates;* from 6095; a *tree* (from its *firmness*); hence *wood* (plur. *sticks*):— + carpenter, gallows, helve, + pine, plank, staff, stalk, stick, stock, timber, tree, wood.

6087. עָצַב **'âtsab,** *aw-tsab´;* a prim. root; prop. to *carve,* i.e. *fabricate* or *fashion;* hence (in a bad sense) to *worry, pain* or *anger:*—displease, grieve, hurt, make, be sorry, vex, worship, wrest.

6088. עֲצַב **'ătsab** (Chald.), *ats-ab´;* corresp. to 6087; to *afflict:*—lamentable.

6089. עֶצֶב **'etseb,** *eh´-tseb;* from 6087; an earthen *vessel;* usually (painful) *toil;* also a *pang* (whether of body or mind):—grievous, idol, labor, sorrow.

6090. עֹצֶב **'ôtseb,** *o´-tseb;* a var. of 6089; an *idol* (as fashioned); also *pain* (bodily or mental):—idol, sorrow, × wicked.

6091. עָצָב **'âtsâb,** *aw-tsawb´;* from 6087; an (idolatrous) *image:*—idol, image.

6092. עָצֵב **'âtsêb,** *aw-tsabe´;* from 6087; a (hired) *workman:*—labour.

6093. עִצָּבוֹן **'itstsâbôwn,** *its-tsaw-bone´;* from 6087; *worrisomeness,* i.e. *labor* or *pain:*—sorrow, toil.

6094. עַצֶּבֶת **'atstsebeth,** *ats-tseh´-beth;* from 6087; an *idol;* also a *pain* or *wound:*—sorrow, wound.

6095. עָצָה **'âtsâh,** *aw-tsaw´;* a prim. root; prop. to *fasten* (or *make firm*), i.e. to *close* (the eyes):—shut.

6096. עָצֶה **'âtseh,** *aw-tseh´;* from 6095; the *spine* (as giving *firmness* to the body):—back bone.

6097. עֵצָה **'êtsah,** *ay-tsaw´;* fem. of 6086; *timber:*—trees.

6098. עֵצָה **'êtsâh,** *ay-tsaw´;* from 3289; *advice;* by impl. *plan;* also *prudence:*—advice, advisement, counsel ([-lor]), purpose.

6099. עָצוּם **'âtsûwm,** *aw-tsoom´;* or עָצֻם **'âtsûm,** *aw-tsoom´;* pass. part. of 6105; *powerful* (spec. a *paw*); by impl. *numerous:*— + feeble, great, mighty, must, strong.

6100. עֶצְיוֹן גֶּבֶר **'Etsyôwn** (shorter עֶצְיֹן **'Etsyôn) Geber,** *ets-yone´; gheh´-ber;* from 6096 and 1397; *backbone-like of a man; Etsjon-Geber,* a place on the Red Sea:—Ezion-gaber, Ezion-geber.

6101. עָצַל **'âtsal,** *aw-tsal´;* a prim. root; to *lean* idly, i.e. to be *indolent* or *slack:*—be slothful.

6102. עָצֵל **'âtsêl,** *aw-tsale´;* from 6101; *indolent:*—slothful, sluggard.

6103. עַצְלָה **'atslâh,** *ats-law´;* fem. of 6102; (as abstr.) *indolence:*—slothfulness.

6104. עַצְלוּת **'atslûwth,** *ats-looth´;* from 6101; *indolence:*—idleness.

6105. עָצַם **'âtsam,** *aw-tsam´;* a prim. root; to *bind* fast, i.e. *close* (the eyes); intrans. to *be* (causat, *make*) *powerful* or *numerous;* denom. (from 6106) to *craunch* the bones:—break the bones, close, be great, be increased, be (wax) mighty (-ier), be more, shut, be (-come, make) strong (-er).

6106. עֶצֶם **'etsem,** *eh´-tsem;* from 6105; a *bone* (as *strong*); by extens. the *body;* fig. the *substance,* i.e. (as pron.) *selfsame:*—body, bone, × life, (self-) same, strength, × very.

6107. עֶצֶם **'Etsem,** *eh´-tsem;* the same as 6106; *bone; Estsem,* a place in Pal.:—Azem, Ezem.

6108. עֹצֶם **'ôtsem,** *o´-tsem;* from 6105; *power;* hence *body:*—might, strong, substance.

עָצֻם **'âtsûm.** See 6099.

6109. עָצְמָה **'otsmâh,** *ots-maw´;* fem. of 6108; *powerfulness;* by extens. *numerousness:*—abundance, strength.

6110. עַצֻּמָה **'atstsûmâh,** *ats-tsoo-maw´;* fem. of 6099; a *bulwark,* i.e. (fig.) *argument:*—strong.

6111. עַצְמוֹן **'Atsmôwn,** *ats-mone´;* or עַצְמֹן **'Atsmôn,** *ats-mone´;* from 6107; *bone-like; Atsmon,* a place near Pal.:—Azmon.

6112. עֵצֶן **'êtsen,** *ay´-tsen;* from an unused root mean. to *be sharp* or *strong;* a *spear:*—Eznite [*from the marg.*].

6113. עָצַר **'âtsâr,** *aw-tsar´;* a prim. root; to *inclose;* by anal. to *hold back;* also to *maintain, rule, assemble:*— × be able, close up, detain, fast, keep (self close, still), prevail, recover, refrain, × reign, restrain, retain, shut (up), slack, stay, stop, withhold (self).

6114. עֶצֶר **'etser,** *eh´-tser;* from 6113; *restraint:*— + magistrate.

6115. עֹצֶר **'ôtser,** *o´-tser;* from 6113; *closure;* also *constraint:*— × barren, oppression, × prison.

6116. עֲצָרָה **'ătsârâh,** *ats-aw-raw´;* or עֲצֶרֶת **'ătsereth,** *ats-eh´-reth;* from 6113; an *assembly,* espec. on a *festival* or *holiday:*—(solemn) assembly (meeting).

6117. עָקַב **'âqab,** *aw-kab´;* a prim. root; prop. to *swell* out or up; used only as denom. from 6119; to *seize by the heel;* fig. to *circumvent* (as if *tripping* up the heels); also to *restrain* (as if holding by the heel):—take by the heel, stay, supplant, × utterly.

6118. עֵקֶב **'êqeb,** *ay´-keb;* from 6117 in the sense of 6119; a *heel,* i.e. (fig.) the *last* of anything (used adv. *for ever*); also *result,* i.e. *compensation;* and so (adv. with prep. or rel.) on *account* of:— × because, by, end, for, if, reward.

6119. עָקֵב **'âqêb,** *aw-kabe´;* or (fem.) עִקְּבָה **'iqqᵉbâh,** *ik-keb-aw´;* from 6117; a *heel* (as *protuberant*); hence a *track;* fig. the *rear* (of an army):—heel, [horse-] hoof, last, lier in wait [*by mistake for* 6120], (foot-) step.

6120. עָקֵב **'âqêb,** *aw-kabe´;* from 6117 in its denom. sense; a *lier in wait:*—heel [*by mistake for* 6119].

6121. עָקֹב **'âqôb,** *aw-kobe´;* from 6117; in the orig. sense, a *knoll* (as *swelling* up); in the denom. sense (trans.) *fraudulent* or (intrans.) *tracked:*—crooked, deceitful, polluted.

6122. עָקְבָה **'oqbâh,** *ok-baw´;* fem. of an unused form from 6117 mean. a *trick; trickery:*—subtilty.

6123. עָקַד **'âqad,** *aw-kad´;* a prim. root; to *tie* with thongs:—bind.

עֵקֶד **'Êqed.** See 1044.

6124. עָקֹד **'âqôd,** *aw-kode´;* from 6123; *striped* (with *bands*):—ring straked.

6125. עָקָה **'âqâh,** *aw-kaw´;* from 5781; *constraint:*—oppression.

6126. עַקּוּב **'Aqqûwb,** *ak-koob´;* from 6117; *insidious; Akkub,* the name of five Isr.:—Akkub.

6127. עָקַל **'âqal,** *aw-kal´;* a prim. root; to *wrest:*—wrong.

6128. עֲקַלְקַל **'ăqalqal,** *ak-al-kal´;* from 6127; *winding:*—by [-way], crooked way.

6129. עֲקַלָּתוֹן **'ăqallâthôwn,** *ak-al-law-thone´;* from 6127; *tortuous:*—crooked.

6130. עָקָן **'Âqân,** *aw-kawn´;* from an unused root mean. to *twist; tortuous; Akan,* an Idumæan:—Akan. Comp. 3292.

6131. עָקַר **'âqar,** *aw-kar´;* a prim. root; to *pluck* up (espec. by the roots); spec. to *hamstring;* fig. to *exterminate:*—dig down, hough, pluck up, root up.

6132. עֲקַר **'ăqar** (Chald.), *ak-ar´;* corresp. to 6131:—pluck up by the roots.

6133. עֵקֶר **'êqer,** *ay´-ker;* from 6131; fig. a *transplanted* person, i.e. naturalized citizen:—stock.

6134. עֵקֶר **'Êqer,** *ay´-ker;* the same as 6133; *Eker,* an Isr.:—Eker.

6135. עָקָר **'âqâr,** *aw-kawr´;* from 6131; *sterile* (as if *extirpated* in the generative organs):—(× male or female) barren (woman).

6136. עִקַּר **'iqqar** (Chald.), *ik-kar´;* from 6132, a *stock:*—stump.

6137. עַקְרָב **'aqrâb,** *ak-rawb´;* of uncert. der.; a *scorpion;* fig. a *scourge* or knotted whip:—scorpion.

6138. עֶקְרוֹן **'Eqrôwn,** *ek-rone´;* from 6131; *eradication; Ekron,* a place in Pal.:—Ekron.

6139. עֶקְרוֹנִי **'Eqrôwnîy,** *ek-ro-nee´;* or עֶקְרֹנִי **'Eqrônîy,** *ek-ro-nee´;* patrial from 6138; an *Ekronite* or inhab. of Ekron:—Ekronite.

6140. עָקַשׁ **'âqash,** *aw-kash´;* a prim. root; to *knot* or *distort;* fig. to *pervert* (act or declare perverse):—make crooked, (prove, that is) perverse (-rt).

6141. עִקֵּשׁ **'iqqêsh,** *ik-kashe´;* from 6140; *distorted;* hence *false:*—crooked, froward, perverse.

6142. עִקֵּשׁ **'Îqqêsh,** *ik-kashe´;* the same as 6141; *perverse; Ikkesh,* an Isr.:—Ikkesh.

6143. עִקְּשׁוּת **'iqqᵉshûwth,** *ik-kesh-ooth´;* from 6141; *perversity:*— × froward.

עַר **'ar.** See 5892.

6144. עָר **'Âr,** *awr;* the same as 5892; a *city; Ar,* a place in Moab:—Ar.

6145. עָר **'âr,** *awr;* from 5782; a *foe* (as *watchful* for mischief):—enemy.

6146. עָר **'âr** (Chald.), *awr;* corresp. to 6145:—enemy.

6147. עֵר **'Êr,** *ayr;* from 5782; *watchful; Er,* the name of two Isr.:—Er.

6148. עָרַב **'ârab,** *aw-rab´;* a prim. root; to *braid,* i.e. *intermix;* techn. to *traffic* (as if by barter); alo to *give* or *be security* (as a kind of exchange):—engage, (inter-) meddle (with), mingle (self), mortgage, occupy, give pledges, be (-come, put in) surety, undertake.

6149. עָרֵב **'ârêb,** *aw-rabe´;* a prim. root [rather identical with 6148 through the idea of close *association*]; to be *agreeable:*—be pleasant (-ing), take pleasure in, be sweet.

6150. עָרַב **'ârab,** *aw-rab´;* a prim. root [rather identical with 6148 through the idea of *covering* with a texture]; to *grow dusky* at sundown:—be darkened, (toward) evening.

6151. עֲרַב **'ărab** (Chald.), *ar-ab´;* corresp. to 6148; to *commingle:*—mingle (self), mix.

6152. עֲרָב **'Ărâb,** *ar-awb´;* or עֲרַב **'Ărab,** *ar-ab´;* from 6150 in the fig. sense of *sterility; Arab* (i.e. *Arabia*), a country E. of Pal.:—Arabia.

6153. עֶרֶב **'ereb,** *eh´-reb;* from 6150; *dusk:*— + day, even (-ing, tide), night.

6154. עֵרֶב **'êreb,** *ay´-reb;* or עֶרֶב **'ereb** (1 Kings 10 : 15), (with the art. pref.), *eh´-reb;* from 6148; the *web* (or transverse threads of cloth); also a *mixture,* (or *mongrel* race):—Arabia, mingled people, mixed (multitude), woof.

6155. עָרָב **'ârâb,** *aw-rawb´;* from 6148; a *willow* (from the use of osiers as wattles):—willow.

6156. עָרֵב **'ârêb,** *aw-rabe´;* from 6149; *pleasant:*—sweet.

6157. עָרֹב **'ârôb,** *aw-robe´;* from 6148; a *mosquito* (from its *swarming*):—divers sorts or flies, swarm.

6158. עֹרֵב **'ôrêb,** *o-rabe´;* or עוֹרֵב **'ôwrêb,** *o-rabe´;* from 6150; a *raven* (from its *dusky* hue):—raven.

6159. עֹרֵב **'Ôrêb,** *o-rabe´;* or עוֹרֵב **'Ôwrêb,** *o-rabe´;* the same as 6158; *Oreb,* the name of a Midianite and of a cliff near the Jordan:—Oreb.

6160. עֲרָבָה **'ărâbâh,** *ar-aw-baw´;* from 6150 *(in the sense of sterility);* a *desert;* espec. (with the art. pref.) the (generally) sterile valley of the Jordan and its continuation to the Red Sea:—Arabah, champaign, desert, evening, heaven, plain, wilderness. See also 1026.

6161. עֲרֻבָּה **'ărubbâh,** *ar-oob-baw´;* fem. pass. part. of 6148 in the sense of a *bargain* or *exchange;* something given as *security,* i.e. (lit.) a *token* (of safety) or (metaph.) a *bondsman:*—pledge, surety.

6162. עֲרָבוֹן **'ărâbôwn,** *ar-aw-bone´;* from 6148 (in the sense of *exchange*); a *pawn* (given as security):—pledge.

6163. עֲרָבִי **'Ărâbîy,** *ar-aw-bee´;* or עַרְבִי **'Arbîy,** *ar-bee´;* patrial from 6152; an *Arabian* or inhab. of Arab (i.e. Arabia):—Arabian.

6164. עַרְבָתִי **'Arbâthîy,** *ar-baw-thee´;* patrial from 1026; an *Arbathite* or inhab. of (Beth-) Arabah:—Arbathite.

6165. עָרַג **'ârag,** *aw-rag´;* a prim. root; to *long for:*—cry, pant.

6166. עֲרָד **'Ărâd,** *ar-awd´;* from an unused root mean. to *sequester* itself; *fugitive; Arad,* the name of a place near Pal., also of a Canaanite and an Isr.:—Arad.

6167. עֲרָד **'ărâd** (Chald.), *ar-awd´;* corresp. to 6171; an *onager:*—wild ass.

6168. עָרָה **'ârâh,** *aw-raw´;* a prim. root; to *be* (caus. *make*) *bare;* hence to *empty, pour* out, *demolish:*—leave destitute, discover, empty, make naked, pour (out), rase, spread self, uncover.

6169. עָרָה **'ârâh,** *aw-raw´;* fem. from 6168; a *naked* (i.e. level) plot:—paper reed.

6170. עֲרוּגָה **'ărûwgâh,** *ar-oo-gaw´;* or עֲרֻגָה **'ărûgâh,** *ar-oo-gaw´;* fem. pass. part. of 6165; something *piled* up (as if [fig.] *raised* by mental aspiration), i.e. a *parterre:*—bed, furrow.

6171. עָרוֹד **'ârôwd,** *aw-rode´;* from the same as 6166; an *onager* (from his *lonesome* habits):—wild ass.

6172. עֶרְוָה **'ervâh,** *er-vaw´;* from 6168; *nudity,* lit. (espec. the *pudenda*) or fig. (*disgrace, blemish*):—nakedness, shame, unclean (-ness).

6173. עַרְוָה **'arvâh** (Chald.), *ar-vaw´;* corresp. to 6172; *nakedness,* i.e. (fig.) *impoverishment:*—dishonour.

6174. עָרוֹם **'ârôwm,** *aw-rome´;* or עָרֹם **'ârôm,** *aw-rome´;* from 6191 (in its orig. sense); *nude,* either partially or totally:—naked.

6175. עָרוּם **'ârûwm,** *aw-room´;* pass. part. of 6191; *cunning* (usually in a bad sense):—crafty, prudent, subtil.

6176. עֲרוֹעֵר **'ărôw'êr,** *ar-o-ayr´;* or עַרְעָר **'ar'âr,** *ar-awr´;* from 6209 redupl.; a *juniper* (from its *nudity* of situation):—heath.

6177. עֲרוֹעֵר **'Ărôw'êr,** *ar-o-ayr´;* or עֲרֹעֵר **'Ărô'êr,** *ar-o-ayr´;* or עַרְעוֹר **'Ar'ôwr,** *ar-ore´;* the same as 6176; *nudity* of situation; *Aroër,* the name of three places in or near Pal.:—Aroer.

6178. עָרוּץ **'ârûwts,** *aw-roots´;* pass. part. of 6206; *feared,* i.e. (concr.) a *horrible* place or *chasm:*—cliffs.

6179. עֵרִי **'Êrîy,** *ay-ree´;* from 5782; *watchful; Eri,* an Isr.:—Eri.

6180. עֵרִי **'Êrîy,** *ay-ree´;* patron. of 6179; an *Erite* (collect.) or desc. of Eri.:—Erites.

6181. עֶרְיָה **'eryâh,** *er-yaw´;* for 6172; *nudity:*—bare, naked, × quite.

6182. עֲרִיסָה **'ărîyçâh,** *ar-ee-saw´;* from an unused root mean. to *comminute; meal:*—dough.

6183. עָרִיף **'ârîyph,** *aw-reef´;* from 6201; the *sky* (as *drooping* at the horizon):—heaven.

6184. עָרִיץ **'ârîyts,** *aw-reets´;* from 6206; *fearful,* i.e. *powerful* or *tyrannical:*—mighty, oppressor, in great power, strong, terrible, violent.

6185. עֲרִירִי **'ărîyrîy,** *ar-e-ree´;* from 6209; *bare,* i.e. destitute (of children):—childless.

6186. עָרַךְ **'ârak,** *aw-rak´;* a prim. root; to set in a *row,* i.e. *arrange,* put in *order* (in a very wide variety of applications):—put (set) (the battle, self) in array, compare, direct, equal, esteem, estimate, expert [in war], furnish, handle, join [battle], ordain, (lay, put, reckon up, set) (in) order, prepare, tax, value.

6187. עֵרֶךְ **'êrek,** *eh´-rek;* from 6186; a *pile, equipment, estimate:*—equal, estimation, (things that are set in) order, price, proportion, × set at, suit, taxation, × valuest.

6188. עָרֵל **'ârêl,** *aw-rale´;* a prim. root; prop. to *strip;* but used only as denom. from 6189; to *expose* or *remove* the *prepuce,* whether lit. (to *go naked*) or fig. (to *refrain* from using):—count uncircumcised, foreskin to be uncovered.

6189. עָרֵל **'ârêl,** *aw-rale´;* from 6188; prop. *exposed,* i.e. projecting loose (as to the prepuce); used only techn. *uncircumcised* (i.e. still having the prepuce uncurtailed):—uncircumcised (person).

6190. עָרְלָה **'orlâh,** *or-law´;* fem. of 6189; the *prepuce:*—foreskin, + uncircumcised.

6191. עָרַם **'âram,** *aw-ram´;* a prim. root; prop. to *be* (or *make*) *bare;* but used only in the der. sense (through the idea perh. of *smoothness*) to *be cunning* (usually in a bad sense):— × very, beware, take crafty [counsel], be prudent, deal subtilly.

6192. עָרַם **'âram,** *aw-ram´;* a prim. root; to *pile* up:—gather together.

6193. עֹרֶם **'ôrem,** *o´-rem;* from 6191; a *stratagem:*—craftiness.

עֵרֹם **'Êrôm.** See 5903.

עָרֹם **'ârôm.** See 6174.

6194. עָרֵם **'ârêm** (Jer. 50 : 26), *aw-rame´;* or (fem.) עֲרֵמָה **'ărêmâh,** *ar-ay-maw´;* from 6192; a *heap;* spec. a *sheaf:*—heap (of corn), sheaf.

6195. עָרְמָה **'ormâh,** *or-maw´;* fem. of 6193; *trickery;* or (in a good sense) *discretion:*—guile, prudence, subtilty, wilily, wisdom.

עֲרֵמָה **'arêmâh.** See 6194.

6196. עַרְמוֹן **'armôwn,** *ar-mone´;* prob. from 6191; the *plane* tree (from its *smooth* and shed bark):—chestnut tree.

6197. עֵרָן **'Êrân,** *ay-rawn´;* prob. from 5782; *watchful; Eran,* an Isr.:—Eran.

6198. עֵרָנִי **'Êrânîy,** *ay-raw-nee´;* patron. from 6197; an *Eranite* or desc. (collect.) of Eran:—Eranites.

עַרְעוֹר **'Ar'ôwr.** See 6177.

6199. עַרְעָר **'ar'âr,** *ar-awr´;* from 6209; *naked,* i.e. (fig.) *poor:*—destitute. See also 6176.

עֲרֹעֵר **'Ărô'êr.** See 6177.

6200. עֲרֹעֵרִי **'Ărô'êrîy,** *ar-o-ay-ree´;* patron. from 6177; an *Aroërite* or inhab. of Aroër:—Aroerite.

6201. עָרַף **'âraph,** *aw-raf´;* a prim. root; to *droop;* hence to *drip:*—drop (down).

6202. עָרַף **'âraph,** *aw-raf´;* a prim. root [rather ident. with 6201 through the idea of *slopping*]; prop. to *bend* downward; but used only as a denom. from 6203; to *break the neck;* hence (fig.) to *destroy:*—that is beheaded, break down, break (cut off, strike off) neck.

6203. עֹרֶף **'ôreph,** *o-ref´;* from 6202; the *nape* or back of the neck (as *declining*); hence the *back* generally (whether lit. or fig.):—back ([stiff-]) neck ([-ed]).

6204. עָרְפָּה **'Orpâh,** *or-paw´;* fem. of 6203; *mane; Orpah,* a Moabitess:—Orpah.

6205. עֲרָפֶל **'ărâphel,** *ar-aw-fel´;* prob. from 6201; *gloom* (as of a *lowering* sky):—(gross, thick) dark (cloud, -ness).

6206. עָרַץ **'ârats,** *aw-rats´;* a prim. root; to *awe* or (intrans.) to *dread;* hence to *harass:*—be affrighted (afraid, dread, feared, terrified), break, dread, fear, oppress, prevail, shake terribly.

6207. עָרַק **'âraq,** *aw-rak´;* a prim. root; to *gnaw,* i.e. (fig.) *eat* (by hyberbole); also (part.) a *pain:*—fleeing, sinew.

6208. עַרְקִי **'Arqîy,** *ar-kee´;* patrial from an unused name mean. a *tush;* an *Arkite* or inhab. of Erek:—Arkite.

6209. עָרַר **'ârar,** *aw-rar´;* a prim. root; to *bare;* fig. to *demolish:*—make bare, break, raise up [*perh. by clerical error for* RAZE], × utterly.

6210. עֶרֶשׂ **'eres,** *eh'-res;* from an unused root mean. perh. to *arch;* a *couch* (prop. with a *canopy*):—bed (-stead), couch.

6211. עָשׁ **'âsh,** *awsh;* from 6244; a *moth:*—moth.
See also 5906.

6211.´ עֲשַׂב **'ăsab** (Chald.), *as-ab´;* 6212:—grass.

6212. עֶשֶׂב **'eseb,** *eh´-seb;* from an unused root mean. to *glisten* (or *be green*); *grass* (or any tender shoot):—grass, herb.

6213. עָשָׂה **'âsâh,** *aw-saw´;* a prim. root; to *do* or *make,* in the broadest sense and widest application (as follows):—accomplish, advance, appoint, apt, be at, become, bear, bestow, bring forth, bruise, be busy, × certainly, have the charge of, commit, deal (with), deck, + displease, do, (ready) dress (-ed), (put in) execute (-ion), exercise, fashion, + feast, [fight-] ing man, + finish, fit, fly, follow, fulfil, furnish, gather, get, go about, govern, grant, great, + hinder, hold ([a feast]), × indeed, + be industrious, + journey, keep, labour, maintain, make, be meet, observe, be occupied, offer, + officer, pare, bring (come) to pass, perform, practise, prepare, procure, provide, put, requite, × sacrifice, serve, set, shew, × sin, spend, × surely, take, × thoroughly, trim, × very, + vex, be [warr-] ior, work (-man), yield, use.

6214. עֲשָׂהאֵל **'Ăsâh'êl,** *as-aw-ale´;* from 6213 and 410; *God has made; Asahel,* the name of four Isr.:—Asahel.

6215. עֵשָׂו **'Êsâv,** *ay-sawv´;* appar. a form of the pass. part. of 6213 in the orig. sense of *handling; rough* (i.e. sensibly *felt*); Esav, a son of Isaac, including his posterity:—Esau.

6216. עָשׁוֹק **'âshôwq,** *aw-shoke´;* from 6231; *oppressive* (as noun, a *tyrant*):—oppressor.

6217. עָשׁוּק **'âshûwq,** *aw-shook´;* or עָשֻׁק **'âshûq,** *aw-shook´;* pass. part. of 6231; used in plur. masc. as abstr. *tyranny:*—oppressed (-ion). [*Doubtful.*]

6218. עָשׂוֹר **'âsôwr,** *aw-sore´;* or עָשֹׂר **'âsôr,** *aw-sore´;* from 6235; *ten;* by abbrev. ten *strings,* and so a *decachord:*—(instrument of) ten (strings, -th).

6219. עָשׁוֹת **'âshôwth,** *aw-shōth´;* from 6245; *shining,* i.e. polished:—bright.

6220. עַשְׁוָת **'Ashvâth** *ash-vawth´;* for 6219; *bright; Ashvath,* an Isr.:—Ashvath.

6221. עֲשִׂיאֵל **'Ăsîy'êl,** *as-ee-ale´;* from 6213 and 410; *made of God; Asiël,* an Isr.:—Asiel.

6222. עֲשָׂיָה **'Ăsâyâh,** *aw-saw-yaw´;* from 6213 and 3050; *Jah has made; Asajah,* the name of three or four Isr.:—Asaiah.

6223. עָשִׁיר **'âshîyr,** *aw-sheer´;* from 6238; *rich,* whether lit. or fig. (*noble*):—rich (man)

6224. עֲשִׂירִי **'ăsîyrîy,** *as-ee-ree´;* from 6235; *tenth;* by abbrev. *tenth month* or (fem.) *part:*—tenth (part.)

6225. עָשַׁן **'âshan,** *aw-shan´;* a prim. root; to *smoke,* whether lit. or fig.:—be angry (be on a) smoke.

6226. עָשֵׁן **'âshên,** *aw-shane´;* from 6225; *smoky:*—smoking.

6227. עָשָׁן **'âshân,** *aw-shawn´;* from 6225; *smoke,* lit. or fig. (*vapor, dust, anger*):—smoke (-ing).

6228. עָשָׁן **'Âshân,** *aw-shawn´;* the same as 6227; *Ashan,* a place in Pal.:—Ashan.

6229. עָשַׂק **'âsaq,** *aw-sak´;* a prim. root (ident. with 6231); to *press upon,* i.e. *quarrel:*—strive with.

6230. עֵשֶׂק **'êseq,** *ay´-sek;* from 6229; *strife:*—Esek.

6231. עָשַׁק **'âshaq,** *aw-shak´;* a prim. root (comp. 6229); to *press* upon, i.e. *oppress, defraud, violate, overflow:*—get deceitfully, deceive, defraud, drink up, (use) oppress ([-ion], -or), do violence (wrong).

6232. עֵשֶׁק **'Êsheq,** *ay-shek´;* from 6231; *oppression; Eshek,* an Isr.:—Eshek.

6233. עֹשֶׁק **'ôsheq,** *o´-shek;* from 6231; *injury, fraud,* (subj.) *distress,* (concr.) *unjust gain:*—cruelly, extortion, oppression, thing [deceitfully gotten].

עָשֻׁק **'âshûq.** See 6217.

6234. עָשְׁקָה **'oshqâh,** *osh-kaw´;* fem. of 6233; *anguish:*—oppressed.

6235. עֶשֶׂר **'eser,** *eh´-ser;* masc. עֲשָׂרָה **'ăsârâh,** *as-aw-raw´;* from 6237; *ten* (as an *accumulation* to the extent of the digits):—ten, [fif-, seven-] teen.

6236. עֲשַׂר **'ăsar** (Chald.), *as-ar´;* masc. עַשְׂרָה **'ăsrâh** (Chald.), *as-raw´;* corresp. to 6235; *ten:*—ten, + twelve.

6237. עָשַׂר **'âsar,** *aw-sar´;* a prim. root (ident. with 6238); to *accumulate;* but used only as denom. from 6235; to *tithe,* i.e. take or give a tenth:— × surely, give (take) the tenth, (have, take) tithe (-ing, -s), × truly.

6238. עָשַׁר **'âshar,** *aw-shar´;* a prim. root; prop. to *accumulate;* chiefly (spec.) to *grow* (caus. *make*) *rich:*—be (-come, en-, make, make self, wax) rich, make [1 Kings 22 : 48 *marg.*]. See 6240.

6239. עֹשֶׁר **'ôsher,** *o´-sher;* from 6238; *wealth:*— × far [richer], riches.

6240. עָשָׂר **'âsâr,** *aw-sawr´;* for 6235; *ten* (only in combination), i.e. *-teen;* also (ordinal) *-teenth;*—[eigh-, fif-, four-, nine-, seven-, six-, thir-] teen (-th), + eleven (-th), + sixscore thousand, + twelve (-th).

עָשֹׂר **'âsôr.** See 6218.

6241. עִשָּׂרוֹן **'issârôwn,** *is-saw-rone´;* or עִשָּׂרֹן **'issârôn,** *is-saw-rone´;* from 6235; (fractional) a *tenth* part:—tenth deal.

6242. עֶשְׂרִים **'esrîym,** *es-reem´;* from 6235; *twenty;* also (ordinal) *twentieth:*—[six-] score, twenty (-ieth).

6243. עֶשְׂרִין **'esrîyn** (Chald.), *es-reen´;* corresp. to 6242:—twenty.

6244. עָשֵׁשׁ **'âshêsh,** *aw-shaysh´;* a prim. root; prob. to *shrink,* i.e. *fail:*—be consumed.

6245. עָשַׁת **'âshath,** *aw-shath´;* a prim. root; prob. to be *sleek,* i.e. *glossy;* hence (through the idea of *polishing*) to *excogitate* (as if *forming* in the mind):—shine, think.

6246. עֲשִׁת **'ăshîth** (Chald.), *ash-eeth´;* corresp. to 6245; to *purpose:*—think.

6247. עֶשֶׁת **'esheth,** *eh´-sheth;* from 6245; a *fabric:*—bright.

6248. עַשְׁתּוּת° **'ashtûwth,** *ash-tooth´;* from 6245; *cogitation:*—thought.

6249. עַשְׁתֵּי **'ashtêy,** *ash-tay´;* appar. masc. plur. constr. of 6247 in the sense of *afterthought;* (used only in connection with 6240 in lieu of 259) *eleven* or (ordinal) *eleventh:*— + eleven (-th).

6250. עֶשְׁתֹּנָה **'eshtônâh,** *esh-to-naw´;* from 6245; *thinking:*—thought.

6251. עַשְׁתְּרָה **'asht^erâh,** *ash-ter-aw´;* prob. from 6238; *increase:*—flock.

6252. עַשְׁתָּרוֹת **'Ashtârôwth,** *ash-taw-rōth´,* or עַשְׁתָּרֹת **'Ashtârôth,** *ash-taw-rōth´;* plur. of 6251; *Ashtaroth,* the name of a Sidonian deity, and of a place E. of the Jordan:—Ashtaroth, Astaroth. See also 1045, 6253, 6255.

6253. עַשְׁתֹּרֶת **'Ashtôreth,** *ash-to´-reth;* prob. for 6251; *Ashtoreth,* the Phœnician goddess of love (and *increase*):—Ashtoreth.

6254. עַשְׁתְּרָתִי **'Asht^erâthîy,** *ash-ter-aw-thee´;* patrial from 6252; an *Ashterathite* or inhab. of Ashtaroth:—Ashterathite.

6255. עַשְׁתְּרֹת קַרְנַיִם **'Asht^erôth Qarnayim,** *ash-ter-ōth´ kar-nah´-yim;* from 6252 and the dual of 7161; *Ashtaroth of* (the) *double horns* (a symbol of the deity); *Ashteroth-Karnaïm,* a place E. of the Jordan:—Ashtoreth Karnaim.

6256. עֵת **'êth,** *ayth;* from 5703; *time,* espec. (adv. with prep.) *now, when,* etc.:— + after, [al-] ways, × certain, + continually, + evening, long, (due) season, so [long] as, [even-, evening-, noon-] tide, ([meal-], what) time, when.

6257. עָתַד **'âthad,** *aw-thad´;* a prim. root; to *prepare:*—make fit, be ready to become.

עַתֻּד **'attûd.** See 6260.

6258. עַתָּה **'attâh,** *at-taw´;* from 6256; at *this time,* whether adv., conj. or expletive:—henceforth, now, straightway, this time, whereas.

6259. עָתוּד **'âthûwd,** *aw-thood´;* pass. part. of 6257; *prepared:*—ready, treasures.

6260. עַתּוּד **'attûwd,** *at-tood´;* or עַתֻּד **'attûd,** *at-tood´;* from 6257; *prepared,* i.e. *full grown;* spoken only (in plur.) of *he-goats,* or (fig.) *leaders* of the people:—chief one, (he) goat, ram.

6261. עִתִּי **'ittîy,** *it-tee´;* from 6256; *timely:*—fit.

6262. עַתַּי **'Attay,** *at-tah'ee;* for 6261; *Attai,* the name of three Isr.:—Attai.

6263. עֲתִיד **'ăthîyd** (Chald.), *ath-eed';* corresp. to 6264; *prepared:*—ready.

6264. עָתִיד **'âthîyd,** *aw-theed';* from 6257; *prepared;* by impl. *skilful;* fem. plur. the *future;* also *treasure:*—things that shall come, ready, treasures.

6265. עֲתָיָה **'Ăthâyâh,** *ath-aw-yaw';* from 5790 and 3050; *Jah has helped; Athajah,* an Isr.:—Athaiah.

6266. עָתִיק **'âthîyq,** *aw-theek';* from 6275; prop. *antique,* i.e. *venerable* or *splendid:*—durable.

6267. עַתִּיק **'attîyq,** *at-teek';* from 6275; *removed* i.e. *weaned;* also *antique:*—ancient, drawn.

6268. עַתִּיק **'attîyq** (Chald.) *at-teek';* corresp. to 6267; *venerable:*—ancient.

6269. עֲתָךְ **'Ăthâk,** *ath-awk';* from an unused root mean. to *sojourn; lodging; Athak,* a place in Pal.:—Athach.

6270. עַתְלַי **'Athlay,** *ath-lah'ee;* from an unused root mean. to *compress; constringent; Athlai,* an Isr.:—Athlai.

6271. עֲתַלְיָה **'Ăthalyâh,** *ath-al-yaw';* or עֲתַלְיָהוּ **'Ăthalyâhûw,** *ath-al-yaw'-hoo;* from the same as 6270 and 3050; *Jah has constrained; Athaljah,* the name of an Israelitess and two Isr.:—Athaliah.

6272. עָתַם **'âtham,** *aw-tham';* a prim. root; prob. to *glow,* i.e. (fig.) *be desolated:*—be darkened.

6273. עָתְנִי **'Othnîy,** *oth-nee';* from an unused root mean. to *force; forcible; Othni,* an Isr.:—Othni.

6274. עָתְנִיאֵל **'Othnîy'êl,** *oth-nee-ale';* from the same as 6273; and 410; *force of God; Othniël,* an Isr.:—Othniel.

6275. עָתַק **'âthaq,** *aw-thak';* a prim. root; to *remove* (intrans. or trans.); fig. to *grow old;* spec. to *transcribe:*—copy out, leave off, become (wax) old, remove.

6276. עָתֵק **'âthêq,** *aw-thake';* from 6275; *antique,* i.e *valued:*—durable.

6277. עָתָק **'âthâq,** *aw-thawk';* from 6275 in the sense of *license; impudent:*—arrogancy, grievous (hard) things, stiff.

6278. עֵת קָצִין **'Êth Qâtsîyn,** *ayth-kaw-tseen';* from 6256 and 7011; *time of a judge; Eth-Katsin,* a place in Pal.:—Ittah-kazin [*by includ. directive enclitic*].

6279. עָתַר **'âthar,** *aw-thar';* a prim. root [rather denom. from 6281]; to burn *incense* in worship, i.e. *intercede* (recipr. *listen* to prayer):—intreat, (make) pray (-er).

6280. עָתַר **'âthar,** *aw-thar';* a prim. root; to *be* (caus. *make*) *abundant:*—deceitful, multiply.

6281. עֶתֶר **'Ether,** *eh'-ther;* from 6280; *abundance; Ether,* a place in Pal.:—Ether.

6282. עָתָר **'âthâr,** *aw-thawr';* from 6280; *incense* (as increasing to a *volume* of smoke); hence (from 6279) a *worshipper:*—suppliant, thick.

6283. עֲתֶרֶת **'ăthereth,** *ath-eh'-reth;* from 6280; *copiousness:*—abundance.

פ

פֹּא **pô'.** See 6311.

6284. פָּאָה **pâ'âh,** *paw-aw';* a prim. root; to *puff,* i.e. *blow* away:—scatter into corners.

6285. פֵּאָה **pê'âh,** *pay-aw';* fem. of 6311; prop. *mouth* in a fig. sense, i.e. *direction, region, extremity:*—corner, end, quarter, side.

6286. פָּאַר **pâ'ar,** *paw-ar';* a prim. root; to *gleam,* i.e. (causat.) *embellish;* fig. to *boast;* also to *explain* (i.e. make clear) oneself; denom. from 6288, to *shake* a tree:—beautify, boast self, go over the boughs, glorify (self), glory, vaunt self.

6287. פְּאֵר **pᵉ'êr,** *peh-ayr';* from 6286; an *embellishment,* i.e. fancy *head-dress:*—beauty, bonnet, goodly, ornament, tire.

6288. פְּאֹרָה **pᵉ'ôrâh,** *peh-o-raw';* or פֹּרָאה **pôrâ'h,** *po-raw';* or פֻּארָה **pû'râh,** *poo-raw';* from 6286; prop. *ornamentation,* i.e. (plur.) *foliage* (includ. the limbs) as *bright* green:—bough, branch, sprig.

6289. פָּארוּר **pâ'rûwr,** *paw-roor';* from 6286; prop. *illuminated,* i.e. a *glow;* as noun, a *flush* (of anxiety):—blackness.

6290. פָּארָן **Pâ'rân,** *paw-rawn';* from 6286; *ornamental; Paran,* a desert of Arabia:—Paran.

6291. פַּג **pag,** *pag;* from an unused root mean. to *be torpid,* i.e. *crude;* an *unripe* fig.:—green fig.

6292. פִּגּוּל **piggûwl,** *pig-gool';* or פִּגֻּל **piggûl,** *pig-gool';* from an unused root mean. to *stink;* prop. *fetid,* i.e. (fig.) *unclean* (ceremonially):—abominable (-tion, thing).

6293. פָּגַע **pâga',** *paw-gah';* a prim. root; to *impinge,* by accident or violence, or (fig.) by importunity:—come (betwixt), cause to entreat, fall (upon), make intercession, intercessor, intreat, lay, light [upon], meet (together), pray, reach, run.

6294. פֶּגַע **pega',** *peh'-gah;* from 6293; *impact* (causal):—chance, occurrent.

6295. פַּגְעִיאֵל **Pag'îy'êl,** *pag-ee-ale';* from 6294 and 410; *accident of God; Pagiël,* an Isr.:—Pagiel.

6296. פָּגַר **pâgar,** *paw-gar';* a prim. root; to *relax,* i.e. become *exhausted:*—be faint.

6297. פֶּגֶר **peger,** *peh'-gher;* from 6296; a *carcase* (as *limp*), whether of man or beast; fig. an idolatrous *image:*—carcase, corpse, dead body.

6298. פָּגַשׁ **pâgash,** *paw-gash';* a prim. root; to *come in contact with,* whether by accident or violence; fig. to *concur:*—meet (with, together).

6299. פָּדָה **pâdâh,** *paw-daw';* a prim. root; to *sever,* i.e. *ransom;* gener. to *release, preserve:*—× at all, deliver, × by any means, ransom, (that are to be, let be) redeem (-ed), rescue, × surely.

6300. פְּדַהְאֵל **Pᵉdah'êl,** *ped-ah-ale';* from 6299 and 410; *God has ransomed; Pedahel,* an Isr.:—Pedahel.

6301. פְּדָהצוּר **Pᵉdâhtsûwr,** *ped-aw-tsoor';* from 6299 and 6697; a *rock* (i.e. God) *has ransomed; Pedahtsur,* an Isr.:—Pedahzur.

6302. פָּדוּי **pâdûwy,** *paw-doo'ee;* pass. part. of 6299; *ransomed* (and so occurring under 6299); as abstr. (in plur. masc.) a *ransom:*—(that are) to be (that were) redeemed.

6303. פָּדוֹן **Pâdôwn,** *paw-done';* from 6299; *ransom; Padon,* one of the Nethinim:—Padon.

6304. פְּדוּת **pᵉdûwth,** *ped-ooth';* or פְּדֻת **pᵉdûth,** *ped-ooth';* from 6929; *distinction;* also *deliverance:*—division, redeem, redemption.

6305. פְּדָיָה **Pᵉdâyâh,** *ped-aw-yaw';* or פְּדָיָהוּ **Pᵉdâyâhûw,** *ped-aw-yaw'-hoo;* from 6299 and 3050; *Jah has ransomed; Pedajah,* the name of six Isr.:—Pedaiah.

6306. פִּדְיוֹם **pidyôwm,** *pid-yome';* or פִּדְיֹם **pidyôm,** *pid-yome';* also פִּדְיוֹן **pidyôwn,** *pid-yone';* or פִּדְיֹן **pidyôn,** *pid-yone';* from 6299; a *ransom:*—ransom, that were redeemed, redemption.

6307. פַּדָּן **Paddân,** *pad-dawn';* from an unused root mean. to *extend;* a *plateau;* or פַּדַּן אֲרָם **Paddan 'Ărâm,** *pad-dan' arawm';* from the same and 758; the *table-land of Aram; Paddan* or *Paddan-Aram,* a region of Syria:—Padan, Padan-aram.

6308. פָּדַע **pâda',** *paw-dah';* a prim. root; to *retrieve:*—deliver.

6309. פֶּדֶר **peder,** *peh'-der;* from an unused root mean. to *be greasy; suet:*—fat.

פְּדֻת **pᵉdûth.** See 6304.

6310. פֶּה **peh,** *peh;* from 6284; the *mouth* (as the means of *blowing*), whether lit. or fig. (particularly *speech*); spec. *edge, portion* or *side;* adv. (with prep.) *according to:*—accord (-ing as, -ing to), after, appointment, assent, collar, command (-ment), × eat, edge, end, entry, + file, hole, × in, mind, mouth, part, portion, × (should) say (-ing), sentence, skirt, sound, speech, × spoken, talk, tenor, × to, + two-edged, wish, word.

6311. פֹּה **pôh,** *po;* or פֹּא **pô'** (Job 38 : 11), *po;* or פּוֹ **pôw,** *po;* prob. from a prim. insep. particle פּ **p** (of demonstrative force) and 1931; *this place* (French *içil*), i.e. *here* or *hence:*—here, hither, the one (other, this, that) side.

פּוֹא **pôw.** See 375.

6312. פּוּאָה **Pûw'âh,** *poo-aw´;* or פֻּוָּה **Puvvâh,** *poov-vaw´;* from 6284; *blast; Puäh* or *Puvvah,* the name of two Isr.:—Phuvah, Pua, Puah.

6313. פּוּג **pûwg,** *poog;* a prim. root; to *be sluggish:*—cease, be feeble, faint, be slacked.

6314. פּוּגָה **pûwgâh,** *poo-gaw´;* from 6313; *intermission:*—rest.

פֻּוָּה **Puvvâh.** See 6312.

6315. פּוּחַ **pûwach,** *poo´-akh;* a prim. root; to *puff,* i.e. blow with the breath or air; hence to *fan* (as a breeze), to *utter,* to *kindle* (a fire), to *scoff:*—blow (upon), break, puff, bring into a snare, speak, utter.

6316. פּוּט **Pûwṭ,** *poot;* or for. or.; *Put,* a son of Ham, also the name of his descendants or their region, and of a Persian tribe:—Phut, Put.

6317. פּוּטִיאֵל **Pûwṭîy'êl,** *poo-tee-ale´;* from an unused root (prob. mean. to *disparage*) and 410; *contempt of God; Putiël,* an Isr.:—Putiel.

6318. פּוֹטִיפַר **Pôwṭîyphar,** *po-tee-far´;* of Eg. der.; *Potiphar,* an Eg.:—Potiphar.

6319. פּוֹטִי פֶרַע **Pôwṭîy Phera',** *po´-tee feh´-rah;* of Eg. der.; *Poti-Phera,* an Eg.:—Poti-pherah.

6320. פּוּךְ **pûwk,** *pook;* from an unused root mean. to *paint; dye* (spec. *stibium* for the eyes):—fair colours, glistering, paint [-ed] (-ing).

6321. פּוֹל **pôwl,** *pole;* from an unused root mean. to *be thick;* a *bean* (as *plump*):—beans.

6322. פּוּל **Pûwl,** *pool;* of for. or.; *Pul,* the name of an Ass. king and of an Ethiopian tribe:—Pul.

6323. פּוּן **pûwn,** *poon;* a prim. root mean. to *turn,* i.e. *be perplexed:*—be distracted.

6324. פּוּנִי **Pûwnîy,** *poo-nee´;* patron. from an unused name mean. a *turn;* a *Punite* (collect.) or desc. of an unknown Pun:—Punites.

6325. פּוּנֹן **Pûwnôn,** *poo-none´;* from 6323; *perplexity; Punon,* a place in the Desert:—Punon.

6326. פּוּעָה **Pûw'âh,** *poo-aw´;* from an unused root mean. to *glitter; brilliancy; Puäh,* an Israelitess:—Puah.

6327. פּוּץ **pûwts,** *poots;* a prim. root; to *dash* in pieces, lit. or fig. (espec. to *disperse*):—break (dash, shake) in (to) pieces, cast (abroad), disperse (selves), drive, retire, scatter (abroad), spread abroad.

6328. פּוּק **pûwq,** *pook;* a prim. root; to *waver:*—stumble, move.

6329. פּוּק **pûwq,** *pook;* a prim. root [rather ident. with 6328 through the idea of *dropping* out; comp. 5312]; to *issue,* i.e. *furnish;* causat. to *secure;* fig. to *succeed:*—afford, draw out, further, get, obtain.

6330. פּוּקָה **pûwqâh,** *poo-kaw´;* from 6328; a *stumbling-block:*—grief.

6331. פּוּר **pûwr,** *poor;* a prim. root; to *crush:*—break, bring to nought, × utterly take.

6332. פּוּר **Pûwr,** *poor;* also (plur.) פּוּרִים **Pûwrîym,** *poo-reem´;* or פֻּרִים **Pûrîym,** *poo-reem´;* from 6331; a *lot* (as by means of a *broken* piece):—Pur, Purim.

6333. פּוּרָה **pûwrâh,** *poo-raw´;* from 6331; a *wine-press* (as *crushing* the grapes):—wine-press.

פּוּרִים **Pûwrîym.** See 6332.

6334. פּוֹרָתָא **Pôwrâthâ',** *po-raw-thaw´;* of Pers. or.; *Poratha,* a son of Haman:—Poratha.

6335. פּוּשׁ **pûwsh,** *poosh;* a prim. root; to *spread;* fig. *act proudly:*—grow up, be grown fat, spread selves, be scattered.

6336. פּוּתִי **Pûwthîy,** *poo-thee´;* patron. from an unused name mean. a *hinge;* a *Puthite* (collect.) or descend. of an unknown Puth:—Puhites [*as if from* 6312].

6337. פָּז **pâz,** *pawz;* from 6338; *pure* (gold); hence *gold* itself (as refined):—fine (pure) gold.

6338. פָּזַז **pâzaz,** *paw-zaz´;* a prim. root; to *refine* (gold):—best [gold].

6339. פָּזַז **pâzaz,** *paw-zaz´;* a prim. root [rather ident. with 6338]; to *solidify* (as if by *refining*); also to *spring* (as if *separating* the limbs):—leap, be made strong.

6340. פָּזַר **pâzar,** *paw-zar´;* a prim. root; to *scatter,* whether in enmity or bounty:—disperse, scatter (abroad).

6341. פַּח **pach,** *pakh;* from 6351; a (metallic) *sheet* (as *pounded* thin); also a spring *net* (as spread out like a *lamina*):—gin, (thin) plate, snare.

6342. פָּחַד **pâchad,** *paw-kkad´;* a prim. root: to *be startled* (by a sudden alarm); hence to *fear* in general:—be afraid, stand in awe, (be in) fear, make to shake.

6343. פַּחַד **pachad,** *pakh´-ad;* from 6342; a (sudden) *alarm* (prop. the object feared, by impl. the feeling):—dread (-ful), fear, (thing) great [fear, -ly feared], terror.

6344. פַּחַד **pachad,** *pakh´-ad;* the same as 6343; a *testicle* (as a cause of *shame* akin to fear):—stone.

6345. פַּחְדָּה **pachdâh,** *pakh-daw´;* fem. of 6343; *alarm* (i.e. *awe*):—fear.

6346. פֶּחָה **pechâh,** *peh-khaw´;* of for. or.; a *prefect* (of a city or small district):—captain, deputy, governor.

6347. פֶּחָה **pechâh** (Chald.), *peh-khaw´;* corresp. to 6346:—captain, governor.

6348. פָּחַז **pâchaz,** *paw-khaz´;* a prim. root; to *bubble* up or *froth* (as boiling water), i.e. (fig.) to *be unimportant:*—light.

6349. פַּחַז **pachaz,** *pakh´-az;* from 6348; *ebullition,* i.e. froth (fig. lust):—unstable.

6350. פַּחֲזוּת **pachăzûwth,** *pakh-az-ooth´;* from 6348; *frivolity:*—lightness.

6351. פָּחַח **pâchach,** *paw-khakh´;* a prim. root; to *batter* out; but used only as denom. from 6341, to *spread a net:*—be snared.

6352. פֶּחָם **pechâm,** *peh-khawm´;* perh. from an unused root prob. mean. to *be black;* a *coal,* whether charred or live:—coals.

6353. פֶּחָר **pechâr** (Chald.), *peh-khawr´;* from an unused root prob. mean. to *fashion;* a *potter:*—potter.

6354. פַּחַת **pachath,** *pakh´-ath;* prob. from an unused root appar. mean. to *dig;* a *pit,* espec. for catching animals:—hole, pit, snare.

6355. פַּחַת מוֹאָב **Pachath Môw'âb,** *pakh´-ath mo-awb´;* from 6354 and 4124; *pit of Moäb; Pachath-Moäb,* an Isr.:—Pahath-moab.

6356. פְּחֶתֶת **pᵉchetheth,** *pekh-eh´-theth;* from the same as 6354; a *hole* (by mildew in a garment):—fret inward.

6357. פִּטְדָה **piṭdâh,** *pit-daw´;* of for. der.; a *gem,* prob. the *topaz:*—topaz.

6358. פָּטוּר **pâṭûwr,** *paw-toor´;* pass. part. of 6362; *opened,* i.e. (as noun) a *bud:*—open.

6359. פָּטִיר **pâṭîyr,** *paw-teer´;* from 6362; *open,* i.e. *unoccupied:*—free.

6360. פַּטִּישׁ **paṭṭîysh,** *pat-teesh´;* intens. from an unused root mean. to *pound;* a *hammer:*—hammer.

6361. פַּטִּישׁ **paṭṭîysh** (Chald.), *pat-teesh´;* from a root corresp. to that of 6360; a *gown* (as if *hammered* out wide):—hose.

6362. פָּטַר **pâṭar,** *paw-tar´;* a prim. root; to *cleave* or burst through, i.e. (caus.) to *emit,* whether lit. or fig. (*gape*):—dismiss, free, let (shoot) out, slip away.

6363. פֶּטֶר **peṭer,** *peh´-ter;* or פִּטְרָה **piṭrâh,** *pit-raw´;* from 6362; a *fissure,* i.e. (concr.) *firstling* (as *opening* the matrix):—firstling, openeth, such as open.

6364. פִּי־בֶסֶת **Pîy-Beçeth,** *pee beh´-seth;* of Eg. or.; *Pi-Beseth,* a place in Eg.:—Pi-beseth.

6365. פִּיד **pîyd,** *peed;* from an unused root prob. mean. to *pierce;* (fig.) *misfortune:*—destruction, ruin.

6366. פֵּיָה **pêyâh,** *pay-aw´;* or פִּיָה **pîyâh,** *pee-yaw´;* fem. of 6310; an *edge:*—(two-) edge (-d).

6367. פִּי הַחִרֹת **Pi ha-Chîyrôth,** *pee hah-khee-rōth´;* from 6310 and the fem. plur. of a noun (from the same root as 2356), with the art. interp.; *mouth of the gorges; Pi-ha-Chiroth,* a place in Eg.:—Pi-hahiroth. [In Num. 14 : 19 without Pi-.]

6368. פִּיחַ **pîyach,** *pee´-akh;* from 6315; a *powder* (as easily *puffed* away), i.e. *ashes* or *dust:*—ashes.

6369. פִּיכֹל **Pîykôl,** *pee-kole´;* appar. from 6310 and 3605; *mouth of all; Picol,* a Philistine:—Phichol.

6370. פִּילֶגֶשׁ **pîylegesh,** *pee-leh´-ghesh;* or פִּלֶגֶשׁ **pîlegesh,** *pee-leh´-ghesh;* of uncert. der.; a *concubine;* also (masc.) a *paramour:*—concubine, paramour.

6371. פִּימָה **pîymâh,** *pee-maw´;* prob. from an unused root mean. to *be plump; obesity:*—collops.

6372. פִּינְחָס **Pîynᵉchâç,** *pee-nekh-aws´;* appar. from 6310 and a var. of 5175; *mouth of a serpent; Pinechas,* the name of three Isr.:—Phinehas.

6373. פִּינֹן **pîynôn,** *pee-none´;* prob. the same as 6325; *Pinon,* an Idumæan:—Pinon.

6374. פִּיפִיָּה **pîyphîyâh,** *pee-fee-yaw´;* for 6366, an *edge* or *tooth:*—tooth, × two-edged

6375. פִּיק **pîyq,** *peek;* from 6329; a *tottering:*—smite together.

6376. פִּישׁוֹן **Pîyshôwn,** *pee-shone´;* from 6335; *dispersive; Pishon,* a river of Eden:—Pison.

6377. פִּיתוֹן **Pîythôwn,** *pee-thone´;* prob. from the same as 6596; *expansive; Pithon,* an Isr.:—Pithon.

6378. פַּךְ **pak,** *pak;* from 6379; a *flask* (from which a liquid may *flow*):—box, vial.

6379. פָּכָה **pâkâh,** *paw-kaw´;* a prim. root; to *pour:*—run out.

6380. פֹּכֶרֶת צְבָיִים **Pôkereth Tsᵉbâyîym,** *po-keh´-reth tseb-aw-yeem´;* from the act. part. (of the same form as the first word) fem. of an unused root (mean. to *entrap*) and plur. of 6643; *trap of gazelles; Pokereth-Tsebajim,* one of the "servants of Solomon":—Pochereth of Zebaim.

6381. פָּלָא **pâlaʼ,** *paw-law´;* a prim. root; prop. perh. to *separate,* i.e. *distinguish* (lit. or fig.); by impl. to *be* (causat. *make*) *great, difficult, wonderful:*—accomplish, (arise . . . too, be too) hard, hidden, things too high, (be, do, do a, shew) marvelous (-ly, -els, things, work), miracles, perform, separate, make singular, (be, great, make) wonderful (-ers, -ly, things, works), wondrous (things, works, -ly).

6382. פֶּלֶא **peleʼ,** *peh´-leh;* from 6381; a *miracle:*—marvellous thing, wonder (-ful, -fully).

6383. פִּלְאִי **pilʼîy,** *pil-ee´;* or פָּלִיא **pâlîyʼ,** *paw-lee´;* from 6381; *remarkable:*—secret, wonderful.

6384. פַּלֻּאִי **Pallûʼîy,** *pal-loo-ee´;* patron. from 6396; a *Palluïte* (collect.) or desc. of Pallu:—Palluites.

פְּלָאיָה **Pᵉlâʼyâh.** See 6411.

פִּלְאֶסֶר **Pilʼeçer.** See 8407.

6385. פָּלַג **pâlag,** *paw-lag´;* a prim. root; to *split* (lit. or fig.):—divide.

6386. פְּלַג **pᵉlag** (Chald.), *pel-ag´;* corresp. to 6385:—divided.

6387. פְּלַג **pᵉlag** (Chald.), *pel-ag´;* from 6386; a *half:*—dividing.

6388. פֶּלֶג **peleg,** *peh´-leg;* from 6385; a *rill* (i.e. small *channel* of water, as in irrigation):—river, stream.

6389. פֶּלֶג **Peleg,** *peh´-leg;* the same as 6388; *earthquake; Peleg,* a son of Shem:—Peleg.

6390. פְּלַגָּה **pᵉlaggâh,** *pel-ag-gaw´;* from 6385; a *runlet,* i.e. *gully:*—division, river.

6391. פְּלֻגָּה **pᵉluggâh,** *pel-oog-gaw´;* from 6385; a *section:*—division.

6392. פְּלֻגָּה **pᵉluggâh** (Chald.), *pel-oog-gaw´;* corresp. to 6391:—division.

פִּלֶגֶשׁ **pîlegesh.** See 6370.

6393. פְּלָדָה **pᵉlâdâh,** *pel-aw-daw´;* from an unused root mean. to *divide;* a *cleaver,* i.e. iron *armature* (of a chariot):—torch.

6394. פִּלְדָּשׁ **Pildâsh,** *pil-dawsh´;* of uncert. der.; *Pildash,* a relative of Abraham:—Pildash.

6395. פָּלָה **pâlâh,** *paw-law´;* a prim. root; to *distinguish* (lit. or fig.):—put a difference, show marvellous, separate, set apart, sever, make wonderfully.

6396. פַּלּוּא **Pallûwʼ,** *pal-loo´;* from 6395; *distinguished; Pallu,* an Isr.:—Pallu, Phallu.

6397. פְּלוֹנִי **Pᵉlôwnîy,** *pel-o-nee´;* patron. from an unused name (from 6395) mean. *separate;* a *Pelonite* or inhab. of an unknown Palon:—Pelonite.

6398. פָּלַח **pâlach,** *paw-lakh´;* a prim. root; to *slice,* i.e. *break* open or *pierce:*—bring forth, cleave, cut, shred, strike through.

6399. פְּלַח **pᵉlach** (Chald.), *pel-akh´;* corresp. to 6398; to *serve* or worship:—minister, serve.

6400. פֶּלַח **pelach,** *peh´-lakh;* from 6398; a *slice:*—piece.

6401. פִּלְחָא **Pilchâʼ,** *pil-khaw´;* from 6400; *slicing; Pilcha,* an Isr.:—Pilcha.

6402. פָּלְחָן **polchân** (Chald.), *pol-khawn´;* from 6399; *worship:*—service.

6403. פָּלַט **pâlaṭ,** *paw-lat´;* a prim. root; to *slip* out, i.e. *escape;* causat. to *deliver:*—calve, carry away safe, deliver, (cause to) escape.

6404. פֶּלֶט **Peleṭ,** *peh´-let;* from 6403; *escape; Pelet,* the name of two Isr.:—Pelet. See also 1046.

פָּלֵט **pâlêṭ.** See 6412.

6405. פַּלֵּט **pallêṭ,** *pal-late´;* from 6403; *escape:*—deliverance, escape.

פְּלֵטָה **pᵉlêṭâh.** See 6413.

6406. פַּלְטִי **Palṭîy,** *pal-tee´;* from 6403; *delivered; Palti,* the name of two Isr.:—Palti, Phalti.

6407. פַּלְטִי **Palṭîy,** *pal-tee´;* patron. from 6406; a *Paltite* or desc. of Palti:—Paltite.

6408. פִּלְטַי **Pilṭay,** *pil-tah´ee;* for 6407; *Piltai,* an Isr.:—Piltai.

6409. פַּלְטִיאֵל **Palṭîyʼêl,** *pal-tee-ale´;* from the same as 6404 and 410; *deliverance of God; Paltiël,* the name of two Isr.:—Paltiel, Phaltiel.

6410. פְּלַטְיָה **Pᵉlaṭyâh,** *pel-at-yaw´;* or פְּלַטְיָהוּ **Pᵉlaṭyâhûw,** *pel-at-yaw´-hoo;* from 6403 and 3050; *Jah has delivered; Pelatjah,* the name of four Isr.:—Pelatiah.

פָּלִיא **pâlîyʼ.** See 6383.

6411. פְּלָיָה **Pᵉlâyâh,** *pel-aw-yaw´;* or פְּלָאיָה **Pᵉlâʼyâh,** *pel-aw-yaw´;* from 6381 and 3050; *Jah has distinguished; Pelajah,* the name of three Isr.:—Pelaiah.

6412. פָּלִיט **pâlîyṭ,** *paw-leet´;* or פָּלֵיט **pâlêyṭ,** *paw-late´;* or פָּלֵט **pâlêṭ,** *paw-late´;* from 6403; a *refugee:*—(that have) escape (-d, -th), fugitive.

6413. פְּלֵיטָה **pᵉlêyṭâh,** *pel-ay-taw´;* or פְּלֵטָה **pᵉlêṭâh,** *pel-ay-taw´;* fem. of 6412; *deliverance;* concr. an *escaped* portion:—deliverance, (that is) escape (-d), remnant.

6414. פָּלִיל **pâlîyl,** *paw-leel´;* from 6419; a *magistrate:*—judge.

6415. פְּלִילָה **pᵉlîylâh,** *pel-ee-law´;* fem. of 6414; *justice:*—judgment.

6416. פְּלִילִי **pᵉlîylîy,** *pel-ee-lee´;* from 6414; *judicial:*—judge.

6417. פְּלִילִיָּה **pᵉlîylîyâh,** *pel-ee-lee-yaw´;* fem. of 6416; *judicature:*—judgment.

6418. פֶּלֶךְ **pelek,** *peh´-lek;* from an unused root mean. to *be round;* a *circuit* (i.e. *district*); also a *spindle* (as *whirled*); hence a *crutch:*—(di-) staff, part.

6419. פָּלַל **pâlal,** *paw-lal´;* a prim. root; to *judge* (officially or mentally); by extens. to *intercede, pray:*—intreat, judge (-ment), (make) pray (-er, -ing), make supplication.

6420. פָּלָל **Pâlâl,** *paw-lawl´;* from 6419; *judge; Palal,* an Isr.:—Palal.

6421. פְּלַלְיָה **Pᵉlalyâh,** *pel-al-yaw´;* from 6419 and 3050; *Jah has judged; Pelaljah,* an Isr.:—Pelaliah.

6422. פַּלְמוֹנִי **palmôwnîy,** *pal-mo-nee´;* prob. for 6423; a *certain* one, i.e. so-and-so:—certain.

פִּלְנְאֶסֶר **Pilnᵉeçer.** See 8407.

6423. פְּלֹנִי **pᵉlônîy,** *pel-o-nee´;* from 6395; *such* a one, i.e. a specified *person:*—such.

פִּלְנֶסֶר **Pilneçer.** See 8407.

6424. פָּלַס **pâlaç,** *paw-las´;* a prim. root; prop. to *roll* flat, i.e. *prepare* (a road); also to *revolve,* i.e. *weigh* (mentally):—make, ponder, weigh.

6425. פֶּלֶס **peleç,** *peh´-les;* from 6424; a *balance:*—scales, weight.

פְּלֶסֶר **Pᵉleçer.** See 8407.

6426. פָּלַץ **pâlats,** *paw-lats´;* a prim. root; prop. perh. to *rend,* i.e. (by impl.) to *quiver:*—tremble.

6427. פַּלָּצוּת **pallâtsûwth,** *pal-law-tsooth´;* from 6426; *affright:*—fearfulness, horror, trembling.

6428. פָּלַשׁ **pâlash,** *paw-lash´;* a prim. root; to *roll* (in dust):—roll (wallow) self.

6429. פְּלֶשֶׁת **Pᵉlesheth,** *pel-eh´-sheth;* from 6428; *rolling,* i.e. *migratory; Pelesheth,* a region of Syria:—Palestina, Palestine, Philistia, Philistines.

6430. פְּלִשְׁתִּי **Pᵉlishtîy,** *pel-ish-tee´;* patrial from 6429; a *Pelishtite* or inhab. of Pelesheth:—Philistine.

6431. פֶּלֶת **Peleth,** *peh´-leth;* from an unused root mean. to *flee; swiftnees; Peleth,* the name of two Isr.:—Peleth.

6432. פְּלֵתִי **Pᵉlêthîy,** *pel-ay-thee´;* from the same form as 6431; a *courier* (collect.) or official *messenger:*—Pelethites.

6433. פֻּם **pûm** (Chald.), *poom;* prob. for 6310; the *mouth* (lit. or fig.):—mouth.

6434. פֵּן **pên,** *pane;* from an unused root mean. to *turn;* an *angle* (of a street or wall):—corner.

6435. פֵּן **pên,** *pane;* from 6437; prop. *removal;* used only (in the constr.) adv. as conj. *lest:*—(lest) (peradventure), that . . . not.

6436. פַּנַּג **pannag,** *pan-nag´;* of uncert. der.; prob. *pastry:*—Pannag.

6437. פָּנָה **pânâh,** *paw-naw´;* a prim. root; to *turn;* by impl. to *face,* i.e. *appear, look,* etc.:—appear, at [even-] tide, behold, cast out, come on, × corner, dawning, empty, go away, lie, look, mark, pass away, prepare, regard, (have) respect (to), (re-) turn (aside, away, back, face, self), × right [early].

פָּנֶה **pâneh.** See 6440.

6438. פִּנָּה **pinnâh,** *pin-naw´;* fem. of 6434; an *angle;* by impl. a *pinnacle;* fig. a *chieftain:*—bulwark, chief, corner, stay, tower.

6439. פְּנוּאֵל **Pᵉnûw'êl,** *pen-oo-ale´;* or (more prop.) פְּנִיאֵל **Pᵉnîy'êl,** *pen-ee-ale´;* from 6437 and 410; *face of God; Penuël* or *Peniël,* a place E. of Jordan; also (as Penuel) the name of two Isr.:—Peniel, Penuel.

פָּנִי° **pânîy.** See 6443.

6440. פָּנִים **pânîym,** *paw-neem´;* plur. (but always as sing.) of an unused noun [פָּנֶה **pâneh,** *paw-neh´;* from 6437]; the *face* (as the part that *turns*); used in a great variety of applications (lit. and fig.); also (with prep. pref.) as a prep. (*before,* etc.):— + accept, a (be-) fore (-time), against, anger, × as (long as), at, + battle, + because (of), + beseech, countenance, edge, + employ, endure, + enquire, face, favour, fear of, for, forefront (-part), form (-er time, -ward), from, front, heaviness, × him (-self), + honourable, + impudent, + in, it, look [-eth] (-s), × me, + meet, × more than, mouth, of, off, (of) old (time), × on, open, + out of, over against, the partial, person, + please, presence, prospect, was purposed, by reason, of, + regard, right forth, + serve, × shewbread, sight, state, straight, + street, × thee, × them (-selves), through (+ -out), till, time (-s) past, (un-) to (-ward), + upon, upside (+ down), with (-in, + stand), × ye, × you.

6441. פְּנִימָה **pᵉnîymâh,** *pen-ee´-maw;* from 6440 with directive enclitic; *faceward,* i.e. *indoors:*—(with-) in (-ner part, -ward).

6442. פְּנִימִי **pᵉnîymîy,** *pen-ee-mee´;* from 6440; *interior:*—(with-) in (-ner, -ward).

6443. פָּנִין **pânîyn,** *paw-neen´;* or פָּנִי° **pânîy,** *paw-nee´;* from the same as 6434; prob. a *pearl* (as *round*):—ruby.

6444. פְּנִנָּה **Pᵉninnâh,** *pen-in-naw´;* prob. fem. from 6443 contr.; *Peninnah,* an Israelitess:—Peninnah.

6445. פָּנַק **pânaq,** *paw-nak´;* a prim. root; to *enervate:*—bring up.

6446. פַּס **paç,** *pas;* from 6461; prop. the *palm* (of the hand) or *sole* (of the foot) [comp. 6447]; by impl. (plur.) a *long and sleeved* tunic (perh. simply a *wide* one; from the orig. sense of the root, i.e. of *many breadths*):—(divers) colours.

6447. פַּס **paç** (Chald.), *pas;* from a root corresp. to 6461; the *palm* (of the hand, as being *spread* out):—part.

6448. פָּסַג **pâçag,** *paw-sag´;* a prim. root; to *cut up,* i.e. (fig.) *contemplate:*—consider.

6449. פִּסְגָּה **Piçgâh,** *pis-gaw´;* from 6448; a *cleft; Pisgah,* a mt. E. of Jordan:—Pisgah.

6450. פַּס דַּמִּים **Paç Dammîym,** *pas dam-meem´;* from 6446 and the plur. of 1818; *palm* (i.e. *dell*) *of bloodshed; Pas-Dammim,* a place in Pal.:—Pas-dammim. Comp. 658.

6451. פִּסָּה **piççâh,** *pis-saw´;* from 6461; *expansion,* i.e. *abundance:*—handful.

6452. פָּסַח **pâçach,** *paw-sakh´;* a prim. root; to *hop,* i.e (fig.) *skip* over (or *spare*); by impl. to *hesitate;* also (lit.) to *limp,* to *dance:*—halt, become lame, leap, pass over.

6453. פֶּסַח **peçach,** *peh´-sakh;* from 6452; a *pretermission,* i.e. *exemption;* used only tech. of the Jewish *Passover* (the festival or the victim):—passover (offering).

6454. פָּסֵחַ **Pâçêach,** *paw-say´-akh;* from 6452; *limping; Paseäch,* the name of two Isr.:—Paseah, Phaseah.

6455. פִּסֵּחַ **piççêach,** *pis-say´-akh;* from 6452; *lame:*—lame.

6456. פְּסִיל **pᵉçîyl,** *pes-eel´;* from 6458; an *idol:*—carved (graven) image, quarry.

6457. פָּסַךְ **Pâçak,** *paw-sak´;* from an unused root mean. to *divide; divider; Pasak,* an Isr.:—Pasach.

6458. פָּסַל **pâçal,** *paw-sal´;* a prim. root; to *carve,* whether wood or stone:—grave, hew.

6459. פֶּסֶל **peçel,** *peh´-sel;* from 6458; an *idol:*—carved (graven) image.

6460. פְּסַנְטֵרִין **pᵉçanṭêrîyn** (Chald.), *pes-an-tay-reen´;* or פְּסַנְתֵּרִין **pᵉçantêrîyn,** *pes-an-tay-reen´;* a transliteration of the Gr. ψαλτήριον *psaltēriŏn;* a *lyre:*—psaltery.

6461. פָּסַס **pâçaç,** *paw-sas´;* a prim. root; prob. to *disperse,* i.e. (intrans.) *disappear:*—cease.

6462. פִּסְפָּה **Piçpâh,** *pis-paw´;* perh. from 6461; *dispersion; Pispah,* an Isr.:—Pispah.

6463. פָּעָה **pâ'âh,** *paw-aw´;* a prim. root; to *scream:*—cry.

6464. פָּעוּ **Pâ'ûw,** *paw-oo´;* or פָּעִי **Pâ'îy,** *paw-ee´;* from 6463; *screaming; Paü* or *Paï,* a place in Edom:—Pai, Pau.

6465. פְּעוֹר **Pᵉ'ôwr,** *peh-ore´;* from 6473; a *gap; Peör,* a mountain E. of Jordan; also (for 1187) a deity worshipped there:—Peor. See also 1047.

פָּעִי **Pâ'îy.** See 6464.

6466. פָּעַל **pâ'al,** *paw-al´;* a prim. root; to *do* or *make* (systematically and habitually), espec. to *practise:*—commit, [evil-] do (-er), make (-r), ordain, work (-er), wrought.

6467. פֹּעַל **pô'al,** *po´-al;* from 6466; an *act* or *work* (concr.):—act, deed, do, getting, maker, work.

6468. פְּעֻלָּה **pᵉ'ullâh,** *peh-ool-law´;* fem. pass. part. of 6466; (abstr.) *work:*—labour, reward, wages, work.

6469. פְּעֻלְּתַי **Pᵉull'thay,** *peh-ool-leh-thah´ee;* from 6468; *laborious; Peüllethai,* an Isr.:—Peulthai.

6470. פָּעַם **pâ'am,** *paw-am´;* a prim. root; to *tap,* i.e. beat regularly; hence (gen.) to *impel* or *agitate:*—move, trouble.

6471. פַּעַם **pa'am,** *pah´-am;* or (fem.) פַּעֲמָה **pa'ămâh,** *pah-am-aw´;* from 6470; a *stroke,* lit. or fig. (in various applications, as follow):—anvil, corner, foot (-step), going, [hundred-] fold, × now, (this) + once, order, rank, step, + thrice, [often-], second, this, two) time (-s), twice, wheel.

6472. פַּעֲמֹן **pa'ămôn,** *pah-am-one´;* from 6471; a *bell* (as *struck*):—bell.

6473. פָּעַר **pâ'ar,** *paw-ar´;* a prim. root; to *yawn,* i.e. *open* wide (lit. or fig.):—gape, open (wide).

6474. פַּעֲרַי **Pa'ăray,** *pah-ar-ah´ee;* from 6473; *yawning; Paarai,* an Isr.:—Paarai.

6475. פָּצָה **pâtsâh,** *paw-tsaw´;* a prim. root; to *rend,* i.e. *open* (espec. the mouth):—deliver, gape, open, rid, utter.

6476. פָּצַח **pâtsach,** *paw-tsakh´;* a prim. root; to *break* out (in joyful sound):—break (forth, forth into joy), make a loud noise.

6477. פְּצִירָה **pᵉtsîyrâh,** *pets-ee-raw´;* from 6484; *bluntness:*— + file.

6478. פָּצַל **pâtsal,** *paw-tsal´;* a prim. root; to *peel:*—pill.

6479. פְּצָלָה **pᵉtsâlâh,** *pets-aw-law´;* from 6478; a *peeling:*—strake.

6480. פָּצַם **pâtsam,** *paw-tsam´;* a prim. root; to *rend* (by earthquake):—break.

6481. פָּצַע **pâtsa'**, *paw-tsah'*; a prim. root; to *split,* i.e. *wound:*—wound.

6482. פֶּצַע **petsa'**, *peh'-tsah;* from 6481; a *wound:*—wound (-ing).

פַּצֵּץ **Patstets.** See 1048.

6483. פִּצֵּץ **Pitstsêts,** *pits-tsates';* from an unused root mean. to *dissever; dispersive; Pitstets,* a priest:—Apses [*includ. the art.*].

6484. פָּצַר **pâtsar,** *paw-tsar';* a prim. root; to *peck* at, i.e. (fig.) *stun* or *dull:*—press, urge, stubbornness.

6485. פָּקַד **pâqad,** *paw-kad';* a prim. root; to *visit* (with friendly or hostile intent); by anal. to *oversee, muster, charge, care for, miss, deposit,* etc.:—appoint, × at all, avenge, bestow, (appoint to have the, give a) charge, commit, count, deliver to keep, be empty, enjoin, go see, hurt, do judgment, lack, lay up look, make × by any means, miss, number, officer, (make) overseer have (the) oversight, punish, reckon, (call to) remember (-brance), set (over), sum, × surely, visit, want.

פִּקֻּד **piqqûd.** See 6490.

6486. פְּקֻדָּה **peqquddâh,** *pek-ood-daw';* fem. pass. part. of 6485; *visitation* (in many senses, chiefly official):—account, (that have the) charge, custody, that which . . . laid up, numbers, office (-r), ordering, oversight, + prison, reckoning, visitation.

6487. פִּקָּדוֹן **piqqâdôwn,** *pik-kaw-done';* from 6485; a *deposit:*—that which was delivered (to keep), store.

6488. פְּקִדֻת **peqîdûth,** *pek-ee-dooth';* from 6496; *supervision:*—ward.

6489. פְּקוֹד **Peqôwd,** *pek-ode';* from 6485; *punishment; Pekod,* a symbol. name for Bab.:—Pekod.

6490. פִּקּוּד **piqqûwd,** *pik-kood';* or פִּקֻּד **piqqûd,** *pik-kood';* from 6485; prop. *appointed,* i.e. a *mandate* (of God; plur. only, collect. for the *Law*):—commandment, precept, statute.

6491. פָּקַח **pâqach,** *paw-kakh';* a prim. root; to *open* (the senses, espec. the eyes); fig. to *be observant:*—open.

6492. פֶּקַח **Peqach,** *peh'-kakh;* from 6491; *watch; Pekach,* an Isr. king:—Pekah.

6493. פִּקֵּחַ **piqqêach,** *pik-kay'-akh;* from 6491; *clear-sighted;* fig. *intelligent:*—seeing, wise.

6494. פְּקַחְיָה **Peqachyâh,** *pek-akh-yaw';* from 6491 and 3050; *Jah has observed; Pekachjah,* an Isr. king:—Pekahiah.

6495. פְּקַח־קוֹחַ **peqach-qôwach,** *pek-akh-ko'-akh;* from 6491 redoubled; *opening* (of a dungeon), i.e. *jail-delivery* (fig. *salvation* from sin):—opening of the prison.

6496. פָּקִיד **pâqîyd,** *paw-keed';* from 6485; a *superintendent* (civil, military or religious):—which had the charge, governor, office, overseer, [that] was set.

6497. פֶּקַע **peqa',** *peh'-kah;* from an unused root mean. to *burst;* only used as an architect. term of an ornament similar to 6498, a *semi-globe:*—knop.

6498. פַּקֻּעָה **paqqû'âh,** *pak-koo-aw';* from the same as 6497; the *wild cucumber* (from *splitting* open to shed its seeds):—gourd.

6499. פַּר **par,** *par;* or פָּר **pâr,** *pawr;* from 6565; a *bullock* (appar. as *breaking* forth in wild strength, or perh. as *dividing* the hoof):— (+ young) bull (-ock), calf, ox.

6500. פָּרָא **pârâ',** *paw-raw';* a prim. root; to *bear fruit:*—be fruitful.

6501. פֶּרֶא **pere',** *peh'-reh;* or פֶּרֶה **pereh** (Jer. 2 : 24), *peh'-reh;* from 6500 in the secondary sense of *running* wild; the *onager:*—wild (ass).

פֹּרָאה **pôrâ'h.** See 6288.

6502. פִּרְאָם **Pir'âm,** *pir-awm';* from 6501; *wildly; Piram,* a Canaanite:—Piram.

6503. פַּרְבָּר **Parbâr,** *par-bawr';* or פַּרְוָר **Parvâr,** *par-vawr';* of for. or.; *Parbar* or *Parvar,* a quarter of Jerus.:—Parbar, suburb.

6504. פָּרַד **pârad,** *paw-rad';* a prim. root; to *break* through, i.e. *spread* or *separate* (oneself):—disperse, divide, be out of joint, part, scatter (abroad), separate (self), sever self, stretch, sunder.

6505. פֶּרֶד **pered,** *peh'-red;* from 6504; a *mule* (perh. from his *lonely* habits):—mule.

6506. פִּרְדָּה **pirdâh,** *pir-daw';* fem. of 6505; a *she-mule;*—mule.

6507. פְּרֻדָה **perûdâh,** *per-oo-daw';* fem. pass. part. of 6504; something *separated,* i.e. a *kernel;*—seed.

6508. פַּרְדֵּס **pardêç,** *par-dace';* of for. or.; a *park:*—forest, orchard.

6509. פָּרָה **pârâh,** *paw-raw';* a prim. root; to *bear fruit* (lit. or fig.):—bear, bring forth (fruit), (be, cause to be, make) fruitful, grow, increase.

6510. פָּרָה **pârâh,** *paw-raw';* fem. of 6499; a *heifer:*—cow, heifer, kine.

6511. פָּרָה **Pârâh,** *paw-raw';* the same as 6510; *Parah,* a place in Pal.:—Parah.

פֶּרֶה **pereh.** See 6501.

6512. פֵּרָה **pêrâh,** *pay-raw';* from 6381; a *hole* (as *broken,* i.e. dug):— + mole. Comp. 2661.

6513. פֻּרָה **Pûrâh,** *poo-raw';* for 6288; *foliage; Purah,* an Isr.:—Phurah.

6514. פְּרוּדָא **Perûwdâ',** *per-oo-daw';* or פְּרִידָא **Perîydâ',** *per-ee-daw';* from 6504; *dispersion; Peruda* or *Perida,* one of "Solomon's servants":—Perida, Peruda.

פְּרוֹזִי° **perôwzîy.** See 6521.

6515. פָּרוּחַ **Pârûwach,** *paw-roo'-akh;* pass. part. of 6524; *blossomed; Paruäch,* an Isr.:—Paruah.

6516. פַּרְוַיִם **Parvayim,** *par-vah'-yim;* of for. or.; *Parvajim,* an Oriental region:—Parvaim.

6517. פָּרוּר **pârûwr,** *paw-roor';* pass. part. of 6565 in the sense of *spreading* out [comp. 6524]; a *skillet* (as *flat* or *deep*):—pan, pot.

פַּרְוָר **Parvâr.** See 6503.

6518. פָּרָז **pârâz,** *paw-rawz';* from an unused root mean. to *separate,* i.e. *decide;* a *chieftain:*—village.

6519. פְּרָזָה **perâzâh,** *per-aw-zaw';* from the same as 6518; an *open* country:—(unwalled) town (without walls), unwalled village.

6520. פְּרָזוֹן **perâzôwn** *per-aw-zone';* from the same as 6518; *magistracy,* i.e. *leadership* (also concr. *chieftains*):—village.

6521. פְּרָזִי **perâzîy,** *per-aw-zee';* or פְּרוֹזִי° **perôwzîy,** *per-o-zee';* from 6519; a *rustic:*—village.

6522. פְּרִזִּי **Perizzîy,** *per-iz-zee';* for 6521; inhab. *of the open country;* a *Perizzite,* one of the Canaanitish tribes:—Perizzite.

6523. פַּרְזֶל **parzel** (Chald.), *par-zel';* corresp. to 1270; *iron:*—iron.

6524. פָּרַח **pârach,** *paw-rakh';* a prim. root; to *break forth as a bud, i.e. bloom;* gen. to *spread;* spec. to *fly* (as extending the wings); fig. to *flourish:*— × abroad, × abundantly, blossom, break forth (out), bud, flourish, make fly, grow, spread, spring (up).

6525. פֶּרַח **perach,** *peh'-rakh;* from 6524; a *calyx* (nat. or artif.); gen. *bloom:*—blossom, bud, flower.

6526. פִּרְחַח **pirchach,** *pir-khakh';* from 6524; *progeny,* i.e. a *brood:*—youth.

6527. פָּרַט **pâraṭ,** *paw-rat';* a prim. root; to *scatter* words, i.e. *prate* (or *hum*):—chant.

6528. פֶּרֶט **pereṭ,** *peh'-ret;* from 6527; a *stray* or *single* berry:—grape.

6529. פְּרִי **perîy,** *per-ee';* from 6409; *fruit* (lit. or fig.):—bough, ([first-]) fruit ([-ful]), reward.

פְּרִידָא **Perîydâ'.** See 6514.

פּוּרִים **Pûrîym.** See 6332.

6530. פְּרִיץ **perîyts,** *per-eets';* from 6555; *violent,* i.e. a *tyrant:*—destroyer, ravenous, robber.

6531. פֶּרֶךְ **perek,** *peh'-rek;* from an unused root mean. to *break* apart; *fracture,* i.e. *severity:*—cruelty, rigour.

6532. פֹּרֶכֶת **pôreketh,** *po-reh'-keth;* fem. act. part. of the same as 6531; a *separatrix,* i.e. (the sacred) *screen:*—vail.

6533. פָּרַם **pâram,** *paw-ram';* a prim. root; to *tear:*—rend.

6534. פַּרְמַשְׁתָּא **Parmashtâ',** *par-mash-taw';* of Pers. or.; *Parmashta,* a son of Haman:—Parmasta.

6535. פַּרְנַךְ **Parnak,** *par-nak';* of uncert. der.; *Parnak,* an Isr.:—Parnach.

6536. פָּרַס **pâraç,** *paw-ras´;* a prim. root; to *break* in pieces, i.e. (usually without violence) to *split, distribute:*—deal, divide, have hoofs, part, tear.

6537. פְּרַס **perac** (Chald.), *per-as´;* corresp. to 6536; to *split* up:—divide, [U-] pharsin.

6538. פֶּרֶס **pereç,** *peh´-res;* from 6586; a *claw;* also a kind of *eagle:*—claw, ossifrage.

6539. פָּרַס **Pâraç,** *paw-ras´;* of for. or.; *Paras* (i.e. *Persia*), an Eastern country, including its inhab.:—Persia, Persians.

6540. פָּרַס **Pâraç** (Chald.), *paw-ras´;* corresp. to 6539:—Persia, Persians.

6541. פַּרְסָה **parçâh,** *par-saw´;* fem. of 6538; a *claw* or split *hoof:*—claw, [cloven-] footed, hoof.

6542. פַּרְסִי **Parçîy,** *par-see´;* patrial from 6539; a *Parsite* (i.e. *Persian*), or inhab. of Peres:—Persian.

6543. פַּרְסִי **Parçîy** (Chald.), *par-see´;* corresp. to 6542:—Persian.

6544. פָּרַע **pâra',** *paw-rah´;* a prim. root; to *loosen;* by impl. to *expose, dismiss;* fig. *absolve, begin:*—avenge, avoid, bare, go back, let, (make) naked, set at nought, perish, refuse, uncover.

6545. פֶּרַע **pera',** *peh´-rah;* from 6544; the *hair* (as *dishevelled*):—locks.

6546. פַּרְעָה **par'âh,** *par-aw´;* fem. of 6545 (in the sense of *beginning*); *leadership* (plur. concr. *leaders*):— + avenging, revenge.

6547. פַּרְעֹה **Par'ôh,** *par-o´;* of Eg. der.; *Paroh,* a gen. title of Eg. kings:—Pharaoh.

6548. פַּרְעֹה חָפְרַע **Par'ôh Chophra',** *par-o´khof-rah´;* of Eg. der.; *Paroh-Chophra,* an Eg. king:—Pharaoh-hophra.

6549. פַּרְעֹה נְכֹה **Par'ôh Nekôh,** *par-o´ nek-o´;* or פַּרְעֹה נְכוֹ **Par'ôh Nekôw,** *par-o´ nek-o´;* of Eg. der.; *Paroh-Nekoh* (or *Neko*), an Eg. king:—Pharaoh-necho, Pharaoh-nechoh.

6550. פַּרְעֹשׁ **par'ôsh,** *par-oshe´;* prob. from 6544 and 6211; a *flea* (as the *isolated insect*):—flea.

6551. פַּרְעֹשׁ **Par'ôsh,** *par-oshe´;* the same as 6550; *Parosh,* the name of four Isr.:—Parosh, Pharosh.

6552. פִּרְעָתוֹן **Pir'âthôwn,** *pir-aw-thone´;* from 6546; *chieftaincy; Pirathon,* a place in Pal.:—Pirathon.

6553. פִּרְעָתוֹנִי **Pir'âthôwnîy,** *pir-aw-tho-nee´;* or פִּרְעָתֹנִי **Pir'âthônîy,** *pir-aw-tho-nee´;* patrial from 6552; a *Pirathonite* or inhab. of Pirathon:—Pirathonite.

6554. פַּרְפַּר **Parpar,** *par-par´;* prob. from 6565 in the sense of *rushing; rapid; Parpar,* a river of Syria:—Pharpar.

6555. פָּרַץ **pârats,** *paw-rats´;* a prim. root; to *break* out (in many applications, direct and indirect, lit. and fig.):— × abroad, (make a) breach, break (away, down, -er, forth, in, up), burst out come (spread) abroad, compel, disperse, grow, increase, open, press, scatter, urge.

6556. פֶּרֶץ **perets,** *peh´-rets;* from 6555; a *break* (lit. or fig.):—breach, breaking forth (in), × forth, gap.

6557. פֶּרֶץ **Perets,** *peh´-rets;* the same as 6556; *Perets,* the name of two Isr.:—Perez, Pharez.

6558. פַּרְצִי **Partsîy,** *par-tsee´;* patron. from 6557; a *Partsite* (collect.) or desc. of Perets:—Pharzites.

6559. פְּרָצִים **perâtsîym,** *per-aw-tseem´;* plur. of 6556; *breaks; Peratsim,* a mountain in Pal.:—Perazim.

6560. פֶּרֶץ עֻזָּא **Perets 'Uzzâ',** *peh´-rets ooz-zaw´;* from 6556 and 5798; *break of Uzza; Perets-Uzza,* a place in Pal.:—Perez-uzza.

6561. פָּרַק **pâraq,** *paw-rak´;* a prim. root; to *break* off or *craunch;* fig. to *deliver:*—break (off), deliver, redeem, rend (in pieces), tear in pieces.

6562. פְּרַק **peraq** (Chald.), *per-ak´;* corresp. to 6561; to *discontinue:*—break off.

6563. פֶּרֶק **pereq,** *peh´-rek;* from 6561; *rapine;* also a *fork* (in roads):—crossway, robbery.

6564. פָּרָק° **pârâq,** *paw-rawk´;* from 6561; *soup* (as full of *crumbed* meat):—broth. See also 4832.

6565. פָּרַר **pârar,** *paw-rar´;* a prim. root; to *break* up (usually fig., i.e. to *violate, frustrate*):—× any ways, break (asunder), cast off, cause to cease, × clean, defeat, disannul, disappoint, dissolve, divide, make of none effect, fail, frustrate, bring (come) to nought, × utterly, make void.

6566. פָּרַשׂ **pâras,** *paw-ras´;* a prim. root; to *break* apart, *disperse,* etc.:—break, chop in pieces, lay open, scatter, spread (abroad, forth, selves, out), stretch (forth, out).

6567. פָּרָשׁ **pârâsh,** *paw-rash´;* a prim. root; to *separate,* lit. (to *disperse*) or fig. (to *specify*); also (by impl.) to *wound:*—scatter, declare, distinctly, shew, sting.

6568. פְּרַשׁ **perash** (Chald.), *per-ash´;* corresp. to 6567; to *specify:*—distinctly.

6569. פֶּרֶשׁ **peresh,** *peh´-resh;* from 6567; *excrement* (as *eliminated*):—dung.

6570. פֶּרֶשׁ **Peresh,** *peh´-resh;* the same as 6569; *Peresh,* an Isr.:—Peresh.

6571. פָּרָשׁ **pârâsh,** *paw-rawsh´;* from 6567; a *steed* (as *stretched* out to a vehicle, not single nor for mounting [comp. 5483]); also (by impl.) a *driver* (in a chariot), i.e. (collect.) cavalry:—horseman.

6572. פַּרְשֶׁגֶן **parshegen,** *par-sheh´-ghen;* or פַּתְשֶׁגֶן **pathshegen,** *path-sheh´-gen;* of for. or.; a *transcript:*—copy.

6573. פַּרְשֶׁגֶן **parshegen** (Chald.), *par-sheh´-ghen;* corresp. to 6572:—copy.

6574. פַּרְשְׁדֹן **parshedôn,** *par-shed-one´;* perh. by compounding 6567 and 6504 (in the sense of *straddling*) [comp. 6576]; the *crotch* (or *anus*):—dirt.

6575. פָּרָשָׁה **pârâshâh,** *paw-raw-shaw´;* from 6567; *exposition:*—declaration, sum.

6576. פַּרְשֵׁז **parshêz,** *par-shaze´;* a root appar. formed by compounding 6567 and that of 6518 [comp. 6574]; to *expand:*—spread.

6577. פַּרְשַׁנְדָּתָא **Parshandâthâ',** *par-shan-daw-thaw´;* of Pers. or.; *Parshandatha,* a son of Haman:—Parshandatha.

6578. פְּרָת **Perâth,** *per-awth´;* from an unused root mean. to *break* forth; *rushing; Perath* (i.e. *Euphrates*), a river of the East:—Euphrates.

פֹּרָת **pôrâth.** See 6509.

6579. פַּרְתַּם **partam,** *par-tam´;* of Pers. or.; a *grandee:*—(most) noble, prince.

6580. פַּשׁ **pash,** *pash;* prob. from an unused root mean. to *disintegrate; stupidity* (as a result of *grossness* or of *degeneracy*):—extremity.

6581. פָּשָׂה **pâsâh,** *paw-saw´;* a prim. root; to *spread:*—spread.

6582. פָּשַׁח **pâshach,** *paw-shakh´;* a prim. root; to *tear* in pieces:—pull in pieces.

6583. פַּשְׁחוּר **Pashchûwr,** *pash-khoor´;* prob. from 6582; *liberation; Pashchur,* the name of four Isr.:—Pashur.

6584. פָּשַׁט **pâshaṭ,** *paw-shat´;* a prim. root; to *spread* out (i.e. *deploy* in hostile array); by anal. to *strip* (i.e. *unclothe, plunder, flay,* etc.):—fall upon, flay, invade, make an invasion, pull off, put off, make a road, run upon, rush, set, spoil, spread selves (abroad), strip (off, self).

6585. פָּשַׂע **pâsa',** *paw-sah´;* a prim. root; to *stride* (from *spreading* the legs), i.e. *rush* upon:—go.

6586. פָּשַׁע **pâsha',** *paw-shah´;* a prim. root [rather ident. with 6585 through the idea of *expansion*]; to *break* away (from just authority), i.e. *trespass, apostatize, quarrel:*—offend, rebel, revolt, transgress (-ion, -or).

6587. פֶּשַׂע **pesa',** *peh´-sah;* from 6585; a *stride:*—step.

6588. פֶּשַׁע **pesha',** *peh´-shah;* from 6586; a *revolt* (national, moral or religious):—rebellion, sin, transgression, trespass.

6589. פָּשַׂק **pâsaq,** *paw-sak´;* a prim. root; to *dispart* (the feet or lips), i.e. *become licentious:*—open (wide).

6590. פְּשַׁר **peshar** (Chald.), *pesh-ar´;* corresp. to 6622; to *interpret:*—make [interpretations], interpreting.

6591. פְּשַׁר **peshar** (Chad.), *pesh-ar´;* from 6590; an *interpretation:*—interpretation.

6592. פֵּשֶׁר **pêsher,** *pay´-sher;* corresp. to 6591:—interpretation.

6593. פִּשְׁתֶּה **pishteh,** *pish-teh´;* from the same as 6580 as in the sense of *comminuting; linen* (i.e. the thread, as *carded*):—flax, linen.

6594. פִּשְׁתָּה **pishtâh,** *pish-taw´;* fem. of 6593; *flax;* by impl. a *wick:*—flax, tow.

6595. פַּת **path,** *path;* from 6626; a *bit:*—meat, morsel, piece.

6596. פֹּת **pôth,** *pohth;* or פֹּתָה **pothâh** (Ezek. 13 : 19), *po-thaw´;* from an unused root mean. to *open;* a *hole,* i.e. *hinge* or the female *pudenda:*—hinge, secret part.

פְּתָאִי **pᵉthâ'îy.** See 6612.

6597. פִּתְאוֹם **pith'ôwm,** *pith-ome´;* or פִּתְאֹם **pith'ôm,** *pith-ome´;* from 6621; *instantly:*—straightway, sudden (-ly).

6598. פַּתְבַּג **pathbag,** *pathbag´;* of Pers. or.; a *dainty:*—portion (provision) of meat.

6599. פִּתְגָּם **pithgâm,** *pith-gawm´;* of Pers. or.; a (judicial) *sentence:*—decree, sentence.

6600. פִּתְגָּם **pithgâm** (Chald.), *pith-gawm´;* corresp. to 6599; a *word, answer, letter* or *decree:*—answer, letter, matter, word.

6601. פָּתָה **pâthâh,** *paw-thaw´;* a prim. root; to *open,* i.e. *be* (causat. *make*) *roomy;* usually fig. (in a mental or moral sense) to *be* (causat. *make*) *simple* or (in a sinister way) *delude:*—allure, deceive, enlarge, entice, flatter, persuade, silly (one).

6602. פְּתוּאֵל **Pᵉthûw'êl,** *peth-oo-ale´;* from 6601 and 410; *enlarged of God; Pethuël,* an Isr.:—Pethuel.

6603. פִּתּוּחַ **pittûwach,** *pit-too´-akh;* or פִּתֻּחַ **pittûach,** *pit-too´-akh;* pass. part. of 6605; *sculpture* (in low or high relief or even intaglio):—carved (work) (are, en-) grave (-ing, -n).

6604. פְּתוֹר **Pᵉthôwr,** *peth-ore´;* of for. or.; *Pethor,* a place in Mesopotamia:—Pethor.

6605. פָּתַח **pâthach,** *paw-thakh´;* a prim. root; to *open* wide (lit. or fig.); spec. to *loosen, begin, plough, carve:*—appear, break forth, draw (out), let go free, (en-) grave (-n), loose (self), (be, beset) open (-ing), put off, ungird, unstop, have vent.

6606. פְּתַח **pᵉthach** (Chad.), *peth-akh´;* corresp. to 6605; to *open:*—open.

6607. פֶּתַח **pethach,** *peh´-thakh;* from 6605; an *opening* (lit.), i.e. *door* (*gate*) or *entrance* way:—door, entering (in), entrance (-ry), gate, opening, place.

6608. פֵּתַח **pêthach,** *pay´-thakh;* from 6605; *opening* (fig.) i.e. *disclosure:*—entrance.

פָּתֻחַ **pâthûach.** See 6603.

6609. פְּתִחָה **pᵉthîchâh,** *peth-ee-khaw´;* from 6605; something *opened,* i.e. a *drawn* sword:—drawn sword.

6610. פִּתְחוֹן **pithchôwn,** *pith-khone´;* from 6605; *opening* (the act):—open (-ing).

6611. פְּתַחְיָה **Pᵉthachyâh,** *peth-akh-yaw´;* from 6605 and 3050; *Jah has opened; Pethachjah,* the name of four Isr.:—Pethakiah.

6612. פְּתִי **pᵉthîy,** *peth-ee´;* or פֶּתִי **pethîy,** *peh´-thee;* or פְּתָאִי **pᵉthâ'îy,** *peth-aw-ee´;* from 6601; *silly* (i.e. *seducible*):—foolish, simple (-icity, one).

6613. פְּתַי **pᵉthay** (Chald.), *peth-ah´ee;* from a root corresp. to 6601, *open,* i.e. (as noun) *width:*—breadth.

6614. פְּתִיגִיל **pᵉthîygîyl,** *peth-eeg-eel´;* of uncert. der.; prob. a figured *mantle* for holidays:—stomacher.

6615. פְּתַיּוּת **pᵉthayûwth,** *peth-ah-yooth´;* from 6612; *silliness* (i.e. *seducibility*):—simple.

6616. פָּתִיל **pâthîyl,** *paw-theel´;* from 6617; *twine:*—bound, bracelet, lace, line, ribband, thread, wire.

6617. פָּתַל **pâthal,** *paw-thal´;* a prim. root; to *twine,* i.e. (lit.) to *struggle* or (fig.) *be* (morally) *tortuous:*—(shew self) froward, shew self unsavoury, wrestle.

6618. פְּתַלְתֹּל **pᵉthaltôl,** *peth-al-tole´;* from 6617; *tortuous* (i.e. crafty):—crooked.

6619. פִּתֹם **Pîthôm,** *pee-thome´;* of Eg. der.; *Pithom,* a place in Eg.:—Pithom.

6620. פֶּתֶן **pethen,** *peh´-then;* from an unused root mean. to *twist;* an *asp* (from its *contortions*):—adder.

6621. פֶּתַע **petha',** *peh´-thah;* from an unused root mean. to *open* (the eyes); a *wink,* i.e. *moment* [comp. 6597] (used only [with or without prep.] adv. *quickly* or *unexpectedly*):—at an instant suddenly, × very.

6622. פָּתַר **pâthar,** *paw-thar´;* a prim. root; to *open* up, i.e. (fig.) *interpret* (a dream):—interpret (-ation, -er).

6623. פִּתְרוֹן **pithrôwn,** *pith-rone´;* or פִּתְרֹן **pithrôn,** *pith-rone´;* from 6622; *interpretation* (of a dream):—interpretation.

6624. פַּתְרוֹס **Pathrôwç,** *path-roce´;* of Eg. der.; *Pathros,* a part of Eg.:—Pathros.

6625. פַּתְרֻסִי **Pathrûçîy,** *path-roo-see´;* patrial from 6624; a *Pathrusite,* or inhab. of Pathros:—Pathrusim.

פַּתְשֶׁגֶן **pathshegen.** See 6572.

6626. פָּתַת **pâthath,** *paw-thath´;* a prim. root; to *open,* i.e. *break:*—part.

צ

6627. צָאָה **tsâ'âh,** *tsaw-aw´;* from 3318; *issue,* i.e. (human) *excrement:*—that (which) cometh from (out).

צֹאָה **tsô'âh.** See 6675.

צְאוֹן° **tsᵉ'ôwn.** See 6629.

6628. צֶאֱל **tse'el,** *tseh´-el;* from an unused root mean. to *be slender;* the *lotus* tree:—shady tree.

6629. צֹאן **tsô'n,** *tsone;* or צְאוֹן° **tsᵉ'ôwn** (Psa. 144 : 13), *tseh-one´;* from an unused root mean. to *migrate;* a collect. name for a *flock* (of sheep or goats); also fig. (of men):—(small) cattle, flock (+ -s), lamb (+ -s), sheep ([-cote, -fold, -shearer, -herds]).

6630. צַאֲנָן **Tsa'ănân,** *tsah-an-awn´;* from the same as 6629 used denom.; *sheep* pasture; *Zaanan,* a place in Pal.:—Zaanan.

6631. צֶאֱצָא **tse'ĕtsâ',** *tseh-ets-aw´;* from 3318; *issue,* i.e. *produce, children:*—that which cometh forth (out), offspring.

6632. צָב **tsâb,** *tsawb;* from an unused root mean. to *establish;* a *palanquin* or *canopy* (as a *fixture*); also a species of *lizard* (prob. as clinging *fast*):—covered, litter, tortoise.

6633. צָבָא **tsâbâ',** *tsaw-baw´;* a prim. root; to *mass* (an army or servants):—assemble, fight, perform, muster, wait upon, war.

6634. צְבָא **tsᵉbâ'** (Chad.), *tseb-aw´;* corresp. to 6633 in the fig. sense of *summoning* one's wishes; to *please:*—will, would.

6635. צָבָא **tsâbâ',** *tsaw-baw´;* or (fem.) צְבָאָה **tsᵉbâ'âh,** *tseb-aw-aw´;* from 6633; a *mass* of persons (or fig. things), espec. reg. organized for war (an *army*); by impl. a *campaign,* lit. or fig. (spec. *hardship, worship*):—appointed time, (+) army, (+) battle, company, host, service, soldiers, waiting upon, war (-fare).

6636. צְבֹאִים **Tsᵉbô'iym,** *tseb-o-eem´;* or (more correctly) צְבִיִּים° **Tsᵉbîyîym,** *tseb-ee-yeem´;* or צְבִיִּם° **Tsᵉbîyîm,** *tseb-ee-yeem´;* plur. of 6643; *gazelles; Tseboïm* or *Tsebijim,* a place in Pal.:—Zeboiim, Zeboim.

6637. צֹבֵבָה **Tsôbêbâh,** *tso-bay-baw´;* fem. act. part. of the same as 6632; the *canopier* (with the art.); *Tsobebah,* an Israelitess:—Zobebah.

6638. צָבָה **tsâbâh,** *tsaw-baw´;* a prim. root; to *amass,* i.e. *grow turgid;* spec. to *array* an army against:—fight, swell.

6639. צָבֶה **tsâbeh,** *tsaw-behy;* from 6638; *turgid:*—swell.

צֹבָה **Tsôbâh.** See 6678.

6640. צְבוּ **tsᵉbûw** (Chald.), *tseb-oo´;* from 6634; prop. *will;* concr. an *affair* (as a matter of *determination*):—purpose.

6641. צָבוּעַ **tsâbûwa',** *tsaw-boo´-ah;* pass. part. of the same as 6648; *dyed* (in stripes), i.e. the *hyena:*—speckled.

6642. צָבַט **tsâbaṭ,** *tsaw-bat´;* a prim. root; to *grasp,* i.e. *hand* out:—reach.

6643. צְבִי **tsᵉbîy,** *tseb-ee´;* from 6638 in the sense of *prominence; splendor* (as *conspicuous*); also a *gazelle* (as *beautiful*):—beautiful (-ty), glorious (-ry), goodly, pleasant, roe (-buck).

6644. צִבְיָא **Tsibyâ',** *tsib-yaw´;* for 6645; *Tsibja,* an Isr.:—Zibia.

6645. צִבְיָה **Tsibyâh,** *tsib-yaw´;* for 6646; *Tsibjah,* an Israelitess:—Zibiah.

6646. צְבִיָּה **ts^{e}bîyâh,** *tseb-ee-yaw´;* fem. of 6643; a *female* gazelle:—roe.

צְבִיִּים° (or צְבִיִם) **Ts^{e}bîyîm.** See 6636.

צְבָיִם° **Ts^{e}bâyîm.** See 6380.

6647. צְבַע **ts^{e}ba'** (Chald.), *tseb-ah´;* a root corresp. to that of 6648; to *dip:*—wet.

6648. צֶבַע **tseba',** *tseh´-bah;* from an unused root mean. to *dip* (into coloring fluid); a *dye:*—divers, colours.

6649. צִבְעוֹן **Tsib'ôwn,** *tsib-one´;* from the same as 6648; *variegated; Tsibon,* an Idumæan:—Zibeon.

6650. צְבֹעִים **Ts^{e}bô'îym,** *tseb-o-eem´;* plur. of 6641; *hyenas; Tseboïm,* a place in Pal.:—Zeboim.

6651. צָבַר **tsâbar,** *tsaw-bar´;* a prim. root; to *aggregate:*—gather (together), heap (up), lay up.

6652. צִבֻּר **tsibbûr,** *tsib-boor´;* from 6551; a *pile:*—heap.

6653. צֶבֶת **tsebeth,** *tseh´-beth;* from an unused root appar. mean. to *grip;* a *lock* of stalks:—handful.

6654. צַד **tsad,** *tsad;* contr. from an unused root mean. to *sidle* off; a *side;* fig. an *adversary:*—(be-) side.

6655. צַד **tsad** (Chald.), *tsad;* corresp. to 6654; used adv. (with prep.) at or upon the *side* of:—against, concerning.

6656. צְדָא **ts^{e}dâ'** (Chald.), *tsed-aw´;* from an unused root corresp. to 6658 in the sense of *intentness;* a (sinister) *design:*—true.

6657. צְדָד **Ts^{e}dad,** *tsed-awd´;* from the same as 6654, a *siding; Tsedad,* a place near Pal.:—Zedad.

6658. צָדָה **tsâdâh,** *tsaw-daw´;* a prim. root; to *chase;* by impl. to *desolate:*—destroy, hunt, lie in wait.

צֵדָה **tsêdâh.** See 6720.

6659. צָדוֹק **Tsâdôwq,** *tsaw-doke´;* from 6663; *just; Tsadok,* the name of eight or nine Isr.:—Zadok.

6660. צְדִיָּה **ts^{e}dîyâh,** *tsed-ee-yaw´;* from 6658; *design* [comp/ 6656]:—lying in wait.

6661. צִדִּים **Tsiddîym,** *tsid-deem´;* plur. of 6654; *sides; Tsiddim* (with the art.), a place in Pal.:—Ziddim.

6662. צַדִּיק **tsaddîyq,** *tsad-deek´;* from 6663; *just:*—just, lawful, righteous (man).

צִדֹנִי° **Tsîdônîy.** See 6722.

6663. צָדַק **tsâdaq,** *tsaw-dak´;* a prim. root; to *be* (causat. *make*) *right* (in a moral or forensic sense):—cleanse, clear self, (be, do) just (-ice, -ify, -ify self), (be, turn to) righteous (-ness).

6664. צֶדֶק **tsedeq,** *tseh´-dek;* from 6663; the *right* (nat., mor. or legal); also (abstr.) *equity* or (fig.) *prosperity:*— × even, (× that which is altogether) just (-ice), ([un-]) right (-eous) (cause, -ly, -ness).

6665. צִדְקָה **tsidqâh** (Chald.), *tsid-kaw´;* corresp. to 6666; *beneficence:*—righteousness.

6666. צְדָקָה **ts^{e}dâqâh,** *tsed-aw-kaw´;* from 6663; *rightness* (abstr.), subj. (*rectitude*), obj. (*justice*), mor. (*virtue*) or fig. (*prosperity*):—justice, moderately, right (-eous) (act, -ly, -ness).

6667. צִדְקִיָּה **Tsidqîyâh,** *tsid-kee-yaw´;* or צִדְקִיָּהוּ **Tsidqîyâhûw,** *tsid-kee-yaw´-hoo;* from 6664 and 3050; *right of Jah; Tsidkijah,* the name of six Isr.:—Zedekiah, Zidkijah.

6668. צָהַב **tsâhab,** *tsaw-hab´;* a prim. root; to *glitter,* i.e. *be golden* in color:— × fine.

6669. צָהֹב **tsâhôb,** *tsaw-obe´;* from 6668; *golden* in color:—yellow.

6670. צָהַל **tsâhal,** *tsaw-hal´;* a prim. root; to *gleam,* i.e. (fig.) *be cheerful;* by transf. to *sound* clear (of various animal or human expressions):—bellow, cry aloud (out), lift up, neigh, rejoice, make to shine, shout.

6671. צָהַר **tsâhar,** *tsaw-har´;* a prim. root; to *glisten;* used only as denom. from 3323, to *press* out *oil:*—make oil.

6672. צֹהַר **tsôhar,** *tso´-har;* from 6671; a *light* (i.e. *window*); dual *double light,* i.e. *noon:*—midday, noon (-day, -tide), window.

6673. צַו **tsav,** *tsav;* or צָו **tsâv,** *tsawv;* from 6680; an *injunction:*—commandment, precept.

6674. צוֹא **tsôw',** *tso;* or צֹא **tsô',** *tso;* from an unused root mean. to *issue; soiled* (as if *excrementitious*):—filthy.

6675. צוֹאָה **tsôw'âh,** *tso-aw´;* or צֹאָה **tsô'âh,** *tso-aw´;* fem. of 6674; *excrement;* gen. *dirt;* fig. *pollution:*—dung, filth (-iness). Marg. for 2716.

6676. צַוַּאר **tsavva'r** (Chad.), *tsav-var´;* corresp. to 6677:—neck.

6677. צַוָּאר **tsavvâ'r,** *tsav-vawr´;* or צַוָּר **tsavvâr** (Neh. 3 : 5), *tsav-vawr´;* or צַוָּרֹן **tsavvârôn** (Cant. 4 : 9), *tsav-vaw-rone´;* or (fem.) צַוָּארָה **tsavvâ'râh** (Mic. 2 : 3), *tsav-vaw-raw´;* intens. from 6696 in the sense of *binding;* the back of the *neck* (as that on which burdens are *bound*):—neck.

6678. צוֹבָא **Tsôwbâ',** *tso-baw´;* or צוֹבָה **Tsôwbâh,** *tso-baw´;* or צֹבָה **Tsôbâh,** *tso-baw´;* from an unused root mean. to *station;* a *station; Zoba* or *Zobah,* a region of Syria:—Zoba, Zobah.

6679. צוּד **tsûwd,** *tsood;* a prim. root; to *lie* alongside (i.e. in wait); by impl. to *catch* an animal (fig. men); (denom. from 6718); to *victual* (for a journey):—chase, hunt, sore, take (provision).

6680. צָוָה **tsâvâh,** *tsaw-vaw´;* a prim. root; (intens.) to *constitute, enjoin:*—apppoint, (for-) bid. (give a) charge, (give a, give in, send with) command (-er, ment), send a messenger, put, (set) in order.

6681. צָוַח **tsâvach,** *tsaw-vakh´;* a prim. root; to *screech* (exultingly):—shout.

6682. צְוָחָה **ts^{e}vâchâh,** *tsev-aw-khaw´;* from 6681; a *screech* (of anguish):—cry (-ing).

6683. צוּלָה **tsûwlâh,** *tsoo-law´;* from an unused root mean. to *sink;* an *abyss* (of the sea):—deep.

6684. צוּם **tsûwm,** *tsoom;* a prim. root; to *cover* over (the mouth), i.e. to *fast:*— × at all, fast.

6685. צוֹם **tsôwm,** *tsome;* or צֹם **tsôm,** *tsome;* from 6684; a *fast:*—fast (-ing).

6686. צוּעָר **Tsûw'âr,** *tsoo-awr´;* from 6819; *small; Tsuär,* an Isr.:—Zuar.

6687. צוּף **tsûwph,** *tsoof;* a prim. root; to *overflow:*—(make to over-) flow, swim.

6688. צוּף **tsûwph,** *tsoof;* from 6687; *comb* of honey (from *dripping*):—honeycomb.

6689. צוּף **Tsûwph,** *tsoof;* or צוֹפַי **Tsôwphay,** *tso-fah´ee;* or צִיף° **Tsîyph,** *tseef;* from 6688; *honey-comb; Tsuph* or *Tsophai* or *Tsiph,* the name of an Isr. and of a place in Pal.:—Zophai, Zuph.

6690. צוֹפַח **Tsôwphach,** *tso-fakh´;* from an unused root mean. to *expand, breadth; Tsophach,* an Isr.:—Zophah.

צוֹפַי **Tsôwphay.** See 6689.

6691. צוֹפַר **Tsôwphar,** *tso-far´;* from 6852; *departing; Tsophar,* a friend of Job:—Zophar.

6692. צוּץ **tsûwts,** *tsoots;* a prim. root; to *twinkle,* i.e. *glance;* by anal. to *blossom* (fig. *flourish*):—bloom, blossom, flourish, shew self.

6693. צוּק **tsûwq,** *took;* a prim. root; to *compress,* i.e. (fig.) *oppress, distress:*—constrain, distress, lie sore, (op-) press (-or), straiten.

6694. צוּק **tsûwq,** *tsook;* a prim. root [rather ident. with 6693 through the idea of *narrowness* (of orifice)]; to *pour* out, i.e. (fig.) *smelt, utter:*—be molten, pour.

6695. צוֹק **tsôwq,** *tsoke;* or (fem.) צוּקָה **tsûwqâh,** *tsoo-kaw´;* from 6693; a *strait,* i.e. (fig.) *distress:*—anguish, × troublous.

6696. צוּר **tsûwr,** *tsoor;* a prim. root; to *cramp,* i.e. *confine* (in many applications, lit. and fig., formative or hostile):—adversary, assault, beset, besiege, bind (up), cast, distress, fashion, fortify, inclose, lay siege, put up in bags.

6697. צוּר **tsûwr,** *tsoor;* or צֻר **tsûr,** *tsoor;* from 6696; prop. a *cliff* (or sharp rock, as *compressed*); gen. a *rock* or *boulder;* fig. a *refuge;* also an *edge* (as *precipitous*):—edge, × (mighty) God (one), rock, × sharp, stone, × strength, × strong. See also 1049.

6698. צוּר **Tsûwr,** *tsoor;* the same as 6697; *rock; Tsur,* the name of a Midianite and of an Isr.:—Zur.

צוֹר **Tsôwr.** See 6865.

צַוָּר **tsavvâr.** See 6677.

6699. צוּרָה **tsûwrâh,** *tsoo-raw´;* fem. of 6697; a *rock* (Job 28 : 10); also a *form* (as if *pressed* out):—form, rock.

צַוָּרֹן **tsavvârôn.** See 6677.

6700. צוּרִיאֵל **Tsûwrîy'êl,** *tsoo-ree-ale´;* from 6697 and 410; *rock of God; Tsuriël,* an Isr.:—Zuriel.

6701. צוּרִישַׁדַּי **Tsûwrîyshadday,** *tsoo-ree-shad-dah´ee;* from 6697 and 7706; *rock of* (the) *Almighty; Tsurishaddai,* an Isr.:—Zurishaddai.

6702. צוּת **tsûwth,** *tsooth;* a prim. root; to *blaze;*—burn.

6703. צַח **tsach,** *tsakh;* from 6705; *dazzling,* i.e. *sunny, bright,* (fig.) *evident:*—clear, dry, plainly, white.

צִחָא **Tsîchâ'.** See 6727.

6704. צִחֶה **tsîcheh,** *tsee-kheh´;* from an unused root mean. to *glow; parched:*—dried up.

6705. צָחַח **tsâchach,** *tsaw-khakh´;* a prim. root; to *glare,* i.e. *be dazzling* white:—be whiter.

6706. צְחִיחַ **tsᵉchîyach,** *tsekh-ee´-akh;* from 6705; *glaring,* i.e. *exposed* to the bright sun:—higher place, top.

6707. צְחִיחָה **tsᵉchîychâh,** *tsekh-ee-khaw´;* fem. of 6706; a *parched* region, i.e. the *desert:*—dry land.

6708. צְחִיחִי° **tsᵉchîychîy,** *tsekh-ee-khee´;* from 6706; *bare* spot, i.e. in the *glaring* sun:—higher place.

6709. צַחֲנָה **tsachănâh,** *tsakh-an-aw´;* from an unused root mean. to *putrefy; stench:*—ill savour.

6710. צַחְצָחָה **tsachtsâchâh,** *tsakh-tsaw-khaw´;* from 6705; a *dry* place, i.e. *desert:*—drought.

6711. צָחַק **tsâchaq,** *tsaw-khak´;* a prim. root; to *laugh* outright (in merriment or scorn); by impl. to *sport:*—laugh, mock, play, make sport.

6712. צְחֹק **tsᵉchôq,** *tsekh-oke´;* from 6711; *laughter* (in pleasure or derision):—laugh (-ed to scorn).

6713. צַחַר **tsachar,** *tsakh´-ar;* from an unused root mean. to *dazzle; sheen,* i.e. *whiteness:*—white.

6714. צֹחַר **Tsôchar,** *tso´-khar;* from the same as 6713; *whiteness; Tsochar,* the name of a Hittite and of an Isr.:—Zohar. Comp. 3328.

6715. צָחֹר **tsâchôr,** *tsaw-khore´;* from the same as 6713; *white:*—white.

6716. צִי **tsîy,** *tsee;* from 6680; a *ship* (as a *fixture*):—ship.

6717. צִיבָא **Tsîybâ',** *tsee-baw´;* from the same as 6678; *station; Tsiba,* an Isr.:—Ziba.

6718. צַיִד **tsayid,** *tsah´-yid;* from a form of 6679 and mean. the same; the *chase;* also *game* (thus taken); (gen.) *lunch* (espec. for a journey):—× catcheth, food, × hunter, (that which he took in) hunting, venison, victuals.

6719. צַיָּד **tsayâd,** *tsah´-yawd;* from the same as 6718; a *huntsman:*—hunter.

6720. צֵידָה **tsêydâh,** *tsay-daw´;* or צֵדָה **tsêdâh,** *tsay-daw´;* fem. of 6718; *food:*—meat, provision, venison, victuals.

6721. צִידוֹן **Tsîydôwn,** *tsee-done´;* or צִידֹן **Tsîydôn,** *tsee-done´;* from 6679 in the sense of *catching* fish; *fishery; Tsidon,* the name of a son of Canaan, and of a place in Pal.:—Sidon, Zidon.

6722. צִידֹנִי (or צִדֹנִי°) **Tsîydônîy,** *tsee-do-nee´;* patrial from 6721; a *Tsidonian* or inhab. of Tsidon:—Sidonian, of Sidon, Zidonian.

6723. צִיָּה **tsîyâh,** *tsee-yaw´;* from an unused root mean. to *parch; aridity;* concr. a *desert:*—barren, drought, dry (land, place), solitary place, wilderness.

6724. צִיוֹן **tsîyôwn,** *tsee-yone´;* from the same as 6723; a *desert:*—dry place.

6725. צִיּוּן **tsîyûwn,** *tsee-yoon´;* from the same as 6723 in the sense of *conspicuousness* [comp. 5329]; a monumental or guiding *pillar:*—sign, title, waymark.

6726. צִיּוֹן **Tsîyôwn,** *tsee-yone´;* the same (reg.) as 6725; *Tsijon* (as a permanent *capital*), a mountain of Jerus.:—Zion.

6727. צִיחָא **Tsîychâ',** *tsee-khaw´;* or צִחָא **Tsîchâ',** *tsee-khaw´;* as if fem. of 6704; *drought; Tsicha,* the name of two Nethinim:—Ziha.

6728. צִיִּי **tsîyîy,** *tsee-ee´;* from the same as 6723; a *desert-dweller,* i.e. *nomad* or wild *beast:*—wild beast of the desert, that dwell in (inhabiting) the wilderness.

6729. צִינֹק **tsîynôq,** *tsee-noke´;* from an unused root mean. to *confine;* the *pillory:*—stocks.

6730. צִיעֹר **Tsîy'ôr,** *tsee-ore´;* from 6819; *small; Tsior,* a place in Pal.:—Zior.

צִיף° **Tsîyph.** See 6689.

6731. צִיץ **tsîyts,** *tseets;* or צִץ **tsîts,** *tseets;* from 6692; prop. *glistening,* i.e. a burnished *plate;* also a *flower* (as *bright* colored); a *wing* (as *gleaming* in the air):—blossom, flower, plate, wing.

6732. צִיץ **Tsîyts,** *tseets;* the same as 6731; *bloom; Tsits,* a place in Pal.:—Ziz.

6733. צִיצָה **tsîytsâh,** *tsee-tsaw´;* fem. of 6731; a *flower:*—flower.

6734. צִיצִת **tsîytsîth,** *tsee-tseeth´;* fem. of 6731; a *floral* or *wing*-like projection, i.e. a *fore-lock* of hair, a *tassel:*—fringe, lock.

צִיקְלַג **Tsîyqᵉlag.** See 6860.

6735. צִיר **tsîyr,** *tseer;* from 6696; a *hinge* (as *pressed* in turning); also a *throe* (as a phys. or mental *pressure*); also a *herald* or errand-doer (as *constrained* by the principal):—ambassador, hinge, messenger, pain, pang, sorrow. Comp. 6736.

6736. צִיר **tsîyr,** *tseer;* the same as 6735; a *form* (of beauty; as if *pressed* out, i.e. carved); hence an (idolatrous) *image:*—beauty, idol.

6737. צָיַר **tsâyar,** *tsaw-yar´;* a denom. from 6735 in the sense of *ambassador;* to *make an errand,* i.e. *betake* oneself:—make as if . . . had been ambassador.

6738. צֵל **tsêl,** *tsale;* from 6751; *shade,* whether lit. or fig.:—defence, shade (-ow).

6739. צְלָא **tsᵉlâ'** (Chald.), *tsel-aw´;* prob. corresp. to 6760 in the sense of *bowing; pray:*—pray.

6740. צָלָה **tsâlâh,** *tsaw-law´;* a prim. root; to *roast:*—roast.

6741. צִלָּה **Tsillâh,** *tsil-law´;* fem. of 6738; *Tsillah,* an antediluvian woman:—Zillah.

6742. צְלוּל° **tsᵉlûwl,** *tsel-ool´;* from 6749 in the sense of *rolling;* a (round or flattened) *cake:*—cake.

6743. צָלַח **tsâlach,** *tsaw-lakh´;* or צָלֵחַ **tsâlêach,** *tsaw-lay´-akh;* a prim. root; to *push* forward, in various senses (lit. or fig., trans. or intrans.):—break out, come (mightily), go over, be good, be meet, be profitable, (cause to, effect, make to, send) prosper (-ity, -ous, -ously).

6744. צְלַח **tsᵉlach** (Chald.), *tsel-akh´;* corresp. to 6743; to *advance* (trans. or intrans.):—promote, prosper.

6745. צֵלָחָה **tsêlâchâh,** *tsay-law-khaw´;* from 6743; something *protracted* or flattened out, i.e. a *platter:*—pan.

6746. צְלֹחִית **tsᵉlôchîyth,** *tsel-o-kheeth´;* from 6743; something *prolonged* or tall, i.e. a *vial* or salt-*cellar:*—cruse.

6747. צַלַּחַת **tsallachath,** *tsal-lakh´-ath;* from 6743; something *advanced* or deep, i.e. a *bowl;* fig. the *bosom:*—bosom, dish.

6748. צָלִי **tsâlîy,** *tsaw-lee´;* pass. part. of 6740; *roasted:*—roast.

6749. צָלַל **tsâlal,** *tsaw-lal´;* a prim. root; prop. to *tumble* down, i.e. *settle* by a waving motion:—sink. Comp. 6750, 6751.

6750. צָלַל **tsâlal,** *tsaw-lal´;* a prim. root [rather ident. with 6749 through the idea of *vibration*]; to *tinkle,* i.e. *rattle* together (as the ears in *reddening* with shame, or the teeth in *chattering* with fear):—quiver, tingle.

6751. צָלַל **tsâlal,** *tsaw-lal´;* a prim. root [rather ident. with 6749 through the idea of *hovering* over (comp. 6754)]; to *shade,* as twilight or an opaque object:—begin to be dark, shadowing.

6752. צֵלֶל **tsêlel,** *tsay´-lel;* from 6751; *shade:*—shadow.

6753. צְלֶלְפּוֹנִי **Tsᵉlelpôwnîy,** *tsel-el-po-nee´;* from 6752 and the act. part. of 6437; *shade-facing; Tselelponi,* an Israelitess:—Hazelelponi [*includ. the art.*].

6754. צֶלֶם **tselem,** *tseh´-lem;* from an unused root mean. to *shade;* a *phantom,* i.e. (fig.) *illusion, resemblance;* hence a representative *figure,* espec. an *idol:*—image, vain shew.

6755. צֶלֶם **tselem** (Chald.), *tseh´-lem;* or צְלֵם **tsᵉlem** (Chald.), *tsel-em´;* corresp. to 6754; an idolatrous *figure:*—form, image.

6756. צַלְמוֹן **Tsalmôwn,** *tsal-mone´;* from 6754; *shady; Tsalmon,* the name of a place in Pal. and of an Isr.:—Zalmon.

6757. צַלְמָוֶת **tsalmâveth,** *tsal-maw´-veth;* from 6738 and 4194; *shade of death,* i.e. the *grave* (fig. *calamity*):—shadow of death.

6758. צַלְמֹנָה **Tsalmônâh,** *tsal-mo-naw´;* fem. of 6757; *shadiness; Tsalmonah,* a place in the Desert:—Zalmonah.

6759. צַלְמֻנָּע **Tsalmunnâʻ,** *tsal-moon-naw´;* from 6738 and 4513; *shade has been denied; Tsalmunna,* a Midianite:—Zalmunna.

6760. צָלַע **tsâlaʻ,** *tsaw-lah´;* a prim. root; prob. to *curve;* used only as denom. from 6763, to *limp* (as if *one*-sided):—halt.

6761. צֶלַע **tselaʻ,** *tseh´-lah;* from 6760; a *limping* or *fall* (fig.):—adversity, halt (-ing).

6762. צֶלַע **Tselaʻ,** *tseh´-lah;* the same as 6761; *Tsela,* a place in Pal.:—Zelah.

6763. צֵלָע **tsêlâʻ,** *tsay-law´;* or (fem.) צַלְעָה **tsalʻâh,** *tsal-aw´;* from 6760; a *rib* (as *curved*), lit. (of the body) or fig. (of a door, i.e. *leaf*); hence a *side,* lit. (of a person) or fig. (of an object or the sky, i.e. *quarter*); arch. a (espec. floor or ceiling) *timber* or *plank* (single or collect., i.e. a *flooring*):—beem, board, chamber, corner, leaf, plank, rib, side (chamber).

6764. צָלָף **Tsâlâph,** *tsaw-lawf´;* from an unused root of unknown mean.; *Tsalaph,* an Isr.:—Zalaph.

6765. צְלָפְחָד **Tsᵉlophchâd,** *tsel-of-chawd´;* from the same as 6764 and 259; *Tselophchad,* an Isr.:—Zelophehad.

6766. צֶלְצַח **Tseltsach,** *tsel-tsakh´;* from 6738 and 6703; *clear shade; Tseltsach,* a place in Pal.:—Zelzah.

6767. צְלָצַל **tsᵉlâtsal,** *tsel-aw-tsal´;* from 6750 redupl.; a *clatter,* i.e. (abstr.) *whirring* (of wings); (concr.) a *cricket;* also a *harpoon* (as *rattling*), a *cymbal* (as *clanging*):—cymbal, locust, shadowing, spear.

6768. צֶלֶק **Tseleq,** *tseh´-lek;* from an unused root mean. to *split; fissure; Tselek,* an Isr.:—Zelek.

6769. צִלְּתַי **Tsillᵉthay,** *tsil-leth-ah´ee;* from the fem. of 6738; *shady; Tsillethai,* the name of two Isr.:—Zilthai.

צֹם **tsôm.** See 6685.

6770. צָמֵא **tsâmêʼ,** *tsaw-may´;* a prim. root; to *thirst* (lit. or fig.):—(be a-, suffer) thirst (-y).

6771. צָמֵא **tsâmêʼ,** *tsaw-may´;* from 6770; *thirsty* (lit. or fig.):—(that) thirst (-eth, -y).

6772. צָמָא **tsâmâʼ,** *tsaw-maw´;* from 6770; *thirst* (lit. or fig.):—thirst (-y).

6773. צִמְאָה **tsimʼâh,** *tsim-aw´;* fem. of 6772; *thirst* (fig. of *libidinousnes*):—thirst.

6774. צִמָּאוֹן **tsimmâʼôwn,** *tsim-maw-one´;* from 6771; a *thirsty* place, i.e. *desert:*—drought, dry ground, thirsty land.

6775. צָמַד **tsâmad,** *tsaw-mad´;* a prim. root; to *link,* i.e. *gird;* fig. to *serve,* (mentally) *contrive:*—fasten, frame, join (self).

6776. צֶמֶד **tsemed,** *tseh´-med;* a *yoke* or *team* (i.e. pair); hence an *acre* (i.e. day's task for a yoke of cattle to plough):—acre, couple, × together, two [asses], yoke (of oxen).

6777. צַמָּה **tsammâh,** *tsam-maw´;* from an unused root mean. to *fasten* on; a *veil:*—locks.

6778. צִמּוּק **tsammûwq,** *tsam-mook´;* from 6784; a cake of *dried* grapes:—bunch (cluster) of raisins.

6779. צָמַח **tsâmach,** *tsaw-makh´;* a prim. root; to *sprout* (trans. or intrans., lit. or fig.):—bear, bring forth, (cause to, make to) bud (forth), (cause to, make to) grow (again, up), (cause to) spring (forth, up).

6780. צֶמַח **tsemach,** *tseh´-makh;* from 6779; a *sprout* (usually concr.), lit. or fig.:—branch, bud, that which (where) grew (upon), spring (-ing).

6781. צָמִיד **tsâmîyd,** *tsaw-meed´;* or צָמִד **tsâmid,** *tsaw-meed´;* from 6775; a *bracelet* or *arm-clasp;* gen. a *lid:*—bracelet, covering.

6782. צַמִּים **tsammîym,** *tsam-meem´;* from the same as 6777; a *noose* (as *fastening*); fig. *destruction:*—robber.

6783. צְמִיתֻת **tsᵉmîythûth,** *tsem-ee-thooth´;* or צְמִתֻת **tsᵉmîthûth,** *tsem-ee-thooth´;* from 6789; *excision,* i.e. *destruction;* used only (adv.) with prep. pref. to *extinction,* i.e. *perpetually:*—ever.

6784. צָמַק **tsâmaq,** *tsaw-mak´;* a prim. root; to *dry* up:—dry.

6785. צֶמֶר **tsemer,** *tseh´-mer;* from an unused root prob. mean. to *be shaggy; wool:*—wool (-len).

6786. צְמָרִי **Tsᵉmârîy,** *tsem-aw-ree´;* patrial from an unused name of a place in Pal.; a *Tsemarite* or branch of the Canaanites:—Zemarite.

6787. צְמָרַיִם **Tsᵉmârayim,** *tsem-aw-rah´-yim;* dual of 6785; *double fleece; Tsemarajim,* a place in Pal.:—Zemaraim.

6788. צַמֶּרֶת **tsammereth,** *tsam-meh´-reth;* from the same as 6785; *fleeciness,* i.e. *foliage:*—highest branch, top.

6789. צָמַת **tsâmath,** *tsaw-math´;* a prim. root; to *extirpate* (lit. or fig.):—consume, cut off, destroy, vanish.

צְמִתֻת **tsᵉmîthûth.** See 6783.

6790. צִן **Tsîn,** *tseen;* from an unused root mean. to *prick;* a *crag; Tsin,* a part of the Desert:—Zin.

6791. צֵן **tsên,** *tsane;* from an unused root mean, to *be prickly;* a *thorn;* hence a thorn-*hedge:*—thorn.

6792. צֹנֵא **tsônêʼ,** *tso-nay´;* or צֹנֶה **tsôneh,** *tso-neh´;* for 6629; a *flock:*—sheep.

6793. צִנָּה **tsinnâh,** *tsin-naw´;* fem. of 6791; a *hook* (as *pointed*); also a (large) *shield* (as if guarding by *prickliness*); also *cold* (as *piercing*):—buckler, cold, hook, shield, target.

6794. צִנּוּר **tsinnûwr,** *tsin-noor´;* from an unused root perh. mean. to *be hollow;* a *culvert:*—gutter, water-spout.

6795. צָנַח **tsânach,** *tsaw-nakh´;* a prim. root; to *alight;* (trans.) to *cause to descend,* i.e. *drive* down:—fasten, light [from off].

6796. צָנִין **tsânîyn,** *tsaw-neen´;* or צָנִן **tsânîn,** *tsaw-neen´;* from the same as 6791; a *thorn:*—thorn.

6797. צָנִיף **tsânîyph,** *tsaw-neef´;* or צָנוֹף° **tsânôwph,** *tsaw-nofe´;* or (fem.) צָנִיפָה **tsânîyphâh,** *tsaw-nee-faw´;* from 6801; a *head-dress* (i.e. piece of cloth *wrapped* around):—diadem, hood, mitre.

6798. צָנַם **tsânam,** *tsaw-nam´;* a prim. root; to *blast* or *shrink:*—withered.

6799. צְנָן **Tsᵉnân,** *tsen-awn´;* prob. for 6630; *Tsenan,* a place near Pal.:—Zenan.

צָנִן **tsânîn.** See 6796.

6800. צָנַע **tsânaʻ,** *tsaw-nah´;* a prim. root; to *humiliate:*—humbly, lowly.

6801. צָנַף **tsânaph,** *tsaw-naf´;* a prim. root; to *wrap,* i.e. *roll* or *dress:*—be attired, × surely, violently turn.

6802. צְנֵפָה **tsᵉnêphâh,** *tsen-ay-faw´;* from 6801; a *ball:*— × toss.

6803. צִנְצֶנֶת **tsintseneth,** *tsin-tseh´-neth;* from the same as 6791; a *vase* (prob. a vial *tapering* at the top):—pot.

6804. צַנְתָּרָה **tsantârâh,** *tsan-taw-raw´;* prob. from the same as 6794; a *tube:*—pipe.

6805. צָעַד **tsâʻad,** *tsaw-ad´;* a prim. root; to *pace,* i.e. *step* regularly; (upward) to *mount;* (along) to *march;* (down and caus.) to *hurl:*—bring, go, march (through), run over.

6806. צַעַד **tsaʻad,** *tsah´-ad;* from 6804; a *pace* or regular *step:*—pace, step.

6807. צְעָדָה **tsᵉʻâdâh,** *tseh-aw-daw´;* fem. of 6806; a *march;* (concr.) an (ornamental) *ankle-chain:*—going, ornament of the legs.

6808. צָעָה **tsâʻâh,** *tsaw-aw´;* a prim. root; to *tip* over (for the purpose of *spilling* or *pouring* out), i.e. (fig.) *depopulate;* by impl. to *imprison* or *conquer;* (reflex.) to *lie down* (for coition):—captive exile, travelling, (cause to) wander (-er).

צָעוֹר° **tsâʻôwr.** See 6810.

6809. צָעִיף **tsâʻîyph,** *tsaw-eef´;* from an unused root mean. to *wrap* over; a *veil:*—vail.

6810. צָעִיר **tsâʻîyr,** *tsaw-eer´;* or צָעוֹר° **tsâʻôwr,** *tsaw-ore´;* from 6819; *little;* (in number) *few;* (in age) *young,* (in value) *ignoble:*—least, little (one), small (one), + young (-er, -est).

6811. צָעִיר **Tsâʻîyr,** *tsaw-eer´;* the same as 6810; *Tsaïr,* a place in Idumæa:—Zair.

6812. צְעִירָה **tseʻîyrâh,** *tseh-ee-raw´;* fem. of 6810; *smallness* (of age), i.e. *juvenility:*—youth.

6813. צָעַן **tsâʻan,** *tsaw-an´;* a prim. root; to *load* up (beasts), i.e. to *migrate:*—be taken down.

6814. צֹעַן **Tsôʻan,** *tso´-an;* of Eg. der.; *Tsoän,* a place in Eg.:—Zoan.

6815. צַעֲנַנִּים **Tsaʻănannîym,** *tsah-an-an-neem´;* or (dual) צַעֲנַיִם° **Tsaʻănayim,** *tsah-an-ah´-yim;* plur. from 6813; *removals; Tsaanannim* or *Tsaanajim,* a place in Pal.:—Zaannannim, Zaanaim.

6816. צַעְצֻעַ **tsaʻtsûaʻ,** *tsah-tsoo´-ah;* from an unused root mean. to *bestrew* with carvings; *sculpture:*—image [work].

6817. צָעַק **tsâʻaq,** *tsaw-ak´;* a prim. root; to *shriek;* (by impl.) to *proclaim* (an assembly):—× at all, call together, cry (out), gather (selves) (together).

6818. צַעֲקָה **tsaʻăqâh,** *tsah-ak-aw´;* from 6817; a *shriek:*—cry (-ing).

6819. צָעַר **tsâʻar,** *tsaw-ar´;* a prim. root; to *be small,* i.e. (fig.) *ignoble:*—be brought low, little one, be small.

6820. צֹעַר **Tsôʻar,** *tso´-ar;* from 6819; *little; Tsoär,* a place E. of the Jordan:—Zoar.

6821. צָפַד **tsâphad,** *tsaw-fad´;* a prim. root; to *adhere:*—cleave.

6822. צָפָה **tsâphâh,** *tsaw-faw´;* a prim. root; prop. to *lean* forward, i.e. to *peer* into the distance; by impl. to *observe, await:*—behold, espy, look up (well), wait for, (keep the) watch (-man).

6823. צָפָה **tsâphâh,** *tsaw-faw´;* a prim. root [prob. rather ident. with 6822 through the idea of *expansion* in outlook transf. to act]; to *sheet* over (espec. with metal):—cover, overlay.

6824. צָפָה **tsâphâh,** *tsaw-faw´;* from 6823; an *inundation* (as *covering*):— × swimmest.

6825. צְפוֹ **Tsephôw,** *tsef-o´;* or צְפִי **Tsephîy,** *tsef-ee´;* from 6822; *observant; Tsepho* or *Tsephi,* an Idumæan:—Zephi, Zepho.

6826. צִפּוּי **tsippûwy,** *tsip-poo´ee;* from 6823; *encasement* (with metal):—covering, overlaying.

6827. צְפוֹן **Tsephôwn,** *tsef-one´;* prob. for 6837; *Tsephon,* an Isr.:—Zephon.

6828. צָפוֹן **tsâphôwn,** *tsaw-fone´;* or צָפֹן **tsâphôn,** *tsaw-fone´;* from 6845; prop. *hidden,* i.e. *dark;* used only of the *north* as a quarter (*gloomy* and *unknown*):—north (-ern, side, -ward, wind).

6829. צָפוֹן **Tsâphôwn,** *tsaw-fone´;* the same as 6828; *boreal; Tsaphon,* a place in Pal.:—Zaphon.

6830. צְפוֹנִי **tsephôwnîy,** *tsef-o-nee´;* from 6828; *northern:*—northern.

6831. צְפוֹנִי **Tsephôwnîy,** *tsef-o-nee´;* patron. from 6827; a *Tsephonite,* or (collect.) descend. of Tsephon:—Zephonites.

6832. צְפוּעַ° **tsephûwaʻ,** *tsef-oo´-ah;* from the same as 6848; *excrement* (as *protruded*):—dung.

6833. צִפּוֹר **tsippôwr,** *tsip-pore´;* or צִפֹּר **tsippôr,** *tsip-pore´;* from 6852; a little *bird* (as *hopping*):—bird, fowl, sparrow.

6834. צִפּוֹר **Tsippôwr,** *tsip-pore´;* the same as 6833; *Tsippor,* a Moabite:—Zippor.

6835. צַפַּחַת **tsappachath,** *tsap-pakh´-ath;* from an unused root mean. to *expand;* a *saucer* (as *flat*):—cruse.

6836. צְפִיָּה **tsephîyâh,** *tsef-ee-yaw´;* from 6822; *watchfulness:*—watching.

6837. צִפְיוֹן **Tsiphyôwn,** *tsif-yone´;* from 6822; *watch*-tower; *Tsiphjon,* an isr.:—Ziphion. Comp. 6827.

6838. צַפִּיחִת **tsappîychîth,** *tsap-pee-kheeth´;* from the same as 6835; a flat thin *cake:*—wafer.

6839. צֹפִים **Tsôphîym,** *tso-feem´;* plur. of act. part. of 6822; *watchers; Tsophim,* a place E. of the Jordan:—Zophim.

6840. צָפִין° **tsâphîyn,** *tsaw-feen´;* from 6845; a *treasure* (as *hidden*):—hid.

6841. צְפִיר **tsephîyr** (Chald.), *tsef-eer´;* corresp. to 6842; a he-*goat:*—he [goat].

6842. צָפִיר **tsâphîyr,** *tsaw-feer´;* from 6852; a male *goat* (as *prancing*):—(he) goat.

6843. צְפִירָה **tsephîyrâh,** *tsef-ee-raw´;* fem. formed like 6842; a *crown* (as *encircling* the head); also a *turn* of affairs (i.e. *mishap*):—diadem, morning.

6844. צָפִית **tsâphîyth,** *tsaw-feeth´;* from 6822; a *sentry:*—watchtower.

6845. צָפַן **tsâphan,** *tsaw-fan´; a prim. root; to hide* (by *covering* over); by impl. to *hoard* or *reserve;* fig. to *deny;* spec. (favorably) to *protect,* (unfavorably) to *lurk:*—esteem, hide (-den one, self), lay up, lurk (be set) privily, (keep) secret (-ly, place).

צָפֹן **tsâphôn.** See 6828.

6846. צְפַנְיָה **Tsephanyâh,** *tsef-an-yaw´;* or צְפַנְיָהוּ **Tsephanyâhûw,** *tsef-an-yaw´-hoo;* from 6845 and 3050; *Jah has secreted; Tsephanjah,* the name of four Isr.:—Zephaniah.

6847. צָפְנַת פַּעְנֵחַ **Tsophnath Paʻnêach,** *tsof-nath´ pah-nay´-akh;* of Eg. der.; *Tsophnath-Paneäch,* Joseph's Eg. name:—Zaphnath-paaneah.

6848. צֶפַע **tsephaʻ,** *tseh´-fah;* or צִפְעֹנִי **tsiphʻônîy,** *tsif-o-nee´;* from an unused root mean. to *extrude;* a *viper* (as *thrusting* out the tongue, i.e. *hissing*):—adder, cockatrice.

6849. צְפִעָה **tsephîʻâh,** *tsef-ee-aw´;* fem. from the same as 6848; an *outcast* thing:—issue.

צִפְעֹנִי **tsiphʻônîy.** See 6848.

6850. צָפַף **tsâphaph,** *tsaw-faf´;* a prim. root; to *coo* or *chirp* (as a bird):—chatter, peep, whisper.

6851. צַפְצָפָה **tsaphtsâphâh,** *tsaf-tsaw-faw´;* from 6687; a *willow* (as growing in *overflowed* places):—willow tree.

6852. צָפַר **tsâphar,** *tsaw-far´;* a prim. root; to *skip* about, i.e. *return:*—depart early.

6853. צְפַר **tsephar** (Chald.), *tsef-ar´;* corresp. to 6833; a *bird.*—bird.

צִפֹּר **tsippôr.** See 6833.

6854. צְפַרְדֵּעַ **tsephardêaʻ,** *tsef-ar-day´-ah;* from 6852 and a word elsewhere unused mean. a *swamp;* a *marsh-leaper,* i.e. *frog:*—frog.

6855. צִפֹּרָה **Tsippôrâh,** *tsip-po-raw´;* fem. of 6833; *bird; Tsipporah,* Moses' wife:—Zipporah.

6856. צִפֹּרֶן **tsippôren,** *tsip-po´-ren;* from 6852 (in the denom. sense [from 6833] of *scratching*); prop. a *claw,* i.e. (human) *nail;* also the *point* of a style (or pen, tipped with adamant):—nail, point.

6857. צְפַת **Tsephath,** *tsef-ath´;* from 6822; *watch*-tower; *Tsephath,* a place in Pal.:—Zephath.

6858. צֶפֶת **tsepheth,** *tseh´-feth;* from an unused root mean. to *encircle;* a *capital* of a column:—chapiter.

6859. צְפָתָה **Tsephâthâh,** *tsef-aw´-thaw;* the same as 6857; *Tsephathah,* a place in Pal.:—Zephathah.

צִץ **tsîts.** See 6732.

6860. צִקְלַג **Tsiqlâg,** *tsik-lag´;* or צִיקְלַג **Tsîyqelag** (1 Chron. 12 : 1, 20), *tsee-kel-ag´;* of uncert. der.; *Tsiklag* or *Tsikelag,* a place in Pal.:—Ziklag.

6861. צִקְלֹן **tsiqlôn,** *tsik-lone´;* from an unused root mean. to *wind;* a *sack* (as *tied* at the mouth):—husk.

6862. צַר **tsar,** *tsar;* or צָר **tsâr,** *tsawr;* from 6887; *narrow;* (as a noun) a *tight* place (usually fig., i.e. *trouble*); also a *pebble* (as in 6864); (trans.) an *opponent* (as *crowding*):—adversary, afflicted (-tion), anguish, close, distress, enemy, flint, foe, narrow, small, sorrow, strait, tribulation, trouble.

6863. צֵר **Tsêr,** *tsare;* from 6887; *rock; Tser,* a place in Pal.:—Zer.

6864. צֹר **tsôr,** *tsore;* from 6696; a *stone* (as if *pressed* hard or to a point); (by impl. of use) a *knife:*—flint, sharp stone.

6865. צֹר **Tsôr,** *tsore;* or צוֹר **Tsôwr,** *tsore;* the same as 6864; a *rock; Tsor,* a place in Pal.:—Tyre, Tyrus.

צֻר **tsûr.** See 6697.

6866. צָרַב **tsârab,** *tsaw-rab´;* a prim. root; to *burn:*—burn.

6867. צָרֶבֶת **tsârebeth,** *tsaw-reh´-beth;* from 6866; *conflagration* (of fire or disease):—burning, inflammation.

6868. צְרֵדָה **Tsᵉrêdâh,** *tser-ay-daw´;* or צְרֵדָתָה **Tsᵉrêdâthâh,** *tser-ay-daw´-thaw;* appar. from an unused root mean. to *pierce; puncture; Tseredah,* a place in Pal.:—Zereda, Zeredathah.

6869. צָרָה **tsârâh,** *tsaw-raw´;* fem. of 6862; *tightness* (i.e. fig. *trouble);* trans. a female *rival:*—adversary, adversity, affliction, anguish, distress, tribulation, trouble.

6870. צְרוּיָה **Tsᵉrûwyâh,** *tser-oo-yaw´;* fem. part. pass. from the same as 6875; *wounded; Tserujah,* an Israelitess:—Zeruiah.

6871. צְרוּעָה **Tsᵉrûwʻâh,** *tser-oo-aw´;* fem. pass. part. of 6879; *leprous; Tseruäh,* an Israelitess:—Zeruah.

6872. צְרוֹר **tsᵉrôwr,** *tser-ore´;* or (shorter) צְרֹר **tsᵉrôr,** *tser-ore´;* from 6887; a *parcel* (as *packed* up); also a *kernel* or *particle* (as if a *package*):—bag, × bendeth, bundle, least grain, small stone.

6873. צָרַח **tsârach,** *tsaw-rakh´;* a prim. root; to *be clear* (in tone, i.e. *shrill*), i.e. to *whoop:*—cry, roar.

6874. צְרִי **Tsᵉrîy,** *tser-ee´;* the same as 6875; *Tseri,* an Isr.:—Zeri. Comp. 3340.

6875. צְרִי **tsᵉrîy,** *tser-ee´;* or צֳרִי **tsŏrîy,** *tsor-ee´;* from an unused root mean. to *crack* [as by *pressure*], hence to *leak; distillation,* i.e. *balsam:*—balm.

6876. צֹרִי **Tsôrîy,** *tso-ree´;* patrial from 6865; a *Tsorite* or inhab. of Tsor (i.e. *Syrian*):—(man) of Tyre.

6877. צְרִיחַ **tsᵉrîyach,** *tser-ee´-akh;* from 6873 in the sense of *clearness* of vision; a *citadel:*—high place, hold.

6878. צֹרֶךְ **tsôrek,** *tso´-rek;* from an unused root mean. to *need; need:*—need.

6879. צָרַע **tsâraʻ,** *tsaw-rah´;* a prim. root; to *scourge,* i.e. (intrans. and fig.) to *be stricken with leprosy:*—leper, leprous.

6880. צִרְעָה **tsirʻâh,** *tsir-aw´;* from 6879; a *wasp* (as *stinging*):—hornet.

6881. צָרְעָה **Tsorʻâh,** *tsor-aw´;* appar. another form for 6880; *Tsorah,* a place in Pal.:—Zareah, Zorah, Zoreah.

6882. צָרְעִי **Tsorʻîy,** *tsor-ee´;* or צָרְעָתִי **Tsorʻâthîy,** *tsor-aw-thee´;* patrial from 6881; a *Tsorite* or *Tsorathite,* i.e. inhab. of Tsorah:—Zorites, Zareathites, Zorathites.

6883. צָרַעַת **tsâraʻath,** *tsaw-rah´-ath;* from 6879; *leprosy:*—leprosy.

6884. צָרַף **tsâraph,** *tsaw-raf´;* a prim. root; to *fuse* (metal), i.e. *refine* (lit. or fig.):—cast, (re-) fine (-er), founder, goldsmith, melt, pure, purge away, try.

6885. צֹרְפִי **Tsôrᵉphîy,** *tso-ref-ee´;* from 6884; *refiner; Tsorephi* (with the art.), an Isr.:—goldsmith's.

6886. צָרְפַת **Tsârᵉphath,** *tsaw-ref-ath´;* from 6884; *refinement; Tsarephath,* a place in Pal.:—Zarephath.

6887. צָרַר **tsârar,** *tsaw-rar´;* a prim. root; to *cramp,* lit. or fig., trans. or intrans. (as follows):—adversary, (be in) afflict (-ion), besiege, bind (up), (be in, bring) distress, enemy, narrower, oppress, pangs, shut up, be in a strait (trouble), vex.

6888. צְרֵרָה **Tsᵉrêrâh,** *tser-ay-raw´;* appar. by erroneous transcription for 6868; *Tsererah* for *Tseredah:*—Zereath.

6889. צֶרֶת **Tsereth,** *tseh´-reth;* perh. from 6671; *splendor; Tsereth,* an Isr.:—Zereth.

6890. צֶרֶת הַשַּׁחַר **Tsereth hash-Shachar,** *tseh´-reth hash-shakh´-ar;* from the same as 6889 and 7837 with the art. interposed; *splendor of the dawn; Tsereth-hash-Shachar,* a place in Pal.:—Zareth-shahar.

6891. צָרְתָן **Tsârᵉthân,** *tsaw-reth-awn´;* perh. for 6868; *Tsarethan,* a place in Pal.:—Zarthan.

ק

6892. קֵא **qêʼ,** *kay;* or קִיא **qîyʼ,** *kee;* from 6958; *vomit:*—vomit.

6893. קָאַת **qâʼath,** *kaw-ath´;* from 6958; prob. the *pelican* (from *vomiting*):—cormorant.

6894. קַב **qab,** *kab;* from 6895; a *hollow,* i.e. vessel used as a (dry) *measure:*—cab.

6895. קָבַב **qâbab,** *kaw-bab´;* a prim. root; to *scoop* out, i.e. (fig.) to *malign* or *execrate* (i.e. *stab* with words):— × at all, curse.

6896. קֵבָה **qêbâh,** *kay-baw´;* from 6895; the *paunch* (as a *cavity*) or first stomach of ruminants:—maw.

6897. קֹבָה **qôbâh,** *ko´-baw;* from 6895; the *abdomen* (as a cavity):—belly.

6898. קֻבָּה **qubbâh,** *koob-baw´;* from 6895; a *pavilion* (as a domed *cavity*):—tent.

6899. קִבּוּץ **qibbûwts,** *kib-boots´;* from 6908; a *throng:*—company.

6900. קְבוּרָה **qᵉbûwrâh,** *keb-oo-raw´;* or קְבֻרָה **qᵉbûrâh,** *keb-oo-raw´;* fem. pass. part. of 6912; *sepulture;* (concr.) a *sepulchre:*—burial, burying place, grave, sepulchre.

6901. קָבַל **qâbal,** *kaw-bal´;* a prim. root; to *admit,* i.e. *take* (lit. or fig.):—choose, (take) hold, receive, (under-) take.

6902. קְבַל **qᵉbal** (Chald.), *keb-al´;* corresp. to 6901; to *acquire:*—receive, take.

6903. קְבֵל **qᵉbêl** (Chald.), *keb-ale´;* or קֳבֵל **qŏbêl** (Chald.), *kob-ale´;* corresp. to 6905; (adv.) *in front of;* usually (with other particles) *on account of, so* as, *since, hence:*— + accounting to, + as, + because, before, + for this cause, + forasmuch as, + by this means, over against, by reason of, + that, + therefore, + though, + wherefore.

6904. קֹבֶל **qôbel,** *ko´-bel;* from 6901 in the sense of *confronting (as standing opposite* in order to receive); a *battering*-ram:—war.

6905. קָבָל **qâbâl,** *kaw-bawl´;* from 6901 in the sense of *opposite* [see 6904]; the *presence,* i.e. (adv.) *in front of:*—before.

6906. קָבַע **qâbaʻ,** *kaw-bah´;* a prim. root; to *cover,* i.e. (fig.) *defraud:*—rob, spoil.

6907. קֻבַּעַת **qubbaʻath,** *koob-bah´-ath;* from 6906; a *goblet* (as deep like a *cover*):—dregs.

6908. קָבַץ **qâbats,** *kaw-bats´;* a prim. root; to *grasp,* i.e. *collect:*—assemble (selves), gather (bring) (together, selves together, up), heap, resort, × surely, take up.

6909. קַבְצְאֵל **Qabtsᵉʼêl,** *kab-tseh-ale´;* from 6908 and 410; *God has gathered; Kabtseël,* a place in Pal.:—Kabzeel. Comp. 3343.

6910. קְבֻצָה **qᵉbûtsâh,** *keb-oo-tsaw´;* fem. pass. part. of 6908; a *hoard:*— × gather.

6911. קִבְצַיִם **Qibtsayim,** *kib-tsah´-yim;* dual from 6908; a *double heap; Kibtsajim,* a place in Pal.:—Kibzaim.

6912. קָבַר **qâbar,** *kaw-bar´;* a prim. root; to *inter:*— × in any wise, bury (-ier).

6913. קֶבֶר **qeber,** *keh´-ber;* or (fem.) קִבְרָה **qibrâh,** *kib-raw´;* from 6912; a *sepulchre:*—burying place, grave, sepulchre.

קְבֻרָה **qᵉbûrâh.** See 6900.

6914. קִבְרוֹת הַתַּאֲוָה **Qibrôwth hat-Taʼăvâh,** *kib-rōth´ hat-tah-av-aw´;* from the fem. plur. of 6913 and 8378 with the art. interposed; *graves of the longing; Kibroth-hat-Taavh,* a place in the Desert:—Kibroth-hattaavah.

6915. קָדַד **qâdad,** *kaw-dad´;* a prim. root; to *shrivel* up, i.e. *contract* or *bend* the body (or neck) in deference:—bow (down) (the) head, stoop.

6916. קִדָּה **qiddâh,** *kid-daw´;* from 6915; *cassia* bark (as in *shrivelled* rolls):—cassia.

6917. קָדוּם **qâdûwm,** *kaw-doom´;* pass. part. of 6923; a *pristine* hero:—ancient.

6918. קָדוֹשׁ **qâdôwsh,** *kaw-doshe´;* or קָדֹשׁ **qâdôsh,** *kaw-doshe´;* from 6942; *sacred* (ceremonially or morally); (as noun) *God* (by eminence), an *angel,* a *saint,* a *sanctuary:*—holy (One), saint.

6919. קָדַח **qâdach,** *kaw-dakh´;* a prim. root to *inflame:*—burn, kindle.

6920. קַדַּחַת **qaddachath,** *kad-dakh´-ath;* from 6919; *inflammation,* i.e. febrile disease:—burning ague, fever.

6921. קָדִים **qâdîym,** *kaw-deem´;* or קָדִם **qâdîm,** *kaw-deem´;* from 6923; the *fore* or front part; hence (by orientation) the *East* (often adv. *eastward,* for brevity the *east wind*):—east (-ward, wind).

6922. קַדִּישׁ **qaddîysh** (Chald.), *kad-deesh´;* corresp. to 6918.—holy (One), saint.

6923. קָדַם **qâdam,** *kaw-dam´;* a prim. root; to *project* (one self), i.e. *precede;* hence to *anticipate, hasten, meet* (usually for help):—come (go, [flee]) before, + disappoint, meet, prevent.

6924. קֶדֶם **qedem,** *keh´-dem;* or קֵדְמָה **qêdmâh,** *kayd´-maw;* from 6923; the *front,* of place (absol. the *fore part,* rel. the *East*) or time (*antiquity*); often used adv. (*before, anciently, eastward*):—aforetime, ancient (time), before, east (end, part, side, -ward), eternal, × ever (-lasting), forward, old, past. Comp. 6926.

6925. קֳדָם **qŏdâm** (Chald.), *kod-awm´;* or קְדָם **qᵉdâm** (Chald.) (Dan. 7 : 13), *ked-awm´;* corresp. to 6924; *before:*— before, × from, × I (thought), × me, + of, × it pleased, presence.

קַדִּים **qâdîm.** See 6921.

6926. קִדְמָה **qidmâh,** *kid-maw´;* fem. of 6924; the *forward* part (or rel.) *East* (often adv. *on the east* or *in front*):—east (-ward).

6927. קַדְמָה **qadmâh,** *kad-maw´;* from 6923; *priority* (in time); also used adv. (*before*):—afore, antiquity, former (old) estate.

6928. קַדְמָה **qadmâh** (Chad.), *kad-maw´;* corresp. to 6927; *former* time:—afore [-time], ago.

קֵדְמָה **qêdmâh.** See 6924.

6929. קֵדְמָה **Qêdᵉmâh,** *kayd´-maw´;* from 6923; *precedence; Kedemah,* a son of Ishmael:—Kedemah.

6930. קַדְמוֹן **qadmôwn,** *kad-mone´;* from 6923; *eastern:*—east.

6931. קַדְמוֹנִי **qadmôwnîy,** *kad-mo-nee´;* or קַדְמֹנִי **qadmônîy,** *kad-mo-nee´;* from 6930; (of time) *anterior* or (of place) *oriental:*—ancient, they that went before, east, (thing of) old.

6932. קְדֵמוֹת **Qᵉdêmôwth,** *ked-ay-mothe´;* from 6923; *beginnings; Kedemoth,* a place in eastern Pal.:—Kedemoth.

6933. קַדְמַי **qadmay** (Chald.), *kad-mah´ee;* from a root corresp. to 6923; *first:*—first.

6934. קַדְמִיאֵל **Qadmîy'êl,** *kad-mee-ale´;* from 6924 and 410; *presence of God; Kadmiël,* the name of three Isr.:—Kadmiel.

קַדְמֹנִי **qadmônîy.** See 6931.

6935. קַדְמֹנִי **Qadmônîy,** *kad-mo-nee´;* the same as 6931; *ancient,* i.e. aboriginal; *Kadmonite* (collect.), the name of a tribe in Pal.:—Kadmonites.

6936. קׇדְקֹד **qodqôd,** *kod-kode´;* from 6915; the *crown* of the head (as the part most *bowed*):—crown (of the head), pate, scalp, top of the head.

6937. קָדַר **qâdar,** *kaw-dar´;* a prim. root; to *be ashy,* i.e. *dark*-colored; by impl. to *mourn* (in sackcloth or sordid garments):—be black (-ish), be (make) dark (-en), × heavily, (cause to) mourn.

6938. קֵדָר **Qêdâr,** *kay-dawr´;* from 6937; *dusky* (of the skin or the tent); *Kedar,* a son of Ishmael; also (collect.) *bedawin* (as his descendants or representatives):—Kedar.

6939. קִדְרוֹן **Qidrôwn,** *kid-rone´;* from 6937; *dusky* place; *Kidron,* a brook near Jerus.:—Kidron.

6940. קַדְרוּת **qadrûwth,** *kad-rooth´;* from 6937; *duskiness:*—blackness.

6941. קְדֹרַנִּית **qᵉdôrannîyth,** *ked-o-ran-neeth´;* adv. from 6937; *blackish ones* (i.e. *in sackcloth*); used adv. in *mourning* weeds:—mournfully.

6942. קָדַשׁ **qâdâsh,** *kaw-dash´;* a prim. root; to *be* (causat. *make, pronounce* or *observe* as) *clean* (ceremonially or morally):—appoint, bid, consecrate, dedicate, defile, hallow, (be, keep) holy (-er, place), keep, prepare, proclaim, purify, sanctify (-ied one, self), × wholly.

6943. קֶדֶשׁ **Qedesh,** *keh´-desh;* from 6942; a *sanctum; Kedesh,* the name of four places in Pal.:—Kedesh.

6944. קֹדֶשׁ **qôdesh,** *ko´-desh;* from 6942; a *sacred* place or thing; rarely abstr. *sanctity:*—consecrated (thing), dedicated (thing), hallowed (thing), holiness, (× most) holy (× day, portion, thing), saint, sanctuary.

6945. קָדֵשׁ **qâdêsh,** *kaw-dashe´;* from 6942; a (quasi) *sacred* person, i.e. (techn.) a (male) *devotee* (by prostitution) to licentious idolatry:—sodomite, unclean.

6946. קָדֵשׁ **Qâdêsh,** *kaw-dashe´;* the same as 6945; *sanctuary; Kadesh,* a place in the Desert:—Kadesh. Comp. 6947.

קָדֹשׁ **qâdôsh.** See 6918.

6947. קָדֵשׁ בַּרְנֵעַ **Qâdêsh Barnêaʻ,** *kaw-dashe´ bar-nay´-ah;* from the same as 6946 and an otherwise unused word (appar. compounded of a correspondent to 1251 and a deriv. of 5128) mean. *desert of a fugitive; Kadesh of* (the) *Wilderness of Wandering; Kadesh-Barneä,* a place in the Desert:—Kadesh-barnea.

6948. קְדֵשָׁה **qᵉdêshâh,** *ked-ay-shaw´;* fem. of 6945; a female *devotee* (i.e. *prostitute*):—harlot, whore.

6949. קָהָה **qâhâh,** *kaw-haw´;* a prim. root; to be *dull:*—be set on edge, be blunt.

6950. קָהַל **qâhal,** *kaw-hal´;* a prim. root; to *convoke:*—assemble (selves) (together), gather (selves) (together).

6951. קָהָל **qâhâl,** *kaw-hawl´;* from 6950; *assemblage* (usually concr.):—assembly, company, congregation, multitude.

6952. קְהִלָּה **qᵉhillâh,** *keh-hil-law´;* from 6950; an *assemblage:*—assembly, congregation.

6953. קֹהֶלֶת **qôheleth,** *ko-heh´-leth;* fem. of act. part. from 6950; a (female) *assembler* (i.e. lecturer); abstr. *preaching* (used as a "nom de plume", *Koheleth*):—preacher.

6954. קְהֵלָתָה **Qᵉhêlâthâh,** *keh-hay-law´-thaw,* from 6950; *convocation; Kehelathah,* a place in the Desert:—Kehelathah.

6955. קְהָת **Qᵉhâth,** *keh-hawth´;* from an unused root mean. to *ally* oneself; *allied; Kehath,* an Isr.:—Kohath.

6956. קֳהָתִי **Qŏhâthîy,** *ko-haw-thee´;* patron. from 6955; a *Kohathite* (collect.) or desc. of Kehath:—Kohathites.

6957. קַו **qav,** *kav;* or קָו **qâv,** *kawv;* from 6960 [comp. 6961]; a *cord* (as *connecting*), espec. for measuring; fig. a *rule;* also a *rim,* a musical *string* or *accord:*—line. Comp. 6978.

6958. קוֹא **qôw',** *ko;* or קָיָה **qâyâh** (Jer. 25 : 27), *kaw-yaw´;* a prim. root; to *vomit:*—spue (out), vomit (out, up, up again).

6959. קוֹבַע **qôwbaʻ,** *ko´-bah* or *ko-bah´;* a form collat. to 3553; a *helmet:*—helmet.

6960. קָוָה **qâvâh,** *kaw-vaw´;* a prim. root; to *bind* together (perh. by *twisting*), i.e. *collect;* (*fig.*) *to expect:*—gather (together), look, patiently, tarry, wait (for, on, upon).

6961. קָוֶה° **qâveh,** *kaw-veh´;* from 6960; a (measuring) *cord* (as if for *binding*):—line.

קוֹחַ **qôwach.** See 6495.

6962. קוּט **qûwṭ,** *koot;* a prim. root; prop. to *cut off,* i.e. (fig.) *detest:*—be grieved, lothe self.

6963. קוֹל **qôwl,** *kole;* or קֹל **qôl,** *kole;* from an unused root mean. to *call* aloud; a *voice* or *sound:*— + aloud, bleating, crackling, cry (+ out), fame, lightness, lowing, noise, + hold peace, [pro-] claim, proclamation, + sing, sound, + spark, thunder (-ing), voice, + yell.

6964. קוֹלָיָה **Qôwlâyâh,** *ko-law-yaw´;* from 6963 and 3050; *voice of Jah; Kolajah,* the name of two Isr.:—Kolaiah.

6965. קוּם **qûwm,** *koom;* a prim. root; to *rise* (in various applications, lit. fig., intens. and caus.):—abide, accomplish, × be clearer, confirm, continue, decree, × be dim, endure, × enemy, enjoin, get up, make good, help, hold, (help to) lift up (again), make, × but newly, ordain, perform, pitch, raise (up), rear (up), remain, (a-) rise (up) (again, against), rouse up, set (up), (e-) stablish, (make to) stand (up), stir up, strengthen, succeed, (as-, make) sure (-ly), (be) up (-hold, -rising).

6966. קוּם **qûwm** (Chald.), *koom;* corresp. to 6965:—appoint, establish, make, raise up self, (a-) rise (up), (make to) stand, set (up).

6967. קוֹמָה **qôwmâh,** *ko-maw´;* from 6965; *height:*— × along, height, high, stature, tall.

6968. קוֹמְמִיּוּת **qôwmᵉmîyûwth,** *ko-mem-ee-yooth´;* from 6965; *elevation,* i.e. (adv.) *erectly* (fig.):—upright.

6969. קוּן **qûwn,** *koon;* a prim. root; to *strike* a musical note, i.e. *chant* or *wail* (at a funeral):—lament, mourning woman.

6970. קוֹעַ **Qôwaʻ,** *ko´-ah;* prob. from 6972 in the orig. sense of *cutting* off; *curtailment; Koä,* a region of Bab.:—Koa.

6971. קוֹף **qôwph,** *kofe;* or קֹף **qôph,** *kofe;* prob. of for. or.; a *monkey:*—ape.

6972. קוּץ **qûwts,** *koots;* a prim. root; to *clip* off; used only as denom. from 7019; to *spend the harvest* season:—summer.

6973. קוּץ **qûwts,** *koots;* a prim. root [rather ident. with 6972 through the idea of *severing* oneself from (comp. 6962)]; to be (caus. *make*) *disgusted* or *anxious:*—abhor, be distressed, be grieved, loathe, vex, be weary.

6974. קוּץ **qûwts,** *koots;* a prim. root [rather ident. with 6972 through the idea of *abruptness* in starting up from sleep (comp. 3364)]; to *awake* (lit. or fig.):—arise, (be) (a-) wake, watch.

6975. קוֹץ **qôwts,** *kotse;* or קֹץ **qôts,** *kotse;* from 6972 (in the sense of *pricking*); a *thorn:*—thorn.

6976. קוֹץ **Qôwts,** *kotse;* the same as 6975; *Kots,* the name of two Isr.:—Koz, Hakkoz [*includ. the art.*].

6977. קְוֻצָּה **q^{e}vutstsâh,** *kev-oots-tsaw´;* fem. pass. part. of 6972 in its orig. sense; a *forelock* (as *shorn*):—lock.

6978. קַו־קַו **qav-qav,** *kav-kav´;* from 6957 (in the sense of a *fastening*); *stalwart:*— × meted out.

6979. קוּר **qûwr,** *koor;* a prim. root; to *trench;* by impl. to *throw forth;* also (denom. from 7023) to *wall up,* whether lit. (to *build* a wall) or fig. (to *estop*):—break down, cast out, destroy, dig.

6980. קוּר **qûwr,** *koor;* from 6979; (only plur.) *trenches,* i.e. a *web* (as if so formed):—web.

6981. קוֹרֵא **Qôwrêʼ,** *ko-ray´;* or קֹרֵא **Qôrêʼ** (1 Chron. 26 : 1), *ko-ray´;* act. part. of 7121; *crier; Korè,* the name of two Isr.:—Kore.

6982. קוֹרָה **qôwrâh,** *ko-raw´;* or קֹרָה **qôrâh,** *ko-raw´;* from 6979; a *rafter* (forming *trenches* as it were); by impl. a *roof:*—beam, roof.

6983. קוֹשׁ **qôwsh,** *koshe;* a prim. root; to *bend; used only as denom. for 3369, to set a trap:*—lay a snare.

6984. קוּשָׁיָהוּ **qûwshâyâhûw,** *koo-shaw-yaw´-hoo;* from the pass. part. of 6983 and 3050; *entrapped of Jah; Kushajah,* an Isr.:—Kushaiah.

6985. קַט **qaṭ,** *kat;* from 6990 in the sense of *abbreviation;* a *little,* i.e. (adv.) *merely:*—very.

6986. קֶטֶב **qeṭeb,** *keh´-teb;* from an unused root mean. to *cut* off; *ruin:*—destroying, destruction.

6987. קֹטֶב **qôṭeb,** *ko´-teb;* from the same as 6986; *extermination:*—destruction.

6988. קְטוֹרָה **q^{e}ṭôwrâh,** *ket-o-raw´;* from 6999; *perfume:*—incense.

6989. קְטוּרָה **Q^{e}ṭûwrâh,** *ket-oo-raw´;* fem. pass. part. of 6999; *perfumed; Keturah,* a wife of Abraham:—Keturah.

6990. קָטַט **qâṭaṭ,** *kaw-tat´;* a prim. root; to *clip* off, i.e. (fig.) *destroy:*—be cut off.

6991. קָטַל **qâṭal,** *kaw-tal´;* a prim. root; prop. to *cut* off, i.e. (fig.) *put to death:*—kill, slay.

6992. קְטַל **q^{e}ṭal** (Chald.), *ket-al´;* corresp. to 6991; to *kill:*—slay.

6993. קֶטֶל **qeṭel,** *keh´-tel;* from 6991; a violent *death:*—slaughter.

6994. קָטֹן **qâṭôn,** *kaw-tone´;* a prim. root [rather denom. from 6996]; to *diminish,* i.e. *be* (caus. *make*) *diminutive* or (fig.) *of no account:*—be a (make) small (thing), be not worthy.

6995. קֹטֶן **qôṭen,** *ko´-ten;* from 6994; a *pettiness,* i.e. the *little finger:*—little finger.

6996. קָטָן **qâṭân,** *kaw-tawn´;* or קָטֹן **qâṭôn,** *kaw-tone´;* from 6962; *abbreviated,* i.e. *diminutive,* lit. (in quantity, size or number) or fig. (in age or importance):—least, less (-ser), little (one), small (-est, one, quantity, thing), young (-er, -est).

6997. קָטָן **Qâṭân,** *kaw-tawn´;* the same as 6996; *small; Katan,* an Isr.:—Hakkatan [*includ. the art.*].

6998. קָטַף **qâṭaph,** *kaw-taf´;* a prim. root; to *strip* off:—crop off, cut down (up), pluck.

6999. קָטַר **qâṭar,** *kaw-tar´;* a prim. root [rather ident. with 7000 through the idea of fumigation in a *close* place and perh. thus *driving* out the occupants]; to *smoke,* i.e. turn into fragrance by fire (espec. as an act of worship):—burn (incense, sacrifice) (upon), (altar for) incense, kindle, offer (incense, a sacrifice).

7000. קָטַר **qâṭar,** *kaw-tar´;* a prim. root; to *inclose:*—join.

7001. קְטַר **q^{e}ṭar** (Chald.), *ket-ar´;* from a root corresp. to 7000; a *knot* (as *tied* up), i.e. (fig.) a *riddle;* also a *vertebra* (as if a knot):—doubt, joint.

7002. קִטֵּר **qiṭṭêr,** *kit-tare´;* from 6999; *perfume:*—incense.

7003. קִטְרוֹן **Qiṭrôwn,** *kit-rone´;* from 6999; *fumigative; Kitron,* a place in Pal.:—Kitron.

7004. קְטֹרֶת **q^{e}ṭôreth,** *ket-o´-reth;* from 6999; a *fumigation:*—(sweet) incense, perfume.

7005. קַטָּת **Qaṭṭâth,** *kat-tawth´;* from 6996; *littleness, Kattath,* a place in Pal.:—Kattath.

7006. קָיָה **qâyâh,** *kaw-yaw´;* a prim. root; to *vomit:*—spue.

7007. קַיִט **qâyiṭ** (Chald.), *kah´-yit;* corresp. to 7019; *harvest:*—summer.

7008. קִיטוֹר **qîyṭôwr,** *kee-tore´;* or קִיטֹר **qîyṭôr,** *kee-tore´;* from 6999; a *fume,* i.e. *cloud:*—smoke, vapour.

7009. קִים **qîym,** *keem;* from 6965; an *opponent* (as *rising* against one), i.e. (collect.) enemies:—substance.

7010. קְיָם **q^{e}yâm** (Chald.), *keh-yawm´;* from 6966; an *edict* (as *arising* in law):—decree, statute.

7011. קַיָּם **qayâm** (Chald.), *kah-yawm´;* from 6966; *permanent* (as *rising* firmly):—stedfast, sure.

7012. קִימָה **qîymâh,** *kee-maw´;* from 6965; an *arising:*—rising up.

קִימוֹשׁ **Qîymôwsh.** See 7057.

7013. קַיִן **qayin,** *kah´-yin;* from 6969 in the orig. sense of *fixity;* a *lance* (as *striking fast*):—spear.

7014. קַיִן **Qayin,** *kah´-yin;* the same as 7013 (with a play upon the affinity to 7069); *Kajin,* the name of the first child, also of a place in Pal., and of an Oriental tribe:—Cain, Kenite (-s).

7015. קִינָה **qîynâh,** *kee-naw´;* from 6969; a *dirge* (as accompanied by *beating* the breasts or on instruments):—lamentation.

7016. קִינָה **Qîynâh,** *kee-naw´;* the same as 7015; *Kinah,* a place in Pal.:—Kinah.

7017. קֵינִי **Qêynîy,** *kay-nee´;* or קִינִי **Qîynîy** (1 Chron. 2 : 55), *kee-nee´;* patron. from 7014; a *Kenite* or member of the tribe of Kajin:—Kenite.

7018. קֵינָן **Qêynân,** *kay-nawn´;* from the same as 7064; *fixed; Kenan,* an antediluvian:—Cainan, Kenan.

7019. קַיִץ **qayits,** *kah´-yits;* from 6972; *harvest* (as the *crop*), whether the product (grain or fruit) or the (dry) season:—summer (fruit, house).

7020. קִיצוֹן **qîytsôwn,** *kee-tsone´;* from 6972; *terminal:*—out- (utter-) most.

7021. קִיקָיוֹן **qîyqâyôwn,** *kee-kaw-yone´;* perh. from 7006; the *gourd* (as *nauseous*):—gourd.

7022. קִיקָלוֹן **qîyqâlôwn,** *kee-kaw-lone´;* from 7036; intense *disgrace:*—shameful spewing.

7023. קִיר **qîyr,** *keer;* or קִר **qîr** (Isa. 22 : 5), *keer;* or (fem.) קִירָה **qîyrâh,** *kee-raw´;* from 6979; a *wall* (as built in a *trench*):— + mason, side, town, × very, wall.

7024. קִיר **Qîyr,** *keer;* the same as 7023; *fortress; Kir,* a place in Ass.; also one in Moab:—Kir. Comp. 7025.

7025. קִיר חֶרֶשׂ **Qîyr Cheres,** *keer kheh´-res;* or (fem. of the latter word) קִיר חֲרֶשֶׂת **Qîyr Chăreseth,** *keer khar-eh´-seth;* from 7023 and 2789; *fortress of earthenware; Kir-Cheres* or *Kir-Chareseth,* a place in Moab:—Kir-haraseth, Kir-hareseth, Kir-haresh, Kir-heres.

7026. קֵירֹס **Qêyrôç,** *kay-roce´;* or קֵרֹס **Qêrôç,** *kay-roce´;* from the same as 7166; *ankled; Keros,* one of the Nethinim:—Keros.

7027. קִישׁ **Qîysh,** *keesh;* from 6983; a *bow; Kish,* the name of five Isr.:—Kish.

7028. קִישׁוֹן **Qîyshôwn,** *kee-shone´;* from 6983; *winding; Kishon,* a river of Pal.:—Kishon, Kison.

7029. קִישִׁי **Qîyshîy,** *kee-shee´;* from 6983; *bowed; Kishi,* an Isr.:—Kishi.

7030. קִיתָרֹס° **qîythârôç** (Chald.), *kee-thaw-roce´;* of Gr. origin (*κιθαρις*); a *lyre:*—harp.

7031. קַל **qal,** *kal;* contr. from 7043; *light;* (by impl.) *rapid* (also adv.):—light, swift (-ly).

7032. קָל **qâl** (Chald.), *kawl;* corresp. to 6963:—sound, voice.

קֹל **qôl.** See 6963.

7033. קָלָה **qâlâh,** *kaw-law´;* a prim. root [rather ident. with 7034 through the idea of *shrinkage* by heat]; to *toast, i.e. scorch* partially or slowly:—dried, loathsome, parch, roast.

7034. קָלָה **qâlâh,** *kaw-law´;* a prim. root; to *be light* (as implied in *rapid* motion), but fig. only (*be* [caus. *hold*] *in contempt*):—base, contemn, despise, lightly esteem, set light, seem vile.

7035. קָלַהּ° **qâlahh,** *kaw-lah´;* for 6950; to *assemble:*—gather together.

7036. קָלוֹן **qâlôwn,** *kaw-lone´;* from 7034; *disgrace;* (by impl.) the *pudenda:*—confusion, dishonour, ignominy, reproach, shame.

7037. קַלַּחַת **qallachath,** *kal-lakh´-ath;* appar. but a form for 6747; a *kettle:*—caldron.

7038. קָלַט **qâlaṭ,** *kaw-lat´;* a prim. root; to *maim:*—lacking in his parts.

7039. קָלִי **qâlîy,** *kaw-lee´;* or קָלִיא **qâlîy',** *kaw-lee´;* from 7033; *roasted* ears of grain:—parched corn.

7040. קַלָּי **Qallay,** *kal-lah´ee;* from 7043; *frivolous; Kallai,* an Isr.:—Kallai.

7041. קֵלָיָה **Qêlâyâh,** *kay-law-yaw´;* from 7034; *insignificance; Kelajah,* an Isr.:—Kelaiah.

7042. קְלִיטָא **Qᵉlîyṭâ',** *kel-ee-taw´;* from 7038; *maiming; Kelita,* the name of three Isr.:—Kelita.

7043. קָלַל **qâlal,** *kaw-lal´;* a prim. root; to *be* (caus. *make*) *light,* lit. (*swift, small, sharp,* etc.) or fig. (*easy, trifling, vile,* etc.):—abate, make bright, bring into contempt, (ac-) curse, despise, (be) ease (-y, -ier), (be a, make, make somewhat, move, seem a, set) light (-en, -er, ly, -ly afflict, -ly esteem, thing), × slight [-ly], be swift (-er), (be, be more, make, re-) vile, whet.

7044. קָלָל **qâlâl,** *kaw-lawl´;* from 7043; *brightened* (as if *sharpened*):—burnished, polished.

7045. קְלָלָה **qᵉlâlâh,** *kel-aw-law´;* from 7043; *vilification:*—(ac-) curse (-d, -ing).

7046. קָלַס **qâlaç,** *kaw-las´;* a prim. root; to *disparage,* i.e. ridicule:—mock, scoff, scorn.

7047. קֶלֶס **qeleç,** *keh´-les;* from 7046; a *laughing-stock:*—derision.

7048. קַלָּסָה **qallâçâh,** *kal-law-saw´;* intens. from 7046; *ridicule:*—mocking.

7049. קָלַע **qâla',** *kaw-lah´;* a prim. root; to *sling;* also to *carve* (as if a *circular* motion, or into *light* forms):—carve, sling (out).

7050. קֶלַע **qela',** *keh´-lah;* from 7049; a *sling;* also a (door) *screen* (as if *slung* across), or the *valve* (of the door) itself:—hanging, leaf, sling.

7051. קַלָּע **qallâ',** *kal-law´;* intens. from 7049; a *slinger:*—slinger.

7052. קְלֹקֵל **qᵉlôqêl,** *kel-o-kale´;* from 7043; *insubstantial:*—light.

7053. קִלְּשׁוֹן **qillᵉshôwn,** *kil-lesh-one´;* from an unused root mean. to *prick;* a *prong,* i.e. hay-fork:—fork.

7054. קָמָה **qâmâh,** *kaw-maw´;* fem. of act. part. of 6965; something that *rises,* i.e. a *stalk* of grain:—(standing) corn, grown up, stalk.

7055. קְמוּאֵל **Qᵉmûw'êl,** *kem-oo-ale´;* from 6965 and 410; *raised of God; Kemuël,* the name of a relative of Abraham, and of two Isr.:—Kemuel.

7056. קָמוֹן **Qâmôwn,** *kaw-mone´;* from 6965; an *elevation; Kamon,* a place E. of the Jordan:—Camon.

7057. קִמּוֹשׁ **qimmôwsh,** *kim-moshe´;* or קִימוֹשׁ **qîymôwsh,** *kee-moshe´;* from an unused root mean. to *sting;* a *prickly* plant:—nettle. Comp. 7063.

7058. קֶמַח **qemach,** *keh´-makh;* from an unused root prob. mean. to *grind; flour:*—flour, meal.

7059. קָמַט **qâmaṭ,** *kaw-mat´;* a prim. root; to *pluck,* i.e. destroy:—cut down, fill with wrinkles.

7060. קָמַל **qâmal,** *kaw-mal´;* a prim. root; to *wither:*—hew down, wither.

7061. קָמַץ **qâmats,** *kaw-mats´;* a prim. root; to *grasp* with the hand:—take an handful.

7062. קֹמֶץ **qômets,** *ko´-mets;* from 7061; a *grasp,* i.e. *handful:*—handful.

7063. קִמָּשׁוֹן **qimmâshôwn,** *kim-maw-shone´;* from the same as 7057; a *prickly* plant:—thorn.

7064. קֵן **qên,** *kane;* contr. from 7077; a *nest* (as *fixed*), sometimes includ. the *nestlings;* fig. a *chamber* or *dwelling:*—nest, room.

7065. קָנָא **qânâ',** *kaw-naw´;* a prim. root; to *be* (caus. *make*) *zealous,* i.e. (in a bad sense) *jealous* or *envious:*— (be) envy (-ious), be (move to, provoke to) jealous (-y), × very, (be) zeal (-ous).

7066. קְנָא **qᵉnâ'** (Chald.), *ken-aw´;* corresp. to 7069; to *purchase:*—buy.

7067. קַנָּא **qannâ',** *kan-naw´;* from 7065; *jealous:*—jealous. Comp. 7072.

7068. קִנְאָה **qin'âh,** *kin-aw´;* from 7065; *jealousy* or *envy:*—envy (-ied), jealousy, × sake, zeal.

7069. קָנָה **qânâh,** *kaw-naw´;* a prim. root; to *erect,* i.e. *create;* by extens. to *procure,* espec. by purchase (caus. *sell*); by impl. to *own:*—attain, buy (-er), teach to keep cattle, get, provoke to jealousy, possess (-or), purchase, recover, redeem, × surely, × verily.

7070. קָנֶה **qâneh,** *kaw-neh´;* from 7069; a *reed* (as *erect*); by resemblance a *rod* (espec. for measuring), *shaft, tube, stem,* the *radius* (of the arm), *beam* (of a steelyard):—balance, bone, branch, calamus, cane, reed, × spearman, stalk.

7071. קָנָה **Qânâh,** *kaw-naw´;* fem. of 7070; *reediness; Kanah,* the name of a stream and of a place in Pal.:—Kanah.

7072. קַנּוֹא **qannôw',** *kan-no´;* for 7067; *jealous* or *angry:*—jealous.

7073. קְנַז **Qᵉnaz,** *ken-az´;* prob. from an unused root mean. to *hunt; hunter; Kenaz,* the name of an Edomite and of two Isr.:—Kenaz.

7074. קְנִזִּי **Qᵉnizzîy,** *ken-iz-zee´;* patron. from 7073; a *Kenizzite* or desc. of Kenaz:—Kenezite, Kenizzites.

7075. קִנְיָן **qinyân,** *kin-yawn´;* from 7069; *creation,* i.e. (concr.) *creatures;* also *acquisition, purchase, wealth:*—getting, goods, × with money, riches, substance.

7076. קִנָּמוֹן **qinnâmôwn,** *kin-naw-mone´;* from an unused root (mean. to *erect*); *cinnamon* bark (as in *upright* rolls):—cinnamon.

7077. קָנַן **qânan,** *kaw-nan´;* a prim. root; to *erect;* but used only as denom. from 7064; to *nestle,* i.e. *build* or *occupy* as a nest:—make . . . nest.

7078. קֶנֶץ **qenets,** *keh´-nets;* from an unused root prob. mean. to *wrench; perversion:*—end.

7079. קְנָת **Qᵉnâth,** *ken-awth´;* from 7069; *possession; Kenath,* a place E. of the Jordan:—Kenath.

7080. קָסַם **qâçam,** *kaw-sam´;* a prim. root; prop. to *distribute,* i.e. *determine* by lot or magical scroll; by impl. to *divine:*—divine (-r, -ation), prudent, soothsayer, use [divination].

7081. קֶסֶם **qeçem,** *keh´-sem;* from 7080; a *lot;* also *divination* (includ. its *fee*), *oracle:*—(reward of) divination, divine sentence, witchcraft.

7082. קָסַס **qâçaç,** *kaw-sas´;* a prim. root; to *lop* off:—cut off.

7083. קֶסֶת **qeçeth,** *keh´-seth;* from the same as 3563 (or as 7185); prop. a *cup,* i.e. an *ink-stand:*—inkhorn.

7084. קְעִילָה **Qᵉ'îylâh,** *keh-ee-law´;* perh. from 7049 in the sense of *inclosing; citadel; Keïlah,* a place in Pal.:—Keilah.

7085. קַעֲקַע **qa'ăqa',** *kah-ak-ah´;* from the same as 6970; an *incision* or gash:— + mark.

7086. קְעָרָה **qᵉ'ârâh,** *keh-aw-raw´;* prob. from 7167; a *bowl* (as *cut* out hollow):—charger, dish.

קֹף **qôph.** See 6971.

7087. קָפָא **qâphâ',** *kaw-faw´;* a prim. root; to *shrink,* i.e. *thicken* (as unracked wine, curdled milk, clouded sky, frozen water):—congeal, curdle, dark°, settle.

7088. קָפַד **qâphad,** *kaw-fad´;* a prim. root; to *contract,* i.e. roll together:—cut off.

7089. קְפָדָה **qᵉphâdâh,** *kef-aw-daw´;* from 7088; *shrinking,* i.e. terror:—destruction.

7090. קִפּוֹד **qippôwd,** *kip-pode´;* or קִפֹּד **qippôd,** *kip-pode´;* from 7088; a species of bird, perh. the *bittern* (from its *contracted* form):—bittern.

7091. קִפּוֹז **qippôwz,** *kip-poze´;* from an unused root mean. to *contract,* i.e. *spring* forward; an *arrow-snake* (as *darting* on its prey):—great owl.

7092. קָפַץ **qâphats,** *kaw-fats´;* a prim. root; to *draw* together, i.e. close; by impl. to *leap* (by *contracting* the limbs); spec. to *die* (from *gathering* up the feet):—shut (up), skip, stop, take out of the way.

7093. קֵץ **qêts,** *kates;* contr. from 7112; an *extremity;* adv. (with prep. pref.) *after:*— + after, (utmost) border, end, [in-] finite, × process.

קֹץ **qôts.** See 6975.

7094. קָצַב **qâtsab,** *kaw-tsab´;* a prim. root; to *clip,* or (gen.) *chop:*—cut down, shorn.

7095. קֶצֶב **qetseb,** *keh´-tseb;* from 7094; *shape* (as if *cut* out); *base* (as if there *cut* off):—bottom, size.

7096. קָצָה **qâtsâh,** *kaw-tsaw´;* a prim. root; to *cut* off; (fig.) to *destroy;* (partially) to *scrape* off:—cut off, cut short, scrape (off).

7097. קָצֶה **qâtseh,** *kaw-tseh´;* or (neg. only) קֵצֶה **qêtseh,** *kay´-tseh;* from 7096; an *extremity* (used in a great variety of applications and idioms; comp. 7093):— × after, border, brim, brink, edge, end, [in-] finite, frontier, outmost coast, quarter, shore, (out-) side, × some, ut (-ter-) most (part).

7098. קָצָה **qâtsâh,** *kaw-tsaw´;* fem. of 7097; a *termination* (used like 7097):—coast, corner, (selv-) edge, lowest, (uttermost) part.

7099. קֶצֶו **qetsev,** *keh´-tsev;* and (fem.) קִצְוָה **qitsvâh,** *kits-vaw´;* from 7096; a *limit* (used like 7097; but with less variety):—end, edge, uttermost part.

7100. קֶצַח **qetsach,** *keh´-tsakh;* from an unused root appar. mean. to *incise; fennel-flower* (from its *pungency*):—fitches.

7101. קָצִין **qâtsîyn,** *kaw-tseen´;* from 7096 in the sense of *determining;* a *magistrate* (as *deciding*) or other *leader:*—captain, guide, prince, ruler. Comp. 6278.

7102. קְצִיעָה **q^etsîyʻâh,** *kets-ee-aw´;* from 7106; *cassia* (as *peeled;* plur. the *bark*):—cassia.

7103. קְצִיעָה **Q^etsîyʻâh,** *kets-ee-aw´;* the same as 7102; *Ketsiah,* a daughter of Job:—Kezia.

7104. קְצִיץ **Q^etsîyts,** *kets-eets´;* from 7112; *abrupt; Keziz,* a valley in Pal.:—Keziz.

7105. קָצִיר **qâtsîyr,** *kaw-tseer´;* from 7114; *severed,* i.e. *harvest* (as *reaped*), the crop, the time, the reaper, or fig.; also a *limb* (of a tree, or simply *foliage*):—bough, branch, harvest (man).

7106. קָצַע **qâtsaʻ,** *kaw-tsah´;* a prim. root; to *strip* off, i.e. (partially) *scrape;* by impl. to *segregate* (as an angle):—cause to scrape, corner.

7107. קָצַף **qâtsaph,** *kaw-tsaf´;* a prim. root; to *crack* off, i.e. (fig.) *burst* out in rage:—(be) anger (-ry), displease, fret self, (provoke to) wrath (come), be wroth.

7108. קְצַף **q^etsaph** (Chald.), *kets-af´;* corresp. to 7107; to *become enraged:*—be furious.

7109. קְצַף **q^etsaph** (Chald.), *kets-af´;* from 7108; *rage:*—wrath.

7110. קֶצֶף **qetseph,** *keh´-tsef;* from 7107; a *splinter* (as *chipped* off); fig. *rage* or *strife:*—foam, indignation, × sore, wrath.

7111. קְצָפָה **q^etsâphâh,** *kets-aw-faw´;* from 7107; a *fragment:*—bark [-ed].

7112. קָצַץ **qâtsats,** *kaw-tsats´;* a prim. root; to *chop* off (lit. or fig.):—cut (asunder, in pieces, in sunder, off), × utmost.

7113. קְצַץ **q^etsats** (Chald.), *kets-ats´;* corresp. to 7112:—cut off.

7114. קָצַר **qâtsar,** *kaw-tsar´;* a prim. root; to *dock* off, i.e. *curtail* (trans. or intrans., lit. or fig.); espec. to *harvest* (grass or grain):— × at all, cut down, much discouraged, grieve, harvestman, lothe, mourn, reap (-er), (be, wax) short (-en, -er), straiten, trouble, vex.

7115. קֹצֶר **qôtser,** *ko´-tser;* from 7114; *shortness* (of spirit), i.e. impatience:—anguish.

7116. קָצֵר **qâtsêr,** *kaw-tsare´;* from 7114; *short* (whether in size, number, life, strength or temper):—few, hasty, small, soon.

7117. קְצָת **q^etsâth,** *kets-awth´;* from 7096; a *termination* (lit. or fig.); also (by impl.) a *portion;* adv. (with prep. pref.) *after:*—end, part, × some.

7118. קְצָת **q^etsâth** (Chald.), *kets-awth´;* corresp. to 7117:—end, partly.

7119. קַר **qar,** *kar;* contr. from an unused root mean. to *chill; cool;* fig. *quiet;*—cold, excellent [*from the marg.*].

קִר **qîr.** See 7023.

7120. קֹר **qôr,** *kore;* from the same as 7119; *cold:*—cold.

7121. קָרָא **qârâʼ,** *kaw-raw´;* a prim. root [rather ident. with 7122 through the idea of *accosting* a person met]; to *call* out to (i.e. prop. *address* by name, but used in a wide variety of applications):—bewray [self], that are bidden, call (for, forth, self, upon), cry (unto), (be) famous, guest, invite, mention, (give) name, preach, (make) proclaim (-ation), pronounce, publish, read, renowned, say.

7122. קָרָא **qârâʼ,** *kaw-raw´;* a prim. root; to *encounter,* whether accidentally or in a hostile manner:—befall, (by) chance, (cause to) come (upon), fall out, happen, meet.

7123. קְרָא **q^erâʼ** (Chald.), *ker-aw´;* corresp. to 7121:—call, cry, read.

7124. קֹרֵא **qôrêʼ,** *ko-ray´;* prop. act. part. of 7121; a *caller,* i.e. *partridge* (from its *cry*):—partridge. See also 6981.

7125. קִרְאָה **qîrʼâh,** *keer-aw´;* from 7122; an *encountering,* accidental, friendly or hostile (also adv. *opposite*):— × against (he come), help, meet, seek, × to, × in the way.

7126. קָרַב **qârab,** *kaw-rab´;* a prim. root; to *approach* (caus. *bring near*) for whatever purpose:—(cause to) approach, (cause to) bring (forth, near), (cause to) come (near, nigh), (cause to) draw near (nigh), go (near), be at hand, join, be near, offer, present, produce, make ready, stand, take.

7127. קְרֵב **q^erêb** (Chald.), *ker-abe´;* corresp. to 7126:—approach, come (near, nigh), draw near.

7128. קְרָב **q^erâb,** *ker-awb´;* from 7126; hostile *encounter:*—battle, war.

7129. קְרָב **q^erâb** (Chald.), *ker-awb´;* corresp. to 7128:—war.

7130. קֶרֶב **qereb,** *keh´-reb;* from 7126; prop. the *nearest* part, i.e. the *centre,* whether lit., fig. or adv. (espec. with prep.):— × among, × before, bowels, × unto charge, + eat (up), × heart, × him, × in, inward (× -ly, part, -s, thought), midst, + out of, purtenance, × therein, × through, × within self.

7131. קָרֵב **qârêb,** *kaw-rabe´;* from 7126; *near:*—approach, come (near, nigh), draw near.

קָרֹב **qârôb.** See 7138.

7132. קְרָבָה **q^erâbâh,** *ker-aw-baw´;* from 7126; *approach:*—approaching, draw near.

7133. קָרְבָּן **qorbân,** *kor-bawn´;* or קֻרְבָּן **qurbân,** *koor-bawn´;* from 7126; something *brought near* the altar, i.e. a sacrificial *present:*—oblation, that is offered, offering.

7134. קַרְדֹּם **qardôm,** *kar-dome´;* perh. from 6923 in the sense of *striking* upon; an *axe:*—ax.

7135. קָרָה **qârâh,** *kaw-raw´;* fem. of 7119; *coolness:*—cold.

7136. קָרָה **qârâh,** *kaw-raw´;* a prim. root; to *light upon* (chiefly by accident); caus. to *bring about;* spec. to *impose* timbers (for roof or floor):—appoint, lay (make) beams, befall, bring, come (to pass unto), floor, [hap] was, happen (unto), meet, send good speed.

7137. קָרֶה **qâreh,** *kaw-reh´;* from 7136; an (unfortunate) *occurrence,* i.e. some accidental (ceremonial) *disqualification:*—uncleanness that chanceth.

קֹרָה **qôrâh.** See 6982.

7138. קָרוֹב **qârôwb,** *kaw-robe´;* or קָרֹב **qârôb,** *kaw-robe´;* from 7126; *near* (in place, kindred or time):—allied, approach, at hand, + any of kin, kinsfolk (-sman), (that is) near (of kin), neighbour, (that is) next, (them that come) nigh (at hand), more ready, short (-ly).

7139. קָרַח **qârach,** *kaw-rakh´;* a prim. root; to *depilate:*—make (self) bald.

7140. קֶרַח **qerach,** *keh´-rakh;* or קֹרַח **qôrach,** *ko´-rakh;* from 7139; *ice* (as if bald, i.e. *smooth*); hence, *hail;* by resemblance, rock *crystal:*—crystal, frost, ice.

7141. קֹרַח **Qôrach,** *ko´-rakh;* from 7139; *ice; Korach,* the name of two Edomites and three Isr.:—Korah.

7142. קֵרֵחַ **qêrêach,** *kay-ray´-akh;* from 7139; *bald* (on the back of the head):—bald (head).

7143. קָרֵחַ **Qârêach,** *kaw-ray´-akh;* from 7139; *bald; Kareäch;* an Isr.:—Careah, Kareah.

7144. קָרְחָה **qorchâh,** *kor-khaw´;* or קָרְחָא **qorchâ'** (Ezek. 27 : 31), *kor-khaw´;* from 7139; *baldness:*—bald (-ness), × utterly.

7145. קָרְחִי **Qorchîy,** *kor-khee´;* patron. from 7141; a *Korchite* (collect.) or desc. of Korach:—Korahite, Korathite, sons of Kore, Korhite.

7146. קָרַחַת **qârachath,** *kaw-rakh´-ath;* from 7139; a *bald* spot (on the back of the head); fig. a *threadbare* spot (on the back side of the cloth):—bald head, bare within.

7147. קְרִי **qᵉrîy,** *ker-ee´;* from 7136; hostile *encounter:*—contrary.

7148. קָרִיא **qârîy',** *kaw-ree´;* from 7121; *called,* i.e. *select:*—famous, renowned.

7149. קִרְיָא **qiryâ'** (Chald.), *keer-yaw´;* or קִרְיָה **qiryâh** (Chald.), *keer-yaw´;* corresp. to 7151:—city.

7150. קְרִיאָה **qᵉrîy'âh,** *ker-ee-aw´;* from 7121; a *proclamation:*—preaching.

7151. קִרְיָה **qiryâh,** *kir-yaw´;* from 7136 in the sense of *flooring,* i.e. building; a *city:*—city.

7152. קְרִיּוֹת **Qᵉrîyôwth,** *ker-ee-yōth´;* plur. of 7151; *buildings; Kerioth,* the name of two places in Pal.:—Kerioth, Kirioth.

7153. קִרְיַת אַרְבַּע **Qiryath 'Arba',** *keer-yath´ ar-bah´;* or (with the art. interposed) קִרְיַת הָאַרְבַּע **Qiryath hâ-'Arba'** (Neh. 11 : 25), *keer-yath´ haw-ar-bah´;* from 7151 and 704 or 702; *city of Arba,* or *city of the four* (giants); *Kirjath-Arba* or *Kirjath-ha-Arba,* a place in Pal.:—Kirjath-arba.

7154. קִרְיַת בַּעַל **Qiryath Ba'al,** *keer-yath´ bah´-al;* from 7151 and 1168; *city of Baal; Kirjath-Baal,* a place in Pal.:—Kirjath-baal.

7155. קִרְיַת חֻצוֹת **Qiryath Chûtsôwth,** *keer-yath´ khoo-tsōth´;* from 7151 and the fem. plur. of 2351; *city of streets; Kirjath-Chutsoth,* a place in Moab:—Kirjath-huzoth.

7156. קִרְיָתַיִם **Qiryâthayim,** *keer-yaw-thah´-yim;* dual of 7151; *double city; Kirjathaïm,* the name of two places in Pal.:—Kiriathaim, Kirjathaim.

7157. קִרְיַת יְעָרִים **Qiryath Yᵉ'ârîym,** *keer-yath´ yeh-aw-reem´;* or (Jer. 26 : 20) with the art. interposed; or (Josh. 18 : 28) simply the former part of the word; or קִרְיַת עָרִים **Qiryath 'Ârîym,** *keer-yath´ aw-reem´;* from 7151 and the plur. of 3293 or 5892; *city of forests,* or *city of towns; Kirjath-Jeärim* or *Kirjath-Arim,* a place in Pal.:—Kirjath, Kirjath-jearim, Kirjath-arim.

7158. קִרְיַת סַנָּה **Qiryath Çannâh,** *keer-yath´ san-naw´;* or קִרְיַת סֵפֶר **Qiryath Çêpher,** *keer-yath´ say´-fer;* from 7151 and a simpler fem. from the same as 5577, or (for the latter name) 5612; *city of branches,* or *of a book; Kirjath-Sannah* or *Kirjath-Sepher,* a place in Pal.—Kirjath-sannah, Kirjath-sepher.

7159. קָרַם **qâram,** *kaw-ram´;* a prim. root; to *cover:*—cover.

7160. קָרַן **qâran,** *kaw-ran´;* a prim. root; to *push* or gore; used only as denom. from 7161, to *shoot out horns;* fig. *rays:*—have horns, shine.

7161. קֶרֶן **qeren,** *keh´-ren;* from 7160; a *horn* (as *projecting*); by impl. a *flask, cornet;* by resembl. an elephant's *tooth* (i.e. *ivory*), a *corner* (of the altar), a *peak* (of a mountain), a *ray* (of light); fig. *power:*— × hill, horn.

7162. קֶרֶן **qeren** (Chald.), *keh´-ren;* corresp. to 7161; a *horn* (lit. or for sound):—horn, cornet.

7163. קֶרֶן הַפּוּךְ **qeren hap-pûwk,** *keh´-ren hap-pook´;* from 7161 and 6320; *horn of cosmetic; Keren-hap-Puk,* one of Job's daughters:—Keren-happuch.

7164. קָרַס **qâraç,** *kaw-ras´;* a prim. root; prop. to *protrude;* used only as denom. from 7165 (for alliteration with 7167), to *hunch,* i.e. be hump-backed:—stoop.

7165. קֶרֶס **qereç,** *keh´-res;* from 7164; a *knob* or belaying-pin (from its swelling form):—tache.

קֵרֹס **Qêrôç.** See 7026.

7166. קַרְסֹל **qarçôl,** *kar-sole´;* from 7164 an *ankle* (as a *protuberance* or joint):—foot.

7167. קָרַע **qâra',** *kaw-rah´;* a prim. root; to *rend,* lit. or fig. (*revile, paint* the eyes, as if enlarging them):—cut out, rend, × surely, tear.

7168. קֶרַע **qera',** *keh´-rah;* from 7167; a *rag:*—piece, rag.

7169. קָרַץ **qârats,** *kaw-rats´;* a prim. root; to *pinch,* i.e. (partially) to *bite* the lips, *blink* the eyes (as a gesture of malice), or (fully) to *squeeze* off (a piece of clay in order to mould a vessel from it):—form, move, wink.

7170. קְרַץ **qᵉrats** (Chald.), *ker-ats´;* corresp. to 7171 in the sense of a *bit* (to "eat the *morsels* of" any one, i.e. *chew* him up [fig.] by *slander*):— + accuse.

7171. קֶרֶץ **qerets,** *keh´-rets;* from 7169; *extirpation* (as if by *constriction*):—destruction.

7172. קַרְקַע **qarqa',** *kar-kah´;* from 7167; *floor* (as if a pavement of pieces or *tesseræ*), of a building or the sea:—bottom, (× one side of the) floor.

7173. קַרְקַע **Qarqa',** *kar-kah´;* the same as 7172; *ground-floor; Karka* (with the art. pref.), a place in Pal.:—Karkaa.

7174. קַרְקֹר **Qarqôr,** *kar-kore´;* from 6979; *foundation; Karkor,* a place E. of the Jordan:—Karkor.

7175. קֶרֶשׁ **qeresh,** *keh´-resh;* from an unused root mean. to *split* off; a *slab* or plank; by impl. a *deck* of a ship:—bench, board.

7176. קֶרֶת **qereth,** *keh´-reth;* from 7136 in the sense of building; a *city:*—city.

7177. קַרְתָּה **Qartâh,** *kar-taw´;* from 7176; *city; Kartah,* a place in Pal.:—Kartah.

7178. קַרְתָּן **Qartân,** *kar-tawn´;* from 7176; *city-plot; Kartan,* a place in Pal.:—Kartan.

7179. קַשׁ **qash,** *kash;* from 7197; *straw* (as *dry*):—stubble.

7180. קִשֻּׁא **qishshû',** *kish-shoo´;* from an unused root (mean. to be *hard*); a *cucumber* (from the difficulty of *digestion*):—cucumber.

7181. קָשַׁב **qâshab,** *kaw-shab´;* a prim. root; to *prick up* the ears, i.e. *hearken:*—attend, (cause to) hear (-ken), give heed, incline, mark (well), regard.

7182. קֶשֶׁב **qesheb,** *keh´-sheb;* from 7181; a *hearkening:*— × diligently, hearing, much heed, that regarded.

7183. קַשָּׁב **qashshâb,** *kash-shawb´;* or קַשֻּׁב **qashshûb,** *kash-shoob´;* from 7181; *hearkening:*—attent (-ive).

7184. קָשָׂה **qâsâh,** *kaw-saw´;* or קַשְׂוָה **qasvâh,** *kas-vaw´;* from an unused root mean. to be *round;* a *jug* (from its shape):—cover, cup.

7185. קָשָׁה **qâshâh,** *kaw-shaw´;* a prim. root; prop. to *be dense,* i.e. tough or *severe* (in various applications):—be cruel, be fiercer, make grievous, be ([ask a], be in, have, seem, would) hard (-en, [labour], -ly, thing), be sore, (be, make) stiff (-en, [-necked]).

7186. קָשֶׁה **qâsheh,** *kaw-sheh´;* from 7185; *severe* (in various applications):—churlish, cruel, grievous, hard ([-hearted], thing), heavy, + impudent, obstinate, prevailed, rough (-ly), sore, sorrowful, stiff ([-necked]), stubborn, + in trouble.

7187. קְשׁוֹט **qᵉshôwṭ** (Chald.), *kesh-ote´;* or קְשֹׁט **qᵉshôṭ** (Chald.), *kesh-ote´;* corresp. to 7189; *fidelity:*—truth.

7188. קָשַׁח **qâshach,** *kaw-shakh´;* a prim. root; to *be* (caus. *make*) *unfeeling:*—harden.

7189. קֹשֶׁט **qôsheṭ,** *ko´-shet;* or קֹשְׁט **qôshṭ,** *kōsht;* from an unused root mean. to *balance; equity* (as evenly *weighed*), i.e. *reality:*—certainty, truth.

קֹשֹׁט **qôshôṭ.** See 7187.

7190. קְשִׁי **qᵉshîy,** *kesh-ee´;* from 7185; *obstinacy:*—stubbornness.

7191. קִשְׁיוֹן **Qishyôwn,** *kish-yone´;* from 7190; *hard ground; Kishjon,* a place in Pal.:—Kishion, Keshon.

7192. קְשִׂיטָה **qᵉsîyṭah,** *kes-ee-taw´;* from an unused root (prob. mean. to *weigh* out); an *ingot* (as definitely *estimated* and stamped for a coin):—piece of money (silver).

7193. קַשְׂקֶשֶׂת **qasqeseth,** *kas-keh´-seth;* by redupl. from an unused root mean. to *shale* off as bark; a *scale* (of a fish); hence a coat of *mail* (as composed of or covered with jointed *plates* of metal):—mail, scale.

7194. קָשַׁר **qâshar,** *kaw-shar´;* a prim. root; to *tie,* phys. (*gird, confine, compact*) or ment. (in *love, league*):—bind (up), (make a) conspire (-acy, -ator), join together, knit, stronger, work [treason].

7195. קֶשֶׁר **qesher,** *keh´-sher;* from 7194; an (unlawful) *alliance:*—confederacy, conspiracy, treason.

7196. קִשֻּׁר **qishshûr,** *kish-shoor´;* from 7194; an (ornamental) *girdle* (for women):—attire, headband.

7197. קָשַׁשׁ **qâshash,** *kaw-shash´;* a prim. root; to *become sapless* through drought; used only as denom. from 7179; to *forage* for straw, stubble or wood; fig. to *assemble:*—gather (selves) (together).

7198. קֶשֶׁת **qesheth,** *keh´-sheth;* from 7185 in the orig. sense of (6983) of *bending;* a *bow,* for *shooting* (hence fig. *strength*) or the *iris:*— × arch (-er), + arrow, bow ([-man, -shot]).

7199. קַשָּׁת **qashshâth,** *kash-shawth´;* intens. (as denom.) from 7198; a *bowman:*— × archer.

ר

7200. רָאָה **râ'âh,** *raw-aw´;* a prim. root; to *see,* lit. or fig. (in numerous applications, direct and implied, trans., intrans. and causat.):—advise self, appear, approve, behold, × certainly, consider, discern, (make to) enjoy, have experience, gaze, take heed, × indeed, × joyfully, lo, look (on, one another, one on another, one upon another, out, up, upon), mark, meet, × be near, perceive, present, provide, regard, (have) respect, (fore-, cause to, let) see (-r, -m, one another), shew (self), × sight of others, (e-) spy, stare, × surely, × think, view, visions.

7201. רָאָה **râ'âh,** *raw-aw´;* from 7200; a *bird of* prey (prob. the *vulture,* from its sharp *sight*):—glede. Comp. 1676.

7202. רָאֶה **râ'eh,** *raw-eh´;* from 7200; *seeing,* i.e. experiencing:—see.

7203. רֹאֶה **rô'eh,** *ro-eh´;* act. part. of 7200; a *seer* (as often rendered); but also (abstr.) a *vision:*—vision.

7204. רֹאֵה **Rô'êh,** *ro-ay´;* for 7203; *prophet; Roëh,* an Isr.:—Haroeh [*includ. the art.*].

7205. רְאוּבֵן **Rᵉ'ûwbên,** *reh-oo-bane´;* from the imper. of 7200 and 1121; *see* ye a *son; Reüben,* a son of Jacob:—Reuben.

7206. רְאוּבֵנִי **Rᵉ'ûwbênîy,** *reh-oo-bay-nee´;* patron. from 7205; a *Reübenite* or desc. of Reüben:—children of Reuben, Reubenites.

7207. רַאֲוָה **ra'ăvâh,** *rah-av-aw´;* from 7200; *sight,* i.e. satisfaction:—behold.

7208. רְאוּמָה **Rᵉ'ûwmâh,** *reh-oo-maw´;* fem. pass. part. of 7213; *raised; Reümah,* a Syrian woman:—Reumah.

7209. רְאִי **rᵉ'îy,** *reh-ee´;* from 7200; a *mirror* (as *seen*):—looking glass.

7210. רֳאִי **rô'îy,** *ro-ee´;* from 7200; *sight,* whether abstr. (*vision*) or concr. (a *spectacle*):—gazingstock, look to, (that) see (-th).

7211. רְאָיָה **Rᵉ'âyâh,** *reh-aw-yaw´;* from 7200 and 3050; *Jah has seen; Reäjah,* the name of three Isr.:—Reaia, Reaiah.

7212. רְאִית° **rᵉ'îyth,** *reh-eeth´;* from 7200; *sight:*—beholding.

7213. רָאַם **râ'am,** *raw-am´;* a prim. root; to *rise:*—be lifted up.

7214. רְאֵם **rᵉ'êm,** *reh-ame´;* or רְאֵים **rᵉ'êym,** *reh-ame´;* or רֵים **rêym,** *rame;* or רֵם **rêm,** *rame;* from 7213; a wild *bull* (from its *conspicuousness*):—unicorn.

7215. רָאמָה **râ'mâh,** *raw-maw´;* from 7213; something *high* in value, i.e. perh. *coral:*—coral.

7216. רָאמוֹת **Râ'môwth,** *raw-mōth´;* or רָאמֹת **Râmôth,** *raw-mōth´;* plur. of 7215; *heights; Ramoth,* the name of two places in Pal.:—Ramoth.

7217. רֵאשׁ **rê'sh** (Chald.), *raysh;* corresp. to 7218; the *head;* fig. the *sum:*—chief, head, sum.

7218. רֹאשׁ **rô'sh,** *roshe;* from an unused root appar. mean. to *shake;* the *head* (as most easily *shaken*), whether lit. or fig. (in many applications, of place, time, rank, etc.):—band, beginning, captain, chapiter, chief (-est place, man, things), company, end, × every [man], excellent, first, forefront, ([be-]) head, height, (on) high (-est part, [priest]), × lead, × poor, principal, ruler, sum, top.

7219. רֹאשׁ **rô'sh,** *roshe;* or רוֹשׁ **rôwsh** (Deut. 32 : 32), *roshe;* appar. the same as 7218; a poisonous *plant,* prob. the *poppy* (from its conspicuous *head*); gen. *poison* (even of serpents):—gall, hemlock, posion, venom.

7220. רֹאשׁ **Rô'sh,** *roshe;* prob. the same as 7218; *Rosh,* the name of an Isr. and of a for. nation:—Rosh.

רֵאשׁ **rê'sh.** See 7389.

7221. רִאשָׁה **rî'shâh,** *ree-shaw´* from the same as 7218; a *beginning:*—beginning.

7222. רֹאשָׁה **rô'shâh,** *ro-shaw´;* fem. of 7218; the *head:*—head [-stone].

7223. רִאשׁוֹן **rî'shôwn,** *ree-shone´;* or רִאשֹׁן **rî'shôn,** *ree-shone´;* from 7221; *first,* in place, time or rank (as adj. or noun):—ancestor, (that were) before (-time), beginning, eldest, first, fore [-father] (-most), former (thing), of old time, past.

7224. רִאשֹׁנִי **rî'shônîy,** *ree-sho-nee´;* from 7223; *first:*—first.

7225. רֵאשִׁית **rê'shîyth,** *ray-sheeth´;* from the same as 7218; the *first,* in place, time, order or rank (spec. a *firstfruit*):—beginning, chief (-est), first (-fruits, part, time), principal thing.

7226. רַאֲשֹׁת **ra'ăshôth,** *rah-ash-ōth´;* from 7218; a *pillow* (being for the *head*):—bolster.

7227. רַב **rab,** *rab;* by contr. from 7231; *abundant* (in quantity, size, age, number, rank, quality):—(in) abound (-undance, -ant, -antly), captain, elder, enough, exceedingly, full, great (-ly, man, one), increase, long (enough, [time]), (do, have) many (-ifold, things, a time), ([ship-]) master, mighty, more, (too, very) much, multiply (-tude), officer, often [-times], plenteous, populous, prince, process [of time], suffice (-ient).

7228. רַב **rab,** *rab;* by contr. from 7232; an *archer* [or perh. the same as 7227]:—archer.

7229. רַב **rab** (Chald.), *rab;* corresp. to 7227:—captain, chief, great, lord, master, stout.

רִב **rîb.** See 7378.

7230. רֹב **rôb,** *robe;* from 7231; *abundance* (in any respect):—abundance (-antly), all, × common [sort], excellent, great (-ly, -ness, number), huge, be increased, long, many, more in number, most, much, multitude, plenty (-ifully), × very [age].

7231. רָבַב **râbab,** *raw-bab´;* a prim. root; prop. to *cast* together [comp. 7241], i.e. *increase,* espec. in number; also (as denom. from 7233) to *multiply by the myriad:*—increase, be many (-ifold), be more, multiply, ten thousands.

7232. רָבַב **râbab,** *raw-bab´;* a prim. root [rather ident. with 7231 through the idea of *projection*]; to *shoot* an arrow:—shoot.

7233. רְבָבָה **rᵉbâbâh,** *reb-aw-baw´;* from 7231; *abundance* (in number), i.e. (spec.) a *myriad* (whether def. or indef.):—many, million, × multiply, ten thousand.

7234. רָבַד **râbad,** *raw-bad´;* a prim. root; to *spread:*—deck.

7235. רָבָה **râbâh,** *raw-baw´;* a prim. root; to *increase* (in whatever respect):—[bring in] abundance (× -antly), + archer [*by mistake for* 7232], be in authority, bring up, × continue, enlarge, excel, exceeding (-ly), be full of, (be, make) great (-er, -ly, × -ness), grow up, heap, increase, be long, (be, give, have, make, use) many (a time), (any, be, give, give the, have) more (in number), (ask, be, be so, gather, over, take, yield) much (greater, more), (make to) multiply, nourish, plenty (-eous), × process [of time], sore, store, thoroughly, very.

7236. רְבָה **rᵉbâh** (Chald.), *reb-aw´;* corresp. to 7235:—make a great man, grow.

7237. רַבָּה **Rabbâh,** *rab-baw´;* fem. of 7227; *great; Rabbah,* the name of two places in Pal., E. and W.:—Rabbah, Rabbath.

7238. רְבוּ **rᵉbûw** (Chald.), *reb-oo´;* from a root corresp. to 7235; *increase* (of dignity):—greatness, majesty.

7239. רִבּוֹ **ribbôw,** *rib-bo´;* from 7231; or רִבּוֹא **ribbôw',** *rib-bo´;* from 7231; a *myriad,* i.e. indef. *large number:*—great things, ten ([eight] -een, [for] -ty, + sixscore, + threescore, × twenty, [twen] -ty) thousand.

7240. רִבּוֹ **ribbôw** (Chald.), *rib-bo´;* corresp. to 7239:— × ten thousand times ten thousand.

7241. רָבִיב **râbîyb,** *raw-beeb´;* from 7231; a *rain* (as an *accumulation* of drops):—shower.

7242. רָבִיד **râbîyd,** *raw-beed´;* from 7234; a *collar* (as *spread* around the neck):—chain.

7243. רְבִיעִי **rᵉbîyʻîy,** *reb-ee-ee´;* or רְבִעִי **rᵉbîʻîy,** *reb-ee-ee´;* from 7251; *fourth;* also (fractionally) a *fourth:*—four-square, fourth (part).

7244. רְבִיעַי **rᵉbîyʻay** (Chald.), *reb-ee-ah´ee;* corresp. to 7243:—fourth.

7245. רַבִּית **Rabbîyth,** *rab-beeth´;* from 7231; *multitude; Rabbith,* a place in Pal.:—Rabbith.

7246. רָבַךְ **râbak,** *raw-bak´;* a prim. root; to *soak* (bread in oil):—baken, (that which is) fried.

7247. רִבְלָה **Riblâh,** *rib-law´;* from an unused root mean. to *be fruitful; fertile; Riblah,* a place in Syria:—Riblah.

7248. רַב־מָג **Rab-Mâg,** *rab-mawg´;* from 7227 and a for. word for a Magian; *chief Magian; Rab-Mag,* a Bab. official:—Rab-mag.

7249. רַב־סָרִיס **Rab-Çârîyç,** *rab-saw-reece´;* from 7227 and a for. word for a eunuch; *chief chamberlain; Rab-Saris,* a Bab. official:—Rab-saris.

7250. רָבַע **râbaʻ,** *raw-bah´;* a prim. root; to *squat* or *lie* out flat, i.e. (spec.) in copulation:—let gender, lie down.

7251. רָבַע **râbaʻ,** *raw-bah´;* a prim. root; [rather ident. with 7250 through the idea of *sprawling* "at all fours" (or possibly the reverse is the order of deriv.); comp. 702]; prop. to *be four* (sided); used only as denom. of 7253; to *be quadrate:*—(four-) square (-d).

7252. רֶבַע **rebaʻ,** *reh´-bah;* from 7250; *prostration* (for sleep):—lying down.

7253. רֶבַע **rebaʻ,** *reh´-bah;* from 7251; a *fourth* (part or side):—fourth part, side, square.

7254. רֶבַע **Rebaʻ,** *reh´-bah;* the same as 7253; *Reba,* a Midianite:—Reba.

7255. רֹבַע **rôbaʻ,** *ro´-bah;* from 7251; a *quarter:*—fourth part.

7256. רִבֵּעַ **ribbêaʻ,** *rib-bay´-ah;* from 7251; a descendant of the *fourth* generation, i.e. *great great grandchild:*—fourth.

רְבִעִי **rᵉbîyʻîy.** See 7243.

7257. רָבַץ **râbats,** *raw-bats´;* a prim. root; to *crouch* (on all four legs folded, like a recumbent animal); by impl. to *recline, repose, brood, lurk, imbed:*—crouch (down), fall down, make a fold, lay (cause to, make to) lie (down), make to rest, sit.

7258. רֵבֶץ **rebets,** *reh´-bets;* from 7257; a *couch* or place of repose:—where each lay, lie down in, resting place.

7259. רִבְקָה **Ribqâh,** *rib-kaw´;* from an unused root prob. mean. to *clog* by tying up the fetlock; *fettering* (by beauty); *Ribkah,* the wife of Isaac:—Rebekah.

7260. רַבְרַב **rabrab** (Chald.), *rab-rab´;* from 7229; *huge* (in size); *domineering* (in character):—(very) great (things).

7261. רַבְרְבָן **rabrᵉbân** (Chald.), *rab-reb-awn´;* from 7260; a *magnate:*—lord, prince.

7262. רַבְשָׁקֵה **Rabshâqêh,** *rab-shaw-kay´;* from 7227 and 8248; *chief butler; Rabshakeh,* a Bab. official:—Rabshakeh.

7263. רֶגֶב **regeb,** *reh´-gheb;* from an unused root mean. to *pile* together; a *lump* of clay:—clod.

7264. רָגַז **râgaz,** *raw-gaz´;* a prim. root; to *quiver* (with any violent emotion, espec. anger or fear):—be afraid, stand in awe, disquiet, fall out, fret, move, provoke, quake, rage, shake, tremble, trouble, be wroth.

7265. רְגַז **rᵉgaz** (Chald.), *reg-az´;* corresp. to 7264:—provoke unto wrath.

7266. רְגַז **rᵉgaz** (Chald.), *reg-az´;* from 7265; violent *anger:*—rage.

7267. רֹגֶז **rôgez,** *ro´-ghez;* from 7264; *commotion, restlessness* (of a horse), *crash* (of thunder), *disquiet, anger:*—fear, noise, rage, trouble, (-ing), wrath.

7268. רַגָּז **raggâz,** *rag-gawz´;* intens. from 7264; *timid:*—trembling.

7269. רָגְזָה **rogzâh,** *rog-zaw´;* fem. of 7267; *trepidation:*—trembling.

7270. רָגַל **râgal,** *raw-gal´;* a prim. root; to *walk* along; but only in spec. applications, to *reconnoitre,* to *be a tale-bearer* (i.e. slander); also (as denom. from 7272) to *lead about:*—backbite, search, slander, (e-) spy (out), teach to go, view.

7271. רְגַל **rᵉgal** (Chald.), *reg-al´;* corresp. to 7272:—foot.

7272. רֶגֶל **regel,** *reh´-gel;* from 7270; a *foot* (as used in *walking*); by impl. a *step;* by euphem. the *pudenda:*— × be able to endure, × according as, × after, × coming, × follow, ([broken-]) foot ([-ed, -stool]), × great toe, × haunt, × journey, leg, + piss, + possession, time.

7273. רַגְלִי **raglîy,** *rag-lee´;* from 7272; a *footman* (soldier):—(on) foot (-man).

7274. רֹגְלִים **Rôgᵉlîym,** *ro-gel-eem´;* plur. of act. part. of 7270; *fullers* (as *tramping* the cloth in washing); *Rogelim,* a place E. of the Jordan:—Rogelim.

7275. רָגַם **râgam,** *raw-gam´;* a prim. root [comp. 7263, 7321, 7551]; to *cast* together (stones), i.e. to *lapidate:*— × certainly, stone.

7276. רֶגֶם **Regem,** *reh´-gem;* from 7275; stone-*heap; Regem,* an Isr.:—Regem.

7277. רִגְמָה **rigmâh,** *rig-maw´;* fem. of the same as 7276; a *pile* (of stones), i.e. (fig.) a *throng:*—council.

7278. רֶגֶם מֶלֶךְ **Regem Melek,** *reh´-gem meh´-lek;* from 7276 and 4428; *king's heap; Regem-Melek,* an Isr.:—Regem-melech.

7279. רָגַן **râgan,** *raw-gan´;* a prim. root; to *grumble,* i.e. *rebel:*—murmur.

7280. רָגַע **râgaʻ,** *raw-gah´;* a prim. root; prop. to *toss* violently and suddenly (the sea with waves, the skin with boils); fig. (in a faborable manner) to *settle,* i.e. quiet; spec. to *wink* (from the motion of the eye-lids):—break, divide, find ease, be a moment, (cause, give, make to) rest, make suddenly.

7281. רֶגַע **regaʻ,** *reh´-gah;* from 7280; a *wink* (of the eyes), i.e. a very *short space* of time:—instant, moment, space, suddenly.

7282. רָגֵעַ **râgêaʻ,** *raw-gay´-ah;* from 7280; *restful,* i.e. peaceable:—that are quiet.

7283. רָגַשׁ **râgash,** *raw-gash´;* a prim. root; to *be tumultuous:*—rage.

7284. רְגַשׁ **rᵉgash** (Chald.), *reg-ash´;* corresp. to 7283; to *gather* tumultuously:—assemble (together).

7285. רֶגֶשׁ **regesh,** *reh´-ghesh;* or (fem.) רִגְשָׁה **rigshâh,** *rig-shaw´;* from 7283; a tumultuous *crowd:*—company, insurrection.

7286. רָדַד **râdad,** *raw-dad´;* a prim. root; to *tread* in pieces, i.e. (fig.) to *conquer,* or (spec.) to *overlay:*—spend, spread, subdue.

7287. רָדָה **râdâh,** *raw-daw´;* a prim. root; to *tread* down, i.e. *subjugate;* spec. to *crumble* off:—(come to, make to) have dominion, prevail against, reign, (bear, make to) rule, (-r, over), take.

7288. רַדַּי **Radday,** *rad-dah´ee;* intens. from 7287; *domineering; Raddai,* an Isr.:—Raddai.

7289. רָדִיד **râdîyd,** *raw-deed´;* from 7286 in the sense of *spreading;* a *veil* (as expanded):—vail, veil.

7290. רָדַם **râdam,** *raw-dam´;* a prim. root; to *stun,* i.e. *stupefy* (with sleep or death):—(be fast a-, be in a deep, cast into a dead, that) sleep (-er, -eth).

7291. רָדַף **râdaph,** *raw-daf´;* a prim. root; to *run after* (usually with hostile intent; fig. [of time] *gone by*):—chase, put to flight, follow (after, on), hunt, (be under) persecute (-ion, -or), pursue (-r).

7292. רָהַב **râhab,** *raw-hab´;* a prim. root; to *urge* severely, i.e. (fig.) *importune, embolden, capture, act insolently:*—overcome, behave self proudly, make sure, strengthen.

7293. רַהַב **rahab,** *rah´-hab;* from 7292; *bluster* (*-er*):—proud, strength.

7294. רַהַב **Rahab,** *rah´-hab;* the same as 7293; *Rahab* (i.e. *boaster*), an epithet of Egypt:—Rahab.

7295. רָהָב **râhâb,** *raw-hawb´;* from 7292; *insolent:*—proud.

7296. רֹהַב **rôhab,** *ro´-hab;* from 7292; *pride:*—strength.

7297. רָהָה **râhâh,** *raw-haw´;* a prim. root; to *fear:*—be afraid.

7298. רַהַט **rahaṭ,** *rah´-hat;* from an unused root appar. mean. to *hollow out; a channel* or watering-box; by resemblance a *ringlet* of hair (as forming parallel lines):—gallery, gutter, trough.

7299. רֵו **rêv** (Chald.), *rave;* from a root corresp. to 7200; *aspect:*—form.

רוּב° **rûwb.** See 7378.

7300. רוּד **rûwd,** *rood;* a prim. root; to *tramp* about, i.e. *ramble* (free or disconsolate):—have the dominion, be lord, mourn, rule.

7301. רָוָה **râvâh,** *raw-vaw´;* a prim. root; to *slake* the thirst (occasionally of other appetites):—bathe, make drunk, (take the) fill, satiate, (abundantly) satisfy, soak, water (abundantly).

7302. רָוֶה **râveh,** *raw-veh´;* from 7301; *sated* (with drink):—drunkenness, watered.

7303. רוֹהֲגָה° **Rôwhăgâh,** *ro-hag-aw´;* from an unused root prob. mean. to *cry* out; *outcry; Rohagah,* an Isr.:—Rohgah.

7304. רָוַח **râvach,** *raw-vakh´;* a prim. root [rather ident. with 7306]; prop. to *breathe* freely, i.e. *revive;* by impl. to *have ample room:*—be refreshed, large.

7305. רֶוַח **revach,** *reh´-vakh;* from 7304; *room,* lit. (an *interval*) or fig. (*deliverance*):—enlargement, space.

7306. רוּחַ **rûwach,** *roo´-akh;* a prim. root; prop. to *blow,* i.e. *breathe;* only (lit.) to *smell* or (by impl. *perceive* (fig. to *anticipate, enjoy*):—accept, smell, × touch, make of quick understanding.

7307. רוּחַ **rûwach,** *roo´-akh;* from 7306; *wind;* by resemblance *breath,* i.e. a sensible (or even violent) exhalation; fig. *life, anger, unsubstantiality;* by extens. a *region* of the sky; by resemblance *spirit,* but only of a rational being (includ. its expression and functions):—air, anger, blast, breath, × cool, courage, mind, × quarter, × side, spirit ([-ual]), tempest, × vain, ([whirl-]) wind (-y).

7308. רוּחַ **rûwach** (Chald.), *roo´-akh;* corresp. to 7307:—mind, spirit, wind.

7309. רְוָחָה **rᵉvâchâh,** *rev-aw-khaw´;* fem. of 7305; *relief:*—breathing, respite.

7310. רְוָיָה **rᵉvâyâh,** *rev-aw-yaw´;* from 7301; *satisfaction:*—runneth over, wealthy.

7311. רוּם **rûwm,** *room;* a prim. root; to *be high* act. to *rise* or *raise* (in various applications, lit. or fig.):—bring up, exalt (self), extol, give, go up, haughty, heave (up), (be, lift up on, make on, set up on, too) high (-er, one), hold up, levy, lift (-er) up, (be) lofty, (× a-) loud, mount up, offer (up), + presumptuously, (be) promote (-ion), proud, set up, tall (-er), take (away, off, up), breed worms.

7312. רוּם **rûwm,** *room;* or רֻם **rûm,** *room;* from 7311; (lit), *elevation* or (fig.) *elation:*—haughtiness, height, × high.

7313. רוּם **rûwm** (Chald.), *room;* corresp. to 7311; (fig. only):—extol, lift up (self), set up.

7314. רוּם **rûwm** (Chald.), *room;* from 7313; (lit.) *altitude:*—height.

7315. רוֹם **rôwm,** *rome;* from 7311; *elevation,* i.e. (adv.) *aloft:*—on high.

7316. רוּמָה **Rûwmâh,** *roo-maw´;* from 7311; *height; Rumah,* a place in Pal.:—Rumah.

7317. רוֹמָה **rôwmâh,** *ro-maw´;* fem. of 7315; *elation,* i.e. (adv.) *proudly:*—haughtily.

7318. רוֹמָם **rôwmâm,** *ro-mawm´;* from 7426; *exaltation,* i.e. (fig. and spec.) *praise:*—be extolled.

7319. רוֹמְמָה **rôwmᵉmâh,** *ro-mem-aw´;* fem. act. part. of 7426; *exaltation,* i.e. *praise:*—high.

7320. רוֹמַמְתִּי עֶזֶר **Rôwmamtîy ʻEzer** (or רֹמַמְתִּי **Rômamtîy**), *ro-mam´-tee eh´-zer;* from 7311 and 5828; *I have raised* up a help; *Romamti-Ezer,* an Isr.:—Romamti-ezer.

7321. רוּעַ **rûwaʻ,** *roo-ah´;* a prim. root; to *mar* (espec. by breaking); fig. to *split* the ears (with sound), i.e. *shout* (for alarm or joy):—blow an alarm, cry (alarm, aloud, out), destroy, make a joyful noise, smart, shout (for joy), sound an alarm, triumph.

7322. רוּף **rûwph,** *roof;* a prim. root; prop. to *triturate* (in a mortar), i.e. (fig.) to *agitate* (by concussion):—tremble.

7323. רוּץ **rûwts,** *roots;* a prim. root; to *run* (for whatever reason, espec. to *rush*):—break down, divide speedily, footman, guard, bring hastily, (make) run (away, through), post, stretch out.

7324. רוּק **rûwq,** *rook;* a prim. root; to *pour* out (lit. or fig.), i.e. *empty:*— × arm, cast out, draw (out), (make) empty, pour forth (out).

7325. רוּר **rûwr,** *roor;* a prim. root; to *slaver* (with spittle), i.e. (by analogy) to *emit* a fluid (ulcerous or natural):—run.

7326. רוּשׁ **rûwsh,** *roosh;* a prim. root; to *be destitute:*—lack, needy, (make self) poor (man).

רוֹשׁ **rôwsh.** See 7219.

7327. רוּת **Rûwth,** *rooth;* prob. for 7468; *friend; Ruth,* a Moabitess:—Ruth.

7328. רָז **râz** (Chald.), *rawz;* from an unused root prob. mean. to *attenuate,* i.e. (fig.) *hide;* a *mystery:*—secret.

7329. רָזָה **râzâh,** *raw-zaw´;* a prim. root; to *emaciate,* i.e. *make* (*become*) *thin* (lit. or fig.):—famish, wax lean.

7330. רָזֶה **râzeh,** *raw-zeh´;* from 7329; *thin:*—lean.

7331. רְזוֹן **Rᵉzôwn,** *rez-one´;* from 7336; *prince; Rezon;* a Syrian:—Rezon.

7332. רָזוֹן **râzôwn,** *raw-zone´;* from 7329; *thinness:*—leanness, × scant.

7333. רָזוֹן **râzôwn,** *raw-zone´;* from 7336; a *dignitary:*—prince.

7334. רָזִי **râzîy,** *raw-zee;* from 7329; *thinness:*—leanness.

7335. רָזַם **râzam,** *raw-zam´;* a prim. root; to *twinkle* the eye (in mockery):—wink.

7336. רָזַן **râzan,** *raw-zan´;* a prim. root; prob. to be *heavy,* i.e. (fig.) *honorable:*—prince, ruler.

7337. רָחַב **râchab,** *raw-khab´;* a prim. root; to *broaden* (intrans. or trans., lit. or fig.):—be an en- (make) large (-ing), make room, make (open) wide.

7338. רַחַב **rachab,** *rakh´-ab;* from 7337; a *width:*—breadth, broad place.

7339. רְחֹב **rᵉchôb,** *rekh-obe´;* or רְחוֹב **rᵉchôwb,** *rekh-obe´;* from 7337; a *width,* i.e. (concr.) *avenue* or *area:*—broad place (way), street. See also 1050.

7340. רְחֹב **Rᵉchôb,** *rekh-obe´;* or רְחוֹב **Rᵉchôwb,** *rekh-obe´;* the same as 7339; *Rechob,* the name of a place in Syria, also of a Syrian and an Isr.:—Rehob.

7341. רֹחַב **rôchab,** *ro´-khab;* from 7337; *width* (lit. or fig.):—breadth, broad, largeness, thickness, wideness.

7342. רָחָב **râchâb,** *raw-khab´;* from 7337; *roomy,* in any (or every) direction, lit. or fig.:—broad, large, at liberty, proud, wide.

7343. רָחָב **Râchâb,** *raw-khawb´;* the same as 7342; *proud; Rachab,* a Canaanitess:—Rahab.

7344. רְחֹבוֹת **Rᵉchôbôwth,** *rekh-o-bōth´;* or רְחֹבֹת **Rᵉchôbôth,** *rekh-o-bōth´;* plur. of 7339; *streets; Rechoboth,* a place in Assyria and one in Pal.:—Rehoboth.

7345. רְחַבְיָה **Rᵉchabyâh,** *rekh-ab-yaw´; or* רְחַבְיָהוּ **Rᵉchabyâhûw,** *rekh-ab-yaw´-hoo;* from 7337 and 3050; *Jah has enlarged; Rechabjah,* an Isr.:—Rehabiah.

7346. רְחַבְעָם **Rᵉchabʻâm,** *rekh-ab-awm´;* from 7337 and 5971; a *people has enlarged; Rechabam,* an Isr. king:—Rehoboam.

רְחֹבֹת **Rᵉchôbôth.** See 7344.

7347. רֵחֶה **rêcheh,** *ray-kheh´;* from an unused root mean. to *pulverize;* a *mill*-stone:—mill (stone).

רְחוֹב **Rᵉchôwb.** See 7339, 7340.

7348. רְחוּם **Rᵉchûwm,** *rekh-oom´;* a form of 7349; *Rechum,* the name of a Pers. and of three Isr.:—Rehum.

7349. רַחוּם **rachûwm,** *rakh-oom´;* from 7355; *compassionate:*—full of compassion, merciful.

7350. רָחוֹק **râchôwq,** *raw-khoke´;* or רָחֹק **râchôq,** *raw-khoke´;* from 7368; *remote,* lit. or fig., of place or time; spec. *precious;* often used adv. (with prep.):—(a-) far (abroad, off), long ago, of old, space, great while to come.

7351. רְחִיט° **rᵉchîyṭ,** *rekh-eet´;* from the same as 7298; a *panel* (as resembling a *trough*):—rafter.

7352. רַחִיק **rachîyq** (Chald.), *rakh-eek´;* corresp. to 7350:—far.

7353. רָחֵל **râchêl,** *raw-kale´;* from an unused root mean. to *journey;* a *ewe* [the *females* being the predominant element of a flock] (as a good *traveller*):—ewe, sheep.

7354. רָחֵל **Râchêl,** *raw-khale´;* the same as 7353; *Rachel,* a wife of Jacob:—Rachel.

7355. רָחַם **râcham,** *raw-kham´;* a prim. root; to *fondle;* by impl. to *love,* espec. to *compassionate:*—have compassion (on, upon), love, (find, have, obtain, shew) mercy (-iful, on, upon), (have) pity, Ruhamah, × surely.

7356. רַחַם **racham,** *rakh´-am;* from 7355; *compassion* (in the plur.); by extens. the *womb* (as *cherishing* the fœtus); by impl. a *maiden:*—bowels, compassion, damsel, tender love, (great, tender) mercy, pity, womb.

7357. רַחַם **Racham,** *rakh´-am;* the same as 7856; *pity; Racham,* an Isr.:—Raham.

7358. רֶחֶם **rechem,** *rekh´-em;* from 7355; the *womb* [comp. 7356]:—matrix, womb.

7359. רְחֵם **rᵉchêm** (Chald.), *rekh-ame´;* corresp. to 7356; (plur.) *pity:*—mercy.

7360. רָחָם **râchâm,** *raw-khawm´;* or (fem.) רָחָמָה **râchâmâh,** *raw-khaw-maw´;* from 7355; a kind of *vulture* (supposed to be *tender* towards its young):—gier-eagle.

7361. רַחֲמָה **rachămâh,** *rakh-am-aw´;* fem. of 7356; a *maiden:*—damsel.

7362. רַחְמָנִי **rachmânîy,** *rakh-maw-nee´;* from 7355; *compassionate:*—pitiful.

7363. רָחַף **râchaph,** *raw-khaf´;* a prim. root; to *brood,* by impl. to *be relaxed:*—flutter, move, shake.

7364. רָחַץ **râchats,** *raw-khats´;* a prim. root; to *lave* (the whole or a part of a thing):—bathe (self), wash (self).

7365. רְחַץ **rᵉchats** (Chald.), *rekh-ats´;* corresp. to 7364 [prob. through the accessory idea of *ministering* as a servant at the bath]; to *attend* upon:—trust.

7366. רַחַץ **rachats,** *rakh´-ats;* from 7364; a *bath:*—wash [-pot].

7367. רַחְצָה **rachtsâh,** *rakh-tsaw´;* fem. of 7366; a *bathing*-place:—washing.

7368. רָחַק **râchaq,** *raw-khak´;* a prim. root; to *widen* (in any [direction), i.e. (intrans.) *recede* or (trans.) *remove* (lit. or fig., of place or relation):—(a, be, cast, drive, get, go, keep [self], put, remove, be too, [wander], withdraw) far (away, off), loose, × refrain, very, (be) a good way (off).

7369. רָחֵק **râchêq,** *raw-khake´;* from 7368; *remote:*—that are far.

רָחֹק **râchôq.** See 7350.

7370. רָחַשׁ **râchash,** *raw-khash´;* a prim. root; to *gush:*—indite.

7371. רַחַת **rachath,** *rakh´-ath;* from 7306; a *winnowing*-fork (as *blowing* the chaff away):—shovel.

7372. רָטַב **râṭab,** *raw-tab´;* a prim. root; to *be moist:*—be wet.

7373. רָטֹב **râṭôb,** *raw-tobe´;* from 7372; *moist* (with sap):—green.

7374. רֶטֶט **reṭeṭ,** *reh´-tet;* from an unused root mean. to *tremble; terror:*—fear.

7375. רֻטֲפַשׁ **rûwṭăphash,** *roo-taf-ash´;* a root compounded from 7373 and 2954; to *be rejuvenated:*—be fresh.

7376. רָטַשׁ **râṭash,** *raw-tash´;* a prim. root; to *dash* down:—dash (in pieces).

7377. רִי **rîy,** *ree;* from 7301; *irrigation,* i.e. a shower:—watering.

7378. רִיב **rîyb,** *reeb;* or רוּב° **rûwb,** *roob;* a prim. root; prop. to *toss,* i.e. *grapple;* mostly fig. to *wrangle,* i.e. *hold a controversy;* (by impl.) to *defend:*—adversary, chide, complain, contend, debate, × ever, × lay wait, plead, rebuke, strive, × thoroughly.

7379. רִיב **rîyb,** *reeb;* or רִב **rib,** *reeb;* from 7378; a *contest* (personal or legal):— + adversary, cause, chiding, contend (-tion), controversy, multitude [*from the marg.*], pleading, strife, strive (-ing), suit.

7380. רִיבַי **Rîybay,** *ree-bah´ee;* from 7378; *contentious; Ribai,* an Isr.:—Ribai.

7381. רֵיחַ **rêyach,** *ray´-akh;* from 7306; *odor* (as if *blown*):—savour, scent, smell.

7382. רֵיחַ **rêyach** (Chald.), *ray´-akh;* corresp. to 7381:—smell.

רֵים **rêym.** See 7214.

רֵיעַ **rêyaʻ.** See 7453.

7383. רִיפָה **rîyphâh,** *ree-faw´;* or רִפָה **rîphâh,** *ree-faw´;* from 7322; (only plur.), *grits* (as *pounded*):—ground corn, wheat.

7384. רִיפַת **Rîyphath,** *ree-fath´;* or (prob. by orth. error)

דִּיפַת **Dîyphath,** *dee-fath´;* of for. or.; *Riphath,* a grandson of Japheth and his desc.:—Riphath.

7385. רִיק **rîyq,** *reek;* from 7324; *emptiness;* fig. a *worthless* thing; adv. *in vain:*—empty, to no purpose, (in) vain (thing), vanity.

7386. רֵיק **rêyq,** *rake;* or (shorter) רֵק **rêq,** *rake;* from 7324; *empty;* fig. *worthless:*—emptied (-ty), vain (fellow, man).

7387. רֵיקָם **rêyqâm,** *ray-kawm´;* from 7386; *emptily;* fig. (obj.) *ineffectually,* (subj.) *undeservedly:*—without cause, empty, in vain, void.

7388. רִיר **rîyr,** *reer;* from 7325; *saliva;* by resemblance *broth:*—spittle, white [of an egg].

7389. רֵישׁ **rêysh,** *raysh;* or רֵאשׁ **rê'sh,** *raysh;* or רִישׁ **rîysh,** *reesh;* from 7326; *poverty:*—poverty.

7390. רַךְ **rak,** *rak;* from 7401; *tender* (lit. or fig.); by impl. *weak:*—faint [-hearted], soft, tender ([-hearted], one), weak.

7391. רֹךְ **rôk,** *roke;* from 7401; *softness* (fig.):—tenderness.

7392. רָכַב **râkab,** *raw-kab´;* a prim. root; to *ride* (on an animal or in a vehicle); caus. to *place upon* (for riding or gen), to *despatch:*—bring (on [horse-] back), carry, get [oneself] up, on [horse-] back, put, (cause to, make to) ride (in a chariot, on, -r), set.

7393. רֶכֶב **rekeb,** *reh´-keb;* from 7392; a *vehicle;* by impl. a *team;* by extens. *cavalry;* by analogy a *rider,* i.e. the upper millstone:—chariot, (upper) millstone, multitude [*from the marg.*], wagon.

7394. רֵכָב **Rêkâb,** *ray-kawb´;* from 7392; *rider; Rekab,* the name of two Arabs and of two Isr.:—Rechab.

7395. רַכָּב **rakkâb,** *rak-kawb´;* from 7392; a *charioteer:*—chariot man, driver of a chariot, horseman.

7396. רִכְבָה **rikbâh,** *rik-baw´;* fem. of 7393; a *chariot* (collect.):—chariots.

7397. רֵכָה **Rêkâh,** *ray-kaw´;* prob. fem. from 7401; *softness; Rekah,* a place in Pal.:—Rechah.

7398. רְכוּב **rᵉkûwb,** *rek-oob´;* from pass. part. of 7392; a *vehicle* (as *ridden* on):—chariot.

7399. רְכוּשׁ **rᵉkûwsh,** *rek-oosh´;* or רְכֻשׁ **rᵉkûsh,** *rek-oosh´;* from pass. part. of 7408; *property* (as *gathered*):—good, riches, substance.

7400. רָכִיל **râkîyl,** *raw-keel´;* from 7402; a *scandal-monger* (as *travelling* about):—slander, carry tales, talebearer.

7401. רָכַךְ **râkak,** *raw-kak´;* a prim. root; to *soften* (intrans. or trans.), used fig.:—(be) faint ([-hearted]), mollify, (be, make) soft (-er), be tender.

7402. רָכַל **râkal,** *raw-kal´;* a prim. root; to *travel* for trading:—(spice) merchant.

7403. רָכָל **Râkâl,** *raw-kawl´;* from 7402; *merchant; Rakal,* a place in Pal.:—Rachal.

7404. רְכֻלָּה **rᵉkullâh,** *rek-ool-law´;* fem. pass. part. of 7402; *trade* (as *peddled*):—merchandise, traffic.

7405. רָכַס **râkaç,** *raw-kas´;* a prim. root; to *tie:*—bind.

7406. רֶכֶס **rekeç,** *reh´-kes;* from 7405; a mountain *ridge* (as of *tied* summits):—rough place.

7407. רֹכֶס **rôkeç,** *ro´-kes;* from 7405; a *snare* (as of *tied* meshes):—pride.

7408. רָכַשׁ **râkash,** *raw-kash´;* a prim. root; to *lay up,* i.e. collect:—gather, get.

7409. רֶכֶשׁ **rᵉkesh,** *reh´-kesh;* from 7408; a *relay* of animals on a post-route (as *stored* up for that purpose); by impl. a *courser:*—dromedary, mule, swift beast.

רְכֻשׁ **rᵉkûsh.** See 7399.

רֵם **rêm.** See 7214.

7410. רָם **Râm,** *rawm;* act. part. of 7311; *high; Ram,* the name of an Arabian and of an Isr.:—Ram. See also 1027.

רֻם **rûm.** See 7311.

7411. רָמָה **râmâh,** *raw-maw´;* a prim. root; to *hurl; spec. to shoot;* fig. to *delude* or *betray* (as if causing to fall):—beguile, betray, [bow-] man, carry, deceive, throw.

7412. רְמָה **rᵉmâh** (Chald.), *rem-aw´;* corresp. to 7411; to *throw, set,* (fig.) *assess:*—cast (down), impose.

7413. רָמָה **râmâh,** *raw-maw´;* fem. act. part. of 7311; a *height* (as a seat of idolatry):—high place.

7414. רָמָה **Râmâh,** *raw-maw´;* the same as 7413; *Ramah,* the name of four places in Pal.:—Ramah.

7415. רִמָּה **rimmâh,** *rim-maw´;* from 7426 in the sense of *breeding* [comp. 7311]; a *maggot* (as rapidly *bred*), lit. or fig.:—worm.

7416. רִמּוֹן **rimmôwn,** *rim-mone´;* or רִמֹּן **rimmôn,** *rim-mone´;* from 7426; a *pomegranate,* the tree (from its *upright* growth) or the fruit (also an artificial ornament):—pomegranate.

7417. רִמּוֹן **Rimmôwn,** *rim-mone´;* or (shorter) רִמֹּן **Rimmôn,** *rim-mone´;* or רִמּוֹנוֹ **Rimmôwnôw** (1 Chron. 6 : 62 [77]), *rim-mo-no´;* the same as 7416; *Rimmon,* the name of a Syrian deity, also of five places in Pal:—Remmon, Rimmon. The addition "-methoar" (Josh 19 : 13) is הַמְּתֹאָר **ham-mᵉthô'âr,** *ham-meth-o-awr´;* pass. part. of 8388 with the art.; *the* (one) *marked off,* i.e. *which pertains;* mistaken for part of the name.

רָמוֹת **Râmôwth.** See 7418, 7433.

7418. רָמוֹת־נֶגֶב **Râmôwth-Negeb,** *raw-mōth-neh´-gheb;* or רָמַת נֶגֶב **Râmath Negeb,** *raw´-math neh´-gheb;* from the plur. or construct. of 7413 and 5045; *heights* (or *height*) *of* the *South: Ramoth-Negeb* or *Ramath-Nebeg,* a place in Pal.:—south Ramoth, Ramath of the south.

7419. רָמוּת **râmûwth,** *raw-mooth´;* from 7311; a *heap* (of carcases):—height.

7420. רֹמַח **rômach,** *ro´-makh;* from an unused root mean. to *hurl;* a *lance* (as *thrown*); espec. the iron *point:*—buckler, javelin, lancet, spear.

7421. רַמִּי **rammîy,** *ram-mee´;* for 761; a *Ramite,* i.e. Aramæan:—Syrian.

7422. רַמְיָה **Ramyâh,** *ram-yaw´;* from 7311 and 3050; *Jah has raised; Ramjah,* an Isr.:—Ramiah.

7423. רְמִיָּה **rᵉmîyâh,** *rem-ee-yaw´;* from 7411; *remissness, treachery:*—deceit (-ful, -fully), false, guile, idle, slack, slothful.

7424. רַמָּךְ **rammâk,** *ram-mawk´;* of for. or.; a brood *mare:*—dromedary.

7425. רְמַלְיָהוּ **Rᵉmalyâhûw,** *rem-al-yaw´-hoo;* from an unused root and 3050 (perh. mean. to *deck*); *Jah has bedecked; Remaljah,* an Isr.:—Remaliah.

7426. רָמַם **râmam,** *raw-mam´;* a prim. root; to *rise* (lit. or fig.):—exalt, get [oneself] up, lift up (self), mount up.

7427. רֹמֵמֻת **rômêmûth,** *ro-may-mooth´;* from the act. part. of 7426; *exaltation:*—lifting up of self.

רִמֹּן **rimmôn.** See 7416.

7428. רִמֹּן פֶּרֶץ **Rimmôn Perets,** *rim-mone´ peh´-rets;* from 7416 and 6556; *pomegranate of the breach; Rimmon-Perets,* a place in the Desert:—Rimmon-parez.

7429. רָמַס **râmaç,** *raw-mas´;* a prim. root; to *tread* upon (as a potter, in walking or abusively):—oppressor, stamp upon, trample (under feet), tread (down, upon).

7430. רָמַשׂ **râmas,** *raw-mas`;* a prim. root; prop. to *glide* swiftly, i.e. to *crawl* or *move* with short steps; by analogy to *swarm:*—creep, move.

7431. רֶמֶשׂ **remes,** *reh´-mes;* from 7430; a *reptile* or any other rapidly moving animal:—that creepeth, creeping (moving) thing.

7432. רֶמֶת **Remeth,** *reh´-meth;* from 7411; *height; Remeth,* a place in Pal.:—Remeth.

7433. רָמֹת (or רָמוֹת **Râmôwth**) גִּלְעָד **Râmôth Gil'âd** (2 Chron. 22 : 5), *raw-mōth´ gil-awd´;* from the plur. of 7413 and 1568; *heights of Gilad, Ramoth-Gilad,* a place E. of the Jordan:—Ramoth-gilead, Ramoth in Gilead. See also 7216.

7434. רָמַת הַמִּצְפֶּה **Râmath ham-Mits-peh,** *raw-math´; ham-mits-peh´;* from 7413 and 4707 with the art. inter.; *height of the watch*-tower; *Ramath-ham-Mitspeh,* a place in Pal.:—Ramath-mizpeh.

7435. רָמָתִי **Râmâthîy,** *raw-maw-thee´;* patron. of 7414; a *Ramathite* or inhab. of Ramah:—Ramathite.

7436. רָמָתַיִם צוֹפִים **Râmâthayim Tsôwphîym,** *raw-maw-thah´-yim tso-feem´;* from the dual of 7413 and the plur. of the act. part. of 6822; *double height of watchers; Ramathajim-Tsophim,* a place in Pal.:—Ramathaim-zophim.

7437. רָמַת לֶחִי **Râmath Lechîy,** *raw´-math lekh´-ee;* from 7413 and 3895; *height of a jaw-bone; Ramath-Lechi,* a place in Pal.:—Ramath-lehi.

רָן **Rân.** See 1028.

7438. רֹן **rôn,** *rone;* from 7442; a *shout* (of deliverance):—song.

7439. רָנָה **rânâh,** *raw-naw´;* a prim. root; to *whiz:*—rattle.

7440. רִנָּה **rinnâh,** *rin-naw´;* from 7442; prop. a *creaking* (or shrill sound), i.e. *shout* (of joy or grief):—cry, gladness, joy, proclamation, rejoicing, shouting, sing (-ing), triumph.

7441. רִנָּה **Rinnâh,** *rin-naw´;* the same as 7440; *Rinnah,* an Isr.:—Rinnah.

7442. רָנַן **rânan,** *raw-nan´;* a prim. root; prop. to *creak* (or emit a stridulous sound), i.e. to *shout* (usually for joy):—aloud for joy, cry out, be joyful, (greatly, make to) rejoice, (cause to) shout (for joy), (cause to) sing (aloud, for joy, out), triumph.

7443. רֶנֶן **renen,** *reh´-nen;* from 7442; an *ostrich* (from its *wail*):— × goodly.

7444. רַנֵּן **rannên,** *ran-nane´;* intens. from 7442; *shouting* (for joy):—singing.

7445. רְנָנָה **rᵉnânâh,** *ren-aw-naw´;* from 7442; a *shout* (for joy):—joyful (voice), singing, triumphing.

7446. רִסָּה **Riççâh,** *ris-saw´;* from 7450; a *ruin* (as *dripping* to pieces); *Rissah,* a place in the Desert:—Rissah.

7447. רָסִיס **râçîyç,** *raw-sees´;* from 7450; prop. *dripping* to pieces, i.e. a *ruin;* also a dew-*drop:*—breach, drop.

7448. רֶסֶן **reçen,** *reh´-sen;* from an unused root mean. to *curb;* a *halter* (as *restraining*); by impl. the *jaw:*—bridle.

7449. רֶסֶן **Reçen,** *reh´-sen;* the same as 7448; *Resen,* a place in Ass.:—Resen.

7450. רָסַס **râçaç,** *raw-sas´;* a prim. root; to *comminute;* used only as denom. from 7447, to *moisten* (with drops):—temper.

7451. רַע **ra',** *rah;* from 7489; *bad* or (as noun) *evil* (nat. or mor.):—adversity, affliction, bad, calamity, + displease (-ure), distress, evil ([-favouredness], man, thing), + exceedingly, × great, grief (-vous), harm, heavy, hurt (-ful), ill (favoured), + mark, mischief, (-vous), misery, naught (-ty), noisome, + not please, sad (-ly), sore, sorrow, trouble, vex, wicked (-ly, -ness, one), worse (-st) wretchedness, wrong. [Incl. fem. רָעָה **râ'âh;** as adj. or noun.]

7452. רֵעַ **rêa',** *ray´-ah;* from 7321; a *crash* (of thunder), *noise* (of war), *shout* (of joy):— × aloud, noise, shouted.

7453. רֵעַ **rêaʻ,** *ray´-ah;* or רֵיעַ **rêyaʻ,** *ray´-ah;* from 7462; an *associate* (more or less close):—brother, companion, fellow, friend, husband, lover, neighbour, × (an-) other.

7454. רֵעַ **rêaʻ,** *ray´-ah;* from 7462; a *thought* (as *association* of ideas):—thought.

7455. רֹעַ **rôaʻ,** *ro´-ah;* from 7489; *badness* (as *marring*); phys. or mor.:— × be so bad, badness, (× be so) evil, naughtiness, sadness, sorrow, wickedness.

7456. רָעֵב **râʻêb,** *raw-abe´;* a prim. root; to *hunger:*—(suffer to) famish, (be, have, suffer, suffer to) hunger (-ry).

7457. רָעֵב **râʻêb,** *raw-abe´;* from 7456; *hungry* (more or less intensely):—hunger bitten, hungry.

7458. רָעָב **râʻâb,** *raw-awb´;* from 7456; *hunger* (more or less extensive):—dearth, famine, + famished, hunger.

7459. רְעָבוֹן **r^{e}ʻâbôwn,** *reh-aw-bone´;* from 7456; *famine:*—famine.

7460. רָעַד **râʻad,** *raw-ad´;* a prim. root; to *shudder* (more or less violently):—tremble.

7461. רַעַד **raʻad,** *rah´-ad;* or (fem.) רְעָדָה **r^{e}ʻâdâh,** *reh-aw-daw´;* from 7460; a *shudder:*—fear, trembling.

7462. רָעָה **râʻâh,** *raw-aw´;* a prim. root; to *tend* a flock, i.e. *pasture* it; intrans. to *graze* (lit. or fig.); gen. to *rule;* by extens. to *associate* with (as a friend):— × break, companion, keep company with, devour, eat up, evil entreat, feed, use as a friend, make friendship with, herdman, keep [sheep] (-er), pastor, + shearing house, shepherd, wander, waste.

7463. רֵעֶה **rê'eh,** *ray-eh´;* from 7462; a (male) *companion:*—friend.

7464. רֵעָה **rêʻâh,** *ray´-aw;* fem. of 7453; a female *associate:*—companion, fellow.

7465. רֹעָה **rôʻâh,** *ro-aw´;* for 7455; *breakage:*—broken, utterly.

7466. רְעוּ **R^{e}ʻûw,** *reh-oo´;* for 7471 in the sense of 7453; *friend; Reü,* a postdiluvian patriarch:—Reu.

7467. רְעוּאֵל **R^{e}ʻûw'êl,** *reh-oo-ale´;* from the same as 7466 and 410; *friend of God; Reüel,* the name of Moses' father-in-law, also of an Edomite and an Isr.:—Raguel, Reuel.

7468. רְעוּת **r^{e}ʻûwth,** *reh-ooth´;* from 7462 in the sense of 7453; a female *associate;* gen. an *additional* one:— + another, mate, neighbour.

7469. רְעוּת **r^{e}ʻûwth,** *reh-ooth´;* prob. from 7462; a *feeding* upon, i.e. grasping after:—vexation.

7470. רְעוּת **r^{e}ʻûwth** (Chald.), *reh-ooth´;* corresp. to 7469; *desire:*—pleasure, will.

7471. רְעִי **r^{e}ʻîy,** *reh-ee´;* from 7462; *pasture:*—pasture.

7472. רֵעִי **Rêʻîy,** *ray-ee´;* from 7453; *social; Reï,* an Isr.:—Rei.

7473. רֹעִי **rôʻîy,** *ro-ee´;* from act. part. of 7462; *pastoral;* as noun, a *shepherd:*—shepherd.

7474. רַעְיָה **raʻyâh,** *rah-yaw´;* fem. of 7453; a female *associate:*—love.

7475. רַעְיוֹן **raʻyôwn,** *rah-yone´;* from 7462 in the sense of 7469; *desire:*—vexation.

7476. רַעְיוֹן **raʻyôwn** (Chald.), *rah-yone´;* corresp. to 7475; a *grasp,* i.e. (fig.) mental *conception:*—cogitation, thought.

7477. רָעַל **râʻal,** *raw-al´;* a prim. root; to *reel,* i.e. (fig.) to *brandish:*—terribly shake.

7478. רַעַל **raʻal,** *rah´-al;* from 7477; a *reeling* (from intoxication):—trembling.

7479. רַעֲלָה **raʻălâh,** *rah-al-aw´;* fem. of 7478; a long *veil* (as *fluttering*):—muffler.

7480. רְעֵלָיָה **R^{e}ʻêlâyâh,** *reh-ay-law-yaw´;* from 7477 and 3050; *made to tremble* (i.e. *fearful*) *of Jah; Reëlajah,* an Isr.:—Reeliah.

7481. רָעַם **râʻam,** *raw-am´;* a prim. root; to *tumble,* i.e. violently *agitated;* spec. to *crash* (of thunder); fig. to *irritate* (with anger):—make to fret, roar, thunder, trouble.

7482. רַעַם **raʻam,** *rah´-am;* from 7481; a *peal* of thunder:—thunder.

7483. רַעְמָה **raʻmâh,** *rah-maw´;* fem. of 7482; the *mane* of a horse (as *quivering* in the wind):—thunder.

7484. רַעְמָה **Raʻmâh,** *rah-maw´;* the same as 7483; *Ramah,* the name of a grandson of Ham, and of a place (perh. founded by him):—Raamah.

7485. רַעַמְיָה **Raʻamyâh,** *rah-am-yaw´;* from 7481 and 3050; *Jah has shaken; Raamjah,* an Isr.:—Raamiah.

7486. רַעְמְסֵס **Raʻm^{e}çêç,** *rah-mes-ace´;* or רַעַמְסֵס **Raʻamçêç,** *rah-am-sace´;* of Eg. or.; *Rameses* or *Raamses,* a place in Egypt:—Raamses, Rameses.

7487. רַעֲנַן **raʻănan** (Chald.), *rah-aw-nan´;* corresp. to 7488; *green,* i.e. (fig.) *prosperous:*—flourishing.

7488. רַעֲנָן **raʻănân,** *rah-an-awn´;* from an unused root mean. to *be green; verdant;* by anal. *new;* fig. *prosperous:*—green, flourishing.

7489. רָעַע **râʻaʻ,** *raw-ah´;* a prim. root; prop. to *spoil* (lit. by *breaking* to pieces); fig. to *make* (or *be*) *good for nothing,* i.e. *bad* (phys., soc. or mor.):—afflict, associate selves [*by mistake for* 7462], break (down, in pieces), + displease, (be, bring, do) evil (doer, entreat, man), show self friendly [*by mistake for* 7462], do harm, (do) hurt, (behave self, deal) ill, × indeed, do mischief, punish, still vex, (do) wicked (doer, -ly), be (deal, do) worse.

7490. רְעַע **r^{e}ʻaʻ** (Chald.), *reh-ah´;* corresp. to 7489:—break, bruise.

7491. רָעַף **râʻaph,** *raw-af´;* a prim. root; to *drip:*—distil, drop (down).

7492. רָעַץ **râʻats,** *raw-ats´;* a prim. root; to *break* in pieces; fig. *harass:*—dash in pieces, vex.

7493. רָעַשׁ **râʻash,** *raw-ash;* a prim. root; to *undulate* (as the earth, the sky, etc.; also a field of grain), partic. through fear; spec. to *spring* (as a locust):—make afraid, (re-) move, quake, (make to) shake, (make to) tremble.

7494. רַעַשׁ **raʻash,** *rah´-ash;* from 7493; *vibration; bounding, uproar:*—commotion, confused noise, earthquake, fierceness, quaking, rattling, rushing, shaking.

7495. רָפָא **râphâ',** *raw-faw´;* or רָפָה **râphâh,** *raw-faw´;* a prim. root; prop. to *mend* (by stitching), i.e. (fig.) to *cure:*—cure, (cause to) heal, physician, repair, × thoroughly, make whole. See 7503.

7496. רָפָא **râphâ',** *raw-faw´;* from 7495 in the sense of 7503; prop. *lax,* i.e. (fig.) a *ghost* (as *dead;* in plur. only):—dead, deceased.

7497. רָפָא **râphâ',** *raw-faw´;* or רָפָה **râphâh,** *raw-faw´;* from 7495 in the sense of *invigorating;* a *giant:*—giant, Rapha, Rephaim (-s). See also 1051.

7498. רָפָא **Râphâ',** *raw-faw´;* or רָפָה **Râphâh,** *raw-faw´;* prob. the same as 7497; *giant; Rapha* or *Raphah,* the name of two Isr.:—Rapha.

7499. רְפֻאָה **r^{e}phû'âh,** *ref-oo-aw´;* fem. pass. part. of 7495; a *medicament:*—heal [-ed], medicine.

7500. רִפְאוּת **riph'ûwth,** *rif-ooth´;* from 7495; a *cure:*—health.

7501. רְפָאֵל **R^{e}phâ'êl,** *ref-aw-ale´;* from 7495 and 410; *God has cured; Rephaël,* an Isr.:—Rephael.

7502. רָפַד **râphad,** *raw-fad´;* a prim. root; to *spread* (a bed); by impl. to *refresh:*—comfort, make [a bed], spread.

7503. רָפָה **râphâh,** *raw-faw´;* a prim. root; to *slacken* (in many applications, lit. or fig.):—abate, cease, consume, draw [toward evening], fail, (be) faint, be (wax) feeble, forsake, idle, leave, let alone (go, down), (be) slack, stay, be still, be slothful, (be) weak (-en). See 7495.

7504. רָפֶה **râpheh,** *raw-feh´;* from 7503; *slack* (in body or mind):—weak.

רָפָה **râphâh, Râphâh.** See 7497, 7498.

רִפָה **riphâh.** See 7383.

7505. רָפוּא **Râphûw',** *raw-foo´;* pass. part. of 7495; *cured; Raphu,* an Isr.:—Raphu.

7506. רֶפַח **Rephach,** *reh´-fakh;* from an unused root appar. mean. to *sustain; support; Rephach,* an Isr.:—Rephah.

7507. רְפִידָה **r^{e}phîydâh,** *ref-ee-daw´;* from 7502; a *railing* (as *spread* along):—bottom.

7508. רְפִידִים **Rᵉphîydîym,** *ref-ee-deem´;* plur. of the masc. of the same as 7507; *ballusters; Rephidim,* a place in the Desert:—Rephidim.

7509. רְפָיָה **Rᵉphâyâh,** *ref-aw-yaw´;* from 7495 and 3050; *Jah has cured; Rephajah,* the name of five Isr.:—Rephaiah.

7510. רִפְיוֹן **riphyôwn,** *rif-yone´;* from 7503; *slackness:*—feebleness.

7511. רָפַס **râphaç,** *raw-fas´;* a prim. root; to *trample,* i.e. *prostrate:*—humble self, submit self.

7512. רְפַס **rᵉphaç,** (Chald.), *ref-as´;* corresp. to 7511:—stamp.

7513. רַפְסֹדָה **raphçôdâh,** *raf-so-daw´;* from 7511; a *raft* (as *flat* on the water):—flote.

7514. רָפַק **râphaq,** *raw-fak´;* a prim. root; to *recline:*—lean.

7515. רָפַשׂ **râphas,** *raw-fas´;* a prim. root; to *trample,* i.e *roil* water:—foul, trouble.

7516. רֶפֶשׁ **rephesh,** *reh´-fesh;* from 7515; *mud* (as *roiled*):—mire.

7517. רֶפֶת **repheth,** *reh´-feth;* prob. from 7503; a *stall* for cattle (from their *resting* there):—stall.

7518. רַץ **rats,** *rats;* contr. from 7533; a *fragment:*—piece.

7519. רָצָא **râtsâʼ,** *raw-tsaw´;* a prim. root; to *run;* also to *delight* in:—accept, run.

7520. רָצַד **râtsad,** *raw-tsad´;* a prim. root; prob. to *look askant,* i.e. (fig.) *be jealous:*—leap.

7521. רָצָה **râtsâh,** *raw-tsaw´;* a prim. root; to *be pleased with;* spec. to *satisfy* a debt:—(be) accept (-able), accomplish, set affection, approve, consent with, delight (self), enjoy, (be, have a) favour (-able), like, observe, pardon, (be, have, take) please (-ure), reconcile self.

7522. רָצוֹן **râtsôwn,** *raw-tsone´;* or רָצֹן **râtsôn,** *raw-tsone´;* from 7521; *delight* (espec. as shown):—(be) acceptable (-ance, -ed), delight, desire, favour, (good) pleasure, (own, self, voluntary) will, as . . . (what) would.

7523. רָצַח **râtsach,** *raw-tsakh´;* a prim. root; prop. to *dash* in pieces, i.e. *kill* (a human being), espec. to *murder:*—put to death, kill, (man-) slay (-er), murder (-er).

7524. רֶצַח **retsach,** *reh´-tsakh;* from 7523; a *crushing;* spec. a *murder*-cry:—slaughter, sword.

7525. רִצְיָא **Ritsyâʼ,** *rits-yaw´;* from 7521; *delight; Ritsjah,* an Isr.:—Rezia.

7526. רְצִין **Rᵉtsîyn,** *rets-een´;* prob. for 7522; *Retsin,* the name of a Syrian and of an Isr.:—Rezin.

7527. רָצַע **râtsaʻ,** *raw-tsah´;* a prim. root; to *pierce:*—bore.

7528. רָצַף **râtsaph,** *raw-tsaf´;* a denom. from 7529; to *tessellate,* i.e. embroider (as if with bright stones):—pave.

7529. רֶצֶף **retseph,** *reh´-tsef;* for 7565; a red-hot *stone* (for baking):—coal.

7530. רֶצֶף **Retseph,** *reh´-tsef;* the same as 7529; *Retseph,* a place in Ass.:—Rezeph.

7531. רִצְפָּה **ritspâh,** *rits-paw´;* fem. of 7529; a hot *stone;* also a tessellated *pavement:*—live coal, pavement.

7532. רִצְפָּה **Ritspâh,** *rits-paw´;* the same as 7531; *Ritspah,* an Israelitess:—Rizpah.

7533. רָצַץ **râtsats,** *raw-tsats´;* a prim. root; to *crack* in pieces, lit. or fig.:—break, bruise, crush, discourage, oppress, struggle together.

7534. רַק **raq,** *rak;* from 7556 in its orig. sense; *emaciated* (as if *flattened* out):—lean ([-fleshed]), thin.

7535. רַק **raq,** *rak;* the same as 7534 as a noun; prop. *leanness,* i.e. (fig.) limitation; only adv. *merely,* or conj. *although:*—but, even, except, howbeit howsoever, at the least, nevertheless, nothing but, notwithstanding, only, save, so [that], surely, yet (so), in any wise.

7536. רֹק **rôq,** *roke;* from 7556; *spittle:*—spit (-ting, -tle).

7537. רָקַב **râqab,** *raw-kab´;* a prim. root; to *decay* (as by worm-eating):—rot.

7538. רָקָב **râqâb,** *raw-kawb´;* from 7537; *decay* (by *caries*):—rottenness (thing).

7539. רִקָּבוֹן **riqqâbôwn,** *rik-kaw-bone´;* from 7538; *decay* (by *caries*):—rotten.

7540. רָקַד **râqad,** *raw-kad´;* a prim. root; prop. to *stamp,* i.e. to *spring* about (wildly or for joy):—dance, jump, leap, skip.

7541. רַקָּה **raqqâh,** *raw-kaw´;* fem. of 7534; prop. *thinness,* i.e. the *side* of the head:—temple.

7542. רַקּוֹן **Raqqôwn,** *rak-kone´;* from 7534 *thinness; Rakkon,* a place in Pal.:—Rakkon.

7543. רָקַח **râqach,** *raw-kakh´;* a prim. root; to *perfume:*—apothecary, compound, make [ointment], prepare, spice.

7544. רֶקַח **reqach,** *reh´-kakh;* from 7543; prop. *perfumery,* i.e. (by impl.) *spicery* (for flavor):—spiced.

7545. רֹקַח **rôqach,** *ro´-kakh;* from 7542; an *aromatic:*—confection, ointment.

7546. רַקָּח **raqqâch** *rak-kawkh´;* from 7543; a male *perfumer:*—apothecary.

7547. רִקֻּחַ **raqqûach,** *rak-koo´-akh;* from 7543; a *scented* substance:—perfume.

7548. רַקָּחָה **raqqâchâh,** *rak-kaw-khaw´;* fem. of 7547; a female *perfumer:*—confectioner.

7549. רָקִיעַ **râqîyaʻ,** *raw-kee´-ah;* frm 7554; prop. an *expanse,* i.e. the *firmament* or (apparently) visible arch of the sky:—firmament.

7550. רָקִיק **râqîyq,** *raw-keek´;* from 7556 in its orig. sense; a thin *cake:*—cake, wafer.

7551. רָקַם **râqam,** *raw-kam´;* a prim. root; to *variegate* color, i.e. *embroider;* by impl. to *fabricate:*—embroiderer, needlework, curiously work.

7552. רֶקֶם **Reqem,** *reh´-kem;* from 7551; *versicolor; Rekem,* the name of a place in Pal., also of a Midianite and an Isr.:—Rekem.

7553. רִקְמָה **riqmâh,** *rikmaw´;* from 7551; *variegation* of color; spec. *embroidery:*—broidered (work), divers colours, (raiment of) needlework (on both sides).

7554. רָקַע **râqaʻ,** *raw-kah´;* a prim. root; to *pound* the earth (as a sign of passion); by analogy to *expand* (by hammering); by impl. to *overlay* (with thin sheets of metal):—beat, make broad, spread abroad (forth, over, out, into plates), stamp, stretch.

7555. רִקֻּעַ **riqqûaʻ,** *rik-koo´-ah;* from 7554; *beaten* out, i.e. a (metallic) *plate:*—broad.

7556. רָקַק **râqaq,** *raw-kak´;* a prim. root; to *spit:*—spit.

7557. רַקַּת **Raqqath,** *rak-kath´;* from 7556 in its orig. sense of *diffusing;* a *beach* (as *expanded* shingle); *Rakkath,* a place in Pal.:—Rakkath.

7558. רִשְׁיוֹן **rîshyôwn,** *rish-yone´;* from an unused root mean. to *have leave;* a *permit:*—grant.

7559. רָשַׁם **râsham,** *raw-sham´;* a prim. root; to *record:*—note.

7560. רְשַׁם **rᵉsham** (Chald.), *resh-am´;* corresp. to 7559:—sign, write.

7561. רָשַׁע **râshaʻ,** *raw-shah´;* a prim. root; to *be* (caus. *do* or *declare*) *wrong:* by impl. to *disturb, violate:*—condemn, make trouble, vex, be (commit, deal, depart, do) wicked (-ly, -ness).

7562. רֶשַׁע **reshaʻ,** *reh´-shah;* from 7561; a *wrong* (espec. moral):—iniquity, wicked (-ness).

7563. רָשָׁע **râshâʻ,** *raw-shaw´;* from 7561; morally *wrong;* concr. an (actively) *bad* person:— + condemned, guilty, ungodly, wicked (man), that did wrong.

7564. רִשְׁעָה **rishʻâh,** *rish-aw´;* fem. of 7562; *wrong* (espec. moral):—fault, wickedly (-ness).

7565. רֶשֶׁף **resheph,** *reh´-shef,* from 8313; a live *coal;* by analogy *lightning;* fig. an *arrow* (as *flashing* through the air); spec. *fever:*—arrow, (burning) coal, burning heat, + spark, hot thunderbolt.

7566. רֶשֶׁף **Resheph,** *reh´-shef;* the same as 7565; *Resheph,* an Isr.:—Resheph.

7567. רָשַׁשׁ **râshash,** *raw-shash´;* a prim. root; to *demolish:*—impoverish.

7568. רֶשֶׁת **resheth,** *reh´-sheth;* from 3423; a *net* (as *catching* animals):—net [-work].

7569. רַתּוֹק **rattôwq** *rat-toke´;* from 7576; a *chain:*—chain.

7570. רָתַח **râthach,** *raw-thakh´;* a prim. root; to *boil:*—boil.

7571. רֶתַח **rethach,** *reh´-thakh;* from 7570; a *boiling:*) × [boil] well.

7572. רַתִּיקָה° **rattîyqâh,** *rat-tee-kaw´;* from 7576; a *chain:*—chain.

7573. רָתַם **râtham,** *raw-tham´;* a prim. root; to *yoke* up (to the pole of a vehicle):—bind.

7574. רֶתֶם **rethem,** *reh´-them;* or רֹתֶם **rôthem,** *ro´-them;* from 7573; the Spanish *broom* (from its pole-like stems):—juniper (tree).

7575. רִתְמָה **Rithmâh,** *rith-maw´;* fem. of 7574; *Rithmah,* a place in the Desert:—Rithmah.

7576. רָתַק **râthaq,** *raw-thak´;* a prim. root; to *fasten:*—bind.

7577. רְתֻקָה **rethûqâh,** *reth-oo-kaw´;* fem. pass. part. of 7576; something *fastened,* i.e. a *chain:*—chain.

7578. רְתֵת **rethêth,** *reth-ayth´;* for 7374; *terror:*—trembling.

ש

7579. שָׁאַב **shâ'ab,** *shaw-ab´;* a prim. root; to *bale* up water:—(woman to) draw (-er, water).

7580. שָׁאַג **shâ'ag,** *shaw-ag´;* a prim. root; to *rumble* or *moan:*— × mightily, roar.

7581. שְׁאָגָה **she'âgâh,** *sheh-aw-gaw´;* from 7580; a *rumbling* or *moan:*— roaring.

7582. שָׁאָה **shâ'âh,** *shaw-aw´;* a prim. root; to *rush;* by impl. to *desolate:*—be desolate, (make a) rush (-ing), (lay) waste.

7583. שָׁאָה **shâ'âh,** *shaw-aw´;* a prim. root [rather ident. with 7582 through the idea of *whirling* to giddiness]; to *stun,* i.e. (intrans.) *be astonished:*—wonder.

7584. שַׁאֲוָה **sha'ăvâh,** *shah-av-aw´;* from 7582; a *tempest* (as *rushing*):—desolation.

7585. שְׁאוֹל **she'ôwl,** *sheh-ole´;* or שְׁאֹל **she'ôl,** *sheh-ole´;* from 7592; *hades* or the world of the dead (as if a subterranean *retreat*), includ. its accessories and inmates:—grave, hell, pit.

7586. שָׁאוּל **Shâ'ûwl,** *shaw-ool´;* pass. part. of 7592; *asked; Shaül,* the name of an Edomite and two Isr.:—Saul, Shaul.

7587. שָׁאוּלִי **Shâ'ûwlîy,** *shaw-oo-lee´;* patron. from 7856; a *Shaülite* or desc. of Shaul:—Shaulites.

7588. שָׁאוֹן **shâ'ôwn,** *shaw-one´;* from 7582; *uproar* (as of *rushing*); by impl. *destruction:*— × horrible, noise, pomp, rushing, tumult (× -uous).

7589. שְׁאָט **she'âṭ,** *sheh-awt´;* from an unused root mean. to *push* aside; *contempt:*—despite (-ful).

7590. שָׁאט **shâ'ṭ,** *shawt;* for act. part. of 7750 [comp. 7589]; one *contemning:*—that (which) despise (-d).

7591. שְׁאִיָּה **she'îyâh,** *sheh-ee-yaw´;* from 7582; *desolation:*—destruction.

7592. שָׁאַל **shâ'al,** *shaw-al´;* or שָׁאֵל **shâ'êl,** *shaw-ale´;* a prim. root; to *inquire;* by impl. to *request;* by extens. to *demand:*—ask (counsel, on), beg, borrow, lay to charge, consult, demand, desire, × earnestly, enquire, + greet, obtain leave, lend, pray, request, require, + salute, × straitly, × surely, wish.

7593. שְׁאֵל **she'êl** (Chald.), *sheh-ale´;* corresp. to 7592:—ask, demand, require.

7594. שְׁאָל **She'âl,** *sheh-awl´;* from 7592; *request; Sheäl,* an Isr.:—Sheal.
שְׁאֹל **she'ôl.** See 7585.

7595. שְׁאֵלָא **she'êlâ'** (Chald.), *sheh-ay-law´;* from 7593; prop. a *question* (at law), i.e. judicial *decision* or mandate:—demand.

7596. שְׁאֵלָה **she'êlâh,** *sheh-ay-law´;* or שֵׁלָה **shêlâh** (1 Sam. 1 : 17), *shay-law´;* from 7592; a *petition;* by impl. a *loan:*—loan, petition, request.

7597. שְׁאַלְתִּיאֵל **She'altîy'êl,** *sheh-al-tee-ale´;* or שַׁלְתִּיאֵל **Shaltîy'êl,** *shal-tee-ale´;* from 7592 and 410; *I have asked God; Sheältiël,* an Isr.:—Shalthiel, Shealtiel.

7598. שְׁאַלְתִּיאֵל **She'altîy'êl** (Chald.), *sheh-al-tee-ale´;* corresp. to 7597:—Shealtiel.

7599. שָׁאַן **shâ'an,** *shaw-an´;* a prim. root; to *loll,* i.e. *be peaceful:*—be at ease, be quiet, rest. See also 1052.

7600. שַׁאֲנָן **sha'ănân,** *shah-an-awn´;* from 7599; *secure;* in a bad sense, *haughty:*—that is at ease, quiet, tumult. Comp. 7946.

7601. שָׁאַס° **shâ'aç,** *shaw-as´;* a prim. root; to *plunder:*—spoil.

7602. שָׁאַף **shâ'aph,** *shaw-af´;* a prim. root; to *inhale* eagerly; fig. to *covet;* by impl. to *be angry;* also to *hasten:*—desire (earnestly), devour, haste, pant, snuff up, swallow up.

7603. שְׂאֹר **se'ôr,** *seh-ore´;* from 7604; *barm* or yeast-cake (as *swelling* by fermentation):—leaven.

7604. שָׁאַר **shâ'ar,** *shaw-ar´;* a prim. root; prop. to *swell* up, i.e. *be* (caus. *make*) *redundant:*—leave, (be) left, let, remain, remnant, reserve, the rest.

7605. שְׁאָר **she'âr,** *sheh-awr´;* from 7604; a *remainder:*— × other, remnant, residue, rest.

7606. שְׁאָר **she'âr** (Chald.), *sheh-awr´;* corresp. to 7605:— × whatsoever more, residue, rest.

7607. שְׁאֵר **she'êr,** *sheh-ayr´;* from 7604; *flesh* (as *swelling* out), as living or for food; gen. *food* of any kind; fig. *kindred* by blood:—body, flesh, food, (near) kin (-sman, -swoman), near (nigh) [of kin]

7608. שַׁאֲרָה **sha'ărâh,** *shah-ar-aw´;* fem. of 7607; female *kindred* by blood:—near kinswomen.

7609. שֶׁאֱרָה **She'ĕrâh,** *sheh-er-aw´;* the same as 7608; *Sheërah,* an Israelitess:—Sherah.

7610. שְׁאָר יָשׁוּב **She'âr Yâshûwb,** *sheh-awr´ yaw-shoob´;* from 7605 and 7725; a ***remnant will return;*** *Sheär-Jashub,* the symbol. name of one of Isaiah's sons:—Shear-jashub.

7611. שְׁאֵרִית **she'êrîyth,** *sheh-ay-reeth´;* from 7604; a *remainder* or residual (surviving, final) portion:—that had escaped, be left, posterity, remain (-der), remnant, residue, rest.

7612. שֵׁאת **shê'th,** *shayth;* from 7582; *devastation:*—desolation.

7613. שְׂאֵת **se'êth,** *seh-ayth´;* from 5375; an *elevation* or leprous scab; fig. *elation* or cheerfulness; *exaltation* in rank or character:—be accepted, dignity, excellency, highness, raise up self, rising.

7614. שְׁבָא **Shebâ',** *sheb-aw´;* of for. or.; *Sheba,* the name of three early progenitors of tribes and of an Ethiopian district:—Sheba, Sabeans.

7615. שְׁבָאִי **Shebâ'îy,** *sheb-aw-ee´;* patron. from 7614; a *Sheabite* or desc. of Sheba:—Sabean.

7616. שָׁבָב **shâbâb,** *shaw-bawb´;* from an unused root mean. to *break* up; a *fragment,* i.e. *ruin:*—broken in pieces.

7617. שָׁבָה **shâbâh,** *shaw-baw´;* a prim. root; to *transport* into captivity:—(bring away, carry, carry away, lead, lead away, take) captive (-s), drive (take) away.

7618. שְׁבוּ **shebûw,** *sheb-oo´;* from an unused root (prob. ident. with that of 7617 through the idea of *subdivision* into flashes or streamers [comp. 7632]) mean. to *flame;* a *gem* (from its sparkle); prob. the *agate:*—agate.

7619. שְׁבוּאֵל **Shebûw'êl,** *sheb-oo-ale´;* or שׁוּבָאֵל **Shûwbâ'êl,** *shoo-baw-ale´;* from 7617 (abbrev.) or 7725 and 410; *captive* (or *returned*) *of God; Shebuël* or *Shubaël,* the name of two Isr.:—Shebuel, Shubael.

7620. שָׁבוּעַ **shâbûwa',** *shaw-boo´-ah;* or שָׁבֻעַ **shâbûa',** *shaw-boo´-ah;* also (fem.) שְׁבֻעָה **shebû'âh,** *sheb-oo-aw´;* prop. pass. part. of 7650 as a denom. of 7651; lit. *sevened,* i.e. a *week* (spec. of years):—seven, week.

7621. שְׁבוּעָה **shebûw'âh,** *sheb-oo-aw´;* fem. pass. part. of 7650; prop. something *sworn,* i.e. an *oath:*—curse, oath, × sworn.

7622. שְׁבוּת **shebûwth,** *sheb-ooth´;* or שְׁבִית **shebîyth,** *sheb-eeth´;* from 7617; *exile:* concr. *prisoners;* fig. a *former state* of prosperity:—captive (-ity).

7623. שָׁבַח **shâbach,** *shaw-bakh´;* a prim. root; prop. to *address* in a loud tone, i.e. (spec.) *loud;* fig. to *pacify* (as if by words):—commend, glory, keep in, praise, still, triumph.

7624. שְׁבַח **shebach** (Chald.), *sheb-akh´;* corresp. to 7623; to *adulate,* i.e. *adore:*—praise.

7625. שְׁבַט **sh^ebaṭ,** (Chald.), *sheb-at´;* corresp. to 7626; a *clan:*—tribe.

7626. שֵׁבֶט **shêbeṭ,** *shay´-bet;* from an unused root prob. mean. to *branch* off, a *scion,* i.e. (lit.) a *stick* (for punishing, writing, fighting, ruling, walking, etc.) or (fig.) a *clan:*— × correction, dart, rod, sceptre, staff, tribe.

7627. שְׁבָט **Sh^ebâṭ,** *sheb-awt´;* of for. or.; *Shebat,* a Jewish month:—Sebat.

7628. שְׁבִי **sh^ebîy,** *sheb-ee´;* from 7618; *exiled; captured;* as noun, *exile* (abstr. or concr. and collect.); by extens. *booty:*—captive (-ity), prisoners, × take away, that was taken.

7629. שֹׁבִי **Shôbîy,** *sho-bee´;* from 7617; *captor; Shobi,* an Ammonite:—Shobi.

7630. שֹׁבַי **Shôbay,** *sho-bah´ee;* for 7629; *Shobai,* an Isr.:—Shobai.

7631. שְׂבִיב **s^ebîyb** (Chald.), *seb-eeb´;* corresp. to 7632:—flame.

7632. שָׁבִיב **shâbîyb,** *shaw-beeb´;* from the same as 7616; *flame* (as *split* into tongues):—spark.

7633. שִׁבְיָה **shibyâh,** *shib-yaw´;* fem. of 7628; *exile* (abstr. or concr. and collect.):—captives (-ity).

7634. שָׁבְיָה **Shobyâh,** *shob-yaw´;* fem. of the same as 7629; *captivation; Shobjah,* an Isr.:—Shachia [*from the marg.*].

7635. שָׁבִיל **shâbîyl,** *shaw-beel´* from the same as 7640; a *track* or passage-way (as if *flowing* along):—path.

7636. שָׁבִיס **shâbîyç,** *shaw-beece´;* from an unused root mean. to *interweave;* a *netting* for the hair:—caul.

7637. שְׁבִיעִי **sh^ebîyʻîy,** *sheb-ee-ee´;* or שְׁבִעִי **sh^ebiʻîy,** *sheb-ee-ee´;* ordinal from 7657; *seventh:*—seventh (time).

שְׁבִית **sh^ebîyth.** See 7622.

7638. שָׂבָךְ **sâbâk,** *saw-bawk´;* from an unused root mean. to *intwine;* a *netting* (ornament to the capital of a column):—net.

שַׂבְּכָא **sabb^ekâʼ.** See 5443.

7639. שְׂבָכָה **s^ebâkâh,** *seb-aw-kaw´;* fem. of 7638; a *net-work,* i.e. (in hunting) a *snare,* (in arch.) a *ballustrade;* also a *reticulated* ornament to a pillar:—checker, lattice, network, snare, wreath (-enwork).

7640. שֹׁבֶל **shôbel,** *show´-bel;* from an unused root mean. to *flow;* a lady's *train* (as *trailing* after her):—leg.

7641. שִׁבֹּל **shibbôl,** *shib-bole´;* or (fem.) שִׁבֹּלֶת **shibbôleth,** *shib-bo´-leth;* from the same as 7640; a *stream* (as *flowing*); also an *ear* of grain (as *growing* out); by anal. a *branch:*—branch, channel, ear (of corn), ([water-]) flood, Shibboleth. Comp. 5451.

7642. שַׁבְלוּל **shablûwl,** *shab-lool´;* from the same as 7640; a *snail* (as if *floating* in its own slime):—snail.

שִׁבֹּלֶת **shibbôleth.** See 7641.

7643. שְׂבָם **S^ebâm,** *seb-awm´;* or (fem.) שִׂבְמָה **Sibmâh,** *sib-maw´;* prob. from 1313; *spice; Sebam* or *Sibmah,* a place in Moab:—Shebam, Shibmah, Sibmah.

7644. שֶׁבְנָא **Shebnâʼ,** *sheb-naw´;* or שֶׁבְנָה **Shebnâh,** *sheb-naw´;* from an unused root mean. to *grow; growth; Shebna* or *Shebnah,* an Isr.:—Shebna, Shebnah.

7645. שְׁבַנְיָה **Sh^ebanyâh,** *sheb-an-yaw´;* or שְׁבַנְיָהוּ **Sh^ebanyâhûw,** *sheb-an-yaw´-hoo;* from the same as 7644 and 3050; *Jah has grown* (i.e. *prospered*); *Shebanjah,* the name of three or four Isr.:—Shebaniah.

7646. שָׂבַע **sâbaʻ,** *saw-bah´;* or שָׂבֵעַ **sâbêaʻ,** *saw-bay´-ah;* a prim. root; to *sate,* i.e. *fill* to satisfaction (lit. or fig.):—have enough, fill (full, self, with), be (to the) full (of), have plenty of, be satiate, satisfy (with), suffice, be weary of.

7647. שָׂבָע **sâbâʻ,** *saw-baw´;* from 7646; *copiousness:*—abundance, plenteous (-ness, -ly).

7648. שֹׂבַע **sôbaʻ,** *so´-bah;* from 7646; *satisfaction* (of food or [fig.] joy):—fill, full (-ness), satisfying, be satisfied.

7649. שָׂבֵעַ **sâbêaʻ,** *saw-bay´-ah;* from 7646; *satiated* (in a pleasant or disagreeable sense):—full (of), satisfied (with).

7650. שָׁבַע **shâbaʻ,** *shaw-bah´;* a prim. root; prop. to *be complete,* but used only as a denom. from 7651; to *seven* oneself, i.e. *swear* (as if by repeating a declaration seven times):—adjure, charge (by an oath, with an oath), feed to the full [*by mistake for* 7646], take an oath, × straitly, (cause to, make to) swear.

7651. שֶׁבַע **shebaʻ,** *sheh´-bah;* or (masc.) שִׁבְעָה **shibʻâh,** *shib-aw´;* from 7650; a prim. cardinal number; *seven* (as the sacred *full* one); also (adv.) *seven times;* by impl. a *week;* by extens. an *indefinite* number:— (+ by) seven ([-fold], -s, [-teen, -teenth], -th, times). Comp. 7658.

7652. שֶׁבַע **shebaʻ,** *sheh´-bah;* the same as 7651; *seven; Sheba,* the name of a place in Pal., and of two Isr.:—Sheba.

שָׁבֻעַ **shâbûaʻ.** See 7620.

7653. שִׂבְעָה **sibʻâh,** *sib-aw´;* fem. of 7647; *satiety:*—fulness.

7654. שָׂבְעָה **sobʻâh,** *sob-aw´;* fem. of 7648; *satiety:*—(to have) enough, × till . . . be full, [un-] satiable, satisfy, × sufficiently.

שִׁבְעָה **shibʻâh.** See 7651.

7655. שִׁבְעָה **shibʻâh** (Chald.), *shib-aw´;* corresp. to 7651:—seven (times).

7656. שִׁבְעָה **Shibʻâh,** *shib-aw´;* masc. of 7651; *seven (-th); Shebah,* a well in Pal.:—Shebah.

שְׁבֻעָה **sh^ebûʻâh.** See 7620.

שְׁבִעִי **sh^ebîyʻîy.** See 7637.

7657. שִׁבְעִים **shibʻîym,** *shib-eem´;* multiple of 7651; *seventy:*—seventy, threescore and ten (+ -teen).

7658. שִׁבְעָנָה **shibʻânâh,** *shib-aw-naw´;* prol. for the masc. of 7651; *seven:*—seven.

7659. שִׁבְעָתַיִם **shibʻâthayim,** *shib-aw-thah´-yim;* dual (adv.) of 7651; *seven-times:*—seven (-fold, times).

7660. שָׁבַץ **shâbats,** *shaw-bats´;* a prim. root; to *interweave* (colored) threads in squares; by impl. (*of reticulation*) to *inchase* germs in gold:—embroider, set.

7661. שָׁבָץ **shâbâts,** *shaw-bats´;* from 7660; *intanglement,* i.e. (fig.) *perplexity:*—anguish.

7662. שְׁבַק **sh^ebaq** (Chald.), *sheb-ak´;* corresp. to the root of 7733; to *quit,* i.e. allow to remain:—leave, let alone.

7663. שָׂבַר **sâbar,** *saw-bar´;* erroneously שָׁבַר **shâbar** (Neh. 2 : 13, 15), *shaw-bar´;* a prim. root; to *scrutinize;* by impl. (of *watching*) to *expect* (with hope and patience):—hope, tarry, view, wait.

7664. שֵׂבֶר **sêber,** *say´-ber;* from 7663; *expectation:*—hope.

7665. שָׁבַר **shâbar,** *shaw-bar´;* a prim. root; to *burst* (lit. or fig.):—break (down, off, in pieces, up), broken ([-hearted]), bring to the birth, crush, destroy, hurt, quench, × quite, tear, view [*by mistake for* 7663].

7666. שָׁבַר **shâbar,** *shaw-bar´;* denom. from 7668; to *deal* in grain:—buy, sell.

7667. שֶׁבֶר **sheber,** *sheh´-ber;* or שֵׁבֶר **shêber,** *shay´-ber;* from 7665; a *fracture,* fig. *ruin;* spec. a *solution* (of a dream):—affliction, breach, breaking, broken [-footed, -handed], bruise, crashing, destruction, hurt, interpretation, vexation.

7668. שֶׁבֶר **sheber,** *sheh´-ber;* the same as 7667; *grain* (as if *broken* into kernels):—corn, victuals.

7669. שֶׁבֶר **Sheber,** *sheh´-ber;* the same as 7667; *Sheber,* an Isr.:—Sheber.

7670. שִׁבְרוֹן **shibrôwn,** *shib-rone´;* from 7665; *rupture,* i.e. a *pang;* fig. *ruin:*—breaking, destruction.

7671. שְׁבָרִים **Sh^ebârîym,** *sheb-aw-reem´;* plur. of 7667; *ruins; Shebarim,* a place in Pal.:—Shebarim.

7672. שְׁבַשׁ **sh^ebash** (Chald.), *sheb-ash´;* corresp. to 7660; to *intangle,* i.e. *perplex:*—be astonished.

7673. שָׁבַת **shâbath,** *shaw-bath´;* a prim. root; to *repose,* i.e. *desist* from exertion; used in many impl. relations (caus., fig. or spec.):—(cause to, let, make to) cease, celebrate, cause (make) to fail, keep (sabbath), suffer to be lacking, leave, put away (down), (make to) rest, rid, still, take away.

7674. שֶׁבֶת **shebeth,** *sheh´-beth;* from 7673; *rest, interruption, cessation:*—cease, sit still, loss of time.

7675. שֶׁבֶת **shebeth,** *sheh´-beth;* infin. of 3427; prop. *session;* but used also concr. an *abode* or *locality:*—place, seat. Comp. 3429.

7676. שַׁבָּת **shabbâth,** *shab-bawth´;* intens. from 7673; *intermission,* i.e. (spec.) the *Sabbath:*— (+ every) sabbath.

7677. שַׁבָּתוֹן **shabbâthôwn,** *shab-baw-thone´;* from 7676; a *sabbatism* or special holiday:—rest, sabbath.

7678. שַׁבְּתַי **Shabbᵉthay,** *shab-beth-ah´ee;* from 7676; *restful; Shabbethai,* the name of three Isr.:—Shabbethai.

7679. שָׂגָא **sâgâ',** *saw-gaw´;* a prim. root; to *grow,* i.e. (caus.) to *enlarge,* (fig.) *laud:*—increase, magnify.

7680. שְׂגָא **sᵉgâ'** (Chald.), *seg-aw´;* corresp. to 7679; to *increase:*—grow, be multiplied.

7681. שָׁגֵא **Shâgê',** *shaw-gay´;* prob. from 7686; *erring; Shagè,* an Isr.:—Shage.

7682. שָׂגַב **sâgab,** *saw-gab´;* a prim. root; to *be* (caus. *make*) *lofty,* espec. *inaccessible;* by impl. *safe, strong;* used lit. and fig.:—defend, exalt, be excellent, (be, set on) high, lofty, be safe, set up (on high), be too strong.

7683. שָׁגַג **shâgag,** *shaw-gag´;* a prim. root; to *stray,* i.e. (fig.) *sin* (with more or less apology):— × also for that, deceived, err, go astray, sin ignorantly.

7684. שְׁגָגָה **shᵉgâgâh,** *sheg-aw-gaw´;* from 7683; a *mistake* or inadvertent *transgression:*—error, ignorance, at unawares, unwittingly.

7685. שָׂגָה **sâgâh,** *saw-gaw´;* a prim. root; to *enlarge* (espec. upward, also fig.):—grow (up), increase.

7686. שָׁגָה **shâgâh,** *shaw-gaw´;* a prim. root; to *stray* (caus. *mislead*), usually (fig.) to *mistake,* espec. (mor.) to *transgress;* by extens. (through the idea of intoxication) to *reel,* (fig.) *be enraptured:*—(cause to) go astray, deceive, err, be ravished, sin through ignorance, (let, make to) wander.

7687. שְׂגוּב **Sᵉgûwb,** *seg-oob´;* from 7682; *aloft; Segub,* the name of two Isr.:—Segub.

7688. שָׁגַח **shâgach,** *shaw-gakh´;* a prim. root; to *peep,* i.e. *glance* sharply at:—look (narrowly).

7689. שַׂגִּיא **saggîy',** *sag-ghee´;* from 7679; (superlatively) *mighty:*—excellent, great.

7690. שַׂגִּיא **saggîy'** (Chald.), *sag-ghee´;* corresp. to 7689; *large* (in size, quantity or number, also adv.):—exceeding, great (-ly), many, much, sore, very.

7691. שְׁגִיאָה **shᵉgîy'âh,** *sheg-ee-aw´;* from 7686; a moral *mistake:*—error.

7692. שִׁגָּיוֹן **shiggâyôwn,** *shig-gaw-yone´;* or שִׁגָּיֹנָה **shiggâyônâh,** *shig-gaw-yo-naw´;* from 7686; prop. *abberation,* i.e. (tech.) a *dithyramb* or rambling poem:—Shiggaion, Shigionoth.

7693. שָׁגַל **shâgal,** *shaw-gal´;* a prim. root; to *copulate* with:—lie with, ravish.

7694. שֵׁגָל **shêgâl,** *shay-gawl´;* from 7693; a *queen* (from cohabitation):—queen.

7695. שֵׁגָל **shêgâl** (Chald.), *shay-gawl´;* corresp. to 7694; a (legitimate) *queen:*—wife.

7696. שָׁגַע **shâga',** *shaw-gah´;* a prim. root; to *rave* through insanity:—(be, play the) mad (man).

7697. שִׁגָּעוֹן **shiggâ'ôwn,** *shig-gaw-yone´;* from 7696; *craziness:*—furiously, madness.

7698. שֶׁגֶר **sheger,** *sheh´-ger;* from an unused root prob. mean. to *eject;* the *fœtus* (as finally *expelled*):—that cometh of, increase.

7699. שַׁד **shad,** *shad;* or שֹׁד **shôd,** *shode;* prob. from 7736 (in its orig. sense) contr.; the *breast* of a woman or animal (as *bulging*):—breast, pap, teat.

7700. שֵׁד **shêd,** *shade;* from 7736; a *dæmon* (as *malignant*):—devil.

7701. שֹׁד **shôd,** *shode;* or שׁוֹד **shôwd** (Job 5 : 21), *shode;* from 7736; *violence, ravage:*—desolation, destruction, oppression, robbery, spoil (-ed, -er, -ing), wasting.

7702. שָׂדַד **sâdad,** *saw-dad´;* a prim. root; to *abrade,* i.e. *harrow* a field:—break clods, harrow.

7703. שָׁדַד **shâdad,** *shaw-dad´;* a prim. root; prop. to *be burly,* i.e. (fig.) *powerful* (pass. *impregnable*); by impl. to *ravage:*—dead, destroy (-er), oppress, robber, spoil (-er), × utterly, (lay) waste.

7704. שָׂדֶה **sâdeh,** *saw-deh´;* or שָׂדַי **sâday,** *saw-dah´ee;* from an unused root mean. to *spread* out; a *field* (as *flat*):—country, field, ground, land, soil, × wild.

7705. שִׁדָּה **shiddâh,** *shid-dah´;* from 7703; a *wife* (as *mistress* of the house):) × all sorts, musical instrument.

7706. שַׁדַּי **Shadday,** *shad-dah´ee;* from 7703, the *Almighty:*—Almighty.

7707. שְׁדֵיאוּר **Shᵉdêy'ûwr,** *shed-ay-oor´;* from the same as 7704 and 217; *spreader of light; Shedejur,* an Isr.:—Shedeur.

7708. שִׂדִּים **Siddîym,** *sid-deem´;* plur. from the same as 7704; *flats; Siddim,* a valley in Pal.:—Siddim.

7709. שְׁדֵמָה **shᵉdêmâh,** *shed-ay-maw´;* appar. from 7704; a cultivated *field:*—blasted, field.

7710. שָׁדַף **shâdaph,** *shaw-daf´;* a prim. root; to *scorch:*—blast.

7711. שְׁדֵפָה **shᵉdêphâh,** *shed-ay-faw´;* or שִׁדָּפוֹן **shiddâphôwn,** *shid-daw-fone´;* from 7710; *blight:*—blasted (-ing).

7712. שְׁדַר **shᵉdar** (Chad.), *shed-ar´;* a prim. root; to *endeavor:*—labour.

7713. שְׂדֵרָה **sᵉdêrâh,** *sed-ay-raw´;* from an unused root mean. to *regulate;* a *row,* i.e. *rank* (of soldiers), *story* (of rooms):—board, range.

7714. שַׁדְרַךְ **Shadrak,** *shad-rak´;* prob. of for. or.; *Shadrak,* the Bab. name of one of Daniel's companions:—Shadrach.

7715. שַׁדְרַךְ **Shadrak** (Chald.), *shad-rak´;* the same as 7714:—Shadrach.

7716. שֶׂה **seh,** *seh;* or שֵׂי **sêy,** *say;* prob. from 7582 through the idea of *pushing* out to graze; a member of a flock, i.e. a *sheep* or *goat:*—(lesser, small) cattle, ewe, lamb, sheep.

7717. שָׂהֵד **sâhêd,** *saw-hade´;* from an unused root mean. to *testify;* a *witness:*—record.

7718. שֹׁהַם **shôham,** *sho´-ham;* from an unused root prob. mean. to *blanch;* a gem, prob. the *beryl* (from its *pale* green color):—onyx.

7719. שֹׁהַם **Shôham,** *sho´-ham;* the same as 7718; *Shoham,* an Isr.:—Shoham.

7720. שַׂהֲרֹן **sahărôn,** *sah-har-one´;* from the same as 5469; a round *pendant* for the neck:—ornament, round tire like the moon.

שַׁו° **shav.** See 7723.

7721. שׂוֹא **sôw',** *so;* from an unused root (akin to 5375 and 7722) mean. to *rise;* a *rising:*—arise.

7722. שׁוֹא **shôw',** *sho;* or (fem.) שׁוֹאָה **shôw'âh,** *sho-aw´;* or שֹׁאָה **shô'âh,** *sho-aw´;* from an unused root mean. to *rush* over; a *tempest;* by impl. *devastation:*—desolate (-ion), destroy, destruction, storm, wasteness.

7723. שָׁוְא **shâv',** *shawv;* or שַׁו° **shav,** *shav;* from the same as 7722 in the sense of *desolating; evil* (as *destructive*), lit. (*ruin*) or mor. (espec. *guile*); fig. *idolatry* (as false, subj.) *uselessness* (as deceptive, obj.; also adv. in *vain*):—false (-ly), lie, lying, vain, vanity.

7724. שְׁוָא **Shᵉvâ',** *shev-aw´;* from the same as 7723; *false; Sheva,* an Isr.:—Sheva.

7725. שׁוּב **shûwb,** *shoob;* a prim. root; to *turn* back (hence, away) trans. or intrans., lit. or fig. (not necessarily with the idea of *return* to the starting point); gen. to *retreat;* often adv. *again:*— ([break, build, circumcise, dig, do anything, do evil, feed, lay down, lie down, lodge, make, rejoice, send, take, weep]) × again, (cause to) answer (+ again), × in any case (wise), × at all, averse, bring (again, back, home again), call [to mind], carry again (back), cease, × certainly, come again (back) × consider, + continually, convert, deliver (again), + deny, draw back, fetch home again, × fro, get [oneself] (back) again, × give (again), go again (back, home), [go] out, hinder, let, [see] more, × needs, be past, × pay, pervert, pull in again, put (again, up again), recall, recompense, recover, refresh, relieve, render (again), × repent, requite, rescue, restore, retrieve, (cause to, make to) return, reverse, reward, + say nay, send back, set again, slide back, still, × surely, take back (off), (cause to, make to) turn (again, self again, away, back, back again, backward, from, off), withdraw.

שׁוּבָאֵל **Shûwbâ'êl.** See 7619.

7726. שׁוֹבָב **shôwbâb,** *sho-bawb´;* from 7725; *apostate,* i.e. idolatrous:—backsliding, frowardly, turn away [*from marg.*].

7727. שׁוֹבָב **Shôwbâb,** *sho-bawb´;* the same as 7726; *rebellious; Shobab,* the name of two Isr.:—Shobab.

7728. שׁוֹבֵב **shôwbêb,** *sho-babe´;* from 7725; *apostate,* i.e. heathenish or (actually) heathen:—backsliding.

7729. שׁוּבָה **shûwbâh,** *shoo-baw´;* from 7725; a *return:*—returning.

7730. שׂוֹבֶךְ **sôwbek,** *so´-bek;* for 5441; a *thicket,* i.e. interlaced branches:—thick boughs.

7731. שׁוֹבָךְ **Shôwbâk,** *sho-bawk´;* perh. for 7730; *Shobak,* a Syrian:—Shobach.

7732. שׁוֹבָל **Shôwbâl,** *sho-bawl´;* from the same as 7640; *overflowing; Shobal,* the name of an Edomite and two Isr.:—Shobal.

7733. שׁוֹבֵק **Shôwbêq,** *sho-bake´;* act. part. from a prim. root mean. to *leave* (comp. 7662); *forsaking; Shobek,* an Isr.:—Shobek.

7734. שׂוּג **sûwg,** *soog;* a prim. root; to *retreat:*—turn back.

7735. שׂוּג **sûwg,** *soog;* a prim. root; to *hedge* in:—make to grow.

7736. שׁוּד **shûwd,** *shood;* a prim. root; prop. to *swell* up, i.e. fig. (by impl. of *insolence*) to *devastate:*—waste.

שׁוֹד **shôwd.** See 7699, 7701.

7737. שָׁוָה **shâvâh,** *shaw-vaw´;* a prim. root; prop. to *level,* i.e. *equalize;* fig. to *resemble;* by impl. to *adjust* (i.e. counterbalance, be suitable, compose, place, yield, etc.):—avail, behave, bring forth, compare, countervail, (be, make) equal, lay, be (make, a-) like, make plain, profit, reckon.

7738. שָׁוָה° **shâvâh,** *shaw-vaw´;* a prim. root; to *destroy:*— × substance [*from the marg.*].

7739. שְׁוָה **sh**e**vâh** (Chald.), *shev-aw´;* corresp. to 7737; to *resemble:*—make like.

7740. שָׁוֵה **Shâvêh,** *shaw-vay´;* from 7737; *plain; Shaveh,* a place in Pal.:—Shaveh.

7741. שָׁוֵה קִרְיָתַיִם **Shâvêh Qiryâthayim,** *shaw-vay´; kir-yaw-thah´-yim;* from the same as 7740 and the dual of 7151; *plain of a double city; Shaveh-Kirjathajim,* a place E. of the Jordan:—Shaveh Kiriathaim.

7742. שׂוּחַ **sûwach,** *soo´-akh;* a prim. root; to *muse* pensively:—meditate.

7743. שׁוּחַ **shûwach,** *shoo´-akh;* a prim. root; to *sink,* lit. or fig.:—bow down, incline, humble.

7744. שׁוּחַ **Shûwach,** *shoo´-akh;* from 7743; *dell; Shuäch,* a son of Abraham:—Shuah.

7745. שׁוּחָה **shûwchâh,** *shoo-khaw´;* from 7743; a *chasm:*—ditch, pit.

7746. שׁוּחָה **Shûwchâh,** *shoo-khaw´;* the same as 7745; *Shuchah,* an Isr.:—Shuah.

7747. שׁוּחִי **Shuchîy,** *shoo-khee´;* patron. from 7744; a *Shuchite* or desc. of Shuach:—Shuhite.

7748. שׁוּחָם **Shûwchâm,** *shoo-khawm´;* from 7743; *humbly; Shucham,* an Isr.:—Shuham.

7749. שׁוּחָמִי **Shûwchâmîy,** *shoo-khaw-mee´;* patron. from 7748; a *Shuchamite* (collect.):—Shuhamites.

7750. שׂוּט **sûwṭ,** *soot;* or (by perm.) סוּט **çûwṭ,** *soot;* a primitive root; to *detrude,* i.e. (intrans. and fig.) *become derelict* (wrongly practise; namely, idolatry):—turn aside to.

7751. שׁוּט **shûwṭ,** *shoot;* a prim. root; prop. to *push* forth; (but used only fig.) to *lash,* i.e. (the sea with oars) to *row;* by impl. to *travel:*—go (about, through, to and fro), mariner, rower, run to and fro.

7752. שׁוֹט **shôwṭ,** *shote;* from 7751; a *lash* (lit. or fig.):—scourge, whip.

7753. שׂוּךְ **sûwk,** *sook;* a prim. root; to *entwine,* i.e. *shut* in (for formation, protection or restraint):—fence. (make an) hedge (up).

7754. שׂוֹךְ **sôwk,** *soke;* or (fem.) שׂוֹכָה **sôwkâh,** *so-kaw´;* from 7753; a *branch* (as *interleaved*):—bough.

7755. שׂוֹכֹה **Sôwkôh,** *so-ko´;* or שֹׂכֹה **Sôkôh,** *so-ko´;* or שׂוֹכוֹ **Sôwkôw,** *so-ko´;* from 7753; *Sokoh* or *Soko,* the name of two places in Pal.:—Shocho, Shochoh, Sochoh, Soco, Socoh.

7756. שׂוּכָתִי **Sûwkâthîy,** *soo-kaw-thee´;* prob. patron. from a name corresp. to 7754 (fem.); a *Sukathite* or desc. of an unknown Isr. named Sukah:—Suchathite.

7757. שׁוּל **shûwl,** *shool;* from an unused root mean. to *hang* down; a *skirt;* by impl. a bottom *edge:*—hem, skirt, train.

7758. שׁוֹלָל **shôwlâl,** *sho-lawl´;* or שֵׁילָל° **shêylâl** (Mic. 1 : 8), *shay-lawl´;* from 7997; *nude* (espec. bare-foot); by impl. *captive:*—spoiled, stripped.

7759. שׁוּלַמִּית **Shûwlammîyth,** *shoo-lam-meeth´;* from 7999; *peaceful* (with the art. always pref., making it a pet name); the *Shulammith,* an epithet of Solomon's queen:—Shulamite.

7760. שׂוּם **sûwm,** *soom;* or שִׂים **sîym,** *seem;* a prim. root; to *put* (used in a great variety of applications, lit., fig., infer. and ellip.):— × any wise, appoint, bring, call [a name], care, cast in, change, charge, commit, consider, convey, determine, + disguise, dispose, do, get, give, heap up, hold, impute, lay (down, up), leave, look, make (out), mark, + name, × on, ordain, order, + paint, place, preserve, purpose, put (on), + regard, rehearse, reward, (cause to) set (on, up), shew, + stedfastly, take, × tell, + tread down, ([over-]) turn, × wholly, work.

7761. שׂוּם **sûwm** (Chald.), *soom;* corresp. to 7760:— + command, give, lay, make, + name, + regard, set.

7762. שׁוּם **shûwm,** *shoom;* from an unused root mean. to *exhale; garlic* (from its rank *odor*):—garlic.

7763. שׁוֹמֵר **Shôwmêr,** *sho-mare´;* or שֹׁמֵר **Shômêr,** *sho-mare´;* act. part. of 8104; *keeper; Shomer,* the name of two Isr.:—Shomer.

7764. שׁוּנִי **Shûwnîy,** *shoo-nee´;* from an unused root mean. to *rest; quiet; Shuni,* an Isr.:—Shuni.

7765. שׁוּנִי **Shûwnîy,** *shoo-nee´;* patron. from 7764; a *Shunite* (collect.) or desc. of Shuni:—Shunites.

7766. שׁוּנֵם **Shûwnêm,** *shoo-name´;* prob. from the same as 7764; *quietly; Shunem,* a place in Pal.:—Shunem.

7767. שׁוּנַמִּית **Shûwnammîyth,** *shoo-nam-meeth´;* patrial from 7766; a *Shunammitess,* or female inhab. of Shunem:—Shunamite.

7768. שָׁוַע **shâva',** *shaw-vah´;* a prim. root; prop. to *be free;* but used only causat. and reflex. to *halloo* (for help, i.e. *freedom* from some trouble):—cry (aloud, out), shout.

7769. שׁוּעַ **shûwa',** *shoo´-ah;* from 7768; a *halloo:*—cry, riches.

7770. שׁוּעַ **Shûwa',** *shoo´-ah;* the same as 7769; *Shuä,* a Canaanite:—Shua, Shuah.

7771. שׁוֹעַ **shôwa',** *sho´-ah;* from 7768 in the orig. sense of *freedom;* a *noble,* i.e. *liberal, opulent;* also (as noun in the derived sense) a *halloo:*—bountiful, crying, rich.

7772. שׁוֹעַ **Shôwa',** *sho´-ah;* the same as 7771; *rich; Shoä,* an Oriental people:—Shoa.

7773. שֶׁוַע **sheva',** *sheh´-vah;* from 7768; a *halloo:*—cry.

7774. שׁוּעָא **Shûw'â',** *shoo-aw´;* from 7768; *wealth; Shuä,* an Israelitess:—Shua.

7775. שַׁוְעָה **shav'âh,** *shav-aw´;* fem. of 7773; a *hallooing:*—crying.

7776. שׁוּעָל **shûw'âl,** *shoo-awl´;* or שֻׁעָל **shû'âl,** *shoo-awl´;* from the same as 8168; a *jackal* (as a *burrower*):—fox.

7777. שׁוּעָל **Shûw'âl,** *shoo-awl´;* the same as 7776; *Shuäl,* the name of an Isr. and of a place in Pal.:—Shual.

7778. שׁוֹעֵר **shôw'êr,** *sho-are´;* or שֹׁעֵר **shô'êr,** *sho-are´;* act. part. of 8176 (as denom. from 8179); a *janitor:*—doorkeeper, porter.

7779. שׁוּף **shûwph,** *shoof;* a prim. root; prop. to *gape,* i.e. *snap* at; fig. to *overwhelm:*—break, bruise, cover.

7780. שׁוֹפָךְ **Shôwphâk,** *sho-fawk´;* from 8210; *poured; Shophak,* a Syrian:—Shophach.

7781. שׁוּפָמִי **Shûwphâmîy,** *shoo-faw-mee´;* patron. from 8197; a *Shuphamite* (collect.) or desc. of Shephupham:—Shuphamite.

שׁוֹפָן **Shôwphân.** See 5855.

7782. שׁוֹפָר **shôwphâr,** *sho-far´;* or שֹׁפָר **shôphâr,** *sho-far´;* from 8231 in the orig. sense of *incising;* a *cornet* (as giving a *clear* sound) or curved horn:—cornet, trumpet.

7783. שׁוּק **shûwq,** *shook;* a prim. root; to *run* after or over, i.e. *overflow:*—overflow, water.

7784. שׁוּק **shûwq,** *shook;* from 7783; a *street* (as *run* over):—street.

7785. שׁוֹק **shôwq,** *shoke;* from 7783; the (lower) *leg* (as a *runner*):—hip, leg, shoulder, thigh.

7786. שׂוּר **sûwr,** *soor;* a prim. root; prop. to *vanquish;* by impl. to *rule* (caus. *crown*):—make princes, have power, reign. See 5493.

7787. שׂוּר **sûwr,** *soor;* a prim. root; [rather ident. with 7786 through the idea of *reducing* to pieces; comp. 4883]; to *saw:*—cut.

7788. שׁוּר **shûwr,** *shoor;* a prim. root; prop. to *turn,* i.e. *travel* about (as a harlot or a merchant):—go, sing. See also 7891.

7789. שׁוּר **shûwr,** *shoor;* a prim. root [rather ident. with 7788 through the idea of *going round* for inspection]; to *spy* out, i.e. (gen.) *survey,* (for evil) *lurk for,* (for good) *care for:*—behold, lay wait, look, observe, perceive, regard, see.

7790. שׁוּר **shûwr,** *shoor;* from 7789; a *foe* (as *lying in wait*):—enemy.

7791. שׁוּר **shûwr,** *shoor;* from 7788; a *wall* (as *going about*):—wall.

7792. שׁוּר **shûwr** (Chald.), *shoor;* corresp. to 7791:—wall.

7793. שׁוּר **Shûwr,** *shoor;* the same as 7791; *Shur,* a region of the Desert:—Shur.

7794. שׁוֹר **shôwr,** *shore;* from 7788; a *bullock* (as a *traveller):*—bull (-ock), cow, ox, wall [*by mistake for* 7791].

7795. שׂוֹרָה **sôwrâh,** *so-raw´;* from 7786 in the prim. sense of 5493; prop. a *ring,* i.e. (by analogy) a *row* (adv.):—principal.

שׂוֹרֵק **sôwrêq.** See 8321.

7796. שׂוֹרֵק **Sôwrêq,** *so-rake´;* the same as 8321; a *vine; Sorek,* a valley in Pal.:—Sorek.

7797. שׂוּשׂ **sûws,** *soos;* or שִׂישׂ **sîys,** *sece;* a prim. root; to *be bright,* i.e. *cheerful:*—be glad, × greatly, joy, make mirth, rejoice.

7798. שַׁוְשָׁא **Shavshâ',** *shav-shaw´;* from 7797; *joyful; Shavsha,* an Isr.:—Shavsha.

7799. שׁוּשַׁן **shûwshan,** *shoo-shan´;* or שׁוֹשָׁן **shôwshân,** *sho-shawn´;* or שֹׁשָׁן **shôshân,** *sho-shawn´;* and (fem.) שׁוֹשַׁנָּה **shôwshannâh,** *sho-shan-naw´;* from 7797; a *lily* (from its *whiteness*), as a flower or arch. ornament; also a (straight) *trumpet* (from the *tubular* shape):—lily, Shoshannim.

7800. שׁוּשַׁן **Shûwshan,** *shoo-shan´;* the same as 7799; *Shushan,* a place in Persia:—Shushan.

7801. שׁוּשַׁנְכִי **Shûwshankîy** (Chald.), *shoo-shan-kee´;* or for. or.; a *Shushankite* (collect.) or inhab. of some unknown place in Ass.:—Susanchites.

7802. שׁוּשַׁן עֵדוּת **Shûwshan 'Êdûwth,** *shoo-shan´ ay-dooth´;* or (plur. of former) שׁוֹשַׁנִּים עֵדוּת **Shôwshannîym 'Êdûwth,** *sho-shan-neem´ ay-dooth´;* from 7799 and 5715; *lily* (or *trumpet*) *of assemblage; Shushan-Eduth* or *Shoshannim-Eduth,* the title of a popular song:—Shoshannim-Eduth, Shushan-eduth.

שׁוּשַׁק° **Shûwshaq.** See 7895.

7803. שׁוּתֶלַח **Shûwthelach,** *shoo-theh´-lakh;* prob. from 7582 and the same as 8520; *crash of breakage; Shuthelach,* the name of two Isr.:—Shuthelah.

7804. שְׁזַב **sh**e**zab** (Chald.) *shez-ab´;* corresp. to 5800; to *leave,* i.e. (caus.) *free:*—deliver.

7805. שָׁזַף **shâzaph,** *shaw-zaf´;* a prim. root; to *tan* (by sun-burning); fig. (as if by a piercing ray) to *scan:*—look up, see.

7806. שָׁזַר **shâzar,** *shaw-zar´;* a prim. root; to *twist* (a thread of straw):—twine.

7807. שַׁח **shach,** *shakh;* from 7817; *sunk,* i.e. *downcast:*— + humble.

7808. שֵׂחַ **sêach,** *say´-akh;* for 7879; *communion,* i.e. (reflex.) *meditation:*—thought.

7809. שָׁחַד **shâchad,** *shaw-khad´;* a prim. root; to *donate,* i.e. *bribe:*—hire, give a reward.

7810. שַׁחַד **shachad,** *shakh´-ad;* from 7809; a *donation* (venal or redemptive):—bribe (-ry), gift, present, reward.

7811. שָׂחָה **sâchâh,** *saw-khaw´;* a prim. root; to *swim;* caus. to *inundate:*—(make to) swim.

7812. שָׁחָה **shâchâh,** *shaw-khaw´;* a prim. root; to *depress,* i.e. *prostrate* (espec. reflex. in homage to royalty or God):—bow (self) down, crouch, fall down (flat), humbly beseech, do (make) obeisance, do reverence, make to stoop, worship.

7813. שָׂחוּ **sâchûw,** *saw´-khoo´;* from 7811; a *pond* (for *swimming*):—to swim in.

7814. שְׂחוֹק **s**e**chôwq,** *sekh-oke´;* or שְׂחֹק **s**e**chôq,** *sekh-oke´;* from 7832; *laughter* (in merriment or defiance):—derision, laughter (-ed to scorn, -ing), mocked, sport.

7815. שְׁחוֹר **sh**e**chôwr,** *shekh-ore´;* from 7835; *dinginess,* i..e. perh. *soot:*—coal.

שִׁחוֹר **shîchôwr.** See 7883.

שָׁחוֹר **shâchôwr.** See 7838.

7816. שְׁחוּת **sh**e**chûwth,** *shekh-ooth´;* from 7812; *pit:*—pit.

7817. שָׁחַח **shâchach,** *shaw-khakh´;* a prim. root; to *sink* or *depress* (reflex. or caus.):—bend, bow (down), bring (cast) down, couch, humble self, be (bring) low, stoop.

7818. שָׂחַט **sâchaṭ,** *saw-khat´;* a prim. root; to *tread* out, i.e. *squeeze* (grapes):—press.

7819. שָׁחַט **shâchaṭ,** *shaw-khat´;* a prim. root; to *slaughter* (in sacrifice or massacre):—kill, offer, shoot out, slay, slaughter.

7820. שָׁחַט **shâchaṭ,** *shaw-khat´;* a prim. root [rather ident. with 7819 through the idea of *striking*]; to *hammer* out:—beat.

7821. שְׁחִיטָה **sh**e**chîyṭâh,** *shekh-ee-taw´;* from 7819; *slaughter:*—killing.

7822. שְׁחִין **sh**e**chîyn,** *shekh-een´;* from an unused root prob. mean. to *burn; inflammation,* i.e. an *ulcer:*—boil, botch.

7823. שָׁחִיס **shâchîyç,** *shaw-khece´;* or סָחִישׁ **çâchîysh,** *saw-kheesh´;* from an unused root appar. mean. to *sprout, after-growth:*—(that) which springeth of the same.

7824. שָׁחִיף **shâchîyph,** *shaw-kheef´;* from the same as 7828; a *board* (as *chipped* thin):—cieled with.

7825. שְׁחִית **sh**e**chîyth,** *shekh-eeth´;* from 7812; a *pit*-fall (lit. or fig.):—destruction, pit.

7826. שַׁחַל **shachal,** *shakh´-al;* from an unused root prob. mean. to *roar;* a *lion* (from his characteristic *roar*):—(fierce) lion.

7827. שְׁחֵלֶת **sh**e**chêleth,** *shekh-ay´-leth;* appar. from the same as 7826 through some obscure idea, perh. that of *peeling* off by concussion of sound; a *scale* or shell, i.e. the aromatic *mussel:*—onycha.

7828. שַׁחַף **shachaph,** *shakh´-af;* from an unused root mean. to *peel,* i.e. *emaciate;* the *gull (as thin)*:—cuckoo.

7829. שַׁחֶפֶת **shachepheth,** *shakh-eh´-feth;* from the same as 7828; *emaciation:*—consumption.

7830. שַׁחַץ **shachats,** *shakh´-ats;* from an unused root appar. mean. to *strut; haughtiness* (as evinced by the attitude):— × lion, pride.

7831. שַׁחֲצוֹם° **Shachatsôwm,** *shakh-ats-ome´;* from the same as 7830; *proudly; Shachatsom,* a place in Pal.:—Shahazimah [*from the marg.*].

7832. שָׂחַק **sâchaq,** *saw-khak´;* a prim. root; to *laugh* (in pleasure or detraction); by impl. to *play:*—deride, have in derision, laugh, make merry, mock (-er), play, rejoice, (laugh to) scorn, be in (make) sport.

7833. שָׁחַק **shâchaq,** *shaw-khak´;* a prim. root; to *comminute* (by trituration or attrition):—beat, wear.

7834. שַׁחַק **shachaq,** *shakh´-ak;* from 7833; a *powder* (as *beaten* small); by anal. a thin *vapor;* by extens. the *firmament:*—cloud, small dust, heaven, sky.

שְׂחֹק **s**e**chôq.** See 7814.

7835. שָׁחַר **shâchar,** *shaw-khar´;* a prim. root [rather ident. with 7836 through the idea of the *duskiness* of early dawn]; to be *dim* or dark (in color):—be black.

7836. שָׁחַר **shâchar,** *shaw-khar´;* a prim. root; prop. to *dawn,* i. e. (fig.) *be* (up) *early* at any task (with the impl. of earnestness); by extens. to *search* for (with painstaking):—[do something] betimes, enquire early, rise (seek) betimes, seek (diligently) early, in the morning).

7837. שַׁחַר **shachar,** *shakh´-ar;* from 7836; *dawn* (lit., fig. or adv.):—day (-spring), early, light, morning, whence riseth.

שִׁחֹר **Shîchôr.** See 7883.

7838. שָׁחֹר **shâchôr,** *shaw-khore´;* or שָׁחוֹר **shâchôwr,** *shaw-khore´;* from 7835; prop. *dusky,* but also (absol.) *jetty:*—black.

7839. שַׁחֲרוּת **shachărûwth,** *shakh-ar-ooth´;* from 7836; a *dawning,* i.e. (fig.) *juvenescence:*—youth.

7840. שְׁחַרְחֹרֶת **sh^{e}charchôreth,** *shekh-ar-kho´-reth;* from 7835; *swarthy:*—black.

7841. שְׁחַרְיָה **Sh^{e}charyâh,** *shekh-ar-yaw´;* from 7836 and 3050; *Jah has sought; Shecharjah,* an Isr.:—Shehariah.

7842. שַׁחֲרַיִם **Shachărayim,** *shakh-ar-ah´-yim;* dual of 7837; *double dawn; Shacharajim,* an Isr.:—Shaharaim.

7843. שָׁחַת **shâchath,** *shaw-khath´;* a prim. root; to *decay,* i.e. (caus.) *ruin* (lit. or fig.):—batter, cast off, corrupt (-er, thing), destroy (-er, -uction), lose, mar, perish, spill, spoiler, × utterly, waste (-r).

7844. שְׁחַת **sh^{e}chath** (Chald.), *shekh-ath´;* corresp. to 7843:—corrupt, fault.

7845. שַׁחַת **shachath,** *shakh´-ath;* from 7743; a *pit* (espec. as a trap); fig. *destruction:*—corruption, destruction, ditch, grave, pit.

7846. שֵׂט **sêṭ,** *sayte;* or סֵט **çêṭ,** *sayt;* from 7750; a *departure* from right, i.e. *sin:*—revolter, that turn aside.

7847. שָׂטָה **sâṭâh,** *saw-taw´;* a prim. root; to *deviate* from duty:—decline, go aside, turn.

7848. שִׁטָּה **shiṭṭâh,** *shit-taw´;* fem. of a deriv. [only in the plur. שִׁטִּים **shiṭṭîym,** *shit-teem´,* mean. the *sticks* of wood] from the same as 7850; the *acacia* (from its *scourging* thorns):—shittah, shittim. See also 1029.

7849. שָׁטַח **shâṭach,** *shaw-takh´;* a prim. root; to *expand:*—all abroad, enlarge, spread, stretch out.

7850. שֹׁטֵט **shôṭêṭ,** *sho-tate´;* act. part. of an otherwise unused root mean. (prop. to *pierce;* but only as a denom. from 7752) to *flog;* a *goad:*—scourge.

7851. שִׁטִּים **Shiṭṭîym,** *shit-teem´;* the same as the plur. of 7848; *acacia* trees; *Shittim,* a place E. of the Jordan:—Shittim.

7852. שָׂטַם **sâṭam,** *saw-tam´;* a prim. root; prop. to *lurk* for, i.e. *persecute:*—hate, oppose self against.

7853. שָׂטַן **sâṭan,** *saw-tan´;* a prim. root; to *attack,* (fig.) *accuse:*—(be an) adversary, resist.

7854. שָׂטָן **sâṭân,** *saw-tawn´;* from 7853; an *opponent:* espec. (with the art. pref.) *Satan,* the arch-enemy of good:—adversary, Satan, withstand.

7855. שִׂטְנָה **siṭnâh,** *sit-naw´;* from 7853; *opposition* (by letter):—accusation.

7856. שִׂטְנָה **Siṭnâh,** *sit-naw´;* the same as 7855; *Sitnah,* the name of a well in Pal.:—Sitnah.

7857. שָׁטַף **shâṭaph,** *shaw-taf´;* a prim. root; to *gush;* by impl. to *inundate, cleanse;* by anal. to *gallop, conquer:*—drown, (over-) flow (-whelm), rinse, run, rush, (throughly) wash (away).

7858. שֶׁטֶף **sheṭeph,** *sheh´-tef;* or שֵׁטֶף **shêṭeph,** *shay´-tef;* from 7857; a *deluge* (lit. or fig.):—flood, outrageous, overflowing.

7859. שְׁטַר **sh^{e}ṭar** (Chald.), *shet-ar´;* of uncert. der.:—a *side:*—side.

7860. שֹׁטֵר **shôṭêr,** *sho-tare´;* act. part. of an otherwise unused root prob. mean. to *write;* prop. a *scribe,* i.e. (by anal. or impl.) an official *superintendent* or *magistrate:*—officer, overseer, ruler.

7861. שִׁטְרַי° **Shiṭray,** *shit-rah´ee;* from the same as 7860; *magisterial; Shitrai,* an Isr.:—Shitrai.

7862. שַׁי **shay,** *shah´ee;* prob. from 7737; a *gift* (as *available*):—present.

7863. שִׂיא **sîy',** *see;* from the same as 7721 by perm,; *elevation:*—excellency.

7864. שְׁיָא° **Sh^{e}yâ',** *sheh-yaw´;* for 7724; *Sheja,* an Isr.:—Sheva [*from the marg.*].

7865. שִׂיאֹן **Sîy'ôn,** *see-ohn´;* from 7863; *peak; Sion,* the summit of Mt. Hermon:—Sion.

7866. שִׁיאוֹן **Shî'yôwn,** *shee-ohn´;* from the same as 7722; *ruin; Shijon,* a place in Pal.:—Shihon.

7867. שִׂיב **sîyb,** *seeb;* a prim. root; prop. to *become aged,* i.e. (by impl.) to *grow gray:*—(be) grayheaded.

7868. שִׂיב **sîyb** (Chald.), *seeb;* corresp. to 7867:—elder.

7869. שֵׂיב **sêyb,** *sabe;* from 7867; old *age:*—age.

7870. שִׁיבָה **shîybâh,** *shee-baw´;* by perm. from 7725; a *return* (of property):—captivity.

7871. שִׁיבָה **shîybâh,** *shee-baw´;* from 3427; *residence:*—while . . . lay.

7872. שֵׂיבָה **sêybâh,** *say-baw´;* fem. of 7869; old *age:*—(be) gray (grey, hoar, -y) hairs (head, -ed), old age.

7873. שִׂיג **sîyg,** *seeg;* from 7734; a *withdrawal* (into a private place):—pursuing.

7874. שִׂיד **sîyd,** *seed;* a prim. root prob. mean. to *boil* up (comp. 7736); used only as denom. from 7875; to *plaster:*—plaister.

7875. שִׂיד **sîyd,** *seed;* from 7874; *lime* (as *boiling* when slacked):—lime, plaister.

7876. שָׁיָה **shâyâh,** *shaw-yaw´;* a prim. root; to *keep* in memory:—be unmindful. [Render Deut. 32 : 18, "A Rock bore thee, *thou must recollect;* and (yet) thou hast forgotten," etc.]

7877. שִׁיזָא **Shîyzâ',** *shee-zaw´;* of unknown der.; *Shiza,* an Isr.:—Shiza.

7878. שִׂיחַ **sîyach,** *see´-akh;* a prim. root; to *ponder,* i.e. (by impl.) *converse* (with oneself, and hence aloud) or (trans.) *utter:*—commune, complain, declare, meditate, muse, pray, speak, talk (with).

7879. שִׂיחַ **sîyach,** *see´-akh;* from 7878, a *contemplation;* by impl. an *utterance:*—babbling, communication, complaint, meditation, prayer, talk.

7880. שִׂיחַ **sîyach,** *see´-akh;* from 7878; a *shoot* (as if *uttered* or put forth), i.e. (gen.) *shrubbery:*—bush, plant, shrub.

7881. שִׂיחָה **sîychâh,** *see-khaw´;* fem. of 7879; *reflection;* by extens. *devotion:*—meditation, prayer.

7882. שִׁיחָה **shîychâh,** *shee-khaw´;* for 7745; a *pit*-fall:—pit.

7883. שִׁיחוֹר **Shîychôwr,** *shee-khore´;* or שִׁחוֹר **Shîchôwr,** *shee-khore´;* or שִׁחֹר **Shîchôr,** *shee-khore´;* prob. from 7835; *dark,* i.e. *turbid; Shichor,* a stream of Egypt:—Shihor, Sihor.

7884. שִׁיחוֹר לִבְנָת **Shîychôwr Libnâth,** *shee-khore´ lib-nawth´;* from the same as 7883 and 3835; *darkish whiteness; Shichor-Libnath,* a stream of Pal.:—Shihor-libnath.

7885. שַׁיִט **shayiṭ,** *shah´yit;* from 7751; an *oar;* also (comp. 7752) a *scourge*° (fig.):—oar, scourge.

7886. שִׁילֹה **Shîylôh,** *shee-lo´;* from 7951; *tranquil; Shiloh,* an epithet of the Messiah:—Shiloh.

7887. שִׁילֹה **Shîylôh,** *shee-lo´;* or שִׁלֹה **Shîlôh,** *shee-lo´;* or שִׁילוֹ **Shîylôw,** *shee-lo´;* or שִׁלוֹ **Shîlôw,** *shee-lo´;* from the same as 7886; *Shiloh,* a place in Pal.:—Shiloh.

7888. שִׁילוֹנִי **Shiylôwnîy,** *shee-lo-nee´;* or שִׁילֹנִי **Shîylônîy,** *shee-lo-nee´;* or שִׁלֹנִי **Shîlônîy,** *shee-lo-nee´;* from 7887; a *Shilonite* or inhab. of Shiloh:—Shilonite.

שֵׁילָל **shêylâl.** See 7758.

7889. שִׁימוֹן **Shîymôwn,** *shee-mone´;* appar. for 3452; *desert; Shimon,* an Isr.:—Shimon.

7890. שַׁיִן° **shayin,** *shah´-yin;* from an unused root mean. to *urinate; urine:*—piss.

7891. שִׁיר **shîyr,** *sheer;* or (the orig. form) שׁוּר° **shûwr** (1 Sam. 18 : 6), *shoor;* a prim. root [rather ident. with 7788 through the idea of *strolling* minstrelsy]; to *sing:*—behold [*by mistake for* 7789], sing (-er, -ing man, -ing woman).

7892. שִׁיר **shîyr,** *sheer;* or fem. שִׁירָה **shîyrâh,** *shee-raw´;* from 7891; a *song;* abstr. *singing:*—musical (-ick), × sing (-er, -ing), song.

שִׁישׁ **sîys.** See 7797.

7893. שַׁיִשׁ **shayish,** *shah´-yish;* from an unused root mean. to *bleach,* i.e. *whiten; white,* i.e. *marble:*—marble. See 8336.

7894. שִׁישָׁא **Shîyshâ',** *shee-shaw´;* from the same as 7893; *whiteness; Shisha,* an Isr.:—Shisha.

7895. שִׁישַׁק **Shîyshaq,** *shee-shak´;* or שׁוּשַׁק° **Shûwshaq,** *shoo-shak´;* of Eg. der.; *Shishak,* an Eg. king:—Shishak.

7896. שִׁית **shîyth,** *sheeth;* a prim. root; to *place* (in a very wide application):—apply, appoint, array, bring, consider, lay (up), let alone, × look, make, mark, put (on), + regard, set, shew, be stayed, × take.

7897. שִׁית **shîyth,** *sheeth;* from 7896; a *dress* (as *put* on):—attire.

7898. שַׁיִת **shayith,** *shah´-yith;* from 7896; *scrub* or *trash,* i.e. wild *growth* of weeds or briers (as if *put* on the field):—thorns.

7899. שֵׂךְ **sêk,** *sake;* from 5526 in the sense of 7753; a *brier* (as of a hedge):—prick.

7900. שֹׂךְ **sôk,** *soke;* from 5526 in the sense of 7753; a *booth* (as *interlaced*):—tabernacle.

7901. שָׁכַב **shâkab,** *shaw-kab´;* a prim. root; to *lie* down (for rest, sexual connection, decease or any other purpose):— × at all, cast down, ([over-]) lay (self) (down), (make to) lie (down, down to sleep, still, with), lodge, ravish, take rest, sleep, stay.

7902. שְׁכָבָה **shᵉkâbâh,** *shek-aw-baw´;* from 7901; a *lying* down (of dew, or for the sexual act):— × carnally, copulation, × lay, seed.

7903. שְׁכֹבֶת **shᵉkôbeth,** *shek-o´-beth;* from 7901; a (sexual) *lying* with:— × lie.

7904. שָׁכָה **shâkâh,** *shaw-kaw´;* a prim. root; to *roam* (through lust):—in the morning [*by mistake for* 7925].

7905. שֻׂכָּה **sukkâh,** *sook-kaw´;* fem. of 7900 in the sense of 7899; a *dart* (as pointed like a *thorn*):—barbed iron.

7906. שֵׂכוּ **Sêkûw,** *say´-koo;* from an unused root appar. mean. to *surmount;* an *observatory* (with the art.); *Seku,* a place in Pal.:—Sechu.

7907. שֶׂכְוִי **sekvîy,** *sek-vee´;* from the same as 7906; *observant,* i.e. (concr.) the *mind:*—heart.

7908. שְׁכוֹל **shᵉkôwl,** *shek-ole´;* infin. of 7921; *bereavement:*—loss of children, spoiling.

7909. שַׁכּוּל **shakkuwl,** *shak-kool´;* or שַׁכֻּל **shakkul,** *shak-kool´;* from 7921; *bereaved:*—barren, bereaved (robbed) of children (whelps).

7910. שִׁכּוֹר **shikkôwr,** *shik-kore´;* or שִׁכֹּר **shikkôr,** *shik-kore´;* from 7937; *intoxicated,* as a state or a habit:—drunk (-ard, -en, -en man).

7911. שָׁכַח **shâkach,** *shaw-kakh´;* or שָׁכֵחַ **shâkêach,** *shaw-kay´-akh,* a prim. root; to *mislay,* i.e. to *be oblivious* of, from want of memory or attention:— × at all, (cause to) forget.

7912. שְׁכַח **shᵉkach** (Chald.), *shek-akh´;* corresp. to 7911 through the idea of disclosure of a *covered* or *forgotten* thing; to *discover* (lit. or fig.):—find.

7913. שָׁכֵחַ **shâkêach,** *shaw-kay´-akh;* from 7911; *oblivious:*—forget.

7914. שְׂכִיָּה **sᵉkîyâh,** *sek-ee-yaw´;* fem. from the same as 7906; a *conspicuous* object:—picture.

7915. שַׂכִּין **sakkîyn,** *sak-keen´;* intens. perh. from the same as 7906 in the sense of 7753; a *knife* (as *pointed* or edged):—knife.

7916. שָׂכִיר **sâkîyr,** *saw-keer´;* from 7936; a man *at wages* by the day or year:—hired (man, servant), hireling.

7917. שְׂכִירָה **sᵉkîyrâh,** *sek-ee-raw´;* fem. of 7916; a *hiring:*—that is hired.

7918. שָׁכַךְ **shâkak,** *shaw-kak´;* a prim. root; to *weave* (i.e. *lay*) a trap; fig. (through the idea of *secreting*) to *allay* (passions; phys. *abate* a flood):—appease, assuage, make to cease, pacify, set.

7919. שָׂכַל **sâkal,** *saw-kal´;* a prim. root; to *be* (caus. *make* or *act*) *circumspect* and hence *intelligent:*—consider, expert, instruct, prosper, (deal) prudent (-ly), (give) skill (-ful), have good success, teach, (have, make to) understand (-ing), wisdom, (be, behave self, consider, make) wise (-ly), guide wittingly.

7920. שְׂכַל **sᵉkal** (Chald.), *sek-al´;* corresp. to 7919:—consider.

7921. שָׁכֹל **shâkôl,** *shaw-kole´;* a prim. root; prop. to *miscarry,* i.e. *suffer abortion;* by anal. to *bereave* (lit. or fig.):—bereave (of children), barren, cast calf (fruit, young), be (make) childless, deprive, destroy, × expect, lose children, miscarry, rob of children, spoil.

7922. שֶׂכֶל **sekel,** *seh´-kel;* or שֵׂכֶל **sêkel,** *say´-kel;* from 7919; *intelligence;* by impl. *success:*—discretion, knowledge, policy, prudence, sense, understanding, wisdom, wise.

שַׁכֻּל **shakkûl.** See 7909.

שִׂכְלוּת **siklûwth.** See 5531.

7923. שִׁכֻּלִים **shikkûlîym,** *shik-koo-leem´;* plur. from 7921; *childlessness* (by continued bereavements):—to have after loss of others.

7924. שָׂכְלְתָנוּ **soklᵉthânûw** (Chad.), *sok-leth-aw-noo´;* from 7920; *intelligence:*—understanding.

7925. שָׁכַם **shâkam,** *shaw-kam´;* a prim. root; prop. to *incline* (the shoulder to a burden); but used only as denom. from 7926; lit. to *load up* (on the back of man or beast), i.e. to *start early* in the morning:—(arise, be up, get [oneself] up, rise up) early (betimes), morning.

7926. שְׁכֶם **shᵉkem,** *shek-em´;* from 7925; the *neck* (between the shoulers) as the place of burdens; fig. the *spur* of a hill:—back, × consent, portion, shoulder.

7927. שְׁכֶם **Shᵉkem,** *shek-em´;* the same as 7926; *ridge; Shekem,* a place in Pal.:—Shechem.

7928. שֶׁכֶם **Shekem,** *sheh´-kem;* for 7926; *Shekem,* the name of a Hivite and two Isr.:—Shechem.

7929. שִׁכְמָה **shikmâh,** *shik-maw´;* fem. of 7926; the *shoulder*-bone:—shoulder blade.

7930. שִׁכְמִי **Shikmîy,** *shik-mee´;* patron. from 7928; a *Shikmite* (collect.), or desc. of Shekem:—Shichemites.

7931. שָׁכַן **shâkan,** *shaw-kan´;* a prim. root [appar. akin (by transm.) to 7901 through the idea of *lodging;* comp. 5531, 7925]; to *reside* or permanently stay (lit. or fig.):—abide, continue, (cause to, make to) dwell (-er), have habitation, inhabit, lay, place, (cause to) remain, rest, set (up).

7932. שְׁכַן **shᵉkan** (Chald.), *shek-an´;* corresp. to 7931:—cause to dwell, have habitation.

7933. שֶׁכֶן **sheken,** *sheh´-ken;* from 7931; a *residence:*—habitation.

7934. שָׁכֵן **shâkên,** *shaw-kane´;* from 7931; a *resident;* by extens. a fellow-*citizen:*—inhabitant, neighbour, nigh.

7935. שְׁכַנְיָה **Shᵉkanyâh,** *shek-an-yaw´;* or (prol.) שְׁכַנְיָהוּ **Shᵉkanyâhûw,** *shek-an-yaw´-hoo;* from 7931 and 3050; *Jah has dwelt; Shekanjah,* the name of nine Isr.:—Shecaniah, Shechaniah.

7936. שָׂכַר **sâkar,** *saw-kar´;* or (by perm.) סָכַר **çâkar** (Ezra 4 : 5), *saw-kar´;* a prim. root [appar. akin (by prosthesis) to 3739 through the idea of temporary *purchase;* comp. 7937]; to *hire:*—earn wages, hire (out self), reward, × surely.

7937. שָׁכַר **shâkar,** *shaw-kar´;* a prim. root; to *become tipsy;* in a qualified sense, to *satiate* with a stimulating drink or (fig.) influence:—(be filled with) drink (abundantly), (be, make) drunk (-en), be merry. [Superlative of 8248.]

7938. שֶׂכֶר **seker,** *seh´-ker;* from 7936; *wages:*—reward, sluices.

7939. שָׂכָר **sâkâr,** *saw-kawr´;* from 7936; *payment* of contract; concr. *salary, fare, maintenance;* by impl. *compensation, benefit:*—hire, price, reward [-ed], wages, worth.

7940. שָׂכָר **Sâkar,** *saw-kar´;* the same as 7939; *recompense; Sakar,* the name of two Isr.:—Sacar.

7941. שֵׁכָר **shêkâr,** *shay-kawr´;* from 7937; an *intoxicant,* i.e. intensely alcoholic *liquor:*—strong drink, + drunkard, strong wine.

שִׁכֹּר **shikkôr.** See 7910.

7942. שִׁכְּרוֹן **Shikkᵉrôwn,** *shik-ker-one´;* for 7943; *drunkenness; Shikkeron,* a place in Pal.:—Shicron.

7943. שִׁכָּרוֹן **shikkârôwn,** *shik-kaw-rone´;* from 7937; *intoxication:*—(be) drunken (-ness).

7944. שַׁל **shal,** *shal;* from 7952 abbrev.; a *fault:*—error.

7945. שֶׁל **shel,** *shel;* for the rel. 834; used with prep. pref., and often followed by some pron. aff.; on *account* of, *what*soever, *which*soever:—cause, sake.

7946. שַׁלְאֲנָן **shal'ănân,** *shal-an-awn´;* for 7600; *tranquil:*—being at ease.

7947. שָׁלַב **shâlab,** *shaw-lab´;* a prim. root; to *space* off; intens. (*evenly*) to *make equi-distant:*—equally distant, set in order.

7948. שָׁלָב **shâlâb,** *shaw-lawb´;* from 7947; a *spacer* or raised *interval,* i.e. the *stile* in a frame or panel:—ledge.

7949. שָׁלַג **shâlag,** *shaw-lag´;* a prim. root; prop. mean. to be *white;* used only as denom. from 7950; to be *snow-white* (with the linen clothing of the slain):—be as snow.

7950. שֶׁלֶג **sheleg,** *sheh´-leg;* from 7949; *snow* (prob. from its *whiteness*):—snow (-y).

7951. שָׁלָה **shâlâh,** *shaw-law´;* or שָׁלַו **shâlav** (Job 3 : 26), *shaw-lav´;* a prim. root; to be *tranquil,* i.e. *secure* or *successful:*—be happy, prosper, be in safety.

7952. שָׁלָה **shâlâh,** *shaw-law´;* a prim. root [prob. rather ident. with 7953 through the idea of *educing*]; to *mislead:*—deceive, be negligent.

7953. שָׁלָה **shâlâh,** *shaw-law´;* a prim. root [rather cognate (by contr.) to the base of 5394, 7997 and their congeners through the idea of *extracting*]; to *draw* out or off, i.e. *remove* (the soul by death):—take away.

7954. שְׁלָה **shᵉlâh** (Chald.), *shel-aw´;* corresp. to 7951; to *be secure:*—at rest.

שִׁלֹה **Shîlôh.** See 7887.

7955. שָׁלָה° **shâlâh** (Chald.), *shaw-law´;* from a root corresp. to 7952; a *wrong:*—thing amiss.

שֵׁלָה **shêlâh.** See 7596.

7956. שֵׁלָה **Shêlâh,** *shay-law´;* the same as 7596 (shortened); *request; Shelah,* the name of a postdiluvian patriarch and of an Isr.:—Shelah.

7957. שַׁלְהֶבֶת **shalhebeth,** *shal-heh´-beth;* from the same as 3851 with sibilant pref.; a *flare* of fire:—(flaming) flame.

שָׁלֵו **shâlav.** See 7951.

7958. שְׂלָו° **sᵉlâv,** *sel-awv´;* or שְׂלָיו **sᵉlâyv,** *sel-awv´;* by orth. var. from 7951 through the idea of *sluggishness;* the *quail* collect. (as *slow* in flight from its weight):—quails.

7959. שֶׁלֶו **shelev,** *sheh´-lev;* from 7951; *security:*—prosperity.

שִׁלוֹ **Shîlôw.** See 7887.

7960. שָׁלוּ **shâlûw** (Chald.), *shaw-loo´;* or שָׁלוּת **shâlûwth** (Chald.), *shaw-looth´;* from the same as 7955; a *fault:*—error, × fail, thing amiss.

7961. שָׁלֵו **shâlêv,** *shaw-lave´;* or שָׁלֵיו **shâlêyv,** *shaw-lave´;* fem. שְׁלֵוָה **shᵉlêvâh,** *shel-ay-vaw´;* from 7951; *tranquil;* (in a bad sense) *careless;* abstr. *security:*—(being) at ease, peaceable, (in) prosper (-ity), quiet (-ness), wealthy.

7962. שַׁלְוָה **shalvâh,** *shal-vaw´;* from 7951; *security* (genuine or false):—abundance, peace (-ably), prosperity, quietness.

7963. שְׁלֵוָה **shᵉlêvâh** (Chald.), *shel-ay-vaw´;* corresp. to 7962; *safety:*—tranquility. See also 7961.

7964. שִׁלּוּחַ **shillûwach,** *shil-loo´-akh;* or שִׁלֻּחַ **shillûach,** *shil-loo´-akh;* from 7971; (only in plur.) a *dismissal,* i.e. (of a wife) *divorce* (espec. the document); also (of a daughter) *dower:*—presents, have sent back.

7965. שָׁלוֹם **shâlôwm,** *shaw-lome´;* or שָׁלֹם **shâlôm,** *shaw-lome´;* from 7999; *safe,* i.e. (fig.) *well, happy, friendly;* also (abstr.) *welfare,* i.e. health, prosperity, peace:— × do, familiar, × fare, favour, + friend, × greet, (good) health, (× perfect, such as be at) peace (-able, -ably), prosper (-ity, -ous), rest, safe (-ly), salute, welfare, (× all is, be) well, × wholly.

7966. שִׁלּוּם **shillûwm,** *shil-loom´;* or שִׁלֻּם **shillûm,** *shil-loom´;* from 7999; a *requital,* i.e. (secure) *retribution,* (venal) a *fee:*—recompense, reward.

7967. שַׁלּוּם **Shallûwm,** *shal-loom´; or (shorter)* שַׁלֻּם **Shallûm,** *shal-loom´;* the same as 7966; *Shallum,* the name of fourteen Isr.:—Shallum.

שְׁלוֹמִית **Shᵉlôwmîyth.** See 8019.

7968. שַׁלּוּן **Shallûwn,** *shal-loon´;* prob. for 7967; *Shallun,* an Isr.:—Shallum.

7969. שָׁלוֹשׁ **shâlôwsh,** *shaw-loshe´;* or שָׁלֹשׁ **shâlôsh,** *shaw-loshe´;* masc. שְׁלוֹשָׁה **shᵉlôwshâh,** *shel-o-shaw´;* or שְׁלֹשָׁה **shᵉlôshâh,** *shel-o-shaw´;* a prim. number; *three;* occasionally (ordinal) *third,* or (multipl.) *thrice:*— + fork, + often [-times], third, thir [-teen, -teenth], three, + thrice. Comp. 7991.

7970. שְׁלוֹשִׁים **shᵉlôwshîym,** *shel-o-sheem´;* or שְׁלֹשִׁים **shᵉlôshîym,** *shel-o-sheem´;* multiple of 7969; *thirty;* or (ordinal) *thirtieth:*— thirty, thirtieth. Comp. 7991.

שָׁלוּת **shâlûwth.** See 7960.

7971. שָׁלַח **shâlach,** *shaw-lakh´;* a prim. root; to *send* away, for, or out (in a great variety of applications):— × any wise, appoint, bring (on the way), cast (away, out), conduct, × earnestly, forsake, give (up), grow long, lay, leave, let depart (down, go, loose), push away, put (away, forth, in, out), reach forth, send (away, forth, out), set, shoot (forth, out), sow, spread, stretch forth (out).

7972. שְׁלַח **shᵉlach** (Chald.), *shel-akh´;* corresp. to 7971:—put, send.

7973. שֶׁלַח **shelach,** *sheh´-lakh;* from 7971; a *missle* of attack, i.e. *spear;* also (fig.) a *shoot* of growth, i.e. *branch:*—dart, plant, × put off, sword, weapon.

7974. שֶׁלַח **Shelach,** *sheh´-lakh;* the same as 7973; *Shelach,* a postdiluvian patriarch:—Salah, Shelah. Comp. 7975.

7975. שִׁלֹּחַ **Shilôach,** *shee-lo´-akh;* or (in imitation of 7974).

שֶׁלַח **Shelach** (Neh. 3 : 15), *sheh´-lakh;* from 7971; *rill; Shiloăch,* a fountain of Jerus.:—Shiloah, Siloah.

שִׁלֻּחַ **shillûach.** See 7964.

7976. שִׁלֻּחָה **shilluchâh,** *shil-loo-khaw´;* fem. of 7964; a *shoot:*—branch.

7977. שִׁלְחִי **Shilchîy,** *shil-khee´;* from 7973; *missive,* i.e. *armed; Shilchi,* an Isr.:—Shilhi.

7978. שִׁלְחִים **Shilchîym,** *shil-kheem´;* plur. of 7973; *javelins* or *sprouts; Shilchim,* a place in Pal.:—Shilhim.

7979. שֻׁלְחָן **shulchân,** *shool-khawn´;* from 7971; a *table* (as *spread* out); by impl. a *meal:*—table.

7980. שָׁלַט **shâlaṭ,** *shaw-lat´;* a prim. root; to *dominate,* i.e. *govern;* by impl. to *permit:*—(bear, have) rule, have dominion, give (have) power.

7981. שְׁלֵט **shᵉlêṭ** (Chald.), *shel-ate´;* corresp. to 7980:—have the mastery, have power, bear rule, be (make) ruler.

7982. שֶׁלֶט **sheleṭ,** *sheh´-let;* from 7980; prob. a *shield* (as *controlling,* i.e. protecting the person):—shield.

7983. שִׁלְטוֹן **shilṭôwn,** *shil-tone´;* from 7980; a *potentate:*—power.

7984. שִׁלְטוֹן **shilṭôwn** (Chald.), *shil-tone´;* or שִׁלְטֹן **shilṭôn,** *shil-tone´;* corresp. to 7983:—ruler.

7985. שָׁלְטָן **sholṭân** (Chald.), *shol-tawn´;* from 7981; *empire* (abstr. or concr.):—dominion.

7986. שַׁלֶּטֶת **shalleṭeth,** *shal-leh´-teth;* fem. from 7980; a *vixen:*—imperious.

7987. שְׁלִי **shᵉlîy,** *shel-ee´;* from 7951; *privacy:*— + quietly.

7988. שִׁלְיָה **shilyâh,** *shil-yaw´;* fem. from 7953; a *fœtus* or *babe* (as *extruded* in birth):—young one.

שְׂלָיו **sᵉlâyv.** See 7958.

שָׁלֵיו **shalêyv.** See 7961.

7989. שַׁלִּיט **shallîyṭ,** *shal-leet´;* from 7980; *potent;* concr. a *prince* or *warrior:*—governor, mighty, that hath power, ruler.

7990. שַׁלִּיט **shallîyṭ** (Chald.), *shal-leet´;* corresp. to 7989; *mighty;* abstr. *permission;* concr. a *premier:*—captain, be lawful, rule (-r).

7991. שָׁלִישׁ **shâlîysh,** *shaw-leesh´;* or שָׁלוֹשׁ° **shâlôwsh** (1 Chron. 11 : 11; 12 : 18). *shaw-loshe´;* or שָׁלשׁ° **shâlôsh** (2 Sam. 23 : 13), *shaw-loshe´;* from 7969; a *triple,* i.e. (as a musical instrument) a *triangle* (or perh. rather *three*-stringed lute); also (as an indef. great quantity) a *three*-fold measure (perh. a *treble* ephah); also (as an officer) a general of the *third* rank (upward, i.e. the highest):—captain, instrument of musick, (great) lord, (great) measure, prince, three [*from the marg.*].

7992. שְׁלִישִׁי **shelîyshîy,** *shel-ee-shee´;* ordinal from 7969; *third;* fem. a *third* (part); by extens. a *third* (day, year or time); spec. a *third*-story cell):—third (part, rank, time), three (years old).

7993. שָׁלַךְ **shâlak,** *shaw-lak´;* a prim. root; to *throw* out, down or away (lit. or fig.):—adventure, cast (away, down, forth, off, out), hurl, pluck, throw.

7994. שָׁלָךְ **shâlâk,** *shaw-lawk´;* from 7993; *bird of prey,* usually thought to be the *pelican* (from *casting* itself into the sea):—cormorant.

7995. שַׁלֶּכֶת **shalleketh,** *shal-leh´-keth;* from 7993; a *felling* (of trees):—when cast.

7996. שַׁלֶּכֶת **Shalleketh,** *shal-leh´-keth;* the same as 7995; *Shalleketh,* a gate in Jerus.:—Shalleketh.

7997. שָׁלַל **shâlal,** *shaw-lal´;* a prim. root; to *drop* or *strip;* by impl. to *plunder:*—let fall, make self a prey, × of purpose, (make a, [take]) spoil.

7998. שָׁלָל **shâlâl,** *shaw-lawl´;* from 7997; *booty:*—prey, spoil.

7999. שָׁלַם **shâlam,** *shaw-lam´;* a prim. root; to *be safe* (in mind, body or estate); fig. to *be* (caus. *make*) *completed;* by impl. to *be friendly;* by extens. to *reciprocate* (in various applications):—make amends, (make an) end, finish, full, give again, make good, (re-) pay (again), (make) (to) (be at) peace (-able), that is perfect, perform, (make) prosper (-ous), recompense, render, requite, make restitution, restore, reward, × surely.

8000. שְׁלַם **shelam** (Chald.), *shel-am´;* corresp. to 7999; to *complete,* to *restore:*—deliver, finish.

8001. שְׁלָם **shelâm** (Chad.), *shel-awm´;* corresp. to 7965; *prosperity:*—peace.

8002. שֶׁלֶם **shelem,** *sheh´-lem;* from 7999; prop. *requital,* i.e. a (voluntary) sacrifice in *thanks:*—peace offering.

8003. שָׁלֵם **shâlêm,** *shaw-lame´;* from 7999; *complete* (lit. or fig.); espec. *friendly:*—full, just, made ready, peaceable, perfect (-ed), quiet, Shalem [*by mistake for a name*], whole.

8004. שָׁלֵם **Shâlêm,** *shaw-lame´;* the same as 8003; *peaceful; Shalem,* an early name of Jerus.:—Salem.

שָׁלֹם **shâlôm.** See 7965.

8005. שִׁלֵּם **shillêm,** *shil-lame´;* from 7999; *requital:*—recompense.

8006. שִׁלֵּם **Shillêm,** *shil-lame´;* the same as 8005; *Shillem,* an Isr.:—Shillem.

שִׁלֻּם **shillûm.** See 7966.

שַׁלֻּם **Shallûm.** See 7967.

8007. שַׂלְמָא **Salmâ',** *sal-maw´;* prob. for 8008; *clothing; Salma,* the name of two Isr.:—Salma.

8008. שַׂלְמָה **salmâh,** *sal-maw´;* transp. for 8071; a *dress:*—clothes, garment, raiment.

8009. שַׂלְמָה **Salmâh,** *sal-maw´;* the same as 8008; *clothing; Salmah,* an Isr.:—Salmon. Comp. 8012.

8010. שְׁלֹמֹה **Shelômôh,** *shel-o-mo´;* from 7965; *peaceful; Shelomoh,* David's successor:—Solomon.

8011. שִׁלֻּמָה **shillumâh,** *shil-loo-maw´;* fem. of 7966; *retribution:*—reward.

8012. שַׂלְמוֹן **Salmôwn,** *sal-mone´;* from 8008; *investiture; Salmon,* an Isr.:—Salmon. Comp. 8009.

8013. שְׁלֹמוֹת **Shelômôwth,** *shel-o-mōth´;* fem. plur. of 7965; *pacifications; Shelomoth,* the name of two Isr.:—Shelomith [*from the marg.*], Shelomoth. Comp. 8019.

8014. שַׂלְמַי **Salmay,** *sal-mah´ee;* from 8008; *clothed; Salmai,* an Isr.:—Shalmai.

8015. שְׁלֹמִי **Shelômîy,** *shel-o-mee´;* from 7965; *peaceable; Shelomi,* an Isr.:—Shelomi.

8016. שִׁלֵּמִי **Shillêmîy,** *shil-lay-mee´;* patron. from 8006; a *Shilemite* (collect.) or desc. of Shillem:—Shillemites.

8017. שְׁלֻמִיאֵל **Shelûmîy'êl,** *shel-oo-mee-ale´;* from 7965 and 410; *peace of God; Shelumiël,* an Isr.:—Shelumiel.

8018. שֶׁלֶמְיָה **Shelemyâh,** *shel-em-yaw´;* or שֶׁלֶמְיָהוּ **Shelemyâhuw,** *shel-em-yaw´-hoo;* from 8002 and 3050; *thank-offering of Jah; Shelemjah,* the name of nine Isr.:—Shelemiah.

8019. שְׁלֹמִית **Shelômîyth,** *shel-o-meeth´;* or שְׁלוֹמִית **Shelôwmiyth** (Ezra 8 : 10), *shel-o-meeth´;* from 7965; *peaceableness; Shelomith,* the name of five Isr. and three Israelitesses:—Shelomith.

8020. שַׁלְמַן **Shalman,** *shal-man´;* of for. der.; *Shalman,* a king appar. of Assyria:—Shalman. Comp. 8022.

8021. שַׁלְמֹן **shalmôn,** *shal-mone´;* from 7999; a *bribe:*—reward.

8022. שַׁלְמַנְאֶסֶר **Shalman'eçer,** *shal-man-eh´-ser;* of for. der.; *Shalmaneser,* an Ass. king:—Shalmaneser. Comp. 8020.

8023. שִׁלֹנִי **Shîlônîy** *shee-lo-nee´;* the same as 7888; *Shiloni,* an Isr.:—Shiloni.

8024. שֵׁלָנִי **Shêlânîy,** *shay-law-nee´;* from 7956; a *Shelanite* (collect.), or desc. of Shelah:—Shelanites.

8025. שָׁלַף **shâlaph,** *shaw-laf´;* a prim. root; to *pull* out, up or off:—draw (off), grow up, pluck off.

8026. שֶׁלֶף **sheleph,** *sheh´-lef;* from 8025; *extract; Sheleph,* a son of Jokthan:—Sheleph.

8027. שָׁלַשׁ **shâlash,** *shaw-lash´;* a prim. root perh. orig. to *intensify,* i.e. *treble;* but appar. used only as denom. from 7969, to *be* (caus. *make*) *triplicate* (by restoration, in portions, strands, days or years):—do the third time, (divide into, stay) three (days, -fold, parts, years old).

8028. שֶׁלֶשׁ **Shelesh,** *sheh´-lesh;* from 8027; *triplet; Shelesh,* an Isr.:—Shelesh.

שָׁלֹשׁ **shâlôsh.** See 7969.

8029. שִׁלֵּשׁ **shillêsh,** *shil-laysh´;* from 8027; a desc. of the *third* degree, i.e. *great grandchild:*—third [generation].

8030. שִׁלְשָׁה **Shilshâh,** *shil-shaw´;* fem. from the same as 8028; *triplication; Shilshah,* an Isr.:—Shilshah.

8031. שָׁלִשָׁה **Shâlîshâh,** *shaw-lee-shaw´;* fem. from 8027; *trebled* land; *Shalishah,* a place in Pal.:—Shalisha.

שְׁלֹשָׁה **shâlôshâh.** See 7969.

8032. שִׁלְשׁוֹם **shilshôwm,** *shil-shome´;* or שִׁלְשֹׁם **shilshôm,** *shil-shome´;* from the same as 8028; *trebly,* i.e. (in time) *day before yesterday:*— + before (that time, -time), excellent things [*from the marg.*], + heretofore, three days, + time past.

שְׁלֹשִׁים **shelôshiym.** See 7970.

שַׁלְתִּיאֵל **Shaltîy'êl.** See 7597.

8033. שָׁם **shâm,** *shawm;* a prim. particle [rather from the rel. 834]; *there* (transf. to time) *then;* often *thither,* or *thence:*—in it, + thence, there (-in, + of, + out), + thither, + whither.

8034. שֵׁם **shêm,** *shame;* a prim. word [perh. rather from 7760 through the idea of definite and conspicuous *position;* comp. 8064]; an *appelation,* as a mark or memorial of individuality; by impl. *honor, authority, character:*— + base, [in-] fame [-ous], name (-d), renown, report.

8035. שֵׁם **Shêm,** *shame;* the same as 8034; *name; Shem,* a son of Noah (often includ. his posterity):—Sem, Shem.

8036. שֻׁם **shum** (Chald.), *shoom;* corresp. to 8034:—name.

8037. שַׁמָּא **Shammâ',** *sham-maw´;* from 8074; *desolation; Shamma,* an Isr.:—Shamma.

8038. שֶׁמְאֵבֶר **Shem'êber,** *shem-ay´-ber;* appar. from 8034 and 83; *name of pinion, i.e. illustrious; Shemeber,* a king of Zeboim:—Shemeber.

8039. שִׁמְאָה **Shim'âh,** *shim-aw´;* perh. for 8093 *Shimah,* an Isr.:—Shimah. Comp. 8043.

8040. שְׂמֹאול **semô'wl,** *sem-ole´;* or שְׂמֹאל **semô'l,** *sem-ole´;* a prim. word [rather perh. from the same as 8071 (by insertion of א) through the idea of *wrapping* up]; prop. *dark* (as *enveloped*), i.e. the *north;* hence (by orientation) the *left* hand:—left (hand, side).

8041. שָׂמַאל **sâma'l,** *saw-mal´;* a prim. root [rather denom. from 8040]; to use the *left* hand or pass in that direction):—(go, turn) (on the, to the) left.

8042. שְׂמָאלִי **s**e**mâ'lîy,** *sem-aw-lee´;* from 8040; situated on the *left* side:—left.

8043. שִׁמְאָם **Shim'âm,** *shim-awm´;* for 8039 [comp. 38]; *Shimam,* an Isr.:—Shimeam.

8044. שַׁמְגַּר **Shamgar,** *sham-gar´;* of uncert. der.; *Shamgar,* an Isr. judge:—Shamgar.

8045. שָׁמַד **shâmad,** *shaw-mad´;* a prim. root; to *desolate:*—destroy (-uction), bring to nought, overthrow, perish, pluck down, × utterly.

8046. שְׁמַד **sh**e**mad** (Chald.), *shem-ad´;* corresp. to 8045:—consume.

שָׁמֶה **shâmeh.** See 8064.

8047. שַׁמָּה **shammâh,** *sham-maw´;* from 8074; *ruin;* by impl. *consternation:*—astonishment, desolate (-ion), waste, wonderful thing.

8048. שַׁמָּה **Shammâh,** *sham-maw´;* the same as 8047; *Shammah,* the name of an Edomite and four Isr.:—Shammah.

8049. שַׁמְהוּת **Shamhûwth,** *sham-hooth´;* for 8048; *desolation; Shamhuth,* an Isr.:—Shamhuth.

8050. שְׁמוּאֵל **Sh**e**mûw'êl,** *shem-oo-ale´;* from the pass. part. of 8085 and 410; *heard of God; Shemuël,* the name of three Isr.:—Samuel, Shemuel.

שְׁמוֹנֶה **sh**e**môwneh.** See 8083.
שְׁמוֹנָה **sh**e**môwnah.** See 8083.
שְׁמוֹנִים **sh**e**môwnîym.** See 8084.

8051. שַׁמּוּעַ **Shammûwa',** *sham-moo´-ah;* from 8074; *renowned; Shammua,* the name of four Isr.:—Shammua, Shammuah.

8052. שְׁמוּעָה **sh**e**mûw'âh,** *shem-oo-aw´;* fem. pass. part. of 8074; something *heard,* i.e. an *announcement:*—bruit, doctrine, fame, mentioned, news, report, rumor, tidings.

8053. שָׁמוּר° **Shâmûwr,** *shaw-moor´;* pass. part. of 8103; *observed; Shamur,* an Isr.:—Shamir [*from the marg.*].

8054. שַׁמּוֹת **Shammôwth,** *sham-mōth´;* plur. of 8047; *ruins; Shammoth,* an Isr.:—Shamoth.

8055. שָׂמַח **sâmach,** *saw-makh´;* a prim. root; prob. to *brighten* up, i.e. (fig.) *be* (caus. make) *blithe* or *gleesome:*—cheer up, be (make) glad, (have make) joy (-ful), be (make) merry, (cause to, make to) rejoice, × very.

8056. שָׂמֵחַ **sâmêach,** *saw-may´-akh;* from 8055; *blithe* or *gleeful:*—(be) glad, joyful, (making) merry ([-hearted]), rejoice (-ing).

8057. שִׂמְחָה **simchâh,** *sim-khaw´;* from 8056 *blithesomeness* or *glee,* (religious or festival):—× exceeding (-ly), gladness, joy (-fulness), mirth, pleasure, rejoice (-ing).

8058. שָׁמַט **shâmaṭ,** *shaw-mat´;* a prim. root; to *fling* down; incipiently to *jostle;* fig. to *let alone, desist, remit:*—discontinue, overthrow, release, let rest, shake, stumble, throw down.

8059. שְׁמִטָּה **sh**e**miṭṭâh,** *shem-it-taw´;* from 8058; *remission* (of debt) or *suspension* of labor):—release.

8060. שַׁמַּי **Shammay,** *sham-mah´ee;* from 8073; *destructive; Shammai,* the name of three Isr.:—Shammai.

8061. שְׁמִידָע **Sh**e**mîydâ',** *shem-ee-daw´;* appar. from 8034 and 3045; *name of knowing; Shemida,* an Isr.:—Shemida, Shemidah.

8062. שְׁמִידָעִי **Sh**e**mîydâ'îy,** *shem-ee-daw-ee´;* patron. from 8061; a *Shemidaïte* (collect.) or desc. of Shemida:—Shemidaites.

8063. שְׂמִיכָה **s**e**mîykâh,** *sem-ee-kaw´;* from 5564; a *rug* (as *sustaining* the Oriental sitter):—mantle.

8064. שָׁמַיִם **shâmayim,** *shaw-mah´-yim;* dual of an unused sing. שָׁמֶה **shâmeh,** *shaw-meh´;* from an unused root mean. to *be lofty;* the *sky* (as *aloft;* the dual perh. alluding to the visible arch in which the clouds move, as well as to the higher ether where the celestial bodies revolve):—air, × astrologer, heaven (-s).

8065. שָׁמַיִן **shâmayin** (Chald.), *shaw-mah´-yin;* corresp. to 8064:—heaven.

8066. שְׁמִינִי **sh**e**mîynîy,** *shem-ee-nee´;* from 8083; *eight:*—eight.

8067. שְׁמִינִית **sh**e**mîynîyth,** *shem-ee-neeth´;* fem. of 8066; prob. an *eight*-stringed lyre:—Sheminith.

8068. שָׁמִיר **shâmîyr,** *shaw-meer´;* from 8104 in the orig. sense of *pricking;* a *thorn;* also (from its *keenness* for scratching) a gem, prob. the *diamond:*—adamant (stone), brier, diamond.

8069. שָׁמִיר **Shâmîyr,** *shaw-meer´;* the same as 8068; *Shamir,* the name of two places in Pal.:—Shamir. Comp. 8053.

8070. שְׁמִירָמוֹת **Sh**e**mîyrâmôwth,** *shem-ee-raw-mōth´;* or שְׁמָרִימוֹת° **Sh**e**mârîymôwth,** *shem-aw-ree-mōth´;* prob. from 8034 and plur. of 7413; *name of heights; Shemiramoth,* the name of two Isr.:—Shemiramoth.

8071. שִׂמְלָה **simlâh,** *sim-law´;* perh. by perm. for the fem. of 5566 (through the idea of a *cover* assuming the shape of the object beneath); a *dress,* espec. a *mantle:*—apparel, cloth (-es, -ing), garment, raiment. Comp. 8008.

8072. שַׂמְלָה **Samlâh,** *sam-law´;* prob. for the same as 8071; *Samlah,* an Edomite:—Samlah.

8073. שַׁמְלַי° **Shamlay,** *sham-lah´ee;* for 8014; *Shamlai,* one of the Nethinim:—Shalmai [*from the marg.*].

8074. שָׁמֵם **shâmêm,** *shaw-mame´;* a prim. root; to *stun* (or intrans. *grow numb*), i.e. *devastate* or (fig.) *stupefy* (both usually in a passive sense):—make amazed, be astonied, (be an) astonish (-ment), (be, bring into, unto, lay, lie, make) desolate (-ion, places), be destitute, destroy (self), (lay, lie, make) waste, wonder.

8075. שְׁמַם **sh**e**mam** (Chald.), *shem-am´;* corresp. to 8074:—be astonied.

8076. שָׁמֵם **shâmêm,** *shaw-mame´;* from 8074; *ruined:*—desolate.

8077. שְׁמָמָה **sh**e**mâmâh,** *shem-aw-maw´;* or שִׁמָמָה **shîmămâh,** *shee-mam-aw´;* fem. of 8076; *devastation;* fig. *astonishment:*—(laid, × most) desolate (-ion), waste.

8078. שִׁמָּמוֹן **shimmâmôwn,** *shim-maw-mone´;* from 8074; *stupefaction:*—astonishment.

8079. שְׂמָמִית **s**e**mâmîyth,** *sem-aw-meeth´;* prob. from 8074 (in the sense of *poisoning*); a *lizard* (from the superstition of its *noxiousness*):—spider.

8080. שָׁמַן **shâmam,** *shaw-man´;* a prim. root; to *shine,* i.e. (by anal.) *be* (caus. *make*) *oily* or *gross:*—become (make, wax) fat.

8081. שֶׁמֶן **shemen,** *sheh´-men;* from 8080; *grease,* espec. liquid (as from the olive, often perfumed); fig. *richness:*—anointing, × fat (things), × fruitful, oil ([-ed]), ointment, olive, + pine.

8082. שָׁמֵן **shâmên,** *shaw-mane´;* from 8080; *greasy,* i.e. *gross;* fig. *rich:*—fat, lusty, plenteous.

8083. שְׁמֹנֶה **sh**e**môneh,** *shem-o-neh´;* or שְׁמוֹנֶה **sh**e**môwneh,** *shem-o-neh´;* fem. שְׁמֹנָה **sh**e**mônâh,** *shem-o-naw´;* or שְׁמוֹנָה **sh**e**môwnâh,** *shem-o-naw´;* appar. from 8082 through the idea of *plumpness;* a cardinal number, *eight* (as if a *surplus* above the "perfect" seven); also (as ordinal) *eighth:*—eight ([-een, -eenth]), eighth.

8084. שְׁמֹנִים **sh**e**mônîym,** *shem-o-neem´;* or שְׁמוֹנִים **sh**e**môwnîym,** *shem-o-neem´;* mult. from 8083; *eighty;* also *eightieth:*—eighty (-ieth), fourscore.

8085. שָׁמַע **shâma',** *shaw-mah´;* a prim. root; to *hear* intelligently (often with impl. of attention, obedience, etc.; caus. to *tell,* etc.):—× attentively, call (gather) together, × carefully, × certainly, consent, consider, be content, declare, × diligently, discern, give ear, (cause to, let, make to) hear (-ken, tell), × indeed, listen, make (a) noise, (be) obedient, obey, perceive, (make a) proclaim (-ation), publish, regard, report, shew (forth), (make a) sound, × surely, tell, understand, whosoever [heareth], witness.

8086. שְׁמַע **sh**e**ma'** (Chald.), *shem-ah´;* corresp. to 8085:—hear, obey.

8087. שֶׁמַע **Shema',** *sheh´-mah;* for the same as 8088; *Shema,* the name of a place in Pal. and of four Isr.:—Shema.

8088. שֵׁמַע **shêma',** *shay´-mah;* from 8085; something *heard,* i.e. a *sound, rumor, announcement;* abstr. *audience:*—bruit, fame, hear (-ing), loud, report, speech, tidings.

8089. שֹׁמַע **shôma'**, *sho'-mah;* from 8085; a *report:*—fame.

8090. שְׁמָע **Shᵉmâ'**, *shem-aw';* for 8087; *Shema,* a place in Pal.:—Shema.

8091. שָׁמָע **Shâmâ'**, *shaw-maw';* from 8085; *obedient; Shama,* an Isr.:—Shama.

8092. שִׁמְעָא **Shim'â'**, *shim-aw';* for 8093; *Shima,* the name of four Isr.:—Shimea, Shimei, Shamma.

8093. שִׁמְעָה **Shim'âh**, *shim-aw';* fem. of 8088; *annunciation; Shimah,* an Isr.:—Shimeah.

8094. שְׁמָעָה **Shᵉmâ'âh**, *shem-aw-aw';* for 8093; *Shemaah,* an Isr.:—Shemaah.

8095. שִׁמְעוֹן **Shim'ôwn**, *shim-ōne';* from 8085; *hearing; Shimon,* one of Jacob's sons, also the tribe desc. from him:—Simeon.

8096. שִׁמְעִי **Shim'iy**, *shim-ee';* from 8088; *famous; Shimi,* the name of twenty Isr.:—Shimeah [*from the marg.*], Shimei, Shimhi, Shimi.

8097. שִׁמְעִי **Shim'iy**, *shim-ee';* patron. from 8096; a *Shimite* (collect.) or desc. of Shimi:—of Shimi, Shimites.

8098. שְׁמַעְיָה **Shᵉma'yâh**, *shem-aw-yaw';* or שְׁמַעְיָהוּ **Shᵉma'yâhûw**, *shem-aw-yaw'-hoo;* from 8085 and 3050; *Jah has heard; Shemajah,* the name of twenty-five Isr.:—Shemaiah.

8099. שִׁמְעֹנִי **Shim'ôniy**, *shim-o-nee';* patron. from 8095; a *Shimonite* (collect.) or desc. of Shimon:—tribe of Simeon, Simeonites.

8100. שִׁמְעָת **Shim'âth**, *shim-awth';* fem. of 8088; *annunciation; Shimath,* an Ammonitess:—Shimath.

8101. שִׁמְעָתִי **Shim'âthiy**, *shim-aw-thee';* patron. from 8093; a *Shimathite* (collect.) or desc. of Shimah:—Shimeathites.

8102. שֶׁמֶץ **shemets**, *sheh'-mets;* from an unused root mean. to *emit* a sound; an *inkling:*—a little.

8103. שִׁמְצָה **shimtsâh**, *shim-tsaw';* fem. of 8102; scornful *whispering* (of hostile spectators):—shame.

8104. שָׁמַר **shâmar**, *shaw-mar';* a prim. root; prop. to *hedge* about (as with thorns), i.e. *guard;* gen. to *protect, attend to,* etc.:—beware, be circumspect, take heed (to self), keep (-er, self), mark, look narrowly, observe, preserve, regard, reserve, save (self), sure, (that lay) wait (for), watch (-man).

8105. שֶׁמֶר **shemer**, *sheh'-mer;* from 8104; something *preserved;* i.e. the *settings* (plur. only) of wine:—dregs, (wines on the) lees.

8106. שֶׁמֶר **Shemer**, *sheh'-mer;* the same as 8105; *Shemer,* the name of three Isr.:—Shamer, Shemer.

8107. שִׁמֻּר **shimmûr**, *shim-moor';* from 8104; an *observance:*— × be (much) observed.

שֹׁמֵר **Shômêr**. See 7763.

8108. שָׁמְרָה **shomrâh**, *shom-raw';* fem. of an unused noun from 8104 mean. a *guard; watchfulness:*—watch.

8109. שְׁמֻרָה **shᵉmûrâh**, *shem-oo-raw';* fem. of pass. part. of 8104; something *guarded,* i.e. an *eye-lid:*—waking.

8110. שִׁמְרוֹן **Shimrôwn**, *shim-rone';* from 8105 in its orig. sense; *guardianship; Shimron,* the name of an Isr. and of a place in Pal.:—Shimron.

8111. שֹׁמְרוֹן **Shômᵉrôwn**, *sho-mer-ōne';* from the act. part. of 8104; *watch-station; Shomeron,* a place in Pal.:—Samaria.

8112. שִׁמְרוֹן מְראוֹן **Shimrôwn Mᵉr'ôwn**, *shim-rone' mer-one';* from 8110 and a der. of 4754; *guard of lashing; Shimron-Meron,* a place in Pal.:—Shimon-meron.

8113. שִׁמְרִי **Shimriy**, *shim-ree';* from 8105 in its orig. sense; *watchful; Shimri,* the name of four Isr.:—Shimri.

8114. שְׁמַרְיָה **Shᵉmaryâh**, *shem-ar-yaw';* or שְׁמַרְיָהוּ **Shᵉmaryâhûw**, *shem-ar-yaw'-hoo;* from 8104 and 3050; *Jah has guarded; Shemarjah,* the name of four Isr.:—Shamariah, Shemariah.

שְׁמָרִימוֹת° **Shᵉmârîymôwth.** See 8070.

8115. שָׁמְרַיִן **Shomrayin** (Chald.), *shom-rah'-yin;* corresp. to 8111; *Shomrain,* a place in Pal.:—Samaria.

8116. שִׁמְרִית **Shimrîyth**, *shim-reeth';* fem. of 8113; *female guard; Shimrith,* a Moabitess:—Shimrith.

8117. שִׁמְרֹנִי **Shimrônîy**, *shim-ro-nee';* patron. from 8110; a *Shimronite* (collect.) or desc. of Shimron:—Shimronites.

8118. שֹׁמְרֹנִי **Shômᵉrônîy**, *sho-mer-o-nee';* patrial from 8111; a *Shomeronite* (collect.) or inhab. of Shomeron:—Samaritans.

8119. שִׁמְרָת **Shimrâth**, *shim-rawth';* from 8104; *guardship; Shimrath,* an Isr.:—Shimrath.

8120. שְׁמַשׁ **shᵉmash** (Chald.), *shem-ash';* corresp. to the root of 8121 through the idea of *activity* implied in day-light; to *serve:*—minister.

8121. שֶׁמֶשׁ **shemesh**, *sheh'-mesh;* from an unused root mean. to be *brilliant;* the *sun;* by impl. the *east;* fig. a *ray,* i.e. (arch.) a notched *battlement:*— + east side (-ward), sun ([rising]), + west (-ward), window. See also 1053.

8122. שֶׁמֶשׁ **shemesh** (Chald.), *sheh'-mesh;* corresp. to 8121; the *sun:*—sun.

8123. שִׁמְשׁוֹן **Shimshôwn**, *shim-shone';* from 8121; *sunlight; Shimshon,* an Isr.:—Samson.

שִׁמְשִׁי **Shimshîy.** See 1030.

8124. שִׁמְשַׁי **Shimshay** (Chald.), *shim-shah'ee;* from 8122; *sunny; Shimshai,* a Samaritan: Shimshai.

8125. שַׁמְשְׁרַי **Shamshᵉray**, *sham-sher-ah'ee;* appar from 8121; *sunlike; Shamsherai,* an Isr.:—Shamsherai.

8126. שֻׁמָתִי **Shûmâthîy**, *shoo-maw-thee';* patron. from an unused name from 7762 prob. mean. *garlic*-smell; a *Shumathite* (collect.) or desc. of Shumah:—Shumathites.

8127. שֵׁן **shên**, *shane;* from 8150; a *tooth* (as *sharp*); spec. (for 8143) *ivory;* fig. a *cliff:*—crag, × forefront, ivory, × sharp, tooth.

8128. שֵׁן **shên** (Chald.), *shane;* corresp. to 8127; a *tooth:*—tooth.

8129. שֵׁן **Shên**, *shane;* the same as 8127; *crag; Shen,* a place in Pal.:—Shen.

8130. שָׂנֵא **sânê'**, *saw-nay';* a prim. root; to *hate* (personally):—enemy, foe, (be) hate (-ful, -r), odious, × utterly.

8131. שְׂנֵא **sᵉnê'** (Chald.), *sen-ay';* corresp. to 8130:—hate.

8132. שָׁנָא **shânâ'**, *shaw-naw';* a prim. root; to *alter:*—change.

8133. שְׁנָא **shᵉnâ'** (Chald.), *shen-aw';* corresp. to 8132:—alter, change, (be) diverse.

שֵׁנָא **shênâ'**. See 8142.

8134. שִׁנְאָב **Shin'âb**, *shin-awb';* prob. from 8132 and 1; a *father has turned; Shinab,* a Canaanite:—Shinab.

8135. שִׂנְאָה **sin'âh**, *sin-aw';* from 8130; *hate:*— + exceedingly, hate (-ful, -red).

8136. שִׁנְאָן **shin'ân**, *shin-awn';* from 8132; *change,* i.e. *repetition:*— × angels.

8137. שֶׁנְאַצַּר **Shenatstsar**, *shen-ats-tsar';* appar. of Bab. or.; *Shenatstsar,* an Isr.:—Senazar.

8138. שָׁנָה **shânâh**, *shaw-naw';* a prim. root; to *fold,* i.e. *duplicate* (lit. or fig.); by impl. to *transmute* (trans. or intrans.):—do (speak, strike) again, alter, double, (be given to) change, disguise, (be) diverse, pervert, prefer, repeat, return, do the second time.

8139. שְׁנָה **shᵉnâh** (Chald.), *shen-aw';* corresp. to 8142:—sleep.

8140. שְׁנָה **shᵉnâh** (Chald.), *shen-aw';* corresp. to 8141:—year.

8141. שָׁנֶה **shâneh** (in plur. only), *shaw-neh';* or (fem.) שָׁנָה **shânâh**, *shaw-naw';* from 8138; a *year* (as a *revolution* of time):— + whole age, × long, + old, year (× -ly).

8142. שֵׁנָה **shênâh**, *shay-naw';* or שֵׁנָא **shênâ'** (Psa. 127 : 2), *shay-naw';* from 3462; *sleep:*—sleep.

8143. שֶׁנְהַבִּים **shenhabbîym**, *shen-hab-beem';* from 8127 and the plur. appar. of a for. word; prob. *tooth of elephants,* i.e. *ivory tusk:*—ivory.

8144. שָׁנִי **shânîy**, *shaw-nee';* of uncert. der.; *crimson,* prop. the insect or its color, also stuff dyed with it:—crimson, scarlet (thread).

8145. שֵׁנִי **shênîy,** *shay-nee´;* from 8138; prop. *double,* i.e. *second;* also adv. *again:*—again, either [of them], (an-) other, second (time).

8146. שָׂנִיא **sânîy',** *saw-nee´;* from 8130; *hated:*—hated.

8147. שְׁנַיִם **shᵉnayim,** *shen-ah´-yim;* dual of 8145; fem. שְׁתַּיִם **shᵉttayim,** *shet-tah´-yim; two;* also (as ordinal) *twofold:*—both, couple, double, second, twain, + twelfth, + twelve, + twenty (sixscore) thousand, twice, two.

8148. שְׁנִינָה **shᵉnîynâh,** *shen-ee-naw´;* from 8150; something *pointed,* i.e. a *gibe:*—byword, taunt.

8149. שְׁנִיר **Shᵉnîyr,** *shen-eer´;* or שְׂנִיר **Sᵉnîyr,** *sen-eer´;* from an unused root mean. to *be pointed; peak; Shenir* or *Senir,* a summit of Lebanon:—Senir, Shenir.

8150. שָׁנַן **shânan,** *shaw-nan´;* a prim. root; to *point* (trans. or intrans); intens. to *pierce;* fig. to *inculcate:*—prick, sharp (-en), teach diligently, whet.

8151. שָׁנַס **shânaç,** *shaw-nas´;* a prim. root; to *compress* (with a belt):—gird up.

8152. שִׁנְעָר **Shinʻâr,** *shin-awr´;* prob. of for. der.; *Shinar,* a plain in Bab.:—Shinar.

8153. שְׁנָת **shᵉnâth,** *shen-awth´;* from 3462; *sleep:*—sleep.

8154. שָׁסָה **shâçâh,** *shaw-saw´;* or שָׁשָׂה **shâsâh** (Isa. 10 : 13), *shaw-saw´;* a prim. root; to *plunder:*—destroyer, rob, spoil (-er).

8155. שָׁסַס **shâçaç,** *shaw-sas´;* a prim. root; to *plunder:*—rifle, spoil.

8156. שָׁסַע **shâçaʻ,** *shaw-sah´;* a prim. root; to *split* or *tear;* fig. to *upbraid:*—cleave, (be) cloven ([footed]), rend, stay.

8157. שֶׁסַע **sheçaʻ,** *sheh´-sah;* from 8156; a *fissure:*—cleft, clovenfooted.

8158. שָׁסַף **shâçaph,** *shaw-saf´;* a prim. root; to *cut* in pieces, i.e. slaughter:—hew in pieces.

8159. שָׁעָה **shâʻâh,** *shaw-aw´;* a prim. root; to *gaze* at or about (prop. for help); by impl. to *inspect, consider, compassionate, be nonplussed* (as looking around in amazement) or *bewildered:*—depart, be dim, be dismayed, look (away), regard, have respect, spare, turn.

8160. שָׁעָה **shâʻâh** (Chald.), *shaw-aw´;* from a root corresp. to 8159; prop. a *look,* i.e. a *moment:*—hour.

שְׂעוֹר **sᵉʻôwr.** See 8184.

שְׂעוֹרָה **sᵉʻôwrâh.** See 8184.

8161. שַׁעֲטָה **shaʻăṭâh,** *shah´-at-aw;* fem. from an unused root mean. to *stamp;* a *clatter* (of hoofs):—stamping.

8162. שַׁעַטְנֵז **shaʻaṭnêz,** *shah-at-naze´;* prob. of for. der.; *linsey-woolsey,* i.e. cloth of linen and wool carded and spun together:—garment of divers sorts, linen and woollen.

8163. שָׂעִיר **sâʻîyr,** *saw-eer´;* or שָׂעִר **sâʻir,** *saw-eer´;* from 8175; *shaggy;* as noun, a *he-goat;* by anal. a *faun:*—devil, goat, hairy, kid, rough, satyr.

8164. שָׂעִיר **sâʻîyr,** *saw-eer´;* formed the same as 8163; a *shower* (as *tempestuous*):—small rain.

8165. שֵׂעִיר **Sêʻîyr,** *say-eer´;* formed like 8163; *rough; Seïr,* a mountain of Idumæa and its aboriginal occupants, also one in Pal.:—Seir.

8166. שְׂעִירָה **sᵉʻîyrâh,** *seh-ee-raw´;* fem. of 8163; a *she-goat:*—kid.

8167. שְׂעִירָה **Sᵉʻîyrâh,** *seh-ee-raw´;* formed as 8166; *roughness; Seïrah,* a place in Pal.:—Seirath.

8168. שֹׁעַל **shôʻal,** *sho´-al;* from an unused root mean. to *hollow* out; the *palm;* by extens. a *handful:*—handful, hollow of the band.

שֻׁעָל **shûʻâl.** See 7776.

8169. שַׁעַלְבִים **Shaʻalbîym,** *shah-al-beem´;* or שַׁעֲלַבִּין **Shaʻălabbîyn,** *shah-al-ab-been´;* plur. from 7776; *fox-holes; Shaalbim* or *Shaalabbin,* a place in Pal.:—Shaalabbin, Shaalbim.

8170. שַׁעַלְבֹנִי **Shaʻalbônîy,** *shah-al-bo-nee´;* patrial from 8169; a *Shaalbonite* or inhab. of Shaalbin:—Shaalbonite.

8171. שַׁעֲלִים **Shaʻălîym,** *shah-al-eem´;* plur. of 7776; *foxes; Shaalim,* a place in Pal.:—Shalim.

8172. שָׁעַן **shâʻan,** *shaw-an´;* a prim. root; to *support* one's self:—lean, lie, rely, rest (on, self), stay.

8173. שָׁעַע **shâʻaʻ,** *shaw-ah´;* a prim. root; (in a good acceptation) to *look* upon (with complacency), i.e. *fondle, please* or *amuse* (self); (in a bad one) to *look* about (in dismay), i.e. *stare:*—cry (out) [*by confusion with* 7768], dandle, delight (self), play, shut.

שָׂעִף **sâʻîph.** See 5587.

8174. שַׁעַף **Shaʻaph,** *shah´-af;* from 5586; *fluctuation; Shaaph,* the name of two Isr.:—Shaaph.

8175. שָׂעַר **sâʻar,** *saw-ar´;* a prim. root; to *storm;* by impl. to *shiver,* i.e. *fear:*—be (horribly) afraid, fear, hurl as a storm, be tempestuous, come like (take away as with) a whirlwind.

8176. שָׁעַר **shâʻar,** *shaw-ar´;* a prim. root; to *split* or *open,* i.e. (lit., but only as denom. from 8179) to *act as gate-keeper* (see 7778); (fig.) to *estimate:*—think.

8177. שְׂעַר **sᵉʻar** (Chald.), *seh-ar´;* corresp. to 8181; *hair:*—hair.

8178. שַׂעַר **saʻar,** *sah´-ar;* from 8175; a *tempest;* also a *terror:*—affrighted, × horribly, × sore, storm. See 8181.

8179. שַׁעַר **shaʻar,** *shah´-ar;* from 8176 in its orig. sense; an *opening,* i.e. *door* or *gate:*—city, door, gate, port (× -er).

8180. שַׁעַר **shaʻar,** *shah´-ar;* from 8176; a *measure* (as a *section*):—[hundred-] fold.

שָׂעִר **sâʻîr.** See 8163.

8181. שֵׂעָר **sêʻâr,** *say-awr´;* or שַׂעַר **saʻar** (Isa. 7 : 20), *sah´-ar;* from 8175 in the sense of *dishevelling; hair* (as if *tossed* or *bristling*):—hair (-y), × rough.

שֹׁעֵר **shôʻêr.** See 7778.

8182. שֹׁעָר **shôʻâr,** *sho-awr´;* from 8176; *harsh* or *horrid,* i.e. *offensive:*—vile.

8183. שְׂעָרָה **sᵉʻârâh,** *seh-aw-raw´;* fem. of 8178; a *hurricane:*—storm, tempest.

8184. שְׂעֹרָה **sᵉʻôrâh,** *seh-o-raw´;* or שְׂעוֹרָה **sᵉʻôwrâh,** *seh-o-raw´* (fem. mean. the *plant*); and (masc. mean. the *grain*); also שְׂעֹר **sᵉʻôr,** *seh-ore´;* or שְׂעוֹר **sᵉʻôwr,** *seh-ore´;* from 8175 in the sense of *roughness; barley* (as *villose*):—barley.

8185. שַׂעֲרָה **saʻărâh,** *sah-ar-aw´;* fem. of 8181; *hairiness:*—hair.

8186. שַׁעֲרוּרָה **shaʻărûwrâh,** *shah-ar-oo-raw´;* or שַׁעֲרִירִיָּה° **shaʻărîyrîyâh,** *shah-ar-ee-ree-yaw´;* or שַׁעֲרֻרִת **shaʻărûrîth,** *shah-ar-oo-reeth´;* fem. from 8176 in the sense of 8175; something *fearful:*—horrible thing.

8187. שְׁעַרְיָה **Shᵉʻaryâh,** *sheh-ar-yaw´;* from 8176 and 3050; *Jah has stormed; Sheärjah,* an Isr.:—Sheariah.

8188. שְׂעֹרִים **Sᵉʻôrîym,** *seh-o-reem´;* masc. plur. of 8184; *barley* grains; *Seörim,* an Isr.:—Seorim.

8189. שַׁעֲרַיִם **Shaʻărayim,** *shah-ar-ah´-yim;* dual of 8179; *double gates; Shaarajim,* a place in Pal.:—Shaaraim.

שַׁעֲרִירִיָּה° **shaʻărîyrîyâh.** See 8186.

שַׁעֲרֻרִת **shaʻărûrîth.** See 8186.

8190. שַׁעַשְׁגַז **Shaʻashgaz,** *shah-ash-gaz´;* of Pers. der.; *Shaashgaz,* a eunuch of Xerxes:—Shaashgaz.

8191. שַׁעְשֻׁעַ **shaʻshûaʻ,** *shah-shoo´-ah;* from 8173; *enjoyment:*—delight, pleasure.

8192. שָׁפָה **shâphâh,** *shaw-faw´;* a prim. root; to *abrade,* i.e. *bare:*—high, stick out.

8193. שָׂפָה **sâphâh,** *saw-faw´;* or (in dual and plur.) שֶׂפֶת **sepheth,** *sef-eth´;* prob. from 5595 or 8192 through the idea of *termination* (comp. 5490); the *lip* (as a natural boundary); by impl. *language;* by anal. a *margin* (of a vessel, water, cloth, etc.):—band, bank, binding, border, brim, brink, edge, language, lip, prating, ([sea-]) shore, side, speech, talk, [vain] words.

8194. שָׁפָה **shâphâh,** *shaw-faw´;* from 8192 in the sense of *clarifying;* a *cheese* (as *strained* from the whey):—cheese.

8195. שְׁפוֹ **Shᵉphôw,** *shef-o´;* or שְׁפִי **Shᵉphîy,** *shef-ee´;* from 8192; *baldness* [comp. 8205]; *Shepho* or *Shephi,* an Idumæan:—Shephi, Shepho.

8196. שְׁפוֹט **shᵉphôwṭ,** *shef-ote´;* or שְׁפוּט **shᵉphûwṭ,** *shef-oot´;* from 8199; a judicial *sentence,* i.e. *punishment:*—judgment.

8197. שְׁפוּפָם **Shᵉphûwphâm,** *shef-oo-fawm´;* or שְׁפוּפָן **Shᵉphuwphân,** *shef-oo-fawn´;* from the same as 8207; *serpent-like; Shephupham* or *Shephuphan,* an Isr.:—Shephuphan, Shupham.

8198. שִׁפְחָה **shiphchâh,** *shif-khaw´;* fem. from an unused root mean. to *spread* out (as a *family;* see 4940); a *female slave* (as a member of the *household*):—(bond-, hand-) maid (-en, -servant), wench, bondwoman, womanservant.

8199. שָׁפַט **shâphaṭ,** *shaw-fat´;* a prim. root; to *judge,* i.e. pronounce *sentence* (for or against); by impl. to *vindicate* or *punish;* by extens. to *govern;* pass to *litigate* (lit. or fig.):— + avenge, × that condemn, contend, defend, execute (judgment), (be a) judge (-ment), × needs, plead, reason, rule.

8200. שְׁפַט **shephaṭ** (Chald.), *shef-at´;* corresp. to 8199; to *judge:*—magistrate.

8201. שֶׁפֶט **shepheṭ,** *sheh´-fet;* from 8199; a *sentence,* i.e. *infliction:*—judgment.

8202. שָׁפָט **Shâphâṭ,** *shaw-fawt´;* from 8199; *judge; Shaphat,* the name of four Isr.:—Shaphat.

8203. שְׁפַטְיָה **Shephaṭyâh,** *shef-at-yaw´;* or שְׁפַטְיָהוּ **Shephaṭyâhûw,** *shef-at-yaw´-hoo;* from 8199 and 3050; *Jah has judged; Shephatjah,* the name of ten Isr.:—Shephatiah.

8204. שִׁפְטָן **Shiphṭân,** *shif-tawn´;* from 8199; *judge-like; Shiphtan,* an Isr.:Shiphtan.

8205. שְׁפִי **shephîy,** *shef-ee´;* from 8192; *bareness;* concr. a *bare* hill or plain:—high place, stick out.

8206. שֻׁפִּים **Shuppîym,** *shoop-peem´;* plur. of an unused noun from the same as 8207 and mean. the same; *serpents; Shuppim,* an Isr.:—Shuppim.

8207. שְׁפִיפֹן **shephîyphôn,** *shef-ee-fone´;* from an unused root mean. the same as 7779; a kind of *serpent* (as *snapping*), prob. the *cerastes* or horned adder:—adder.

8208. שָׁפִיר **Shaphîyr,** *shaf-eer´;* from 8231; *beautiful; Shaphir,* a place in Pal.:—Saphir.

8209. שַׁפִּיר **shappîyr** (Chald.), *shap-peer´;* intens. of a form corresp. to 8208; *beautiful:*—fair.

8210. שָׁפַךְ **shâphak,** *shaw-fak´;* a prim. root; to *spill* forth (blood, a libation, liquid metal; or even a solid, i.e. to *mound* up); also (fig.) to *expend* (life, soul, complaint, money, etc.); intens. to *sprawl* out:—cast (up), gush out, pour (out), shed (-der, out), slip.

8211. שֶׁפֶךְ **shephek,** *sheh´-fek;* from 8210; an *emptying* place, e.g. an ash-*heap:*—are poured out.

8212. שָׁפְכָה **shophkâh,** *shof-kaw´;* fem. of a der. from 8210; a *pipe* (for *pouring* forth, e.g. wine), i.e. the *penis:*—privy member.

8213. שָׁפֵל **shâphêl,** *shaw-fale´;* a prim. root; to *depress* or *sink* (espec. fig. to *humiliate,* intrans. or trans.):—abase, bring (cast, put) down, debase, humble (self), be (bring, lay, make, put) low (-er).

8214. שְׁפַל **shephal** (Chald.), *shef-al´;* corresp. to 8213:—abase, humble, put down, subdue.

8215. שְׁפַל **shephal** (Chald.), *shef-al´;* from 8214; *low:*—basest.

8216. שֶׁפֶל **shêphel,** *shay´-fel;* from 8213; an *humble* rank:—low estate (place).

8217. שָׁפָל **shâphâl,** *shaw-fawl´;* from 8213; *depressed,* lit. or fig.:—base (-st), humble, low (-er, -ly).

8218. שִׁפְלָה **shiphlâh,** *shif-law´;* fem. of 8216; *depression:*—low place.

8219. שְׁפֵלָה **shephêlâh,** *shef-ay-law´;* from 8213; *Lowland,* i.e. (with the art.) the maritime slope of Pal.:—low country, (low) plain, vale (-ley).

8220. שִׁפְלוּת **shiphlûwth,** *shif-looth´;* from 8213; *remissness:*—idleness.

8221. שְׁפָם **Shephâm,** *shef-awm´;* prob. from 8192; *bare* spot; *Shepham,* a place in or near Pal.:—Shepham.

8222. שָׂפָם **sâphâm,** *saw-fawm´;* from 8193; the *beard* (as a *lip-piece*):—beard, (upper) lip.

8223. שָׁפָם **Shâphâm,** *shaw-fawm´;* formed like 8221; *baldly; Shapham,* an Isr.:—Shapham.

8224. שִׂפְמוֹת **Siphmôwth,** *sif-mōth´;* fem. plur. of 8221; *Siphmoth,* a place in Pal.:—Siphmoth.

8225. שִׁפְמִי **Shiphmîy,** *shif-mee´;* patrial from 8221; a *Shiphmite* inhab. of Shepham:—Shiphmite.

8226. שָׂפַן **sâphan,** *saw-fan´;* a prim. root; to *conceal* (as a valuable):—treasure.

8227. שָׁפָן **shâphân,** *shaw-fawn´;* from 8226; a species of *rock-rabbit* (from its *hiding*), i.e. prob. the *hyrax:*—coney.

8228. שֶׁפַע **shepha',** *sheh´-fah;* from an unused root mean. to *abound; resources:*—abundance.

8229. שִׁפְעָה **shiph'âh,** *shif-aw´;* fem. of 8228; *copiousness:*—abundance, company, multitude.

8230. שִׁפְעִי **Shiph'îy,** *shif-ee´;* from 8228; *copious; Shiphi,* an Isr.:—Shiphi.

שָׂפַק **sâphaq.** See 5606.

8231. שָׁפַר **shâphar,** *shaw-far´;* a prim. root; to *glisten,* i.e. (fig.) *be* (caus. *make*) *fair:*— × goodly.

8232. שְׁפַר **shephar** (Chald.), *shef-ar´;* corresp. to 8231; to *be beautiful:*—be acceptable, please, + think good.

8233. שֶׁפֶר **shepher,** *sheh´-fer;* from 8231; *beauty:*— × goodly.

8234. שֶׁפֶר **Shepher,** *sheh´-fer;* the same as 8233; *Shepher,* a place in the Desert:—Shapper.

שֹׁפָר **shôphâr.** See 7782.

8235. שִׁפְרָה **shiphrâh,** *shif-raw´;* from 8231; *brightness:*—garnish.

8236. שִׁפְרָה **Shiphrâh,** *shif-raw´;* the same as 8235; *Shiphrah,* an Israelitess:—Shiphrah.

8237. שַׁפְרוּר° **shaphrûwr,** *shaf-roor´;* from 8231; *splendid,* i.e. a *tapestry* or *canopy.*—royal pavilion.

8238. שְׁפַרְפַר **shepharphar** (Chald.), *shef-ar-far´;* from 8231; the *dawn* (as *brilliant* with aurora):— × very early in the morning.

8239. שָׁפַת **shâphath,** *shaw-fath´;* a prim. root; to *locate,* i.e. (gen.) *hang* on or (fig.) *establish, reduce:*—bring, ordain, set on.

8240. שָׁפָת **shâphâth,** *shaw-fawth´;* from 8239; a (double) *stall* (for cattle); also a (two-pronged) *hook* (for flaying animals on):—hook, pot.

8241. שֶׁצֶף **shetseph,** *sheh´-tsef;* from 7857 (for alliteration with 7110); an *outburst* (of anger):—little.

8242. שַׂק **saq,** *sak;* from 8264; prop. a *mesh* (as allowing a liquid to *run* through), i.e. coarse loose cloth or *sacking* (used in mourning and for bagging); hence a *bag* (for grain, etc.):—sack (-cloth, -clothes).

8243. שָׁק **shâq** (Chald.), *shawk;* corresp. to 7785; the *leg:*—leg.

8244. שָׂקַד **sâqad,** *saw-kad´;* a prim. root; to *fasten:*—bind.

8245. שָׁקַד **shâqad,** *shaw-kad´;* a prim. root; to *be alert,* i.e. *sleepless;* hence to *be on the lookout* (whether for good or ill):—hasten, remain, wake, watch (for).

8246. שָׁקַד **shâqad,** *shaw-kad´;* a denom. from 8247; to *be* (intens. *make*) *almond-shaped:*—make like (unto, after the fashion of) almonds.

8247. שָׁקֵד **shâqêd,** *shaw-kade´;* from 8245; the *almond* (tree or nut; as being the *earliest* in bloom):—almond (tree).

8248. שָׁקָה **shâqâh,** *shaw-kaw´;* a prim. root; to *quaff,* i.e. (caus.) to *irrigate* or *furnish a potion* to:—cause to (give, give to, let, make to) drink, drown, moisten, water. See 7937, 8354.

8249. שִׁקֻּו **shiqqûv,** *shik-koov´;* from 8248; (plur. collect.) a *draught:*—drink.

8250. שִׁקּוּי **shiqqûwy,** *shik-koo´ee;* from 8248; a *beverage; moisture,* i.e. (fig.) *refreshment:*—drink, marrow.

8251. שִׁקּוּץ **shiqqûwts,** *shik-koots´;* or שִׁקֻּץ **shiqqûts,** *shik-koots´;* from 8262; *disgusting,* i.e. *filthy;* espec. *idolatrous* or (concr.) an *idol:*—abominable filth (idol, -ation), detestable (thing).

8252. שָׁקַט **shâqaṭ,** *shaw-kat´;* a prim. root; to *repose* (usually fig.):—appease, idleness, (at, be at, be in, give) quiet (-ness), (be at, be in, give, have, take) rest, settle, be still.

8253. שֶׁקֶט **sheqeṭ,** *sheh´-ket;* from 8252; *tranquillity:*—quietness.

8254. שָׁקַל **shâqal,** *shaw-kal´;* a prim. root; to *suspend* or *poise* (espec. in trade):—pay, receive (-r), spend, × throughly, weigh.

8255. שֶׁקֶל **sheqel,** *sheh´-kel;* from 8254; prob. a *weight;* used as a commercial standard:—shekel.

8256. שָׁקָם **shâqâm,** *shaw-kawm´;* or (fem.) שִׁקְמָה **shiqmâh,** *shik-maw´;* of uncert. der.; a *sycamore* (usually the tree):—sycamore (fruit, tree).

8257. שָׁקַע **shâqaʻ,** *shaw-kah´;* (abbrev. ° Am. 8 : 8); a prim. root; to *subside;* by impl. to *be overflowed, cease;* caus. to *abate, subdue:*—make deep, let down, drown, quench, sink.

8258. שְׁקַעֲרוּרָה **sheqaʻrûwrâh,** *shek-ah-roo-raw´;* from 8257; a *depression:*—hollow strake.

8259. שָׁקַף **shâqaph,** *shaw-kaf´;* a prim. root; prop. to *lean out* (of a window), i.e. (by impl.) *peep* or *gaze* (pass. *be a spectacle*):—appear, look (down, forth, out).

8260. שֶׁקֶף **sheqeph,** *sheh´-kef;* from 8259; a *loophole* (for looking *out*), to admit light and air:—window.

8261. שָׁקֻף **shâqûph,** *shaw-koof´;* pass. part. of 8259; an *embrasure* or opening [comp. 8260] with bevelled jam:—light, window.

8262. שָׁקַץ **shâqats,** *shaw-kats´;* a prim. root; to *be filthy,* i.e. (intens.) to *loathe, pollute:*—abhor, make abominable, have in abomination, detest, × utterly.

8263. שֶׁקֶץ **sheqets,** *sheh´kets;* from 8262; *filth,* i.e. (fig. and spec.) an *idolatrous* object:—abominable (-tion).

שִׁקֻּץ **shiqqûts.** See 8251.

8264. שָׁקַק **shâqaq,** *shaw-kak´;* a prim. root; to *course* (like a beast of prey); by impl. to *seek* greedily:—have appetite, justle one against another, long, range, run (to and fro).

8265. שָׂקַר **sâqar,** *saw-kar´;* a prim. root; to *ogle,* i.e. *blink* coquettishly:—wanton.

8266. שָׁקַר **shâqar,** *shaw-kar´;* a prim. root; to *cheat,* i.e. *be untrue* (usually in words):—fail, deal falsely, lie.

8267. שֶׁקֶר **sheqer,** *sheh´-ker;* from 8266; an *untruth;* by impl. a *sham* (often adv.):—without a cause, deceit (-ful), false (-hood, -ly), feignedly, liar, + lie, lying, vain (thing), wrongfully.

8268. שֹׁקֶת **shôqeth,** *sho´-keth;* from 8248; a *trough* (for *watering*):—trough.

8269. שַׂר **sar,** *sar;* from 8323; a *head* person (of any rank or class):—captain (that had rule), chief (captain), general, governor, keeper, lord, ([-task-]) master, prince (-ipal), ruler, steward.

8270. שֹׁר **shôr,** *shore;* from 8324; a *string* (as *twisted* [comp. 8306]), i.e. (spec.) the umbilical cord (also fig. as the centre of strength):—navel.

8271. שְׁרֵא **sherê'** (Chald.), *sher-ay´;* a root corresp. to that of 8293; to *free, separate;* fig. to *unravel, commence;* by impl. (of unloading beasts) to *reside:*—begin dissolve, dwell, loose.

8272. שַׁרְאֶצֶר **Shar'etser,** *shar-eh´-tser;* of for. der.; *Sharetser,* the name of an Ass. and an Isr.:—Sharezer.

8273. שָׁרָב **shârâb,** *shaw-rawb´;* from an unused root mean. to *glare;* quivering *glow* (of the air), espec. the *mirage:*—heat, parched ground.

8274. שֵׁרֵבְיָה **Shêrêbyâh,** *shay-rayb-yaw´;* from 8273 and 3050; *Jah has brought heat; Sherebjah,* the name of two Isr.:—Sherebiah.

8275. שַׁרְבִיט **sharbîyṭ,** *shar-beet´;* for 7626; a *rod* of empire:—sceptre.

8276. שָׂרַג **sârag,** *saw-rag´;* a prim. root; to *intwine:*—wrap together, wreath.

8277. שָׂרַד **sârad,** *saw-rad´;* a prim. root; prop. to *puncture* [comp. 8279], i.e. (fig. through the idea of *slipping* out) to *escape* or survive:—remain.

8278. שְׂרָד **serâd,** *ser-awd´;* from 8277; *stitching* (as *pierced* with a needle):—service.

8279. שֶׂרֶד **sered,** *seh´-red;* from 8277; a (carpenter's) *scribing-awl* (for *pricking* or scratching measurements):—line.

8280. שָׂרָה **sârâh,** *saw-raw´;* a prim. root; to *prevail:*—have power (as a prince).

8281. שָׁרָה **shârâh,** *shaw-raw´;* a prim. root; to *free:*—direct.

8282. שָׂרָה **sârâh,** *saw-raw´;* fem. of 8269; a *mistress,* i.e. female noble:—lady, princess, queen.

8283. שָׂרָה **Sârâh,** *saw-raw´;* the same as 8282; *Sarah,* Abraham's wife:—Sarah.

8284. שָׁרָה **shârâh,** *shaw-raw´;* prob. fem. of 7791; a *fortification* (lit. or fig.):—sing [*by mistake for* 7891], wall.

8285. שֵׁרָה **shêrâh,** *shay-raw´;* from 8324 in its orig. sense of *pressing;* a wrist-*band* (as *compact* or *clasping*):—bracelet.

8286. שְׂרוּג **Serûwg,** *ser-oog´;* from 8276; *tendril; Serug,* a postdiluvian patriarch:—Serug.

8287. שָׁרוּחֶן **Shârûwchen,** *shaw-roo-khen´;* prob. from 8281 (in the sense of *dwelling* [comp. 8271]) and 2580; *abode of pleasure; Sharuchen,* a place in Pal.:—Sharuhen.

8288. שְׂרוֹךְ **serôwk,** *ser-oke´;* from 8308; a *thong* (as *laced* or *tied*):—([shoe-]) latchet.

8289. שָׁרוֹן **Shârôwn,** *shaw-rone´;* prob. abridged from 3474; *plain; Sharon,* the name of a place in Pal.:—Lasharon, Sharon.

8290. שָׁרוֹנִי **Shârôwnîy,** *shaw-ro-nee´;* patrial from 8289; a *Sharonite* or inhab. of Sharon:—Sharonite.

8291. שַׂרוּק **sarûwq,** *sar-ook´;* pass. part. from the same as 8321; a *grapevine:*—principal plant. See 8320, 8321.

8292. שְׁרוּקָה° **sherûwqâh,** *sher-oo-kaw´;* or (by perm.) שְׁרִיקָה **sherîyqâh,** *sher-ee-kaw´;* fem. pass. part. of 8319; a *whistling* (in scorn); by anal. a *piping:*—bleating, hissing.

8293. שֵׁרוּת° **shêrûwth,** *shay-rooth´;* from 8281 abbrev.; *freedom:*—remnant.

8294. שֶׂרַח **Serach,** *seh´-rakh;* by perm. for 5629; *superfluity; Serach,* an Israelitess:—Sarah, Serah.

8295. שָׂרַט **sâraṭ,** *saw-rat´;* a prim. root; to *gash:*—cut in pieces, make [cuttings] pieces.

8296. שֶׂרֶט **sereṭ,** *seh´-ret;* and שָׂרֶטֶת **sâreṭeth,** *saw-reh´-teth;* from 8295; an *incision:*—cutting.

8297. שָׂרַי **Sâray,** *saw-rah´ee;* from 8269; *dominative; Sarai,* the wife of Abraham:—Sarai.

8298. שָׁרַי **Shâray,** *shaw-rah´ee;* prob. from 8324; *hostile; Sharay,* an Isr.:—Sharai.

8299. שָׂרִיג **sârîyg,** *saw-reeg´;* from 8276; a *tendril* (as *intwining*):—branch.

8300. שָׂרִיד **sârîyd,** *saw-reed´;* from 8277; a *survivor:*— × alive, left, remain (-ing), remnant, rest.

8301. שָׂרִיד **Sârîyd,** *saw-reed´;* the same as 8300; *Sarid,* a place in Pal.:—Sarid.

8302. שִׁרְיוֹן **shiryôwn,** *shir-yone´;* or שִׁרְיֹן **shiryôn,** *shir-yone´;* and שִׁרְיָן **shiryân,** *shir-yawn´;* also (fem.) שִׁרְיָה **shiryâh,** *shir-yaw´;* and שִׁרְיֹנָה **shiryônâh,** *shir-yo-naw´;* from 8281 in the orig. sense of *turning;* a *corslet* (as if *twisted*):—breastplate, coat of mail, habergeon, harness. See 5030.

8303. שִׁרְיוֹן **Shiryôwn,** *shir-yone´;* and שִׂרְיֹן **Siryôn,** *sir-yone´;* the same as 8302 (i.e. *sheeted* with snow); *Shirjon* or *Sirjon,* a peak of the Lebanon:—Sirion.

8304. שְׂרָיָה **Serâyâh,** *ser-aw-yaw´;* or שְׂרָיָהוּ **Serâyâhûw,** *ser-aw-yaw´-hoo;* from 8280 and 3050; *Jah has prevailed; Serajah,* the name of nine Isr.:—Seraiah.

8305. שְׂרִיקָה **serîyqâh,** *ser-ee-kaw´;* from the same as 8321 in the orig. sense of *piercing; hetchelling* (or combing flax), i.e. (concr.) *tow* (by extens. *linen* cloth):—fine.

8306. שָׁרִיר **shârîyr,** *shaw-reer´;* from 8324 in the orig. sense as in 8270 (comp. 8326); a *cord,* i.e. (by anal.) *sinew:*—navel.

8307. שְׁרִירוּת **sherîyrûwth,** *sher-ee-rooth´;* from 8324 in the sense of *twisted,* i.e. *firm; obstinacy:*—imagination, lust.

8308. שָׂרַךְ **sârak,** *saw-rak´;* a prim. root; to *interlace:*—traverse.

8309. שְׁרֵמָה° **sherêmâh,** *sher-ay-maw´;* prob. by orth. error for 7709; a *common:*—field.

8310. שַׂרְסְכִים **Sarçekîym,** *sar-seh-keem´;* of for. der.; *Sarsekim,* a Bab. general:—Sarsechim.

8311. שָׂרַע **sâraʻ,** *saw-rah´;* a prim. root; to *prolong,* i.e. (reflex.) *be deformed* by excess of members:—stretch out self, (have any) superfluous thing.

8312. שַׂרְעַף **sar'aph,** *sar-af´;* for 5587; *cogitation:*—thought.

8313. שָׂרַף **sâraph,** *saw-raf´;* a prim. root; to *be* (caus. *set*) *on fire:*—(cause to, make a) burn ([-ing], up), kindle, × utterly.

8314. שָׂרָף **sârâph,** *saw-rawf´;* from 8313; *burning,* i.e. (fig.) *poisonous* (serpent); spec. a *saraph* or symbol. creature (from their copper color):—fiery (serpent), seraph.

8315. שָׂרָף **Sâraph,** *saw-raf´;* the same as 8314; *Saraph,* an Isr.:—Saraph.

8316. שְׂרֵפָה **s^erêphâh,** *ser-ay-faw´;* from 8313; *cremation:*—burning.

8317. שָׁרַץ **shârats,** *shaw-rats´;* a prim. root; to *wriggle,* i.e. (by impl.) *swarm* or *abound:*—*breed (bring forth, increase) abundantly (in abundance), creep, move.*

8318. שֶׁרֶץ **sherets,** *sheh´-rets;* from 8317; a *swarm,* i.e. active mass of minute animals:—creep (-ing thing), move (-ing creature).

8319. שָׁרַק **shâraq,** *shaw-rak´;* a prim. root; prop. to *be shrill,* i.e. to whistle or *hiss* (as a call or in scorn):—hiss.

8320. שָׂרֻק **sâruq,** *saw-rook´;* from 8319; *bright red* (as *piercing* to the sight), i.e. *bay:*—speckled. See 8291.

8321. שֹׂרֵק **sôrêq,** *so-rake´;* or שׂוֹרֵק **sôwrêq,** *so-rake´;* and (fem.) שֹׂרֵקָה **sôrêqâh,** *so-ray-kaw´;* from 8319 in the sense of *redness* (comp. 8320); a *vine* stock (prop. one yielding *purple* grapes, the richest variety):—choice (-st, noble) wine. Comp. 8291.

8322. שְׁרֵקָה **sh^erêqâh,** *sher-ay-kaw´;* from 8319; a *derision:*—hissing.

8323. שָׂרַר **sârar,** *saw-rar´;* a prim. root; to *have* (trans. *exercise;* reflex. *get*) *dominion:*— × altogether, make self a prince, (bear) rule.

8324. שָׁרַר **shârar,** *shaw-rar´;* a prim. root; to *be hostile* (only act. part. an *opponent*):—enemy.

8325. שָׁרָר **Shârâr,** *shaw-rawr´;* from 8324; *hostile; Sharar,* an Isr.:—Sharar.

8326. שֹׁרֶר **shôrer,** *sho´-rer;* from 8324 in the sense of *twisting* (comp. 8270); the umbilical *cord,* i.e. (by extens.) a *bodice:*—navel.

8327. שָׁרַשׁ **shârash,** *shaw-rash´;* a prim. root; to *root;* i.e. strike into the soil, or (by impl.) to pluck from it:—(take, cause to take) root (out).

8328. שֶׁרֶשׁ **sheresh,** *sheh´-resh;* from 8327; a *root* (lit. or fig.):—bottom, deep, heel, root.

8329. שֶׁרֶשׁ **Sheresh,** *sheh´-resh;* the same as 8328; *Sheresh,* an Isr.:—Sharesh.

8330. שֹׁרֶשׁ **shôresh** (Chald.), *sho´-resh;* corresp. to 8328:—root.

8331. שַׁרְשָׁה **sharshâh,** *shar-shaw´;* from 8327; a *chain* (as *rooted,* i.e. *linked*):—chain. Comp. 8333.

8332. שְׁרֹשׁוּ° **sh^erôshûw** (Chald.), *sher-o-shoo´* from a root corresp. to 8327; *eradication,* i.e. (fig.) *exile:*—banishment.

8333. שַׁרְשְׁרָה **sharsh^erâh,** *shar-sher-aw´;* from 8327 [comp. 8331]; a *chain;* (arch.) prob. a *garland:*—chain.

8334. שָׁרַת **shârath,** *shaw-rath´;* a prim. root; to *attend* as a menial or worshipper; fig. to *contribute* to:—minister (unto), (do) serve (-ant, -ice, -itor), wait on.

8335. שָׁרֵת **shârêth,** *shaw-rayth´;* infin. of 8334; *service* (in the Temple):—minister (-ry).

8336. שֵׁשׁ **shêsh,** *shaysh;* or (for alliteration with 4897) שְׁשִׁי **sh^eshiy,** *shesh-ee´;* for 7893; *bleached* stuff, i.e. *white* linen or (by anal.) marble:— × blue, fine [(twined)] linen, marble, silk.

8337. שֵׁשׁ **shêsh,** *shaysh;* masc. שִׁשָּׁה **shishshâh,** *shish-shaw´;* a prim. number; *six* (as an overplus [see 7797] beyond five or the fingers of the hand); as ord. *sixth:*—six ([-teen, -teenth]), sixth.

8338. שָׁשָׁא **shâwshâw,** *shaw-shaw´;* a prim. root; appar. to *annihilate:*—leave but the sixth part [*by confusion with* 8341].

8339. שֵׁשְׁבַּצַּר **Shêshbatstsar,** *shaysh-bats-tsar´;* or for. der.; *Sheshbatstsar,* Zerubbabel's Pers. name:—Sheshbazzar.

8340. שֵׁשְׁבַּצַּר **Shêshbatstsar** (Chald.), *shaysh-bats-tsar´;* corresp. to 8339:—Sheshbazzar.

שָׁשָׂה **shâsâh.** See 8154.

8341. שָׁשָׁה **shâshâh,** *shaw-shaw´;* a denom. from 8337; to *sixth* or divide into sixths:—give the sixth part.

8342. שָׂשׂוֹן **sâsôwn,** *saw-sone´;* or שָׂשֹׂן **sâsôn,** *saw-sone´;* from 7797; *cheerfulness;* spec. *welcome:*—gladness, joy, mirth, rejoicing.

8343. שָׁשַׁי **Shâshay,** *shaw-shah´ee;* perh. from 8336; *whitish; Shashai,* an Isr.:—Shashai.

8344. שֵׁשַׁי **Shêshay,** *shay-shah´ee;* prob. for 8343; *Sheshai,* a Canaanite:—Sheshai.

8345. שִׁשִּׁי **shishshîy,** *shish-shee´;* from 8337; *sixth,* ord. or (fem.) fractional:—sixth (part).

8346. שִׁשִּׁים **shishshîym,** *shish-sheem´;* multiple of 8337; *sixty:*—sixty, three score.

8347. שֵׁשַׁךְ **Shêshak,** *shay-shak´;* of for. der.; *Sheshak,* a symbol. name of Bab.:—Sheshach.

8348. שֵׁשָׁן **Shêshân,** *shay-shawn´;* perh. for 7799; *lily; Sheshan,* an Isr.:—Sheshan.

שֹׁשָׁן **Shôshân.** See 7799.

8349. שָׁשַׁק **Shâshaq,** *shaw-shak´;* prob. from the base of 7785; *pedestrian; Shashak,* an Isr.:—Shashak.

8350. שָׁשַׁר **shâshar,** *shaw-shar´;* perh. from the base of 8324 in the sense of that of 8320; *red* ochre (from its *piercing* color):—vermillion.

8351. שֵׁת **shêth** (Num. 24 : 17), *shayth;* from 7582; *tumult:*—Sheth.

8352. שֵׁת **Shêth,** *shayth;* from 7896; *put,* i.e. *substituted; Sheth,* third son of Adam:—Seth, Sheth.

8353. שֵׁת **shêth** (Chald.), *shayth;* or שִׁת **shîth** (Chald.), *sheeth;* corresp. to 8337:—six (-th).

8354. שָׁתָה **shâthâh,** *shaw-thaw´;* a prim. root; to *imbibe* (lit. or fig.):— × assuredly, banquet, × certainly, drink (-er, -ing), drunk (× -ard), surely. [Prop. intensive of 8248.]

8355. שְׁתָה **sh^ethâh** (Chald.), *sheth-aw´;* corresp. to 8354:—drink.

8356. שָׁתָה **shâthâh,** *shaw-thaw´;* from 7896; a *basis,* i.e. (fig.) political or moral *support:*—foundation, purpose.

8357. שֵׁתָה **shêthâh,** *shay-thaw´;* from 7896; the *seat* (of the person):—buttock.

8358. שְׁתִי **sh^ethîy,** *sheth-ee´;* from 8354; *intoxication:*—drunkenness.

8359. שְׁתִי **sh^ethîy,** *sheth-ee´;* from 7896; a *fixture,* i.e. the *warp* in weaving:—warp.

8360. שְׁתִיָּה **sh^ethîyâh,** *sheth-ee-yaw´;* fem. of 8358; *potation:*—drinking.

שְׁתַּיִם **sh^ettayim.** see 8147.

8361. שִׁתִּין **shittîyn** (Chald.), *shit-teen´;* corresp. to 8346 [comp. 8353]; *sixty:*—three-score.

8362. שָׁתַל **shâthal,** *shaw-thal´;* a prim. root; to *transplant:*—plant.

8363. שְׁתִל **sh^ethîyl,** *sheth-eel´;* from 8362; a *sprig* (as if *transplanted*), i.e. *sucker:*—plant.

8364. שֻׁתַלְחִי **Shûthalchîy,** *shoo-thal-kee´;* patron. from 7803; a *Shuthalchite* (collect.) or desc. of Shuthelach:—Shuthalhites.

שָׂתַם **sâtham.** See 5640.

8365. שָׁתַם **shâtham,** *shaw-tham´;* a prim. root; to *unveil* (fig.):—be open.

8366. שָׁתַן **shâthan,** *shaw-than´;* a prim. root; (caus.) to *make water,* i.e. *urinate:*—piss.

8367. שָׁתַק **shâthaq,** *shaw-thak´;* a prim. root; to *subside:*—be calm, cease, be quiet.

8368. שָׂתַר **sâthar,** *saw-thar´;* a prim. root; to *break* out (as an eruption):—have in [one's] secret parts.

8369. שֵׁתָר **Shêthâr,** *shay-thawr´;* of for. der.; *Shethar,* a Pers. satrap:—Shethar.

8370. שְׁתַר בּוֹזְנַי **Sh^ethar Bôwz^enay,** *sheth-ar´ bo-zen-ah´ee;* of for. der.; *Shethar-Bozenai,* a Pers. officer:—Shethar-boznai.

8371. שָׁתַת **shâthath,** *shaw-thath´;* a prim. root; to *place,* i.e. *array;* reflex. to *lie:*—be laid, set.

ת

8372. תָּא **tâ',** *taw;* and (fem.) תָּאָה **tâ'âh** (Ezek. 40 : 12), *taw-aw´;* from (the base of) 8376; a *room* (as *circumscribed*):—(little) chamber.

8373. תָּאַב **tâ'ab,** *taw-ab´;* a prim. root; to *desire:*—long.

8374. תָּאַב **tâ'ab,** *taw-ab´;* a prim. root [prob. rather ident. with 8373 through the idea of *puffing* disdainfully at; comp. 340]; to *loathe* (mor.):—abhor.

8375. תַּאֲבָה **ta'ăbâh,** *tah-ab-aw´;* from 8374 [comp. 15]; *desire:*—longing.

8376. תָּאָה **tâ'âh,** *taw-aw´;* a prim. root; to *mark* off, i.e. (intens.) *designate:*—point out.

8377. תְּאוֹ **te'ôw,** *teh-o´;* and תּוֹא **tôw'** (the orig. form), *toh;* from 8376; a species of *antelope* (prob. from the white *stripe* on the cheek):—wild bull (ox).

8378. תַּאֲוָה **ta'ăvâh,** *tah-av-aw´;* from 183 (abbrev.); a *longing;* by impl. a *delight* (subj. *satisfaction,* obj. a *charm*):—dainty, desire, × exceedingly, × greedily, lust (ing), pleasant. See also 6914.

8379. תַּאֲוָה **ta'ăvâh,** *tah-av-aw´;* from 8376; a *limit,* i.e. full extent:—utmost bound.

8380. תָּאוֹם **tâ'ôwm,** *taw-ome´;* or תָּאֹם **tâ'ôm,** *taw-ome´;* from 8382; a *twin* (in plur. only), lit. or fig.:—twins.

8381. תַּאֲלָה **ta'ălâh,** *tah-al-aw´;* from 422; an *imprecation:*—curse.

8382. תָּאַם **tâ'am,** *taw-am´;* a prim. root; to *be complete;* but used only as denom. from 8380; to *be* (caus. *make*) *twinned,* i.e. (fig.) *duplicate* or (arch.) *jointed:*—coupled (together), bear twins.

תָּאֹם **tâ'ôm.** See 8380.

8383. תְּאֻן **te'ûn,** *teh-oon´;* from 205; *naughtiness,* i.e. *toil:*—lie.

8384. תְּאֵן **te'ên,** *teh-ane´;* or (in the sing., fem.) תְּאֵנָה **te'ênâh,** *teh-ay-naw´;* perh. of for. der.; the *fig.* (tree or fruit):—fig (tree).

8385. תַּאֲנָה **ta'ănâh,** *tah-an-aw´;* or תֹּאֲנָה **tô'ănâh,** *to-an-aw´;* from 579; an *opportunity* or (subj.) *purpose:*—occasion.

8386. תַּאֲנִיָּה **ta'ănîyâh,** *tah-an-ee-yaw´;* from 578; *lamentation:*—heaviness, mourning.

8387. תַּאֲנַת שִׁלֹה **Ta'ănath Shîlôh,** *tah-an-ath´ shee-lo´;* from 8385 and 7887; *approach of Shiloh; Taanath-Shiloh,* a place in Pal.:—Taanath-shiloh.

8388. תָּאַר **tâ'ar,** *taw-ar´;* a prim. root; to *delineate;* reflex. to *extend:*—be drawn, mark out, [Rimmon-] methoar [*by union with* 7417].

8389. תֹּאַר **tô'ar,** *to´-ar;* from 8388; *outline,* i.e. *figure* or *appearance:*— + beautiful, × comely, countenance, + fair, × favoured, form, × goodly, × resemble, visage.

8390. תַּאֲרֵעַ **Ta'ărêa',** *tah-ar-ay´-ah;* perh. from 772; *Taareä,* an Isr.:—Tarea. See 8475.

8391. תְּאַשּׁוּר **te'ashshûwr,** *teh-ash-shoor´;* from 833; a species of *cedar* (from its *erectness*):—box (tree).

8392. תֵּבָה **têbâh,** *tay-baw´;* perh. of for. der.; a *box:*—ark.

8393. תְּבוּאָה **tebûw'âh,** *teb-oo-aw´;* from 935; *income,* i.e. *produce* (lit. or fig.):—fruit, gain, increase, revenue.

8394. תָּבוּן **tâbûwn,** *taw-boon´;* and (fem.) תְּבוּנָה **tebûwnâh,** *teb-oo-naw´;* or תּוֹבֻנָה° **tôwbûnâh,** *to-boo-naw´;* from 995; *intelligence;* by impl. an *argument;* by extens. *caprice:*—discretion, reason, skilfulness, understanding, wisdom.

8395. תְּבוּסָה **tebûwçâh,** *teb-oo-saw´;* from 947: a *treading down,* i.e. *ruin:*—destruction.

8396. תָּבוֹר **Tâbôwr,** *taw-bore´;* from a root corresp. to 8406; *broken* region; *Tabor,* a mountain in Pal., also a city adjacent:—Tabor.

8397. תֶּבֶל **tebel,** *teh´-bel;* appar. from 1101; *mixture,* i.e. *unnatural* bestiality:—confusion.

8398. תֵּבֵל **têbêl,** *tay-bale´;* from 2986; the *earth* (as *moist* and therefore inhabited); by extens. the *globe;* by impl. its *inhabitants;* spec. a partic. *land,* as Babylonia, Pal.:—habitable part, world.

תֻּבַל **Tûbal.** See 8422.

8399. תַּבְלִית **tablîyth,** *tab-leeth´;* from 1086; *consumption:*—destruction.

8400. תְּבַלֻּל **teballûl,** *teb-al-lool´;* from 1101 in the orig. sese of *flowing;* a *cataract* (in the eye):—blemish.

8401. תֶּבֶן **teben,** *teh´-ben;* prob. from 1129; prop. *material,* i.e. (spec.) refuse *haum* or stalks of grain (as *chopped* in threshing and used for fodder):—chaff, straw, stubble.

8402. תִּבְנִי **Tibni,** *tib-nee´;* from 8401; *strawy; Tibni,* an Isr.:—Tibni.

8403. תַּבְנִית **tabnîyth,** *tab-neeth´;* from 1129; *structure;* by impl. a *model, resemblance:*—figure, form, likeness, pattern, similitude.

8404. תַּבְעֵרָה **Tab'êrâh,** *tab-ay-raw´;* from 1197; *burning; Taberah,* a place in the Desert:—Taberah.

8405. תֵּבֵץ **Têbêts,** *tay-bates´;* from the same as 948; *whiteness; Tebets,* a place in Pal.:—Thebez.

8406. תְּבַר **tebar** (Chald.), *teb-ar´;* corresp. to 7665; to *be fragile* (fig.):—broken.

8407. תִּגְלַת פִּלְאֶסֶר **Tiglath Pil'eçer,** *tig-lath´ pil-eh´-ser;* or תִּגְלַת פְּלֶסֶר **Tiglath Peleçer,** *tig-lath pel-eh-ser;* or תִּלְּגַת פִּלְנְאֶסֶר **Tilgath Pilne'eçer,** *til-gath´ pil-neh-eh´-ser;* or תִּלְּגַת פִּלְנֶסֶר **Tilgath Pilneçer,** *til-gath´ pil-neh´-ser;* of for. der.; *Tiglath-Pileser* or *Tilgath-pilneser,* an Assyr. king:—Tiglath-pileser, Tilgath-pilneser.

8408. תַּגְמוּל **tagmûwl,** *tag-mool´;* from 1580; a *bestowment:*—benefit.

8409. תִּגְרָה **tigrâh,** *tig-raw´;* from 1624; *strife,* i.e. *infliction:*—blow.

תֹּגַרְמָה **Tôgarmâh.** See 8425.

8410. תִּדְהָר **tidhâr,** *tid-hawr´;* appar. from 1725; *enduring;* a species of hard-wood or *lasting* tree (perh. *oak*):—pine (tree).

8411. תְּדִירָא **tedîyrâ'** (Chald.), *ted-ee-raw´;* from 1753 in the orig. sense of *enduring; permanence,* i.e. (adv.) *constantly:*—continually.

8412. תַּדְמֹר **Tadmôr,** *tad-more´;* or תַּמֹּר° **Tammôr** (1 Kings 9 : 18), *tam-more´;* appar. from 8558; *palm*-city; *Tadmor,* a place near Pal.:—Tadmor.

8413. תִּדְעָל **Tid'âl,** *tid-awl´;* perh. from 1763; *fearfulness; Tidal,* a Canaanite:—Tidal.

8414. תֹּהוּ **tôhûw,** *to´-hoo;* from an unused root mean. to lie *waste;* a *desolation* (of surface), i.e. *desert;* fig. a *worthless* thing; adv. in *vain:*—confusion, empty place, without form, nothing, (thing of) nought, vain, vanity, waste, wilderness.

8415. תְּהוֹם **tehôwm,** *teh-home´;* or תְּהֹם **tehôm,** *teh-home´;* (usually fem.) from 1949; an *abyss* (as a *surging* mass of water), espec. the *deep* (the *main* sea or the subterranean *water-supply*):—deep (place), depth.

8416. תְּהִלָּה **tehillâh,** *teh-hil-law´;* from 1984; *laudation;* spec. (concr.) a *hymn:*—praise.

8417. תָּהֳלָה **tohŏlâh,** *to-hol-aw´;* fem. of an unused noun (appar. from 1984) mean. *bluster; braggadocio,* i.e. (by impl.) *fatuity:*—folly.

8418. תַּהֲלֻכָה **tahălûkâh,** *tah-hal-oo-kaw´;* from 1980; a *procession:*— × went.

תְּהֹם **tehôm.** See 8415.

8419. תַּהְפֻּכָה **tahpûkâh,** *tah-poo-kaw´;* from 2015; a *perversity* or *fraud:*— (very) froward (-ness, thing), perverse thing.

8420. תָּו **tâv,** *tawv;* from 8427; a *mark;* by impl. a *signature:*—desire, mark.

8421. תּוּב **tûwb** (Chald.), *toob;* corresp, to 7725; to *come back;* spec. (trans. and ellip.) to *reply:*—answer, restore, return (an answer).

8422. תּוּבַל **Tûwbal,** *too-bal´;* or תֻּבַל **Tûbal,** *too-bal´;* prob. of for. der.; *Tubal,* a postdiluvian patriarch and his posterity:—Tubal.

8423. תּוּבַל קַיִן **Tûwbal Qayin,** *too-bal´ kah´-yin;* appar. from 2986 (comp. 2981) and 7014; *offspring of Cain; Tubal-Kajin,* an antediluvian patriarch:—Tubal-cain.

תּוֹבֻנָה° **tôwbûnâh.** See 8394.

8424. תּוּגָה **tûwgâh,** *too-gaw´;* from 3013; *depression* (of spirits); concr. a *grief:*—heaviness, sorrow.

8425. תּוֹגַרְמָה **Tôwgarmâh,** *to-gar-maw´;* or תֹּגַרְמָה **Tôgarmâh,** *to-gar-maw´;* prob. of for. der.; *Togarmah,* a son of Gomer and his posterity:—Togarmah.

8426. תּוֹדָה **tôwdâh,** *to-daw´;* from 3034; prop. an *extension* of the hand, i.e. (by impl.) *avowal,* or (usually) *adoration;* spec. a *choir* of worshippers:—confession, (sacrifice of) praise, thanks (-giving, offering).

8427. תָּוָה **tâvâh,** *taw-vaw´;* a prim. root; to *mark* out, i.e. (prim.) *scratch* or (def.) *imprint:*—scrabble, set [a mark].

8428. תָּוָה **tâvâh,** *taw-vaw´;* a prim. root [or perh. ident. with 8427 through a similar idea from *scraping* to pieces]; to *grieve:*—limit [*by confusion with* 8427].

8429. תְּוַהּ **tᵉvahh** (Chald.), *tev-ah´;* corresp. to 8539 or perh. to 7582 through the idea of *sweeping* to ruin [comp. 8428]; to *amaze,* i.e. (reflex. by impl.) *take alarm:*—be astonied.

8430. תּוֹחַ **Tôwach,** *to´-akh;* from an unused root mean. to *depress; humble; Toäch,* an Isr.:—Toah.

8431. תּוֹחֶלֶת **tôwcheleth,** *to-kheh´-leth;* from 3176; *expectation:*—hope.

תּוֹךְ **tôwk.** See 8496.

8432. תָּוֶךְ **tâvek,** *taw´-vek;* from an unused root mean. to *sever;* a *bisection,* i.e. (by impl.) the *centre:*—among (-st), × between, half, × (there-, where-) in (-to), middle, mid [-night], midst (among), × out (of), × through, × with (-in).

8433. תּוֹכֵחָה **tôwkêchâh,** *to-kay-khaw´;* and תּוֹכַחַת **tôwkachath,** *to-kakh´-ath;* from 3198; *chastisement;* fig. (by words) *correction, refutation, proof* (even in defence):—argument, × chastened, correction, reasoning, rebuke, reproof, × be (often) reproved.

תּוּכִּי **tûwkkîy.** See 8500.

8434. תּוֹלָד **Tôwlâd,** *to-lawd´;* from 3205; *posterity; Tolad,* a place in Pal.:—Tolad. Comp. 513.

8435. תּוֹלְדָה **tôwlᵉdâh,** *to-led-aw´;* or תֹּלְדָה **tôlᵉdâh,** *to-led-aw´;* from 3205; (plur. only) *descent,* i.e. *family;* (fig.) *history:*—birth, generations.

8436. תּוּלוֹן° **Tûwlôn,** *too-lone´;* from 8524; *suspension; Tulon,* an Isr.:—Tilon [*from the marg.*].

8437. תּוֹלָל **tôwlâl,** *to-lawl´;* from 3213; *causing* to *howl,* i.e. an *oppressor:*—that wasted.

8438. תּוֹלָע **tôwlâʻ,** *to-law´;* and (fem.) תּוֹלֵעָה **tôwlêʻâh,** *to-lay-aw´;* or תּוֹלַעַת **tôwlaʻath,** *to-lah´-ath;* or תֹּלַעַת **tôlaʻath,** *to-lah´-ath;* from 3216; a *maggot* (as *voracious*); spec. (often with ellips. of 8144) the crimson-*grub,* but used only (in this connection) of the color from it, and cloths dyed therewith:—crimson, scarlet, worm.

8439. תּוֹלָע **Tôwlâʻ,** *to-law´;* the same as 8438; *worm; Tola,* the name of two Isr.:—Tola.

8440. תּוֹלָעִי **Tôwlâʻîy,** *to-law-ee´;* patron. from 8439; a *Toalite* (collect.) or desc. of Tola:—Tolaites.

8441. תּוֹעֵבָה **tôwʻêbâh,** *to-ay-baw´;* or תֹּעֵבָה **tôʻêbâh,** *to-ay-baw´;* fem. act. part. of 8581; prop. something *disgusting* (mor.), i.e. (as noun) (an *abhorrence;* espec. *idolatry* or (concr.) an *idol:*—abominable (custom, thing), abomination.

8442. תּוֹעָה **tôwʻâh,** *to-aw´;* fem. act. part. of 8582; *mistake,* i.e. (mor.) *impiety,* or (political) *injury:*—error, hinder.

8443. תּוֹעָפָה **tôwʻâphâh,** *to-aw-faw´;* from 3286; (only in plur. collect.) *weariness,* i.e. (by impl.) *toil* (*treasure* so obtained) or *speed:*—plenty, strength.

8444. תּוֹצָאָה **tôwtsâʼâh,** *to-tsaw-aw´;* or תֹּצָאָה **tôtsâʼâh,** *to-tsaw-aw´;* from 3318; (only in plur. collect.) *exit,* i.e. (geographical) *boundary,* or (fig.) *deliverance,* (act.) *source:*—border (-s), going (-s) forth (out), issues, outgoings.

8445. תּוֹקַהַת° **Tôwqahath,** *to-kah´-ath;* from the same as 3349; *obedience; Tokahath,* an Isr.:—Tikvath [*by correction for* 8616].

8446. תּוּר **tûwr,** *toor;* a prim. root; to *meander* (caus. *guide*) about, espec. for trade or reconnoitring:—chap [-man], sent to descry, be excellent, merchant [-man], search (out), seek, (e-) spy (out).

8447. תּוֹר **tôwr,** *tore;* or תֹּר **tôr,** *tore;* from 8446; a *succession,* i.e. a *string* or (abstr.) *order;*—border, row, turn.

8448. תּוֹר **tôwr,** *tore;* prob. the same as 8447; a *manner* (as a sort of *turn*):—estate.

8449. תּוֹר **tôwr,** *tore;* or תֹּר **tôr,** *tore;* prob. the same as 8447; a *ring*-dove, often (fig.) as a term of endearment:—(turtle) dove.

8450. תּוֹר **tôwr** (Chald.), *tore;* corresp. (by perm.) to 7794; a *bull:*—bullock, ox.

8451. תּוֹרָה **tôwrâh,** *to-raw´;* or תֹּרָה **tôrâh,** *to-raw´;* from 3384; a *precept* or *statute,* espec. the *Decalogue* or *Pentateuch:*—law.

8452. תּוֹרָה **tôwrâh,** *to-raw´;* prob. fem. of 8448; a *custom:*—manner.

8453. תּוֹשָׁב **tôwshâb,** *to-shawb´;* or תֹּשָׁב **tôshâb** (1 Kings 17 : 1), *to-shawb´;* from 3427; a *dweller* but not outlandish [5237]); espec. (as distinguished from a native citizen [act. part. of 3427] and a temporary inmate [1616] or mere lodger [3885]) resident *alien:*—foreigner-inhabitant, sojourner, stranger.

8454. תּוּשִׁיָּה **tûwshîyâh,** *too-shee-yaw´;* or תֻּשִׁיָּה **tûshîyâh,** *too-shee-yaw´;* from an unused root prob. mean. to *substantiate; support* or (by impl.) *ability,* i.e. (direct) *help,* (in purpose) an *undertaking,* (intellectual) *understanding:*—enterprise, that which (thing as it) is, substance, (sound) wisdom, working.

8455. תּוֹתָח **tôwthâch,** *to-thawkh´;* from an unused root mean. to *smite;* a *club:*—darts.

8456. תָּזַז **tâzaz,** *taw-zaz´;* a prim. root; to *lop* off:—cut down.

8457. תַּזְנוּת **taznûwth,** *taz-nooth´;* or תַּזְנֻת **taznûth,** *taz-nooth´;* from 2181; *harlotry,* i.e. (fig.) *idolatry:*—fornication, whoredom.

8458. תַּחְבֻּלָה **tachbûlâh,** *takh-boo-law´;* or תַּחְבּוּלָה **tachbûwlâh,** *takh-boo-law´;* from 2254 as denom. from 2256; (only in plur.) prop. *steerage* (as a management of *ropes*), i.e. (fig.) *guidance* or (by impl.) a *plan:*—good advice, (wise) counsels.

8459. תֹּחוּ **Tôchûw,** *to´-khoo;* from an unused root mean. to *depress; abasement, Tochu,* an Isr.:—Tohu.

8460. תְּחוֹת **tᵉchôwth** (Chald.), *tekh-ōth´;* or תְּחֹת **tᵉchôth** (Chald.), *tekh-ōth´;* corresp. to 8478; *beneath:*—under.

8461. תַּחְכְּמֹנִי **Tachkᵉmônîy,** *takh-kem-o-nee´;* prob. for 2453; *sagacious; Tachkemoni,* an Isr.:—Tachmonite.

8462. תְּחִלָּה **tᵉchillâh,** *tekh-il-law´;* from 2490 in the sense of *opening;* a *commencement;* rel. *original* (adv. *-ly*):—begin (-ning), first (time).

8463. תַּחֲלוּא **tachălûwʼ,** *takh-al-oo´;* or תַּחֲלֻא **tachălûʼ,** *takh-al-oo´;* from 2456; a *malady:*—disease, × grievous, (that are) sick (-ness).

8464. תַּחְמָס **tachmâç,** *takh-mawce´;* from 2554; a species of unclean bird (from its *violence*), perh. an *owl:*—night hawk.

8465. תַּחַן **Tachan,** *takh´-an;* prob. from 2583; *station; Tachan,* the name of two Isr.:—Tahan.

8466. תַּחֲנָה **tachănâh,** *takh-an-aw´;* from 2583; (only plur. coll.) an *encampment:*—camp.

8467. תְּחִנָּה **tᵉchinnâh,** *tekh-in-naw´;* from 2603; *graciousness;* caus. *entreaty:*—favour, grace, supplication.

8468. תְּחִנָּה **Tᵉchinnâh,** *tekh-in-naw´;* the same as 8467; *Techinnah,* an Isr.:—Tehinnah.

8469. תַּחֲנוּן **tachănûwn,** *takh-an-oon´;* or (fem.) תַּחֲנוּנָה **tachănûwnâh,** *takh-an-oo-naw´;* from 2603; earnest *prayer:*—intreaty, supplication.

8470. תַּחֲנִי **Tachănîy,** *takh-an-ee´;* patron. from 8465; a *Tachanite* (collect.) or desc. of Tachan:—Tahanites.

8471. תַּחְפַּנְחֵס **Tachpanchêç,** *takh-pan-khace´;* or תְּחַפְנְחֵס **Tᵉchaphnᵉchêç** (Ezek. 30 : 18), *tekh-af-nekh-ace´;* or תַּחְפְּנֵס° **Tachpᵉnêç** (Jer. 2 : 16), *takh-pen-ace´;* of Eg. der.; *Tachpanches, Techaphneches* or *Tachpenes,* a place in Egypt:—Tahapanes, Tahpanhes, Tehaphnehes.

8472. תַּחְפְּנֵיס **Tachpᵉnêyç,** *takh-pen-ace´;* of Eg. der.; *Tachpenes,* an Eg. woman:—Tahpenes.

8473. תַּחֲרָא **tachărâʼ,** *takh-ar-aw´;* from 2734 in the orig. sense of 2352 or 2353; a linen *corslet* (as *white* or *hollow*):—habergeon.

8474. תַּחָרָה **tachârâh,** *takh-aw-raw´;* a factitious root from 2734 through the idea of the *heat* of jealousy; to *vie* with a rival:—close, contend.

8475. תַּחְרֵעַ **Tachrêaʻ,** *takh-ray´-ah;* for 8390; *Tachreä,* an Isr.:—Tahrea.

8476. תַּחַשׁ **tachash,** *takh´-ash;* prob. of for. der.; a (clean) animal with fur, prob. a species of *antelope:*—badger.

8477. תַּחַשׁ **Tachash,** *takh´-ash;* the same as 8476; *Tachash,* a relative of Abraham:—Thahash.

8478. תַּחַת **tachath,** *takh´-ath;* from the same as 8430; the *bottom* (as *depressed*); only adv. *below* (often with prep. pref. *underneath*), in *lieu of,* etc.:—as, beneath, × flat, in (-stead), (same) place (where . . . is), room, for . . . sake, stead of, under, × unto, × when . . . was mine, whereas, [where-] fore, with.

8479. תַּחַת **tachath** (Chald.), *takh´-ath;* corresp. to 8478:—under.

8480. תַּחַת **Tachath,** *takh´-ath;* the same as 8478; *Tachath,* the name of a place in the Desert, also of three Isr.:—Tahath.

תְּחֹת **t^echôth.** See 8460.

8481. תַּחְתּוֹן **tachtôwn,** *takh-tone´;* or תַּחְתֹּן **tachtôn,** *takh-tone´;* from 8478; *bottommost:*—lower (-est), nether (-most).

8482. תַּחְתִּי **tachtîy,** *takh-tee´;* from 8478; *lower most;* as noun (fem. plur.) the *depths* (fig. a *pit,* the *womb*):—low (parts, -er, -er parts, -est), nether (part).

8483. תַּחְתִּים חָדְשִׁי **Tachtîym Chodshîy,** *takh-teem´ khod-shee´;* appar. from the plur. masc. of 8482 or 8478 and 2320; *lower* (ones) *monthly; Tachtim-Chodshi,* a place in Pal.:—Tahtim-hodshi.

8484. תִּיכוֹן **tîykôwn,** *tee-kone´;* or תִּיכֹן **tîykôn,** *tee-kone´;* from 8432; *central:*—middle (-most), midst.

8485. תֵּימָא **Têymâ',** *tay-maw´;* or תֵּמָא **Têmâ',** *tay-maw´;* prob. of for. der.; *Tema,* a son of Ishmael, and the region settled by him:—Tema.

8486. תֵּימָן **têymân,** *tay-mawn´;* or תֵּמָן **têmân,** *tay-mawn´;* denom. from 3225; the *south* (as being on the *right* hand of a person facing the east):—south (side, -ward, wind).

8487. תֵּימָן **Têymân,** *tay-mawn´;* or תֵּמָן **Têmân,** *tay-mawn´;* the same as 8486; *Teman,* the name of two Edomites, and of the region and desc. of one of them:—south, Teman.

8488. תֵּימְנִי **Têym^enîy,** *tay-men-ee´;* prob. for 8489; *Temeni,* an Isr.:—Temeni.

8489. תֵּימָנִי **Têymânîy,** *tay-maw-nee´;* patron. from 8487; a *Temanite* or desc. of Teman:—Temani, Temanite.

8490. תִּימָרָה **tîymârâh,** *tee-maw-raw´;* or תִּמָרָה **tîmârâh,** *tee-maw-raw´;* from the same as 8558; a *column,* i.e. cloud:—pillar.

8491. תִּיצִי **Tîytsîy,** *tee-tsee´;* patrial or patron. from an unused noun of uncert. mean.; a *Titsite* or desc. or inhab. of an unknown Tits:—Tizite.

8492. תִּירוֹשׁ **tîyrôwsh,** *tee-roshe´;* or תִּירֹשׁ **tîyrôsh,** *tee-roshe´;* from 3423 in the sense of *expulsion; must* or fresh grape-juice (as just *squeezed* out); by impl. (rarely) fermented *wine:*—(new, sweet) wine.

8493. תִּירְיָא **Tîyr^eyâ',** *tee-reh-yaw´;* prob. from 3372; *fearful; Tirja,* an Isr.:—Tiria.

8494. תִּירָס **Tîyrâç,** *tee-rawce´;* prob. of for. der.; *Tiras,* a son of Japheth:—Tiras.

תִּירֹשׁ **tîyrôsh.** See 8492.

8495. תַּיִשׁ **tayish,** *tah´-yeesh;* from an unused root mean. to *butt;* a *buck* or he-goat (as given to *butting*):—he goat.

8496. תֹּךְ **tôk,** *toke;* or תּוֹךְ **tôwk** (Psa. 72 : 14), *toke;* from the same base as 8432 (in the sense of *cutting* to pieces); *oppression:*—deceit, fraud.

8497. תָּכָה **tâkâh,** *taw-kaw´;* a prim. root; to *strew,* i.e. *encamp:*—sit down.

8498. תְּכוּנָה **t^ekûwnâh,** *tek-oo-naw´;* fem. pass. part. of 8505; *adjustment,* i.e. *structure;* by impl. *equipage:*—fashion, store.

8499. תְּכוּנָה **t^ekûwnâh,** *tek-oo-naw´;* from 3559; or prob. ident. with 8498; something *arranged* or *fixed,* i.e. a *place:*—seat.

8500. תֻּכִּי **tukkîy,** *took-kee´;* or תּוּכִּי **tûwkkîy,** *took-kee´;* prob. of for. der.; some imported creature, prob. a *peacock:*—peacock.

8501. תָּכָךְ **tâkâk,** *taw-kawk´;* from an unused root mean. to *dissever,* i.e. *crush:*—deceitful.

8502. תִּכְלָה **tiklâh,** *tik-law´;* from 3615; *completeness:*—perfection.

8503. תַּכְלִית **taklîyth,** *tak-leeth´;* from 3615; *completion;* by impl. an *extremity:*—end, perfect (-ion).

8504. תְּכֵלֶת **t^ekêleth,** *tek-ay´-leth;* prob. for 7827; the cerulean *mussel,* i.e. the color (*violet*) obtained therefrom or stuff dyed therewith:—blue.

8505. תָּכַן **tâkan,** *taw-kan´;* a prim, root; to *balance,* i.e. *measure* out (by weight or dimension); fig. to *arrange, equalize,* through the idea of *levelling* (ment, *estimate, test*):—bear up, direct, be ([un-]) equal, mete, ponder, tell, weigh.

8506. תֹּכֶן **tôken,** *to´-ken;* from 8505; a fixed *quantity:*—measure, tale.

8507. תֹּכֶן **Tôken,** *to´-ken;* the same as 8506; *Token,* a place in Pal.:—Tochen.

8508. תָּכְנִית **toknîyth,** *tok-neeth´;* from 8506; *admeasurement,* i.e. *consummation:*—pattern, sum.

8509. תַּכְרִיךְ **takrîyk,** *tak-reek´;* appar. from an unused root mean. to *encompass;* a *wrapper* or robe:—garment.

8510. תֵּל **têl,** *tale;* by contr. from 8524; a *mound:*—heap, × strength.

8511. תָּלָא **tâlâ',** *taw-law´;* a prim. root; to *suspend;* fig. (through *hesitation*) to *be uncertain;* by impl. (of ment. *dependence*) to *habituate:*—be bent, hang (in doubt).

8512. תֵּל אָבִיב **Têl 'Âbîyb,** *tale-aw-beeb´;* from 8510 and 24; *mound* of *green* growth; *Tel-Abib,* a place in Chaldæa:—Tel-abib.

8513. תְּלָאָה **t^elâ'âh,** *tel-aw-aw´;* from 3811; *distress:*—travail, travel, trouble.

8514. תַּלְאוּבָה **tal'ûwbâh,** *tal-oo-baw´;* from 3851; *desiccation:*—great drought.

8515. תְּלַאשַּׂר **T^ela'ssar,** *tel-as-sar´;* or תְּלַשַּׂר **T^elassar,** *tel-as-sar´;* of for. der.; *Telassar,* a region of Assyria:—Telassar.

8516. תַּלְבֹּשֶׁת **talbôsheth,** *tal-bo´-sheth;* from 3847; a *garment:*—clothing.

8517. תְּלַג **t^elag** (Chald.), *tel-ag´;* corresp. to 7950; *snow:*—snow.

תִּלְגַת **Tilgath.** See 8407.

תֹּלְדָה **tôl^edâh.** See 8435.

8518. תָּלָה **tâlâh,** *taw-law´;* a prim. root; to *suspend* (espec. to *gibbet*):—hang (up).

8519. תְּלוּנָה **t^elûwnâh,** *tel-oo-naw´;* or תְּלֻנָּה **t^elunnâh,** *tel·oon-naw´;* from 3885 in the sense of *obstinacy;* a *grumbling:*—murmuring.

8520. תֶּלַח **Telach,** *teh´-lakh;* prob. from an unused root mean. to *dissever; breach; Telach,* an Isr.:—Telah.

8521. תֵּל חַרְשָׁא **Têl Charshâ',** *tale kharshaw´;* from 8510 and the fem. of 2798; *mound of workmanship; Tel-Charsha,* a place in Bab.:—Tel-haresha, Tel-harsa.

8522. תְּלִי **t^elîy,** *tel-ee´;* prob. from 8518; a *quiver* (as *slung*):—quiver.

8523. תְּלִיתַי **t^elîythay** (Chald.), *tel-ee-thah´ee;* or תַּלְתִּי **taltîy** (Chald.), *tal-tee´;* ordinal from 8532; *third:*—third.

8524. תָּלַל **tâlal,** *taw-lal`;* a prim. root; to *pile* up, i.e. *elevate:*—eminent. Comp. 2048.

8525. תֶּלֶם **telem,** *teh´-lem;* from an unused root mean. to *accumulate;* a *bank* or *terrace:*—furrow, ridge.

8526. תַּלְמַי **Talmay,** *tal-mah´ee;* from 8525; *ridged; Talmai,* the name of a Canaanite and a Syrian:—Talmai.

8527. תַּלְמִיד **talmîyd,** *tal-meed´;* from 3925; a *pupil:*—scholar.

8528. תֵּל מֶלַח **Têl Melach,** *tale meh´-lakh;* from 8510 and 4417; *mound of salt; Tel-Melach,* a place in Bab.:—Tel-melah.

תְּלֻנָּה **t^elunnâh.** See 8519.

8529. תָּלַע **tâla',** *taw-law´;* a denom. from 8438; to *crimson,* i.e. dye that color:— × scarlet.

תֹּלַעַת **tôla'ath.** See 8438.

8530. תַּלְפִּיָּה **talpîyâh,** *tal-pee-yaw´;* fem. from an unused root mean. to *tower;* something *tall,* i.e. (plur. collect.) *slenderness:*—armoury.

תְּלַשַּׂר **T^elassar.** See 8515.

8531. תְּלַת **t^elath** (Chald.), *tel-ath´;* from 8532; a *tertiary* rank:—third.

8532. תְּלָת **t^elâth** (Chald.), *tel-awth´;* masc. תְּלָתָה **t^elâthâh** (Chald.), *tel-aw-thaw´;* or תְּלָתָא **t^elâthâ'** (Chald.), *tel-aw-thaw´;* corresp. to 7969; *three* or *third:*—third, three.

תַּלְתִּי **taltîy.** See 8523.

8533. תְּלָתִין t^{e}lâthîyn (Chald.), *tel-aw-theen´;* mult. of 8532; *ten times three:*—thirty.

8534. תַּלְתַּל taltal, *tal-tal´;* by redupl. from 8524 through the idea of *vibration;* a trailing *bough* (as *pendulous*):—bushy.

8535. תָּם tâm, *tawm;* from 8552; *complete;* usually (mor.) *pious;* spec. *gentle, dear:*—coupled together, perfect, plain, undefiled, upright.

8536. תָּם tâm (Chald.), *tawm;* corresp. to 8033; *there:*— × thence, there, × where.

8537. תֹּם tôm, *tome;* from 8552; *completeness;* fig. *prosperity;* usually (mor.) *innocence:*—full, integrity, perfect (-ion), simplicity, upright (-ly, -ness), at a venture. See 8550.

תֵּמָא Têmâ'. See 8485.

8538. תֻּמָּה tummâh, *toom-maw´;* fem. of 8537; *innocence:*—integrity.

8539. תָּמַהּ tâmahh, *taw-mah´;* a prim. root; to *be in consternation:*—be amazed, be astonished, marvel (-lously), wonder.

8540. תְּמַהּ t^{e}mahh (Chald.), *tem-ah´;* from a root corresp. to 8539; a *miracle:*—wonder.

8541. תִּמָּהוֹן timmâhôwn, *tim-maw-hone´;* from 8539; *consternation:*—astonishment.

8542. תַּמּוּז Tammûwz, *tam-mooz´;* of uncert. der.; *Tammuz,* a Phœnician deity:—Tammuz.

8543. תְּמוֹל t^{e}môwl, *tem-ole´;* or תְּמֹל t^{e}môl, *tem-ole´;* prob. for 865; prop. *ago,* i.e. a (short or long) *time since;* espec. *yesterday,* or (with 8032) *day before* yesterday:— + before (-time), + these [three] days, + heretofore, + time past, yesterday.

8544. תְּמוּנָה t^{e}mûwnâh, *tem-oo-naw´;* or תְּמֻנָה t^{e}mûnâh, *tem-oo-naw´;* from 4327; *something portioned* (i.e. *fashioned*) out, as a *shape,* i.e. (indef.) *phantom,* or (spec.) *embodiment,* or (fig.) *manifestation* (of favor):—image, likeness, similitude.

8545. תְּמוּרָה t^{e}mûwrâh, *tem-oo-raw´;* from 4171; *barter, compensation:*— (ex-) change (-ing), recompense, restitution.

8546. תְּמוּתָה t^{e}mûwthâh, *tem-oo-thaw´;* from 4191; *execution* (as a doom):—death, die.

8547. תֶּמַח Temach, *teh´-makh;* of uncert. der.; *Temach,* one of the Nethinim:—Tamah, Thamah.

8548. תָּמִיד tâmîyd, *taw-meed´;* from an unused root mean. to *stretch;* prop. *continuance* (as indef. *extension*); but used only (attributively as adj.) *constant* (or adv. *constantly*); ellipt. the *regular* (daily) sacrifice:— alway (-s), continual (employment, -ly), daily, ([n-]) ever (-more), perpetual.

8549. תָּמִים tâmîym, *taw-meem´;* from 8552; *entire* (lit., fig. or mor.); also (as noun) *integrity, truth:*—without blemish, complete, full, perfect, sincerely (-ity), sound, without spot, undefiled, upright (-ly), whole.

8550. תֻּמִּים Tummîym, *toom-meem´;* plur. of 8537; *perfections,* i.e. (techn.) one of the epithets of the objects in the high-priest's breastplate as an emblem of *complete* Truth:—Thummim.

8551. תָּמַךְ tâmak, *taw-mak´;* a prim. root; to *sustain;* by impl. to *obtain, keep fast;* fig. to *help, follow close:*—(take, up-) hold (up), maintain, retain, stay (up).

תְּמֹל t^{e}môl. See 8543.

8552. תָּמַם tâmam, *taw-mam´;* a prim. root; to *complete;* in a good or a bad sense, lit. or fig., trans. or intrans. (as follows):—accomplish, cease, be clean [pass-] ed, consume, have done, (come to an, make an) end, fail, come to the full, be all gone, × be all here, be (make) perfect, be spent, sum, be (shew self) upright, be wasted, whole.

תֵּמָן têmân, Têmân. see 8486; 8487.

8553. תִּמְנָה Timnâh, *tim-naw´;* from 4487; a *portion* assigned; *Timnah,* the name of two places in Pal.:—Timnah, Timnath, Thimnathah.

תְּמֻנָה t^{e}mûnâh. See 8544.

8554. תִּמְנִי Timnîy, *tim-nee´;* patrial from 8553; a *Timnite* or inhab. of Timnah:—Timnite.

8555. תִּמְנָע Timnâ', *tim-naw´;* from 4513; *restraint; Timna,* the name of two Edomites:—Timna, Timnah.

8556. תִּמְנַת חֶרֶס Timnath Chereç, *tim-nath kheh´-res;* or תִּמְנַת סֶרַח Timnath Çerach, *tim-nath seh´-rakh;* from 8553 and 2775; *portion of* (the) *sun; Timnath-Cheres,* a place in Pal.:—Timnath-heres, Timnath-serah.

8557. תֶּמֶס temeç, *teh´-mes;* from 4529; *liquefaction,* i.e. *disappearance:*—melt.

8558. תָּמָר tâmâr, *taw-mawr´;* from an unused root mean. to *be erect;* a *palm* tree:—palm (tree).

8559. תָּמָר Tâmâr, *taw-mawr´;* the same as 8558; *Tamar,* the name of three women and a place:—Tamar.

8560. תֹּמֶר tômer, *to´-mer;* from the same root as 8558; a *palm* trunk:—palm tree.

8561. תִּמֹּר timmôr (plur. only), *tim-more´;* or (fem.) תִּמֹּרָה timmôrâh (sing. and plur.), *tim-mo-raw´;* from the same root as 8558; (arch.) a *palm*-like pilaster (i.e. umbellate):—palm tree.

תַּמֹּר Tammôr. See 8412.

תִּמָרָה tîmârâh. See 8490.

8562. תַּמְרוּק tamrûwq, *tam-rook´;* or תַּמְרֻק tamrûq, *tam-rook´;* or תַּמְרִיק° tamrîyq, *tam-reek´;* from 4838; prop. a *scouring,* i.e. *soap* or *perfumery* for the bath; fig. a *detergent:*— × cleanse, (thing for) purification (-fying).

8563. תַּמְרוּר tamrûwr, *tam-roor´;* from 4843; *bitterness* (plur. as collect.):— × most bitter (-ly).

תַּמְרֻק tamrûq, and תַּמְרִיק tamrîyq. See 8562.

8564. תַּמְרוּר tamrûwr, *tam-roor´;* from the same root as 8558; an *erection,* i.e. *pillar* (prob. for a guide-board):—high heap.

8565. תַּן tan, *tan;* from an unused root prob. mean. to *elongate;* a *monster* (as preternaturally formed), i.e. a *sea-serpent* (or other huge marine animal); also a *jackal* (or other hideous land animal):—dragon, whale. Comp. 8577.

8566. תָּנָה tânâh, *taw-naw´;* a prim. root; to *present* (a mercenary inducement), i.e. *bargain* with (a harlot):—hire.

8567. תָּנָה tânâh, *taw-naw´;* a prim. root [rather ident. with 8566 through the idea of *attributing* honor]; to *ascribe* (praise), i.e. *celebrate, commemorate:*—lament, rehearse.

8568. תַּנָּה tannâh, *tan-naw´;* prob. fem. of 8565; a female *jackal:*—dragon.

8569. תְּנוּאָה t^{e}nûw'âh, *ten-oo-aw´;* from 5106; *alienation;* by impl. *enmity:*—breach of promise, occasion.

8570. תְּנוּבָה t^{e}nûwbâh, *ten-oo-baw´;* from 5107; *produce:*—fruit, increase.

8571. תְּנוּךְ t^{e}nûwk, *ten-ook´;* perh. from the same as 594 through the idea of *protraction;* a *pinnacle,* i.e. *extremity:*—tip.

8572. תְּנוּמָה t^{e}nûwmâh, *ten-oo-maw´;* from 5123; *drowsiness,* i.e. *sleep:*—slumber (-ing).

8573. תְּנוּפָה t^{e}nûwphâh, *ten-oo-faw´;* from 5130; a *brandishing* (in threat); by impl. *tumult;* spec. the official *undulation* of sacrificial offerings:—offering, shaking, wave (offering).

8574. תַּנּוּר tannûwr, *tan-noor´;* from 5216; a *fire-pot:*—furnace, oven.

8575. תַּנְחוּם tanchûwm, *tan-khoom´;* or תַּנְחֻם tanchûm, *tan-khoom´;* and (fem.) תַּנְחוּמָה tanchûwmâh, *tan-khoo-maw´;* from 5162; *compassion, solace:*—comfort, consolation.

8576. תַּנְחֻמֶת Tanchûmeth, *tan-khoo´-meth;* for 8575 (fem.); *Tanchumeth,* an Isr.:—Tanhumeth.

8577. תַּנִּין tannîyn, *tan-neen´;* or תַּנִּים tannîym (Ezek. 29 : 3), *tan-neem´;* intens. from the same as 8565; a marine or land *monster,* i.e. *sea-serpent* or *jackal:*—dragon, sea-monster, serpent, whale.

8578. תִּנְיָן tinyân (Chald.), *tin-yawn´;* corresp. to 8147; *second:*—second.

8579. תִּנְיָנוּת tinyânûwth (Chald.), *tin-yaw-nooth´;* from 8578; a *second time:*—again.

8580. תַּנְשֶׁמֶת tanshemeth, *tan-sheh´-meth;* from 5395; prop. a hard *breather,* i.e. the name of two unclean creatures, a lizard and a bird (both perh. from changing color through their *irascibility*), prob. the *tree-toad* and the *water-hen:*—mole, swan.

8581. תָּעַב tâ'ab, *taw-ab´;* a prim. root; to *loathe,* i.e. (mor.) *detest:*—(make to be) abhor (-red), (be, commit more, do) abominable (-y), × utterly.

תֹּעֵבָה tô'êbâh. See 8441.

8582. תָּעָה **tâ'âh,** *taw-aw´;* a prim. root; to *vacillate,* i.e. *reel* or *stray* (lit. or fig.); also caus. of both:—(cause to) go astray, deceive, dissemble, (cause to, make to) err, pant, seduce, (make to) stagger, (cause to) wander, be out of the way.

8583. תֹּעוּ **Tô'ûw,** *to´-oo;* or תֹּעִי **Tô'îy,** *to´-ee;* from 8582; *error; Toü* or *Toï,* a Syrian king:—Toi, Tou.

8584. תְּעוּדָה **te'ûwdâh,** *teh-oo-daw´;* from 5749; *attestation,* i.e. a *precept, usage:*—testimony.

8585. תְּעָלָה **te'âlâh,** *teh-aw-law´;* from 5927; a *channel* (into which water is *raised* for irrigation); also a *bandage* or *plaster* (as placed *upon* a wound):—conduit, cured, healing, little river, trench, watercourse.

8586. תַּעֲלוּל **ta'ălûwl,** *tah-al-ool´;* from 5953; *caprice* (as a fit *coming on*), i.e. *vexation;* concr. a *tyrant:*—babe, delusion.

8587. תַּעֲלֻמָּה **ta'ălummâh,** *tah-al-oom-maw´;* from 5956; a *secret:*—thing that is hid, secret.

8588. תַּעֲנוּג **ta'ănûwg,** *tah-an-oog´;* or תַּעֲנֻג **ta'ănûg,** *tah-an-oog´;* and (fem.) תַּעֲנֻגָה **ta'ănûgâh,** *tah-an-oog-aw´;* from 6026; *luxury:*—delicate, delight, pleasant.

8589. תַּעֲנִית **ta'ănîyth,** *tah-an-eeth´;* from 6031; *affliction* (of self), i.e. *fasting:*—heaviness.

8590. תַּעֲנָךְ **Ta'ănâk,** *tah-an-awk´;* or תַּעְנָךְ **Ta'nâk,** *tah-nawk´;* of uncert. der.; *Taanak* or *Tanak,* a place in Pal.:—Taanach, Tanach.

8591. תָּעַע **tâ'a',** *taw-ah´;* a prim. root; to *cheat;* by anal. to *maltreat:*—deceive, misuse.

8592. תַּעֲצֻמָה **ta'ătsûmâh,** *tah-ats-oo-maw´;* from 6105; *might* (plur. collect.):—power.

8593. תַּעַר **ta'ar,** *tah´-ar;* from 6168; a *knife* or *razor* (as *making* bare); also a *scabbard* (as *being bare,* i.e. empty):—[pen-] knife, rasor, scabbard, shave, sheath.

8594. תַּעֲרֻבָה **ta'ărûbâh,** *tah-ar-oo-baw´;* from 6148; *suretyship,* i.e. (concr.) a *pledge:*— + hostage.

8595. תַּעְתֻּעַ **ta'tûa',** *tah-too´-ah;* from 8591; a *fraud:*—error.

8596. תֹּף **tôph,** *tofe;* from 8608 contr.; a *tambourine:*—tabret, timbrel.

8597. תִּפְאָרָה **tiph'ârâh,** *tif-aw-raw´;* or תִּפְאֶרֶת **tiph'ereth,** *tif-eh´-reth;* from 6286; *ornament* (abstr. or concr., lit. or fig.):—beauty (-iful), bravery, comely, fair, glory (-ious), honour, majesty.

8598. תַּפּוּחַ **tappûwach,** *tap-poo´-akh;* from 5301; an *apple* (from its *fragrance*), i.e. the fruit or the tree (prob. includ. others of the *pome* order, as the quince, the orange, etc.):—apple (tree). See also 1054.

8599. תַּפּוּחַ **Tappûwach,** *tap-poo´-akh;* the same as 8598; *Tappuäch,* the name of two places in Pal., also of an Isr.:—Tappuah.

8600. תְּפוֹצָה **tephôwtsâh,** *tef-o-tsaw´;* from 6327; a *dispersal:*—dispersion.

8601. תֻּפִין **tûphîyn,** *too-feen´;* from 644; *cookery,* i.e. (concr.) a *cake:*—baked piece.

8602. תָּפֵל **tâphêl,** *taw-fale´;* from an unused root mean. to *smear; plaster* (as *gummy*) or *slime;* (fig.) *frivolity:*—foolish things, unsavoury, untempered.

8603. תֹּפֶל **Tôphel,** *to´-fel;* from the same as 8602; *quagmire; Tophel,* a place near the Desert:—Tophel.

8604. תִּפְלָה **tiphlâh,** *tif-law´;* from the same as 8602; *frivolity:*—folly, foolishly.

8605. תְּפִלָּה **tephillâh,** *tef-il-law´;* from 6419; *intercession, supplication;* by impl. a *hymn:*—prayer.

8606. תִּפְלֶצֶת **tiphletseth,** *tif-leh´-tseth;* from 6426; *fearfulness:*—terrible.

8607. תִּפְסַח **Tiphçach,** *tif-sakh´;* from 6452; *ford; Tiphsach,* a place in Mesopotamia:—Tipsah.

8608. תָּפַף **tâphaph,** *taw-faf´;* a prim. root; to *drum,* i.e. play (as) on the tambourine:—taber, play with timbrels.

8609. תָּפַר **tâphar,** *taw-far´;* a prim. root; to *sew:*—(women that) sew (together).

8610. תָּפַשׂ **tâphas,** *taw-fas´;* a prim. root; to *manipulate,* i.e. *seize;* chiefly to *capture, wield;* spec. to *overlay;* fig. to *use* unwarrantably:—catch, handle, (lay, take) hold (on, over), stop, × surely, surprise, take.

8611. תֹּפֶת **tôpheth,** *to´-feth;* from the base of 8608; a *smiting,* i.e. (fig.) *contempt:*—tabret.

8612. תֹּפֶת **Tôpheth,** *to´-feth;* the same as 8611; *Topheth,* a place near Jerus.:—Tophet, Topheth.

8613. תָּפְתֶּה **Tophteh,** *tof-teh´;* prob. a form of 8612; *Tophteh,* a place of cremation:—Tophet.

8614. תִּפְתַּי **tiphtay** (Chald.), *tif-tah´ee;* perh. from 8199; *judicial,* i.e. a *lawyer:*—sheriff.

תֹּצָאָה **tôtsâ'âh.** See 8444.

8615. תִּקְוָה **tiqvâh,** *tik-vaw´;* from 6960; lit. a *cord* (as an *attachment* [comp. 6961]); fig. *expectancy:*—expectation ([-ted]), hope, live, thing that I long for.

8616. תִּקְוָה **Tiqvâh,** *tik-vaw´;* the same as 8615; *Tikvah,* the name of two Isr.:—Tikvah.

8617. תְּקוּמָה **teqûwmâh,** *tek-oo-maw´;* from 6965; *resistfulness:*—power to stand.

8618. תְּקוֹמֵם **teqôwmêm,** *tek-o-mame´;* from 6965; an *opponent:*—rise up against.

8619. תָּקוֹעַ **tâqôwa',** *taw-ko´-ah;* from 8628 (in the musical sense); a *trumpet:*—trumpet.

8620. תְּקוֹעַ **Teqôwa',** *tek-o´-ah;* a form of 8619; *Tekoä,* a place in Pal.:—Tekoa, Tekoah.

8621. תְּקוֹעִי **Teqôw'îy,** *tek-o-ee´;* or תְּקֹעִי **Teqô'îy,** *tek-o-ee´;* patron. from 8620, a *Tekoïte* or inhab. of Tekoah:—Tekoite.

8622. תְּקוּפָה **teqûwphâh,** *tek-oo-faw´;* or תְּקֻפָה **teqûphâh,** *tek-oo-faw´;* from 5362; a *revolution,* i.e. (of the sun) *course,* (of time) *lapse:*—circuit, come about, end.

8623. תַּקִּיף **taqqîyph,** *tak-keef´;* from 8630; *powerful:*—mightier.

8624. תַּקִּיף **taqqîyph** (Chald.), *tak-keef´;* corresp. to 8623:—mighty, strong.

8625. תְּקַל **teqal** (Chald.), *tek-al´;* corresp. to 8254; to *balance:*—Tekel, be weighed.

8626. תָּקַן **tâqan,** *taw-kan´;* a prim. root; to *equalize,* i.e. *straighten* (intrans. or trans.); fig. to *compose:*—set in order, make straight.

8627. תְּקַן **teqan** (Chald.), *tek-an´;* corresp. to 8626; to *straighten* up, i.e. *confirm:*—establish.

8628. תָּקַע **tâqa',** *taw-kah´;* a prim. root; to *clatter,* i.e. *slap* (the hands together), *clang* (an instrument); by anal. to *drive* (a nail or tent-pin, a dart, etc.); by impl. to *become bondsman* (by hand-clasping):—blow ([a trumpet]), cast, clap, fasten, pitch [tent], smite, sound, strike, × suretiship, thrust.

8629. תֵּקַע **têqa',** *tay-kah´;* from 8628; a *blast* of a trumpet:—sound.

תְּקֹעִי **Teqô'îy.** See 8621.

8630. תָּקַף **tâqaph,** *taw-kaf´;* a prim. root; to *overpower:*—prevail (against.).

8631. תְּקֵף **teqêph** (Chald.), *tek-afe´;* corresp. to 8630; to *become* (caus. *make*) *mighty* or (fig.) *obstinate:*—make firm, harden, be (-come) strong.

8632. תְּקֹף **teqôph** (Chald.), *tek-ofe´;* corresp. to 8633; *power:*—might, strength.

8633. תֹּקֶף **tôqeph,** *to´-kef;* from 8630; *might* or (fig.) *positiveness:*—authority, power, strength.

תְּקֻפָה **teqûphâh.** See 8622.

תֹּר **tôr.** See 8447, 8449.

8634. תַּרְאֲלָה **Tar'ălâh,** *tar-al-aw´;* prob. for 8653; a *reeling; Taralah,* a place in Pal.:—Taralah.

8635. תַּרְבּוּת **tarbûwth,** *tar-booth´;* from 7235; *multiplication,* i.e. *progeny:*—increase.

8636. תַּרְבִּית **tarbîyth,** *tar-beeth´;* from 7235; *multiplication,* i.e. *percentage* or *bonus* in addition to principal:—increase, unjust gain.

8637. תִּרְגַּל **tirgal,** *teer-gal´;* a denom. from 7270; to *cause* to *walk:*—teach to go.

8638. תִּרְגַּם **tirgam,** *teer-gam´;* a denom. from 7275 in the sense of *throwing* over; to *transfer,* i.e. *translate:*—interpret.

תֹּרָה **tôrâh.** See 8451.

8639. תַּרְדֵּמָה **tardêmâh,** *tar-day-maw´;* from 7290; a *lethargy* or (by impl.) *trance:*—deep sleep.

8640. תִּרְהָקָה **Tirhâqâh,** *teer-haw-kaw;* of for. der.; *Tirhakah,* a king of Kush:—Tirhakah.

8641. תְּרוּמָה **t**e**rûwmâh,** *ter-oo-maw´;* or תְּרֻמָה **t**e**rûmâh** (Deut. 12 : 11), *ter-oo-maw´;* from 7311; a *present* (as offered *up*), espec. in *sacrifice* or as *tribute:*—gift, heave offering ([shoulder]), oblation, offered (-ing).

8642. תְּרוּמִיָּה **t**e**rûwmîyâh,** *ter-oo-mee-yaw´;* formed as 8641; a sacrificial *offering:*—oblation.

8643. תְּרוּעָה **t**e**rûw'âh,** *ter-oo-aw´;* from 7321; *clamor,* i.e. *acclamation* of joy or a *battle-cry;* espec. *clangor* of trumpets, as an *alarum:*—alarm, blow (-ing) (of, the) (trumpets), joy, jubile, loud noise, rejoicing, shout (-ing), (high, joyful) sound (-ing).

8644. תְּרוּפָה **t**e**rûwphâh,** *ter-oo-faw´;* from 7322 in the sense of its congener 7495; a *remedy:*—medicine.

8645. תִּרְזָה **tirzâh,** *teer-zaw´;* prob. from 7329; a species of tree (appar. from its *slenderness*), perh. the *cypress:*—cypress.

8646. תֶּרַח **Terach,** *teh´-rakh;* of uncert. der.; *Terach,* the father of Abraham; also a place in the Desert:—Tarah, Terah.

8647. תִּרְחֲנָה **Tirchănâh,** *teer-khan-aw´;* of uncert. der.; *Tirchanah,* an Isr.:—Tirhanah.

8648. תְּרֵין **t**e**rêyn** (Chald.), *ter-ane´;* fem. תַּרְתֵּין **tartêyn,** *tar-tane´;* corresp. to 8147; *two:*—second, + twelve, two.

8649. תָּרְמָה **tormâh,** *tor-maw´;* and תַּרְמוּת° **tarmûwth,** *tar-mooth´;* or תַּרְמִית **tarmîyth,** *tar-meeth´;* from 7411; *fraud:*—deceit (-ful), privily.

תְּרֻמָה **t**e**rûmâh.** See 8641.

8650. תֹּרֶן **tôren,** *to´-ren;* prob. for 766; a *pole* (as a mast or flag-staff):—beacon, mast.

8651. תְּרַע **t**e**ra'** (Chald.), *ter-ah´;* corresp. to 8179; a *door;* by impl. a *palace:*—gate mouth.

8652. תָּרָע **târâ'** (Chald.), *taw-raw´;* from 8651; a *doorkeeper:*—porter.

8653. תַּרְעֵלָה **tar'êlâh,** *tar-ay-law´;* from 7477; *reeling:*—astonishment, trembling.

8654. תִּרְעָתִי **Tir'âthîy,** *teer-aw-thee´;* patrial from an unused name mean. *gate;* a *Tirathite* or inhab. of an unknown Tirah:—Tirathite.

8655. תְּרָפִים **t**e**râphîym,** *ter-aw-feme´;* plur. per. from 7495; a *healer; Teraphim* (sing. or plur.) a family idol:—idols (-atry), images, teraphim.

8656. תִּרְצָה **Tirtsâh,** *teer-tsaw´; from 7521; delightsomeness; Tirtsah,* a place in Pal.:—also an Israelitess:—Tirzah.

8657. תֶּרֶשׁ **Teresh,** *teh´-resh;* of for. der.; *Teresh,* a eunuch of Xerxes:—Teresh.

8658. תַּרְשִׁישׁ **tarshîysh,** *tar-sheesh´;* prob. of for. der. [comp. 8659]; a gem, perh. the *topaz:*—beryl.

8659. תַּרְשִׁישׁ **Tarshîysh,** *tar-sheesh´;* prob. the same as 8658 (as the region of the stone, or the reverse); *Tarshish,* a place on the Mediterranean, hence the epithet of a *merchant* vessel (as if for or from that port); also the name of a Persian and of an Isr.:—Tarshish, Tharshish.

8660. תִּרְשָׁתָא **Tirshâthâ',** *teer-shaw-thaw´;* of for. der.; the title of a Pers. deputy or *governor:*—Tirshatha.

תַּרְתֵּין **tartêyn.** See 8648.

8661. תַּרְתָּן **Tartân,** *tar-tawn´;* of for. der.; *Tartan,* an Assyrian:—Tartan.

8662. תַּרְתָּק **Tartâq,** *tar-tawk´;* of for. der.; *Tartak,* a deity of the Avvites:—Tartak.

8663. תְּשֻׁאָה **t**e**shû'âh,** *tesh-oo-aw´;* from 7722; a *crashing* or loud *clamor:*—crying, noise, shouting, stir.

תֹּשָׁב **tôshâb.** See 8453.

8664. תִּשְׁבִּי **Tishbîy,** *tish-bee´;* patrial from an unused name mean. *recourse;* a *Tishbite* or inhab. of Tishbeh (in Gilead):—Tishbite.

8665. תַּשְׁבֵּץ **tashbêts,** *tash-bates´;* from 7660; *checkered* stuff (as *reticulated*):—broidered.

8666. תְּשׁוּבָה **t**e**shûwbâh,** *tesh-oo-baw´;* or תְּשֻׁבָה **t**e**shûbâh,** *tesh-oo-baw´;* from 7725; a *recurrence* (of time or place); a *reply* (as *returned*):—answer, be expired, return.

8667. תְּשׂוּמֶת **t**e**sûwmeth,** *tes-oo-meth´;* from 7760; a *deposit,* i.e. *pledging:*— + fellowship.

8668. תְּשׁוּעָה **t**e**shûw'âh,** *tesh-oo-aw´;* or תְּשֻׁעָה **t**e**shû'âh,** *tesh-oo-aw´;* from 7768 in the sense of 3467; *rescue* (lit. or fig., pers., national or spir.):—deliverance, help, safety, salvation, victory.

8669. תְּשׁוּקָה **t**e**shûwqâh,** *tesh-oo-kaw´;* from 7783 in the orig. sense of *stretching* out after; a *longing:*—desire.

8670. תְּשׁוּרָה **t**e**shûwrâh,** *tesh-oo-raw´;* from 7788 in the sense of *arrival;* a *gift:*—present.

תַּשְׁחֵת **taschêth.** See 516.

תֻּשִׁיָּה **tûshîyâh.** See 8454.

8671. תְּשִׁיעִי **t**e**shîy'îy,** *tesh-ee-ee´;* ord. from 8672; *ninth:*—ninth.

תְּשֻׁעָה **t**e**shû'âh.** See 8668.

8672. תֵּשַׁע **têsha',** *tay´-shah;* or (masc.) תִּשְׁעָה **tish'âh,** *tish-aw´;* perh. from 8159 through the idea of a *turn* to the next or full number ten; *nine* or (ord.) *ninth:*—nine (+ -teen, + -teenth, -th).

8673. תִּשְׁעִים **tish'îym,** *tish-eem´;* multiple from 8672; *ninety:*—ninety.

8674. תַּתְּנַי **Tatt**e**nay,** *tat-ten-ah´ee;* of for. der.; *Tattenai,* a Persian:—Tatnai.

PLACES WHERE THE HEBREW AND THE ENGLISH BIBLES DIFFER IN THE DIVISION OF CHAPTERS AND VERSES

	English	*Hebrew*
Genesis	31:55	32:1
	32:1-32	2-33
Exodus	8:1-4	7:26-29
	5-32	8:1-28
	22:1	21:37
	2-31	22:1-30
Leviticus	6:1-7	5:20-26
	8-30	6:1-23
Numbers	16:36-50	17:1-15
	17:1-13	16-28
	26:1 (first clause)	25:19
	29:40	30:1
	30:1-16	2-17
Deuteronomy	5:18-33	5:17-30
	12:32	13:1
	13:1-18	2-19
	22:30	23:1
	23:1-25	2-26
	29:1	28:69
	2-29	29:1-28
Joshua	21:36, 37.. (not in most copies)	
	38-45	21:36-43
1 Samuel	19:2 (first clause)	19:1
	20:42	21:1
	21:1-15	2-16
	23:29	24:1
	24:1-22	2-23
2 Samuel	17:28 (first word)...	29 (middle)
	18:33	19:1
	19:1-43	2-44
1 Kings	4:21-34	5:1-14
	5:1-18	15-32
	18:33 (l. half).. (first half)	18:34
	20: 2 (l. half... (first half)	20:3
	22:22 (f. clause)... (l. cl.)	22:21
	43 (last half)	44
	44-53	45-54
2 Kings	11:21	12:1
	12:1-21	2-22
1 Chronicles	6:1-15	5:27-41
	16-81	6:1-66
2 Chronicles	2:1	1:18
	2-18	2:1-17
	14:1	13:23
	2-15	14:1-14
Nehemiah	4:1-6	3:33-38
	7-23	4: 1-17
	9:38	10:1
	10:1-39	2-40
Job	41:1-8	40:25-32
	9-34	41:1-26
Psalms	3:*title*	3:1
	1-8	3-9
	4:*title*	4:1
	1-8	2-9
	5:*title*	5:1
	1-12	2-13
	6:*title*	6:1
	1-10	2-11
	7:*title*	7:1
	1-17	2-18
	8:*title*	8:1
	1-9	2-10
	9:*title*	9:1
	1-20	2-21
	11:*title* (first clause)	11:1

	English	Hebrew
Psalms	12:*title*	12:1
	1-8	2-9
	13:*title*	13:1
	1-5	2-6
	6 (last half)	6
	14:*title* (first clause)	14:1
	15:*title* (first clause)	15:1
	16:*title* (first clause)	16:1
	17:*title* (first clause):	17:1
	18:*title*	18:1&(f.c.)2
	1-50	2-51
	19:*title*	19:1
	1-14	2-15
	20:*title*	20:1
	1-9	2-10
	21:*title*	21:1
	1-13	2-14
	22:*title*	22:1
	1-31	2-32
	23:*title* (first clause)	23:1
	24-28:*title* (first clause)	24-28:1
	29:*title* (first clause)	29:1
	30:*title*	30:1
	1-12	2-13
	31:*title*	31:1
	1-24	2-25
	32:*title* (first clause)	32:1
	34:*title*	34:1
	1-22	2-23
	35&37:*title* (first word)	35&37:1
	36:*title*	36:1
	1-12	2-13
	38:*title*	38:1
	1-22	2-23
	39:*title*	39:1
	1-13	2-14
	40:*title*	40:1
	1-17	2-18
	41:*title*	41:1
	1-13	2-14
	42:*title*	42:1
	1-11	2-12
	44:*title*	44:1
	1-26	2-27
	45:*title*	45:1
	1-17	2-18
	46:*title*	46:1
	1-11	2-12
	47:*title*	47:1
	1-9	2-10
	48:*title*	48:1
	1-14	2-15
	49:*title*	49:1
	1-20	2-21
	50:*title* (first clause)	50:1
	51:*title*	51:1&2
	1-19	2-21
	52:*title* (first clause)	52:1 & 2
	1-9	2-11
	53:*title*	53:1
	1-6	2-7
	54:*title*	54:1 & 2
	1-7	2-9
	55:*title*	55:1
	1-23	2-24

	English	Hebrew
Psalms	56:*title*	56:1
	1-23	2-24
	57:*title*	57:1
	1-11	2-12
	58:*title*	58:1
	1-11	2-12
	59:*title*	59:1
	1-17	2-18
	60:*title*	60:1 & 2
	1-12	3-14
	61:*title*	61:1
	1-8	2-9
	62:*title*	62:1
	1-12	2-13
	63:*title*	63:1
	1-11	2-12
	64:*title*	64:1
	1-10	2-11
	65:*title*	65:1
	1-13	2-14
	66:*title* (first clause)	66:1
	67:*title*	67:1
	1-7	2-8
	68:*title*	68:1
	1-35	2-36
	69:*title*	69:1
	1-36	2-37
	70:*title*	70:1
	1-5	2-6
	72:*title* (first word)	72:1
	73:*title* (first clause)	73:1
	74:*title* (first clause)	74:1
	1-10	2-11
	76:*title*	76:1
	1-12	2-13
	77:*title*	77:1
	1-20	2-21
	78:79:*title*. (f. clause)	78&79:1
	80:*title*	80:1
	1-19	2-20
	81:*title*	81:1
	1-16	2-17
	82:*title* (first clause)	82:1
	83:*title*	83:1
	1-18	2-19
	84:*title*	84:1
	1-12	2-13
	85:*title*	85:1
	1-13	2-14
	86&87:*title* (first cl.)	86 & 87:1
	88:*title*	88:1
	1-18	2-19
	89:*title*	89:1
	1-52	2-53
	90:*title* (first clause)	90:1
	92:*title*	92:1
	11-5	2-16
	98:*title* (first word)	98:1
	100&101:*title*...(1st cl.)	100 & 101:1
	102:*title*	102:1
	1-28	2-29
	103:*title* (first word)	103:1
	108:*title*	108:1
	1-13	2-14
	109,110, 120-134, 138 and 139:*title*..... (first cl.)	same 1

(Continued)

Book	*English*	*Hebrew*
Psalms	140:*title*	140:1
	1-13	2-14
	141:*title* (first clause)	141:1
	142:*title*	142:1
	1-6	2-7
	143:*title* (first clause)	143:1
	144:*title* (first word)	144:1
	145:*title* (first clause)	145:1
Ecclesiastes	5:1	4:17
	2-20	5:1-19
Canticles	6:13	7:1
	7:1-13	2-14
Isaiah	9:1	8:23
	2-21	9:1-20
Isaiah	64:1	63:19
	2-12	64:1-11
Jeremiah	9:1	8:23
	2-26	9:1-25
Ezekiel	20:45-49	21:1-5
	21:1-32	6-37
Daniel	4:1-3	3:31-33
	4-37	4:1-34
	5:31	6:1
	6:1-28	2-29
Hosea	1:10, 11	2:1, 2
	2:1-23	3-25
	11:12	12:1
	12:1-14	2-15
	13:16	14:1
	14:1-9	2-10
Joel	2:28-32	3:1-5
	3:1-21	4:1-21
Jonah	1:17	2:1
	2:1-10	2-11
Micah	5:1	4:14
	2-15	5:1-14
Nahum	1:15	2:1
	2:1-13	2-14
Zechariah	1:18	2:1-4
	2:1-13	2-17
Malachi	4:1-6	3:19-24

A Concise Dictionary
of the Words in the
Greek/New Testament

---

with their Renderings in the King James Version

PREFACE

THIS work is entirely similar in origin, method, and design, to the author's HEBREW DICTIONARY, and may be employed separately, for a corresponding purpose and with a like result, namely, to be serviceable to many who have not the wish or the ability to use a more copious Lexicon of New-Testament Greek. In this case also even scholars will find many suggestions and explanations not unworthy their attention.

PLAN OF THE DICTIONARY

All the original words are treated in their alphabetical Greek order, and are numbered regularly from the first to the last, each being known throughout by its appropriate number. This renders reference easy without recourse to the Greek characters.

Immediately after each word is given its exact equivalent in English letters, according to the system of transliteration laid down in the scheme here following, which is substantially that adopted in the King James Version, only more consistently and uniformly carried out; so that the word could readily be turned back again into Greek from the form thus given it.

Next follows the precise pronunciation, according to the usual English mode of sounding syllables, so plainly indicated that none can fail to apprehend and apply it. The most approved sounds are adopted, as laid down in the annexed scheme of articulation, and in such a way that any good Græcist would immediately recognise the word if so pronounced, notwithstanding the minor variations current among scholars in this respect.

Then ensues a tracing of the etymology, radical meaning, and applied significations of the word, justly but tersely analyzed and expressed, with any other important peculiarities in this regard.

In the case of proper names, the same method is pursued, and at this point the regular mode of Anglicizing it, after the general style of the King James Version, is given, and a few words of explanation are added to identify it.

Finally (after the punctuation-mark :—) are given all the different renderings of the word in the King James Version, arranged in the alphabetical order of the leading terms, and conveniently condensed according to the explanations given below.

By searching out these various renderings in the MAIN CONCORDANCE, to which this Dictionary is designed as a companion, and noting the passages to which the same number corresponding to that of any given Greek word is attached in the marginal column, the reader, whether acquainted with the original language or not, will obtain a complete *Greek Concordance* also, expressed in the words of the King James Version. This is an advantage which no other Concordance or Lexicon affords.

GREEK ARTICULATION

THE following explanations are sufficient to show the mode of writing and pronouncing Greek words in English adopted in this *Dictionary.*

The *Alphabet* is as follows:

No.	*Form*	*Name*	*Transliteration and Power*
1.	Α α	Alpha (*al´-fah*)	**a,** as in A*rm* or
2.	Β β	Bēta (*bay´-tah*)	**b** [*m*A*n*[1]
3.	Γ γ	Gamma (*gam´-mah*)	**g** hard[2]
4.	Δ δ	Dĕlta (*del´-tah*)	**d**
5.	Ε ε	Ĕpsilŏn (*ep´-see-lon*)	**ĕ,** as in *m*E*t*[3]
6.	Ζ ζ	Zēta (*dzay´-tah*)	**z,** as in *a*DZ*e*‡
7.	Η η	Ēta (*ay´-tah*)	**ē,** as in *th*E*y*
8.	Θ θ or ϑ	Thēta (*thay´-tah*)	**th,** as in TH*in*[4]
9.	Ι ι	Iōta (*ee-o´-tah*)	**i,** as in *ma-*
10.	Κ κ or ϰ	Kappa (*cap´-pah*)	**k** [*ch*I*ne*[5]
11.	Λ λ	Lambda (*lamb´-dah*)	**l**
12.	Μ μ	Mu (*moo*)	**m**
13.	Ν ν	Nu (*noo*)	**n**
14.	Ξ ξ	Xi (*ksee*)	**x** = *ks*
15.	Ο ο	Omikrŏn (*om´-e-cron*)	**ŏ,** as in *n*O*t*
16.	Π π	Pi (*pee*)	**p**
17.	Ρ ρ	Rhō (*hro*)	**r**
18.	Σ σ, final ς	Sigma (*sig´-mah*)	**s** sharp
19.	Τ τ	Tau (*tŏw*)	**t** [6]
20.	Υ υ	Upsilŏn (*u´-pse-lon*)	**u,** as in *f*U*ll*
21.	Φ φ	Phi (*fee*)	**ph** = *f*
22.	Χ χ	Chi (*khee*)	German **ch**[7]
23.	Ψ ψ	Psi (*psee*)	**ps**
24.	Ω ω	Omĕga (*o´-meg-ah*)	**ō,** as in *n*O.

The mark ῾, placed over the *initial* vowel of a word, is called the *Rough Breathing,* and is equivalent to the English *h,* by which we have accordingly represented it. Its *absence* over an initial vowel is indicated by the mark ᾿, called the *Smooth Breathing,* which is unappreciable or silent, and is therefore not represented in our method of transliteration.[8]

The following are the Greek diphthongs, properly so called:[9]

Form	*Transliteration and Power*	*Form*	*Transliteration and Power*
αι	**ai (ah´ee)** [ă + ē]	αυ	**ow,** as in nOW
ει	**ei,** as in hEIght	ευ	**eu,** as in fEUd
οι	**oi,** as in OIl	ου	**ou,** as in thrOUgh.
υι	**we,**as in sWEet		

The accent (stress of voice) falls on the syllable where it is written.[10] It is of three forms: the acute (´), which is the only true accent; the grave (`) which is its substitute; and the circumflex (˜ or ˆ), which is the union of the two. The acute may stand on any one of the last three syllables, and in case it occurs on the final syllable, before another word in the same sentence, it is written as a grave. The grave is understood (but never written as such) on every other syllable. The circumflex is written on any syllable (necessarily the last or next to the last one of a word), formed by the contraction of two syllables, of which the first would properly have the acute.

The following punctuation-marks are used: the comma (**,**), the semicolon (**;**), the colon or period (**.**), the interrogation-point (**?**), and by some editors, also the exclamation-point, parentheses and quotation-marks.

---

[1] α, when final, or before ρ final or followed by any other consonant, is sounded like α in Arm; elsewhere like α in mAn.

[2] γ, when followed by γ, κ, χ, or ξ, is sounded like ng in kING.

[3] ζ is always sounded like dz.

[4] θ never has the guttural sound, like th in THis.

[5] ι has the sound of ee when it ends an accented syllable; in other situations a more obscure sound, like i in amIable or Imbecile.

[6] τ never has a sibilant sound, like t in naTion, naTure.

[7] From the difficulty of producing the true sound of χ, it is generally sounded like k.

[8] These signs are placed over the second vowel of a diphthong. The same is true of the accents.

The Rough Breathing always belongs to υ initial.

The Rough Breathing is always used with ρ, when it begins a word. If this letter be doubled in the middle of a word, the first takes the Smooth, and the second the Rough, Breathing.

As these signs cannot conveniently be written over the first letter of a word, when a capital, they are in such cases placed before it. This observation applies also to the accents. The aspiration always begins the syllable.

Occasionally, in consequence of a contraction (crasis), the Smooth Breathing is made to stand in the middle of a word, and is then called Coro´nis.

[9] The above are combinations of two short vowels, and are pronounced like their respecative elements, but in more rapid succession than otherwise. Thus αι is midway between i in hIgh, and ay in SAY.

Besides these, there are what are called improper diphthongs, in which the former is a long vowel. In these,

ᾳ sounds like α   ηυ sounds like η + υ

ῃ sounds like υ   ωυ sounds like ω + υ.

ῳ sounds like ω

the second vowel, when ι, is written under the first (unless that be a capital), and is silent; when υ, it is sounded separately. When the initial is a capital, the ι is placed after it, but does not take the breathing nor accent.

The sign ¨, called diær´esis, placed over the latter of two vowels, indicates that they do not form a diphthong.

[10] Every word (except a few monosyllables, called Aton´ics) must have one accent; several small words (called Enclit´ics) throw their accent (always as an acute) on the last syllable of the preceding word (in addition to its own accent, which still has the principal stress), where this is possible.

ABBREVIATIONS EMPLOYED

abst. = abstract (-ly)
acc. = accusative (case)
adv. = adverb (-ial) (-ly)
aff. = affinity
alt. = alternate (-ly)
anal. = analogy
app. = apparent (-ly)
caus. = causative (-ly)
cer. = ceremony / ceremonial (-ly)
Chald. = Chaldee
Chr. = Christian
coll. = collective (-ly)
comp. = comparative / comparatively / compare / compound (-s)
concr. = concrete (-ly)
corr. = corresponding
dat. = dative (case)
der. = derivation / derivative / derived
dim. = diminutive
dir. = direct (-ly)
E. = East
eccl. = ecclesiastical (-ly)
Eg. = Egypt (-ian)
ell. = ellipsis / elliptical (-ly)
eq. = equivalent
esp. = especially
euph. = euphemism / euphemistic / euphemistically
ext. = extension
fem. = feminine
fig. = figurative (-ly)
for. = foreign
gen. = genitive (case)
Gr. = Greek
Heb. = Hebraism / Hebrew
i.e. = *id est* / that is
imper. = imperative
imperf. = imperfect
impers. = impersonal (-ly)
impl. = implication / implied
incl. = including
ind. = indicative (-ly)
indiv. = individual (-ly)
inf. = infinitive
inh. = inhabitant (-s)
intens. = intensive (-ly)
intr. = intransitive (-ly)
invol. = involuntary / involuntarily
irr. = irregular (-ly)
Isr. = Israelite (-s) / Israelitish
Jer. = Jerusalem
Lat. = Latin
lit. = literal (-ly)
mean. = meaning
ment. = mental (-ly)
mid. = middle (voice)
mor. = moral (-ly)
mult. = multiplicative
nat. = natural (-ly)
neg. = negative (-ly)
neut. = neuter
obj. = objective (-ly)
obs. = obsolete
or. = origin (-al) (-ly)
Pal. = Palestine
part. = participle
pass. = passive (-ly)
perh. = perhaps
pers. = person (-al) (-ly)
phys. = physical (-ly)
pl. = plural
pref. = prefix (-ed)
pos. = positive (-ly)
prim. = primary
prob. = probably
prol. = prolongation / prolonged
pron. = pronominal (-ly) / pronoun
prop. = properly
redupl. = reduplicated / reduplication
refl. = reflexive (-ly)
rel. = relative (-ly)
Rom. = Roman
sing. = singular
spec. = special (-ly)
subj. = subjective (-ly)
sup. = superlative (-ly)
tech. = technical
term. = termination
trans. = transitive (-ly)
transp. = transposed / transposition
typ. = typical (-ly)
unc. = uncertain
var. = variation / various
voc. = vocative
vol. = voluntarily / voluntary

SIGNS EMPLOYED

\+ (*addition*) denotes a rendering in the KJV of one or more Greek words in connection with the one under consideration.

× (*multiplication*) denotes a rendering in the KJV that results from an idiom peculiar to the Greek.

( ) (*parenthesis*), in the renderings from the KJV denotes a word or syllable sometimes given in connection with the principal word to which it is annexed.

[ ] (*bracket*), in the rendering from the KJV denotes the inclusion of an additional word in the Greek.

Italics, at the end of a rendering from the KJV, denote an explanation of the variations from the usual form.

NOTE

Owing to changes in the enumeration while in progress, there were no words left for Nos. *2717* and *3203-3302*, which were therefore silently dropped out of the vocabulary and references as redundant. This will occasion no practical mistake or inconvenience.

Greek Dictionary of The New Testament

A

N. B.—The numbers *not in italics* refer to the words in the *Hebrew Dictionary.* Significations within quotation-marks are derivative representatives of the Greek.

1. A **a,** *al-fah;* of Heb. or.; the first letter of the alphabet; fig. only (from its use as a numeral) the *first;*—Alpha. Often used (usually *ἀν* **an,** before a vowel) also in composition (as a contraction from *427*) in the sense of *privation;* so in many words beginning with this letter; occasionally in the sense of *union* (as a contraction of *200*).

2. Ἀαρών **Aarōn,** *ah-ar-ōhn´;* of Heb. or. [175]; *Aaron,* the brother of Moses:—Aaron.

3. Ἀβαδδών **Abaddōn** *ab-ad-dōhn´;* of Heb. or. [11]; a destroying *angel:*—Abaddon.

4. ἀβαρής **abarēs,** *ab-ar-ace´;* from *1* (as a neg. particle) and *922; weightless,* i.e. (fig.) *not burdensome:*—from being burdensome.

5. Ἀββᾶ **Abba,** *ab-bah´;* of Chald. or. [2]; *father* (as a voc.):—Abba.

6. Ἄβελ **Abĕl,** *ab'-el;* of Heb. or. [1893]; *Abel,* the son of Adam:—Abel.

7. Ἀβιά **Abia,** *ab-ee-ah´;* of Heb. or. [29]; *Abijah,* the name of two Isr.:—Abia.

8. Ἀβιάθαρ **Abiathar,** *ab-ee-ath´-ar;* of Heb. or. [54]; *Abiathar,* an Isr.:—Abiathar.

9. Ἀβιληνή **Abilēnē,** *ab-ee-lay-nay';* of for. or. [comp. 58]; *Abilene,* a region of Syria:—Abilene.

10. Ἀβιούδ **Abiŏud,** *ab-ee-ood´;* of Heb. or. [31]; *Abihud,* an Isr:—Abiud.

11. Ἀβραάμ **Abraam,** *ab-rah-am´;* of Heb. or. [85]; *Abraham,* the Heb. patriarch:—Abraham. [In Acts 7 : 16 the text should prob. read *Jacob.*]

12. ἄβυσσος **abussŏs,** *ab´-us-sos;* from *1* (as a neg. particle) and a var. of *1037; depthless,* i.e. (spec.) (infernal) *"abyss":*—deep, (bottomless) pit.

13. Ἄγαβος **Agabŏs,** *ag´-ab-os;* of Heb. or. [comp. *2285*]; *Agabus,* an Isr.:—Agabus.

14. ἀγαθοεργέω **agathŏĕrgĕō,** *ag-ath-er-gheh´-o;* from *18* and *2041;* to *work good:*—do good.

15. ἀγαθοποιέω **agathŏpŏiĕō,** *ag-ath-op-oy-eh´-o;* from *17;* to be a *well-doer* (as a favor or a duty):—(when) do good (well).

16. ἀγαθοποιΐα **agathŏpŏiia,** *ag-ath-op-oy-ee´-ah;* from *17; well-doing,* i.e. *virtue:*—well-doing.

17. ἀγαθοποιός **agathŏpŏiŏs,** *ag-ath-op-oy-os´;* from *18* and *4160;* a *well-doer,* i.e. *virtuous:*—them that do well.

18. ἀγαθός **agathŏs,** *ag-ath-os´;* a prim. word; *"good"* (in any sense, often as noun):—benefit, good (-s, things), well. Comp. *2570.*

19. ἀγαθωσύνη **agathōsunē,** *ag-ath-oo-soo´-nay;* from *18; goodness,* i.e. *virtue* or *beneficence:*—goodness.

20. ἀγαλλίασις **agalliasis,** *ag-al-lee´-as-is;* from *21; exultation;* spec. *welcome:*—gladness, (exceeding) joy.

21. ἀγαλλιάω **agalliaō,** *ag-al-lee-ah´-o;* from ἄγαν **agan** (*much*) and *242;* prop. to *jump for joy,* i.e. *exult:*—be (exceeding) glad, with exceeding joy, rejoice (greatly).

22. ἄγαμος **agamŏs,** *ag´-am-os;* from *1* (as a neg. particle) and *1002; unmarried:*—unmarried.

23. ἀγανακτέω **aganaktĕo,** *ag-an-ak-teh´-o;* from ἄγαν **agan** (*much*) and ἄχθος **achthŏs** (*grief;* akin to the base of *43*); to *be greatly afflicted,* i.e. (fig.) *indignant:*—be much (sore) displeased, have (be moved with, with) indignation.

24. ἀγανάκτησις **aganaktēsis,** *ag-an-ak´-tay-sis;* from *23; indignation:*—indignation.

25. ἀγαπάω **agapaō,** *ag-ap-ah´-o;* perh. from ἄγαν **agan** (*much*) [or comp. 5689]; to *love* (in a social or moral sense):—(be-) love (-ed). Comp. *5368.*

26. ἀγάπη **agapē,** *ag-ah´-pay;* from *25; love,* i.e. *affection* or *benevolence;* spec. (plur.) a *love-feast:*—(feast of) charity ([-ably]), dear, love.

27. ἀγαπητός **agapētŏs,** *ag-ap-ay-tos´;* from *25; beloved:*—(dearly, well) beloved, dear.

28. Ἄγαρ **Agar,** *ag´-ar;* of Heb. or. [1904]; *Hagar,* the concubine of Abraham:—Hagar.

29. ἀγγαρεύω **aggarĕuō,** *ang-ar-yew´-o;* of for. or. [comp. 104]; prop. to *be a courier,* i.e., (by impl.) to *press* into public service:—compel (to go).

30. ἀγγεῖον **aggĕiŏn,** *ang-eye´-on;* from ἄγγος **aggŏs** (a *pail,* perh. as *bent;* comp. the base of *43*); a *receptacle:*—vessel.

31. ἀγγελία **aggĕlia,** *ang-el-ee´-ah;* from *32;* an *announcement,* i.e. (by impl.) *precept:*—message.

32. ἄγγελος **aggĕlŏs,** *ang´-el-os;* from ἀγγέλλω **aggĕllō** [prob. der. from *71;* comp. *34*] (to *bring tidings*); a *messenger;* esp. an *"angel";* by impl. a *pastor:*—angel, messenger.

33. ἄγε **agĕ,** *ag´-eh;* imper. of *71;* prop. *lead,* i.e. *come* on:—go to.

34. ἀγέλη **agĕlē,** *ag-el'-ay;* from *71* [comp. *32*]; a *drove:*—herd.

35. ἀγενεαλόγητος **agĕnĕalŏgētŏs,** *ag-en-eh-al-og´-ay-tos;* from *1* (as neg. particle) and *1075; unregistered* as to birth:—without descent.

36. ἀγενής **agĕnēs,** *ag-en-ace´;* from *1* (as neg. particle) and *1085;* prop. *without kin,* i.e. (of unknown descent, and by impl.) *ignoble:*—base things.

37. ἁγιάζω **hagiazō,** *hag-ee-ad´-zo;* from *40;* to *make holy,* i.e. (cer.) *purify* or *consecrate;* (mentally) to *venerate:*—hallow, be holy, sanctify.

38. ἁγιασμός **hagiasmŏs,** *hag-ee-as-mos´;* from *37;* prop. *purification,* i.e. (the state) *purity;* concr. (by Hebr.) a *purifier:*—holiness, sanctification.

39. ἅγιον **hagiŏn,** *hag´-ee-on;* neut. of *40;* a *sacred* thing (i.e. spot):—holiest (of all), holy place, sanctuary.

40. ἅγιος **hagiŏs,** *hag´-ee-os;* from ἅγος **hagŏs** (an *awful* thing) [comp. *53, 2282*]; *sacred* (phys. *pure,* mor. *blameless* or *religious,* cer. *consecrated*):—(most) holy (one, thing), saint.

41. ἁγιότης **hagiŏtēs,** *hag-ee-ot´-ace;* from *40; sanctity* (i.e. prop. the state):—holiness.

42. ἁγιωσύνη **hagiōsunē,** *hag-ee-o-soo´-nay;* from *40; sacredness* (i.e. prop. the quality):—holiness.

43. ἀγκάλη **agkalē,** *ang-kal´-ay;* from ἄγκος **agkŏs** (a *bend,* "ache"); an *arm* (as *curved*):—arm.

44. ἄγκιστρον **agkistrŏn,** *ang´-kis-tron;* from the same as *43;* a *hook* (as *bent*):—hook.

45. ἄγκυρα **agkura,** *ang´-koo-rah;* from the same as *43;* an *"anchor"* (as *crooked*):—anchor.

46. ἄγναφος **agnaphŏs,** *ag´-naf-os;* from *1* (as a neg. particle) and the same as *1102;* prop. *unfulled,* i.e. (by impl.) *new* (cloth):—new.

47. ἁγνεία **hagnĕia,** *hag-ni´-ah;* from *53; cleaniness* (the quality), i.e. (spec.) *chastity:*—purity.

48. ἁγνίζω **hagnizō,** *hag-nid´-zo;* from *53;* to *make clean,* i.e. (fig.) *sanctify* (cer. or mor.):—purity (self).

49. ἁγνισμός **hagnismŏs,** *hag-nis-mos´;* from *48;* a *cleansing* (the act), i.e. (cer.) *lustration:*—purification.

50. ἀγνοέω **agnŏĕō,** *ag-no-eh´-o;* from *1* (as a neg. particle) and *3539; not to know* (through lack of information or intelligence); by impl. to *ignore* (through disinclination):—(be) ignorant (-ly), not know, not understand, unknown.

51. ἀγνόημα **agnŏēma,** *ag-no´-ay-mah;* from *50;* a thing *ignored,* i.e. *shortcoming:*—error.

52. ἄγνοια **agnŏia,** *ag´-noy-ah;* from *50; ignorance* (prop. the quality):—ignorance.

53. ἁγνός **hagnŏs,** *hag-nos´;* from the same as *40;* prop. *clean,* i.e. (fig.) *innocent, modest, perfect:*—chaste, clean, pure.

54. ἁγνότης **hagnŏtēs,** *hag-not´-ace;* from *53; cleanness* (the state), i.e. (fig.) *blamelessness:*—pureness.

55. ἁγνῶς **hagnōs,** *hag-noce´;* adv. from *53; purely,* i.e. *honestly:*—sincerely.

56. ἀγνωσία **agnōsia,** *ag-no-see´-ah;* from *1* (as neg. particle) and *1108; ignorance* (prop. the state):—ignorance, not the knowledge.

57. ἄγνωστος **agnōstŏs,** *ag´-noce-tos;* from *1* (as neg. particle) and *1110; unknown:*—unknown.

58. ἀγορά **agŏra,** *ag-or-ah´;* from ἀγείρω **agĕirō** (to *gather;* prob. akin to *1453*); prop. the *town-square* (as a place of public resort); by impl. a *market* or *thoroughfare:*—market (-place), street.

59. ἀγοράζω **agŏrazō,** *ag-or-ad´-zo;* from *58;* prop. to *go to market,* i.e. (by impl.) to *purchase;* spec. to *redeem:*—buy, redeem.

60. ἀγοραῖος **agŏraiŏs,** *ag-or-ah´-yos;* from *58; relating to the market-place,* i.e. *forensic* (times); by impl. *vulgar:*—baser sort, low.

61. ἄγρα **agra,** *ag´-rah;* from *71;* (abstr.) a *catching* (of fish); also (concr.) a *haul* (of fish):—draught.

62. ἀγράμματος **agrammatŏs,** *ag-ram´-mat-os;* from *1* (as neg. particle) and *1121; unlettered,* i.e. *illiterate:*—unlearned.

63. ἀγραυλέω **agraulĕō,** *ag-row-leh´-o;* from *68* and *832* (in the sense of *833*); to *camp out:*—abide in the field.

64. ἀγρεύω **agrĕuō,** *ag-rew´-o;* from *61;* to *hunt,* i.e. (fig.) to *entrap:*—catch.

65. ἀγριέλαιος **agriĕlaiŏs,** *ag-ree-el´-ah-yos;* from *66* and *1636;* an *oleaster:*—olive tree (which is) wild.

66. ἄγριος **agriŏs,** *ag´-ree-os;* from *68; wild* (as pertaining to the *country*), lit, *(natural),* or fig. (*fierce*):—wild, raging.

67. Ἀγρίππας **Agrippas,** *ag-rip´-pas;* appar. from *66* and *2402; wild-horse* tamer; *Agrippas,* one of the Herods:—Agrippa.

68. ἀγρός **agrŏs,** *ag-ros´;* from *71;* a *field* (as a *drive* for cattle); gen. the *country;* spec. a *farm,* i.e. *hamlet:*—country, farm, piece of ground, land.

69. ἀγρυπνέω **agrupnĕō,** *ag-roop-neh´-o;* ultimately from *1* (as neg. particle) and *5258;* to *be sleepless,* i.e. *keep awake:*—watch.

70. ἀγρυπνία **agrupnia,** *ag-roop-nee´-ah;* from *69; sleeplessness,* i.e. a *keeping awake:*—watch.

71. ἄγω **agō,** *ag´-o;* a prim. verb; prop. to *lead;* by impl. to *bring, drive,* (reflex.) *go,* (spec.) *pass* (time), or (fig.) *induce:*—be, bring (forth), carry, (let) go, keep, lead away, be open.

72. ἀγωγή **agōgē,** *ag-o-gay´;* redupl. from *71;* a *bringing up,* i.e. *mode of living:*—manner of life.

73. ἀγών **agōn,** *ag-one´;* from *71;* prop. a place of *assembly* (as if *led*), i.e. (by impl.) a *contest* (held there); fig. an *effort* or *anxiety:*—conflict, contention, fight, race.

74. ἀγωνία **agōnia,** *ag-o-nee´-ah;* from *73;* a *struggle* (prop. the state), i.e. (fig.) *anguish:*—agony.

75. ἀγωνίζομαι **agōnizŏmai,** *ag-o-nid´-zom-ahee;* from *73;* to *struggle,* lit. (to *compete* for a prize), fig. (to *contend* with an adversary), or gen. (to *endeavor* to accomplish something):—fight, labor fervently, strive.

76. Ἀδάμ **Adam,** *ad-am´;* of Heb. or. [121]; *Adam,* the first man; typ. (of Jesus) *man* (as his representative):—Adam.

77. ἀδάπανος **adapanŏs,** *ad-ap´-an-os;* from *1* (as neg. particle) and *1160; costless,* i.e. *gratuitous:*—without expense.

78. Ἀδδί **Addi,** *ad-dee´;* prob. of Heb. or. [comp. *5716*]; *Addi,* an Isr.:—Addi.

79. ἀδελφή **adĕlphē,** *ad-el-fay´;* fem. of *80;* a *sister* (nat. or eccles.):—sister.

80. ἀδελφός **adĕlphŏs,** *ad-el-fos´;* from *1* (as a connective particle) and δελφύς **dĕlphus** (the *womb*); a *brother* (lit. or fig.) near or remote [much like 1]:—brother.

81. ἀδελφότης **adĕlphŏtēs,** *ad-el-fot´-ace;* from *80; brotherhood* (prop. the feeling of *brotherliness*), i.e. the (Christian) *fraternity:*—brethren, brotherhood.

82. ἄδηλος **adēlŏs,** *ad´-ay-los;* from *1* (as a neg. particle) and *1212; hidden,* fig. *indistinct:*—appear not, uncertain.

83. ἀδηλότης **adēlŏtēs,** *ad-ay-lot´-ace;* from *82; uncertainty:*—× uncertain.

84. ἀδήλως **adēlōs,** *ad-ay´-loce;* adv. from *82; uncertainly:*—uncertainly.

85. ἀδημονέω **adēmŏnĕō,** *ad-ay-mon-eh´-o:* from a der. of ἀδέω **adĕō,** (to be *sated* to loathing); to *be in distress* (of mind):—be full of heaviness, be very heavy.

86. ᾅδης **haidēs,** *hah´-dace;* from *1* (as a neg. particle) and *1492;* prop. *unseen,* i.e. *"Hades"* or the place (state) of departed souls:—grave, hell.

87. ἀδιάκριτος **adiakritŏs,** *ad-ee-ak-´ree-tos;* from *1* (as a neg. particle) and a der. of *1252;* prop. *undistinguished,* i.e. (act.) *impartial:*—without partiality.

88. ἀδιάλειπτος **adialĕiptŏs,** *ad-ee-al´-ipe-tos;* from *1* (as a neg. particle) and a der. of a compound of *1223* and *3007; unintermitted,* i.e. *permanent:*—without ceasing, continual.

89. ἀδιαλείπτως **adialĕiptōs,** *ad-ee-al-ipe´-toce;* adv. from *88; uninterruptedly,* i.e. *without omission* (on an appropriate occasion):—without ceasing.

90. ἀδιαφθορία **adiaphthŏria,** *ad-ee-af-thor-ee´-ah;* from a der. of a compound of *1* (as a neg. particle) and a der. of *1311; incorruptibleness,* i.e. (fig.) *purity* (of doctrine):—uncorruptness.

91. ἀδικέω **adikĕō,** *ad-ee-keh´-o;* from *94;* to *be unjust,* i.e. (act.) *do wrong* (mor., socially or phys.):—hurt, injure, be an offender, be unjust, (do, suffer, take) wrong.

92. ἀδίκημα **adikēma,** *ad-eek´-ay-mah;* from *91;* a *wrong* done:—evil doing, iniquity, matter of wrong.

93. ἀδικία, **adikia,** *ad-ee-kee´-ah;* from *94;* (legal) *injustice* (prop. the quality, by impl. the act); mor. *wrongfulness* (of character, life or act):—iniquity, unjust, unrighteousness, wrong.

94. ἄδικος **adikŏs,** *ad´-ee-kos;* from *1* (as a neg. particle) and *1349; unjust;* by extens. *wicked;* by impl. *treacherous;* spec. *heathen:*—unjust, unrighteous.

95. ἀδίκως **adikōs,** *ad-ee´-koce;* adv. from *94; unjustly:*—wrongfully.

96. ἀδόκιμος **adŏkimŏs,** *ad-ok´-ee-mos;* from *1* (as a neg. particle) and *1384; unapproved,* i.e. *rejected;* by impl. *worthless* (lit. or mor.):—castaway, rejected, reprobate.

97. ἄδολος **adŏlŏs,** *ad´-ol-os;* from *1* (as a neg. particle) and *1388; undeceitful,* i.e. (fig.) *unadulterated:*—sincere.

98. Ἀδραμυττηνός **Adramuttēnŏs,** *ad-ram-oot-tay-nos´;* from Ἀδραμύττειον **Adramuttĕiŏn** (a place in Asia Minor); *Adramyttene* or belonging to Adramyttium:—of Adramyttium.

99. Ἀδρίας **Adrias,** *ad-ree´-as;* from Ἀδρία **Adria** (a place near its shore); the *Adriatic* sea (including the Ionian):—Adria.

100. ἁδρότης **hadrŏtēs,** *had-rot´-ace;* from ἁδρός **hadrŏs** (*stout*); *plumpness,* i.e. (fig.) *liberality:*—abundance.

101. ἀδυνατέω **adunatĕō,** *ad-oo-nat-eh´-o;* from *102;* to *be unable,* i.e. (pass.) *impossible:*—be impossible.

102. ἀδύνατος **adunatŏs,** *ad-oo´-nat-os;* from *1* (as neg. particle) and *1415; unable,* i.e. *weak* (lit. or fig.); pass. *impossible:*—could not do, impossible, impotent, not possible, weak.

103. ᾄδω **a̧dō,** *ad´-o;* a prim. verb; to *sing:*—sing.

104. ἀεί **aĕi,** *ah-eye´;* from an obs. prim. noun (appar. mean. continued *duration*); *"ever;"* by qualification *regularly;* by impl. *earnestly:—always, ever.*

105. ἀετός **aĕtŏs,** *ah-et-os´;* from the same as *109;* an *eagle* (from its *wind-like flight):—eagle.*

106. ἄζυμος **azumŏs,** *ad´-zoo-mos;* from *1* (as a neg. particle) and *2219; unleavened,* i.e. (fig.) *uncorrupted;* (in the neut. plur.) spec. (by impl.) the *Passover* week:—unleavened (bread).

107. Ἀζώρ **Azōr,** *ad-zore´;* of Heb. or. [comp. 5809], *Azor,* an Isr.:—Azor.

108. Ἄζωτος **Azōtŏs,** *ad´-zo-tos;* of Heb. or. [795]; *Azotus* (i.e. Ashdod), a place in Pal.:—Azotus.

109. ἀήρ **aēr,** *ah-ayr´;* from ἄημι **aēmi** (to *breathe* unconsciously, i.e. *respire;* by anal. to *blow*); *"air"* (as naturally *circumambient*): —air. Comp. *5594.*

ἀθά **atha.** See *3134.*

110. ἀθανασία **athanasia,** *ath-an-as-ee´-ah;* from a compound of *1* (as a neg. particle) and *2288; deathlessness:*—immortality.

111. ἀθέμιτος **athĕmitŏs,** *ath-em´-ee-tos;* from *1* (as a neg. particle) and a der. of θέμις **thĕmis** (*statute:* from the base of *5087*); *illegal;* by impl. *flagitious:*—abominable, unlawful thing.

112. ἄθεος **athĕŏs,** *ath´-eh-os;* from *1* (as a neg. particle) and *2316; godless:*—without God.

113. ἄθεσμος **athĕsmŏs,** *ath´-es-mos;* from *1* (as a neg. particle) and a der. of *5087* (in the sense of *enacting*); *lawless,* i.e. (by impl.) *criminal:*—wicked.

114. ἀθετέω **athĕtĕō,** *ath-et-eh´-o;* from a compound of *1* (as a neg. particle) and a der. of *5087;* to *set aside,* i.e. (by impl.) to *disesteem, neutralize* or *violate:*—cast off, despise, disannul, frustrate, bring to nought, reject.

115. ἀθέτησις **athĕtēsis,** *ath-et´-ay-sis;* from *114; cancellation* (lit. or fig.):—disannulling, put away.

116. Ἀθῆναι **Athēnai,** *ath-ay´-nahee;* plur. of Ἀθήνη **Athēnē** (the goddess of wisdom, who was reputed to have founded the city); *Athenæ,* the capital of Greece:—Athens.

117. Ἀθηναῖος **Athēnaiŏs,** *ath-ay-nah´-yos;* from *116;* an *Athenaean* or inhab. of Athenae:—Athenian.

118. ἀθλέω **athlĕō,** *ath-leh´-o;* from ἄθλος **athlŏs** (a *contest* in the public lists); to *contend* in the competitive games:—strive.

119. ἄθλησις **athlēsis,** *ath´-lay-sis;* from *118;* a *struggle* (fig.):—fight.

120. ἀθυμέω **athumĕō,** *ath-oo-meh´-o;* from a comp. of *1* (as a neg. particle) and *2372;* to *be spiritless,* i.e. *disheartened:*—be dismayed.

121. ἄθωος **athōŏs,** *ath´-o-os;* from *1* (as a neg. particle) and a prob. der. of *5087* (mean. a *penalty*); *not guilty:*—innocent.

122. αἴγειος **aigĕŏs,** *ah´-ee-ghi-os;* from αἴξ **aix,** (a *goat*); belonging to a *goat:*—goat.

123. αἰγιαλός **aigialŏs,** *ahee-ghee-al-os´;* from ἀΐσσω **aïssō** (to *rush*) and *251* (in the sense of the *sea*); a *beach* (on which the *waves dash*):—shore.

124. Αἰγύπτιος **Aiguptiŏs,** *ahee-goop´-tee-os;* from *125;* an *AEgyptian* or inhab. of *AEgyptus:*—Egyptian.

125. Αἴγυπτος **Aiguptŏs,** *ah´ee-goop-tos;* of uncert. der.; *AEgyptus,* the land of the Nile:—Egypt.

126. ἀΐδιος **aïdiŏs,** *ah-id´-ee-os;* from *104; everduring* (forward and backward, or forward only):—eternal, everlasting.

127. αἰδώς **aidōs,** *ahee-doce´;* perh. form *1* (as a neg. particle) and *1492* (through the idea of *downcast* eyes); *bashfulness, i.e. (towards men), modesty* or (towards God) *awe:*—reverence, shamefacedness.

128. Αἰθίοψ **Aithiŏps,** *ahee-thee´-ops;* from αἴθω **aithō** (to *scorch*) and ὤψ **ōps** (the *face,* from *3700*); an *AEthiopian* (as a *blackamoor*):—Ethiopian.

129. αἷμα **haima,** *hah´-ee-mah;* of uncert. der.; *blood,* lit. (of men or animals), fig. (the *juice* of grapes) or spec. (the atoning *blood* of Christ); by impl. *bloodshed,* also *kindred:*—blood.

130. αἱματεκχυσία **haimatĕkchusia,** *hahee-mat-ek-khoo-see´-ah;* from *129* and a der. of *1632;* an *effusion of blood:*—shedding of blood.

131. αἱμοῤῥέω **haimŏrrhĕō,** *hahee-mor-hreh´-o;* from *129* and *4482;* to *flow blood,* i.e. *have a haemorrhage:*—diseased with an issue of blood.

132. Αἰνέας **Ainĕas,** *ahee-neh´-as;* of uncert. der.; *AEnĕas,* an Isr.:—AEneas.

133. αἴνεσις **ainĕsis,** *ah´ee-nes-is;* from *134;* a *praising* (the act), i.e. (spec.) a *thank* (-offering):—praise.

134. αἰνέω **ainĕō,** *ahee-neh´-o;* from *136;* to *praise* (God):—praise.

135. αἴνιγμα **ainigma,** *ah´ee-nig-ma;* from a der. of *136* (in its prim. sense); an *obscure* saying ("enigma"), i.e. (abstr.) *obscureness:*— × darkly.

136. αἶνος **ainŏs,** *ah´ee-nos;* appar. a prim. word; prop. a *story,* but used in the sense of *1868; praise* (of God):—praise.

137. Αἰνών **Ainōn,** *ahee-nohn´;* of Hebr. or. [a der. of 5869, *place of springs*]; *AEnon,* a place in Pal.:—AEnon.

138. αἱρέομαι **hairĕŏmai,** *hahee-reh´-om-ahee;* prob. akin to *142;* to *take for oneself,* i.e. to *prefer:*—choose. Some of the forms are borrowed from a cognate ἕλλομαι **hellŏmai,** *hel´-lom-ahee;* which is otherwise obsolete.

139. αἵρεσις **hairĕsis,** *hah´ee-res-is;* from *138;* prop. a *choice,* i.e. (spec.) a *party* or (abstr.) *disunion:*—heresy [*which is the Gr. word itself*], sect.

140. αἱρετίζω **hairĕtizō,** *hahee-ret-id´-zo;* from a der. of *138;* to *make a choice:*—choose.

141. αἱρετικός **hairĕtikŏs,** *hahee-ret-ee-kos´;* from the same as *140;* a *schismatic:*—heretic [*the Gr. word itself*].

142. αἴρω **airō,** *ah´ee-ro;* a prim. verb; to *lift;* by impl. to *take up* or *away;* fig. to *raise* (the voice), *keep in suspense* (the mind); spec. to *sail* away (i.e. *weigh anchor*); by Heb. [comp. 5375] to *expiate* sin:—away with, bear (up), carry, lift up, loose, make to doubt, put away, remove, take (away, up).

143. αἰσθάνομαι **aisthanŏmai,** *ahee-sthan´-om-ahee;* of uncert. der.; to *apprehend* (prop. by the senses):—perceive.

144. αἴσθησις **aisthēsis,** *ah´ee-sthay-sis;* from *143; perception,* i.e. (fig.) *discernment:*—judgment.

145. αἰσθητήριον **aisthētēriŏn,** *ahee-sthay-tay´-ree-on;* from a der. of *143;* prop. an *organ of perception,* i.e. (fig.) *judgment:*—senses.

146. αἰσχροκερδής **aischrŏkĕrdēs,** *ahee-skhrok-er-dace´;* from *150* and κέρδος **kerdos** (*gain*); *sordid:*—given to (greedy of) filthy lucre.

147. αἰσχροκερδῶς **aischrŏkĕrdōs,** *ahee-skhrok-er-doce´;* adv. from *146; sordidly:*—for filthy lucre's sake.

148. αἰσχρολογία **aischrŏlŏgia,** *ahee-skhrol-og-ee´-ah;* from *150* and *3056; vile conversation:*—filthy communication.

149. αἰσχρόν **aischrŏn,** *ahee-skhron´;* neut. of *150;* a *shameful thing,* i.e. *indecorum:*—shame.

150. αἰσχρός **aischrŏs,** *ahee-skhros´;* from the same as *153; shameful,* i.e. *base* (spec. *venal*):—filthy.

151. αἰσχρότης **aischrŏtēs,** *ahee-skhrot´-ace;* from *150; shamefulness,* i.e. *obscenity:*—filthiness.

152. αἰσχύνη **aischunē,** *ahee-skhoo´-nay;* from *153; shame* or *disgrace* (abstr. or concr.):—dishonesty, shame.

153. αἰσχύνομαι **aischunŏmai,** *ahee-skhoo´-nom-ahee;* from αἶσχος **aischŏs** (*disfigurement,* i.e. *disgrace*); to *feel shame* (for oneself):—be ashamed.

154. αἰτέω **aitĕō,** *ahee-teh´-o;* of uncert. der.; to *ask* (in gen.):—ask, beg, call for, crave, desire, require. Comp. *4441.*

155. αἴτημα **aitēma,** *ah´ee-tay-mah;* from *154;* a *thing asked* or (abstr.) an *asking:*—petition, request, required.

156. αἰτία **aitia,** *ahee-tee´-a;* from the same as *154;* a *cause* (as if *asked* for), i.e. (logical) *reason* (motive, matter), (legal) *crime* (alleged or proved):—accusation, case, cause, crime, fault, [wh-]ere[-fore].

157. αἰτίαμα **aitiama,** *ahee-tee´-am-ah;* from a der. of *156;* a *thing charged:*—complaint.

158. αἴτιον **aitiŏn,** *ah´ee-tee-on;* neut. of *159;* a *reason* or *crime* [like *156*]:—cause, fault.

159. αἴτιος **aitiŏs,** *ah´ee-tee-os;* from the same as *154; causative,* i.e. (concr.) a *causer:*—author.

160. αἰφνίδιος **aiphnidiŏs,** *aheef-nid´-ee-os;* from a comp. of *1* (as a neg. particle) and *5316* [comp. *1810*] (mean. *non-apparent*); *unexpected,* i.e. (adv.) *suddenly:*—sudden, unawares.

161. αἰχμαλωσία **aichmalōsia,** *aheekh-mal-o-see´-ah;* from *164; captivity:*—captivity.

162. αἰχμαλωτεύω **aichmalōtĕuō,** *aheekh-mal-o-tew´-o;* from *164;* to *capture* [like *163*]:—lead captive.

163. αἰχμαλωτίζω **aichmalōtizō,** *aheekh-mal-o-tid´-zo;* from *164:* to *make captive:*—lead away captive, bring into captivity.

164. αἰχμαλωτός **aichmalōtŏs,** *aheekh-mal-o-tos´;* from αἰχμή **aichmē** (a *spear*) and a der. of the same as *259;* prop. a *prisoner of war,* i.e. (gen.) a *captive:*—captive.

165. αἰών **aiōn,** *ahee-ohn´;* from the same as *104;* prop. an *age;* by extens. *perpetuity* (also past); by impl. the *world;* spec. (Jewish) a Messianic period (present or future):—age, course, eternal, (for) ever (-more), [n-]ever, (beginning of the, while the) world (began, without end). Comp. *5550.*

166. αἰώνιος **aiōniŏs,** *ahee-o´-nee-os;* from *165; perpetual* (also used of past time, or past and future as well):—eternal, for ever, everlasting, world (began).

167. ἀκαθαρσία **akatharsia,** *ak-ath-ar-see´-ah;* from *169; impurity* (the quality), phys. or mor.:—uncleanness.

168. ἀκαθάρτης **akathartēs,** *ak-ath-ar´-tace;* from *169; impurity* (the state), mor.:—filthiness.

169. ἀκάθαρτος **akathartŏs,** *ak-ath´-ar-tos;* from *1* (as a neg. particle) and a presumed der. of *2508* (mean, *cleansed*); *impure* (cer., mor. [*lewd*] or spec. [*dæmonic*]):—foul, unclean.

170. ἀκαιρέομαι **akairĕŏmai,** *ak-ahee-reh´-om-ahee:* from a comp. of *1* (as a neg. particle) and *2540* (mean. *unseasonable); to be inopportune* (for oneself), i.e. to *fail of a proper occasion:*—lack opportunity.

171. ἀκαίρως **akairōs,** *ak-ah´-ee-roce;* adv. from the same as *170; inopportunely:*—out of season.

172. ἄκακος **akakŏs,** *ak´-ak-os;* from *1* (as a neg. particle) and *2556; not bad,* i.e. (obj.) *innocent* or (subj.) *unsuspecting:*—harmless, simple.

173. ἄκανθα **akantha,** *ak´-an-thah;* prob. from the same as *188;* a *thorn:*—thorn.

174. ἀκάνθινος **akanthinŏs,** *ak-an´-thee-nos;* from *173; thorny:*—of thorns.

175. ἄκαρπος **akarpŏs,** *ak´-ar-pos;* from *1* (as a neg. particle) and *2590; barren* (lit. or fig.):—without fruit, unfruitful.

176. ἀκατάγνωστος **akatagnōstŏs,** *ak-at-ag´-noce-tos;* from *1* (as a neg. particle) and a der. of *2607; unblamable:*—that cannot be condemned.

177. ἀκατακάλυπτος **akatakaluptŏs,** *ak-at-ak-al´-oop-tos;* from *1* (as a neg. particle) and a der. of a comp. of *2596* and *2572; unveiled:*—uncovered.

178. ἀκατάκριτος **akatakritŏs,** *ak-at-ak´-ree-tos;* from *1* (as a neg. particle) and a der. of *2632; without* (legal) *trial:*—uncondemned.

179. ἀκατάλυτος **akatalutŏs,** *ak-at-al´-oo-tos;* from *1* (as a neg. particle) and a der. of *2647; indissoluble,* i.e. (fig.) *permanent:*—endless.

180. ἀκατάπαυστος **akatapaustŏs,** *ak-at-ap´-ŏw-stos;* from *1* (as a neg. particle) and a der. of *2664; unrefraining:*—that cannot cease.

181. ἀκαταστασία **akatastasia,** *ak-at-as-tah-see´-ah;* from *182; instability,* i.e. *disorder:*—commotion, confusion, tumult.

182. ἀκατάστατος **akatastatŏs,** *ak-at-as´-tat-os;* from *1* (as a neg. particle) and a der. of *2525; inconstant:*—unstable.

183. ἀκατάσχετος **akataschĕtŏs,** *ak-at-as´-khet-os;* from *1* (as a neg. particle) and a der. of *2722; unrestrainable:*—unruly.

184. Ἀκελδαμά **Akeldama,** *ak-el-dam-ah´;* of Chald. or. [mean. *field of blood;* corresp. to 2506 and 1818]; *Akeldama,* a place near Jerus.:—Aceldama.

185. ἀκέραιος **akĕraiŏs,** *ak-er´-ah-yos;* from *1* (as a neg. particle) and a presumed der. of *2767: unmixed,* i.e. (fig.) *innocent:*—harmless, simple.

186. ἀκλινής **aklinēs,** *ak-lee-nace´;* from *1* (as a neg. particle) and *2827; not leaning,* i.e. (fig.) *firm.:*—without wavering.

187. ἀκμάζω **akmazō,** *ak-mad´-zo;* from the same as *188;* to *make a point,* i.e. (fig.) *mature:*—be fully ripe.

188. ἀκμήν **akmēn,** *ak-mane´;* accus. of a noun (*"acme"*) akin to ἀκή **akē** (a *point*) and mean. the same; adv. *just* now, i.e. *still:*—yet.

189. ἀκοή **akŏē,** *ak-ŏ-ay´;* from *191; hearing* (the act, the sense or the thing heard):—audience, ear, fame, which ye heard, hearing, preached, report, rumor.

190. ἀκολουθέω **akŏlŏuthĕō,** *ak-ol-oo-theh´-o;* from *1* (as a particle of union) and κέλευθος **kĕlĕu-thŏs** (a *road*); prop. to *be in the same way with,* i.e. to *accompany* (spec. as a disciple):—follow, reach.

191. ἀκούω **akŏuō,** *ak-oo´-o;* a prim. verb; to *hear* (in various senses):—give (in the) audience (of), come (to the ears), ([shall]) hear (-er, -ken), be noised, be reported, understand.

192. ἀκρασία **akrasia,** *ak-ras-ee´-a;* from *193; want of self-restraint:*—excess, incontinency.

193. ἀκράτης **akratēs,** *ak-rat´-ace;* from *1* (as a neg. particle) and *2904; powerless,* i.e. *without self-control:*—incontinent.

194. ἄκρατος **akratŏs,** *ak´-rat-os;* from *1* (as a neg. particle) and a presumed der. of *2767; undiluted:*—without mixture.

195. ἀκρίβεια **akribĕia,** *ak-ree´-bi-ah;* from the same as *196; exactness:*—perfect manner.

196. ἀκριβέστατος **akribĕstatŏs,** *ak-ree-bes´-ta-tos;* superlative of ἀκρίβης **akribēs** (a der. of the same as *206*); *most exact:*—most straitest.

197. ἀκριβέστερον **akribĕstĕrŏn,** *ak-ree-bes´-ter-on;* neut. of the comparative of the same as *196;* (adv.) *more exactly:*—more perfect (-ly).

198. ἀκριβόω **akribŏō,** *ak-ree-bŏ´-o;* from the same as *196;* to *be exact,* i.e. *ascertain:*—enquire diligently.

199. ἀκριβῶς **akribōs,** *ak-ree-boce´;* adv. from the same as *196; exactly:*—circumspectly, diligently, perfect (-ly).

200. ἀκρίς **akris,** *ak-rece´;* appar. from the same as *206;* a *locust* (as *pointed,* or as *lighting* on the *top* of vegetation):—locust.

201. ἀκροατήριον **akrŏateriŏn,** *ak-rŏ-at-ay´-ree-on;* from *202;* an *audience-room:*—place of hearing.

202. ἀκροατής **akrŏatēs,** *ak-rŏ-at-ace´;* from ἀκροάομαι **akrŏaŏmai** (to *listen;* appar. an intens. of *191*); a *hearer* (merely):—hearer.

203. ἀκροβυστία **akrŏbustia,** *ak-rob-oos-tee´-ah;* from *206* and prob. a modified form of πόσθη **pŏsthē** (the *penis* or male sexual organ); the *prepuce;* by impl. an *uncircumcised* (i.e. *gentile,* fig. *unregenerate*) state or person:—not circumcised, uncircumcised [*with 2192*], uncircumcision.

204. ἀκρογωνιαῖος **akrŏgōniaiŏs,** *ak-rog-o-nee-ah´-yos;* from *206* and *1137;* belonging to the extreme *corner:*—chief corner.

205. ἀκροθίνιον **akrŏthiniŏn,** *ak-roth-in´-ee-on;* from *206* and θίς **this** (a *heap*); prop. (in the plur.) the *top of the heap,* i.e. (by impl.) *best of the booty:*—spoils.

206. ἄκρον **akrŏn,** *ak´-ron;* neut. of an adj. prob. akin to the base of *188;* the *extremity:*—one end . . . other, tip, top, uttermost part.

207. Ἀκύλας **Akulas,** *ak-oo´-las;* prob. for Lat. *aquila* (an *eagle*); *Akulas,* an Isr.:—Aquila.

208. ἀκυρόω **akurŏō,** *ak-oo-rŏ´-o;* from *1* (as a neg. particle) and *2964;* to *invalidate:*—disannul, make of none effect.

209. ἀκωλύτως **akōlutōs,** *ak-o-loo´-toce;* adv. from a compound of *1* (as a neg. particle) and a der. of *2967;* in *an unhindered manner,* i.e. *freely:*—no man forbidding him.

210. ἄκων **akōn,** *ak´-ohn;* from *1* (as a neg. particle) and *1635; unwilling:*—against the will.

211. ἀλάβαστρον **alabastrŏn,** *al-ab´-as-tron;* neut. of ἀλάβαστρος **alabastrŏs** (of uncert. der.), the name of a stone; prop. an *"alabaster"* box, i.e. (by extens.) a perfume *vase* (of any material):—(alabaster) box.

212. ἀλαζονεία **alazŏnĕia,** *al-ad-zon-i´-a;* from *213; braggadocio,* i.e. (by impl.) *self-confidence:*—boasting, pride.

213. ἀλαζών **alazōn,** *al-ad-zone´;* from ἄλη **alē** *(vagrancy); braggart:*—boaster.

214. ἀλαλάζω **alalazō,** al-al-ad´-zo; from ἀλαλή **alalē** (a *shout, "halloo"*); to *vociferate,* i.e. (by impl.) to *wail;* fig. to *clang:*—tinkle, wail.

215. ἀλάλητος **alalētŏs,** *al-al´-ay-tos;* from *1* (as a neg. particle) and a der. of *2980; unspeakable:*—unutterable, which cannot be uttered.

216. ἄλαλος **alalŏs,** *al´-al-os;* from *1* (as a neg. particle) and *2980; mute:*—dumb.

217. ἅλας **halas,** *hal´-as;* from *251; salt;* fig. *prudence:*—salt.

218. ἀλείφω **alĕiphō,** *al-i´-fo;* from *1* (as particle of union) and the base of *3045;* to *oil* (with perfume):—anoint.

219. ἀλεκτοροφωνία **alektŏrŏphōnia,** *alek-tor-of-o-nee´-ah;* from *220* and *5456; cockcrow,* i.e. the third night-watch:—cockcrowing.

220. ἀλέκτωρ **alĕktōr,** *al-ek´-tore;* from ἀλέκω (to *ward* off); a *cock* or male fowl:—cock.

221. Ἀλεξανδρεύς **Alĕxandrĕus,** *al-ex-and-reuce´;* from Ἀλεξάνδρεια (the city so called); an *Alexandreian* or inhab. of Alexandria:—of Alexandria, Alexandrian.

222. Ἀλεξανδρῖνος **Alĕxandrinŏs,** *al-ex-an-dree´-nos;* from the same as 221; *Alexandrine,* or belonging to Alexandria:—of Alexandria.

223. Ἀλέξανδρος **Alĕxandrŏs,** *al-ex´-an-dros;* from the same as (the first part of) *220* and *435; man-defender; Alexander,* the name of three Isr. and one other man:—Alexander.

224. ἄλευρον **alĕurŏn,** *al´-yoo-ron;* from ἀλέω **alĕō** (to *grind*); *flour:*—meal.

225. ἀλήθεια **alēthĕia,** *al-ay´-thi-a;* from *227; truth:*—true, × truly, truth, verity.

226. ἀληθεύω **alēthĕuō,** *al-ayth-yoo´-o;* from *227;* to *be true* (in doctrine and profession):—speak (tell) the truth.

227. ἀληθής **alēthēs,** *al-ay-thace´;* from *1* (as a neg. particle) and *2990; true* (as *not concealing*):—true, truly, truth.

228. ἀληθινός **alēthinŏs,** *al-ay-thee-nos´;* from *227; truthful:*—true.

229. ἀλήθω **alēthō,** *al-ay´-tho;* from the same as *224;* to *grind:*—grind.

230. ἀληθῶς **alēthōs,** *al-ay-thoce´;* adv. from *227; truly:*—indeed, surely, of a surety, truly, of a (in) truth, verily, very.

231. ἁλιεύς **haliĕus,** *hal-ee-yoos´;* from *251;* a *sailor* (as engaged on the *salt* water), i.e. (by impl.) a *fisher:*—fisher (-man).

232. ἁλιεύω **haliĕuō,** *hal-ee-yoo´-o;* from *231;* to *be a fisher,* i.e. (by impl.) to *fish:*—go a-fishing.

233. ἁλίζω **halizō,** *hal-id´-zo;* from *251;* to *salt:*—salt.

234. ἀλίσγεμα **alisgĕma,** *al-is´-ghem-ah;* from ἀλισγέω **alisgĕō** (to *soil*); (cer.) *defilement:*—pollution.

235. ἀλλά **alla,** *al-lah´;* neut. plur. of *243;* prop. *other* things, i.e. (adv.) *contrariwise* (in many relations):—and, but (even), howbeit, indeed, nay, nevertheless, no, notwithstanding, save, therefore, yea, yet.

236. ἀλλάσσω **allassō,** *al-las´-so;* from *243;* to *make different:*—change.

237. ἀλλαχόθεν **allachŏthĕn,** *al-lakh-oth´-en;* from *243; from elsewhere:*—some other way.

238. ἀλληγορέω **allēgŏrĕo,** *al-lay-gor-eh´-o;* from *243* and ἀγορέω **agŏrĕō** (to *harangue* [comp. *58*]); to *allegorize:*—be an allegory [*the Gr. word itself*].

239. ἀλληλουϊα **allēlŏuïa,** *al-lay-loo´-ee-ah;* of Heb. or. [imper. of 1984 and 3050]; *praise ye Jah!,* an adoring exclamation:—alleluiah.

240. ἀλλήλων **allēlōn,** *al-lay´-lone;* Gen. plur. from *243* redupl.; *one another:*—each other, mutual, one another, (the other), (them-, your-) selves, (selves) together [*sometimes with 3326 or 4314*].

241. ἀλλογενής **allŏgĕnēs,** *al-log-en-ace´;* from *243* and *1085; foreign,* i.e. not a Jew:—stranger.

242. ἅλλομαι **hallŏmai,** *hal´-lom-ahee;* mid. of appar. a prim. verb; to *jump;* fig. to *gush:*—leap, spring up.

243. ἄλλος **allŏs,** *al´-los;* a prim. word; *"else,"* i.e. *different* (in many applications):—more, one (another), (an-, some an-) other (-s, -wise).

244. ἀλλοτριεπίσκοπος **allotriĕpiskŏpŏs,** *al-lot-ree-ep-is´-kop-os;* from *245* and *1985; overseeing others'* affairs, i.e. a *meddler* (spec. in Gentile customs):—busybody in other men's matters.

245. ἀλλότριος **allŏtriŏs,** *al-lot´-ree-os;* from *243; another's,* i.e. not one's own; by extens. *foreign, not akin, hostile:*—alien, (an-) other (man's, men's), strange (-r).

246. ἀλλόφυλος **allŏphulŏs,** *al-lof´-oo-los;* from *243* and *5443; foreign,* i.e. (spec.) *Gentile:*—one of another nation.

247. ἄλλως **allōs,** *al´-loce;* adv. from *243; differently:*—otherwise.

248. ἀλοάω **alŏaō,** *al-o-ah´-o;* from the same as *257;* to *tread* out grain:—thresh, tread out the corn.

249. ἄλογος **alŏgŏs,** *al´-og-os;* from *1* (as a neg. particle) and *3056; irrational:*—brute, unreasonable.

250. ἀλοή **alŏē,** *al-ŏ-ay´;* of for. or. [comp. 174]; *aloes* (the gum):—aloes.

251. ἅλς **hals,** *halce;* a prim. word; *"salt":*—salt.

252. ἁλυκός **halukŏs,** *hal-oo-kos´;* from *251; briny:*—salt.

253. ἀλυπότερος **alupŏtĕrŏs,** *al-oo-pot´-er-os;* compar. of a comp. of *1* (as a neg. particle) and *3077; more without grief:*—less sorrowful.

254. ἅλυσις **halusis,** *hal´-oo-sis;* of uncert. der.; a *fetter* or *manacle:*—bonds, chain.

255. ἀλυσιτελής **alusitĕlēs,** *al-oo-sit-el-ace´;* from *1* (as a neg. particle) and the base of *3081; gainless,* i.e. (by impl.) *pernicious:*—unprofitable.

256. Ἀλφαῖος **Alphaiŏs,** *al-fah´-yos;* of Heb. or. [comp, 2501]; *Alphæus,* an Isr.:—Alpheus.

257. ἅλων **halōn,** *hal´-ohn;* prob. from the base of *1507;* a threshing-*floor* (as *rolled* hard), i.e. (fig.) the *grain* (and chaff, as just threshed):—floor.

258. ἀλώπηξ **alōpĕx,** *al-o´-pakes;* of uncert. der.; a *fox,* i.e. (fig.) a *cunning* person:—fox

259. ἅλωσις **halōsis,** *hal´-o-sis;* from a collateral form of *138; capture:*—be taken.

260. ἅμα **hama,** *ham´-ah;* a prim. particle; prop. *at the "same" time,* but freely used as a prep. or adv. denoting close association:—also, and, together, with (-al).

261. ἀμαθής **amathēs,** *am-ath-ace´;* from *1* (as a neg. particle) and *3129; ignorant:*—unlearned.

262. ἀμαράντινος **amarantinŏs,** *am-ar-an´-tee-nos;* from *263; "amaranthine",* i.e. (by impl.) *fadeless:*—that fadeth not away.

263. ἀμάραντος **amarantŏs,** *am-ar´-an-tos;* from *1* (as a neg. particle) and a presumed der. of *3133; unfading,* i.e. (by impl.) *perpetual:*—that fadeth not away.

264. ἁμαρτάνω **hamartanō,** *ham-ar-tan´-o;* perh. from *1* (as a neg. particle) and the base of *3313;* prop. to *miss* the mark (and so *not share* in the prize), i.e. (fig.) to *err,* esp. (mor.) to *sin.*—for your faults, offend, sin, trespass.

265. ἁμάρτημα **hamartēma,** *ham-ar´-tay-mah;* from *264;* a *sin* (prop. concr.):—sin.

266. ἁμαρτία **hamartia,** *ham-ar´-tee´-ah;* from *264; sin* (prop. abstr.):—offence, sin (-ful).

267. ἀμάρτυρος **amarturŏs,** *am-ar´-too-ros;* from *1* (as a neg. particle) and a form of *3144; unattested:*—without witness.

268. ἁμαρτωλός **hamartōlŏs,** *ham-ar-to-los´;* from *264; sinful,* i.e. a *sinner:*—sinful, sinner.

269. ἄμαχος **amachŏs,** *am´-akh-os;* from *1* (as a neg. particle) and *3163; peaceable:*—not a brawler.

270. ἀμάω **amaō,** *am-ah´-o;* from *260;* prop. to *collect,* i.e. (by impl.) *reap:*—reap down.

271. ἀμέθυστος **amĕthustŏs,** *am-eth´-oos-tos;* from *1* (as a neg. particle) and a der. of *3184;* the *"amethyst"* (supposed to *prevent intoxication*):—amethyst.

272. ἀμελέω **amĕlĕō,** *am-el-eh´-o;* from *1* (as a neg. particle) and *3199;* to *be careless* of:—make light of, neglect, be negligent, not regard.

273. ἄμεμπτος **amĕmptŏs,** *am´-emp-tos;* from *1* (as a neg. particle) and a der. of *3201; irreproachable:*—blameless, faultless, unblamable.

274. ἀμέμπτως **amĕmptōs,** *am-emp´-toce;* adv. from *273; faultlessly:*—blameless, unblamably.

275. ἀμέριμνος **amĕrimnŏs,** *am-er´-im-nos;* from *1* (as a neg. particle) and *3308; not anxious:*—without care (-fulness), secure.

276. ἀμετάθετος **amĕtathĕtŏs,** *am-et-ath´-et-os;* from *1* (as a neg. particle) and a der. of *3346; unchangeable,* or (neut. as abstr.) *unchangeability:*—immutable (-ility).

277. ἀμετακίνητος **amĕtakinētŏs,** *am-et-ak-in´-ay-tos;* from *1* (as a neg. particle) and a der. of *3334; immovable:*—unmovable.

278. ἀμεταμέλητος **amĕtamĕlētŏs,** *am-et-am-el´-ay-tos;* from *1* (as a neg. particle) and a presumed der. of *3338; irrevocable:*—without repentance, not to be repented of.

279. ἀμετανόητος **amĕtanŏētŏs,** *am-et-an-ŏ´-ay-tos;* from *1* (as a neg. particle) and a presumed der. of *3340; unrepentant:*—impenitent.

280. ἄμετρος **amĕtrŏs,** *am´-et-ros;* from *1* (as a neg. particle) and *3358; immoderate:*—(thing) without measure.

281. ἀμήν **amēn,** *am-ane´;* of Heb. or. [543]; prop. *firm,* i.e. (fig.) *trustworthy;* adv. *surely* (often as interj. *so be it*):—amen, verily.

282. ἀμήτωρ **amētōr,** *am-ay´-tore;* from *1* (as a neg. particle) and *3384; motherless,* i.e. *of unknown maternity:*—without mother.

283. ἀμίαντος **amiantŏs,** *am-ee´-an-tos;* from *1* (as a neg. particle) and a der. of *3392; unsoiled,* i.e. (fig.) *pure:*—undefiled.

284. Ἀμιναδάβ **Aminadab,** *am-ee-nad-ab´;* of Heb. or. [5992]; *Aminadab,* an Isr.:—Aminadab.

285. ἄμμος **ammŏs,** *am´-mos;* perh. from *260; sand* (as *heaped* on the beach):—sand.

286. ἀμνός **amnŏs,** *am-nos´;* appar. a prim. word; a *lamb:*—lamb.

287. ἀμοιβή **amŏibē,** *am-oy-bay´;* from ἀμείβω **amĕibō** (to *exchange*); *requital:*—requite.

288. ἄμπελος **ampĕlŏs,** *am´-pel-os;* prob. from the base of *297* and that of *257;* a *vine* (as *coiling about* a support):—vine.

289. ἀμπελουργός **ampĕlŏurgŏs,** *am-pel-oor-gos´;* from *288* and *2041;* a *vine-worker,* i.e. *pruner:*—vine-dresser.

290. ἀμπελών **ampĕlōn,** *am-pel-ohn´;* from *288;* a *vineyard:*—vineyard.

291. Ἀμπλίας **Amplias,** *am-plee´-as;* contr. for Lat. *ampliatus* [*enlarged*]; *Amplias,* a Rom. Chr.:—Amplias.

292. ἀμύνομαι **amunŏmai,** *am-oo´-nom-ahee;* mid. of a prim. verb; to *ward off* (for oneself), i.e. *protect:*—defend.

293. ἀμφίβληστρον **amphiblēstrŏn,** *am-fib´-lace-tron;* from a comp. of the base of *297* and *906;* a (fishing) *net* (as *thrown about* the fish):—net.

294. ἀμφιέννυμι **amphiĕnnumi,** *am-fee-en´-noo-mee;* from the base of *297* and ἕννυμι **hĕnnumi** (to *invest*); to *enrobe:*—clothe.

295. Ἀμφίπολις **Amphipŏlis,** *am-fip´-ol-is;* from the base of *297* and *4172;* a *city surrounded* by a river; *Amphipolis,* a place in Macedonia:—Amphipolis.

296. ἄμφοδον **amphŏdŏn,** *am´-fod-on;* from the base of *297* and *3598;* a *fork* in the road:—where two ways meet.

297. ἀμφότερος **amphŏtĕrŏs,** *am-fot´-er-os;* compar. of ἀμφί **amphi** *(around);* (in plur.) *both:*—both.

298. ἀμώμητος **amōmētŏs,** *am-o´-may-tos;* from *1* (as a neg. particle) and a der. of *3469; unblameable:*—blameless.

299. ἄμωμος **amōmŏs,** *am´-o-mos;* from *1* (as a neg. particle) and *3470; unblemished* (lit. or fig.):—without blame (blemish, fault, spot), faultless, unblameable.

300. Ἀμών **Amōn,** *am-one´;* of Heb. or. [526]; *Amon,* an Isr.:—Amon.

301. Ἀμώς **Amōs,** *am-oce´;* of Heb. or. [531]; *Amos,* an Isr.:—Amos.

302. ἄν **an,** *an;* a prim. particle, denoting a *supposition, wish, possibility* or *uncertainty:*—[what-, where-, whither-, who-]soever. Usually unexpressed except by the subjunctive or potential mood. Also contr. for *1437.*

303. ἀνά **ana,** *an-ah´;* a prim. prep. and adv.; prop. *up;* but (by extens.) used (distributively) *severally,* or (locally) *at* (etc.):—and, apiece, by, each, every (man), in, through. In compounds (as a prefix) it often means (by impl.) *repetition, intensity, reversal,* etc.

304. ἀναβαθμός **anabathmŏs,** *an-ab-ath-mos´;* from *305* [comp. *898*]; a *stairway:*—stairs.

305. ἀναβαίνω **anabainō,** *an-ab-ah´ee-no;* from *303* and the base of *939;* to *go up* (lit. or fig.):—arise, ascend (up), climb (go, grow, rise, spring) up, come (up).

306. ἀναβάλλομαι **anaballŏmai,** *an-ab-al´-lom-ahee;* mid. from *303* and *906;* to *put off* (for oneself):—defer.

307. ἀναβιβάζω **anabibazō,** *an-ab-ee-bad´-zo;* from *303* and a der. of the base of *939;* to *cause to go up,* i.e. *haul* (a net):—draw.

308. ἀναβλέπω **anablĕpō,** *an-ab-lep´-o;* from *303* and *991:* to *look up;* by impl. to *recover sight:*—look (up), see, receive sight.

309. ἀνάβλεψις **anablĕpsis,** *an-ab´-lep-sis;* from *308; restoration of sight:*—recovering of sight.

310. ἀναβοάω **anabŏaō,** *an-ab-o-ah´-o;* from *303* and *994;* to *halloo:*—cry (aloud, out).

311. ἀναβολή **anabŏlē,** *an-ab-ol-ay´;* from *306;* a *putting off:*—delay.

312. ἀναγγέλλω **anaggĕllō,** *an-ang-el´-lo;* from *303* and the base of *32;* to *announce* (in detail):—declare, rehearse, report, show, speak, tell.

313. ἀναγεννάω **anagĕnnaō,** *an-ag-en-nah´-o;* from *303* and *1080;* to *beget* or (by extens.) *bear* (again):—beget, (bear) × again.

314. ἀναγινώσκω **anaginōskō,** *an-ag-in-oce´-ko;* from *303* and *1097;* to *know again,* i.e. (by extens.) to *read;*—read.

315. ἀναγκάζω **anagkazō,** *an-ang-kad´-zo;* from *318;* to *necessitate;*—compel, constrain.

316. ἀναγκαῖος **anagkaiŏs,** *an-ang-kah´-yos;* from *318; necessary;* by impl. *close* (of kin):—near, necessary, necessity, needful.

317. ἀναγκαστῶς **anagkastŏs,** *an-ang-kas-toce´;* adv. from a der. of *315; compulsorily:*—by constraint.

318. ἀναγκή **anagkē,** *an-ang-kay´;* from *303* and the base of *43; constraint* (lit. or fig.); by impl. *distress:*—distress, must needs, (of) necessity (-sary), neededth, needful.

319. ἀναγνωρίζομαι **anagnōrizŏmai,** *an-ag-no-rid´-zom-ahee;* mid. from *303* and *1107;* to *make* (oneself) *known:*—be made known.

320. ἀνάγνωσις **anagnōsis,** *an-ag´-no-sis;* from *314;* (the act of) *reading:*—reading.

321. ἀνάγω **anagō,** *an-ag´-o;* from *303* and *71;* to *lead up;* by extens. to *bring out;* spec. to *sail* away:—bring (again, forth, up again), depart, launch (forth), lead (up), loose, offer, sail, set forth, take up.

322. ἀναδείκνυμι **anadĕiknumi,** *an-ad-ike´-noo-mee;* from *303* and *1166;* to *exhibit,* i.e. (by impl.) to *indicate, appoint:*—appoint, shew.

323. ἀνάδειξις **anadĕixis,** *an-ad´-ike-sis;* from *322;* (the act of) *exhibition:*—shewing.

324. ἀναδέχομαι **anadĕchŏmai,** *an-ad-ekh´-om-ahee;* from *303* and *1209;* to *entertain* (as a guest):—receive.

325. ἀναδίδωμι **anadidōmi,** *an-ad-eed´-om-ee;* from *303* and *1325;* to *hand over:*—deliver.

326. ἀναζάω **anazaō,** *an-ad-zah´-o;* from *303* and *2198;* to *recover life* (lit. or fig.):—(be a-) live again, revive.

327. ἀναζητέω **anazētĕō,** *an-ad-zay-teh´-o;* from *303* and *2212;* to *search* out:—seek.

328. ἀναζώννυμι **anazōnnumi,** *an-ad-zone´-noo-mee;* from *303* and *2224;* to *gird afresh:*—gird up.

329. ἀναζωπυρέω **anazōpurĕō,** *an-ad-zo-poor-eh´-o;* from *303* and a comp. of the base of *2226* and *4442;* to *re-enkindle:*—stir up.

330. ἀναθάλλω **anathallō,** *an-ath-al´-lo;* from *303* and θάλλω **thallō** (to *flourish*); to *revive:*—flourish again.

331. ἀνάθεμα **anathĕma,** *an-ath´-em-ah;* from *394;* a (religious) *ban* or (concr.) *excommunicated* (thing or person):—accursed, anathema, curse, × great.

332. ἀναθεματίζω **anathĕmatizō,** *an-ath-em-at-id´-zo;* from *331;* to *declare* or *vow* under penalty of execration:—(bind under a) curse, bind with an oath.

333. ἀναθεωρέω **anathĕōrĕō,** *an-ath-eh-o-reh´-o;* from *303* and *2334;* to *look again* (i.e. *attentively*) at (lit. or fig.):—behold, consider.

334. ἀνάθημα **anathēma,** *an-ath´-ay-mah;* from *394* [like *331,* but in a good sense]; a *votive* offering:—gift.

335. ἀναίδεια **anaidĕia,** *an-ah´ee-die-ah;* from a comp. of *1* (as a neg. particle [comp. *427*]) and *127; impudence,* i.e. (by impl.) *importunity:*—importunity.

336. ἀναίρεσις **anairĕsis,** *an-ah´ee-res-is;* from *337;* (the act of) *killing:*—death.

337. ἀναιρέω **anairĕō,** *an-ahee-reh´-o;* from *303* and (the act. of) *138;* to *take up,* i.e. *adopt;* by impl. to *take away* (violently), i.e. *abolish, murder:*—put to death, kill, slay, take away, take up.

338. ἀναίτιος **anaitiŏs,** *an-ah´-ee-tee-os;* from *1* (as a neg. particle) and *159* (in the sense of *156*); *innocent:*—blameless, guiltless.

339. ἀνακαθίζω **anakathizō,** *an-ak-ath-id´-zo;* from *303* and *2523;* prop. to *set up,* i.e. (reflex.) to *sit up:*—sit up.

340. ἀνακαινίζω **anakainizō,** *an-ak-ahee-nid´-zo;* from *303* and a der. of *2537;* to *restore:*—renew.

341. ἀνακαινόω **anakainŏō,** *an-ak-ahee-nŏ´-o;* from *303* and a der. of *2537;* to *restore:*—renew.

342. ἀνακαίνωσις **anakainōsis,** *an-ak-ah´ee-no-sis;* from *341; renovation:*—renewing.

343. ἀνακαλύπτω **anakaluptō,** *an-ak-al-oop´-to;* from *303* (in the sense of *reversal*) and *2572;* to *unveil:*—open, ([un-]) taken away.

344. ἀνακάμπτω **anakamptō,** *an-ak-amp´-to;* from *303* and *2578;* to *turn back:*—(re-) turn.

345. ἀνακεῖμαι **anakĕimai,** *an-ak-i´-mahee;* from *303* and *2749;* to *recline* (as a corpse or at a meal):—guest, lean, lie, sit (down, at meat), at the table.

346. ἀνακεφαλαίομαι **anakĕphalaiŏmai,** *an-ak-ef-al-ah´ee-om-ahee;* from *303* and *2775* (in its or. sense); to *sum up:*—briefly comprehend, gather together in one.

347. ἀνακλίνω **anaklinō,** *an-ak-lee´-no;* from *303* and *2827;* to *lean back:*—lay, (make) sit down.

348. ἀνακόπτω **anakŏptō,** *an-ak-op´-to;* from *303* and *2875;* to *beat back,* i.e. *check:*—hinder.

349. ἀνακράζω **anakrazō,** *an-ak-rad´-zo;* from *303* and *2896;* to *scream up* (aloud):—cry out.

350. ἀνακρίνω **anakrinō,** *an-ak-ree´-no;* from *303* and *2919;* prop. to *scrutinize,* i.e. (by impl.) *investigate, interrogate, determine:*—ask, question, discern, examine, judge, search.

351. ἀνάκρισις **anakrisis,** *an-ak´-ree-sis;* from *350;* a (judicial) *investigation:*—examination.

352. ἀνακύπτω **anakuptō,** *an-ak-oop´-to;* from *303* (in the sense of *reversal*) and *2955;* to *unbend,* i.e. *rise;* fig. *be elated:*—lift up, look up.

353. ἀναλαμβάνω **analambanō,** *an-al-am-ban´-o;* from *303* and *2983;* to *take up:*—receive up, take (in, unto, up).

354. ἀνάληψις **analēpsis,** *an-al´-ape-sis;* from *353; ascension:*—taking up.

355. ἀναλίσκω **analiskō,** *an-al-is´-ko;* from *303* and a form of the alternate of *138;* prop. to *use up,* i.e. *destroy:*—consume.

356. ἀναλογία **analŏgia,** *an-al-og-ee´-ah;* from a comp. of *303* and *3056; proportion:*—proportion.

357. ἀναλογίζομαι **analŏgizŏmai,** *an-al-og-id´-zom-ahee;* mid. from *356;* to *estimate,* i.e. (fig.) *contemplate:*—consider.

358. ἄναλος **analŏs,** *an´-al-os:* from *1* (as a neg. particle) and *251; saltless,* i.e. *insipid:*— × lose saltness.

359. ἀνάλυσις **analusis,** *an-al´-oo-sis;* from *360; departure:*—departure.

360. ἀναλύω **analuō,** *an-al-oo´-o;* from *303* and *3089;* to *break up,* i.e. *depart* (lit. or fig.):—depart, return.

361. ἀναμάρτητος **anamartētŏs,** *an-am-ar´-tay-tos;* from *1* (as a neg. particle) and a presumed der. of *264; sinless:*—that is without sin.

362. ἀναμένω **anemĕnō,** *an-am-en´-o;* from *303* and *3306;* to *await:*—wait for.

363. ἀναμιμνήσκω **anamimnēskō,** *an-am-im-nace´-ko;* from *303* and *3403;* to *remind;* reflex. to *recollect:*—call to mind, (bring to, call to, put in), remember (-brance).

364. ἀνάμνησις **anamnēsis,** *an-am´-nay-sis;* from *363; recollection:*—*remembrance* (again).

365. ἀνανεόω **ananĕŏō,** *an-an-neh-ŏ´-o;* from *303* and a der of 3501; to *renovate;* i.e. *reform:*—renew.

366. ἀνανήφω **ananēphō,** *an-an-ay´-fo;* from *303* and *3525;* to become *sober again,* i.e. (fig.) *regain* (one's) *senses:*—recover self.

367. Ἀνανίας **Ananias,** *an-an-ee´-as;* of Heb. or. [2608]; *Ananias,* the name of three Isr.:—Ananias.

368. ἀναντίῤῥητος **anantirrhētŏs,** *an-an-tir´-hray-tos;* from *1* (as a neg. particle) and a presumed der. of a comp. of *473* and *4483; indisputable:*—cannot be spoken against.

369. ἀναντιῤῥήτως **anantirrhētŏs,** *an-an-tir-hray´-toce;* adv. from *368; promptly:*—without gainsaying.

370. ἀνάξιος **anaxiŏs,** *an-ax´-ee-os;* from *1* (as a neg. particle) and *514; unfit:*—unworthy.

371. ἀναξίως **anaxiōs,** *an-ax-ee´-oce;* adv. from *370; irreverently:*—unworthily.

372. ἀνάπαυσις **anapausis,** *an-ap´-ŏw-sis;* from *373; intermission;* by impl. *recreation:*—rest.

373. ἀναπαύω **anapauō,** *an-ap-ŏv´-o;* from *303* and *3973;* (reflex.) to *repose* (lit. or fig. [*be exempt*], *remain*); by impl. to *refresh:*—take ease, refresh, (give, take) rest.

374. ἀναπείθω **anapĕithō,** *an-ap-i´-tho;* from *303* and *3982;* to *incite;*—persuade.

375. ἀναπέμπω **anapĕmpō,** *an-ap-em´-po;* from *303* and *3992;* to *send up* or *back:*—send (again).

376. ἀνάπηρος **anapĕrŏs,** *an-ap´-ay-ros;* from *303* (in the sense of *intensity*) and πῆρος **pērŏs** *(maimed); crippled:*—maimed.

377. ἀναπίπτω **anapipto,** *an-ap-ip´-to;* from *303* and *4098;* to *fall back,* i.e. *lie down, lean back:*—lean, sit down (to meat).

378. ἀναπληρόω **anaplērŏō,** *an-ap-lay-rŏ´-o;* from *303* and *4137;* to *complete;* by impl. to *occupy, supply;* fig. to *accomplish* (by coincidence or obedience):—fill up, fulfil, occupy, supply.

379. ἀναπολόγητος **anapŏlŏgētŏs,** *an-ap-ol-og´-ay-tos;* from *1* (as a neg. particle) and a presumed der. of *626; indefensible:*—without excuse, inexcuseable.

380. ἀναπτύσσω **anaptussō,** *an-ap-toos´-so;* from *303* (in the sense of *reversal*) and *4428;* to *unroll* (a scroll or volume):—open.

381. ἀνάπτω **anaptō,** *an-ap´-to;* from *303* and *681;* to *enkindle:*—kindle, light.

382. ἀναρίθμητος **anarithmētŏs,** *an-ar-ith´-may-tos;* from *1* (as a neg. particle) and a der. of *705; unnumbered,* i.e. *without number:*—innumerable.

383. ἀνασείω **anasĕiō,** *an-as-i´-o;* from *303* and *4579;* fig. to *excite:*—move, stir up.

384. ἀνασκευάζω **anakĕuazō,** *an-ask-yoo-ad´-zo;* from *303* (in the sense of *reversal*) and a der. of *4632* prop. to *pack up* (baggage), i.e. (by impl. and fig.) to *upset:*—subvert.

385. ἀνασπάω **anaspaō,** *an-as-pah´-o;* from *303* and *4685;* to *take up* or *extricate:*—draw up, pull out.

386. ἀνάστασις **anastasis,** *an-as´-tas-is;* from *450;* a *standing up* again, i.e. (lit.) a *resurrection* from death (individual, gen. or by impl. [its author]), or (fig.) a (moral) *recovery* (of spiritual truth):—raised to life again, resurrection, rise from the dead, that should rise, rising again.

387. ἀναστατόω **anastatŏō,** *an-as-tat-ŏ´-o;* from a der. of *450* (in the sense of *removal*); prop. to *drive out* of home, i.e. (by impl.) to *disturb* (lit. or fig.):—trouble, turn upside down, make an uproar.

388. ἀνασταυρόω **anastaurŏō,** *an-as-tŏw-rŏ´-o;* from *303* and *4717;* to *recrucify* (fig.):—crucify afresh.

389. ἀναστενάζω **anastĕnazō,** *an-as-ten-ad´-zo;* from *303* and *4727;* to *sigh deeply:*—sigh deeply.

390. ἀναστρέφω **anastrĕphō**, *an-as-tref´-o;* from *303* and *4762;* to *overturn;* also to *return;* by impl. to *busy* oneself, i.e. *remain, live:*—abide, behave self, have conversation, live, overthrow, pass, return, be used.

391. ἀναστροφή **anastrŏphē**, *an-as-trof-ay´;* from *390; behavior:*—conversation.

392. ἀνατάσσομαι **anatassŏmai**, *an-at-as´-som-ahee;* from *303* and the mid. of *5021;* to *arrange:*—set in order.

393. ἀνατέλλω **anatĕllō**, *an-at-el´-lo;* from *303* and the base of *5056;* to (*cause* to) *arise:*—(a-, make to) rise, at the rising of, spring (up), be up.

394. ἀνατίθεμαι **anatithĕmai**, *an-at-ith´-em-ahee;* from *303* and the mid. of *5087;* to *set forth* (for oneself), i.e. *propound:*—communicate, declare.

395. ἀνατολή **anatŏlē**, *an-at-ol-ay´;* from *393;* a *rising* of light, i.e. *dawn* (fig.); by impl. the *east* (also in plur.):—dayspring, east, rising.

396. ἀνατρέπω **anatrĕpō**, *an-at-rep´-o;* from *303* and the base of *5157;* to *overturn* (fig.):—overthrow, subvert.

397. ἀνατρέφω **anatrĕphō**, *an-at-ref´-o;* from *303* and *5142;* to *rear* (phys. or ment.):—bring up, nourish (up).

398. ἀναφαίνω **anaphainō**, *an-af-ah´ee-no;* from *303* and *5316;* to *show,* i.e. (reflex.) *appear,* or (pass.) *have pointed* out:—(should) appear, discover.

399. ἀναφέρω **anaphĕrō**, *an-af-er´-o;* from *303* and *5342;* to *take up* (lit. or fig.):—bear, bring (carry, lead) up, offer (up).

400. ἀναφωνέω **anaphōnĕō**, *an-af-o-neh´-o;* from *303* and *5455;* to *exclaim:*—speak out.

401. ἀνάχυσις **anachusis**, *an-akh´-oo-sis;* from a comp. of *303* and χέω **chĕō** (to *pour*); prop. *effusion,* i.e. (fig.) *license:*—excess.

402. ἀναχωρέω **anachōrĕō**, *an-akh-o-reh´-o;* from *303* and *5562;* to *retire:*—depart, give place, go (turn) aside, withdraw self.

403. ἀνάψυξις **anapsuxis**, *an-aps´-ook-sis;* from *404;* prop. a *recovery of breath,* i.e. (fig.) *revival:*—revival.

404. ἀναψύχω **anapsuchō**, *an-aps-oo´-kho;* from *303* and *5594;* prop. to *cool off,* i.e. (fig.) *relieve:*—refresh.

405. ἀνδραποδιστής **andrapŏdistēs**, *an-drap-od-is-tace´;* from a der. of a comp. of *435* and *4228;* an *enslaver* (as bringing *men* to his *feet*):—men-stealer.

406. Ἀνδρέας **Andrĕas**, *an-dreh´-as;* from *435; manly; Andreas,* an Isr.:—Andrew.

407. ἀνδρίζομαι **andrizŏmai**, *an-drid´-zom-ahee;* mid. from *435;* to *act manly:*—quit like men.

408. Ἀνδρόνικος **Andrŏnikŏs**, *an-dron´-ee-kos;* from *435* and *3534; man of victory; Andronicos,* an Isr.:—Andronicus.

409. ἀνδροφόνος **andrŏphŏnŏs**, *an-drof-on´-os;* from *435* and *5408;* a *murderer:*—manslayer.

410. ἀνέγκλητος **anĕgklētŏs**, *an-eng´-klay-tos;* from *1* (as a neg. particle) and a der. of *1458; unaccused,* i.e. (by impl.) *irreproachable:*—blameless.

411. ἀνεκδιήγητος **anĕkdiēgētŏs**, *an-ek-dee-ay´-gay-tos;* from *1* (as a neg. particle) and a presumed der. of *1555; not expounded* in full, i.e. *indescribable:*—unspeakable.

412. ἀνεκλάλητος **anĕklalētŏs**, *an-ek-lal´-ay-tos;* from *1* (as a neg. particle) and a presumed der. of *1583; not spoken out,* i.e. (by impl.) *unutterable:*—unspeakable.

413. ἀνέκλειπτος **anĕklĕiptŏs**, *an-ek´-lipe-tos;* from *1* (as a neg. particle) and a presumed der. of *1587; not left out,* i.e. (by impl.) *inexhaustible:*—that faileth not.

414. ἀνεκτότερος **anĕktŏtĕrŏs**, *an-ek-tot´-er-os;* compar. of a der. of *430; more endurable:*—more tolerable.

415. ἀνελεήμων **anĕlĕēmōn**, *an-eleh-ay´-mone;* from *1* (as a neg. particle) and *1655; merciless:*—unmerciful.

416. ἀνεμίζω **anemizō**, *an-em-id´-zo;* from *417;* to *toss with the wind:*—drive with the wind.

417. ἄνεμος **anĕmŏs**, *an´-em-os;* from the base of *109; wind;* (plur.) by impl. (the four) *quarters* (of the earth):—wind.

418. ἀνένδεκτος **anĕndĕktŏs**, *an-en´-dek-tos;* from *1* (as a neg. particle) and a der. of the same as *1735; unadmitted,* i.e. (by impl.) *not supposable:*—impossible.

419. ἀνεξερεύνητος **anĕxĕrĕunētŏs**, *an-ex-er-yoo´-nay-tos;* from *1* (as a neg. particle) and a presumed der. of *1830; not searched out,* i.e. (by impl.) *inscrutable:*—unsearchable.

420. ἀνεξίκακος **anĕxikakŏs**, *an-ex-ik´-ak-os;* from *430* and *2556; enduring of ill,* i.e. *forbearing:*—patient.

421. ἀνεξιχνίαστος **anĕxichniastŏs**, *an-ex-ikh-nee´-as-tos;* from *1* (as a neg. particle) and a presumed der. of a comp. of *1537* and a der. of *2487; not tracked out,* i.e. (by impl.) *untraceable:*—past finding out, unsearchable.

422. ἀνεπαίσχυντος **anĕpaischuntŏs**, *an-ep-ah´-ee-skhoon-tos;* from *1* (as a neg. particle) and a presumed der. of a comp. of *1909* and *153; not ashamed,* i.e. (by impl.) *irreprehensible:*—that needeth not to be ashamed.

423. ἀνεπίληπτος **anĕpilēptŏs**, *an-ep-eel´-ape-tos;* from *1* (as a neg. particle) and a der. of *1949; not arrested,* i.e. (by impl.) *inculpable:*—blameless, unrebukeable.

424. ἀνέρχομαι **anĕrchŏmai**, *an-erkh´-om-ahee;* from *303* and *2064;* to *ascend:*—go up.

425. ἄνεσις **anĕsis**, *an´-es-is;* from *447; relaxation* or (fig.) *relief:*—eased, liberty, rest.

426. ἀνετάζω **anĕtazō**, *an-et-ad´-zo;* from *303* and ἐτάζω **ĕtazō** (to *test*); to *investigate* (judicially):—(should have) examine (-d).

427. ἄνευ **anĕu**, *an´-yoo;* a prim. particle; *without:*—without. Comp. *1.*

428. ἀνεύθετος **anĕuthĕtŏs**, *an-yoo´-the-tos;* from *1* (as a neg. particle) and *2111; not well set,* i.e. *inconvenient:*—not commodious.

429. ἀνευρίσκω **anĕuriskō**, *an-yoo-ris´-ko;* from *303* and *2147;* to *find out:*—find.

430. ἀνέχομαι **anĕchŏmai**, *an-ekh´-om-ahee;* mid. from *303* and *2192;* to *hold oneself up* against, i.e. (fig.) *put up* with:—bear with endure, forbear, suffer.

431. ἀνέψιος **anĕpsiŏs**, *an-eps´-ee-os;* from *1* (as a particle of union) and an obsolete νέπος **nĕpŏs** (a *brood*); prop. *akin,* i.e. (spec.) a *cousin:*—sister's son.

432. ἄνηθον **anēthŏn**, *an´-ay-thon;* prob. of for. or.; *dill:*—anise.

433. ἀνήκω **anēkō**, *an-ay´-ko;* from *303* and *2240;* to *attain to,* i.e. (fig.) *be proper:*—convenient, be fit.

434. ἀνήμερος **anēmĕrŏs**, *an-ay´-mer-os;* from *1* (as a neg. particle) and ἥμερος **hēmĕrŏs** *(lame); savage:*—fierce.

435. ἀνήρ **anēr**, *an´-ayr;* a prim. word [comp. *444*]; a *man* (prop. as an individual male):—fellow, husband, man, sir.

436. ἀνθίστημι **anthistēmi**, *anth-is´-tay-mee;* from *473* and *2476;* to *stand against,* i.e. *oppose:*—resist, withstand.

437. ἀνθομολογέομαι **anthŏmŏlŏgĕŏmai**, *anth-om-ol-og-eh´-om-ahee;* from *473* and the mid. of *3670;* to *confess in turn,* i.e. *respond* in praise:—give thanks.

438. ἄνθος **anthŏs**, *anth´-os;* a prim. word; a *blossom:*—flower.

439. ἀνθρακιά **anthrakia**, *anth-rak-ee-ah´;* from *440;* a bed of burning *coals:*—fire of coals.

440. ἄνθραξ **anthrax**, *anth´-rax;* of uncert. der.; a live *coal:*—coal of fire.

441. ἀνθρωπάρεσκος **anthrōparĕskŏs**, *anth-ro-par´-es-kos;* from *444* and *700; man-courting,* i.e., *fawning:*—men-pleaser.

442. ἀνθρώπινος **anthrōpinŏs**, *anth-ro´-pee-nos;* from *444; human:*—human, common to man, man[-kind], [man-]kind, men's, after the manner of men.

443. ἀνθρωποκτόνος **anthrōpŏktŏnŏs**, *anth-ro-pok-ton´-os;* from *444* a κτείνω **ktĕinō** (to *kill*); a *manslayer:*—murderer. Comp. *5406.*

444. ἄνθρωπος **anthrōpŏs**, *anth´-ro-pos;* from *435* and ὤψ **ōps** (the *countenance;* from *3700*); *man-faced,* i.e. a *human* being:—certain, man.

445. ἀνθυπατεύω **anthupatĕuō**, *anth-oo-pat-yoo´-o;* from *446;* to *act as proconsul:*—be the deputy.

446. ἀνθύπατος **anthupatŏs**, *anth-oo´-pat-os;* from *473* and a superlative of *5228; instead* of the *highest* officer, i.e. (spec.) a Roman *proconsul:*—deputy.

447. ἀνίημι **aniēmi,** *an-ee´-ay-mee;* from *303* and ἵημι **hiēmi** (to *send*); to *let up,* i.e. (lit.) *slacken,* or (fig.) *desert, desist* from:—forbear, leave, loose.

448. ἀνίλεως **anilĕōs,** *an-ee´-leh-oce;* from *1* (as a neg. particle) and *2436; inexorable:*—without mercy.

449. ἄνιπτος **aniptŏs,** *an´-ip-tos;* from *1* (as a neg. particle) and a presumed der. of *3538; without ablution:*—unwashen.

450. ἀνίστημι **anistēmi,** *an-is´-tay-mee;* from *303* and *2476;* to *stand up* (lit. or fig., trans. or intrans.):—arise, lift up, raise up (again), rise (again), stand up (-right).

451. Ἄννα **Anna,** *an´-nah;* of Heb. or. [2584]; *Anna,* an Israelitess:—Anna.

452. Ἄννας **Annas,** *an´-nas;* of Heb. or. [2608]; *Annas* (i.e. *367*), an Isr.:—Annas.

453. ἀνόητος **anŏētŏs,** *an-ŏ´-ay-tos;* from *1* (as a neg. particle) and a der. of *3539; unintelligent;* by impl. *sensual:*—fool (-ish), unwise.

454. ἄνοια **anŏia,** *an´-oy-ah;* from a comp. of *1* (as a neg. particle) and *3563; stupidity;* by impl. *rage:*—folly, madness.

455. ἀνοίγω **anŏigō,** *an-oy´-go;* from *303* and οἴγω **ŏigō** (to *open*); to *open up* (lit. or fig., in various applications):—open.

456. ἀνοικοδομέω **anŏikŏdŏmĕō,** *an-oy-kod-om-eh´-o;* from *303* and *3618;* to *rebuild:*—build again.

457. ἄνοιξις **anŏixis,** *an´-oix-is;* from *455; opening* (throat):—× open.

458. ἀνομία **anŏmia,** *an-om-ee´-ah;* from *459; illegality,* i.e. *violation of law* or (gen.) *wickedness:*—iniquity, × transgress (-ion of) the law, unrighteousness.

459. ἄνομος **anŏmŏs,** *an´-om-os;* from *1* (as a neg. particle) and *3551; lawless,* i.e. (neg.) *not subject to* (the Jewish) *law;* (by impl. a *Gentile*), or (pos.) *wicked:*—without law, lawless, transgressor, unlawful, wicked.

460. ἀνόμως **anŏmōs,** *an-om´-oce;* adv. from *459; lawlessly,* i.e. (spec.) *not amenable to* (the Jewish) *law:*—without law.

461. ἀνορθόω **anŏrthŏō,** *an-orth-ŏ´-o;* from *303* and a der. of the base of *3717;* to *straighten up:*—lift (set) up, make straight.

462. ἀνόσιος **anŏsiŏs,** *an-os´-ee-os;* from *1* (as a neg. particle) and *3741; wicked:*—unholy.

463. ἀνοχή **anŏchē,** *an-okh-ay´;* from *430; self-restraint,* i.e. *tolerance:*—forbearance.

464. ἀνταγωνίζομαι **antagōnizŏmai,** *an-tag-o-nid´-zom-ahee;* from *473* and *75;* to *struggle against* (fig.) ["antagonize"]:—strive against.

465. ἀντάλλαγμα **antallagma,** *an-tal´-ag-mah;* from a comp. of *473* and *236;* an *equivalent* or *ransom:*—in exchange.

466. ἀνταναπληρόω **antanaplērŏō,** *an-tan-ap-lay-rŏ´-o;* from *473* and *378;* to *supplement:*—fill up.

467. ἀνταποδίδωμι **antapŏdidōmi,** *an-tap-od-ee´-do-mee;* from *473* and *591;* to *requite* (good or evil):—recompense, render, repay.

468. ἀνταπόδομα **antapŏdŏma,** *an-tap-od´-om-ah;* from *467;* a *requital* (prop. the thing):—recompense.

469. ἀνταπόδοσις **antapŏdŏsis,** *an-tap-od´-os-is;* from *467; requital* (prop. the act):—reward.

470. ἀνταποκρίνομαι **antapŏkrinŏmai,** *an-tap-ok-ree´-nom-ahee;* from *473* and *611;* to *contradict* or *dispute:*—answer again, reply against.

471. ἀντέπω **antĕpō,** *an-tep´-o;* from *473* and *2036;* to *refute* or *deny:*—gainsay, say against.

472. ἀντέχομαι **antĕchŏmai,** *an-tekh´-om-ahee;* from *473* and the mid. of *2192;* to *hold* oneself *opposite* to, i.e. (by impl.) *adhere to;* by extens. to *care for:*—hold fast, hold to, support.

473. ἀντί **anti,** *an-tee´;* a prim. particle; *opposite,* i.e. *instead* or *because* of (rarely *in addition* to):—for, in the room of. Often used in composition to denote *contrast, requital, substitution, correspondence,* etc.

474. ἀντιβάλλω **antiballō,** *an-tee-bal´-lo;* from *473* and *906;* to *bandy:*—have.

475. ἀντιδιατίθεμαι **antidiatithĕmai,** *an-tee-dee-at-eeth´-em-ahee;* from *473* and *1303;* to *set oneself opposite,* i.e. *be disputatious:*—that oppose themselves.

476. ἀντίδικος **antidikŏs,** *an-tid´-ee-kos;* from *473* and *1349;* and *opponent* (in a lawsuit); spec. *Satan* (as the arch-enemy):—adversary.

477. ἀντίθεσις **antithĕsis,** *an-tith´-es-is;* from a comp. of *473* and *5087; opposition,* i.e. a *conflict* (of theories):—opposition.

478. ἀντικαθίστημι **antikathistēmi,** *an-tee-kath-is´-tay-mee;* from *473* and *2525;* to *set down* (troops) *against,* i.e. *withstand:*—resist.

479. ἀντικαλέω **antikalĕō,** *an-tee-kal-eh´-o;* from *473* and *2564;* to *invite in return:*—bid again.

480. ἀντίκειμαι **antikĕimai,** *an-tik´-i-mahee;* from *473* and *2749;* to *lie opposite,* i.e. *be adverse* (fig. *repugnant*) to:—adversary, be contrary, oppose.

481. ἀντικρύ **antikru,** *an-tee-kroo´;* prol. from *473; opposite:*—over against.

482. ἀντιλαμβάνομαι **antilambanŏmai,** *an-tee-lam-ban´-om-ahee;* from *473* and the mid. of *2983;* to *take* hold of *in turn,* i.e. *succor;* also to *participate:*—help, partaker support.

483. ἀντίλεγω **antilĕgō,** *an-til´-eg-o;* from *473* and *3004;* to *dispute, refuse:*—answer again, contradict, deny, gainsay (-er), speak against.

484. ἀντίληψις **antilēpsis,** *an-til´-ape-sis;* from *482; relief:*—help.

485. ἀντιλογία **antilŏgia,** *an-tee-log-ee´-ah;* from a der. of *483; dispute, disobedience:*—contradiction, gainsaying, strife.

486. ἀντιλοιδορέω **antilŏidŏrĕō,** *an-tee-loy-dor-eh´-o;* from *473* and *3058;* to *rail in reply:*—revile again.

487. ἀντίλυτρον **antilutrŏn,** *an-til´-oo-tron;* from *473* and *3083;* a *redemption-price:*—ransom.

488. ἀντιμετρέω **antimĕtrĕō,** *an-tee-met-reh´-o;* from *473* and *3354;* to *mete in return:*—measure again.

489. ἀντιμισθία **antimisthia,** *an-tee-mis-thee´-ah;* from a comp. of *473* and *3408; requital, correspondence;*—recompense.

490. Ἀντιόχεια **Antiŏchĕia,** *an-tee-okh´-i-ah;* from Ἀντίοχος **Antiŏchus** (a Syrian king); *Antiochia,* a place in Syria:—Antioch.

491. Ἀντιοχεύς **Antiŏchĕus,** *an-tee-okh-yoos´;* from *490;* an *Antiochian* or inhab. of Antiochia:—of Antioch.

492. ἀντιπαρέρχομαι **antiparĕrchŏmai,** *an-tee-par-er´-khom-ahee;* from *473* and *3928;* to *go along opposite:*—pass by on the other side.

493. Ἀντίπας **Antipas,** *an-tee´-pas;* contr. for a comp. of *473* and a der. of *3962; Antipas,* a Chr.:—Antipas.

494. Ἀντιπατρίς **Antipatris,** *an-tip-at-rece´;* from the same as *493; Antipatris,* a place in Pal.:—Antipatris.

495. ἀντιπέραν **antipĕran,** *an-tee-per´-an;* from *473* and *4008; on the opposite side:*—over against.

496. ἀντιπίπτω **antipiptō,** *an-tee-pip´-to;* from *473* and *4098* (includ. its alt.); to *oppose:*—resist.

497. ἀντιστρατεύομαι **antistratĕuŏmai,** *an-tee-strat-yoo´-om-ahee;* from *473* and *4754;* (fig.) to *attack,* i.e. (by impl.) *destroy:*—war against.

498. ἀντιτάσσομαι **antitassŏmai,** *an-tee-tas´-som-ahee;* from *473* and the mid. of *5021;* to *range oneself against,* i.e. *oppose:*—oppose themselves, resist.

499. ἀντίτυπον **antitupŏn,** *an-teet´-oo-pon;* neut. of a comp. of *473* and *5179; corresponding* ["an titype"], i.e. a *representative, counterpart:*—(like) figure (whereunto).

500. ἀντίχριστος **antichristŏs,** *an-tee´-khris-tos:* from *473* and *5547;* an *opponent of the Messiah:*—antichrist.

501. ἀντλέω **antlĕō,** *ant-leh-o;* from ἄντλος **antlŏs** (the *hold* of a ship); to *bale* up (prop. bilge water), i.e. *dip* water (with a bucket, pitcher, etc.):—draw (out).

502. ἄντλημα **antlēma,** *ant´-lay-mah;* from *501;* a *baling-vessel:*—thing to draw with.

503. ἀντοφθαλμέω **antŏphthalmĕō,** *ant-of-thal-meh´-o;* from a comp. of *473* and *3788;* to *face:*—bear up into.

504. ἄνυδρος **anudrŏs,** *an´-oo-dros;* from *1* (as a neg. particle) and *5204; waterless,* i.e. *dry:*—dry, without water.

505. ἀνυπόκριτος **anupŏkritŏs,** *an-oo-pok´-ree-tos;* from *1* (as a neg. particle) and a presumed der. of *5271; undissembled,* i.e. *sincere:*—without dissimulation (hypocrisy), unfeigned.

506. ἀνυπότακτος **anupŏtaktŏs,** *an-oo-pot´-ak-tos;* from *1* (as a neg. particle) and a presumed der. of *5293; unsubdued,* i.e. *insubordinate* (in fact or temper):—disobedient, that is not put under, unruly.

507. ἄνω **anō,** *an´-o;* adv. from *473; upward* or *on the top:*—above, brim, high, up.

508. ἀνώγεον **anōgĕŏn,** *an-ogue´-eh-on;* from *507* and *1093; above* the *ground,* i.e. (prop.) the *second floor* of a building; used for a *dome* or a *balcony* on the upper story:—upper room.

509. ἄνωθεν **anōthĕn,** *an´-o-then;* from *507; from above;* by anal. *from the first;* by impl. *anew:*—from above, again, from the beginning (very first), the top.

510. ἀνωτερικός **anōtĕrikŏs,** *an-o-ter-ee-kos´;* from *511; superior,* i.e. (locally) *more remote:*—upper.

511. ἀνώτερος **anōtĕrŏs,** *an-o´-ter-os;* comp. degree of *507; upper,* i.e. (neut. as adv.) to a *more conspicuous* place, in a *former* part of the book:—above, higher.

512. ἀνωφέλες **anōphĕlĕs,** *an-o-fel´-ace;* from *1* (as a neg. particle) and the base of *5624; useless* or (neut.) *inutility:*—unprofitable (-ness).

513. ἀξίνη **axinē,** *ax-ee´-nay;* prob. from ἄγνυμι **agnumi** (to *break;* comp. *4486*); an *axe:*—axe.

514. ἄξιος **axiŏs,** *ax´-ee-os;* prob. from *71; deserving, comparable* or *suitable* (as if *drawing* praise):—due reward, meet, [un-] worthy.

515. ἀξιόω **axiŏō,** *ax-ee-ŏ´-o;* from *514;* to *deem entitled* or *fit:*—desire, think good, count (think) worthy.

516. ἀξίως **axiōs,** *ax-ee´-oce;* adv. from *514; appropriately:*—as becometh, after a godly sort, worthily (-thy).

517. ἀόρατος **aŏratŏs,** *ah-or´-at-os;* from *1* (as a neg. particle) and *3707; invisible:*—invisible (thing).

518. ἀπαγγέλλω **apaggĕllō,** *ap-ang-el´-lo;* from *575* and the base of *32;* to *announce:*—bring word (again), declare, report, shew (again), tell.

519. ἀπάγχομαι **apagchŏmai,** *ap-ang´-khom-ahee;* from *575* and ἄγχω **agchō** (to *choke;* akin to the base of *43*); to *strangle oneself off* (i.e. to death):—hang himself.

520. ἀπάγω **apagō,** *ap-ag´-o;* from *575* and *71;* to *take off* (in various senses):—bring, carry away, lead (away), put to death, take away.

521. ἀπαίδευτος **apaidĕutŏs,** *ap-ah´ee-dyoo-tos;* from *1* (as a neg. particle) and a der. of *3811; uninstructed,* i.e. (fig.) *stupid:*—unlearned.

522. ἀπαίρω **apairō,** *ap-ah´ee-ro;* from *575* and *142;* to *lift off,* i.e. *remove:*—take (away).

523. ἀπαιτέω **apaitĕō,** *ap-ah´ee-teh-o;* from *575* and *154;* to *demand back:*—ask again, require.

524. ἀπαλγέω **apalgĕō,** *ap-alg-eh´-o;* from *575* and ἀλγέω **algĕō** (to *smart*); to *grieve out,* i.e. *become apathetic:*—be past feeling.

525. ἀπαλλάσσω **apallassō,** *ap-al-las´-so;* from *575* and *236;* to *change away,* i.e. release, (reflex.) *remove:*—deliver, depart.

526. ἀπαλλοτριόω **apallŏtriŏō,** *ap-al-lot-ree-ŏ´-o;* from *575* and a der. of *245;* to *estrange away,* i.e. (pass. and fig.) to *be non-participant:*—alienate, be alien.

527. ἁπαλός **apalŏs,** *ap-al-os´;* of uncert. der.; *soft:*—tender.

528. ἀπαντάω **apantaō,** *ap-an-tah´-o;* from *575* and a der. of *473;* to *meet away,* i.e. *encounter:*—meet.

529. ἀπάντησις **apantēsis,** *ap-an´tay-sis;* from *528;* a (friendly) *encounter:*—meet.

530. ἅπαξ **hapax,** *hap´-ax;* prob. from *537; one* (or a *single*) *time* (numerically or conclusively):—once.

531. ἀπαράβατος **aparabatŏs,** *ap-ar-ab´-at-os;* from *1* (as a neg. particle) and a der. of *3845; not passing away,* i.e. *untransferable* (perpetual):—unchangeable.

532. ἀπαρασκεύαστος **aparaskĕunastŏs,** *ap-ar-ask-yoo´-as-tos;* from *1* (as a neg. particle) and a der. of *3903; unready:*—unprepared.

533. ἀπαρνέομαι **aparnĕŏmai,** *ap-ar-neh´-om-ahee;* from *575* and *720;* to *deny utterly,* i.e. *disown, abstain:*—deny.

534. ἀπάρτι **aparti,** *ap-ar´-tee;* from *575* and *737; from now,* i.e. *henceforth (already):*—from henceforth.

535. ἀπαρτισμός **apartismŏs,** *ap-ar-tis-mos´;* from a der. of *534; completion:*—finishing.

536. ἀπαρχή **aparchē,** *ap-ar-khay´;* from a comp. of *575* and *756;* a *beginning* of sacrifice, i.e. the (Jewish) *first-fruit* (fig.):—first-fruits.

537. ἅπας **hapas,** *hap´-as;* from *1* (as a particle of union) and *3956;* absolutely *all* or (sing.) *every* one:—all (things), every (one), whole.

538. ἀπατάω **apataŏ,** *ap-at-ah´-o;* of uncert. der.; to *cheat,* i.e. *delude:*—deceive.

539. ἀπάτη **apatē,** *ap-at´-ay;* from *538; delusion:*—deceit (-ful, -fulness), deceivableness (-ving).

540. ἀπάτωρ **apatōr,** *ap-at´-ore;* from *1* (as a neg. particle) and *3962; fatherless,* i.e. *of unrecorded paternity:*—without father.

541. ἀπαύγασμα **apaugasma,** *ap-ŏw´-gas-mah;* from a comp. of *575* and *826;* an *off-flash,* i.e. *effulgence:*—brightness.

542. ἀπείδω **apĕidō,** *ap-i´-do;* from *575* and the same as *1492;* to *see* fully:—see.

543. ἀπείθεια **apĕithĕia,** *ap-i´-thi-ah;* from *545; disbelief* (obstinate and rebellious):—disobedience, unbelief.

544. ἀπειθέω **apĕithĕō,** *ap-i-theh´-o;* from *545;* to *disbelieve* (wilfully and perversely):—not believe, disobedient, obey not, unbelieving.

545. ἀπειθής **apĕithēs,** *ap-i-thace´;* from *1* (as a neg. particle) and *3982; unpersuadable,* i.e. *contumacious:*—disobedient.

546. ἀπειλέω **apĕilĕō,** *ap-i-leh´-o;* of uncert. der.; to *menace;* by impl. to *forbid:*—threaten.

547. ἀπειλή **apĕilē,** *ap-i-lay´;* from *546;* a *menace:*—× straitly, threatening.

548. ἄπειμι **apĕimi,** *ap´-i-mee;* from *575* and *1510;* to *be away:*—be absent. Comp. *549.*

549. ἄπειμι **apĕimi,** *ap´-i-mee;* from *575* and εἶμι **ĕimi** (to *go*); to *go away:*—go. Comp. *548.*

550. ἀπειπόμην **apĕipŏmēn,** *ap-i-pom´-ane;* reflex. past of a comp. of *575* and *2036;* to *say off* for oneself, i.e. *disown:*—renounce.

551. ἀπείραστος **apĕirastŏs,** *ap-i´-ras-tos;* from *1* (as a neg. particle) and a presumed der. of *3987; untried,* i.e. *not temptable:*—not to be tempted.

552. ἄπειρος **apĕirŏs,** *ap´-i-ros;* from *1* (as a neg. particle) and *3984; inexperienced,* i.e. *ignorant:*—unskilful.

553. ἀπεκδέχομαι **apĕkdĕchŏmai,** *ap-ek-dekh´-om-ahee;* from *575* and *1551;* to *expect fully:*—look (wait) for.

554. ἀπεκδύομαι **apĕkduŏmai,** *ap-ek-doo´-om-ahee;* mid. from *575* and *1562;* to *divest wholly* oneself, or (for oneself) *despoil:*—put off, spoil.

555. ἀπέκδυσις **apĕkdusis,** *ap-ek´-doo-sis;* from *554; divestment:*—putting off.

556. ἀπελαύνω **apĕlaunō,** *ap-el-ŏw´-no;* from *575* and *1643;* to *dismiss:*—drive.

557. ἀπελεγμός **apĕlĕgmŏs,** *ap-el-eg-mos´;* from a comp. of *575* and *1651; refutation,* i.e. (by impl.) *contempt:*—nought.

558. ἀπελεύθερος **apĕlĕuthĕrŏs,** *ap-el-yoo´-ther-os;* from *575* and *1658;* one *freed away,* i.e. a *freedman:*—freeman.

559. Ἀπελλῆς **Apĕllēs,** *ap-el-lace´;* of Lat. or.; *Apelles,* a Chr.:—Apelles.

560. ἀπελπίζω **apĕlpizō,** *ap-el-pid´-zo;* from *575* and *1679;* to *hope out,* i.e. *fully expect:*—hope for again.

561. ἀπέναντι **apĕnanti,** *ap-en´-an-tee;* from *575* and *1725; from in front,* i.e. *opposite, before* or *against:*—before, contrary, over against, in the presence of.

ἀπέπω **apĕpō.** See *550.*

562. ἀπέραντος **apĕrantŏs,** *ap-er´-an-tos;* from *1* (as a neg. particle) and a secondary der. of *4008; unfinished,* i.e. (by impl.) *interminable:*—endless.

563. ἀπερισπάστως **apĕrispastōs,** *ap-er-is-pas´-toce;* adv. from a comp. of *1* (as a neg. particle) and a presumed der. of *4049; undistractedly,* i.e. *free from* (domestic) *solicitude:*—without distraction.

564. ἀπερίτμητος **apĕritmētŏs,** *ap-er-eet´-may-tos;* from *1* (as a neg. particle) and a presumed der. of *4059; uncircumcised* (fig.):—uncircumcised.

565. ἀπέρχομαι **apĕrchŏmai,** *ap-erkh´-om-ahee;* from *575* and *2064;* to *go off* (i.e. *depart*), *aside* (i.e. *apart*) or *behind* (i.e. *follow*), lit. or fig.:—come, depart, go (aside, away, back, out, . . . ways), pass away, be past.

566. ἀπέχει **apĕchĕi,** *ap-ekh´-i;* 3d pers. sing. pres. indic. act. of *568* used impers.; *it is sufficient:*—it is enough.

567. ἀπέχομαι **apĕchŏmai,** *ap-ekh´-om-ahee;* mid. (reflex.) of *568;* to *hold oneself off,* i.e., *refrain:*—abstain.

568. ἀπέχω **apĕchō,** *ap-ekh´-o;* from *575* and *2192;* (act.) to *have out,* i.e. *receive in full;* (intrans.) to *keep* (oneself) *away,* i.e. *be distant* (lit. or fig.):—be, have, receive.

569. ἀπιστέω **apistĕō,** *ap-is-teh´-o;* from *571;* to *be unbelieving,* i.e. (trans.) *disbelieve,* or (by impl.) *disobey:*—believe not.

570. ἀπιστία **apistia,** *ap-is-tee´-ah;* from *571; faithlessness,* i.e. (neg.) *disbelief* (*want* of Chr. *faith*), or (pos.) *unfaithfulness (disobedience):*—unbelief.

571. ἄπιστος **apistŏs,** *ap´-is-tos;* from *1* (as a neg. particle) and *4103;* (act.) *disbelieving,* i.e. *without* Chr. *faith* (spec. a *heathen*); (pass.) *untrustworthy* (person), or *incredible* (thing):—that believeth not, faithless, incredible thing, infidel, unbeliever (-ing).

572. ἁπλότης **haplŏtēs,** *hap-lot´-ace;* from *573; singleness, i.e. (subj.) sincerity* (*without dissimulation* or *self-seeking*), or (obj.) *generosity (copious bestowal):*—bountifulness, liberal (-ity), simplicity, singleness.

573. ἁπλοῦς **haplŏus,** *hap-looce´;* prob. from *1* (as a particle of union) and the base of *4120;* prop. *folded together,* i.e. *single* (fig. *clear*):—single.

574. ἁπλῶς **haplōs,** *hap-loce´;* adv. from *573* (in the obj. sense of *572*); *bountifully:*—liberally.

575. ἀπό **apŏ,** *apŏ´;* a prim. particle; *"off,"* i.e. *away* (from something near), in various senses (of place, time, or relation; lit. or fig.):—(× here-) after, ago, at, because of, before, by (the space of), for (-th), from, in, (out) of, off, (up-) on (-ce), since, with. In composition (as a prefix) it usually denotes *separation, departure, cessation, completion, reversal,* etc.

576. ἀποβαίνω **apŏbainō,** *ap-ob-ah´-ee-no;* from *575* and the base of *939;* lit. to *disembark;* fig. to *eventuate:*—become, go out, turn.

577. ἀποβάλλω **apŏballō,** *ap-ob-al´-lo;* from *575* and *906;* to *throw off;* fig. to *lose:*—cast away.

578. ἀποβλέπω **apŏblĕpō,** *ap-ob-lep´-o;* from *575* and *991;* to *look away* from everything else, i.e. (fig.) intently *regard:*—have respect.

579. ἀπόβλητος **apŏblētŏs,** *ap-ob´-lay-tos;* from *577; cast off,* i.e. (fig.) such as *to be rejected:*—be refused.

580. ἀποβολή **apŏbŏlē,** *ap-ob-ol-ay´;* from *577; rejection;* fig. *loss:*—casting away, loss.

581. ἀπογενόμενος **apŏgĕnŏmĕnŏs,** *ap-og-en-om´-en-os;* past part. of a comp. of *575* and *1096; absent,* i.e. *deceased* (fig. *renounced*):—being dead.

582. ἀπογραφή **apŏgraphē,** *ap-og-raf-ay´;* from *583;* an *enrollment;* by impl. an *assessment:*—taxing.

583. ἀπογράφω **apŏgraphō,** *ap-og-raf´-o;* from *575* and *1125;* to *write off* (a copy or list), i.e. *enroll:*—tax, write.

584. ἀποδείκνυμι **apŏdĕiknumi,** *ap-od-ike´-noo-mee;* from *575* and *1166;* to *show off,* i.e. *exhibit;* fig. to *demonstrate,* i.e. *accredit:*—(ap-) prove, set forth, shew.

585. ἀπόδειξις **apŏdĕixis,** *ap-od´-ike-sis;* from *584; manifestation:*—demonstration.

586. ἀποδεκατόω **apŏdĕkatŏō,** *ap-od-ek-at-ŏ´-o;* from *575* and *1183;* to *tithe* (as debtor or creditor):—(give, pay, take) tithe.

587. ἀπόδεκτος **apŏdĕktŏs,** *ap-od´-ek-tos;* from *588; accepted,* i.e. *agreeable:*—acceptable.

588. ἀποδέχομαι **apŏdĕchŏmai,** *ap-od-ekh´-om-ahee;* from *575* and *1209;* to *take fully,* i.e. *welcome* (persons), *approve* (things):—accept, receive (gladly).

589. ἀποδημέω **apŏdēmĕō,** *ap-od-ay-meh´-o;* from *590;* to *go abroad,* i.e. *visit a foreign land:*—go (travel) into a far country, journey.

590. ἀπόδημος **apŏdēmŏs,** *ap-od´-ay-mos;* from *575* and *1218; absent from* one's own *people,* i.e. a *foreign traveller:*—taking a far journey.

591. ἀποδίδωμι **apŏdidōmi,** *ap-od-eed´-o-mee;* from *575* and *1325;* to *give away,* i.e. *up, over, back,* etc. (in various applications):—deliver (again), give (again), (re-) pay (-ment be made), perform, recompense, render, requite, restore, reward, sell, yield,

592. ἀποδιορίζω **apŏdiŏrizō,** *ap-od-ee-or-id´-zo;* from *575* and a comp. of *1223* and *3724;* to *disjoin* (by a boundary, fig. a party):—separate.

593. ἀποδοκιμάζω **apŏdŏkimazō,** *ap-od-ok-ee-mad´-zo;* from *575* and *1381;* to *disapprove,* i.e. (by impl.) to *repudiate:*—disallow, reject.

594. ἀποδοχή **apŏdŏchē,** *ap-od-okh-ay´;* from *588; acceptance:*—acceptation.

595. ἀπόθεσις **apŏthĕsis,** *ap-oth´-es-is;* from *659;* a *laying aside* (lit. or fig.):—putting away (off).

596. ἀποθήκη **apŏthēkē,** *ap-oth-ay´-kay;* from *659;* a *repository,* i.e. *granary:*—barn, garner.

597. ἀποθησαυρίζω **apŏthēsaurizō,** *ap-oth-ay-sŏw-rid´-zo;* from *575* and *2343;* to *treasure away:*—lay up in store.

598. ἀποθλίβω **apŏthlibō,** *ap-oth-lee´-bo;* from *575* and *2346;* to *crowd* from (every side):—press.

599. ἀποθνήσκω **apŏthnēskō,** *ap-oth-nace´-ko;* from *575* and *2348;* to *die* off (lit. or fig.):—be dead, death, die, lie a-dying, be slain (× with).

600. ἀποκαθίστημι **apŏkathistēmi,** *ap-ok-ath-is´-tay-mee;* from *575* and *2525;* to *reconstitute* (in health, home or organization):—restore (again).

601. ἀποκαλύπτω **apŏkaluptō,** *ap-ok-al-oop´-to;* from *575* and *2572;* to take *off the cover,* i.e. *disclose:*—reveal.

602. ἀποκάλυψις **apŏkalupsis,** *ap-ok-al´-oop-sis;* from *601; disclosure:*—appearing, coming, lighten, manifestation, be revealed, revelation.

603. ἀποκαραδοκία **apŏkaradŏkia,** *ap-ok-ar-ad-ok-ee´-ah;* from a comp. of *575* and a comp. of *κάρα* **kara** (the *head*) and *1380* (in the sense of *watching*); *intense anticipation:*—earnest expectation.

604. ἀποκαταλλάσσω **apŏkatallassō,** *ap-ok-at-al-las´-so;* from *575* and *2644;* to *reconcile fully:*—reconcile.

605. ἀποκατάστασις **apŏkatastasis,** *ap-ok-at-as´-tas-is;* from *600; reconstitution:*—restitution.

606. ἀπόκειμαι **apŏkĕimai,** *ap-ok´-i-mahee;* from *575* and *2749;* to *be reserved;* fig. to *await:*—be appointed, (be) laid up.

607. ἀποκεφαλίζω **apŏkĕphalizō,** *ap-ok-ef-al-id´-zo;* from *575* and *2776;* to *decapitate:*—behead.

608. ἀποκλείω **apŏklĕiō,** *ap-ok-li´-o;* from *575* and *2808;* to *close fully:*—shut up.

609. ἀποκόπτω **apŏkŏptō,** *ap-ok-op´-to;* from *575* and *2875;* to *amputate;* reflex. (by irony) to *mutilate* (the privy parts):—cut off. Comp. *2699.*

610. ἀπόκριμα **apŏkrima,** *ap-ok´-ree-mah;* from *611* (in its orig. sense of *judging*); a judicial *decision:*—sentence.

611. ἀποκρίνομαι **apŏkrinŏmai,** *ap-ok-ree´-nom-ahee;* from *575* and *κρινω* **krino;** to *conclude for oneself,* i.e. (by impl.) to *respond;* by Hebr. [comp. 6030] to *begin to speak* (where an address is expected):—answer.

612. ἀπόκρισις **apŏkrisis,** *ap-ok´-ree-sis;* from *611;* a *response:*—answer.

613. ἀποκρύπτω **apŏkruptō,** *ap-ok-roop´-to;* from *575* and *2928;* to *conceal away* (i.e. *fully*); fig. to *keep secret:*—hide.

614. ἀπόκρυφος **apŏkruphŏs,** *ap-ok´-roo-fos;* from *613; secret;* by impl. *treasured:*—hid, kept secret.

615. ἀποκτείνω **apŏktĕinō,** *ap-ok-ti´-no;* from *575* and κτείνω **ktĕinō** (to *slay*); to *kill* outright; fig. to *destroy:*—put to death, kill, slay.

616. ἀποκυέω **apŏkuĕō,** *ap-ok-oo-eh´o;* from *575* and the base of *2949;* to *breed forth,* i.e. (by transf.) to *generate* (fig.):—beget, bring forth.

617. ἀποκυλίω **apŏkuliō,** *ap-ok-oo-lee´-o;* from *575* and *2947;* to *roll away:*—roll away (back).

618. ἀπολαμβάνω **apŏlambanō,** *ap-ol-am-ban´-o;* from *575* and *2983;* to *receive* (spec. in *full,* or as a host); also to *take aside:*—receive, take.

619. ἀπόλαυσις **apŏlausis,** *ap-ol´-ŏw-sis;* from a comp. of *575* and λαύω **lauō** (to *enjoy*); full *enjoyment:*—enjoy (-ment).

620. ἀπολείπω **apŏlĕipō,** *ap-ol-ipe´-o;* from *575* and *3007;* to *leave* behind (pass, *remain*); by impl. to *forsake:*—leave, remain.

621. ἀπολείχω **apŏlĕichō,** *ap-ol-i´-kho;* from *575* and λείχω **lĕichō** (to *"lick"*); to *lick* clean:—lick.

622. ἀπόλλυμι **apŏllumi,** *ap-ol´-loo-mee;* from *575* and the base of *3639;* to *destroy* fully (reflex. to *perish,* or *lose*), lit. or fig.:—destroy, die, lose, mar, perish.

623. Ἀπολλύων **Apŏlluŏn,** *ap-ol-loo´-ohn;* act. part. of *622;* a *destroyer* (i.e. *Satan*);—Apollyon.

624. Ἀπολλωνία **Apŏllōnia,** *ap-ol-lo-nee´-ah;* from the pagan deity Ἀπόλλων **Apŏllōn** (i.e. the *sun;* from *622*); *Apollonia,* a place in Macedonia:—Apollonia.

625. Ἀπολλώς **Apŏllōs,** *ap-ol-loce´;* prob. from the same as *624; Apollos,* an Isr.:—Apollos.

626. ἀπολογέομαι **apŏlŏgĕŏmai,** *ap-ol-og-eh´-om-ahee:* mid. from a comp. of *575* and *3056;* to give an *account* (legal *plea*) of oneself, i.e. *exculpate* (self):—answer (for self), make defence, excuse (self), speak for self.

627. ἀπολογία **apŏlŏgia,** *ap-ol-og-ee´-ah;* from the same as *626;* a *plea* ("apology"):—answer (for self), clearing of self, defence.

628. ἀπολούω **apŏlŏuō,** *ap-ol-oo´-o;* from *575* and *3068;* to *wash* fully, i.e. (fig.) *have remitted* (reflex.):—wash (away).

629. ἀπολύτρωσις **apŏlutrōsis,** *ap-ol-oo´-tro-sis;* from a comp. of *575* and *3083;* (the act) *ransom* in full, i.e. (fig.) *riddance,* or (spec.) Chr. *salvation:*—deliverance, redemption.

630. ἀπολύω **apŏluō,** *ap-ol-oo´-o;* from *575* and *3089;* to *free* fully, i.e. (lit.) *relieve, release, dismiss* (reflex. *depart*), or (fig.) *let die, pardon,* or (spec.) *divorce:*—(let) depart, dismiss, divorce, forgive, let go, loose, put (send) away, release, set at liberty.

631. ἀπομάσσομαι **apŏmassŏmai,** *ap-om-as´-som-ahee;* mid. from *575* and μάσσω **massō** (to *squeeze, knead, smear*); to *scrape away:*—wipe off.

632. ἀπονέμω **apŏnĕmō,** *ap-on-em´-o;* from *575* and the base of *3551;* to *apportion,* i.e. *bestow:*—give.

633. ἀπονίπτω **apŏniptō,** *ap-on-ip´-to;* from *575* and *3538;* to *wash off* (reflex. one's own hands symbolically):—wash.

634. ἀποπίπτω **apŏpiptō,** *ap-op-ip´-to;* from *575* and *4098;* to *fall off:*—fall.

635. ἀποπλανάω **apŏplanaō,** *ap-op-lan-ah´-o;* from *575* and *4105;* to *lead astray* (fig.); pass. to *stray* (from truth):—err, seduce.

636. ἀποπλέω **apŏplĕō,** *ap-op-leh´-o;* from *575* and *4126;* to *set sail:*—sail away.

637. ἀποπλύνω **apŏplunō,** *ap-op-loo´-no;* from *575* and *4150;* to *rinse off:*—wash.

638. ἀποπνίγω **apŏpnigō,** *ap-op-nee´-go;* from *575* and *4155;* to *stifle* (by drowning or overgrowth):—choke.

639. ἀπορέω **apŏrĕō,** *ap-or-eh´-o;* from a comp. of *1* (as a neg. particle) and the base of *4198;* to *have no way out,* i.e. *be at a loss* (mentally):—(stand in) doubt, be perplexed.

640. ἀπορία **apŏria,** *ap-or-ee´-a;* from the same as *639;* a (state of) *quandary:*—perplexity.

641. ἀποῤῥίπτω **apŏrrhiptō,** *ap-or-hrip´-to;* from *575* and *4496;* to *hurl off,* i.e. *precipitate* (oneself):—cast.

642. ἀπορφανίζω **apŏrphanizō,** *ap-or-fan-id´-zo;* from *575* and a der. of *3737;* to *bereave wholly,* i.e. (fig.) *separate* (from intercourse):—take.

643. ἀποσκευάζω **apŏskĕuazō,** *ap-osk-yoo-ad´-zo;* from *575* and a der. of *4632;* to *pack up* (one's) *baggage:*—take up . . . carriages.

644. ἀποσκίασμα **apŏskiasma,** *ap-os-kee´-as-mah;* from a comp. of *575* and a der. of *4639;* a *shading off,* i.e. *obscuration:*—shadow.

645. ἀποσπάω **apŏspaō,** *ap-os-pah´-o;* from *575* and *4685;* to *drag forth,* i.e. (lit.) *unsheathe* (a sword), or rel. (with a degree of force implied) *retire* (pers. or factiously):—(with-) draw (away), after we were gotten from.

646. ἀποστασία **apŏstasia,** *ap-os-tas-ee´-ah;* fem. of the same as *647; defection* from truth (prop. the state) ["apostasy"]:—falling away, forsake.

647. ἀποστάσιον **apŏstasiŏn,** *ap-os-tas´-ee-on;* neut. of a (presumed) adj. from a der. of *868;* prop. something *separative,* i.e. (spec.) *divorce:*—(writing of) divorcement.

648. ἀποστεγάζω **apŏstĕgazō,** *ap-os-teg-ad´-zo;* from *575* and a der. of *4721;* to *unroof:*—uncover.

649. ἀποστέλλω **apŏstĕllō,** *ap-os-tel´-lo;* from *575* and *4724; set apart,* i.e. (by impl.) to *send out* (prop. on a mission) lit. or fig.:—put in, send (away, forth, out), set [at liberty].

650. ἀποστερέω **apŏstĕrĕō,** *ap-os-ter-eh´-o;* from *575* and στερέω **stĕrĕō** (to *deprive*); to *despoil:*—defraud, destitute, kept back by fraud.

651. ἀποστολή **apŏstŏlē,** *ap-os-tol-ay´;* from *649, commission,* i.e. (spec.) *apostolate:*—apostleship.

652. ἀπόστολος **apŏstŏlŏs,** *ap-os´-tol-os;* from *649;* a *delegate;* spec. an *ambassador* of the Gospel; officially a *commissioner* of Christ ["*apostle*"] (with miraculous powers):—apostle, messenger, he that is sent.

653. ἀποστοματίζω **apŏstŏmatizō,** *ap-os-tom-at-id´-zo;* from *575* and a (presumed) der. of *4750;* to *speak off-hand* (prop. *dictate*), i.e. to *catechize* (in an invidious manner):—provoke to speak.

654. ἀποστρέφω **apŏstrĕphō,** *ap-os-tref´-o;* from *575* and *4762;* to *turn away* or *back* (lit. or fig.):—bring again, pervert, turn away (from).

655. ἀποστυγέω **apŏstugĕō,** *ap-os-toog-eh´-o;* from *575* and the base of *4767;* to *detest* utterly:—abhor.

656. ἀποσυνάγωγος **apŏsunagōgŏs,** *ap-os-oon-ág´-o-gos;* from *575* and *4864; excommunicated:*—(put) out of the synagogue (-s).

657. ἀποτάσσομαι **apŏtassŏmai,** *ap-ot-as´-som-ahee;* mid. from *575* and *5021;* lit. to *say adieu* (by departing or dismissing); fig. to *renounce:*—bid farewell, forsake, take leave, send away.

658. ἀποτελέω **apŏtĕlĕō,** *ap-ot-el-eh´-o;* from *575* and *5055;* to *complete entirely,* i.e. *consummate:*—finish.

659. ἀποτίθημι **apŏtithēmi,** *ap-ot-eeth´-ay-mee;* from *575* and *5087;* to *put away* (lit. or fig.):—cast off, lay apart (aside, down), put away (off).

660. ἀποτινάσσω **apŏtinassō,** *ap-ot-in-as´-so;* from *575* and τινάσσω **tinassō** (to *jostle*); to *brush off:*—shake off.

661. ἀποτίνω **apŏtinō,** *ap-ot-ee´-no;* from *575* and *5099;* to *pay* in full:—repay.

662. ἀποτολμάω **apŏtŏlmaō,** *ap-ot-ol-mah´-o;* from *575* and *5111;* to *venture* plainly:—be very bold.

663. ἀποτομία **apŏtŏmia,** *ap-ot-om-ee´-ah;* from the base of *664;* (fig.) *decisiveness,* i.e. *rigor:*—severity.

664. ἀποτόμως **apŏtŏmōs,** *ap-ot-om´-oce;* adv. from a der. of a comp. of *575* and τέμνω **tĕmnō** (to *cut*); *abruptly,* i.e. *peremptorily:*—sharply (-ness).

665. ἀποτρέπω **apŏtrĕpō,** *ap-ot-rep´-o;* from *575* and the base of *5157;* to *deflect,* i.e. (reflex.) *avoid:*—turn away.

666. ἀπουσία **apŏusia,** *ap-oo-see´-ah;* from the part of *548;* a *being away:*—absence.

667. ἀποφέρω **appŏhĕrō,** *ap-of-er´-o;* from *575* and *5342;* to *bear off* (lit. or rel.):—bring, carry (away).

668. ἀπυφεύγω **apŏphĕugō,** *ap-of-yoo´-go;* from *575* and *5343;* (fig.) to *escape:*—escape.

669. ἀποφθέγγομαι **apŏphthĕggŏmai,** *ap-of-theng´-om-ahee;* from *575* and *5350;* to *enunciate* plainly, i.e. *declare:*—say, speak forth, utterance.

670. ἀποφορτίζομαι **apŏphŏrtizŏmai,** *ap-of-or-tid´-zom-ahee;* from *575* and the mid. of *5412;* to *unload:*—unlade.

671. ἀπόχρησις **apŏchrēsis,** *ap-okh´-ray-sis;* from a comp. of *575* and *5530;* the act of *using up,* i.e. *consumption:*—using.

672. ἀποχωρέω **apŏchōrĕō,** *ap-okh-o-reh´-o;* from *575* and *5562;* to *go away:*—depart.

673. ἀποχωρίζω **apŏchōrizō,** *ap-okh-o-rid´-zo;* from *575* and *5563;* to *rend apart;* reflex. to *separate:*—depart (asunder).

674. ἀποψύχω **apŏpsuchō,** *ap-ops-oo´-kho;* from *575* and *5594;* to *breathe out,* i.e. *faint:*—hearts failing.

675. Ἄππιος **'Appiŏs,** *ap´-pee-os;* of Lat. or.; (in the genitive, i.e. possessive case) of *Appius,* the name of a Roman:—Appii.

676. ἀπρόσιτος **aprŏsitŏs,** *ap-ros´-ee-tos;* from *1* (as a neg. particle) and a der. of a comp. of *4314* and εἶμι **ĕimi** (to *go*); *inaccessible:*—which no man can approach.

677. ἀπρόσκοπος **aprŏskŏpŏs,** *ap-ros´-kop-os;* from *1* (as a neg. particle) and a presumed der. of *4350;* act. *inoffensive,* i.e. *not leading into sin;* pass. *faultless,* i.e. *not led into sin:*—none (void of, without) offence.

678. ἀπροσωπολήπτως **aprŏsōpŏlēptōs,** *ap-ros-o-pol-ape´-toce;* adv. from a comp. of *1* (as a neg. particle) and a presumed der. of a presumed comp. of *4383* and *2983* [comp. *4381*]; in a way *not accepting the person,* i.e. *impartially:*—without respect of persons.

679. ἄπταιστος **aptaistŏs,** *ap-tah´-ee-stos;* from *1* (as a neg. particle) and a der. of *4417; not stumbling,* i.e. (fig.) *without sin:*—from falling.

680. ἅπτομαι **haptŏmai,** *hap´-tom-ahee;* reflex. of *681;* prop. to *attach* oneself to, i.e. to *touch* (in many implied relations):—touch.

681. ἅπτω **haptō,** *hap´-to;* a prim. verb; prop. to *fasten* to, i.e. (spec.) to *set* on fire:—kindle, light.

682. Ἀπφία **Apphia,** *ap-fee´-a;* prob. of for. or.; *Apphia,* a woman of Colossæ:—Apphia.

683. ἀπωθέομαι **apōthĕŏmai,** *ap-o-theh´-om-ahee;* or ἀπώθομαι **apōthŏmai,** *ap-o´-thom-ahee;* from *575* and the mid. of ὠθέω **ōthĕō** or ὤθω **ōthō** (to *shove*); to *push off,* fig. to *reject:*—cast away, put away (from), thrust way (from).

684. ἀπώλεια **apōlĕia,** *ap-o´-li-a;* from a presumed der. of *622; ruin* or *loss* (phys., spiritual or eternal):—damnable (-nation), destruction, die, perdition, × perish, pernicious ways, waste.

685. ἀρά **ara,** *ar-ah´;* prob. from *142;* prop. *prayer* (as *lifted* to Heaven), i.e. (by impl.) *imprecation:*—curse.

686. ἄρα **ara,** *ar´-ah;* prob. from *142* (through the idea of *drawing* a conclusion); a particle denoting an *inference* more or less decisive (as follows):—haply, (what) manner (of man), no doubt, perhaps, so be, then, therefore, truly, wherefore. Often used in connection with other particles, especially *1065* or *3767* (after) or *1487* (before). Comp. also *687.*

687. ἆρα **ara,** *ar´-ah;* a form of *686,* denoting an *interrogation* to which a negative answer is presumed:—therefore.

688. Ἀραβία **Arabia,** *ar-ab-ee´-ah;* of Heb. or. [6152]; *Arabia,* a region of Asia:—Arabia.

ἄραγε **aragĕ.** See *686* and *1065.*

689. Ἀράμ **Aram,** *ar-am´;* of Heb. or. [7410]; *Aram* (i.e. *Ram*), an Isr.:—Aram.

690. Ἄραψ **'Araps,** *ar´-aps;* from *688;* an *Arab* or native of Arabia:—Arabian.

691. ἀργέω **argĕō,** *arg-eh´-o;* from *692;* to *be idle,* i.e. (fig.) to *delay:*—linger.

692. ἀργός **argŏs,** *ar-gos´;* from *1* (as a neg. particle) and *2041; inactive,* i.e. *unemployed;* (by impl.) *lazy, useless:*—barren, idle, slow.

693. ἀργύρεος **argurĕŏs,** *ar-goo´-reh-os;* from *696;* made *of silver:*—(of) silver.

694. ἀργύριον **arguriŏn,** *ar-goo´-ree-on;* neut. of a presumed der. of *696; silvery,* i.e. (by impl.) *cash;* spec. a *silverling* (i.e. *drachma* or *shekel*):—money, (piece of) silver (piece).

695. ἀργυροκόπος **argurŏkŏpŏs,** *ar-goo-rok-op´-os;* from *696* and *2875;* a *beater* (i.e. *worker*) *of silver:*—silversmith.

696. ἄργυρος **argurŏs,** *ar´-goo-ros;* from ἀργός **argŏs** (*shining*); *silver* (the metal, in the articles or coin):—silver.

697. Ἄρειος Πάγος **Arĕiŏs Pagŏs,** *ar´-i-os pag´-os;* from Ἄρης **Arēs** (the name of the Greek deity of war) and a der. of *4078; rock of Ares,* a place in Athens:—Areopagus, Mars' Hill.

698. Ἀρεοπαγίτης **Arĕŏpagitēs,** *ar-eh-op-ag-ee´-tace;* from *697;* an *Areopagite* or member of the court held on Mars' Hill:—Areopagite.

699. ἀρέσκεια **arĕskĕia,** *ar-es´-ki-ah;* from a der. of *700; complaisance:*—pleasing.

700. ἀρέσκω **arĕskō,** *ar-es´-ko;* prob. from *142* (through the idea of *exciting* emotion); to *be agreeable* (or by impl. to seek to be so):—please.

701. ἀρεστός **arĕstŏs,** *ar-es-tos´;* from *700; agreeable;* by impl. *fit:*—(things that) please (-ing), *reason.*

702. Ἀρέτας **Arĕtas,** *ar-et´-as;* of for. or.; *Aretas,* an Arabian:—Aretas.

703. ἀρετή **arĕtē,** *ar-et´-ay;* from the same as *730;* prop. *manliness* (*valor*), i.e. *excellence* (intrinsic or attributed):—praise, virtue.

704. ἀρήν **arēn,** *ar-ane´;* perh. the same as *730;* a *lamb* (as a *male*):—lamb.

705. ἀριθμέω **arithmĕō,** *ar-ith-meh´-o;* from *706;* to *enumerate* or *count:*—number.

706. ἀριθμός **arithmŏs,** *ar-ith-mos´;* from *142;* a *number* (as reckoned *up*):—number.

707. Ἀριμαθαία **Arimathaia,** *ar-ee-math-ah´ee-ah;* of Heb. or. [7414]; *Arimathæa* (or *Ramah*), a place in Pal.:—Arimathæa.

708. Ἀρίσταρχος **Aristarchŏs,** *ar-is´-tar-khos;* from the same as *712* and *757; best ruling; Aristarchus,* a Macedonian:—Aristarchus.

709. ἀριστάω **aristaō,** *ar-is-tah´-o;* from *712;* to *take the principal meal:*—dine.

710. ἀριστερός **aristĕrŏs,** *ar-is-ter-os´;* appar. a comp. of the same as *712;* the *left* hand (as *second-best*):—left [hand].

711. Ἀριστόβουλος **Aristŏbŏulŏs,** *ar-is-tob´-oo-los;* from the same as *712* and *1012; best counseling; Aristoboulus,* a Chr.:—Aristobulus.

712. ἄριστον **aristŏn,** *ar´-is-ton;* appar. neut. of a superlative from the same as *730;* the *best* meal [or *breakfast;* perh. from ἦρι **ēri** ("*early*")], i.e. *luncheon:*—dinner.

713. ἀρκετός **arkĕtŏs,** *ar-ket-os´;* from *714; satisfactory:*—enough, suffice (-ient).

714. ἀρκέω **arkĕō,** *ar-keh´-o;* appar. a prim. verb [but prob. akin to *142* through the idea of *raising* a barrier]; prop. to *ward off,* i.e. (by impl.) to *avail* (fig. *be satisfactory*):—be content, be enough, suffice, be sufficient.

715. ἄρκτος **arktŏs,** *ark´-tos;* prob. from *714;* a *bear* (as *obstructing* by ferocity):—bear.

716. ἅρμα **harma,** *har´-mah;* prob. from *142* [perh. with *1* (as a particle of union) prefixed]; a *chariot* (as *raised* or fitted *together* [comp. *719*]):—chariot.

717. Ἀρμαγεδδών **Armagĕddōn,** *ar-mag-ed-dohn´;* of Heb. or [2022 and 4023]; *Armageddon* (or *Har-Megiddon*), a symbol. name:—Armageddon.

718. ἁρμόζω **harmŏzō,** *har-mod´-zo;* from *719;* to *joint,* i.e. (fig.) to *woo* (reflex. to *betroth*):—espouse.

719. ἁρμός **harmŏs,** *har-mos´;* from the same as *716;* an *articulation* (of the body):—joint.

720. ἀρνέομαι **arnĕŏmai,** *ar-neh´-om-ahee;* perh. from *1* (as a neg. particle) and the mid. of *4483;* to *contradict,* i.e. *disavow, reject, abnegate:*—deny, refuse.

721. ἀρνίον **arniŏn,** *ar-nee´-on;* diminutive from *704;* a *lambkin:*—lamb.

722. ἀροτριόω **arŏtriŏō,** *ar-ot-ree-ŏ´-o;* from *723;* to *plough:*—plow.

723. ἄροτρον **arŏtrŏn,** *ar´-ot-ron;* from ἀρόω **arŏō** (to *till*); a *plough:*—plow.

724. ἁρπαγή **harpagē,** *har-pag-ay´;* from *726; pillage* (prop. abstr.):—extortion, ravening, spoiling.

725. ἁρπαγμός **harpagmŏs,** *har-pag-mos´;* from *726; plunder* (prop. concr.):—robbery.

726. ἁρπάζω **harpazō,** *har-pad´-zo;* from a der. of *138;* to *seize* (in various applications):—catch (away, up), pluck, pull, take (by force).

727. ἅρπαξ **harpax,** *har´-pax;* from *726; rapacious:*—extortion, ravening.

728. ἀῤῥαβών **arrhabōn,** *ar-hrab-ohn´;* of Heb. or. [6162]; a *pledge,* i.e. part of the purchase-money or property given in advance as *security* for the rest:—earnest.

729. ἄῤῥαφος **arrhaphŏs,** *ar´-hhraf-os;* from *1* (as a neg. particle) and a presumed der. of the same as *4476; unsewed,* i.e. of a single piece:—without seam.

730. ἄῤῥην **arrhēn,** *ar´-hrane;* or
αρσην **arsēn,** *ar´-sane;* prob. from *142; male* (as stronger for *lifting*):—male, man.

731. ἄῤῥητος **arrhētŏs,** *ar´-hray-tos;* from *1* (as a neg. particle) and the same as *4490; unsaid,* i.e. (by impl.) *inexpressible:*—unspeakable.

732. ἄῤῥωστος **arrhōstŏs,** *ar´-hroce-tos;* from *1* (as a neg. particle) and a presumed der. of *4517; infirm:*—sick (folk, -ly).

733. ἀρσενοκοίτης **arsĕnŏkŏitēs,** *ar-sen-ok-oy´-tace;* from *730* and *2845;* a *sodomite:*—abuser of (that defile) self with mankind.

734. Ἀρτεμᾶς **Artĕmas,** *ar-tem-as´;* contr. from a comp. of *735* and *1435; gift of Artemis; Artemas* (or *Artemidorus*), a Chr.:—Artemas.

735. Ἄρτεμις **Artĕmis,** *ar´-tem-is;* prob. from the same as *736; prompt; Artemis,* the name of a Grecian goddess borrowed by the Asiatics for one of their deities:—Diana.

736. ἀρτέμων **artĕmōn,** *ar-tem´-ohn;* from a der. of *737:* prop. something *ready* [or else more remotely from *142* (comp. *740*); something *hung* up], i.e. (spec.) the *topsail* (rather *foresail* or *jib*) of a vessel:—mainsail.

737. ἄρτι **arti,** *ar´-tee;* adv. from a der. of *142* (comp. *740*) through the idea of *suspension;* just *now:*—this day (hour), hence [-forth], here [-after], hither [-to], (even) now, (this) present.

738. ἀρτιγέννητος **artigĕnnētŏs,** *ar-teeg-en´-nay-tos;* from *737* and *1084; just born,* i.e. (fig.) a *young convert:*—new born.

739. ἄρτιος **artiŏs,** *ar´-tee-os;* from *737; fresh,* i.e. (by impl.) *complete:*—perfect.

740. ἄρτος **artos,** *ar´-tos;* from *142; bread* (as *raised*) or a *loaf:*—(shew-) bread, loaf.

741. ἀρτύω **artuō,** *ar-too´-o;* from a presumed der. of *142;* to *prepare,* i.e. *spice* (with *stimulating* condiments):—season.

742. Ἀρφαξάδ **Arphaxad,** *ar-fax-ad´;* of Heb. or. [775]; *Arphaxad,* a post-diluvian patriarch:—Arphaxad.

743. ἀρχάγγελος **archaggĕlŏs,** *ar-khang´-el-os;* from *757* and *32;* a *chief angel:*—archangel.

744. ἀρχαῖος **archaiŏs,** *ar-khah´-yos;* from *746; original* or *primeval:*—(them of) old (time).

745. Ἀρχέλαος **Archĕlaŏs,** *ar-khel´-ah-os;* from *757* and *2994; people-ruling; Archelaus,* a Jewish king:—Archelaus.

746. ἀρχή **archē,** *ar-khay´;* from *756;* (prop. abstr.) a *commencement,* or (concr.) *chief* (in various applications of order, time, place or rank):—beginning, corner, (at the, the) first (estate), magistrate, power, principality, principle, rule.

747. ἀρχηγός **archēgŏs,** *ar-khay-gos´;* from *746* and *71;* a *chief leader:*—author, captain, prince.

748. ἀρχιερατικός **archiĕratikŏs,** *ar-khee-er-at-ee-kos´;* from *746* and a der. of *2413; high-priestly:*—of the high-priest.

749. ἀρχιερεύς **archiĕrĕus,** *ar-khee-er-yuce´;* from *746* and *2409;* the *high-priest* (lit. of the Jews, typ. Christ); by extens. a *chief priest:*—chief (high) priest, chief of the priests.

750. ἀρχιποίμην **archipŏimēn,** *ar-khee-poy´-mane;* from *746* and *4166;* a *head shepherd:*—chief shepherd.

751. Ἄρχιππος **Archippŏs,** *ar´-khip-pos;* from *746* and *2462; horse-ruler; Archippus,* a Chr.:—Archippus.

752. ἀρχισυνάγωγος **archisunagōgŏs,** *ar-khee-soon-ag´-o-gos;* from *746* and *4864; director of* the *synagogue* services:—(chief) ruler of the synagogue.

753. ἀρχιτέκτων **architĕktōn,** *ar-khee-tek´-tone;* from *746* and *5045;* a *chief constructor,* i.e. "*architect*":—masterbuilder.

754. ἀρχιτελώνης **architĕlōnēs,** *ar-khee-tel-o´-nace;* from *746* and *5057;* a *principal tax-gatherer:*—chief among the publicans.

755. ἀρχιτρίκλινος **architriklinŏs,** *ar-khee-tree´-klee-nos;* from *746* and a comp. of *5140* and *2827* (a *dinner-bed,* because composed of three couches); *director of* the *entertainment:*—governor (ruler) of the feast.

756. ἄρχομαι **archŏmai,** *ar´-khom-ahee;* mid. of *757* (through the impl. of *precedence*); to *commence* (in order of time):—rehearse from the) begin (-ning).

757. ἄρχω **archō,** *ar´-kho;* a prim. verb; to be *first* (in political rank or power):—reign (rule) over.

758. ἄρχων **archōn,** *ar´-khone;* pres. part. of *757;* a *first* (in rank or power):—chief (ruler), magistrate, prince, ruler.

759. ἄρωμα **"arōma,"** *ar´-o-mah;* from *142* (in the sense of *sending* off scent); an *aromatic:*—(sweet) spice.

760. Ἀσά **Asa,** *as-ah´;* of Heb. or. [609]; *Asa,* an Isr.:—Asa.

761. ἀσάλευτος **asalĕutŏs,** *as-al´-yoo-tos;* from *1* (as a neg. particle) and a der. of *4531; unshaken,* i.e. (by impl.) *immovable* (fig.):—which cannot be moved, unmovable.

762. ἄσβεστος **asbĕstŏs,** *as´-bes-tos;* from *1* (as a neg. particle) and a der. of *4570; not extinguished,* i.e. (by impl.) *perpetual:*—not to be quenched, unquenchable.

763. ἀσέβεια **asĕbĕia,** *as-eb´-i-ah;* from *765; impiety,* i.e. (by impl.) *wickedness:*—ungodly (-liness).

764. ἀσεβέω **asĕbĕō,** *as-eb-eh´-o;* from *765;* to *be* (by impl. *act*) *impious* or *wicked:*—commit (live, that after should live) ungodly.

765. ἀσεβής **asĕbēs,** *as-eb-ace´;* from *1* (as a neg. particle) and a presumed der. of *4576; irreverent,* i.e. (by extens.) *impious* or *wicked:*—ungodly (man).

766. ἀσέλγεια **asĕlgĕia,** *as-elg´-i-a;* from a comp. of *1* (as a neg. particle) and a presumed σελγής **sĕlgēs** (of uncert. der., but appar. mean. *continent*); *licentiousness* (sometimes including other vices):—filthy, lasciviousness, wantonness.

767. ἄσημος **asēmŏs,** *as´-ay-mos;* from *1* (as a neg. particle) and the base of *4591; unmarked,* i.e. (fig.) *ignoble:*—mean.

768. Ἀσήρ **Asēr,** *as-ayr´;* of Heb. or [836]; *Aser* (i.e. *Asher*), an Isr. tribe:—Aser.

769. ἀσθένεια **asthĕnĕia,** *as-then´-i-ah;* from *772; feebleness* (of body or mind); by impl. *malady;* mor. *frailty:*—disease, infirmity, sickness, weakness.

770. ἀσθενέω **asthĕnĕō,** *as-then-eh´-o;* from *772;* to *be feeble* (in any sense):—be diseased, impotent folk (man), (be) sick, (be, be made) weak.

771. ἀσθένημα **asthĕnēma,** *as-then´-ay-mah;* from *770;* a *scruple* of conscience:—infirmity.

772. ἀσθενής **asthĕnēs,** *as-then-ace´;* from *1* (as a neg. particle) and the base of *4599; strengthless* (in various applications, lit., fig. and mor.):—more feeble, impotent, sick, without strength, weak (-er, -ness, thing).

773. Ἀσία **Asia,** *as-ee´-ah;* of uncert. der.; *Asia,* i.e. *Asia Minor,* or (usually) only its western shore:—Asia.

774. Ἀσιανός **Asianŏs,** *as-ee-an-os´;* from *773;* an *Asian* (i.e. *Asiatic*) or inhab. of Asia:—of Asia.

775. Ἀσιάρχης **Asiarchēs,** *as-ee ar´-khace;* from *773* and *746;* an *Asiarch* or president of the public festivities in a city of Asia Minor:—chief of Asia.

776. ἀσιτία **asitia,** *as-ee-tee´-ah;* from *777; fasting* (the state):—abstinence.

777. ἄσιτος **asitŏs,** *as´-ee-tos;* from *1* (as a neg. particle) and *4621; without* (taking) *food:*—fasting.

778. ἀσκέω **askĕō,** *as-keh´-o;* prob. from the same as *4632;* to *elaborate,* i.e. (fig.) *train* (by impl. *strive*):—exercise.

779. ἀσκός **askŏs,** *as-kos´;* from the same as *778;* a leathern (or skin) *bag* used as a bottle:—bottle.

780. ἀσμένως **asmĕnōs,** *as-men´-oce;* adv. from a der. of the base of *2237; with pleasure:*—gladly.

781. ἄσοφος **asŏphŏs,** *as´-of-os;* from *1* (as a neg. particle) and *4680; unwise:*—fool.

782. ἀσπάζομαι **aspazŏmai,** *as-pad´-zom-ahee;* from *1* (as a particle of union) and a presumed form of *4685;* to *enfold* in the arms, i.e. (by impl.) to *salute,* (fig.) to *welcome:*—embrace, greet, salute, take leave.

783. ἀσπασμός **aspasmŏs,** *as-pas-mos´;* from *782;* a *greeting* (in person or by letter):—greeting, salutation.

784. ἄσπιλος **aspilŏs,** *as´-pee-los;* from *1* (as a neg. particle) and *4695; unblemished* (phys. or mor.):—without spot, unspotted.

785. ἀσπίς **aspis,** *as-pece´;* of uncert. der.; a *buckler* (or *round* shield); used of a serpent (as *coiling* itself), prob. the *"asp"*:—asp.

786. ἄσπονδος **aspŏndŏs,** *as´-pon-dos;* from *1* (as a neg. particle) and a der. of *4689;* lit. *without libation* (which usually accompanied a treaty), i.e. (by impl.) *truceless:*—implacable, truce-breaker.

787. ἀσσάριον **assariŏn,** *as-sar´-ee-on;* of Lat. or.; an *assarius* or *as,* a Roman coin:—farthing.

788. ἆσσον **assŏn,** *as´-son;* neut. comparative of the base of *1451; more nearly,* i.e. *very near:*—close.

789. Ἆσσος **Assŏs,** *as´-sos;* prob. of for. or.; *Assus,* a city of Asia Minor:—Assos.

790. ἀστατέω **astatĕō,** *as-tat-eh´-o;* from *1* (as a neg. particle) and a der. of *2476;* to *be non-stationary,* i.e. (fig.) *homeless:*—have no certain dwelling-place.

791. ἀστεῖος **astĕiŏs,** *as-ti´-os;* from ἄστυ **astu** (a *city*); *urbane,* i.e. (by impl.) *handsome:*—fair.

792. ἀστήρ **astēr,** *as-tare´;* prob. from the base of *4766;* a *star* (as *strown* over the sky), lit. or fig.:—star.

793. ἀστήρικτος **astēriktŏs,** *as-tay´-rik-tos;* from *1* (as a neg. particle) and a presumed der. of *4741; unfixed,* i.e. (fig.) *vacillating:*—unstable.

794. ἄστοργος **astŏrgŏs,** *as´-tor-gos;* from *1* (as a neg. particle) and a presumed der. of στέργω **stĕrgō** (to *cherish* affectionately); *hard-hearted* towards kindred:—without natural affection.

795. ἀστοχέω **astŏchĕō** *as-tokh-eh´-o;* from a comp. of *1* (as a neg. particle) and στοίχος **stŏichŏs** (an *aim*); to *miss* the mark, i.e. (fig.) *deviate* from truth:—err, swerve.

796. ἀστραπή **astrapē,** *as-trap-ay´;* from *797; lightning;* by anal. *glare:*—lightning, bright shining.

797. ἀστράπτω **astraptō,** *as-trap´-to;* prob. from *792;* to *flash* as lightning:—lighten, shine.

798. ἄστρον **astrŏn,** *as´-tron;* neut. from *792;* prop. a *constellation;* put for a single *star* (nat. or artificial):—star.

799. Ἀσύγκριτος **Asugkritŏs,** *as-oong´-kree-tos;* from *1* (as a neg. particle) and a der. of *4793; incomparable; Asyncritus,* a Chr.:—Asyncritus.

800. ἀσύμφωνος **asumphōnŏs,** *as-oom´-fo-nos;* from *1* (as a neg. particle) and *4859; inharmonious* (fig.):—agree not.

801. ἀσύνετος **asunĕtŏs,** *as-oon´-ay-tos;* from *1* (as a neg. particle) and *4908; unintelligent;* by impl. *wicked:*—foolish, without understanding.

802. ἀσύνθετος **asunthĕtŏs,** *as-oon´-thet-os;* from *1* (as a neg. particle) and a der. of *4934;* prop. *not agreed,* i.e. *treacherous* to compacts:—covenant-breaker

803. ἀσφάλεια **asphalĕia,** *as-fal´-i-ah;* from *804; security* (lit. or fig.):—certainty, safety.

804. ἀσφαλής **asphalēs,** *as-fal-ace´;* from *1* (as a neg. particle) and σφάλλω **sphallō** (to *"fail"*); *secure* (lit. or fig.):—certain (-ty), safe, sure.

805. ἀσφαλίζω **asphalizō,** *as-fal-id´-zo;* from *804;* to *render secure:*—make fast (sure).

806. ἀσφαλῶς **asphalōs,** *as-fal-oce´;* adv. from *804; securely* (lit. or fig.):—assuredly, safely.

807. ἀσχημονέω **aschēmŏnĕō,** *as-kay-mon-eh´-o;* from *809;* to *be* (i.e. *act*) *unbecoming:*—behave self uncomely (unseemly).

808. ἀσχημοσύνη **aschēmŏsunē,** *as-kay-mos-oo´-nay;* from *809;* an *indecency;* by impl. the *pudenda:*—shame, that which is unseemly.

809. ἀσχήμων **askēmōn,** *as-kay´-mone;* from *1* (as a neg. particle) and a presumed der. of *2192* (in the sense of its congener *4976*); prop. *shapeless,* i.e. (fig.) *inelegant:*—uncomely.

810. ἀσωτία **asōtia,** *as-o-tee´-ah;* from a comp. of *1* (as a neg. particle) and a presumed der. of *4982;* prop. *unsavedness,* i.e. (by impl.) *profligacy:*—excess, riot.

811. ἀσώτως **asōtōs,** *as-o´-toce;* adv. from the same as *810; dissolutely:*—riotous.

812. ἀτακτέω **ataktĕō,** *at-ak-teh´-o;* from *813;* to *be* (i.e. *act*) *irregular:*—behave self disorderly.

813. ἄτακτος **ataktōs,** *at´-ak-tos;* from *1* (as a neg. particle) and a der. of *5021; unarranged,* i.e. (by impl.) *insubordinate* (religiously):—unruly.

814. ἀτάκτως **ataktōs,** *at-ak´-toce;* adv. from *813; irregularly* (mor.):—disorderly.

815. ἄτεκνος **atĕknŏs,** *at´-ek-nos;* from *1* (as a neg. particle) and *5043; childless:*—childless, without children.

816. ἀτενίζω **atĕnizō,** *at-en-id´-zo;* from a comp. of *1* (as a particle of union) and τείνω **tĕinō** (to *stretch*); to *gaze* intently:—behold earnestly (stedfastly), fasten (eyes), look (earnestly, stedfastly, up stedfastly), set eyes.

817. ἄτερ **atĕr,** *at´-er;* a particle prob. akin to *427; aloof,* i.e. *apart* from (lit. or fig.):—in the absence of, without.

818. ἀτιμάζω **atimazō,** *at-im-ad´-zo;* from *820;* to *render infamous,* i.e. (by impl.) *contemn* or *maltreat:*—despise, dishonour, suffer shame, entreat shamefully.

819. ἀτιμία **atimia,** *at-ee-mee´-ah;* from *820; infamy,* i.e. (subj.) comparative *indignity,* (obj.) *disgrace:*—dishonour, reproach, shame, vile.

820. ἄτιμος **atimŏs,** *at´-ee-mos;* from *1* (as a neg. particle) and *5092;* (neg.) *unhonoured* or (pos.) *dishonoured:*—despised, without honour, less honourable [*comparative degree*].

821. ἀτιμόω **atimŏō,** *at-ee-mŏ´-o;* from *820;* used like *818,* to *maltreat:*—handle shamefully.

822. ἀτμίς **atimis,** *at-mece´;* from the same as *109; mist:*—vapour.

823. ἄτομος **atŏmŏs,** *at´-om-os;* from *1* (as a neg. particle) and the base of *5114; uncut,* i.e. (by impl.) *indivisible* [an *"atom"* of time]:—moment.

824. ἄτοπος **atŏpŏs,** *at´-op-os;* from *1* (as a neg. particle) and *5117; out of place,* i.e. (fig.) *improper, injurious, wicked:*—amiss, harm, unreasonable.

825. Ἀττάλεια **Attalĕia,** *at-tal´-i-ah;* from Ἄτταλος **Attalŏs** (a king of Pergamus); *Attaleia,* a place in Pamphylia:—Attalia.

826. αὐγάζω **augazō,** *ŏw-gad´-zo;* from *827;* to *beam* forth (fig.):—shine.

827. αὐγή **augē,** *ŏwg´-ay;* of uncert. der.; a *ray* of light, i.e. (by impl.) *radiance, dawn:*—break of day.

828. Αὔγουστος **Augŏustŏs,** *ŏw´-goos-tos;* from Lat. ["august"]; *Augustus,* a title of the Rom. emperor:—Augustus.

829. αὐθάδης **authadēs,** *ŏw-thad´-ace;* from *846* and the base of *2237; self-pleasing,* i.e. *arrogant:*—self-willed.

830. αὐθαίρετος **authairĕtŏs,** *ŏw-thah´ee-ret-os;* from *846* and the same as *140; self-chosen,* i.e. (by impl.) *voluntary:*—of own accord, willing of self.

831. αὐθεντέω **authĕntĕō,** *ŏw-then-teh´-o;* from a comp. of *846* and an obsol. ἕντης **hĕntēs** (a *worker*); to *act of oneself,* i.e. (fig.) *dominate:*—usurp authority over.

832. αὐλέω **aulĕō,** *ŏw-leh´-o;* from *836;* to play the *flute:*—pipe.

833. αὐλή **aulē,** *ŏw-lay´;* from the same as *109;* a *yard* (as open to the *wind*); by impl. a *mansion:*—court, ([sheep-]) fold, hall, palace.

834. αὐλητής **aulētēs,** *ŏw-lay-tace´;* from *832;* a *flute-player:*—minstrel, piper.

835. αὐλίζομαι **aulizŏmai,** *ŏw-lid´-zom-ahee;* mid. from *833;* to *pass the night* (prop. in the open air):—abide, lodge.

836. αὐλός **aulŏs,** *ŏw-los´;* from the same as *109,* a *flute* (as *blown*):—pipe.

837. αὐξάνω **auxanō,** *ŏwx-an´-o;* a prolonged form of a prim. verb; to *grow* (*"wax"*), i.e. *enlarge* (lit. or fig., act. or pass.):—grow (up), (give the) increase.

838. *αὔξησις* **auxēsis,** *ŏwx´-ay-sis;* from *837; growth:*—increase.

839. *αὔριον* **auriŏn,** *ŏw´-ree-on;* from a der. of the same as *109* (mean, a *breeze,* i.e. the morning *air*); prop. *fresh,* i.e. (adv. with ellipsis of *2250*) *to-mor-row:*—(to-) morrow, next day.

840. *αὐστηρός* **austērŏs,** *ŏw-stay-ros´;* from a (presumed) der. of the same as *109* (mean. *blown*); *rough* (prop. as a *gale*), i.e. (fig.) *severe:*—austere.

841. *αὐτάρκεια* **autarkeia,** *ŏw-tar´-ki-ah;* from *842; self-satisfaction,* i.e. (abstr.) *contentedness,* or *(concr.)* a *competence:*—contentment, sufficiency.

842. *αὐτάρκης* **autarkēs,** *ŏw-tar´-kace;* from *846* and *714; self-complacent,* i.e. *contented:*—content.

843. *αὐτοκατάκριτος* **autŏkatakritŏs,** *ŏw-tok-at-ak´-ree-tos;* from *846* and a der. of *2632; self-condemned:*—condemned of self.

844. *αὐτόματος* **autŏmatŏs,** *ŏw-tom´-at-os;* from *846* and the same as *3155; self-moved* ["automatic"], i.e. *spontaneous:*—of own accord, of self.

845. *αὐτόπτης* **autŏptēs,** *ŏw-top´-tace;* from *846* and *3700; self-seeing,* i.e. an *eye-witness:*—eye-witness.

846. *αὐτός* **autŏs,** *ŏw-tos´;* from the particle *αὖ* **au** [perh. akin to the base of *109* through the idea of a *baffling* wind] (*backward*); the reflex. pron. *self,* used (alone or in the comp. *1438*) of the third pers., and (with the prop. pers. pron.) of the other persons:—her, it (-self), one, the other, (mine) own, said, ([self-], the) same, ([him-, my-, thy-]) self, [your-] selves, she, that, their (-s), them ([-selves]), there [-at, -by, -in, -into, -of, -on, -with], they, (these) things, this (man), those, together, very, which. Comp. *848.*

847. *αὐτοῦ* **autŏu,** *ŏw-too´;* genitive (i.e. possessive) of *846,* used as an adv. of location; prop. belonging to the *same* spot, i.e. *in this* (or *that*) *place:*—(t-) here.

848. *αὑτοῦ* **hautŏu,** *how-too´;* contr. for *1438; self* (in some oblique case or reflex. relation):—her (own), (of) him (-self), his (own), of it, thee, their (own), them (-selves), they.

849. *αὐτόχειρ* **autŏchĕir,** *ŏw-tokh´-ire;* from *846* and *5495; self-handed,* i.e. doing *personally:*—with . . . own hands.

850. *αὐχμηρός* **auchmērŏs,** *ŏwkh-may-ros´;* from *αὐχμός* **auchmŏs** [prob. from a base akin to that of *109*] (*dust,* as *dried* by wind); prop. *dirty,* i.e. (by impl.) *obscure:*—dark.

851. *ἀφαιρέω* **aphairĕō,** *af-ahee-reh´-o;* from *575* and *138;* to *remove* (lit. or fig.):—cut (smite) off, take away.

852. *ἀφανής* **aphanēs,** *af-an-ace´;* from *1* (as a neg. particle) and *5316; non-apparent:*—that is not manifest.

853. *ἀφανίζω* **aphanizō,** *af-an-id´-zo;* from *852;* to *render unapparent,* i.e. (act.) *consume* (*becloud*), or (pass.) *disappear* (*be destroyed*):—corrupt, disfigure, perish, vanish away.

854. *ἀφανισμός* **aphanismŏs,** *af-an-is-mos´;* from *853; disappearance,* i.e. (fig.) *abrogation:*—vanish away.

855. *ἄφαντος* **aphantŏs,** *af´-an-tŏs;* from *1* (as a neg. particle) and a der. of *5316; non-manifested,* i.e. *invisible:*—vanished out of sight.

856. *ἀφεδρών* **aphĕdrōn,** *af-ed-rone´;* from a comp. of *575* and the base of *1476;* a place of *sitting apart,* i.e. a *privy:*—draught.

857. *ἀφειδία* **aphĕidia,** *af-i-dee´-ah;* from a comp. of *1* (as a neg. particle) and *5339; unsparingness,* i.e. *austerity* (*ascetism*):—neglecting.

858. *ἀφελότης* **aphĕlŏtēs,** *af-el-ot´-ace;* from a comp. of *1* (as a neg. particle) and *φέλλος* **phĕllŏs** (in the sense of a *stone* as *stubbing* the foot); *smoothness,* i.e. (fig.) *simplicity:*—singleness.

859. *ἄφεσις* **aphĕsis,** *af´-es-is;* from *863; freedom;* (fig.) *pardon:*—deliverance, forgiveness, liberty, remission.

860. *ἁφή* **haphē,** *haf-ay´;* from *680;* prob. a *ligament* (as *fastening*):—joint.

861. *ἀφθαρσία* **aphtharsia,** *af-thar-see´-ah;* from *862; incorruptibility;* gen. *unending existence;* (fig.) *genuineness:*—immortality, incorruption, sincerity.

862. *ἄφθαρτος* **aphthartŏs,** *af´-thar-tos;* from *1* (as a neg. particle) and a der. of *5351; undecaying* (in essence or continuance):—not (in-, un-) corruptible, immortal.

863. *ἀφίημι* **aphiēmi,** *af-ee´-ay-mee;* from *575* and *ἵημι* **hiemi** (to *send;* an intens. form of *εἶμι* **ĕimi,** to *go*); to *send forth,* in various applications (as follow):—cry, forgive, forsake, lay aside, leave, let (alone, be, go, have), omit, put (send) away, remit, suffer, yield up.

864. *ἀφικνέομαι* **aphiknĕŏmai,** *af-ik-neh´-om-ahee;* from *575* and the base of *2425;* to *go* (i.e. *spread*) *forth* (by rumor):—come abroad.

865. *ἀφιλάγαθος* **aphilagathŏs,** *af-il-ag´-ath-os;* from *1* (as a neg. particle) and *5358; hostile to virtue:*—depiser of those that are good.

866. *ἀφιλάργυρος* **aphilargurŏs,** *af-il-ar´-goo-ros;* from *1* (as a neg. particle) and *5366; unavaricious:*—without covetousness, not greedy of filthy lucre.

867. *ἄφιξις* **aphixis,** *af´-ix-is;* from *864;* prop. *arrival,* i.e. (by impl.) *departure:*—departing.

868. *ἀφίστημι* **aphistēmi,** *af-is´-tay-mee;* from *575* and *2476;* to *remove,* i.e. (act.) *instigate* to revolt.; usually (reflex.) to *desist, desert,* etc.:—depart, draw (fall) away, refrain, withdraw self.

869. *ἄφνω* **aphnō,** *af´-no;* adv. from *852* (contr.); *unawares,* i.e. *unexpectedly:*—suddenly.

870. *ἀφόβως* **aphŏbōs,** *af-ob´-oce;* adv. from a comp. of *1* (as a neg. particle) and *5401; fearlessly:*—without fear.

871. *ἀφομοιόω* **aphŏmŏiŏō,** *af-om-oy-ŏ´-o;* from *575* and *3666;* to *assimilate* closely:—make like.

872. *ἀφοράω* **aphŏraō,** *af-or-ah´-o;* from *575* and *3708;* to *consider* attentively:—look.

873. *ἀφορίζω* **aphŏrizō,** *af-or-id´-zo;* from *575* and *3724;* to *set off* by boundary, i.e. (fig.) *limit, exclude, appoint,* etc.:—divide, separate, sever.

874. *ἀφορμή* **aphŏrmē,** *af-or-may´;* from a comp. of *575* and *3729;* a *starting*-point, i.e. (fig.) an *opportunity:*—occasion.

875. *ἀφρίζω* **aphrizō,** *af-rid´-zo;* from *876;* to *froth* at the mouth (in epilepsy):—foam.

876. *ἀφρός* **aphrŏs,** *af-ros´;* appar. a prim. word; *froth,* i.e. *slaver:*—foaming.

877. *ἀφροσύνη* **aphrŏsunē,** *af-ros-oo´-nay;* from *878; senselessness,* i.e. (euphem.) *egotism;* (mor.) *recklessness:*—folly, foolishly (-ness).

878. *ἄφρων* **aphrōn,** *af´-rone;* from *1* (as a neg. particle) and *5424;* prop. *mindless,* i.e. *stupid,* (by impl.) *ignorant,* (spec.) *egotistic,* (practically) *rash,* or (mor.) *unbelieving:*—fool (-ish), unwise.

879. *ἀφυπνόω* **aphupnŏō,** *af-oop-nŏ´-o;* from a comp. of *575* and *5258;* prop. to *become awake,* i.e. (by impl.) to *drop* (off) in slumber:—fall asleep.

880. *ἄφωνος* **aphōnŏs,** *af´-o-nos;* from *1* (as a neg. particle) and *5456; voiceless,* i.e. *mute* (by nature or choice); fig. *unmeaning:*—dumb, without signification.

881. *Ἀχάζ* **Achaz,** *akh-adz´;* of Heb. or. [271]; *Achaz,* an Isr.:—Achaz.

882. *Ἀχαΐα* **Achaïa,** *ach-ah-ee´-ah;* of uncert. der.; *Achaïa* (i.e. *Greece*), a country of Europe:—Achaia.

883. *Ἀχαϊκός* **Achaïkŏs,** *ach-ah-ee-kos´;* from *882;* an *Achaïan; Achaicus,* a Chr.:—Achaicus.

884. *ἀχάριστος* **acharistŏs,** *ach-ar´-is-tos;* from *1* (as a neg. particle) and a presumed der. of *5483; thankless,* i.e. *ungrateful:*—unthankful.

885. *Ἀχείμ* **Achĕim,** *akh-ime´;* prob. of Heb. or. [comp. 3137]; *Achim,* an Isr.:—Achim.

886. *ἀχειροποίητος* **achĕirŏpŏiētŏs,** *akh-i-rop-oy´-ay-tos;* from *1* (as a neg. particle) and *5499; unmanufactured,* i.e. *inartificial:*—made without (not made with) hands.

887. *ἀχλύς* **achlus,** *akh-looce´;* of uncert. der.: *dimness* of sight, i.e. (prob.) a *cataract:*—mist.

888. *ἀχρεῖος* **achrĕiŏs,** *akh-ri´-os;* from *1* (as a neg. particle) and a der. of *5534* [comp. *5532*]; *useless,* i.e. (euphem.) *unmeritorious:*—unprofitable.

889. *ἀχρειόω* **achrĕiŏō,** *akh-ri-ŏ´-o;* from *888;* to *render useless,* i.e. *spoil:*—become unprofitable.

890. ἄχρηστος **achrēstŏs,** *akh´-race-tos;* from *1* (as a neg. particle) and *5543; inefficient,* i.e. (by impl.) *detrimental:*—unprofitable.

891. ἄχρι **achri,** *akh´-ree;* or ἄχρις **achris,** *akh´-rece;* akin to *206* (through the idea of a *terminus*); (of time) *until* or (of place) *up to:*—as far as, for, in (-to), till, (even, un-) to, until, while. Comp. *3360.*

892. ἄχυρον **achurŏn,** *akh´-oo-ron;* perh. remotely from χέω **chĕō** (to *shed* forth); *chaff* (as *diffusive*):—chaff.

893. ἀψευδής **apsĕudēs,** *aps-yoo-dace´;* from *1* (as a neg. particle) and *5579; veracious:*—that cannot lie.

894. ἄψινθος **apsinthŏs,** *ap´-sin-thos;* of uncert. der.; *wormwood* (as a type of *bitterness,* i.e. [fig.] *calamity*):—wormwood.

895. ἄψυχος **apsuchŏs,** *ap´-soo-khos;* from *1* (as a neg. particle) and *5590; lifeless,* i.e. *inanimate* (mechanical):—without life.

B

896. Βάαλ **Baal,** *bah´-al;* of Heb. or. [1168]; *Baal,* a Phœnician deity (used as a symbol of idolatry):—Baal.

897. Βαβυλών **Babulōn,** *bab-oo-lone´;* of Heb. or. [894]; *Babylon,* the capital of Chaldæa (lit. or fig. [as a type of tyranny]):—Babylon.

898. βαθμός **bathmŏs,** *bath-mos´;* from the same as *899;* a *step,* i.e. (fig.) *grade* (of dignity):—degree.

899. βάθος **bathŏs,** *bath´-os;* from the same as *901; profundity,* i.e. (by impl.) *extent;* (fig.) *mystery:*—deep (-ness, things), depth.

900. βαθύνω **bathunō,** *bath-oo´-no;* from *901;* to *deepen:*—deep.

901. βαθύς **bathus,** *bath-oos´;* from the base of *939; profound* (as *going* down), lit. or fig.:—deep, very early.

902. βαΐον **baïŏn,** *bah-ee´-on;* a diminutive of a der. prob. of the base of *939;* a palm *twig* (as *going* out far):—branch.

903. Βαλαάμ **Balaam,** *bal-ah-am´;* of Heb. or. [1109]; *Balaam,* a Mesopotamian (symb. of a false teacher):—Balaam.

904. Βαλάκ **Balak,** *bal-ak´;* of Heb. or. [1111]; *Balak,* a Moabite:—Balac.

905. βαλάντιον **balantiŏn,** *bal-an´-tee-on;* prob. remotely from *906* (as a *depository*); a *pouch* (for money):—bag, purse.

906. βάλλω **ballō,** *bal´-lo;* a prim. verb; to *throw* (in various applications, more or less violent or intense):—arise, cast (out), × dung, lay, lie, pour, put (up), send, strike, throw (down), thrust. Comp. *4496.*

907. βαπτίζω **baptizō,** *bap-tid´-zo;* from a der. of *911;* to *make whelmed* (i.e. *fully wet*); used only (in the N.T.) of ceremonial *ablution,* espec. (techn.) of the ordinance of Chr. *baptism:*—baptist, baptize, wash.

908. βάπτισμα **baptisma,** *bap´-tis-mah;* from *907; baptism* (techn. or fig.):—baptism.

909. βαπτισμός **baptismŏs,** *bap-tis-mos´;* from *907; ablution* (cerem. or Chr.):—baptism, washing.

910. Βαπτιστής **Baptistēs,** *bap-tis-tace´;* from *907;* a *baptizer,* as an epithet of Christ's forerunner:—Baptist.

911. βάπτω **baptō,** *bap´-to;* a prim. verb; to *whelm,* i.e. cover wholly with a fluid; in the N.T. only in a qualified or spec. sense, i.e. (lit.) to *moisten* (a part of one's person), or (by impl.) to *stain* (as with dye):—dip.

912. Βαραββᾶς **Barabbas,** *bar-ab-bas´;* of Chald. or. [1247 and *5*]; *son of Abba; Bar-abbas,* an Isr.:—Barabbas.

913. Βαράκ **Barak,** *bar-ak´;* of Heb. or. [1301]; *Barak,* an Isr.:—Barak.

914. Βαραχίας **Barachias,** *bar-akh-ee´-as;* of Heb. or. [1296]; *Barachias* (i.e. *Berechijah*), an Isr.:—Barachias.

915. βάρβαρος **barbarŏs,** *bar´-bar-os;* of uncert. der.; a *foreigner* (i.e. *non-Greek*):—barbarian (-rous).

916. βαρέω **barĕō,** *bar-eh´-o;* from *926;* to *weigh* down (fig.):—burden, charge, heavy, press.

917. βαρέως **barĕōs,** *bar-eh´-oce;* adv. from *926; heavily* (fig.):—dull.

918. Βαρθολομαῖος **Barthŏlŏmaiŏs,** *bar-thol-om-ah´-yos; of Chald. or. [1247 and 8526]; son of Tolmai, Bar-tholomæus,* a Chr. apostle:—Bartholomeus.

919. Βαριησοῦς **Bariēsŏus,** *bar-ee-ay-sooce´;* of Chald. or. [1247 and 3091]; *son of Jesus* (or *Joshua*); *Bar-jesus,* an Isr.:—Barjesus.

920. Βαριωνᾶς **Bariōnas,** *bar-ee-oo-nas´;* of Chald. or. [1247 and 3124]; *son of Jonas* (or *Jonah*); *Bar-jonas,* an Isr.:—Bar-jona.

921. Βαρνάβας **Barnabas,** *bar-nab´-as;* of Chald. or. [1247 and 5029]; *son of Nubas* (i.e. *prophecy*); *Barnabas,* an Isr.:—Barnabas.

922. βάρος **barŏs,** *bar´-os;* prob. from the same as *939* (through the notion of *going* down; comp. *899*); *weight;* in the N.T. only fig. a *load, abundance, authority:*—burden (-some), weight.

923. Βαρσαβᾶς **Barsabas,** *bar-sab-as´;* of Chald. or. [1247 and prob. 6634]; *son of Sabas* (or *Tsaba*); *Bar-sabas,* the name of two Isr.:—Barsabas.

924. Βαρτιμαῖος **Bartimaiŏs,** *bar-tim-ah´-yos;* of Chald. or. [1247 and 2931]; *son of Timæus* (or the *unclean*); *Bar-timæus,* an Isr.:—Bartimæus.

925. βαρύνω **barunō,** *bar-oo´-no;* from *926;* to *burden* (fig.):—overcharge.

926. βαρύς **barus,** *bar-ooce´;* from the same as *922; weighty,* i.e. (fig.) *burdensome, grave:*—grievous, heavy, weightier.

927. βαρύτιμος **barutimŏs,** *bar-oo´-tim-os;* from *926* and *5092;* highly *valuable:*—very precious.

928. βασανίζω **basanizō,** *bas-an-id´-zo;* from *931;* to *torture:*—pain, toil, torment, toss, vex.

929. βασανισμός **basanismŏs,** *bas-an-is-mos´;* from *928; torture:*—torment.

930. βασανιστής **basanistēs,** *bas-an-is-tace´;* from *928;* a *torturer:*—tormentor.

931. βάσανος **basanŏs,** *bas´-an-os;* perh. remotely from the same as *939* (through the notion of *going* to the bottom); a *touch-stone,* i.e. (by anal.) *torture:*—torment.

932. βασιλεία **basilĕia,** *bas-il-i´-ah;* from *935;* prop. *royalty,* i.e. (abstr.) *rule,* or (concr.) a *realm* (lit. or fig.):—kingdom, + reign.

933. βασίλειον **basilĕiŏn,** *bas-il´-i-on;* neut. of *934;* a *palace:*—king's court.

934. βασίλειος **basilĕiŏs,** *bas-il´-i-os;* from *935; kingly* (in nature):—royal.

935. βασιλεύς **basilĕus,** *bas-il-yooce´;* prob. from *939* (through the notion of a *foundation* of power); a *sovereign* (abs., rel. or fig.):—king.

936. βασιλεύω **basilĕuō,** *bas-il-yoo´-o;* from *935;* to *rule* (lit. or fig.):—king, reign.

937. βασιλικός **basilikŏs,** *bas-il-ee-kos´;* from *935; regal* (in relation), i.e. (lit.) belonging to (or befitting) the sovereign (as land, dress, or a *courtier*), or (fig.) *preeminent:*—king's, nobleman, royal.

938. βασίλισσα **basilissa,** *bas-il´-is-sah;* fem. from *936;* a *queen:*—queen.

939. βάσις **basis,** *bas´-ece;* from βαίνω **bainō** (to *walk*); a *pace* ("base"), i.e. (by impl.) the *foot:*—foot.

940. βασκαίνω **baskainō,** *bas-kah´ee-no;* akin to *5335;* to *malign,* i.e. (by extens.) to *fascinate* (by false representations):—bewitch.

941. βαστάζω **bastazō,** *bas-tad´-zo;* perh. remotely der. from the base of *939* (through the idea of *removal*); to *lift,* lit. or fig. (*endure, declare, sustain, receive,* etc.):—bear, carry, take up.

942. βάτος **batŏs,** *bat´-os;* of uncert. der.; a *brier* shrub:—bramble, bush.

943. βάτος **batŏs,** *bat´-os;* of Heb. or. [1324]; a *bath,* or measure for liquids:—measure.

944. βάτραχος **batrachŏs,** *bat´-rakh-os;* of uncert. der.; a *frog:*—frog.

945. βαττολογέω **battŏlŏgĕō,** *bat-tol-og-eh´-o;* from βάττος **Battŏs** (a proverbial stammerer) and *3056;* to *stutter,* i.e. (by impl.) to *prate* tediously:—use vain repetitions.

946. βδέλυγμα **bdĕlugma,** *bdel´-oog-mah;* from *948;* a *detestation,* i.e. (spec.) *idolatry:*—abomination.

947. βδελυκτός **bdĕluktŏs,** *bdel-ook-tos´;* from *948; detestable,* i.e. (spec.) *idolatrous:*—abominable.

948. βδελύσσω **bdĕlussō,** *bdel-oos´-so;* from a (presumed) der. of βδέω **bdĕō** (to *stink*); to be *disgusted,* i.e. (by impl.) *detest* (espec. of idolatry):—abhor, abominable.

949. βέβαιος **bĕbaiŏs,** *beb´-ah-yos;* from the base of *939* (through the idea of *basality*); *stable* (lit. or fig.):—firm, of force, stedfast, sure.

950. βεβαιόω **bĕbaiŏō,** *beb-ah-yŏ´-o;* from *949;* to *stabilitate* (fig.):—confirm, (e-) stablish.

951. βεβαίωσις **bĕbaiōsis,** *beb-ah´-yo-sis;* from *950; stabiliment:*—confirmation.

952. βέβηλος **bĕbēlŏs,** *beb´-ay-los;* from the base of *939* and βηλός **bēlŏs** (a *threshold*); *accessible* (as by *crossing the door-way*), i.e. (by impl. of Jewish notions) *heathenish, wicked:*—profane (person).

953. βεβηλόω **bĕbēlŏō,** *beb-ay-lŏ´-o;* from *952;* to *desecrate:*—profane.

954. βεελζεβούλ **Bĕĕlzĕbŏul,** *beh-el-zeb-ool´;* of Chald. or [by parody upon 1176]; *dung-god; Beel-zebul,* a name of Satan:—Beelzebub.

955. Βελίαλ **Bĕlial,** *bel-ee´-al;* of Heb. or. [1100]; *worthlessness; Belial,* as an epithet of Satan:—Belial.

956. βέλος **bĕlŏs,** *bel´-os;* from *906;* a *missile,* i.e. *spear* or *arrow:*—dart.

957. βελτίον **bĕltiŏn,** *bel-tee´-on;* neut. of a comp. of a der. of *906* (used for the comp. of *18*); *better:*—very well.

958. Βενιαμίν **Bĕniamin,** *ben-ee-am-een´;* of Heb. or. [1144]; *Benjamin,* an Isr.:—Benjamin.

959. Βερνίκη **Bĕrnikē,** *ber-nee´-kay;* from a provincial form of *5342* and *3529; victorious; Bernicè,* a member of the Herodian family:—Bernice.

960. Βέροια **Bĕrŏia,** *ber´-oy-ah;* perh. a provincial from a der. of *4008* [*Peræa,* i.e. the region *beyond* the coast-line]; *Beræa,* a place in Macedonia:—Berea.

961. Βεροιαῖος **Bĕrŏiaiŏs,** *ber-oy-ah´-yos;* from *960;* a *Berœæan* or native of Berœea:—of Berea.

962. Βηθαβαρά **Bēthabara,** *bay-thab-ar-ah´;* of Heb. or. [1004 and 5679]; *ferry-house; Bethabara* (i.e. *Bethabarah*), a place on the Jordan:—Bethabara.

963. Βηθανία **Bēthania,** *bay-than-ee´-ah;* of Chald. or; *date-house; Beth-any,* a place in Pal.:—Bethany.

964. Βηθεσδά **Bēthĕsda,** *bay-thes-dah´;* of Chald. or. [comp. 1004 and 2617]; *house of kindness; Beth-esda,* a pool in Jerus.:—Bethesda.

965. Βηθλεέμ **Bēthlĕĕm,** *bayth-leh-em´;* of Heb. or. [1036]; *Bethleem* (i.e. *Beth-lechem*), a place in Pal.:—Bethlehem.

966. Βηθσαϊδά **Bēthsaïda,** *bayth-sahee-dah´;* of Chald. or. [comp. 1004 and 6719]; *fishing-house; Bethsaïda,* a place in Pal.:—Bethsaida.

967. Βηθφαγή **Bēthphagē,** *bayth-fag-ay´;* of Chald. or. [comp. 1004 and 6291]; *fig-house; Bethphagè,* a place in Pal.:—Bethphage.

968. βῆμα **bēma,** *bay´-ma;* from the base of *939;* a *step,* i.e. *foot-breath;* by impl. a *rostrum,* i.e. *tribunal:*—judgment-seat, set [foot] on, throne.

969. βήρυλλος **bērullŏs,** *bay´-rool-los;* of uncert. der.; a *"beryl":*—beryl.

970. βία **bia,** *bee´-ah;* prob. akin to *979* (through the idea of *vital* activity); *force:*—violence.

971. βιάζω **biazō,** *bee-ad´-zo;* from *970;* to *force,* i.e. (reflex.) to *crowd oneself* (into), or (pass.) to *be seized:*—press, suffer violence.

972. βίαιος **biaiŏs,** *bee´-ah-yos;* from *970; violent:*—mighty.

973. βιαστής **biastēs,** *bee-as-tace´;* from *971;* a *forcer,* i.e. (fig.) *energetic:*—violent.

974. βιβλιαρίδιον **bibliaridiŏn,** *bib-lee-ar-id´-ee-on;* a dimin. of *975;* a *booklet:*—little book.

975. βιβλίον **bibliŏn,** *bib-lee´-on;* a dimin. of *976;* a *roll:*—bill, book, scroll, writing.

976. βίβλος **biblŏs,** *bib´-los;* prop. the inner *bark* of the papyrus plant, i.e. (by impl.) a *sheet* or *scroll* of writing:—book.

977. βιβρώσκω **bibrōskō,** *bib-ro´-sko;* a reduplicated and prolonged form of an obsol. prim. verb [perh. causative of *1006*]; to *eat:*—eat.

978. Βιθυνία **Bithunia,** *bee-thoo-nee´-ah;* of uncert. der.; *Bithynia,* a region of Asia:—Bithynia.

979. βίος **biŏs,** *bee´-os;* a prim. word; *life,* i.e. (lit.) the present state of existence; by impl. the means of *livelihood:*—good, life, living.

980. βιόω **biŏō,** *bee-ŏ´-o; from 979;* to *spend* existence:—live.

981. βίωσις **biōsis,** *bee´-o-sis;* from *980; living* (prop. the act, by impl. the mode):—manner of life

982. βιωτικός **biōtikŏs,** *bee-o-tee-kos´;* from a der. of *980; relating to* the present *existence:*—of (pertaining to, things that pertain to) this life.

983. βλαβερός **blabĕrŏs,** *blab-er-os´;* from *984; injurious:*—hurtful.

984. βλάπτω **blaptō,** *blap´-to;* a prim. verb; prop. to *hinder,* i.e. (by impl.) to *injure:*—hurt.

985. βλαστάνω **blastanō,** *blas-tan´-o;* from βλαστός **blastŏs** (a *sprout*); to *germinate;* by impl. to *yield* fruit:—bring forth, bud, spring (up).

986. βλάστος **Blastŏs,** *blas´-tos;* perh. the same as the base of *985; Blastus,* an officer of Herod Agrippa:—Blastus.

987. βλασφημέω **blasphēmĕō,** *blas-fay-meh´-o;* from *989;* to *vilify;* spec. to *speak impiously:*—(speak) blaspheme (-er, -mously, -my), defame, rail on, revile, speak evil.

988. βλασφημία **blasphēmia,** *blas-fay-me´-ah;* from *989; vilification* (espec. against God):—blasphemy, evil speaking, railing.

989. βλάσφημος **blasphēmŏs,** *blas´-fay-mos;* from a der. of *984* and *5345; scurrilous, i.e. calumnious* (against man), or (spec.) *impious* (against God):—blasphemer (-mous), railing.

990. βλέμμα **blemma,** *blem´-mah;* from *991; vision* (prop. concr.; by impl. abstr.):—seeing.

991. βλέπω **blĕpō,** *blep´-o;* a prim. verb; to *look* at (lit. or fig.):—behold, beware, lie, look (on, to), perceive, regard, see, sight, take heed. Comp. *3700.*

992. βλητέος **blētĕŏs,** *blay-teh´-os;* from *906;* fit *to be cast* (i.e. *applied*):—must be put.

993. Βοανεργές **Bŏanĕrgĕs,** *bŏ-an-erg-es´;* of Chald. or. [1123 and 7266]; *sons of commotion; Boänerges,* an epithet of two of the Apostles:—Boanerges.

994. βοάω **bŏaō,** *bŏ-ah´-o;* appar. a prol. form of a prim. verb; to *halloo,* i.e. *shout* (for help or in a tumultuous way):-cry.

995. βοή **bŏē,** *bŏ-ay´;* from *994;* a *halloo,* i.e. *call* (for aid, etc.):—cry.

996. βοήθεια **bŏēthĕia,** *bŏ-ay´-thi-ah;* from *998; aid;* spec. a rope or chain for *frapping* a vessel:—help.

997. βοηθέω **bŏēthĕō,** *bŏ-ay-theh´-o;* from *998;* to *aid* or *relieve:*—help, succour.

998. βοηθός **bŏēthŏs,** *bŏ-ay-thos´;* from *995* and θέω **thĕō** (to *run*); a *succorer:*—helper.

999. βόθυνος **bŏthunŏs,** *both´-oo-nos;* akin to *900;* a *hole* (in the ground); spec. a *cistern:*—ditch, pit.

1000. βολή **bŏlē,** *bol-ay´;* from *906;* a *throw* (as a measure of distance):—cast.

1001. βολίζω **bŏlizō,** *bol-id´-zo;* from *1002;* to *heave the lead:—sound.*

1002. βολίς **bŏlis,** *bol-ece´;* from *906;* a *missile,* i.e. *javelin:*—dart.

1003. Βοόζ **Bŏŏz.** *bŏ-oz´;* of Heb. or. [1162]; *Boöz,* (i.e. *Boäz*), an Isr.:—Booz.

1004. βόρβορος **bŏrbŏrŏs,** *bor´-bor-os;* of uncert. der.; *mud:*—mire.

1005. βοῤῥᾶς **borrhas,** *bor-hras´;* of uncert. der.; the *north* (prop. wind):—north.

1006. βόσκω **bŏskō,** *bos´-ko;* a prol. form of a prim. verb [comp. *977, 1016*]; to *pasture;* by extens. to *fodder;* reflex. to *graze:*—feed, keep.

1007. Βοσόρ **Bŏsŏr,** *bos-or´;* of Heb. or. [1160]; *Bosor* (i.e. *Beör*), a Moabite:—Bosor.

1008. βοτάνη **bŏtanē,** *bot-an´-ay;* from *1006; herbage* (as if for *grazing*):—herb.

1009. βότρυς **bŏtrus,** *bot´-rooce;* of uncert. der.; a *bunch* (of grapes):—(vine) cluster (of the vine).

1010. βουλευτής **bŏulĕutēs,** *bool-yoo-tace´;* from *1011;* an *adviser,* i.e. (spec.) a *councillor* or member of the Jewish Sanhedrim:—counsellor.

1011. *βουλεύω* **bŏulĕuō,** *bool-yoo´-o;* from *1012;* to *advise,* i.e. (reflex.) *deliberate,* or (by impl.) *resolve:*—consult, take counsel, determine, be minded, purpose.

1012. *βουλή* **bŏulē,** *boo-lay´;* from *1014; volition,* i.e. (obj.) *advice,* or (by impl.) *purpose:*— + advise, counsel, will.

1013. *βούλημα* **bŏulēma,** *boo´-lay-mah;* from *1014;* a *resolve:*—purpose, will.

1014. *βούλομαι* *boo´-lom-ahee;* mid. of a prim. verb; to *"will,"* i.e. (reflex.) *be willing:*—be disposed, minded, intend, list (be, of own) will (-ing). Comp. *2309.*

1015. *βουνός* **bŏunŏs,** *boo-nos´;* prob. of for. or.; a *hillock:*—hill.

1016. *βοῦς* **bŏus,** *booce;* prob. from the base of *1006;* an *ox* (as *grazing*), i.e. an animal of that species ("beef"):—ox.

1017. *βραβεῖον* **brabĕiŏn,** *brab-i´-on;* from *βραβεύς* **brabĕus** (an *umpire;* of uncert. der.); an *award* (of arbitration), i.e. (spec.) a *prize* in the public games:—prize.

1018. *βραβεύω* **brabĕuō,** *brab-yoo´-o;* from the same as *1017;* to *arbitrate,* i.e. (gen.) to *govern* (fig. *prevail*):—rule.

1019. *βραδύνω* **bradunō,** *brad-oo´-no;* from *1021;* to *delay:*—be slack, tarry.

1020. *βραδυπλοέω* **braduplŏĕō,** *brad-oo-plŏ-eh´-o;* from *1021* and a prol. form of *4126;* to *sail slowly:*—sail slowly.

1021. *βραδύς* **bradus,** *brad-ooce´;* of uncert. affin.; *slow;* fig. *dull:*—slow.

1022. *βραδύτης* **bradutēs,** *brad-oo´-tace;* from *1021; tardiness:*—slackness.

1023. *βραχίων* **brachiōn,** *brakh-ee´-own;* prop. comp. of *1024,* but appar. in the sense of *βράσσω* **brassō** (to *wield*); the *arm,* i.e. (fig.) *strength:*—arm.

1024. *βραχύς* **brachus,** *brakh-ooce´;* of uncert. affin.; *short* (of time, place, quantity, or number):—few words, little (space, while).

1025. *βρέφος* **brĕphŏs,** *bref´-os;* of uncert. affin.; an *infant* (prop. unborn) lit. or fig.:—babe, (young) child, infant.

1026. *βρέχω* **brĕchō,** *brekh´-o;* a prim. verb; to *moisten* (espec. by a shower):—(send) rain, wash.

1027. *βροντή* **brŏntē,** *bron-tay´;* akin to *βρέμω* **brĕmō** (to *roar*); *thunder:*—thunder (-ing).

1028. *βροχή* **brŏchē,** *brokh-ay´;* from 1026; *rain:*—rain.

1029. *βρόχος* **brŏchŏs,** *brokh´-os;* of uncert. der.; a *noose:*—snare.

1030. *βρυγμός* **brugmŏs,** *broog-mos´;* from *1031;* a *grating* (of the teeth):—gnashing.

1031. *βρύχω* **bruchō,** *broo´-kho;* a prim. verb; to *grate* the teeth (in pain or rage):—gnash.

1032. *βρύω* **bruō,** *broo´-o;* a prim. verb; to *swell* out, i.e. (by impl.) to *gush:*—send forth.

1033. *βρῶμα* **brōma,** *bro´-mah;* from the base of *977; food* (lit. or fig.), espec. (cer.) articles allowed or forbidden by the Jewish law:—meat, victuals.

1034. *βρώσιμος* **brōsimos,** *bro´-sim-os;* from *1035; eatable:*—meat.

1035. *βρῶσις* **brōsis,** *bro´-sis;* from the base of *977;* (abstr.) *eating* (lit. or fig.); by extens. (concr.) *food* (lit. or fig.):—eating, food, meat.

1036. *βυθίζω* **buthizō,** *boo-thid´-zo;* from *1937;* to *sink;* by impl. to *drown:*—begin to sink, drown.

1037. *βυθός* **buthŏs,** *boo-thos´;* a var. of *899; depth,* i.e. (by impl.) the *sea:*—deep.

1038. *βυρσεύς* **bursĕus,** *boorce-yooce´;* from *βύρσα* **bursa** (a *hide*); a *tanner:*—tanner.

1039. *βύσσινος* **bussinŏs,** *boos´-see-nos;* from *1040;* made of *linen* (neut. a linen *cloth*):—fine linen.

1040. *βύσσος* **bussŏs,** *boos´-sos;* of Heb. or. [948]; white *linen:*—fine linen.

1041. *βῶμος* **bōmŏs,** *bo´-mos;* from the base of *939;* prop. a *stand,* i.e. (spec.) an *altar:*—altar.

Γ

1042. *γαββαθά* **gabbatha,** *gab-bath-ah´;* of Chald. or. [comp. 1355]; *the knoll; gabbatha,* a vernacular term for the Roman tribunal in Jerus.:—Gabbatha.

1043. *Γαβριήλ* **Gabriēl,** *gab-ree-ale´;* of Heb. or. [1403]; *Gabriel,* an archangel:—Gabriel.

1044. *γάγγραινα* **gaggraina,** *gang´-grahee-nah;* from *γραίνω* **grainō** (to *gnaw*); an *ulcer* ("gangrene"):—canker.

1045. *Γάδ* **Gad,** *gad;* of Heb. or. [1410]; *Gad,* a tribe of Isr.:—Gad.

1046. *Γαδαρηνός* **Gadarēnŏs,** *gad-ar-ay-nos´;* from *Γαδαρά* (a town E. of the Jordan); a *Gadarene* or inhab. of Gadara:—Gadarene.

1047. *γάζα* **gaza,** *gad´-zah;* of for. or.; a *treasure:*—treasure.

1048. *Γάζα* **Gaza,** *gad´-zah;* of Heb. or. [5804]; *Gazah* (i.e. *Azzah*), a place in Pal.:—Gaza.

1049. *γαζοφυλάκιον* **gazŏphulakiŏn,** *gad-zof-oo-lak´-ee-on;* from *1047* and *5438;* a *treasure-house,* i.e. a court in the temple for the collection-boxes:—treasury.

1050. *Γάϊος* **Gaïŏs,** *gah´-ee-os;* of Lat. or.; *Gaïus* (i.e. *Caius*), a Chr.:—Gaius.

1051. *γάλα* **gala,** *gal´-ah;* of uncert. affin.; *milk* (fig.):—milk.

1052. *Γαλάτης* **Galatēs,** *gal-at´-ace;* from *1053;* a *Galatian* or inhab. of Galatia:—Galatian.

1053. *Γαλατία* **Galatia,** *gal-at-ee´-ah;* of for. or.; *Galatia,* a region of Asia:—Galatia.

1054. *Γαλατικός* **Galatikŏs,** *gal-at-ee-kos´;* from *1053; Galatic* or relating to Galatia:—of Galatia.

1055. *γαλήνη* **galēnē,** *gal-ay´-nay;* of uncert. der.; *tranquillity:*—calm.

1056. *Γαλιλαία* **Galilaia,** *gal-il-ah´-yah;* of Heb. or. [1551]; *Galilæa* (i.e. the heathen *circle*), a region of Pal.:—Galilee.

1057. *Γαλιλαῖος* **Galilaiŏs,** *gal-ee-lah´-yos;* from *1056; Galilæan* or belonging to Galilæa:—Galilæan, of Galilee.

1058. *Γαλλίων* **Galliōn,** *gal-lee´-own;* of Lat. or.; *Gallion* (i.e. *Gallio*), a Roman officer:—Gallio

1059. *Γαμαλιήλ* **Gamaliēl,** *gam-al-ee-ale´;* of Heb. or. [1583]; *Gamaliel* (i.e. *Gamliel*), an Isr.:—Gamaliel.

1060. *γαμέω* **gamĕō,** *gam-eh´-o;* from *1062;* to *wed* (of either sex):—marry (a wife).

1061. *γαμίσκω* **gamiskō,** *gam-is´-ko;* from *1062;* to *espouse* (a daughter to a husband):—give in marriage.

1062. *γάμος* **gamŏs,** *gam´-os;* of uncert. affin.; *nuptials:*—marriage, wedding.

1063. *γάρ* **gar,** *gar;* a prim. particle; prop. assigning a *reason* (used in argument, explanation or intensification; often with other particles):—and, as, because (that), but, even, for indeed, no doubt, seeing, then, therefore, verily, what, why, yet.

1064. *γαστήρ* **gastēr,** *gas-tare´;* of uncert. der.; the *stomach;* by anal. the *matrix;* fig. a *gourmand:*—belly, + with child, womb.

1065. *γέ* **gĕ,** *gheh;* a prim. particle of *emphasis* or *qualification* (often used with other particles prefixed):—and besides, doubtless, at least, yet.

1066. *Γεδεών* **Gĕdĕōn,** *ghed-eh-own´;* of Heb. or. [1439]; *Gedeon* (i.e. *Gid[e]on*), an Isr.:—Gedeon.

1067. *γέεννα* **gĕĕnna,** *gheh´-en-nah;* of Heb. or [1516 and 2011]; *valley of* (the son of) *Hinnom; gehenna* (or *Ge-Hinnom*), a valley of Jerus., used (fig.) as a name for the place (or state) of everlasting punishment:—hell.

1068. *Γεθσημανῆ* **Gĕthsēmanē,** *gheth-say-man-ay´;* of Chald. or. [comp. 1660 and 8081]; *oil-press; Gethsemane,* a garden near Jerus.:—Gethsemane.

1069. *γείτων* **gĕitōn,** *ghi´-tone;* from *1093;* a *neighbor* (as adjoining one's *ground*); by impl. a *friend:*—neighbour.

1070. *γελάω* **gĕlaō,** *ghel-ah´-o;* of uncert. affin.; to *laugh* (as a sign of joy or satisfaction):—laugh.

1071. *γέλως* **gĕlōs,** *ghel´-oce;* from *1070; laughter* (as a mark of gratification):—laughter.

1072. *γεμίζω* **gĕmizō,** *ghem-id´-zo;* trans. from *1073,* to *fill* entirely:—fill (be) full.

1073. *γέμω* **gĕmō,** *ghem´-o;* a prim. verb; to *swell* out, i.e. *be full:*—be full.

1074. γενεά **gĕnĕa,** *ghen-eh-ah´;* from (a presumed der. of) *1085;* a *generation;* by impl. an *age* (the period or the persons):—age, generation, nation, time.

1075. γενεαλογέω **gĕnĕalŏgĕō,** *ghen-eh-al-og-eh´-o;* from *1074* and *3056;* to *reckon by generations,* i.e. *trace in genealogy:*—count by descent.

1076. γενεαλογία **gĕnĕalŏgia,** *ghen-eh-al-og-ee´-ah;* from the same as *1075; tracing by generations,* i.e. *"genealogy":*—genealogy.

1077. γενέσια **gĕnĕsia,** *ghen-es´-ee-ah;* neut. plur. of a der. of *1078; birthday* ceremonies:—birthday.

1078. γένεσις **genesis,** *ghen´-es-is;* from the same as *1074; nativity;* fig. *nature:*—generation, nature (-ral).

1079. γενετή **gĕnĕtē,** *ghen-et-ay´;* fem. of a presumed der. of the base of *1074; birth:*—birth.

1080. γεννάω **gĕnnaō,** *ghen-nah´-o;* from a var. of *1085;* to *procreate* (prop. of the father, but by extens. of the mother); fig. to *regenerate:*—bear, beget, be born, bring forth, conceive, be delivered of, gender, make, spring.

1081. γέννημα **gĕnnēma,** *ghen´-nay-mah;* from *1080; offspring;* by anal. *produce* (lit. or fig.):—fruit, generation.

1082. Γεννησαρέτ **Gĕnnēsarĕt,** *ghen-nay-sar-et´;* of Heb. or. [comp. 3672]; *Gennesaret* (i.e. *Kinnereth*), a lake and plain in Pal.:—Gennesaret.

1083. γέννησις **gĕnnēsis,** *ghen´-nay-sis;* from *1080; nativity:*—birth.

1084. γεννητός **gĕnnētŏs,** *ghen-nay-tos´;* from *1080; born:*—they that are born.

1085. γένος **gĕnŏs,** *ghen´-os;* from *1096; "kin"* (abstr. or concr., lit. or fig., indiv. or coll.):—born, country (-man), diversity, generation, kind (-red), nation, offspring, stock.

1086. Γεργεσηνός **Gĕrgĕsēnŏs,** *gher-ghes-ay-nos´;* of Heb. or. [1622]; a *Gergesene* (i.e. *Girgashite*) or one of the aborigines of Pal.:—Gergesene.

1087. γερουσία **gĕrŏusia,** *gher-oo-see´-ah;* from *1088;* the *eldership,* i.e. (collect.) the Jewish *Sanhedrim:*—senate.

1088. γέρων **gĕrōn,** *gher´-own;* of uncert. affin. [comp. *1094*]; *aged:*—old.

1089. γεύομαι **gĕuŏmai,** *ghyoo´-om-ahee;* a prim. verb; to *taste;* by impl. to *eat;* fig. to *experience* (good or ill):—eat, taste.

1090. γεωργέω **gĕōrgĕō,** *gheh-ore-gheh´-o;* from *1092;* to *till* (the soil):—dress.

1091. γεώργιον **gĕōrgiŏn,** *gheh-ore´-ghee-on;* neut. of a (presumed) der. of *1092; cultivable,* i.e. a *farm:*—husbandry.

1092. γεωργός **gĕōrgŏs,** *gheh-ore-gos´;* from 1093 and the base of *2041;* a *land-worker,* i.e. *farmer:*—husbandman.

1093. γῆ **gē,** *ghay;* contr. from a prim. word; *soil;* by extens. a *region,* or the solid part or the whole of the *terrene* globe (includ. the occupants in each application):—country, earth (-ly), ground, land, world.

1094. γῆρας **gēras,** *ghay´-ras;* akin to *1088; senility:*—old age.

1095. γηράσκω **gēraskō,** *ghay-ras´-ko;* from *1094;* to *be senescent:*—be (wax) old.

1096. γίνομαι **ginŏmai,** *ghin´-om-ahee;* a prol. and mid. form of a prim. verb; to *cause to be* (*"gen"-erate*), i.e. (reflex.) to *become* (*come into being*), used with great latitude (lit. fig., intens., etc.):—arise be assembled, be (come, -fall, -have self), be brought (to pass), (be) come (to pass), continue, be divided, be done, draw, be ended, fall, be finished, follow, be found, be fulfilled, + God forbid, grow, happen, have, be kept, be made, be married, be ordained to be, partake, pass, be performed, be published, require, seem, be showed, × soon as it was, sound, be taken, be turned, use, wax, will, would, be wrought.

1097. γινώσκω **ginōskō,** *ghin-oce´-ko;* a prol. form of a prim. verb; to *"know"* (absol.), in a great variety of applications and with many impl. (as follow, with others not thus clearly expressed):—allow, be aware (of), feel, (have) known (-ledge), perceive, be resolved, can speak, be sure, understand.

1098. γλεῦκος **glĕukŏs,** *glyoo´-kos;* akin to *1099; sweet* wine, i.e. (prop.) *must* (fresh juice), but used of the more saccharine (and therefore highly inebriating) fermented *wine:*—new wine.

1099. γλυκύς **glukus,** *gloo-koos´;* of uncert. affin.; *sweet* (i.e. not bitter nor salt):—sweet, fresh.

1100. γλῶσσα **glōssa,** *gloce´-sah;* of uncert. affin.; the *tongue;* by impl. a *language* (spec. one naturally unacquired):—tongue.

1101. γλωσσόκομον **glōssŏkŏmŏn,** *gloce-sok´-om-on;* from *1100* and the base of *2889;* prop. a *case* (to keep mouthpieces of wind-instruments in), i.e. (by extens.) a *casket* or (spec.) *purse:*—bag.

1102. γναφεύς **gnaphĕus,** *gnaf-yuce´;* by var. for a der. from κνάπτω **knaptō** (to *tease* cloth); a cloth-*dresser:*—fuller.

1103. γνήσιος **gnēsiŏs,** *gnay´-see-os;* from the same as *1077; legitimate* (of birth), i.e. *genuine:*—own, sincerity, true.

1104. γνησίως **gnēsiōs,** *gnay-see´-oce;* adv. from *1103; genuinely,* i.e. *really:*—naturally.

1105. γνόφος **gnŏphŏs,** *gnof´-os;* akin to *3509; gloom* (as of a storm):—blackness.

1106. γνώμη **gnōmē,** *gno´-may;* from *1097; cognition,* i.e. (subj.) *opinion,* or (obj.) *resolve* (*counsel, consent,* etc.):—advice, + agree, judgment, mind, purpose, will.

1107. γνωρίζω **gnōrizō,** *gno-rid´-zo;* from a der. of *1097;* to *make known;* subj. to *know:*—certify, declare, make known, give to understand, do to wit, wot.

1108. γνῶσις **gnōsis,** *gno´-sis;* from *1097; knowing* (the act), i.e. (by impl.) *knowledge:*—knowledge, science.

1109. γνώστης **gnōstēs,** *gnoce´-tace;* from *1097;* a *knower:*—expert.

1110. γνωστός **gnōstŏs,** *gnoce-tos´;* from *1097;* well *known:*—acquaintance, (which may be) known, notable.

1111. γογγύζω **gŏgguzō,** *gong-good´-zo;* of uncert. der.; to *grumble:*—murmur.

1112. γογγυσμός **gŏggusmŏs,** *gong-goos-mos´;* from *1111;* a *grumbling:*—grudging, murmuring.

1113. γογγυστής **gŏggustēs,** *gong-goos-tace´;* from *1111;* a *grumbler:*—murmurer.

1114. γόης **gŏēs,** *gŏ´-ace;* from γοάω **gŏaō** (to *wail*); prop. a *wizard* (as *muttering* spells), i.e. (by impl.) an *impostor:*—seducer.

1115. Γολγοθᾶ **Golgŏtha,** *gol-goth-ah´;* of Chald. or. [comp. 1538]; *the skull; Golgotha,* a knoll near Jerus.:—Golgotha.

1116. Γόμοῤῥα **Gŏmŏrrha,** *gom´-or-hrhah;* of Heb. or. [6017]; *Gomorrha* (i.e. *'Amorah*), a place near the Dead Sea:—Gomorrha.

1117. γόμος **gŏmŏs,** *gom´-os;* from *1073;* a *load* (as *filling*), i.e. (spec.) a *cargo,* or (by extens.) *wares:*—burden, merchandise.

1118. γονεύς **gŏnĕus,** *gon-yooce´;* from the base of *1096;* a *parent:*—parent.

1119. γονύ **gŏnu,** *gon-oo´;* of uncert. affin.; the *"knee":*—knee (× -l).

1120. γονυπετέω **gŏnupĕtĕō,** *gon-oo-pet-eh´-o;* from a comp. of *1119* and the alt. of *4098;* to *fall* on the *knee:*—bow the knee, kneel down.

1121. γράμμα **gramma,** *gram´-mah;* from *1125;* a *writing,* i.e. a *letter, note, epistle, book,* etc.; plur. *learning:*—bill, learning, letter, scripture, writing, written.

1122. γραμματεύς **grammatĕus,** *gram-mat-yooce´;* from *1121;* a *writer,* i.e. (professionally) *scribe* or *secretary:*—scribe, town-clerk.

1123. γραπτός **graptŏs,** *grap-tos´;* from *1125; inscribed* (fig.):—written.

1124. γραφή **graphē,** *graf-ay´;* from *1125;* a *document,* i.e. holy *Writ* (or its contents or a statement in it):—scripture.

1125. γράφω **graphō,** *graf´-o;* a prim. verb; to *"grave",* espec. to *write;* fig. to *describe:*—describe, write (-ing, -ten).

1126. γραώδης **graōdēs,** *grah-o´-dace;* from γραῦς **graus** (an *old woman*) and *1491; crone-like,* i.e. *silly:*—old wives'.

1127. γρηγορεύω **grēgŏrĕuō,** *gray-gor-yoo´-o;* from *1453;* to *keep awake,* i.e. *watch* (lit. or fig.):—be vigilant, wake, (be) watch (-ful).

1128. γυμνάζω **gumnazō,** *goom-nad´-zo;* from *1131;* to *practise naked* (in the games), i.e. *train* (fig.):—exercise.

1129. γυμνασία **gumnasia,** *goom-nas-ee´-ah;* from *1128; training,* i.e. (fig.) *asceticism:*—exercise.

1130. γυμνητεύω **gumnētĕuō,** *goom-nayt-yoo´-o;* from a der. of *1131;* to *strip,* i.e. (reflex.) *go poorly clad:*—be naked.

1131. γυμνός **gumnŏs,** *goom-nos´;* of uncert. affin.; *nude* (absol. or rel., lit. or fig.):—naked.

1132. γυμνότης **gumnŏtēs,** *goom-not´-ace;* from *1131; nudity* (absol. or comp.):—nakedness.

1133. γυναικάριον **gunaikariŏn,** *goo-nahee-kar´-ee-on;* a dimin. from *1135;* a *little* (i.e. *foolish*) *woman:*—silly woman.

1134. γυναικεῖος **gunaikĕiŏs,** *goo-nahee-ki´-os;* from *1135; feminine:*—wife.

1135. γυνή **gunē,** *goo-nay´;* prob. from the base of *1096;* a *woman;* spec. a *wife:*—wife, woman.

1136. Γώγ **Gōg,** *gogue;* of Heb. or. [1463]; *Gog,* a symb. name for some future Antichrist:—Gog.

1137. γωνία **gōnia,** *go-nee´-ah;* prob. akin to *1119;* an *angle:*—corner, quarter.

Δ

1138. Δαβίδ **Dabid,** *dab-eed´;* of Heb. or. [1732]; *Dabid* (i.e. *David*), the Isr. king:—David.

1139. δαιμονίζομαι **daimŏnizŏmai,** *dahee-mon-id´-zom-ahee;* mid. from *1142;* to *be exercised by a dæmon:*—have a (be vexed with, be possessed with) devil (-s).

1140. δαιμόνιον **daimŏniŏn,** *dahee-mon´-ee-on;* neut. of a der. of *1142;* a *dæmonic being;* by extens. a *deity:*—devil, god.

1141. δαιμονιώδης **daimŏniōdēs,** *dahee-mon-ee-o´-dace;* from *1140* and *1142; dæmon-like:*—devilish.

1142. δαίμων **daimōn,** *dah´-ee-mown;* from δαίω **daiō** (to *distribute* fortunes); a *dæmon* or supernatural spirit (of a bad nature):—devil.

1143. δάκνω **daknō,** *dak´-no;* a prol. form of a prim. root: to *bite,* i.e. (fig.) *thwart:*—bite.

1144. δάκρυ **dakru,** *dak´-roo;* or
δάκρυον **dakruŏn,** *dak´-roo-on;* of uncert. affin.; a *tear:*—tear.

1145. δακρύω **dakruō,** *dak-roo´-o;* from *1144;* to *shed tears:*—weep. Comp. *2799.*

1146. δακτύλιος **daktuliŏs,** *dak-too´-lee-os;* from *1147;* a *finger*-ring:—ring.

1147. δάκτυλος **daktulŏs,** *dak´-too-los;* prob. from *1176;* a *finger:*—finger.

1148. Δαλμανουθά **Dalmanŏutha,** *dal-man-oo-thah´;* prob. of Chald. or.; *Dalmanūtha,* a place in Pal.:—Dalmanutha.

1149. Δαλματία **Dalmatia,** *dal-mat-ee´-ah;* prob. of for. der.; *Dalmatia,* a region of Europe:—Dalmatia.

1150. δαμάζω **damazō,** *dam-ad´-zo;* a var. of an obs. prim. of the same mean.; to *tame:*—tame.

1151. δάμαλις **damalis,** *dam´-al-is;* prob. from the base of *1150;* a *heifer* (as *tame*):—heifer.

1152. Δάμαρις **Damaris,** *dam´-ar-is;* prob. from the base of *1150;* perh. *gentle; Damaris,* an Athenian woman:—Damaris.

1153. Δαμασκηνός **Damaskēnŏs,** *dam-as-kay-nos´;* from *1154;* a *Damascene* or inhab. of Damascus:—Damascene.

1154. Δαμασκός **Damaskŏs,** *dam-as-kos´;* of Heb. or. [1884]; *Damascus,* a city of Syria:—Damascus.

1155. δανείζω **danĕizō,** *dan-ide´-zo;* from *1156;* to *loan* on interest; reflex. to *borrow:*—borrow, lend.

1156. δάνειον **danĕiŏn,** *dan´-i-on;* from δάνος **danŏs** (a *gift*); prob. akin to the base of *1325;* a *loan:*—debt.

1157. δανειστής **danĕistēs,** *dan-ice-tace´;* from *1155;* a *lender:*—creditor.

1158. Δανιήλ **Daniēl,** *dan-ee-ale´;* of Heb. or [1840]; *Daniel,* an Isr.:—Daniel.

1159. δαπανάω **dapanaō,** *dap-an-ah´-o;* from *1160;* to *expend,* i.e. (in a good sense) to *incur cost,* or (in a bad one) to *waste:*—be at charges, consume, spend.

1160. δαπάνη **dapanē,** *dap-an´-ay;* from δάπτω **daptō** (to *devour*); *expense* (as *consuming*):—cost.

1161. δέ **dĕ,** *deh;* a prim. particle (adversative or continuative); *but, and,* etc.:—also, and, but, moreover, now [*often unexpressed in English*].

1162. δέησις **dĕēsis,** *deh´-ay-sis;* from *1189;* a *petition:*—prayer, request, supplication.

1163. δεῖ **dĕi,** *die;* 3d pers. sing. act. pres. of *1210;* also δεόν **dĕŏn,** *deh-on´;* neut. act. part. of the same; both used impers.; *it is* (*was,* etc.) *necessary* (as *binding*):—behoved, be meet, must (needs), (be) need (-ful), ought, should.

1164. δεῖγμα **dĕigma,** *dīgh´-mah;* from the base of *1166;* a *specimen* (as *shown*):—example.

1165. δειγματίζω **dĕigmatizō,** *dīgh-mat-id´-zo;* from *1164;* to *exhibit:*—make a shew.

1166. δεικνύω **dĕiknuō,** *dike-noo´-o;* a prol. form of an obs. prim. of the same mean.; to *show* (lit. or fig.):—shew.

1167. δειλία **dĕilia,** *di-lee´-ah;* from *1169; timidity:*—fear.

1168. δειλιάω **dĕiliaō,** *di-lee-ah´-o;* from *1167;* to *be timid:*—be afraid.

1169. δειλός **dĕilŏs,** *di-los´;* from δέος **dĕŏs** (*dread*); *timid,* i.e. (by impl.) *faithless:*—fearful.

1170. δεῖνα **dĕina,** *di´-nah;* prob. from the same as *1171* (through the idea of forgetting the name as *fearful,* i.e. *strange*); *so and so* (when the person is not specified):—such a man.

1171. δεινῶς **dĕinōs,** *di-noce´;* adv. from a der. of the same as *1169; terribly,* i.e. *excessively:*—grievously, vehemently.

1172. δειπνέω **dĕipnĕō,** *dipe-neh´-o;* from *1173;* to *dine,* i.e. take the principal (or evening) meal:—sup (× -per).

1173. δεῖπνον **dĕipnŏn,** *dipe´-non;* from the same as *1160; dinner,* i.e. the chief meal (usually in the evening):—feast, supper.

1174. δεισιδαιμονέστερος **dĕisidaimŏnĕstĕrŏs,** *dice-ee-dahee-mon-es´-ter-os;* the comp. of a der. of the base of *1169* and *1142; more religious* than others:—too superstitious.

1175. δεισιδαιμονία **dĕisidaimŏnia,** *dice-ee-dahee-mon-ee´-ah;* from the same as *1174; religion:*—superstition.

1176. δέκα **dĕka,** *dek´-ah;* a prim. number; *ten:*—[eight-] een, ten.

1177. δεκαδύο **dĕkaduŏ,** *dek-ad-oo´-ō;* from *1176* and *1417; two* and *ten,* i.e. *twelve:*—twelve.

1178. δεκαπέντε **dĕkapĕntĕ,** *dek-ap-en´-teh;* from *1176* and *4002; ten* and *five,* i.e. *fifteen:*—fifteen.

1179. Δεκάπολις **Dĕkapŏlis,** *dek-ap´-ol-is;* from *1176* and *4172;* the *ten-city* region; the *Decapolis,* a district in Syria:—Decapolis.

1180. δεκατέσσαρες **dĕkatĕssarĕs,** *dek-at-es´-sar-es;* from *1176* and *5064; ten* and *four,* i.e. *fourteen:*—fourteen.

1181. δεκάτη **dĕkatē,** *dek-at´-ay;* fem. of *1182;* a *tenth,* i.e. as a percentage or (tech.) *tithe:*—tenth (part), tithe.

1182. δέκατος **dĕkatŏs,** *dek´-at-os;* ordinal from *1176; tenth:*—tenth.

1183. δεκατόω **dĕkatŏō,** *dek-at-ŏ´-o;* from *1181;* to *tithe,* i.e. to *give* or *take a tenth:*—pay (receive) tithes.

1184. δεκτός **dĕktŏs,** *dek-tos´;* from *1209; approved;* (fig.) *propitious:*—accepted (-table).

1185. δελεάζω **dĕlĕazō,** *del-eh-ad´-zo;* from the base of *1388;* to *entrap,* i.e. (fig.) *delude:*—allure, beguile, entice.

1186. δένδρον **dĕndrŏn,** *den´-dron;* prob. from δρύς **drus** (an *oak*); a *tree:*—tree.

1187. δεξιολάβος **dĕxiŏlabŏs,** *dex-ee-ol-ab´-os;* from *1188* and *2983;* a *guardsman* (as if *taking the right*) or light-armed soldier:—spearman.

1188. δεξιός **dĕxiŏs,** *dex-ee-os´;* from *1209;* the *right* side or (fem.) hand (as that which usually *takes*):—right (hand, side).

1189. δέομαι **dĕŏmai,** *deh´-om-ahee;* mid. of *1210;* to *beg* (as *binding oneself*), i.e. *petition:*—beseech, pray (to), make request. Comp. *4441.*

δεόν **dĕŏn.** See *1163.*

1190. Δερβαῖος **Dĕrbaiŏs,** *der-bah´ee-os;* from *1191;* a *Derbæan* or inhab. of Derbe:—of Derbe.

1191. Δέρβη **Dĕrbē,** *der´-bay;* of for. or.; *Derbè,* a place in Asia Minor:—Derbe.

1192. δέρμα **dĕrma,** *der´-mah;* from 1194; a *hide:*—skin.

1193. δερμάτινος **dĕrmatinŏs,** *der-mat´-ee-nos;* from *1192;* made of *hide:*—leathern, of a skin.

1194. δέρω **dĕrō,** *der´-o;* a prim. verb; prop. to *flay,* i.e. (by impl.) to *scourge,* or (by anal.) to *thrash:*—beat, smite.

1195. δεσμεύω **dĕsmĕuō,** *des-myoo´-o;* from a (presumed) der. of *1196;* to *be a binder* (*captor*), i.e. to *enchain* (a prisoner), to *tie on* (a load):—bind.

1196. δεσμέω **dĕsmĕō,** *des-meh´-o;* from *1199;* to *tie,* i.e. *shackle:*—bind.

1197. δεσμή **dĕsmē,** *des-may´;* from *1196;* a *bundle:*—bundle.

1198. δέσμιος **dĕsmiŏs,** *des´-mee-os;* from *1199;* a *captive* (as *bound*):—in bonds, prisoner.

1199. δεσμόν **dĕsmŏn,** *des-mon´;* or
δεσμός **dĕsmŏs,** *des-mos´;* neut. and masc. respectively from *1210;* a *band,* i.e. *ligament* (of the body) or *shackle* (of a prisoner); fig. an *impediment* or *disability:*—band, bond, chain, string.

1200. δεσμοφύλαξ **dĕsmŏphulax,** *des-mof-oo´-lax;* from *1199* and *5441;* a *jailer* (as *guarding* the *prisoners*):—jailer, keeper of the prison.

1201. δεσμωτήριον **dĕsmōtēriŏn,** *des-mo-tay´-ree-on;* from a der. of *1199* (equiv. to *1196*); a *place of bondage,* i.e. a *dungeon:*—prison.

1202. δεσμώτης **dĕsmōtēs,** *des-mo´-tace;* from the same as *1201;* (pass.) a *captive:*—prisoner.

1203. δεσπότης **dĕspŏtēs,** *des-pot´-ace;* perh. from *1210* and πόσις **pŏsis** (a *husband*); an absolute *ruler* ("despot"):—Lord, master.

1204. δεῦρο **dĕurŏ,** *dyoo´-rŏ;* of uncert. affin.; *here;* used also imper. *hither!;* and of time, *hitherto:*—come (hither), hither [-to].

1205. δεῦτε **dĕutĕ,** *dyoo´-teh;* from *1204* and an imper. form of εἶμι **ĕimi** (to *go*); *come hither!:*—come, × follow.

1206. δευτεραῖος **dĕutĕraiŏs,** *dyoo-ter-ah´-yos;* from *1208; secondary,* i.e. (spec.) on the *second* day:—next day.

1207. δευτερόπρωτος **dĕutĕrŏprōtŏs,** *dyoo-ter-op´-ro-tos;* from *1208* and *4413; second-first,* i.e. (spec.) a designation of the Sabbath immediately after the Paschal week (being the *second* after Passover day, and the *first* of the seven Sabbaths intervening before Pentecost):—second . . . after the first.

1208. δεύτερος **dĕutĕrŏs,** *dyoo´-ter-os;* as the comp. of *1417;* (ordinal) *second* (in time, place, or rank; also adv.):—afterward, again, second (-arily, time).

1209. δέχομαι **dĕchŏmai,** *dekh´-om-ahee;* mid. of a prim. verb; to *receive* (in various applications, lit. or fig.):—accept, receive, take. Comp. *2983.*

1210. δέω **dĕō,** *deh´-o;* a prim. verb; to *bind* (in various applications, lit. or fig.):—bind, be in bonds, knit, tie, wind. See also *1163, 1189.*

1211. δή **dē,** *day;* prob. akin to *1161;* a particle of emphasis or explicitness; *now, then,* etc.:—also, and, doubtless, now, therefore.

1212. δῆλος **dēlŏs,** *day´-los;* of uncert. der.; *clear:*— + bewray, certain, evident, manifest.

1213. δηλόω **dēlŏō,** *day-lŏ´-o;* from *1212;* to *make plain* (by words):—declare, shew, signify.

1214. Δημᾶς **Dēmas,** *day-mas´;* prob. for *1216; Demas,* a Chr.:—Demas.

1215. δημηγορέω **dēmēgŏrĕō,** *day-may-gor-eh´-o;* from a comp. of *1218* and *58;* to *be a people-gatherer,* i.e. to *address* a public assembly:—make an oration.

1216. Δημήτριος **Dēmētriŏs,** *day-may´-tree-os;* from Δημήτηρ **Dēmētēr** (*Ceres*); *Demetrius,* the name of an Ephesian and of a Chr.:—Demetrius.

1217. δημιουργός **dēmiŏurgŏs,** *day-me-oor-gos´;* from *1218* and *2041;* a *worker* for the *people,* i.e. *mechanic* (spoken of the *Creator*):—maker.

1218. δῆμος **dēmŏs,** *day´-mos;* from *1210;* the *public* (as *bound* together socially):—people.

1219. δημόσιος **dēmŏsiŏs,** *day-mos´-ee-os;* from *1218; public;* (fem. sing. dat. as adv.) *in public:*—common, openly, publickly.

1220. δηνάριον **dēnariŏn,** *day-nar´-ee-on;* of Lat. or.; a *denarius* (or *ten asses*):—pence, penny [-worth].

1221. δήποτε **dēpŏtē,** *day´-pot-eh;* from *1211* and *4218;* a particle of generalization; *indeed, at any time:*—(what-) soever.

1222. δήπου **dēpŏu,** *day´-poo;* from *1211* and *4225;* a particle of asseveration; *indeed doubtless:*—verily.

1223. διά **dia,** *dee-ah´;* a prim. prep. denoting the *channel* of an act; *through* (in very wide applications, local, causal or occasional):—after, always, among, at, to avoid, because of (that), briefly, by, for (cause) . . . fore, from, in, by occasion of, of, by reason of, for sake, that, thereby, therefore, × though, through (-out), to, wherefore, with (-in). In composition it retains the same general import.

Δία **Dia.** See *2203.*

1224. διαβαίνω **diabainō,** *dee-ab-ah´ee-no;* from *1223* and the base of *939;* to *cross:*—come over, pass (through).

1225. διαβάλλω **diaballō,** *dee-ab-al´-lo;* from *1223* and *906;* (fig.) to *traduce:*—accuse.

1226. διαβεβαιόομαι **diabĕbaiŏŏmai,** *dee-ab-eb-ahee-ŏ´-om-ahee;* mid. of a comp. of *1223* and *950;* to *confirm thoroughly* (by words), i.e. *asseverate:*—affirm constantly.

1227. διαβλέπω **diablĕpō,** *dee-ab-lep´-o;* from *1223* and *991;* to *look through,* i.e. *recover* full *vision;*—see clearly.

1228. διάβολος **diabŏlŏs,** *dee-ab´-ol-os;* from *1225;* a *traducer;* spec. *Satan* [comp. 7854]:—false accuser, devil, slanderer.

1229. διαγγέλλω **diaggĕllō,** *de-ang-gel´-lo;* from *1223* and the base of *32;* to *herald thoroughly:*—declare, preach, signify.

1230. διαγίνομαι **diaginŏmai,** *dee-ag-in´-om-ahee;* from *1223* and *1096;* to *elapse meanwhile:*— × after, be past, be spent.

1231. διαγινώσκω **diaginōskō,** *dee-ag-in-o´-sko;* from *1223* and *1097;* to *know thoroughly,* i.e. *ascertain exactly:*—(would) enquire, know the uttermost.

1232. διαγνωρίζω **diagnōrizō,** *dee-ag-no-rid´-zo;* from *1123* and *1107;* to *tell abroad:*—make known.

1233. διάγνωσις **diagnōsis,** *dee-ag´-no-sis;* from *1231;* (magisterial) *examination* ("diagnosis"):—hearing.

1234. διαγογγύζω **diagŏgguzō,** *dee-ag-ong-good´-zo;* from *1223* and *1111;* to *complain throughout* a crowd:—murmur.

1235. διαγρηγορέω **diagrēgŏrĕō,** *dee-ag-ray-gor-eh´-o;* from *1223* and *1127;* to *waken thoroughly:*—be awake.

1236. διάγω **diagō,** *dee-ag´-o;* from *1223* and *71;* to *pass* time or life:—lead life, living.

1237. διαδέχομαι **diadĕchŏmai,** *dee-ad-ekh´-om-ahee;* from *1223* and *1209;* to *receive in turn,* i.e. (fig.) *succeed to:*—come after.

1238. διάδημα **diadēma,** *dee-ad´-ay-mah;* from a comp. of *1223* and *1210;* a *"diadem"* (as *bound about* the head):—crown. Comp. *4735.*

1239. διαδίδωμι **diadidōmi,** *dee-ad-id´-o-mee;* from *1223* and *1325;* to *give throughout* a crowd, i.e. *deal out;* also to *deliver* over (as to a successor):—(make) distribute (-ion), divide, give.

1240. διάδοχος **diadŏchŏs,** *dee-ad´-okh-os;* from *1237;* a *successor* in office:—room.

1241. διαζώννυμι **diazōnnumi,** *dee-az-own´-noo-mee;* from *1223* and *2224;* to *gird tightly:*—gird.

1242. διαθήκη **diathēkē,** *dee-ath-ay´-kay;* from *1303;* prop. a *disposition,* i.e. (spec.) a *contract* (espec. a devisory *will*):—covenant, testament.

1243. διαίρεσις **diairĕsis,** *dee-ah´-ee-res-is;* from *1244;* a *distinction* or (concr.) *variety:*—difference, diversity.

1244. διαιρέω **diairĕō,** *dee-ahee-reh´-o;* from *1223* and *138;* to *separate,* i.e. *distribute:*—divide.

1245. διακαθαρίζω **diakatharizō,** *dee-ak-ath-ar-id´-zo;* from *1223* and *2511;* to *cleanse perfectly,* i.e. (spec.) *winnow:*—throughly purge.

1246. διακατελέγχομαι **diakatĕlĕgchŏmai,** *dee-ak-at-el-eng´-khom-ahee;* mid. from *1223* and a comp. of *2596* and *1651;* to *prove downright,* i.e. *confute:*—convince.

1247. διακονέω **diakŏnĕō,** *dee-ak-on-eh´-o;* from *1249;* to *be an attendant,* i.e. *wait upon* (menially or as a host, friend or [fig.] teacher); techn. to *act as a* Chr. *deacon:*—(ad-) minister (unto), serve, use the office of a deacon.

1248. διακονία **diakŏnia,** *dee-ak-on-ee´-ah;* from *1249; attendance* (as a servant, etc.); fig. (eleemosynary) *aid,* (official) *service* (espec. of the Chr. teacher, or techn. of the *diaconate*):—(ad-) minister (-ing, -tration, -try), office, relief, service (-ing).

1249. διάκονος **diakŏnŏs,** *dee-ak´-on-os;* prob. from an obs. διάκω **diakō** (to *run* on errands; comp. *1377*); an *attendant,* i.e. (gen.) a *waiter* (at table or in other menial duties); spec. a Chr. *teacher* and *pastor* (techn. a *deacon* or *deaconess*):—deacon, minister, servant.

1250. διακόσιοι **diakŏsiŏi,** *dee-ak-os´-ee-oy;* from *1364* and *1540; two hundred:*—two hundred.

1251. διακούομαι **diakŏuŏmai,** *dee-ak-oo´-om-ahee;* mid. from *1223* and *191;* to *hear throughout,* i.e. *patiently listen* (to a prisoner's plea):—hear.

1252. διακρίνω **diakrinō,** *dee-ak-ree´-no;* from *1223* and *2919;* to *separate thoroughly,* i.e. (lit. and reflex.) to *withdraw* from, or (by impl.) *oppose;* fig. to *dscriminate* (by impl. *decide*), or (reflex.) *hesitate:*—contend, make (to) differ (-ence), discern, doubt, judge, be partial, stagger, waver.

1253. διάκρισις **diakrisis,** *dee-ak´-ree-sis;* from *1252;* judicial *estimation:*—discern (-ing), disputation.

1254. διακωλύω **diakōluō,** *dee-ak-o-loo´-o;* from *1223* and *2967;* to *hinder altogether,* i.e. *utterly prohibit:*—forbid.

1255. διαλαλέω **dialalĕō,***dee-al-al-eh´-o;* from *1223* and *2980;* to *talk throughout* a company, i.e. *converse* or (gen.) *publish:*—commune, noise abroad.

1256. διαλέγομαι **dialĕgŏmai,** *dee-al-eg´-om-ahee;* mid. from *1223* and *3004;* to *say thoroughly,* i.e. *discuss* (in argument or exhortation):—dispute, preach (unto), reason (with), speak.

1257. διαλείπω **dialĕipō,** *dee-al-i´-po;* from *1223* and *3007;* to *leave off in the middle,* i.e. *intermit:*—cease.

1258. διάλεκτος **dialĕktŏs,** *dee-al´-ek-tos;* from *1256;* a (mode of) *discourse,* i.e. *"dialect":*—language, tongue.

1259. διαλλάσσω **diallassō,** *dee-al-las´-so;* from *1223* and *236;* to *change thoroughly,* i.e. (ment.) to *conciliate:*—reconcile.

1260. διαλογίζομαι **dialŏgizŏmai,** *dee-al-og-id´-zom-ahee;* from *1223* and *3049;* to *reckon thoroughly,* i.e. (gen.) to *deliberate* (by reflection or discussion):—cast in mind, consider, dispute, muse, reason, think.

1261. διαλογισμός **dialŏgismŏs,** *dee-al-og-is-mos´;* from *1260; discussion,* i.e. (internal) *consideration* (by impl. *purpose*), or (external) *debate:*—dispute, doubtful (-ing), imagination, reasoning, thought.

1262. διαλύω **dialuō,** *dee-al-oo´-o;* from *1223* and *3089;* to *dissolve utterly:*—scatter.

1263. διαμαρτύρομαι **diamarturŏmai,** *dee-amar-too´-rom-ahee;* from *1223* and *3140;* to *attest* or *protest earnestly,* or (by impl.) *hortatively:*—charge, testify (unto), witness.

1264. διαμάχομαι **diamachŏmai,** *dee-am-akh´-om-ahee;* from *1223* and *3164;* to *fight fiercely* (in altercation):—strive.

1265. διαμένω **diamĕnō,** *dee-am-en´-o;* from *1223* and *3306;* to *stay constantly* (in being or relation):—continue, remain.

1266. διαμερίζω **diamĕrizō,** *dee-am-er-id´-zo;* from *1223* and *3307;* to *partition thoroughly* (lit. in distribution, fig. in dissension):—cloven, divide, part.

1267. διαμερισμός **diamĕrismŏs,** *dee-am-er-is-mos´;* from *1266; disunion* (of opinion and conduct):—division.

1268. διανέμω **dianĕmō,** *dee-an-em´-o;* from *1223* and the base of *3551;* to *distribute,* i.e. (of information) to *disseminate:*—spread.

1269. διανεύω **dianĕuō,** *dee-an-yoo´-o;* from *1223* and *3506;* to *nod* (or *express* by signs) *across* an intervening space:—beckon.

1270. διανόημα **dianŏēma,** *dee-an-ŏ´-ay-mah;* from a comp. of *1223* and *3539;* something *thought through,* i.e. a *sentiment:*—thought.

1271. διάνοια **dianŏia,** *dee-an´-oy-ah;* from *1223* and *3563; deep thought,* prop. the faculty (*mind* or its *disposition*), by impl. its exercise:—imagination, mind, understanding.

1272. διανοίγω **dianŏigō,** *dee-an-oy´-go;* from *1223* and *455;* to *open thoroughly,* lit. (as a first-born) or fig. (to *expound*):—open.

1273. διανυκτερεύω **dianuktĕrĕuō,** *dee-an-ook-ter-yoo´-o;* from *1223* and a der. of *3571;* to *sit up the whole night:*—continue all night.

1274. διανύω **dianuō,** *dee-an-oo´-o;* from *1223* and ἀνύω **anuō** (to *effect*); to *accomplish thoroughly:*—finish.

1275. διαπαντός **diapantŏs,** *dee-ap-an-tos´;* from *1223* and the genit. of *3956; through all* time, i.e. (adv.) *constantly:*—alway (-s), continually.

1276. διαπεράω **diapĕraō,** *dee-ap-er-ah´-o;* from *1223* and a der. of the base of *4008;* to *cross entirely:*—go over, pass (over), sail over.

1277. διαπλέω **diaplĕō,** *dee-ap-leh´-o;* from *1223* and *4126;* to *sail through:*—sail over.

1278. διαπονέω **diapŏnĕō,** *dee-ap-on-eh´-o;* from *1223* and a der. of *4192;* to *toil through,* i.e. (pass.) *be worried:*—be grieved.

1279. διαπορεύομαι **diapŏrĕuŏmai,** *dee-ap-or-yoo´-om-ahee;* from *1223* and *4198;* to *travel through:*—go through, journey in, pass by.

1280. διαπορέω **diapŏrĕō,** *dee-ap-or-eh´-o;* from *1223* and *639;* to *be thoroughly nonplussed:*—(be in) doubt, be (much) perplexed.

1281. διαπραγματεύομαι **diapragmatĕuŏmai,** *dee-ap-rag-mat-yoo´-om-ahee;* from *1223* and *4231;* to *thoroughly occupy oneself,* i.e. (trans. and by impl.) to *earn* in business:—gain by trading.

1282. διαπρίω **diapriō,** *dee-ap-ree´-o;* from *1223* and the base of *4249;* to *saw asunder,* i.e. (fig.) to *exasperate:*—cut (to the heart).

1283. διαρπάζω **diarpazō,** *dee-ar-pad´-zo;* from *1223* and *726;* to *seize asunder,* i.e. *plunder:*—spoil.

1284. διαῤῥήσσω **diarrhēssō,** *dee-ar-hrayce´-so;* from *1223* and *4486;* to *tear asunder:*—break, rend.

1285. διασαφέω **diasaphĕō,** *dee-as-af-eh´-o;* from *1223* and σαφής **saphēs** (*clear*); to *clear thoroughly,* i.e. (fig.) *declare:*—tell unto.

1286. διασείω **diasĕiō,** *dee-as-i´-o;* from *1223* and *4579;* to *shake thoroughly,* i.e. (fig.) to *intimidate:*—do violence to.

1287. διασκορπίζω **diaskŏrpizō,** *dee-as-kor-pid´-zo;* from *1223* and *4650;* to *dissipate,* i.e. (gen.) to *rout* or *separate;* spec. to *winnow;* fig. to *squander:*—disperse, scatter (abroad), strew, waste.

1288. διασπάω **diaspaō,** *dee-as-pah´-o;* from *1223* and *4685;* to *draw apart,* i.e. *sever* or *dismember:*—pluck asunder, pull in pieces.

1289. διασπείρω **disapĕirō,** *dee-as-pi´-ro;* from *1223* and *4687;* to *sow throughout,* i.e. (fig.) *distribute* in foreign lands:—scatter abroad.

1290. διασπορά **diaspŏra,** *dee-as-por-ah´;* from *1289; dispersion,* i.e. (spec. and concr.) the (converted) Isr. *resident* in Gentile countries:—(which are) scattered (abroad).

1291. διαστέλλομαι **diastĕllŏmai,** *dee-as-tel´-lom-ahee;* mid. from *1223* and *4724;* to *set* (oneself) *apart* (fig. *distinguish*), i.e. (by impl.) to *enjoin:*—charge, that which was (give) commanded (-ment).

1292. διάστημα **diastēma,** *dee-as´-tay-mah;* from *1339;* an *interval:*—space.

1293. διαστολή **diastŏlē,** *dee-as-tol-ay´;* from *1291;* a *variation:*—difference, distinction.

1294. διαστρέφω **diastrĕphō,** *dee-as-tref´-o;* from *1223* and *4762;* to *distort,* i.e. (fig.) *misinterpret,* or (mor.) *corrupt:*—perverse (-rt), turn away.

1295. διασώζω **diasōzō,** *dee-as-odze´-o;* from *1223* and *4982;* to *save thoroughly,* i.e. (by impl. or anal.) to *cure, preserve, rescue,* etc.:—bring safe, escape (safe), heal, make perfectly whole, save.

1296. διαταγή **diatagē,** *dee-at-ag-ay´;* from *1299; arrangement,* i.e. *institution:*—instrumentality.

1297. διάταγμα **diatagma,** *dee-at´-ag-mah;* from *1299;* an *arrangement,* i.e. (authoritative) *edict:*—commandment.

1298. διαταράσσω **diatarassō**, *dee-at-ar-as´-so;* from *1223* and *5015;* to *disturb wholly,* i.e. *agitate* (with alarm):—trouble.

1299. διατάσσω **diatassō**, *dee-at-as´-so;* from *1223* and *5021;* to *arrange thoroughly,* i.e. (spec.) *institute, prescribe,* etc.:—appoint, command, give, (set in) order, ordain.

1300. διατελέω **diatĕlĕō**, *dee-at-el-eh´-o;* from *1223* and *5055;* to *accomplish thoroughly,* i.e. (subj.) to *persist:*—continue.

1301. διατηρέω **diatērĕō**, *dee-at-ay-reh´-o;* from *1223* and *5083;* to *watch thoroughly,* i.e. (pos. and trans.) to *observe* strictly, or (neg. and reflex.) to *avoid* wholly:—keep.

1302. διατί **diati**, *dee-at-ee´;* from *1223* and *5101; through what* cause ?, i.e. *why?:*—wherefore, why.

1303. διατίθεμαι **diatithĕmai**, *dee-at-ith´-em-ahee;* mid. from *1223* and *5087;* to *put apart,* i.e. (fig.) *dispose* (by assignment, compact or bequest):—appoint, make, testator.

1304. διατρίβω **diatribō**, *dee-at-ree´-bo;* from *1223* and the base of *5147;* to *wear through* (time), i.e. *remain:*—abide, be, continue, tarry.

1305. διατροφή **diatrŏphē**, *dee-at-rof-ay´;* from a comp. of *1223* and *5142; nourishment:*—food.

1306. διαυγάζω **diaugazō**, *dee-ŏw-gad´-zo;* from *1223* and *826;* to *glimmer through,* i.e. *break* (as day):—dawn.

1307. διαφανής **diaphanēs**, *dee-af-an-ace´;* from *1223* and *5316; appearing through,* i.e. *"diaphanous":*—transparent.

1308. διαφέρω **diaphĕrō**, *dee-af-er´-o;* from *1223* and *5342;* to *bear through, i.e. (lit.) transport;* usually to *bear apart,* i.e. (obj.) to *toss about* (fig. *report*); subj. to *"differ,"* or (by impl.) *surpass:*—be better, carry, differ from, drive up and down, be (more) excellent, make matter, publish, be of more value.

1309. διαφεύγω **diaphĕugō**, *dee-af-yoo´-go;* from *1223* and *5343;* to *flee through,* i.e. *escape:*—escape.

1310. διαφημίζω **diaphēmizō**, *dee-af-ay-mid´-zo;* from *1223* and a der. of *5345;* to *report thoroughly,* i.e. *divulgate:*—blaze abroad, commonly report, spread abroad, fame.

1311. διαφθείρω **diaphthĕirō**, *dee-af-thi´-ro;* from *1225* and *5351;* to *rot thoroughly,* i.e. (by impl.) to *ruin* (pass. *decay* utterly, fig. *pervert*):—corrupt, destroy, perish.

1312. διαφθορά **diaphthŏra**, *dee-af-thor-ah´;* from *1311; decay:*—corruption.

1313. διάφορος **diaphŏrŏs**, *dee-af´-or-os;* from *1308; varying;* also *surpassing:*—differing, divers, more excellent.

1314. διαφυλάσσω **diaphulassō**, *dee-af-oo-las´-so;* from *1223* and *5442;* to *guard thoroughly,* i.e. *protect:*—keep.

1315. διαχειρίζομαι **diachĕirizŏmai**, *dee-akh-i-rid´-zom-ahee;* from *1223* and a der. of *5495;* to *handle thoroughly,* i.e. *lay* violent *hands* upon:—kill, slay.

1316. διαχωρίζομαι **diachōrizŏmai**, *dee-akh-o-rid´-zom-ahee;* from *1223* and the mid. of *5563;* to *remove* (oneself) *wholly,* i.e. *retire:*—depart.

1317. διδακτικός **didaktikŏs**, *did-ak-tik-os´;* from *1318; instructive* ("didactic"):—apt to teach.

1318. διδακτός **didaktŏs**, *did-ak-tos´;* from *1321;* (subj.) *instructed* or (obj.) *communicated* by teaching:—taught, which . . . teacheth.

1319. διδασκαλία **didaskalia**, *did-as-kal-ee´-ah;* from *1320; instruction* (the function or the information):—doctrine, learning, teaching.

1320. διδάσκαλος **didaskalŏs**, *did-as´-kal-os;* from *1321;* an *instructor* (gen. or spec.):—doctor, master, teacher.

1321. διδάσκω **didaskō**, *did-as´-ko;* a prol. (caus.) form of a prim. verb δάω **daō** (to *learn*); to *teach* (in the same broad application):—teach.

1322. διδαχή **didachē**, *did-akh-ay´;* from *1321; instruction* (the act or the matter):—doctrine, hath been taught.

1323. δίδραχμον **didrachmŏn**, *did´-rakh-mon;* from *1364* and *1406;* a *double drachma* (*didrachm*):—tribute.

1324. Δίδυμος **Didumŏs**, *did´-oo-mos;* prol. from *1364; double,* i.e. *twin; Didymus,* a Chr.:—Didymus.

1325. δίδωμι **didōmi**, *did´-o-mee;* a prol. form of a prim. verb (which is used as an altern. in most of the tenses); to *give* (used in a very wide application, prop. or by impl. lit. or fig.; greatly modified by the connection):—adventure, bestow, bring forth, commit, deliver (up), give, grant, hinder, make, minister, number, offer, have power, put, receive, set, shew, smite (+ with the hand), strike (+ with the palm of the hand), suffer, take, utter, yield.

1326. διεγείρω **diĕgĕirō**, *dee-eg-i´-ro;* from *1223* and *1453;* to *wake fully,* i.e. *arouse* (lit. or fig.):—arise, awake, raise, stir up.

1327. διέξοδος **diĕxŏdŏs**, *dee-ex´-od-os;* from *1223* and *1841;* an *outlet through,* i.e. prob. an open *square* (from which roads diverge):—highway.

1328. διερμηνευτής **diĕrmēnĕutēs**, *dee-er-main-yoo-tace´;* from *1329;* an *explainer:*—*interpreter.*

1329. διερμηνεύω **diĕrmēnĕuō**, *dee-er-main-yoo´ o;* from *1223* and *2059;* to *explain thoroughly;* by impl. to *translate:*—expound, interpret (-ation).

1330. διέρχομαι **diĕrchŏmai**, *dee-er´-khom-ahee;* from *1223* and *2064;* to *traverse* (lit):—come, depart, go (about, abroad, every where, over, through, throughout), pass (by, over, through, throughout), pierce through, travel, walk through.

1331. διερωτάω **diĕrōtaō**, *dee-er-o-tah´-o;* from *1223* and *2065;* to *question throughout,* i.e. *ascertain* by interrogation:—make enquiry for.

1332. διετής **diĕtēs**, *dee-et-ace´;* from *1364* and *2094; of two years* (in age):—two years old.

1333. διετία **diĕtia**, *dee-et-ee´-a;* from *1332;* a space of *two years* (*biennium*):—two years.

1334. διηγέομαι **diēgĕŏmai**, *dee-ayg-eh´-om-ahee;* from *1223* and *2233;* to *relate fully:*—declare, shew, tell.

1335. διήγεσις **diēgĕsis**, *dee-ayg´-es-is;* from *1334;* a *recital:*—declaration.

1336. διηνεκές **diēnĕkĕs**, *dee-ay-nek-es´;* neut. of a comp. of *1223* and a der. of an alt. of *5342; carried through,* i.e. (adv. with *1519* and *3588* pref.) *perpetually:*— + continually, for ever.

1337. διθάλασσος **dithalassŏs**, *dee-thal´-as-sos;* from *1364* and *2281; having two seas,* i.e. a *sound* with a double outlet:—where two seas met.

1338. διϊκνέομαι **diïknĕŏmai**, *dee-ik-neh´-om-ahee;* from *1223* and the base of *2425;* to *reach through,* i.e. *penetrate:*—pierce.

1339. διΐστημι **diïstēmi**, *dee-is´-tay-mee;* from *1223* and *2476;* to *stand apart,* i.e. (reflex.) to *remove, intervene:*—go further, be parted, after the space of.

1340. διϊσχυρίζομαι **diïschurizŏmai**, *dee-is-khoo-rid´-zom-ahee;* from *1223* and a der. of *2478:* to *stout* it *through,* i.e. *asseverate:*—confidently (constantly) affirm.

1341. δικαιοκρισία **dikaiŏkrisia**, *dik-ah-yok-ris-ee´-ah;* from *1342* and *2920;* a *just sentence:*—righteous judgment.

1342. δίκαιος **dikaiŏs**, *dik´-ah-yos;* from *1349; equitable* (in character or act); by impl. *innocent, holy* (absol. or rel.):—just, meet, right (-eous).

1343. δικαιοσύνη **dikaiŏsunē**, *dik-ah-yos-oo´-nay;* from *1342; equity* (of character or act); spec. (Chr.) *justification:*—righteousness.

1344. δικαιόω **dikaiŏō**, *dik-ah-yo´-o;* from *1342;* to *render* (i.e. *show* or *regard* as) *just* or *innocent:*—free, justify (-ier), be righteous.

1345. δικαίωμα **dikaiōma**, *dik-ah´-yo-mah;* from *1344;* an *equitable deed;* by impl. a *statute* or *decision:*—judgment, justification, ordinance, righteousness.

1346. δικαίως **dikaiōs**, *dik-ah´-yoce;* adv. from *1342; equitably:*—justify, (to) righteously (-ness).

1347. δικαίωσις **dikaiōsis**, *dik-ah´-yo-sis;* from *1344; acquittal* (for Christ's sake):—justification.

1348. δικαστής **dikastēs**, *dik-as-tace´;* from a der. of *1349;* a *judger:*—judge.

1349. δίκη **dikē**, *dee´-kay;* prob. from *1166; right* (as self-*evident*), i.e. *justice* (the principle, a decision, or its execution):—judgment, punish, vengeance.

1350. δίκτυον **diktuŏn,** *dik´-too-on;* prob. from a prim. verb δίκω **dikō** (to *cast*); a *seine* (for fishing):—net.

1351. δίλογος **dilŏgŏs,** *dil´-og-os;* from *1364* and *3056; equivocal,* i.e. telling a different story:—double-tongued.

1352. διό **diŏ,** *dee-ŏ´;* from *1223* and *3739; through which* thing, i.e. *consequently:*—for which cause, therefore, wherefore.

1353. διοδεύω **diŏdĕuō,** *dee-od-yoo´-o;* from *1223* and *3593; to travel through:*—go throughout, pass through.

1354. Διονύσιος **Diŏnusiŏs,** *dee-on-oo´-see-os;* from Διόνυσος **Diŏnusŏs** (*Bacchus*); *reveller; Dionysius,* an Athenian:—Dionysius.

1355. διόπερ **diŏpĕr,** *dee-op´-er;* from *1352* and *4007; on which very account:*—wherefore.

1356. διοπετής **diŏpĕtēs,** *dee-op-et´-ace;* from the alt. of *2203* and the alt. of *4098; sky-fallen* (i.e. an *aerolite*):—which fell down from Jupiter.

1357. διόρθωσις **diŏrthōsis,** *dee-or´-tho-sis;* from a comp. of *1223* and a der. of *3717,* mean. to *straighten thoroughly; rectification,* i.e. (spec.) the Messianic *restauration:*—reformation.

1358. διορύσσω **diŏrussō,** *dee-or-oos´-so;* from *1223* and *3736;* to *penetrate* burglariously:—break through (up).

Διός **Diŏs.** See *2203.*

1359. Διόσκουροι **Diŏskŏurŏi,** *dee-os´-koo-roy;* from the alt. of *2203* and a form of the base of *2877; sons of Jupiter,* i.e. the twins *Dioscuri:*—Castor and Pollux.

1360. διότι **diŏti,** *dee-ot´-ee;* from *1223* and *3754; on the very account that,* or *inasmuch as:*—because (that), for, therefore.

1361. Διοτρεφής **Diŏtrĕphēs,** *dee-ot-ref-ace´;* from the alt. of *2203* and *5142; Jove-nourished; Diotrephes,* an opponent of Christianity:—Diotrephes.

1362. διπλοῦς **diplŏus,** *dip-looce´;* from *1364* and (prob.) the base of *4119; two-fold:*—double, two-fold more.

1363. διπλόω **diplŏō,** *dip-lŏ´-o;* from *1362;* to *render two-fold:*—double.

1364. δίς **dis,** *dece;* adv. from *1417; twice:*—again, twice.

Δίς **Dis.** See *2203.*

1365. διστάζω **distazō,** *dis-tad´-zo;* from *1364;* prop. to *duplicate,* i.e. (ment.) to *waver* (in opinion):—doubt.

1366. δίστομος **distŏmŏs,** *dis´-tom-os;* from *1364* and *4750; double-edged:*—with two edges, two-edged.

1367. δισχίλιοι **dischiliŏi,** *dis-khil´-ee-oy;* from *1364* and *5507: two thousand:*—two thousand.

1368. διϋλίζω **diulizō,** *dee-oo-lid´-zo;* from *1223* and ὑλίζω **hulizō,** *hoo-lid´-zo* (to *filter*); to *strain out:*—strain at [*prob. by misprint*].

1369. διχάζω **dichazō,** *dee-khad´-zo;* from a der. of *1364;* to *make apart,* i.e. *sunder* (fig. *alienate*):—set at variance.

1370. διχοστασία **dichŏstasia,** *dee-khos-tas-ee´-ah;* from a der. of *1364* and *4714; disunion,* i.e. (fig.) *dissension:*—division, sedition.

1371. διχοτομέω **dichŏtŏmĕō,** *dee-khot-om-eh´-o;* from a comp. of a der. of *1364* and a der. of τέμνω **tĕmnō** (to *cut*); to *bisect,* i.e. (by extens.) to *flog* severely:—cut asunder (in sunder).

1372. διψάω **dipsaō,** *dip-sah´-o;* from a var. of *1373;* to *thirst* for (lit. or fig.):—(be, be a-) thirst (-y).

1373. δίψος **dipsŏs,** *dip´-sos;* of uncert. affin.; *thirst:*—thirst.

1374. δίψυχος **dipsuchŏs,** *dip´-soo-khos;* from *1364* and *5590; two-spirited,* i.e. *vacillating* (in opinion or purpose):—double minded.

1375. διωγμός **diōgmŏs,** *dee-ogue-mos´;* from *1377; persecution:*—persecution.

1376. διώκτης **diōktēs,** *dee-oke´-tace;* from *1377;* a *persecutor:*—persecutor.

1377. διώκω **diōkō,** *dee-o´-ko;* a prol. (and caus.) form of a prim. verb δίω **diō** (to *flee;* comp. the base of *1169* and *1249*); to *pursue* (lit. or fig.); by impl. to *persecute:*—ensue, follow (after), given to, (suffer) persecute (-ion), press toward.

1378. δόγμα **dŏgma,** *dog´-mah;* from the base of *1380;* a *law* (civil, cer. or eccl.):—decree, ordinance.

1379. δογματίζω **dŏgmatizō,** *dog-mat-id´-zo;* from *1378;* to *prescribe* by statute, i.e. (reflex.) to *submit* to cer. *rule:*—be subject to ordinances.

1380. δοκέω **dŏkĕō,** *dok-eh´-o;* a prol. form of a prim. verb δόκω **dŏkō,** *dok´-o* (used only as an alt. in certain tenses: comp. the base of *1166*) of the same mean.; to *think;* by impl. to *seem* (truthfully or uncertainly):—be accounted, (of own) please (-ure), be of reputation, seem (good), suppose, think, trow.

1381. δοκιμάζω **dŏkimazō,** *dok-im-ad´-zo;* from *1384;* to *test* (lit. or fig.); by impl. to *approve:*—allow, discern, examine, × like, (ap-) prove, try.

1382. δοκιμή **dŏkimē,** *dok-ee-may´;* from the same as *1384; test* (abstr. or concr.); by impl. *trustiness:*—experience (-riment), proof, trial.

1383. δοκίμιον **dŏkimiŏn,** *dok-im´-ee-on;* neut. of a presumed der. of *1382;* a *testing;* by impl. *trustworthiness:*—trial, trying.

1384. δόκιμος **dŏkimŏs,** *dok´-ee-mos;* from *1380;* prop. *acceptable* (*current* after assayal), i.e. *approved:*—approved, tried.

1385. δοκός **dŏkŏs,** *dok-os´;* from *1209* (through the idea of *holding* up); a *stick* of timber:—beam.

δόκω **dŏkō.** See *1380.*

1386. δόλιος **dŏliŏs,** *dol´-ee-os;* from *1388; guileful:*—deceitful.

1387. δολιόω **dŏliŏō,** *dol-ee-ŏ´-o;* from *1386;* to *be guileful:*—use deceit.

1388. δόλος **dŏlŏs,** *dol´-os;* from an obs. prim. δέλλω **dĕllō** (prob. mean. to *decoy;* comp. *1185*); a *trick* (*bait*), i.e. (fig.) *wile:*—craft, deceit, guile, subtilty.

1389. δολόω **dŏlŏō,** *dol-ŏ´-o;* from *1388;* to *ensnare,* i.e. (fig.) *adulterate:*—handle deceitfully.

1390. δόμα **dŏma,** *dom´-ah;* from the base of *1325;* a *present:*—gift.

1391. δόξα **dŏxa,** *dox´-ah;* from the base of *1380; glory* (as very *apparent*), in a wide application (lit. or fig., obj. or subj.):—dignity, glory (-ious), honour, praise, worship.

1392. δοξάζω **dŏxazō,** *dox-ad´-zo;* from *1391;* to *render* (or *esteem*) *glorious* (in a wide application):—(make) glorify (-ious), full of (have) glory, honour, magnify.

1393. Δορκάς **Dŏrkas,** *dor-kas´; gazelle; Dorcas,* a Chr. woman:—Dorcas.

1394. δόσις **dŏsis,** *dos´-is;* from the base of *1325;* a *giving;* by impl. (concr.) a *gift:*—gift, giving.

1395. δότης **dŏtēs,** *dot´-ace;* from the base of *1325;* a *giver:*—giver.

1396. δουλαγωγέω **dŏulagŏgĕō,** *doo-lag-ogue-eh´-o;* from a presumed comp. of *1401* and *71;* to *be a slave-driver,* i.e. to *enslave* (fig. *subdue*):—bring into subjection.

1397. δουλεία **dŏulĕia,** *doo-li´-ah;* from *1398; slavery* (cer. or fig.):—bondage.

1398. δουλεύω **dŏulĕuō,** *dool-yoo´-o;* from *1401;* to *be a slave* to (lit. or fig., invol. or vol.):—be in bondage, (do) serve (-ice).

1399. δούλη **dŏulē,** *doo´-lay;* fem. of *1401;* a *female slave* (invol. or vol.):—handmaid (-en).

1400. δοῦλον **dŏulŏn,** *doo´-lon;* neut. of *1401; subservient:*—servant.

1401. δοῦλος **dŏulŏs,** *doo´-los;* from *1210;* a *slave* (lit. or fig., invol. or vol.; frequently therefore in a qualified sense of *subjection* or *subserviency*):—bond (-man), servant.

1402. δουλόω **dŏulŏō,** *doo-lŏ´-o;* from *1401;* to *enslave* (lit. or fig.):—bring into (be under) bondage, × given, become (make) servant.

1403. δοχή **dŏchē,** *dokh-ay´;* from *1209;* a *reception,* i.e. convivial *entertainment:*—feast.

1404. δράκων **drakōn,** *drak´-own;* prob. from an alt. form of δέρκομαι **dĕrkŏmai** (to *look*); a fabulous kind of *serpent* (perh. as supposed to *fascinate*):—dragon.

1405. δράσσομαι **drassŏmai,** *dras´-som-ahee;* perh. akin to the base of *1404* (through the idea of *capturing*); to *grasp,* i.e. (fig.) *entrap:*—take.

1406. δραχμή **drachmē,** *drakh-may´;* from *1405;* a *drachma* or (silver) coin (as *handled*):—piece (of silver).

δρέμω **drĕmō.** See *5143.*

1407. δρέπανον **drĕpanŏn,** *drep´-an-on;* from δρέπω **drĕpō** (to *pluck*); a gathering *hook* (espec. for harvesting):—sickle.

1408. δρόμος **drŏmŏs,** *drom´-os;* from the alt. of *5143;* a *race,* i.e. (fig.) *career:*—course.

1409. Δρούσιλλα **Drŏusilla,** *droo´-sil-lah;* a fem. dimin. of *Drusus* (a Rom. name); *Drusilla,* a member of the Herodian family:—Drusilla.

δῦμι **dumi.** See *1416.*

1410. δύναμαι **dunamai,** *doo´-nam-ahee;* of uncert. affin.; to *be able* or *possible:*—be able, can (do, + -not), could, may, might, be possible, be of power.

1411. δύναμις **dunamis,** *doo´-nam-is;* from *1410; force* (lit. or fig.); spec. miraculous *power* (usually by impl. a *miracle* itself):—ability, abundance, meaning, might (-ily, -y, -y deed), (worker of) miracle (-s), power, strength, violence, mighty (wonderful) work.

1412. δυναμόω **dunamŏō,** *doo-nam-ŏ´-o;* from *1411;* to *enable:*—strengthen.

1413. δυνάστης **dunastēs,** *doo-nas´-tace;* from *1410;* a *ruler* or *officer:*—of great authority, mighty, potentate.

1414. δυνατέω **dunatĕō,** *doo-nat-eh´-o;* from *1415;* to *be efficient* (fig.):—be mighty.

1415. δυνατός **dunatŏs,** *doo-nat-os´;* from *1410; powerful* or *capable* (lit. or fig.); neut. *possible:*—able, could, (that is) mighty (man), possible, power, strong.

1416. δύνω **dunō,** *doo´-no;* or

δῦμι **dumi,** *doo´-mee;* prol. forms of an obs. prim. δύω **duō,** *doo´-o* (to *sink*); to *go "down":*—set.

1417. δύο **duŏ,** *doo´-ŏ;* a prim. numeral; *"two":*—both, twain, two.

1418. δυσ- **dus-,** *doos;* a prim. inseparable particle of uncert. der.; used only in composition as a pref.; *hard,* i.e. *with difficulty:*— + hard, + grievous, *etc.*

1419. δυσβάστακτος **dusbastaktŏs,** *doos-bas´-tak-tos;* from *1418* and a der. of *941; oppressive:*—grievous to be borne.

1420. δυσεντερία **dusĕntĕria,** *doos-en-ter-ee´-ah;* from *1418* and a comp. of *1787* (mean. a *bowel*); a *"dysentery":*—bloody flux.

1421. δυσερμήνευτος **dusĕrmēnĕutŏs,** *doos-er-mane´-yoo-tos;* from *1418* and a presumed der. of *2059; difficult of explanation:*—hard to be uttered.

1422. δύσκολος **duskŏlŏs,** *doos´-kol-os;* from *1418* and κόλον **kŏlŏn** (*food*); prop. *fastidious about eating* (*peevish*), i.e. (gen.) *impracticable:*—hard.

1423. δυσκόλως **duskŏlōs,** *doos-kol´-oce;* adv. from *1422; impracticably:*—hardly.

1424. δυσμή **dusmē,** *doos-may´;* from *1416;* the sun-*set,* i.e. (by impl.) the *western* region:—west.

1425. δυσνόητος **dusnŏētŏs,** *doos-nŏ´-ay-tos;* from *1418* and a der. of *3539; difficult of perception:*—hard to be understood.

1426. δυσφημία **dusphēmia,** *doos-fay-mee´-ah;* from a comp. of *1418* and *5345; defamation:*—evil report.

δύω **duō.** See *1416.*

1427. δώδεκα **dōdĕka,** *do´-dek-ah;* from *1417* and *1176; two* and *ten,* i.e. a *dozen:*—twelve.

1428. δωδέκατος **dōdĕkatŏs,** *do-dek´-at-os;* from *1427; twelfth:*—twelfth.

1429. δωδεκάφυλον **dōdĕkaphulŏn,** *do-dek-af´-oo-lon;* from *1427* and *5443;* the *commonwealth* of Israel:—twelve tribes.

1430. δῶμα **dōma,** *do´-mah;* from δέμω **dĕmō** (to *build*); prop. an *edifice,* i.e. (spec.) a *roof:*—housetop.

1431. δωρεά **dōrĕa,** *do-reh-ah´;* from *1435;* a *gratuity:*—gift.

1432. δωρεάν **dōrĕan,** *do-reh-an´;* acc. of *1431* as adv.; *gratuitously* (lit. or fig.):—without a cause, freely, for naught, in vain.

1433. δωρέομαι **dōrĕŏmai,** *do-reh´-om-ahee;* mid. from *1435;* to *bestow* gratuitously:—give.

1434. δώρημα **dōrēma,** *do´-ray-mah;* from *1433;* a *bestowment:*—gift.

1435. δῶρον **dōrŏn,** *do´-ron;* a *present;* spec. a *sacrifice:*—gift, offering.

E

1436. ἔα **ĕa,** *eh´-ah;* appar. imper. of *1439;* prop. *let* it *be,* i.e. (as interj.) *aha!:*—let alone.

1437. ἐάν **ĕan,** *eh-an´;* from *1487* and *302;* a *conditional* particle; *in case* that, *provided,* etc.; often used in connection with other particles to denote *indefiniteness* or *uncertainty:*—before, but, except, (and) if, (if) so, (what-, whither-) soever, though, when (-soever), whether (or), to whom, [who-] so (-ever). See *3361.*

ἐάν μή **ĕan mē.** See *3361.*

1438. ἑαυτοῦ **hĕautŏu,** *heh-ŏw-too´* (incl. all the other cases); from a reflex. pron. otherwise obsol. and the gen. (dat. or acc.) of *846; him-* (*her-, it-, them-,* also [in conjunction with the pers. pron. of the other persons] *my-, thy-, our-, your-*) *self* (*selves*), etc.:—alone, her (own, -self), (he) himself, his (own), itself, one (to) another, our (thine) own (-selves), + that she had, their (own, own selves), (of) them (-selves), they, thyself, you, your (own, own conceits, own selves, -selves).

1439. ἐάω **ĕaō,** *eh-ah´-o;* of uncert. affin.; to *let be,* i.e. *permit* or *leave* alone:—commit, leave, let (alone), suffer. See also *1436.*

1440. ἑβδομήκοντα **hĕbdŏmēkŏnta,** *heb-dom-ay´-kon-tah;* from *1442* and a modified form of *1176, seventy:*—seventy, three score and ten.

1441. ἑβδομηκοντακίς **hĕbdŏmēkŏntakis,** *heb-dom-ay-kon-tak-is´;* multiple adv. from *1440; seventy times:*—seventy times.

1442. ἕβδομος **hĕbdŏmŏs,** *heb´-dom-os;* ordinal from *2033; seventh:*—seventh.

1443. Ἐβέρ **Ĕbĕr,** *eb-er´;* of Heb. or. [5677]; *Eber,* a patriarch:—Eber.

1444. Ἑβραϊκός **Hĕbraïkŏs,** *heb-rah-ee-kos´;* from *1443; Hebraïc* or the *Jewish* language:—Hebrew.

1445. Ἑβραῖος **Hĕbraiŏs,** *heb-rah´-yos;* from *1443;* a *Hebræan* (i.e. Hebrew) or *Jew:*—Hebrew.

1446. Ἑβραΐς **Hĕbraïs,** *heb-rah-is´;* from *1443;* the *Hebraistic* (i.e. *Hebrew*) or *Jewish* (*Chaldee*) language:—Hebrew.

1447. Ἑβραϊστί **Hĕbraïsti,** *heb-rah-is-tee´;* adv. from *1446; Hebraistically* or in the Jewish (Chaldee) language:—in (the) Hebrew (tongue).

1448. ἐγγίζω **ĕggizō,** *eng-id´-zo;* from *1451;* to make *near,* i.e. (reflex.) *approach:*—approach, be at hand, come (draw) near, be (come, draw) nigh.

1449. ἐγγράφω **ĕggraphō,** *eng-graf´-o;* from *1722* and *1125;* to *"engrave",* i.e. *inscribe:*—write (in).

1450. ἔγγυος **ĕgguŏs,** *eng´-goo-os;* from *1722* and γυῖον **guiŏn** (a *limb*); *pledged* (as if *articulated* by a member), i.e. a *bondsman:*—surety.

1451. ἐγγύς **ĕggus,** *eng-goos´;* from a prim. verb ἄγχω **agchō** (to *squeeze* or *throttle;* akin to the base of *43*); *near* (lit. or fig., of place or time):—from, at hand, near, nigh (at hand, unto), ready.

1452. ἐγγύτερον **ĕggutĕrŏn,** *eng-goo´-ter-on;* neut. of the comp. of *1451; nearer:*—nearer.

1453. ἐγείρω **ĕgĕirō,** *eg-i´-ro;* prob. akin to the base of *58* (through the idea of *collecting* one's faculties); to *waken* (trans. or intrans.), i.e. *rouse* (lit. from sleep, from sitting or lying, from disease, from death; or fig. from obscurity, inactivity, ruins, nonexistence):—awake, lift (up), raise (again, up), rear up, (a-) rise (again, up), stand, take up.

1454. ἔγερσις **ĕgĕrsis,** *eg´-er-sis;* from *1453;* a *resurgence* (from death):—resurrection.

1455. ἐγκάθετος **ĕgkathĕtŏs,** *eng-kath´-et-os;* from *1722* and a der. of *2524; subinduced,* i.e. surreptitiously *suborned* as a lier-in-wait:—spy.

1456. ἐγκαίνια **ĕgkainia,** *eng-kah´ee-nee-ah;* neut. plur. of a presumed comp. from *1722* and *2537; innovatives,* i.e. (spec.) *renewal* (of religious services after the Antiochian interruption):—dedication.

1457. ἐγκαινίζω **ĕgkainizō,** *eng-kahee-nid´-zo;* from *1456;* to *renew,* i.e. *inaugurate:*—consecrate, dedicate.

1458. ἐγκαλέω **ĕgkalĕō,** *eng-kal-eh´-o;* from *1722* and *2564;* to *call in* (as a debt or demand), i.e. *bring to account* (*charge, criminate,* etc.):—accuse, call in question, implead, lay to the charge.

1459. ἐγκαταλείπω **ĕgkatalĕipō,** *en-kat-al-i´-po;* from *1722* and *2641;* to *leave behind in* some place, i.e. (in a good sense) *let remain over,* or (in a bad one) to *desert:*—forsake, leave.

1460. ἐγκατοικέω **ĕgkatŏikĕō,** *eng-kat-oy-keh´-o;* from *1722* and *2730;* to *settle down in* a place, i.e. *reside:*—dwell among.

1461. ἐγκεντρίζω **ĕgkĕntrizō,** *eng-ken-trid´-zo;* from *1722* and a der. of *2759;* to *prick in,* i.e. *ingraft:*—graff in (-to).

1462. ἔγκλημα **ĕgklēma,** *eng´-klay-mah;* from *1458;* an *accusation,* i.e. *offence* alleged:—crime laid against, laid to charge.

1463. ἐγκομβόομαι **ĕgkŏmbŏŏmai,** *eng-kom-bŏ´-om-ahee;* mid. from *1722* and κομβόω **kŏmbŏō** (to *gird*); to *engirdle* oneself (for labor), i.e. fig. (the apron being a badge of servitude) to *wear* (in token of mutual deference):—be clothed with.

1464. ἐγκοπή **ĕgkŏpē,** *eng-kop-ay´;* from *1465;* a *hindrance:*—× hinder.

1465. ἐγκόπτω **ĕgkŏptō,** *eng-kop´-to;* from *1722* and *2875;* to *cut into,* i.e. (fig.) *impede, detain:*—hinder, be tedious unto.

1466. ἐγκράτεια **ĕgkratĕia,** *eng-krat´-i-ah;* from *1468; self-control* (espec. *continence*):—temperance.

1467. ἐγκρατεύομαι **ĕgkratĕuŏmai,** *eng-krat-yoo´-om-ahee;* mid. from *1468;* to *exercise self-restraint* (in diet and chastity):—can([-not]) contain, be temperate.

1468. ἐγκρατής **ĕgkratēs,** *eng-krat-ace´;* from *1722* and *2904; strong in* a thing (*masterful*), i.e. (fig. and reflex.) *self-controlled* (in appetite, etc.):—temperate.

1469. ἐγκρίνω **ĕgkrinō,** *eng-kree´-no;* from *1722* and *2919;* to *judge in,* i.e. *count* among:—make of the number.

1470. ἐγκρύπτω **ĕkgruptō,** *eng-kroop´-to;* from *1722* and *2928;* to *conceal in,* i.e. *incorporate with:*—hid in.

1471. ἔγκυος **ĕgkuŏs,** *eng´-koo-os;* from *1722* and the base of *2949; swelling inside,* i.e. *pregnant:*—great with child.

1472. ἐγχρίω **ĕgchriō,** *eng-khree´-o;* from *1722* and *5548;* to *rub in* (oil), i.e. *besmear:*—anoint.

1473. ἐγώ **ĕgō,** *eg-o´;* a prim. pron. of the first pres. *I* (only expressed when emphatic):—I, me. For the other cases and the plur. see *1691, 1698, 1700, 2248, 2249, 2254, 2257,* etc.

1474. ἐδαφίζω **ĕdaphizō,** *ed-af-id´-zo;* from *1475;* to *raze:*—lay even with the ground.

1475. ἔδαφος **ĕdaphŏs,** *ed´-af-os;* from the base of *1476;* a *basis* (*bottom*), i.e. the *soil:*—ground.

1476. ἑδραῖος **hĕdraiŏs,** *hed-rah´-yos;* from a der. of ἕζομαι **hĕzŏmai** (to *sit*); *sedentary,* i.e. (by impl.) *immovable:*—settled, stedfast.

1477. ἑδραίωμα **hĕdraiōma,** *hed-rah´-yo-mah;* from a der. of *1476;* a *support,* i.e. (fig.) *basis:*—ground.

1478. Ἐζεκίας **Ĕzĕkias,** *ed-zek-ee´-as;* of Heb. or. [2396]; *Ezekias* (i.e. *Hezekiah*), an Isr.:—Ezekias.

1479. ἐθελοθρησκεία **ĕthĕlŏthrēskĕia,** *eth-el-oth-race-ki´-ah;* from *2309* and *2356; voluntary* (*arbitrary* and *unwarranted*) *piety,* i.e. *sanctimony:*—will worship.

ἐθέλω **ĕthĕlō.** See *2309.*

1480. ἐθίζω **ĕthizō,** *eth-id´-zo;* from *1485;* to *accustom,* i.e. (neut. pass. part.) *customary:*—custom.

1481. ἐθνάρχης **ĕthnarchēs,** *eth-nar´-khace;* from *1484* and *746;* the *governor* [not king] *of a district:*—ethnarch.

1482. ἐθνικός **ĕthnikŏs,** *eth-nee-kos´;* from *1484; national* ("*ethnic*"), i.e. (spec.) a *Gentile:*—heathen (man).

1483. ἐθνικῶς **ĕthnikōs,** *eth-nee-koce´;* adv. from *1482; as a Gentile:*—after the manner of Gentiles.

1484. ἔθνος **ĕthnŏs,** *eth´-nos;* prob. from *1486;* a *race* (as of the same *habit*), i.e. a *tribe;* spec. a *foreign* (*non-Jewish*) one (usually by impl. *pagan*):—Gentile, heathen, nation, people.

1485. ἔθος **ĕthŏs,** *eth´-os;* from *1486;* a *usage* (prescribed by habit or law):—custom, manner, be wont.

1486. ἔθω **ĕthō,** *eth´-o;* a prim. verb; to *be used* (by habit or conventionality); neut. perf. part. *usage:*—be custom (manner, wont).

1487. εἰ **ĕi,** *i;* a prim. particle of conditionality; *if, whether, that,* etc.:—forasmuch as, if, that, ([al-]) though, whether. Often used in connection or composition with other particles, espec. as in *1489, 1490, 1499, 1508, 1509, 1512, 1513, 1536, 1537.* See also *1437.*

1488. εἶ **ĕi,** *i;* second pers. sing. pres. of *1510;* thou *art:*—art, be.

1489. εἴγε **ĕigē,** *i´-gheh;* from *1487* and *1065; if indeed, seeing that, unless,* (with neg.) *otherwise:*—if (so be that, yet).

1490. εἰ δὲ μή(γε) **ĕi dĕ mē(gĕ),** *i deh may´(gheh);* from *1487, 1161* and *3361 (sometimes with 1065* added); *but if not:*—(or) else, if (not, otherwise), otherwise.

1491. εἶδος **ĕidŏs,** *i´-dos;* from *1492;* a *view,* i.e. *form* (lit. or fig.):—appearance, fashion, shape, sight.

1492. εἴδω **ĕidō,** *i´-do;* a prim. verb; used only in certain past tenses, the others being borrowed from the equiv. *3700* and *3708;* prop. to *see* (lit. or fig.); by impl. (in the perf. only) to *know:*—be aware, behold, × can (+ not tell), consider, (have) known (-ledge), look (on), perceive, see, be sure, tell, understand, wist, wot. Comp. *3700.*

1493. εἰδωλεῖον **ĕidōlĕiŏn,** *i-do-li´-on;* neut. of a presumed der. of *1497;* an *image-fane:*—idol's temple.

1494. εἰδωλόθυτον **ĕidōlŏthutŏn,** *i-do-loth´-oo-ton;* neut. of a comp. of *1497* and a presumed der. of *2380;* an *image-sacrifice,* i.e. part of an *idolatrous offering:*—(meat, thing that is) offered (in sacrifice, sacrificed) to (unto) idols.

1495. εἰδωλολατρεία **ĕidōlŏlatrĕia,** *i-do-lol-at ri´-ah;* from *1497* and *2999; image-worship* (lit. or fig.):—idolatry.

1496. εἰδωλολάτρης **ĕidōlŏlatrēs,** *i-do-lol-at´-race;* from *1497* and the base of *3000;* an *image-* (*servant* or) *worshipper* (lit. or fig.):—idolater.

1497. εἴδωλον **ĕidōlŏn,** *i´-do-lon;* from *1491;* an *image* (i.e. for worship); by impl. a heathen *god,* or (plur.) the *worship* of such:—idol.

1498. εἴην **ĕiēn,** *i´-ane;* optative (i.e. Eng. subjunctive) pres. of *1510* (includ. the other pers.); *might* (*could, would* or *should*) *be:*—mean, + perish, should be, was, were.

1499. εἰ καί **ĕi kai,** *i kahee;* from *1487* and *2532; if also* (or *even*):—if (that), though.

1500. εἰκῇ **ĕikē,** *i-kay´;* prob. from *1502* (through the idea of *failure*); *idly,* i.e. *without reason* (or *effect*):—without a cause, (in) vain (-ly.)

1501. εἴκοσι **ĕikŏsi,** *i´-kos-ee;* of uncert. affin.; a *score:*—twenty.

1502. εἴκω **ĕikō,** *i´-ko;* appar. a prim. verb; prop. to *be weak,* i.e. *yield:*—give place.

1503. εἴκω **ĕikō,** *i´-ko;* appar. a prim. verb [perh. akin to *1502* through the idea of *faintness* as a copy]; to *resemble:*—be like.

1504. εἰκών **ĕikōn,** *i-kone´;* from *1503;* a *likeness,* i.e. (lit.) *statute, profile,* or (fig.) *representation, resemblance:*—image.

1505. εἰλικρίνεια **ĕilikrinĕia,** *i-lik-ree´-ni-ah;* from *1506; clearness,* i.e. (by impl.) *purity* (fig.):—sincerity.

1506. εἰλικρινής **ĕilikrinēs,** *i-lik-ree-nace´;* from εἵλη **hĕilē** (the sun's *ray*) and *2919; judged by sunlight,* i.e. tested as *genuine* (fig.):—pure, sincere.

1507. εἱλίσσω **hĕilissō,** *hi-lis´-so;* a prol. form of a prim. but defective verb εἴλω **hĕilō** (of the same mean.); to *coil* or *wrap:*—roll together. See also *1667.*

1508. εἰ μή **ĕi mē,** *i may;* from *1487* and *3361; if not:*—but, except (that), if not, more than, save (only) that, saving, till.

1509. εἰ μή τι **ĕi mē ti,** *i may tee;* from *1508* and the neut. of *5100; if not somewhat:*—except.

1510. εἰμί **ĕimi,** *i-mee´;* first, pers. sing. pres. indic.; a prol. form of a prim. and defective verb; I *exist* (used only when emphatic):—am, have been, × it is I, was. See also *1488, 1498, 1511, 1527, 2258, 2071, 2070, 2075, 2076, 2771, 2468, 5600.*

1511. εἶναι **ĕinai,** *i´-nahee;* pres. infin. from *1510; to exist:*—am, are, come, is, × lust after, × please well, there is, to be, was.

εἵνεκεν **hĕinĕkĕn.** See *1752.*

1512. εἴ περ **ĕi pĕr,** *i per;* from *1487* and *4007; if perhaps:*—if so be (that), seeing, though.

1513. εἴ πως **ĕi pōs,** *i poce;* from *1487* and *4458; if somehow:*—if by any means.

1514. *εἰρηνεύω* **ěirēněuō,** *i-rane-yoo´-o;* from *1515;* to *be* (*act*) *peaceful:*—be at (have, live in) peace, live peaceably.

1515. *εἰρήνη* **ěirēnē,** *i-ray´-nay;* prob. from a prim. verb *εἴρω* **ěirō** (to *join*); *peace* (lit. or fig.); by impl. *prosperity:*—one, peace, quietness, rest, + set at one again.

1516. *εἰρηνικός* **ěirēnikŏs,** *i-ray-nee-kos´;* from *1515; pacific;* by impl. *salutary:*—peaceable.

1517. *εἰρηνοποιέω* **ěirēnŏpŏiěō,** *i-ray-nop-oy-eh´-o;* from *1518;* to *be a peace-maker,* i.e. (fig.) to *harmonize:*—make peace.

1518. *εἰρηνοποιός* **ěirēnŏpŏiŏs,** *i-ray-nop-oy-os´;* from *1515* and *4160; pacificatory,* i.e. (subj.) *peaceable:*—peacemaker.

εἴρω **ěirō.** See *1515, 4483, 5346.*

1519. *εἰς* **ěis,** *ice;* a prim. prep.; *to* or *into* (indicating the point reached or entered), of place, time, or (fig.) purpose (result, etc.); also in adv. phrases:—[abundant-] ly, against, among, as, at, [back-] ward, before, by, concerning, + continual, + far more exceeding, for [intent, purpose], fore, + forth, in (among, at unto, -so much that, -to), to the intent that, + of one mind, + never, of, (up-) on, + perish, + set at one again, (so) that, therefore (-unto), throughout, till, to (be, the end, -ward), (here-) until (-to), . . . ward, [where-] fore, with. Often used in composition with the same general import, but only with verbs (etc.) expressing motion (lit. or fig.).

1520. *εἷς* **hěis,** *hice;* (includ. the neut. [etc.] *ἕν* **hěn**); a prim. numeral; *one:*—a (-n, -ny, certain), + abundantly, man, one (another), only, other, some. See also *1527, 3367, 3391, 3762.*

1521. *εἰσάγω* **ěisagō,** *ice-ag´-o;* from *1519* and *71;* to *introduce* (lit. or fig.):—bring in (-to), (+ as to) lead into.

1522. *εἰσακούω* **ěisakŏuō,** *ice-ak-oo´-o;* from *1519* and *191;* to *listen* to:—hear.

1523. *εἰσδέχομαι* **ěisděchŏmai,** *ice-dekh´-om-ahee;* from *1519* and *1209;* to *take into* one's favor:—receive.

1524. *εἴσειμι* **ěisěimi,** *ice´-i-mee;* from *1519* and *εἶμι* **ěimi** (to *go*); to *enter:*—enter (go) into.

1525. *εἰσέρχομαι* **ěisěrchŏmai,** *ice-er´-khom-ahee;* from *1519* and *2064;* to *enter* (lit. or fig.):—× arise, come (in, into), enter in (-to), go in (through).

1526. *εἰσί* **ěisi,** *i-see´;* 3d pers. plur. pres. indic. of *1510;* they *are:*—agree, are, be, dure, × is, were.

1527. *εἷς καθ' εἷς* **hěis kath' hěis,** *hice kath hice;* from *1520* repeated with *2596* inserted; *severally:*—one by one.

1528. *εἰσκαλέω* **ěiskalěō,** *ice-kal-eh´-o;* from *1519* and *2564;* to *invite* in:—call in.

1529. *εἴσοδος* **ěisŏdŏs,** *ice´-od-os;* from *1519* and *3598;* an *entrance* (lit. or fig.):—coming, enter (-ing) in (to).

1530. *εἰσπηδάω* **ěispēdaō,** *ice-pay-dah´-o;* from *1519* and *πηδάω* **pēdaō** (to *leap*); to *rush in:*—run (spring) in.

1531. *εἰσπορεύομαι* **ěispŏrěuŏmai,** *ice-por-yoo´-om-ahee;* from *1519* and *4198;* to *enter* (lit. or fig.):—come (enter) in, go into.

1532. *εἰστρέχω* **ěistrěchō,** *ice-trekh´-o;* from *1519* and *5143;* to *hasten inward:*—run in.

1533. *εἰσφέρω* **ěisphěrō,** *ice-fer´-o;* from *1519* and *5342;* to *carry inward* (lit. or fig.):—bring (in), lead into.

1534. *εἶτα* **ěita,** *i´-tah;* of uncert. affin.; a particle of *succession* (in time or logical enumeration), *then, moreover:*—after that (-ward), furthermore, then. See also *1899.*

1535. *εἴτε* **ěitě,** *i´-teh;* from *1487* and *5037; if too:*—if, or, whether.

1536. *εἴ τις* **ěi tis,** *i tis;* from *1487* and *5100; if any:*—he that, if a (-ny) man ('s thing, from any, ought), whether any, whosoever.

1537. *ἐκ* **ěk,** *ek;* or

ἐξ **ěx,** *ex;* a prim. prep. denoting *origin* (the point *whence* motion or action proceeds), *from, out* (of place, time or cause; lit. or fig.; direct or remote):—after, among, × are, at betwixt (-yond), by (the means of), exceedingly, (+ abundantly above), for (-th), from (among, forth, up), + grudgingly, + heartily, × heavenly, × hereby, + very highly, in, . . . ly, (because, by reason) of, off (from), on, out among (from, of), over, since, × thenceforth, through, × unto, × vehemently, with (-out). Often used in composition, with the same general import; often of *completion.*

1538. *ἕκαστος* **hěkastŏs,** *hek´-as-tos;* as if a superlative of *ἕκας* **hěkas** (*afar*); *each* or *every:*—any, both, each (one), every (man, one, woman), particularly.

1539. *ἑκάστοτε* **hěkastŏtě,** *hek-as´-tot-eh;* as if from *1538* and *5119;* at *every time:*—always.

1540. *ἑκατόν* **hěkatŏn,** *hek-at-on´;* of uncert. affin.; a *hundred:*—hundred.

1541. *ἑκατονταέτης* **hěkatŏntaětēs,** *hek-at-on-tah-et´-ace;* from *1540* and *2094; centenarian:*—hundred years old.

1542. *ἑκατονταπλασίων* **hěkatŏntaplasiōn,** *hek-at-on-ta-plah-see´-own;* from *1540* and a presumed der. of *4111;* a *hundred times:*—hundredfold.

1543. *ἑκατοντάρχης* **hěkatŏntarchēs,** *hek-at-on-tar´-khace;* or

ἑκατόνταρχος **hěkatŏntarchŏs,** *hek-at-on´-tar-khos;* from *1540* and *757;* the *captain of one hundred men:*—centurion.

1544. *ἐκβάλλω* **ěkballō,** *ek-bal´-lo;* from *1537* and *906;* to *eject* (lit. or fig.):—bring forth, cast (forth, out), drive (out), expel, leave, pluck (pull, take, thrust) out, put forth (out), send away (forth, out).

1545. *ἔκβασις* **ěkbasis,** *ek´-bas-is;* from a comp. of *1537* and the base of *939* (mean, to *go out*); an *exit* (lit. or fig.):—end, way to escape.

1546. *ἐκβολή* **ěkbŏlē,** *ek-bol-ay´;* from *1544; ejection,* i.e. (spec.) a *throwing overboard* of the cargo:— + lighten the ship.

1547. *ἐκγαμίζω* **ěkgamizō,** *ek-gam-id´-zo;* from *1537* and a form of *1061* [comp. *1548*]; to *marry off* a daughter:—give in marriage.

1548. *ἐκγαμίσκω* **ěkgamiskō,** *ek-gam-is´-ko;* from *1537* and *1061;* the same as *1547:*—give in marriage.

1549. *ἔκγονον* **ěkgŏnŏn,** *ek´-gon-on;* neut. of a der. of a comp. of *1537* and *1096;* a *descendant,* i.e. (spec.) *grandchild:*—nephew.

1550. *ἐκδαπανάω* **ěkdapanaō,** *ek-dap-an-ah´-o;* from *1537* and *1159;* to *expend* (wholly), i.e. (fig.) *exhaust:*—spend.

1551. *ἐκδέχομαι* **ěkděchŏmai,** *ek-dekh´-om-ahee;* from *1537* and *1209;* to *accept from* some source, i.e. (by impl.) to *await:*—expect, look (tarry) for, wait (for).

1552. *ἔκδηλος* **ěkdēlŏs,** *ek´-day-los;* from *1537* and *1212; wholly evident:*—manifest.

1553. *ἐκδημέω* **ěkdēměō,** *ed-day-meh´-o;* from a comp. of *1537* and *1218;* to *emigrate,* i.e. (fig.) *vacate* or *quit:*—be absent.

1554. *ἐκδίδωμι* **ěkdidōmi,** *ek-did´-o-mee;* from *1537* and *1325;* to *give forth,* i.e. (spec.) to *lease:*—let forth (out).

1555. *ἐκδιηγέομαι* **ěkdiēgěŏmai,** *ek-dee-ayg-eh´-om-ahee;* from *1537* and a comp. of *1223* and *2233;* to *narrate* through wholly:—declare.

1556. *ἐκδικέω* **ěkdikěō,** *ek-dik-eh´-o;* from *1558;* to *vindicate, retaliate, punish:*—a (re-) venge.

1557. *ἐκδίκησις* **ěkdikēsis,** *ek-dik´-ay-sis;* from *1556; vindication, retribution:*—(a-, re-) venge (-ance), punishment.

1558. *ἔκδικος* **ěkdikŏs,** *ek´-dik-os;* from *1537* and *1349;* carrying *justice out,* i.e. a *punisher:*—a (re-) venger.

1559. *ἐκδιώκω* **ěkdiōkō,** *ek-dee-o´-ko;* from *1537* and *1377;* to *pursue out,* i.e. *expel* or *persecute* implacably:—persecute.

1560. *ἔκδοτος* **ěkdŏtŏs,** *ek´-dot-os;* from *1537* and a der. of *1325; given out* or *over,* i.e. *surrendered:*—delivered.

1561. *ἐκδοχή* **ěkdŏchē,** *ek-dokh-ay´;* from *1551; expectation:*—looking for.

1562. *ἐκδύω* **ěkduō,** *ek-doo´-o;* from *1537* and the base of *1416;* to cause to *sink out* of, i.e. (spec. as of clothing) to *divest:*—strip, take off from, unclothe.

1563. *ἐκεῖ* **ěkěi,** *ek-i´;* of uncert. affin.; *there;* by extens. *thither:*—there, thither (-ward), (to) yonder (place).

1564. *ἐκεῖθεν* **ěkěithěn,** *ek-i´-then;* from *1563; thence:*—from that place, (from) thence, there.

1565. ἐκεῖνος **ĕkĕinŏs,** *ek-i´-nos;* from *1563; that* one (or [neut.] thing); often intensified by the art. prefixed:—he, it, the other (same), selfsame, that (same, very), × their, × them, they, this, those. See also *3778.*

1566. ἐκεῖσε **ĕkĕisĕ,** *ek-i´-seh;* from *1563; thither:*—there.

1567. ἐκζητέω **ĕkzētĕō,** *ek-zay-teh´-o;* from *1537* and *2212;* to *search out,* i.e. (fig.) *investigate, crave, demand,* (by Hebr.) *worship:*—en- (re-) quire, seek after (carefully, diligently).

1568. ἐκθαμβέω **ĕkthambĕō,** *ek-tham-beh´-o;* from *1569;* to *astonish* utterly:—affright, greatly (sore) amaze.

1569. ἔκθαμβος **ĕkthambŏs,** *ek´-tham-bos;* from *1537* and *2285; utterly astounded:*—greatly, wondering.

1570. ἔκθετος **ĕkthĕtŏs,** *ek´-thet-os;* from *1537* and a der. of *5087; put out,* i.e. *exposed* to perish:—cast out.

1571. ἐκκαθαίρω **ĕkkathairō,** *ek-kath-ah´ee-ro;* from *1537* and *2508;* to *cleanse thoroughly:*—purge (out).

1572. ἐκκαίω **ĕkkaiō,** *ek-kah´-yo;* from *1537* and *2545;* to *inflame* deeply:—burn.

1573. ἐκκακέω **ĕkkakĕō,** *ek-kak-eh´-o;* from *1537* and *2556;* to *be* (*bad* or) *weak,* i.e. (by impl.) to *fail* (in heart):—faint, be weary.

1574. ἐκκεντέω **ĕkkĕntĕō,** *ek-ken-teh´-o;* from *1537* and the base of *2759;* to *transfix:*—pierce.

1575. ἐκκλάω **ĕkklaō,** *ek-klah´-o;* from *1537* and *2806;* to *exscind:*—break off.

1576. ἐκκλείω **ĕkklĕiō,** *ek-kli´-o;* from *1537* and *2808;* to *shut out* (lit. or fig.):—exclude.

1577. ἐκκλησία **ĕkklēsia,** *ek-klay-see´-ah;* from a comp. of *1537* and a der. of *2564; a calling out,* i.e. (concr.) a popular *meeting,* espec. a religious *congregation* (Jewish *synagogue,* or Chr. community of members on earth or saints in heaven or both):—assembly, church.

1578. ἐκκλίνω **ĕkklinō,** *ek-klee´-no;* from *1537* and *2827;* to *deviate,* i.e. (absol.) to *shun* (lit. or fig.), or (rel.) to *decline* (from piety):—avoid, eschew, go out of the way.

1579. ἐκκολυμβάω **ĕkkŏlumbaō,** *ek-kol-oom-bah´-o;* from *1537* and *2860;* to *escape* by *swimming:*—swim out.

1580. ἐκκομίζω **ĕkkŏmizō,** *ek-kom-id´-zo;* from *1537* and *2865;* to *bear forth* (to burial):—carry out.

1581. ἐκκόπτω **ĕkkŏptō,** *ek-kop´-to;* from *1537* and *2875;* to *exscind;* fig. to *frustrate:*—cut down (off, out), hew down, hinder.

1582. ἐκκρέμαμαι **ĕkkrĕmamai,** *ek-krem´-am-ahee;* mid. from *1537* and *2910;* to *hang upon* the lips of a speaker, i.e. *listen closely:*—be very attentive.

1583. ἐκλαλέω **ĕklalĕō,** *ek-lal-eh´-o;* from *1537* and *2980;* to *divulge:*—tell.

1584. ἐκλάμπω **ĕklampō,** *ek-lam´-po;* from *1537* and *2989;* to *be resplendent:*—shine forth.

1585. ἐκλανθάνομαι **ĕklanthanŏmai,** *ek-lan-than´-om-ahee;* mid. from *1537* and *2990;* to *be* utterly *oblivious* of:—forget.

1586. ἐκλέγομαι **ĕklĕgŏmai,** *ek-leg´-om-ahee;* mid. from *1537* and *3004* (in its prim. sense); to *select:*—make choice, choose (out), chosen.

1587. ἐκλείπω **ĕklĕipō,** *ek-li´-po;* from *1537* and *3007;* to *omit,* i.e. (by impl.) *cease* (*die*):—fail.

1588. ἐκλεκτός **ĕklĕktŏs,** *ek-lek-tos´;* from *1586; select;* by impl. *favorite:*—chosen, elect.

1589. ἐκλογή **ĕklŏgē,** *ek-log-ay´;* from *1586;* (divine) *selection* (abstr. or concr.):—chosen, election.

1590. ἐκλύω **ĕkluō,** *ek-loo´-o;* from *1537* and *3089;* to *relax* (lit. or fig.):—faint.

1591. ἐκμάσσω **ĕkmassō,** *ek-mas´-so;* from *1537* and the base of *3145;* to *knead out,* i.e. (by anal.) to *wipe dry:*—wipe.

1592. ἐκμυκτερίζω **ĕkmuktĕrizō,** *ek-mook-ter-id´-zo;* from *1537* and *3456;* to *sneer* outright at:—deride.

1593. ἐκνεύω **ĕknĕuō,** *ek-nyoo´-o;* from *1537* and *3506;* (by anal.) to *slip off,* i.e. quietly *withdraw:*—convey self away.

1594. ἐκνήφω **ĕknēphō,** *ek-nay´-fo;* from *1537* and *3525;* (fig.) to *rouse* (oneself) *out* of stupor:—awake.

1595. ἑκούσιον **hĕkŏusiŏn,** *hek-oo´-see-on;* neut. of a der. from *1635; voluntariness:*—willingly.

1596. ἑκουσίως **hĕkŏusiōs,** *hek-oo-see´-oce;* adv. from the same as *1595; voluntarily:*—wilfully, willingly.

1597. ἔκπαλαι **ĕkpalai,** *ek´-pal-ahee;* from *1537* and *3819; long ago, for a long while:*—of a long time, of old.

1598. ἐκπειράζω **ĕkpĕirazō,** *ek-pi-rad´-zo;* from *1537* and *3985;* to *test thoroughly:*—tempt.

1599. ἐκπέμπω **ĕkpĕmpō,** *ek-pem´-po;* from *1537* and *3992;* to *despatch:*—send away (forth).

ἐκπερισσοῦ **ĕkpĕirissŏu.** See *1537* and *4053.*

1600. ἐκπετάννυμι **ĕkpĕtannumi,** *ek-pet-an´-noo-mee;* from *1537* and a form of *4072;* to *fly out,* i.e. (by anal.) *extend:*—stretch forth.

1601. ἐκπίπτω **ĕkpiptō,** *ek-pip´-to;* from *1537* and *4098;* to *drop away;* spec. *be driven out* of one's course; fig. to *lose, become inefficient:*—be cast, fail, fall (away, off), take none effect.

1602. ἐκπλέω **ĕkplĕō,** *ek-pleh´-o;* from *1537* and *4126;* to *depart* by ship:—sail (away, thence).

1603. ἐκπληρόω **ĕkplērŏō,** *ek-play-rŏ´-o;* from *1537* and *4137;* to *accomplish* entirely:—fulfill.

1604. ἐκπλήρωσις **ĕkplērōsis,** *ek-play´-ro-sis;* from *1603; completion:*—accomplishment.

1605. ἐκπλήσσω **ĕkplēssō,** *ek-place´-so;* from *1537* and *4141;* to *strike* with astonishment:—amaze, astonish.

1606. ἐκπνέω **ĕkpnĕō,** *ek-pneh´-o;* from *1537* and *4154;* to *expire:*—give up the ghost.

1607. ἐκπορεύομαι **ĕkpŏrĕuŏmai,** *ek-por-yoo´-om-ahee;* from *1537* and *4198;* to *depart, be discharged, proceed, project:*—come (forth, out of), depart, go (forth, out), issue, proceed (out of).

1608. ἐκπορνεύω **ĕkpŏrnĕuō,** *ek-porn-yoo´-o;* from *1537* and *4203;* to *be utterly unchaste:*—give self over to fornication.

1609. ἐκπτύω **ĕkptuō,** *ek-ptoo´-o;* from *1537* and *4429;* to *spit out,* i.e. (fig.) *spurn:*—reject.

1610. ἐκριζόω **ĕkrizŏō,** *ek-rid-zŏ´-o;* from *1537* and *4492;* to *uproot:*—pluck up by the root, root up.

1611. ἔκστασις **ĕkstasis,** *ek´-stas-is;* from *1839;* a *displacement* of the mind, i.e. *bewilderment, "ecstasy":*— + be amazed, amazement, astonishment, trance.

1612. ἐκστρέφω **ĕkstrĕphō,** *ek-stref´-o;* from *1537* and *4762;* to *pervert* (fig.):—subvert.

1613. ἐκταράσσω **ĕktarassō,** *ek-tar-as´-so;* from *1537* and *5015;* to *disturb wholly:*—exceedingly trouble.

1614. ἐκτείνω **ĕktĕinō,** *ek-ti´-no;* from *1537* and τείνω **tĕinō** (to *stretch*); to *extend:*—cast, put forth, stretch forth (out).

1615. ἐκτελέω **ĕktĕlĕō,** *ek-tel-eh´-o;* from *1537* and *5055;* to *complete* fully:—finish.

1616. ἐκτένεια **ĕktĕnĕia,** *ek-ten´-i-ah;* from *1618; intentness:*— × instantly.

1617. ἐκτενέστερον **ĕktĕnĕstĕrŏn,** *ek-ten-es´-ter-on;* neut. of the comp. of *1618; more intently:*—more earnestly.

1618. ἐκτενής **ĕktĕnēs,** *ek-ten-ace´;* from *1614; intent:*—without ceasing, fervent.

1619. ἐκτενῶς **ĕktĕnōs,** *ek-ten-oce´;* adv. from *1618; intently:*—fervently.

1620. ἐκτίθημι **ĕktithēmi,** *ek-tith´-ay-mee;* from *1537* and *5087;* to *expose;* fig. to *declare:*—cast out, expound.

1621. ἐκτινάσσω **ĕktinassō,** *ek-tin-as´-so;* from *1537* and τινάσσω **tinassō** (to *swing*); to *shake* violently:—shake (off).

1622. ἐκτός **ĕktŏs,** *ek-tos´;* from *1537;* the *exterior;* fig. (as a prep.) *aside from, besides:*—but, except (-ed), other than, out of, outside, unless, without.

1623. ἕκτος **hĕktŏs,** *hek´-tos;* ordinal from *1803; sixth:*—sixth.

1624. ἐκτρέπω **ĕktrĕpō,** *ek-trep´-o;* from *1537* and the base of *5157;* to *deflect,* i.e. *turn away* (lit. or fig.):—avoid, turn (aside, out of the way).

1625. ἐκτρέφω **ĕktrĕphō,** *ek-tref´-o;* from *1537* and *5142;* to *rear up* to maturity, i.e. (gen.) to *cherish* or *train:*—bring up, nourish.

1626. ἔκτρωμα **ĕktrōma,** *ek´-tro-mah;* from a comp. of *1537* and τιτρώσκω **titrōskō** (to *wound*); a *miscarriage* (*abortion*), i.e. (by anal.) *untimely birth:*—born out of due time.

1627. ἐκφέρω **ĕkphĕrō,** *ek-fer´-o;* from *1537* and *5342;* to *bear out* (lit. or fig.):—bear, bring forth, carry forth (out).

1628. ἐκφεύγω **ĕkphĕugō,** *ek-fyoo´-go;* from *1537* and *5343;* to *flee out:*—escape, flee.

1629. ἐκφοβέω **ĕkphŏbĕō,** *ek-fob-eh´-o;* from *1537* and *5399;* to *frighten utterly:*—terrify.

1630. ἔκφοβος **ĕkphŏbŏs,** *ek´-fob-os;* from *1537* and *5401; frightened out* of one's wits:—sore afraid, exceedingly fear.

1631. ἐκφύω **ĕkphuō,** *ek-foo´-o;* from *1537* and *5453;* to *sprout up:*—put forth.

1632. ἐκχέω **ĕkchĕō,** *ek-kheh´-o;* or (by var.)
ἐκχύνω **ĕkchunō,** *ek-khoo´-no;* from *1537* and χέω **chĕō** (to *pour*); to *pour forth;* fig. to *bestow:*—gush (pour) out, run greedily (out), shed (abroad, forth), spill.

1633. ἐκχωρέω **ĕkchōrĕō,** *ek-kho-reh´-o;* from *1537* and *5562;* to *depart:*—depart out.

1634. ἐκψύχω **ĕkpsuchō,** *ek-psoo´-kho;* from *1537* and *5594;* to *expire:*—give (yield) up the ghost.

1635. ἑκών **hĕkōn,** *hek-own´;* of uncert. affin.; *voluntary:*—willingly.

1636. ἐλαία **ĕlaia,** *el-ah´-yah;* fem. of a presumed der. from an obsol. prim.; an *olive* (the tree or the fruit):—olive (berry, tree).

1637. ἔλαιον **ĕlaiŏn,** *el´-ah-yon;* neut. of the same as *1636;* olive *oil:*—oil.

1638. ἐλαιών **ĕlaiōn,** *el-ah-yone´;* from *1636;* an *olive-orchard,* i.e. (spec.) the *Mt. of Olives:*—Olivet.

1639. Ἐλαμίτης **Ĕlamitēs,** *el-am-ee´-tace;* of Heb. or. [5867]; an *Elamite* or Persian:—Elamite.

1640. ἐλάσσων **ĕlassōn,** *el-as´-sone;* or
ἐλάττων **ĕlattōn,** *el-at´-tone;* comp. of the same as *1646; smaller* (in size, quantity, age or quality):—less, under, worse, younger.

1641. ἐλαττονέω **ĕlattŏnĕō,** *el-at-ton-eh´-o;* from *1640;* to *diminish,* i.e. *fall short:*—have lack.

1642. ἐλαττόω **ĕlattŏō,** *el-at-tŏ´-o;* from *1640;* to *lessen* (in rank or influence):—decrease, make lower.

1643. ἐλαύνω **ĕlaunō,** *el-ŏw´-no;* a prol. form of a prim. verb (obsol. except in certain tenses as an altern. of this) of uncert. affin.; to *push* (as wind, oars or dæmoniacal power):—carry, drive, row.

1644. ἐλαφρία **ĕlaphria,** *el-af-ree´-ah;* from *1645; levity* (fig.), i.e. *fickleness:*—lightness.

1645. ἐλαφρός **ĕlaphrŏs,** *el-af-ros´;* prob. akin to *1643* and the base of *1640; light,* i.e. *easy:*—light.

1646. ἐλάχιστος **ĕlachistŏs,** *el-akh´-is-tos;* superl. of ἔλαχυς **ĕlachus** (*short*); used as equiv. to *3398; least* (in size, amount, dignity, etc.):—least, very little (small), smallest.

1647. ἐλαχιστότερος **ĕlachistŏtĕrŏs,** *el-akh-is-tot´-er-os;* comp. of *1646; far less:*—less than the least.

1648. Ἐλεάζαρ **Ĕlĕazar,** *el-eh-ad´-zar;* of Heb. or. [499]; *Eleazar,* an Isr.:—Eleazar.

1649. ἔλεγξις **ĕlĕgxis,** *el´-eng-xis;* from *1651; refutation,* i.e. *reproof:*—rebuke.

1650. ἔλεγχος **ĕlĕgchŏs,** *el´-eng-khos;* from *1651; proof, conviction:*—evidence, reproof.

1651. ἐλέγχω **ĕlĕgchō,** *el-eng´-kho;* of uncert. affin.; to *confute, admonish:*—convict, convince, tell a fault, rebuke, reprove.

1652. ἐλεεινός **ĕlĕĕinŏs,** *el-eh-i-nos´;* from *1656; pitiable:*—miserable.

1653. ἐλεέω **ĕlĕĕō,** *el-eh-eh´-o;* from *1656;* to *compassionate* (by word or deed, spec. by divine grace):—have compassion (pity on), have (obtain, receive, shew) mercy (on).

1654. ἐλεημοσύνη **ĕlĕēmŏsunē,** *el-eh-ay-mos-oo´-nay;* from *1656; compassionateness,* i.e. (as exercised towards the poor) *beneficence,* or (concr.) a *benefaction:*—alms (-deeds).

1655. ἐλεήμων **ĕlĕēmōn** *el-eh-ay´-mone;* from *1653; compassionate* (actively):—merciful.

1656. ἔλεος **ĕlĕŏs,** *el´-eh-os;* of uncert. affin.; *compassion* (human or divine, espec. active):—(+ tender) mercy.

1657. ἐλευθερία **ĕlĕuthĕria,** *el-yoo-ther-ee´ah;* from *1658; freedom* (legitimate or licentious, chiefly mor. or cer.):—liberty.

1658. ἐλεύθερος **ĕlĕuthĕrŏs,** *el-yoo´-ther-os;* prob. from the alt. of *2064; unrestrained* (to *go* at pleasure), i.e. (as a citizen) *not a slave* (whether *freeborn* or *manumitted*), or (gen.) *exempt* (from obligation or liability):—free (man, woman), at liberty.

1659. ἐλευθερόω **ĕlĕuthĕrŏō,** *el-yoo-ther-ŏ´-o;* from *1658;* to *liberate,* i.e. (fig.) to *exempt* (from mor., cer. or mortal liability):—deliver, make free.

ἐλεύθω **ĕlĕuthō.** See *2064.*

1660. ἔλευσις **ĕlĕusis,** *el´-yoo-sis;* from the alt. of *2064;* an *advent:*—coming.

1661. ἐλεφάντινος **ĕlĕphantinŏs,** *el-ef-an´-tee-nos;* from ἔλεφας **ĕlĕphas** (an "*elephant*"); *elephantine,* i.e. (by impl.) composed of *ivory:*—of ivory.

1662. Ἐλιακείμ **Ĕliakĕim,** *el-ee-ak-ime´;* of Heb. or. [471]; *Eliakim,* an Isr.:—Eliakim.

1663. Ἐλιέζερ **Ĕliĕzĕr,** *el-ee-ed´-zer;* of Heb. or. [461]; *Eliezer,* an Isr.:—Eliezer.

1664. Ἐλιούδ **Ĕliŏud,** *el-ee-ood´;* of Heb. or. [410 and 1935]; *God of majesty; Eliud,* an Isr.:—Eliud.

1665. Ἐλισάβετ **Ĕlisabĕt,** *el-ee-sab´-et;* of Heb. or. [472]; *Elisabet,* an Israelitess:—Elisabeth.

1666. Ἐλισσαῖος **Ĕlissaiŏs,** *el-is-sah´-yos;* of Heb. or. [477]; *Elissæus,* an Isr.:—Elissæus.

1667. ἑλίσσω **hĕlissō,** *hel-is´-so;* a form of *1507;* to *coil* or *wrap:*—fold up.

1668. ἕλκος **hĕlkŏs,** *hel´-kos;* prob. from *1670;* an *ulcer* (as if drawn together):—sore.

1669. ἑλκόω **hĕlkŏō,** *hel-kŏ´-o;* from *1668;* to *cause to ulcerate,* i.e. (pass.) *be ulcerous:*—full of sores.

1670. ἑλκύω **hĕlkuō,** *hel-koo´-o;* or
ἕλκω **hĕlkō,** *hel´-ko;* prob. akin to *138;* to *drag* (lit. or fig.):—draw. Comp. *1667.*

1671. Ἑλλάς **Hĕllas,** *hel-las´;* of uncert. affin.; *Hellas* (or *Greece*), a country of Europe:—Greece.

1672. Ἕλλην **Hĕllēn,** *hel´-lane;* from *1671;* a *Hellen* (*Grecian*) or inhab. of Hellas; by extens. a *Greek-speaking* person, espec. a *non-Jew:*—Gentile, Greek.

1673. Ἑλληνικός **Hĕllēnikŏs,** *hel-lay-nee-kos´;* from *1672; Hellenic,* i.e. *Grecian* (in language):—Greek.

1674. Ἑλληνίς **Hĕllēnis,** *hel-lay-nis´;* fem. of *1672;* a *Grecian* (i.e. *non-Jewish*) woman:—Greek.

1675. Ἑλληνιστής **Hĕllēnistēs,** *hel-lay-nis-tace´;* from a der. of *1672;* a *Hellenist* or Greek-speaking Jew:—Grecian.

1676. Ἑλληνιστί **Hĕllēnisti,** *hel-lay-nis-tee´;* adv. from the same as *1675; Hellenistically,* i.e. in the Grecian language:—Greek.

1677. ἐλλογέω **ĕllŏgĕō,** *el-log-eh´-o;* from *1722* and *3056* (in the sense of *account*); to *reckon in,* i.e. *attribute:*—impute, put on account.

ἔλλομαι **hĕllŏmai.** See *138.*

1678. Ἐλμωδάμ **Ĕlmōdam,** *el-mo-dam´;* of Heb. or. [perh. for 486]; *Elmodam,* an Isr.:—Elmodam.

1679. ἐλπίζω **ĕlpizō,** *el-pid´-zo;* from *1680;* to *expect* or *confide:*—(have, thing) hope (-d) (for), trust.

1680. ἐλπίς **ĕlpis,** *el-pece´;* from a prim. ἔλπω **ĕlpō** (to *anticipate,* usually with pleasure); *expectation* (abstr. or concr.) or *confidence:*—faith, hope.

1681. Ἐλύμας **Ĕlumas,** *el-oo´-mas;* of for. or.; *Elymas,* a wizard:—Elymas.

1682. ἐλοΐ **ĕlōï,** *el-o-ee´;* of Chald. or. [426 with pron. suff.]; *my God:*—Eloi.

1683. ἐμαυτοῦ **ĕmautŏu,** *em-ŏw-too´;* gen. comp. of *1700* and *846; of myself* (so likewise the dat.

ἐμαυτῷ **ĕmautōi,** *em-ow-tō´;* and acc.
ἐμαυτόν **ĕmautŏn,** *em-ow-ton´*):—me, mine own (self), myself.

1684. ἐμβαίνω **ĕmbainō,** *em-ba´hee-no;* from *1722* and the base of *939;* to *walk on,* i.e. *embark* (aboard a vessel), *reach* (a pool):—come (get) into, enter (into), go (up) into, step in, take ship.

1685. ἐμβάλλω **ĕmballō,** *em-bal´-lo;* from *1722* and *906;* to *throw on,* i.e. (fig.) *subject to* (eternal punishment):—cast into.

1686. ἐμβάπτω **ĕmbaptō,** *em-bap´-to;* from *1722* and *911;* to *whelm on,* i.e. *wet* (a part of the person, etc.) by contact with a fluid:—dip.

1687. ἐμβατεύω **ĕmbatĕuō,** *em-bat-yoo´-o;* from *1722* and a presumed der. of the base of *939;* equiv. to *1684;* to *intrude on* (fig.):—intrude into.

1688. ἐμβιβάζω **ĕmbibazō,** *em-bib-ad´-zo;* from *1722* and βιβάζω **bibazō** (to *mount;* causat. of *1684*); to *place on,* i.e. *transfer* (aboard a vessel):—put in.

1689. ἐμβλέπω **ĕmblĕpō,** *em-blep´-o;* from *1722* and *991;* to *look on,* i.e. (rel.) to *observe* fixedly, or (absol.) to *discern* clearly:—behold, gaze up, look upon, (could) see.

1690. ἐμβριμάομαι **ĕmbrimaŏmai,** *em-brim-ah´-om-ahee;* from *1722* and βριμάομαι **brimaŏmai** (to *snort* with anger); to have *indignation on,* i.e. (trans.) to *blame,* (intrans.) to *sigh* with chagrin, (spec.) to sternly *enjoin:*—straitly charge, groan, murmur against.

1691. ἐμέ **ĕmĕ,** *em-eh´;* a prol. form of *3165; me:*—I, me, my (-self).

1692. ἐμέω **ĕmĕō,** *em-eh´-o;* of uncert. affin.; to *vomit:*—(will) spue.

1693. ἐμμαίνομαι **ĕmmainŏmai,** *em-mah´-ee-nom-ahee;* from *1722* and *3105;* to *rave on,* i.e. *rage at:*—be mad against.

1694. Ἐμμανουήλ **Ĕmmanŏuēl,** *em-man-oo-ale´;* of Heb. or. [6005]; *God with us; Emmanuel,* a name of Christ:—Emmanuel.

1695. Ἐμμαούς **Ĕmmaŏus,** *em-mah-ooce´;* prob. of Heb. or. [comp. 3222]; *Emmaüs,* a place in Pal.:—Emmaus.

1696. ἐμμένω **ĕmmĕnō,** *em-men´-o;* from *1722* and *3306;* to *stay in* the same place, i.e. (fig.) to *persevere:*—continue.

1697. Ἐμμόρ **Ĕmmŏr,** *em-mor´;* of Heb. or, [2544]; *Emmor* (i.e. *Chamor*), a Canaanite:—Emmor.

1698. ἐμοί **ĕmŏi,** *em-oy´;* a prol. form of *3427; to me:*—I, me, mine, my.

1699. ἐμός **ĕmŏs,** *em-os´;* from the oblique cases of *1473* (*1698, 1700, 1691*); *my:*—of me, mine (own), my.

1700. ἐμοῦ **ĕmŏu,** *em-oo´;* a prol. form of *3450; of me:*—me, mine, my.

1701. ἐμπαιγμός **ĕmpaigmŏs,** *emp-aheeg-mos´;* from *1702; derision:*—mocking.

1702. ἐμπαίζω **ĕmpaizō,** *emp-aheed´-zo;* from *1722* and *3815;* to *jeer at,* i.e. *deride:*—mock.

1703. ἐμπαίκτης **ĕmpaiktēs,** *emp-aheek-tace´;* from *1702;* a *derider,* i.e. (by impl.) a *false teacher:*—mocker, scoffer.

1704. ἐμπεριπατέω **ĕmpĕripatĕō,** *em-per-ee-pat-eh´-o;* from *1722* and *4043;* to *perambulate on* a place, i.e. (fig.) to *be occupied among persons:*—walk in.

1705. ἐμπίπλημι **ĕmpiplēmi,** *em-pip´-lay-mee;*

or

ἐμπλήθω **ĕmplēthō,** *em-play´-tho;* from *1722* and the base of *4118;* to *fill in* (*up*), i.e. (by impl.) to *satisfy* (lit. or fig.):—fill.

1706. ἐμπίπτω **ĕmpiptō,** *em-pip´-to;* from *1722* and *4098;* to *fall on,* i.e. (lit.) *be entrapped by,* or (fig.) *be overwhelmed with:*—fall among (into).

1707. ἐμπλέκω **ĕmplĕkō,** *em-plek´-o;* from *1722* and *4120;* to *entwine,* i.e. (fig.) *involve* with:—entangle (in, self with).

ἐμπλήθω **ĕmplēthō.** See *1705.*

1708. ἐμπλοκή **ĕmplŏkē,** *em-plok-ay´;* from *1707;* elaborate *braiding* of the hair:—plaiting.

1709. ἐμπνέω **ĕmpnĕō,** *emp-neh´-o;* from *1722* and *4154;* to *inhale,* i.e. (fig.) to *be animated by* (*bent upon*):—breathe.

1710. ἐμπορεύομαι **ĕmpŏrĕuŏmai,** *em-por-yoo´-om-ahee;* from *1722* and *4198;* to *travel in* (a country as a pedlar), i.e. (by impl.) to *trade:*—buy and sell, make merchandise.

1711. ἐμπορία **ĕmpŏria,** *em-por-ee´-ah;* fem. from *1713; traffic:*—merchandise.

1712. ἐμπόριον **ĕmpŏriŏn,** *em-por´-ee-on;* neut. from *1713;* a *mart* (*"emporium"*):—merchandise.

1713. ἔμπορος **ĕmpŏrŏs,** *em´-por-os;* from *1722* and the base of *4198;* a (wholesale) *tradesman:*—merchant.

1714. ἐμπρήθω **ĕmprēthō,** *em-pray´-tho;* from *1722* and πρήθω **prēthō** (to *blow* a flame); to *enkindle,* i.e. *set on fire:*—burn up.

1715. ἔμπροσθεν **ĕmprŏsthĕn,** *em´-pros-then;* from *1722* and *4314; in front of* (in place, [lit. or fig.] or time):—against, at, before, (in presence, sight) of.

1716. ἐμπτύω **ĕmptuō,** *emp-too´-o;* from *1722* and *4429;* to *spit at* or *on:*—spit (upon).

1717. ἐμφανής **ĕmphanēs,** *em-fan-ace´;* from a comp. of *1722* and *5316; apparent in* self:—manifest, openly.

1718. ἐμφανίζω **ĕmphanizō,** *em-fan-id´-zo;* from *1717;* to *exhibit* (in person) or *disclose* (by words):—appear, declare (plainly), inform, (will) manifest, shew, signify.

1719. ἔμφοβος **ĕmphŏbŏs,** *em´-fob-os;* from *1722* and *5401; in fear,* i.e. *alarmed:*—affrighted, afraid, tremble.

1720. ἐμφυσάω **ĕmphusaō,** *em-foo-sah´-o;* from *1722* and φυσάω **phusaō** (to *puff*) [comp. *5453*]; to *blow at* or *on:*—breathe on.

1721. ἔμφυτος **ĕmphutŏs,** *em´-foo-tos;* from *1722* and a der. of *5453; implanted* (fig.):—engrafted.

1722. ἐν **ĕn,** *en;* a prim. prep. denoting (fixed) *position* (in place, time or state), and (by impl.) *instrumentality* (medially or constructively), i.e. a relation of *rest* (intermediate between *1519* and *1537*); *"in," at,* (up-) *on, by,* etc.:—about, after, against, + almost, × altogether, among, × as, at, before, between, (here-) by (+ all means), for (. . . sake of), + give self wholly to, (here-) in (-to, -wardly), × mightily, (because) of, (up-) on, [open-] ly, × outwardly, one, × quickly, × shortly, [speedi-] ly, × that, × there (-in, -on), through (-out), (un-) to(-ward), under, when, where (-with), while, with (-in). Often used in compounds, with substantially the same import; rarely with verbs of motion, and then not to indicate direction, except (elliptically) by a separate (and different) prep.

1723. ἐναγκαλίζομαι **ĕnagkalizŏmai,** *en-ang-kal-id´-zom-ahee;* from *1722* and a der. of *43;* to *take in* one's *arms,* i.e. *embrace:*—take up in arms.

1724. ἐνάλιος **ĕnaliŏs,** *en-al´-ee-os;* from *1722* and *251; in* the *sea,* i.e. *marine:*—thing in the sea.

1725. ἔναντι **ĕnanti,** *en´-an-tee;* from *1722* and *473; in front* (i.e. fig. *presence*) *of:*—before.

1726. ἐναντίον **ĕnantiŏn,** *en-an-tee´-on;* neut. of *1727;* (adv.) *in* the *presence* (*view*) *of:*—before, in the presence of.

1727. ἐναντίος **ĕnantiŏs,** *en-an-tee´-os;* from *1725; opposite;* fig. *antagonistic:*—(over) against, contrary.

1728. ἐνάρχομαι **ĕnarchŏmai,** *en-ar´-khom-ahee;* from *1722* and *756;* to *commence on:*—rule [*by mistake* for *757*].

1729. ἐνδεής **ĕndĕēs,** *en-deh-ace´;* from a comp. of *1722* and *1210* (in the sense of *lacking*); *deficient in:*—lacking.

1730. ἔνδειγμα **ĕndĕigma,** *en´-dighe-mah;* from *1731;* an *indication* (concr.)—manifest token.

1731. ἐνδείκνυμι **ĕndĕiknumi,** *en-dike´-noo-mee;* from *1722* and *1166;* to *indicate* (by word or act):—do, show (forth).

1732. ἔνδειξις **ĕndĕixis,** *en´-dike-sis;* from *1731; indication* (abstr.):—declare, evident token, proof.

1733. ἕνδεκα **hĕndĕka,** *hen´-dek-ah;* from (the neut. of) *1520* and *1176; one* and *ten,* i.e. *eleven:*—eleven.

1734. ἑνδέκατος **hĕndĕkatŏs,** *hen-dek´-at-os* ord. from *1733; eleventh:*—eleventh.

1735. ἐνδέχεται **ĕndĕchĕtai,** *en-dekh´-et-ahee;* third pers. sing. pres. of a comp. of *1722* and *1209;* (impers.) *it is accepted in,* i.e. *admitted* (*possible*):—can (+ not) be.

1736. ἐνδημέω **ĕndēmĕō,** *en-day-meh´-o;* from a comp. of *1722* and *1218;* to *be in* one's own *country,* i.e. *home* (fig.):—be at home (present).

1737. ἐνδιδύσκω **ĕndiduskō,** *en-did-oos´-ko;* a prol. form of *1746;* to *invest* (with a garment):—clothe in, wear.

1738. ἔνδικος **ĕndikŏs,** *en´-dee-kos;* from *1722* and *1349; in* the *right,* i.e. *equitable:*—just.

1739. ἐνδόμησις **ĕndŏmēsis,** *en-dom´-ay-sis;* from a comp. of *1722* and a der. of the base of *1218;* a *housing in* (*residence*), i.e. *structure:*—building.

1740. ἐνδοξάζω **ĕndŏxazō,** *en-dox-ad´-zo;* from *1741;* to *glorify:*—glorify.

1741. ἔνδοξος **ĕndŏxŏs,** *en´-dox-os;* from *1722* and *1391; in glory,* i.e. *splendid,* (fig.) *noble:*—glorious, gorgeous [-ly], honourable.

1742. ἔνδυμα **ĕnduma,** *en´-doo-mah;* from *1746, apparel* (espec. the outer *robe*):—clothing, garment, raiment.

1743. ἐνδυναμόω **ĕndunamŏō,** *en-doo-nam-ŏ´-o;* from *1722 and 1412;* to *empower:*—enable, (increase in) strength (-en), be (make) strong.

1744. ἐνδύνω **ĕndunō,** *en-doo´-no;* from *1772* and *1416;* to *sink* (by impl. *wrap* [comp. *1746*]) *on,* i.e. (fig.) *sneak:*—creep.

1745. ἔνδυσις **ĕndusis,** *en´-doo-sis;* from *1746; investment* with clothing:—putting on.

1746. ἐνδύω **ĕnduō,** *en-doo´-o;* from *1722* and *1416* (in the sense of *sinking* into a garment); to *invest* with clothing (lit. or fig.):—array, clothe (with), endue, have (put) on.

ἐνέγκω **ĕnĕgkō.** See *5342.*

1747. ἐνέδρα **ĕnĕdra,** *en-ed´-rah;* fem. from *1722* and the base of *1476;* an *ambuscade,* i.e. (fig.) murderous *purpose:*—lay wait. See also *1749.*

1748. ἐνεδρεύω **ĕnĕdrĕuō,** *en-ed-ryoo´-o;* from *1747;* to *lurk,* i.e. (fig.) *plot* assassination:—lay wait for.

1749. ἔνεδρον **ĕnĕdrŏn,** *en´-ed-ron;* neut. of the same as *1747;* an *ambush,* i.e. (fig.) murderous *design:*—lying in wait.

1750. ἐνειλέω **ĕnĕilĕō,** *en-i-leh´-o;* from *1772* and the base of *1507;* to *enwrap:*—wrap in.

1751. ἔνειμι **ĕnĕimi,** *en´-i-mee:* from *1772* and *1510;* to *be within* (neut. part. plur.):—such things as . . . have. See also *1762.*

1752. ἕνεκα **hĕnĕka,** *hen´-ek-ah;* or ἕνεκεν **hĕnĕkĕn,** *hen´-ek-en;* or εἵνεκεν **hĕinĕkĕn,** *hi´-nek-en;* of uncert. affin.; *on account of:*—because, for (cause, sake), (where-) fore, by reason of, that.

1753. ἐνέργεια **ĕnĕrgĕia,** *en-erg´-i-ah;* from *1756; efficiency* ("energy"):—operation, strong, (effectual) working.

1754. ἐνεργέω **ĕnĕrgĕō,** *en-erg-eh´-o;* from *1756;* to *be active, efficient:*—do, (be) effectual (fervent), be mighty in, shew forth self, work (effectually in).

1755. ἐνέργημα **ĕnĕrgēma,** *en-erg´-ay-mah;* from *1754;* an *effect:*—operation, working.

1756. ἐνεργής **ĕnĕrgēs,** *en-er-gace´;* from *1722* and *2041: active, operative:*—effectual, powerful.

1757. ἐνευλογέω **ĕnĕulŏgĕō,** *en-yoo-log-eh´-o;* from *1722* and *2127;* to *confer a benefit on:*—bless.

1758. ἐνέχω **ĕnĕchō,** *en-ekh´-o;* from *1722* and *2192;* to *hold in* or *upon,* i.e. *ensnare;* by impl. to *keep a grudge:*—entangle with, have a quarrel against, urge.

1759. ἐνθάδε **ĕnthadĕ,** *en-thad´-eh;* from a prol. form of *1722;* prop. *within,* i.e. (of place) *here, hither:*—(t-) here, hither.

1760. ἐνθυμέομαι **ĕnthumĕŏmai,** *en-thoo-meh´-om-ahee;* from a comp. of *1722* and *2372;* to *be inspirited,* i.e. *ponder:*—think.

1761. ἐνθύμησις **ĕnthumēsis,** *en-thoo´-may-sis;* from *1760; deliberation:*—device, thought.

1762. ἔνι **ĕni,** *en´-ee;* contr. for third pers. sing. pres. indic. of *1751;* impers. *there is* in or among:—be, (there) is.

1763. ἐνιαυτός **ĕniautŏs,** *en-ee-ŏw-tos´;* prol. from a prim. ἔνος **ĕnŏs** (a *year*); a *year:*—year.

1764. ἐνίστημι **ĕnistēmi,** *en-is´-tay-mee;* from *1722* and *2476;* to *place on* hand, i.e. (reflex.) *impend,* (part.) be *instant:*—come, be at hand, present.

1765. ἐνισχύω **ĕnischuō,** *en-is-khoo´-o;* from *1722* and *2480;* to *invigorate* (trans. or reflex.):—strengthen.

1766. ἔννατος **ĕnnatŏs,** *en´-nat-os;* ord. from *1767; ninth:*—ninth.

1767. ἐννέα **ĕnnĕa,** *en-neh´-ah;* a prim. number; *nine:*—nine.

1768. ἐννενηκονταεννέα **ennĕnēkŏntaĕnnĕa,** *en-nen-ay-kon-tah-en-neh´-ah;* from a (tenth) multiple of *1767* and *1767* itself; *ninety-nine:*—ninety and nine.

1769. ἐννεός **ĕnnĕŏs,** *en-neh-os´;* from *1770; dumb* (as *making signs*), i.e. *silent* from astonishment:—speechless.

1770. ἐννεύω **ĕnnĕuō,** *en-nyoo´-o;* from *1722* and *3506;* to *nod at,* i.e. *beckon* or *communicate by gesture:*—make signs.

1771. ἔννοια **ĕnnŏia,** *en´-noy-ah;* from a comp. of *1722* and *3563; thoughtfulness,* i.e. moral *understanding:*—intent, mind.

1772. ἔννομος **ĕnnŏmŏs,** *en´-nom-os;* from *1722* and *3551;* (subj.) *legal,* or (obj.) *subject* to:—lawful, under law.

1773. ἔννυχον **ĕnnuchŏn,** *en´-noo-khon;* neut. of a comp. of *1722* and *3571;* (adv.) *by night:*—before day.

1774. ἐνοικέω **ĕnŏikĕō,** *en-oy-keh´-o;* from *1722* and *3611;* to *inhabit* (fig.):—dwell in.

1775. ἑνότης **hĕnŏtēs,** *hen-ot´-ace;* from *1520; oneness,* i.e. (fig.) *unanimity:*—unity.

1776. ἐνοχλέω **ĕnŏchlĕō,** *en-okh-leh´-o;* from *1722* and *3791* to *crowd in,* i.e. (fig.) to *annoy:*—trouble.

1777. ἔνοχος **ĕnŏchŏs,** *en´-okh-os;* from *1758; liable* to (a condition, penalty or imputation):—in danger of, guilty of, subject to.

1778. ἔνταλμα **ĕntalma,** *en´-tal-mah;* from *1781;* an *injunction,* i.e. religious *precept:*—commandment.

1779. ἐνταφιάζω **ĕntaphiazō,** *en-taf-ee-ad´-zo;* from a comp. of *1722* and *5028;* to *inswathe* with cerements for interment:—bury.

1780. ἐνταφιασμός **ĕntaphiasmŏs,** *en-taf-ee-as-mos´;* from *1779; preparation* for interment:—burying.

1781. ἐντέλλομαι **ĕntĕllŏmai,** *en-tel´-lom-ahee;* from *1722* and the base of *5056;* to *enjoin:*—(give) charge, (give) command (-ments), injoin.

1782. ἐντεῦθεν **ĕntĕuthĕn,** *ent-yoo´-then;* from the same as *1759; hence* (lit. or fig.); (repeated) *on both sides:*—(from) hence, on either side.

1783. ἔντευξις **ĕntĕuxis,** *ent´-yook-sis;* from *1793;* an *interview,* i.e. (spec.) *supplication:*—intercession, prayer.

1784. ἔντιμος **ĕntimŏs,** *en´-tee-mos;* from *1722* and *5092; valued* (fig.):—dear, more honourable, precious, in reputation.

1785. ἐντολή **ĕntŏlē,** *en-tol-ay´;* from *1781; injunction,* i.e. an authoritative *prescription:*—commandment, precept.

1786. ἐντόπιος **ĕntŏpiŏs,** *en-top´-ee-os;* from *1722* and *5117;* a *resident:*—of that place.

1787. ἐντός **ĕntŏs,** *en-tos´;* from *1722; inside* (adv. or noun):—within.

1788. ἐντρέπω **ĕntrĕpō,** *en-trep´-o;* from *1722* and the base of *5157;* to *invert,* i.e. (fig. and reflex.) in a good sense, to *respect;* or in a bad one, to *confound:*—regard, (give) reverence, shame.

1789. ἐντρέφω **ĕntrĕphō,** *en-tref´-o;* from *1722* and *5142;* (fig.) to *educate:*—nourish up in.

1790. ἔντρομος **ĕntrŏmŏs,** *en´-trom-os;* from *1722* and *5156; terrified:*— × quake, × trembled.

1791. ἐντροπή **ĕntrŏpē,** *en-trop-ay´;* from *1788; confusion:*—shame.

1792. ἐντρυφάω **ĕntruphaō,** *en-troo-fah´-o;* from *1722* and *5171;* to *revel in:*—sporting selves.

1793. ἐντυγχάνω **ĕntugchanō,** *en-toong-khan´-o;* from *1722* and *5177;* to *chance upon,* i.e. (by impl.) *confer with;* by extens. to *entreat* (in favor or against):—deal with, make intercession.

1794. ἐντυλίσσω **ĕntulissō,** *en-too-lis´-so;* from *1722* and τυλίσσω **tulissō** (to *twist;* prob. akin to *1507*); to *entwine,* i.e. *wind* up in:—wrap in (together).

1795. ἐντυπόω **ĕntupŏō,** *en-too-pŏ´-o;* from *1722* and a der. of *5179;* to *enstamp,* i.e. *engrave:*—engrave.

1796. ἐνυβρίζω **ĕnubrizō,** *en-oo-brid´-zo;* from *1722* and *5195;* to *insult:*—do despite unto.

1797. ἐνυπνιάζομαι **ĕnupniazŏmai,** *en-oop-nee-ad´-zom-ahee;* mid. from *1798;* to *dream:*—dream (-er).

1798. ἐνύπνιον **ĕnupniŏn,** *en-oop´-nee-on;* from *1722* and *5258;* something seen *in sleep,* i.e. a *dream* (*vision* in a dream):—dream.

1799. ἐνώπιον **ĕnōpiŏn,** *en-o´-pee-on;* neut. of a comp. of *1722* and a der. of *3700; in* the *face* of (lit. or fig.):—before, in the presence (sight) of, to.

1800. Ἐνώς **Ĕnōs,** *en-oce´;* of Heb. or. [583]; *Enos* (i.e. *Enosh*), a patriarch:—Enos.

1801. ἐνωτίζομαι **ĕnōtizŏmai,** *en-o-tid´-zom-ahee;* mid. from a comp. of *1722* and *3775;* to take *in one's ear,* i.e. to *listen:*—hearken.

1802. Ἐνώχ **Ĕnōk,** *en-oke´;* of Heb. or. [2585]; *Enoch* (i.e. *Chanok*), an antediluvian:—Enoch.

ἐξ **ĕx.** See *1537.*

1803. ἕξ **hĕx,** *hex;* a prim. numeral; *six:*—six.

1804. ἐξαγγέλλω **ĕxaggĕllō,** *ex-ang-el´-lo;* from *1537* and the base of *32;* to *publish,* i.e. *celebrate:*—shew forth.

1805. ἐξαγοράζω **ĕxagŏrazō,** *ex-ag-or-ad´-zo;* from *1537* and *59;* to *buy up,* i.e. *ransom;* fig. to *rescue* from loss (*improve* opportunity):—redeem.

1806. ἐξάγω **ĕxagō,** *ex-ag´-o;* from *1537* and *71;* to *lead forth:*—bring forth (out), fetch (lead) out.

1807. ἐξαιρέω **ĕxairĕō,** *ex-ahee-reh´-o;* from *1537* and *138;* act. to *tear out;* mid. to *select;* fig. to *release:*—deliver, pluck out, rescue.

1808. ἐξαίρω **ĕxairō,** *ex-ah´ee-ro;* from *1537* and *142;* to *remove:*—put (take) away.

1809. ἐξαιτέομαι **ĕxaitĕŏmai,** *ex-ahee-teh´-om-ahee;* mid. from *1537* and *154;* to *demand* (for trial):—desire.

1810. ἐξαίφνης **ĕxaiphnēs,** *ex-ah´eef-nace;* from *1537* and the base of *160; of* a *sudden* (*unexpectedly*):—suddenly. Comp. *1819.*

1811. ἐξακολουθέω **ĕxakŏlŏuthĕō,** *ex-ak-ol-oo-theh´-o;* from *1537* and *190;* to *follow out,* i.e. (fig.) to *imitate, obey,* yield to:—follow.

1812. ἑξακόσιοι **hĕxakŏsiŏi,** *hex-ak-os´-ee-oy;* plur. ordinal from *1803* and *1540; six hundred:*—six hundred.

1813. ἐξαλείφω **ĕxalĕiphō,** *ex-al-i´-fo;* from *1537* and *218;* to *smear out,* i.e. *obliterate* (*erase* tears, fig. *pardon* sin):—blot out, wipe away.

1814. ἐξάλλομαι **ĕxallŏmai,** *ex-al´-lom-ahee;* from *1537* and *242;* to *spring forth:*—leap up.

1815. ἐξανάστασις **ĕxanastasis,** *ex-an-as´-tas-is;* from *1817;* a *rising from* death:—resurrection.

1816. ἐξανατέλλω **ĕxanatĕllō,** *ex-an-at-el´-lo;* from *1537* and *393;* to *start up out* of the ground, i.e. *germinate:*—spring up.

1817. ἐξανίστημι **ĕxanistēmi,** *ex-an-is´-tay-mee;* from *1537* and *450;* obj. to *produce,* i.e. (fig.) *beget;* subj. to *arise,* i.e. (fig.) *object:*—raise (rise) up.

1818. ἐξαπατάω **ĕxapataō,** *ex-ap-at-ah´-o;* from *1537* and *538;* to *seduce wholly:*—beguile, deceive.

1819. ἐξάπινα **ĕxapina,** *ex-ap´-ee-nah;* from *1537* and a der. of the same as *160; of* a *sudden,* i.e. *unexpectedly:*—suddenly. Comp. *1810.*

1820. ἐξαπορέομαι **ĕxapŏrĕŏmai,** *ex-ap-or-eh´-om-ahee;* mid. from *1537* and *639;* to *be utterly at a loss,* i.e. *despond:*—(in) despair.

1821. ἐξαποστέλλω **ĕxapŏstĕllō,** *ex-ap-os-tel´-lo;* from *1537* and *649;* to *send away forth,* i.e. (on a mission) to *despatch,* or (peremptorily) to *dismiss:*—send (away, forth, out).

1822. ἐξαρτίζω **ĕxartizō,** *ex-ar-tid´-zo;* from *1537* and a der. of *739;* to *finish out* (time); fig. to *equip fully* (a teacher):—accomplish, thoroughly furnish.

1823. ἐξαστράπτω **ĕxastraptō,** *ex-as-trap´-to;* from *1537* and *797;* to *lighten forth,* i.e. (fig.) to *be radiant* (of very white garments):—glistening.

1824. ἐξαύτης **ĕxautēs,** *ex-ŏw´-tace;* from *1537* and the gen. sing. fem. of *846* (*5610* being understood); *from that* hour, i.e. *instantly:*—by and by, immediately, presently, straightway.

1825. ἐξεγείρω **ĕxĕgĕirō,** *ex-eg-i´-ro;* from *1537* and *1453;* to *rouse fully,* i.e. (fig.) to *resuscitate* (from death), *release* (from infliction):—raise up.

1826. ἔξειμι **ĕxĕimi,** *ex´-i-mee;* from *1537* and εἶμι **ĕimi** (to *go*); to *issue,* i.e. *leave* (a place), *escape* (to the shore):—depart, get [*to land*], go out.

1827. ἐξελέγχω **ĕxĕlĕgchō,** *ex-el-eng´-kho;* from *1537* and *1651;* to *convict fully,* i.e. (by impl.) to *punish:*—convince.

1828. ἐξέλκω **ĕxĕlkō,** *ex-el´-ko;* from *1537* and *1670;* to *drag forth,* i.e. (fig.) to *entice* (to sin):—draw away.

1829. ἐξέραμα **ĕxĕrama,** *ex-er´-am-ah;* from a comp. of *1537* and a presumed ἐράω **ĕraō** (to *spue*); *vomit,* i.e. *food disgorged:*—vomit.

1830. ἐξερευνάω **ĕxĕrĕunaō,** *ex-er-yoo-nah´-o;* from *1537* and *2045;* to *explore* (fig.):—search diligently.

1831. ἐξέρχομαι **ĕxĕrchŏmai,** *ex-er´-khom-ahee;* from *1537* and *2064;* to *issue* (lit. or fig.):—come-(forth, out), depart (out of), escape, get out, go (abroad, away, forth, out, thence), proceed (forth), spread abroad.

1832. ἔξεστι **ĕxĕsti,** *ex´-es-tee;* third pers. sing. pres. indic. of a comp. of *1537* and *1510;* so also

ἐξόν **ĕxŏn,** *ex-on´;* neut. pres. part. of the same (with or without some form of *1510* expressed); impers. *it is right* (through the fig. idea of *being out* in public):—be lawful, let, × may (-est).

1833. ἐξετάζω **ĕxĕtazō,** *ex-et-ad´-zo;* from *1537* and ἐτάζω **ĕtazō** (to *examine*); to *test thoroughly* (by questions), i.e. *ascertain* or *interrogate:*—ask, enquire, search.

1834. ἐξηγέομαι **ĕxēgĕŏmai,** *ex-ayg-eh´-om-ahee;* from *1537* and *2233;* to *consider out* (aloud), i.e. *rehearse, unfold.*—declare, tell.

1835. ἑξήκοντα **hĕxēkŏnta,** *hex-ay´-kon-tah;* the tenth multiple of *1803; sixty:*—sixty [-fold], threescore.

1836. ἑξῆς **hĕxēs,** *hex-ace´;* from *2192* (in the sense of *taking hold* of, i.e. *adjoining*); *successive:*—after, following, × morrow, next.

1837. ἐξηχέομαι **ĕxēchĕŏmai,** *ex-ay-kheh´-om-ahee;* mid. from *1537* and *2278;* to *"echo" forth,* i.e. *resound* (*be* generally *reported*):—sound forth.

1838. ἕξις **hĕxis,** *hex´-is;* from *2192; habit,* i.e. (by impl.) *practice:*—use.

1839. ἐξίστημι **ĕxistēmi,** *ex-is´-tay-mee;* from *1537* and *2476;* to *put* (*stand*) *out* of wits, i.e. *astound,* or (reflex.) *become astounded, insane:*—amaze, be (make) astonished, be beside self (selves), bewitch, wonder.

1840. ἐξισχύω **ĕxischuō,** *ex-is-khoo´-o;* from *1537* and *2480;* to *have full strength,* i.e. *be entirely competent:*—be able.

1841. ἔξοδος **ĕxŏdŏs,** *ex´-od-os;* from *1537* and *3598;* an *exit,* i.e. (fig.) *death:*—decease, departing.

1842. ἐξολοθρεύω **ĕxŏlŏthrĕuō,** *ex-ol-oth-ryoo´-o;* from *1537* and *3645;* to *extirpate:*—destroy.

1843. ἐξομολογέω **ĕxŏmŏlŏgĕō,** *ex-om-ol-og-eh´-o;* from *1537* and *3670;* to *acknowledge* or (by impl. of *assent*) *agree fully:*—confess, profess, promise.

ἐξόν **ĕxŏn.** See *1832.*

1844. ἐξορκίζω **ĕxŏrkizō,** *ex-or-kid´-zo;* from *1537* and *3726;* to *exact an oath,* i.e. *conjure:*—adjure.

1845. ἐξορκιστής **ĕxŏrkistēs,** *ex-or-kis-tace´;* from *1844; one that binds by an oath* (or *spell*), i.e. (by impl.) an *"exorcist"* (*conjurer*);—exorcist.

1846. ἐξορύσσω **ĕxŏrussō,** *ex-or-oos´-so;* from *1537* and *3736;* to *dig out,* i.e. (by extens.) to *extract* (an eye), *remove* (a roofing):—break up, pluck out.

1847. ἐξουδενόω **ĕxŏudĕnŏō,** *ex-oo-den-ŏ´-o;* from *1537* and a der. of the neut. of *3762;* to *make utterly nothing of,* i.e. *despise:*—set at nought. See also *1848.*

1848. ἐξουθενέω **ĕxŏuthĕnĕō,** *ex-oo-then-eh´-o;* a var. of *1847* and mean. the same:—contemptible, despise, least esteemed, set at nought.

1849. ἐξουσία **ĕxŏusia,** *ex-oo-see´-ah;* from *1832* (in the sense of *ability*); *privilege,* i.e. (subj.) *force, capacity, competency, freedom,* or (obj.) *mastery* (concr. *magistrate, superhuman, potentate, token of control*), delegated *influence:*—authority, jurisdiction, liberty, power, right, strength.

1850. ἐξουσιάζω **ĕxŏusiazō,** *ex-oo-see-ad´-zo;* from *1849;* to *control:*—exercise authority upon, bring under the (have) power of.

1851. ἐξοχή **ĕxŏchē,** *ex-okh-ay´;* from a comp. of *1537* and *2192* (mean. to *stand out*); *prominence* (fig.):—principal.

1852. ἐξυπνίζω **ĕxupnizō,** *ex-oop-nid´-zo;* from *1853;* to *waken:*—awake out of sleep.

1853. ἔξυπνος **ĕxupnŏs,** *ex´-oop-nos;* from *1537* and *5258; awake:*—× out of sleep.

1854. ἔξω **ĕxō** *ex´-o;* adv. from *1537; out* (*-side, of doors*), lit. or fig.:—away, forth, (with-) out (of, -ward), strange.

1855. ἔξωθεν **ĕxōthĕn,** *ex´-o-then;* from *1854; external* (*-ly*):—out (-side, -ward, -wardly), (from) without.

1856. ἐξωθέω **ĕxōthĕō,** *ex-o-theh´-o;* or ἐξώθω **ĕxōthō,** *ex-o´-tho;* from *1537* and ὠθέω **ōthĕō** (to *push*); to *expel;* by impl. to *propel:*—drive out, thrust in.

1857. ἐξώτερος **ĕxōtĕrŏs,** *ex-o´-ter-os;* comp. of *1854; exterior:*—outer.

1858. ἑορτάζω **hĕŏrtazō,** *heh-or-tad´-zo;* from *1859;* to *observe a festival:*—keep the feast.

1859. ἑορτή **hĕŏrtē,** *heh-or-tay´;* of uncert. affin.; a *festival:*—feast, holyday.

1860. ἐπαγγελία **ĕpaggĕlia,** *ep-ang-el-ee´-ah;* from *1861;* an *announcement* (for information, assent or pledge; espec. a divine *assurance* of good):—message, promise.

1861. ἐπαγγέλλω **ĕpaggĕllō,** *ep-ang-el´-lo;* from *1909* and the base of *32;* to *announce upon* (reflex.), i.e. (by impl.) to *engage* to do something, to *assert* something respecting oneself:—profess, (make) promise.

1862. ἐπάγγελμα **ĕpaggĕlma,** *ep-ang´-el-mah;* from *1861;* a *self-committal* (by *assurance* of conferring some good):—promise.

1863. ἐπάγω **ĕpagō,** *ep-ag´-o;* from *1909* and *71;* to *superinduce,* i.e. *inflict* (an evil), *charge* (a crime):—bring upon.

1864. ἐπαγωνίζομαι **ĕpagōnizŏmai,** *ep-ag-o-nid´-zom-ahee;* from *1909* and *75;* to *struggle for:*—earnestly contend for.

1865. ἐπαθροίζω **ĕpathrŏizō,** *ep-ath-roid´-zo;* from *1909* and ἀθροίζω **athrŏizō** (to *assemble*); to *accumulate:*—gather thick together.

1866. Ἐπαίνετος **Ĕpainĕtŏs,** *ep-a´hee-net-os;* from *1867; praised; Epænetus,* a Chr.:—Epenetus.

1867. ἐπαινέω **ĕpainĕō,** *ep-ahee-neh´-o;* from *1909* and *134;* to *applaud:*—commend, laud, praise.

1868. ἔπαινος **ĕpainŏs,** *ep´-ahee-nos;* from *1909* and the base of *134; laudation;* concr. a *commendable* thing:—praise.

1869. ἐπαίρω **ĕpairō,** *ep-ahee´-ro;* from *1909* and *142;* to *raise up* (lit. or fig.):—exalt self, poise (lift, take) up.

1870. ἐπαισχύνομαι **ĕpaischunŏmai,** *ep-ahee-skhoo´-nom-ahee;* from *1909* and *153;* to *feel shame for* something:—be ashamed.

1871. ἐπαιτέω **ĕpaitĕō,** *ep-ahee-teh´-o;* from *1909* and *154;* to *ask for:*—beg.

1872. ἐπακολουθέω **ĕpakŏlŏuthĕō,** *ep-ak-ol-oo-theh´-o;* from *1909* and *190;* to *accompany:*—follow (after).

1873. ἐπακούω **ĕpakŏuō,** *ep-ak-oo´-o;* from *1909* and *191;* to *hearken* (favorably) *to:*—hear.

1874. ἐπακροάομαι **ĕpakrŏaŏmai,** *ep-ak-rŏ-ah´-om-ahee;* from *1909* and the base of *202;* to *listen* (intently) *to:*—hear.

1875. ἐπάν **ĕpan,** *ep-an´;* from *1909* and *302;* a particle of indef. contemporaneousness; *whenever, as soon as:*—when.

1876. ἐπάναγκες **ĕpanagkĕs,** *ep-an´-ang-kes;* neut. of a presumed comp. of *1909* and *318;* (adv.) *on necessity,* i.e. *necessarily:*—necessary.

1877. ἐπανάγω **ĕpanagō,** *ep-an-ag´-o;* from *1909* and *321;* to *lead up on,* i.e. (techn.) to *put out* (to sea); (intrans.) to *return:*—launch (thrust) out, return.

1878. ἐπαναμιμνήσκω **ĕpanamimnēskō,** *ep-an-ah-mim-nace´-ko;* from *1909* and *363;* to *remind of:*—put in mind.

1879. ἐπαναπαύομαι **ĕpanapauŏmai,** *ep-an-ah-pŏw´-om-ahee;* mid. from *1909* and *373;* to *settle on;* lit. (*remain*) or fig. (*rely*):—rest in (upon).

1880. ἐπανέρχομαι **ĕpanĕrchŏmai,** *ep-an-er´-khom-ahee;* from *1909* and *424;* to *come up on,* i.e. *return:*—come again, return.

1881. ἐπανίσταμαι **ĕpanistamai,** *ep-an-is´-tam-ahee;* mid. from *1909* and *450;* to *stand up on,* i.e. (fig.) to *attack:*—rise up against.

1882. ἐπανόρθωσις **ĕpanŏrthōsis,** *ep-an-or´-tho-sis;* from a comp. of *1909* and *461;* a *straightening up again,* i.e. (fig.) *rectification* (*reformation*):—correction.

1883. ἐπάνω **ĕpanō,** *ep-an´-o;* from *1909* and *507; up above,* i.e. *over* or *on* (of place, amount, rank, etc.):—above, more than, (up-) on, over.

1884. ἐπαρκέω **ĕparkĕō,** *ep-ar-keh´-o;* from *1909* and *714;* to *avail for,* i.e. *help:*—relieve.

1885. ἐπαρχία **ĕparchia,** *ep-ar-khee´-ah;* from a comp. of *1909* and *757* (mean. a *governor* of a district, "eparch"); a special *region* of government, i.e. a Roman *præfecture:*—province.

1886. ἔπαυλις **ĕpaulis,** *ep´-ŏw-lis;* from *1909* and an equiv. of *833;* a *hut over* the head, i.e. a *dwelling.*

1887. ἐπαύριον **ĕpauriŏn,** *ep-ow´-ree-on;* from *1909* and *839;* occurring *on* the *succeeding* day, i.e. (*2250* being implied) *to-morrow:*—day following, morrow, next day (after).

1888. ἐπαυτοφώρῳ **ĕpautŏphōrō̤,** *ep-ow-tof-o´-ro;* from *1909* and *846* and (the dat. sing. of) a der. of φώρ **phōr** (a *thief*); *in theft itself,* i.e. (by anal.) *in actual crime:*—in the very act.

1889. Ἐπαφρᾶς **Ĕpaphras,** *ep-af-ras´;* contr. from *1891; Epaphras,* a Chr.:—Epaphras.

1890. ἐπαφρίζω **ĕpaphrizō,** *ep-af-rid´-zo;* from *1909* and *875;* to *foam upon,* i.e. (fig.) to *exhibit* (a vile passion):—foam out.

1891. Ἐπαφρόδιτος **Ĕpaphrŏditŏs,** *ep-af-rod´-ee-tos;* from *1909* (in the sense of *devoted* to) and Ἀφροδίτη **Aphrŏditē** (*Venus*); *Epaphroditus,* a Chr.:—Epaphroditus. Comp. *1889.*

1892. ἐπεγείρω **ĕpĕgĕirō,** *ep-eg-i´-ro;* from *1909* and *1453;* to *rouse upon,* i.e. (fig.) to *excite* against:—raise, stir up.

1893. ἐπεί **ĕpĕi,** *ep-i´;* from *1909* and *1487; thereupon,* i.e. *since* (of time or cause):—because, else, for that (then, -asmuch as), otherwise, seeing that, since, when.

1894. ἐπειδή **ĕpĕidē,** *ep-i-day´;* from *1893* and *1211; since now,* i.e. (of time) *when,* or (of cause) *whereas:*—after that, because, for, (that, -asmuch as), seeing, since.

1895. ἐπειδήπερ **ĕpĕidēpĕr,** *ep-i-day´-per;* from *1894* and *4007; since indeed* (of cause):—forasmuch.

1896. ἐπεῖδον **ĕpĕidŏn,** *ep-i´-don;* and other moods and persons of the same tense; from *1909* and *1492;* to *regard* (favorably or otherwise):—behold, look upon.

1897. ἐπείπερ **ĕpĕipĕr,** *ep-i´-per;* from *1893* and *4007; since* indeed (of cause):—seeing.

1898. ἐπεισαγωγή **ĕpĕisagōgē,** *ep-ice-ag-o-gay´;* from a comp. of *1909* and *1521;* a *superintroduction:*—bringing in.

1899. ἔπειτα **ĕpĕita,** *ep´-i-tah;* from *1909* and *1534; thereafter:*—after that (-ward), then.

1900. ἐπέκεινα **ĕpĕkĕina,** *ep-ek´-i-nah;* from *1909* and (the acc. plur. neut. of) *1565; upon those* parts of, i.e. *on the further side of:*—beyond.

1901. ἐπεκτείνομαι **ĕpĕktĕinŏmai,** *ep-ek-ti´-nom-ahee;* mid. from *1909* and *1614;* to *stretch* (oneself) forward *upon:*—reach forth.

1902. ἐπενδύομαι **ĕpĕnduŏmai,** *ep-en-doo´-om-ahee;* mid. from *1909* and *1746;* to *invest upon* oneself:—be clothed upon.

1903. ἐπενδύτης **ĕpĕndutēs,** *ep-en-doo´-tace;* from *1902;* a *wrapper,* i.e. outer garment:—fisher's coat.

1904. ἐπέρχομαι **ĕpĕrchŏmai,***ep-er´-khom-ahee;* from *1909* and *2064;* to *supervene,* i.e. *arrive, occur, impend, attack,* (fig.) *influence:*—come (in, upon).

1905. ἐπερωτάω **ĕpĕrōtaō,** *ep-er-o-tah´-o;* from *1909* and *2065;* to *ask for,* i.e. *inquire, seek:*—ask (after, questions), demand, desire, question.

1906. ἐπερώτημα **ĕpĕrōtēma,** *ep-er-o´-tay-mah;* from *1905;* an *inquiry:*—answer.

1907. ἐπέχω **ĕpĕchō,** *ep-ekh´-o;* from *1909* and *2192;* to *hold upon,* i.e. (by impl.) to *retain;* (by extens.) to *detain;* (with impl. of *3563*) to *pay attention to:*—give (take) heed unto, hold forth, mark, stay.

1908. ἐπηρεάζω **ĕpērĕazō,** *ep-ay-reh-ad´-zo;* from a comp. of *1909* and (prob.) ἀρειά **arĕia** (*threats*); to *insult, slander:*—use despitefully, falsely accuse.

1909. ἐπί **ĕpi,** *ep-ee´;* a prim. prep. prop. mean. *superimposition* (of time, place, order, etc.), as a relation of *distribution* [with the gen.], i.e. *over, upon,* etc.; of *rest* (with the dat.) *at, on,* etc.; of *direction* (with the acc.) *towards, upon,* etc.:—about (the times), above, after, against, among, as long as (touching), at, beside, × have charge of, (be-, [where-]) fore, in (a place, as much as, the time of, -to), (because) of, (up-) on (behalf of) over, (by, for) the space of, through (-out), (un-) to (-ward), with. In compounds it retains essentially the same import, *at, upon,* etc. (lit. or fig.).

1910. ἐπιβαίνω **ĕpibainō,** *ep-ee-bah´ee-no;* from *1909* and the base of *939;* to *walk upon,* i.e. *mount, ascend, embark, arrive:*—come (into), enter into, go abroad, sit upon, take ship.

1911. ἐπιβάλλω **ĕpiballō,** *ep-ee-bal´-lo;* from *1909* and *906;* to *throw upon* (lit. or fig., trans. or reflex.; usually with more or less force); spec. (with *1438* implied) to *reflect;* impers. to *belong to:*—beat into, cast (up-), on, fall, lay (on), put (unto), stretch forth, think on.

1912. ἐπιβαρέω **ĕpibarĕō,** *ep-ee-bar-eh´-o;* from *1909* and *916;* to *be heavy upon,* i.e. (pecuniarily) to *be expensive to;* fig. to *be severe towards:*—be chargeable to, overcharge.

1913. ἐπιβιβάζω **ĕpibibazō,** *ep-ee-bee-bad´-zo;* from *1909* and a redupl. deriv. of the base of *939* [comp. *307*]; to *cause to mount* (an animal):—set on.

1914. ἐπιβλέπω **ĕpiblĕpō,** *ep-ee-blep´-o;* from *1909* and *991;* to *gaze at* (with favor, pity or partiality):—look upon, regard, have respect to.

1915. ἐπίβλημα **ĕpiblēma,** *ep-ib´-lay-mah;* from *1911;* a *patch:*—piece.

1916. ἐπιβοάω **ĕpibŏaō,** *ep-ee-bo-ah´-o;* from *1909* and *994;* to *exclaim against:*—cry.

1917. ἐπιβουλή **ĕpibŏulē,** *ep-ee-boo-lay´;* from a presumed comp. of *1909* and *1014;* a *plan against* someone, i.e. a *plot:*—laying (lying) in wait.

1918. ἐπιγαμβρεύω **ĕpigambrĕuō,** *ep-ee-gam-bryoo´-o;* from *1909* and a der. of *1062;* to *form affinity with,* i.e. (spec.) in a levirate way:—marry.

1919. ἐπίγειος **ĕpigĕiŏs,** *ep-ig´-i-os;* from *1909* and *1093;* *worldly* (phys. or mor.):—earthly, in earth, terrestrial.

1920. ἐπιγίνομαι **ĕpiginŏmai,** *ep-ig-in´-om-ahee;* from *1909* and *1096;* to *arrive upon,* i.e. *spring up* (as a wind):—blow.

1921. ἐπιγινώσκω **ĕpiginōskō,** *ep-ig-in-oce´-ko;* from *1909* and *1097;* to *know upon* some mark, i.e. *recognise;* by impl. to *become fully acquainted with,* to *acknowledge:*—(ac-, have, take) know (-ledge, well), perceive.

1922. ἐπίγνωσις **epignōsis,** *ep-ig´-no-sis;* from *1921;* *recognition,* i.e. (by impl.) full *discernment, acknowledgment:*—(ac-) knowledge (-ing, -ment).

1923. ἐπιγραφή **ĕpigraphē,** *ep-ig-raf-ay´;* from *1924;* an *inscription:*—superscription.

1924. ἐπιγράφω **ĕpigraphō,** *ep-ee-graf´-o;* from *1909* and *1125;* to *inscribe* (phys. or ment.):—inscription, write in (over, thereon).

1925. ἐπιδείκνυμι **ĕpidĕiknumi,** *ep-ee-dike´-noo-mee;* from *1909* and *1166;* to *exhibit* (phys. or ment.):—shew.

1926. ἐπιδέχομαι **ĕpidĕchŏmai,** *ep-ee-dekh´-om-ahee;* from *1909* and *1209;* to *admit* (as a guest or [fig.] teacher):—receive.

1927. ἐπιδημέω **ĕpidēmĕō,** *ep-ee-day-meh´-o;* from a comp. of *1909* and *1218;* to *make oneself at home,* i.e. (by extens.) to *reside* (in a foreign country:—[be] dwelling (which were) there, stranger.

1928. ἐπιδιατάσσομαι **ĕpidiatassŏmai,** *ep-ee-dee-ah-tas´-som-ahee;* mid. from *1909* and *1299;* to *appoint besides,* i.e. *supplement* (as a codicil):—add to.

1929. ἐπιδίδωμι **ĕpididōmi,** *ep-ee-did´-o-mee;* from *1909* and *1325;* to *give over* (by hand or surrender):—deliver unto, give, let (+ [her drive]), offer.

1930. ἐπιδιορθόω **ĕpidiŏrthŏō,** *ep-ee-dee-or-thŏ´-o;* from *1909* and a der. of *3717;* to *straighten further,* i.e. (fig.) *arrange additionally:*—set in order.

1931. ἐπιδύω **ĕpiduō,** *ep-ee-doo´-o;* from *1909* and *1416;* to *set* fully (as the sun):—go down.

1932. ἐπιείκεια **ĕpiĕikĕia,** *ep-ee-i´-ki-ah;* from *1933;* *suitableness,* i.e. (by impl.) *equity, mildness:*—clemency, gentleness.

1933. ἐπιεικής **ĕpiĕikēs,** *ep-ee-i-kace´;* from *1909* and *1503;* *appropriate,* i.e. (by impl.) *mild:*—gentle, moderation, patient.

1934. ἐπιζητέω **ĕpizētĕō,** *ep-eed-zay-teh´-o;* from *1909* and *2212;* to *search* (*inquire*) *for;* intens to *demand,* to *crave:*—desire, enquire, seek (after, for).

1935. ἐπιθανάτιος **ĕpithanatiŏs,** *ep-ee-than-at´-ee-os;* from *1909* and *2288;* doomed *to death:*—appointed to death.

1936. ἐπίθεσις **ĕpithĕsis,** *ep-ith´-es-is;* from *2007;* an *imposition* (of hands officially):—laying (putting) on.

1937. ἐπιθυμέω **ĕpithumĕō,** *ep-ee-thoo-meh´-o;* from *1909* and *2372;* to set the *heart upon,* i.e. *long* for (rightfully or otherwise):—covet, desire, would fain, lust (after).

1938. ἐπιθυμητής **ĕpithumētēs,** *ep-ee-thoo-may-tace´;* from *1937;* a *craver:*—+ lust after.

1939. ἐπιθυμία **ĕpithumia,** *ep-ee-thoo-mee´-ah;* from *1937;* a *longing* (espec. for what is forbidden):—concupiscence, desire, lust (after).

1940. ἐπικαθίζω **ĕpikathizō,** *ep-ee-kath-id´-zo;* from *1909* and *2523;* to *seat upon:*—set on.

1941. ἐπικαλέομαι **ĕpikalĕŏmai,** *ep-ee-kal-eh´-om-ahee;* mid. from *1909* and *2564;* to *entitle;* by impl. to *invoke* (for aid, worship, testimony, decision, etc.):—appeal (unto), call (on, upon), surname.

1942. ἐπικάλυμα **ĕpikaluma,** *ep-ee-kal´-oo-mah;* from *1943;* a *covering,* i.e. (fig.) *pretext:*—cloke.

1943. ἐπικαλύπτω **ĕpikaluptō,** *ep-ee-kal-oop´-to;* from *1909* and *2572;* to *conceal,* i.e. (fig.) *forgive:*—cover.

1944. ἐπικατάρατος **ĕpikataratŏs,** *ep-ee-kat-ar´-at-os;* from *1909* and a der. of *2672;* *imprecated,* i.e. *execrable:*—accursed.

1945. ἐπίκειμαι **ĕpikĕimai,** *ep-ik´-i-mahee;* from *1909* and *2749;* to *rest upon* (lit. or fig.):—impose, be instant, (be) laid (there-, up-) on, (when) lay (on), lie (on), press upon.

1946. Ἐπικούρειος **Ĕpikŏurĕiŏs,** *ep-ee-koo´-ri-os;* from Ἐπίκουρος **Ĕpikŏurŏs** [comp. *1947*] (a noted philosopher); an *Epicurean* or follower of Epicurus:—Epicurean.

1947. ἐπικουρία **ĕpikŏuria,** *ep-ee-koo-ree´-ah;* from a comp. of *1909* and a (prol.) form of the base of *2877* (in the sense of *servant*); *assistance:*—help.

1948. ἐπικρίνω **ĕpikrinō,** *ep-ee-kree´-no;* from *1909* and *2919;* to *adjudge:*—give sentence.

1949. ἐπιλαμβάνομαι **ĕpilambanŏmai,** *ep-ee-lam-ban´-om-ahee;* mid. from *1909* and *2983;* to *seize* (for help, injury, attainment or any other purpose; lit. or fig.):—catch, lay hold (up-) on, take (by, hold of, on).

1950. ἐπιλανθάνομαι **ĕpilanthanŏmai,** *ep-ee-lan-than´-om-ahee;* mid. from *1909* and *2990;* to *lose out* of mind; by impl. to *neglect:*—(be) forget (-ful of).

1951. ἐπιλέγομαι **ĕpilĕgŏmai,** *ep-ee-leg´-om-ahee;* mid. from *1909* and *3004;* to *surname, select:*—call, choose.

1952. ἐπιλείπω **ĕpilĕipō,** *ep-ee-li´-po;* from *1909* and *3007;* to *leave upon,* i.e. (fig.) to *be insufficient for:*—fall.

1953. ἐπιλησμονή **ĕpilēsmŏnē,** *ep-ee-lace-mon-ay´;* from a der. of *1950;* *negligence:*—× forgetful.

1954. ἐπίλοιπος **ĕpilŏipŏs,** *ep-il´-oy-pos;* from *1909* and *3062;* *left over,* i.e. *remaining:*—rest.

1955. ἐπίλυσις **ĕpilusis,** *ep-il´-oo-sis;* from *1956; explanation,* i.e. *application:*—interpretation.

1956. ἐπιλύω **ĕpiluō,** *ep-ee-loo´-o;* from *1909* and *3089;* to *solve further,* i.e. (fig.) to *explain, decide:*—determine, expound.

1957. ἐπιμαρτυρέω **ĕpimarturĕō,** *ep-ee-mar-too-reh´-o;* from *1909* and *3140;* to *attest further,* i.e. *corroborate:*—testify.

1958. ἐπιμέλεια **ĕpimĕlĕia,** *ep-ee-mel´-i-ah;* from *1959; carefulness,* i.e. kind *attention* (*hospitality*):— + refresh self.

1959. ἐπιμελέομαι **ĕpimĕlĕŏmai,** *ep-ee-mel-eh´-om-ahee;* mid. from *1909* and the same as *3199;* to *care for* (phys. or otherwise):—take care of.

1960. ἐπιμελῶς **ĕpimĕlōs,** *ep-ee-mel-oce´;* adv. from a der. of *1959; carefully:*—diligently.

1961. ἐπιμένω **ĕpimĕnō,** *ep-ee-men´-o;* from *1909* and *3306;* to *stay over,* i.e. *remain* (fig. *persevere*):—abide (in), continue (in), tarry.

1962. ἐπινεύω **ĕpinĕnō,** *ep-een-yoo´-o;* from *1909* and *3506;* to *nod at,* i.e. (by impl.) to *assent:*—consent.

1963. ἐπίνοια **ĕpinŏia,** *ep-in´-oy-ah;* from *1909* and *3563; attention* of the mind, i.e. (by impl.) *purpose:*—thought.

1964. ἐπιορκέω **ĕpiŏrkĕō,** *ep-ee-or-keh´-o;* from *1965;* to *commit perjury:*—forswear self.

1965. ἐπίορκος **ĕpiŏrkŏs,** *ep-ee´-or-kos;* from *1909* and *3727; on oath,* i.e. (falsely) a *forswearer:*—perjured person.

1966. ἐπιοῦσα **ĕpiŏusa,** *ep-ee-oo´-sah;* fem. sing. part. of a comp. of *1909* and εἶμι **hĕimi** (to *go*); *supervening,* i.e. (*2250* or *3571* being expressed or implied) the *ensuing* day or night:—following, next.

1967. ἐπιούσιος **ĕpiŏusiŏs,** *ep-ee-oo´-see-os;* perh. from the same as *1966; to-morrow's;* but more prob. from *1909* and a der. of the pres. part. fem. of *1510; for subsistence,* i.e. *needful:*—daily.

1968. ἐπιπίπτω **ĕpipiptō,** *ep-ee-pip´-to;* from *1909* and *4098;* to *embrace* (with affection) or *seize* (with more or less violence; lit. or fig.):—fall into (on, upon), lie on, press upon.

1969. ἐπιπλήσσω **ĕpiplēssō,** *ep-ee-place´-so;* from *1909* and *4141;* to *chastise,* i.e. (with words) to *upbraid:*—rebuke.

1970. ἐπιπνίγω **ĕpipnigō,** *ep-ee-pnee´-go;* from *1909* and *4155;* to *throttle upon,* i.e. (fig.) *overgrow:*—choke.

1971. ἐπιποθέω **ĕpipŏthĕō,** *ep-ee-poth-eh´-o;* from *1909* and ποθέω **pŏthĕō** (to *yearn*); to *dote upon,* i.e. *intensely crave* possession (lawfully or wrongfully):—(earnestly) desire (greatly), (greatly) long (after), lust.

1972. ἐπιπόθησις **ĕpipŏthēsis,** *ep-ee-poth´-ay-sis;* from *1971;* a *longing for:*—earnest (vehement) desire.

1973. ἐπιπόθητος **ĕpipŏthētŏs,** *ep-ee-poth´-ay-tos;* from *1909* and a der. of the latter part of *1971; yearned upon,* i.e. *greatly loved:*—longed for.

1974. ἐπιποθία **ĕpipŏthia,** *ep-ee-poth-ee´-ah;* from *1971; intense longing:*—great desire.

1975. ἐπιπορεύομαι **ĕpipŏrĕuŏmai,** *ep-ee-por-yoo´-om-ahee;* from *1909* and *4198;* to *journey further,* i.e. *travel on* (*reach*):—come.

1976. ἐπιῤῥάπτω **ĕpirrhaptō,** *ep-ir-hrap´-to;* from *1909* and the base of *4476;* to *stitch upon,* i.e. *fasten with the needle:*—*sew on.*

1977. ἐπιῤῥίπτω **ĕpirrhiptō,** *ep-ir-hrip´-to;* from *1909* and *4496;* to *throw upon* (lit. or fig.):—cast upon.

1978. ἐπίσημος **ĕpisēmŏs,** *ep-is´-ay-mos;* from *1909* and some form of the base of *4591; remarkable,* i.e. (fig.) *eminent:*—notable, of note.

1979. ἐπισιτισμός **ĕpisitismŏs,** *ep-ee-sit-is-mos´;* from a comp. of *1909* and a der. of *4621;* a *provisioning,* i e. (concr.) *food:*—victuals.

1980. ἐπισκέπτομαι **ĕpiskĕptŏmai,** *ep-ee-skep´-tom-ahee;* mid. from *1909* and the base of *4649;* to *inspect,* i.e. (by impl.) to *select;* by extens. to *go to see, relieve:*—look out, visit.

1981. ἐπισκηνόω **ĕpiskēnŏō,** *ep-ee-skay-nŏ´-o;* from *1909* and *4637;* to *tent upon,* i.e. (fig.) *abide with:*—rest upon.

1982. ἐπισκιάζω **ĕpiskiazō,** *ep-ee-skee-ad´-zo;* from *1909* and a der. of *4639;* to *cast a shade upon,* i.e. (by anal.) to *envelop* in a haze of brilliancy; fig. to *invest* with preternatural influence:—overshadow.

1983. ἐπισκοπέω **ĕpiskŏpĕō,** *ep-ee-skop-eh´-o;* from *1909* and *4648;* to *oversee;* by impl. to *beware:*—look diligently, take the oversight.

1984. ἐπισκοπή **ĕpiskŏpē,** *ep-is-kop-ay´;* from *1980; inspection* (for relief); by impl. *superintendence;* spec. the Chr. *"episcopate":*—the office of a "bishop", bishoprick, visitation.

1985. ἐπίσκοπος **ĕpiskŏpŏs,** *ep-is´-kop-os;* from *1909* and *4649* (in the sense of *1983*); a *superintendent,* i.e. Chr. officer in gen. charge of a (or the) church (lit. or fig.):—bishop, overseer.

1986. ἐπισπάομαι **ĕpispaŏmai,** *ep-ee-spah´-om-ahee;* from *1909* and *4685;* to *draw over,* i.e. (with *203* implied) *efface* the mark of *circumcision* (by recovering with the foreskin):—become uncircumcised.

1987. ἐπίσταμαι **ĕpistamai,** *ep-is´-tam-ahee;* appar. a mid. of *2186* (with *3563* implied); to *put* the mind *upon,* i.e. *comprehend,* or *be acquainted with:*—know, understand.

1988. ἐπιστάτης **ĕpistatēs,** *ep-is-tat´-ace;* from *1909* and a presumed der. of *2476;* an *appointee over,* i.e. *commander* (*teacher*):—master.

1989. ἐπιστέλλω **ĕpistĕllō,** *ep-ee-stel´-lo;* from *1909* and *4724;* to *enjoin* (by writing), i.e. (gen.) to *communicate by letter* (for any purpose):—write (a letter, unto).

1990. ἐπιστήμων **ĕpistēmōn,** *ep-ee-stay´-mone;* from *1987; intelligent:*—endued with knowledge.

1991. ἐπιστηρίζω **ĕpistērizō,** *ep-ee-stay-rid´-zo;* from *1909* and *4741;* to *support further,* i.e. *reëstablish:*—confirm, strengthen.

1992. ἐπιστολή **ĕpistŏlē,** *ep-is-tol-ay´;* from *1989;* a *written message:*—"epistle", letter.

1993. ἐπιστομίζω **ĕpistŏmizō,** *ep-ee-stom-id´-zo;* from *1909* and *4750;* to put something *over* the *mouth,* i.e. (fig.) to *silence:*—stop mouths.

1994. ἐπιστρέφω **ĕpistrĕphō,** *ep-ee-stref´-o;* from *1909* and *4762;* to *revert* (lit., fig. or mor.):—come (go) again, convert, (re-) turn (about, again).

1995. ἐπιστροφή **ĕpistrŏphē,** *ep-is-trof-ay´;* from *1994; reversion,* i.e. mor. *revolution:*—conversion.

1996. ἐπισυνάγω **ĕpisunagō,** *ep-ee-soon-ag´-o;* from *1909* and *4863;* to *collect upon* the same place:—gather (together).

1997. ἐπισυναγωγή **ĕpisunagōgē,** *ep-ee-soon-ag-o-gay´;* from *1996;* a complete *collection;* spec. a Chr. *meeting* (for worship):—assembling (gathering) together.

1998. ἐπισυντρέχω **ĕpisuntrĕchō,** *ep-ee-soon-trekh´-o;* from *1909* and *4936;* to *hasten together upon* one place (or a partic. occasion):—come running together.

1999. ἐπισύστασις **ĕpisustasis,** *ep-ee-soo´-stas-is;* from the mid. of a comp. of *1909* and *4921;* a *conspiracy,* i.e. *concourse* (riotous or friendly):—that which cometh upon, + raising up.

2000. ἐπισφαλής **ĕpisphalēs,** *ep-ee-sfal-ace´;* from a comp. of *1909* and σφάλλω **sphallō** (to *trip*); fig. *insecure:*—dangerous.

2001. ἐπισχύω **ĕpischuō,** *ep-is-khoo´-o;* from *1909* and *2480;* to *avail further,* i.e. (fig.) *insist stoutly:*—be the more fierce.

2002. ἐπισωρεύω **ĕpisōrĕuō,** *ep-ee-so-ryoo´-o;* from *1909* and *4987;* to *accumulate further,* i.e. (fig.) *seek* additionally:—heap.

2003. ἐπιταγή **ĕpitagē,** *ep-ee-tag-ay´;* from *2004;* an *injunction* or *decree;* by impl. *authoritativeness:*—authority, commandment.

2004. ἐπιτάσσω **ĕpitassō,** *ep-ee-tas´-so;* from *1909* and *5021;* to *arrange upon,* i.e. *order:*—charge, command, injoin.

2005. ἐπιτελέω **ĕpitĕlĕō,** *ep-ee-tel-eh´-o;* from *1909* and *5055;* to *fulfill further* (or *completely*), i.e. *execute;* by impl. to *terminate, undergo:*—accomplish, do, finish, (make) (perfect), perform (× -ance).

2006. ἐπιτήδειος **ĕpitēdĕiŏs,** *ep-ee-tay´-di-os;* from ἐπιτηδές **ĕpitēdĕs** (*enough*); *serviceable,* i.e. (by impl.) *requisite:*—things which are needful.

2007. ἐπιτίθημι **ĕpitithēmi,** *ep-ee-tith´-ay-mee;* from *1909* and *5087;* to *impose* (in a friendly or hostile sense):—add unto, lade, lay upon, put (up) on, set on (up), + surname, × wound.

2008. ἐπιτιμάω **ĕpitimaō,** *ep-ee-tee-mah´-o;* from *1909* and *5091;* to *tax upon,* i.e. *censure* or *admonish;* by impl. *forbid:*—(straitly) charge, rebuke.

2009. ἐπιτιμία **ĕpitimia,** *ep-ee-tee-mee´-ah;* from a comp. of *1909* and *5092;* prop. *esteem,* i.e. *citizenship;* used (in the sense of *2008*) of a *penalty:*—punishment.

2010. ἐπιτρέπω **ĕpitrĕpō,** *ep-ee-trep´-o;* from *1909* and the base of *5157;* to *turn over* (*transfer*), i.e. *allow:*—give leave (liberty, license), let, permit, suffer.

2011. ἐπιτροπή **ĕpitrŏpē,** *ep-ee-trop-ay´;* from *2010; permission,* i.e. (by impl.) full *power:*—commission.

2012. ἐπίτροπος **ĕpitrŏpŏs,** *ep-it´-rop-os;* from *1909* and *5158* (in the sense of *2011*); a *commissioner,* i.e. domestic *manager, guardian:*—steward, tutor.

2013. ἐπιτυγχάνω **ĕpitugchanō,** *ep-ee-toong-khan´-o;* from *1909* and *5177;* to *chance upon,* i.e. (by impl.) *attain:*—obtain.

2014. ἐπιφαίνω **ĕpiphainō,** *ep-ee-fah´ee-no;* from *1909* and *5316;* to *shine upon,* i.e. *become* (lit.) *visible* or (fig.) *known:*—appear, give light.

2015. ἐπιφάνεια **ĕpiphanĕia,** *ep-if-an´-i-ah;* from *2016;* a *manifestation,* i.e. (spec.) the *advent* of Christ (past or fut.):—appearing, brightness.

2016. ἐπιφανής **ĕpiphanēs,** *ep-if-an-ace´;* from *2014; conspicuous,* i.e. (fig.) *memorable:*—notable.

2017. ἐπιφαύω **ĕpiphauō,** *ep-ee-fōw´-o;* a form of *2014;* to *illuminate* (fig.):—give light.

2018. ἐπιφέρω **ĕpiphĕrō,** *ep-ee-fer´-o;* from *1909* and *5342;* to *bear upon* (or *further*), i.e. *adduce* (pers. or judicially [*accuse, inflict*]), *superinduce:*—add, bring (against), take.

2019. ἐπιφωνέω **ĕpiphōnĕō,** *ep-ee-fo-neh´-o;* from *1909* and *5455;* to *call at* something, i.e. *exclaim:*—cry (against), give a shout.

2020. ἐπιφώσκω **ĕpiphōskō,** *ep-ee-foce´-ko;* a form of *2017;* to begin to *grow light:*—begin to dawn, × draw on.

2021. ἐπιχειρέω **ĕpichĕirĕō,** *ep-ee-khi-reh´-o;* from *1909* and *5495;* to put the *hand upon,* i.e. *undertake:*—go about, take in hand (upon).

2022. ἐπιχέω **ĕpichĕō,** *ep-ee-kheh´-o;* from *1909* and χέω **chĕō** (to *pour*); to *pour upon:*—pour in.

2023. ἐπιχορηγέω **ĕpichŏrēgĕō,** *ep-ee-khor-ayg-eh´-o;* from *1909* and *5524;* to *furnish besides,* i.e. fully *supply,* (fig.) *aid* or *contribute:*—add, minister (nourishment, unto).

2024. ἐπιχορηγία **ĕpichŏrēgia,** *ep-ee-khor-ayg-ee´-ah;* from *2023; contribution:*—supply.

2025. ἐπιχρίω **ĕpichriō,** *ep-ee-khree´-o;* from *1909* and *5548;* to *smear over:*—anoint.

2026. ἐποικοδομέω **ĕpŏikŏdŏmĕō,** *ep-oy-kod-om-eh´-o;* from *1909* and *3618;* to *build upon,* i.e. (fig.) to *rear up:*—build thereon (thereupon, on, upon).

2027. ἐποκέλλω **ĕpŏkĕllō,** *ep-ok-el´-lo;* from *1909* and ὀκέλλω **ŏkĕllō** (to *urge*); to *drive upon* the shore, i.e. to *beach* a vessel:—run aground.

2028. ἐπονομάζω **ĕpŏnŏmazō,** *ep-on-om-ad´-zo;* from *1909* and *3687;* to *name further,* i.e. *denominate:*—call.

2029. ἐποπτεύω **ĕpŏptĕuō,** *ep-opt-yoo´-o;* from *1909* and a der. of *3700;* to *inspect,* i.e. *watch:*—behold.

2030. ἐπόπτης **ĕpŏptēs,** *ep-op´-tace;* from *1909* and a presumed der. of *3700;* a *looker-on:*—eye-witness.

2031. ἔπος **ĕpŏs,** *ep´-os;* from *2036;* a *word:*—× say.

2032. ἐπουράνιος **ĕpŏuraniŏs,** *ep-oo-ran´-ee-os;* from *1909* and *3772; above* the *sky:*—celestial, (in) heaven (-ly), high.

2033. ἑπτά **hĕpta,** *hep-tah´;* a prim. number; *seven:*—seven.

2034. ἑπτακίς **hĕptakis,** *hep-tak-is´;* adv. from *2033; seven times:*—seven times.

2035. ἑπτακισχίλιοι **hĕptakischiliŏi,** *hep-tak-is-khil´-ee-oy;* from *2034* and *5507; seven times a thousand:*—seven thousand.

2036. ἔπω **ĕpō,** *ep´-o;* a prim. verb (used only in the def. past tense, the others being borrowed from *2046, 4483* and *5346*); to *speak* or *say* (by word or writing):—answer, bid, bring word, call, command, grant, say (on), speak, tell. Comp. *3004.*

2037. Ἔραστος **Ĕrastŏs,** *er´-as-tos;* from ἐράω **ĕraō** (to *love*); *beloved; Erastus,* a Chr.:—Erastus.

2038. ἐργάζομαι **ĕrgazŏmai,** *er-gad´-zom-ahee;* mid. from *2041;* to *toil* (as a task, occupation, etc.), (by impl.) *effect, be engaged in* or *with,* etc.:—commit, do, labor for, minister about, trade (by), work.

2039. ἐργασία **ĕrgasia,** *er-gas-ee´-ah;* from *2040; occupation;* by impl. *profit, pains:*—craft, diligence, gain, work.

2040. ἐργάτης **ĕrgatēs,** *er-gat´-ace;* from *2041;* a *toiler;* fig. a *teacher:*—labourer, worker (-men).

2041. ἔργον **ĕrgŏn,** *er´-gon;* from a prim. (but obsol.) ἔργω **ĕrgō** (to *work*); *toil* (as an effort or occupation); by impl. an *act:*—deed, doing, labour, work.

2042. ἐρεθίζω **ĕrĕthizō,** *er-eth-id´-zo;* from a presumed prol. form of *2054;* to *stimulate* (espec. to anger):—provoke.

2043. ἐρείδω **ĕrĕidō,** *er-i´-do;* of obscure affin.; to *prop,* i.e. (reflex.) *get fast:*—stick fast.

2044. ἐρεύγομαι **ĕrĕugŏmai,** *er-yoog´-om-ahee;* of uncert. affin.; to *belch,* i.e. (fig.) to *speak out:*—utter.

2045. ἐρευνάω **ĕrĕunaō,** *er-yoo-nah´-o;* appar. from *2046* (through the idea of *inquiry*); to *seek,* i.e. (fig.) to *investigate:*—search.

2046. ἐρέω **ĕrĕō,** *er-eh´-o;* prob. a fuller form of *4483;* an alt. for *2036* in cert. tenses; to *utter,* i.e. *speak* or *say:*—call, say, speak (of), tell.

2047. ἐρημία **ĕrēmia,** *er-ay-mee´-ah;* from *2048; solitude* (concr.):—desert, wilderness.

2048. ἔρημος **ĕrēmŏs,** *er´-ay-mos;* of uncert. affin.; *lonesome,* i.e. (by impl.) *waste* (usually as a noun, *5561* being implied):—desert, desolate, solitary, wilderness.

2049. ἐρημόω **ĕrēmŏō,** *er-ay-mŏ´-o;* from *2048;* to *lay waste* (lit. or fig.):—(bring to, make) desolate (-ion), come to nought.

2050. ἐρήμωσις **ĕrēmōsis,** *er-ay´-mo-sis;* from *2049; despoliation:*—desolation.

2051. ἐρίζω **ĕrizō,** *er-id´-zo;* from *2054;* to *wrangle:*—strive.

2052. ἐριθεία **ĕrithĕia,** *er-ith-i´-ah;* perh. from the same as *2042;* prop. *intrigue,* i.e. (by impl.) *faction:*—contention (-ious), strife.

2053. ἔριον **ĕriŏn,** *er´-ee-on;* of obscure affin.; *wool:*—wool.

2054. ἔρις **ĕris,** *er´-is;* of uncert. affin.; a *quarrel,* i.e. (by impl.) *wrangling:*—contention, debate, strife, variance.

2055. ἐρίφιον **ĕriphiŏn,** *er-if´-ee-on;* from *2056;* a *kidling,* i.e. (gen.) *goat* (symbol, *wicked* person):—goat.

2056. ἔριφος **ĕriphŏs,** *er´-if-os;* perh. from the same as *2053* (through the idea of *hairiness*); a *kid* or (gen.) *goat:*—goat, kid.

2057. Ἑρμᾶς **Hĕrmas,** *her-mas´;* prob. from *2060; Hermas,* a Chr.:—Hermas.

2058. ἑρμηνεία **hĕrmēnĕia,** *her-may-ni´-ah;* from the same as *2059; translation:*—interpretation.

2059. ἑρμηνεύω **hĕrmēnĕuō,** *her-mayn-yoo´-o;* from a presumed der. of *2060* (as the god of language); to *translate:*—interpret.

2060. Ἑρμῆς **Hĕrmēs,** *her-mace´;* perh. from *2046; Hermes,* the name of the messenger of the Gr. deities; also of a Chr.:—Hermes, Mercury.

2061. Ἑρμογένης **Hĕrmŏgĕnēs,** *her-mog-en´-ace;* from *2060* and *1096; born of Hermes; Hermogenes,* an apostate Chr.:—Hermogenes.

2062. ἑρπετόν **hĕrpĕtŏn,** *her-pet-on´;* neut. of a der. of ἕρπω **hĕrpō** (to *creep*); a *reptile,* i.e. (by Hebr. [comp. 7431]) a small *animal:*—creeping thing, serpent.

2063. ἐρυθρός **ĕruthrŏs,** *er-oo-thros´;* of uncert. affin.; *red,* i.e. (with *2281*) the *Red* Sea:—red.

2064. *ἔρχομαι* **ĕrchŏmai,** *er´-khom-ahee;* mid. of a prin. verb (used only in the pres. and imperf. tenses, the others being supplied by a kindred [mid.]

ἐλεύθομαι **ĕlĕuthŏmai,** *el-yoo´-thom-ahee;* or [act.]

ἔλθω **ĕlthō,** *el´-tho;* which do not otherwise occur); to *come* or *go* (in a great variety of applications, lit. and fig.):—accompany, appear, bring, come enter, fall out, go, grow, × light, × next, pass, resort, be set.

2065. *ἐρωτάω* **ĕrōtaō,** *er-o-tah´-o;* appar. from *2046* [comp. *2045*]; to *interrogate;* by impl. to *request:*—ask, beseech, desire, intreat, pray. Comp. *4441.*

2066. *ἐσθής* **ĕsthēs,** *es-thace´;* from *ἕννυμι* **hĕnnumi** (to *clothe*); *dress:*—apparel, clothing, raiment, robe.

2067. *ἔσθησις* **ĕsthēsis,** *es´-thay-sis;* from a der. of *2066; clothing* (concr.):—garment.

2068. *ἐσθίω* **ĕsthiō,** *es-thee´-o;* strengthened for a prim. *ἔδω* **ĕdō** (to *eat*); used only in certain tenses, the rest being supplied by *5315;* to *eat* (usually lit.):—devour, eat, live.

2069. *Ἐσλί* **Ĕsli,** *es-lee´;* of Heb. or. [prob. for 454]; *Esli,* an Isr.:—Esli.

2070. *ἐσμέν* **ĕsmĕn,** *es-men´;* first pers. plur. indic. of *1510;* we *are:*—are, be, have our being, × have hope, + [the gospel] was [preached unto] us.

2071. *ἔσομαι* **ĕsŏmai,** *es´-om-ahee;* fut. of *1510; will be:*—shall (should) be (have), (shall) come (to pass), × may have, × fall, what would follow, × live long, × sojourn.

2072. *ἔσοπτρον* **ĕsŏptrŏn,** *es´-op-tron;* from *1519* and a presumed der. of *3700;* a *mirror* (for *looking into*):—glass. Comp. *2734.*

2073. *ἑσπέρα* **hĕspĕra,** *hes-per´-ah;* fem. of an adj. *ἑσπερός* **hĕspĕrŏs** (*evening*); the *eve* (*5610* being impl.):—evening (-tide).

2074. *Ἐσρώμ* **Ĕsrōm,** *es-rome;* of Heb. or. [2696]; *Esrom* (i.e. *Chetsron*), an Isr.:—Esrom.

2075. *ἐστέ* **ĕstĕ,** *es-teh´;* second pers. plur. pres. indic. of *1510;* ye *are:*—be, have been, belong.

2076. *ἐστί* **ĕsti,** *es-tee´;* third pers. sing. pres. indic. of *1510;* he (she or it) *is;* also (with neut. plur.) they *are:*—are, be (-long), call, × can [-not], come, consisteth, × dure for awhile, + follow, × have, (that) is (to say), make, meaneth, × must needs, + profit, + remaineth, + wrestle.

2077. *ἔστω* **ĕstō,** *es´-to;* second pers. sing. pres. imper. of *1510; be* thou; also

ἔστωσαν **ĕstōsan,** *es´-to-san;* third pers. of the same; *let* them *be:*—be.

2078. *ἔσχατος* **ĕschatŏs,** *es´-khat-os;* a superl. prob. from *2192* (in the sense of *contiguity*); *farthest, final* (of place or time):—ends of, last, latter end, lowest, uttermost.

2079. *ἐσχάτως* **ĕschatōs,** *es-khat´-oce;* adv. from *2078; finally,* i.e. (with *2192*) *at the extremity* of life:—point of death.

2080. *ἔσω* **ĕsō,** *es´-o;* from *1519; inside* (as prep. or adj.):—(with-) in (-ner, -to, -ward).

2081. *ἔσωθεν* **ĕsōthĕn,** *es´-o-then;* from *2080; from inside;* also used as equiv. to *2080* (*inside*):—inward (-ly), (from) within, without.

2082. *ἐσώτερος* **ĕsōtĕrŏs,** *es-o´-ter-os;* compar. of *2080; interior:*—inner, within.

2083. *ἑταῖρος* **hĕtairŏs,** *het-ah´-ee-ros;* from *ἔτης* **ĕtēs** (a *clansman*); a *comrade:*—fellow, friend.

2084. *ἑτερόγλωσσος* **hĕtĕrŏglōssŏs,** *het-er-og´-loce-sos;* from *2087* and *1100; other-tongued,* i.e. a *foreigner:*—man of other tongue.

2085. *ἑτεροδιδασκαλέω* **hĕtĕrŏdidaskalĕō,** *het-er-od-id-as-kal-eh´-o;* from *2087* and *1320;* to *instruct differently:*—teach other doctrine (-wise).

2086. *ἑτεροζυγέω* **hĕtĕrŏzugĕō,** *het-er-od-zoog-eh´-o;* from a comp. of *2087* and *2218;* to *yoke* up *differently,* i.e. (fig.) to *associate discordantly:*—unequally yoke together with.

2087. *ἕτερος* **hĕtĕrŏs,** *het´-er-os;* of uncert. affin.; (an-, the) *other* or *different:*—altered, else, next (day), one, (an-) other, some, strange.

2088. *ἑτέρως* **hĕtĕrōs,** *het-er´-oce;* adv. from *2087; differently:*—otherwise.

2089. *ἔτι* **ĕti,** *et´-ee;* perh. akin to *2094; "yet," still* (of time or degree):—after that, also, ever, (any) further, (t-) henceforth (more), hereafter, (any) longer, (any) more (-one), now, still, yet.

2090. *ἑτοιμάζω* **hĕtŏimazō,** *het-oy-mad´-zo;* from *2092;* to *prepare:*—prepare, provide, make ready. Comp. *2680.*

2091. *ἑτοιμασία* **hĕtŏimasia,** *het-oy-mas-ee´-ah;* from *2090; preparation:*—preparation.

2092. *ἑτοίμος* **hĕtŏimŏs,** *het-oy´-mos;* from an old noun *ἕτεος* **hĕtĕŏs** (*fitness*); *adjusted,* i.e. *ready:*—prepared, (made) ready (-iness, to our hand).

2093. *ἑτοίμως* **hĕtŏimōs,** *het´-oy-moce;* adv. from *2092; in readiness:*—ready.

2094. *ἔτος* **ĕtŏs,** *et´-os;* appar. a prim. word; a *year:*—year.

2095. *εὖ* **ĕu,** *yoo;* neut. of a prim. *εὖς* **ĕus** (*good*); (adv.) *well:*—good, well (done).

2096. *Εὔα* **Ĕua,** *yoo´-ah;* of Heb. or. [2332]; *Eua* (or *Eva,* i.e. *Chavvah*), the first woman:—Eve.

2097. *εὐαγγελίζω* **ĕuaggĕlizō,** *yoo-ang-ghel-id´-zo*); from *2095* and *32;* to *announce good* news ("evangelize") espec. the gospel:—declare, bring (declare, show) glad (good) tidings, preach (the gospel).

2098. *εὐαγγέλιον* **ĕuaggĕliŏn,** *yoo-ang-ghel´-ee-on;* from the same as *2097;* a *good message,* i.e. the *gospel:*—gospel.

2099. *εὐαγγελιστής* **ĕuaggĕlistēs,** *yoo-ang-ghel-is-tace´;* from *2097;* a *preacher* of the gospel:—evangelist.

2100. *εὐαρεστέω* **ĕuarĕstĕō,** *yoo-ar-es-teh´-o;* from *2101;* to *gratify entirely:*—please (well).

2101. *εὐάρεστος* **ĕuarĕstŏs,** *yoo-ar´-es-tos;* from *2095* and *701; fully agreeable:*—acceptable (-ted), wellpleasing.

2102. *εὐαρέστως* **ĕuarĕstōs,** *yoo-ar-es´-toce;* adv. from *2101; quite agreeably:*—acceptably, + please well.

2103. *Εὔβουλος* **Ĕubŏulŏs,** *yoo´-boo-los;* from *2095* and *1014; good-willer; Eubulus,* a Chr.:—Eubulus.

2104. *εὐγένης* **ĕugĕnēs,** *yoog-en´-ace;* from *2095* and *1096; well born,* i.e. (lit.) *high* in rank, or (fig.) *generous:*—more noble, nobleman.

2105. *εὐδία* **ĕudia,** *yoo-dee´-ah;* fem. from *2095* and the alt. of *2203* (as the god of the weather); a *clear sky,* i.e. *fine weather:*—fair weather.

2106. *εὐδοκέω* **ĕudŏkĕō,** *yoo-dok-eh´-o;* from *2095* and *1380;* to *think well* of, i.e. *approve* (an act); spec. to *approbate* (a person or thing):—think good, (be well) please (-d), be the good (have, take) pleasure, be willing.

2107. *εὐδοκία* **ĕudŏkia,** *yoo-dok-ee´-ah;* from a presumed comp. of *2095* and the base of *1380; satisfaction,* i.e. (subj.) *delight,* or (obj.) *kindness, wish, purpose:*—desire, good pleasure (will), × seem good.

2108. *εὐεργεσία* **ĕuĕrgĕsia,** *yoo-erg-es-ee´-ah;* from *2110; beneficence* (gen. or spec.):—benefit, good deed done.

2109. *εὐεργετέω* **ĕuĕrgĕtĕō,** *yoo-erg-et-eh´-o;* from *2110;* to *be philanthropic:*—do good.

2110. *εὐεργέτης* **ĕuĕrgĕtēs,** *yoo-erg-et´-ace;* from *2095* and the base of *2041;* a *worker of good,* i.e. (spec.) a *philanthropist:*—benefactor.

2111. *εὔθετος* **ĕuthĕtŏs,** *yoo´-thet-os;* from *2095* and a der. of *5087; well placed,* i.e. (fig.) *appropriate:*—fit, meet.

2112. *εὐθέως* **ĕuthĕōs,** *yoo-theh´-oce;* adv. from *2117; directly,* i.e. *at once* or *soon:*—anon, as soon as, forthwith, immediately, shortly, straightway.

2113. *εὐθυδρομέω* **ĕuthudrŏmĕō,** *yoo-thoo-drom-eh´-o;* from *2117* and *1408;* to *lay a straight course,* i.e. *sail direct:*—(come) with a straight course.

2114. *εὐθυμέω* **ĕuthumĕō,** *yoo-thoo-meh´-o;* from *2115;* to *cheer up,* i.e. (intrans.) *be cheerful;* neut. comp. (adv.) *more cheerfully:*—be of good cheer (merry).

2115. *εὔθυμος* **ĕuthumŏs,** *yoo´-thoo-mos;* from *2095* and *2372;* in *fine spirits,* i.e. *cheerful:*—of good cheer, the more cheerfully.

2116. *εὐθύνω* **ĕuthunō,** *yoo-thoo´-no;* from *2117;* to *straighten* (*level*); tech. to *steer:*—governor, make straight.

2117. *εὐθύς* **ĕuthus,** *yoo-thoos´;* perh. from *2095* and *5087; straight,* i.e. (lit.) *level,* or (fig.) *true;* adv. (of time) *at once:*—anon, by and by, forthwith, immediately, straightway.

2118. *εὐθύτης* **ĕuthutēs,** *yoo-thoo´-tace;* from *2117; rectitude:*—righteousness.

2119. *εὐκαιρέω* **ĕukairĕō,** *yoo-kahee-reh´-o;* from *2121;* to *have good time,* i.e. *opportunity* or *leisure:*—have leisure (convenient time), spend time.

2120. *εὐκαιρία* **ĕukairia,** *yoo-kahee-ree´-ah;* from *2121;* a favorable *occasion:*—opportunity.

2121. *εὔκαιρος* **ĕukairŏs,** *yoo´-kahee-ros;* from *2095* and *2540; well-timed,* i.e. *opportune:*—convenient, in time of need.

2122. *εὐκαίρως* **ĕukairōs,** *yoo-kah´ee-roce;* adv. from *2121; opportunely:*—conveniently, in season.

2123. *εὐκοπώτερος* **ĕukŏpōtĕrŏs,** *yoo-kop-o´-ter-os;* comp. of a comp. of *2095* and *2873; better for toil,* i.e. *more facile:*—easier.

2124. *εὐλάβεια* **ĕulabĕia,** *yoo-lab´-i-ah;* from *2126;* prop. *caution,* i.e. (religiously) *reverence* (*piety*); by impl. *dread* (concr.):—fear (-ed).

2125. *εὐλαβέομαι* **ĕulabĕŏmai,** *yoo-lab-eh´-om-ahee;* mid. from *2126;* to *be circumspect,* i.e. (by impl.) to *be apprehensive;* religiously, to *reverence:*—(moved with) fear.

2126. *εὐλαβής* **ĕulabēs,** *yoo-lab-ace´;* from *2095* and *2983; taking well* (*carefully*), i.e. *circumspect* (religiously, *pious*):—devout.

2127. *εὐλογέω* **ĕulŏgĕō,** *yoo-log-eh´-o;* from a comp. of *2095* and *3056;* to *speak well of,* i.e. (religiously) to *bless* (*thank* or *invoke a benediction upon, prosper*):—bless, praise.

2128. *εὐλογητός* **ĕulŏgētŏs,** *yoo-log-ay-tos´;* from *2127; adorable:*—blessed.

2129. *εὐλογία* **ĕulŏgia,** *yoo-log-ee´-ah;* from the same as *2127; fine speaking,* i.e. *elegance of language; commendation* (*"eulogy"*), i.e. (reverentially) *adoration;* religiously, *benediction;* by impl. *consecration;* by extens. *benefit* or *largess:*—blessing (a matter of) bounty (× -tifully), fair speech.

2130. *εὐμετάδοτος* **ĕumĕtadŏtŏs,** *yoo-met-ad´-ot-os;* from *2095* and a presumed der. of *3330; good at imparting,* i.e. *liberal:*—ready to distribute.

2131. Εὐνίκη **Ĕunikē,** *yoo-nee´-kay;* from *2095* and *3529; victorious; Eunice,* a Jewess:—Eunice.

2132. *εὐνόεω* **ĕunŏĕō,** *yoo-nŏ´-eh-o;* from a comp. of *2095* and *3563;* to *be well-minded,* i.e. *reconcile:*—agree.

2133. *εὔνοια* **ĕunŏia,** *yoo´-noy-ah;* from the same as *2132; kindness;* euphem. *conjugal duty:*—benevolence, good will.

2134. *εὐνουχίζω* **ĕunŏuchizō,** *yoo-noo-khid´-zo,* from *2135;* to *castrate* (fig. *live unmarried*):—make . . . eunuch.

2135. *εὐνοῦχος* **ĕunŏuchŏs,** *yoo-noo´-khos;* from *εὐνή* **ĕunē** (a *bed*) and *2192;* a *castrated* person (such being employed in Oriental bed-chambers); by extens. an *impotent* or *unmarried* man; by impl. a *chamberlain* (*state-officer*):—eunuch.

2136. Εὐοδία **Ĕuŏdia,** *yoo-od-ee´-ah;* from the same as *2137; fine travelling; Euodia,* a Chr. woman:—Euodias.

2137. *εὐοδόω* **ĕuŏdŏō,** *yoo-od-ŏ´-o;* from a comp. of *2095* and *3598;* to *help* on the *road,* i.e. (pass.) *succeed in reaching;* fig. to *succeed* in business affairs:—(have a) prosper (-ous journey).

2138. *εὐπειθής* **ĕupĕithēs,** *yoo-pi-thace´;* from *2095* and *3982; good* for *persuasion,* i.e. (intrans.) *compliant:*—easy to be intreated.

2139. *εὐπερίστατος* **ĕupĕristatŏs,** *yoo-per-is´-tat-os;* from *2095* and a der. of a presumed comp. of *4012* and *2476; well standing around,* i.e. (a *competitor*) *thwarting* (a racer) in every direction (fig. of sin in gen.):—which doth so easily beset.

2140. *εὐποιΐα* **ĕupŏiïa,** *yoo-poy-ee´-ah;* from a comp. of *2095* and *4160; well doing,* i.e. *beneficence:*—to do good.

2141. *εὐπορέω* **ĕupŏrĕō,** *yoo-por-eh´-o;* from a comp. of *2090* and the base of *4197;* (intrans.) to *be good* for *passing* through, i.e. (fig.) *have* pecuniary *means:*—ability.

2142. *εὐπορία* **ĕupŏria,** *yoo-por-ee´-ah;* from the same as *2141;* pecuniary *resources:*—wealth.

2143. *εὐπρέπεια* **ĕuprĕpĕia,** *yoo-prep´-i-ah;* from a comp. of *2095* and *4241; good suitableness,* i.e. *gracefulness:*—grace.

2144. *εὐπρόσδεκτος* **ĕuprŏsdĕktŏs,** *yoo-pros´-dek-tos;* from *2095* and a der. of *4327; well-received,* i.e. *approved, favorable:*—acceptable (-ted).

2145. *εὐπρόσεδρος* **ĕuprŏsĕdrŏs,** *yoo-pros´-ed-ros;* from *2095* and the same as *4332; sitting well towards,* i.e. (fig.) *assiduous* (neut. *diligent service*):—× attend upon.

2146. *εὐπροσωπέω* **ĕuprŏsōpĕō,** *yoo-pros-o-peh´-o;* from a comp. of *2095* and *4383;* to *be of good countenance,* i.e. (fig.) to *make a display:*—make a fair show.

2147. *εὑρίσκω* **hĕuriskō,** *hyoo-ris´-ko;* a prol. form of a prim.

εὕρω **hĕurō,** *hyoo´-ro;* which (together with another cognate form

εὑρέω **hĕurĕō,** *hyoo-reh´-o*) is used for it in all the tenses except the pres. and imperf.; to *find* (lit. or fig.):—find, get, obtain, perceive, see.

2148. Εὐροκλύδων **Ĕurŏkludōn,** *yoo-rok-loo´-dohn;* from Εὖρος **Ĕurŏs** (the *east* wind) and *2830;* a *storm from the East* (or S. E.), i.e. (in modern phrase) a *Levanter:*—Euroklydon.

2149. *εὐρύχωρος* **ĕuruchōrŏs,** *yoo-roo´-kho-ros;* from *εὐρύς* **ĕurus** (*wide*) and *5561; spacious:*—broad.

2150. *εὐσέβεια* **ĕusĕbĕia,** *yoo-seb´-i-ah;* from *2152; piety;* spec. the *gospel* scheme:—godliness, holiness.

2151. *εὐσεβέω* **ĕusĕbĕō,** *yoo-seb-eh´-o;* from *2152;* to *be pious;* i.e. (towards God) to *worship,* or (towards parents) to *respect* (*support*):—show piety, worship.

2152. *εὐσεβής* **ĕusĕbēs,** *yoo-seb-ace´;* from *2095* and *4576; well-reverent,* i.e. *pious:*—devout, godly.

2153. *εὐσεβῶς* **ĕusĕbōs,** *yoo-seb-oce´;* adv. from *2152; piously:*—godly.

2154. *εὔσημος* **ĕusēmŏs,** *yoo´-say-mos;* from *2095* and the base of *4591; well indicated,* i.e. (fig.) *significant:*—easy to be understood.

2155. *εὔσπλαγχνος* **ĕusplagchnŏs,** *yoo´-splangkh-nos;* from *2095* and *4698; well compassioned,* i.e. *sympathetic:*—pitiful, tender-hearted.

2156. *εὐσχημόνως* **ĕuschēmŏnōs,** *yoo-skhay-mon´-oce;* adv. from *2158; decorously:*—decently, honestly.

2157. *εὐσχημοσύνη* **ĕuschēmŏsunē,** *yoo-skhay-mos-oo´-nay;* from *2158; decorousness:*—comeliness.

2158. *εὐσχήμων* **ĕuschēmōn,** *yoo-skhay´-mone;* from *2095* and *4976; well-formed,* i.e. (fig.) *decorous, noble* (in rank):—comely, honourable.

2159. *εὐτόνως* **ĕutŏnōs,** *yoo-ton´-oce;* adv. from a comp. of *2095* and a der. of *τείνω* **tĕinō** (to *stretch*); *in a well-strung manner,* i.e. (fig.) *intensely* (in a good sense, *cogently;* in a bad one, *fiercely*):—mightily, vehemently.

2160. *εὐτραπελία* **ĕutrapĕlia,** *yoo-trap-el-ee´-ah;* from a comp. of *2095* and a der. of the base of *5157* (mean. *well-turned,* i.e. *ready at repartee, jocose*); *witticism,* i.e. (in a vulgar sense) *ribaldry:*—jesting.

2161. Εὔτυχος **Ĕutuchŏs,** *yoo´-too-khos;* from *2095* and a der. of *5177; well-fated,* i.e. *fortunate; Eutychus,* a young man:—Eutychus.

2162. *εὐφημία* **ĕuphēmia,** *yoo-fay-mee´-ah;* from *2163; good language* (*"euphemy"*), i.e. *praise* (*repute*):—good report.

2163. *εὔφημος* **ĕuphēmŏs,** *yoo´-fay-mos;* from *2095* and *5345; well spoken of,* i.e. *reputable:*—of good report.

2164. *εὐφορέω* **ĕuphŏrĕō,** *yoo-for-eh´-o;* from *2095* and *5409;* to *bear well,* i.e. *be fertile:*—bring forth abundantly.

2165. *εὐφραίνω* **ĕuphrainō,** *yoo-frah´ee-no;* from *2095* and *5424;* to *put* (mid. or pass. *be*) *in a good* frame of *mind,* i.e. *rejoice:*—fare, make glad, be (make) merry, rejoice.

2166. Εὐφράτης **Ĕuphratēs,** *yoo-frat´-ace;* of for. or. [comp. 6578]; *Euphrates,* a river of Asia:—Euphrates.

2167. *εὐφροσύνη* **ĕuphrŏsunē,** *yoo-fros-oo´-nay;* from the same as *2165; joyfulness:*—gladness, joy.

2168. *εὐχαριστέω* **ĕucharistĕō,** *yoo-khar-is-teh´-o;* from *2170;* to *be grateful,* i.e. (act.) to *express gratitude* (towards); spec. to *say grace* at a meal:—(give) thank (-ful, -s).

2169. εὐχαριστία **ĕucharistia,** *yoo-khar-is-tee´-ah;* from *2170; gratitude;* act. *grateful language* (to God, as an act of worship):—thankfulness, (giving of) thanks (-giving).

2170. εὐχάριστος **ĕucharistŏs,** *yoo-khar´-is-tos;* from *2095* and a der. of *5483; well favored,* i.e. (by impl.) *grateful:*—thankful.

2171. εὐχή **ĕuchē,** *yoo-khay´;* from *2172;* prop. a *wish,* expressed as a *petition* to God, or in *votive* obligation:—prayer, vow.

2172. εὔχομαι **ĕuchŏmai,** *yoo´-khom-ahee;* mid. of a prim. verb; to *wish;* by impl. to *pray* to God:—pray, will, wish.

2173. εὔχρηστος **ĕuchrēstŏs,** *yoo´-khrays-tos;* from *2095* and *5543; easily used,* i.e. *useful:*—profitable, meet for use.

2174. εὐψυχέω **ĕupsuchĕō,** *yoo-psoo-kheh´-o;* from a comp. of *2095* and *5590;* to *be in good spirits,* i.e. *feel encouraged:*—be of good comfort.

2175. εὐωδία **ĕuōdia,** *yoo-o-dee´-ah;* from a comp. of *2095* and a der. of *3605; good-scentedness,* i.e. *fragrance:*—sweet savour (smell, -smelling).

2176. εὐώνυμος **ĕuōnumŏs,** *yoo-o´-noo-mos;* from *2095* and *3686;* prop. *well-named* (*good-omened*), i.e. the *left* (which was the *lucky* side among the pagan Greeks); neut. as adv. *at the left* hand:—(on the) left.

2177. ἐφάλλομαι **ĕphallŏmai,** *ef-al´-lom-ahee;* from *1909* and *242;* to *spring upon:*—leap on.

2178. ἐφάπαξ **ĕphapax,** *ef-ap´-ax;* from *1909* and *530; upon one occasion* (only):—(at) once (for all).

2179. Ἐφεσῖνος **Ĕphĕsinŏs,** *ef-es-ee´-nos;* from *2181; Ephesine,* or situated at Ephesus:—of Ephesus.

2180. Ἐφέσιος **Ĕphĕsiŏs,** *ef-es´-ee-os;* from *2181;* an *Ephesian* or inhab. of Ephesus:—Ephesian, of Ephesus.

2181. Ἔφεσος **Ĕphĕsŏs,** *ef´-es-os;* prob. of for. or.; *Ephesus,* a city of Asia Minor:—Ephesus.

2182. ἐφευρέτης **ĕphĕurĕtēs,** *ef-yoo-ret´-ace;* from a comp. of *1909* and *2147;* a *discoverer,* i.e. *contriver:*—inventor.

2183. ἐφημερία **ĕphēmĕria,** *ef-ay-mer-ee´-ah;* from *2184; diurnality,* i.e. (spec.) the quotidian *rotation* or *class* of the Jewish priests' service at the Temple, as distributed by families:—course.

2184. ἐφήμερος **ĕphēmĕrŏs,** *ef-ay´-mer-os;* from *1909* and *2250; for a day* ("ephemeral"), i.e. *diurnal:*—daily.

2185. ἐφικνέομαι **ĕphiknĕŏmai,** *ef-ik-neh´-om-ahee;* from *1909* and a cognate of *2240;* to *arrive upon,* i.e. *extend to:*—reach.

2186. ἐφίστημι **ĕphistēmi,** *ef-is´-tay-mee;* from *1909* and *2476;* to *stand upon,* i.e. *be present* (in various applications, friendly or otherwise, usually lit.):—assault, come (in, to, unto, upon), be at hand (instant), present, stand (before, by, over).

2187. Ἐφραΐμ **Ĕphraïm,** *ef-rah-im´; of Heb. or. [669 or better 6085]; Ephraïm,* a place in Pal.:—Ephraim.

2188. ἐφφαθά **ĕphphatha,** *ef-fath-ah´;* of Chald. or. [6606]; *be opened!:*—Ephphatha.

2189. ἔχθρα **ĕchthra,** *ekh´-thrah;* fem. of *2190; hostility;* by impl. a reason for *opposition:*—enmity, hatred.

2190. ἐχθρός **ĕchthrŏs,** *ekh-thros´;* from a prim. ἔχθω **ĕchthō** (to *hate*); *hateful* (pass. *odious,* or act. *hostile*); usually as a noun, an *adversary* (espec. *Satan*):—enemy, foe.

2191. ἔχιδνα **ĕchidna,** *ekh´-id-nah;* of uncert. or.; an *adder* or other poisonous snake (lit. or fig.):—viper.

2192. ἔχω **ĕchō,** *ekh´-o;* (includ. an alt. form σχέω **schĕō,** *skheh´-o;* used in certain tenses only); a prim. verb; to *hold* (used in very various applications, lit. or fig., direct or remote; such as *possession, ability, contiguity, relation* or *condition*):—be (able, × hold, possessed with), accompany, + begin to amend, can (+ -not), × conceive, count, diseased, do, + eat, + enjoy, + fear, following, have, hold, keep, + lack, + go to law, lie, + must needs, + of necessity, + need, next, + recover, + reign, + rest, return, × sick, take for, + tremble, + uncircumcised, use.

2193. ἕως **hĕōs,** *heh´-oce;* of uncert. affin.; a conj., prep. and adv. of continuance, *until* (of time and place):—even (until, unto), (as) far (as), how long, (un-) til (-l), (hither-, un-, up) to, while (-s).

Z

2194. Ζαβουλών **Zabŏulōn,** *dzab-oo-lone´;* of Heb. or. [2074]; *Zabulon* (i.e. *Zebulon*), a region of Pal.:—Zabulon.

2195. Ζακχαῖος **Zakchaiŏs,** *dzak-chah´ee-yos;* of Heb. or. [comp. 2140]; *Zacchæus,* an Isr.:—Zacchæus.

2196. Ζαρά **Zara,** *dzar-ah´;* of Heb. or. [2226]; *Zara* (i.e. *Zerach*), an Isr.:—Zara.

2197. Ζαχαρίας **Zacharias,** *dzakh-ar-ee´-as;* of Heb. or. [2148]; *Zacharias* (i.e. *Zechariah*), the name of two Isr.:—Zacharias.

2198. ζάω **zaō,** *dzah´-o;* a prim. verb; to *live* (lit. or fig.):—life (-time), (a-) live (-ly), quick.

2199. Ζεβεδαῖος **Zĕbĕdaiŏs,** *dzeb-ed-ah´-yos;* of Heb. or. [comp. 2067]; *Zebedæus,* an Isr.:—Zebedee.

2200. ζεστός **zĕstŏs,** *dzes-tos´;* from *2204; boiled,* i.e. (by impl.) *calid* (fig. *fervent*):—hot.

2201. ζεῦγος **zĕugŏs,** *dzyoo´-gos;* from the same as *2218;* a *couple,* i.e. a *team* (of oxen yoked together) or *brace* (of birds tied together):—yoke, pair.

2202. ζευκτηρία **zĕuktēria,** *dzyook-tay-ree´-ah;* fem. of a der. (at the second stage) from the same as *2218;* a *fastening* (*tiller-rope*):—band.

2203. Ζεύς **Zĕus,** *dzyooce;* of uncert. affin.; in the oblique cases there is used instead of it a (prob. cognate) name

Δίς **Dis,** *deece,* which is otherwise obsolete; *Zeus* or *Dis* (among the Latins *Jupiter* or *Jove*), the supreme deity of the Greeks:—Jupiter.

2204. ζέω **zĕō,** *dzeh´-o;* a prim. verb; to *be hot* (*boil,* of liquids; or *glow,* of solids), i.e. (fig.) *be fervid* (*earnest*):—be fervent.

2205. ζῆλος **zēlŏs,** *dzay´-los;* from *2204;* prop. *heat,* i.e. (fig.) *"zeal"* (in a favorable sense, *ardor;* in an unfavorable one, *jealousy,* as of a husband [fig. of God], or an enemy, *malice*):—emulation, envy (-ing), fervent mind, indignation, jealousy, zeal.

2206. ζηλόω **zēlŏō,** *dzay-lŏ´-o;* from *2205;* to *have warmth* of feeling for or against:—affect, covet (earnestly), (have) desire, (move with) envy, be jealous over, (be) zealous (-ly affect).

2207. ζηλωτής **zēlōtēs,** *dzay-lo-tace´;* from *2206;* a *"zealot":*—zealous.

2208. Ζηλωτής **Zēlōtēs,** *dzay-lo-tace´;* the same as *2207;* a *Zealot,* i.e. (spec.) *partisan* for Jewish political independence:—Zelotes.

2209. ζημία **zēmia,** *dzay-mee´-ah;* prob. akin to the base of *1150* (through the idea of *violence*); *detriment:*—damage, loss.

2210. ζημιόω **zēmiŏō,** *dzay-mee-ŏ´-o;* from *2209;* to *injure,* i.e. (reflex. or pass.) to *experience detriment:*—be cast away, receive damage, lose, suffer loss.

2211. Ζηνᾶς **Zēnas,** *dzay-nas´;* prob. contr. from a poetic form of *2203* and *1435; Jove-given; Zenas,* a Chr.:—Zenas.

2212. ζητέω **zētĕō,** *dzay-teh´-o;* of uncert. affin.; to *seek* (lit. or fig.); spec. (by Heb.) to *worship* (God), or (in a bad sense) to *plot* (against life):—be (go) about, desire, endeavour, enquire (for), require, (× will) seek (after, for, means). Comp. *4441.*

2213. ζήτημα **zētēma,** *dzay´-tay-mah;* from *2212;* a *search* (prop. concr.), i.e. (in words) a *debate:*—question.

2214. ζήτησις **zētēsis,** *dzay´-tay-sis;* from *2212;* a *searching* (prop. the act), i.e. a *dispute* or its *theme:*—question.

2215. ζιζάνιον **zizaniŏn,** *dziz-an´-ee-on;* of uncert. or.; *darnel* or false grain:—tares.

2216. Ζοροβάβελ **Zŏrŏbabĕl,** *dzor-ob-ab´-el;* of Heb. or. [2216]; *Zorobabel* (i.e. *Zerubbabel*), an Isr.:—Zorobabel.

2217. ζόφος **zŏphŏs,** *dzof´-os;* akin to the base of *3509; gloom* (as shrouding like a *cloud*):—blackness, darkness, mist.

2218. ζυγός **zugŏs,** *dzoo-gos´;* from the root of ζεύγνυμι **zĕugnumi** (to *join* espec. by a "yoke"); a *coupling,* i.e. (fig.) *servitude* a *law* or *obligation*); also (lit.) the *beam* of the balance (as *connecting* the scales):—pair of balances, yoke.

2219. ζύμη **zumē,** *dzoo´-may;* prob. from *2204; ferment* (as if *boiling* up):—leaven.

2220. ζυμόω **zumŏō,** *dzoo-mŏ´-o;* from *2219;* to *cause to ferment:*—leaven.

2221. ζωγρέω **zōgrĕō,** *dzogue-reh´-o;* from the same as *2226* and *64;* to *take alive* (*make a prisoner of war*), i.e. (fig.) to *capture* or *ensnare:*—take captive, catch.

2222. ζωή **zōē,** *dzo-ay´;* from *2198; life* (lit. or fig.):—life (-time). Comp. *5590.*

2223. ζώνη **zōnē,** *dzo´-nay;* prob. akin to the base of *2218;* a *belt;* by impl. a *pocket:*—girdle, purse.

2224. ζώννυμι **zōnnumi,** *dzone´-noo-mi;* from *2223;* to *bind about* (espec. with a belt):—gird.

2225. ζωογονέω **zōŏgŏnĕō,** *dzo-og-on-eh´-o;* from the same as *2226* and a der. of *1096;* to *engender alive* i.e. (by anal.) to *rescue* (pass. *be saved*) from death:—live, preserve.

2226. ζῷον **zōŏn,** *dzo´-on;* neut. of a der. of *2198;* a *live* thing, i.e. an *animal:*—beast.

2227. ζωοποιέω **zōŏpŏiĕō,** *dzo-op-oy-eh´-o;* from the same as *2226* and *4160;* to *(re-) vitalize* (lit. or fig.):—make alive, give life, quicken.

H

2228. ἤ **ē,** *ay;* a prim. particle of distinction between two connected terms; disjunctive, *or;* comparative, *than:*—and, but (either), (n-) either, except it be, (n-) or (else), rather, save, than, that, what, yea. Often used in connection with other particles. Comp. especially *2235, 2260, 2273.*

2229. ἦ **ē,** *ay;* an adv. of *confirmation;* perh. intens. of *2228;* used only (in the N.T.) before *3303; assuredly:*—surely.

ἡ **hē.** See *3588.*

ἥ **hē.** See *3739.*

ᾗ **ēı.** See *5600.*

2230. ἡγεμονεύω **hēgĕmŏnĕuō,** *hayg-em-on-yoo´-o;* from *2232;* to *act as ruler:*—be governor.

2231. ἡγεμονία **hēgĕmŏnia,** *hayg-em-on-ee´-ah;* from *2232; government,* i.e. (in time) official *term:*—reign.

2232. ἡγεμών **hēgĕmōn,** *hayg-em-ohn´;* from *2233;* a *leader,* i.e. *chief* person (or fig. place) of a province:—governor, prince, ruler.

2233. ἡγέομαι **hēgĕŏmai,** *hayg-eh´-om-ahee;* mid. of a (presumed) strengthened form of *71;* to *lead,* i.e. *command* (with official authority); fig. to *deem,* i.e. *consider:*—account, (be) chief, count, esteem, governor, judge, have the rule over, suppose, think.

2234. ἡδέως **hēdĕōs,** *hay-deh´-oce;* adv. from a der. of the base of *2237; sweetly,* i.e. (fig.) *with pleasure:*—gladly.

2235. ἤδη **ēdē,** *ay´-day;* appar. from *2228* (or possibly *2229*) and *1211; even now:*—already, (even) now (already), by this time.

2236. ἥδιστα **hēdista,** *hay´-dis-tah;* neut. plur. of the superl. of the same as *2234; with great pleasure:*—most (very) gladly.

2237. ἡδονή **hēdŏnē,** *hay-don-ay´;* from ἁνδάνω **handanō** (to *please*); sensual *delight;* by impl. *desire:*—lust, pleasure.

2238. ἡδύοσμον **hēduŏsmŏn,** *hay-doo´-os-mon;* neut. of a comp. of the same as *2234* and *3744;* a *sweet-scented* plant, i.e. *mint:*—mint.

2239. ἦθος **ēthŏs,** *ay´-thos;* a strengthened form of *1485; usage,* i.e. (plur.) moral *habits:*—manners.

2240. ἥκω **hēkō,** *hay´-ko;* a prim. verb; to *arrive,* i.e. *be present* (lit. or fig.):—come.

2241. ἠλί **ēli,** *ay-lee´;* of Heb. or. [410 with pron. suffix]; *my God:*—Eli.

2242. Ἡλί **Hēli,** *hay-lee´;* of Heb. or. [5941]; *Heli* (i.e. *Eli*), an Isr.:—Heli.

2243. Ἡλίας **Hēlias,** *hay-lee´-as;* of Heb. or. [452]; *Helias* (i.e. *Elijah*), an Isr.:—Elias.

2244. ἡλικία **hēlikia,** *hay-lik-ee´-ah;* from the same as *2245; maturity* (in years or size):—age, stature.

2245. ἡλίκος **hēlikŏs,** *hay-lee´-kos;* from ἧλιξ **hēlix** (a *comrade,* i.e. one of the same age); *as big as,* i.e. (interjectively) *how much:*—how (what) great.

2246. ἥλιος **hēliŏs,** *hay´-lee-os;* from ἕλη **hĕlē** (a *ray;* perh. akin to the alt. of *138*); the *sun;* by impl. *light:*— + east, sun.

2247. ἧλος **hēlŏs,** *hay´-los;* of uncert. affin.; a *stud,* i.e. *spike:*—nail.

2248. ἡμᾶς **hēmas,** *hay-mas´;* acc. plur. of *1473; us:*—our, us, we.

2249. ἡμεῖς **hēmĕis,** *hay-mice´;* nom. plur. of *1473; we* (only used when emphatic):—us, we (ourselves).

2250. ἡμέρα **hēmĕra,** *hay-mer´-ah;* fem. (with *5610* implied) of a der. of ἧμαι **hēmai** (to *sit;* akin to the base of *1476*) mean. *tame,* i.e. *gentle; day,* i.e. (lit.) the time space between dawn and dark, or the whole 24 hours (but several days were usually reckoned by the Jews as inclusive of the parts of both extremes); fig. a *period* (always defined more or less clearly by the context):—age, + alway, (mid-) day (by day, [-ly]), + for ever, judgment, (day) time, while, years.

2251. ἡμέτερος **hēmĕtĕrŏs,** *hay-met´-er-os;* from *2349; our:*—our, your [*by a different reading*].

2252. ἤμην **ēmēn,** *ay´-mane;* a prol. form of *2358;* I *was:*—be, was. [*Sometimes unexpressed.*]

2253. ἡμιθανής **hēmithanēs,** *hay-mee-than-ace´;* from a presumed comp. of the base of *2255* and *2348; half dead,* i.e. *entirely exhausted:*—half dead.

2254. ἡμῖν **hēmin,** *hay-meen´;* dat. plur. of *1473; to* (or *for, with, by*) *us:*—our, (for) us, we.

2255. ἥμισυ **hēmisu,** *hay´-mee-soo;* neut. of a der. from an inseparable pref. akin to *260* (through the idea of *partition* involved in *connection*) and mean. *semi-;* (as noun) *half:*—half.

2256. ἡμιώριον **hēmiōriŏn,** *hay-mee-o´-ree-on;* from the base of *2255* and *5610;* a *half-hour:*—half an hour.

2257. ἡμῶν **hēmōn,** *hay-mone´;* gen. plur. of *1473; of* (or *from*) *us:*—our (company), us, we.

2258. ἦν **ēn,** *ane;* imperf. of *1510; I* (*thou,* etc.) *was* (*wast* or *were*):— + agree, be, × have (+ charge of), hold, use, was (-t), were.

2259. ἡνίκα **hēnika,** *hay-nee´-kah;* of uncert. affin.; *at which time:*—when.

2260. ἤπερ **ēpēr,** *ay´-per;* from *2228* and *4007; than at all* (or *than perhaps, than indeed*):—than.

2261. ἤπιος **ēpiŏs,** *ay´-pee-os;* prob. from *2031;* prop. *affable,* i.e. *mild* or *kind:*—gentle.

2262. Ἤρ **Ēr,** *ayr;* of Heb. or. [6147]; *Er,* an Isr.:—Er.

2263. ἤρεμος **ērĕmŏs,** *ay´-rem-os;* perh. by transposition from *2048* (through the idea of *stillness*); *tranquil:*—quiet.

2264. Ἡρώδης **Hērōdēs,** *hay-ro´-dace;* comp. of ἥρως **hērōs** (a *"hero"*) and *1491; heroic; Herodes,* the name of four Jewish kings:—Herod.

2265. Ἡρωδιανοί **Hērōdianŏi,** *hay-ro-dee-an-oy´;* plur. of a der. of *2264; Herodians,* i.e. partisans of Herodes:—Herodians.

2266. Ἡρωδιάς **Hērōdias,** *hay-ro-dee-as´;* from *2264; Herodias,* a woman of the Herodian family:—Herodias.

2267. Ἡρωδίων **Hērōdiōn,** *hay-ro-dee´-ohn;* from *2264; Herodion,* a Chr.:—Herodion.

2268. Ἡσαΐας **Hēsaïas,** *hay-sah-ee´as;* of Heb. or. [3470]; *Hesaias* (i.e. *Jeshajah*), an Isr.:—Esaias.

2269. Ἡσαῦ **Ēsau,** *ay-sŏw´;* of Heb. or. [6215]; *Esau,* an Edomite:—Esau.

2270. ἡσυχάζω **hēsuchazō,** *hay-soo-khad´-zo;* from the same as *2272;* to *keep still* (intrans.), i.e. *refrain* from labor, meddlesomeness or speech:—cease, hold peace, be quiet, rest.

2271. ἡσυχία **hēsuchia,** *hay-soo-khee´-ah;* fem. of *2272;* (as noun) *stillness,* i.e. desistance from bustle or language:—quietness, silence.

2272. ἡσύχιος **hēsuchiŏs,** *hay-soo´-khee-os;* a prol. form of a comp. prob. of a der. of the base of *1476* and perh. *2192;* prop. *keeping* one's *seat* (*sedentary*), i.e. (by impl.) *still* (*undisturbed, undisturbing*):—peaceable, quiet.

2273. ἤτοι **ētŏi,** *ay´-toy;* from *2228* and *5104; either indeed:*—whether.

2274. ἡττάω **hēttaō,** *hayt-tah´-o;* from the same as *2276;* to *make worse,* i.e. *vanquish* (lit. or fig.); by impl. to *rate lower:*—be inferior, overcome.

2275. ἥττημα **hēttēma,** *hayt´-tay-mah;* from *2274;* a *deterioration,* i.e. (obj.) *failure* or (subj.) *loss:*—diminishing, fault.

2276. ἥττον **hēttŏn,** *hate´-ton;* neut. of comp. of ἧκα **hēka** (*slightly*) used for that of *2556; worse* (as noun); by impl. *less* (as adv.):—less, worse.

2277. ἤτω **ētō,** *ay´-to;* third pers. sing. imperative of *1510; let him* (or *it*) *be:*—let . . . be.

2278. ἠχέω **ēchĕō,** *ay-kheh´-o;* from *2279;* to *make a* loud *noise,* i.e. *reverberate:*—roar, sound.

2279. ἦχος **ēchŏs,** *ay´-khos;* of uncert. affin.; a loud or confused *noise* ("*echo*"), i.e. *roar;* fig. a *rumor:*—fame, sound.

Θ

2280. Θαδδαῖος **Thaddaiŏs,** *thad-dah´-yos;* of uncert. or.; *Thaddæus,* one of the Apostles:—Thaddæus.

2281. θάλασσα **thalassa,** *thal´-as-sah;* prob. prol. from *251;* the *sea* (gen. or spec.):—sea.

2282. θάλπω **thalpō,** *thal´-po;* prob. akin to θάλλω **thallō** (to *warm*); to *brood,* i.e. (fig.) to *foster:*—cherish.

2283. Θάμαρ **Thamar,** *tham´-ar;* of Heb. or. [8559]; *Thamar* (i.e. *Tamar*), an Israelitess:—Thamar.

2284. θαμβέω **thambĕō,** *tham-beh´-o;* from *2285;* to *stupefy* (with surprise), i.e. *astound:*—amaze, astonish.

2285. θάμβος **thambŏs,** *tham´-bos;* akin to an obsol. τάφω **taphō** (to *dumbfound*); *stupefaction* (by surprise), i.e. *astonishment:*—× amazed, + astonished, wonder.

2286. θανάσιμος **thanasimŏs,** *than-as´-ee-mos;* from *2288; fatal,* i.e. *poisonous:*—deadly.

2287. θανατήφορος **thanatēphŏrŏs,** *than-at-ay´-for-os;* from (the fem. form of) *2288* and *5342; death-bearing,* i.e. *fatal:*—deadly.

2288. θάνατος **thanatŏs,** *than´-at-os;* from *2348;* (prop. an adj. used as a noun) *death* (lit. or fig.):—× deadly, (be . . .) death.

2289. θανατόω **thanatŏō,** *than-at-ŏ´-o;* from *2288;* to *kill* (lit. or fig.):—become dead, (cause to be) put to death, kill, mortify.

θάνω **thanō.** See *2348.*

2290. θάπτω **thaptō,** *thap´-to;* a prim. verb; to *celebrate funeral rites,* i.e. *inter:*—bury.

2291. Θάρα **Thara,** *thar´-ah;* of Heb. or. [8646]; *Thara* (i.e. *Terach*), the father of Abraham:—Thara.

2292. θαῤῥέω **tharrhĕō,** *thar-hreh´-o;* another form for *2293;* to *exercise courage:*—be bold, × boldly, have confidence, be confident. Comp. *5111.*

2293. θαρσέω **tharsĕō,** *thar-seh´-o;* from *2294;* to *have courage:*—be of good cheer (comfort). Comp. *2292.*

2294. θάρσος **tharsŏs,** *thar´-sos;* akin (by transp.) to θράσος **thrasŏs** (*daring*); *boldness* (subj.):—courage.

2295. θαῦμα **thauma,** *thŏu´-mah;* appar. from a form of *2300; wonder* (prop. concr.; but by impl. abstr.):—admiration.

2296. θαυμάζω **thaumazō,** *thŏu-mad´-zo;* from *2295;* to *wonder;* by impl. to *admire:*—admire, have in admiration, marvel, wonder.

2297. θαυμάσιος **thaumasiŏs,** *thŏw-mas´-ee-os;* from *2295; wondrous,* i.e. (neut. as noun) a *miracle:*—wonderful thing.

2298. θαυμαστός **thaumastŏs,** *thŏw-mas-tos´;* from *2296; wondered* at, i.e. (by impl.) *wonderful:*—marvel (-lous).

2299. θεά **thĕa,** *theh-ay´;* fem. of *2316;* a female *deity:*—goddess.

2300. θεάομαι **thĕaŏmai,** *theh-ah´-om-ahee;* a prol. form of a prim. verb; to *look* closely at, i.e. (by impl.) to *perceive* (lit. or fig.); by extens. to *visit:*—behold, look (upon), see. Comp. *3700.*

2301. θεατρίζω **thĕatrizō,** *theh-at-rid´-zo;* from *2302;* to *expose as a spectacle:*—make a gazing stock.

2302. θέατρον **thĕatrŏn,** *theh´-at-ron;* from *2300; a place for public show* ("*theatre*"), i.e. general *audience-room;* by impl. a *show* itself (fig.):—spectacle, theatre.

2303. θεῖον **thĕiŏn,** *thi´-on;* prob. neut. of *2304* (in its or. sense of *flashing*); *sulphur:*—brimstone.

2304. θεῖος **thĕiŏs,** *thi´-os;* from *2316; godlike* (neut. as noun, *divinity*):—divine, godhead.

2305. θειότης **thĕiŏtēs,** *thi-ot´-ace;* from *2304; divinity* (abstr.):—godhead.

2306. θειώδης **thĕiōdēs,** *thi-o´-dace;* from *2303* and *1491; sulphur-like,* i.e. *sulphurous:*—brimstone.

θελέω **thĕlĕō.** See *2309.*

2307. θέλημα **thĕlēma,** *thel´-ay-mah;* from the prol. form of *2309;* a *determination* (prop. the thing), i.e. (act.) *choice* (spec. *purpose, decree;* abstr. *volition*) or (pass.) *inclination:*—desire, pleasure, will.

2308. θέλησις **thĕlēsis,** *thel´-ay-sis;* from *2309; determination* (prop. the act), i.e. *option:*—will.

2309. θέλω **thĕlō,** *thel´-o;* or ἐθέλω **ĕthĕlō,** *eth-el´-o;* in certain tenses θελέω **thĕlĕō,** *thel-eh´-o;* and ἐθελέω **ĕthĕlĕō,** *eth-el-eh´-o,* which are otherwise obsol.; appar. strengthened from the alt. form of *138;* to *determine* (as an act. *option* from subj. impulse; whereas *1014* prop. denotes rather a pass. *acquiescence* in obj. considerations), i.e. *choose* or *prefer* (lit. or fig.); by impl. to *wish,* i.e. *be inclined* to (sometimes adv. *gladly*); impers. for the fut. tense, to *be about to;* by Heb. to *delight in:*—desire, be disposed (forward), intend, list, love, mean, please, have rather, (be) will (have, -ling, -ling [ly]).

2310. θεμέλιος **thĕmĕliŏs,** *them-el´-ee-os;* from a der. of *5087;* something *put* down, i.e. a *substruction* (of a building, etc.), (lit. or fig.):—foundation.

2311. θεμελιόω **thĕmĕliŏō,** *them-el-ee-ŏ´-o;* from *2310;* to *lay a basis* for, i.e. (lit.) *erect,* or (fig.) *consolidate:*—(lay the) found (-ation), ground, settle.

2312. θεοδίδακτος **thĕŏdidaktŏs,** *theh-od-id´-ak-tos;* from *2316* and *1321; divinely instructed:*—taught of God.

2312´. θεολόγος **thĕŏlŏgŏs,** *theh-ol-og´-os;* from *2316* and *3004;* a "*theologian*":—divine.

2313. θεομαχέω **thĕŏmachĕō,** *theh-o-makh-eh´-o;* from *2314;* to *resist deity:*—fight against God.

2314. θεόμαχος **thĕŏmachŏs,** *theh-om´-akh-os;* from *2316* and *3164;* an *opponent of deity:*—to fight against God.

2315. θεόπνευστος **thĕŏpnĕustŏs,** *theh-op´-nyoo-stos;* from *2316* and a presumed der. of *4154; divinely breathed* in:—given by inspiration of God.

2316. θεός **thĕŏs,** *theh´-os;* of uncert. affin.; a *deity, espec. (with 3588)* the supreme *Divinity;* fig. a *magistrate;* by Heb. *very:*—× exceeding, God, god [-ly, -ward].

2317. θεοσέβεια **thĕŏsĕbĕia,** *theh-os-eb´-i-ah;* from *2318; devoutness,* i.e. *piety:*—godliness.

2318. θεοσεβής **thĕŏsĕbēs,** *theh-os-eb-ace´;* from *2316* and *4576; reverent of God,* i.e. *pious:*—worshipper of God.

2319. θεοστυγής **thĕŏstugēs,** *theh-os-too-gace´;* from *2316* and the base of *4767; hateful to God,* i.e. *impious:*—hater of God.

2320. θεότης **thĕŏtēs,** *theh-ot´-ace;* from *2316; divinity* (abstr.):—godhead.

2321. Θεόφιλος **Thĕŏphilŏs,** *theh-of´-il-os;* from *2316* and *5384; friend of God; Theophilus,* a Chr.:—Theophilus.

2322. θεραπεία **thĕrapĕia,** *ther-ap-i´-ah;* from *2323; attendance* (spec. medical, i.e. *cure*); fig. and collec. *domestics:*—healing, household.

2323. θεραπεύω **thĕrapĕuō,** *ther-ap-yoo´-o;* from the same as *2324;* to *wait upon* menially, i.e. (fig.) to *adore* (God), or (spec.) to *relieve* (of disease):—cure, heal, worship.

2324. θεράπων **thĕrapōn,** *ther-ap´-ohn;* appar. a part. from an otherwise obsol. der. of the base of *2330;* a menial *attendant* (as if *cherishing*):—servant.

2325. θερίζω **thĕrizō,** *ther-id´-zo;* from *2330* (in the sense of the *crop*); to *harvest:*—reap.

2326. θερισμός **thĕrismŏs,** *ther-is-mos´;* from *2325; reaping,* i.e. the *crop:*—harvest.

2327. θεριστής **thĕristēs,** *ther-is-tace´;* from *2325;* a *harvester:*—reaper.

2328. θερμαίνω **thĕrmainō,** *ther-mah´ee-no;* from *2329;* to *heat* (oneself):—(be) warm (-ed, self).

2329. θέρμη **thĕrmē,** *ther´-may;* from the base of *2330; warmth:*—heat.

2330. θέρος **thĕrŏs,** *ther´-os;* from a prim. θέρω **thĕrō** (to *heat*); prop. *heat,* i.e. *summer:*—summer.

2331. Θεσσαλονικεύς **Thĕssalŏnikĕus,** *thes-sal-on-ik-yoos´;* from *2332;* a *Thessalonican,* i.e. inhab. of Thessalonice:—Thessalonian.

2332. Θεσσαλονίκη **Thĕssalŏnikē,** *thes-sal-on-ee´-kay;* from Θεσσαλός **Thĕssalŏs** (a *Thessalian*) and *3529; Thessalonice,* a place in Asia Minor:—Thessalonica.

2333. Θευδᾶς **Thĕudas,** *thyoo-das´;* of uncert. or.; *Theudas,* an Isr.:—Theudas.

θέω **thĕō.** See *5087.*

2334. θεωρέω **thĕōrĕō,** *theh-o-reh´-o;* from a der. of *2300* (perh. by add. of *3708*); to *be a spectator* of, *i.e. discern,* (lit., fig. [*experience*] or intens. [*acknowledge*]):—behold, consider, look on, perceive, see. Comp. *3700.*

2335. θεωρία **thĕōria,** *theh-o-ree´-ah;* from the same as *2334; spectatorship,* i.e. (concr.) a *spectacle:*—sight.

2336. θήκη **thēkē,** *thay´-kay;* from *5087;* a *receptacle,* i.e. *scabbard:*—sheath.

2337. θηλάζω **thēlazō,** *thay-lad´-zo;* from θηλή **thēlē** (the *nipple*); to *suckle;* by impl. to *suck:*—(give) suck (-ling).

2338. θῆλυς **thēlus,** *thay´-loos;* from the same as *2337; female:*—female, woman.

2339. θήρα **thēra,** *thay´-rah;* from θήρ **thēr** (a wild *animal,* as *game*); *hunting,* i.e. (fig.) *destruction:*—trap.

2340. θηρεύω **thērĕuō,** *thay-ryoo´-o;* from *2339;* to *hunt* (an animal), i.e. (fig.) to *carp at:*—catch.

2341. θηριομαχέω **thēriŏmachĕō,** *thay-ree-om-akh-eh´-o;* from a comp. of *2342* and *3164;* to *be a beast-fighter* (in the gladiatorial show), i.e. (fig.) to *encounter* (furious men):—fight with wild beasts.

2342. θηρίον **thēriŏn,** *thay-ree´-on;* dimin. from the same as *2339;* a *dangerous animal:*—(venomous, wild) beast.

2343. θησαυρίζω **thēsaurizō,** *thay-sŏw-rid´-zo;* from *2344;* to *amass* or *reserve* (lit. or fig.):—lay up (treasure), (keep) in store, (heap) treasure (together, up).

2344. θησαυρός **thēsaurŏs,** *thay-sow-ros´;* from *5087;* a *deposit,* i.e. *wealth* (lit. or fig.):—treasure.

2345. θιγγάνω **thigganō,** *thing-gan´-o;* a prol. form of an obsol. prim. θίγω **thigō** (to *finger*); to *manipulate,* i.e. *have to do with;* by impl. to *injure:*—handle, touch.

2346. θλίβω **thlibō,** *thlee´-bo;* akin to the base of *5147;* to *crowd* (lit. or fig.):—afflict, narrow, throng, suffer tribulation, trouble.

2347. θλίψις **thlipsis,** *thlip´-sis;* from *2346; pressure* (lit. or fig.):—afflicted, (-tion), anguish, burdened, persecution, tribulation, trouble.

2348. θνήσκω **thnēskō,** *thnay´-sko;* a strengthened form of a simpler prim. θάνω **thanō,** *than´-o* (which is used for it only in certain tenses); to *die* (lit. or fig.):—be dead, die.

2349. θνητός **thnētŏs,** *thnay-tos´;* from *2348; liable to die:*—mortal (-ity).

2350. θορυβέω **thŏrubĕō,** *thor-oo-beh´-o;* from *2351;* to *be in tumult,* i.e. *disturb, clamor:*—make ado (a noise), trouble self, set on an uproar.

2351. θόρυβος **thŏrubŏs,** *thor´-oo-bos;* from the base of *2360;* a *disturbance:*—tumult, uproar.

2352. θραύω **thrauō,** *thrŏw´-o;* a prim. verb; to *crush:*—bruise. Comp. *4486.*

2353. θρέμμα **thrĕmma,** *threm´-mah;* from *5142; stock* (as *raised* on a farm):—cattle.

2354. θρηνέω **thrēnĕō,** *thray-neh´-o;* from *2355;* to *bewail:*—lament, mourn.

2355. θρῆνος **thrēnŏs,** *thray´-nos;* from the base of *2360; wailing:*—lamentation.

2356. θρησκεία **thrēskĕia,** *thrace-ki´-ah;* from a der. of *2357;* ceremonial *observance:*—religion, worshipping.

2357. θρῆσκος **thrēskŏs,** *thrace´-kos;* prob. from the base of *2360; ceremonious* in worship (as *demonstrative*), i.e. *pious:*—religious.

2358. θριαμβεύω **thriambĕuō,** *three-am-byoo´-o;* from a prol. comp. of the base of *2360* and a der. of *680* (mean. a *noisy iambus,* sung in honor of Bacchus); to *make an acclamatory procession,* i.e. (fig.) to *conquer* or (by Hebr.) to *give victory:*—(cause) to triumph (over).

2359. θρίξ **thrix,** *threeks;* gen. τριχός **trichŏs,** etc.; of uncert. der.; *hair:*—hair. Comp. *2864.*

2360. θροέω **thrŏĕō,** *thrŏ-eh´-o;* from θρέομαι **thrĕŏmai** (to *wail*); to *clamor,* i.e. (by impl.) to *frighten:*—trouble.

2361. θρόμβος **thrŏmbŏs,** *throm´-bos;* perh. from *5142* (in the sense of *thickening*); a *clot:*—great drop.

2362. θρόνος **thrŏnŏs,** *thron´-os;* from θράω **thraō** (to *sit*); a stately *seat* ("*throne*"); by impl. *power* or (concr.) a *potentate:*—seat, throne.

2363. Θυάτειρα **Thuatĕira,** *thoo-at´-i-rah;* of uncert. der.; *Thyatira,* a place in Asia Minor:—Thyatira.

2364. θυγάτηρ **thugatēr,** *thoo-gat´-air;* appar. a prim. word [comp. "daughter"]; a *female child,* or (by Hebr.) *descendant* (or *inhabitant*):—daughter.

2365. θυγάτριον **thugatriŏn,** *thoo-gat´-ree-on;* from *2364;* a *daughterling:*—little (young) daughter.

2366. θύελλα **thuĕlla,** *thoo´-el-lah;* from *2380* (in the sense of *blowing*) a storm:—tempest.

2367. θύϊνος **thuïnŏs,** *thoo´-ee-nos;* from a der. of *2380* (in the sense of *blowing;* denoting a certain *fragrant* tree); made of *citron*-wood:—thyine.

2368. θυμίαμα **thumiama,** *thoo-mee´-am-ah;* from *2370;* an *aroma,* i.e. fragrant *powder* burnt in religious service; by impl. the *burning* itself:—incense, odour.

2369. θυμιαστήριον **thumiastēriŏn,** *thoo-mee-as-tay´-ree-on;* from a der. of *2370;* a *place of fumigation,* i.e. the *altar of incense* (in the Temple):—censer.

2370. θυμιάω **thumiaō,** *thoo-mee-ah´-o;* from a der. of *2380* (in the sense of *smoking*); to *fumigate,* i.e. *offer* aromatic *fumes:*—burn incense.

2371. θυμομαχέω **thumŏmachĕō,** *thoo-mom-akh-eh´-o;* from a presumed comp. of *2372* and *3164;* to *be in a furious fight,* i.e. (fig.) to *be exasperated:*—be highly displeased.

2372. θυμός **thumŏs,** *thoo-mos´;* from *2380; passion* (as if *breathing* hard):—fierceness, indignation, wrath. Comp. *5590.*

2373. θυμόω **thumŏō,** *thoo-mŏ´-o;* from *2372;* to *put in a passion,* i.e. *enrage:*—be wroth.

2374. θύρα **thura,** *thoo´-rah;* appar. a prim. word [comp. "door"]; a *portal* or entrance (the opening or the closure, lit. or fig.):—door, gate.

2375. θυρεός **thurĕŏs,** *thoo-reh-os´;* from *2374;* a large *shield* (as *door*-shaped):—shield.

2376. θυρίς **thuris,** *thoo-rece´;* from *2374;* an *aperture,* i.e. *window:*—window.

2377. θυρωρός **thurōrŏs,** *thoo-ro-ros´;* from *2374* and οὖρος **ŏurŏs** (a *watcher*); a *gate-warden:*—that kept the door, porter.

2378. θυσία **thusia,** *thoo-see´-ah;* from *2380; sacrifice* (the act or the victim, lit. or fig.):—sacrifice.

2379. θυσιαστήριον **thusiastēriŏn,** *thoo-see-as-tay´-ree-on;* from a der. of *2378;* a *place of sacrifice,* i.e. an *altar* (spec. or gen., lit. or fig.):—altar.

2380. θύω **thuō,** *thoo´-o;* a prim. verb; prop. to *rush* (*breathe* hard, *blow, smoke*), i.e. (by impl.) to *sacrifice* (prop. by fire, but gen.); by extens. to *immolate* (*slaughter* for any purpose):—kill, (do) sacrifice, slay.

2381. Θωμᾶς **Thōmas,** *tho-mas´;* of Chald. or. [comp. 8380]; *the twin; Thomas,* a Chr.:—Thomas.

2382. θώραξ **thōrax,** *tho´-rax;* of uncert. affin.; the *chest* ("*thorax*"), i.e. (by impl.) a *corslet:*—breastplate.

I

2383. Ἰάειρος **Iaĕirŏs,** *ee-ah´-i-ros;* of Heb. or. [2971]; *Jäïrus* (i.e. *Jair*), an Isr.:—Jairus.

2384. Ἰακώβ **Iakōb,** *ee-ak-obe´;* of Heb. or. [3290]; *Jacob* (i.e. *Ja'akob*), the progenitor of the Isr.; also an Isr.:—Jacob.

2385. Ἰάκωβος **Iakōbŏs,** *ee-ak´-o-bos;* the same as *2384* Græcized; *Jacobus,* the name of three Isr.:—James.

2386. ἴαμα **iama,** *ee´-am-ah;* from *2390;* a *cure* (the effect):—healing.

2387. Ἰαμβρῆς **Iambrēs,** *ee-am-brace´;* of Eg. or.; *Jambres,* an Eg.:—Jambres.

2388. Ἰαννά **Ianna,** *ee-an-nah´;* prob. of Heb. or. [comp. 3238]; *Janna,* an Isr.:—Janna.

2389. Ἰαννῆς **Iannēs,** *ee-an-nace´;* of Eg. or.; *Jannes,* an Eg.:—Jannes.

2390. ἰάομαι **iaŏmai,** *ee-ah´-om-ahee;* mid. of appar. a prim. verb; to *cure* (lit. or fig.):—heal, make whole.

2391. Ἰάρεδ **Iarĕd,** *ee-ar´-ed;* of Heb. or. [3382]; *Jared* (i.e. *Jered*), an antediluvian:—Jared.

2392. ἴασις **iasis,** *ee´-as-is;* from *2390; curing* (the act):—cure, heal (-ing).

2393. ἴασπις **iaspis,** *ee´-as-pis;* prob. of for. or. [see 3471]; *"jasper",* a gem:—jasper.

2394. Ἰάσων **Iasōn,** *ee-as´-oan;* fut. act. part. masc. of *2390; about to cure; Jason,* a Chr.:—Jason.

2395. ἰατρός **iatrŏs,** *ee-at-ros´;* from *2390;* a *physician:*—physician.

2396. ἴδε **idĕ,** *id´-eh;* second pers. sing. imper. act. of *1492;* used as interj. to denote *surprise; lo!:*—behold, lo, see.

2397. ἰδέα **idĕa,** *id-eh´-ah;* from *1492;* a *sight* [comp. fig. "idea"], i.e. *aspect:*—countenance.

2398. ἴδιος **idiŏs,** *id´-ee-os;* of uncert. affin.; *pertaining to self,* i.e. one's *own;* by impl. *private* or *separate:*—× his acquaintance, when they were alone, apart, aside, due, his (own, proper, several), home, (her, our, thine, your) own (business), private (-ly), proper, severally, their (own).

2399. ἰδιώτης **idiōtēs,** *id-ee-o´-tace;* from *2398;* a *private* person, i.e. (by impl.) an *ignoramus* (comp. "idiot"):—ignorant, rude, unlearned.

2400. ἰδού **idŏu,** *id-oo´;* second pers. sing. imper. mid. of *1492;* used as imper. *lo!:*—behold, lo, see.

2401. Ἰδουμαία **Idŏumaia,** *id-oo-mah´-yah;* of Heb. or. [123]; *Idumæa* (i.e. *Edom*), a region E. (and S.) of Pal.:—Idumæa.

2402. ἱδρώς **hidrōs,** *hid-roce´;* a strengthened form of a prim. ἴδος **idŏs** (*sweat*); *perspiration:*—sweat.

2403. Ἰεζαβήλ **Iĕzabēl,** *ee-ed-zab-ale´;* of Heb. or. [348]; *Jezabel* (i.e. *Jezebel*), a Tyrian woman (used as a synonym of a termagant or false teacher):—Jezabel.

2404. Ἱεράπολις **Hiĕrapŏlis,** *hee-er-ap´-ol-is;* from *2413* and *4172; holy city; Hierapolis,* a place in Asia Minor:—Hierapolis.

2405. ἱερατεία **hiĕratĕia,** *hee-ar-at-i´-ah;* from *2407; priestliness,* i.e. the *sacerdotal function:*—office of the priesthood, priest's office.

2406. ἱεράτευμα **hiĕratĕuma,** *hee-er-at´-yoo-mah;* from *2407;* the *priestly fraternity,* i.e. a *sacerdotal order* (fig.):—priesthood.

2407. ἱερατεύω **hiĕratĕuō,** *hee-er-at-yoo´-o;* prol. from *2409;* to *be a priest,* i.e. *perform his functions:*—execute the priest's office.

2408. Ἱερεμίας **Hiĕrĕmias,** *hee-er-em-ee´-as;* of Heb. or. [3414]; *Hieremias* (i.e. *Jermijah*), an Isr.:—Jeremiah.

2409. ἱερεύς **hiĕrĕus,** *hee-er-yooce´;* from *2413;* a *priest* (lit. or fig.):—(high) priest.

2410. Ἱεριχώ **Hiĕrichō,** *hee-er-ee-kho´;* of Heb. or. [3405]; *Jericho,* a place in Pal.:—Jericho.

2411. ἱερόν **hiĕrŏn,** *hee-er-on´;* neut. of *2413;* a *sacred* place, i.e. the entire precincts (whereas *3485* denotes the central *sanctuary* itself) of the *Temple* (at Jerus. or elsewhere):—temple.

2412. ἱεροπρεπής **hiĕrŏprĕpēs,** *hee-er-op-rep-ace´;* from *2413* and the same as *4241; reverent:*—as becometh holiness.

2413. ἱερός **hiĕrŏs,** *hee-er-os´;* of uncert. affin.; *sacred:*—holy.

2414. Ἱεροσόλυμα **Hiĕrŏsŏluma,** *hee-er-os-ol´-oo-mah;* of Heb. or. [3389]; *Hierosolyma* (i.e. *Jerushalaïm*), the capital of Pal.:—Jerusalem. Comp. *2419.*

2415. Ἱεροσολυμίτης **Hiĕrŏsŏlumitēs,** *hee-er-os-ol-oo-mee´-tace;* from *2414;* a *Hierosolymite,* i.e. inhab. of Hierosolyma:—of Jerusalem.

2416. ἱεροσυλέω **hiĕrŏsulĕō,** *hee-er-os-ool-eh´-o;* from *2417;* to *be a temple-robber* (fig.):—commit sacrilege.

2417. ἱερόσυλος **hiĕrŏsulŏs,** *hee-er-os´-oo-los;* from *2411* and *4813;* a *temple-despoiler:*—robber of churches.

2418. ἱερουργέω **hiĕrŏurgĕō,** *hee-er-oorg-eh´-o;* from a comp. of *2411* and the base of *2041;* to *be a temple-worker,* i.e. *officiate as a priest* (fig.):—minister.

2419. Ἱερουσαλήμ **Hiĕrŏusalēm,** *hee-er-oo-sal-ame´;* of Heb. or. [3389]; *Hierusalem* (i.e. *Jerushalem*), the capital of Pal.:—Jerusalem. Comp. *2414.*

2420. ἱερωσύνη **hiĕrōsunē,** *hee-er-o-soo´-nay;* from *2413; sacredness,* i.e. (by impl.) the *priestly office:*—priesthood.

2421. Ἰεσσαί **Iĕssai,** *es-es-sah´-ee;* of Heb. or. [3448]; *Jessæ* (i.e. *Jishai*), an Irs.:—Jesse.

2422. Ἰεφθάε **Iĕphthaĕ,** *ee-ef-thah´-eh;* of Heb. or. [3316]; *Jephthaë* (i.e. *Jiphtach*), an Isr.:—Jephthah.

2423. Ἰεχονίας **Iĕchŏnias,** *ee-ekh-on-ee´-as;* of Heb. or. [3204]; *Jechonias* (i.e. *Jekonjah*), an Isr.:—Jechonias.

2424. Ἰησοῦς **Iēsŏus,** *ee-ay-sooce´;* of Heb. or. [3091]; *Jesus* (i.e. *Jehoshua*), the name of our Lord and two (three) other Isr.:—Jesus.

2425. ἱκανός **hikanŏs,** *hik-an-os´;* from ἵκω **hikō** [ἱκάνω or ἱκνέομαι, akin to *2240*] (to *arrive*): *competent* (as if *coming* in season), i.e. *ample* (in amount) or *fit* (in character):—able, + content, enough, good, great, large, long (while), many, meet, much, security, sore, sufficient, worthy.

2426. ἱκανότης **hikanŏtēs,** *hik-an-ot´-ace;* from *2425; ability:*—sufficiency.

2427. ἱκανόω **hikanŏō,** *hik-an-ŏ´-o;* from *2425;* to *enable,* i.e. *qualify:*—make able (meet).

2428. ἱκετηρία **hikĕtēria,** *hik-et-ay-ree´-ah;* from a der. of the base of *2425* (through the idea of *approaching* for a favor); *intreaty:*—supplication.

2429. ἰκμάς **hikmas,** *hik-mas´;* of uncert. affin.; *dampness:*—moisture.

2430. Ἰκόνιον **Ikŏniŏn,** *ee-kon´-ee-on;* perh. from *1504; image-like; Iconium,* a place in Asia Minor:—Iconium.

2431. ἱλαρός **hilarŏs,** *hil-ar-os´;* from the same as *2436; propitious* or *merry* ("*hilarious*"), i.e. *prompt* or *willing:*—cheerful.

2432. ἱλαρότης **hilarŏtēs,** *hil-ar-ot´-ace;* from *2431; alacrity:*—cheerfulness.

2433. ἱλάσκομαι **hilaskŏmai,** *hil-as´-kom-ahee;* mid. from the same as *2436;* to *conciliate,* i.e. (trans.) to *atone* for (sin), or (intrans.) *be propitious:*—be merciful, make reconciliation for.

2434. ἱλασμός **hilasmŏs,** *hil-as-mos´; atonement,* i.e. (concr.) an *expiator:*—propitiation.

2435. ἱλαστήριον **hilastēriŏn,** *hil-as-tay´-ree-on;* neut. of a der. of *2433;* an *expiatory* (place or thing), i.e. (concr.) an atoning *victim,* or (spec.) the *lid* of the Ark (in the Temple):—mercyseat, propitiation.

2436. ἵλεως **hilĕōs,** *hil´-eh-oce;* perh. from the alt. form of *138; cheerful* (as *attractive*), i.e. *propitious;* adv. (by Hebr.) God be *gracious!,* i.e. (in averting some calamity) *far* be it:—be it far, merciful.

2437. Ἰλλυρικόν **Illurikŏn,** *il-loo-ree-kon´;* neut. of an adj. from a name of uncert. der.; (the) *Illyrican* (shore), i.e. (as a name itself) *Illyricum,* a region of Europe:—Illyricum.

2438. ἱμάς **himas,** *hee-mas´;* perh. from the same as *260;* a *strap,* i.e. (spec.) the *tie* (of a sandal) or the *lash* (of a scourge):—latchet, thong.

2439. ἱματίζω **himatizō,** *him-at-id-´zo;* from *2440;* to *dress:*—clothe.

2440. ἱμάτιον **himatiŏn,** *him-at´-ee-on;* neut. of a presumed der. of ἕννυμι **ĕnnumi** (to *put on*); a *dress* (inner or outer):—apparel, cloke, clothes, garment, raiment, robe, vesture.

2441. ἱματισμός **himatismŏs,** *him-at-is-mos´;* from *2439; clothing:*—apparel (× -led), array, raiment, vesture.

2442. ἱμείρομαι **himĕirŏmai,** *him-i´-rom-ahee;* mid. from ἵμερος **himĕrŏs** (a *yearning;* of uncert. affin.); to *long for:*—be affectionately desirous.

2443. ἵνα **hina,** *hin´-ah;* prob. from the same as the former part of *1438* (through the *demonstrative* idea; comp. *3588*); in order *that* (denoting the *purpose* or the *result*):—albeit, because, to the intent (that), lest, so as, (so) that, (for) to. Comp. *3363.*

ἵνα μή **hina mē.** See *3363.*

2444. ἱνατί **hinati,** *hin-at-ee´;* from *2443* and *5101; for what reason?,* i.e. *why?:*—wherefore, why.

2445. Ἰόππη **Iŏppē,** *ee-op´-pay;* of Heb. or. [3305]: *Joppe* (i.e. *Japho*), a place in Pal.:—Joppa.

2446. Ἰορδάνης **Iŏrdanēs,** *ee-or-dan´-ace;* of Heb. or. [3383]; the *Jordanes* (i.e. *Jarden*), a river of Pal.:—Jordan.

2447. ἰός **iŏs,** *ee-os´;* perh. from εἶμι **ĕimi** (to *go*) or ἵημι **hiēmi** (to *send*); *rust* (as if *emitted* by metals); also *venom* (as *emitted* by serpents):—poison, rust.

2448. Ἰουδά **Iŏuda,** *ee-oo-dah´;* of Heb. or. [3063 or perh. 3194]; *Judah* (i.e. *Jehudah* or *Juttah*), a part of (or place in) Pal.:—Judah.

2449. Ἰουδαία **Iŏudaia,** *ee-oo-dah´-yah;* fem. of *2453* (with *1093* impl.); the *Judæan* land (i.e. *Judæa*), a region of Pal.:—Judæa.

2450. Ἰουδαΐζω **Iŏudaïzō,** *ee-oo-dah-id´-zo;* from *2453;* to *become a Judæan,* i.e. *"Judaize":*—live as the Jews.

2451. Ἰουδαϊκός **Iŏudaïkŏs,** *ee-oo-dah-ee-kos´;* from *2453; Judaïc,* i.e. *resembling a Judæan:*—Jewish.

2452. Ἰουδαϊκῶς **Iŏudaïkōs,** *ee-oo-dah-ee-koce´;* adv. from *2451; Judaïcally* or *in a manner resembling a Judæan:*—as do the Jews.

2453. Ἰουδαῖος **Iŏudaiŏs,** *ee-oo-dah´-yos;* from *2448* (in the sense of *2455* as a country); *Judæan,* i.e. belonging to *Jehudah:*—Jew (-ess), of Judæa.

2454. Ἰουδαϊσμός **Iŏudaismŏs,** *ee-oo-dah-is-mos´;* from *2450; "Judaïsm",* i.e. the *Jewish faith* and usages:—Jews' religion.

2455. Ἰουδάς **Iŏudas,** *ee-oo-das´;* of Heb. or. [3063]; *Judas* (i.e. *Jehudah*), the name of ten Isr.; also of the posterity of one of them and its region:—Juda (-h, -s); Jude.

2456. Ἰουλία **Iŏulia,** *ee-oo-lee´-ah;* fem. of the same as *2457; Julia,* a Chr. woman:—Julia.

2457. Ἰούλιος **Iŏuliŏs,** *ee-oo´-lee-os;* of Lat. or.; *Julius,* a centurion:—Julius.

2458. Ἰουνίας **Iŏunias,** *ee-oo-nee´-as;* of Lat. or.; *Junias,* a Chr.:—Junias.

2459. Ἰοῦστος **Iŏustŏs,** *ee-ooce´-tos;* of Lat. or. (*"just"*); *Justus,* the name of three Chr.:—Justus.

2460. ἱππεύς **hippĕus,** *hip-yooce´;* from *2462;* an *equestrian,* i.e. member of a *cavalry* corps:—horseman.

2461. ἱππικόν **hippikŏn,** *hip-pee-kon´;* neut. of a der. of *2462;* the *cavalry* force:—horse [-men].

2462. ἵππος **hippŏs,** *hip´-pos;* of uncert. affin.; a *horse:*—horse.

2463. ἶρις **iris,** *ee´-ris;* perh. from *2046* (as a symb. of the female *messenger* of the pagan deities); a *rainbow* (*"iris"*):—rainbow.

2464. Ἰσαάκ **Isaak,** *ee-sah-ak´;* of Heb. or. [3327]; *Isaac* (i.e. *Jitschak*), the son of Abraham—:Isaac.

2465. ἰσάγγελος **isaggĕlŏs,** *ee-sang´-el-los;* from *2470* and *32; like an angel,* i.e. *angelic:*—equal unto the angels.

2466. Ἰσαχάρ **Isachar,** *ee-sakh-ar´;* of Heb. or. [3485]; *Isachar* (i.e. *Jissaskar*), a son of Jacob (fig. his desc.):—Issachar.

2467. ἴσημι **isēmi,** *is´-ay-mee;* assumed by some as the base of cert. irreg. forms of *1492;* to *know:*—know.

2468. ἴσθι **isthi,** *is´-thee;* sec. pers. imper. pres. of *1510; be* thou:—+ agree, be, × give thyself wholly to.

2469. Ἰσκαριώτης **Iskariōtēs,** *is-kar-ee-o´-tace;* of Heb. or. [prob. 377 and 7149]; *inhab. of Kerioth; Iscariotes* (i.e. *Keriothite*), an epithet of Judas the traitor:—Iscariot.

2470. ἴσος **isŏs,** *ee´-sos;* prob. from *1492* (through the idea of *seeming*); *similar* (in amount or kind):—+ agree, as much, equal, like.

2471. ἰσότης **isŏtēs,** *ee-sot´-ace; likeness* (in condition or proportion); by impl. *equity:*—equal (-ity).

2472. ἰσότιμος **isŏtimŏs,** *ee-sot´-ee-mos;* from *2470* and *5092; of equal value* or *honor:*—like precious.

2473. ἰσόψυχος **isŏpsuchŏs,** *ee-sop´-soo-khos;* from *2470* and *5590; of similar spirit:*—likeminded.

2474. Ἰσραήλ **Israēl,** *is-rah-ale´;* of Heb. or. [3478]; *Israel* (i.e. *Jisrael*), the adopted name of Jacob, includ. his desc. (lit. or fig.):—Israel.

2475. Ἰσραηλίτης **Israēlitēs,** *is-rah-ale-ee´-tace;* from *2474;* an *"Israelite",* i.e. desc. of Israel (lit. or fig.):—Israelite.

2476. ἵστημι **histēmi,** *his´-tay-mee;* a prol. form of a prim. στάω **staō,** *stah´-o* (of the same mean., and used for it in certain tenses); to *stand* (trans. or intrans.), used in various applications (lit. or fig.):—abide, appoint, bring, continue, covenant, establish, hold up, lay, present, set (up), stanch, stand (by, forth, still, up). Comp. *5087.*

2477. ἱστορέω **histŏrĕō,** *his-tor-eh´-o;* from a der. of *1492;* to *be knowing* (*learned*), i.e. (by impl.) to *visit* for information (*interview*):—see.

2478. ἰσχυρός **ischurŏs,** *is-khoo-ros´;* from *2479; forcible* (lit. or fig.):—boisterous, mighty (-ier), powerful, strong (-er, man), valiant.

2479. ἰσχύς **ischus,** *is-khoos´;* from a der. of ἰς **is** (*force;* comp. ἔσχον **ĕschŏn,** a form of *2192*); *forcefulness* (lit. or fig.):—ability, might ([-ily]), power, strength.

2480. ἰσχύω **ischuō,** *is-khoo´-o;* from *2479;* to *have* (or *exercise*) *force* (lit. or fig.):—be able, avail, can do ([-not]), could, be good, might, prevail, be of strength, be whole, + much work.

2481. ἴσως **isōs,** *ee´-soce;* adv. from *2470; likely,* i.e. *perhaps:*—it may be.

2482. Ἰταλία **Italia,** *ee-tal-ee´-ah;* prob. of for. or.; *Italia,* a region of Europe:—Italy.

2483. Ἰταλικός **Italikŏs,** *ee-tal-ee-kos´;* from *2482; Italic,* i.e. belonging to Italia:—Italian.

2484. Ἰτουραῖα **Itŏuraia,** *ee-too-rah´-yah;* of Heb. or. [3195]; *Ituræa* (i.e. *Jetur*), a region of Pal.:—Ituræa.

2485. ἰχθύδιον **ichthudiŏn,** *ikh-thoo´-dee-on;* dimin. from *2486;* a *petty fish:*—little (small) fish.

2486. ἰχθύς **ichthus,** *ikh-thoos´;* of uncert. affin.; a *fish:*—fish.

2487. ἴχνος **ichnŏs,** *ikh´-nos;* from ἰκνέομαι **iknĕŏmai** (to *arrive;* comp. *2240*); a *track* (fig.):—step.

2488. Ἰωάθαμ **Iōatham,** *ee-o-ath´-am;* of Heb. or. [3147]; *Joatham* (i.e. *Jotham*), an Isr.:—Joatham.

2489. Ἰωάννα **Iōanna,** *ee-o-an´-nah;* fem. of the same as *2491; Joanna,* a Chr.:—Joanna.

2490. Ἰωαννᾶς **Iōannas,** *ee-o-an-nas´;* a form of *2491; Joannas,* an Isr.:—Joannas.

2491. Ἰωάννης **Iōannēs,** *ee-o-an´-nace;* of Heb. or. [3110]; *Joannes* (i.e. *Jochanan*), the name of four Isr.:—John.

2492. Ἰώβ **Iōb,** *ee-obe´;* of Heb. or. [347]; *Job* (i.e. *Ijob*), a patriarch:—Job.

2493. Ἰωήλ **Iōēl,** *ee-o-ale´;* of Heb. or. [3100]; *Joel,* an Isr.:—Joel.

2494. Ἰωνάν **Iōnan,** *ee-o-nan´;* prob. for *2491* or *2495; Jonan,* an Isr.:—Jonan.

2495. Ἰωνᾶς **Iōnas,** *ee-o-nas´;* of Heb. or. [3124]; *Jonas* (i.e. *Jonah*), the name of two Isr.:—Jonas.

2496. Ἰωράμ **Iōram,** *ee-o-ram´;* of Heb. or. [3141]; *Joram,* an Isr.:—Joram.

2497. Ἰωρείμ **Iōrĕim,** *ee-o-rime´;* perh. for *2496; Jorim,* an Isr.:—Jorim.

2498. Ἰωσαφάτ **Iōsaphat,** *ee-o-saf-at´;* of Heb. or. [3092]; *Josaphat* (i.e. *Jehoshaphat*), an Isr.:—Josaphat.

2499. Ἰωσή **Iōsē,** *ee-o-say´;* gen. of *2500; Jose,* an Isr.:—Jose.

2500. Ἰωσῆς **Iōsēs,** *ee-o-sace´;* perh. for *2501; Joses,* the name of two Isr.:—Joses. Comp. *2499.*

2501. Ἰωσήφ **Iōsēph,** *ee-o-safe´;* of Heb. or. [3130]; *Joseph,* the name of seven Isr.:—Joseph.

2502. Ἰωσίας **Iōsias,** *ee-o-see´-as;* of Heb. or. [2977]; *Josias* (i.e. *Joshiah*), an Isr.:—Josias.

2503. ἰῶτα **iōta,** *ee-o´-tah;* of Heb. or. [the tenth letter of the Heb. alphabet]; *"iota"*, the name of the ninth letter of the Gr. alphabet, put (fig.) for a very small part of anything:—jot.

K

2504. κἀγώ **kagō,** *kag-o´;* from *2532* and *1473* (so also the dat.

κἀμοί **kamŏi,** *kam-oy´;* and acc.

κἀμέ **kamĕ,** *kam-eh´*); *and* (or *also, even,* etc.) *I,* (*to*) *me:*—(and, even, even so, so) I (also, in like wise), both me, me also.

2505. καθά **katha,** *kath-ah´;* from *2596* and the neut. plur. of *3739; according to which* things, i.e. *just as:*—as.

2506. καθαίρεσις **kathairĕsis,** *kath-ah´ee-res-is;* from *2507; demolition;* fig. *extinction:*—destruction, pulling down.

2507. καθαιρέω **kathairĕō,** *kath-ahee-reh´-o;* from *2596* and *138* (includ. its alt.); to *lower* (or with violence) *demolish* (lit. or fig.):—cast (pull, put, take) down, destroy.

2508. καθαίρω **kathairō,** *kath-ah´ee-ro;* from *2513;* to *cleanse,* i.e. (spec.) to *prune;* fig. to *expiate:*—purge.

2509. καθάπερ **kathapĕr,** *kath-ap´-er;* from *2505* and *4007; exactly as:*—(even, as well) as.

2510. καθάπτω **kathaptō,** *kath-ap´-to;* from *2596* and *680;* to *seize upon:*—fasten on.

2511. καθαρίζω **katharizō,** *kath-ar-id´-zo;* from *2513;* to *cleanse* (lit. or fig.):—(make) clean (-se), purge, purify.

2512. καθαρισμός **katharismŏs,** *kath-ar-is-mos´;* from *2511;* a *washing* off, i.e. (cer.) *ablution,* (mor.) *expiation:*—cleansing, + purge, purification, (-fying).

2513. καθαρός **katharŏs,** *kath-ar-os´;* of uncert. affin.; *clean* (lit. or fig.):—clean, clear, pure.

2514. καθαρότης **katharŏtēs,** *kath-ar-ot´-ace;* from *2513; cleanness* (cer.):—purification.

2515. καθέδρα **kathĕdra,** *kath-ed´-rah;* from *2596* and the same as *1476;* a *bench* (lit. or fig.):—seat.

2516. καθέζομαι **kathĕzŏmai,** *kath-ed´-zom-ahee;* from *2596* and the base of *1476;* to *sit down:*—sit.

2517. καθεξῆς **kathĕxēs,** *kath-ex-ace´;* from *2596* and *1836; thereafter,* i.e. *consecutively;* as a noun (by ell. of noun) a *subsequent* person or time:—after (-ward), by (in) order.

2518. καθεύδω **kathĕudō,** *kath-yoo´-do;* from *2596* and εὕδω **hĕudō** (to *sleep*); to lie *down* to *rest,* i.e. (by impl.) to *fall asleep* (lit. or fig.):—(be a-) sleep.

2519. καθηγητής **kathēgētēs,** *kath-ayg-ay-tace´;* from a comp. of *2596* and *2233;* a *guide,* i.e. (fig.) a *teacher:*—master.

2520. καθήκω **kathēkō,** *kath-ay´-ko;* from *2596* and *2240;* to *reach to,* i.e. (neut. of pres. act. part., fig. as adj.) *becoming:*—convenient, fit.

2521. κάθημαι **kathēmai,** *kath´-ay-mahee;* from *2596* and ἧμαι **hēmai** (to *sit;* akin to the base of *1476*); to *sit down;* fig. to *remain, reside:*—dwell, sit (by, down).

2522. καθημερινός **kathēmĕrinŏs,** *kath-ay-mer-ee-nos´;* from *2596* and *2250; quotidian:*—daily.

2523. καθίζω **kathizō,** *kath-id´-zo;* another (act.) form for *2516;* to *seat down,* i.e. *set* (fig. *appoint*); intrans. to *sit* (down); fig. to *settle* (*hover, dwell*):—continue, set, sit (down), tarry.

2524. καθίημι **kathiēmi,** *kath-ee´-ay-mee;* from *2596* and ἵημι **hiēmi** (to *send*); to *lower:*—let down.

2525. καθίστημι **kathistēmi,** *kath-is´-tay-mee;* from *2596* and *2476;* to *place down* (permanently), i.e. (fig.) to *designate, constitute, convoy:*—appoint, be, conduct, make, ordain, set.

2526. καθό **kathŏ,** *kath-ŏ´;* from *2596* and *3739; according to which* thing, i.e. *precisely as, in proportion as:*—according to that, (inasmuch) as.

2526´. καθολικός, **kathŏlikŏs,** *kath-ol-ee-kos´;* from *2527; universal:*—general.

2527. καθόλου, **kathŏlŏu,** *kath-ol´-oo;* from *2596* and *3650; on* the *whole,* i.e. *entirely:*—at all.

2528. καθοπλίζω **kathŏplizō,** *kath-op-lid´-zo;* from *2596* and *3695;* to *equip fully* with armor:—arm.

2529. καθοράω **kathŏraō,** *kath-or-ah´-o;* from *2596* and *3708;* to *behold fully,* i.e. (fig.) *distinctly apprehend:*—clearly see.

2530. καθότι **kathŏti,** *kath-ot´-ee;* from *2596* and *3739* and *5100; according to which certain* thing, i.e. *as far* (or *inasmuch*) *as:*—(according, forasmuch) as, because (that).

2531. καθώς **kathōs,** *kath-oce´;* from *2596* and *5613; just* (or *inasmuch*), *as, that:*—according to, (according, even) as, how, when.

2532. καί **kai,** *kahee;* appar. a prim. particle, having a *copulative* and sometimes also a *cumulative* force; *and, also, even, so, then, too,* etc.; often used in connection (or composition) with other particles or small words:—and, also, both, but, even, for, if, indeed, likewise, moreover, or, so, that, then, therefore, when, yea, yet.

2533. Καϊάφας **Kaïaphas,** *kah-ee-af´-as;* of Chald. or.; *the dell; Caïaphas* (i.e. *Cajepha*), an Isr.:—Caiaphas.

2534. καίγε **kaigĕ,** *ka´-hee-gheh;* from *2532* and *1065; and at least* (or *even, indeed*):—and, at least.

2535. Κάϊν **Kaïn,** *kah´-in;* of Heb. or. [7014]; *Caïn* (i.e. *Cajin*), the son of Adam:—Cain.

2536. Καϊνάν **Kaïnan,** *kah-ee-nan´;* of Heb. or. [7018]; *Caïnan* (i.e. *Kenan*), the name of two patriarchs:—Cainan.

2537. καινός **kainŏs,** *kahee-nos´;* of uncert. affin.; *new* (espec. in *freshness;* while *3501* is prop. so with respect to *age*):—new.

2538. καινότης **kainŏtēs,** *kahee-not´-ace;* from *2537; renewal* (fig.):—newness.

2539. καίπερ **kaipĕr,** *kahe´ee-per;* from *2532* and *4007; and indeed,* i.e. *nevertheless* or *notwithstanding:*—and yet, although.

2540. καιρός **kairŏs,** *kahee-ros´;* of uncert. affin.; an *occasion,* i.e. *set* or *proper* time:— × always, opportunity, (convenient, due) season, (due, short, while) time, a while. Comp. *5550.*

2541. Καῖσαρ **Kaisar,** *kah´-ee-sar;* of Lat. or.; *Cæsar,* a title of the Rom. emperor:—Cæsar.

2542. Καισάρεια **Kaisarĕia,** *kahee-sar´-i-a;* from *2541; Cæsaria,* the name of two places in Pal.:—Cæsarea.

2543. καίτοι **kaitŏi,** *kah´-ee-toy;* from *2532* and *5104; and yet,* i.e. *nevertheless:*—although.

2544. καίτοιγε **kaitŏigĕ,** *kah´ee-foyg-eh;* from *2543* and *1065; and yet indeed,* i.e. *although really:*—nevertheless, though.

2545. καίω **kaiō,** *kah´-yo;* appar. a prim. verb; to *set on fire,* i.e. *kindle* or (by impl.) *consume:*—burn, light.

2546. κἀκεῖ **kakĕi,** *kak-i´;* from *2532* and *1563; likewise in that place:*—and there, there (thither) also.

2547. κἀκεῖθεν **kakĕithĕn,** *kak-i´-then;* from *2532* and *1564; likewise from that place* (or *time*):—and afterward (from) (thence), thence also.

2548. κἀκεῖνος **kakĕinŏs,** *kak-i´-nos;* from *2532* and *1565; likewise that* (or *those*):—and him (other, them), even he, him also, them (also), (and) they.

2549. κακία **kakia,** *kak-ee´-ah;* from *2556; badness,* i.e. (subj.) *depravity,* or (act.) *malignity,* or (pass.) *trouble:*—evil, malice (-iousness), naughtiness, wickedness.

2550. κακοήθεια **kakŏēthĕia,** *kak-ŏ-ay´-thi-ah;* from a comp. of *2556* and *2239; bad character,* i.e. (spec.) *mischievousness:*—malignity.

2551. κακολογέω **kakŏlŏgĕō,** *kak-ol-og-eh´-o;* from a comp. of *2556* and *3056;* to *revile:*—curse, speak evil of.

2552. κακοπάθεια **kakŏpathĕia,** *kak-op-ath´-i-ah;* from a comp. of *2556* and *3806; hardship:*—suffering affliction.

2553. κακοπαθέω **kakŏpathĕō,** *kak-op-ath-eh´-o;* from the same as *2552;* to *undergo hardship:*—be afflicted, endure afflictions (hardness), suffer trouble.

2554. κακοποιέω **kakŏpŏiĕō,** *kak-op-oy-eh´-o;* from *2555;* to *be a bad-doer,* i.e. (obj.) to *injure,* or (gen.) to *sin:*—do (-ing) evil.

2555. κακοποιός **kakŏpŏiŏs,** *kak-op-oy-os´;* from *2556* and *4160;* a *bad-doer;* (spec.) a *criminal:*—evil-doer, malefactor.

2556. κακός **kakŏs,** *kak-os´;* appar. a prim. word; *worthless* (*intrinsically* such; whereas *4190* prop. refers to *effects*), i.e. (subj.) *depraved,* or (obj.) *injurious:*—bad, evil, harm, ill, noisome, wicked.

2557. κακοῦργος **kakŏurgŏs,** *kak-oor´-gos;* from *2556* and the base of *2041;* a *wrong-doer,* i.e. *criminal:*—evil-doer, malefactor.

2558. κακουχέω **kakŏuchĕō,** *kak-oo-kheh´-o;* from a presumed comp. of *2556* and *2192;* to *maltreat:*—which suffer adversity, torment.

2559. κακόω **kakŏō,** *kak-ŏ´-o;* from *2556;* to *injure;* fig. to *exasperate:*—make evil affected, entreat evil, harm, hurt, vex.

2560. κακῶς **kakōs,** *kak-oce´;* adv. from *2556; badly* (phys. or mor.):—amiss, diseased, evil, grievously, miserably, sick, sore.

2561. κάκωσις **kakōsis,** *kak´-o-sis;* from *2559; maltreatment:*—affliction.

2562. καλάμη **kalamē,** *kal-am´-ay;* fem. of *2563;* a *stalk* of grain, i.e. (collect.) *stubble:*—stubble.

2563. κάλαμος **kalamŏs,** *kal´-am-os;* of uncert. affin.; a *reed* (the plant or its stem, or that of a similar plant); by impl. a *pen:*—pen, reed.

2564. καλέω **kalĕō,** *kal-eh´-o;* akin to the base of *2753;* to *"call"* (prop. aloud, but used in a variety of applications, dir. or otherwise):—bid, call (forth), (whose, whose sur-) name (was [called]).

2565. καλλιέλαιος **kalliĕlaiŏs,** *kal-le-el´-ah-yos;* from the base of *2566* and *1636;* a *cultivated olive* tree, i.e. a *domesticated* or *improved* one:—good olive tree.

2566. καλλίον **kalliŏn,** *kal-lee´-on;* neut. of the (irreg.) comp. of *2570;* (adv.) *better* than many:—very well.

2567. καλοδιδάσκαλος **kalŏdidaskalŏs,** *kal-od-id-as´-kal-os;* from *2570* and *1320;* a *teacher of* the *right:*—teacher of good things.

2568. Καλοὶ Λιμένες **Kalŏi Limĕnĕs,** *kal-oy´-lee-men´-es;* plur. of *2570* and *3040; Good Harbors,* i.e. *Fairhaven,* a bay of Crete:—fair havens.

2569. καλοποιέω **kalŏpŏiĕō,** *kal-op-oy-eh´-o;* from *2570* and *4160;* to *do well,* i.e. live virtuously:—well doing.

2570. καλός **kalŏs,** *kal-os´;* of uncert. affin.; prop. *beautiful,* but chiefly (fig.) *good* (lit. or mor.), i.e. *valuable* or *virtuous* (for *appearance* or *use,* and thus distinguished from *18,* which is prop. *intrinsic*):—× better, fair, good (-ly), honest, meet, well, worthy.

2571. κάλυμα **kaluma,** *kal´-oo-mah;* from *2572;* a *cover,* i.e. *veil:*—vail.

2572. καλύπτω **kaluptō,** *kal-oop´-to;* akin to *2813* and *2928;* to *cover* up (lit. or fig.):—cover, hide.

2573. καλῶς **kalōs,** *kal-oce´;* adv. from *2570; well* (usually mor.):—(in a) good (place), honestly, + recover, (full) well.

2574. κάμηλος **kamēlŏs,** *kam´-ay-los;* of Heb. or. [1581]; a *"camel":*—camel.

2575. κάμινος **kaminŏs,** *kam´-ee-nos;* prob. from *2545;* a *furnace:*—furnace.

2576. καμμύω **kammuō,** *kam-moo´-o;* for a comp. of *2596* and the base of *3466;* to *shut down,* i.e. *close* the eyes:—close.

2577. κάμνω **kamnō,** *kam´-no;* appar. a prim. verb; prop. to *toil,* i.e. (by impl.) to *tire* (fig. *faint, sicken*):—faint, sicken, be wearied.

2578. κάμπτω **kamptō,** *kamp´-to;* appar. a prim. verb; to *bend:*—bow.

2579. κἄν **kan,** *kan;* from *2532* and *1437; and* (or *even*) *if:*—and (also) if (so much as), if but, at the least, though, yet.

2580. Κανᾶ **Kana,** *kan-ah´;* of Heb. or. [comp. 7071]; *Cana,* a place in Pal.:—Cana.

2581. Κανανίτης **Kananitēs,** *kan-an-ee´-tace;* of Chald. or. [comp. 7067]; *zealous; Cananitès,* an epithet:—Canaanite [*by mistake for a der. from 5477*].

2582. Κανδάκη **Kandakē,** *kan-dak´-ay;* of for. or.; *Candacè,* an Eg. queen:—Candace.

2583. κανών **kanōn,** *kan-ohn´;* from κάνη **kanē** (a straight *reed,* i.e. *rod*); a *rule* (*"canon"*), i.e. (fig.) a *standard* (of faith and practice); by impl. a *boundary,* i.e. (fig.) a *sphere* (of activity):—line, rule.

2584. Καπερναούμ **Kapĕrnaŏum,** *cap-er-nah-oom´;* of Heb. or. [prob. 3723 and 5151]; *Capernaüm* (i.e. *Caphanachum*), a place in Pal.:—Capernaum.

2585. καπηλεύω **kapēlĕuō,** *kap-ale-yoo´-o;* from κάπηλος **kapēlŏs** (a *huckster*); to *retail,* i.e. (by impl.) to *adulterate* (fig.):—corrupt.

2586. καπνός **kapnŏs,** *kap-nos´;* of uncert. affin.; *smoke:*—smoke.

2587. Καππαδοκία **Kappadŏkia,** *kap-pad-ok-ee´-ah;* of for. or.; *Cappadocia,* a region of Asia Minor:—Cappadocia.

2588. καρδία **kardia,** *kar-dee´-ah;* prol. from a prim. κάρ **kar** (Lat. *cor, "heart"*); the *heart,* i.e. (fig.) the *thoughts* or *feelings* (*mind*); also (by anal.) the *middle:*—(+ broken-) heart (-ed).

2589. καρδιογνώστης **kardiŏgnōstēs,** *kar-dee-og-noce´-tace;* from *2588* and *1097;* a *heart-knower:*—which knowest the hearts.

2590. καρπός **karpŏs,** *kar-pos´;* prob. from the base of *726; fruit* (as *plucked*), lit. or fig.:—fruit.

2591. Κάρπος **Karpŏs,** *kar´-pos;* perh. for *2590; Carpus,* prob. a Chr.:—Carpus.

2592. καρποφορέω **karpŏphŏrĕō,** *kar-pof-or-eh´-o;* from *2593;* to *be fertile* (lit. or fig.):—be (bear, bring forth) fruit (-ful).

2593. καρποφόρος **karpŏphŏrŏs,** *kar-pof-or´-os;* from *2590* and *5342; fruitbearing* (fig.):—fruitful.

2594. καρτερέω **kartĕrĕō,** *kar-ter-eh´-o;* from a der. of *2904* (transp.); to *be strong,* i.e. (fig.) *steadfast* (*patient*):—endure.

2595. κάρφος **karphŏs,** *kar´-fos;* from κάρφω **karphō** (to *wither*); a dry *twig* or *straw:*—mote.

2596. κατά **kata,** *kat-ah´;* a prim. particle; (prep.) *down* (in place or time), in varied relations (according to the case [gen. dat. or acc.] with which it is joined):—about, according as (to), after, against, (when they were) × alone, among, and, × apart, (even, like) as (concerning, pertaining to, touching), × aside, at, before, beyond, by, to the charge of, [charita-] bly, concerning, + covered, [dai-] ly, down, every, (+ far more) exceeding, × more excellent, for, from . . . to, godly, in (-asmuch, divers, every, -to, respect of), . . . by, after the manner of, + by any means, beyond (out of) measure, × mightily, more, × natural, of (up-) on (× part), out (of every), over against, (+ your) × own, + particularly, so, through (-oughout, -oughout every), thus, (un-) to (-gether, -ward), × uttermost, where (-by), with. In composition it retains many of these applications, and frequently denotes *opposition, distribution* or *intensity.*

2597. καταβαίνω **katabainō,** *kat-ab-ah´ee-no;* from *2596* and the base of *939;* to *descend* (lit. or fig.):—come (get, go, step) down, descend, fall (down).

2598. καταβάλλω **kataballō,** *kat-ab-al´lo;* from *2596* and *906;* to *throw down:*—cast down, descend, fall (down).

2599. καταβαρέω **katabarĕō,** *kat-ab-ar-eh´-o;* from *2596* and *916;* to *impose upon:*—burden

2600. κατάβασις **katabasis,** *kat-ab´-as-is;* from *2597;* a *declivity:*—descent.

2601. καταβιβάζω **katabibazō,** *kat-ab-ib-ad´-zo;* from *2596* and a der. of the base of *939;* to *cause to go down,* i.e. *precipitate:*—bring (thrust) down.

2602. καταβολή **katabŏlē,** *kat-ab-ol-ay´;* from *2598;* a *deposition,* i.e. *founding;* fig. *conception:*—conceive, foundation.

2603. καταβραβεύω **katabrabĕuō,** *kat-ab-rab-yoo´-o;* from *2596* and *1018* (in its orig. sense); to *award* the prize *against,* i.e. (fig.) to *defraud* (of salvation):—beguile of reward.

2604. καταγγελεύς **kataggĕlĕus,** *kat-ang-gel-yooce´;* from *2605;* a *proclaimer:*—setter forth.

2605. καταγγέλλω **kataggĕllō,** *kat-ang-gel´-lo;* from *2596* and the base of *32;* to *proclaim, promulgate:*—declare, preach, shew, speak of, teach.

2606. καταγελάω **katagĕlaō,** *kat-ag-el-ah´-o;* to *laugh down,* i.e. *deride:*—laugh to scorn.

2607. καταγινώσκω **kataginōskō,** *kat-ag-in-o´-sko;* from *2596* and *1097;* to *note against,* i.e. *find fault with:*—blame, condemn.

2608. κατάγνυμι **katagnumi,** *kat-ag´-noo-mee;* from *2596* and the base of *4486;* to *rend in pieces, i.e. crack apart:*—break.

2609. *κατάγω* **katagō,** *kat-ag´-o;* from *2596* and *71;* to *lead down;* spec. to *moor* a vessel:—bring (down, forth), (bring to) land, touch.

2610. *καταγωνίζομαι* **katagōnizŏmai,** *kat-ag-o-nid´-zom-ahee;* from *2596* and *75;* to *struggle against,* i.e. (by impl.) to *overcome:*—subdue.

2611. *καταδέω* **katadĕō,** *kat-ad-eh´-o;* from *2596* and *1210;* to *tie down,* i.e. *bandage* (a wound):—bind up.

2612. *κατάδηλος* **katadēlŏs,** *kat-ad´-ay-los;* from *2596* intens. and *1212; manifest:*—far more evident.

2613. *καταδικάζω* **katadikazō,** *kat-ad-ik-ad´-zo;* from *2596* and a der. of *1349;* to *adjudge against,* i.e. *pronounce guilty:*—condemn.

2614. *καταδιώκω* **katadiōkō,** *kat-ad-ee-o´-ko;* from *2596* and *1377;* to *hunt down,* i.e. *search for:*—follow after.

2615. *καταδουλόω* **katadŏulŏō,** *kat-ad-oo-lŏ´-o;* from *2596* and *1402;* to *enslave utterly:*—bring into bondage.

2616. *καταδυναστεύω* **katadunastĕuō,** *kat-ad-oo-nas-tyoo´-o;* from *2596* and a der. of *1413;* to *exercise dominion against,* i.e. *oppress:*—oppress.

2617. *καταισχύνω* **kataischunō,** *kat-ahee-skhoo´-no;* from *2596* and *153;* to *shame down,* i.e. *disgrace* or (by impl.) *put to the blush:*—confound, dishonour, (be a-, make a-) shame (-d).

2618. *κατακαίω* **katakaiō,** *kat-ak-ah´ee-o;* from *2596* and *2545;* to *burn down* (to the ground), i.e. *consume wholly:*—burn (up, utterly).

2619. *κατακαλύπτω* **katakaluptō,** *kat-ak-al-oop´-to;* from *2596* and *2572;* to *cover wholly,* i.e. *veil:*—cover, hide.

2620. *κατακαυχάομαι* **katakauchaŏmai,** *kat-ak-ŏw-khah´-om-ahee;* from *2596* and *2744;* to *exult against* (i.e. *over*):—boast (against), glory, rejoice against.

2621. *κατάκειμαι* **katakĕimai,** *kat-ak´-i-mahee;* from *2596* and *2749;* to *lie down,* i.e. (by impl.) *be sick;* spec. to *recline* at a meal:—keep, lie, sit at meat (down).

2622. *κατακλάω* **kataklaō,** *kat-ak-lah´-o;* from *2596* and *2806;* to *break down,* i.e. *divide:*—break.

2623. *κατακλείω* **kataklĕiō,** *kat-ak-li´-o;* from *2596* and *2808;* to *shut down* (in a dungeon), i.e. *incarcerate:*—shut up.

2624. *κατακληροδοτέω* **kataklērŏdŏtĕō,** *kat-ak-lay-rod-ot-eh´-o;* from *2596* and a der. of a comp. of *2819* and *1325;* to *be a giver of lots to each,* i.e. (by impl.) to *apportion an estate:*—divide by lot.

2625. *κατακλίνω* **kataklinō,** *kat-ak-lee´-no;* from *2596* and *2827;* to *recline down,* i.e. (spec.) to *take a place* at table:—(make) sit down (at meat).

2626. *κατακλύζω* **katakluzō,** *kat-ak-lood´-zo;* from *2596* and the base of *2830;* to *dash* (*wash*) *down,* i.e. (by impl.) to *deluge:*—overflow.

2627. *κατακλυσμός* **kataklusmŏs,** *kat-ak-looce-mos´;* from *2626;* an *inundation:*—flood.

2628. *κατακολουθέω* **katakŏlŏuthĕō,** *kat-ak-ol-oo-theh´-o;* from *2596* and *190;* to *accompany closely:*—follow (after).

2629. *κατακόπτω* **katakŏptō,** *kat-ak-op´-to;* from *2596* and *2875;* to *chop down,* i.e. *mangle:*—cut.

2630. *κατακρημνίζω* **katakrēmnizō,** *kat-ak-rame-nid´-zo;* from *2596* and a der. of *2911;* to *precipitate down:*—cast down headlong.

2631. *κατάκριμα* **katakrima,** *kat-ak´-ree-mah;* from *2632;* an *adverse sentence* (the verdict):—condemnation.

2632. *κατακρίνω* **katakrinō,** *kat-ak-ree´-no;* from *2596* and *2919;* to *judge against,* i.e. *sentence:*—condemn, damn.

2633. *κατάκρισις* **katakrisis,** *kat-ak´-ree-sis;* from *2632; sentencing adversely* (the act):—condemn (-ation).

2634. *κατακυριεύω* **katakuriĕuō,** *kat-ak-oo-ree-yoo´-o;* from *2596* and *2961;* to *lord against,* i.e. *control, subjugate:*—exercise dominion over (lordship), be lord over, overcome.

2635. *καταλαλέω* **katalalĕō,** *kat-al-al-eh´-o;* from *2637;* to *be a traducer,* i.e. to *slander:*—speak against (evil of).

2636. *καταλαλία* **katalalia,** *kat-al-al-ee´-ah;* from *2637; defamation:*—backbiting, evil speaking.

2637. *κατάλαλος* **katalalŏs,** *kat-al´-al-os;* from *2596* and the base of *2980; talkative against,* i.e. a *slanderer:*—backbiter.

2638. *καταλαμβάνω* **katalambanō,** *kat-al-am-ban´-o;* from *2596* and *2983;* to *take eagerly,* i.e. *seize, possess,* etc. (lit. or fig.):—apprehend, attain, come upon, comprehend, find, obtain, perceive, (over-) take.

2639. *καταλέγω* **katalĕgō,** *kat-al-eg´-o;* from *2596* and *3004* (in its orig. mean.); to *lay down,* i.e. (fig.) to *enrol:*—take into the number.

2640. *κατάλειμμα* **katalĕimma,** *kat-al´-ime-mah;* from *2641;* a *remainder,* i.e. (by impl.) a *few:*—remnant.

2641. *καταλείπω* **katalĕipō,** *kat-al-i´-po;* from *2596* and *3007;* to *leave down,* i.e. *behind;* by impl. to *abandon, have remaining:*—forsake, leave, reserve.

2642. *καταλιθάζω* **katalithazō,** *kat-al-ith-ad´-zo;* from *2596* and *3034;* to *stone down,* i.e. *to death:*—stone.

2643. *καταλλαγή* **katallagē,** *kat-al-lag-ay´;* from *2644; exchange* (fig. *adjustment*), i.e. *restoration* to (the divine) favor:—atonement, reconciliation (-ing).

2644. *καταλλάσσω* **katallassō,** *kat-al-las´-so;* from *2596* and *236;* to *change mutually,* i.e. (fig.) to *compound* a difference:—reconcile.

2645. *κατάλοιπος* **katalŏipŏs,** *kat-al´-oy-pos;* from *2596* and *3062; left down* (*behind*), i.e. *remaining* (plur. the *rest*):—residue.

2646. *κατάλυμα* **kataluma,** *kat-al´-oo-mah;* from *2647;* prop. a *dissolution* (breaking up of a journey, i.e. (by impl.) a *lodging-place:*—guest-chamber, inn.

2647. *καταλύω* **kataluō,** *kat-al-oo´-o;* from *2596* and *3089;* to *loosen down* (*disintegrate*), i.e. (by impl.) to *demolish* (lit. or fig.); spec. [comp. *2646*] to *halt* for the night:—destroy, dissolve, be guest, lodge, come to nought, overthrow, throw down.

2648. *καταμανθάνω* **katamanthanō,** *kat-am-an-than´-o;* from *2596* and *3129;* to *learn thoroughly,* i.e. (by impl.) to *note carefully:*—consider.

2649. *καταμαρτυρέω* **katamarturĕō,** *kat-am-ar-too-reh´-o;* from *2596* and *3140;* to *testify against:*—witness against.

2650. *καταμένω* **katamĕnō,** *kat-am-en´-o;* from *2596* and *3306;* to *stay fully,* i.e. *reside:*—abide.

2651. *καταμόνας* **katamŏnas,** *kat-am-on´-as;* from *2596* and acc. plur. fem. of *3441* (with *5561* impl.); *according to sole* places, i.e. (adv.) *separately:*—alone.

2652. *κατανάθεμα* **katanathĕma,** *kat-an-ath´-em-ah;* from *2596* (intens.) and *331;* an *imprecation:*—curse.

2653. *καταναθεματίζω* **katanathĕmatizō,** *kat-an-ath-em-at-id´-zo;* from *2596* (intens.) and *332;* to *imprecate:*—curse.

2654. *καταναλίσκω* **katanaliskō,** *kat-an-al-is´-ko;* from *2596* and *355;* to *consume utterly:*—consume.

2655. *καταναρκάω* **katanarkaō,** *kat-an-ar-kah´-o;* from *2596* and *ναρκάω* **narkaō** (to *be numb*); to *grow utterly torpid,* i.e. (by impl.) *slothful* (fig. *expensive*):—be burdensome (chargeable).

2656. *κατανεύω* **kataneuō,** *kat-an-yoo´-o;* from *2596* and *3506;* to *nod down* (*towards*), i.e. (by anal.) to *make signs* to:—beckon.

2657. *κατανοέω* **katanŏĕō,** *kat-an-o-eh´-o;* from *2596* and *3539;* to *observe fully:*—behold, consider, discover, perceive.

2658. *καταντάω* **katantaō,** *kat-an-tah´-o;* from *2596* and a der. of *473;* to *meet against,* i.e. *arrive* at (lit. or fig.):—attain, come.

2659. *κατάνυξις* **katanuxis,** *kat-an´-oox-is;* from *2660;* a *prickling* (sensation, as of the limbs *asleep*), i.e. (by impl. [perh. by some confusion with *3506* or even with *3571*]) *stupor* (*lethargy*):—slumber.

2660. *κατανύσσω* **katanussō,** *kat-an-oos´-so;* from *2596* and *3572;* to *pierce thoroughly,* i.e. (fig.) to *agitate* violently ("sting to the quick"):—prick.

2661. *καταξιόω* **kataxiŏō,** *kat-ax-ee-ŏ´-o;* from *2596* and *515;* to *deem entirely deserving:*—(ac-) count worthy.

2662. καταπατέω **katapatĕō,** *kat-ap-at-eh´-o;* from *2596* and *3961;* to *trample down;* fig. to *reject* with disdain:—trample, tread (down, underfoot).

2663. κατάπαυσις **katapausis,** *kat-ap´ŏw-sis;* from *2664; reposing down,* i.e. (by Hebr.) *abode:*—rest.

2664. καταπαύω **katapauō,** *kat-ap-ŏw´-o;* from *2596* and *3973;* to *settle down,* i.e. (lit.) to *colonize,* or (fig.) to (*cause to*) *desist:*—cease, (give) rest (-rain).

2665. καταπέτασμα **katapĕtasma,** *kat-ap-et´-as-mah;* from a comp. of *2596* and a congener of *4072;* something *spread thoroughly,* i.e. (spec.) the door *screen* (to the Most Holy Place) in the Jewish Temple:—vail.

2666. καταπίνω **katapinō,** *kat-ap-ee´-no;* from *2596* and *4095;* to *drink down,* i.e. *gulp entire* (lit. or fig.):—devour, drown, swallow (up).

2667. καταπίπτω **katapiptō,** *kat-ap-ip´-to;* from *2596* and *4098;* to *fall down:*—fall (down).

2668. καταπλέω **kataplĕō,** *kat-ap-leh´-o;* from *2596* and *4126;* to *sail down* upon a place, i.e. to *land* at:—arrive.

2669. καταπονέω **katapŏnĕō,** *kat-ap-on-eh´-o;* from *2596* and a der. of *4192;* to *labor down,* i.e. *wear with toil* (fig. *harass*):—oppress, vex.

2670. καταποντίζω **katapŏntizō,** *kat-ap-on-tid´-zo;* from *2596* and a der. of the same as *4195;* to *plunge down,* i.e. *submerge:*—drown, sink.

2671. κατάρα **katara,** *kat-ar´-ah;* from *2596* (intens.) and *685; imprecation, execration:*—curse (-d, -ing).

2672. καταράομαι **kataraŏmai,** *kat-ar-ah´-om-ahee;* mid. from *2671;* to *execrate;* by anal. to *doom:*—curse.

2673. καταργέω **katargĕō,** *kat-arg-eh´-o;* from *2596* and *691;* to *be* (*render*) *entirely idle* (*useless*), lit. or fig.:—abolish, cease, cumber, deliver, destroy, do away, become (make) of no (none, without) effect, fail, loose, bring (come) to nought, put away (down), vanish away, make void.

2674. καταριθμέω **katarithmĕō,** *kat-ar-ith-meh´-o;* from *2596;* and *705;* to *reckon among:*—number with.

2675. καταρτίζω **katartizō,** *kat-ar-tid´-zo;* from *2596* and a der. of *739;* to *complete thoroughly,* i.e. *repair* (lit. or fig.) or *adjust:*—fit, frame, mend, (make) perfect (-ly join together), prepare, restore.

2676. κατάρτισις **katartisis,** *kat-ar´-tis-is;* from *2675; thorough equipment* (subj.):—perfection.

2677. καταρτισμός **katartismŏs,** *kat-ar-tis-mos´;* from *2675; complete furnishing* (obj.):—perfecting.

2678. κατασείω **katasĕiō,** *kat-as-i´-o;* from *2596* and *4579;* to *sway downward,* i.e. *make a signal:*—beckon.

2679. κατασκάπτω **kataskaptō,** *kat-as-kap´-to;* from *2596* and *4626;* to *undermine,* i.e. (by impl.) *destroy:*—dig down, ruin.

2680. κατασκευάζω **kataskĕuazō,** *kat-ask-yoo-ad´-zo;* from *2596* and a der. of *4632;* to *prepare thoroughly* (prop. by external *equipment;* whereas *2090* refers rather to internal *fitness*); by impl. to *construct, create:*—build, make, ordain, prepare.

2681. κατασκηνόω **kataskēnŏō,** *kat-as-kay-nŏ´-o;* from *2596* and *4637;* to *camp down,* i.e. *haunt;* fig. to *remain:*—lodge, rest.

2682. κατασκήνωσις **kataskēnōsis,** *kat-as-kay´-no-sis;* from *2681;* an *encamping,* i.e. (fig.) a *perch:*—nest.

2683. κατασκιάζω **kataskiazō,** *kat-as-kee-ad´-zo;* from *2596* and a der. of *4639;* to *overshade,* i.e. *cover:*—shadow.

2684. κατασκοπέω **kataskŏpĕō,** *kat-as-kop-eh´-o;* from *2685;* to *be a sentinel,* i.e. to *inspect* insidiously:—spy out.

2685. κατάσκοπος **kataskŏpŏs,** *kat-as´-kop-os;* from *2596* (intens.) and *4649* (in the sense of a *watcher*); a *reconnoiterer:*—spy.

2686. κατασοφίζομαι **katasŏphizŏmai,** *kat-as-of-id´-zom-ahee;* mid. from *2596* and *4679;* to *be crafty against,* i.e. *circumvent:*—deal subtilly with.

2687. καταστέλλω **katastĕllō,** *kat-as-tel´-lo;* from *2596* and *4724;* to *put down,* i.e. *quell:*—appease, quiet.

2688. κατάστημα **katastēma,** *kat-as´-tay-mah;* from *2525;* prop. a *position* or *condition,* i.e. (subj.) *demeanor:*—behaviour.

2689. καταστολή **katastŏlē,** *kat-as-tol-ay´;* from *2687;* a *deposit,* i.e. (spec.) *costume:*—apparel.

2690. καταστρέφω **katastrĕphō,** *kat-as-tref´-o;* from *2596* and *4762;* to *turn* upside *down,* i.e. *upset:*—overthrow.

2691. καταστρηνιάω **katastrēniaō,** *kat-as-tray-nee-ah´-o;* from *2596* and *4763;* to *become voluptuous against:*—begin to wax wanton against.

2692. καταστροφή **katastrŏphē,** *kat-as-trof-ay´;* from *2690;* an *overturn* ("*catastrophe*"), i.e. *demolition;* fig. *apostasy:*—overthrow, subverting.

2693. καταστρώννυμι **katastrōnnumi,** *kat-as-trone´-noo-mee;* from *2596* and *4766;* to *strew down,* i.e. (by impl.) to *prostrate* (*slay*):—overthrow.

2694. κατασύρω **katasurō,** *kat-as-oo´-ro;* from *2596* and *4951;* to *drag down,* i.e. *arrest* judicially:—hale.

2695. κατασφάττω **katasphattō,** *kat-as-fat´-to;* from *2596* and *4969;* to *kill down,* i.e. *slaughter:*—slay.

2696. κατασφραγίζω **katasphragizō,** *kat-as-frag-id´-zo;* from *2596* and *4972;* to *seal closely:*—seal.

2697. κατάσχεσις **kataschĕsis,** *kat-as´-khes-is;* from *2722;* a *holding down,* i.e. *occupancy:*—possession.

2698. κατατίθημι **katatithēmi,** *kat-at-ith´-ay-mee;* from *2596* and *5087;* to *place down,* i.e. *deposit* (lit. or fig.):—do, lay, shew.

2699. κατατομή **katatŏmē,** *kat-at-om-ay´;* from a comp. of *2596* and τέμνω **tĕmnō** (to *cut*); a *cutting down* (*off*), i.e. *mutilation* (ironically):—concision. Comp. *609.*

2700. κατατοξεύω **katatŏxĕuō,** *kat-at-ox-yoo´-o;* from *2596* and a der. of *5115;* to *shoot down* with an arrow or other missile:—thrust through.

2701. κατατρέχω **katatrĕchō,** *kat-at-rekh´-o;* from *2596* and *5143;* to *run down,* i.e. *hasten* from a tower:—run down.

καταφάγω **kataphagō.** See *2719.*

2702. καταφέρω **kataphĕrō,** *kat-af-er´-o;* from *2596* and *5342* (includ. its alt.); to *bear down,* i.e. (fig.) *overcome* (with drowsiness); spec. to *cast* a vote:—fall, give, sink down.

2703. καταφεύγω **kataphĕugō,** *kat-af-yoo´-go;* from *2596* and *5343;* to *flee down* (*away*):—flee.

2704. καταφθείρω **kataphthĕirō,** *kat-af-thi´-ro;* from *2596* and *5351;* to *spoil entirely,* i.e. (lit.) to *destroy;* or (fig.) to *deprave:*—corrupt, utterly perish.

2705. καταφιλέω **kataphilĕō,** *kat-af-ee-leh´-o;* from *2596* and *5368;* to *kiss earnestly:*—kiss.

2706. καταφρονέω **kataphrŏnĕō,** *kat-af-ron-eh´-o;* from *2596* and *5426;* to *think against,* i.e. *disesteem:*—despise.

2707. καταφροντής **kataphrŏntēs,** *kat-af-ron-tace´;* from *2706;* a *contemner:*—despiser.

2708. καταχέω **katachĕō,** *kat-akh-eh´-o;* from *2596* and χέω **chĕō** (to *pour*); to *pour down* (*out*):—pour.

2709. καταχθόνιος **katachthŏniŏs,** *kat-akh-thon´-ee-os;* from *2596* and χθών **chthōn** (the *ground*); *subterranean,* i.e. *infernal* (belonging to the world of departed spirits):—under the earth.

2710. καταχράομαι **katachraŏmai,** *kat-akh-rah´-om-ahee;* from *2596* and *5530;* to *overuse,* i.e. *misuse:*—abuse.

2711. καταψύχω **katapsuchō,** *kat-ap-soo´-kho;* from *2596* and *5594;* to *cool down* (*off*), i.e. *refresh:*—cool.

2712. κατείδωλος **katĕidōlŏs,** *kat-i´-do-los;* from *2596* (intens.) and *1497; utterly idolatrous:*—wholly given to idolatry.

κατελεύθω **katĕlĕuthō.** See *2718.*

2713. κατέναντι **katĕnanti,** *kat-en´-an-tee;* from *2596* and *1725; directly opposite:*—before, over against.

κατενέγκω **katĕnĕgkō.** See *2702.*

2714. κατενώπιον **katĕnōpiŏn,** *kat-en-o´-pee-on;* from *2596* and *1799; directly in front of:*—before (the presence of), in the sight of.

2715. κατεξουσιάζω **katĕxŏusiazō,** *kat-ex-oo-see-ad´-zo;* from *2596* and *1850;* to *have* (*wield*) *full privilege over:*—exercise authority.

2716. κατεργάζομαι **katĕrgazŏmai,** *kat-er-gad´-zom-ahee;* from *2596* and *2038;* to *work fully,* i.e. *accomplish;* by impl. to *finish, fashion:*—cause, do (deed), perform, work (out).

2717. See note, page 4.

2718. κατέρχομαι **katĕrchŏmai,** *kat-er´-khom-ahee;* from *2596* and *2064* (includ. its alt.); to *come* (or *go*) *down* (lit. or fig.):—come (down), depart, descend, go down, land.

2719. κατεσθίω **katĕsthiō,** *kat-es-thee´-o;* from *2596* and *2068* (includ. its alt.); to *eat down,* i.e. *devour* (lit. or fig.):—devour.

2720. κατευθύνω **katĕuthunō,** *kat-yoo-thoo´-no;* from *2596* and *2116;* to *straighten fully,* i.e. (fig.) *direct:*—guide, direct.

2721. κατεφίστημι **katĕphistēmi,** *kat-ef-is´-tay-mee;* from *2596* and *2186;* to *stand over against,* i.e. *rush upon* (*assault*):—make insurrection against.

2722. κατέχω **katĕchō,** *kat-ekh´-o;* from *2596* and *2192;* to *hold down* (*fast*), in various applications (lit. or fig.):—have, hold (fast), keep (in memory), let, × make toward, possess, retain, seize on, stay, take, withhold.

2723. κατηγορέω **katēgŏrĕō,** *kat-ay-gor-eh´-o;* from *2725;* to *be a plaintiff,* i.e. to *charge* with some offence:—accuse, object.

2724. κατηγορία **katēgŏria,** *kat-ay-gor-ee´-ah;* from *2725;* a *complaint* ("category"), i.e. criminal *charge:*—accusation (× -ed).

2725. κατήγορος **katēgŏrŏs,** *kat-ay´-gor-os;* from *2596* and *58;* *against* one in the *assembly,* i.e. a *complainant* at law; spec. *Satan:*—accuser.

2726. κατήφεια **katēphĕia,** *kat-ay´-fi-ah;* from a comp. of *2596* and perh. a der. of the base of *5316* (mean. *downcast* in look); *demureness,* i.e. (by impl.) *sadness:*—heaviness.

2727. κατηχέω **katēchĕō,** *kat-ay-kheh´-o;* from *2596* and *2279;* to *sound down* into the ears, i.e. (by impl.) to *indoctrinate* ("catechize") or (gen.) to *apprise* of:—inform, instruct, teach.

2728. κατιόω **katiŏō,** *kat-ee-ŏ´-o;* from *2596* and a der. of *2447;* to *rust down,* i.e. *corrode:*—canker.

2729. κατισχύω **katischuō,** *kat-is-khoo´-o;* from *2596* and *2480;* to *overpower:*—prevail (against).

2730. κατοικέω **katŏikĕō,** *kat-oy-keh´-o;* from *2596* and *3611;* to *house permanently,* i.e. *reside* (lit. or fig.):—dwell (-er), inhabitant (-ter).

2731. κατοίκησις **katŏikēsis,** *kat-oy´-kay-sis;* from *2730;* *residence* (prop. the act; but by impl. concr. the mansion):—dwelling.

2732. κατοικητήριον **katŏikētēriŏn,** *kat-oy-kay-tay´-ree-on;* from a der. of *2730;* a *dwelling-place*—habitation.

2733. κατοικία **katŏikia,** *kat-oy-kee´-ah; residence* (prop. the condition; but by impl. the abode itself):—habitation.

2734. κατοπτρίζομαι **katŏptrizŏmai,** *kat-op-trid´-zom-ahee;* mid. from a comp. of *2596* and a der. of *3700* [comp. *2072*]; to *mirror oneself,* i.e. to *see reflected* (fig.):—behold as in a glass.

2735. κατόρθωμα **katŏrthōma,** *kat-or´-tho-mah;* from a comp. of *2596* and a der. of *3717* [comp. *1357*]; something *made fully upright,* i.e. (fig.) *rectification* (spec. *good* public *administration*):—very worthy deed.

2736. κάτω **katō,** *kat´-o;* also (comp.) κατωτέρω **katōtĕrō,** *kat-o-ter´-o* [comp. *2737*]; adv. from *2596;* *downwards:*—beneath, bottom, down, under.

2737. κατώτερος **katōtĕrŏs,** *kat-o´-ter-os;* comp. from *2736;* *inferior* (locally, of Hades):—lower.

2738. καῦμα **kauma,** *kŏw´-mah;* from *2545;* prop. a *burn* (concr.), but used (abstr.) of a *glow:*—heat.

2739. καυματίζω **kaumatizō,** *kŏw-mat-id´-zo;* from *2738;* to *burn:*—scorch.

2740. καῦσις **kausis,** *kŏw´-sis;* from *2545;* *burning* (the act):—be burned.

2741. καυσόω **kausŏō,** *kŏw-sŏ´-o;* from *2740;* to *set on fire:*—with fervent heat.

2742. καύσων **kausōn,** *kŏw´-sone;* from *2741;* a *glare:*—(burning) heat.

2743. καυτηριάζω **kautēriazō,** *kŏw-tay-ree-ad´-zo;* from a der. of *2545;* to *brand* ("*cauterize*"), i.e. (by impl.) to *render unsensitive* (fig.):—sear with a hot iron.

2744. καυχάομαι **kauchaŏmai,** *kŏw-khah´-om-ahee;* from some (obsol.) base akin to that of αὐχέω **auchĕō** (to *boast*) and *2172;* to *vaunt* (in a good or a bad sense):—(make) boast, glory, joy, rejoice.

2745. καύχημα **kauchēma,** *kŏw´-khay-mah;* from *2744;* a *boast* (prop. the object; by impl. the act) in a good or a bad sense:—boasting, (whereof) to glory (of), glorying, rejoice (-ing).

2746. καύχησις **kauchēsis,** *kŏw´-khay-sis;* from *2744;* *boasting* (prop. the act; by impl. the object), in a good or a bad sense:—boasting, whereof I may glory, glorifying, rejoicing.

2747. Κεγχρεαί **Kĕgchrĕai,** *keng-khreh-a´hee;* prob. from κέγχρος **kĕgchrŏs** (*millet*); *Cenchreæ,* a port of Corinth:—Cenchrea.

2748. Κεδρών **Kĕdrōn,** *ked-rone´;* of Heb. or. [6939]; *Cedron* (i.e. *Kidron*), a brook near Jerus.:—Cedron.

2749. κεῖμαι **kĕimai,** *ki´-mahee;* mid. of a prim. verb; to *lie* outstretched (lit. or fig.):—be (appointed, laid up, made, set), lay, lie. Comp. *5087.*

2750. κειρία **kĕiria,** *ki-ree´-ah;* of uncert. affin.; a *swathe,* i.e. *winding-sheet:*—grave-clothes.

2751. κείρω **kĕirō,** *ki´-ro;* a prim. verb; to *shear:*—shear (-er).

2752. κέλευμα **kĕlĕuma,** *kel´-yoo-mah;* from *2753;* a *cry* of incitement:—shout.

2753. κελεύω **kĕlĕuō,** *kel-yoo´-o;* from a prim. κέλλω **kĕllō** (to *urge* on); "hail"; to *incite* by word, i.e. *order:*—bid, (at, give) command (-ment).

2754. κενοδοξία **kĕnŏdŏxia,** *ken-od-ox-ee´-ah;* from *2755;* *empty glorying,* i.e. *self-conceit:*—vain-glory.

2755. κενόδοξος **kĕnŏdŏxŏs,** *ken-od´-ox-os;* from *2756* and *1391;* *vainly glorifying,* i.e. *self-conceited:*—desirous of vain-glory.

2756. κενός **kĕnŏs,** *ken-os´;* appar. a prim. word; *empty* (lit. or fig.):—empty, (in) vain.

2757. κενοφωνία **kĕnŏphōnia,** *ken-of-o-nee´-ah;* from a presumed comp. of *2756* and *5456;* *empty sounding,* i.e. *fruitless discussion:*—vain.

2758. κενόω **kĕnŏō,** *ken-ŏ´-o;* from *2756;* to *make empty,* i.e. (fig.) to *abase, neutralize, falsify:*—make (of none effect, of no reputation, void), be in vain.

2759. κέντρον **kĕntrŏn,** *ken´-tron;* from κεντέω **kĕntĕō** (to *prick*); a *point* ("centre"), i.e. a *sting* (fig. *poison*) or *goad* (fig. divine *impulse*):—prick, sting.

2760. κεντυρίων **kĕnturiōn,** *ken-too-ree´-ohn;* of Lat. or.; a *centurion,* i.e. *captain* of one hundred soldiers:—centurion.

2761. κενῶς **kĕnōs,** *ken-oce´;* adv. from *2756;* *vainly,* i.e. *to no purpose:*—in vain.

2762. κεραία **kĕraia,** *ker-ah´-yah;* fem. of a presumed der. of the base of *2768;* something *horn-like,* i.e. (spec.) the *apex* of a Heb. letter (fig. the least *particle*):—tittle.

2763. κεραμεύς **kĕramĕus,** *ker-am-yooce´;* from *2766;* a *potter:*—potter.

2764. κεραμικός **kĕramikŏs,** *ker-am-ik-os´;* from *2766;* *made of clay,* i.e. *earthen:*—of a potter.

2765. κεράμιον **kĕramiŏn,** *ker-am´-ee-on;* neut. of a presumed der. of *2766;* an *earthenware* vessel, i.e. *jar:*—pitcher.

2766. κέραμος **kĕramŏs,** *ker´-am-os;* prob. from the base of *2767* (through the idea of *mixing* clay and water); *earthenware,* i.e. a *tile* (by anal. a thin *roof* or *awning*):—tiling.

2767. κεράννυμι **kĕrannumi,** *ker-an´-noo-mee;* a prol. form of a more prim. κεράω **kĕraō,** *ker-ah´-o* (which is used in certain tenses); to *mingle,* i.e. (by impl.) to *pour* out (for drinking):—fill, pour out. Comp. *3396.*

2768. κέρας **kĕras,** *ker´-as;* from a prim. κάρ **kar** (the *hair* of the head); a *horn* (lit. or fig.):—horn.

2769. κεράτιον **kĕratiŏn,** *ker-at´-ee-on;* neut. of a presumed der. of *2768;* something horned i.e. (spec.) the *pod* of the carob-tree:—husk.

κεράω **kĕraō.** See *2767.*

2770. κερδαίνω **kĕrdainō,** *ker-dah´-ee-no,* from *2771;* to *gain* (lit. or fig.):—(get) gain, win.

2771. κέρδος **kĕrdŏs,** *ker´-dos;* of uncert. affin.; *gain* (pecuniary or gen.):—gain, lucre.

2772. κέρμα **kĕrma,** *ker´-mah;* from *2751,* a *clipping* (*bit*), i.e. (spec.) a *coin:*—money.

2773. κερματιστής **kĕrmatistēs,** *ker-mat-is-tace´;* from a der. of *2772;* a *handler of coins,* i.e. *money-broker:*—changer of money.

2774. κεφάλαιον **kĕphalaiŏn,** *kef-al´-ah-yon;* neut. of a der. of *2776;* a *principal* thing, i.e. *main point;* spec. an *amount* (of money):—sum.

2775. κεφαλαιόω **kĕphalaiŏō,** *kef-al-ahee-ŏ´-o;* from the same as *2774;* (spec.) to *strike on the head:*—wound in the head.

2776. κεφαλή **kĕphalē,** *kef-al-ay´;* prob. from the prim. κάπτω **kaptō** (in the sense of *seizing*); the *head* (as the part most readily *taken* hold of), lit. or fig.:—head.

2777. κεφαλίς **kĕphalis,** *kef-al-is´;* from *2776;* prop. a *knob,* i.e. (by impl.) a *roll* (by extens. from the *end* of a stick on which the MS. was rolled):—volume.

2778. κῆνσος **kēnsŏs,** *kane´-sos;* of Lat. or.; prop. an *enrolment* ("*census*"), i.e. (by impl.) a *tax:*—tribute.

2779. κῆπος **kēpŏs,** *kay´-pos;* of uncert. affin.; a *garden:*—garden.

2780. κηπουρός **kēpŏurŏs,** *kay-poo-ros´;* from *2779* and οὖρος **ŏurŏs** (a *warden*); a *garden-keeper,* i.e. *gardener:*—gardener.

2781. κηρίον **kēriŏn,** *kay-ree´-on;* dimin. from κηός **kēŏs** (*wax*); a *cell* for honey, i.e. (collect.) the *comb:*—[honey-] comb.

2782. κήρυγμα **kērugma,** *kay´-roog-mah;* from *2784;* a *proclamation* (espec. of the gospel; by impl. the *gospel* itself):—preaching.

2783. κήρυξ **kērux,** *kay´-roox;* from *2784;* a *herald,* i.e. of divine truth (espec. of the gospel):—preacher.

2784. κηρύσσω **kērussō,** *kay-roos´-so;* of uncert. affin.; to *herald* (as a public *crier*), espec. divine truth (the gospel):—preach (-er), proclaim, publish.

2785. κῆτος **kētŏs,** *kay´-tos;* prob. from the base of *5490;* a huge *fish* (as *gaping* for prey):—whale.

2786. Κηφᾶς **Kēphas,** *kay-fas´;* of Chad. or. [comp. 3710]; *the Rock; Cephas* (i.e. *Kepha*), a surname of Peter:—Cephas.

2787. κιβωτός **kibōtŏs,** *kib-o-tos´;* of uncert. der.; a *box,* i.e. the sacred *ark* and that of Noah:—ark.

2788. κιθάρα **kithara,** *kith-ar´-ah;* of uncert. affin.; a *lyre:*—harp.

2789. κιθαρίζω **kitharizō,** *kith-ar-id´-zo;* from *2788;* to *play on a lyre:*—harp.

2790. κιθαρῳδός **kitharōidŏs,** *kith-ar-o-dos´;* from *2788* and a der. of the same as *5603;* a *lyresinger (-player),* i.e. *harpist:*—harper.

2791. Κιλικία **Kilikia,** *kil-ik-ee´-ah;* prob. of for. or.; *Cilicia,* a region of Asia Minor:—Cilicia.

2792. κινάμωμον **kinamōmon,** *cin-am´-o-mon;* of for. or. [comp. 7076]; *cinnamon:*—cinnamon.

2793. κινδυνεύω **kinduneŭō,** *kin-doon-yoo´-o;* from *2794;* to *undergo peril:*—be in danger, be (stand) in jeopardy.

2794. κίνδυνος **kindunŏs,** *kin´-doo-nos;* of uncert. der.; *danger:*—peril.

2795. κινέω **kinĕō,** *kin-eh´-o;* from κίω **kiō** (poetic for εἶμι **ĕimi,** to *go*); to *stir* (trans.), lit. or fig.:—(re-) move (-r), wag.

2796. κίνησις **kinēsis,** *kin´-ay-sis;* from *2795;* a *stirring:*—moving.

2797. Κίς **Kis,** *kis;* of Heb. or. [7027]; *Cis* (i.e. *Kish*), an Isr.:—Cis.

κίχρημι **kichrēmi.** See *5531.*

2798. κλάδος **kladŏs,** *klad´-os;* from *2866;* a *twig* or *bough* (as if broken off):—branch.

2799. κλαίω **klaiō,** *klah´-yo;* of uncert. affin.; to *sob,* i.e. *wail* aloud (whereas *1145* is rather to *cry* silently):—bewail. weep.

2800. κλάσις **klasis,** *klas´-is;* from *2806; fracture* (the act):—breaking.

2801. κλάσμα **klasma,** *klash´-mah;* from *2806;* a *piece* (*bit*):—broken, fragment.

2802. Κλαύδη **Klaudē,** *klŏw´-day;* of uncert. der.; *Claude,* an island near Crete:—Clauda.

2803. Κλαυδία **Klaudia,** *klŏw-dee´-ah;* fem. of *2804; Claudia,* a Chr. woman:—Claudia.

2804. Κλαύδιος **Klaudiŏs,** *klŏw´-dee-os;* of Lat. or.; *Claudius,* the name of two Romans:—Claudius.

2805. κλαυθμός **klauthmŏs,** *klŏwth-mos´;* from *2799; lamentation:*—wailing, weeping, × wept.

2806. κλάω **klaō,** *klah´-o;* a prim. verb; to *break* (spec. of bread):—break.

2807. κλείς **klĕis,** *klice;* from *2808;* a *key* (as *shutting* a lock), lit. or fig.:—key.

2808. κλείω **klĕiō,** *kli´-o;* a prim. verb; to *close* (lit. or fig.):—shut (up).

2809. κλέμμα **klĕmma,** *klem´-mah;* from *2813; stealing* (prop. the thing stolen, but used of the act):—theft.

2810. Κλεόπας **Klĕŏpas,** *kleh-op´-as;* prob. contr. from Κλεόπατρος **Klĕŏpatrŏs** (comp. of *2811* and *3962*); *Cleopas,* a Chr.:—Cleopas.

2811. κλέος **klĕŏs,** *kleh´-os;* from a shorter form of *2564; renown* (as if *being called*):—glory.

2812. κλέπτης **klĕptēs,** *klep´-tace;* from *2813;* a *stealer* (lit. or fig.):—thief. Comp. *3027.*

2813. κλέπτω **klĕptō,** *klep´-to;* a prim. verb; to *filch:*—steal.

2814. κλῆμα **klēma,** *klay´-mah;* from *2806;* a *limb* or *shoot* (as if *broken* off):—branch.

2815. Κλήμης **Klēmēs,** *klay´-mace;* of Lat. or.; *merciful; Clemes* (i.e. *Clemens*), a Chr.:—Clement.

2816. κληρονομέω **klērŏnŏmĕō,** *klay-ron-om-eh´-o;* from *2818;* to *be* an *heir* to (lit. or fig.):—be heir, (obtain by) inherit (-ance).

2817. κληρονομία **klērŏnŏmia,** *klay-ron-om-ee´-ah;* from *2818; heirship,* i.e. (concr.) a *patrimony* or (gen.) a *possession:*—inheritance.

2818. κληρονόμος **klērŏnŏmŏs,** *klay-ron-om´-os;* from *2819* and the base of *3551* (in its orig. sense of *partitioning,* i.e. [reflex.] *getting* by apportionment); a *sharer by lot,* i.e. an *inheritor* (lit. or fig.); by impl. a *possessor:*—heir.

2819. κλῆρος **klērŏs,** *klay´-ros;* prob. from *2806* (through the idea of using *bits* of wood, etc., for the purpose); a *die* (for drawing chances); by impl. a *portion* (as if so secured); by extens. an *acquisition* (espec. a *patrimony,* fig.):—heritage, inheritance, lot, part.

2820. κληρόω **klērŏō,** *klay-rŏ´-o;* from *2819;* to *allot,* i.e. (fig.) to *assign* (a privilege):—obtain an inheritance.

2821. κλῆσις **klēsis,** *klay´-sis;* from a shorter form of *2564;* an *invitation* (fig.):—calling, vocation.

2822. κλητός **klētŏs,** *klay-tos´;* from the same as *2821; invited,* i.e. *appointed,* or (spec.) a *saint:*—called.

2823. κλίβανος **klibanŏs,** *klib´-an-os;* of uncert. der.; an earthen *pot* used for baking in:—oven.

2824. κλίμα **klima,** *klee´-mah;* from *2827;* a *slope,* i.e. (spec.) a "*clime*" or *tract* of country:—part, region.

2825. κλίνη **klinē,** *klee´-nay;* from *2827;* a *couch* (for sleep, sickness, sitting or eating):—bed, table.

2826. κλινίδιον **klinidiŏn,** *klin-id´-ee-on;* neut. of a presumed der. of *2825;* a *pallet* or *little couch:*—bed.

2827. κλίνω **klinō,** *klee´-no;* a prim. verb; to *slant* or *slope,* i.e. *incline* or *recline* (lit. or fig.):—bow (down), be far spent, lay, turn to flight, wear away.

2828. κλισία **klisia,** *klee-see´-ah;* from a der. of *2827;* prop. *reclination,* i.e. (concr. and spec.) a *party* at a meal:—company.

2829. κλοπή **klŏpē,** *klop-ay´;* from *2813; stealing:*—theft.

2830. κλύδων **kludōn,** *kloo´-dohn;* from κλύζω **kluzō** (to *billow* or *dash* over); a *surge* of the sea (lit. or fig.):—raging, wave.

2831. κλυδωνίζομαι **kludōnizŏmai,** *kloo-do-nid´-zom-ahee;* mid. from 2830; to *surge,* i.e. (fig.) to *fluctuate:*—toss to and fro.

2832. Κλωπᾶς **Klōpas,** *klo-pas´;* of Chald. or. (corresp. to *256*); *Clopas,* an Isr.:—Clopas.

2833. κνήθω **knēthō,** *knay´-tho;* from a prim. κνάω **knaō** (to *scrape*); to *scratch,* i.e. (by impl.) to *tickle:*—× itching.

2834. Κνίδος **Knidŏs,** *knee´-dos;* prob. of for. or.; *Cnidus,* a place in Asia Minor:—Cnidus.

2835. κοδράντης **kŏdrantēs,** *kod-ran´-tace;* of Lat. or.; a *quadrans,* i.e. the fourth part of an as:—farthing.

2836. κοιλία **kŏilia,** *koy-lee´-ah; from* κοῖλος **kŏilŏs** ("*hollow*"); a *cavity,* i.e. (spec.) the *abdomen;* by impl. the *matrix;* fig. the *heart:*—belly, womb.

2837. κοιμάω **kŏimaō,** *koy-mah´-o;* from *2749;* to *put to sleep,* i.e. (pass. or reflex.) to *slumber;* fig. to *decease:*—(be a-, fall a-, fall on) sleep, be dead.

2838. κοίμησις **kŏimēsis,** *koy´-may-sis;* from *2837; sleeping,* i.e. (by impl.) *repose:*—taking of rest.

2839. κοινός **kŏinŏs,** *koy-nos´;* prob. from *4862; common,* i.e. (lit.) shared by all or several, or (cer.) *profane:*—common, defiled, unclean, unholy.

2840. κοινόω **kŏinŏō,** *koy-nŏ´-o;* from *2839;* to *make* (or *consider*) *profane* (cer.):—call common, defile, pollute, unclean.

2841. κοινωνέω **kŏinōnĕō,** *koy-no-neh´-o;* from *2844;* to *share* with others (obj. or subj.):—communicate, distribute, be partaker.

2842. κοινωνία **kŏinōnia,** *koy-nohn-ee´-ah;* from *2844; partnership,* i.e. (lit.) *participation,* or (social) *intercourse,* or (pecuniary) *benefaction:*—(to) communicate (-ation), communion, (contri-), distribution, fellowship.

2843. κοινωνικός **kŏinōnikŏs,** *koy-no-nee-kos´;* from *2844; communicative,* i.e. (pecuniarily) *liberal:*—willing to communicate.

2844. κοινωνός **kŏinōnŏs,** *koy-no-nos´;* from *2839;* a *sharer,* i.e. *associate:*—companion, × fellowship, partaker, partner.

2845. κοίτη **kŏitē,** *koy´-tay;* from *2749;* a *couch;* by extens. *cohabitation;* by impl. the male *sperm:*—bed, chambering, × conceive.

2846. κοιτών **kŏitōn,** *koy-tone´;* from *2845;* a *bedroom:*— + chamberlain.

2847. κόκκινος **kŏkkinŏs,** *kok´-kee-nos;* from *2848* (from the *kernel*-shape of the insect); *crimson*-colored:—scarlet (colour, coloured).

2848. κόκκος **kŏkkŏs,** *kok´-kos;* appar. a prim. word; a *kernel* of seed:—corn, grain.

2849. κολάζω **kŏlazō,** *kol-ad´-zo;* from κόλος **kŏlos** (*dwarf*); prop. to *curtail,* i.e. (fig.) to *chastise* (or *reserve* for infliction):—punish.

2850. κολακεία **kŏlakĕia,** *kol-ak-i´-ah;* from a der. of κόλαξ **kŏlax** (a *fawner*); *flattery:*— × flattering.

2851. κόλασις **kŏlasis,** *kol´-as-is;* from *2849;* penal *infliction:*—punishment, torment.

2852. κολαφίζω **kŏlaphizō,** *kol-af-id´-zo;* from a der. of the base of *2849;* to *rap* with the fist:—buffet.

2853. κολλάω **kŏllaō,** *kol-lah´-o;* from κόλλα **kŏlla** ("*glue*"); to *glue,* i.e. (pass. or reflex.) to *stick* (fig.):—cleave, join (self), keep company.

2854. κολλούριον **kŏllŏuriŏn,** *kol-loo´-ree-on;* neut. of a presumed der. of κολλύρα **kŏllura** (a *cake;* prob. akin to the base of *2853*); prop. a *poultice* (as made of or in the form of *crackers*), i.e. (by anal.) a *plaster:*—eyesalve.

2855. κολλυβιστής **kŏllubistēs,** *kol-loo-bis-tace´;* from a presumed der. of κόλλυβος **kŏllubŏs** (a small *coin;* prob. akin to *2854*); a *coindealer:*—(money-) changer.

2856. κολοβόω **kŏlŏbŏō,** *kol-ob-ŏ´-o;* from a der. of the base of *2849;* to *dock,* i.e. (fig.) *abridge:*—shorten.

2857. Κολοσσαί **Kŏlŏssai,** *kol-os-sah´-ee;* appar. fem. plur. of κολοσσός **kŏlŏssŏs** ("*colossal*"); *Colossæ,* a place in Asia Minor:—Colosse.

2858. Κολοσσαεύς **Kŏlŏssaĕus,** *kol-os-sayoos´;* fr. *2857;* a *Colossæan,* i.e. inh. of Colossæ:—Colossian.

2859. κόλπος **kŏlpŏs,** *kol´-pos;* appar. a prim. word; the *bosom;* by anal. a *bay:*—bosom, creek.

2860. κολυμβάω **kŏlumbaō,** *kol-oom-bah´-o;* from κόλυμβος **kŏlumbŏs** (a *diver*): to *plunge* into water:—swim.

2861. κολυμβήθρα **kŏlumbēthra,** *kol-oom-bay´-thrah;* from *2860;* a *diving-place,* i.e. pond for bathing (or swimming):—pool.

2862. κολωνία **kŏlōnia,** *kol-o-nee´-ah;* of Lat. or.; a Roman *"colony"* for veterans:—colony.

2863. κομάω **kŏmaō,** *kom-ah´-o;* from *2864;* to *wear tresses* of hair:—have long hair.

2864. κόμη **kŏmē,** *kom´-ay;* appar. from the same as *2865;* the *hair* of the head (*locks,* as *ornamental,* and thus differing from *2359,* which prop. denotes merely the *scalp*):—hair.

2865. κομίζω **kŏmizō,** *kom-id´-zo;* from a prim. κομέω **kŏmĕō** (to *tend,* i.e. take care of); prop. to *provide* for, i.e. (by impl.) to *carry* off (as if from harm; gen. *obtain*):—bring, receive.

2866. κομψότερον **kŏmpsŏtĕrŏn,** *komp-sot´-er-on;* neut. compar. of a der. of the base of *2865* (mean. prop. *well dressed,* i.e. *nice*); fig. *convalescent:*— + began to amend.

2867. κονιάω **kŏniaō,** *kon-ee-ah´-o;* from κονία **kŏnia** (*dust;* by anal. *lime*); to *whitewash:*—whiten.

2868. κονιορτός **kŏniŏrtŏs,** *kon-ee-or-tos´;* from the base of *2867* and ὄρνυμι **ŏrnumi** (to "*rouse*"); *pulverulence* (as *blown* about):—dust.

2869. κοπάζω **kŏpazō,** *kop-ad´-zo;* from *2873;* to *tire,* i.e. (fig.) to *relax:*—cease.

2870. κοπετός **kŏpĕtŏs,** *kop-et-os´;* from *2875; mourning* (prop. by *beating* the breast):—lamentation.

2871. κοπή **kŏpē,** *kop-ay´;* from *2875; cutting;* i.e. *carnage:*—slaughter.

2872. κοπιάω **kŏpiaō,** *kop-ee-ah´-o;* from a der. of *2873;* to *feel fatigue;* by impl. to *work hard:*—(bestow) labour, toil, be wearied.

2873. κόπος **kŏpŏs,** *kop´-os;* from *2875;* a *cut,* i.e. (by anal.) *toil* (as *reducing* the strength), lit. or fig.; by impl. *pains:*—labour, + trouble, weariness.

2874. κοπρία **kŏpria,** *kop-ree´-ah;* from κόπρος **kŏprŏs** (*ordure;* perh. akin to *2875*); *manure:*—dung (-hill).

2875. κόπτω **kŏptō,** *kop´-to;* a prim. verb; to "*chop*"; spec. to *beat* the breast in grief:—cut down, lament, mourn, (be-) wail. Comp. the base of *5114.*

2876. κόραξ **kŏrax,** *kor´-ax;* perh. from *2880;* a *crow* (from its *voracity*):—raven.

2877. κοράσιον **kŏrasiŏn,** *kor-as´-ee-on,* neut. of a presumed der. of κόρη **kŏrē** (a *maiden*); a (little) *girl:*—damsel, maid.

2878. κορβᾶν **kŏrban,** *kor-ban´;* and κορβανᾶς **kŏrbanas,** *kor-ban-as´;* of Heb. and Chald. or. respectively [7133]; a votive *offering* and *the offering;* a *consecrated present* (to the Temple fund); by extens. (the latter term) the *Treasury* itself, i.e. the room where the contribution boxes stood:—Corban, treasury.

2879. Κορέ **Kŏrĕ,** *kor-eh´;* of Heb. or [7141]; *Corè* (i.e. *Korach*), an Isr.:—Core.

2880. κορέννυμι **kŏrĕnnumi,** *kor-en´-noo-mee;* a prim. verb; to *cram,* i.e. *glut* or *sate:*—eat enough, full.

2881. Κορίνθιος **Kŏrinthiŏs,** *kor-in´-thee-os;* from *2882;* a *Corinthian,* i.e. inhab. of Corinth:—Corinthian.

2882. Κόρινθος **Kŏrinthŏs,** *kor´-in-thos;* of uncert. der.; *Corinthus,* a city of Greece:—Corinth.

2883. Κορνήλιος **Kŏrnēliŏs,** *kor-nay´-lee-os;* of Lat. or.; *Cornelius,* a Roman:—Cornelius.

2884. κόρος **kŏrŏs,** *kor´-os;* of Heb. or. [3734]; a *cor,* i.e. a specific measure:—measure.

2885. κοσμέω **kŏsmĕō,** *kos-meh´-o;* from *2889;* to *put in* proper *order,* i.e. *decorate* (lit. or fig.); spec. to *snuff* (a wick):—adorn, garnish, trim.

2886. κοσμικός **kŏsmikŏs,** *kos-mee-kos´;* from *2889* (in its secondary sense); *terrene* ("*cosmic*"), lit. (*mundane*) or fig. (*corrupt*):—worldly.

2887. κόσμιος **kŏsmiŏs,** *kos´-mee-os;* from *2889* (in its prim. sense); *orderly,* i.e. *decorous:*—of good behaviour, modest.

2888. κοσμοκράτωρ **kŏsmŏkratōr,** *kos-mok-rat´-ore;* from *2889* and *2902;* a *world-ruler,* an epithet of Satan:—ruler.

2889. κόσμος **kŏsmŏs,** *kos´-mos;* prob. from the base of *2865;* orderly *arrangement,* i.e. *decoration;* by impl. the *world* (in a wide or narrow sense, includ. its inhab., lit. or fig. [mor.]):—adorning, world.

2890. Κούαρτος **Kŏuartŏs,** *koo´-ar-tos;* of Lat. or. (*fourth*); *Quartus,* a Chr.:—Quartus.

2891. κοῦμι **kŏumi,** *koo´-mee;* of Chald. or. [6966]; *cumi* (i.e. *rise!*):—cumi.

2892. κουστωδία **kŏustōdia,** *koos-to-dee´-ah;* of Lat. or.; *"custody",* i.e. a Roman *sentry:*—watch.

2893. κουφίζω **kŏuphizō,** *koo-fid´-zo;* from κοῦφος **kŏuphŏs** (*light* in weight); to *unload:*—lighten.

2894. κόφινος **kŏphinŏs,** *kof´-ee-nos;* of uncert. der.; a (small) *basket:*—basket.

2895. κράββατος **krabbatŏs,** *krab´-bat-os;* prob. of for. or.; a *mattress:*—bed.

2896. κράζω **krazō,** *krad´-zo;* a prim. verb; prop. to *"croak"* (as a raven) or *scream,* i.e. (gen.) to *call* aloud (*shriek, exclaim, intreat*):—cry (out).

2897. κραιπάλη **kraipalē,** *krahee-pal´-ay;* prob. from the same as *726;* prop. a *headache* (as a *seizure* of pain) from drunkenness, i.e. (by impl.) a *debauch* (by anal. a *glut*):—surfeiting.

2898. κρανίον **kraniŏn,** *kran-ee´-on;* dimin. of a der. of the base of *2768;* a *skull* (*"cranium"*):—Calvary, skull.

2899. κράσπεδον **kraspĕdŏn,** *kras´-ped-on;* of uncert. der.; a *margin,* i.e. (spec.) a *fringe* or *tassel:*— border, hem.

2900. κραταιός **krataiŏs,** *krat-ah-yos´;* from *2904; powerful:*—mighty.

2901. κραταιόω **krataiŏō,** *krat-ah-yŏ´-o;* from *2900;* to *empower,* i.e. (pass.) *increase in vigor:*—be strenghtened, be (wax) strong.

2902. κρατέω **kratĕō,** *krat-eh´-o;* from *2904;* to *use strength,* i.e. *seize* or *retain* (lit. or fig.):—hold (by, fast), keep, lay hand (hold) on, obtain, retain, take (by).

2903. κράτιστος **kratistŏs,** *krat´-is-tos;* superl. of a der. of *2904; strongest,* i.e. (in dignity) *very honorable:*—most excellent (noble).

2904. κράτος **kratŏs,** *krat´-os;* perh. a prim. word; *vigor* ["great"] (lit. or fig.):—dominion, might [-ily], power, strength.

2905. κραυγάζω **kraugazō,** *krŏw-gad´-zo;* from *2906;* to *clamor:*—cry out.

2906. κραυγή **kraugē,** *krŏw-gay´;* from *2896;* an *outcry* (in notification, tumult or grief):—clamour, cry (-ing).

2907. κρέας **krĕas,** *kreh´-as;* perh. a prim. word; (butcher's) *meat:*—flesh.

2908. κρεῖσσον **krĕissŏn,** *krice´-son;* neut. of an alt. form of *2909;* (as noun) *better,* i.e. *greater advantage:*—better.

2909. κρείττων **krĕittōn,** *krite´-tohn;* compar. of a der. of *2904; stronger,* i.e. (fig.) *better,* i.e. *nobler:*—best, better.

2910. κρεμάννυμι **krĕmannumi,** *krem-an´-noo-mee;* a prol. form of a prim. verb; to *hang:*—hang.

2911. κρημνός **krēmnŏs,** *krame-nos´;* from *2910; overhanging,* i.e. a *precipice:*—steep place.

2912. Κρής **Krēs,** *krace;* from *2914;* a *Cretan,* i.e. inhab. of Crete:—Crete, Cretian.

2913. Κρήσκης **Krēskēs,** *krace´-kace;* of Lat. or.; *growing; Cresces* (i.e. *Crescens),* a Chr.:—Crescens.

2914. Κρήτη **Krētē,** *kray´-tay;* of uncert. der.; *Cretè,* an island in the Mediterranean:—Crete.

2915. κριθή **krithē,** *kree-thay´;* of uncert. der.; *barley:*—barley.

2916. κρίθινος **krithinŏs,** *kree´-thee-nos;* from *2915;* consisting *of barley:*—barley.

2917. κρίμα **krima,** *kree´-mah;* from *2919;* a *decision* (the function or the effect, for or against ["crime"]):—avenge, condemned, condemnation, damnation, + go to law, judgment.

2918. κρίνον **krinŏn,** *kree´-non;* perh. a prim. word; a *lily:*—lily.

2919. κρίνω **krinō,** *kree´-no;* prop. to *distinguish,* i.e. *decide* (mentally or judicially); by impl. to *try, condemn, punish:*—avenge, conclude, condemn, damn, decree, determine, esteem, judge, go to (sue at the) law, ordain, call in question, sentence to, think.

2920. κρίσις **krisis,** *kree´-sis; decision* (subj. or obj., for or against); by extens. a *tribunal;* by impl. *justice* (spec. divine *law*):—accusation, condemnation, damnation, judgment.

2921. Κρίσπος **Krispŏs,** *kris´-pos;* of Lat. or.; *"crisp"; Crispus,* a Corinthian:—Crispus.

2922. κριτήριον **kritēriŏn,** *kree-tay´-ree-on;* neut. of a presumed der. of *2923;* a *rule* of judging (*"criterion"*), i.e. (by impl.) a *tribunal:*—to judge, judgment (seat).

2923. κριτής **kritēs,** *kree-tace´;* from *2919;* a *judge* (gen. or spec.):—judge.

2924. κριτικός **kritikŏs,** *krit-ee-kos´;* from *2923; decisive* (*"critical"*), i.e. *discriminative:*—discerner.

2925. κρούω **krŏuō,** *kroo´-o;* appar. a prim. verb; to *rap:*—knock.

2926. κρυπτή **kruptē,** *kroop-tay´;* fem. of *2927;* a *hidden* place, i.e. *cellar* (*"crypt"*):—secret.

2927. κρυπτός **kruptŏs,** *kroop-tos´;* from *2928; concealed,* i.e. *private:*—hid (-den), inward [-ly], secret.

2928. κρύπτω **kruptō,** *kroop´-to;* a prim. verb; to *conceal* (prop. by *covering*):—hide (self), keep secret, secret [-ly].

2929. κρυσταλλίζω **krustallizō,** *kroos-tal-lid´-zo;* from *2930;* to *make* (i.e. intrans. *resemble*) *ice* ("crystallize"):—be clear as crystal.

2930. κρύσταλλος **krustallŏs,** *kroos´-tal-los;* from a der. of κρύος **kruŏs** (*frost*); *ice,* i.e. (by anal.) rock *"crystal":*—crystal.

2931. κρυφῆ **kruphē,** *kroo-fay´;* adv. from *2928; privately:*—in secret.

2932. κτάομαι **ktaŏmai,** *ktah´-om-ahee;* a prim. verb; to *get,* i.e. *acquire* (by any means; *own*):—obtain, possess, provide, purchase.

2933. κτῆμα **ktēma,** *ktay´-mah;* from *2932;* an *acquirement,* i.e. *estate:*—possession.

2934. κτῆνος **ktēnŏs,** *ktay´-nos;* from *2932; property,* i.e. (spec.) a domestic *animal:*—beast.

2935. κτήτωρ **ktētōr,** *ktay´-tore;* from *2932;* an *owner:*—possessor.

2936. κτίζω **ktizō,** *ktid´-zo;* prob. akin to *2932* (through the idea of the *proprietorship* of the *manufacturer*); to *fabricate,* i.e. *found* (*form* originally):—create, Creator, make.

2937. κτίσις **ktisis,** *ktis´-is;* from *2936;* original *formation* (prop. the act; by impl. the thing, lit. or fig.):—building, creation, creature, ordinance.

2938. κτίσμα **ktisma,** *ktis´-mah;* from *2936;* an original *formation* (concr.), i.e. *product* (created thing):—creature.

2939. κτιστής **ktistēs,** *ktis-tace´;* from *2936;* a *founder,* i.e. *God* (as author of all things):—Creator.

2940. κυβεία **kubĕia,** *koo-bi´-ah;* from κύβος **kubŏs** (a *"cube",* i.e. *die* for playing); *gambling,* i.e. (fig.) *artifice* or *fraud:*—sleight.

2941. κυβέρνησις **kubĕrnēsis,** *koo-ber´-nay-sis;* from κυβερνάω **kubĕrnaō** (of Lat. or., to *steer*); *pilotage,* i.e. (fig.) *directorship* (in the church):—government.

2942. κυβερνήτης **kubĕrnētēs,** *koo-ber-nay´-tace;* from the same as *2941; helmsman,* i.e. (by impl.) *captain:*—(ship) master.

2943. κυκλόθεν **kuklŏthĕn,** *koo-kloth´-en;* adv. from the same as *2945; from* the *circle,* i.e. *all around:*—(round) about.

κυκλός **kuklŏs.** See *2945.*

2944. κυκλόω **kuklŏō,** *koo-klŏ´-o;* from the same as *2945;* to *encircle,* i.e. *surround:*—compass (about), come (stand) round about.

2945. κύκλῳ **kuklōi,** *koo´-klo;* as if dat. of κύκλος **kuklŏs** (a *ring, "cycle";* akin to *2947*); i.e. *in a circle* (by impl. of *1722*), i.e. (adv.) *all around:*—round about.

2946. κύλισμα **kulisma,** *koo´-lis-mah;* from *2947;* a *wallow* (the effect of *rolling*), i.e. *filth:*—wallowing.

2947. κυλιόω **kuliŏō,** *koo-lee-ŏ´-o;* from the base of *2949* (through the idea of *circularity;* comp. *2945, 1507*); to *roll* about:—wallow.

2948. κυλλός **kullŏs,** *kool-los´;* from the same as *2947; rocking* about, i.e. *crippled* (*maimed,* in feet or hands):—maimed.

2949. κῦμα **kuma,** *koo´-mah;* from κύω **kuō** (to *swell* [with young], i.e. *bend, curve*); a *billow* (as *bursting* or *toppling*):—wave.

2950. κύμβαλον **kumbalŏn,** *koom´-bal-on;* from a der. of the base of *2949;* a *"cymbal"* (as *hollow*):—cymbal.

2951. κύμινον **kuminŏn,** *koo´-min-on;* of for. or. [comp. 3646]; *dill* or *fennel* ("cummin"):—cummin.

2952. κυνάριον **kunariŏn,** *koo-nar´-ee-on;* neut. of a presumed der. of *2965;* a *puppy:*—dog.

2953. Κύπριος **Kupriŏs,** *koo´-pree-os;* from *2954;* a *Cyprian (Cypriot),* i.e. inhab. of Cyprus:—of Cyprus.

2954. Κύπρος **Kuprŏs,** *koo´-pros;* of uncert. or.; *Cyprus,* an island in the Mediterranean:—Cyprus.

2955. κύπτω **kuptō,** *koop´-to;* prob. from the base of *2949;* to *bend* forward:—stoop (down).

2956. Κυρηναῖος **Kurēnaiŏs,** *koo-ray-nah´-yos;* from *2957;* a *Cyrenæan,* i.e. inhab. of Cyrene:—of Cyrene, Cyrenian.

2957. Κυρήνη **Kurēnē,** *koo-ray´-nay;* of uncert. der.; *Cyrenè,* a region of Africa:—Cyrene.

2958. Κυρήνιος **Kurēniŏs,** *koo-ray´-nee-os;* of Lat. or.; *Cyrenius* (i.e. *Quirinus*), a Roman:—Cyrenius.

2959. Κυρία **Kuria,** *koo-ree´-ah;* fem. of *2962; Cyria,* a Chr. woman:—lady.

2960. κυριακός **kuriakŏs,** *koo-ree-ak-os´;* from *2962; belonging to* the *Lord* (Jehovah or Jesus):—Lord's.

2961. κυριεύω **kuriĕuō,** *koo-ree-yoo´-o;* from *2962;* to *rule:*—have dominion over, lord, be lord of, exercise lordship over.

2962. κύριος **kuriŏs,** *koo´-ree-os;* from κῦρος **kurŏs** (*supremacy*); *supreme* in authority, i.e. (as noun) *controller;* by impl. *Mr.* (as a respectful title):—God, Lord, master, Sir.

2963. κυριότης **kuriŏtēs,** *koo-ree-ot´-ace;* from *2962; mastery,* i.e. (concr. and coll.) *rulers:*—dominion, government.

2964. κυρόω **kurŏō,** *koo-rŏ´-o;* from the same as *2962;* to *make authoritative,* i.e. *ratify:*—confirm.

2965. κύων **kuōn,** *koo´-ohn;* a prim. word; a *dog* ["*hound*"] (lit. or fig.):—dog.

2966. κῶλον **kōlŏn,** *ko´-lon;* from the base of *2849;* a *limb* of the body (as if *lopped*):—carcase.

2967. κωλύω **kōluō,** *ko-loo´-o;* from the base of *2849;* to *estop,* i.e. *prevent* (by word or act):—forbid, hinder, keep from, let, not suffer, withstand.

2968. κώμη **kōmē,** *ko´-may;* from *2749;* a *hamlet* (as if *laid* down):—town, village.

2969. κωμόπολις **kōmŏpŏlis,** *ko-mop´-ol-is;* from *2968* and *4172;* an unwalled *city:*—town.

2970. κῶμος **kōmŏs,** *ko´-mos;* from *2749;* a *carousal* (as if a *letting loose*):—revelling, rioting.

2971. κώνωψ **kōnōps,** *ko´-nopes;* appar. from a der. of the base of *2759* and a der. of *3700;* a *mosquito* (from its *stinging proboscis):*—gnat.

2972. Κῶς **Kōs,** *koce;* of uncert. or.; *Cos,* an island in the Mediterranean:—Cos.

2973. Κωσάμ **Kōsam,** *ko-sam´;* of Heb. or. [comp. 7081]; *Cosam* (i.e. *Kosam*), an Isr.:—Cosam.

2974. κωφός **kōphŏs,** *ko-fos´;* from *2875; blunted,* i.e. (fig.) of hearing *(deaf)* or speech (*dumb*):—deaf, dumb, speechless.

Λ

2975. λαγχάνω **lagchanō,** *lang-khan´-o;* a prol. form of a prim. verb, which is only used as an alt. in certain tenses; to *lot,* i.e. *determine* (by impl. *receive*) espec. by lot:—his lot be, cast lots, obtain.

2976. Λάζαρος **Lazarŏs,** *lad´-zar-os;* prob. of Heb. or. [499]; *Lazarus* (i.e. *Elazar*), the name of two Isr. (one imaginary):—Lazarus.

2977. λάθρα **lathra,** *lath´-rah;* adv. from *2990; privately:*—privily, secretly.

2978. λαῖλαψ **lailaps,** *lah´-ee-laps;* of uncert. der.; a *whirlwind* (*squall*):—storm, tempest.

2979. λακτίζω **laktizō,** *lak-tid´-zo;* from adv. λάξ **lax** (*heelwise*); to *recalcitrate:*—kick.

2980. λαλέω **lalĕō,** *lal-eh´-o;* a prol. form of an otherwise obsol. verb; to *talk,* i.e. *utter* words:—preach, say, speak (after), talk, tell, utter. Comp. *3004.*

2981. λαλιά **lalia,** *lal-ee-ah´;* from *2980; talk:*—saying, speech.

2982. λαμά **lama,** *lam-ah´;* or
λαμμᾶ **lamma,** *lam-mah´;* of Heb. or. [4100 with prep. pref.]; *lama* (i.e. *why*):—lama.

2983. λαμβάνω **lambanō,** *lam-ban´-o;* a prol. form of a prim. verb, which is used only as an alt. in certain tenses; to *take* (in very many applications, lit. and fig. [prop. obj. or act., to *get hold* of; whereas *1209* is rather subj. or pass., to *have offered* to one; while *138* is more violent, to *seize* or *remove*]):—accept, + be amazed, assay, attain, bring, × when I call, catch, come on (× unto), + forget, have, hold, obtain, receive (× after), take (away, up).

2984. Λάμεχ **Lamĕch,** *lam´-ekh;* of Heb. or. [3929]; *Lamech* (i.e. *Lemek*), a patriarch:—Lamech.

λαμμᾶ **lamma.** See *2982.*

2985. λαμπάς **lampas,** *lam-pas´;* from *2989;* a "*lamp*" or *flambeau:*—lamp, light, torch.

2986. λαμπρός **lamprŏs,** *lam-pros´;* from the same as *2985; radiant;* by anal. *limpid;* fig. *magnificent* or *sumptuous* (in appearance):—bright, clear, gay, goodly, gorgeous, white.

2987. λαμπρότης **lamprŏtēs,** *lam-prot´-ace;* from *2896; brilliancy:*—brightness.

2988. λαμπρῶς **lamprōs,** *lam-proce´;* adv. from *2986; brilliantly,* i.e. (fig.) *luxuriously:*—sumptuously.

2989. λάμπω **lampō,** *lam´-po;* a prim. verb; to *beam,* i.e. *radiate* brilliancy (lit. or fig.):—give light, shine.

2990. λανθάνω **lanthanō,** *lan-than´-o;* a prol. form of a prim. verb, which is used only as an alt. in certain tenses; to *lie hid* (lit. or fig.); often used adv. *unwittingly:*—be hid, be ignorant of, unawares.

2991. λαξευτός **laxĕutŏs,** *lax-yoo-tos´;* from a comp. of λᾶς **las** (a *stone*) and the base of *3584* (in its orig. sense of *scraping*); *rock-quarried:*—hewn in stone.

2992. λαός **laŏs,** *lah-os´;* appar. a prim. word; a *people* (in gen.; thus differing from *1218,* which denotes one's *own* populace):—people.

2993. Λαοδίκεια **Laŏdikĕia,** *lah-od-ik´-i-ah;* from a comp. of *2992* and *1349; Laodicia,* a place in Asia Minor:—Laodicea.

2994. Λαοδικεύς **Laŏdikĕus,** *lah-od-ik-yooce´;* from *2993;* a *Laodicean,* i.e. inhab. of Laodicia:—Laodicean.

2995. λάρυγξ **larugx,** *lar´-oongks;* of uncert. der.; the *throat* ("*larynx*"):—throat.

2996. Λασαία **Lasaia,** *las-ah´-yah;* of uncert. or.; *Lasæa,* a place in Crete:—Lasea.

2997. λάσχω **laschō,** *las´-kho;* a strengthened form of a prim. verb, which only occurs in this and another prol. form as alt. in certain tenses; to *crack* open (from a fall):—burst asunder.

2998. λατομέω **latŏmĕō,** *lat-om-eh´-o;* from the same as the first part of *2991* and the base of *5114;* to *quarry:*—hew.

2999. λατρεία **latrĕia,** *lat-ri´-ah;* from *3000; ministration* of God, i.e. *worship:*—(divine) service.

3000. λατρεύω **latrĕuō,** *lat-ryoo´-o;* from λάτρις **latris** (a hired *menial*); to *minister (to God), i.e. render* religious *homage:*—serve, do the service, worship (-per).

3001. λάχανον **lachanŏn,** *lakh´-an-on;* from λαχαίνω **lachainō** (to *dig*); a *vegetable:*—herb.

3002. Λεββαῖος **Lĕbbaiŏs,** *leb-bah´-yos;* of uncert. or.; *Lebbæus,* a Chr.:—Lebbæus.

3003. λεγεών **lĕgĕōn,** *leg-eh-ohn´;* of Lat. or.; a "*legion*", i.e. Rom. *regiment* (fig.):—legion.

3004. λέγω **lĕgō,** *leg´-o;* a prim. verb; prop. to "*lay*" forth, i.e. (fig.) *relate* (in words [usually of systematic or set *discourse;* whereas *2036* and *5346* generally refer to an *individual* expression or speech respectively; while *4483* is prop. to *break silence* merely, and *2980* means an *extended* or random harangue]); by impl. to *mean:*—ask, bid, boast, call, describe, give out, name, put forth, say (-ing, on), shew, speak, tell, utter.

3005. λεῖμμα **lĕimma,** *lime´-mah;* from 3007; a *remainder:*—remnant.

3006. λεῖος **lĕiŏs,** *li´-os;* appar. a prim. word; *smooth,* i.e. "*level*":—smooth.

3007. λείπω **lĕipō,** *li´-po;* a prim. verb; to *leave,* i.e. (intrans. or pass.) to *fail* or *be absent:*—be destitute (wanting), lack.

3008. λειτουργέω **lĕitŏurgĕō,** *li-toorg-eh´-o;* from *3011;* to be a *public servant,* i.e. (by anal.) to *perform* religious or charitable *functions* (*worship, obey, relieve*):—minister.

3009. λειτουργία **lĕitŏurgia,** *li-toorg-ee´-ah;* from *3008; public function* (as priest ["liturgy"] or almsgiver):—ministration (-try), service.

3010. λειτουργικός **lĕitŏurgikŏs,** *li-toorg-ik-os´;* from the same as *3008; functional publicly* ("liturgic"), i.e. *beneficent:*—ministering.

3011. λειτουργός **lĕitŏurgŏs,** *li-toorg-os´;* from a der. of *2992* and *2041;* a *public servant,* i.e. a *functionary* in the Temple or Gospel, or (gen.) a *worshipper* (of God) or *benefactor* (of man):—minister (-ed).

3012. λέντιον **lĕntiŏn,** *len´-tee-on;* of Lat. or.; a *"linen"* cloth, i.e. *apron:*—towel.

3013. λεπίς **lĕpis,** *lep-is´;* from λέπω **lĕpō** (to *peel*); a *flake:*—scale.

3014. λέπρα **lĕpra,** *lep´-rah;* from the same as *3013; scaliness,* i.e. *"leprosy":*—leprosy.

3015. λεπρός **lĕprŏs,** *lep-ros´;* from the same as *3014; scaly,* i.e. *leprous* (a *leper*):—leper.

3016. λεπτόν **lĕptŏn,** *lep-ton´;* neut. of a der. of the same as *3013;* something *scaled* (*light*), i.e. a small *coin:*—mite.

3017. Λευΐ **Lĕuï,** *lyoo-ee´;* of Heb. or. [3878]; *Levi,* the name of three Isr.:—Levi. Comp. *3018.*

3018. Λευΐς **Lĕuïs,** *lyoo-is´;* a form of *3017; Lewis* (i.e. *Levi*), a Chr.:—Levi.

3019. Λευΐτης **Lĕuïtēs,** *lyoo-ee´-tace;* from *3017;* a *Levite,* i.e. desc. of Levi:—Levite.

3020. Λευϊτικός **Lĕuïtikŏs,** *lyoo-it-ee-kos´;* from 3019; *Levitic,* i.e. relating to the Levites:—Levitical.

3021. λευκαίνω **lĕukainō,** *lyoo-kah´ee-no;* from *3022;* to *whiten:*—make white, whiten.

3022. λευκός **lĕukŏs,** *lyoo-kos´;* from λύκη **lukē** ("*light*"); *white:*—white.

3023. λεών **lĕōn,** *leh-ohn´;* a prim. word. a *"lion":*—lion.

3024. λήθη **lēthē,** *lay´-thay;* from *2990; forgetfulness:*—+ forget.

3025. ληνός **lēnŏs,** *lay-nos´;* appar. a prim. word; a *trough,* i.e. wine-*vat:*—winepress.

3026. λῆρος **lērŏs,** *lay´-ros;* appar. a prim. word; *twaddle,* i.e. an *incredible* story:—idle tale.

3027. λῃστής **lēistēs,** *lace-tace´;* from ληΐζομαι **lēïzŏmai** (to *plunder*); a *brigand:*—robber, thief.

3028. λῆψις **lēpsis,** *lape´-sis;* from *2983; receipt* (the act):—receiving.

3029. λίαν **lian,** *lee´-an;* of uncert. affin.; *much* (adv.):—exceeding, great (-ly), sore, very (+ chiefest).

3030. λίβανος **libanŏs,** *lib´-an-os;* of for. or. [3828]; the *incense*-tree, i.e. (by impl.) *incense* itself:—frankincense.

3031. λιβανωτός **libanōtŏs,** *lib-an-o-tos´;* from *3030; frankincense,* i.e. (by extens.) a *censer* for burning it:—censer.

3032. Λιβερτῖνος **Libĕrtinŏs,** *lib-er-tee´-nos;* of Lat. or.; a Rom. *freedman:*—Libertine.

3033. Λιβύη **Libuē,** *lib-oo´-ay;* prob. from *3047; Libye,* a region of Africa:—Libya.

3034. λιθάζω **lithazō,** *lith-ad´-zo;* from *3037;* to *lapidate:*—stone.

3035. λίθινος **lithinŏs,** *lith´-ee-nos;* from *3037; stony,* i.e. made of *stone:*—of stone.

3036. λιθοβολέω **lithŏbŏlĕō,** *lith-ob-ol-eh´-o;* from a comp. of *3037* and *906;* to *throw stones,* i.e. *lapidate:*—stone, cast stones.

3037. λίθος **lithŏs,** *lee´-thos;* appar. a prim. word; *a stone* (lit. or fig.):—(mill-, stumbling-) stone.

3038. λιθόστρωτος **lithŏstrōtŏs,** *lith-os´-tro-tos;* from *3037* and a der. of *4766; stone-strewed,* i.e. a tessellated *mosaic* on which the Rom. tribunal was placed:—Pavement.

3039. λικμάω **likmaō,** *lik-mah´-o;* from λικμός **likmŏs,** the equiv. of λίκνον **liknŏn** (a winnowing *fan* or basket); to *winnow,* i.e. (by anal.) to *triturate:*—grind to powder.

3040. λιμήν **limēn,** *lee-mane´;* appar. a prim. word; a *harbor:*—haven. Comp. *2568.*

3041. λίμνη **limnē,** *lim´-nay;* prob. from *3040* (through the idea of the nearness of shore); a *pond* (large or small):—lake.

3042. λιμός **limŏs,** *lee-mos´;* prob. from *3007* (through the idea of *destitution*); a *scarcity* of food:—dearth, famine, hunger.

3043. λίνον **linŏn,** *lee´-non;* prob. a prim. word; *flax,* i.e. (by impl.) *"linen":*—linen.

3044. Λῖνος **Linŏs,** *lee´-nos;* perh. from *3043; Linus,* a Chr.:—Linus.

3045. λιπαρός **liparŏs,** *lip-ar-os´;* from λίπος **lipŏs** (*grease*); *fat,* i.e. (fig.) *sumptuous:*—dainty.

3046. λίτρα **litra,** *lee´-trah;* of Lat. or. [*libra*]; a pound in weight:—pound.

3047. λίψ **lips,** *leeps;* prob. from λείβω **lĕibō** (to *pour* a "libation"); the *south* (-west) wind (as bringing rain, i.e. (by extens.) the *south* quarter:—southwest.

3048. λογία **lŏgia,** *log-ee´-ah;* from *3056* (in the commercial sense); a *contribution:*—collection, gathering.

3049. λογίζομαι **lŏgizŏmai,** *log-id´-zom-ahee;* mid. from *3056;* to *take an inventory,* i.e. *estimate* (lit. or fig.):—conclude, (ac-) count (of), + despise, esteem, impute, lay, number, reason, reckon, suppose, think (on).

3050. λογικός **lŏgikŏs,** *log-ik-os´;* from *3056; rational* ("*logical*"):—reasonable, of the word.

3051. λόγιον **lŏgiŏn,** *log´-ee-on;* neut. of *3052;* an *utterance* (of God):—oracle.

3052. λόγιος **lŏgiŏs,** *log´-ee-os;* from *3056; fluent,* i.e. an *orator:*—eloquent.

3053. λογισμός **lŏgismŏs,** *log-is-mos´;* from *3049; computation,* i.e. (fig.) *reasoning* (*conscience, conceit*):—imagination, thought.

3054. λογομαχέω **lŏgŏmachĕō,** *log-om-akh-eh´-o;* from a comp. of *3056* and *3164;* to *be disputatious* (on trifles):—strive about words.

3055. λογομαχία **lŏgŏmachia,** *log-om-akh-ee´-ah;* from the same as *3054; disputation* about trifles ("*logomachy*"):—strife of words.

3056. λόγος **lŏgŏs,** *log´-os;* from *3004;* something *said* (including the *thought*); by impl. a *topic* (subject of discourse), also *reasoning* (the mental faculty) or *motive;* by extens. a *computation;* spec. (with the art. in John) the Divine *Expression* (i.e. *Christ*):—account, cause, communication, × concerning, doctrine, fame, × have to do, intent, matter, mouth, preaching, question, reason, + reckon, remove, say (-ing), shew, × speaker, speech, talk, thing, + none of these things move me, tidings, treatise, utterance, word, work.

3057. λόγχη **lŏgchē,** *long´-khay;* perh. a prim. word; a *"lance":*—spear.

3058. λοιδορέω **lŏidŏrĕō,** *loy-dor-eh´-o;* from *3060;* to *reproach,* i.e. *vilify:*—revile.

3059. λοιδορία **lŏidŏria,** *loy-dor-ee´-ah;* from *3060; slander* or *vituperation:*—railing, reproach [-fully].

3060. λοίδορος **lŏidŏrŏs,** *loy´-dor-os;* from λοιδός **lŏidŏs** (*mischief*); *abusive,* i.e. a *blackguard:*—railer, reviler.

3061. λοιμός **lŏimŏs,** *loy-mos´;* of uncert. affin.; a *plague* (lit. the *disease,* or fig. a *pest*):—pestilence (-t).

3062. λοιποί **lŏipŏy,** *loy-poy´;* masc. plur. of a der. of *3007; remaining* ones:—other, which remain, remnant, residue, rest.

3063. λοιπόν **lŏipŏn,** *loy-pon´;* neut. sing. of the same as *3062;* something *remaining* (adv.):—besides, finally, furthermore, (from) henceforth, moreover, now, + it remaineth, then.

3064. λοιποῦ **lŏipŏu,** *loy-poo´;* gen. sing. of the same as *3062; remaining* time:—from henceforth.

3065. Λουκᾶς **Lŏukas,** *loo-kas´;* contr. from Lat. *Lucanus; Lucas,* a Chr.:—Lucas, Luke.

3066. Λούκιος **Lŏukiŏs,** *loo´-kee-os;* of Lat. or.; *illuminative; Lucius,* a Chr.:—Lucius.

3067. λουτρόν **lŏutrŏn,** *loo-tron´;* from *3068;* a *bath,* i.e. (fig.) *baptism:*—washing.

3068. λούω **lŏuō,** *loo´-o;* a prim. verb; to *bathe* (the *whole* person; whereas *3538* means to wet a *part* only, and *4150* to wash, cleanse *garments* exclusively):—wash.

3069. Λύδδα **Ludda,** *lud´-dah;* of Heb. or. [3850]; *Lydda* (i.e. *Lod*), a place in Pal.:—Lydda.

3070. Λυδία **Ludia,** *loo-dee´-ah;* prop. fem. of Λύδιος **Ludiŏs** [of for. or.] (a *Lydian,* in Asia Minor); *Lydia,* a Chr. woman:—Lydia.

3071. Λυκαονία **Lukaŏnia,** *loo-kah-on-ee´-ah;* perh. remotely from 3074; *Lycaonia,* a region of Asia Minor:—Lycaonia.

3072. Λυκαονιστί **Lukaŏnisti,** *loo-kah-on-is-tee´;* adv. from a der. of *3071; Lycaonistically,* i.e. in the language of the Lycaonians:—in the speech of Lycaonia.

3073. Λυκία **Lukia,** *loo-kee´-ah;* prob. remotely from *3074; Lycia,* a province of Asia Minor:—Lycia.

3074. λύκος **lukŏs,** *loo´-kos;* perh. akin to the base of *3022* (from the *whitish* hair); a *wolf:*—wolf.

3075. λυμαίνομαι **lumainŏmai,** *loo-mah´-ee-nom-ahee;* mid. from a prob. der. of *3089* (mean. *filth*); prop. to *soil,* i.e. (fig.) *insult* (*maltreat*):—make havock of.

3076. λυπέω **lupĕō,** *loo-peh´-o;* from *3077;* to *distress;* reflex. or pass. to *be sad:*—cause grief, grieve, be in heaviness, (be) sorrow (-ful), be (make) sorry.

3077. λύπη **lupē,** *loo´-pay;* appar. a prim. word; *sadness:*—grief, grievous, + grudgingly, heaviness, sorrow.

3078. Λυσανίας **Lusanias,** *loo-san-ee´-as;* from *3080* and ἀνία **ania** *(trouble); grief-dispelling; Lysanias,* a governor of Abilene:—Lysanias.

3079. Λυσίας **Lusias,** *loo-see´-as;* of uncert. affin.; *Lysias,* a Rom.:—Lysias.

3080. λύσις **lusis,** *loo´-sis;* from *3089;* a *loosening,* i.e. (spec.) *divorce:*—to be loosed.

3081. λυσιτελεῖ **lusitĕlĕi,** *loo-sit-el-i´;* third pers. sing. pres. indic. act. of a der. of a comp. of *3080* and *5056;* impers. it *answers* the *purpose,* i.e. *is advantageous:*—it is better.

3082. Λύστρα **Lustra,** *loos´-trah;* of uncert. or.; *Lystra,* a place in Asia Minor:—Lystra.

3083. λύτρον **lutrŏn,** *loo´-tron;* from *3089;* something to *loosen* with, i.e. a redemption *price* (fig. *atonement*):—ransom.

3084. λυτρόω **lutrŏō,** *loo-trŏ´-o;* from *3083;* to *ransom* (lit. or fig.):—redeem.

3085. λύτρωσις **lutrōsis,** *loo´-tro-sis;* from *3084;* a *ransoming* (fig.):— + redeemed, redemption.

3086. λυτρωτής **lutrōtēs,** *loo-tro-tace´;* from *3084;* a *redeemer* (fig.):—deliverer.

3087. λυχνία **luchnia,** *lookh-nee´-ah;* from *3088;* a *lamp-stand* (lit. or fig.):—candlestick.

3088. λύχνος **luchnŏs,** *lookh´-nos;* from the base of *3022;* a portable *lamp* or other *illuminator* (lit. or fig.):—candle, light.

3089. λύω **luō,** *loo´-o;* a prim. verb; to *"loosen"* (lit. or fig.):—break (up), destroy, dissolve, (un-) loose, melt, put off. Comp. *4486.*

3090. Λωΐς **Lōïs,** *lo-ece´;* of uncert. or.; *Loïs,* a Chr. woman:—Lois.

3091. Λώτ **Lōt,** *lote;* of Heb. or. [3876]; *Lot,* a patriarch:—Lot.

M

3092. Μαάθ **Maath,** *mah-ath´;* prob. of Heb. or.; *Maath,* an Isr.:—Maath.

3093. Μαγδαλά **Magdala,** *mag-dal-ah´;* of Chald. or. [comp. 4026]; *the tower; Magdala* (i.e. *Migdala*), a place in Pal.:—Magdala.

3094. Μαγδαληνή **Magdalēnē,** *mag-dal-ay-nay´;* fem. of a der. of *3093;* a female *Magdalene,* i.e. inhab. of Magdala:—Magdalene.

3095. μαγεία **magĕia,** *mag-i´-ah;* from *3096; "magic":*—sorcery.

3096. μαγεύω **magĕuō,** *mag-yoo´-o;* from *3097;* to *practice magic:*—use sorcery.

3097. μάγος **magŏs,** *mag´-os;* of for. or. [7248]; a *Magian,* i.e. Oriental *scientist;* by impl. a *magician:*—sorcerer, wise man.

3098. Μαγώγ **Magōg,** *mag-ogue´;* of Heb. or. [4031]; *Magog,* a for. nation, i.e. (fig.) an Antichristian party:—Magog.

3099. Μαδιάν **Madian,** *mad-ee-an´;* of Heb. or. [4080]; *Madian* (i.e. *Midian*), a region of Arabia:—Madian.

3100. μαθητεύω **mathētĕuō,** *math-ayt-yoo´-o;* from *3101;* intrans. to *become a pupil;* trans. to *disciple,* i.e. enrol as scholar:—be disciple, instruct, teach.

3101. μαθητής **mathētēs,** *math-ay-tes´;* from *3129;* a *learner,* i.e. *pupil:*—disciple.

3102. μαθήτρια **mathētria,** *math-ay´-tree-ah;* fem. from *3101;* a female *pupil:*—disciple.

3103. Μαθουσάλα **Mathŏusala,** *math-oo-sal´-ah;* of Heb. or. [4968]; *Mathusala* (i.e. *Methushelach*), an antediluvian:—Mathusala.

3104. Μαϊνάν **Maïnan,** *mahee-nan´;* prob. of Heb. or.; *Maïnan,* an Isr.:—Mainan.

3105. μαίνομαι **mainŏmai,** *mah´ee-nom-ahee;* mid. from a prim. μάω **maō** (to *long* for; through the idea of insensate *craving*); to *rave* as a "maniac":—be beside self (mad).

3106. μακαρίζω **makarizō,** *mak-ar-id´-zo;* from *3107;* to *beatify,* i.e. *pronounce* (or *esteem*) *fortunate:*—call blessed, count happy.

3107. μακάριος **makariŏs,** *mak-ar´-ee-os;* a prol. form of the poetical μάκαρ **makar** (mean. the same); supremely *blest;* by extens. *fortunate, well off:*—blessed, happy (× -ier).

3108. μακαρισμός **makarismŏs,** *mak-ar-is-mos´;* from *3106; beatification,* i.e., *attribution of good fortune:*—blessedness.

3109. Μακεδονία **Makĕdŏnia,** *mak-ed-on-ee´-ah;* from *3110; Macedonia,* a region of Greece:—Macedonia.

3110. Μακεδών **Makĕdōn,** *mak-ed-ohn´;* of uncert. der.; a *Macedon* (*Macedonian*), i.e. inhab. of Macedonia:—of Macedonia, Macedonian.

3111. μάκελλον **makĕllŏn,** *mak´-el-lon;* of Lat. or. [*macellum*]; a *butcher's stall, meat market* or *provision-shop:*—shambles.

3112. μακράν **makran,** *mak-ran´;* fem. acc. sing. of *3117* (*3598* being implied); *at a distance* (lit. or fig.):—(a-) far (off), good (great) way off.

3113. μακρόθεν **makrŏthĕn,** *mak-roth´-en;* adv. from *3117; from a distance* or *afar:*—afar off, from far.

3114. μακροθυμέω **makrŏthumĕō,** *mak-roth-oo-meh´-o;* from the same as *3116;* to *be long-spirited,* i.e. (obj.) *forbearing* or (subj.) *patient:*—bear (suffer) long, be longsuffering, have (long) patience, be patient, patiently endure.

3115. μακροθυμία **makrŏthumia,** *mak-roth-oo-mee´-ah;* from the same as *3116; longanimity,* i.e. (obj.) *forbearance* or (subj.) *fortitude:*—longsuffering, patience.

3116. μακροθυμώς **makrŏthumōs,** *mak-roth-oo-moce´;* adv. of a comp. of *3117* and *2372; with long* (*enduring*) *temper,* i.e. *leniently:*—patiently.

3117. μακρός **makrŏs,** *mak-ros´;* from *3372; long* (in place [*distant*] or time [neut. plur.]):—far, long.

3118. μακροχρόνιος **makrŏchrŏniŏs,** *mak-rokh-ron´-ee-os;* from *3117* and *5550; long-timed,* i.e. *long-lived:*—live long.

3119. μαλακία **malakia,** *mal-ak-ee´-ah;* from *3120; softness,* i.e. *enervation* (*debility*):—disease.

3120. μαλακός **malakŏs,** *mal-ak-os´;* of uncert. affin.; *soft,* i.e. *fine* (clothing); fig. a *catamite:*—effeminate, soft.

3121. Μαλελεήλ **Malĕlĕēl,** *mal-el-eh-ale´;* of Heb. or [4111]; *Maleleël* (i.e. *Mahalalel*), an antediluvian:—Maleleel.

3122. μάλιστα **malista,** *mal´-is-tah;* neut. plur. of the superl. of an appar. prim. adv. μάλα **mala** (*very*); (adv.) *most* (*in the greatest degree*) or *particularly:*—chiefly, most of all, (e-) specially.

3123. μᾶλλον **mallŏn,** *mal´-lon;* neut. of the compar. of the same as *3122;* (adv.) *more* (*in a greater degree*) or *rather:*— + better, × far, (the) more (and more), (so) much (the more), rather.

3124. Μάλχος **Malchŏs,** *mal´-khos;* of Heb. or. [4429]; *Malchus,* an Isr.:—Malchus.

3125. μάμμη **mammē,** *mam´-may;* of nat. or. ["mammy"]; a *grandmother:*—grandmother.

3126. μαμμωνᾶς **mammōnas,** *mam-mo-nas´;* of Chald. or. (*confidence,* i.e. fig. *wealth,* personified); *mammonas,* i.e. *avarice* (deified):—mammon.

3127. Μαναήν **Manaēn,** *man-ah-ane´;* of uncert. or.; *Manaën,* a Chr.:—Manaen.

3128. Μανασσῆς **Manassēs,** *man-as-sace´;* of Heb. or. [4519]; *Manasses* (i.e. *Menashsheh*), an Isr.:—Manasses.

3129. μανθάνω **manthanō,** *man-than´-o;* prol. from a prim. verb, another form of which, μαθέω **mathĕō,** is used as an alt. in cert. tenses; to *learn* (in any way):—learn, understand.

3130. μανία **mania,** *man-ee´-ah;* from *3105; craziness:*—[+ make] × mad.

3131. μάννα **manna,** *man´-nah;* of Heb. or. [4478]; *manna* (i.e. *man*), an edible gum:—manna.

3132. *μαντεύομαι* **mantěuŏmai,** *mant-yoo´-om-ahee;* from a der. of *3105* (mean. a *prophet,* as supposed to *rave* through *inspiration*); to *divine,* i.e. *utter spells* (under pretence of foretelling):—by soothsaying.

3133. *μαραίνω* **marainō,** *mar-ah´ee-no;* of uncert. affin.; to *extinguish* (as fire), i.e. (fig. and pass.) to *pass away:*—fade away.

3134. *μαρὰν ἀθά* **maran atha,** *mar´-an ath´-ah;* of Chald. or. (mean. *our Lord has come*); *maranatha,* i.e. an exclamation of the approaching *divine judgment:*—Maran-atha.

3135. *μαργαρίτης* **margaritēs,** *mar-gar-ee´-tace;* from *μάργαρος* **margarŏs** (a pearl-*oyster*); a *pearl:*—pearl.

3136. Μάρθα **Martha,** *mar´-thah;* prob. of Chald. or. (mean. *mistress*); *Martha,* a Chr. woman:—Martha.

3137. Μαρία **Maria,** *mar-ee´-ah;* or
Μαριάμ **Mariam,** *mar-ee-am´;* of Heb. or. [4813]; *Maria* or *Mariam* (i.e. *Mirjam*), the name of six Chr. females:—Mary.

3138. Μάρκος **Markŏs,** *mar´-kos;* of Lat. or.; *Marcus,* a Chr:—Marcus, Mark.

3139. *μάρμαρος* **marmarŏs,** *mar´-mar-os;* from *μαρμαίρω* **marmairō** (to *glisten*); *marble* (as sparkling *white*):—marble.

μάρτυρ **martur.** See *3144.*

3140. *μαρτυρέω* **marturěō,** *mar-too-reh´-o;* from *3144;* to *be a witness,* i.e. *testify* (lit. or fig.):—charge, give [*evidence*], bear record, have (obtain, of) good (honest) report, be well reported of, testify, give (have) testimony, (be, bear, give, obtain) witness.

3141. *μαρτυρία* **marturia,** *mar-too-ree´-ah;* from *3144; evidence given (judicially or gen.):*—*record, report, testimony, witness.*

3142. *μαρτύριον* **marturiŏn,** *mar-too´-ree-on;* neut. of a presumed der. of *3144;* something *evidential,* i.e. (gen.) *evidence* given or (spec.) the *Decalogue* (in the sacred Tabernacle):—to be testified, testimony, witness.

3143. *μαρτύρομαι* **marturŏmai,** *mar-too´-rom-ahee;* mid. from *3144;* to *be adduced* as *a witness,* i.e. (fig.) to *obtest* (in affirmation or exhortation):—take to record, testify.

3144. *μάρτυς* **martus,** *mar´-toos;* of uncert. affin.; a *witness* (lit. [judicially] or fig. [gen.]); by anal. a *"martyr":*—martyr, record, witness.

3145. *μασσάομαι* **massaŏmai,** *mas-sah´-om-ahee;* from a prim. *μάσσω* **massō** (to *handle* or *squeeze*); to *chew:*—gnaw.

3146. *μαστιγόω* **mastigŏō,** *mas-tig-ŏ´-o;* from *3148;* to *flog* (lit. or fig.):—scourge.

3147. *μαστίζω* **mastizō,** *mas-tid´-zo;* from *3149;* to *whip* (lit.):—scourge.

3148. *μάστιξ* **mastix,** *mas´-tix;* prob. from the base of *3145* (through the idea of *contact*); a *whip* (lit. the Roman *flagellum* for criminals; fig. a *disease*):—plague, scourging.

3149. *μαστός* **mastŏs,** *mas-tos´;* from the base of *3145;* a (prop. female) *breast* (as if *kneaded* up):—pap.

3150. *ματαιολογία* **mataiŏlŏgia,** *mat-ah-yol-og-ee´-ah;* from *3151; random talk,* i.e. *babble:*—vain jangling.

3151. *ματαιολόγος* **mataiŏlŏgŏs,** *mat-ah-yol-og´-os;* from *3152* and *3004;* an *idle* (i.e. *senseless* or *mischievous*) *talker,* i.e. a *wrangler:*—vain talker.

3152. *μάταιος* **mataiŏs,** *mat´-ah-yos;* from the base of *3155; empty,* i.e. (lit.) *profitless,* or (spec.) an *idol:*—vain, vanity.

3153. *ματαιότης* **mataiŏtēs,** *mat-ah-yot´-ace;* from *3152; inutility;* fig. *transientness;* mor. *depravity:*—vanity.

3154. *ματαιόω* **mataiŏō,** *mat-ah-yŏ´-o;* from *3152;* to *render* (pass. *become*) *foolish,* i.e. (mor.) *wicked* or (spec.) *idolatrous:*—become vain.

3155. *μάτην* **matēn,** *mat´-ane;* accus. of a der. of the base of *3145* (through the idea of tentative *manipulation,* i.e. unsuccessful *search,* or else of *punishment*); *folly,* i.e. (adv.) *to no purpose:*—in vain.

3156. Ματθαῖος **Matthaiŏs,** *mat-thah´-yos;* a shorter form of *3161; Matthæus* (i.e. *Matthitjah*), an Isr. and Chr.:—Matthew.

3157. Ματθάν **Matthan,** *mat-than´;* of Heb. or. [4977]; *Matthan* (i.e. *Mattan*), an Isr.:—Matthan.

3158. Ματθάτ **Matthat,** *mat-that´;* prob. a shortened form of *3161; Matthat* (i.e. *Mattithjah*), the name of two Isr.:—Mathat.

3159. Ματθίας **Matthias,** *mat-thee´-as;* appar. a shortened form of *3161; Matthias* (i.e. *Mattithjah*), an Isr.:—Matthias.

3160. Ματταθά **Mattatha,** *mat-tath-ah´;* prob. a shortened form of *3161* [comp. 4992]; *Mattatha* (i.e. *Mattithjah*), an Isr.:—Mattatha.

3161. Ματταθίας **Mattathias,** *mat-tath-ee´-as;* of Heb. or. [4993]; *Mattathias* (i.e. *Mattithjah*), an Isr. and Chr.:—Mattathias.

3162. *μάχαιρα* **machaira,** *makh´-ahee-rah;* prob. fem. of a presumed der. of *3163;* a *knife,* i.e. *dirk;* fig. *war,* judicial *punishment:*—sword.

3163. *μάχη* **machē,** *makh´-ay;* from *3164;* a *battle,* i.e. (fig.) *controversy:*—fighting, strive, striving.

3164. *μάχομαι* **machŏmai,** *makh´-om-ahee;* mid. of an appar. prim. verb; to *war,* i.e. (fig.) to *quarrel, dispute:*—fight, strive.

3165. *μέ* **mě,** *meh;* a shorter (an prob. orig.) form of *1691; me:*—I, me, my.

3166. *μεγαλαυχέω* **měgalauchěō,** *meg-al-ŏw-kheh´-o;* from a comp. of *3173* and *αὐχέω* **auchěō** (to *boast;* akin to *837* and *2744*); to *talk big,* i.e. *be grandiloquent* (*arrogant, egotistic*):—boast great things.

3167. *μεγαλεῖος* **měgalěiŏs,** *meg-al-i´-os;* from *3173; magnificent,* i.e. (neut. plur. as noun) a conspicuous *favor,* or (subj.) *perfection:*—great things, wonderful works.

3168. *μεγαλειότης* **měgalěiŏtēs,** *meg-al-i-ot´-ace;* from *3167; superbness,* i.e. *glory* or *splendor:*—magnificence, majesty, mighty power.

3169. *μεγαλοπρεπής* **měgalŏprěpēs,** *meg-al-op-rep-ace´;* from *3173* and *4241; befitting greatness* or *magnificence* (*majestic*):—excellent.

3170. *μεγαλύνω* **měgalunō,** *meg-al-oo´-no;* from *3173;* to *make* (or *declare*) *great,* i.e. *increase* or (fig.) *extol:*—enlarge, magnify, shew great.

3171. *μεγάλως* **měgalōs,** *meg-al´-oce;* adv. from *3173; much:*—greatly.

3172. *μεγαλωσύνη* **měgalōsunē,** *meg-al-o-soo´-nay;* from *3173; greatness,* i.e. (fig.) *divinity* (often *God* himself):—majesty.

3173. *μέγας* **měgas,** *meg´-as* [includ. the prol. forms, fem. *μεγάλη* **měgalē,** plur. *μεγάλοι* **měgalŏi,** etc.; comp. also *3176, 3187*]; *big* (lit. or fig., in a very wide application):—(+ fear) exceedingly, great (-est), high, large, loud, mighty, + (be) sore (afraid), strong, × to years.

3174. *μέγεθος* **měgěthŏs,** *meg´-eth-os;* from *3173; magnitude* (fig.):—greatness.

3175. *μεγιστᾶνες* **měgistaněs,** *meg-is-tan´-es;* plur. from *3176; grandees:*—great men, lords.

3176. *μέγιστος* **měgistŏs,** *meg´-is-tos;* superl. of *3173; greatest* or *very great:*—exceeding great.

3177. *μεθερμηνεύω* **měthěrmēněuō,** *meth-er-mane-yoo´-o;* from *3326* and *2059;* to *explain over,* i.e. *translate:*—(by) interpret (-ation).

3178. *μέθη* **měthē,** *meth´-ay;* appar. a prim. word; an *intoxicant,* i.e. (by impl.) *intoxication:*—drunkenness.

3179. *μεθίστημι* **měthistēmi,** *meth-is´-tay-mee;* or (1 Cor. 13:2)
μεθιστάνω **měthistanō,** *meth-is-tan´-o;* from *3326* and *2476;* to *transfer,* i.e. *carry away, depose* or (fig.) *exchange, seduce:*—put out, remove, translate, turn away.

3180. *μεθοδεία* **měthŏděia,** *meth-od-i´-ah;* from a comp. of *3326* and *3593* [comp. "method"]; *travelling over,* i.e. *travesty* (*trickery*):—wile, lie in wait.

3181. *μεθόριος* **měthŏriŏs,** *meth-or´-ee-os;* from *3326* and *3725; bounded alongside,* i.e. *contiguous* (neut. plur. as noun, *frontier*):—border.

3182. *μεθύσκω* **měthuskō,** *meth-oos´-ko;* a prol. (trans.) form of *3184;* to *intoxicate:*—be drunk (-en).

3183. *μέθυσος* **měthusŏs,** *meth´-oo-sos;* from *3184; tipsy,* i.e. (as noun) a *sot:*—drunkard.

3184. μεθύω **mĕthuō,** *meth-oo´-o;* from another form of *3178;* to *drink* to *intoxication,* i.e. *get drunk:*—drink well, make (be) drunk (-en).

3185. μεῖζον **mĕizŏn,** *mide´-zon;* neut. of *3187;* (adv.) in a *greater* degree:—the more.

3186. μειζότερος **mĕizŏtĕrŏs,** *mide-zot´-er-os;* continued compar. of *3187; still larger* (fig.):—greater.

3187. μείζων **mĕizōn,** *mide´-zone;* irreg. compar. of *3173; larger* (lit. or fig., spec. in age):—elder, greater (-est), more.

3188. μέλαν **mĕlan,** *mel´-an;* neut. of *3189* as noun; *ink:*—ink.

3189. μέλας **mĕlas,** *mel´-as;* appar. a prim. word; *black:*—black.

3190. Μελεᾶς **Mĕlĕas,** *mel-eh-as´;* of uncert. or.; *Meleas,* an Isr.:—Meleas.

μέλει **mĕlĕi.** See *3199.*

3191. μελετάω **mĕlĕtaō,** *mel-et-ah´-o;* from a presumed der. of *3199;* to *take care of,* i.e. (by impl.) *revolve* in the mind:—imagine, (pre-) meditate.

3192. μέλι **mĕli,** *mel´-ee;* appar. a prim. word; *honey:*—honey.

3193. μελίσσιος **mĕlissiŏs,** *mel-is´-see-os;* from *3192; relating to honey,* i.e. *bee* (comb):—honeycomb.

3194. Μελίτη **Mĕlitē,** *mel-ee´-tay;* of uncert. or.; *Melita,* an island in the Mediterranean:—Melita.

3195. μέλλω **mĕllō,** *mel´-lo;* a strengthened form of *3199* (through the idea of *expectation*); to *intend,* i.e. *be about* to be, do, or suffer something (of persons or things, espec. events; in the sense of *purpose, duty, necessity, probability, possibility,* or *hestitation*):—about, after that, be (almost), (that which is, things, + which was for) to come, intend, was to (be), mean, mind, be at the point, (be) ready, + return, shall (begin), (which, that) should (after, afterwards, hereafter) tarry, which was for, will, would, be yet.

3196. μέλος **mĕlŏs,** *mel´-os;* of uncert. affin.; a *limb* or *part* of the body:—member.

3197. Μελχί **Mĕlchi,** *mel-khee´;* of Heb. or. [4428 with pron. suf., *my king*]; *Melchi* (i.e. *Malki*), the name of two Isr.:—Melchi.

3198. Μελχισεδέκ **Mĕlchisĕdĕk,** *mel-khis-ed-ek´;* of Heb. or. [4442]; *Melchisedek* (i.e. *Malkitsedek*), a patriarch:—Melchisedec.

3199. μέλω **mĕlō,** *mel´-o;* a prim. verb; to *be of interest* to, i.e. to *concern* (only third pers. sing. pres. indic. used impers. *it matters*):—(take) care.

3200. μεμβράνα **mĕmbrana,** *mem-bran´-ah;* of Lat. or. ("*membrane*"); a (written) sheep-*skin:*—parchment.

3201. μέμφομαι **mĕmphŏmai,** *mem´-fom-ahee;* mid. of an appar. prim. verb; to *blame:*—find fault.

3202. μεμψίμοιρος **mĕmpsimŏirŏs,** *mem-psim´-oy-ros;* from a presumed der. of *3201* and *μοῖρα* **mŏira** (*fate;* akin to the base of *3313*); *blaming fate,* i.e. *querulous* (*discontented*):—complainer.

3203-3302. See note, page 4.

3303. μέν **mĕn,** *men;* a prim. particle; prop. indic. of *affirmation* or *concession* (*in fact*); usually followed by a *contrasted* clause with *1161* (*this* one, the *former,* etc.):—even, indeed, so, some, truly, verily. Often compounded with other particles in an *intensive* or *asseverative* sense.

3304. μενοῦνγε **mĕnŏungĕ,** *men-oon´-geh;* from *3303* and *3767* and *1065; so then at least:*—nay but, yea doubtless (rather, verily).

3305. μέντοι **mĕntŏi,** *men´-toy;* from *3303* and *5104; indeed though,* i.e. *however:*—also, but, howbeit, nevertheless, yet.

3306. μένω **mĕnō,** *men´-o;* a prim. verb; to *stay* (in a given place, state, relation or expectancy):—abide, continue, dwell, endure, be present, remain, stand, tarry (for), × thine own.

3307. μερίζω **mĕrizō,** *mer-id´-zo;* from *3313;* to *part,* i.e. (lit.) to *apportion, bestow, share,* or (fig.) to *disunite, differ:*—deal, be difference between, distribute, divide, give part.

3308. μέριμνα **mĕrimna,** *mer´-im-nah;* from *3307* (through the idea of *distraction*); *solicitude:*—care.

3309. μεριμνάω **mĕrimnaō,** *mer-im-nah´-o;* from *3308;* to *be anxious* about:—(be, have) care (-ful), take thought.

3310. μερίς **mĕris,** *mer-ece´;* fem. of *3313;* a *portion,* i.e. *province, share* or (abstr.) *participation:*—part (× -akers).

3311. μερισμός **mĕrismŏs,** *mer-is-mos´;* from *3307;* a *separation* or *distribution:*—dividing asunder, gift.

3312. μεριστής **mĕristēs,** *mer-is-tace´;* from *3307;* an *apportioner* (*administrator*):—divider.

3313. μέρος **mĕrŏs,** *mer´-os;* from an obsol. but more prim. form of *μείρομαι* **mĕirŏmai** (to *get* as a *section* or *allotment*); a *division* or *share* (lit. or fig., in a wide application):—behalf, coast, course, craft, particular (+ -ly), part (+ -ly), piece, portion, respect, side, some sort (-what).

3314. μεσημβρία **mĕsēmbria,** *mes-ame-bree´-ah;* from *3319* and *2250; midday;* by impl. the *south:*—noon, south.

3315. μεσιτεύω **mĕsitĕuō,** *mes-it-yoo´-o;* from *3316;* to *interpose* (as arbiter), i.e. (by impl.) to *ratify* (as surety):—confirm.

3316. μεσίτης **mĕsitēs,** *mes-ee´-tace;* from *3319;* a *go-between,* i.e. (simply) an *internunciator,* or (by impl.) a *reconciler* (*intercessor*):—mediator.

3317. μεσονύκτιον **mĕsŏnuktiŏn,** *mes-on-ook´-tee-on;* neut. of a comp. of *3319* and *3571; midnight* (espec. as a watch):—midnight.

3318. Μεσοποταμία **Mĕsŏpŏtamia,** *mes-op-ot-am-ee´-ah;* from *3319* and *4215; Mesopotamia* (as lying between the Euphrates and the Tigris; comp. 763), a region of Asia:—Mesopotamia.

3319. μέσος **mĕsŏs,** *mes´-os;* from *3326; middle* (as adj. or [neut.] noun):—among, × before them, between, + forth, mid [-day, -night], midst, way.

3320. μεσότοιχον **mĕsŏtŏichŏn,** *mes-ot´-oy-khon;* from *3319* and *5109;* a *partition* (fig.):—middle wall.

3321. μεσουράνημα **mĕsŏuranēma,** *mes-oo-ran´-ay-mah;* from a presumed comp. of *3319* and *3772; mid-sky:*—midst of heaven.

3322. μεσόω **mĕsŏō,** *mes-ŏ´-o;* from *3319;* to *form* the *middle,* i.e. (in point of time), to *be half-way* over:—be about the midst.

3323. Μεσσίας **Mĕssias,** *mes-see´-as;* of Heb. or. [4899]; the *Messias* (i.e. *Mashiach*), or Christ:—Messias.

3324. μεστός **mĕstŏs,** *mes-tos´;* of uncert. der.; *replete* (lit. or fig.):—full.

3325. μεστόω **mĕstŏō,** *mes-tŏ´-o;* from *3324;* to *replenish,* i.e. (by impl.) to *intoxicate:*—fill.

3326. μετά **mĕta,** *met-ah´;* a prim. prep. (often used adv.); prop. denoting *accompaniment;* "*amid*" (local or causal); modified variously according to the case (gen. *association,* or acc. *succession*) with which it is joined; occupying an intermediate position between *575* or *1537* and *1519* or *4314;* less intimate than *1722,* and less close than *4862*):—after (-ward), × that he again, against, among, × and, + follow, hence, hereafter, in, of, (up-) on, + our, × and setting, since, (un-) to, + together, when, with (+ -out). Often used in composition, in substantially the same relations of *participation* or *proximity,* and *transfer* or *sequence.*

3327. μεταβαίνω **mĕtabainō,** *met-ab-ah´ee-no;* from *3326* and the base of *939;* to *change place:*—depart, go, pass, remove.

3328. μεταβάλλω **mĕtaballō,** *met-ab-al´-lo;* from *3326* and *906;* to *throw over,* i.e. (mid. fig.) to *turn about* in opinion:—change mind.

3329. μετάγω **mĕtagō,** *met-ag´-o;* from *3326* and *71;* to *lead over,* i.e. *transfer* (*direct*):—turn about.

3330. μεταδίδωμι **mĕtadidōmi,** *met-ad-id´-o-mee;* from *3326* and *1325;* to *give over,* i.e. *share:*—give, impart.

3331. μετάθεσις **mĕtathĕsis,** *met-ath´-es-is;* from *3346; transposition,* i.e. *transferral* (to heaven), *disestablishment* (of a law):—change, removing, translation.

3332. μεταίρω **mĕtairō,** *met-ah´ee-ro;* from *3326* and *142;* to *betake* oneself, i.e. *remove* (locally):—depart.

3333. μετακαλέω **mĕtakalĕō,** *met-ak-al-eh´-o;* from *3326* and *2564;* to *call elsewhere,* i.e. *summon:*—call (for, hither).

3334. *μετακινέω* **mĕtakinĕō,** *met-ak-ee-neh´-o;* from *3326* and *2795;* to *stir* to a place *elsewhere,* i.e. *remove* (fig.):—move away.

3335. *μεταλαμβάνω* **mĕtalambanō,** *met-al-am-ban´-o;* from *3326* and *2983;* to *participate;* gen. to *accept* (and use):—eat, have, be partaker, receive, take.

3336. *μετάληψις* **mĕtalēpsis,** *met-al´-ape-sis;* from *3335; participation:*—taking.

3337. *μεταλλάσσω* **mĕtallassō,** *met-al-las´-so;* from *3326* and *236;* to *exchange:*—change.

3338. *μεταμέλλομαι* **mĕtamĕllŏmai,** *met-am-el´-lom-ahee;* from *3326* and the mid. of *3199;* to *care afterwards,* i.e. *regret:*—repent (self).

3339. *μεταμορφόω* **mĕtamŏrphŏō,** *met-am-or-fŏ´-o;* from *3326* and *3445;* to *transform* (lit. or fig. "metamorphose"):—change, transfigure, transform.

3340. *μετανοέω* **mĕtanŏĕō,** *met-an-ŏ-eh´-o;* from *3326* and *3539;* to *think differently* or *afterwards,* i.e. *reconsider* (mor. *feel compunction*):—repent.

3341. *μετάνοια* **mĕtanŏia,** *met-an´-oy-ah;* from *3340;* (subj.) *compunction* (for guilt, includ. *reformation*); by impl. *reversal* (of [another's] decision):—repentance.

3342. *μεταξύ* **mĕtaxu,** *met-ax-oo´;* from *3326* and a form of *4862; betwixt* (of place or person); (of time) as adj. *intervening,* or (by impl.) *adjoining:*—between, mean while, next.

3343. *μεταπέμπω* **mĕtapĕmpō,** *met-ap-emp´-o;* from *3326* and *3992;* to *send* from *elsewhere,* i.e. (mid.) to *summon* or *invite:*—call (send) for.

3344. *μεταστρέφω* **mĕtastrĕphō,** *met-as-tref´-o;* from *3326* and *4762;* to *turn across,* i.e. *transmute* or (fig.) *corrupt:*—pervert, turn.

3345. *μετασχηματίζω* **mĕtaschēmatizō,** *met-askh-ay-mat-id´-zo;* from *3326* and a der. of *4976;* to *transfigure* or *disguise;* fig. to *apply* (by accommodation):—transfer, transform (self); to *change.*

3346. *μετατίθημι* **mĕtatithēmi,** *met-at-ith´-ay-mee;* from *3326* and *5087;* to *transfer,* i.e. (lit.) *transport,* (by impl.) *exchange,* (reflex.) *change sides,* or (fig.) *pervert:*—carry over, change, remove, translate, turn.

3347. *μετέπειτα* **mĕtĕpĕita,** *met-ep´-i-tah;* from *3326* and *1899; thereafter:*—afterward.

3348. *μετέχω* **mĕtĕchō,** *met-ekh´-o;* from *3326* and *2192;* to *share* or *participate;* by impl. *belong* to, *eat* (or *drink*):—be partaker, pertain, take part, use.

3349. *μετεωρίζω* **mĕtĕōrizō,** *met-eh-o-rid´-zo;* from a comp. of *3326* and a collat. form of *142* or perh. rather of *109* (comp. "meteor"); to *raise in mid-air,* i.e. (fig.) *suspend* (pass. *fluctuate* or *be anxious*):—be of doubtful mind.

3350. *μετοικεσία* **mĕtŏikĕsia,** *met-oy-kes-ee´-ah;* from a der. of a comp. of *3326* and *3624;* a *change of abode,* i.e. (spec.) *expatriation:*—× brought, carried (-ying) away (in-) to.

3351. *μετοικίζω* **mĕtŏikizō,** *met-oy-kid´-zo;* from the same as *3350;* to *transfer* as a *settler* or *captive,* i.e. *colonize* or *exile:*—carry away, remove into.

3352. *μετοχή* **mĕtŏchē,** *met-okh-ay´;* from *3348; participation,* i.e. *intercourse:*—fellowship.

3353. *μέτοχος* **mĕtŏchŏs,** *met´-okh-os;* from *3348; participant,* i.e. (as noun) a *sharer;* by impl. an *associate:*—fellow, partaker, partner.

3354. *μετρέω* **mĕtrĕō,** *met-reh´-o;* from *3358;* to *measure* (i.e. ascertain in size by a fixed standard); by impl. to *admeasure* (i.e. allot by rule); fig. to *estimate:*—measure, mete.

3355. *μετρητής* **mĕtrētēs,** *met-ray-tace´;* from *3354;* a *measurer,* i.e. (spec.) a certain standard *measure* of capacity for liquids:—firkin.

3356. *μετριοπαθέω* **mĕtriŏpathĕō,** *met-ree-op-ath-eh´-o;* from a comp. of the base of *3357* and *3806;* to *be moderate in passion,* i.e. *gentle* (to *treat indulgently*):—have compassion.

3357. *μετρίως* **mĕtriōs,** *met-ree´-oce;* adv. from a der. of *3358; moderately,* i.e. *slightly:*—a little.

3358. *μέτρον* **mĕtrŏn,** *met´-ron;* an appar. prim. word; a *measure* ("metre"), lit. or fig.; by impl. a limited *portion* (*degree*):—measure.

3359. *μέτωπον* **mĕtōpŏn,** *met´-o-pon;* from *3326* and *ὤψ* **ōps** (the *face*); the *forehead* (as *opposite* the *countenance*):—forehead.

3360. *μέχρι* **mĕchri,** *mekh´-ree;* or
μεχρίς **mĕchris,** *mekh-ris´;* from *3372; as far as,* i.e. *up to* a certain point (as prep. of extent [denoting the *terminus,* whereas *891* refers espec. to the *space of time or place intervening] or conj.):—till, (un-) to, until.*

3361. *μή* **mē,** *may;* a prim. particle of qualified *negation* (whereas *3756* expresses an absolute denial); (adv.) *not,* (conj.) *lest;* also (as interrog. implying a *neg.* answer [whereas *3756* expects an *affirm.* one]) *whether:*—any, but, (that), × forbear, + God forbid, + lack, lest, neither, never, no (× wise in), none, nor, [can-] not, nothing, that not, un [-taken], without. Often used in compounds in substantially the same relations. See also *3362, 3363, 3364, 3372, 3373, 3375, 3378.*

3362. *ἐὰν μή* **ĕan mē,** *eh-an´ may;* i.e. *1437* and *3361; if not,* i.e. *unless:*—× before, but, except, if no, (if, + whosoever) not.

3363. *ἵνα μή* **hina mē,** *hin´-ah may;* i.e. *2443* and *3361; in order* (or *so*) *that not:*—albeit not, lest, that no (-t, [-thing]).

3364. *οὐ μή* **ŏu mē,** *oo may;* i.e. *3756* and *3361;* a double neg. strengthening the denial; *not at all:*—any more, at all, by any (no) means, neither, never, no (at all), in no case (wise), nor ever, not (at all, in any wise). Comp. *3378.*

3365. *μηδαμῶς* **mēdamōs,** *may-dam-oce´;* adv. from a comp. of *3361* and *ἀμός* **amŏs** (*somebody*); *by no means:*—not so.

3366. *μηδέ* **mēdĕ,** *may-deh´;* from *3361* and *1161; but not, not even;* in a continued negation, *nor:*—neither, nor (yet), (no) not (once, so much as).

3367. *μηδείς* **mēdĕis,** *may-dice´;* includ. the irreg. fem. *μηδεμία* **mēdĕmia,** *may-dem-ee´-ah,* and the neut. *μηδέν* **mēdĕn,** *may-den´;* from *3361* and *1520; not even one* (man, woman, thing):—any (man, thing), no (man), none, not (at all, any man, a whit), nothing, + without delay.

3368. *μηδέποτε* **mēdĕpŏtĕ,** *may-dep´-ot-eh;* from *3366* and *4218; not even ever:*—never.

3369. *μηδέπω* **mēdĕpō,** *may-dep´-o;* from *3366* and *4452; not even yet:*—not yet.

3370. *Μῆδος* **Mēdŏs,** *may´-dos;* of for. or. [comp. 4074]; a *Median,* or inhab. of Media:—Mede.

3371. *μηκέτι* **mēkĕti,** *may-ket´-ee;* from *3361* and *2089; no further:*—any longer, (not) henceforth, hereafter, no henceforward (longer, more, soon), not any more.

3372. *μῆκος* **mēkŏs,** *may´-kos;* prob. akin to *3173; length* (lit. or fig.):—length.

3373. *μηκύνω* **mēkunō,** *may-koo´-no;* from *3372;* to *lengthen,* i.e. (mid.) to *enlarge:*—grow up.

3374. *μηλωτή* **mēlōtē,** *may-lo-tay´;* from *μῆλον* **mēlŏn** (a *sheep*); a *sheep-skin:*—sheepskin.

3375. *μήν* **mēn,** *mane;* a stronger form of *3303;* a particle of affirmation (only with *2229*); *assuredly:*— + surely.

3376. *μήν* **mēn,** *mane;* a prim. word; a *month:*—month.

3377. *μηνύω* **mēnuō,** *may-noo´-o;* prob. from the same base as *3145* and *3415* (i.e. *μάω* **maō,** to *strive*); to *disclose* (through the idea of mental *effort* and thus calling to *mind*), i.e. *report, declare, intimate:*—shew, tell.

3378. *μὴ οὐκ* **mē ŏuk,** *may ook;* i.e. *3361* and *3756;* as interrog. and neg. *is it not that?:*—neither (followed by *no*), + never, not. Comp. *3364.*

3379. *μήποτε* **mēpŏtĕ,** *may´-pot-eh;* or
μή ποτε **mē pŏtĕ,** *may pot´-eh;* from *3361* and *4218; not ever;* also *if* (or *lest*) *ever* (or *perhaps*):—if peradventure, lest (at any time, haply), not at all, whether or not.

3380. *μήπω* **mēpō,** *may´-po;* from *3361* and *4452; not yet:*—not yet.

3381. *μήπως* **mēpōs,** *may´-poce;* or
μή πως **mē pōs,** *may poce;* from *3361* and *4458; lest somehow:*—lest (by any means, by some means, haply, perhaps).

3382. *μηρός* **mērŏs,** *may-ros´;* perh. a prim. word; a *thigh:*—thigh.

3383. *μήτε* **mētĕ,** *may´-teh;* from *3361* and *5037; not too,* i.e. (in continued negation) *neither* or *nor;* also, *not even:*—neither, (n-) or, so much as.

3384. *μήτηρ* **mētēr,** *may´-tare;* appar. a prim. word; a *"mother"* (lit. or fig., immed. or remote):—mother.

3385. *μήτι* **mēti,** *may´-tee;* from *3361* and the neut. of *5100; whether at all:*—not [*the particle usually not expressed, except by the form of the question*].

3386. *μήτιγε* **mētigĕ,** *may´-tig-eh;* from *3385* and *1065; not at all then,* i.e. *not to say* (*the rather still*):—how much more.

3387. *μήτις* **mētis,** *may´-tis;* or *μή τις* **mē tis,** *may tis;* from *3361* and *5100; whether any:*—any [*sometimes unexpressed except by the simple interrogative form of the sentence*].

3388. *μήτρα* **mētra,** *may´-trah;* from *3384;* the *matrix:*—womb.

3389. *μητραλῴας* **mētralōias,** *may-tral-o´-as;* from *3384* and the base of *257;* a *mother-thresher,* i.e. *matricide:*—murderer of mothers.

3390. *μητρόπολις* **mētrŏpŏlis,** *may-trop´-ol-is;* from *3384* and *4172;* a *mother city,* i.e. *"metropolis"*:—chiefest city.

3391. *μία* **mia,** *mee´-ah;* irreg. fem. of *1520; one* or *first:*—a (certain), + agree, first, one, × other.

3392. *μιαίνω* **miainō,** *me-ah´ee-no;* perh. a prim. verb; to *sully* or *taint,* i.e. *contaminate* (cer. or mor.):—defile.

3393. *μίασμα* **miasma,** *mee´-as-mah;* from *3392* (*"miasma"*); (mor.) *foulness* (prop. the effect):—pollution.

3394. *μιασμός* **miasmŏs,** *mee-as-mos´;* from *3392;* (mor.) *contamination* (prop. the act):—uncleanness.

3395. *μίγμα* **migma,** *mig´-mah;* from *3396;* a *compound:*—mixture.

3396. *μίγνυμι* **mignumi,** *mig´-noo-mee;* a prim. verb; to *mix:*—mingle.

3397. *μικρόν* **mikrŏn,** *mik-ron´;* masc. or neut. sing. of *3398* (as noun); a *small* space of *time* or *degree:*—a (little) (while).

3398. *μικρός* **mikrŏs,** *mik-ros´;* includ. the comp. *μικρότερος* **mikrŏtĕrŏs,** *mik-rot´-er-os;* appar. a prim. word; *small* (in size, quantity, number or (fig.) dignity):—least, less, little, small.

3399. Μίλητος **Milētŏs,** *mil´-ay-tos;* of uncert. or.; *Miletus,* a city of Asia Minor:—Miletus.

3400. *μίλιον* **miliŏn,** *mil´-ee-on;* of Lat. or.: a *thousand* paces, i.e. a *"mile"*:—mile.

3401. *μιμέομαι* **mimĕŏmai,** *mim-eh´-om-ahee;* mid. from *μῖμος* **mimŏs** (a *"mimic"*); to *imitate:*—follow.

3402. *μιμητής* **mimētēs,** *mim-ay-tace´;* from *3401;* an *imitator:*—follower.

3403. *μιμνήσκω* **mimnēskō,** *mim-nace´-ko;* a prol. form of *3415* (from which some of the tenses are borrowed); to *remind,* i.e. (mid.) to *recall to mind:*—be mindful, remember.

3404. *μισέω* **misĕō,** *mis-eh´-o;* from a prim. *μῖσος* **misŏs** (*hatred*); to *detest* (espec. to *persecute*); by extens. to *love less:*—hate (-ful).

3405. *μισθαποδοσία* **misthapŏdŏsia,** *mis-thap-od-os-ee´ah;* from *3406; requital* (good or bad):—recompence of reward.

3406. *μισθαποδότης* **misthapŏdŏtēs,** *mis-thap-od-ot´-ace;* from *3409* and *591;* a *remunerator:*—rewarder.

3407. *μίσθιος* **misthiŏs,** *mis´-thee-os;* from *3408;* a *wage-earner:*—hired servant.

3408. *μισθός* **misthŏs,** *mis-thos´;* appar. a prim. word; *pay* for service (lit. or fig.), good or bad:—hire, reward, wages.

3409. *μισθόω* **misthŏō,** *mis-tho´-o;* from *3408;* to *let* out for wages, i.e. (mid.) to *hire:*—hire.

3410. *μίσθωμα* **misthōma,** *mis´-tho-mah;* from *3409;* a *rented* building:—hired house.

3411. *μισθωτός* **misthōtŏs,** *mis-tho-tos´;* from *3409;* a *wage-worker* (good or bad):—hired servant, hireling.

3412. Μιτυλήνη **Mitulēnē,** *mit-oo-lay´-nay;* for *μυτιλήνη* **mutilēnē** (*abounding in shell-fish*); *Mitylene* (or *Mytilene*), a town in the island Lesbos:—Mitylene.

3413. Μιχαήλ **Michaēl,** *mikh-ah-ale´;* of Heb. or. [4317]; *Michaël,* an archangel:—Michael.

3414. *μνᾶ* **mna,** *mnah;* of Lat. or.; a *mna* (i.e. *mina*), a certain *weight:*—pound.

3415. *μνάομαι* **mnaŏmai,** *mnah´-om-ahee;* mid. of a der. of *3306* or perh. of the base of *3145* (through the idea of *fixture* in the mind or of mental *grasp*); to *bear in mind,* i.e. *recollect;* by impl. to *reward* or *punish:*—be mindful, remember, come (have) in remembrance. Comp. *3403.*

3416. Μνάσων **Mnasōn,** *mnah´-sohn;* of uncert. or.; *Mnason,* a Chr.:—Mnason.

3417. *μνεία* **mnĕia,** *mni´-ah;* from *3415* or *3403; recollection;* by impl. *recital:*—mention, remembrance.

3418. *μνῆμα* **mnēma,** *mnay´-mah;* from *3415;* a *memorial,* i.e. sepulchral *monument* (*burial-place*):—grave, sepulchre, tomb.

3419. *μνημεῖον* **mnēmĕiŏn,** *mnay-mi´-on;* from *3420;* a *remembrance,* i.e. *cenotaph* (*place of interment*):—grave, sepulchre, tomb.

3420. *μνήμη* **mnēmē,** *mnay´-may;* from *3403; memory:*—remembrance.

3421. *μνημονεύω* **mnēmŏnĕuō,** *mnay-mon-yoo´-o;* from a der. of *3420;* to *exercise memory,* i.e. *recollect;* by impl. to *punish;* also to *rehearse:*—make mention, be mindful, remember.

3422. *μνημόσυνον* **mnēmŏsunŏn,** *mnay-mos´-oo-non;* from *3421;* a *reminder* (*memorandum*), i.e. *record:*—memorial.

3423. *μνηστεύω* **mnēstĕuō,** *mnace-tyoo´-o;* from a der. of *3415;* to *give a souvenir* (engagement present), i.e. *betroth:*—espouse.

3424. *μογιλάλος* **mŏgilalŏs,** *mog-il-al´-os;* from *3425* and *2980; hardly talking,* i.e. *dumb* (*tongue-tied*):—having an impediment in his speech.

3425. *μόγις* **mŏgis,** *mog´-is;* adv. from a prim. *μόγος* **mŏgŏs** (*toil*); *with difficulty:*—hardly.

3426. *μόδιος* **mŏdiŏs,** *mod´-ee-os;* of Lat. or.; a *modius,* i.e. certain measure for things dry (the quantity or the utensil):—bushel.

3427. *μοί* **mŏi,** *moy;* the simpler form of *1698; to me:*—I, me, mine, my.

3428. *μοιχαλίς* **mŏichalis,** *moy-khal-is´;* a prol. form of the fem. of *3432;* an *adulteress* (lit. or fig.):—adulteress (-ous, -y).

3429. *μοιχάω* **mŏichaō,** *moy-khah´-o;* from *3432;* (mid.) to *commit adultery:*—commit adultery.

3430. *μοιχεία* **mŏichĕia,** *moy-khi´-ah;* from *3431; adultery:*—adultery.

3431. *μοιχεύω* **mŏichĕuō,** *moy-khyoo´-o;* from *3432;* to *commit adultery:*—commit adultery.

3432. *μοιχός* **mŏichŏs,** *moy-khos´;* perh. a prim. word; a (male) *paramour;* fig. *apostate:*—adulterer.

3433. *μόλις* **mŏlis,** *mol´-is;* prob. by var. for *3425; with difficulty:*—hardly, scarce (-ly), + with much work.

3434. Μολόχ **Mŏlŏch,** *mol-okh´;* of Heb. or. [4432]; *Moloch* (i.e. *Molek*), an idol:—Moloch.

3435. *μολύνω* **mŏlunō,** *mol-oo´-no;* prob. from *3189;* to *soil* (fig.):—defile.

3436. *μολυσμός* **mŏlusmŏs,** *mol-oos-mos´;* from *3435;* a *stain,* i.e. (fig.) *immorality:*—filthiness.

3437. *μομφή* **mŏmphē,** *mom-fay´;* from *3201; blame,* i.e. (by impl.) a *fault:*—quarrel.

3438. *μονή* **mŏnē,** *mon-ay´;* from *3306;* a *staying,* i.e. *residence* (the act or the place):—abode, mansion.

3439. *μονογενής* **mŏnŏgĕnēs,** *mon-og-en-ace´;* from *3441* and *1096; only-born,* i.e. *sole:*—only (begotten, child).

3440. *μόνον* **mŏnŏn,** *mon´-on;* neut. of *3441* as adv.; *merely:*—alone, but, only.

3441. *μόνος* **mŏnŏs,** *mon´-os;* prob. from *3306; remaining,* i.e. *sole* or *single;* by impl. *mere:*—alone, only, by themselves.

3442. *μονόφθαλμος* **mŏnŏphthalmŏs,** *mon-of´-thal-mos;* from *3441* and *3788; one-eyed:*—with one eye.

3443. *μονόω* **mŏnŏō,** *mon-ŏ´-o;* from *3441;* to *isolate,* i.e. *bereave:*—be desolate.

3444. μορφή **mŏrphē,** *mor-fay´;* perh. from the base of *3313* (through the idea of *adjustment* of parts); *shape;* fig. *nature:*—form.

3445. μορφόω **mŏrphŏō,** *mor-fŏ´-o;* from the same as *3444;* to *fashion* (fig.):—form.

3446. μόρφωσις **mŏrphōsis,** *mor´-fo-sis;* from *3445; formation,* i.e. (by impl.) *appearance* (*semblance* or [concr.] *formula*):—form.

3447. μοσχοποιέω **mŏschŏpŏiĕō,** *mos-khop-oy-eh´-o;* from *3448* and *4160;* to *fabricate* the image of a *bullock:*—make a calf.

3448. μόσχος **mŏschŏs,** *mos´-khos;* prob. strengthened for ὄσχος **ŏschŏs** (a *shoot*); a young *bullock:*—calf.

3449. μόχθος **mŏchthŏs,** *mokh´-thos;* from the base of *3425; toil,* i.e. (by impl.) *sadness:*—painfulness, travail.

3450. μοῦ **mŏu,** *moo;* the simpler form of *1700; of me:*—I, me, mine (own), my.

3451. μουσικός **mŏusikŏs,** *moo-sik-os´;* from Μοῦσα **Mŏusa** (a *Muse*); *"musical",* i.e. (as noun) a *minstrel:*—musician.

3452. μυελός **muĕlŏs,** *moo-el-os´;* perh. a prim. word; the *marrow:*—marrow.

3453. μυέω **muĕō,** *moo-eh´-o;* from the base of *3466;* to *initiate,* i.e. (by impl.) to *teach:*—instruct.

3454. μῦθος **muthŏs,** *moo-´thos;* perh. from the same as *3453* (through the idea of *tuition*); a *tale,* i.e. *fiction* (*"myth"*):—fable.

3455. μυκάομαι **mukaŏmai,** *moo-kah´-om-ahee;* from a presumed der. of μύζω **muzō** (to *"moo"*); to *bellow* (*roar*):—roar.

3456. μυκτηρίζω **muktērizō,** *mook-tay-rid´-zo;* from a der. of the base of *3455* (mean. *snout,* as that whence *lowing* proceeds); to *make mouths* at, i.e. *ridicule:*—mock.

3457. μυλικός **mulikŏs,** *moo-lee-kos´;* from *3458; belonging to a mill:*—mill [-stone].

3458. μύλος **mulŏs,** *moo´-los;* prob. ultimately from the base of *3433* (through the idea of *hardship*); a *"mill",* i.e. (by impl.) a *grinder* (*millstone*):—millstone.

3459. μύλων **mulōn,** *moo´-lone;* from *3458;* a *mill-house:*—mill.

3460. Μύρα **Mura,** *moo´-rah;* of uncert. der.; *Myra,* a place in Asia Minor:—Myra.

3461. μυριάς **murias,** *moo-ree´-as;* from *3463;* a *ten-thousand;* by extens. a *"myriad"* or indefinite number:—ten thousand.

3462. μυρίζω **murizō,** *moo-rid´-zo;* from *3464;* to *apply* (perfumed) *unguent* to:—anoint.

3463. μύριοι **muriŏi,** *moo´-ree-oi;* plur. of an appar. prim. word (prop. mean. *very many*); *ten thousand;* by extens. *innumerably* many:—ten thousand.

3464. μύρον **murŏn,** *moo´-ron;* prob. of for. or. [comp. 4753, *4666*]; *"myrrh",* i.e. (by impl.) *perfumed oil:*—ointment.

3465. Μυσία **Musia,** *moo-see´-ah;* of uncert. or.; *Mysia,* a region of Asia Minor:—Mysia.

3466. μυστήριον **mustēriŏn,** *moos-tay´-ree-on;* from a der. of μύω **muō** (to *shut* the mouth); a *secret* or *"mystery"* (through the idea of *silence* imposed by *initiation* into religious rites):—mystery.

3467. μυωπάζω **muōpazō,** *moo-ope-ad´-zo;* from a comp. of the base of *3466* and ὤψ **ōps** (the *face:* from *3700*); to *shut* the *eyes,* i.e. *blink* (*see indistinctly*):—cannot see afar off.

3468. μώλωψ **mōlōps,** *mo´-lopes;* from μῶλος **mōlŏs** (*"moil";* prob. akin to the base of *3433*) and prob. ὤψ **ōps** (the *face;* from *3700*); a *mole* ("black eye") or *blow-mark:*—stripe.

3469. μωμάομαι **mōmaŏmai,** *mo-mah´-om-ahee;* from *3470;* to *carp* at, i.e. *censure* (*discredit*):—blame.

3470. μῶμος **mōmŏs,** *mo´-mos;* perh. from *3201;* a *flaw* or *blot,* i.e. (fig.) *disgraceful* person:—blemish.

3471. μωραίνω **mōrainō,** *mo-rah´-ee-no;* from *3474;* to *become insipid;* fig. to *make* (pass. *act*) as a *simpleton:*—become fool, make foolish, lose savour.

3472. μωρία **mōria,** *mo-ree´-ah;* from *3474; silliness,* i.e. *absurdity:*—foolishness.

3473. μωρολογία **mōrŏlŏgia,** *mo-rol-og-ee´-ah;* from a comp. of *3474* and *3004; silly talk,* i.e. *buffoonery:*—foolish talking.

3474. μωρός **mōrŏs,** *mo-ros´;* prob. from the base of *3466; dull* or *stupid* (as if *shut* up), i.e. *heedless,* (mor.) *blockhead,* (appar.) *absurd:*—fool (-ish, × -ishness).

3475. Μωσεύς **Mōsĕus,** *moce-yoos´;* or
Μωσῆς **Mōsēs,** *mo-sace´;* or
Μωϋσῆς **Mōüsēs,** *mo-oo-sace´;* of Heb. or.; [4872]; *Moseus, Moses* or *Moüses* (i.e. *Mosheh*), the Heb. lawgiver:—Moses.

N

3476. Ναασσών **Naassōn,** *nah-as-sone´;* of Heb. or. [5177]; *Naasson* (i.e. *Nachshon*), an Isr.:—Naasson.

3477. Ναγγαί **Naggai,** *nang-gah´ee;* prob. of Heb. or. [comp. 5052]; *Nangæ* (i.e. perh. *Nogach*), an Isr.:—Nagge.

3478. Ναζαρέθ **Nazarĕth,** *nad-zar-eth´;* or
Ναζαρέτ **Nazarĕt,** *nad-zar-et´;* of uncert. der.; *Nazareth* or *Nazaret,* a place in Pal.:—Nazareth.

3479. Ναζαρηνός **Nazarēnŏs,** *nad-zar-ay-nos´;* from *3478;* a *Nazarene,* i.e. inhab. of Nazareth:—of Nazareth.

3480. Ναζωραῖος **Nazōraiŏs,** *nad-zo-rah´-yos;* from *3478;* a *Nazoræan,* i.e. inhab. of Nazareth; by extens. a *Christian:*—Nazarene, of Nazareth.

3481. Ναθάν **Nathan,** *nath-an´;* of Heb. or. [5416]; *Nathan,* an Isr.:—Nathan.

3482. Ναθαναήλ **Nathanaēl,** *nath-an-ah-ale´;* of Heb. or. [5417]; *Nathanaël* (i.e. *Nathanel*), an Isr. and Chr.:—Nathanael.

3483. ναί **nai,** *nahee;* a prim. particle of strong affirmation; *yes:*—even so, surely, truth, verily, yea, yes.

3484. Ναΐν **Naïn,** *nah-in´;* prob. of Heb. or. [comp. 4999]; *Naïn,* a place in Pal.:—Nain.

3485. ναός **naŏs,** *nah-os´;* from a prim. ναίω **naiō** (to *dwell*); a *fane, shrine, temple:*—shrine, temple. Comp. *2411.*

3486. Ναούμ **Naŏum,** *nah-oom´;* of Heb. or. [5151]; *Naüm* (i.e. *Nachum*), an Isr.:—Naum.

3487. νάρδος **nardŏs,** *nar´-dos;* of for. or. [comp. 5373]; *"nard":*—[spike-] nard.

3488. Νάρκισσος **Narkissŏs,** *nar´-kis-sos;* a flower of the same name, from ναρκη **narkē** (*stupefaction,* as a "narcotic"); *Narcissus,* a Roman:—Narcissus.

3489. ναυαγέω **nauagĕō,** *nŏw-ag-eh´-o;* from a comp. of *3491* and *71;* to *be shipwrecked* (*stranded,* "navigate"), lit. or fig.:—make (suffer) shipwreck.

3490. ναύκληρος **nauklērŏs,** *nŏw´-klay-ros;* from *3491* and *2819* ("clerk"); a *captain:*—owner of a ship.

3491. ναῦς **naus,** *nŏwce;* from νάω **naō** or νέω **nĕō** (to *float*); a *boat* (of any size):—ship.

3492. ναύτης **nautēs,** *now´-tace;* from *3491;* a *boatman,* i.e. *seaman:*—sailor, shipman.

3493. Ναχώρ **Nachōr,** *nakh-ore´;* of Heb. or. [5152]; *Nachor,* the grandfather of Abraham:—Nachor.

3494. νεανίας **nĕanias,** *neh-an-ee´-as;* from a der. of *3501;* a *youth* (up to about forty years):—young man.

3495. νεανίσκος **nĕaniskŏs,** *neh-an-is´-kos;* from the same as *3494;* a *youth* (under forty):—young man.

3496. Νεάπολις **Nĕapŏlis,** *neh-ap´-ol-is;* from *3501* and *4172; new town; Neäpolis,* a place in Macedonia:—Neapolis.

3497. Νεεμάν **Nĕĕman,** *neh-eh-man´;* of Heb. or. [5283]; *Neëman* (i.e. *Naaman*), a Syrian:—Naaman.

3498. νεκρός **nĕkrŏs,** *nek-ros´;* from an appar. prim. νέκυς **nĕkus** (a *corpse*); *dead* (lit. or fig.; also as noun):—dead.

3499. νεκρόω **nĕkrŏō,** *nek-rŏ´-o;* from *3498;* to *deaden,* i.e. (fig.) to *subdue:*—be dead, mortify.

3500. νέκρωσις **nĕkrōsis,** *nek´-ro-sis;* from *3499; decease;* fig. *impotency:*—deadness, dying.

3501. νέος **nĕŏs,** *neh´-os;* includ. the comp.
νεώτερος **nĕōtĕrŏs,** *neh-o´-ter-os;* a prim. word; *"new",* i.e. (of persons) *youthful,* or (of things) *fresh;* fig. *regenerate:*—new, young.

3502. νεοσσός **nĕŏssŏs,** *neh-os-sos´;* from *3501;* a *youngling* (*nestling*):—young.

3503. νεότης **nĕŏtēs,** *neh-ot´-ace;* from *3501; newness,* i.e. *youthfulness:*—youth.

3504. *νεόφυτος* **nĕŏphutŏs,** *neh-of´-oo-tos;* from *3501* and a der. of *5453; newly planted,* i.e. (fig.) a *young convert* (*"neophyte"*):—novice.

3505. Νέρων **Nĕrōn,** *ner´-ohn;* of Lat. or.; *Neron* (i.e. *Nero*), a Rom. emperor:—Nero.

3506. *νεύω* **nĕuō,** *nyoo´-o;* appar. a prim. verb; to *"nod"*, i.e. (by anal.) to *signal:*—beckon.

3507. *νεφέλη* **nĕphĕlē,** *nef-el´-ay;* from *3509;* prop. *cloudiness,* i.e. (concr.) a *cloud:*—cloud.

3508. Νεφθαλείμ **Nĕphthalĕim,** *nef-thal-ime´;* of Heb. or. [5321]; *Nephthaleim* (i.e. *Naphthali*), a tribe in Pal.:—Nephthalim.

3509. *νέφος* **nĕphŏs,** *nef´-os;* appar. a prim. word; a *cloud:*—cloud.

3510. *νεφρός* **nĕphrŏs,** *nef-ros´;* of uncert. affin.; a *kidney* (plur.), i.e. (fig.) the inmost *mind:*—reins.

3511. *νεωκόρος* **nĕōkŏrŏs,** *neh-o-kor´-os;* from a form of *3485* and *κορέω* **kŏrĕō** (to *sweep*); a *temple-servant,* i.e. (by impl.) a *votary:*—worshipper.

3512. *νεωτερικός* **nĕōtĕrikŏs,** *neh-o-ter´-ik-os;* from the comp. of *3501; appertaining to younger* persons, i.e. *juvenile:*—youthful.

νεώτερος **nĕōtĕrŏs.** See *3501.*

3513. *νή* **nē,** *nay;* prob. an intens. form of *3483;* a particle of attestation (accompanied by the object invoked or appealed to in confirmation); *as sure as:*—I protest by.

3514. *νήθω* **nēthō,** *nay´-tho;* from *νέω* **nĕō** (of like mean.); to *spin:*—spin.

3515. *νηπιάζω* **nēpiazō,** *nay-pee-ad´-zo;* from *3516;* to *act* as a *babe,* i.e. (fig.) *innocently:*—be a child.

3516. *νήπιος* **nēpiŏs,** *nay´-pee-os;* from an obsol. particle *νη-* **nē-** (implying *negation*) and *2031; not speaking,* i.e. an *infant* (*minor*); fig. a *simple-minded* person, an *immature* Christian:—babe, child (+ -ish).

3517. Νηρεύς **Nērĕus,** *nare-yoos´;* appar. from a der. of the base of *3491* (mean. *wet*); *Nereus,* a Chr.:—Nereus.

3518. Νηρί **Nēri,** *nay-ree´;* of Heb. or. [5374]; *Neri* (i.e. *Nerijah*), an Isr.:—Neri.

3519. *νησίον* **nēsiŏn,** *nay-see´-on;* dimin. of *3520;* an *islet:*—island.

3520. *νῆσος* **nēsŏs,** *nay´-sos;* prob. from the base of *3491;* an *island:*—island, isle.

3521. *νηστεία* **nēstĕia,** *nace-ti´-ah;* from *3522; abstinence* (from lack of food, or voluntary and religious); spec. the *fast* of the Day of Atonement:—fast (-ing.)

3522. *νηστεύω* **nēstĕuō,** *nace-tyoo´-o;* from *3523;* to *abstain* from food (religiously):—fast.

3523. *νῆστις* **nēstis,** *nace´-tis;* from the insep. neg. particle *νη-* **nē-** (*not*) and *2068; not eating,* i.e. *abstinent* from food (religiously):—fasting.

3524. *νηφάλεος* **nēphalĕŏs,** *nay-fal´-eh-os;* or *νηφάλιος* **nēphaliŏs,** *nay-fal´-ee-os;* from *3525; sober,* i.e. (fig.) *circumspect*—sober, vigilant.

3525. *νήφω* **nēphō,** *nay´-fo;* of uncert. affin.; to *abstain* from wine (*keep sober*), i.e. (fig.) *be discreet:*—be sober, watch.

3526. Νίγερ **Nigĕr,** *neeg´-er;* of Lat. or.; *black; Niger,* a Chr.:—Niger.

3527. Νικάνωρ **Nikanōr,** *nik-an´-ore;* prob. from *3528; victorious; Nicanor,* a Chr.:—Nicanor.

3528. *νικάω* **nikaō,** *nik-ah´-o;* from *3529;* to *subdue* (lit. or fig.):—conquer, overcome, prevail, get the victory.

3529. *νίκη* **nikē,** *nee´-kay;* appar. a prim. word; *conquest* (abstr.), i.e. (fig.) the *means of success:*—victory.

3530. Νικόδημος **Nikŏdēmŏs,** *nik-od´-ay-mos;* from *3534* and *1218; victorious* among his *people; Nicodemus,* an Isr.:—Nicodemus.

3531. Νικολαΐτης **Nikŏlaïtēs,** *nik-ol-ah-ee´-tace;* from *3532;* a *Nicolaïte,* i.e. adherent of *Nicolaüs:*—*Nicolaitane.*

3532. Νικόλαος **Nikŏlaŏs,** *nik-ol´-ah-os;* from *3534* and *2992; victorious* over the *people; Nicolaüs,* a heretic:—Nicolaus.

3533. Νικόπολις **Nikŏpŏlis,** *nik-op´-ol-is;* from *3534* and *4172; victorious city; Nicopolis,* a place in Macedonia:—Nicopolis.

3534. *νῖκος* **nikŏs,** *nee´-kos;* from *3529;* a *conquest* (concr.), i.e. (by impl.) *triumph:*—victory.

3535. Νινευΐ **Ninĕuï,** *nin-yoo-ee´;* of Heb. or. [5210]; *Ninevi* (i.e. *Nineveh*), the capital of Assyria:—Nineve.

3536. Νινευΐτης **Ninĕuïtēs,** *nin-yoo-ee´-tace;* from *3535;* a *Ninevite,* i.e. inhab. of Nineveh:—of Nineve, Ninevite.

3537. *νιπτήρ* **niptēr,** *nip-tare´;* from *3538;* a *ewer:*—bason.

3538. *νίπτω* **niptō,** *nip´-to;* to *cleanse* (espec. the hands or the feet or the face); cer. to *perform ablution:*—wash. Comp. *3068.*

3539. *νοιέω* **nŏiĕō,** *noy-eh´-o;* from *3563;* to *exercise* the *mind* (*observe*), i.e. (fig.) to *comprehend, heed:*—consider, perceive, think, understand.

3540. *νόημα* **nŏēma,** *nŏ´-ay-mah;* from *3539;* a *perception,* i.e. *purpose,* or (by impl.) the *intellect, disposition,* itself:—device, mind, thought.

3541. *νόθος* **nŏthŏs,** *noth´-os;* of uncert. affin.; a *spurious* or *illegitimate* son:—bastard.

3542. *νομή* **nŏmē,** *nom-ay´;* fem. from the same as *3551; pasture,* i.e. (the act) *feeding* (fig. *spreading* of a gangrene), or (the food) *pasturage:*—× eat, pasture.

3543. *νομίζω* **nŏmizō,** *nom-id´-zo;* from *3551;* prop. to *do* by *law* (*usage*), i.e. to *accustom* (pass. *be usual*); by extens. to *deem* or *regard:*—suppose, think, be wont.

3544. *νομικός* **nŏmikŏs,** *nom-ik-os´;* from *3551; according* (or *pertaining*) *to law,* i.e. *legal* (cer.); as noun, an *expert* in the (Mosaic) *law:*—about the law, lawyer.

3545. *νομίμως* **nŏmimōs,** *nom-im´-oce;* adv. from a der. of *3551; legitimately* (spec. agreeably to the rules of the lists):—lawfully.

3546. *νόμισμα* **nŏmisma,** *nom´-is-mah;* from *3543; what is reckoned* as of value (after the Lat. *numisma*), i.e. current *coin:*—money.

3547. *νομοδιδάσκαλος* **nŏmŏdidaskalŏs,** *nom-od-id-as´-kal-os;* from *3551* and *1320;* an *expounder of* the (Jewish) *law,* i.e. a *Rabbi:*—doctor (teacher) of the law.

3548. *νομοθεσία* **nŏmŏthĕsia,** *nom-oth-es-ee´-ah;* from *3550; legislation* (spec. the *institution of* the Mosaic *code*):—giving of the law.

3549. *νομοθετέω* **nŏmŏthĕtĕō,** *nom-oth-et-eh´-o;* from *3550;* to *legislate,* i.e. (pass.) to *have* (the Mosaic) *enactments* injoined, be *sanctioned* (by them):—establish, receive the law.

3550. *νομοθέτης* **nŏmŏthĕtēs,** *nom-oth-et´-ace;* from *3551* and a der. of *5087;* a *legislator:*—lawgiver.

3551. *νόμος* **nŏmŏs,** *nom´-os;* from a prim. *νέμω* **nĕmō** (to *parcel* out, espec. *food* or *grazing* to animals); *law* (through the idea of prescriptive *usage*), gen. (*regulation*), spec. (of Moses [includ. the volume]; also of the Gospel), or fig. (a *principle*):—law.

3552. *νοσέω* **nŏsĕō** *nos-eh´-o;* from *3554;* to *be sick,* i.e. (by impl. of a diseased appetite) to *hanker* after (fig. to *harp* upon):—dote.

3553. *νόσημα* **nŏsēma,** *nos´-ay-ma;* from *3552;* an *ailment:*—disease.

3554. *νόσος* **nŏsŏs,** *nos´-os;* of uncert. affin.; a *malady* (rarely fig. of mor. *disability*):—disease, infirmity, sickness.

3555. *νοσσιά* **nŏssia,** *nos-see-ah´;* from *3502;* a *brood* (of chickens):—brood.

3556. *νοσσίον* **nŏssiŏn,** *nos-see´-on;* dimin. of *3502;* a *birdling:*—chicken.

3557. *νοσφίζομαι* **nŏsphizŏmai,** *nos-fid´-zom-ahee;* mid. from *νοσφί* **nŏsphi** (*apart* or *clandestinely*); to *sequestrate* for oneself, i.e. *embezzle:*—keep back, purloin.

3558. *νότος* **nŏtŏs,** *not´-os;* of uncert. affin.; the *south* (*-west*) *wind;* by extens. the *southern quarter* itself:—south (wind).

3559. *νουθεσία* **nŏuthĕsia,** *noo-thes-ee´-ah;* from *3563* and a der. of *5087;* calling *attention* to, i.e. (by impl.) mild *rebuke* or *warning:*—admonition.

3560. *νουθετέω* **nŏuthĕtĕō,** *noo-thet-eh´-o;* from the same as *3559;* to *put in mind,* i.e. (by impl.) to *caution* or *reprove* gently:—admonish, warn.

3561. *νουμηνία* **nŏumēnia,** *noo-may-nee´-ah;* fem. of a comp. of *3501* and *3376* (as noun by impl. of *2250*); the festival of *new moon:*—new moon.

3562. νουνεχῶς **nŏunĕchōs,** *noon-ekh-oce´;* adv. from a comp. of the acc. of *3563* and *2192;* in a *mind-having* way, i.e. *prudently:*—discreetly.

3563. νοῦς **nŏus,** *nooce;* prob. from the base of *1097;* the *intellect,* i.e. *mind* (divine or human; in thought, feeling, or will); by impl. *meaning:*—mind, understanding. Comp. *5590.*

3564. Νυμφᾶς **Numphas,** *noom-fas´;* prob. contr. for a comp. of *3565* and *1435; nymph-given* (i.e. *-born*); *Nymphas,* a Chr.:—Nymphas.

3565. νύμφη **numphē,** *noom-fay´;* from a prim. but obsol. verb *νύπτω* **nuptō** (to *veil* as a bride; comp. Lat. *"nupto,"* to *marry*); a young *married* woman (as *veiled*), includ. a *betrothed* girl; by impl. a *son's wife:*—bride, daughter in law.

3566. νυμφίος **numphiŏs,** *noom-fee´-os;* from *3565;* a *bride-groom* (lit. or fig.):—bridegroom.

3567. νυμφών **numphōn,** *noom-fohn´;* from *3565;* the *bridal* room:—bridechamber.

3568. νῦν **nun,** *noon;* a prim. particle of present time; *"now"* (as adv. of date, a transition or emphasis); also as noun or adj. *present* or *immediate:*—henceforth, + hereafter, of late, soon, present, this (time). See also *3569, 3570.*

3569. τανῦν **tanun,** *tan-oon´;* or
τὰ νῦν **ta nun,** *tah noon;* from neut. plur. of *3588* and *3568; the* things *now,* i.e. (adv.) *at present:*—(but) now.

3570. νυνί **nuni,** *noo-nee´;* a prol. form of *3568* for emphasis; *just now:*—now.

3571. νύξ **nux,** *noox;* a prim. word; *"night"* (lit. or fig.):—(mid-) night.

3572. νύσσω **nussō,** *noos´-so;* appar. a prim. word; to *prick* ("nudge"):—pierce.

3573. νυστάζω **nustazō,** *noos-tad´-zo;* from a presumed der. of *3506;* to *nod,* i.e. (by impl.) to *fall asleep;* fig. to *delay:*—slumber.

3574. νυχθήμερον **nuchthēmĕrŏn,** *nookh-thay´-mer-on;* from *3571* and *2250;* a *day*-and-*night,* i.e. full *day* of twenty-four hours:—night and day.

3575. Νῶε **Nōĕ,** *no´-eh;* of Heb. or. [5146]; *Noë,* (i.e. *Noäch*), a patriarch:—Noe.

3576. νωθρός **nōthrŏs,** *no-thros´;* from a der. of *3541; sluggish,* i.e. (lit.) *lazy,* or (fig.) *stupid:*—dull, slothful.

3577. νῶτος **nōtŏs,** *no´-tos;* of uncert. affin.; the *back:*—back.

3578. ξενία **xĕnia,** *xen-ee´-ah;* from *3581; hospitality,* i.e. (by impl.) a *place of entertainment:*—lodging.

3579. ξενίζω **xĕnizō,** *xen-id´-zo;* from *3581;* to *be a host* (pass. a *guest*); by impl. *be* (*make, appear*) *strange:*—entertain, lodge, (think it) strange.

3580. ξενοδοχέω **xĕnŏdŏchĕō,** *xen-od-okh-eh´-o;* from a comp. of *3581* and *1209;* to *be hospitable:*—lodge strangers.

3581. ξένος **xĕnŏs,** *xen´-os;* appar. a prim. word; *foreign* (lit. *alien,* or fig. *novel*); by impl. a *guest* or (vice-versa) *entertainer:*—host, strange (-r).

3582. ξέστης **xĕstēs,** *xes´-tace;* as if from *ξέω* **xĕō** (prop. to *smooth;* by impl. [of *friction*] to *boil* or *heat*); a *vessel* (as *fashioned* or for *cooking*) [or perh. by corruption from the Lat. *sextarius,* the *sixth* of a modius, i.e. about a *pint*], i.e. (spec.) a *measure* for liquids or solids, (by anal. a *pitcher*):—pot.

3583. ξηραίνω **xērainō,** *xay-rah´ee-no;* from *3584;* to *desiccate;* by impl. to *shrivel,* to *mature:*—dry up, pine away, be ripe, wither (away).

3584. ξηρός **xērŏs,** *xay-ros´;* from the base of *3582* (through the idea of *scorching*); *arid;* by impl. *shrunken, earth* (as opposed to water):—dry, land, withered.

3585. ξύλινος **xulinŏs,** *xoo´-lin-os;* from *3586; wooden:*—of wood.

3586. ξύλον **xulŏn,** *xoo´-lon;* from another form of the base of *3582; timber* (as fuel or material); by impl. a *stick, club* or *tree* or other wooden article or substance:—staff, stocks, tree, wood.

3587. ξυράω **xuraō,** *xoo-rah´-o;* from a der. of the same as *3586* (mean. a *razor*); to *shave* or *"shear"* the hair:—shave.

O

3588. ὁ **hŏ,** *hŏ;* includ. the fem.
ἡ **hē,** *hay;* and the neut.
τό **tŏ,** *tŏ,* in all their inflections; the def. article; *the* (sometimes to be supplied, at others omitted in English idiom):—the, this, that, one, he, she, it, etc.
ὅ **hŏ.** See *3739.*

3589. ὀγδοήκοντα **ŏgdŏēkŏnta,** *og-dŏ-ay´-kon-tah;* from *3590; ten times eight:*—fourscore.

3590. ὄγδοος **ŏgdŏŏs,** *og´-dŏ-os;* from *3638;* the *eighth:*—eighth.

3591. ὄγκος **ŏgkŏs,** *ong´-kos;* prob. from the same as *43;* a *mass* (as *bending* or *bulging* by its load), i.e. *burden* (*hindrance*):—weight.

3592. ὅδε **hŏdĕ,** *hod´-eh;* includ. the fem.
ἥδε **hēdĕ,** *hay´-deh;* and the neut.
τόδε **tŏdĕ,** *tod´-e;* from *3588* and *1161;* the *same,* i.e. *this* or *that* one (plur. *these* or *those*); often used a pers. pron.:—he, she, such, these, thus.

3593. ὁδεύω **hŏdĕuō,** *hod-yoo´-o;* from *3598;* to *travel:*—journey.

3594. ὁδηγέω **hŏdēgĕō,** *hod-ayg-eh´-o;* from *3595;* to *show* the *way* (lit. or fig. [*teach*]):—guide, lead.

3595. ὁδηγός **hŏdēgŏs,** *hod-ayg-os´;* from *3598* and *2233;* a *conductor* (lit. or fig. [*teacher*]):—guide, leader.

3596. ὁδοιπορέω **hŏdŏipŏrĕō,** *hod-oy-por-eh´-o;* from a comp. of *3598* and *4198;* to *be a wayfarer,* i.e. *travel:*—go on a journey.

3597. ὁδοιπορία **hŏdŏipŏria,** *hod-oy-por-ee´-ah;* from the same as *3596; travel:*—journey (-ing).

3598. ὁδός **hŏdŏs,** *hod-os´;* appar. a prim. word; a *road;* by impl. a *progress* (the route, act or distance); fig. a *mode* or *means:*—journey, (high-) way.

3599. ὀδούς **ŏdŏus,** *od-ooce´;* perh. from the base of *2068;* a *"tooth":*—tooth.

3600. ὀδυνάω **ŏdunaō,** *od-oo-nah´-o;* from *3601;* to *grieve:*—sorrow, torment.

3601. ὀδύνη **ŏdunē,** *od-oo´-nay;* from *1416; grief* (as *dejecting*):—sorrow.

3602. ὀδυρμός **ŏdurmŏs,** *od-oor-mos´;* from a der. of the base of *1416; moaning,* i.e. *lamentation:*—mourning.

3603. ὅ ἐστι **hŏ esti,** *hŏ es-tee´;* from the neut. of *3739* and the third pers. sing. pres. ind. of *1510; which is:*—called, which is (make), that is (to say).

3604. Ὀζίας **Ŏzias,** *od-zee´-as;* of Heb. or. [5818]; *Ozias* (i.e. *Uzzijah*), an Isr.:—Ozias.

3605. ὄζω **ŏzō,** *od´-zo;* a prim. verb (in a strengthened form); to *scent* (usually an ill "odor"):—stink.

3606. ὅθεν **hŏthĕn,** *hoth´-en;* from *3739* with the directive enclitic of source; *from which* place or source or cause (adv. or conj.):—from thence, (from) whence, where (-by, -fore, -upon).

3607. ὀθόνη **ŏthŏnē,** *oth-on´-ay;* of uncert. affin.; a *linen* cloth, i.e. (espec.) a *sail:*—sheet.

3608. ὀθόνιον **ŏthŏniŏn,** *oth-on´-ee-on;* neut. of a presumed der. of *3607;* a linen *bandage:*—linen clothes.

3609. οἰκεῖος **ŏikĕiŏs,** *oy-ki´-os;* from *3624; domestic,* i.e. (as noun), a *relative, adherent:*—(those) of the (his own) house (-hold).

3610. οἰκέτης **ŏikĕtēs,** *oy-ket´-ace;* from *3611;* a fellow *resident,* i.e. menial *domestic:*—(household) servant.

3611. οἰκέω **ŏikĕō,** *ay-keh´-o;* from *3624;* to *occupy a house,* i.e. *reside* (fig. *inhabit, remain, inhere*); by impl. to *cohabit:*—dwell. See also *3625.*

3612. οἴκημα **ŏikēma,** *oy´-kay-mah;* from *3611;* a *tenement,* i.e. (spec.) a *jail:*—prison.

3613. οἰκητήριον **ŏikētēriŏn,** *oy-kay-tay´-ree-on;* neut. of a presumed der. of *3611* (equiv. to *3612*); a *residence* (lit. or fig.):—habitation, house.

3614. οἰκία **ŏikia,** *oy-kee´-ah;* from *3624;* prop. *residence* (abstr.), but usually (concr.) an *abode* (lit. or fig.); by impl. a *family* (espec. *domestics*):—home, house (-hold).

3615. οἰκιακός **ŏikiakŏs,** *oy-kee-ak-os´;* from *3614; familiar,* i.e. (as noun) *relatives:*—they (them) of (his own) household.

3616. οἰκοδεσποτέω **ŏikŏdĕspŏtĕō,** *oy-kod-es-pot-eh´-o;* from *3617;* to *be* the *head of* (i.e. *rule*) *a family:*—guide the house.

3617. οἰκοδεσπότης **ŏikŏdĕspŏtēs,** *oy-kod-es-pot´-ace;* from *3624* and *1203; the head of a family:*—goodman (of the house), householder, master of the house.

3618. οἰκοδομέω **ŏikŏdŏmĕō,** *oy-kod-om-eh´-o;* from the same as *3619;* to *be* a *house-builder,* i.e. *construct* or (fig.) *confirm:*—(be in) build (-er, -ing, up), edify, embolden.

3619. οἰκοδομή **ŏikŏdŏmē,** *oy-kod-om-ay´;* fem. (abstr.) of a comp. of *3624* and the base of *1430; architecture,* i.e. (concr.) a *structure;* fig. *confirmation:*—building, edify (-ication, -ing).

3620. οἰκοδομία **ŏikŏdŏmia,** *oy-kod-om-ee´-ah;* from the same as *3619; confirmation:*—edifying.

3621. οἰκονομέω **ŏikŏnŏmĕō,** *oy-kon-om-eh´-o;* from *3623;* to *manage* (a house, i.e. an estate):—be steward.

3622. οἰκονομία **ŏikŏnŏmia,** *oy-kon-om-ee´-ah;* from *3623; administration* (of a household or estate); spec. a (religious) *"economy"*:—dispensation, stewardship.

3623. οἰκονόμος **ŏikŏnŏmŏs,** *oy-kon-om´-os;* from *3624* and the base of *3551;* a *house-distributor* (i.e. *manager*), or *overseer,* i.e. an employee in that capacity; by extens. a fiscal *agent* (*treasurer*); fig. a *preacher* (of the Gospel):—chamberlain, governor, steward.

3624. οἶκος **ŏikŏs,** *oy´-kos;* of uncert. affin.; a *dwelling* (more or less extensive, lit. or fig.); by impl. a *family* (more or less related, lit. or fig.):—home, house (-hold), temple.

3625. οἰκουμένη **ŏikŏumĕnē,** *oy-kou-men´-ay;* fem. part. pres. pass. of *3611* (as noun, by impl. of *1093*); *land,* i.e. the (terrene part of the) *globe;* spec. the Roman *empire:*—earth, world.

3626. οἰκουρός **ŏikŏurŏs,** *oy-koo-ros´;* from *3624* and οὖρος **ŏurŏs** (a *guard;* be "ware"); a *stayer at home,* i.e. *domestically inclined* (a "good housekeeper"):—keeper at home.

3627. οἰκτείρω **ŏiktĕirō,** *oyk-ti´-ro;* also (in certain tenses) prol.

οἰκτερέω **ŏiktĕrĕō,** *oyk-ter-eh´-o;* from οἶκτος **ŏiktŏs** (*pity*); to *exercise pity:*—have compassion on.

3628. οἰκτιρμός **ŏiktirmŏs,** *oyk-tir-mos´;* from *3627; pity:*—mercy.

3629. οἰκτίρμων **ŏiktirmōn,** *oyk-tir´-mone;* from *3627; compassionate:*—merciful, of tender mercy.

οἶμαι **ŏimai.** See *3633.*

3630. οἰνοπότης **ŏinŏpŏtēs,** *oy-nop-ot´-ace;* from *3631* and a der. of the alt. of *4095;* a *tippler:*—winebibber.

3631. οἶνος **ŏinŏs,** *oy´-nos;* a prim. word (or perh. of Heb. or. [3196]); *"wine"* (lit. or fig.):—wine.

3632. οἰνοφλυγία **ŏinŏphlugia,** *oy-nof-loog-ee´-ah;* from *3631* and a form of the base of *5397;* an *overflow* (or surplus) of *wine,* i.e. *vinolency* (*drunkenness*):—excess of wine.

3633. οἴομαι **ŏiŏmai,** *oy´-om-ahee;* or (shorter)

οἶμαι **ŏimai,** *oy´-mahee;* mid. appar. from *3634;* to *make like* (oneself), i.e. *imagine* (*be of* the *opinion*):—suppose, think.

3634. οἷος **hŏiŏs,** *hoy´-os;* prob. akin to *3588, 3739,* and *3745; such* or *what sort* of (as a correl. or exclamation); espec. the neut. (adv.) with neg. not *so:*—so (as), such as, what (manner of), which.

οἴω **ŏiō.** See *5342.*

3635. ὀκνέω **ŏknĕō,** *ok-neh´-o;* from ὄκνος **ŏknŏs** (*hesitation*); to *be slow* (fig. *loath*):—delay.

3636. ὀκνηρός **ŏknērŏs,** *ok-nay-ros´;* from *3635; tardy,* i.e. *indolent;* (fig.) *irksome:*—grievous, slothful.

3637. ὀκταήμερος **ŏktaēmĕrŏs,** *ok-tah-ay´-mer-os;* from *3638* and *2250;* an *eight-day* old person or act:—the eighth day.

3638. ὀκτώ **ŏktō,** *ok-to´;* a prim. numeral; *"eight"*:—eight.

3639. ὄλεθρος **ŏlĕthrŏs,** *ol´-eth-ros;* from a prim. ὄλλυμι **ŏllumi** (to *destroy;* a prol. form); *ruin,* i.e. *death, punishment:*—destruction.

3640. ὀλιγόπιστος **ŏligŏpistŏs,** *ol-ig-op´-is-tos;* from *3641* and *4102; incredulous,* i.e. *lacking confidence* (in Christ):—of little faith.

3641. ὀλίγος **ŏligŏs,** *ol-ee´-gos;* of uncert. affin.; *puny* (in extent, degree, number, duration or value); espec. neut. (adv.) *somewhat:*— + almost, brief [-ly], few, (a) little, + long, a season, short, small, a while.

3642. ὀλιγόψυχος **ŏligŏpsuchŏs,** *ol-ig-op´-soo-khos;* from *3641* and *5590; little-spirited,* i.e. *faint-hearted:*—feebleminded.

3643. ὀλιγωρέω **ŏligōrĕō,** *ol-ig-o-reh´-o;* from a comp. of *3641* and ὤρα **ōra** (*"care"*); to *have little regard* for, i.e. to *disesteem:*—despise.

3644. ὀλοθρευτής **ŏlŏthrĕutēs,** *ol-oth-ryoo-tace´;* from *3645;* a *ruiner,* i.e. (spec.) a venomous *serpent:*—destroyer.

3645. ὀλοθρεύω **ŏlŏthrĕuō,** *ol-oth-ryoo´-o;* from *3639;* to *spoil,* i.e. *slay:*—destroy.

3646. ὁλοκαύτωμα **hŏlŏkautōma,** *hol-ok-ŏw´-to-mah;* from a der. of a comp. of *3650* and a der. of *2545;* a *wholly-consumed* sacrifice ("holocaust"):—(whole) burnt offering.

3647. ὁλοκληρία **hŏlŏklēria,** *hol-ok-lay-ree´-ah;* from *3648; integrity,* i.e. physical *wholeness:*—perfect soundness.

3648. ὁλόκληρος **hŏlŏklērŏs,** *hol-ok´-lay-ros;* from *3650* and *2819; complete* in every *part,* i.e. perfectly *sound* (in body):—entire, whole.

3649. ὀλολύζω **ŏlŏluzō,** *ol-ol-ood´-zo;* a redupl. prim. verb; to *"howl"* or *"halloo",* i.e. *shriek:*—howl.

3650. ὅλος **hŏlŏs,** *hol´-os;* a prim. word; *"whole"* or *"all",* i.e. *complete* (in extent, amount, time or degree), espec. (neut.) as noun or adv.:—all, altogether, every whit, + throughout, whole.

3651. ὁλοτελής **hŏlŏtĕlēs,** *hol-ot-el-ace´;* from *3650* and *5056; complete* to the *end,* i.e. *absolutely perfect:*—wholly.

3652. Ὀλυμπᾶς **Olumpas,** *ol-oom-pas´;* prob. a contr. from Ὀλυμπιόδωρος **Olumpiŏdōrŏs** (*Olympian-bestowed,* i.e. *heaven-descended*); *Olympas,* a Chr.:—Olympas.

3653. ὄλυνθος **ŏlunthŏs,** *ol´-oon-thos;* of uncert. der.; an *unripe* (because out of season) *fig:*—untimely fig.

3654. ὅλως **hŏlōs,** *hol´-oce;* adv. from *3650; completely,* i.e. *altogether;* (by anal.) *everywhere;* (neg.) not *by any means:*—at all, commonly, utterly.

3655. ὄμβρος **ŏmbrŏs,** *om´-bros;* of uncert. affin.; a thunder *storm:*—shower.

3656. ὁμιλέω **hŏmilĕō,** *hom-il-eh´-o;* from *3658;* to *be in company* with, i.e. (by impl.) to *converse:*—commune, talk.

3657. ὁμιλία **hŏmilia,** *hom-il-ee´-ah;* from *3658; companionship* ("homily"), i.e. (by impl.) *intercourse:*—communication.

3658. ὅμιλος **hŏmilŏs,** *hom´-il-os;* from the base of *3674* and a der. of the alt. of *138* (mean. a *crowd*); *association together,* i.e. a *multitude:*—company.

3659. ὄμμα **ŏmma,** *om´-mah;* from *3700;* a *sight,* i.e. (by impl.) the *eye:*—eye.

3660. ὀμνύω **ŏmnuō,** *om-noo´-o;* a prol. form of a prim. but obsol. ὄμω **ŏmō,** for which another prol. form (ὀμόω **ŏmŏō,** *om-ŏ´-o*) is used in certain tenses; to *swear,* i.e. *take* (or *declare on*) *oath:*—swear.

3661. ὁμοθυμαδόν **hŏmŏthumadŏn,** *hom-oth-oo-mad-on´;* adv. from a comp. of the base of *3674* and *2372; unanimously:*—with one accord (mind).

3662. ὁμοιάζω **hŏmŏiazō,** *hom-oy-ad´-zo;* from *3664;* to *resemble:*—agree.

3663. ὁμοιοπαθής **hŏmŏiŏpathēs,** *hom-oy-op-ath-ace´;* from *3664* and the alt. of *3958; similarly affected:*—of (subject to) like passions.

3664. ὅμοιος **hŏmŏiŏs,** *hom´-oy-os;* from the base of *3674; similar* (in appearance or character):—like, + manner.

3665. ὁμοιότης **hŏmŏiŏtēs,** *hom-oy-ot´-ace;* from *3664; resemblance:*—like as, similitude.

3666. ὁμοιόω **hŏmŏiŏō,** *hom-oy-ŏ´-o;* from *3664;* to *assimilate,* i.e. *compare;* pass. to *become similar:*—be (make) like, (in the) liken (-ess), resemble.

3667. ὁμοίωμα **hŏmŏiōma,** *hom-oy´-o-mah;* from *3666;* a *form;* abstr. *resemblance:*—made like to, likeness, shape, similitude.

3668. ὁμοίως **hŏmŏiōs,** *hom-oy´-oce;* adv. from *3364; similarly:*—likewise, so.

3669. ὁμοίωσις **hŏmŏiōsis,** *hom-oy´-o-sis;* from *3666; assimilation,* i.e. *resemblance:*—similitude.

3670. ὁμολογέω **hŏmŏlŏgĕō,** *hom-ol-og-eh´-o;* from a comp. of the base of *3674* and *3056;* to *assent,* i.e. *covenant, acknowledge:*—con- (pro-) fess, confession is made, give thanks, promise.

3671. ὁμολογία **hŏmŏlŏgia,** *hom-ol-og-ee´-ah;* from the same as *3670; acknowledgment:*—con- (pro-) fession, professed.

3672. ὁμολογουμένως **hŏmŏlŏgŏumĕnōs,** *hom-ol-og-ŏw-men´-oce;* adv. of pres. pass. part. of *3670; confessedly:*—without controversy.

3673. ὁμότεχνος **hŏmŏtĕchnŏs,** *hom-ot´-ekh-nos;* from the base of *3674* and *5078;* a *fellow-artificer:*—of the same craft.

3674. ὁμοῦ **hŏmŏu,** *hom-oo´;* gen. of ὁμός **hŏmŏs** (the *same;* akin to *260*) as adv.; *at* the *same* place or time:—together.

3675. ὁμόφρων **hŏmŏphrōn,** *hom-of´-rone;* from the base of *3674* and *5424; like-minded,* i.e. *harmonious:*—of one mind.

ὀμόω **ŏmŏō.** See *3660.*

3676. ὅμως **hŏmŏs,** *hom´-oce;* adv. from the base of *3674; at* the *same* time, i.e. (conj.) *notwithstanding, yet still:*—and even, nevertheless, though but.

3677. ὄναρ **ŏnar,** *on´-ar;* of uncert. der.; a *dream:*—dream.

3678. ὀνάριον **ŏnariŏn,** *on-ar´-ee-on;* neut. of a presumed der. of *3688;* a *little ass:*—young ass.

ὀνάω **ŏnaō.** See *3685.*

3679. ὀνειδίζω **ŏnĕidizō,** *on-i-did´-zo;* from *3681;* to *defame,* i.e. *rail at, chide, taunt:*—cast in teeth, (suffer) reproach, revile, upbraid.

3680. ὀνειδισμός **ŏnĕidismŏs,** *on-i-dis-mos´;* from *3679; contumely:*—reproach.

3681. ὄνειδος **ŏnĕidŏs,** *on´-i-dos;* prob. akin to the base of *3686; notoriety,* i.e. a *taunt* (*disgrace*):—reproach.

3682. Ὀνήσιμος **Ŏnēsimŏs,** *on-ay´-sim-os;* from *3685; profitable; Onesimus,* a Chr.:—Onesimus.

3683. Ὀνησίφορος **Ŏnēsiphŏrŏs,** *on-ay-sif´-or-os;* from a der. of *3685* and *5411; profit-bearer; Onesiphorus,* a Chr.:—Onesiphorus.

3684. ὀνικός **ŏnikŏs,** *on-ik-os´;* from *3688; belonging to* an *ass,* i.e. *large* (so as to be turned by an ass):—millstone.

3685. ὀνίνημι **ŏninēmi,** *on-in´-ay-mee;* a prol. form of an appar. prim. verb.

(ὄνομαι **ŏnŏmai,** to *slur*); for which another prol. form (ὀνάω **ŏnaō**) is used as an alt. in some tenses [unless indeed it be identical with the base of *3686* through the idea of *notoriety*]; to *gratify,* i.e. (mid.) to *derive pleasure* or *advantage* from:—have joy.

3686. ὄνομα **ŏnŏma,** *on´-om-ah;* from a presumed der. of the base of *1097* (comp. *3685*); a *"name"* (lit. or fig.) [*authority, character*]:—called, (+ sur-) name (-d).

3687. ὀνομάζω **ŏnŏmazō,** *on-om-ad´-zo;* from *3686;* to *name,* i.e. *assign an appellation;* by extens. to *utter, mention, profess:*—call, name.

3688. ὄνος **ŏnŏs,** *on´-os;* appar. a prim. word; a *donkey:*—ass.

3689. ὄντως **ŏntōs,** *on´-toce;* adv. of the oblique cases of *5607; really:*—certainly, clean, indeed, of a truth, verily.

3690. ὄξος **ŏxŏs,** *ox-os´;* from *3691; vinegar,* i.e. *sour* wine:—vinegar.

3691. ὀξύς **ŏxus,** *ox-oos´;* prob. akin to the base of *188* [*"acid"*]; *keen;* by anal. *rapid:*—sharp, swift.

3692. ὀπή **ŏpē,** *op-ay´;* prob. from *3700;* a *hole* (as if for light), i.e. *cavern;* by anal. a *spring* (of water):—cave, place.

3693. ὄπισθεν **ŏpisthĕn,** *op´-is-then;* from ὄπις **ŏpis** (*regard;* from *3700*) with enclitic of source; *from the rear* (as a secure *aspect*), i.e. *at* the *back* (adv. and prep. of place or time):—after, backside, behind.

3694. ὀπίσω **ŏpisō,** *op-is´-o;* from the same as *3693* with enclitic of direction; *to* the *back,* i.e. *aback* (as adv. or prep. of time or place; or as noun):—after, back (-ward), (+ get) behind, + follow.

3695. ὁπλίζω **hŏplizō,** *hop-lid´-zo;* from *3696;* to *equip* (with weapons [mid. and fig.]):—arm self.

3696. ὅπλον **hŏplŏn,** *hop´-lon;* prob. from a prim. ἕπω **hĕpō** (to be *busy* about); an *implement* or *utensil* or *tool* (lit. or fig., espec. offensive for war):—armour, instrument, weapon.

3697. ὁποῖος **hŏpŏiŏs,** *hop-oy´-os;* from *3739* and *4169;* of *what* kind *that,* i.e. *how* (*as*) *great* (*excellent*) (spec. as indef. correl. to anteced. def. *5108* of quality):—what manner (sort) of, such as, whatsoever.

3698. ὁπότε **hŏpŏtĕ,** *hop-ot´-eh;* from *3739* and *4218; what* (-ever) *then,* i.e. (of time) *as soon as:*—when.

3699. ὅπου **hŏpŏu,** *hop´-oo;* from *3739* and *4225; what* (-ever) *where,* i.e. *at whichever* spot:—in what place, where (-as, -soever), whither (+ soever).

3700. ὀπτάνομαι **ŏptanŏmai,** *op-tan´-om-ahee;* a (mid.) prol. form of the prim. (mid.)

ὄπτομαι **ŏptŏmai,** *op´-tom-ahee,* which is used for it in certain tenses; and both as alt. of *3708;* to *gaze* (i.e. with wide-open eyes, as at something remarkable; and thus differing from *991,* which denotes simply *voluntary* observation; and from *1492,* which expresses merely mechanical, passive or casual vision; while *2300,* and still more emphatically its intens. *2334,* signifies an earnest but more continued *inspection;* and *4648* a watching *from a distance*):—appear, look, see, shew self.

3701. ὀπτασία **ŏptasia,** *op-tas-ee´-ah;* from a presumed der. of *3700; visuality,* i.e. (concr.) an *apparition:*—vision.

ὄπτομαι **ŏptŏmai.** See *3700.*

3702. ὀπτός **ŏptŏs,** *op-tos´;* from an obsol. verb. akin to ἕψω **hĕpsō** (to *"steep"*); *cooked,* i.e. *roasted:*—broiled.

3703. ὀπώρα **ŏpōra,** *op-o´-rah;* appar. from the base of *3796* and *5610;* prop. *even-tide* of the (summer) season *(dog-days),* i.e. (by impl.) *ripe* fruit:—fruit.

3704. ὅπως **hŏpōs,** *hop´-oce;* from *3739* and *4459; what* (-ever) *how,* i.e. *in* the *manner that* (as adv. or conj. of coincidence, intentional or actual):—because, how, (so) that, to, when.

3705. ὅραμα **hŏrama,** *hor´-am-ah;* from *3708; something gazed at,* i.e. a *spectacle* (espec. supernat.):—sight, vision.

3706. ὅρασις **hŏrasis,** *hor´-as-is;* from *3708;* the act of *gazing,* i.e. (external) an *aspect* or (intern.) an inspired *appearance:*—sight, vision.

3707. ὁρατός **hŏratŏs,** *hor-at-os´;* from *3708; gazed at,* i.e. (by impl.) *capable of being seen:*—visible.

3708. ὁράω **hŏraō,** *hor-ah´-o;* prop. to *stare* at [comp. *3700*], i.e. (by impl.) to *discern* clearly (phys. or ment); by extens. to *attend* to; by Hebr. to *experience;* pass. to *appear:*—behold, perceive, see, take heed.

3709. ὀργή **ŏrgē,** *or-gay´;* from *3713;* prop. *desire* (as a *reaching* forth or *excitement* of the mind), i.e. (by anal.) violent *passion* (*ire,* or [justifiable] *abhorrence*); by impl. *punishment:*—anger, indignation, vengeance, wrath.

3710. ὀργίζω **ŏrgizō,** *or-gid´-zo;* from *3709;* to *provoke* or *enrage,* i.e. (pass) *become exasperated:*—be angry (wroth).

3711. ὀργίλος **ŏrgilŏs,** *org-ee´-los;* from *3709; irascible:*—soon angry.

3712. ὀργυιά **ŏrguia,** *org-wee-ah´;* from *3713;* a *stretch* of the arms, i.e. a *fathom:*—fathom.

3713. ὀρέγομαι **ŏrĕgŏmai,** *or-eg´-om-ahee;* mid. of appar. a prol. form of an obsol. prim. [comp. *3735*]; to *stretch* oneself, i.e. *reach* out after (*long* for):—covet after, desire.

3714. ὀρεινός **ŏrĕinŏs,** *or-i-nos´;* from *3735; mountainous,* i.e. (fem. by impl. of *5561*) the *Highlands* (of Judæa):—hill country.

3715. ὄρεξις **ŏrĕxis,** *or´-ex-is;* from *3713; excitement* of the mind, i.e. *longing* after:—lust.

3716. ὀρθοποδέω **ŏrthŏpŏdĕō,** *or-thop-od-eh´-o;* from a comp. of *3717* and *4228;* to *be straight-footed,* i.e. (fig.) to *go directly* forward:—walk uprightly.

3717. ὀρθός **ŏrthŏs,** *or-thos´;* prob. from the base of *3735; right* (as *rising*), i.e. (perpendicularly) *erect* (fig. *honest*), or (horizontally) *level* or *direct:*—straight, upright.

3718. ὀρθοτομέω **ŏrthŏtŏmĕō,** *or-thot-om-eh´-o;* from a comp. of *3717* and the base of *5114;* to *make* a *straight cut,* i.e. (fig.) to *dissect* (*expound*) *correctly* (the divine message):—rightly divide.

3719. ὀρθρίζω **ŏrthrizō,** *or-thrid´-zo;* from *3722,* to *use* the *dawn,* i.e. (by impl.) to *repair betimes:*—come early in the morning.

3720. ὀρθρινός **ŏrthrinŏs,** *or-thrin-os´;* from *3722; relating to* the *dawn,* i.e. *matutinal* (as an epithet of Venus, espec. brilliant in the early day):—morning.

3721. ὄρθριος **ŏrthriŏs,** *or´-three-os;* from *3722; in* the *dawn,* i.e. up *at day-break:*—early.

3722. ὄρθρος **ŏrthrŏs,** *or´-thros;* from the same as *3735; dawn* (as *sun-rise, rising* of light); by extens. *morn:*—early in the morning.

3723. ὀρθῶς **ŏrthōs,** *or-thoce´;* adv. from *3717; in a straight* manner, i.e. (fig.) *correctly* (also mor.):—plain, right (-ly).

3724. ὁρίζω **hŏrizō,** *hor-id´-zo;* from *3725;* to *mark* out or *bound* ("horizon"), i.e. (fig.) to *appoint, decree, specify:*—declare, determine, limit, ordain.

3725. ὅριον **hŏriŏn,** *hor´-ee-on;* neut. of a der. of an appar. prim. ὅρος **hŏrŏs** (a *bound* or *limit*); a *boundary*-line, i.e. (by impl.) a *frontier* (*region*):—border, coast.

3726. ὁρκίζω **hŏrkizō,** *hor-kid´-zo;* from *3727;* to *put on oath,* i.e. *make swear;* by anal. to solemnly *enjoin:*—adjure, charge.

3727. ὅρκος **hŏrkŏs,** *hor´-kos;* from ἕρκος **hĕrkŏs,** (a *fence;* perh. akin to *3725*); a *limit,* i.e. (sacred) *restraint (spec. oath):*—oath.

3728. ὁρκωμοσία **hŏrkōmŏsia,** *hor-ko-mos-ee´-ah;* from a comp. of *3727* and a der. of *3660; asseveration on oath:*—oath.

3729. ὁρμάω **hŏrmaō,** *hor-mah´-o;* from *3730;* to *start, spur* or *urge* on, i.e. (reflex.) to *dash* or *plunge:*—run (violently), rush.

3730. ὁρμή **hŏrmē,** *hor-may´;* of uncert. affin.; a violent *impulse,* i.e. *onset:*—assault.

3731. ὅρμημα **hŏrmēma,** *hor´-may-mah;* from *3730;* an *attack,* i.e. (abstr.) *precipitancy:*—violence.

3732. ὄρνεον **ŏrnĕŏn,** *or´-neh-on;* neut. of a presumed der. of *3733;* a *birdling:*—bird, fowl.

3733. ὄρνις **ŏrnis,** *or´-nis;* prob. from a prol. form of the base of *3735;* a *bird* (as *rising* in the air), i.e. (spec.) a *hen* (or female domestic fowl):—hen.

3734. ὁροθεσία **hŏrŏthĕsia,** *hor-oth-es-ee´-ah;* from a comp. of the base of *3725* and a der. of *5087;* a *limit-placing,* i.e. (concr.) *boundary-line:*—bound.

3735. ὄρος **ŏrŏs,** *or´-os;* prob. from an obsol. ὄρω **ŏrō** (to *rise* or *"rear";* perh. akin to *142;* comp. *3733*); a *mountain* (as *lifting* itself above the plain):—hill, mount (-ain).

3736. ὀρύσσω **ŏrussō,** *or-oos´-so;* appar. a prim. verb; to *"burrow"* in the ground, i.e. *dig.:*—dig.

3737. ὀρφανός **ŏrphanŏs,** *or-fan-os´;* of uncert. affin.; *bereaved* (*"orphan"*), i.e. *parentless:*—comfortless, fatherless.

3738. ὀρχέομαι **ŏrchĕŏmai,** *or-kheh´-om-ahee;* mid. from ὄρχος **ŏrchŏs** (a *row* or *ring*); to *dance* (from the *ranklike* or *regular* motion):—dance.

3739. ὅς **hŏs,** *hos;* includ. fem.

ἥ **hē,** *hay;* and neut.

ὅ **hŏ,** *hŏ;* prob. a prim. word (or perh. a form of the art. *3588*); the rel. (sometimes demonstrative) pron., *who, which, what, that:*—one, (an-, the) other, some, that, what, which, who (-m, -se), etc. See also *3757.*

3740. ὁσάκις **hŏsakis,** *hos-ak´-is;* multiple adv. from *3739; how* (i.e. with *302, so*) *many times* as:—as oft (-en) as.

3741. ὅσιος **hŏsiŏs,** *hos´-ee-os;* of uncert. affin.; prop. *right* (by intrinsic or divine character; thus distinguished from *1342,* which refers rather to *human* statutes and relations; from *2413,* which denotes formal *consecration;* and from *40,* which relates to *purity* from defilement), i.e. *hallowed* (*pious, sacred, sure*):—holy, mercy, shalt be.

3742. ὁσιότης **hŏsiŏtēs,** *hos-ee-ot´-ace;* from *3741; piety:*—holiness.

3743. ὁσίως **hŏsiōs,** *hos-ee´-oce;* adv. from *3741; piously:*—holily.

3744. ὀσμή **ŏsmē,** *os-may´;* from *3605; fragrance* (lit. or fig.):—odour, savour.

3745. ὅσος **hŏsŏs,** *hos´-os;* by redupl. from *3739; as* (*much, great, long,* etc.) *as:*—all (that), as (long, many, much) (as), how great (many, much), [in-] asmuch as, so many as, that (ever), the more, those things, what (great, -soever), wheresoever, wherewithsoever, which, × while, who (-soever).

3746. ὅσπερ **hŏspĕr,** *hos´-per;* from *3739* and *4007; who especially:*—whomsoever.

3747. ὀστέον **ŏstĕŏn,** *os-teh´-on;* or contr.

ὀστοῦν **ŏstŏun,** *os-toon´;* of uncert. affin.; a *bone:*—bone.

3748. ὅστις **hŏstis,** *hos´-tis;* includ. the fem.

ἥτις **hētis,** *hay´-tis;* and the neut.

ὅ,τι **hŏ,ti,** *hot´-ee;* from *3739* and *5100; which some,* i.e. *any that;* also (def.) *which same:*—× and (they), (such) as, (they) that, in that they, what (-soever), whereas ye, (they) which, who (-soever). Comp. *3754.*

3749. ὀστράκινος **ŏstrakinŏs,** *os-tra´-kin-os;* from ὄστρακον **ŏstrakŏn** ["oyster"] (a *tile,* i.e. *terra cotta*); *earthen*-ware, i.e. *clayey;* by impl. *frail:*—of earth, earthen.

3750. ὄσφρησις **ŏsphrēsis,** *os´-fray-sis;* from a der. of *3605; smell* (the sense):—smelling.

3751. ὀσφύς **ŏsphus,** *os-foos´;* of uncert. affin.; the *loin* (extern.), i.e. the *hip;* intern. (by extens.) *procreative power:*—loin.

3752. ὅταν **hŏtan,** *hot´-an;* from *3753* and *302; whenever* (implying *hypothesis* or more or less *uncertainty*); also caus. (conj.) *inasmuch as:*—as long (soon) as, that, + till, when (-soever), while.

3753. ὅτε **hŏtĕ,** *hot´-eh;* from *3739* and *5037;* at *which* (thing) *too,* i.e. *when:*—after (that), as soon as, that, when, while.

ὅ,τε **hŏ,tĕ,** *hŏ,t´-eh;* also fem.

ἥ,τε **hē,tĕ,** *hay´-teh;* and neut.

τό,τε **tŏ,tĕ,** *tot´-eh;* simply the art. *3588* followed by *5037;* so written (in some editions) to distinguish them from *3752* and *5119.*

3754. ὅτι **hŏti,** *hot´-ee;* neut. of *3748* as conj.; demonst. *that* (sometimes redundant); caus. *because:*—as concerning that, as though, because (that), for (that), how (that), (in) that, though, why.

3755. ὅτου **hŏtŏu,** *hot´-oo;* for the gen. of *3748* (as adv.); during *which same* time, i.e. *whilst:*—whiles.

3756. οὐ **ŏu,** *oo;* also (before a vowel)

οὐκ **ŏuk,** *ook;* and (before an aspirate)

οὐχ **ŏuch,** *ookh;* a prim. word; the absol. neg. [comp. *3361*] adv.; *no* or *not:*— + long, nay, neither, never, no (× man), none, [can-] not, + nothing, + special, un ([-worthy]), when, + without, + yet but. See also *3364, 3372.*

3757. οὗ **hŏu,** *hoo;* gen. of *3739* as adv.; at *which* place, i.e. *where:*—where (-in), whither ([-soever]).

3758. οὐά **ŏua,** *oo-ah´;* a prim. exclamation of surprise; *"ah":*—ah.

3759. οὐαί **ŏuai,** *oo-ah´ee;* a prim. exclamation of grief: *"woe":*—alas, woe.

3760. οὐδαμῶς **ŏudamōs,** *oo-dam-oce´;* adv. from (the fem.) of *3762; by no means:*—not.

3761. οὐδέ **ŏudĕ,** *oo-deh´;* from *3756* and *1161; not however,* i.e. *neither, nor, not even:*—neither (indeed), never, no (more, nor, not), nor (yet), (also, even, then) not (even, so much as), + nothing, so much as.

3762. οὐδείς **ŏudĕis,** *oo-dice´;* includ. fem.

οὐδεμία **ŏudĕmia,** *oo-dem-ee´-ah;* and neut.

οὐδέν **ŏudĕn,** *oo-den´;* from *3761* and *1520; not even one* (man, woman or thing), i.e. *none, nobody, nothing:*—any (man), aught, man, neither any (thing), never (man), no (man), none (+ of these things), not (any, at all, -thing), nought.

3763. οὐδέποτε **ŏudĕpŏtĕ,** *oo-dep´-ot-eh;* from *3761* and *4218; not even at any time,* i.e. *never at all:*—neither at any time, never, nothing at any time.

3764. οὐδέπω **ŏudĕpō,** *oo-dep´-o;* from *3761* and *4452; not even yet:*—as yet not, never before (yet), (not) yet.

3765. οὐκέτι **ŏukĕti,** *ook-et´-ee;* also (separately)

οὐκ ἔτι **ŏuk ĕti,** *ook et´-ee;* from *3756* and *2089; not yet, no longer:*—after that (not), (not) any more, henceforth (hereafter), not, no longer (more), not as yet (now), now no more (not), yet (not).

3766. οὐκοῦν **ŏukŏun,** *ook-oon´;* from *3756* and *3767;* is it *not therefore* that, i.e. (affirm.) *hence* or *so:*—then.

3767. *οὖν* **ŏun,** *oon;* appar. a prim. word; (adv.) *certainly,* or (conj.) *accordingly:*—and (so, truly), but, now (then), so (likewise then), then, therefore, verily, wherefore.

3768. *οὔπω* **ŏupō,** *oo´-po;* from *3756* and *4452; not yet:*—hitherto not, (no . . .) as yet, not yet.

3769. *οὐρά* **ŏura,** *oo-rah´;* appar. a prim. word; a *tail:*—tail.

3770. *οὐράνιος* **ŏuraniŏs,** *oo-ran´-ee-os;* from *3772; celestial,* i.e. *belonging to* or *coming from* the *sky:*—heavenly.

3771. *οὐρανόθεν* **ŏuranŏthĕn,** *oo-ran-oth´-en;* from *3772* and the enclitic of source; *from* the *sky:*—from heaven.

3772. *οὐρανός* **ŏuranŏs,** *oo-ran-os´;* perh. from the same as *3735* (through the idea of *elevation*); the *sky;* by extens. *heaven* (as the abode of God); by impl. *happiness, power, eternity;* spec. the *Gospel* (*Christianity*):—air, heaven ([-ly]), sky.

3773. *Οὐρβανός* **Ŏurbanŏs,** *oor-ban-os´;* of Lat. or.; *Urbanus* (*of* the *city, "urbane"*), a Chr.:—Urbanus.

3774. *Οὐρίας* **Ŏurias,** *oo-ree´-as;* of Heb. or. [223]; *Urias* (i.e. *Urijah*), a Hittite:—Urias.

3775. *οὖς* **ŏus,** *ooce;* appar. a prim. word; the *ear* (phys. or ment.):—ear.

3776. *οὐσία* **ŏusia,** *oo-see´-ah;* from the fem. of *5607; substance,* i.e. *property* (*possessions*):—goods, substance.

3777. *οὔτε* **ŏutĕ,** *oo´-teh;* from *3756* and *5037; not too,* i.e. *neither* or *nor;* by anal. *not even:*—neither, none, nor (yet), (no, yet) not, nothing.

3778. *οὗτος* **hŏutŏs,** *hoo´-tos;* includ. nom. masc. plur.

οὗτοι **hŏutŏi,** *hoo´-toy;* nom. fem. sing.

αὕτη **hautē,** *hŏw´-tay;* and nom. fem. plur.

αὗται **hautai,** *hŏw´-tahee;* from the art. *3588* and *846; the he* (*she* or it), i.e. *this* or *that* (often with art. repeated):—he (it was that), hereof, it, she, such as, the same, these, they, this (man, same, woman), which, who.

3779. *οὕτω* **hŏutō,** *hoo´-to;* or (before a vowel)

οὕτως **hŏutōs,** *hoo´-toce;* adv. from *3778; in this way* (referring to what precedes or follows):—after that, after (in) this manner, as, even (so), for all that, like (-wise), no more, on this fashion (-wise), so (in like manner), thus, what.

3780. *οὐχί* **ŏuchi,** *oo-khee´;* intens. of *3756; not indeed:*—nay, not.

3781. *ὀφειλέτης* **ŏphĕilĕtēs,** *of-i-let´-ace;* from *3784;* an *ower,* i.e. person *indebted;* fig. a *delinquent;* mor. a *transgressor* (against God):—debtor, which owed, sinner.

3782. *ὀφειλή* **ŏphĕilē,** *of-i-lay´;* from *3784; indebtedness,* i.e. (concr.) a *sum* owed; fig. *obligation,* i.e. (conjugal) *duty:*—debt, due.

3783. *ὀφείλημα* **ŏphĕilēma,** *of-i´-lay-mah;* from (the alt. of) *3784; something owed,* i.e. (fig.) a *due;* mor. a *fault:*—debt.

3784. *ὀφείλω* **ŏphĕilō,** *of-i´-lo;* or (in cert. tenses) its prol. form

ὀφειλέω **ŏphĕilĕō,** *of-i-leh´-o;* prob. from the base of *3786* (through the idea of *accruing*); to *owe* ((pecuniarily); fig. to *be under obligation* (*ought, must, should*); mor. to *fail* in duty:—behove, be bound, (be) debt (-or), (be) due (-ty), be guilty (indebted), (must) need (-s), ought, owe, should. See also *3785.*

3785. *ὄφελον* **ŏphĕlŏn,** *of´-el-on;* first pers. sing. of a past tense of *3784; I ought* (*wish*), i.e. (interj.) *oh that!:*—would (to God).

3786. *ὄφελος* **ŏphĕlŏs,** *of´-el-os;* from *ὀφέλλω* **ŏphĕllō** (to *heap* up, i.e. *accumulate* or *benefit*); *gain:*—advantageth, profit.

3787. *ὀφθαλμοδουλεία* **ŏphthalmŏdŏulĕia,** *of-thal-mod-oo-li´-ah;* from *3788* and *1397; sight-labor,* i.e. that needs watching (*remissness*):—eye-service.

3788. *ὀφθαλμός* **ŏphthalmŏs,** *of-thal-mos´;* from *3700;* the *eye* (lit. or fig.); by impl. *vision;* fig. *envy* (from the jealous side-glance):—eye, sight.

3789. *ὄφις* **ŏphis,** *of´-is;* prob. from *3700* (through the idea of *sharpness* of vision); a *snake,* fig. (as a type of sly cunning) an artful *malicious* person, espec. *Satan:—serpent.*

3790. *ὀφρύς* **ŏphrus,** *of-roos´;* perh. from *3700* (through the idea of the shading or proximity to the organ of *vision*); the eye-*"brow"* or *forehead,* i.e. (fig.) the *brink* of a precipice:—brow.

3791. *ὀχλέω* **ŏchlĕō,** *okh-leh´-o;* from *3793;* to *mob,* i.e. (by impl.) to *harass:*—vex.

3792. *ὀχλοποιέω* **ŏchlŏpŏiĕō,** *okh-lop-oy-eh´-o;* from *3793* and *4160;* to *make a crowd,* i.e. *raise a* public *disturbance:*—gather a company.

3793. *ὄχλος* **ŏchlŏs,** *okh´-los;* from a der. of *2192* (mean. a *vehicle*); a *throng* (as *borne* along); by impl. the *rabble;* by extens. a *class* of people; fig. a *riot:*—company, multitude, number (of people), people, press.

3794. *ὀχύρωμα* **ŏchurōma,** *okh-oo´-ro-mah;* from a remote der. of *2192* (mean. to *fortify,* through the idea of *holding* safely); a *castle* (fig. *argument*):—stronghold.

3795. *ὀψάριον* **ŏpsariŏn,** *op-sar´-ee-on;* neut. of a presumed der. of the base of *3702;* a *relish* to other food (as if cooked *sauce*), i.e. (spec.) *fish* (presumably salted and dried as a condiment):—fish.

3796. *ὀψέ* **ŏpsĕ,** *op-seh´;* from the same as *3694* (through the idea of *backwardness*); (adv.) *late* in the day; by extens. *after the close* of the day:—(at) even, in the end.

3797. *ὄψιμος* **ŏpsimŏs,** *op´-sim-os;* from *3796; later,* i.e. *vernal* (showering):—latter.

3798. *ὄψίος* **ŏpsiŏs,** *op´-see-os;* from *3796; late;* fem. (as noun) *afternoon* (early eve) or *nightfall* (later eve):—even (-ing, [-tide]).

3799. *ὄψις* **ŏpsis,** *op´-sis;* from *3700;* prop. *sight* (the act), i.e. (by impl.) the *visage,* an external *show:*—appearance, countenance, face.

3800. *ὀψώνιον* **ŏpsōniŏn,** *op-so´-nee-on;* neut. of a presumed der. of the same as *3795; rations* for a soldier, i.e. (by extens.) his *stipend* or *pay:*—wages.

3801. *ὁ ὢν καὶ ὁ ἦν καὶ ὁ ἐρχόμενος* **hŏ ōn kai hŏ ēn kai hŏ ĕrchŏmĕnŏs,** *hŏ own kahee hŏ ane kahee hŏ er-khom´-en-os;* a phrase combining *3588* with the pres. part. and imperf. of *1510* and the pres. part of *2064* by means of *2532; the* one *being and the* one that *was and the* one *coming,* i.e. *the Eternal,* as a divine epithet of Christ:—which art (is, was), and (which) wast (is, was), and art (is) to come (shalt be).

Π

3802. *παγιδεύω* **pagidĕuō,** *pag-id-yoo´-o;* from *3803;* to *ensnare* (fig.):—entangle.

3803. *παγίς* **pagis,** *pag-ece´;* from *4078;* a *trap* (as *fastened* by a noose or notch); fig. a *trick* or *stratagem* (*temptation*):—snare

Πάγος **Pagŏs.** See *697.*

3804. *πάθημα* **pathēma,** *path´-ay-mah;* from a presumed der. of *3806;* something *undergone,* i.e. *hardship* or *pain;* subj. an *emotion* or *influence:*—affection, affliction, motion, suffering.

3805. *παθητός* **pathētŏs,** *path-ay-tos´;* from the same as *3804; liable* (i.e. *doomed*) *to* experience *pain:*—suffer.

3806. *πάθος* **pathŏs,** *path´-os;* from the alt. of *3958;* prop. *suffering* (*"pathos"*), i.e. (subj.) a *passion* (espec. *concupiscence*):—(inordinate) affection, lust.

πάθω **pathō.** See *3958.*

3807. *παιδαγωγός* **paidagōgŏs,** *pahee-dag-o-gos´;* from *3816* and a redupl. form of *71;* a *boy-leader,* i.e. a servant whose office it was to take the children to school; (by impl. [fig.] a *tutor* [*"pædagogue"*]):—instructor, schoolmaster.

3808. *παιδάριον* **paidariŏn,** *pahee-dar´-ee-on;* neut. of a presumed der. of *3816;* a *little boy:*—child, lad.

3809. *παιδεία* **paidĕia,** *pahee-di´-ah;* from *3811; tutorage;* i.e. *education* or *training;* by impl. disciplinary *correction:*—chastening, chastisement, instruction, nurture.

3810. *παιδευτής* **paidĕutēs,** *pahee-dyoo-tace´;* from *3811;* a *trainer,* i.e. *teacher* or (by impl.) *discipliner:*—which corrected, instructor.

3811. *παιδεύω* **paidĕuō,** *pahee-dyoo´-o;* from *3816;* to *train* up a child, i.e. *educate,* or (by impl.) *discipline* (by punishment):—chasten (-ise), instruct, learn, teach.

3812. *παιδιόθεν* **paidiŏthĕn,** *pahee-dee-oth´-en;* adv. (of *source*) from *3813; from infancy:*—of a child.

3813. *παιδίον* **paidiŏn,** *pahee-dee´-on;* neut. dimin. of *3816;* a *childling* (of either sex), i.e. (prop.) an infant, or (by extens.) a half-grown *boy* or girl; fig. an *immature* Christian:—(little, young) child, damsel.

3814. παιδίσκη **paidiskē,** *pahee-dis´-kay;* fem. dimin. of *3816;* a *girl,* i.e. (spec.) a *female slave* or *servant:*—bondmaid (-woman), damsel, maid (-en).

3815. παίζω **paizō,** *paheed´-zo;* from *3816;* to *sport* (as a boy):—play.

3816. παῖς **pais,** *paheece;* perh. from *3817;* a *boy* (as often *beaten* with impunity), or (by anal.) a *girl,* and (gen.) a *child;* spec. a *slave* or *servant* (espec. a *minister* to a king; and by eminence to God):—child, maid (-en), (man) servant, son, young man.

3817. παίω **paiō,** *pah´-yo;* a prim. verb; to *hit* (as if by a single blow and less violently than *5180*); spec. to *sting* (as a scorpion):—smite, strike.

3818. Πακατιανή **Pakatianē,** *pak-at-ee-an-ay´;* fem. of an adj. of uncert. der.; *Pacatianian,* a section of Phrygia:—Pacatiana.

3819. πάλαι **palai,** *pal´-ahee;* prob. another form for *3825* (through the idea of *retrocession*); (adv.) *formerly,* or (by rel.) *sometime since;* (ellipt. as adj.) *ancient:*—any while, a great while ago, (of) old, in time past.

3820. παλαιός **palaiŏs,** *pal-ah-yos´;* from *3819; antique,* i.e. *not recent, worn out:*—old.

3821. παλαιότης **palaiŏtēs,** *pal-ah-yot´-ace;* from *3820; antiquatedness:*—oldness.

3822. παλαιόω **palaiŏō,** *pal-ah-yŏ´-o;* from *3820;* to *make* (pass *become*) *worn out,* or *declare obsolete:*—decay, make (wax) old.

3823. πάλη **palē,** *pal´-ay;* from πάλλω **pallō** (to *vibrate;* another form for *906*); *wrestling:*— + wrestle.

3824. παλιγγενεσία **paliggĕnĕsia,** *pal-ing-ghen-es-ee´-ah;* from *3825* and *1078;* (spiritual) *rebirth* (the state or the act), i.e. (fig.) spiritual *renovation;* spec. Messianic *restoration:*—regeneration.

3825. πάλιν **palin,** *pal´-in;* prob. from the same as *3823* (through the idea of *oscillatory* repetition); (adv.) *anew,* i.e. (of place) *back,* (of time) *once more,* or (conj.) *furthermore* or *on the other hand:*—again.

3826. παμπληθεί **pamplēthĕi,** *pam-play-thi´;* dat. (adv.) of a comp. of *3956* and *4128; in full multitude,* i.e. *concertedly* or *simultaneously:*—all at once.

3827. πάμπολυς **pampŏlus,** *pam-pol-ooce;* from *3956* and *4183; full many,* i.e. *immense:*—very great.

3828. Παμφυλία **Pamphulia,** *pam-fool-ee´-ah;* from a comp. of *3956* and *5443; every-tribal,* i.e. *heterogeneous* (*5561* being impl.); *Pamphylia,* a region of Asia Minor:—Pamphylia.

3829. πανδοχεῖον **pandŏchĕiŏn,** *pan-dokh-i´-on;* neut. of a presumed comp. of *3956* and a der. of *1209; all-receptive,* i.e. a public *lodging-place* (*caravanserai* or *khan*):—inn.

3830. πανδοχεύς **pandŏchĕus,** *pan-dokh-yoos´;* from the same as *3829;* an *innkeeper* (*warden of a caravanserai*):—host.

3831. πανήγυρις **panēguris,** *pan-ay´-goo-ris;* from *3956* and a der. of *58;* a *mass-meeting,* i.e. (fig.) *universal companionship:*—general assembly.

3832. πανοικί **panŏiki,** *pan-oy-kee´;* adv. from *3956* and *3624; with* the *whole family:*—with all his house.

3833. πανοπλία **panŏplia,** *pan-op-lee´-ah;* from a comp. of *3956* and *3696; full armor* (*"panoply"*):—all (whole) armour.

3834. πανουργία **panŏurgia,** *pan-oorg-ee´-ah;* from *3835; adroitness,* i.e. (in a bad sense) *trickery* or *sophistry:*—(cunning) craftiness, subtilty.

3835. πανοῦργος **panŏurgŏs,** *pan-oor´-gos;* from *3956* and *2041; all-working,* i.e. *adroit* (*shrewd*):—crafty.

3836. πανταχόθεν **pantachŏthĕn,** *pan-takh-oth´-en;* adv. (of *source*) from *3837; from all* directions:—from every quarter.

3837. πανταχοῦ **pantachŏu,** *pan-takh-oo´;* gen. (as adv. of *place*) of a presumed der. of *3956; universally:*—in all places, everywhere.

3838. παντελής **pantĕlēs,** *pan-tel-ace´;* from *3956* and *5056; full-ended,* i.e. *entire* (neut. as noun, *completion*):— + in [no] wise, uttermost.

3839. πάντη **pantē,** *pan´-tay;* adv. (of *manner*) from *3956; wholly:*—always.

3840. παντόθεν **pantŏthĕn,** *pan-toth´-en;* adv. (of *source*) from *3956; from* (i.e. *on*) *all* sides:—on every side, round about.

3841. παντοκράτωρ **pantŏkratōr,** *pan-tok-rat´-ore;* from *3956* and *2904;* the *all-ruling,* i.e. *God* (as absolute and universal *sovereign*):—Almighty, Omnipotent.

3842. πάντοτε **pantŏtĕ,** *pan´-tot-eh;* from *3956* and *3753; every when,* i.e. *at all* times:—always (-s), ever (-more).

3843. πάντως **pantōs,** *pan´-toce;* adv. from *3956; entirely;* spec. *at all events,* (with neg. following) *in* no *event:*—by all means, altogether, at all, needs, no doubt, in [no] wise, surely.

3844. παρά **para,** *par-ah´;* a prim. prep.; prop. *near,* i.e. (with gen.) *from beside* (lit. or fig.), (with dat.) *at* (or *in*) the *vicinity* of (obj. or subj.), (with acc.) to the *proximity* with (local [espec. *beyond* or *opposed* to] or causal [*on account* of]):—above, against, among, at, before, by, contrary to, × friend, from, + give [such things as they], + that [she] had, × his, in, more than, nigh unto, (out) of, past, save, side . . . by, in the sight of, than, [there-] fore, with. In compounds it retains the same variety of application.

3845. παραβαίνω **parabainō,** *par-ab-ah´ee-no;* from *3844* and the base of *939;* to *go contrary to,* i.e. *violate* a command:—(by) transgress (-ion).

3846. παραβάλλω **paraballō,** *par-ab-al´-lo;* from *3844* and *906;* to *throw alongside,* i.e. (reflex.) to *reach* a place, or (fig.) to *liken:*—arrive, compare.

3847. παράβασις **parabasis,** *par-ab´-as-is;* from *3845; violation:*—breaking, transgression.

3848. παραβάτης **parabatēs,** *par-ab-at´-ace;* from *3845;* a *violator:*—breaker, transgress (-or).

3849. παραβιάζομαι **parabiazŏmai,** *par-ab-ee-ad´-zom-ahee;* from *3844* and the mid. of *971;* to *force contrary* to (nature), i.e. *compel* (by entreaty):—constrain.

3850. παραβολή **parabŏlē,** *par-ab-ol-ay´;* from *3846; a similitude* (*"parable"*), i.e. (symbol.) *fictitious narrative* (of common life conveying a moral), *apothegm* or *adage:*—comparison, figure, parable, proverb.

3851. παραβουλεύομαι **parabŏulĕuŏmai,** *par-ab-ool-yoo´-om-ahee;* from *3844* and the mid. of *1011;* to *misconsult,* i.e. *disregard:*—not (to) regard (-ing).

3852. παραγγελία **paraggĕlia,** *par-ang-gel-ee´-ah;* from *3853;* a *mandate:*—charge, command.

3853. παραγγέλλω **paraggĕllō,** *par-ang-gel´-lo;* from *3844* and the base of *32;* to *transmit a message,* i.e. (by impl.) to *enjoin:*—(give in) charge, (give) command (-ment), declare.

3854. παραγίνομαι **paraginŏmai,** *par-ag-in´-om-ahee;* from *3844* and *1096;* to *become near,* i.e. *approach* (*have arrived*); by impl. to *appear* publicly:—come, go, be present.

3855. παράγω **paragō,** *par-ag´-o;* from *3844* and *71;* to *lead near,* i.e. (reflex. or intrans.) to *go along* or *away:*—depart, pass (away, by, forth).

3856. παραδειγματίζω **paradĕigmatizō,** *par-ad-igue-mat-id´-zo;* from *3844* and *1165;* to *show alongside* (the public), i.e. *expose to infamy:*—make a public example, put to an open shame.

3857. παράδεισος **paradĕisŏs,** *par-ad´-i-sos;* of Oriental or. [comp. 6508]; a *park,* i.e. (spec.) an *Eden* (place of future happiness, *"paradise"*):—paradise.

3858. παραδέχομαι **paradĕchŏmai,** *par-ad-ekh´-om-ahee;* from *3844* and *1209;* to *accept near,* i.e. *admit* or (by impl.) *delight* in:—receive.

3859. παραδιατριβή **paradiatribē,** *par-ad-ee-at-ree-bay´;* from a comp. of *3844* and *1304; misemployment,* i.e. *meddlesomeness:*—perverse disputing.

3860. παραδίδωμι **paradidōmi,** *par-ad-id´-o-mee;* from *3844* and *1325;* to *surrender,* i.e. *yield up, intrust, transmit:*—betray, bring forth, cast, commit, deliver (up), give (over, up), hazard, put in prison, recommend.

3861. παράδοξος **paradŏxŏs,** *par-ad´-ox-os;* from *3844* and *1391* (in the sense of *seeming*); *contrary to expectation,* i.e. *extraordinary* (*"paradox"*):—strange.

3862. παράδοσις **paradŏsis,** *par-ad´-os-is;* from *3860; transmission,* i.e. (concr.) a *precept;* spec. the Jewish *traditionary law:*—ordinance, tradition.

3863. παραζηλόω **parazēlŏō,** *par-ad-zay-lŏ´-o;* from *3844* and *2206;* to *stimulate alongside,* i.e. *excite to rivalry:*—provoke to emulation (jealousy).

3864. παραθαλάσσιος **parathalassiŏs,** *par-ath-al-as´-see-os;* from *3844* and *2281; along* the *sea,* i.e. *maritime* (*lacustrine*):—upon the sea coast.

3865. παραθεωρέω **parathĕōrĕō,** *par-ath-eh-o-reh´-o;* from *3844* and *2334;* to *overlook* or *disregard*:—neglect.

3866. παραθήκη **parathēkē,** *par-ath-ay´-kay;* from *3908;* a *deposit,* i.e. (fig.) *trust:*—committed unto.

3867. παραινέω **parainĕō,** *par-ahee-neh´-o;* from *3844* and *134;* to *mispraise;* i.e. *recommend* or *advise* (a different course):—admonish, exhort.

3868. παραιτέομαι **paraitĕŏmai,** *par-ahee-teh´-om-ahee;* from *3844* and the mid. of *154;* to *beg off,* i.e. *deprecate, decline, shun:*—avoid, (make) excuse, intreat, refuse, reject.

3869. παρακαθίζω **parakathizō,** *par-ak-ath-id´-zo;* from *3844* and *2523;* to *sit down near:*—sit.

3870. παρακαλέω **parakalĕō,** *par-ak-al-eh´-o;* from *3844* and *2564;* to *call near,* i.e. *invite, invoke* (by *imploration, hortation* or *consolation*):—beseech, call for, (be of good) comfort, desire, (give) exhort (-ation), intreat, pray.

3871. παρακαλύπτω **parakaluptō,** *par-ak-al-oop´-to;* from *3844* and *2572;* to *cover alongside,* i.e. *veil* (fig.):—hide.

3872. παρακαταθήκη **parakatathēkē,** *par-ak-at-ath-ay´-kay;* from a comp. of *3844* and *2698;* something *put down alongside,* i.e. a *deposit* (sacred *trust*):—that (thing) which is committed (un-) to (trust).

3873. παράκειμαι **parakĕimai,** *par-ak´-i-mahee;* from *3844* and *2749;* to *lie near,* i.e. *be at hand* (fig. *be prompt* or *easy*):—be present.

3874. παράκλησις **paraklēsis,** *par-ak´-lay-sis;* from *3870; imploration, hortation, solace:*—comfort, consolation, exhortation, intreaty.

3875. παράκλητος **paraklētŏs,** *par-ak´-lay-tos;* an *intercessor, consoler:*—advocate, comforter.

3876. παρακοή **parakŏē,** *par-ak-ŏ-ay´;* from *3878; inattention,* i.e. (by impl.) *disobedience:*—disobedience.

3877. παρακολουθέω **parakŏlŏuthĕō,** *par-ak-ol-oo-theh´-o;* from *3844* and *190;* to *follow near,* i.e. (fig.) *attend* (as a result), *trace out, conform* to:—attain, follow, fully know, have understanding.

3878. παρακούω **parakŏuō,** *par-ak-oo´-o;* from *3844* and *191;* to *mishear,* i.e. (by impl.) to *disobey:*—neglect to hear.

3879. παρακύπτω **parakuptō,** *par-ak-oop´-to;* from *3844* and *2955;* to *bend beside,* i.e. *lean over* (so as to *peer within*):—look (into), stoop down.

3880. παραλαμβάνω **paralambanō,** *par-al-am-ban´-o;* from *3844* and *2983;* to *receive near,* i.e. *associate with* oneself (in any familiar or intimate act or relation); by anal. to *assume* an office; fig. to *learn:*—receive, take (unto, with).

3881. παραλέγομαι **paralĕgŏmai,** *par-al-eg´-om-ahee;* from *3844* and the mid. of *3004* (in its orig. sense); (spec.) to *lay* one's course *near,* i.e. *sail past:*—pass, sail by.

3882. παράλιος **paraliŏs,** *par-al´-ee-os;* from *3844* and *251; beside* the *salt* (*sea*), i.e. *maritime:*—sea coast.

3883. παραλλαγή **parallagē,** *par-al-lag-ay´;* from a comp. of *3844* and *236; transmutation* (of phase or orbit), i.e. (fig.) *fickleness:*—variableness.

3884. παραλογίζομαι **paralŏgizŏmai,** *par-al-og-id´-zom-ahee;* from *3844* and *3049;* to *misreckon,* i.e. *delude:*—beguile, deceive.

3885. παραλυτικός **paralutikŏs,** *par-al-oo-tee-kos´;* from a der. of *3886;* as if *dissolved,* i.e. *"paralytic":*—that had (sick of) the palsy.

3886. παραλύω **paraluō,** *par-al-oo´-o;* from *3844* and *3089;* to *loosen beside,* i.e. *relax* (perf. pas. part. *paralyzed* or *enfeebled*):—feeble, sick of the (taken with) palsy.

3887. παραμένω **paramĕnō,** *par-am-en´-o;* from *3844* and *3306;* to *stay near,* i.e. *remain* (lit. *tarry;* or fig. *be permanent, persevere*):—abide, continue.

3888. παραμυθέομαι **paramuthĕŏmai,** *par-am-oo-theh´-om-ahee;* from *3844* and the mid. of a der. of *3454;* to *relate near,* i.e. (by impl.) *encourage, console*:—comfort.

3889. παραμυθία **paramuthia,** *par-am-oo-thee´-ah;* from *3888; consolation* (prop. abstr.):—comfort.

3890. παραμύθιον **paramuthiŏn,** *par-am-oo´-thee-on;* neut. of *3889; consolation* (prop. concr.):—comfort.

3891. παρανομέω **paranŏmĕō,** *par-an-om-eh´-o;* from a comp. of *3844* and *3551;* to *be opposed to law,* i.e. to *transgress:*—contrary to law.

3892. παρανομία **paranŏmia,** *par-an-om-ee´-ah;* from the same as *3891; transgression:*—iniquity.

3893. παραπικραίνω **parapikrainō,** *par-ap-ik-rah´ee-no;* from *3844* and *4087;* to *embitter alongside,* i.e. (fig.) to *exasperate:*—provoke.

3894. παραπικρασμός **parapikrasmŏs,** *par-ap-ik-ras-mos´;* from *3893; irritation:*—provocation.

3895. παραπίπτω **parapiptō,** *par-ap-ip´-to;* from *3844* and *4098;* to *fall aside,* i.e. (fig.) to *apostatize:*—fall away.

3896. παραπλέω **paraplĕō,** *par-ap-leh´-o;* from *3844* and *4126;* to *sail near:*—sail by.

3897. παραπλήσιον **paraplēsiŏn,** *par-ap-lay´-see-on;* neut. of a comp. of *3844* and the base of *4139* (as adv.); *close by,* i.e. (fig.) *almost:*—nigh unto.

3898. παραπλησίως **paraplēsiōs,** *par-ap-lay-see´-oce;* adv. from the same as *3897; in a manner near by,* i.e. (fig.) *similarly:*—likewise.

3899. παραπορεύομαι **parapŏrĕuŏmai,** *par-ap-or-yoo´-om-ahee;* from *3844* and *4198;* to *travel near:*—go, pass (by).

3900. παράπτωμα **paraptōma,** *par-ap´-to-mah;* from *3895;* a *side-slip* (*lapse* or *deviation*), i.e. (unintentional) *error* or (wilful) *transgression:*—fall, fault, offence, sin, trespass.

3901. παραῤῥυέω **pararrhuĕō,** *par-ar-hroo-eh´-o;* from *3844* and the alt. of *4482;* to *flow by,* i.e. (fig.) carelessly *pass* (*miss*):—let slip.

3902. παράσημος **parasēmŏs,** *par-as´-ay-mos;* from *3844* and the base of *4591; side-marked,* i.e. *labelled* (with a *badge* [*figure-head*] of a ship):—sign.

3903. παρασκευάζω **paraskĕuazō,** *par-ask-yoo-ad´-zo;* from *3844* and a der. of *4632;* to *furnish aside,* i.e. *get ready:*—prepare self, be (make) ready.

3904. παρασκευή **paraskĕuē,** *par-ask-yoo-ay´;* as if from *3903; readiness:*—preparation.

3905. παρατείνω **paratĕinō,** *par-at-i´-no;* from *3844* and τείνω **tĕinō** (to *stretch*); to *extend along,* i.e. *prolong* (in point of time):—continue.

3906. παρατηρέω **paratērĕō,** *par-at-ay-reh´-o;* from *3844* and *5083;* to *inspect alongside,* i.e. *note insidiously* or *scrupulously:*—observe, watch.

3907. παρατήρησις **paratērēsis,** *par-at-ay´-ray-sis;* from *3906; inspection,* i.e. *ocular evidence:*—observation.

3908. παρατίθημι **paratithēmi,** *par-at-ith´-ay-mee;* from *3844* and *5087;* to *place alongside,* i.e. *present* (food, truth); by impl. to *deposit* (as a trust or for protection):—allege, commend, commit (the keeping of), put forth, set before.

3909. παρατυγχάνω **paratugchanō,** *par-at-oong-khan´-o;* from *3844* and *5177;* to *chance near,* i.e. *fall in with:*—meet with.

3910. παραυτίκα **parautika,** *par-ŏw-tee´-kah;* from *3844* and a der. of *846; at* the *very* instant, i.e. *momentary:*—but for a moment.

3811. παραφέρω **paraphĕrō,** *par-af-er´-o;* from *3844* and *5342* (includ. its alt. forms); to *bear along* or *aside,* i.e. *carry off* (lit. or fig.); by impl. to *avert:*—remove, take away.

3912. παραφρονέω **paraphrŏnĕō,** *par-af-ron-eh´-o;* from *3844* and *5426;* to *misthink,* i.e. *be insane* (*silly*):—as a fool.

3913. παραφρονία **paraphrŏnia,** *par-af-ron-ee´-ah;* from *3912; insanity,* i.e. *foolhardiness:*—madness.

3914. παραχειμάζω **parachĕimazō,** *par-akh-i-mad´-zo;* from *3844* and *5492;* to *winter near,* i.e. *stay* with over the *rainy* season:—winter.

3915. παραχειμασία **parachĕimasia,** *par-akh-i-mas-ee´-ah;* from *3914;* a *wintering* over:—winter in.

3916. παραχρῆμα **parachrēma,** *par-akh-ray´-mah;* from *3844* and *5536* (in its orig. sense); *at the thing* itself, i.e. *instantly:*—forthwith, immediately, presently, straightway, soon.

3917. πάρδαλις **pardalis,** *par´-dal-is;* fem. of πάρδος **pardŏs** (a *panther*); a *leopard:*—leopard.

3918. πάρειμι **parĕimi,** *par´-i-mee;* from *3844* and *1510* (includ. its various forms); to *be near,* i.e. *at hand;* neut. pres. part. (sing.) *time being,* or (plur.) *property:*—come, × have, be here, + lack, (be here) present.

3919. παρεισάγω **parĕisagō,** *par-ice-ag´-o;* from *3844* and *1521;* to *lead in aside,* i.e. *introduce surreptitiously:*—privily bring in.

3920. παρείσακτος **parĕisaktŏs,** *par-ice´-ak-tos;* from *3919; smuggled in:*—unawares brought in.

3921. παρεισδύνω **parĕisdunō,** *par-ice-doo´-no;* from *3844* and a comp. of *1519* and *1416;* to *settle in alongside,* i.e. *lodge stealthily:*—creep in unawares.

3922. παρεισέρχομαι **parĕisĕrchŏmai,** *par-ice-er´-khom-ahee;* from *3844* and *1525;* to *come in alongside,* i.e. *supervene additionally* or *stealthily:*—come in privily, enter.

3923. παρεισφέρω **parĕisphĕrō,** *par-ice-fer´-o;* from *3844* and *1533;* to *bear in alongside,* i.e. *introduce simultaneously:*—give.

3924. παρεκτός **parĕktŏs,** *par-ek-tos´;* from *3844* and *1622; near outside,* i.e. *besides:*—except, saving, without.

3925. παρεμβολή **parĕmbŏlē,** *par-em-bol-ay´;* from a comp. of *3844* and *1685;* a *throwing in beside* (*juxtaposition*), i.e. (spec.) *battle-array, encampment* or *barracks* (tower Antonia):—army, camp, castle.

3926. παρενοχλέω **parĕnŏchlĕō,** *par-en-okh-leh´-o;* from *3844* and *1776;* to *harass further,* i.e. *annoy:*—trouble.

3927. παρεπίδημος **parĕpidēmŏs,** *par-ep-id´-ay-mos;* from *3844* and the base of *1927;* an *alien alongside,* i.e. a *resident foreigner:*—pilgrim, stranger.

3928. παρέρχομαι **parĕrchŏmai,** *par-er´-khom-ahee;* from *3844* and *2064;* to *come near* or *aside,* i.e. to *approach* (*arrive*), *go by* (or *away*), (fig.) *perish* or *neglect,* (caus.) *avert:*—come (forth), go, pass (away, by, over), past, transgress.

3929. πάρεσις **parĕsis,** *par´-es-is;* from *3935; prætermission,* i.e. *toleration:*—remission.

3930. παρέχω **parĕchō,** *par-ekh´-o;* from *3844* and *2192;* to *hold near,* i.e. *present, afford, exhibit, furnish occasion:*—bring, do, give, keep, minister, offer, shew, + trouble.

3931. παρηγορία **parēgŏria,** *pay-ay-gor-ee´-ah;* from a comp. of *3844* and a der. of *58* (mean. to *harangue* an assembly); an *address alongside,* i.e. (spec.) *consolation:*—comfort.

3932. παρθενία **parthĕnia,** *par-then-ee´-ah;* from *3933; maidenhood:*—virginity.

3933. παρθένος **parthĕnŏs,** *par-then´-os;* of unknown or.; a *maiden;* by impl. an unmarried *daughter:*—virgin.

3934. Πάρθος **Parthŏs,** *par´-thos;* prob. of for. or.; a *Parthian,* i.e. inhab. of Parthia:—Parthian.

3935. παρίημι **pariēmi,** *par-ee´-ay-mi;* from *3844* and ἵημι **hiēmi** (to *send*); to *let by,* i.e. *relax:*—hang down.

3936. παρίστημι **paristēmi,** *par-is´-tay-mee;* or prol. παριστάνω **paristanō,** *par-is-tan´-o;* from *3844* and *2476;* to *stand beside,* i.e. (trans.) to *exhibit, proffer,* (spec.) *recommend,* (fig.) *substantiate;* or (intrans.) to *be at hand* (or *ready*), *aid:*—assist, bring before, command, commend, give presently, present, prove, provide, shew, stand (before, by, here, up, with), yield.

3937. Παρμενᾶς **Parmĕnas,** *par-men-as´;* prob. by contr. for Παρμενίδης **Parmĕnidēs** (a der. of a comp. of *3844* and *3306*); *constant; Parmenas,* a Chr.:—Parmenas.

3938. πάροδος **parŏdŏs,** *par´-od-os;* from *3844* and *3598;* a *by-road,* i.e. (act.) a *route:*—way.

3939. παροικέω **parŏikĕō,** *par-oy-keh´-o;* from *3844* and *3611;* to *dwell near,* i.e. *reside* as a *foreigner:*—sojourn in, be a stranger.

3940. παροικία, **parŏikia,** *par-oy-kee´-ah;* from *3941; foreign residence:*—sojourning, × as strangers.

3941. πάροικος **parŏikŏs,** *par´-oy-kos;* from *3844* and *3624;* having a *home near,* i.e. (as noun) a *by-dweller* (*alien resident*):—foreigner, sojourn, stranger.

3942. παροιμία **parŏimia,** *par-oy-mee´-ah;* from a comp. of *3844* and perh. a der. of *3633;* appar. a state *alongside of supposition,* i.e. (concr.) an *adage;* spec. an engimatical or fictitious *illustration:*—parable, proverb.

3943. πάροινος **parŏinŏs,** *par´-oy-nos;* from *3844* and *3631;* staying *near wine,* i.e. *tippling* (a *toper*):—given to wine.

3944. παροίχομαι **parŏichŏmai,** *par-oy´-khom-ahee;* from *3844* and οἴχομαι **ŏichŏmai** (to *depart*); to *escape along,* i.e. *be gone:*—past.

3945. παρομοιάζω **parŏmŏiazō,** *par-om-oy-ad´-zo;* from *3946;* to *resemble:*—be like unto.

3946. παρόμοιος **parŏmŏiŏs,** *par-om´-oy-os;* from *3844* and *3664; alike nearly,* i.e. *similar:*—like.

3947. παροξύνω **parŏxunō,** *par-ox-oo´-no;* from *3844* and a der. of *3691;* to *sharpen alongside,* i.e. (fig.) to *exasperate:*—easily provoke, stir.

3948. παροξυσμός **parŏxusmŏs,** *par-ox-oos-mos´;* from *3947* (*"paroxysm"*); *incitement* (to good), or *dispute* (in anger):—contention, provoke unto.

3949. παροργίζω **parŏrgizō,** *par-org-id´-zo;* from *3844* and *3710;* to *anger alongside,* i.e. *enrage:*—anger, provoke to wrath.

3950. παροργισμός **parŏrgismŏs,** *par-org-is-mos´;* from *3949; rage:*—wrath.

3951. παροτρύνω **parŏtrunō,** *par-ot-roo´-no;* from *3844* and ὀτρύνω **ŏtrunō,** (to *spur*); to *urge along,* i.e. *stimulate* (to hostility):—stir up.

3952. παρουσία **parŏusia,** *par-oo-see´-ah;* from the pres. part. of *3918;* a *being near,* i.e. *advent* (often, *return;* spec. of Christ to punish Jerusalem, or finally the wicked); (by impl.) phys. *aspect:*—coming, presence.

3953. παροψίς **parŏpsis,** *par-op-sis´;* from *3844* and the base of *3795;* a *side-dish* (the receptacle):—platter.

3954. παῤῥησία **parrhēsia,** *par-rhay-see´-ah;* from *3956* and a der. of *4483; all* out-*spokenness,* i.e. *frankness, bluntness, publicity;* by impl. *assurance:*—bold (× -ly, -ness, -ness of speech), confidence, × freely, × openly, × plainly (-ness).

3955. παῤῥησιάζομαι **parrhēsiazŏmai,** *par-hray-see-ad´-zom-ahee;* mid. from *3954;* to *be frank* in utterance, or *confident* in spirit and demeanor:—be (wax) bold, (preach, speak) boldly.

3956. πᾶς **pas,** *pas;* includ. all the forms of declension; appar. a prim. word; *all, any, every,* the *whole:*—all (manner of, means) alway (-s), any (one), × daily, + ever, every (one, way), as many as, + no (-thing), × throughly, whatsoever, whole, whosoever.

3957. πάσχα **pascha,** *pas´-khah;* of Chald. or. [comp. 6453]; the *Passover* (the meal, the day, the festival or the special sacrifices connected with it):—Easter, Passover.

3958. πάσχω **paschō,** *pas´-kho;* includ. the forms

πάθω (**pathō,** *path´-o*) and

πένθω (**pĕnthō,** *pen´-tho*), used only in certain tenses for it; appar. a prim. verb; to *experience* a sensation or impression (usually painful):—feel, passion, suffer, vex.

3959. Πάταρα **Patara,** *pat´-ar-ah;* prob. of for. or.; *Patara,* a place in Asia Minor:—Patara.

3960. πατάσσω **patassō,** *pat-as´-so;* prob. prol. from *3817;* to *knock* (gently or with a weapon or fatally):—smite, strike. Comp. *5180.*

3961. πατέω **patĕō,** *pat-eh´-o;* from a der. prob. of *3817* (mean. a *"path"*); to *trample* (lit. or fig.):—tread (down, under foot).

3962. πατήρ **patēr,** *pat-ayr´;* appar. a prim. word; a *"father"* (lit. or fig., near or more remote):—father, parent.

3963. Πάτμος **Patmŏs,** *pat´-mos;* of uncert. der.; *Patmus,* an islet in the Mediterranean:—Patmos.

3964. πατραλῴας **patralōias,** *pat-ral-o´-as;* from *3962* and the same as the latter part of *3389;* a *parricide:*—murderer of fathers.

3965. πατριά **patria,** *pat-ree-ah´;* as if fem. of a der. of *3962;* paternal *descent,* i.e. (concr.) a *group* of families or a whole *race* (*nation*):—family, kindred, lineage.

3966. πατριάχης **patriarchēs,** *pat-ree-arkh´-ace;* from *3965* and *757;* a *progenitor* ("patriarch"):—patriarch.

3967. πατρικός **patrikŏs,** *pat-ree-kos´;* from *3962; paternal,* i.e. *ancestral:*—of fathers.

3968. πατρίς **patris,** *pat-rece´;* from *3962;* a *father-land,* i.e. *native town;* (fig.) heavenly *home:*—(own) country.

3969. Πατρόβας **Patrŏbas,** *pat-rob´-as;* perh. contr. for Πατρόβιος **Patrŏbiŏs,** (a comp. of *3962* and *979*); *father's life; Patrobas,* a Chr.:—Patrobas.

3970. πατροπαράδοτος **patrŏparadŏtŏs,** *pat-rop-ar-ad´-ot-os;* from *3962* and a der. of *3860* (in the sense of *handing over* or *down*); *traditionary:*—received by tradition from fathers.

3971. πατρῷος **patrōịŏs,** *pat-ro´-os;* from *3962; paternal,* i.e. *hereditary:*—of fathers.

3972. Παῦλος **Paulŏs,** *pŏw´-los;* of Lat. or.; (*little;* but remotely from a der. of *3973,* mean. the same); *Paulus,* the name of a Rom. and of an apostle:—Paul, Paulus.

3973. παύω **pauō,** *pŏw´-o;* a prim. verb. ("*pause*"); to *stop* (trans. or intrans.), i.e. *restrain, quit, desist, come to an end:*—cease, leave, refrain.

3974. Πάφος **Paphŏs,** *paf´-os;* of uncert. der.; *Paphus,* a place in Cyprus:—Paphos.

3975. παχύνω **pachunō,** *pakh-oo´-no;* from a der. of *4078* (mean. *thick*); to *thicken,* i.e. (by impl.) to *fatten* (fig. *stupefy* or *render callous*):—wax gross.

3976. πέδη **pĕdē,** *ped´-ay;* ultimately from *4228;* a *shackle* for the feet:—fetter.

3977. πεδινός **pĕdinŏs,** *ped-ee-nos´;* from a der. of *4228* (mean. the *ground*); *level* (as easy for the *feet*):—plain.

3978. πεζεύω **pĕzĕuō,** *ped-zyoo´-o;* from the same as *3979;* to *foot* a journey, i.e. *travel* by land:—go afoot.

3979. πεζῇ **pĕzēị,** *ped-zay´;* dat. fem. of a der. of *4228* (as adv.); *foot-wise,* i.e. by *walking:*—a-(on) foot.

3980. πειθαρχέω **pĕitharchĕō,** *pi-tharkh-eh´-o;* from a comp. of *3982* and *757;* to *be persuaded* by a *ruler,* i.e. (gen.) to *submit* to authority; by anal. to *conform* to advice:—hearken, obey (magistrates).

3981. πειθός **pĕithŏs,** *pi-thos´;* from *3982; persuasive:*—enticing.

3982. πείθω **pĕithō,** *pi´-tho;* a prim. verb; to *convince* (by argument, true or false); by anal. to *pacify* or *conciliate* (by other fair means); reflex. or pass. to *assent* (to evidence or authority), to *rely* (by inward certainty):—agree, assure, believe, have confidence, be (wax) content, make friend, obey, persuade, trust, yield.

3983. πεινάω **pĕinaō,** *pi-nah´-o;* from the same as *3993* (through the idea of pinching *toil;* "*pine*"); to *famish* (absol. or comparatively); fig. to *crave:*—be an hungered.

3984. πεῖρα **pĕira,** *pi´-rah;* from the base of *4008* (through the idea of *piercing*); a *test,* i.e. *attempt, experience:*—assaying, trial.

3985. πειράζω **pĕirazō,** *pi-rad´-zo;* from *3984;* to *test* (obj.) i.e. *endeavor, scrutinize, entice, discipline:*—assay, examine, go about, prove, tempt (-er), try.

3986. πειρασμός **pĕirasmŏs,** *pi-ras-mos´;* from *3985;* a putting to *proof* (by experiment [of good], *experience* [of evil], solicitation, discipline or provocation); by impl. *adversity:*—temptation, × try.

3987. πειράω **pĕiraō,** *pi-rah´-o;* from *3984;* to *test* (subj.), i.e. (reflex.) to *attempt:*—assay.

3988. πεισμονή **pĕismŏnē,** *pice-mon-ay´;* from a presumed der. of *3982; persuadableness,* i.e. *credulity:*—persuasion.

3989. πέλαγος **pĕlagŏs,** *pel´-ag-os;* of uncert. affin.; deep or open *sea,* i.e. the *main:*—depth, sea.

3990. πελεκίζω **pĕlĕkizō,** *pel-ek-id´-zo;* from a der. of *4141* (mean. an *axe*); to *chop* off (the head), i.e. *truncate:*—behead.

3991. πέμπτος **pĕmptŏs,** *pemp´-tos;* from *4002; fifth:*—fifth.

3992. πέμπω **pĕmpō,** *pem´-po;* appar. a prim. verb; to *dispatch* (from the subj. view or point of *departure,* whereas ἵημι **hiēmi** [as a stronger form of εἶμι **ĕimi**] refers rather to the obj. point or *terminus ad quem,* and *4724* denotes prop. the *orderly* motion involved), espec. on a temporary errand; also to *transmit, bestow,* or *wield:*—send, thrust in.

3993. πένης **pĕnēs,** *pen´-ace;* from a prim. πένω **pĕnō** (to *toil* for daily subsistence); *starving,* i.e. *indigent:*—poor. Comp. *4434.*

3994. πενθερά **pĕnthĕra,** *pen-ther-ah´;* fem. of *3995;* a *wife's mother:*—mother in law, wife's mother.

3995. πενθερός **pĕnthĕrŏs,** *pen-ther-os´;* of uncert. affin.; a *wife's father:*—father in law.

3996. πενθέω **pĕnthĕō,** *pen-theh´-o;* from *3997;* to *grieve* (the feeling or the act):—mourn, (be-) wail.

3997. πένθος **pĕnthŏs,** *pen´-thos;* strengthened from the alt. of *3958; grief:*—mourning, sorrow.

3998. πεντιχρός **pĕntichrŏs,** *pen-tikh-ros´;* prol. from the base of *3993; necessitous:*—poor.

3999. πεντακίς **pĕntakis,** *pen-tak-ece´;* mult. adv. from *4002; five times:*—five times.

4000. πεντακισχίλιοι **pĕntakischiliŏi,** *pen-tak-is-khil´-ee-oy;* from *3999* and *5507; five times a thousand:*—five thousand.

4001. πεντακόσιοι **pĕntakŏsiŏi,** *pen-tak-os´-ee-oy;* from *4002* and *1540; five hundred:*—five hundred.

4002. πέντε **pĕntĕ,** *pen´-teh;* a prim. number; "*five*":—five.

4003. πεντεκαιδέκατος **pĕntĕkaidĕkatŏs,** *pen-tek-ahee-dek´-at-os;* from *4002* and *2532* and *1182; five and tenth:*—fifteenth.

4004. πεντήκοντα **pĕntēkŏnta,** *pen-tay´-kon-tah;* mult. of *4002; fifty:*—fifty.

4005. πεντηκοστή **pĕntēkŏstē,** *pen-tay-kos-tay´;* fem. of the ord. of *4004; fiftieth* (*2250* being implied) from Passover, i.e. the festival of "*Pentecost*":—Pentecost.

4006. πεποίθησις **pĕpŏithēsis,** *pep-oy´-thay-sis;* from the perf. of the alt. of *3958; reliance:*—confidence, trust.

4007. περ **pĕr,** *per;* from the base of *4008;* an enclitic particle significant of *abundance* (*thoroughness*), i.e. *emphasis; much, very* or *ever:*—[whom-] soever.

4008. πέραν **pĕran,** *per´-an;* appar. acc. of an obsol. der. of πείρω **pĕirō** (to "*pierce*"); *through* (as adv. or prep.), i.e. *across:*—beyond, farther (other) side, over.

4009. πέρας **pĕras,** *per´-as;* from the same as *4008;* an *extremity:*—end, ut- (ter-) most part.

4010. Πέργαμος **Pĕrgamŏs,** *per´-gam-os;* from *4444; fortified; Pergamus,* a place in Asia Minor:—Pergamos.

4011. Πέργη **Pĕrgē,** *perg´-ay;* prob. from the same as *4010;* a *tower; Perga,* a place in Asia Minor:—Perga.

4012. περί **pĕri,** *per-ee´;* from the base of *4008;* prop. *through* (all *over*), i.e. *around;* fig. *with respect* to; used in various applications, of place, cause or time (with the gen. denoting the *subject* or *occasion* or *superlative* point; with the acc. the *locality, circuit, matter, circumstance* or general *period*):—(there-) about, above, against, at, on behalf of, × and his company, which concern, (as) concerning, for, × how it will go with, ([there-, where-]) of, on, over, pertaining (to), for sake, × (e-) state, (as) touching, [where-] by (in), with. In comp. it retains substantially the same mean. of circuit (*around*), excess (*beyond*), or completeness (*through*).

4013. περιάγω **pĕriagō,** *per-ee-ag´-o;* from *4012* and *71;* to *take around* (as a companion); reflex. to *walk around:*—compass, go (round) about, lead about.

4014. περιαιρέω **pĕriairĕō,** *per-ee-ahee-reh´-o;* from *4012* and *138* (incl. its alt.); to *remove* all *around,* i.e. *unveil, cast off* (anchor); fig. to *expiate:*—take away (up).

4015. περιαστράπτω **pĕriastraptō,** *per-ee-as-trap´-to;* from *4012* and *797;* to *flash* all *around,* i.e. *envelop in light:*—shine round (about).

4016. περιβάλλω **pĕriballō,** *per-ee-bal´-lo;* from *4012* and *906;* to *throw* all *around,* i.e. *invest* (with a palisade or with clothing):—array, cast about, clothe (-d me), put on.

4017. περιβλέπω **pĕriblĕpō,** *per-ee-blep´-o;* from *4012* and *991;* to *look* all *around:*—look (round) about (on).

4018. περιβόλαιον **pĕribŏlaiŏn,** *per-ib-ol´-ah-yon;* neut. of a presumed der. of *4016;* something *thrown around* one, i.e. a *mantle, veil:*—covering, vesture.

4019. περιδέω **pĕridĕō,** *per-ee-deh´-o;* from *4012* and *1210;* to *bind around* one, i.e. *enwrap:*—bind about.

περιδρέμω **pĕridrĕmō.** See *4063.*
περιέλλω **pĕriĕllō.** See *4014.*
περιέλθω **pĕriĕlthō.** See *4022.*

4020. περιεργάζομαι **pĕriĕrgazŏmai,** *per-ee-er-gad´-zom-ahee;* from *4012* and *2038;* to *work* all *around,* i.e. *bustle about* (*meddle*):—be a busybody.

4021. περίεργος **pĕriĕrgŏs,** *per-ee´-er-gos;* from *4012* and *2041; working all around,* i.e. *officious* (*meddlesome,* neut. plur. *magic*):—busybody, curious arts.

4022. περιέρχομαι **pĕriĕrchŏmai,** *per-ee-er´-khom-ahee;* from *4012* and *2064* (includ. its alt.); to *come* all *around,* i.e. *stroll, vacillate, veer:*—fetch a compass, vagabond, wandering about.

4023. περιέχω **pĕriĕchō,** *per-ee-ekh´-o;* from *4012* and *2192;* to *hold* all *around,* i.e. *include, clasp* (fig.):—+ astonished, contain, after [this manner].

4024. περιζώννυμι **pĕrizŏnnumi,** *per-id-zone´-noo-mee;* from *4012* and *2224;* to *gird* all *around,* i.e. (mid. or pass.) to *fasten on one's belt* (lit. or fig.):—gird (about, self).

4025. περίθεσις **pĕrithĕsis,** *per-ith´-es-is;* from *4060;* a *putting* all *around,* i.e. *decorating* oneself with:—wearing.

4026. περιΐστημι **pĕriistēmi,** *per-ee-is´-tay-mee;* from *4012* and *2476;* to *stand* all *around,* i.e. (near) to *be a bystander,* or (aloof) to *keep away* from:—avoid, shun, stand by (round about).

4027. περικάθαρμα **pĕrikatharma,** *per-ee-kath´-ar-mah;* from a comp. of *4012* and *2508;* something *cleaned* off all *around,* i.e. *refuse* (fig.):—filth.

4028. περικαλύπτω **pĕrikaluptō,** *per-ee-kal-oop´-to;* from *4012* and *2572;* to *cover* all *around,* i.e. *entirely* (the face, a surface):—blindfold, cover, overlay.

4029. περίκειμαι **pĕrikĕimai,** *per-ik´-i-mahee;* from *4012* and *2749;* to *lie* all *around,* i.e. *inclose, encircle, hamper* (lit. or fig.):—be bound (compassed) with, hang about.

4030. περικεφαλαία **pĕrikĕphalaia,** *per-ee-kef-al-ah´-yah;* fem. of a comp. of *4012* and *2776; encirclement of* the *head,* i.e. a *helmet:*—helmet.

4031. περικρατής **pĕrikratēs,** *per-ee-krat-ace´;* from *4012* and *2904; strong* all *around,* i.e. a *master* (*manager*):—+ come by.

4032. περικρύπτω **pĕrikruptō,** *per-ee-kroop´-to;* from *4012* and *2928;* to *conceal* all *around,* i.e. *entirely:*—hide.

4033. περικυκλόω **pĕrikuklŏō,** *per-ee-koo-klŏ´-o;* from *4012* and *2944;* to *encircle* all *around,* i.e. *blockade completely:*—compass round.

4034. περιλάμπω **pĕrilampō,** *per-ee-lam´-po;* from *4012* and *2989;* to *illuminate* all *around,* i.e. *invest with a halo:*—shine round about.

4035. περιλείπω **pĕrilĕipō,** *per-ee-li´-po;* from *4012* and *3007;* to *leave* all *around,* i.e. (pass.) *survive:*—remain.

4036. περίλυπος **pĕrilupŏs,** *per-il´-oo-pos;* from *4012* and *3077; grieved* all *around,* i.e. *intensely sad:*—exceeding (very) sorry (-owful).

4037. περιμένω **pĕrimĕnō,** *per-ee-men´-o;* from *4012* and *3306;* to *stay around,* i.e. *await:*—wait for.

4038. πέριξ **pĕrix,** *per´-ix;* adv. from *4012;* all *around,* i.e. (as adj.) *circumjacent:*—round about.

4039. περιοικέω **pĕriŏkĕō,** *per-ee-oy-keh´-o;* from *4012* and *3611;* to *reside around,* i.e. *be* a *neighbor:*—dwell round about.

4040. περίοικος **pĕriŏikŏs,** *per-ee´-oy-kos;* from *4012* and *3624; housed around,* i.e. *neighboring* (ellipt. as noun):—neighbour.

4041. περιούσιος **pĕriŏusiŏs,** *per-ee-oo´-see-os;* from the pres. part. fem. of a comp. of *4012* and *1510; being beyond* usual, i.e. *special* (one's *own*):—peculiar.

4042. περιοχή **pĕriŏchē,** *per-ee-okh-ay´;* from *4023;* a *being held around,* i.e. (concr.) a *passage* (of Scripture, as *circumscribed*):—place.

4043. περιπατέω **pĕripatĕō,** *per-ee-pat-eh´-o;* from *4012* and *3961;* to *tread* all *around,* i.e. *walk* at large (espec. as proof of ability); fig. to *live, deport oneself, follow* (as a companion or votary):—go, be occupied with, walk (about).

4044. περιπείρω **pĕripĕirō,** *per-ee-pi´-ro;* from *4012* and the base of *4008;* to *penetrate entirely,* i.e. *transfix* (fig.):—pierce through.

4045. περιπίπτω **pĕripiptō,** *per-ee-pip´-to;* from *4012* and *4098;* to *fall* into something that is all *around,* i.e. *light among* or *upon, be surrounded with:*—fall among (into).

4046. περιποιέομαι **pĕripŏiĕŏmai,** *per-ee-poy-eh´-om-ahee;* mid. from *4012* and *4160;* to *make around oneself,* i.e. *acquire* (*buy*):—purchase.

4047. περιποίησις **pĕripŏiēsis,** *per-ee-poy´-ay-sis;* from *4046; acquisition* (the act or the thing); by extens. *preservation:*—obtain (-ing), peculiar, purchased, possession, saving.

4048. περιῤῥήγνυμι **pĕrirrhĕgnumi,** *per-ir-hrayg´-noo-mee;* from *4012* and *4486;* to *tear* all *around,* i.e. *completely away:*—rend off.

4049. περισπάω **pĕrispaō,** *per-ee-spah´-o;* from *4012* and *4685;* to *drag* all *around,* i.e. (fig.) to *distract* (with care):—cumber.

4050. περισσεία **pĕrissĕia,** *per-is-si´-ah;* from *4052; surplusage,* i.e. *superabundance:*—abundance (-ant, [-ly]), superfluity.

4051. περίσσευμα **pĕrissĕuma,** *per-is´-syoo-mah;* from *4052;* a *surplus,* or *superabundance:*—abundance, that was left, over and above.

4052. περισσεύω **pĕrissĕuō,** *per-is-syoo´-o;* from *4053;* to *superabound* (in quantity or quality), *be in excess, be superfluous;* also (trans.) to *cause to superabound* or *excel:*—(make, more) abound, (have, have more) abundance, (be more) abundant, be the better, enough and to spare, exceed, excel, increase, be left, redound, remain (over and above).

4053. περισσός **pĕrissŏs,** *per-is-sos´;* from *4012* (in the sense of *beyond*); *superabundant* (in quantity) or *superior* (in quality); by impl. *excessive;* adv. (with 1537) *violently;* neut. (as noun) *preeminence:*—exceeding abundantly above, more abundantly, advantage, exceedingly, very highly, beyond measure, more, superfluous, vehement [-ly].

4054. περισσότερον **pĕrissŏtĕrŏn,** *per-is-sot´-er-on;* neut. of *4055* (as adv.); in a *more superabundant* way:—more abundantly, a great deal, far more.

4055. περισσότερος **pĕrissŏtĕrŏs,** *per-is-sot´-er-os;* comp. of *4053; more superabundant* (in number, degree or character):—more abundant, greater (much) more, overmuch.

4056. περισσοτέρως **pĕrissŏtĕrōs,** *per-is-sot-er´-oce;* adv. from *4055; more superabundantly:*—more abundant (-ly), × the more earnest, (more) exceedingly, more frequent, much more, the rather.

4057. περισσῶς **pĕrissōs,** *per-is-soce´;* adv. from *4053; superabundantly:*—exceedingly, out of measure, the more.

4058. περιστερά **pĕristĕra,** *per-is-ter-ah´;* of uncert. der.; a *pigeon:*—dove, pigeon.

4059. περιτέμνω **pĕritĕmnō,** *per-ee-tem´-no;* from *4012* and the base of *5114;* to *cut around,* i.e. (spec.) to *circumcise:*—circumcise.

4060. περιτίθημι **pĕritithēmi,** *per-ee-tith´-ay-mee;* from *4012* and *5087;* to *place around;* by impl. to *present:*—bestow upon, hedge round about, put about (on, upon), set about.

4061. περιτομή **pĕritŏmē,** *per-it-om-ay´;* from *4059; circumcision* (the rite, the condition or the people, lit. or fig.):—× circumcised, circumcision.

4062. περιτρέπω **pĕritrĕpō,** *per-ee-trep´-o;* from *4012* and the base of *5157;* to *turn around,* i.e. (ment.) to *craze:*—+ make mad.

4063. περιτρέχω **pĕritrĕchō,** *per-ee-trekh´-o;* from *4012* and *5143* (includ. its alt.); to *run around,* i.e. *traverse:*—run through.

4064. περιφέρω **pĕriphĕrō,** *per-ee-fer´-o;* from *4012* and *5342;* to *convey around,* i.e. *transport hither* and *thither:*—bear (carry) about.

4065. περιφρονέω **pĕriphrŏnĕō,** *per-ee-fron-eh´-o;* from *4012* and *5426;* to *think beyond,* i.e. *depreciate* (*contemn*):—despise.

4066. περίχωρος **pĕrichōrŏs,** *per-ikh´-o-ros;* from *4012* and *5561; around* the *region,* i.e. *circumjacent* (as noun, with *1093* impl. *vicinity*):—country (round) about, region (that lieth) round about.

4067. περίψωμα **pĕripsōma,** *per-ip´-so-mah;* from a comp. of *4012* and ψάω **psaō** (to *rub*); something *brushed* all *around,* i.e. *off-scrapings* (fig. *scum*):—offscouring.

4068. περπερεύομαι **pĕrpĕrĕuŏmai,** *per-per-yoo´-om-ahee;* mid. from πέρπερος **pĕrpĕrŏs,** (*braggart;* perh. by redupl. of the base of *4008*); to *boast:*—vaunt itself.

4069. Περσίς **Pĕrsis,** *per-sece´;* a *Persian* woman; *Persis,* a Chr. female:—Persis.

4070. πέρυσι **pĕrusi,** *per´-oo-si;* adv. from *4009;* the *by-gone,* i.e. (as noun) *last year:*—+ a year ago.

πετάομαι **pĕtaŏmai.** See *4072.*

4071. πετεινόν **pĕtĕinŏn,** *pet-i-non´;* neut. of a der. of *4072;* a *flying* animal, i.e. *bird:*—bird, fowl.

4072. πέτομαι **pĕtŏmai,** *pet´-om-ahee;* or prol.

πετάομαι **pĕtaŏmai,** *pet-ah´-om-ahee;* or contr. πτάομαι **ptaŏmai,** *ptah´-om-ahee;* mid. of a prim. verb; to *fly:*—fly (-ing).

4073. πέτρα **pĕtra,** *pet´-ra;* fem. of the same as *4074;* a (mass of) *rock* (lit. or fig.):—rock.

4074. Πέτρος **Pĕtrŏs,** *pet´-ros;* appar. a prim. word; a (piece of) *rock* (larger than *3037*); as a name, *Petrus,* an apostle:—Peter, rock. Comp. *2786.*

4075. πετρώδης **pĕtrōdēs,** *pet-ro´-dace;* from *4073* and *1491; rock-like,* i.e. *rocky:*—stony.

4076. πήγανον **pēganŏn,** *pay´-gan-on;* from *4078; rue (from its thick* or *fleshy* leaves):—rue.

4077. πηγή **pēgē,** *pay-gay´;* prob. from *4078* (through the idea of *gushing* plumply); a *fount* (lit. or fig.), i.e. *source* or *supply* (of water, blood, enjoyment) (not necessarily the original spring):—fountain, well.

4078. πήγνυμι **pēgnumi,** *payg´-noo-mee;* a prol. form of a prim. verb (which in its simpler form occurs only as an alt. in certain tenses); to *fix* ("*peg*"), i.e. (spec.) to *set up* (a tent):—pitch.

4079. πηδάλιον **pēdaliŏn,** *pay-dal´-ee-on;* neut. of a (presumed) der. of πηδόν **pēdŏn** (the *blade* of an oar; from the same as *3976*); a "*pedal*", i.e. *helm:*—rudder.

4080. πηλίκος **pēlikŏs,** *pay-lee´-kos;* a quantitative form (the fem.) of the base of *4225; how much* (as indef.), i.e. in size or (fig.) dignity:—how great (large).

4081. πηλός **pēlŏs,** *pay-los´;* perh. a prim. word; *clay:*—clay.

4082. πήρα **pēra,** *pay´-rah;* of uncert. affin.; a *wallet* or leather *pouch* for food:—scrip.

4083. πῆχυς **pēchus,** *pay´-khoos;* of uncert. affin.; the *fore-arm,* i.e. (as a measure) a *cubit:*—cubit.

4084. πιάζω **piazō,** *pee-ad´-zo;* prob. another form of *971;* to *squeeze,* i.e. *seize* (gently by the hand [*press*], or officially (*arrest*], or in hunting [*capture*]):—apprehend, catch, lay hand on, take. Comp. *4085.*

4085. πιέζω **piĕzō,** *pee-ed´-zo;* another form for *4084;* to *pack:*—press down.

4086. πιθανολογία **pithanŏlŏgia,** *pith-an-ol-og-ee´-ah;* from a comp. of a der. of *3982* and *3056; persuasive language:*—enticing words.

4087. πικραίνω **pikrainō,** *pik-rah´ee-no;* from *4089;* to *embitter* (lit. or fig.):—be (make) bitter.

4088. πικρία **pikria,** *pik-ree´-ah;* from *4089; acridity* (espec. *poison*), lit. or fig:—bitterness.

4089. πικρός **pikrŏs,** *pik-ros´;* perh. from *4078* (through the idea of *piercing*); *sharp* (*pungent*), i.e. *acrid* (lit. or fig.):—bitter.

4090. πικρῶς **pikrōs,** *pik-roce´;* adv. from *4089; bitterly,* i.e. (fig.) *violently:*—bitterly.

4091. Πιλάτος **Pilatŏs,** *pil-at´-os;* of Lat. or.; *close-pressed,* i.e. *firm; Pilatus,* a Rom.:—Pilate.

πίμπλημι **pimplēmi.** See *4130.*

4092. πίμπρημι **pimprēmi,** *pim´-pray-mee;* a redupl. and prol. form of a prim.

πρέω **prĕō,** *preh´-o* (which occurs only as an alt. in certain tenses); to *fire,* i.e. *burn* (fig. and pass. *become inflamed* with fever):—be (× should have) swollen.

4093. πινακίδιον **pinakidiŏn,** *pin-ak-id´-ee-on;* dimin. of *4094;* a *tablet* (for writing on):—writing table.

4094. πίναξ **pinax,** *pin´-ax;* appar. a form of *4109;* a *plate:*—charger, platter.

4095. πίνω **pinō,** *pee´-no;* a prol. form of

πίω **piō,** *pee´-o;* which (together with another form πόω **pŏō,** *pŏ´-o*) occurs only as an alt. in cert. tenses; to *imbibe* (lit. or fig.):—drink.

4096. πιότης **piŏtēs,** *pee-ot´-ace;* from πίων **piōn** (*fat;* perh. akin to the alt. of *4095* through the idea of *repletion*); *plumpness,* i.e. (by impl.) *richness* (*oiliness*):—fatness.

4097. πιπράσκω **pipraskō,** *pip-ras´-ko;* a redupl. and prol. form of

πράω **praō,** *prah´-o* (which occurs only as an alt. in cert. tenses); contr. from περάω **pĕraō** (to *traverse;* from the base of *4008*); to *traffic* (by *travelling*), i.e. *dispose* of as merchandise or into slavery (lit. or fig.):—sell.

4098. πίπτω **piptō,** *pip´-to;* a redupl. and contr. form of πέτω **pĕtō,** *pet´-o* (which occurs only as an alt. in cert. tenses); prob. akin to *4072* through the idea of *alighting;* to *fall* (lit. or fig.):—fail, fall (down), light on.

4099. Πισιδία **Pisidia,** *pis-id-ee´-ah;* prob. of for. or.; *Pisidia,* a region of Asia Minor:—Pisidia.

4100. πιστεύω **pistĕuō,** *pist-yoo´-o;* from *4102;* to *have faith* (in, upon, or with respect to, a person or thing), i.e. *credit;* by impl. to *entrust* (espec. one's spiritual well-being to Christ):—believe (-r), commit (to trust), put in trust with.

4101. πιστικός **pistikŏs,** *pis-tik-os´;* from *4102; trustworthy,* i.e. *genuine* (*unadulterated*):—spike-[nard].

4102. πίστις **pistis,** *pis´-tis;* from *3982; persuasion,* i.e. *credence;* mor. *conviction* (of *religious* truth, or the truthfulness of God or a religious teacher), espec. *reliance* upon Christ for salvation; abstr. *constancy* in such profession; by extens. the system of religious (Gospel) *truth* itself:—assurance, belief, believe, faith, fidelity.

4103. πιστός **pistŏs,** *pis-tos´;* from *3982;* obj. *trustworthy;* subj. *trustful;*—believe (-ing, -r), faithful (-ly), sure, true.

4104. πιστόω **pistŏō,** *pis-tŏ´-o;* from *4103;* to *assure:*—assure of.

4105. πλανάω **planaō,** *plan-ah´-o;* from *4106;* to (prop. *cause* to) *roam* (from safety, truth, or virtue):—go astray, deceive, err, seduce, wander, be out of the way.

4106. πλάνη **planē,** *plan´-ay;* fem. of *4108* (as abstr.); obj. *fraudulence;* subj. a *straying* from orthodoxy or piety:—deceit, to deceive, delusion, error.

4107. πλανήτης **planētēs,** *plan-ay´-tace;* from *4108;* a *rover* ("planet"), i.e. (fig.) an *erratic* teacher:—wandering.

4108. πλάνος **planŏs,** *plan´-os;* of uncert. affin.; *roving* (as a *tramp*), i.e. (by impl.) an *impostor* or *misleader:*—deceiver, seducing.

4109. πλάξ **plax,** *plax;* from *4111;* a *moulding-board,* i.e. *flat* surface ("*plate*", or *tablet,* lit. or fig.):—table.

4110. πλάσμα **plasma,** *plas´-mah;* from *4111;* something *moulded:*—thing formed.

4111. πλάσσω **plassō,** *plas´-so;* a prim. verb; to *mould,* i.e. *shape* or *fabricate:*—form.

4112. πλαστός **plastŏs,** *plas-tos´;* from *4111; moulded,* i.e. (by impl.) *artificial* or (fig.) *fictitious* (*false*):—feigned.

4113. πλατεῖα **platĕia,** *plat-i´-ah;* fem. of *4116;* a *wide* "*plat*" or "*place*", i.e. open *square:*—street.

4114. πλάτος **platŏs,** *plat´-os;* from *4116; width:*—breadth.

4115. πλατύνω **platunō,** *plat-oo´-no;* from *4116;* to *widen* (lit. or fig.):—make broad, enlarge.

4116. πλατύς **platus,** *plat-oos´;* from *4111;* spread out "*flat*" ("plot"), i.e. *broad:*—wide.

4117. πλέγμα **plĕgma,** *pleg´-mah;* from *4120;* a *plait* (of hair):—broidered hair.

πλεῖον **plĕiŏn.** See *4119.*

4118. πλεῖστος **plĕistŏs,** *plice´-tos;* irreg. superl. of *4183;* the *largest number* or *very large:*—very great, most.

4119. πλείων **plĕiōn,** *pli-own;* neut. πλεῖον **plĕiŏn,** *pli´-on;* or πλέον **plĕŏn,** *pleh´-on;* compar. of *4183;* *more* in quantity, number, or quality; also (in plur.) the *major portion:*—× above, + exceed, more excellent, further, (very) great (-er), long (-er), (very) many, greater (more) part, + yet but.

4120. πλέκω **plĕkō,** *plek´-o;* a prim. word; to *twine* or *braid:*—plait.

πλέον **plĕŏn.** See 4119.

4121. πλεονάζω **plĕŏnazō,** *pleh-on-ad´-zo;* from *4119;* to *do, make* or *be more,* i.e. *increase* (trans. or intrans.); by extens. to *superabound:*—abound, abundant, make to increase, have over.

4122. πλεονεκτέω **plĕŏnĕktĕō,** *pleh-on-ek-teh´-o;* from *4123;* to *be covetous,* i.e. (by impl.) to *overreach:*—get an advantage, defraud, make a gain.

4123. πλεονέκτης **plĕŏnĕktēs,** *pleh-on-ek´-tace;* from *4119* and *2192;* *holding* (*desiring*) *more,* i.e. *eager for gain* (*avaricious,* hence a *defrauder*):—covetous.

4124. πλεονεξία **plĕŏnĕxia,** *pleh-on-ex-ee´-ah;* from *4123;* *avarice,* i.e. (by impl.) *fraudulency, extortion:*—covetous (-ness) practices, greediness.

4125. πλευρά **plĕura,** *plyoo-rah´;* of uncert. affin.; a *rib,* i.e. (by extens.) *side:*—side.

4126. πλέω **plĕō,** *pleh´-o;* another form for πλεύω **plĕuō,** *plyoo´-o;* which is used as an alt. in certain tenses; prob. a form of *4150* (through the idea of *plunging* through the water); to *pass* in a vessel:—sail. See also *4130.*

4127. πληγή **plēgē,** *play-gay´;* from *4141;* a *stroke;* by impl. a *wound;* fig. a *calamity:*—plague, stripe, wound (-ed).

4128. πλῆθος **plēthŏs,** *play´-thos;* from *4130;* a *fulness,* i.e. a *large number, throng, populace:*—bundle, company, multitude.

4129. πληθύνω **plēthunō,** *play-thoo´-no;* from another form of *4128;* to *increase* (trans. or intrans.):—abound, multiply.

4130. πλήθω **plēthō,** *play´-tho;* a prol. form of a prim. πλέω **plĕō,** *pleh´-o* (which appears only as an alt. in certain tenses and in the redupl. form πίμπλημι **pimplēmi**); to *"fill"* (lit. or fig. [*imbue, influence, supply*]); spec. to *fulfil* (time):—accomplish, full (. . . come), furnish.

4131. πλήκτης **plēktēs,** *plake´-tace;* from *4141;* a *smiter,* i.e. *pugnacious* (*quarrelsome*):—striker.

4132. πλημμύρα **plēmmura,** *plame-moo´-rah;* prol. from *4130;* *flood-tide,* i.e. (by anal.) a *freshet:*—flood.

4133. πλήν **plēn,** *plane;* from *4119;* *moreover* (*besides*), i.e. *albeit, save that, rather, yet:*—but (rather), except, nevertheless, notwithstanding, save, than.

4134. πλήρης **plērēs,** *play´-race;* from *4130;* *replete,* or *covered* over; by anal. *complete:*—full.

4135. πληροφορέω **plērŏphŏrĕō,** *play-rof-or-eh´-o;* from *4134* and *5409;* to *carry* out *fully* (in evidence), i.e. *completely assure* (or *convince*), *entirely accomplish:*—most surely believe, fully know (persuade), make full proof of.

4136. πληροφορία **plērŏphŏria,** *play-rof-or-ee´-ah;* from *4135;* *entire confidence:*—(full) assurance.

4137. πληρόω **plērŏō,** *play-rŏ´-o;* from *4134;* to *make replete,* i.e. (lit.) to *cram* (a net), *level* up (a hollow), or (fig.) to *furnish* (or *imbue, diffuse, influence*), *satisfy, execute* (an office), *finish* (a period or task), *verify* (or *coincide* with a prediction), etc.:—accomplish, × after, (be) complete, end, expire, fill (up), fulfil, (be, make) full (come), fully preach, perfect, supply.

4138. πλήρωμα **plērōma,** *play´-ro-mah;* from *4137;* *repletion* or *completion,* i.e. (subj.) what *fills* (as contents, supplement, copiousness, multitude), or (obj.) what is *filled* (as container, performance, period):—which is put in to fill up, piece that filled up, fulfilling, full, fulness.

4139. πλησίον **plēsiŏn,** *play-see´-on;* neut. of a der. of πέλας **pĕlas** (*near*); (adv.) *close* by; as noun, a *neighbor,* i.e. *fellow* (as man, countryman, Chr. or friend):—near, neighbour.

4140. πλησμονή **plēsmŏnē,** *place-mon-ay´;* from a presumed der. of *4130;* a *filling* up, i.e. (fig.) *gratification:*—satisfying.

4141. πλήσσω **plēssō,** *place´-so;* appar. another form of *4111* (through the idea of *flattening out*); to *pound,* i.e. (fig.) to *inflict* with (calamity):—smite. Comp. *5180.*

4142. πλοιάριον **plŏiariŏn,** *ploy-ar´-ee-on;* neut. of a presumed der. of *4143;* a *boat:*—boat, little (small) ship.

4143. πλοῖον **plŏiŏn,** *ploy´-on;* from *4126;* a *sailer,* i.e. *vessel:*—ship (-ping).

4144. πλόος **plŏŏs,** *plŏ´-os;* from *4126;* a *sail,* i.e. *navigation:*—course, sailing, voyage.

4145. πλούσιος **plŏusiŏs,** *ploo´-see-os;* from *4149;* *wealthy;* fig. *abounding* with:—rich.

4146. πλουσίως **plŏusiōs,** *ploo-see´-oce;* adv. from *4145;* *copiously:*—abundantly, richly.

4147. πλουτέω **plŏutĕō,** *ploo-teh´-o;* from *4148;* to *be* (or *become*) *wealthy* (lit. or fig.):—be increased with goods, (be made, wax) rich.

4148. πλουτίζω **plŏutizō,** *ploo-tid´-zo;* from *4149;* to *make wealthy* (fig.):—en- (make) rich.

4149. πλοῦτος **plŏutŏs,** *ploo´-tos;* from the base of *4130;* *wealth* (as *fulness*), i.e. (lit.) *money, possessions,* or (fig.) *abundance, richness,* (spec.) valuable *bestowment:*—riches.

4150. πλύνω **plunō,** *ploo´-no;* a prol. form of an obsol. πλύω **pluō** (to *"flow"*); to *"plunge"*, i.e. *launder* clothing:—wash. Comp. *3068, 3538.*

4151. πνεῦμα **pnĕuma,** *pnyoo´-mah;* from *4154;* a *current* of air, i.e. *breath* (*blast*) or a *breeze;* by anal. or fig. a *spirit,* i.e. (human) the rational *soul,* (by impl.) *vital principle,* mental *disposition,* etc., or (superhuman) an *angel, dæmon,* or (divine) *God,* Christ's *spirit,* the Holy *Spirit:*—ghost, life, spirit (-ual, -ually), mind. Comp. *5590.*

4152. πνευματικός **pnĕumatikŏs,** *pnyoo-mat-ik-os´;* from *4151;* *non-carnal,* i.e. (humanly) *ethereal* (as opposed to gross), or (dæmoniacally) a *spirit* (concr.), or (divinely) *supernatural, regenerate, religious:*—spiritual. Comp. *5591.*

4153. πνευματικῶς **pnĕumatikōs,** *pnyoo-mat-ik-oce´;* adv. from *4152;* *non-physically,* i.e. *divinely, figuratively:*—spiritually.

4154. πνέω **pnĕō,** *pneh´-o;* a prim. word; to *breathe* hard, i.e. *breeze:*—blow. Comp. *5594.*

4155. πνίγω **pnigō,** *pnee´-go;* strengthened from *4154;* to *wheeze,* i.e. (caus. by impl.) to *throttle* or *strangle* (*drown*):—choke, take by the throat.

4156. πνικτός **pniktŏs,** *pnik-tos´;* from *4155;* *throttled,* i.e. (neut. concr.) an animal *choked* to death (*not bled*):—strangled.

4157. πνοή **pnŏē,** *pno-ay´;* from *4154;* *respiration,* a *breeze:*—breath, wind.

4158. ποδήρης **pŏdērēs,** *pod-ay´-race;* from *4228* and another element of uncert. affin.; a *dress* (*2066* implied) *reaching* the *ankles:*—garment down to the foot.

4159. πόθεν **pŏthĕn,** *poth´-en;* from the base of *4213* with enclitic adv. of origin; *from which* (as interrog.) or *what* (as rel.) place, state, source or cause:—whence.

4160. ποιέω **pŏiĕō,** *poy-eh´-o;* appar. a prol. from of an obsol. prim.; to *make* or *do* (in a very wide application, more or less direct):—abide, + agree, appoint, × avenge, + band together, be, bear, + bewray, bring (forth), cast out, cause, commit, + content, continue, deal, + without any delay, (would) do (-ing), execute, exercise, fulfil, gain, give, have, hold, × journeying, keep, + lay wait, + lighten the ship, make, × mean, + none of these things move me, observe, ordain, perform, provide, + have purged, purpose, put, + raising up, × secure, shew, × shoot out, spend, take, tarry, + transgress the law, work, yield. Comp. *4238.*

4161. ποίημα **pŏiēma,** *poy´-ay-mah;* from *4160;* a *product,* i.e. *fabric* (lit. or fig.):—thing that is made, workmanship.

4162. ποίησις **pŏiēsis,** *poy´-ay-sis;* from *4160;* *action,* i.e. *performance* (of the law):—deed.

4163. ποιητής **pŏiētēs,** *poy-ay-tace´;* from *4160;* a *performer;* spec. a *"poet"*;—doer, poet.

4164. ποικίλος **pŏikilŏs,** *poy-kee´-los;* of uncert. der.; *motley,* i.e. *various* in character:—divers, manifold.

4165. ποιμαίνω **pŏimainō,** *poy-mah´ee-no;* from *4166;* to *tend* as a shepherd (or fig. *superviser*):—feed (cattle), rule.

4166. ποιμήν **pŏimēn,** *poy-mane´;* of uncert. affin.; a *shepherd* (lit. or fig.):—shepherd, pastor.

4167. ποίμνη **pŏimnē,** *poym´-nay;* contr. from *4165;* a *flock* (lit. or fig.):—flock, fold.

4168. ποίμνιον **pŏimniŏn,** *poym´-nee-on;* neut. of a presumed der. of *4167;* a *flock,* i.e. (fig.) *group* (of believers):—flock.

4169. ποῖος **pŏiŏs,** *poy´-os;* from the base of *4226* and *3634;* individualizing interrog. (of character) *what* sort of, or (of number) *which* one:—what (manner of), which.

4170. πολεμέω **pŏlĕmĕō,** *pol-em-eh´-o;* from *4171;* to *be* (engaged) in *warfare,* i.e. to *battle* (lit. or fig.):—fight, (make) war.

4171. πόλεμος **pŏlĕmŏs,** *pol´-em-os;* from πέλομαι **pĕlŏmai** (to *bustle*); *warfare* (lit. or fig.; a single encounter or a series):—battle, fight, war.

4172. πόλις **pŏlis,** *pol´-is;* prob. from the same as *4171,* or perh. form *4183;* a *town* (prop. with walls, of greater or less size):—city.

4173. πολιτάρχης **pŏlitarchēs,** *pol-it-ar´-khace;* from *4172* and *757;* a *town-officer,* i.e. *magistrate:*—ruler of the city.

4174. πολιτεία **pŏlitĕia,** *pol-ee-ti´-ah;* from *4177* ("*polity*"); *citizenship;* concr. a *community:*—commonwealth, freedom.

4175. πολίτευμα **pŏlitĕuma,** *pol-it´-yoo-mah;* from *4176;* a *community,* i.e. (abstr.) *citizenship* (fig.):—conversation.

4176. πολιτεύομαι **pŏlitĕuŏmai,** *pol-it-yoo´-om-ahee;* mid. of a der. of *4177;* to *behave* as a citizen (fig.):—let conversation be, live.

4177. πολίτης **pŏlitēs,** *pol-ee´-tace;* from *4172;* a *townsman:*—citizen.

4178. πολλάκις **pŏllakis,** *pol-lak´-is;* mult. adv. from *4183; many times,* i.e. *frequently:*—oft (-en, -en-times, -times).

4179. πολλαπλασίων **pŏllaplasiōn,** *pol-lap-las-ee´-ohn;* from *4183* and prob. a der. of *4120; manifold,* i.e. (neut. as noun) *very much more:*—manifold more.

4180. πολυλογία **pŏlulŏgia,** *pol-oo-log-ee´-ah;* from a comp. of *4183* and *3056; loquacity,* i.e. *prolixity:*—much speaking.

4181. πολυμέρως **pŏlumĕrōs,** *pol-oo-mer´-oce;* adv. from a comp. of *4183* and *3313; in many portions,* i.e. *variously* as to time and agency (*piecemeal*):—at sundry times.

4182. πολυποίκιλος **pŏlupŏikilos,** *pol-oo-poy´-kil-os;* from *4183* and *4164; much variegated,* i.e. *multifarious:*—manifold.

4183. πολύς **pŏlus,** *pol-oos´;* includ. the forms from the alt. πολλός **pŏllŏs;** (sing.) *much* (in any respect) or (plur.) *many;* neut. (sing.) as adv. *largely;* neut. (plur.) as adv. or noun *often, mostly, largely:*—abundant, + altogether, common, + far (passed, spent), (+ be of a) great (age, deal, -ly, while), long, many, much, oft (-en [-times]), plenteous, sore, straitly. Comp. *4118, 4119.*

4184. πολύσπλαγχνος **pŏlusplagchnos,** *pol-oo´-splankh-nos;* from *4183* and *4698* (fig.); *extremely compassionate:*—very pitiful.

4185. πολυτελής **pŏlutĕlēs,** *pol-oo-tel-ace´;* from *4183* and *5056; extremely expensive:*—costly, very precious, of great price.

4186. πολύτιμος **pŏlutimŏs,** *pol-oot´-ee-mos;* from *4183* and *5092; extremely valuable:*—very costly, of great price.

4187. πολυτρόπως **pŏlutrŏpōs,** *pol-oot-rop´-oce;* adv. from a comp. of *4183* and *5158; in many ways,* i.e. *variously* as to method or form:—in divers manners.

4188. πόμα **pŏma,** *pom´-ah;* from the alt. of *4095;* a *beverage:*—drink.

4189. πονηρία **pŏnēria,** *pon-ay-ree´-ah;* from *4190; depravity,* i.e. (spec.) *malice;* plur. (concr.) *plots, sins:*—iniquity, wickedness.

4190. πονηρός **pŏnērŏs,** *pon-ay-ros´;* from a der. of *4192; hurtful,* i.e. *evil* (prop. in effect or influence, and thus differing from *2556,* which refers rather to *essential* character, as well as from *4550,* which indicates *degeneracy* from original virtue); fig. *calamitous;* also (pass.) *ill,* i.e. *diseased;* but espec. (mor.) *culpable,* i.e. *derelict, vicious, facinorous;* neut. (sing.) *mischief, malice,* or (plur.) *guilt;* masc. (sing.) the *devil,* or (plur.) *sinners:*—bad, evil, grievous, harm, lewd, malicious, wicked (-ness). See also *4191.*

4191. πονηρότερος **pŏnērŏtĕrŏs,** *pon-ay-rot´-er-os;* compar. of *4190; more evil:*—more wicked.

4192. πόνος **pŏnŏs,** *pon´-os;* from the base of *3993; toil,* i.e. (by impl.) *anguish:*—pain.

4193. Ποντικός **Pŏntikŏs,** *pon-tik-os´;* from *4195;* a *Pontican,* i.e. native of Pontus:—born in Pontus.

4194. Πόντιος **Pŏntiŏs,** *pon´-tee-os;* of Lat. or.; appar. *bridged; Pontius,* a Rom.:—Pontius.

4195. Πόντος **Pŏntŏs,** *pon´-tos;* a *sea; Pontus,* a region of Asia Minor:—Pontus.

4196. Πόπλιος **Pŏpliŏs,** *pop´-lee-os;* of Lat. or.; appar. "*popular*"; *Poplius* (i.e. *Publius*), a Rom.:—Publius.

4197. πορεία **pŏrĕia,** *por-i´-ah;* from *4198; travel* (by land); fig. (plur.) *proceedings,* i.e. *career:*—journey [-ing], ways.

4198. πορεύομαι **pŏrĕuŏmai,** *por-yoo´-om-ahee;* mid. from a der. of the same as *3984;* to *traverse,* i.e. *travel* (lit. or fig.; espec. to *remove* [fig. *die*], *live,* etc.);—depart, go (away, forth, one's way, up), (make a, take a) journey, walk.

4199. πορθέω **pŏrthĕō,** *por-theh´-o;* prol. from πέρθω **pĕrthō** (to *sack*); to *ravage* (fig.):—destroy, waste.

4200. πορισμός **pŏrismŏs,** *por-is-mos´;* from a der. of πόρος **pŏrŏs** (a *way,* i.e. *means*); *furnishing* (*procuring*), i.e. (by impl.) *money-getting* (*acquisition*):—gain.

4201. Πόρκιος **Pŏrkiŏs,** *por´-kee-os;* of Lat. or.; appar. *swinish; Porcius,* a Rom.:—Porcius.

4202. πορνεία **pŏrnĕia,** *por-ni´-ah;* from *4203; harlotry* (includ. *adultery* and *incest*); fig. *idolatry:*—fornication.

4203. πορνεύω **pŏrnĕuō,** *porn-yoo´-o;* from *4204;* to *act* the *harlot,* i.e. (lit.) *indulge* unlawful *lust* (of either sex), or (fig.) *practise idolatry:*—commit (fornication).

4204. πόρνη **pŏrnē,** *por´-nay;* fem. of *4205;* a *strumpet;* fig. an *idolater:*—harlot, whore.

4205. πόρνος **pŏrnŏs,** *por´-nos;* from πέρνημι **pĕrnēmi** (to *sell;* akin to the base of *4097*); a (male) *prostitute* (as *venal*), i.e. (by anal.) a *debauchee* (*libertine*):—fornicator, whoremonger.

4206. πόῤῥω **pŏrrhō,** *por´-rho;* adv. from *4253; forwards,* i.e. *at a distance:*—far, a great way off. See also *4207.*

4207. πόῤῥωθεν **pŏrrhōthĕn,** *por´-rho-then;* from *4206* with adv. enclitic of source; *from far,* or (by impl.) *at a distance,* i.e. *distantly:*—afar off.

4208. ποῤῥωτέρω **pŏrrhōtĕrō,** *por-rho-ter´-o;* adv. compar. of *4206; farther,* i.e. *a greater distance:*—further.

4209. πορφύρα **pŏrphura,** *por-foo´-rah;* of Lat. or.; the "*purple*" mussel, i.e. (by impl.) the *red-blue* color itself, and finally a garment dyed with it:—purple.

4210. πορφυροῦς **pŏrphurŏus,** *por-foo-rooce´;* from *4209; purpureal,* i.e. *bluish red:*—purple.

4211. πορφυρόπωλις **pŏrphurŏpōlis,** *por-foo-rop´-o-lis;* fem. of a comp. of *4209* and *4453;* a *female trader in purple* cloth:—seller of purple.

4212. ποσάκις **pŏsakis,** *pos-ak´-is;* mult. from *4214; how many times:*—how oft (-en).

4213. πόσις **pŏsis,** *pos´-is;* from the alt. of *4095;* a *drinking* (the act), i.e. (concr.) a *draught:*—drink.

4214. πόσος **pŏsŏs,** *pos´-os;* from an obsol. πός **pŏs** (*who, what*) and *3739;* interrog. pron. (of amount) *how much* (*large, long* or [plur.] *many*):—how great (long, many), what.

4215. ποταμός **pŏtamŏs,** *pot-am-os´;* prob. from a der. of the alt. of *4095* (comp. *4224*); a *current, brook* or *freshet* (as *drinkable*), i.e. *running water:*—flood, river, stream, water.

4216. ποταμοφόρητος **pŏtamŏphŏrētŏs,** *pot-am-of-or´-ay-tos;* from *4215* and a der. of *5409; riverborne,* i.e. *overwhelmed by a stream:*—carried away of the flood.

4217. ποταπός **pŏtapŏs,** *pot-ap-os´;* appar. from *4219* and the base of *4226;* interrog. *whatever,* i.e. of *what possible* sort:—what (manner of).

4218. ποτέ **pŏtĕ,** *pot-eh´;* from the base of *4225* and *5037;* indef. adv., at *some time, ever:*—afore- (any, some-) time (-s), at length (the last), (+ n-) ever, in the old time, in time past, once, when.

4219. ´*πότε* **pŏtĕ,** *pot´-eh;* from the base of *4226* and *5037;* interrog. adv., at *what time:*— + how long, when.

4220. *πότερον* **pŏtĕrŏn,** *pot´-er-on;* neut. of a compar. of the base of *4226;* interrog. as adv., *which* (of two), i.e. *is it* this or that:—whether.

4221. *ποτήριον* **pŏtēriŏn,** *pot-ay´-ree-on;* neut. of a der. of the alt. of *4095;* a *drinking-vessel;* by extens. the contents thereof, i.e. a *cupful* (*draught*); fig. a *lot* or *fate:*—cup.

4222. *ποτίζω* **pŏtizō,** *pot-id´-zo;* from a der. of the alt. of *4095;* to *furnish drink, irrigate:*—give (make) to drink, feed, water.

4223. Ποτίολοι **Pŏtiŏlŏi,** *pot-ee´-ol-oy;* of Lat. or.; *little wells,* i.e. *mineral springs; Potioli* (i.e. *Puteoli*), a place in Italy:—Puteoli.

4224. *πότος* **pŏtŏs,** *pot´-os;* from the alt. of *4095;* a *drinking-bout* or *carousal:*—banqueting.

4225. *πού* **pŏu,** *poo;* gen. of an indef. pron. *πός* **pŏs** (*some*) otherwise obsol. (comp. *4214*); as adv. of place, *somewhere,* i.e. *nearly:*—about, a certain place.

4226. *ποῦ* **pŏu,** *poo;* gen. of an interrog. pron. *πός* **pŏs** (*what*) otherwise obsol. (perh. the same as *4225* used with the rising slide of inquiry); as adv. of place; *at* (by impl. *to*) *what* locality:—where, whither.

4227. Πούδης **Pŏudēs,** *poo´-dace;* of Lat. or.; *modest; Pudes* (i.e. *Pudens*), a Chr.:—Pudens.

4228. *πούς* **pŏus,** *pooce;* a prim word; a *"foot"* (fig. or lit.):—foot (-stool).

4229. *πρᾶγμα* **pragma,** *prag´-mah;* from *4238;* a *deed;* by impl. an *affair;* by extens. an *object* (material):—business, matter, thing, work.

4230. *πραγματεία* **pragmatĕia,** *prag-mat-i´-ah;* from *4231;* a *transaction,* i.e. *negotiation:*—affair.

4231. *πραγματεύομαι* **pragmatĕuŏmai,** *prag-mat-yoo´-om-ahee;* from *4229;* to *busy oneself* with, i.e. to *trade:*—occupy.

4232. *πραιτώριον* **praitōriŏn,** *prahee-to´-ree-on;* of Lat. or.; the *prætorium* or governor's *courtroom* (sometimes includ. the whole *edifice* and *camp*):—(common, judgment) hall (of judgment), palace, prætorium.

4233. *πράκτωρ* **praktōr,** *prak´-tore;* from a der. of *4238;* a *practiser,* i.e. (spec.) an official *collector:*—officer.

4234. *πρᾶξις* **praxis,** *prax´-is;* from *4238; practice,* i.e. (concr.) an *act;* by extens. a *function:*—deed, office, work.

4235. *πρᾷος* **praịŏs,** *prah´-os;* a form of *4239,* used in cert. parts; *gentle,* i.e. *humble:*—meek.

4236. *πρᾳότης* **praịŏtēs,** *prah-ot´-ace;* from *4235; gentleness;* by impl. *humility:*—meekness.

4237. *πρασιά* **prasia,** *pras-ee-ah´;* perh. from *πράσον* **prasŏn** (a *leek,* and so an *onion-patch*); a garden-*plot,* i.e. (by impl. of regular *beds*) a *row* (repeated in plur. by Hebr. to indicate an arrangement):—in ranks.

4238. *πράσσω* **prassō,** *pras´-so;* a prim. verb; to *"practise",* i.e. *perform repeatedly* or *habitually* (thus differing from *4160,* which prop. refers to a *single* act); by impl. to *execute, accomplish,* etc.; spec. to *collect* (dues), *fare* (personally):—commit, deeds, do, exact, keep, require, use arts.

4239. *πραΰς* **praüs,** *prah-ooce´;* appar. a prim. word; *mild,* i.e. (by impl.) *humble:*—meek. See also *4235.*

4240. *πραΰτης* **praütēs,** *prah-oo´-tace;* from *4239; mildness,* i.e. (by impl.) *humility:*—meekness.

4241. *πρέπω* **prĕpō,** *prep´-o;* appar. a prim. verb; to *tower* up (*be conspicuous*), i.e. (by impl.) to *be suitable* or *proper* (third pers. sing. pres. indic., often used impers., it is *fit* or *right*):—become, comely.

4242. *πρεσβεία* **prĕsbĕia,** *pres-bi´-ah;* from *4243; seniority* (*eldership*), i.e. (by impl.) an *embassy* (concr. *ambassadors*):—ambassage, message.

4243. *πρεσβεύω* **prĕsbĕuō,** *pres-byoo´-o;* from the base of *4245;* to be a *senior,* i.e. (by impl.) *act as a representative* (fig. *preacher*):—be an ambassador.

4244. *πρεσβυτέριον* **prĕsbutĕriŏn,** *pres-boo-ter´-ee-on;* neut. of a presumed der. of *4245;* the *order of elders,* i.e. (spec.) Isr. *Sanhedrim* or Chr. *"presbytery":*—(estate of) elder (-s), presbytery.

4245. *πρεσβύτερος* **prĕsbutĕrŏs,** *pres-boo´-ter-os;* compar. of *πρέσβυς* **prĕsbus** (*elderly*); *older;* as noun, a *senior;* spec. an Isr. *Sanhedrist* (also fig. member of the celestial council) or Chr. *"presbyter":*—elder (-est), old.

4246. *πρεσβύτης* **prĕsbutēs,** *pres-boo´-tace;* from the same as *4245;* an *old man:*—aged (man), old man.

4247. *πρεσβῦτις* **prĕsbutis,** *pres-boo´-tis;* fem. of *4246;* an *old woman:*—aged woman.

πρήθω **prēthō.** See *4092.*

4248. *πρηνής* **prēnēs,** *pray-nace´;* from *4253; leaning* (*falling*) *forward* (*"prone"*), i.e. *head foremost:*—headlong.

4249. *πρίζω* **prizō,** *prid´-zo;* a strengthened form of a prim. *πρίω* **priō** (to *saw*); to *saw* in two:—saw asunder.

4250. *πρίν* **prin,** *prin;* adv. from *4253; prior, sooner:*—before (that), ere.

4251. Πρίσκα **Priska,** *pris´-kah;* of Lat. or.; fem. of *Priscus, ancient; Priska,* a Chr. woman:—Prisca. See also *4252.*

4252. Πρίσκιλλα **Priscilla,** *pris´-cil-lah;* dimin. of *4251; Priscilla* (i.e. *little Prisca*), a Chr. woman:—Priscilla.

4253. *πρό* **prŏ,** *prŏ;* a prim. prep.; *"fore",* i.e. *in front of, prior* (fig. *superior*) *to:*—above, ago, before, or ever. In comp. it retains the same significations.

4254. *προάγω* **prŏagō,** *prŏ-ag´-o;* from *4253* and *71;* to *lead forward* (magisterially); intrans. to *precede* (in place or time [part. *previous*]):—bring (forth, out), go before.

4255. *προαιρέομαι* **prŏairĕŏmai,** *prŏ-ahee-reh´-om-ahee;* from *4253* and *138;* to *choose* for oneself *before* another thing (*prefer*), i.e. (by impl.) to *propose* (*intend*):—purpose.

4256. *προαιτιάομαι* **prŏaitiaŏmai,** *prŏ-ahee-tee-ah´-om-ahee;* from *4253* and a der. of *156;* to *accuse already,* i.e. *previously charge:*—prove before.

4257. *προακούω* **prŏakŏuō,** *prŏ-ak-oo´-o;* from *4253* and *191;* to *hear already,* i.e. *anticipate:*—hear before.

4258. *προαμαρτάνω* **prŏamartanō,** *prŏ-am-ar-tan´-o;* from *4253* and *264;* to *sin previously* (to conversion):—sin already, heretofore sin.

4259. *προαύλιον* **prŏauliŏn,** *prŏ-ŏw´-lee-on;* neut. of a presumed comp. of *4253* and *833;* a *forecourt,* i.e. *vestibule* (*alley-way*):—porch.

4260. *προβαίνω* **prŏbainō,** *prob-ah´ee-no;* from *4253* and the base of *939;* to *walk forward,* i.e. *advance* (lit. or in years):— + be of a great age, go farther (on), be well stricken.

4261. *προβάλλω* **prŏballō,** *prob-al´-lo;* from *4253* and *906;* to *throw forward,* i.e. *push to the front, germinate:*—put forward, shoot forth.

4262. *προβατικός* **prŏbatikŏs,** *prob-at-ik-os´;* from *4263; relating to sheep,* i.e. (a *gate*) through which they were led into Jerusalem:—sheep (market).

4263. *πρόβατον* **prŏbatŏn,** *prob´-at-on;* prop. neut. of a presumed der. of *4260; something that walks forward* (a *quadruped*), i.e. (spec.) a *sheep* (lit. or fig.):—sheep ([-fold]).

4264. *προβιβάζω* **prŏbibazō,** *pro-ib-ad´-zo;* from *4253* and a redupl. form of *971;* to *force forward,* i.e. *bring to the front, instigate:*—draw, before instruct.

4265. *προβλέπω* **prŏblĕpō,** *prob-lep´-o;* from *4253* and *991;* to *look* out *beforehand,* i.e. *furnish in advance:*—provide.

4266. *προγίνομαι* **prŏginŏmai,** *prog-in´-om-ahee;* from *4253* and *1096;* to *be already,* i.e. *have previously transpired:*—be past.

4267. *προγινώσκω* **prŏginōskō,** *prog-in-oce´-ko;* from *4253* and *1097;* to *know beforehand,* i.e. *foresee:*—foreknow (ordain), know (before).

4268. *πρόγνωσις* **prŏgnōsis,** *prog´-no-sis;* from *4267; forethought:*—foreknowledge.

4269. *πρόγονος* **prŏgŏnŏs,** *prog´-on-os;* from *4266;* an *ancestor,* (*grand-*) *parent:*—forefather, parent.

4270. *προγράφω* **prŏgraphō,** *prog-raf´-o;* from *4253* and *1125;* to *write previously;* fig. to *announce, prescribe:*—before ordain, evidently set forth, write (afore, aforetime).

4271. *πρόδηλος* **prŏdēlŏs,** *prod´-ay-los;* from *4253* and *1212; plain before* all men, i.e. *obvious:*—evident, manifest (open) beforehand.

4272. *προδίδωμι* **prŏdidōmi,** *prod-id´-o-mee;* from *4253* and *1325;* to *give before* the other party has given:—first give.

4273. προδότης **prŏdŏtēs,** *prod-ot´-ace;* from *4272* (in the sense of *giving forward* into another's [the enemy's] hands); a *surrender:*—betrayer, traitor.

προδρέμω **prŏdrĕmō.** See *4390.*

4274. πρόδρομος **prŏdrŏmŏs,** *prod´-rom-os;* from the alt. of *4390;* a *runner ahead,* i.e. *scout* (fig. *precursor*):—forerunner.

4275. προείδω **prŏĕidō,** *pro-i´-do;* from *4253* and *1492; foresee:*—foresee, saw before.

προειρέω **prŏĕirĕō.** See *4280.*

4276. προελπίζω **prŏĕlpizō,** *prŏ-el-pid´-zo;* from *4253* and *1679; to hope in advance* of other confirmation:—first trust.

4277. προέπω **prŏĕpō,** *prŏ-ep´-o;* from *4253* and *2036; to say already,* to *predict:*—forewarn, say (speak, tell) before. Comp. *4280.*

4278. προενάρχομαι **prŏĕnarchŏmai,** *prŏ-en-ar´-khom-ahee;* from *4253* and *1728;* to *commence already:*—begin (before).

4279. προεπαγγέλλομαι **prŏĕpaggĕllŏmai,** *prŏ-ep-ang-ghel´-lom-ahee;* mid. from *4253* and *1861;* to *promise of old:*—promise before.

4280. προερέω **prŏĕrĕō,** *prŏ-er-eh´-o;* from *4253* and *2046;* used as alt. of *4277;* to *say already, predict:*—foretell, say (speak, tell) before.

4281. προέρχομαι **prŏĕrchŏmai,** *prŏ-er´-khom-ahee;* from *4253* and *2064* (includ. its alt.); to *go onward, precede* (in place or time):—go before (farther, forward), outgo, pass on.

4282. προετοιμάζω **prŏĕtŏimazō,** *prŏ-et-oy-mad´-zo;* from *4253* and *2090;* to *fit* up *in advance* (lit. or fig.):—ordain before, prepare afore.

4283. προευαγγελίζομαι **prŏĕuaggĕlizŏmai,** *prŏ-yoo-ang-ghel-id´-zom-ahee;* mid. from *4253* and *2097;* to *announce* glad news *in advance:*—preach before the gospel.

4284. προέχομαι **prŏĕchŏmai,** *prŏ-ekh-om-ahee;* mid. from *4253* and *2192;* to *hold* oneself *before* others, i.e. (fig.) to *excel:*—be better.

4285. προηγέομαι **prŏēgĕŏmai,** *prŏ-ay-geh´-om-ahee;* from *4253* and *2233;* to *lead the way* for others, i.e. *show deference:*—prefer.

4286. πρόθεσις **prŏthĕsis,** *proth´-es-is;* from *4388;* a *setting forth,* i.e. (fig.) *proposal* (*intention*); spec. the *show*-bread (in the Temple) as *exposed* before God:—purpose, shew [-bread].

4287. προθέσμιος **prŏthĕsmiŏs,** *proth-es´-mee-os;* from *4253* and a der. of *5087; fixed beforehand,* i.e. (fem. with *2250* impl.) a *designated* day:—time appointed.

4288. προθυμία **prŏthumia,** *proth-oo-mee´-ah;* from *4289; predisposition,* i.e. *alacrity:*—forwardness of mind, readiness (of mind), ready (willing) mind.

4289. πρόθυμος **prŏthumŏs,** *proth´-oo-mos;* from *4253* and *2372; forward* in *spirit,* i.e. *predisposed;* neut. (as noun) *alacrity:*—ready, willing.

4290. προθύμως **prŏthumōs,** *proth-oo´-moce;* adv. from *4289; with alacrity:*—willingly.

4291. προΐστημι **prŏïstēmi,** *prŏ-is´-tay-mee;* from *4253* and *2476;* to *stand before,* i.e. (in rank) to *preside,* or (by impl.) to *practise:*—maintain, be over, rule.

4292. προκαλέομαι **prŏkalĕŏmai,** *prok-al-eh´-om-ahee;* mid. from *4253* and *2564;* to *call forth to oneself* (*challenge*), i.e. (by impl.) to *irritate:*—provoke.

4293. προκαταγγέλλω **prŏkataggĕllō,** *prok-at-ang-ghel´-lo;* from *4253* and *2605;* to *announce beforehand,* i.e. *predict, promise:*—foretell, have notice (shew) before.

4294. προκαταρτίζω **prŏkatartizō,** *prok-at-ar-tid´-zo;* from *4253* and *2675;* to *prepare in advance:*—make up beforehand.

4295. πρόκειμαι **prŏkĕimai,** *prok´-i-mahee;* from *4253* and *2749;* to *lie before* the view, i.e. (fig.) to *be present* (to the mind), to *stand forth* (as an example or reward):—be first, set before (forth).

4296. προκηρύσσω **prŏkērussō,** *prok-ay-rooce´-so;* from *4253* and *2784;* to *herald* (i.e. *proclaim*) *in advance:*—before (first) preach.

4297. προκοπή **prŏkŏpē,** *prok-op-ay´;* from *4298; progress,* i.e. *advancement* (subj. or obj.):—furtherance, profit.

4298. προκόπτω **prŏkŏptō,** *prok-op´-to;* from *4253* and *2875;* to *drive forward* (as if by beating), i.e. (fig. and intrans.) to *advance* (in amount, to *grow;* in time, to *be well along*):—increase, proceed, profit, be far spent, wax.

4299. πρόκριμα **prŏkrima,** *prok´-ree-mah;* from a comp. of *4253* and *2919;* a *prejudgment* (*prejudice*), i.e. *prepossession:*—prefer one before another.

4300. προκυρόω **prŏkurŏō,** *prok-oo-rŏ´-o;* from *4253* and *2964;* to *ratify previously:*—confirm before.

4301. προλαμβάνω **prŏlambanō,** *prol-am-ban´-o;* from *4253* and *2983;* to *take in advance,* i.e. (lit.) *eat before* others have an opportunity; (fig.) to *anticipate, surprise:*—come aforehand, overtake, take before.

4302. προλέγω **prŏlĕgō,** *prol-eg´-o;* from *4253* and *3004;* to *say beforehand,* i.e. *predict, forewarn:*—foretell, tell before.

4303. προμαρτύρομαι **prŏmarturŏmai,** *prom-ar-too´-rom-ahee;* from *4253* and *3143;* to *be a witness in advance,* i.e. *predict:*—testify beforehand.

4304. προμελετάω **prŏmĕlĕtaō,** *prom-el-et-ah´-o;* from *4253* and *3191;* to *premeditate:*—meditate before.

4305. προμεριμνάω **prŏmĕrimnaō,** *prom-er-im-nah´-o;* from *4253* and *3309;* to *care* (anxiously) *in advance:*—take thought beforehand.

4306. προνοέω **prŏnŏĕō,** *pron-ŏ-eh´-o;* from *4253* and *3539;* to *consider in advance,* i.e. *look* out for *beforehand* (act. by way of *maintenance* for others; mid. by way of *circumspection* for oneself):—provide (for).

4307. πρόνοια **prŏnŏia,** *pron´-oy-ah;* from *4306; forethought,* i.e. provident *care* or *supply:*—providence, provision.

4308. προοράω **prŏŏraō,** *prŏ-or-ah´-o;* from *4253* and *3708;* to *behold in advance,* i.e. (act.) to *notice* (another) *previously,* or (mid.) to *keep in* (one's own) *view:*—foresee, see before.

4309. προορίζω **prŏŏrizō,** *prŏ-or-id´-zo;* from *4253* and *3724;* to *limit in advance,* i.e. (fig.) *predetermine:*—determine before, ordain, predestinate.

4310. προπάσχω **prŏpaschō,** *prop-as´-kho;* from *4253* and *3958;* to *undergo* hardship *previously:*—suffer before.

4311. προπέμπω **prŏpĕmpō,** *prop-em´-po;* from *4253* and *3992;* to *send forward,* i.e. *escort* or *aid* in travel:—accompany, bring (forward) on journey (way), conduct forth.

4312. προπετής **prŏpĕtēs,** *prop-et-ace´;* from a comp. of *4253* and *4098; falling forward,* i.e. *headlong* (fig. *precipitate*):—heady, rash [-ly].

4313. προπορεύομαι **prŏpŏrĕuŏmai,** *prop-or-yoo´-om-ahee;* from *4253* and *4198;* to *precede* (as guide or herald):—go before.

4314. πρός **prŏs,** *pros;* a strengthened form of *4253;* a prep. of direction; *forward to,* i.e. *toward* (with the genit. *the side* of, i.e. *pertaining to;* with the dat. *by the side of,* i.e. *near to;* usually with the accus. the place, time, occasion, or respect, which is the *destination* of the relation, i.e. *whither* or *for* which it is predicated):—about, according to, against, among, at, because of, before, between, ([where-]) by, for, × at thy house, in, for intent, nigh unto, of, which pertain to, that, to (the end that), + together, to ([you]) -ward, unto, with (-in). In comp. it denotes essentially the same applications, namely, motion *towards,* accession *to,* or nearness *at.*

4315. προσάββατον **prŏsabbatŏn,** *pros-ab´-bat-on;* from *4253* and *4521;* a *fore-sabbath,* i.e. the *Sabbath-eve:*—day before the sabbath. Comp. *3904.*

4316. προσαγορεύω **prŏsagŏrĕuō,** *pros-ag-or-yoo´-o;* from *4314* and a der. of *58* (mean. to *harangue*); to *address,* i.e. salute by *name:*—call.

4317. προσάγω **prŏsagō,** *pros-ag´-o;* from *4314* and *71;* to *lead towards,* i.e. (trans.) to *conduct near* (*summon, present*), or (intrans.) to *approach:*—bring, draw near,

4318. προσαγωγή **prŏsagōgē,** *pros-ag-ogue-ay´;* from *4317* (comp. *72*); *admission:*—access.

4319. προσαιτέω **prŏsaitĕō** *pros-ahee-teh´-o;* from *4314* and *154;* to *ask repeatedly* (*importune*), i.e. *solicit:*—beg.

4320. προσαναβαίνω **prŏsanabainō,** *pros-an-ab-ah´ee-no;* from *4314* and *305;* to *ascend farther,* i.e. *be promoted* (*take an upper* [*more honourable*] *seat*):—go up.

4321. προσαναλίσκω **prŏsanaliskō,** *pros-an-al-is´-ko;* from *4314* and *355;* to *expend further:*—spend.

4322. προσαναπληρόω **prŏsanaplērŏō,** *pros-an-ap-lay-rŏ´-o;* from *4314* and *378;* to *fill up further,* i.e. *furnish fully:*—supply.

4323. προσανατίθημι **prŏsanatithēmi,** *pros-an-at-ith´-ay-mee;* from *4314* and *394;* to *lay up in addition,* i.e. (mid. and fig.) to *impart* or (by impl.) to *consult:*—in conference add, confer.

4324. προσαπειλέω **prŏsapĕilĕō,** *pros-ap-i-leh´-o;* from *4314* and *546;* to *menace additionally:*—threaten further.

4325. προσδαπανάω **prŏsdapanaō,** *pros-dap-an-ah´-o;* from *4314* and *1159;* to *expend additionally:*—spend more.

4326. προσδέομαι **prŏsdĕŏmai,** *pros-deh´-om-ahee;* from *4314* and *1189;* to *require additionally,* i.e. *want further:*—need.

4327. προσδέχομαι **prŏsdĕchŏmai,** *pros-dekh´-om-ahee;* from *4314* and *1209;* to *admit* (to intercourse, hospitality, credence or [fig.] endurance); by impl. to *await* (with confidence or patience):—accept, allow, look (wait) for, take.

4328. προσδοκάω **prŏsdŏkaō,** *pros-dok-ah´-o;* from *4314* and δοκεύω **dŏkĕuō** (to *watch*); to *anticipate* (in thought, hope or fear); by impl. to *await:*—(be in) expect (-ation), look (for), when looked, tarry, wait for.

4329. προσδοκία **prŏsdŏkia,** *pros-dok-ee´-ah;* from *4328; apprehension* (of evil); by impl. *infliction* anticipated:—expectation, looking after.

προσδρέμω **prŏsdrĕmō.** See *4370.*

4330. προσεάω **prŏsĕaō,** *pros-eh-ah´-o;* from *4314* and *1439;* to *permit further* progress:—suffer.

4331. προσεγγίζω **prŏsĕggizō,** *pros-eng-ghid´-zo;* from *4314* and *1448;* to *approach near:*—come nigh.

4332. προσεδρεύω **prŏsĕdrĕuō,** *pros-ed-ryoo´-o;* from a comp. of *4314* and the base of *1476;* to *sit near,* i.e. *attend* as a servant:—wait at.

4333. προσεργάζομαι **prŏsĕrgazŏmai,** *pros-er-gad´-zom-ahee;* from *4314* and *2038;* to *work additionally,* i.e. (by impl.) *acquire besides:*—gain.

4334. προσέρχομαι **prŏsĕrchŏmai,** *pros-er´-khom-ahee;* from *4314* and *2064* (includ. its alt.); to *approach,* i.e. (lit.) *come near, visit,* or (fig.) *worship, assent to:*—(as soon as he) come (unto), come thereunto, consent, draw near, go (near, to, unto).

4335. προσευχή **prŏsĕuchē,** *pros-yoo-khay´;* from *4336; prayer* (*worship*); by impl. an *oratory* (*chapel*):—× pray earnestly, prayer.

4336. προσεύχομαι **prŏsĕuchŏmai,** *pros-yoo´-khom-ahee;* from *4314* and *2172;* to *pray to* God, i.e. *supplicate, worship:*—pray (× earnestly, for), make prayer.

4337. προσέχω **prŏsĕchō,** *pros-ekh´-o;* from *4314* and *2192;* (fig.) to *hold* the mind (*3563* impl.) *towards,* i.e. *pay attention to, be cautious about, apply oneself* to, *adhere to:*—(give) attend (-ance, -ance at, -ance to, unto), beware, be given to, give (take) heed (to, unto) have regard.

4338. προσηλόω **prŏsēlŏō,** *pros-ay-lŏ´-o;* from *4314* and a der. of *2247;* to *peg to,* i.e. *spike* fast:—nail to.

4339. προσήλυτος **prŏsēlutŏs,** *pros-ay´-loo-tos;* from the alt. of *4334;* an *arriver* from a foreign region, i.e. (spec.) an *acceder* (*convert*) to Judaism (*"proselyte"*):—proselyte.

4340. πρόσκαιρος **prŏskairŏs,** *pros´-kahee-ros;* from *4314* and *2540; for* the *occasion* only, i.e. *temporary:*—dur- [eth] for awhile, endure for a time, for a season, temporal.

4341. προσκαλέομαι **prŏskalĕŏmai,** *pros-kal-eh´-om-ahee;* mid. from *4314* and *2564;* to *call toward oneself,* i.e. *summon, invite:*—call (for, to, unto).

4342. προσκαρτερέω **prŏskartĕrĕō,** *pros-kar-ter-eh´-o;* from *4314* and *2594;* to *be earnest towards,* i.e. (to a thing) to *persevere, be constantly* diligent, or (in a place) to *attend* assiduously all the exercises, or (to a person) to *adhere* closely *to* (as a servitor):—attend (give self) continually (upon), continue (in, instant in, with), wait on (continually).

4343. προσκαρτέρησις **prŏskartĕrēsis,** *pros-kar-ter´-ay-sis;* from *4342; persistency:*—perseverance.

4344. προσκεφάλαιον **prŏskĕphalaiŏn,** *pros-kef-al´-ahee-on;* neut. of a presumed comp. of *4314* and *2776;* something *for* the *head,* i.e. a *cushion:*—pillow.

4345. προσκληρόω **prŏsklērŏō,** *pros-klay-rŏ´-o;* from *4314* and *2820;* to *give* a common *lot to,* i.e. (fig.) to *associate with:*—consort with.

4346. πρόσκλισις **prŏsklisis,** *pros´-klis-is;* from a comp. of *4314* and *2827;* a *leaning towards,* i.e. (fig.) *proclivity* (*favoritism*):—partiality.

4347. προσκολλάω **prŏskŏllaō,** *pros-kol-lah´-o;* from *4314* and *2853;* to *glue to,* i.e. (fig.) to *adhere:*—cleave, join (self).

4348. πρόσκομμα **prŏskŏmma,** *pros´-kom-mah;* from *4350;* a *stub,* i.e. (fig.) *occasion of apostasy:*—offence, stumbling (-block, [-stone]).

4349. προσκοπή **prŏskŏpē,** *pros-kop-ay´;* from *4350;* a *stumbling,* i.e. (fig. and concr.) *occasion of sin:*—offence.

4350. προσκόπτω **prŏskŏptō,** *pros-kop´-to;* from *4314* and *2875;* to *strike at,* i.e. *surge against* (as water); spec. to *stub on,* i.e. *trip up* (lit. or fig.):—beat upon, dash, stumble (at).

4351. προσκυλίω **prŏskuliō,** *pros-koo-lee´-o;* from *4314* and *2947;* to *roll towards,* i.e. *block against:*—roll (to).

4352. προσκυνέω **prŏskunĕō,** *pros-koo-neh´-o;* from *4314* and a prob. der. of *2965* (mean. to *kiss,* like a dog *licking* his master's hand); to *fawn* or *crouch to,* i.e. (lit. or fig.) *prostrate* oneself in homage (*do reverence* to, *adore*):—worship.

4353. προσκυνητής **prŏskunētēs,** *pros-koo-nay-tace´;* from *4352;* an *adorer:*—worshipper.

4354. προσλαλέω **prŏslalĕō,** *pros-lal-eh´-o;* from *4314* and *2980;* to *talk to,* i.e. *converse with:*—speak to (with).

4355. προσλαμβάνω **prŏslambanō,** *pros-lam-ban´-o;* from *4314* and *2983;* to *take to* oneself, i.e. *use* (food), *lead* (aside), *admit* (to friendship or hospitality):—receive, take (unto).

4356. πρόσληψις **prŏslēpsis,** *pros´-lape-sis;* from *4355; admission:*—receiving.

4357. προσμένω **prŏsmĕnō,** *pros-men´-o;* from *4314* and *3306;* to *stay further,* i.e. *remain* in a place, with a person; fig. to *adhere* to, *persevere* in:—abide still, be with, cleave unto, continue in (with).

4358. προσορμίζω **prŏsŏrmizō,** *pros-or-mid´-zo;* from *4314* and a der. of the same as *3730* (mean. to *tie* [*anchor*] or *lull*); to *moor to,* i.e. (by impl.) *land at:*—draw to the shore.

4359. προσοφείλω **prŏsŏphĕilō,** *pros-of-i´-lo;* from *4314* and *3784;* to *be indebted additionally:*—over besides.

4360. προσοχθίζω **prŏsŏchthizō,** *pros-okh-thid´-zo;* from *4314* and a form of ὀχθέω **ŏchthĕō** (to *be vexed* with something irksome); to *feel indignant at:*—be grieved with.

4361. πρόσπεινος **prŏspĕinŏs,** *pros´-pi-nos;* from *4314* and the same as *3983; hungering further,* i.e. *intensely hungry:*—very hungry.

4362. προσπήγνυμι **prŏspēgnumi,** *pros-payg´-noo-mee;* from *4314* and *4078;* to *fasten to,* i.e. (spec.) to *impale* (on a cross):—crucify.

4363. προσπίπτω **prŏspiptō,** *pros-pip´-to;* from *4314* and *4098;* to *fall towards,* i.e. (gently) *prostrate* oneself (in supplication or homage), or (violently) to *rush* upon (in storm):—beat upon, fall (down) at (before).

4364. προσποιέομαι **prŏspŏiĕŏmai,** *pros-poy-eh´-om-ahee;* mid. from *4314* and *4160;* to *do forward for oneself,* i.e. *pretend* (as if about to do a thing):—make as though.

4365. προσπορεύομαι **prŏspŏrĕuŏmai,** *pros-por-yoo´-om-ahee;* from *4314* and *4198;* to *journey towards,* i.e. *approach* [not the same as *4313*]:—go before.

4366. προσρήγνυμι **prŏsrēgnumi,** *pros-rayg´-noo-mee;* from *4314* and *4486;* to *tear towards,* i.e. *burst upon* (as a tempest or flood):—beat vehemently against (upon).

4367. προστάσσω **prŏstassō,** *pros-tas´-so;* from *4314* and *5021;* to *arrange towards,* i.e. (fig.) *enjoin:*—bid, command.

4368. προστάτις **prŏstatis,** *pros-tat´-is;* fem. of a der. of *4291;* a *patroness,* i.e. *assistant:*—succourer.

4369. προστίθημι **prŏstithēmi,** *pros-tith´-ay-mee;* from *4314* and *5087;* to *place additionally,* i.e. *lay beside, annex, repeat:*—add, again, give more, increase, lay unto, proceed further, speak to any more.

4370. προστρέχω **prŏstrĕchō,** *pros-trekh´-o;* from *4314* and *5143* (includ. its alt.); to *run towards,* i.e. *hasten* to meet or join:—run (thither to, to).

4371. προσφάγιον **prŏsphagiŏn,** *pros-fag´-ee-on;* neut. of a presumed der. of a comp. of *4314* and *5315;* something *eaten in addition* to bread, i.e. a *relish* (spec. *fish;* comp. *3795*):—meat.

4372. πρόσφατος **prŏsphatŏs,** *pros´-fat-os;* from *4253* and a der. of *4969; previously* (*recently*) *slain* (*fresh*), i.e. (fig.) *lately made:*—new.

4373. προσφάτως **prŏsphatōs,** *pros-fat´-oce;* adv. from *4372; recently:*—lately.

4374. προσφέρω **prŏsphĕrō,** *pros-fer´-o;* from *4314* and *5342* (includ. its alt.); to *bear towards,* i.e. *lead to, tender* (espec. to God), *treat:*—bring (to, unto), deal with, do, offer (unto, up), present unto, put to.

4375. προσφιλής **prŏsphilēs,** *pros-fee-lace´;* from a presumed comp. of *4314* and *5368; friendly towards,* i.e. *acceptable:*—lovely.

4376. προσφορά **prŏsphŏra,** *pros-for-ah´;* from *4374; presentation;* concr. an *oblation* (bloodless) or *sacrifice:*—offering (up).

4377. προσφωνέω **prŏsphōnĕō,** *pros-fo-neh´-o;* from *4314* and *5455;* **to** *sound towards,* i.e. *address, exclaim, summon:*—call unto, speak (un-) to.

4378. πρόσχυσις **prŏschusis,** *pros´-khoo-sis;* from a comp. of *4314* and χέω **chĕō** (to *pour*); a *shedding forth,* i.e. *affusion:*—sprinkling.

4379. προσψαύω **prŏspsauō,** *pros-psŏw´-o;* from *4314* and ψαύω **psauō** (to *touch*); to *impinge,* i.e. *lay a finger on* (in order to relieve):—touch.

4380. προσωποληπτέω **prŏsōpŏlēptĕō,** *pros-o-pol-ape-teh´-o;* from *4381;* to *favor an individual,* i.e. *show partiality:*—have respect to persons.

4381. προσωπολήπτης **prŏsōpŏlēptēs,** *pros-o-pol-ape´-tace;* from *4383 and 2983;* an *accepter* of *a face* (*individual*), i.e. (spec.) one *exhibiting partiality:*—respecter of persons.

4382. προσωποληψία **prŏsōpŏlēpsia,** *pros-o-pol-ape-see´-ah;* from *4381; partiality,* i.e. *favoritism:*—respect of persons.

4383. πρόσωπον **prŏsōpŏn,** *pros´-o-pon;* from *4314* and ὤψ **ōps** (the *visage;* from *3700*); the *front* (as being *towards view*), i.e. the *countenance, aspect, appearance, surface;* by impl. *presence, person:*—(outward) appearance, × before, countenance, face, fashion, (men's) person, presence.

4384. προτάσσω **prŏtassō,** *prot-as´-so;* from *4253* and *5021;* to *pre-arrange,* i.e. *prescribe:*—before appoint.

4385. προτείνω **prŏtĕinō,** *prot-i´-no;* from *4253* and τείνω **tĕinō** (to *stretch*); to *protend,* i.e. *tie prostrate* (for scourging):—bind.

4386. πρότερον **prŏtĕrŏn,** *prot´-er-on;* neut. of *4387* as adv. (with or without the art.); *previously:*—before, (at the) first, former.

4387. πρότερος **prŏtĕrŏs,** *prot´-er-os;* compar. of *4253; prior* or *previous:*—former.

4388. προτίθεμαι **prŏtithĕmai,** *prot-ith´-em-ahee;* mid. from *4253* and *5087;* to *place before,* i.e. (for oneself) to *exhibit;* (to oneself) to *propose* (*determine*):—purpose, set forth.

4389. προτρέπομαι **prŏtrĕpŏmai,** *prot-rep´-om-ahee;* mid. from *4253* and the base of *5157;* to *turn forward* for oneself, i.e. *encourage:*—exhort.

4390. προτρέχω **prŏtrĕchō,** *prot-rekh´-o;* from *4253* and *5143* (includ. its alt.); to *run forward,* i.e. *outstrip, precede:*—outrun, run before.

4391. προϋπάρχω **prŏüparchō,** *prŏ-oop-ar´-kho;* from *4253* and *5225;* to *exist before,* i.e. (adv.) to *be* or *do* something *previously:*— + be before (-time).

4392. πρόφασις **prŏphasis,** *prof´-as-is;* from a comp. of *4253* and *5316;* an *outward showing,* i.e. *pretext:*—cloke, colour, pretence, show.

4393. προφέρω **prŏphĕrō,** *prof-er´-o;* from *4253* and *5342;* to *bear forward,* i.e. *produce:*—bring forth.

4394. προφητεία **prŏphētĕia,** *prof-ay-ti´-ah;* from *4396* ("*prophecy*"); *prediction* (scriptural or other):—prophecy, prophesying.

4395. προφητεύω **prŏphētĕuō,** *prof-ate-yoo´-o;* from *4396;* to *foretell* events, *divine, speak* under *inspiration, exercise* the prophetic *office:*—prophesy.

4396. προφήτης **prŏphētēs,** *prof-ay´-tace;* from a comp. of *4253* and *5346;* a *foreteller* ("*prophet*"); by anal. an *inspired speaker;* by extens. a *poet:*—prophet.

4397. προφητικός **prŏphētikŏs,** *prof-ay-tik-os´;* from *4396; pertaining to a foreteller* ("*prophetic*"):—of prophecy, of the prophets.

4398. προφῆτις **prŏphētis,** *prof-ay´-tis;* fem. of *4396;* a *female foreteller* or an *inspired woman:*—prophetess.

4399. προφθάνω **prŏphthanō,** *prof-than´-o;* from *4253* and *5348;* to *get* an *earlier start of,* i.e. *anticipate:*—prevent.

4400. προχειρίζομαι **prŏchĕirizŏmai,** *prokh-i-rid´-zom-ahee;* mid. from *4253* and a der. of *5495;* to *handle* for oneself *in advance,* i.e. (fig.) to *purpose:*—choose, make.

4401. προχειροτονέω **prŏchĕirŏtŏnĕō,** *prokh-i-rot-on-eh´-o;* from *4253* and *5500;* to *elect in advance:*—choose before.

4402. Πρόχορος **Prŏchŏrŏs,** *prokh´-or-os;* from *4253* and *5525; before* the *dance; Prochorus,* a Chr.:—Prochorus.

4403. πρύμνα **prumna,** *proom´-nah;* fem. of πρυμνύς **prumnus** (*hindmost*); the *stern* of a ship:—hinder part, stern.

4404. πρωΐ **prōï,** *pro-ee´;* adv. from *4253;* at *dawn;* by impl. the *day-break* watch:—early (in the morning), (in the) morning.

4405. πρωΐα **prōïa,** *pro-ee´-ah;* fem. of a der. of *4404* as noun; *day-dawn:*—early, morning.

4406. πρώϊμος **prōïmŏs,** *pro´-ee-mos;* from *4404; dawning,* i.e. (by anal.) *autumnal* (showering, the first of the rainy season):—early.

4407. πρωϊνός **prōïnŏs,** *pro-ee-nos´;* from *4404;* pertaining to the *dawn,* i.e. *matutinal:*—morning.

4408. πρώρα **prōra,** *pro´-ra;* fem. of a presumed der. of *4253* as noun; the *prow,* i.e. forward part of a vessel:—forepart (-ship).

4409. πρωτεύω **prōtĕuō,** *prote-yoo´-o;* from *4413;* to *be first* (in rank or influence):—have the preeminence.

4410. πρωτοκαθεδρία **prōtŏkathĕdria,** *pro-tok-ath-ed-ree´-ah;* from *4413* and *2515;* a *sitting first* (in the front row), i.e. *preeminence* in council:—chief (highest, uppermost) seat.

4411. πρωτοκλισία **prōtŏklisia,** *pro-tok-lis-ee´-ah;* from *4413* and *2828;* a *reclining first* (in the place of honor) at the dinner-bed, i.e. *preeminence* at meals:—chief (highest, uppermost) room.

4412. πρῶτον **prōtŏn,** *pro´-ton;* neut. of *4413* as adv. (with or without *3588*); *firstly* (in time, place, order, or importance):—before, at the beginning, chiefly, (at, at the) first (of all).

4413. πρῶτος **prōtŏs,** *pro´-tos;* contr. superl. of *4253; foremost* (in time, place, order or importance):—before, beginning, best, chief (-est), first (of all), former.

4414. πρωτοστάτης **prōtŏstatēs,** *pro-tos-tat´-ace;* from *4413* and *2476;* one *standing first* in the ranks, i.e. a *captain* (*champion*):—ringleader.

4415. πρωτοτόκια **prōtŏtŏkia,** *pro-tot-ok´-ee-ah;* from *4416; primogeniture* (as a privilege):—birthright.

4416. πρωτοτόκος **prōtŏtŏkŏs,** *pro-tot-ok´-os;* from *4413* and the alt. of *5088; first-born* (usually as noun, lit. or fig.):—firstbegotten (-born).

4417. πταίω **ptaiō,** *ptah´-yo;* a form of *4098;* to *trip,* i.e (fig.) to *err, sin, fail* (of salvation):—fall, offend, stumble.

4418. πτέρνα **ptĕrna,** *pter´-nah;* of uncert. der.; the *heel* (fig.):—heel.

4419. πτερύγιον **ptĕrugiŏn,** *pter-oog´-ee-on;* neut. of a presumed der. of *4420;* a *winglet,* i.e. (fig.) *extremity* (top corner):—pinnacle.

4420. πτέρυξ **ptĕrux,** *pter´-oox;* from a der. of *4072* (mean. a *feather*); a *wing:*—wing.

4421. πτηνόν **ptēnŏn,** *ptay-non´;* contr. for *4071;* a *bird:*—bird.

4422. πτοέω **ptŏĕō,** *ptŏ-eh´-o;* prob. akin to the alt. of *4098* (through the idea of causing to *fall*) or to *4072* (through that of causing to *fly* away); to *scare:*—frighten.

4423. πτόησις **ptŏēsis,** *ptŏ´-ay-sis;* from *4422; alarm:*—amazement.

4424. Πτολεμαΐς **Ptŏlĕmaïs,** *ptol-em-ah-is´;* from Πτολεμαῖος **Ptŏlĕmaiŏs** (*Ptolemy,* after whom it was named); *Ptolemaïs,* a place in Pal.:—Ptolemais.

4425. πτύον **ptuŏn,** *ptoo´-on;* from *4429;* a *winnowing-fork* (as *scattering* like spittle):—fan.

4426. πτύρω **pturō,** *ptoo´-ro;* from a presumed der. of *4429* (and thus akin to *4422*); to *frighten:*—terrify.

4427. πτύσμα **ptusma,** *ptoos´-mah;* from *4429; saliva:*—spittle.

4428. πτύσσω **ptussō,** *ptoos´-so;* prob. akin to πετάννυμι **pĕtannumi** (to *spread;* and thus appar. allied to *4072* through the idea of *expansion,* and to *4429* through that of *flattening;* comp. *3961*); to *fold,* i.e. *furl* a scroll:—close.

4429. πτύω **ptuō,** *ptoo´-o;* a prim. verb (comp. *4428*); to *spit:*—spit.

4430. πτῶμα **ptōma,** *pto´-mah;* from the alt. of *4098;* a *ruin,* i.e. (spec.) lifeless *body* (*corpse, carrion*):—dead body, carcase, corpse.

4431. πτῶσις **ptōsis,** *pto´-sis;* from the alt. of *4098;* a *crash,* i.e. *downfall* (lit. or fig.):—fall.

4432. πτωχεία **ptōchĕia,** *pto-khi´-ah;* from *4433; beggary,* i.e. *indigence* (lit. or fig.):—poverty.

4433. πτωχεύω **ptōchĕuō,** *pto-khyoo´-o;* from *4434;* to *be a beggar,* i.e. (by impl.) to *become indigent* (fig.):—become poor.

4434. πτωχός **ptōchŏs,** *pto-khos´;* from πτώσσω **ptōssō** (to *crouch;* akin to *4422* and the alt. of *4098*); a *beggar* (as *cringing*), i.e. *pauper* (strictly denoting absolute or public *mendicancy,* although also used in a qualified or relative sense; whereas *3993* prop. means only *straitened* circumstances in private), lit. (often as noun) or fig. (*distressed*):—beggar (-ly), poor.

4435. πυγμή **pugmē,** *poog-may´;* from a prim. πύξ **pux** (the *fist* as a weapon); the clenched *hand,* i.e. (only in dat. as adv.) *with* the *fist* (hard *scrubbing*):—oft.

4436. Πύθων **Puthōn,** *poo´-thone;* from Πυθώ **Puthō** (the name of the region where Delphi, the seat of the famous *oracle,* was located); a *Python,* i.e. (by anal. with the supposed *diviner* there) *inspiration* (*soothsaying*):—divination.

4437. πυκνός **puknŏs,** *pook-nos´;* from the same as *4035; clasped* (*thick*), i.e. (fig.) *frequent;* neut. plur. (as adv.) *frequently:*—often (-er).

4438. πυκτέω **puktĕō,** *pook-teh´-o;* from a der. of the same as *4435;* to *box* (with the fist), i.e. *contend* (as a boxer) at the games (fig.):—fight.

4439. πύλη **pulē,** *poo´-lay;* appar. a prim. word; a *gate,* i.e. the leaf or wing of a folding *entrance* (lit. or fig.):—gate.

4440. πυλών **pulōn,** *poo-lone´;* from *4439;* a *gateway, door-way* of a building or city; by impl. a *portal* or *vestibule:*—gate, porch.

4441. πυνθάνομαι **punthanŏmai,** *poon-than´-om-ahee;* mid. prol. from a prim. πύθω **puthō** (which occurs only as an alt. in certain tenses); to *question,* i.e. *ascertain* by inquiry (as a matter of *information* merely; and thus differing from *2065,* which prop. means a *request* as a favor; and from *154,* which is strictly a *demand* of something due; as well as from *2212,* which implies a *search* for something hidden; and from *1189,* which involves the idea of urgent *need*); by impl. to *learn* (by casual intelligence):—ask, demand, enquire, understand.

4442. πῦρ **pur,** *poor;* a prim. word; *"fire"* (lit. or fig., spec. *lightning*):—fiery, fire.

4443. πυρά **pura,** *poo-rah´;* from *4442;* a *fire* (concr.):—fire.

4444. πύργος **purgŏs,** *poo´-gos;* appar. a prim. word (*"burgh"*); a *tower* or *castle:*—tower.

4445. πυρέσσω **purĕssō,** *poo-res´-so;* from *4443;* to *be on fire,* i.e. (spec.) to *have a fever:*—be sick of a fever.

4446. πυρετός **purĕtŏs,** *poo-ret-os´;* from *4445; inflamed,* i.e. (by impl.) *feverish* (as noun, *fever*):—fever.

4447. πύρινος **purinŏs,** *poo´-ree-nos;* from *4443; fiery,* i.e. (by impl.) *flaming:*—of fire.

4448. πυρόω **purŏō,** *poo-rŏ´-o;* from *4442;* to *kindle,* i.e. (pass.) to *be ignited, glow* (lit.), *be refined* (by impl.), or (fig.) to *be inflamed* (with anger, grief, lust):—burn, fiery, be on fire, try.

4449. πυῤῥάζω **purrhazō,** *poor-hrad´-zo;* from *4450;* to *redden* (intrans.):—be red.

4450. πυῤῥός **purrhŏs,** *poor-hros´;* from *4442; fire-like,* i.e. (spec.) *flame-colored:*—red.

4451. πύρωσις **purōsis,** *poo´-ro-sis;* from *4448; ignition,* i.e. (spec.) *smelting* (fig. *conflagration, calamity* as a *test*):—burning, trial.

4452. -πω **-pō,** *po;* another form of the base of *4458;* an enclitic particle of indefiniteness; *yet, even;* used only in comp. See *3369, 3380, 3764, 3768, 4455.*

4453. πωλέω **pōlĕō,** *po-leh´-o;* prob. ultimately from πέλομαι **pĕlŏmai** (to *be busy,* to *trade*); to *barter* (as a *pedlar*), i.e. to *sell:*—sell, whatever is sold.

4454. πῶλος **pōlŏs,** *po´-los;* appar. a prim. word; a *"foal"* or *"filly",* i.e. (spec.) a *young ass:*—colt.

4455. πώποτε **pōpŏtĕ,** *po´-pot-e;* from *4452* and *4218; at any time,* i.e. (with neg. particle) *at no time:*—at any time, + never (. . . to any man), + yet never man.

4456. πωρόω **pōrŏō,** *po-rŏ´-o;* appar. from πῶρος **pōrŏs** (a kind of *stone*); to *petrify,* i.e. (fig.) to *indurate* (*render stupid* or *callous*):—blind, harden.

4457. πώρωσις **pōrōsis,** *po´-ro-sis;* from *4456; stupidity* or *callousness:*—blindness, hardness.

4458. -πώς **-pōs,** *poce;* adv. from the base of *4225;* an enclitic particle of indefiniteness of manner; *somehow* or *anyhow;* used only in comp.:—haply, by any (some) means, perhaps. See *1513, 3381.* Comp. *4459.*

4459. πῶς **pōs,** *poce;* adv. from the base of *4426;* an interrog. particle of manner; *in what way?* (sometimes the question is indirect, *how?*); also as exclamation, *how* much!:—how, after (by) what manner (means), that. [*Occasionally unexpressed in English.*]

P

4460. Ῥαάβ **Rhaab,** *hrah-ab´;* of Heb. or. [7343]; *Raab* (i.e. *Rachab*), a Canaanitess:—Rahab. See also *4477.*

4461. ῥαββί **rhabbi,** *hrab-bee´;* of Heb. or. [7227 with pron. suffix]; *my master,* i.e. *Rabbi,* as an official title of honor:—Master, Rabbi.

4462. ῥαββονί **rhabbŏni,** *hrab-bon-ee´;* or ῥαββουνί **rhabbŏuni,** *hrab-boo-nee´;* of Chald. or.; corresp. to *4461:*—Lord, Rabboni.

4463. ῥαβδίζω **rhabdizō,** *hrab-did´-zo;* from *4464;* to *strike with a stick,* i.e. *bastinado:*—beat (with rods).

4464. ῥάβδος **rhabdŏs,** *hrab´-dos;* from the base of *4474;* a *stick* or *wand* (as a *cudgel,* a *cane* or a *baton* of royalty):—rod, sceptre, staff.

4465. ῥαβδοῦχος **rhabdŏuchŏs,** *hrab-doo´-khos;* from *4464* and *2192;* a *rod-* (the Lat. *fasces*) *holder,* i.e. a Rom. *lictor* (*constable* or *executioner*):—serjeant.

4466. Ῥαγαῦ **Rhagau,** *hrag-ŏw;* of Heb. or. [7466]; *Ragau* (i.e. *Reü*), a patriarch:—Ragau.

4467. ῥᾳδιούργημα **rhaidiŏurgēma,** *hrad-ee-oorg´-ay-mah;* from a comp. of ῥᾴδιος **rhaidiŏs** (*easy,* i.e. *reckless*) and *2041; easy-going behavior,* i.e. (by extens.) a *crime:*—lewdness.

4468. ῥᾳδιουργία **rhaidiŏurgia,** *hrad-ee-oorg-ee´-a;* from the same as *4467; recklessness,* i.e. (by extens.) *malignity:*—mischief.

4469. ῥακά **rhaka,** *rhak-ah´;* of Chald. or. [comp. 7386]; O *empty* one, i.e. thou *worthless* (as a term of utter vilification):—Raca.

4470. ῥάκος **rhăkŏs,** *hrak´-os;* from *4486;* a *"rag,"* i.e. *piece* of cloth:—cloth.

4471. Ῥαμᾶ **Rhama,** *hram-ah´;* of Heb. or. [7414]; *Rama* (i.e. *Ramah*), a place in Pal.:—Rama.

4472. ῥαντίζω **rhantizō,** *hran-tid´-zo;* from a der. of ῥαίνω **rhainō** (to *sprinkle*); to *render besprinkled,* i.e. *asperse* (cer. or fig.):—sprinkle.

4473. ῥαντισμός **rhantismŏs,** *hran-tis-mos´;* from *4472; aspersion* (cer. or fig.):—sprinkling.

4474. ῥαπίζω **rhapizō** *hrap-id´-zo;* from a der. of a prim. ῥέπω **rhĕpō** (to *let fall, "rap"*); to *slap:*—smite (with the palm of the hand). Comp. *5180.*

4475. *ῥάπισμα* **rhapisma,** *hrap´-is-mah;* from *4474;* a *slap:*—(+ strike with the) palm of the hand, smite with the hand.

4476. *ῥαφίς* **rhaphis,** *hraf-ece´;* from a prim. *ῥάπτω* **rhaptō** (to *sew;* perh. rather akin to the base of *4474* through the idea of *puncturing*); a *needle:*—needle.

4477. *Ῥαχάβ* **Rhachab,** *hrakh-ab´;* from the same as *4460; Rachab,* a Canaanitess:—Rachab.

4478. *Ῥαχήλ* **Rhachēl,** *hrakh-ale´;* of Heb. or [7354]; *Rachel,* the wife of Jacob:—Rachel.

4479. *Ῥεβέκκα* **Rhĕbĕkka,** *hreb-bek´-kah;* of Heb. or [7259]; *Rebecca* (i.e. *Ribkah*), the wife of Isaac:—Rebecca.

4480. *ῥέδα* **rhĕda,** *hred´-ah;* of Lat. or.; a *rheda,* i.e. four-wheeled *carriage* (*wagon* for riding):—chariot.

4481. *Ῥεμφάν* **Rhĕmphan,** *hrem-fan´;* by incorrect transliteration for a word of Heb. or. [3594]; *Remphan* (i.e. *Kijun*), an Eg. idol:—Remphan.

4482. *ῥέω* **rhĕō,** *hreh´-o;* a prim. verb; for some tenses of which a prol. form

ῥεύω **rhĕuō,** *hryoo´-o,* is used; to *flow* (*"run"*, as water):—flow.

4483. *ῥέω* **rhĕō,** *hreh´-o;* for certain tenses of which a prol. form

ἐρέω **ĕrĕō,** *er-eh´-o,* is used; and both as alt. for *2036;* perh. akin (or ident.) with *4482* (through the idea of *pouring* forth); to *utter,* i.e. *speak* or *say:*—command, make, say, speak (of). Comp. *3004.*

4484. *Ῥήγιον* **Rhēgiŏn,** *hrayg´-ee-on;* of Lat. or.; *Rhegium,* a place in Italy:—Rhegium.

4485. *ῥῆγμα* **rhēgma,** *hrayg´-mah;* from *4486;* something *torn,* i.e. a *fragment* (by impl. and abstr. a *fall*):—ruin.

4486. *ῥήγνυμι* **rhēgnumi,** *hrayg´-noo-mee;* or *ῥήσσω* **rhēssō,** *hrace´-so;* both prol. forms of *ῥήκω* **rhēkō** (which appears only in certain forms, and is itself prob. a strengthened form of *ἄγνυμι* **agnumi** [see in *2608*]); to *"break"*, *"wreck"* or *"crack"*, i.e. (espec.) to *sunder* (by *separation* of the parts; *2608* being its intensive [with the prep. in comp.], and *2352* a *shattering* to minute fragments; but not a *reduction* to the constituent particles, like *3089*) or *disrupt, lacerate;* by impl. to *convulse* (with *spasms*); fig. to *give vent* to joyful emotions:—break (forth), burst, rend, tear.

4487. *ῥῆμα* **rhēma,** *hray´-mah;* from *4483;* an *utterance* (individ., collect. or spec.); by impl. a *matter* or *topic* (espec. of narration, command or dispute); with a neg. *naught* whatever:—+ evil, + nothing, saying, word.

4488. *Ῥησά* **Rhēsa,** *hray-sah´;* prob. of Heb. or. [appar. for 7509]; *Resa* (i.e. *Rephajah*), an Isr.:—Rhesa.

4489. *ῥήτωρ* **rhētōr,** *hray´-tore;* from *4483;* a *speaker,* i.e. (by impl.) a forensic *advocate:*—orator.

4490. *ῥητῶς* **rhētōs,** *hray-toce´;* adv. from a der. of *4483;* out-*spokenly,* i.e. *distinctly:*—expressly.

4491. *ῥίζα* **rhiza,** *hrid´-zah;* appar. a prim. word; a *"root"* (lit. or fig.):—root.

4492. *ῥιζόω* **rhizŏō,** *rhid-zŏ´-o;* from *4491;* to *root* (fig. *become stable*):—root.

4493. *ῥιπή* **rhipē,** *hree-pay´;* from *4496;* a *jerk* (of the eye, i.e. [by anal.] an *instant*):—twinkling.

4494. *ῥιπίζω* **rhipizō,** *hrip-id´-zo;* from a der. of *4496* (mean. a *fan* or *bellows*); to *breeze up, i.e. (by anal.) to agitate* (into waves):—toss.

4495. *ῥιπτέω* **rhiptĕō,** *hrip-teh´-o;* from a der. of *4496;* to *toss* up:—cast off.

4496. *ῥίπτω* **rhiptō,** *hrip´-to;* a prim. verb (perh. rather akin to the base of *4474,* through the idea of sudden *motion*); to *fling* (prop. with a quick *toss,* thus differing from *906,* which denotes a *deliberate* hurl; and from *τείνω* **tĕinō** [see in *1614*], which indicates an *extended* projection); by qualification, to *deposit* (as if a load); by extens. to *disperse:*—cast (down, out), scatter abroad, throw.

4497. *Ῥοβοάμ* **Rhŏbŏam,** *hrob-ŏ-am´;* of Heb. or. [7346]; *Roboäm* (i.e. *Rechabam*), an Isr.:—Roboam.

4498. *Ῥόδη* **Rhŏdē,** *hrod´-ay;* prob. for *ῥοδή* **rhŏdē** (a *rose*); *Rodè,* a servant girl:—Rhoda.

4499. *Ῥόδος* **Rhŏdŏs,** *hrod´-os;* prob. from *ῥόδον* **rhŏdŏn** (a *rose*); *Rhodus,* an island of the Mediterranean:—Rhodes.

4500. *ῥοιζηδόν* **rhŏizēdŏn,** *hroyd-zay-don´;* adv. from a der. of *ῥοῖζος* **rhŏizŏs** (a *whir*); *whizzingly,* i.e. *with a crash:*—with a great noise.

4501. *ῥομφαία* **rhŏmphaia,** *hrom-fah´-yah;* prob. of for. or.; a *sabre,* i.e. a long and broad *cutlass* (any *weapon* of the kind, lit. or fig.):—sword.

4502. *Ῥουβήν* **Rhŏubēn,** *hroo-bane´;* of Heb. or. [7205]; *Ruben* (i.e. *Reuben*), an Isr.:—Reuben.

4503. *Ῥούθ* **Rhŏuth,** *hrooth;* of Heb. or. [7327]; *Ruth,* a Moabitess:—Ruth.

4504. *Ῥοῦφος* **Rhŏuphŏs,** *hroo´-fos;* of Lat. or.; *red; Rufus,* a Chr.:—Rufus.

4505. *ῥύμη* **rhumē,** *hroo´-may;* prol. from *4506* in its orig. sense; an *alley* or *avenue* (as crowded):—lane, street.

4506. *ῥύομαι* **rhuŏmai,** *hroo´-om-ahee;* mid. of an obsol. verb, akin to *4482* (through the idea of a *current;* comp. *4511*); to *rush* or *draw* (for oneself), i.e. *rescue:*—deliver (-er).

4507. *ῥυπαρία* **rhuparia,** *hroo-par-ee´-ah;* from *4508; dirtiness* (mor.):—filthiness.

4508. *ῥυπαρός* **rhuparŏs,** *hroo-par-os´;* from *4509; dirty,* i.e. (rel.) *cheap* or *shabby;* mor. *wicked:*—vile.

4509. *ῥύπος* **rhupŏs,** *hroo´-pos;* of uncert. affin.; *dirt,* i.e. (mor.) *depravity:*—filth.

4510. *ῥυπόω* **rhupŏō,** *hroo-pŏ´-o;* from *4509;* to *soil,* i.e. (intrans.) to *become dirty* (mor.):—be filthy.

4511. *ῥύσις* **rhusis,** *hroo´-sis;* from *4506* in the sense of its congener *4482;* a *flux* (of blood):—issue.

4512. *ῥυτίς* **rhutis,** *hroo-tece´;* from *4506;* a *fold* (as *drawing* together), i.e. a *wrinkle* (espec. on the face):—wrinkle.

4513. *Ῥωμαϊκός* **Rhōmaïkŏs,** *hro-mah-ee-kos´;* from *4514; Romaïc,* i.e. *Latin:*—Latin.

4514. *Ῥωμαῖος* **Rhōmaiŏs,** *hro-mah´-yos;* from *4516; Romæan,* i.e. *Roman* (as noun):—Roman, of Rome.

4515. *Ῥωμαϊστί* **Rhōmaïsti,** *hro-mah-is-tee´;* adv. from a presumed der. of *4516; Romaïstically,* i.e. *in* the *Latin* language:—Latin.

4516. *Ῥώμη* **Rhōmē,** *hro´-may;* from the base of *4517; strength; Roma,* the capital of Italy:—Rome.

4517. *ῥώννυμι* **rhōnnumi,** *hrone´-noo-mee;* prol. from *ῥώομαι* **rhōŏmai** (to *dart;* prob. akin to *4506*); to *strengthen,* i.e. (imper. pass.) *have health* (as a parting exclamation, *good-bye*):—farewell.

Σ

4518. *σαβαχθανί* **sabachthani,** *sab-akh-than-ee´;* of Chald. or. [7662 with pron. suff.]; *thou hast left me; sabachthani* (i.e. *shebakthani*), a cry of distress:—sabachthani.

4519. *σαβαώθ* **sabaōth,** *sab-ah-ōwth´;* of Heb. or. [6635 in fem. plur.]; *armies; sabaoth* (i.e. *tsebaoth*), a military epithet of God:—sabaoth.

4520. *σαββατισμός* **sabbatismŏs,** *sab-bat-is-mos´;* from a der. of *4521;* a *"sabbatism"*, i.e. (fig.) the *repose* of Christianity (as a type of heaven):—rest.

4521. *σάββατον* **sabbatŏn,** *sab´-bat-on;* of Heb. or [7676]; the *Sabbath* (i.e. *Shabbath*), or day of weekly *repose* from secular avocations (also the observance or institution itself); by extens. a *se'nnight,* i.e. the interval between two Sabbaths; likewise the plur. in all the above applications:—sabbath (day), week.

4522. *σαγήνη* **sagēnē,** *sag-ay´-nay;* from a der. of *σάττω* **sattō** (to *equip*) mean. *furniture,* espec. a *pack-saddle* (which in the East is merely a bag of *netted* rope); a *"seine"* for fishing:—net.

4523. *Σαδδουκαῖος* **Saddŏukaiŏs,** *sad-doo-kah´-yos;* prob. from *4524;* a *Sadducæan* (i.e. *Tsadokian*), or follower of a certain heretical Isr.:—Sadducee.

4524. *Σαδώκ* **Sadōk,** *sad-oke´;* of Heb. or. [6659]; *Sadoc* (i.e. *Tsadok*), an Isr.:—Sadoc.

4525. *σαίνω* **sainō,** *sah´-ee-no;* akin to *4579:* to *wag* (as a dog its tail fawningly), i.e. (gen.) to *shake* (fig. *disturb*):—move.

4526. *σάκκος* **sakkŏs,** *sak´-kos;* of Heb. or. [8242]; *"sack"-cloth,* i.e. *mohair* (the material or garments made of it, worn as a sign of grief):—sackcloth.

4527. *Σαλά* **Sala,** *sal-ah´;* of Heb. or. [7974]; *Sala* (i.e. *Shelach*), a patriarch:—Sala.

4528. *Σαλαθιήλ* **Salathiēl,** *sal-ath-ee-ale´;* of Heb. or. [7597]; *Salathiël* (i.e. *Sheältiël*), an Isr.:—Salathiel.

4529. *Σαλαμίς* **Salamis,** *sal-am-ece´;* prob. from *4535* (from the *surge* on the shore); *Salamis,* a place in Cyprus:—Salamis.

4530. *Σαλείμ* **Salĕim,** *sal-ime´;* prob. from the same as *4531; Salim,* a place in Pal.:—Salim.

4531. *σαλεύω* **salĕuō,** *sal-yoo´-o;* from *4535;* to *waver,* i.e. *agitate, rock, topple* or (by impl.) *destroy;* fig. to *disturb, incite:*—move, shake (together), which can [-not] be shaken, stir up.

4532. *Σαλήμ* **Salēm,** *sal-ame´;* of Heb. or [8004]; *Salem* (i.e. *Shalem*), a place in Pal.:—Salem.

4533. *Σαλμών* **Salmōn,** *sal-mone´;* of Heb. or. [8012]; *Salmon,* an Isr.:—Salmon.

4534. *Σαλμώνη* **Salmōnē,** *sal-mo´-nay;* perh. of similar or. to *4529; Salmone,* a place in Crete:—Salmone.

4535. *σάλος* **salŏs,** *sal´-os;* prob. from the base of *4525;* a *vibration,* i.e. (spec.) *billow:*—wave.

4536. *σάλπιγξ* **salpigx,** *sal´-pinx;* perh. from *4535* (through the idea of *quavering* or *reverberation*): a *trumpet:*—trump (-et).

4537. *σαλπίζω* **salpizō,** *sal-pid´-zo;* from *4536;* to *trumpet,* i.e. *sound a blast* (lit. or fig.):—(which are yet to) sound (a trumpet).

4538. *σαλπιστής* **salpistēs,** *sal-pis-tace´;* from *4537;* a *trumpeter:*—trumpeter.

4539. *Σαλώμη* **Salōmē,** *sal-o´-may;* prob. of Heb. or. [fem. from 7965]; *Salomè* (i.e. *Shelomah*), an Israelitess:—Salome.

4540. *Σαμάρεια* **Samarĕia,** *sam-ar´-i-ah;* of Heb. or. [8111]; *Samaria* (i.e. *Shomeron*), a city and region of Pal.:—Samaria.

4541. *Σαμαρείτης* **Samarĕitēs,** *sam-ar-i´-tace;* from *4540;* a *Samarite,* i.e. inhab. of Samaria:—Samaritan.

4542. *Σαμαρεῖτις* **Samarĕitis,** *sam-ar-i´-tis;* fem. of *4541;* a *Samaritess,* i.e. woman of Samaria:—of Samaria.

4543. *Σαμοθρᾴκη* **Samŏthra$_i$kē,** *sam-oth-rak´-ay;* from *4544* and *Θρᾴκη* **Thra$_i$kē** (*Thrace*); *Samo-thracè* (*Samos of Thrace*), an island in the Mediterranean:—Samothrace.

4544. *Σάμος* **Samŏs,** *sam´-os;* of uncert. affin.; *Samus,* an island of the Mediterranean:—Samos.

4545. *Σαμουήλ* **Samŏuēl,** *sam-oo-ale´;* of Heb. or. [8050]; *Samuel* (i.e. *Shemuel*), an Isr.:—Samuel.

4546. *Σαμψών* **Sampsōn,** *samp-sone´;* of Heb. or. [8123]; *Sampson* (i.e. *Shimshon*), an Isr.:—Samson.

4547. *σανδάλιον* **sandaliŏn,** *san-dal´-ee-on;* neut. of a der. of *σάνδαλον* **sandalŏn** (a *"sandal"*; of uncert. or.); a *slipper* or *sole-pad:*—sandal.

4548. *σανίς* **sanis,** *san-ece´;* of uncert. affin.; a *plank:*—board.

4549. *Σαούλ* **Saŏul,** *sah-ool´;* of Heb. or. [7586]; *Saül* (i.e. *Shaül*), the Jewish name of *Paul:*—Saul. Comp. *4569.*

4550. *σαπρός* **saprŏs,** *sap-ros´;* from *4595; rotten,* i.e. *worthless* (lit. or mor.):—bad, corrupt. Compt. *4190.*

4551. *Σαπφείρη* **Sapphĕirē,** *sap-fi´-ray;* fem. of *4552; Sapphirè,* an Israelitess:—Sapphira.

4552. *σάπφειρος* **sapphĕirŏs,** *sap´-fi-ros;* of Heb. or. [5601]; a *"sapphire"* or *lapis-lazuli* gem:—sapphire.

4553. *σαργάνη* **sarganē,** *sar-gan´-ay;* appar. of Heb. or. [8276]; a *basket* (as *interwoven* or *wicker*-work):—basket.

4554. *Σάρδεις* **Sardĕis,** *sar´-dice;* plur. of uncert. der.; *Sardis,* a place in Asia Minor:—Sardis.

4555. *σάρδινος* **sardinŏs,** *sar´-dee-nos;* from the same as *4556; sardine* (*3037* being impl.), i.e. a gem, so called:—sardine.

4556. *σάρδιος* **sardiŏs,** *sar´-dee-os;* prop. adj. from an uncert. base; *sardian* (*3037* being impl.), i.e. (as noun) the gem so called:—sardius.

4557. *σαρδόνυξ* **sardŏnux,** *sar-don´-oox;* from the base of *4556* and *ὄνυξ* **ŏnux** (the *nail* of a finger; hence the *"onyx"* stone); a *"sardonyx"*, i.e. the gem so called:—sardonyx.

4558. *Σάρεπτα* **Sarĕpta,** *sar´-ep-tah;* of Heb. or. [6886]; *Sarepta* (i.e. *Tsarephath*), a place in Pal.:—Sarepta.

4559. *σαρκικός* **sarkikŏs,** *sar-kee-kos´;* from *4561; pertaining to flesh,* i.e. (by extens.) *bodily, temporal,* or (by impl.) *animal, unregenerate:*—carnal, fleshly.

4560. *σάρκινος* **sarkinŏs,** *sar´-kee-nos;* from *4561; similar to flesh,* i.e. (by anal.) *soft:*—fleshly.

4561. *σάρξ* **sarx,** *sarx;* prob. from the base of *4563; flesh* (as *stripped* of the skin), i.e. (strictly) the *meat* of an animal (as food), or (by extens.) the *body* (as opposed to the soul [or spirit], or as the symbol of what is external, or as the means of kindred), or (by impl.) *human nature* (with its frailties [phys. or mor.] and passions), or (spec.) a *human being* (as such):—carnal (-ly, + -ly minded), flesh ([-ly]).

4562. *Σαρούχ* **Sarŏuch,** *sar-ooch´;* of Heb. or. [8286]; *Saruch* (i.e. *Serug*), a patriarch:—Saruch.

4563. *σαρόω* **sarŏō,** *sar-ŏ´-o;* from a der. of *σαίρω* **sairō** (to *brush* off; akin to *4951*) mean. a *broom;* to *sweep:*—sweep.

4564. *Σάῤῥα* **Sarrha,** *sar´-hrah;* of Heb. or. [8283]; *Sarra* (i.e. *Sarah*), the wife of Abraham:—Sara, Sarah.

4565. *Σάρων* **Sarōn,** *sar´-one;* of Heb. or. [8289]; *Saron* (i.e. *Sharon*), a district of Pal.:—Saron.

4566. *Σατᾶν* **Satan,** *sat-an´;* of Heb. or. [7854]; *Satan,* i.e. the *devil:*—Satan. Comp. *4567.*

4567. *Σατανᾶς* **Satanas,** *sat-an-as´;* of Chald. or. corresp. to *4566* (with the def. affix); *the accuser,* i.e. the *devil:*—Satan.

4568. *σάτον* **satŏn,** *sat´-on;* of Heb. or. [5429]; a certain *measure* for things dry:—measure.

4569. *Σαῦλος* **Saulŏs,** *sŏw´-los;* of Heb. or., the same as *4549; Saulus* (i.e. *Shaül*), the Jewish name of *Paul:*—Saul.

σαυτοῦ **sautŏu,** etc. See *4572.*

4570. *σβέννυμι* **sbĕnnumi,** *sben´-noo-mee;* a prol. form of an appar. prim. verb; to *extinguish* (lit. or fig.):—go out, quench.

4571. *σέ* **sĕ,** *seh;* accus. sing. of *4771; thee:*—thee, thou, × thy house.

4572. *σεαυτοῦ* **sĕautŏu,** *seh-ŏw-too´;* gen. from *4571* and *846;* also dat. of the same,
σεαυτῷ **sĕautō$_i$,** *seh-ŏw-to´;* and acc.
σεαυτόν **sĕautŏn,** *seh-ŏw-ton´;* likewise
contr. *σαυτοῦ* **sautŏu,** *sŏw-too´;*
σαυτῷ **sautō$_i$,** *sŏw-to´;* and
σαυτόν **sautŏn,** *sŏw-ton´;* respectively; of (*with, to*) *thyself:*—thee, thine own self, (thou) thy (-self).

4573. *σεβάζομαι* **sĕbazŏmai,** *seb-ad´-zom-ahee;* mid. from a der. of *4576;* to *venerate,* i.e. *adore:*—worship.

4574. *σέβασμα* **sĕbasma,** *seb´-as-mah;* from *4573;* something *adored,* i.e. an *object of worship* (god, altar, etc.):—devotion, that is worshipped.

4575. *σεβαστός* **sĕbastŏs,** *seb-as-tos´;* from *4573; venerable* (*august*), i.e. (as noun) a title of the Rom. *Emperor,* or (as adj.) *imperial:*—Augustus (-').

4576. *σέβομαι* **sĕbŏmai,** *seb´-om-ahee;* mid. of an appar. prim. verb; to *revere,* i.e. *adore:*—devout, religious, worship.

4577. *σειρά* **sĕira,** *si-rah´;* prob. from *4951* through its congener *εἴρω* **ĕirō** (to *fasten;* akin to *138*); a *chain* (as *binding* or *drawing*):—chain.

4578. *σεισμός* **sĕismŏs,** *sice-mos´;* from *4579;* a *commotion,* i.e. (of the air) a *gale,* (of the ground) an *earthquake:*—earthquake, tempest.

4579. *σείω* **sĕiō,** *si´-o;* appar. a prim. verb; to *rock* (*vibrate,* prop. sideways or to and fro), i.e. (gen.) to *agitate* (in any direction; cause to *tremble*); fig. to throw into a *tremor* (of fear or concern):—move, quake, shake.

4580. *Σεκοῦνδος* **Sĕkŏundŏs,** *sek-oon´-dos;* of Lat. or.; *"second"*; *Secundus,* a Chr.:—Secundus.

4581. Σελεύκεια **Sĕlĕukĕia,** *sel-yook´-i-ah;* from Σέλευκος **Sĕlĕukŏs,** (*Seleucus,* a Syrian king); *Seleuceia,* a place in Syria:—Seleucia.

4582. σελήνη **sĕlēnē,** *sel-ay´-nay;* from σέλας **sĕlas** (*brilliancy;* prob. akin to the alt. of *138,* through the idea of *attractiveness*); the *moon:*—moon.

4583. σεληνιάζομαι **sĕlēniazŏmai,** *sel-ay-nee-ad´-zom-ahee;* mid. or pass. from a presumed der. of *4582;* to *be moon-struck,* i.e. *crazy:*—be lunatic.

4584. Σεμεΐ **Sĕmĕï,** *sem-eh-ee´;* of Heb. or. [8096]; *Semeï* (i.e. *Shimi*), an Isr.:—Semei.

4585. σεμίδαλις **sĕmidalis,** *sem-id´-al-is;* prob. of for. or.; fine wheaten *flour:*—fine flour.

4586. σεμνός **sĕmnŏs,** *sem-nos´;* from *4576; venerable,* i.e. *honorable:*—grave, honest.

4587. σεμνότης **sĕmnŏtēs,** *sem-not´-ace;* from *4586; venerableness,* i.e. *probity:*—gravity, honesty.

4588. Σέργιος **Sĕrgiŏs,** *serg´-ee-os;* of Lat. or.; *Sergius,* a Rom.:—Sergius.

4589. Σήθ **Sēth,** *sayth;* of Heb. or. [8352]; *Seth* (i.e. *Sheth*), a patriarch:—Seth.

4590. Σήμ **Sēm,** *same;* of Heb. or. [8035]; *Sem* (i.e. *Shem*), a patriarch:—Sem.

4591. σημαίνω **sēmainō,** *say-mah´-ee-no;* from σῆμα **sēma** (a *mark;* of uncert. der.); to *indicate:*—signify.

4592. σημεῖον **sēmĕiŏn,** *say-mi´-on;* neut. of a presumed der. of the base of *4591;* an *indication,* espec. cer. or supernat.:—miracle, sign, token, wonder.

4593. σημειόω **sēmĕiŏō,** *say-mi-ŏ´-o;* from *4592;* to *distinguish,* i.e. *mark* (for avoidance):—note.

4594. σήμερον **sēmĕrŏn,** *say´-mer-on;* neut. (as adv.) of a presumed comp. of the art. *3588* (τ changed to σ) and *2250;* on *the* (i.e. *this*) *day* (or *night* current or just passed); gen. *now* (i.e. *at present, hither-to*):—this (to-) day.

4595. σήπω **sēpō,** *say´-po;* appar. a prim. verb; to *putrefy,* i.e. (fig.) *perish:*—be corrupted.

4596. σηρικός **sērikŏs,** *say-ree-kos´;* from Σήρ **Sēr** (an Indian tribe from whom *silk* was procured; hence the name of the *silk-worm*); *Seric,* i.e. *silken* (neut. as noun, a *silky* fabric):—silk.

4597. σής **sēs,** *sace;* appar. of Heb. or. [5580]; a *moth:*—moth.

4598. σητόβρωτος **sētŏbrōtŏs,** *say-tob´-ro-tos;* from *4597* and a der. of *977; moth-eaten:*—motheaten.

4599. σθενόω **sthĕnŏō,** *sthen-ŏ´-o;* from σθένος **sthĕnŏs,** (bodily *vigor;* prob. akin to the base of *2476*); to *strengthen,* i.e. (fig.) *confirm* (in spiritual knowledge and power):—strengthen.

4600. σιαγών **siagōn,** *see-ag-one´;* of uncert. der.; the *jaw*-bone, i.e. (by impl.) the *cheek* or side of the face:—cheek.

4601. σιγάω **sigaō,** *see-gah´-o;* from *4602;* to *keep silent* (trans. or intrans.):—keep close (secret, silence), hold peace.

4602. σιγή **sigē,** *see-gay´;* appar. from σίζω **sizō** (to *hiss,* i.e. *hist* or *hush*); *silence:*—silence. Comp. *4623.*

4603. σιδήρεος **sidērĕŏs,** *sid-ay´-reh-os;* from *4604;* made *of iron:*—(of) iron.

4604. σίδηρος **sidērŏs,** *sid´-ay-ros;* of uncert. der.; *iron:*—iron.

4605. Σιδών **Sidōn,** *sid-one´;* of Heb. or. [6721]; *Sidon* (i.e. *Tsidon*), a place in Pal.:—Sidon.

4606. Σιδώνιος **Sidōniŏs,** *sid-o´-nee-os;* from *4605;* a *Sidonian,* i.e. inhab. of Sidon:—of Sidon.

4607. σικάριος **sikariŏs,** *sik-ar´-ee-os;* of Lat. or.; a *dagger-man* or *assassin;* a *freebooter* (Jewish *fanatic* outlawed by the Romans):—murderer. Comp. *5406.*

4608. σίκερα **sikĕra,** *sik´-er-ah;* of Heb. or. [7941]; an *intoxicant,* i.e. intensely fermented *liquor:*—strong drink.

4609. Σίλας **Silas,** *see´-las;* contr. for *4610; Silas,* a Chr.:—Silas.

4610. Σιλουανός **Silŏuanŏs,** *sil-oo-an-os´;* of Lat. or.; *"silvan"; Silvanus,* a Chr.:—Silvanus. Comp. *4609.*

4611. Σιλωάμ **Silōam,** *sil-o-am´;* of Heb. or. [7975]; *Siloäm* (i.e. *Shiloäch*), a pool of Jerus.:—Siloam.

4612. σιμικίνθιον **simikinthiŏn,** *sim-ee-kin´-thee-on;* of Lat. or.; a *semicinctium* or *half-girding,* i.e. narrow covering (*apron*):—apron.

4613. Σίμων **Simōn,** *see´-mone;* of Heb. or. [8095]; *Simon* (i.e. *Shimon*), the name of nine Isr.:—Simon. Comp. *4826.*

4614. Σινᾶ **Sina,** *see-nah´;* of Heb. or. [5514]; *Sina (i.e. Sinai*), a mountain in Arabia:—Sina.

4615. σίναπι **sinapi,** *sin´-ap-ee;* perh. from σίνομαι **sinŏmai** (to *hurt,* i.e. *sting*); *mustard* (the plant):—mustard.

4616. σινδών **sindōn,** *sin-done´;* of uncert. (perh. for.) or.; *byssos,* i.e. bleached *linen* (the cloth or a garment of it):—(fine) linen (cloth).

4617. σινιάζω **siniazō,** *sin-ee-ad´-zo;* from σινίον **siniŏn** (a *sieve*); to *riddle* (fig.):—sift.

σῖτα **sita.** See *4621.*

4618. σιτευτός **sitĕutŏs,** *sit-yoo-tos´;* from a der. of *4621; grain-fed,* i.e. *fattened:*—fatted.

4619. σιτιστός **sitistŏs,** *sit-is-tos´;* from a der. of *4621; grained,* i.e. *fatted:*—fatling.

4620. σιτόμετρον **sitŏmĕtrŏn,** *sit-om´-et-ron;* from *4621* and *3358;* a *grain-measure,* i.e. (by impl.) *ration* (*allowance* of food):—portion of meat.

4621. σῖτος **sitŏs,** *see´-tos;* plur. irreg. neut. σῖτα **sita,** *see´-tah;* of uncert. der.; *grain,* espec. *wheat:*—corn, wheat.

4622. Σιών **Siōn,** *see-own´;* of Heb. or. [6726]; *Sion* (i.e. *Tsijon*), a hill of Jerus.; fig. the *Church* (militant or triumphant):—Sion.

4623. σιωπάω **siōpaō,** *see-o-pah´-o;* from σιωπή **siōpē** (*silence,* i.e. a *hush;* prop. *muteness,* i.e. *involuntary* stillness, or *inability* to speak; and thus differing from *4602,* which is rather a voluntary *refusal* or *indisposition* to speak, although the terms are often used synonymously); to *be dumb* (but not *deaf* also, like *2974* prop.); fig. to *be calm* (as *quiet* water):—dumb, (hold) peace.

4624. σκανδαλίζω **skandalizō,** *skan-dal-id´-zo* ("scandalize"); from *4625;* to *entrap,* i.e. *trip* up (fig. *stumble* [trans.] or *entice* to sin, apostasy or displeasure):—(make to) offend.

4625. σκάνδαλον **skandalŏn,** *skan´-dal-on* ("scandal"); prob. from a der. of *2578;* a *trap-stick* (*bent* sapling), i.e. *snare* (fig. *cause* of displeasure or sin):—occasion to fall (of stumbling), offence, thing that offends, stumbling-block.

4626. σκάπτω **skaptō,** *skap´-to;* appar. a prim. verb; to *dig:*—dig.

4627. σκάφη **skaphē,** *skaf´-ay;* a *"skiff"* (as if *dug* out), or *yawl* (carried aboard a large vessel for landing):—boat.

4628. σκέλος **skĕlŏs,** *skel´-os;* appar. from σκέλλω **skĕllō** (to *parch;* through the idea of *leanness*); the *leg* (as *lank*):—leg.

4629. σκέπασμα **skĕpasma,** *skep´-as-mah;* from a der. of σκέπας **skĕpas,** (a *covering;* perh. akin to the base of *4649* through the idea of *noticeableness*); *clothing:*—raiment.

4630. Σκευᾶς **Skĕuas,** *skyoo-as´;* appar. of Lat. or.; *left-handed; Scevas* (i.e. *Scævus*), an Isr.:—Sceva.

4631. σκευή **skĕuē,** *skyoo-ay´;* from *4632; furniture,* i.e. spare *tackle:*—tackling.

4632. σκεῦος **skĕuŏs,** *skyoo´-os;* of uncert. affin.; a *vessel, implement, equipment* or *apparatus* (lit. or fig. [spec. a *wife* as contributing to the usefulness of the husband]):—goods, sail, stuff, vessel.

4633. σκηνή **skēnē,** *skay-nay´;* appar. akin to *4632* and *4639;* a *tent* or cloth hut (lit. or fig.):—habitation, tabernacle.

4634. σκηνοπηγία **skēnŏpēgia,** *skay-nop-ayg-ee´-ah;* from *4636* and *4078;* the *Festival of Tabernacles* (so called from the custom of erecting booths for temporary homes):—tabernacles.

4635. σκηνοποιός **skēnŏpŏiŏs,** *skay-nop-oy-os´;* from *4633* and *4160;* a *manufacturer of tents:*—tentmaker.

4636. σκῆνος **skēnŏs,** *skay´-nos;* from *4633;* a *hut* or temporary residence, i.e. (fig.) the human *body* (as the abode of the spirit):—tabernacle.

4637. σκηνόω **skēnŏō,** *skay-nŏ´-o;* from *4636;* to *tent* or *encamp,* i.e. (fig.) to *occupy* (as a mansion) or (spec.) to *reside* (as God did in the Tabernacle of old, a symbol of protection and communion):—dwell.

4638. *σκήνωμα* **skēnōma,** *skay´-no-mah;* from *4637;* an *encampment,* i.e. (fig.) the *Temple* (as God's residence), the *body* (as a tenement for the soul):—tabernacle.

4639. *σκία* **skia,** *skee´-ah;* appar. a prim. word; *"shade"* or a shadow (lit. or fig. [darkness of *error* or an *adumbration*]):—shadow.

4640. *σκιρτάω* **skirtaō,** *skeer-tah´-o;* akin to *σκαίρω* **skairō** (to *skip*); to *jump,* i.e. sympathetically *move* (as the *quickening* of a fœtus):—leap (for joy).

4641. *σκληροκαρδία* **sklērŏkardia,** *sklay-rok-ar-dee´-ah;* fem. of a comp. of *4642* and *2588; hard-heartedness,* i.e. (spec.) *destitution of* (spiritual) *perception:*—hardness of heart.

4642. *σκληρός* **sklērŏs,** *sklay-ros´;* from the base of *4628; dry,* i.e. *hard* or *tough* (fig. *harsh, severe*):—fierce, hard.

4643. *σκληρότης* **sklērŏtēs,** *sklay-rot´-ace;* from *4642; callousness,* i.e. (fig.) *stubbornness:*—hardness.

4644. *σκληροτράχηλος* **sklērŏtrachēlŏs,** *sklay-rot-rakh´-ay-los;* from *4642* and *5137; hardnaped,* i.e. (fig.) *obstinate:*—stiffnecked.

4645. *σκληρύνω* **sklērunō,** *sklay-roo´-no;* from *4642;* to *indurate,* i.e. (fig.) *render stubborn:*—harden.

4646. *σκολιός* **skŏliŏs,** *skol-ee-os´;* from the base of *4628; warped,* i.e. *winding;* fig. *perverse:*—crooked, froward, untoward.

4647. *σκόλοψ* **skŏlŏps,** *skol´-ops;* perh. from the base of *4628* and *3700; withered* at the *front,* i.e. a *point* or *prickle* (fig. a bodily *annoyance* or *disability*):—thorn.

4648. *σκοπέω* **skŏpĕō,** *skop-eh´-o;* from *4649;* to take *aim* at (*spy*), i.e. (fig.) *regard:*—consider, take heed, look at (on), mark. Comp. *3700.*

4649. *σκοπός* **skŏpŏs,** *skop-os´* ("scope"); from *σκέπτομαι* **skĕptŏmai** (to *peer* about ["skeptic"]; perh. akin to *4626* through the idea of *concealment;* comp. *4629*); a *watch* (*sentry* or *scout*), i.e. (by impl.) a *goal:*—mark.

4650. *σκορπίζω* **skŏrpizō,** *skor-pid´-zo;* appar. from the same as *4651* (through the idea of *penetrating*); to *dissipate,* i.e. (fig.) *put to flight, waste, be liberal:*—disperse abroad, scatter (abroad).

4651. *σκορπίος* **skŏrpiŏs,** *skor-pee´-os;* prob. from an obsol. *σκέρπω* **skĕrpō** (perh. strengthened from the base of *4649* and mean. to *pierce*); a *"scorpion"* (from its *sting*):—scorpion.

4652. *σκοτεινός* **skŏtĕinŏs,** *skot-i-nos´;* from *4655; opaque,* i.e. (fig.) *benighted:*—dark, full of darkness.

4653. *σκοτία* **skŏtia,** *skot-ee´-ah;* from *4655; dimness, obscurity* (lit. or fig.):—dark (-ness).

4654. *σκοτίζω* **skŏtizō,** *skot-id-zo;* from *4655;* to *obscure* (lit. or fig.):—darken.

4655. *σκότος* **skŏtŏs,** *skot´-os;* from the base of *4639; shadiness,* i.e. *obscurity* (lit. or fig.):—darkness.

4656. *σκοτόω* **skŏtŏō,** *skot-ŏ´-o;* from *4655;* to *obscure* or *blind* (lit. or fig.):—be full of darkness.

4657. *σκύβαλον* **skubalŏn,** *skoo´-bal-on;* neut. of a presumed der. of *1519* and *2965* and *906;* what is *thrown to* the *dogs,* i.e. *refuse* (*ordure*):—dung.

4658. *Σκύθης* **Skuthēs,** *skoo´-thace;* prob. of for. or.; a *Scythene* or *Scythian,* i.e. (by impl.) a *savage:*—Scythian.

4659. *σκυθρωπός* **skuthrōpŏs,** *skoo-thro-pos´;* from *σκυθρός* **skuthrŏs,** (*sullen*) and a der. of *3700; angry-visaged,* i.e. *gloomy* or affecting a *mournful* appearance:—of a sad countenance.

4660. *σκύλλω* **skullō,** *skool´-lo;* appar. a prim. verb; to *flay,* i.e. (fig.) to *harass:*—trouble (self).

4661. *σκῦλον* **skulŏn,** *skoo´-lon;* neut. from *4660;* something *stripped* (as a *hide*), i.e. *booty:*—spoil.

4662. *σκωληκόβρωτος* **skōlēkŏbrōtŏs,** *sko-lay-kob´-ro-tos;* from *4663* and a der. of *977; worm-eaten,* i.e. *diseased with maggots:*—eaten of worms.

4663. *σκώληξ* **skōlēx,** *sko´-lakes;* of uncert. der.; a *grub, maggot* or *earth-worm:*—worm.

4664. *σμαράγδινος* **smaragdinŏs,** *smar-ag´-dee-nos;* from *4665;* consisting *of emerald:*—emerald.

4665. *σμάραγδος* **smaragdŏs,** *smar´-ag-dos;* of uncert. der.; the *emerald* or green gem so called:—emerald.

4666. *σμύρνα* **smurna,** *smoor´-nah;* appar. strengthened for *3464; myrrh:*—myrrh.

4667. *Σμύρνα* **Smurna,** *smoor´-nah;* the same as *4666; Smyrna,* a place in Asia Minor:—Smyrna.

4668. *Σμυρναῖος* **Smurnaiŏs,** *smoor-nah´-yos;* from *4667;* a *Smyrnæan:*—in Smyrna.

4669. *σμυρνίζω* **smurnizō,** *smoor-nid´-zo;* from *4667;* to *tincture with myrrh,* i.e. *embitter* (as a narcotic):—mingle with myrrh.

4670. *Σόδομα* **Sŏdŏma,** *sod´-om-ah;* plur. of Heb. or. [5467]; *Sodoma* (i.e. *Sedom*), a place in Pal.:—Sodom.

4671. *σοί* **sŏi,** *soy;* dat. of *4771; to thee:*—thee, thine own, thou, thy.

4672. *Σολομών* or *Σολομῶν* **Sŏlŏmōn,** *sol-om-one´;* of Heb. or. [8010]; *Solomon* (i.e. *Shelomoh*), the son of David:—Solomon.

4673. *σορός* **sŏrŏs,** *sor-os´;* prob. akin to the base of *4987;* a *funereal receptacle* (*urn, coffin*), i.e. (by anal.) a *bier:*—bier.

4674. *σός* **sŏs,** *sos;* from *4771; thine:*—thine (own), thy (friend).

4675. *σοῦ* **sŏu,** *soo;* gen. of *4771; of thee, thy:*—× home, thee, thine (own), thou, thy.

4676. *σουδάριον* **sŏudariŏn,** *soo-dar´-ee-on;* of Lat. or.; a *sudarium* (*sweat-cloth*), i.e. *towel* (for wiping the perspiration from the face, or binding the face of a corpse):—handerchief, napkin.

4677. *Σουσάννα* **Sŏusanna,** *soo-san´-nah;* of Heb. or. [7799 fem.]; *lily; Susannah* (i.e. *Shoshannah*), an Israelitess:—Susanna.

4678. *σοφία* **sŏphia,** *sof-ee´-ah;* from *4680; wisdom* (higher or lower, worldly or spiritual):—wisdom.

4679. *σοφίζω* **sŏphizō,** *sof-id´-zo;* from *4680;* to *render wise;* in a sinister acceptation, to *form "sophisms",* i.e. *continue plausible error:*—cunningly devised, make wise.

4680. *σοφός* **sŏphŏs,** *sof-os´;* akin to *σαφής* **saphēs,** (*clear*); *wise* (in a most gen. application):—wise. Comp. *5429.*

4681. *Σπανία* **Spania,** *span-ee´-ah;* prob. of for. or.; *Spania,* a region of Europe:—Spain.

4682. *σπαράσσω* **sparassō,** *spar-as´-so;* prol. from *σπαίρω* **spairō** (to *gasp;* appar. strengthened from *4685* through the idea of *spasmodic* contraction); to *mangle,* i.e. *convulse* with epilepsy:—rend, tear.

4683. *σπαργανόω* **sparganŏō,** *spar-gan-ŏ´-o;* from *σπάργανον* **sparganŏn** (a *strip;* from a der. of the base of *4682* mean. to *strap* or *wrap* with strips); to *swathe* (an infant after the Oriental custom):—wrap in swaddling clothes.

4684. *σπαταλάω* **spatalaō,** *spat-al-ah´-o;* from *σπατάλη* **spatalē** (*luxury*); to *be voluptuous:*—live in pleasure, be wanton.

4685. *σπάω* **spaō,** *spah´-o;* a prim. verb; to *draw:*—draw (out).

4686. *σπεῖρα* **spĕira,** *spi´-rah;* of immed. Lat. or., but ultimately a der. of *138* in the sense of its cogn. *1507;* a *coil* (*spira,* "spire"), i.e. (fig.) a *mass* of men (a Rom. military *cohort;* also [by anal.] a *squad* of Levitical janitors):—band.

4687. *σπείρω* **spĕirō,** *spi´-ro;* prob. strengthened from *4685* (through the idea of *extending*); to *scatter,* i.e. *sow* (lit. or fig.):—sow (-er), receive seed.

4688. *σπεκουλάτωρ* **spĕkŏulatōr,** *spek-oo-lat´-ore;* of Lat. or.; a *speculator,* i.e. military *scout* (*spy* or [by extens.] *life-guardsman*):—executioner.

4689. *σπένδω* **spĕndō,** *spen´-do;* appar. a prim. verb; to *pour* out as a libation, i.e. (fig.) to *devote* (one's life or blood, as a sacrifice) (*"spend"*):—(be ready to) be offered.

4690. *σπέρμα* **spĕrma,** *sper´-mah;* from *4687;* something *sown,* i.e. *seed* (includ. the male *"sperm"*); by impl. *offspring;* spec. a *remnant* (fig. as if kept over for planting):—issue, seed.

4691. *σπερμολόγος* **spĕrmŏlŏgŏs,** *sper-mol-og´-os;* from *4690* and *3004;* a *seed-picker* (as the crow), i.e. (fig.) a *sponger, loafer* (spec. a *gossip* or *trifler* in talk):—babbler.

4692. σπεύδω **spĕudō,** *spyoo´-do;* prob. strengthened from *4228;* to *"speed"* ("study"), i.e. *urge* on (diligently or earnestly); by impl. to *await* eagerly:—(make, with) haste unto.

4693. σπήλαιον **spēlaiŏn,** *spay´-lah-yon;* neut. of a presumed der. of σπέος **spĕŏs** (a *grotto*); a *cavern;* by impl. a *hiding-place* or *resort:*—cave, den.

4694. σπιλάς **spilas,** *spee-las´;* of uncert. der.; a *ledge* or *reef* of rock in the sea:—spot [*by confusion with 4696*].

4695. σπιλόω **spilŏō,** *spee-lŏ´-o;* from *4696;* to *stain* or *soil* (lit. or fig.):—defile, spot.

4696. σπίλος **spilŏs,** *spee´-los;* of uncert. der.; a *stain* or *blemish,* i.e. (fig.) *defect, disgrace:*—spot.

4697. σπλαγχνίζομαι **splagchnizŏmai,** *splangkh-nid´-zom-ahee;* mid. from *4698;* to have the *bowels* yearn, i.e. (fig.) *feel sympathy,* to *pity:*—have (be moved with) compassion.

4698. σπλάγχνον **splagchnŏn,** *splangkh´-non;* prob. strengthened from σπλήν **splēn,** (the *"spleen"*); an *intestine* (plur.); fig. *pity* or *sympathy:*—bowels, inward affection, + tender mercy.

4699. σπόγγος **spŏggŏs,** *spong´-gos;* perh. of for. or.; a *"sponge":*—spunge.

4700. σποδός **spŏdŏs,** *spod-os´;* of uncert. der.; *ashes:*—ashes.

4701. σπορά **spŏra,** *spor-ah´;* from *4687;* a *sowing,* i.e. (by impl.) *parentage:*—seed.

4702. σπόριμος **spŏrimŏs,** *spor´-ee-mos;* from *4703; sown,* i.e. (neut. plur.) a planted *field:*—corn (-field).

4703. σπόρος **spŏrŏs,** *spor´-os;* from *4687;* a *scattering* (of seed), i.e. (concr.) *seed* (as sown):—seed (× sown).

4704. σπουδάζω **spŏudazō,** *spoo-dad´-zo;* from *4710;* to *use speed,* i.e. to *make effort, be prompt* or *earnest:*—do (give) diligence, be diligent (forward), endeavour, labour, study.

4705. σπουδαῖος **spŏudaiŏs,** *spoo-dah´-yos;* from *4710; prompt, energetic, earnest:*—diligent.

4706. σπουδαιότερον **spŏudaiŏtĕrŏn,** *spoo-dah-yot´-er-on;* neut. of *4707* as adv.; *more earnestly* than others), i.e. very *promptly:*—very diligently.

4707. σπουδαιότερος **spŏudaiŏtĕrŏs,** *spoo-dah-yot´-er-os;* compar. of *4705; more prompt, more earnest:*—more diligent (forward).

4708. σπουδαιοτέρως **spŏudaiŏtĕrōs,** *spoo-dah-yot-er´-oce;* adv. from *4707; more speedily,* i.e. *sooner* than otherwise:—more carefully.

4709. σπουδαίως **spŏudaiōs,** *spoo-dah´-yoce;* adv. from *4705; earnestly, promptly:*—diligently, instantly.

4710. σπουδή **spŏudē,** *spoo-day´;* from *4692; "speed",* i.e. (by impl.) *despatch, eagerness, earnestness:*—business, (earnest) care (-fulness), diligence forwardness, haste.

4711. σπυρίς **spuris,** *spoo-rece´;* from *4687* (as *woven*); a *hamper* or *lunch-receptacle:*—basket.

4712. στάδιον **stadiŏn,** *stad´-ee-on;* or masc. (in plur.) στάδιος **stadiŏs,** *stad´-ee-os;* from the base of *2476* (as *fixed*); a *stade* or certain measure of distance; by impl. a *stadium* or *race-course:*—furlong, race.

4713. στάμνος **stamnŏs,** *stam´-nos;* from the base of *2476* (as *stationary*); a *jar* or earthen *tank:*—pot.

4714. στάσις **stasis,** *stas´-is;* from the base of *2476;* a *standing* (prop. the act), i.e. (by anal.) *position* (*existence*); by impl. a popular *uprising;* fig. *controversy:*—dissension, insurrection, × standing, uproar.

4715. στατήρ **statēr,** *stat-air´;* from the base or *2746;* a *stander* (*standard* of value), i.e. (spec.) *a stater* or certain coin:—piece of money.

4716. σταυρός **staurŏs,** *stŏw-ros´;* from the base of *2476;* a *stake* or *post* (as *set* upright), i.e. (spec.) a *pole* or *cross* (as an instrument of capital punishment); fig. *exposure to death,* i.e. *self-denial;* by impl. the *atonement* of Christ:—cross.

4717. σταυρόω **staurŏō,** *stŏw-rŏ´-o;* from *4716;* to *impale* on the cross; fig. to *extinguish* (*subdue*) passion or selfishness:—crucify.

4718. σταφυλή **staphulē,** *staf-oo-lay´;* prob. from the base of *4735;* a *cluster* of grapes (as if *intertwined*):—grapes.

4719. στάχυς **stachus,** *stakh´-oos;* from the base of *2476;* a *head* of grain (as *standing* out from the stalk):—ear (of corn).

4720. Στάχυς **Stachus,** *stakh´-oos;* the same as *4719; Stachys,* a Chr.:—Stachys.

4721. στέγη **stĕgē,** *steg´-ay;* strengthened from a prim. τέγος **tĕgŏs** (a *"thatch"* or *"deck"* of a building); a *roof:*—roof.

4722. στέγω **stĕgō,** *steg´-o;* from *4721;* to *roof* over, i.e. (fig.) to *cover* with silence (*endure* patiently):—(for-) bear, suffer.

4723. στεῖρος **stĕirŏs,** *sti´-ros;* a contr. from *4731* (as *stiff* and *unnatural*); *"sterile":*—barren.

4724. στέλλω **stĕllō,** *stel´-lo;* prob. strengthened from the base of *2476;* prop. to *set* fast ("*stall*"), i.e. (fig.) to *repress* (reflex. *abstain* from associating with):—avoid, withdraw self.

4725. στέμμα **stĕmma,** *stem´-mah;* from the base of *4735;* a *wreath* for show:—garland.

4726. στεναγμός **stĕnagmŏs,** *sten-ag-mos´;* from *4727;* a *sigh:*—groaning.

4727. στενάζω **stĕnazō,** *sten-ad´-zo;* from *4728;* to *make* (intrans. *be*) *in straits,* i.e. (by impl.) to *sigh, murmur, pray* inaudibly:—with grief, groan, grudge, sigh.

4728. στενός **stĕnŏs,** *sten-os´;* prob. from the base of *2476; narrow* (from obstacles *standing* close about):—strait.

4729. στενοχωρέω **stĕnŏchōrĕō,** *sten-okh-o-reh´-o;* from the same as *4730;* to *hem* in closely, i.e. (fig.) *cramp:*—distress, straiten.

4730. στενοχωρία **stĕnŏchōria,** *sten-okh-o-ree´-ah;* from a comp. of *4728* and *5561; narrowness of room,* i.e. (fig.) *calamity:*—anguish, distress.

4731. στερεός **stĕrĕŏs,** *ster-eh-os´;* from *2476; stiff,* i.e. *solid, stable* (lit. or fig.):—stedfast, strong, sure.

4732. στερεόω **stĕrĕŏō,** *ster-eh-ŏ´-o;* from *4731;* to *solidify,* i.e. *confirm* (lit. or fig.):—establish, receive strength, make strong.

4733. στερέωμα **stĕrĕōma,** *ster-eh´-o-mah;* from *4732;* something *established,* i.e. (abstr.) *confirmation* (*stability*):—stedfastness.

4734. Στεφανᾶς **Stĕphanas,** *stef-an-as´;* prob. contr. for στεφανωτός **stĕphanōtŏs,** (*crowned;* from *4737*); *Stephanas,* a Chr.:—Stephanas.

4735. στέφανος **stĕphanŏs,** *stef´-an-os;* from an appar. prim. στέφω **stĕphō,** (to *twine* or *wreathe*); a *chaplet* (as a badge of royalty, a prize in the public games or a symbol of honor gen.; but more conspicuous and elaborate than the simple *fillet, 1238*), lit. or fig.:—crown.

4736. Στέφανος **Stĕphanŏs,** *stef´-an-os;* the same as *4735; Stephanus,* a Chr.:—Stephen.

4737. στεφανόω **stephanŏō,** *stef-an-ŏ-o;* from *4735;* to *adorn with* an honorary *wreath* (lit. or fig.):—crown.

4738. στῆθος **stēthŏs,** *stay´-thos;* from *2476* (as *standing* prominently); the (entire extern.) *bosom,* i.e. *chest:*—breast.

4739. στήκω **stēkō,** *stay´-ko;* from the perf. tense of *2476;* to *be stationary,* i.e. (fig.) to *persevere:*—stand (fast).

4740. στηριγμός **stērigmŏs,** *stay-rig-mos´;* from *4741; stability* (fig.):—stedfastness

4741. στηρίζω **stērizō,** *stay-rid´-zo;* from a presumed der. of *2476* (like *4731*); to *set fast,* i.e. (lit.) to *turn resolutely* in a certain direction, or (fig.) to *confirm:*—fix, (e-) stablish, stedfastly set, strengthen.

4742. στίγμα **stigma,** *stig´-mah;* from a prim. στίζω **stizō** (to *"stick",* i.e. *prick*); a *mark* incised or punched (for recognition of ownership), i.e. (fig.) *scar* of service:—mark.

4743. στιγμή **stigmē,** *stig-may´;* fem. of *4742;* a *point* of time, i.e. an *instant:*—moment.

4744. στίλβω **stilbō,** *stil´-bo;* appar. a prim. verb; to *gleam,* i.e. *flash* intensely:—shining.

4745. στοά **stŏa,** *stŏ-ah´;* prob. from *2476;* a *colonnade* or interior *piazza:*—porch.

4746. στοιβάς **stŏibas,** *stoy-bas´;* from a prim. 163steîqv **stĕibō** (to *"step"* or *"stamp"*); a *spread* (as if *tramped* flat) of loose materials for a couch, i.e. (by impl.) a *bough* of a tree so employed:—branch.

4747. στοιχεῖον **stŏichĕiŏn,** *stoy-khi´-on;* neut. of a presumed der. of the base of *4748;* something *orderly* in arrangement, i.e. (by impl.) a *serial* (*basal, fundamental, initial*) constituent (lit.), proposition (fig.):—element, principle, rudiment.

4748. *στοιχέω* **stŏichĕō,** *stoy-kheh´-o;* from a der. of *στείχω* **stĕichō** (to *range* in regular line); to *march* in (military) rank (*keep step*), i.e. (fig.) to *conform* to virtue and piety:—walk (orderly).

4749. *στολή* **stŏlē,** *stol-ay´;* from *4724; equipment,* i.e. (spec.) a *"stole"* or long-fitting *gown* (as a mark of dignity):—long clothing (garment), (long) robe.

4750. *στόμα* **stŏma,** *stom´-a;* prob. strengthened from a presumed der. of the base of *5114;* the *mouth* (as if a *gash* in the face); by impl. *language* (and its relations); fig. an *opening* (in the earth); spec. the *front* or *edge* (of a weapon):—edge, face, mouth.

4751. *στόμαχος* **stŏmachŏs,** *stom´-akh-os;* from *4750;* an *orifice* (the *gullet*), i.e. (spec.) the *"stomach"*:—stomach.

4752. *στρατεία* **stratĕia,** *strat-i´-ah;* from *4754;* military *service,* i.e. (fig.) the apostolic *career* (as one of hardship and danger):—warfare.

4753. *στράτευμα* **stratĕuma,** *strat´-yoo-mah;* from *4754;* an *armament,* i.e. (by impl.) a body of *troops* (more or less extensive or systematic):—army, soldier, man of war.

4754. *στρατεύομαι* **stratĕuŏmai,** *strat-yoo´-om-ahee;* mid. from the base of *4756;* to *serve* in a military campaign; fig. to *execute the apostolate* (with its arduous duties and functions), to *contend* with carnal inclinations:—soldier, (go to) war (-fare).

4755. *στρατηγός* **stratēgŏs,** *strat-ay-gos´;* from the base of *4756* and *71* or *2233;* a *general,* i.e. (by impl. or anal.) a (military) *governor* (*prætor*), the *chief* (*præfect*) of the (Levitical) temple-wardens:—captain, magistrate.

4756. *στρατία* **stratia,** *strat-ee´-ah;* fem. of a der. of *στρατός* **stratŏs** (an *army;* from the base of *4766,* as *encamped*); *camp-likeness,* i.e. an *army,* i.e. (fig.) the *angels,* the celestial *luminaries:*—host.

4757. *στρατιώτης* **stratiōtēs,** *strat-ee-o´-tace;* from a presumed der. of the same as *4756;* a *camperout,* i.e. a (common) *warrior* (lit. or fig.):—soldier.

4758. *στρατολογέω* **stratŏlŏgĕō,** *strat-ol-og-eh´-o;* from a comp. of the base of *4756* and *3004* (in its orig. sense); to *gather* (or *select*) as a *warrior,* i.e. *enlist* in the army:—choose to be a soldier.

4759. *στρατοπεδάρχης* **stratŏpĕdarchēs,** *strat-op-ed-ar´-khace;* from *4760* and *757;* a *ruler of an army,* i.e. (spec.) a Praetorian *præfect:*—captain of the guard.

4760. *στρατόπεδον* **stratŏpĕdŏn,** *strat-op´-ed-on;* from the base of *4756* and the same as *3977;* a *camping-ground,* i.e. (by impl.) a body of *troops:*—army.

4761. *στρεβλόω* **strĕblŏō,** *streb-lŏ´-o;* from a der. of *4762;* to *wrench,* i.e. (spec.) to *torture* (by the rack), but only fig. to *pervert:*—wrest.

4762. *στρέφω* **strĕphō,** *stref´-o;* strengthened from the base of *5157;* to *twist,* i.e. *turn* quite around or *reverse* (lit. or fig.):—convert, turn (again, back again, self, self about).

4763. *στρηνιάω* **strēniaō,** *stray-nee-ah´-o;* from a presumed der. of *4764;* to *be luxurious:*—live deliciously.

4764. *στρῆνος* **strēnŏs,** *stray´-nos;* akin to *4731;* a *"straining", "strenuousness"* or "strength", i.e. (fig.) *luxury* (*voluptuousness*):—delicacy.

4765. *στρουθίον* **strŏuthiŏn,** *stroo-thee´-on;* dimin. of *στρουθός* **strŏuthŏs,** (a *sparrow*); a *little sparrow:*—sparrow.

4766. *στρώννυμι* **strōnnumi,** *strone´-noo-mee;* or simpler

στρωννύω **strōnnuō,** *strone-noo´-o;* prol. from a still simpler

στρόω **strŏō,** *strŏ´-o* (used only as an alt. in certain tenses; prob. akin to *4731* through the idea of *positing*); to *"strew"*, i.e. *spread* (as a carpet or couch):—make bed, furnish, spread, strew.

4767. *στυγνητός* **stugnētŏs,** *stoog-nay-tos´;* from a der. of an obsol. appar. prim. *στύγω* **stugō** (to *hate*); *hated,* i.e. *odious:*—hateful.

4768. *στυγνάζω* **stugnazō,** *stoog-nad´-zo;* from the same as *4767;* to *render gloomy,* i.e. (by impl.) *glower* (*be overcast* with clouds, or *sombreness* of speech):—lower, be sad.

4769. *στύλος* **stulŏs,** *stoo´-los;* from *στύω* **stuō** (to *stiffen;* prop. akin to the base of *2476*); a *post* (*"style"*), i.e. (fig.) *support:*—pillar.

4770. *Στωϊκός* **Stōikŏs,** *sto-ik-os´;* from *4745;* a *"Stoïc"* (as occupying a particular porch in Athens), i.e. adherent of a certain philosophy:—Stoick.

4771. *σύ* **su,** *soo;* the pers. pron. of the sec. pers. sing.; *thou:*—thou. See also *4571, 4671, 4675;* and for the plur. *5209, 5210, 5213, 5216.*

4772. *συγγένεια* **suggĕnĕia,** *soong-ghen´-i-ah;* from *4773; relationship,* i.e. (concr.) *relatives:*—kindred.

4773. *συγγενής* **suggĕnēs,** *soong-ghen-ace´;* from *4862* and *1085:* a *relative* (by blood); by extens. a fellow *countryman:*—cousin, kin (-sfolk, -sman).

4774. *συγγνώμη* **suggnōmē,** *soong-gno´-may;* from a comp. of *4862* and *1097; fellow knowledge,* i.e. *concession:*—permission.

4775. *συγκάθημαι* **sugkathēmai,** *soong-kath´-ay-mahee;* from *4862* and *2521;* to *seat oneself* in company *with:*—sit with.

4776. *συγκαθίζω* **sugkathizō,** *soong-kath-id´-zo;* from *4862* and *2523;* to *give* (or *take*) a *seat* in company *with:*—(make) sit (down) together.

4777. *συγκακοπαθέω* **sugkakŏpathĕō,** *soong-kak-op-ath-eh´-o;* from *4862* and *2553;* to *suffer hardship* in company *with:*—be partaker of afflictions.

4778. *συγκακουχέω* **sugkakŏuchĕō,** *soong-kak-oo-kheh´-o;* from *4862* and *2558;* to *maltreat* in company *with,* i.e. (pass.) *endure persecution together:*—suffer affliction with.

4779. *συγκαλέω* **sugkalĕō,** *soong-kal-eh´-o;* from *4862* and *2564;* to *convoke:*—call together.

4780. *συγκαλύπτω* **sugkaluptō,** *soong-kal-oop´-to;* from *4862* and *2572;* to *conceal altogether:*—cover.

4781. *συγκάμπτω* **sugkamptō,** *soong-kamp´-to;* from *4862* and *2578;* to *bend together,* i.e. (fig.) to *afflict:*—bow down.

4782. *συγκαταβαίνω* **sugkatabainō,** *soong-kat-ab-ah´ee-no;* from *4862* and *2597;* to *descend* in company *with:*—go down with.

4783. *συγκατάθεσις* **sugkatathĕsis,** *soong-kat-ath´-es-is;* from *4784;* a *deposition* (of sentiment) in company *with,* i.e. (fig.) *accord* with:—agreement.

4784. *συγκατατίθεμαι* **sugkatatithĕmai,** *soong-kat-at-ith´-em-ahee;* mid. from *4862* and *2698;* to *deposit* (one's vote or opinion) in company *with,* i.e. (fig.) to *accord* with:—consent.

4785. *συγκαταψηφίζω* **sugkatapsēphizō,** *soong-kat-aps-ay-fid´-zo;* from *4862* and a comp. of *2596* and *5585;* to *count down* in company *with,* i.e. *enroll among:*—number with.

4786. *συγκεράννυμι* **sugkĕrannumi,** *soong-ker-an´-noo-mee;* from *4862* and *2767;* to *commingle,* i.e. (fig.) to *combine* or *assimilate:*—mix with, temper together.

4787. *συγκινέω* **sugkinĕō,** *soong-kin-eh´-o;* from *4682* and *2795;* to *move together,* i.e. (spec.) to *excite* as a mass (to sedition):—stir up.

4788. *συγκλείω* **sugklĕiō,** *soong-kli´-o;* from *4862* and *2808;* to *shut together,* i.e. *include* or (fig.) *embrace* in a common subjection to:—conclude, inclose, shut up.

4789. *συγκληρονόμος* **sugklērŏnŏmŏs,** *soong-klay-ron-om´-os;* from *4862* and *2818;* a *co-heir,* i.e. (by anal.) *participant in common:*—fellow (joint) -heir, heir together, heir with.

4790. *συγκοινωνέω* **sugkŏinōnĕō,** *soong-koy-no-neh´-o;* from *4862* and *2841;* to *share* in company *with,* i.e. *co-participate* in:—communicate (have fellowship) with, be partaker of.

4791. *συγκοινωνός* **sugkŏinōnŏs,** *soong-koy-no-nos´;* from *4862* and *2844;* a *co-participant:*—companion, partake (-r, -r with).

4792. *συγκομίζω* **sugkŏmizō,** *soong-kom-id´-zo;* from *4862* and *2865;* to *convey together,* i.e. *collect* or *bear* away in company *with* others:—carry.

4793. *συγκρίνω* **sugkrinō,** *soong-kree´-no;* from *4862* and *2919;* to *judge* of one thing in connection *with* another, i.e. *combine* (spiritual ideas with appropriate expressions) or *collate* (one person with another by way of contrast or resemblance):—compare among (with).

4794. *συγκύπτω* **sugkuptō,** *soong-koop´-to;* from *4862* and *2955;* to *stoop altogether,* i.e. *be completely overcome* by:—bow together.

4795. συγκυρία **sugkuria,** *soong-koo-ree´-ah;* from a comp. of *4862* and κυρέω **kurĕō** (to *light* or *happen;* from the base of *2962*); *concurrence,* i.e. *accident:*—chance.

4796. συγχαίρω **sugchairō,** *soong-khah´ee-ro;* from *4862* and *5463;* to *sympathize in gladness, congratulate:*—rejoice in (with).

4797. συγχέω **sugchĕō,** *soong-kheh´-o;* or συγχύνω **sugchunō,** *soong-khoo´-no;* from *4862* and χέω **chĕō** (to *pour*) or its alt.; to *commingle* promiscuously, i.e. (fig.) to *throw* (an assembly) *into disorder,* to *perplex* (the mind):—confound, confuse, stir up, be in an uproar.

4798. συγχράομαι **sugchraŏmai,** *soong-khrah´-om-ahee;* from *4862* and *5530;* to *use jointly,* i.e. (by impl.) to *hold intercourse in common:*—have dealings with.

4799. σύγχυσις **sugchusis,** *soong´-khoo-sis;* from *4797; commixture,* i.e. (fig.) riotous *disturbance:*—confusion.

4800. συζάω **suzaō,** *sood-zah´-o;* from *4862* and *2198;* to continue to *live* in common *with,* i.e. *co-survive* (lit. or fig.):—live with.

4801. συζεύγνυμι **suzĕugnumi,** *sood-zyoog´-noo-mee;* from *4862* and the base of *2201;* to *yoke together,* i.e. (fig.) *conjoin* (in marriage):—join together.

4802. συζητέω **suzētĕō,** *sood-zay-teh´-o;* from *4862* and *2212;* to investigate *jointly,* i.e. *discuss, controvert, cavil:*—dispute (with), enquire, question (with), reason (together).

4803. συζήτησις **suzētēsis,** *sood-zay´-tay-sis;* from *4802; mutual questioning,* i.e. *discussion:*—disputation (-ting), reasoning.

4804. συζητητής **suzētētēs,** *sood-zay-tay-tace´;* from *4802;* a *disputant,* i.e. *sophist:*—disputer.

4805. σύζυγος **suzugŏs,** *sood´-zoo-gos;* from *4801; co-yoked,* i.e. (fig.) as noun, a *colleague;* prob. rather as prop. name; *Syzygus,* a Chr.:—yokefellow.

4806. συζωοποιέω **suzōŏpŏiĕō,** *sood-zo-op-oy-eh´-o;* from *4862* and *2227;* to *reanimate conjointly* with (fig.):—quicken together with.

4807. συκάμινος **sukaminŏs,** *soo-kam´-ee-nos;* of Heb. or. [8256] in imitation of *4809;* a *sycamore*-fig tree:—sycamine tree.

4808. συκῆ **sukē,** *soo-kay´;* from *4810;* a *fig-tree:*—fig tree.

4809. συκομωραία **sukŏmōraia,** *soo-kom-o-rah´-yah;* from *4810* and μόρον **mŏrŏn** (the *mulberry*); the "*sycamore*"-fig tree:—sycamore tree. Comp. *4807.*

4810. σῦκον **sukŏn,** *soo´-kon;* appar. a prim. word; a *fig:*—fig.

4811. συκοφαντέω **sukŏphantĕō,** *soo-kof-an-teh´-o;* from a comp. of *4810* and a der. of *5316;* to *be a fig-informer* (reporter of the law forbidding the exportation of figs from Greece), "*sycophant*", i.e. (gen. and by extens.) to *defraud* (*exact* unlawfully, *extort*):—accuse falsely, take by false accusation.

4812. συλαγωγέω **sulagōgĕō,** *soo-lag-ogue-eh´-o;* from the base of *4813* and (the redupl. form of) *71;* to *lead* away as *booty,* i.e. (fig.) *seduce:*—spoil.

4813. συλάω **sulaō,** *soo-lah´-o;* from a der. of σύλλω **sullō** (to *strip;* prob. akin to *138;* comp. *4661*); to *despoil:*—rob.

4814. συλλαλέω **sullalĕō,** *sool-lal-eh´-o;* from *4862* and *2980;* to *talk together,* i.e. *converse:*—commune (confer, talk) with, speak among.

4815. συλλαμβάνω **sullambanō,** *sool-lam-ban´-o;* from *4862* and *2983;* to *clasp,* i.e. *seize* (*arrest, capture*); spec. to *conceive* (lit. or fig.); by impl. to *aid:*—catch, conceive, help, take.

4816. συλλέγω **sullĕgō,** *sool-leg´-o;* from *4862* and *3004* in its orig. sense; to *collect:*—gather (together, up).

4817. συλλογίζομαι **sullŏgizŏmai,** *sool-log-id´-zom-ahee;* from *4862* and *3049;* to *reckon together* (with oneself), i.e. *deliberate:*—reason with.

4818. συλλυπέω **sullupĕō,** *sool-loop-eh´-o;* from *4862* and *3076;* to *afflict jointly,* i.e. (pass.) *sorrow at* (on account of) some one:—be grieved.

4819. συμβαίνω, **sumbainō,** *soom-bah´-ee-no;* from *4862* and the base of *939;* to *walk* (fig. *transpire*) *together,* i.e. *concur* (*take place*):—be (-fall), happen (unto).

4820. συμβάλλω **sumballō,** *soom-bal´-lo;* from *4862* and *906;* to *combine,* i.e. (in speaking) to *converse, consult, dispute,* (mentally) to *consider,* (by impl.) to *aid,* (personally) to *join, attack:*—confer, encounter, help, make, meet with, ponder.

4821. συμβασιλεύω **sumbasilĕuō,** *soom-bas-il-yoo´-o;* from *4862* and *936;* to *be co-regent* (fig.):—reign with.

4822. συμβιβάζω **sumbibazō,** *soom-bib-ad´-zo;* from *4862* and βιβάζω **bibazō** (to *force;* caus. [by redupl.] of the base of *939*); to *drive together,* i.e. *unite* (in association or affection), (mentally) to *infer, show, teach:*—compact, assuredly, gather, instruct, knit together, prove.

4823. συμβουλεύω **sumbŏulĕuō,** *soom-bool-yoo´-o;* from *4862* and *1011;* to *give* (or *take*) *advice jointly,* i.e. *recommend, deliberate* or *determine:*—consult, (give, take) counsel (together).

4824. συμβούλιον **sumbŏuliŏn,** *soom-boo´-lee-on;* neut. of a presumed der. of *4825; advisement;* spec. a *deliberative* body, i.e. the provincial *assessors* or lay-court:—consultation, counsel, council.

4825. σύμβουλος **sumbŏulŏs,** *soom´-boo-los;* from *4862* and *1012;* a *consultor,* i.e. *adviser:*—counsellor.

4826. Συμεών **Sumĕōn,** *soom-eh-one´;* from the same as *4613; Symeon* (i.e. *Shimon*), the name of five Isr.:—Simeon, Simon.

4827. συμμαθητής **summathētēs,** *soom-math-ay-tace´;* from a comp. of *4862* and *3129;* a *co-learner* (of Christianity):—fellowdisciple.

4828. συμμαρτυρέω **summarturĕō,** *soom-mar-too-reh´-o;* from *4862* and *3140;* to *testify jointly,* i.e. *corroborate* by (concurrent) evidence:—testify unto, (also) bear witness (with).

4829. συμμερίζομαι **summĕrizŏmai,** *soom-mer-id´-zom-ahee;* mid. from *4862* and *3307;* to *share jointly,* i.e. *participate* in:—be partaker with.

4830. συμμέτοχος **summĕtŏchŏs,** *soom-met´-okh-os;* from *4862* and *3353;* a *co-participant:*—partaker.

4831. συμμιμητής **summimētēs,** *soom-mim-ay-tace´;* from a presumed comp. of *4862* and *3401;* a *co-imitator,* i.e. *fellow votary:*—follower together.

4832. σύμμορφος **summŏrphŏs,** *soom-mor-fos´;* from *4862* and *3444; jointly formed,* i.e. (fig.) *similar:*—conformed to, fashioned like unto.

4833. συμμορφόω **summŏrphŏō,** *soom-mor-fŏ´-o;* from *4832;* to *render like,* i.e. (fig.) to *assimilate:*—make conformable unto.

4834. συμπαθέω **sumpathĕō,** *soom-path-eh´-o;* from *4835;* to *feel "sympathy"* with, i.e. (by impl.) to *commiserate:*—have compassion, be touched with a feeling of.

4835. συμπαθής **sumpathēs,** *soom-path-ace´;* from *4841; having a fellow-feeling* ("*sympathetic*"), i.e. (by impl.) *mutually commiserative:*—having compassion one of another.

4836. συμπαραγίνομαι **sumparaginŏmai,** *soom-par-ag-in´-om-ahee;* from *4862* and *3854;* to *be present together,* i.e. to *convene;* by impl. to *appear in aid:*—come together, stand with.

4837. συμπαρακαλέω **sumparakalĕō,** *soom-par-ak-al-eh´-o;* from *4862* and *3870;* to *console jointly:*—comfort together.

4838. συμπαραλαμβάνω **sumparalambanō,** *soom-par-al-am-ban´-o;* from *4862* and *3880;* to *take along in company:*—take with.

4839. συμπαραμένω **sumparamĕnō,** *soom-par-am-en´-o;* from *4862* and *3887;* to *remain in company,* i.e. *still live:*—continue with.

4840. συμπάρειμι **sumparĕimi,** *soom-par´-i-mee;* from *4862* and *3918;* to *be at hand together,* i.e. *now present:*—be here present with.

4841. συμπάσχω **sumpaschō,** *soom-pas´-kho;* from *4862* and *3958* (includ. its alt.); to *experience pain jointly* or of the *same kind* (spec. *persecution;* to "*sympathize*"):—suffer with.

4842. συμπέμπω **sumpĕmpō,** *soom-pem´-po;* from *4862* and *3992;* to *despatch in company:*—send with.

4843. συμπεριλαμβάνω **sumpĕrilambanō,** *soom-per-ee-lam-ban´-o;* from *4862* and a comp. of *4012* and *2983;* to *take by inclosing altogether,* i.e. *earnestly throw the arms about one:*—embrace.

4844. συμπίνω **sumpinō,** *soom-pee´-no;* from *4862* and *4095;* to *partake a beverage in company:*—drink with.

4845. συμπληρόω **sumplērŏō,** *soom-play-rŏ´-o;* from *4862* and *4137;* to *implenish completely,* i.e. (of space) to *swamp* (a boat), or (of time) to *accomplish* (pass. be *complete*):—(fully) come, fill up.

4846. συμπνίγω **sumpnigō,** *soom-pnee´-go;* from *4862* and *4155;* to *strangle completely,* i.e. (lit.) to *drown,* or (fig.) to *crowd:*—choke, throng.

4847. συμπολίτης **sumpŏlitēs,** *soom-pol-ee´-tace;* from *4862* and *4177;* a *native of the same town,* i.e. (fig.) *co-religionist* (*fellow-Christian*):—fellow-citizen.

4848. συμπορεύομαι **sumpŏrĕuŏmai,** *soom-por-yoo´-om-ahee;* from *4862* and *4198;* to *journey together;* by impl. to *assemble:*—go with, resort.

4849. συμπόσιον **sumpŏsiŏn,** *soom-pos´-ee-on;* neut. of a der. of the alt. of *4844;* a *drinking*-party ("*symposium*"), i.e. (by extens.) a *room* of guests:—company.

4850. συμπρεσβύτερος **sumprĕsbutĕrŏs,** *soom-pres-boo´-ter-os;* from *4862* and *4245;* a *co-presbyter:*—presbyter, also an elder.

συμφάγω **sumphagō.** See *4906.*

4851. συμφέρω **sumphĕrō,** *soom-fer´-o;* from *4862* and *5342* (includ. its alt.); to *bear together* (*contribute*), i.e. (lit.) to *collect,* or (fig.) to *conduce;* espec. (neut. part. as noun) *advantage:*—be better for, bring together, be expedient (for), be good, (be) profit (-able for).

4852. σύμφημι **sumphēmi,** *soom´-fay-mee;* from *4862* and *5346;* to *say jointly,* i.e. *assent to:*—consent unto.

4853. συμφυλέτης **sumphulĕtēs,** *soom-foo-let´-ace;* from *4862* and a der. of *5443;* a *co-tribesman,* i.e. *native of the same country:*—countryman.

4854. σύμφυτος **sumphutŏs,** *soom´-foo-tos;* from *4862* and a der. of *5453; grown* along *with* (*connate*), i.e. (fig.) closely *united* to:—planted together.

4855. συμφύω **sumphuō,** *soom-foo´-o;* from *4862* and *5453;* pass. to *grow jointly:*—spring up with.

4856. συμφωνέω **sumphōnĕō,** *soom-fo-neh´-o;* from *4859;* to be *harmonious,* i.e. (fig.) to *accord* (*be suitable, concur*) or *stipulate* (by compact):—agree (together, with).

4857. συμφώνησις **sumphōnēsis,** *soom-fo´-nay-sis;* from *4856; accordance:*—concord.

4858. συμφωνία **sumphōnia,** *soom-fo-nee´-ah;* from *4859; unison* of sound ("*symphony*"), i.e. a *concert* of instruments (harmonious *note*):—music.

4859. σύμφωνος **sumphōnŏs,** *soom´-fo-nos;* from *4862* and *5456; sounding together* (*alike*), i.e. (fig.) *accordant* (neut. as noun, *agreement*):—consent.

4860. συμψηφίζω **sumpsēphizō,** *soom-psay-fid´-zo;* from *4862* and *5585;* to *compute jointly:*—reckon.

4861. σύμψυχος **sumpsuchŏs,** *soom´-psoo-khos;* from *4862* and *5590; co-spirited,* i.e. *similar in sentiment:*—like-minded.

4862. σύν **sun,** *soon;* a prim. prep. denoting *union; with* or *together* (but much closer than *3326* or *3844*), i.e. by association, companionship, process, resemblance, possession, instrumentality, addition etc.:—beside, with. In comp, it has similar applications, includ. *completeness.*

4863. συνάγω **sunagō,** *soon-ag´-o;* from *4862* and *71;* to *lead together,* i.e. *collect* or *convene;* spec. to *entertain* (hospitably):— + accompany, assemble (selves, together), bestow, come together, gather (selves together, up, together), lead into, resort, take in.

4864. συναγωγή **sunagōgē,** *soon-ag-o-gay´;* from (the redupl. form of) *4863;* an *assemblage* of persons; spec. a Jewish "*synagogue*" (the meeting or the place); by anal. a Christian *church:*—assembly, congregation, synagogue.

4865. συναγωνίζομαι **sunagōnizŏmai,** *soon-ag-o-nid´-zom-ahee;* from *4862* and *75;* to *struggle* in company *with,* i.e. (fig.) to *be a partner* (*assistant*):—strive together with.

4866. συναθλέω **sunathlĕō,** *soon-ath-leh´-o;* from *4862* and *118;* to *wrestle* in company *with,* i.e. (fig.) to *seek jointly:*—labour with, strive together for.

4867. συναθροίζω **sunathrŏizō,** *soon-ath-royd´-zo;* from *4862* and ἀθροίζω **athrŏizō** (to *hoard*); to *convene:*—call (gather) together.

4868. συναίρω **sunairō,** *soon-ah´-ee-ro;* from *4862* and *142;* to *make up together,* i.e. (fig.) to *compute* (an account):—reckon, take.

4869. συναιχμάλωτος **sunaichmalōtŏs,** *soon-aheekh-mal´-o-tos;* from *4862* and *164;* a *co-captive:*—fellowprisoner.

4870. συνακολουθέω **sunakŏlŏuthĕō,** *soon-ak-ol-oo-theh´-o;* from *4862* and *190;* to *accompany:*—follow.

4871. συναλίζω **sunalizō,** *soon-al-id´-zo;* from *4862* and ἁλίζω **halizō** (to *throng*); to *accumulate,* i.e. *convene:*—assemble together.

4872. συναναβαίνω **sunanabainō,** *soon-an-ab-ah´-ee-no;* from *4862* and *305;* to *ascend* in company *with:*—come up with.

4873. συνανάκειμαι **sunanakĕimai,** *soon-an-ak´-i-mahee;* from *4862* and *345;* to *recline* in company *with* (at a meal):—sit (down, at the table, together) with (at meat).

4874. συναναμίγνυμι **sunanamignumi,** *soon-an-am-ig´-noo-mee;* from *4862* and a comp. of *303* and *3396;* to *mix up together,* i.e. (fig.) *associate with:*—(have, keep) company (with).

4875. συναναπαύομαι **sunanapauŏmai,** *soon-an-ap-ŏw´-om-ahee;* mid. from *4862* and *373;* to *recruit oneself* in company *with:*—refresh with.

4876. συναντάω **sunantaō,** *soon-an-tah´-o;* from *4862* and a der. of *473;* to *meet with;* fig. to *occur:*—befall, meet.

4877. συνάντησις **sunantēsis,** *soon-an´-tay-sis;* from *4876;* a *meeting with:*—meet.

4878. συναντιλαμβάνομαι **sunantilambanŏmai,** *soon-an-tee-lam-ban´-om-ahee;* from *4862* and *482;* to *take* hold of *opposite together,* i.e. *co-operate* (*assist*):—help.

4879. συναπάγω **sunapagō,** *soon-ap-ag´-o;* from *4862* and *520;* to *take off together,* i.e. *transport with* (*seduce,* pass. *yield*):—carry (lead) away with, condescend.

4880. συναποθνήσκω **sunapŏthnēskō,** *soon-ap-oth-nace´-ko;* from *4862* and *599;* to *decease* (lit.) in company *with,* or (fig.) similarly *to:*—be dead (die) with.

4881. συναπόλλυμι **sunapŏllumi,** *soon-ap-ol´-loo-mee;* from *4862* and *622;* to *destroy* (mid. or pass. *be slain*) in company *with:*—perish with.

4882. συναποστέλλω **sunapŏstĕllō,** *soon-ap-os-tel´-lo;* from *4862* and *649;* to *despatch* (on an errand) in company *with:*—send you.

4883. συναρμολογέω **sunarmŏlŏgĕō,** *soon-ar-mol-og-eh´-o;* from *4862* and a der. of a comp. of *719* and *3004* (in its orig. sense of *laying*); to *render close-jointed together,* i.e. *organize compactly:*—be fitly framed (joined) together.

4884. συναρπάζω **sunarpazō,** *soon-ar-pad´-zo;* from *4862* and *726;* to *snatch together,* i.e. *seize:*—catch.

4885. συναυξάνω **sunauxanō,** *soon-ŏwx-an´-o;* from *4862* and *837;* to *increase* (*grow up*) *together:*—grow together.

4886. σύνδεσμος **sundĕsmŏs,** *soon´-des-mos;* from *4862* and *1199;* a *joint tie,* i.e. *ligament,* (fig.) *uniting principle, control:*—band, bond.

4887. συνδέω **sundĕō,** *soon-deh´-o;* from *4862* and *1210;* to *bind with,* i.e. (pass.) *be a fellow-prisoner* (fig.):—be bound with.

4888. συνδοξάζω **sundŏxazō,** *soon-dox-ad´-zo;* from *4862* and *1392;* to *exalt* to dignity in company (i.e. *similarly*) *with:*—glorify together.

4889. σύνδουλος **sundŏulŏs,** *soon´-doo-los;* from *4862* and *1401;* a *co-slave,* i.e. *servitor* or *ministrant of the same master* (human or divine):—fellowservant.

συνδρέμω **sundrĕmō.** See *4936.*

4890. συνδρομή **sundrŏmē,** *soon-drom-ay´;* from (the alt. of) *4936;* a *running together,* i.e. (riotous) *concourse:*—run together.

4891. συνεγείρω **sunĕgĕirō,** *soon-eg-i´-ro;* from *4862* and *1453;* to *rouse* (from death) in company *with,* i.e. (fig.) to *revivify* (spiritually) in resemblance to:—raise up together, rise with.

4892. συνέδριον **sunĕdriŏn,** *soon-ed´-ree-on;* neut of a presumed der. of a comp. of *4862* and the base of *1476;* a *joint session,* i.e. (spec.) the Jewish *Sanhedrim;* by anal. a subordinate *tribunal:*—council.

4893. συνείδησις **suněidēsis,** *soon-i´-day-sis;* from a prol. form of *4894; co-perception,* i.e. moral *consciousness:*—conscience.

4894. συνείδω **suněidō,** *soon-i´-do;* from *4862* and *1492;* to *see completely;* used (like its prim.) only in two past tenses, respectively mean. to *understand* or *become aware,* and to *be conscious* or (clandestinely) *informed of:*—consider, know, be privy, be ware of.

4895. σύνειμι **suněimi,** *soon´-i-mee;* from *4862* and *1510* (includ. its various inflections); to *be* in company *with,* i.e. *present* at the time:—be with.

4896. σύνειμι **suněimi,** *soon´-i-mee;* from *4862* and εἶμι **ěimi** (to *go*); to *assemble:*—gather together.

4897. συνεισέρχομαι **suněisěrchŏmai,** *soon-ice-er´-khom-ahee;* from *4862* and *1525;* to *enter* in company *with:*—go in with, go with into.

4898. συνέκδημος **suněkdēmŏs,** *soon-ek´-day-mos;* from *4862* and the base of *1553;* a *co-absentee* from home, i.e. *fellow-traveller:*—companion in travel, travel with.

4899. συνεκλεκτός **suněklěktŏs,** *soon-ek-lek-tos´;* from a comp. of *4862* and *1586; chosen* in company *with,* i.e *co-elect* (*fellow Christian*):—elected together with.

4900. συνελαύνω **suněllaunō,** *soon-el-ow´-no;* from *4862* and *1643;* to *drive together,* i.e. (fig.) *exhort* (to reconciliation):— + set at one again.

4901. συνεπιμαρτυρέω **suněpimarturěō,** *soon-ep-ee-mar-too-reh´-o;* from *4862* and *1957;* to *testify further jointly,* i.e. *unite in adding evidence:*—also bear witness.

4902. συνέπομαι **suněpŏmai,** *soon-ep´-om-ahee;* mid. from *4862* and a prim. ἕπω **hěpō** (to *follow*); to *attend* (*travel*) in company *with:*—accompany.

4903. συνεργέω **suněrgěō,** *soon-erg-eh´-o;* from *4904;* to *be a fellow-worker,* i.e. *co-operate:*—help (work) with, work (-er) together.

4904. συνεργός **suněrgŏs,** *soon-er-gos´;* from a presumed comp. of *4862* and the base of *2041;* a *colaborer,* i.e. *coadjutor:*—companion in labour, (fellow-) helper (-labourer, -worker), labourer together with, workfellow.

4905. συνέρχομαι **suněrchŏmai,** *soon-er´-khom-ahee;* from *4862* and *2064;* to *convene, depart* in company *with, associate* with, or (spec.) *cohabit* (conjugally):—accompany, assemble (with), come (together), come (company, go) with, resort.

4906. συνεσθίω **suněsthiō,** *soon-es-thee´-o;* from *4862* and *2068* (includ. its alt.); to *take food* in company *with:*—eat with.

4907. σύνεσις **suněsis,** *soon´-es-is;* from *4920;* a mental *putting together,* i.e. *intelligence* or (concr.) the *intellect:*—knowledge, understanding.

4908. συνετός **suněttŏs,** *soon-et´-os;* from *4920;* mentally *put* (or *putting*) *together,* i.e. *sagacious:*—prudent. Comp. *5429.*

4909. συνευδοκέω **suněudŏkěō,** *soon-yoo-dok-eh´-o;* from *4862* and *2106;* to *think well of in common,* i.e. *assent* to, *feel gratified with:*—allow, assent, be pleased, have pleasure.

4910. συνευωχέω **suněuōchěō,** *soon-yoo-o-kheh´-o;* from *4862* and a der. of a presumed comp. of *2095* and a der. of *2192* (mean. to *be in good condition,* i.e. [by impl.] to *fare well,* or *feast*); to *entertain* sumptuously in company *with,* i.e. (mid. or pass.) to *revel together:*—feast with.

4911. συνεφίστημι **suněphistēmi,** *soon-ef-is´-tay-mee;* from *4862* and *2186;* to *stand up together,* i.e. to *resist* (or *assault*) *jointly:*—rise up together.

4912. συνέχω **suněchō,** *soon-ekh´-o;* from *4862* and *2192;* to *hold together,* i.e. to *compress* (the ears, with a crowd or siege) or *arrest* (a prisoner); fig. to *compel, perplex, afflict, preoccupy:*—constrain, hold, keep in, press, lie sick of, stop, be in a strait, straiten, be taken with, throng.

4913. συνήδομαι **sunēdŏmai,** *soon-ay´-dom-ahee;* mid. from *4862* and the base of *2237;* to *rejoice* in *with* oneself, i.e. *feel satisfaction* concerning:—delight.

4914. συνήθεια **sunēthěia,** *soon-ay´-thi-ah;* from a comp. of *4862* and *2239; mutual habituation,* i.e. *usage:*—custom.

4915. συνηλικιώτης **sunēlikiōtēs,** *soon-ay-lik-ee-o´-tace;* from *4862* and a der. of *2244;* a *co-aged* person, i.e. *alike* in years:—equal.

4916. συνθάπτω **sunthaptō,** *soon-thap´-to;* from *4862* and *2290;* to *inter* in company *with,* i.e. (fig.) to *assimilate* spiritually (to Christ by a sepulture as to sin):—bury with.

4917. συνθλάω **sunthlaō,** *soon-thlah´-o;* from *4862* and θλάω **thlaō** (to *crush*); to *dash together,* i.e. *shatter:*—break.

4918. συνθλίβω **sunthlibō,** *soon-thlee´-bo;* from *4862* and *2346;* to *compress,* i.e. *crowd* on all sides:—throng.

4919. συνθρύπτω **sunthruptō,** *soon-throop´-to;* from *4862* and θρύπτω **thruptō,** (to *crumble*); to *crush together,* i.e. (fig.) to *dispirit:*—break.

4920. συνίημι **suniēmi,** *soon-ee´-ay-mee;* from *4862* and ἵημι **hiēmi** (to *send*); to *put together,* i.e. (mentally) to *comprehend;* by impl. to *act piously:*—consider, understand, be wise.

4921. συνιστάω **sunistaō,** *soon-is-tah´-o;* or (strengthened)

συνιστάνω **sunistanō,** *soon-is-tan´-o;* or

συνίστημι **sunistēmi,** *soon-is´-tay-mee;* from *4862* and *2476* (includ. its collat. forms); to *set together,* i.e. (by impl.) to *introduce* (favorably), or (fig.) to *exhibit;* intrans. to *stand near,* or (fig.) to *constitute:*—approve, commend, consist, make, stand (with).

4922. συνοδεύω **sunŏdĕuō,** *soon-od-yoo´-o;* from *4862* and *3593;* to *travel* in company *with:*—journey with.

4923. συνοδία **sunŏdia,** *soon-od-ee´-ah;* from a comp. of *4862* and *3598* ("*synod*"); *companionship* on a journey, i.e. (by impl.) a *caravan:*—company.

4924. συνοικέω **sunŏikěō,** *soon-oy-keh´-o;* from *4862* and *3611;* to *reside together* (as a family):—dwell together.

4925. συνοικοδομέω **sunŏikŏdŏměō,** *soon-oy-kod-om-eh´-o;* from *4862* and *3618;* to *construct,* i.e. (pass.) to *compose* (in company with other Christians, fig.):—build together.

4926. συνομιλέω **sunŏmilěō,** *soon-om-il-eh´-o;* from *4862* and *3656;* to *converse* mutually:—talk with.

4927. συνομορέω **sunŏmŏrěō,** *soon-om-or-eh´-o;* from *4862* and a der. of a comp. of the base of *3674* and the base of *3725;* to *border together,* i.e. *adjoin:*—join hard.

4928. συνοχή **sunŏchē,** *soon-okh-ay´;* from *4912; restraint,* i.e. (fig.) *anxiety:*—anguish, distress.

4929. συντάσσω **suntassō,** *soon-tas´-so;* from *4862* and *5021;* to *arrange jointly,* i.e. (fig.) to *direct:*—appoint.

4930. συντέλεια **suntělěia,** *soon-tel´-i-ah; from 4931; entire completion,* i.e. *consummation* (of a dispensation):—end.

4931. συντελέω **suntělěō,** *soon-tel-eh´-o;* from *4862* and *5055;* to *complete entirely;* gen. to *execute* (lit. or fig.):—end, finish, fulfil, make.

4932. συντέμνω **suntěmnō,** *soon-tem´-no;* from *4862* and the base of *5114;* to *contract* by cutting, i.e. (fig.) *do concisely* (*speedily*):—(cut) short.

4933. συντηρέω **suntērěō,** *soon-tay-reh´-o;* from *4862* and *5083;* to *keep* closely *together,* i.e. (by impl.) to *conserve* (from ruin); ment. to *remember* (and *obey*):—keep, observe, preserve.

4934. συντίθεμαι **suntithěmai,** *soon-tith´-em-ahee;* mid. from *4862* and *5087;* to *place jointly,* i.e. (fig.) to *consent* (*bargain, stipulate*), *concur:*—agree assent, covenant.

4935. συντόμως **suntŏmōs,** *soon-tom´-oce;* adv. from a der. of *4932; concisely* (*briefly*):—a few words.

4936. συντρέχω **suntrěchō,** *soon-trekh´-o;* from *4862* and *5143* (includ. its alt.); to *rush together* (hastily *assemble*) or *headlong* (fig.):—run (together, with).

4937. συντρίβω **suntribō,** *soon-tree´-bo;* from *4862* and the base of *5147;* to *crush completely,* i.e. to *shatter* (lit. or fig.):—break (in pieces), broken to shivers (+ -hearted), bruise.

4938. σύντριμμα **suntrimma,** *soon-trim´-mah;* from *4937; concussion* or utter *fracture* (prop. concr.), i.e. complete *ruin:*—destruction.

4939. σύντροφος **suntrŏphŏs,** *soon´-trof-os;* from *4862* and *5162* (in a pass. sense); a *fellow-nursling,* i.e. *comrade:*—brought up with.

4940. συντυγχάνω **suntugchanō,** *soon-toong-khan´-o;* from *4862* and *5177;* to *chance together,* i.e. *meet* with (*reach*):—come at.

4941. Συντύχη **Suntuchē,** *soon-too´-khay;* from *4940;* an *accident; Syntyche,* a Chr. female:—Syntyche.

4942. συνυποκρίνομαι **sunupŏkrinŏmai,** *soon-oo-pok-rin´-om-ahee;* from *4862* and *5271;* to *act hypocritically* in concert *with:*—dissemble with.

4943. συνυπουργέω **sunupŏurgĕō,** *soon-oop-oorg-eh´-o;* from *4862* and a der. of a comp. of *5259* and the base of *2041;* to *be a co-auxiliary,* i.e. *assist:*—help together.

4944. συνωδίνω **sunōdinō,** *soon-o-dee´-no;* from *4862* and *5605;* to *have* (parturition) *pangs* in company (concert, simultaneously) *with,* i.e. (fig.) to *sympathize* (in expectation of relief from suffering):—travail in pain together.

4945. συνωμοσία **sunōmŏsia,** *soon-o-mos-ee´-ah,* from a comp. of *4862* and *3660;* a *swearing together,* i.e. (by impl.) a *plot:*—conspiracy.

4946. Συράκουσαι **Surakŏusai,** *soo-rak´-oo-sahee;* plur. of uncert. der.; *Syracusæ,* the capital of Sicily:—Syracuse.

4947. Συρία **Suria,** *soo-ree´-ah;* prob. of Heb. or. [6865]; *Syria* (i.e. *Tsyria* or *Tyre*), a region of Asia:—Syria.

4948. Σύρος **Surŏs,** *soo´-ros;* from the same as *4947;* a *Syran* (i.e. prob. *Tyrian*), a native of Syria:—Syrian.

4949. Συροφοίνισσα **Surŏphŏinissa,** *soo-rof-oy´-nis-sah;* fem. of a comp. of *4948* and the same as *5403;* a *Syro-phœnician* woman, i.e. a female native of Phœnicia in Syria:—Syrophenician.

4950. σύρτις **surtis,** *soor´-tis;* from *4951;* a *shoal* (from the sand *drawn* thither by the waves), i.e. the *Syrtis* Major or great bay on the N. coast of Africa:—quicksands.

4951. σύρω **surō,** *soo´-ro;* prob. akin to *138;* to *trail:*—drag, draw, hale.

4952. συσπαράσσω **susparassō,** *soos-par-as´-so;* from *4862* and *4682;* to *rend completely,* i.e. (by anal.) to *convulse* violently:—throw down.

4953. σύσσημον **sussēmŏn,** *soos´-say-mon;* neut. of a comp. of *4862* and the base of *4591;* a *sign in common,* i.e. preconcerted *signal:*—token.

4954. σύσσωμος **sussōmŏs,** *soos´-so-mos;* from *4862* and *4983;* *of a joint body,* i.e. (fig.) a *fellow-member* of the Christian community:—of the same body.

4955. συστασιαστής **sustasiastēs,** *soos-tas-ee-as-tace´;* from a comp. of *4862* and a der. of *4714;* a *fellow-insurgent:*—make insurrection with.

4956. συστατικός **sustatikŏs,** *soos-tat-ee-kos´;* from a der. of *4921;* *introductory,* i.e. *recommendatory:*—of commendation.

4957. συσταυρόω **sustaurŏō,** *soos-tow-rŏ´-o;* from *4862* and *4717;* to *impale* in company *with* (lit. or fig.):—crucify with.

4958. συστέλλω **sustĕllō,** *soos-tel´-lo;* from *4862* and *4724;* to *send* (*draw*) *together,* i.e. *enwrap* (*enshroud* a corpse for burial), *contract* (an interval):—short, wind up.

4959. συστενάζω **sustĕnazō,** *soos-ten-ad´-zo;* from *4862* and *4727;* to *moan jointly,* i.e. (fig.) *experience a common calamity:*—groan together.

4960. συστοιχέω **sustŏichĕō,** *soos-toy-kheh´-o;* from *4862* and *4748;* to *file together* (as soldiers in ranks), i.e. (fig.) to *correspond* to:—answer to.

4961. συστρατιώτης **sustratiōtēs,** *soos-trat-ee-o´-tace;* from *4862* and *4757;* a *co-campaigner,* i.e. (fig.) an *associate* in Christian toil:—fellow-soldier.

4962. συστρέφω **sustrĕphō,** *soos-tref´-o;* from *4862* and *4762;* to *twist together,* i.e. *collect* (a bundle, a crowd):—gather.

4963. συστροφή **sustrŏphē,** *soos-trof-ay´;* from *4962;* a *twisting together,* i.e. (fig.) a secret *coalition,* riotous *crowd:*— + band together, concourse.

4964. συσχηματίζω **suschēmatizō,** *soos-khay-mat-id´-zo;* from *4862* and a der. of *4976;* to *fashion alike,* i.e. *conform* to the same pattern (fig.):—conform to, fashion self according to.

4965. Συχάρ **Suchar,** *soo-khar´;* of Heb. or. [7941]; *Sychar* (i.e. *Shekar*), a place in Pal.:—Sychar.

4966. Συχέμ **Suchĕm,** *soo-khem´;* of Heb. or. [7927]; *Sychem* (i.e. *Shekem*), the name of a Canaanite and of a place in Pal.:—Sychem.

4967. σφαγή **sphagē,** *sfag-ay´;* from *4969;* *butchery* (of animals for food or sacrifice, or [fig.] of men [*destruction*]):—slaughter.

4968. σφάγιον **sphagiŏn,** *sfag´-ee-on;* neut. of a der. of *4967;* a *victim* (in sacrifice):—slain beast.

4969. σφάζω **sphazō,** *sfad´-zo;* a prim. verb; to *butcher* (espec. an animal for food or in sacrifice) or (gen.) to *slaughter,* or (spec.) to *maim* (violently):—kill, slay, wound.

4970. σφόδρα **sphŏdra,** *sfod´-rah;* neut. plur. of σφοδρός **sphŏdrŏs** (*violent;* of uncert. der.) as adv.; *vehemently,* i.e. in *a high degree, much:*—exceeding (-ly), greatly, sore, very.

4971. σφοδρῶς **sphŏdrōs,** *sfod-roce´;* adv. from the same as *4970;* *very much:*—exceedingly.

4972. σφραγίζω **sphragizō,** *sfrag-id´-zo;* from *4973;* to *stamp* (with a signet or private mark) for security or preservation (lit. or fig.); by impl. to *keep secret,* to *attest:*—(set a, set to) seal up.

4973. σφραγίς **sphragis,** *sfrag-ece´;* prob. strengthened from *5420;* a *signet* (as *fencing* in or protecting from misappropriation); by impl. the *stamp* impressed (as a mark of privacy, or genuineness), lit. or fig.:—seal.

4974. σφυρόν **sphurŏn,** *sfoo-ron´;* neut. of a presumed der. prob. of the same as σφαῖρα **sphaira** (a *ball, "sphere";* comp. the fem. σφῦρα **sphura,** a *hammer*); the *ankle* (as *globular*):—ancle bone.

4975. σχεδόν **schĕdŏn,** *skhed-on´;* neut. of a presumed der. of the alt. of *2192* as adv.; *nigh,* i.e. *nearly:*—almost.

σχέω **schĕō.** See *2192.*

4976. σχῆμα **schēma,** *skhay´-mah;* from the alt. of *2192;* a *figure* (as a *mode* or *circumstance*), i.e. (by impl.) external *condition:*—fashion.

4977. σχίζω **schizō,** *skhid´-zo;* appar. a prim. verb; to *split* or *sever* (lit. or fig.):—break, divide, open, rend, make a rent.

4978. σχίσμα **schisma,** *skhis´-mah;* from *4977;* a *split* or *gap* ("*schism*"), lit. or fig.:—division, rent, schism.

4979. σχοινίν **schŏiniŏn,** *skhoy-nee´-on;* dimin. of σχοῖνος **schŏinŏs** (a *rush* or *flag*-plant; of uncert. der.); a *rushlet,* i.e. *grass-withe* or *tie* (gen.):—small cord, rope.

4980. σχολάζω **schŏlazō,** *skhol-ad´-zo;* from *4981;* to *take a holiday,* i.e. *be at leisure* for (by impl. *devote oneself* wholly to); fig. to *be vacant* (of a house):—empty, give self.

4981. σχολή **schŏlē,** *skhol-ay´;* prob. fem. of a presumed der. of the alt. of *2192;* prop. *loitering* (as a *withholding* of oneself from work) or *leisure,* i.e. (by impl.) a "*school*" (as *vacation* from phys. employment):—school.

4982. σώζω **sōzō,** *sode´-zo;* from a prim. σῶς **sōs** (contr. for obsol. σάος **saŏs,** "*safe*"); to *save,* i.e. *deliver* or *protect* (lit. or fig.):—heal, preserve, save (self), do well, be (make) whole.

4983. σῶμα **sōma,** *so´-mah;* from *4982;* the *body* (as a *sound* whole), used in a very wide application, lit. or fig.:—bodily, body, slave.

4984. σωματικός **sōmatikŏs,** *so-mat-ee-kos´;* from *4983;* *corporeal* or *physical:*—bodily.

4985. σωματικῶς **sōmatikōs,** *so-mat-ee-koce´;* adv. from *4984;* *corporeally* or *physically:*—bodily.

4986. Σώπατρος **Sōpatrŏs,** *so´-pat-ros;* from the base of *4982* and *3962;* *of a safe father; Sopatrus,* a Chr.:—Sopater. Comp. *4989.*

4987. σωρεύω **sōrĕuō,** *sore-yoo´-o;* from another form of *4673;* to *pile* up (lit. or fig.):—heap, load.

4988. Σωσθένης **Sōsthĕnēs,** *soce-then´-ace;* from the base of *4982* and that of *4599;* *of safe strength; Sosthenes,* a Chr.:—Sosthenes.

4989. Σωσίπατρος **Sōsipatrŏs,** *so-sip´-at-ros;* prol. for *4986;* *Sosipatrus,* a Chr.:—Sosipater.

4990. σωτήρ **sōtēr,** *so-tare´;* from *4982;* a *deliverer,* i.e. God or Christ:—saviour.

4991. σωτηρία **sōtēria,** *so-tay-ree´-ah;* fem. of a der. of *4990* as (prop. abstr.) noun; *rescue* or *safety* (phys. or mor.):—deliver, health, salvation, save, saving.

4992. σωτήριον **sōtēriŏn,** *so-tay´-ree-on;* neut. of the same as *4991* as (prop. concr.) noun; *defender* or (by impl.) *defence:*—salvation.

4993. σωφρονέω **sōphrŏnĕō,** *so-fron-eh´-o;* from *4998;* to *be of sound mind,* i.e. *sane,* (fig.) *moderate:*—be in right mind, be sober (minded), soberly.

4994. σωφρονίζω **sōphrŏnizō,** *so-fron-id´-zo;* from *4998;* to *make of sound mind,* i.e. (fig.) to *discipline* or *correct:*—teach to be sober.

4995. σωφρονισμός **sōphrŏnismŏs,** *so-fron-is-mos´;* from *4994; discipline,* i.e. *self-control:*—sound mind.

4996. σωφρόνως **sōphrŏnōs,** *so-fron´-oce;* adv. from *4998; with sound mind,* i.e. *moderately:*—soberly.

4997. σωφροσύνη **sōphrŏsunē,** *so-fros-oo´-nay;* from *4998; soundness of mind,* i.e. (lit.) *sanity* or (fig.) *self-control:*—soberness, sobriety.

4998. σώφρων **sōphrōn,** *so´-frone;* from the base of *4982* and that of *5424; safe* (*sound*) in *mind,* i.e. *self-controlled* (*moderate* as to opinion or passion):—discreet, sober, temperate.

T

τά **ta.** See *3588.*

4999. Ταβέρναι **Tabĕrnai,** *tab-er´-nahee;* plur. of Lat. or.; *huts* or *wooden-walled* buildings; *Tabernæ:*—taverns.

5000. Ταβιθά **Tabitha,** *tab-ee-thah´;* of Chald. or. [comp. 6646]; *the gazelle; Tabitha* (i.e. *Tabjetha*), a Chr. female:—Tabitha.

5001. τάγμα **tagma,** *tag´-mah;* from *5021;* something orderly in *arrangement* (a *troop*), i.e. (fig.) a *series* or *succession:*—order.

5002. τακτός **taktŏs,** *tak-tos´;* from *5021; arranged,* i.e. *appointed* or *stated:*—set.

5003. ταλαιπωρέω **talaipōrĕō,** *tal-ahee-po-reh´-o,* from *5005;* to *be wretched,* i.e. *realize* one's own *misery:*—be afflicted.

5004. ταλαιπωρία **talaipōria,** *tal-ahee-po-ree´-ah;* from *5005; wretchedness,* i.e. *calamity:*—misery.

5005. ταλαίπωρος **talaipōrŏs,** *tal-ah´ee-po-ros;* from the base of *5007* and a der. of the base of *3984; enduring trial,* i.e. *miserable:*—wretched.

5006. ταλαντιαῖος **talantiaiŏs,** *tal-an-tee-ah´-yos;* from *5007; talent-like* in weight:—weight of a talent.

5007. τάλαντον **talantŏn,** *tal´-an-ton;* neut. of a presumed der. of the orig. form of τλάω **tlaō** (to *bear;* equiv. to *5342*); a *balance* (as *supporting* weights), i.e. (by impl.) a certain *weight* (and thence a *coin* or rather *sum* of money) or *"talent":*—talent.

5008. ταλιθά **talitha,** *tal-ee-thah´;* of Chald. or. [comp. 2924]; *the fresh,* i.e. young *girl; talitha* (*O maiden*):—talitha.

5009. ταμεῖον **taměiŏn,** *tam-i´-on;* neut. contr. of presumed der. of ταμίας **tamias** (a *dispenser* or *distributor;* akin to τέμνω **tĕmnō,** to *cut*); a *dispensary* or *magazine,* i.e. a chamber on the ground-floor or interior of an Oriental house (gen. used for *storage* or *privacy,* a spot for retirement):—secret chamber, closet, storehouse.

ταννῦν **tanun.** See *3568.*

5010. τάξις **taxis,** *tax´-is;* from *5021;* regular *arrangement,* i.e. (in time) fixed *succession* (of rank or character), official *dignity:*—order.

5011. ταπεινός **tapĕinŏs,** *tap-i-nos´;* of uncert. der.; *depressed,* i.e. (fig.) *humiliated* (in circumstances or disposition):—base, cast down, humble, of low degree (estate), lowly.

5012. ταπεινοφροσύνη **tapĕinŏphrŏsunē,** *tap-i-nof-ros-oo´-nay;* from a comp. of *5011* and the base of *5424; humiliation of mind,* i.e. *modesty:*—humbleness of mind, humility (of mind), lowliness (of mind).

5013. ταπεινόω **tapĕinŏō,** *tap-i-nŏ´-o;* from *5011;* to *depress;* fig. to *humiliate* (in condition or heart):—abase, bring low, humble (self).

5014. ταπείνωσις **tapĕinōsis,** *tap-i´-no-sis;* from *5013; depression* (in rank or feeling):—humiliation, be made low, low estate, vile.

5015. ταράσσω **tarassō,** *tar-as´-so;* of uncert. affin.; to *stir* or *agitate* (*roil* water):—trouble.

5016. ταραχή **tarachē,** *tar-akh-ay´;* fem. from *5015; disturbance,* i.e. (of water) *roiling,* or (of a mob) *sedition:*—trouble (-ing).

5017. τάραχος **tarachŏs,** *tar´-akh-os;* masc. from *5015;* a *disturbance,* i.e. (popular) *tumult:*—stir.

5018. Ταρσεύς **Tarsĕus,** *tar-syoos´;* from *5019;* a *Tarsean,* i.e. native of Tarsus:—of Tarsus.

5019. Ταρσός **Tarsŏs,** *tar-sos´;* perh. the same as ταρσός **tarsŏs** (a *flat* basket); *Tarsus,* a place in Asia Minor:—Tarsus.

5020. ταρταρόω **tartarŏō,** *tar-tar-ŏ´-o;* from Τάρταρος **Tartarŏs** (the deepest *abyss* of Hades); to *incarcerate* in eternal torment:—cast down to hell.

5021. τάσσω **tassō,** *tas´-so;* a prol. form of a prim. verb (which latter appears only in certain tenses); to *arrange* in an orderly manner, i.e. *assign* or *dispose* (to a certain position or lot):—addict, appoint, determine, ordain, set.

5022. ταῦρος **taurŏs,** *tŏw´-ros;* appar. a prim. word [comp. 8450, *"steer"*]; a *bullock:*—bull, ox.

5023. ταῦτα **tauta,** *tŏw´-tah;* nom. or acc. neut. plur. of *3778; these* things:— + afterward, follow, + hereafter, × him, the same, so, such, that, then, these, they, this, those, thus.

5024. ταὐτά **tauta,** *tow-tah´;* neut. plur. of *3588* and *846* as adv.; in *the same* way:—even thus, (manner) like, so.

5025. ταύταις **tautais,** *tŏw´-toheece;* and
ταύτας **tautas,** *tŏw´-tas;* dat. and acc. fem. plur. respectively of *3778;* (*to* or *with* or *by,* etc.) *these:*—hence, that, then, these, those.

5026. ταύτῃ **tautēi,** *tŏw´-tay;* and
ταύτην **tautēn,** *tŏw´-tane;* and
ταύτης **tautēs,** *tŏw´-tace;* dat., acc. and gen. respectively of the fem. sing. of *3778;* (*towards* or *of*) *this:*—her, + hereof, it, that, + thereby, the (same), this (same).

5027. ταφή **taphē,** *taf-ay´;* fem. from *2290; burial* (the act):— × bury.

5028. τάφος **taphŏs,** *taf´-os;* masc. from *2290;* a *grave* (the place of interment):—sepulchre, tomb.

5029. τάχα **tacha,** *takh´-ah;* as if neut. plur. of *5036* (adv.); *shortly,* i.e. (fig.) *possibly:*—peradventure (-haps).

5030. ταχέως **tachĕōs,** *takh-eh´-oce;* adv. from *5036; briefly,* i.e. (in time) *speedily,* or (in manner) *rapidly:*—hastily, quickly, shortly, soon, suddenly.

5031. ταχινός **tachinŏs,** *takh-ee-nos´;* from *5034; curt,* i.e. *impending:*—shortly, swift.

5032. τάχιον **tachiŏn,** *takh´-ee-on;* neut. sing. of the compar. of *5036* (as adv.); *more swiftly,* i.e. (in manner) *more rapidly,* or (in time) *more speedily:*—out [run], quickly, shortly, sooner.

5033. τάχιστα **tachista,** *takh´-is-tah;* neut. plur. of the superl. of *5036* (as adv.); *most quickly,* i.e. (with *5613* pref.) *as soon* as possible:— + with all speed.

5034. τάχος **tachŏs,** *takh´-os;* from the same as *5036;* a *brief* space (of time), i.e. (with *1722* pref.) in *haste:*— + quickly, + shortly, + speedily.

5035. ταχύ **tachu,** *takh-oo´;* neut. sing. of *5036* (as adv.); *shortly,* i.e. *without delay, soon,* or (by surprise) *suddenly,* or (by impl. of ease) *readily:*—lightly, quickly.

5036. ταχύς **tachus,** *takh-oos´;* of uncert. affin.; *fleet,* i.e. (fig.) *prompt* or *ready:*—swift.

5037. τε **tĕ,** *teh;* a prim. particle (enclitic) of connection or addition; *both* or *also* (prop. as correl. of *2532*):—also, and, both, even, then whether. Often used in comp., usually as the latter part.

5038. τεῖχος **tĕichŏs,** *ti´-khos;* akin to the base of *5088;* a *wall* (as *formative* of a house):—wall.

5039. τεκμήριον **tĕkmēriŏn,** *tek-may´-ree-on;* neut. of a presumed der. of τεκμάρ **tĕkmar** (a *goal* or fixed *limit*); a *token* (as *defining* a fact), i.e. *criterion* of certainty:—infallible proof.

5040. τεκνίον **tĕkniŏn,** *tek-nee´-on;* dimin. of *5043;* an *infant,* i.e. (plur. fig.) *darlings* (Christian *converts*):—little children.

5041. τεκνογονέω **tĕknŏgŏnĕō,** *tek-nog-on-eh´-o;* from a comp. of *5043* and the base of *1096;* to *be a child-bearer,* i.e. *parent* (*mother*):—bear children.

5042. τεκνογονία **tĕknŏgŏnia,** *tek-nog-on-ee´-ah;* from the same as *5041; childbirth* (*parentage*), i.e. (by impl.) *maternity* (the performance of *maternal duties*):—childbearing.

5043. τέκνον **tĕknŏn,** *tek´-non;* from the base of *5088;* a *child* (as *produced*):—child, daughter, son.

5044. τεκνοτροφέω **tĕknŏtrŏphĕō,** *tek-not-rof-eh´-o;* from a comp. of *5043* and *5142;* to *be a childrearer,* i.e. *fulfil* the duties of *a female parent:*—bring up children.

5045. τέκτων **tĕktōn,** *tek´-tone;* from the base of *5088;* an *artificer* (as *producer* of fabrics), i.e. (spec.) a *craftsman* in wood:—carpenter.

5046. τέλειος **tĕlĕiŏs,** *tel´-i-os;* from *5056; complete* (in various applications of labor, growth, mental and moral character, etc.); neut. (as noun, with *3588*) *completeness:*—of full age, man, perfect.

5047. τελειότης **tĕlĕiŏtēs,** *tel-i-ot´-ace;* from *5046;* (the state) *completeness* (ment. or mor.):—perfection (-ness).

5048. τελειόω **tĕlĕiŏō,** *tel-i-ŏ´-o;* from *5046;* to *complete,* i.e. (lit.) *accomplish,* or (fig.) *consummate* (in character):—consecrate, finish, fulfil, (make) perfect.

5049. τελείως **tĕlĕiōs,** *tel-i´-oce;* adv. from *5046; completely,* i.e. (of hope) *without wavering:*—to the end.

5050. τελείωσις **tĕlĕiōsis,** *tel-i´-o-sis;* from *5448;* (the act) *completion,* i.e. (of prophecy) *verification,* or (of expiation) *absolution:*—perfection, performance.

5051. τελειωτής **tĕlĕiōtēs,** *tel-i-o-tace´;* from *5048;* a *completer,* i.e. *consummater:*—finisher.

5052. τελεσφορέω **tĕlĕsphŏrĕō,** *tel-es-for-eh´-o;* from a comp. of *5056* and *5342;* to *be a bearer to completion* (maturity), i.e. to *ripen* fruit (fig.):—bring fruit to perfection.

5053. τελευτάω **tĕlĕutaō,** *tel-yoo-tah´-o;* from a presumed der. of *5055;* to *finish* life (by impl. of *979*), i.e. *expire* (*demise*):—be dead, decease, die.

5054. τελευτή **tĕlĕutē,** *tel-yoo-tay´;* from *5053; decease:*—death.

5055. τελέω **tĕlĕō,** *tel-eh´-o;* from *5056;* to *end,* i.e. *complete, execute, conclude, discharge* (a debt):—accomplish, make an end, expire, fill up, finish, go over, pay, perform.

5056. τέλος **tĕlŏs,** *tel´-os;* from a prim. τέλλω **tĕllō** (to *set out* for a definite point or *goal*); prop. the point aimed at as a *limit,* i.e. (by impl.) the *conclusion* of an act or state (*termination* [lit., fig. or indef.], *result* [immed., ultimate or prophetic], *purpose*); spec. an *impost* or *levy* (as *paid*):—+ continual, custom, end (-ing), finally, uttermost. Comp. *5411.*

5057. τελώνης **tĕlōnēs,** *tel-o´-nace;* from *5056* and *5608;* a *tax-farmer,* i.e. *collector of* public *revenue:*—publican.

5058. τελώνιον **tĕlōniŏn,** *tel-o´-nee-on;* neut. of a presumed der. of *5057;* a *tax-gatherer's* place of business:—receipt of custom.

5059. τέρας **tĕras,** *ter´-as;* of uncert. affin.; a *prodigy* or *omen:*—wonder.

5060. Τέρτιος **Tĕrtiŏs,** *ter´-tee-os;* of Lat. or.; *third; Tertius,* a Chr.:—Tertius.

5061. Τέρτυλλος **Tĕrtullŏs,** *ter´-tool-los;* of uncert. der.; *Tertullus,* a Rom.:—Tertullus.

τέσσαρα **tĕssara.** See *5064.*

5062. τεσσαράκοντα **tĕssarakŏnta,** *tes-sar-ak´-on-tah;* the decade of *5064; forty:*—forty.

5063. τεσσαρακονταετής **tĕssarakŏntaĕtēs,** *tes-sar-ak-on-tah-et-ace´;* from *5062* and *2094; of forty years* of age:—(+ full, of) forty years (old).

5064. τέσσαρες **tĕssarĕs,** *tes´-sar-es;* neut. τέσσαρα **tĕssara,** *tes´-sar-ah;* a plur. number; *four:*—four.

5065. τεσσαρεσκαιδέκατος **tĕssarĕskaidĕkatŏs,** *tes-sar-es-kahee-dek´-at-os;* from *5064* and *2532* and *1182; fourteenth:*—fourteenth.

5066. τεταρταῖος **tĕtartaiŏs,** *tet-ar-tah´-yos;* from *5064;* pertaining to the *fourth* day:—four days.

5067. τέταρτος **tĕtartŏs,** *tet´-ar-tos;* ord. from *5064; fourth:*—four (-th).

5068. τετράγωνος **tĕtragōnŏs,** *tet-rag´-o-nos;* from *5064* and *1137; four-cornered,* i.e. *square:*—foursquare.

5069. τετράδιον **tĕtradiŏn,** *tet-rad´-ee-on;* neut. of a presumed der. of τέτρας **tĕtras** (a *tetrad;* from *5064*); a *quaternion* or squad (picket) of four Rom. soldiers:—quaternion.

5070. τετρακισχίλιοι **tĕtrakischiliŏi,** *tet-rak-is-khil´-ee-oy;* from the mult. adv. of *5064* and *5507; four times a thousand:*—four thousand.

5071. τετρακόσιοι **tĕtrakŏsiŏi,** *tet-rak-os´-ee-oy;* neut. τετρακόσια **tĕtrakŏsia,** *tet-rak-os´-ee-ah;* plur. from *5064* and *1540; four hundred:*—four hundred.

5072. τετράμηνον **tĕtramēnŏn,** *tet-ram´-ay-non;* neut. of a comp. of *5064* and *3376;* a *four months'* space:—four months.

5073. τετραπλόος **tĕtraplŏŏs,** *tet-rap-lŏ´-os;* from *5064* and a der. of the base of *4118; quadruple:*—fourfold.

5074. τετράπους **tĕtrapŏus,** *tet-rap´-ooce;* from *5064* and *4228;* a *quadruped:*—fourfooted beast.

5075. τετραρχέω **tĕtrarchĕō,** *tet-rar-kheh´-o;* from *5076;* to *be a tetrarch:*—(be) tetrarch.

5076. τετράρχης **tĕtrarchēs,** *tet-rar´-khace;* from *5064* and *757;* the *ruler of a fourth* part of a country ("*tetrarch*"):—tetrarch.

τεύχω **tĕuchō.** See *5177.*

5077. τεφρόω **tĕphrŏō,** *tef-rŏ´-o;* from τέφρα **tephra** (*ashes*); to *incinerate,* i.e. *consume:*—turn to ashes.

5078. τέχνη **tĕchnē,** *tekh´-nay;* from the base of *5088; art* (as *productive*), i.e. (spec.) a *trade,* or (gen.) *skill:*—art, craft, occupation.

5079. τεχνίτης **tĕchnitēs,** *tekh-nee´-tace;* from *5078;* an *artisan;* fig. a *founder* (*Creator*):—builder, craftsman.

5080. τήκω **tēkō,** *tay´-ko;* appar. a prim. verb; to *liquefy:*—melt.

5081. τηλαυγῶς **tēlaugōs,** *tay-lŏw-goce´;* adv. from a comp. of a der. of *5056* and *827;* in a *far-shining* manner, i.e. *plainly:*—clearly.

5082. τηλικοῦτος **tēlikŏutŏs,** *tay-lik-oo´-tos;* fem. τηλικαύτη **tēlikautē,** *tay-lik-ŏw´-tay;* from a comp. of *3588* with *2245* and *3778; such as this,* i.e. (in [fig.] magnitude) *so vast:*—so great, so mighty.

5083. τηρέω **tērĕō,** *tay-reh´-o;* from τηρός **tērŏs** (a *watch;* perh. akin to *2334*); to *guard* (from *loss* or *injury,* prop. by keeping *the eye* upon; and thus differing from *5442,* which is prop. to *prevent* escaping; and from *2892,* which implies a *fortress* or full military lines of apparatus), i.e. to *note* (a prophecy; fig. to *fulfil* a command); by impl. to *detain* (in custody; fig. to *maintain*); by extens. to *withhold* (for personal ends; fig. to *keep unmarried*):—hold fast, keep (-er), (ob-, pre-, re) serve, watch.

5084. τήρησις **tērēsis,** *tay´-ray-sis;* from *5083;* a *watching,* i.e. (fig.) *observance,* or (concr.) a *prison:*—hold.

τῇ **tēi,** τήν **tēn,** τῆς **tēs.** See *3588.*

5085. Τιβεριάς **Tibĕrias,** *tib-er-ee-as´;* from *5086; Tiberias,* the name of a town and a lake in Pal.:—Tiberias.

5086. Τιβέριος **Tibĕriŏs,** *tib-er´-ee-os;* of Lat. or.; prob. *pertaining to the* river *Tiberis* or *Tiber; Tiberius,* a Rom. emperor:—Tiberius.

5087. τίθημι **tithēmi,** *tith´-ay-mee;* a prol. form of a prim.

θέω **thĕō,** *theh´-o* (which is used only as alt. in cert. tenses); to *place* (in the widest application, lit. and fig.; prop. in a passive or horizontal posture, and thus different from *2476,* which prop. denotes as upright and active position, while *2749* is prop. reflexive and utterly prostrate):—+ advise, appoint, bow, commit, conceive, give, × kneel down, lay (aside, down, up), make, ordain, purpose, put, set (forth), settle, sink down.

5088. τίκτω **tiktō,** *tik´-to;* a strengthened form of a prim. τέκω **tĕkō,** *tek´-o* (which is used only as alt. in certain tenses); to *produce* (from seed, as a mother, a plant, the earth, etc.), lit. or fig.:—bear, be born, bring forth, be delivered, be in travail.

5089. τίλλω **tillō,** *til´-lo;* perh. akin to the alt. of *138,* and thus to *4951;* to *pull* off:—pluck.

5090. Τίμαιος **Timaiŏs,** *tim´-ah-yos;* prob. of Chald. or. [comp. 2931]; *Timæus* (i.e. *Timay*), an Isr.:—Timæus.

5091. τιμάω **timaō,** *tim-ah´-o;* from *5093;* to *prize,* i.e. *fix* a *valuation* upon; by impl. to *revere:*—honour, value.

5092. τιμή **timē,** *tee-may´;* from *5099;* a *value,* i.e. *money* paid, or (concr. and collect.) *valuables;* by anal. *esteem* (espec. of the highest degree), or the *dignity* itself:—honour, precious, price, some.

5093. τίμιος **timiŏs,** *tim´-ee-os;* includ. the comp.

τιμιώτερος **timiōtĕrŏs,** *tim-ee-o´-ter-os;* and the superl.

τιμιώτατος **timiōtatŏs,** *tim-ee-o´-tat-os;* from *5092; valuable,* i.e. (obj.) *costly,* or (subj.) *honored, esteemed,* or (fig.) *beloved:*—dear, honourable, (more, most) precious, had in reputation.

5094. τιμιότης **timiŏtēs,** *tim-ee-ot´-ace;* from *5093; expensiveness,* i.e. (by impl.) *magnificence:*—costliness.

5095. Τιμόθεος **Timŏthĕŏs,** *tee-moth´-eh-os;* from *5092* and *2316; dear to God; Timotheus,* a Chr.:—Timotheus, Timothy.

5096. Τίμων **Timōn,** *tee´-mone;* from *5092; valuable; Timon,* a Chr.:—Timon.

5097. τιμωρέω **timōrĕō,** *tim-o-reh´-o;* from a comp. of *5092* and οὖρος **ŏurŏs** (a *guard*); prop. to *protect* one's *honor,* i.e. to *avenge* (*inflict a penalty*):—punish.

5098. τιμωρία **timōria,** *tee-mo-ree´-ah;* from *5097; vindication,* i.e. (by impl.) a *penalty:*—punishment.

5099. τίνω **tinō,** *tee´-no;* strengthened for a prim.

τίω **tiō,** *tee´-o* (which is only used as an alt. in certain tenses); to *pay* a price, i.e. as a *penalty:*—be punished with.

5100. τὶς **tis,** *tis;* an enclit. indef. pron.; *some* or *any* person or object:—a (kind of), any (man, thing, thing at all), certain (thing), divers, he (every) man, one (× thing), ought, + partly, some (man, -body, -thing, -what), (+ that no-) thing, what (-soever), × wherewith, whom [-soever], whose ([-soever]).

5101. τίς **tis,** *tis;* prob. emphat. of *5100;* an interrog. pron., *who, which,* or *what* (in direct or indirect questions):—every man, how (much), + no (-ne, thing), what (manner, thing), where ([-by, -fore, -of, -unto, -with, -withal]), whether, which, who (-m, -se), why.

5102. τίτλος **titlŏs,** *tit´-los;* of Lat. or.; a *titulus* or *"title"* (*placard*):—title.

5103. Τίτος **Titŏs,** *tee´-tos,* of Lat. or. but uncert. signif.; *Titus,* a Chr.:—Titus.

τίω **tiō.** See *5099.*

τό **tŏ.** See *3588.*

5104. τοί **tŏi,** *toy;* prob. for the dat. of *3588;* an enclit. particle of *asseveration* by way of contrast; *in sooth:*—[*used only with other particles in comp., as 2544, 3305, 5105, 5106,* etc.]

5105. τοιγαροῦν **tŏigarŏun,** *toy-gar-oon´;* from *5104* and *1063* and *3767; truly for then,* i.e. *consequently:*—there- (where-) fore.

τοίγε **tŏigĕ.** See *2544.*

5106. τοίνυν **tŏinun,** *toy´-noon;* from *5104* and *3568; truly now,* i.e. *accordingly:*—then, therefore.

5107. τοιόσδε **tŏiŏsdĕ,** *toy-os´-deh* (includ. the other inflections); from a der. of *5104* and *1161; such-like then,* i.e. *so great:*—such.

5108. τοιοῦτος **tŏiŏutŏs,** *toy-oo´-tos* (includ. the other inflections); from *5104* and *3778; truly this,* i.e. *of this sort* (to denote character or individuality):—like, such (an one).

5109. τοῖχος **tŏichŏs,** *toy´-khos;* another form of *5038;* a *wall:*—wall.

5110. τόκος **tŏkŏs,** *tok´-os;* from the base of *5088; interest* on money loaned (as a *produce*):—usury.

5111. τολμάω **tŏlmaō,** *tol-mah´-o;* from τόλμα **tŏlma** (*boldness;* prob. itself from the base of *5056* through the idea of *extreme* conduct); to *venture* (obj. or in *act;* while *2292* is rather subj. or in *feeling*); by impl. to be *courageous:*—be bold, boldly, dare, durst.

5112. τολμηρότερον **tŏlmērŏtĕrŏn,** *tol-may-rot´-er-on;* neut. of the comp. of a der. of the base of *5111* (as adv.); *more daringly,* i.e. *with greater confidence* than otherwise:—the more boldly.

5113. τολμητής **tŏlmētēs,** *tol-may-tace´;* from *5111;* a *daring* (*audacious*) man:—presumptuous.

5114. τομώτερος **tŏmōtĕrŏs,** *tom-o´-ter-os;* comp. of a der. of the prim. τέμνω **tĕmnō** (to *cut;* more comprehensive or decisive than *2875,* as if by a *single* stroke; whereas that implies repeated blows, like *hacking*); *more keen:*—sharper.

5115. τόξον **tŏxŏn,** *tox´-on;* from the base of *5088;* a *bow* (appar. as the simplest fabric):—bow.

5116. τοπάζιον **tŏpaziŏn,** *top-ad´-zee-on;* neut. of a presumed der. (alt.) of τόπαζος **tŏpazŏs** (a *"topaz"*; of uncert. or.); a gem, prob. the *chrysolite:*—topaz.

5117. τόπος **tŏpŏs,** *top´-os;* appar. a prim. word; a *spot* (gen. in *space,* but limited by occupancy; whereas *5561* is a larger but partic. *locality*), i.e. *location* (as a position, home, tract, etc.); fig. *condition, opportunity;* spec. a *scabbard:*—coast, licence, place, × plain, quarter, + rock, room, where.

5118. τοσοῦτος **tŏsŏutŏs,** *tos-oo´-tos;* from τόσος **tŏsŏs** (*so much;* appar. from *3588* and *3739*) and *3778* (includ. its variations); so *vast as this,* i.e. *such* (in quantity, amount, number or space):—as large, so great (long, many, much), these many.

5119. τότε **tŏtĕ,** *tot´-eh;* from (the neut. of) *3588* and *3753; the when,* i.e. *at the time* that (of the past or future, also in consecution):—that time, then.

5120. τοῦ **tŏu,** *too;* prop. the gen. of *3588;* sometimes used for *5127; of this person:*—his.

5121. τοὐναντίον **tŏunantiŏn,** *too-nan-tee´-on;* contr. for the neut. of *3588* and *1726; on the contrary:*—contrariwise.

5122. τοὔνομα **tŏunŏma,** *too´-no-mah;* contr. for the neut. of *3588* and *3686; the name* (is):—named.

5123. τουτέστι **tŏutĕsti,** *toot-es´-tee;* contr. for *5124* and *2076; that is:*—that is (to say).

5124. τοῦτο **tŏutŏ,** *too´-tŏ;* neut. sing. nom. or acc. of *3778; that* thing:—here [-unto], it, partly, self [-same], so, that (intent), the same, there [-fore, -unto], this, thus, where [-fore].

5125. τούτοις **tŏutŏis,** *too´-toice;* dat. plur. masc. or neut. of *3778; to* (*for, in, with* or *by*) *these* (persons or things):—such, them, there [-in, -with], these, this, those.

5126. τοῦτον **tŏutŏn,** *too´-ton;* acc. sing. masc. of *3778; this* (person, as obj. of verb or prep.):—him, the same, that, this.

5127. τούτου **tŏutŏu,** *too´-too;* gen. sing. masc. or neut. of *3778; of* (*from* or *concerning*) *this* (person or thing):—here [-by], him, it, + such manner of, that, thence [-forth], thereabout, this, thus.

5128. τούτους **tŏutŏus,** *too´-tooce;* acc. plur. masc. of *3788; these* (persons, as obj. of verb or prep.):—such, them, these, this.

5129. τούτῳ **tŏutō₁,** *too´-to;* dat. sing. masc. or neut. of *3778; to* (*in, with* or *by*) *this* (person or thing):—here [-by, -in], him, one, the same, there [-in], this.

5130. τούτων **tŏutōn,** *too´-tone;* gen. plur. masc. or neut. of *3778; of* (*from* or *concerning*) *these* (persons or things):—such, their, these (things), they, this sort, those.

5131. τράγος **tragŏs,** *trag´-os;* from the base of *5176;* a *he-goat* (as a *gnawer*):—goat.

5132. τράπεζα **trapĕza,** *trap´-ed-zah;* prob. contr. from *5064* and *3979;* a *table* or *stool* (as being *four-legged*), usually for food (fig. a *meal*); also a *counter* for money (fig. a broker's *office* for loans at interest):—bank, meat, table.

5133. τραπεζίτης **trapĕzitēs,** *trap-ed-zee´-tace;* from *5132;* a money-*broker* or *banker:*—exchanger.

5134. τραῦμα **trauma,** *trŏw´-mah;* from the base of τιτρώσκω **titrōskō** (to *wound;* akin to the base of *2352, 5147, 5149,* etc.); a *wound:*—wound.

5135. τραυματίζω **traumatizō,** *trŏw-mat-id´-zo;* from *5134;* to *inflict a wound:*—wound.

5136. τραχηλίζω **trachēlizō,** *trakh-ay-lid´-zo;* from *5137;* to *seize* by *the throat* or *neck,* i.e. to *expose* the *gullet* of a victim for killing (gen. to *lay bare*):—opened.

5137. τράχηλος **trachēlŏs,** *trakh´-ay-los;* prob. from *5143* (through the idea of *mobility*); the *throat* (*neck*), i.e. (fig.) *life:*—neck.

5138. τραχύς **trachus,** *trakh-oos´;* perh. strengthened from the base of *4486* (as if *jagged* by rents); *uneven, rocky* (*reefy*):—rock, rough.

5139. Τραχωνῖτις **Trachōnitis,** *trakh-o-nee´-tis;* from a der. of *5138; rough* district; *Trachonitis,* a region of Syria:—Trachonitis.

5140. τρεῖς **trĕis,** *trice;* neut.

τρία **tria,** *tree´-ah;* a prim. (plur.) number; *"three"*:—three.

5141. τρέμω **trĕmō,** *trem´-o;* strengthened from a prim. τρέω **trĕō** (to *"dread", "terrify"*); to *"tremble"* or *fear:*—be afraid, trembling.

5142. τρέφω **trĕphō,** *tref´-o;* a prim. verb (prop. θρέφω **thrĕphō;** but perh. strength. from the base of *5157* through the idea of *convolution*); prop. to *stiffen*, i.e. *fatten* (by impl. to *cherish* [with food, etc.], *pamper, rear*):—bring up, feed, nourish.

5143. τρέχω **trĕchō,** *trekh´-o;* appar. a prim. verb (prop. θρέχω **thrĕchō;** comp. *2359*); which uses δρέμω **drĕmō,** *drem´-o* (the base of *1408*) as alt. in certain tenses; to *run* or *walk hastily* (lit. or fig.):—have course, run.

5144. τριάκοντα **triakŏnta,** *tree-ak´-on-tah;* the decade of *5140; thirty:*—thirty.

5145. τριακόσιοι **triakŏsiŏi,** *tree-ak-os´-ee-oy;* plur. from *5140* and *1540; three hundred:*—three hundred.

5146. τρίβολος **tribŏlŏs,** *trib´-ol-os;* from *5140* and *956;* prop. a *crow-foot* (*three-pronged* obstruction in war), i.e. (by anal.) a *thorny* plant (*caltrop*):—brier, thistle.

5147. τρίβος **tribŏs,** *tree´-bos;* from τρίβω **tribō** (to *"rub"*; akin to τείρω **tĕirō,** τρύω **truō,** and the base of *5131, 5134*); a *rut* or worn *track:*—path.

5148. τριετία **triĕtia,** *tree-et-ee´-ah;* from a comp. of *5140* and *2094;* a *three years' period* (*triennium*):—space of three years.

5149. τρίζω **trizō,** *trid´-zo;* appar. a prim. verb; to *creak* (*squeak*), i.e. (by anal.) to *grate* the teeth (in frenzy):—gnash.

5150. τρίμηνον **trimēnŏn,** *trim´-ay-non;* neut. of a comp. of *5140* and *3376* as noun; a *three months'* space:—three months.

5151. τρίς **tris,** *trece;* adv. from *5140; three times:*—three times, thrice.

5152. τρίστεγον **tristĕgŏn,** *tris´-teg-on;* neut. of a comp. of *5140* and *4721* as noun; a *third roof* (*story*):—third loft.

5153. τρισχίλιοι **trischiliŏi,** *tris-khil´-ee-oy;* from *5151* and *5507; three times a thousand:*—three thousand.

5154. τρίτος **tritŏs,** *tree´-tos;* ord. from *5140; third;* neut. (as noun) a *third part*, or (as adv.) a (or the) *third* time, *thirdly:*—third (-ly).

τρίχες **trichĕs,** etc. See *2359.*

5155. τρίχινος **trichinŏs,** *trikh´-ee-nos;* from *2359; hairy,* i.e. made *of hair* (*mohair*):—of hair.

5156. τρόμος **trŏmŏs,** *trom´-os;* from *5141;* a *"trembling"*, i.e. quaking with *fear:*— + tremble (-ing).

5157. τροπή **tropē,** *trop-ay´;* from an appar. prim. τρέπω **trĕpō** (to *turn*); a *turn* ("trope"), i.e. *revolution* (fig. *variation*):—turning.

5158. τρόπος **trŏpŏs,** *trop´-os;* from the same as *5157;* a *turn,* i.e. (by impl.) *mode* or *style* (espec. with prep. or rel. pref. as adv. *like*); fig. *deportment* or *character:*—(even) as, conversation, [+ like] manner (+ by any) means, way.

5159. τροποφορέω **trŏpŏphŏrĕō,** *trop-of-or-eh´-o;* from *5158* and *5409;* to *endure* one's *habits:*—suffer the manners.

5160. τροφή **trŏphē,** *trof-´ay;* from *5142; nourishment* (lit. or fig.); by impl. *rations* (*wages*):—food, meat.

5161. Τρόφιμος **Trŏphimŏs,** *trof´-ee-mos;* from *5160; nutritive; Trophimus,* a Chr.:—Trophimus.

5162. τροφός **trŏphŏs,** *trof-os´;* from *5142;* a *nourisher,* i.e. *nurse:*—nurse.

5163. τροχιά **trŏchia,** *trokh-ee-ah´;* from *5164;* a *track* (as a wheel-*rut*), i.e. (fig.) a *course* of conduct:—path.

5164. τροχός **trŏchŏs,** *trokh-os´;* from *5143;* a *wheel* (as a *runner*), i.e. (fig.) a *circuit* of phys. effects:—course.

5165. τρύβλιον **trubliŏn,** *troob´-lee-on;* neut. of a presumed der. of uncert. affin.; a *bowl:*—dish.

5166. τρυγάω **trugaō,** *troo-gah´-o;* from a der. of τρύγω **trugō** (to *dry*) mean. ripe *fruit* (as if *dry*); to *collect* the vintage:—gather.

5167. τρυγών **trugōn,** *troo-gone´;* from τρύζω **truzō** (to *murmur;* akin to *5149,* but denoting a *duller* sound); a *turtle-dove* (as *cooing*):—turtle-dove.

5168. τρυμαλιά **trumalia,** *troo-mal-ee-ah´;* from a der. of τρύω **truō** (to *wear* away; akin to the base of *5134, 5147* and *5176*); an *orifice,* i.e. a needle's *eye:*—eye. Comp. *5169.*

5169. τρύπημα **trupēma,** *troo´-pay-mah;* from a der. of the base of *5168;* an *aperture,* i.e. a needle's *eye:*—eye.

5170. Τρύφαινα **Truphaina,** *troo´-fahee-nah;* from *5172; luxurious; Tryphœna,* a Chr. woman:—Tryphena.

5171. τρυφάω **truphaō,** *troo-fah´-o;* from *5172;* to *indulge in luxury:*—live in pleasure.

5172. τρυφή **truphē,** *troo-fay´;* from θρύπτω **thruptō** (to *break* up or [fig.] *enfeeble,* espec. the mind and body by indulgence); *effeminacy,* i.e. *luxury* or *debauchery:*—delicately, riot.

5173. Τρυφῶσα **Truphōsa,** *troo-fo´-sah;* from *5172; luxuriating; Tryphosa,* a Chr. female:—Tryphosa.

5174. Τρωάς **Trōas,** *tro-as´;* from Τρός **Trŏs** (a *Trojan*); the *Troad* (or plain of Troy), i.e. *Troas,* a place in Asia Minor:—Troas.

5175. Τρωγύλλιον **Trōgulliŏn,** *tro-gool´-lee-on;* of uncert. der.; *Trogyllium,* a place in Asia Minor:—Trogyllium.

5176. τρώγω **trōgō,** *tro´-go;* prob. strength from a collat. form of the base of *5134* and *5147* through the idea of *corrosion* or *wear;* or perh. rather of a base of *5167* and *5149* through the idea of a *craunching* sound; to *gnaw* or *chew,* i.e. (gen.) to *eat:*—eat.

5177. τυγχάνω **tugchanō,** *toong-khan´-o;* prob. for an obsol. τύχω **tuchō** (for which the mid. of another alt. τεύχω **tĕuchō** (to *make ready* or *bring to pass*] is used in cert. tenses; akin to the base of *5088* through the idea of *effecting;* prop. to *affect;* or (spec.) to *hit* or *light upon* (as a mark to be reached), i.e. (trans.) to *attain* or *secure* an object or end, or (intrans.) to *happen* (as if *meeting* with); but in the latter application only impers. (with *1487*), i.e. *perchance;* or (pres. part.) as adj. *usual* (as if commonly *met with,* with *3756, extraordinary*), neut. (as adv.) *perhaps;* or (with another verb) as adv. by *accident* (*as it were*):—be, chance, enjoy, little, obtain, × refresh . . . self, + special. Comp. *5180.*

5178. τυμπανίζω **tumpanizō,** *toom-pan-id´-zo;* from a der. of *5180* (mean. a *drum, "tympanium"*); to stretch on an instrument of *torture* resembling a drum, and thus *beat* to death:—torture.

5179. τύπος **tupŏs,** *too´-pos;* from *5180;* a *die* (as *struck*), i.e. (by impl.) a *stamp* or *scar;* by anal. a *shape,* i.e. a *statue,* (fig.) *style* or *resemblance;* spec. a *sampler* (*"type"*), i.e. a *model* (for imitation) or *instance* (for warning):—en- (ex-) ample, fashion, figure, form, manner, pattern, print.

5180. τύπτω **tuptō,** *toop´-to;* a prim. verb (in a strength. form); to *"thump"*, i.e. *cudgel* or *pummel* (prop. with a stick or *bastinado*), but in any case by *repeated* blows; thus differing from *3817* and *3960,* which denote a [usually single] blow with the hand or any instrument, or *4141* with the *fist* [or a *hammer*], or *4474* with the *palm;* as well as from *5177,* an *accidental* collision); by impl. to *punish;* fig. to *offend* (the conscience):—beat, smite, strike, wound.

5181. Τύραννος **Turannŏs,** *too´-ran-nos;* a provincial form of the der. of the base of *2962;* a *"tyrant"; Tyrannus,* an Ephesian:—Tyrannus.

5182. τυρβάζω **turbazō,** *toor-bad´-zo;* from τύρβη **turbē** (Lat. *turba,* a *crowd;* akin to *2351*); to *make "turbid"*, i.e. *disturb:*—trouble.

5183. Τύριος **Turiŏs,** *too´-ree-os;* from *5184;* a *Tyrian,* i.e. inhab. of Tyrus:—of Tyre.

5184. Τύρος **Turŏs,** *too´-ros;* of Heb. or. [6865]: *Tyrus* (i.e. *Tsor*), a place in Pal.:—Tyre.

5185. τυφλός **tuphlŏs,** *toof-los´;* from *5187; opaque* (as if *smoky*), i.e. (by anal.) *blind* (phys. or ment.):—blind.

5186. τυφλόω **tuphlŏō,** *toof-lŏ´-o;* from *5185;* to *make blind,* i.e. (fig.) to *obscure:*—blind.

5187. τυφόω **tuphŏō,** *toof-ŏ´-o;* from a der. of *5188;* to envelop with *smoke,* i.e. (fig.) to *inflate* with self-conceit:—high-minded, be lifted up with pride, be proud.

5188. τυφώ **tuphō,** *too´-fo;* appar. a prim. verb; to make a *smoke,* i.e. slowly *consume* without flame:—smoke.

5189. τυφωνικός **tuphōnikŏs,** *too-fo-nee-kos´;* from a der. of *5188; stormy* (as if *smoky*):—tempestuous.

5190. Τυχικός **Tuchikŏs,** *too-khee-kos´;* from a der. of *5177; fortuitous,* i.e. *fortunate; Tychicus,* a Chr.:—Tychicus.

Υ

5191. ὑακίνθινος **huakinthinŏs,** *hoo-ak-in´-thee-nos;* from *5192; "hyacinthine"* or *"jacinthine",* i.e. deep *blue:*—jacinth.

5192. ὑάκινθος **huakinthŏs,** *hoo-ak´-in-thos;* of uncert. der.; the *"hyacinth"* or *"jacinth",* i.e. some gem of a deep *blue* color, prob. the *zirkon:*—jacinth.

5193. ὑάλινος **hualinŏs,** *hoo-al´-ee-nos;* from *5194; glassy,* i.e. *transparent:*—of glass.

5194. ὕαλος **hualŏs,** *hoo´-al-os;* perh. from the same as *5205* (as being transparent like *rain*); *glass:*—glass.

5195. ὑβρίζω **hubrizō,** *hoo-brid´-zo;* from *5196;* to *exercise violence,* i.e. *abuse:*—use despitefully, reproach, entreat shamefully (spitefully).

5196. ὕβρις **hubris,** *hoo´-bris;* from *5228; insolence* (as *over*-bearing), i.e. *insult, injury:*—harm, hurt, reproach.

5197. ὑβριστής **hubristēs,** *hoo-bris-tace´;* from *5195;* an *insulter,* i.e. *maltreater:*—despiteful, injurious.

5198. ὑγιαίνω **hugiainō,** *hoog-ee-ah´ee-no;* from *5199;* to *have* sound *health,* i.e. *be well* (in body); fig. to be *uncorrupt* (*true* in doctrine):—be in health, (be safe and) sound, (be) whole (-some).

5199. ὑγιής **hugiēs,** *hoog-ee-ace´;* from the base of *837; healthy,* i.e. *well* (in body); fig. *true* (in doctrine):—sound, whole.

5200. ὑγρός **hugrŏs,** *hoo-gros´;* from the base of *5205; wet* (as if with *rain*), i.e. (by impl.) *sappy* (*fresh*):—green.

5201. ὑδριά **hudria,** *hoo-dree-ah´;* from *5204;* a *water-jar,* i.e. *receptacle* for family supply:—waterpot.

5202. ὑδροποτέω **hudrŏpŏtĕō,** *hoo-drop-ot-eh´-o;* from a comp. of *5204* and a der. of *4095;* to *be* a *water-drinker,* i.e. to *abstain from vinous beverages:*—drink water.

5203. ὑδρωπικός **hudrōpikŏs,** *hoo-dro-pik-os´;* from a comp. of *5204* and a der. of *3700* (as if *looking watery*); to *be "dropsical":*—have the dropsy.

5204. ὕδωρ **hudōr,** *hoo´-dore;* gen.
ὕδατος **hudatŏs,** *hoo´-dat-os;* etc.; from the base of *5205; water* (as if *rainy*) lit. or fig.:—water.

5205. ὑετός **huĕtŏs,** *hoo-et-os´;* from a prim. ὕω **huō** (to *rain*); *rain,* espec. a *shower:*—rain.

5206. υἱοθεσία **huiŏthĕsia,** *hwee-oth-es-ee´-ah;* from a presumed comp. of *5207* and a der. of *5087;* the *placing* as a *son,* i.e. *adoption* (fig. Chr. *sonship* in respect to God):—adoption (of children, of sons).

5207. υἱός **huiŏs,** *hwee-os´;* appar. a prim. word; a *"son"* (sometimes of animals), used very widely of immed., remote or fig. kinship:—child, foal, son.

5208. ὕλη **hulē,** *hoo-lay´;* perh. akin to *3586;* a *forest, i.e. (by impl.) fuel:*—matter.

5209. ὑμᾶς **humas,** *hoo-mas´;* acc. of *5210; you* (as the obj. of a verb or prep.):—ye, you, (+ -ward), your (+ own).

5210. ὑμεῖς **humĕis,** *hoo-mice´;* irreg. plur. of *4771; you* (as subj. of verb):—ye (yourselves), you.

5211. Ὑμεναῖος **Humĕnaiŏs,** *hoo-men-ah´-yos;* from Ὑμήν **Humēn** (the god of *weddings*); *"hymenæal"; Hymenæus,* an opponent of Christianity:—Hymenæus.

5212. ὑμέτερος **humĕtĕrŏs,** *hoo-met´-er-os;* from *5210; yours,* i.e. *pertaining to you:*—your (own).

5213. ὑμῖν **humin,** *hoo-min´;* irreg. dat. of *5210; to* (*with* or *by*) *you:*—ye, you, your (-selves).

5214. ὑμνέω **humnĕō,** *hoom-neh´-o;* from *5215;* to *hymn,* i.e. sing a religious ode; by impl. to *celebrate* (God) in song:—sing an hymn (praise unto).

5215. ὕμνος **humnŏs,** *hoom´-nos;* appar. from a simpler (obsol.) form of ὕδέω **hudĕō** (to *celebrate;* prob. akin to *103;* comp. *5567*); a *"hymn"* or religious ode (one of the Psalms):—hymn.

5216. ὑμῶν **humōn,** *hoo-mone´;* gen. of *5210; of* (*from* or *concerning*) *you:*—ye, you, your (own, -selves).

5217. ὑπάγω **hupagō,** *hoop-ag´-o;* from *5259* and *71;* to *lead* (oneself) *under,* i.e. *withdraw* or *retire* (as if *sinking* out of sight), lit. or fig.:—depart, get hence, go (a-) way.

5218. ὑπακοή **hupakŏē,** *hoop-ak-ŏ-ay´;* from *5219; attentive hearkening,* i.e. (by impl.) *compliance* or *submission:*—obedience, (make) obedient, obey (-ing).

5219. ὑπακούω **hupakŏuō,** *hoop-ak-oo´-o;* from *5259* and *191;* to *hear under* (as a *subordinate*), i.e. to *listen attentively;* by impl. to *heed* or *conform* to a command or authority:—hearken, be obedient to, obey.

5220. ὕπανδρος **hupandrŏs,** *hoop´-an-dros;* from *5259* and *435;* in subjection *under a man,* i.e. a *married* woman:—which hath an husband.

5221. ὑπαντάω **hupantaō,** *hoop-an-tah´-o;* from *5259* and a der. of *473;* to *go opposite* (*meet*) *under* (*quietly*), i.e. to *encounter, fall in with:*—(go to) meet.

5222. ὑπάντησις **hupantēsis,** *hoop-an´-tay-sis;* from *5221;* an *encounter* or *concurrence* (with *1519* for infin., in order to *fall in with*):—meeting.

5223. ὕπαρξις **huparxis,** *hoop´-arx-is;* from *5225; existency* or *proprietorship,* i.e. (concr.) *property, wealth:*—goods, substance.

5224. ὑπάρχοντα **huparchŏnta,** *hoop-ar´-khon-tah;* neut. plur. of pres. part. act. of *5225* as noun; things *extent* or *in hand,* i.e. *property* or *possessions:*—goods, that which one has, things which (one) possesseth, substance, that hast.

5225. ὑπάρχω **huparchō,** *hoop-ar´-kho;* from *5259* and *756;* to *begin under* (*quietly*), i.e. *come into existence* (*be present* or *at hand*); expletively, to *exist* (as copula or subordinate to an adj., part., adv. or prep., or as auxil. to principal verb):—after behave, live.

5226. ὑπείκω **hupĕikō,** *hoop-i´-ko;* from *5259* and εἴκω **ĕikō** (to *yield,* be *"weak"*); to *surrender:*—submit self.

5227. ὑπεναντίος **hupĕnantiŏs,** *hoop-en-an-tee´-os;* from *5259* and *1727; under* (*covertly*) *contrary* to, i.e. *opposed* or (as noun) an *opponent:*—adversary, against.

5228. ὑπέρ **hupĕr,** *hoop-er´;* a prim. prep.; *"over",* i.e. (with the gen.) of place, *above, beyond, across,* or causal, *for* the sake of, *instead, regarding;* with the acc. *superior to,* more *than:*—(+ exceeding abundantly) above, in (on) behalf of, beyond, by, + very chiefest, concerning, exceeding (above, -ly), for, + very highly, more (than), of, over, on the part of, for sake of, in stead, than, to (-ward), very. In comp. it retains many of the above applications.

5229. ὑπεραίρομαι **hupĕrairŏmai,** *hoop-er-ah´ee-rom-ahee;* mid. from *5228* and *142;* to *raise* oneself *over,* i.e. (fig.) to *become haughty:*—exalt self, be exalted above measure.

5230. ὑπέρακμος **hupĕrakmŏs,** *hoop-er´-ak-mos;* from *5228* and the base of *188; beyond* the *"acme",* i.e. fig. (of a daughter) *past* the *bloom* (*prime*) of youth:—+ pass the flower of (her) age.

5231. ὑπεράνω **hupĕranō,** *hoop-er-an´-o;* from *5228* and *507; above upward,* i.e. *greatly higher* (in place or rank):—far above, over.

5232. ὑπεραυξάνω **hupĕrauxanō,** *hoop-er-ŏwx-an´-o;* from *5228* and *837;* to *increase above* ordinary degree:—grow exceedingly.

5233. ὑπερβαίνω **hupĕrbainō,** *hoop-er-bah´-ee-no;* from *5228* and the base of *939;* to *transcend,* i.e. (fig.) to *overreach:*—go beyond.

5234. ὑπερβαλλόντως **hupĕrballŏntōs,** *hoop-er-bal-lon´-toce;* adv. from pres. part. act. of *5235; excessively:*—beyond measure.

5235. ὑπερβάλλω **hupĕrballō,** *hoop-er-bal´-lo;* from *5228* and *906;* to *throw beyond* the usual mark, i.e. (fig.) to *surpass* (only act. part. *supereminent*):—exceeding, excel, pass.

5236. ὑπερβολή **hupĕrbŏlē,** *hoop-er-bol-ay´;* from *5235;* a *throwing beyond* others, i.e. (fig.) *supereminence;* adv. (with *1519* or *2596*) *pre-eminently:*—abundance, (far more) exceeding, excellency, more excellent, beyond (out of) measure.

5237. ὑπερείδω **hupĕrĕidō,** *hoop-er-i´-do;* from *5228* and *1492;* to *overlook,* i.e. *not punish:*—wink at.

5238. ὑπερέκεινα **hupĕrĕkĕina,** *hoop-er-ek´-i-nah;* from *5228* and the neut. plur. of *1565; above those* parts, i.e. *still farther:*—beyond.

5239. ὑπερεκτείνω **hupĕrĕktĕinō,** *hoop-er-ek-ti´-no;* from *5228* and *1614;* to *extend inordinately:*—stretch beyond.

5240. ὑπερεκχύνω **hupĕrekchunō,** *hoop-er-ek-khoo´-no;* from *5228* and the alt. form of *1632;* to *pour out over,* i.e (pass.) to *overflow:*—run over.

ὑπερεκπερισσοῦ **hupĕrĕkpĕrissŏu.** See *5228* and *1537* and *4053.*

5241. ὑπερεντυγχάνω **hupĕrĕntugchanō,** *hoop-er-en-toong-khan´-o;* from *5228* and *1793;* to *intercede in behalf of:*—make intercession for.

5242. ὑπερέχω **hupĕrĕchō,** *hoop-er-ekh´-o;* from *5228* and *2192;* to *hold* oneself *above,* i.e. (fig.) to *excel;* part. (as adj., or neut. as noun) *superior, superiority:*—better, excellency, higher, pass, supreme.

5243. ὑπερηφανία **hupĕrēphania,** *hoop-er-ay-fan-ee´-ah;* from *5244; haughtiness:*—pride.

5244. ὑπερήφανος **hupĕrēphanŏs,** *hoop-er-ay´-fan-os;* from *5228* and *5316; appearing above* others (*conspicuous*), i.e. (fig.) *haughty:*—proud.

ὑπερλίαν **hupĕrlian.** See *5228* and *3029.*

5245. ὑπερνικάω **hupĕrnikaō,** *hoop-er-nik-ah´-o;* from *5228* and *3528;* to *vanquish beyond,* i.e. *gain* a decisive *victory:*—more than conquer.

5246. ὑπέρογκος **hupĕrŏgkŏs,** *hoop-er´-ong-kos;* from *5228* and *3591; bulging over,* i.e. (fig.) *insolent:*—great swelling.

5247. ὑπεροχή **hupĕrŏchē,** *hoop-er-okh-ay´;* from *5242; prominence,* i.e. (fig.) *superiority (in rank or character):—authority, excellency.*

5248. ὑπερπερισσεύω **hupĕrpĕrissĕuō,** *hoop-er-per-is-syoo´-o;* from *5228* and *4052;* to *superabound:*—abound much more, exceeding.

5249. ὑπερπερισσῶς **hupĕrpĕrissōs,** *hoop-er-per-is-soce´;* from *5228* and *4057; superabundantly,* i.e. *exceedingly:*—beyond measure.

5250. ὑπερπλεονάζω **hupĕrplĕŏnazō,** *hoop-er-pleh-on-ad´-zo;* from *5228* and *4121;* to *superabound:*—be exceeding abundant.

5251. ὑπερυψόω **hupĕrupsŏō,** *hoop-er-oop-sŏ´-o;* from *5228* and *5312;* to *elevate above* others, i.e. *raise* to the *highest* position:—highly exalt.

5252. ὑπερφρονέω **hupĕrphrŏnĕō,** *hoop-er-fron-eh´-o;* from *5228* and *5426;* to *esteem* oneself *overmuch,* i.e. *be vain* or *arrogant:*—think more highly.

5253. ὑπερῷον **hupĕrōiŏn,** *hoop-er-o´-on;* neut. of a der. of *5228;* a *higher* part of the house, i.e. apartment in the *third story:*—upper chamber (room).

5254. ὑπέχω **hupĕchō,** *hoop-ekh´-o;* from *5259* and *2192;* to *hold* oneself *under,* i.e. *endure* with patience:—suffer.

5255. ὑπήκοος **hupēkŏŏs,** *hoop-ay´-kŏ-os;* from *5219; attentively listening,* i.e. (by impl.) *submissive:*—obedient.

5256. ὑπηρετέω **hupērĕtĕō,** *hoop-ay-ret-eh´-o;* from *5257;* to *be a subordinate,* i.e. (by impl.) *subserve:*—minister (unto), serve.

5257. ὑπηρέτης **hupērĕtēs,** *hoop-ay-ret´-ace;* from *5259* and a der. of ἐρέσσω **ĕrĕssō** (to *row*); an *under-oarsman,* i.e. (gen.) *subordinate* (*assistant, sexton, constable*):—minister, officer, servant.

5258. ὕπνος **hupnŏs,** *hoop´-nos;* from an obsol. prim. (perh. akin to *5259* through the idea of *subsilience*); *sleep,* i.e. (fig.) spiritual *torpor:*—sleep.

5259. ὑπό **hupŏ,** *hoop-ŏ´;* a prim. prep.; *under,* i.e. (with the gen.) of place (*beneath*), or with verbs (the agency or means, *through*); (with the acc.) of place (whither [*underneath*] or where [*below*]) or time (when [*at*]):—among, by, from, in, of, under, with. In comp. it retains the same gen. applications, espec. of *inferior* position or condition, and spec. *covertly* or *moderately.*

5260. ὑποβάλλω **hupŏballō,** *hoop-ob-al´-lo;* from *5259* and *906;* to *throw* in *stealthily,* i.e. *introduce* by collusion:—suborn.

5261. ὑπογραμμός **hupŏgrammŏs,** *hoop-og-ram-mos´;* from a comp. of *5259* and *1125;* an *underwriting,* i.e. *copy* for imitation (fig.):—example.

5262. ὑπόδειγμα **hupŏdĕigma,** *hoop-od´-igue-mah;* from *5263;* an *exhibit* for imitation or warning (fig. *specimen, adumbration*):—en- (ex-) ample, pattern.

5263. ὑποδείκνυμι **hupŏdĕiknumi,** *hoop-od-ike´-noo-mee;* from *5259* and *1166;* to *exhibit under* the eyes, i.e. (fig.) to *exemplify* (*instruct, admonish*):—show, (fore-) warn.

5264. ὑποδέχομαι **hupŏdĕchŏmai,** *hoop-od-ekh´-om-ahee;* from *5259* and *1209;* to *admit under* one's roof, i.e. *entertain* hospitably:—receive.

5265. ὑποδέω **hupŏdĕō,** *hoop-od-eh´-o;* from *5259* and *1210;* to *bind under* one's feet, i.e. *put on* shoes or sandals:—bind on, (be) shod.

5266. ὑπόδημα **hupŏdēma,** *hoop-od´-ay-mah;* from *5265;* something *bound under* the feet, i.e. a *shoe* or *sandal:*—shoe.

5267. ὑπόδικος **hupŏdikŏs,** *hoop-od´-ee-kos;* from *5259* and *1349; under sentence,* i.e. (by impl.) *condemned:*—guilty.

5268. ὑποζύγιον **hupŏzugiŏn,** *hoop-od-zoog´-ee-on;* neut. of a comp. of *5259* and *2218;* an animal *under* the *yoke* (*draught-beast*), i.e. (spec.) a *donkey:*—ass.

5269. ὑποζώννυμι **hupŏzōnnumi,** *hoop-od-zone´-noo-mee;* from *5259* and *2224;* to *gird under,* i.e. *frap* (a vessel with cables across the keel, sides and deck):—undergirt.

5270. ὑποκάτω **hupŏkatō,** *hoop-ok-at´-o;* from *5259* and *2736; down under,* i.e. *beneath:*—under.

5271. ὑποκρίνομαι **hupŏkrinŏmai,** *hoop-ok-rin´-om-ahee;* mid. from *5259* and *2919;* to *decide* (*speak* or *act*) *under* a false part, i.e. (fig.) *dissemble* (*pretend*):—feign.

5272. ὑπόκρισις **hupŏkrisis,** *hoop-ok´-ree-sis;* from *5271; acting under* a feigned part, i.e. (fig.) *deceit* ("*hypocrisy*"):—condemnation, dissimulation, hypocrisy.

5273. ὑποκριτής **hupŏkritēs,** *hoop-ok-ree-tace´;* from *5271;* an *actor under* an assumed character (*stage-player*), i.e. (fig.) a *dissembler* ("*hypocrite*"):—hypocrite.

5274. ὑπολαμβάνω **hupŏlambanō,** *hoop-ol-am-ban´-o;* from *5259* and *2983;* to *take* from *below,* i.e. *carry upward;* fig. to *take up,* i.e. *continue* a discourse or topic; ment. to *assume* (*presume*):—answer, receive, suppose.

5275. ὑπολείπω **hupŏlĕipō,** *hoop-ol-i´-po;* from *5295* and *3007;* to *leave under* (*behind*), i.e. (pass.) to *remain* (*survive*):—be left.

5276. ὑπολήνιον **hupŏlēniŏn,** *hoop-ol-ay´-nee-on;* neut. of a presumed comp. of *5259* and *3025;* vessel or receptacle *under* the *press,* i.e. lower *winevat:*—winefat.

5277. ὑπολιμπάνω **hupŏlimpanō,** *hoop-ol-im-pan´-o;* a prol. form for *5275;* to *leave behind,* i.e. *bequeath:*—leave.

5278. ὑπομένω **hupŏmĕnō,** *hoop-om-en´-o;* from *5259* and *3306;* to *stay under* (*behind*), i.e. *remain;* fig. to *undergo,* i.e. *bear* (trials), *have fortitude, persevere:*—abide, endure, (take) patient (-ly), suffer, tarry behind.

5279. ὑπομιμνήσκω **hupŏmimnēskō,** *hoop-om-im-nace´-ko;* from *5259* and *3403;* to *remind quietly,* i.e. *suggest* to the (mid. one's own) memory:—put in mind, remember, bring to (put in) remembrance.

5280. ὑπόμνησις **hupŏmnēsis,** *hoop-om´-nay-sis;* from *5279;* a *reminding* or (reflex.) *recollection:*—remembrance.

5281. ὑπομονή **hupŏmŏnē,** *hoop-om-on-ay´;* from *5278;* cheerful (or hopeful) *endurance, constancy:*—enduring, patience, patient continuance (waiting).

5282. ὑπονοέω **hupŏnŏĕō,** *hoop-on-ŏ-eh´-o;* from *5259* and *3539;* to *think under* (*privately*), i.e. to *surmise* or *conjecture:*—think, suppose, deem.

5283. ὑπόνοια **hupŏnŏia,** *hoop-on´-oy-ah;* from *5282; suspicion:*—surmising.

5284. ὑποπλέω **hupŏplĕō,** *hoop-op-leh´-o;* from *5259* and *4126;* to *sail under* the lee of:—sail under.

5285. ὑποπνέω **hupŏpnĕō,** *hoop-op-neh´-o;* from *5259* and *4154;* to *breathe gently,* i.e. *breeze:*—blow softly.

5286. ὑποπόδιον **hupŏpŏdiŏn,** *hoop-op-od´-ee-on;* neut. of a comp. of *5259* and *4228;* something *under* the *feet,* i.e. a *foot-rest* (fig.):—footstool.

5287. ὑπόστασις **hupŏstasis,** *hoop-os´-tas-is;* from a comp. of *5259* and *2476;* a *setting under* (*support*), i.e. (fig.) concr. *essence,* or abstr. *assurance* (obj. or subj.):—confidence, confident, person, substance.

5288. ὑποστέλλω **hupŏstĕllō,** *hoop-os-tel´-lo;* from *5259* and *4724;* to *withhold under* (*out of sight*), i.e. (reflex.) to *cower* or *shrink,* (fig.) to *conceal* (*reserve*):—draw (keep) back, shun, withdraw.

5289. ὑποστολή **hupŏstŏlē,** *hoop-os-tol-ay´;* from *5288; shrinkage* (*timidity*), i.e. (by impl.) *apostasy:*—draw back.

5290. ὑποστρέφω **hupŏstrĕphō,** *hoop-os-tref´-o;* from *5259* and *4762;* to *turn under* (*behind*), i.e. to *return* (lit. or fig.):—come again, return (again, back again), turn back (again).

5291. ὑποστρώννυμι **hupŏstrōnnumi,** *hoop-os-trone´-noo-mee;* from *5259* and *4766; to strew underneath* (the feet as a carpet):—spread.

5292. ὑποταγή **hupŏtagē,** *hoop-ot-ag-ay´;* from *5293; subordination:*—subjection.

5293. ὑποτάσσω **hupŏtassō,** *hoop-ot-as´-so;* from *5259* and *5021;* to *subordinate;* reflex. to *obey:*—be under obedience (obedient), put under, subdue unto, (be, make) subject (to, unto), be (put) in subjection (to, under), submit self unto.

5294. ὑποτίθημι **hupŏtithēmi,** *hoop-ot-ith´-ay-mee;* from *5259* and *5087;* to *place underneath,* i.e. (fig.) to *hazard,* (reflex.) to *suggest:*—lay down, put in remembrance.

5295. ὑποτρέχω **hupŏtrĕchō,** *hoop-ot-rekh´-o;* from *5259* and *5143* (includ. its alt.); to *run under,* i.e. (spec.) to *sail past:*—run under.

5296. ὑποτύπωσις **hupŏtupōsis,** *hoop-ot-oop´-o-sis;* from a comp. of *5259* and a der. of *5179; typification under* (*after*), i.e. (concr.) a *sketch* (fig.) for imitation:—form, pattern.

5297. ὑποφέρω **hupŏphĕrō,** *hoop-of-er´-o;* from *5259* and *5342;* to *bear* from *underneath,* i.e. (fig.) to *undergo* hardship:—bear, endure.

5298. ὑποχωρέω **hupŏchōrĕō,** *hoop-okh-o-reh´-o;* from *5259* and *5562;* to *vacate down,* i.e. *retire* quietly:—go aside, withdraw self.

5299. ὑπωπιάζω **hupōpiazō,** *hoop-o-pee-ad´-zo;* from a comp. of *5259* and a der. of *3700;* to hit *under* the *eye* (*buffet* or *disable* an antagonist as a pugilist), i.e. (fig.) to *tease* or *annoy* (into compliance), *subdue* (one's passions):—keep under, weary.

5300. ὗς **hus,** *hoos;* appar. a prim. word; a *hog* ("*swine*"):—sow.

5301. ὕσσωπος **hussōpŏs,** *hoos´-so-pos;* of for. or. [231]; *"hyssop":*—hyssop.

5302. ὑστερέω **hustĕrĕō,** *hoos-ter-eh´-o;* from *5306;* to *be later,* i.e. (by impl.) to *be inferior;* gen. to *fall short* (*be deficient*):—come behind (short), be destitute, fall, lack, suffer need, (be in) want, be the worse.

5303. ὑστέρημα **hustĕrēma,** *hoos-ter´-ay-mah;* from *5302;* a *deficit;* spec. *poverty:*—that which is behind, (that which was) lack (-ing), penury, want.

5304. ὑστέρησις **hustĕrēsis,** *hoos-ter´-ay-sis;* from *5302;* a *falling short,* i.e. (spec.) *penury:*—want.

5305. ὕστερον **hustĕrŏn,** *hoos´-ter-on;* neut. of *5306* as adv.; *more lately,* i.e. *eventually:*—afterward, (at the) last (of all).

5306. ὕστερος **hustĕrŏs,** *hoos´-ter-os;* compar. from *5259* (in the sense of *behind*); *later:*—latter.

5307. ὑφαντός **huphantŏs,** *hoo-fan-tos´;* from ὑφαίνω **huphainō** (to *weave*); *woven,* i.e. (perh.) *knitted:*—woven.

5308. ὑψηλός **hupsēlŏs,** *hoop-say-los´;* from *5311; lofty* (in place or character):—high (-er, -ly) (esteemed).

5309. ὑψηλοφρονέω **hupsēlŏphrŏnĕō,** *hoop-say-lo-fron-eh´-o;* from a comp. of *5308* and *5424;* to *be lofty in mind,* i.e. *arrogant:*—be highminded.

5310. ὕψιστος **hupsistŏs,** *hoop´-sis-tos;* superl. from the base of *5311; highest,* i.e. (masc. sing.) the *Supreme* (God), or (neut. plur.) the *heavens:*—most high, highest.

5311. ὕψος **hupsŏs,** *hoop´-sos;* from a der. of *5228; elevation,* i.e. (abstr.) *altitude,* (spec.) the *sky,* or (fig.) *dignity:*—be exalted, height, (on) high.

5312. ὑψόω **hupsŏō,** *hoop-sŏ´-o;* from *5311;* to *elevate* (lit. or fig.):—exalt, lift up.

5313. ὕψωμα **hupsōma,** *hoop´-so-mah;* from *5312;* an *elevated* place or thing, i.e. (abstr.) *altitude,* or (by impl.) a *barrier* (fig.):—height, high thing.

Φ

5314. φάγος **phagŏs,** *fag´-os;* from *5315;* a *glutton:*—gluttonous.

5315. φάγω **phagō,** *fag´-o;* a prim. verb (used as an alt. of *2068* in cert. tenses); to *eat* (lit. or fig.):—eat, meat.

5316. φαίνω **phainō,** *fah´ee-no;* prol. for the base of *5457;* to *lighten* (*shine*), i.e. *show* (trans. or intrans., lit. or fig.):—appear, seem, be seen, shine, × think.

5317. Φάλεκ **Phalĕk,** *fal´-ek;* of Heb. or. [6389]; *Phalek* (i.e. *Peleg*), a patriarch:—Phalec.

5318. φανερός **phanĕrŏs,** *fan-er-os´;* from *5316; shining,* i.e. *apparent* (lit. or fig.); neut. (as adv.) *publicly, externally:*—abroad, + appear, known, manifest, open [+ -ly], outward ([+ -ly]).

5319. φανερόω **phanĕrŏō,** *fan-er-ŏ´-o;* from *5318;* to *render apparent* (lit. or fig.):—appear, manifestly declare, (make) manifest (forth), shew (self).

5320. φανερῶς **phanĕrōs,** *fan-er-oce´;* adv. from *5318; plainly,* i.e. *clearly* or *publicly:*—evidently, openly.

5321. φανέρωσις **phanĕrōsis,** *fan-er´-o-sis;* from *5319; exhibition,* i.e. (fig.) *expression,* (by extens.) a *bestowment:*—manifestation.

5322. φανός **phanŏs,** *fan-os´;* from *5316;* a *lightener,* i.e. *light; lantern:*—lantern.

5323. Φανουήλ **Phanŏuēl,** *fan-oo-ale´;* of Heb. or. [6439]; *Phanuël* (i.e. *Penuël*), an Isr.:—Phanuel.

5324. φαντάζω **phantazō,** *fan-tad´-zo;* from a der. of *5316;* to *make apparent,* i.e. (pass.) to *appear* (neut. part. as noun, a *spectacle*):—sight.

5325. φαντασία **phantasia,** *fan-tas-ee´-ah;* from a der. of *5324;* (prop. abstr.) a (vain) *show* ("fantasy"):—pomp.

5326. φάντασμα **phantasma,** *fan´-tas-mah;* from *5324;* (prop. concr.) a (mere) *show* ("phantasm"), i.e. *spectre:*—spirit.

5327. φάραγξ **pharagx,** *far´-anx;* prop. strength. from the base of *4008* or rather of *4486;* a *gap* or *chasm,* i.e. *ravine* (*winter-torrent*):—valley.

5328. Φαραώ **Pharaō,** *far-ah-o´;* of for. or. [6547]; *Pharaö* (i.e. *Pharoh*), an Eg. king:—Pharaoh.

5329. Φαρές **Pharĕs,** *far-es´;* of Heb. or. [6557]; *Phares* (i.e. *Perets*), an Isr.:—Phares.

5330. Φαρισαῖος **Pharisaiŏs,** *far-is-ah´-yos;* of Heb. or. [comp. 6567]; a *separatist,* i.e. exclusively *religious;* a *Pharisæan,* i.e. Jewish sectary:—Pharisee.

5331. φαρμακεία **pharmakĕia,** *far-mak-i´-ah;* from *5332; medication* ("pharmacy"), i.e. (by extens.) *magic* (lit. or fig.):—sorcery, witchcraft.

5332. φαρμακεύς **pharmakĕus,** *far-mak-yoos´;* from φάρμακον **pharmakŏn** (a *drug,* i.e. spell-giving *potion*); a *druggist* ("pharmacist") or *poisoner,* i.e. (by extens.) a *magician:*—sorcerer.

5333. φαρμακός **pharmakŏs,** *far-mak-os´;* the same as *5332:*—sorcerer.

5334. φάσις **phasis,** *fas´-is;* from *5346* (not the same as "phase", which is from *5316*); a *saying,* i.e. *report:*—tidings.

5335. φάσκω **phaskō,** *fas´-ko;* prol. from the same as *5346;* to *assert:*—affirm, profess, say.

5336. φάτνη **phatnē,** *fat´-nay;* from πατέομαι **patĕŏmai** (to *eat*); a *crib* (for fodder):—manger, stall.

5337. φαῦλος **phaulŏs,** *fŏw´-los;* appar. a prim. word; *"foul"* or *"flawy",* i.e. (fig.) *wicked:*—evil.

5338. φέγγος **phĕggŏs,** *feng´-gos;* prob. akin to the base of *5457* [comp. *5350*]; *brilliancy:*—light.

5339. φείδομαι **phĕidŏmai,** *fi´-dom-ahee;* of uncert. affin.; to *be chary* of, i.e. (subj.) to *abstain* or (obj.) to *treat leniently:*—forbear, spare.

5340. φειδομένως **phĕidŏmĕnōs,** *fi-dom-en´-oce;* adv. from part. of *5339; abstemiously,* i.e. *stingily:*—sparingly.

5341. φελόνης **phĕlŏnēs,** *fel-on´-ace;* by transp. for a der. prob. of *5316* (as *showing* outside the other garments); a *mantle* (*surtout*):—cloke.

5342. φέρω **phĕrō,** *fer´-o;* a prim. verb (for which other and appar. not cognate ones are used in certain tenses only; namely,
οἴω **ŏiō,** *oy´-o;* and
ἐνέγκω **ĕnĕgkō,** *en-eng´-ko*); to *"bear"* or *carry* (in a very wide application, lit. and fig., as follows):—be, bear, bring (forth), carry, come, + let her drive, be driven, endure, go on, lay, lead, move, reach, rushing, uphold.

5343. φεύγω **phĕugō,** *fyoo´-go;* appar. a prim. verb; to *run away* (lit. or fig.); by impl. to *shun;* by anal. to *vanish:*—escape, flee (away).

5344. Φῆλιξ **Phēlix,** *fay´-lix;* of Lat. or.; *happy; Phelix* (i.e. *Felix*), a Rom.:—Felix.

5345. φήμη **phēmē,** *fay´-may;* from *5346;* a *saying,* i.e. *rumor* ("fame"):—fame.

5346. φημί **phēmi,** *fay-mee´;* prop. the same as the base of *5457* and *5316;* to *show* or *make known* one's thoughts, i.e. *speak* or *say:*—affirm, say. Comp. *3004.*

5347. Φῆστος **Phēstŏs,** *face´-tos;* of Lat. der.; *festal; Phestus* (i.e. *Festus*), a Rom.:—Festus.

5348. φθάνω **phthanō,** *fthan´-o;* appar. a prim. verb; to *be beforehand,* i.e. *anticipate* or *precede,* by extens. to *have arrived* at:—(already) attain, come, prevent.

5349. φθαρτός **phthartŏs,** *fthar-tos´;* from *5351; decayed,* i.e. (by impl.) *perishable:*—corruptible.

5350. φθέγγομαι **phthĕggŏmai,** *ftheng´-gom-ahee;* prob. akin to *5338* and thus to *5346;* to *utter* a clear sound, i.e. (gen.) to *proclaim:*—speak.

5351. φθείρω **phthĕirō,** *fthi´-ro;* prob. strength. from φθίω **phthiō** (to *pine* or *waste*); prop. to *shrivel* or *wither,* i.e. to *spoil* (by any process) or (gen.) to *ruin* (espec. fig. by mor. influences, to *deprave*):—corrupt (self), defile, destroy.

5352. φθινοπωρινός **phthinŏpōrinŏs,** *fthin-op-o-ree-nos´;* from a der. of φθίνω **phthinō** (to *wane;* akin to the base of *5351*) and *3703* (mean. *late autumn*); *autumnal* (as *stripped* of leaves):—whose fruit withereth.

5353. φθόγγος **phthŏggŏs,** *fthong´-gos;* from *5350; utterance,* i.e. a *musical* note (vocal or instrumental):—sound.

5354. φθονέω **phthŏnĕō,** *fthon-eh´-o;* from *5355;* to *be jealous* of:—envy.

5355. φθόνος **phthŏnŏs,** *fthon´-os;* prob. akin to the base of *5351; ill-will* (as *detraction*), i.e. *jealousy* (*spite*):—envy.

5356. φθορά **phthŏra,** *fthor-ah´;* from *5351; decay,* i.e. *ruin* (spontaneous or inflicted, lit. or fig.):—corruption, destroy, perish.

5357. φιάλη **phialē,** *fee-al´-ay;* of uncert. affin.; a broad shallow *cup* ("phial"):—vial.

5358. φιλάγαθος **philagathŏs,** *fil-ag´-ath-os;* from *5384* and *18; fond to good,* i.e. a *promoter of virtue:*—love of good men.

5359. Φιλαδέλφεια **Philadĕlphĕia,** *fil-ad-el´-fee-ah;* from Φιλάδελφος **Philadĕlphōs** (the same as *5361*), a king of Pergamos; *Philadelphia,* a place in Asia Minor:—Philadelphia.

5360. φιλαδελφία **philadĕlphia,** *fil-ad-el-fee´ah;* from *5361; fraternal affection:*—brotherly love (kindness), love of the brethren.

5361. φιλάδελφος **philadĕlphŏs,** *fil-ad´-el-fos;* from *5384* and *80; fond of brethren,* i.e. *fraternal:*—love as brethren.

5362. φίλανδρος **philandrŏs,** *fil´-an-dros;* from *5384* and *435; fond of man,* i.e. *affectionate* as a wife:—love their husbands.

5363. φιλανθρωπία **philanthrōpia,** *fil-an-thro-pee´-ah;* from the same as *5364; fondness of mankind,* i.e. *benevolence* (*"philanthropy"*):—kindness, love towards man.

5364. φιλανθρώπως **philanthrōpōs,** *fil-an-thro´-poce;* adv. from a comp. of *5384* and *444; fondly to man* ("philanthropically"), i.e. *humanely:*—courteously.

5365. φιλαργυρία **philarguria,** *fil-ar-goo-ree´ah;* from *5366; avarice:*—love of money.

5366. φιλάργυρος **philargurŏs,** *fil-ar´-goo-ros;* from *5384* and *696; fond of silver* (*money*), i.e. *avaricious:*—covetous.

5367. φίλαυτος **philautŏs,** *fil´-ŏw-tos;* from *5384* and *846; fond of self,* i.e. *selfish:*—lover of own self.

5368. φιλέω **philĕō,** *fil-eh´-o;* from *5384;* to *be a friend to* (*fond of* [an individual or an object]), i.e. *have affection* for (denoting *personal* attachment, as a matter of sentiment or feeling; while *25* is wider, embracing espec. the judgment and the *deliberate* assent of the will as a matter of principle, duty and propriety: the two thus stand related very much as *2309* and *1014,* or as *2372* and *3563* respectively; the former being chiefly of the *heart* and the latter of the *head*); spec. to *kiss* (as a mark of tenderness):—kiss, love.

5369. φιλήδονος **philēdŏnŏs,** *fil-ay´-don-os;* from *5384* and *2237; fond of pleasure,* i.e. *voluptuous:*—lover of pleasure.

5370. φίλημα **philēma,** *fil´-ay-mah;* from *5368;* a *kiss:*—kiss.

5371. Φιλήμων **Philēmōn,** *fil-ay´-mone;* from *5368; friendly; Philemon,* a Chr.:—Philemon.

5372. Φιλητός **Philētŏs,** *fil-ay-tos´;* from *5368; amiable; Philetus,* an opposer of Christianity:—Philetus.

5373. φιλία **philia,** *fil-ee´-ah;* from *5384; fondness:*—friendship.

5374. Φιλιππήσιος **Philippēsiŏs,** *fil-ip-pay´-see-os;* from *5375;* a *Philippesian* (*Philippian*), i.e. native of Philippi:—Philippian.

5375. Φίλιπποι **Philippŏi,** *fil´-ip-poy;* plur. of *5376; Philippi,* a place in Macedonia:—Philippi.

5376. Φίλιππος **Philippŏs,** *fil´-ip-pos;* from *5384* and *2462; fond of horses; Philippus,* the name of four Isr.:—Philip.

5377. φιλόθεος **philŏthĕŏs,** *fil-oth´-eh-os;* from *5384* and *2316; fond of God,* i.e. *pious:*—lover of God.

5378. Φιλόλογος **Philŏlŏgŏs,** *fil-ol´-og-os;* from *5384* and *3056; fond of words,* i.e. *talkative* (*argumentative, learned, "philological"*); *Philologus,* a Chr.:—Philologus.

5379. φιλονεικία **philŏnĕikia,** *fil-on-i-kee´-ah;* from *5380; quarrelsomeness,* i.e. a *dispute:*—strife.

5380. φιλόνεικος **philŏnĕikŏs,** *fil-on´-i-kos;* from *5384* and νεῖκος **nĕikŏs** (a *quarrel;* prob. akin to *3534*); *fond of strife,* i.e. *disputatious:*—contentious.

5381. φιλονεξία **philŏnĕxia,** *fil-on-ex-ee´-ah;* from *5382; hospitableness:*—entertain strangers, hospitality.

5382. φιλόξενος **philŏxĕnŏs,** *fil-ox´-en-os;* from *5384* and *3581; fond of guests,* i.e. *hospitable:*—given to (lover of, use) hospitality.

5383. φιλοπρωτεύω **philŏprōtĕuō,** *fil-op-rote-yoo´-o;* from a comp. of *5384* and *4413;* to *be fond of being first,* i.e. *ambitious* of distinction:—love to have the preeminence.

5384. φίλος **philŏs,** *fee´-los;* prop. *dear,* i.e. a *friend;* act. *fond,* i.e. *friendly* (still as a noun, an *associate, neighbor,* etc.):—friend.

5385. φιλοσοφία **philŏsŏphia,** *fil-os-of-ee´-ah;* from *5386; "philosophy",* i.e. (spec.) Jewish *sophistry:*—philosophy.

5386. φιλόσοφος **philŏsŏphŏs,** *fil-os´-of-os;* from *5384* and *4680; fond of wise* things, i.e. a *"philosopher":*—philosopher.

5387. φιλόστοργος **philŏstŏrgŏs,** *fil-os´-tor-gos;* from *5384* and στοργή **stŏrgē** (*cherishing* one's kindred, espec. parents or children); *fond of* natural *relatives,* i.e. *fraternal* towards fellow Chr.:—kindly affectioned.

5388. φιλότεκνος **philŏtĕknŏs,** *fil-ot´-ek-nos;* from *5384* and *5043; fond of* one's *children,* i.e. *maternal:*—love their children.

5389. φιλοτιμέομαι **philŏtimĕŏmai,** *fil-ot-im-eh´-om-ahee;* mid. from a comp. of *5384* and *5092;* to be *fond of honor,* i.e. *emulous* (*eager* or *earnest* to do something):—labour, strive, study.

5390. φιλοφρόνως **philŏphrŏnōs,** *fil-of-ron´-oce;* adv. from *5391; with friendliness of mind,* i.e. *kindly:*—courteously.

5391. φιλόφρων **philŏphrōn,** *fil-of´-rone;* from *5384* and *5424; friendly of mind,* i.e. *kind:*—courteous.

5392. φιμόω **phimŏō,** *fee-mŏ´-o;* from φιμός **phimŏs** (a *muzzle*); to *muzzle:*—muzzle.

5393. Φλέγων **Phlĕgōn,** *fleg´-one;* act. part. of the base of *5395; blazing; Phlegon,* a Chr.:—Phlegon.

5394. φλογίζω **phlŏgizō,** *flog-id´-zo;* from *5395;* to *cause a blaze,* i.e. *ignite* (fig. to *inflame* with passion):—set on fire.

5395. φλόξ **phlŏx,** *flox;* from a prim. φλέγω **phlĕgō** (to *"flash"* or *"flame"*); a *blaze:*—flame (-ing).

5396. φλυαρέω **phluarĕō,** *floo-ar-eh´-o;* from *5397;* to *be a babbler* or *trifler,* i.e. (by impl.) to *berate* idly or mischievously:—prate against.

5397. φλύαρος **phluarŏs,** *floo´-ar-os;* from φλύω **phluō** (to *bubble*); a *garrulous* person, i.e. *prater:*—tattler.

5398. φοβερός **phŏbĕrŏs,** *fob-er-os´;* from *5401; frightful,* i.e. (obj.) *formidable:*—fearful, terrible.

5399. φοβέω **phŏbĕō,** *fob-eh´-o;* from *5401;* to *frighten,* i.e. (pass.) to *be alarmed;* by anal. to *be in awe* of, i.e. *revere:*—be (+ sore) afraid, fear (exceedingly), reverence.

5400. φόβητρον **phŏbētrŏn,** *fob´-ay-tron;* neut. of a der. of *5399;* a *frightening* thing, i.e. *terrific* portent:—fearful sight.

5401. φόβος **phŏbŏs,** *fob´-os;* from a prim. φέβομαι **phĕbŏmai** (to *be* put in *fear*); *alarm* or *fright:*—be afraid, + exceedingly, fear, terror.

5402. Φοίβη **Phŏibē,** *foy´-bay;* fem. of φοῖβος **phŏibŏs** (*bright;* prob. akin to the base of *5457*); *Phœbe,* a Chr. woman:—Phebe.

5403. Φοινίκη **Phŏinikē,** *foy-nee´-kay;* from *5404; palm-*country; *Phœnice* (or *Phœnicia*), a region of Pal.:—Phenice, Phenicia.

5404. φοῖνιξ **phŏinix,** *foy´-nix;* of uncert. der.; a *palm-*tree:—palm (tree).

5405. Φοῖνιξ **Phŏinix,** *foy´-nix;* prob. the same as *5404; Phœnix,* a place in Crete:—Phenice.

5406. φονεύς **phŏnĕus,** *fon-yooce´;* from *5408;* a *murderer* (always of *criminal* [or at least *intentional*] homicide; which *443* does not necessarily imply; while *4607* is a spec. term for a *public* bandit):—murderer.

5407. φονεύω **phŏnĕuō,** *fon-yoo´-o;* from *5406;* to *be a murderer* (of):—kill, do murder, slay.

5408. φόνος **phŏnŏs,** *fon´-os;* from an obsol. prim. φένω **phĕnō** (to *slay*); *murder:*—murder, + be slain with, slaughter.

5409. φορέω **phŏrĕō,** *for-eh´-o;* from *5411;* to *have a burden,* i.e. (by anal.) to *wear* as clothing or a constant accompaniment:—bear, wear.

5410. Φόρον **Phŏrŏn,** *for´-on;* of Lat. or.; a *forum* or market-place; only in comp. with *675;* a *station* on the Appian road:—forum.

5411. φόρος **phŏrŏs,** *for´-os;* from *5342; a load* (as *borne*), i.e. (fig.) a *tax* (prop. an individ. *assessment* on persons or property; whereas *5056* is usually a gen. *toll* on goods or travel):—tribute.

5412. φορτίζω **phŏrtizō,** *for-tid´-zo;* from *5414;* to *load* up (prop. as a vessel or animal), i.e. (fig.) to *overburden* with ceremony (or spiritual anxiety):—lade, be heavy laden.

5413. φορτίον **phŏrtiŏn,** *for-tee´-on;* dimin. of *5414;* an *invoice* (as part of *freight*), i.e. (fig.) a *task* or *service:*—burden.

5414. φόρτος **phŏrtŏs,** *for´-tos;* from *5342;* something *carried,* i.e. the *cargo* of a ship:—lading.

5415. Φορτουνάτος **Phŏrtŏunatŏs,** *for-too-nat´-os;* of Lat. or.; *"fortunate"; Fortunatus,* a Chr.:—Fortunatus.

5416. φραγέλλιον **phragĕlliŏn,** *frag-el´-le-on;* neut. of a der. from the base of *5417;* a *whip,* i.e. Rom. *lash* as a public punishment:—scourge.

5417. φραγελλόω **phragĕllŏō,** *frag-el-lŏ´-o;* from a presumed equiv. of the Lat. *flagellum;* to *whip,* i.e. *lash* as a public punishment:—scourge.

5418. φραγμός **phragmŏs,** *frag-mos´;* from *5420;* a *fence,* or inclosing *barrier* (lit. or fig.):—hedge (+ round about), partition.

5419. φράζω **phrazō,** *frad´-zo;* prob. akin to *5420* through the idea of *defining;* to *indicate* (by word or act), i.e. (spec.) to *expound:*—declare.

5420. φράσσω **phrassō,** *fras´-so;* appar. a strength. form of the base of *5424;* to *fence* or inclose, i.e. (spec.) to *block* up (fig. to *silence*):—stop.

5421. φρέαρ **phrĕar,** *freh´-ar;* of uncert. der.; a *hole* in the ground (dug for obtaining or holding water or other purposes), i.e. a *cistern* or *well;* fig. an *abyss* (as a *prison*):—well, pit.

5422. φρεναπατάω **phrĕnapataō,** *fren-ap-at-ah´-o;* from *5423;* to *be a mind-misleader,* i.e. *delude:*—deceive.

5423. φρεναπάτης **phrĕnapatēs,** *fren-ap-at´-ace;* from *5424* and *539;* a *mind-misleader,* i.e. *seducer:*—deceiver.

5424. φρήν **phrēn,** *frane;* prob. from an obsol. φράω **phraō** (to *rein* in or *curb;* comp. *5420*); the *midrif* (as a *partition* of the body), i.e. (fig. and by impl. of sympathy) the *feelings* (or sensitive nature; by extens. [also in the plur.] the *mind* or cognitive faculties):—understanding.

5425. φρίσσω **phrissō,** *fris´-so;* appar. a prim. verb; to *"bristle"* or *chill,* i.e. *shudder* (*fear*):—tremble.

5426. φρονέω **phrŏnĕō,** *fron-eh´-o;* from *5424;* to *exercise* the *mind,* i.e. *entertain* or *have* a *sentiment* or *opinion;* by impl. to *be* (mentally) *disposed* (more or less earnestly in a certain direction); intens. to *interest oneself* in (with concern or obedience):—set the affection on, (be) care (-ful), (be like-, + be of one, + be of the same, + let this) mind (-ed, regard, savour, think.

5427. φρόνημα **phrŏnēma,** *fron´-ay-mah;* from *5426;* (mental) *inclination* or *purpose:*—(be, + be carnally, + be spiritually) mind (-ed).

5428. φρόνησις **phrŏnēsis,** *fron´-ay-sis;* from *5426;* mental *action* or *activity,* i.e. intellectual or mor. *insight:*—prudence, wisdom.

5429. φρόνιμος **phrŏnimŏs,** *fron´-ee-mos;* from *5424; thoughtful,* i.e. *sagacious* or *discreet* (implying a *cautious* character; while *4680* denotes *practical* skill or acumen; and *4908* indicates rather *intelligence* or mental acquirement); in a bad sense *conceited* (also in the compar.):—wise (-r).

5430. φρονίμως **phrŏnimōs,** *fron-im´-oce;* adv. from *5429; prudently:*—wisely.

5431. φροντίζω **phrŏntizō,** *fron-tid´-zo;* from a der. of *5424;* to *exercise thought,* i.e. *be anxious:*—be careful.

5432. φρουρέω **phrŏurĕō,** *froo-reh´-o;* from a comp. of *4253* and *3708;* to *be a watcher in advance,* i.e. to *mount guard* as a sentinel (*post spies* at gates); fig. to *hem in, protect:*—keep (with a garrison). Comp. *5083.*

5433. φρυάσσω **phruassō,** *froo-as´-so;* akin to *1032, 1031;* to *snort* (as a spirited horse), i.e. (fig.) to *make a tumult:*—rage.

5434. φρύγανον **phruganŏn,** *froo´-gan-on;* neut. of a presumed der. of φρύγω **phrugō** (to *roast* or *parch;* akin to the base of *5395*); something *desiccated,* i.e. a dry *twig:*—stick.

5435. Φρυγία **Phrugia,** *froog-ee´-ah;* prob. of for. or; *Phrygia,* a region of Asia Minor:—Phrygia.

5436. Φύγελλος **Phugĕllŏs,** *foog´-el-los;* prob. from *5343; figitive; Phygellus,* an apostate Chr.:—Phygellus.

5437. φυγή **phugē,** *foog-ay´;* from *5343;* a *fleeing,* i.e. *escape:*—flight.

5438. φυλακή **phulakē,** *foo-lak-ay´;* from *5442;* a *guarding* or (concr. *guard*), the act, the person; fig. the place, the condition, or (spec.) the time (as a division of day or night), lit. or fig.:—cage, hold, (im-) prison (-ment), ward, watch.

5439. φυλακίζω **phulakizō,** *foo-lak-id´-zo;* from *5441;* to *incarcerate:*—imprison.

5440. φυλακτήριον **phulaktēriŏn,** *foo-lak-tay´-ree-on;* neut. of a der. of *5442;* a *guard-case,* i.e. *"phylactery"* for wearing slips of Scripture texts:—phylactery.

5441. φύλαξ **phulax,** *foo´-lax;* from *5442;* a *watcher* or *sentry:*—keeper.

5442. φυλάσσω **phulassō,** *foo-las´-so;* prob. from *5443* through the idea of *isolation;* to *watch,* i.e. *be on guard* (lit. or fig.); by impl. to *preserve, obey, avoid:*—beware, keep (self), observe, save. Comp. *5083.*

5443. φυλή **phulē,** *foo-lay´;* from *5453* (comp. *5444*); an *offshoot,* i.e. *race* or *clan:*—kindred, tribe.

5444. φύλλον **phullŏn,** *fool´-lon;* from the same as *5443;* a *sprout,* i.e. *leaf:*—leaf.

5445. φύραμα **phurama,** *foo´-ram-ah;* from a prol. from of φύρω **phurō** (to *mix* a liquid with a solid; perh. akin to *5453* through the idea of *swelling* in bulk), mean to *knead;* a *mass* of dough:—lump.

5446. φυσικός **phusikŏs,** *foo-see-kos´;* from *5449; "physical",* i.e. (by impl.) *instinctive:*—natural. Comp. *5591.*

5447. φυσικῶς **phusikōs,** *foo-see-koce´;* adv. from *5446; "physically",* i.e. (by impl.) *instinctively:*—naturally.

5448. φυσιόω **phusiŏō,** *foo-see-ŏ´-o;* from *5449* in the prim. sense of *blowing;* to *inflate,* i.e. (fig.) *make proud* (*haughty*):—puff up.

5449. φύσις **phusis,** *foo´-sis;* from *5453; growth* (by *germination* or *expansion*), i.e. (by impl.) natural *production* (lineal *descent*); by extens. a *genus* or *sort;* fig. native *disposition, constitution* or *usage:*—([man-]) kind, nature ([-al]).

5450. φυσίωσις **phusiōsis,** *foo-see´-o-sis;* from *5448; inflation,* i.e. (fig.) *haughtiness:*—swelling.

5451. φυτεία **phutĕia,** *foo-ti´-ah;* from *5452;* trans-*planting,* i.e. (concr.) a *shrub* or *vegetable:*—plant.

5452. φυτεύω **phutĕuō,** *foot-yoo´-o;* from a der. of *5453;* to *set out* in the earth, i.e. *implant;* fig. to *instil* doctrine:—plant.

5453. φύω **phuō,** *foo´-o;* a prim. verb; prob. orig. to *"puff"* or *blow,* i.e. to *swell* up; but only used in the impl. sense, to *germinate* or *grow* (*sprout, produce*), lit. or fig.:—spring (up).

5454. φωλεός **phōlĕŏs,** *fo-leh-os´;* of uncert. der.; a *burrow* or *lurking-place:*—hole.

5455. φωνέω **phōnĕō,** *fo-neh´-o;* from *5456;* to emit a *sound* (animal, human or instrumental); by impl. to *address* in words or by name, also in imitation:—call (for), crow, cry.

5456. φωνή **phōnē,** *fo-nay´;* prob. akin to *5316* through the idea of *disclosure;* a *tone* (articulate, bestial or artificial); by impl. an *address* (for any purpose), *saying* or *language:*—noise, sound, voice.

5457. φῶς **phōs,** *foce;* from an obsol. φάω **phaō** (to *shine* or make *manifest,* espec. by *rays;* comp. *5316, 5346*); *luminousness* (in the widest application, nat. or artificial, abstr. or concr., lit. or fig.):—fire, light.

5458. φωστήρ **phōstēr,** *foce-tare´;* from *5457;* an *illuminator,* i.e. (concr.) a *luminary,* or (abstr.) *brilliancy:*—light.

5459. φωσφόρος **phōsphŏrŏs,** *foce-for´-os;* from *5457* and *5342; light-bearing* ("phosphorus"), i.e. (spec.) the *morning-star* (fig.):—day star.

5460. φωτεινός **phōtĕinŏs,** *fo-ti-nos´;* from *5457; lustrous,* i.e. *transparent* or *well-illuminated* (fig.):—bright, full of light.

5461. φωτίζω **phōtizō,** *fo-tid´-zo;* from *5457;* to *shed rays,* i.e. to *shine* or (trans.) to *brighten* up (lit. or fig.):—enlighten, illuminate, (bring to, give) light, make to see.

5462. φωτισμός **phōtismŏs,** *fo-tis-mos´;* from *5461; illumination* (fig.):—light.

X

5463. χαίρω **chairō,** *khah´ee-ro;* a prim. verb; to be *"cheer"ful,* i.e. calmly *happy* or well-off; impers. espec. as salutation (on meeting or parting), *be well:*—farewell, be glad, God speed, greeting, hail, joy (-fully), rejoice.

5464. χάλαζα **chalaza,** *khal´-ad-zah;* prob. from *5465; hail:*—hail.

5465. χαλάω **chalaō,** *khal-ah´-o;* from the base of *5490;* to *lower* (as into a *void*):—let down, strike.

5466. Χαλδαῖος **Chaldaiŏs,** *khal-dah´-yos;* prob. of Heb. or. [3778]; a *Chaldæan* (i.e. *Kasdi*), or native of the region of the lower Euphrates:—Chaldæan.

5467. χαλεπός **chalĕpŏs,** *khal-ep-os´;* perh. from *5465* through the idea of *reducing* the strength; *difficult,* i.e. *dangerous,* or (by impl.) *furious:*—fierce, perilous.

5468. χαλιναγωγέω **chalinagōgĕō,** *khal-in-ag-ogue-eh´-o;* from a comp. of *5469* and the redupl. form of *71;* to *be a bit-leader,* i.e. to *curb* (fig.):—bridle.

5469. χαλινός **chalinŏs,** *khal-ee-nos´;* from *5465;* a *curb* or *head-stall* (as *curbing* the spirit):—bit, bridle.

5470. χάλκεος **chalkĕŏs,** *klal´-keh-os;* from *5475; coppery:*—brass.

5471. χαλκεύς **chalkĕus,** *khalk-yooce´;* from *5475;* a *copper-worker* or *brazier:*—coppersmith.

5472. χαλκηδών **chalkēdōn,** *khal-kay-dōhn´;* from *5475* and perh. *1491; copper-like,* i.e. *"chalcedony":*—chalcedony.

5473. χαλκίον **chalkiŏn,** *khal-kee´-on;* dimin. from *5475;* a *copper dish:*—brazen vessel.

5474. χαλκολίβανον **chalkŏlibanŏn,** *khal-kol-ib´-an-on;* neut. of a comp. of *5475* and *3030* (in the impl. mean. of *whiteness* or *brilliancy*); *burnished copper,* an alloy of copper (or gold) and silver having a brilliant lustre:—fine brass.

5475. χαλκός **chalkŏs,** *khal-kos´;* perh. from *5465* through the idea of *hollowing* out as a vessel (this metal being chiefly used for that purpose); *copper* (the substance, or some implement or coin made of it):—brass, money.

5476. χαμαί **chamai,** *kham-ah´-ee;* adv. perh. from the base of *5490* through the idea of a *fissure* in the soil; *earthward,* i.e. *prostrate:*—on (to) the ground.

5477. Χαναάν **Chanaan,** *khan-ah-an´;* of Heb. or. [3667]; *Chanaan* (i.e. *Kenaan*), the early name of Pal.:—Chanaan.

5478. Χαναναῖος **Chanaanaiŏs,** *khan-ah-an-ah´-yos;* from *5477;* a *Chanaanœan* (i.e. *Kenaanite*), or native of gentile Pal.:—of Canaan.

5479. χαρά **chara,** *khar-ah´;* from *5463; cheerfulness,* i.e. calm *delight:*—gladness, × greatly, (× be exceeding) joy (-ful, -fully, -fulness, -ous).

5480. χάραγμα **charagma,** *khar´-ag-mah;* from the same as *5482;* a *scratch* or *etching,* i.e. *stamp* (as a *badge* of servitude), or *sculptured* figure (*statue*):—graven, mark.

5481. χαρακτήρ **charaktēr,** *khar-ak-tare´;* from the same as *5482;* a *graver* (the tool or the person), i.e. (by impl.) *engraving* ([*"character"*], the *figure* stamped, i.e. an exact *copy* or [fig.] *representation*):—express image.

5482. χάραξ **charax,** *khar´-ax;* from χαράσσω **charassō** (to *sharpen* to a point; akin to *1125* through the idea of *scratching*); a *stake,* i.e. (by impl.) a *palisade* or *rampart* (military *mound* for circumvallation in a siege):—trench.

5483. χαρίζομαι **charizŏmai,** *khar-id´-zom-ahee;* mid. from *5485;* to grant as a *favor,* i.e. gratuitously, in kindness, pardon or rescue:—deliver, (frankly) forgive, (freely) give, grant.

5484. χάριν **charin,** *khar´-in;* acc. of *5485* as prep.; through *favor* of, i.e. *on account* of:—be-(for) cause of, for sake of, + . . . fore, × reproachfully.

5485. χάρις **charis,** *khar´-ece;* from *5463; graciousness* (as *gratifying*), of manner or act (abstr. or concr.; lit., fig. or spiritual; espec. the divine influence upon the heart, and its reflection in the life; including *gratitude*):—acceptable, benefit, favour, gift, grace (-ious), joy liberality, pleasure, thank (-s, -worthy).

5486. χάρισμα **charisma,** *khar´-is-mah;* from *5483;* a (divine) *gratuity,* i.e. *deliverance* (from danger or passion); (spec.) a (spiritual) *endowment,* i.e. (subj.) religious *qualification,* or (obj.) miraculous *faculty:*—(free) gift.

5487. χαριτόω **charitŏō,** *khar-ee-tŏ´-o;* from *5485;* to *grace,* i.e. indue with special *honor:*—make accepted, be highly favoured.

5488. Χαῤῥάν **Charrhan,** *khar-hran´;* of Heb. or. [2771]; *Charrhan* (i.e. *Charan*), a place in Mesopotamia:—Charran.

5489. χάρτης **chartēs,** *khar´-tace;* from the same as *5482;* a *sheet* ("chart") of writing-material (as to be *scribbled* over):—paper.

5490. χάσμα **chasma,** *khas´-mah;* from a form of an obsol. prim. χάω **chaō** (to *"gape"* or *"yawn"*); a *"chasm"* or *vacancy* (impassable *interval*):—gulf.

5491. χεῖλος **chĕilŏs,** *khi´-los;* from a form of the same as *5490;* a *lip* (as a *pouring* place); fig. a *margin* (of water):—lip, shore.

5492. χειμάζω **chĕimazō,** *khi-mad´-zo;* from the same as *5494;* to *storm,* i.e. (pass) to *labor under a gale:*—to tossed with tempest.

5493. χείμαῤῥος **chĕimarrhŏs,** *khi´-mar-hros;* from the base of *5494* and *4482;* a *storm-runlet,* i.e. *winter-torrent:*—brook.

5494. χειμών **chĕimōn,** *khi-mone´;* from a der. of χέω **chĕō** (to *pour;* akin to the base of *5490* through the idea of a *channel*), mean. a *storm* (as *pouring* rain); by impl. the *rainy* season, i.e. *winter:*—tempest, foul weather, winter.

5495. χείρ **chĕir,** *khire;* perh. from the base of *5494* in the sense of its congener the base of *5490* (through the idea of *hollowness* for grasping); the *hand* (lit. or fig. [*power*]; espec. [by Heb.] a *means* or *instrument*):—hand.

5496. χειραγωγέω **chĕiragōgĕō,** *khi-rag-ogue-eh´-o;* from *5497;* to be a *hand-leader,* i.e. to *guide* (a blind person):—lead by the hand.

5497. χειραγωγός **chĕiragōgŏs,** *khi-rag-o-gos´;* from *5495* and a redupl. form of *71;* a *hand-leader,* i.e. personal *conductor* (of a blind person):—some to lead by the hand.

5498. χειρόγραφον **chĕirŏgraphŏn,** *khi-rog´-raf-on;* neut. of a comp. of *5495* and *1125;* something *hand-written* ("*chirograph*"), i.e. a *manuscript* (spec. a legal *document* or *bond* [fig.]):—handwriting.

5499. χειροποίητος **chĕirŏpŏiētŏs,** *khi-rop-oy´-ay-tos;* from *5495* and a der. of *4160; manufactured,* i.e. *of human construction:*—made by (make with)— hands.

5500. χειροτονέω **chĕirŏtŏnĕō,** *khi-rot-on-eh´-o;* from a comp. of *5495* and τείνω **tĕinō** (to *stretch*); to be a *hand-reacher* or *voter* (by raising the hand), i.e. (gen.) to *select* or *appoint:*—choose, ordain.

5501. χείρων **chĕirōn,** *khi´-rone;* irreg. comp. of *2556;* from an obsol. equiv. χέρης **chĕrēs** (of uncert. der.); *more evil* or *aggravated* (phys., ment. or mor.):—sorer, worse.

5502. χερουβίμ **chĕrŏubim,** *kher-oo-beem´;* plur. of Heb. or. [3742]; "*cherubim*" (i.e. *cherubs* or *kerubim*):—cherubims.

5503. χήρα **chēra,** *khay-rah;* fem. of a presumed der. appar. from the base of *5490* through the idea of *deficiency;* a *widow* (as *lacking* a husband), lit. or fig.:—widow.

5504. χθές **chthĕs,** *khthes;* of uncert. der.; "*yesterday*"; by extens. *in time past* or *hitherto:*—yesterday.

5505. χιλιάς **chilias,** *khil-ee-as´;* from *5507;* one *thousand* ("*chiliad*"):—thousand.

5506. χιλίαρχος **chiliarchŏs,** *khil-ee´-ar-khos;* from *5507* and *757;* the *commander of a thousand* soldiers ("*chiliarch*"), i.e. *colonel:*—(chief, high) captain.

5507. χίλιοι **chiliŏi,** *khil´-ee-oy;* plur. of uncert. affin.; a *thousand:*—thousand.

5508. Χίος **Chiŏs,** *khee´-os;* of uncert. der.; *Chios,* an island in the Mediterranean:—Chios.

5509. χιτών **chitōn,** *khee-tone´;* of for. or. [3801]; a *tunic* or *shirt:*—clothes, coat, garment.

5510. χιών **chiōn,** *khee-one´;* perh. akin to the base of *5490* (*5465*) or *5494* (as *descending* or *empty*); *snow:*—snow.

5511. χλαμύς **chlamus,** *khlam-ooce´;* of uncert. der.; a military *cloak:*—robe.

5512. χλευάζω **chlĕuazō,** *khlyoo-ad´-zo;* from a der. prob. of *5491; to throw out* the *lip,* i.e. *jeer* at:—mock.

5513. χλιαρός **chliarŏs,** *khlee-ar-os´;* from χλίω **chliō** (to *warm*); *tepid:*—lukewarm.

5514. Χλόη **Chlŏē,** *khlŏ´-ay;* fem. of appar. a prim. word; "*green*"; *Chloë,* a Chr. female:—Chloe.

5515. χλωρός **chlōrŏs,** *khlo-ros´;* from the same as *5514; greenish;* i.e. *verdant, dun-colored:*—green, pale.

5516. χξς **chi xi stigma,** *khee xee stig´-ma;* the 22d, 14th and an obsol. letter (*4742* as a *cross*) of the Greek alphabet (intermediate between the 5th and 6th), used as numbers; denoting respectively 600, 60 and 6; 666 as a numeral:—six hundred threescore and six.

5517. χοϊκός **chŏïkŏs,** *khŏ-ik-os´;* from *5522; dust* or *dirty* (*soil*-like), i.e. (by impl.) *terrene:*—earthy.

5518. χοῖνιξ **chŏinix,** *khoy´-nix;* of uncert. der.; a *chœnix* or cert. dry measure:—measure.

5519. χοῖρος **chŏirŏs,** *khoy´-ros;* of uncert. der.; a *hog:*—swine.

5520. χολάω **chŏlaō,** *khol-ah´-o;* from *5521;* to *be bilious,* i.e. (by impl.) *irritable* (*enraged,* "choleric"):—be angry.

5521. χολή **chŏlē,** *khol-ay´;* fem. of an equiv. perh. akin to the same as *5514* (from the *greenish* hue); "*gall*" or *bile,* i.e. (by anal.) *poison* or an *anodyne* (wormwood, poppy, etc.):—gall.

5522. χόος **chŏŏs,** *khŏ´-os;* from the base of *5494;* a *heap* (as *poured* out), i.e. *rubbish;* loose *dirt:*—dust.

5523. Χοραζίν **Chŏrazin,** *khor-ad-zin´;* of uncert. der.; *Chorazin,* a place in Pal.:—Chorazin.

5524. χορηγέω **chŏrēgĕō,** *khor-ayg-eh´-o;* from a comp. of *5525* and *71;* to be a *dance-leader,* i.e. (gen.) to *furnish:*—give, minister.

5525. χορός **chŏrŏs,** *khor-os´;* of uncert. der.; a *ring,* i.e. round *dance* ("choir"):—dancing.

5526. χορτάζω **chŏrtazō,** *khor-tad´-zo;* from *5528;* to *fodder,* i.e. (gen.) to *gorge* (*supply food* in abundance):—feed, fill, satisfy.

5527. χόρτασμα **chŏrtasma,** *khor´-tas-mah;* from *5526; forage,* i.e. *food:*—sustenance.

5528. χόρτος **chŏrtŏs,** *khor´-tos;* appar. a prim. word; a "*court*" or "*garden*", i.e. (by impl. of *pasture*) *herbage* or *vegetation:*—blade, grass, hay.

5529. Χουζᾶς **Chŏuzas,** *khood-zas´;* of uncert. or.; *Chuzas,* an officer of Herod:—Chuza.

5530. χράομαι **chraŏmai,** *khrah´-om-ahee;* mid. of a prim. verb (perh. rather from *5495,* to *handle*); to *furnish* what is needed; (give an *oracle,* "*graze*" [touch slightly], *light* upon, etc.), i.e. (by impl.) to *employ* or (by extens.) to *act towards* one in a given manner:—entreat, use. Comp. *5531, 5534.*

5531. χράω **chraō,** *khrah´-o;* prob. the same as the base of *5530;* to *loan:*—lend.

5532. χρεία **chrĕia,** *khri´-ah;* from the base of *5530* or *5534; employment,* i.e. an *affair;* also (by impl.) *occasion, demand, requirement* or *destitution:*—business, lack, necessary (-ity), need (-ful), use, want.

5533. χρεωφειλέτης **chrĕōphĕilĕtēs,** *khreh-o-fi-let´-ace;* from a der. of *5531* and *3781;* a *loan-ower,* i.e. *indebted* person:—debtor.

5534. χρή **chrē,** *khray;* third pers. sing. of the same as *5530* or *5531* used impers.; it *needs* (*must* or *should*) be:—ought.

5535. χρῄζω **chrēizō,** *khrade´-zo;* from *5532;* to *make* (i.e. *have*) *necessity,* i.e. *be in want* of:—(have) need.

5536. χρῆμα **chrēma,** *khray´-mah;* something *useful* or *needed,* i.e. *wealth, price:*—money, riches.

5537. χρηματίζω **chrēmatizō,** *khray-mat-id´-zo;* from *5536;* to *utter an oracle* (comp. the orig. sense of *5530*), i.e. divinely *intimate;* by impl. (comp. the secular sense of *5532*) to constitute a *firm* for business, i.e. (gen.) *bear* as a *title:*—be called, be admonished (warned) of God, reveal, speak.

5538. χρηματισμός **chrēmatismŏs,** *khray-mat-is-mos´;* from *5537;* a divine *response* or *revelation:*—answer of God.

5539. χρήσιμος **chrēsimŏs,** *khray´-see-mos;* from *5540; serviceable:*—profit.

5540. χρῆσις **chrēsis,** *khray´-sis;* from 5530; *employment,* i.e. (spec.) sexual *intercourse* (as an *occupation* of the body):—use.

5541. χρηστεύομαι **chrēstĕuŏmai,** *khraste-yoo´-om-ahee;* mid. from *5543;* to *show oneself useful,* i.e. *act benevolently:*—be kind.

5542. χρηστολογία **chrēstŏlŏgia,** *khrase-tol-og-ee´-ah;* from a comp. of *5543* and *3004; fair speech,* i.e. *plausibility:*—good words.

5543. χρηστός **chrēstŏs,** *khrase-tos´;* from *5530; employed,* i.e. (by impl.) *useful* (in manner or morals):—better, easy, good (-ness), gracious, kind.

5544. χρηστότης **chrēstŏtēs,** *khray-stot´-ace;* from *5543; usefulness,* i.e. mor. *excellence* (in character or demeanor):—gentleness, good (-ness), kindness.

5545. χρίσμα **chrisma,** *khris´-mah;* from *5548;* an *unguent* or *smearing,* i.e. (fig.) the spec. *endowment* ("chrism") of the Holy Spirit:—anointing, unction.

5546. Χριστιανός **Christianŏs,** *khris-tee-an-os´;* from *5547;* a *Christian,* i.e. follower of Christ:—Christian.

5547. Χριστός **Christŏs,** *khris-tos´;* from *5548; anointed,* i.e. the *Messiah,* an epithet of Jesus:—Christ.

5548. χρίω **chriō,** *khree´-o;* prob. akin to *5530* through the idea of *contact;* to *smear* or *rub* with oil, i.e. (by impl.) to *consecrate* to an office or religious service:—anoint.

5549. χρονίζω **chrŏnizō,** *khron-id´-zo;* from *5550;* to *take time,* i.e. *linger:*—delay, tarry.

5550. χρόνος **chrŏnŏs,** *khron´-os;* of uncert. der.; a space of *time* (in gen., and thus prop. distinguished from *2540,* which designates a *fixed* or special occasion; and from *165,* which denotes a particular *period*) or *interval;* by extens. an individ. *opportunity;* by impl. *delay:*— + years old, season, space, (× often-) time (-s), (a) while.

5551. χρονοτριβέω **chrŏnŏtribĕō,** *khron-ot-rib-eh´-o;* from a presumed comp. of *5550* and the base of *5147;* to be a *time-wearer,* i.e. to *procrastinate* (*linger*):—spend time.

5552. χρύσεος **chrusĕŏs,** *khroo´-seh-os;* from *5557;* made *of gold:*—of gold, golden.

5553. χρυσίον **chrusiŏn,** *khroo-see´-on;* dimin. of *5557;* a *golden* article, i.e. gold plating, ornament, or coin:—gold.

5554. χρυσοδακτύλιος **chrusŏdaktuliŏs,** *khroo-sod-ak-too´-lee-os;* from *5557* and *1146; gold-ringed,* i.e. *wearing* a golden finger-ring or similar *jewelry:*—with a gold ring.

5555. χρυσόλιθος **chrusŏlithŏs,** *khroo-sol´-ee-thos;* from *5557* and *3037; gold-stone,* i.e. a *yellow gem* (*"chrysolite"*):—chrysolite.

5556. χρυσόπρασος **chrusŏprasŏs,** *khroo-sop´-ras-os;* from *5557* and πράσον **prasŏn** (a *leek*); a *greenish-yellow* gem (*"chrysoprase"*):—chrysoprase.

5557. χρυσός **chrusŏs,** *khroo-sos´;* perh. from the base of *5530 (through the idea of the utility* of the metal); *gold;* by extens. a *golden* article, as an ornament or coin:—gold.

5558. χρυσόω **chrusŏō,** *khroo-sŏ´-o;* from *5557;* to *gild,* i.e. *bespangle* with golden ornaments:—deck.

5559. χρώς **chrōs,** *khroce;* prob. akin to the base of *5530* through the idea of *handling;* the *body* (prop. its *surface* or *skin*):—body.

5560. χωλός **chōlŏs,** *kho-los´;* appar. a prim. word; *"halt",* i.e. *limping:*—cripple, halt, lame.

5561. χώρα **chōra,** *kho´-rah;* fem. of a der. of the base of *5490* through the idea of *empty* expanse; *room,* i.e. a space of *territory* (more or less extensive; often includ. its inhab.):—coast, county, fields, grounds, land, region. Comp. *5117.*

5562. χωρέω **chōrĕō,** *kho-reh´-o;* from *5561;* to *be* in (*give*) *space,* i.e. (intrans.) to *pass, enter,* or (trans.) to *hold, admit* (lit. or fig.):—come, contain, go, have, place, (can, be room to) receive.

5563. χωρίζω **chōrizō,** *kho-rid´-zo;* from *5561;* to *place room* between, i.e. *part;* reflex. to *go away:*—depart, put asunder, separate.

5564. χωρίον **chōriŏn,** *kho-ree´-on;* dimin. of *5561;* a *spot* or *plot* of ground:—field, land, parcel of ground, place, possession.

5565. χωρίς **chōris,** *kho-rece´;* adv. from *5561; at* a *space,* i.e. *separately* or *apart* from (often as prep.):—beside, by itself, without.

5566. χῶρος **chōrŏs,** *kho´-ros;* of Lat. or.; the *north-west* wind:—north west.

Ψ

5567. ψάλλω **psallō,** *psal´-lo;* prob. strengthened from ψάω **psaō** (to *rub* or *touch* the surface; comp. *5597*); to *twitch* or *twang,* i.e. to *play* on a stringed instrument (*celebrate* the divine worship *with music* and accompanying odes):—make melody, sing (psalms).

5568. ψαλμός **psalmŏs,** *psal-mos´;* from *5567;* a set piece of *music,* i.e. a sacred *ode* (accompanied with the voice, harp or other instrument; a *"psalm"*); collect. the book of the *Psalms:*—psalm. Comp. *5603.*

5569. ψευδάδελφος **psĕudadĕlphŏs,** *psyoo-dad´-el-fos;* from *5571* and *80;* a *spurious brother,* i.e. *pretended associate:*—false brethren.

5570. ψευδαπόστολος **psĕudapŏstŏlŏs,** *psyoo-dap-os´-tol-os;* from *5571* and *652;* a *spurious apostle,* i.e. *pretended preacher:*—false teacher.

5571. ψευδής **psĕudēs,** *psyoo-dace´;* from *5574; untrue,* i.e. *erroneous, deceitful, wicked:*—false, liar.

5572. ψευδοδιδάσκαλος **psĕudŏdidaskalŏs,** *psyoo-dod-id-as´-kal-os;* from *5571* and *1320;* a *spurious teacher,* i.e. *propagator* of *erroneous* Chr. *doctrine:*—false teacher.

5573. ψευδολόγος **psĕudŏlŏgŏs,** *psyoo-dol-og´-os;* from *5571* and *3004; mendacious,* i.e. *promulgating erroneous* Chr. *doctrine:*—speaking lies.

5574. ψεύδομαι **psĕudŏmai,** *psyoo´-dom-ahee;* mid. of an appar. prim. verb; to *utter an untruth* or attempt to *deceive* by falsehood:—falsely, lie.

5575. ψευδομάρτυρ **psĕudŏmartur,** *psyoo-dom-ar´-toor;* from *5571* and a kindred form of *3144;* a *spurious witness,* i.e. *bearer of untrue testimony:*—false witness.

5576. ψευδομαρτυρέω **psĕudŏmarturĕō,** *psyoo-dom-ar-too-reh´-o;* from *5575;* to *be an untrue testifier,* i.e. offer *falsehood in evidence:*—be a false witness.

5577. ψευδομαρτυρία **psĕudŏmarturia,** *psyoo-dom-ar-too-ree´-ah;* from *5575; untrue testimony:*—false witness.

5578. ψευδοπροφήτης **psĕudŏprŏphētēs,** *psyoo-dop-rof-ay´-tace;* from *5571* and *4396;* a *spurious prophet,* i.e. *pretended foreteller* or religious *impostor:*—false prophet.

5579. ψεῦδος **psĕudŏs,** *psyoo´-dos;* from *5574;* a *falsehood:*—lie, lying.

5580. ψευδόχριστος **psĕudŏchristŏs,** *psyoo-dokh´-ris-tos;* from *5571* and *5547;* a *spurious Messiah:*—false Christ.

5581. ψευδώνυμος **psĕudōnumŏs,** *psyoo-do´-noo-mos;* from *5571* and *3686; untruly named:*—falsely so called.

5582. ψεῦσμα **psĕusma,** *psyoos´-mah;* from *5574;* a *fabrication,* i.e. *falsehood:*—lie.

5583. ψεύστης **psĕustēs,** *psyoos-tace´;* from *5574;* a *falsifier:*—liar.

5584. ψηλαφάω **psēlaphaō,** *psay-laf-ah´-o;* from the base of *5567* (comp. *5586*); to *manipulate,* i.e. *verify* by contact; fig. to *search* for:—feel after, handle, touch.

5585. ψηφίζω **psēphizō,** *psay-fid´-zo;* from *5586;* to *use pebbles* in enumeration, i.e. (gen.) to *compute:*—count.

5586. ψῆφος **psēphŏs,** *psay´-fos;* from the same as *5584;* a *pebble* (as worn smooth by *handling*), i.e. (by impl. of use as a *counter* or *ballot*) a *verdict* (of acquittal) or *ticket* (of admission); a *vote:*—stone, voice.

5587. ψιθυρισμός **psithurismŏs,** *psith-oo-ris-mos´;* from a der. of ψίθος **psithŏs** (a *whisper;* by impl. a *slander;* prob. akin to *5574*); *whispering,* i.e. secret *detraction:*—whispering.

5588. ψιθυριστής **psithuristēs,** *psith-oo-ris-tace´;* from the same as *5587;* a secret *calumniator:*—whisperer.

5589. ψιχίον **psichiŏn,** *psikh-ee´-on;* dimin. from a der. of the base of *5567* (mean. a *crumb*); a *little bit* or *morsel:*—crumb.

5590. ψυχή **psuchē,** *psoo-khay´;* from *5594; breath,* i.e. (by impl.) *spirit,* abstr. or concr. (the *animal* sentient principle only; thus distinguished on the one hand from *4151,* which is the rational and immortal *soul;* and on the other from *2222,* which is mere *vitality,* even of plants: these terms thus exactly correspond respectively to the Heb. 5315, 7307 and 2416):—heart (+ -ily), life, mind, soul, + us, + you.

5591. ψυχικός **psuchikŏs,** *psoo-khee-kos´;* from *5590; sensitive,* i.e. *animate* (in distinction on the one hand from *4152,* which is the higher or *renovated* nature; and on the other from *5446,* which is the lower or *bestial* nature):—natural, sensual.

5592. ψύχος **psuchŏs,** *psoo´-khos;* from *5594; coolness:*—cold.

5593. ψυχρός **psuchrŏs,** *psoo-chros´;* from *5592; chilly* (lit. or fig.):—cold.

5594. ψύχω **psuchō,** *psoo´-kho;* a prim. verb; to *breathe* (*voluntarily* but *gently;* thus differing on the one hand from *4154,* which denotes prop. a *forcible* respiration; and on the other from the base of *109,* which refers prop. to an inanimate *breeze*), i.e. (by impl. of reduction of temperature by evaporation) to *chill* (fig.):—wax cold.

5595. ψωμίζω **psōmizō,** *pso-mid´-zo;* from the base of *5596;* to *supply* with *bits,* i.e. (gen.) to *nourish:*—(bestow to) feed.

5596. ψωμίον **psōmiŏn,** *pso-mee´-on;* dim. from a der. of the base of *5597;* a *crumb* or *morsel* (as if *rubbed* off), i.e. a *mouthful:*—sop.

5597. ψώχω **psōchō,** *pso´-kho;* prol. from the same base as *5567;* to *triturate,* i.e. (by anal.) to *rub* out (kernels from husks with the fingers or hand):—rub.

Ω

5598. Ω **ō,** i.e. ὦμεγα **ōmĕga,** *o´-meg-ah;* the last letter of the Gr. alphabet, i.e. (fig.) the *finality:*—Omega.

5599. ὦ **ō,** *o;* a prim. interj.; as a sign of the voc. *O;* as a note of exclamation, *oh:*—O.

5600. ὦ **ō,** *o;* includ. the oblique forms, as well as ᾗς **ēs,** *ace;* ᾗ **ē,** *ay,* etc.; the subjunctive of *1510;* (*may, might, can, could, would, should, must,* etc.; also with *1487* and its comp., as well as with other particles) *be:*—+ appear, are, (may, might, should) be, × have, is, + pass the flower of her age, should stand, were.

5601. Ὠβήδ **Obēd,** *o-bade´;* of Heb. or. [5744]; *Obed,* an Isr.:—Obed.

5602. ὧδε **hōdĕ,** *ho´-deh;* from an adv. form of *3592; in this* same spot, i.e. *here* or *hither:*—here, hither, (in) this place, there.

5603. ᾠδή **ōidē,** *o-day´;* from *103;* a *chant* or "*ode*" (the gen. term for any words sung; while *5215* denotes espec. a *religious* metrical composition, and *5568* still more spec. a *Heb.* cantillation):—song.

5604. ὠδίν **ōdin,** *o-deen´;* akin to *3601;* a *pang* or *throe,* esp. of childbirth:—pain, sorrow, travail.

5605. ὠδίνω **ōdinō,** *o-dee´-no;* from *5604;* to *experience* the *pains* of parturition (lit. or fig.):—travail in (birth).

5606. ὦμος **ōmŏs,** *o´-mos;* perh. from the alt. of *5342;* the *shoulder* (as that on which burdens are *borne*):—shoulder.

5607. ὤν **ōn,** *oan;* includ. the fem.
οὖσα **ŏusa,** *oo´-sah;* and the neut.
ὄν **ŏn,** *on;* pres. part. of *1510; being:*—be, come, have.

5608. ὠνέομαι **ōnĕŏmai,** *o-neh´-om-ahee;* mid. from an appar. prim. ὦνος **ōnŏs** (a *sum* or *price*); to *purchase* (synon. with the earlier *4092*):—buy.

5609. ὠόν **ōŏn,** *o-on´;* appar. a prim. word; an "*egg*":—egg.

5610. ὥρα **hōra,** *ho´-rah;* appar. a prim. word; an "*hour*" (lit. or fig.):—day, hour, instant, season, × short, [even-] tide, (high) time.

5611. ὡραῖος **hōraiŏs,** *ho-rah´-yos;* from *5610; belonging* to the right *hour* or *season* (*timely*), i.e. (by impl.) *flourishing* (*beauteous* [fig.]):—beautiful.

5612. ὠρύομαι **ōruŏmai,** *o-roo´-om-ahee;* mid. of an appar. prim. verb; to "*roar*":—roar.

5613. ὡς **hōs,** *hoce;* prob. adv. of comp. from *3739; which how,* i.e. *in that manner* (very variously used, as follows):—about, after (that), (according) as (it had been, it were), as soon (as), even as (like), for, how (greatly), like (as, unto), since, so (that), that, to wit, unto, when ([-soever]), while, × with all speed.

5614. ὡσαννά **hōsanna,** *ho-san-nah´;* of Heb. or. [3467 and 4994]; *oh save!; hosanna* (i.e. *hoshia-na*), an exclamation of adoration:—hosanna.

5615. ὡσαύτως **hōsautōs,** *ho-sŏw´-toce;* from *5613* and an adv. from *846; as thus,* i.e. *in the same way:*—even so, likewise, after the same (in like) manner.

5616. ὡσεί **hōsĕi,** *ho-si´;* from *5613 and 1487; as if:*—about, as (it had been, it were), like (as).

5617. Ὡσηέ **Hōsēĕ,** *ho-say-eh´;* of Heb. or. [1954]; *Hoseë,* (i.e. *Hosheä*), an Isr.:—Osee.

5618. ὥσπερ **hōspĕr,** *hoce´-per;* from *5613* and *4007; just as,* i.e. *exactly like:*—(even, like) as.

5619. ὡσπερεί **hōspĕrĕi,** *hoce-per-i´;* from *5618* and *1487; just as if,* i.e. *as it were:*—as.

5620. ὥστε **hōstĕ,** *hoce´-teh;* from *5613* and *5037; so too,* i.e. *thus therefore* (in various relations of *consecution,* as follow):—(insomuch) as, so that (then), (insomuch) that, therefore, to, wherefore.

5621. ὠτίον **ōtiŏn,** *o-tee´-on;* dimin. of *3775;* an *earlet,* i.e. *one* of the ears, or perh. the *lobe* of the ear:—ear.

5622. ὠφέλεια **ōphĕlĕia,** *o-fel´-i-ah;* from a der. of the base of *5624; usefulness,* i.e. *benefit:*—advantage, profit.

5623. ὠφελέω **ōphĕlĕō,** *o-fel-eh´-o;* from the same as *5622;* to *be useful,* i.e. to *benefit:*—advantage, better, prevail, profit.

5624. ὠφέλιμος **ōphĕlimŏs,** *o-fel´-ee-mos;* from a form of *3786; helpful* or *serviceable,* i.e. *advantageous:*—profit (-able).

VARIATIONS

IN THE NUMBERING OF VERSES IN THE GREEK AND ENGLISH NEW TESTAMENT

English	*Greek*
Mark 13: 8 (last clause)......(first clauses)	9
Luke 22:66 (last word).........(first word)	67
John 1:38 (all after first clause)..............	39
39	40
40	41
41	42
42	43

English	*Greek*
John 1:43	44
44	45
45	46
46	47
47	48
48	49
49	50

English	*Greek*
John 1:50	51
51	52
Acts 4: 6 (last clause)...................(in)	5
13:33 (former half).........(latter half)	32
1 Pet 2: 8 (first two clauses) (last two clauses)	7

Bible Study Helps

CHRONOLOGY OF BIBLICAL EVENTS

The accompanying table includes both precise dates—some quite certain and others less provable which may be a year or two off—and round numbers, indicated by italic type, which indicate general periods or approximations. To this italic class must belong most of the dates included for the biblical and other books.

CHRONOLOGICAL TABLE

Dates in italics represent periods rather than exact years. Names of persons mentioned in the Bible are printed in boldface type at their first appearance.

BC ***The Background of the Patriarchs***

8000 Stone Age inhabitants of Palestine leave evidences of village life and agriculture.

5500 Pottery invented.

4500 Use of metals begins with gold and copper.

3500 Sumerians settle in S Mesopotamia and develop complex civilization, including pictographic writing.

3300 Bronze is discovered as harder metal for tools and weapons.

3200 Sumerians adapt pictographs to cuneiform system of punching syllabic characters in clay tablets.

3000 Egyptians become united under first dynasty and develop advanced civilization. They adapt pictographs to hieroglyphic writing, invent papyrus.

2300 Sargon, a Semite, conquers Sumer and builds vast Akkadian Empire. His people learn Sumerian arts and culture.

2000 Ur-Nammu, Sumerian king of Ur, gains control of all Sumer and Akkad, issues earliest known code of laws.

1900 Abraham migrates to S Palestine. Sodom and Gomorrah destroyed.

1750 Hyksos invaders seize control of Palestine and Egypt. Hammurabi, Semitic ruler of first Babylonian Empire, issues elaborate law code. Kings of Mari preserve archive of cuneiform tablets which reveal customs like some in Genesis stories and mention Habiru (Hebrews?) and Benjaminites.

1650 Alphabet invented, probably by Canaanites.

1570 Ahmose I of Egypt expels Hyksos, destroying many Palestinian cities.

1468 Thutmose III of Egypt reconquers Palestine, establishes empire soon reaching the Euphrates.

1400 At Nuzi, Hurrians (Horites) leave cuneiform tablets revealing customs like some in Genesis stories and mentioning Habiru. At Ugarit (Ras Shamra) in N Syria, Canaanites leave tablets, especially of Baal myths, in a language much like Hebrew.

1360 Palestinian vassals ask Pharaoh Akhenaton, in cuneiform letters preserved at his capital, Akhetaton (Tell el-Amarna), for protection against Habiru, apparently Hebrew tribes entering Palestine, possibly with **Jacob** as a leader. Perhaps it is under Akhenaton that **Joseph** holds office and some Hebrew tribes settle in Egypt.

The Exodus and Settlement in Palestine

1302 Seti I accedes in Egypt, revives empire in Palestine, and undertakes to drive Hittites from Syria.

1290 Ramses II succeeds Seti, continues his father's military compaigns in Syria-Palestine, begins extensive building projects in Delta region with enforced labor that includes Apiru, i.e., Habiru or Hebrews.

1250 **Moses** leads exodus of Hebrews from Egypt.

1225 Hebrew tribes under **Joshua** destroy a number of major Canaanite cities.

1220 Merneptah, Ramses' son and successor, erects victory stele naming Israel among peoples defeated in Palestine.

1200 Iron comes into use.

1188 Invasion of Egypt by Sea Peoples is turned back. Part of them, the Philistines, settle on the S Palestinian coast.

1120 N Israelite tribes join in defeating **Sisera**.

1100 **Abimelech** destroys Shechem.

1075 Gibeah destroyed in intertribal war against Benjamin.

1050 Philistines destroy temple at Shiloh, also other Israelite and Canaanite cities.

The United Kingdom

1020 **Saul** unites Israelite tribes as first king.

1009/8 Saul dies. **David** is chosen king of Judah in Hebron.

1002/1 David is anointed king of Israel, captures Jerusalem and makes it his capital.

990 David's interest in poetry stimulates written collections of old poems as well as new compositions.

970/69 **Solomon** anointed king. David dies.

965 Building of temple is begun in April/May.

959 Temple completed in October/November.

950 Solomon encourages collection and composition of wisdom sayings. Literature flourishes, e.g., stories of Saul and David.

The Divided Kingdom

931/30 **Rehoboam** succeeds Solomon. N tribes secede, choose **Jeroboam** king of Israel.

926/25 Egyptian invader **Shishak** (Sheshonk I) despoils Jerusalem, destroys several cities of both Israel and Judah.

920 Gezer calendar, earliest example of written Hebrew yet found.

913 **Abijam** succeeds Rehoboam in Judah.

911/10 **Asa** succeeds Abijam in Judah.

910/9 **Nadab** succeeds Jeroboam in Israel.

909/8 Nadab killed; **Baasha** usurps in Israel.

886/85 **Elah** succeeds Baasha in Israel.

885/84 Elah killed by **Zimri,** who reigns seven days. **Omri** and **Tibni** lay rival claims to throne of Israel.

880 Omri overcomes Tibni, builds Samaria as his capital.

874/73 **Ahab** succeeds Omri in Israel.

873/72 **Jehoshaphat** coregent with Asa in Judah.

870/69 Asa dies; Jehoshaphat sole ruler in Judah.

865 Prophet **Elijah** sparks revival of Yahwism in Israel.

854/53 **Jehoram** (Joram) coregent with Jehoshaphat in Judah.

853 Assyrian record of Shalmaneser III mentions Ahab of Israel at Battle of Qarqar. **Ahaziah** succeeds Ahab.

852 **Jehoram** (Joram) succeeds Ahaziah in Israel.

850 **Elisha** succeeds Elijah as influential prophet of Yahwism in Israel. King **Mesha** of Moab erects stele to commemorate his winning independence from Israel.

848 Jehoshaphat dies; Jehoram (Joram) sole ruler in Judah.

841 **Ahaziah** succeeds Jehoram in Judah. He and Jehoram of Israel are killed in revolt of **Jehu.** Assyrian obelisk shows Jehu as king of Israel paying tribute to Shalmaneser III. **Athaliah** seizes rule in Judah.

835 Athaliah killed; **Jehoash** (Joash) enthroned in Judah.

830 Yahwist revival in Israel stimulates collection and writing of traditions of judges and beginning of monarchy.

814/13 **Jehoahaz** (Joahaz) succeeds Jehu in Israel.

798 **Jehoash** (Joash) succeeds Jehoahaz in Israel.

796 Jehoash of Judah assassinated; **Amaziah** succeeds.

793/92 **Jeroboam II** coregent with Jehoash in Israel.

792/91 War between Israel and Judah results in capture of Amaziah of Judah. **Azariah** (Uzziah) is enthroned in his place.

782/81 Jehoash of Israel dies; Jeroboam II sole ruler. He frees Amaziah, who resumes rule in Judah.

767 Amaziah assassinated; Azariah sole ruler in Judah.

755 **Amos** is banished from Bethel. **Hosea** begins to prophesy.

753 **Zechariah** succeeds Jeroboam II in Israel.

752 Zechariah killed; **Shallum** usurps, reigns one month; **Menahem** usurps.

750 **Jotham** coregent in Judah when Azariah becomes leper.

742/41 Menahem of Israel pays tribute to **Tiglath-pileser III** of Assyria. **Pekahiah** succeeds Menahem.

740/39 Pekahiah killed in Israel; **Pekah** usurps, dates reign from 752. Azariah dies in Judah; Jotham sole ruler. **Isaiah** called to prophesy.

735 **Ahaz** coregent with Jotham in Judah.

734 Syro-Ephraimitic War sets Israel and Syria (Aram-Damascus) against Judah. Ahaz asks help from Tiglath-pileser.

733/32 Tiglath-pileser invades Israel, seizes Galilee and **Transjordan,** exiles many of inhabitants.

732/31 Pekah of Israel is killed; **Hoshea** usurps as Assyrian vassal. Jotham of Judah dies; Ahaz sole ruler.

725/24 Hoshea revolts. **Shalmaneser V** of Assyria besieges Samaria. **Micah** prophesies the city's destruction.

723/22 Fall of Samaria brings end to N kingdom, exile to many Israelites.

The Southern Kingdom Alone

716/15 **Hezekiah** succeeds Ahaz in Judah.

710 Hezekiah encourages immigration of N Yahwists who escaped exile. They bring traditions and documents, which stimulate literary activity, e.g., probably compiling of core of Deuteronomy.

701 Assyrian record of **Sennacherib** reports his siege of Jerusalem.

697/96 **Manasseh** coregent with Hezekiah.

687/86 Hezekiah dies; Manasseh sole ruler. As Assyrian vassal he promotes Assyrian cults, represses Yahwism.

663 Ashurbanipal **(Osnappar)** destroys Thebes and adds Egypt to the Assyrian Empire, bringing it to its widest extent.

643/43 **Amon** succeeds Manasseh.

641/40 **Josiah** succeeds Amon.

630 **Zephaniah** prophesies.

628/27 **Jeremiah** called to prophesy.

623/22 Law scroll found in temple is made basis for drastic Yahwist reform. Josiah extends rule to N as Assyrian power is weakened by revolts.

615 Editors under influence of Deuteronomy compile historical records of Israel.

612 **Nahum** prophesies destruction of Assyrian capital, Nineveh, which is accomplished by Cyaxares, king of Media.

609 Josiah killed in June/July as indicated by Babylonian record of expedition of **Pharaoh Neco** to support Assyrian forces holding out in W. **Jehoahaz** succeeds, is deposed by Neco after three months. **Jehoiakim** is enthroned as Egyptian vassal.

607 **Habakkuk** begins to prophesy.

605 **Nebuchadrezzar** defeats Neco and Assyrian remnants at Carchemish in May/June, takes Palestine from Egypt. In September he accedes as Babylonian king.

604/3 Jeremiah dictates oracles to **Baruch** in December/January.

601 Nebuchadrezzar suffers heavy losses in attempt to invade Egypt. As a result Jehoiakim withholds tribute.

598/97 **Jehoiachin** succeeds Jehoiakim in December/January, approx. when Nebuchadrezzar besieges Jerusalem.

597 Babylonian Chronicle dates Nebuchadrezzar's capture of Jerusalem March 16. Jehoiachin and many leading citizens exiled; **Zedekiah** made regent as Babylonian puppet.

593 **Ezekiel** called to prophesy July 31.

589 Pro-Egyptian party forces Zedekiah to revolt.

588 Nebuchadrezzar besieges Jerusalem January 15. Later the siege is lifted for a time as the Babylonians drive back invasion of Palestine by **Pharaoh Hophra.**

586 Wall of Jerusalem breached July 18; Zedekiah flees and is captured. Destruction of city and temple begins August 14 or 17. Many more are exiled.

The Exile and Persian Rule

562 **Evil-merodach** succeeds Nebuchadrezzar in September.

561 Jehoiachin released from prison March 31 or April 2.

550 **Cyrus** the Persian gains control of Median Empire.

546 Cyrus conquers Lydia in Asia Minor.

540 Isaiah prophesies Cyrus will free exiles for return to Jerusalem.

539 Cyrus' army takes Babylon without a battle.

538 Cyrus authorizes return to ancestral lands of displaced peoples. **Sheshbazzar** leads a body of Jews to Jerusalem.

530 Cambyses succeeds Cyrus.

525 Cambyses adds Egypt to Persian Empire.

522 **Darius I** overcomes rival to secure Persian throne.

520 **Zerubbabel** begins rebuilding of temple in August/September at urging of **Haggai** and **Zechariah.**

515 Temple completed March 12.

486 Xerxes I **(Ahasuerus)** succeeds Darius.

480 Xerxes attempts conquest of Greece.

465 **Artaxerxes I** succeeds Xerxes.

450 Malachi composed.

445 **Nehemiah** appointed governor of Judea, plans rebuilding of walls of Jerusalem.

433 Nehemiah ends first term as governor.

404 Accession of **Artaxerxes II.**

397 **Ezra** brings the Law, probably the completed Pentateuch, to Jerusalem and gains its acceptance as the constitution of the Jewish state.

380 I, II Chronicles, Ezra, Nehemiah, Joel composed.

Hellenistic Rule and the Maccabean Revolt

334 **Alexander** the Great begins his conquest of the Persian Empire.

332 Alexander conquers Syria-Palestine, taking Tyre by a seven-month siege.

331 Alexander conquers Egypt, founds Alexandria.

323 Alexander dies, leaving his empire for his generals to squabble over. Ptolemy, founder of the Ptolemaic dynasty, gets control of Egypt, claims but is unable to hold Palestine.

312 Seleucus, founder of the Seleucid dynasty, gets control of Babylonia. He dates his reign, on which the Seleucid Era is based, from October.

301 Seleucus adds Syria to his realm. Ptolemy secures firm hold on Palestine.

300 Seleucus founds Antioch in Syria as his capital.

250 LXX, Greek translation of the Law (Pentateuch), is made in Alexandria, followed in time by translation of other books. Regular readings in the synagogues accord them wide familiarity and acceptance.

198 Seleucid **Antiochus III,** the Great, takes Palestine from Ptolemy V.

190 Romans defeat Antiochus the Great at Magnesia, remove Asia Minor from his control, impose heavy tribute and hostages.

187 **Seleucus IV** succeeds his father, Antiochus the Great.

180 **Jeshua ben Sira** writes Ecclesiasticus.

175 **Antiochus IV Epiphanes** succeeds his brother, Seleucus IV. He deposes the Jewish high priest, **Onias III,** appointing **Jason.**

172 **Menelaus** outbids Jason for the high priesthood.

169 Antiochus invades Egypt. Jason makes armed attack on Jerusalem. Antiochus brings army to quell revolt, enters temple, takes some of its treasures.

168 Roman ultimatum halts Antiochus in another invasion of Egypt.

167 Antiochus bans Jewish religious practices, desecrates temple on December 6.

166 **Judas Maccabeus** takes lead in Jewish revolt, organizes guerrilla force.

165 Antiochus sets out on campaign in E, leaves **Lysias** in charge of Syria and Palestine. Daniel is written.

164 Judas defeats Lysias, enters Jerusalem, rededicates the temple on December 14.

163 Antiochus IV dies in the E. His young son, **Antiochus V Eupator,** succeeds with Lysias as regent.

162 **Demetrius I,** son of Seleucus IV, seizes the throne.

160 Judas killed in battle. His brother **Jonathan** takes command of the revolt.

152 **Alexander Balas,** pretender to the Seleucid throne, appoints Jonathan high priest.

150 Qumran community formed. Judith, Testaments of the Twelve Patriarchs written.

143 Jonathan murdered. His brother **Simon** takes over.

Judean Independence and Conquest by Rome

142 Simon secures from **Demetrius II** recognition as high priest and ruler of an independent state of Judea.

134 Simon murdered; his son **John Hyrcanus I** succeeds.

130 Jeshua ben Sira's grandson translates Ecclesiasticus into Greek.

120 Jubilees written.

110 Hyrcanus conquers most of Palestine, forcibly proselytizes many. Pharisees gain wide following as opponents of aristocratic Sadducees. **Simon of Cyrene** writes five-volume history of Maccabean revolt.

104 Aristobulus I succeeds Hyrcanus, conquers Galilee.

103 Alexander Janneus succeeds his brother Aristobulus, issues coins with title "king," completes conquest of Palestine.

100 I Maccabees written.

90 Pharisees lead six-year revolt against Janneus, ended by his crucifying eight hundred rebels.

80 Epitomist condenses Simon of Cyrene's history to form II Maccabees. Main part of Enoch written.

76 Janneus dies; his widow, Alexandra, rules as queen, favors Pharisees.

67 Alexandra dies; bequeathing rule to her elder son, Hyrcanus II; but the younger, Aristobulus II, backed by the Sadducees, seizes it by force.

65 Hyrcanus is incited by Antipater, an Idumean, to besiege Jerusalem. Both parties seek Roman support.

63 Pompey captures Jerusalem, brings Palestine under Roman rule, appoints Hyrcanus II high priest.

50 Wisdom of Solomon written.

48 Julius Caesar defeats Pompey, becomes absolute Roman ruler. Antipater appointed governor of Palestine.

44 Caesar assassinated by Brutus, Cassius, and others. Palestine comes under control of Cassius.

42 Mark Antony and Octavius Caesar defeat Brutus and Cassius. Palestine under Antony.

40 Parthians invade Palestine, help Antigonus, son of Aristobulus II, to seize control. Roman Senate proclaims **Herod,** son of Antipater, king of the Jews.

37 Herod defeats Antigonus, establishes himself as king.

31 Octavius defeats Antony, becomes master of Roman world.

27 Octavius proclaimed **Augustus** Octavianus, Roman emperor.

120/19 Rebuilding of temple begun.

The Life of Jesus

7 Jesus is born.

4 Herod dies in April. His realm is divided among three sons: Judea, Samaria to **Archelaus;** Galilee, Perea to **Herod** Antipas; NE region to **Philip.**

AD

6 Augustus deposes Archelaus, puts Judea under Roman prefect.

14 **Tiberius Caesar** succeeds Augustus August 19.

25 Philo of Alexandria writes to harmonize Judaism and Greek philosophy.

26 **Pontius Pilate** becomes prefect of Judea.

28 **John** begins baptizing in fifteenth year of Tiberius.

30 Jesus crucified Friday, April 7.

The Career of Paul

33 **Paul** is converted, goes into Nabatean Arabia.

36 Paul visits Jerusalem, goes to Syria and Cilicia. Pilate replaced as prefect of Judea.

37 Caligula succeeds Tiberius March 16.

41 **Claudius** succeeds Caligula January 25. **Herod** Agrippa I appointed king of Judea, executes **James,** imprisons **Peter.**

44 Herod Agrippa dies. Judea put under procuratorship.

47 Paul and **Barnabas** begin "first missionary journey," to Cyprus, S Galatia.

49 Paul confers with apostles in Jerusalem, wins approval of Gentile mission. He and **Silas** begin "second missionary journey," going overland through Asia Minor and crossing to Macedonia. Claudius expels Jews from Rome.

50 Paul works in Macedonia, Athens. He arrives in Corinth, meets **Aquila** and **Prisca,** recent refugees from Rome, writes I Thessalonians.

51 Paul is hailed before proconsul **Gallio** after eighteen months in Corinth.

52 Paul leaves Corinth, sails for Ephesus, then Syria.

53 Paul arrives at Ephesus on "third missionary journey," beginning three-year residence there.

54 Nero succeeds Claudius.

55 Paul perhaps writes Philippians, Colossians, Philemon while imprisoned for a time in Ephesus.

56 Paul writes I Corinthians. He makes a brief "painful" visit to Corinth, returns to Ephesus, writes a "severe" letter to the Corinthians (II Corinthians 10-13 in the view of some scholars). Perhaps at this time he writes Galatians, Philippians 3. He goes to Macedonia, where he writes part or all of II Corinthians. He begins three-month stay in Corinth.

57 Paul writes Romans at Corinth, spends Passover at Philippi, arrives at Jerusalem for Pentecost. He is arrested and sent to the procurator **Felix** at Caesarea.

59 **Festus** replaces Felix as procurator. Paul appeals to Caesar, is sent to Rome.

60 Paul arrives in Rome, perhaps writes Philippians, Colossians, Philemon while imprisoned there. I Peter written approx. this time if by Peter.

64 Fire destroys much of Rome in July. Christians are blamed and persecuted. Perhaps Peter and Paul are among the martyrs.

The Period of the Later NT Books

66 Jews revolt against Rome.

68 Nero commits suicide; Galba succeeds. Roman troops destroy Qumran community.

69 Galba succeeded by Otho, Vitellius, and finally Vespasian, the general besieging Jerusalem.

70 Vespasian's son Titus takes Jerusalem in August, destroys temple, and razes city.

73 Last Jewish rebels commit suicide at Masada.

75 Mark written. Josephus writes an account of the war in Aramaic, later translates it into Greek.

79 Titus succeeds Vespasian.

81 Domitian succeeds Titus.

85 Matthew written.

90 Luke-Acts written. Rabbis at Jamnia close Hebrew canon.

92 Paul's letters collected and circulated together.

93 Josephus writes his Antiquities of the Jews.

95 Hebrews, Revelation written.

96 Nerva succeeds Domitian. I Clement written, perhaps also I Peter if pseudonymous.

98 Trajan succeeds Nerva.

100 John, James, and main part of II Esdras written.

110 Letters of John written.

115 Letters of Ignatius and Polycarp written.

117 Hadrian succeeds Trajan.

125 Jude written. Oldest extant NT manuscript copied—a papyrus fragment of John.

130 Pastorals, Letter of Barnabas written.

132 Hadrian's plan to rebuild Jerusalem as Roman colony incites second Jewish revolt, led by Simon ben Koseba.

135 Romans put down revolt, proceed to build Aelia Capitolina on site of Jerusalem.

138 Hadrian succeeded by Antoninus Pius.

140 Shepherd of Hermas written.

144 Marcion promotes his expurgated version of Luke and Paul's letters to replace the OT in Christian usage.

150 II Peter, Teaching of the Twelve Apostles (Didache) written.

ARCHAEOLOGICAL PERIODS OF PALESTINE

Mesolithic (Natufian)	approx. 8000-6000 B.C.
Pre-Pottery Neolithic	approx. 6000-5000 B.C.
Pottery Neolithic	approx. 5000-4000 B.C.
Chalcolithic	approx. 4000-3200 B.C.
Esdraelon	approx. 3200-3000 B.C.
Early Bronze	
EB I	approx. 3000-2800 B.C.
EB II	approx. 2800-2600 B.C.
EB III	approx. 2600-2300 B.C.
EB IV (or III B)	approx. 2300-2100 B.C.
Middle Bronze	
MB I (or EB-MB)	approx. 2100-1900 B.C.
MB II*a*	approx. 1900-1700 B.C.
MB II*b*	approx. 1700-1600 B.C.
MB II*c*	approx. 1600-1550 B.C.
Late Bronze	
LB I	approx. 1550-1400 B.C.
LB II*a*	approx. 1400-1300 B.C.
LB II*b*	approx. 1300-1200 B.C.
Iron I or Early Iron	
I*a*	approx. 1200-1150 B.C.
I*b*	approx. 1150-1025 B.C.
I*c*	approx. 1025- 950 B.C.
I*d*	approx. 950- 900 B.C.
Iron II or Middle Iron	
II*a*	approx. 900-800 B.C.
II*b*	approx. 800-700 B.C.
II*c*	approx. 700-600 B.C.
Iron III, Late Iron, or Persian	approx. 600-300 B.C.
Hellenistic	approx. 300-63 B.C.
Roman	approx. 63 B.C.-A.D. 323
Byzantine	approx. A.D. 323-636
Islamic	approx. A.D. 636-present

GENEALOGY OF THE EARLY PATRIARCHS

Patriarch	Age at Successor's Birth	Remaining Years	Total Years
Adam	130	800	930
Seth	105	807	912
Enosh	90	815	905
Kenan	70	840	910
Mahalalel	65	830	895
Jared	162	800	962
Enoch	65	300	365
Methuselah	187	782	969
Lamech	182	595	777
Noah	500	450	950
Shem	100	500	
Total years at the Flood	1656		
Arpachshad	35	403	
Kainan			
Shelah	30	403	
Eber	34	430	
Peleg	30	209	
Reu	32	207	
Serug	30	200	
Nahor	29	119	
Terah	70		205
Total years at Abraham's birth	1946		
Plus the 2 years of Gen. 11:10	1948		

YEARS FROM ABRAHAM'S BIRTH TO THE EXODUS

Period	Years
From Abraham's birth to his entry into Canaan (Gen. 12:4)	75
From Abraham's entry into Canaan to the birth of Isaac (Gen. 21:5)	25
From Isaac's birth to the birth of Jacob (Gen. 25:26)	60
From Jacob's birth to his descent into Egypt (Gen. 47:9)	130
From the descent into Egypt to the Exodus (Exod. 12:40-41)	430
Total duration	720

THE PLAGUES OF EGYPT

	Exod. 7:8–12:30	Psalm 78:43-57	Psalm 105:28-36
1. Water to blood	(7:14-15*a*, 16-17*a*, 17*c*-18, 20*c*-21*a*, 23-25) (7:15*b*, 17*b*, 20*b*) (7:19-20*a*, 21*b*-22)	Vs. 44 (1)	Vs. 29 (2)
2. Frogs	(8:1-4, 8-15*a* 7:26-29; 8:4-11*a*) (8:5-7, 15*b*; 8:1-3, 11*b*)	Vs. 45 (3)	Vs. 30 (3)
3. Gnats	(8:16-19; 8:12-15)		Vs. 31 (5)
4. Flies	(8:20-32; 8:16-28)	Vs. 45 (2)	Vs. 31 (4)
5. Murrain	(9:1-7)	Cattle slain by hail and flocks by lightning (6)	No mention of any harm to cattle
6. Boils	(9:8-12)		
7. Hail	(9:13-21, 23*b*, 24*b*, 25*b*-34) (9:22-23*a*, 24*a*, 25*a*, 35)	Vs. 48 (5)	Vs. 32 (6)
8. Locusts	(10:1-11, 13*b*, 14*b*-15*a*, 15*c*-19, 24-26, 28-29) (10:12-13*a*, 14*a*, 15*b*, 20)	Vs. 46 (4)	Vs. 34 (7)
9. Darkness	(10:21-23, 27)		Vs. 28 (1)
10. Death of the first-born	(11:4-8; 12:21-27, 29 ff) (11:1-3) (11:9-10; 12:1-20, 28)	Vs. 51 (7)	Vs. 36 (8)

YEARS FROM THE EXODUS TO THE FOUNDING OF SOLOMON'S TEMPLE

Intervals Associated With	Years
The wilderness wandering (Num. 32:13)	40
Period of Joshua and the elders (Judg. 2:7; duration not stated)	*x*
Oppression of Cushan-rishathaim (Judg. 3:8)	8
Othniel (Judg. 3:11)	40
Oppression of Eglon (Judg. 3:14)	18
Ehud (Judg. 3:30)	80
Oppression of Jabin (Judg. 4:3)	20
Deborah-Barak (Judg. 5:31)	40
Oppression of the Midianites (Judg. 6:1)	7
Gideon (Judg. 8:28)	40
Abimelech (Judg. 9:22)	3
Tola (Judg. 10:2)	23
Jair (Judg. 10:3)	22

Oppression of the Ammonites (Judg. 10:8)	18
Jephthah (Judg. 12:7)	6
Ibzan (Judg. 12:9)	7
Elon (Judg. 12:11)	10
Abdon (Judg. 12:14)	8
Oppression of the Philistines (Judg. 13:1)	40
Samson (Judg. 15:20; 16:31)	20
Eli (I Sam. 4:18)	40
Samuel; ark in Kirjath-jearim (I Sam. 7:2)	20
Saul (I Sam. 13:1; full number lacking)	*y*
David (I Kings 2:11; 7 years in Hebron, 33 years in Jerusalem)	40
Solomon (to building of temple; I Kings 6:1)	4
Total duration	554 plus *x* plus *y*
Remaining years of Solomon (total reign, 40 years; I Kings 11:42)	36

FAMILY OF JESSE

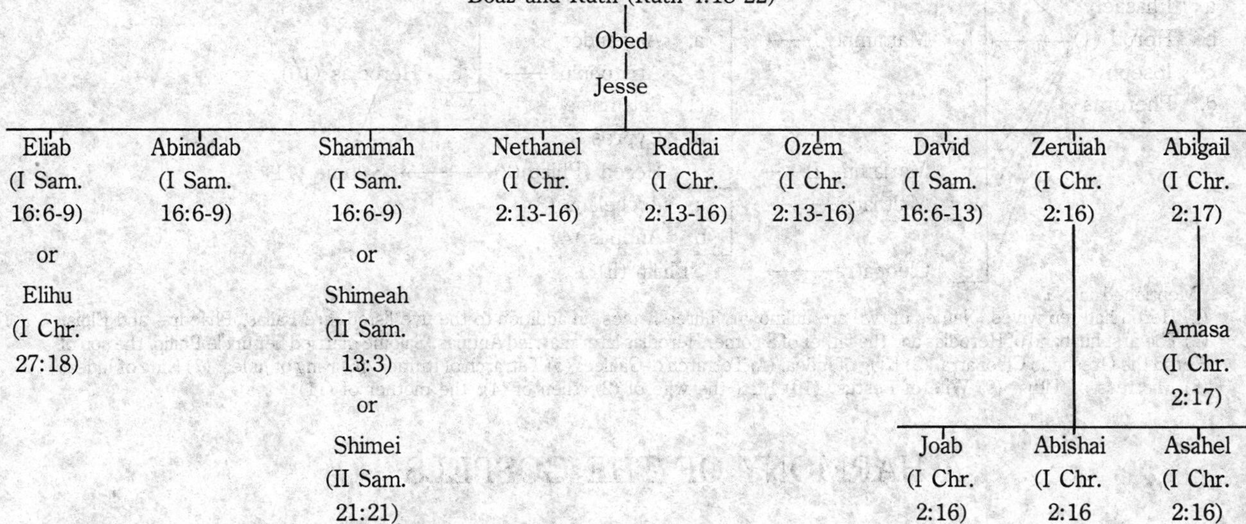

DAVID'S WIVES AND SONS

Michal (I Sam. 18:27)	Abigail (I Sam. 25:42)	Ahinoam (I Sam. 25:43)	Maacah (I Chr. 3:2)	Haggith (I Chr. 3:2)	Abital (I Chr. 3:3)	Eglah (I Chr. 3:3)	Bath-shua/Bathsheba (I Chr. 3:5)	Others
	Daniel (I Chr. 3:1)	Amnon (I Chr. 3:1)	Absalom (I Chr. 3:2)	Adonijah (I Chr. 3:2)	Shephatiah (I Chr. 3:3)	Ithream (I Chr. 3:3)	Shimea/Shammua Shobab Nathan Solomon (II Sam. 5:14; I Chr. 3:5)	Ibhar Elishua/Elishama Nogah Nepheg Japhia Elishama Beelida/Eliada Eliphelet/Elpelet (II Sam. 5:14; I Chr. 3:6-8; 14:4-7)

THE LISTS OF DAVID'S SONS

Born at Hebron		**Born at Jerusalem**					
II Sam. 3:2-5	*I Chr. 3:1-4*	*II Sam. 5:14*		*1 Chr. 3:5-9*		*1 Chr. 14:4-7*	
1. Amnon	Amnon	1. Shammua	7. ________	Shimea	Eliphelet	Shammua	Elpelet
2. Chileab	Daniel	2. Shobab	8. ________	Shobab	Nogah	Shobab	Nogah
3. Absalom	Absalom	3. Nathan	9. Nepheg	Nathan	Nepheg	Nathan	Nepheg
4. Adonijah	Adonijah	4. Solomon	10. Japhia	Solomon	Japhia	Solomon	Japhia
5. Shephatiah	Shephatiah	5. Ibhar	11. Elishama	Ibhar	Elishama	Ibhar	Elishama
6. Ithream	Ithream	6. Elishua	12. Eliada	Elishama	Eliada	Elishua	Beeliada
		13. Eliphelet		Eliphelet		Eliphelet	

A PARTIAL GENEALOGY OF THE FAMILY OF HEROD

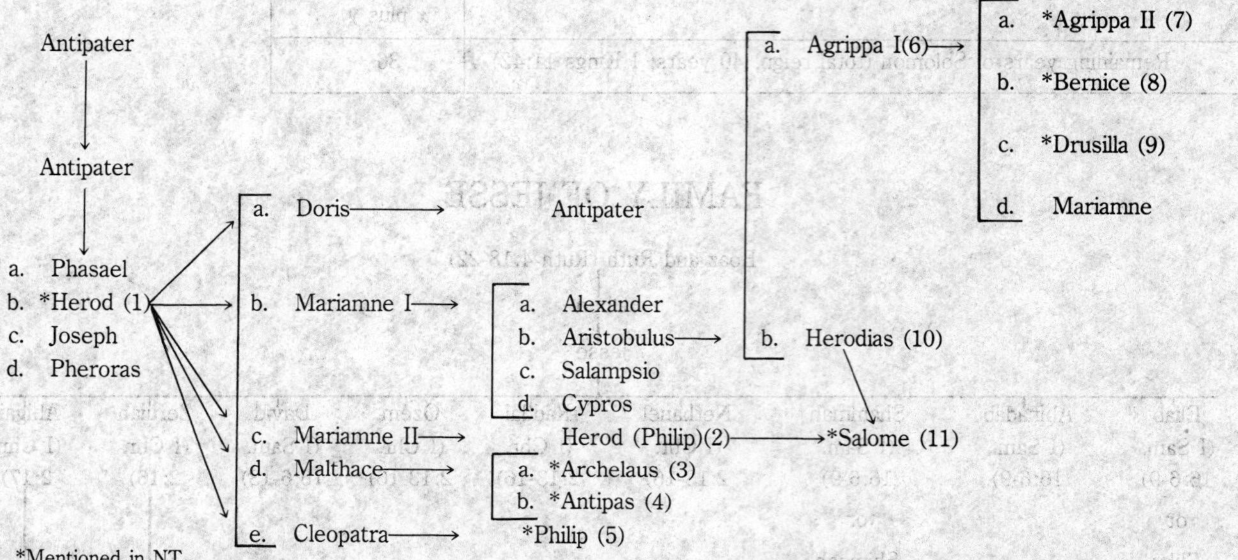

(1) Herod had ten wives. Names of two are unknown. Three names, in addition to the five listed, are Pallas, Phaedra, and Elpis. (2) The first husband of Herodias and the father of Salome. Herodias later married Antipas. Salome married her uncle Philip, the son of Herod the Great and Cleopatra. (3) King of Judea. (4) Tetrarch of Galilee. (5) Tetrarch of Ituraea. (6) King of Judea. (7) King of Judea. (8) Mistress of Titus. (9) Wife of Festus. (10) First the wife of (2), then of (4); the mother of (11)

A HARMONY OF THE GOSPELS

Jesus' Infancy (Matthew 1–2; Luke 1–2)

Jesus in Galilee (Matthew 3–18; Mark 1–9; Luke 3:1–9:50)

The Sermon on the Mount (Matthew 5–7)

The Sermon on the Plain (Luke 6:20-49)

Jesus' Parables (Luke 9:51–18:14)

Jesus in Judea (Matthew 19–27; Mark 10–15; Luke 18:15–23:40)

Jesus' Journey to Jerusalem (Matthew 19–20; Mark 10; Luke 18:15–19:27)

Jesus' Days in Jerusalem (Matthew 21–25; Mark 11–13; Luke 19:28–21:7)

Jesus and the End (Matthew 24:4-36; Mark 13:5-37; Luke 21:8-36)

Jesus' Betrayal (Matthew 26–27; Mark 14–15; Luke 22–23)

Jesus' Last Supper (Matthew 26:20-29; Mark 14:17-25; Luke 22:14-18)

Jesus' Resurrection (Matthew 28:11-20; Mark 16:9-20; Luke 24:13-53)

WEIGHTS AND MEASURES

Lengths

UNIT	RELATION TO CUBIT	APPROXIMATE EQUIVALENT
finger	÷24	.75 inch
handbreadth	÷6	3 inches
span	÷2	9 inches
cubit		1.5 feet

Dry Volumes

UNIT	RELATION TO EPHAH	APPROXIMATE EQUIVALENT
kab	÷18	.89 quart
omer	÷10	1.6 quart
seah	÷3	.67 peck
ephah		.5 bushel
lethech	×5	2.5 bushel
homer	×10	5 bushels
cor	×10	5 bushels

Liquid Volumes

UNIT	RELATION TO BATH	APPROXIMATE EQUIVALENT
log	÷72	.56 pint
hin	÷6	3.33 quarts
bath		5 gallons
cor	×10	50 gallons

Weights, Sanctuary Standard

UNIT	RELATION TO SHEKEL	APPROXIMATE EQUIVALENT
gerah	÷20	.017 ounce
beka	÷2	.17 ounce
shekel		.33 ounce
mina	×60	1.25 pounds
talent	×3,000	62.5 pounds

Weights, Commercial Standard

UNIT	RELATION TO SHEKEL	APPROXIMATE EQUIVALENT
gerah	÷24	.017 ounce
beka	÷2	.2 ounce
pim	÷1.5	.267 ounce
shekel		.4 ounce
mina	×50	1.25 pounds
talent	×2,500	62.5 pounds

A SELECTED LIST OF OBSOLETE TERMS AND THEIR MEANINGS

No attempt is here made to give a complete list of obsolete terms in the King James Version. Their number is well over a thousand, and in a complete list account must be taken of a wide variety of contexts. The Revised Standard Version replaces these terms with their equivalent in living English.

Term	Reference	Meaning
abhor	I Sam. 2:17	treat with contempt
abide	Acts 20:23	await
abroad	Deut. 24:11	outside
addicted	I Cor. 16:15	devoted
admiration	Rev. 17:6	astonishment
admire	II Thess. 1:10	marvel at
advertise	Ruth 4:4	tell
advise thyself	I Chr. 21:12	decide
affect	Gal. 4:17	make much of
affections	Gal. 5:24	passions
affinity	I Kings 3:1	marriage alliance
after	Ps. 28:4	according to
again	Gen. 24:5	back
allege	Acts 17:3	prove
allow	Rom. 14:22	approve
all to brake	Judg. 9:53	crushed
amazed	Mark 14:33	distressed
amazement	I Pet. 3:6	terror
amiable	Ps. 84:1	lovely
ancients	Isa. 3:14	old men, elders
and	Matt. 24:48	if

Term	Reference	Meaning
angle	Isa. 19:8	hook
anon	Matt. 13:20	immediately
any	Jas. 5:19	any one
any thing	Judg. 11:25	any
any thing at all	Acts 25:8	at all
any ways	Lev. 20:4	at all
apparently	Num. 12:8	clearly
appointed	Judg. 18:11	armed
apprehend	Phil. 3:12	make one's own
armholes	Jer. 38:12	armpits
artillery	I Sam. 20:40	weapons
ask at	Dan. 2:10	ask of
assay	Acts 9:26	attempt
assuaged	Gen. 8:1	subsided
attain to	Acts 27:12	reach
attendance	I Tim. 4:13	attend to
attire	Ezek. 23:15	headdress, turban
audience	I Sam. 25:24	hearing, ears
avoid	I Sam. 18:11	evade
away with	Isa. 1:13	endure
backside	Exod. 26:12	back
bands	Judg. 15:14	bonds
bank	II Sam. 20:15	mound
barbarian	I Cor. 14:11	foreigner
base	I Cor. 1:28	lowly, humble
because	Matt. 20:31	in order that
beside	Josh. 22:19	besides, other than
bestow	Luke 12:17	store
bewray	Matt. 26:73	reveal, betray
blow up	Ps. 81:3	blow
book	Job 31:35	indictment
botch	Deut. 28:27	boils
bottle	Matt. 9:17	wineskin
bowels	Phil. 1:8	affection
breaking up	Exod. 22:2	breaking in
broided	I Tim. 2:9	braided
broken up	Matt. 24:43	broken into
bruit	Jer. 10:22	rumor
bunch	Isa. 30:6	hump
bursting	Isa. 30:14	fragments
but	Amos 3:7	except, without
by	I Cor. 4:4	against
by and by	Matt. 13:21	immediately
by that	Exod. 22:26	before
by the space of	Acts 19:10	for
cabin	Jer. 37:16	cell
captivity	Judg. 5:12	captives
careful	Luke 10:41	anxious
carefully	Phil. 2:28	eagerly
carefulness	I Cor. 7:32	anxiety
careless	Judg. 18:7	free from care
carelessly	Isa. 47:8	securely
carriage	I Sam. 17:22	baggage
cast	Jer. 38:11	castoff
cast	Luke 1:29	consider
cast about	Jer. 41:14	turned about
castaway	I Cor. 9:27	disqualified
certify	Gal. 1:11	make known to
challenge	Exod. 22:9	say
chambering	Rom. 13:13	debauchery
chapman	II Chr. 9:14	trader

Term	Reference	Meaning
chargeable	II Sam. 13:25	burdensome
charged	I Tim. 5:16	burdened
charger	Matt. 14:8	platter
charges	I Cor. 9:7	expense
charity	I Cor. 13:13	love
check	Job 20:3	censure
churl	Isa. 32:5	knave
cieled	Ezek. 41:16	paneled
closet	Matt. 6:6	room
clothed upon	II Cor. 5:4	further clothed
clouted	Josh. 9:5	patched
clouts	Jer. 38:11	rags
coasts	Acts 19:1	country
come at	Luke 8:19	reach
comely	Eccl. 5:18	fitting
comfortably	Isa. 40:2	tenderly
comfortless	John 14:18	desolate
commune	Luke 6:11	discuss
communicate	Gal. 6:6	share
communications	I Cor. 15:33	company
compact	Ps. 122:3	bound firmly
compacted	Eph. 4:16	knit together
compass	Josh. 6:3	march around
compass, fetch a	Acts 28:13	make a circuit
compel	I Sam. 28:23	urge
comprehend	John 1:5	overcome
concupiscence	I Thess. 4:5	lust
condescend	Rom. 12:16	associate
confection	Exod. 30:35	incense blended
confectionaries	I Sam. 8:13	perfumers
confidences	Jer. 2:37	those in whom you trust
confound	I Cor. 1:27	shame
confusion	Ps. 44:15	disgrace
conscience	Heb. 10:2	consciousness
consist	Col. 1:17	hold together
consort with	Acts 17:4	join
constant	I Chr. 28:7	resolute
constantly	Acts 12:15	confidently
contain	I Cor. 7:9	exercise self-control
convenient	Prov. 30:8	needful
not convenient	Rom. 1:28	improper
were conversant	I Sam. 25:15	went
conversation	Heb. 13:7	life, behavior
convert	Isa. 6:10	turn
convince	John 8:46	convict
corn	Ps. 65:13	grain
corn of wheat	John 12:24	grain of wheat
corrupt	Luke 12:33	destroy
corruptible	I Cor. 9:25	perishable
cousin	Luke 1:36	kinswoman
covet	I Cor. 12:31	earnestly desire
creature	Rom. 8:19	creation
cumber	Luke 13:7	use up
cumbered	Luke 10:40	distracted
cumbrance	Deut. 1:12	weight
cunning	Gen. 25:27	skilful
cunning	I Kings 7:14	skill
curious	Acts 19:19	magical
curiously	Ps. 139:15	intricately
daily	Ps. 56:1	all day long

Term	Reference	Meaning
damnable	II Pet. 2:1	destructive
damnation	I Cor. 11:29	judgment
damned	Rom. 14:23	condemned
in danger of	Mark 3:29	guilty
darling	Ps. 22:20	life
daysman	Job 9:33	umpire
dayspring	Job 38:12	dawn
deal to	Isa. 58:7	share with
dearth	Acts 7:11	famine
debate	Rom. 1:29	strife
declare	Matt. 13:36	explain
decline	Ps. 44:18	depart
degree	I Tim. 3:13	standing
degrees	II Kings 20:9	steps
delectable	Isa 44:9	that they delight in
delicacies	Rev. 18:3	wantonness
delicately	I Sam. 15:32	cheerfully
delicates	Jer. 51:34	delicacies
deliciously	Rev. 18:9	wantonly
demand	Luke 17:20	ask
denounce	Deut. 30:18	declare
descry	Judg. 1:23	spy out
desire	II Chr. 21:20	regret
despite	Ezek. 25:6	malice
despitefully use	Luke 6:28	abuse
do despite unto	Heb. 10:29	outrage
device	Jer. 51:11	purpose
devotions	Acts 17:23	objects of worship
diet	Jer. 52:34	allowance
dig up	Prov. 16:27	plot
disallow	I Pet. 2:4	reject
disannul	Isa. 14:27	annul
discomfit	Judg. 4:15	rout
discover	Mic. 1:6	uncover
disorderly	II Thess. 3:6	in idleness
dispensation	Eph. 3:2	stewardship
by disposition of	Acts 7:53	as delivered by
dispute	Mark 9:33	discuss
dissolve doubts	Dan. 5:12	solve problems
divers	Mark 1:34	various
doctor	Luke 2:46	teacher
doctrine	Matt. 7:28	teaching
done away	Num. 27:4	taken away
dote	Jer. 50:36	become fools
doubt	Acts 10:17	be perplexed
doubtful mind	Luke 12:29	anxious mind
doubting nothing	Acts 10:20	without hesitation
draught	Matt. 15:17	privy
draught house	II Kings 10:27	latrine
duke	Gen. 36:15	chief
dure	Matt. 13:21	endure
ear	I Sam. 8:12	plow
eared	Deut. 21:4	plowed
earing	Gen. 45:6	plowing
earnest	Eph. 1:14	guarantee
edification	I Cor. 14:3	upbuilding
edify	Eph. 4:16	upbuild
either	Lev. 10:1	each
either	Luke 6:42	or
eminent	Ezek. 16:24	lofty
emulation	Gal. 5:20	jealousy
enable	I Tim. 1:12	give strength

Term	Reference	Meaning
end	Jer. 31:17	future
enlargement	Esth. 4:14	relief
ensue	I Pet. 3:11	pursue
entreat	Matt. 22:6	treat
equal	Ezek. 18:25	just
equal	Lam. 2:13	liken
espoused	Matt. 1:18	betrothed
estate	Acts 22:5	council
estate	Col. 4:8	state, condition
every	II Sam. 21:20	each
evidence	Jer. 32:10	deed
evidently	Acts 10:3	clearly
example	Heb. 8:5	copy
exceed	Job 36:9	behave arrogantly
exchanger	Matt. 25:27	banker
exercise	I Tim. 4:7	train
exercise myself	Acts 24:16	take pains
expect	Heb. 10:13	wait
expectation	Ps. 62:5	hope
fable	I Tim. 1:4	myth
faint	II Cor. 4:16	lose heart
fair	Zech. 3:5	clean
fame	Gen. 45:16	report
familiars	Jer. 20:10	familiar friends
fan	Jer. 4:11	winnow
fan	Matt. 3:12	winnowing fork
fanners	Jer. 51:2	winnowers
fashion	II Kings 16:10	model
fast	Ruth 2:8	close
fat	Joel 2:24	vat
feebleminded	I Thess. 5:14	faint-hearted
fenced	Num. 32:17	fortified
fine	Job 28:1	refine
fining pot	Prov. 17:3	crucible
flagons	Song of S. 2:5	raisins
flood	Josh. 24:3	river
floor	Matt. 3:12	threshing floor
flux	Acts 28:8	dysentery
follow	Heb. 13:7	imitate
footmen	Jer. 12:5	men on foot
for all	John 21:11	although
for because	Gen. 22:16	because
forecast	Dan. 11:24	devise
forepart	Acts 27:41	bow
foreship	Acts 27:30	bow
foretell	II Cor. 13:2	warn
for that	I Tim. 1:12	because
for to	Luke 4:16	to
forward	Gal. 2:10	eager
forwardness	II Cor. 9:2	readiness
fowl	Gen. 1:20	birds
fray	Deut. 28:26	frighten
freely	Matt. 10:8	without pay
froward	Deut. 32:20	perverse
furniture	Gen. 31:34	saddle
gainsay	Luke 21:15	contradict
gender	Gal. 4:24	bear children
generation	Matt. 3:7	brood
glass	I Cor. 13:12	mirror
go about	John 7:19	seek
go aside	Num. 5:12	go astray
go beyond	I Thess. 4:6	transgress

Term	Reference	Meaning
go to	Gen. 11:3	come
governor	Jas. 3:4	pilot
grace	Ruth 2:2	favor
grief	Job 6:2	vexation
grieve	Gen. 49:23	attack
grudge	Jas. 5:9	grumble
be guilty of	Matt. 26:66	deserve
hale	Luke 12:58	drag
halt	Matt. 18:8	lame
halt	I Kings 18:21	go limping
hardly	Matt. 19:23	it is hard for
hardness	II Tim. 2:3	suffering
harness	I Kings 20:11	armor
headstone	Zech. 4:7	top stone
heady	II Tim. 3:4	reckless
on heaps	Ps. 79:1	in ruins
heavily	Ps. 35:14	in mourning
heaviness	Prov. 12:25	anxiety
heavy	I Kings 20:43	resentful
herb	Gen. 1:29	plant
high	Prov. 21:4	haughty
highminded	Rom. 11:20	proud
his	I Cor. 15:38	its
hitherto	Job 38:11	thus far
hold	I Sam. 22:4	stronghold
hold peace at	Num. 30:11	say nothing to
honest	Phil. 4:8	honorable
honestly	Rom. 13:13	becomingly
honourable	I Sam. 9:6	held in honor
hough	Josh 11:6	hamstring
howbeit	II Sam. 12:14	nevertheless
how that	Matt. 16:12	that
husbandman	II Tim. 2:6	farmer
husbandry	I Cor. 3:9	field
if so be	Rom. 8:9	if
illuminated	Heb. 10:32	enlightened
imagination	Deut. 29:19	stubbornness
imagine	Gen. 11:6	propose
impart	Luke 3:11	share
implead	Acts 19:38	accuse
impotent	Acts 14:8	crippled
incontinent	II Tim. 3:3	profligate
inn	Gen. 42:27	lodging place
inquisition	Esth. 2:23	investigation
instant	Luke 23:23	urgent
instantly	Luke 7:4	earnestly
have intelligence with	Dan. 11:30	give heed to
be intreated	I Chr. 5:20	grant an entreaty
inward	Job 19:19	intimate
inwards	Exod. 29:13	entrails
jangling	I Tim. 1:6	vain discussion
judge	Luke 19:22	condemn
kerchief	Ezek. 13:18	veil
latchet	Mark 1:7	thong
laugh on	Job 29:24	smile on
lay at	Job 41:26	reach
lay away	Ezek. 26:16	remove
lay from	Jonah 3:6	remove
lay out	II Kings 12:11	pay out
leasing	Ps. 5:6	lies
left	Acts 21:32	stopped

Term	Reference	Meaning
let	Isa. 43:13	hinder
lewd	Acts 17:5	wicked
lewdness	Acts 18:14	crime
light	Judg. 9:4	reckless
light	I Kings 7:4	window
light bread	Num. 21:5	worthless food
lightly	Gen. 26:10	easily
lightness	Jer. 23:32	recklessness
liketh him	Deut. 23:16	pleases him
in good liking	Job 39:4	strong
worse liking	Dan. 1:10	in poorer condition
limit	Heb. 4:7	set
list	John 3:8	choose, will
lively	Acts 7:38	living
lover	Ps. 38:11	friend
lucre	I Tim. 3:3	gain
lunatick	Matt. 4:24	epileptic
lust after	Deut. 12:15	desire
mad	Eccl. 7:7	foolish
make	Judg. 18:3	do
make for	Ezek. 17:17	help
with the manner	Num. 5:13	in the act
man of war	Luke 23:11	soldier
mansion	John 14:2	room
mar	I Sam. 6:5	ravage
master	Matt. 10:24	teacher
maul	Prov. 25:18	war club
mean	Prov. 22:29	obscure
meat	Gen. 1:29	food
meat offering	Lev. 2:1	cereal offering
meet	Gen. 2:18	fit
memorial	Ps. 9:6	memory
merchantman	I Kings 10:15	trader
me thinketh	II Sam. 18:27	I think
minding	Acts 20:13	intending
minister	Luke 4:20	attendant
minister	II Cor. 9:10	to supply
mock	Jer. 38:19	abuse
moderation	Phil. 4:5	forbearance
the more part	Acts 27:12	the majority
mortify	Rom. 8:13	put to death
motions	Rom. 7:5	passions
munition	Isa. 29:7	stronghold
murrain	Exod. 9:3	plague
muse	Luke 3:15	question
naughtiness	Jas. 1:21	wickedness
naughty	Jer. 24:2	bad
neesing	Job 41:8	sneezing
nephew	Judg. 12:14	grandson
noisome	Ps. 91:3	deadly
set at nought	Prov. 1:25	ignore
nourish	Gen. 45:11	provide for
nursing father	Num. 11:12	nurse
nurture	Eph. 6:4	discipline
observe	Mark 6:20	keep safe
occupier	Ezek. 27:27	dealer
occupy	Judg. 16:11	use
occupy	Luke 19:13	trade
occurrent	I Kings 5:4	misfortune
odd	Num. 3:48	excess
offence	Gal. 5:11	stumbling block

Term	Reference	Meaning
offend	Matt. 18:8	cause to sin
often	I Tim. 5:23	frequent
once	Jer. 13:27	ever
open	Acts 17:3	explain
ordain	Ps. 8:3	establish
order	I Kings 20:14	begin
or ever	Prov. 8:23	before
outgoings	Josh. 17:18	farthest borders
outlandish	Neh. 13:26	foreign
out of hand	Num. 11:15	immediately
overcharged	Luke 21:34	weighed down
overlive	Josh. 24:31	outlive
overpass	Jer. 5:28	know no bounds
overrun	II Sam. 18:23	outrun
pap	Luke 11:27	breast
part	Acts 2:45	distribute
in particular	I Cor. 12:27	individually
particularly	Acts 21:19	one by one
passage	Judg. 12:6	ford
passengers	Prov. 9:15	those who pass by
pastor	Jer. 23:1	shepherd
pattern	Heb. 9:23	copy
a peculiar people	I Pet. 2:9	God's own people
peradventure	Gen. 24:5	perhaps
persecute	Ps. 71:11	pursue
persuade	I Kings 22:20	entice
persuaded	Rom. 8:38	sure
persuading	Acts 28:23	trying to convince
pillow	Ezek. 13:18	magic band
pitiful	Jas. 5:11	compassionate
plead	Judg. 6:31	contend
plagued	Ps. 73:5	stricken
plain	Gen. 25:27	quiet
possess	Deut. 1:8	take possession of
post	II Chr. 30:6	courier
power	II Chr. 32:9	forces
have power with	Gen. 32:28	have striven with
prefer	Esth. 2:9	advance
presently	Matt. 21:19	immediately
pressfat	Hag. 2:16	winevat
prevent	I Thess. 4:15	precede
prey	Josh. 8:2	booty
prick	Acts 26:14	goad
printed	Job. 19:23	inscribed
privily	Acts 16:37	secretly
privy to	Acts 5:2	with knowledge of
profane	Ezek. 22:26	common, ordinary
profess	Matt. 7:23	declare
prolong	Ezek. 12:25	delay
proper	Heb. 11:23	beautiful
prove	I Thess. 5:21	test
provide	Heb. 11:40	foresee
provoke	II Cor. 9:2	stir up
publican	Mark 2:15	tax collector
publish	Deut. 32:3	proclaim
pulse	Dan. 1:12	vegetables
purchase	I Tim. 3:13	gain, obtain
purge	John 15:2	prune
purtenance	Exod. 12:9	inner parts
put down	II Chr. 36:3	depose
put to	Ezra 6:12	put forth

Term	Reference	Meaning
quarrel	Mark 6:19	grudge
question	Mark 9:16	discuss
quick	Num 16:30	alive
quicken	Eph. 2:1	make alive
reap down	Jas. 5:4	mow
rear up	Exod. 26:30	erect
reason	Acts 6:2	right
reasoning	Luke 9:46	argument
record	Phil. 1:8	witness
recover	II Kings 5:7	cure
refrain	Job 7:11	restrain
refuse	Ps. 118:22	reject
rehearse	I Sam. 17:31	repeat
reins	Jer. 12:2	heart
remembrance	Job 13:12	maxim
remove	Ps. 46:2	change
repent himself	Ps. 135:14	have compassion
replenish	Gen. 1:28	fill
report	Acts 6:3	repute
reprobate	Jer. 6:30	refuse
require	Ezra 8:22	ask
resemble	Luke 13:18	compare
residue	Zech. 8:11	remnant
respect persons	Deut. 1:17	be partial
rid	Gen. 37:22	rescue
ringstraked	Gen. 30:35	striped
riot	I Pet 4:4	profligacy
rioting	Rom. 13:13	reveling
riotous	Prov. 23:20	gluttonous
road	I Sam. 27:10	raid
room	Luke 14:7	place
safeguard	I Sam. 22:23	safekeeping
scall	Lev. 13:30	itch
scrip	Matt. 10:10	bag
search	Ezek. 34:11	search for
secure	Judg. 8:11	unsuspecting
seethe	Exod. 16:23	boil
sentence	Acts 15:19	judgment
set by	I Sam. 18:30	esteemed
settle	Ezek. 43:14	ledge
sever	Exod. 9:4	make a distinction
several	II Kings 15:5	separate
severally	I Cor. 12:11	individually
shambles	I Cor. 10:25	meat market
shamefacedness	I Tim. 2:9	modesty
simple	Rom. 16:19	guileless
simplicity	Rom. 12:8	liberality
sincere	I Pet. 2:2	pure
can skill	I Kings 5:6	know how
could skill of	II Chr. 34:12	were skilful with
sleight	Eph. 4:14	cunning
slime	Gen. 11:3	bitumen
so as	Rev. 8:12	so that
sober	I Tim. 3:2	sensible
sod	Gen. 25:29	boiled
sodden	Exod. 12:9	boiled
softly	Isa. 8:6	gently
some	Rom. 5:7	one
sometime	Col. 3:7	once
sometimes	Eph. 2:13	once
sop	John 13:26	morsel
sore	Gen. 19:9	hard

Term	Reference	Meaning
sore	Ps. 38:11	plague
sorer	Heb. 10:29	worse
so that	I Kings 8:25	if only
sottish	Jer. 4:22	stupid
space	Acts 5:34	while
spare	Job 30:10	hesitate
special	Acts 19:11	extraordinary
specially	Acts 25:26	especially
sped	Judg. 5:30	succeeded
speed	Gen. 24:12	success
spend up	Prov. 21:20	devour
spitefully	Matt. 22:6	shamefully
spoil	Gen. 34:27	plunder
spoil	Col. 2:8	make a prey of
stagger	Rom. 4:20	waver
stand to	Deut. 25:8	persist
stand to	II Kings 23:3	join in
stand upon	II Sam. 1:9	stand beside
stay	Job 37:4	restrain
still	Ps. 84:4	ever
stoutness	Isa. 9:9	arrogance
strain at	Matt. 23:24	strain out
strait	Job 36:16	distress
strait	Matt. 7:13	narrow
straitly	Gen. 43:7	carefuly
straitness	Jer. 19:9	distress
strake	Gen. 30:37	streak
strength	Ezek. 30:15	stronghold
strike his hand	II Kings 5:11	wave his hand
strike hands	Prov. 22:26	give pledges
study	II Tim. 2:15	do your best
stuff	I Sam. 30:24	baggage
substance	Deut. 11:6	living thing
succour	II Sam. 8:5	help
succourer	Rom. 16:2	helper
such like	Mark 7:13	such
suddenly	I Tim. 5:22	hastily
suffer	Matt. 19:14	let
to supple	Ezek. 16:4	to cleanse
surely	Prov. 10:9	securely
surfeiting	Luke 21:34	dissipation
swellings	II Cor. 12:20	conceit
taber upon	Nah. 2:7	beat
table	Luke 1:63	tablet
tablet	Exod. 35:22	armlet
take thought	Matt. 6:25	be anxious
take wrong	I Cor. 6:7	suffer wrong
tale	I Sam. 18:27	number
target	I Sam. 17:6	javelin
tell	Gen. 15:5	number
temperance	Acts 24:25	self-control
tempered	Exod. 29:2	mixed
tempt	Gen. 22:1	test
temptation	Deut. 4:34	trial
thankworthy	I Pet. 2:19	approved
tire	II Kings 9:30	adorn
tire	Ezek. 24:17	turban

Term	Reference	Meaning
translate	II Sam. 3:10	transfer
translation	Heb. 11:5	was taken
true	Gen. 42:11	honest
turtle	Song of S. 2:12	turtledove
tutor	Gal. 4:2	guardian
twain	I Sam. 18:21	a second time
at unawares	Num. 35:11	without intent
uncomely	I Cor. 7:36	not properly
uncorruptness	Tit. 2:7	integrity
unction	I John 2:20	anointing
unjust	Luke 16:8	dishonest
unspeakable	II Cor. 9:15	inexpressible
unto	Gen. 3:21	for
unto	Num. 35:25	until
untoward	Acts 2:40	crooked
usury	Matt. 25:27	interest
vagabond	Gen. 4:12	wanderer
vain	Judg. 9:4	worthless
vanity	Rom. 8:20	futility
venison	Gen. 25:28	game
vex	Exod. 22:21	wrong
vile	Phil. 3:21	lowly
virtue	Mark 5:30	power
vocation	Eph. 4:1	calling
void place	I Kings 22:10	threshing floor
volume	Ps. 40:7	roll
wait upon	Ps. 123:2	look to
want	II Cor. 11:9	be in want
to the mercy seatward	Exod. 37:9	toward the mercy seat
to us-ward	Ps. 40:5	toward us
to thee-ward	I Sam. 19:4	to you
to you-ward	II Cor. 1:12	toward you
waster	Isa. 54:16	ravager
wasting	Isa. 59:7	desolation
wax	Luke 13:19	become
wealth	I Cor. 10:24	good
wealthy	Jer. 49:31	at ease
went for	I Sam. 17:12	was
when as	Matt. 1:18	when
whether	Matt. 21:31	which
which	Matt. 6:9	who
whiles	Matt. 5:25	while
wholesome	Prov. 15:4	gentle
willing	Heb. 13:18	desiring
win	Phil. 3:8	gain
winefat	Isa. 63:2	wine press
wink at	Acts 17:30	overlook
without	II Cor. 10:13	beyond
witty inventions	Prov. 8:12	discretion
woe worth	Ezek. 30:2	alas for
work	Rom. 5:3	produce
have worship	Luke 14:10	be honored
worthy	Rom. 1:32	deserve
would God	II Kings 5:3	would that
would to God	Josh 7:7	would that
wrest	Deut. 16:19	pervert